Who'sWho of American Women®

Published by Marquis Who's Who®

Titles in Print

Who's Who in America®
Who's Who in America Junior & Senior High School Version
Who Was Who in America®
  Historical Volume (1607–1896)
  Volume I (1897–1942)
  Volume II (1943–1950)
  Volume III (1951–1960)
  Volume IV (1961–1968)
  Volume V (1969–1973)
  Volume VI (1974–1976)
  Volume VII (1977–1981)
  Volume VIII (1982–1985)
  Volume IX (1985–1989)
  Volume X (1989–1993)
  Volume XI (1993–1996)
  Index Volume (1607–1996)
Who's Who in the World®
Who's Who in the East®
Who's Who in the Midwest®
Who's Who in the South and Southwest®
Who's Who in the West®
Who's Who in American Education®
Who's Who in American Law®
Who's Who in American Nursing®
Who's Who in Entertainment®
Who's Who in Finance and Industry®
Who's Who in Medicine and Healthcare™
Who's Who in Religion®
Who's Who in Science and Engineering®
Who's Who in the Media and Communications™
Who's Who of American Women®
Who's Who of Emerging Leaders in America®
Index to Marquis Who's Who® Publications
The *Official* ABMS Directory of Board Certified Medical Specialists®

Available on CD-ROM

The Complete Marquis Who's Who® on CD-ROM
ABMS Medical Specialists *PLUS*™

Who's Who of American Women®

1997~1998

20th Edition

MARQUIS Who's Who® 121 Chanlon Road
New Providence, NJ 07974 U.S.A.

Who's Who of American Women®

Marquis Who's Who®

Vice President & Co-publisher Sandra S. Barnes   **Vice President, Database Production & Co-publisher** Dean Hollister
Editorial & Marketing Director Paul Canning   **Research Director** Judy Redel   **Managing Editor** Lisa Weissbard

Editorial

Senior Editor	Kathleen Litzenberg
Associate Editor	Hazel Conner
Assistant Editors	Alison Butkiewicz
	Jennifer Cox
	Launa Heron
	Francine Richardson
	Josh Samber

Editorial Services

Manager	Nadine Hovan
Supervisors	Mary Lyn Koval
	Debra Krom
Coordinator	Anne Marie C. Calcagno

Editorial Support

Manager	Sharon L. Gonzalez
Coordinator	J. Hector Gonzalez

Mail Processing

Supervisor	Kara A. Seitz
Staff	Cheryl A. Rodriguez
	Jill S. Terbell

Database Operations

Production Manager	Ren Reiner
Production Editor	Matthew O'Connell

Research

Managing Research Editor	Tanya Hurst
Senior Research Editor	Robert J. Docherty
Associate Research Editors	Christian Loeffler
	Oscar Maldonado
Assistant Editor	Ingrid Hsia

Support Services

Assistant	Jeanne Danzig

Table of Contents

Preface

In 1958, Marquis Who's Who published the first edition of *Who's Who of American Women*. Since that time there has been an increasing interest and need for the biographical data of successful American women.

Many of the Biographees in the premier edition were volunteer workers involved in civic, religious, and club activities. This, the twentieth edition, features Biographees in a broader range of endeavors and varying levels of responsibility. Listed in this volume are outstanding women from the fields of business, education, government, law, medicine, the performing and visual arts, the sciences, and many more.

The Marquis researchers have drawn on a wide range of sources in identifying listees: newspapers, magazines, trade publications, professional association rosters, and nominations by current Biographees, among others, were consulted in the preparation of the more than 29,000 sketches found in this edition. The result is a wealth of personal and professional biographical facts concerning women in virtually every important field of endeavor.

To supplement the efforts of Marquis researchers, and to ensure comprehensive coverage of important professionals, members of the distinguished Board of Advisors have nominated outstanding individuals in their own geographic regions or professional fields for inclusion in this volume.

As in all Marquis Who's Who biographical volumes, the principle of current reference value determines selection of Biographees. Reference interest is based either on position of responsibility or noteworthy achievement. In the editorial evaluation that resulted in the ultimate selection of the names in this directory, an individual's desire to be listed was not sufficient reason for inclusion.

The twentieth edition of *Who's Who of American Women* continues the tradition of excellence established in 1899 with the publication of the first edition of *Who's Who in America*. Each candidate is invited to submit biographical data about her life and professional career. Submitted information is reviewed by the Marquis editorial staff before being written in sketch form, and a prepublication proof of the composed sketch is sent to potential Biographees for verification. Every verified sketch returned by a candidate and accepted by the editorial staff is written in the final Marquis Who's Who format. This process ensures a high degree of accuracy.

In the event that an individual of significant reference interest fails to submit biographical data, the Marquis staff compiles the needed information through independent research. Brief key information is provided in the sketches of selected individuals, new to this edition, who did not submit data. Such sketches are denoted by an asterisk.

Marquis Who's Who editors exercise the utmost care in preparing each biographical sketch for publication. Occasionally, however, errors do appear. Users of this directory are requested to notify the publisher of any errors found so that corrections can be made in a subsequent edition.

Board of Advisors

Marquis Who's Who gratefully acknowledges the following distinguished individuals who have made themselves available for review, evaluation, and general comment with regard to the publication of the twentieth edition of *Who's Who of American Women.* The advisors have enhanced the reference value of this edition by the nomination of outstanding individuals for inclusion. However, the Board of Advisors, either collectively or individually, is in no way responsible for the final selection of names appearing in this volume, nor does the Board of Advisors bear responsibility for the accuracy or comprehensiveness of the biographical information or other material contained herein.

Standards of Admission

The foremost consideration in selecting Biographees for *Who's Who of American Women* is the extent of an individual's reference interest. Such reference interest is judged on either of two factors: (1) the position of responsibility held, or (2) the level of achievement attained by the individual.

Admissions based on the factor of position include:

High-level federal officials

Specified elected and appointed state officials

Mayors of major cities

Principal officers of selected businesses

Outstanding educators from major universities and colleges

Principal figures of cultural and artistic institutions

Heads of major women's organizations

Recipients of major awards and honors

Members of selected honorary organizations

Other women chosen because of incumbency or membership

Admission for individual achievement is based on qualitative criteria. To be selected, a person must have attained conspicuous achievement.

Key to Information

[1] **CHAMBERS, ELIZABETH BATES,** [2] lawyer; [3] b. Mitchell, S.D., July 19, 1940; [4] d. Oscar William and Judith (Strait) Bates; [5] m. Richard T. Chambers, Dec. 11, 1967; [6] children: Christopher Dwight, Mary Beth. [7] BA, U. Okla., 1962, MA, 1967; JD, Rice U., 1970. [8] Bar: Tex. 1970, S.D. 1973, U.S. Dist. Ct. S.D. 1982, U.S. Supreme Ct. 1982. [9] Assoc. Newman, Calvin & Swain, Houston, 1967-73, ptnr., 1973-74; ptnr. Hadley, Ellis, Chambers & Gonzalez, Amarillo, Tex., 1974-78; sole practice, Rapid City, S.D., 1978-82; ptnr. Chambers & Costner, Rapid City, 1982-90, sr. ptnr., 1990—; [10] lectr. Black Hills State Coll., Spearfish, S.D., 1987; mem. Gov.'s Task Force on Constl. Revision, Pierre, S.D., 1996—; bd. dirs. Custer Nat. Bank. [11] Contbr. articles to profl. jours. [12] Trustee The Grove Sch., Rapid City, 1982—; active Pennington County United Way. [13] Served with WAC, 1962-63. [14] Named Outstanding Woman of Yr., Amarillo C. of C., 1975; Lincoln Found. grantee, 1980. [15] Mem. ABA, S.D. Bar Assn., S.D. Assn. Def. Counsel, Pennington County Bar Assn., World Wildlife Fedn., Rushmore Hills Country Club, Noontime Club, Order Eastern Star. [16] Democrat. [17] Lutheran. [18] Home: 527 Woodbine Way Rapid City SD 57702 [19] Office: Chambers & Costner 964 N Omaha St Rapid City SD 57701

KEY

[1] Name
[2] Occupation
[3] Vital statistics
[4] Parents
[5] Marriage
[6] Children
[7] Education
[8] Professional certifications
[9] Career
[10] Career-related
[11] Writings and creative works
[12] Civic and political activities
[13] Military service
[14] Awards and fellowships
[15] Professional and association memberships, clubs and lodges
[16] Political affiliation
[17] Religion
[18] Home address
[19] Office address

Table of Abbreviations

The following abbreviations and symbols are frequently used in this book.

*An asterisk following a sketch indicates that it was researched by the Marquis Who's Who editorial staff and has not been verified by the Biographee.
A Associate (used with academic degrees only)
AA, A.A. Associate in Arts, Associate of Arts
AAAL American Academy of Arts and Letters
AAAS American Association for the Advancement of Science
AACD American Association for Counseling and Development
AACN American Association of Critical Care Nurses
AAHA American Academy of Health Administrators
AAHP American Association of Hospital Planners
AAHPERD American Alliance for Health, Physical Education, Recreation, and Dance
AAS Associate of Applied Science
AASL American Association of School Librarians
AASPA American Association of School Personnel Administrators
AAU Amateur Athletic Union
AAUP American Association of University Professors
AAUW American Association of University Women
AB, A.B. Arts, Bachelor of
AB Alberta
ABA American Bar Association
ABC American Broadcasting Company
AC Air Corps
acad. academy, academic
acct. accountant
acctg. accounting
ACDA Arms Control and Disarmament Agency
ACHA American College of Hospital Administrators
ACLS Advanced Cardiac Life Support
ACLU American Civil Liberties Union
ACOG American College of Ob-Gyn
ACP American College of Physicians
ACS American College of Surgeons
ADA American Dental Association
a.d.c. aide-de-camp
adj. adjunct, adjutant
adj. gen. adjutant general
adm. admiral
adminstr. administrator
adminstrn. administration
adminstrv. administrative
ADN Associate's Degree in Nursing
ADP Automatic Data Processing
adv. advocate, advisory
advt. advertising
AE, A.E. Agricultural Engineer
A.E. and P. Ambassador Extraordinary and Plenipotentiary

AEC Atomic Energy Commission
aero. aeronautical, aeronautic
aerodyn. aerodynamic
AFB Air Force Base
AFL-CIO American Federation of Labor and Congress of Industrial Organizations
AFTRA American Federation of TV and Radio Artists
AFSCME American Federation of State, County and Municipal Employees
agr. agriculture
agrl. agricultural
agt. agent
AGVA American Guild of Variety Artists
agy. agency
A&I Agricultural and Industrial
AIA American Institute of Architects
AIAA American Institute of Aeronautics and Astronautics
AIChE American Institute of Chemical Engineers
AICPA American Institute of Certified Public Accountants
AID Agency for International Development
AIDS Acquired Immune Deficiency Syndrome
AIEE American Institute of Electrical Engineers
AIM American Institute of Management
AIME American Institute of Mining, Metallurgy, and Petroleum Engineers
AK Alaska
AL Alabama
ALA American Library Association
Ala. Alabama
alt. alternate
Alta. Alberta
A&M Agricultural and Mechanical
AM, A.M. Arts, Master of
Am. American, America
AMA American Medical Association
amb. ambassador
A.M.E. African Methodist Episcopal
Amtrak National Railroad Passenger Corporation
AMVETS American Veterans of World War II, Korea, Vietnam
ANA American Nurses Association
anat. anatomical
ANCC American Nurses Credentialing Center
ann. annual
ANTA American National Theatre and Academy
anthrop. anthropological
AP Associated Press
APA American Psychological Association
APGA American Personnel Guidance Association
APHA American Public Health Association
APO Army Post Office
apptd. appointed
Apr. April
apt. apartment

AR Arkansas
ARC American Red Cross
arch. architect
archeol. archeological
archtl. architectural
Ariz. Arizona
Ark. Arkansas
ArtsD, ArtsD. Arts, Doctor of
arty. artillery
AS American Samoa
AS Associate in Science
ASCAP American Society of Composers, Authors and Publishers
ASCD Association for Supervision and Curriculum Development
ASCE American Society of Civil Engineers
ASHRAE American Society of Heating, Refrigeration, and Air Conditioning Engineers
ASME American Society of Mechanical Engineers
ASNSA American Society for Nursing Service Administrators
ASPA American Society for Public Administration
ASPCA American Society for the Prevention of Cruelty to Animals
assn. association
assoc. associate
asst. assistant
ASTD American Society for Training and Development
ASTM American Society for Testing and Materials
astron. astronomical
astrophys. astrophysical
ATLA Association of Trial Lawyers of America
ATSC Air Technical Service Command
AT&T American Telephone & Telegraph Company
atty. attorney
Aug. August
AUS Army of the United States
aux. auxiliary
Ave. Avenue
AVMA American Veterinary Medical Association
AZ Arizona
AWHONN Association of Women's Health Obstetric and Neonatal Nurses

B. Bachelor
b. born
BA, B.A. Bachelor of Arts
BAgr, B.Agr. Bachelor of Agriculture
Balt. Baltimore
Bapt. Baptist
BArch, B.Arch. Bachelor of Architecture
BAS, B.A.S. Bachelor of Agricultural Science
BBA, B.B.A. Bachelor of Business Administration
BBB Better Business Bureau
BBC British Broadcasting Corporation

BC, B.C. British Columbia
BCE, B.C.E. Bachelor of Civil Engineering
BChir, B.Chir. Bachelor of Surgery
BCL, B.C.L. Bachelor of Civil Law
BCLS Basic Cardiac Life Support
BCS, B.C.S. Bachelor of Commercial Science
BD, B.D. Bachelor of Divinity
bd. board
BE, B.E. Bachelor of Education
BEE, B.E.E. Bachelor of Electrical Engineering
BFA, B.F.A. Bachelor of Fine Arts
bibl. biblical
bibliog. bibliographical
biog. biographical
biol. biological
BJ, B.J. Bachelor of Journalism
Bklyn. Brooklyn
BL, B.L. Bachelor of Letters
bldg. building
BLS, B.L.S. Bachelor of Library Science
BLS Basic Life Support
Blvd. Boulevard
BMI Broadcast Music, Inc.
BMW Bavarian Motor Works (Bayerische Motoren Werke)
bn. battalion
B.&O.R.R. Baltimore & Ohio Railroad
bot. botanical
BPE, B.P.E. Bachelor of Physical Education
BPhil, B.Phil. Bachelor of Philosophy
br. branch
BRE, B.R.E. Bachelor of Religious Education
brig. gen. brigadier general
Brit. British, Brittanica
Bros. Brothers
BS, B.S. Bachelor of Science
BSA, B.S.A. Bachelor of Agricultural Science
BSBA Bachelor of Science in Business Administration
BSChemE Bachelor of Science in Chemical Engineering
BSD, B.S.D. Bachelor of Didactic Science
BSEE Bachelor of Science in Electrical Engineering
BSN Bachelor of Science in Nursing
BST, B.S.T. Bachelor of Sacred Theology
BTh, B.Th. Bachelor of Theology
bull. bulletin
bur. bureau
bus. business
B.W.I. British West Indies

CA California
CAA Civil Aeronautics Administration
CAB Civil Aeronautics Board
CAD-CAM Computer Aided Design–Computer Aided Model
Calif. California
C.Am. Central America
Can. Canada, Canadian
CAP Civil Air Patrol
capt. captain
cardiol. cardiological
cardiovasc. cardiovascular
CARE Cooperative American Relief Everywhere
Cath. Catholic
cav. cavalry
CBC Canadian Broadcasting Company
CBI China, Burma, India Theatre of Operations
CBS Columbia Broadcasting Company
C.C. Community College
CCC Commodity Credit Corporation
CCNY City College of New York

CCRN Critical Care Registered Nurse
CCU Cardiac Care Unit
CD Civil Defense
CE, C.E. Corps of Engineers, Civil Engineer
CEN Certified Emergency Nurse
CENTO Central Treaty Organization
CEO chief executive officer
CERN European Organization of Nuclear Research
cert. certificate, certification, certified
CETA Comprehensive Employment Training Act
CFA Chartered Financial Analyst
CFL Canadian Football League
CFO chief financial officer
CFP Certified Financial Planner
ch. church
ChD, Ch.D. Doctor of Chemistry
chem. chemical
ChemE, Chem.E. Chemical Engineer
ChFC Chartered Financial Consultant
Chgo. Chicago
chirurg. chirurgical
chmn. chairman
chpt. chapter
CIA Central Intelligence Agency
Cin. Cincinnati
cir. circle, circuit
CLE Continuing Legal Education
Cleve. Cleveland
climatol. climatological
clin. clinical
clk. clerk
C.L.U. Chartered Life Underwriter
CM, C.M. Master in Surgery
CM Northern Mariana Islands
CMA Certified Medical Assistant
cmty. community
CNA Certified Nurse's Aide
CNOR Certified Nurse (Operating Room)
C.&N.W.Ry. Chicago & North Western Railway
CO Colorado
Co. Company
COF Catholic Order of Foresters
C. of C. Chamber of Commerce
col. colonel
coll. college
Colo. Colorado
com. committee
comd. commanded
comdg. commanding
comdr. commander
comdt. commandant
comm. communications
commd. commissioned
comml. commercial
commn. commission
commr. commissioner
compt. comptroller
condr. conductor
Conf. Conference
Congl. Congregational, Congressional
Conglist. Congregationalist
Conn. Connecticut
cons. consultant, consulting
consol. consolidated
constl. constitutional
constn. constitution
constrn. construction
contbd. contributed
contbg. contributing
contbn. contribution
contbr. contributor
contr. controller
Conv. Convention
COO chief operating officer

coop. cooperative
coord. coordinator
CORDS Civil Operations and Revolutionary Development Support
CORE Congress of Racial Equality
corp. corporation, corporate
corr. correspondent, corresponding, correspondence
C.&O.Ry. Chesapeake & Ohio Railway
coun. council
CPA Certified Public Accountant
CPCU Chartered Property and Casualty Underwriter
CPH, C.P.H. Certificate of Public Health
cpl. corporal
CPR Cardio-Pulmonary Resuscitation
C.P.Ry. Canadian Pacific Railway
CRT Cathode Ray Terminal
C.S. Christian Science
CSB, C.S.B. Bachelor of Christian Science
C.S.C. Civil Service Commission
CT Connecticut
ct. court
ctr. center
ctrl. central
CWS Chemical Warfare Service
C.Z. Canal Zone

D. Doctor
d. daughter
DAgr, D.Agr. Doctor of Agriculture
DAR Daughters of the American Revolution
dau. daughter
DAV Disabled American Veterans
DC, D.C. District of Columbia
DCL, D.C.L. Doctor of Civil Law
DCS, D.C.S. Doctor of Commercial Science
DD, D.D. Doctor of Divinity
DDS, D.D.S. Doctor of Dental Surgery
DE Delaware
Dec. December
dec. deceased
def. defense
Del. Delaware
del. delegate, delegation
Dem. Democrat, Democratic
DEng, D.Eng. Doctor of Engineering
denom. denomination, denominational
dep. deputy
dept. department
dermatol. dermatological
desc. descendant
devel. development, developmental
DFA, D.F.A. Doctor of Fine Arts
D.F.C. Distinguished Flying Cross
DHL, D.H.L. Doctor of Hebrew Literature
dir. director
dist. district
distbg. distributing
distbn. distribution
distbr. distributor
disting. distinguished
div. division, divinity, divorce
divsn. division
DLitt, D.Litt. Doctor of Literature
DMD, D.M.D. Doctor of Dental Medicine
DMS, D.M.S. Doctor of Medical Science
DO, D.O. Doctor of Osteopathy
docs. documents
DON Director of Nursing
DPH, D.P.H. Diploma in Public Health
DPhil, D.Phil. Doctor of Philosophy
D.R. Daughters of the Revolution
Dr. Drive, Doctor
DRE, D.R.E. Doctor of Religious Education
DrPH, Dr.P.H. Doctor of Public Health, Doctor of Public Hygiene
D.S.C. Distinguished Service Cross

DSc, D.Sc. Doctor of Science
DSChemE Doctor of Science in Chemical Engineering
D.S.M. Distinguished Service Medal
DST, D.S.T. Doctor of Sacred Theology
DTM, D.T.M. Doctor of Tropical Medicine
DVM, D.V.M. Doctor of Veterinary Medicine
DVS, D.V.S. Doctor of Veterinary Surgery

E, E. East
ea. eastern
E. and P. Extraordinary and Plenipotentiary
Eccles. Ecclesiastical
ecol. ecological
econ. economic
ECOSOC Economic and Social Council (of the UN)
ED, E.D. Doctor of Engineering
ed. educated
EdB, Ed.B. Bachelor of Education
EdD, Ed.D. Doctor of Education
edit. edition
editl. editorial
EdM, Ed.M. Master of Education
edn. education
ednl. educational
EDP Electronic Data Processing
EdS, Ed.S. Specialist in Education
EE, E.E. Electrical Engineer
E.E. and M.P. Envoy Extraordinary and Minister Plenipotentiary
EEC European Economic Community
EEG Electroencephalogram
EEO Equal Employment Opportunity
EEOC Equal Employment Opportunity Commission
E.Ger. German Democratic Republic
EKG Electrocardiogram
elec. electrical
electrochem. electrochemical
electrophys. electrophysical
elem. elementary
EM, E.M. Engineer of Mines
EMT Emergency Medical Technician
ency. encyclopedia
Eng. England
engr. engineer
engring. engineering
entomol. entomological
environ. environmental
EPA Environmental Protection Agency
epidemiol. epidemiological
Episc. Episcopalian
ERA Equal Rights Amendment
ERDA Energy Research and Development Administration
ESEA Elementary and Secondary Education Act
ESL English as Second Language
ESPN Entertainment and Sports Programming Network
ESSA Environmental Science Services Administration
ethnol. ethnological
ETO European Theatre of Operations
Evang. Evangelical
exam. examination, examining
Exch. Exchange
exec. executive
exhbn. exhibition
expdn. expedition
expn. exposition
expt. experiment
exptl. experimental
Expy. Expressway
Ext. Extension

F.A. Field Artillery
FAA Federal Aviation Administration
FAO Food and Agriculture Organization (of the UN)
FBA Federal Bar Association
FBI Federal Bureau of Investigation
FCA Farm Credit Administration
FCC Federal Communications Commission
FCDA Federal Civil Defense Administration
FDA Food and Drug Administration
FDIA Federal Deposit Insurance Administration
FDIC Federal Deposit Insurance Corporation
FE, F.E. Forest Engineer
FEA Federal Energy Administration
Feb. February
fed. federal
fedn. federation
FERC Federal Energy Regulatory Commission
fgn. foreign
FHA Federal Housing Administration
fin. financial, finance
FL Florida
Fl. Floor
Fla. Florida
FMC Federal Maritime Commission
FNP Family Nurse Practitioner
FOA Foreign Operations Administration
found. foundation
FPC Federal Power Commission
FPO Fleet Post Office
frat. fraternity
FRS Federal Reserve System
FSA Federal Security Agency
Ft. Fort
FTC Federal Trade Commission
Fwy. Freeway

G-1 (or other number) Division of General Staff
GA, Ga. Georgia
GAO General Accounting Office
gastroent. gastroenterological
GATE Gifted and Talented Educators
GATT General Agreement on Tariffs and Trade
GE General Electric Company
gen. general
geneal. genealogical
geod. geodetic
geog. geographic, geographical
geol. geological
geophys. geophysical
geriat. geriatrics
gerontol. gerontological
G.H.Q. General Headquarters
GM General Motors Corporation
GMAC General Motors Acceptance Corporation
G.N.Ry. Great Northern Railway
gov. governor
govt. government
govtl. governmental
GPO Government Printing Office
grad. graduate, graduated
GSA General Services Administration
Gt. Great
GTE General Telephone and Electric Company
GU Guam
gynecol. gynecological

HBO Home Box Office
hdqs. headquarters

HEW Department of Health, Education and Welfare
HHD, H.H.D. Doctor of Humanities
HHFA Housing and Home Finance Agency
HHS Department of Health and Human Services
HI Hawaii
hist. historical, historic
HM, H.M. Master of Humanities
HMO Health Maintenance Organization
homeo. homeopathic
hon. honorary, honorable
Ho. of Dels. House of Delegates
Ho. of Reps. House of Representatives
hort. horticultural
hosp. hospital
H.S. High School
HUD Department of Housing and Urban Development
Hwy. Highway
hydrog. hydrographic

IA Iowa
IAEA International Atomic Energy Agency
IATSE International Alliance of Theatrical and Stage Employees and Moving Picture Operators of the United States and Canada
IBM International Business Machines Corporation
IBRD International Bank for Reconstruction and Development
ICA International Cooperation Administration
ICC Interstate Commerce Commission
ICCE International Council for Computers in Education
ICU Intensive Care Unit
ID Idaho
IEEE Institute of Electrical and Electronics Engineers
IFC International Finance Corporation
IGY International Geophysical Year
IL Illinois
Ill. Illinois
illus. illustrated
ILO International Labor Organization
IMF International Monetary Fund
IN Indiana
Inc. Incorporated
Ind. Indiana
ind. independent
Indpls. Indianapolis
indsl. industrial
inf. infantry
info. information
ins. insurance
insp. inspector
insp. gen. inspector general
inst. institute
instl. institutional
instn. institution
instr. instructor
instrn. instruction
instrnl. instructional
internat. international
intro. introduction
IRE Institute of Radio Engineers
IRS Internal Revenue Service
ITT International Telephone & Telegraph Corporation

JAG Judge Advocate General
JAGC Judge Advocate General Corps
Jan. January
Jaycees Junior Chamber of Commerce
JB, J.B. Jurum Baccalaureus

JCB, J.C.B. Juris Canoni Baccalaureus
JCD, J.C.D. Juris Canonici Doctor, Juris Civilis Doctor
JCL, J.C.L. Juris Canonici Licentiatus
JD, J.D. Juris Doctor
jg. junior grade
jour. journal
jr. junior
JSD, J.S.D. Juris Scientiae Doctor
JUD, J.U.D. Juris Utriusque Doctor
jud. judicial

Kans. Kansas
K.C. Knights of Columbus
K.P. Knights of Pythias
KS Kansas
K.T. Knight Templar
KY, Ky. Kentucky

LA, La. Louisiana
L.A. Los Angeles
lab. laboratory
L.Am. Latin America
lang. language
laryngol. laryngological
LB Labrador
LDS Latter Day Saints
LDS Church Church of Jesus Christ of Latter Day Saints
lectr. lecturer
legis. legislation, legislative
LHD, L.H.D. Doctor of Humane Letters
L.I. Long Island
libr. librarian, library
lic. licensed, license
L.I.R.R. Long Island Railroad
lit. literature
litig. litigation
LittB, Litt.B. Bachelor of Letters
LittD, Litt.D. Doctor of Letters
LLB, LL.B. Bachelor of Laws
LLD, L.L.D. Doctor of Laws
LLM, L.L.M. Master of Laws
Ln. Lane
L.&N.R.R. Louisville & Nashville Railroad
LPGA Ladies Professional Golf Association
LPN Licensed Practical Nurse
LS, L.S. Library Science (in degree)
lt. lieutenant
Ltd. Limited
Luth. Lutheran
LWV League of Women Voters

M. Master
m. married
MA, M.A. Master of Arts
MA Massachusetts
MADD Mothers Against Drunk Driving
mag. magazine
MAgr, M.Agr. Master of Agriculture
maj. major
Man. Manitoba
Mar. March
MArch, M.Arch. Master in Architecture
Mass. Massachusetts
math. mathematics, mathematical
MATS Military Air Transport Service
MB, M.B. Bachelor of Medicine
MB Manitoba
MBA, M.B.A. Master of Business Administration
MBS Mutual Broadcasting System
M.C. Medical Corps
MCE, M.C.E. Master of Civil Engineering
mcht. merchant
mcpl. municipal
MCS, M.C.S. Master of Commercial Science

MD, M.D. Doctor of Medicine
MD, Md. Maryland
MDiv Master of Divinity
MDip, M.Dip. Master in Diplomacy
mdse. merchandise
MDV, M.D.V. Doctor of Veterinary Medicine
ME, M.E. Mechanical Engineer
ME Maine
M.E.Ch. Methodist Episcopal Church
mech. mechanical
MEd., M.Ed. Master of Education
med. medical
MEE, M.E.E. Master of Electrical Engineering
mem. member
meml. memorial
merc. mercantile
met. metropolitan
metall. metallurgical
MetE, Met.E. Metallurgical Engineer
meteorol. meteorological
Meth. Methodist
Mex. Mexico
MF, M.F. Master of Forestry
MFA, M.F.A. Master of Fine Arts
mfg. manufacturing
mfr. manufacturer
mgmt. management
mgr. manager
MHA, M.H.A. Master of Hospital Administration
M.I. Military Intelligence
MI Michigan
Mich. Michigan
micros. microscopic, microscopical
mid. middle
mil. military
Milw. Milwaukee
Min. Minister
mineral. mineralogical
Minn. Minnesota
MIS Management Information Systems
Miss. Mississippi
MIT Massachusetts Institute of Technology
mktg. marketing
ML, M.L. Master of Laws
MLA Modern Language Association
M.L.D. Magister Legnum Diplomatic
MLitt, M.Litt. Master of Literature, Master of Letters
MLS, M.L.S. Master of Library Science
MME, M.M.E. Master of Mechanical Engineering
MN Minnesota
mng. managing
MO, Mo. Missouri
moblzn. mobilization
Mont. Montana
MP Northern Mariana Islands
M.P. Member of Parliament
MPA Master of Public Administration
MPE, M.P.E. Master of Physical Education
MPH, M.P.H. Master of Public Health
MPhil, M.Phil. Master of Philosophy
MPL, M.P.L. Master of Patent Law
Mpls. Minneapolis
MRE, M.R.E. Master of Religious Education
MRI Magnetic Resonance Imaging
MS, M.S. Master of Science
MS, Ms. Mississippi
MSc, M.Sc. Master of Science
MSChemE Master of Science in Chemical Engineering
MSEE Master of Science in Electrical Engineering

MSF, M.S.F. Master of Science of Forestry
MSN Master of Science in Nursing
MST, M.S.T. Master of Sacred Theology
MSW, M.S.W. Master of Social Work
MT Montana
Mt. Mount
MTO Mediterranean Theatre of Operation
MTV Music Television
mus. museum, musical
MusB, Mus.B. Bachelor of Music
MusD, Mus.D. Doctor of Music
MusM, Mus.M. Master of Music
mut. mutual
MVP Most Valuable Player
mycol. mycological

N. North
NAACOG Nurses Association of the American College of Obstetricians and Gynecologists
NAACP National Association for the Advancement of Colored People
NACA National Advisory Committee for Aeronautics
NACDL National Association of Criminal Defense Lawyers
NACU National Association of Colleges and Universities
NAD National Academy of Design
NAE National Academy of Engineering, National Association of Educators
NAESP National Association of Elementary School Principals
NAFE National Association of Female Executives
N.Am. North America
NAM National Association of Manufacturers
NAMH National Association for Mental Health
NAPA National Association of Performing Artists
NARAS National Academy of Recording Arts and Sciences
NAREB National Association of Real Estate Boards
NARS National Archives and Record Service
NAS National Academy of Sciences
NASA National Aeronautics and Space Administration
NASP National Association of School Psychologists
NASW National Association of Social Workers
nat. national
NATAS National Academy of Television Arts and Sciences
NATO North Atlantic Treaty Organization
NATOUSA North African Theatre of Operations, United States Army
nav. navigation
NB, N.B. New Brunswick
NBA National Basketball Association
NBC National Broadcasting Company
NC, N.C. North Carolina
NCAA National College Athletic Association
NCCJ National Conference of Christians and Jews
ND, N.D. North Dakota
NDEA National Defense Education Act
NE Nebraska
NE, N.E. Northeast
NEA National Education Association
Nebr. Nebraska
NEH National Endowment for Humanities
neurol. neurological
Nev. Nevada
NF Newfoundland

NFL National Football League
Nfld. Newfoundland
NG National Guard
NH, N.H. New Hampshire
NHL National Hockey League
NIH National Institutes of Health
NIMH National Institute of Mental Health
NJ, N.J. New Jersey
NLRB National Labor Relations Board
NM New Mexico
N.Mex. New Mexico
No. Northern
NOAA National Oceanographic and Atmospheric Administration
NORAD North America Air Defense
Nov. November
NOW National Organization for Women
N.P.Ry. Northern Pacific Railway
nr. near
NRA National Rifle Association
NRC National Research Council
NS, N.S. Nova Scotia
NSC National Security Council
NSF National Science Foundation
NSTA National Science Teachers Association
NSW New South Wales
N.T. New Testament
NT Northwest Territories
nuc. nuclear
numis. numismatic
NV Nevada
NW, N.W. Northwest
N.W.T. Northwest Territories
NY, N.Y. New York
N.Y.C. New York City
NYU New York University
N.Z. New Zealand

OAS Organization of American States
ob-gyn obstetrics-gynecology
obs. observatory
obstet. obstetrical
occupl. occupational
oceanog. oceanographic
Oct. October
OD, O.D. Doctor of Optometry
OECD Organization for Economic Cooperation and Development
OEEC Organization of European Economic Cooperation
OEO Office of Economic Opportunity
ofcl. official
OH Ohio
OK Oklahoma
Okla. Oklahoma
ON Ontario
Ont. Ontario
oper. operating
ophthal. ophthalmological
ops. operations
OR Oregon
orch. orchestra
Oreg. Oregon
orgn. organization
orgnl. organizational
ornithol. ornithological
orthop. orthopedic
OSHA Occupational Safety and Health Administration
OSRD Office of Scientific Research and Development
OSS Office of Strategic Services
osteo. osteopathic
otol. otological
otolaryn. otolaryngological

PA, Pa. Pennsylvania

P.A. Professional Association
paleontol. paleontological
path. pathological
PBS Public Broadcasting System
P.C. Professional Corporation
PE Prince Edward Island
pediat. pediatrics
P.E.I. Prince Edward Island
PEN Poets, Playwrights, Editors, Essayists and Novelists (international association)
penol. penological
P.E.O. women's organization (full name not disclosed)
pers. personnel
pfc. private first class
PGA Professional Golfers' Association of America
PHA Public Housing Administration
pharm. pharmaceutical
PharmD, Pharm.D. Doctor of Pharmacy
PharmM, Pharm.M. Master of Pharmacy
PhB, Ph.B. Bachelor of Philosophy
PhD, Ph.D. Doctor of Philosophy
PhDChemE Doctor of Science in Chemical Engineering
PhM, Ph.M. Master of Philosophy
Phila. Philadelphia
philharm. philharmonic
philol. philological
philos. philosophical
photog. photographic
phys. physical
physiol. physiological
Pitts. Pittsburgh
Pk. Park
Pky. Parkway
Pl. Place
P.&L.E.R.R. Pittsburgh & Lake Erie Railroad
Plz. Plaza
PNP Pediatric Nurse Practitioner
P.O. Post Office
PO Box Post Office Box
polit. political
poly. polytechnic, polytechnical
PQ Province of Quebec
PR, P.R. Puerto Rico
prep. preparatory
pres. president
Presbyn. Presbyterian
presdl. presidential
prin. principal
procs. proceedings
prod. produced (play production)
prodn. production
prodr. producer
prof. professor
profl. professional
prog. progressive
propr. proprietor
pros. atty. prosecuting attorney
pro tem. pro tempore
PSRO Professional Services Review Organization
psychiat. psychiatric
psychol. psychological
PTA Parent-Teachers Association
ptnr. partner
PTO Pacific Theatre of Operations, Parent Teacher Organization
pub. publisher, publishing, published
pub. public
publ. publication
pvt. private

quar. quarterly
qm. quartermaster

Q.M.C. Quartermaster Corps
Que. Quebec

radiol. radiological
RAF Royal Air Force
RCA Radio Corporation of America
RCAF Royal Canadian Air Force
RD Rural Delivery
Rd. Road
R&D Research & Development
REA Rural Electrification Administration
rec. recording
ref. reformed
regt. regiment
regtl. regimental
rehab. rehabilitation
rels. relations
Rep. Republican
rep. representative
Res. Reserve
ret. retired
Rev. Reverend
rev. review, revised
RFC Reconstruction Finance Corporation
RFD Rural Free Delivery
rhinol. rhinological
RI, R.I. Rhode Island
RISD Rhode Island School of Design
Rlwy. Railway
Rm. Room
RN, R.N. Registered Nurse
roentgenol. roentgenological
ROTC Reserve Officers Training Corps
RR Rural Route
R.R. Railroad
rsch. research
rschr. researcher
Rt. Route

S. South
s. son
SAC Strategic Air Command
SAG Screen Actors Guild
SALT Strategic Arms Limitation Talks
S.Am. South America
san. sanitary
SAR Sons of the American Revolution
Sask. Saskatchewan
savs. savings
SB, S.B. Bachelor of Science
SBA Small Business Administration
SC, S.C. South Carolina
SCAP Supreme Command Allies Pacific
ScB, Sc.B. Bachelor of Science
SCD, S.C.D. Doctor of Commercial Science
ScD, Sc.D. Doctor of Science
sch. school
sci. science, scientific
SCLC Southern Christian Leadership Conference
SCV Sons of Confederate Veterans
SD, S.D. South Dakota
SE, S.E. Southeast
SEATO Southeast Asia Treaty Organization
SEC Securities and Exchange Commission
sec. secretary
sect. section
seismol. seismological
sem. seminary
Sept. September
s.g. senior grade
sgt. sergeant
SHAEF Supreme Headquarters Allied Expeditionary Forces
SHAPE Supreme Headquarters Allied Powers in Europe
S.I. Staten Island

S.J. Society of Jesus (Jesuit)
SJD Scientiae Juridicae Doctor
SK Saskatchewan
SM, S.M. Master of Science
SNP Society of Nursing Professionals
So. Southern
soc. society
sociol. sociological
S.P.Co. Southern Pacific Company
spkr. speaker
spl. special
splty. specialty
Sq. Square
S.R. Sons of the Revolution
sr. senior
SS Steamship
SSS Selective Service System
St. Saint, Street
sta. station
stats. statistics
statis. statistical
STB, S.T.B. Bachelor of Sacred Theology
stblzn. stabilization
STD, S.T.D. Doctor of Sacred Theology
std. standard
Ste. Suite
subs. subsidiary
SUNY State University of New York
supr. supervisor
supt. superintendent
surg. surgical
svc. service
SW, S.W. Southwest
sys. system

TAPPI Technical Association of the Pulp and Paper Industry
tb. tuberculosis
tchg. teaching
tchr. teacher
tech. technical, technology
technol. technological
tel. telephone
Tel. & Tel. Telephone & Telegraph
telecom. telecommunications
temp. temporary
Tenn. Tennessee
Ter. Territory
Ter. Terrace
TESOL Teachers of English to Speakers of Other Languages
Tex. Texas
ThD, Th.D. Doctor of Theology
theol. theological

ThM, Th.M. Master of Theology
TN Tennessee
tng. training
topog. topographical
trans. transaction, transferred
transl. translation, translated
transp. transportation
treas. treasurer
TT Trust Territory
TV television
TVA Tennessee Valley Authority
TWA Trans World Airlines
twp. township
TX Texas
typog. typographical

U. University
UAW United Auto Workers
UCLA University of California at Los Angeles
UDC United Daughters of the Confederacy
U.K. United Kingdom
UN United Nations
UNESCO United Nations Educational, Scientific and Cultural Organization
UNICEF United Nations International Children's Emergency Fund
univ. university
UNRRA United Nations Relief and Rehabilitation Administration
UPI United Press International
U.P.R.R. United Pacific Railroad
urol. urological
U.S. United States
U.S.A. United States of America
USAAF United States Army Air Force
USAF United States Air Force
USAFR United States Air Force Reserve
USAR United States Army Reserve
USCG United States Coast Guard
USCGR United States Coast Guard Reserve
USES United States Employment Service
USIA United States Information Agency
USMC United States Marine Corps
USMCR United States Marine Corps Reserve
USN United States Navy
USNG United States National Guard
USNR United States Naval Reserve
USO United Service Organizations
USPHS United States Public Health Service
USS United States Ship
USSR Union of the Soviet Socialist Republics
USTA United States Tennis Association

USV United States Volunteers
UT Utah

VA Veterans Administration
VA, Va. Virginia
vet. veteran, veterinary
VFW Veterans of Foreign Wars
VI, V.I. Virgin Islands
vice pres. vice president
vis. visiting
VISTA Volunteers in Service to America
VITA Volunteers in Technical Assistance
vocat. vocational
vol. volunteer, volume
v.p. vice president
vs. versus
VT, Vt. Vermont

W, W. West
WA Washington (state)
WAC Women's Army Corps
Wash. Washington (state)
WATS Wide Area Telecommunications Service
WAVES Women's Reserve, US Naval Reserve
WCTU Women's Christian Temperance Union
we. western
W. Ger. Germany, Federal Republic of
WHO World Health Organization
WI Wisconsin
W.I. West Indies
Wis. Wisconsin
WSB Wage Stabilization Board
WV West Virginia
W.Va. West Virginia
WWI World War I
WWII World War II
WY Wyoming
Wyo. Wyoming

YK Yukon Territory
YMCA Young Men's Christian Association
YMHA Young Men's Hebrew Association
YM & YWHA Young Men's and Young Women's Hebrew Association
yr. year
YT, Y.T. Yukon Territory
YWCA Young Women's Christian Association

zool. zoological

Alphabetical Practices

Names are arranged alphabetically according to the surnames, and under identical surnames according to the first given name. If both surname and first given name are identical, names are arranged alphabetically according to the second given name.

Surnames beginning with De, Des, Du, however capitalized or spaced, are recorded with the prefix preceding the surname and arranged alphabetically under the letter D.

Surnames beginning with Mac and Mc are arranged alphabetically under M.

Surnames beginning with Saint or St. appear after names that begin Sains, and are arranged according to the second part of the name, e.g. St. Clair before Saint Dennis.

Surnames beginning with Van, Von, or von are arranged alphabetically under the letter V.

Compound surnames are arranged according to the first member of the compound.

Many hyphenated Arabic names begin Al-, El-, or al-. These names are alphabetized according to each Biographee's designation of last name. Thus Al-Bahar, Neta may be listed either under Al- or under Bahar, depending on the preference of the listee.

Also, Arabic names have a variety of possible spellings when transposed to English. Spelling of these names is always based on the practice of the Biographee. Some Biographees use a Western form of word order, while others prefer the Arabic word sequence.

Similarly, Asian names may have no comma between family and given names, but some Biographees have chosen to add the comma. In each case, punctuation follows the preference of the Biographee.

Parentheses used in connection with a name indicate which part of the full name is usually deleted in common usage. Hence Chambers, E(lizabeth) Anne indicates that the usual form of the given name is E. Anne. In such a case, the parentheses are ignored in alphabetizing and the name would be arranged as Chambers, Elizabeth Anne. However, if the name is recorded Chambers, (Elizabeth) Anne, signifying that the entire name Elizabeth is not commonly used, the alphabetizing would be arranged as though the name were Chambers, Anne. If an entire middle or last name is enclosed in parentheses, that portion of the name is used in the alphabetical arrangement. Hence Chambers, Elizabeth (Anne) would be arranged as Chambers, Elizabeth Anne.

Where more than one spelling, word order, or name of an individual is frequently encountered, the sketch has been entered under the form preferred by the Biographee, with cross-references under alternate forms.

Who'sWho of American Women®

Biographies

AADALEN, SHARON PRICE, nursing educator, researcher; b. Manchester, N.H., June 26, 1940; d. Trevor Alaric Pryce and Beatrice (Dinsmore) Price; m. Richard Jerome Aadalen, July 27, 1963; children: Richard Andrew, Kirk Jeremy, Lora Elizabeth. BA magna cum laude, Radcliffe Coll., 1962; BS in Nursing, Western Res. U., 1967; MS in Pub. Health, U. Minn., 1979, PhD in Edn., 1983; cert. Reflective Leadership Program Hubert Humphrey Inst. Pub. Affairs, 1984. RN, cert. pub. health nursing, Minn. Staff nurse pub. health Vis. Nurse Assn., Roxbury Dist. Boston, 1964-65; staff and charge nurse, Lakeside Hosp., Univ. Hosps., Cleve., 1965-66; staff and charge nurse neurol. rehab. Benjamin Rose Hosp., Univ. Hosps., Cleve., 1966; staff nurse coronary rehab., coronary ICU, Mt. Sinai Hosp., Mpls., 1974-76; instr. Sch. Nursing SUNY-Plattsburgh, 1967-69; instr. Sch. Pub. Health, U. Minn., Mpls., 1979-82, adj. faculty, 1982-86, adj. asst. prof. maternal child health program Sch. Pub. Health, 1986—, adj. asst. prof. Sch. Nursing, 1986—; community faculty mem. nursing edn. program Met. State Univ., Mpls., 1986—; prin. investigator Minn. Sudden Infant Death Ctr., 1978-85; dir. nursing edn. and research United Hosp., St. Paul, 1985—; cons. div. nursing and health scis. mgmt. Minot State Coll. (N.D.), 1982; workshop coordinator dept. family social sci. U. Minn., St. Paul, 1983, cons., 1983; instr. sch. nurse achievement program U. Colo., 1983; mem. maternal and child health external grants rev. com. Minn. Dept. Health, 1983; bd. dirs., exec. com. Midwest Alliance in Nursing, 1982-83; mem. task force Gov.'s White House Conf. on Family Stress and Work, 1981; speaker profl. confs. U.S.; invited speaker USSR, 1983. Contbr. chpts. to books, articles to profl. jours. Bd. dirs. YWCA, Cleveland Heights, Ohio, 1969-73; speakers bur. Minn. affiliate Am. Heart Assn., 1975-77; mem. Citizens League, 1979—; mem. subcom. Citizens Adv. Task Force on Edn., Edina, Minn., 1975-77; v.p. Edina Community Lutheran Ch., 1983-84, pres. 1984-85, mem. Council of Ministers; mem. allocation and evaluation panels United Way Mpls., 1983-86; mem. Edina Health Adv. Bd., 1985-87, chmn., 1985-86; mem. State Community Health Services Adv. Com., 1985-86. Thompson scholar, 1960-61, Mass. Gen. Hosp. Sch. Nursing scholar, 1962-64; Ruth Sherman fellow, 1962; trainee div. nursing USPHS, HEW, Frances Payne Bolton Sch. Nursing, Western Res. U., 1966-67, Sch. Pub. Health, U. Minn., 1977-78; scholar reflective leadership seminar Hubert H. Humphrey Inst. Pub. Affairs, U. Minn., 1983-84. Mem. Am. Nurses Assn. (council nurse researchers, council continuing edn., council on computer applications), Minn. Nurses Assn., Am. Pub. Health Assn., Minn. Pub. Health Assn. (future directions task force 1980-81), Am. Assn. Adult and Continuing Edn., Am. Assn. Nurse Execs., Minn. Assn. Nurse Execs. (edn. com. 1985—, chmn. 1986—), Twin Cities Assn. Nurse Execs., Midwest Nursing Research Soc., Minn. Mental Health Assn., World Futures Soc., U. Minn. Alumni Assn. (interim bd. dirs. Constituent Soc. Sch. Pub. Health), Sigma Theta Tau (bd. dirs. 1980-82, research award 1984, distinguished lectr. 1988—), Phi Delta Kappa, Phi Kappa Phi. Home: 4924 Dale Dr Minneapolis MN 55424-1150 Office: United Hosp Nursing Edn and Research Dept 333 Smith Ave N Saint Paul MN 55102-2344

AARON, BETSY, journalist; b. N.Y.C., Nov. 11, 1938; d. Bertram Henry and Evelyn (Horner) Siegeltuch; m. Richard Threlkeld, 1983. BA, Am. U., 1960. Researcher, writer, field producer, reporter, corr. ABC News, Washington, N.Y.C., Chgo., 1960-76; network corr. CBS News, Atlanta, N.Y.C., 1976-80; corr. CBS News, N.Y.C., 1988—; network corr. NBC Mag., NBC News, N.Y.C., 1980-82; Nightline corr. ABC News, N.Y.C., 1980-84; corr. World News Tonight ABC News, 1985-88; corr. CBS Evening News, N.Y.C., 1989-91, CBS Sunday Morning, 1991-93; Moscow corr. CNN, Atlanta, 1996—. Mem. Amnesty Internat. (dep. exec. dir. comms. 1995). Office: CNN Moscow Bur 1 CNN Ctr Atlanta GA 30303

AARON, CYNTHIA G., judge; b. Mpls., May 3, 1957; d. Allen Harold and Barbara Lois (Perlman) A.; m. Craig D. Higgs, May 15, 1993. Student, Brandeis U., 1975-77; BA with honors and distinction, Stanford U., 1979; JD cum laude, Harvard U., 1984. Bar: Calif. 1984, U.S. Dist. Ct. (so. dist.) Calif. 1984, U.S. Ct. Appeals (9th cir.) 1984, U.S Dist. Ct. (no. dist.) Calif. 1986, U.S. Dist. Ct. (ctrl. dist.) Calif. 1988, U.S. Supreme Ct. 1991. Law clerk Topel & Goodman, San Francisco, 1982; rsch. asst. to Prof. Alan Dushowitz law sch. Harvard U., 1982-83; law clerk Coblentz, Cahen, McCabe & Breyer, San Francisco, 1983; trial atty. Fed. Defenders San Diego, Inc., 1984-88; ptnr. Aaron & Cortez, 1988-94; U.S. magistrate judge U.S. Dist. Ct. (so. dist.) Calif., San Diego, 1994—; guest instr. law sch. U. San Diego, 1988-90; instr. pacific regional program Nat. Inst. for Trial Advocacy, 1988-91, instr. deposition skills workshop, 1993; adj. prof. Calif. We. Sch. Law, San Diego, 1990-93; instr., critiquer baskic trial skills workshop Continuing Edn. Bar, San Diego, 1991; instr. advocacy trial skills acad. Inst. for Criminal Def., San Diego, 1992-94; adj. prof. law sch. U. San Diego, 1993, 95. Mem. Nat. Assn. Women Judges, Lawyers Club San Diego, U.J.F. Downtown Breakfast Club, City Club San Diego, Phi Beta Kappa. Office: US Dist Ct (So Dist) Calif Edward J Schwartz US Courthouse 940 Front St Rm E San Diego CA 92101-8994

AARON, SHIRLEY MAE, tax consultant; b. Covington, La., Feb. 28, 1935; d. Morgan and Pearl (Jenkins) King; m. Richard L. King, Feb. 16, 1952 (div. Feb. 1965); children: Deborah, Richard, Roberta, Keely; m. Michael A. Aaron, Nov. 27, 1976 (dec. July 1987). Adminstrv. asst. South Central Bell, Covington, La., 1954-62; acct. Brown & Root, Inc., Houston, 1962-75; timekeeper Alyeska Pipeline Co., Fairbanks, Alaska, 1975-77; adminstrv. asst. Boeing Co., Seattle, 1979-93; pres. Aaron Enterprises, Seattle, 1977—; owner Gabriel's Dinner Club, La., 1993—. Contbr.: Who's Cooking What in America by Phyllis Hanes, 1993. Bd. dirs. Burien 146 Homeowners Assn., Seattle, 1979—, pres., 1980-83, 92. Mem. NAFE. Avocation: singing, art. Home: 131 Gerard St Mandeville LA 70448-5808

AARONS, CECILIA, retired secondary school educator; b. Louisville, Oct. 26, 1911; d. Raphael Louis and Jenny (Leff) A. BA, U. Miss., 1932, MA, 1935; postgrad., Columbia U., 1937, U. Chgo., 1944. Cert. tchr., Miss. Tchr. Shelby (Miss.) Spl. Consol. H.S., 1933-43; English tchr., Latin and French tchr. Carr Ctrl. H.S., Vicksburg, 1943-61; English tchr. H.V. Cooper H.S., Vicksburg, 1963-76; math. tchr. St. Aloysius H.S., Vicksburg, 1976-78, English tchr., 1976-87; ret., 1987; cons. in field; mem. workshop U.S. Dept. of State, Washington. Recipient Gold Key award Columbia Scholastic Press Assn., 1971. Democrat. Jewish. Home: 2520 1/2 Cherry St Vicksburg MS 39180-4108

AARON-TAYLOR, SUSAN WENDY, sculptor, educator; b. Bklyn., July 11, 1947; d. Irving and Frances Estelle (Sidorofsky) Aaron; m. Harry William Taylor, June 27, 1971; 1 child, Jay Philip Aaron Taylor. BS, Wayne State U., 1969; MFA, Cranbrook Acad. Art, 1973. Tchr. h.s. art Groves H.S., Birmingham, Mich., 1969-71; prof. art Ctr. for Creative Studies Coll. Art and Design, 1973—; studio artist, sculptor Pleasant Ridge, Mich., 1969—. One person shows include Xochipilli Gallery, Birmingham, Mich., 1988, 92, 95, Cranbrook Acad. Art Mus., Bloomfield Hills, Mich., 1994; exhibited in group shows Inst. Culture, Zacateca City, Zacateca, Mex., 1989, Detroit Inst. Arts, 1995, others. Assn. Ind. Colls. Art grantee, 1981, 83. Mem. Am. Crafts Coun., Surface Design Assn. Home: 51 Fairwood Pleasant Ridge MI 48069 Office: Ctr Creative Studies Coll Art and Design 201 E Kirby Detroit MI 48202

AASEN-HULL, AUDREY AVIS, music educator; b. Coquille, Oreg., July 9, 1916; d. John Lawrence and Orra Amy (Kelley) Aasen; m. James Byrne Hull, Sept. 15, 1962. BA, U. Oreg., 1939; MA, Stanford U., 1946. Music tchr. Monroe (Oreg.) H.S., 1939-40, Estacada (Oreg.) Union Sch., 1940-41; performer of solo violin program Sta. KOOS, Coos Bay, Oreg., 1941-43; supr. instrumental music San Francisco Pub. Schs., 1944-45; tchr. violin and piano Menlo Sch. & Coll., Menlo Park, Calif., 1947-48, Sacred Heart Convent Sch., Menlo Park, Calif., 1948-49. Performances of string quartets, trios, quintets and sextets for San Francisco Musical Club and Palo Alto Fortnightly Music Club, 1947-89; performed with People's Symphony, San Francisco, 1945, Calif. Mfrs. Assn., San Francisco, 1950, Palo Alto String quartet, 1958, String Orch. Televised Concert, Innsbruck, Austria, 1982, Queen Elizabeth Hall, Belgium, Internat. String Tchrs. Workshop, Brussels, 1984, and numerous others; soloist at Soroptimist Internat. Conv. for Am. Fedn. Soroptimist Clubs, Can., 1954; concertmistress Penisula Symphony, 1958-59. Adv. bd. mem. Calif. Summer Music at Pebble Beach, initiating mem., 1996—; patron San Francisco Symphony, underwriter violin chair position, 1989—. Recipient citation for Disting. Svc. USO, 1943-44, 45-46. Mem. Am. Fed. Musicians (life), Am. String Tchrs. Assn., Soroptimist Club (life), Fortnightly Music Club.

ABAJIAN, WENDY ELISSE, writer, producer, educator; b. Selma, Calif., Mar. 16, 1955; d. Mesik Nishon and Blanche Peggy (Emerzian) A. AA, Kings River Community Coll., 1975; BA, Calif. State U., Fresno, 1978; MS, U. So. Calif., 1981, EdD, 1986. Instr., tchr. various sch. dists., Burbank, Fresno & L.A., Calif., 1981—; free-lance writer various corps., Los Angeles area, 1984—; pres., ind. producer Abhawk Prodns., Inc., Long Beach, Calif., 1986-91; ind. writer/producer for TV, cable and video, 1991—; owner, pres. Gold Giraffe, 1995—; cons. multi-media projects. Contbr. articles to profl. jours. Active Rep. Nat. Com., Washington, 1983—, Statue of Liberty Ellis Island Found., 1984—, Women Appointees Coun., Sacramento, 1988-93, Burbank Ctr. for Retarded; gubernatorial appointee to adv. bd. Lanterman State Hosp., 1986-93; gubernatorial appointee to bd. dirs. Protection and Advocacy, Inc., 1990-93. Mem. Ednl. Grad. Orgn., Am. Film Inst., Farm Bur. Fedn., Film Adv. Bd., Nat. Com. Prevention Child Abuse, U.S. Com. for UN Devel. Fund for Women, World Affairs Coun. Armenian. Apostolic.

ABARBANELL, GAYOLA HAVENS, financial planner; b. Chgo., Oct. 21, 1939; d. Leonard Milton and Lillian Love (Leviten) Havens; m. Burton J. Abarbanell, June 1, 1965 (div. 1972); children: Jeffrey J. Reddick, Dena Reddick Lamb. Student, UCLA, 1975; student, San Joaquin Coll. Law, 1976-77. Cert. fin. planner; lic. real estate rep. Calif.; lic. life ins. broker, Calif., Wash., Nev., N.Y., Ill., S.C.; lic. securities broker. Postal clk. Van Nuys, Calif., 1966-69; regional mgr. Niagara Cyclo Massage, Fresno, Calif., 1969-72; owner, mgr. AD Enterprises, Fresno, 1970-72; agt., field supr. Equitable of Iowa, Fresno, 1972-73; rep. Ciba Pharms., Fresno, 1973-75; owner, operator Creativity Unltd., Fresno, 1975-76; registered fin. advisor Univ. Securities Corp., L.A., 1976-83, Fin. Network Investment Corp., L.A., 1983—; lectr. seminars for civic orgns.; mem. adv. bd. Fin. Network, Torrance, Calif., 1985-88. Co-author: Guidelines to Feminist Consciousness Raising, 1985. Mem. bus. adv. bd. of 2d careers. Recipient award Women in Ins., 1972. Mem. Bus. and Profl. Assn., L.A. Internat. Assn. Fin. Planners (bd. dirs. 1993-94), Inst. Cert. Fin. Planners, So. Calif. Socially Responsible Investment Profls., ACLU, NOW (nat. consciousness raising coord. 1975-76), Gay Acad. Union, Nat. Gay Task Force, Culver City C. of C., Internat. Assn. Fin. Planners, Social Investment Forum, Rotary (founding mem. L.A. Westside Sunrise Club sgt. at arms 1990-91, community svc. chair 1991-94, v.p. 1992-93, found. chair 1993-94). Democrat. Jewish. Home: 57124 Mono Wind Way North Fork CA 93643-9797 Office: Fin Network Investment Corp 5625 Green Valley Cir Apt 103 Culver City CA 90230-7120

ABATO, F. ROZANN, federal government administrator, nurse; b. Morrilton, Ark., Dec. 23, 1946; d. Vernon James Morris and Naomi Ruth (Williams) Hampton; m. Cosimo Carl Abato, May 28, 1983 (div. 1989). RN, Bapt. Hosp. Sch. Nursing, 1967. Hosp. staff nurse, 1967-68, surg. nurse for pvt. physicians, 1968-74, state health planning, 1974-76; program analyst Medicaid and Medicare Health Care Financing Adminstrn., Washington and Balt., 1976-81, staff dir. task force for regulatory relief, 1981-82, dir. Office Regulations Mgmt., 1982-86, dir. Office Exec. Ops., 1986-90, dep. dir. Medicaid bur., 1990-96, dir. office fin. and human resources, 1996—. Presbyterian. Home: 10 E Lee St Baltimore MD 21202-6003 Office: Health Care Financing Adminstrn 7500 Security Blvd Baltimore MD 21244

ABBEY, MARGARITA JAVELLANA, cardiology nurse; b. Iloilo, Philippines; came to U.S., 1970; d. Manuel Advincula Javellana and Cecilia Cumpaga Villalon; m. Francis Edmund Abbey, Mar. 26, 1977; children: Francis Manuel, Mark Edmund. Diploma, St. Paul Sch. Nursing, Iloilo, 1969; BSN, St. Paul Coll., Manila, 1970; MSN, Cath. U. Am., 1972. RN, D.C., Md., Mich.; cert. nurse practitioner, adult nurse practitioner, ACLS; cert. med.-surg. nursing ANCC. Staff nurse Sibley Meml. Hosp., Washington, 1972-73; staff nurse Washington Hosp. Ctr., 1973-77, staff nurse, cardiology, 1982-85, nurse clinician, cardiology, 1985-91; nurse practitioner, cardiology Washington Cardiology Ctr., 1991-93; nurse practitioner B-cardiology Washington Hosp. Ctr., 1993—. Author patient guides. Parent vol. St. Jerome's Sch., Hyattsville, Md., 1983-94. Mem. ANA, Am. Acad. Nurse Practitioners, Nurse Practitioners Assn. D.C. Roman Catholic. Home: 5805 Queens Chapel Rd Hyattsville MD 20782-3867 Office: Washington Hosp Ctr 110 Irving St NW Washington DC 20010-2931

ABBOTT, FRANCES ELIZABETH DOWDLE, journalist, civic worker; b. Rome, Ga., Mar. 21, 1924; d. John Wesley and Lucille Elizabeth (Field) Dowdle; m. Jackson Miles Abbott, May 15, 1948; children: Medora Frances, David Field, Elizabeth Stockton, Robert Jackson; m. Archibald W. Lyon, Oct. 15, 1993. Student, Draughon's Bus. Coll., Columbia, S.C.. Feature writer Mt. Vernon corr. Alexandria Gazette, Va., 1967-75; libr., rsch. assoc. Gadsby's Tavern Mus., Alexandria, 1977—. Chmn. ann. George Washington Birthnight Ball, Mt. Vernon, 1974-82; sec. George Washington 250th Birthday Celebration Commn., 1979-82; mem. steering com. Neighborhood Friends Hist. Mt. Vernon, 1988-92; chmn. publicity Waynewood Woman's Club, Waynewood Citizens Assn.; treas. Mt. Vernon Citizens Assn., 1967-82; dist. chmn. Mt. Vernon March of Dimes, 1960-62; sec. Waynewood Sch. PTA, 1962-64; tchr. 1st aid Girl Scouts U.S., 1964-65; den mother Cub Scouts, 1966; registrar DAR, 1968-77; chmn. publicity Mt. Vernon Women's Rep. Club, 1955. Named Mrs. Waynewood by Community Vote, 1969. Mem. Audubon Naturalist Soc., Nat. Trust Hist. Preservation. Episcopalian. Home: 9110 Belvoir Woods Pky # J-414 Fort Belvoir VA 22060-2716 Office: 134 N Royal St Alexandria VA 22314-3226

ABBOTT, MARY ELAINE, photographer, lecturer, researcher; b. LaGrange, Ill., Apr. 23, 1922; d. Vergil and Goldie (Wright) Schwarzkopf; m. Harry Edward Abbott, Oct. 8, 1949; children: John Edward, Jane Ann. BA in English, Psychology, U. Iowa, 1944. With child welfare dept. Montgomery County Children's Home, Dayton, Ohio, 1944-47, Mich. Children's Inst., Ann Arbor, 1947-49; photographer, lectr., researcher, 1978—; researcher, lectr. in field. Documentary photography for regional history books, mags., calendars and brochures; commd. Taft Sculpture, Sculpture Jackson County; artistic dir. James Agee's Knoxville, Summer, 1915 Potter Ctr., Jackson Hillsdale Coll., 1996; Claire Allen Architecture for Mich. State Hist. Soc.; commd. by Jackson Historic Dist. Commn. and State Hist. Soc., Mich. Dance Assn.; hist. dist. commn. advisor Dance for the Handicapped, Savs. and Loan "40 Doors", Amitech, Jackson Alliance of Businessmen; works hung in various exhbns. and juried shows; photographs in many pvt., pub. and bus. collections; permanent commissions: Ella Sharp Mus., Jackson Symphony, St. Paul's Episcopal Ch., Carnegie Libr., others. Mem. Jr. League, Jackson Chorale, Nat. Trust for Hist. Preservation; panel participant on creative process Ella Sharp Mus.; advisor Jackson Hist. Commn. Lorado Taft Scholarship; tchr. Gt. Books, U. Chgo.; participant in enrichment for advanced children, also others; participant Save Outdoor Sculpture for Nat. Inst. Conservation Cultural Property, Smithsonian Instn. Recipient photography award Our Town Exhibit, Ella Sharp Mus., Hist. Trinity Ch., Detroit, Cert. of Honor, Spl. Recognitions Excellence Luth. Ctr. Assn.; Lorado Taft scholar. Mem. Internat. Platform Assn. (mem. arts com., arts adv. bd., photography award, Juror's Choice in art exhibit, Inner Cir. Merit award 1993, 2d prize for photography 1994, 1st prize art show), Log Cabin Soc. Mich., Nat. Mus. Women in Arts, Arts Midwest, Kappa Alpha Theta. Republican. Episcopalian. Home and Office: 721 Oakridge Dr Jackson MI 49203-3914

ABBOTT, REBECCA PHILLIPS, museum director; b. Giessen, Germany, Jan. 10, 1950; d. Charles Leonard and Janet Alice (Praeger) Phillips. BA, Emory and Henry Coll., 1973; postgrad., Georgetown U., 1975, Am. U., 1982-88. Assoc. univ. registrar Am. U., Washington, 1977-81, assoc. dir. adminstrv. computing, 1981-84, dir. adminstrv. computing, 1984-88; dir. membership Nat. Mus. of Women in the Arts, Washington, 1988-89, dir., 1989—; fine arts photographer. Photographs exhibited in numerous solo and group exhbns., 1988—. Mem. Am. Assn. Mus., Mid-Atlantic Assn. Mus. Office: National Museum of Women in Arts 1250 New York Ave NW Washington DC 20005-3920

ABBOTT, REGINA A., neurodiagnostic technologist, consultant, business owner; b. Haverhill, Mass., Mar. 5, 1950; d. Frank A. and Ann (Drelick) A. Student, Pierce Bus. Sch., Boston, 1967-70, Seizure Unit Children's Hosp. Med. Ctr. Sch. EEG Tech., Boston, 1970-71. Registered technologist. Tech. dir. electrodiagnostic labs. Salem Hosp., 1972-76; lab. dir. clin. neurophysiology Tufts U. New Eng. Med. Ctr., Boston, 1976-78; clin. instr. EEG program Laboure Coll., Boston, 1977-81; adminstrv. dir. dept. Neurology Mt. Auburn Hosp., Cambridge, Mass., 1978-81; tech. dir. clin. neurophysiology Drs. Diagnostic Service, Virginia Beach, Va.; tech. dir. neurodiagnostic ctr. Portsmouth Psychiatric Ctr., 1981-87; founder, pres., owner Commonwealth Neurodiagnostic Services, Inc., 1986—; co-dir. continuing edn. program EEG Tech., Boston, 1977-78; mem. adv. com. sch. neurodiagnostic tech. Laboure Coll., 1977-81, Sch. EEG Tech. Children's Hosp. Med. Ctr., Boston, 1980-81; assoc. examiner Am. Bd. Registration of Electroencephalographic Technologists, 1977-83; mem. guest faculty Oxford Medilog Co., 1986; cons. Nihon Kohden Am., 1981-83; cons., educator Teca Corp., Pleasantville, N.Y., 1981-87; allied health profl. staff mem. Virginia Beach Gen. Hosp., Humana Hosp. Bayside, Virginia Beach; clin. evaluator Calif. Coll. for Health Scis., 1995—. Contbr. articles to profl. jours. EIL scholar, Poland/USSR, 1970; recipient Internat. Woman of Yr. award in bus. and sci. Internat. Biographical Ctr., London, 1993-94, Woman of Yr. award Am. Biographical Inst., 1993. Mem. NAFE, Am. Soc. Electroneurodiagnostic Technologists, New Eng. Soc. EEG Technologists (bd. dirs., sec., tng. and edn. com., faculty tng. and edn.), Am. Assn. Electrodiagnostic Technologists, Epilepsy Soc. Mass. Office: Commonwealth Neurodiagnostic Svcs Inc 400 Biltmore Ct Virginia Beach VA 23454-3459

ABBOTT, SUSAN ALICIA, elementary education educator; b. Easton, Pa., July 8, 1947; d. Solomon and Edith Mae (Cooper) Bergstein; m. William Walter Wood, Aug. 28, 1971 (div. Mar. 1976); m. Karl Richard Abbott, Feb. 19, 1977 (div.); 1 child, Tracie Ellen. BA in Psychology, Pa. State U., 1969; MS in Edn., Nazareth Coll. of Rochester, N.Y., 1976. Cert. nursery/elem. and spl. edn. tchr., N.Y. Tchr. Penn Yan (N.Y.) Cen. Schs., 1970; learning disabilities tchr. Wayne-Finger Lakes Bd. Coop. Schs., Stanley, N.Y., 1970-79; spl. edn. tchr. Victor (N.Y.) Cen. Schs., 1979—; tchr. rep. com. on handicapped Com. Spl. Edn., Victor, 1987-91, coord. grades 4-6, 1991-94, chmn. grades 5-6, 1991-93. Bd. dirs. Genesee Valley Orch. and Chorus, 1994-96, Sta. WXXI, pub. TV, Rochester, 1978—; leader Girl Scouts Am., Fairport, N.Y., 1987-90; chmn. publicity program Seneca Zool. Soc., Rochester, 1974-77, bd. dirs., 1975-78, mem. 1982—; supt. ch. sch., asst. supt. Sunday sch. Ref. Ch. Women, 1990-94; mem. Trinity Reformed Ch., 1990—. Mem. ASCD, Coun. for Exceptional Children (divsn. learning disabilities), Am. Fedn. Tchrs., Nature Conservancy, Whale Adoption Project, Internat. Assn. Children and Adults with Learning Disabilities, N.Y. State Assn. Learning Disabilities, N.Y. State United Tchrs., Monroe County Learning Disabilities Assn., Greenpeace, Rochester Mus. Sci. Ctr., Pa. State U. Alumni Assn., Habitat for Humanity, Fairport PTSA, Nat. Coun. Tchrs. Math., Victor Tchrs. Assn., Psi Chi. Home: 58 Alina St Fairport NY 14450-2843 Office: Victor Cen Schs 953 High St Victor NY 14564-1168

ABDELLAH, FAYE GLENN, retired public health service executive; b. N.Y.C., Mar. 13; d. H.B. and Margaret (Glenn) A. BS in Teaching, Columbia U., 1945, MA in Teaching, 1947, EdD, 1955; LLD (hon.), Case Western Res. U., 1967, Rutgers U., 1973; DSc (hon.), U. Akron, 1978, Cath. U. Am., 1981, Monmouth Coll., 1982, Ea. Mich U., 1987, U. Bridgeport, 1987, Georgetown U., 1989; D Pub. Svc. (hon.), Am. U., 1987; LHD (hon.), Georgetown U., 1989, U. S.C., 1991; D Pub. Svc., U. S.C., 1991. RN. Commd. officer USPHS, Rockville, Md., 1949, advanced through grades to rear adm., 1970, asst. surgeon gen., chief nurse officer, 1970-87, dep. surgeon gen., 1981-89, chief nursing edn. br., div. nursing, 1949-59; surgeon gen. USPHS, 1989; chief rsch. grants br. Bur. Health Manpower Edn., NIH, HEW, Rockville, 1959-69; dir. Office Rsch. Tng. Nat. Ctr. for Health Svcs. R & D, Health Svcs. Mental Health Adminstrn., Rockville, 1969; acting dep. dir. Nat. Ctr. for Health Svcs. R & D, Rockville, 1971, Bur. Health Svcs. Rsch. and Evaluation, Health Resources Adminstrn., Rockville, 1973; dir. Office Long-Term Care, Office Asst. Sec. for Health, HEW, Rockville, 1973-80; exec. dir. grad. sch. nursing uniformed svcs., dean, prof. U. Health Scis., Bethesda, Md., 1993—; exec. dir., acting dean; prof. nursing, Emily Smith chair U. S.C., Columbia, 1990-91; dean, prof. Grad. Sch. Nursing, Uniformed Srvs. U. Health Scis., 1993—. Author: Effect of Nurse Staffing on Satisfactions with Nursing Care, 1959, Patient Centered Approaches to Nursing, 1960, Better Patient Care Through Nursing Research, 1965, 2d edit., 1979, 3d edit., 1986, Intensive Care, Concepts and Practices for Clinical Nurse Specialists, 1969, New Directions in Patient Centered Nursing, 1972, Preparing Nursing Research for the 21st Century, 1994; contbr. articles to profl. jours. Recipient Mary Adelaide Nutting award, 1983, hon. recognition ANA, 1986, Oustanding Leadership award U. Pa., 1987, 99, Disting. Svc. award, 1973-89, Surgeon Gen.'s medal and medallion, 1989, Allied-Signal Achievement award in aging, 1989, Gustav O. Lienhard award Inst. Medicine, NAS, 1992. Fellow Am. Acad. Nursing (charter, past v.p., pres.); mem. Am. Psychol. Assn., AAAS, Assn. Mil. Surgeons U.S., Sigma Theta Tau (Disting. Rsch. Fellow award 1989), Phi Lambda Theta. Home: 3713 Chanel Rd Annandale VA 22003-2024

ABDOLALI, NASRIN, political scientist, educator; b. Tehran, Iran, June 28, 1957; came to U.S., 1983; d. Nematollah and Molouk Akram (Miraftab) A. BA in Polit. Sci., Tehran U., Iran, 1978; MA in Politics, NYU, 1986, PhD in Polit. Sci., 1990. Dir. devel. project. Simin Lang. Inst., Tehran, Iran, 1978-81; legal advisor Bur. D'Etude d'Avocat, Tehran, Iran, 1981-83; asst. prof. NYU, N.Y.C., 1989-92; analytical svcs. exec. Nielsen Mktg. Rsch., Wilton, Conn., 1992-93; analytical svcs. mgr. Nielsen Mktg. Rsch., N.Y.C.,

1993, analytical svcs. sr. mgr., 1994; asst. prof. C.W. Post Coll., Long Island U., 1994—; cons. Office for Internat. Students and Scholars NYU, 1995—; cons. Office for Internat. students and scholars NYU, 1995—. Recipient Grad. Studies award Pahlavi Found. Iran, 1978, Penfield Dissertation grant NYU, 1988, Best Paper award N.E. Polit. Sci. Assn., 1988, GFUSA Productivity award Kraft Gen. Foods, 1993. Mem. Am. Polit. Sci. Assn., Internat. Studies Assn., Asia Soc., Phi Eta Sigma (hon.). Home: 1 Washington Sq Village Apt 11R New York NY 10012-1608 Office: Long Island U CW Post Coll Dept Polit Sci/Internat Studies Brookville NY 11548

ABDUL, CORINNA GAY, software engineer, consultant; b. Honolulu, Aug. 10, 1961; d. Daniel Lawrence and Katherine Yoshie (Kanada) A. BS in Computer Sci., U. Hawaii, 1984. Programmer, analyst, adminstrv. and fiscal svcs. U. Hawaii, Honolulu, 1982-84, software engr. libr. of divsn. of planetary geoscis., 1984; sys. software engr. II dept. space and tech. group TRW Inc., Redondo Beach, Calif., 1985-89; systems software engr. II, Sierra On-Line, Inc., Oakhurst, Calif., 1989-90; sr. programmer, analyst Decision Rsch. Corp., Honolulu, 1990-92; ind. computer cons. Honolulu, 1992-94; computer cons. Wailuku, Hawaii, 1994—. Recipient The 20th Century award for achievement, 1994. Home: 856 W Kaena Pl Wailuku HI 96793-9620

ABEL, ANNE ELIZABETH SUTHERLAND, pediatrician; b. Milw., June 16, 1945; d. David Hollingsworth and Mildred June (Nees) Sutherland; m. Francis Lee Abel; 1 child, Jonathan Earl. BA, Pasadena Coll., 1967; MS, Ind. U., Indpls., 1969, MD, 1973. Diplomate Am. Bd. Pediatrics. Resident in pediat. Meth. Hosp., Indpls., 1973-75, Richland Meml. Hosp., Columbia, S.C., 1975-76; pediatrician Moncrief Army Hosp., Ft. Jackson, S.C., 1976-80; child and adolescent psychiatry fellow William S. Hall Psychiat. Inst., Columbia, 1981, 82-83, U. B.C.-Vancouver Gen. Hosp., 1982; pvt. practice Columbia, S.C., 1983—; pediatrician Children's Rehabilitative Svcs., Orangeburg, S.C., 1984-91, 92—; chief med. sect. Columbia Area Mental Health Ctr., 1987-92; assoc. prof. neuropsychiatry, behavioral sci. and pediats. Sch. Medicine U. S.C., Columbia, 1992-95, clin. assoc. prof. neuropsychiatry, behavioral sci. and pediats. Sch. Medicine, 1995—; cons. behavioral pediatrics Epworth Children's Home, Columbia, 1983-86, 90—; mem. med. adv. com., children's health rehabilitative svcs. S.C. Dept. Health & Environ. Control, Columbia, 1986-92, mem. maternal and child health adv. com., 1989-91; behavioral/devel. pediatrician Orangeburg Health Dept., 1994—. Contbr. articles to profl. jours. Mem. S.C. Gov.'s Youth Unemployment Coun., Columbia, 1987. Recipient Alumni award Pasadena Coll., 1977, Vol. of Yr. award Mayor's Com. Employment Handicapped, 1988; grantee Ctr. Family Soc., U. S.C., 1993—. Fellow Am. Acad. Pediatrics; mem. AMA, Am. Acad. Cerebral Palsy and Devel. Medicine, Am. Profl. Soc. on Abuse of Children, S.C. Med. Assn., S.C. Pediatric Soc., Columbia Med. Soc. Office: 1 Harbison Way Ste 108 Columbia SC 29212-3408

ABEL, ELIZABETH A., dermatologist; b. Hartford, Conn., Mar. 16, 1940; d. Frederick A. and Rose (Borovicka) A.; m. Barton Lane; children: Barton, Geoffrey, Suzanne. Student, Colby-Sawyer Coll., 1957-60; BS, Wash. Hosp. Ctr. Sch. Med. Tech., 1961, U. Md., 1965; MD cum laude, U. Md., 1967. Diplomate Am. Bd. Dermatology. Intern San Francisco Gen. Hosp., 1967-68; resident in medicine, fellow in oncology U. Calif. Med. Ctr., San Francisco, 1968-69; resident in dermatology NYU Med. Ctr., 1969-72, chief resident, 1971-72, USPHS research trainee in dermatology, 1972-73; dep. chief dept. dermatology USPHS Hosp., S.I., N.Y., 1973-74; instr. clin. dermatology Columbia U. Coll. Physicians and Surgeons, N.Y.C., 1974-75; instr. clin. dermatology Stanford (Calif.) U. Sch. Medicine, 1975-77, clin. asst. prof. dermatology, 1977-82, asst. prof. dermatology, 1982-90, clin. assoc. prof., 1990—; asst. editor Jour. Am. Acad. Dermatology; mem. med. adv. bd. The Nat. Psoriasis Found. Contbr. articles to sci. jours. Mellon Found. fellow, 1983, 87. Fellow Am. Acad. Dermatology; mem. N.Am. Clin. Dermatologic Soc., Soc. Investigative Dermatology, San Francisco Dermatologic Soc., Internat. Soc. Dermatology Surgery, Dermatology Found., Pacific Dermatologic Assn., Women's Dermatologic Soc., Noah Worcester Dermatologic Soc., Alpha Omega Alpha. Episcopalian. Office: 525 South Dr Ste 115 Mountain View CA 94040-4211

ABEL, MARY, state legislator; m. Richard Abel; 1 child, Jason. BS, MSJ, Ohio U. Mem. Ohio Ho. of Reps., 1989—. Mem. adv. coun. exec. programs Capitol U.; bd. dirs. Big Bros.-Big Sisters. Mem. AAUW, LWV, Inst. Local Govt. Adminstrn. and Rural Devel. (mem. adv. com.), Delta Kappa Gamma. Democrat. Home: PO Box 113 Athens OH 45701-1480 Office: OH Ho of Reps State House Columbus OH 43215

ABEL, MARY ELLEN KATHRYN, quality control executive, chemist; b. Cleve., Nov. 3, 1949; d. Arthur L. and Dorothy Virginia (DeLura) Jaklic; m. Burton E. Abel, June 22, 1990; 2 stepchildren: Stephanie, Russell E.; 1 child, Matthew Anthony. A.A. with honors Lakeland Community Coll., 1985, BS in Chem. magna cum laude, Lake Erie Coll., Painesville, Ohio, 1991. Lab technician W.S. Tyler, Inc., Cleve., 1969-71, C-E Tyler, Cleve., 1974-76; quality control mgr., environ. coord, Morton Salt, Painesville, Ohio, 1977—. Treas. com. mem. Boy Scouts Am., 1988-90, sr. mem. explorer scouts marksmanship post, 1987-90, sec. local com., 1987-90; mem. Lake County Indsl. Community Awareness Emergency Response Adv. Panel, 1987-90. Mem. NAFE, Am. Chem. Soc, Gold Wing Road Riders Assn. Republican. Roman Catholic. Avocations: traveling, photography, tutoring math. Home: 391 Manhattan Pky Painesville OH 44077-5024 Office: Morton Salt Divsn Morton Internat Inc PO Box 428 Grand River OH 44045-0428

ABELL, JAN MARY, architect; b. Chgo.; d. Philip and Dolores (Krumdick) Meisterheim. BArch, Ohio U., 1969. Registered architect, N.Y., Fla. Architect apprentice Verster, Djikstra, Cannegieter, Amsterdam, The Netherlands, 1970-72, Stevens, Bertin, O'Connell, Rochester, N.Y., 1972-76; architect McElvy, Jennewein Stefany, Howard, Tampa, Fla., 1976-79; prin., owner Abell Garcia Partnership Architects, Tampa, 1980—; adj. faculty mem. U. South Fla., Tampa, 1989-96; Beinecke Reeves disting. chair in archtl. preservation U. Fla., 1995-97. Prin. works include B.C. Graham Elem. Sch. (Outstanding Preservation Project award), restoration of St. Paul AME Ch., Leiman Wilson House (Gt. Am. Home award Nat. Trust for Hist. Preservation, Outstanding Preservation Project award Hillsborough County Planning Commn.), Edson Keith Estate, Sarasota, Fla. (Fla. Preservation award), Founder's House, Koreshan State Hist. Park, Estero, Fla. (Outsanding award for Restoration, Fla. Trust for Hist. Preservation); exhbns. include Women in Arch., Washington, 1987, Fla./Caribbean Arch., San Juan, P.R. Recipient numerous awards for arch., 1979—, Women of Achievement award Bus. and Profl. Women's Assn., 1982, Fla. Trust award, 1995, Design award Writer's Studio, 1995. Fellow AIA (juror Broward County chpt. Honor awards 1990, Nat. AIA Honor awards 1993, Nat. Com. on Design co-chmn. publs., Medal of Honor Fla. Cen. chpt. 1990), AIA Fla. Assn. (Comty. Svc. award 1979). Office: Abell Garcia Architects 2201 W Dekle Ave Tampa FL 33606-3118

ABELL, MARY ELLEN, art history educator; b. Dayton, Ohio, Nov. 2, 1949; d. George Haigh and Cindorella (Miller) A.; m. Carmen Louis Cicero, July 29, 1995. BA, Miami U., Oxford, Ohio, 1978; MA, NYU, 1991. Asst. conf. mgr. ARTnews mag., N.Y.C., 1982-84; dir. Art Views Lecture Bur., N.Y.C., 1984-87; dir. Long Point Gallery, Provincetown, Mass., 1987-94, cons., 1995; adj. lectr. Dowling Coll., Oakdale, N.Y., 1991-94, instr. visual arts, 1994—. Contbr. articles to profl. jours. Scholar and fellow CUNY Grad. Ctr., 1994. Home: 268 Bowery New York NY 10012 Office: Dowling Coll Oakdale NY 11769

ABELLA, MARISELA CARLOTA, business executive; b. Havana, Cuba, Feb. 5, 1943; d. Carlos and Angela (Acosta) A.; m. Alberto Herrera Nogueira, Apr. 6, 1968 (div. Apr. 1986); 1 child, Carlos Alberto Herrera Abella. Asst. to v.p. and gen. mgr. bonding dept. Manuel San Juan (P.R.) Co. Inc., 1962-64; asst. corp. sec. and exec. sec. to pres. and stockholder Interstate Gen. Corp., Hato Rey, P.R., 1964-72, corp. sec. and pvt. sec. to corp. pres., 1972-79; sec.-treas., dir. A. H. Enterprises Inc., Caparra Heights, P.R., 1979-86; v.p., sec., bd. dirs. El Viajero Inc.; bd. dirs. A. H. Enterprises Inc., San Juan; pres. Marisela Abella Mktg. and Selling Promotional Items and Ideas, Caparra Heights, 1986—. Roman Catholic. Clubs: Caribe Hilton Swimming and Tennis, Barry U. Alumnae Assn. Home: 909 Borinquen Towers 2 Caparra Heights PR 00920 Office: PO Box 10510 Caparra Heights San Juan PR 00922-0510

ABER, ITA, curator, artist; b. Montreal, Que., Can., Mar. 27, 1932; arrived in U.S., 1954; d. Tudick and Fannie (Zabitsky) Hershcovich; m. M. Joshua Aber, Dec. 8, 1954; children: Mindy Ann Barad, Judah David, Harry Asher. Cert. textile honors, Valentine Mus., Richmond, Va., 1975; BA in Cultural Studies, Empire State Coll., 1982. Asst. curator history Hudson River Mus., Yonkers, N.Y., 1969-70; asst. curator textiles The Jewish Mus., N.Y.C., 1971; guest curator Yeshiva U. Mus., N.Y.C., 1976-77, 82, Jewish Comty. Centennial, Mpls., 1983; curator of collection Park Ave. Synagogue, N.Y.C., 1983—; curator Hebrew Home for Aged, Riverdale, N.Y., 1989-93; bd. dirs. Pomegranate Guild, L.A., Judaica Mus., Riverdale; chair ethnography Am. Friends Israel Mus., N.Y.C., 1980—; N.Am. rep. Ctr. for Jewish Art, Jerusalem, 1983-93. Author: The Art of Judaic Needlework, 1979; contbr. articles to art publs. and mus. catalogs. Bd. dirs. Landmarks Bd., Yonkers, N.Y., 1991-94; mem. mayor's adv. commn. Housing Bd., Yonkers, 1988-90; mem. design com. Low Cost Housing, Yonkers, 1989. Mem. Am. Inst. for Cons., N.Y. Artists Equity, Internat. Soc. for Jewish Art (bd. dirs.), Women's Caucus for Art, Fiber Artists with Nerve, West Side Arts Coalition (N.Y.C.). Home: # 3GE 11 Riverside Dr New York NY 10023 Office: Ita Aber Co 20 W 72d St New York NY 10023

ABERCROMBIE, CHARLOTTE MANNING, reading specialist, supervisor; b. Swampscott, Mass., Oct. 25, 1915; d. Fredric Wilbur and Mary Sayer (Delano) Manning; m. Alexander Vaughan Abercrombie, Oct. 17, 1937; children: Lois A. Street, Paul M., David M., Lucia A. Harvilchuck. BA, Marietta Coll., 1937; MA, Columbia U., 1974, EdD, 1976. Cert. tchr. R.I., Wash., Wis., N.J.; cert. reading specialist, supr. N.J. Tchr. elem. schs. Tacoma (Wash.) Pub. Schs., 1958-62, Warwick (R.I.) Pub. Schs., 1957; tchr., reading specialist Milw. Pub. Schs., 1966-69; elem. tchr. and reading specialist, supr. East Orange (N.J.) Pub. Schs., 1969-79; dir. Fla. Ctr. for Philosophy for Children, Pensacola, 1994—. Mem. Nat. Assn. Congregational Chs. (exec. com. 1980-84). Mem. AAUW (v.p. Marco Island, Fla. chpt. 1988-89, bd. dirs. State of Fla. 1990, bd. dirs. Pensacola br. Coll. Univ., 1992). Repulican. Home: 10100 Hillview Rd Apt 616 Pensacola FL 32514-5460

ABERNATHY, SUE EURY, physical education educator; b. Washington, N.C., July 28, 1947; d. Craig Stanford and Lelia Frances (McHarney) Eury; m. Dean Judson Abernathy Jr., Dec. 27, 1970; children: Kristan Joanna, Dean Judson III. BS in Health and Phys. Edn., Campbell U., 1969; MA in Tchg., U. N.C., 1970; DA in Phys. Edn., Middle Tenn. State U., 1995. Cert. tchr. Tchr. Lee County Schs., Lemon Springs, N.C., 1970-71, Weatherford County Schs., Reno, Tex., 1971-73, Prince George's County Schs., Suitland, Md., 1973-75, Duval County Schs., Jacksonville, Fla., 1975-84, Akiva Sch., Nashville, 1984-92, Metro Nashville (Tenn.) Schs., Lakeview Elem Sch., 1992—; 4th degree black belt World Tae Kwon Do Fedn., Seoul, Korea, 1987—; writer Tenn. Elem. Tae Kwon Do curriculum, 1993; mem. adv. team Lakeview Elem. Sch., 1993-94; presenter in field. Youth dir., tchr. Brentwood (Tenn.) Bapt. Sunday Sch., 1984—; active tchg. mission trip Brentwood Bapt. Ch., Scotland, 1990, 92. Recipient Mayor's Acts of Excellence award Mayor of Nashville, 1994, 95, Tchr. award grant Hosp. Corp. Am., 1994, Eskind Ednl. grant, 1995, 96, Am. South Excellence in Edn. grant, 1995, Letter of Commendation, World Tae Kwon Do Fedn., 1994. Mem. AAHPERD (presenter so. dist. 1994-95, sec. hist. coun. 1995-96), Tenn. AHPERD (presenter 1994, 95, 96), N.Am. Assn. Sport History, All-Am. Scholar, Phi Epsilon Kappa, Kappa Delta Pi, Phi Kappa Phi. Home: 1020 Highland Rd Brentwood TN 37027-5528

ABERNATHY, VICKI MARIE, nurse; b. L.A., Feb. 14, 1949; d. James David and Margaret Helen (Quider) Abernathy; m. Dirk Klaus Ernst Wiese, Aug. 15, 1968 (div. 1973); 1 child, Zoe Erde. Student, U. Calif., Riverside, 1966-67, L.A. City Coll., 1968-69; AA in Nursing, Riverside City Coll., 1971-74. RN, Calif.; cert. med.-surg. nurse; cert. ACLS. Staff nurse Riverside (Calif.) County Hosp., 1974, Oceanside (Calif.) Community Hosp., 1974-76; with Scripps Hosp., Encinitas, Calif., 1976—, ambulatory surgery unit and endoscopy coord., 1981-94, staff nurse short stay unit, 1994—. Mem. ACLU, Calif. Nurses Assn., San Diego Zool. Soc., San Elijo Lagoon Conservancy. Democrat.

ABERNETHY, ANN LAWSON, retired elementary education educator; b. Pa., July 19, 1937; d. Samuel Chrisman Abernethy and Josephine Crozer Ludlow II. BS in Edn., SUNY, Oneonta, 1959. Cert. early childhood tchr., N.Y. Tchr. grade 1 Mineola (N.Y.) Sch. Dist., 1959-93, primary dir. summer recreation program, 1954-64, winter recreation dir., 1967, dir. sci. curriculum writing, 1972; strategic plan writer, 1990-91; chair grade level Mineola (N.Y.) Sch. Dist., 1985-93; substitute tchr., 1993-94, ret.,, 1993—. Staff liaison PTA, 1980-93; sec. Northville Beach Civic Assn., 1982—; sec. bd. elders Cmty. Ch. of East Williston, chair mem. personnel and relationships com. Recipient Jenkins Meml. award. Mem. N.Y. State United Tchrs. (del. rep.), Mineola Tchrs. Assn. (bldg. rep., co-chmn. assn. ret. staff 1993—). Home: 371 Feather Ln East Williston NY 11596-2545

ABERNETHY, IRENE MARGARET, county official; b. Ord, Nebr., Mar. 28, 1924; d. Glen Dayton and Margaret Lillian (Jones) Auble; m. Don R. Abernethy, Aug. 8, 1954 (dec. Nov. 1980); children: Jill Adele Abernethy Johnson, Ted Verne. BA cum laude, Hastings Coll., 1946; postgrad., U. Nebr., 1950-53. Tchr. Ord High Sch., 1946-50, Scottsbluff (Nebr.) High Sch., 1950-55, Grand Island (Nebr.) Sr. High Sch., 1961-62; mem. Hall County Bd. Suprs., Grand Island, 1979—, chair, 1984, 95. Vice chair Hall County Rep. Ctrl. Com., Grand Island, 1971-73; chair campaign Congresswoman Virginia Smith for Hall County, 1974-80; sr. v.p. Nebr. Rep. Founders Day, Lincoln, 1981; chair Gov.'s Juv. Justice Adv. Group, Lincoln, 1981-91; mem. Nebr. Commn. on Law Enforcement and Criminal Justice, Lincoln, 1970-91; mem. Nebr. Commn. on Local Govt. Innovation and Restructuring; bd. dirs. Head Start, 1979—, Hall County Leadership Tomorrow, 1990-94, Indsl. Found., 1991, College Park, 1991—, Community Help Ctr., 1991—, Family Violence Coalition, 1993—, Midland Area Agy. on Aging, 1993-95; adv. com. Region III Mental Health Adv. Bd.; active Nat. Coalition State Juvenile Justice Adv. Groups, 1988-91, Partners in Community Planning, 1994—, Grand Island Area Edn. 2000; mem. task force on needs Heartland United Way. Named Woman of Yr., Grand Island Independent, 1980, Bus. and Profl. Woman, Grand Island, 1980, Beta Sigma Phi, 1982, Nebr. chpt. NASW, 1983; recipient Svc. to Mankind award Sertoma, 1994, recognition award PTA, 1988, Outstanding Cmty. Svc. award Rotary, 1985, Cmty. Leadership award Ak-Sar-Ben, 1995, Outstanding Alumni award Hastings Coll., 1996. Mem. LWV (local pres. 1962-64, state bd. dirs. 1965-69), AAUW (local pres. 1966-68, state bd. dirs. 1970-71), YWCA (local pres. 1974-75, Woman of Distinction award 1988). Republican. Methodist. Home: 707 S Blaine St Grand Island NE 68803-6146 Office: Hall County Adminstrn 121 S Pine St Grand Island NE 68801-6076

ABERT, AMBER CHRISTINE, home remodeling contractor; b. East Alton, Ill., Sept. 15, 1969; d. Jerry Lee Abert and Bette Lee (Gause) Schenk. AS in Radio Broadcasting, Lewis & Clark C.C., Godfrey, Ill., 1990; B in Gen. Studies, S.E. Mo. State U., 1992. V.p. sales Jerry Abert Siding & Window Co., East Alton, Ill., 1990—. Mem. NAFE, Jr. League of Greater Alton (pub. rels. chair, 1994-96), Nat. Auctioneer Assn., Ill. State Auctioneer Assn. Office: Jerry Abert Siding & Window 631 Broadway East Alton IL 62024

ABID, ANN B., art librarian; b. St. Louis, Mar. 17, 1942; d. Clarence Frederick and Luella (Niehaus) Bartelsmeyer; m. Amor Abid (div. 1969); children: Rod, Kady; m. Cleon R. Yohe, Aug. 10, 1974 (div.); m. Roldo S. Bartimole, Feb. 1, 1991. Cert. in Librarianship, Washington U., St. Louis, 1976. Asst. to libr. St. Louis Art Mus., 1963-68, libr., 1968-85; head libr. Cleve. Mus. Art, 1985—; vis. com. univ. librs. Case We. Res.U., 1987-90, co-chairperson, 1990. Co-author: Documents of Surrealism, 1918-1942, 1981; contbr. articles to profl. jours. Grantee Mo. Coun. Arts, 1978, Mo. Com. Humanities, 1980, Nat. Hist. Pubs. and Records Commn., 1981, Reinberger Found., 1987, Japan Found., 1996. Mem. ALA, Art Librs. Soc. N. Am. (Ohio and nat. chpts. chairperson Mus.-Type-of-Libr. group 1979-81, chair New Orleans 1980, nominating com. 1980, 84, Wittenborn awards com. 1981, 90, v.p., pres. elect 1987-88, pres. 1988-89, past pres. 1989-90, chairperson N. Am. art libr. resources com. 1991-93, search com. new exec. dir. 1993-94. chair fin. adv. com. 1996—, presenter numerous papers), Soc. Am. Archivists, Midwest Mus. Conf. (co-chairperson program com. ann. meeting 1982), Spl. Librs. Assn. (shares exec. group, rsch. librs. group). Office: Cleve Mus of Art 11150 East Blvd Cleveland OH 44106-1711

ABISH, CECILE, artist; b. N.Y.C.; m. Walter Abish. B.F.A., Bklyn. Coll., 1953. Instr. art Queens Coll.; vis. artist U. Mass, Amherst, Cooper Union, Harvard U. Solo exhbns. include Newark Coll. Engring., 1968, Inst. Contemporary Art, Boston, 1974, U. Md., 1975, Alessandra Gallery, N.Y.C., 1977, Wright State U., Dayton, Ohio, 1978, Carpenter Ctr., Cambridge, Mass., 1979, Anderson Gallery, Va. Commonwealth U., Richmond, 1981, SUNY-Stony Brook, 1982, Ctr. for Creative Photography, Tucson, 1984, Books & Co., N.Y.C., 1996; group exhbns.: Detroit Inst. Art, 1969, Aldrich Mus. Art, 1971, 10 Bleecker St., N.Y.C., 1972, Lakeview Ctr. Arts, Peoria, Ill., 1972, Bykert Gallery, N.Y.C., 1971-74, Michael Walls Gallery, N.Y.C., 1975, Fine Arts Bldg. Gallery, N.Y.C., 1976, Mus. Modern Art, N.Y.C., 1976, Hudson River Mus., 1979, Atlanta Arts Festival, 1980, New Mus., N.Y.C., 1980, 81, Kuntsgebaude, Stuttgart, Fed. Republic Germany, 1981, Long Beach (Calif.) Mus., 1983, Edith C. Blum Art Inst., Bard Coll., Annandale-on-Hudson, N.Y., 1984, Mus. Modern Kunst, Vienna, Austria, 1985, U. R.I., Kingston, 1985, Art Defense Galleries, Paris, 1993, Architektur Zentrum, Vienna, 1993, Artists Space, N.Y.C., 1994, Islip Art Mus., N.Y., 1995; numerous commns.; represented in permanent collections; published photo works: Firsthand, 1978, Chinese Crossing, 1986, 99: The New Meaning, 1990. Nat. Endowment Arts fellow, 1975, 77, 80; CAPS fellow, 1975. Mem. Coll. Art Assn. Office: Cooper Station 4th Ave PO Box 485 New York NY 10276-5204

ABLES, NANCY BUMSTEAD, sales executive; b. Galesburg, Ill., Mar. 9, 1948; d. Charles Heath Bumstead and Thelma Delta (Hughes) McDonald; m. Laurence Clifton Greenwold, June 4, 1966 (div. Feb. 1987); children: Laurie J. Greenwold Campos, Charles Howard Greenwold; m. David Stephen Ables, Mar. 15, 1987. With, Knox Coll., 1965-69. Assembler printed circuit bd. Astro Internat. Corp., League City, Tex., 1987, spare parts sales mgr., 1987-95, parts cons., 1995-96; edn. coord. Astro Internat. Corp., League City, 1996—; printed cir. bd. assembler Gadget Electronics, Pasadena, Tex., 1986—; v.p. Gadget Electronics, Pasadena, 1987—; cons. parts bus., Houston, 1995—. Chmn. Environ. Commn., Park Forest South, Ill., 1971-74; v.p. Balmoral Elem. P.T.O., Crete, Ill., 1980-81, pres., 1981-83; campaign mgr. J. Gustafson Sch. Bd. mem., Crete, 1980. Home: 9800 Hollock St Apt 1009 Houston TX 77075-1833 Office: Earth Found 5151 Mitchelldale Houston TX 77092

ABLOW, ROSELYN KAROL, painter, curator; b. Allentown, Pa.. BA, Bennington Coll., 1954; student, Boston U. Instr. Bunting Inst., 1988, Newton Arts Ctr., Mass., 1989-92, New Arts Ctr., Newtown, Mass., 1993-95; curator New Arts Ctr., Newton, Mass., 1994. Exhbns. include Smithsonian Traveling Exhbn., 1978-80, Fitchburg Art Mus., 1988, The Bunting Inst., Radcliffe Coll., 1988, David Brown Gallery, Provincetown, Mass., 1988, Gallery 30, Burlingame, Calif., 1993, New Art Ctr., Newton, Mass., 1994, others; represented in permanent collections Mobil Corp., Chemical Bank, N.Y., New Eng. Mutual Life Ins. Co., Boston, Conn. Gen. Life, Hartford, Sears, Roebuck & Co., Chgo., Broadway Crown Plaza Hotel, N.Y. Bunting Inst. fellow Radcliffe Coll., 1988; grantee Mass. Arts Lottery Coun., 1990-91. •

ABRAHAM, HILARY LISA, professional association administrator; b. Chgo., Mar. 21, 1971; d. Henry David and Susan Leslie (Spinner) A. BA, U. Wisc., 1993. Mid-atlantic regional dir. Nurses Strategic Action Team Am. Nurses Assn., Washington, 1993-94; western regional dir. Nurses Strategic Action Team Am. Nurses Assn., Portland, Oreg., 1994-95; health policy coord. Oreg. Nurses Assn., Portland, 1995—; orgnl. liaison Health Svcs. comm., Portland, 1995-96, Oreg. Leadership coalition, Portland, 1996—; orgnl. liaison Oreg. Health Plan coalition, Portland, 1995—. Active The City Club of Portland, Oreg. Women's Health and Wellness Alliance, Portland. Mem. NOW, The Nature Conservancy. Home: 4234 SW Viewpoint Terr # C Portland OR 97201 Office: Oreg Nurses Assn 9600 SW Oak St # 550 Portland OR 97223

ABRAHAMSEN, VALERIE ANN, institute official, theologian, educator; b. Norwood, Mass., Oct. 5, 1954; d. Frederick Henry and Ruth Eleanor (Pierce) A. BA, U. S.C., 1975; M Theol. Studies, Harvard U., 1979, ThD, 1986. Cert. secondary social studies tchr., Mass. Adminstrv. sec. Joslin Diabetes Ctr., Boston, 1982-84; adminstrv. asst. Harvard Med. Sch., Boston, 1984-86; adminstr. Harvard U., Cambridge, Mass., 1986-89; exec. office mgr. Mass. Gen. Hosp., Boston, 1990-93, mgr. spl. projects, 1993; registrar, bursar MGH Inst. Health Professions, Boston, 1993—; mem. adj. faculty Bunker Hill C.C., Boston, 1995—; reviewer NEH, Washington, 1994—; editor Fortress Press, Phila., 1977-79. Author: Women and Worship at Philippi, 1995; contbr. articles and revs. to profl. publs. Mem. anti-racism task force Episcopal Diocese Mass., Boston, 1993—, co-chmn. congl. resources and devel. com., 1995-98; mem. choir Cathedral Ch. of St. Paul, 1991—. Pfeiffer fellow Harvard Div. sch., 1979, 80; travel grantee Kittridge Found., 1990, Am. Coun. Learned Socs., 1995. Mem. Am. Acad. Religion, Soc. Bibl. Lit., Nat. Assn. Student Pers. Adminstrs. (state adv. bd. 1995—).

ABRAHAMSON, SHIRLEY SCHLANGER, state supreme court justice; b. N.Y.C., Dec. 17, 1933; d. Leo and Ceil (Sauerteig) Schlanger; m. Seymour Abrahamson, Aug. 26, 1953; 1 son, Daniel Nathan. AB, NYU, 1953; JD, Ind. U., 1956; SJD, U. Wis., 1962. Bar: Ind. 1956, N.Y. 1961, Wis. 1962. Asst. dir. Legis. Drafting Research Fund, Columbia U. Law Sch., 1957-60; since practiced in Madison, Wis., 1962-76; mem. firm LaFollette, Sinykin, Anderson & Abrahamson, 1962-76; justice Supreme Ct. Wis., Madison, 1976-96, chief justice, 1996—; prof. U. Wis. Sch. Law, 1966-92; bd. visitors Ind. U. Sch. Law, 1972—, U. Miami Sch. Law, 1982—, U. Chgo. Law Sch., 1988-92, Brigham Young U., Sch. Law, 1986-88, Northwestern U. Law Sch., 1989-94; chmn. Wis. Rhodes Scholarship Com., 1992—; chmn. nat. adv. com. on ct.-adjudicated and ct.-ordered health care George Washington U. Ctr. Health Policy, Washington, 1993—; mem. DNA adv. bd. FBI, U.S. Dept. Justice, 1995—. Editor: Constitutions of the United States (National and State) 2 vols, 1962. Mem. study group program of rsch., mental health and the law John D. and Catherine T. MacArthur Found., 1988—; mem. coun. fund for rsch. on dispute resolution Ford Found., 1987-91; bd. dirs. Wis. Civil Liberties Union, 1968-72; mem. ct. reform adv. panel Internat. Human Rights Law Group Cambodia Project, 1995—. Mem. ABA (coun., sect. legal edn. and admissions to bar 1976-86, mem. commn. on undergrad. edn. in law and the humanities 1978-79, standing com. on pub. edn. 1991—, mem. commn. on access to justice/2000 1993—, mem. adv. bd. Ctrl. and East European law intiative 1994—), Wis. Bar Assn., Dane County Bar Assn., 7th Cir. Bar Assn., Nat. Assn. Women Judges, Am. Law Inst. (mem. coun. 1985—), Order of Coif, Phi Beta Kappa. Home: 2012 Waunona Way Madison WI 53713-1616 Office: Wis Supreme Ct PO Box 1688 Madison WI 53701-1688

ABRAHM, JANET LEE, hematologist, oncologist, educator; b. San Francisco, Mar. 14, 1949; d. Paul Milton and Helen Lesser Abrahm; m. David Rytman Slavitt, Apr. 16, 1978. Student, U. Calif., Berkeley, 1969; BA, U. Calif., San Francisco, 1970, MD, 1973. Diplomate Am. Bd. Internal Medicine. Intern and resident medicine Mass. Gen. Hosp., Boston, 1973-75, hematology fellow, 1975-76; chief resident medicine Moffitt Hosp. U. Calif., San Francisco, 1976-77; hematology/oncology fellow Hosp. U. Pa., Phila., 1977-80; postdoctoral fellow medicine U. Pa., Phila., 1977-78, postdoctoral trainee medicine, 1977-80, asst. prof. medicine, 1980-86; asst. prof. medicine Hosp. U. Pa. and VA Med. Ctr., Phila., 1986-89, assoc. prof. medicine, 1989—; attending physician Hosp. U. Pa., Phila., 1980-93; staff physician Phila. VA Med. Ctr., 1982—, dir. Hematology/Oncology Clinic, 1983-94, chief hematology and oncology sect., 1984-94, med. oncologist Hospice Consultation Team, 1993—, chief med. svc., 1994—; prin. investigator, Palliative Care Fellowship Grant, 1996-2001; chmn. adv. com. Cancer Care VA Dist. 4, 1987-90; sec. subspecialty bd. hematology Am. Bd. Internal Medicine, 1987-92, sec. SEP subcom. Hematology Am. Bd. Internal Medicine, 1993-95; vis. asst. prof. medicine Med. Coll. Pa., 1988—; adj. asst. prof. clin. pharmacy Phila. Coll. Pharmacy and Sci., 1988—; mem. tech. adv. group Cancer Care Region 1, 1990-95; med. oncology cons. cancer pain consultation panel Ctr. for Continuing Edn. U. Pa. Sch. Nursing, 1990—; mem. quality of life and cancer edn. com. of Pan. Cancer Adv. Bd., 1994—; mem. human resources coun. of VHA VISN, 1996—, councillor Region 1, AUOCOM, 1996—; invited lectr. Mt. Zion Med. Ctr. U. Calif., San

Francisco, 1992, 95, Women in Medicine, Phila., 1993, Pa. Hosp., 1993, Sacred Heart Hosp., Allentown, Pa., 1993, Med. Coll. Pa., Phila., 1993-96, Mercy Hosp., Wilkes-Barre, Pa., 1993, Wilkes-Barre VA Hosp., 1993, Delaware Valley Geriatrics Soc., King of Prussia, Pa., 1993, Am. Cancer Soc. MCP, Phila., 1993, Family Practice Group Bryn Mawr (Pa.) Hosp., 1994, Pa. Cancer Control Program, Phila., 1994, Hospice Conf. Phila. VA Med. Ctr., 1994, Washington VA Med. Ctr., 1994, Phila. Corp. for Aging, 1994, Mercy Cath. Med. Ctr., 1995, Mt. Sinai Med. Ctr., Miami, 1995, U. Chgo. Med. Sch., 1995, Northwestern U. Sch. of Med., Chgo., 1995, San Diego, Calif. 1995, Stanford U., 1995, others. Author: (with others) Handbook of Experimental Pharmacology, 1980, Vivo and In Vitro Erythropoiesis: The Friend System, 1980, Clinical Care of the Terminal Patient, 1982, Yearbook of Medicine, 1984, Yearbook of Cancer, 1984, Vitamins and Cancer - Human Cancer Prevention by Vitamins and Micronutrients, 1985, Biological Regulation of Cell Proliferation, vol. 34, 1986, Pain Management in Hematology: Basic Principles and Practice, 1990, 94, Internal Medicine for Dentistry, 2d edit., 1990, Textbook of Internal Medicine, 1996, Geriatric Secrets, 1996; contbr. (booklets) Caring for the Terminally Ill Patient at Home - A Guide for Family Caregivers, 1986, Caring for the Cancer Patient at Home - A Guide for Patients and Families, 1986; reviewer JAMA, Cancer, Archives Internal Medicine, Annals Internal Medicine, Jour. Cancer Edn., Resident and Staff Physician; contbr. numerous articles to profl. jours. Vol. lectr. Am. Cancer Soc. Pain Control in Cancer Patients; mem. edn. com. Greater Phila. Pain Soc., 1993. Recipient Manual award Merck, 1973; Fife Medicine scholar, 1973. Fellow ACP (lectr. Pa. chpt. 1994); mem. Am. Soc. Hematology, Am. Fedn. Clin. Rsch., Am. Soc. Clin. Hypnosis, Am. Soc. Clin. Oncology, Am. Assn. Cancer Edn. (program com. 1993), Am. Pain Soc., Phi Beta Kappa, Alpha Omega Alpha. Home: 523 S 41st St Philadelphia PA 19104-4501 Office: Phila VA Med Ctr 111 Chief Medical Service University and Woodland Aves Philadelphia PA 19104

ABRAM, PRUDENCE BEATTY, federal judge; b. Kingston, R.I., Nov. 19, 1942; d. Kenneth Orion and Mary Catharine (Carter) Beatty; 1 child, Andrea Beatty. B.A., U. Mich., 1964, J.D. cum laude, 1968. Bar: Mich. 1969, N.Y. 1971, U.S. Dist. Ct. for so. dist. N.Y. 1972, U.S. Dist. Ct. for eastern dist. N.Y. 1972, U.S. Ct. Appeals for 2d circuit 1972, U.S. Supreme Ct. 1979. Assoc. firm Breed Abbott & Morgan, N.Y.C., 1970-72, Weil Gotshal & Manges, N.Y.C., 1972-78, Krause, Hirsch & Gross, N.Y.C., 1978-79; ptnr. firm Stroock & Stroock & Lavan, N.Y.C., 1980-82; judge U.S. Bankruptcy Ct. (so. dist.) N.Y., N.Y.C., 1982—. Mem. ABA. Office: US Bankruptcy Ct US Custom House One Bowling Green 6th Fl New York NY 10004-1408

ABRAMOVITZ, ANITA ZELTNER BROOKS (MRS. MAX ABRAMOVITZ), writer; b. Long Island, N.Y., January 7, 1914; d. Charles Frederick and Amelia (Koch) Zeltner. grad. Sarah Lawrence Coll., 1932, BA, 1962; m. Thomas Vail Brooks, Sept. 25, 1937 (div. July 1957); children: Antoinette Brooks-Floyd, Cora Vail Brooks, Henry Stanford Brooks II; m. Max Abramovitz, Feb. 29, 1964. Editl. asst. The New Yorker mag., N.Y.C., 1943-46; editor alumni mag. Sarah Lawrence Coll., 1947-48, asst. to prof. history, 1958-60, asst. in writing to lectr. courses, 1960-62; tchr. remedial reading, 1950; asst. to dir. Sarah Lawrence Paris Summer Sch., 1963. Democratic Party Insp. 18th Dist. Hastings-on-Hudson, N.Y., 1958-61; founding mem. Village League, 1950. Author series Picture Aids to World Geography, Picture Book of Fisheries, 1961, Picture Book of Tea and Coffee, 1962, Picture Book of Grains, 1963, Picture Book of Salt, 1964, Picture Book of Oil, 1965, Picture Book of Timber, 1966, A Small Bird Sang, 1967, Winifred, 1970, Picture Book of Metals, 1972, People and Spaces: A View of History Through Architecture, 1979; contbr. stories to children's books. Home: 176 Honey Hollow Rd Pound Ridge NY 10576-1105

ABRAMOWICZ, JANET, painter, print-maker; b. N.Y.C.; children: Alex, Anna. Student, Art Students League, 1948-50, Columbia U., 1948-50; BFA, Accademia di Belle Arti, Bologna, Italy, 1952, MFA, 1953. Teaching asst. to Giorgio Morandi Acad. di Belle Art, 1953-55; instr. dept. art and architecture U. Ill., 1955-57, Sch. Worcester, Mass., 1957-58; sr. lectr. fine arts Harvard U., Cambridge, Mass., 1971-91; former lectr. on spl. exhibits Mus. Fine Arts, Boston; vis. artist Am. Acad. Rome, 1984, 85, 94; fellow Japan Found., 1979-80; advisor Calcografia Nazionale, Rome, 1989-90; hon. fellow Accademia Clementina, Bologna, Italy, 1990—. Contbg. editor: Opera Grafiche di Morandi, 1990; contbr. articles to profl. jours. Sr. Fulbright fellow, 1977-79, 89, Rockefeller Found., 1989—, Am. Coun. Learned Socs. fellow, 1990, John Simon Guggenheim fellow, 1992. Democrat.

ABRAMS, ELIZABETH, educator, singer; b. Oceanside, N.Y., Apr. 26, 1960; d. Bernard and Barbara Gay (Borsuk) Segaloff; m. Dore Joseph Abrams, July 20, 1986. BFA in Drama, NYU, 1982, MA in Music Edn., 1990. Cert. music tchr. N.Y. Prodr. BCS Prodns., N.Y.C., 1983-85; adminstrv. asst. FAS dean's office NYU, 1987-88, adminstrv. asst. dept. journalism, 1988-90; music tchr. 3rd St Music Settlement, N.Y.C., 1989-90, summers 90-95; music tchr. grades 1-8 Grace Ch. Sch., N.Y.C., 1990—, also faculty rep. Lo bd. dirs. Appeared in How Could He Lie Like That, 1986, 87, Only Love, 1993, 94. Mem. N.Y. State Sch. Music Assn., Kodaly Orgn. N.Y. (bd. dirs. 1990-94). Office: Grace Ch Sch 86 4th Ave New York NY 10003

ABRAMS, LINDA, marketing executive. BS, Syracuse U. Promotion mgr. CBS Records, Arista Records, 1980-85; acct. supr. Lucker & Co., 1985-86; acct. supr. Ruder, Finn & Rotman, 1986-88, dir. pub. rels., sr. acct. mgr., 1988-89; sr. acct. supr. Ruder Finn, 1989-90, v.p., 1990-93; dir. affiliate mktg., 1993—. Office: MTV 1515 Broadway New York NY 10036

ABRAMS, OSSIE EKMAN, fundraiser; b. Olofström, Blekinge, Sweden, Jan. 8, 1952; came to the U.S., 1972; d. Ossian B. and Margit A. (Adolfsson) Ekman; m. Howard L. Abrams, Nov. 17, 1973 (div. Sept. 1983); m. David B. Orser, Aug. 1992. Student, Lärarhögskolan, 1972, New Sch. for Social Rsch., 1975; BA (hon.), Rocky Mountain Coll., 1994. Dental asst., sec. Samuel Meyer DDS, N.Y.C., 1973-74; office mgr., adminstr. Irving Peress DDS, N.Y.C., 1974-81; chief adminstr. Allen Kozin DDS, N.Y.C., 1981-87; head devel. Rocky Mountain Coll., Billings, Mont., 1991-92; owner, operator Davoss Ranch, Park City, Mont.; bd. mem. Mental Health Found., Billings, 1991, 92, bd. pres., 1993, 94. Active in Met. Opera Guild, N.Y.C., N.Y.C. Ballet Guild, N.Y. Philharm. Soc.; supporter Alberta Bair Theater, Billings Symphony, Billings Studio Theater; mem. selection com. Orser Chair, Coll. Bus., Mont. State U., Bozeman, 1988-96; fundraiser ann. campaign Yellowstone Art Ctr., Billings, 1989; fundraiser bus. drive Rocky Mountain Coll., Billings, 1990, vol. Rocky Mountain Coll. Black Tie Blue Jeans Ball, mem. auction com. 1990-93, chair auction com. 1994, 95, chair ball, 1996; mem. Nat. Adv. Coun., 1993-96. Recipient Alumni Hall of Fame award Rocky Mountain Coll., 1993, Leadership award Mental Health Found., Billings, 1994. Home: 1420 Granite Ave Billings MT 59102-0716 Office: 10 Douglas Ct, London NW64QA, England

ABRAMS, ROBERTA BUSKY, hospital administrator, nurse; b. Bklyn., Feb. 16, 1937; d. Albert H. and Gladys Busky; m. Robert L. Abrams, June 28, 1959 (div. 1977); children: Susan Abrams Federman, David B. BSN, U. Rochester, 1959; MA, Fairfield U., 1977. Asst. head nurse Jewish Hosp., Bklyn., 1959-60; instr. medicine/surgery Bklyn. Hosp., 1960-62, U. Rochester, N.Y., 1963-64; instr. ob-gyn Malden (Mass.) Hosp. Sch. Nursing, 1965-66; instr. prospective parents ARC, San Rafael, Calif., 1968-69; instr. ob-gyn SUNY, Farmingdale, 1970-71; instr. maternal/child health Stamford (Conn.) Hosp., 1971-75; clinician maternal/child health Lawrence Hosp., Bronxville, N.Y., 1975-78; asst. prof. nursing Ohio Wesleyan U., Delaware, 1981-84; dir. Elizabeth Blackwell Hosp. at Riverside Meth., Columbus, Ohio, 1978-86; dir. nursing Henry Ford Hosp., Detroit, 1986-87, assoc. adminstr. nursing, 1988-92; cons. Henry Ford Health Systems, Detroit, 1993—; cons. maternal/child nursing currents Ross Labs., 1984-94; cons. women's children's health Henry Ford Health Systems, 1993-94, cons. at large, 1994—; state coord. maternal/child health First Am. Home Care Co., 1994-96; co-dir. women's and children's health Arcadia Health Systems, 1996—; lectr. in field. Contbr. articles to profl. jours. Mem. NAACOG (vice-chmn. Ohio chpt. 1984-87), Am. Soc. Psychoprophylaxsis, Greater Detroit Orgn. Nurses Execs., LWV, Sigma Theta Tau. Home and Office: 32478 Dunford St Farmington Hills MI 48334-2724

ABRAMS, RONI, business education educator, communications consultant, trainer; b. N.Y.C.; d. William and Edith Lillian (Monkarsh) Abrams. BA, U. Miami, 1971. Mng. editor Corset, Bra and Lingerie Mag., N.Y.C., 1972-75; assoc. advt. dir. TV World Mag., N.Y.C., 1976-80; pres. Roni Abrams Assocs., Ltd., Bklyn., 1981—; founder The Ctr. for Networking, Bklyn., 1982—; design and conduct tng. programs in field of perception, interpersonal comm., negotiations, mgmt., sales, orgnl. devel. and personal transformation. Contbg. author: (textbook) Basic Sales Skills Business to Business, 1995; contbr. articles to profl. jours. Asst. to dir. Impact on Hunger, N.Y.C, 1980; coord. campaign com. to elect Paul Wrablica for state assembly, N.Y.C., 1988. Mem. Sales and Mktg. Execs. of Greater N.Y. (faculty). Home and Office: Roni Abrams Assocs Ltd 2820 Avenue J Brooklyn NY 11210-3736

ABRAMS, ROSALIE SILBER, retired state agency official; b. Balt.; d. Isaac and Dora (Rodbell) Silber. R.N., Sinai Hosp.; postgrad., Columbia U.; BS, Johns Hopkins U., 1963, MA in Polit. Sci.; 1 child, Elizabeth Joan. Public health nurse, USNR, 1945-46; bus. mgr. Sequoia Med. Group, Calif., 1946-47; asst. bus. mgr. Silber's Bakery, Balt., 1947-53; mem. Md. Ho. of Dels., 1967-70; mem. Md. Senate, 1970-83, majority leader, 1978-82; chmn. Dem. Party of Md., 1978-83, chmn. fin. com., 1982-83; dir. Office on Aging, State of Md., 1983-95, retired 1995, chair dept. human resources, dept. health and mental hygiene, trans., housing and community devel., econ. and employment devel., Interagency Com., 1984-95; host Outlook TV show, 1983-90; guest lectr., witness before congl. coms. Platform com. on nat. health care Dem. Nat. Com., 1979—; chmn. Md. Humane Practices Commn., 1978-83, mem., 1971-74; mem. New Coalition, 1979-83, State-Fed. Assembly Com. on Human Resources, 1977-83, Md. Comprehensive Health Planning Agency, 1972-75, Md. Commn. on Status of Women, 1968— , Am. Jewish Com.; bd. dirs. Sinai Hosp., Balt., 1973—, Balt. Jewish Coun., Cross Country Improvement Assn., 1969—, Fifth Dist. Reform Democrats, 1967—; chmn. legis. com. Balt. Area Coun. on Alcoholism, 1973-75; mem. adv. bd. long term care project U. Md., Balt., 1986; mem. Md. Adv. Com. for Adult and Community Svcs., 1984; mem. nat. adv. bd. Pre-Retirement Edn. Planning, 1986—; mem. State Adv. Coun. on Nutrition, 1988—;bd. dir. Sinai Hosp., 1973—; special trustee Sheppard-Pratt Hosp., 1992—. With Nurse Corps USN, 1944-46. Recipient Louise Waterman Wise Community Svc. award, 1969, award Am. Acad. Comprehensive Health Planning, 1971, Balt. News Am. award, Women of Distinction in Medicine, 1971, traffic safety award, Safety First Club of Md., 1971, Ann London Scott Meml. award for legis. excellence, Md. Chpt. NOW, 1975, Md. Nurses Assn., 1975, svc. award Balt. Area Coun. on Alcoholism, 1975; named to Md. Women's Hall of Fame, Md. Commn. for Women and Women Legislators of Md. Gen. Assembly, 1994, numerous others. Mem. AARP, Md. Order Women Legislators (pres., 1973-75), Nat. Conf. State Legislatures (human resources and urban affairs steering com. 1977-83), Nat. Legis. Conf. (human resources task force, intergovt. rels. com. 1975-83), Md. Gerontol. Assn. (bd. dirs. 1984—), Nat. Fedn. Dem. Women, Am. Jewish Congress, Am. Soc. on Aging, Md. Gerontological Assn. Home: 66 Olmstead Green Ct Baltimore MD 21210-1508

ABRAMS, RUTH IDA, state supreme court justice; b. Boston, Dec. 26, 1930; d. Samuel and Matilda A. BA, Radcliffe Coll., 1953; LLB, Harvard U., 1956; hon. degree, Mt. Holyoke Coll., 1977, Suffolk U., 1977, New Eng. Sch. Law, 1978. Bar: Mass. 1957. Ptnr. Abrams Abrams & Abrams, Boston, 1957-60; asst. dist. atty. Middlesex County, Mass., 1961-69; asst. atty. gen. Mass., chief appellate sect. criminal div., 1969-71; spl. counsel Supreme Jud. Ct. Mass., 1971-72; assoc. justice Superior Ct. Commonwealth of Mass., 1972-77, Supreme Jud. Ct. Mass., Boston, 1977—; mem. Gov.'s Commn. on Child Abuse, 1970-71, Mass. Law Revision Commn. Proposed Criminal Code for Mass., 1969-71; trustee Radcliffe Coll., from 1981. Editor: Handbook for Law Enforcement Officers, 1969-71. Recipient Radcliffe Coll. Achievement award, 1976, Radcliffe Grad. Soc. medal, 1977. Mem. ABA (com. on proposed fed. code from 1977), Mass. Bar Assn., Am. Law Inst., Am. Judicature Soc. (dir. 1978), Am. Judges Assn., Mass. Assn. Women Lawyers. Office: Mass Supreme Jud Ct 1300 New Courthouse Boston MA 02108*

ABRAMS-COLLENS, VIVIEN, artist; b. Cleve.. BFA, Carnegie-Mellon U.; MFA, Instituto Allende, San Miguel de Allende, Mex. Art tchr. Biblioteca Publica, San Miguel de Allende, Mex., 1969, Cleve. Mus. Art, 1971-72; instr. watercolor Dept. Community Svcs., Cleveland Heights, Univ. Heights, Ohio, 1974; instr. drawing Cuyahoga C.C., Cleve., 1974; design instr. Manhattanville Coll., Purchase, N.Y., 1985-86; artist-in-residence Bennington (Vt.) Coll., 1980; vis. artist in painting SUNY, Purchase, N.Y., 1983; lectr. in field. One-woman shows include Akron (Ohio) Art Inst., 1976, The New Gallery Contemporary Art, Cleve., 1977, 80, Luise Ross Gallery, N.Y.C., 1984, Coup de Grâce Gallery, N.Y.C., 1992, 100 Church Street, N.Y.C., 1992, Lisa Stern Gallery, Mountainville, N.Y., 1993, Lycian Ctr. Galleries, Sugarloaf, N.Y., 1994, Mus. Hudson Highlands, Cornwall-on-Hudson, N.Y., 1995; selected group exhbns. include Butler Inst. Am. Art, Ohio, 1976, 77, Cleve. Mus. Art, 1976, 77, 79, 81, 84 (1st Prize in Painting 1981), Akron Inst. Art, 1977, Harbourfront Gallery, Toronto, 1978, Marilyn Pearl Gallery, N.Y.C., 1978, 82, Phoenix Mus. Art, 1979, Soho Ctr. Visual Artists, N.Y.C., 1979, Washington Sq. East Galleries, N.Y.C., 1980, Little Rock (Ark.) Art Mus., 1982, Steven Rosenberg Gallery, N.Y.C., 1983, Ericson Gallery, N.Y.C., 1983, Sculpture Ctr., N.Y.C., 1983, A.I.R. Gallery, N.Y.C., 1983, Aldrich Mus. Contemporary Art, Ridgefield, Conn., 1984, 86, 92, Luise Ross Gallery, 1984, Mus. of the Hudson Highlands, 1985, City Gallery, N.Y.C., 1987, Squibb Gallery, Princeton, N.J., 1988, Cleve. Inst. Art, 1988, Mansfield Art Ctr., Ohio, 1989, OIA Salon, N.Y.C., 1991, Middletown Art Ctr., 1994 (Oil/Acrylic award 1994), Dietrich Contemporary Arts, N.Y.C., 1994, Cleve. Ctr. for Contemporary Art, 1994, Mansfield (Ohio) Art Ctr., 1995; permanent collections include Cleve. Found., Cleve. Art Assn., The Currier Gallery Art, Home Ins. Co., We. Electric, J.P. Morgan & Co., Continental Corp., Progressive Ins. Co., Nat. City Bank Cleve., Sohio, Walter & Samuels, Inc., Columbus Mus. Arts & Scis., Cleve. Mus. Art, Aldrich Mus. Contemporary Art; commns. include AT&T Longlines. Mem. fellows exec. com. MacDowell Colony, 1982-85. Cleve. Found. grantee, 1976, Athena Found. grantee, 1984; Hand Follow Found. fellow, 1983, fellow MacDowell Colony, Peterborough, N.H., 1979, 81, 85; recipient 1st prize Cleve. Mus. Art 62nd May Show, 1981, award Middletown Art Ctr., 1994; named to Shaker Heights H.S. Hall of Fame, 1994. Office: 196 Mountain Rd Cornwall On Hudson NY 12520 also: 11 Worth St New York NY 10013

ABRAMSON, SARA JANE, radiologist, educator; b. New Orleans, La., May 12, 1945; m. Walter Squire; children: Harrison, Russell, Zachary, Andrew. BA, Sarah Lawrence Coll., 1967; postgrad., Tulane U., 1967-69; MD, Mt. Sinai Sch. Medicine, 1971. Diplomate Am. Bd. Radiology, cert. added qualifications pediat. radiology. Intern in pediatrics Mt. Sinai Hosp., N.Y.C., 1971-72, resident in pediatrics, 1972-73; resident in radiology St. Luke's Children's Mercy Hosp., Kansas City, Mo., 1973-76; asst. prof. radiology U. Mo., 1976-79, Harvard U. Med. Sch., Cambridge, Mass., 1979-81; fellow in pediatric radiology Children's Hosp., Boston, 1979-81; asst. prof. radiology Columbia Coll. Physicians & Surgeons, N.Y.C., 1981-88, assoc. prof. radiology, 1988-93; assoc. attending radiologist Babies Hosp. Columbia Presbyn. Med. Ctr., N.Y.C., 1981-93, dep. dir. Div. Pediatric Radiology, 1992-93; assoc. prof. radiology Med. Coll. Cornell U., Ithaca, N.Y., 1993—; assoc. attending radiologist, assoc. mem. Mem. Sloan-Kettering Cancer Ctr. Mem. Hosp., N.Y.C., 1993—; apptd. to radiology elective program Columbia U. Med. Sch., N.Y.C., 1981-93, radiology residency program reevaluation, 1984-93, affirmative action com., 1987-90, program coord. affiliated hosps. teaching program, 1991-93, med. student advisor, 1991-93; mem. faculty coun. Columbia U., 1987-93; mem. resident selection com. Columbia-Presbyn. Med. Ctr., N.Y.C., 1985-93, quality assurance com., 1987-91, practice rev. com., 1991-93; cons. in pediatric radiology Blythedale Children's Hosp., 1982—, Bet Israel Hosp., N.Y.C., 1983—, Harlem Hosp., N.Y.C., 1983—, N.Y. Foundling Hosp., 1988—, Lenox Hill Hosp., 1990—, Morristown Meml. Hosp., 1990—; lectr., presenter in field. Contbr. over 40 articles to profl. jours., chpts. to books. Named Radiology Tchr. of Yr., Columbia Coll. Physicians and Surgeons, 1992. Fellow Am. Coll. Radiology (del. N.Y. chpt. 1991—, alt. del. 1984-91); mem. AMA, Soc. for Pediat. Radiology, Radiology Soc. N.Am., European Soc. for Pediat. Radiology, Soc. Thoracic Radiology, Am. Assn. Ultrasound in Medicine, Am. Assn. Women in Radiology, N.Y. Roentgen Soc. (sec.-treas. 1991-94, v.p. 1996—, moderator, pediat. program chair spring conf. 1991, guest lectr. spring conf. 1990), Nat. Children's Cancer Study Group, Caffey Soc., Neuhauser Soc., Kirkpatrick Soc. Office: Sloan-Kettering Cancer Ctr 1175 York Ave New York NY 10021-7169

ABREU, SUE HUDSON, physician, army officer; b. Indpls., May 24, 1956; d. M.B. Hudson and Wilma (Jones) Hudson Black. BS in Engring., Purdue U., 1978; MD, Uniformed Services U., 1982. Grad. U.S. Army Command & Gen. Staff Coll, 1988, Armed Forces Staff Coll., 1990. Commd. 2d lt. U.S. Army, 1978, advanced to lt. col., 1993; intern Walter Reed Army Med. Ctr., Washington, 1982-83, resident in diagnostic radiology, 1983-85, fellow in nuclear medicine, 1985-87, staff nuclear medicine physician, 1987-88, med. research fellow, 1988-89; chief Nuclear Medicine Svc., 1990-96; chief Dept. Radiology Womack Army Med. Ctr., Ft. Bragg, N.C., 1991-92, 96—. Fellow Am. Coll. Nuclear Physicians; mem. Am. Coll. Radiology, Soc. Nuclear Medicine, Am. Coll. Nuclear Physicians, Soc. Women Engrs., U.S. Parachute Assn., Tau Beta Pi, Omicron Delta Kappa, Phi Kappa Phi. Avocations: calligraphy, parachuting. Home: 613 Saddlebred Ln Raeford NC 28376-9075 Office: Dept Radiology Womack Army Med Ctr Fort Bragg NC 28307

ABT, SYLVIA HEDY, dentist; b. Chgo., Oct. 7, 1957; d. Wendel Peter and Hedi Lucie (Wieder) A. Student, Loyola U., Chgo., 1975-77; cert. dental hygiene, Loyola U., Maywood, Ill., 1979, DDS, 1983. Registered dental hygienist. Dental asst. Office Dr. Baran and Dr. O'Neill, DDS, Chgo., 1977-78; dental hygienist Drs. Spiro, Sudakoff, Kadens, Weidman, DDS, Skokie, Ill., 1979-83, Dr. Laudando, DiFranco, Rosemont, Ill., 1980-83; gen. practice dentistry Chgo., 1983—. Vol. Community Health Rotations, VA Hosps., grammar schs., convalescent ctrs., mental health ctrs., Maywood, Ill. and Chgo., 1978-82. Recipient 1st Pl. award St. Apollonia Art Show Loyola U., 1982. Mem. ADA, PETA, Ill. Dental Soc., Chgo. Dental Soc., Loyola Dental Alumni Assn. (golf outing registration chmn. 1987, awards in golf and tennis 1987), Ill. Dentists 99th Club (legis. interest com.), Psi Omega (historian, editor Kappa chpt.). Office: 6509 W Higgins Ave Chicago IL 60656-2204

ABU-LUGHOD, JANET LIPPMAN, sociologist, educator; b. Newark, Aug. 3, 1928; d. Irving O. and Tessie Lippman; m. Ibrahim Abu-Lughod, Dec. 8, 1951 (div. 1992); children: Lila, Mariam, Deena, Jawad. BA, U. Chgo., 1947, MA, 1950; PhD (NSF fellow), U. Mass., 1966. Dir. research Am. Soc. Planning Ofcls., 1950-52; sociologist-cons. Am. Council to Improve Our Neighborhoods, 1953-57; asst. prof. sociology Am. U., Cairo, 1958-60, Smith Coll., 1963-66; assoc. prof. Northwestern U., Evanston, Ill., 1967-71; prof. sociology, urban affairs Northwestern U., 1971-87, dir. comparative urban studies program, 1974-77, dir. urban studies program, 1984-87; prof. sociology Grad. Faculty The New Sch. for Social Research, N.Y.C., 1986—; dir. Rsch. Ctr. on Lower Manhattan, N.Y.C., 1988-91, chmn. dept. of sociology, 1990-92; cons. UN, 1971—, UNESCO, 1979-80. Author: (with Nelson Foote, others) Housing Choices and Constraints, 1960, Cairo-1001 Years of the City Victorious, 1971, (with Richard Hay, Jr.) Third World Urbanization, 1977, Rabat: Urban Apartheid in Morocco, 1980, Before European Hegemony, 1989, Changing Cities, 1991, From Urban Village to East Village, 1994; contbr. chpts. to books, articles, revs. to profl. jours.; also monographs. Radcliffe Inst. scholar, 1963-64; Ford Faculty fellow, 1971-72, Guggenheim fellow, 1976-77, NEH fellow, 1977-78, ACLS fellow, 1994; Getty Sr. scholar, 1994-96. Mem. Internat. Sociol. Assn., Am. Sociol. Assn. (governing coun. 1994—), Social Sci. History Assn., Chgo. Coun. on Fgn. Rels. (dir. 1973-76), Social Sci. Rsch. Coun. (com. on Near East 1973-75.), Phi Beta Kappa. Office: New Sch for Social Rsch Grad Faculty 65 Fifth Ave New York NY 10003-4520

ABZUG, BELLA SAVITZKY, lawyer, former congresswoman; b. N.Y.C., July 24, 1920; d. Emanuel and Esther Savitzky; m. Maurice M. Abzug, June 4, 1944 (dec.); children: Eve Gail, Isobel Jo. B.A., Hunter Coll., 1942; LL.B., Columbia U., 1947; hon. degree, Hunter Coll., Hobart Coll., Manhattanville Coll. Bar: N.Y. 1947. Private law practice in N.Y.C., 1944-70, 1980—; legislative dir. Women Strike for Peace, 1961-70; mem. 92d Congress from 19th Dist. N.Y., 1970-72, 93d-94th Congresses from 20th Dist. N.Y., 1972-76; presiding officer Nat. Commn. on Observance of Internat. Women's Year, 1977; presided Nat. Women's Conf., Houston, 1977; co-chmn. Pres.'s Nat. Adv. Com. for Women, 1978; pres. The Women's Enviro. & Devel. Org., N.Y.C.; cable news commentator; speaker numerous coll. campuses; Congl. advisor to U.S. Del. to UN Conf. on the Decade for Women, Mexico City, 1975; fellow Inst. Politics, John F. Kennedy Sch. Govt., Harvard U., 1987; founder Nat. Women's Polit. Caucus, co-chair Women's Environment & Devel. Org., 1991; presided over World Women's Congress for a Healthy Planet, 1991; mem. Internat. Facilitating Com. of Nongovtl. Orgns. and Ind. Sectors, UN Conf. on Environment and Devel., Brazil, 1992; sr. adv. to UNCED sec. gen. for UN Conf. on Environment & Devel., 1992. Editor: Columbia Law Rev.; author: Bella! Ms. Abzug Goes to Washington, 1972, Gender Gap: Bella Abzug's Guide to Political Power for American Women, 1984. Apptd. chair of Commn. on Status of Women by Mayor Dinkins, 1992. Mem. Women Strike for Peace, Nat. Urban League, NOW, Nat. Women's Polit. Caucus, ACLU, Women U.S.A. (pres.), UN Assn. U.S., Ams. for Democratic Action (v.p.), Am. Jewish Congress, Women's Environment & Devel. Orgn. (co-chair). Office: The Women's Enviro & Devel Org 845 3rd Ave 15th Fl New York NY 10022

ACERS, PATSY PIERCE, financial seminars company executive; b. Muskogee, Okla., Mar. 10, 1933; d. Claude James and Clara B. (Chaney) Pierce, m. Thomas Edward Acers, Apr. 9, 1955 (div. Feb. 1980); children: Alison Ann, Angela Lynn, Ann Pierce, Ashley French. BA, U. Okla., 1955. Tchr. Oklahoma City Pub. Schs., 1955-58; dir. spl. events Am. Cancer Soc., 1980-86, dir. legacies and planned giving, 1983-86; ins. agt. life and health Conn. Mut., Oklahoma City, 1986-90; pres., owner Bag Lady Fin. Svcs., Inc., Oklahoma City, 1987—. Developer slide seminars: Do You Really Want to Be a Bag Lady, 1987, The Bag Lady Returns With Who Do You Trust, 1991, There Is Financial Life for Singles, 1989. Mem. Women Life Underwriters (pres. 1989-90), High Noon Profl. Women (pres. 1990-91), Women's Exec. Network (pres. 1988-89), Million Dollar Round Table, Am. Bus. Women's Assn., Okla. Spkrs. Assn., Nat. Spkrs. Assn., Nat. Leaders Club. Methodist. Home: 1413 Sims Ave Edmond OK 73013-6355 Office: Bag Lady Fin Seminars Inc PO Box 20213 Oklahoma City OK 73156-0213

ACKALUSKY, HAZEL ETHEL, artist; b. Pottsville, Pa., May 24, 1929; d. William Martin and Eleanor (Edden) Frankenstein; m. James Martin Ackalusky, June 25, 1949; children: Eleanor Charlotte, Ramona. Grad. high sch. One-woman shows include Frames Etc., Frackville, Pa., 1991, Am. Savs. Bank, Tamaqua, Pa., 1992, The Gallery, Schuylkill Haven, Pa., 1993, Schuylkill County Coun. of the Arts, Pottsville, Pa., 1993, First Fed. Bank, Pottsville, 1994; group exhbns. include Allied Artists of Schuylkill County, Pottsville, 1982-95, Schuykill C. of C., Pottsville, 1991-95, Berks Art Alliance-Reading (Pa.) Area C.C., 1993. Mem. Anthracite Concert Assn., 1966—, Hist. Soc. Schuylkill County, 1993-95, Schuylkill County Coun. for the Arts, 1977-95; charter mem. Nat. Mus. Women in the Arts, 1989-95. Mem. Pa. Watercolor Soc., Allied Artists of Schulkill County (hon. life, v.p. 1983-84, pres. 1985-86, bd. dirs. 1987-96), Schuylkill River Group. Roman Catholic. Home: 701 Pierce St Pottsville PA 17901

ACKER, LORETTA LYNN, pilot; b. Colorado Springs, Colo., Nov. 17, 1965; d. Norman Lofgren and Patricia Ann (Slater) Smith; m. Donald Ward Acker, May 1, 1993; 1 child, Christian Austin Acker. BS in Human Factors Engirng., U.S. Airforce Acad., 1989; undergrad pilot tng., USAF, 1990. Joined USAF, Charleston AFB, S.C., 1985, advanced through ranks to capt., 1993, sq. tng. officer, 1992-94, wing tng. officer, 1994, sq. mission scheduler, pilot chief, 1994-95, air refueling aircraft comdr., C-141 instr. pilot, command post duty officer, 1995—; instr. aerobics. DJ 96 Wave WAVF, Charleston. Home: 11312 Wonderland Tr Dallas TX 75229 Office: 15AS Charleston AFB Charleston SC 29404

ACKER, VIRGINIA MARGARET, nursing educator; b. Madison, Wis., Aug. 11, 1946; d. Paul Peter and Lucille (Klein) A. Diploma in Nursing, St. Mary's Med. Ctr., Madison, 1972; BS in Nursing, Incarnate Work Coll., San Antonio, 1976; MS in Health Professions, S.W. Tex. State U., 1980; postgrad., U. Tex., 1992-93. RN, Wis., Tex. Staff nurse St. Mary's Hosp., Milw., 1972-73, Kenosha Meml. Hosp., Wis., 1973-74, S.W. Tex. Meth. Hosp., San Antonio, 1974-75, Met. Gen. Hosp., San Antonio, 1975-76; instr. Bapt. Meml. Hosp. System Sch. Nursing, San Antonio, 1976-83; dir. nursing Meml. Hosp., Gonzales, Tex., 1983-84; instr., dir. nursing Victoria Coll.,

Cuero, Tex., 1984-86; dir. nursing Rocky Knoll Health Care Facility, Plymouth, Wis., 1986-87, Unicare Health Facilities, Milw., 1987-88; coord. nursing edn. St. Nicholas Hosp., Sheboygan, Wis., 1989-90; instr. U. Wis., Oshkosh, 1990-92, St. David's Hosp., Austin, Tex., 1992-95, Bailey Sq. Surg. Ctr., 1995—. Roman Catholic. Avocations: cross-stiching, reading, camping, fishing. Home: 2103 Four Oaks Ln Austin TX 78704-4624

ACKERLY, WENDY SAUNDERS, computer systems analyst; b. Chgo., July 23, 1960; d. Robert S. Jr. and Linda Ackerly. BS in Atmospheric Sci., U. Calif., Davis, 1982; postgrad., U. Nev., Reno, 1985. Programmer U. Calif, Davis, 1982-83; cons. software Tesco, Sacramento, 1983; software engr. Bently Nev. Corp., Minden, Nev., 1984-85; mgr. computer scis. Jensen Electric Co., Reno, 1985-86; software engr. Jensen Electric Co., Cameron Park, Calif., 1986-89; sr. engr. Aerojet, Sacramento, 1989-96, test ops. specialist, 1996—; sec.-treas. Kerry King Constrn. Co., Inc., 1991—. Pres. Four Springs Homeowners Assn., 1993-96. Mem. Nat. Space Soc., Am. Meteorol. Soc., Planetary Soc., U.S. Tennis Assn., Calif. Aggie Alumni Assn. Republican. Office: Aerojet PO Box 13222 Sacramento CA 95813-6000

ACKERMAN, ANN, mathematics educator; b. Oklahoma City, Aug. 12, 1950. BS in Math., Okla. State U., 1972; MEd, U. Okla., 1974, PhD in Math. Edn., 1980; postdoctoral student, Cen. State U., 1982-83. Prof. math Okla. City C. C., 1977-89; dean of science and math Okla. City C. C., 1986-96, assoc. v.p. external edn., 1996—; speaker at profl. confs. Contbr. to profl. publs. Mem. Am. Math. Assn. Two-Yr. Colls., Nat. Coun. Tchrs. Math., Cen. Okla. Assn. Tchrs. Math. (v.p. 1987-89), Okla. Assn. Community and Jr. Colls. (pres. 1986-87), Okla. Coun. Tchrs. Math. (sec. 1988-90, conv. chair 1988). Office: Oklahoma City Cmty Coll 7777 S May Ave Oklahoma City OK 73159-4419

ACKERMAN, ARLENE ALICE, accountant, business consultant, artist, writer; b. Omaha, Mar. 24, 1936; d. Walter Nelson and Mildred Eleanor (Krimlofski) A. BA in Social Sci. and Econs., San Francisco State U., 1962; MA in Polit. Sci., Purdue U., 1967; grad., U.S. Dept. Def. Info. Sch., 1973, U.S. Army Command-Gen. Staff Coll., 1977. CPA, Ind. Acct., adminstr. Peeples & MacDonald, CPAs, Sacramento, 1961-66; acct. Chief Acct.'s Office, Purdue U., West Lafayette, Ind., 1966-67; adj. gen. and info. officer, editor newspaper 123d Army Res. Command, Ind., 1972-75; mng. ptnr. Piano Showcase, Indpls., 1975-83; adminstr. Bennett Thrasher & Co. CPAs, Atlanta, 1983-86, Melvin Belli Law Offices, San Francisco, 1990; bus. cons. Ackerman & Assocs., Indpls., 1986-90; acctg. mgr., acting CFO, Lera Dynalectric, San Francisco, 1991-94; CFO Nat. Home Bus. Assn., St. Helena, Calif., 1994-96; prin. Ackerman & Assocs., Fairfax, Calif. Editor Mus. Indian Heritage Newsletter, Indpls., 1971-77; group shows include Marin Agrl. Land Trust, San Rafael, Calif., 1993, Marin County Fair & Exposition, San Rafael, 1993, 96, Marin Soc. Artists, Ross, Calif., 1993, 94, Monterey Peninsula Mus. Art Christmas Miniature Show, 1993, Artisans Gallery, Mill Valley, Calif., 1993, 94, 95, Sonoma-Marin Fair, Petaluma, Calif., 1993, 94, San Mateo (Calif.) County Fair, 1992, 93, 94, Sonoma County Fair, Santa Rosa, Calif., 1993, 94, 95; contbr. articles to Army profl. jours. Officer U.S. Army, 1956-61, 67-71; col. USAR, 1961-67, 71-88. Home: 255 Scenic Rd Fairfax CA 94930 Office: Ackerman & Assocs PO Box 663 Fairfax CA 94978-0663

ACKERMAN, DIANE, author, educator; b. Waukegan, Ill., Oct. 7, 1948; d. Sam and Marcia Molly (Tischler) Fink; student Boston U., 1966-67; B.A. in English, Pa. State U., 1970; M.F.A., Cornell U., 1973, M.A. in English, 1976, Ph.D., 1978. Editorial asst. Library Jour., N.Y.C., 1970; teaching fellow Cornell U., Ithaca, N.Y., 1971-78; asst. prof. U. Pitts., 1980—; vis. writer-in-residence Coll. William and Mary, Williamsburg, Va., 1982-83, Ohio U., Athens, 1983; writer-in-residence Washington U., St. Louis, 1984—, dir. Writing Programs, 1982—; vis. writer Columbia U., N.Y.C., 1986, NYU, 1986; mem. lit. panel N.Y. State Council on Arts, 1980—; mem. poetry panel Pa. Arts Council, 1980, Creative Artists Pub. Service Program, 1978; mem. adv. bd. Planetary Soc., 1980—; host (TV series) Mystery of the Senses. Recipient Black Warrior Rev. Poetry prize, 1981; Abbie Copps Poetry prize, 1974; Pushcart prize, 1983; Peter I.B. Lavan Poetry prize, 1985; CAPS creative writing fellow, 1980; Rockefeller fellow, 1974-75; Nat. Endowment Arts fellow, 1976, 85; Nat. Book Cir. Critics nomination, 1991; Wordsmith award, 1992; Literary Lion award N.Y. Pub. Libr., 1994. Mem. PEN. Author: (poetry) The Planets: A Cosmic Pastoral, 1976, 80, Wife of Light, 1978, Lady Faustus, 1983, Jaguar of Sweet Laughter, 1990; (prose memoir) Twilight of the Tenderfoot, 1980; (drama) Reverse Thunder, 1988; (nonfiction) On Extended Wings, 1985, A Natural History of the Senses, 1990, The Moon by Whale Light, and Other Adventures Among Bats, Penguins, Crocadilians and Whales, 1990, A Natural History of Love, 1994, The Rarest of the Rare, 1995; (children's nonfiction) Monk Seal Hideaway, 1995; contbr. poetry and prose to various lit. jours. Office: care Janklaw & Nesbit 598 Madison Ave New York NY 10022

ACKERMAN, HELEN PAGE, librarian, educator; b. Evanston, Ill., June 30, 1912; d. John Bernard and Florence Page. B.A., Agnes Scott Coll., Decatur, Ga., 1933; B.L.S., U. N.C., 1940. Cataloger Columbia Theol. Sem., 1942-43; post librarian U.S. Army, Aberdeen Proving Ground, Md., 1943-45; asst. librarian Union Theol. Sem., Richmond, Va., 1945-49; reference librarian UCLA, 1949-54, asst. univ. librarian, 1954-65, asso. univ. librarian, 1965-73, univ. librarian, 1973-77, prof. Sch. Info. and Library Sci., 1973-77, 82, 83; vis. prof. Sch. Librarianship, U. Calif., Berkeley, 1978, 80. Recipient award of distinction in libr. sci. UCLA Alumnae Assn., 1977, Disting. Career Citation, Assn. Coll. and Rsch. Librs., 1989. Mem. ALA, AAUW (Status of Women award 1973), Calif. Libr. Assn., Coun. on Libr. Resources (bd. dirs. 1975-90). Home: 310 20th St Santa Monica CA 90402-2414

ACKERMAN, LOUISE MAGAW, civic worker, writer; b. Topeka, July 9, 1904; d. William Glenn and Anna Mary (Shaler) Magaw; BS, Kans. State U., 1926; MA, U. Nebr., 1942; m. Grant Albert Ackerman, Dec. 27, 1926; children—Edward Shaler, Anita Louise. Free lance writer, 1930—. Mem. Nat. Soc. Daus. Colonial Wars (nat. pres. 1977-80), Daus. Am. Colonists (regent Nebr. 1970-72), DAR (past v.p. gen.), Americans of Armorial Ancestry (sec. 1976-82), Nat. Huguenot Soc. (2d v.p. 1977-81), Nebr. Writers Guild (past sec.-treas.), Nat. League Am. Pen Women, Colonial Lords in Am., Nat. Gavel Soc., Soc. Descs. of Founders of Hartford, Conn., Phi Kappa Phi. Republican. Club: Nat. Writers. Lodge: Order Eastern Star. Home: 6315 O St Rm 509 Lincoln NE 68510-2237

ACKERMANN, KATHLEEN SEDLACK, lawyer, musician; b. Atlanta, June 12, 1949; d. James Joseph and Patricia Ann (Doyle) Sedlack; m. Steven John Reidy, Mar. 20, 1971 (div. Dec. 1980); 1 child, Melissa Lauren Reidy; m. James Joseph Ackermann, Apr. 14, 1984. MusB cum laude, Fla. State U., Tallahasee, 1971, MusM, 1972; JD, Coll. Law, Ga. State U., Atlanta, 1994. Bar: Ga., 1994. Instr. music E. Carolina U., Greenville, 1972-75; pvt. piano tchr. Atlanta, 1976-90; pianist Roberts Restaurante, Alpharetta, Ga., 1984-90; assoc. atty. Deming, Born & Parker, Norcross, Ga., 1994-95; atty. King & Spalding, Atlanta, 1995—; pres. N. DeKalb Music Tchrs., Atlanta, 1989-91. Mem. bd. trustees Embry Hills Club, Chamblee, Ga., 1986-88; pianist The Nostalgics, Atlanta, 1994—; sec. Embry Hills Twigs-Egleton Aux., Chamblee, 1995-96. Mem. Atlanta Bar Assn., Alpha Phi Sorority. Democrat. Mem. Unitarian Ch. Home: 3248 Embry Cir Atlanta GA 30341

ACORD-SKELTON, BARBARA BURROWS, counselor, educator, artist; b. L.A., Dec. 26, 1928; d. Harry and Sophia (Dittman) Burrows; m. Benjamin Raddatz, June 11, 1949 (div. Dec. 1970); children: Randolph, Marjorie, Thomas, Deborah; m. William A. Acord, Feb. 26, 1974 (dec.); m. Gerald Skelton, 1989. AA, Riverside City Coll., 1956; BA, Calif. State U., San Bernardino, 1970; MA, Pacific Oaks Coll., 1974; postgrad., Claremont Coll., 1976-91. Lic. marriage, family and child counselor, Calif., 1974. Dir. pvt. nursery sch. Headstart, Riverside, Calif., 1964-66; career devel., coord. Riverside County Head Start and Corono Norco Sch. Dist., Riverside, 1966-72; instr. Chaffey Community Coll., Alta Loma, Calif., 1971-82; class room coord., family counselor Casa Colina Hosp., Pomona, Calif., 1973-79; counselor LaVerne (Calif.) Ctr. for Edn. Counseling, 1976-82; social worker III San Andreas Regional Ctr., Salinas, Calif., 1984-87; pvt. practice family and individual counseling Medford, 1987-92; cons. Pomona U. Sch. Dist., Calif., 1973-80, San Gabriel Valley Regional Ctr., Covina, Calif., 1976-82, Nat. Council Alcoholism, Covina, 1980-82; instr. U. LaVerne, 1976-82. Author: On Learning and Growing, 1974; co-author: Parent Advocacy Training, 1977, Creative Competency, 1978. Vol. Day Springs Hospice, Medford, 1987-90; bd. dirs. Gold Coast Arab Horse Assn., Santa Clara County, Calif., 1983-85. Riverside County Headstart scholar, 1967, Ednl. Profl. Devel. Act scholar, 1971-74. Mem. Am. Assn. Marriage and Family Therapists, Upper Rogue Art Assn., Arab Horse Assn. (So. Oreg. bd. dirs. 1988, pres. 1989), Women Artists Cascades Mountains, Region III Arab Horse Assn. (bd. dirs. 1983-85). Home: 13856 Weowna Way White City OR 97503-9572

ACTON, PATRICIA NASSIF (LADY ACTON), lawyer, educator; b. Cedar Rapids, Iowa, June 7, 1949; d. M. Morey and Barbara (Lindsey) Nassif; m. Richard Gerald Lyon Dalberg Acton (Lord Acton), Mar. 19, 1988. BA in history with highest distinction, U. Iowa, 1971, JD with high distinction, 1974. Admitted to Iowa bar, 1974; assoc. atty. Simmons, Perrine, Albright & Ellwood, Cedar Rapids, 1974-78; sole practice, Cedar Rapids 1978-80; Bigelow teaching fellow, lectr. law U. Chgo. Law Sch., 1980-81; vis. assoc. prof. Coll. Law, U. Iowa, 1981-84, clin. assoc. prof., 1984-85, clin. prof., 1985—; vis. prof. U. Fla. Coll. Law, 1985; dir. London Law Consortium, 1994—. Mem. ABA, Iowa Bar Assn., Order of Coif, Phi Beta Kappa. Author: Invasion of Privacy: The Cross Creek Trial of Marjorie Kinnan Rawlings, 1988, (with Selz & Simensky) Entertainment Law, 2nd edit. 1992, (with Lord Acton) To Go Free: A Treasury of Iowa's Legal Heritage, 1995; editor notes and comments The Iowa Law Rev. 1973-74; contbr. articles to profl. jours. and books on lit. and entertainment law. Office: U Iowa College of Law Iowa City IA 52242

ADAIR, BARBARA REED, psychotherapist, administrator; b. Chgo., July 26, 1939; d. Robert Chamberlain Adair and Eleanor Louise (Kaul) Kriss; children: Christopher S., Jeffrey L., Catherine L. BA, Northwestern U., Evanston, Ill., 1962; MA, Stetson U., Deland, Fla., 1987. RN, CS, LPC. Dir. Fern Park (Fla.) Nursery/Kindergarten, 1967-74; tchr., counselor The Center, Leverett, Mass., 1974-77; DON Am. Red Cross, Daytona Beach, Fla., 1978-85; counselor ACT, Daytona Beach, 1985-90; counselor psychiatric evaluation Halifax Med. Ctr., 1991-95; co-dir. St. Francis of the Woods, Coyle, Okla., 1995—; trustee St. Francis of the Woods, Coyle, 1993—; lectr. on bereavement and other topics; workshop presenter dreams, fairy tales, journaling, metaphors. Instr. Am. Red Cross, Fla., 1964-85; lectr., co-leader Scouts, Fla., Mass., 1971-76; organist, Sunday sch. tchr. Church, Fern Park, Fla. and Mass., 1967-77. Mem. ANA, Am. Counselor's Assn. Republican. Mem. Ea. Orthodox Ch. Home: PO Box 105 Coyle OK 73027 Office: PO Box 400 Coyle OK 73027

ADAMAK, JEANELLE, broadcast executive; b. Odessa, Tex., Aug. 18, 1952; d. E.W. and Jo Martin; m. Russell J. Adamak, July 19, 1973; children: Aaron, Ashley. BS in Mgmt./Telecom., Ind. Wesleyan U. Dir. devel. Odessa Coll., 1986-90; v.p. devel. and comm. WFYI TelePlex, Indpls., 1990—; chair Exec. Women's Leadership Program, Indpls., 1994—, Vol. Action Ctr. Com., Indpls., 1996—. Mem. Vol. Action Ctr., United Way, 1996—; bd. dirs. YWCA, Indpls., 1995—, Cmty. Svc. Coun.-United Way, Indpls., 1996—, Prevent Blindness, Ind., 1996—. Recipient Devel. award So. Ednl. Comm. Assn., 1988. Mem. Nat. Fundraisers Coun., Ind. Fundraisers Coun. Office: WFYI TelePlex 1401 N Meridian Indianapolis IN 46202

ADAMCZESKI, MADELINE MARIE, chemistry educator, researcher; b. Staten Island, N.Y., Apr. 5, 1961; d. John Anthony and Barbara Margaret (Dudley) Prestia; m. Walter Thomas Adamczeski, Sept. 14, 1985 (div. Dec. 1993). BS in Marine Sci. cum laude, L.I. U., 1983; student, SUNY, Stony Brook, 1983-84; PhD in Chemistry, U. Calif., Santa Cruz, 1989. Sea grant trainee, grad. rsch. & teaching asst. U. Calif., Santa Cruz, 1984-89; sr. scientist, natural product scientist Takasago Inst., Walnut Creek, Calif., 1990-91; part-time chemistry instr. Diablo Valley Coll., Pleasant Hill, Calif., 1991-93, Las Positas Coll., Livermore, Calif., 1992-93; mem. staff BIOCAD Corp. (A.K.A. Biosym Technologies), Mountain View, Calif., 1993; postdoctoral U. Calif., Santa Cruz, 1993-94; asst. prof. Am. Univ., Washington, 1994—. Contbr. articles to profl. jours.; patentee in field. Mem. Am. Chem. Soc. (preceptor 1995), Am. Assn. Pharm. Scientists, Am. Soc. Pharmacognosy. Office: Am Univ Dept Chemistry 4400 Massachusetts Ave NW Washington DC 20016-8014

ADAMOVICH, SHIRLEY GRAY, retired librarian, state official; b. Pepperell, Mass., May 8, 1927; d. Willard Ellsworth and Carrie (Shattuck) Gray; m. Frank Walter Adamovich, Aug. 31, 1960; children: Carrie Rose, Elizabeth Maude. BA, U. N.H., 1954; MS, Simmons Coll., Boston, 1955; LittD, New Eng. Coll., 1991. Cons. Vt. State Libr ., Montpelier, 1955-58; head cataloger Bentley Coll., Boston, 1958-60; tchr. U. N.H. System, Durham, 1965-79; asst. state librarian N.H. State Libr., Concord, 1979-81; state librarian N.H. State Library, Concord, 1981-85; commr. cultural affairs N.H. Dept. Cultural Affairs, Concord, 1985-92. Editor: A Reader in Library Technology, 1975, The Road Taken, 1989. Served in USAF, 1949-53. Mem. ALA, Nat. Commn. Librs. and Info. Scis., New Eng. Libr. Assn., N.H. Libr. Assn.

ADAMS, ALGALEE POOL, college dean, art educator; b. Columbia, Mo., Nov. 6, 1919; d. William I. and Anna Ethelene (Dunning) Pool; 1 dau., Judith Dean Adams. B.S. in Art and English, U. Mo., 1941, M.A. in Art, 1951; Ed.D. in Fine Arts and Art Edn, Pa. State U., 1960; postgrad. Inst. Advminstrv. Advancement, for Women, U. Mich.; postgrad., Inst. Ednl. Mgmt., Harvard U. Tchr. art Cuba (Mo.) High Sch., 1941-42, Hickman High Sch., Columbia, 1942-43; art specialist elementary schs. St. Joseph, Mo., 1943-45; tchr. art St. Clair (Mo.) High Sch., 1946-49; pub. sch. art supr. Webb City, Mo., 1949-51; instr. dept. of art St. Cloud (Minn.) State Coll., 1951-58, asst. prof., 1958-60, assoc. prof., 1960-63, prof., 1963-64, chmn. dept. art, 1959-64; prof. art edn. Mass. Coll. Art, Boston, 1964-77; also chmn. div. of edn. Mass. Coll. Art, 1967-70, dir. tchr. placement, 1964-70, dir. grad. programs in edn., 1970-77; chmn. grad. council, 1970-74; dean Firelands Coll. Bowling Green State U., Huron, Ohio, 1977-85; owner Adams Miniature Fiber Arts, Columbia, Mo., 1989; liaison with bus. and industry; mem. gov.'s adv. commn. on edn. in arts, 1958, 67; asso. dir. Project Renewal Mass. State Coll. System, 1974-76; art curriculum cons. to numerous pub. schs. in, Minn., 1951-64; art cons. to Minn. Ins. Info. Center, 1960-62; chmn. Eastern Arts Student Conf., N.Y.C., 1968; participant Internat. Conf., Notre Dame U., 1968; field reader HEW, 1966-70. Vol. tutor state literacy program; docent Detroit Inst. Arts. Recipient Artisian Status award Internat. Guild Miniature Artisians, 1991, Fellow status award, 1995. Club: Zonta. Home: 2604 Grant Ln Columbia MO 65203-0652

ADAMS, ALICE, sculptor; b. N.Y.C., Nov. 16, 1930; d. Charles P. and Loretto G. (Tobin) A.; m. William D. Gordy, Feb. 7, 1969; 1 dau., Katherine Adams Gordy. Student, Adelphi Coll., 1948-50; BFA, Columbia U., 1953; postgrad. (French Govt. fellow), 1953-54; postgrad. Fulbright Travel grantee, L'Ecole Nat d'Art Decoratif, Aubusson, France, 1953-54. Lectr. Manhattanville Coll., Purchase, N.Y., 1960-79; instr. sculpture Sch. Visual Arts, 1980-87. One-woman shows N.Y.C., 1972, 74, 75, Hal Bromm Gallery, N.Y.C., 1979, 80; group shows include Whitney Mus. Am. Art, N.Y.C., 1971, 73, Indpls. Mus. Art, 1974, Nassau County Mus. Fine Arts, Roslyn, N.Y., 1977, Wave Hill, Riverdale, N.Y., 1979, Mus. Modern Art, N.Y.C., 1984; represented in permanent collections Weatherspoon Gallery U. N.C., Greensboro, U. Nebr., Everson Mus., Syracuse, N.Y., Haags Gemetemuseum, The Hague, Netherlands, Edwin I. Ulrich Mus., Wichita, Kans.; pub. commissions include Bot. Garden, Toledo, Ohio, Design Team Seattle Transit Project, St. Louis Metro-Link Project, Midland Metro, Birmingham, Eng., Port Authority of N.Y. and N.J., Thomas Jefferson U., Phila., N.Y.C. Bd. Edn., State of Conn., Denver Internat. Airport, N.Y.C. Metro. Transp. Authority. Creative Artists Pub. Service grantee, 1973-74, 76-77; Nat. Endowment for Arts Artists grantee, 1978-79; Guggenheim fellow, 1981-82. Home: 3370 Fort Independence St Bronx NY 10463-4502

ADAMS, ALICE, writer; b. Fredericksburg, Va., Aug. 14, 1926; d. Nicholson Barney and Agatha Erskine (Boyd) A.; 1 son, Peter Adams Linenthal. A.B., Radcliffe Coll., 1946. Author: (novels) Careless Love, 1966, Families and Survivors, 1975, Listening to Billie, 1978, Rich Rewards, 1980, Superior Women, 1984, Second Chances, 1988, Caroline's Daughters, 1991, Almost Perfect, 1993, A Southern Exposure, 1995; (short story collections) Beautiful Girl, 1979, To See You Again, 1982, Return Trips, 1985, After You've Gone, 1989, (travel) Mexico: Some Travels and Travellers There, 1991; editor: Best American Short Stories, 1991; contbr. short stories to New Yorker mag., others. Recipient Best Am. Short Stories award, 1976, 92, 96, O. Henry awards, 1971-82, 84-96, Acad. and Inst. award in lit. Am. Acad. and Inst. of Arts and Letters, 1992; grantee NEA, 1976; Guggenheim fellow, 1978-79. Mem. PEN. Democratic Socialist. Office: Alfred A Knopf Inc Press Rels 201 E 50th St New York NY 10022-7703

ADAMS, BARBARA, English language educator, poet, writer; b. N.Y.C., Mar. 23, 1932; d. David S. Block and Helen (Taxter) Block Tyler; m. Elwood Adams, June 6, 1952 (dec. 1993); children: Steven, Amy, Anne, Samuel. BS, SUNY-New Paltz, 1962, MA, 1970; PhD, NYU, 1981. Prof. English Pace U., N.Y.C., 1984—, dir. bus. communications, 1984—; poet in residence Cape Cod Writers' Conf., 1988. Author: Double Solitaire, 1982, The Enemy Self: The Poetry & Criticism of Laura Riding, 1990, Hapax legomena, 1990; contbr. poems, stories, articles to various mags. and jours. Recipient 1st prize for poetry NYU and Acad. Am. Poets, 1975; Penfield fellow NYU, 1977. Mem. PEN, Poetry Soc. Am., Assn. Bus. Communication, Poets and Writers. Home: 57 Coach Ln Newburgh NY 12550-3818 Office: Pace U Pace Plz New York NY 10038

ADAMS, BEEJAY (MEREDITH ELISABETH JANE J. ADAMS), sales executive; b. Jefferson Banks, Mo., June 9, 1920; d. Alden Humphrey and Louise Marion (Banta) Seabury; m. Merlin Francis Adams, July 10, 1948 (dec. 1977); children: S(tephen) Kent, Mark Francis. AB, Bradley U., 1942. Svc. editor Peoria (Ill.) Jour. Star, 1942-46; women's program dir. Sta. WEEK-AM, Peoria, 1946-47; on air personality Sta. KSD-AM, St. Louis, 1948; lectr. Sch. Assembly Svc., Chgo., 1948-49; pres. M.F. Adams, Inc., Quincy, Ill., 1977-85; commodities broker Quincy, 1985-87; pres. MarKent, Inc., Quincy, 1975—; sec., treas. Miss. Belle Distbn. Co., Inc., Quincy, 1976—, v.p., treas., 1979—. Active Quincy Svc. League, 1949-57, local polit. campaigns, co-chmn. local presdl. campaigns, 1952-77; founder, past pres. Quincy Jr. Theatre, 1953-78; charter mem. Quincy Community Theatre; co-chmn. coll. fund drive Quincy Coll., 1988, chmn. 1989. Mem. Quincy C. of C., Adams County Red Cross Bd., Sales and Mktg. Execs. Club, Quincy Art Club, Atlantis Study Club, Quincy Country Club, Phi Beta Phi. Anglican. Home: 2303 Jersey St Quincy IL 62301-4343 Office: Miss Belle Distbn Co Inc PO Box 768 Quincy IL 62306-0768

ADAMS, BELINDA JEANETTE SPAIN, nursing administrator; b. Rome, Ga., Dec. 5; d. Oscar Joe and Eleanor (Camacho) Spain. Diploma, Ga. Bapt. Hosp. Sch. Nursing, Atlanta, 1974; BS in Nursing, Med. Coll. Ga., Augusta, 1976; MS in Nursing, Ga. State U., Atlanta, 1980, postgrad., 1990—. Cert. clin. specialist in med.-surg. nursing, intravenous nurse. Critical care flight nurse Critical Care Medflight, Inc., Atlanta, 1984-88; intravenous therapy coord. DeKalb Gen. Hosp., Atlanta, 1974-81; asst. prof. Mercer U., Atlanta, 1981-87; corp. dir. infusion/high tech. svcs. Kimberly Quality Care, Atlanta, 1988-92; cons. Profl. Learning Systems, 1992—; asst. prof. Clayton State Coll., Morrow, Ga., 1992-94, Ga. Bapt. Coll. Nursing, Atlanta, 1994-95. Mem. ANA, Intravenous Nurses Soc. (rsch. com.), Ga. Nurses Assn. Home: 5979 Eton Ct Norcross GA 30071-2030

ADAMS, BEVERLY JOSEPHINE, data processing specialist; b. Kansas City, Kans., Nov. 29, 1951; d. Cecil and Eula Laverne (Lynch) Brown; m. Theodore Lavern Adams, Sept. 20, 1969; children: Theodore Lavern Jr., Terry Levar, Traveon LeVar. AA in Data Processing, Kansas City Kans. Community Coll., 1980; BS in Mgmt. and Computers, Park Coll., Parkville, Mo., 1986; postgrad., Rockhurst Coll.; MA, Webster U., 1991. Sr. data processor AT&T, Kansas City, Mo., 1984-86, computer programmer, 1987—; profl. devel. and career devel. facilitator tng. orgn. AT&T, 1991-96; lectr. in field. Editor: (newspaper) Courier, 1969, (newsletter) Kansas City Link, 1987. Cons. Youth of Am., Kansas City, 1983; mem. Kansas City Chief's Football, 1968-72, Coalition Labor Union Women, Washington, 1984, AFL-CIO City Labor Coun., Kansas City, 1984; dir. ch. adult and youth choir, Kansas City, 1982—; Kans. state advisor Young Women's Christian Coun. Named one of Outstanding Young Women of Am., 1981-96. Mem. NAFE, Alliance AT&T Employees (chairperson 1987, treas. 1988-89, regional dir.), Profl. Women's Fedn., Young People's Willing workers, Nat. The. Alliance (nat. outstanding mem. award), Alpha Kappa Alpha (exec. bd., philacter, chairperson Debutante Ball), Gamma Mu Gamma (program chmn. 1985, exec. bd., pres.). Republican. Pentacostal. Clubs: Wecomo (svcs. award 1983), Young Adults Action (bd. dirs., Leadership award 1980), YWCA (Kansas City). Home: 2635 N 22nd St Kansas City KS 66104-4514 Office: AT&T Comms 2121 E 63rd St Kansas City MO 64130-3440

ADAMS, CAROL ANN, hairstylist; b. Fontana, Calif., June 2, 1970; d. Alfred Floyd and Rita Clara (Boyer) A.. Grad., DeLoux Sch Cosmotology, 1988. Lic. cosmotologist, 1988. Hair designer Duanes Hair Designs, Redlands, Calif., 1988-92; hairstylist Redlands Hair Co., 1992; receptionist H&R Block, Redlands, 1989-95; hairstylist The Rose of Sharon, Redlands, 1992—; fashon show stylist Jr. Assistance League, Redlands, 1994-96; vol. hairstylist Leukemia Soc., Redlands, 1995. Model for hairstyle competitions, 1989-92. Mem. Nat. Cosmotology Assn. Republican. Baptist. Office: The Rose of Sharon 101 E Redlands Blvd Ste 130 Redlands CA 92373

ADAMS, CAROLINE JEANETTE H., writer; b. Dallas, June 15, 1951; d. Bill Gene and Anita N. (Murrah) Hickey. BFA, So. Meth. U., 1973. Media buyer Jim Leslie & Assocs., Dallas, 1973; continuity dir. Sta. KZEW-FM, Dallas, 1973-75; adminstrv. asst. Neiman-Marcus Co., Dallas, 1975-77; exec. sec. Harris Data Communications, Dallas, 1978-80; mgr. classified sales ADWEEK/Southwest mag., Dallas, 1980-91; freelance copywriter, editor, proofreader, 1992-95; exec. asst. to pres., gen. mgr. KDFW-TV, 1995—. Editor, writer Dallas Advt. League newsletter, 1987-89. Mem. Press Club Dallas (editor bulletin 1993). Methodist. Avocations: travel, antiques, collecting soundtrack and rare record albums, restoring classic automobiles.

ADAMS, CHRISTINE BEATE LIEBER, psychiatrist, educator; b. Greensboro, N.C., June 20, 1949; d. Paul Lieber Adams and Marjorie Pinckney (Quackenbos) Ould; 1 child, Justin McKendree Adams-Tucker. Student, Agnes Scott Coll., 1967-69; BA in English Lit. with honors, U. Fla., 1971, MD, 1976. Diplomate Am. Bd. Psychiatry and Neurology (examiner 1985), Am. Bd. Child Psychiatry (examiner 1984, 91), Nat. Bd. Med. Examiners. Resident in gen. psychiatry U. Louisville Sch. Medicine, 1976-78, fellow in child psychiatry, 1978-80, asst. clin. prof. dept. psychiatry and behavioral scis., 1981—, attending psychiatrist consultation-liaison svc., 1992, 93; pvt. practice, Louisville, 1980—; med. advisor Social Security Adminstrn., HHS, Louisville, 1986—; child psychiatry cons. Seven Counties Svcs., Ky. Dept. Human Resources, 1989,, 93; physician advisor Healthcare Rev. Corp., Louisville, 1993—; reviewer Am. Jour. Psychiatry, 1983—; cons. So. Ind. Mental Health and Guidance Ctr., Jeffersonville, 1981-83, U. Fla., 1982; presenter in field. Contbr. articles to med. jours., chpts. to books. Bd. dirs. Gainesville (Fla.) Women's Health Ctr., 1973-75; mem. Jefferson County (Ky.) Juvenile Justice Commn., 1982-86. Recipient award Nat. Psychiat. Endowment Fund, 1980. Fellow Am. Acad. Child and Adolescent Psychiatry (com. on rights and legal matters 1984-92); mem. Am. Psychiat. Assn. (mem. com. family violence and child sexual abuse 1987-94), Am. Orthopsychiat. Assn., Am. Acad. Psychiatry and Law, Nat. Com. for Prevention Child Abuse, Ky. Psychiat. Assn., Ky. Acad. Child Psychiatry (sec.-treas. 1980-81, pres.-elect 1981-82, pres. 1982-83). Office: Med Arts Bldg Ste 3364 1169 Eastern Pky Louisville KY 40217-1417

ADAMS, CHRISTINE HANSON, advertising executive; b. Hackensack, N.J., May 24, 1950; d. Kenwood Alwin and Doris (Rogers) Hanson; m. L. Ashby Adams III, June 1, 1974 (div. Aug. 1993). BA, Lafayette Coll., 1972; MBA, Duke U., 1979. Med. sales rep. Hoffman-LaRoche, Nutley, N.J., 1972-75; sr. market rsch. analyst Burroughs Wellcome Co., Research Triangle Park, N.C., 1976-77, product planner, 1978; dir. market research Sterling Drug Inc., N.Y.C., 1979-81; group product mgr. Pfizer Inc., N.Y.C., 1981-83; account supr. Kallir Philips Ross Inc., N.Y.C., 1983, v.p., account group supr., 1984-86; v.p., account supr. Baxter Gurian and Mazzei Inc., Beverly Hills, Calif., 1987-89, account group v.p., 1990-91, sr. v.p. account group, supr., 1991-93, sr. v.p. mgmt. supr., 1994; sr. v.p. group acct. dir. Kallir Philips Ross Inc, N.Y., 1994-96; sr. v.p. mgmt. supr. Torre Renta Lazur Comm., Parsippany, N.J., 1996—; cons. advt. Wellness Cmty., Santa Monica, Calif., 1988-92. Active membership com. St. Michael's Episcopal Ch., Studio City, Calif., 1987-93, altar guild, 1988-93, tchr. Sunday sch., 1990-91. Named Young Career Woman Bus. Profl. Women's Assn., Chapel

Hill, N.C., 1978. Mem. Am. Mgmt. Assn., Healthcare Mktg. and Comms. Coun., Healthcare Businesswomen's Assn. Republican. Home: 8 Villa Dr Princeton Junction NJ 08550-1241 Office: Torre Renta Lazur Comms 20 Waterview Blvd Parsippany NJ 07054-1295

ADAMS, CONSTANCE EWING, school psychologist, art therapist; b. Troy, N.Y., Oct. 15, 1946; d. Walter Duncan and Gabrielle Roberts (Solomon) Ewing; m. Robert Maurice Adams, Aug. 23, 1969; children: Karen Gayle, Louise Katherine, Robert Ewing. BA, Denison U., 1968; MA, Ft. Hays (Kans.) State U., 1977; MS, Ea. Ky. U., 1988. Cert. art therapist, sch. counselor, Ky. Psychologist High Plains Comprehensive Cmty. Mental Health Ctr., Hays, 1970-72, art therapist, 1974-75; instr. Ft. Hays State U., 1974-79; sch. psychologist Madison County Schs., Richmond, Ky., 1987—; presenter in field; mem. adv. bd. Richmond Youth Svcs. Ctr., 1994—; mem.-at-large Sch. Psychology Coun., Ky. Dept. Edn., Frankfort, 1993—. Paintings exhibited in one-woman show, other invitational and juried exhbns., 1975-79. Mem. Kans. Gov.'s Commn. on Criminal Adminstrn., Hays, 1975; chair, pers. dir. Friendship Home, Youth Care, Inc., Kans., 1970-77; responder Ky. Cmty. Crisis Respnse Team, 1993. Mem. LWV (pres., bd. dirs. Hays chpt. 1970-79, bd. dirs., bull. editor, 2d v.p. Madison County chpt. 1980—), Nat. Assn. Sch. Psychologists (cert., Govtl. and Profl. Rels. award 1996), Am. Art Therapy Assn. (registered), Ky. Assn. for Psychology in Schs. (exec. coun. 1990—, program chair 1990-91, legis. chair 1991—, Ky. Sch. Psychologist of Yr. 1991), Am. Ednl. Rsch. Assn. Home: 390 Adams Ln Richmond KY 40475 Office: Madison County Schs 707 N 2d St Richmond KY 40475

ADAMS, DARLENE AGNES, secondary education educator; b. Prague, Okla., Aug. 23, 1952; d. Carney and Bertha Ellen (Capps) A. AS, Murray State Coll., 1972; BA, East Ctrl. State Coll., 1974, MEd, 1978. Tchr., libr. Carney Pub. Schs., 1974-75, Paden (Okla.) Pub. Schs., 1975—; staff devel com. Paden Pub. Schs., 1985-90, curriculum guidelines com., 1985—, career counseling com., 1990—, gifted and talented com., 1993—, sponsor jr. and sr. class plays and proms. Pres. The Chem. People, Paden, 1983—; sponsor Beta Club, 1990-91, 95-96. Mem. ALA, NEA, Okla. Library Assn., Okla. Edn. Assn., Smithsonian, Phi Theta Kappa. Republican. Pentacostal. Home: RR 1 Box 82 Paden OK 74860-9766 Office: Paden Pub Schs PO Box 370 Paden OK 74860-0370

ADAMS, DEBRA ANN, accountant; b. Cherryvale, Kans., Feb. 24, 1950; d. John LeRoy and Betty Jean (Carson) Hanchett; m. Tommy Wayne Adams, June 26, 1971. AA, Independence (Kans.) C.C., 1970; BBA, U. Hawaii-Manoa, Honolulu, 1978. CPA, Wash. Tax preparer Whidbey Tax Svc., Oak Harbor, Wash., 1978-79, 79-80; instr. acctg. Skagit Valley Coll., Oak Harbor, 1978-81; staff acct. Cascade Savings & Loan, Everett, Wash., 1982-84; trust tax preparer Bank of Calif., Seattle, 1985; gen. ledger acct. The Squire Shops, Seattle, 1985-86; acct. Mgmt. Northwest, Inc., Lynnwood, Wash., 1988-89, acctg. supr., 1989-95; acct. Wash. State Ferries-DOT, Seattle, 1995—. Mem. Inst. Mgmt. Acct., Phi Theta Kappa. Mem. Ch. of the Nazarene. Home: 20624 3d Place W Lynnwood WA 98036

ADAMS, ELAINE, art agent, publicist; b. L.A., Sept. 15, 1960; d. Mikhael Nikitovich Perieva-Shelby and Emma (Davidian) Shelby; m. Peter Seitz Adams, Mar. 12, 1990. BA in Econs. and Math., U. So. Calif., 1982. Stock broker Crowell, Weedon & Co., L.A., 1983-89; art agt., artist rep. Peter Adams Studio, Pasadena, Calif., 1990—; publicity chmn. Calif. Art Club, Pasadena, 1993. Editor Calif. Art Club newsletter, 1994—. Assoc. trustee Pacific Asia Mus., Pasadena, 1993, chmn. Festival of the Autumn Moon, 1994; bd. dirs. Pasadena Symphony, 1994. Mem. Am. Art Coun. (steering com.), Art Ctr. One-Hundred (bd. mem.). Republican. Russian Orthodox. Office: Calif Art Club PO Box 92555 Pasadena CA 91109-2555

ADAMS, JANE, actress. Diploma, Julliard Sch. performances include (Broadway) An Inspector Calls (Antoinette Perry award 1994), I Hate Hamlet, The Crucible (off-Broadway) The Nice and the Nasty, Psychoneurotic Phantasies, Mutterschaft (regional) Careless Love, Our Town, Love Diatribe, The Glass Menagerie (T.V.) The Rising Sun, Family Ties (film) Vital Signs, Light Sleeper, Mrs. Parker and the Vicious Circle, I Love Trouble, Father of the Bride II. Office: ICM care Lisa Loosemore 40 W 57th St New York NY 10019*

ADAMS, JEAN RUTH, entomologist, researcher; b. Edgewater Park, N.J., Aug. 17, 1928; d. Herbert Raymond and Gertrude Gladys (Budd) A. BS, Rutgers U., 1950, PhD (Trubeck fellow), 1962. Registered profl. entomologist. Lab. technician Rohm & Haas Co., Bristol, Pa., 1951-57; postdoctoral fellow U. Pa., Phila., 1961-62; rsch. entomologist U.S. Dept. Agr., Agr. Rsch. Ctr., Beltville, Md., 1962-96, collaborator, 1996—; cons. insect pathology, electron microscopy. Mem. nominating com. D.C. Bapt. Conv., 1977-79, dir. Acteens, Mission Youth Orgn., D.C. Bapt. Conv., 1972-87, 88—, Sunday sch. tchr. 1st Bapt. Ch., Hyattsville, Md., 1962—, chmn. Christian edn. bd., 1973-74, mem. nominating com., 1974-77, mem. bd. missions, 1977-80, ch. treas., 1973-74, mem. choir, 1979—, diaconate, 1980-86, 90—, vice chmn., 1981-82, chmn., 1982-91, trustee Bapt. Home, 1982-91, sec., 1985-91; trustee Sunday sch. bd. SBC, 1991—. Mem. editorial bd. Jour. of Invertebrate Pathology, 1986-89. Mem. Am. Registered Profl. Entomologists (bd. dirs. Chesapeake chpt. 1989—, pres. 1991-93), Electron Microscopy Soc. Am. (chmn. sci. exhibits ann. meeting 1982), Entomol. Soc. Am., Am. Soc. for Cell Biology, Soc. for Invertebrate Pathology (sec. 1982-84), Washington Soc. for Electron Microscopy (coun. 1976-83, sec.-treas. 1976-78, 80-82), Washington Entomol. Soc., Md. Entomol. Soc., Sigma Xi, Sigma Delta Epsilon. Editor: Atlas of Invertebrate Viruses, 1991, Insect Potpourri: Adventures in Entomology, 1992; contbr. articles to profl. jours. Home: 6004 41st Ave Hyattsville MD 20782-3058 Office: USDA Agr Rsch Ctr Bldg 011A W Insect Biocontrol Lab Rm 214 Beltsville MD 20705

ADAMS, JOANNE ATHENA, international public policy consultant; b. Houston, June 3, 1956; d. John A. S. Adams Sr. and Anne Donchin. BA in Philosophy, Rice U., 1981; MPA, Harvard U., 1994. Adminstrv. asst. Office of the Mayor, Houston, 1980-81, from asst. dir. to dir. communications, 1982-88, chief of staff, 1988-91.

ADAMS, JUANITA KAY (NITA ADAMS), public service administrator; b. Charleston, Ill., July 27, 1944; d. Charles Edward Gregory and Lois Juanita (Taylor) Wood; 1 child, April Lyn; m. Kenneth Roy Adams, Dec. 6, 1991. BA, Sangamon State U., 1980. Supr. fiscal mgmt. dept. adminstrn. svcs. State of Ill., Springfield, 1976-80, supr. gen. acctg. dept. commerce, 1980, supr. support svcs. dept. pub. health, 1980-84, audit mgr. dept. corrections, 1984-85, asst. chief of audit dept. pub. aid, 1985-94, asst. chief of audit dept. profl. regulation, 1994-96, pgm exec. adminstrv. svcs. profl. regulation, 1996—. Mem. NAFE, Assn. Info. Sys. Profls., Inst. Internal Auditors, Women in Mgmt., Capitol City Republican Women, Exec. Women in State Govt., Order of Eastern Star. Home: 2800 E Lake Shore Dr Springfield IL 62707-8912

ADAMS, JULIE KAREN, clinical psychologist; b. Portland, Oreg., Dec. 12, 1955; d. Allen Hays and Susanna Angelina (Meyers) A. B degree, Willamette U., 1977; M degree, Ctrl. Wash. U., 1982; cert. in bus. adminstrn., U. Wash., 1986; D degree, Pacific U., 1992. Lic. clin. psychologist; cert. counselor, sch. psychologist, Wash. Sch. psychologist Highline Sch. Dist., Seattle, 1987-90; psychology intern Elmcrest Psychiat. Hosp., Portland, Conn., 1990, clinician, 1991; rsch. asst. Yale U., New Haven, Conn., 1991; clinician Advanced Clin. Svcs., Seattle, 1991-93; postdoctoral fellow U. Wash., Seattle, 1991-93; acad. counselor Johns Hopkins U., Balt., 1993; behavior intervention specialist Edmonds (Wash.) Sch. Dist., 1993-94, Marysville Sch. Dist., Marysville, Wash., 1994—; instr. Seattle U., 1995—; guest spkr. in field to profl. assns., also Pacific U., U. Oreg., 1989—. Contbr. articles to profl. jours. Mem. tng. com., kids week com., nursing home com., pub. policy com. Jr. League of Seattle, 1988—; health care researcher Wash. State Legis., Olympia, 1993; campaigner Bush for Pres., Seattle, 1988, 92; rsch. asst. to state senator Oreg. State Legis., Salem, 1985; press page nat. conv. Rep. Nat. Com., Detroit, 1980; student grad. v.p., faculty rep. com. Pacific U. Sch. of Profl. Psychology, 1989-90. Mem. APA (health psychology com. student rep. 1992-93), Wash. Psychol. Assn., Willamette U. Alumni Assn. (bd. dirs. 1983-88), Vols. for Outdoor Wash. (bd. dirs. 1986-87), City Club of Seattle (membership com. 1986-88), Jr. League Seattle, Psi Chi, Beta Alpha Gamma. Home: 1038 NE 125th St Seattle WA 98125-4000

ADAMS, KAREN HOEVE, university administrator; b. Holland, Mich., Jan. 3, 1961; d. Erville Wayne and Nella Ruth (Heemstra) Hoeve; m. James Franklin Adams Jr., July 1, 1989; children: Lucas James, Matthew Wayne (twins). BA, Calvin Coll., 1983; MS in Edn., Ind. U., 1985, EdD, 1995. Asst. dir. student fin. assistance Bloomington Office Student Fin. Assistance, Ind. U., 1985-89; computing edn. trainer Ind. U. Computing Svcs., Bloomington, 1989-91, planning and comms. adminstr., 1991—. Bd. dirs. Bloomington Pops, 1993—. Home: 214 S Bryan St Bloomington IN 47408 Office: Ind U Computing Svcs 750 N SR 46 Bloomington IN 47405

ADAMS, KATHLEEN QUINN, pharmaceutical marketing executive; b. Southington, Conn., Aug. 28, 1963; d. Thomas Edward and Chrystene Ann (Curtis) A. AB in Biology and Philosophy, Bryn Mawr (Pa.) Coll., 1985; MPPM, Yale Sch. of Mgmt., New Haven, Conn., 1994. Project mgr. Genetics Inst., Cambridge, Mass., 1986-92; mgmt. assoc. Schering-Plough Internat., Kenilworth, N.J., 1994-96; assoc. prodn. mgr. Schering Oncology/Biotech, Kenilworth, N.J., 1996—. Mem. Healthcare Businesswomen's Assn. Office: Schering Oncology/Biotech 2000 Galloping Hill Rd K-5-2 Kenilworth NJ 07033

ADAMS, KELLY LYNN, emergency physician; b. High Point, N.C., Oct. 17, 1959; d. Roger Lee and Kathryn Maxine (Floyd) A. AA in Gen. Studies, U. Md., 1979; BA in Biology, Va. Intermont Coll., 1980; DO, Southeastern Coll. Osteo. Med., 1988. Cert. Am. Coll. Osteopathic Family Physicians. Emergency physician Humana South Broward, Hollywood, Fla., 1989-91; family practice physician Adams and Herzog, DO, PA, Plantation, Fla., 1990-91; emergency physician Homestead (Fla.) AFB, 1991-92, Mariners Hosp., Tavernier, Fla., 1991-93, Meml. Hosp., Pembroke Pines, Fla., 1992-96, Comp Health, Salt Lake City, 1996—. Recipient Cert. of Merit, State of Fla. and Fla. N.G., 1992. Mem. AMA, Am. Osteo. Assn., Fla. Osteo. Med. Assn., Broward County Osteo. Med. Assn., Assn. Emergency Physicians, Mensa. Republican. Home and Office: 5722 S Flamingo Rd #273 Cooper City FL 33330

ADAMS, LILIANA OSSES, music performer, harpist; b. Poznan, Poland, May 16, 1939; came to U.S., 1978, naturalized, 1990; d. Sylwester and Helena (Koswenda) O.; m. Edmund Pietryk, Sept. 4, 1965 (div. Aug. 1970); m. Bruce Meredith Adams, Feb. 3, 1978. MA, Music Acad. Poznan, Poland, 1971. Prin. harpist Philharm. Orch. of Szczecin, Poland, 1964-72, Imperial Opera and Ballet Orch., Tehran, Iran, 1972-78; pvt. music tchr. Riyadh, Saudi Arabia, 1979-81; soloist Austrian Radio, 1981-86; solo harpist, pvt. tchr. harp and piano Antioch, Calif., 1986—; music cons. Schs. and Librs., Calif., 1991—. Contbr. articles to profl. jours. Mem. Am. Fedn. of Musicians, Am. Harp Soc., Music Tchrs. Assn. Calif., Internat. Soc. of Harpers, U.K. Harp Assn., Internat. Harp Ctr. (Switzerland). Home: PO Box 233 Antioch CA 94509-0023

ADAMS, LINDA RUTH, elementary school educator; b. Canton, Ill., Feb. 21, 1948; d. Robert Linn and Annalee (Post) Haggerty; m. Gary Lee Adams, Mar. 11, 1967; children: Colin, Heather, Dawn. BA in Music, So. Ill. U., 1971; MS in Elem. Edn., Western Ill. U., 1992. Cert. elem. tchr., Ill. Music tchr. Bunker Hill, Ill., 1969-73, Dunfermline (Ill.) Sch. Dist., 1992-93; elem. tchr. Canton Christian Sch., 1991—; project facilitator Project Wild, Ill., 1991—, Project Wild/Aquatics, Ill., 1991—. Dir. Christian edn. Covenant Comty. Fellowship Ch., Canton, 1992—; bd. dirs. Comty. Concert Assn., Canton, 1982—; sec. Canton Christian Sch. Bd., 1992-95. Mem. Nat. Coun. Tchrs. Math., Ill. Sci. Tchrs. Assn., Lamoine Emergency Amateur Radio Club, Fulton County Amateur Radio Club, Phi Kappa Phi. Home: 35 Sycamore Terr Canton IL 61520

ADAMS, LINETTE M., principal. Prin. Benjamin Banneker High Sch., Washington. Recipient Blue Ribbon Sch. award U.S. Dept. Edn., 1990-92. Office: Benjamin Banneker High Sch 800 Euclid St NW Washington DC 20001-2296

ADAMS, LORRAINE, reporter. BA in English, Princeton U., 1981, MA in English, 1982. With The Concord (N.H.) Monitor, 1983, 84, The Dallas Morning News; now projects reporter The Washington Post, now metro reporter. Recipient Pulitzer Prize for investigative reporting, 1992. Office: Washington Post 1150 15th St NW Washington DC 20071-0001*

ADAMS, MARGARET BERNICE, retired museum official; b. Toronto, Ont., Can., Apr. 29, 1936; came to U.S., 1948, naturalized, 1952; d. Robert Russell and Kathleen Olive (Buffin) A.; m. Alberto Enrique Sánchez-Quiñonez, Nov. 30, 1956 (div. 1960). AA, Monterey Peninsula Coll., 1969; BA, San Jose State U., 1971; MA, U. Utah, 1972. Curator ethnic arts Civic Art Gallery, San Jose, 1971; staff asst. Utah Mus. Fine Arts, Salt Lake City, 1972; lectr./curator Coll. Seven, U. Calif., Santa Cruz, 1972-74; part-time educator Cabrillo Coll., Aptos, Calif., 1973, Monterey Peninsula Coll., 1973-84; dir. U.S. Army Mus., Presidio of Monterey, 1974-83; chief. mus. br. Ft. Ord Mil. Complex, 1983-88; Guest curator Am. Indian arts Monterey Peninsula Mus. Art, 1975-88. Author: Indian Tribes of North America and Chronology of World Events in Prehistoric Pueblo Times, 1975, Historic Old Monterey, 1976; cntbg. editor Indian Am., (exhibit catalogue) Writing on the Wall: WWII Patriotic Posters, 1987; contbr. articles to jours. Mem. native Am. adv. panel AAAS, Washington, 1972-78; mem. rev. and adv. com. Project Media, Nat. Indian Edn. Assn., Mpls., 1973-78; working mem. Program for Tng. Am. Indian Counsellors in Alcoholism Counselling and Rehab. Programs, 1972-74; mem. hist. adv. com. Montery County Bd. Suprs., 1987-89. Grad. fellow, dean's scholar U. Utah, 1972; dean's scholar Monterey (Calif.) Peninsula Coll., 1969, San Jose (Calif.) State U., 1971. Mem. Am. Anthrop. Assn., Am. Assn. Museums, Soc. for Applied Anthropology, Soc. Am. Archeology, Am. Ethnol. Soc., Nat., Calif., Indian edn. assns. Home: PO Box 51983 Pacific Grove CA 93950

ADAMS, MARIE JANE REED, naturopathic physician; b. Cleve., Oct. 14, 1925; d. David Clifford and Irene Lucille (Spilker) Reed; m. Raymond John Adams, Dec. 31, 1949 (div. Sept. 1983); children: Leslie Jane, Leah Rae, Jeanne Marie, Anne Kathryn. BS in Occupl. Therapy, Ohio State U., 1946; Cert. in Phys. Therapy, Stanford U., 1947; Dr. Naturopathic Medicine, Bastyr Coll.Naturopathic Med., Seattle, 1990. Phys. therapist Asheville (N.C.) Orthop. Home, 1948-49; head dept. occupl. therapy dept. orthop. U. Ill. Hosps., Chgo., 1949-52; self-employed naturopathic physician Seattle, 1990—. Coord. in-sch. program Seattle Art Mus., 1972-73, docent chmn., 1973-75, touring docent, 1965-80. Mem. Am. Assn. Naturopathic Physicians, Wash. Assn. Naturopathic Physicians. Home: 4209 2d Ave NE Seattle WA 98105 Office: The Vitality Clinic 3931 Bridge Way N Seattle WA 98103

ADAMS, MARY RAPRICH, retired nursing education administrator; b. Lonoke, Ark., July 25, 1918; d. Fred A. and Katie (Kittler) Raprich; children: Richard, Dorothy A. Grad., St. Vincent Infirmary, Little Rock; BSN, Case Western Res. U., 1951, MSN, 1953. Sr. asst. nurse officer USPHS, 1944-48; head nurse, supr. Ohio USPHS, Ohio, 1954-58; instr. nursing edn. Akron (Ohio) City Hosp. Sch. Nursing, 1954-58, Akron Gen. Hosp. Sch. Nursing, 1958-60; dir. nursing edn. affiliate program pediatrics Children's Hosp., Akron, 1961-83, ret. Sr. asst. nurse officer USPHS, 1944-48. Mem. Nat. League for Nursing, Sigma Theta Tau. Home: 1146 Raprich Rd Lonoke AR 72086-9271

ADAMS, NANCY R., nurse, military officer. BSN, Cornell U., N.Y. Hosp. Sch. Nursing; MSN, Cath. U. Am.; grad., Command and Gen. Staff Coll., U.S. Army War Coll. Commd. Nurse Corps, U.S. Army, 1968, advanced through grades to brig. gen., 1991; chief nurse Army Regional Med. Ctr., Frankfurt, Germany, 1987-89; nursing adminstr. various locations; nurse cons. to U.S. Surgeon Gen., 1989-91; chief Nurse Corps Ctr. for Health Promotion and Preventive Medicine, U.S. Army, 1991—, asst. surgeon gen., comdr., 1993—; now Army Nurse Corps Office of Chief, Surgeon Gen. U.S. Army, 1994—. Author textbooks; contbr. articles to profl. jours. Fellow Am. Acad. Nursing; mem. ANA, Assn. Mil. Surgeons of U.S., Am. Orgn. Nurse Execs., Sigma Theta Tau. Office: Army Nurse Corp Office of Chief 5111 Leesburg Pike # 5 Falls Church VA 22041-3206

ADAMS, PATRICIA MURPHY, special education educator; b. Mt. Kisco, N.Y., Aug. 12, 1947; d. John A. and Natalie (Coffey) Murphy; m. Gerald N. Adams, July 29, 1989; children: Frank R. Mattoni, Christopher T. Mattoni, Howard M. Adams, Melissa J. Adams. BA in Psychology, Mercy Coll., Dobbs Ferry, N.Y., 1978; MS in Reading, L.I. U., Dobbs Ferry, 1983. Cert. in elem. edn., reading, spl. edn., N.Y. Spl. edn. tchr. North Salem (N.Y.) Schs., 1980—; bd. dirs., chair No. Westchester Tchr. Ctr., North Salem, 1982-89; tchr. critical thinking, effective teaching program N.Y. State United Tchrs., Albany, 1985-89; tchr. writing Fairfield (Conn.) U., 1985. Bd. dirs., sec. Mt. Kisco (N.Y.) Recreation Commn., 1987-89; mem. com. Mt. Kisco Meml. Day Com., 1985-89. Coun. for Ednl. Children lending libr. grantee, 1980s; Danbury News Times/Union Carbide Learning Links grantee, 1994. Mem. Coun. for Exceptional Children, Internat. Reading Assn., Assn. for Learning Disabilities, Autism Soc. Am., Kappa Delta Pi. Democrat. Roman Catholic. Home: 105 Horseshoe Hill Rd Pound Ridge NY 10576-1636 Office: Pequenakonck Elem Sch 173 June Rd North Salem NY 10560

ADAMS, PHOEBE, sculptor; b. Greenwich, Conn., 1953. BFA, Phila. Coll. Art, 1972; postgrad., Skowhegan Sch. Painting, Maine, 1977; MFA, SUNY, Albany, 1978. Solo shows include Lawrence Oliver Gallery, Phila., 1984, 86, 90, Curt Marcus Gallery, N.Y.C., 1987, 90, 94, Pence Gallery, Santa Monica, Calif., 1988, 91, Locks Gallery, Phila., 1993; exhibited in group shows at Sophia's House, Morris Gallery, Pa. Acad. Fine Arts, Phila., 1983, New Horizons in Am. Art, Exxon Nat. Exhibit, Solomon R. Guggenheim Mus., N.Y.C., 1985, Sculpture on the Wall, Aldrich Mus. Contemporary Art, Ridgefield, Conn., 1987, Sculpture Inside/Out (with catalog) Walker Art Ctr., Mpls., 1988, Works on Paper, 92, Curt Marcus Gallery, N.Y.C., 1993, Process to Presence: Issues in Sculpture 1960-1990, 1992, Les Objects d'artistes: Objects of Domestic Elegence for the Home, Locks Gallery, Phila., 1994, Small Sculpture Triennial 1993 (with catalog) Walker Hill Art Ctr., Seoul, Korea, 1993; two person exhibit Ind. U. Pa., 1993, N.S. Art and Design, Halifax, 1994, others; works in permanent collections at Solomon R. Guggenheim Met. Mus. Art, N.Y.C., Bklyn. Mus., AT&T, Chgo., Pa. Acad. Fine Arts, Phila., Pa. Conv. Ctr., Phila. Mus. Art, Storm King Art Ctr., Mountainville, N.Y., Prudential Ins. Co., Walker Art Ctr., Mpls., Harn Mus., Fla., others; commns. include: Sculpture for outdoor garden, Walker Art Ctr., Mpls., 1988, Intaglio print, Friends of the Phila. Mus. Art, 1991, sculpture Pa. Conv. Ctr., Phila., 1993. Recipient Pa. Coun. Arts awards, 1982, 84, Guggenheim Sculptor in Residence award, Chesterwood, Stockbridge, Mass., 1986; Nat. Endowment Arts fellow, 1986. Office: Locks Gallery 600 S Washington Sq Philadelphia PA 19106-4155*

ADAMS, PHOEBE-LOU, journalist; b. Hartford, Conn., Dec. 18, 1918; d. Harold Irving and Alice (Burlingame) A. A.B. cum laude, Radcliffe Coll., 1939. Reporter Hartford Courant, 1942-45; with editorial staff Atlantic Monthly, Boston, 1945—. Author: A Rough Map of Greece, 1965. Office: The Atlantic 77 N Washington St Boston MA 02114

ADAMS, REBECCA ANNE, elementary education educator; b. Portsmouth, N.H., Nov. 14, 1951; d. William Willard Leonard; m. Charles Roberts Adams, Sept. 12, 1970; children: Tanya C., Kara J., Chay. BS in Edn., U. So. Maine, 1985. Tchr. elem. sch. S.A.D. #60, Berwick, Maine, 1985—. Co-author: (curriculum) Primary K-3 Curriculum, 1994. Mem. Phi Kappa Phi. Home: RFD #2 Box 104 Alfred ME 04002 Office: Hussey Primary PO Box 1156 Berwick ME 03901-1156

ADAMS, ROSE ANN, management consultant; b. McHenry, Ill., Apr. 4, 1952; d. Clemens Jacob and Marguerite Elizabeth (Freund) A. BS in Edn., Ill. State U., 1974; MEd, U. Ark., 1979. Supt., exec. dir. Clinton County Children's Services, Wilmington, Ohio, 1979-81; dir. ednl. and adult svcs. Bost Human Devel. Svcs., Ft. Smith, Ark., 1981-87; adminstrv. officer Cen. Ark. Devel. Coun., Benton, 1987; adminstrv. officer, interim Head Start dir., dir. resource devel. Community Orgn. Poverty Elimination Pulaski, Lonoke Counties, Little Rock, 1987-93; exec. dir. So. Early Childhood Assn., 1993-94; cons. Earl Moore and Assocs., Little Rock, 1994—. Active Welfare Adv. Bd., Clinton County, 1979-81, Home Econs. Extension Svcs. Adv. Com., 1979-81, adv. bd. U. Ark. Women's Ctr., 1979; coord. White House Conf. on Families, 1980; mem. Task Force Child Abuse, 1985; trustee Multiple Sclerosis Soc., Ark.; bd. dirs. Morris Found.; chair Ark. Health Promotion Coalition; vice-chair Pulaski County Local Planning Group; chair Ark. Com. on Women's Concerns; charter mem. Am. Lung Assn. of Ark. Aux.; adv. com. Ark. Mentors; pres., v.p. Ark. Single Parent Scholarship Fund. Named one of Outstanding Young Women of Am., 1982. Mem. Am. Bus. Women's Assn. (Woman of Yr. Avant Garde chpt. 1992). Home: Sonata Trl # 1 Little Rock AR 72205-1632 Office: Earl Moore and Assocs 300 S Spring St Ste 612 Little Rock AR 72201-2422

ADAMS, SALLYANN KELLY, chiropractor; b. Omaha, Aug. 28, 1952; d. Paul Samuel and Sally Mae (Hayman) Kelly; m. Larry Leon Adams, Dec. 27, 1985; children: Laurie, Ryan, Mica, Kelly, Sarah, Paul, Levi, Jana, Benjamin, Samuel. D. of Chriopractic, Palmer Coll., 1976; AA, Parkland Coll., Champaign, Ill., 1977. Bd. cert. chiropractic orthopedist. Dir. Moore Chiropractic Family Ctr., Danville, Ill., 1977-84; assoc. Barrow Chriopractic Ctr., Hattiesburg, Miss., 1984-86; owner, pres. Adams Chiropractic, Gautier, Miss., 1986—; mem. Miss. State Bd. Chiropractic Examiners, 1992—. Mem. NAFE, Miss. Assn. Chiropractors (chmn. worker's comp PPO 1990-91, Spl. Recognition award 1990, Achievement award 1991, Clinician of Yr. 1993), Am. Bus. Women's Assn. (Spl. Recognition 1991), Am. Chiropractic Assn. Latter Day Saints. Office: Adams Chiropractic 1408 Hwy 90 Gautier MS 39553-5449

ADAMS, SARA JANE, artist; b. Ozark, Ala., Jan. 9, 1963; d. William Carey and Cassie B. (Smith) A.; m. Farrell Bedsole, May 5, 1989 (div. Apr. 1994); 1 child, Sierra Michele. Student, Lurleen B. Wallace Coll., Andalusia, Ala., 1994—. Vet. helper Barr's Veteranarian, Ozark, 1979-81; sales person Avon, Tuscaloosa, Ala., 1981-82; cashier Busy Bee, Birmingham, Ala., 1981-82; dancer Baby Doe's, Birmingham, 1981-83; farmer Hog Farm, Columbia, La., 1985-86; nursery worker Campground Bapt., Ozark, 1988; bakery worker Bruno's, Dothan, Ala., 1987-88; window worker McDonalds, Ozark, 1986-89. Designer Art Club, Ozark, 1976-81. Recipient Performance Scholarship Art Work, Andalusia, 1995, 96. Home: 501 7th St PO Box 185 Opp AL 36467

ADAMS, SUSAN MEZGER, chiropractor; b. Lansing, Mich., Oct. 8, 1962; d. Marvin Arthur and Joanne (Burgie) Mezger; m. D. Kurt Adams. Student, U. Mich.; D of Chiropractic, Palmer Coll., Davenport, Iowa. Chiropractor Summit Family Chiropractic, Lexington, Ky. Mem. BBB, Bus. and Profl. Women (past pres. Lexington chpt.), Progressive Execs. (past pres. Lexington chpt.), Ky. Chiropractic Soc. (pres. ctrl. regional chpt.), Rotary (Lexington), Greater Lexington C. of C. Office: Summit Family Chiropractic 3167 Custer Dr Ste 202 Lexington KY 40517

ADAMS, VICTORIA ELEANOR, retired realty company executive; b. San Francisco, Feb. 8, 1941; d. George Mulford and Sarah Louise (Dearborn) A.; m. Gene M. Richardson, 1965 (div. 1972); 1 child, Raymond; m. Franklin Carlisle Boosman, 1972 (div. 1990); 1 child, Eric; m. Harold Glen Kirchner, Mar. 14, 1992. AA, Palomar Coll., 1976; BBA summa cum laude, Nat. U., 1978. Sales adminstr. Evergreen Internat. Airlines, McMinnville, Oreg., 1983; corp. adminstr. N.N. Jaeschke, Inc., San Diego, 1984—; adminstrv. mgr. Tomlinson Agy., Inc., Spokane, Wash., 1980-86; v.p. Champion Realty Inc., Spokane, 1987-93; pub. dir. Champion Pubs., 1987-93; ret., 1993. Editor: Bravura, 1976; (text) Science Among Us, 1965, Principles in Action Newsletter, 1992—; author: No More than 4 Ingredients Cookbook, 1994; designer Astrology game, 1974. Contbr. articles to profl. jours. Solicitor, Am. Heart Assn., 1985. Recipient Cert. Real Estate Sales Achievment, 1978, 1982, 85, 86, 88, 89, 91; Cert. Outstanding Contbn. to Real Estate Edn., 1980. Avocations: writing, ednl. rsch., fishing, camping, traveling. Home: Apt 3433 6110 Pleasant Ridge Rd Arlington TX 76016-4307

ADAMS-ANDERSON, NIKI MARIA, communications company executive; b. Baytown, Tex., Oct. 18, 1954; d. Fred Elester and Carl Juanita (Brown) A. BS in Speech Pathology, Lamar U., Beaumont, Tex., 1978. Cert. tchr., Tex.; cert.engring. planning. Speech therapist South Park Ind. Sch. Dist., Beaumont, 1978-79; mgr. engring. design Southwestern Bell Telephone Co., Beaumont, 1979-85; mgr. engring. planning Southwestern Bell Telephone Co., Dallas, 1985-90, Houston, 1990—; tutor, mentor Harlem Elem. Sch.,

Baytown, Tex., 1995; mentor Duncanville (Tex.) Mid. Sch., 1989-90; tutor Furr H.S., Houston, 1990-91. Mem. NAACP (membership recruitment nat. conv.), Telephone Pioneers Am., Tex. Soc. Telephone Engrs. Home: PO Box 1932 Baytown TX 77522

ADAMSEN, JULIA MAHLER, account executive; b. Mineola, N.Y., Oct. 23, 1960; d. John Francis and Nancy (Badyna) Mahler; m. William Ross Adamsen, Oct. 11, 1986. BS in Bus. Mktg., SUNY, Stony Brook, 1984; degree in direct mktg., NYU, 1988. Account exec. Advo System, Inc., Hartford, Conn., 1984-88; account mgr. Donnelly Mktg., Stamford, Conn., 1988—; sr. v.p. & dir. corp. mktg. KeyCorp, Cleveland, OH. Mem. Hammond Mus., N. Salem, N.Y., 1986—, Wilton (Conn.) Hist. Soc., 1987—, United Way, Wilton, 1987—. Mem. Women's Direct Response Group, Retail Advt. Conf., NAFE, Ad Club of N.Y. Office: Donnelly Mktg 70 Seaview Ave Stamford CT 06902-6040*

ADAMSON, JANE NAN, elementary school educator; b. Amarillo, Tex., Feb. 5, 1931; d. Carl W. and Lydie O. (Martin) Ray; 1 child, Dave R. Student, Amarillo Coll., Richland Coll. Univ. Dallas, North Tex. State U.; BS, West Tex. A&M U., Canyon, 1953; MEd, Tex. A&M U., Commerce, 1975; diploma, Inst. Children's Lit., 1991; cert., Bur. Edn. and Rsch., 1995. Cert. elem. tchr., Tex.; lic. real estate salesman. Tchr. Dallas Ind. Sch. Dist. Mem. Alliance of Dallas Educators, Navy League U.S.

ADAMSON, MARY ANNE, geographer, systems engineer; b. Berkeley, Calif., June 25, 1954; d. Arthur Frank and Frances Isobel (Key) A.; m. Richard John Harrington, Sept. 20, 1974. BA with highest honors and great distinction U. Calif., Berkeley, 1975, MA, 1976, postgrad., 1976-78. Cert. tchr. earth scis., Calif.; cert. cave rescue ops. and mgmt., Calif.; lic. emergency med. technician, Contra Costa (Calif.) County, 1983. Teaching asst. dept. geography U. Calif., Berkeley, 1976; geographer, environ. and fgn. area analyst Lawrence Livermore Nat. Lab., Livermore, Calif., 1978-83, cons., 1983-86; systems engr. ESL, Sunnyvale, Calif., 1986-90; rsch. analyst, rsch. devel. and analysis P.G. & E., San Francisco, 1990-93; admin. asst. Internal Audit Dept., 1993—. Contbr. articles to profl. jours. With USNR, 1983—, lt. comdr., 1993—. Recipient Navy Achievement medal, 1992. Staff mem. ARC/Am. Trauma Soc/Sierra Club Urgent Care and Mountain Medicine seminars, 1983—. Asst. editor Vulcan's Voice, 1982. Mem. Assn. Am. Geographers (life), Assn. Pacific Coast Geographers, Nat. Speleol. Soc. (geology, geography sects., sec., editor newsletter Diablo Grotto chpt. 1982-86), Toastmasters Internat. Club (adminstrv. v.p. Blue Monday Club 1991), Sierra Club (life), Nature Conservancy (life), U. Calif. Alumnae Assn., Phi Beta Kappa. Home: 4603 Lakewood St Pleasanton CA 94588-4342 Office: PG&E Internal Auditing 245 Market St San Francisco CA 94105-2230

ADAN, SUZANNE, painter; b. Woodland, Calif., Feb. 12, 1946. BA, Calif. State U., Sacramento, 1969; MA, 1971. Instr. drawing Am. River Coll., Sacramento, 1975-76; represented by Michael Himovitz Gallery, Sacramento. Exhbns. include San Francisco Mus. Modern Art, 1971, Whitney Mus. Art, 1973-74; one-woman shows include Womanspace, L.A., 1974, Betsy Rosenfield Gallery, Chgo., 1983, 85, Himovitz-Salomon Gallery, Sacramento, 1984, 86, 93, John Berggruen Gallery, San Francisco, 1987; group shows include Meml. Union Gallery, U. Calif., Davis, 1990, 94, Crocker Art Mus., Sacramento, 1991, 94, Spectrum/Himovitz Gallery, San Francisco, 1991, Am. Cult. Ctr., Brussels, 1992, Holmes Fine Art Gallery, San Jose, Calif., 1993, many others; represented in permanent collections Crocker Art Mus., Sacramento, Continental Bank, Houston, Lexecon, Inc., Chgo., Impact Commun, Bloomington, Ill., Livingston & Mattesich, Sacramento, U. Calf. Med. Ctr., Sacramento, Nat. Sta., Folsom, Calif. Recipient Hardison, Komatsu, Ivelich & Tucker award Richmond Art Ctr., 1980, James D. Phelan Art award San Francisco Found. Kala Inst., Berkely, 1991; New Works grantee Sacramento Met. Arts Commn., 1990. Mem. Coll. Art Assn. Address: 3977 Rosemary Cir Sacramento CA 95821 Office: Michael Himovitz Gallery 1020 10th St Sacramento CA 95814*

ADATO, LINDA JOY, artist, educator; b. London, Oct. 24, 1942; d. John and Renee (Katz) Falber; m. Albert Adato, June 26, 1966; 1 child, Vanessa. Student, Hornsey (Eng.) Coll. of Art, 1960-61; BA in Pictorial Arts, UCLA, 1966, MA in Art Edn., 1967. Adj. lectr. in art Manhattanville Coll., Purchase, N.Y., 1987—; printmaking tchr. Silvermine Sch. of Art, New Canaan, Conn., 1995—. Exhibitions include Achenbach Found. for Graphic Arts, Fine Arts Mus., San Francisco, 1987, Decordova Mus., Lincoln, Mass., 1990, Portland (Oreg.) Art Mus., 1994, Art Complex Mus., Duxbury, Mass., 1994, Newark Pub. Libr., 1994. Recipient anonymous prize for prints Nat. Acad. Design, 1990, Karlene Cusick Purchase award print Club of Albany, 1995. Mem. Soc. Am. Graphic Artists (treas. 1995—, Purchase award 1985). Home: 20 Pratt St New Rochelle NY 10801

ADATO, PERRY MILLER, documentary producer, director, writer; b. Yonkers, N.Y.; d. Perry and Ida (Block) Miller; m. Neil M. Adato, Sept. 11, 1955; children: Laurie, Michelle. Student, Marshalov Sch. Drama, N.Y.C., New Sch. Social Research; L.H.D. hon., Ill. Wesleyan U., 1984. Film research coordinator CBS-TV, N.Y.C., 1959-64, producer, 1964; assoc. producer NET (became WNET Thirteen, Pub. Broadcasting System 1972, N.Y.C., 1964-68, producer dir., 1968-92; lectr. Fairfield U., Conn., 1974-75; exec. prodr. Alvin H. Perlmutter Inc./Ind. Prodn. Fund, 1992-96, 13/WNET, Westport, Conn., 1996—; guest lectr. on film Harvard U., Columbia U., NYU, Yale U., others, 1970—; mem. film award jury Am. Film Inst., Beverly Hills, Calif., 1974; judge film award Creative Artists Pub. Svc., N.Y.C., 1976; first chmn. UN Women in the Arts Film Com., 1976-77; pres. jury Montreal Internat. Film Festival, 1990; mem. jury Pompidou Ctr., Paris Internat. Festival of Films on Art, 1994. Producer, dir.: (TV documentary films) Dylan Thomas: The World I Breathe, 1968 (Emmy award for outstanding achievement in cultural documentary 1968), Gertrude Stein: When This You See, Remember Me, 1970 (Montreal Festival Diplome d'Excellence 1970, Am. Film Festival Blue Ribbon award 1970, 2 Emmy nominations for outstanding direction and outstanding achievement in cultural documentary 1971), The Great Radio Comedians, 1972 (Am. Film Festival Red Ribbon award 1975), An Eames Celebration: Several Worlds of Charles and Ray Eames, 1973 (Chgo. Internat. Film Festival Silver Hugo award 1973, Am. Film Festival Red Ribbon award 1973), Mary Cassatt: Impressionist From Philadelphia, 1974 (Women in Communications Clarion award 1974), Georgia O'Keeffe, 1977 (Dirs. Guild Am. award for documentary achievement 1977-1st woman to receive any Dirs. Guild Am. award, NCCJ Christopher award 1978, Com. for Internat. Events Golden Eagle award 1978, Women in Communications Clarion award 1978, Alfred I. DuPont/Columbia U. citation 1978), Frankenthaler: Toward a New Climate, 1978 (Am. Film Festival Blue Ribbon award in fine arts 1979), Picasso: A Painter's Diary, 1980 (Dirs. Guild Am. award for directorial achievement in TV documentary 1980, Alfred I. DuPont/Columbia U. award for excellence in broadcast journalism 1980, Com. for Internat. Events Golden Eagle award 1980, Am. Film Festival Blue Ribbon award in fine arts 1980, Montreal Internat. Festival of Films on Art First prize for Best Biography of an Artist 1981), Carl Sandburg: Echoes and Silences, 1982 (Women in Communications Matrix award 1982, American Women in Radio and TV (Pinnacle award for TV documentary 1982), Dirs. Guild Am. award for achievement in TV documentary 1983), Eugene O'Neill: A Glory of Ghosts, 1984-85, Broadcast, 1986 (Most Outstanding Achievement in TV Documentary award Dirs. Guild Am. 1986, Spl. Jury award San Francisco Film Festival 1985, Internat. Film and TV Festival of N.Y. Silver medal 1986); exec. producer (9-hour TV series): Art of the Western World, 1985-89; producer, dir., writer: A White Garment of Churches, 1989 (Clarion award 1990, Silver Plaque award Chgo. Internat. Film Festival 1990, Silver Cindy award 1990); exec. prodr. 3 part series Asian Art, 1990-94; prodr., dir. Great Tales in Asian Art, 1993-94; writer Dream Journeys-Nature in East Asian Art, 1994-95; prodr. R & D Alfred Stieglitz, 1996. Hon. bd. dirs. Weston-Westport (Conn.) Arts Coun., 1981-89. Poynter fellow Yale U., 1976; grantee NEA, 1977-78, 93, NEH, 1980, 83, 91, 93; Calhoun Coll. fellow Yale U., 1993—; subject tribute, Montreal Internat. Art Film Festival, 1990; recipient Westport (Conn.) Arts Coun. award in visual arts category, 1996. Mem. NATAS, Dirs. Guild Am., Writers Guild Am., Women in Communications, N.Y. Women in Film and TV.

ADCOCK, MURIEL W., special education educator; b. Chgo.. BA, U. Calif. Sonoma State, Rohnert Park, 1979. Cert. spl. edn. tchr., Calif., Montessori spl. edn. tchr. Tchr. The Concordia Sch., Concord, Calif., 1980-85; tchr., cons. Tenderloin Community Children's Ctr., San Francisco, 1985-86; adminstr. Assn. Montessori Internat.-USA, San Francisco, 1988, tchr., advisor, 1989—; course asst. Montessori Spl. Edn. Inst., San Francisco, 1985-87, tchr. spl. edn., 1990, tchr. cons., 1991—, rschr. 1992—. Contbr. articles to profl. jour. Sec. Internat. Forum World Affairs Coun., San Francisco, 1990-95, program chair, 1993-95. Mem. ASCD, Coun. for Exceptional Children, Nat. Assn. Edn. Young Children, Am. Orthopsychiat. Assn., Am. Assn. Mental Retardation, Assn. Montessori Internat., N.Am. Montessori Tchrs. Assn., Assn. Childhood Edn. Internat., Smithsonian Assocs., N.Y. Acad. Scis., Nat. Geog. Soc., Menninger Found. Office: PO Box 424519 San Francisco CA 94142-4519

ADDIS, DEBORAH JANE, management consultant; b. Rahway, N.J., Jan. 29, 1950; d. Emmanuel and Stella (Oles) Addis; m. James Eldin Reed, Apr. 14, 1983. BA, Bowling Green State U., 1972; MA in Orgn., Mgmt. and Pub. Policy, Lesley Coll., Cambridge, Mass., 1992. Pub. info. officer Dept. Transp., State of Ohio, 1972-73; dir. pub. info. and edn. Dept. Commerce, State of Ohio, 1973-75; press sec. Atty. Gen., State of Ohio, 1975-77; dep. press sec. Office of Gov., Commonwealth of Mass., Boston, 1978-79; sr. account exec. Miller Communications, Boston, 1979-80; v.p., prin. Addis & Reed Cons., Inc., Boston, 1981-91, pres., 1992—; adj. faculty Lesley Coll. Grad. Sch., 1992—. Author monograph and articles, congl. testimony; mng. editor The American Canada Watch, 1995. Bd. govs. Women's City Club of Boston, 1982-85; mem. Ohio Task Force on Domestic Violence, Columbus, 1976. Mem. New Eng.-Can. Bus. Coun. (bd. dirs. 1994—), Harvard Club of Boston. Democrat. Home: 25 Holly Ln Chestnut Hill MA 02167-2156 Office: Addis & Reed Cons Inc PO Box 85 Chestnut Hill MA 02167

ADDIS, MARGUERITE CHRISTJOHN (CHRIS ADDIS), physical therapist; b. Pitts., Sept. 14, 1930; d. Preston Arthur and Marguerite Elizabeth (Shirley) Christjohn; m. Richard Barton Addis, Feb. 9, 1957 (div. Oct. 1989); children: Jacqueline Carol Addis, Barton David. BS in Phys. Therapy, Boston U., 1952. Phys. therapist Ohio State U. Hosp., Columbus, 1952-57, Pa. Easter Seals Camp, White Haven, 1954, 55, 56, Canton (Ohio) Rehab. Ctr., 1957-58, Tinken-Mercy Hosp., Canton, 1959-62, Lovelace Med. Ctr., Albuquerque, 1987-89, Ednl. Assessment Systems, Albuquerque, 1990-94, Rehab. Ctr. Inc., 1994-96. Mem. Am. Phys. Therapy Assn., N.Mex. Phys. Therapy Assn.. Home: 3708 Hannett Ave NE Albuquerque NM 87110-4914

ADDISON, DONNA MARIE, artist, art therapist; b. Franklin Park, Ill., June 24, 1962; d. John Thomas and Maryann (Guarascio) Addison; m. Matthew Vincent, Sept. 29, 1984 (div. Mar. 1986). BFA in Ceramics and Drawing cum laude, Rockford (Ill.) Coll., 1984; MS in Art Therapy, No. Ill. U., 1993, postgrad., 1993-95. Program specialist/seasonal employee Rockford Park Dist., 1987-93; art therapist Rockford Meml. Hosp., 1993-95; crisis intervention officer of the day Janet Wattles Ctr., Rockford, 1994—. Artist/author mo. newspaper col.: Women's Sports Corner, Rock River News, 1991—; artist in drawing and ceramics. Vol. AIDS Care Network, Rockford, 1991-92; co-founder Lesbian/Bisexual Counselors Networking Group, Rockford, 1995—; vol. campaign Barb Gioletto, Rockford, 1994, John Cox, Rockford, 1992, others; mem. Ill. Gay and Lesbian Task Force. Recipient David McKay award No. Ill. U., 1994. Mem. ACLU, Am. Art Therapy Assn. (student editor newsletter 1991-93, student concerns co-chair 1991-92), Ill. Art Therapy Assn. Democrat. Office: Janet Wattles Ctr 526 W State St Rockford IL 61101

ADDISON, HELEN KATHERINE, marketing professional, art dealer; b. N.Y.C., June 4, 1954; d. Arthur Michael and Helen Irene (Ernst) Weber; m. Keith Robert Scott, Oct. 1, 1979 (div. Oct. 1986). BA, Syracuse U., 1973; MBA, Cornell U., 1978. Prin. Addison & Assoc., Orleans, Mass., 1980—, Addison Holmes Gallery, Orleans, Mass., 1995—; bd. dirs. Cape Cod Arts Found., Hyannis, Mass., Ctr. for Coastal Studies, Provincetown, Mass. Bd. corporators Seamens Bank, Provincetown, 1995—. Recipient Creative Excellence award Hotel Sales and Mktg. Assn., 1993-94, South Shore Ad Club, 1990-93, Cape Cod Ad Club, 1989-92. Mem. Orleans C. of C. (v.p. 1992), Provincetown Bus. Guild, Provincetown C. of C., Cape Cod C. of C., Cape Mus. Fine Arts, Provincetown Art Assn. and Mus., Addison Holmes Fine Art Gallery (pres.), Boston Mus. of Fine Arts. Unitarian. Office: Addison & Assoc PO Box 2756 43 S Orleans Rd Orleans MA 02653

ADDISON, SARAH, cosmetics executive; b. Chgo., Apr. 12, 1953; d. James and Elnora (Murrell) Russell; m. Ronald Merritt Sr., Sep. 21, 1971 (div. 1984); children: Ronald Merritt Jr., Shantell Merritt, Chevette Merritt; m. Stephen Jospeh Addison, Nov. 14, 1994; children Dontele L. Addison, Donyele L. Addison. Diploma, Debbie Sch. of Beauty Cult., 1986; BS in cosmetology, Dudley UNC, 1992. Barber Goldie's Barber Shop, Chgo., 1984-85; hair stylist, barber Dynasty, Chgo., 1985-86, Mrs. Curry's, Chgo., 1990-94, Lady Sarah's Hair Salon, Chgo., 1994—. Office: Lady Sarahs Hair Salon 6114 W Roosevelt Rd Oak Park IL 60304

ADDISS, SUSAN SILLIMAN, public health consultant; b. New Haven, Apr. 3, 1931; d. Thomas North Tracy and Susan Silliman (Bennett) Pearson; m. James M. Addiss, Apr. 21, 1956 (div. July 1967); children: Justus Joseph, Susan Silliman. BA, Smith Coll., 1951; MPH, M. Urban Studies, Yale U., 1969. Health educator New Haven Health Dept., 1969-72; health dir. Naugatuck Valley Health Dist., Ansonia, Conn., 1972-76; health planning bur. chief Conn. Dept. Health Svcs., Hartford, Conn., 1976-85; health dir. Quinnipiack Valley Health Dist., Hamden, Conn., 1985-91; health commr. Conn. Dept. of Pub. Health and Addiction Svcs., Hartford, 1991-95; lectr. Dept. of Epidemiology & Pub. Health, Yale Univ., 1970—, Univ. Conn. Health Ctr., Farmington, 1978—; asst. clin. prof. Yale Sch. of Nursing, 1988—. Chair bd. Pub. Health Found., 1996. Mem. APHA (pres. 1984), Conn. Pub. Health Assn. (pres. 1985-87, C.E.A. Winslow award 1994), Nat. Assn. for Pub. Health Policy (treas. 1978-93), Quota Internat. New Haven (pres. 1996-97), Phi Beta Kappa (Smith Coll. medal 1981).

ADDY, JAN ARLENE, clinical nurse, educator; b. Balt., Apr. 16, 1951; d. James Anderson and June Annette (Windsor) Briggle; m. Rick Edward Addy, Feb. 26, 1988; children: Brittany Anissa, Richard Michael. AA in Nursing, Essex Community Coll., Balt., 1972; BSN, U. San Francisco, 1976; MS, U. Md., Balt., 1979; postgrad., Nova Southeastern U. Cert. sch. health nurse, pub. health nurse. Sr. staff nurse Francis Scott Key Med. Ctr., Balt., 1980-87; clin. instr. Harford Community Coll., Bel Air, Md., 1987-88; primary nurse and nurse educator U. Md., Balt., 1987—; asst. prof. Baltimore City C.C., 1994—; mem. rev. faculty for Nat. State Bd. Exam. for Nursing; mem. adj. faculty Catonsville C.C., 1994; instr. jr. students St. Joseph's Hosp. Sch. Nursing, Towson, Md., 1979-80; clin. instr., skills instr. Essex C.C., 1978-79; mem. U. Md. Med. Sys. Partnership Program, Frederick Douglas H.S. Contbr. articles to profl. jours. Mem. ASCD, Nat. Soc. Trauma Nurses, Nat. Nursing Staff Devel. Orgn., Emergency Nurses Assn., C.A.R.E., Sigma Theta Tau (program com. Pi chpt.).

ADE, BARBARA JEAN, secondary education educator; b. Youngstown, Ohio, Nov. 6, 1951; d. Donald Eugene Sr. and Louise Ann (Bodnark) Kihm; m. Robert Randal Ade, Mar. 17, 1973. BS in Edn., Youngstown State U., 1975, MS in Edn., 1987. High sch. media specialist Springfield Local High Sch., New Middletown, Ohio, 1975—. Active Youngstown Area YWCA. Grad. Sch. scholar Youngstown State U., 1986-87; named Woman of the Yr., Youngstown Area YWCA, 1993. Mem. Ohio Ednl. Libr./Media Assn., Nat. Edn. Assn., Ohio Edn. Assn., Delta Kappa Gamma, Phi Delta Kappa. Democrat. Roman Catholic. Office: Springfield Local High Sch 11335 Youngstown Pittsburgh Rd New Middletown OH 44442-9738

ADEKSON, MARY OLUFUNMILAYO, therapist; b. Ogbomoso, Nigeria; came to U.S., 1988; d. Gabriel and Deborah Williams; children: Adedayo, Babatunde. BA in English and Am. Lit., Brandeis U., 1975; MEd in Guidance and Counseling, Obafemi Awolowo U., Ile-Ife, Nigeria, 1987; PhD, Ohio U., 1996. English tchr. Cen. Sch. Bd., Ibadan, Nigeria, 1976-88; acting prin. Abe Tech. Coll., Ibadan, 1978; coord. guidance svcs. Min. Edn., Ile-Ife, 1984-88; part-time lectr. Obafemi Awolowo U., Ile-Ife, 1986-88; vice prin. Olubuse Meml. High Sch., Ile-Ife, 1987-88; grad. asst. Ohio U., Athens, 1988-91; vol. contract worker, trainer Careline, Tri-County Mental Health Ctr., Athens, 1988-92; vol. My Sister's Place, Athens, 1989, Good Works Athens, 1989, Montgomery County Hotline, 1994; contract worker Tri County Activity Ctr., Athens, 1989-92, therapist II Woodland Ctr., Gallipolis, Ohio, 1991-92; part-time lectr. U. Md., 1993, coord. tutorial svcs.; dir. Christian Book Ctr., Ile-Ife; vol., part-time counselor DWI program Prince George's County Health Dept., Hyattsville, Md.; counselor Potomac Healthcare Found. Mountain Manor Treatment Program. Vol. Montgomery County Police Dept.; mem. Alcohol and Other Drug Abuse Adv. Coun., Montgomery County, Md.; mem. adv. com. Germantown (Md.) Libr.; mem. Gaithersburg (Md.) City Adv. Com.; chmn. bd. dirs. Faith Enterprises, Germantown. Recipient Gold medal West African Athletic Assn., 1965; Internat. Peace scholar P.E.O., 1990-91, Wien Internat. scholar Brandeis U., 1973-75. Mem. ACA, Am. Mental Health Counselors Assn. Network on Children and Teens (membership chair 1991-92, chair 1993—), Am. Assn. Counseling and Devel. (award for internat. grad. students 1990), Counseling Assn. Nigeria (planning com. 1986), Am. Rehab. Counselors Assn., Am. Mental Health Counseling Assn., Assn. Multicultural Counseling and Devel., Oyo State Assn. Guidance Counselors (chmn. Oranmiyan local govt. area 1986-88), Chi Sigma Iota (program coord. ou chpt. 1990).

ADELEKAN, PATRICIA ANN, school administrator; b. Columbus, Ohio, Mar. 13, 1942; d. Arthur H. and Betty Jane Isbell; children: Adebola, Adetokunbo, Aderemi, Adegboyega. BA, Ohio State U., 1966; MA, U. San Francisco, 1975; PhD, U. Ibadan, 1983. Cert. coll. adminstr., secondary tchr. Tchr. various schs., Hartford, Conn. and Oakland, Calif., 1968-75; v.p. Lagos State Coll. Edn., Nigeria, 1976-80; dept. head Ogun State Poly. U., Nigeria, 1980-84; rsch. specialist Sacramento City (Calif.) Unified Sch. Dist., 1985-87; lectr. Sierra Coll., Rocklin, Calif., 1988-89; founder, pres. Youth-on-the-Move, Inc., Sacramento, 1986—; cons. Gifted and Talented Edn., Sacramento, 1985-86; columnist Sacramento Observer, 1987—; founder Youth-on-the-Move, Inc. Prep. Acad. and Family Learning Ctr., 1992, Youth-on-the-Move, Inc. African Am. Multicultural Hall of Fame, 1993. Author: Hall of Fame Educators, 1993, Multicultural Hall of Fame Educators, 1993, 94, 95; prodr. Youth Talk, a live youth radio program, 1993; editor: Multicultural Hall of Fame Educators, 1995, numerous articles; contbr. articles to profl. jours.; pub./editor Youth-on-the-News, monthly newspaper, 1989—. V.p. YWCA, Sacramento, 1988-89; commr. County Children's Commn., Sacremento, 1989—; mem. Leadership Sacramento, 1988-89; program coord. World Exch., 1991—; chairperson Juneteenth Art & Music Festival, 1991-95. Recipient Cert. of Recognition award, Assemblyman Norman Waters, 1981, Proclamation award City of Sacramento Mayor, 1989, Plaque of Achievement award, 1989, Love and Help Children award, Luminary of the Yr. award Coors, 1992, Outstanding Woman Cmty. Leader YWCA, 1991-95, over 25 awards and honors, 1992—; named to African Am. Educators' Hall of Fame, 1993. Mem. Calif. Tchr.'s Assn., Nat. Assn. French Tchrs., Nat. Mensa Soc., AAUW (chair edn. com.), NAFE, Nat. Coun. of Negro Women, Inc. (life), Friends of Marva Collins (founder), Phi Delta Kappa. Home: PO Box 22106 Sacramento CA 95822-0106

ADELMAN, IRMA GLICMAN, economics educator; b. Cernowitz, Rumania, Mar. 14, 1930; came to U.S., 1949, naturalized, 1955; d. Jacob Max and Raissa (Ettinger) Glicman; m. Frank L. Adelman, Aug. 16, 1950 (div. 1979); 1 son, Alexander. BS, U. Calif., Berkeley, 1950, MA, 1951, PhD, 1955. Teaching assoc. U. Calif., Berkeley, 1955-56; instr. U. Calif., 1956-57, lectr. with rank asst. prof., 1957-58; vis. asst. prof. Mills Coll., 1958-59; acting asst. prof. Stanford, 1959-61, asst. prof., 1961-62; assoc. prof. Johns Hopkins, Balt., 1962-65; prof. econs. Northwestern U., Evanston, Ill., 1966-72, U. Md., 1972-78; prof. econs. and agrl. econs. U. Calif. at Berkeley, 1979-94; prof. emeritus, 1994—; cons. divsn. indsl. devel. UN, 1962-63, AID U.S. Dept. State, Washington, 1963-72, World Bank, 1968—, ILD, Geneva, 1973—. Author: Theories of Economic Growth and Development, 1961, Institutions and Development Strategies: Selected Essays of Irma Adelman Volume I, 1994, Dynamics and Income Distribution: Selected Essays of Irma Adelman Volume II, 1994, Selected Essays (in Spanish), 1994, (with A. Pepelasis and L. Mears), Village Economies: Design, Estimation and Application of Village Wide Economic Models, New York, Cambridge U. Press, 1996, Economic Development: Analysis and Case Studies, 1961, (with Eric Thorbecke) The Theory and Design of Economic Development, 1966, (with C.T. Morris) Society, Politics and Economic Development—A Quantitative Approach, 1967, Practical Approaches to Development Planning-Korea's Second Five Year Plan, 1969, (with C.T. Morris) Economic Development and Social Equity in Developing Countries, 1973, (with Sherman Robinson) Planning for Income Distribution, 1977-78, (with C. T. Morris) Comparative Patterns of Economic Growth, 1850-1914, 1987. Fellow Center Advanced Study Behavioral Scis., 1970-71. Fellow Am. Acad. Arts and Scis., Econometric Soc., Royal Soc. Encouragement Arts, Mfgs. & Commerce; mem. Am. Econ. Assn. (mem. exec. com., v.p. 1969-71). Office: Univ Calif Dept Agr & Natural Resources 207 Giannini Hall #3310 Berkeley CA 94720-3310

ADELSON, GLORIA ANN, financial executive; b. Savannah, Ga., Aug. 3, 1944; d. Lee Roy and Edith Thelma (Horovitz) Schraibman; m. Joseph Harvey Adelson, Mar. 19, 1967 (dec.). BA in Polit. Sci., U. Fla., 1965; MA in Bus., Webster U., 1991. Budget analyst U.S. Dept. Labor, Silver Spring, Md., 1967; mgmt. analyst U.S. Naval Supply Ctr., Charleston, S.C., 1967-69, budget analyst, 1969-70, head fin. mgmt. staff, 1970-73, head. ops. and maintenance br., 1973-75; mgmt. coord. officer So. Divsn. Naval Facilities Engring. Commd., Charleston, 1975-80, dir. budget br., 1980-85, dir. budget and programs divsn., 1985-88, dep. dir. programs and comptroller dept., 1988—. Fin. sec., treas. Synagogue Emanu-El, Charleston, 1982-88; pres. Sisterhood Emanu-El, Charleston, 1993-94, 95-96; active patron com. Am. Cancer Soc., Charleston, 1989, 91, 95; mem. fed. sector com. United Way, Charleston, 1991. Mem. Am. Soc. Mil. Comptrollers (Charleston chpt., chair coms. 1987—, v.p. Navy, 1990-91, pres., 1991-92), Trident Area Cmty. Excellence Comm. Team. Home: 4 Berwick Cir Charleston SC 29407 Office: So Divsn Naval Facilities Engring Commd 2155 Eagle Dr Charleston SC 29406-4804

ADENIRAN, DIXIE DARLENE, library administrator; b. L.A., May 26, 1943; d. Alfred and Madge (Clare) Harvey. BA, U. Calif., Santa Barbara, 1965; MA, Mich. State U., 1968; MLS, U. Mich., 1970. Libr. Free Libr. of Phila., 1970-72, Coll. Sci. and Tech., Port Harcourt, Nigeria, 1972-73; libr. Ventura (Calif.) County Libr. Svcs. Agy., 1974-79, libr. dir., 1979—; chair Black Gold Coop. Libr. Sys., 1995—. Pres. Ventura County Master Chorale and Opera Assn., 1985. Mem. ALA, Calif. Libr. Assn. (assembly 1994—), Calif. County Librs. Assn. (pres. 1988), Soroptimists (pres. Ventura club 1984). Home: 5548 Rainier St Ventura CA 93003-1135 Office: Ventura County Libr Svcs 4274 Telegraph Rd Ventura CA 93003-3706

ADICKES, SANDRA ELAINE, English language educator, writer; b. N.Y.C., July 14, 1933; d. August Ernst and Edythe Louise (Oberschlake) A.; 1 child, Delores, Sept. 16, 1966. BA, Douglass Coll., 1954; MA, CUNY, 1964; PhD, NYU, 1977. Asst. registrar NYU, 1954-55; sec. McCann Erickson, J. Walter Thompson Cos., N.Y.C., 1955-60; English tchr. N.Y.C. Bd. Edn., 1960-70, 1980-88; instr. edn. N.Y.C. Tech. Coll., 1970-72; asst. prof. English S.I. C.C., N.Y.C., 1972-77; dir. project chance Bklyn. Coll., 1977-80; from assoc. prof. to prof. English Winona State U., Minn., 1988—; cons. Antioch Coll. N.Y.C., 1970; guest tutor London U., 1979. Author: The Social Quest, 1991, Legends of Good Women, 1992; editor: By A Woman Writt, 1973; contbr. articles to profl. jours. Co-founder Tchrs'. Freedom Sch. Project, Miss., 1963-64, Tchrs'. Com. for Peace Vietnam, 1965-66. Named Woman of Yr. Nat. Assn. Negro Bus. Profl. Women, N.J., 1966. Mem. MLA, Midwest Modern Lang. Assn., Nat Coun. Tchrs. of English. Democrat. Home: 579 W 7th St Winona MN 55987-4226 Office: Winona State U Dept English Winona MN 55987

ADILETTA, DEBRA JEAN OLSON, business analyst consultant; b. Gloucester, Mass., Oct. 1, 1959; d. Melvin Porter Jr. and Ruth Margaret (Dahlmer) Olson; m. Mark Anthony Adiletta, Aug. 25, 1984; children: Christopher Michael, Nichole Brianna, Mark Andrew. BA, Coll. of Holy Cross, Worcester, Mass., 1981; MBA, U. Rochester, 1986. Systems analyst Eastman Kodak Co., Rochester, N.Y., 1981-85, infosystems specialist, 1985-86, personal computer area mgr., 1986-87, bus. analyst cons., 1987—. seminar instr., Rochester, 1987. Fin. advisor Sts. Peter and Paul Ch., Rochester, 1985-86; div. chairperson United Way, Rochester, 1987. Mem. Assn. Systems Mgmt., Holy Cross Alumni Assn. (class agt. 1981—, sec. 1983-84, treas. 1984-88, v.p. 1988-90, pres. 1990-91, bd. dirs. 1992—). Office: Eastman Kodak Co 343 State St Rochester NY 14650-0001

ADILETTO, ROSEMARY A., community prevention educator, consultant; b. Honolulu, Oct. 9, 1943; d. Alfred L. Boardman and Annamarie (Trimarco) Hummel; m. Stephen J. Adiletto Jr., Sept. 15, 1962; children: Stephen III, Daniel. Student, Thomas A. Edison State Coll., 1990—. Cert. prevention specialist, PA. Cmty. organizing cons. Bucks County (Pa.) Drug and Alcohol Commn., New Britain, 1983-84, prevention specialist, 1984-88, prevention program supr., 1988-95; prevention program coord. TODAY, Inc., Newtown, Pa., 1995—; tng. cons. Pa. Dept. Health, Harrisburg, 1985—; co-developer SkillBuilders comty. devel. tng., 1989; developer, author Project MEDS (medication edn. designed for srs.), 1991, Many Voices, One Choir comty. planning model, 1993, Comty. Visions, Pa. ofcl. comty. mobilization model, 1995, Pa. Ofcl. Prevention Protocols Tng., 1996. Chmn. bd. Children's Cultural Ctr., Doylestown, Pa., 1993-96, Bensalem (Pa.) Coun. on Arts and Culture, 1994—, Bensalem Pride Days, 1990—; bd. dirs. Bucks County Anti-Violence Coalition, 1996; bd. dirs. nominating com. Lower Bucks YWCA; co-chmn. Bensalem Tricentennial, 1988-92; mem. Bensalem Comty. Devel. Bd., 1994—; chairperson risk assessment Bucks County (Pa.) Violence Prevention Task Force, 1995-96; bd. dirs. Bucks County Ret. Sr. Vol. Program, Doylestown, 1990-94. Recipient Presdl. Vol. Program Action award Pres. George Bush, 1991; named Vol. of Yr., Bucks County, 1984, Bensalem Twp., 1994. Mem. Commonwealth Prevention Alliance (bd. dirs. 1986-93), Nat. Assn. Prevention Profls. and Advocates, Pa. Prevention Dirs. Assn. Comty. Anti-Drug Coalition of Am. Democrat. Roman Catholic. Home: 4450 Yates Rd Bensalem PA 19020 Office: TODAY Inc P O Box 908 Newtown PA 18940

ADKERSON, DONYA LYNN, clinical counselor; b. Mattoon, Ill., Oct. 5, 1959; d. Edwin Dwayne and Sonya Jeanne (Abernathie) Adkerson; m. George Anthony Ferguson, May 20, 1990; 1 child, Tiana Jo Berry. MA, So. Ill. U., Edwardsville, 1983. Outpatient dir. Children's Ctr. for Behavioral Devel., Centerville, Ill., 1983-90; pvt. practice psychotherapy Evaluation & Therapy Svc., Edwardsville, 1991-92; dir. Alternatives Counseling, Inc., 1993—; cons. St. Louis City Juvenile Ct., 1991-94, Covenant Children's Home, 1991-93. Co-author: Adult Sexual Offender Assessment Packet, 1994. Pres. Ill. Network for Mgmt. Abusive Sexuality, 1991; clin. mem. Assn. for Treatment of Sex Abusers, exec. bd., 1994—, mem. ethics and stds. com., founding mem. Ill. chpt., 1996; mem. Cmty. Coordinating Coun. Domestic Violence, 1996—; mem. Adolescent Perpetrator Network, 1987-95; exec. bd. Arts League Players Theatre, Edwardsville, 1986—; former chmn. Metro-East Task Force on Sexual Offenders. Mem. ACA, Ill. Counseling Assn., Ill. Mental Health Counselors Assn. Office: Alternatives Counseling 1 Mark Twain Plz Edwardsville IL 62025

ADKINS, BETTY A., state legislator; b. Mpls., June 4, 1934; d. John Edward and Barbara (Graff) Whalen; m. Wally Adkins, 1956; children—Patrick, Susan, Michael, Kathleen, Caroline, Nancy. Student North Hennepin Community Coll.; student U. Minn., 1952-53. Formerly dep. clk. Otsego Twp., vice chmn. Wright County Bd. Adjustment, Minn.; mem. Minn. Senate, St. Paul, 1982—. Formerly chmn. Wright County Democratic-Farmer-Labor Party. Home: 200 Grand Ave NE Saint Michael MN 55376-9722 Office: State Senate State Capital Building Saint Paul MN 55155-1606 also: 550 Central Ave E Saint Michael MN 55376-9522

ADKINS, GERRY WHITLOCK, elementary school educator; b. Brevard, N.C., Dec. 28, 1946; d. Dean Crane and Geneva Burnice (Hunter) Whitlock; m. Cary Neil Adkins, June 15, 1973; 1 child, Sarah Elizabeth (Betsy). BS in Health and Phys. Edn., Berea Coll., 1970; MA in Health and Phys. Edn., Western Carolina U., 1975. Cert. phys. edn. tchr., N.C., W.Va., Tenn., Ariz.; cert. spl. edn. tchr., Tenn., N.C. Spl. edn. tchr. Canton (N.C.) Jr. H.S., 1971-73, Gilvert (W.Va.) Elem. Sch., 1973-74, Keystone & Fairmont Elem. Sch., Johnson City, Tenn., 1974-78; health and phys. edn. tchr. Phoenix Christian H.S., 1978-85; spl. edn. tchr. Emma Elem., Asheville, N.C., 1985-87; elem. tchr. phys. edn. Weaverville (N.C.) Elem. and Primary Sch., 1987-95, coach jump rope team, 1988—; counselor, co-dir. Buncombe County Camp for Mentally Handicapped, Asheville, summers 1967-70; presenter, demonstrator at state conv., Activities in Elem. Phys. Edn., 1989. Coord. Jump Rope for Heart Am. Heart Assn., Asheville, 1989, 91, 93-95; organizer Soccer Youth League, 1988. Mem. AAHPERD, N.C. Alliance Health, Phys. Edn., Recreation and Dance, N.C. Edn. Assn., Profl. Educators N.C. Baptist. Home: 869 Fletcher Martin Rd Alexander NC 28701-8746

ADKINS, JEANNE M., state legislator; b. North Platte, Nebr., May 2, 1949. BA, U. Nebr. Journalist; mem. Colo. Ho. of Reps., chairwoman judiciary com., vice-chairwoman legal svcs. com., mem. fin. com., regional air quality control coun., state edn. accountability commn. Founding sec. Douglas County Econ. Devel. Coun., bd. dirs., 1988. Fellow Vanderbilt U. Govt., Gates fellow JFK Sch. Govt. State/Local Program, Toll fellow. Mem. Am. Soc. Newspaper Editors, Soc. Profl. Journalists, Suburban Newspaper Assn. Republican. Baptist. Home: 6505 E Alcorn Ave Parker CO 80134-8003 also: 11086 Rodeo Cir Parker CO 80134-7344 Office: House of Reps State Capitol Rm 271 Denver CO 80203*

ADKINS, ROSANNE BROWN, speech and language pathologist, myofunctional therapist; b. Norfolk, Va., Jan. 10, 1944; d. Melvin Dillard and Mattye Marie (Cox) Brown; BS, U. Ga., 1968, MEd, 1971; m. Steve Bunker, Aug. 24, 1962 (div.); children: Steve, Amy Bunker Patterson; m. Jon Adkins, May 27, 1988. Speech pathologist Barrow County Schs., Winder, Ga., 1968-69, Madison County Schs., Danielsville, Ga., 1969-70, Hall County Schs., Gainesville, Ga., 1971-72, Hope Haven Sch. for Retarded Children, Athens, Ga., 1972-73, Buford (Ga.) City Schs., 1973-75, Duval County Bd. Pub. Instrn., Jacksonville, Fla., 1975-79, Orange County Pub. Schs., Orlando, Fla., 1979—. Sallie Maude Jones scholar, U. Ga., 1966-68; USPHS grad. fellow, 1970-71. Mem. Am. Speech-Lang.-Hearing Assn. (cert. of clin. competence), Fla. Lang. Speech and Hearing Assn. Delta Zeta, Zeta Phi Eta, Kappa Delta Pi, Phi Kappa Phi. Mem. Disciples of Christ. Clubs: Order Amaranth (past Royal Matron). Editor, Speakeasy, Speech and Language Newsletter, 1982—. Home: 2997 Carlsbad Ct Oviedo FL 32765-8438 Office: Orange County Sch System 434 N Tampa Ave Orlando FL 32805-1220

ADKINS, SUSAN IRENE, pediatric orthopedic nurse; b. Miami, Fla., Aug. 28, 1953; d. Robert Count Adkins and Mary Louise Craig. Student, Tex. Women's U., 1976. Cert. Am. Oper. Rm. Staff nurse St. Luke's Hosp., Houston, 1976-80; ICU/PACU dialysis nurse Med. Plz. Hosp., Ft. Worth, 1980-81; OR nurse spl. project St. Luke's Hosp., Houston, 1982-89; customer support rep. Enterprise Sys., Inc., Bannockbum, Ill., 1989-90; mgr. surgical support scheduling St. Lukes Hosp., Houston, 1990-91; nurse Fondren Orthopedic Group, Houston, 1991—. Mem. Am. Oper. Rm. Nurses. Republican. Roman Catholic. Home: 3310 Sansford Cir Katy TX 77449-6639

ADKISON, LINDA RUSSELL, geneticist, consultant; b. Columbia, S.C., Apr. 28, 1951; d. George Palmer Russell, Jr. and Annie Frances (Ingram) White; m. Daniel Lee Adkison, Jan. 28, 1978; children: Emily Kathleen, Seth Adams Russell. BS, Ga. So. U., 1973, MS, 1977; PhD, Tex. A&M U., 1986. Lab. tech. VA Hosp., Gainesville, 1973-75, Shands Teaching Hosp., Gainesville, Fla., 1973-75; grad. teaching asst. Ga. So. U., Statesboro, 1975-77; rsch. assoc. U. South Ala. Med. Sch., Mobile, 1978-80; instr. St. Mary's Dominican Coll., New Orleans, 1980-81; grad. rsch. asst. Tulane Med. Sch., New Orleans, 1980-82, Tex. A&M U., College Station, 1982-86; postdoctoral fellow Jackson Lab., Bar Harbor, Maine, 1986-89; asst. prof. genetics Mercer U. Sch. Medicine, Macon, Ga., 1989-94, assoc. prof. genetics, 1994, assoc. prof. ob-gyn., 1995—, asst. prof. ob-gyn., 1991-95, assoc. prof. ob-gyn., 1995—. contbr. more than 40 articles to profl. jours. Vol. Girl Scouts Mid. Ga., Macon, 1990—, Abnaki Girl Scout Coun., Bar Harbor, 1986-89, Ctrl. Ga. Boy Scouts, Macon, 1993—. Mem. AAAS, Am. Soc. Human Genetics, Grad. Women in Sci., Internat. Mammalian Genome Soc., S.E. Regional Genetics Group, Genetics Soc. Ga. (bd. dirs. 1990—), Ga. Acad. Sci., Am. Men and Women in Sci., Sigma Xi. Home: 1699 Wesleyan Bowman Rd Macon GA 31210-1037 Office: Mercer Univ Sch Medicine 1550 College St Macon GA 31201-1554

ADLER, ADRIENNE EDNA-LOIS, art dealer, gallery owner, publisher; b. Stillwater, Okla., Mar. 9, 1947; d. Wayne L. Brake and Lois K. (Fisk) Kyle; m. Gary G. Wilcox, Aug. 4, 1964 (div. 1974); children: Troy V., Trisha J.; m. Frederick Peter Adler, Oct. 11, 1991. Butler County Jr. Coll., Richland Coll. From asst. to pres. H.J. Gruy & Assocs., Dallas, 1972-75; from asst. to v.p. econs. dept. DeGolyer and MacNaughton, Dallas, 1975-80; sales mgr. Telecommunications Specialists, Inc., Dallas, 1980-85; dir., cons. various art galleries in Calif., Wash., Colo., Tex. & Hawaii, 1985-90; owner Genestar Internat., Santa Barbara, Calif., 1990-95, Galerie Adrienne & Adrienne Editions, San Francisco, 1995—. Chmn. tri-counties adv. bd. Jefferson Ctr. Character Edn., Santa Barbara 1993-95; v.p., pres., mem. women's bd. Santa Barbara Mus. Art, 1995; v.p., chmn. of ball Symphony League, Santa Barbara, 1994-95; advocate, mem. Calif. Assn. Mentally Ill, 1993-95. Mem. NAFE. Office: Galerie Adrienne and Adrienne Editions 377 Geary St San Francisco CA 94102

ADLER, BARBARA ANN, social worker, consultant; b. Chgo., July 6, 1938; d. Joe and Sarah (Kesselman) Moret; widowed; 1 child, Karyn A. AA with honors, Lake Mich. Coll., 1976; BA cum laude, Western Mich. U., 1978, MSW, 1981. Cert. social worker, Mich.; lic. marriage and family therapist. Dir. Coll. Vocat. Edn. Rasmussen Bus. Coll., St. Paul; pres. The Fashion Mart, Inc., South Haven, Mich.; dir. Coll. Vocat. Edn. Mich. Dunes Correctional Facility, 1985-87; pvt. practice South Haven; adj. faculty Southwestern Mich. Coll., Dowagiac, Mich., Lake Mich. Coll., Benton Harbor, Mich. Active Citizen Amb. Program-Law Enforcement Adminstrn. Delegation, Shanghai and Manila, 1987, China, 1987, 88; citizen amb. to Russia, 1990; mem. City Coun., South Haven, 1993—. Recipient award of Appreciation, Commendation Dept. Social Svc. State of Mich., 1979, hon. fellowship Office Substance Abuse Western Mich. U. Mem. NASW, Internat. Soc. Prevention Child Abuse, Am. Assn. Marriage and Family Therapists, Am. Soc. Criminology, Mich. League for Human Svcs. (chair S.W. Mich. Total Living Ctrs.). Home: 38 Lake Shore Dr South Haven MI 49090-1131

ADLER, ELIZABETH M., biologist, educator; b. N.Y.C., Aug. 25, 1954; d. Edward and Ruth (Woods) A.; m. Paul J. Schwartz, May 20, 1995. BS, Antioch Coll., 1975; PhD, U. Pa., 1986. Postdoctoral fellow U. Toronto, Ont., Can., 1987-89, Mass. Gen. Hosp., Boston, 1990-93; asst. prof. Williams Coll., Williamstown, Mass., 1994—. Contbr. chpt. in book and articles to profl. jours. Mem. AAAS, Soc. Neurosci. Office: Williams Coll Dept Biology Williamstown MA 01267

ADLER, LOUISE DECARL, bankruptcy judge; b. 1945. BA, Chatham Coll., Pitts.; JD, Loyola U., Chgo. Bar: Ill., 1970, Calif., 1972. Practicing atty. San Diego, 1972-84; standing trustee Bankruptcy Ct. So. Dist. Calif., San Diego, 1974-79, chief judge bankruptcy, 1984—. Mem. editorial bd. Calif. Bankruptcy Jour., 1991-92. Fellow Am. Coll. Bankruptcy; mem. San Diego County Bar Assn. (chair bus. law study sect. 1979, fed. ct. com. 1983-84), Lawyers Club of San Diego (bd. dirs. 1972-73, treas. 1972-75, sec. 1972-74, v.p. 1974-75), San Diego Bankruptcy Forum (bd. dirs. 1989-92), Nat. Conf. Bankruptcy Judges (bd. dirs. 1989-91, sec. 1992-93, v.p. 1993-94, pres. 1994-95). Office: US Bankruptcy Ct 325 W F St San Diego CA 92101-6017

ADLER, MADELEINE WING, academic administrator; d. George and Bette Wing; m. Frederick S. Lane; children: J. Peter Adler, Rand Lane, Cary Lane. BA in Polit. Sci., Northwestern U., 1962; MA in Polit. Sci., U. Wis., 1963, PhD in Polit. Sci., 1969. Asst. prof. polit. sci. Am. U., Washington, 1965-67; cons. Charles Nelson Assoc., N.Y.C., 1967-68; asst. prof. Queens Coll. CUNY, N.Y.C., 1969-74, assoc. prof. Queens Coll., 1974-86, assoc. dean, 1983-86; v.p. acad. affairs, prof. polit. sci. Framingham (Mass.) State Coll., 1986-92; pres. West Chester (Pa.) U., 1993 ; staff mem. Joint Com. Orgn. Congress, Washington, 1965-66; vis. asst. prof. Pa. State U., summers 1967-71; dir. profl. staff recruitment N.Y.C. Urban Acad., 1975-78; pres. Ctr. Applied Rsch. and Analysis Social Scis., Inc., 1976-86; mem. crosscutting rsch. panel, office rsch. and evaluation U.S. HEW, 1978-80; program coord. N.E. region Soc. Coll. and Univ. Planning, 1987-89; mem. exec. bd. Am. Coun. Edn./Nat. Identification Project, State of Mass., 1987-92, vice chair exec. bd., 1991—. Author: (with Harold Savitch) Decentralization at the Grassroots: Political Innovation in New York City and London, 1974; contbr. article to profl. jours. Mem. Comty. Bd. 14, Bklyn., 1978-81, Gov.'s Award Panel for Humanities, 1993—, Gov.'s Comty. Svc. Adv. Bd., 1994—, Chester County Comty. Found., 1994—; appointee Bklyn. Econ. Devel. Corp., 1982-86; bd. advisors Acad. Search Consultation Svcs., 1994—. Mem. Pa. Assn. Colls. and Univs. (com. acad. issues 1993—). Home: 100 E Rosedale Ave West Chester PA 19382-4927 Office: Office of Pres West Chester University West Chester PA 19383*

ADLER, MARGOT SUSANNA, journalist, radio producer; b. Little Rock, Apr. 16, 1946; d. Kurt Alfred and Freyda (Nacque) A. BA, U. Calif.-Berkeley, 1968, MS, Columbia U., 1970. Newscaster Sta. WBAI-FM, N.Y.C., 1968-71, host talk show, 1972—; chief Washington bur. Pacifica News Svc. Network, 1971-72; corr., prodr. All Things Considered, Morning Edit., Nat. Pub. Radio, N.Y.C., 1978—; instr. radio comms. Goddard Coll., Plainfield, Vt., 1977; instr. religion and ecology Inst. for Social Ecology, Vt., 1986-93. Author: Drawing Down the Moon, 1979. Co-prodr., dir. (radio drama) War Day, 1985. Contbr. articles to jours. Nieman fellow Harvard U., 1982. Mem. Phi Beta Kappa. Avocations: swimming, running, bird watching. Home: 333 Central Park W New York NY 10025-7145 Office: Nat Pub Radio 801 2nd Ave Rm 701 New York NY 10017-4706

ADLER, NADIA C., lawyer; b. Salford, Lancashire, Eng., Feb. 26, 1945; came to U.S., 1948; d. David Colin and Rose (Bolton) Cohen; m. David Jonathan Adler, Mar. 13, 1977 (div. 1992). BA, CCNY, 1966; JD, N.Y.U., 1973. Bar: N.Y. 1974, U.S. Dist. Ct. (so. and ea. dists.) N.Y. 1974, U.S. Ct. Appeals (2d cir.) 1975, U.S. Supreme Ct. 1983. Assoc. Rosenman Colin Freund Lewis & Cohen and predecessor firms, N.Y.C., 1973-82; ptnr. Rosenman & Colin, N.Y.C., 1983-87; v.p., gen. counsel Montefiore Med. Ctr., N.Y.C., 1987-89, sr. v.p., gen. counsel, 1989—; mem. legal affairs com. Greater N.Y. Hosp. Assn., N.Y.C., 1987—; mem. bioethics task force, subcoms. on patient decision making, reproductive techs. and physician-assisted suicide, commn. women's equality Am. Jewish Congress, N.Y.C., 1989—. Bd. dirs. Berkeley-in-Scarsdale (N.Y.) Assn., 1989-91. Mem. ABA (mem. forum on health care), Assn. of Bar of City of N.Y., Am. Acad. Hosp. Attys., Am. Hosp. Assn., Nat. Health Lawyers Assn., N.Y. State Bar Assn. (co-chair in-house com. health law sect., mem. com. health law sect. 1996—). Democrat. Office: Montefiore Med Ctr 111 E 210th St Bronx NY 10467-2490

ADLER, NAOMI SAMUEL, real estate counselor; b. N.Y.C., Sept. 30, 1931; d. Jacob Alexander and Madeline Samuel; m. Gerson Adler, Aug. 1, 1950; children: Don A., Samson Y., Nathan Tzvi, Eliyohu, Hillel M., Ezra, William Martin Selman, Zahava Sara. Student, 1945-50, John Carroll U., 1980-82, Bais Yaakov Tchrs. Sem. Am., Bklyn., 1945-49. Real estate agt. B.O.D. Milliken, Cleveland Heights, Ohio, 1981-82, The Kenny Co., University Heights, Ohio, 1982-84, Century 21 Crysler-Kenny, Cleve., 1984-90; gen. mgr. Fialkoff Bungalow Colony Real Estate, Monticello, N.Y., 1981—; real estate counselor HKS Realty, Inc., Shaker Heights, Ohio, 1993-96; real estate counselor Realty One, Lyndhurst, Ohio, 1990-93. Bd. dirs. Monticello Bungalow Assn., Bur. Jewish Edn., Jewish Cmty. Fedn. Cleve.; child adv. Jewish Children's Foster Family, Jewish Day Nursery, Shaker Heights, 1970-93, Traditional Fund, Jewish Welfare, Hebrew Free Loan Assn., sec., 1992-94, treas., 1989-90; pres. Shorme Shabbas Sisterhood, 1978-82, pres. N'shei Agudah Women, 1990-92, Hebrew Acad., Cleve., 1972-75, Union Orthodox Jewish Congregations, 1975-77, pres. Mosdos Ohr Hatora Sch., 1977-80; founding charter mem., safety chairperson Chofetz Chaim Heritage Found., 1994—; vol. Chevra Kadisha Jewish Boriel Soc., 1963-86. Named Woman of Valor, Hebrew Acad., Woman of Yr., Beth Jacob High Sch. of Denver. Mem. Grad. Realtors Inst., Cleve. Area Bd. Realtors (RPAC com.), Nat. Assn. Parliamentarians, Post Office Adv. Home: 3595 Severn Rd Cleveland Heights OH 44118-1999 Office: Crysler Kenny Realty 4589 Mayfield Rd South Euclid OH 44121

ADLER, PEGGY See ROBOHM, PEGGY ADLER

ADLER, TRACY, film company executive; b. Feb. 2, 1963. BS in Econs., U. Pa., 1985. Staff acct. Ernst & Young, N.Y.C., 1985-87; asst. contr. New Line Cinema Corp., N.Y.C., 1987-89, contr., 1989-91, v.p. and contr., 1991-96, sr. v.p. and contr., 1996—. Office: New Line Cinema Corp 888 Seventh Ave 20th fl New York NY 10106

ADNAN, ETEL, writer, poet; b. Beirut, Lebanon, Feb. 24, 1925; came to U.S., 1955; d. Assaf Kadri and Rose Lily (Lacorté) A. Licence ès lettres, U. Paris Sorbonne, 1952, Diplome Etudes Philosophy, 1952; postgrad. in philosophy, U. Calif. Berkeley, 1955-57, Harvard U., 1957-58. Prof. philosophy Dominican Coll., San Rafael, Calif., 1958-72; cultural editor Safa, Beirut, Lebanon, 1972-74; cultural reporter L'Orient-le Jour, Beirut, Lebanon, 1974-76; writer, painter Sausalito, Calif., 1976—. Author: (book) Sitt Marie Rose, 1978, The Indian Never Had a Horse, 1985, The Spring Flowers Own, 1990, (essays) Paris, When It's Naked, 1993, (book of letters) Of Cities and Women, 1993. Recipient prize France-Pays Arabes, Paris. Home: 35 Marie St Sausalito CA 94965

ADREON, BEATRICE MARIE RICE, pharmacist; b. Huntington, W.Va., July 23, 1929; d. Lloyd Emerson and Beatrice (Odell) Rice; student Mary Washington Coll., 1947-49; B.S. in Pharmacy, Med. Coll. Va., 1952; M.A. in Spl. Studies and Women's Studies, George Washington U., 1976; m. Harry Barnes Adreon, Jr., Dec. 27, 1952. Summer vol. worker pharmacies De Paul Hosp., Norfolk, Va., 1949, U.S. Marine Hosp., Norfolk, 1950; pharmacist Washington Clinic, 1954-71; counselor George Washington U., 1976-77, cons. gerontology health scis. dept., 1977—; cons. medicine control traffic patterns nursing homes Cross & Adreon, Washington, 1962-87; founder, pres. Pharmacy Counseling Services, Inc., 1978—. Instr. advanced first aid ARC, 1952—, civil def. instr., 1952—; vol. Spanish Edn. Devel. Center, Washington, 1972; mem. Arlington (Va.) Community Services Bd., 1980-83; chmn. com. substance abuse. Recipient Arnold and Marie Schwartz award in pharmacy, 1980. Mem. Acad. Pharmacy Practice and Mgmt., Am. Pharm. Assn., Va. Pharm. Assn., Potomac Pharmacists Assn., Am. Inst. History of Pharmacy, Nat. Council Patient Info. and Edn. (task force pub. info.), Panhellenic Assn., Kappa Epsilon. Episcopalian (mem. bishop's com. neighborhood services 1967-69, chmn. services for aged div. 1967-69). Contbr. articles in field to profl. jours. Home: 4524 19th Rd N Arlington VA 22207-2352 Office: Pharmacy Counseling Svcs Inc 950 N Glebe Rd # 140 Arlington VA 22203-1824

ADRI (ADRIENNE STECKLING), fashion designer; b. St. Joseph, Mo.. Ed., Sch. Fine Arts, Washington U., St. Louis, Parson Sch. Design. With B.H. Wragge; owner, pres. Adri Studio, Ltd., N.Y.C., 1983—; with Claire McCardell in 2-person showing, Innovative Contemporary Fashion, Smithsonian Instn., Washington, 1971. Recipient Coty award, 1982, Internat. Best Five award, Tokyo, 1986. Office: Adri 143 W 20th St New York NY 10011-3630

ADRIANOPOLI, BARBARA CATHERINE, librarian; b. Fort Dodge, Iowa, January 27, 1943; d. Daniel Joseph and Mary Dolores (Coleman) Hogan; m. Carl David Adrianopoli, June 28, 1968; children: Carlin, Laurie. BS, Mundeline Coll., 1966; M.L.S., Rosary Coll., 1975. Tchr., Father Bertrand H.S., Memphis, 1966-68; caseworker Dept. Pub. Aid Chgo., 1968; tchr. North Chicago Jr. H.S. (Ill.), 1968-70, Austin Middle Sch., Chgo., 1970-73; libr. Barrington Pub. Libr. (Ill.), 1976-79, Schaumburg Twp. Dist. Library (Ill.), 1979—; diversity com. N. Suburban/Suburban Libr. Systems, LaGrange, Ill., 1995—. Contbr. articles to jours. Mem. Com. Schaumburg Twp. Disabled, 1981—; historian Village of Hoffman Estates, 1986—; adv. com. Hoffman Estates Sister Cities, 1988-96; advisor Boy Scout Am. handicapped badge, Schaumburg Twp., 1981—; mem. adv. bd. Cmty. Nutrition Network, 1994—; organizer, mem. Northwest Corridor-St. Patrick's Day Parade com., 1986—; bd. dirs. Children's Mus. and Imaginasium, 1990-93; trainer A World of Difference Anti-Defamation League, 1995; speaker on library outreach svcs., 1995—; mem. Com. For Choices For Success-Seminars For Young Women, 1996—. Grantee Sears Community Project for Literacy; recipient Hoffman Estates Citizen of Yr. award VFW, 1995. Mem. ALA, Ill. Libr. Assn. Democrat. Roman Catholic. Home: 1105 Kingsdale Rd Schaumburg IL 60194-2378 Office: Schaumburg Twp Pub Libr 32 W Library Ln Schaumburg IL 60194-3421

ADRIAZOLA, ANA, Spanish and Latin American culture educator; b. Arequipa, Peru, July 7, 1945; came to U.S., 1990; d. Jorge-Roberto Adriazola del Carpio and Maria-Luz (Corrales) de Adriazola; m. Jose O. Rodriguez, Dec. 6, 1974; children: Ana Maria Rodriguez, Aurora-Luz Rodriguez. EdD, Nat. U. San Agustin, Arequipa, 1985, D History and Anthropology, 1989. Cert. prof. secondary history and social scis. Prof. h.s. Colegio Mayta Capac, Cayma-Arequipa, 1967-71; prin. pvt. schs. So. Peru Cooper Co., Tacna, 1972-76, coord. ednl. and technol., 1976-81; conservator, curator Museo San Agustin U., Arequipa, 1982-83; prof. Colls. Edn. and History U. Nat. San Agustin, 1984-89; tchr. Spanish and culture Fla. Atlantic U., Boca Radon; dir. ballet group S.P.C.C., Tacna, 1972-86; dir. choir group Mayta Capac Sch., Arequipa, 1967-71; advisor textiles Kontisuyo Archaeol. Program, Moquegua, Peru, 1984-89. Active Sister Cities-Arequipa-Charlotte, 1986-91. Mem. Sigma Delta (pres. 1994-95). Home: 21443 Fairfield Ln Boca Raton FL 33486

AEHLERT, BARBARA JUNE, health services executive; b. San Antonio, June 17, 1956; d. Bobby Ray and Ronella Su (Light) Mahoney; m. Dean A. Aehlert, Sept. 6, 1980; children: Andrea, Sherri. AA in Nursing, Glendale (Ariz.) Community Coll., 1976. Cert. ACLS instr., affiliate faculty, BLS instr., Pre-Hosp. Trauma Life Support instr., Basic Trauma Life Support instr., emergency med. tng./parametic instr., ATLS course coord. Gen. mgr. Hosp. Ambulance Svc., Phoenix, 1982-83; critical care nurse Samaritan Health Svcs., Phoenix, 1978-80, coord. patient transp., 1980-82, mgr. clin. programs, 1983-92; dir. emergency med. svcs. edn. EMS Edn. and Rsch., 1992—. Author: ACLS Quick Review Study Guide, 1994, ACLS Quick Review Slide Set, 1994, ACLS Quick Review Study Cards, 1994, PALS Study Guide, 1994, ECG's Made Easy, 1995, ECG's Made Easy Lesson Plans, 1996, Mosby's Computerized Paramedic Test Generator, 1996. Republican. Office: Samaritan Health System EMS 1500 E Thomas Rd Phoenix AZ 85014-5731

AELION, C. MARJORIE, educator. BS summa cum laude, U. Mass., 1980; MSCE, MIT, 1983; PhD, U. N.C., 1988. Park ranger Nat. Park Svc., Cape Cod Nat. Seashore, South Wellfleet, Mass., 1976-78; biologist, resource assessment divsn. Nat. Marine Fisheries, Woods Hole, Mass., 1978-84; rsch. asst. MIT, Cambridge, Mass., 1981-83, U. Mass.-Amherst, Amherst, Peru, 1983-84; rsch. asst. U. N.C., Chapel Hill, 1986-88, teaching asst., 1987; hydrologist U.S. Geol. Survey, Water Resources Divsn., Columbia, S.C., 1988-91, faculty mem., 1991—; asst. prof. dept. environ. health scis. U. S.C., Columbia, 1991—; presenter in field. contbr. articles to profl. jours. Fulbright-Hayes scholar, 1980-81; Bd. Govs.' fellow U. N.C., 1984-86, Dissertation fellow, 1988, NSF fellow in engring., 1993; grantee U.S. EPA, 1991-93, Hazardous Waste Mgmt. Rsch. Fund, 1991-94, Nat. Geographic Soc., 1992, S.C. Dept. Health and Environ. Control and Hazardous Waste Mgmt. Rsch. Fund, 1991-94, U. S.C., 1993-94, NSF, 1993—; recipient Grad. Student Travel award U. N.C., 1988. Mem. Am. Chem. Soc., Am. Soc. Microbiology, Soc. Women Engrs., Soc. Environ. Toxicology and Chemistry, Water Environ. Fedn., Phi Kappa Phi, Delta Omega. Office: U SC Environ Health Scis Dept Columbia SC 29208

AERY, SHAILA ROSALIE, legislative staff member; b. Tulsa, Dec. 4, 1938; d. Silas Cleveland and Billie (Brewer) A. BS, U. Okla., 1964; MS, Okla. State U., 1972, EdD, 1975. Spl. asst., chancellor Okla. Regents for Higher Edn., Oklahoma City, 1977; spl. asst., chancellor U. Mo., Columbia, 1978-80, asst. provost acad. affairs, 1980-81; dep. commr. higher edn. State of Mo., Jefferson City, 1981, commr., 1982-89; sec. higher edn., Md., 1989-95; chief of staff U.S. Senator Barbara A. Mikulski, Washington, 1995—; dir. Mo. Higher Edn. Loan Authority, St. Louis, 1982-89; commr. Edn. Commn. of the States, Denver, 1983-95, nat. steering com., nat. treas. 1993; mem. exec. bd. State Higher Edn. Officers, Denver, 1983—, So. Regionals Edn. Bd., 1990-95. Contbr. articles to profl. jours. Mem. AAUW, Women Execs. in State Govt. (bd. dirs.). Democrat. Episcopalian. Office: 709 Senate Hart Bldg Washington DC 20002

AFFONSO, DYANNE D., dean, nursing educator. BSN, U. Hawaii, 1966; MN in Nursing, U. Wash., 1967; MA in Clin. Psychology, U. Ariz., 1980, PhD in Clin. Psychology, 1982. Asst. prof. sch. nursing U. Miss., 1967-68; OB staff nurse, night charge nurse Kinchloe AFB Hosp., Mich., 1968-70; instr. sch. nursing U. Hawaii, 1970-73; asst. prof. coll. nursing U. Ariz., 1974-77, assoc. prof. coll. nursing, 1978, coord. psychiatric mental health nursing coll. nursing, 1982-84, joint appointment in psychology dept.

psychology, 1983; assoc. prof. sch. nursing U. Calif., San Francisco, 1984-87, prof. sch. nursing, 1988; prof., dean sch. nursing Emory U., Atlanta, 1993—, assoc. prof. women's & children's divsn. sch. pub. health, 1993—. Contbr. articles to profl. jours.; presenter in field. Mem. NAS (mem. inst. medicine 1994), NIH (mem. adv. coun. nat. inst. child health & human devel. 1979-83, mem. agenda com. nat. inst. child health & human devel. 1982, mem. scientific rev. com. nat. ctr. nursing rsch. 1986, mem. adv. coun. nat. ctr. nursing rsch. 1986-88, mem. steering com. rsch. patient outcomes nat. ctr. nursing rsch. 1991, sec.'s conf. 1993, charter mem. adcv. coun. office rsch. on women's health 1995). Office: Emory U Sch Nursing Atlanta GA 30322-1100*

AFTOORA, PATRICIA JOAN, transportation executive; b. Cleve., Jan. 2, 1940; d. Joseph Patrick and Frances Dolores (Fabis) Hunady; m. Albert B. Aftoora, Feb. 17, 1989; 1 child, Christopher Hunady; stepchildren: Melissa, Matthew, Richard. Student, Fenn Coll., Cleve., 1957-59, UCLA, 1959-61, John Carroll U., Cleve., 1961-63. Various positions Chesapeake and Ohio Ry. Co., Balt. and Ohio R.R. Co., Cleve., 1962-73; asst. corp. sec. Chessie System, Inc., Cleve., 1973-79; dept. corp. sec. Chessie System Inc. and Affiliates, Cleve., 1979-80; corp. sec. Chesapeake and Ohio Ry. Co., Balt. and Ohio R.R. Co., Cleve., 1980-87, CSX Transp. Inc., Balt., 1986-87; asst. v.p., asst. corp. sec. CSX Corp., Richmond, Va., 1987-89, v.p., corp. sec., from 1989; now v.p., corp. sec. CSX Transp., Inc., Jacksonville, Fla. Mem. Am. Soc. Corp. Secs. Inc., Nat. Assn. Records Mgrs. and Adminstrs. Home: 1211 Creek View Way Ponte Vedra Beach FL 32082-2509 Office: CSX Transp Inc 500 Water St Jacksonville FL 32202-4422*

AGARD, EMMA ESTORNEL, psychotherapist; b. Bronx, N.Y.. BA, Queens Coll.; MSW, Fordham U., 1962; cert. in Psychoanalytic Psychotherapy, Tng. Inst. for Mental Health, 1979; cert. in Child and Adolescent Psychotherapy, Postgrad. Ctr. for Mental Health, 1982. Supr. social work Foster Care Div., N.Y.C., 1968-72; asst. dir. Henry St. Settlement Urban Family Ctr., N.Y.C., 1972-74; tng. analyst, sr. supr. Tng. Inst. for Mental Health, N.Y.C., 1974—; pvt. practice psychotherapist N.Y.C., 1974—; lectr. social work Columbia U., N.Y.C., 1977-80; adj. asst. prof. NYU, 1978-80; field instr. N.Y.C. Housing Authority, 1974-80; dist. dir., cons. Am. Consultation Ctrs., Bklyn. and N.Y.C., 1985—, dir. Park Slope br. Mem. Albemarle-Kenmore Neighborhood Assn., Bklyn., 1974—, dir. Park Slope br. Fellow N.Y. State Soc. Clin. Social Work Psychotherapists (pres. Bklyn. chpt. 1988-91); mem. Profl. Soc. Tng. Inst. for Mental Health (sec.), Nat. Assn. Social Workers (diplomate), Acad. Cert. Social Workers, Nat. Coalition 100 Black Women, Delta Sigma Theta. Address: 221 E 21st St Brooklyn NY 11226-3903

AGARD, NANCEY PATRICIA, nursing administrator; b. Amsterdam, N.Y., Mar. 3, 1955; d. Richard Edward and Jean Elizabeth (Sweet) A.; m. Robert Frank Whittaker, Nov. 16, 1991. Diploma, St. Mary's Hosp. Sch. Nursing, 1976; BS, SUNY, 1981; MS, Syracuse U., 1986. RN N.Y. Staff nurse St. Mary's Hosp., Amsterdam, N.Y., 1976-77; nurse teaching & rsch. SUNY Health Sci. Ctr., Syracuse, N.Y., 1977-80; staff nurse St. Luke's Hosp., Utica, N.Y., 1980-81; clin. edn. specialist SUNY Health Sci. Ctr., 1981-84, lectr., 1984-90, nurse tchg. and rsch. ctr., 1984-90, cons., 1986; assoc. dir. nursing practice N.Y. State Nurses Assn., Latham, N.Y., 1990—; mem. immunization action plan com. N.Y. State Dept. Health, Albany, 1993—, mem. immunization info. sys. com., 1994—, mem. medicaid managed care adv. com., 1993—; mem. health family com. N.Y. State Fedn. to Prevent Child Abuse, 1993—. Vol. Karen Burstein and Mary Eileen Callan Campaigns, Albany, 1994. Rural immunization grantee Merck Vaccine Div., 1992-93. Mem. ANA, AACN, N.Y. State Nurses Assn., N.E. Safety Coun., Rural Nurse Orgn., Sigma Theta Tau (media award 1993). Democrat. Office: NY State Nurses Assn 46 Cornell Rd Latham NY 12110

AGEE, NELLE HULME, art history educator; b. Memphis, May 22, 1940; d. John Eulice and Nelle (Ray) Hulme; m. Bob R. Agee, June 7, 1958; children: Denise, Robyn. Student Memphis State U., 1971-72; BA, Union U., Jackson, Tenn., 1978; postgrad. Seminole Okla. Coll., 1982, Okla. Bapt. U., 1984; MEd Cen. State U., Edmond, Okla., 1989. Cert. tchr. art, history, Ky., Tenn., Okla. Offices services supr. So. Bapt. Theol. Sem., Louisville, 1961-64; kindergarten tchr. Shively Heights Bapt. Ch., Louisville, 1965-70; editorial asst. Little Publs., agrl. mags., Memphis, 1973-75; tchr. art Humboldt High Sch., Tenn., 1978-82; vis. artist-in-schs. Tenn. Arts Commn., Nashville, 1978, 81, 82; adj. prof. art history Seminole Coll., Okla., 1985-86, 87, 89; instr. art Okla. Baptist U., 1989, asst. prof. art and edn., 1989—; frequent speaker art orgns., ch. groups; tchr. art workshops Humboldt City Sch. system; tchr. Cultural Arts Day Camp, Jackson, Tenn., 1982; nat. pres. ministers' wives conf. So. Bapt. Conv., 1987-88; vol. Mabee-Gerrer Mus., Shawnee. Exhibited art in various shows. Bd. dirs. Robert Dotson Found., Mabee-Gerrer Mus., Family Resource Ctr. 1993—; active Salvation Army Aux., Shawnee; v.p. Union U. Woman's Club, 1976-77, pres., 1978. Recipient Disting. Classroom Tchr. award Tenn. Edn. Assn., 1982. Mem. Univ. Alliance, Okla Bapt. U., Goals 2000, Delta Kappa Gamma, Alpha Delta Kappa. Democrat. Baptist. Avocations: stained glass, pottery making, travel. Home: 616 University Pky Shawnee OK 74801-1711

AGLER, VICKIE LYN, state legislator; b. St. Joseph, Mo., July 14, 1946; d. Harry Ernest and Fern Dorothy (Hart) Kerr; m. Rex Duane Agler, June 7, 1968; children: Kristen Michelle, Stephanie Dianne. Assoc. degree, Mo. Western Jr. Coll., St. Joseph, 1966; BS in Edn., U. Mo., 1968. Secondary sch. tchr. Topeka (Kans.) Pub. Sch., 1968-70; paralegal Dan Moran, Atty. at Law, Huntsville, Ala., 1970-76; stained glass artist Agler's Arts & Glass, Littleton, Colo., 1980-86; planning commr. Jefferson Co. Planning Commn., Littleton, 1983-87; staff asst. Congressman Joel Hefley, Littleton, 1987-90; state rep. Colo. Gen. Assembly, Denver, 1990—; coun. mem., v.p. Arapahoe C.C. Coun., 1989-92. Mem. Colo. Fedn. Rep. Women, Littleton, Am. Legis. Exchange Coun., Washington, So. Jefferson County Rep. Club, Littleton, Rep. Leadership Program, Colo.; dir. Foothills Found. Bd.; bd. mem., legis. liaison Chatfield P.T.S.A., 1989-92; del., v.p. Coun. Homeowners for Planned Environment, 1984-89. Named Woman of Yr., Sentinal Newspaper, Jefferson County, Colo., 1984, Outstanding Legislator, Colo. Counties, 1992. Mem. West C. of C. (Community Svc. award 1992), Beta Sigma Phi. Methodist. Home: 10289 W Burgundy Ave Littleton CO 80127-5532 Office: Colo House of Reps State Capitol Rm 271 Denver CO 80203*

AGONITO, ROSEMARY, executive; b. Syracuse, N.Y., Feb. 22, 1937; d. Mariangelo and Filomena (Albanese) Giambattista; m. Joseph Agonito, July 1, 1961; children: Giancarlo, Mae Lee. BA, LeMoyne Coll., 1959; MA, Niagara U., 1961; PhD, Syracuse U., 1975. Asst. instr. Syracuse (N.Y.) U., 1969-75; instr. Colgate U., Hamilton, N.Y., 1973-75; assoc. prof. Rochester (N.Y.) Inst. Tech., 1976-83; pres. New Futures Enterprises, Syracuse, 1983—. Author: History of Ideas on Women, 1977, Promoting Seld Esteem in Young Women, 1988, No More "Nice Girl", 1993. Commr. Mayor's Commn. Women, Syracuse, 1986-92; co-chair City-County Human Rights Commn., Syracuse, 1988-93; mem. N.Y. State Adv. Coun. Equal Opportunity for Women, Albany, N.Y., 1988-92. Mem. NAFE. Independent.

AGOSTA, CAROLYN ANN, writer; b. Detroit, Oct. 8, 1947; d. Carl John and Veronica Mary (Mondello) A.; m. Terry Frances Albertson, May 8, 1987. AA, Met. State Coll., Denver, 1974, BS in Human Svcs., 1976; MSW in Cmty. Svcs./Social Planning, U. Denver, 1978. Lic. clin. social worker. Co-founder, program developer Detroit Transient Alternative Shelter for Runaways, 1971-73; cmty. worker police cmty. rels. Denver Police Dept., 1974-75; field faculty instr. U. Denver, 1978-79; faculty mem. Met. State Coll., Denver, 1978-86; program dir. Safe House for Battered Women, Denver, 1978-79, exec. dir., 1979-81; co-founder, co-dir., therapist, cons., expert witness Ending Violence Effectively, Denver, 1981-92; staff writer, cmty. affairs editor Coast Mag., Gualala, Calif., 1993-95, freelance writer, 1995—; v.p. Abusive Men Exploring New Directions, Denver, 1979-81; mem. conf. planning com. Colo. Mental Health Conf., 1979-87; chairwoman Victim Rights Week, Colo., 1986, 87, 88. Contbg. author: Post-Traumatic Stress Disorder: A Handbook for Clinicians, 1987, Evaluation & Treatment of Sexually Abused: Vulnerable Populations, vol. 1, 1988; contbr. articles to profl. jours. and chpts. to books. Vol. organizer Norm Early Campaign for Mayor, Denver, 1991. Recipient Pres.'s Appreciation award Denver Victim's Svc. Ctr., 1989, honorable mention Colo. Orgn. for Victim Assistance, 1990, Outstanding Victim Advocate award Colo. Orgn. for Victim Assistance, 1991, Spl. Recognition award U.S. Dept. Justice Office of Justice Programs Office of Crime Victims, 1991, The Norm Early Victim Rights award, 1993. Mem. Nat. Assn. Social Workers, Acad. Cert. Social Workers. Office: Agosta Consulting PO Box 5103 Anchor Bay CA 95445-5103

AGOSTINI, ROSEMARIE CONIGLIO, human services administrator; b. N.Y.C., Aug. 13, 1939; d. Louis and Frances (Licata) Coniglio; m. Remo P. Agostini, Oct. 24, 1959; children: Peter L. Agostini, Francesca G. Agostini. Cert. cmty. svc. profl. gerontologist, bereavement counselor/Lazarus min. Exec. dir. Dept. Aging, Parsippany, N.J., 1973-91, Sussex County (N.J.) Office on Aging, 1991-93; del. Nat. coun. Aging., NISC. Author, pub. (newsletter) Golden Gazette, 1974—; producer, host (cable TV) Horizons Unltd., 1976—, Sincerely Yours, 1991—. Bd. dirs., trustee Hospice of Morris County, N.J., 1982—; founder, leader Parkinsons and Caregiver Support Group, Parsippany, 1980; co-founder Parsippany Area Legis. Task Force, 1980; founder chpt. 3070 AARP, Parsippany, 1976; chair interdenominational com. of Parsippany; chair cmty. rels. St. Christophers Ch., chair cmty. svc.; candidate for mayor Parsippany-Troy Hills, N.J., 1993; mem. bd. dirs. Mental Health Assn.; bd. mgrs., v.p., treas. Am. Cancer Soc., 1994—; mem. Twp. Coun., 1996—; mem. Twp. Coun.; eucharistic min. Named Woman of Distinction Cath. War Vets., 1988. Mem. N.J. Assn. Sr. Ctr. Dirs. (founder, pres.), Jaycees (Disting. Svc. 1976, Outstanding Pub. Health award 1980), N.J. Gerontol. Soc. (bd. dirs.), Morris County Svc. Providers (founder, chair), LWV (pres. Parsippany chpt.), Rotary Club (Outstanding Citizen 1978), Unico Nat. (co-founder 1976, Citizen of Yr. 1986), Human Svcs. Assn. Home: 79 Jean Ter Parsippany NJ 07054-1719

AGRESTI, MIRIAM MONELL, psychologist; b. N.Y.C., Mar. 23, 1926; d. James McCloud and Marion Henrietta (Zippel) Monell; children: Robert, Carol. BS, Queens Coll., 1947; MA in Sci. Edn., Columbia U., 1949; PhD in Clin. Psychology, Yeshiva U., 1976; postgrad., Ackerman Inst. Family Therapy, 1977-81, L.I. Jewish Hosp. Human Sexuality Ctr. Psychology intern Creedmoor Psychiat. Center, Queens, N.Y., 1963-64, family therapist, 1964-69; psychologist Northeast Nassau Psychiat. Ctr., Kings Park, N.Y., 1969-72; adminstrv. dir. Friendship House Day Hosp., Glen Cove, N.Y., 1972-74; psychologist and team leader Ctrl. Islip (N.Y.) Psychiat. Ctr., 1974-75; tchr., coord. family therapy program Pilgrim Psychiat. Ctr., West Brentwood, N.Y., 1976-80; pvt. practice psychotherapy, 1977—; pres. Nassau County Med. Ctr., 1990-95; co-dir. L.I. Family Inst., 1976-79; cons. family therapy Cath. Charities, 1979, St. Vincent's Hall, 1979, Nassau County Mental Health Assn., 1980; adj. faculty Sch. Edn., C.W. Post Coll., L.I. U., 1972, CUNY, 1978-80, St. John's U., 1983, Hofstra U., 1985-88. Exec. dir. movie/videotape Beware the Gaps in Medical Care for Older People (1st prize Am. Film Festival). Lic. psychologist, N.Y. Diplomate Am. Bd. Family Psychology (fellow, pres. 1984-85). Fellow Am. Orthopsychiat. Assn., Internat. Council Sex Edn. and Parenthood of Am. U.; mem. APA, N.Y. State Psychol. Assn., Nassau County Psychol. Assn., Suffolk County Psychol. Assn., Am. Assn. for Marriage and Family Therapy (pres. L.I. chpt. 1981-83, sec. N.Y. state divsn. 1996—), Am. Orthopsychiat. Assn., Pi Lambda Theta. Unitarian. Address: 11 Wren Dr Woodbury NY 11797-3212

AGRONICK, GAIL S., psychologist; b. Providence, R.I., July 12, 1966; d. Jordan and Cynthia A.; m. Steven Schwartz, June 11, 1995. BA with high honors, Wesleyan U., Middletown, Conn., 1988; postgrad., U. Calif., Berkeley. Costume character Chuck-E-Cheese, Warwick, R.I., 1984; rsch. asst. Psychology Dept. Wesleyan U., Middletown, 1986-88; mgmt. cons. Iamco, Wayland, Mass., 1988-90; rsch. asst. infant study Harvard U., Cambridge, Mass., 1990-92; rschr. Inst. of Personality & Social Psychology U. Calif., Berkeley, 1992—. Contbr. chpt. to book, articles to profl. jours. Parental aide, vol. counselor Watertown Multi-Counseling Ctr., 1992. Mem. APA, Am. Psychol. Soc., Cmty. Women's Orch. Office: IPSR Dept Psychology U Calif Tolman Hall Berkeley CA 94720

AGUILAR, DIANA GUERRERO, elementary school educator; b. San Antonio, Dec. 9, 1956; d. Jose S. and Maria (Perez) Guerrero; m. Jose Aldo Aguilar, Nov. 17, 1984; children: Marisa A., Cristina A. BA, U. Tex., San Antonio, 1978, MA, 1982. Cert. tchr. bilingual edn. Tex. Edn. Agy.; cert. profl. counselor. Bilingual tchr. Forest Hills Elem. Sch., Northside Ind. Sch. Dist., San Antonio, 1978-80; bilingual tchr. grade 2 Govalle Elem. Sch., Austin (Tex.) Ind. Sch. Dist., 1984-86, Windcrest Elem. Sch., N.E. Ind. Sch. Dist., San Antonio, 1980-84; bilingual tchr. grades 2-4 Olmos Elem. Sch., N.E. Ind. Sch. Dist., San Antonio, 1986-88, tchr. English to speakers of other langs. grades K-5, 1988—; bilingual campus coord. Windcrest Elem. Sch., 1980-84; bilingual/English to speakers of other langs. coord. Olmos Elem. Sch., 1991-93, mem. lang. proficiency com., 1991—; mem. writing team ESOL (English to speakers of other langs.) Curriculum Guide, N.E. Ind. Sch. Dist., 1989. Fin. chairperson Colonial Hills PTA, San Antonio, 1994-95, sec., 1995-96; active Olmos Elem. PTA, 1986—, Phobia Clinic of San Antonio Vol. Hotline; eucharistic min. St. Gregory the Gt.; registration chair San Antonio Area Assn. for Bilingual Educators-Bilingual Conf., 1996. Recipient Outstanding Contbn. to Bilingual Edn. award Austin and Travis County Hispanic C. of C., 1985, Supt.'s Appreciation award Colonial Hills PTA, 1991-92, Cert. of Appreciation, Olmos Elem. PTA, 1991-92, Recognition award Region 20 Edn. Svc. Ctr., 1994, Human Rels. award Northeast Tchrs. Assn., 1995. Mem. N.E. Tchrs. Assn., Alamo Reading Coun., Tex. TESOL II, Tex. Assn. Bilingual Edn., San Antonio Area Assn. Bilingual Edn. (v.p. 1994-95, bd. dirs., sec. 1995-96, ho. of dels.). Democrat. Roman Catholic.

AGUILAR-POSADA, GLADYS MARIA, counselor; b. Mérida, Mexico, Mar. 16, 1965; came to the U.S., 1968; d. Francisco Javier and Gladys Maria (Salazar) Aguilar; m. Ramón Jorge Posada, June 30, 1990; children: Emmanuel, Daniel. BS cum laude, Loyola Marymount U., 1987; MS, Calif. State U., 1990. Cert. in pupil personnel svcs. Youth min. St. Francis of Assisi Parish, L.A., 1987-88; sch. counselor Concern Counseling Svcs., Fullerton, Calif., 1988-89; bilingual behavioral therapist Inst. for Applied Behavioral Analysis, L.A., 1988-89; sch. counselor, tchr. St. Lucy's Priory High Sch., Glendora, Calif., 1989-90; intern Cath. Psychol. Svcs. Cath. Charities of L.A., L.A., 1990-93; marriage, family and child counseling intern Brown & Assocs., Whittier, Calif., 1989-93; bilingual elem. sch. counselor L.A. Unified Sch. Dist., 1993—. Eucharistic min., lector St. Francis of Assisi Cath. Ch., 1986-92. Mem. Calif. Assn. Marriage and Family Therapists, L.A. Sch. Counselors Assn., Psi Chi, Alpha Sigma Nu. Home: 836 Forest Hills Dr Covina CA 91724

AGUILERA, JULIE, social services administrator. BBA, Hunter Coll. Pres. Coun. Adoptable Children, N.Y.C.; ptnr. in edn. spkr. N.Y.C. Bd. Edn., 1991—. Recipient Latina Excellence Family award, 1995. Office: Coun Adoptable Children 666 Broadway St New York NY 10012*

AGUIRRE, LINDA G., state legislator; b. Flagstaff, Ariz., July 12, 1951; m. John Aguirre; children: Eric, Stephanie. BA, Ariz. State U., 1978. Educator; mem. Ariz. Ho. of Reps., mem. banking and ins., human svcs. and transp. coms., mem. banking and ins., environmental, transp., & economic dev coms. Active Ariz. Sch. Bd., Nat. Sch. Bd., Nat. Hispanic Sch. Bd., Ariz. Citizens Edn. Mem. South Mountain C. of C. Democrat. Office: Ariz House of Reps 1700 W Washington State Capitol Phoenix AZ 85007*

AGUIRRE-BATTY, MERCEDES, Spanish and English language and literature educator; b. Cd Juarez, Mex., Dec. 20, 1952; came to U.S., 1957.; d. Alejandro M. and Mercedes (Péon) Aguirre; m. Hugh K. Batty, Mar. 17, 1979; 1 child, Henry B. BA, U. Tex., El Paso, 1974, MA, 1977. Instr. ESL Paso del Norte- Prep Sch., Cd Juarez, 1973-74; teaching asst. ESL and English U. Tex., El Paso, 1974-77; instr. ESL English Lang. Svcs., Bridgeport, Conn., 1977-80; instr. Spanish and English, coord. modern lang. Sheridan (Wyo.) Coll., 1980—, pres. faculty senate, 1989-90; pres. faculty senate, chair dist. coun. No. Wyo. C.C. Dist., 1995-96; advanced placement faculty Spanish cons. The College Bd. Ednl. Testing Svc.; adj. prof. Spanish, U. Autonoma Cd Juarez, 1975; adj. prof. Spanish and English, Sacred Heart U., Fairfield, Conn., 1977-80; spkr. in field. Bd. dirs. Wyo. Coun. for the Humanities, 1988-92; translator county and dist. cts., Sheridan. NEH fellow, 1991, 92; Wyo. State Dept. Edn. grantee, 1991. Mem. Wyo. Fgn. Lang. Tchrs. Assn. (pres. 1990-92), Am. Assn. Tchrs. Spanish and Portuguese (founder, 1st pres. Wyo. chpt. 1987-90), TESOL, Sigma Delta Mu (v.p. 1992—), Sigma Delta Pi (pres. 1974-75). Office: Sheridan Coll NWCCD 3059 Coffeen Ave Sheridan WY 82801-9133

AHALT, MARY JANE, management consultant; b. Elizabethville, Pa., Oct. 11, 1914; d. George Lewis and Grace Eva (Cooper) Zeigler; m. Arthur Montraville Ahalt, Mar. 29, 1935 (dec. Sept. 1958); children: Mary Jane Ahalt Barker, Arthur Montraville Monty. Student, U. Md., 1949-51, 63-65. Relief tchr., dir. Calvert Nursery Sch., Riverdale, Md., 1943-45; off-campus housemother U. Md., College Park, 1939-93, typist, 1951-58, prin. stenographer Coll. Agr., 1958-59, sec. I, III, and IV coll. Edn., 1959-68, 68-78, sec. to dean, 1960-76; sec., bookkeeper Entomology Soc. Am., College Park & Washington, 1951-53; cons. office practice and mgmt. College Park, 1978—; panel mem. College Park Bus. and Profl. Women, St. Louis, 1994, College Park, 1995; cons. Project Return, Prince George's County Mental Health Assn., 1970-72. Historian archivist History of Maryland Business and Professional Women, 1983-86; co-prodr. cable TV program Women's Changing Roles: Finding a Balance, 1991. Sec. coun. Hope Luth. Ch., College Park, 1956-61, 69-74, pres. Luth. Ch. Women, 1952, 74, 87, mem. adv. bd. dist. bd., 1975-87; mem. Prince George's County Internat. Women's Task Force, 1974-76; mem. aux. Nat. Luth. Home for Aged, 1960-96; asst. leader Jr. H.S. Girl Scout troop, 1951-54; chair publicity com. Prince George's County Internat. Women's Yr. Task Force, 1974-76, mem. recognition of woman of month com., 1974-76; mem. by-laws com. Women's Action Coalition of Prince George's County, 1976-77; chair parish-staff rels. com. Hope Luth. Ch., 1988; judge Most Beautiful Youth, Prince George's County. Named Prince Georgian of Yr., Prince George County Citizens, 1989, Womanof Hist. Note Prince George County Bus. and Profl. Women, 1988, Woman of Achievement in Prince George's County History, 1994; named to Women's Hall of Fame, Prince George's County, Commn. for Women, 1990; recipient Beautification award Com. for a Beter Environ., College Park, 1990. Mem. College Park Bus. and Profl. Women, Inc. (charter mem., historian, archivist 1964—, mem. Cable TV 1983-89, 89—, pres. 1966-68, Woman of Yr. 1975), Md. Fedn. Bus. and Profl. Women's Clubs Inc. (bd. mem. 1967—, pres. 1973-74, Woman of Yr. 1976), Nat. Fedn. Bus. and Profl. Women's Clubs (nat. bd. 1973-74), U. Md. Heritage Club and Pres. Club, Md. Classified Employees Assn. Home: Apt 215 717 Maiden Choice Ln Catonsville MD 21228

AHART-WALLS, PAMELA, elementary school principal; b. Sacramento, Calif., May 31, 1950; d. Eury Anthony and Mercedes (Brown) Ahart; children: Courtney Ahart James, Howell Burl Walls. BA in English, Edn., Our Lady of the Lake Coll., 1971; MA Comm. Disorders, Lrning. Disabilities, Our Lady of the Lake U., 1973. Tchr. H.K. Williams Elem. Sch. Edgewood Ind. Sch. Dist., San Antonio, Tex., 1971-73; cons. spl. edn. and materials specialist Edn. Svc. Ctr., Region 20, San Antonio, 1973-79, project mgr. metric edn., 1979-81; tchr. lang. and learning disabilites San Antonio Ind. Sch. Dist., 1981-88, peer tchr. evaluator, 1988-89, elem. prin., 1989-95; cons., speaker on elem. edn., various cities, Tex., 1985—. Author: (edn. kit) Metric Education Made Easy, Kindergarten to 5th Grade, 1980. Mem. exec. com. Met. Alliance, San Antonio, 1994—; mem. Lit. Commn. of San Antonio, 1994—. School recognized as Smart Sch., Trinity Univ., San Antonio, 1991-95; grantee Tex. Edn. Agy., 1992-95. Mem. ASCD, Tex. Elem. Prins. and Suprs. Assn., Jack and Jill of Am., LINKS, Nat. Coalition of 100 Black Women. Home: 9626 Cloverdale San Antonio TX 78250 Office: Samuel Houston Gates Elem San Antonio Ind Sch Dist 510 Morning View San Antonio TX 78220

AHERN, JODIE LUCEY, writer, editor; b. Haverhill, Mass., Mar. 30, 1951; d. Edmund Francis and Joan Margaret (Everett) Lucey; m. Philip Muller Ahern, May 6, 1973 (div. Feb. 1992); children: Andrea Lucey, Samuel Joseph. BA, Conn. Coll., 1973. Writer, editor Mpls., 1980-84; assoc. editor Garden Supply Retailer, Mpls., 1984-86; editor Minn. Home and Design, Mpls., 1986-89; mng. editor Minn. Monthly, Mpls., 1989-94; editor Midwest Home and Design, Mpls., 1989-94, Casino Mag., Mpls., 1994-95; writer, editor St. Paul, 1995—. Author (editorials) St. Paul Pioneer Press, 1993, Mpls. Star Tribune, 1980—, (home sect.) Mpls. St. Paul Mag., 1995—. Scholarship Conn. Coll., 1969-73. Mem. Assn. of Women Journalists, Women in the Arts. Home: 3422 43rd Ave S Minneapolis MN 55406

AHERN, MARGARET ANN, nun, nursing educator; b. Manchester, N.H., Nov. 23, 1931; d. Timothy Joseph and Helen Bridget (Kearns) Ahern. Diploma, Sacred Heart Hosp. Sch. Nursing, 1952; BSN, Mt. St. Mary Coll., 1957; MSN, Cath. U. Am., 1965. Entered Sisters of Mercy, Roman Cath. Ch., 1953. Staff nurse Sacred Heart Hosp., Manchester, 1954-57, oper. rm. supr., 1957-62, med.-surg. nursing instr., 1962-66, dir. Sch. Nursing, 1966-75; dir. Sch. Nursing Cath. Med. Ctr., Manchester, 1975-79, dir. dept. edn. and mem. sr. mgmt., 1979-87; pres. Cath. Med. Ctr. Networks, Inc., Manchester, 1987-94; mng. dir. Optima Health Systems, Inc., Manchester, N.H., 1994—. Contbr. articles to profl. jours. Chmn. bd. dirs. Health Edn. Consortium, 1977-89; bd. dirs. Vis. Nurse Assn., 1981-87; adv. bd. Hesser Coll., 1980—, N.H. Vocat.-Tech. Coll., 1979-87; mem. United Health Systems Agy., 1977-83; mem. adv. council on continuing edn. St. Anselm Coll., 1978-89; mem. gen. chpt. Sisters of Mercy, 1968-70, 79-81, chmn. fin. bd., 1981-86, chmn. Bd. Consolidation and Arbitration, 1981-86, 1991—. Recipient Disting. Women Leaders award YWCA, 1986, Pres.'s award Fidelity Health Alliance, 1992. Mem. ANA, N.H. Nurses Assn., Nat. League for Nursing, New Eng. Cath. Hosp. Assn., N.H. Heart Assn., Sigma Theta Tau (Leadership Recognition award Epsilon Tau chpt. 1989, Disting. Leaders award 1989). Democrat. Roman Catholic. Home: 647 Amoskeag Pl Manchester NH 03101-1224 Office: Optima Health Cmty Svcs 77 Pearl St Manchester NH 03101-1464

AHERN, RANDI ELLEN BORENSTEIN, marketing manager; b. Summit, N.J., Nov. 5, 1961; d. Herbert and Dorothy (Borowick) Borenstein; m. James Walter Ahern, May 31, 1987 (div. Sept. 1993). BSEE, Trenton State Coll., 1994; MBA in Mktg., Fairleigh Dickenson U., 1988. Tech. writer network systems AT&T, Morristown, N.J., 1984-86; product planner tech. systems AT&T, Holmdel, N.J., 1986-87; mktg. mgr. consumer comm. AT&T, Basking Ridge, N.J., 1987-93; sys. devel. mgr. Unitel/AT&T Consumer Mktg., Toronto, Ont., Can., 1994-95; event mktg. mgr. mktg. comm. AT&T, Basking Ridge, 1995—. Vol. Nat. MS Soc., 1992—. Mem. U.S. Holocaust Mus., AT&T Pioneers, Rails-to-Trails, Beminster Flyers. Democrat. Jewish. Office: AT&T 295 N Maple Ave Basking Ridge NJ 07920

AHL, JANYCE BARNWELL, historian, writer, speaker, retired educator; b. St. Augustine, Fla., Oct. 13, 1911; d. Carlos Drew and Martha Rebecca (Adams) A. BS in English and Biology, Fla. Southern Coll., Lakeland, Fla., 1939. Tchr., sci. Lake Wales Jr. High, Fla. Author: Early History of Lake Wales Woman's Club, 1989, Crown Jewel of the Highlands: Lake Wales, Florida, 1983 (donated proceeds from book to Lake Wales Libr. Assn.), Early History of the Lake Wales Cemetery, 1984; co-author Late History of the First Presbyterian Church of Lake Wales Florida, 1989. Mem. Prayer and Care Group, Sunday Afternoon Circle (life mem.), Lakes Wales Hist. Soc. (life mem.), Lake Wales Mus. and Culture Ctr. (charter mem.), Polk County Hist. Soc., Friends of Bok Tower, Polk County Hist. Commn., 1992—; campaigned for Gov. Lawton Chiles; guest spkr. various schs., civic and social orgns. Named Pioneer of the Yr. City of Lake Wales, 1979, citizen of the Yr. Lake Wales Masonic Lodge, 1990; recipient key to the City of Lake Wales, 1979, Gold pin Woman's Soc., 1982, Lifetime Achievement award Polk County Sch. Bd., 1992, Disting. svc. to Humanity award Fla. So. Coll. Ann. Alumni Awards, 1996. Mem. Am. Legion Aux. (pres. 1988, 89, past pres. pin), Polk County Ret. Tchrs. Assn., Fla. Ret. Educators Assn., Nat. Edn. Assn., Lake Wales Dem. Club. Democrat. Presbyterian.

AHLGREN, MADELYN, state legislator; b. Manchester, N.H., Feb. 6, 1915; m. Adler R. (dec.); 3 children. BA, U. N.H., 1936; attended, Northeastern, Wesleyan, U. N.H. Del. Dem. Nat. Convention, 1988; treas. Ward 4 Dem. Com., 1991—; Dem. presdl. elector, 1988. Mem. N.H. Ret. Tchrs., Manchester Hist. Assn., Manchester Ret. Tchrs., Manchester Women's Club, ADK Tchr's Sorority. Roman Catholic. Office: NH Ho of Reps State Capitol Concord NH 03301*

AHLRICHS, NANCY SURRATT, marketing professional; b. Harrisburg, Pa., Oct. 13, 1952; d. Joe Free and Mary Alice (Norris) Surratt; m. Karl J. Ahlrichs, Sept. 10, 1983. BA in Anthropology, Purdue U., 1974, MS in Phys. Anthropology, 1976. With dept. prodn. Steuben Printing Co., Angola, Ind., 1977-78; project specialist A.B. Dick Co., Chgo., 1978-81, sr. instructional designer, 1981-82; mgr. tng. and devel. Equitable Relocation Mgmt. Corp., Chgo. and Orlando, 1982-83; v.p. Todd Persons Communications,

Inc., Orlando, 1984-87, Gary Bitner Pub. Rels., Orlando, 1987-89; v.p. client svcs. Right Assocs., San Diego, 1989-90; v.p. profl. svcs. Right Assocs., Indpls., 1992-94; mktg. cons., entrepreneur Indpls., 1994—; sr. orgnl. devel. cons. RCI, Indpls., 1995—. Producer videotape: The Big Push, 1983; author/ghost writer over 50 mag. and trade jour. articles; writer, producer, dir. over 50 corp. videotapes. Vol. Steve Goldsmith for Mayor, Indpls., 1991; major gifts chmn. Am. Heart Assn., San Diego, 1990-91. Recipient Pres.'s award Cen. Fla. Zool. Soc., 1988. Mem. Kiwanis Indpls. (mktg. com., chmn. downtown program 1994-95, numerous other coms. 1994-95, bd. dirs. 1995—), Phi Kappa Phi. Democrat. Lutheran. Office: 6160 N Meridian St Indianapolis IN 46208-1536

AHO, BARBARA, accountant; b. Pitts., July 19, 1955; d. Martin Francis and Barbara Ann (Pelkofer) Gaynord; m. Gary Ralph Westman, Nov. 22, 1975 (div. Dec. 1983); children: Melissa Ann Westman, Wendolyn Joan Westman (dec.); m. John David Aho, Aug. 7, 1987 (div. July 1995); children: Erika Valentine, Edward Ross. BA, Seton Hill Coll., 1978. enrolled agt. U.S. Dept Treasury. Adminstrv. asst. H&R Block, North Palm Beach, Fla., 1984-86; staff acct. Accts. Unltd., Ft. Lauderdale, Fla., 1986-90; owner, cons. Barbara Westman, Inc., Lantana, Fla., 1990-93; ptnr. Wallis & Aho Enrolled Agts., Lake Worth, Fla., 1993—; adj. faculty Palm Beach C.C., Lake Worth, 1988-94. Vol. Girl Scouts U.S., Glade Mills, Pa., 1973-75, Pompano Beach, Fla., 1986-88. Mem. Nat. Assn. Enrolled Agts., Fla. Soc. Enrolled Agts., Nat. Soc. Pub. Accts., Nat. Assn. Tax Profls., Am. Soc. Women Accts. Democrat. Office: Wallis & Aho Enrolled Agts 1776 Lake Worth Rd #103 Lake Worth FL 33460

AHRENS, KAREN RAPPAPORT, therapist; b. Johnson AFB, Japan, Sept. 28, 1954; d. Burton F. and Betty J. (Reaves) Rappaport; m. Mario E. Ahrens, July 16, 1975; children: Caroline E., Lucia V. BA in Criminal Justice, St. Martin's Coll., 1989, MA in Cmty. Psychology, 1995. Cert. domestic violence treatment provider, Wash. Probation officer Mason County, Shelton, Wash., 1988-91; coord. victim assistance program City of Olympia, Wash., 1991-93; domestic violence program therapist Shelton, 1993—, mental health therapist, 1994—; cons. City of Shelton, 1995—. Mem. ACA, Washington Domestic Violence Treatment Providers Assn. Office: Counseling Resources PO Box 457 Shelton WA 98584

AHWINONA, CYNTHIA A., legislative professional staff; b. Nome, Alaska, Dec. 12, 1952; d. Jacob and Hannah (Anagick) A. Student, U. Alaska, 1972-73, U. Alaska, Anchorage, 1988. With Green Constrn. Co., 1973-76; mem. staff Senator Mike Gravel, 1976-80, Rep. Don Young, 1980-87; regional planner, with pub. rels. Bering Sea Fishermen's Assn., Anchorage, 1988-89; profl. staff Ho. Com. Natural Resources. Mem. Nat. Conf. State Socs. (regional dir. 1994), Alaska State Soc. (pres., bd. dirs.). Office: Rm 819 O'Neill House Office Bldg Washington DC 20515

AIELLO, ELIZABETH ANN, public relations liaison; b. Pitts., Apr. 10, 1922; d. Edward Aloysius and Sarah Marie (Short) Maroney; m. William Peter Aiello, June 4, 1946 (dec. Nov. 1989); children: David Robert, Beverly Ann Aiello Reecer. BA, Chatham Coll., 1943; MA, St. John's Coll., Santa Fe, N.Mex., 1969; postgrad., U. N.Mex., 1970—. Cert. tchr. elem./secondary English, history, social studies, govt., civics. Secondary instr. history Moon Twp. Schs., Coraopolis, Pa., 1943-44; secondary instr. English, Latin Blawnox (Pa.) Schs., 1944-49; elementary instr. upper primary Los Alamos (N.Mex.) Schs., 1949-59, secondary instr. advanced placement English/history, 1959-82; chair English dept. U. N.Mex., Los Alamos, 1982-90, head humanities div., 1986-90, dir. reentry program for women in sci., 1984-89, dir. reentry program for Native Am./Hispanic students, 1987-90; ednl. pub. rels. liaison Los Alamos Nat. Lab., 1984—; Great Books discussion groups coord. No. N.Mex., 1992—; adv. bd. N.Mex. Women in Sci., Santa Fe, 1980-84, Los Alamos Women in Sci., 1984-90; Fulbright teaching fellow U.S. Dept. Edn., Washington, 1971-72. Author: Perigrinations at Pokesdown, 1974, Consumation and Other Poems, 1984, New Hope for Dying Muse, 1986, Perceptions and Reality, 1991, Perceptions I-IV. Phoebe Brashear Soc. scholar, Pitts., 1939-43; Am. Hist. Soc.-NEH joint fellow, 1976, William Robertson Coe fellow, 1981; rsch. grantee AAUW, 1982, Carl Perkins grantee N.Mex. Dept. Vocat.-Tech. Edn., 1986-90; named Outstanding N.Mex. History Tchr., DAR, 1976, One of 80 Women to Watch in 80's, N.Mex. Women's Polit. Caucus, 1980; recipient N.Mex. Women at Work award Nat. Coun. Working Women and Minority Affairs, Washington, 1975, Gov.'s award Gov. N.Mex., N.Mex. Commn. Status of Women, 1986, 89. Mem. NEA, AAUW (div. adv. bd. 1985-90, nat. adv. bd. 1985-89, June B. West fellow N.Mex. div. 1969, Grace Braker Wilson award 1990), Los Alamos Nat. Edn. Assn. (adv. bd., pres. 1975-80), Delta Kappa Gamma. Office: Los Alamos Nat Lab Box 1663 MS C330 Los Alamos NM 87545

AIGNER, EMILY BURKE, lay worker; b. Henrico, Va., Oct. 28, 1920; d. William Lyne and Susie Emily (Willson) Burke; m. Louis Cottrell Aigner, Nov. 27, 1936; children: Lyne, Betty, D. Muriel (dec.), Willson, Norman, William, Randolph, Dorothy. Cert. in Bible, U. Richmond, 1969; postgrad., So. Bapt. Sem. Extension, Nashville, 1987, Va. Commonwealth U., 1981; diploma in Bible, Liberty Home Bible Inst., 1992. Deacon Four Mile Creek Bapt. Ch., Richmond, Va., 1972—, trustee, 1991, dir. Woman's Missionary Union, 1986-94, treas., 1984-89, dir. Sunday sch., 1993—; chaplain Richmond Meml. Hosp., 1996—; spl. edn. tchr.; acctg. tech., 1959-80. Prodr. Dial-A-Devotion for pub. by telephone, 1978-85. Solicitor ARC, Henrico County, 1947-49, induction ctr. vol., 1994—; solicitor, United Givers' Fund, Henrico County, 1945-48; sec.-treas. soliciting funds Bible Edn. in Varina Sch., 1946-49; singer Bellwood Choir, Chesterfield County, Va., 1965-70; telephone counselor Richmond Contact, 1980-82, Am. Cancer Soc., Richmond, 1980-82; program chmn. Varina (Va.) Home Demonstration Club, 1950-53; worker Vol. Visitor Program Westport Convalescent Home, 1983—; vol. patient rep. Richmond Meml. Hosp., 1994—; vol. Crisis Pregnancy Ctr., 1995—; jail min. Richmond City Jail, 1973—; chaplain Richmond Meml. Hosp., 1996—. Named Woman of Yr., Henrico Farm Bur., 1996. Mem. Gideons Internat. (sec. Va. aux. 1977-80, 82-84, new mem. plan rep. 1981, 85, 91, 94, zone leader 1988-89, 90-91, state cabinet rep. 1989-90, pres. Richmond N.E. Camp 1976-78, sec.-treas. 1980-82, 93, scripture sec. 1973-75, 87-89, chmn. Va. state widows com. 1993—), Henrico Farm Bur. (women's com. 1994—), Farm Bur. Fedn. (Henrico Farm Woman of Yr. 1996), Alpha Phi Sigma. Home: 9717 Varina Rd Richmond VA 23231-8428

AIKEN, BETTY JEANNE JENKINS, elementary education educator; b. Old Fort, N.C., July 4, 1928; d. Charles McBryde and Nan Margaret Edwards Jenkins; m. Francis James Aiken Jr., Dec. 19, 1956 (div. Aug. 1979); children: Nancy, James Michael, John Patrick, Charles Franklin. BA, Winthrop U., 1949; MEd, Columbus Coll., 1979, EdS, 1985; postgrad., Clemson U., 1950-52, Ga. So. U., 1986, 87. Tchr. cert. N.C., S.C., Ga. Tchr. Johnston (S.C.) Pub. Schs., 1949-52, Gastonia (N.C.) Schs., 1952-53, Charleston County Schs., Mt. Pleasant, S.C., 1953-54, Pickens County Schs., Easley, S.C., 1954-60, Greenville (S.C.) County Schs., 1960-61, Muscogee County Sch. Dist., Columbus, Ga., 1978-93; part-time tchr. Midlands Tech. Coll., Columbia, 1994-95, Columbus Coll., 1993, ADD Meadows Jr. Coll., 1980-84, BSEP and ESL programs at Fort Benning, 1979, 80. Editor: Paw Prints, 1982-83, TV Tempo, 1975-76, (church newsletter) Morningside News, 1977-79. Mem. PAGE, Ga., 1978-93, PTA, S.C. and Ga., 1949-93; leader Brownie Scouts, Girl Scouts U.S., S.C., 1967-70, den mother Cub Scouts, Boy Scouts Am., Ga., 1971-72. Mem. DAR, AAUW, Nat. Fgn. Langs Profls., Ga. Fgn. Lang. Profls., Columbia World Affairs Coun., S.C. Hist. Soc., Hist. Columbia Found., Mensa. Presbyterian.

AIKEN, DOROTHY LOUISE, secondary education educator; b. Washington, Apr. 27, 1924; d. Willard Ross and Gertrude (Rucker) Snyder; m. William David Aiken, May 22, 1948 (dec. 1988); children: Katherine Aiken Schwartz, Mary Aiken Fishback, Sally Aiken Fitterer, Jerome. BS, George Washington U., 1946; postgrad., Wash. State U., 1946-47. Teaching fellow Wash. State U., Pullman, 1946-47; tchr. secondary sch. D.C. Schs., Washington, 1947-50; tchr. Sunnyside (Wash.) Sch. Dist. 201, 1962-80. Sec. vestry Holy Trinity Ch., 1968-70; staff Evergreen Girls State, 1972-81; Dem. precinct committeeman, Sunnyside, 1980-86; mem. com. Margaret Rayburn Legislator campaign, Grandview, Wash., 1990; vice chair Yakima Valley C.C., 1994-95, trustee; trustee Assn. Cmty. and Tech. Colls., mem. conf. com., 1992; co-producer Valley Mus. Comedy Co. Prodns., 1989-91; chmn. Hospice Light Up a Life, 1991; vol., program head ARC. Mem. Am. Legion Aux. (pres. 1974-76, meritorious svc. citation 1983, 88), Nouvella Federated Women's Club (2d v.p. 1984-86), Women's Golf Assn. (pres.). Episcopalian. Home: 1241 Sunset Pl Sunnyside WA 98944-1720

AIKEN, LINDA HARMAN, nurse, sociologist, educator; b. Roanoke, Va., July 29, 1943; d. William Jordan and Betty Philips (Warner) Harman; children: June Elizabeth, Alan James. BSN, U. Fla., 1964, M in Nursing, 1966; PhD in Sociology, U. Tex., 1973. Nurse Med. Ctr. U. Fla., Gainesville, 1964-65, instr. coll. nursing, 1966-67; instr. sch. of nursing U. Mo., Columbia, 1967-70, clin. nurse specialist sch. of nursing, 1967-70; program officer Robert Wood Johnson Found., Princeton, N.J., 1974-76, dir. rsch., 1976-79, asst. v.p., 1979-81, v.p., 1981-87; trustee prof. nursing and sociology U. Pa., Phila., 1988—; dir. Ctr. for Health Svcs. and Policy Rsch. U. Pa.; rsch. assoc. population studies ctr. U. Pa.; mem. Sec. Health and Human Svcs. Commn. on Nursing, 1988, Pres. Clinton's Nat. Health Care Reform Task Force, 1993; commr. Physician Payment Rev. Commn. nat. adv. coun. U.S. Agy. for Health Care Care Policy and Rsch. Author: Health Policy and Nursing Practice, 1981, Nursing in the 1980s, 1982, Applications of Social Science to Clinical Medicine and Health Policy, 1986, Evaluation Studies Rev. Ann., 1985, Charting Nursing's Future, 1991; assoc. editor Jour. Health and Social Behavior, 1979-81, Transaction Soc., 1985—; mem. editorial bd. Evaluation Quar., 1979-80, Med. Care, 1983—; contbr. articles to profl. jours. Mem. Adv. Council Social Security, 1982-83. Recipient Joint Secretarial commendation U.S. Dept. Health and Human Services and HUD, 1987; NIH Nurse Scientist fellow, 1970-73. Mem. ANA (Jessie M. Scott award 1984), Inst. Medicine, Nat. Acad. Scis., Nat. Acad. Social Ins., Am. Acad. Nursing (pres. 1979-80), Am. Sociol. Assn. (chair med. sociology sect. 1983-84), Sociol. Rsch. Assn., Coun. Nurse Rschrs. (Nurse Scientist of Yr. 1991), Sigma Theta Tau, Phi Kappa Phi. Home: 2209 Lombard St Philadelphia PA 19146-1107 Office: U Pa 420 Service Dr Philadelphia PA 19104-6020

AIKEN, LOUISETTE ADRIENNE, psychotherapist; b. Moineville, France, Dec. 29, 1929; came to U.S., 1947; d. Nicolas and Julia (Dautremont) Tarnus; m. Thomas C. Aiken, Aug. 5, 1947; children: Thomas, Michael. BA, Canisius Coll., 1976; ED, SUNY, 1983. Real estate broker Aiken Real Estate, Inc., Lancaster, N.Y., 1960-80; exec. dir. Alden (N.Y.) Area Counseling Ctr., 1980-85; psychotherapist pvt. practice, Alden, 1985—; educator Nardin Acad., Buffalo, 1976-78. Mem. Pi Lambda Theta. Home and Office: 347 S Exchange St Alden NY 14004

AIKENS, JOAN DEACON, government official; b. Lansdowne, Pa.; d. Robert Wallace and Bessie (Crook) Deacon; m. Donald R. Aikens (div.); 1 son, Donald R. BA, Ursinus Coll., 1950, LLD, 1979. Fashion cons. Park Ave. Shop, Swarthmore, Pa., 1971-73; v.p. Lew Hodges Communications, Inc., Valley Forge, Pa., 1974-75; mem. Fed. Election Commn., Washington, 1975—, vice chmn., 1977-78, 85, 91, chmn., 1978-79, 85-86, 92, now commr.; Chmn. women's div. Washington conf. Republican Nat. Com., 1966; hospitality chmn. Pa. del. Rep. Nat. Conf., 1968, alt.-at-large, 1972; bd. dirs. Nat. Fedn. Rep. Women, 1972-75; active Pa. Council Rep. Women, 1960-74, pres., 1972-74; co-chmn. Women for McCorkle-Williams, Pa. Rep. State Com., 1970; mem. exec. com. Pa. Rep. State Com., 1972-74, elected mem., 1974; vice chmn. Citizens for Nixon-Agnew, Delaware County (Pa.) Rep. Party, 1968, Com. to Re-Elect the Pres., 1972; precinct committeewoman Swarthmore (Pa.) Rep. Party, 1960-75; pres. Swarthmore Council Rep. Women, 1970-72; chmn. various campaigns Swarthmore Rep. Hdqrs., 1960-74. Active Swarthmore Presbyn. Ch., 1955-64; bd. dirs. Women's Assn., 1956-60; active Riddle Meml. Hosp., Delaware County, Pa., 1958-74; pres. Women's Bd. Assoc. Auxs., 1970-72; mem. women's bd. Women's Med. Coll., Phila., 1978-98; bd. dirs. Ursinus Coll., 1985—, Nat. League Ctr. for the Pub. Interest, Washington, 1995—. Mem. Exec. Women in Govt. (pres. 1989-91), Washington Host Lions Club (King lion 1993-94). Office: Fed Election Commn 999 E St NW Washington DC 20463-0001

AIKMAN, ROSALIE H., state legislator. Mem. Maine Ho. of Reps., mem. appropriations & fin. affairs com. Republican. Home: HCR Box 420 Poland ME 04273 Office: Maine State Capital House Rep Office State House Sta #2 Augusta ME 04333

AILLONI-CHARAS, MIRIAM CLARA, interior designer, consultant; b. Veere, The Netherlands, July 31, 1935; came to U.S., 1958; d. Maurits and Elzina (De Groot) Taytelbaum; m. Dan Ailloni-Charas, Oct. 8, 1957; children: Ethan Benjamin, Orrin, Adam. Degree in Interiors, Pratt Inst., 1962; BSc, SUNY, Albany, 1978. Interior designer S.J. Miller Assocs., N.Y.C., 1960-63; interior design cons. Rye Brook, N.Y., 1963-88, 90—; exec. v.p. Contract 2000 Inc., Port Chester, N.Y., 1988-90. Treas. Temple Guild, Congregation Emanu-El, Rye, N.Y., 1979-88, co-chmn., 1988-96, chair, 1996—, trustee, 1986-92, pres., 1996—. Recipient Cert. of Merit, U.S. Jaycees, 1962, March of Dimes, 1989, 91. Mem. Am. Soc. Interior Designers, Allied Bd. Trade, Westchester Assn. Women Bus. Owners (bd. dirs. 1988-93), Nat. Trust for Historic Preservation, Westchester C. of C. (area devel. coun. 1988-90). Home and Office: 23 Woodland Dr Rye Brook NY 10573-1797

AINSWORTH, HARRIET CRAWFORD, journalist, public relations consultant; b. Columbus, Ohio, Nov. 27, 1914; d. Harry Hoskins and Pansy Lucy (Graham) Crawford; m. J. Gordon Ainsworth, Oct. 6, 1945; children: J. Gordon Jr., Adeline Ainsworth Forrest. BA, Ohio Wesleyan U., 1934; postgrad., Columbia U. Sch. Journalism, 1934-35, Gonzaga U., 1940, Calif. Coll. Arts and Crafts, 1968; life adult edn.-C.C. tchg. credential, U. Calif., Berkeley, 1967. Reporter Portland Oregonian, 1936-37; ind. pub. rels. writer, 1937-42; fgn. corr. Oakland Tribune, Indpls. Star, Japan, China, The Philippines, 1946; pub. info. dir. Am. Cancer Soc., Contra Costa County, Calif., 1958-89; cons. Calif. divsn. Am. Cancer Soc., 1965-77; pres. Ainsworth-Powell Pub. Rels., 1965-77; v.p. Corp. Identity Assocs., Orinda, Calif., 1968-94, pres., 1994—; columnist (Sunbeams), feature writer Contra Costa Sun, Contra Costa Times, 1990—. Co-author: The Road Back, 1968; contbr. articles to profl. jours., newspaper columns. Mem. Citizen's Recreation Commn., dist. 6, Orinda, 1974-79; founder, pres. Orinda Found., 1975; chmn. spl. events Calif. Shakespeare Festival Amphitheater campaign, 1988-92. Lt. comdr. USNR, 1942-58. Named Orinda Citizen of Yr., 1976; recipient Plaque and Resolution Commendation Recreation Dist. 6, Orinda, 1979, Recognition award Plaque Pres. U.S. People-to-People Sports Com. Mem. San Francisco Pub. Rels. Round Table, Contra Costa Press Club, East Bay Women's Press Club (pres.), Orinda Country Club, Orindawoods Tennis Club, Orinda Tennis Club, Kappa Alpha Theta (co-founder Diablo Valley chpt.).

AINSWORTH, JOAN HORSBURGH, university development director; b. Cleve., Dec. 30, 1942; d. Donald Francis and Elaine Mildred Horsburgh; m. Richard B. Ainsworth Jr., Oct. 30, 1965; children: Richard B. III, Alison. BA, Wells Coll., 1965; MBA, Case Western Res. U., 1986. CFRE. Social worker San Diego County (Calif.) Welfare Dept., 1966-68; social worker, vol. coord. Washtenaw County (Mich.) Juvenile Ct., Ann Arbor, 1968-70; adminstrv. asst. to pres. Med. Ventures, Ltd., Cleve., 1985-86; dir. Project MOVE, Office of Mayor City of Cleve., 1986-89; dir. devel. and pres.'s programs Case Western Res. U., Cleve., 1989—. Trustee, v.p. Children's Aid Soc., Cleve., 1989—; trustee, chair devel. Project: LEARN, Cleve., 1990—; past trustee, cmty. vol. Jr. League Cleve., Inc., 1971—; mem. Vol. Ohio, 1987—. Named Hon. Mayor City of Cleve., 1989. Mem. Nat. Assn. Fundraising Execs. (cert.; chair publicity Greater Cleve. chpt. 1994—), Coun. for Advancement and Support of Edn. Home: 2023 Lyndway Rd Cleveland OH 44121 Office: Case Western Res U 10900 Euclid Ave Cleveland OH 44106-7035

AIRES, JULIET LYNN, screenwriter; b. Ann Arbor, Mich., Feb. 13, 1962; d. Randolf Hess and Virginia Catherine (Peters) Aires; m. Keith Louis Giglio, Apr. 29, 1989; 1 child, Sabrina Aires. BA, Dartmouth Coll., 1984; MFA in Film and TV, NYU, 1990. Screenwriter: Archie, 1995, The Broadway Brawler, 1996—, Gabrielle, 1996, Welcome to the Family, 1996—. Mem. Writers Guild of Am. Democrat. Presbyterian.

AITCHISON, ANNE CATHERINE, environmental activist; b. Pontiac, Mich., Dec. 27, 1939; d. Willard Francis and Elizabeth (Smith) Speer; m. Robert Terrington Aitchison, Aug. 10, 1963; children: Hannah, Guy, Will. MusB, U. Mich., 1963, MusM, 1965. Chair Naperville (Ill.) Area Recycling Ctr., 1980-89, exec. dir., 1989-93; exec. dir. Sun Shares, Durham, N.C., 1994-96; mem. Citizen's Solid Waste Adv. Com., Will County, Ill., 1989-90, Task Force on Solid Waste, Ill., 1989-90, Task Force on Degradable Plastic, Ill., 1990-91, Mayor's Adv. Com. on Plastic Recycling, Chgo., 1990, Solid Waste Adv. Com., Durham, N.C., 1994—, Chmn.'s Environ. Com., DuPage County, 1993. Co-author: Resource Recycling, 1991, Environmental Policy for DuPage County, 1993. Founding mem. Naperville Chamber Winds, 1981-93; dir. DuPage Environ. Awareness Ctr., 1987-93; mem. Chmn.'s Environ. Commn., DuPage County, 1992-93; mem. Durham County Solid Waste Adv. Bd., 1994—; bd. dirs. Durham Symphony, 1994—. Named Individual Recycler of Yr. Keep Am. Beautiful, 1987, Outstanding Woman Leader YWCA, 1988. Mem. Ill. Recycling Assn. (co-pres. 1987-90, founding dir. 1980—, Pied Piper of Recycling 1989), Women in Waste, Ill. Environ. Coun. (bd. dirs. 1989-90), LWV (bd. dirs. Naperville chpt. 1977-93), Kiwanis (Disting. Svc. award 1987). Office: Sun Shares Inc 1215 S Briggs Ave # 100 Durham NC 27703-5047

AITCHISON, SUANN, elementary school educator; b. Paterson, N.J., Oct. 1, 1941; d. Archie Wilson and Isabell (Farrow) A. BA, William Paterson Coll., 1963, MEd, 1976; student, Fairleigh Dickinson U., summer 1991, St. Peter's Coll., 1996. Cert. elem. edn., reading tchr., elem. reading specialist. Tchr. 3d grade Fair Lawn (N.J.) Pub. Schs., 1963-64, 70-71, tchr. 2d grade, 1964-70, 71-87, tchr. reading, 1987-95; adj. prof. William Paterson Coll., 1977; developer curriculum guides for remedial reading, 1989, lang. arts and reading for ESL children, 1989, lang. arts and reading for gifted children, 1989, libr. skills and lit. for neurologically impaired children, 1991. Mem. Fair Lawn Pride Com. Assn. N.J. Edn., 1994-95, mem. Observation and Evaluation Revision Com., 1995—; com. person Fair Lawn Rep. County Com., 1986, rec. sec., 1994; trustee Fair Lawn Rep. Club, 1991-93, rec. sec., 1993, mem. nominating com., 1994-95; mem. choir Ch. in Radburn, 1993-95; mem. Garretson Forge Found., 1993-95; vol. Gov. Whitman primary and gen. election campaigns, 1992; assoc. Cerebral Palsy Ctr., 1993-95; mem. com. for Bergen County Celebrate Excellence and Pride in Our Pub. Schs., 1996; mem. Fair Lawn mayor and coun. adv. com. Ams. With Disabilities Act, 1996. Mem. AAHPERD, ASCD (premium mem. 1995—), AAUW, N.J. Reading Assn. (North Jersey coun. 1987-95), Tchrs. English to Students of Other Langs., Coun. Exceptional Children, N.J. Assn. Supervision and Curriculum Devel., Nat. Coun. Tchrs. of English, Coun. Ednl. Diagnostic Svcs. Home: 38-56 Van Duren Ave Fair Lawn NJ 07410 Office: Fair Lawn Bd Edn Fair Lawn NJ 07410

AIZEN, RACHEL K., clinical psychologist; b. Tel-Aviv, Israel; d. Aron and Jochewed L. Klotz; m. Icek Aizen; children: Ron, Elie, Jonathan. MA, U. Ill., 1968, PhD, 1970; postgrad. in clin. psychology, U. Mass., 1980-83. Lic. psychologist, Mass.; nat. cert. sch. psychologist. Asst. prof. Tel-Aviv U., 1972-73; psychologist Northampton (Mass.) State Hosp., 1971-72; clin. psychologist Amherst (Mass.) Sch. System, 1974—; pvt. practice Amherst, Mass, 1974—; intern VA Med. Ctr., Northampton, 1982-83; clin. psychologist Shieba Med. Ctr., Israel, 1985-86; fellow in neuropsychology Mass. Mental Health Hosp., Boston, 1987-88; cons. psychologist Mass. Rehab., 1974—, various local agys. and cts. Cons. editor The Am. Psychologist, 1974; co-author: Psychological Counseling: Principles, Strategies and Intervention, 1990; contbr. articles to profl. jours. With Israeli Air Force, 1960-62. Mem. APA (divsn. clin. and psychoanalysis), NEA, Nat. Assn. Sch. Psychologists. Office: 48 N Pleasant St Ste 204 Amherst MA 01002-1740

AJAMI, JOCELYN M., filmmaker, artist; b. Caracas, Venezuela, June 18, 1950; came to U.S., 1961; d. Alfred M. and Selma M. (Bojalad) A. BA in French, BFA in Studio Art, Manhattanville Coll., Purchase, N.Y., 1972; MA in Painting, Rosary Coll., River Forest, Ill., 1973, MA in Art History, 1974. Dir. Studio 36/Gallery, Boston, 1977-87; ind. filmmaker Boston, 1987—; lectr. in field. Prodr. video: Tiger and Cube, 1993; solo exhibits in art include Mus. Modern Art, N.Y.C., 1995, Newton (Mass.) Libr., 1993. Recipient Merit Finalist award Houston Film Festival, 1995; Leadership Found. fellow Internat. Women's Forum, 1996; Ministry of Culture (Bucharest, Romania) grantee, 1992. Mem. Boston Film and Video Found., Newton TV Found., Radius Arab Am. Writers, Women Inc. Taoist. Home and Office: 250 Beacon St Boston MA 02116

AJELLO, EDITH H., state legislator; b. Apr. 26, 1944; d. Kenneth Aaron and Rozella Christina (Ewoldt) Hanover; children: Linell, Aaron. BA, Bucknell U., 1966. Store mgr. V George Rustigian Rugs, Inc., 1981-93, 94—; interim exec. dir. Providence Schs., 1993—; mem. R.I. Ho. of Reps., 1993—. Democrat. Office: RI Ho of Reps 29 Benefit St State House Providence RI 02904*

AKABAS, SHEILA HELENE, social work educator; b. N.Y.C., Apr. 24, 1931; d. Louis Arnold and Lillian (Lefrak) Epstein; BS, Cornell U., 1951; PhD, NYU, 1970; m. Aaron Louis Akabas, Sept. 27, 1953; children: Myles, Seth, Miriam. Assoc. dir. Just One Break, 1953-55; rsch. dir. mental health rehab. program Amalgamated Clothing & Textile Workers Union, 1963-69; rsch. dir. Ctr. for Social Policy and Practice in the Workplace, Columbia U., N.Y.C., 1969-75, dir., 1975—, prof. Sch. Social Work, 1975—; adv. bd. Work in Am. Inst., 1988—, N.Y. State Sch. Indsl. Labor Rels., Cornell U., 1989—, chair, 1992-93, 93-94; dir. Mcpl. Employees Legal Svcs., 1973-83. Bd. dirs. Westchester Symphony Orch., 1965-80; mem. Pres.'s Com. Employment of Persons with Disabilities, 1975—, chair med. and ins. com., 1988-94, exec. com., 1994—. NIMH Manpower Demonstration Rev. Com., 1980-85, exec. com. NIMH Manpower Demonstration Rev. Com., 1994—, Cornell U. Coun., 1971-86, 1988-92, 94—; bd. dirs. Internat. Com. on Occupational Mental Health, 1982-86, 94—; mem. adv. bd. Menninger Found. Rehab. Inst., 1984-88; mem. tech. adv. com. Dole Found., 1984—, chair, 1992—; mem. adv. bd. Washington Bus. Group on Health Inst. Rehab. and Disability Mgmt., 1985—; editorial advisor Employee Assistance, 1988—; mem. editorial bd. Jour. Disability Policy Studies, 1988—; mem. adv. workplace policy panel Nat. Inst. Drug Abuse, 1990-94; fund rep. Cornell U. Class Assn.; active Temple B'nai Jeshurum, N.Y.C. Switzer fellow, 1980; recipient Research in Rehab. award, 1982, Rehab. Project of Yr. award NRA, 1992; World Rehab. Fund fellow, 1983, 88; HHS grantee; NIMH grantee; Nat. Inst. Disability and Rehab. Research grantee, U.S. Dept. Edn. grantee, 1985—, Nat. Inst. on Drug Abuse grantee, others. Mem. Council Social Work Edn. Club: Hadassah (N.Y.C.). Co-author: Mental Health Care in the World of Work, 1973, Disability Management, 1992; co-editor: Work, Workers & Work Organizations, 1982, Work and Well-Being, 1993; guest editor Practice Digest issue, 1982; contbr. articles to jours. Office: Columbia U Ctr Social Policy in Workplace 622 W 113th St New York NY 10025-7982

AKAGI, LEORA JEAN, marketing consultant; b. Clarita, Okla., Mar. 14, 1939; d. Percy Alfred and Viola Violet (Lane) Ennis; m. Kaku Akagi, Jan. 24, 1959 (div. May 1985); children: Kay Lynn, Patrick Gregg. Student, Shasta Coll., 1994. Profl. model Touch of Class, Denver, 1958-90; deputy treas. Stanton County, Johnson, Kans., 1970's; sec., bookkeeper Stanton County Schs., Johnson, Kans., 1970's; co-owner Red Tree Farms, Inc., Johnson, Kans., 1961-85; animal nutritionist Continental Grain, N.Y.C., 1986-90; owner, editor Meeting Place for Friends, Redding, Calif., 1990-96; sales mgr. Avanti, Redding, Calif., 1990-92; mktg. dir. Bijan Corp., Redding, Calif., 1992-94; records dept. clk. Calif. Dept. Corrections, Delano, 1995—. Author: Page Day USA, 1980, Single & Fre2beme, 1990, Let the Kids Cook, 1992, I'm One of those Ennis Kids, 1994. Bd. dirs. Shasta County symphony, 1993-94, Tumbleweed Girl Scout Coun., Garden City, Kans., 1970, Southwest Kans. Area Mental Health, Garden City, 1978-85. Mem. VFW Aux. (chmn. Americanism for Kans. 1980-81), Bus. Profl. Women Kans. (dir. dir. 1970-72), Ladies of Moose, Emblem Club Elks, Am. Legion Aux. Republican. Methodist. Office: Calif Dept Corrections 2737 W Cecil Delano CA 93216

AKERS, KAREN ELIZABETH, research organization official; b. Marion, Ohio, June 1, 1961; d. Cecil Joseph and Renate T. (Binder) A.; m. John Philip King, Aug. 3, 1991. BA in Comm., Miami U., Oxford, Ohio, 1987; MA in Higher Edn. Adminstrn., George Washington U., 1994. Interpreter Roscoe Village Found., Coshocton, Ohio, 1976-79; customer svc. rep. M. Jacobs Furniture, Springfield, Oreg., 1980-81; word processor Miami U., 1981-84; receptionist Infotxt Corp., Cin., 1985; waitress TGI Fridays, Cin., 1986; dept. head TGI Fridays, Alexandria, Va., 1987; adminstrv. assoc.

Brookings Instn., Washington, 1988-95; outreach mgr. Brookins Instn., 1996—. Roman Catholic. Office: Brookings Instn 1775 Massachusetts Ave NW Washington DC 20036

AKERS, MICHELLE ANNE, soccer player; b. Santa Clara, Calif., Feb. 1, 1966. Forward Tyreso Football Club, Sweden, 1990, 92, 94, Orlando (Fla.) Calibre Soccer Club, 1993. Recipient Hermann Trophy, Golden Boot award FIFA Women's World Championship, 1991, Silver Ball award, 1991, Gold medal Atlanta Olympics, 1996; named All-Am., Ctrl. Fla. Athlete of Yr., 1988-89, MVP CONCACAF Qualifying Championship, 1994, U.S. Soccer Female Athlete of Yr., 1990, 91. Office: US Soccer Fedn US Soccer House 1801-1811 S Prairie Ave Chicago IL 60616*

AKIWUMI, VIKI, English language educator, writer; b. Bklyn., N.Y., June 30, 1965; d. Joseph and Beatrice (Jacobs) A. BA, Hunter Coll., N.Y.C., 1992; Cert. Interfaith Minister, The New Seminary, N.Y.C., 1993; MFA in English, Bklyn. Coll., 1995. Cert. clergy N.Y. Writing cons. Poets in Public Svc., N.Y.C., 1990-94; ednl. cons., trainer Tchrs. and Writers Collaborative, N.Y.C., 1990—; adj. prof. Bklyn. Coll., 1993—, Medgar Evers Coll., Bklyn., 1996—; mem. adv. bd., cons. Ariane Co., N.Y.C., 1993—. Contbr. articles and poems to books and mags. Ednl. cons, speaker Ctr. for Urban Youth and Technology Tchrs. Coll. N.Y., 1990—; vol speaker on motivation and self esteem for youth Ancient Image Productions, N.Y.C., 1991-96. Recipient Honor cert. award State of N.Y. Dept. of Law, Assn. Black Educators, 1983, Pres'. Task Force on HIV/AIDS award CUNY, 1990, Cert. of Recognition award Les Brown Unlimited, Inc., 1993, Girl Scouts Scholars Program, 1996. Mem. Assn. Interfaith Ministers. Mem. Ecumenical Ch. Office: Ancient Image Prodns Ste 180 61 E 8th St New York NY 10003

ALAFOUZO, ANTONIA, marketing and image making professional; b. Cairo, Egypt, Oct. 13, 1952; came to U.S., 1982; d. Pano Antony and Agni-Maria (Ranos) A.; m. Thomas D'Ambola Jr., May 29, 1988; 1 child. BSC in Econs., Brunel U., London, 1975; Diploma in Econs. and Politics, Oxford (Eng.) U., 1977, M of Philosophy, PhD, 1980. Staff reporter The Economist, London, 1973-75, contbg. writer, 1975-82; communications exec. Rubenstein, Wolfson Co., N.Y.C., 1982-87; founder, pres. Markcom Ltd., N.Y.C., 1987—; contbg. writer Fin. Report, London, 1975-82; cons. writer Fin. Times, London, 1980-82; cons. communications and econs. World Gold Council, N.Y.C., 1982—. Contbr. reports to fin. publs. Mem. Inst. Journalism Internat., Oxford Union Soc. Office: Markcom Ltd 277 Broadway New York NY 10007-2001

ALARIE, PEGGY SUE, physician assistant; b. Flint, Mich., Feb. 8, 1957; d. Albert Joseph Jr. and Elizabeth Anna (Eksten) A.; m. John L. McAttee III, Oct. 30, 1980 (div. Aug. 1987). AAS, Mott C.C., 1983; BS, Mich. State U., 1988; MS, U. Detroit-Mercy, 1994. Physician asst. Hurley Med. Ctr., Flint, Mich., 1996—. Fellow Am. Acad. Physician Assts., Mich. Acad. Physician Assts.; mem. Soc. Emergency Pysician Assts., Sigma Theta Tau. Home: 2769 Brandon St Flint MI 48503-3469 Office: Hurley Med Ctr 1 Hurley Plz Flint MI 48502

ALBA, BENNY, artist; b. Columbus, Ohio, May 7, 1949; d. Louis Peter and Marjorie Helen (Post) Benua. Student, Kent State U., 1968-70; BA in Psychology, U. Mich., 1982. artist-in-residence St. Charles Boy's Pres. Sch., Columbus, 1982-85; represented by numerous cons., Calif., Fla., Ill., Tex., Md., N.J., N.Y., Va., Mass.; lectr. Columbus Cultural Arts Ctr., 1983, 84, 93; presenter workshops in field; panelist Calif. Inst. for Intergral Studies, San Francisco, 1995. Solo shows include Columbus Cultural Arts Ctr., 1993, Apprentice Alliance, San Francisco, 1994, Las Vegas (Nev.) Mus., 1994, Artist TV Access, San Francisco, 1994, Western Wyo. Coll., Rock Springs, 1994, A Gallery in the Clock Tower, San Francisco, 1994, Ctr. for Psychol. Studies, Albany, Calif., 1994, Idyllwild (Calif.) Sch. Music and Art, 1995, Saffron Cafe, Berkeley, Calif., 1996, Mimosa Cafe, Oakland, Calif., 1996, Edible Complex, Berkeley, 1996, Brewberry's, Oakland, 1996; exhibited in group shows at Informative Edge, San Francisco, 1992, YWCA Youngstown, Ohio, 1992, Mus. Without Walls, Bemis Pt., N.Y., 1993, Church St. Gallery, San Francisco, 1993, Davis (Calif.) Art Ctr., 1993, Kunst für Begegnungen, Munich, 1993, Ednl. Testing Svc., Emeryville, Calif., 1993-94, Diablo (Calif.) Valley Coll. Gallery, 1994, N. Mex. Art League, Albuquerque, 1995, Nat. Congress Art & Design, Salt Lake City, 1995, Danville (Calif.) Fine Arts, 1995, Lillian Paley Ctr. Visual Arts, Oakland, 1995, Lamar U., Beaumont, Tex., 1996, John Jay Coll. of Criminal Justice, N.Y., 1996, Serra House, Stanford U., 1996, Fed. Bldgs. Window Project, Oakland, 1996; represented in private and public collections Nat. Mus. Women in Arts, Ark. A Ctr., Little Rock, U. Mich. Mus. Art, Kalamazoo (Mich.) Inst. Arts, Greenpeace, Ulli Wachter (Germany), Las Vegas (N. Mex.) Art Mus., Ctr. for Psychol. Studies, Albany, Calif., Birmingham (Ala.) Mus. Art, Portland (Oreg.) Art Mus., others. Bd. dirs. no. Calif. Women's Caucus for Art, 1991, sec. 1991-92, phone liaison, 1991-93. Recipient Lenore Miles award North Platte Valley Art Gallery, 1991, Body of Work award Women Artists, A Celebration, 1990, Merit award San Francisco Women Artist Gallery, 1986. Mem. Women's Caucus for Art (bd. dirs. No. Calif. 1991-94, sec. 1991, 92). Studio: 4400 Market St Oakland CA 94608-3424

ALBAGLI, LOUISE MARTHA, psychologist; b. Queens, N.Y., Jan. 15, 1954; d. Meyer Nathan and Leah (Bleier) Greenberg; m. Eli S. Albagli, July 31, 1977. BA in Psychology summa cum laude, CUNY, 1976; D of Clin. Psychology, Rutgers U., 1983. Clin. psychology intern Postgrad. Ctr. Mental Health, N.Y.C., 1980-81; staff psychologist Queens County Neuropsychiat. Inst., Jackson Heights, N.Y., 1981-83, Bklyn. Community Counseling Ctr., 1981-84; sr. clin. psychologist Richard Hall Community Mental Health Ctr., Bridgewater, N.J., 1984-86; pvt. practice specializing in women's reproductive health issues cen. N.J., 1985—; adj. faculty mem. Rutgers U., 1990—. Mem. Nat. Register Health Care Providers, Am. Psychol. Assn., N.J. Psychol. Assn. (com. inter-profl. rels.), Internat. Childbirth Edn. Assn., RESOLVE, Raritans, Phi Beta Kappa.

ALBANESE, ELLEN LOUISE, newspaper editor; b. Cohasset, Mass., Sept. 17, 1949; d. Francis Joseph and Louise (Whittredge) A.; m. William P. Landers, Oct. 23, 1971; children: Abby Jean, Tracy Ellen. Cert., Sorbonne U., Paris, 1970; BA in Sociology and French, Tufts U., 1971; MS in Pub. Rels., Boston U., 1975. Editor MIT Press, Cambridge, 1971-73; publicity dir. Cahners Books, Boston, 1973-75; pub. rels. dir. Ea. Mass. and R.I. dists. Weight Watchers, Attleboro, Mass., 1976-78; editor The Country GAZETTE, Franklin, Mass., 1980-92; editor-in-chief Norfolk Newspaper Co., Franklin, 1992-96; regional editor Middlesex News, 1996—. Publicity chair Women's Success Network, Franklin, 1986-88; leader Girl Scouts U.S.A., Franklin, 1988-89; mem. community coun. Dean Jr. Coll., Franklin, 1989—. Recipient 1st pl. column writing award N.Eng. Press Assn., Boston, 1987. Mem. Internat. Soc. Weekly Newspaper Editors (bd. dirs., pres. 1993-94, Golden Dozen award 1986, 94, Golden Quill award 1987), Am. Press Inst. (mem. Weekly Adv. Track), Mass. Press Assn. (treas. 1986-88, pres. 1989, 1st Place in Editl. Writing award 1994), Phi Beta Kappa.

ALBARRAN, JACQUELINE, architect; b. Havana, Mar. 22, 1949; came to U.S., 1959; d. Eugenio Jorge and Maria Luisa (de los Reyes) A.; m. Mario G. de Mendoza, Sept. 16, 1989. MArch, U. de los Andes, 1973; postgrad., U. London, 1975. Registered architect. Architect I.N.C.O.L, Bogota, Colombia, 1974, ARK, Madrid, 1974, Bur. D'Architecture et Urbanisme, Vevey, Switzerland, 1975, Suarez & Assoc., San Salvador, El Salvador, 1976, Panelfab Internat., Miami, Fla., 1976-77, Harry Weese & Assoc., Miami, 1977-78, Steel Partnership, Palm Beach, Fla., 1979-85, SKA Architect & Planner, Palm Beach, 1985—. Commr. Landmarks Preservation Commn., Palm Beach, 1992—. Mem. AIA. Republican. Roman Catholic. Office: SKA Architect & Planner Inc 204 Phipps Plz Palm Beach FL 33480

ALBAUM, JEAN STIRLING, psychologist, educator; b. Beijing, China, Jan. 11, 1932; came to U.S., 1936; d. Richard Henry and Emma Bowyer (Lueders) Ritter; m. B. Taylor Stirling, Aug. 15, 1953 (div. 1965); 1 child, Christopher Taylor Stirling; m. Joseph H. Albaum; stepchildren: Thomas Gary, Lauren Jean. BA, Beloit (Wis.) Coll., 1953; MS, Danbury (Conn.) State U., 1964, U. La Verne, Calif., 1983; PhD, Claremont (Calif.) Grad. Sch., 1985. Lic. ednl. psychologist, Calif. Spl. edn. tchr. Charter Oak (Calif.) Sch. Dist., 1966-80; psychologist, coord. elem. counseling Claremont Sch. Dist., 1980—; pvt. practice ednl. psychologist Encino, Calif., 1987—; clin. supr. Marriage, Family and Child Counselor Interns, Claremont, 1987—; sr. adj. prof. U. La Verne, 1988—; oral commr. Bd. Behavioral Sci. Examiners, Sacramento, 1989—. Contbr. articles to profl. jours. Hostess L.A. World Affairs Coun., 1980—; pres. Woodley Homeowner's Assn., Encino, 1986-89. Grantee Durfee Found., 1986, 92. Mem. Am. Psychol. Assn., Calif. Assn. Marriage, Family and Child Therapists, Calif. Assn. Lic. Ednl. Psychologists. Office: Edn Ctr 2080 N Mountain Ave Claremont CA 91711-2643

ALBERG, MILDRED FREED, film and television producer, writer; b. Montreal, Jan. 15, 1921; d. Harry and Florence (Goldstein) Freed; m. Somer Alberg, Jan. 28, 1940 (dec.). Grad., high sch. Assoc. producer N.Y.C. Radio, 1940-43; writer radio shows AFL-CIO Community Services Com., N.Y.C., 1944-46; dir. info. CARE, Inc., N.Y.C., 1947-51; lectr. univs. Producer: Hallmark Hall of Fame, N.Y.C., 1953-60; TV series Our Am. Heritage, assoc. with Am. Heritage mag., N.Y.C., 1961-62; Broadway show Little Moon of Alban, 1961; (films) Hot Millions, 1968, M.G.M.; film series on Bibl. archaeology, ABC-TV, 1972-75; producer, co-dir., co-writer: PBS documentary The Royal Archives of Ebla, 1981; contbr. articles, N.Y. Post. Trustee Am. Schs. Oriental Rsch., Albright Inst. Archaeol. Rsch.; former bd. dirs. Holy Land Conservation Fund. Recipient numerous awrds for radio, TV and film prodns.; NEH grantee, 1978-80. Home: 3333 NE 34th St Apt 801 Fort Lauderdale FL 33308-6909

ALBERGA, ALTA WHEAT, artist; b. Ala.; d. James Richard and Leila Savannah (Sullivan) Wheat; BA, MA, Wichita State U., 1954; BFA, Washington U., St. Louis, 1961; MFA, U. Ill., 1964; m. Alvyn Clyde Alberga, Dec. 3, 1930. Mem. faculty Wichita (Kans.) State U., 1955-56, Webster Coll., St. Louis, 1969. art tchr. Ossining (N.Y.) High Sch., 1968; asst. prof., head visual arts Presbyn. Coll., Clinton, S.C., 1969-74; pvt. art tchr., Greenville, S.C., 1972—; substitute tchr. Greenville County Schs.; tchr. painting Tempo Gallery Sch., Greenville, 1974—, Greenville County Mus. Sch., 1975—, Tryon (N.C.) Fine Arts Ctr., 1986 (merit award 1987); tchr. Tri-County Tech. Coll., Pendleton, S.C., 1975. One-woman shows include Greenville County Mus., 1979, Greenville Artists Guild Gallery, 1979, 83, Wichita State U., 1954, St. Louis Artists Guild, 1956, N.C. State U., 1965, 66, Met. Arts Council, Greenville, 1980, 83, 85, Tryon Fine Arts Ctr., 1988, S.C. State U., 1992, 93; exhibited in group shows at Pickens County Mus., 1979, 88-89, Internation, Washington, 1981-82, Greenville Artists Guild, 1982, 88, Art/7, Washington, 1983, N.C. Univ., Charlotte invitational, 1989, Furman U. Women's Show, 1989, S.C. State U., 1992, Upstate Visual Arts, 1993, S.C. State U., 1993, Rolling Green Gallery, 1993, Internationale Grafiek Biennale, Maastricht, the Netherlands, 1993, S.C. Watercolor Soc., 1994 (award), Greenville County Mus. Art, 1995; represented in permanent collections S.C. State Mus., Columbia, S.C. Arts Commn., Pickens County Mus.; represented in pvt. collections; bd. dirs. Greenville Artists Guild, 1977-79, pres., 1985; bd. dirs. Guild Gallery, 1978, Guild Greenville Symphony, 1989-90. Recipient Richard K. Weil award St. Louis Mus., 1957; Purchase prize S.C. Arts Commn., 1972; Merritt award Greenville Mus., 1986, Pickens County Mus., 1987, 88; Cash award S.C. Water Color Assn. Mem. Artists Equity (pres. St. Louis chpt. 1962), Internat. Platform Assn. (life), Art Students League (life), Guild Greenville Artists (pres. 1984-85), S.C. Artists Guild, Southeastern Council Printmakers, Greenville Symphony Guild, Mus. Assn. (invited Greenville County Mus. 1993), Kappa Pi, Kappa Delta Pi. Democrat. Home: 11 Overton Ave Greenville SC 29609-2612

ALBERGHENE, JANICE MARIE, English literature educator; b. Lowell, Mass., Jan. 20, 1949; d. Derrin Michael and Loretta Mary (Curran) A.; m. David Harper Watters, Aug. 23, 1980; 1 child, D. Harper. BA, U. Mass., Amherst, 1970; PhD, Brown U., Providence, R.I., 1980. Vis. instr. Wheaton Coll., Norton, Mass., 1978-79; instr. Bowling Green (Ohio) State U., 1979-80, asst. prof., 1980-85, assoc. prof., 1985-88; asst. dir. New Hampshire Humanities Coun., Concord, 1985-86; assoc. prof. Fitchburg (Mass.) State Coll., 1988-95, prof., 1995—; adv. bd. mem. Children's Literature, 1989—; editl. cons. Children's Literature Assn. Quarterly, 1983—. Contbr. articles to profl. jours. Sec. Strafford County Democrats, 1987-88. Recipient Summer Study grantee NEH, 1995. Mem. MLA (chair exec. com. divsn. children's lit. 1989), Children's Lit. Assn. (sec. 1986-88, exec. bd. 1988-90, v.p. 1990-91, pres. 1991-92). Democrat. Roman Catholic. Office: English Dept Fitchburg State Coll 160 Pearl St Fitchburg MA 01420

ALBERS, DOLORES MARY, physical education educator; b. Lander, Wyo., June 2, 1949; d. Russell Henry and Adrienne Gladys (Coderko) A. AS, Casper Jr. Coll., 1969; BA, U. No. Colo., 1972. Sci. and phys. edn. tchr., coach Bent County Sch. Dist. RE-2, McClave, Colo., 1972-75; health and phys. edn. tchr., coach Sweetwater County Sch. Dist., Green River, Wyo., 1975—; mem., chairperson Green River Pks. and Recreation Bd., 1978-81; v.p. recreation Wyo. Alliance for Health, Phys. Edn., Recreation and Dance. Recipient Secondary Phys. Edn. Tchr. of Yr. award Wyo. Alliance of Health, Phys. Edn., Recreation and Dance, 1985, 94. Mem. NEA, AAHPERD (Ctrl. Dist. Secondary Phys. Edn. Tchr. of Yr. 1995), Nat. Assn. Sport and Phys. Edn. (Nat. Secondary Phys. Edn. Tchr. of Yr. 1995), Nat. Fedn. Interscholastic Ofcls. Assn., Wyo. Edn. Assn. (Outstanding Wyo. Ofcl. 1992), Green River Edn. Assn. Roman Catholic. Home: PO Box 868 Green River WY 82935 Office: Sweetwater County Sch Dist 300 Monroe Ave Green River WY 82935

ALBERS, LUCIA BERTA, land developer; b. Guatemala, Feb. 10, 1943; d. Jose Luis De Leon Polanco and Maria Marta (Vasquez) De Leon; m. Ray Cisneros, Nov. 2, 1968 (div. 1972); 1 child, Elizabeth Ann Albers Cisneros; m. Monte Dean Albers, June 12, 1974; 1 child, Monte Roberto. Grad. in Acctg., Sacred Heart, Guatemala, 1963; student in Econs., San Carlos, Guatemala, 1964; student, Diablo Valley Coll., 1975, 76. Chief acct. Discovery Bay, Byron, Calif., 1971-76; asst. fin. dir. City of Pittsburg, Calif., 1976-78, corporate contr. Conco Cement, Concord, Calif., 1981-90; land developer Contra Costa County, Calif., 1990—. Mem. adv. coun. City of Byron, Calif., 1991-94; dir. Ctr. for New Ams., Concord, 1994—. Mem. Nat. Assn. Accts., Nat. Assn. Exec. Women, Nat. Assn. Women, Mex.-Am. Polit. Assn. Home: 9601 Deer Valley Rd Brentwood CA 94513-4907

ALBERS-CISNEROS, ELIZABETH ANN, mental health services professional; b. Conconrd, Calif., Apr. 13, 1971; d. Ray B. Cisneros and Lucia B. De Leon. BA, St. Mary's Coll., 1992, MA, 1994; postgrad., Calif. Sch. Profl. Psychology, 1996. Counselor Battered Women's Alternatives, Concord, Calif., 1993-94; counselor, coord. Ctr. for New Ams., Concord, Calif., 1993-95; mental health clin. specialist Contra Costa County Mental Health, Antioch, Calif., 1995—. Mem. Am. Counseling Assn., Mexican-Am. Cultural Assn. (Dow Chem. award 1989). Home: 9601 Deer Valley Rd Brentwood CA 94513

ALBERT, ANN MARIE, sales executive; b. Ft. Kent, Maine, Mar. 25, 1961; d. Jean Claude and Rita Simone (Picard) A.; m. David Leonard Nack, Aug. 6, 1983 (div. July 1989). Sales profl. Zayre, Madawaska, Maine, 1977-80, Bullocks, San Diego, 1980-83; outside sales exec. La France (S.C.) Fabrics, 1983-85, Robert Allen Fabrics, Mansfield, Mass., 1985-87, Kravet Fabrics, Bethpage, N.Y., 1987, 90, F. Schumacher Co., N.Y.C., 1990—. Mem. Am. Soc. Interior Designers (bd. dirs. L.A. chpt. 1994-95, Presdl. citation 1995). Republican. Roman Catholic. Office: F Schumacher & Co 3997 Pacific Coast Hwy Torrance CA 90505

ALBERT, CHRISTINE LYNNETTE, accountant; b. Stillman Valley, Ill., May 21, 1965; d. Charles Ralph and June Ruth (Freeman) Peterson; m. James Howard Albert, May 28, 1988. AAS in Bus., Rock Valley Coll., 1986; BS in Acctg., Rockford Coll., 1992. CPA, Ill. Bookkeeper, supr. Harwood Aviation, Inc., Rockford, Ill., 1984-86; comml. lending credit analyst Bank One 1st Nat. Bank, Rockford, 1986-92; acct. Ringdahl's, Inc., Rockford, 1992-95; treas. analyst Woods Equipment Co., 1995—; owner, pres. CLA Fin. Svcs., Rockford, 1996—. Student mem. Coast Guard Aux., Ill., 1994; fundraiser Chgo. Children's Hosp., 1992—. Mem. Ill. CPA Soc., Inst. Mgmt. Accts. (bd. dirs.), Golf League (treas.). Home: 7170 S Main St Rockford IL 61102-5114

ALBERT, MARGARET COOK, communications executive; b. Madison, Wis., Aug. 25, 1933; d. Hulet Hall and Esther Frances (Marhoefer) Cook; m. Walter E. Albert, Jan. 24, 1959; children: Jennifer Ann, Bryan Walter. AB in Journalism, Ind. U., 1955; postgrad., U. Bordeaux, France, 1957-58. Reporter Daily Herald-Telephone, Bloomington, Ind., 1953-55, 59-60; copy editor Cosmopolitan Mag., N.Y.C., 1955-57; copy chief, coll. advt. Houghton Mifflin, Boston, 1960-62, freelance writer, 1962-70; pub. rels. coord., editor Allegheny County Med. Soc., Pitts., 1970-75; dir. pub. info. Urban League Pitts., 1975-86; pres., owner Matrix Comms. Assocs., Pitts., 1986—; cons. West Penn Hosp.: James I. McGuire Antiquity Ctr., Pitts., 1989-91; cons., sr. writer Comms. 2000, Agy. for Instnl. Tech., Bloomington, 1994—; cons. Family Comms., Pitts., 1992—; writer, editor 651-Arts, Bklyn. Acad. Music, 1992-95. Rschr., ghost writer: Day Breakers: The Story of the Urban League of Pittsburgh, 1983 (Matrix award 1984); author: A Practical Vision: The Story of Blue Cross of West Pennsylvania, 1987; contbr. articles to profl. publs.; prodr. computer graphics program African-Am. Computer Graphics, 1994; guest editor Mademoiselle Mag., 1955. Bd. dirs. Health Sys. Agy. of S.W. Pa., Pitts., 1976-86, Pa. Med. Care Found., Camp Hill, 1981-86, Animal Rescue League of S.W. Pa., Pitts., 1988-93; mem. Pa. Blue Shield Corp., Camp Hill, 1982-90. Fulbright scholar, 1957-58; recipient Disting. Svc. award Urban League of Pitts., 1977, Harold B. Gardner Citizens award Allegheny County Med. Soc., 1981, 1st place award Women in Comms., Inc., Pa. Assn. for Nonprofit Homes for Aging, Brotherhood award. Mem. Phi Beta Kappa. Democrat.

ALBERTO, MARGARET L., art educator, researcher; b. Paterson, N.J.; d. Joseph P. and Elizabeth (Kempasky) Sweeney; m. Louis M. Alberto, June 15, 1969; 1 child, Lisa. BA in Fine Arts, Kean Coll. N.J., 1972, MA in Fine Arts, 1975. Office mgr. Passaic County Welfare Bur., Passaic, N.J., 1960-72; tchr. fine arts Clifton (N.J.) H.S., 1972-86; tchr. Seminole H.S. Seminole (Fla.) H.s. Pinellas Bd. Edn., 1990—; dir. World Friendship Art Exhibit; pvt. art instr., Seminole, Fla., 1986—; instr. adult edn. programs; chairperson Kean Coll. Art Workshop; spkr. in field. Mem. Paterson (N.J.) Cultural Commn.; vol. sch.sys. Seminole, Fla., 1990—. Mem. Greater Paterson (N.J.) Art League (initiator art scholarship fund, past pres. Home: 10377 Barry Dr Largo FL 34644

ALBERTS, CELIA ANNE, lawyer; b. Denver, May 3, 1953; d. Robert Edward and Barbara Ellen (Wedge) A. BA in French, U. Colo., 1975, JD, 1979; LLM in Taxation, U. Denver, 1984. Bar: Colo. 1979, U.S. Dist. Ct. Colo. 1979, U.S. Ct. Appeals (10th cir.) 1979. Assoc. Dietze, Davis & Porter, Boulder, Colo., 1979-82; sole practice Boulder, 1983-84; assoc. George, Davies and Assocs., Denver, 1984-86, Loser, Davies, Magoon & Fitzgerald, Denver, 1986-87; sole practice Denver, 1987-89; v.p., sr. counsel Merrill Lynch, Denver, 1989—. Mem. ABA (tax div., real estate div., corp. div.), Colo. Bar Assn. (tax div.), Denver Bar Assn. (tax, corp., real estate, estate/probate divs.). Home: 237 S Lamb Ln Golden CO 80401-9426 Office: Merrill Lynch Legal Advisory 3840 S Wadsworth Blvd Denver CO 80235-2107

ALBERTSEN, RANDI LONDON, early childhood educator; b. Balt., Apr. 4, 1967; d. Fred S. and Phyllis Rona (Bloom) London; m. William James Albertsen, Oct. 27, 1990. BS in Early Childhood Edn., U. Md., 1989; MBA, Loyola Coll., Balt., 1994. Kindergarten tchr. Montgomery County Pub. Schs., Wheaton, Md., 1990—. Mem. NEA, ASCD, Nat. Assn. for Edn. of Young Children, Nat. Coalition Edn. Activists, Montgomery County Edn. Assn. (co-chair bargaining support network 1993-94), Md. Com. for Children, Phi Kappa Phi. Democrat. Home: 7720 Old Woodstock Ln Ellicott City MD 21043-6981 Office: Highland Elem Sch 3100 Medway St Silver Spring MD 20902-2225

ALBERT-SHERIDAN, LENORE LUANN, legal research fellow; b. Coldwater, Mich.; d. Samuel George and Carol Louise (Huttenen) Albert; m. James Christopher Sheridan, Feb. 23, 1991. AA in Liberal Arts, Long Beach City Coll.; BA in Econs., Calif. State U., Long Beach, 1992; postgrad., U. of the Pacific, 1994—. Asst. purchasing agt., supr. warehouse assembly, head inventory control Neill Aircraft Co., Long Beach, 1987-89; head inventory control/regional purchasing & receiving supr. Internat. Paper, Inc., L.A., 1989-91; fin./gen. ledger acct. Port of Long Beach, 1991-92; corp. acct. Weber Aircraft Inc., Fullerton, Calif., 1993; fin. analyst Sizzler Internat., L.A., 1993; rsch. fellow McGeorge Sch. Law, Sacramento, Calif., 1994—; participant Nat. Inst. Judicial Hearsay Study, McGeorge/U. Calif.-Davis, Sacramento, 1994; tutor minority bus. program Calif. State U., Long Beach, 1992. Back stage mgr. San Pedro (Calif.) Theatre Performing Arts, 1987. Mem. ABA (internat. law and antitrust sects., export control and econ. sects. com. mem., internat. intellectual property rights com.), Inst. Managerial Accts., Internat. Platform Assn., Phi Alpha Delta, Phi Alpha Delta ((Clair Engle chpt. alumni com. 1994-95). Lutheran. Home: 2701 Corabel Ln # 70 Sacramento CA 95821

ALBERTSON, SUSAN L., retired federal government official; b. Washington, Dec. 3, 1929; d. J. Mark and Alice (Myers) A. BS, Purdue U., 1952; postgrad. in internat. rels., George Washington U., 1956-58. Numerous profl. positions CIA, Washington, 1952-88; ret., 1988. Republican.

ALBINO, JUDITH E.N., university president; b. Jackson, Tenn.; m. Salvatore Albino; children: Austin, Adrian. BJ, U. Tex., 1967, PhD, 1973. Mem. faculty sch. dental medicine SUNY, Buffalo, 1972-90, assoc. provost, 1984-87, dean sch. arch. and planning, 1987-89, dean grad. sch., 1989-90; v.p. acad. affairs and rsch, dean system grad. sch. U. Colo., Boulder, 1990-91, pres., 1991-95, pres. emeritus, prof. psychiatry, 1995—. Contbr. articles to profl. jours. Acad. Adminstrn. fellow Am. Coun. on Edn., 1983; grantee NIH. Fellow APA (treas., bd. dirs.); mem. Behavioral Scientists in Dental Rsch. (past pres.), Am. Assn. Dental Rsch. (bd. dirs.). Office: U Colo System Office of President 4200 E 9th Ave Camp Box C249-46 Denver CO 80262*

ALBRECHT, BEVERLY JEAN, special education educator; b. Dixon, Ill., Sept. 8, 1936; d. Harold Ivan Foster and Grace Gertrude Tracy Freed; m. Marvin Blackert Albrecht, Aug. 13, 1960; children: Bradley K., Brent D., Kimberly S. Albrecht Schluns. BS, Manchester Coll., North Manchester, Ind., 1958; MS, No. Ill. U., 1978. Cert. in elem. edn., educable mentally handicapped, learning disabled, supervision and early childhood edn., Ill. Kindergarten tchr. Sch. Dist. 300, Carpentersville, Ill, 1958-60; thcr. 5th grade Sch. Dist. 5, Sterling, Ill., 1960-61, 64-65, kindergarten tchr., 1962-64, substitute tchr., 1965-71; dir. nursery sch. Sterling YWCA, 1971-75; program dir. Ctr. for Human Devel., Sterling, 1975-76; family advocate Ill. Dept. Child and Family Svcs., Rock Falls, 1977-78; learning disablities and behavior disorders spl. edn. tchr. Sch. Dist. 289, Mendota, Ill., 1978-84, devel. pre-sch. tchr., 1984-89; clinician, case mgr., family preservation Sinnissippi Ctrs. Inc., Sterling, 1989—; replication specialist PEECH project U. Ill., Champaign, 1985-88; supervisory faculty Ill. State U., Normal, 1983-85, Ill. Valley C.C., Oglesby 1985-89. Host family Rock River Valley Internat. Fellowships, Sterling, 1975-92; chair coun. on edn. United Meth. Ch., Rock Falls, 1973-75, supt., chr. ch. sch., 1968-88. Spl. Edn. fellow Ill. Office of Pub. Instrn., 1966; name grant honoree United Meth. Women, Rock Falls. Mem. NEA, Ill. Edn. Assn., Coun. for Exceptional Children. Republican. Home: 3254 Mineral Springs Rd Sterling IL 61081-4107

ALBRECHT, CAROL HEATH, artist, educator; b. Lafayette, Ind., May 26, 1921; d. Donald Leroy and Zula Elpha (Whicker) Heath; m. Edward Mathews Albrecht, May 25, 1944; children: Lynn, Catherine. Grad. high sch., Lafayette, Ind. Sec. U.S. Maritime Commn., San Francisco, 1941-44; mem. faculty art dept. Pensacola (Fla.) Jr. Coll., 1984-86, Eastern Shore Fine Arts Acad., Fairhope, Ala., 1986-91; presenter workshops in field, including oriental brush painting workshop/seminar, Sarasota, Fla., Clearwater, Fla., Pensacola. One-woman shows include Maison Le Cel, Ft. Walton Beach, Fla., 1976, 77, Whiting Gallery, Fairhope, 1989, Estate Gallery, Pensacola, 1991, Elliott Mus., Stuart, Fla., 1983; group shows include Fla. Watercolor Soc., Tallahassee, 1982, Pensacola Mus. Art, 1983-93, Sumi-e Soc. Am., Washington, 1982-94, Fla. Gulf Coast Art Ctr., Belleair, 1983, Asheville (N.C.) Mus. Art, 1983, Yosemite (Calif.) Renaissance Nat. Art Exhibit, 1987. Recipient purchase award Elliot Mus., 1983. Mem. Sumi-e Soc. Am. (pres. White Lotus chpt., Best in Show award 1990, Grumbacher gold medal 1991, Winsor-Newton award 1992, Sarasota chpt. award 1993, Shaffer award for brush mastery 1994, Reba Dickerson Hill Meml. award 1994). Home and Studio: 2026 Copley Dr Pensacola FL 32503-3349

ALBRECHT, KATHE HICKS, art historian, visual resources manager; b. Ann Arbor, Mich., Aug. 21, 1952; d. Richard Brian and Mafalda (Brasile) Hicks; m. Mark Jennings Albrecht, July 20, 1973; children: Nicole, Alexander, Olivia. BA in Art History, UCLA, 1975; MA in Art History, Am. U., 1989. Slide libr. asst. Am. U., Washington, 1986-88, visual resources mgr., 1991—; panel mem. Forum on Career Options in Art History, Am. Univ., 1994; co-coord. Mus. Ednl. Site Licensing Project (Nat. Initiative Getty), 1994; presenter Southeastern Coll. Art Conf., Georgetown U., 1995; mem. Conf. on Fair Use represents VRA rep. to Digital Future Coalition, 1996. Vol. Fairfax County Pub. Sch. System, 1980—; re-election com. Rep. Nat. Com., Washington, 1984; Rep. precinct worker Mason dist., 1980s. Grantee: Getty Art History Info. Program, 1994-97; Am. U. (image processing, database devel.), 1995 (2). Mem. Art Librs. Soc. N. Am., Coll. Art Assn., Mus. Computer Network, Southeastern Coll. Art Conf., Visual Resources Assn. (pres. Mid-Atlantic region 1995-96, chair nat. membership com., 1995-97). Presbyterian. Office: Am Univ 4400 Massachusetts Ave NW Washington DC 20016

ALBRECHT, WENDY A., financial analysis administrator; b. Berwyn, Ill., Mar. 26, 1964; d. William P. and Nancy M. (Churan) Albrecht. BBA, Augusta (Ga.) Coll., 1990, MBA, 1995. Computer cons. Career Pers., Augusta, 1989-90; data specialist Mr/Ms Temps, Augusta, 1988-89; bus. mgr. Oakwood Devel. Co., Chgo., 1986-88; sr. project specialist Hutchens Co. Inc., Aiken, S.C., 1990-91; acct. Aiken County Govt., Aiken, 1991; fin. analyst Westinghouse, Aiken, 1991-95; fin. analysis adminstr. D.C. Chartered Health Plan, Inc., Washington, 1995—. Named to Outstanding Young Women of Am., 1991. Mem. Inst. Mgmt. Accts., Nat. Mgmt. Assn. (spl. events team 1994-96). Office: DC Chartered Helath Plan Inc 820 1st St NE U100 Washington DC 20002

ALBRIGHT, ANNAROSE M., secondary school educator; b. Norton, Va., May 8, 1944; d. Joseph Paul and Dorothy Mae (Woody) Cooch; m. William J. Albright, Mar. 28, 1975; children: Angela Rose, Marisa Rose. BS in Edn., Millersville (Pa.) U., 1965; MS in Edn., Temple U., 1968. Cert. English and history tchr., supr., Pa. Tchr. Eastern Lancaster County Sch. Dist., New Holland, Pa., 1965-67, Lancaster County Sch. Dist., 1967-70; tchr. Conestoga Valley Sch. Dist., Lancaster, Pa., 1970-84, chief negotiator for union, 1978-80; supr. English dept. Hempfield Sch. Dist., Landisville, Pa., 1984-91, tchr., 1992—. Rep. People to People, 1981-90; chairperson Christian edn. adv. com. St. John Neumann Cath. Ch., 1991-96; tchr., catechism, 1987—; mem. pub. policy com. YWCA, Pa., 1991-95. Recipient journalistic recognition from local and state edn. assns. Mem. NEA, Pa. Edn. Assn., HEA, AAUW (chair local chpt. pub. policy com.), ASCD, Nat. Coun. Tchrs. English (hospitality com. 1990), Conf. on English Leadership (program com. 1991), Pa. Coun. Tchrs. English, Landis Valley Mus. Assn. (chmn. Christmas program, bd. dirs.), Mission Hills Civic Assn. Home: 2636 Breezewood Dr Lancaster PA 17601-4804

ALBRIGHT, APRIL LYNN, librarian, entrepreneur; b. Plainfield, N.J., May 17, 1960; d. Ralston J. and Eileen M. (Creed) Nelson; m. Gregory Richard Albright, Sept. 12, 1992. BA in Econs., Kean Coll. N.J., 1983; MPA, Calif. State U., 1986; MLS, Rutgers U., 1988. Collection devel. asst. Georgian Court Coll., Lakewood, N.J., 1987; reference libr. County of L.A. Pub. Libr. Manhattan Beach Br. Libr., 1989-93; pres. Déjà Vu Gifts, Inc., Brant Beach, N.J., 1993—; sr. libr. Ocean County Libr., N.J., 1994—. Author: pub. awareness media slogans. Life mem. Long Beach Hist. Soc., Beach Haven, N.J., dir. pub. service announcements, WKNJ AM Radio Sta., Union, 1982-83. Mem. Calif. State U. Sailing Assn. Republican. Episcopalian. Office: Déjà Vu Gifts Inc 6003 Long Beach Blvd Brant Beach NJ 08008-3738

ALBRIGHT, CAROL BONOMO, journal editor; b. N.Y.C.; d. Salvatore and Michela (Guerrieri) Bonomo; m. Edward James Ahearn, Aug. 20, 1960 (div.); children: Edward Michael, Sally Ann; m. Birge Albright, June 27, 1992. BA, Coll. Mt. St. Vincent, Riverdale, N.Y.; MA, Brown U., 1970. Editor, instr. Coll. of Continuing Edn. U. R.I., Providence, 1990—; Adv. bd. Italian Am. Ency., Garland Press, N.Y.C., 1995—. Series editor: Italian Immigrant Autobiographies, 1993; contbr.: (book) The Dream Book: Writings by Italian American Women, 1985; contbr. articles to profl. jours. Pres. John Russell Bartlett Soc., Providence, 1987-88; exec. bd. Higher Edn. Cable TV Coun., Providence, 1980-84; state chair Heart Sunday, Am. Heart Assn., R.I., 1979; bd. dirs. Lippitt Hill Tutorial, 1975-82; R.I. State committeewoman, 1982-84. State Coun. on the Arts grantee, 1988, Danforth Found. for Higher Edn. Assoc. Fellow grantee, 1974, NSF Study grantee, 1978; Roger Williams U. Fiction fellow, 1987. Mem. Am. Italian Hist. Assn. (exec. coun. 1990—).

ALBRIGHT, DIANNE ELIZABETH, counseling educator; b. Phila., Dec. 20, 1944; d. William Henry Walters and Eleanor Florence (Astfalk) Walters Schmidt; m. Paul Robert Albright, June 1966 (div. Sept. 1973); children: Cherie Lynnette, Lisa Renee. BMus, Ea. Nazarene Coll., 1967; postgrad., Rivier Coll., 1978-79; MEd, Plymouth State U., 1990; PhD, Ohio U., 1994. Cert. tchr. music K-12, elem. K-6, guidance counselor, N.H., Mass., Conn.; lic. profl. clin. counselor, Ohio. Social worker Mass. Dept. Welfare, Dedham, 1968-70; sustitute tchr. Braintree/Quincy (Mass.) Pub. Schs., 1970-77; music tchr. Nashua (N.H.) Pub. Schs., 1976-80, classroom tchr., 1980-90; clin. counselor Backus Hosp., Norwich, Conn., 1990-91; sch. counselor Plainfield (Conn.) Pub. Schs., 1990-91; instr. Ohio U., Athens, 1991-94; asst. prof., coord. counselor edn. Cen. Mo. State U., 1994—; ednl. cons. IBM, Bedford, N.H., 1983-84; rsch. asst. NASA Mascot Project, Ohio U. Athens, 1992-93. Author: (booklet) Am. Counseling Assn., 1993; contbr. articles to profl. jours. Recipient scholarship grad. assn. Ohio. U., Athens, 1991-94, fellowship Chi Sigma Iota, 1992. Mem. ACA, Ohio Counseling Assn., Assn. for Humanistic Edn. and Devel. (editl. asst. 1992-94, sec.-elect 1993-94, sec. 1994-95, treas. 1996—, editl. bd. 1994—), Mo. Counseling Assn., Internat. Assn. Marriage and Family Counselors, Assn. for Counselor Edn. and Supervision, Am. Sch. Counselors Assn., Phi Delta Kappa, Phi Kappa Phi, Chi Sigma Iota (assoc. editor 1993-96, pres. Alpha chpt. Ohio U. 1992-93, Outstanding Chpt. award 1993). Home: 616 S Main St Apt 5 Warrensburg MO 64093-1550 Office: Central Mo State Univ Dept Psych Warrensburg MO 64093

ALBRIGHT, MADELEINE KORBEL, diplomat, political scientist; b. Prague, Czechoslovakia, May 15, 1937; d. Josef and Anna (Speeglova) Korbel; m. Joseph Medill Patterson Albright, June 11, 1959 (div. 1983); children: Anne Korbel, Alice Patterson, Katharine Medill. BA with honors, Wellesley Coll., 1959; MA, Columbia U., 1968; cert., Russian Inst., 1968, PhD, 1976. Washington coord. Maine for Muskie, 1975-76; chief legis. asst. to U.S. Senator Muskie, 1976-78; mem. staff NSC, 1978-81; fellow Woodrow Wilson Internat. Ctr. for Scholars, Washington, 1981-82; Donner prof. internat. affairs, dir. women in fgn. service Sch. Fgn. Service Georgetown U., 1982-93, sr. fellow in Soviet and Eastern European Affairs Ctr. for Strategic and Internat. Studies,, 1981; fgn. policy coord. Mondale for Pres. campaign, 1984, to Geraldine A. Ferraro, 1984; vice chmn. Nat. Dem. Inst. for Internat. Affairs, Washington, 1984-93; perm. rep. of the U.S. UN, N.Y.C., 1993—; sr. fgn. policy advisor Dukakis for Pres. Campaign, 1988; mem. Pres.'s Cabinet, Nat. Security Coun. Author: Poland: The Role of the Press in Political Change, 1983; contbr. articles to profl. jours., chpts. to books. Bd. dirs. Beauvoir Sch., Washington, 1968-76, chmn., 1978-83; trustee Black Student Fund, 1969-78, 82-93, Dem. Forum, 1976-78, Williams Coll., 1978-82, Wellesley Coll., 1983-89; mem. exec. com. D.C. Citizens for Better Pub. Edn., 1975-76; bd. dirs. Washington Urban League, 1982-84, Atlantic Coun., 1984-93, Ctr. for Nat. Policy, 1985-93, Chatham House Fedn., 1986-88. Mem. Council Fgn. Relations, Am. Polit. Sci. Assn., Czeckoslovak Soc. Arts and Scis. Am., Atlantic Council U.S. (dir.), Am. Assn. for Advancement Slavic Studies. Office: US Mission to the UN 799 United Nations Plz New York NY 10017-3505*

ALBRIGHT, MELISSA MAY, elementary school educator; b. Marshall, Mo., Dec. 2, 1966; d. Benjamin Richard Jr. and Carol Louise (Biggs) Pemberton; m. Garret Eugene Albright, July 10, 1993. BS in Elem. Edn., N.E. Mo. State U., 1989, MS in Elem. Adminstrn., 1993. Cert. elem. tchr. grades 1-8, cert. elem. adminstr. grades kindergarten-8, Mo.; cert. specialist in edn.-superintendency. Tchr. St. Joseph (Mo.) Pub. Schs., 1989—; homebound tutor St. Joseph Pub. Schs., 1992-93, designer/implementer summer sch. program Summer Acad., '94, '95, '96, 1993-96, prin. Summer Acad., 1994, 95, 96; coach Accelerated Schs., St. Joseph, 1993—. Active local PTA, 1989—; vol. Trails West, St. Joseph, 1994. Mem. NEA (conv. del. 1987—), ASCD, PEO (treas. sisterhood 1991—), Sigma Kappa (adv. bd. 1994-96). Democrat. Presbyterian. Home: 3412 N 35th Pl Saint Joseph MO 64506-1462 Office: Noyes Elem Sch 1415 N 26th St Saint Joseph MO 64506

ALBRINK, MARGARET JORALEMON, medical educator; b. Warren, Ariz., Jan. 6, 1920; d. Ira Beaman and Dorothy (Rieber) Joralemon; m. Wilhelm Stockman Albrink, Sept. 16, 1944 (dec. July 1991); children: Frederick Henry, Jonathan Wilhelm, Peter Varick. MA in Psychology cum laude, Radcliffe Coll., 1941; MS in Physiol. Chemistry, Yale U., 1943, MD, 1946, MPH, 1951. Diplomate Am. Bd. Med. Examiners, Am. Bd. Nutrition; lic. physician and surgeon, W.Va., Calif. Intern New Haven (Conn.) Hosp., 1946-47; NIH postdoctoral fellow Yale U., New Haven, 1947-49, fellow pub. health, 1950-51, instr. medicine, 1952-58, asst. prof. medicine, 1958-61; assoc. prof. W.Va. U., Morgantown, 1961-66, prof. medicine, 1966-90, prof. emeritus, 1990—, mem. grad. faculty, 1977-92; mem. med. and dental staff W.Va. U. Hosp., Morgantown, 1961—; vis. scientist Donner Lab., U. Calif., Berkeley, 1993-96; assoc. physician Grace-New Haven Cmty. Hosp., 1952-61; cons. nutrition study sect. NIH; vis. scholar U. Calif., Berkeley, 1977-78; established investigator Am. Heart Assn., 1958-63. Guest editor: Clinics in Endocrinology and Metabolism, 1976; guest editor Am. Jour. Clin. Nutrition, 1968, mem. editorial bd., 1963-68; mem. editorial adv. bd. Jour. Am. Coll. Nutrition, 1988-89; reviewer jours.; contbr. articles, chpts. and abstracts to profl. jours. Recipient Rsch. Career award Nat. Heart, Lung and Blood Inst., 1963-90. Fellow ACP, Am. Coll. Nutrition; mem. Am. Fedn. Clin. Rsch., Am. Soc. Clin. Investigation, Am. Soc. Clin. Nutrition, Am. Heart Assn. (fellow arteriosclerosis coun., fellow coun. epidemiology), Am. Diabetes Assn. (epidemiology coun.), Alpha Omega Alpha, Sigma Xi, Phi Beta Kappa. Democrat. Home: 817 Augusta Ave Morgantown WV 26505-6237 Office: WVa U Dept Medicine Box 9159 Morgantown WV 26506-9159

ALCON, SONJA LEE DE BEY GEBHARDT RYAN, retired medical social worker; b. Orange City, Iowa, Aug. 2, 1937; d. Albert Lee Gerard and Clarice Victoria (Brown) deBey; m. Richard J. Gebhardt, June 6, 1959; children: Russell, Cheryl, Kurt Gebhardt Ryan; m. George W. Ryan, Dec. 28, 1968; 1 dau., Alanna (dec.); m. David E. Alcon, July 20, 1985. C BA, Western Md. Coll., 1959; MSW, U. Md., 1973. Caseworker, Springfield State Hosp., Sykesville, Md., 1959-61; dir. social work dept. Hanover (Pa.) Gen. Hosp., 1966-96, ret., 1996; field instr. We. Md. Coll., 1967-96; clin. assoc. prof. sch. social work and social planning U. Md., 1987-92; cons. Golden Age Nursing Home, Hanover, 1973-76, Carlisle (Pa.) Hosp., 1974-78, Hanover Vis. Nurse Assn., 1977-83, emergency svcs. Mental Health Clinic, 1972; chmn. profl. adv. com. Vis. Nurse Assn. of Hanover and Spring Grove, Inc., 1986-89; mem. social work adv. coun. Western Md. Coll., 1979, 80, 81, 94—. Bd. dirs. Hospice of York, 1980-82, Hanover chpt. ARC, 1976-79, Adams-Hanover Mental Health, 1973-76; pres. Human Svcs. Orgn., 1980, v.p., 1985-86; mem. adv. coun. Hanover Hospice, 1982-85; treas. Hanover Cmty. Progress Com., 1976-80; mem. Adams-Hanover Sheltered Workshop Com., 1968-70; bd. dirs. Hanover Cmty. Players, 1974-77, sec., 1982; organizer local chpt. Make Today Count and Preemie Parent Support Group, 1979; initiator, co-trustee Children's Cardiac Fund, 1979-92; mem. Hanover Oratorio Soc., 1964-85, adv. bd. United Cerebral Palsy South Cen. Pa., 1989-90; active YWCA, 1979-84; co-organizer Adams-Hanover chpt. Compassionate Friends, 1983; mem. vestry All Saints Episcopal Ch., 1973-74, 76-79, 83-86, vestry sec., 1975, diocesan del. Ctrl. Pa., 1978, 80-86, mem. altar guild, 1968-86, 92-95, treas. ch. women, 1979-83, ch. choir, soloist, 1975—, life mem.; life mem. Hanover Gen. Hosp. Aux.; mem. adv. group Inst. Pastoral Care, 1976-77; mem. adv. coun. Parents Anonymous, 1976-79, 85-92; adminstr. Hanover Gen. Hosp. Spl. Needs Fund, 1986—; cmty. adv. com. Healthsouth Rehab. York; co-facilitator I Can Cope classes Am. Cancer Soc., 1989-92; active Cmty. Needs Coalition, 1990—, South Ctrl. Pa. Orgn./Time Donation Coalition, 1994—; mem. Case Mgmt. Network South Ctrl. Pa., 1994-96; vol. Hanover Gen. Hosp., Hanover Gen. Hosp. Aux., South Ctrl. Pa. Coalition Organ/Tissue Donation, Hanover Area Coun. Chs., York unit NASW, Hanover Area Cmty. Needs Coalition. Recipient York Daily Record Exceptional Citizen award, 1979, Spl. Recognition cert. Col. Richard McAllister chpt. DAR, 1980; finalist YWCA Salute to Women, 1986, 87. Mem. Nat. Assn. Social Workers, Acad. Cert. Social Workers (lic. social worker), Ea. Pa. Soc. Hosp. Social Workers, Am. Hosp. Assn. Soc. Hosp. Social Work Adminstrs., Hosp. Assn. Pa. Soc. for Social Work Adminstrs. in Health Care, Ctrl. Pa. Hosp. Social Workers (treas. 1981-85, v.p. 1987, pres. 1988), Md. Alumni Assn. (bd. dirs. 1983), Order Eastern Star (worthy matron 1985-86), Order of Amaranth (royal patron 1988-89, royal matron, 1995-96), Order of the White Shrine of Jerusalem (worthy high priestess 1994-95), Social Order of Beauceant (line officer 1996—), Commandery Ladies Aux. (pres. 1989-90), Elks Aux. (v.p. local club 1986-88). Home: RD # 3 Box 3305-M Spring Grove PA 17362

ALCORN, KAREN ZEFTING HOGAN, artist, art educator, analyst; b. Hartford, Conn., Sept. 29, 1949; d. Edward C. and Doris V. (Anderson) Zefting; m. Wendell R. Alcorn, Apr. 12, 1985. BS, Skidmore Coll., 1971; MFA, Boston U., 1976. Secondary art tchr. Scituate (Mass.) High Sch., 1971-73, Milton (Mass.) High Sch., 1973-79; engr. VEDA, Inc., Arlington, Va., 1979-80; analyst Info. Spectrum, Inc., Arlington, Va., 1980-82, Pacer Systems, Inc., Arlington, Va., 1982-84; dir. ops., mgr. tng. program Starmark Corp., Arlington, Va., 1984; sr. systems analyst VSE Corp., Arlington, Va., 1984-85; analyst, tech. writer Allen Corp., Las Vegas, 1987-88; mem. faculty Western Nev. C.C., 1989; instr. Newport (R.I.) Art Mus., 1990-92; dir. North Tahoe (Calif.) Art Ctr., 1994; dir. Artward Bound, 1994; instr. Sierra Nevada Coll., 1995—. Exhbns. include Skidmore Coll., 1970, 71, Boston U., 1975, Newport Art Mus., 1990, 91, 92, Naval War Coll., R.I., 1989, 90, 91, Pogan Gallery, Tahoe City, Calif., Corridor Gallery, Truckee, Calif., 1993-95, Am. Artists Profl. League Grand. Nat., N.Y.C., 1995, Nev. Artists Assn., 1996, Nev. Biennial, 1996. Recipient Silver medal All-Media Competition, 1994, Calif. Discovery Awards finalist, Artists' Mag., 1994, Coun. Am. Artist Socs. award Graphic Am. Artists Profl. League, 1995. Mem. AAUW, Sierra Artists Network, Nev. Artists Assn., Allied Artists Am. (assoc.). Home: 2221 Manhattan Dr Carson City NV 89703

ALDAVE, BARBARA BADER, law educator, lawyer; b. Tacoma, Dec. 28, 1938; d. Fred A. and Patricia W. (Burns) Bader; m. Ralph Theodore Aldave, Apr. 2, 1966; children—Anna Marie, Anthony John. B.S., Stanford U., 1960; J.D., U. Calif.-Berkeley, 1966. Bar: Oreg. 1966, Tex. 1982. Assoc. law firm Eugene, Oreg., 1967-70; asst. prof. U. Oreg., 1970-73; vis. prof. U. Calif., Berkeley, 1973-74; from vis. prof. to prof. U. Tex., Austin, 1974-89, co-holder James R. Dougherty chair for faculty excellence, 1981-82, Piper prof., 1982, Joe A. Worsham centennial prof., 1984-89, Liddell, Sapp, Zivley, Hill and LaBoon prof. banking financial and comml. law, 1989; dean sch. law St. Mary's U., San Antonio, 1989—; vis. prof. Northeastern U., 1985-88; ABA rep. to Coun. Inter-ABA, 1995—; NAFTA chpt. 19 panelist, 1994—. Pres. NETWORK, 1985-89; chair Gender Bias Task Force of Supreme Ct. Tex., 1991-94; bd. dirs. Partnership for Hope, Tex. Resource Ctr., Assn. Religiously Affiliated Law Schs., Lawyer's com. for Civil Rights Under Law of Tex., Mex. Am. Legal Def. and Ednl. Fund. Recipient Tchg. Excellence award U. Tex. Student Bar Assn., 1976, Appreciation awards Thurgood Marshall Legal Soc. of U. Tex., 1979, 81, 85, 87, Tchg. Excellence award Chicano Law Students Assn. of U. Tex., 1984, Hermine Tobolowsky award Women's Law Caucus of U. Tex., 1985, Ethics award Kugle, Stewart, Dent & Frederick, 1988, Leadership award Women's Law Assn. St. Mary's U., 1989, Ann. Inspirational award Women's Advocacy Project, 1989, Appreciation award San Antonio Black Lawyers Assn., 1990, Spl. Recognition award Nat. Conv. Nat. Lawyers Guild, 1990, Spirit of the Am. Woman award J. C. Penney Co., 1992, Sarah T. Hughes award Women and the Law sect. State Bar Tex., 1994, Ann. Tchg. award Soc. Am. Law Tchrs., 1996. Mem. ABA (com. on corp. laws sect., banking and bus. law 1982-88), Bexar County Women's Bar Assn. (Belva Lockwood Outstanding Lawyer award 1991), San Antonio Bar Assn., Nat. Lawyers Guild, William S. Sessions Inn of Ct., World Affairs Coun. San Antonio, Harlan Soc., Tex. Women's Forum, Stanford U. Alumni Assn., Order of Coif, Phi Delta Phi, Iota Sigma Pi, Omicron Delta Kappa, Delta Theta Phi (Outstanding Law Prof. award St. Mary's U. chpt. 1990, 91). Roman Catholic. Home: 323 W Woodlawn Ave San Antonio TX 78212-3312 Office: St Mary's U 1 Camino Santa Maria St San Antonio TX 78228-5433

ALDAY, MARTA PERDOMO, library director, media specialist; b. Havana, Cuba, Mar. 24, 1945; d. Jose E. and Celia (Gutierrez) Perdomo; m. Gonzalo Alday, Nov. 23, 1963; children: Marta Elena, Gonzalo Luis, Juan Antonio, Carolina Maria. AA, U. Fla., 1964, BA cum laude, 1973; MLS, Fla. State U., 1980. Cert. media specialist, Fla. Media specialist Heritage Christian, Miami, Fla., 1982-83, Palmer Acaad., Miami, 1983-91; libr. dir., media specialist Jones Coll., Miami, 1991-92, Belen Jesuit Prep. Sch., Miami, 1992—; mem. adv. bd dor libr. stds. Fla. Coun. Ind. Schs., Miami, 1990—; panel mem. Archdiocese of Miami Schs., 1992—. Author: Handbook of Philosophy and Procedures, 1990. Coord. youth activities Big Five Club, Miami, 1988; chmn. St. Mary Cath. Hispanic Club, Miami, 1994. Recipient Outstanding Svc. award St. Mary Cathedral, Miami, 1989. Mem. ALA, Am. Assn. Sch. Librs., Fla. Assn. Media Edn., Dade County Libr. Assn., Phi Kappa Phi. Democrat. Office: Belen Prep Sch 500 SW 127th Ave Miami FL 33184

ALDEA, PATRICIA, architect; b. Bucharest, Romania, Mar. 18, 1947; came to U.S., 1976; d. Dan Jasmin Negreanu and Sonia (Friedgant) Philip-Negreanu; m. Val O. Aldea, Feb. 17, 1971; 1 child, Donna-Dana. MArch, Ion Mincu, Bucharest, 1970. Registered architect, N.Y. Architect, project. mgr. The Landmark Preservation Inst., Bucharest, 1971-76; architect Edward Durell Stone Assn., N.Y.C., 1977-79; assoc. architect, project mgr. Alan Lapidus P.C., N.Y.C., 1980—. Columnist Contemporanul art jour., 1969-73. Hist. landmarks study fellow Internationes Fed. Republic of Germany, 1974. Office: Alan Lapidus PC 1841 Broadway New York NY 10023-7603

ALDER, JENNIFER SEICH, primary education educator; b. Cleve., Sept. 8, 1970; d. Richard Arpad Seich and Paulette Christine (Antonace) Grenzebach; m. Jonathan Douglas Alder, July 21, 1995. BS, Bowling Green (Ohio) State, 1992. Cert. tchr., Ohio. Asst. tchr. Bay Village Montesorri, Ohio, 1994. Roman Catholic. Home: 49 Woodbury Ln Northfield Center OH 44067

ALDERDICE, CYNTHIA LOU, artist; b. Des Moines, Mar. 16, 1932; d. Charles Lloyd and Marion Maxine (Hinn) Sandahl; m. Lee Edward Alderdice, Jan. 30, 1954; children: Cheryl Lynn, Kirk Bryan. BA, U. Tex., 1957. Pres. Am. Art Assocs., Inc., Bethesda, Md., 1966-92; v.p. Am. Art Make-A-Frame, Inc., Rockville, Md., 1972—; v.p., bd. dirs. Pyramid Atlantic, Inc., Riverdale, Md., 1994—; com. mem. Jewelry from Walters Art Gallery and Zucker Family Collection, 1987, Greek Gold from Beenaki Mus., 1991; com. mem. tarnished vistas Hist. Annapolis, Md., 1988. One-woman shows include: Touchstone Gallery, Washington, 1993, 95, Marion Price Contemporary Fine Art Gallery, Centreville, Md., 1995, U. Md., University College, Annapolis, 1996; exhibited in group shows Mus. Contemporary Art, Chamalieres, France, 1991, Walters Art Gallery, Balt., 1991, Inst. of the Arts George Mason U., Fairfax, Va., 1995, Montpelier Cultural Arts Ctr., Laurel, Md., 1995, Tarrytown Gallery, Austin, Tex., 1995; permanent collections incl. Musee d'Art Contemporain of Chamalieres, France, Artist Book Collection Balt. Mus. Art, Md. Fedn. Art, 1991, Internat. Monetary Fund Collection, Washington, Freedie Mac's Collection Honoring Washington Artists, U. Md., The Jane Voorhees Silmmerli Art Mus., N.J. Recipient individual artist award Md. Arts Coun., 1992. Mem. Md. Fedn. Art (pres., bd. dirs. 1985-87), Md. Printmakers, So. Graphics Art Coun., Washington Guild Goldsmiths, Friends Cardinal Gallery (hon.). Studio: Annapolis Bus Pk 2104 Renard Ct Annapolis MD 21401-6748

ALDERMAN, MINNIS AMELIA, psychologist, educator, small business owner; b. Douglas, Ga., Oct. 14, 1928; d. Louis Cleveland Sr. and Minnis Amelia (Wooten) A. AB in Music, Speech and Drama, Ga. State Coll., Milledgeville, 1949; MA in Supervision and Counseling Psychology, Murray State U., 1960; postgrad. Columbia Pacific U., 1987—. Tchr. music Lake County Sch. Dist., Umatilla, Fla., 1949-50; instr. vocal and instrumental music, dir. band, orch. and choral Fulton County Sch. Dist., Atlanta, 1950-54; instr. English, speech, debate, vocal and instrumental music, dir. drama, band, choral and orch. Elko County Sch. Dist., Wells, Nev., 1954-59; tchr. English and social studies Christian County Sch. Dist., Hopkinsville, Ky., 1960, instr. psychology, counselor critic prof. Murray (Ky.) State U., 1961-63, U. Nev., Reno, 1963-67; owner Minisizer Exercising Salon, Ely, Nev., 1969-71, Knit Knook, Ely, 1969—, Minimimeo, Ely, 1969—, Gift Gamut, Ely, 1977—; prof. dept. fine arts Wassuk Coll., Ely, 1986-91, assoc. dean, 1986-87, dean, 1987-90; counselor White Pine County Sch. Dist., Ely, 1960-68; dir. Child and Family Ctr., Ely Indian Tribe, 1988-93, Family and Community Ctr., Ely Shoshone Indian Tribe, 1988-93; adv. Ely Shoshone Tribal Youth Coun., 1990-93, Budge Stanton Meml. Scholarship, 1991-93, Budge Stanton Meml. Living Mus. and Cultural Ctr., 1991-93; fin. aid contracting officer Ely Shoshone Tribe, 1990-93; instr. No. Nev. C.C., 1995—; supr. testing Ednl. Testing Svc., Princeton, N.J., 1960-68, Am. Coll. Testing Program, Iowa, 1960-68, U. Nev., Reno, 1960-68; chmn. bd. White Pine Sch. Dist. Employees Fed. Credit Union, Ely, 1961-69; psychologist mental hygiene div. Nev. Pers., Ely, 1969-75, dept. employment security, 1975-80; sec.-treas. bd. dirs. Gt. Basin Enterprises, Ely, 1969-71; speaker at confs. Author various news articles, feature stories, pamphlets, handbooks and grants in field. Pvt. instr. piano, violin, voice and organ, Ely, 1981—; bd. dirs. band Sacred Heart Sch., Ely, 1982—; mem. Gov.'s Mental Health State Commn., 1963-65, Ely Shoshone Tribal Youth Camp, 1991-92, Elys Shoshone Tribal Unity Conf., 1991-92, Tribal Parenting Skills Coord., 1991; bd. dirs. White Pine County Sch. Employees Fed. Credit Union, 1961-68, pres., 1963-68; 2d v.p. White Pine Community Concert Assn., 1965-67, pres., 1967, 85—, treas., 1975-79, dr. chmn., 1981-85; chmn. of bd., 1984; bd. dirs. White Pine chpt. ARC, 1978-82; mem. Nev. Hwy. Safety Leaders Bd., 1979-82; mem. Gov.'s Commn. on Status Women, 1968-74, Gov.'s Nevada State Juvenile Justice Adv. Commn., 1992-94, White Pine Overall Econ. Devel. Plan Coun., 1992-94; sec.-treas. White Pine Rehab. Tng. Ctr. for Retarded Persons, 1973-75; mem. Gov.'s Commn. on Hwy. Safety, 1979-81, Gov.'s Juvenile Justice Program; sec.-treas. White Pine County Juvenile Problems Cabinet, 1994—; dir. Ret. Sr. Vol. Program, 1973-74; vice chmn. Gt. Basin Health Coun., 1973-75, Home Extension Adv. Bd., 1977-80; sec.-treas. Great Basin chpt. Nev. Employees Assn.; bd. dirs. United Way, 1970-76; vice chmn. White Pine Coun. on Alcoholism and Drug Abuse, 1975-76, chmn., 1976-77; grants author 3 yrs. Indian Child Welfare Act; originator Community Tng. Ctr. for Retarded People, 1972, Ret. Sr. Vol. Program, 1974, Nutrition Program for Sr. Citizens, 1974, Sr. Citizens Ctr., 1974, Home Repairs for Sr. Citizens, 1974, Sr. Citizens Home Assistance Program, 1977, Creative Crafters Assns., 1976, Inst. Current World Affairs, 1989, Victims of Crime, 1990-92, grants author Family Resource Ctr., 1995; bd. dirs. Family coalition, 1990-92, Sacred Heart Parochial Sch., 1982—, dir. band, 1982—; candidate for diaconal ministry, 1982-93; dir. White Pine Community Choir, 1962—, Ely Meth. Ch. Choir, 1960-84; choir dir., organist Sacred Heart Ch., 1984—. Precinct reporter ABC News 1966; speaker U.S. Atty. Gen. Conf. Bringing Nev. Together; bd. dirs. White Pine Juvenile Cabinet, 1993—. Recipient Recognition rose Alpha Chi State Delta Kappa Gamma, 1994; mem. adv. com. William Bee Ririe Hosp., 1996—, Ea. Nev. Child and Family Svcs., 1996—. Fellow Am. Coll. Musicians, Nat. Guild Piano Tchrs.; mem. NEA (life), UDC, DAR, Nat. Fedn. Ind. Bus. (dist. chair 1971-85, nat. guardian coun. 1985—, state guardian coun. 1987—), AAUW (pres. Wells br. 1957-58, pres. White Pine br. 1965-66, 86-87, 89-91, 93—, bd. dirs. 1965-87, rep. edn. 1965-67, implementation chair 1967-69, area advisor 1969-73, 89-91), Nat. Fedn. Bus. and Profl. Women (1st v.p. Ely chpt. 1965-66, pres. Ely chpt. 1966-68, 74-76, 85—, bd. dirs. Nev. chpt. 1966—, 1st v.p. Nev. Fedn. 1970-71, pres. Nev. chpt. 1972-73, nat. bd. dirs. 1972-73), White Pine County Mental Health Assn. (pres. 1960-63, 78—), Mensa (supr. testing 1965—), Delta Kappa Gamma (br. pres. 1968-72, 94—, state bd. 1967—, chpt. parliamentarian 1974-78, state 1st v.p. 1967-69, state pres. 1969-71, nat. bd. 1969-71, state parliamentarian 1971-73, chmn. state nominating com. 1995—, workshop presenter S.W. Regional Conf. 1995), White Pine Knife and Fork Club (1st v.p. 1969-70, pres. 1970-71, bd. dirs. 1979—), Soc. Descendants of Knights of Most Noble Order of Garter, Nat. Soc. Magna Charta Dames. Office: 1280 Avenue F East Ely NV 89301-2511

ALDERMAN, SHARON DAVIS, artist, writer, lecturer; b. Tulare, Calif., Oct. 17, 1941; d. Ronald Everett and Ida Oriet (Nelson) Davis; m. Donald Wesley Alderman, Feb. 4, 1964 (div. Apr. 1988); 1 child, Susan Elizabeth. BS in Chemistry, Harvey Rudd Coll., 1963; Harvey Mudd Coll. Testing chemist Hornkohl Lab., Bakersfield, Calif., 1963; rsch. asst. Cornell U., Ithaca, N.Y., 1964-66; lectr., writer, weaver Salt Lake City, 1970—. Author: Handwoven, Tailormade, 1982, A Handweaver's Notebook, 1990; contbr. articles to Handwoven, Shuttle Spindle and Dyepot mags. Vice chair

Ctrl. City Cmty. Coun., Salt Lake City, 1991-92; mem. bd. Salt Lake City Arts Coun., 1988—; del. Dem. county-state convs., Salt Lake City, 1992—. Recipient Purchase award Salt Lake City, 1985, Utah Arts Coun., 1986, Salt Lake County, 1990, Gov.'s award in the arts, 1996. Democrat. Home and Office: 753 South Fifth East Salt Lake City UT 84102

ALDERSON, GLORIA FRANCES DALE, rehabilitation specialist; b. Rainelle, W.Va., May 11, 1945; d. Orval Rupert and Juanita Rose (Nelson) Dale; m. Grayson Raines Alderson, June 3, 1964; children: John Grayson, James Leslie, Kathy LeDawn. ADN, U. Charleston; BS, W.Va. U. DON Charleston Area Med. Ctr., Charleston, 1977-84; head nurse Eye & Ear Clinic, Charleston, 1981-84; owner, operator ABZ Nursing, Kanawha County, W.Va., 1983-87; rehab. specialist W.Va., 1983—; bd. dirs. Profl. and Social Com. on Nursing. Bd. dirs. Urban Politics Symposium, Charleston, 1978; election campaign mgr. Rep. Party, Charleston. Scholarship Bd. Regents, 1974-77. Mem. AAUW, Am. Rehab. Profls., Internat. Platform Assn., Order Ea. Star. Home and Office: 1089 Highland Dr Saint Albans WV 25177-3675

ALDERSON, KAREN ANNETTE, bank examiner; b. Springfield, Mo., Mar. 24, 1962; d. Jerry E. and Pauline M. (Kastendieck) Gipson; m. Mark Reed Alderson, Nov. 4, 1995. BS, S.W. Mo. State U., 1984. Computer conversion technician Fed. Deposit Ins. Corp., Kansas City, 1985-87; nat. bank examiner Comptr. of the Currency, Kansas City, 1987—. Presbyterian.

ALDERSON, MARGARET NORTHROP, arts administrator, educator, artist; b. Washington, Nov. 28, 1936; d. Vernon D. and Margaret (Lloyd) Northrop; m. Donald Marr Alderson, Jr., June 4, 1955; children: Donald Marr III, Barbara Lynn Hennesy, Brian, Graham. Student George Washington U., 1954-55; A.A., Monterey Peninsula Jr. Coll., 1962. Staff, tchr. Galerie Jaclande, Springfield, Va. 1972-73; artist/tchr. Studio 7, Torpedo Factory Art Ctr., Alexandria, 1974—, dir. ctr., 1979-85; tchr. Fairfax County Recreation, 1972-73, Art League Schs., Alexandria, 1978—, ann. Feb. workshop, Accapulco, Mex., 1985—, English Painting Workshop, 1989, 90, 91, 93, 95, Santa Fe Workshop, 1991, 92, 95, Provence, France Workshop, 1995; cons. in field; project supr. City of Alexandria for Torpedo Factory Art Ctr., 1978-83; ptnr. Soho Hubris Art Gallery (N.Y.), 1977-78; pres. Touchstone Gallery, Washington. One woman shows include Way Up Gallery, Livermore, Calif., 1971, Lynchburg Coll. (Va.), 1978, Farm House Gallery, Rehobeth, Del., 1979, Art League Gallery, Alexandria, Va., 1980, 86, 93, Lyceum Mus., Alexandria, 1987, Alexandria Mus., 1987-88, William Ris Gallery, Stone Harbor, N.J., 1988, Touchstone Gallery, Washington, 1992, 94; exhibited in group shows at Art League Gallery, Alexandria, 1972—, Lynchburg (Va.) Coll., 1978, Montgomery (Ala.) Mus., 1980, Art Barn, 1989, Moscow-Washington Art Exch. Exhibit Internat., Moscow, 1990, Washington, 1991; represented in permanent collections Texaco, Inc., Phillip Morse Collection, United Va. Bank, CSX Corp., Fannie Mae Corp., Acacia Fin. Group, Office U.S. Atty. Gen., Office of Ins. Gen. EPA, Aerospace Corp., Texaco Corp. Festival chmn. City Festival Cultural Arts, Livermore, Calif., 1971; bd. dirs., Cultural Alliance Greater Washington, 1982—; bd. dirs. Torpedo Factory Art Ctr., 1978—; mem. Partners for Liveable Places, 1979—; mem. Catherine Llorilard Wolfe Art Soc.; pres. Touchstone Art Coop. Recipient Md. found. award Balt. watercolor regional annual, 1989, Elgie and David Ject Kay award Audubon Artists annual, 1989, 1st Place Awards in Watercolor, Art League, 1975, 76, 77, 82, 84-85, also numerous purchase awards, Jane Morton Norman award Ky. Nat. Watercolor Show, 1986, Adirondack Nat. Watercolor Show, 1987, 3d award Catherine Lorillard Show, N.Y.C., 1987, Albert Ehringer award, 1989, Holbein award Mid Atlantic Watercolor Regional show, 1992, Purchase award d'Arches Paper Co., Knickerbocker Exhibit, Best in Show award Deland Mus. Art, 1993, Catherine Lovell award, 1993; nominated Woman of Yr. Alexandria C. of C., 1992, 93; travel show include Chrysler Mus. Biennial, 1988, Audubon Artists Nat. Show, 1989 (Elsie & Davis Ject Key award 1989), Balt. Regional Watercolor Annual, 1989 (Md. Found. award 1989). Mem. Fed. Nat. Mortgage Assn., Va. Watercolor Soc. (pres. 1982, 1st place awards ann. exhibit 1980, 82, excellence award 1989, 94), Potomac Valley Watercolorists (pres. 1978), Torpedo Factory Artists Assn. (pres. 1977-78), Springfield Art Guild (pres. 1977), Artists Equity, Am. Council on Arts, Am. Watercolor Soc., Am. Council of Univ. and Community Arts Ctrs., Phila. Watercolor Club, Watercolor West, Soc. Layerists Multi-Media, Va. Watercolor Soc., Am. Profl. Artist's League, Am. Mgmt. Assn., Nat. Hist. Trust, Ga. Watercolor Soc., Miss. Watercolor Soc., La. Watercolor Soc., Ky. Watercolor Soc., Catherine Llorilard Wolfe Club. Republican. Home: 2204 Windsor Rd Alexandria VA 22307-1018 Studio: Torpedo Factory Art Ctr 105 N Union St # 7 Alexandria VA 22314-3217

ALDOUS, JOAN, sociology educator. BS, Kans. State U., 1948; MA, U. Tex., 1949; PhD, U. Minn., 1963. With U. Notre Dame, Ind., 1976—, now William R. Kenan Jr. prof. sociology; mem. adv. coun. Coll. Human Ecol. Cornell U., 1987-92. Author: Family Careers: Rethinking Family Development, 1996. Trustee St. Joseph County Libr. Bd., 1991-95. Recipient Ernest W. Burgess award, 1988. Mem. Nat. Coun. Family Rels. (pres. 1986), Am. Sociol. Assn. (mem. coun. 1990-93). Office: U of Notre Dame Dept Of Sociology Notre Dame IN 46556

ALDREDGE, THEONI VACHLIOTIS, costume designer; b. Athens, Greece, Aug. 22, 1932; d. Gen. Athanasios and Meropi (Gregoriades) Vachliotis; m. Thomas E. Aldredge, Dec. 10, 1953. Student, Am. Sch., Athens, 1949-53, Goodman Theatre, Chgo.; LHD, De Paul U., 1985. Mem. design staff Goodman Theatre, 1951-53; head designer N.Y. Shakespeare Festival, 1962—. Designer numerous Broadway and off Broadway shows, ballet, opera, TV spls.; films include Girl of the Night, You're a Big Boy Now, No Way to Treat a Lady, Uptight, Last Summer, I Never Sang for My Father, Promise at Dawn, The Great Gatsby (Brit. Motion Picture Acad. award 1976), Network, The Cheap Detective, The Fury, The Eyes of Laura Mars (Acad. Sci. Fiction Films award), The Champ, Semi-Tough, The Rose, Monsignor, Annie, Ghostbusters, Moonstruck, We're No Angels, Stanley and Iris, Other People's Money, Night and the City, Addams Family Values, Milk Money, Mrs. Winterbourne, The Mirror Has Two Faces, The First Wives Club; Broadway shows include A Chorus Line (Theatre World award 1976), Annie (Tony award 1977), Barnum (Tony award 1979), Dream Girls, Woman of the Year, Onward Victoria, La Cage Aux Folles (Tony award 1984), 42d Street, A Little Family Business, Merlin, Private Lives, The Corn Is Green, The Rink, Blithe Spirit, Chess, Gypsy (1989 revival), Oh, Kay, The Secret Garden, Nick and Nora, High Rollers, Putting It Together, Annie Warbucks, The Flowering Peach, School for Scandal, "EFX" MGM Grand. Recipient Obie award for Disting. Svc. to Off-Broadway Theatre Village Voice, Maharam award for Peer Gynt, N.Y.C. Liberty medal, 1986, numerous Drama Desk and Critic awards; inducted into Theatre Hall of Fame. Mem. United Scenic Artists, Costume Designers Guild, Acad. Motion Picture Arts Scis. (Oscar award Great Gatsby 1975).

ALDRICH, ANN, federal judge; b. Providence, June 28, 1927; d. Allie C. and Ethel M. (Carrier) A.; m. Chester Aldrich, 1960 (dec.); children: Martin, William; children by previous marriage: James, Allen; m. John H. McAllister III, 1986. BA cum laude, Columbia U., 1948; LLB cum laude, NYU, 1950, LLM, 1964, JSD, 1967. Bar: D.C. bar, N.Y. bar 1952, Conn. bar 1966, Ohio bar 1973, Supreme Ct. bar 1956. Research asst. to mem. faculty N.Y. U. Sch. Law; atty. IBRD, 1952; atty., rsch. asst. Samuel Nakasian, Esq., Washington, 1952-53; mem. gen. counsel's staff FCC, Washington, 1953-60; U.S. del. to Internat. Radio Conf., Geneva, 1959; practicing atty. Darien, Conn., 1961-68; asso. prof. law Cleve. State U., 1968-71, prof., 1971-80; judge U.S. Dist. Ct. (no. dist.) Ohio, Cleveland, 1980—; bd. govs. Citizens' Communications Center, Inc., Washington; mem. litigation com.; guest lectr. Calif. Inst. Tech., Pasadena, summer 1971. Mem. Fed. Bar Assn., Nat. Assn. of Women Judges, Fed. Communications Bar Assn., Fed. Judge Assn. Episcopalian. Office: US Dist Ct 201 Superior Ave E Cleveland OH 44114-1201

ALDRICH, JOSEPHINE DIANE, science, religion, band educator; b. Kansas City, Mo., Apr. 16, 1970; d. Joseph Albert and Diane Patricia (Blee) A. BS in Edn., N.W. Mo. State U., 1993. Cert. elem. tchr., Mo. Daycare tchr. Kirksville (Mo.) Daycare Ctr., 1989-90; 5th-8th grade sci. and 6th grad. relgion tchr., 6th-8th grade band dir. Cath. Diocese of Jefferson City, Moberly, Mo., 1993—; aftercare dir. Mary Immaculate Ch., Kirksville, 1993, St. Pius X Ch., Moberly, 1994—. Mem. ASCD, Nat. Coun. Tchrs. of Math., Sci. Tchr. Mo., Mo. Assn. Sch. Coun. Dirs. Republican. Roman Catholic. Home: 415 E Ashley St Apt B Jefferson City MO 65101-3484

ALDRICH, NANCY ARMSTRONG, psychotherapist, clinical social worker; b. Taylorville, Ill., Oct. 4, 1925; d. Guy L. and Alice Irene (Hicks) Armstrong; m. Paul Harwood Aldrich, Sept. 30, 1949; children: Gregory Paul, Mark Douglas, Alice Ann Aldrich White, Ruth Lynne Aldrich Sammis. AB with highest honors, U. Ill., 1947, BS in Chemistry, 1948, MS in Chemistry, 1949; MSS, Bryn Mawr Coll., 1986. Lic. clin. social worker, Del., Pa. Parole bd. mem. State of Del., Dover, 1970-74; instr. continuing edn. U. Del., Newark, 1976-78, program specialist, 1978-83; founder Acad. Lifelong Learning; v.p. Aldrich Assocs. Inc., Landenberg, Pa., 1983—, psychotherapist, 1987—; psychotherapist Family Community Service Del. County, Media, Pa., 1986, Tressler Ctr. for Human Growth, Wilmington, Del., 1987-93; clin. affiliate Personal Performance Cons., 1990-94, Acorn, 1990—, CMG Health, 1991—, Inst. for Human Resources, 1993—, employee assistance program DuPont, 1992—, Champus, 1988—, HAI/Aetna, 1994—, Value Behavioral Health, 1993—, OPTUM, 1993—, Accord, 1996—; coord. human resources devel. program Tressler Ctr. for Human Growth, 1983-84. Pres. YWCA New Castle County, Wilmington, 1974-76; mem. Statewide Health Coordinating Coun., Del., 1978-79; bd. dirs., com. mem. United Way Del., Wilmington, 1975-84; trustee Unitarian Universalist House, Phila., 1992-94. Mem. AAUW (pres. Wilmington br. 1968-70, nat. resolutions com. 1971-72, fellowship gift named in her honor 1970), Del. Soc. Lic. Clin. Social Workers (pres. 1990-91), Del. Gerontol. Soc., Mental Health Assn. Del., Internat. Soc. Bioenergetic Analysis, Phi Beta Kappa, Phi Kappa Phi, Iota Sigma Pi. Office: 625 Chambers Rock Rd Landenberg PA 19350-1041 also: 1601 Milltown Rd Ste 8 Wilmington DE 19808-4047

ALDRICH, PATRICIA ANNE RICHARDSON, retired magazine editor; b. St. Paul, Apr. 6, 1926; d. James Calvin and Anna Catherine (Eskra) Richardson; m. Edwin Chauncey Aldrich, July 31, 1948; 1 son, Mason Calvin. Student, Stout Inst., 1944-45; BS in Journalism; scholar, Northwestern U., 1948. Editor Child's World News, The Child's World, Inc., Chgo., 1952-57; assoc. editor Home Life mag. Advt. Div., Inc., Chgo., 1957-71, editor, 1971-90, ret., 1990; pres. Aldrich Enterprises, Inc., Chgo. Mem. steering com., publicity chmn. Evanston Urban League, 1961-64. Democrat.

ALDRIDGE, GEANIE BLACK, bank executive; b. Holyoke, Mass., July 6, 1942; d. Edward Dewey and Mary Virginia (Johnson) Black; m. Robert Patten Aldridge, Jan. 16, 1969; 1 child, Ruth Johnson. Student, U. N.C., 1960-61, Gonzaga U., 1977-81; grad., Pacific Coast Banking Sch., 1983. Asst. cashier N.C. Nat. Bank, Chapel Hill, 1967-69; mgmt. trainee Seafirst Bank, Spokane, 1976-78, br. mgr., 1978-82; v.p., mgr. Seafirst Bank, Moses Lake, Wash., 1982-85, Wenatchee, Wash., 1985-89; v.p., mgr. Seafirst Bank, Yakima, Wash., 1989-92, sr. v.p., mgr., 1992-95, exec. v.p., divsn. mgr., 1995—; mem. steering com. Wash. State Agrl. Showcase, Yakima, 1992—. Bd. dirs. Yakima County Devel. Assn., 1994—; mem. sel. jury Freedom Found., Valley Forge, Pa., 1986; pres. coun. Heritage Coll., Toppenish, Wash., 1996; bd. dirs. United Way Yakima County, 1996. Mem. Am. Bus. Women's Assn. (nat. pres. 1985-86, nat. sec.-treas. 1984-85, dist. v.p. 1982-83), Rotary. Presbyterian. Office: Seafirst Bank 101 N 2d St Yakima WA 98901

ALEANDRI, EMELISE FRANCESCA, producer, director, television personality, actress; b. Riva del Garda, Italy; d. John Baptist and Elodia (Lutterotti) A. AB in French, Coll. of New Rochelle, N.Y.; MA in Theater, Hunter Coll., N.Y.C., 1975; MPhil in Theater, CUNY, 1976, PhD in Theater, 1983. Drama instr. N.Y.C. Tech. Coll., Bklyn., Hunter Coll., N.Y.C., Borough of Manhattan C.C., N.Y.C., Bennington (Vt.) Coll., NYU, N.Y.C., 1977-78; dir. Ctr. Italian-Am. Studies, Bklyn. Coll., 1984-87; producer Italics Mag. Show CUNY/TV, N.Y.C., 1987—; producer videodocumentary TEATRO CUNY/TV, 1995; artistic dir. Frizzi Lazzi: Olde Time Italian-Am. Music & Theatre Co., 1994—. Actress (TV) Loving, Our Family Honor, Internal Affairs, Tattingers, Eischeid, Donohue, Nurse, MTV, Another World, Equalizer, Mathnet, Law and Order, America's Most Wanted, (films) Crooklyn, Paper Blood, Sleepers, Godfather III, My New Gun, Age of Innocence, Teenage Mutant Ninja Turtles, Cookie, Married to the Mob, Jerky Boys, Moonstruck, Jumping Jack Flash, Car 54, Turk 182, All That Jazz, Ft. Apache, John and Yoko, Raging Bull, Danger Adrift, Regarding Henry, The World According to Garp, King of the Gypsies, Night of the Juggler, Defiance, Danger Adrift, Willie and Phil, Rooftops; author: Italian-American Theatre, 1983, host (TV show) Italics; prodr., dir. TEATRO: The Legacy of Italian-American Theatre, 1995; appeared in numerous plays, concerts, operas, including Italian Funerals and other Festive Occasions, Phila.; translator various plays from Italian to English; contbr. articles on theater to profl. jours.; stage dir. numerous plays & musicals. Recipient N.Y. State Hist. award; NEA grantee Bklyn. Coll., CUNY, Ctr. for Italian-Am. Studies, Bklyn. Coll., Recreation Assn. for Handicapped, Milan, InterCities Performing Arts, N.J. Mem. AGVA, AFTRA, SAG, Actors Equity Assn., Soc. Stage Dirs. and Choreographers, Italian Actors Union, Am. Italian Hist. Assn., Ind. Feature Project.

ALEFF, ANDREA LEE (ANDY ALEFF), newspaper editor; b. Sheboygan, Wis., Oct. 2, 1946; d. Howard Joseph and Phyllis Leanne (Perkins) A.; m. David L. Nelson, Apr. 18, 1970 (div. 1981); 1 child, Andrew. AA, Christian Coll., Columbia, Mo., 1965; BJ, U. Mo., 1967. Reporter AP, N.Y.C., 1967-68, Chgo. Tribune, 1968-69, Sta. WTVJ-TV, Miami, Fla., 1969-70, Sta. WLS-TV, Chgo., 1970-73; instr. journalism Northwestern U., Evanston, Ill., 1975-76; dir. advt. and pub. rels. Expn. Corp. Am., Coral Gables, Fla., 1979-81; shoreline editor Sun-Sentinel, Ft. Lauderdale, Fla., 1981-84, assoc. editor, 1984-94, spl. projects mgr., 1995; media mgr. Sun-Sentinel, Ft. Lauderdale, 1996—. Mem. Am. Soc. Newspaper Editors, Navy League of the U.S., Ocean Watch. Episcopalian. Home: 3064 NE 49th St Fort Lauderdale FL 33308-4915 Office: Sun-Sentinel 200 E Las Olas Blvd Fort Lauderdale FL 33301-2248

ALEMAN, MINDY R., event marketing, advertising and public relations consultant, freelance writer and columnist; b. N.Y.C., Nov. 23, 1950; d. Lionel and Jocelyn (Cohen) Luskin; m. Gary Aleman, Aug. 27, 1983. BA, U. Akron, 1972, MA, 1975. Instr. speech U. Akron, 1973-83; car salesperson Dave Towell Cadillac, Akron, 1977-79, mgr. fin. and ins., 1979; account exec., pub. rels. dir. Loos, Edwards & Sexauer, Akron, 1980-82; mktg. svcs. coord. Century Products, Stow, Ohio, 1982-83; mgr. advt., pub. rels. Century Products, Gerber Furniture Group, Stow, 1983-86, Macedonia, Ohio, 1986-89; dir. rsch. and promotion Akron Beacon Jour., 1989-95; owner Mindy Aleman Mktg. and promotion Showbiz and Speak-On Workshops, 1995—; instr. comm. U. Akron, 1975-95, part-time faculty mem., 1975-96, instr. com. and advt., 1973-82, 95—; instr. Walsh U., 1996—. Playwright Danny's Choice, 1972; weekly columnist Ready or Not Sunday Beacon Mag., 1991-95. Mem. Internat. Newspaper Mktg. Assn. (various awards 1989-93), Am. Mktg. Assn., Newspaper Assn. Am., Pub. Rels. Soc. Am. (accredited), Akron Advt. Club (various awards 1983-94), Cleve. Advt. Assn., Women's Network. Office: 2891 Saybrooke Blvd Stow OH 44224-2899

ALES, BEVERLY GLORIA, artist; b. Laplace, La., Aug. 16, 1925; d. William Pinckney and Clementine Marie (Madere) Rushing; m. Warren Vincent Ales, Dec. 29, 1946 (dec. June 1991); children: Merrick Vance Patrick, Sheryl Ann, Lori Patrice. BA, Felt & Tarrant, New Orleans, 1943. Civil svc. clerk Am. Agrl., Baton Rouge, 1943-44, U.S. Naval Depot, New Orleans, 1944-45; office mgr. Nat. Auto Assn., New Orleans, 1958-59; cosmetician Labiche's Inc., New Orleans, 1959-68; art gallery owner, mgr. Gallery Toulouse, New Orleans, 1976-80, Village D'Artiste, Metairie, La., 1980-82; pvt. practice Metairie, 1980—; past pres. Metairie Art Guild, 1983, Le Petit Art Guild, New Orleans, 1986-87, 94, New Orleans Art Assn., 1991-93. Author poetry. Mem. Rep. Nat. Com., 1988, Rep. Pres. Trust, 1996; past pres. La Soc. De Femme, Metairie, 1984. Recipient Great Lady award East Jefferson Hosp. Aux., 1990, Legion of Merit award, 1994. Mem. Nat. Mus. Women in Arts (charter), Nat. Authors Registry, Internat. Soc. Poets (bd. dirs.), Workers of Magnolia Spl. Sch. (pres. 1983-84), New Orleans Garden Soc., Heart Ambassadors (v.p., 1995-96). Roman Catholic. Home: 1149 Melody Dr Metairie LA 70002

ALESCHUS, JUSTINE LAWRENCE, real estate broker; b. New Brunswick, N.J., Aug. 13, 1925; d. Walter and Mildred Lawrence; student Rutgers U.; m. John Aleschus, Jan. 23, 1949; children: Verdene Jan, Janine Kimberley, Joanna Lauren. Dept. sec. Am. Baptist Home Mission Soc., N.Y.C., 1947-49; claims examiner Republic Ins. Co., Dallas, 1950-52; broker Damon Homes, L.I., 1960-72; exclusive broker estate of Kenneth H. Leeds, L.I., 1980-90; pres. Justine Aleschus Real Estate, 1975—. Past-pres. Nassau-Suffolk Coun. of Hosp. Aux., 1981-82; hon. mem. aux. of St. John's Episcopal Hosp., Smithtown, N.Y., past pres., hosp. adv. bd.; past pres. L.I. Coalition for Sensible Growth, Inc.; mem. exec. bd. dirs. Suffolk County coun. Boy Scouts Am.; mem. adv. bd. Suffolk County coun. Girl Scouts U.S. Mem. Suffolk County Real Estate Bd. (v.p., past pres., treas., sec.), L.I. Builders Inst. (bd. dirs.), L.I. Mid-Suffolk Business Assn. (past pres.), Roundtable Eastern L.I. (bd. dirs.), Smithtown Bus. and Profl. Women's Network, New L.I. Partnership, L.I. Econ. Summit Coord. Coun., S.C. Women's Bus. Enterprise Coalition, Sky Island Club (gov.). Republican. Lutheran. Office: PO Box 267 Smithtown NY 11787-0267

ALESHIRE, SHIRLEY ANN, bank executive, rancher; b. Mena, Ark., Jan. 13, 1945; d. Owen and Madine (Howard) Cole; m. JOe M. Aleshire, Mar. 7, 1964; children: Whitney Ann, Lindsey Jo. Diploma, So. Meth. U., 1982. Bookkeeper 1st Nat. Bank, Mena, Ark., 1962; teller 1st Nat. Bank, loan clk., loan officer, cashier, v.p., cashier, v.p., cashier, mgmt. info. sys. Home: PO Box 421 5211 Hwy 8 E Mena AR 71953 Office: 1st Nat Bank 1 Fin Ctr 600 Hwy 71 S Mena AR 71953

ALEWINE, BETT C., telecommunications executive. Pres. Comsat Internat. Comm., Bethesda, Md. Office: Comsat Internat Comm 6560 Rock Spring Dr Bethesda MD 20817*

ALEXANDER, BARBARA LEAH SHAPIRO, clinical social worker; b. St. Louis, May 6, 1943; d. Harold Albert and Dorothy Miriam (Leifer) Shapiro; m. Richard E. Alexander. B in Music Edn., Washington U., St. Louis, 1964; postgrad., U. Ill., 1964-66; MSW, Smith Coll., 1970; postgrad., Inst. Psychoanalysis, Chgo., 1971-73, grad., child therapy program, 1976-80; cert. therapist Sex Dysfunction Clinic, Loyola U., Chgo., 1975. Diplomate in Clin. Social Work. Rsch. asst., NIMH grantee Smith Coll., 1968-70; probation officer Juvenile Ct. Cook County, Chgo., 1966-68, 70; therapist Madden Mental Health Ctr., Hines, Ill., 1970-72; supr., therapist, field instr. U. Chgo., U. Ill. Grad. Schs. Social Work; therapist Pritzker Children's Hosp., Chgo., 1972-82; therapist, cons., also pvt. practice, 1973—; pres. On Good Authority, 1992—; intern Divorce Conciliation Svc., Circuit Ct. Cook County, 1976-77. Contbr. articles to profl. jours. Bd. dirs., Grant Park Concerts Soc.; sec. Art Resources in Teaching. Recipient Sterling Achievement award Mu Phi Epsilon, 1964. Mem. Nat. Fed. Soc. for Clin. Social Work (chmn. 20th ann. conf., exec. bd.), Ill. Soc. Clin. Social Work (pres. 1986-90, bd. dirs., chmn. svcs. to mems. com., dir. pvt. practitioners' referral service), Assn. Child Psychotherapists, Amateur Chamber Music Players Assn., Jewish Geneal. Soc., Smith Coll. Alumni Assn. (bd. dirs., v.p. 1992-94). Home and Office: 6 Horizon Ln Galena IL 61036-9258

ALEXANDER, BARBARA TOLL, investment banker; b. Little Rock, Dec. 18, 1948; d. Lawrence Jesser and Geraldine Best (Proctor) Toll; m. Lawrence Allen Alexander, Jan. 25, 1969 (div. 1980); m. Thomas Beveridge Stiles, II, Mar. 7, 1981; stepchildren: Thomas B. Stiles III, Jonathan E. Stiles. BS, U. Ark., 1969, MS, 1970. Asst. v.p. Wachovia Bank & Trust Co., Winston-Salem, N.C., 1972-77; security analyst Investors Diversified Services, Mpls., 1977-78; 1st v.p. Smith Barney Inc., N.Y.C., 1978-84; mng. dir. Salomon Bros., N.Y.C., 1984-91, Dillon Read & Co., 1992—; chmn. policy adv. bd. Joint Ctr. for Housing Studies of Harvard U.; mem. N.Y. adv. bd. Enterprise Found; bd. dir. Covenant House; chmn. audit com. Covenant House. Presbyterian. Home: 18 Tuttle Ave Spring Lake NJ 07762-1564 Office: Dillon Read & Co Inc 535 Madison Ave New York NY 10022-4212

ALEXANDER, CEOLA JUNE, paralegal; b. New Orleans, May 5, 1951; d. Bishop King Solomon and Ceola (Smith) Jordan; m. Cleveland Ferguson, Nov. 17, 1967 (div. 1975); 1 child, Jordan Christopher; m. Buford Miller Alexander, Oct. 31, 1982; children: Sydney Renee, Marc-Anthony. Degree in paralegal, Souther Career Inst., 1990. Pvt. practice Port Allen, La. V.p. asst. Youth, Adult Polit. Orgn., Baton Rouge, 1989. Mem. NAFE. Democrat.

ALEXANDER, CONSTANCE JOY (CONNIE ALEXANDER), stone sculptor; b. Hillsboro, Ohio, Oct. 13, 1939; d. Laurence Adair and Martha Ellen (Hill-Overman) Lucas; m. Anfred Agee Alexander, June 6, 1959; children: Troy Arthur, Andrea Ellen. Grad., Cin. Art Acad., 1961, postgrad., 1962; postgrad., Atlanta Coll. of Art, 1977. represented by Miller Gallery Cin., also various galleries in Ga. and Fla. Exhibited in group exhibitions at Southeastern Artists Ga. Jubilee Festival (1st in sculpture award 1974), Southeastern Arts & Crafts Festival, Macon (Ga.) Colisuem, 1977 (1st in sculpture), World's Fair, Knoxville, Tenn., 1982, David Schaeffer Gallery, Alpharetta, Ga., 1988-93, Ga. Marble Festival, Jasper, 1989 (1st place award), Ariel Gallery, Soho, N.Y., 1989 (award of excellence), 90, 45th Ann. Pen & Brush Sculpture Exhbn., Soho, N.Y., 1991 (Excalibur Bronze Sculpture Foundry award), Ariel Gallery, Soho, 1989-91, Tim Verstegen's The Dutch Framer Gallery, Canton, Ga., 1989-93, Artistic Frames & Gallery, Jasper, Ga., 1991-93, Buckhead Trinity Arts Group, Atlanta, Ga., 1994, Gallery 300, Atlanta, 1994; represented in permanent collections Cin. Pub. Libr., Ga. Inst. Tech., Atlanta, Hartsfield Internat. Airport, North Dekalb Coll., Coca-Cola Internat. Hdqs. Mem. Soc. of Friends. Home: PO Box 67 Canton GA 30114-0067 Office: Trinity Arts Gallery 315 E Paces Ferry Rd NE Atlanta GA 30305-2307

ALEXANDER, DONNA MARIE, tax specialist, accountant; b. St. Louis, Mar. 18, 1965; d. Kenneth Raymond and Rose Marie (Huck) Hirth; m. Scott Alexander, Oct. 14, 1989 (div. Feb. 1995). BS in Accountancy, So. Ill. U., Edwardsville, 1988; MBA, St. Louis U., 1995. CPA, Mo., Ill. Tax mgr. KPMG Peat Marwick, St. Louis, 1988-92; internat. tax mgr. Emerson Electric Co., St. Louis, 1992-96, fed. and internat. tax mgr., 1996—. Mem. AICPA. Home: 17 Briarhill Ln Columia IL 62236 Office: Emerson Electric Co AA4 X3486 8000 Florissant Ave Saint Louis MO 63136

ALEXANDER, EDNA M. DEVEAUX, elementary education educator; d. Richard and Eva (Musgrove) DeVeaux. BBA, Fla. A & M U., 1943; BS in Elem. Edn., Fla. A&M U., 1948; MS in Supervision and Adminstrn., U. Pa., 1954; cert., U. Madrid, 1961; postgrad., Dade Jr. Coll., U. Miami. Sec. Dunbar Elem. Sch., 1943-46, tchr., 194-55; tchr. Orchard Villa Elem., 1959-66; prin. A. L. Lewis Elem. Sch., 1955-57; reading specialist North Cen. Dist., 1966-69; tchr. L. C. Evans Elem. Sch., 1969-71; first black woman newscaster in Miami, Sta. WBAY, 1948. V.p. Fla. Council on Human Relations Dade County, Coun. for Internat. Visitors Greater Miami; past pres. Episcopal Churchwomen of Christ Ch., Miami; bd. dirs. YWCA; vice chmn. Community Action Agy. Dade County; chmn. Dade County Minimum Housing Appeals Bd.; active Vol. Unltd. Project Nat. Coun. Negro Women; sponsor Am. Jr. Red Cross, Girl Scouts U.S.; trustee Fla. Internat. U. Found., 1974-79; mem. Jacksonville Symphony Assn. Guild. Named to Miami Centennial Women's Hall of Fame, 1996. Mem. AAUW (life, Edna M. DeVeaux Alexander fellowship named in her honor Miami br.), NEA (life), LWV, Fla. Edn. Assn., Classroom Tchrs. Assn., Dade County Edn. Assn. (chmn. pub. rels. com.), Dade County Reading Assn., Assn. for Childhood Edn., Internat. Reading Tchr. Assn., U. Pa. Alumni Assn., Alpha Kappa Alpha. Home: 805 Blue Gill Rd PO Box 26063 Jacksonville FL 32226

ALEXANDER, JANE, federal agency administrator, actress, producer; b. Boston, Oct. 28, 1939; d. Thomas Bartlett and Ruth (Pearson) Quigley; m. Robert Alexander, July 23, 1962 (div. 1969); 1 child, Jason; m. Edwin Sherin, Mar. 29, 1975. Student, Sarah Lawrence Coll., 1957-59, U. Edinburgh, 1959-60; LHD, Wilson Coll., 1984; DFA (hon.), The Julliard Sch., 1994, N.C. Sch. Arts, 1994, N.C. Sch. Arts, 1994, U. Pa., 1995; PhD (hon.), U. Pa., 1995; DFA, The New Sch. Social Rsch., 1996. Ind. TV, film and theatrical actress, 1962—; chmn. Nat. Endowment for Arts, Washington, 1993—; guest artist in residence Okla. Arts Inst., 1982, tchr. adult theatre workshop, 1984, 91, tchr. master class, 1990; mem. adv. bd. Nat. Wildlife Art Mus., hon. group, 1992—; mem. adv. bd. Women for a Meaningful Summit, 1985-90, The Acting Co., 1980-93, The Video Project, 1990-93, Nat. Stroke Assn., 1984-91, Women's Action for New Directions, 1981-90, N.Y. Zool. Soc./Wildlife Conservation Soc., 1985-93, The Am. Bird

Conservancy, 1995. Author: (with Greta Jacobs) The Bluefish Cookbook, 5 edits., 1979-95, 5th edit., 1996; translator: (with Sam Engelstad) The Master Builder (Henrik Ibsen), 1978; appeared in prodns.: Charles Playhouse Boston, 1964-65, Arena Stage, Washington, 1965-68, 70—, Am. Shakespeare Festival; plays include Major Barbara, Mourning Becomes Electra, Merry Wives of Windsor, Stratford, Conn., summers 1971-72; Broadway prodns. include The Great White Hope, 1968-69 (Tony award 1969, Drama Desk award, Theatre World award), 6 Rms Riv Vu, 1972-73 (Tony nomination), Find Your Way Home, 1974 (Tony nomination), Hamlet, 1975, The Heiress, 1976, First Monday in October, 1978 (Tony nomination), Goodbye Fidel, 1980, Monday After the Miracle, 1982, Night of the Iguana, 1988, Shadowlands, 1990-91, The Visit, 1992 (Tony nomination), The Sisters Rosensweig, 1993 (Drama Desk award 1992-93, Tony award nomination, Obie award 1993); also appeared in plays The Time of Your Life, Present Laughter, 1975, The Master Builder, 1977, Losing Time, 1980, Antony and Cleopatra, 1981, Hedda Gabler, 1981, Old Times, 1984, Approaching Zanzibar, 1989, Mystery of the Rose Bouquet, 1989; appeared in films The Great White Hope, 1970 (Acad. award nomination), A Gunfight, 1970, The New Centurions, 1972, All the President's Men, 1976 (Acad. award nomination), The Betsy, 1978, Kramer vs. Kramer, 1979 (Acad. award nomination), Brubaker, 1980, Night Crossing, 1981, Testament, 1983 (Acad. award nomination), City Heat, 1984, Sweet Country, 1986, Square Dance, 1987, Glory, 1989; appeared in TV films Welcome Home Johny Bristol, 1971, Miracle on 34th Street, 1973, Death Be Not Proud, 1974, This Was the West That Was, 1974, Eleanor and Franklin, 1976 (Emmy nomination), Eleanor and Franklin: The White House Years, 1977 (Emmy nomination, TV Critics Circle award), Lovey, 1977, A Question of Love, 1978, Playing for Time, 1980 (Emmy award 1980), Calamity Jane: The Diary of a Frontier Woman, 1981, Dear Liar, 1981, Kennedy's Children, 1981, In the Custody of Strangers, 1982, When She Says No, 1983, Mountainview, 1989, Daughter of the Streets, 1990, A Marriage: Georgia O'Keeffe and Alfred Stieglitz, 1991; appeared in TV spls. A Circle of Children, 1977, Blood and Orchids, 1986, Calamity Jane, 1984 (Emmy nomination), Malice in Wonderland, 1985 (Emmy nomination), In Love and War, 1987, Open Admissions, 1988, A Friendship in Vienna, 1988, Stay the Night, 1992. Recipient Achievement in Dramatic Arts award St. Botolph Club, 1979, Israel Cultural award, 1982, Western Heritage Wrangler award, 1985, Helen Caldicott Leadership award, 1984, Living Legacy award Women's Internat. Ctr., San Diego, 1988, Environ. Leadership award Eco-Expo, 1991, Muse award N.Y. Women in Film, 1993, Torch of Hope award, 1992, Lectureship award NIH, 1994, Houseman award The Acting Co., 1994, medal UCLA, 1994, Outer Critics Circle award Disting. Voice in Theatre, 1994, Helen Hayes award Am. Express Tribute, 1994, Women of Achievement award Anti-Defamation League, 1994, Margo Jones award, 1995, Mass. Soc. award, 1995, N.Am. Mont Blanc de la Culture award, 1995, Commonwealth award, 1995. Mem. AFTRA, SAG, Actors Equity Assn., Acad. Motion Picture Arts and Scis., Actors Fund. Office: Nat Endowment for Arts Nancy Hanks Bldg 1100 Pennsylvania Ave NW Washington DC 20004-2501*

ALEXANDER, JANE TYLOR FIELD, retired secondary education educator, writer; b. Whittier, Calif., May 31, 1915; d. Archibald Ray and Agnes (Withey) Tylor; m. Clifton Harold Field, Sept. 1, 1938 (dec. Oct. 1985); children: Pamela Field West, Melinda Field Bus, D. Robin Field; m. Luther Allen Alexander, July 14, 1988. BA, U. So. Calif., 1935; MA, San Diego State U., 1963. Lifetime secondary tchg. credential, Calif. Tchr. El Centro (Calif.) City Schs., 1936-41, San Diego City Schs., La Jolla, Calif., 1942-44, San Diego City Coll., 1958-61, Sweetwater Unified H.S. Dist., Chula Vista, Calif., 1961-75. Author, photographer: Naked Ladies and Other California Garden Exotica, 1994; editor classroom tips NEA Jour./Today's Edn., 1965-80; contbr. articles to popular mags. V.p., pres. El Centro Jr. Women's Club, 1938-41; co-leader, leader Girl Scouts Am., Salt Lake City and La Mesa, Calif., 1952-56; pink lady hosps., Highland Park, Ill. and La Mesa, 1957-70; mem. Silverwood com. San Diego Audubon Soc., 1981-95; bd. dirs., pres. Buena Vista Audubon Soc., Oceanside, Calif., 1993-96; mem. Zero Population Growth. Mem. AAUW (edn. chair, pres. 1982-85, sec. 1994-95), Defenders of Wildlife, Sierra Club, Wilderness Soc., Nature Conservancy (life), Project Wildlife, Common Cause.

ALEXANDER, JANICE HOEHNER, physician, educator; b. Detroit; d. Robert Paul and Leafy Edna (Phillips) Hoehner; m. Michael Alexander; children: Jason, Janelle Collins. BSN, Wayne State U., 1971, MD, 1979. Resident in family practice, emergency rm. Providence Hosp., Southfield, Mich., 1980-86; resident in ob-gyn. Saginaw (Mich.) Gen. Hosp., 1986-88; staff surgeon ob-gyn. Columbia and St. Joseph Hosps., Milw., 1988—; clin. instr. Mich. State U., Lansing, 1986-88, Med. Coll. Wis., Milw., 1988—; physician, tchr. Women's Med. Internat. People to People, Russia, Latvia, Lithuania, 1993. Instr. CPR ARC, Milw., 1991—. Fellow AAFP; mem. ACOG, AMA, AFS, SLS, MGynS, Milw. Med. Soc., Wis. Med. Soc. Office: 2025 E Newport Ave Ste 129 Milwaukee WI 53211-2906

ALEXANDER, JOYCE LONDON, judge. BA, Howard Univ., D.C.; JD, New Eng. Law Sch., 1972; LLD, Northeastern Univ., New Eng. Law Sch., Bridgewater State Coll. Staff atty. Greater Boston Legal Assistance Project, 1972-74; legal counsel Youth Activities Commn., Boston, 1974-76; gen. counsel Mass. Bd. of Higher Edn., 1976-79; magistrate judge U.S. Dist. Ct. (Mass. dist.), 1st circuit, Boston, 1979-96, chief magistrate judge, 1996—; asst. prof. Tufts Univ., 1974-75; legal editor WBZ-TV, Boston, 1978-79. Trustee Boys & Girls Club of Greater Boston. Recipient Martin Luther King Jr. Drum Major for Justice award So. Christian Leadership Conf., 1985, Raymond Pace Alexander award Nat. Bar Assn.; named Outstanding Young Leader of Mass. Boston Jaycees, 1980. Mem. Am. Judicature Soc., Nat. Bar Assn., Nat. Coun. of U.S. Magistrate, Mass. Black Judges Conf., Urban League of Ea. Mass. (co-founder, pres. emeritus), World Peace Through Law Conf., Orgn. of Black Airline Pilots. Office: John W McCormack Courthouse 90 Devonshire St Rm 932 Boston MA 02109-4501*

ALEXANDER, JOYCE MARY, illustrator; b. Pepin, Wis., Mar. 31, 1927; d. Colonel and Martha (Varnum) Yochem; m. Don Tocher, June 27, 1955 (div. 1962); m. Dorsey Potter Alexander, Nov. 1, 1963. Student, Coll. Arts and Crafts, 1946, Acad. of Art, 1961-62. Co-founder, owner Turtle's Quill Scriptorium Publishers, Berkeley, Calif., 1963—. Author: Thaddeus, 1972, Happy Bird Day, 1980; illustrator numerous books including: Soil and Plant Analysis, A Practical Guide for the Home Gardener, 1963, CAlifornia Farm and Ranch Law, 1967, Chinatown, A Legend of Old Cannery Row, 1968, The Sea: Excerpts from Herman Melville, 1969, Of Mice, 1966, David: Psalm Twenty-Four, 1970, Shakespeare: Selected Sonnets, 1974, The Blue-Jay Yarn, 1975, Psalm One Hundred Four, 1978, Messiah: Choruses from Handel's Messiah, 1985, A Flurry of Angels, Angels in Literature, 1986, Eleven Poems by Emily Dickinson, A Packet of Rhymes, 1989, Psalm Eight (A Nature Psalm), 1991, Poems, Emily Dickenson, 1992, Comfort Me With Apples-Excerpts From Literature Involving Food, 1993, Father William, 1994; work represented in permanent collections Hunt Botan. Libr. at Carnegie-Mellon U. Republican. Office: Turtle's Quill Scriptorium PO Box 643 Mendocino CA 95460-0643

ALEXANDER, KATHRYN JEAN (KAY ALEXANDER), retired art education consultant, art curriculum writer; b. Oakland, Calif., July 31, 1924; d. Haskell Seward Bennett and Ruth (Simpson) Bennett Macaulay; m. Earl Bryan Alexander, Aug. 12, 1945; children: Steven Bryan , Lauren Alexander Marks, Douglas Brandon. BA in Art with honors, U. Calif., Berkeley, 1946; MA in Edn. Adminstr. with honors, Calif. State U., Long Beach, 1959; postgrad., Oxford (Eng.) U., 1984. Cert. tchr., adminstr., supr. Elem. tchr. Anaheim (Calif.) Sch. Dist., 1956-60, coord. gifted edn., 1960-63, art edn. coord., 1963-67; art edn. coord. Palo Alto (Calif.) Unified Sch. Dist., 1967-85; ind. art edn. cons. Los Altos, Calif., 1984—; adj. prof. Hayward (Calif.) State U., 1971-73; chair interdisciplinary com. State of Calif. Arts Framework, Sacramento, 1980-82; dir. Curriculum Devel. Inst., Getty Ctr. for Edn., L.A., 1986-89. Author: (series of 9 books) Learning to Look and Create: The SPECTRA Program, 1986-94, (40 annotated posters) Take Five, 1988-90, (2 video-filmstrip sets) The Skills of Art, 1987; editor (handbook) Discipline Based Art Education, A Curriculum Sampler, 1990, (multimedia H.S. program) Native American Arts & Crafts, 1995; contbg. editor Arts and Activities, 1988—. Assoc. dir. J. Paul Getty Ctr. for Edn. in Arts Curriculum Devel. Inst., 1987-89; vol. Stanford Com. for Art, 1971—. Recipient Humanities award Calif. Humanities Assn., 1984, Emerson award Cultural Arts Peninsula Area, Calif., 1986. Mem. Nat. Art Edn. Assn. (chair publs. com. 1974-78, Outstanding Art Educator award 1983, Pacific region Outstanding Art Supr. 1984), Pacific Art League (sec. bd. trustees 1983-85), Calif. Art Edn. Assn. (various exec. positions 1964—, Disting. Art Educator 1988), Photog. Soc. Am., Phi Beta Kappa. Home and Office: 800 El Monte Ave Los Altos CA 94022-3960

ALEXANDER, LENORA COLE, business executive, educator; b. Buffalo, Mar. 9, 1935; d. John L. and Susie (Stamper) Cole; m. T.M. Alexander Sr., June 22, 1976. BS, SUNY, Buffalo, 1957, MEd, 1969, PhD, 1974. Lic. elem. tchr., elem. sch. prin. Tchr. pub. schs. Chgo. and Lancaster, N.Y., 1957-68; v.p. student life Am. U., Washington, 1974-77; v.p. student affairs U. D.C., 1978-81; dir. Women's Bur. Dept. Labor, Washington, 1981-86; Commonwealth prof. George Mason U., Fairfax, Va., 1986-88; pres. LCA and Assocs., Inc., Washington, 1986—; cons. div. student affairs U. Calif. Irvine, 1971, CCNY, 1972, Temple U., 1973; advisor regional and city planning colloquium U. Pa., 1973; panel on selection fellow HEW, 1976-77; cons. advanced instrl. devel. program Dillard U., 1977-81; mem. mayor's blue ribbon panel on reorgn. Dept. Human Resources, Washington, 1977; mem. selection com. fellows program Am. Council on Edn., 1982; lectr. in field. Author tech. reports for U.S. Govt. Printing Office. Trustee Wider Opportunities for Women, 1975-77; del. Internat. Commn. on Status Women, 1982, Columbia, 1983, Women in World Prep. Conf., 1983; apptd. del. Decade for Women in World Conf., UN, Vienna, Austria, 1984, Kenya, 1986; U.S. rep. on role women on economy Orgn. Econ. Devel., Paris, 1982-86; mem. adv. com. on women vets VA, 1983; participant Jerusalem Internat. Forum, Am.-Israel Friendship League, 1986; mem. D.C. Bd. Elections and Ethics, 1986-88, Def. Adv. Com. On Women in Mil., def. adv. com. Women in the Svc., 1989—; bd. dirs. Legal Aid Soc., Washington, 1975-77, D.C. Rental Accommodations Commn., 1978-79, McAuley Inst., Silver Spring, Va., 1987—; pres. bd. dirs. Found. for Exceptional Children, Reston, Va., 1987—. SUNY grad. fellow, 1968; recipient Disting. Alumnus award SUNY-Buffalo, 1983, Pauline Weeden Maloney award in nat. trends and Services The Links, Phila., 1984, Disting. Service Citation Nat. MBA Assn., 1984, Outstanding Woman award DC chpt. Federally Employed Women, Washington, 1984, Outstanding Polit. Achievement award Nat. Assn. Minortiy Polit. Women, 1985, Outstanding Career Woman award women's activities com. Alpha Phi Alpha, Washington, 1986, Woman of Achievement award Women's City Club Cleve., 1986. Mem. Delta Sigma Theta. Republican. Home and Office: 3020 Brandywine St NW Washington DC 20008-2140*

ALEXANDER, LYNN See MARGULIS, LYNN

ALEXANDER, MARJORIE ANNE, artist, hand papermaker, consultant; b. Chgo., Apr. 16, 1928; d. Alexander and Nancy Rebecca (Cordrey) Roberts; m. Harold Harman Alexander, June 13, 1948; children: Jeffrey C., Cassandra J., Peter B., Timothy C., Patrick J. Student, Wilson Jr. Coll., 1946-47; MFA in Painting, U. Ill., 1968, MA in Art Edn., 1972. cert. tchr. K-12: Ill., Minn. Graphic artist Barry Martin Studio, Rumson, N.J., 1963-65; instr. painting, drawing U. YMCA, Champaign, Ill., 1968-72; teaching asst. U. Ill., Urbana, 1968-72, rsch. assoc., 1972-76; instr. art Champaign High Sch., 1973-75, Urbana High Sch., 1976-80, Concordia Acad., St. Paul, Minn., 1982-84, U. Minn., Mpls., 1984-87; design, housing and apparel artist in residence U. Minn., St. Paul, 1984-88; craft cons. and educator tech. asstance program USAID, OAS, U. Minn., Kingtson, Jamaica, 1986—; design cons. J.A.M. Corp., Mpls., 1988—; tech. cons. OAS, Kingston, 1990-91, Blandin Found. grantee, Minn., 1989—; rsch. and product devel. agrl. unilization rsch. inst., 1992-95; tech. cons. Zabbaleen Paper Project, Assn. for the Protection of the Environment, Cairo, 1993—. Works have appeared in over 20 solo shows, 1960—, over 19 invitational shows nationally and internationally, 1985—; co-author (book): Selected Papers, 1994; contbr. articles to profl. jours. Vestry mem. St. John's Episcopal Ch., Champaign, 1975-78, St. Matthew's Episcopal Ch., St. Paul, 1989—. Recipient Celebrity award Minn. State Fair, 1984, book First award 1986, Honorable mention 3rd Onn/Off Paper Nat., Wis., 1984; grantee Blandin Found. U. Minn., 1989-90, OAS, 1990-91, Agrl. Utilization Rsch. Inst. grantee, 1992-95. Mem. Nat. League Am. Penwomen (Minn. art chair 1990-94, state v.p. 1994—), Internat. Assn. Hand Papermakers and Paper Artists, Friends of Dard Hunter Paper Mus. (com. chair 1990—). Episcopalian. Home: Graybridge 3251 Fernwood St Arden Hills MN 55112

ALEXANDER, MARTHA SUE, librarian; b. Washington, June 8, 1945; d. Lyle Thomas and Helen (Goodwin) Alexander; m. David Henry Bowman, June 11, 1965 (div. 1982); 1 child, Elaine. B.A., U. Md., 1967; M.S. in Library Sci., Cath. U. Am., 1969. Librarian U. Md., College Park, 1969-72, head acquisitions, 1973-75; asst. univ. librarian George Washington U., Washington, 1975-78, assoc. univ. librarian, 1978-82; univ. librarian U. Louisville, 1983-90; dir. libraries U. Mo., Columbia, 1990—; chmn. bd. dirs. SOLINET (Southeastern Library Network), 1987-88. Coord. U. Louisville United Way, 1987; bd. dirs. Mo. Libr. Network Corp., 1990—. Mem. ALA (chmn. poster sessions 1983-85, co-chmn. nat. conf. in Cin. 1989), Am. Assn. Higher Edn., Athletic Assn. U. Louisville (vice chmn., bd. dirs. 1989-90), D.C. Library Assn. (pres. 1981-82), Women Acad. Libr. Dirs. Exch. Network. Episcopalian. Home: 100 Mumford Dr Columbia MO 65203-0226 Office: Univ Mo Columbia-Ellis Libr Columbia MO 65201

ALEXANDER, MARY ELSIE, lawyer; b. Chgo., Nov. 16, 1947; d. Theron and Marie (Bailey) A.; m. Lyman Saunders Faulkner, Jr., Dec. 1, 1984; 1 child, Michelle. BA, U. Iowa, 1969; MPH, U. Calif.-Berkeley, 1975; JD, U. Santa Clara, 1982. Bar: Calif. 1982, U.S. Dist. Ct. (no. dist.) Calif. 1982, U.S. ct. Appeals (9th cir.) 1982. Rschr., U. Cin., 1969-74; dept. dir., sr. environ. health scientist Stanford Rsch. Inst., Menlo Park, Calif., 1975-80; cons. Alexander Assocs., Ambler, Pa., 1980-82; assoc. Caputo, Liccardo Rossi Sturges & McNeil, San Jose, Calif., 1982-84; assoc. Cartwright, Slobodin, Bokelman, et al, San Francisco, 1984-88, ptnr., 1988—. Com. mem. Cancer Soc., San Jose, 1983; elder Valley Presbyn. Ch., Portola Valley, 1987-90; active Am. Heart Assn., Santa Clara County. Named one of top 10 Trial Lawyers San Francisco Bay Area, San Francisco Chronicle, 1990. Nat. Inst. Occpational Safety and Health scholar U. Calif., Berkeley, 1975. Mem. ABA, Assn. Trial Lawyers Am. (state del.), pres. 1996. Consumer Attys. Calif. (formerly Calif. Trial Lawyers Assn.) (PAC bd. 1989—, parliamentarian 1991, v.p. 1992, chair mem. com., editor Forum, pres. elect 1995), San Francisco Trial Lawyers Assn., Trial Lawyers for Pub. Justice, Calif. Women Lawyers, Am. Indsl. Hygiene Assn. (bd. dirs. 1979-81, treas. 1977-79), Nat. Assn. Advancement of Sci., Santa Clara Trial Lawyers Assn. (bd. dirs. 1983-84). Democrat. Office: Alexander 101 California St Fl 26 San Francisco CA 94111-5802

ALEXANDER, MONICA MARY HARRIET, laboratory analyst; b. Manama, Bahrain, May 4, 1942; came to U.S., 1967; d. Emidio Simplicio and Sabina Isabela (De-Rego) Simoes; divorced; children: Robert, Mark. Student, Midland Tech. Inst., 1975, U. S.C., 1978, Dale Carnegie Inst., 1980. Receiver/contr. Carolina Eastman Kodak, Columbia, S.C., 1972-87, lab. fiber analyst, 1987-90; environ. lab. analyst, operator second incinerator Carolina Eastman Chem. Co., Columbia, 1990—. Vol. Floyd Spence campaign Rep. Party, Columbia, 1985, Bob Dole campaign, Columbia, 1988, Dole presdl. campaign, 1996, Sen. Joe Wilson, 1993—; vol. Lexington County Hosp., West Columbia, S.C., 1993, S.C. State Mus./docent; mem. host family internat. students Columbia Coun. Internats. Mem. NAFE, Springdale Woman's Club. Roman Catholic. Office: Carolina Eastman Chemical Co PO Box 1782 Columbia SC 29202-1782

ALEXANDER, MYRNA B., psychologist, counselor; b. Phila., Apr. 13, 1949. BA, U. Md., 1971, MA, 1972, AGS, 1973; EdD, George Washington U., 1981; BS, Am. Holistic Coll. Nutrition, 1995; postgrad., various training insts. Cert. clinical mental health counselor; nationally cert. counselor; cert. employee assistance profl.; cert. marriage and family therapist; lic. profl. counselor, Va., Washington. Rehab. counselor Learning Disability Ctr., Clinton, Md., 1973; program dir., vocat. rehab. counselor Walden Res., Kensington, Md., 1974; sr. crisis intervention therapist Emergency Psychiatric Svc., Md., 1974-79; employee assistance program adminstr., counselor U.S. Dept. Energy, Washington, 1980-81; counseling dir. Profl. Counseling Svcs., Arlington, Va., 1973—; regional mgr. counseling AT&T, Oakton, Va., 1984-96; asst. prof. U. Md., 1976, George Washington U., Washington, 1992, 94, 96; vis. prof. George Mason U., Va., 1990; employee assistance profl. cons. Contbr. articles to profl. jours; guest spkr. public radio and public T.V. Outstanding Cmty. Effort award Cmty. Leaders and Noteworthy Ams., 1979-80. Mem. Employee Assistance Profl. Assn., Am. Counselors Assn., Assn. of Employee Assitance Program Profls. (pres. 1994-95). Home and Office: 3850 South 9th Rd Arlington VA 22204

ALEXANDER, PATRICIA ANN, education educator; b. Washington; d. William Cecil and Rosina Angelina (Munari) Mullins; 1 child, John F. BA, Bethel Coll., 1970; MEd, James Madison U., 1979; PhD, U. Md., 1981. Tchr. St. Thomas More Sch., Arlington, Va., 1970-71, Shenandoah County Pub. Schs., Woodstock, Va., 1973-79; prof. edn. Tex. A&M U., College Station, 1981-95, interim head dept. ednl. psychology, 1992-95; prof. human devel. U. Md., College Park; presenter, spkr. in field. Mem. editl. bd. 3 jours.; ad hoc reviewer 8 jours.; co-editor: Beliefs About Text and Instruction With Text, 1994; co-author: Adults' Views About Knowing and Believing, 1994; contbr. articles to profl. jours. Spencer fellow Nat. Acad. Edn., 1987, Disting. Rsch. Fellow Coll. Edn. Tex. A&M U., 1990—. Mem. Am. Ednl. Rsch. Assn. (chair nominations com. 1994), S.W. Ednl. Rsch. Assn. (pres. 1988), Nat. Reading Conf. (editl. bd. 1994). Office: Dept Human Devel U Md College Park MD 20742

ALEXANDER, PATRICIA ROSS, administrative assistant; b. Blue Ridge, Ga., May 19, 1955; d. Ernest B. and Sara P. (Williams) Ross; m. Robert W. Alexander, Jr., June 24, 1978; children: Sarah E., Robert R. AA, Young Harris (Ga.) Coll., 1975; BA, North Ga. Coll., 1978, postgrad.; postgrad., Emory U. Fiber artist Morganton, Ga.; clk., postmaster relief U.S. Postal Svc., Mineral Bluff, Ga., 1987-96; adminstrv. asst. Indsl. Strength Art, Morganton. Contbr. articles to publs. Recipient cert. of Appreciation and Pride in Performance Gold medal, U.S. Postal Svc., 1992; grantee Ga. Coun. for Arts, 1984, NSF, 1979. Mem. NAPUS, So. Highlands Handicraft Guild, Ga. Mountain Crafts (bd. dirs. 1981-84), Copper Basin/Fannin C. of C., Blue Ridge Mountains Arts Assn. (v.p. 1979-80, coord. 1980-81, bd. dirs. 1993-96), Basket Weavers Guild Ga., Fannin County Heritage Found., Fannin County Tree League (bd. dirs. 1993-95), Ga. Pub. TV Leadership Cir. Baptist. Home: PO Box 599 Morganton GA 30560-0599 Office: US Post Office Mineral Bluff GA 30559

ALEXANDER, TRACY LOUISE, elementary school educator; b. Boston, Dec. 15, 1969; d. Richard Roth and Louise Elizabeth (Mooney) A. BS in Edn. magna cum laude, Lesley Coll., 1991, M in Edn. summa cum laude, 1994. Cert. elem. tchr. 1-6. consulting reading tchr, grades K-12. Extended day tchr Daniel Butler Elem. Sch., Belmont, Mass., 1987-91; profl. aide Belmont H.S., 1991-93; 6th grade tchr. Chenery Mid. Sch., 1993—. Mem. NEA, Nat. Coun. Tchrs. of English.

ALEXANDER, VERA, dean, marine science educator; b. Budapest, Hungary, Oct. 26, 1932; came to U.S., 1950; d. Paul and Irene Alexander; div.; children: Graham Alexander Dugdale, Elizabeth Alexander. BA in Zoology, U. Wis., 1955, MS in Zoology, 1962; PhD in Marine Sci., U. Alaska, 1965. From asst. prof. to assoc. prof. marine sci. U. Alaska, Fairbanks, 1965-74, prof., 1974—, dean Coll. Environ. Scis., 1977-78, 80-81, dir. Inst. Marine Sci., 1979-93, acting dean Sch. Fisheries and Ocean Scis., 1987-89, dean, 1989—; mem. adv. com. to Ocean Scis. divsn. NSF, 1980-84, chairperson adv. com., 1983-84; mem. com. to evaluate outer continental shelf environ. assessment program Minerals Mgmt. Svc., Bd. Environ. Sci. and Tech. NRC, 1987-91, mem. com. on geophys. and environ. Data, 1993—; mem. adv. com. Office Health and Environ. Rsch. U.S. Dept. Energy, Washington, 1987-90; vice chmn. Arctic Ocean Scis. Bd., 1988-89; commr. U.S. Marine Mammal Commn., 1995—; U.S. del. to North Pacific Marine Sci. Orgn. Editor: Marine Biological Systems of the Far North (W.L. Rey), 1989. Sec. Fairbanks Light Opera Theatre Bd., 1987-88; chairwoman Rhodes Scholar Selection Com., Ak., 1986—. Research grantee U. Alaska. Fellow AAAS, Arctic Inst. N.Am., Explorers Club (sec., treas. Alaska/Yukon chpt. 1987-89, 91—, pres. 1990-91); mem. Am. Soc. Limnology and Oceanography, Am. Geophysical Union, Oceanography Soc., Rotary. Office: PO Box 80650 Fairbanks AK 99708-0650 also: U Alaska PO Box 707220 Fairbanks AK 99775

ALEXANDER, VIRGINIA GLAZE, religious organization administrator; b. Decatur, Ala., Nov. 6, 1955; d. Author Jerome and Alice Marie (Sims) Glaze; m. William Michael Alexander, Apr. 5, 1975; children: Crystal Marie, Cassie Michelle. Student, U. North Ala., 1974, Calhoun Coll., 1977-79. Cert. mcpl. ofcl. Assistance mgr. Behr'ss Women Clothing Store, Decatur, 1990-92; drug technician Medicine Shoppe Drug Store, Decatur, 1992-94; coun. mem. City of Hartselle, Ala., 1992—; Bapt. campus ministry dir. Calhoun Coll. Ala. Bapt. State Conv./Morgan & Lawrence County Bapt. Assn., Decatur, 1994—. Active, tchr. First Bapt. Ch., Hartselle, 1990—; mem. coun. com. Bd. Edn., Hartselle, 1991; coun. mem. Hartselle City, 1992—; mem. North-Ctrl. Ala. Regional Coun. of Govt., Decatur, 1993—; cons. Jr. Achievement, Hartselle, 1996; leader for leadership tng. Campus Ministries, Montgomery, Ala., 1996; pres. PTO Hartselle Sch. Scholar Calhoun Coll., Decatur, 1977-79. Mem. Nat. League Cities, North Ctrl. Coun. Govt., Ala. League Municipalities, Clean City-Hartselle, New Comers Club-Hartselle, C. of C. Home: 910 Tunsel Rd Hartselle AL 35640

ALEXANDRE, KRISTIN KUHNS, public relations executive; b. Dayton, Ohio, July 15, 1948; d. James Edward and Faith (Colgan) Kuhns; m. Dick Gerrity (div. 1984); m. DeWitt Loomis Alexandre; children: James Andrew, Cynthia Lenox Banks. BA, Sweet Briar, 1968. Editor C.I.T. Finance Corp., N.Y.C., 1970-73; newscaster Channel 5 News, N.Y.C., 1973-74, Channel 13 News, N.Y.C., 1974-75; editor champion Internat., N.Y.C., 1975-76; copy editor House Beautiful, N.Y.C., 1975-76; pub. rels. officer Economic Devel. Adminstrn. Puerto Rico, N.Y.C., 1976-80; pres. Kristin Alexandre Pub. Rels., N.Y.C., 1980—. Mem. New York Jr. League. Home: PO Box 367 Far Hills NJ 07931-0367

ALF, MARTHA JOANNE, artist; b. Berkeley, Calif., Aug. 13, 1930; d. Foster Wise and Julia Vivian (Kane) Powell; m. Edward Franklin Alf, Mar. 17, 1951; 1 child, Richard Franklin. BA with distinction, San Diego State U., 1953, MA in Painting, 1963, jr. coll. teaching credential, 1969; MFA in Pictorial Arts, UCLA, 1970. Rsch. asst. Health and Welfare Assn., Seattle, 1956; teaching asst. in drawing, instr. design San Diego State U., 1963; instr. drawing L.A. Valley Coll., 1970-73, El Camino Coll., Hawthorne, Calif., 1971; instr. drawing and painting L.A. Harbor Coll., Wilmington, Calif., 1971-75; instr. art UCLA Extension, 1971-79; instr. contemporary art Brand Library Art Ctr., Glendale, Calif., 1973; vis. artist Calif. State Coll., Bakersfield, 1980; freelance art critic Artweek, Oakland, Calif., 1974-77; guest curator Lang Art Gallery, Scripps Coll., Claremont, Calif., 1974. Retrospective exhbn. Fellows Contemporary Art, L.A. Municipal Art Gallery, San Francisco Art Inst., 1984; represented in permanent collections L.A. County Mus. Art; one woman shows include John Berggruen Gallery, San Francisco, 1977, The Forth Worth Art Mus., 1988, Dorothy Rosenthal Gallery, Chgo., 1982, Eloise Pickard Smith Gallery Cowell Coll. U. Calif., Santa Cruz, 1983, Newspace Gallery, L.A., 1985, ann. 1976-84, 1990, 91, Tortue Gallery, Santa Monica, 1986, Jan Baum Gallery, L.A., 1988, 871 Fine Arts, San Francisco, 1991, Art Inst. of So. Calif., Laguna Beach, Calif., 1991; exhibited in group shows at San Diego Mus. of Art, 1964, 67, 68, 70, 71, 77, 78, 83, Whitney Mus. of Contemporary Art Biennial, 1975, Newport Harbor Art Mus., 1975, Marion Koogler McNay Art Inst., San Antonio, 1976, Long Beach Mus. of art, 1972, 82, 86, Henry Art Gallery U. Wash., Seattle, 1985, L.A. County Mus. of Art , 1979, 82; rep. in permanent collections Chem. Bank of N.Y., Ga. Mus. of Art, Israel Mus. Art, Jerusalem, L.A. County Mus. of Art., McCrory Corp., N.Y., Metromedic Inc., L.A., N.Y., San Diego Mus. of Art, Santa Barbara Mus. of Art, Southland Corp., Dallas, Spencer Mus. of Art U. Kanas., Lawrence. Nat. Endowment for Arts grantee, 1979, 89. Home and Studio: 5701 Waring Rd San Diego CA 92120 also: 103 Brooks Ave Venice CA 90291-3254*

ALFORD, JOAN FRANZ, entrepreneur; b. St. Louis, Sept. 16, 1940; d. Henry Reisch and Florence Mary (Shaughnessy) Franz; m. Charles Hebert Alford, Dec. 28, 1978; stepchildren: Terry, David, Paul. BS, St. Louis U., 1962; postgrad. Consortium of State U., Calif., 1975-77; MBA, Pepperdine U., 1987, postgrad., Fielding Inst., 1988-90. Head user svcs. Lawrence Berkeley Lab., Calif., 1977-78, head software support and devel. Computer Ctr., 1978-82, dep. head, 1980-81; regional site analyst mgr. Cray Rsch., Inc., Pleasanton, Calif., 1982-83; owner, pres. Innovative Leadership, Oakland, Calif., 1983-91; realtor, assoc. Mason-McDuffie Real Estate, Inc., 1991-96, Coldwell Banker, 1996—; bd. dirs. Oakland Multiple Listing Svc., 1994, 96—, treas., 1994—; co-chair computer user com. OAR, 1992-93, chair,

1993-94; bd. dirs. Oakland Assn. Realtors, 1995—, chair of bus. and tech., 1996—. Contbr. articles to profl. jours. Bd. dirs., sec. Vol. Ctrs. of Alameda County, 1985, chair nominating com., 1990-91, pres. bd. dirs., 1991—; campaign mem. Marge Gibson for County Supr., Oakland, 1984; pres. bd. dirs. Vol. Ctrs. Alameda City, 1991-92; mem. Oakland Piedmont Rep. Orgn., Alameda County Apt. Owners Assn., 1982. Mem. Assn. Computing Machinery, Spl. Interest Group on Computer Pers. Rsch. (past chmn.), Nat. Assn. Realtors, Calif. Assn. Realtors, Oakland Assn. Realtors, Internat. Platform Assn., Small Owners for Fair Treatment. Republican. Clubs: Claremont Pool and Tennis, Lakeview, San Francisco Opera Guild. Avocations: swimming, skiing, opera, horseback riding, gardening. Home: 2605 Beaconsfield Pl Piedmont CA 94611-2501 Office: Coldwell Banker 6137 La Salle Oakland CA 94611

ALFORD, PAULA N., federal agency administrator; b. Monterey, Calif., Nov. 18, 1952; d. Paul and Thelma Nuschke; m. James K. Alford; 1 child, Karen Louise. BA, Scripps Coll., 1974; MPA, George Washington U., 1978. Fed. rels. assoc. Adv. Commn. Intergovernmental Rels., 1979-81; dir. fed. legislation and regulations Nat. Assn. Towns and Twps., 1982-86; cons. hazardous materials transp. and environ. issues, 1986-88; dir. external affairs Monitored Retrievable Storage Rev. Commn., 1988-89, Nuclear Waste Tech. Rev. Bd., Arlington, Va. Author various publs. in field. Mem. Pi Alpha Alpha. Office: Nuclear Waste Tech Review Bd 1100 Wilson Blvd Arlington VA 22209-2297

ALGASE, SARA JEANNE, editor; b. N.Y.C., Aug. 31, 1967; d. Roger Carl Algase and Helen Frances (Wertheimer) Hubler. Student, Rutgers-Mason Gross Sch. Arts, 1986-87; BFA, NYU, 1990. Asst. to mng. editor Archie Comics, Inc., Mamaroneck, N.Y., 1990-93; editl. asst. Scholastic, Inc., N.Y.C., 1994-95; asst. editor Daniel Weiss Assocs., N.Y.C., 1995—. Author, actress: (play) Childhood and Other Natural Disasters, 1990; author: (novel) Missing Marc, 1993, (children's advice column) Archie Comic Books, 1991—; contbr. articles to profl. publs. and newspapers. Adoption vol. ASPCA, 1995—. Recipient Sr. award Old Tappan H.S. Dance Troupe, 1985. Mem. Soka Gokkai Internat. (dist. leader 1986—, mem. young woman's chorus 1993—). Buddhist. Home: # 4C 320 W 30th St New York NY 10001 Office: Daniel Weiss Assocs 11th Fl 33 W 17th St New York NY 10011

ALICE, MARY (MARY ALICE SMITH), actress; b. Indianola, Miss., Dec. 3, 1941; d. Sam and Ozelar (Jurnakin) Smith. BE, Chgo. State U.; studied with Lloyd Richards, Negro Ensemble Co., N.Y.C. Sch. tchr. Chgo. Theater debut Purlie Victorious, Chgo.; off-Broadway debut Trials of Brother Jero and the StrongBreed, Greenwich Mews Theatre, 1967; Broadway debut No Place to Be Somebody, Morosco Theatre, 1971; other N.Y.C. appearances include A Rat's Mass, 1969, The Duplex, 1972, Miss Julie, 1973, House Party, 1973, Black Sunlight, 1974, Terraces, 1974, Heaven and Hell's Agreement, 1974, In the Deepest Part of Sleep, 1974, Cockfight, 1977, Nongogo, 1978 (Obie award Village Voice 1979), Julius Caesar, N.Y. Shakespeare Festival, 1979 (Obie award Village Voice 1979), Player # 9, Spell # 7, N.Y. Shakespeare Festival, 1979, Zooman and the Sign, 1980, Glasshouse, 1984, Take Me Along, 1984, Fences, Goodman Theatre, Chgo., 1986, 46th St. Theatre, N.Y.C., 1987 (Tony award for best featured actress in a play, Drama Desk award 1987), The Shadow Box, 1994, Having Our Say, 1995 (Tony award nominee for lead actress in a play 1995); other theater appearances include Open Admissions, Long Wharf Theatre, New Haven, 1982, A Raisin in the Sun, Yale Repertory Theatre, 1984; film debut The Education of Sonny Carson, 1974; other film appearances include Sparkle, 1976, Teachers, 1984, Brat Street, 1984, To Sleep With Anger, 1990, Awakenings, 1990, Bonfire of the Vanities, 1990, A Perfect World, 1992, Life with Mikey, 1993, The Inkwell, 1994; appeared in TV films The Sty of the Blind Pig, 1974, Just an Old Sweet Song, 1976, This Man Stands Alone, 1979, Joshua's World, 1980, The Color of Friendship, 1981, The Killing Floor, 1984, Concealed Burmies, 1984, Charlotte Forten's Mission: Experiment on Freedom, 1984, The Women of Brewster Place, 1989, Laurel Avenue, 1993, The Mother, 1994, The Vernon Johns Story, 1994; TV series include: Sanford and Son, 1972, A Different World, 1988-89, I'll Fly Away (Emmy Award, Outstanding Supporting Actress in a Drama Series, 1993), 1991-1993. Mem. AFTRA, SAG, Actors' Equity Assn. Office: Ambrosio/Mortimer and Assocs Inc 9150 Wilshire Blvd Ste 175 Beverly Hills CA 90212-3428*

ALKON, ELLEN SKILLEN, physician; b. Los Angeles, Apr. 10, 1936; d. Emil Bogen and Jane (Skillen) Rost; m. Paul Kent Alkon, Aug. 30, 1957; children: Katherine Ellen, Cynthia Jane, Margaret Elaine. BA, Stanford U., 1955; MD, U. Chgo., 1961; MPH, U. Calif., Berkeley, 1968. Diplomate Nat. Bd. Med. Examiners, Am. Bd. Pediatrics, Am. Bd. Preventive Medicine in Pub. Health. Chief sch. health Anne Arundel County Health Dept., Annapolis, Md., 1970-71; practice medicine specializing in pediatrics Mpls. Health Dept., 1971-73, dir. MCH, 1973-75, commr. health, 1975-80; chief preventive and pub. health Coastal Region of Los Angeles County Dept. Health Services, 1980-81; chief pub. health West Area Los Angeles County Dept. Health Services, 1981-85; acting med. dir. pub. health Los Angeles County Dept. Health, 1986-87, med. dir. pub. health, 1987-93; med. dir. Coastal Cluster Health Ctrs. L.A. County Dept. Pub. Health Svcs., 1993-96, CEO, med. dir., 1996—; adj. prof. UCLA Sch. Pub. Health, 1981—; adminstr. vis. nurses service, Mpls., 1975-80. Fellow Am. Coll. Preventive Medicine, Am. Acad. Pediatrics; mem. So. Calif. Pub. Health Assn. (pres. 1985-86), Minn. Pub. Health Assn. (pres. 1978-79), Am. Pub. Health Assn., Calif. Conf. Local Health Officers (pres. 1990-91), Delta Omega. Office: Comprehensive Health Ctr 1333 Chestnut Ave Long Beach CA 90813-2944

ALLAMONG, BETTY D., academic administrator; b. Morgantown, W.Va., Apr. 8, 1935; d. Lonnie R. and Jessie R. (Hoffman) Davis; m. Joseph K. Allamong, Sept. 12, 1954; 1 child, John Bradley. BS, W.Va. U., 1961, MA, 1964, PhD, 1971; student, Inst. for Ednl. Mgmt. Harvard U., 1984. Instr. biology Morgantown High Sch., W.Va., 1961-67; instr. edn. W.Va. U., Morgantown, 1965-67, instr. biology, 1967-72; asst. to full prof. Ball State U., Muncie, Ind., 1972-87, assoc. dean, scis. and humanities, 1981-86, acting dean, scis. and humanities, 1986-87; provost and v.p. acad. affairs Bloomsburg U., Pa., 1987-92; mem. Ind. Corp. for Sci. & Tech., 1983-87. Coauthor: Energy for Life, 1976; author numerous lab. manuals; contbr. articles to profl.jours. Mem. Ind. Corp. Sci. & Tech., 1983-87. Recipient Women of Achievement edn. award Women in Comms. Inc., Muncie, 1981. Mem. Muncie-Del. County C. of C. (various coms.), AAAS, NSF (rev. Panel), Am. Soc. Plant Physiologists (midwest div.), Ind. Coll. Biology Tchrs. Assn., Sigma Xi; fellow Ind. Acad. Sci. Home: PO Box 577 Dellslow WV 26531-0577

ALLARD, LINDA MARIE, fashion designer; b. Akron, Ohio, May 27, 1940; d. Carroll Preston and Zella Viola (Indoe) A. BFA, Kent State U., 1962, LHD (hon.), 1992. Designer Ellen Tracy, N.Y.C., 1962—; design critic Fashion Inst. Tech., N.Y.C.; vis. prof. Internat. Acad. Merchandising and Design, Chgo. Author: Absolutely Delicious cookbook, 1994. Bd. dirs. N. Y. adv. bd. Kent State U.; bd. dirs. Kent State U. Found. Bd. Recipient Dallas Fashion award Dallas Apparel Mart, 1986, 87, 94. Mem. Fashion Group Internat., Inc. (past bd. dirs.), Coun. Fashion Designers Am. Office: Ellen Tracy 575 7th Ave New York NY 10018-1805

ALLBRIGHT, KARAN ELIZABETH, psychologist, consultant; b. Oklahoma City, Okla., Jan. 28, 1948; d. Jack Gahnal and Irma Lolene (Keesee) A. BA, Oklahoma City U., 1970, MAT, 1972; PhD, U. So. Miss., 1981. Cert. sch. psychologist, psychometrist; lic. psychologist, Okla., Ark. Psychol. technician Donald J. Bertoch, Ph.D., Oklahoma City, 1973-76; asst. adminstr. Parents' Assistance Ctr., Oklahoma City, 1976-77; psychology intern Burwell Psycho-ednl. Ctr., Carrollton, Ga., 1980-81; staff psychologist Griffin Area Psychoednl. Ctr., Ga., 1981-85; clinic dir. Sequoyah County Guidance Clinic, Sallisaw, Okla., 1985-88; psychologist Baker Psychiatric Clinic, Ft. Smith, Ark., 1988-90; cons. Harbor View Mercy Hosp., 1988-90, Columbia Med. Ctr., 1992—; pvt. practice, Oklahoma City, 1990—; lectr. various orgns.; bd. dirs. workshops. Mem. Task Force to Prevent Child Abuse, Fayette County, Ga., 1984-85, Task Force on Family Violence, Spalding County, Ga., 1983-85; cons. Family Alliance (Parents Anonymous) Sequoyah County, Okla., 1985-88; assoc. bd. dirs. Lyric Theatre. Named Outstanding Young Women in Am., 1980. Mem. APA, Southeastern Psychol. Assn., Nat. Assn. Sch. Psychologists (cert. sch. psychologist), Okla. Psychol. Assn., Play Therapy Assn., Nat. Assn. Health Svc. Providers in Psychology, Psi Chi, Delta Zeta (chpt. dir. 1970-72). Democrat. Presbyterian. Home: 3941 NW 44th St Oklahoma City OK 73112-2517 Office: Northwest Mental Health Assocs 3832 N Meridian Ave Oklahoma City OK 73112-2820

ALLEBACA, ANNA MARIE HERZFELD, small business owner; b. Galveston, Tex., Feb. 23, 1949; d. Heinerich Frederich Ernest and Anna Augusta (Schmidt) Herzfeld; m. William Craig Allebach; 1 child, Merry Anna. BS, U. Houston, 1973; MLS, Sam Houston State U., 1978, MA, 1993. Math tchr. Spring Forest Mid. Sch., Houston, 1973-78; libr. Thornwood Elem. Sch. Spring Branch Ind. Sch. Dist., Houston, 1978-82; libr. Yorkshire Acad., Houston, 1985-86; libr. Frostwood Elem. Sch. Spring Branch Ind. Sch. Dist., Houston, 1989-91; owner Cargill's Custom Ltd., Houston, 1984-96. Mem. Girl Scouts U.S., Houston, 1988-92, North Houston, Greenspoint C. of C., 1995-96, Westwick Homeowners Assn., Houston, 1993-96. Mem. NOW, Document Mgmt. Industries Assn., Advt. Specialties Inst., AAUW. Methodist. Office: Cargills Custom Ltd 1737 Stebbins # 230 Houston TX 77043-2830

ALLEMAN, ROMONA ANN, cable company administrator; b. Rayne, La., Feb. 24, 1958; d. Leo Jr. and Mae Belle (Fields) A. BA in Broadcast Prodn./Polit. Sci., U. Southwestern La., 1993. Lic. cosmetologist, La.; registered radio telephone operator, FCC. Tech. advisor, mktg. coord. Frank Fuhrer Internat., Coraopolis, Pa., 1985-89; dir. edn. RSK of Tex., Dallas, 1989-90; spl. orders adminstr. Neiman Marcus, Dallas, 1990-91; master control administr. Acadiana Open Channel, Lafayette, La., 1991-92, KLFY TV 10, Lafayette, La., 1992-93; prodr., prodn. mgr. Calbetime, Lafayette, La., 1993—. Prodn. grip WFAA-TV/ABC affiliate Rep. Nat. Conv., Houston, 1992, Inauguration of Pres. Clinton, 1993. Bd. dirs., pres. Acadiana Open Channel, 1996-97; chmn. mem. com. La. Icegators Booster Club, 1996-97. Recipient scholarship The Washington Ctr., 1992. Mem. Acadiana Open Channel (vol. chair 1994-95, bd. dirs. 1995—, Prodr. Best Series 1994, Prodr. Best Entertainment Program 1994), ABWA (Bus. Assn. of Yr. 1996), U. Southwestern La. Alumni Assn. Republican. Home: 2358 Mire Hwy Rayne LA 70578

ALLEMANN, SABINA, ballet dancer; b. Bern, Switzerland. Student, Nat. Ballet Sch., Toronto, Ont., Can., 1971-80. With Nat. Ballet Can., 1980-89, 2d soloist, 1982-84, 1st soloist, 1984-88, prin. dancer, 1988-89; prin. guest artist San Francisco Ballet Co., 1988-89, prin. dancer, 1989—; Performed in Toronto's Internat. Festival, 1984; in Reykjavik Arts Festival, Iceland, 1990. Repertoire includes (with San Francisco Ballet) The Sleeping Beauty, Swan Lake, Con Brio, Valses Poeticos, Menuetto, Reflections of Saint Joan, Handel -- A Celebration, Le Quattro Stagioni, Forevermore, La pavane Rouge, Tagore, Dark Elegies, Filling Station, La fille mal gardée, Job, The End, Nutcracker, Rodeo, Serenade, Symphony in C, Glinka Pas de Trois, The Four Temperaments, Who Cares?, Pulcinella, Seeing Stars, Connotations; (with other companies) Napoli, Symphony in C, The Four Temperaments, Serenade, La Bayadere, Act II, Alice, The Merry Widow, Les Sylphides, La Ronde; appeared in film Onegin, 1986. Office: San Francisco Ballet 455 Franklin St San Francisco CA 94102-4438*

ALLEN, ALICE, communications, public relations and marketing executive; b. N.Y.C., May 31, 1943; d. C. Edmonds and Helen (McCreery) A.; 1 child, Helen. Student, Conn. Coll., 1961. Sr. v.p. Alice Allen, Inc., N.Y.C., 1970-83, Robert Marston, N.Y.C., 1983-84, Cunningham & Walsh, N.Y.C., 1984-86, Carl Byoir (acquired by Hill & Knowlton), N.Y.C., 1986, Hill & Knowlton, N.Y.C., 1986-88; pres., owner Allen Comms. Group, Inc., N.Y.C., 1988-95, Alice Allen Comms, 1995—. Bd. dirs. Family Dynamics, N.Y.C., 1976-78, Veritas, 1980-85; v.p. Junior League, N.Y.C., 1975-76; mem. adv. bd. Enterprise Found., 1992—; mem. Women's Media Group. Mem. Women in in Comms., Assn. Book Travelers, Pub. Rels. Soc. Am., Pub. Publicity Assn. (pres. 1969-71). Office: Alice Allen Comms 320 E 72 New York NY 10021

ALLEN, ALICE CATHERINE TOWSLEY, public relations professional, writer, consultant; b. N.Y.C., July 26, 1924; d. George Everett and Alice Sophia (Kunkeli) Goldsmith; m. Harold Dulmage Towsley, Jan. 4, 1940 (div. 1942); m. Charles Kissam Allen, Jan. 20, 1973. Student, U. Hawaii, 1941-42. Writer Honolulu Advertiser, 1942-47; advt. mgr. Paterson Morning Call, Paterson, N.J., 1949-52; publ. cons. N.Y. (N.Y.C.) Herald Tribune, 1953; assoc. editor Mayfair, Travel, Fashion mags., N.Y.C., 1953-54; pub. editor Assoc. Jr. Leagues, Inc., N.Y.C., 1954-59; editor, asst. pub. Doctor's Wife mag., N.Y.C., 1959-65; pub. relations dir., editor Am. Field Svc. Internat., N.Y.C., 1967-72; free-lance writer, pub. cons. N.Y.C., 1973—. Recipient award for outstanding copy promotion Blood Bank Hawaii, 1944, Golden Poet award World of Poetry, 1989, Editor's Choice award for Outstanding Achievement, Nat. Libr. of Poetry, 1994. Mem. Overseas Press Club Am., ASCAP. Republican. Home and Office: 325 E 41st St New York NY 10017-5955

ALLEN, BARBARA, state legislator. Atty.; mem. Kans. Ho. of Reps. Republican. Home: 8136 Rosewood Dr Prairie Village KS 66208-5008 Office: Kansas House of Representatives State Capitol Topeka KS 66612*

ALLEN, BEATRICE, music educator, pianist; b. N.Y.C., June 30, 1917; d. Samuel and Rose (Krell) Hyman; m. Eugene Murray Allen, Jan. 23, 1937; children: Marlene Allen Galzin, Julian Lewis. Student NYU, 1933-36; diploma (scholar), Inst. Musical Arts, N.Y.C., 1939, postgrad. (scholar), 1939-40; diploma (fellow, letter commendation), Juilliard Grad. Sch., N.Y.C., 1943; BA magna cum laude Cedar Crest Coll., 1980. Mem. faculty prep. div. Juilliard Sch. Music, 1957-69, Moravian Coll., 1967-68, Northampton County Area Community Coll., 1968-70, Manhattan Sch. Music, 1969-89; mem. founding faculty Community Music Sch., Allentown, Pa., 1982—; artist-in-residence, condr. Tchrs. Workshop, Antioch Coll., Yellow Springs, Ohio, 1966; Bach lectr., recitals various univs.; concert appearances Town Hall, N.Y.C., Chautauqua, N.Y., others. Winner N.J. Artists contest, 1936. Mem. Music Tchrs. Nat. Assn. (program chmn. Lehigh Valley chpt. 1981-82), Pa. Music Tchrs. Assn. Address: 2100 Main St Bethlehem PA 18017-3752

ALLEN, BELLE, management consulting firm executive, communications company executive; b. Chgo.; d. Isaac and Clara (Friedman) A. Student, U. Chgo. Cert. conf. mgr. Internat. Inst. Conf. Planning and Mgmt., 1989. Report, spl. correspondent The Leader Newspapers, Chgo., Washington, 1960-64; Cons., v.p., treas., dir. William Karp Cons. Co. Inc., Chgo., 1961-79, chmn. bd., pres., treas., 1979—; pres. Belle Allen Comms., Chgo., 1961—; nat. corr. CCA Press, 1990—; v.p., treas., bd. dirs. Cultural Arts Survey Inc., Chgo., 1965-79; cons., bd. dirs. Am. Diversified Rsch. Corp., Chgo., 1967-70; v.p., sec., bd. dirs. Mgmt. Performance Systems Inc., 1976-77; cons. City Club Chgo., 1962-65, Ill. Commn. on Tech. Progress, 1965-67; mem. Ill. Gov.'s Grievance Panel for State Employees, 1979—; mem. grievance panel Ill. Dept. Transp., 1985—; mem. adv. governing bd. Ill. Coalition on Employment of Women, 1980-88; spl. program advisor President's Project Partnership, 1980-88; mem. consumer adv. coun. FRS, 1979-82; reporter CCA Press Svc., 1990—; panel mem. Free Press vs. Fair Trial Nat. Ctr. Freedom of Info. Studies Loyola U. Law Sch., 1993, mem. planning com. Freedom of Info. awards, 1993; conf. chair The Swedish Inst. Press Ethics: How to Handle, 1993. Editor: Operations Research and the Management of Mental Health Systems, 1968; contbr. articles to profl. jours. Mem. campaign staff Adlai E. Stevenson II, 1952, 56, John F. Kennedy, 1960; founding mem. women's bd. United Cerebral Palsy Assn., Chgo., 1954, bd. dirs., 1954-58; pres. Dem. Fedn. Ill., 1958-61; pres. conf. staff Eleanor Roosevelt, 1960; mem. Welfare Pub. Rels. Forum, 1960-61; bd. dirs., mem. exec. com., chmn. pub. rels. com. Regional Ballet Ensemble, Chgo., 1961-63; bd. dirs. Soc. Chgo. Strings, 1963-64; mem. Ind. Dem. Coalition, 1968-69; bd. dirs. Citizens for Polit. Change, 1969; campaign mgr. aldermanic election 42d ward Chgo. City Coun., 1969; mem. selection com. Robert Aragon Scholarship, 1991; planning com. mem. Hutchins Era reunion U. Chgo., 1995; mem. reunion planning com. U. Chgo., 1995. Recipient Outstanding Svc. award United Cerebral Palsy Assn., Chgo., 1954, 55, Chgo. Lighthouse for Blind, 1986, Spl. Comms. award The White House, 1961, cert. of appreciation Ill. Dept. Human Rights, 1985, Internat. Assn. Ofcl. Human Rights Agys., 1985; selected as reference source Am. Bicentennial Rsch. Inst. Libr. Human Resources, 1973; named Hon. Citizen, City of Alexandria, Va., 1985. Mem. AAAS, NOW, AAAU, Affirmative Action Assn. (bd. dirs. 1981-85, chmn. mem. and programs com. 1981-85, pres. 1983—), Fashion Group (bd. dirs. 1981-83, chmn. Restrospective View of an Hist. Decade 1960-70, editor The Bull. 1981), Indsl. Rels. Rsch. Assn. (bd. dirs., chmn. pers. placement com. 1960-61), Sarah Siddons Soc., Soc. Pers. Adminstrs., Women's Equity Action League, Nat. Assn. Inter-Group Rels. Ofcls. (nat. conf. program 1959), Publicity Club Chgo. (chmn. inter-city rels. com. 1960-61, Disting. Svc. award 1968), Ill. C. of C. (cmty. rels. com., alt. mem. labor rels. com. 1971-74), Chgo. C. of C. and Industry (merit employment com. 1961-63), Internat. Press Club Chgo. (charter 1992—, bd. dirs. 1992—), Chgo. Press Club (chmn. women's activities 1969-71), U. Chgo. Club of Met. Chgo. (program com. 1993—, chair summer quarter programs 1994), Soc. Profl. Journalists (Chgo. Headline Club 1992—, regional conf. planning com. 1993, co-chair Peter Lisagor awards 1993, program com. 1992—). Office: 111 E Chestnut St Ste # 36G Chicago IL 60611-2051

ALLEN, BETTY (MRS. RITTEN EDWARD LEE, III), mezzo-soprano; b. Campbell, Ohio, Mar. 17, 1930; d. James Corr and Dora Catherine (Mitchell) A.; m. Ritten Edward Lee, III, Oct. 17, 1953; children: Anthony Edward, Juliana Catherine. Student, Wilberforce U., 1944-46; certificate, Hartford Sch. Music, 1953; pupil voice, Sarah Peck More, Zinka Milanov, Paul Ulanowsky, Carolina Segrera Holden; LHD (hon.), Wittenberg U., 1971; MusD (hon.), Union Coll., 1981; DFA (hon.), Adelphi U., 1990, Bklyn. Coll., 1991; LittD (hon.), Clark U., 1993; MusD (hon.), New Sch. Social Rsch., 1994. Faculty Phila. Mus. Acad., 1979, Manhattan Sch. Music, 1971, N.C. Sch. Arts, 1978-87; now faculty Harlem Sch. Arts; tchr. master classes Inst. Teatro Colon, 1985-86, Curtis Inst. Music, 1987—; exec. dir. Harlem Sch. Arts, 1979, now pres.; vis. faculty Sibelius Akademie, Helsinki, Finland, 1976; mem. adv. bd. music panel Amherst Coll.; mem. music panel N.Y. State Council of the Arts, Dept. State Office Cultural Presentations, Nat. Endowment Arts.; bd. dirs. Arts Alliance, Karl Weigl Found., Diller-Quaile Sch. Music, U.S. Com. for UNICEF, Manhattan Sch. Music, Theatre Devel. Fund, Children's Storefront; mem. adv. bd. Bloomingdale House of Music; bd. vis. artists Boston U.; bd. dirs., mem. exec. com. Carnegie Hall, Nat. Found. for Advancement in the Arts; bd. dirs. Chamber Music Soc. of Lincoln Ctr., N.Y.C. Housing Authority Orch., Independent Sch. Orch., N.Y.C. Opera CO., Joy in Singing, Arts & Bus. Coun.; mem. Mayor's adv. commn. Cultural Affairs. Appeared as soloist: Leonard Bernstein's Jeremiah Symphony, Tanglewood, 1951, Virgil Thomson's Four Saints in Three Acts, N.Y.C. and Paris, 1952, N.Y.C. Light Opera Co., 1954; recitalist, also soloist with major symphonies on tours including ANTA-State Dept. tours, Europe, N. Africa, Caribbean, Can., U.S., S.Am., Far East, 1954-, S.Am. tour, 1968, Bellas Artes Opera, Mexico City, 1970; recital debut, Town Hall, N.Y.C., 1958, ofcl. debuts, London, Berlin, 1958, formal opera debut, Teatro Colon, Buenos Aires, Argentina, 1964; U.S. opera debut San Francisco Opera, 1966; N.Y.C. opera debut, 1973, Mini-Met. debut, 1973; Broadway debut in Treemonisha, 1975; opened new civic theaters in San Jose, Calif., and Regina, Sask., Can., concert hall, Lyndon Baines Johnson Library, Austin, Tex., 1971; artist-in-residence, Phila. Opera Co.; appeared with Caramoor Music Festival, summer 1965, 71, Cin. May Festival, 1972, Santa Fe Opera, 1972, 75, Canadian Opera Co., Winnipeg, Man., 1972, 77, Washington Opera Co., 1971, Tanglewood Festival, 1951, 52, 53, 67, 74, Oslo, The Hague, Montreal, Kansas City, Houston and Santa Fe operas, 1975, Saratoga Festival, 1975, Casals Festival, 1967, 68, 69, 76, Helsinki Festival, 1976, Marlboro Festival, 1967-74, numerous radio and TV performances, U.S., Can., Mex., Eng., Germany, Scandinavia; rec. artist, London, Vox, Capitol, Odeon-Pathe, Decca, Deutsche Grammophon, Columbia Records, RCA Victor records; represented U.S. in Cultural Olympics, Mexico City, 1968. Recipient Marian Anderson award, 1953-54, Nat. Music League Mgmt. award, 1953, 52 St Am. Festival Duke Ellington Meml. award, 1989, Bowery award Bowery Bank, 1989, Harlem Sch. of the Arts award Harlem Sch. and Isaac Stern, 1990, Womans Day Celebration award St. Thomas Episcopal Ch., 1990, St. Thomas Ch. award St. Thomas Catholic Ch., 1990, Men's Day Celebration award St. Paul's Ch., 1990, Martell House of Segram award Avery Fisher Hall, 1990; named Best Singer of Season Critics' Circle, Argentina and Chile, 1959, Best Singer of Season Critics' Circle, Uruguay, 1961; Martha Baird Rockefeller Aid to Music grantee, 1953, 58; John Hay Whitney fellow, 1953-54; Ford Found. concert soloist grantee, 1963-64. Mem. NAACP, Urban League, Hartford Mus. Club (life), Am. Guild Mus. Artists, Actors Equity, AFTRA, Silvermine Guild Artists, Jeunesses Musicales, Gioventu Musicale, Student Sangverein Trondheim, Unitarian-Universalist Women's Fedn., Nat. Negro Musicians Assn. (life), Concert Artists Guild,Met. Opera Guild, Amherst Glee Club (hon. life), Union Coll. Glee Club (hon. life), Met. Mus. Art, Mus. Modern Art, Am. Mus. Natural History, Century Assn., Sigma Alpha Iota (hon.). Unitarian-Universalist. Clubs: Cosmopolitan, Second. Office: Harlem Sch of Arts 645 Saint Nicholas Ave New York NY 10030-1001*

ALLEN, BRENDA JOYCE, management consultant, editor in chief; b. Detroit, June 10, 1950; d. William Howard and Ottie Fay (Mills) A.; m. Robert Edward Arthur Lightbourne, Mar. 2 (div. Jan., 1980); 1 child, Shonja Diane; m. Thomas M. Kyle, May 19, 1984; children: Portia Lynne Allen Kyle, Tomantha Mercedes Allen Kyle. AB in Math., U. Calif., 1976; MS in Engring., George Washington U., D.C., 1981. Cert. profl. logistician, Soc. Logistics Engrs. Sci. data analyst Lawrence Berkeley Lab., Berkeley, Calif., 1972-76; lectr. Howard U., Washington, 1977-78; sr. fellow Logistics Mgmt. Inst., Washington; sr. logistics engr., sr. systems analyst TASC, Reading, Mass., 1983-85; program logistics enrg. ITT Defense Comm. Divsn., Nutley, N.J., 1985-87; adj. prof. Bergen C.C., Paramus, N.J., 1989-94; sr. cons. AT&T GIS, Warren, N.J., 1984-85, NCR, Warren, N.J., 1985—; cons. UN, World Bank, AT&T, Bankers Trust, Washington and N.Y.C., 1983—. Editor in chief Global Digest mag., 1995—. Sec., bd. dirs., exec. Teaneck (N.J.) Jr. Soccer League, 1995—; mem. exec. bd. Working Parents Assn., Teaneck, 1995-96; mem. exec. bd. Gifted and Talented Parents, Teaneck, 1995—. Mem. Calif. Scholarship Fedn., (life), N. Jersey Soc. Logistics Engrs., Nat. Assn. Self Employed, Delta Sigma Theta (local chpt. treas. 1972—, Montgomery County alumni treas. 1977-78, Golden Life 1975). Home: 585 Ramapo Rd Teaneck NJ 07666 Office: BJ Assocs PO Box 222 Teaneck NJ 07666

ALLEN, BRENDA KAYE, guidance counselor; b. Waxahachie, Tex., June 24, 1968; d. Archie Lynn and Patsy Ruth (Harper) Heard; m. Robert Edward Allen; 1 child: Paige Whitney. AS, Navarro Coll., 1988; BS, Lamar U., 1990. Cert. secondary tchr., Tex. Tchr., coach Grand Prarie Sch Dist., 1991-93; tchr. Ennis (Tex.) Sch. Dist., 1993-95, guidance counselor, 1995—. Mem. Am. Counseling Assn., Am. Sch. Counselor Assn., Assn. of Tex. Profl. Educators. Office: Ennis High Sch 1405 Lake Bardwell Ennis TX 75119

ALLEN, CAROL LINNEA OSTROM, art educator; b. Phila., Apr. 23, 1936; d. Gustaf Adolph Ostrom and Anne Marie (Scheib) Heckman; m. David Wilford Allen Sr., Mar. 8, 1932; children: Jonathan Ostrom, David Wilford. BS in Art Edn. with honors, Kutztown U., 1958; MA in Art Edn., U. of the Arts, 1991. Cert. tchr., supr. art, English. Jr. H.S. art tchr. West York (Pa.) Sch. Dist., 1958-60; elem. art supr. Colonial Sch. Dist., Plymouth Meeting, Pa., 1960-62; substitute tchr., art tchr., English tchr. Phoenixville (Pa.) Area Sch. Dist., 1968—, art dept. head, yearbook advisor, 1991—, mem. strategic planning com., 1992-94; presenter at state and nat. art confs., 1986—. Exhibited in group shows at Nat. Art Edn. Assn. Electronic Gallery, 1989, 95. Mem. LWV, Valley Forge, 1992—. Mem. AAUW, NOW, Nat. Art Edn. Assn., Pa. Art Edn. Assn., Phoenixville Area Edn. Assn. (polit. action com. for edn. chair 1992—). Office: Phoenixville Area Sch Dist 1120 Gay St Phoenixville PA 19460-4417

ALLEN, CATHERINE ANN, management consultant; b. Hannibal, Mo., June 21, 1946; d. Robert E. and Catherine (Sullivan) A.; m. Gary L. Johansen, Nov. 21, 1980. BS, U. Mo., 1968; MS, U. Md., 1975; postgrad., George Washington U., 1979-84. Retail mgr. Highees, Cleve., 1968-70, Woodward and Lothrop, Washington, 1970-71; instr. bus. adminstrn. Marymount Coll., Arlington, Va., 1971-73; instr. Mt. Vernon H.S., Alexandria, Va., 1973-74; asst. prof., dept. chair Mt. Vernon Coll., Washington, 1974-78; instr. bus. adminstrn. George Washington U., Washington, 1978-80; asst. prof. bus. adminstrn. Am. U., Washington, 1980-85; asst. v.p., mktg. Donnelley Dir./Dun and Bradstreet, N.Y.C., 1985-87; asst. v.p., dir. planning Dun and Bradstreet, N.Y.C., 1987-88; v.p. mktg. bus devel. Citibank NA, N.Y.C., 1988-96; pres., CEO The Santa Fe Group, 1996—; chair, bd. dirs. The Smart Card Forum, Tampa. Co-author: Smart Cards: Strategies and Benefits, 1996, The Artists Way for Business, 1996; contbr. articles to profl. jours. Active Emilys List. Mem. Info. Industry Assn. (bd. dirs. 1985-89), Am. Mktg. Assn. (pres., bd. dirs. 1978-80), Washington Internat. Trade Assn. (bd. dirs., v.p. 1980-85), Electronic Yellow Pages Assn. (pres., bd. dirs. 1986-88), Santa Fe Inst. Bus. Network. Democrat. Home: Rte 3 Box 97 Santa Fe NM 87505

ALLEN, CHERI, legislative staff director; b. Washington, Feb. 14, 1953. BA in Psychology, U. Md., 1983. Program asst. gen. revenue sharing U.S. Dept. Treas., 1972-81; customer svc. rep. City of North Miami Beach, Fla., 1984-87; computer applications asst., statistician Congl. Rsch. Svc., 1987-89; exec. dir. Sen. Rep. Policy Com., 1991—; now dir. info sys. Sec. of Senate. Office: Sec of Senate Capitol Bldg 5208 Washington DC 20510*

ALLEN, CHERYL HAMILTON, software engineer; b. Columbus, Ohio, Oct. 22, 1952; d. Charles William and Doris Louise (Varming) Hamilton; children: Nathaniel, Olivia. BA in Psychology Peace Studies, Manchester Coll., 1974, BS in Computer Sci., 1990. Software engr. Adaptive MicroWare, Ft. Wayne, Ind., 1986-89; sr. software engr. Tokheim, Ft. Wayne, Ind., 1990-92, 95-96, Adaptive MicroWare, Ft. Wayne, Ind., 1992-95; owner Hamilton Allen Computer Solutions, Ft. Wayne, 1994—. Independent.

ALLEN, CYNTHIA LYNN, social services administrator; b. Grundy Center, Iowa, Aug. 2, 1956; d. James Terrill and Pauline Jean (Hanson) Irwin; m. Duane R. Allen, June 26, 1976; children: Lindsey Morgan, Lauren Terrill. BS in Human Svcs., Lindenwood Coll., 1979; MPA, U. Mo., 1996. Youth asst. U. Mo. Extension Svc., St. Charles, 1979; program dir. ARC, Kansas City, 1981-83, exec. dir., 1983—; new mgr. faculty ARC, Des Moines, 1996. Chmn. Leadership 2000, Kansas City, 1987—; bd. dirs. Women's C. of C., Kansas City, 1984-87; pub. support divsn. chair United Way, Kansas City, 1988; pres. Agy. Execs. Coun., Kansas City, 1987. Mem. Nat. Soc. Fund Raising Execs., Greater Kansas City Coun. Philanthropy, Rotary, Phi Alpha Alpha. Office: ARC 1600 Washington Blvd Kansas City KS 66102

ALLEN, DEBORAH COLLEEN, state legislator; b. Denver, Jan. 25, 1950; d. Anton Jr. and Esther Ochs; m. Bob Allen; 1 child, Dallas. Student, Aurora C.C. Jr. acct. Am. TV & Comm.; bus mgr. Deer Trail Pub. Schs., sch. bus driver; data entry clk. United Banking Svcs.; caretaker Evergreen Cemetery; owner, mgr. Custom Data Sys. Specialists, Aurora, 1979—; mem. Colo. Ho. of Reps., 1992—, mem. various coms., 1993—. Former sec., vice chmn., chmn. Arapahoe County Rep. Party; past pres. Aurora Rep. Forum; active Arapahoe County Chmn.'s Cir.; block capt. Am. Cancer Soc., Am. Arthritis Found. Recipient 5 Yr. Award as Leathercraft Instr., 4-H. Mem. Nat. Fedn. Rep. Women, Colo. Fedn. Rep. Women, South Metro C. of C., Colo. Rep. 250 Club, Arapahoe Rep. Men's Club. Republican. Home: 923 S Ouray St Aurora CO 80017-3152 Office: Colo House of Reps 200 E Colfax State Capitol Denver CO 80203*

ALLEN, DIANA D., insurance agent, author; b. Dallas, Nov. 26, 1945; d. William S. and Pearl P. (Sessions) Dandridge; m. Edwin Richard Allen, Dec. 23, 1966; children: Reagan, Ryan. BS, U. Ark., 1967. Tchr. elem. sch. Lincoln/McKinley Sch., Enid, Okla., 1967-72; real estate agent House of Hough Agy., Enid, 1972-75; ins. agent Dick Allen Ins. Co., Inc., Enid, 1990—. Author: Gourmet: The Quick and Easy Way, 1992. Asst. pack master, den leader Boy Scouts Am., Glenwood Sch., Enid, 1981-85; sustaining chmn. Jr. Welfare League, Enid, 1979, 94; head Parent of Okla. Tiger Football Parents Orgn., Columbia, Mo., 1994—; bd. dirs. Arts and Humanities Coun., Enid, 1994—; mem. Rep. Women's Club; tchr. Bible and Sunday Sch.; sponsor Bravettes Pep Club, 1993-95; pres. Enid High Sch. Parent Tchr. Student Assn., 1993-94, parliamentarian, 1994-95. Mem. PEO (pres. 1987-88), DAR, Ladies Shrine (v.p. 1970), Oakwood Ladies Golf Assn. (v.p. 1992-93), Bravettes Pep Club (sponsor 1994—), PTA (pres. 1993-94), Circle Two (nurturing com.), Kappa Alpha Theta (alumni pres. 1969, 85). Presbyterian. Home: 1614 Quailwood Dr Enid OK 73703-2047

ALLEN, DORIS BROWN, principal; b. Redfield, N.Y., Sept. 30, 1921; d. David Richard and Agnes Jane (Aldridge) Brown; m. Edwin Miles Allen, Nov. 2, 1946 (dec.); children: Elisabeth Allen Cody, John David, Phyllis Jane. BE, SUNY, 1942; MA, Columbia U., 1946. Cert. tchr., N.Y. From kindergarten tchr. to 3rd and 4th grade tchr. Whitesboro (N.Y.) Pub. Sch., 1942-46; kindergarten supr. Oswego (N.Y.) Coll., 1946-47; 5th grade tchr. Oswego Pub. Sch., 1957, tchr., 1957-76, prin., 1976—; lectr. in field. Author: Stories & Studies, 1948, 4, 5, 6 Grade Social Studies, 1963; (halloween operetta) Flap, Rattle and Moan, 1980; contbg. editor Day Care and Early Edn., 1976-80. Alderman City of Oswego, 1952-54, planning commn., 1954-57; del. Dem. Nat. Conv., N.Y., 1976, planning com., 1980; active Salt City ofr Performing Arts, 1982—, Oswego Players, 1983—, pres., 1950-52; vol. publicity ARC, Girl Scouts Am. Mem. AAUW (v.p. legis. com., program com.), Ret. Officers Assn. Aux., Womens Dem. Club. Democrat. Roman Catholic. Home: 123 Alanson Rd Syracuse NY 13207

ALLEN, DORIS ILDA (LUCKI ALLEN), psychologist; b. El Paso, Tex., May 9, 1927; d. Richard Minor and Stella May (Davis) A. BS in Phys. Edn., Tuskegee Inst., 1959; MS in Counseling, Ball State U., 1976; PhD in Psychology, Wright Inst., 1986. Tchr. Stone St. H.S., Greenwood, Miss., 1949-50; journalist U.S. Army, 1950-63; interrogator, linguist, analyst U.S. Army, Vietnam, 1963-70; counterintelligence officer U.S. Army, 1971-80; pvt. investigator Bruce Haskett & Assocs., Long Beach, Oakland, Calif., 1980—; psychologist Oakland, 1986—; mem. adv. bd. Vets. Coalition League, San Francisco, 1993—; bd. dirs. 505 Inc., Oakland. Co-author: A Piece of My Heart, 1985. Decorated Bronze Star with 3 oak leaf clusters, Vietnam Cross Gallantry. Mem. VFW, Disabled Am. Vets., Vietnam Vets. Am., Mil. Order Cootie (hosp. chair 1994-96), Elks, Masons, Heroines of Jericho.

ALLEN, DORIS RENSHAW, music educator; b. East McKeesport, Pa., Apr. 6, 1928; d. William Blair and Margaret (Croushore) Renshaw; m. Theo C. Allen (div.); children: Lenore Kennedy, Blair, Scott M. MusB, Westminster Coll., 1950; MS, Goddard Coll., 1970. Instr. Westminster Choir Coll., Princeton, N.J., 1965-75; assoc. prof. U. Oreg., Eugene, 1975—; lectr. in field. Author: Creative Keyboard for Adult Beginner's, 1982, Blue Book - Kids at the Keyboard, 1990; contbr. articles to profl.jours. Ctr. for Study of Women in Soc. grantee, U. Oreg., 1976. Mem. Oreg. Music Tchrs. Assn., Dalcroze Soc. Am., Music Educators Conf. Office: U Oreg Dept Music Eugene OR 97403

ALLEN, DOROTHEA, secondary education educator; b. Rockaway, N.J., Apr. 30, 1919; d. Harrison Engleman and Caroline (Tierney) A. AB, Montclair U., 1941, MA, 1949. Cert. secondary, sci., math. tchr., counselor, supr., prin., N.J. Tchr. sci. and math. Denville (N.J.) Jr. High Sch., 1942-46; tchr. sci. Boonton (N.J.) High Sch., 1946-94, supr. sci. dept., 1978-94; lab. technician Drew Chem. Corp., Boonton, 1942-47; tech. asst. Bell Telecom. Lab., Whippany, N.J., 1956; rsch. scientist Warner Lambert Rsch. Inst., Morris Plains, N.J., 1959-62; tchr. sci. enrichment Boonton Summer Sch., 1963-85; curriculum developer Morris County Vocat.-Tech. Sch., Denville, 1987; conf. program presenter, 1978, 85; project evaluator sci. fairs, N.J., 1970—; program evaluator Mid. States Assn., 1973, 79; facilitator Ptnrs. in Edn. Program; spkr., promoter Media Ctr. Open House; cons., reviewer Am. Biol. Tchr. mag., 1975—; com. mem. Sch. Articulation Program, Boonton Schs., 1991-94; spkr., resource person Career Confs.; media ctr. spkr. Meet the Author; sponsor Student Showcase of Excellence in Sci., 1990-94, faculty sponsor, mentor h.s. students, 1966-94; mentor Alt. Rt. Program Tchrs., N.J. Organizer Am. Dental Health Clinic, Boonton, 1968-72; mem. career com. N.J. divsn. Theobald Smith Soc., 1975-76; fundraiser Am. Hemophilia Found., Rockaway, N.J., 1985—, Am. Heart Assn., 1995—, Muscular Dystrophy Found., 1995—; cons. Cmty. Mid. Sch. Planning Com., Boonton, 1988-90. Recipient Disting. Citizen's award Town of Rockaway, 1984, Gov.'s and Edn. award N.J. Dept. Edn., 1984, Morris County Tchr. of Yr. award, 1990, Presdl. award NSF, 1984, Cert. of Honor State of N.J., 1985, World Lifetime Achievement award, 1994, Internat. Order of Merit, 1994, Spotlight award Boonton Bd. Edn., 1980-86, Tchr. of Yr., 1984, 90, Women's Inner Circle of Achievement award, 1995; named outstanding Biology Tchr. Nat. Assn. Biology Tchrs., 1972, Outstanding Sci. Tchr. Rsch. Assn. N.Am., 1980, 86, Woman of Yr., 1993, 94, 95, Sci. Edn. Hall of Fame, 1994, 95. Mem. NEA, NEA Ret., ASCD, NSTA, Morris County Ret. Educators Assn., Nat. Assn. Secondary Sch. Prins., Assn. Presdl. Award Winners in Sci. Tchg., N.J. Edn. Assn., N.J. Prins. and Suprs. Assn., N.J. Acad. Alliance for Math. and Sci., N.J. Dept. Edn. Exec. Acad., Morris Area Sci. Alliance. Home: 115 Jackson Ave Rockaway NJ 07866-3039

ALLEN, DOTTIE RUTH MITCHELL, artist, educator; b. Corona, Calif., Apr. 11, 1956; d. Albert Vaughan and Lula Maedell (Love) Mitchell; m. Thomas Fancher Sale, Mar. 11, 1989; 1 child from previous marriage, Colin Andrew (dec.). BFA in Photography, North Tex. State U., 1985; MFA in Photography, U. North Tex., 1988. Art program coord. Hill Coll., Hillsboro, Tex., 1989—; artist-in-residence Brookhaven Coll., Dallas, 1991; lectr. infield. Exhibited in group shows at 500X Gallery, Dallas, 1987, North Tex. State U., Denton, 1987; work featured in film Ninth Life, also in various publs.; represented in permanent collections at Tex. Women's U., Denton, U. North Tex., Mus. Fine Arts, Mus. Fine Arts, Houston, also numerous pvt. collections; juror numerous exhbns. Mem. Tex. Assn. Schs. of Art, Emergency Artists Support League, Dallas Artists Rsch. and Exhbn., Phi Kappa Phi. Home: 711 N Dallas Ave Lancaster TX 75146 Office: Hill Coll PO Box 619 Hillsboro TX 76645

ALLEN, ELIZABETH MARESCA, marketing executive; b. Red Bank, N.J., Jan. 4, 1958; d. Paul William Michael and Roberta Gertrude (Abbes) Maresca; m. David D. Allen; 1 son, Brandon D. Student, Brookdale Community Coll., 1976-77; A Bus. Adminstrn., Tidewater C.C., 1988; student, Va. Wesleyan Coll., 1994—. Systems analyst Methods Research Corp., Farmingdale, N.J., 1977-79; div. mgr. Abacus Bus. Svcs., Inc., Virginia Beach, Va., 1979—. Bd. dirs. Arthritis Found., Norfolk, Va., 1986-90; v.p. Charlestowne Civic League, Virginia Beach, 1983-84, Plantation Lakes Homeowners Assn., Chesapeake, Va., 1992—; advisor Commonwealth Coll., Norfolk, 1984-91; del. Va. Rep. Conv., 1993—. Mem. Women's Network Hampton Roads (publicity chmn. 1988-91, chmn. publicity for Job Fair 1989), Hampton Roads C. of C. (com. chmn. 1985, 88), Williamsburg Area C. of C. (exhibit chmn. 1987). Republican. Roman Catholic. Office: Abacus Bus Svcs Inc 5620 Virginia Beach Blvd Virginia Beach VA 23462-5631

ALLEN, FRANCES ELIZABETH, computer scientist; b. Peru, N.Y., Aug. 4, 1932; d. John Abram and Ruth Genevieve (Downs) A. BS, State U. N.Y., Albany, 1954; MA, U. Mich., 1957; DSc (hon.), U. Alta., 1991. Fellow IBM Research Lab., Yorktown Heights, N.Y., 1957—; adj. assoc. prof. N.Y. U., 1970-72; mem. computer sci. adv. bd. NSF, 1972-75, cons., 1975-78; lectr. Chinese Acad. Scis., 1973, 77; IEEE disting. visitor, 1973-74; cons. prof. Stanford U., 1977-78; chancellor's disting. vis. lectr., U. Calif., Berkeley, 1988-89. IBM Corp. fellow, 1989. Fellow IEEE, Am. Acad. Arts and Scis., Assn. Computing Machinery (nat. lectr. 1972-73); mem. NAE, Programming Sys. and Langs. (Paper award 1976). Home: Finney Farm Croton On Hudson NY 10520 Office: IBM Corp PO Box 704 Yorktown Heights NY 10598-0704

ALLEN, FRANCES MICHAEL, publisher; b. Charlotte, N.C., Apr. 7, 1939; d. Thomas Wilcox and Lola Frances (Horne) A.; m. Joseph Taylor Lisenbee, Feb. 24, 1955 (div. 1957); 1 child, Leslie Autice. Abilene (Tex.) Christian Coll., 1954-56, Chico (Calif.) State U., 1957-59. Art dir. B&E Publs., L.A., 1963-65; editor B&E Publs., 1969-70; art dir. Tiburon Corp., Chgo., 1970-75; founder, editor Boxers, Internat., L.A., 1970-76; editor The Hound's Tale, 1974, Saints, Incorp., 1974-76; founder, editor Setters, Incorp., Costa Mesa, Calif., 1975-85; founder, owner Michael Enterprises, Midway City, Calif., 1976—; editor Am. Cocker Rev., Midway City, 1980-81; editor, publisher, ptnr. Am. Cocker Mag., 1981—; editor, co-publisher Sporting Life, 1991. Author: The American Cocker Book, 1989; editor The Sporting Life, 1991—; editor, pub. The Royal Spaniels, 1995— (Dogs Writer's Assn. 1995 winner); illustrator: The First Five Years, 1970, The Aftercare of the Ear, 1975, The Shenn Simplicity Collection, 1976, The Miniature Pinscher, 1967; prin. works include mag. and book covers for USA, most widely published show dog artist world wide, past 20 yrs. Recipient Dog World Award Top Producer, 5 times, 1966-88, numerous 1st awards in art fairs. Mem. Dog Writers Assn. Am. Republican. Mem. Ch. of Christ. Home and Office: 14531 Jefferson St Midway City CA 92655-1030

ALLEN, JANE ADAMS, editor, curator; b. Chgo.. BA, U. Chgo., MFA; student, San Francisco Sch. Fine Arts. Art and photography critic Chgo. Tribune, 1971-73; editor New Art Examiner, 1973-82; art critic Washington Times, 1982-88; cons., curator Sasakawa Peace Found-U.S.A., 1993-94; sr. resident fellow Smithsonian, Washington, 1994-95. Curator collections including Chgo. Civic Ctr., 1969, Sasakawa Peace Found.-U.S.A., Washington, 1994, 95; contbr. articles to profl. jours. Critics fellow NEA, 1975, 80; recipient Art World award Mfrs. Hanover, 1984, 89. Mem. Chgo. New Art Assn. (pres. 1970-82), Coll. Art Assn. Office: 2718 Ontario Rd NW Washington DC 20009*

ALLEN, JANICE FAYE CLEMENT, nursing administrator; b. Norfolk, Nebr., Aug. 19, 1946; d. Allen Edward and Hilda Bernice (Stange) Reeves; m. Roger Allen Clement, Oct. 6, 1968 (dec. July 1974).; m. August H. Allen, Sept. 17, 1988. RN, Meth. Sch. Nursing, Omaha, 1967; BS in Nursing, magna cum laude, Creighton U., 1978; MS in Nursing, U. Nebr., 1981; cert. in nursing adminstrn. With Meth. Hosp., 1967-68, 72-83, asst. head nurse, 1974-77, staff devel. nurse, 1977-81, dir. staff adminstrv. services, 1981-83; pub. health nurse Wichita-Sedgwick County Health Dept., Wichita, Kans., 1970-72; dir. nursing Meth. Med. Ctr., St. Joseph, Mo., 1983-84, Broadlawns Med. Ctr., Des Moines, 1984-93; dir. staff mgmt./infection control Ea. N.Mex. Med. Ctr., Roswell, 1993—; adj. clin. faculty nursing Drake U. Nursing, Des Moines, 1986-93, mem. adv. bd., 1984-93, Cen. Campus Practical Nursing, 1984-93; mem. adv. bd. Des Moines Area Community Coll. Dist., 1987—, Des Moines Area C.C. Nursing Bd., 1987-93, Grandview Coll., 1988-93; bd. dirs. Vis. Nurse Svcs., 1988-93; assoc. Am. Coll. Healthcare Execs. Mem. Am. Nurses Assn., Am. Orgn. Nurse Execs., N.Mex. Nurses Assn. (bd. dirs. 1995), Cen. Iowa Nursing Leadership Conf. (pres. 1985), Colloquium Nursing Leaders Cen. Iowa, Iowa League for Nursing (treas. 1987-89, pres. 1989), Iowa Orgn. Nurse Execs. (treas. 1987, sec. 1989, pres.-elect 1993), Assn. Infection Control and Epidemiology, Sigma Theta Tau (pres. Zeta Chi chpt. 1990-92). Democrat. Presbyterian. Avocations: flying, sewing, golf, walking, reading. Home: 3201 Allison Dr Roswell NM 88201-1011 Office: Ea NMex Med Ctr 405 W Country Club Rd Roswell NM 88201-5209

ALLEN, JANICE MANDABACH, interior designer, nurse, office manager, actress, model; b. Evanston, Ill., May 29, 1953; d. Paul John and Claudia Stroman (White) Mandabach; m. George Whitaker Allen, Apr. 26, 1980. Student, Syracuse U., 1971-72; BSN, Tex. Christian U., 1976. Nurse oper. rm., circulating nurse oper. rm. Northwestern Meml. Hosp., Chgo., 1976-78; model and actress Chgo., 1978-86, 94—; nurse, office mgr. George W. Allen, MD, Chgo., 1986—. Mem. Carlton Club, Sand Creek Country Club. Republican. Methodist. Home: 1503 Sand Creek Dr Chesterton IN 46304-9373 Office: George W Allen MD 150 E Huron St Chicago IL 60611-2912

ALLEN, JEANETTE MARIE, reading specialist; b. Ft. Wayne, Ind., June 17, 1963; d. Richard Alan and Romelle Agnes (Mayhood) Durand; m. Mark Vernon Allen, June 10, 1989; 1 child, Jennifer. BA, U. Maine, Farmington, 1985; M of Reading and Learning Disabilities, No. Ariz. U., 1990. Tchr. spl. edn. Parker (Ariz.) Sch. Dist., 1985-90; elem. tchr. spl. edn. Cottonwood (Ariz.)-Oak Creek Schs., 1990-93, reading specialist, 1993-95; elem. spl. edn. tchr. Mancos Sch. Dist., 1995—; presenter workshop in sch. dist. Vol., coach Spl. Olympics, Maine and Ariz., 1984-92. Mem. ASCD, Internat. Reading Assn. (presenter 40th ann. conv.). Home: PO Box 444 Dolores CO 81323 Office: Cottonwood-Oak Creek Sch Dt 1 N Willard St Cottonwood AZ 86326

ALLEN, JOAN, actress; b. Rochelle, Ill., Aug. 20, 1956. Student, Ea. Ill. U., No. Ill. U. Founding mem. Steppenwolf Theatre Co., Chgo.; theater appearances include (debut) And A Nightingale Sang, N.Y.C. (Clarence Derwent award, Drama Desk award, Outer Critics Circle award 1984), Steppenwolf Theatre Co., also Hartford, 1983, The Marriage of Bette and Boo, N.Y. Shakespeare Festival, 1986, Burn This! (Tony awrd for Best Actress 1988) Mark Taper Forum, L.A., also N.Y.C., 1987, The Heidi Chronicles, N.Y.C., 1988, 89; film appearances include Compromising Positions, 1985, Peggy Sue Got Married, 1986, Manhunter, 1986, Tucker: The Man and His Dream, 1988, In Country, 1989, Ethan Frome, 1993, Searching for Bobbie Fischer, 1993, Josh and S.A.M., 1993, Nixon, 1995 (Acad. award nominee for best supporting actress 1996), Mad Love, 1995, The Crucible, 1996, Ice Storm, 1996; TV appearances include miniseries Evergreen, 1985, All My Sons, 1986, Am. Playhouse, PBS, 1987, Robert Frost, Voices and Visions, PBS, 1988, TV film The Room Upstairs, 1987, Without Warning: The James Brady Story, 1991, Say Goodnight, Gracie, PBS. Office: Internat Creative Mgmt care Brian Mann 8942 Wilshire Blvd Beverly Hills CA 90211 also: ICM Agy Inc 8942 Wilkshire Blvd Beverly Hills CA 90211*

ALLEN, JOYCE SMITH, librarian; b. Englewood, N.J., Aug. 1, 1939; d. Harold Willard and Mary Elizabeth Smith; m. Jim Frank Allen, Mar. 1974 (div. 1982); 1 child, Shani Jamilla. BA, Howard U., 1961; MLS, Atlanta U., 1966; cert. in advanced studies, U. Ill., 1974. Reference librarian Howard U., Washington, 1966-73; mgr. libr. Meth. Hosp. Ind., Indpls., 1974-94; libr. Aenon Bible Coll., Indpls., 1994—, Rowland Design Inc., 1995—; instr. Ind. Vocat. Tech. Coll., 1979, 85, Med. Library Assn., 1982—, Martin Ctr. Coll., Indpls., 1983-84. Author career materials. Vol. Indpls. Police Dept. Libr., 1977, Children's Mus., Indpls., 1987-88. Recipient Minority Bus. and Profl. Achiever award Ctr. for Leadership Devel., Indpls., 1981, Central Ind. Area Libr. Svcs. Authority cert. of Excellence, 1990. Mem. ALA, Internat. Tng. In Comm., Ch. and Synagogue Libr. Assn. (pres. 1992-93, 95-96), Med. Libr. Assn., Coun. on Libr. Technicians, Spl. Librs. Assn., Indpls. Interdenominational Ch. Users' Assn. Democrat. Home: 3815 N Bolton Ave Indianapolis IN 46226-4826 Office: Aenon Bible Coll 3939 Meadows Dr Indianapolis IN 46205-3113 also: Rowland Design Inc 701 E New York St Indianapolis IN 46202

ALLEN, KAREN ALFSTAD, management consultant; b. Wichita, Kans., Nov. 21, 1942; d. Harold Daniel and Myrtle (Creach) Keefer; m. Richard Allen, Dec. 16, 1962 (dec. 1994). AS, Oreg. Inst. of Tech., L.A., 1964; AA, Pasadena City, 1973; BS, Calif. State U., Pasadena City, 1974. Administra. asst. Transamerica, Los Angeles, 1974-75; v.p. Calif. Fed., Los Angeles, 1975-86; mgmt. cons. Coopers & Lybrand, Los Angeles, 1986-90; mgr. large accounts J.D. Edwards, Denver, 1990-92; v.p. Insecon Computer Sys., Encino, Calif., 1992-95; project dir. SHL Systemhouse, Cerritos, Calif., 1995—. Bd. dirs. Polit. Action Com. Calif. Fed., L.A., 1984-86, Arcadia Arts Coun., 1993—; vol. Youth Motivation Task Force, L.A., 1982-86. Recipient Honors Calif. State U., Los Angeles, 1974. Mem. Nat. Trust for Historic Preservation, Internat. Facility Mgmt., So. Calif. Emergency Assn., NAFE, NOW, U. Club L.A. Democrat. Home: 1632 Hyland Ave Arcadia CA 91006-1810 Office: SHL Systemhouse 12720 Center Ct Dr Cerritos CA 90852

ALLEN, KAREN JANE, actress; b. Carrollton, Ill., Oct. 5, 1951; d. Carroll Thompson and Patricia (Howell) A. Student, George Washington U., 1974-76. Mem. Washington Theatre Lab., 1973-77. Appeared in films The Whidjit-Maker, 1977, National Lampoon's Animal House, 1978, The Wanderers, 1979, Manhattan, 1979, A Small Circle of Friends, 1979, Cruising, 1979, Raiders of the Lost Ark, 1981, Shoot The Moon, 1981, Split Image, 1981, Strange Invaders, 1983, Until September, 1984, Starman, 1984, The End of the Line, 1986, The Glass Menagerie, 1987, Backfire, 1987, Scrooged, 1988, Animal Behavior, 1989, Sweet Talker, 1991, Malcolm X, 1992, Secret Places of the Heart, Confidence, Exile, The Sandlot, 1993, King of the Hill, 1993, Ghost in the Machine, 1994; TV films Lovey: A Circle of Children, Part II, 1978, East of Eden, 1980, Secret Weapon, 1990, Challenge, 1990, Rapture, 1993, Voyage, 1993; TV series Knots Landing, 1979, The Road Home, 1994; Broadway debut as Helen Keller in Monday After the Miracle, 1982; other stage appearances include Two For the Seesaw, 1981, Monday After The Miracle, Actors Studio (N.Y.C.), Kennedy Ctr. (Washington), (Theatre World award 1983), Tennessee Williams: A Celebration, Williamstown Theatre Festival, 1982, Extremities, West Side Arts Theatre, N.Y.C., 1983, The Glass Menagerie, Williamstown Theatre Festival, 1985, Longwharf Theatre, New Haven, Ct., 1986, The Miracle Worker, Roundabout Theatre, N.Y.C., 1987, Beautiful Bodies, The Whole Theatre, 1987, As You Like It, Mount Theatre, 1988, The Country Girl, Roundabout Theatre, N.Y.C., 1990-91. Mem. Screen Actors Guild, Actor's Equity Assn. Office: The Gersh Agy 232 N Canon Dr Beverly Hills CA 90210-5302*

ALLEN, KATHERINE SPICER, writer, former chemist; b. Plainfield, N.J., Apr. 29, 1919; d. Arthur Joseph and Linda Varner (Morrison) Spicer; m. Carl Holley Allen, Sept. 24, 1943; children: Carl Holley, Jr., David Randolph, Katherine Allen Fehn, Linda Ruth Allen Taylor. BA, U. Del., 1942. Libr. asst. State Libr., Dover, Del., summers 1936-41; typist U. Del., Newark, 1940-42; chemist Esso Rsch. Divsn., Bayway and Elizabeth, N.J., 1942-46; analyst Azoplate Corp., Murray Hill, N.J., 1963-67; enumerator U.S. Census Bur., Somerset County, N.J., 1980, 90; contbg. writer Bernardsville (N.J.) News, 1982—. Co-author: A History of the Presbyterian Church of Liberty Corner, 1837-1937, 1987, (booklet) Christian Education Goals and Objectives, 1991 (with others) Past and Present Lives of New Jersey Women, 1990. Mem. Bernards Twp. Local Assistance Bd., 1972—, sec., 1974-89, chmn., 1990; mem. Bernards Twp. Mcpl. Alliance, 1992—; mem. Somerset County Rep. Com., 1972-93; mem. personnel com. Mcpls. Com. Bernards Twp., 1990-93, mem. comm. com. am. Cancer Soc., 1990-94, vol. Reach to Recovery, 1985—, Somerset County coord. programs, 1987-89; ordained elder Presbyn. Ch. U.S.A., 1980; mem. justice for women com. Elizabeth Presbytery, 1988—, mem. comm. com., 1992—, commr. to Synod of N.E., 1991, 92-93, mem. media com. 1988-90, mem. nominating com. 1987-92, vice chairperson 1990-92, mem. search com. for assoc. exec. 1993; pres. Liberty Corner Presbyn. Ch. Women's Assn., 1973, 74, 84, ch. sch. tchr., 1952-81, ruling elder, 1980-82; mission chair United Presbyn. Ch., Plainfield; dir. Ch. Women United Somerset County, 1979-81; state chmn. Ecumenical Action, 1982-83. Named Somerset County Reach to Recovery Vol. of Yr., Am. Cancer Soc., 1991; recipient svc. pins. Mem. N.J. Press Women (various awards for articles written in Bernardsville News), AAUW, Bernard Twp. Mcpl. Alliance. Home: 218 Lurline Dr Basking Ridge NJ 07920-2624

ALLEN, KATHY S., physical therapist; b. Bartlesville, Okla., Oct. 10, 1969; d. George Nathan Keyser and Doris Ann Morrison; m. Andrew H. Allen, May 9, 1992. BBA, U. Ctrl. Okla., 1991; BS, U. Okla., 1994. Patient questionnaire coord. Bapt. Med. Ctr., Okla. City, 1991-92; physical therapist St. Anthony Hosp., Okla. City, 1994-95, Contract Therapy Svcs., Inc., Okla. City, 1995—. Mem. Am. Physical Therapy Assn.

ALLEN, LEATRICE DELORICE, psychologist; b. Chgo., July 15, 1948; d. Burt and Mildred Floy (Taylor) Hawkins; m. Allen Moore, Jr., July 30, 1965 (div. Oct. 1975); children: Chandra, Valarie, Allen; m. Armstead Allen, May 11, 1978 (div. May 1987). AA in Bus. Edn., Olive Harvey Coll., Chgo., 1975; BA in Psychology cum laude, Chgo. State U., 1977; M.Clin. Psychology, Roosevelt U., 1980; MA in Health Care Adminstrn., Coll. St. Francis, Joliet, Ill., 1993. Clk., U.S. Post Office, Chgo., 1967-72; clin. therapist Bobby Wright Mental Health Ctr., Chgo., 1979-80; clin. therapist Community Mental Health Council, Chgo., 1980-83, assoc. dir., 1983—; cons. Edgewater Mental Health, Chgo., 1984—, Project Pride, Chgo., 1985—; victim services coordinator Community Mental Health Council, Chgo., 1986-87; mgr. youth family services Mile Square Health Ctr., Chgo., 1987-88; coord. Evang. Health Systems, Oakbrook, Ill., 1988-93; adminstr. Human Enrichment Devel. Assn., Hazel Crest, Ill., 1993-96; dir. Ada S. McKinley, Chgo., 1996—. Scholar Chgo. State U., 1976, Roosevelt U., 1978; fellow Menninger Found., 1985. Mem. Am. Profl. Soc. on Abuse of Children, Nat. Orgn. for Victim Assistance, Ill. Coalition Against Sexual Assault (del. 1985—), Soc. Traumatic Stress Studies (treatment innovations task force), Chgo. Sexual Assault Svcs. Network (vice-chair, bd. dirs.), Chgo. Coun. Fgn. Rels. Avocations: aerobics, reading, theatre, dining.

ALLEN, LEILANI ELEANOR, data processing executive; b. Rudesheim, Rhein, Fed. Republic Germany, Nov. 27, 1949; d. John Kaleiapu and Ilse Eva (Ritter) A. BA, San Francisco State U., 1971, MA, 1973; PhD, U. Conn., 1978. Sr. analyst VISA, U.S.A., San Mateo, Calif., 1978-81; asst. gen. mgr. Inst. for Info. Mgmt., Sunnyvale, Calif., 1981-85; pres. Knowledge Consortium, Oakland, Calif., 1985-87; sr. cons. Amdahl Corp., Sunnyvale, 1987-88; v.p. Aon Corp., Chgo., 1988-91; sr. v.p. PNC Mortgage Corp., Vernon Hills, Ill., 1991-95; dir. Tenex Consulting, Burlington, Mass.,

1995—; chmn. No Cal Computer Measurement Group, San Francisco, 1982-84, chmn. MBA tech. com., 1994-95. Co-author: Management Handbook of Information Center and End User Computer, 1987, (survey) Strategic Planning for Info. Sys., 1987, (cartoon) Tech Tales, 1993; editor: Executive Perspectives on Info. Sys., 1985; contbr. articles to profl. jours.; columnist Software mag., 1991-94, Computerworld. Mem. NAFE, Mensa, Mortgage Bankers Assn. (chair tech. com.).

ALLEN, LOUISE, writer, educator; b. Alliance, Ohio, Sept. 21, 1910; d. Earl Wayne and Ella Celesta (Goodall) Allerton; m. Benjamin Yukl, June 27, 1936; children: Katherine Anne Yukl Johnston, Kenneth Allen, Richard Lee, Margaret Louise Yukl Border. Student, Cleve. Coll. Western Res. U., 1963, Lakeland C.C., 1981-84. Co-founder Sch. Writing, Cleve., 1961-62; founder, dir. Allen Writers' Agy., Wickliffe, Ohio, 1963-84; editorial assoc. criticism service Writer's Digest mag., 1967-69; instr. Cuyahoga C.C., 1965-81, Lakeland C.C., Mentor, Ohio, 1973-81, Scottsdale C.C., 1984-88; writer. Author: (poems) Confetti, 1987; contbr. articles to mags.; composer (hymn) The Foot of the Cross. Mem. AAUW, Mensa, Assn. Mundial de Mujeres Periodistas y Escritoras, Women in Communications, Nat. League Am. Pen Women, DAR, Shore Writers Club (founder), Euclid Three Arts Club, Women's City Club (Cleve.). Republican. Congregationalist. Address: 2609 W Southern Ave Lot 11 Tempe AZ 85282-4208

ALLEN, MARCIA DEE, special education educator; b. Schenectady, N.Y., July 15, 1949; d. Joseph and Angelia Frances (Loucks) A. BA in Art, SUNY, Oneonta, 1971; MS Edn. in Spl. Edn., Bank St. Coll. Edn., 1994. 1st-12th grade art tchr. Gilboa (N.Y.)-Conesville C.S., 1973-78; English tchr. Bank of Bilbao, Bank of Vizcaya, Spain, 1982-84; substitute art tchr., spl. edn. grades 1-6 Schenectady, Saratoga and Albany County Pub. Schs., N.Y., 1985, 89-90; asst. tchr. Churchill Sch., N.Y.C., 1991-92; lang. tchr. St. Luke's-Roosevelt Hosp. Lang. Learning Clinic, N.Y.C., 1992-93; spl. edn. tchr. grades 9-12 day treatment program Pub. Sch. 186 at N.Y. State Psychiat. Inst., N.Y.C., 1993-95; spl. edn. tchr. grades 8-12 Chester (N.Y.) Union Free Sch. Dist., 1995—. Mem. N.Y.C. ASCD, Internat. Reading Assn. Home: PO Box 161 Wurtsboro NY 12790

ALLEN, MARGARET ELIZABETH, elementary education educator; b. Auburn, Maine, May 20, 1952; d. Bernal Bryan and Grace Jane (Hunt) A.; divorced; children: Gardner Gregory Seekins, M. Elizabeth Seekins. BS in Edn., U. Maine, 1974; M Ednl. Adminstrn., U. South Maine, 1989. Cert. tchr. and prin., Maine. Tchr. South Portland (Maine) Schs., 1970—; workshop facilitator, presenter in field; cons. Many Rivers Sch., Portland, 1994. Mem. Maine Gov.'s Goals 2000 Task Force, 1995. Named Pine Tree Educator of Yr., Pine Tree Burn Found., 1990. Mem. ASCD, Partnership Tchrs. Network (bd. dirs. 1994—). Home: RR 2 Box 205 Bath ME 94530 Office: Skillin Sch 180 Westcott Rd South Portland ME 04106

ALLEN, MARILYN MYERS POOL, theater director, video producer; b. Fresno, Calif., Nov. 2, 1934; d. Laurence B. and Asa (Griggs) Myers; BA, Stanford U., 1955, postgrad., 1955-56; postgrad. U. Tex., 1957-60, West Tex. State U. summers 1962, 63, Odessa Coll., 1987-88; m. Joseph Harold Pool, Dec. 28, 1955; children: Pamela Elizabeth, Victoria Anne, Catherine Marcia; m. Neal R. Allen, Apr. 1982. Pvt. tchr. drama, speech, acting, directing, speech correction, Amarillo, Tex., 1960-82, Midland, Tex., 1982—; free-lance radio and TV actress; asst. mng. dir. Amarillo Little Theatre, 1964-66, mng. dir., 1966-68; mng. dir. Horseshoe Players, touring profl. theater, 1969-73; actress, multi-media prodn. Palo Duro Canyon, 1971; dir. touring children's theatre, 1978-79 guest actress in Medea, Amarillo Coll., 1981; guest reciter Amarillo Symphony, 1972, Midland-Odessa Symphony, 1984. Pres. Tex. Non-Profit Theatres, 1972-74, 75-77, bd. dirs., 1988-91; 1st v.p. High Plains Center for Performing Arts, 1969-73; adv. mem. dept. fine arts Amarillo Coll., 1980-82. Adv. mem. Tex. Constnl. Revision Commn., 1973-75; mem. adv. coun. U. Tex. Coll. Fine Arts, 1969-72; cmty. adv. com. for women Amarillo Coll., 1975-79; conv. program com. Am. Theatre Assn., 1978, program participant 1978-80, bd. dirs., 1980-83; bd. dirs. Amarillo Found. Health and Sci. Edn., 1976-82, program v.p., 1979-81; bd. dirs. Domestic Violence Coun., 1979-82, March of Dimes, 1979-81, Tex. Panhandle Heritage Found., 1964-82, Friends of Fine Arts, W. Tex. State U. (now West Tex. A&M U.), 1980-82, Amarillo Pub. Libr., 1980-82, Amarillo Symphony, 1981-82; publicity chmn. Midland Cmty. Theatre, 1984-87, bd. govs., 1986-92, sec., 1987-88, v.p., 1988-92; mem. Mus. of S.W., Midland Arts Assembly; bd. dirs. Midland County Rep. Women, Ways and Means Ch., 1991, 1st v.p., 1992, publicity chair, 1994; mem. Midland County Redistricting com., 1991; cultural exchange del. from Midland, Tex., to Dong Ying, China, 1993; Tex. UIL one act play adjudicator, 1974—. Recipient cert. of appreciation Woman of Year, Amarillo Bus. and Profl. Women's Club, 1966; Best Actress award for Hedda Gabler role Amarillo Little Theatre 1965, Best Dir. award for Rashomon, 1967, 1st Pl. award for video spl. Tex. Press Conf., 1988, 1st Pl. award for news Tex. Press Conf., 1989, Disting. Svc. award Tex. Non-Profit Theatres, 1992; named Amarillo Woman of Yr., Beta Sigma Phi, 1980, Broadcaster of the Yr., Rocky Mountain Press Conf., 1988, Hamhock of Yr., Midland Cmty. Theatre, 1992, Outstanding Svc. award Midland Arts Assembly, 1992; Travel fellow AAUW, 1973, 78. Fellow Am. Assn. Cmty. Theatre (dir. 1969-72, 82-84, v.p. planning and devel. 1985-87, co-chair AACT/Fest '95); mem. USTA (sr. women's team sect. winner 1993, 94), S.W. Theatre Conf. (dir. 1973-76, 82-84, exec. com. 1982-84, Disting. Svc. award 1985), Tex. Theatre Council (dir. 1974-78, exec. com., pres. 1975-76), AAUW (br. pres. 1973-75, state chmn. cultural interests 1975-77, 86-88, state program v.p. 1977-79, state bd. dirs. 1984-88, program v.p. Midland 1988-89), Episc. Ch. Women (program v.p. Midland 1988-89, outreach chair 1996), DAR (chpt. chaplain 1971-75, historian 1975-77), C. of C. (fine arts coun.), U.S. Judo Assn., Symphony Guild, Amarillo Art Assn., Midland Symphony Guild (arrangements chmn. 1983-84), Act IX, Shakespeare As We Like It, Amarillo Law Wives Club (pres. 1976-77), Midland Law Wives, Hamhocks (v.p. 1985-86).

ALLEN, MARY LOUISE HOOK, physical education educator; b. Ironwood, Mich., July 18, 1930; d. Frank Eugene and Elsie Clara (Schneider) Hook; m. Dale Sanson Allen, June 30, 1955; children: Jack Eugene, Bradley Arthur. BS in Phys. Edn. cum laude, U. Mich., 1951; MA in Phys. Edn., U. Minn., 1970, postgrad., 1987—. Life teaching cert., coaching lic., Minn. Secondary edn. tchr. New Trier Twp. High Sch., Winnetka, Ill., 1951-55, Richfield (Minn.) Sch. Dist., 1955-59; teaching assoc. U. Minn., Mpls., 1969-70; part-time lectr. U. Minn., 1985-86; tchr. Bloomington (Minn.) Sch. Dist., 1961-85; adj. prof. Concordia Coll., St. Paul, Minn., 1987-92; officiator U.S. Synchro Minn. Assn., Minn. State High Sch. League, Pan-Am. Trials Swimming Co-Chair, others; past officiating bd. chmn. North Shore (Winnetka) Basketball/Volleyball, Ill. State Basketball com., others. Co-author: Soccer/Speedball Rule Book - Creative Game, 1952. Mem. Atonement Luth. Ch., Bloomington, 1956—; worker Dem. Party, Bloomington, 1988—; dir. Synchronized Swimming Camp, 1980-87. Recipient numerous athletic awards. Mem. AAHPERD (mem. com. 1949—), Minn. Assn. Health, Phys. Edn., Recreation and Dance (sec. 1982-83, pres.-elect 1984, pres. 1985, past pres. 1986, conv. chmn. 1984, 86, student confs. 1988-92), Synchronized Swim Coaches Assn. (state chmn. 1980-82), Athletic Fedn. Coll. Women (chmn. nat. conv. 1951), Phi Beta Kappa, Phi Kappa Phi, Mortarboard, Pi Lambda Theta, others. Home: 10312 Wentworth Ave Bloomington MN 55420-5249

ALLEN, MARYON PITTMAN, former senator, journalist, lecturer, interior and clothing designer; b. Meridian, Miss., Nov. 30, 1925; d. John D. and Tellie (Chism) Pittman; m. Joshua Sanford Mullins, Jr., Oct. 17, 1946 (div. Jan. 1959); children: Joshua Sanford III, John Pittman, Maryon Foster; m. James Browning Allen, Aug. 7, 1964 (dec. June 1978). Student, U. Ala., 1944-47, Internat. Inst. Interior Design, 1970. Office mgr. for Dr. Alston Callahan, Birmingham, Ala., 1959-60; bus. mgr. psychiat. clinic U. Ala. Med. Center, Birmingham, 1960-61; life underwriter Protective Life Ins. Co., Birmingham, 1961-62; women's editor Sun Newspapers, Birmingham, 1962-64; v.p., ptnr. Pittman family cos., J.D. Pittman Partnership Co., J.D. Pittman Tractor Co., Emerald Valley Corp., Mountain Lake Farms, Inc., Birmingham; mem. U.S. Senate (succeeding late husband James B. Allen), 1978; dir. pub. rels. and advt. C.G. Sloan & Co. Auction House, Washington, 1981; feature writer Birmingham News, 1964; writer syndicated column Reflections of a News Hen, Washington, 1969-78; feature writer, columnist Maryon Allen's Washington, Washington Post, 1979-81; columnist McCall's Needlework Mag., 1993—; owner The Maryon Allen Co. Cliff House (Restoration/Design), Birmingham. Contbg. editor So. Accents Mag., 1976-78. Mem. Ladies of U.S. Senate unit ARC, Former Mems. of Congress, Ala. Hist. Commn., Blair House Fine Arts Commn.; charter mem. Birmingham Com. of 100 for Women; trustee Children's Fresh Air Farm; trustee, deacon, elder Ind. Presbyn. Ch., Birmingham; Democratic Presdl. elector, Ala., 1968. Recipient 1st place award for best original column Ala. Press Assn., 1962, 63, also various press state and nat. awards for typography, fashion writing, food pages, also several awards during Senate service; sponsor, U.S. Navy Nuclear submarine, U.S.S. Birmingham, S.S.N. 695, launched Newport News, Va., 1977, commissioned 1978. Mem. Nat. Press Club, 1925 F Street Club, 91st Congress Club, Congl. Club, Birmingham Country Club. Home: Cliff House 3215 Cliff Rd S Birmingham AL 35205-1405

ALLEN, NANCY, vocational rehabilitation counselor; b. Louisville, Oct. 16, 1945; d. James William and Genevieve (Hambrick) A. BA, U. Miami, 1968; MA, Spalding U., 1969. Counseling supervisor Fla. Job Svc., Miami, 1969-76; dir. rehab. Crawford & Co., Miami, 1976-85; admissions rep. South Miami Hosp., 1985-89; sr. vocat. rehab. counselor State Fla. Dept. Labor, Miami, 1989—; treas. Project YES, Miami, 1996. V.p. Fla. Rehab. Assn. Home: 6770 SW 59th St Miami FL 33143-1906

ALLEN, NANCY SCHUSTER, librarian, director information resources; b. Buffalo, Jan. 10, 1948; d. Joseph E. and Margaret (Cormack) Schuster; m. Richard R. Allen, Sept. 2, 1967; children: Seth Cormack, Emily Margaret, Laura Jean. BA, U. Rochester, 1971, MA in Art History, 1973; MLS, Rutgers U., 1973. Asst. libr. Mus. Fine Arts, Boston, 1975-76, chief libr., 1976—; reference libr. Medford (Mass.) Pub. Libr., 1973-75; dir. info. resources Mus. Fine Arts, Boston, 1995—; lectr. Grad. Sch. Libr. and Info. Scis., Simmons Coll., Boston, 1984—; mem. preservation adv. group Rsch. Librs. Group, 1993—. Mem. art history scholarly adv. com. and joint task force Commn. on Preservation and Access, 1990-92. Mem. Art Libr. Soc. N.Am. (chmn. 1983-84), Soc. Am. Archivists, Rsch. Librs. Info. Network (chmn. art and architecture program com. 1985-88, mem. preservation adv. coun. 1993—), Internat. Fedn. Librs. (fin. officer sect. art librs. 1985-89), Fenway Librs. Online (v.p. 1987-89, pres. 1989-91), Rsch. Librs. Group (bd. dirs. 1995—). Office: Mus Fine Arts Dept Info Resources 465 Huntington Ave Boston MA 02115-5519

ALLEN, ORPHIA JANE, English language educator; b. La Mesa, N.Mex., Sept. 14, 1937; d. Clifford Lee and Rachel Emma (Corpening) A.; m. William Pierce Mooney, May 26, 1954 (div. Sept. 1963); children: Martin Pierce Mooney, James Patrick Mooney; m. Joseph Henry Forsyth. BA in English, N.Mex. State U., 1972, BA in Philosophy, 1974, MA in English, 1974; PhD in English, U. Okla., 1979. Assoc. prof. English N.Mex. State U., Las Cruces, 1976—. Author: Barbara Pym: Writing a Life, 1994; co-editor, contbr.: Publications Management, 1994 (NCTE award 1995); contbr. articles to profl. pubis. Office: N Mex State U English Dept PO Box 30001 Las Cruces NM 88003

ALLEN, PATRICIA CAROL, elementary education educator; b. Charleston, W.Va., Oct. 19, 1951; d. William Edgar and Freida Marie (Blake) Winters; m. Dewey Wayne Miller, June 30, 1972 (div. Dec. 1982); m. Bobby Edd Allen, June 7, 1984; 1 child, Blake Edward Allen. BS, Lee Coll., 1973. Cert. elem. edn. grades 1-9 career level III. Tchr. grade 4 Waterville Elem., Cleveland, Tenn., 1973-77; tchr. grade 5 Perry (Ga.) Elem., 1977-79; tchr. grade 6 Waterville Elem., Cleveland, 1979-84; tchr. grades 5-8 North Cumberland Elem., Crossville, Tenn., 1984-95; tchr. grade 7 Cumberland Elem. Sch., Crossville, Tenn., 1995—; sch. coord. Ptnrs.-In-Edn., Crossville, 1993-95. Ch. soloist Bethlehem Bapt., Crossville, 1991—, VBS dir., 1994, tchr. Sunday sch. grades 5, 6 Vacation Bible Sch. Mem. Delta Kappa Gamma (Beta Lambda chpt. 1st v.p. 1994-96). Home: Rt 12 Box 490W Creekway Ct Crossville TN 38555 Office: South Cumberland Elem Sch Rt 11 Box 319 Crossville TN 38555

ALLEN, PATRICIA J., library director; b. McLean County, Ky., Nov. 10, 1941; d. Richard Louis and Helen (Hancock) Jones; m. Jerry M. Mize, Mar. 19, 1960 (div. 1978); children: Martin P., Elizabeth M. Atherton; m. Lawrence A. Allen, Nov. 24, 1983 (div. 1985). Student, Murray (Ky.) State U., 1959-60; BA, Ky. Wesleyan Coll., 1962; MA, Western Ky. U., 1974; MLS, U. Ky., 1982; postgrad., U. N.C., 1983-84. Libr. pub. elem. schs. Daviess County, Ky., 1963-70; media specialist pub. elem., mid. and high schs. McLean County, Ky., 1970-78; head pub. svcs., assoc. prof. libr. sci. Ky. Wesleyan Coll., Owensboro, 1978-83; asst. dir. Evansville (Ind.) Vanderburgh County Pub. Libr., 1985-89; dir. Carmel (Ind.) Clay Pub. Libr., 1989-91, Sanibel (Fla.) Pub. Libr., 1991—; mem. adj. faculty Western Ky. U., Bowling Green, 1977-78, Ind. U., Bloomington, 1988; workshop presenter Nursing Home Activities Dirs. Assn., Owensboro, Ky., 1981; cons. Ky. Dept. Librs. and Archives, Frankfort, 1982, Purchase (Ky.) Regional Libr. Sys., Murray, 1983, Henderson (Ky.) C.C. Libr., 1988. Editor: Emergency Handbook, 1987, Circulation Policies and Procedures, 1988, Sanibel Public Library Building Program Statement, 1992; contbr. article to profl. jours. Pres. Ret. Sr. Vol. Program Adv. Coun., Evansville, 1986-88; bd. dirs. Evansville Goodwill Industries, 1987-89. Named Outstanding Citizen of the Yr., Sanibel-Captiva Islands C. of C., 1995; Caroline M. Hewins scholar U. Ky., 1982, Margaret Ellen Kalp scholar U. N.C., 1983-84; hon. Ky. Col., 1981. Mem. ALA, Ky. Libr. Assn., Fla. Libr. Assn. (Transformer award 1996), Pub. Libr. Assn., Libr. Adminstrs. and Mgrs. Assn., P.E.O., Altrusa Club (bd. dirs. Evansville chpt. 1988, treas. Hamilton County chpt. 1990-91), Tales and Scales (pres. Evansville chpt. 1986), Beta Phi Mu. Democrat. Baptist. Office: Sanibel Pub Libr 770 Dunlop Rd Sanibel FL 33957-4016

ALLEN, PEGGY, broadcast executive. Grad. cum laude, Carlton Coll., Northfield, Minn. Prodn. of "You!" WMAQ TV; prodr. "Good Day!" WCVB-TV, 1983-89; exec. prodr. Hearst/ABC News Svcs., 1989-91; dir. program devel. Heart Broadcasting Prodns., 1991-93; v.p. produced programming and prodn. Lifetime Television, N.Y.C., 1993—. Development daily live talk shows including Queens, Girls' Night Out, The Marriage Counselor, Our Home, Growing Up Funny with Brett Butler, Christy Turlington Backstage; prodr.: Your Baby and Child with Penelope Leach, Your Child Six to Twelve with Dr. Kyle Pruett. Recipient CableACE award for Your Baby and Child with Penelope Leach, 1992, Emmy awards (4), Iris award. Office: Lifetime Tel 16th 17th Fls 309 W 49th St New York NY 10019-7316

ALLEN, PINNEY L., lawyer; b. Marshalltown, Iowa, Jan. 26, 1953; d. Walker Woodrow and Doris (Pinney) A.; m. Charles C. Miller, III, Aug. 20, 1977; children: Linden, Doria. AB summa cum laude, Harvard U., 1976; JD cum laude, Harvard Law Sch., 1979. Bar: Ga., 1976; U.S. Tax Ct. 1984. Assoc. Alston & Bird, Atlanta, 1979-86, ptnr., 1986—. Contbr. articles to profl. jours., 1981—. Mem. ABA, Nat. Soc. Accts. for Coops., Ga. Bar Assn., Atlanta Bar Assn., Atlant Tax Forum. Office: Alston & Bird 1 Atlantic Ctr 1201 W Peachtree St NW Atlanta GA 30309-3400*

ALLEN, RAYE VIRGINIA, cultural historian; b. Temple, Tex., May 27, 1929; d. Irvin and Vivian (Arnold) McCreary; m. Henry Kiper Allen, June 9, 1951; children: Henry Kiper, Irvin McCreary, Rave Virginia. BA, U. Tex.-Austin, 1951, MA in Am. Civilization, 1975, postgrad. Mem. Am. Folklife Ctr. in Libr. of Congress, Washington, 1976-84, chmn., 1978-79; trustee, Future Homemakers of Am. Found., 1983-91; bd. dirs. Future Homemakers Am., 1978-85; trustee U.S.-N.Z. Arts Found.; vice chmn., trustee Fund for Folk Culture Found.; chmn., coord. com. for Ellis Island; bd. dirs. Centennial Commn. of U. Tex.-Austin and chmn. continuing edn. com., 1981-84, bd. visitors U. Tex. astronomy dept. and McDonald Obs., 1984—; bd. dirs. 500 Yrs. of Am. Clothing; adv. coun. Inst. Texan Cultures, 1980-91; mem. Am. Revolution Bicentennial Commn. of Tex., 1971-75; co-founder, 1st pres. Cultural Activities Ctr. of Temple, Tex., 1957-59; bd. dirs. Tex. State Soc. of Washington, 1980-83, Tex. Breakfst Club D.C., Inst. Humanities, Salado, Tex. Bd., Tex. Folklife Resources. Recipient Outstanding Citizen of Temple award, 1973; Raye Virginia Allen State Pres. scholarship established in her honor Future Homemakers Am., 1986. Mem. Am. Studies Assn., Costume Soc. Am., Am. News Women's Club, Nat. Mus. Women in Arts, Tex. State Hist. Assn. Episcopalian.

ALLEN, RITA F., secondary education educator; b. Athens, Tex., Feb. 25, 1944; d. Ernest R. Herd and Opal F. (Mayfield) Suitt; div.; children: Steve, Keith, Kevin, Quentin. AA, Bee County Coll., 1980; BS, Corpus Christi State U., 1989. Cert. comm., secondary edn., English. Tchr. E.M. Smith Jr. H.S., Sinton, Tex. Mem. Smith Jr. High Parent-Tchr. Involvement Orgn., Sinton, 1989-94, Sinton (Tex.) Athletic Booster Club, 1990-94; instr. for merit badge Boy Scouts Am., Sinton, 1992-94. Recipient Sinton ISD Secondary Sch. Tchr. of Yr., 1996. Mem. Assn. Tex. Profl. Educators. Lutheran. Home: PO Box 388 Skidmore TX 78389-0388 Office: E M Smith Jr High Sch 900 S San Patricio St Sinton TX 78387-3506

ALLEN, ROBERTA L., fiction and nonfiction writer, conceptual artist; b. N.Y.C., Oct. 6, 1945; d. Sol and Jeanette (Waldner) A. A.A.S., Fashion Inst. Tech., N.Y.C., 1964; student, Instituto de Bellas Artes, Mex. Lectr. Corcoran Sch. Art, Washington, 1975, Kutztown State Coll., 1979, C.W. Post Coll., 1979; instr. creative writing Parsons Sch. Design, N.Y.C., 1986; instr. The Writer's Voice, 1992-96, The New Sch. Social Rsch., 1993-96, Dept. Continuing Edn., NYU, 1993-96. Author: Partially Trapped Lines, 1975, Pointless Arrows, 1976, Pointless Acts, 1977, Everything In The World There Is To Know Is Known By Somebody, But Not By the Same Knower, 1981, The Traveling Woman (fiction collection), 1986, (nouvella) The Daughter, 1992, Amazon Dream (travel memoir), 1993; one woman shows include Galerie 845, Amsterdam, The Netherlands, 1967, John Weber Gallery, N.Y.C., 1974, 75, 77, 79, Inst. for Art and Urban Resources, N.Y.C., 1977, 80, Galerie Maier-Hahn, Dusseldorf, W. Ger., 1977, MTL Galerie, Brussels, 1978, C.W. Post Coll., Glenvale, N.Y., 1978, Galerie Walter Storms, Munich, W. Ger., 1981, Kunstforum, Stadt. Galerie in Lenbachhaus, Munich, 1981, Galleria Primo Piano, Rome, Italy, 1981, Perth Inst. Contemporary Arts, 1989. Fellow MacCowell Colony, 1971, 72, Ossabaw I. Project fellow, 1972, Yaddo fellow, 1983, 87, 93, Va. Ctr. for Creative Arts fellow, 1985, 94; grantee LINE, 1985, Creative Artists Pub. Svc., 1978-79. Home and Office: 5 W 16th St New York NY 10011-6307

ALLEN, ROSE LETITIA, special education educator; b. Dayton, Ohio, Oct. 10, 1960; d. Billie Wesley and Elisabeth Julia (Coler) Taylor; m. Randolph Eugene Allen, June 27, 1987. BSN, Wright State U., 1982; MS in Edn., U. Bridgeport, 1987. Cert. elem., K-12 handicapped edn., developmentally handicapped and specific LD tchr. Tchr. Hawaii Dept. of Edn., Honolulu, 1989-91; substitute tchr. Montgomery County Bd. Mental Retardation and Devel. Disabilities, Dayton, Ohio, 1993; tchr. Dayton Pub. Schs., 1994—; mem. Faculty Coun., Dayton, 1994-95. 2d lt. USAF, 1983-84. Mem. AAUW, Alpha Xi Delta. Home: 2421 Orange Ave Moraine OH 45439

ALLEN, SANDRA KAY, costume historian; b. Little Rock, Sept. 25, 1954; d. John Herbert and Mary Marcella (Gray) A. Student, U. Okla., 1973, U. Ark., 1973; BFA, U. Tex., 1979, BA with honors, 1979. Costume/textile identification specialist Lane County Hist. Mus., Eugene, Oreg., 1987-88; stitcher Santa Fe (N.Mex.) Opera, 1988; asst. pattern maker Denver Ctr. Theatre Co., 1980, 83, 88-89; costume designer Living History Farm, Littleton, Colo., 1989-93, Living History Ranch, Boulder, Colo., 1990-91; pattern maker Skea, Ltd., Denver, 1990-93; costume history educator EGOS Adult Edn., Denver, 1991-93. Northwest corr. Region V Costume Soc. Am. newsletter, 1996. Prentice Hall scholar, 1978. Mem. Costume Soc. Am. Home: 1169 Lincoln St Eugene OR 97401

ALLEN, SHEILA HILL, nursing executive, counselor, consultant; b. Imperial, Nebr., Sept. 28, 1935; d. Roger William and Lois Marion (Clayton) Hill; children: Steven Morgan, Lee-Ann Hill, Todd Everett, Andrew James. R.N., St. Lukes Sch. Nursing, 1958; BS, U. Denver, 1959. Cert. alcohol drug counselor, Calif. Asst. head nurse St. Lukes Hosp., Denver, 1959-62; dir. nursing Ridge Vista Mental Health, San Jose, Calif., 1973-75; dir. nursing svcs. Westwood Mental Health Facility, Fremont, Calif., 1975-89, dir. nursing svcs. Chem. Dependency Inst. No. Calif., Campbell, 1989-90; program dir. O'Connor Hosp. Recovery Ctr., San Jose, 1991-94; health facilities evaluator nurse State of Calif. Dept. Health Svcs. Licensing and Certification, 1995—. Bd. dirs., sec., Health Acctg. Svcs., Calif., 1984-89; co-founder, partner Health Acctg. Svcs., Fremont, 1984-89; co-owner Westwood Mental Health, 1984-89. Contbr. articles to profl jours. Mem. Calif. Assn. Alcoholism and Drug Abuse Counselors, Nat. Consortium Chem. Dependency Nurses, Brookridge Inst. Serving Addiction and Consciousness Profls., San Francisco Acad. Hypnosis, Nat. Coun. Alcoholism and Drug Dependence, Delta Gamma.

ALLEN, SUSAN DAVIS, chemistry and electrical engineering educator, academic administrator, dean; b. Jacksonville, Fla., Sept. 13, 1943; d. James E. and Eleanor H. Davis; m. Charles C. Allen, Dec. 23, 1962; children: Harold, Eleanor. BS, Colo. Coll., 1966; PhD in Chem. Physics, U. So. Calif., 1971. Postdoctoral rsch. assoc. dept. chemistry U. So. Calif., L.A., 1971-73, rsch. scientist Ctr. for Laser Studies, 1977-82, sr. rsch. scientist, 1983-84, rsch. asst. prof. elec. engring., 1981-84, rsch. assoc. prof., assoc. dir. Ctr. for Laser Studies, 1984-87; mem. tech. staff Hughes Rsch. Labs., Malibu, Calif., 1973-77; prof. chemistry and elec. and computer engring. U. Iowa, Iowa City, 1987-92, dir. laser microfabrication facility, 1988-92; co-dir. Inst. for Environ. Remediation and Waste Mgmt. Tulane U. and Xavier U., New Orleans, 1992-94, interim dir. Ctr. for Bioenviron. Rsch., 1993-94; prof. chemistry and elec. engring. Tulane U., 1992—, v.p. for rsch., dean Grad. Sch., 1992—; mem. adv. bd. on elec., comm. and sys. engring. NSF, 1988-90, div. materials rsch., 1991-93, ad hoc com. on materials rsch. labs. and materials rsch. groups, 1993; mem. exec. com. Assn. Grad. Schs., 1993-96, v.p., 1996; bd. dirs. Oak Ridge (Tenn.) Assoc. Univs., 1994-97, mem. found. bd., 1994—, chmn., 1995—; numerous presentations in field; cons. Hughes Rsch. Labs., Malibu, 1977-78, Xerox Corp., Webster, N.Y., 1979-82, TRW, El Segundo, Calif., 1982-84, Jet Propulsion Lab., 1982-88, Hughes Aircraft Co., 1986-90, Army Missile Command, 1988-93, Microbeam, Newbury Park, Calif., 1988-89, Teltech, 1991—, also others. Contbr. over 100 articles to sci. jours.; patentee for method and apparatus for removing minute particles from a surface, laser fabricated fiber optic tap structures and devices. Grantee Air Force Materials Lab., Def. Advanced Rsch. Projects Agy., 1991, Amoco Corp., 1992, L.A. Bd. Regents, 1996—, NSF, 1996—, also others. Mem. IEEE (sr.), Am. Phys. Soc., Am. Chem. Soc., Optical Soc. Am. (chmn. tech. group 1990-92, mem. edn. coun. 1991-94), Assn. Women in Sci. (founding E. Iowa chpt.), Materials Rsch. Soc., Soc. Women Engrs. (faculty advisor U. Iowa chpt. 1988-92), Internat. Soc. for Optical Engring., Am. Vacuum Soc. (trustee 1979-81, 86-88, chmn. 1988, sec.-treas. thin film divsn. 1980-82, bd. dirs. 1982-84, exec. com. electronic materials and processing divsn. 1992-95), Women in Engring. Program Advs. Network, Sigma Xi. Home: 1640 Palmer Ave New Orleans LA 70118-6114 Office: Tulane U 327 Gibson Hall New Orleans LA 70118

ALLEN, SYLVIA CAROL, internet trainer, writer, consultant; b. Nacogdoches, Tex., May 21, 1943; m. Thomas Harrell Allen, Dec. 26, 1967 (Div. Dec. 20, 1984); 1 child, Maston Thomas Allen. BS, East Tex. State U., Commerce, 1964; MA, U. Tex., El Paso, 1968. Coord. Women's Health Care Svcs., San Bernadino, Calif., 1976-81; exec. dir. Adv. Health Care Systems, Anaheim, Calif., 1981-83; buyer Southland Corp., San Bernadino, 1983-89; franchisee 7-Eleven Southland Corp., Rialto, 1989-95; staff educator Valley Health Systems, Hemet, Calif., 1992-95; book author, newsletter editor Aaron-Stone Publishing, Yucca Valley, Calif., 1992-95; internet trainer Skill Path Seminars, Inc., Mission, Kans., 1995; cons., trainer in field. Author: (book) How To Successfully Run a BBS For Profit, 1992, A Business Guide To BBS, Internet, Online Services, 1995; editor: (newsletter) Online Profits, 1994-95.

ALLEN, THERESA OHOTNICKY, neurobiologist, consultant; b. Torrington, Conn., Apr. 27, 1948; d. Frank Richard and Helen Theresa (Drozdenko) Ohotnicky; m. Thomas Atherton Allen, Aug. 12, 1972; children: Melanie Atherton, Abigail Baldwin. BA, U. Conn., 1970; MS, Villanova U., 1975; PhD, Duke U., 1978; cert. in bus. adminstrn., U. Pa., 1983. Realtor. Rsch. assoc. U. Pa., Phila., 1981-83; sci. dir. Drexel U., Phila., 1983-84; cons. on neurobiology to sci.-oriented cos., 1984—. Contbr. articles to profl. jours., also chpts. to books. Bd. dirs. Gladwyne (Pa.) Libr. League, 1986—, Athena Inst. for Women's Wellness, Haverford, Pa., 1989-93; trustee Gladwyne Libr., 1988—, pres., 1991-93; com. chmn. Jr. League Phila., 1989-90. Fellow Inst. Neurol. Scis., U. Pa., 1978-80, NIH, 1980-81. Mem. Phila. Skating Club, Humane Soc., Phi Beta Kappa. Episcopalian. Home: 1433

Waverly Rd Gladwyne PA 19035-1224 Office: 336 Conshohocken State Rd Gladwyne PA 19035-1336

ALLEN, VICKY, marketing professional; b. Springfield, Pa., May 27, 1957; d. James Joseph and Ann Marie (Cifone) Cattafesta; m. James Francis DeLeone, Aug. 11, 1979 (div. 1982); m. Dennis Ronald Allen, June 30, 1990; 1 child, Amber. BBA in Computer Sci., Temple U., 1979. Quality assurance Burroughs Corp., Downingtown, Pa., 1977, software QA, 1978, systems analyst, 1979-81; program analyst Crocker Internal Systems, San Jose, Calif., 1981-83; sr. systems analyst Avantek, Inc., Santa Clara, Calif., 1983-84; product mktg. program specialist Micro Focus, Palo Alto, Calif., 1984—; programmer cons. Fin. Group, Palo Alto, 1985-86. Active Sierra Club. Mem. Phi Sigma Sigma (sec. 1978-79). Democrat. Roman Catholic. Office: Micro Focus 2465 E Bayshore Rd Palo Alto CA 94303-3205

ALLEN-MEARES, PAULA, social work educator, dean; b. Buffalo, N.Y., Feb. 29; d. Joe N. and Mary T. (Hienz) Allen; married; children: Tracey, Nikki, Shannon. BS, SUNY, Buffalo, 1969; MSW in Child Welfare, U. Ill., Urbana-Champaign, 1971, PhD in Social Work and Ednl. Adminstrn., 1975; cert. in mgmt., Harvard U., 1990; cert. mgmt. of mgrs., U. Mich., 1993. Lic. cert. social worker, Ill.; lic. clin. social worker, Ill. Rsch. asst. SUNY, Buffalo, 1966-69; child welfare worker Dept. Children and Family Svcs., Champaign, Ill., 1970-71; sch. social worker Urbana (Ill.) Sch. Dist. 116, 1971-78; supt. Sch. Social Work U. Ill., Urbana-Champaign, 1973-78, asst. prof. Sch. Social Work, 1978-83, chair Sch. Social Work Specialization, 1978-84, dir. doctoral program Sch. Social Work, 1985-88, 89, assoc. prof. Sch. Social Work, 1983-89, acting dean Sch. Social Work, 1989-90, prof. Sch. Social Work, 1989-93, dean, prof. Sch. Social Work, 1990-93; dean, prof. Sch. Social Work U. Mich., Ann Arbor, 1993—; scholars forum vis. lectr. U. Tex., Austin, 1992; vis. minority scholar Sch. Social Work, U. S.C., 1994; manuscript and book reviewer; reviewer Social Casework, summers 1988, 89, 90, Children & Youth Svcs. Rev., 1988, 89, 90, Jour. Ethnic and Multicultural Concerns in Social Work, 1990, among others; cons. Ill. Office Edn., Pupil Pers. Svc. Unit, Springfield, 1977, Detroit Pub. Schs., 1979, Decatur (Ill.) Pub. Schs., 1979, Family Svcs. Champaign County, 1979, Dept. Pub. Instrn., State of N.C., 1979, Urbana Sch. Dist. 116, 1978-80, Ill. State Bd. Edn., 1979-81, Chgo. Pub. Schs., 1981, Champaign Pub. Schs., 1981, Vermilion County Spl. Edn. Coop., Danville, 1982, Pembroke Sch. Dist., Kankakee, Ill., 1982, Champaign Pub. Schs., 1982, Defferin-Peel Sch. Dist., Mississauga, Ont., Can., 1982, Mid-State Spl. Edn., 1983, Milw. Wis. Office Edn., 1983, D.C. Sch. Social Work, 1984, Ind. Office Edn. Pupil Pers. Divsn., Indpla., 1984, Glenbrook (Ill.) Sch. Dist., 1984, 85, 86, Kankakee Spl. Edn. Coop., 1985, N.J. State Dept. Edn. Office Cert., Trenton, 1985, Pub. Sch. Disvn., Mississauga, Can., 1985, Budapest, Hungary, 1990, Dept. Def., 1991, Cath. Social Svcs., Indpls., 1991, Bd. Sch. Commrs., Indpls. Pub. Schs., 1991, Brown U. and Lilly Endowment, Indpls., 1992. Author: Intervention with Children & Adolescents, 1995, (with others) Social Work Services in Schools, 1986, Controversial Issues in Social Work Research, 1995; co-editor: Methods and Issues--Evaluating Social Services in Education Settins, 1988, Adolescent Sexuality--An Overview and Principles of Intervention, 1986; mem. editl. bd. Jour. of Women in Social Work, 1990-93, Arete, 1989—, Sch. Jour. Social Work, 1986—, Jour. NASW, 1984-88, Ednl. and Psychol. Rsch., 1983-89, Jour. Social Svc. Rsch., 1993—, Children and Youth Svcs. Rev., 1991—, Jour. Tchg. Social Work, 1990—; cons. editor Social Work in Edn., 1978-84; editor-in-chief Social Work in Edn., 1989-93; mem. editl. adv. bd. Families in Contemporary Soc., 1991—; contbr. articles to profl. jours. Human rels. dir. Urbana Edn., 1973-75; mem. regional adv. bd. Gifted, 1977-78; mem. planning com. for Ill. March of Dimes, 1978; bd. dirs. Vol. Action Ctr. Champaign County, 1978-80, chair nomination com., ad hoc com. on bd. policy; mem. program com. Girls Club of Champaign, 1978-81; mem. adv. bd. Ambulatory Care Ctr., Mercy Hosp., 1981-82; bd. dirs. devel. svcs. Champaign County, 1973-75; moderator black adoptions Children's Home & Aid Soc. Ill. and Dept. Children and Family Svcs., 1984; mem. policy com. Regional Ill. Children's Home and Aid Soc., 1980-84; bd. dirs. Family Svc. Champaign County, 1988-89; mem. Champaign county child placement rev. com. Champaign County Cir. Ct., 1985-93. Recipient scholarship SUNY, 1966, Alumni of Yr. U. Ill., 1993, Human Rels. award Ill. Edn. Assn., 1975; fellow U. Ill., 1969-71; grantee Urban Sch. Dist. 116, 1976, Dept. Children and Family Svcs., 1983, Workshops on Prevention of Teenage Pregnancy, 1985, Dept. Edn., 1986, 89, U. Ill. 1986—, NASW, 1988-92, Mich. Dept. Social Svcs., 1994. Mem. NASW (chair comms. com. 1993—, comms. bd. dirs. 1990—, coun. editors bd. 1990—, cert., editor-in-chief Social Work in Edn. 1990—; Social Worker of Yr. Illini dist. 1992), Nat. Assn. Black Social Workers, Nat. Assn. Deans and Dirs. (v.p. 1993—, bd. dirs. 1991-93), Coun. on Social Work Edn. (treas. 1992—, bd. dirs. 1989-91, del. assembly 1988-89), Rotary, Phi Delta Kappa, Delta Mu, Delta Kappa Gamma (Xi chpt.). Office: U Mich Sch Social Work 1065 Freize Bldg Ann Arbor MI 48109

ALLENSON, MIRIAM S., marketing manager; b. N.Y.C., Oct. 20, 1942; d. Herman M. and Helen C. (Konigsberg) Schulman; m. Andrew J. Allenson, Oct. 10, 1964; children: Michael Ian, Aron David, Herman Mayer. BA, Syracuse U., 1964. Office mgr., sales rep. Donna Shops, New Bern, N.C., 1977-85; air staff, program dir., asst. gen. mgr., gen. mgr. WTEB-FM/NPR, APR Affiliate, New Bern, N.C., 1985-89; listener's club mktg. mgr. WNCN-FM, N.Y.C., 1990-93; mgr. mktg. and promotions WAXQ FM, N.Y.C., 1993—. Mem. NAFE, Promax, Women in Comms. Democrat. Jewish. Home: 52 Franklin St Tenafly NJ 07670-2005

ALLENSWORTH, DOROTHY ALICE, education foundation administrator; b. Willoughby, Ohio, Aug. 12, 1907; d. William and Effie Alice (Minthorn) Etzensperger; m. Carl Allensworth, Jan. 12, 1944; children: Stephen Edward, Robert Minthorn. BA, Smith Coll., Northampton, Mass., 1929; MA, Western Res. U., 1935. Various positions, 1935-41; program dir. Cleve. Festival of Freedom, 1939-41; costume designer Shrine Circus, Cleve., 1941, 49th St. Circus, Rockefeller Ctr., N.Y.C., 1942, Shubert Costume Co., N.Y.C., 1942-44; co-producer Cedarhurst (N.Y.C) Summer Theatre, 1943; costumer Chgo. Ice Circus, 1944; dir. neighborhood youth corps Westchester Community Opportunity Program, U.S. Dept. Labor, Westchester County, N.Y., 1965-68; founder, exec. dir. Coll. Careers Fund of Westchester, Westchester County, 1967-91, ret., 1991. Co-author: The Complete Play Production Handbook, 1973; co-author (play) Interurban, 1947-48. Pres. Rye Neck Sch. Dist. Community Coun., Mamaroneck, N.Y., 1953-57; mem., co-founder recreation coun. Village of Mamaroneck, 1957-59, chmn. recreation commn., 1960-65; co-founder Village Fours pre-school program for 4-yr. olds. Recipient Award for Improving Human Rels., B'nai B'rith Tri-Town chpt., Larchmont, Mamaroneck, Harrison, N.Y., 1967, Woman of Achievement award Westchester County, 1975, Jesse Hill Meml. award Ionic 108 lodge Prince Hall Masons, Westchester County, 1977, Onward and Upward award New Rochelle (N.Y.) Urban League, 1978, Humanitarian award United Bapt. Deacon's Union and Deaconess' Aux., Westchester County, 1979, Disting. Alumna medal Smith Coll., 1980, citation Gov. of N.Y., 1989, Edn. for the Poor award Westchester County, 1991, Award for Educating Poor Minority Youth Westchester Clubmen, 1991, State Senator Suzi Oppenheimer award for edn., 1991, Congresswoman Nita Lowey spl. award for dedication to the poor, 1991. Mem. Westchester Coun. on Crime and Delinquency (bd. dirs.), Westchester Coalition for Legal Abortion (bd. dirs.), Westchester Alliance for Juvenile and Criminal Justice (Marjorie Johnson Margolis award 1985). Home: 220 S Barry Ave Mamaroneck NY 10543-4103

ALLER, MARGO FRIEDEL, astronomer; b. Springfield, Ill., Aug. 27, 1938; d. Jules and Claire (Cornick) Friedel; m. Hugh Duncan Aller, Aug. 17, 1964; 1 child, Monique Christine. BA, Vassar Coll., 1960; postgrad., Harvard U., 1961-62; MS, U. Mich., 1964, PhD, 1969. Mathematician programmer Smithsonian Astrophys. Obs., Cambridge, Mass., 1960-62; rsch. assoc. U. Mich., Ann Arbor, 1970-76, assoc. rsch. scientist, 1976-85, rsch. scientist, 1985—; mem. users' com. Nat. Radio Astronomy Observatory, 1984-86. Mem. Am. Astron. Soc., Internat. Astron. Union, Sigma Xi. Office: U Mich Dept Astronomy 817 Dennison Bldg Ann Arbor MI 48109-1090

ALLEY, KIRSTIE, actress; b. Wichita, Kans., Jan. 12, 1955; m. Parker Stevenson; 1 child, William True. Student, U. Kans., Kans. State U. Actress: (stage prodns.) Cat on a Hot Tin Roof, Answers; (feature films) Star Trek II: The Wrath of Khan, 1982, Blind Date, 1984, Champions, 1984, Runaway, 1984, Summer School, 1987, Shoot to Kill, 1988, Look Who's Talking, 1989, Daddy's Home, 1989, One More Chance, 1990, Madhouse, 1990, Sibling Rivalry, 1990, Look Who's Talking Too, 1990, Look Who's Talking Now, 1993, Village of the Damned, 1995; (TV mini-series) North and South Book I, 1985, North and South, Book II, 1986; (TV movies) Sins of the Past, 1984, A Bunny's Tale, 1984, The Prince of Bel Air, 1985, Stark: Mirror Image, 1986, Infidelity, 1987, David's Mother, 1994 (Emmy award, Lead Actress - Special, 1994); (TV series) Masquerade, 1984-85, Cheers, 1987-1993 (Emmy award as Outstanding Lead Actress in a Comedy Series 1991). Office: Met Travel Agy 4526 Wilshire Blvd Los Angeles CA 90010-3801*

ALLEY-BARROS, ELIZABETH DALEIN, law enforcement training educator; b. New Bedford, Mass., Oct. 18, 1958; children: Vincent, Lisa. AS in Criminal Justice, Bristol C.C., 1979; BS in Adminstrn. of Criminal Justice, Roger Williams Coll., 1982. Court transp. officer New Bedford 3rd Dist. Ct., 1980-81; police officer U.S. Dept. Defense Police, Mass. and R.I., 1981-86; corrections officer S.E. Correctional Ctr., Bridgewater, Mass., 1986-87; police instr. Police Survival Def. Tactics Tng., New Bedford, 1982—; specialized training include Training Rsch. Validation, 1989, Use of Force Reporting Systems, 1989, Monadnock PR-24 Police Baton instr., 1988, Court Room Survival, 1989, Edges Weapon Defense, 1989, Street Survival, 1982-87 and others. Author: Who's Who in Law Enforcement Collecting and Police Trainers, 1988; editor, pub.: Who's Who in Law Enforcement Institutes and Schools, Trainers, and Training Organizations, 1995. Office: Police Survival Def Tactics PO Box 6454 New Bedford MA 02742-6454

ALLGAIER, SUSANN, artist, educator; b. Zurich, Switzerland, Aug. 9, 1968; d. Robert and Margreth (Knöll) A.; m. David Michael Davidson, June 30, 1995. Diploma, Art Sch. Zurich, 1989, Art Sch. Bern, Switzerland, 1989; Cert., Art Sch. Bern, Switzerland, 1992; MFA, N.Y. Acad. Art, 1994. Gilder, art restorer, conservator Zurich, Florence, London, N.Y.C., 1986—; instr. Ctr. for Gilding Arts, N.Y.C., 1994—. Exhibited in group and solo shows at Hunter Coll., N.Y.C.,Y. Acad. Art, N.Y.C., 1994, 4 World Trade Ctr., N.Y.C., 1994, Ctr. for Visual Arts, Denton, Tex., 1994, 95, Stamford (Conn.) Hist. Soc., 1994, Nat. Arts Club, N.Y.C., 1994, 95, Salmagundi Club, N.Y.C., 1994, Wichita (Kans.) Ctr. for Arts, 1994, Griffin Gallery, Miami Beach, Fla., 1995, Rockland Ctr. for Arts, West Nyack, N.Y., 1995, St. John's Univ. Gallery, Jamaica, N.Y., 1995, Lamar U., Beaumont, Tex., 1995, Stonington Gallery, Anchorage, 1995, Palm Springs (Calif.) Desert Mus., 1995, Gadsden (Ala.) Ctr. for Cultural Arts, 1995, Creative Arts Workshop, New Haven, Conn., 1995, N.Y. Law Sch., N.Y.C., 1995, Nat. Art League, Douglaston, N.Y., 1995, Icon Factory, Sacramento, Calif., 1995, Perry House Galleries, Alexandria, Va., 1995, 96, Pump House Gallery, Hartford, Conn., 1995, Orson (Pa.) Summer Gallery, 1995, Pleiades Gallery, N.Y.C., 1995, Medici Ctr. for Visual Arts, Phila., 1995, Nicolet Coll. Gallery, Rhinelander, Wis., 1995, Columbia Coll. Lake Campus, Osage Beach, Mo., 1995, State of the Art Gallery, Ithaca, N.Y., 1995, Studio 109 Sculpture Gallery, Bklyn., 1995, Kaki Bassi Gallery, Cabo San Lucas, Mex., 1995, Lichtenstein Ctr. for Arts, Pitts., 1996, Parkersburg (W.Va.) Art Ctr., 1996, Corvallis (Oreg.) Art Ctr., 1996, Emerging Collector, N.Y.C., 1996, Studio 109 Sculpture Gallery, Bklyn., 1996, Gallery Q, Tucson, Tex., 1996, Perry House Galleries, Alexandria, Va., 1996, Heckscher Mus. Art, N.Y., 1996, QCC Art Gallery, N.Y., 1996, Viridian Gallery, N.Y.C., Jacob Javits Fed. Bldg., N.Y.C., 1996. Recipient grant Elizabeth Greenshields Found., Montreal, 1993, grant Ludwig Vogelstein Found., 1995, Robert and June Heck award No. Nat. Art Competition, 1995, Award of Merit, Stonington Gallery, 1995, award of merit Manhattan Arts Internat., 1994, critic's pick award, 1995, 3d pl. Splash II, Cabo San Lucas, Mexico, 1996, Domenico Facci meml. award Audubon Artists, 1996, Leo Brooks Meml. award Nat. Art League, 1995. Home: 90 Bedford St # 5D New York NY 10014-3785

ALLGOOD, MARILYN JANE, mathematics educator; b. Nebraska City, Nebr., Nov. 11, 1939; d. William Andrew and Margaret M. (Parriott) Tynon; m. Clyde Eldon Allgood, July 23, 1960; children: Steven, Teresa, Mark, Bret. BS in Edn., Peru (Nebr.) State Coll., 1960. Math/sci. tchr. Bratton-Union H.S., Humboldt, Nebr., 1960-62; math./physics tchr. Johnson (Nebr.) Brock H.S., 1963-64; math./sci. tchr. Lourdes Ctrl. H.S., Nebraska City, Nebr., 1968-72; math./computer tchr. Fremont-Mills Cmty. Sch., Tabor, Iowa, 1972—. Mem. NEA, Nat. Coun. Tchrs. Math., Iowa State Edn. Assn., Fremont-Mills Edn. Assn. Democrat. Roman Catholic.

ALLIGOOD, MARY SALE, special education educator; b. Richmond, Va., Oct. 28, 1942; d. Charles Latané and Virginia Carter (Elmer) Sale; m. Frederick Marvin Alligood, Jr., June 12, 1965; children: Anne Hassell Alligood Tadlock, Frederick Carter. BA in Psychology, Mary Washington Coll., 1965; MEd in Spl. Edn./Learning Disabilities, Va. Commonwealth U., 1982. 2d grade tchr. West Columbia-Cayce Schs., Columbia, S.C., 1965-67; 3d/4th grade tchr. Riverside Sch., Richmond, Va., 1972-79; 1st/2d grade tchr. Steward Sch., Richmond, Va., 1979-83; learning disabilities tchr. Chesterfield County Schs., Richmond, Va., 1983-85; spl. edn. educator Powhatan (Va.) County Schs., 1985-96. Bd. dirs., sec., chair Redeemer Episcopal Day Sch., Midlothian, Va., 1992—; mem., treas. Episcopal Ch. Women, Richmond, 1967—; mem. vestry Episcopal Ch. of Redeemer, Midlothian, 1975-78, 81-83, mem. search com., 1994, stewardship co-chair, 1996—. Mem. ASCD, Coun. for Learning Disabilities, Assn. for Children/Adults with Learning Disabilities, Powhatan County Edn. Assn. (pres. 1989-91), Delta Kappa Gamma (membership com., programs 1989-92, pres. 1996-98). Home: 2841 River Oaks Dr Midlothian VA 23113-2226 Office: Powhatan Elem Sch 4111 Old Buckingham Rd Powhatan VA 23139

ALLISON, ANNE MARIE, librarian; b. Oak Park, Ill., Oct. 3, 1931; d. Gerald Patrick and Anna Evelyn (Beam) Myers; m. James Dixon Alison, Aug. 28, 1954; children: Mark, Mary, Clare, Ruth, Edward. BA in French, St. Mary of the Woods Coll., 1951; postgrad., U. Fribourg, 1952-53; MLS, Rosary Coll., 1968. Asst. libr. Triton Coll., River Grove, Ill., 1967-68; asst. libr. tech. svcs. Moraine Valley Community Coll., Palos Hills, Ill., 1968-69; dir. learning resources, head libr. Coll. Lake County, Grayslake, Ill., 1969-71; asst. head catalog dept. Kent (Ohio) State U. Librs., 1971-73, head processing dept., 1973-79, asst. dir. libr. svcs., 1979-81; acting dir. Fla. Atlantic U. Libr., Boca Raton, 1980-81; asst. dir., head tech. svcs. Wayne State U. Librs., Detroit, 1981-83; dir. librs. U. Cen. Fla., Orlando, 1983—; past chair, bd. dirs. Fla. Extension Libr., Tampa; bd. dirs. Ctr. for Libr. Automation, Gainesville, Fla., Cen. Fla. Holocaust Meml. Resource Ctr., Orlando; adj. prof. Libr. and Info. Sci., U. S. Fla., Tampa. Editor: OCLC: A National Library Network, 1979; contbr. articles to profl. jours. Arbitrator alternative dispute resolution program Better Bus. Bur. Cen. Fla., Maitland, 1985—; active Friends Winter Park Pub. Libr., Friends of Orlando Pub. Libr. Recognized for Outstanding Leadership in Edn. Cen. Fla. Ednl. Consortium for Women, 1990. Mem. ALA (chair profl. ethics com.), Fla. Libr. Assn., Fla. Assn. Coll. and Rsch. Librs. (pres. bd. dirs.). Office: U Cen Fla PO Box 25000 Orlando FL 32816-0001

ALLISON, BRENDA JOYCE, secondary education educator; b. Greenville, Ky., Mar. 23, 1941; d. Oather William and Jessie Ferrell (Furman) Welborn; m. Hugh Louis Allison, Aug. 12, 1961; children: Cheryl, Michael, Kimberly, Darren. BA, Western Ky. U., 1969; MA, Austin Peay U., 1975, Murray State U., 1981. Tchr. Todd County Bd. Edn., Elkton, Ky., 1969-70; tchr. Christian County Bd. Edn., Hopkinsville, Ky., 1970—; adv. bd. Christian County Credit Union, Hopkinsville, 1992-94. Recipient computer grant Christian County Bd. Edn. Tech. Ctr., 1994. Mem. NEA, Ky. Edn. Assn., Christian County Edn. Assn., Nat. Coun. Tchrs. Math., Nat. Coun. Math. Tchrs., Delta Acad. Republican. Baptist. Home: 832 North Dr Hopkinsville KY 42240-2619 Office: Christian County H S 220 Glass Ave Hopkinsville KY 42240-2471

ALLISON, JOAN KELLY, music educator, pianist; b. Denison, Iowa, Jan. 25, 1935; d. Ivan Martin and Esther Cecelia (Newborg) K.; m. Guy Hendrick Allison, July 25, 1954 (div. Apr. 1973); children: David, Dana, Douglas, Diane. MusB, St. Louis Inst. of Music, 1955; MusM, So. Meth. U., 1976. Korrepetitor Corpus Christi (Tex.) Symphony, 1963-85; staff pianist Am. Inst. Mus. Studies, Graz, Austria, 1974-89; prof. Del Mar Coll., Corpus Christi, 1976—; adj. prof. Del Mar Coll., 1959-75, Corpus Christi State U., 1978-93, Tex. A&M U., Corpus Christi, 1993—; program dir. Corpus Christi Chamber Music Soc., 1986—; piano chmn. Corpus Christi Young Artists' Competition, 1987—; chmn. Del Mar Coll. Student Programs Com., 1986-88, 91-92, 94-95; chmn. radio commn., S.Tex. Pub. Broadcasting Svc., Corpus Christi, 1987-88; asst. mus. dir. Little Theater, Corpus Christi, 1970-74; judge, Houston Symphony Auditions, 1988, S.C. Young Artist Competition, Columbia, 1990; freelance accompanist, 1955—, adjudicator, 1960—; v.p. united fac., Del Mar Coll., 1986-88; pianist with Del Mar Trio, 1965-95, Young Audiences, Inc., 1975-83; recital tours in U.S., Mex., Austria, 1954-88. Piano soloist, St. Louis Symphony, 1956, 57, Bach Festival Orch., St. Louis, 1955, Corpus Christi Symphony; recipient Artist Presentation award, Artist Presentation Soc., St. Louis, 1956. Co-chmn. Mayor's Com. on Recycling, Corpus Christi, 1989-91; bd. dirs. Corpus Christi Symphony; adv. bd. Corpus Christi Concert Ballet; mem. steering com. cultural devel. plan City of Corpus Christi, 1995-96. Mem. Music Tchrs. Nat. Assn., Tex. Music Tchrs. Assn., Corpus Christi Music Tchrs. Assn., Liszt Soc. (contbr. to jour.). Home: 4709 Curtis Clark Dr Corpus Christi TX 78411-4801 Office: Del Mar Coll Baldwin & Ayers Corpus Christi TX 78404

ALLISON, LOYETTE E., construction company executive; b. Delano, Calif., July 7, 1946; d. Dempsey Willard and Billie Wanda (Fink) Bogard; m. Robert Lee, Nov. 30, 1963; children: Cindy Kay, Ann Rena. Photography student Northwestern U., 1963 student Pima Coll., 1979, U. Denver, 1983; AA in Gen. Edn. Pima Coll., 1995; postgrad. U. Ariz., 1995—. Sales mgr. K-Mart, Tucson, 1975-78; clk.-typist Fairfield Green Valley, Ariz., 1978-81; purchasing agt. Tobin Homes, Tucson, 1981-83; constrn. mgr. Fairfield La Cholla Hills, Tucson, 1983-86; v.p. ops. Fairfield Sunrise, 1986-91, Fairfield Pusch Ridge, 1989, Fairfield comml. divsn.; spkr. on cause of child abuse and how to help prevent multiple personality dissociative disorders. Author: Living and Coping with D.I.D.: Managing Life With Multiple Personality Disorder, 1995. Notary public State of Ariz; civic leader on behalf of women and community; spkr. on causes of child abuse, disorders. Recipient Persuasive Comm. award Dept. Real Estate State of Ariz., 1989, Women on the Move Leadership award YMCA, Citizens for a Sound Economy award. Mem. NAFE, Am. Bus. Inst. (2000 notable women), Bus. on the Move, Toastmasters. Baptist. Avocations: stock car racing; aerobics, modern dance. Home: 2151 W Felicia Pl Tucson AZ 85741-3101

ALLISON, TOMILEA, former mayor; b. Madera, Calif., Mar. 28, 1934; d. John and Edna (Archer) Radosevich; m. James Allison, 1958; children: Devon, Leigh. B.A. in Sociology, Occidental Coll., 1955; postgrad. Fresno State Coll., 1956. City council mem. City of Bloomington, Ind., 1977-82, mayor, 1983-96; pres. Ind. Assn. Cities and Towns, 1994. Active Citizens for Good Govt., Bloomington, 1960-65, Community Progress Council, 1980-85. Mem. LWV, Bloomington C. of C. Recipient Russell G. Lloyd Dist. Svc. award. Democrat. Home: 1127 E First St Bloomington IN 47402 Office: 220 E 3rd St Bloomington IN 47401-3513

ALLMAND, LINDA F(AITH), library director; b. Port Arthur, Tex., Jan. 31, 1937; d. Clifton James and Jewel Etoile (Smith) A. BA, North Tex. State U., 1960; MA, U. Denver, 1962. Clerical asst. Gates Meml. Libr., 1953-55; libr. asst. Houston Pub. Libr., 1955-58; children's libr. Denver Pub. Libr., 1960-63; children's coord. Anaheim Pub. Libr., Calif., 1963-65; br. mgr. Dallas Pub. Libr, 1965-71, chief br. svcs., 1971-81; dir. Ft. Worth Pub. Libr., 1981—; instr. North Tex. State U., Denton, 1967—; instr. Dallas County C.C., 1981; bldg. cons. Dallas Pub. Libr., 1974-80, Hurst Pub. Libr., 1977-78, Jacksonville (Tex.) Pub. Libr., 1976-79, Carrollton Pub. Libr., 1979-81, Haltom (Tex.) City Pub. Libr., 1984, Iowa Park (Tex.) Pub. Libr., 1985, S.W. Regional Libr., Ft. Worth, 1987. Author: 1981-2000, Ft. Worth Public Library—Facilities and Long-Range Planning Study, 1982; contbr. chpts. to books, articles to profl. jours. Bd. dirs. City of Dallas Credit Union, 1973-81, Sr. Citizen's Ctrs., Inc., 1982; com. chmn. Goals for Dallas, 1967-69; mem. Forum Ft. Worth, 1983. Pilot Club of Port Arthur scholar, 1954, Libr. Binding Inst. scholar, 1958; recipient Disting. Alumnus award North Tex. State U., 1983, Leadership Ft. Worth, 1982-83; named Tarrant County Newsmaker of the Yr., 1984, Outstanding Leader, Ft. Worth Star Telegram, 1989, Outstanding Woman of the Yr., Mayor's Commn. on Status of Women, 1989, North Tex. Pub. Adminstr. of the Yr., 1990. Mem. ALA, AAUP, AAUW, Tex. Libr. Assn. (pres. pub. libr. divsn. 1980-81, chmn. planning com. 1982-84, pres.-elect 1985-86, pres. 1986-87, Libr. of Yr. award 1985, North Tex. Pub. Adminstr. of Yr. award 1990), Tarrant Regional Librs. Assn., Am. Mgmt. Assn., Dallas County Librs. Assn. (pres. 1968-69), Downtown Ft. Worth (mem. edn. info. task force 1992-93), Freedom to Read Found., Ft. Worth C. of C. (bd. dirs. 1993—), Rotary, Sister Cities, Inc., Ft. Worth Pub. Libr. Found. Home: 701 Timberview Ct N Fort Worth TX 76112-1715 Office: Fort Worth Pub Libr 300 Taylor St Fort Worth TX 76102-7309

ALLMON, REBECCA LEA, marketing executive; b. San Antonio, Apr. 18, 1956; d. Jack Dale and Dorothy Ruth (Norris) A. BS in Bus., Trinity U., San Antonio, 1980; BS in Journalism/Broadcasting/Film, 1980. News anchor, producer Sta. KTBC-TV, Austin, Tex., 1980-82; pub. rels. dir. Topletz Devel. Co., Austin, 1982-86; pub. rels. account exec. DBG&H Unltd., Inc., Austin and Houston, 1986-88; chief media rels. Tex. Dept. Commerce, Austin, 1988-89; dir. mktg. communications Cycle Sat, Inc., Forest City, Iowa, 1990-93; dir. corp. comm. Expeditors Internat., Seattle, 1993—. Bd. dirs. Big Bros./Big Sisters, Austin, 1987-88, mem. Leadership Iowa Class of 1991, Des Moines, mktg. adv. com. Iowa Dept. Econ. Devel., Des. Moines, 1990-93, adv. com. Hospice of Forest City, 1991-93; mem. Des Moines Symphony Guild, 1991-93, Austin Symphony League, 1984-89,. Named Outstanding Woman in Tex. Govt., State of Tex., 1989. Mem. Am. Mktg. Assn. Republican. Office: Expeditors Internat 19119 16th Ave S Seattle WA 98188-5157

ALLRED, GLORIA RACHEL, lawyer; b. Phila., July 3, 1941; d. Morris and Stella Bloom; m. William Allred (div. Oct. 1987); 1 child, Lisa. BA, U. Pa., 1963; MA, NYU, 1966; JD, Loyola U., L.A., 1974; JD (hon.), U. West Los Angeles, 1981. Bar: Calif. 1975, U.S. Dist. Ct. (cen. dist.) Calif. 1975, U.S. Ct. Appeals (9th cir.) 1976, U.S. Supreme Ct. 1979. Ptnr. Allred, Maroko, Goldberg & Ribakoff (now Allred, Maroko & Goldberg), L.A., 1976—. Contbr. articles to profl. jours. Pres. Women's Equal Rights Legal Def. and Edn. Fund, L.A., 1978—, Women's Movement Inc., L.A. Recipient Commendation award L.A. Bd. Suprs., 1986, Mayor of L.A., 1986, Pub. Svc. award Nat. Assn. Fed. Investigators, 1986, Vol. Action award Pres. of U.S., 1986. Mem. ABA, Calif. Bar Assn., Nat. Assn. Women Lawyers, Calif. Women Lawyers Assn., Women Lawyers L.A. Assn., Friars (Beverly Hills, Calif.), Magic Castle Club (Hollywood, Calif.). Office: Allred Maroko & Goldberg 6300 Wilshire Blvd Ste 1500 Los Angeles CA 90048-5217*

ALLRED, RITA REED, artist; b. Davenport, Iowa, Apr. 12, 1935; d. Edward Platt and Delia Marie (Quinn) Reed; m. Glenn Charles Scott, June 9, 1956 (div. Nov. 1977); children: Sheryl Marie, Laura Ann; m. Robert Yates Allred, Dec. 9, 1977. Student Marycrest Coll., Davenport, 1953-56; BS in Art Edn., Drake U., 1958; MFA in Painting, Winthrop U., 1995. Art tchr. Fayetteville City Schs., N.C., 1961-64, Charlotte-Mecklenburg Schs., N.C., 1967-71; cons., project dir. PCA Internat., Matthews, N.C., 1981; artist, art cons., dir. workshops, 1976—; civilian artist USCG, 1981—; instr. portrait painting Cen. Piedmont Community Coll., 1986—; instr. drawing and painting Mint Mus. Art, 1991—; courtroom sketch artist WBTV, 1991-92; adj. prof. art Gardner-Webb U., Boiling Springs, N.C., 1993—; painter in oils; recent comms. include paintings for U.S. Army, USCG, portraits for ABCO Industries, U.S. Naval Inst. Service Head Portrait Series, NASA Art Team; pres. Willow Reed Studios, 1986-90. Bd. dirs. Internat. House, Charlotte, 1985-86; mem. Sister Cities Com., Charlotte, 1984-85. Recipient George Gray award USCG, 1983. Democrat. Mem. Cedarwood Country Club. Avocation: golf. Home and Studio: 7217 Quail Meadow Ln Charlotte NC 28210-5124 Office: Willow Reed Studios 7217 Quail Meadow Ln Charlotte NC 28210-5124

ALLRED, SANDRA LYNN, elementary education educator; b. Tyler, Tex., Aug. 21, 1946; d. Joe Douglas and Bennie George (Vance) Lawson; m. Danny W. Allred, May 1, 1966; children: Charles Winfield, Matthew Thomas. BS, Phillips U., 1968. Cert. elem. tchr., Okla. Classroom tchr. Enid (Okla.) Pub. Schs., 1968-74, Putnam City Schs., Oklahoma City, 1975—. Mem. NEA, Okla. Edn. Assn., Putnam City Assn. Classroom Tchrs., Okla. Reading Coun. Republican. Roman Catholic. Office: Ralph Downs Elem Sch 7501 W Hefner Rd Oklahoma City OK 73162-4432

ALLSUP, DONNA CAROL, secondary education educator; b. Macon, Miss., Feb. 6, 1957; d. Dwayne Arthur and Jo Carolyn (Haley) A. BS, Miss. Univ. for Women, Columbus, 1979. Cert. in math. and English, Miss. Tchr. math. Lowndes County Schs., Columbus, Miss., 1979—; head dept. math. New Hope Middle Sch., Columbus, 1987—. Weyerhaeuser Co. Found. grantee; named OTE Tchr. of Yr., New Hope Mid. Sch., 1995. Mem. ASCD, Nat. Coun. Tchrs. Math., Miss. Profl. Educators. Home: 206 E Manor Dr Apt 3 Columbus MS 39702-5210 Office: Lowndes County Schs 201 Airline Rd Columbus MS 39702-6303

ALLUM, JERRI LYNN, financial company representative; b. Burke, S.D., Mar. 22, 1965; d. Oscar Warren and Irene Elaine (Mayer) A. BS, No. State U., Aberdeen, S.D., 1987; MS, S.D. State U., 1994. Customer svc. profl. Citibank, Sioux Falls, S.D., 1988-90, case rev. specialist, 1990-93, fraud investigator, 1993—; counselor-intern McKennan Hosp., Sioux Falls, 1994; pvt. practice mental health counselor Sioux Falls. Vol. children's advocate, domestic violence counselor Children's Inn, Sioux Falls, 1995—; advocate for abused and neglected children Ct. Approved Spl. Advocate, Sioux Falls, 1995—. Mem. ACA, Am. Assn. Marriage and Family Therapists. Home: 2013 W 15th St Apt 5 Sioux Falls SD 57104

ALLWOOD, RHONDA MARIE, middle school educator; b. Boston, July 23, 1961; d. Kenneth Dudley and Lena Theodosia (Stewart) A.; 1 child, Hashabiah Y.O. Nelson. BA in Psychology, Coll. of the Holy Cross, 1982; MA in Indsl. Orgnl. Psychology, U. New Haven, 1986. Cert. elem. tchr., cert. tchr. psychology, N.J. Client relation mgr. People Express Airlines, Newark, N.J., 1987; owner, operator Just Hearts Internat., West Haven, Conn., 1988-91; substitute tchr. West Haven Bd. of Edn., 1990-91; substitute tchr. Newark Bd. of Edn., 1991-92, 8th grade math. tchr., 1992—; cons. Homeschoolers, East Orange, N.J., 1993—. Mng. bd. dirs. YMCA, East Orange, 1994—. Recipient Very Important Parent award Clark Sch., 1993. Mem. Nat. Coun. Tchrs. Math., Assn. Math. Tchrs. N.J., Assn. Supervision and Curriculum Devel., Psi Chi. Office: Thirteenth Ave Elem Sch 359 13th Ave Newark NJ 07103-2125

ALMAN, EMILY ARNOW, lawyer, sociologist; b. N.Y.C., Jan. 20, 1922; d. Joseph Michael and Cecilia (Greenstone) Arnow; B.A., Hunter Coll., 1948; Ph.D., New Sch. for Social Research, 1963; J.D., Rutgers U., Newark, 1977; m. David Alman, Aug. 1, 1940; children: Michelle Alman Harrison, Jennifer Alman Michaels. Bar: N.J. 1978, U.S. Supreme Ct. 1987. Probation officer, N.Y.C., 1945-48; assoc. prof. sociology Douglass Coll. Rutgers U., Newark, 1960-86, prof. emeritus, 1986—; sr. ptnr. Alman & Michaels, Highland Park, N.J., 1978—. Candidate for mayor, City of East Brunswick, 1972; chmn. Concerned Citizens of East Brunswick, 1970-78; pres. bd. trustees Concerned Citizens Environ. Fund., East Brunswick, 1977-78. Mem. ABA (com. family law) N.J. Bar Assn. (bd. dirs. legal svcs), Middlesex County Bar Assn. (Ann. Aldona Appleton award women lawyers sect. 1990, Ann. Svc. to Families award 1993), Am. Sociol. Assn., Assn. Fed. Bar State of N.J., Assn. Trial Lawyers Am., Trial Lawyers Assn. Middlesex County, Law and Soc. Assn., Am. Judicature Soc., Nat. Assn. Women Lawyers, N.J. Assn. Women Lawyers, ACLU, AAUP, Women Helping Women. Author: Ride The Long Night, 1963; screenplay, The Ninety-First Day, 1963. Home: 611 S Park Ave Highland Park NJ 08904-2928

ALMEDA MUÑOZ, FLOR ADRIANA, payroll manager; b. Del Rio, Tex., Oct. 16, 1971; d. Florentino Almeda Alvarado and Juanita Almeda Clark; m. Manuel Muñoz III, Sept. 3, 1994. AA magna cum laude, S.W. Tex. Jr. Coll., 1991, BA, 1996. Acctg. clk. Tecnol, Inc., Del Rio, Tex., 1993, payroll mgr. Mex. plant, 1993—; acct. Jerry Horne, CPA, Del Rio. Roman Catholic. Home: 110 Sombrero Dr Del Rio TX 78840 Office: Tecnol Inc 14 Finegan Rd Del Rio TX 76640

ALMEKINDER, LEISA ANN, general contracting company executive; b. Rochester, N.Y., Sept. 24, 1952; d. Eugene Almekinder and John C. (Lewis) Morse; m. Edward K. Courter, July 24, 1986; 1 child, William H. AS in Forestry, Paul Smiths Coll., N.Y., 1975. Cartographer Adirondack Park Agy., Ray Brook, N.Y., 1976-79; glazier Bloomingdale, N.Y., 1979-91; owner, mgr. A.G. Constrn., Bloomingdale, N.Y., 1991—. Art glass displayed in Profl. Stained Glass, Adirondack Life, Archtl. Digest. Home and Office: HCR 1 Box 37 Bloomingdale NY 12913

ALMES, JUNE, retired education educator, librarian; b. Pitts., Feb. 14, 1934; d. Donald John Rowbottom and Marie Catherine (Linz) Douglas; widowed; children: Lawrence John, Douglas Alan. BS in Edn., Ind. U. of Pa., 1955; MLS, U. Pitts., 1969. Tchr. Shippensburg (Pa.) Area High Sch., 1964-68; assoc. prof. Lock Haven (Pa.) U., 1971-94; ret., 1990; instr. Changsha U. Electric Power, Hunan, China, 1989-90, 95. Trustee Ross Pub. Libr., Lock Haven, 1975-88, community story programs, 1973-86; tutor Clinton City Literacy Found., Lock Haven, 1979. Mem. Am. Assn. Sch. Librs., Pa. Assn. Sch. Librs., ACLU, Phi Kappa Phi, Phi Delta Kappa. Democrat. Home: 227 Hillside Dr Lock Haven PA 17745-1731

ALMLOFF, BETHANY DAWN, physical education educator; b. Springfield, Mo., June 2, 1967; d. John D. Berry and Carolyn F. (Means) Dykes; m. Kevin Almloff, July 27, 1991. AA, Johnson County C.C., Overland Park, Kans., 1988; BS, Kansas State U., 1991. Cert. phys. edn. and adapted phys. edn. tchr., Kans. Tchr. adapted phys. edn. New Horizons Day Camp Johnson County Parks and Recreation, Overland Park, Kans., 1992 summer, Lakemary Ctr., Paolo, Kans., 1992—; spl. olympics coach Lakemary Ctr. Paola, Kans., 1992-95. Mem. AAHPERD, Kans. Assn. Health, Phys. Edn., Recreation and Dance (chair student br. Kans. State U. 1990-91), Golden Key. Office: Lakemary Ctr 100 Lakemary Dr Paola KS 66071-1855

ALMORE-RANDLE, ALLIE LOUISE, special education educator; b. Jackson, Miss., Apr. 20; d. Thomas Carl and Theressa Ruth (Garrett) Almore; m. Olton Charles Randle, Sr., Aug. 3, 1974. BA, Tougaloo (Miss.) Coll., 1951; MS in Edn., U. So. Calif., L.A., 1971. Recreation leader Pasadena (Calif.) Dept. Recreation, 1954-56; demonstration tchr. Pasadena Unified Schs., 1956-63; cons. spl. edn. Temple City (Calif.) Sch. Dist., 1967; supr. tchr. edn. U. Calif., Riverside, 1971; tchr. spl. edn. Pasadena Unified Sch. Dist., 1955-70, dept. chair spl. edn. Pasadena High Sch., 1972—; also adminstrv. asst. Pasadena High Sch., 1993—; supr. Evelyn Frieden Ctr., U. So. Calif., L.A., 1970; mem. Coun. Exceptional Children, 1993—. Organizer Northwest Project, Camp Fire Girls, Pasadena, 1963; leader Big Sister Program, YWCA, Pasadena, 1966; organizer, dir. March on The Boys' Club, the Portrait of a Boy, 1966; pub. souvenir jours. Women's Missionary Soc., AME Ch., State of Wash. to Mo.; mem. NAACP, Ch. Women United, Afro-Am. Quilters L.A. Recipient Cert. of Merit, Pasadena City Coll., 1963, Outstanding Achievement award Nat. Coun. Negro Women, Pasadena, 1965, Earnest Thompson Seton award Campfire Girls, Pasadena, 1968, Spl. Recognition, Outstanding Community Svc. award The Tuesday Morning Club, 1967, Dedicated Svc. award AME Ch., 1983, Educator of Excellence award Rotary Club of Pasadena, 1993, Edn. award Altadena NAACP, 1994; named Tchr. of Yr., Pasadena Masonic Bodies, 1967, Woman of the Yr. for Community Svc. and Edn., Zeta Phi Beta, 1992; grad. fellow U. So. Calif., L.A., 1970. Mem. NAACP (bd. mem., chmn. ch. workers com. 1955-63, Fight for Freedom award West Coast region 1957, NAACP Edn. award Altadena, Calif. chpt. 1994), ASCD, Calif. Tchrs. Assn., Nat. Coun. Negro Women, Phi Delta Gamma (hospitality chair 1971—), Alpha Kappa Alpha (membership com.), Phi Delta Phi (founder, organizer 1961). Democrat. Mem. AME Ch. Home: 1710 La Cresta Dr Pasadena CA 91103-1261

ALOFF, MINDY, writer; b. Phila., Dec. 20, 1947; d. Jacob and Selma (Album) A.; m. Martin Steven Cohen, June 16, 1968; 1 child, Ariel Nikiya. AB in English, Vassar Coll., 1969; MA in English, SUNY, Buffalo, 1972. Asst. prof. English U. Portland, Oreg., 1973-75; editor Encore Mag. of the Arts, Portland, 1977-80, Vassar Quar., Poughkeepsie, N.Y., 1980-88; free-lance writer Bklyn., 1988—; coord. Portland Poetry Festival, 1974-75. Author: (poems) Night Lights, 1979; author essays and revs. theatrical dancing and lit. for N.Y. Times Book Rev., New Republic mag., Nation mag., Threepenny Rev., Dance magn., New Yorker mag., ann. Ency. Britannica, others. Mem. urgent action com. Amnesty Internat. Recipient Whiting Writers award Mrs. Giles Whiting Found., N.Y.C., 1987; Woodrow Wilson Found. fellow, 1969, Woodburn fellow SUNY-Buffalo, 1972, Am. Dance Festival Dance Critics Inst. fellow, New London, Conn., 1977, John Simon Guggenheim Meml. Found. fellow, 1990. Mem. Dance Critics Assn. (pres. 1984-85), Nat. Book Critics Circle (bd. dirs. 1988-91), Phi Beta Kappa.

ALOISI, CAROL ANN, marketing executive; b. Plainfield, N.J., Nov. 29, 1953; d. Edward Charles and Evelyn Helen (Nowhark) Schaffernoth; m. Michael Francis Aloisi, Jan. 20, 1979. BA, Rutgers the State U., 1979; MBA, Rutgers the State U., Newark, 1991. Mgr. employment Bamberger's/Macy's, Newark, 1975-78; pers. adminstr. John Wiley & Sons., N.Y.C., 1978-79, corp. pers. mgr., 1979-81; mgr. pers. adminstrn. Ortho Diagnostic Sys., Inc., N.Y.C., 1981-82, mgr. employee rels., 1982-83, dir. employee rels., 1984-85, nat. account exec., 1985-87, product mgr., 1987-89; dir. mktg. Ortho Diagnostic Sys., Inc., Raritan, N.J., 1989-92; gen. mgr. Ortho Diagnostic Systems Inc., Raritan, N.J., 1992-93; pres. Career Mgmt. Cons., Inc., Bound Brook, N.J., 1994—. Recipient Tribute to Women in Industry award YWCA/TWIN of Cen. N.J., 1987. Mem. Tribute to Women in Industry, BioMed Mktg. Assn., Internat. Assn. Career Mgmt. Profls. Office: Career Mgmt Cons Inc 20 W Maple Ave Bound Brook NJ 08805-1734

ALONSO, MARIA CONCHITA, actress, singer; b. Cuba, 1957; d. Joséand Conchita Alonso. Appeared in films Moscow on the Hudson, 1984, A Fine Mess, 1986, Touch and Go, 1986, Extreme Prejudice, 1987, The Running Man, 1987, Colors, 1988, Vampire's Kiss, 199, Predator II, 1990, House of the Spirits, 1994; appeared in numerous Venezuelan films and soap operas; TV appearances include Blood Ties, 1986, One of the Boys, 1989; recording artist, albums include: Maria Conchita, 1984 (Grammy award nomination for Best Latin Artist 1985), O ella o yo, 1985. Named Miss World Teenager, 1971, Miss Venezuela, 1975. Office: ICM 8942 Wilshire Blvd Beverly Hills CA 90211*

ALONZO, LISA BELTRAN, accounting technician; b. San Antonio, July 29, 1966; d. Jesse Castillo and Mary Louise (Landavazo) Beltran; m. Rene Garcia Alonzo, Aug. 16, 1986. BBA, St. Mary's U., 1988. Acctg. tech. USAA, San Antonio, 1993—. Home: 914 Briarcliff Dr San Antonio TX 78213

ALONZO-SNYDER, MARIE CARMEN, dance educator, choreographer; b. Manila, The Philippines, July 4, 1964; came to U.S., 1981; d. Domingo Cruz and Carmen Reloj Alonzo; m. W. Kirk Synder, Jul. 16, 1988; 1 child, Gregory. BFA, Tisch Sch. of the Arts, NYU, 1985, MFA, 1986; EdD, Tchrs. Coll. Columbia U., 1995. Teacher, dancer Elec. Body Art Ctr. for Dance and Movement, Albany, N.Y., 1987-88, Arts Gate Ctr., N.Y.C., 1988-89; teacher, dancer Asian Am. Arts Ctr., N.Y.C., 1988-89, prodn. and program mgr., 1988-90; producer, choreographer, dancer Marie Alonzo-Choreographer, N.Y.C., 1986-95; sch. asst. New Ballet Sch., Feld Ballet, N.Y.C., 1991; Dance Edn. Prop Asst., Tchrs. Coll., Columbia U., N.Y.C., 1992. Choreographer, producer (dance prodns.) An Evening of Dance, 1989, Impressions of A Woman, 1991. Recipient Minority Merit scholarship Tchrs. Coll., Columbia U., 1989-92. Mem. Congress on Rsch. in Dance (moderator conf. 1995), Nat. Dance Assn. Roman Catholic.

ALPERN, LINDA LEE WEVODAU, health agency administrator; b. Harrisburg, Pa., July 16, 1949; d. William Irvin Wevodau and Maretia Christine (Mills) Staley; m. Neil Stephen Alpern, Apr. 12, 1985; 1 child, Philip Wevodau. BS in Edn., Shippensburg (Pa.) U., 1971. Unit program coord. Pa. Div. Am. Cancer Soc., Harrisburg, 1973-75, unit exec. dir., 1975-76, div. svc. dir., 1976-81; div. med. affairs dir. Pa. Div. Am. Cancer Soc., Hershey, 1981-83; div. crusade dir. Md. Div. Am. Cancer Soc., Balt., 1983-87, div. v.p. for field ops., 1988, div. dep., exec. v.p. ops., 1988-95, divsn. chief oper. officer, 1995—. Bd. dirs., sec. Cmty. Assn.; treas. PTA. Democrat. Methodist. Home: 4108 Colonial Rd Baltimore MD 21208-6042

ALPERN, MILDRED, history educator, consultant; b. Boston, Sept. 10, 1931; d. Samuel and Mary (Poncewicz) Rosoff; m. Hale Nissen Alpern, Aug. 27, 1954; children: Merry, Spenser. BA summa cum laude, Boston U., 1953; MA, Columbia U., 1966. Cert. tchr. social studies. Tchr. history and econs. Spring Valley (N.Y.) Sr. H.S., 1966-96, Manhattan H.S. Girls, 1996—; adj. instr. Rockland C.C., Suffern, N.Y., 1973-76; instr. Manhattan Coll., Riverdale, N.Y., summers 1983, 84, 85, 87, LaSalle U., summer 1988, Columbia U. Tchrs. Coll., 1988; mem. advanced placement European history test devel. com., Coll. Bd. 1979-82, chmn. 1982-86, mem. Coll. Bd. history and social scis. adv. com., 1983-85, chmn., 1985-88, chmn. acad. adv. coun., 1987-89, middle states regional assembly, 1993-96; master tchr. summer inst. Sarah Lawrence Coll., Bronxville, N.Y., 1984; mem. faculty Coll. Bd. Project Equality Inst., 1986, 87; adj. instr. econs. Syracuse U., 1988—. Co-editor (history column) Am. Hist. Assn. Perspectives, 1982-88; co-author (teaching guide) Household and Kin, 1981; author: Longman's Guide to the Advanced Placement European History Examination, 1993; contbr. articles to profl. publs. Recipient award for contbns. in edn. Rockland County Women's Network, 1984, Tchr. of Yr. award Jr. Achievement, 1989, 90; Finalist N.Y. State Tchr. of Yr., 1988; Fulbright Commn. study grantee, Italy, 1980, NEH grantee Tufts U., 1983. Mem. Orgn. Am. Historians (chmn. teaching div. 1982-83), Am. Hist. Assn. (teaching div.), Phi Beta Kappa, Pi Gamma Mu. Democrat. Home: 13 Cragmere Rd Suffern NY 10901-7515 Office: Manhattan HS Girls 154 E 70th St New York NY 10021

ALPERT, ANN SHARON, insurance claims examiner; b. Indpls., Feb. 24, 1938; d. Oscar and Adele Alpert. BS in Edn., Ind. U., 1959. Tchr. Indpls. Pub. Schs., 1959-60; libr. George Fry & Assocs., Chgo., 1960-62, DeLeuw, Cather & Co., Chgo., 1962-65, Arthur Young & Co., CPAs, Chgo., 1965-74; statis. asst. Sargent & Lundy, Chgo., 1974-81, computer liaison agt., 1981-83, tech. editor, 1983-87; sales assoc. Jewelmaster, Inc., Chgo., 1987-88; claims processor Benefit Trust Life Ins. Co., Chgo., 1988-90; claims examiner Ft. Dearborn Life Ins. Co., 1990-91, sr. claims examiner, 1991—. Fellow Life Mgmt. Inst. (assoc. customer svc.); mem. Chgo. Claims Assn., Women in Workers' Compensation.

ALPERT, DEIRDRE WHITTLETON, state legislator; b. N.Y.C., Oct. 6, 1945; d. Harry Mark and Dorothy (Lehn) Whittleton; m. Michael Edward Alpert, Jan. 1, 1964; children: Lehn, Kristin, Alison. Student, Pomona Coll., 1963-65; LLD (hon.), Western Am. U., 1994. Mem. from 78th dist. Calif. State Assembly, Sacramento, 1990—; chairwoman Women's Legislators Caucus, Sacramento, 1993; active Calif. Tourism Commn., Sacramento, 1990—, Calif. Libr. Allocations Bd., Sacramento, 1993—. dist. rep., troop leader Girl Scouts Am., San Diego, 1977-83; spl. advocate Voices for Children, San Diego, 1982-90; mem. bd. Solana Beach (Calif.) Sch. Bd., 1983-90, also pres.; pres. beach and county guild United Cerebral Palsy, San Diego, 1986. Recipient Legis. award Calif. Regional Occupation Program, 1991-92, Am. Acad. Pediats., 1991-92, San Diego Psychol. Assn., 1993-94, Commitment to Children award Calif. Assn. for Edn. of Young Children, 1993-94; named Legis. Commendation award Nat. Assn. for Yr.-Round Edn., 1991-92, State Commn. on Status of Women, 1993-94; named Friend of Yr., Children's PKU Network, 1991-92, Woman of Yr., Nat. Women's Polit. Caucus San Diego, 1991-92, Orgn. for Rehab. through Tng., 1993-94, Legislator of Yr., Am. Electronics Assn., 1991-92, 1993-94, Calif. Sch.-Age Consortium, 1993-94, Women of Distinction, Soropimists Internat. of La Jolla, 1993-94, Assemblymember of Yr., Calif. Assn. Edn. Young Children, 1993-94. Mem. Charter 100 of San Diego, Calif. Elected Women's Assn. for Edn. and Rsch. (v.p. 1994—). Democrat. Mem. Congregation Ch. Office: 1350 Front St Ste 6013 San Diego CA 92101-3607*

ALSMEYER, MARSHA ANN, underwriter; b. Tuscola, Ill., May 22, 1962; d. Elmer C. and Elizabeth J. Alsmeyer. BBA, St. Mary's U., San Antonio, 1988; Assoc. in Risk Mgmt., Ins. Inst. Am., 1993. With EPIC, Indpls. Mem. Am. Soc. Safety Engrs. Office: American States Insurance 500 N Meridian St Indianapolis IN 46240

ALSOP, MARIN, conductor; d. LaMar and Ruth A. Student, Yale Univ., Julliard Sch. Debut with Symphony Space, N.Y.C., 1984; founder, artistic dir. Concordia Chamber Orchestra, N.Y.C., 1984—; asst. condr. Richmond Symphony, Va., 1987; music dir. Eugene Symphony Orchestra, Oreg., 1989—, Long Island Philharmonic, N.Y., 1990-94; principal condr. Colorado Symphony Orchestra, Denver, 1993—; guest condr. San Francisco Symphony Orchestra, Boston Pops, Los Angeles Philharmonic Orchestra, 1991, City Ballet Orchestra, 1992; dir. Cabrillo Music Festival, Calif., 1991—; concertmaster Northeastern Pennsylvania Philharmonic, Scranton; founder, mem. String Fever (swing band), 1980—. Recipient Koussevitzky Conducting prize Tanglewood Music Festival, 1988. Office: Long Island Philharmonic Tilles Ctr for the Performing Arts 1 Huntington Quadrangle Ste LL-09 Melville NY 11747*

ALSTON, LELA, state senator; b. Phoenix, June 26, 1942; d. Virgil Lee and Frances Mae Koonse Mulkey; B.S., U. Ariz., 1967; M.S., Ariz. State U., 1971; children—Brenda Susan, Charles William. Tchr. high sch., 1968—; mem. Ariz. State Senate, 1977—. Named Disting. Citizen, U. Ariz. Alumni Assn., 1978. Mem. NEA, Ariz. Edn. Assn., Am. Home Econs. Assn., Ariz. Home Econs. Assn., Am. Vocat. Assn. Methodist. Office: Ariz State Sen State Capitol Phoenix AZ 85007-2812

ALT, BETTY L., sociology educator; b. Walsenburg, Colo., Nov. 12, 1931; d. Cecil R. and Mary M. (Giordano) Sowers; m. William E. Alt, June 19, 1960; 1 child, Eden Jeanette Alt Murrie. BA, Colo. Coll., 1960; MA, NE Mo. State U., 1968. Instr. sociology Indian Hills Community Coll., Centerville, Iowa, 1965-70; dept. chmn. Middlesex Community Coll., Bedford, Mass., 1971-75; instr. sociology Auburn U., Montgomery, 1975-76; div. chmn. Tidewater Community Coll., Virginia Beach, Va., 1976-80; program coord. Pikes Peak Community Coll., Woomera, Australia, 1980-83; instr. sociology Hawaii Pacific Coll., Honolulu, 1983-86, U. Md., Okinawa, Japan, 1987-88, Christopher Newport Coll., Newport News, Va., 1988-89, U. Colo., Colorado Springs, 1989—. Co-author: Uncle Sam's Brides, 1990, Campfollowing: A History of the Military Wife, 1991, Weeping Violins: The Gypsy Tragedy in Europe, 1996. Mem. AAUW, AAUP, Pen Women, N.E. Mo. State U. Alumni Assn. (bd. dirs. 1993—). Home: 2460 N Interstate 25 Pueblo CO 81008-9614 Office: U So Colo 2200 Bonforte Pueblo CO 81001

ALT, MARGARET, reading specialist; b. Chgo., Sept. 18, 1919; d. Hugo and Anna (Kleer) A.; m. Erwin Lionel Ruff, Mar. 29, 1944; children: Stephen M., Nancy E. Mercer; m. William Carrington Levy, Dec. 31, 1977. BA, U. Chgo., 1942; MA, NYU, 1963. Cert. elem. educator, reading specialist, sch. adminstr. Tchr., reading specialist Onteora Unified Sch. Dist., Boiceville, N.Y., 1954-65; reading specialist San Bruno, Calif., 1965-66, Berkeley Unified Sch. Dist., Calif., 1966-77; prof. remedial reading San Francisco State U., 1967-68. Author: (short story) Expanding Horizons, 1984, The Villager, 1984; editor, writer (newspaper) Catskill Mountain Star, 1951-54, Clearlake Observer, 1980-81. Workshop presenter LWV, Woodstock, N.Y., 1955-60; publicity, pres. Clear Lake Performing Arts, Lakeport, Calif., 1990-96; mem. Women's Nat. Book Assn., San Francisco, 1983-96. Recipient scholarship Remedial Reading Inst., Title XI Nat. Def. Edn. Act, 1965. Mem. Clear Lake Performing Arts (pres. 1994-96). Home: 13950 Lakeview Pl Clearlake CA 95422

ALTEKRUSE, JOAN MORRISSEY, retired preventive medicine educator; b. Cohoes, N.Y., Nov. 15, 1928; d. William T. Dee and Agnes Kay (Fitzgerald) Morrissey; m. Ernest B. Altekruse, Dec. 17, 1950; children—Philip, Clifford, Lisa, Janice, Charles, Sean, Lowell, Patrick, E. Caitlin. AB, Vassar Coll., N.Y., 1949; MD, Stanford U., Calif., 1960; MPH, Harvard U., Cambridge, 1965; DPH, U. Calif., Berkeley, 1973. Cons., program dir. Calif. State Health Dept., 1966-69; mem. faculty U. Heidelberg, Germany, 1970-72; med. dir. regional office Fla. State Health Dept., 1972-75; prof., dir. health adminstrn. Sch. Pub. Health, U. S.C., Columbia, 1975-77; prof. preventive medicine Univ. S.C. Sch. of Medicine, Columbia, 1975-94, chmn. dept., 1979-89, disting. prof. emerita, 1994—; fellow, assoc. dir. Irish Peace Inst., U. LImerick, Ireland, 1990—; vis. scholar Ctr. for Rsch. in Disease Prevention, Stanford U., 1992; women in medicine liaison officer Assn. Am. Med. Colls., 1980-94; editl. bd. Aspen Publs. Mem. editorial bd. Family and Community Health Jour., Jour. Community Health; editorial adv. bd. VA Practitioner. Alumni councillor Harvard Sch. Pub. Health; docent, vol. bd. mem. Hunter Mus. Am. Art, Chattanooga. Lt. USMC, 1949-51; sr. surgeon USPHS, 1960-64. Recipient Adminstrn. award Women in Higher Edn., 1989, Achievement award S.C. Commn. on Women, 1990, Ann. award, 1991, Life Achievement award Emma Willard Sch., 1996; WHO travel fellow, Eng., 1974; grantee NIH, NCI, Ctr. for Disease Control, pvt. founds. Fellow Assn. Tchrs. Preventive Medicine (Spl. Recognition award 1995); mem. Am. Bd. Preventive Medicine (trustee 1984-93), Am. Bd. Med. specialities (del. 1990-93), Am. Heart Assn. (S.C. affiliate pres. 1986, agenda planning com. 1987-89, women and minorities leadership 1989-92, Lifetime Achievement award 1992), Nat. Bd. Med. Examiners (comprehensive test com. 1986-92), Am. Womens Med. Assn. Democrat. Catholic.

ALTENHOFEN, JANE ELLEN, federal agency administrator, auditor; b. Seneca, Kans., Sept. 4, 1952; d. Justin Leo and Marva Mae (Sextro) A.; m. John Dean Arnette, Sept. 12, 1975 (div. Mar. 1978). BBA cum laude, Wichita (Kans.) State U., 1973; MPA, Am. U., 1982; cert., Inst. Internal Auditors, 1986. Cert. internal auditor, cert. fraud examiner, cert. govt. fin. mgr. Auditor U.S. Gen. Acctg. Office, Kansas City, Kans., 1974-76, Honolulu, 1976-80, Washington, 1980-84; auditor Fed. Emergency Mgmt. Agy., Washington, 1984-89; insp. gen. U.S. Internat. Trade Commn., Washington, 1989—. Mem. Adopt a Grandparent Program, Wichita, 1973; vol. reading course work to blind students, Wichita, 1973; vol. Vis. Nurse Assn., Washington, 1986—; host, traveler, Wash. area rep. SERVAS, 1987—; commr. Adv. Neighborhood Commn., Washington, 1986-89; troop leader Girl Scouts U.S., Washington, 1983-85; foster home Washington Humane Soc., 1994—. Mem. Inst. Internal Auditors, Nat. Intergovtl. Audit Forum, Assn. Govt. Accouts, Nat. Assn. Cert. Fraud Examiners, Phi Kappa Phi, Pi Alpha Pi. Home: 507 2nd St SE Washington DC 20003-1928 Office: US Internat Trade Commn 500 E St NW Ste 515 Washington DC 20436-0003

ALTER, ELEANOR BREITEL, lawyer; b. N.Y.C., Nov. 10, 1938; d. Charles David and Jeanne (Hollander) Breitel; children: Richard B. Zabel, David B. Zabel. BA with honors, U. Mich., 1960; postgrad., Harvard U., 1960-61; LLB, Columbia U., 1964. Bar: N.Y. 1965. Atty., office of gen. counsel, ins. dept. State of N.Y., 1964-66; assoc. Miller & Carlson, N.Y.C., 1966-68, Marshall, Bratter, Greene, Allison & Tucker, N.Y.C., 1968-74; mem. firm Marshall, Bratter, Greene, Allison & Tucker, 1974-82, Rosenman & Colin, 1982—; fellow U. Chgo. Law Sch., 1988; adj. prof. law NYU Sch. Law, 1983-87; vis. prof. law U. Chgo., 1990-91, 93; lectr. in field. Editorial bd.: N.Y. Law Jour. Contbr. articles to profl. jours. Trustee Lawyers' Fund for Client Protection of the State of N.Y., 1983—, chmn., 1985—; bd. visitors U. Chgo. Law Sch., 1984-87. Mem. ABA, Am. Law Inst., Am. Coll. Family Trial Lawyers, N.Y. State Bar Assn., Assn. of Bar of City of N.Y. (libr. com. 1978-80, com. on matrimonial law 1977-81, 87-88, judiciary com. 1981-84, 94, 95, 96, com. 1988-92), Am. Acad. Matrimonial Lawyers. Office: Rosenman & Colin 575 Madison Ave New York NY 10022-2511

ALTER, SHIRLEY JACOBS, jewelry store owner; b. Beaumont, Tex., June 23, 1929; d. Morris Louis and Helen (Dow) Jacobs; m. Nelson Tobias Alter, June 12, 1949; children: Dennis, Keith, Brian, Wendy. Student, U. Tex., Austin, 1950. Owner Gem Jewelry Co., Beaumont, 1950—. Pres. Nat. Coun. Jewish Women, Beaumont, 1965, 66, Sisterhood of Temple Emanuel, Beaumont, 1967, 68, Buckner Bapt. Benevolence Aux., Beaumont, 1970-72; bd. dirs. Temple Emanuel, pres. elect, 1994-96, pres. 1996-98; active Beaumont Music Commn., 1990; founder Beaumont Reach to Recovery, 1973; trustee Beaumont Heritage Soc.; mem. adv. bd. Bapt. Hosp., 1989—. Democrat. Office: Gem Jewelry Co 795 N 11th St Beaumont TX 77702-1501

ALTFEST, KAREN CAPLAN, financial planning executive; b. Mont., Que., Can.; d. Philip and Betty (Gamer) Caplan; m. Lewis Jay Altfest; children: Ellen Wendy, Andrew Gamer. Tchr.'s diploma, McGill U.; BA cum laude, Hunter Coll., 1970, MA, 1972; PhD, CUNY, 1979. CFP, N.Y. V.p. L. J. Altfest & Co., Inc., N.Y.C., 1985—; dir. fin. planning program New Sch. for Social Rsch., N.Y.C., 1989—; dir. CFP program Pace U., White Plains, N.Y., 1988-90. Author: Robert Owen, 1978; co-author: Lew Altfest Answers Almost All Your Questions about Money, 1992; contbr. articles to fin. jours. Founding chmn. Yorkville Common Pantry, N.Y.C., 1980-84; v.p. PS 6 PTA, N.Y.C., 1991-92; bd. dirs. Temple Shaaray Tefila, 1993—. Recipient Community Svc. award Temple Shaaray Tefila, N.Y.C., 1985; named one of 200 best fin. planners in U.S. Worth mag., 1996. Mem. Nat. Assn. Women Bus. Owners (bd. dirs., chmn. FOCUS 1993-95), Assn. for Can. Studies in U.S., Assn. for Women's Econ. Devel., Inst. CFP (bd. dirs. N.Y. chpt. 1994—), Nat. Assn. Personal Fin. Advisors (chair Northeast-Mid Atlantic Conf. 1995, bd. dirs. Northeast region 1996—, Achievement cert. Northeast

Region 1995), CUNY PhD Alumni Assn. (v.p. 1982-84), Fin. Women's Assn., Women's Econ. Round Table, Phi Alpha Theta. Office: L J Altfest & Co Inc 116 John St Ste 1120 New York NY 10038-3801

ALTMAN, ADELE ROSENHAIN, radiologist; b. Tel Aviv, Israel, June 4, 1924; came to U.S., 1933, naturalized, 1939; d. Bruno and Salla (Silberzweig) Rosenhain; m. Emmett Altman, Sept. 3, 1944; children: Brian R., Alan L., Karen D. Diplomate Am. Bd. Radiology. Intern Queens Gen. Hosp., N.Y.C., 1949-51; resident Hosp. for Joint Diseases, N.Y.C., 1951-52, Roosevelt Hosp., N.Y.C., 1955-57; clin. instr. radiology Downstate Med. Ctr., SUNY, Bklyn., 1957-61; asst. prof. radiology N.Y. Med. Coll., N.Y.C., 1961-65, assoc. prof., 1965-68; assoc. prof. radiology U. Okla. Health Sci. Ctr., Oklahoma City, 1968-78; assoc. prof. dept. radiology U. N.Mex. Sch. Medicine, Albuquerque, 1978-85. Author: Radiology of the Respiratory System: A Basic Review, 1978; contbr. articles to profl. jours. Fellow Am. Coll. Angiology, N.Y. Acad. Medicine; mem. Am. Coll. Radiologist, Am. Roentgen Ray Soc., Assn. Univ. Radiologists, Radiol. Soc. N.Am., B'nai B'rith Anti-Defamation League (bd. dirs. N.Mex. state bd.), Hadassah Club.

ALTMAN, EDITH G., sculptor; b. Altenberg, Germany, May 5, 1931; arrived in U.S.; BA, Wayne State U., 1949; student, Marygrove Coll., 1956-57. Instr. visual arts and printing project U. Omaha, 1984; asst. prof. painting, grad. advisor U. Chgo., 1984-85; vis. asst. prof. painting Sch. Art Inst. Chgo., 1985-86; lectr. painting U. Ill., Columbia Coll., Oakton C.C., Chgo. Exhbns. include Art Inst. Chgo., 1975, 79, 81, 85, Mus. Contemporary Art, Chgo., 1976, 81, 83; NAME Gallery, 1987; one-woman shows include Spertus Mus. Gallery Contemporary Art, 1988, Rockford Art Mus., 1989, State of Ill. Mus. Gallery, Chgo., 1992, Loyola U. Fine Arts Gallery, 1993, Peace Mus., Chgo., 1993, Mitchell Mus., Ill., 1995, Minn. Mus. Am. Art, 1995, others; represented in permanent collections Standard Oil Co., Mus. Contemporary Art, Chgo., State of Ill., Yale U. Mus., Holocaust Mus., Peace Mus.; contbr. articles to profl. jours., newspapers. Individual Artist fellow Ill. Arts. Coun., 1984; Individual Artist Fellow grantee NEA, 1990-91, Art Matters fellow, 1994. Mem. Chgo. Artist Coalition (founding mem., mem. com. artists rights, 1988). Address: 811 W 16th St Chicago IL 60608*

ALTMAN, JEANNETTE MEHR, pharmaceutical sales specialist; b. N.Y.C., Dec. 19, 1938; d. Charles and Gertrude (Handelsman) Mehr; m. Martin Lee Altman, Aug. 7, 1960 (div. July 1974); children: Michael David, Sharyn Ann. Student, SUNY, 1956-59, Washington U., St. Louis, 1961-63. RN, N.Y., Mo. Staff nurse Barnes Hosp., St. Louis, 1960-68; staff nurse Jewish Hosp., St. Louis, 1968-74, nurse adminstr., 1974-76; sales rep. Adria Labs., Columbus, Ohio, 1976-79, Key Pharms., Miami, Fla., 1979-86; cardiovasc. specialist Schering Corp., Kenilworth, N.J., 1986—; mem. sales adv. bd. Warrenteed Labs., Columbus, 1977-78. Pres. B'nai B'rith Women, St. Louis, 1972. Nat. Merit scholar State of N.Y., 1956. Mem. Jewish Women Internat. (life), St. Louis Imperial Dance Club (life, pres. 1985-86). Home: 270 Carmel Woods Ballwin MO 63021

ALTOBELLI, MARY T., artist; b. Yonkers, N.Y., Mar. 5, 1954; d. Anthony M. and Susan (LaGaccia) A.; divorced; 1 child, Gabriella Murphy. BS in Art History, Empire State Coll., 1979. Art dir: Critical Mass, 1995; organizer (installation) This is Our Tribe for Earth Day, 1995; painter (exhbns.) Installation, Billboard, 1993, N.Y. State Regional Women's Art, 1989. Mem. Chester Hist. Soc., N.Y., 1996, Orange Environment, Goshen, N.Y., 1996, Women's Studio Workshop, Rosendale, 1996. Decentralization grantee Arts Coun. of Orange County, 1993; Master Class, Mini Sink Sch. Dist., 1994; recipient prize The Art of Rockland and Orange, 1986; travel grantee German Acad. Exch., 1978.

ALTSCHUL, B. J., public relations counselor; b. Norfolk, Va., Jan. 28, 1948; d. Lemuel and Sylva (Behr) A. Student, Goucher Coll., 1965-67; BA, U. South Fla., MA, U. Md., 1995. Reporter St. Petersburg Times, Fla., 1973-74; dir. pub. rels. Valkyrie Press, Inc., St. Petersburg, 1974-77; founding editor Bay Life, Clearwater, Fla., 1977-79, Tampa Bay Monthly, Clearwater, 1977-79; mng. editor Fla. Tourist News, Tampa and Orlando, 1981; founder Capital Communications of Tampa, 1981, since owner, prin., name changed to b j Altschul & Assocs., 1985—; mgr. editorial and info. svcs. Va. Port Authority, Norfolk, 1985-88; dir. pub. rels. Va. Dept. Agr. and Consumer Svcs., Richmond, 1988-93; adj. faculty Old Dominion U., Norfolk, 1986-88, U. Richmond, 1990, Washington Ctr. for Internships, 1995—. Author: Cracker Cookin' & Other Favorites, 1984; editor: The Underground Gourmet, 1983; contbg. author: Virginia: A Commonwealth Comes of Age, 1988. Bd. dirs. Pinellas County Big Bros.-Big Sisters, 1980-82, Fla. Folklore Soc., 1984-85. Grant rev. panelist Fla. Fine Arts Coun., 1981. Mem. Fla. Motion Picture and TV Assn. (treas. 1976-78), Hampton Rds. C. of C. (co-chmn. pub. rels. Internat. Azalea Festival 1986, chmn. publs. 1987), Va. Conf. on World Trade (chmn. pub. relations com.), Downtown Norfolk Devel. Corp. (chmn. urban living com.), Mensa, Pub. Rels. Soc. Am. (chmn. Mid-Atlantic Dist. 1988, chmn. govt. sect. 1989, bd. dirs. accreditation chmn. Old Dominion chpt. 1988—), Va. State Agy. Pub. Affairs Assn. (pres. 1990), Internat. Assn. Bus. Communicators (v.p. mem. svcs. Richmond chpt. 1996), Forum Agriculture and Consumer Topics (founder, chmn. 1992). Avocations: sailing, classical music, folk music, jazz. Office: B J Altschul & Assocs 2226 Rockwater Ter Richmond VA 23233-3622

ALTSCHWAGER, ANNETTE JEAN, insurance company executive; b. Valparaiso, Ind., June 3, 1957; d. Rudolph and Helen Dolezal; m. Steven Louis Altschwager, May 27, 1978; children: Matthew, Katie, Kurt, Andrew. BS in zoology, U. Wisc., Milw., 1980. Claim svc. rep. Wisc. Physicians Svc., Madison, Wisc., 1988-90; supr. claim entry Wisc. Physicians Svc., Madison, 1990-91, supr. customer svc., 1991, mgr. trainee, 1991-92, asst. mgr. claim support, 1992-94; mgr. group claim support Wausau Ins. Co., Wausau, Wisc., 1994-95; mgr. group claim ops. Wausau Ins. Co., Wausau, 1995—. Loaned exec. Marathon Co. United Way, Wausau, 1995—. Office: Wausau Ins Co 115 W Wausau Ave Wausau WI 54402

ALTURA, BELLA T., physiologist, educator; b. Solingen, Germany; came to U.S., 1948; d. Sol and Rosa (Brandstetter) Tabak; m. Burton M. Altura, Dec. 27, 1961; 1 child, Rachel Allison. BA, CUNY, 1953, MA, 1962, PhD, 1968. Instr. exptl. anesthesiology Albert Einstein Coll. Medicine, Bronx, 1970-74; asst. prof. physiology SUNY Health Sci Ctr., Bklyn., 1974-82, assoc. prof. physiology, 1982—; vis. prof. Beijing Coll. of Traditional Chinese Medicine, 1988, Jiangsu (China) Med. Coll., 1988, Tokyo U. Med. Sch., 1993, U. Brussels Esramè Hosp., 1995, Humboldt U.-Charitè Hosp., 1995, U. Birmingham, U.K., 1996; mem. Nat. Coun. on Magnesium and Cardiovascular Disease, 1991—; cons. NOVA Biomedical, 1989, Nichè pharm. cons. Protina GmbH, Munich, 1992—, Otsuka Pharm. Co., Japan, 1995—; co-prin. investigator NIH, MIMH, NIAAA. Contbr. over 500 articles to profl. jours. Fellowship NASA, 1966-67, CUNY, 1968; recipient Gold-Silver medal French Nat. Acad. Medicine, 1984, Silver medal Mayor of Paris, 1984. Mem. Am. Physiol. Soc., Am. Soc. Pharmacology and Exptl. Therapeutics, Am. Soc. for Magnesium Rsch. (founder, treas. 1984—), Hungarian Soc. Electrochemistry (hon. co-pres. 1995—), Phi Beta Kappa, Sigma Xi. Office: SUNY Health Sci Ctr Box 31 450 Clarkson Ave Brooklyn NY 11203-2012

ALUMBAUGH, JOANN MCCALLA, magazine editor; b. Ann Arbor, Mich., Sept. 16, 1952; d. William Samuel and Jean Arliss (Guy) McCalla; m. Lyle Ray Alumbaugh, Apr. 30, 1974; children: Brent William, Brandon Jess, Brooke Louise. BA, Ea. Mich. U., 1974. Cert. elem. tch., Mich. Assoc. editor Chester White Swine Record Assn., Rochester, Ind., 1974-77; prodn. editor United Duroc Swine Registry, Peoria, Ill., 1977-79; dir., pres. Nat. Assn. Swine Records, Macomb, Ill., 1979-82; free-lance writer, artist Ill. and Nat. Specific Pathogen Free Assn., Ind. producers, Good Hope, Emden, Ill., 1982-85; editor The Hog Producer, Farm Progress Publs., Urbandale, Iowa, 1985—; coord. Master Farm Homemaker Program, Pub. div. Cap Cities ABC, Urbandale, 1985—, Family Living Program, Farm Progress Show, 1985—; mem. U.S. Agrl. Export Devel. Coun., Washington, 1979-82, apptd. mem. Blue Ribbon Com. on Agr., 1980-81. Contbr. numerous articles to profl. jours. Precinct chmn. Rep. Party, Linden, Iowa, 1988; mem. Keep Improving Dist. Schs., Panora, Iowa, 1990-91; v.p. Sunday sch. com. Sunset Circle, United Meth. Ch., Linden, 1990-91; pres. PTA, Panorama Schs., Panora, 1993-94. Mem. Am. Agrl. Editors Assn. (Outstanding Young Women Am. award 1988, chmn. dist. svc. com. 1991, co-chmn. Info-Expo com. 1994—), U.S. Animal Health Assn. (pseudorabies, identification coms. 1989—), Farm Found., Iowa Pork Producers Assn. (legis. com. 1990-95, hon. master pork producer), Nat. Pork Producers Coun. (product devel. com. 1980-81), McDonough County and Ill. Porkettes (county pres. 1978-79, Belleringer award 1979), Guthrie County Pork Prodrs. Home: 2644 Amarillo Ave Linden IA 50146-8029 Office: Farm Progress Publs/Wallaces Farmer 6200 Aurora Ave Ste 609E Urbandale IA 50322-2863

ALVA, MARLENE J., lawyer; b. Rochester, N.Y., Apr. 6, 1948. BA, Barnard Coll., 1970; JD, Columbia U., 1974. Bar: N.Y. 1975; admitted as Conseil Juridique France 1979, 89, avocat France 1992. Ptnr. Davis Polk & Wardell, N.Y.C. Mem. ABA, Assn. of the Bar of the City of N.Y., Am. Soc. of Internat. Law. Office: Davis Polk & Wardwell 450 Lexington Ave New York NY 10017-3911*

ALVARADO, REBECCA JANE, secondary education educator; b. LeMars, Iowa, Apr. 17, 1955; d. Robert Joseph and Beverly Anne (Smith) Meylor; m. John Frederick Clair, June 10, 1974 (div. June 24, 1987); 1 child, Christopher L. Clair; m. Hector Abel Alvarado, Sept. 5, 1987; children: David M. Strait, Randee M. Alvarado. BS in Edn., Ea. Mont. Coll., 1985. Cert. K-12 tchr., Mont. Pharmacy technician St. Anthony Hosp., Denver, Colo., 1972-78; sec. to pharmacy dir. Mercy Med. Ctr., Denver, 1980; with radio sales advt. Sta. KLYC, Laurel, Mont., 1981; realtor ERA Leuthold, Billings, Mont., 1981-84; art tchr. gifted and talented Lockwood (Mont.) Intermediate Sch., 1985-86; substitute tchr. Billings (Mont.) Pub. Schs., 1986-87; art tchr. Hardin (Mont.) Mid. Sch., 1987—, curriculum coord., 1993—; cons., judge Jailhouse Art Gallery, Hardin, 1991; postal cancellation designer Big Horn Days, Hardin, 1992—. Watercolor, photography exhibited in Metrapark Art Gallery, 1985-94, Nothcutt Gallery, 1985, Jailhouse Art Gallery, 1994; Appeared in film: Son of the Morningstar, 1990. With upward bound Ea. Mont. Coll., Billings, 1991-94; acting cmty. theatre Der Schwartzwald Dinner Theatre, Billings Studio Theatre, Alberta Bair Theatre. Mem. NEA, Mont. Edn. Assn., Nat. Art Edn. Assn., Kappa Delta Epsilon (hon.), Alpha Psi Omega (hon.). Home: Rt 1 Box 1223 C Hardin MT 59034 Office: Hardin Mid Sch 611 W 5th St Hardin MT 59034

ALVARADO, SANDRA EDGA, mental health nurse, psychotherapist; b. Adjuntas, P.R., Dec. 3, 1952; d. Pedro Antonio Alvarado and Julia (Altoro) Gonzalez; m. Samuel Soto, Dec. 23, 1985; children: Jeremy Michael, Jonathan Matthew. BSN cum laude, City Coll., N.Y.C., 1973; MSN, Columbia U., N.Y.C., 1976; cert. psychoanalytic psychotherapy, Washington Sq. Inst., N.Y.C., 1980, cert. group psychotherapy, 1985. Cert. clin. specialist adult psychiat. nurse; cert. group psychotherapist. Staff nurse Met. Hosp., N.Y.C., 1973-77, head nurse, 1977-79; staff therapist psychotherapy dept. Washington Sq. Inst., N.Y.C., 1980-87, staff therapist group dept., 1984-88; nurse clinician Mt. Sinai Hosp., N.Y.C., 1979—. Vol. med. support team N.Y.C. (N.Y.) Marathon, 1985. Recipient Regents Nursing Scholarship award N.Y. State, N.Y.C., 1970-73, Fellowship award NIMH, 1974-75. Mem. ANA, Am. Group Psychotherapy Assn., Ea. Group Psychotherapy Soc., N.Y. State Nurses Assn., Phi Betta Kappa (award 1970). Roman Catholic. Office: Mt Sinai Hosp 1 Gustave L Levy Pl New York NY 10029-6504

ALVARADO, SANDRA JACQUELINE, television director; b. Santiago, Chile, July 18, 1964; d. Abraham S. and Fresia C. (Gomez) A.; children: Jordan Alexander Korcowicz, Brandon Michael Korcowicz. AA cum laude, Valley Coll., 1983; BA, Calif. State U., Northridge, 1986. Fl. dir. Univision Network, L.A., 1987-88; casting coord. Ralph Edwards/Stu Billet Prodns., L.A., 1988-89; with several prodn. cos., L.A., 1989-90; dir. Sta. KWHY-TV, L.A., 1990-93, prodr., 1993-94; assoc. dir., dir. Sta. KMEX-TV, L.A., 1994—. Mem. Nat. Assn. Broadcast Employees & Technicians/Comms. Workers of Am. Office: Sta KMEX-TV 6701 Center Dr 2nd Fl Los Angeles CA 90045-5073

ALVAREZ, MERCEDES, advertising executive; b. Havana, Cuba; d. José Manuel and Teresita (Rionda) A. BBA, U. Miami, 1963; postgrad., Manhattanville Coll., Purchase, N.Y., 1964. Sr. rsch. analyst J. Walter Thompson, N.Y.C., 1966-78; v.p. rsch. dir. Isidore, Lefkowitz & Elgort, N.Y.C., 1978-79, Bozell & Jacobs, N.Y.C., 1979-85; sr. v.p. assoc. rsch. dir., rsch. dir. Latin Am. BBDO, Inc., N.Y.C., 1985—; sec., treas. Rsch. Dirs. Coun., 1979-80, Communications Rsch. Coun., 1988-89, pres., 1989—. Recipient BBDO Founders award, 1996. Mem. Am. Mktg. Assn. (Effie Judge, 1978-85). Office: BBDO NY 1285 Avenue Of The Americas New York NY 10019-6028

ALVAREZ, OFELIA AMPARO, medical educator; b. Havana, Cuba, Mar. 29, 1958; d. Alvaro Venancio and Lydia Caridad (Folgueras) A.; m. Manuel Sanabria, Mar. 9, 1985; children: Marian Paola, David Manuel, Gabriel Jesus. BS, U. Puerto Rico, 1978, MD, 1982. Diplomate Nat. Bd. Med. Examiners, Am. Bd. Pediat., Sub-bd. Pediatric Hematology-Oncology. Pediatric residency Univ. Children's Hosp., San Juan, P.R., 1982-85; fellow pediatric hematology, oncology Children's Hosp. L.A., 1985-88; asst. prof. pediat. Loma Linda (Calif.) U., 1988-95, assoc. prof., 1995—; med. advisor Candlelighter, Inland Empire, 1988—. Contbr. articles to profl. jours. Bd. mem., med. advisor Make-A-Wish Found., Inland Empire, 1994-95. Clin. oncology fellow Am. Cancer Soc., 1985-86; pediatric rsch. fund Loma Linda U., 1993-95. Fellow Am. Acad. Pediat.; mem. Am. Soc. Clin. Oncology, Am. Soc. Pediatric Hematology/Oncology, Calif. Med. Assn., AAUW, Histiocyte Soc., Beta Beta Beta. Roman Catholic. Office: Loma Linda Children's Hosp 11262 Campus St Rm 166 Loma Linda CA 92350

ALVES, LISA CYNTHIA, secondary school educator; b. Fall River, Mass., Mar. 10, 1969; d. Manuel Louis and Hilda (Garcia) A. BS in Music Edn. cum laude, R.I. Coll., 1991. Cert. tchr., R.I. Waitress, cook McGovern's Restaurant, Fall River, 1985-92; music educator Woonsocket (R.I.) Pub. Schs., 1991—; asst. choral dir. Woonsocket H.S. Vocal Ensemble, 1991—, mem. sch. improvement team, 1993—; vocal soloist, R.I. and Mass., 1988—; piano accompanist, R.I. and Mass., 1989—; pvt. instr. voice and piano, Cumberland, R.I., 1992—. Choral dir. Woonsocket All-City Children's Chorus, 1992—. Recipient scholarship R.I. Coll., 1990, 91, 1st Pl. Singing Competition Nat. Assn. Tchrs. Singing, 1990. Mem. R.I. Music Educators Assn., Music Educators Nat. Conf.

ALWARD, RUTH ROSENDALL, nursing consultant; d. Henry Rosendall and Freda Jonkman; m. Samuel Alward, Jan. 17, 1976. Diploma, Butterworth Hosp. Sch. Nursing, Grand Rapids, Mich.; RN, Hunter-Bellevue Sch. Nursing, N.Y.; BSN summa cum laude, Columbia U., MA, 1982, EdM, 1983; EdD, 1986. Sr. clin. nurse Wadsworth VA Hosp., L.A., 1966-68; exec. dir. nursing Care Corp, Grand Rapids, Mich., 1968-71; nursing cons. Humana Inc., Louisville, 1972-76; asst. prof., dir. nursing adminstrn. grad. prog. Hunter Coll., CUNY, N.Y.C., 1986-90; pres. Nurse Exec. Assocs., Inc., Washington, 1990—; series editor Delmar Pubs. Inc., Albany, 1993-96. Co-author: The Nurse's Shift Work Handbook, 1993, The Nurse's Guide to Marketing, 1991; contbr. articles to profl. jours.; mem. editorial adv. bd. Jour. of Nursing Adminstrn. Mem. Va Nurses Assn. (chair fin. com.), Nat. League Nursing (treas. D.C. chpt.), Coun. on Grad. Edn. for Adminstrn. in Nursing, Am. Orgn. Nurse Execs., Sigma Theta Tau. Home and Office: 2011 N St NW Washington DC 20036-2301

AMADIO, BARI ANN, metal fabrication executive, former nurse; b. Phila., Mar. 26, 1949; d. Fred Deutscher and Celena (Lusky) Garber; m. Peter Colby Amadio, June 24, 1973; children: P. Grant, Jamie Blair. BA in Psychology, U. Miami, 1970; diploma in Nursing, Thomas Jefferson U., 1973, Johnston-Willis Sch. Nursing, 1974; BS in Nursing, Northeastern U., 1977; MS in Nursing, Boston U., 1978; JD, U. Bridgeport, 1983. Faculty Johnston-Willis Sch. Nursing, Richmond, Va., 1974-75; staff, charge nurse Mass. Gen. Hosp., Boston, 1975-78; faculty New Eng. Deaconess, Boston, 1978-80, Lankenau Hosp. Sch. of Nursing, Phila., 1980-81; pres. Original Metals, Inc., Phila., 1985—, also bd. dirs.; owner Silver Carousel Antiques, Rochester, Minn. Treas. Women's Assn. Minn. Orch., Rochester, 1986-87, pres., 1987-89, life advisor, 1989—, editor newsnotes, 1985-87; mem. mayor's coms. All Am. City Award Com., Rochester, 1984-88; bd. dirs. Rochester Civic League, 1988-94, pres.-elect, 1990-91, pres., 1991-92; pres. Rochester Friends of Mpls. Inst. Arts, 1989-90, Folwell PTA, 1990-91; state liaison Gateway, 1990-91; bd. dirs. Rochester Civic Theatre, 1993—, v.p., 1994-95, pres., 1995-96. Mem. Am. Soc. Law and Medicine, Zumbro Valley Med. Soc. Aux. (Rochester, fin. chmn. 1986-90, treas. 1988-90), NAFE, Nat. Assn. Food Equipment Mfrs., Friends of Mayowood, Phi Alpha Delta, Sigma Theta Tau.

AMADO, HONEY KESSLER, lawyer; b. Bklyn., July 20, 1949; d. Bernard and Mildred Kessler; m. Ralph Albert Amado, Oct. 24, 1976; children: Jessica Reina, Micah Solomon, Gabrielle Beth. BA in Polit. Sci., Calif. State Coll., Long Beach, 1971; JD, Western State U., Fullerton, Calif., 1976. Bar: Calif. 1977, U.S. Dist. Ct. (ctrl. dist.) Calif. 1981, U.S. Ct. Appeals (9th cir.) 1981, U.S. Supreme Ct. 1994. Assoc. Law Offices of Jack M. Lasky, Beverly Hills, Calif., 1977-78; pvt. practice Beverly Hills, Calif., 1978—; lectr. in field. Contbr. articles to profl. jours. Mem. Com. Concerned Lawyers for Soviet Jewry, 1979-90; nat. v.p. Jewish Nat. Fund, 1995—; bd. dirs. Jewish Nat. Fund L.A., 1990—; sec. L.A. region, bd. dirs. Sephardic Temple Tifereth Israel, 1991-94, Am. Jewish Congress, Jewish Feminist Ctr., 1992—; mem. Commn. on Soviet Jewry of Jewish Fedn. Coun. Greater L.A., 1977-83, chmn., 1979-81, commn. on edn., 1982-83, cmty. rels. com., 1979-83. Mem. Calif. Women Lawyers (bd. govs. 1988-90, 1st v.p. 1989-90, jud. evaluations co-chair 1988-90), San Fernando Valley Bar Assn. (family law mediators and arbitrators planel 1983-94, judge pro-tem panel 1987-94), Beverly Hills Bar Assn. (family law mediators panel 1985-94), L.A. County Bar Assn. (family law sect., appellate cts. com. 1987—, chmn. subcom. to examine reorgn. Calif. Supreme Ct. 1990-94, judge pro tem panel 1985-95, appellate jud. evaluations com. 1989—, editl. bd. L.A. Lawyer mag. 1996—, chmn. dist. 2 settlement program 1996—), Calif. State Bar. Democrat. Jewish. Office: 261 S Wetherly Dr Beverly Hills CA 90211-2515

AMATO, BARBARA BROUGH, English language educator; b. Detroit, June 24, 1953; d. Frederick Aubrey and Marian Jane (Cooper) Jones; m. Richard Brough Jr., June 26, 1976 (div. Dec. 1983); m. Philip Martin Amato, July 3, 1993. BS in Edn., Miami U., 1975; MA in Edn., No. Ky. U., 1996. Cert. secondary tchr., Ohio. Tchr. h.s. English Forest Hills Sch. Dist., Cin., 1975—. Contbr. articles to profl. jours. Mem. Mensa, Delta Kappa Gamma (pres. 1992-94, comms. chair 1992—). Office: Forest Hills Sch Dist Forest Rd Cincinnati OH 45255

AMATO, CAMILLE JEAN, manufacturing executive; b. N.Y.C., Aug. 6, 1942; d. William and Mary Carmela (Lombardi) Tuorto; m. Thomas Amato, June 1, 1963; children: Dawn, Thomas. Assoc. Sci., SUNY-Albany, 1981, B.S., 1983; B.S., Empire State Coll., 1983, M. Bus. and Policy, 1986. Lic. realtor, notary, N.Y. Controller, owner Island Marine Inc., Bellmore, N.Y., 1977—; account mgr. L.I. Luth. Assn., Brookville, N.Y., 1983-84, Borden Inc. Chem., Glen Cove, N.Y., 1984-85; real estate agt. N. of 25A R.E. Inc., Locust Valley, N.Y., 1986—; owner, pres. Penn Yan (N.Y.) Marine Mfg. Inc., 1986—; pres., owner Camille Properties, Inc., Penn Yan, 1986—; pres. Pendragon Co., 1991—; cons. various areas. Cons. sub-com. edn. and safety N.Y. State Senate, 1976-77; exec. trustee Pen Yan Boat Mus., 1990—. Mem. Nat. Assn. Female Execs. Roman Catholic. Avocation: classical piano. Home: Woodstock Manor Muttontown Oyster Bay NY 11771

AMATO, ISABELLA ANTONIA, real estate executive; b. Noto, Italy, July 17, 1942; d. Raimondo and Giuseppa (Pinna) Sesta; m. Vincent Amato; children: Alice, Claudine. Acctg. diploma, Inst. Tech. and Commerce, 1962. Cert. Comml. Investment Mgr., Comml. Investment Inst., Specialist Real Estate Securities, Real Estate Securities and Syndication Inst. V.p., dir. Thomas F. Seay & Assocs., Chgo., 1977-81; treas. Seay & Thomas Inc., Chgo., 1979-81; CFO Group One Investments, Chgo., 1981—; exec. v.p., registered prin. First Group Securities, Ltd., Chgo., 1983-95, pres., 1995—. Vol. translator Altrusa Lang. Bank, Chgo., 1980-86; v.p. Jr. Woman Club, Elk Grove Village, Ill., 1977; chairperson Atty. Exec. Forum, Chgo., 1985. Mem. Nat. Assn. Securities Dealers (prin.), Nat. Assn. Realtors, Chgo. Real Estate Bd., Real Estate Fin. Forum, Altrusa Profl. Woman (treas. Chgo. club 1984-85). Office: Group One Investments 77 W Washington St Ste 1005 Chicago IL 60602-2805

AMAYA, PATRICIA MOJARRO, elementary education educator; b. Orange, Calif., Feb. 25, 1965; d. Guillermo Jimenez and Maria Angelina (Avalos) Mojarro; m. Elias Amaya, Oct. 22, 1988 (dec. Oct. 1993); 1 child, Eliana Ashley. BA in Spanish, U. Calif., Irvine, 1987; postgrad. in writing, Inst. Children's Lit., West Redding, Conn., 1996. Cert. elem. tchr., bilingual, cert. bilingual competence, Calif., 1989. Biliterate instrnl. asst. Franklin Elem. Sch., Santa Ana, Calif., 1986-89, bilingual tchr., 1989-91; bilingual tchr. Alcott Elem. Sch., Pomona, Calif., 1991—. Mem. ASCD, NEA, Calif. Tchrs. Assn., U. Calif.-Irvine Alumnae Assn. Home: 12836 Tehama Cir Riverside CA 92503-4501 Office: Alcott Elem Sch 1600 S Towne Ave Pomona CA 91766-5367

AMBROSE, DIANE MARIE, financial analyst; b. Troy, N.Y., Feb. 21, 1951; d. Edward John and Wanda M. (Zmijewski) Krawetz; m. Gregory Dole Ambrose, Jan. 27, 1973; children: Ken, Gareth. BA in Math., MA in Math., SUNY, Potsdam, 1969; MA in Internat. Mgmt., U. Tex., 1981. Cert. mgmt. acct. Sys. analyst US West, Denver, 1981-83, budget mgr., 1983-84, regulation acct., 1984-85, internal cons., 1985-87, fin. syss. mgr., 1987-88, regulatory compliance mgr., 1988-93, bus. analyst, 1993—. Co-author: (course) International Free Trade, 1995. Mem. Inst. Mgmt. Accts., Pacific Asian Am. Network (dir. 1993-96), Project Mgmt. Inst.

AMBROSE, DONETTA W., federal judge; b. 1945. BA, Duquesne U., 1967, JD cum laude, 1970. Law clerk to Hon. Louis L. Manderino Commonwealth Ct. Pa., 1970-71, Supreme Ct. Pa., 1972; asst. atty. gen. Pa. Dept. Justice, 1972-74; pvt. practice atty. Ambrose & Ambrose, Kensington, Pa., 1974-81; asst. dist. atty. Westmoreland County, Pa., 1977-81; judge Ct. Common Pleas Westmoreland County, 1982-93, U.S. Dist. Ct. (we. dist.) Pa., Pitts., 1994—; resident advisor Duquesne U., 1967-70. Scholar Pa. Conf. State Trial Judges, 1992, State Justice Inst., 1993. Mem. ABA, Nat. Assn. Women Judges, Am. Judicature Soc., Pa. Bar Assn., Women's Bar Assn. Western Pa., Pa. Conf. State Trial Judges (sec. 1992-93), Westmoreland County Bar Assn., Italian Sons and Daus. Am., William Penn Fraternal Assn., New Kensington Women's Club, Delta Kappa Gamma. Office: 620 US Post Office & Courthouse 7th Ave Grant Pittsburgh PA 15219*

AMBRUS, CLARA MARIA, physician; b. Rome, Dec. 28, 1924; came to U.S., 1949, naturalized, 1955; d. Anthony and Charlotte (Schneider) Bayer; m. Julian Lawrence Ambrus, Feb. 17, 1945; children: Madeline Ambrus Lillie, Peter, Julian, Linda Ambrus-Broenniman, Steven, Katherine Ambrus-Cheney, Charles. Student, U. Budapest (Hungary), 1943-47; M.D., U. Zurich, Switzerland, 1949; postgrad., U. Paris, 1949; Ph.D., Jefferson Med. Coll., 1955. Diplomate: Am. Bd. Clin. Chemists. Research asst. Inst. Histology, Embryology and Biology U. Budapest, 1943-45; demonstrator in pharmacology U. Budapest Med. Sch., 1946-47; asst. dept. pharmacology U. Zurich Med. Sch., 1947-49; asst. dept. therapeutic chemistry and virology Inst. Pasteur, Paris, 1949; asst. prof. pharmacology Phila. Coll. Pharmacy and Sci., 1950-52, asso. prof., 1952-55; research asso. Roswell Park Meml. Inst., Buffalo, 1955-58; sr. cancer research scientist Roswell Park Meml. Inst., 1958-64, asso. scientist, 1964-69, prin. cancer research scientist, 1969-85; prof. pharmacology State U. N.Y.; prof. pharmacology Buffalo Med. and Grad. Schs., 1955—, asso. prof. pediatrics, 1955-76, prof. pediatrics, 1976, research prof. ob-gyn, 1983—; chmn., founder, chief of R&D Hemex Inc., 1984—. Contbr. articles to med. and sci. jours. Trustee Nichols Sch., Buffalo, Community Music Sch. Named Outstanding Woman of Western N.Y. Community Adv. Council, SUNY, Buffalo, 1980. Fellow ACP, Internat. Soc. Hematology; mem. Am. Soc. Pharmacology and Exptl. Therapeutics, Am. Soc. Cancer Rsch., Am. Fedn. Clin. Rsch., Am. Physiol. Soc., Am. Soc. Hematology, Buffalo Acad. Medicine, Am. Med. Women's Assn., Clarksburg Country Club, Saturn Club, Garrett Club, Sigma Xi. Home: 143 Windsor Ave Buffalo NY 14209-1020 also: West Hill Farm Boston NY 14025 Office: Buffalo Gen Hosp 100 High St Buffalo NY 14203-1126

AMBRUS, LORNA, medical, surgical and geriatrics nurse; b. Phila., June 17, 1956; d. Walter C. and Joan B. (Watts) Beilfuss; 1 child, Victoria Ambrus. LPN, Upper Bucks Vo-Tech., Perkasie, Pa., 1976; diploma, Gwynedd Mercy Coll., Gwynedd Valley, Pa., 1989. RN. Nurse Grandview Hosp., Sellersville, Pa., Quality Care, Allentown, Pa., Comprehensive Home Care, Doylestown, Pa., Doylestown Manor. Home: 118 Jefferson Ct Quakertown PA 18951-1417

AMEND, KATE, film editor, educator; b. San Francisco, June 27, 1947; d. Carroll Conrad and Mary Florence (Saller) A. BA, U. Calif., Berkeley, 1969; MA, Calif. State U., San Francisco, 1973. Instr. humanities City Coll. San Francisco, 1973-78; instr. humanities and women's studies Diablo Valley Coll., Pleasant Hill, Calif., 1973-78; adminstr. Through the Flower Corp., Santa Monica, Calif., 1978-81; rschr., adminstr. Judy Chicago's Dinner Party, Santa Monica, Calif., 1978-81; film editor L.A., 1982-95; adj. prof. Sch. Cinema & Tv U. So. Calif., L.A., 1992-95. Film editor Metamorphosis: Man Into Woman, 1989, Legends, 1990, Asylum, 1992, Skinheads, USA, 1993, Spread The Word, 1994, Arrested Development: In The House, 1995, From The Ashes, 1996. Pres., bd. trustees Nat. Repertory Theatre Found., L.A., 1994-95. Mem. Internat. Documentary Assn. Democrat.

AMENDT, MARILYN JOAN, personnel director; b. Marshalltown, Iowa, June 21, 1928; d. Floyd Wilford and Helen Mary (Scheid) Peterson; m. Virgil E. Amendt, Sept. 4, 1949 (div. Aug. 1971); children: Gregory F., Scott R., Brad A. AA, Stephens Coll., Columbia, Mo., 1948; postgrad., U. Mich., 1978, U. Wis., Superior, 1980-83. Cert. personnel mgr. Office mgr. S&O Products, Inc., Marshalltown, Iowa, 1961-71; life underwriter Lincoln Liberty Life Ins. Co., Marshalltown, Iowa, 1971-72; retail store mgr. Amy's Fashions, Marshalltown, Iowa, 1972-74, Maurices, Inc., Marshalltown, Iowa, 1974-76; corp. personnel dir. Maurices, Inc., Duluth, Minn., 1976-84; sr. v.p., dir. human resources Ohrbach's, Inc., N.Y.C., 1984-87; dir. personnel adminstrn. AMCENA Corp., N.Y.C., 1970-91; pres., owner Success Strategies, Des Moines, 1992—; lectr. U. Wis, Superior, 1981-82, U. Minn., Duluth, 1981-82. Founder, pres., bd. dirs. Mid-Iowa Sheltered Workshop, Marshalltown, 1968-76; mem. Hostess com. Duluth (Minn.) Day Luncheon, 1983; keynote speaker Am. Bus. Women's Day, Mpls. and Duluth, 1984, 85, 86, 90. Mem. Am. Bus. Women's Assn. (dist. v.p. 1982, nat. v.p. 1983, nat. pres. 1984, woman of the yr. 1978), Am. Soc. Exec. and Profl. Women. Home: 2233 Country Club Blvd Des Moines IA 50325-8602

AMENTA, JOYCE ANN, United Nations executive; b. Washington, Oct. 26, 1943; d. Kenneth John and Hildegard (Klinge) McCallister; m. Howard Richard Schmidt, Aug. 9, 1986. BA in Sociology with honors, George Washington U., 1967; MPA, Am. Univ., 1987. Cert. pvt. pilot. Computer programmer U.S. Dept. Commerce, Suitland, Md., 1967-74; tech. rep. Informatics, Inc., Rockville, Md., 1974-77; sr. analyst com. rules and adminstrn. U.S. Senate, Washington, 1977-80; dir. computer ctr. U.S. Dept. Transp., Washington, 1981-90; dir. info. resources mgmt. Nuc. Regulatory Commn., Washington, 1987-90; dir. sci. & tech. info. IAEA, Vienna, Austria, 1990-96; dir. info. tech. svcs. UN, N.Y.C., 1996—. Pres. Women's Forum, Vienna, 1992-95. Mem. Am. Nuc. Soc. (chmn. Austria local sect. 1994-95), Toastmasters Internat. Office: UN Electronic Svcs Divsn S1912B New York NY 10017

AMERO, JANE ADAMS, state legislator; b. Rumford, Maine, Aug. 6, 1941; d. William Anthony and Evangeline Jean (McInnis) Adams; m. Gerald M. Amero, Sept. 4, 1961; children: Scott Martin, Brett Douglas, Melanie Jane. BA, Cornell U., 1963. Tchr. South Portland (Maine) Sch. Dist., 1965-67; mem. Cape Elizabeth (Maine) Sch. Bd., 1975-81, Maine Bd. Edn., Augusta, 1987-92; asst. majority leader, chair state & local govt. com., chair legis. coun. Maine Bd. Edn., 1989-92; elected to Maine senate Maine Senate, 1992; re-elected, 1994; elected asst. majority leader Maine senate, chair legis. coun., state and local govt. com.; mem. senate edn. com., reapportionment com., 1992-94; mem. Maine Coalition for Excellence in Edn., 1990—, Commn. to Evaluate Tech. Coll. System, Augusta, 1990-91, 3 sch. funding task forces, Augusta, 1987, 88, 90-91. Mem. coun. Town of Cape Elizabeth, 1983-92, chmn., 1987; mem., pres. Catherine Morrill Day Nursery, Portland, 1981-87; mem. Commn. on Restructuring State Govt., Augusta, 1991—; corporator Maine Med. Ctr., Portland, 1989—; active Vol. Lawyers Project, Portland, 1984-90; mem. Ptnrs. for Progress in Portland Leadership Initiative, 1990—. Recipient Svc. Above Self award Rotary Clubs, Cape Elizabeth, South Portland, 1991; named Regional Citizen of Yr. in Greater Portland Area, 1993. Mem. Nat. Assn. State Bds. of Edn. (mem. nat. study com. on parent and cmty. invilvement in schs. 1989, Disting. Svc. award 1993), Maine Mcpl. Assn., Nat. League Cities, Maine Assn. Ptnrs. in Edn. (bd. dirs. 1988—), LWV (Emily Farley award Portland chpt. 1989), Phi Beta Kappa, Phi Kappa Phi. Republican. Home: 44 Old Ocean House Rd Cape Eliz ME 04107-2625 Office: Maine State Senate State Capitol Augusta ME 04330

AMES, SANDRA L., library media specialist, elementary education educator, reading consultant; b. Iowa City, Nov. 13, 1951; d. Ernest F. and Erlean F. Skare; m. Richard D. Ames; children: Caroline K., Julia M. BS in Library Sci., Elem. Edn., U. S.D., 1972; MA in Reading, U. Nebr., 1985. Teaching cert. in reading, library sci., elem. edn. Tchr. 2d grade Linden Elem., Fremont, Nebr., 1977-79; tchr. 2d and 3d grades Shelden Elem., Fremont, 1973-75; tchr. 2d grade Howard Elem., Fremont, 1975-76; reading tchr. Willa Cather Elem., Millard, 1979-82, kindergarten tchr., 1982-85; tchr. computers Metro Cmty. Coll., Omaha, 1981; prin. Summer sch. Cody Elem., Millard, 1983; library media specialist Scarborough Elem., Olathe, Kans., 1985-95, Heatherstone Elem., Olathe, Kans., 1995—; mem. bd. dirs. Nebr. Assn. of Edn. Data, 1982-85; mem. tech. cadre Olathe (Kans.) Unified Dist. Com., 1990-94; com. mem. Kans. Tchrs. Award, Topeka, 1993-95. Contbr. chpts. to textbook. Sun. sch. tchr. Atonement Lutheran, Overland Park, Kans., 1986-95, dir. Christmas programs, 1988-89, 94. Mem. ALA, NEA, Am. Assn. Sch. Libraries, Kans. Assn. Sch. Libraries (mem. profl. rels. com. 1990-94), Kans. Ednl. Assn., Olathe Ednl. Assn. Office: Heatherstone Elem 13745 W 123d St Olathe KS 66062

AMEY, RAE, television and video developer, producer; b. Shreveport, La., Sept. 26, 1947; d. Bruce Harold and Genevieve (Amey) Gentry; m. John E. Scarborough, Dec. 18, 1971 (div. Nov. 1979). Student, La. State U., 1968-70, U. Houston, 1972-74; BA in Liberal Arts, Antioch U., 1985; grad., U. So. Calif., 1988—. Freelance photographer Calif., 1973—; adminstrn. coord. Y.E.S. Inc., Sta. KCET-TV, L.A., 1980-83; freelande ednl. TV writer, cons. L.A., 1983-84; asst. to pres. prodn. So. Calif. Consortium, Cypress, 1984, project mgr., dir. devel., project dir. The Human Condition, 1985-87; v.p. devel. and outreach The California Channel, L.A., 1990-92, project dir., 1991, 92; pres. Video Nexus, L.A., 1987—. Editor TV guide book, 1985; photography exhbns. include: Contemporary Art Mus., Houston, 1973, Galveston (Tex.) Arts Ctr., 1975, Cameravision Gallery, L.A.,1980, Aloft, Pasadena, 1989. Co-founder Harbor Arts Alliance; mem., bd. dirs. African Am. Arts Coun.; founder, chair, bd. dirs. CIVICS: a video project for cmty. edn. and conversation, 1993—; advisor Congress on Racial Equality. Ellen Torgenson Shaw scholar Annenberg Sch. Communications, U. So. Calif., 1989. Mem. Women in Communications (bd. dirs., v.p. campus svcs. 1987-88, exec. v.p. 1988-89, bd. dirs. scholarship and edn. fund L.A. chpt.). Democrat. Home and Office: 255 S Grand Ave Apt 1914 Los Angeles CA 90012-6017

AMIDEI, NANCY JEAN, social service agency executive, writer, speaker, media commentator; b. Lake Forest, Ill., Mar. 27, 1942; d. Natale and Dema (Capitani) A. BS in Humanities, Loyola U., Chgo., 1963; MSW, U. Mich., 1968. Vol., Peace Corps, Nigeria, 1964-65; mem. staff, then staff dir. U.S. Senate Com. on Nutrition and Human Needs, Washington, 1969-72; dep. asst. sec. HEW, Washington, 1977-79; dir. Food Research Action Ctr., Washington, 1980-84; weekly columnist; Washington corr. Commonweal Mag.; commentator All Things Considered program Nat. Pub. Radio, 1985; vis. prof. Sch. Social Work, U. Mich., Ann Arbor, 1985, Sch. Social Work, Catholic U., Washington, 1986-89, 93—; Belle Spafford prof. U. Utah, Salt Lake City, 1990-92; coord univ. dist. univ. partnership for youth. Co-author: Protest, Politics and Prosperity: Black Americans and White Institutions, 1940-75, 1978; prin. author: Hunger in the Eighties: A Primer, 1984; author: So You Want to Make a Difference, 1992; also numerous articles. Commn. mem. Hunger Watch, N.Y. State, 1983; mem. adv. bd. Project Vote, KCTS Seattle; bd. dirs. OMB Watch; originator The Decency Principles. Recipient Disting. Alumni award U. Mich. Sch. Social Work, 1984, Spl. Achievement award Kenny and Marianne Rogers Hunger Awards, 1984; alumna in residence U. Mich. Alumnae Assn., 1985. Mem. Nat. Assn. Social Workers, Nat. Anti-Hunger Coalition.

AMISANO, BERNADETTE PARKER, artist; b. Flint, Mich., June 30, 1954; d. Wayne L. and Doloris J. (Anderson) Parker; m. James A. Moses, June 1, 1973 (div. 1984); m. Albert D. Amisano, May 21, 1994. AA, San Jacinto Coll., 1979; BA magna cum laude, Elmira Coll., 1993. Intern Nat. Portrait Gallery Smithsonian Inst., Washington, 1993. Exhibited paintings at numerous shows including Shows at the George, Waters, West End and Arnot Art Mus., 1993-95. Vol. Arnot Art Mus., Elmira, N.Y., 1992, Rockwell Art Mus., Corning, N.Y., 1993-96. Mem. Women You Want to Know, Arts of So. Tier Finger Lakes. Republican. Home: 736 W Clinton St Elmira NY 14905

AMM, SOPHIA J., artist, educator; b. Czestochowa, Poland, June 13, 1932; arrived in Can., 1948; came to U.S., 1962-66, 87—; d. Romuald Witold and Jadwiga Wactawa (Kotowska) Sulatycki; m. Bruce Campbell Amm, Aug. 5, 1961; children: Alicia, Alexander, Christopher, Bruce Jr., Gregory. Diploma in nursing, Ont. Hosp., 1953; cert. pub. health nurse, U. Toronto, 1961; BFA with honours, York U., 1980. RN, 1953; diploma in nursing Ont. Hosp., 1953; cert. pub. health nursing U. Toronto, 1960. Pvt. duty nurse Allied Registry, Toronto, Ont., Can., 1954-56; asst. head nurse Reddy Meml. Hosp., Mont., Que., Can., 1957-59; pub. health nurse Dist. of Subbury, Ont., Can., 1960-62; counselor to new immigrants Ont. Welcome House, Toronto, 1982; vis. nurse St. Elizabeth Vis. Nurses Assn., Toronto, 1983-87; artist, tchr. of art in studio YMCA, Appleton, Wis., 1994—; vol. art tchr. children with devel. disabilities, Appleton, 1988-89, disabled srs. Colony Oaks Nursing Home, Appleton, 1988-91; condr. art workshops Very Spl. Arts Wis. festivals, state and regional, 1989, 90, 92. One person show Bergstrom Mahler Mus., Neenah, Wis., 1991; exhibited in group shows at Harbourfront Exhbn. Gallery, Toronto, 1978, Simpson's Art Gallery, Toronto, 1984, City Hall, Toronto, 1984, Ukrainian Art Found., Toronto, 1984, Art Gallery of Hamilton, Can., 1985, 86, Pastel Soc. Can., Ottawa, 1985, IDA Gallery, York U., Toronto, 1980, 81, 86, Carnegie Gallery, Dundas, Can., 1986, Calumet Coll., York U., 1986, Gallery 68, Burlington, Can., 1986, Charles A. Wustum Mus. Fine Arts, Racine, Wis., 1990-91, 94, Gallery Ten, Rockford, Ill., 1992, 94, 95 (3d Pl. award 1992), New Vision Gallery, Marshfield, Wis., 1992, Neville Pub. Mus., Green Bay, Wis., 1987, 88, 89, 92, 94, 95, 96, Lakeland Coll., Wis., 1994, U. Wis. Gallery, Madison, 1992, 94, Consilium Pl., Scarborough, Can., 1987, 89, 92, 93, Del Bello Gallery, Toronto, 1986-93, Butler Inst. Am. Art, Youngstown, Ohio, 1993, Alverno Coll., Milw., 1994, Appleton Gallery of Arts, 1995, Bergstrom Mahler Mus., 1995 (1st pl. award 1995). Recipient Award of Excellence, North York (Can.) Arts Coun., 1982, 86, Best in Show Etobicoke (Can.) Arts Coun., 1982, 87; project grantee (2) Very Spl. Arts Wis., 1989. Mem. AAUW, Nat. Mus. Women in Arts, Arts, Scarborough, Wis. Women in the Arts, Wis. Painters and Sculptors. Roman Catholic. Home: 1109 Briarcliff Dr Appleton WI 54915

AMMAN, E(LIZABETH) JEAN, university official; b. Hoyleton, Ill., July 13, 1941; d. James Kerr and Marie Fern (Schnake) White; m. Douglas Dorrance Amman, Aug. 12, 1962; children: Mark, Kirk, Jill, Drew, Gwen. BA in English, Ill. Wesleyan U., 1963; MA in English, U. Cin., 1975. Cert. tchr., Ill. Tchr. lang. arts John Greer Jr. High Sch., Hoopeston, Ill., 1963-64, Pleasant Hill Sch., East Peoria, Ill., 1966-67; tchr. English, chmn. Am. studies Anderson Sr. High Sch., Cin., 1967-69; instr. English, No. Mich. U., Marquette, 1976-82; instr. English, Ball State U., Muncie, Ind., 1982-86, adminstrv. intern, 1983-84, asst. to chmn. dept., 1984-86, adminstrv. asst., 1986, asst. to provost, coord. provost's lecture series, 1986—, exec. sec. student and campus life coun., 1986—. Editor: Provost's Lecture Series: Perspectives on Culture and Society, Vol. I, 1988, Vol. II, 1991, The Associator, 1983-86. Mem. choir College Ave. Meth. Ch., Muncie, 1989—; fundraiser Delaware County Coalition for Literacy, 1989, 90; flutist Muncie Sinfonietta Orch., 1989—, Am.'s Hometown Band, 1991—. Recipient recognition Black Student Assn., Ball State U., 1988, cert. of svc. for minority student devel., 1990, 91, 92. Mem. AAUW (pres.-elect Muncie chpt. 1996—), Ind. Coll. English Assn. (editor 1993-95, exec. bd. 1983-86), P.E.O. (pres. Muncie 1985-87), Sigma Alpha Iota (v.p. 1993-94, pres. 1994—, Sword of Honor 1995), Kappa Delta (Ind. Kappa Delta of Yr. 1994, advisor 1992-95, collegiate province pres. 1995—), Phi Kappa Phi. Democrat. Home: 4305 Castleton Ct Muncie IN 47304-2476 Office: Ball State U 2000 W University Ave Muncie IN 47306-1022

AMMERMAN, CHARLENE, religious organization administrator. Dep. dir. Chaplaincy of Full Gospel Chs. Office: 2721 Whitewood Dr Dallas TX 75233-2713*

AMNEUS, D. A., English language educator; b. Beverly, Mass., Oct. 15, 1919; d. Nils A. and Harriet S. (Anchersen) Amneus; divorced; children: Paul, Pamela. AB, U. Calif. Berkeley, 1941; MA, U. So. Calif., 1947, PhD, 1953. From asst. prof. to prof. Calif. State U., L.A., 1950-86, prof. emeritus, 1986—; pub. Primrose Press, Alhambra, Calif. Author: Back to Patriarchy, 1979, The Mystery of Macbeth, 1983, The Three Othellos, 1986, The Garbage Generation, 1990; contbr. articles to profl. jours. Mem. NOW. Republican. Home: 2131 S Primrose Ave Alhambra CA 91803-3834 Office: Calif State U English Dept 5151 State University Dr Los Angeles CA 90032-4221

AMODIO, BARBARA ANN, philosophy educator, educational administrator; b. Middletown, N.Y., Feb. 14, 1948; d. Arthur West and Dorothy Elizabeth (Curran) Amodio. BA, Thomas More Coll., Fordham U., 1970; MA, Fordham U., 1972, PhD, 1979; student, U. Aix-Marseille, Aix-en-Provence, France, 1968; diploma in Bus. French & Euromkt. Instn., U. Strasbourg (France), 1992. Mediator, Chgo. Bar Assn. Ctr. for Conflict Resolution, Am. Acad. Family Mediators. Teaching fellow Fordham U., Bronx, N.Y., 1971-73; from lectr. to instr. philosophy Loyola U., Chgo., 1975-76, 79-83; contract monitor Pres.'s Office of Manpower Adminstrn., Chgo., 1976-78; acad. career advisor, vis. prof. U. Chgo., 1985-88; mediator Chgo. Bar Assn., 1985-87; pvt. mediation practice, 1985-89; coord. adminstrv. programs, adminstrv. intern to campus dir. U. Conn., Stamford, 1989-90, coord. student community svc. programs, lectr. French lang., 1990-93; lectr. Oriental philosophies and philosophy Fairfield (Conn.) U., 1990—; lectr. Grad. Sch. Pub. Mgmt., U. New Haven, 1990; researcher China, 1994—; dir. Scarlet Bird Internat. Expeditions in Learning and Intelligent Travel, Asia, Europe, Mediterranean Basin, 1994—. Contbr. articles to profl. jours. Mem. Norwalk (Conn.) Human Rights and Rels. Commn., 1987—; mem. Conn. Gov.'s Adv. Com. on Am. and Francophone Affairs, 1992-96, adv. commr., 1996—. French Embassy Cultural Svcs. grantee, 1971, 92; invited Philosophy Edn. del. P.R. China, 1993; Fordham U. fellow, Woodrow Wilson fellow and finalist; Danforth Found. fellow and finalst, numerous other grants. Mem. Metaphys. Soc. Am., Internat. Soc. for Chinese Philosophy, Soc. for Study of Process Philosophies, Am. Maritain Soc., Yves Simon Inst., Am. Philos. Assn., Alliance Francaise, Am. Assn. Tchrs. French, Am. Acad. Divorce and Family Mediators. Home: PO Box 533 Westport CT 06881-0533

AMON, CAROL BAGLEY, federal judge; b. 1946. BS, Coll. William and Mary, 1968; JD, U. Va., 1971. Bar: Va. 1971, D.C. 1972, N.Y. 1980. Staff atty. Communications Satellite Corp., Washington, 1971-73; trial atty. U.S. Dept. Justice, Washington, 1973-74; asst. U.S. atty. Ea. Dist. N.Y., 1974-86, U.S. magistrate, 1986-90, dist. ct. judge, 1990—. Recipient John Marshall award U.S. Dept. Justice, 1983. Mem. ABA, Assn. of Bar of City of N.Y., Va. State Bar Assn., D.C. Bar Assn. Office: US District Court US Courthouse 225 Cadman Plz E Brooklyn NY 11201-1818*

AMONSON, JOHANNE LESLIE, barrister, solicitor; b. Edmonton, Alta., Can., Mar. 28, 1949. BA, U. Oreg., 1970; LLB, U. Alta., 1977. Bar: Alta. 1978. Assoc. Weeks Joyce, Edmonton, 1978-85; ptnr. Peterson Ross, Edmonton, 1985-89, McLennan Ross, Edmonton, 1989—; appointed Queen's Counsel Lt. Gov. of Alberta, 1992; appointee fed. jud. appointments com. Province of Alberta, 1991-93, appointed a fellow of the Am. Coll, of Estates and Trusts Coun., 1995; mem. Atty. Gen. Alberta Surrogate Rules Amendment Project; panel chmn. Legal Edn. Soc. Alberta; tchr., lectr. on legal edn. tchr. Bavarian Ministry of Edn., Germany, 1972-73; sessional lectr. U. Alberta Law Sch., 1987, 88. Exhbns. registrar Glenbow Mus. Calgary, 1973-74. Named to Dean's List, U. Ore., 1969-70, U. Alta. Law Rev., 1975-77; recipient of fgn. student scholarship, U. Ore., 1967-70. Fellow Am. Coll. Trust and Estate Counsel (mem. fiduciary litigation com., estate and gift tax com. 1996—); mem. Law Soc. Alta. (mentor), Can. Bar Assn. (panelist, nat. coun. and provincial exec. com., coord. no. sects., past chair wills and trusts sect.), Edmonton Bar Assn., Internat. Commn. Jurists, Can. Tax Found. (surrogate rules com.). Conservative. Lutheran. Office: McLennan Ross, POB 12040 12220 Stony Plain Rd, Edmonton, AB Canada T5J 3L2

AMOROSI, TERESA, artist; b. Gioiosa Ionica, Reggio Calabria, Italy, Nov. 17, 1932; d. Natale and Marianna (Quartiere) Fazzolare; m. Nicholas A. Amorosi, Apr. 22, 1956 (dec. 1988); children: Thomas, Elizabeth, Joseph. BA, Pratt Inst., 1956. Art dir. Norcross Greeting Card Co., 1950-57; artist Charmcraft Greetings, 1957-62, Manhattan Greeting Card Co., 1978-89, Magic Moments Greeting Card Co., 1989—, Sunshine Artists, 1990—. Illustrator: International Mother's Book, 1980. Recipient awards Washington Square Outdoor Art Show, N.Y.C., 1976, 82, 85. Mem. Tri-County Artists L.I. (treas. 1994), Fortnightly of Rockville Ctr., (art dir. 1996). Roman Catholic. Office: Intaglio Dimension 93 Mill River Ave Lynbrook NY 11563

AMOS, LINDA K., nursing educator, college dean; b. Findlay, Ohio, Sept. 7, 1940; d. Blond G. and Dorotha (Brinkman) A. BS, Ohio State U., 1962, MS, 1964; EdD, Boston U., 1977. Asst. dean of baccalaureate affairs Boston U. Coll. Nursing, 1971-74, dean, prof., 1975-80; dean, prof. U. Utah Coll. Nursing, Salt Lake City, 1980—; chair Presdl. Commn. Status of Women U. Utah, 1995—; cons. Social Sci. Rsch. Inst., Boston. Contbr. articles to profl. jours. Chair Presdl. Commn. on Status of Women, U. Utah; bd. dirs. Utah Heart Assn. SErved with USPHS. Named for Outstanding Contbns. to the Nursing Profession, Utah Citizen's League for Nursing, 1989; recipient VA Chief Nurse award for promoting unity between edn. and practice, Mary Tolle Wright award for excellence in leadership Sigma Theta Tau, 1991. Fellow Am. Acad. Nursing (governing coun. 1986-90, selection com. 1995—); mem. ANA, Am. Assn. Colls. of Nursing (pres. 1984-86), Nat. Adv. Coun. on Nurse Tng., Sigma Theta Tau (internat. nominating com. 1995—).

AMPOLA, MARY G., pediatrician, geneticist; b. Syracuse, N.Y., Nov. 2, 1934; d. Mariangelo and Filomena (Albanese) Giambattista; m. Vincent G. Ampola, Aug. 7, 1966; children: Leanna, David. BA cum laude, Syracuse U., 1956; MD, SUNY, Syracuse, 1960. Diplomate Am. Bd. Pediatrics. Intern George Washington Univ. Hosp., Washington, 1960-61; pediatric resident Children's Nat. Med. Ctr., Washington, 1961-63, chief resident in pediatrics, 1963-64; genetics fellow Children's Hosp. Med. Ctr., Boston, 1964-66; metabolic diseases fellow Mass. Gen. Hosp., Boston, 1966-67; cytogeneticist New Eng. Med. Ctr., Boston, 1967-69, dir. pediatric amino acid lab., 1969—, pediatrician, 1969—, acting chief clin. genetics divsn. dept. pediatrics, 1989—, chief divsn. metabolism, dept. pediatrics, 1996—; from asst. to assoc. prof. pediatrics New Eng. Med. Ctr./Tufts U. Sch. Medicine, Boston, 1967-92, prof., 1992—; chmn. PL-1 selection com. dept. pediatrics New Eng. Med. Ctr., 1975—, chnm. residency com., 1981-87, mem. residency com. 1987—, bd. dirs. Ctr. Children Spl. Needs, 1990—, mem. hosp. quality assurance com., 1982-92; mem. curriculum com., various others sch. medicine Tufts U., 1981—. Editor: Early Detection and Management of Inborn Errors, 1976; author: Metabolic Diseases in Pediatric Practice, 1982; contbr. chpts. to books and articles to profl. jours. Named Alumna of Yr., SUNY Coll. Medicine, 1980. Fellow Am. Acad. Pediatrics (sect. genetics); mem. Am. Soc. Human Genetics, New Eng. Pediatric Soc. (sec.-treas. 1993—), Soc. Inherited Metabolic Disorders, Soc. Study Inborn Errors Metabolism, Phi Beta Kappa. Republican. Office: New Eng Med Ctr 750 Washington St Boston MA 02111-1533

AMSLER, BEVERLY ANN, broadcast journalist; b. Clarion, Pa., Nov. 2, 1961; d. Robert Lee and Bessie Earlene (Sheesley) A. BS in Music Edn., Clarion U., 1983; postgrad. in Broadcast Comms., U. Pitts., Bradford, 1987; diploma in Journalism, Internat. Corr. Sch., 1991; MFA in Mass Comm., Towson State U., 1995. News dir. WWCH/WCCR, Clarion, 1984-86; morning news anchor WESB, Bradford, Pa., 1986-87; news and pub. affairs coord. WKYN, St. Marys, Pa., 1987-89; anchor, reporter WKBO, Harrisburg, Pa., 1989-91; news and sports dir. WQLV, Millersburg, Pa., 1992-95; reporter WHAG-TV, Hagerstown, Md., 1995; anchor/reporter Ind. Pub. Radio and WIPB-TV, Muncie, 1995—. Recipient News Series award Ctrl. Pa. Woman in Comms., 1993, 94, Best Local Newscast award Pa. Assn. Broadcasters, 1992, 94, 95, numerous awards Pa. AP, 1985, 86, 87, 89, 90, 95, Best Newscast SPJ-Ind., 1995. Mem. Pa. AP Broadcasters Assn., Soc. Profl. Jouralists. Democrat. United Methodist. Home: 422 S Manning Ave Apt 15 Muncie IN 47303 Office: Ball Bldg Ball State U Muncie IN 47306

AMSTER, LINDA EVELYN, newspaper executive, consultant; b. N.Y.C., May 21, 1938; d. Abraham and Belle Shirley (Levine) Meyerson; m. Robert L. Amster, Feb. 18, 1961 (dec. Feb. 1974). B.A., U. Mich., 1960; M.L.S., Columbia U., 1968. Tchr. English Stamford High Sch., Conn., 1961-63; research librarian The Detroit News, 1965-67; research librarian The N.Y. Times, N.Y.C., 1967-69, supr. news research, 1969-74, news research mgr., 1974—; bd. dirs. Council for Career Planning, N.Y.C., 1982—. Contbr. articles to books, N.Y. Times and other publs. Mem. Spl. libraries Assn. Club: Coffee House. Home: 336 Central Park W New York NY 10025-7111 Office: The NY Times 229 W 43rd St New York NY 10036-3913

AMSTUTZ, MARY LOIS, music educator; b. Bluffton, Ind., Dec. 24, 1942; d. Glenn Daniel and Ruby Lois (McDonald) Masterson; m. Stanley J. Amstutz, June 3, 1967; children: Jeffrey, Scott. B of Music Edn., Ft. Wayne Bible Coll., 1965; MA, Ball State U., 1969. Music tchr. 1st-12th grades So. Wells Community, Poneto, Ind., 1965-69; music tchr. K-5th grades Adams Ctrl. Community, Monroe, Ind., 1969-72, 81—; music tchr. K-8th grades Montpelier (Ind.) Mid. Sch., 1979-81. Office: Adams Ctrl Community Sch 222 W Washington St Monroe IN 46772-9436

ANABLE, ANNE CURRIER STEINERT, journalist; b. Boston, Feb. 18; d. Robert Shuman and Lucy Pettingill (Currier) Steinert; m. Anthony Anable, Jr., 1962 (div. 1965); m. Robert C. Henriques, 1973 (div. 1980). Grad. West Hill Jr. Coll., Boston, 1951. Reporter women's pages N.Y. Jour. Am., N.Y.C., 1961-66, World Jour. Tribune, N.Y.C., 1966-67; fashion editor Cleve. Plain Dealer, 1967-73; fashion and beauty editor New Woman mag., Ft. Lauderdale, Fla., 1973-75, 78-79; contbg. editor Com. sect. N.Y. Times, 1977-81, New Choices Mag., 1991-92; beauty editor L'Officiel/USA, 1979, New Woman mag., 1982; fashion editor Am. Salon, 1984-87; contbg. editor Playbill, N.Y.C., 1985—, Harris Publs., 1987-90, Weight Watchers Mag., 1996—. Recipient Fashion Reporting award N.Y., 1970. Mem. Soc. Profl. Journalists, Fashion Group, Fashion's Inner Circle, Editorial Free Lancers Assn. Home and Office: 7 Flower Hill Pl Port Washington NY 11050-3608

ANANG, AMMA CECILIA, dance company administrator. MFA in Dance, Mills Coll. Co-founder, mgr, costume designer, dancer, make-up artist Ocheami Dance Co., Seattle. Office: PO Box 31635 Seattle WA 98103-1635

ANARGYROS, NEDRA HARRISON, cytotechnologist; b. N.Y.C., Dec. 3, 1915; d. Leverette Roland and Florence Martha (Pickard) Harrison; student Emerson Coll., 1936; cert. in cytology U. Calif., San Francisco, 1957; m. Spero Drosos Anargyros, Oct. 21, 1940 (div. 1969). Supr. cytology San Francisco Gen. Hosp., 1957-88; ret. 1988. Mem. Am. Soc. Clin. Pathologists (affiliate mem.), Am. Soc. for Cytotech. (affiliate mem., cert. cytologist), Women Flyers of Am., DAR (past regent, 1990-91, 1st vice regent La Puerta de Ora chpt., San Francisco), Nat. Soc. Colonial Dames of Am. in Calif., Huguenot Soc. of Calif. Republican. Christian Scientist. Club: Presidents of Mercer U. (Macon, Ga.). Home: 2503 Clay St San Francisco CA 94115-1810 also: 1400 Geary Blvd Apt 5N San Francisco CA 94109-6561

ANAS, JULIANNE KAY, administrative laboratory director; b. Detroit, Oct. 31, 1941; d. Theodore John and Lorraine (Comment) Knechtges; m. Donald Cartwright, Jan. 25, 1965 (div. June 1968); m. Daniel James Anas, Jan. 6, 1979. BS, Ea. Mich. U., 1969; MA, Cen. Mich. U., 1978. Cert. specialist in chemistry and med. tech. Am Soc. Clin. Pathologists. Med. technologist W.A. Foote Hosp., Jackson, Mich., 1962-63; med. technologist PCHA Annapolis Hosp., Wayne, Mich., 1964-65, supr. spl. chemistry and nuclear medicine, 1969-71; med. technologist Herrick Hosp., Tecumseh, Mich., 1965, Emma L. Bixby Hosp., Adrian, Mich., 1965-68; asst. clin. chemist Peoples Community Hosp. Authority, Wayne, 1971-81; adminstrv. lab. dir. Metro Med. Group Health Alliance Plan Henry Ford Health System, Detroit, 1981—; lab. adv. coun. Highland Pk. Cmty. Coll., 1994—;

adv. panel Medicalab Observor mag., 1988—. Contbr. articles to profl. publs. Mem. Am. Soc. Med. Tech. (bd. dirs. Mich. sect. 1972-73, pres. Detroit sect. 1972), Hosp. Lab. Mgrs. Assn. (membership chmn. 1984, 85, 90), Detroit Soc. Med. Technologists (Med. Technologist of Yr. 1975), Am. Assn. Clin. Chemists (nominations chair Mich. sect. 1992), Founders Art Inst. Republican. Home: 6369 Mabley Hill Rd Fenton MI 48430-9999

ANASTAS, JEANE WIENER, social work educator; b. Boston, Jan. 31, 1946; d. Francis M. and Britta G. (Gunther) Wiener; m. Peter N. Anastas, Nov., 1964 (div. Nov. 1972); children: Jonathan, Benjamin, Rhea. BLS, Boston U., 1976; MSW, Boston Coll., 1978; PhD, Brandeis U., 1982. Adj. asst. prof. Boston U. Sch. Social Work, 1978-80; asst. prof. Simmons Coll. Grad. Sch. Social Work, Boston, 1980-83; assoc. prof. Smith Coll. Sch. for Social Work, Northampton, Mass., 1983-89, prof., 1989—; sr. lectr. Met. Coll., Boston U., 1980-83; project evaluator Daybreak/Brightside, West Springfield, Mass., 1991-96, Adolescent Family Life Project/Brightside, West Springfield; cons. in field; vis. rsch. scholar Ctr. for Rsch. on Women, Wellesley (Mass.) Coll., 1992-93. Co-author: Research Design for Social Work and the Human Services, 1994, (book chpts.) Social Work: A Profession of Many Faces, 1992, Women as Social Work Leaders and Managers, 1994. Project evaluator Ctr. for Substance Abuse Prevention, Washington, 1991—, Office of Adolescent Pregnancy and Parenting Programs, Washington, 1985-91. Fellow Am. Orthopsychiat. Assn.; mem. NASW (pres. Mass. chpt., mem. nat. nominating com. 1993-96, nat. com. on women's issues, chair 1992-95), Coun. on Social Work Edn. Office: Smith Coll Sch Social Work Lilly Hall Northampton MA 01063

ANASTASI, ANNE (MRS. JOHN PORTER FOLEY, JR.), psychology educator; b. N.Y.C., Dec. 19, 1908; d. Anthony and Theresa (Gaudiosi) A.; m. John Porter Foley, Jr., July 26, 1933. A.B., Barnard Coll., 1928; Ph.D., Columbia U., 1930; Litt.D. (hon.), U. Windsor, Can., 1967; Sc.D. (hon.), Cedar Crest Coll., 1971, La Salle Coll., 1979, Fordham U., 1979; Paed.D. (hon.), Villanova U., 1971. Instr. psychology Barnard Coll., N.Y.C., 1930-39; asst. prof., chmn. dept. Queens Coll., N.Y.C., 1939-46; assoc. prof. psychology Fordham U., N.Y.C., 1947-51; prof. Fordham U., 1951-79, prof. emeritus, 1979—, chmn. dept. psychology, 1968-74; mem. NRC, 1952-55; pres. Am. Psychol. Found., 1965-67. Author: Differential Psychology, 1937, rev. edit., 1949, 58, Psychological Testing, 1954, 6th edit., 1988, Fields of Applied Psychology, 1964, 2d edit., 1979; also articles in field.; editor: Individual Differences, 1965, Testing Problems in Perspective, 1966; Contributions to Differential Psychology, 1982. Recipient award for disting. svc. to measurement Ednl. Testing Svc., 1977, award disting. contbns. to rsch. Am. Ednl. Rsch. Assn., 1983, Gold medal Am. Psychol. Found., 1984, Nat. medal of Sci., 1987; James McKeen Cattell fellow Am. PSychol. Soc., 1993. Mem. APA (rec. sec. 1952-55, pres. divsn. gen. psychology 1956-57, bd. dirs. 1956-59, 68-70, pres. divsn. evaluation and measurement 1965-66, pres. 1971-72, Disting. Sci. award 1981, E.L. Thorndike medal divsn. ednl. psychology 1984, Lifetime Contbn. award 1994), Ea. Psychol. Assn. (pres. 1946-47, bd. dirs. 1948-50), Psychonomic Soc., Phi Beta Kappa, Sigma Xi.

ANASTASIA, PAULA JEAN, oncological nurse; b. Lawrenceburg, Ind., Nov. 16, 1960; d. Peter Francis and Ruth Evelyn (Gill) A.; m. Martin James Davis, Dec. 31, 1988. BS, Hanover (Ind.) Coll., 1983; BSN, Rush U., 1983; M in Nursing, UCLA, 1993. RN, Calif., La. Gynecology/oncology clin. nurse specialist UCLA, 1993—, clin. instr., 1993—, assoc. prof. Sch. Nursing, 1995—. Contbr. articles to profl. jours. Vol. Am. Cancer Soc., Culver City, Calif. Mem. Oncology Nursing Soc., Soc. Gynecologic Nurse Oncologists, Calif. Nurses Assn., Nat. League for Nursing, Sigma Theta Tau. Democrat. Roman Catholic. Office: UCLA Med Ctr 10833 Le Conte Ave Los Angeles CA 90095

ANASTOLE, DOROTHY JEAN, electronics company executive; b. Akron, Ohio, Mar. 26, 1932; d. Leonard L. and Helen (Sagedy) Dice; children: Kally, Dennis, Christopher. Student, De Anza Jr. Coll., Cupertino, Calif., 1969. Various secretarial positions in mfg., 1969-75; office mgr. Sci. Devices Co., Mountain View, Calif., 1975-76; exec. adminstrv. sec. corp. office Cezar Industries, Palo Alto, Calif., 1976-77; office and personnel mgr. AM Bruning Co., Mountain View, 1977-81; dir. employee relations Consol. Micrographics, Mountain View, 1981-83; personnel mgmt. cons., 1983-84; mgr. adminstrn./employee relations Mitsubishi Electronics Am., Inc., Sunnyvale, Calif., 1984-89, sr. mgr., 1989-91, corp./nat. v.p., 1991-96, ret., 1996. Bd. dirs. Agnew State Hosp., San Jose, Calif., 1966-72, div. chmn. program mentally retarded, 1966-72, staff tutor, 1966-72; bd. dirs. Project Hired, Sunnyvale, 1991-93; bd. advisors The Senior Staff, 1994—. Recipient Scv. award Agnew State Hosp., 1972.

ANASTOS, ANNA VEDOURAS, federal lawyer; b. Cleveland, Ohio, Feb. 21, 1960; d. John and Emily (Peters) Vedouras; m. Thomas L. Anastos, July 21, 1984. BA, U. Mich., 1981; JD, Cleve. State U., 1985. Bar: Ohio 1989. Atty. LIGHTNET, New Haven, Conn., 1985-86; contract adminstr. Constrn. Control Svcs., Inc., Boston, 1986-87; project mgr. Legal Support Svcs., Boston, 1987-89; sr. assoc. counsel Dept. of Defense, Cleveland, Ohio, 1989—. Pres. Young Friends Cleve. Mus. Art, 1993-95; trustee, v.p. Ctr. for Prevention of Domestic Violence, 1993—; trustee Cleve. Play House, 1991-96; Cleve. Film Soc., 1993—, Cleve. Ctr. Contemporary Arts, 1996—; bd. mem. Near West Theatre, 1996—. Mem. Cleve. Bar Assn.

ANASTOS, ROSEMARY PARK, retired higher education educator; b. Andover, Mass., 1907. AB, Radcliffe Coll., 1928, AM, 1929; PhD, U. Cologne, Germany, 1934; 25 hon. degrees, Yale U., Columbia U., NYU, Brown U., Syracuse U., U. Notre Dame, Claremont Coll., U. Pa., Oberlin Coll., others. Prof. German, acad. dean Conn. Coll., New London, 1943-47, pres., 1947-62; pres. Barnard Coll., dean Columbia U., 1962-67; vice-chancellor UCLA, 1967-70, prof. higher edn. Grad. Sch. Edn., 1967-74, prof. emeritus, 1974—, prof. on recall, 1974-75; pres. United Chpts. Phi Beta Kappa, 1970-73. Author: Das Bild Richard Wagner's Tristan und Isolde, 1935, two textbooks; articles in field; contbg. editor Change mag. Trustee Mt. St. Mary's Coll., L.A.; former chmn. bd. visitors Def. Intelligence Coll., U.S. Dept. Def.; former trustee Robert Coll., Istanbul, Turkey, New Sch. for Social Rsch., N.Y., Danforth Found., U. Hartford, Scripps Coll., Marlborough Sch., U. Notre Dame, Carnegie Found. for Advancement of Teaching; former mem. adv. coun. and chmn. rsch. com. NEH; former mem. adv. coun. Fund for Improvement of Post-secondary Edn.; former dir. Am. Coun. on Edn. Recipient Woman of Yr. award L.A. Times, 1967, Radcliffe Coll. Alumnae award, 1974, medal U.S. Dept. Def. Fellow Am. Acad. Arts and Scis. Home: 10501 Wilshire Blvd Apt 2101 Los Angeles CA 90024-6330

ANAWALT, PATRICIA RIEFF, anthropologist; b. Ripon, Calif., Mar. 10, 1924; d. Edmund Lee and Anita Esto (Capps) Rieff; m. Richard Lee Anawalt, June 8, 1945; children: David, Katherine Anawalt Arnoldi, Harmon Fred. BA in Anthropology, UCLA, 1957, MA in Anthropology, 1971, PhD in Anthropology, 1975. Cons. curator costumes and textiles Mus. Cultural History UCLA, 1975-90, dir. Ctr. for Study Regional Dress, Fowler Mus. Cultural History, 1990—; trustee S.W. Mus., L.A., 1978-92; rsch. assoc. UCLA Inst. Archaeology, 1994—; trustee Archaeol. Inst. Am., U.S., Can., 1983-95, traveling lectr., 1975-86, 94-96, Pres.'s Lectureship, 1993-94, Charles E. Norton lectureship, 1996—; cons. Nat. Geog. Soc., 1980-82, Denver Mus. Natural History, 1992-93; apptd. by U.S. Pres. to Cultural Property Adv. Com., Washington, 1984-93; fieldwork Guatemala, 1961, 70, 72, Spain, 1975, Sierra Norte de Puebla, Mex., 1983, 85, 88, 89, 91. Author: Indian Clothing Before Cortés: Mesoamerican Costumes from the Codices, 1981, paperback edit., 1990; co-author: The Codex Mendoza, 4 vols., 1992 (winner Archaeol. Inst. Am. 1994 James Wiseman Book award). Adv. com Textile Mus., Washington, 1983-87. Recipient NEH grant, J. Paul Getty Found. grant, Nat. Geog. Soc. grants, 1983, 85, 88, 89, 91, Guggenheim fellowship, 1988-89. Fellow Am. Anthrop. Assn., L.A. County Mus. Natural History; mem. Centre Internat. D'Etude Des Textiles Anciens, Am. Ethnol. Soc., Soc. Am. Archaeology, Soc. Women Geographers (Outstanding Achievement award 1993), Textile Soc. Am. (bd. dirs. 1992-96, co-coord. 1994 biennial symposium), Patrons Cir. L.A. County Mus. Art, Archaeol. Inst. Am. So. Calif. Soc. (pres. 1986-89, v.p. 1983-86, sec. 1979-83). Office: Fowler Mus Cultural History Ctr Study of Regional Dress Los Angeles CA 90095-1549

ANCHIE, TOBY LEVINE, health facility administrator; b. New Haven, Conn., Jan. 21, 1944; d. Solomon and Mary (Karlins) Levine; children: Michael D. Anchie, Robert P. Anchie. BSN, U. of Conn., 1966; MA in Edn. magna cum laude, Nor. Ariz. U., 1984. RN Ariz., Conn. Coord. spl. projects, nurse coord., adult day hosp. Barrow Neurol. Inst. of St. Joseph's Hosp. and Med. Ctr., Phoenix, 1984-87, mgr., 1985-92; mgr. adminstrv. and support svcs., neuroscis. Barrow Neurol. Inst. of St. Joseph's Hosp. and Med. Ctr., 1992-94; mgr. clin. rsch., 1994—; cons.; presenter in field; mem. faculty U. Phoenix; adv. bd. mem. Myasthenia Gravis Assn.; mem. adv. coun. Office Disability Prevention Ariz. Dept. Health Svcs., mem. strategic planning com. Contbr. articles to profl. jours., chpts. Mem. NAFE, Am. Assn. Neurosci. Nurses (bd. dirs., pres.), Assocs. Clinical Pharmacology, Am. Bd. Neurosci. Nursing (treas. 1995-96), World Fedn. Splty. Nursing Orgn. (chair membership com. 1993-95), Assn. Clin. Rsch. Coords. (Ariz chpt.), Ariz. Assn. Neurosci. Nurses. Home: 3112 S Los Feliz Dr Tempe AZ 85282-2854

ANCKER-JOHNSON, BETSY, physicist, engineer, retired automotive company executive; b. St. Louis, Apr. 29, 1927; d. Clinton James and Fern (Lalan) A.; m. Harold Hunt Johnson, Mar. 15, 1958; children: Ruth P. Johnson, David H. Johnson, Paul A. Johnson, Marti H. Johnson. B.A. in Physics with high honors (Pendleton scholar), Wellesley Coll., 1949; Ph.D. magna cum laude, U. Tuebingen, Germany, 1953; D.Sc. (hon.), Poly. Inst. N.Y., 1979, Trinity Coll., 1981, U. So. Calif., 1984, Alverno Coll., 1984; LL.D. (hon.), Bates Coll., 1980. Instr., jr. research physicist U. Calif., Berkeley, 1953-54; physicist Sylvania Microwave Physics Lab., 1956-58; mem. tech. staff RCA Labs., 1958-61; research specialist Boeing Co., 1961-70, exec., 1970-73; asst. sec. U.S. Dept. Commerce for Sci. and Tech., 1973-77; dir. phys. research Argonne Nat. Lab., Ill., 1977-79; v.p. environ. activities staff GM, Warren, Mich., 1979-92; affiliate prof. elec. engring. U. Wash., 1961-73; bd. dirs. Gen. Mills; mem. Energy Rsch. Adv. Bd., adv. com. on inertial confinement fusion Dept. Energy, 1993—, U.S. Safety Rev. Panel NSF, 1987-88; cons. Inland Steel Inc., 1991—; bd. dirs. Enterprise Devel., Inc., 1992—; mem. adv. com. Rowan Sch. Engring., 1993—. Author of 80 sci. papers; patentee in field. Mem. staff Inter-Varsity Christian Fellowship, 1954-56; mem. vis. com. elec. and computer divsn. MIT, U.S. Dept. Def. Sci. Bd.; mem. adv. bd. Stanford U. Sch. Engring., Fla. State U., Fla. A&M U., Congl. Caucus for Sci. and Tech.; trustee Wellesley Coll., 1971-77; chair bd. dirs. World Environ. Ctr., 1988-93, dir., 1988—. AAUW fellow, 1950-51; Horton Hollowell fellow, 1951-52; NSF grantee, 1967-72. Fellow AAAS, IEEE, Am. Phys. Soc. (councillor-at-large 1973-76); mem. NRC (bd. engring. edn. 1991—, com. on women in sci. and engring. 1990—, office sci. and engring. pers. adv. com. 1993—), Nat. Acad. Engring. (councillor 1995—), Air Pollution Control Assn., Soc. Automotive Engrs. (bd. dirs. 1979-81), Phi Beta Kappa, Sigma Xi. Home: 222 Harbour Dr Apt 311 Naples FL 34103

ANCRUM, CHERYL DENISE, dentist; b. Bklyn., Sept. 28, 1958; d. Ida Jackson. BA in Psychology, Harvard U., Cambridge, 1980; DDS, Columbia U., N.Y., 1986, MPH, 1989. Dentist. Credit analyst Hartford (Conn.) Nat. Bank, 1980-81; statistical coding instr./analyst Aetna Ins. Co., Hartford, Conn., 1981-82; dental asst. Gouverneur Hosp., N.Y.C., 1983; clk. typist Columbia Presbyn. Med. Ctr., N.Y.C., 1984-86; gen. practice resident Beth Israel Med. Ctr., N.Y.C., 1986-87; dental attending Montefiore Med. Ctr., Bronx, 1987-90; rsch. assoc./dentist North Central Bronx Hosp., 1989-90; dental dir. Manhattan Men's Ho. of Detention, N.Y.C., 1989—; dental extern N. Central Bronx. Hosp., 1985-86. Vol. St. John Episc. Hosp., Bklyn., 1974-75, Mt. Auburn Hosp., Cambridge, 1978, Harlem Hosp., N.Y.C., 1987-88; health adv. Harvard U., Cambridge, 1977-80; active Sutton for Mayor Campaign, Bklyn., 1977; mem. Girl Scouts U.S., Bklyn., 1969-75, Operation PUSH, Hartford, 1981-82, Hartford Black Women Network, 1980-82, Kuumba Singers, Harvard U., 1977-80, New Temple Singers, Cambridge, 1977-80; mem. tape commn. Bridge St. A.M.E. Ch., Bklyn., 1987-88; fin. sec. Flower Guild, Allen A.M.E. Church, Queens, 1994—; bd. dirs. F.I.S.H. of Uniondale, 1991-96. Recipient scholarship A Better Chance, 1973-76, Am. Fund for Dental Health, 1982-84, Clark Found., 1983-86, selected profl. fellowship AAUW, 1985-86, Letter of Commendation, Columbia U., 1983, Applewhite award, 1986, William Bailey Dunning award, 1986, Lester R. Cain Pathology prize, 1986; named to Outstanding Young Women of Am., 1983. Mem. ADA, N.Y. State Dental Soc., Acad. of Gen. Dentistry, Am. Assn. of Pub. Health Dentistry, Am. Profl. Practice Assn., Order of the Ea. Star (Elizabeth Moore chpt. sec. 1996—), Delta Sigma Theta (Nassau alumnae chpt. journalist, 1992-96, 2d v.p., 1995-96). Democrat. Mem. African Methodist Episcopal Ch. Home: 1043 Tulsa St Uniondale NY 11553-1615

ANCUTA, KATHLEEN MADELINE, financial executive; b. Kineley AFB, St. George, Bermuda, Sept. 7, 1953; (parents Am. citizens); d. Daniel Philip and Beatrice Madeline (Murphy) Allen; m. Len Ancuta, Jan. 29, 1977; 1 child, Leonard Daniel. BS, Ramapo Coll., 1975; MBA, Fairleigh Dickenson U., 1981. Acct. Merrill Lynch Pierce Fenner & Smith, N.Y.C., 1976-77, fin. analyst, acctg. supr., 1977-78; asst. mgr. Young & Rubicam Inc., N.Y.C., 1978-79, fin. mgr., 1979-82, asst. contr., 1982-84, v.p., 1984-86, dir. compensation and equity, 1984-91, sr. v.p., 1986-91, sr. v.p. corp. fin., 1991—. Named to Acad. Women Achievers, YWCA, N.Y.C., 1987. Mem. NAFE, Am. Mgmt. Assn., Fin. Execs. Inst. Republican. Roman Catholic. Home: 457 Shadyside Rd Ramsey NJ 07446-1732 Office: Young & Rubicam Inc 285 Madison Ave New York NY 10017-6401*

ANDELL, NANCY, artist; b. Boston, Nov. 14, 1953. Diploma, Sch. Mus. Fine Arts, Boston, 1974, Cert., 1976; BS in Edn., Tufts U., 1975; MFA, Vt. Coll., 1994. tchg. faculty Exptl. Etching Studio, Boston, 1979-80, Albany Inst. History and Art, 1989-90, Berkshire Mus., Pittsfield, Mass., 1989, Rensselaer County Coun. for Arts, Troy, 1989-92, Taconic Hills H.S., Philmont, N.Y., 1990-96. Solo exhbns. include New Work, Flag Gallery, Boston, 1978, Impressions Gallery, Boston, 1979, 80, Shaker Mus., Old Chatham, N.Y., 1991, Vt. Coll., Montpelier, 1994, Simon's Rock Coll., Great Barrington, Mass.; group shows include Albany (N.Y.) Inst. History and Art, 1989, Rensselaer County Coun. for Arts, Troy, N.Y., 1991, Smithy Pioneer Gallery, Cooperstown, N.Y., 1992, Exptl. Etching Studio, Boston, 1992-94, Westbeth Gallery, N.Y., 1994, others; works in permanent collections at Met. Mus. Art, New Mus. Contemporary Art, N.Y., Bklyn. Mus., Worcester (Mass.) Art Mus., Provincetown (Mass.) Mus. Art. Visual Arts fellow NEA, 1987. Home: PO Box 46 Chatham NY 12037-0046*

ANDERHUB, BETH MARIE, medical educator; b. St. Louis, Feb. 7, 1953; d. Anthony Pierre and Eleanor (Corich) A. A in Applied Sci., Forest Park C.C., St. Louis, 1974; BS in Radiologic Tech., U. Mo., 1975; MEd, St. Louis U., 1989, postgrad., 1989—. Cert. radiologic tech., nuclear medicine, abdominal sonography, ob-gyn sonography. Nuclear medicine and ultrasound technician VA Hosp., St. Louis, 1976-79; ultrasound technologist, sr. sonographer Deaconess Hosp., St. Louis, 1979-82, chief sonographer, 1982-83; assoc. prof., dir. ultrasound program St. Louis C.C., 1983—; chmn. accreditation com. Ultrasound Program, Englewood, Colo., 1990-95; v.p. Commn. on Accreditation for Allied Health Program, 1994-1996; lectr., presenter programs in field confs., symposia, colls., univs. Author: Manual on Abdominal Sonography, 1983, General Sonography, 1994; contbr. articles to profl. jours. Fellow Soc. Diagnostic Med. Sonographers (chmn. edn. com. 1984-86, contbg. editor Jour. Diagnostic Med. Sonography 1984-89, bd. dirs. 1986-89, v.p. 1989-91, pres.-elect 1991-93, pres. 1993-95, treas. ednl. found. 1988-91, other coms.), Am. Soc. Radiologic Technologists (bd. dirs. 1982-85, task force modality del. roles 1988-89, rep. sonography summit 1988, chmn. ultrasound com. 1980, 82-85, others), Am. Inst. Ultrasound in Medicine, Mo. Soc. Radiologic Technologists (pres. 1979-80, pres. 4th dist. 1978-79). Home: 12449 Dawn Hill Dr Maryland Hts MO 63043-3636 Office: St Louis C C 5600 Oakland Ave Saint Louis MO 63110-1316

ANDERS, CAMILLE SHEPHARD, director of adult and family ministries; b. Meridian, Miss., Dec. 28, 1938; m. Dan Raney Anders, Sept. 3, 1994; children: Christel Camille Funk, Lisa Leah Funk Nied, Melanie Maria Funk Futch, Wendi Wanita Funk. BA, U. Miss., 1960; Lang. Cert., Yale Inst. Far Ea. Langs., 1962. Speech pathologist Quincy (Mass.) City Schs., 1960-61; lay ednl. missionary Gen. Bd. Global Ministries, Un. Meth. Ch., Kapit and Sibu, Sarawak, Malaysia, 1962-71; sec. Gen. Bd. Global Ministries, Un. Meth. Ch., Atlanta, 1976-84, mission educator, 1985, southeastern mission devel. field rep., 1986-94; gen. sec. Global Mission Ptnrs., 1994—; mem., organizer U.S.-China Peoples Friendship Assn., Atlanta, 1974—; leader mission edn. workshops. Author (study book guide) 10 Sessions for 3d-4th Grade, 1989, (study book guide) Winds Across China, 1985 (study program) God, Our World, and Me, 1989, Leader's Guide to The Enduring Church, an ecumenical Mission study on China/Hong Kong, 1996; contbr. articles to publs. Democrat. Home: 3216 Prince William Dr Fairfax VA 22031-3020

ANDERSEN, ETHEL DUGGAN, lawyer; b. Perry, Ga., May 6, 1949; d. James Powell and Mary (Lawson) Duggan; m. Thomas J. Andersen, Dec. 28, 1973; children: David S., James T. BA in Psychology, Duke U., Durham, N.C., 1971; attended, U. Ga. Law Sch., Athens, 1972-73; JD Sch. Law, Emory U., 1975. Bar: Ga. Lawyer Troutman Sanders, Atlanta, 1975-77; asst. atty. gen. Ga. A.G. Office, Atlanta, 1977-83; adminstrv. law judge State of Ga., Atlanta, 1983—; lawyer Anderson, Davidson & Tate, Lawrenceville, Ga., 1988—. Pres. Gwinnett Coun. Arts, Lawrenceville, Ga., 1982; founding bd. mem. Jr. League North Fulton & Gwinnett, 1985, mem. planned giving com. Gwinnett Hosp. Found., 1996. Mem. Ga. Bar Assn. (fiduciary law sect.), Gwinnett County Bar Assn. Methodist. Home: 6210 Blackberry Hill Norcross GA 30092 Office: Andersen Davidson & Tate 324 W Pike St Lawrenceville GA 30245

ANDERSEN, FRANCES ELIZABETH GOLD, religious leadership educator; b. Hot Springs, Ark., Feb. 11, 1916; d. Benjamin Knox and Pearl Scott (Smith) Gold; m. Robert Thomas Andersen, June 27, 1942; children: Nancy Ruth (Mrs. Bernd Neumann), Robert Thomas. BA, UCLA, 1936, sec. teaching credential, 1937. Tchr. math. L.A. City Schs., 1937-42, 46-48; faculty Ariz. State Coll., Tempe, 1943-45; mem. nat. bd. missions United Meth. Ch., 1940-44; dir. Christian edn. 1st Presbyn. Ch., Phoenix, 1943-45, Trinity Meth. ch., L.A., 1953-55, 1st Bapt. Ch., Lakewood, Calif., 1955-57; dir. Christian edn. Grace Bapt. Ch., Riverside, 1958-83, chmn. nursery sch. bd., 1969-83; mem. nat. bd. Bible sch. and youth Bapt. Gen. Conf., 1966-71; coord. leadership tng. insts. Greater L.A. Sunday Sch. Assn., 1956-80; exec. dir. San Bernardino-Riverside Sunday Sch. Assn., 1959—; prin. Riverside Christian Sch., 1985-87, bd. dirs., 1985—; mem. Christian edn. bd. S.W. Bapt. Conf., 1956-59, 63-66, 72-75, 80-83; bd. dirs. GLASS, 1956—; dir. Women's guild, Calif. Bapt. Coll., Riverside, 1983—. Author: How to Organize Area Leadership Training Institutes, 1964. Pres. Univ. Jr. H.S., PTA, Riverside, 1963-64, Poly. H.S., PTA, 1965-67; life mem. PTA; judge Nat. Sunday Sch. Tchrs. Awards, 1993-95. Named Grace Bapt. Mother of Yr., 1981, People Who Make a Difference Press-Enterprise, 1984, One of Outstanding Women of Riverside, Calif. Bapt. Coll., 1985. Mem. Sons of Norway, Alpha Delta Chi (nat. pres. 1950-51, exec. sec. 1952-54), Pi Mu Epsilon. Home: 1787 Prince Albert Dr Riverside CA 92507-5852

ANDERSEN, MARGARET LOUISE, sociology educator, academic administrator; b. Oakland, Calif., Aug. 24, 1948; d. Milton Andersen and Emma Louise Wangberg; m. Richard Morris Rosenfeld, Apr. 19, 1984. BA, Ga. State U., 1970; MS, U. Mass., 1973, PhD, 1976. From instr. to asst. prof. to assoc. prof. U. Del., Newark, 1974-88, prof., 1988—, vice provost for acad. affairs, 1990—. Author: Thinking About Women, 1982, 88, 93, Race, Class and Gender, 1992, 95; editor: (periodical) Gender and Society, 1990-95. Mem. Phi Kappa Phi. Office: U Del Office of the Provost Newark DE 21921

ANDERSEN, MARIANNE SINGER, clinical psychologist; b. Baden nr. Vienna, Austria; came to U.S., 1940, naturalized, 1946; d. Richard L. and Jolanthe (Garda) Singer; 1 son, Richard Esten. BA, CUNY, 1950, MA, 1974; PhD, Fla. Inst. Tech., 1980. Rsch. assoc. Inst. for Rsch. in Hypnosis, N.Y.C., 1974-76, fellow in clin. hypnosis, 1976, dir. seminars, 1978-82, dir. edn., 1982—; psychotherapist specializing in hypnotherapy Morton Prince Ctr. for Hypnotherapy, dir. clin. services, 1981-82; dir. adminstrn. Internat. Grad. U., N.Y.C., 1974-77; pvt. practice psychotherapy, 1977—; adminstrv. coordinator Internat. Grad. Sch. Behavior Sci., Fla. Inst. Tech., 1978; co-dir. The Melbourne Group, 1983—; clin. instr. hypnotherapy Mt. Sinai Sch. Medicine, N.Y.C., 1996; lectr. hypnosis and hypnotherapy to mental and phys. health profls., 1977—; Author: (with Louis Savary) Passages: A Guide for Pilgrims of the Mind, 1972; rsch. on treatment obesity with hypnotherapy; book editor specializing in psychology and psychiatry including W.W. Norton Co., Sterling Pub. Co., E.P. Dutton Co., 1950-71. Fellow Soc. for Clin. and Exptl. Hypnosis; mem. Internat. Soc. for Clin. and Exptl. Hypnosis, Am. Psychol. Assn., N.Y. Acad. Scis. Home: 60 W 57th St New York NY 10019-3911

ANDERSEN, SUSAN HACKES, early childhood educator; b. Mt. Vernon, N.Y., Apr. 20, 1927; d. John R. and Ruth Edna (Misch) Hackes; m. Birger G. Andersen, Aug. 29, 1959; children: Jon, Kristi. BS magna cum laude, U. Wis., 1949; MA, Hunter Coll., 1954. Tchg. credential, N.Y.; life diploma, Calif. Profl. modern dancer various cos., N.Y.C., 1949-54; presch. tchr., dir. Walt Whitman Sch.-Peter Pan Nursery Sch., N.Y.C., 1951-55; kindergarten tchr. various schs., Calif., 1955-59; child care ctr. dir. Atonement Presch., San Diego, 1971-80, various schs., Calif., 1983-84, Little Beginnings Child Devel. Ctr., Arlington, Va., 1985-92; early childhood educator various schs., Conn., 1993—; cons. M/A-Com. Linkabit, San Diego, 1982-83. Co-founder Arlington (Va.) Dirs. Assn., 1986; child adv., activist Worthy Wage Campaign, Washington, 1992—; bd. mem. East Lyme (Conn.) Pub. Trust Found., 1994—; mem. Vision 2000: People Dedicated to Cmty. Svcs., East Lyme, 1994—. Mem. Nat. Mus. for Women in the Arts (charter), Children's Mus. of S.E. Conn. (charter mem.), Nat. Assn. for the Edn. Young Children, Phi Kappa Phi, Pi Lambda Theta. Democrat. Unitarian. Home: 17 Stone Cliff Dr Niantic CT 06357

ANDERSON, ADRIENNE MARIE, publishing executive; b. San Francisco, Apr. 3, 1968; d. Vincent Michael Anderson and Frances Delores Parham. AA, City Coll. San Francisco, 1988; BA, San Francisco State U., 1993. Publ. Ile-Nommo Publ. co., Oakland, Calif., 1994—; computer instr., entrepreneurship program instr. East Oakland (Calif.) Youth Devel. Ctr., 1996—; staff writer 4080 Mag., Berkeley, Calif., 1994—. Editor: The Ujima Newsletter, 1994-95; contbr. articles to profl. jours. Active Wo'se Cmty. Ch., 1995—. Mem. Nat. Assn. Exec. Women, Iota Phi Lambda Sorority (debutante 1986). African Methodist Episcopal. Office: Ile-Nommo Publ Co 484 Lake Park Ave # 409 Oakland CA 94610

ANDERSON, ALLAMAY EUDORIS, health educator, home economist; b. N.Y.C., July 18, 1933; d. John Samuel and Charlotte Jane (Harrigan) Richardson; B.A., Queens Coll., CUNY, 1975; profl. mgmt. cert. Adelphi U., 1978; M.S. in Edn., Fordham U., 1984; m. Edgar Leopold Anderson, Jr., Apr. 14, 1957; 1 son, David Lancelot. Mem. staff sch. food service, dietitian Bd. Edn., N.Y.C., 1968-88; tchr. home and career skills Louis Armstrong Middle Sch., 1988; spl. edn. tchr. Manhattan High Sch., N.Y.C., 1989-95, coord AIDS resource, 1995, ret. 1995; profl. devel. cons., N.Y.C., 1978—; ptnr. Masiba Bldg. Corp., Corona, N.Y., 1975-82; adj. lectr. home econs. Queens Coll., 1987; owner AEA Devel. Svc., 1987—. Devel. coord. League for Better Community Life, Inc., 1977; treas. exec. bd., 1970-76; officer N.Y.C. Community Devel. Agy., 1980-83; mem. Kwanzaa Adv. Com. (P.R.) Urban Coalition, 1983, L.I. # 28 Episcopal Cursillo, 1991; vestry mem. youth ministries Grace Episcopal Ch., 1982-85, vestry mem., 1996—; mem. NAACP (local Women's History Month honoree). Recipient Elmcor Community Svc. award Elmcor Youth and Adult Activities, Inc., 1989. Mem. Nat. Soc. Fund Raising Execs., Langston Hughes Libr. Action Com. (bd. dirs. 1987—, treas. 1989), Queens Coll. Home Econs. Alumni Assn. (v.p., chmn. bylaws com. 1982), United Fedn. Tchrs./Retired Tchrs. Chpt., Libr. Action Com. (chair Kwanzaa 1994-96), Phi Delta Kappa. Office: 10013 34th Ave Flushing NY 11368-1052

ANDERSON, AMY LEE, realtor; b. Tampa, Fla., July 24, 1950; d. Ernest William and Gloria June (Terrell) Denham; m. Arnold Albin Anderson Jr., Dec. 21, 1986; children: Melissa Lee, Nancy Marie. BA, U. Tampa, 1971. Lic. realtor Nat. Bd. Realtors. Sys. analyst Nat. CSS, Tampa, 1971-79; field analyst Digital Equipment Corp., Meriden, Conn., 1979-84; dir. nat. accounts Canaan Computer Corp., Stratford, Conn., 1981-92; realtor Prudential Carolinas Realty, Raleigh, N.C., 1992-95, Block & Assocs., Raleigh, 1995—; exec. staff Canaan Computer Corp., Stratford, 1987-92. Editor (manual) Corporate Policies, 1986; co-author: Start at the Top, 1989. Treas. PTA, Basking Ridge, N.J., 1989; advisor Tarheel Challenge Acad., Clinton, N.C., 1995; participant Paws Walk for Cancer, Raleigh, 1995. Mem. Data Processing Mgmt. Assn. (publicity com. 1978-92), Capital City Club (membership com. 1993—). Republican. Episcopalian. Office: Block and Assocs Realty Ste 1600 805 Spring Forest Rd Raleigh NC 27609

ANDERSON, ANN, state legislator; b. Yakima, Wash., 1952; married Eric Anderson; 1 child, Cori. Former tchr., mem. Wash. State Senate, majority whip. Republican. Office: Senate House PO Box 40482 Olympia WA 98504-0482*

ANDERSON, ANN DAVIS, curriculum and staff development specialist; b. Washington, Mar. 24, 1946; d. George Perry and Irene Delores (Stewart) Davis; m. Ronald Clifford Anderson, Oct. 13, 1973; 1 child, Tahira Mali. BS in Edn., Bucknell U., Lewisburg, Pa., 1968; MA in Edn., George Washington U., 1972. Cert. reading specialist, Va. Tchr. grades 2-5 D.C. Pub. Schs., 1968-73; reading specialist Alexandria (Va.) City Pub. Schs., 1973-93, curriculum/staff devel. specialist, 1993—; cons. NEA, Washington, 1986-88; reviewer of grants Nat. Found. for Improvement of Edn., Washington, 1993—; mem. nat. rev. panel for blue ribbon schs. U.S. Dept. Edn., Washington, 1992—; staff devel. presenter Alexandria City Pub. Schs., 1989—. Co-author: A Research Framework for the Middle Grades. Recipient Award of Excellence in Edn., Alexandria C. of C., 1986, Am. Tchr. award Walt Disney Corp., L.A., 1990; Washington Post grantee, 1987, Readers Choices 1000 Women for the Nineties, 1994, Reader's Choices 1000 Women for the Nineties, Mirabella mag., 1994. Mem. ASCD, NEA, Internat. Reading Assn., Nat. Coun. for Social Studies, Nat. Coun. Negro Women, Nat. Tots and Teens Inc. (v.p., youth coord. Prince Georges County chpt. 1991-93), Va. Edn. Assn., Edn. Assn. Alexandria, Phi Delta Kappa, Kappa Pi. Home: 12802 Berwick Cir Fort Washington MD 20744-6409 Office: Alexandria City Pub Schs 2000 N Beauregard St Alexandria VA 22311-1712

ANDERSON, ANN STEWART, artist, foundation administrator; b. Frankfort, Ky., Mar. 3, 1935; d. Olof and Martha Ward (Jones) A.; m. Ronald J. Mikulak, June 13, 1981. BA, Wellesley Coll., 1957; MA, Am. U., 1961. Sec. to asst. dir. Corcoran Gallery of Art, Washington, 1957-58, registrar, 1958-59; art cons. Montgomery County Schs., Rockville, Md., 1960-64; admissions counselor Sch. of Art Inst., Chgo., 1964-66, dean of students, 1966-75, asst. prof., 1973-75; freelance lectr., 1976; artist in residence St. Francis H.S., Louisville, 1977-91; exec. dir. Ky. Found. for Women, Louisville, 1991—; acad. coord. Experiment in Internat. Living, Putney, Vt., 1971-72; adjudicator in visual art Nat. Found. for Advancement in Arts, 1994—. One-woman shows at Olney (Md.) Gallery, 1961, Art Ctr. Gallery, Louisville, 1963, Montgomery Gallery, Rockville, Md., 1973, Spalding Coll. Gallery, Louisville, 1977, 79, Bellarmine Gallery, Louisville, 1981, J.b. Speed Mus., Louisville, 1981, Swearingen Gallery, Louisville, 1985, SoHo 20 Gallery, N.Y.C., 1988, McGrath Gallery, Louisville, 1989, Headley Whitney Mus., Lexington, Ky., 1990, Liberty Gallery, Louisville, 1994, Steinway Gallery, Chapel Hill, N.C., 1995, UPS Corp. Hdqrs., Louisville, 1995; exhibited in numerous group shows, including Indpls. Art League, 1989, Zephyr Gallery, 1991, Louisville Visual Art Assn., 1989, 91, 93, Headley-Whitney Mus., 1991, Trumbull Art Gallery, Ohio, 1991, Contemporary Art Gallery, New Harmony, Ind., 1992, Ashland (Ky.) Area Art Gallery, 1993, Ga. Art Festival, Decatur, 1994, Huntsville (Ala.) Mus. of Art, 1994, Woman Made Gallery, Chgo., 1994, Eagle Gallery, Murray, Ky., 1995, Art Ctr. Douglas County, Castle Rock, Colo., 1995, numerous others; contbr. articles, essays to profl. publs. Bd. dirs., program chair Louisville Visual Art Assn., 1979-83; bd. dirs. Shelby Park Neighborhood Assn., Louisville, 1993—. Mary Elvira Stevens fellow Wellesley Coll., 1975; grantee Ky. Found. for Women, 1987, So. Arts Fedn., 1991. Mem. Louisville Donor's Forum. Home: 600 E St Catherine St Louisville KY 40203 Office: Ky Found for Women 332 W Broadway # 1215 Louisville KY 40202

ANDERSON, ANNELISE GRAEBNER, economist; b. Oklahoma City, Nov. 19, 1938; d. Elmer and Dorothy (Zilisch) Graebner; m. Martin Anderson, Sept. 25, 1965. B.A., Wellesley Coll., 1960; M.A., Columbia U., 1965, Ph.D., 1974. Assoc. editor McKinsey and Co., Inc., 1963-65; researcher Nixon Campaign Staff, 1968-69; project mgr. Dept. Justice, 1970-71; from asst. prof. bus. adminstrn. to assoc. prof. Calif. State U.-Hayward, 1975-80; sr. policy adviser Reagan Presdl. campaign and transition, Washington, 1980; assoc. dir. econs. and govt. Office Mgmt. and Budget, Washington, 1981-83; sr. rsch. fellow Hoover Instn., Stanford U., Calif., 1983—, assoc. dir., 1989-90; mem. Nat. Sci. Bd., 1985-90; Author: The Business of Organized Crime: A Cosa Nostra Family, 1979, Illegal Aliens and Employer Sanctions: Solving the Wrong Problem, 1986, The Ruble Problem: A Competitive Solution, 1992; co-editor: Thinking About America: The United States in the 1990's, 1988; contbr. articles to profl. jours., chpts. to books. Mem. bd. overseers Rand/UCLA Ctr. for Soviet Studies, L.A., 1987-91. Mem. Am. Econ. Assn., Western Econ. Assn., Beta Gamma Sigma. Office: Stanford U Hoover Institution Stanford CA 94305

ANDERSON, BARBARA ANN, property manager; b. Springfield, Ill., July 16, 1940; d. Robert F. and Maurine (Ehringer) Engel; m. William J. Tewksbury, July 13, 1963 (div. Apr. 1978); children: Allison L. Heiduk, Maurine; m. Norman K. Anderson, July 1, 1978; children: Amy Lynn Mayfield, Barry. BA, U. Ariz., 1962. Cert. elem. tchr., Calif. Tchr. Jefferson Sch. Dist., Santa Clara, Calif., 1962-63; tchr. dist. 102 LaGrange (Ill.) Sch. Dist., 1963-66; dir. Family Svc. Agy., George AFB, Calif., 1967-69; pres. Pretzel 'n Cheese, Solvang, Calif., 1979—; property mgr. Solvang, 1990—. Dir. Direct Link for Disabled, Solvang, 1994—; nat. treas. Nat. Charity League, L.A., 1986-90; asst. treas. Vis. Nurse Assn., Santa Barbara, 1989-91; v.p. Jr. League Santa Barbara, 1977-78; regional dir. Assistance League, Santa Barbara, 1989-91; dir. Santa Ynez Valley-Cottage Hosp. Aux., 1992-96; mem. Episc. Ch. Women, pres., 1996-97. Named one of Outstanding Young Women of Am., 1971. Mem. Kappa Kappa Gamma (advisor house bd. Epsilon Psi chpt. 1982-94, founder, pres., v.p., sec., treas., advisor 1972-95). Republican. Home: 281 Oster Sted Solvang CA 93463

ANDERSON, BARBARA GRAHAM, philanthropic resources development consultant; b. Detroit, Dec. 2, 1934; d. Neill Edwin and Elizabeth (Blackwood) Graham; m. Donald L. Wells, Jan. 31, 1960 (div. Apr. 1976); m. K. Bruce Anderson, Apr. 1, 1978. AB in Speech/Comms., Fla. State U., Tallahassee, 1956. Dir. devel. Adoption Svc. of Westchester, White Plains, N.Y., 1966-68; founder, devel. chair The Art Barn, Greenwich, Conn., 1966-69; assoc. dir. for corp. appeals and maj. individual gifts Nat. Staff/YWCA, N.Y.C., 1969-70; project dir. Nat. Clearinghouse for Alcohol Info., Gaithersburg, Md., 1974-76; sr. assoc. The Oram Group, Inc., N.Y.C., 1973-74, 76-78; counseling and profl. svcs. various clients in, San Francisco, 1978-86; with Coviello and Assocs., Chevy Chase, Md., 1986-94, Joyaux Assocs., R.I., 1994—; organizer workshops and seminars for orgns. including The Fund Raising Sch., 1982-86, The Found. Ctr., Washington, 1991-93. Housing Authority commr. Town of Chatham, Mass., 1995—. Mem. Nat. Soc. Fund Raising Execs. (cert. fund raising exec., bd. dirs. San Francisco 1980-86, bd. dirs., officer Greater Washington chpt. 1988-92, mem. nat. cert. bd. 1983-90). Democrat. Episcopalian. Home and Office: 101 Riverview Dr Chatham MA 02633-1233

ANDERSON, BEVERLY ANN, nurse administrator, educator; b. Somerville, Mass., Nov. 16, 1937; d. Joseph J. Mercurio and Angela B. (Russo) Castle; m. Richard H. Anderson, June 15, 1958; children: Linda M. Anderson Green, Mark R., Karen E. Diploma in Nursing, Mt. Auburn Hosp. Sch. Nursing, 1959; BS, New Eng. Coll., 1982, MS, 1986. RN, Mass. Staff, charge nurse Mt. Auburn Hosp., Cambridge, Mass., 1959-60; staff nurse med.-surg. Beverly (Mass.) Hosp., 1960-73, IV therapist, 1973-76; health nurse Bd. of Health, Georgetown, 1976-77; dir. nursing Baldpate Hosp., Georgetown, 1977-79; psychiat. nurse clinician North Essex Mental Health Ctrs., Haverhill, 1979-82; dir. geriatric and consult Dept. Mental Health, Amesbury, 1982-90; dir. edn., clin. specialist Dept. Mental Health, Tewksbury, 1990-94; psychiat. clin. nurse specialist pvt. practice, Newburyport, 1992—. Mem. ANA, Mass. Nurse Assn. (co-chair psychiat. mental health coun. 1982—), Nurses United for Responsible Svcs., Am. Psychiat. Nurses Assn. (New Eng. chpt. 1992—). Home: PO Box 495 West Boxford MA 01885-0495 Office: Harris St Assocs 44 Merrimac St Newburyport MA 01950-2580

ANDERSON, BEVERLY JACQUES, dean; b. New Orleans, Sept. 10, 1943; d. alvin Joseph and Dorothy Ann (Angelety) Jacques; m. Ronald Lee Anderson, Sept. 6, 1967; children: Montina Jacquel, Monique Jamee, Montez Jacques. BS cum laude, Dillard U., 1965; MS, Howard U., 1967; PhD, Cath. U. Am., 1978. Instr. math. Howard U., Washington, 1967-69; from instr. to prof. U. D.C., Washington, 1969-94, dean coll. arts & scis., 1994—; instr. math. upward bound program Dillard U., Howard U., and Coll. of V.I., summers 1965-69; dir. minority affairs NRC, Washington, 1988-92; dir. instl. self-study U. D.C., Washington, 1992-94; bd. dirs. Prince Georges C.C., 1993—, also chmn.; bd. dirs. Foxcroft Sch., Middleburg, Va., 1995—; spkr. and presenter in field. Columnist Prince Georges News, 1991—; contbr. articles to profl. jours. Bd. dirs., treas. Greater S.E. Healthcare Sys. Found., Washington, 1994—; chair bd. dirs. Ft. Washington Hosp., 1988—; bd. dirs. YMCA, Metro. Washington, 1992-95; chair FDA Adv. Com., Washington, 1989—. Grantee Office Naval Rsch., NASA, Office Post Secondary Edn. Nat. Security Agy.; recipient White House Initiative Faculty award, 1988, Outstanding Cmty. Svc. award Washington View Mag., 1990, Citation, Assn. Women in Math., 1991, Cmty. Svc. award Greater S.E. Healthcare Sys., 1993, Stewardship award UNCF, 1996. Mem. Nat. Assn. Math., Math. Assn. Am. (chair faculty devel. com. 1992-94), Benjamin Banneker Soc., Beta Kappa Chi, Phi Delta Kappa. Democrat. Roman Catholic. Home: 705 Muirfield Cir Fort Washington MD 20744 Office: Univ DC 4200 Connecticut Ave NW Washington DC 20008

ANDERSON, CARLIS MAE, retired music educator; b. Luverne, Minn., Jan. 8, 1929; d. Carl Henry and Agnes Rachel (McEachran) A. BFA, U. S.D., 1951; M in Music Edn., U. Colo., 1958; postgrad., U. Mich., 1969-70, U. Wis., 1980, 84, Northwestern U., 1966. Tchr. vocal music grades K-12 Scotland (S.D.) Pub. Schs., 1951-52; tchr. vocal music grades 1-8 Sioux Falls (S.D.) Pub. Schs., 1952-54; tchr. vocal music grades 5-6, sr. high chorus Douglas (Ariz.) Pub. Sch., 1954-59; tchr. vocal music grades 1-6 USAF in Europe Dependent Schs., Chateauroux, France, 1959-60, USAFE Dependent Schs., Weisbaden, Germany, 1960-61; vocal music jr. high, sr. high and C.C. Ely (Minn.) Pub. Schs., 1961-63; tchr. music edn., piano, music of the Far East Winona (Minn.) State U., 1963-91; ret., 1991. City voter registration com., Winona, 1988, 89, 90; mem. fin. bd. Winona Area Hopsice Svcs., Cmty. Meml. Hosp., Winona, 1992—; co-chair Winona Pub. Edn., Mr. Rogers Neighborhood, Winona, 1992—, co-chair Save Our Symphony, Winona, 1994-95; ch. organist, elder, deacon Presby. Ch. Mem. AAUW, The Learning Club (steering com., curriculum com.), Order Ea. Star, Alumni U. S.D., Pi Beta Phi. Presbyterian.

ANDERSON, CAROL PATRICIA, chemistry educator; b. Bluefield, W.Va., May 19, 1946; d. Carroll Curtis and Naomi Bessie (Bowles) A.; m. James Brent Anderson, Sept. 9, 1978. BS, Concord Coll., Athens, W.Va., 1968; PhD, U. Tenn., 1973. Post-doctoral instr. U. Conn., Storrs, 1973-75, asst. prof., 1975-80, assoc. prof., 1980—, dir. Marine Environ. Analysis Labs. Svc., 1994—; cons. R&D USCG, 1976-90. Contbr. articles to profl. jours. Mem. Am. Chem. Soc., Nat. Sci. Tchrs. Assn., New Eng. Chemistry Tchrs. Assn. Episcopalian. Home: 143 Pequot Ave Mystic CT 06355-1728 Office: U Conn Avery Point Groton CT 06340

ANDERSON, CAROLE ANN, nursing educator; b. Chgo., Feb. 21, 1938; d. Robert and Marian (Harrity) Irving; m. Clark Anderson, Feb. 14, 1973; 1 child, Julie. Diploma, St. Francis Hosp., 1958; BS, U. Colo., 1962, MS, 1963, PhD, 1977. Group psychotherapist Dept. Vocat. Rehab., Denver, 1963-72; psychotherapist Prof. Psychiatry and Guidance Clinic, Denver, 1970-71; asst. prof., chmn. nursing sch. U. Colo., Denver, 1971-75; therapist, coordinator The Genessee Mental Health, Rochester, N.Y., 1977-78; assoc. dean U. Rochester, N.Y., 1978-86; dean, prof. Coll. Nursing Ohio State U., Columbus, 1986—; lectr. nursing sch. U. Colo., Denver, 1970-71; prin. investigator biomed. rsch. support grant, 1986-93, clin. rsch. facilitation grant, 1981-82; program dir. profl. nurse traineeship, 1978-86, advanced nurse tng. grant, 1982-85. Author: (with others) Women as Victims, 1986, Violence Toward Women, 1982, Substance Abuse of Women, 1982; editor Nursing Outlook, 1993—. Pres., bd. dirs. Health Assn., Rochester, 1984-86; mem. north sub area council Finger Lakes Health Systems Agy., 1983-86, longrange planning com., 1981-82; mem. Columbus Bd. Health; dir. Netcare Mental Health Ctr. Am. Acad. Nursing fellow. Mem. ANA, Am. Sociol. Assn., Ohio Nurses Assn., Am. Assn. Colls. Nursing (bd. dirs. 1992-94, pres.-elect 1994-96, pres. 1996—), Sigma Theta Tau. Home: 406 W 6th Ave Columbus OH 43201-3137 Office: The Ohio State Univ Coll Nursing 1585 Neil Ave Columbus OH 43210-1216

ANDERSON, CAROLE J., lawyer; b. Davenport, Iowa, Aug. 7, 1947; d. Robert Hallin and Margaret Dorothy (Johnson) A.; m. Daniel Kim Prescott, May 24, 1975; children: Thomas Lee Waltz, Kristina Kim Prescott, Anna Tekla Prescott. BA in Sociology, Augustana Coll., 1970; MSW, U. Iowa, 1974, JD, 1985. Bar: Iowa 1985, Ill. 1987. Casework supr. Ill. Dept. Pub. Aid, Rock Island, Ill., 1971-79; dir. Black Hawk County Youth Shelter, Waterloo, Iowa, 1979-82; law clk. to Justice Mark McCormick Iowa Supreme Ct., Des Moines, 1985-86; assoc. Lane & Waterman, Davenport, 1986-91, ptnr., 1992—. Contbr. to books: Parental Loss of a Child, 1986, Women's Legal Guide, 1996; editor jour. Cub Communicator, 1979-93, 94-95; author many booklets and articles on adoption. Treas. Child Abuse Coun., Moline, 1994-96; bd. dirs. Ctr. for Cultural Arts, Bettendorf, Iowa, 1991-96. Mem. NOW, Am. Adoption Congress, Origins, Vasa Order of Am., Iowa Coun. of Sch. Bd. Attys. (chair 1995-96), Concerned United Birthparents (v.p. 1980-84, 88-90, 94-96, pres. 1984-88, sec. 1990-94). Democrat. Office: Lane & Waterman 220 N Main St Ste 600 Davenport IA 52801

ANDERSON, CAROLE LEWIS, investment banker; b. East Stroudsburg, Pa., Oct. 7, 1944; d. William A. and Rosamonde (Lewis) A.; m. John Mason Lee Sweet, Apr. 9, 1983; children: John Mason Lee Anderson-Sweet, Dunn Lewis Anderson-Sweet. B.A. in Polit. Sci., Pa State U., 1966; M.B.A. in Fin., NYU, 1976. Securities analyst PaineWebber, Jackson & Curtis, N.Y.C., 1971-73, assoc. v.p., 1973-75, v.p. research, 1975-77; v.p. PaineWebber, Inc., N.Y.C., 1977-82, mng. dir., 1982-85; sr. v.p. corp. devel. Hasbro, Inc., N.Y.C., 1985-87; also dir. Hasbro, Inc., Pawtucket, R.I., 1985-87; mng. dir. MNC Investment Bank, Washington, 1987-88, pres., chief exec. officer, 1988-90; pres. MASDUN Capital Advisors, 1991—; ptnr. Suburban Capital Mkts., Inc., 1995—; bd. dirs. VICORP Restaurants, Inc., Master Media Ltd., AARP Mutual Funds. County com. person Democratic Party, N.Y.C., 1975-82; chmn. Hasbro Children's Found., 1985-88, mem. exec. com., 1988-91, trustee, 1985—; mem. N.Y. com. U.S. Commn. on Civil Rights, 1980-84; trustee Mary Baldwin Coll., Staunton, Va., 1987—, Pa. State U. Alumni Coun., 1987-93; mem. corp. adv. coun. Women's Rsch. and Edn. Inst. Named to Acad. Women Achievers, YWCA, N.Y.C., 1982; recipient Disting. Alumna award Pa. State U., 1987, apptd. Alumni fellow, 1990. Mem. Nat. Women's Econ. Alliance Resource Coun., Internat. Alliance, Comml. Real Estate Women of Md., Pa. State U. Alumni Coun., City Tavern Club.

ANDERSON, CAROLYN ANNE, clinical psychologist; b. San Diego, Oct. 18, 1964; d. Fredric Clifford and Joan (Brownell) A.; m. Michael John Sundermeyer, May 5, 1991. BA, U. Calif., Davis, 1986; MA, UCLA, 1989, PhD, 1993. Post doctoral fellow Stanford (Calif.) U. Sch. of Medicine, 1993-94, staff psychologist, 1994—. Contbr. articles Jour. Cons. & Clin. Psychology, Jour. Clin. Child Psychology. Recipient Disting. Tchg. Award, UCLA Psychology Dept., 1989; U. fellow,. Mem. APA. Office: Dept of Psychiatry Stanford U School of Med Stanford CA 94305

ANDERSON, CAROLYN RUTH, executive recruiter; b. Manchester, Conn., July 9, 1939; d. Carl Theodore and Helen Margaret (Modean) Johnson; m. James Richard Anderson, June 24, 1961; children: James Michael, Kristen Elizabeth, Amory Kane. BA, Upsala Coll., East Orange, N.J., 1961. Cert. temp. specialist. With Social Security Adminstrn., Newark, 1961-62; svc. coord. People Unltd., Reading, Pa., 1981-84; ops.mgr. Am. Staffing Resources, Feasterville, Pa., 1984-92, v.p. ops., 1992—; notary pub., Pa., 1994; TQM facilitator TIA Assn. Stds. and Rsch., 1994. Pub. rels. mem. Assn. of Jr. Leagues, Lubbock, Tex., 1976-86. Mem. Human Resource Mgmt. Assn. (v.p. pub. rels. 1992—), Soc. for Human Resource Mgmt. Republican. Lutheran. Office: American Staffing Resources 255 E Street Rd Feasterville PA 19053

ANDERSON, CATHERINE, artist; b. Chgo., Aug. 12, 1947; d. William Joseph and Dorothy Virginia Anderson; 1 child, Scott Russell. Student, Am. Acad. Art, Chgo., 1967-70, U. Cin., 1970-77, Acad. Art Coll., San Francisco, 1982-85. Represented by Trailside Americana Fine Art Galleries, Carmel, Calif., 1992-95, Pogan Gallery, Tahoe City, Calif., Quast Gallery, Taos, N.Mex.; lectr. Falkirk Art Ctr., San Rafael, Calif., 1992, Calif. Inst. Integral Studies, San Francisco, 1993; juror various art shows. Exhbns. include Elk Grove Village (Ill.) Art Festival, 1980, 81, 24th Gold Coast Art Fair, Chgo., 1981, Mill Valley City Hall, 1986, Westamerica Bank, Sausalito, Calif., 1990-95, Marin County Fair, San Rafael, Calif., 1990, 92, 93, 94, Lenten Arts Festival, San Anselmo, Calif., 1991. Spirit Wings de Santa Fe, 1991. Artisans Gallery, Mill Valley, Calif., 1991, 94, 96, Sausalito Arts Festival, 1991, 92, 93, 94, 95, JCC, San Rafael, 1991, Green Gulch Farm, Muir Beach, Calif., 1991, Gallery One, Petaluma, Calif., 1991, Poudre Valley Art League, Ft. Collins, Colo., 1992, Saratoga (Calif.) Rotary Art Show, 1992, La Quinta (Calif.) Arts Festival, 1993, Canessa Gallery, San Francisco, 1993, Santa Barbara Mus. of Natural History, Santa Barbara, Calif., 1993, Art Concepts Gallery, Walnut Creek, Calif., 1993, Scottsdale (Ariz.) Arts Festival, 1994, CCC, Tiburon, Calif., 1994, Blue Heron Gallery, Yountville, Calif., 1994, Buena Vista Winery, Sonoma, Calif., 1994, Springfield (Mo.) Art Mus., 1995, 96, Foothills Art Ctr., Golden, Colo., 1995, Gallery Concord, Concord, Calif., 1995, 96, Catharine Lorillard Wolfe Art Club, N.Y., 1995, The Salmagundi Club, N.Y.C., 1995, Neville Pub. Mus., Green Bay, Wis., 1996, Denver Rotary Club Artists of Am. (AOA) Invitational Show, 1996, No. Colorado Artists Assn. Nat. Art Exhibit, GAA Exhibit, Cin. Mus. Ctr., Great Artists of Am. Invitational Show, 1996, Colo. History Mus., Denver; and numerous pvt. collections; columnist Watercolor Magic. Recipient Tony Couch award Western Colo. Watercolor Soc., 1991, 1st Pl. award Affaire in the Gardens, 1993, Blue ribbon Santa Barbara Mus. Natural History, 1994, 1st Pl. award Scottsdale Arts Festival, 1994, 1st Pl. award Marin County Fair, 1994, 95, 1st Pl. award Rocky Mountain Nat. Watermedia Exhibit, 1995, Anna Hyatt Huntington Bronze medal Catharine Lorillard Wolfe Art Club, 1995, Nat. Galleries Endowment award, 1995, Nat. Watercolor Soc. 75th Ann. Exhibit, 1995. Mem. Am. Watercolor Soc. (Winsor-Newton award), Nat. Watercolor Soc., Calif. Watercolor Assn. Home: 4900 Trinity Rd Glen Ellen CA 95442

ANDERSON, CATHERINE M., consulting company executive; b. N.Y.C., Feb. 28, 1937; d. Edward Charles and Elizabeth (O'Shea) McElligott; m. Robert Brown Anderson, June 22, 1963; children: Mark Robert, Jennifer Elizabeth. BA, Douglass Coll., 1959; MA, Rutgers U., 1960. Staff asst. to pres. Chatham Coll., Pitts., 1960-61; instr. urban studies ctr. Rutgers U., New Brunswick, N.J., 1961-63; prin. urban renewal coord. City of Cleve., Cleve., 1963-64; regional admisions counselor Am. Inst. Fgn. Study, Pitts., 1964-74; chief planner, mgr. emergency ops. ctr. Allegheny County Govt., Pitts., 1975-79; dir. accreditation svcs. Energy Cons., Inc., Pitts., 1981-83; pub. involvement cons. Pitts., 1983—. Contbr. articles to profl. jours. Committeewoman Mt. Lebanon (Pa.) Mcpl. Dem. Com., 1970-85; active United Way Allegheny County, Pitts., mem. rev. com., 1980—, chmn. rev. com., 1986-89; bd. dirs. Mt. Lebanon Nature Conservancy, v.p., 1985-88, pres., 1988-92; bd. dirs. Conservation Cons. Inc., v.p., 1983-92, pres., 1992-95; bd. dirs. Pitts. chpt. Women's Transp. Seminar, v.p., 1992-94, pres. 1994-95; bd. dirs. Exec. Women's Coun. Greater Pitts., v.p., 1986-88; bd. dirs. Carnegie-Mellon U. Art Gallery, 1986-89. Recipient Robert L. Wells award Mt. Lebanon Nature Conservancy, 1991, Outstanding Svc. award Exec. Women's Coun., 1988; Eagleton Inst. Politics grad. fellow Rutgers U., 1960. Mem. Am. Soc. Hwy Engrs. (sr. mem.), Exec. Women's Coun. (charter mem., v.p., 1987-88, Outstanding Svc. award 1988), Women's Transp. Seminar (v.p. 1992-94, pres. 94-95, nat. bd. dirs. com. co-chair), Women's Press Club Pitts. Home and Office: 2061 Outlook Dr Upper Saint Clair PA 15241

ANDERSON, CATHERINE MOORE, marketing professional. BA in Radio/TV/Film, U. Mich., 1973, M in Radio/TV/Film, 1974. Media coord. Inst. for Study of Mental Retardation & Related Disabilities, Ann Arbor, Mich., 1974; exec. prodr. Ann Arbor Sesquicentennial Commn. & Ann Arbor Pub. Libr., 1974; prodr., dir. Med. TV, U. Hosp., U. Mich., Ann Arbor, 1975-76, Ctr. for Forensic Psychiatry, Ypsilanti, Mich., 1976-77; rsch. coord. Living History Project Group, Washington, 1977-78, project coord., 1979-80; dir. devel. ELI Prodns., Washington, 1978-81; mgr. nat. program underwriting WOED-TV, Pitts., 1981-84, dir. nat. program mktg., 1984-87; v.p. mktg. and project devel. WTVS-TV, Detroit, 1987—; bd. dirs. Mich. Contemporary Glass Group; chpt. co-founder, first v.p. Women in Film and Video, Inc., Washington, 1980-81; panelist Nat. Endowment for the Arts, 1983, Nat. Endowment for the Humanities, 1984, 87, 89, 94; judge Rose d'Or, 1987; N.Am. cons. Euro Aim Screenings, 1990; presenter at internat. conf. Bd. dirs. Parental Stress Ctr., Pitts., 1982-87, Mich. Humanities Coun., 1988—. Recipient first place award for Best 16mm Film and Best Film Entry, Health Edn. Media Assn., 1977. Office: WTVS/Channel 56 7441 Second Blvd Detroit MI 48202-2796

ANDERSON, CHERINE ESPERANZA, television and film production manager, special events planner; b. Kingston, Jamaica, Mar. 21, 1964; d. Percival and Joyce A. (Brown) A. BS, Fordham U., 1986. Community rels. assoc. N.Y.C. Pks. and Recreation Dept., 1986; employee activities coord. The Rockefeller Group, N.Y.C., 1986-87, employment interviewer, 1987-88; licensing coord. DC Comics-a Div. of Time-Warner, N.Y.C., 1988-90; employee rels. coord. ARC, N.Y.C., 1990; freelance spl. events planner N.Y.C., 1990—; auditor N.Y.C. Bd. Edn., 1991-94; mem. mktg. staff for Nickelodeon MTV Networks, 1996—; prodn. mgr. Bklyn. Shakespeare Co., 1991—; assoc. producer Sports Desk Program-WNYE-FM, Bklyn., 1989-91; prodn. mgr. for film The Best Kept Secret, 1992; mng. dir. (13 week TV series) African Theatre and Drama Prodn., 1993; line producer and asst. dir. for film Angel Walk Prodn., 1993; v.p. ops. and prodn. mgmt. In Stitches Entertainment, 1994—. Contbr. articles to profl. jours. Bd. dirs. N.Y. Dist. Circle K - An Internat. Collegiate Svc. Orgn., N.Y.C., 1983-87; vol. mem. Vol. Svcs. for Children, 1986—. Named Disting. Sec. L.P. Merridew Award Circle K Internat., 1987, Outstanding Dist. Bd. Mem., 1987. Mem. Am. Mgmt. Assn. (cert. 1988, mgmt. cert. 1990). Democrat. Home: 153 Bennett Ave New York NY 10040-4012

ANDERSON, D. JANE, secondary school educator; b. Chillicothe, Ohio, Mar. 30, 1943; d. Henry Branch and Beatrice Clara (Trainer) Ellsworth: m. George Leonard Anderson, Jr., Sept. 9, 1964; children: Doug, Jeff, Michelle. BS in Edn., Ohio State U., 1983, MS in Edn., 1994. Cert. tchr. grades 7-12, Ohio. Long distance operator Ohio Bell Telephone Co., Dayton, 1962-64; real estate agt. Donna Vaughn Realtors, Dayton, 1965-67; sales rep., mgr. Tupperware Dayton Party Sales, 1972-74; sales, office clk. Sears Dept. Stores, Columbus, Dayton, Ohio, 1976-79; tchr. Westerville (Ohio) City Schs., 1984—; advisor Westerville H.S. Yearbook, Golden Warrior, 1986 (1st pl. award), 1987 (1st pl. award). Sec., pres. etc. Englewood Hills Elem. Sch. PTA, Englewood, Ohio, 1971-76; youth dir. Unity Ch., Columbus, Ohio, 1978-80; phone counselor Bridge Counseling Ctr., Columbus, 1980-81. Mem. NEA, Ohio Edn. Assn., Westerville Edn. Assn. Office: Westerville City Schs 346 Otterbein Ave Westerville OH 43081

ANDERSON, DELLA JEAN, secondary school educator; b. Hardin, Mont., Aug. 11, 1956; d. Edward Frank and Lorraine M. (Bergquist) Pattyn; m. Michael Henry Anderson, June 5, 1982. BS in Bus. Edn., Mont. State U., 1979. Cert. vocat. tchr. Tchr. Poplar (Mont.) H.S., 1979-80, Campbell County H.S., Gillette, Wyo., 1980-81; tchr. bus. and computer sci. Lodge Grass (Mont.) H.S., 1985—; adult edn. instr. Ft. Peck C.C., Poplar, 1979-80, Lodge Grass Pub. Schs., 1985—, Little Big Horn Coll., Crow Agency, Mont., 1987-88, Sheridan (Wyo.) Coll., 1994—. Carl Perkins Vocat. grantee, 1985—. Mem. Mont. Edn. Assn., Lodge Grass Tchrs. Assn. (treas. 1991—), Mont. Bus. Edn. Assn. (state historian 1979-80), Alpha Delta Kappa (Iota chpt. v.p. 1990-92, pres. 1992-94). Democrat. Roman Catholic. Home: 465 3d Ave W Ranchester WY 82839 Office: Lodge Grass High Sch 124 N George St Lodge Grass MT 59050

ANDERSON, DENICE ANNA, editor; b. Detroit, Nov. 11, 1947; d. Carl Magnus and Geraldine Elizabeth (Willer) A. BA in Journalism, Mich. State U., 1970. Copy editor/reporter The State News, East Lansing, Mich., 1965-70; reporter/copy editor/photographer The Tecumseh (Mich.) Herald, 1966-68; copy editor/entertainment editor The State Jour., Lansing, Mich., 1970-76; freelance writer State Jour./Lansing Mag., 1977-79; freelance corr. Collier's Year Book, N.Y.C., 1977-79; copy editor, proofreader Booz, Allen & Hamilton, N.Y.C., 1980-81, Rogers & Wells, N.Y.C., 1981-83, Advanced Therapeutic Communications, N.Y.C., 1983-84; freelance editor N.Y.C., Santa Fe, 1984—. Contbr. articles to profl. jours. Bd. dirs., sec. March of Dimes, Lansing, 1972-76; vol./writer Polio Info. Ctr., N.Y.C., 1984-88; vol.

Vol. Involvement Svcs., Santa Fe, N.M., 1989. Mem. Editorial Freelancers Assn. Lutheran. Home: 941 Calle Mejia Apt 304 Santa Fe NM 87501-1463

ANDERSON, DIANA B., library director; b. Eagle River, Wisc., Nov. 6, 1934; d. Uno Mathius and Elsa Sylvia (Ahola) Bloom; m. Carl L. Anderson, Dec. 27, 1958; children: Carl (dec.), Barbara Neddo, Jennifer. BS in secondary edn., U. Wisc., Stevens Point, 1957. Cert. grade 1 libr., Wisc. Tchr. English Waupun (Wisc.) H.S., 1957-59, Eagle River (Wisc.) Union High, 1967-70; asst. libr. Eagle River Pub. Libr., 1972-74; teller, bookkeeper, personal banker First Nat. Bank, Eagle River, 1974-90; dir. Walter E. Olson Meml. Libr., Eagle River, 1993—; bd. dirs. W.E. Olson Meml. Libr.; founder youth adv. bd. First Nat. Bank, Eagle River, 1987-89; libr. adv. bd. Northern Waters Libr. Svc., 1994—. Co-editor: Primipara (poetry jour.), 1974. Bd. dirs., vice chair Vilas Credit Union, Eagle River, 1995—; bd. dirs. WXPR Pub. Radio (White Pine Broadcasting, Inc.), Rhinelander, Wisc., 1996—; mem. Ecumenical Cmty. Health Outreach, Rhinelander, 1996—. Mem. Wisc. Libr. Assn. Democrat. Protestant. Office: Walter E Olson Meml Libr PO Box 69 203 N Main St Eagle River WI 54521

ANDERSON, DIANNE JEAN, nursing administrator; b. Glen Cove, N.Y., Mar. 9, 1956; d. Lionel J. and Jeannette L. (Forest) Audette; m. Scott Wilson Anderson, June 25, 1976. BS, Boston U., 1978, MS, 1988. RN, Mass. Primary nurse New England Med. Ctr., Boston, 1978-79, sr. staff nurse pediatrics, 1979-80, nurse mgr., 1980-86; nurse mgr. The Children's Hosp. Med. Ctr., Boston, 1987-93; dir. patient svcs. Health Care Internat. Med. Ctr., Clydebank, Scotland, 1993-95; v.p. patient svcs., chief nursing officer Glens Falls (N.Y.) Hosp., 1995—; lectr. in field. Author: About Eppendymoma, Case Management, Finance for Nurse Managers, 1990; contbr. articles to profl. jours. Recipient Mass. Coun. Nurse Mgrs. Spl. award for Outstanding Contbn., 1987. Mem. Am. Orgn. Nurse Execs. (founding pres. coun. nurse mgrs. 1988-89, pres. 1989, bd. dirs. 1988—, fin. com. 1989, nominating com. 1991, chair interim nurse mgr. study group 1987, Spl. Award for Outstanding Leadership 1989), Mass. Orgn. Nurse Execs. (chmn. nominating com. 1987, pres. coun. nurse mgrs. 1986), Sigma Theta Tau.

ANDERSON, DOROTHY FISHER, social worker, psychotherapist; b. Funchal, Madeira, May 31, 1924; d. Lewis Mann Anker and Edna (Gilbert) Fisher (adoptive father David Henry Fisher); m. Theodore W. Anderson, July 8, 1950; children: Robert Lewis, Janet Anderson Yang, Jeanne Elizabeth. BA, Queens Coll., 1945; AM, U. Chgo., 1947. Diplomate Am. Bd. Examiners in Clin. Social Work; lic. clin. social worker, Calif.; registered cert. social worker, N.Y. Intern Cook County (Ill.) Bur. Pub. Welfare, Chgo., 1945-46, Ill. Neuropsychiat. Inst., Chgo., 1946; clin. caseworker, Neurol. Inst. Presbyn. Hosp., N.Y.C., 1947; therapist, Mental Hygiene Clinic VA, N.Y.C., 1947-50; therapist, Child Guidance Clinic Pub. Elem. Sch. 42, N.Y.C., 1950-53; social worker, counselor Cedarhurst (N.Y.) Family Service Agy., 1954-55; psychotherapist, counselor Family Service of the Midpeninsula, Palo Alto, Calif., 1971-73, 79-86, George Hexter, M.D., Inc., 1972-83; clin. social worker Tavistock Clinic, London, 1974-75, El Camino Hosp., Mountain View, Calif., 1979; pvt. practice clin. social work, 1978-92, ret., 1992; cons. Human Resource Services, Sunnyvale, Calif., 1981-86. Hannah G. Solomon scholar U. Chgo., 1945-46; Commonwealth fellow U. Chgo., 1946-47. Fellow Soc. Clin. Social Work (Continuing Edn. Recognition award 1980-83); mem. Nat. Assn. Social Workers (diplomate in clin. social work).

ANDERSON, ELLEN RUTH, state senator; b. Gary, Ind., Nov. 25, 1959; d. John Ernest Anderson and Marion Jane (Reeves) Martin; m. Andrew J. Dawkins. BA in History, Carleton Coll., 1982; JD, U. Minn., 1986. Bar: Minn., 1987, U.S. Dist. Ct. Minn. 1988. Jud. law clk. Minn. Ct. Appeals, St. Paul, 1987-88; atty. Hennepin County Pub. Defender, Mpls., 1988-91; staff atty. Minn. Edn. Assn., St. Paul, 1991-92; state senator State of Minn., St. Paul, 1993—. Democrat. Office: State of Minn G27 State Capitol Saint Paul MN 55155-1002

ANDERSON, ELSIE MINERS, mathematics educator; b. Harare, Zimbabwe, July 4, 1931; came to U.S., 1961; d. William James and Winifred Ethel (Lowe) Miners; m. Larry Vance Anderson, Dec. 22, 1961; children: Winifred Jean Whitmore, Margaret Elizabeth Daly. BS, Rhodes U., Grahamstown, South Africa, 1951, EdD, 1952, MLS, East Tex. State U., 1966. Tchr. geography and math. Govt. Cen. African Fedn., Salisbury, 1953-61; tchr. math. Desdemona (Tex.) Ind. Sch. Dist., 1962-64; head libr. Holding Inst., Laredo, Tex., 1971-72; instr. math. Western Tex. Coll., Snyder, 1973-74, prof. math., 1974—; exchange tchr. in geography Mill Hill, North London, Eng., 1957. Active Girl Scouts U.S., Abilene, Tex., 1972—. Recipient Theater Patron award Western Tex. Coll. Drama Dept., Snyder, 1986. Mem. Tex. Jr. Coll. Tchrs. Assn., Tex. Math. Assn. 2-Yr. Colls., Am. Math. Assn. 2-Yr. Colls., Math. Assn. Am., Order of Eastern Star. Baptist. Home: 600 29th St Snyder TX 79549-3614 Office: Western Tex Coll Snyder TX 79549

ANDERSON, ETHEL AVARA, retired retail executive; b. Meridian, Miss.; d. Thomas Franklin and Annie Ethel (Jones) Avara.; m. Theron Young Anderson, Aug. 2, 1940 (dec. Aug. 1964); 1 child, Brenda Anderson Jackson. Grad. high sch., Meridian. Mem. exec. bd., sec. United Way of Meridian, Industries for Developmentally Disabled, Meridian, 1984-93, Lauderdale Assn. Retarded Children, Meridian, 1983-91; mem. exec. bd. Lauderdale County Mental Health, 1991, 92, 93, v.p., 1993-94; bd. dirs. 1st Ladies Civitan of Meridian, 1980-93. Mem. Meridian C. of C. (liaison 1985-87), Xi Gamma, Beta Sigma Phi (life). Methodist. Home: 3400 20th St Meridian MS 39301-2834

ANDERSON, FRANCES SWEM, nuclear medical technologist; b. Grand Rapids, Mich., Nov. 27, 1913; d. Frank Oscar and Carrie (Strang) Swem; m. Clarence A.F. Anderson, Apr. 9, 1934; children: Robert Curtis, Clarelyn Christine (Mrs. Roger L. Schmelling), Stanley Herbert. Student, Muskegon Sch. Bus., 1959-60; cert., Muskegon Community Coll., 1964; cert. adult edn. computer course, Fruitport Cmty. Schs., 1992. Registered nuclear med. technologist Am. Registry Radiol. Technologists. X-ray file clk., film librarian Hackley Hosp., Muskegon, Mich., 1957-59, radioisotope technologist and sec., 1959-65; nuclear med. technologist Butler Meml. Hosp., Muskegon Heights, Mich., 1966-70; nuclear med. technologist Mercy Hosp., Muskegon, 1970-79, ret., 1979. Mem. Muskegon Civic A Capella choir, 1932-39; mem. Mother-Tchr. Singers, PTA, Muskegon, 1941-48, treas. 1944-48; with Muskegon Civic Opera Assn., 1950-51; office vol. Alive '88 Crusade; mem. com. for 60th H.S. Class Reunion; mem. Sr. Harvest Day Com., Muskegon County, 1995; active Forest Park Covenant Ch., mem. choir, 1953-79, 83—, choir pres. 1992, 93, choir sec. 1963-69, Sunday Sch. tchr. 1954-75, supt. Sunday Sch., 1975-78, sec., treas. 1981-86, sec. 1991, 92, 93, mem. support team, sec. 1993, chmn. master planning coun., 1982; coord. centennial com. to 1981, ch. sec. 1982-84, 87, 91, 95-96, registrar vacation Bible sch. 1988, 89, 90, 91, treas., 1995, 96; co-chmn. Jackson Hill Old Timer's Reunion, 1982, 83, 85. Mem. Am. Registry Radiologic Technologists, Soc. Nuclear Medicine (cert. nuclear medicine technologist). Home: 5757 Sternberg Rd Fruitport MI 49415-9740

ANDERSON, GERALDINE LOUISE, laboratory scientist; b. Mpls., July 7, 1941; d. George M. and Viola Julia-Mary (Abel) Havrilla; m. Henry Clifford Anderson, May 21, 1966; children: Bruce Henry, Julie Lynne. BS, U. Minn., 1963. Med. technologist Swedish Hosp., Mpls., 1963-68; hematology supr. Glenwood Hills Hosp. lab., Golden Valley, Minn., 1968-70; assoc. scientist dept. pediatrics U. Minn. Hosps., Mpls., 1970-74; instr. health occupations Hennepin Tech. Coll., Brooklyn Park, Minn., 1974—, St. Paul Tech. Vocat. Inst., 1978-81; rsch. med. technologist Miller Hosp., St. Paul, 1975-78; rsch. assoc. Children's and United Hosps., St. Paul, 1979-88; sr. lab. analyst Cascade Med. Inc., Eden Prairie, Minn., 1989-90; lab. mgr. VA Med. Ctr., Mpls., 1990; technical support scientist INCSTAR Corp., 1990-94; reg. affairs product analysis coord. Medtronic Neurological, Mpls., 1995; quality assurance documentation coord. Lectec Corp., Stillwater, MN., Minnetonka, Minn.; clin. rsch. monitor, Eli Lilly Rsch. Labs., Indpls., 1995—; mem. health occupations adv. com. Hennepin Tech. Ctrs., 1975-90, chairperson, 1978-79; mem. hematology slide edn. rev. bd. Am. Soc. Hematology, 1976—; mem. flow cytometry and clin. chemistry quality control subcoms. Nat. Com. for Clin. Lab. Standards, 1988-92; cons. FCM Specialists, 1989—. Mem. rev. bd. Clin. Lab. Sci., 1990-91, The Learning Laboratorian Series 1991; contbr. and presenter In Svc. Rev. in Clin. Lab. Sci., audio taped study program for ASMT, 1992; contbr. articles to profl. jours. Mem. Med. Lab. Tech. Polit. Action Com., 1978—; charter orgns. rep. troop #534 Boy Scouts Am., Viking Coun., 1988-90; resource person lab. careers Robbinsdale Sch. Dist., Minn., 1970-79; del. Crest View Home Assn., 1981—; mem. sci. and math. subcom. Minn. High Tech. Council, 1983-88, mem. Women Scientists Speakers Bur., 1989-92; observer UN 4th World Conf. on Women, Beijing, 1995. Recipient svc. awards and honors Omicron Sigma. Mem. AAAS, AAUW, NAFE (Twin Cities network), Am. Med. Writers Assn., Women in Com. Inc., Assn. Clin. Pharmacology, Soc. Tech. Comm., Nat. Assn. Women Cons., Inc., Minn. Emerging Med. Orgns., Minn. Soc. Med. Tech. (sec. 1969-71), Am. Soc. Profl. and Exec. Women, Am. Soc. Clin. Lab. Sci. (del. to ann. meetings 1972—, chmn. hematology sci. assembly 1977-79, nomination com. 1979-81, bd. dirs. 1985-88), Twin City Hosp. Assn. (speakers bur. 1968-70), Assn. Women in Sci., World Future Soc., Minn. Med. Tech. Alumni, Am. Soc. Hematology, Internat. Soc. Analytical Cytology, Great Lakes Internat. Flow Cytometry Assn. (charter mem. 1992), Sigma Delta Epsilon (corr. sec. Xi chpt. 1980-82, pres. 1982-84, membership com. 1990-92, nat. nominations chair 1991-92, nat. v.p. 1992-93, nat. pres.-elect 1993-94, nat. pres. 1994-95), Alpha Mu Tau. Lutheran. Office: FCM Specialists 8400-33 Pl N Minneapolis MN 55427

ANDERSON, GLORIA LONG, chemistry educator; b. Altheimer, Ark., Nov. 5, 1938; d. Charley and Elsie Lee (Foggie) L.; 1 child, Gerald Leavell. BS, Ark. Agr. Mech. & Normal Coll., 1958; MS, Atlanta U., 1961; PhD, U. Chgo., 1968. Instr. S.C. State Coll., Orangeburg, 1961-62, Morehouse Coll., Atlanta, 1962-64; teaching and rsch. asst. U. Chgo., 1964-68; assoc. prof., chmn. Morris Brown Coll., Atlanta, 1968-73, Callaway prof., chmn., 1973-84, acad. dean, 1984-89, United Negro Coll. Fund disting. scholar, 1989-90, Callaway prof. chemistry, 1990—; interim pres. Morris Brown Coll., 1992-93, Fuller E. Callaway prof. chemistry, 1993—. Contbr. articles to profl. jours. Bd. dirs. Corp. for Pub. Broadcasting, Washington, 1972-79, vice chmn. 1977-79; Pub. Broadcasting Atlanta, 1980—; mem. Pub. Telecommunications Task Force, Atlanta, 1980. Postdoctoral rsch. fellow NSF, 1969, faculty industry fellow, 1981, faculty rsch. fellow Southeastern Sci. Ctr. for Elec. Engring and Edn., 1984. Fellow Nat. Sci. Tchrs. Assn.; mem. Am. Chem. Soc., Am. Inst. Chemists, Sigma Xi. Baptist. Home: 560 Lynn Valley Rd SW Atlanta GA 30311-2331 Office: Morris Brown Coll 643 Martin Luther King Jr Dr NW Atlanta GA 30314-4140

ANDERSON, HOLLY GEIS, women's health facility administrator, commentator, educator; b. Waukesha, Wis., Oct. 23, 1946; d. Henry H. and Hulda (Sebroff) Geis; m. Richard Kent Anderson, June 6, 1969. BA, Azusa Pacific U., 1970. CEO Oak Tree Antiques, San Gabriel, Calif., 1975-82; pres., founder, CEO Premenstrual Syndrome Treatment Clinic, Arcadia, Calif., 1982—, Breast Healthcare Ctr., 1986-89, Hormonal Treatment Ctrs., Inc., Arcadia, 1992-94; lectr. radio and TV shows, L.A.; on-air radio personality Women's Clinic with Holly Anderson, 1990—. Author: What Every Woman Needs to Know About PMS (audio cassette), 1987, The PMS Treatment Program (video cassette), 1989, PMS Talk (audio cassette), 1989. Mem. NAFE, The Dalton Soc. Republican. Office: PMS Treatment Clinic 150 N Santa Anita Ave Ste 755 Arcadia CA 91006-3113

ANDERSON, IRENE SABINE, business owner; b. Bevern, Germany, Apr. 15, 1931; arrived in U.S., 1956; d. Otto Herman and Hermine (Koss) Magnus; m. James Russell Anderson, Dec. 15, 1956 (dec. Nov. 1989); children: Ray, Mark, Jason. Grad. h.s., Germany. Owner antique shop Edgewater, Md., 1972-96; owner deli Edgewater, 1979-89, owner auction house, 1984-86. Republican. Lutheran. Home: 3911 W Shore Dr Edgewater MD 21037 Office: 3106 Solomon's Island Rd Edgewater MD 21037

ANDERSON, IRIS ANITA, retired secondary education educator; b. Forks, Wash., Aug. 18, 1930; d. James Adolphus and Alma Elizabeth (Haase) Gilbreath; m. Donald Rene Anderson, 1951; children: Karen Christine, Susan Adele, Gayle Lynne, Brian Dale. BA in Teaching, U. Wash., 1969; MA in English, Seattle U., 1972. Cert. English tchr., adminstr., Calif. Tchr. Issaquah (Wash.) Sr. High Sch., 1969-77, L.A. Sr. High Sch., 1977-79. Contbr. article to Skeptic mag. Nutrition vol. Santa Monica (Calif.) Hosp. Aux., Jules Stein Eye Inst., L.A.; mem. Desert Beautiful, Palm Springs Panhellenic; mem. Rancho Mirage Reps. W-Key activities scholar U. Wash. Mem. NEA, DAR (vice regent Palm Springs, 1st vice regent Cahuilla chpt.), AAUW, LEV, Wash. Speech Assn., Nat. Thespians, Bob Hope Cultural Ctr., Palm Springs Press Women, Desert Music Guild, Coachella Valley Hist. Soc., Palm Desert Womens Club, Calif. Ret. Tchrs. Assn., CPA Wives Club, Desert Celebrities, Rancho Mirage Womens Club, Round Table West, World Affairs Coun., Living Desert Wildlife and Bot. Preserve. Republican.

ANDERSON, ISABEL, artist, educator; b. N.Y.C., Apr. 10, 1931; d. William and Mary Elizabeth (Doerr) Smith; m. Hugh Riddell Anderson, Feb. 4, 1955 (div. Jan. 1968); m. William Anthony Dietz, Apr. 29, 1978. Student, Art Students' League, 1951-52; BA, Antioch Coll., 1954; postgrad., UCLA, 1956; MFA, State U. of Iowa, 1956. Cert. h.s. tchr., Calif. C.C. standard teaching credential, instr. credential. Stained glass artist Paul L. Phillips Studio, Altadena, Calif., 1960-64, Roger Daricarrere Studio, L.A., 1965-66; h.s. art tchr. L.A. Unified Sch. Dist., 1967-76; instr. art Glendale (Calif.) C.C., 1979-80; asst. prof. screen printing Pasadena (Calif.) City Coll., 1980-90; artist, writer, 1990—; invited spkr., panelist in field. Exhbns., prints, drawings, paintings, 1965—; represented in permanent collections Boston Coll. Art, Home Savs. and Loan, Antioch Coll., Pasadena City Coll., Kerala State U., India, Hanover Bank, L.A.; contbr. articles and art revs. to profl. jours. Recipient Award of Merit 11th All-City Art Exhbn., 1963, Purchase award State Coll. Art, 1963, Spl. award Inland XII Art Exhbn., 1981, James Jones Purchae award Ink & Clay Exhbn. Calif. Poly., 1982; grantee Screen Printing Assn. Internat., 1985-88. Mem. L.A. Printmaking Soc. (sec. 1978-79, newsletter editor 1978-79), Women's Caucus for Art, SITE (mem. exhbn. com.), Beyond Baroque Found., Wednesday Poetry Workshop. Office: 1564 Talmadge St Los Angeles CA 90027-1543

ANDERSON, JANE A., scriptwriter. TV series include: Raising Miranda, 1988, The Wonder Years, 1989; TV movies include: The Positively True Adventures of the Alleged Texas Cheerleader-Murdering Mom, 1992 (Emmy award outstanding individual achievement in writing in a miniseries or special); film: It Could Happen to You; plays: The Baby Dance, Food and Shelter, Hotel Oubliette, Lynette at 3 A.M. *

ANDERSON, JANE ANN (JANIE ANDERSON), fund developer, consultant; b. Waukesha, Wis., Oct. 19, 1943; d. Robert Stanley Hopson and Elsie Jane (Gray) Taylor; m. Terry Grant Anderson, Sept. 11, 1965 (div. Aug. 22, 1990); children: Kristin Noel Anderson Locke, Jeffrey Grant. BA in Zoology, Rockford Coll., 1965; Certificate Fund Raising, Ind. U., 1986; Cert. Mgmt. Devel., San Diego State U., 1987. Owner To The Point, San Diego, 1981-86; dir. fund raising programs Vista Hill Found., San Diego, 1985-88; exec. dir. Camp Fire Coun. of San Diego County, San Diego, 1988-89; dir. devel. Francis Parker Sch., San Diego, 1990-95; v.p., dir. devel. Scripps Found. Medicine and Sci., San Diego, 1995—; adv., guest faculty Am. Humanics U. San Diego, 1988-93; cons. to non-profit agys.; mem. faculty Support Ctr./Exec. Svc. Corps., San Diego, 1991—; spkr. in field. Exhbns. include San Diego Fellow Calligraphers Show, 1983, 84. Mem. numerous coms. LEAD San Diego, 1988—, v.p., sec., spl. projects chair Children's Hosp. and Health Ctr., San Diego, 1976-81; chair sch. site couns. Wangenheim Jr. H.S., Mira Mesa H.S., San Diego, 1982-86; mem. dist. adv. com. San Diego Unified Sch. Dist., 1983-84; bd. dirs. The Writing Ctr., San Diego, 1996—. Mem. Nat. Soc. Fundraising Execs., Assn. Healthcare Philanthropy, Planned Giving Round Table. Office: Scripps Found Medicine and Sci PO Box 2669 La Jolla CA 92038

ANDERSON, JANE WILHOIT, elementary education educator; b. Johnson City, Tenn., Oct. 14, 1942; d. Kenneth Earney and Katherine (Young) Wilhoit; children: Judy Brandt, Janna. BS, Ea. Tenn. State U., 1976. Cert. tchr. Fingerprint technician F.B.I., Washington, 1961-62; bank bookkeeper Equitable Savs. and Loan, Washington, 1962-63; with stats. dept. State Dept. Mental Health, Columbia, S.C., 1972-73; tchr. South Side Elem. Sch., Johnson City, Tenn., 1976—; peer tutor, evaluator Completed Course in Johnson City Schs., 1985. Mem. bd., PTA advisor South Side PTA, Johnson City, 1978; mem. Woman's Rep. Orgn., Johnson City, 1991—, First United Meth. Ch., Johnson City, 1942—. Mem. NEA, Tenn. Edn. Assn. (bldg. rep. 1989), Johnson City Edn. Assn., Alpha Delta Kappa (sec., v.p. 1978—). Home: 1009 Crocus St Johnson City TN 37601

ANDERSON, JANET ALM, librarian; b. Lafayette, Ind., Dec. 20, 1952; d. Charles Henry and Lenore Elaine Alm; m. Jay Allan Anderson, May 21, 1983. BS, Bemidji State U., 1975; MA in Folklore, Western Ky. U., 1981, MSLS in Libr. Sci., 1982; PhD in Recreation Resources Mgmt., Utah State U., 1994. Cert. elem. tchr., sch. libr. and media specialist. Storyteller, puppeteer North Country Arts Coun., Bemidji, Minn., 1975-76; head children's libr. Bemidji State U., 1976-77; mid. sch. libr. Custer County Sch. Dist., Miles City, Mont., 1977-79; tchr. of gifted and talented Custer County Sch. Dist., Miles City, 1979-80; folklore archivist Western Ky. U., Bowling Green, 1981-83; head children's and young adults' svcs. Bowling Green Pub. Libr., 1983-85; head of serials Utah State U., Logan, 1986-91, campus svcs. libr., 1991—, adj. asst. prof. forestry, 1995—, chmn. adv. bd. Women's Ctr., 1988-92; adj. instr. Miles Community Coll., 1978-80; cons. to various Am. outdoor museums; speaker Utah Endowment for the Humanities Speakers Bur., Salt Lake City, 1987-90. Author: Old Fred, 1972, A Taste of Kentucky, 1986 (Ky. State Book Fair award), Bounty, 1990, (with others) Advances in Serials Management, Vol. 3, 1989, Vendors and Library Acquisitions, 1991; contbr. to Ency. of Am. Popular Beliefs and Superstitions, articles on folklore, librarianship, museology, and natural resource mgmt. to mags. and periodicals; assoc. editor: (jour.) InterpEdge; delivered radio and TV presentations on folklore and librarianship. Co-founder, past pres. Rosebud chpt. Nat. Audubon Soc., Miles City, Mont., 1978-80; mem. Providence/River Hts. Libr. Bd.; trustee Cache County Libr. Bd.; bd. dirs. Denzil Stewart Nature Park; invited author Ky. State Book Fair, 1986, Utah Arts Festival, 1991; life mem. Women and Gender Rsch. Inst., Friends of Brooks Free Libr. Recipient Exhibit and Program Grant Nat. Endowment for the Arts, Bowling Green, Ky., 1984-85. Mem. ALA, Nat. Audubon Soc. (trustee Bridgerland chpt. 1994-97), Nat. Assn. Interpretation, John Muir Assn. (founding mem. environ. ctr.), Utah Libr. Assn., Consortium of Utah Women in Higher Edn. (campus coord. 1989-91), Am. Folklore Soc., Utah Folklore Soc., Assn. Living Hist. Farms and Agrl. Mus., Visitor Studies Assn., Am. Assn. Mus., Assn. Coll. and Rsch. Librs., Old Main Soc., Xi Sigma Pi. Democrat. Lutheran. Home: 1090 S 400 E Providence UT 84332-9461 Office: Utah State U Merrill Libr Logan UT 84322-3000

ANDERSON, JANET ANN, women's health care nurse practitioner; b. Warrington, Eng., Aug. 13, 1946; came to U.S., 1953; d. William Henry and Eileen (Upton) Harold; m. Roger Eric Anderson, May 25, 1968; children: Glenn Michael, Erica Lynn. Diploma in Nursing, St. Luke's Hosp., Cleve., 1968; student, S.W. Med. Sch., Dallas. RN, Tex.; cert. women's health care nurse practitioner, sexual assault nurse examiner. Staff nurse Swedish Covenant Hosp., Chgo., 1968; office nurse Dr. Pohle, Tempe, Ariz., 1968-69, Dr. Gililand, Mesa, Ariz., 1969-70; charge nurse Flagstaff (Ariz.) Cmty. Hosp., 1971-74; staff float nurse Brackenridge Hosp., Austin, Tex., 1980-85; field nurse Girling Health Care, Burnet, Tex., 1985-88; discharge planner Sheppard Hosp., Burnet, 1985-88; pub. health nurse Tex. Dept. Health, Llano, 1988-91; nurse practitioner Tex. Dept. Health, Burnet, 1991-95; nurse practitioner cmty. clinic. Llano (Tex.) Meml. Hosp., 1995—; chair Llano County Interagy. coun. Pres. Barrington Elem. Sch. PTA, Austin, 1982-84. Mem. AWHONN, Austin Assn. Nurse Practitioners, Tex. Nurse Practitioners Assn. Home: RR 2 Box 16G Burnet TX 78611-9744 Office: Llano Meml Cmty Clinic P O Box 29 Llano TX 78643

ANDERSON, JANICE LORAINE, rehabilitation nurse; b. Litchfield, Ill., Sept. 20, 1968; d. John Arthur and Patricia Ann (Elbus) Link; m. Richard Charles Anderson, May 16, 1992. BS cum laude, Rush U., 1990. RN, Ill.; cert. rehab. registered nurse. Staff nurse level B Rush Presbyn. St. Luke's Med. Ctr., Chgo., 1990-93; staff nurse Meth. Med. Ctr. of Ill., Peoria, Ill., 1993-95; charge nurse Apostolic Christian Restmor, Inc., Morton, Ill., 1995—. Mem. Assn. Rehab. Nurses, Heart of Ill. Jr. Med. Aux., Sigma Theta Tau. Roman Catholic. Home: 206 N Kansas Ave Morton IL 61550-2218 Office: Apostolic Christian Restmor 935 E Jefferson Morton IL 61550

ANDERSON, JEWELLE LUCILLE, musician, educator; b. Alexandria, La., Jan. 4, 1932; d. William Andrew and Ethel Dee (Hall) A. Student, Springfield Coll., 1981-82; MusB, Boston U., 1984; postgrad., Harvard U., 1995—. Cert. music and social studies tchr., Mass. Soloist Ch. of the Redeemer Episcopal Ch., Chestnut Hill, Mass., 1964-69, St. James Episcopal Ch., Cambridge, Mass., 1970-75; kindergarten tchr. and music dir. Trinity Episcopal Ch., Boston, 1984-86; chorus music dir. Spencer for Hire, Boston, 1986; music dir. Days in the Arts summer program Boston Symphony Orch., Tanglewood, Mass., summer 1991, 92; music tchr. Clarence Edwards Mid. Sch., Charlestown, Mass., 1984-96; founder Jewelle Anderson Found., Inc., Boston, 1996. Vol. ARC, Boston, 1994—; bd. dirs. Mattapan Cmty. Health Ctr., Boston, 1990-92; founder, pres. Dr. William and Ethel Hall Anderson Scholarship, 1989—. Recipient Am. Music award Nat. Fedn. Music, 1970, Spl. Individual award Nat. Fedn. Music, 1969, Outstanding Contbn. to Humanity award Alexandria Civic Improvement Coun., 1967. Mem. AAUW, Amnesty Internat., Black Educators Alliance of Mass., 464 Women Svc. Club (head youth group 1989—), Alpha Kappa Alpha. Democrat. Baptist. Office: Jewelle Anderson Found Inc PO Box 1181 Boston MA 02103

ANDERSON, JO DORRIS, educational consultant; b. Little Rock, Jan. 8, 1938; d. John Paul and Josephine Elizabeth (White) Jones; m. Robert William Anderson, Aug. 18, 1959; children: Robert W. Jr. (dec.), Jeffrey Lee, Laura Jo, Matthew Charles. BA, George Peabody Coll., 1960, Master's degree, 1976. Tchr. English and Spanish Dearborn County Schs., Lawrenceburg, Ind., 1960-63; cons. State of Tenn. Tng., Nashville, 1977—, Metro Gov. Tng., 1979—; group tester Metro Schs., Nashville, 1977—; substitute tchr. Brentwood (Tenn.) Acad., 1977-90; sec. adminstrv. bd. Forest Hills United Meth. Ch., Nashville, 1985—, mem. adv. bd. for scholarship, 1990—, pres. United Meth. Women, 1995—. Mem. Children's Hosp. Friends, Nashville, 1985—; vol. Mother's March on Birth Defects, Nashville, 1990—; bd. dirs. Anthony Wayne Nursery Sch., Ft. Wayne, Ind., 1968. Mem. Pi Gamma, Gamma Phi Beta. Home: 205 River Oaks Rd Brentwood TN 37027

ANDERSON, JOAN WELLIN FREED, communications executive, consultant, freelance journalist, writer; b. Shreveport, La., Aug. 18, 1945; d. Cyril and Rose (Friedman) F.; m. J. Warren Anderson, July 21, 1984 (div. 1991). BA in Gen. Studies, Tex. Christian U. Freelance reporter Sta. KERA-TV, Dallas, 1979-80, Fort Worth Star-Telegram, 1980-83, Fort Worth bur. Dallas Morning News, 1980-82; pub. rels. coord. Amon Carter Mus., Fort Worth, 1982; med. writer Tex. Coll. Osteo. Medicine, Fort Worth, 1982-85; freelance writer, 1985-87; producer video programs for pub. access cable channel, Ft. Worth, 1987-90; cmty. programming coord. cable TV channel City of Ft. Worth, 1988-90, chair; v.p. corp. comms. & health svcs. Comm. Osteo. Health System of Tex., 1990—; co-owner, playwright, actress Catered Theater, Character Acts. Bd. dirs. Am. Cancer Soc., 1982-84, Am. Heart Assn. 1993-94, Leadership Texas Class 1993, active Cancer Hotline, Cmty. Programming Adv. Coun.; facilitator for fair housing edn. and info. for Cmty. Housing Resource Bd., Ft. Worth; bd. dirs. Women's Haven of Tarrant County (Tex.) Inc., 1987-88, chmn. cmty. rels. com., 1988, Dispute Resolutions Svcs. Tarrant County (bd. dirs., chmn. cmty. rels. 1989-90); mem. Court Apptd. Spl. Adv. for Foster Children, 1986-88. Mem. Women in Comm., Inc. (past dir.), Internat. Assn. Bus. Communicators, Soc. for Theatrical Artists' Guidance and Enhancement, Advt. Club, Sigma Delta Chi. Author: (juvenile) Diggy Armadillo Goes to the Rodeo, Arnie Armadillo Goes to Cowtown; playwright: 1-800-4ADVICE, 1994; contbr. articles to popular mags. Office: Osteopathic Health System of Tex 3715 Camp Bowie Blvd Fort Worth TX 76107-3353

ANDERSON, JOLENE SLOVER, small business owner, publishing executive, consultant; b. Tulare, Calif.; James P. Sr., and Helen B. (Walters) Slover; m. Douglas R. Anderson, June 14, 1975; 1 child by previous marriage, Sabrina Jo. Student, Victor Valley Coll., Riverside City Coll. Model Connor Sch. Modeling, Fresno, Calif., 1955-65; actress M. Kosloff Studios, Hollywood, Calif., 1965; nat. sales mgr. Armed Services Publs., Hollywood, Calif., 1966-68; pres., dir. Sullivan Publs., Inc., Riverside, Calif., 1970-82; pres., chief exec. officer Heritage House Publs., Riverside, 1983-84; pres. Jolene S. Anderson Pub. Cons., Inc., Riverside, 1987—; bd. dirs. Riverside

County Econ. Devel. Coun. Co-comdr. March AFB, Riverside Tourists and Conv.; mem. YWCA, City of Riverside Cultural Heritage Bd., Yr. 2000 Com., 1988, Riverside County Philharm. Bd., Temecula-Murrieta Econ. Devel. Corp. Named Woman of Achievement YWCA, 1989, Humanitarian of Yr. Rotary, 1990. Mem. Riverside Downtown Assn., Sun City/Menifee Valley C. of C., Greater Riverside C. of C., Temecula Valley C. of C., Soroptimists (Riverside chpt.). Office: PO Box 800 Riverside CA 92502-0800

ANDERSON, JOYCE PATRICIA, special education coordinator; b. Springfield, Mass., Mar. 19, 1939; d. Thomas and Eunice Barbara (Maher) Ryan; m. Richard Thomas Anderson, July 8, 1972. BA in Elem. Edn., U. Mass., 1960; MEd in Elem./Spl. Edn., Springfield Coll., 1964; PhD in Ednl. Psychology/Spl. Edn., Fordham U., 1983. Lic. profl. educator level II, Vt.; cert. gen. elem./spl. edn. grades kindergarten through 12, cert. cons. tchr./learning specialist grades kindergarten through 12, Conn.; cert. elem./spl. edn. tchr., Mass. Tchr. grade 3 Fairfield (Conn.) Woods Sch., 1960-63, Pleasant View Sch., East Longmeadow, Mass., 1964-67; tchr. grade 4 Mountain View Sch., East Longmeadow, 1967-69; tchr. kindergarten Meadow Brook Sch., East Longmeadow, 1969-70, tchr. spl. edn./emotionally disturbed, 1970-72; tchr. emotionally disturbed Wellesley (Mass.) area schs., 1972-73; 1st and 2d grade tchr. Hunnewell Elem. Sch., Wellesley, Mass., 1973-74; tchr. spl. edn. resource rm. Ridgebury Elem. Sch., Ridgefield, Conn., 1974-84; asst. prof. spl. edn. St. Thomas Aquinas Coll., Sparkhill, N.Y., 1984-89; spl. edn. coord. Woodstock (Vt.) Elem. Sch., 1984—; dir. grad. program in spl. edn. St. Thomas Aquinas Coll., 1986-89; adj. prof. assessment and lang. devel. Fordham U., Tarrytown, N.Y., Fordham, 1983-86; adj. prof. on exceptional children Castleton (Vt.) State Coll., 1991; adj. prof. assessment U. Vt., Burlington, 1991; adj. prof. attention deficit disorcer St. Joseph's Coll., Rutland, Vt., 1991-94; presenter in field. Mem. profl. bd. Rockland Children's Psychiat. Hosp., Rockland County, N.Y., 1987-89; mem. ednl. adv. com. Hartland (Vt.) Elem. Sch. Mem. ASCD, Coun. for Exceptional Children, Learning Disability Assn. Home: PO Box 61 Hartland Four Corners VT 05049-0061

ANDERSON, JUDITH ANNE, academic dean; b. Little Falls, Minn., June 23, 1943; d. Thomas Martin and Elda Rose Ethel (Klapel) McDonnell; m. Gene Wesley Anderson, Aug. 12, 1961 (div. 1993); children: Jeffery Thomas, Gregory Carl, Joel Michael, Julie Ann. AA, Cambridge (Minn.) Anoka-Ramsey C.C., 1982; BA, Met. State U., St. Paul, 1987; MS, Cardinal Stritch Coll., Milw., 1990. Bookkeeper Peoples State Bank, Cambridge, 1971-77; bus. mgr. Cambridge Anoka-Ramsey C.C., 1979-90; ednl. coord. Barnes Bus. Coll., Denver, 1991-92, dir., 1994—, acad. dean, 1995—; cons. for low-income families U. Minn. Extension Dept., Isanti County, 1987-90. Treas. Govt. Maple Ridge Twp., Isanti County, Minn., 1978-91; chmn. United Charities Dr., Maple Ridge Twp., 1980-85, Jefferson County Ext. Adv. Bd., 1994—. Named State Vol. Gov. of Minn., 1987, 88, 89, 90. Mem. AAUW (Denver), Muskies Inc., Women for Fishing, Hunting and Wildlife, Lady Ducks, Nat. Outdoors Women, Phi Theta Kappa (Alpha Minn. chpt.). Republican. Mem. Covenant Ch. Home: 6836 S Everett Ct Littleton CO 80123-4023

ANDERSON, JUDY, consultant; b. Waukegan, Ill., Jan. 10, 1943; d. Raymond K. and Eleanor (Kozak) Schaaf. BBA with honors, U. Wis., 1965; MS, L.I. U., 1982; PhD, Southeastern U., 1983. Asst. registrar, adj. instr. Gateway Tech. Inst., Kenosha, Wis., 1971-79; assoc. registrar L.I. U., Greenvale, 1979-85; fin. planner Am. Express Fin. Svcs., Mineola, N.Y., 1985-86; trainer, counselor Dime Savings Bank N.Y., Uniondale, 1986-93; trainer, speaker, cons. Anderson Consulting and Tng., Farmingdale, N.Y., 1991—. Author: Teeing Off to the Green: Using Golf as a Business Tool, 1995. Mem. Internat. Spkrs. Network, Nat. Spkrs. Assn., L.I. Ctr. Bus. and Profl. Women, U.S. Golf Assn., Exec. Women's Golf League, Cons. Bur., Women in Sports and Events. *

ANDERSON, KAREN LYNN, educator; b. Oak Park, Ill., Oct. 29, 1956; d. Ralph Lewis and Barbara Ann (Caspers) Brown; m. Timothy William Anderson, June 7, 1980 (dec. Nov. 1990). BA, U. No. Colo., 1978, MA, 1985. Intern Cherry Creek Schs., Walnut Hills Elem. Sch., Englewood, Colo., 1978-79; customer svc. rep. United Bank Am., Denver, 1979-80; substitute tchr. Cherry Creek Schs., Aurora (Colo.) Pub. Schs., 1980-82; advisor of Master's prog. in Whole Learning Regis U., Denver, 1991—; tchr. Cherry Creek Schs., Independence Elem. Sch., Aurora, 1982-85, Cherry Creek Schs., Indian Ridge Elem. Sch., Aurora, Colo., 1985—; dir. steering com. Regis U. Literacy Inst., 1985-94; mem. steering com., Regis U. Early Childhood Inst., 1990-93; staff devel. liaison Cherry Creek Schs., 1991-96. Recipient Cherry Creek Schools Tchr. of Yr., 1988, Tchr. Who Makes a Difference award Channel 4, 1989. Mem. ASCD, Internat. Reading Assn., Young Life (com. chair 1990-96, vol. leader 1990-96). Republican. Presbyterian. Home: 5558 S Telluride St Aurora CO 80015 Office: Indian Ridge Elem 16501 E Progress Dr Aurora CO 80015

ANDERSON, KATHERYN LUCILLE, language arts educator and author; b. Aberdeen, Md., Aug. 17, 1949; d. Boyd Frederick and Lucy Charlotte Anderson. BS in Edn., U. Md., 1973; MA in Spl. Edn., Adams State Coll., Alamosa, Colo., 1977; MA in Ednl. Tech., U. Colo., 1986. Lic. profl. tchr., Colo. Mental health paraprofl. Prince George's County Mental Health, Landover, Md., 1970-73; spl. edn. tchr. Fountain/Ft. Carson (Colo.) Sch. Dist., 1973-75; instr. mil. program Pikes Peak Cmty. Coll., Colorado Springs, Colo., 1977-78; spl. edn. tchr. Harrison Sch. Dist., Colorado Springs, 1978-88, tchr. lang. arts, 1988—, team leader lang. arts, 1989—, dept. chair, 1992—; lectr. in field. Author: English and American Culture, 1991, English and American Culture 6, 1993, English and American Culture 7, 1993, A Writing Companion, 1993; co-author: The Sound of the Apple IIe, 1986, The Shape of the Apple IIe, 1986. Chpt. II Ednl. Program Devel. grantee Harrison Sch. Dist., 1991, 92, 93; recipient 1996 Colo. State A World of Difference Educator of Yr. award. Mem. AAUW, ASCD, Colo. Assn. Middle Level Educators, Colo. Lang. Arts Soc., Nat. Coun. Tchrs. English, Nat. Women's History Project Network, Tenn. Walking Horse Assn. (rep., stock show and horse exposition 1993-94), Tenn. Walking Horse Breeders and Exhibitors Assn. Democrat. Office: Carmel Middle Sch 1740 Pepperwood Dr Colorado Springs CO 80910-1525

ANDERSON, KATHLEEN CALLAHAN, lawyer; b. Milw., May 26, 1953; d. Edgar Fred and Sally Ann (Conley) Callahan; m. Christopher P. Anderson, June 27, 1987. BA, Marquette U., 1975; MBA, U. Calif., 1989, JD, 1978. Assoc. Jackson Tufts Cole Block (formerly Petty Andrews Tufts & Jackson), San Francisco, 1978-83; v.p., gen. counsel, sec. We. Community, Walnut Creek, Calif., 1983-85, ACA Joe, San Francisco, 1986-88, Esprit, San Francisco, 1988—. Bd. dirs., gen. counsel Leadership Calif., 1989-95. Mem. ABA (gov. bd. franchising forum 1992—). Home: 524 Dalewood Dr Orinda CA 94563-1207 Office: Esprit 900 Minnesota St San Francisco CA 94107-3050

ANDERSON, KATHRYN DUNCAN, surgeon; b. Ashton-Under-Lyne, Lancashire, Eng., Mar. 14, 1939; came to U.S., 1961; m. French Anderson, June 24, 1961. BA, Cambridge (Eng.) U., 1961, MA, 1964; MD, Harvard U., 1964. Diplomate Am. Bd. Surgery. Intern in pediat. Children's Hosp., Boston, 1964-65; resident in surgery Georgetown U. Hosp., Washington, 1965-69, chief resident in surgery, 1969-70, attending surgeon, 1972-74, vice chmn. surgery, 1984-92; chief resident in pediat. surgery Children's Hosp., Washington, 1970-72, sr. attending surgeon, 1974-84; surgeon-in-chief Children's Hosp., L.A., 1992—; prof. surgery U. So. Calif. Fellow ACS (sec. 1992—), Am. Acad. Pediatrics (sec. surg. sect. 1982-85, chmn. 1985-86), Am. Pediatric Surg. Assn. (sec. 1988-91); Am. Surg. Assn., Soc. Univ. Surgeons. Office: Childrens Hosp 4650 W Sunset Blvd Los Angeles CA 90027-6016

ANDERSON, KATHRYN LOUISE, women's studies educator; b. Newton, Iowa, Dec. 8, 1943; d. Lawrence Wilmer and Ruby Josephine (Gist) A.; m. Leonard M. Helfgott, Sept. 10, 1971; children: Isadora, Alexander, Jonathan. BA, U. Iowa, 1965, MA, 1967; PhD, U. Wash., 1978. Rsch. asst. U. Iowa, Iowa City, 1966-67; instr. U. Md., College Park, 1967-70; tchg. asst. U. Wash., Seattle, 1970-72; asst. prof. Fairhaven Coll., Western Wash. U., Bellingham, 1972-79, dir. women's studies, 1977-96, assoc. prof., 1979-94, acting asst. dean, 1992-93, prof. women's studies, 1994—; prin. investigator Wash. Women's Heritage Project, 1980-82. Contbr. articles to profl. publs. Bd. dirs. N.W. Women Svcs., Bellingham, 1988-90, Wash. Assn for Children and Adults with Learning Disabilities, 1984-88. NEH grantee, 1980-82. Mem. Nat. Women's Studies Assn. (mem. nat. coord. coun. 1982-92), N.W. Women's Studies Assn (co-coord. 1992—), Coalition Western Women's History (program chair 1984). Democrat. Home: 109 S Forest Bellingham WA 98225 Office: Western Wash U Fairhaven Coll Bellingham WA 98225 also: 33 Lawton St Brookline MA 02146

ANDERSON, LAURA JEAN, aviation maintenance technician; b. Mpls., Sept. 23, 1962; d. Roger Wayne and Susan Eleanor (Swanson) A. Grad. in Field Artillery Digital Sys. Repair, U.S. Army Field Artillery Sch., Ft. Sill, Okla., 1987; grad. in Electronics Tech., Northwestern Electronics Inst., Columbia Heights, Minn., 1992; grad. in Aviation Maintenance, Red Wing Winona Tech. Coll., Winona, Minn., 1994. Cashier/cook Zantigo Restaurants, Mpls., 1980-85; electronic assembly Lee Data, Eden Prairie, Minn., 1988-89; house painter J&M Painting, Big Lake, Minn., 1985-93; electronic technician Electrosonic, Minnetonka, Minn., 1989-93; delivery driver Air Vantage, Mpls., 1993-94; fund raiser Hudson Bay, Lincoln, Nebr., 1994-95; aviation maintenance technician Duncan Aviation, Lincoln, 1994—; spkr. Career Day, Winona Tech. Coll., 1994, Women in Aviation Conf., Mpls., 1996. Mem. unit Morale Support Fund Coun., USAR, Faribault, Minn., 1990, retention NCO, 1992. Sgt. E-5 USAR, 1986—. Recipient David Stumpf Aviation scholarship Winona Tech. Coll., 1993, Equity Program scholarship Winona Tech. Coll., 1994. Mem. Women in Aviation, Profl. Aviation Maintenance Assn., Toastmasters (treas. 1995), Vo-Tec Honor Soc. Home: 5001 Vine St Apt 317 Lincoln NE 68504 Office: Duncan Aviation PO Box 81887 Lincoln Airport Lincoln NE 68501

ANDERSON, LEE, secondary school educator; b. Chgo., Jan. 26, 1938; d. Raymond A. and Adeline (Zabel) Girlock; children: Gail Elaine Tompkins, Donna Lee Nuger, Susan Lynn Lockwood. BA, Northeastern Ill. U., 1979, MA in Reading, 1984; cert. advance studies, Nat. Louis U., 1992. Cert. K-9 tchr., K-12 reading tchr., mid. sch. curriculum and instrn., Ill. Tchr. Dist. 401, Elmwood Park, Ill., 1979-82, North Chgo. H.S., 1984-89, Dist. 60, Waukegan, Ill., 1989—; adj. faculty Coll. of Lake County, Grayslake, Ill., 1985—. Home: 1228 N Streamwood Ln Vernon Hills IL 60061

ANDERSON, LINDA (LYNN ANDERSON), radio executive; b. Detroit, Dec. 24; d. Robert A. and Lucille A. Tower; children: Kierstyn R. Anderson, Gretchen N. Anderson. BA in Bus., Mich. State U., 1968; post-grad., UCLA, 1968-70. Cert. radio mktg. cons. Tchr. pub. schs. L.A. and Chgo., 1968-70; mgr. display ads Frontier Publs., 1970-71; broadcaster Sta. WVVX, Chgo., 1971-72; account exec. Metromedia Radio, Sta. WDHF, Chgo., 1972-76; v.p. sales Metro Radio Sales Metromedia Radio, L.A., 1976-79; sr. account exec. RKO Radio/Sta. KHJ, L.A., 1979-80; with Gannett Radio/Sta. KIIS AM-FM, L.A., 1980-90, v.p. sales, 1984-85, v.p., sta. mgr., 1986, v.p., gen. mgr., 1986-87, pres., 1987-90; exec. v.p. mktg. and sales worldwide Radio Express, L.A., 1991—; v.p., gen. mgr. Southwestern region Metro Networks, L.A., 1995, v.p. internat. devel., 1996. Mem. bd. visitors Southwestern Coll. Law, Los Angeles, 1987. Recipient Jim Dunkan awards 1987, 88; named Gen. Mgr. Yr. Poe Music Survey, 1989. Mem. Nat. Assn. Broadcasters (steering com. 1987—), Am. Women Radio & TV (Broadcaster of Yr. 1990), Hollywood Radio & TV Soc. (IBA awards chair), Hollywood Arts Com. (bd. dirs. 1986—), So. Calif. Broadcasters Assn. (sec. 1989, bd. dirs. 1986—), Hollywood Women's Polit. Com., Hollywood C. of C. (spl. events com. 1987—). Clubs: Los Angeles Ad; Calif. Yacht; Santa Monica Yacht. Office: Metro Networks Los Angeles CA 90068-1366

ANDERSON, LINDA LOUISE, management professional; b. Chgo., Dec. 11, 1963; d. Raymond Bertram and Mary Louise (Stutenroth) A. BA, Iowa State U., 1986. Front desk clk. Best Western, Des Plaines, Ill., 1987; baggage systems investigator United Airlines, Elk Grove, Ill., 1987-89, bus. travel coord., 1989-90, acct. contr., 1990-92, specialist informational sys. analyst, 1992-93; buyer-kitchen United Airlines, Miami, Fla., 1993-95; adminstrv. rep. United Airlines, Elk Grove, 1995-96, staff rep. meal mgmt., 1996—. Home: 1506 Park Ave River Forest IL 60305 Office: United Airlines 1200 E Algonquin Elk Grove Village IL 60007

ANDERSON, LOUISE STOUT, crime analyst; b. Wellsville, N.Y., Aug. 11, 1952; d. Carlton C. and Mary (Gasdik) Stout; m. Leonard M. Anderson, June 2, 1973. BA in German Lit., Polit. Sci., Mt. Holyoke Coll., 1974; MA in Polit. Sci., San Diego State U., 1977; MS Human Resources and Organizational Devel., 1994. Cert. C.C. tchr., Calif. Statistician Grossmont Coll., El Cajon, Calif., 1976-78; crime analyst San Diego Police Dept., 1978-80; crime analyst Career Criminal Apprehension Program, Marin County Sheriff's Office, San Rafael, Calif., 1980-83; crime analyst CCAP Unit, Sonoma County Sheriff's Office, Santa Rosa, Calif., 1983-85; mgr. mktg. svcs. Command Data Systems, Dublin, Calif., 1985-87, client svcs. mgr., 1988-92; contracts mgr. Tiburon Inc., 1992; mgr. field svcs. OCS Techs., 1992-95, v.p. nat. customers support, 1994—; project mgr. Integrated Systems Solution Corp., 1995—; cons. Search Group Inc. for Automated Crime Analysis. Contbr. articles in field. Owner Acacia Assocs., public safety cons. and training orgn.; project mgmt. profl. Project Mgmt. Inst., 1994; bd. dirs. Mltc. Club So. Calif., 1996—. Mem. Antioch Police Commn.; alumna recruiter Mt. Holyoke Club No. Calif., 1981-86.

ANDERSON, LYNDA GOULD, fine arts dealer; b. N.Y.C., Oct. 20, 1957; d. George A. and Suzanne (Metzler) Gould; divorced; 1 child, colin Gray. Student, Hofstra U., NYU, N.Y. Sch. Design. Pres. Lynda Gould Bus. Cons., N.Y.C., 1976-92; pres., dir. Anderson Gould Fine Arts, N.Y.C., 1985-92, Anderson Galleries, Locust Valley, N.Y., 1992—; creator, producer Bravo Networks "Art Profiles", 1995—. Fundraiser Friends Acad., Locust Valley, 1993-95, Nassau County Mus., Roslyn, n.Y., 1994—. Office: Anderson Galleries Box 85 Locust Valley NY 11560

ANDERSON, MARGARET ALLYN, retired carpet showroom manager; b. Meeker, Okla., Aug. 1, 1922; d. Edgar Allen and Maggie May (Smith) Martin; m. Ralph Carlos Huffman, Dec. 23, 1939 (div. Dec. 1954); children: Ronald Carlos, Darrell Duane; m. Walter Monroe Anderson, June 4, 1956. Student, San Antonio Jr. Coll., 1950-51. Clk. stenographer Sinclair Oil Co., Tulsa, 1947-48; clk. stenographer to sec. U.S. Govt. Civil Svc., San Antonio, 1948-55, Wiesbaden, Germany, 1956, Denver, 1956-57, Boise, Idaho, 1957-64; co-owner, sec./treas. Anthane, Inc., Boise, Idaho, 1964-87; co-owner, showroom mgr., sec. Anthane, Inc., San Francisco, 1987-94; ret., 1994. Mem. Am. Bus. Womens Assn. Democrat. Mem. Christian Ch.

ANDERSON, MARGARET TAYLER, real estate broker, career consultant; b. Castle Rock, Wash., May 1, 1918; d. George Lawrence and Frances Tressie (Huntington) Tayler; m. James Kress Anderson, Dec. 31, 1940; children: Bret Douglas, Blythe Rebecca, Beth Lynn Murray, Burke Stuart. AB, Willamette U., 1939, MA, 1940; MA, Columbia U., 1967; profl. diploma, Columbia U., 1970; DHL (hon.), Dominican Coll. Blauvelt, 1970. Cert. English, social studies tchr., N.Y. Asst. travelling libr. Oreg. State Libr., Salem, 1940; chemist Reynolds Metals, Longview, Wash., 1941; electronic technician Sperry Gyroscope, Lake Success, N.Y., 1942-43; adminstrv. asst. New Sch. Social Rsch., N.Y.C., 1944-49; real estate broker Palisades, N.Y., 1952—; dir. Rockland County Guidance Ctr. Women, Nyack, N.Y., 1969-91; career counselor N.Y. State Dept. Adult and Continuing Edn., Albany, 1985-90; pres. Rockland County Bd. Realtors, 1968-69. Editor, co-author From Here to My Goal, 1979-80; co-author, co-editor N.Y. Adult Career Counseling Manual, 1988-91. Mem. com. Rockland County Dems., 1952-56; co-chair Orangetown Dems.; fundraiser Palisades Free Libr., 1960—; mem. alumni coun., devel., fundraising Columbia U. Tchrs. Coll., 1994—. Recipient Woman of Yr. award Bus. & Profl. Women, 1977, Disting. Alumni award Columbia U. Tchrs. Coll., 1992. Mem. AAUW (v.p. 1995—, Woman of Achievement award Rockland County sect. 1979), Nat. Assn. Women Edn., League Women Voters. Home and Office: 286 Rt 9 W Palisades NY 10964

ANDERSON, MARIAN LEA, administrative assistant; b. Hillsboro, Oreg., Nov. 8, 1957; d. Charles Frank and Geraldine Susan (Shebuski) Dubbels; m. Ansel Emil Anderson, Aug. 30, 1979; children: Heather Mae, Candice Sue. Grad. high sch., Hillsboro, Oreg. Computer operator Wel Pland Ins., Lake Grove, Oreg., 1976-79; adminstrv. asst. Anderson's Pro Office Svc., Beaverton, Oreg., 1993—. Democrat.

ANDERSON, MARILYN NELLE, elementary education educator, librarian, counselor; b. Las Animas, Colo., May 5, 1942; d. Mason Hadley Moore and Alice Carrie (Dwyer) Coates; m. George Robert Anderson, Sept. 4, 1974; children: Lisa Lynn, Edward Alan, Justin Patrick. BEd magna cum laude, Adams State Coll., 1962, postgrad., 1965; MEd, Ariz. State U., 1967; postgrad., Idaho State U., 1971, 86, Columbia Pacific U., 1991—. Cert. elem. tchr., K-12 sch. counselor. Tchr. Wendell (Idaho) Sch. Dist. 232, 1962-66, Union-Endicott (N.Y.) Sch. Dist., 1967-68; counselor, librarian West Yuma (Colo.) Sch. Dist., 1968-69; elem. sch. counselor Am. Falls (Idaho) Sch. Dist. 381, 1969-73; project dir. Gooding County (Idaho) Sr. Citizens Orgn., 1974-75; tchr. Castleford (Idaho) Sch. Dist. 417, 1982-92; placement specialist, referral counselor Idaho Child Care Program S. Cen. Idaho Community Action Agy., Twin Falls, 1992—; mem. Castleford Schs. Merit Pay Devel. program, 1983-84, Accreditation Evaluation com., 1984-85, Math. Curriculum Devel. com., 1985-86. Leader Brownie Scouts, Endicott, 1967-68; chmn. fundraising com. Am. Falls Kindergarten, 1971-73. Recipient Leader's award Nat. 4-H Conservation Natural Resources Program, 1984. Mem. NEA, ASCD, Nat. Assn. Edn. Young Children, Assn. Childhood Edn. Internat., Idaho Edn. Assn., Idaho Coun. Internat. Reading Assn., Magic Valley Reading Assn., Support Unltd. Providers and Parents. Republican. Baptist. Home: 1675 BBH Wendell ID 83355-9801 Office: S Ctrl Idaho Community A Twin Falls ID 83301

ANDERSON, MARILYN RUTH, library media specialist; b. Storm Lake, Iowa, Oct. 2, 1934; d. Ernest F. and Elvira (Getzmier) Otto; m. Leland A. Anderson, June 23, 1957; children: Pamela, Mitchell, Darren. BA, U. No. Iowa, 1975. Cert. tchr., Iowa. Tchr. 1st grade Holstein (Iowa) Comty. Sch., 1954-55, Humboldt (Iowa) Comty. Sch., 1955-57; substitute tchr. Aurelia (Iowa) Comty. Sch., 1958-66, Kanawha (Iowa) Comty. Sch., 1966-74; libr. media specialist, reading tchr. Marcus-Meriden-Cleghorn Sch., Meriden, Iowa, 1974—; h.s. libr. media specialist Willow Comty. Sch., Quimby, Iowa, 1984-89; mem. Cleghorn (Iowa) Pub. Libr. Trustees, 1976-86, chair, 1982-86. Mem. planning com., leader Meriden-Cleghorn New Libr. Bldg. Campaign, 1983-85, chmn. libr. design and fed. grant-writing coms.; spkr. dedication ceremony for new libr. Meriden-Cleghorn Comty. Libr., 1986. Mem. Internat. Reading Assn., Area Edn. Agy. 4 Media Specialists (sec. 1980-82, pres. 1984-86), Iowa Edn. Media Assn. (Children's Choice award com.. 1976—), N.W. Iowa Reading Coun., Iowa Reading Assn. Republican. Lutheran. Home: 206 E Front St Cleghorn IA 51014 Office: Marcus-Meriden-Cleghorn Sch 305 Eagle St Meriden IA 51037

ANDERSON, MARTHA ALENE, safety and security executive; b. Monessen, Pa., June 15, 1945; d. Jesse Lee and Helen Frances (Daugherty) Cain; m. James O. Anderson, Sept. 9, 1966; 1 child, Heather Linn. BS in Biology, U. Calif. of Pa., 1967. Rsch. asst. W.Va. U., Morgantown, 1967-72; tchr. Hokkaido Internat. Sch., Sapporo, Japan, 1972-73; research asst. Pa. State U., 1974-75, Trudeau Inst., 1975-76; research assoc. U. Ariz., Tucson, 1976-80; mgr. chem. waste Dept. Risk Mgmt., U. Ariz., Tucson, 1980-81, asst. dir., 1981-85, dir., 1985-87; dir. environ. health and safety Thomas Jefferson U., Phila., 1987-90, asst. v.p. for safety and security, 1990—; chmn. Phila. Local Emergency Planning Com. Mem. Am. Soc. Hosp. Engrs., Bus. and Profl. Women, Campus Safety Assn. Avocations: Japanese literature, sewing. Office: Thomas Jefferson U Edison 1630 Philadelphia PA 19107-5233

ANDERSON, MARTHA JEAN, media specialist; b. Greenville, S.C., May 15, 1946; d. Benjamin Mason and Gladys (Harling) A. BS, Appalachian State U., Boone, N.C., 1968; M.Librarianship, Emory U., Atlanta, 1974, D.A.S.L., 1983. Libr. Arlington Schs., Atlanta, 1968-70, Archer Public High Sch., Atlanta, 1970-74; media specialist Woodmont High Sch. Greenville County Sch. Dist., Piedmont, S.C., 1974-76; media specialist Berea High Sch. Greenville County Sch. Dist., Greenville, S.C., 1976-80; media specialist Hillcrest High Sch. Greenville County Sch. Dist., Simpsonville, S.C., 1980—. Recipient Citation award S.C. Occupational Info. Coord. Com., 1988. Mem. NEA, S.C. Assn. Sch. Librs., S.C. Edn. Assn., Greenville County Edn. Assn., Riedville (S.C.) Hist. Soc. (charter mem., historian), Rotary, Iota Alpha Delta Kappa (historian 1978-80, 88-90, 92-94, v.p. 1980-82, pres. 1982-84, 94-96, sgt.-at-arms 1990-92). Methodist. Home: 537 Harrison Bridge Rd Simpsonville SC 29680-7004 Office: Hillcrest High Sch 3665 S Industrial Dr Simpsonville SC 29681-3238

ANDERSON, MARY ELIZABETH (BETH ANDERSON), nursing administrator; b. Salem, Mass., Feb. 17, 1945; d. Richard Thomas Fanning and Mary Anne (Wright) Fanning-Oldrieve; m. Joseph Lawrence Anderson, Sept. 14, 1965; children: Kathleen Marie, Gregory Michael. ADN, Sinclair C.C., 1980; BSN, Wright State U., 1988, MSN, 1992. CCRN. Staff nurse telemetry Miami Valley Hosp., Dayton, Ohio, 1980-81, primary nurse II ICU, 1981-90, primary nurse II post anesthesia care unit, 1990-91; dir. for nursing svc. The Children's Med. Ctr., Dayton, 1991-95; dir. sub-acute care Bethany Luth. Village, Dayton, 1995-96; co-owner Dynamic Visions of Nursing, Bellbrook, Ohio, 1994—. Co-author: Planning Care in Specialty Practices Inpatient Pediatrics, 1994; co-editor Jour. Shared Governance; contbr. articles to nursing jours. Active United Way, Dayton, 1992—. With U.S. Army, 1963-66. Mem. Respiratory Nursing Soc., Coun. Nurse Mgr. Affiliates (pres. Dayton chpt. 1994), N.Am. Nursing Diagnosis Assn. (chair nominating com.), Sigma Theta Tau (pres. chpt. 1995—). Roman Catholic. Home: 2300 S Linda Dr Bellbrook OH 45305-1559

ANDERSON, MARY JANE, public library director; b. Des Moines, Jan. 23, 1935; d. William Kenneth and Margaret Louise (Snider) McPherson; m. Charles Robert Anderson, Oct. 21, 1965 (div. Oct. 24, 1989); 1 child, Mary Margaret. B.A. in Edn., U. Fla., 1957; MLS, Fla. State U., 1963. Elem. sch. librarian Dade County Schs., Miami, Fla., 1957-61; children's/young adult librarian Santa Fe Regional Library, Gainesville, Fla., 1961-63; br. librarian Jacksonville (Fla.) Pub. Library, 1963-64, chief of children's services, 1964-66, head of circulation, 1966-67; pub. library cons. Fla. State Library, Tallahassee, 1967-70; dir. tech. processing St. Mary's Coll. of Md., St. Mary's City, 1970-72; coordinator children's services Balt. County Pub. Library, Towson, Md., 1972-73; exec. dir. young adult services div. ALA, Chgo., 1973-75, exec. dir. assn. for library service to children, 1973-82; pres. Answers Unltd., Inc., Deerfield, Ill., 1982-92; dir. Wilmington (Ill.) Pub. Libr., 1993—; instr. and cons. in field; part-time faculty No. Ill. U., 1985-86, Nat. Coll. Edn., Evanston, Ill., 1989; head youth svcs. Waukegan (Ill.) Pub. Libr., 1988-93; mem. exec. com. U.S. sect. Internat. Bd. on Books for Young People, 1973-82; mem. adv. bd. Reading Rainbow, TV series, 1981-84; mem. sch. bd. Avoca Sch. Dist. 37, 1985-87; mem. ALSC Newbery Medal Com., 1991. Editor: Top of the News, 1971-73, Fla. State Library Newsletter, 1967-70, Nor'Easter (North Suburban Library System Newsletter), 1984-88; contbr. articles to profl. jours. Bd. dirs. Child Devel. Assocs. Consortium, 1975-83, Coalition for Children and Youth, 1978-80; mem. exec. bd. NSLS Youth Librs., 1991-93, Episcopal Diocese Chgo. Diocesan Coun., 1988-94, standing com., 1994—, dep. to gen. conv., 1997. Mem. ALA (coun. 1992—), Ill. Libr. Assn., Rotary (Island City chpt., sec.-treas. 1994-96, pres. 1996—), Wilmington C. of C. (bd. dirs. 1996), Beta Phi Mu, Sigma Kappa. Episcopalian. Office: Wilmington Pub Libr 201 S Kankakee St Wilmington IL 60481-1338

ANDERSON, MARY THERESA, investment manager; b. Flushing, N.Y., Mar. 30, 1945; d. William John and Loretta (Lent) Donovan; m. Anders Franklin Anderson, Oct. 4, 1964; children: Krista J., A. Erik. BS magna cum laude, So. Oreg. State Coll., 1981; MBA, Fairleigh Dickinson U., 1996. Dir. sales and mktg. Riverside Conf. Ctr., Grants Pass, Oreg., 1981-82; sales mgr. Ashland (Oreg.) Hills Inn, 1982-84; fin. cons. Prudential Ins. Co., Portland, Oreg., 1984-87; investment counselor Vancouver (Wash.) Fed. Savs. Bank, 1987-89; fin. svcs. counselor United Brokerage Svcs. Inc., Lawrenceville, N.J., 1990; fin. svcs. assoc. United Jersey Bank, Hackensack, N.J., 1990-92, asst. v.p., mgr., 1992—; cons. Pegnato Cons. Group Internat., Nutley, N.J., 1993—. Vol. Josephine County Welfare Office, Grants Pass. Named Most Valuable Producer Mktg. One Inc., 1988. Mem. NAFE, Nat. Life Underwriters Assn.

ANDERSON, MELISSA JANE, business consultant; b. Brockton, Mass., July 2, 1958; d. Robert Henning and Judith Ann (Capen) A.; m. Alex Michael Santoski Jr., Oct. 17, 1987; children: Laura Catherine, David Michael. Diploma from ministry of higher edn., Pushkin Inst. of Russian Lang., Moscow, 1978; BA, Middlebury (Vt.) Coll., 1980; MBA, U. Mich., 1986. Paralegal specialist U.S. Dept. of Labor, Washington, 1980-84; market analyst Internat. Resource Network, Inc., Grand Rapids, Mich., 1986-88, dir. rsch., 1988-92, v.p., 1992—. Contbg. editor (monthly column) Inside Automotives mag., 1995—. Mem. AAUW (br. membership v.p. 1990-95, ednl. found. honoree 1995, co-pres. 1996), Soc. Competitive Intelligent Profls., Phi Beta Kappa, Beta Gamma Sigma, Dobro Slovo. Home: 1581 Laraway Lake Dr SE Grand Rapids MI 49546

ANDERSON, NANCY ELAINE, home economics educator; b. Chgo., Feb. 11, 1941; d. Ralph Daniel and Ruth Louise (Johanson) A. BS, So. Ill. U., 1963; postgrad., Mich. State U., 1966-67; Cert. of Advanced Grad. Studies, Am. Internat. Coll., 1994; MEd, Springfield Coll., 1980. Cert. tchr., Mass. Tchr. home econs. and spl. edn. Hennepin (Ill.) Sch., 1963-65; tchr. home econs. East Jordan (Mich.) Sch., 1965-67, Tech. High Sch., Springfield, Mass., 1967-68, Chicopee (Mass.) High Sch., 1968—; tchr. adult edn. Bobbin Shop Fabric Store, South Hadley, Mass., 1982-94. Mem. nat. edn. bd. Covenant Ch. Women's Group, Chgo., 1986-89; mem. edn. bd. Springfield Covenant Ch., 1970-73, mem. mission bd., 1981-87, mem. fin. bd., 1987-90, trustee, 1995—. Mem. NEA, Mass. Edn. Assn., Chicopee Edn. Assn. Home: 113 Fuller Rd Extension Chicopee MA 01020-3726 Office: Chicopee High Sch 650 Front St Chicopee MA 01013-3115

ANDERSON, NANCY MARIE GREENWOOD, special education educator; b. Roanoke, Va., Aug. 19, 1944; d. John Reese and Alice T. (Powell) Greenwood; m. Samuel Edward Anderson, Apr. 30, 1960; children: Sheryl L. Anderson Wicklund, Samuel Edward Jr., Donna M. BS, SUNY, Empire State Coll., Auburn, 1988; postgrad., SUNY, Oswego, 1989-90, SUNY, Geneseo, 1991-93; MS in Reading Edn., SUNY, Oswego, 1996. Cert. spl. edn., elem. tchr. K-6, reading tchr., N.Y. Libr., dir. Wolcott (N.Y.) Civic Free Libr., 1977-89; spl. edn. tchr. North Rose (N.Y.) Wolcott Mid. Sch., 1990-96, North Rose Elem. Sch., 1996—. Mem. Nat. Fedn. Bus. and Profl. Women (chair issues mgmt. 1990), N.Y. State Assn. Tchrs. Handicapped, Rose Bus. and Profl. Womens Club (pres. 1993-95), Oswego Reading Coun., Whole Lang. Tchrs. Assn., Coun. for Exceptional Children. Home: 14640 Lake St Sterling NY 13156-3229 Office: North Rose Elem Sch North Rose NY 14590

ANDERSON, PAULA D.J., pharmacist; b. Yankton, S.D., Nov. 1, 1949; d. Ervin Marion and Ivy Lucille (Christiansen) A. BS in Biology, S.D. State U., Brookings, 1973; MEd, Northeastern Okla. U., Tahlequah, 1977; BS in Pharmacy, S.D. State U., Brookings, 1983; postgrad., U. Colo. Reg. pharmacist Tex., N.Mex., Colo. Pharmacist, store mgr. Revco, Tex. and N.Mex., 1984-92; pharmacist immunizations AIDS, STD, HIV Dept. of Health, Santa Fe, N.Mex., 1993-95; dir. pharmacy Value Rx, Santa Fe, 1995—; mem. sci. adv. bd. Ptnrs. in Rsch., N.Mex.; coord. HIV Pharmacy Bur. of HIV/STD/AIDS Dept. Health, N.Mex.; guest spkr., presenter numerous confs. in field. Pres. NOW (N.Mex. chpt.), Nat. Breast Cancer Coalition. Mem. NAFE, Am. Pharmaceutical Assn., Am. Soc. Health System Pharmacist. Democrat. Home: 1675 Quince Denver CO 80220

ANDERSON, PEGGY REES, accountant; b. Casper, Wyo., Sept. 8, 1958; d. John William and Pauline Marie (Harris) Rees; m. Steven R. Anderson, May 26, 1984 (div. Sept. 1990). BS in Acctg. with honors, U. Wyo., 1980. CPA. Audit staff to sr. Price Waterhouse, Denver, 1980-84; asst. contr. to contr. Am. Investments, Denver, 1984-88; cons. ADI Residential, Denver, 1988-89; contr., treas. Plante Properties, Inc., Denver, 1989-92; acctg. mgr. Woodward-Clyde Group, Inc., Denver, 1992—. Recipient diving scholarship U. Wyo., 1976-77, 77-78. Mem. Colo. Soc. CPAs. Roman Catholic. Office: Woodward-Clyde Group Inc 4582 S Ulster St Ste 600 Denver CO 80237-2635

ANDERSON, PHILLIPA LOIS, lawyer, clothing store owner; b. Charleston, S.C., Sept. 21, 1951; d. Louis Pierce and Sarah Lee (Johnson) A. BA, Newcomb Coll., Tulane U., 1973; JD, George Washington U., 1976. Bar: S.C. 1976. Atty. Westinghouse Hanford Corp., Richland, Wash., 1976-78; contract analyst Westinghouse Electric Corp., Pitts., 1978-80; staff atty. Gen. Svcs. Adminstrn. Bd. Contract Appeals, Washington, 1980-82; sr. trial atty. Office of Gen. Counsel, Dept. Vet. Affairs, Washington, 1982-88, dep. asst. gen. counsel, 1988-95, asst. gen. counsel, 1995—; owner Phillipa's, African-Inspired Fashions, 1991—; lectr. Dept. Justice, Legal Edn. Inst., Washington, 1989—. Featured designer 17th and 18th Ann. Congl. Black Caucus Spouses Fashion Shows, Essence mag. Bd. dirs., treas. D.C.-Dakar Capital Cities Friendship Coun., Washington, 1993—. Mem. ABA (vice chair constrn. claims com. pub. contract law sect. 1994—), Bd. Contract Appeals Bar Assn., Am. Arbitration Assn. (panel of arbitrators 1994—). Democrat. Mem. African Methodist Episcopal Ch. Home: 6213 16th St NW Washington DC 20011-8009 Office: Dept Vets Affairs Office of Gen Counsel 810 Vermont Ave NW Washington DC 20420-0001

ANDERSON, RACHAEL KELLER, library administrator; b. N.Y.C., Jan. 15, 1938; d. Harry and Sarah Keller; 1 child, Rebecca. A.B., Barnard Coll., 1959; M.S., Columbia U., 1960. Librarian CCNY, 1960-62; librarian Mt. Sinai Med. Ctr., N.Y.C., 1964-73, dir. library, 1973-79; dir. Health Scis Libr. Columbia U., N.Y.C., 1979-91, acting v.p., univ. libr., 1982; dir. Ariz. Health Scis. Libr., U. Ariz., Tucson, 1991—; bd. dirs. Med. Libr. Ctr. of N.Y., N.Y.C., 1983-91; mem. biomed. libr. rev. com. Nat. Libr. Medicine, Bethesda, Md., 1984-88, chmn., 1987-88; mem. bd. regents Nat. Libr. Medicine, 1990-94, chmn., 1993-94; pres. Ariz. Health Info. Network, 1995. Contbr. articles to profl. jours. Mem. Med. Libr. Assn. (pres. elect 1996, bd. dirs. 1983-86), Assn. Acad. Health Scis. Libr. Dirs. (bd. dirs. 1983-86, pres. 1991-92). Office: Ariz Health Scis Libr 1501 N Campbell Ave Tucson AZ 85724-0001

ANDERSON, RACHEL LYN, behavior researcher; b. Sacramento, Calif., Apr. 9, 1955; d. Melvin and Regina (Viteri) A.; m. Ralph Everett Dodson, Oct. 19, 1985 (div. July 1990). BA, Calif. State U., Sacramento, 1988. Drug treatment counselor The Effort, Sacramento, 1980-88, Sierra Family Svcs., Roseville, Calif., 1988-89; staff rsch. assoc. U. Calif., Davis, 1989—. Contbr. chpt. to book. Mem. bd. dirs. Harm Reducation Svcs., Sacramento, 1993—, Mending, 1994—; adminstr. Sacramento Area Needle Exchg., 1993—. Mem. APHA. Democrat. Home: 8015 Freeport Blvd Sacramento CA 95832 Office: U Calif Davis Rm 2410 4301 X St Sacramento CA 95817

ANDERSON, RAYLANA SUE, human resources consultant; b. Peoria, Ill., Nov. 27, 1959; d. George Arthur and DeAnn Yvonne (Krebs) A.; m. Robert P. Doyle III, Nov. 27, 1982 (div. Mar. 1985). BA, Bradley U., 1981, MBA, 1988. Cert. employee benefits specialist Internat. Found. Employee enefit Plans and U. Pa. Wharton Sch. Sr. pers. adminstr. RLI Ins. Co., Peoria, 1983-88; dir. employee rels. Customer Devel. Corp., Peoria, 1989-90; human resources cons. McGladrey & Pullen, LLP, Peoria, 1990—, also mgr. cons. svcs., 1993—. Co-author: Americans with Disabilities Act: Complying with the Regulations, 1992, The Family and Medical Leave Act of 1993, 1993, Mandated Benefits: A Practical Guide to Cost-Effective Compliance, 1995. Mem. Peoria Area C. of C. Cmty. Leadership Sch., 1988, 90-94, chmn., 1994; mem. Peoria Fire and Police Commn., 1991—, vice chmn., 1995-96; mem. Ctrl. Ill. Pvt. Industry Coun., 1994—, vice chmn., 1996; bd. dirs. Peoria unit Am. Cancer Soc., 1993—. Recipient Athena award Athena Found.-Peoria Area C. of C., 1994; named One of 40 Leaders under 40, WMBD, 1996. Mem. Soc. for Human Resource Mgmt. (nat. compensation and benefits com. 1994—, chpt. planning com. 1996). Office: McGladrey & Pullen LLP 401 Main St Ste 1200 Peoria IL 61602

ANDERSON, RHONDA VALERIE, home health care coordinator; b. Vansant, Va., May 8, 1962; d. Ronnie Andrew and Myrtle (Rife) Daniels; m. Billy Victor Anderson Jr., Feb. 2, 1985; children: Sara Elizabeth, Rhea Kaye. LPN, Buchanan County Sch., 1983; student, East Tenn. State U., 1983-84; ADN, S.W. Va. C.C., 1992. RN, Va.; BLS. Nursing asst. pvt. practice pediatrics office, Grundy, Va., 1982, pvt. practice obstetrics office, Grundy, 1982-83; LPN pvt. practice physician's office, Grundy, 1984; LPN Buchanan Gen. Hosp., Grundy, 1983, 84-86, LPN obstetrics unit, 1987, charge nurse, 1990-91, oncology nurse coord., 1992-96; staff nurse Buchanan Gen. Hosp. Home Health Agy., Grundy, 1991-92, oncology nurse coord., 1992-96; substitute instr. Buchanan County Sch. Practical Nursing, 1996—; patient care coord. Total Home Care, Med. Svcs. Am., Richlands, Va., 1996—; established only nurse-model outpatient oncology dept. in rural S.W. Va.; presenter in field; mem. adv. bd. Women's Health Coalition on Breast and Cervical Cancer, Grundy, 1994—. Mem. Am. Cancer Soc., Oncology Nursing Soc. Mem. Ch. of Christ. Office: Total Home Care PO Box 937 Richlands VA 24641

ANDERSON, ROBERTA JUNE, computer engineer; b. Widen, W.Va., Mar. 13, 1938; d. Virgil Arthur and Fanny Rebecca (Frame) Davis; m. William Douglas Anderson, Dec. 23, 1956 (div. 1981); children: Gaya Lynne Anderson Harriman, William Michael; m. Lewis Edward Boyle, Feb. 5, 1983; stepchildren: Rhonda Boyle Nelson, Brian Edward. BS in Math., Old Dominion U., 1973, MS in Math. Edn., 1979. Assoc. systems engr. Comptek Rsch. Inc., Virginia Beach, Va., 1979-80; systems analyst Sperry-Univac, Virginia Beach, 1980-84; computer programmer/analyst USAF, Langley, Va., 1984; instr. Tidewater C.C., Virginia Beach, 1984-85; sr. computer scientist Computer Scis. Corp., King George, Va., 1985-90; sr. program engr. Syscon Corp., Dahlgren, Va., 1990-94; prin. engr. Planning Cons. Inc., Dahlgren, 1994—; adj. instr. Germanna C.C., Locust Grove, Va., 1991—, Tidewater C.C., 1981-84; tchr. Chesapeake (Va.) Pub. Schs., 1976-79, Virginia Beach Pub. Schs., 1973-76. Home: 5 Pawnee Dr Fredericksburg VA 22401

ANDERSON, ROCHELLE LOUISE, clinical psychologist; b. Washington, May 16, 1964; d. Joseph Edward and Anne Rene Anderson. BS in Psychology, U. Md., 1986; MA in Psychology, SUNY, Stony Brook, 1988, PhD in Psychology, 1994. Lic. psychologist, Pa. Staff psychologist Bronx (N.Y.) Mcpl. Hosp., 1992-95, North Phila. Health Sys., 1995—. Contbr. articles to profl. jours. Mem. APA, Assn. for Advancement Behavior Therapy.

ANDERSON, RUTH CARRINGTON, retired secondary education educator; b. Lake Hopatcong, N.J., Jan. 7, 1915; d. Harry Porter and Mary Lamberetta (Cook) Carrington; m. Lee Silas Anderson, Nov. 9, 1942 (dec. Dec. 1972); children: Lawrence Lee, Lynette G. Anderson Esposito, Leslie Carl. BA in English, Iowa State Tchrs. Coll., 1938; MS in Edn. and English, Western Ill. U., 1970; postgrad., U. Iowa, 1954, U. Ill., 1958. Cert. elem. tchr., Ill. Tchr. rural schs. Henry County, Ill., 1933-36; jr. high sch. tchr. Woodhull (Ill.) Grade Sch., 1936-42; interviewer U.S. Employment Svc., Galesburg, Ill., 1942-44; English, lit. and govt. tchr. Geneseo (Ill.) Jr. High Sch., 1952-76; ret., 1976; speaker in field; sr. svcs. planning com. Hammond Henry Hosp., Geneseo, Ill., 1992-93; co-chmn. tchr. welfare com. Geneseo Community Unit Dist. 228, 1975-76. Mem. Western Ill. Sr. Advocacy Coun., Kewanee, Ill., 1988-94, Rock Island Sr. Coun., 1988-94, Henry County Farm Bur.; pres Henry County Sr. Advocacy Coun., Geneseo, 1987-94, chmn. pub. info. meetings and programs, 1987-94, moderator Ill. legis. candidate forum, 1992; sec.-treas. Andover, Ill. Sr. Citizens, 1989—; mem. Henry County Sr. Citizens Bd., Kewanee, 1993—; del. to Ill. Conf. on Aging, Springfield, 1990; bd. dirs. Augustana Luth. Ch., Andover, 1989-95, chmn. congl. learning com.; edn. chmn. Augustana Luth. Ch. Women, 1985, mem. peace circle, 1965—; pianist United Meth. Ch., Woodhull, 1931-42; active Evang. Luth. Ch. Women. Mem. DAR, Ill. Ret. Tchrs. Assn. (life, legis. com. 1989-92), Am. Assn. Ret. Persons, Nat. Ret. Tchrs. Assn., Andover Hist. Assn. (life), Am. Legion Aux. (1st v.p. 1979—, pres. 1976-79), U. No. Iowa Alumni Assn., We. Ill. U. Alumni Assn., Kappa Delta Pi, Sigma Tau Delta. Home: PO Box 137 507 5th St Andover IL 61233-0137

ANDERSON, RUTH GRATHWOHL, education educator; b. Cin., Oct. 22, 1937; d. George August and Catherine Cecilia (Pucke) G.; m. William Thomas Anderson, Sept. 1, 1978. BS, U. Dayton, 1959; MA, NYU, 1969; PhD, Tex. Woman's U., 1987. Lic. profl. counselor, Tex., lic. marriage and family counselor, Tex.; nat. counselor cert. Counselor Tex. Woman's U., Denton, 1987-89, prof., 1989—. Contbg. author: (book) Play Therapy in Action, 1993; contbr. articles to profl. jours. Grantee Tex. Woman's U., 1993, 95. Mem. ACA, Tex. Counseling Assn., Tex. Assn. Counselor Educators and Supervisors, Am. Assn. Marriage and Family Therapists, Nat. Assn. Play Therapists.

ANDERSON, SHARON ANNE, gas company executive, auditing manager; d. DeWayne C. and Edith (Walker) A. BSBA, U. Tulsa, 1977. CPA, Okla. With Okla. Natural Gas Co., Tulsa, 1965—, asst. mgr. corp. responsibility and community affairs, 1979-80, asst. mgr. fin. reporting, 1980-83, mgr. fin. reporting, 1983-96, mgr. auditing, 1996—. Mem. Skiatook Reservoir Authority, Tulsa, 1980-84. Mem. AICPA, Okla. Soc. CPA's, LWV (pres. Met. Tulsa chpt. 1991-92, treas. Okla. 1990-93), Toastmasters. Office: Okla Natural Gas Co 100 W 5th St Tulsa OK 74103-4240

ANDERSON, SHARON KAY, special education educator; b. Cookeville, Tenn., Apr. 6, 1959; d. Henry Harlie and Ruby Neil (Gunnels) A. BS in History, Tenn.. Tech. U., 1982. Cert. secondary social studies, secondary history, Tenn. Tchr. Bowman (S.C.) H.S., 1983-84, Bennett Mid. Sch., Orangeburg, S.C., 1984-86, Orangeburg-Wilkinson H.S., Orangeburg, 1986—; coord. artistically gifted program Orangeburg Dist. 5, 1989—. REACH grantee Rockefeller Found./CHART, 1989-94. Mem. NEA, Nat. Coun. for Social Studies, Alpha Zeta chpt. Alpha Delta Kappa (historian 1990-92, pres.-elect 1992-94, pres. 1994-96). Home: 690 Webster St NE Orangeburg SC 29115-4856 Office: Orangeburg-Wilkinson H S 601 Bruin Pky Orangeburg SC 29115-1460

ANDERSON, SHARON LYNN, food technologist; b. Ft. Worth, Dec. 27, 1964; d. Johnnie Victor Langley and Julia Isabell (Turney) Jarmusz; m. Robert Laurence Anderson, Mar. 31, 1984; children: Brittany Dane, William Robert (dec.), Morgen Shay. Student, Tarrant County Jr. Coll., Ft. Worth, 1984, Am. Inst. Baking, 1995—. Receptionist, clk. Indsl. Accident Bd., Liberty Mut. Ins., Ft. Worth, 1982-87; product acct. Assoc. Milk Producers Inc., Sulphur Springs, Tex., 1987-93; ops. and freight coord. Kohler Mix Spltys., Sulphur Springs, office mgr., safety coord., quality control mgr., 1993—. Mem. NAFE, Am. Tae Kwon Do Assn. (red belt). Methodist. Home: Rt 1 Box 142 Como TX 75431

ANDERSON, SUSAN STUEBING, business equipment company executive; b. Cin., Nov. 7, 1951; d. Edward Norman and Ruth Marcella Stuebing; m. Randall Anderson, 1988. B.A., Western Ky. U., 1973, M.A., 1975. Legis. aide U.S. Ho. of Reps., 1975-80; legis. cons. Harvard U., 1981; spl. asst. Nat. Telecommunications and Info. Adminstrn.-U.S. Dept. Commerce, Washington, 1981, dept. asst. sec., 1982-85, acting asst. sec. for communications and info., 1983; dir. Computer and Bus. Equipment Mfrs. Assn., Washington, 1985-86; mgr. govt. affairs Xerox Corp., Washington, 1987-92; mgr. Office of the Corp. Sec., Stamford, Conn., 1992—; U.S. rep. Gen. Assembley-Atlantic Treaty Assn., Funchal, Madeira, 1980. Presbyterian. Office: Xerox Corp 800 Long Ridge Rd Stamford CT 06902-1227

ANDERSON, TYRA JAYDE, occupational therapist; b. Lubbock, Tex., June 9, 1955; d. Jack Edward and Josephine Adele Tayerle Krisle. AS, Richland C.C., Richardson, Tex., 1975; BS in Occupl. Therapy, Tex. Woman's U., 1984. Lic. occupl. therapist, Tex. Staff occupl. therapist Presbyn. Hosp. of Dallas, 1984-85, Vis. Nurse Assn. Kaufman County, Kaufman, Tex., 1985-86, 88-92; owner, therapist Functional Rehab. Svcs., Kaufman, 1986-88; dir. occupl. therapy Rehab. Assocs. of N.E. Tex., Greenville, 1992—; cons. Stroke Support Group, Terrell, Tex., 1990-92, Terrell Cmty. Hosp., 1990-92; contract cons. various home health agencies, 1988. Vol. Soc. for Prevention of Cruelty to Animals, Dallas, 1995—, Meals on Wheels, Dallas, 1988—, Chance Ctr., Dallas, 1989-90; mem. Am. Soc. Prevention of Cruelty to Animals, Washington, 1995—, People for Ethical Treatment of Animals, Washington, 1995—. Mem. Am. Occupl. Therapy Assn., Pi Theta Epsilon. Episcopalian. Office: Rehab Assocs of NE Texas 2824 Terrell Rd #106 Greenville TX 75402

ANDERSON, VIOLET HENSON, artist, educator; b. June 8, 1931; m. Charles A. Anderson, 1953. Grad., U. Tenn., Knoxville. Tchr. art Oak Ridge (Tenn.) Sch. System, 1953-54, Andrew Jackson Elem. Sch., Nashville, 1969-79; originator, dir. Andrew Jackson Art Show, Old Hickory, Tenn., 1972-79. One-woman shows include Nashville Bd. Edn., 1972, Cookeville (Tenn.) Art Ctr., 1972, Tenn. Art Gallery, 1983, 88, Brentwood (Tenn.) Libr., 1991; exhibited in group shows at Falls Creek Falls State Park, Tenn., 1984, 86, Castner Knott Art Festival, Nashville, 1983-89, 90, Downtown Arts Gallery, Nashville, 1989, Dogwood Art Festival, Knoxville, 1993, 94, 95, Summer Lights Art Festival, Nashville, 1989, 92, 93, 94; also 1928 paintings and prints in pvt. and pub. collections in 38 states and 9 fgn. countries; work featured in Nashville Banner, Chattanooga Free Press, Knoxville News Sentinel, others. Named Golden Poet, World of Poetry, 1989-92; included in Best Poems of 90s and Disting. Poets of Am., 1993 Nat. Libr. Poetry, Best Poems of 95, Nat. Libr. Poetry, 1996 Best Poems. Mem. Tenn. Watercolor Soc., Tenn. Art League (past officer), Friends of Tenn. Art League (bd. dirs., 1st v.p.), Cumberland Art Soc., Tenn. Artists Assn., Artists Guild, Hendersonville, Nat. Women's Caucus for Art, Mid. Tenn. Com., Nat. Mus. of Women in the Arts (charter mem., slides and photos in libr. archives), Knoxville Arts Coun., Donelson-Hermitage C. of C., Stones River Woman's Club, Internat. Soc. Poets (charter mem.), Delta Zeta (past province alumnae dir.), Alpha Delta Kappa.

ANDERSON, VIRGINIA HOMEIER, special education administrator; b. Detroit, Dec. 4, 1938; d. George Armstrong Custer and Myrtle Anne (Sandstrom) Homeier; m. Robert Allen Anderson, Nov. 16, 1957; children: David Paul, Daniel Edward, Kathryn Anderson Porterfield, Christine Anderson Carlson, Erika Anderson Harris. BSEd, Portland State U., 1968, MSEd, 1971, EdD, 1990. Cert. sch. adminstr., Oreg. Tchr. Portland (Oreg.) Sch. Dist. # 3, 1968-75, coord. gifted and talented, 1975-78, bldg. prin., 1976-81, spl. edn. adminstr., 1981-84, assessment dir., 1985-90, student svcs. dir., 1990—; edn. cons., Pacific N.W.; bd. dirs. OACOA, Oreg. Contbr. articles to profl. jours. Citizen advisor Portland Police Bur., 1993-95; chmn. health and welfare com. Portland First United Meth. Ch., 1995-97. Ann Leu scholar Portland State U., 1988, Ea. Star scholar, 1968, others. Mem. Coun. for Exceptional Children, Am. Edn. Rsch. Assn., Assn. for Suprs. and Curriculum, Phi Delta Kappa. Republican. Office: Portland Sch Dist 10636 NE Prescott Portland OR 97220

ANDERSON, YASMIN LYNN MULLIS, educational consultant, small business owner; b. Roanoke, Va., Oct. 5, 1953; d. Lonnie Cecil Jr. and Sarah Frances (Cunningham) Mullis; m. Jerry Doyle Anderson, Mar. 1, 1991; 1 child from previous marriage, R. Allen. BS in Edn., U Tenn., 1975, postgrad., 1989-90, 93. Employment counselor State Dept. Employment Security, Knoxville, Tenn., 1975-79; GED instr. Loudon (Tenn.) County Schs., 1979-81; edn. specialist Tenn. Valley Authority, Knoxville, 1979-94; pvt. practice Knoxville, 1991—; ednl. cons. Acad. Innovations, Santa Barbara, Calif., 1991—; edn. specialist Inclusion for All Children Task Force, Nashville, 1992—; advisor tech./Prep. Consortium, Tenn., 1993—; presenter in field; sr. cons. Mary Kay Cosmetics. Mem. ASCD, AAUW, Am. Vocat. Assn. (presenter). Baptist. Home and Office: 1236 Lovell View Dr Knoxville TN 37932-2591

ANDERSON-CERMIN, CHERYL KAY, orthodontics educator; b. Osceola, Wis., Aug. 28, 1956; d. Darrell Duane and Barbara Carolyn (Paulson) Peterson; m. Paul Bradley Anderson, Aug. 12, 1978 (div. June 1986); m. Jonathan A. Cermin, Dec. 31, 1995; 1 child, Hayley Kristine. AA, Normandale C.C., Bloomington, Minn., 1977; BS, U. Minn., 1985, DDS, 1986; cert. in advanced grad. studies, Boston U., 1990. Intern Sch. Dental Medicine Harvard U., Boston, 1986-87; pvt. practice, Boston, 1988-90; rsch. fellow U. Tex. S.W. Med. Sch., Dallas, 1990-91, asst. prof. orthodontics, dir. orthodontics, 1991—. Bd. dirs. Life Enhancement for People, Dallas, 1993-94; sec. ch. coun. Shepherd of Life Luth. Ch., Arlington, Tex., 1993-94. Mem. ADA, Am. Assn. Orthodontists, Am. Cleft Palate Assn.

ANDERSON-MANN, SHELLEY N., institutional review specialist; b. Cleve., Jan. 21, 1964; d. William Henry and Frances Louise (Anderson) Mann. AS in Computer Sci., El Centro, 1990, AA in Acctg., 1990; BS in Sociology, Paul Quinn Coll., 1992, BSBA, 1992; MSI in Interdisciplinary Study, Dallas Bapt. U.-U. Tex., Arlington, 1993. Youth supr. City of Dallas Park and Recreation, 1979-87; instnl. rev. officer U.S. Dept. Edn., 1979-87; acct. asst. Dallas County Sheriff Adult Probation Dept., Dallas, 1984-89; claims asst. Social Security Adminstrn., Dallas, 1989—; founder Shelley Anderson-Mann Computer Ctr., Paul Quinn Coll., 1992; exec. dir. Shelley's Enterprises, Inc.; founder, pres. Grant Me the Freedom Domestic Violence Rape Recovery Tng. Unit, Let's Make it Safe, In my Brother's House, Helping Hands Found., Lancaster, Tex. Author: DQB Procedural Manual, 1991 (Yes award 1991), EPA Archive Manual, 1991 (Promotion award 1991). Mem. exec. bd., vol. City of Dallas Parks and Recreation; vol. Youth Village Criminal Justice, Dallas Ind. Sch. Dist., Dallas County Juvenile Assn., Youth in Action, Dallas. Recipient commendation Dallas Police Dept., 1988, Dept. of Treasury, 1988, award City of Dallas Vol. of the Dallas, 1989, Am. Disting. Women, 1990, Bronze medal for gymnastics, Admired Women of Decade award, 1996-97. Mem. NAFE, NOW, Am. Mgmt. Assn. (1st place 1991), Nat. Coun. Colored Women, Nat. Assn. Negro Women, Liberty U. Charter, Student Free Enterprise (1st place 1991), Distributive Edn. Club (1st place 1991), Internat. Platform Assn., Grant Me the Freedom Let's Make It Safe in My Brother's Place Helping Hand Found. (founder). Democrat. Baptist. Home: PO Box 41247 Dallas TX 75241-0247

ANDERT-SCHMIDT, DARLENE, management consultant and trainer. BA in Bus. Mgmt. and Communications, Alverno Coll., Milw., 1983; M in Adminstrn., Cen. Mich. U., 1993. Cert. fin. mgr.; cert. mgmt. cons. Pres., owner Dance in Exercise, Inc., Milw., 1980-85; security sales Prudential Bache and The Equitable, Milw., 1985-86; stockbroker Merrill Lynch, Ft. Myers, Fla., 1986-89; trainer, cons. Bus. & Industry Svcs., Ft. Myers, 1989; pres. mgmt. Concepts Mgmt., Cape Coral, Fla., 1989—; pres. mgmt. Concepts Mgmt., Cape Coral, Fla. Author: Diversity at Work, 1994. Trustee Lee County Electric Coop., Inc., 1994—. Mem. ASTD, Inst. Mgmt. Cons. (cert.). Office: PO Box 150904 Cape Coral FL 33915-0904

ANDRAU, MAYA HEDDA, physical therapist; b. Digboi, Assam, India, Apr. 15, 1936; came to U.S., 1946; d. William Henry and Klara Irén Judit (Sima) Andrau; married, Sept. 1971 (div. July 1989); children: Francis Meher Traver, Darwin Meher Traver. BS in Phys. Therapy, Columbia U., 1958; MA in Social Anthropology, NYU, 1966. Lamaze cert. childbirth educator; lic. and registered phys. therapist. Phy. therapist Beekman-Downtown Hosp., N.Y.C., 1959-60; physiotherapist Stamford (Conn.) Hosp., 1963-64, Benedictine Hosp., Kingston, N.Y., 1966-69; pvt. practice in phys. therapy and lamaze Woodstock, N.Y., 1968-71; chief phy. therapist No. Duchess Hosp., Rhinebeck, N.Y., 1970-71; phy. therapist Waccamaw Pub. Health Dist., S.C. Dept. Health, Myrtle Beach, 1982-84; pain clinic specialist Pain Therapy Ctr. of Columbia (S.C.), Richland Meml. Hosp., 1986-87; phy. therapist Comprehensive Med. Rehab. Ctr., Conway, S.C., 1988-92; phys. therapist, instr. conditioning program Pawleys Island (S.C.) Wellness Inst., 1993; phys. therapist Total Care, Inc., 1993—; instr. phys. conditioning and therapeutic exercise courses, 1980—. Instr. Conditioning Program, Health Focus Brief for TV, 1990. Mem. Meher Spiritual Ctr., Inc., Alpha Kappa Delta. Follower of Avatar Meher Baba.

ANDREA, ELMA WILLIAMS, retail executive; b. Carroll County, Va.; d. Preston and Macy (Goad) Williams; m. Mario I. Andrea, Nov. 29, 1986; AB with spl. honors, George Washington U., 1953; MA in Public Adminstrn., Am. U., 1961. Asst. program dir., asst. dir. ops. WTOP, CBS-Radio and TV, 1947-51; mem. pub. relations staff George Washington U., 1951-52; registrar Washington Sch. for Secs., 1953; exec. sec. Joint Econ. Com. of U.S. Congress, 1956-59; legis. info. specialist NEA, Washington, 1960-84; asst. mgr. Gem Tree Jewelry Store, Bethesda, Md., 1984—. Bd. dirs. Edn. Assocs. Fed. Credit Union, 1973-83, pres., 1975-77; bd. dirs. Met. Area Credit Union Mgmt. Assn., 1977-82, sec., 1977-82; bd. dirs. Kenwood Beach (Md.) Citizens Assn., 1981-84. Recipient Alumni Service award George Washington U., 1970. Mem. AAUW (br. publicity chmn. 1956-59), NEA (life), Columbian Women George Washington U. (pres. 1965-67), George Washington U. Alumni Assn. (dir. 1965-67, 69-70), Edn. Writers Assn., The Jamestowne Soc., DAR, Gemological Inst. Am., Women's Joint Congl. Com. (chmn. 1974-76), Am. News Women's Club, Twentieth Century Club, Nat. Woman's Party, Md. Free State Doll Study Club (v.p. 1993-94, pres. 1995—), United Fedn. Doll Clubs, Phi Delta Gamma (chpt. pres. 1973-74, nat. conv. chmn. 1980, nat. treas. 1980-84, nat. pres. 1984-86, trustee 1980-86, nat. bylaws 1986-92), Pi Sigma Alpha. Address: 11 Bel Tramonto White Sands MD 20657

ANDREAE, CHRISTINE EWING, author; b. Stamford, Conn., July 13, 1942; d. William and Mary (Challinor) Ewing; m. Frederick Shedd Andreae, Aug. 19, 1967; children: Morgan MacKenzie, Timothy Ewing. BA, Manhattanville Coll., 1964; MAT, Yale U., 1967. Author: (novels) Trail of

Murder, 1992, Grizzly, 1994, A Small Target, 1996, (non-fiction) Seances and Spiritualists, 1974, One Woman's Death, 1996. Bd. dirs. Blue Ridge Hospice, 1989-95, vol., 1990—. Recipient Founder's award Blue Ridge Hospice, 1994. Mem. Mystery Writers Am., Sisters in Crime, Internat. Assn. Crime Writers, Women Writing the West.

ANDREAS, CAROL, sociologist, educator; b. Newton, kans., Nov. 10, 1933; d. Willis Everett and Hulda Suzanne (Penner) Rich; m. Carl Andreas, May 1951 (div. Aug. 1971); children: Joel, Ronald, Peter. BA, Bethel Coll., 1953; MA, U. Minn., 1954; PhD, Wayne State U., 1967. Instr. Oakland Cmty. Coll., 1971-72; hon. lectr. U. Colo., 1981-84; prof. sociology U. No. Colo., Greeley, 1988-94; prof. emeritus sociology U. No. Colo., Greeley, Can., 1994—; journalist Nat. U. Ctrl. Peru, Huancayo, 1973—; prof. emeritus sociology U. No. Colo., Greeley, 1994—; vis. prof. U. Nacional del Centro del Peru, 1974-75; adj. assoc. prof. U. Colo., 1981-84; vis. assoc. prof. Ea. Washington U., 1985; Disting. prof. Simon Fraser U., Vancouver, B.C., Can., 1989. Author: Sex and Caste in America, 1971, Nothing Is AsIt Should Be, 1976, When Women Rebel, 1985, Meatpackers and Beef Barons, 1994. Activist Anti-War Movement, Vietnam and U.S., Women's Movements, U.S. and L.Am., Farmworkers' Unions, Labor and Civil Rights. Mem. Union of Radical Sociologists (founder, jour. The Insurgent Sociologist). Home: 131 S Sherwood St Fort Collins CO 80521

ANDREASEN, NANCY COOVER, psychiatrist, educator; d. John A. Sr. and Pauline G. Coover; children: Robin, Susan. BA summa cum laude, U. Nebr., 1958, PhD, 1963; MA, Radcliffe Coll., 1959; MD, U. Iowa, 1970. Instr. English Nebr. Wesleyan Coll., 1960-61, U. Nebr., Lincoln, 1962-63; asst. prof. English U. Iowa, Iowa City, 1963-66; resident U. Iowa, 1970-73; asst. prof. psychiatry U. Iowa, Iowa City, 1973-77, assoc. prof., 1977-81, Andrew H. Woods prof. psychiatry, 1981—, dir. Mental Health Clin. Rsch. Ctr., 1987—; sr. cons. Northwick Pk. Hosp., London, 1983; acad. visitor Maudsley Hosp., London, 1986. Author: The Broken Brain, 1984, Introductory Psychiatry Textbook, 1991; editor: Can Schizophrenia be Localized to the Brain?, 1986, Brain Imaging: Applications in Psychiatry, 1988; book forum editor: Am. Jour. Psychiatry, 1988—, dep. editor, 1989-93, editor, 1993—. Woodrow Wilson fellow, 1958-59, Fulbright fellow Oxford U., London, 1959-60. Fellow Royal Coll. Physicians Surgeons Can. (hon.), Am. Psychiat. Assn., Am. Coll. Neuropharmacologists; mem. Am. Psychopathol. Assn. (pres. 1989-90), Inst. of Medicine of NAS. Office: U Iowa Hosps & Clinics 200 Hawkins Dr Iowa City IA 52242-1009

ANDREASON, SHARON LEE, sculptor; b. Lebanon, Oreg., Mar. 20, 1937; d. LeRoy and Galdys Edwina (Wells) A.; m. Raymond Locke Eller, Aug. 30, 1957 (div. 1981); 1 child, Jordan Lee; m. Stoddard Pintard Johnston, Dec. 21, 1985; children: Bruce, Azile, John. Student Art, Pierce Jr. Coll., Canoga Park, Calif., 1963-65, Santa Barbara City Coll., Calif., 1980, UCLA, 1983. Lic. real estate broker, Calif. Performing artist Screen Extras Guild, Hollywood, Calif., 1962-70; profl. artist pvt. practice, Carmel, Calif., 1971—. Sculptor: solo shows include Pacific Grove Art Ctr., 1984—, Zantman Art Gallery, Carmel, 1989, Highlands Sculpture Gallery, Carmel, 1991, 92, 93, Galeria Brisamar, Marbella, Spain, 1993, Mack Galleries, Seattle, 1993, Smith Cosby Gallery, Carmel, Silver Light Gallery, Carmel, 1996; group exhbns. include Monterey County (Calif.) Mus. Art, 1984, Am. Acad. Equine Art, Ky. Horse Park, Lexington, 1993, 94, 95, Galeria Brisamar, Marbella, 1995, Galeria Sculpture, Paris, 1995, 96, Signature Gallery, Del Mar, Calif., 1995, Signature Gallery, San Diego, 1995, Galeria Iris Ryman, Marbella, 1996, Nova Galeria De Arte, Milaga, Spain, 1996, Ky. Derby Mus., Louisville, 1996; some of her works are reproduced in bronze and sold for pvt. and pub. collections; represented in collections internationally. Pres., founder Horse Power Internat., Inc., 1991; founder Horse Power Sanctuaries, Inc.; founder Horse Power Protection Projects, Inc., 1991—, pres. currently; authored horse protection legislation Monterey, Calif., 1993-94. Recipient Gwendolyn May award, Monterey County SPCA, Monterey, Calif., 1994. Mem. Artists Equity, Am. Acad. Equinine Artists, Women's Mus. of Art, Soc. for Prevention of Cruelty to Animals (mem. Monterey County aux.), Conv. on the Welfare and Protection of Animals in Transit (N.Am. Free Trade Agreement animal legis. group), Internat. Sculpture Ctr., Pacific Rim Sculptors Group, Monterey Peninsula Mus. of Art. Studio: PO Box 998 Carmel CA 93921

ANDREEN, AVIVA LOUISE, academic administrator, educator; b. Frankfurt, Fed. Republic of Germany, Jan. 6, 1952; d. Robert Benjamin Andreen and Margie Corinne (LaPointe) Marshall; m. Merrill R. Penn, Nov. 8, 1987 (div.); children: Robert Morton Salkin and Elizabeth Aliza Penn. BA, NYU, 1975; DDS, NYU Coll. Dentistry, 1996; postgrad., Laser Inst. Am., 1980; AS, Westchester C.C., 1992. Cert. mobile laser operator, N.Y. Tchr. Kibbutz Regavim, D.N. Menasche, Israel, 1975-76; account rep. Traveler's Ins. Co., N.Y.C., 1976; spl. projects coordinator Sapan Engring. Co., N.Y.C., 1976-78; sec., treas. founder J. Sapan Holographic Studios, N.Y.C., 1979; owner, pres. Universal Media Cons., White Plains, N.Y., 1980-84; dir. edn., owner Am. Ctr. for Laser Edn., Bronx, N.Y., 1984—; pres. Penn Laser Systems Inc., 1994—; lectr. Hudson River Mus., Yonkers, N.Y., 1986-87; producer laser light show, Andrus Planetarium; taught 1st laser safety course in Am. high sch., 1980; designed laser safety course for Westchester C.C., 1992. Curator Holography A New Dimension White Plains Mus. Gallery, Hudson River Mus., Yonkers, Troster Hall Sci. Mem. Am. Student Dental Assn., Internat. Soc. Optical Engring., Acad. Gen. Dentistrey, Van Courtland Park Jewish Ctr., Alpha Omega. Office: Am Ctr Laser Edn 3835 Sedgwick Ave Bronx NY 10463-4452

ANDRESS, CATHY, psychologist, educator; b. Akron, Ohio, June 17, 1960; d. Samuel Coe and Joan (Ferguson) A. BA, Randolph-Macon Woman's Coll., 1982; MA, So. Ill. U., Edwardsville, 1985; PsyD, Chgo. Sch. Profl. Psychology, 1991. Child and family therapist No. Wyo. Mental Health Ctr., Newcastle, 1988-89; sr. therapist Tri-City Community Mental Health Ctr., East Chicago, Ind., 1990; part-time instr. Oakton C.C., Des Plaines, Ill., 1989-91, adj. counselor, 1991; part-time instr. Northeastern Ill. Univ., Chgo., 1990-91; instr. psychology Big Bend C.C., Moses Lake, Wash., 1991—. Mem. NEA, Assn. for Humanistic Psychology, Assn. for Transpersonal Psychology, Wash. Edn. Assn. (mem. minority affairs commn. 1992-96, mem. woman's caucus steering com. 1995—), Wash. State Psychol. Assn. Office: Big Bend CC 7662 Chanute St NE Moses Lake WA 98837-3293

ANDRESS, CYNTHIA GAYLE, school administrator; b. Oklahoma City, Nov. 23, 1962; d. David Arthur and Linda Jean (Yount) Carroll; m. Vance Corbet Andress, Feb. 12, 1988; children: Regan Courtney, Timothy Trey. BS, East Ctrl. U., Ada, Okla., 1985; MEd, Baylor U., 1988. Cert. tchr. elem., spl. edn., adminstrn. Tchr. Killeen (Tex.) Ind. Sch. Dist., 1985-90, behavior specialist, 1985-90; tchr. Mesquite (Tex.) Ind. Sch. Dist., 1990—; asst. prin. Wilkinson Mid. Sch., Mesquite, 1994—. Mem. ASCD, Nat. Mid. Sch. Adminstrs., Tex. Mid. Sch. Assn., Assn. Tex. Profl. Educators. Office: Wilkinson Middle Sch 2100 Crest Park Dr Mesquite TX 75149-1507

ANDRESS, LUCRETIA ANN KING, health care exectutive; b. Durham, N.C., May 10, 1942; d. James Thomas and Gladys Virginia (Burgamy) King; m. Wayne Edward Andress, Aug. 26, 1961 (div. June 1979); children: Kevin Edward Andress, Jason Thomas Andress. BSBA, Tampa Coll., 1994. Br. mgr. Trust Co. Bank, Atlanta, 1974-81; dir. lending coord. Barnett Bank of Polk County, Fla., 1981-89; br. mgr. First Fla. Bank, Polk County, 1989-91; mktg. dir. Olsten Healthcare Svcs., Lakeland, Fla., 1991-93; field devel. rep. First Am. Home Care, Winter Haven, Fla., 1994—; bd. dir. Polk County Assn. for Handicapped Citizens, Inc., Lakeland, Olsten Healthcare, Lakeland. Bd. dirs. Am. Heart Assn., Lakeland, Ret. Sr. Vol. Program, Lakeland, Spouse Abuse Coun., Polk County, Resource Ctr. for Women, Polk County; mem. Polk Hardy Highland AIDS Svc. and Edn., client svcs. com.; mem. Polk County Aging Svcs., Polk County Cmty. Svcs. Coun., United Way of Ctrl. Fla., Sr. Orphans of Polk County; host task force Lakeland Ch., of Commerce. Recipient Membership award United Way of Ctrl. Fla., 1991. Mem. Sertoma, C. of C., Winter Haven C. of C. (amb.). Democrat. Episcopalian. Home: 865 S Oakwood Loop Bartow FL 33830-7042

ANDREW, DOLORES MOLCAN, artist, educator; b. Corning, N.Y., July 11, 1928; d. Ferdinand Joseph and Evelyn Mae (Marnin) Molcan; m. R. Hugh Andrew, June 12, 1954; children: Julia, Douglas, Catherine. BFA in Painting, Syracuse U., 1951; postgrad., Towson State U., 1975-77; MFA in Art Edn., Md. Inst., 1982. Cert. tchr. embroidery, mixed media. Adult edn. tchr. Columbia (Md.) Assoc., 1971-72; adult edn. tchr. Essex C.C., Balt., 1976-80, from. asst. to assoc. prof. art, 1980—; tchr. Rehoboth Art League, Rehoboth Beach, Del., 1985—, Goucher Coll., Towson, Md., 1990-95; supr. paintings & photography Md. State Fair, Timonium, 1987—; Judge, lectr. in field. Author: Italian Renaissance Textiles, 1986, Medieval Tapestry Designs, 1992, American Sampler Designs, 1996; designer copyrights for crewel designs; exhbns. include Gibson Island, Md., 1993, Garrett C.C., McHenry, Md., 1994, others; contbr. illustrations to Balt. Sun, 1988—. Nat. dir. judging certification Nat. Acad. Needlearts, 1988-94, nat. pres., 1990-94. em. NLAPW (pres. Carroll br. 1976-78, Md. state pres. 1992-94), Artists Equity Assn. (corr. sec. Md. chpt. 1987-92, recording sec. 1987-92), Md. Pastel Soc. (charter, pres. 1985-87), Embroiderers Guild Am. (charter). Democrat. Episcopalian.

ANDREWS, ALICE FRENCH, neonatologist educator; b. Alma, Mich., June 22, 1948; d. Lloyd Henry and Gladys (Schneider) French; m. Charles Andrew Andrews, July 15, 1972; children: Rebecca Kirstin, Kimberly Rose. BA, Messiah Coll., 1970; MD, U. Mich., 1974. Asst. prof. pediatrics U. Mich., Ann Arbor, 1983-85; with staff Macha Hospital, Zambia, 1986-88; neonatologist Blodgett Meml. Med. Ctr., Grand Rapids Neonatology, Grand Rapids, Mich., 1988—. Contbr. articles to profl. jours. Mem. Brethren in Christ Ch. Office: Grand Rapids Neonatology 1840 Wealthy St SE Grand Rapids MI 49506-2921

ANDREWS, BARBARA HARCOURT, retired elementary educator; b. Clintondale, N.Y., May 24, 1934; d. Ralph Palmer and Lillian Sophia (Fowler) H.; m. Adolph Alexander Lanauskas, Sept. 21, 1957 (div. Sept. 1974); m. Louis Peter Andrews, July 9, 1976. BS in Acctg., Rider Coll., 1955; MA in Early Childhood Edn., Kean Coll., 1963. Cert. tchr., N.J. Asst. to treas. Rider Coll., Trenton, 1955-59; educator Manville (N.J.) Pub. Sch., 1959-94; retired, 1994. Trustee, house/ fair clk., pers. clk. Yearly Meeting friends Home, North Plainfield, N.J., 1977—; active PTA, 1959—, life mem., 1978—; treas. Manville Edn. Assn., 1980-92; women in edn. com. N.J. Edn. Assn., Trenton, 1980-95; pres. Ctrl. Jersey Reading Assn., 1974-76; asst. clk. long range conf. planning com. Friends Gen. Conf. Mem. AAUW, Internat. Reading Assn., Somerset County Retired Educators (membership chair 1995—), N.J. Reading Assn., Lambda Alpha Zeta (Rose award 1995). Democrat. Home: 23 Forest Hill Dr Flemington NJ 08822

ANDREWS, BETHLEHEM KOTTES, research chemist; b. New Orleans, Sept. 18, 1936; d. George Leonidas and Anna Mercedes (Russell) Kottes; B.A. with honors in Chemistry, Newcomb Coll., Tulane U., 1957; m. William Edward Andrews, May 9, 1959 (dec.); children—Sharon Leslie, Keith Edward. Chemist wash wear investigation, So. Regional Research Center, Sci. and Edn. Adminstrn., Dept. Agr., New Orleans, 1958-63, research chemist wash wear investigation, cotton textile chemistry lab., 1968-70, research chemist spl. products research, cotton textile chemistry lab., 1976-83, sr. research chemist cotton chem. reactions research, 1983-85, lead scientist textile finishing chemistry research, 1985—; scientist-supr. Grace King High Sch. Lab. Tech. Tng. Program; U.S. del. ISO Meeting on Textiles, 1984—, head U.S. Delegation, 1992. Recipient outstanding professionalism citation New Orleans Fedn. Businessman's Assn., 1977, Disting. Service award in med./sci. category, 1983, named Women of Yr. award in profl. category, 1978; recipient Profl. Excellence award Ita Sigma Pi, 1990, Miles award Cotton Found., 1991, Tech. Transfer award USDA-ARS, 1992; La. Heart Assn. grantee, 1957. Mem. Am. Chem. Soc., Am. Assn. Textile Chemists and Colorists (v.p. 1990, 91, exec. com. on research, Olney medal 1992), Fiber Soc., Phi Beta Kappa, Sigma Xi, Phi Mu. Democrat. Greek Orthodox. Clubs: P.E.O., Southern Yacht. Contbr. chpts. to books, articles to sci. jours.; patentee. Office: So Regional Rsch Ctr 1100 Robert E Lee Blvd New Orleans LA 70124-4305

ANDREWS, DEBORAH CREHAN, English studies educator; b. Hartford, Conn., Sept. 1, 1942; d. Mark J. and Gertrude (Parsons) Crehan; m. William D. Andrews, May 16, 1970; 1child, Christopher S. BA, Middlebury (Vt.) Coll., 1964; MA, U. Wyo., 1965, U. Pa., 1969. Instr. Utah State U., Logan, 1966-68; lectr., instr. Ohio State U., Columbus, 1970-77; asst. prof. Drexel U., Phila., 1977-82; asst. prof. English U. Del., Newark, 1982-85, assoc. prof., 1985-88, prof., 1988—; cons. to various orgns. including Am. Chem. Soc., Sun Refining, Batelle Labs., NSF, Hercules Inc. Co-author: Technical Writing: Principles and Forms, 1978, 2d edit. 1982, Write for Results, 1982, Business Communication, 1988, 2d edit., 1992; editor: (anthology) International Dimensions of Technical Communication, 1996; assoc. editor Tech. Comm., 1992—. Unidel Found. grantee, 1986-89. Mem. Soc. for Tech. Comm. (sr. mem.; pres. Ohio chpt.), Assn. Tchrs. Tech. Writing (exec. com. 1986-88). Home: 735 Stevens Ave Portland ME 04103-2624 Office: U Del Dept English Newark DE 19716-2537

ANDREWS, GLORIA MAXINE, fundraiser; b. Cleve., Feb. 23, 1927; d. George Charles and Isabel Maxine (Bryden) Sternad; m. J. Melvin Andrews, July 15, 1950; children: Charles Melvin, Scott Michael, Countess Judith De Maleissye Melun. Student, San Miguel de Allende, Mex., 1947, Queen's U., Kingston, Ont., Can., 1948; BFA, Ohio Wesleyan U., 1949. Pres., trustee Lake County (Ohio) Hist. Soc., 1965-85; trustee Old Mentor (Ohio) Found., 1970's, Lawnfield Civic Com., 1988—; v.p. bd. trustees Western Res. Hist. Soc., Cleve., 1980—; hist. tour guide Lantern Ct. Holden Arboretum, Lake Country, 1970—, bd. dirs., 1989; pres. adv. com. Lake Erie Coll., Painesville, Ohio, 1980-87, Lakeland Coll. Found.; foreman Lake County Grand Jury, 1969. Recipient Liberty Bell award Lake County Bar Assn., 1980. Republican. Episcopalian. Home and Office: Echo Hill 8188 Garfield Rd Mentor OH 44060-5931

ANDREWS, JEAN, artist, writer; b. Kingsville, Tex., Dec. 23, 1923; d. Herbert and Katharine Keith (Smith) A.; divorced; children: Robert Fleming Wasson Jr., Jean Andrews Wasson (dec.). BS in Home Economics, U. Tex., 1944; MS in Edn., Tex. A & I Univ., 1966; PhD in Fine Arts, U. North Tex., 1976. Cert. home economist. Artist, writer Austin, Tex.; vis. scholar dept. botany U. Tex., Austin, also mem. adv. coun. Coll. Natural Sci., mem. exec. com., 1986—, chmn. botany dept. vis. com.; presenter to seminars and confs. in field. Author: Sea Shells of the Texas Coast, 1971, Shells and Shores of Texas, 1977, Tesax Shells: A Field Guide, 1981, Peppers: The Domesticated Capsicums, 1984, rev. edit., 1995, The Texas Bluebonnet, 1985, rev. edit., 1993, An American Wildflower: Florilegium, 1992, Texas Monthly Field Guide to Shells of the Texas Coast, 1992, Red Hot Peppers, 1993, Texas Monthly Field Guide to the Shells of the Florida Coast, 1994; also articles; one-woman shows include RGK Found. Gallery, Austin, 1993, numerous others. Nat. adv. bd. Leadership Am., 1988-95; trustee Laguna Gloria Art Mus., 1985-91, Nat. Wildflower Rsch. Ctr., 1987-94, adv. coun. 1995—; past trustee Art Mus. of S. Tex.; past bd. dirs. Planned Parenthood; mem. Austin Symphony Soc., Friends of Huntington Gallery/Univ. Tex., others. Recipient Disting. Alumna award U.North Tex., 1991, Hall of Honor award U. Tex. Coll. Natural Sci., 1991; endowments include Jean Andrews vis. professorship in human nutrition U. Tex., vis. professorship in tropical and econ. botany, endowed scholar Tex. Found. for Women's Resources, also others; named Tex. Inst. Letters. Mem. DAR, Am. Malacol. Union, Tex. Pepper Found. (life), Tex. State Tchrs. Assn. (life), U. Tex. Alumni Assn. (life), U. North Tex. Alumni Assn. (life), Colonial Dames of 17th Century, Nat. Soc. Ams. of Royal Descent, Nat. Soc. Colonial Dames in Am., Nat. Soc. Magna Charta Dames, Daus. of Cin., Huguenot Soc., Order of Descendants of Ancient Planters, Daus. of the Confederacy.

ANDREWS, JILL C., association executive; b. Clinton, Iowa, June 28, 1943; d. Jack Jackells and Priscilla DeMiller (Bell) A.; divorced; children: Karen, Michael, David, Laura, Lisa. BA in Mgmt., U. Phoenix, 1992. Campaign mgr., dist. rep. U.S. Rep. Eldon Rudd, Phoenix, 1976-77; campaign mgr. Stan Akers Corp. Commn., Phoenix, 1978; exec. dir. Rep. Legis. Campaign Com., Phoenix, 1979-80; dir. pub. relations Circle K Corp., Phoenix, 1980-82; pres. Impact S.W. Inc., Phoenix, 1982-86; exec. dir. Rocky Mountain region Reagan-Bush campaign, Phoenix, 1983-84; dir. pub. affairs Ariz. chpt. Assoc. Gen. Contractors, Phoenix, 1986-90; state dir. Nat. Fedn. of Independent Bus., Phoenix, 1991; exec. dir. Small Bus. Alliance on Comm., Phoenix, 1991-94, Ariz. Landscape Contractors Assn., 1996—; trustee Ariz. Laborers Teamsters, Cement Masons and Operating Engrs., 1986-90. Editor Views and News mag., 1986-90, News Notes newsletter, 1986-90, Supervision, 1986-90. Ariz. chmn. Bus. and Industry Coalitions Bush-Quayle '92; co-chmn. Jane Dee Hull Ariz. Sec. of State. Mem. Ariz. Launderers and Dry Cleaners Assn. Office: 1802 E Thomas Rd #14 Phoenix AZ 85016-5303

ANDREWS, JUDY COKER, electronics company executive; b. Hot Springs, Ark., Dec. 19, 1940; d. Leon G. and Bobbie (Randles) Coker; m. William Campbell Andrews, June 27, 1961; children: Alan Campbell Andrews, Theresa Lee Andrews Mills. BSE, Henderson State U., 1961; MEd, U. N.C., 1973. Instr. math. High Point (N.C.) Coll., 1973, Greensboro (N.C.) Pub. Schs., 1974, Richland Coll., Dallas, 1974-78; systems analyst J.C. Penney Co., Dallas, 1978-80; systems analyst Texas Instruments, Dallas, 1980-83, info. ctr. mgr., 1983-85, customer svc. mgr., 1986-90, bus. devel. mgr., 1990-92; corp. acct. mgr. Telecom Sys., Tex. Instruments, Dallas, 1993-95, corp. acct. mgr. comm. and electronic sys., 1995—. Inventor: system and method for securing cellular telephone access through a cellular telephone network using voice verification (pat. pending). Adult advisor Explorer Post 444, Boy Scouts Am., Richardson, Tex., 1980-82. U. N.C. fellow, 1971-73. Mem. Assn. for Systems Mgmt. (chpt. pres. 1984-85, chair internat. ann. conf. 1989, chair internat. corp. ptnr. com. 1992, Disting. Svc. award 1992). Office: Texas Instruments 6550 Chase Oaks Blvd Plano TX 75023-2308

ANDREWS, JULIE, actress, singer; b. Walton-on-Thames, Eng., Oct. 1, 1935; d. Edward C. and Barbara Wells; m. Tony Walton, May 10, 1959 (div.); 1 dau., Emma; m. Blake Edwards, 1969. Studied with pvt. tutors, studied voice with Mme. Stiles-Allen. Debut as singer, Hippodrome, London, 1947; appeared in pantomime Cinderella, London, 1953; appearences include (Broadway prodns.) The Boy Friend, N.Y.C., 1954, My Fair Lady, 1956-60 (N.Y. Drama Critics award 1956), Camelot, 1960-62, Putting It Together, 1993, Victor/Victoria, 1995 (Tony award nominee Best Actress in a Musical); films include Mary Poppins, 1964 (Acad. award for Best Actress 1964), The Americanization of Emily, 1964, Torn Curtain, 1966, The Sound of Music, 1966, Hawaii, 1966, Thoroughly Modern Millie, 1967, Star!, 1968, Darling Lili, 1970, The Tamarind Seed, 1973, 10, 1979, Little Miss Marker, 1980, S.O.B, 1981, Victor/Victoria, 1982, The Man Who Loved Women, 1983, That's Life!, 1986, Duet For One, 1986, A Fine Romance, 1992; TV debut in High Tor, 1956; star TV series The Julie Andrews Hour, 1972-73 (Emmy award for Best Variety Series), Julie, 1992; also spls.; TV movies include Our Sons, 1991; author: (as Julie Edwards): Mandy, 1971, The Last of the Really Great Whangdoodles, 1974; recs.: The King and I, 1992. Recipient Golden Globe award Hollywood Fgn. Press Assn., 1964, 65; named World Film Favorite (female), 1967. *

ANDREWS, LAUREEN E., foundation administrator; b. Seneca Falls, N.Y., July 28, 1954; d. Lawrence J. and Anita A.; m. Craig T. Scherer, Oct. 4, 1983; children: Casey Alena, Lindsey Adele. BA, George Washington U., 1976; MA in Law and Diplomacy, Fletcher Sch. Law and Diplomacy, Mass., 1978. Lobbyist, editor League of Women Votersof the U.S.A., Washington, 1978-80; dir. internat. rels. League of Women Voters Edn. Fund, Washington, 1980-85; dep. dir. def. budget project Ctr. Budget & Policy Priorities, Washington, 1985—; dep. dir. Ctr. for Stategic & Budgetary Assessments, Washington. Editor: (legis. newsletter) Report from the Hill, 1978-80. Mem. Phi Beta Kappa. Office: Ctr for Strategic & Budgetary Assessments 1730 Rhode Island Ave NW Ste 912 Washington DC 20036*

ANDREWS, LAVONE DICKENSHEETS, architect; b. Beaumont, Tex., Sept. 18, 1912; d. Charles and Lavone (Lowman) Dickensheets; m. Mark Edwin Andrews, July 23, 1948; 1 son, Mark Edwin III. Student, Miss Hamlin's Sch., San Francisco, Marlborough Sch., L.A.; AB, Rice Inst., 1933, BS in Architecture, 1934. Assoc. with outstanding architects in Southwest, 1934-37; opened own office Houston, 1937-41; architect firm Anderson, Clayton & Co. (cotton firm), 1941-51; v.p. Ancon Oil & Gas, Inc. Also pvt. work, museum in, Washington, Naval Hist. Found. & Health Center, schs. for City of Houston. Trustee Mus. Fine Arts in Houston; mem. YWCA World Service Council. Selected as 3d of the 10 outstanding women architects in Am. Archtl. Record, 1947. Fellow AIA, Royal Inst. Architects Ireland; mem. Pallas Athene Lit. Soc. of Rice Inst., Colony Club (N.Y.C.), Houston Club, River Oaks Country Club, Garden of Houston Club, Bayou Club, Garden of Am. Club. Episcopalian. Home: 2121 Kirby Dr Apt 109 Houston TX 77019-6067 also (summer): Knappogue Castle, County Clare Ireland Office: Lavone Dickensheets Andrews 2001 Kirby Dr Ste 805 Houston TX 77019-6033

ANDREWS, MARGARET LOVE, nurse, educator; b. Alamo, Tenn., Jan. 20, 1955; d. Elzie and Ada Mai (Smith) Love; m. Samuel Andrews Jr., Dec. 28, 1992; children: William Anthony, Marcus Anthony. BSN, Howard U., 1979; MA, Webster U., St. Louis, 1982; MSN, San Jose (Calif.) State U., 1994. Head nurse USAF, San Antonio, 1980-82; dir. nursing Eskaton Glenwood, Sacramento, 1988-90; commd. capt. U.S. Army, 1989, promoted to major, 1992; nursing adminstr. U.S. Army, Ft. Ord, Calif., 1990-92; head nurse U.S. Army, Ft. Gordon, Ga., 1994—; staff nurse Hospice, Augusta, Ga., 1994—; home care nurse Hospice, Monterey, Calif., 1992-94. Served to maj. U.S. Army, 1989—. Decorated Army Commendation medal. Mem. Nat. Black Nurses Assn., NAFE, The Rock, Inc. (Most Notable Women of Tex. 1982), Chi Eta Phi (pres. 1977-79). Home: 558 Waterford Dr Evans GA 30809-8516

ANDREWS, MARIA JOSEPHA, diplomat; b. Superior, Wis., June 27, 1954; d. Earl Raymond and Louise Maria (Jongbloed) A. BBA, Ga. So. U., 1977; MBA, Ga. State U., 1979. From sales mgr. to product planner Motorola, Inc., Schaumburg, Ill., 1979-83; cons. Technomic Cons., Chgo., 1983-84; comml. attaché U.S. Embassy, Jakarta, Indonesia, 1985-88, Paris, 1988-91, Helsinki, Finland, 1991-94; comml. counselor U.S. Comml. Svc., Warsaw, Poland, 1995—. Recipient Silver medal U.S. Dept. Commerce, Washington, 1989. Mem. Am. C. of C. Warsaw (bd. dirs. 1995—). Office: US Comml Svc, Al Jerozolimskie 56 C, 00-803 Warsaw Poland also: US Embassy Warsaw Comml Sect Dept State Washington DC 20521-5010

ANDREWS, MARIE STAYLOR, special education educator; b. Farmville, Va., Oct. 29, 1959; d. Luther Presley and Betty Jean (Strum) Staylor; m. Gary Hilton Andrews, Dec. 22, 1990; children: Brian Edward, Forrest Presley. BM, Mars Hill Coll., 1982; postgrad., So. Bapt. Theol. Sem., 1982-89, Longwood Coll., 1989-90. Cert. music tchr., Va. Spl. edn. tchr. Bacon Dist. Elem. Sch., Charlotte County Pub. Schs., Charlotte Court House, Va., 1990—. Leader, receptionist Weight Watchers, Southside, Va., 1988-91; mem. choir, choir dir., pianist Crewe (Va.) Bapt. Ch., 1988-90. Republican. Home: Rt 1 Box 424-C Keysville VA 23947-0723 Office: Bacon Dist Sch RR 1 Box 134 Saxe VA 23967-9533

ANDREWS, ROWENA, public relations executive; b. Chattanooga, Dec. 31, 1944; d. Mose Porter and Waudie Tarvin; married, 1966 (div. 1971); 1 child, Elizabeth Paige Andrews. BA in Journalism, U. Ga., 1974. Info. specialist NASA-Cosmic, Athens, Ga., 1967-74; pub. rels. and photography freelancer Chattanooga, 1974-76; comm. specialist Providence Life Ins., Chattanooga, 1976-78; dir. pub. info. Aid United Givers, L.A., 1978-80; corp. comm. mgr. Informatics Gen. Corp., Woodland Hills, Calif., 1980-81; dir. pub. rels. Candle Corp., L.A., 1981-83; pub. rels. cons. Andrews Pub. Rels., L.A., Ga., 1983-94, Newnan, Ga., 1994—. Home and Office: Andrews PR 24 Stonehaven Dr Newnan GA 30265

ANDREWS, SALLY MAY, healthcare administrator; b. Westfield, Mass., Feb. 29, 1956; d. Roger N. and Dorothy M. (Goodhind) A. Student, U. Conn., 1974-76; BA, Simmons Coll., Boston, 1978; MBA, Boston U., 1986. Payroll clk. Children's Hosp., Boston, 1978-79, asst. payroll supr., 1979-81, staff analyst dept. medicine, 1981-83, asst. adminstr. dept. medicine, 1983-86, adminstr. dept. medicine, 1986—. Bd. overseers Lasell Coll., Newton, Mass. Mem. Am. Mgmt. Assn., Adminstrs. of Internal Medicine, Assn. Adminstrs. in Acad. Pediatrics (pres. 1996—). Congregationalist. Office: Children's Hosp Dept Medicine 300 Longwood Ave Boston MA 02115-5724

ANDREWS, THEODORA ANNE, retired librarian, educator; b. Carroll County, Ind., Oct. 14, 1921; d. Harry Floyd and Margaret Grace (Walter) Ulrey; B.S. with distinction, Purdue U., 1953; M.S., U. Ill., 1955; m. Robert William Andrews, July 18, 1940 (div. 1946); 1 son, Martin Harry. Asst. reference libr. Purdue U., West Lafayette, Ind., 1955-56, pharmacy libr. , instr., 1956-60, pharmacy libr., asst. prof., 1960-65, pharmacy libr. an, assoc.

prof. libr. sci., 1965-71, prof. libr. sci., pharmacy libr., 1971-79, prof. libr. sci., pharmacy, nursing and health scis. libr., 1979-90, prof. libr. sci., spl. bibliographer, 1991-92, prof. emerita of libr. sci., 1992—. Mem. Purdue Women's Caucus, 1973—, v.p., 1975-76, pres., 1976-77; mem. Internat. Women's Yr. Regional Planning Com., 1977; del. Ind. Gov.'s Conf. Librs. and Info. Svcs., 1978. U. Ill. grad. fellow, 1954-55. Mem. Spl. Libr. Assn. (John H. Moriarty award Ind. chpt. 1972), ALA, Med. Libr. Assn., AAUP, Am. Assn. Colls. Pharmacy, Kappa Delta Pi, Delta Rho Kappa. Baptist. Author: A Bibliography of the Socioeconomic Aspects of Medicine, 1975; A Bibliography of Drug Abuse Including Alcohol and Tobacco, 1977; A Bibliography of Drug Abuse, Supplement 1977-1980, 1981; Bibliography on Herbs, Herbal Remedies and Natural Foods, 1982; Substance Abuse Materials for School Libraries, an Annotated Bibliography, 1985; Guide to the Literature of Pharmacy and the Pharmaceutical Sciences, 1986; sect. editor Advances in Alcohol and Substance Abuse, 1981-92; contbr. articles to profl. jours. Office: Purdue U Sch Pharmacy West Lafayette IN 47907

ANDRUK, MARJORIE DEAN, artist, educator; b. Norfolk, Va., Aug. 11, 1922; d. Carl Chadbourne and Bessie Jane (Overman) Dean; m. Richard Andruk, June 5, 1944; children: Richard Dean (dec.), Kenneth Francis. BA, Md. Inst. Coll. Art, 1942; postgrad., Eastman Sch. Photography, Winona Lake, 1943, Inst. Allende, San Miguel de Allende, Guanajuato, Mex., 1968-72; MFA, U. S.C., 1976. 1st woman press photographer Balt. Sun, 1943-45; organizer art dept. Cath. Diocese St. Petersburg, St. Petersburg, Fla., 1957-58; prof. art Gertrude Herbert Art Inst., Augusta, Ga., 1972-76; tchg. assoc. U. S.C., Aiken, 1975-76; panelist DSAC Grant Rev. Panel, 1984-85; condr. workshops Inst. Allende and Centro cultural El Nigromante. One-woman shows include Coyle & Richardson Gallery, Charleston, W.Va., Learning Founds. Gallery, Athens, Ga., Town and Gown Gallery, Athens, Arts and Sci. Mus., Macon, Ga., The Augusta (Ga.)-Richmond County Mus., 1973, 74, Quinlan Art Ctr., Gainesvile, Ga., La Galeria Gaudi, Maracaibo, Venezuela, 1973, Huntington Gallery, U. S.C., 1976, Gertrude Herbert Art Inst., Augusta, 1976, Grande Gallery, Wilmington, Del., 1978, Ware Gallery, Arden, Del., 1979, 81, Casa Carmen Gallery, San Miguel de Allende, 1980, 84, Rodney Square Gallery, Wilmington, Del., 1981, Longwood Gardens Gallery, 1983, The Highland Gallery, Atlanta, 1983, Del. Ctr. for Contemporary Arts, Wilmington, 1983, Evelyn Cobb Gallery, St. Petersburg, Fla., 1994, Lighthouse Gallery, Tequesta, Fla., 1995, many others; group shows include Corcoran Mus., Washington, 1974, Inst. Allende, Russell House Gallery, U. S.C., 1975, Ware Gallery, Rodney Square Gallery, Upham Gallery, St. Petersburg Beach, Fla., 1989, The Arts Ctr., St. Petersburg, Arts on Pk., Lakeland, Fla., 1995, Ridge Art Assn., Winter Haven, Fla., Northwood U., West Palm Beach, 1996, and many others; permanent collections include Centro Cultural "El Nigromante," San Miguel de Allende, Cathedral Ch. of St. John, Wilmington, Del., Gertrude Herbert Art Inst., Augusta, Augusta-Richmond County Mus., Venice (Fla.) Golf and Country Club., also pvt. collections. Active Studio 1212, Clearwater, Fla., Suntan Art Ctr., St. Pete Beach, Fla., The Ctr. for the Arts, St. Petersburg, World Art Workshop, Ocean Hills, Calif. Mem. Nat. Assn. Women Artists, Del. State Arts Coun., Fla. Artist Group, Fla. Watercolor Soc. Episcopal. Studio: 4101 Belle Vista Dr Saint Petersburg Beach FL 33706

ANDRUS, LUCY, art therapist, art educator; b. Newark, Oct. 25, 1951; d. John Joseph and Lucia (Gazzo) Lessa; 1 child, Sasha. BA in Art, Kean Coll. N.J., 1975; MS in Edn., SUNY, Buffalo, 1982. Freelance art educator, cons. Chautauqua County, N.Y., 1978—; founder, dir. Creative Arts for Learning, Westfield, N.Y., 1979-81; dir. Matter at Hand program for spl. needs populations Albright-Knox Art Gallery, Buffalo, N.Y., 1981-85; pvt. practice art therapist Erie County, N.Y., 1986-95; dir. grad. art therapy program Buffalo State Coll., 1985-94, asst. prof. art edn., 1982-95, assoc. prof. art edn. and art therapy, 1996—; founder, dir. Art Ptnr.s Buffalo City Schs., 1994—; cons. Inst. for Addictions Studies, Amherst, N.Y., 1987—. Contbr. chpt. to book and articles to profl. jours. Recipient Cmty. Svc. award Assn. for Retarded Children, Niagara County, N.Y., 1984; fellowship grantee N.Y. State Edn. Dept., Albany, 1980, Ctr. for Devel. Human Svc., Buffalo, 1990, 91, 95. Mem. Am. Art Therapy Assn. (registered art therapist, bd. mem. 1991-94), Nat. Art Edn. Assn. Office: Buffalo State Coll Dept Art Edn Buffalo NY 14222

ANDRUS, THERESA KESTER, photojournalist, communications specialist; b. Manchester, Iowa, Aug. 2, 1953; d. Francis Alfred and Mary Veronica (Keegan) Kester; m. Douglas Burton Andrus, Dec. 23, 1978; children: Ian, Ross. AA in Applied Arts, Hawkeye Inst. Tech., 1975; BS summa cum laude, St. Cloud State U., 1992. Chief photographer Larson Publs., Osseo, Minn., 1978-86; reporter, photographer Monticello (Minn.) Times, 1992-94; comm. dir. Maple Lake (Minn.) Pub. Schs., 1994—. Photographer: (books) Full Circle Five, 1984, A Sampler of Women, 1984, Full Circle Seven, 1986. Ctrl. Minn. Mother's March chairperson March of Dimes, St. Cloud, 1988, Porch Light Night chairperson, 1988-91; gen. coord. for Centennial Playground, Maple Lake (Minn.) Schs., 1989-90, Blandin Cmty. Leadership Program, 1991-92; co-chairperson Irish Summer Fest, Maple Lake, 1992, 95, 96; mem. sch. bd. Mple Lake Schs., 1992-94. Recipient Maple Lake (Minn.) Disting. Svc. award, 1990, Mpls. Aquatennial Assn. Commodore's award, 1993, numerous state and nat. awards for photojournalism, 1980-95. Mem. Maple Lake (Minn.) Jaycees (v.p. for pub. rels. 1989-91, pres. 1991-92, chair bd., Jaycee of Yr. 1990), Phi Kappa Phi. Office: Maple Lake Pub Schs 200 State Hwy 55 E Maple Lake MN 55358

ANDRUZZI, ELLEN ADAMSON, nurse, marital and family therapist; b. Colon, Panama, Dec. 15, 1917; d. Charles and Annie Isabel (Grinder) Adamson; m. Francis Victor Andruzzi, May 28, 1941; children: Barbara F., Francis C., Judith E., Antonette T., John J. BS in Pub. Health Nursing, Cath. U. Am., 1947, MS in Nursing, 1951. Cert. clin. specialist, psychiat. nurse. Pub. health nurse Washington Health Dept., 1942-44; instr. psychiat. nursing St. Elizabeth's Hosp., Washington, 1948-57; dir. nursing Glenn Dale Hosp., Md., 1961-67; chief mental health nurse dept. human resources D.C. Govt., 1967-73; cons. NIMH, HHS, Rockville, Md., 1973-81; marital and family therapist TA Assocs., Camp Springs, Md., 1973-94; assoc. GWITA, Rockville, 1975-79; instr. Charles County C.C., LaPlata, Md., 1976-78, Prince George Community Coll., Largo, Md., 1973-81; assoc. Ctr. for Study of Human Systems, Chevy Chase, Md., 1976-94; nurse, psychotherapist pvt. practice. Author chpts. in books. Dist. co-capt. Prince Georgians for Glendening, Prince George County, Md., 1985-86; chmn. plan devel. com. So. Md. Health Systems Agy., Clinton, 1984-89, sec. governing body, 1978-80; chmn. Mental Health Adv. Com. Prince George County, Cheverly, Md., 1983-85; mem. Blue Ribbon Commn. on Health, Prince George's County, 1991-92; mem. Commn. Health, Prince George's County, 1992-94; mem. health com. and voter reporter League Women Voters. Recipient Disting. Nurse award St. Elizabeths Hosp., 1985, Paula Hamburger Vol. award Mental Health Assn. Md., 1985, Recognition of Service award Md. Nurses Assn., 1983, Prince Georgian of the Yr. award, 1994, Vol. award Prince George's County, 1995. Fellow Am. Acad. Nursing, Am. Orthopsychiat. Assn.; mem. Internat. Transactional Analysis Assn. (clin.), Am. Nurses Assn., World Fedn. for Mental Health, Am. Assn. for Marriage and Family Therapy (clin.), Nat. Mental Health Assn. (v.p. 1984-87, bd. dirs. 1982-87), Mental Health Assn. Prince George County (pres. 1974-76, 87-88, Vol. of Yr. award 1993), Sigma Theta Tau (Kappa chpt., Excellence in Nursing award 1984). Democrat. Roman Catholic. Avocations: theatre, ballet, swimming, foreign travel.

ANGEL, MARINA, law educator; b. N.Y.C., July 21, 1944. BA, Barnard Coll., N.Y.C., 1965; JD, Columbia U., 1969; LLM, U. Pa., Phila., 1977. Bar: N.Y. 1969, Pa. 1971, U. S. Dist. Ct. (ea. dist.) Pa. 1971, U.S. Dist. Ct. (so. and ea. dists.) N.Y. 1973, U.S. Supreme Ct. 1974. Assoc. prof. law Hofstra U. Law Sch., L.I., N.Y., 1971-78; assoc. Gordon & Shectman, P.C., N.Y.C., 1973-75; prof. law Temple U. Law Sch., Phila., 1979—, assoc. dean grad. legal studies, 1983-84; dir. summer sessions abroad Greece Temple U. Law Sch., Athens, 1981-83, 85, 87, 89; vis. prof. Queensland U. Tech. and Wollongong U., Australia, 1992; gen. counsel Modern Greek Studies Assn., 1995—, Greek Am. Women's Network, 1995—. Sec. bd. St. George Sr. Housing Corp., Phila., 1980-88; mem. exec. com. Community Legal Svcs., Phila., 1979-88. Named Most Outstanding Prof., Temple Law Sch., Phila., 1989. Mem. ABA, Phila. Bar Assn. (Sandra Day O'Connor award 1996), Assn. of Bar of City of N.Y. Office: Temple U Law Sch 1719 N Broad St Philadelphia PA 19122-2504

ANGELL, M(ARY) FAITH, federal magistrate judge; b. Buffalo, May 7, 1938; d. San S. and Marie B. (Caboni) A.; m. Kenneth F. Carobus, Oct. 27, 1973; children: Andrew M. Carobus, Alexander P. Carobus. AB, Mt. Holyoke Coll., 1959; MSS, Bryn Mawr Coll., 1965; JD, Temple U., 1971. Bar: Pa. 1971, U.S. Dist. Ct. (ea. dist) Pa. 1971, U.S. Ct. Appeals (3rd cir.) Pa. 1974, U.S. Supreme Ct. 1979; Acad. Cert. Social Workers. Dir. social work, vol. svcs. Wills Eye Hosp., Phila., 1961-64, 65-69; dir. soc. work dept. juvenile divsn. Defender Assoc., Phila., 1969-71; asst. dist. atty. City of Phila., 1971-72; asst. atty. gen. Commonwealth of Pa., Phila., 1972-74, deputy atty. gen., 1974-78; regional counsel ICC, Phila., 1978-80, regional dir., 1980-88; administrv. law judge Social Security Administrn., Phila., 1988-90; U.S. magistrate judge Ea. Dist. Pa., Phila., 1990—; adj. prof. Temple U. Law Sch., Phila., 1976-94, clin. instr., 1973-76; co-chmn. Commn. on Gender, 3d Cir. Task Force on Equal Treatment in Cts., 1994—. Federal trustee Defender Assn. Phila., 1985-90; bd. dirs. Child Welfare Adv. Bd., Phila., 1984-90, Federal Cts. 200 Adv. Bd., Phila., 1987-88, Phila. Woman's Network, 1986-88. Recipient Sr. Exec. Svc. award U.S. Govt., 1980. Mem. NASW, FBA (chair exec. com., pres. 1990-92, recognition 1992), Nat. Assn. Women Judges, Fed. Magistrate Judges Assn. (dist. dir. 1994—), Phila. Bar Assn. (chmn. com. 1976-77), Temple Am. Inn of Cts. (master 1993—). Office: US District Court 4316 US Courthouse 601 Market St Philadelphia PA 19106

ANGELL, ROBIN L., speech language pathologist; b. Pitts., Oct. 21, 1964; d. Kirk J. and Barbara J. (Neff) Metzger; m. Andrew N. Angell, Mar. 26, 1988; children: Joshua, Brianne. BS, Clarion U. Pa., 1986; MS, Bowling Green State U., 1987. Speech lang. pathologist InSpeech, Inc., Akron, Ohio, 1987-88, Akron Gen. Med. Ctr., Ohio, 1988-90; ptnr., owner pvt. practice Comprehensive Comm. Specialists, Medina, Ohio, 1990—. Jr. h.s. youth group leader Stow Alliance Fellowship, Stow, Ohio, 1990—. Mem. Am. Speech Lang. Hearing Assn. (cert. clin. competence), Coun. of Smaller Enterprises. Office: Comprehensive Comm Specialists 750 E Washington St A-6 Medina OH 44256

ANGELOU, MAYA, author; b. St. Louis, Apr. 4, 1928; d. Bailey and Vivian (Baxter) Johnson; 1 son, Guy Johnson. Studied dance with, Pearl Primus, N.Y.C.; hon. degrees, Smith Coll., 1975, Mills Coll., 1975, Lawrence U., 1976. Taught modern dance The Rome Opera House and Hambina Theatre, Tel Aviv; writer-in-residence U. Kans.-Lawrence, 1970; disting. vis. prof. Wake Forest U., 1974, Wichita State U., 1974, Calif. State U.-Sacramento, 1974; apptd. mem. Am. Revolution Bicentennial Council by Pres. Ford, 1975-76; 1st Reynolds prof. Am. Studies, Wake Forest U. since 1981, a lifetime appointment. Author: I Know Why the Caged Bird Sings, 1970, Just Give Me A Cool Drink of Water 'Fore I Diiie, 1971, Georgia, Georgia, 1972, Gather Together in My Name, 1974, Oh Pray My Wings are Gonna Fit Me Well, 1975, Singin' and Swingin' and Gettin' Merry Like Christmas, 1976, And Still I Rise, 1978, The Heart of a Woman, 1981, Shaker, Why Don't You Sing?, 1983, All God's Children Need Traveling Shoes, 1986, Now Sheba Sings the Song, 1987, I Shall Not Be Moved, 1990, On the Pulse of Morning: The Inaugural Poem, 1992, Lessons in Living, 1993, Wouldn't Take Nothing for My Journey Now, 1993, My Painted House, My Friendly Chicken, and Me, 1994, The Complete Collected Poems of Maya Angelou, 1994; prodr.: Moon on a Rainbow Shawl, 1988 (by Errol John); appeared on TV in The Richard Pryor Special; author/prodr. Three Way Choice, Afro-American in the Arts (Golden Eagle award), in ltd. series Roots; appeared in revue Cabaret for Freedom and The Blacks (Obie award) with Godfrey Cambridge; adatped Ajax for Mark Taper Forum in L.A.; librettist, lyricist and composer: And Still I Rise, 1976; wrote and presented Trying to Make it Home, 1988; writer for Oprah Winfrey's Harpo Prodns.; poetry writer for film Poetic Justice, 1993; also numerous appearances on network and local talk shows; articles, short stories, poems to Black Scholar, Chgo. Daily News, Cosmopolitan, Harper's Bazaar, Life Mag., Redbook, Sunday N.Y. Times, others. Mem. adv. bd. Women's Prison Assn.; No. Coord. So. Christian Leadership Conf.; apptd. by Pres. Ford to Bicentennal Commn., by Pres. Carter to Nat. Commn. on Obnservance of Internat. Women's Yr. Named Woman of Yr. in Comm., 1976; Ladies Home Jour. Top 100 Most Influential Women, 1983, The Matric award, 1983, The North Carolina Award in Lit., 1987; named 1st Reynolds prof. Wake Forest U., 1981, a lifetime appointment, Woman of the Yr. Essence Mag., 1992, Disting. Woman of N.C., 1992, Horatio Alger award, 1992, Grammy award Best Spoken Word or Non-Traditional Album, 1994 (for recording of "On the Pulse of the Morning"). Mem. AFTRA, Dirs. Guild Am., Equity, Harlem Writers Guild, Am. Film Inst. (trustee), Women's Prison Assn. Office: care Dave La Camera Lordly and Dame Inc 51 Church St Boston MA 02116-5417

ANGEVINE, ERMA BATRECE, writer, genealogist, consultant, researcher; b. Moffat, Colo., Mar. 8, 1917; d. Silas Bergen and Audrey Erma (Parsons) Miller; m. Ralph Allen Smith, Dec. 24, 1939 (div. Jan. 1951); m. David Walker Angevine, May 24, 1952. BA, Friends U., Wichita, Kans., 1939; postgrad., U. Kans., 1941, 45, U. Chgo., 1948, U. Mo., Kansas City, 1951-52. Cert. tchr., Kans. Elem. sch. libr. Wichita Pub. Libr., 1939; relief tchr. Kingman County H.S., Kingman, Kans., 1940-42; asst. program sec. Kans. Dist. YWCA, Wichita, 1942-43; clk.-typist ARC, Chgo., 1943-44, Employers' Group Ins. Cos., Chgo., 1948-49; sec. Alumni Assn. Office, Tex. A&M U., College Station, 1944; bookeeper, dispatcher Harris Concrete Co., Corpus Christi, Tex., 1944; bookkeeper, office mgr. Weaver Constrn. Co., Corpus Christi, 1944-45; instr. English, U. Kans., Lawrence, 1946-48; reporter, deptl. sec. Consumers Coop. Assn. (now Farmland Industries), Kansas City, 1949-50, editor employee newsletter, libr., 1950-52; asst. editor, libr. Coop. League USA (now Nat. Coop: Bus. Assn.), Chgo., 1954-62; dir. women's activities, coord. assn. meetings Nat. Rural Electric Coop. Assn., Washington, 1962-68; exec. dir. Consumer Fedn. Am., Washington, 1968-73; consumer cons., genealogist, 1973—; housemother Harmon House, Lawrence, 1946-47, Henley House, Lawrence, 1947-48; mem. Orgns. Adv. Com., 1969-73; mem. task force on consumer concerns com. Nat. Health Coun., 1970-76; bd. dirs. Nat. Coop. Bus. Found., 1985-88. Author: In League with the Future, 1959, In America, the Angevines, 1976, Miller and Related Families, 1976, Ellis, Taylor and Certain Related Families, 1979, History of the National Consumers League, 1899-1979, 1979, People-Their Power, the Rural Electric Fact Book, 1980, Instructions for Beginners in Genealaogy, 1986, rev. edit., 1993; contbg. author: The Humanistic Approach to Pharmaccutical Scrvices, 1975; co-author: Consumer Participation in Federal Decision Making, 1981; editor, contbg. author: Consumer Activists, They Made a Difference, 1982; columnist, contbr. articles to coop. and union papers and mags. Election judge Monee Twp., Will County, Ill., 1953-60; campaign worker Paul Douglas for Senator, 1954, 60; mem. President's Com. on Consumer Affairs, 1966-72; bd. dirs. Western States Water and Power Consumer Conf., 1968-74; mem. adv. com. Corp. for Pub. Broadcasting, 1969-73, Conservation Found., 1969-70, Pub. Broadcasting Environ. Ctr., 1970, Nat. Health Coun., 1970-76, FPC Nat. Power Survey, 1972-74, Ctr. for Sci. in Pub. Interest, 1972-76; chmn. consumer concerns com. White House Conf. on Aging, 1971; mem. pub. policy deliberative com. Washington Forum of Am. U., 1973-75; bd. dirs. Citizens Com. for Paperwork Reduction, 1978-79; bd. dirs. Nat. Consumers League, 1976—, pres., 1977-82; Vol. Handley Regional Libr. Archives, 1992—; appeal judge Coun. Rural Electric Communicators, 1990—. Recipient Florence Kelley Consumer Leadership award Nat. Consumers League, 1995. Fellow Nat. Geneal. Soc. (v.p. 1983-86, pres. 1986-86, dir. edn. 1983-90, Disting. Svc. award 1985); mem. AAUW, Internat. Soc. Brit. Genealogy and Family History, Nat. Inst. on Geneal. Rsch. Alumni Assn., Nat. Coop. Bus. Assn. (life), Friends Handley Libr., Friends U. Alumni Assn. Democrat. Mem. Soc. of Friends. Home and Office: 107 Wineberry Dr Winchester VA 22603

ANGIER, NATALIE MARIE, science journalist; b. N.Y.C., Feb. 16, 1958; d. Keith and Adele Bernice (Rosenthal) A.; m. Richard Steven Weiss, July 27, 1991. Student, U. Mich., 1974-76; BA, Barnard Coll., 1978. Staff writer Discover Mag., N.Y.C., 1980-83, Time Mag., N.Y.C., 1984-86; editor Savvy Mag., N.Y.C., 1983-84; journalism educator NYU, N.Y.C., 1987-89; became reporter N.Y. Times, N.Y.C., 1990; now science correspondent N.Y. Times, Washington. Author: Natural Obsessions, 1988, The Beauty of the Beastly, 1995. Recipient Pulitzer Prize for beat reporting, 1991, Journalism award GM Ind. Bd., 1991, Lewis Thomas award Marine Biol. Labs., 1990, Journalism award AAAS, 1992, Disting. Alumna award Barnard Coll., 1993. Mem. Nat. Assn. Sci. Writers. Office: NY Times Washington Bureau 1627 I St NW Fl 7 Washington DC 20006-4007*

ANGLIN, FLORENCE See **AQUINO-KAUFMAN, FLORENCE**

ANGSTADT, F. V., language arts and theatre arts educator; b. Dover, Del., Oct. 11, 1953; d. T. Richard Sr. and Frances Virginia (Kohout) A. BA, Del. State U., 1976; MFA, Cath. U. Am., 1982. Lighting designer, assoc. dir. écarté dance Theatre, Dover, 1981-93; alternative tchr. Lake Forest H.S., Felton, Del., 1982-87; English tchr. Dover H.S., 1987-89; lang. arts and theater tchr. Ctrl. Mid. Sch., Dover, 1989—; lighting designer Harrisburg (Pa.) Ballet, 1991-93; lighting designer, artistic advisor Act I Players, Dover, 1983-93, lighting designer Kimberly McFarlin Dance Co., Balt., Axis Theatre, 1996—; adj. faculty Del. State U., Dover, 1985-89, Wilmington Coll., Dover, 1996—; tech. advisor, bd. dirs. 2nd St. Players, Milford, Del., 1993—; lighting designer Balt. Shakespeare Festival, 1994; mem. dance leadership Visual and Performing Arts Commn., Dover, 1994—. Mem. Vietnam Vets. Meml. Com., Dover, 1985-87; sec., founding mem. Dover Arts Coun., 1988-93, tech. advisor, 1988-94; sec. Capital Educators Assn., Dover, 1993 . Recipient scholarship All Am. Youth Honor Band, 1972, Del. State U., Dover, 1974-76; apptd. to adjudicator Del. Theatre Assn., 1986. Mem. ACLU, Nat. Coun. Tchrs. English, Theatre Communicators Group. Home: 117 Wyoming Ave Dover DE 19904 Office: Ctrl Mid Sch Delaware and Pennsylvania Dover DE 19901

ANGUIANO, LUPE, business executive; b. La Junta, Colo., Mar. 12, 1929; d. Jose and Rosario (Gonzalez) A. Student, Ventura (Calif.) Jr. Coll., 1948, Victory Noll Jr. Coll., Huntington, Ind., 1949-52, Marymount Coll., Palos Verdes, Calif., 1958-59, Calif. State U., L.A., 1965-67; M.A., Antioch-Putney-Yellow Springs, Ohio, 1978. S.W. regional dir. NAACP Legal Def. and Ednl. Fund, L.A., 1965-69; civil rights specialist HEW, Washington, 1969-73; S.W. regional dir. Nat. Coun. Cath. Bishops, Region X, San Antonio, 1973-77; pres. Nat. Women's Employment and Edn., Inc., L.A., 1979-91; pres., cons. Lupe Anguiano & Assocs., 1981—; cons. Tex. Dept. Human Resources, Dept. Labor, Women's Bur.; proposal reader U.S. Office Edn.-Women's Equity Act; mem. Tex. Adv. Coun. on Tech.-Vocat. Edn. Calif. del. White House Conf. on Status Mexican-Ams. in U.S., 1967; founding mem. policy coun. Nat. Women's Polit. Caucus, from 1971; Tex. and nat. del. Internat. Women's Year, 1976-77; chmn. Nat. Women's Polit. Caucus Welfare Reform Task Force, from 1977; co-chmn. Nat. Peace Acad. Campaign, 1977-81; founder, bd. dirs. Nat. Chicana Found., Inc., 1971-78; bd. dirs. Calif. Coun. Children and Youth, 1967, Rio Grande Fedn. Chicano Health Ctrs., S.W. Rural States, 1974-76, Women's Lobby, Washington, 1974-77, Rural Am. Women, Washington, from 1978, Small Bus. Coun. Greater San Antonio; mem. Pres.'s Coun. on Pvt. Sector Initiatives, 1983. Recipient Community award Coalition Mexican-Am. Orgns., 1967, Outstanding Svc. award Washington, 1968, Thanksgiving award Boys' Club, 1976, Outstanding Svc. award Tex. Women's Polit. Caucus, 1977, Liberty Bell award San Antonio Young Lawyers, 1981, Vista award for exceptional svc. to end poverty, 1980, Headliner award San Antonio Women in Communications, 1978, Woman of Yr. award Tex. Women's Polit. Caucus, 1978, Pres.'s Vol. Action award 1983, Leadership award Nat. Network Hispanic Women, 1989; named Outstanding Woman of Yr., L.A. County, 1972, Woman of the 80s Ms. mag., 1980; Nat. Pres.'s award Nat. Image, Inc., 1981, Wonder Woman Found. award, 1982, Pres.' Vol. Action award 1983, Adv. of Yr. San Antonio SBA, 1984; selected Am. 100 Most Important Women, Ladies Home Jour., 1988, 89; featured in CBS TV series An Am. Portrait, 1985, Leadership award Nat. Network Hispanic Women, 1989. Mem. Assn. Female Execs., Pres.'s Assn., Am. Mgmt. Assn. Republican. Roman Catholic. Author: (with others) U.S. Bilingual Education Act, 1967, Texas A.F.D.C. Employment and Education Act, 1977; manuals Women's Employment and Education Model Program.

ANHALT, KAREN SUE, critical care nurse, ambulatory surgery, nursing administration; b. Evanston, Ill., Aug. 10, 1950; d. John K. and Ruth Ann (Ketter) A. ADN, Triton Coll., 1975; BSN, St. Francis Coll., 1987; MSM, National-Louis U., 1995. RN, Ill., cert. post-anesthesia nurse. Dir. patient care, Post Anesthesia Care Unit, Ambulatory Surgery Unit, Pre-Admission Testing Unit St. Francis Hosp., Evanston, Ill., 1981-95. Mem. Am. Soc. Post Anesthesia Nurses (charter, bd. dirs. Ill. chpt.), Ill. Soc. Post Anesthesia Nurses (pres.). Home: 1334 Main St Evanston IL 60202-1653

ANISTON, JENNIFER, actress; b. Sherman Oaks, Calif., Mar. 11; d. John Aniston. Actress Friends, 1994—. Stage appearances include For Dear Life, Dancing on Checkers' Grave; TV appearances include Molloy, The Edge, Ferris Bueller, Herman's Head, Quantum Leap, Burke's Law. Office: The Gersh Agy 232 N Canon Dr Beverly Hills CA 90210

ANJUR, SOWMYA SRIRAM, research scientist, educator; b. Ahmadi, Kuwait, Oct. 4, 1962; came to U.S. 1987; d. V.S. Krishna and Saraswathi (Venkitachalam) Moorthi; m. Sriram Padmanabhan Anjur, Aug. 22, 1991. BS in Biochemistry, Madras U., India, 1982; MS in Biochemistry, Bharathar U., India, 1984, MPhil in Biochemistry/Microbiology, 1986; PhD, Iowa State U., 1992. Biochemist ICCU, Modern Hosp., Salem, India, 1983-84; biochemist R&D Symbiotic Labs, Madras, India, 1984-85; chemistry lectr OCF High Sch., Madras, India, 1985-86; asst. prof. biochemistry Kongunadu Arts & Scis. Coll., Coimbatore, India, 1987; teaching asst. biology/zoology Iowa State U., Ames, 1987-92; lectr. U. Wis., Oshkosh, 1992; rsch. scientist Kimberly-Clark Corp., Neenah, Wis., 1993—; dietary cons. Hosp. Bd. Nutrition, Coimbatore, India, 1978-82; wastewater treatment cons. U. Madras, 1985-87, microbiology cons., 1984-86. Choreographer/performer solo Indian dance fundraisers: Bharathanatyam, 1979-82 (Best Dancer 1980, 81); dir. drama troupe: The Funsters, 1978-80. Group leader Nat. Adult Edn. Program, India, 1978-84; mgr. Nat. Svc. Scheme, India, 1978-84; team leader Community Social Svc. Projects, India, 1978-84; chief fundraiser Solo Bharathanatyam, 1979-82. Recipient Gold medal for proficiency Bharathiar U., India, 1984. Mem. IEEE, Soc. Engrs. in Medicine and Biology, Iowa Acad. Sci., Am. Soc. Animal Sci., Am. Dairy Sci. Assn., Soc. of Biol. Chemists (India), Am. Mensa, Gamma Sigma Delta. Home: 624 E Capitol Dr Appleton WI 54911-1209

ANNENBERG, MARCIA, art educator; b. N.Y.C., Apr. 25, 1950; d. Morton and Frances (Roberts) A.; m. Robert Scher. BA, City Coll. N.Y., 1972; MA, NYU, 1982. Exhibited work in numerous shows including The Rockland Ctr. for Holocaust Studies, N.Y., 1995, Limner Gallery, N.Y.C., 1993, 55 Mercer Street Gallery, 1987, Westbroadway Gallery, N.Y.C., 1983, 84, Alternative Space at Westbroadway Gallery, 1982, Nat. Arts Club, N.Y.C., 1977; represented in pvt. and pub. collections including The Rockland Ctr. for Holocaust Studies, Bob Blackburn Printmaking Workshop, Christopher Monahan, Prof. Andrew McDonough. Mem. Artists Equity, Nat. Assn. Women Artists, Women's Caucus for Art.

ANNESE, BETSY JANE, public relations executive; b. Scranton, Pa., Sept. 26, 1949; d. Frank Nicholas and Ruth Elizabeth (Pillow) A. BA in Journalism, U. S.C., 1971. Reporter The (Columbia, S.C.) State, 1971-73, The (Anderson, S.C.) Ind., 1973-74; mgr. pub. rels Bigelow Carpets, Inc., Greenville, S.C., 1974-80; from sr. pub. rels. rep. to v.p. pub. affairs R. J. Reynolds Tobacco Co., Winston-Salem, N.C., 1980-94; v.p., deputy external rels. R.J. Reynolds Internat., Winston-Salem, N.C., 1994-95; sr. v.p. internat. external rels. R.J. Reynolds Internat., Geneva, 1995—. Bd. dirs. Family Svc., Inc., Winston-Salem, 1990—, Multiple Sclerosis Soc., Winston-Salem, 1990—, Horizons Residential Care, Inc., Winston-Salem, 1991-93, Winston-Salem Urban League, 1993—. Mem. Twin City Club (bd. dirs. 1989-93), Piedmont Club, Forsyth Country Club, Wild Dunes Beach and Racquet Club, Ad 2 Club (hon.). Office: RJ Reynolds Internat, 12-14 Chemin Rieu, CH-1211 Geneva 17, Switzerland

ANNS, ARLENE EISERMAN, publishing company executive; b. Pearl River, N.Y.; d. Frederick Joel and Anna (Behnke) E.; student Bergen Jr. Coll., 1946-48; BS, Utah State U., 1950; postgrad. Traphagen Sch. Design, 1957, NYU, 1958, Hunter Coll., 1959-60. Rsch. and promotion asst. Archtl. Record, N.Y.C., 1952-56; asst. rsch. dir. Esquire Mag., N.Y.C., 1956-62; rsch. mgr. Am. Machinist, publ. McGraw-Hill, Inc., N.Y.C., 1962-67, mktg. svc. mgr., 1967-69, 1969-71, sales mgr., 1976-77, dir. mktg., 1977-78; v.p. mktg. svcs. Morgan-Gramplan, Inc., N.Y.C., 1971-72; mktg. dir. Family Health & Diversion mag., 1972-74; dist. sales mgr. Postgrad. Medicine, 1974-76; advt. sales mgr. Contemporary Ob/Gyn, 1976-78; dir. profl. devel., 1978-80; pub. graduating engr. and dir. mktg. Aviation Week Group, 1980-90; pub. World Aviation Directory; dir. communications Aviation Week Group,

1990-92; v.p., Phase, Ltd., 1993—. Mem. Am. Mktg. Assn., Pharm. Advt. Club, Advt. Women N.Y., Advt. Club N.Y., Sales Exec. Club, Employment Mgmt. Assn., Am. Soc. Pers. Adminstrs., Nat. Orgn. Disability (bd. dirs.), Internat. Platform Assn., Coll. Placement Coun., Svc. Corps Ret. Execs., Wings Club, Dir. Assn., Pi Sigma Alpha. Home: Barnahill Farm Rt # 1 Box 162 Stanardsville VA 22973

ANSAY, A. MANETTE, English language educator; b. Lapeer, Mich., Aug. 15, 1964; d. Dick and Sylvia J. Ansay; m. Jake Smith, May 12, 1990. MFA, Cornell U., 1991. Lectr. Cornell U., 1991-92; asst. prof. English Vanderbilt U., Nashville, 1993—; instr. Sewanee Younger Writer's Conf., Northshore Younger Writer's Conf.; reader Vis. Writers Series Butler U., U. So. Maine, Wells Coll.; resident Mac Dowell Colony, Peterborough, N.H., 1991, 95, Va. Colony for the Creative Arts, 1994, Yaddo, 1994, Ragdale Found., 1995. Author: Vinegar Hill, 1994 (2nd Place Friends of Am. Writers prize competition 1995), (short stories) Read This and Tell Me What It Says, 1995 (Nelson Algren award for Short Fiction Chgo. Tribune 1992, AWP Short Fiction prize, One of Best Books of Yr. Citation Chgo. Tribune 1994, 2nd Place in Friends of Am. Writers prize competition, 1995); (poems) Poetry Northwest (Theodore Roethke prize for poetry, 1995), American Family Values, The Road Ends at the Orchards; work featured in Best American Stories, 1992, 94; assoc. editor EPOCH, 1989-92, Willow Springs, 1995—; contbr. stories to Story, N.Am. Review, Ind. Review, Am. Fiction, others. George Bennett fellow Phillips Exeter Acad., 1992-93, Bread Loaf Writers fellow; recipient Pushcart prize for fiction, 1994. Office: Vanderbilt U Box 1654 Sta B Nashville TN 37235 also: Deborah Schneider Gelfman Schneider Lit Agent 250 W 57th St New York NY 10107*

ANSELMI, TINA RASPANTI, secondary school educator; b. Pitts., May 21, 1968; d. John J. and Mary M. (Mangone) Raspanti; m. Michael Paul Anselmi, Sept. 1, 1990; 1 child, Carli. BS in Edn., Clarion (Pa.) U., 1989; MEd, Coll. William and Mary, 1996. Tchr. social studies Warwick H.S., Newport News, Va., 1991-92, Toano (Va.) Mid. Sch., 1993—; presenter William & Mary Resource Collaborating Tchr. Symposium, Williamsburg, Va., 1995, Va. Coun. Learning Disabilities Conf., Roanoke, 1996. Grantee Kappa Delta Pi, 1996. Mem. ASCD (featured in video), NEA, Coun. for Learning Disabilities, Mid. Sch. Assn. Home: 2926 Forge Rd Toano VA 23168-9119 Office: Toano Mid Sch 7817 Richmond Rd Toano VA 23168-9024

ANSHAW, CAROL, writer; b. Grosse Pointe Shores, Mich., Mar. 22, 1946; d. Henry G. and Virginia (Anshaw) Stanley; m. Charles J. White III, Mar. 15, 1969. BA, Mich. State U., 1968. Book reviewer, Voice Literary Supplement. Author: They Do It All With Mirrors, 1978, Aquamarine, 1992, Seven Moves, 1996. Tutor Literacy Council of Chgo., 1989—. Recipient Nat. Book Critics Circle citation for excellence in reviewing, 1989. Mem. Nat. Book Critics Cir., Nat. Writers Union. Democrat. Office: 3139 N Lincoln Ave Ste 202 Chicago IL 60657

ANSLEY, JUDITH A., legislative staff member; b. Somerville, Mass., Feb. 25, 1958; d. Emilio J. and Gilda C. (Piccoli) Scalesse. BA summa cum laude, Tufts U., 1979; MA, Fletcher Sch. Law and Diplomacy, 1980. Rsch. asst. Congl. Rsch. Svc. Libr. Congress, 1980-83; mem. profl. staff Senate Com. Armed Svcs., 1983-93, Senate Select Com. Intelligence, 1993—; legis. asst. Senator Warner's Office. Mem. Phi Beta Kappa. Office: Rm 225 Russel Senate Office Bldg Washington DC 20510*

ANSLEY, JULIA ETTE, elementary school educator, consultant, poet, writer; b. Malvern, Ark., Nov. 10, 1940; d. William Harold and Dorothy Mae (Hamm) Smith; m. Miles Ansley, Nov. 8, 1964 (div. June 1976); children: Felicia Dianne, Mark Damon. BA in Edn., Calif. State U., Long Beach, 1962; postgrad., UCLA Ext. Early childhood edn., life, Miller-Unruh reading specialist credentials, Calif. Elem. tchr. L.A. Unified Sch. Dist., 1962—; coord. Proficiency in English Program, L.A., 1991-93; mem., advisor P.E.P. instrnl. tchrs. network, 1993—, workshop presenter in field; also poetry presentations, L.A., 1989—; owner Poetry Expressions, L.A.; self-markets own poetry posters; creator, presenter KidChess integrated lang. arts program, 1987—. Author: (poetry vols.) Out of Heat Comes Light, From Dreams to Reality. Bd. dirs. New Frontier Dem. Club, L.A., 1990-93; mem. exec. bd. L.A. Panhellenic Coun., rec. sec., 1993-95. Honored by Teacher mag., 1990; recipient Spirit of Edn. award Sta. KNBC-TV, L.A., 1990; grantee L.A. Ednl. Partnership, 1985, 87, 89, 93. Mem. L.A. Alliance African-Am. Educators (exec. bd. 1991-94, parliamentarian 1992-94), Black Women's Forum, Black Am. Polit. Assn. (edn. co-chair 1993-95), Sigma Gamma Rho. Mem. FAME Ch. Home: 3739 S Gramercy Pl Los Angeles CA 90018 Office: Hillcrest Dr Sch 4041 Hillcrest Dr Los Angeles CA 90008-2902

ANSORGE, IONA MARIE, retired real estate agent, musician, high school and college instructor; b. Nov. 3, 1927; d. Edgar B. and Marie Louise (Bleeke) Bohn; m. Edwin James Ansorge, Sept. 13, 1949; children: Richard, Michelle. BS, Valparaiso U., 1949; cert. teaching, Drake U., 1964; MA, U. Iowa, 1976. Min. of music Our Savior Luth. Ch., Des Moines, 1949-63; tchr. Johnston (Iowa) High Sch., 1964-75; instr. Iowa Meth. Sch. Nursing, Des Moines, 1978-87; owner, pres. Bed and Breakfast in Iowa, Ltd., 1982-86; realtor Better Homes and Gardens First Realty, Des Moines, 1986-92. Pres. Des Moines Jaycee-ettes; fundraiser Des Moines Zoo; founder Messiah Luth. Ch., Des Moines, 1978; started Iowa Bed and Breakfast Industry, 1982; owner, pres. Bed and Breakfast in Iowa, Ltd.; mem. Faith Luth. Ch. Mem. LWV, AAUW, Des Moines Bd. Realtors, Women's Coun. Realtors, Realtor's Million Dollar Club, Jaycee-ettes (pres. Des Moines chpt. 1957-58), Valparaiso U. Guild (charter mem. Des Moines chpt.). Home: 8345 Twinberry Point Colorado Springs CO 80920

ANSPACH, JUDITH FORD, law librarian, law educator; b. Akron, Ohio, Oct. 29, 1940; m. Stephen Fredrick Anspach, Apr. 10, 1963; 1 child, Erich Stephen. BS in Edn., Kent State U., 1962, MLS, 1977; JD, Miss. Coll., 1983. Pub. svcs. librarian Miss. Coll. Law Library, Jackson, 1978-84; assoc. law librarian Law Library, U. Conn., Hartford, 1984-89; assoc. prof., dir. library svcs. Thomas M. Cooley Law Sch., Lansing, Mich., 1989-93; prof., dir. U. N.Mex. Law Sch., Albuquerque, 1993—; paralegal instr. U. Miss., Jackson, 1983. Mem. Am. Assn. Law Schs. (exec. com. sect. on law librs. 1994-96), Am. Assn. Law Librs. (chmn. scholarship com. 1988-89, publs. rev. com. 1993-95), Mich. Assn. Law Librs. (v.p. 1991-92, pres. 1992-93), Ohio Regional Assn. Law Librs., Govt. Documents Roundtable Conn. (chmn. 1988-89). Episcopalian. Office: U NMex Sch Law Libr 1117 Stanford Dr NE Albuquerque NM 87106-3721

ANTHONY, CAROL A., judge; b. 1953. Student, Trinity Univ., 1971-73; BA, Univ. of Ark., Fayetteville, 1976; JD, Univ. of Ark. Sch. of Law, 1979. Law clk. to Hon. Marian Penix, 1979-80, law clk. to Hon. Oren Harris, 1981-84; with Compton, Prewett, Thomas & Hickey, 1984—; magistrate judge U.S. Dist. Ct. (Ark. we. dist.), 8th circuit, El Dorado, 1987—; cir. chancery judge 13th Dist. Ct., El Dorado; instr. Southern Ark. Univ. Mem. Ark. Bar Assn., Am. Trial Lawyers Assn., Ark. Trial Lawyers. Office: US Dist Ct 101 N Washington Ave Ste 306 El Dorado AR 71730*

ANTHONY, ELAINE, artist; b. N.Y.C., June 5, 1943; d. Jack Murray and Elaine Carol (Schleicher) A.; children: Pedro, Tessa. BFA, Stephen Coll., 1963, R.I. Sch. of Design, 1966. lectr. in field. Many one-person shows; prin. works include Merril Lynch, Euro-Disney, Paris, Albright-Knox Mus., Buffalo, others. Named Artist of Yr. Art Place Gallery, 1995; grantee Pollock-Krasner Found., 1991, European Honors Program, 1965; other art awards.

ANTHONY, KATHRYN HARRIET, architecture educator; b. N.Y.C., Sept. 11, 1955; d. Harry Antoniades and Anne (Skoufis) A.; m. Barry Daniel Riccio, May 24, 1980. AB in Psychology, U. Calif., Berkeley, 1976, PhD in Architecture, 1981. Rsch. promotion Kaplan/McLaughlin/Diaz Architects and Planners, San Francisco, 1980-81; vis. lectr. U. Calif., Berkeley, 1980-81, 82-83, San Francisco State U., 1981; assoc. prof. Calif. State Poly. U., Pomona, 1981-84; asst. prof. U. Ill., Urbana-Champaign, 1984-89, assoc. prof., 1989-96, chair bldg. rsch. coun., 1994—, prof. architecture, 1996—; guest lectr. numerous orgns., colls. and univs.; mem. numerous comms. Coll. of Fine and Applied Arts, Sch. Architecture, Housing Rsch. and Devel. Program, Dept. Landscape Architecture. Author: Design Juries on Trial: The Renaissance of the Design Studio, 1991; co-editor Jour. Archtl. Edn. 47:1, 1993; mem. editl. bd. Jour. Archtl. and Planning Rsch., 1989—, Jour. Archtl. Edn., 1990-95, Environ. and Behavior Jour., 1991—; reviewer Landscape Jour., 1990; contbr. articles to profl. jours; co-designer, co-prodr. (exhibit) Shattering the Glass Ceiling: The Role of Gender and Race in the Archtl. Profession, Nat. Conv. AIA, 1996. Recipient Creative Achievement award Assn. Collegiate Sch. Architecture, 1992, grant U.S. Army C.E.R.L., 1993, grant U. Ill., 1984, 87, 92, 93, 95, grant Graham Found., 1989-91, 93-96, grant Decatur Housing Authority, 1988, grant Upgrade Co., Peoria, Ill., 1987, grant Nat. Endowment for Arts, 1986-87, grant L.A. County Community Devel. Commn., 1984, grant Calif. State U. and Colls., 1982, 83, summer grant U. Calif., Berkeley, 1980. Mem. AIA (Champaign Urbana sect.), Environ. Design Rsch. Assn. (bd. dirs. 1989-92, treas. 1990-92, co-editor Coming of Age: Proceedings of 21st Ann. Conf. 1990), Chgo. Women in Architecture, Women in Info. Tech. and Scholarship. Home: 309 W Pennsylvania Ave Urbana IL 61801-4918 Office: U Ill Sch Architecture 611 Taft Dr Champaign IL 61820-6922

ANTHONY, SHEILA F., federal official; b. Hope, Ark., Nov. 8, 1940; m. Beryl F. Anthony; children: Alison, Lauren. BA, U. Ark., 1962; JD, Am. U., 1984. Bar: Ark. 1985, D.C. 1985, U.S. Ct. Appeals (D.C. cir.) 1987, U.S. Supreme Ct. 1992. Tchr. Ark. Pub. Schs., 1962-63, 74-76; with Dow, Lohnes & Albertson, Washington, 1985-93; asst. atty. gen. Dept. of Justice, Washington, 1993-95. Del. Dem. Nat. Conv., 1980; justice of the peace Union County, Ark., 1969; trustee South Ark. U., 1971-75, Wash. Ctr. Seminars and Acad. Internships, 1993—. Office: 3900 Macomb St NW Washington DC 20016-3742

ANTHONY, SUSAN MAE, entrepreneur; b. Elmhurst, Ill., Oct. 11, 1959; d. Neil Jack and Shirley Mae (Deckard) A.; m. Mark Stephan Rogers, Jan. 28, 1989 (div. May 1993); 1 child, Ryan James Rogers. Student, Edison C.C., 1977-82; AS, Internat. Corr. Sch., 1982. Clk. Lee County Elec. Coop., North Ft. Myers, Fla., 1975-78, apprentice journeyman, 1978-82; spl. agt. Northwestern Mut. Life, Ft. Myers, Fla., 1982-86; broker rep. Paul Revere Ins. Co., Ft. Myers, 1986-88; owner Anthony Ins. Svcs., Ft. Myers, 1982-92; co-owner Soil Plus, Ft. Myers, 1988-92; pres. Crews Sanitation Co., Ft. Myers, 1993—; owner Anthony Contracting Svcs., Ft. Myers, 1992—. Author: (guidebook) Guide and Checklist for Starting a Small Business, 1993. Founder, organizer New Directions, Am. Cancer Soc., Ft. Myers, 1986-88, crusade chmn., bd. officer, 1986-88; organizer, co-chmn., pres. Interfaith Vol. Caregivers Project, Ft. Myers, 1993—; founder, chmn. Elder Abuse Task Force, Ft. Myers, 1993-95; elder abuse prevention coord. Area Agy. on Aging of S.W. Fla., Ft. Myers, 1993-95; mem. steering com. for minority task force Horizon Coun. on Econ. Devel., Ft. Myers, 1991-93; active Fla. and Nat. Women's Polit. Caucus, 1991-93. Mem. NRA, Fla. Septic Tank Assn., Fla. Restaurant Assn., Ft. Myers Womens Network (steering com., bd. dirs. 1984-92). Republican. Home: PO Box 2031 Fort Myers FL 33902-2031 Office: Crews Sanitation Co PO Box 27 Fort Myers FL 33902-0027

ANTICH, ROSE ANN, state legislator. Grad., Hammond Bus. Coll.; postgrad., Ind. U. N.W. Radio and TV personality, lectr. positive mental attitude and stress control, astrologist; mem. Ind. State Senate from 4th dist., 1991—. Mem. town coun., 1983-87. Democrat. Roman Catholic. Home: 5401 Lincoln St Merrillville IN 46410-1926 Office: Ind State House 200 W Washington St Indianapolis IN 46204-2728

ANTILLA, SUSAN, journalist; b. New Rochelle, N.Y., May 18, 1954; d. Oscar E. Antilla and Gloria (Jennings) Claudet; m. James Harlan Burdsall, Sept. 26, 1981 (div. Nov. 1995). BA, Manhattanville Coll., 1976; MA, NYU, 1981. Reporter Dun's Bus. Month, N.Y.C., 1978-81, asst. editor, 1981-82; contbg. editor Working Woman Mag., N.Y.C., 1980-86; fin. bur. chief Balt. Sun., N.Y.C., 1985-86; stock market reporter USA Today, N.Y.C., 1982-85, chief Money bur., columnist, 1986-92; columnist, reporter N.Y. Times, 1992-95; columnist Bloomberg Bus. News, 1995—; guest lectr. Marymount Manhattan Coll., 1984, 85; guest lectr. NYU, 1985, adj. prof., 1987-88. Contbr. Savvy mag., 1986-88, also articles to other mags. and profl. jours. Cons. Girls Club Am., N.Y.C., 1983. Mem. N.Y. Fin. Writers Assn. Office: Bloomberg Bus News 499 Park Ave New York NY 10022

ANTOKOL-MECKLER, SHIRLEY, humanities educator; b. Altoona, Pa., Oct. 8, 1940; d. Julius and Faye (Falk) Antokol; m. Jack Meckler, Dec. 1, 1963; children: Janine Lynn, Philip Richard (dec.), David Zvi. Degree in Nursing, U. Md., 1960; AA, Catonsville C.C., Balt., 1978; BS, Towson State U., 1989; MA, Morgan State U., 1995. Staff nurse Md. Ge. Hosp., Balt., 1961-64; mkt. rsch. interviewer Venick Assocs., Balt., 1980-83; pub. rels. staff Shaare Zedek Med. Ctr. in Jerusalem, Balt., 1989-92; instr. English Coppin State Coll., Balt., 1995—; tutor Towson State U., 1988-89. Contbr. articles to newspapers. Mem. steering com. Jewish Am. Festival, Balt., 1979-84, auction com. co-chair, 1979-80, chair raffle com., 1981-84; donor, chair, bd. dirs. Amit Women, Balt., 1978-86. All-Am. Scholar Collegiate award, 1994. Mem. Phi Alpha Theta (past pres.), Lambda Iota Tau. Democrat. Jewish. Office: Coppin State College 2500 W North Ave Baltimore MD 21216

ANTON, CHERYL L., sales executive; b. Toledo, Nov. 3, 1953; d. Ralph Herbert Snyder and Coletta Marie Piekut Nickerson; 1 child, John Daniel. Student U. Toledo, 1971-73. With Kroger Co., Toledo, 1972-80, dept. supr. merchandising; sales dir. Growth Unltd., Toledo, 1979-80; owner CJ's Bar, Toledo, 1980-82; sales rep. Armour Food Co., Orlando, Fla., 1983-85; dist. sales mgr. Jones Dairy Farm, 1985-87; regional sales mgr. Southland Corp., 1987-92; Southeast regional sales mgr. McLane Co., Orlando, 1995—. Mem. NAFE (network dir. 1979—), Nat. Assn. for Women. Democrat. Address: PO Box 593521 Orlando FL 32859-3521

ANTONACCI, LORI (LORETTA MARIE ANTONACCI), marketing executive, consultant; b. Riverton, Ill., Mar. 31, 1947; d. Antonio and Gena Marie A. BA, Bradley U., 1969. Broadcast copywriter Sta. WIRL-TV, Peoria, Ill., 1969; communications specialist Walgreen Co., Chgo., 1970-72; creative supr. Nat. Assn. Realtors, Chgo., 1973; creative dir., producer Steve Sohmer, Inc., N.Y.C., 1974-78; promotion specialist Ziff-Davis Publs., 1979-80; promotion mgr. Psychology Today, 1980-81; sales devel. cons. Antonacci Prodns., N.Y.C., 1982-84; promotion dir. Crain's N.Y. Bus., N.Y.C., 1984-85; pres. Antonacci & Assocs., 1985—; advisor, instr. Gallatin Sch. NYU, 1986—; co-founder, bd. advisors Artists Talk on Art Inc., 1974, Artists Comm. Fed. Credit Union, 1986, N.Y. Women's Agenda, 1992, bd. dirs., v.p. events 1993-95; bd. dirs. Women's City Club N.Y., v.p. devel. 1994-95. Recipient Golden Eagle award CINE, 1976; award U.S. Indsl. Film Festival, 1977; CEBA award, 1979; Bronze medal Internat. Film and TV Festival N.Y., 1979. Mem. Advt. Women N.Y. (profl. devel. com. 1983-85, program com. 1986-90, chmn. speakers bur. 1988-90, chmn. pub. policy com. 1991-95), Women in Comm., Am. Women in Radio and TV. Address: 15 E 10th St New York NY 10003-5930

ANTOS, MARA MELINDA, sales professional; b. San Juan, Puerto Rico, Apr. 27, 1966; d. John M. and Mary Claire (Miller) Slais; m. Ted Justin Antos, July 10, 1993. BA in comparative philosophy and religion, Calif. Luth. U., 1991. Asst. mgr. Frames By You Inc., Thousand Oaks, Calif., 1980-90; ops. mgr. Career Uniforms, North Hollywood, Calif., 1991-94; with sales dept. Pella Archtl. Products, Studio City, Calif., 1994—. Cmty. rels. dir. Rotaract, Thousand Oaks, Calif., 1989-91; mem. planning com. City of Thousand Oaks Crime Task Force, 1994, 96; chair young adult task force Conejo Future Found., 1993-94; commr. Ventura (Calif.) County Commn. for Women, 1995—.

ANTOUN, ANNETTE AGNES, newspaper editor, publisher; b. Franklin, Pa., Mar. 7, 1927; d. Adrien Uriel and Charlotte Mary (McMullen) Adelman; student Allegheny Coll., Meadville, Pa.; m. Frederic George Antoun, July 19, 1947 (dec.); children: Frederic G., Gregory S., Lawrence J., Mark J. (dec.), Laureace A., Scott J., Jonathan M., Lisa A. Founder, editor-pub. Paxton Herald, Harrisburg, Pa., 1960—; founder, owner Graphic Services, advt. and graphics, Harrisburg, 1972—; owner Communications System Design, 1978—; pres. Susquehanna Valley Assos., Inc., 1978—; co-editor French Creek Patriot, community newspaper, Cochranton, Pa., 1972. Bd. dirs. Am. Lung Assn. Assn. Cen. Pa., 1967-89, 92—, exec. bd., 1967-89, sec., 1972-79, treas., 1975-89; mem. communications com. Tri-County United Fund, 1973, mem. com. children's services, 1975-79; bd. dirs. Pa. Am. Lung Assn., 1973—, treas., 1976, sec., 1979-80, v.p., 1980-81, treas. 1996—; counselor to bd. Am. Lung Assn., 1989-90; bd. dirs. Harris Commn., 1975-79, Cath. Social Service Harrisburg, 1972-76; mem. extension planning com. YMCA, 1975-79; bd. govs. Camp Curtin YMCA, 1980-85; exec. bd. Lower Paxton Coalition Community Groups, 1973-93; mem. communications bd. Catholic Diocese Harrisburg, 1971-80; co-chmn. Dauphin County Ethics Com., 1979-81; chmn. bldg. com. Juvenile Detention Home, 1976-80; chmn. fund raising com. Greater Harrisburg Arts Council, 1977-79; mem. Dauphin County bd. Com. Children and Youth, 1982-85; vice chmn. Dauphin County Election Voting Machine Com., 1982—; mem. Tri-County Solid Waste Mgmt. Com., 1983-87; bd. idrs. Salvation Army Rehab. Svcs., 1992—, Capitol Pavilion Rehab., 1992—; mem. exec. com. spl. events United Negro Coll. Fund, 1993—; spl. events chmn. Ctrl. Pa. UNCF, 1993-94. Recipient Advocate award Paxton Area Jaycees, 1969, 73; citation Am. Legion Pa., 1971, 74, CAP, 1972, medallion Am. Legion Pa., 1972; award Am. Cancer Soc., 1969-89, March of Dimes award, 1969-89, AARP award, 1988, MADD award, Historical Preservation award, All America City Participation award, Nat. award Am. Lung Assn., 1992, Am. Legion Regional award, 1994, Pioneer award John Heinz Ctr., 1996, Cmty. Svc. award VFW, 1996; numerous others. Mem. Am. Lung Assn. Pa. (treas. 1995—), Internat. Platform Assn. Home: 4910 Earl Dr Harrisburg PA 17112-2123 Office: 101 Lincoln St Harrisburg PA 17112

ANZALDUA, CYNTHIA VERONICA, artist; b. Brownsville, Tex., Jan. 29, 1956; d. Adolfo Anthony and Ofelia (Flores) A. BFA, U. North Tex., 1980, postgrad., 1996—. Art tchr. K-6th grade John J. Pershing Elem., Dallas, 1980-85, Mark Twain Vanguard, Dallas, 1985-88; art tchr. 7-8th grade Greiner Art Acad., Dallas, 1988-90; arts chair, instr. 9-12th grade Skyline H.S., Dallas, 1990—; art tchr. Evening Alternative H.S., Dallas, 1995—. Dallas Dept. Cultural Affairs grantee, 1995-96; recipient Arts in Edn. award Lincoln Mercury, Dallas, 1995. Mem. Art Edn. Assn., Artist Relating Together and Exhibiting (coord. 1994), Latino Artist Dallas (coord.). Home: 6163 Belmont Ave Dallas TX 75214

APEGIAN CELUCH, DIANE HELENE, organizational development consultant; b. Pasadena, Calif., Sept. 8, 1957; d. Joseph Artine and Helen Louise (Janbaz) Apegian; m. Paul Joseph Celuch; 1 child, Jonathan. BA in Home Econs., Calif. State U., Long Beach, 1984; MA in Psychology, Pepperdine U., 1995. Human resources adminstr. Honeywell, Inc., West Covina, Calif., 1985-88; sales rep. Zeneca Pharms., Glendale, Calif., 1989-94; sr. cons. Drake Beam Morin, Inc., Woodland Hills, Calif., 1995, Lee Hecht Harrison, San Marino, Calif., 1996—; pres. Diane's Spell Mania, Pasadena, 1995—; facilitator U. Phoenix human resources devel. classes. Counselor for women Pasadena Rape Crisis Ctr., 1993-95; baseball team asst. Pasadena Am. Little League. Mem. APA, ASTD, NOW, L.A. Orgnl. Devel. Network, Profls. in Human Resources Assn., Psi Chi. Democrat.

APEL-BRUEGGEMAN, MYRNA L., entrepreneur; b. Cleve., July 19, 1942; d. Melvin Arthur and Merle Ruth (Hoffman) Rehlender; children: Timothy, Kristen, Michelle, Kim; m. Earl L. Brueggeman, May 7, 1994. BS in Edn., Kent State U., 1965, M. in Edn. Counseling, 1987. Cert. tchr., Ohio; lic. minister, Ohio. Owner, mgr. real estate investments Kent, Ohio; owner, founder IHS Counseling Ctr., Ravenna, Ohio; owner, mgr. Winning Edge, Kent, Ohio; founder, pres. IHS Sch. Personal Devel., Ravenna, Ohio; owner IHS Bookstore; co-owner Chapel on the Lakes. Mem. NAFE, Ohio Manufactured Housing Assn. (pres. We. Res. chpt.), Internat. Soc. Profl. Hypnotists, Sigma Epsilon, Chi Sigma Iota.

APELSKOG, KATHLEEN ANN, primary education educator; b. Sept. 27, 1964; d. Herbert Edward and Camille Ann (Ambrosini) A. BA, Molloy Coll., 1988; MA, Hofstra U., 1993. Cert. elem. tchr., N.Y. Jr. then sr. counselor Big Chief Day Camp and Nursery Sch., East Meadow, N.Y., 1982-83; tutor St. Thomas Aquinas program Molloy Coll., Rockville Centre, N.Y., 1987-88; tchr. nursery St. Kilian Cath. Sch., Farmingdale, N.Y., 1988-89; substitute tchr. Nassau & Suffolk Counties, N.Y., 1989-93; tchr. nursery and pre-kindergarten Little Pebbles Nursery Sch., East Rockaway, N.Y., 1993—; asst. counselor Bright Star Country Day Sch. and Camp, Ocean Harbor, N.Y., summers 1995, 96. Author and editor: Healthy Foods and Junk Foods, 1988, Pink Bear, Pink Bear, 1993; contbr. articles to prof. jours. Vol. Anchor Program, Lido Beach, N.Y., summers 1979-80, Mid-Island Hosp., Bethpage, N.Y., 1980-83, Nassau C.C., Uniondale, N.Y., 1986; tutor St. Thomas Aquinas program Molloy Coll., Rockville Centre, N.Y., 1987-88; mem. adv. bd., pub. rels. com. Luth. Singles Orgn., L.I., 1993—. Paul Douglas scholar, 1986-88. Mem. AAUW, Assn. Childhood Edn. Internat. (nominating com. 1991-92), Nassau Assn. Edn. Young Children, Delta Epsilon Sigma, Kappa Delta Pi, Chi Beta Phi, Omicron Alpha Zeta. Republican. Lutheran.

APGAR, BARBARA SUE, physician, educator; b. Guthrie, Okla., Oct. 4, 1943; d. Wallace Duke and Gloria Jayne (Glover) McMillin; 1 child, Larisa Ann. BA in Biology, Loretto Heights Coll., 1965; MS in Anatomy, U. Mich., 1968; MD, Tex. Tech. Med. Sch., 1976. Diplomate Am. Bd. Family Practice, Am. Bd. Med. Examiners; cert. instr. advanced life support sys. Rsch. asst. Parke Davis, Ann Arbor, Mich., 1965-66, Aerospace Med. Labs Wright-Patterson AFB, Ohio, 1968-70; instr. anatomy dept. Tex. Tech. U. Med. Sch., Lubbock, 1972-74, resident in family practice, 1976-79, clin. asst. prof., 1980-83; physician The Pavilion, Lubbock, 1981-83; sr. physician, dir. gynecology clinic U. Mich., 1983-86, instr. dept. family practice, 1984-89, med. dir. Briarwood Health Ctr., 1986—, also mem. steering com. for ambulatory care, asst. prof. dept. family practice, 1989-93, assoc. prof Dept Family Practice, 1993—; dir. women's health, 1989—, asst. residency dir. dept. family practice, 1991—; dir. women's health course Am. Acad. Family Practice; mem. staff Meth. Hosp., St. Mary of the Plains Hosp., U. Mich. Hosp.; mem. med. exec. com. dept. of family practice U. Mich.; advanced life support in obstetrics instr., 1995—. Editl. reviewer Jour. Am. Bd. Family Practice, 1991—; assoc. editor: American Family Physician, 1993, editor, 1994-95, editor gynecologic care, 1996; editl. bd., co-editor primary care series The Female Patient. Mem. adv. bd. Lubbock chpt. March of Dimes, 1972-74. Recipient Upjohn Achievement award, 1976, Psychiatry Achievement award, 1976; Soroptimist Internat. grantee, 1978-79, U. Mich. Dept. Family Practice Resident Teaching award, 1985, 87, 88, 89, 91, 95; fellow Mich. State U., 1989-90. Mem. Am. Acad. Family Practice (task force on clin. policy 1991, mem. faculty procedural skills), Am. Assn. of Med. Writers, Lubbock County Med. Soc., Tex. Med. Assn., Mich. Acad. Family Practice (perinatal com. 1987—, sci. assembly program com.), Soc. of Tchrs. of Family Medicine, Am. Soc. Colposcopy and Cervical Pathology (task force on resident edn., mem. com. on colposcopy recognition award), Alpha Omega Alpha. Democrat. Home: 883 Scio Meadows Dr Ann Arbor MI 48103-1586 Office: U Mich Family Practice Dept 775 S Main St Chelsea MI 48118-1370

APODACA, CLARA R., federal official; b. Las Cruces, N.Mex., Sept. 24, 1934; d. A.D. and Sally H. Melendres; children: Cindy Sherman, Carolyn Folkman, Jerry, Jeff, Judy. Degree in elem. edn., N.Mex. State U., 1955. Mgr. family bus., 1964-74; First Lady N.Mex., 1975-79; owner, mgr. Apodaca Co., Santa Fe, 1979-83; sales dir. City of Santa Fe, 1983-84; dir. office cultural affairs State N.Mex., Santa Fe, 1984-88; dep. Dukakis for Pres., Boston, 1988; gen. asst. to chmn. Dem. Nat. Com., Washington, 1989-93; sr. advisor, asst. sec. Dept. Treasury, Washington, 1993—; bd. dirs. Hitachi Found., Washington. Bd. dirs. Washington Performing Arts Soc., 1993-96, Women in Philanthropy, Washington, 1994-96, Hispanics in Philanthropy, Calif., 1993-96. Roman Catholic. Home: 6223 Utah Ave NW Washington DC 20015 Office: Dept Treasury 1500 Pennsylvania Ave NW Washington DC 20220

APPEL, GLORIA, advertising executive. Exec. v.p. Grey Advt. Inc., N.Y.C. Office: Grey Advt Inc 777 3rd Ave New York NY 10017*

APPEL, NINA SCHICK, law educator, dean; b. Feb. 17, 1936, Prague, Czech Republic; d. Leo and Nora Schick; m. Alfred Appel Jr.; children: Karen Oshman, Richard. Student, Cornell U.; JD, Columbia U., 1959. Instr. Columbia Law Sch., 1959-60; adminstr. Stanford U.; mem. faculty, prof. law, 1973—, assoc. dean 1976-83, dean Sch. Law, Loyola U., 1983—; mem. Ill. Compensation Rev. Bd. Mem. ABA (chair legal edn. and adminstrn. to

Bar 1992-93), Am. Bar Found., Chgo. Bar Found., Ill. State Bar Found.; mem. Chgo. Legal Club, Chgo. Network. Jewish. Office: Loyola U Sch Law 1 E Pearson St Chicago IL 60611-2055

APPELBAUM, ANN HARRIET, lawyer; b. Decatur, Ill., Oct. 31, 1948; d. Irving and Cecelia (Hecht) A.; m. Neal Borovitz, July 4, 1982; children: Abby, Jeremy. BA, Barnard Coll., 1970; JD, Boston U., 1973. Bar: N.Y. 1974, U.S. Dist. Ct. (so. dist.) N.Y. 1975, U.S. Ct. Appeals (2nd cir.) 1975, U.S. Supreme Ct. 1978. Assoc. Hart & Hume, N.Y.C., 1974-76, Warshaw, Burstein, N.Y.C., 1976-80; counsel Jewish Theol. Sem. & Jewish Mus., N.Y.C., 1980—. V.p. Solomon Schechter Day Sch., N.J., 1992—. Mem. Nat. Assn. Coll. & Univ. Attys. Office: The Jewish Theological Seminary 3080 Broadway New York NY 10027

APPELBAUM, JUDITH PILPEL, editor, consultant, educator; b. N.Y.C., Sept. 26, 1939; d. Robert Cecil and Harriet Florence (Fleischl) Pilpel; m. Alan Appelbaum, Apr. 16, 1961; children: Lynn Stephanie, Alexander Eric. BA with honors Vassar Coll., 1960. Editor, Harper's Mag., N.Y.C., 1960-74; mng. editor Harper's Weekly, 1974-76; sr. cons. Atlas World Press Rev., 1977; mng. editor Pubs. Weekly, 1978-81; founder Sensible Solutions, Inc., 1979; contbg. editor Publishers Weekly, 1981-82; columnist N.Y. Times Book Rev., 1982-84; mng. dir. Sensible Solutions, Inc., 1984—; assoc. dir. Ctr. for Book Rsch., U. Scranton, 1985-88; book rev. editor Publishing Research Quar., 1984-86, editor in chief, 1986-88, cons. editor, 1988—, chair book industry systems adv. com. royalty subcom., 1996—; contbg. editor Small Press mag. 1991-96; mem. faculty Pub. Inst. of U. Denver, 1981—, CUNY edn. in pub. program, 1982—; adv. com. Book Industry Study Group Publs., 1980—; mem. stats. com. Book Industry Study Group, 1984—; adv. bd. Coordinating Coun. Lit. Mags., 1980-84, PEN Ctr. USA West, 1988-90. Mem. Authors Guild, Women's Media Group (bull. editor 1990-92), PEN, Com. Small Mag./Press Editors & Pubs., Pubs. Mktg. Assn. (bd. dirs. 1990-92, Benjamin Franklin Lifetime Achievement award 1995). Author: How to Get Happily Published, 1978, 4th edit., 1992; co-author: The Writer's Workbook: A Full and Friendly Guide to Boosting Your Book's Soles, 1991; editor: (with Tony Jones and Gwyneth Cravens) The Big Picture: A Wraparound Book, 1976; The Question of Size in the Book Industry Today, 1978; Getting a Line on Backlist, 1979; Paperback Primacy, 1981; Small Publisher Power, 1982. Office: Sensible Solutions Inc 271 Madison Ave Ste 1007 New York NY 10016-1001

APPELHOF, RUTH STEVENS, museum director, curator, art historian; b. Washington, Feb. 14, 1945. BFA in Painting and Art History, Syracuse U., 1965, MA in Art History, 1974, MPhil, 1980, PhD in Humanities, 1988. Assoc. prof. art SUNY, Cayuga Coll., Auburn, 1971-80, gallery dir., 1977-79; asst. prof. museology grad. divsn. Sch. Art Coll. Visual and Performing Arts, Syracuse (N.Y.) U., 1981-84; curator exhbns. Lowe Art Gallery, Syracuse, 1981-84; curator painting, sculpture and graphic arts Birmingham (Ala.) Mus. Art, 1984-89; exec. dir. Art Mus. Western Va. (formerly Roanoke (Va.) Mus. Fine Arts), 1989-94; dir. Minn. Mus. Am. Art, St. Paul, 1994—; adj. prof. art dept. U. Ala., Birmingham, 1984-89; lectr. in field. Exhbns. curated include Margaret Bourke-White, Syracuse, 1983, The New Figure, Birmingham, 1985, The Expressionist Landscape, Birmingham, 1988, Looking South, Birmingham, 1988, The Commonwealth, Roanoke, 1990, Bill Dunlap, Roanoke, 1992, Hunt Slonem, 1993, Fritz Bultman, Roanoke, 1994, Watershed, St. Paul, 1996. Chair Mus. and the Artist, AAM, 1993; mem. bd. continuing edn. U. Va. Fellow Whitney Mus. Am. Art, N.Y.C., 1980-81. Mem. Am. Assn. Mus., Va. Assn. Mus., Coll. Art Assn., Women's Caucus Art, Roanoke Valley-Va. Tech. Adv. Coun. Office: Minnesota Mus Am Art Landmark Ctr 75 West 5th St Saint Paul MN 55102-1431

APPEL-KAGAN, VALERIE MILLICENT, retired guidance counselor; b. Passaic, N.J., Dec. 18, 1935; d. Murray and Minnie (Geminder) Appel; m. Clarence (Larry) Kagan, June 30, 1963 (dec. Feb. 1982); 1 child, Josh. AA, Rider Coll., Trenton, N.J., 1955, BS in Edn., 1957; MA, Seton Hall U., South Orange, N.J., 1961; 6th yr. cert., NYU, N.Y.C., 1965. Cert. secretarial studies/social bus. studies, bus. dept. head, guidance counselor, pupil svcs. and sch. psychologist. Bus. edn. tchr. South Plainfield (N.J.) H.S., 1957-67; guidance counselor Eastern H.S., Voorhees, N.J., 1967-92. Mem. NEA (life), N.J. Edn. Assn. (life), South Jersey Camera Club, Animal Welfare Assn., Inc., NOW, Am. Assn. Retired Persons, Zonta Club of Tri-County Area (Cherry Hill, N.J.). Democrat. Jewish.

APPELL, KATHLEEN MARIE, management consultant, legal administrator; b. Phila., Apr. 20, 1943; d. Joseph F. and Catherine (Laing) Hudson; m. Vincent M. Mandes (div. Apr. 1968); children: Carren Lee, Vincent, Lori. Cert., Phila. Modeling Sch., 1960-61, Horsham Found., 1979-81, Behavioral Acad., 1981, Fashion Acad., 1984. Adminstr. Phila. Modeling and Career Sch., 1965-68; pres. KMA Enterprises Ltd., Rosemont, Pa., 1968—; exec. asst. Horsham Psychiat. Hosp., Ambler, Pa., 1976-84; cons. Horsham Psychiat. Hosp., Ambler, 1976-84; dir. admissions Career Inst., Phila., 1986-87; legal adminstr. Howson & Howson, Spring House, Pa., 1990-92; northeast regional dir. Gly Derm, Inc., Bloomfield Hills, Mich., 1992-94; pres. Preventif, Rosemont, Pa., 1994—; cons. Resource Spectrum, Ambler, 1979-82, Horsham Mgmt. Corp., Ambler, 1978-84. Contbr. articles to profl. jours. Mem. Rep. Task Force Com., Washington, 1981; mem. Ch. of Bethesda-By-the-Sea Episcopal Ch. Mem. Women's Econ. Devel., Assn. Fashion and Image Cons., Profl. and Exec. Women. Office: Cosmeceutical Resource Specialist 1030 E Lancaster Ave # 1031 Bryn Mawr PA 19010

APPERSON, JEAN, psychologist; b. Durham, N.C., June 8, 1934; d. James Harry and Dorothy Elizabeth (Johnson) Apperson; m. Calvin Adams Pope, Mar. 23, 1956 (div. 1967); 1 child, Richard Allan. BA, U. S. Fla., 1966; MA, Mich. State U., 1970, PhD, 1973. Cert. in psychoanalysis Mich. Psychoanalytic Coun., 1990. Teaching asst. Mich. State U., E. Lansing, 1968-69; psychiatric technician St. Lawrence Community Mental Health Ctr., Lansing, Mich., 1968-69; psychology intern St. Lawrence Community Mental Health Ctr., 1969-71, Mich. State U. Counseling Ctr., 1971-73; clin. psychologist U. Mich. Counseling Ctr., Ann Arbor, 1973-81; pvt. practice psychology and psychoanalysis Ann Arbor, 1974—; mem., chmn. Mich. Bd. Psychology, Lansing, 1984-91. Contbr. articles to profl. jours.; cons. editor Am. Psychol. Assn. Catalog of Selected Documents, 1975-80. USPHS grantee, 1969-70; NIMH grantee, 1970-71. Fellow Mich. Psychol. Assn. (chmn. women's issues com. 1981-83); mem. APA (com. on sci. and profl. ethics and conduct 1977-80), Mich. Soc. Psychoanalytic Psychology (treas. 1982-86), Mich. Psychoanalytic Coun. (teaching and supervising analyst, mem. at large 1991-93, tng. com. 1992—, pres.-elect 1993-95, pres. 1995-97), Assn. for Advancement Psychology, Am. Women in Psychology, Mich. Women Psychologists. Democrat. Unitarian. Home: 7224 Chelsea Manchester Rd Manchester MI 48158-9407 Office: 555 E William St Apt 23E Ann Arbor MI 48104-2428

APPLE, DAINA DRAVNIEKS, government agency official; b. Latvia, Latvia, July 6, 1944; came to U.S., 1951; d. Albins Dravnieks and Alina A. (Bergs) Zelmenis; divorced; 1 child, Almira Moronne; m. Martin A. Apple, Sept. 2, 1986. BSc, U. Calif., Berkeley, 1977, MA, 1980. Economist USDA Pacific S.W. Rsch., Berkeley, 1976-85; mgr. regional land use appeals USDA Forest Svc., San Francisco, 1986-88, program analysis officer, engring., 1988-90; asst. regulatory officer USDA Forest Svc., 1990-95, strategic planner nat. forest sys. resources program, 1995—. Author: Public Involvement in the Forest Service-Methodologies, 1977, Public Involvement, Selected Abstracts for Natural Resource Managers, 1979, The Management of Policy and Direction in the Forest Service, 1982, An Analysis of the Forest Service Human Resource Management Program, 1984, Organization Design—Abstracts for Natural Resources Users, 1985; contbg. editor Jour. Women in Natural Resources, 1987—. Mem. Am. Forestry Assn., Soc. Am. Foresters (sec. nat. capital chpt.), Am. Latvian Assn. (bd. dirs.), Phi Beta Kappa Assocs. (nat. sec. 1985-88, pres. No. Calif. chpt. 1982-84), Sigma Xi. Office: USDA Forest Svc Resources Prog/Assess Staff PO Box 96090 Washington DC 20090-6090

APPLEBY, JOYCE OLDHAM, historian; b. Omaha, Apr. 9, 1929; d. Junius G. and Edith (Cash) Oldham; children: Ann Lansburgh Caylor, Mark Lansburgh, Frank Bell Appleby. B.A., Stanford U., 1950; M.A., U. Calif., Santa Barbara, 1959; Ph.D., Claremont Grad. Sch., 1966. With Mademoiselle mag., 1950-52; asst. prof. history San Diego State U., 1967-70, asso. prof., 1970-73; prof. history, asso. dean Coll. Arts and Letters, 1973-75, prof., 1976-81; vis. asso. prof. U. Calif., Irvine, 1975-76; vis. prof. UCLA, 1978-79, prof. history, 1981—; vis. fellow St. Catherine's Coll., U. Oxford, 1983; Harmsworth prof. Am. History, U. Oxford, 1990-91; Bd. fellows Claremont Grad. Sch. and U. Center, 1970-73. Author: Economic Thought and Ideology in Seventeenth-Century England, 1978, Capitalism and a New Social Order, 1983, Liberalism and Republicanism in the Historical Imagination, 1992; co-author: Telling the Truth about History, 1994; co-editor: Knowledge and Postmodernism in Historical Perspective; mem. bd. editors Democracy, 1980-83, William and Mary Quar., 1980-83, 18th Century Studies, 1982-87, Ency. Am. Polit. History, Am. Hist. Rev., 1988—, Jour. Interdisciplinary History, 1989—, The Papers of Thomas Jefferson, 1988—, The Adams Papers, 1990—; contbr. articles to profl. jours.; mem. adv. bd. Am. Nat. Biography. Mem. Am. Acad. Arts and Scis., Am. Philos. Soc., Smithsonian Inst. (coun.), Am. Hist. Assn. (coun.), Orgn. Am. Historians (pres.), Inst. Early Am. History and Culture (coun. 1980-86, chmn. coun. 1983-86). Home: 615 Westholme Ave Los Angeles CA 90024-3209 Office: UCLA Dept History Los Angeles CA 90024

APPLEGATE, CHRISTINA, actress; b. Hollywood, Calif.; d. Nancy Priddy. Film appearances include: Jaws of Satan, 1980, Streets, 1990, Don't Tell Mom the Babysitter's Dead, 1991; TV appearances include: (series) Days of Our Lives, 1974, Washingtoon, 1985, Heart of the City, 1986, Married...With Children, 1987—, (TV movies) Grace Kelly, 1983, Dance 'til Dawn, 1988, (spls.) Rate the '80's Awards, 1989, MTV's 1989 Ann. Emmy Awards, 1989, Time Warner Presents the Earth Day Special, 1990, The 4th Ann. Am. Comedy Awards, 1990, The 43d Ann. Primetime Emmy Awards Presentation, 1991, (episodes) Father Murphy, 1981, Quincy, 1983, Charles in Charge, 1984, 84, All Is Forgiven, 1986, Leave It to Beaver, 1986, Amazing Stories, 1986, Silver Spoons, 1986, Family Ties, 1987, 21 Jump St., 1988, Animal Crack-Ups, 1988, Hour Magazine, 1988, Win, Lose, or Draw, 1988, The Pat Sajak Show, 1989, Live with Regis and Kathy Lee, 1989, The Arsenio Hall Show, 1989. Office: care Fox Inc PO Box 900 Beverly Hills CA 90213 also: Tami Lynn Mgmt 4527 Park Allegra Calabasas CA 91302*

APPLEMAN, MARJORIE (M. H. APPLEMAN), playwright, educator, poet; b. Ft. Wayne, Ind.; d. Theodore E. and Martha C. Haberkorn; m. Philip Appleman. BA, Northwestern U.; MA, Ind. U.; degré supérieur, U. Paris, Sorbonne. Prof. in English and French Ind. U.; prof. English, playwriting NYU, Columbia U., N.Y.C.; mem. playwrights unit Circle Repertory Co., N.Y.C., 1978—. Author: (plays produced) Nice Place You Have Here, 1971, The Best Is Yet to Be, 1975, The Bedroom, 1978, Seduction Duet, 1982, Fox-Trot by the Bay, 1982, The Commuter, 1982, Thirty-Nine Seconds and Counting, 1983, Space, 1983, Intermission, 1985, Penelope's Odyssey, 1986, The Country House, 1988, Seduction Triangle, 1988, On the Edge, 1989, Happy New Year, 1990, Fox-Trot on Gardiner's Bay, 1991-92, Love Puzzles, 1992, Secrets, 1993, The Black Staircase, 1994, The Salt of Love, 1995, The Brunette, The Blonde, and the Mounties, 1996, Try, Try Again, 1996, (plays published) Seduction Duet, 1982, The Commuter, 1985, (poetry) Against Time, 1994. Recipient Eugene O'Neill award Nat. Playwrights Conf., 1979, Double Image Short Play award Samuel French, Inc., 1981, 12th Ann. Playwriting award Jacksonville U., 1982, New Play Contest award John Drew Theatre, 1987; Hartford Found. fellow. Mem. PEN (membership com. Am. Ctr. 1980—), Dramatists Guild, Author's League Am., Acad. Am. Poets, Women's Project and Prodns., League Profl. Theatre Women (bd. dirs. 1989—), Poets and Writers, Inc. Home: PO Box 39 Sagaponack NY 11962

APREA, SHARON MARTIN, merchandiser; b. Portsmouth, Va., July 17, 1956; d. Addison Berkley and Nancy Carolyn (Kiser) M.; m. Marc Angelo Aprea, Dec. 24, 1985. AS in Bus. Adminstrn., Va. Intermont, 1976; BSBA, Va. Tech., 1978. Ill. regional sales rep. Broyhill Furniture, Lenoir, N.C., 1979-82; sales mgr., acct. rep. Economon & Assocs., Dallas, 1982-87; nat. sales dir. Cavendish Furnitures, Dallas, Ipswich, England, 1987-88; accessories buyer J.C. Penney, Portfolio, Dallas, 1988-90, Breuners, Pleasant Hill, Calif., 1991-92; with Schnadig Internat. Corp., Chgo., Calif., 1992—. Columnist profl. mag., 1990—. Campaign rep. Judge Superior Ct., Rep. party, Dallas, 1990; active Winner's Cir./Schnadig, 1994. Mem. Ill. Home Furnishings Reps. Assn. (treas. 1980-82), Internat. Trade Club (com. leader 1985-88), Southwest Trade Commn. (assoc. mem. 1982-85), Cimarron Club (dir. programs 1986-87, 1st v.p. and social chmn. 1987-88, pres. 1988-90), 500, Inc. (organizing com. mem. 1988-90). Republican. Baptist. Home: 171 Tomlinson Dr Folsom CA 95630-7406

APSELOFF, MARILYN FAIN, English language and literature educator; b. Attleboro, Mass.; d. Arthur A. and Eva (Lubchansky) Fain; m. Stanford S. Apseloff, Nov. 21, 1956; children: Roy, Stan and Glen (twins), Lynn Susan. Attended, Bryn Mawr Coll., 1952-54; BA, U. Cin., 1956, MA, 1957. English instr. Kent (Ohio) State U., 1968-75, asst. prof. English, 1975-85, assoc. prof. English, 1985-92, prof., 1992—; dir. Children's Lit. Assn. Harvard U. Conf., 1978. Author: They Wrote for Children, Too, 1989, Elizabeth George Speare, 1991; co-author: Nonsense Literature for Children, 1989 (Children's Lit. Assn. Honor Book award 1990); editor New and Noteworthy sect. Children's Lit. Assoc. Quar., 1984-87. Mem. adv. bd. Parents' Choice, Waban, Mass., 1978—. Fellow U. Cin., 1956-57. Mem. MLA (session chair 1977-78), Children's Lit. Assn. (pres. 1979-80). Office: Kent State U English Dept Kent OH 44242

APSON, JANE R., public health educator; b. N.Y.C., Feb. 17, 1946; d. Philip and Anna (Rosenweig) Rahl; m. Bernard Apson, Oct. 21, 1968. BA in Math., Skidmore Coll., 1967; MS in Pub. Health, Johns Hopkins U., 1978; PhD in Human Devel., U. Md., 1990. Cert. health edn. specialist Nat. Commn. for Health Edn. Credentialing, Inc. Computer programmer GE Co., Schenectady, N.Y., 1967-68; rsch. assoc. Sch. Hygiene Johns Hopkins U., Balt., 1975-79; pub. health educator Worcester County Health Dept., Snow Hill, Md., 1979—; assoc. prof. Salisbury (Md.) State U., 1995—; adj. faculty mem. Wor-Wic Tech. C.C., Berlin, Md., 1985, 82, 88. Cmty. vol. John F. Kennedy Inst., Balt., 1973; cmty. organizer, v.p., pres. Logan Village Improvement Assn., Balt., 1973-79; cmty. organizer, v.p. Greater Dundalk (Md.) Cmty. Coun., 1975-79; mem. AIDS curriculum com. Worcester County Bd. Edn., Snow Hill, 1989-95; bd. dirs. Jerusalem Day Care Ctr., Snow Hill, 1994—; officer, bd. dirs. Worcester Chorale, Berlin and Ocean City, Md., 1995—. N.Y. State Regents scholar, 1963-67. Mem. APHA, Soc. Pub. Health Edn., Nat. Headache Found. Office: Worcester County Health 6040 Public Landing Rd PO Box 249 Snow Hill MD 21863

AQUILA, DENISE LEE, realtor; b. Omaha, July 4, 1953; d. James Oliver and Dorothy Ree (Summers) Howell; m. John F. Aquila, Jr., Oct. 12, 1974; children: Lyndie, Lee. Student, Am. River Coll., 1971-74, Coll. San Mateo, 1990-92. Lic. real estate broker Calif. Assn. Realtors, Nat. Assn. Realtors. Asst. distbn. mgr. Mercedes-Benz of N.Am., San Francisco, 1974-79; exec. adminstrv. asst. Sully Assoc., Half Moon Bay, Calif., 1982-92; broker assoc. realtor Cornish & Carey, Half Moon Bay, 1992—; tech. com. mem. SAMCAR, San Mateo, 1995—; treas. Women's Coun. Realtors, San Mateo, 1995—. Bd. mem. Half Moon Bay Sports Club, 1984— ; regional commr. Am. Youth Soccer Orgn., Half Moon Bay, 1995—. Named Sports Mom of Yr., Women's Sports Found., San Francisco Bay Area, 1994, Young Women of Yr., Soroptomist Club, Half Moon Bay, 1994. Mem. NAFE, San Mateo County Assn. Realtors (Circle of Excellence 1993, 94, 95), Coastside Women's Club. Methodist. Home: PO Box 370983 Montara CA 94037 Office: Cornish & Carey Ste H 80 N Cabrillo Hwy Half Moon Bay CA 94019

AQUINO-KAUFMAN, FLORENCE (FLORENCE ANGLIN), actress, playwright; b. Bklyn., Sept. 21, 1918; d. Michael and Rebecca (Kaplan) Aquino; m. S. Jay Kaufman, June 3, 1945 (dec. June 1957). Studied acting, Lee Strasberg, Uta Hagan, Sandy Meisner; student, Empire State Coll., 1975. Legal sec., N.Y.C., 1936-43, freelance actress,, 1944—; founder, artistic and mng. dir. Knickerbocker Creative Theatre Found., Inc., N.Y.C., 1964-73; former co-prodr. Promenade Theatre, Bklyn.; crew chief Neighborhood Youth Corp., N.Y.C., 1964-73; dir. Urban Corps, N.Y.C., 1972-73. Author: (plays) It's Up to You!, 1964, The Winner!, 1971, Calling All Heroes/Shattered Idol, 1989, (with Ann Curry) I'd Rather Be Dead Than Alone, 1972; appeared on Broadway in Goodbye Fidel, Gideon, A Bell for Adano, Skipper Next to God, Winged Victory, Lower North; appeared in Romeo and Juliet, As You Like It, Much Ado About Nothing Shakespeare Theatre Workshop (now N.Y. Shakespeare Festival); TV appearances include Mrs. Pappas in Guiding Light, Felicia in One Life To Live, also Lucy Scheff in Love of Life, Freida in The Goldbergs, Naked City, Studio I, Philco TV Playhouse, Hallmark, U.S. Steel Hour, Late Night with Conan O'Brien, Staurday Night Live, also others; appeared in feature and TV films Law and Order, Falling in Love, Out of the Darkness, Trading Places, Author, Author, Lovers and Other Strangers, Mirage, Penelope, Cancel My Reservation, Giovanni and Ben; appeared on tour and summer stock in Prisoner of Second Avenue, Time of the Cuckoo, Middle of the Night, Man and Superman, Picnic, Gigi, Bad Seed, Harvey, Two Queens of Love and Beauty, also others; appearances in regional theatre and off-Broadway include Wrinkles, Steel Magnolias, You Can't Take It with You, Liliom, Bright and Golden Land, Coward in Two Keys, Medea, The Little Foxes, also others. Former mem. bd. dirs. Greenwich Mews Theatre; vol. 55th Street Block Assn. Grantee N.Y. State Coun. on Arts, 1970-72. Mem. AFTRA, SAG, Actors Equity Assn., Dramatists Guild, Inst. Noetic Scis.

ARANDA, MARY KATHRYN, state legislator; b. Nassawadox, Va., Sept. 28, 1945; d. John McCallister and Frances Esther (Mausteller) Copper; m. Ronald William Meyer, Dec. 28, 1965 (dec. June 1966); m. Rembert Aranda, Feb. 4, 1973; 1 child, Olivia Kathryn. BA, Goucher Coll., 1969. Jr. planner Balt. Regional Planning Coun., 1968-71; asst. planner edn. sect. N.Y.C. Dept. City Planning, 1971-74, assoc. dir. edn. and social svcs. sect., 1974-76; rep. Gen. Ct. State of N.H., Concord, 1993—. Commr. Derry House and Devel. Authority, 1983-95, treas., 1986-87, vice chmn., 1987-90, chmn., 1990-95; incorporator Alexander-Eastman Found., Derry and Concord, 1993—; mem. Derry Planning Bd., 1984-88; mem. fiscal adv. com. Derry Coop. Sch. Dist., 1986-89. Republican. Home: 24 Redfield Cir Derry NH 03038-4839

ARAPIAN, LINDA, pediatrics nurse; b. Portsmouth, N.H., July 7, 1949; d. William A. and Esther A. (Carlson) Niland; m. Stephen Graham Arapian, May 2, 1975; children: Stephanie, Michael, Jennifer. BSN, Boston Coll., 1971; MSN, Cath. U. Am., 1984. RN, D.C., Md.; cert. BLS, PALS instr., CPR instr.; RN cert. in pediat. nursing ANCC. Staff nurse Portsmouth Regional Hosp., 1971-74; staff nurse II George Washington Univ. Hosp., Washington, 1974-75; sr. staff nurse emergency rm. Childrens Nat. Med. Ctr., Washington, 1975-80, with rheumatology clinic, 1980-83, clin. nurse III emergency rm., 1983-89, mem. float pool emergency rm., 1990-93, mem. pediatric transport team, 1993—; agy. nurse Md. Profl. Staffing, Bethesda, 1989-91; quality assurance specialist Dept. of Def. project Children's Nat. Med. Ctr., 1990-92, 93-94; health dir. Boy Scouts Goshen (Va.) Scout Camps, 1990, 91, 92; instr. emergency nursing pediatric course Emergency Nurses Assn. Author: (with others) Pediatric Emergencies: A Handbook for Nurses, 1990. Asst. scoutmaster Trrop 926 Boys Scouts Am., Gaithersburg, Md., 1990—, active Order of Arrow; mem. Pastoral coun. Our Lady of the Visitation Parish, Darnestown, Md., 1993-94, chair liturgical life com., 1994—. Recipient St. George medal Nat. Cath. Com. Boy Scouts, 1990, St. Eliz Seton medal Nat. Cath. Com. Girl Scouts, 1993. Mem. Emergency Nurses Assn. (cert. emergency nurse, Emergency Nursing Pediat. Course), Soc. Pediat. Nurses, Am. Acad. Pediat. (affiliate mem. sect. on transport medicine). Democrat. Roman Catholic. Home: 12451 Quail Woods Dr Germantown MD 20874-1545 Office: Children's Nat Med Ctr 111 Michigan Ave NW Washington DC 20010-2970

ARBELBIDE, C(INDY) L(EA), historian; b. Stockton, Calif., Aug. 4, 1949; d. Garrett Walter and Fern Mable (Lea) A. AA in History, Santa Barbara City Coll., Calif., 1969; BS in Health & Phys. Edn., Oreg. State U., 1972; M in Libr. Sci., Emporia State U., 1980; cert., Nat. Crisis Response Team Tng. Inst., 1991. Tchr. Petersburg (Ala.) Sch. System, 1972-73, Santa Barbara (Calif.) Sch. System, 1973-74, Linn Benton Community Coll., Oreg. State U., Albany, Corvallis, 1974-75, Can. Acad., Kobe, Japan, 1975-76; tchr., libr. Wichita (Kans.) Pub. Schs., 1976-81; mgr. Geol. Info. Libr., Dallas, 1982-84; coord., cons. North Tex. Libr. System, Ft. Worth, 1984-86; dir. libr., rsch. svcs. Nat. Victim Ctr., Ft. Worth, 1986-91; dir. tng., coord. tng. all insts. Nat. Orgn. for Victim Assistance, Washington, 1991-95; cons. Nat. Cmty. Response Team, N.J., Tex., 1992, FBI, Washington, 1994, NOVA, 1995. Author: Librarian's PLanning Handbook, 1986, National Library Resource Project on Crime Victimization, 1988, 89, Child Safety Curriculum Standards, 1989, The Story of Presidential Christmas Cards and Gift Prints, 1996, Diary of a White House Squirrel, 1996. Named Woman of the Month Ladies Home Jour., 1973; recipient Yellow Rose of Tex. award Gov. Tex., 1992, Outstanding Contbn. letter U.S. Army, 1993, Recognition and Appreciation cert. Concerns of Police Survivors, 1994. Mem. ALA, Am. Assn. Law Librs., Spl. Librs. Assn. (chairperson catalog com. 1990-91, chairperson social sci. div. roundtable health and human svcs. 1990), Nat. Victim Ctr., Tex. Libr. Assn. (vice chairperson div. spl. librs. 1987-88, chairperson 1988-89), Critical Incident Stress Debriefing Soc. Internat. Assn. Trauma Counselors, Nat. Cmty. Crisi Response Team.

ARBITELL, MICHELLE RENEÉ, clinical psychologist; b. Trenton, N.J., Oct. 24, 1962; d. John A. and Adele M. Arbitell. BA, Lehigh U., 1984; MA, Indiana U. of Pa., 1986, D Psychology, 1988. Diplomate Am. Bd. Forensic Examiners; lic. psychologist, Pa.; cert. counselor; cert. eye movement desensitization reprocessing. Clin. pscyhology intern Geisinger Med. Ctr., Danville, Pa., 1987-88; dir. behavioral medicine and neuropsychology HealthSouth Rehab. Hosp., 1988—; mem. adv. bd. Blair County Pain Support Groups, Altoona, 1988—; pvt. practice psychology, cons., Altoona and State College, Pa., 1991-94; mem. Am. Bd. Forensic Examiners; invited lectr. Pa. State U., University Park, 1991—; presenter in field. Author: (with others) On Spouse Abuse..., 1985; (with others) Bulimics' Perceptions..., 1991. Fellow Pa. Psychol. Assn.; mem. APA, NAFE, Nat. Acad. Neuropsychology, Soc. Behavioral Medicine, Am. Bd. Forensic Examiners, Phi Beta Kappa, Psi Chi (v.p., sec. 1980-84). Office: HealthSouth Rehab Hosp Altoona Valley View Blvd Altoona PA 16602

ARBOLEDA, BARBARA MARIE WILSON, playwright, director; b. Troy, N.Y., Apr. 25, 1968; d. Robert Michael Sr. and Deborah Louise (Schlegel) Wilson; m. Teja J.M. Arboleda, June 21, 1992. BA, Simmons Coll., 1990. Freelance stage mgr. Newton, Mass.; freelance theatrical dir.; co-founder, CFO, mktg. dir. Entertaining Diversity, Dedham, Mass.; individual budget counselor. Author: (plays) The Matter of the Table, 1994 (Hon. Mention award Writer's Digest 1995), The Spice of Life, 1995, Save a Prayer, 1995 (N.Y.C. Prodn. award 1996), others. Recipient Rank # 66 award for short story Writer's Digest, 1995. Mem. AAUW, StageSource (seminar com. 1995), Simmons Coll. Young Alumnae Club. Office: Entertaining Diversity PO Box 126 Dedham MA 02027

ARBUTHNOT, JEANETTE JAUSSAUD, educator, researcher; b. Walla Walla, Wash., Feb. 17, 1934; d. Andre P. and Lena Mae (Fox) Jaussaud; m. Alfred Harold Arbuthnot, Aug. 20, 1953 (div. July 1981); children: Kristi Noel Arbuthnot Bronkema, Lisa Gaye, Douglas Randal. BS, Fla. Internat. U., Miami, 1980; MS, Colo. State U., Ft. Collins, 1984; PhD, Okla. State U., 1990. Sect. mgr. The Treasury Dept. Store divsn. J.C. Penney, Miami, 1980-81; dept. mgr. The Denver, Boulder, Colo., 1981-82; lectr. U. Nev.-Reno, 1984-85; asst. prof. Utah State U., Logan, 1988-96, assoc. prof., 1996—, dir. grad. rsch., 1990—, coord. apparel merchandising and design program, 1990—; reviewer for pubs. McMillan, Fairchild and Delmar, 1994, 95. Contbr. articles to profl. jours. Bd. dirs. Utah State U./Cmty. Assocs., Logan, 1995—; mem. exec. bd. Citizens Agains Phys. and Sexual Abuse, Logan, 1995—. Named Advisor of Yr., Coll. Family Life, Utah State U., 1990, 92; USDA rsch. grantee, 1993—. Mem. Internat. Textile and Apparel Assn. (strategic planning com. 1991-93), Costume Soc. Am. (membership adv. com. 1992-93), Am. Collegiate Retailing Assn., Am. Assn. Family and Consumer Scis., Internat. Fedn. Home Econs., Soroptimists Internat., Phi Upsilon Omicron, Kappa Omicron Nu. Episcopalian. Home: 242 North 200 East Logan UT 84321 Office: Utah State U 303A Coll of Family Life Logan UT 84322-2910

ARCHABAL, NINA M(ARCHETTI), historical society director; b. Long Branch, N.J., Apr. 11, 1940; d. John William and Santina Matilda (Giuffre) Marchetti; m. John William Archabal, Aug. 8, 1964; 1 child, John Fidel. BA in Music History cum laude, Radcliffe Coll., 1962; MAT in Music History, Harvard U., 1963; PhD in Music History, U. Minn., 1979. Asst. dir. humanities art mus. U. Minn., Mpls., 1975-77; asst. supr. edn. div. Minn. Hist. Soc., St. Paul, 1977-78, dep. dir. for program mgmt., 1978-86, acting dir., 1986-87, dir., 1987—. Trustee, bd. dirs. Am. Folklife Ctr., Libr. of Congress, 1989—; bd. dirs. N.W. Area Found., 1989—, St. Paul Acad.

and Summit Sch., 1993—; v.p. Friends of St. Paul Pub. Libr., 1983-93. NDEA fellow U. Minn., 1969-72, U. Minn. grad. fellow, 1974-75. Mem. Am. Assn. State and Local History (sec. 1986-88), Am. Assn. Mus. (v.p. 1991-94, chair bd. dirs. 1994-96). Office: Minn Hist Soc 345 Kellogg Blvd W Saint Paul MN 55102-1906

ARCHACKI-STONE, CYNTHIA SUE, marriage and family therapist; b. Toledo, July 23, 1955; d. Henry and Helen (Plementosh) Archacki; m. David Ward Stone, Sept. 21, 1985. BA, Alliance Coll., 1977; MS, Gannon U., 1982. Social svc. program developer Unity Inst., Meadville, Pa., 1978-79; child care counselor Bethesda Children's Home, Meadville, 1979-80, Crawford County Emergency Shelter, Meadville, 1980-82; outpatient mental health therapist Dickinson Mental Health Ctr., Ridgeway, Pa., 1982-84; adminstr., therapist Odd Fellows Home, Meadville, 1984-88; supr. Family Based MH Porgram, Meadville Med. Ctr., 1988—; trainer Children and Youth Competency Program, Shippensburg (Pa.) U., 1993-96; trainer, cons. Drawbridge, Inc., Pitts., 1992—; spkr. in field. Author: (with others) Children in Families at Risk, 1995. Mem. ACA (clin. mem., approved supr.), Am. Assn. Marriage and Family Therapists. Democrat. Roman Catholic. Home: 16238 Harmonsburg Rd Meadville PA 16335 Office: Meadville Med Ctr 1034 Grove St Meadville PA 16335

ARCHER, ANNE, actress; b. L.A., Aug. 25, 1949; d. John and Marjorie (Lord) A.; m. Terry Jastrow; children: Thomas, Jeffrey. Appearances include (theatre) A Coupla White Chicks Sitting Around Talking, 1981, Les Liaisons Dangeruses, 1988, (films) The Honkers, 1972, Cancel My Reservation, 1972, The All-American Boy, 1973, Trackdown, 1976, Lifeguard, 1976, Paradise Valley, 1978, Good Guys Wear Black, 1978, Raise the Titanic, 1980, Hero At Large, 1980, Green Ice, 1981, Waltz Across Texas, 1983, Too Scared to Scream, 1985, The Naked Face, 1985, The Check Is in the Mail, 1985, Fatal Attraction, 1987 (Golden Globe nominee 1987, Acad. award nominee 1988), Love at Large, 1990, Narrow Margin, 1990, Eminent Domain, 1991, Patroit Games, 1992, Body of Evidence, 1993, Short Cuts, 1993, Clear and Present Danger, 1994; (TV series) Bob and Carol and Ted and Alice, 1973, The Family Tree, 1983, Falcon Crest, 1985, (TV movies) The Blue Knight, 1973, The Mark of Zorro, 1974, The Log of the Black Pearl, 1975, A Matter of Wife...and Death, 1976, The Dark Side of Innocence, 1976, Seventh Avenue, 1977, The Pirate, 1978, The Sky's No Limit, 1984, A Different Affair, 1987, A Leap of Faith, 1988, The Last of His Tribe, 1992, Nails, 1992, Jane's House, 1994, Because Mommy Works, 1994, The Man in the Attic, 1995, Jake's Women, 1996. Office: care ICM 8942 Wilshire Blvd Los Angeles CA 90211*

ARCHER, CLAIRE REYNAUD, artist, nurse; b. Glen Ridge, N.J., Nov. 10, 1932; d. James Robert and Marion Claire (Fitzpatrick) Reynaud; m. Robert Bruce Archer (dec. Sept. 1995); children: R. Bruce, Lauree Fawn, Heather Ellen, Holly Beth, Beryl Lynn, Stuart Owen. LPN, Monmouth County Vocat. Sch., 1974. Freelance artist indsl. concept illustrations Aircruisers divsn. Garrett Corp., Wall Twp., N.J., 1967-72; nursing asst. Tower Lodge, Wall, N.J., 1971-74; practical nurse Jersey Shore Med. Ctr., 1974-75, Monmouth hosps., 1975-81; unit charge nurse Tinton Falls (N.J.) Conva-Ctr., 1981-93; freelance artist, 1952—; spkr. at various local schs.; presenter workshops and demonstrations Brookdale Coll., Monmouth County Park Sys., other orgns. Included in Centennial Art Collection, Statue of Liberty Nat. Monument, N.Y.C., 1986; mural commd. by Am. Legion for chapel N.J. Vets. Meml. Home, Paramus, 1991; watercolor selected as UNICEF holiday card; designer poster for Belmar C. of C., 1995. Challenger mcpl. elections Rep. Party, Belmar, 1995. Recipient award for contbn. artwork Am. Legion, 1986. Mem. Monmouth Arts Found. (v.p. exhbns. 1991), Guild Am. Papercutters, Ocean Artists Guild, Nat. Mus. Women in the Arts, Manasquan River Group of Artists. Presbyterian. Home: 215 3d Ave Belmar NJ 07719-2013

ARCHER, MARY JANE, state agency administrator; b. Oakland, Calif., Aug. 23, 1949; d. Doris Marlene (Howard) Wood; m. Bradley Eugene Archer; Nov. 10, 1984. BS in Acctg., Calif. State U., Hayward, 1971, MBA in Acctg., 1977. Cert. govtl. fin. mgr. Auditor Calif. State Controller's Office, Sacramento, 1972-81, supr., 1981-84, asst. div. chief, divsn. tax adminstrn., 1984-90, acting div. chief, 1990-95; bur. chief div. acctg. and reporting Calif. State Controller;s Office, Sacramento, 1995; chief acctg. Dept. Justice, Sacramento, 1996—. Tutor Sacramento Literacy Ctr. Mem. Calif. Assn. Mgmt., Assn. Govtl. Accountants. Republican. Office: Dept Justice Acctg Office 1300 I St 12th Fl Sacramento CA 95814

ARCHER, SUSAN DAVISON, minister, religious education consultant; b. Kansas City, Mo., Dec. 15, 1946; d. Owen Richards and Jean Carol (Long) Davison; m. Vance Dolven Archer III, Oct. 11, 1975; children: Asa Dolven, Carrie Eliza, Ethan Richard. BA in Religion, DePauw U., 1969; MST, U. Chgo., 1970; MDiv equivalent cert., Meadville Lombard Theol. Sch., 1993; postgrad., Drew Theol. Sch., 1990-92. Tchr. Chgo. Pub. Schs., 1970-72, Hyde Park Coop. Sch., Chgo., 1971-72; asst. dir. youth edn. ABA, Chgo., 1972-76; dir. religious edn. 1st Unitarian Ch. of Monmouth County, Lincroft, N.J., 1982-94; religious edn. cons. Unitarian Universalist Dist. Met. N.Y., Fair Haven, N.J., 1994—; cons. law-related edn., 1976-82. Prin. author: (curriculum) Educating for Citizenship, 1981. Sec., bd. dirs., newsletter editor 1st Unitarian Ch. Monmouth County, Lincraft, 1979-81; bd. dirs. Tower Hill Coop. Nursery, Red Bank, N.J., 1981-86; chair orgn. com. Lincroft Ctr. for Children, 1983-85. Mem. Unitarian Universalist Assn. (min. fellow), Liberal Religious Educators Assn. (bd. dirs. 1994—). Democrat. Office: Univ Unitarian Met NY 41 Church St Fair Haven NJ 07704-3320

ARCHER-SIMONS, JEANNETTE JOANN, association administrator; b. Iowa City, Apr. 19, 1960. BA in Econs., U. Iowa, 1990; postgrad., St. Ambrose U., Davenport. Cert. Girl Scout exec. dir., non-profit mgr. Indsl. sales rep. Electrical Equipment Co., Davenport, Iowa, 1979-83; field underwriter Mutual N.Y., Davenport, Iowa City, 1983-85; bus. mgr., sales mgr. Fin. Planning Svcs., Cedar Rapids, Iowa, 1985-88; cons., sales rep. Rsch. Inst. Am., N.Y.C., 1988-89; advt. rep. Iowa City Press Citizen, 1990-91; asst. exec. dir. Miss. Valley Girl Scout Coun., Rock Island, Ill., 1991-94; exec. dir. Girl Scouts Broward County, Fort Lauderdale, Fla., 1994—; presenter in field. Bd. dirs., 2d v.p. Planned Giving Coun., 1995-96; 1st v.p. coun. agy. execs. Broward County United Way, 1995-96, chair small bus. fund drive, 1986-88, campaign cabinet East Ctrl. Iowa, 1988-89, allocation panel mem., 1990-91, chair edn. com., 1994-95; vol mgmt. systems com. Broward Mentoring Coun., strategic planning com., 1995, membership chair, 1996; accountability com. mem. Greater Fort Lauderdale C. of C., 1995; girl mem. Miss. Vallery Girl Scout Coun., 1967-78, sr. advisor, 1978-81, day camp dir., 1979-81, svc. unit dir., 1980-82, fin. com., fund devel. com., 1984-87, at large bd. dirs., chair nominating com., 1987-88, pres. bd. dirs., 1988-91; bd. dirs. Iowa City Downtown Bus. Assn., 1990-91; bd. dirs. Profl. Women's Network, 1988-91, chair women's conf., 1989. Named Woman of Distinction March of Dimes, 1996. Mem. Nat. Soc. Fund Raising Execs. (Broward County chpt.), Broward Women's Alliance. Democrat. Lutheran. Office: Girl Scouts Broward County PO Box 490450 5255 NW 33d Ave Fort Lauderdale FL 33349-0450

ARCHIBALD, CLAUDIA JANE, parapsychologist, consultant; b. Atlanta, Nov. 14, 1939; d. Claud Bernard and Doris Evelyn (Linch) A. B in Psychology, Georgia State U., 1962; BTh., Emory U., 1964; DD, Stanton Coll., 1969. Pvt. practice psycho-spiritual counselor Atlanta, 1960—; minister Nat. Spiritualist Assn., Atlanta, 1969-72; parapsychologist Ctr. for Life, Atlanta, 1985-86; parapsychologist Inst. of Metaphysical Inquiry, Atlanta, 1980—, also bd. dirs., founder, 1980—. Author: (book) Quantitative Symbolism, 1980, short stories; dir. Phoenix Dance Unltd., 1984-90; choregrapher (dance) Phoenix Rising, 1985. Vol. Aid Atlanta, 1987-89. Recipient City Grant award Bur. Cultural Affairs, Atlanta, 1985, 86. Mem. Am. Psychical Rsch. Assn., Soc. Metaphysicians (corr. Eng. chpt.), Am. Assn. Parapsychology, Nat. Assn. Alcoholism and Drug Abuse Counselors, Ga. Addiction Counselors' Assn., N.Am. Ballet Assn., Nat. Leather Assn., Echoes of the People, Native Am. Orgn., Sun Dancer. Home: 2638 Valmar Dr Atlanta GA 30340-1945

ARCHIBALD, JANE MARTYN, secondary education educator; b. Springfield, Mass., May 30, 1943; d. Lyndon Sanford and Dorothy Loomis (Clapp) Martyn; m. Robert Alan Archibald, June 26, 1965; 1 child, Elizabeth. AB, Mount Holyoke Coll., 1965; MA, U. Oreg., 1968, postgrad., 1969. Tchr. English and Latin Agawam (Mass.) High Sch., 1965-66; Latin instr. U. Oreg., Eugene, 1966-68; tchr. Latin and English Miss Porter's Sch., Farmington, Conn., 1968-73, English tchr., 1982-87; English tchr. Loomis Chaffee Sch., Windsor, Conn., 1973-76, 87—, Milton (Mass.) Acad., 1976-81; speaker in field. Mem. Phi Beta Kappa. Home: 15 Mount Vernon Dr East Granby CT 06026-9553 Office: Loomis Chaffee Sch Batchelder Rd Windsor CT 06095

ARCHIBALD, JEANNE S., lawyer; b. Jan. 30, 1951; d. George R. Stokes and Eleanore (Moran) L.; m. Thomas P. Archibald, Aug. 19, 1972; children: Charles Edward. BA, SUNY, Stony Brook, 1973; JD, Georgetown U., 1977. D.C. bar: 1977. Staff asst. House Com. on Ways and Means, 1975-77, profl. staff mem., 1977-80; assoc. gen. counsel, chmn. sect. 301 com. U.S. Trade Rep., 1980-86; dep. asst. gen. counsel internat. affairs Dept. of Treasury, 1986-88; dep. gen. counsel Dept. of Treasury, 1988-90, gen. counsel, 1990-93; ptnr. Hogan & Hartson, Washington, 1993—. Office: Hogan & Hartson Columbia Sq 555 13th St NW Washington DC 20004-1109*

ARCHIBALD, LARITA JEAN, counselor; b. Harlan County, Nebr., Nov. 14, 1931; d. Alvin Victor and Marian Eleanor (Parker) Vincent; m. Eldon Eugene Archibald, Nov. 25, 1950; children: Craig Eugene, Roger Kent, Karen Jane, Curtis Allen, Kevin Stuart. Cert., Brown-Mackie Coll. Bus., 1950; student, Pikes Peak C.C., Colorado Springs, Colo., 1984. Cert. crisis worker. Founder, exec. dir. HEARTBEAT/Survivors After Suicide, Colorado Springs, 1980-96, suicide bereavement counselor, 1980—; co-founder Suicide Prevention Partnership, Colorado Springs, 1993, internat. crisis response trainer, 1994—. Contbr. articles to profl. jours. Trainer, victim's assistance vol. El Paso County Sheriff Dept., 1991-96. Recipient Cmty. Svc. award Women's Recognition com., 1988, Woman of Distinction award Wagon Wheel Coun. Girl Scouts, 1994, Meritorious Svc. award El Paso County Sheriff Dept., 1995. Fellow Am. Assn. Suicidology (co-founder nat. survivor divsn., co-chair 1990-92, conf. chair 1989, Outstanding Contbr. 1995), Am. Suicide Found., Order Eastern Star. Home: 2015 Devon St Colorado Springs CO 80909

ARCHIE, CAROL LOUISE, obstetrician and gynecologist, educator; b. Detroit, May 18, 1957; d. Frank and Mildred (Barmore) A.; m. Edward Louis Keenan III, Mar. 7, 1993. BA in History, U. Mich., 1979, postgrad. in Pub. Health Adminstrn., 1979-83; MD, Wayne State U., 1983. Diplomate Am. Bd. Ob-Gyn., Am. Bd. Maternal-Fetal Medicine. Resident ob-gyn. Wayne State U., Detroit, 1983-87; fellow in maternal fetal medicine UCLA, 1987-89, asst. prof. ob-gyn., 1987—; cons. Office Substance Abuse Prevention, Washington, 1989—, NIH, Bethesda, Md., 1990—, RAND, 1995—. Peer reviewer jours. Obstetrics and Gynecology, 1989—, Am. Jour. Pub. Health, 1994—, Am. Jour. Obstetrics and Gynecology, 1993—; contbr. chpts. to books. Mem. internal rev. bd. Friends Med. Rsch., 1991—; bd. dirs. Matrix Inst. on Addictions, L.A., 1993—; bd. dirs., vice chair Calif. Advocates for Pregnant Women, 1993—; bd. dirs., asst. v.p. med. svcs. Venice (Calif.) Free Clinic, 1994—. Clin. Tng. grantee UCLA, 1993—; recipient Faculty Devel. award Berlex Found., 1992. Fellow ACOG; mem. AMA, APHA, Soc. Perinatal Obstetricians, Royal Soc. of Medicine (Eng.), Assn. Profs. of Gynecology and Obstetrics. Office: Dept Ob-gyn UCLA Sch Medicine Rm 22-132 10833 Le Conte Ave Los Angeles CA 90024

ARCURIA, JANICE MARIE, children's librarian; b. Kansas City, Kans., Dec. 29, 1948; d. Arthur Joseph and Dorothy Elizabeth (Mallicoat) Van Daele; m. Bill Arcuria, Aug., 1968 (div. 1982); children: Anthony, Philip. BS in Edn., Kans. State Tchrs. Coll., Emporia, 1969; MLS, UCLA, 1986. Children's librarian Glendale (Calif.) Pub. Libr., 1969-73; co-owner, mgr. New Horizons Ednl. Supply Store, Thousand Oaks, Calif., 1976-78; owner, mgr. Story Hour Children's Book Store, Thousand Oaks, Calif., 1978-79; mgmt. trainee Sears Roebuck, Thousand Oaks, Calif., 1979-82; owner licensed child care home, Newbury Park, Calif., 1982-84; children's and young adult librarian Thousand Oaks Pub. Libr., 1986-93; children's svcs. coord. Arlington (Tex.) Pub. Libr., 1993—. Author LSCA Grant Project STAR Svc. to the At Risk, 1995-96. Vol. libr. work Arlington Social Svcs. Providers Network, shelters, Headstart, Children's Museum Inst., Austin, Tex., 1995—. Recipient grants AAUW, 1984, Tall Texan Leadership Inst., 1994. Mem. Nat. Assn. for the Edn. of Young Children, Tex. Libr. Assn., Tarrant Area Guild of Storytellers. Democrat. Office: Arlington Public Library 101 E Abram St Arlington TX 76017

ARDEN, DEBORAH ELINOR, personal property appraiser; b. Corvallis, Oreg., Dec. 31, 1946; d. Norris Elwell and Lenore Alma (Wilcox) Van Wyk; m. Jerry Allen Arden, July 22, 1972 (div. Mar. 1992). BA in Psychology, Chapman Coll., 1972; MA in Edn., Calif. State U., L.A., 1973. Tchr. deaf and hard of hearing Jackson Hearing Ctr., Palo Alto, 1973-80; owner Arden Van Wijk Gallery, Saratoga, Calif., 1980-85; appraiser personal property Arden Van Wijk Assoc. Inc., Cupertino, Calif., 1985-91, Morrison, Colo., 1995—; spkr. in field. Bd. dirs. Euphrat Gallery, DeAnza Coll., Cupertino, 1985-91, pres. bd. dirs., 1986-87; apptd. mem. Cupertino (Calif.) Fine Arts Commn., 1987-91, chairperson, 1988. Mem. Internat. Soc. Appraisers (cert. appraiser personal property-prints, legis. chair 1990-93, fine art divsn. chairperson 1995-96, Leadership award 1991, Outstanding Mem. award 1991, Disting. Svc. award 1993). Home: 1466 Saddleridge Dr Evergreen CO 80439

ARDEN, SHERRY W., publishing company executive; b. N.Y.C., Oct. 18, 1930; d. Abraham and Rose (Bellak) Waretnick; m. Hal Marc Arden (div. 1974); children: Doren, Cathy; m. George Bellak, Oct. 20, 1979. Student, Columbia U. Publicity dir. Coward-McCann, N.Y.C., 1965-67; producer Allan Foshko Assoc., ABC-TV, N.Y.C., 1967-68; sr. v.p., pub. William Morrow & Co., N.Y.C., 1968-85; pres., pub. William Morrow & Co., 1985-89; owner Sherry W. Arden Lit. Agy., 1990—. Mem. Assn. Am. Pubs. (dir.). Club: Pubs. Lunch.

ARDIS, SUSAN BARBER, librarian, educator; b. Holly, Mich., Feb. 21, 1947; d. Raymond Walker and Joan Violet (Grove) Barber; m. Thomas John Ardis, Aug. 18, 1968; children: Jessica, Andrew. BA, U. Mich., 1968, AMLS, 1969. Head natural sci. libr. U. Mich., Ann Arbor, 1969-78; head reference Rosenberg Libr., Galveston, Tex., 1978-79; head Engring. Libr. U. Tex., Austin, 1979—. Author: An Introduction to Patent Searching, 1991, Electrical Electronic Engineering Information Sources, 1987, Toward the Electronic Library, 1994; contbr. articles to profl. jours. Mem. Spl. Librs. Assn., Am. Soc. Engring. Edn. Office: U Tex Austin Engring Libr Gen Librs ECJ 1.300 Austin TX 78713-7330

ARDISON, LINDA G., author, writing educator; b. Ft. Smith, Ark., Apr. 11, 1940; d. Bill Eugene and Mildred M. (Fry) Tanner; m. Gary Winship Ardison, June 10, 1962; children: Amy Roberts, Elizabeth Winship, Matthew Tanner. AA, Stephens Coll., 1960; student, Middlebury Coll., 1960-61; postgrad., Bread Loaf Sch. of English, 1960; BA, U. Ark., 1962. Adminstrv. asst. Wachovia Nat. Bank, Winston-Salem, N.C., 1962-63; English tchr. Wiley Jr. High Sch., Winston-Salem, 1963-64; writing instr. York Coll. of Pa., 1984—; vis. poet York Country Day Sch., 1986, instr. poetry workshop, 1993. Editor Standard lit. mag., 1959-60; asst. editor Keystone News, 1980-82; contbr. articles, poems, plays, short stories to jours. Bd. dirs. York County Med. Soc. Aux., York, 1978-80; mem. Jr. League of York, 1974-75; adult educator Living Word Cmty. Ch., York, 1980-90; bd. dirs. Human Life Svcs., York, 1989-93. Recipient 3d place for fiction in annual coll. contest The Atlantic Monthly, 1960; Bread Loaf scholar The Atlantic Monthly, 1960; Pa. Arts Coun. fellowship grantee, 1990-91. Mem. York County Med. Soc. Aux., Pa. Med. Soc. Aux., Med. Soc. Alliance, Pa. Med. Soc.. Alliance. Republican. Home: 260 School St York PA 17402-9543 Office: York Coll of Pa Country Club Rd York PA 17403

ARDOLF, DEBORAH ANN, speech pathologist; b. Mpls., Apr. 12, 1960; d. Bernard Joseph and Mary Ann (Snyder) A. BS cum laude, Moorhead State U., 1982; MA, U. Northern Colo., 1986. Cert. speech lang. pathologist, Minn., Hawaii. Speech pathologist Pelican Rapids (Minn.) Pub. Schs., 1982-84; speech pathologist intern Vet. Adminstrn. Medical Ctr., Seattle, Washington, 1985-86; speech pathologist Rehabilitation Hosp. Pacific, Honolulu, 1986-87, Dept. Edn., Honolulu, 1987-89, Queen's Med. Ctr., Honolulu, 1989-95; pvt. practice speech pathologist Honolulu, 1987—; instr. U. Hawaii, 1993-94. Recipient Search for Excellence award U. Northern Colo., 1984-85. Mem. Hawaii Speech, Lang. Hearing Assn. (spkr. at conf. 1993, com. mem., pres.-elect 1995-96), Am. Hearing and Speech Assn., Autistic Soc. Hawaii, Hawaii Bicycle League, Mid-Pacific Road Runners Club (vol. 1991—), Hawaii Venture Capital Assn. Address: Ohana Speech Lang Conss 350 Ward Ave Ste 106-87 Honolulu HI 96814-4004

AREEN, JUDITH CAROL, law educator; b. Chgo., Aug. 2, 1944; d. Gordon Eric and Pauline Jeanette (Payberg) A.; m. Richard M. Cooper, Feb. 17, 1979; children: Benjamin Eric, Jonathan Gordon. AB, Cornell U., 1966; JD, Yale U., 1969. Bar: Mass. 1970, D.C. 1972. Program planner for higher edn. Mayor's Office City of N.Y., 1969-70; dir. edn. voucher study Ctr. for Study Pub. Policy, Cambridge, Mass., 1970-72; mem. faculty Georgetown U., Washington, 1971—, assoc. prof. law, 1972-76, prof., 1976—, prof. community and family medicine, 1980-89, assoc. dean Law Ctr., 1984-87; dean, exec. v.p. for law affairs Georgetown U, Washington, 1989—; gen. counsel, coord. domestic reorgn. Office of Mgmt. and Budget, Washington, 1977-80; spl. counsel White House Task Force on Regulatory Reform, Washington, 1978-80; cons. NIH, 1984; cons. NRC, 1985, mem. com. film badge dosimetry; bd. dirs. MCI. Author: Youth Service Agencies, 1977, Cases and Materials on Family Law, 3d edit., 1992, Law, Science and Medicine, 1984, 2d edit., 1996. Mem. Def. Adv. Com. Women In Svcs., Washington, 1979-82. Woodrow Wilson Internat. Ctr. for Scholars fellow, 1988-89, Kennedy Inst. Ethics Sr. Rsch. fellow, Washington, 1982—. Mem. ABA, D.C. Bar Assn., Am. Law Inst.

AREGLADO, NANCY, elementary education educator, consultant; b. Boston, Dec. 10, 1946; d. William Vincent and Julia Marie (Dierkes) Hyland; m. Ronald James Areglado, Aug. 24, 1968; children: Kristin Holly, Kimberly Anne, Julie Lynn. BS, Boston State Coll., 1968; MEd, U. Mass., 1982. Tchr. Quincy (Mass.) Pub. Schs., 1968-70; lang. specialist Mass. Migrant Edn. Program, Holyoke, 1981-83; spl. edn. tutor Greenfield (Mass.) Sch. Dept., 1984; tchr. North Adams (Mass.) Pub. Schs., 1986-89, early childhood coord., 1987-89; adj. instr. North Adams State Coll., 1988-89; pvt. practice as integrated lang. arts cons. Mass., 1987—; 1st grade tchr. Village Sch., West Stockbridge, Mass., 1989-90; whole lang. coord. Berkshire Hills Schs., Stockbridge, 1990; reading specialist Fairfax County Pub. Schs., 1990—. Co-author: Portfolios in the Classroom: A Teacher's Sourcebook. Co-organizer Cambodia Assistance Dr., Franklin County, Mass., 1979; bd. dirs. Big Bros./Big Sisters Assn., Greenfield, Mass., 1975-85. Recipient Exemplary Svc. award Big Bros./Big Sisters, 1976, Celebrate Literacy award, Berkshire Reading Coun., 1990. Mem. Whole Lang. Tchrs. Assn. (networking chair Berkshires 1987-89, mem. Whole Lang. Umbrella 1986—), Nat. Coun. Tchrs. English, Internat. Reading Assn. Democrat. Roman Catholic. Home: 11107 Robert Carter Rd Fairfax VA 22039-1316 Office: Reading Ctr Rolling Valley Sch Fairfax County Pub Schs Springfield VA 22152

ARENA, JUDITH ROXANNE, dietetic technician; b. Elizabeth, N.J., June 6, 1956; d. Samuel and Antoinette (Bentivenga) A. AAS in Hotel and Restaurant Mgmt., Middlesex County Coll., Edison, N.J., 1976; AAS in Dietetic Tech., Camden County Coll., Blackwood, N.J., 1992. Registered dietetic technician. Asst. mgr. Burger King Restaurant, Avenel, N.J., 1978-83; mgr. Howard Johnson's Restaurant, Old Bridge, N.J., 1983-88; real estate processor John B. Canuso, Inc., Voorhees, N.J., 1988-90; food svc. supr. Kennedy Meml. Hosp., Turnersville, N.J., 1990-92; dietetic technician Shore Meml. Hosp., Somers Point, N.J., 1992—. Contbr. abstracts to profl. jours. Mem. NOW, Am. Dietetic Assn. (chair-elect tech. practice group 1996-97, Dietetic Technician of Yr 1995),, N.J. Dietetic Assn. (mem. awards com. 1995, Dietetic Technician of Yr. 1995), Dietetic Out Reach Group (editor 1995—). Home: 8 Lenore Ct Hammonton NJ 08037 Office: Shore Meml Hosp 1 E New York Ave Somers Point NJ 08244

ARENA, KELLI, news correspondent; b. Bklyn., N.Y., Dec. 17, 1963; d. Melvin Mullins and Mary Ann (Scafa) Tracy. BFA, NYU, 1985. Prodr. various shows CNN, N.Y.C., 1985-89, prodr. spl. reports, 1988-89, line prodr., 1989-90, supervising prodr., 1990-92; exec. prodr. CNN, London, 1992; news editor CNN, N.Y.C., 1992-93, reporter, anchor, 1993—. Youth dir. St. George's Ch., N.Y.C., 1989-93. Recipient Peabody award U. Ga., 1987, Cable Ace award, 1987, Gold award Houston Internat. Film Festival, 1987; named Topten Fin. Journalist Jour. Fin. Reporting, 1989-92. Mem. Soc. Am. Bus. Editors and Writers, Internat. Womens Media Found., N.Y. Fin. Writers Assn. Office: CNN Bus News 820 1st St NE Washington DC 20002

ARES, PATRICIA JANE, counselor; b. Texarkana, Ark., July 26, 1937; d. James Edward and Leota Christina (Fleming) Cunningham; m. David Austin Metts, July 21, 1957 (div. Dec. 1979); children: Alison Elizabeth, Leslie Christine; m. Albert Louie Ares, May 10, 1991. BA, UTPB, 1974, MA, 1977. Lic. chem. dependency counselor, Tex. Co-owner Talk It Over Counseling Svc., Midland, Tex., 1980-90; with Odessa Coll., 1985-90; owner Star Counseling Ctr., Arlington, Tex., 1990—. Author: Say Yes to Yourself, 1988; one women show Midland Coll. Mus. S.W., Tex. Mem. NAFE (network dir. 1985-95), Bus. Prof. Women (pres. 1989, woman of yr. 1989), Tex. Assn. Drug & Alcohol Counselor (pres. 1988, counselor of yr. 1994). Office: Star Counseling Ste K 1615 W Abram Arlington TX 76013

ARGERS, HELEN, writer; b. Valisburg, N.J.. BA; graduate studies, Europe. Writer advtsg. copy; workshop lectr. 6th Ann. Metro. Writers Conf. Seton Hall U., South Orange, N.J., 1996. Author: A Lady of Independence, 1982, Noblesse Oblique, 1994, (play) The Home Visit, 1986 (Winner Nat. One-Act-Play Competition 1986, Weisbrod award 1987), A Scandalous Lady, 1991, A Captain's Lady, 1991, An Unlikely Lady, 1992, The Gilded Lily, (short story) The Ozymandias Bush (Nelson Algren award finalist 1990), Repossession (Writer's Digest Short Story Competition award); author (under pseudonym Helen Archery) The Age of Elegance, 1992, The Season of Loving, 1992, Lady Adventuress, 1994, Duel of Hearts, 1994. Recipient Resolution on Honer State of N.J., 1994. Mem. Nat. Hist. Soc., Jane Austen Soc. N. Am., N.J. State Opera Guild. Office: Margit Bolland Creatorwrites Lit Agy 78 Woodbine Ave Newark NJ 07106*

ARGOT, ADELE R., journalist; b. Westersode, Germany, Jan. 16, 1943; d. Amandus A. Tiedemann and Sophie A. (Lühmann) Ewe; m. Robert G. Argot, June 19, 1965; children: Robert G. Jr., Ryan E. BS in Secondary Edn., East Stroudsburg U., 1964; postgrad., U. Mont., 1967. Cert. English, elem. edn., German, Pa. Tchr. English Belvidere (N.J.) H.S., 1964-65; tchr. German Stroudsburg (Pa.) Sch. Dist., 1965-69; part time tchr. German Pleasant Valley Sch. Dist., Brodheadsville, Pa., 1983-86; subagt. Erie Ins./Argot Agy., McMichaels, Pa., 1983-86; corr. Times News, Lehighton, Pa., 1986-89; staff mem. Times News, Lehighton, 1989-90; editl. asst. Pocono Post, Gilbert, Pa., 1990-93; editor Pocono Post, Gilbert, 1993—. Author of poetry. Cub scout den mother Boy Scouts Am., McMichaels, 1981-85; 4-H leader Pa. 4H, McMichaels, 1986—. Recipient Keystone Writing awards Pa. Newspaper Pubs. Assn., Harrisburg. Mem. Pa. Women's Press Assn. (writing awards), West End Rotary (Paul Harris fellow). Home: RR 2 Box 2290 Saylorsburg PA 18353 Office: Pocono Post PO Box 100 Gilbert PA 18331

ARGRETT, LORETTA COLLINS, assistant attorney general, educator; b. Carlisle, Miss., Oct. 7, 1937; d. Joseph Daniel and Katie Marie (Jones) C.; m. James H. Argrett Jr., Mar. 28, 1959 (div.); children: Lisa Argrett Ahmad, Brian E.; m. Vantile E. Whitfield, May 29, 1993. BS cum laude, Howard U., 1958; student, Technische Hochschule, Zurich, Switzerland, 1958; postgrad., Howard U., 1966-67, George Washington U., 1968; JD, Harvard U., 1976. Bar: D.C. Ct. Appeals 1976, U.S. Dist. Ct. D.C. 1977, U.S. Ct. Appeals D.C. 1977, U.S. Tax Ct. 1977. Chemist NIH, 1958-59, 59-61; tchr. Duval County Bd. Instrn., Fla., 1961-62; chemist Hazleton Labs., Reston, Va., 1965-66, FDA, 1966-68; chemist, supr. lab. Walter Reed Army Inst. of Rsch., 1968-73; summer assoc. Mahoney, Hadlow, Chambers & Adams, Jacksonville, Fla., summer 1975; summer assoc. Arent, Fox, Kintner, Plotkin & Kahn, Washington, summer 1975, assoc., 1976-78; assoc. Stroock & Stroock & Lavan, Washington, 1978-79; legis. atty. Joint Com. on Taxation U.S. Congress, 1979-81; ptnr. Wald, Harkrader & Ross, Washington, 1981-86; pvt. practice Washington, 1986; assoc. prof., then prof. Sch. Law, Howard U., Washington, 1986—; Asst. Atty. Gen. in Tax Div. U.S. Dept. of Justice; sec. bd. meetings Opportunity Funding Corp., 1984-93; adj. prof. Georgetown

Law Ctr., Washington Coll. Law, 1986-88, Am. U., 1988; mem. vis. com. Harvard Law Sch., 1987-93; apptd. mem. adv. com. grad. tax program U. Balt. Law Sch., 1986—; mem. spl. com. on gender D.C. Cir. Task Froce on Gender, Race and Ethnic Bias, 1992-95. Contbr. articles to profl. jours. Bd. trustees Free the Children Trust; bd. dirs. Jubilee Enterprise of Greater Washington, Inc.; adv. bd. Jubilee Support Alliance; mem. NAACP, Pub. Defender Svc. of D.C. Lucy Moten fellow, 1958. Fellow Am. Bar Found.; mem. ABA (sect. on taxation, chair task force capital cost recovery 1985, vice chair com. women and minorities 1993-95, lobbyist), Nat. Bar Assn., Washington Bar Assn., D.C. Bar Assn. (mem. atty. client arbitration bd. 1984-90, legal ethics com. 1993—), Harvard Law Sch. Alumni Assn., Sigma Xi (assoc.), Beta Kappa Chi. Office: US Dept JusticeTax Div 950 Penn Ave NW Rm 4143 Washington DC 20530*

ARGUN, FATIMA HATICE, international trade and marketing consultant, specialist. BA in Polit. Sci. and Internat. Studies, U. Tex., 1983; student, U. Paris-Sorbonne, 1983; MPA, U. Tex., 1985. With Office of the U.S. Trade Rep., Washington, 1986; freelance writer Internat. Reports, N.Y.C., 1986-87; dir. internat. trade Competitive Enterprise Inst., Washington, 1987-88; campaign liaison George Bush for President and Bush-Quayle '88 campaigns, Washington, 1987-88; coord. transition office contacts Office of the Pres.-Elect, Washington, 1988-89; asst. to dir. internat. trade Minority Bus. Devel. Agy. U.S. Dept. Commerce, Washington, 1989-91; legis. fellow U.S. Sen. Arlen Specter, Washington, 1991-92; adviser to chmn. U.S. Merit Systems Protection Bd., Washington, 1992—. Co-author: U.S. Trade with Newly Industrializing Countries. Mem. Women in Internat. Trade (charter, bd. dirs., spl. events chmn. 1987-88), World Affairs Coun. Washington, Fgn. Policy Assn. N.Y., Gt. Decisions Fgn. Policy Discussion Group, Washington Internat. Trade Assn., LBJ Sch. Alumni Assn. (v.p. 1989—), Les Compagnery (France). Republican.

ARKIN, MARA J., social studies educator; b. Jackson Heights, N.Y., Apr. 9, 1968; d. Stuart Platt and Joan (Arkin) Scolnick. BA, The George Washington U., 1990, MA, 1992; MEd, U. Md., 1995. Cert. sec. social studies and spl. edn. Resident asst., adminstr. The George Washington U., Washington, 1989-92; tchr. religion Temple Sinai, Washington, 1990-96; peer tutoring coord. The George Washington U., 1991-92; adult edn. tchr. Montgomery County Pub., Rockville, Md., 1992; spl. edn. tchr. Alexandria (Va.) Pub. Schs., 1992, Prince Georges Pub. Schs., Upper Marlboro, Md., 1992-93; tutor Lab Sch. Washington, 1992—; spl. edn. tchr. Howard County Pub. Schs., Elliott City, Md., 1993-96, social studies tchr., 1996—. Troop leader Girl Scouts of Am., 1994-95. Mem. ASCD, Coun. for Exceptional Children, Nat. Coun. for the Social Studies, Phi Kappa Phi, Omicron Delta Kappa.

ARKIN, MARIANGELA, elementary education educator; b. N.Y.C., Mar. 26, 1954; d. Frank and Marietta (Vellucci) Bambino; children: Thomas and Dana DeMattia; m. Zachary Arkin. BA in Sociology, Molloy Coll., 1993; MA in Elem. Edn., Adelphi U. Cert. tchr., cert. in whole lang., N.Y. 5th grade tchr. Oceanside (N.Y.) Sch. Dist., 1993—; travel cons./agt., 1996—. Pres. Oceanside Mid. Sch. PTA, 1987-89; pres. Oceanside Mid. Sch. PTA, 1989-91, hon. life mem. Mem. Nat. Coun. Tchrs. of English. Republican. Roman Catholic. Home: 510 Glen Ct Oceanside NY 11572

ARLINGHAUS, SANDRA JUDITH LACH, mathematical geographer, educator; b. Elmira, N.Y., Apr. 18, 1943; d. Donald Frederick and Alma Elizabeth (Satorius) Lach; m. William Charles Arlinghaus, Sept. 3, 1966; 1 child, William Edward. AB in Math., Vassar Coll., 1964; postgrad., U. Chgo., 1964-66, U. Toronto, Ont., Can., 1966-67, Wayne State U., 1968-70; MA in Geography, Wayne State U., 1976; PhD in Geography, U. Mich., 1977. Vis. instr. math. U. Ill., Chgo., 1966; vis. asst. prof. geography Ohio State U., Columbus, 1977-78, lectr. math., 1978-79; lectr. math. Loyola U., Chgo., 1979-81, asst. prof. math., 1981-82; lectr. math. and geography U. Mich., Dearborn and Ann Arbor, 1982-83; founding dir. Inst. Math. Geography, Ann Arbor, 1985—; guest lectr. U. Chgo., 1979, 87, U. Calif., 1979, Syracuse U., 1991, U. No. Iowa, 1991; guest lectr. U. Mich., Ann Arbor, 1983, 90-93, adj. prof. math. geography, population-environ. dynamics Sch. Natural Resources and Environ., 1994—; cons. Transp. Rsch. Inst., Coll. Architecture, 1985-86, Coll. Edn., 1992, Cmty. Sys. Found., 1993—; prodr. Ann Arbor Cmty. Access TV, 1988-90; dir. spatial analysis divsn. Cmty. Systems Found., 1996—, dir. fellowship tng. divsn., 1996—. Author: Down the Mail Tubes: The Pressured Postal Era, 1853-1984, Essays on Mathematical Geography, 1986, Essays on Mathematical Geography-II, 1987, An Atlas of Steiner Networks, 1989, Essays on Mathematical Geography-III, 1991; co-author: Population-Environment Dynamics, Sectors in Transition, 1992, Mathematical Geography and Global Art, 1986, Environmental Effects on Bus Durability, 1990, Fractals in Geography, 1993; founder, editor, co-author Solstice, 1990—, Image Interactive Atlases, Image Game Series, Image Discussion Papers, Internat. Soc. Spatial Scis., 1995—; author, editor-in-chief Practical Handbook of Curve Fitting, 1994; co-author, editor-in-chief Practical Handbook of Digital Mapping: Terms and Concepts, 1994; editor-in-chief Practical Handbook of Spatial Stats., 1995; editor internat. monograph series; reviewer Mathematical Reviews, 1992—; contbr. articles, book reviews to profl. jours. in field of geography, psychology, math., biology, history, philately. Planning commr. City of Ann Arbor, 1995—; bd. dirs., mem. chmn. Bromley Homeowners Assn., Ann Arbor, 1989-93, pres., 1990-93, 95-96; bd. dirs. World Jr. Bridge Championships, Ann Arbor, 1990-91; bd. dirs. Dolfins Inc., 1993-96; artist Math. Awareness Week, Lawrence Tech. U., 1988; mem. bd. trustees Cmty. Sys. Found., 1995—. Fellow Am. Geog. Soc. (rep. search com. for curator of collection in Golda Meir Libr. U. Wis.-Milw. Libr. 1993-94); mem. AAAS, Am. Math. Soc., Math. Assn. Am., Assn. Am. Geographers, Internat. Soc. Spatial Scis. (founder), N.Y. Acad. Scis., Engring. Soc. Detroit, Regional Sci. Assn. Office: Inst Math Geography 2790 Briarcliff St Ann Arbor MI 48105-1429 also: Sch Natural Resources U Mich Ann Arbor MI 48109

ARMACOST, MARY-LINDA SORBER MERRIAM, former college president; b. Jeannette, Pa., May 31, 1943; d. Everett Sylvester Calvin and Madeleine (Case) Sorber; m. E. William Merriam, Dec. 13, 1969 (div. 1975); m. Peter H. Armacost, July 10, 1993. Student, Grove City Coll., 1961-63; BA, Pa. State U., 1963-65, MA, 1965-67, PhD, 1967-70; HHD (hon.), Carroll Coll., 1991; LLD (hon.), Wilson Coll., 1994. Rsch. assoc. Pa. State U., University Park, 1970-72; asst. prof. speech Emerson Coll., Boston, 1972-79, dir. continuing edn., 1974-77, spl. asst. to pres., 1977-78, v.p. adminstrn., 1978-79; asst. to pres. Boston U., 1979-81; pres. Wilson Coll., Chambersburg, Pa., 1981-91, Moore Coll. Art and Design, Phila., 1991-93; sr. fellow Office of Women in Higher Edn. Am. Coun. on Edn., 1994—; cons. Govt. Edn. and Secondary Edn. Act Title III, Alameda County, Calif., 1968. Bd. dirs. Sta. WITF, Inc., Harrisburg, Pa., 1982-91, chmn. bd., 1988-91; bd. dirs. Chambersburg Hosp., 1984-89, vice chmn. bd., 1987-89; bd. dirs. Sta. WHYY-FM-TV, Phila., 1992-93, Boston Zool. Soc., 1980-81, Arts Boston, 1979-81, Scotland Sch. Vets. Children, Pa., 1984-90, Fla. Orch., 1993-96; mem. exec. com. Found. for Ind. Colls., 1989-91; pres. Chambersburg Area Coun. Arts, 1988-90; chmn. higher edn. com. Gen. Assembly Presbyn. Ch., 1987-90; elder Falling Spring Presbyn. Ch., 1988-90. Recipient Disting. Alumna award Pa. State U., 1984, Disting. Dau. of Pa., 1986, Athena award Chambersburg C. of C., 1988, Outstanding Alumnae award Sch. Dist. Jeannette, 1991. Mem. NATAS (bd. govs. New Eng. chpt. 1980-81), AAUW, Am. Coun. Edn. (commn. on women 1992-93, commn. on govtl. rels. 1985-89, fellow 1977-78), Speech Comm. Assn., Pa. Assn. Colls. and Univs. (exec. com. 1984-90), Assn. Presbyn. Colls. and Univ. (exec. com. 1983-88, pres. 1986-87), Am. Assn. Higher Edn., Nat. Soc. Arts and Letters, Forum for Exec. Women, WEDU (bd. dirs. Tampa, Fla. 1995—), Phi Kappa Phi, Rho Tau Sigma, Phi Delta Kappa.

ARMAGOST, ELSA GAFVERT, retired computer industry communications consultant; b. Duluth, Minn.; d. Axel Justus and Martina Emelia (Magnuson) Gafvert; m. Byron William Armagost, Dec. 8, 1945; children: David Byron, Laura Martina. Grad. with honors, Duluth Jr. Coll., 1936; BJ, U. Minn., 1938, postgrad. in pub. rels., bus. mgmt. and computer tech., 1965-81; PhD in Computer Comm. Cons. Sci. (hon.), Internat. U. Found. Freelance editor, Duluth, 1939-42; procedure editor and analyst U.S. Steel, Duluth, 1942-45; fashion advt. staff Dayton Co., Mpls., 1945-48; systems applications and documentation mgr. Control Data Corp., Mpls., 1969-74, promotion specialist, mktg. editor, 1974-76, corp. staff coord. info. on edn., 1976-78; instr. comm., publ. specialist, 1978-79; commn. cons. peripheral products group, 1979-83; industry comm. cons., 1983-88, ret., 1988; mem. steering com. U.S. Senatorial Bus. Adv. Bd., 1962-68; mem. U.S. Congrl. Adv. Bd., 1958-62. V.p. Sewickley (Pa.) Valley Hosp. Aux.; bd. dirs. Sewickley Valley Mental Health Coun., LWV Pitts.; bd. dirs. publicity chmn. Sacred Arts Expo; mem. World Affairs Coun. radio program, Pitts. Recipient Medal of Merit Rep. Presdl. Task Force. Mem. AAUW (1st v.p. Caracas, Venezuela), Women in Communication (bd. dir. job mart), Marsh Pk. Condominium Assn. (bd. mem.), Toastmasters (Comm. award 1984), N. Ctrl. Deming Mgmt. Forum, Ctr. of the Am. Expt., Internat. Platform Assn., Friends of Mpls. Inst. Art., Walker Art Inst., Ceridian Corp. Retirees Assn. (bd. dirs.), Minn. Alumni Assn. (life), Am. Swedish Inst., Internat. Soc. Newspaper Editors, Phi Beta Nat. Profl. Arts Frat., Internat. Bible Study Fellowship. Nominated for Alumni Notable Achievement, U. Minn. Coll. Liberal Arts, 1995. Home and Office: 9500 Collegeview Rd Apt 312 Minneapolis MN 55437-2158

ARMANI, AIDA MARY, small business executive; b. Amman, Jordan, Apr. 13, 1952; came to U.S., 1956; d. Raji Naiem and Wardeh Elias (Kazanjian) Kawar; m. Steven Earl McBride, Apr. 7, 1973 (div. July 1983); children: Nathaniel Joseph, Aaron Keith. Beauty lic., Martin Anthony Beauty Sch., 1970; cert. in hypnotherapy, Sidona Inst. Hypnotherapy, 1995; cert. imagery therapist, Internat. Inst. Visualization, 1996. Stylist/colorist Jean-Madeline, Phila., 1970-74; colorist Hair Impulse, Media, Pa., 1975-80; colorist/stylist Talent, Bryn Mawr, 1980-83; colorist Salon 600, Bryn Mawr, Pa., 1983-86, James & Co., Wayne, Pa., 1986-87; colorist, cons., head dept., artistic dir. Raya-Haig Salon, Bala Cynwyd, Pa., 1987—; intrepreneur, owner Aida, Inc., West Chester, Pa., 1995—; mem. artistic team Goldwell of Pa., 1995-96, educator, 1990-96; pvt. practice dream interpreter, hypnotherapy counselor, West Chester, Pa., 1995—. Inventor hair styling devices; appeared in opera Acad. of Music., Pa., 1996. Sunday sch. tchr. Ch. of the Savior, Wayne, Pa., 1981-86, leader divorced/singles group, 1987-92; mem. Internat. Inst. Visualization & Rsch., 1995-96. Mem. Internat. Beauty Soc., Art & Fashion, Intercoiffure Internat., Hair Color Exch. Home: 308 Everest Cir West Chester PA 19382 Office: Aida Inc PO Box 937 Edgemont PA 19082 also: Raya-Haig Beauty Ctr 401 City Line Ave Bala Cynwyd PA 19010

ARMAS, JENNIFER VILLAREAL, nurse; b. Manila, July 27, 1967; (parents Am. citizens); d. Ferdinand and Erlinda (Villareal) A. AS in Nursing, Chattanooga State Tech. Community Coll., 1989; student, Ellsworth Aviation Sch., 1990—. RN, Tenn. Pediatric emergency rm. nurse Erlanger Med. Ctr., Chattanooga, 1990—; nurse hematology/oncology unit Egleston Children's Hosp. at Emory U., Atlanta, 1993—. Vol. Riverbend, Chattanooga, 1990; vol. nurse Chattanooga Sports CLinic, 1990-93. Mem. ANA, Emergency Nurses Assn., Soc. Pediatric Nurses, Chattanooga Jaycees.

ARMISTEAD, KATHERINE KELLY (MRS. THOMAS B. ARMISTEAD, III), interior designer, travel consultant, civic worker; b. Pitts., Apr. 14, 1926; d. Joseph Anthony and Katherine Arnold (Manning) Kelly; grad. Finch Jr. Coll., 1946; m. Thomas Boyd Armistead, III, Nov. 29, 1952; children: Katherine Kelly (Mrs. W. Michael Roark), Thomas Boyd IV. Editor news Sta. WOR, N.Y.C., 1946-51; with Dumont TV, 1951-52; editor Social Service Rev., 1956-57; interior designer, L.A., 1963—; travel cons. Gilner Internat. Travels, Beverly Hills, Calif., 1980—. Editorial bd. Previews Mag., 1984-87. Pres. Jrs. Social Svc.,L.A., 1962-64; nat. chpt. chmn. Associated Alumnae of Sacred Heart, 1960-66; pres. Las Floristas, 1967-68; pres. L.A. Orphanage Guild, 1969-70; coord. Jr. Mannequin Assisteens, Assistance League So. Calif., 1971-72; pres. docent coun. L.A. County Mus. Art, 1976-77, pres. decorative arts coun., 1977-80, chmn. Am. Antiques Conf., 1979-81, mem. costume coun., mem. past pres.' coun., 1981—, mem. capital gifts campaign com.; bd. dirs. L.A. Orphanage Guild, 1970—; Cert. travel cons. Recipient Eve award Assistance League So. Calif. Mem. Am. Soc. Travel Agts., Inst. Cert. Travel Agts. (cert.), Equestrian Order of the Holy Sepulchre of Jerusalem. Republican. Roman Catholic. Clubs: Birnam Wood Golf (Santa Barbara, Calif.), Bel Air Garden.

ARMOCIDA, PATRICIA ANNE, managed health care official; b. Portland, Maine, July 29, 1956; d. Gerald Arthur and Aileen Patricia (Malone) Faneuf; m. William Joseph Armocida, June 21, 1986. BS, Purdue U., 1980; MBA, Boston U., 1983. RN, Mass. Staff nurse New Eng. Med. Ctr., Boston, 1980-81, Mass. Gen. Hosp., Boston, 1981; cons. Deloitte, Haskins & Sells, Boston, 1981, Health Data Inst., Boston, 1981-82; cons. Blue Cross/Blue Shield Assn., Chgo., 1983, asst. to the pres., 1983-85; mgr. health svcs. Blue Cross/Blue Shield Ill., 1985-86, dir. HMO, dir. utilization mgmt., 1987-90; v.p. mktg. Health Mgmt. Strategies, Alexandria, Va., 1990-91; dir. med. mgmt. Blue Cross and Blue Shield of the Nat. Capital Area, Washington, 1991-92; pres. Health Dimensions, Inc., Seattle, 1992—; lectr. George Washington U., 1991-94; mem. bd. dirs. Washington Case Mgmt. Assn., 1996. Vol. Exchange Club, Chgo., 1987; vol. instr. Handicapped Riders, Chgo., 1986; mem. rev. com. Nat. Inst. Drug Abuse Project; campaign vol. United Way, Chgo., 1988. Boston U. scholar, 1983; recipient Leadership award YWCA and Blue Cross/Blue Shield, 1988. Mem. Am. Assn. Health Plans (com.). Roman Catholic.

ARMS, ANNELI (ANNA ELIZABETH ARMS), artist, educator; b. N.Y.C., May 23, 1935; d. William Emil and Elizabeth Maria (Bodanzky) Muschenheim; m. John M. Arms, Sept. 1, 1956; 1 child, Thomas C. BA, U. Mich., 1958. Recipient Nora Mirmont award Heckscher Mus., 1984, Guild Hall Sculpture award, 1987; scholar Art Students League N.Y., 1958. Mem. Nat. Drawing Assn., Fedn. Modern Painters and Sculptors (bd. dirs. 1988-96,, v.p. 1996—), Manhattan Graphics Ctr. (bd. dirs. 1995-96), Jimmy Ernst Artists Alliance (exhbns. com. 1988-95), Artists Equity. Gallery: 113 Greene St New York NY 10012

ARMSTRONG, ANNE ELIZABETH, management company executive; b. Birmingham, Ala., Jan. 6, 1961; d. Charles Harris Jr. and Anne Marie (Collier) A. BS in Comms., U. Tenn., 1991. Dist. tng. mgr. Ormond Shops, Inc., Nashville, 1984-89; cmty. rels. rep. Martin Marietta Energy Sys., Oak Ridge, Tenn., 1992-95; cmty. rels. adminstr. M4 Environ. Mgmt. Inc., Oak Ridge, 1995—. Editor newsletter The Armstrong Chronicles, 1989-91. U. Tenn. legis. alumni intern Tenn. Gen. Assembly, Nashville, 1991; unit III chair, cabinet mem. United Way of Anderson County, Inc., 1996—. Recipient Cmty. Rels. Nat. Bellringer award Team Recognition, 1993, K-25 Site Silver Dollar award, 1993, award Pub. Rels. Soc. Am., 1992, 93, 94. Mem. Nat. Assn. Environ. Profls., Women in Comms., Armstrong Clan Soc. (bd. dirs. 1996&), Delta Zeta. Episcopalian. Office: M4 Environ Mgmt Inc 1000 Clearview Ct Oak Ridge TN 37830

ARMSTRONG, ANNE LEGENDRE (MRS. TOBIN ARMSTRONG), former ambassador, corporate director; b. New Orleans, Dec. 27, 1927; d. Armant and Olive (Martindale) Legendre; m. Tobin Armstrong, Apr. 12, 1950; children: John Barclay, Katharine A. Idsal, Sarita A. Hixon, Tobin and James L. (twins). BA in English, Vassar Coll., 1949. Co-chmn. Rep. Nat. Com., 1971-73; del. Rep. Nat. Conv., 1964-88; counsellor to U.S. Pres., 1973-74; U.S. amb. to Gt. Britain and No. Ireland, London, Gt. Britain, No. Ireland, 1976-77; chmn. adv. bd. Ctr. for Strategic and Internat. Studies (formerly affiliated with Georgetown U.), 1981-87, chmn. bd. trustees, 1987—; chmn. Pres.'s Fgn. Intelligence Adv. Bd., 1981-90; commn. on Integrated Long Term Strategy, 1987; pres. Nat. Thanksgiving Commn., 1986-94; bd. dirs. GM Corp., Halliburton Co., Boise Cascade Corp., Am. Express Co., Glaxo Wellcome. Bd. regents Smithsonian Instn., 1978-94, emeritus, 1994; bd. overseers Hoover Instn., 1978—; co-chmn. Reagan-Bush Campaign, 1980. Recipient Rep. Woman of Yr. award, 1979, Texan of Yr. award, 1981, Presdl. Medal of Freedom award, 1987, Golden Plate award Am. Acad. Achievement, 1989; named to Tex. Women's Hall of Fame, 1986. Mem. English-Speaking Union (chmn. 1978-80), Coun. Fgn. Rels., Tex. Women's Alliance (chmn. 1985-89, chmn. emeritus), Am. Assocs. of Royal Acad. Trust (trustee 1985—, vice chmn. 1996), Phi Beta Kappa. Clubs: Alfalfa Club, Washington, F St. (Washington).

ARMSTRONG, BARBARA MIDDLETON, accountant; b. Enterprise, Ala., Aug. 24, 1958; d. Charlie Madison and Verlon (Salter) Middleton; m. Clifford Boyd Armstrong, Sept. 2, 1978 (div. Sept. 1989); children: Charles Luther, Amy Elise. BSBA, Troy State U., 1994, postgrad., 1995—. Mgr. advt. sales Ark. Jour., Little Rock, 1980-82; mgr. fuel systems Walker Oil Co., Inc., Pensacola, Fla., 1982-83; inventory control Wayne Akers Ford, Inc., Lake Worth, Fla., 1983-85; staff acct. Marsh & Carr, Enterprise, Ala., 1985-86; office mgr., bookkeeper Wiregrass Petroleum Svc., Dothan, Ala., 1986-91; fuel sys. mgr. Collier Oil Co., Inc., Ozark, Ala., 1991-95; acct. Jackson Thronton & Co., Dothan, Ala., 1995—. Youth leader Mt. Pleasant Bapt. Ch., Enterprise, 1993—; student advisor Troy State U. Effectiveness Com., Dothan, 1994-95. Mem. Inst. Mgmt. Accts. (pres. student chpt. 1994-95, 95-96). Home: Rte 1 Box 358 Chancellor AL 36316 Office: Jackson Thornton & Co PO Box 6965 Enterprise AL 36302

ARMSTRONG, BESS, actress; b. Balt., Dec. 11, 1953; m. John Fiedler. Student, Brown U. Appeared in films House of God, 1979, The Four Seasons, Jekyll and Hyde-Together Again, High Road to China, Jaws 3-D, Nothing In Common, Second Sight, Mother Mother, The Skateboard Kid; appeared in TV series On Our Own, All Is Forgiven, Married People, My So-Called Life; appeared in t.v. movies: Getting Married, How to Pick Up Girls, Walking Through the Fire, 11th Victim, This Girl For Hire, Lace, Take Me Home Again, She Stood Alone: The Tailhook Scandal, Stolen Innocence; spl. Barefoot in the Park. Office: c/o William Morris Agy 151 El Camino Beverly Hills CA 90212*

ARMSTRONG, CAROLYN PALMER, rancher, investor; b. Muskogee, Okla., Oct. 26, 1941; d. William Henry and Lizzie Lou (Ross) Palmer; m. Helmuth J. Naumer, May 7, 1963; children: Kirsten Naumer, Tatiana Naumbel Percival; m. John Barclay Armstrong. Attended, William Woods Coll. for Women, 1959-60, U. Okla., 1960-62, Tex. Christian U., 1969-70, Bellview, Washington Cmty. Coll. for Computer Studies, Am. Coll. Real Estate, U. Mexico, San Antonio, 1994-96. Real Estate lic. Tex., 1984. Adminstr. Kimbell Art Mus., Ft. Worth, Tex., 1966-75; mgr. J.J. Meeker Investments, Ft. Worth, 1976-77; v.p. Meeker Contemporary Art Investment Co., Ft. Worth, 1976-77; ptnr., cons. Dimensions, Seattle, 1977-79; cons. Design Group, N.Y., 1979-80; dir. Retama Polo Ctr., 1980-86; investor, rancher, 1986—; trustee, sec. bd. dirs. Tex. and Southwestern Cattle Raisers Found., 1995—; trustee Los Compadres, 1995—. Apptd. mem. commn. by Gov. Clements Tex. State Libr. and Archives, 1989, reappointed by Gov. Bush, 1995; mem. Hoover Inst., Leadership Tex., Jr. League, Bexar County Rep. Women; chair Tex. South-Australia Polo Exch., San Antonio, Sesquicentennial Sports Com., St. Mary's Hall Summer Arts Program and English as a 2d Lang.; bd. dirs. Ft. Worth Painted Spaces; chair Orch. Hall project for Symphony; chair Bicentennial Com., Ft. Worth Arrangements Com., Pub. Rels. Com. Ft. Worth Jr. League. Mem. Delta Delta Delta. Home: 223 Allen St PO Box 6109 San Antonio TX 78209

ARMSTRONG, DEANNA FRANCES, engineer; b. Winchester, Va., July 14, 1962; d. Gerald Francis and Reta Marie (Wyatt) A. AS in Mech. Engring. Tech., W.Va. Inst. Tech., 1982, AS in Elec. Engring. Tech. cum laude, 1983, BS in Electronics Engring. Tech. cum laude, 1984. Student engring. asst. Monongahela Power Co., Elkins, W.Va., summers 1980-83; machine shop lab. asst. W.Va. Inst. Tech., Montgomery, 1982-83, acad. asst., 1983-84; engring. technician Monongahela Power Co., Elkins, 1984—; competition judge Vocat. and Indsl. Club. Am., Elkins, 1985—; mem. Partnership in Edn. Com. Corr. Monongahela News, 1993—. Mem. adv. coun. Randolph County Vocat. Tech. Ctr., Partnership in Edn. Com.; vol. Mountain State Forest Festival. Mem. Elkins Jr. C. of C., Alpha Chi Nat. Honor Soc. Republican. Home: 508 Center St Elkins WV 26241-3729 Office: Monongahela Power Co US Rte 215 & 250 Elkins WV 26241

ARMSTRONG, JANE BOTSFORD, sculptor; b. Buffalo; d. Samuel Booth and Edith (Pursel) Botsford; m. Robert Thexton Armstrong, July 3, 1960. Student, Middlebury Coll., 1939-40, Pratt Inst., 1940-41, Art Students' League, 1962-64. One-man shows Frank Rehn Gallery, N.Y.C., 1971, 73, 75, 77, Columbus (Ohio) Gallery Fine Arts, 1972, Columbia (S.C.) Mus. Art, 1975, New Britain (Conn.) Mus. Am. Art, 1972, Johnson Gallery, Middlebury Coll., 1973, Mary Duke Biddle Gallery for Blind N.C. Mus. Art, 1974, J.B. Speed Art Mus., Louisville, 1975, Buffalo State U., 1975, Marjorie Parr Gallery, London, 1976, Ark. Art Center, 1977, Dallas Mus. Fine Art, 1978, Wichita (Kans.) Art Mus., 1978, 82, Wadsworth Atheneum, 1979, Foster Harmon Gallery Am. Art, 1979, 81, 92, Washington County (Md.) Mus. Fine Arts, Hagerstown, 1979, Chautauqua (N.Y.) Nat. Exhbn. Am. Art, 1980, Southeastern Center Contemporary Art, Winston-Salem, N.C., 1980, Rollins Coll., Winter Park, Fla., 1981, The Sculpture Center, N.Y.C., 1981, Sid Deutsch Gallery, N.Y.C., 1983, Boca Raton Mus. (Fla.), 1983, Burchfield Ctr., Buffalo, 1985, Glass Art Gallery, Toronto, 1985, Schiller-Wapner Galleries, N.Y.C., 1987, St. Gaudens Gallery, St. Gaudens Nat. Hist. Site, 1988, Middlebury Coll., Vt., 1988, Grand Cen. Art Galleries, N.Y.C., 1989, Nautical Arts Club, 1996; exhibited in USIA group exhbn., Europe, 1975-76, Artists of Am., Denver, 1981, 82, 83, 84, 85, 86, 87, 88, 90 (U.S. Art mag. award 1990), 91, 92, 93, 94, 95; represented in numerous acad., indsl., pub. and pvt. collections. Recipient Pauline Law prize Allied Artists Am., 1969, 70, Porton award, 1981, Gold medal, 1976, Ralph Fabri medal of honor, 1978, Chaim Gross Found. award, 1980, Helen Apen Oehler Meml. award, 1988, Meiselman award, 1993, cert. merit NAD, 1973, Coun. Am. Artists' Socs. prize Nat. Sculpture Soc., 1973, gold medal of honor Knickerbocker Artists, 1986, Elliott Lisking Meml. award, 1991, Alumni Achievement award Middlebury Coll., 1993. Fellow Nat. Sculpture Soc. (bronze medal 1976, 78, Tallix Foundry award 1985, Percival Dietsch prize, 1986, Proskauer prize 1995); mem. Nat. Arts Club (gold medal 1968, 69, 71, Best in Show award 1973, Edith W. MacGuire award 1975, plaque of honor 1977, Alexander Saltzman award 1983, Exhbn. Com. award 1990), Audubon Artists (medal of honor 1972, Vincent Glinsky Meml. award 1992, gold medal 1994), Sculptors Guild, Allied Artists Am., Nat. Assn. Women Artists (Charles N. Whinston Meml. prize 1973, Anonymous Meml. prize 1979, Elizabeth S. Blake prize 1980, Amelia Peabody award 1985, Freelander-Sawyer Meml. award 1993). Home: RR Box 684 Dorset Hill Rd East Dorset VT 05253 Studio: 401 E 34th St New York NY 10016

ARMSTRONG, JOANNA, education educator; b. Vienna, Austria, Feb. 3, 1915; came to U.S., 1946; m. David B. Armstrong, Mar. 12, 1946 (dec. Feb. 1992). Diploma, Kindergarten Tchr. State Coll., Vienna, 1933; diploma French Lit., Sorbonne, Paris, 1935; MA, U. Utah, 1951; EdD, U. Houston, 1959. Caseworker, interpreter Czech Refugee Trust Fund, London, 1939-41; tchr. French Gt. Missenden, Bucks, Eng., 1941-43; sec., translator-interpreter U.S. Army, England and France, 1943-46; instr. Coll. William and Mary, Williamsburg, Va., 1951-55, U. St. Thomas, Houston, 1957-59; chmn. langs. sect. South Tex. Coll., Houston, 1961-62; assoc. prof. fgn. langs. Tex. So. U., Houston, 1962-68, dir. NDEA Inst., summer 1964, 65; assoc. prof. sch. edn. tng. Headstart tchrs. U. Tex., El Paso, 1968-71; cons. office Child Devel. HEW, Kansas City, Mo., 1973-75; ret., 1975; cons. Tex. Edn. Agy., Austin, 1965; sec. U.S. Forest Svc., Ely, Nev., 1948; dir. summer programs U. Bordeaux, Pau, U. Zaragoza at Jaca. Author: (book) A European Excursion-From the Mediterranean to the Alps, 1967, Surprising Encounters, 1994; contbr. articles to profl. publs. Vol. Long Beach (Calif.) Symphony, 1978-81, Long Beach Opera, 1982-88, Long Beach Cambodian Scs., 1983-85; mem. Normandy Found. (participant 50th D-Day anniversary 1994). Decorated chevalier Ordre des Palmes Académiques; recipient award Heart Start, 1971, Pres. plaque Alliance Francaise El Paso, 1971, Commemorative Medal of Freedom, Coun. of Normandy, France, 1994. Mem. Long Beach Women's Music Club (program chmn. 1986-88, mem. choral sect. 1989-96, 1st v.p. 1990-92, rec. sec., chmn. opera sect. 1993-94), U.S.-China Peoples Friendship Assn. (rec. sec. 1987—). Home: 120 Alamitos Ave Apt 34 Long Beach CA 90802-5330

ARMSTRONG, KAREN LEE, special education educator; b. Schenectady, N.Y., Dec. 6, 1941; d. William James and Rita Mae (Peabody) Safford; m. John Edward Armstrong, July 14, 1962; 1 child, Lori Ellen. BA in English, SUNY, Albany, 1963, MS in Spl. Edn., 1968. Tchr. English Ballston Lake High Sch., Burnt Hills, N.Y., 1963-66; tchr. spl. edn. Oak Hill Sch., Scotia, N.Y., 1975-88, Schenectady City Schs., 1988—; chair spl. edn. curriculum com., lead tng. sessions Schenectady Schs., 1988—; mem. Shared Decision Making Team, 1994—, chair, 1996-97; mem. spl. edn. del. People's Republic ofChina, 1993; mem. U.S. Del. to South Africa, 1995. Founder Schenectady br. Amnesty Internat., 1990. Mem. Coun. for Exceptional Children, Coun. for Children with Behavioral Disorders. Sufi. Home: 642 Swaggertown Rd Scotia NY 12302-9628

ARMSTRONG, LEE KELLETT, special education teacher; b. Summerville, Ga., Feb. 25, 1958; d. Gordon Lee and Mary Lavonia (Whitehead) Kellett; m. Randall Ladel Armstrong, Mar. 16, 1980; 1 child, Robert Byron

Lee. BA French, Berry Coll., 1980; MEd Spl. Edn., West Ga. Coll., 1986. Cert. tchr. French, Spl. Edn. Spl. edn. tchr. Bartow County Bd. Edn., Cartersville, Ga., 1981-85; dept. chmn. Cass High Sch., Cartersville, 1984-85; spl. edn. tchr. Adairsville High Sch., Adairsville, 1985-89, 1989—; debate coach Adairsville High Sch., 1995—. Area rep., local sec. Ga. Assn. Educators, Atlanta, 1992-94. Mem. NEA, Coun. for Exceptional Children, Order of Robert E. Lee/Ladies' Aux. of Sons of Confederate Vets., 9th Ga. Artillery/Civil War Reenactment Unit. Democrat. Presbyterian. Home: 129 Folsom Rd NW Adairsville GA 30103 Office: Adairsville High Sch 100 College St Adairsville GA 30103

ARMSTRONG, LENNI, animator; b. Euclid, Ohio, Mar. 5, 1954; d. Robert Campbell and Geraldine Agnes (Chesmar) A. BS in Chemistry, Simmons Coll., 1979. Rsch. asst. in biochem. and biophys. scis. various New Eng. univ. labs., Mass., Conn., 1979-86; founder, pres. The Hatchery Animation, Cambridge, Mass., 1986—. Designer, animator children's ednl. software The Human Body, 1991, Storybook Theater, 1992, Exploring Math with Manipulatives, 1993, The SoftKey KeyKids Logo, 1995, Postcards, 1995. Mem. NOW, Graphic Artists Guild, Women's Entrepreneurs Homebased, Boston Computer Soc.

ARMSTRONG, LEONA MAY BOTTRELL, counselor, teacher; b. Rochester, Ill., Aug. 14, 1930; d. Vernon Sampson Bottrell and Leonia Ruth (Meeks) Cooper; m. Bryce Glenn Armstrong, June 11, 1950 (div. 1975); children: Steven Lee, Rebecca Sue, Paul Bryce, (twins) Kevin John and Brian Mark. BS, Ind. Ctrl. U., 1952; MS, U. Wis., 1967. Tchr. Dayton, Ohio, 1952-55; sch. counselor Oshkosh, Verona, West Allis, Wis., 1967-88; pvt. practice as counselor, astrologer, tchr. Milw., 1988—; Reiki master Reiki Healers Internat., 1992; guest spkr. in area of parapsychology and metaphysics U. Minn., U., Wis., Milw., other schs., 1980—; spkr. World Peace Program, Milw., 1987. Ecumenical spkr. United Ch. Women, 1966. Named Outstanding Sr. Woman, Philalethea Lit. Soc., 1952, one of Outstanding Personalities in Midwest, 1968. Mem. Nat. Coun. for Geocosmic Rsch. Home and Office: 2706 S 112th St Milwaukee WI 53227-3023

ARMSTRONG, MARGARET COURY, small business owner; b. Las Vegas, Nev., July 6, 1937; d. Isidore John and Mona Craine Coury; m. Edwin Guy Armstrong Jr., June 3, 1961; children: Edwin Coury, Robert James. Student, U. N.Mex, 1954-57, Tobe Coburn, 1959. Buyer Sanger-Harris, Dallas, 1960-65; bookkeeper Armstrong/Coury Ins., Farmington, N.Mex., 1973-85; sec., treas. Armstrong, Inc. (formerly Armstrong/Coury Ins.), Farmington, 1986—, Valley Constrn. & Devel., Farmington, 1974—; owner M's Ladies Apparel, Farmington, 1988—. Sec. N.Mex. Amateur Baseball Congress, 1978-91; bd. dirs. San Juan Econ. Devel. Svc., 1991, Farmington Conv. and Visitors Bur., 1991; mem. Sacred Heart Sch. Bd., 1976-79, rec. sec., 1977-79; com. mem. Gov.'s Immunization Bd., 1978; v.p. Title I Dist. Parent Adv. Com., 1977; mem. Library Found. Bd., 1994—; chair credentials GFWC, 1996—. Named Amateur Baseball Woman of Yr. Oscar Mayer, 1987, Regional Woman of Yr. Am. Amateur Baseball Congress, 1991. Mem. N.Mex. Fedn. Women's Clubs (pres. 1988-90), Farmington Women's Club (pres. 1973, 90-91), Farmington Redcoats Goodwill Ambs., Gen. Fedn. Women's Clubs (South Ctrl. region sec./treas., regional SOAR chmn. 1992-94), Gen. Fedn. Women's Clubs Home Life Econs. (div. chmn.), Downtown Merchants (sec. 1991), Farmington C. of C. (bd. dirs. 1981-91, v.p. 1988, pres. elect 1989, pres. 1990), Gen. Fedn. Women's Clubs (South Ctrl. region sec./treas. 1992, v.p. 1993, pres. 1994—), San Juan Plz. Merchants Assn. (sec. 1993). Democrat. Roman Catholic. Home: 5310 Hallmarc Dr Farmington NM 87402-5108 Office: M's Ladies Apparel 3030 W Main St Farmington NM 87401

ARMSTRONG, SAUNDRA BROWN, federal judge; b. Oakland, Calif., Mar. 23, 1947; d. Coolidge Logan and Pauline Marquette (Bearden) Brown; m. George Walter Armstrong, Apr. 18, 1982. B.A., Calif. State U.-Fresno, 1969; J.D., U. San Francisco, 1977. Bar: Calif. 1977, U.S. Supreme Ct. 1984. Policewoman Oakland Police Dept., 1970-77; prosecutor, dep. dist. atty. Alameda County Dist. Atty., Oakland, 1978-79, 80-82; staff atty. Calif. Legis. Assembly Com. on Criminal Justice, Sacramento, 1979-80; trial atty. Dept. Justice, Washington, 1982-83; vice chmn. U.S. Consumer Product Safety Commn., Washington, 1984-86; commr. U.S. Parole Commn., Washington, 1986-89; judge Alameda Superior Ct., 1989-91, U.S. Dist. Ct. (no. dist.) Calif., San Francisco, 1991—. Recipient commendation Calif. Assembly, 1980. Mem. Nat. Bar Assn., ABA, Calif. Bar Assn., Charles Houston Bar Assn., Black C. of C., Phi Alpha Delta. Democrat. Baptist. Office: US Dist Ct 1301 Clay StSte 400 S Tower Oakland CA 94612*

ARNAUD, SANDRA, financial advisor; b. Arnaudville, La., July 6, 1945; d. Clarence and Nola (Artigue) A.; divorced; children: Andrea, Geralyn. Attended, U. Southwestern La. Cert. fin. planner. Bus. mgr. Schexnaider Farms, Arnaudville, 1969-81; fin. planner Apex Investors Corp., Lafayette, La., 1981-86, IDS Fin. Svcs., Ft. Myers, Fla., 1986; acct. exec. Securicorp., Inc., Ft. Myers, 1986-88; mgmt. cons. Profl. Strategies, Houston, 1988-89; fin. cons. Shearson Lehman Bros., Houston, 1989-93; fin. advisor Investment Mgmt. & Rsch., Inc., Houston, 1993—; developer, producer ednl. program on retirement planning and mng. retirement plan distbns.; conductor retirement planning program for various colls. and chem., aerospace and mfg. cos. in Houston area. Contbr. fin. articles to Bay Area Times newspaper, Houston. Featured in Wall Street Transcript. Mem. Internat. Bd. Standards and Practices for Cert. Fin. Planners. Office: Investment Mgmt & Rsch Inc 1560 W Bay Area Blvd Ste 195 Friendswood TX 77546-2668

ARNDT, CARMEN GLORIA, secondary education educator; b. N.Y.C., Mar. 29, 1942; d. Charles Joseph and Pura María (Rios) A. BA in Spanish, Pace U., 1968; MA in Spanish, NYU, 1970; profl. diploma, Fordham U., 1975. Lic. asst. prin., prin. Simultaneous translator UN, N.Y.C., 1968; instr. Marymount Manhattan Coll., N.Y.C., 1968-70; tchr. Bd. Edn., N.Y.C., 1970—, dir. Bilingual Comprehensive H.S., 1975-78; chairperson sch. based mgmt./shared decision com. L.D. Brandeis H.S., N.Y.C., 1990—, asst. prin., 1984, interim acting asst. prin., 1994, coord. coop. tech./trades, 1993-94; chairperson restructuring com. Bd. Edn., N.Y.C., 1990—; bd. dirs. First N.Y.C. Vomprehensive Bilingual Program, 1975-79; adj. faculty Fordham U., N.Y.C., 1972-75, City Coll., N.Y.C., 1985—; coord. ESL and Fgn. Lang. Dept. Author: Conversational Spanish, 1975, Native Language Art K-8, 1975; contbr. articles to profl. jours. Electioneer, Dem. Party, N.Y.C. Mem. P.R. Edn. Assn. (chairperson-mentor 1988, del.), United Fedn. Tchr. (del. 1985-88), State Assn. Bilingual Edn., Am. Assn. Tchrs. of Spanish and Portuguese, Assn. Suprs. Curriculum Devel., Phi Beta Kappa. Roman Catholic. Home: 110 W 90th St Apt 4C New York NY 10024-1209 Office: 145 W 84th St New York NY 10024-4603

ARNDT, DIANNE JOY, artist, photographer; b. Springfield, Mass., Dec. 20, 1939; d. Samuel Vincent and Carrie Lillian Annino. Student, Art Students League, 1965-71; BFA with honors in Painting, Pratt Inst., 1974; postgrad., Columbia U., 1979-86; MFA, Hunter Coll., 1981; m. Joseph Vincent Bower, June 16, 1979; 1 child by previous marriage, Christabelle Nita Arndt. Photojournalist, photo cons. to mags. and bus., N.Y.C., 1978—; artist, filmmaker, 1962—; exhbns. include Am. Cultural Ctr., U.S., New Delhi and Bombay, 1987, Bathurst Arms Installation, Eng., 1987, Camden Arts, London, 1987, Nat. Inst. of Archtl. Edn., 1988, Phillip Morris Traveling Photo Exhibit, 1988, Centennial Libr. Gallery, Isca Graphics, Edmonton, Alta., Can., 1988, Nat. Inst. Archtl. Edn., 1988, N.Y. Sci. & Tech. Gallery, N.Y., USSR, 1989, Mercer Gallery, 1989, Circolo Pickwick, Alessandria, Italy, 1989, Balt. Mus. Industry, 1992, Aaron Davis Hall, 1992, N.Y. City Coll., Alijira Gallery, Newark, 1994, UN, 1994, Phila. Art Alliance, Phila., 1995, Columbia U., 1995, Severoceske Mus., Liberec, Bohemia, 1996, Naproskovo Mus., Prague, 1996, Modern Age, N.Y.C., 1996, Lever House, N.Y.C., 1996. Mem. Am. Soc. Media Photographers, Am. Soc. Picture Profls., Artists Talk on Art (bd. dirs.), Profl. Women Photographers, Working Press Nation.

ARNDT, SUSAN ELIZABETH, telecommunications industry executive; b. New Castle, Pa., Aug. 11, 1958; d. Walter William and Helen Elizabeth (Bowditch) Leonard; m. Randall Stewart Arndt, Sept. 26, 1992. BA, Stephens Coll., Columbia, Mo., 1980; MBA, So. Ill. U., Edwardsville, Ill., 1983. Resdl. market specialist CONTEL, Wentzville, Mo., 1980-82, analyst market support, 1982-84, coord. telemarketing, 1984-85, coord. market support, 1985-86; adminstr. product planning CONTEL, St. Louis, 1986-90; mgr. product devel. CONTEL Svc. Corp., Wentzville, Mo., 1990-92; v.p. mktg. GLA Internat., St. Louis, 1992—; adv. bd. mem. U.S. Distance Learning Assn., San Ramon, Calif., 1992—. Mem. Am. Mktg. Assn., Nat. Emergency Number Assn., Nat. Jr. Achievement (adv. and judge 1984—), Direct Mktg. Assn., The Greyhound Found. (v.p. publicity 1993—). Office: GLA Internat 17998 Chesterfield Airport Rd Ste 100 Chesterfield MO 63005

ARNESEN, ANNE SCHMITZ, child advocacy director; b. Allegan, Mich., May 21, 1932; d. William Emil and Dorothy (Blanchard) Schmitz; m. Richard Byron Arnesen, June 22, 1957; children: Katherine, Richard. AB, Univ. Mich., 1954. Tchr. Ann Arbor (Mich.) Schs., 1958-59, Cleveland (Ohio) Pub. Schs., 1959-61, 1961-63; dir. Wis. Coun. on Children Family, Madison, 1981—. Bd. dirs., chair Madison Children's Mus., Madison, 1990—; bd. dirs., v.p. Dane County Mental Health Ctr., Madison, 1991—; v.p., bd. dirs. League of Women Voters of Wis., 1970; mem. bd. edn. Madison Met. Sch. Dist., 1981-89. Recipient Women Distinction award YWCA, 1996, Disting. Svc. award Madison Met. Sch. Dist., 1989. Home: 920 Castle Pl Madison WI 53703 Office: 16 N Carroll St Rm 420 Madison WI 53703

ARNOLD, BARBARA EILEEN, state legislator; b. N. Adams, Mass., Aug. 3, 1924; d. Lester Flemming and Sarah (Van Hagen) Smith; m. William E. Arnold, Dec. 5, 1946; children: Wynn, Jeffrey, Gayle, Christopher. B.A. in Psychology, U. Mass.; postgrad. Keene State Coll. Spl. Edn. Clinic tchr. Keene State Coll., N.H., 1964-67; spl. edn. tchr. Easter Seal Rehab. Ctr., Manchester, N.H., 1967-74; state legislator N.H., 1982-95, now Republican floor leader Ho. of Reps., 1989-95; mem. N.H. Coun. Vocat. Tech. Edn., 1986—; mem. Ways and Means com., vice chmn., 1992-95; mem. State and Fed. Rels. commn.; chmn. Manchester Rep. Del.; Del. Bd. dirs. ARC, 1975—, chmn. bd. dirs., 1977-80; Manchester chair Dole for President Campaign, 1995—; del. Rep. Conf., Calif., 1996; Manchester campaign chmn. Warren Rudman for U.S. Senate, 1980, 86, Gov. Judd Gregg for U.S. Senate, 1992; chair Manchester Rep. Com., 1993—; sec. N.E. State Coun. Vocational Edn.; mem. adv. bd. Greater Manchester Federated Women's Club; mem. adv. coun. adult rehab Easter Seal Soc., N.H., 1990—; mem. vestry, registered lay leader, mem. diocesan commns., del. gen. conv. Episcopal Ch.; mem. com. for children, families, social svcs. on the Nat. Conf. of State Legislatures; state adv. com. Vocat. Child Care Programs; chmn. Manchester Rep. Com., 1992—. Recipient Norris Colton Republican of Yr. award, 1989. Mem. Kappa Kappa Gamma. Address: 374 Pickering St Manchester NH 03104-2744

ARNOLD, CLAIRE GROEMLING, administrator; b. Chgo., Dec. 1, 1962; d. Robert Max and Dorothy Irene (Messerschmidt) Groemling; m. Daniel Lee Arnold, June 23, 1990; 1 child, Christopher Alan. BS in Health Adminstrn., We. Ky. U., 1985; MBA, U. Louisville, 1989. Profl. rels. rep. Met Life Healthcare Network, Louisville, 1988-89; network devel. specialist Humana Inc., Louisville, 1989-90; program coord. U. Louisville Sch. Medicine, 1990-93, program mgr., 1993-95; dir. devel. Ky. Acad. Family Physicians Found., Louisville, 1995—. Contbr. articles to profl. jours. Bd. dirs. Goals for Greater Louisville, 1992, The Louisville Orch. Bd., 1993, Jr. League of Louisville, 1994, Tom Sawyer Park Found. Bd., 1996—. Mem. Am. Coll. Healthcare Execs., Ky. Soc. Hosp. Planning and Mktg., Acad. for Health Svcs. Mktg. (pres. 1993-94), Discover the Louisville Orch. (sec. 1989-91, chmn. 1992-93), Western Ky. U. Alumni Assn., Phi Mu (pres. 1991-93). Democrat. Presbyterian. Office: Ky Acad Family Physicians Found 3323 Med Arts Bldg Louisville KY 40217

ARNOLD, CONNIE JEAN, marketing executive; b. Washington. BA, Dunbarton Coll.; grad., U. Md. Editorial asst. Foreign Policy Mag., Washington, 1973-75; membership promotion mgr. USN Inst., Annapolis, Md., 1975-78; mktg. mgr. Gov. Info. Services, Washington, 1979-81, Community Devel. Pubs., Silver Spring, Md., 1981-82; membership dir. Nat. Apt. Assn., Washington, 1982-83; mktg. mgr. Bus. Pubs. Inc., 1984-93; mktg. dir. Bus. Info. Svcs., Inc., 1993-94; mktg. mgr. Capitol Pubs., Inc., 1994-95; mgr. ann. fund Cath. Charities, 1995-96; cons. Acad. Info. Service, Bowie, Md., 1980--. Mem. Friends of Freddy (sec. treas. 1984--). Democrat. Roman Catholic.

ARNOLD, JANET NINA, health care consultant; b. Poughkeepsie, N.Y., Apr. 23, 1933; d. Paul Dudley and Pauline Katherine (Board) Bartram; AB, Vassar Coll., 1955; postgrad. Sch. Med. Tech., Albany Med. Center, 1955-56; MS, Vassar Coll., 1963; MHSM, Webster Coll., 1981; m. Robert William Arnold, Dec. 19, 1954; children: Paul Dudley, Janet Elizabeth. Rsch. asst., med. technologist H. Aird Boswell, M.D., Troy, N.Y., 1956-59; teaching supr., adminstrv. cons. Vassar Bros. Hosp., Poughkeepsie, N.Y., 1959-69; adv. to med. lab., lectr. med. mycology Vassar Coll., Poughkeepsie, 1961-66; asst. adminstr., lab. mgr. Boulder (Colo.) Meml. Hosp., 1975-80; cons. hosp. planning Mercy Med. Center, Denver, 1981-82; clin. lab. dir./adminstr. Humana, 1982-85, cons. health care mgmt., 1982-85; with MRI, 1985—, ptnr., 1988; pres. Arnold and Assocs., 1992—; ptnr. InterExec (divsn. MRI), 1994—; acad./adminstrv. cons. U. Guam, Vassar Coll., Boulder Cmty. Hosp., Humana Int., 1990—, others. Sec., bd. dirs. Sanitas Fed. Credit Union, 1977-78, pres., 1979-82; teaching fellow Vassar Coll., 1961-63, unrestricted fund chmn., 1989-96. Contbr. NMC, 1988-92. NSF rsch. fellow, 1960-62. Mem. Am. Acad. Microbiology, Soc. for Gen. Microbiology, Am. Soc. Med. Technologists, Colo. Public Health Assn., Med. Mycological Soc. of the Ams. Republican. Episcopalian. Asso. editor Am. Jour. Med. Tech., 1980-88; contbr. articles to profl. jours. Home: 4195 Chippewa Dr Boulder CO 80303-3610

ARNOLD, KAREN ELIZABETH, elementary educator; b. St. Charles, Ill., Apr. 20, 1948; d. Marvin Everett and Shirley (Sanders) Heinz; m. Alan Paul Arnold, Mar. 26, 1988; m. Armand Richard Levesque, July 3, 1971 (div. 1985); children: Stacy, Kevin. BA in English, Calif. State U. Stanislaus, Turlock, 1983. Cert. tchr. single subject English, multiple subject K-12. Sec. Forest E. Olson Co., Sana Ana, Calif., 1970-74; exec. sec. Coldwell Banker, L.A., 1974-80; mentor tchr. Atwater (Calif.) Elem. Sch. Dist., 1988-90, 93-96, tchr., 1984—. Mem. AAUW, Calif. League Mid. Schs. (finalist Educator of Yr. 1996). Roman Catholic. Office: Mitchell Sr Elem 1753 Fifth St Atwater CA 95340

ARNOLD, LESLIE BISGER, educational administrator; b. Cheyenne, Wyo., Aug. 26, 1956; d. Fred Bennett and Natalie Sylvia (Cohen) B.; m. Kevin Durkin Arnold, July 6, 1980. BS in Spl. Edn. cum laude, Old Dominion U., 1978, MS in Edn. cum laude, 1984. Cert. spl. educator, emotionally disturbed, mentally retarded, presch. handicapped, severly and profoundly handicapped. Tchr. multiple handicapped Virginia Beach (Va.) Pub. Schs., 1978-81; tchr. autistic Southeastern Coop. Ednl. Programs, Norfolk, Va., 1981-82; tchr. emotionally disturbed/mentally retarded Norfolk Pub. Schs., 1983-86, tchr. specialist, 1986-89, ednl. diagnostician, 1989-90, liaison program mgr., 1990-95, ednl. adminstr., 1995—, coord. pupil pers., 1995—; mental health worker Tidewater Psychiat. Inst., Virginia Beach, 1985-86; curriculum coord. CHANCE program Old Dominion U., Norfolk, 1986-91; ednl. cons. St. Croix, V.I., 1991; speaker in field. Author: Behavioral Disorders, 1987, Developmental Skills Attainment Sequence Guide, 1989, ERIC-CEC, 1991, Programming for Behaviorally Disordered Adolescents, 1991, CHIME (Clearinghouse for Immigrant Education), 1993. Recipient Sch. Bell award Norfolk Pub. Sch. Bd., 1989, 91, 94; Nat. Found. for Improvement of Edn. grantee, 1992. Mem. ASCD, Assn. Ctrl. Office Adminstrs., Autism Soc. Am., Tidewater Soc. Autistic Children (pres. 1980-82), Nat. Alliance for Mentally Ill, Optimists Internat. Home: 1920 Hunters Trail Norfolk VA 23518-4919

ARNOLD, MARGARET MORELOCK, music specialist, educator, performer; b. Craig AFB, Ala., May 12, 1959; d. William Daniel Morelock and Margaret Haynie Morelock Stapleton; m. Barry Raynor Arnold, Aug. 15, 1984. B of Music Edn., U. Montevallo, 1981; MEd in Music, U. South Ala., 1996. Cert. tchr., Fla., Ala. Tchr. music Staley Mid. Sch., Americus, Ga., 1981-82, Eastview Elem. Sch., Americus, Ga., 1982-84; tchr. music/mass prep. St. Thomas More Schs., Pensacola, Fla., 1984-85; tchr. music W.H. Rhodes Elem., Milton, Fla., 1985—; pvt. voice instr., Americus, 1981-84, Milton, 1989—; guest condr. Santa Rosa All-County Chorus, Milton, 1989, 95. Asst. dir. arts festivals W.H. Rhodes Elem., 1993, 94, 95. Dir. elem. chorus performing for Santa Rosa Convalescent Ctr., Milton, 1985—, Live at the Capital, Tallahassee, 1986, Ptnrs. in Edn.-K-Mart and City of Milton and WEAR-TV, 1990—. Recipient 2d Alt. award Nat. Assn. Tchrs. of Singing, 1993, Computer Software grant Santa Rosa Ednl. Found., 1994. Mem. NEA, Santa Rosa Profl. Educators, Music Educators Nat. Conf., Delta Kappa Gamma (music chair 1988-94), Kappa Delta Pi, Phi Kappa Phi. Presbyterian. Home: 5820 Kirkland Dr Milton FL 32570 Office: WH Rhodes Elem 800 Byrom St Milton FL 32570

ARNOLD, MARIE COLLETTE, elementary bilingual education educator; b. Dayton, Ohio, May 21, 1968; d. Clinton Anthony and Lula Theresa (Conner) A. BA cum laude, St. Edward's U., 1990; MS, Trinity Coll., 1996. Cert. bilingual tchr., Tex., Va., ESL tchr., Tex. Bilingual/gifted tchr. Beacon Hill Elem. Sch., San Antonio, Tex., 1990-93; bilingual tchr. Annunciation Sch., Washington, 1993-94; bilingual/inclusion tchr. Alexander Henderson Sch., Dumfries, Va., 1994-96; edn. specialist Region 20 Edn. Svc. Ctr., San Antonio, 1996—; tchr. trainer N.J. Writing Project in Tex., San Antonio, 1993; staff devel. facilitator San Antonio Ind. Sch. Dist., 1992-93. Mem. NEA, Nat. Assn. Bilingual Edn., Tex. Assn. Bilingual Edn., Tex. TESOL, San Antonio Area Assn. for Bilingual Edn. (bilingual tchr. hall of fame 1991), Kappa Gamma Psi, Pi Lambda Theta. Home: 9215 Northchase Blvd San Antonio TX 78250 Office: Region 20 Edn Svc Ctr Hines St San Antonio TX 78202

ARNOLD, MARSHA DIANE, writer; b. Kingman, Kans., July 7, 1948; d. Eugene Willard Krehbiel and Elsie Irene (Lippincott) Raymond; m. Frederick Oak Arnold, Jan. 25, 1970; children: Amy Marie, Calvin Diedrich Oak. BA in English cum laude, Kans. State U., 1970. Cert. secondary English tchr., Kans., standard elem. tchr., Calif. Eligibility worker Dept. Social Svcs., San Mateo, Calif., 1970-71, San Rafael, Calif., 1971-79; eligibility worker Calif. Children Svcs., Dept. of Health, San Rafael, 1979-81; kindergym tchr. Calif. Parenting Inst., Petaluma, 1981; writer children's books, columnist Sebastopol, Calif., 1985—; tchr.'s aide Twin Hills Sch. Dist., Sebastopol, 1991-94; spkr. in field. Author: Heart of a Tiger, 1995 (Jr. Lib. Guild selection 1995), Quick, Quack, Quick, 1996; contbr. columns, stories and articles to mags. Animal care vol. Boyd Mus. Sci., San Rafael, 1974-75, Calif. Marin Mammal Rehab. Ctr., Marin County, Calif., 1976; v.p. PTA, Sebastopol, 1985. Recipient Best Local Columnist award Calif. Newspaper Pubs. Assn., 1986, 87, 93, Marion Vannett Ridgway award for outstanding first published picture book for children by an author or illustrator, 1996. Mem. Soc. Childrens' Book Writers and Illustrators, Phi Kappa Phi, Kappa Delta Pi. Home: 3350 McGregor Sebastopol CA 95472

ARNOLD, MINNIE JEAN, dance educator, researcher; b. Texarkana, Tex., July 3, 1942; d. Charles W. and Theda Inez (Crow) A.; m. Douglas Gehrig, June 15, 1961 (div. Jan. 1966); children: Ann Kimberly Campbell Carver, Kelli Jean Campbell Burgess,. Student U. Tex., Hanson Conservatory Arts, Texarkana, 1966, North Lake Coll., Irving, Tex., 1977-94; student, U. Tex., 1982. Tchr., owner Minnie Arnold Sch. Dance, Irving, 1966—; office clk. D & Z, Texarkana, 1966-69; saleswoman S.W. Airlines, Dallas, 1971. Fundraiser Marc. of Dimes, Dallas and Texarkana, Nat. Kidney Found., Dallas, 1994—; mem. pub. affairs com. The Family Place, Dallas, 1994—; bd. dirs. Parks Cities Rep. Women, 1986-90, Women's Law Ctr., Dallas, 1983-86, Dallas Ballet, 1991-96, North Wood U., Dallas, 1993—; mem. com. Dallas Symphony League, 1988—, Dallas Opera Guild and League, 1987—, Dallas Theater Ctr., 1993—. Recipient various certs. and letters of appreciation. Mem. Nat. Assn. Edn. Young Children, Tex. Assn. Edn. Young Children, Dallas Assn. Edn. Young Children, Dallas Hist. Soc., Dallas Dance Coun. Presbyterian. Home and Office: 609 Cimarron Trail Irving TX 75063

ARNOLD, P. A., special education educator; b. Toledo; d. Mattie Spear; m. Earl E. Arnold. BA, BS, David Lipscomb Coll., 1960; MA, Wayne State U., 1962; MS, Nova U., 1986. Cert. spl. edn., psychology, speech, mental retardation, emotional disturbance, Bible tchr., Fla. Tchr. dactyology, interpreter for deaf, 1960—; tchr. Hobbs (N.Mex.) Mcpl. Schs., 1981-82; tchr. spl. edn. City Systems, Rockford and Warren, Mich., 1960-67; dir. Four-County Ctr. Handicapped, Ark., 1977-81; dir. model project ACTION; Project TREE Tech. Resources Exceptional Edn.; instr. Little Red Schoolhouse. Author: Light for Deaf, 1992, Ol' Time Preacher Man, 1995. Bd. dirs., deaf advisor Hearing Soc. Volusia County; mem. project TREE-Tech. Resources in Exceptional Edn.-SY 2000, Dept. Edn., Fla. State U. Ctr. Ednl. Tech. Grantee Pub. Welfare, Nat. Gardening Assn., FUTURES, Newspapers in Edn. Mem. NEA, ARC, ASCD, VEA, Fla. Edn. Assn., Coun. for Exceptional Children, Am. Assn. on Mental Deficiency, Nat. Assn. Deaf.

ARNOLD, ROSE MARY, county commissioner; b. Richmond, Minn., Dec. 9, 1935; d. Anton and Marie (Brunner) Brisse; m. Richard H. Arnold, June 18, 1955; children: Tom, Cheryl, Charles, Joseph. Grad. high sch., Cold Spring, Minn. Reporter St. Cloud (Minn.) Daily Times, 1970-78; steno clk. Burlington No., 1980-88; loan clk. Liberty Loan, St. Cloud, 1978-80; commr. County of Stearns, St. Cloud, 1988—; chmn. Stearns County Planning Commn., St. Cloud, 1989. Mem. Minn. Dept. of Transp. Dist. 3; past chair AMC Human Svcs. com., chair Stearns County Bd., 1995, Tri County Solid Waste Com.; chmn. Welfare Bd., 1991. Mem. Nat Assn. Counties, Assn. Minn. Counties (chair dist. V 1995—). Home: 29353 Lindbergh Ln Avon MN 56310-9672 Office: Stearns County Courthouse Saint Cloud MN 56301

ARNOLD, ROXANNE, post-anesthesia nurse; b. Connellsville, Pa.; d. Tyree Franklin Sr. and Reva Gayle (Thieler) A. AAS, Gloucester County Coll., 1983; BSN, Widener U., 1989. RN, Fla.; cert. critical care nurse; cert. emergency nurse; cert. trauma nurse, BLS-provider, ACLS provider. Staff devel. instr., nursing supr., cardiac care nurse Meth. Hosp., Phila., 1982-89; emergency nurse Underwood Meml. Hosp., Woodbury, N.J., 1988-89; critical care nurse Jupiter (Fla.) Hosp., 1989-91; emergency clin. nurse III Indian River Meml. Hosp., Vero Beach, Fla., 1990-92; EMT/paramedic instr. Indian River Community Coll., Ft. Pierce, Fla., 1990-92; emergency asst. nurse mgr. Holmes Regional Med. Ctr., Melbourne, Fla., 1992-94; post anesthesia clin. nurse III Indian River Meml. Hosp., Vero Beach, Fla., 1994—. Mem. Am. Soc. Post Anesthesia Nurses, Am. Assn. Critical Care Nurses, , Sigma Theta Tau, Eta Beta. Home: 301 SE Walton Lakes Dr Port Saint Lucie FL 34952

ARNOLD, SANDRA RUTH KOUNS, healthcare marketing executive; b. Cleburne, Tex., Jan. 20, 1941; d. Wyatt Allen and Ethel Louise (Gandillon) Kouns; m. William Patrick Arnold, Feb. 27, 1960; children: Allyson Arnold House, Lynn Ann Workman. Student, Hill Coll., Cleburne, Tex., 1975, 78-79, 95, Richland Coll., Dallas, 1986, 94. Lic. realtor, Tex. With Howell's Dept. Store, Cleburne, 1959-64; decorator Baileys Home Improvements, Cleburne, 1971-77; realtor Red Carpet and Holliday Assocs., Cleburne, 1979-94; pub./patient rels. Meml. Hosp., Cleburne, 1982-86; mktg./patient rels. staff Walls Regional Hosp., Cleburne, 1986; mktg. mgr. Harris Meth. Health System, Ft. Worth, 1986-88; mktg./physician recruiting mgr. Kimbro Med. Ctr., Cleburne, 1988-92; profl. photographer, 1994-96; antique shop owner My Favorite Things, 1995-96; v.p. A&A Plastic Co., 1969—; vocalist weddings, theaters, and chs., Cleburne, 1959—. Contbr. articles to profl. jours. Coord. Area Alzheimer Support Group, Cleburne, 1984; active St. Mark Meth. Ch., Cleburne; coord., cons. Adopt-A-Sch./Cleburne Schs., 1984—; mem. actress Carnegie Theater; active Johnson County Hist. Commn., PTA. Named one of Outstanding Women of S.W., 1979. Mem. Cleburne C. of C. (dir. 1991-93), Women's Forum, Heritage Assembly (charter), Beta Sigma Phi (pres., Woman of Yr. 1963, 81). Home and Office: PO Box 63 Cleburne TX 76033-0063

ARNOLD, SHEILA, former state legislator; b. N.Y.C., Jan. 15, 1929; d. Michael and Eileen (Lynch) Keddy; coll. courses; m. George Longan Arnold, Nov. 12, 1960; 1 child, Peter; 1 child by previous marriage, Michael C. Young (dec.); stepchildren: Drew, George Longan, Joe. Mem. Wyo. Ho. of Reps., 1978-93, vice chmn. Laramie Regional Airport Bd. Former mem., sec. Wyo. Land Use Adv. Coms.; past pres. Dem. Women's Club, Laramie; past chmn. Albany County Dem. Party; past mem. Dem. State Com.; mem. adv. bd. Wyo. Home Health Care; former mem. Nat. Conf. State Legislatures Com. on Fiscal Affairs and Oversight Com. Recipient Spl. Recognition award from Developmentally Disabled Citizens of Wyo., 1985. Mem. Laramie Area C. of C. (pres. 1982; Top Hand award 1977), LWV (Laramie bd. dirs. 1993-94), Internat. Platform Assn., Faculty Women's Club (past pres.), VFW Ladies Aux. (pres. Post 2221), Zonta (Laramie bd. dirs.), Laramie Women's Club.

ARNOLD, TONI LAVALLE, engineering specialist; b. N.Y.C., Nov. 29, 1947; d. Aldo Peter and Margaret E. (Tessitore) Lavalle; m. Asbury Rembert Arnold, July 26, 1975. Student, Marymount Coll., 1965-67. Electro-mech. drafter PRD Electronics, Syosset, N.Y., 1973-74; electro-mech. designer/drafter Cadre Corp., Atlanta, 1974-79; EDA libr. resource mgr. Harris Corp., Palm Bay, Fla., 1982—. Stained glass artist represented in galleries in Fla., N.Y. Vol., leader Camp Fire Sunshine Coun., Lakeland, Fla., 1984-87, bd. dirs., 1993—; mem. Brevard County Dem., 1994-95, exec. com., 1993-96, chair environ. com., 1994—; vol. south Brevard Habitat for Humanity. Recipient scholarship N.Y. State Bd. regents, 1964, Blue Riboon award, Sebago award 1995, Camp Fire Nat., Kansas City, 1985. Democrat. Home: 1670 Heartwellville St NW Palm Bay FL 32907-7119 Office: Harris Corp Govt Com Divsn PO Box 91000 Melbourne FL 32902-3001

ARNOLD-BIUCCHI, CARMEN, museum curator; b. Lugano, Switzerland; Came to the U.S., 1977.; d. Basilio Mario and Noemi (Weibel) Biucchi; m. R. Bruce Arnold, 1977; children: Emma B., Philip V. Attended, U. Heidelberg, Germany, 1971-74; D, U. Fribourg, Switzerland, 1976. Investigator Lexicon Iconographicum Mythologiae Classicae, Basle, Switzerland, 1974-77; cons. Lexicon Iconographicum Mythologiae Classicae Rutgers U., 1979-81; asst. curator Am. Numismatic Soc., N.Y.C., 1982-89, Margaret Thompson curator of Greek coins, 1989—; mem. mng. com. Am. Sch. Classical Studies at Athens, 1989—; vis. scholar U. Padova, Italy, 1993; adj. prof. Columbia U., N.Y.C., 1995. Author: (book) The Randazzo Hoard and Sicilian Chronology, 1990; contbr. articles to profl. jours. Fellow Am. Numismatic Soc. Office: Am Numismatic Soc Broadway & 155th St New York NY 10032

ARNOLD HUBERT, NANCY KAY, writer; b. Kalamazoo, Mich., May 9, 1951; d. Byron Lyle and Ada (Doorlag) Arnold; m. Louis Scott Hubert, May 5, 1989. BFA in Painting, Western Mich. U., 1983, postgrad., 1985-86. Writer Advanced Systems & Designs, Inc., Farmington Hills, Mich., 1987-89; pres., owner TechWrite, Kalamazoo, 1989—. Author: (poetry) Tetragonal Pyramids, 1982; exhibited in group shows, Kalamazoo, 1983, Western Mich. U., 1982, 85. Mem. AAUW, NAFE, Humane Farming Assn. Am. People for Ethical Treatment of Animals. Libertarian. Office: 3857 Wolf Dr Kalamazoo MI 49009-8527

ARNOLD-MASSEY, HELEN PHYLLIS, health education educator, motivational speaker; b. Chgo., Aug. 10, 1949; d. William Jesse and Alyce Mary (Hauck) Arnold; m. Rodney Glenn Massey; children: Jahmann Yendor Massey, Rashon Amiel Massey, Sharieff Carter Massey. BS in Phys. Edn., DePaul U., 1972; MS in Kinesiology, U. Ill., Chgo., 1993. Cert. phys. edn. tchr. K-12, Ill. Phys. edn. tchr. Chgo. Bd. Edn., 1972-81, tchr. health edn., 1989—; fitness cons. Affordable Fitness, Chgo., 1983-85; with corp. health svc. Hurley Med. Ctr., Flint, Mich., 1986-87; spl. projects coord. Jefferson & Williams Cmty. Schs., Flint, Mich., 1988-89. Recipient Kathy Osterman Superior Pub. Svc. award City Chgo., 1994, Those Who Excel award Ill. State Bd. Edn., 1995, Excellence in Teaching award Nat. Coun. Negro Women/Shell Oil, 1995, Milken Nat. Educator award Milken Family Found., 1995, City Ptnr. award U. Ill., Chgo., 1996. Mem. AAUW, Nat. Coun. Negro Women, Ill. Coalition Adapted Phys. Edn., Ill. Assn. Health, Phys. Edn., Recreation & Dance (Honor Fellow award 1993), Parents United Responsible Edn. Home: 637 E Woodland Pk #612 Chicago IL 60616 Office: Chgo Bd Edn 1819 W Pershing Blvd Chicago IL 60609

ARNOT-HEANEY, SUSAN EILEEN, cosmetics executive; b. East Orange, N.J., Aug. 10, 1957; d. Robert B. and Mae (Cockcroft) A.; m. Kevin Barry Heaney, Mar. 28, 1992. BA, Coll. William and Mary, 1979; postgrad., Cambridge U., 1977; cert., NYU, 1979. Promotion asst. Viking Press/Penguin Books, N.Y.C., 1979-82; mgr. promotion Rizzoli Internat. Publs., N.Y.C., 1982-83; mgr. advt. promotion USA Today, N.Y.C., 1983-85; promotion dir. 50 Plus mag., N.Y.C., 1985-88, In Fashion mag., N.Y.C., 1988-89; mktg. svcs. mgr. TAXI mag., N.Y.C., 1989-90; dir. pub. rels. and spl. events Elizabeth Arden, N.Y.C., 1990—; career adv. Coll. William and Mary, 1980—. Writer/editor quar.: (newsletter) 50 Plus Market Update, 1985-88. Vol. cook, fundraiser Cathedral Soup Kitchen, St. John the Divine Cathedral, 1983-85, vol. Women in Need Image Workshops, 1990-94; mem. nat. leadership com. Save the Children Fedn., 1993—. Recipient Best of N.Y. Addy award for advt., 1986. Mem. Cosmetic, Toiletries and Fragrance Assn. (chair pub. rels. com., ex officio bd. dirs. 1994-96), Cosmetic Exec. Women, Women in Communications Inc. (chpt. publicity com. 1985-86, fin. com. 1986-87, spl. events com. 1986-87), NOW, Fashion Group Internat., William and Mary Alumni Soc. (chpt. pres. 1986-90, exec. bd. 1983-86, 90-92), AAUW (chpt. corr. sec. 1983-86, chair com. on women's work 1984-86), Mcpl. Art Soc. Methodist. Avocations: travel, music, theater, reading, art collecting, film. Home: 230 W 107th St Apt 2C New York NY 10025-3041

ARNOTT, ELLEN MARIE, medical case management and occupational health executive; b. Berwyn, Ill., Apr. 28, 1945; d. Howard Thomas and Catherine Marie (Stauber) Simon; m. John Michael Arnott, Dec. 16, 1967; children: John Michael II, Michelle Marie. BSN, Seton Hall U., 1981; MA, Tex. Woman's U., 1991. Cert. occupational health nurse, case mgr. Staff nurse oncology, med.-surgery, ICU, CCU, recovery, 1981-83, community health nurse, 1982-83; disability health nurse AT&T, 1983-84; mgr. health svcs. Lone Star Gas Co., 1985-86, Abbott Labs., 1986-88; corp. nursing supr. J.C. Penney, 1988-89; pres. Arnott & Assocs., Grapevine, Tex., 1989—, New Vision Nursecare, 1996—; wellness cons.; cons. health fair; occupl. health mgmt. cons.; workers compensation case mgmt. cons.; spkr. in field. CPR instr. trainer Am. Heart Assn.; vol. and facilitator SBE and smoking cessation Am. Cancer Soc., edn. com., skin cancer com.; CPR instr. to cmty.; first aid vol.; local rescue squad vol.; bd. dirs. Ctr. for Computer Assistance to the Disabled. Recipient Tex. State Achievement award for excellence in occupational health, 1990; named one of the Great One-Hundred Nurses of 1991, Dallas/Ft. Worth. Mem. Am. Assn. Occupational Health Nurses, Nat. Assn. Women Bus. Owners, Case Mgmt. Soc. Am., Tex. Assn. Occupational Health Nurses (fin. com. 1989-90, v.p. 1989-91), Dallas Tex. Assn. Occupational Health Nurses (hospitality com. 1985, edn. com. 1986-87, dir.-newsletter editor 1987, v.p. 1988-90, pres. 1991-93), ANA, Tex. Nurses Assn., Ctr. Computer Assistance to the Disabled (bd. dirs.), Omicron Delta Epsilon. Roman Catholic. Office: New Vision NurseCare PO Box 923 Grapevine TX 76099

ARNOWITT, LINDA JEAN, secondary education educator; b. Pitts., Sept. 3, 1952; d. Gerald A. and Naomi S. (Spencer) A. AA, U. South Fla.; BA, Pa. State U.; MS, Villanova U. Tchr. Sch. Dist. Phila., Pa., Centennial Sch. Dist., Warminster, Pa., Pennridge Sch. Dist., Perkasie, Pa. Mem. NEA, Pa. State Edn. Assn., Perkasie Edn. Assn. Home: 2245 Rowland Ln Coopersburg PA 18036 Office: Pennridge Sch Dist 1228 N Fifth St Perkasie PA 18944

ARNTSON, AMY E., artist, art educator; b. Frankfort, Mich., Mar. 24, 1947; d. Otto and Marguerite (Johnson) A. BFA, Mich. State U., 1969; MFA, U. Wis., Milw., 1981. Art dir., photographer, designer Ohio, Okla., Ky., Wis., 1970-81; prof. art dept. U. Wis., Whitewater, 1982—, interim assoc. dean Coll. Arts, 1990-91; art dept. chair U. Wis., Whitewater, 1991-96; presenter in field. Author: Graphic Design Basics, 1987, 2d edit., 1993; exhibited in group shows including Royal Coll. Art, London, 1992, Wustum Mus., Racine, Wis., 1992-93, 95, Wright Art Mus., Beloit (Wis.) Coll., 1993, 95, The Adirondacks Nat. Exhbn. Am. Watercolors, N.Y., 1993, 4th Internat. Symposium on Elec. Arts, Mpls. Coll. Art and Design, 1993, Soc. Illustrators, Otis Coll., L.A., 1993, Fla. State U. Gallery and Mus., Tallahasee, 1994, 5th Internat. Symposium on Elec. Arts, Helsinki, Finland, 1994, NGO Forum, Beijing, 1995, others. Recipient Addy award Am. Advt. Fedn., 1983, Watercolor Wis. award Wutsum Mus., 1984, 95, Juror's Choice award Midwest Photography Competition, Artlink, 1988, Artist in Residency award Exptl. TV Ctr., Oswego, N.Y., 1989, Seymour Chwast award Design Milw., MIAD, 1992, 95, Cert. of Merit award Soc. Illustrators, 1993; grantee U. Wis., Whitewater, 1985-86, 88-89, 94. Recipient Addy award Am. Advt. Fedn., 1983, Watercolor Wis. award Wutsum Mus., 1984, 95, Juror's Choice award Midwest Photography Competition, Artlink, 1988, Artist in Residency award Exptl. TV Ctr., Oswego, N.y., 1989, Seymour Chwast award Design Milw., MIAD, 1992, 95, Cert. of Merit award Soc. of Illustrators, 1993. Mem. Nat. Coun. Art Adminstrs., Illustrators and Designers of Milw., Internat. Soc. for the Arts, Scis. & Tech., Coll. Art Assn., Found. in Art and Theory Edn., Women's Caucus for Art, Graphic Design Eductor's Assn. Home: N6475 Shorewood Hills Rd Lake Mills WI 53551 Office: Art Dept U Wis-Whitewater Whitewater WI 53190

AROMIN, MERCEDES FUNG, portfolio manager, investment advisor, consultant; b. Kowloon, Hong Kong, Dec. 1, 1956; came to U.S., 1974; d. Remigio N. and Josephine (Fung) A. BS in Bus. Adminstrn., U. Tenn., Knoxville, 1978; MBA, Ga. State U., 1989. Mgr. Ramada Inn, Scottsburg, Ind., 1978; asst. mgr. York Steak House, Nashville, 1978-80; asst. terminal mgr. Greyhound Lines Inc., Atlanta, 1980-84; staff asst. The Coca-Cola Co., Atlanta, 1985-87; staff asst. Coca-Cola Enterprises Inc., Atlanta, 1987-89, shareholder rels. mgr., 1989-92; pres., CEO MFA Fin. Asset Mgmt., Atlanta, 1992—; sec.-treas. Coca-Cola Enterprises Inc. Employee Nonpartisan Com. for Good Govt., Atlanta, 1989-91. William Way scholar, 1976, Alcoa Found. scholar, 1977. Mem. Atlanta Investment Group (founder, chief investment officer 1990, exec. com., adv. com.), Ga. State U. MBA Alumni Group (charter). Roman Catholic. Office: 2040 Bascomb Carmel Rd Woodstock GA 30189-3545

ARON, EVE GLICKA SERENSON, personal care industry executive; b. N.Y.C., Sept. 5, 1937; d. Max and Edith (Gitelson) Serenson; m. Joel Edward Aron, Dec. 13, 1964; children: Jennifer, Joshua, Eric. BS, CCNY, 1958; MS, Yeshiva U., 1960; MBA with honors, Iona Coll., 1985. Med. technician Albert Einstein Coll. Medicine, Bronx, N.Y., 1959-60; chemist Strasenburgh labs., Belleville, N.J., 1961-63, Roche Labs., Nutley, N.J., 1963-67; sr. chemist Pantene Labs. div. Roche, Nutley, 1967-69; mgr. R&D Combe Inc., White Plains, N.Y., 1978-85, assoc. dir. R&D, 1985-95, dir. tech., 1995—. Contbr. articles and book revs. to profl. jours. Tutor Literacy Vols. of Am. mem. NOW, Am. Chem. Soc., Soc. Cosmetic Chemists (sec. Conn. chpt. 1989-90, chair 1992, hospitality/membership chair Conn. chpt. 1994-96, chpt. advisor 1993). Home: 470 Park Ave Rye NY 10580-1213 Office: Combe Inc 1101 Westchester Ave White Plains NY 10604-3503

ARONOW, INA GLORIA BRODY, journalist; b. Chgo., July 3, 1937; d. Meyer and Mildred (Paretzky) Brody; m. Wilbert S. Aronow, Sept. 20, 1958; children: Michael S., Janice S. BA, U. Chgo., 1959; MA in English, Calif. State U., Long Beach, 1974. Cert. secondary tchr., N.Y., Calif. English tchr. Harrison Tech. High Sch., Chgo., 1959-61; freelance writer for Weekend sect. Ind. Press-Telegram, Long Beach, 1978-82; intern, freelance contbr. L.A. Times, 1979-83; staff writer Mag. of the Midlands Omaha World-Herald, 1983-84; feature editor, news and feature writer Riverdale Press, Bronx, N.Y., 1984-85; staff writer Gannett Westchester Rockland Newspapers, 1986-88; freelance corr. N.Y. Times, N.Y.C., 1988—; journalism tchr., newspaper advisor Woodlands H.S., Hartsdale, N.Y., 1994—. Pres. LWV, Long Beach, Calif., 1975-77. Mem. Women in Comm., Nat. Writers Union. Jewish. Home: 23 Pebbleway Rd New Rochelle NY 10804-3914

ARONOW, JANI ALLISON, public relations executive; b. N.Y.C., Aug. 9, 1957; d. William and Audrey (Lipsky) A. BA in Journalism, Pub. Rels., Ohio State U., 1979. Pub. rels. asst. Union Am. Hebrew Congregations, N.Y.C., 1980-81; asst. pub. rels. dir. Pub. Rels. Soc. Am., N.Y.C., 1981-83; sr. v.p., group mgr. Ketchum Pub. Rels., N.Y.C., 1983-91—; pres. Aronow and Pollock Communications, Inc., N.Y.C., 1991—. Recipient Gold Leaf award Food Mktg. Inst./Family Circle mag., 1988, Best award Nat. Agr. Mktg. Assn., 1988, Golden Circle cert. Am. Soc. Assn. Execs., 1988, 95, Excellence in Advt. award AMA, 1989, 95, Ace award Internat. Assn. Bus. Communicators, 1995, Excellence in Advt. award for Postgrad. Medicine, Jour. AMA, 1995. Mem. Pub. Rels Soc. Am. (Silver Anvil award 1988, 94, 95, judge Silver Anvil awards competition 1993, 94, 95), N.Y. Pub. Rels. Soc. (publicity com. chmn. 1985, honors and awards com. 1989, Big Apple award 1995, 96), Ohio State Alumni Club. Office: Aronow & Pollock Comms Inc 3d Flr 524 Broadway Fl 3 New York NY 10012-4408

ARONS-BARRON, MARJORIE MYERS, television producer; b. Cambridge, Mass.; m. James H. Barron; children from previous marriage: Edward Arons, Daniel Arons. BA, Wellesley Coll., 1960. Political editor Newton (Mass.) Times, 1972-78; nat. polit. affairs writer Boston Phoenix, 1975-79; chief editl. writer WCVB-TV, Boston, 1979-82; editl. dir. WCVB-TV, Needham, 1982—; assoc. producer PBS, Boston, 1978. Contbr. articles to newspapers and mags. Overseer Boston Symphony Orch., 1993—. Recipient N.E. Emmy (3 times), Assoc. Press award, United Press Internat. award, Mass. Trial Lawyers award, Mass. Tchrs. Assn. award, Mass. Broadcasters award, Alliance for Mentally Ill award. Mem. Nat. Broadcast Editl. Assn. (various positions 1985-88, pres. 1988, 5 time nat. winner). Office: WCVB-TV 5 TV Place Boston MA 01292

ARONSON, DANA LYNNE, program/public relations executive; b. Newark, Nov. 12, 1960; d. Stephen Earl and Lila Muriel (Seletsky) A. BS, Boston U., 1982. Asst. acct. exec. Doremus & Co., N.Y.C., 1982-84; sr. acct. exec. Manning Selvage & Lee, N.Y.C., 1984-85; mgr. pub. rels. United Media, N.Y.C., 1985-91; v.p. pub. rels. Am. Diabetes Assn., Somerset, N.J., 1991-94, v.p. programs, 1994—. Recipient Silver Anvil award Pub. Rels. Soc., 1988. Office: Am Diabetes Assn 200 Cottontail Ln Somerset NJ 08873

ARONSON, ESTHER LEAH, association administrator, psychotherapist; b. Bklyn., Sept. 8, 1941; d. Nathan and Nellie (Borack) A.; m. Joel Allen Bernstein, Sept. 8, 1967 (div. 1978). BA, Bklyn. Coll., 1965; MA, New Sch. for Social Rsch., N.Y.C., 1982; MSW, NYU, 1984, PhD, 1996. Lic. social worker, N.Y. Resource cons. N.Y.C. Human Resources Adminstrn., 1965-82; counselor Fordham-Tremont Community Mental Health Ctr., Bronx, 1982-83, South Beach Psychiat. Ctr., Bklyn., 1983-84; social worker Alfred Adler Clinic, N.Y.C., 1984-85; pvt. practice clin. social work psychotherapist N.Y.C., 1986—; program developer Emanu-El Midtown YM-YWHA, N.Y.C., 1987-88, dir. ret. adult div., 1988—; lectr. Am. Mus. Natural History, N.Y.C., 1978. Contbr. articles to profl. jours. Mem. Am. Orthopsychiat. Assn., Inc., N.Y. State Soc. Clin. Social Work Psychotherapists, Inc., Soc. for Pub. Health Edn., NAFE, Phi Delta Kappa, Kappa Delta Pi. Home: 2 Fifth Ave Apt 31 New York NY 10011

ARONSON, LUANN MARIE, actress; b. Ithaca, N.Y., Nov. 18, 1964; d. Arthur Lawrence and Marilyn Ann (Lundeen) A. MusB, Ithaca Coll., 1986; MusM, Southern Meth. U., Dallas, 1988. Appeared as Guenevere in the Nat. Tour of Camelot, 1991; originated the role of Betty Schaefer in the workshop prodn. of Sunset Boulevard at Andrew Lloyd Webber's Sydmonton Festival, London, 1992; features soloist in the Music of Andrew Lloyd Webber, Radio City Music Hall, N.Y.C., 1992; as Maria in the Far East Tour of the Sound of Music, 1992; as Christine Daaé on Broadway in Phantom of the Opera, N.Y.C., 1992-94; as Christine Daaé in the Internat. Tour of The Phantom of the Opera, 1995. Recipient Outstanding Young Alumni award Ithaca Coll. Alumni Assn., 1994; Blossom Music Festival scholar, 1988, Tanglewood Summer Music Festival scholar, 1986. Mem. Actor's Equity Assn.

ARONSON, MARILYN RUTH, English language and literature educator; b. S.I., N.Y., June 14, 1942; d. Nicholas George and Ruth (Schaaf) Rubcich; m. Donald Louis Aronson, Nov. 20, 1965. BA in English Lit., Hunter Coll., 1964; MA in Am. Lit., Wagner Coll., 1969; D in English Lit., St. John's U., 1989. 0 Tottenville High Sch., S.I., 1972-90; tchr. English S.I. Tech. High Sch., 1990—; assoc. prof. English lit. and composition Wagner Coll., S.I., 1975—; advanced placement reader Ednl. Testing Svc.-Coll. Bd. Program, Princeton, N.J., 1986—; reader Nat. Tchrs. English, 1994—; coord. 1st borough-wide conf. N.Y. State Assn. Tchrs. English, S.I., 1990; judge annoration and debate competition Am. Legion Oratorical Contest, 1977—; mem. com. Comprehensive Sch. Improvement Program, 1987—; regional dir. N.Y. State English Coun. and State Edn. Dept., 1989—; nat. head cons. for pub. of advanced placement textbook, 1992. Contbg. author: The English Teacher. Chair polit. and legal coms. Lighthouse Hill Civic Assn., S.I., 1968—; exec. bd. mem. Greenbelt Stewardship Coun., 1980—. Recipient Tchr. of Excellence award N.Y. State English coun., 1985, 94, Borough Pres.'s Honor award, 1987, Outstanding Educator award Am. Legion, 1994; doctoral fellow St. John's U., 1986-87, NEH, 1990, Oxford U, 1990, N.Y.C. Humanities Inst., 1993; grantee A.B.S., 1992, 94. Episcopalian. Home: 375 Lighthouse Ave Staten Island NY 10306-1218

ARONSON, VIRGINIA RUTH, music educator, conductor; b. Glens Falls, N.Y., May 31, 1931; d. Irving Milton and Florence Estelle (Orcutt) Falkenbury; m. Andrew Thomas Murphy, June 12, 1955 (div. 1970); children: Marion Elizabeth, Katherine Annette, Patricia Lynn, Andrew Thomas; m. Chester Samuel Aronson, July 21, 1984 (dec. 1992). BA, Colby Coll., Waterville, 1953; Music Cert., U. Pacific, Stockton, 1955; MM, Westminster Choir, Princeton, 1977; ORFF cert., Conn. Cen. State Coll., Hartford, 1987; Kindermusik cert., Westminster Choir Coll., 1989, 90, 94. Classroom tchr. Wash. Sch., Stockton, Calif., 1955-56, Bellemeade Sch., Richmond, Va., 1956-57; bookstore mgr. Union Theol. Sem., Richmond, 1958-60; adminstrv. sec. Wash. Cathedral, Wash., 1970-73; product mgr. Mr. Rogers Neighborhood, Princeton, N.J., 1973-74; music tchr. The Hun Sch., 1975-77, Millstone Sch., N.J., 1978-89; pvt. music tchr., 1989—; dir. music St. John's Luth. Ch., Morrisville, Pa., 1990-92; dir. Colbyettes, Waterville, 1952-53; pres. Glee Club Colby Coll., 1952-53. Arranger: Songs of the Rain, 1952, Thank God I'm Old, 1985; composer Early in the Morn, 1940. Soprano Peace Odyssey Chorus, 1988; laborer World Coun. Chs., France, 1952; recreation dir. Am. Friends Svc. Com., Rapid City, 1951; seminar leader World Coun. Chs., N.Y.C., 1948; music dir. Unitarian Ch., Princeton, 1980-90. Mem. Unitarian Universalist Musicians Network (chmn. profl. concerns com. 1987-89), Am. Orff Schulwerk Assn. (v.p. ctrl. N.J. chpt. 1989-91), Am. Choral Dirs. Assn., Music Edn. Nat. Conf., N.J. Edn. Assn., Princeton Ski Club, Princeton Pro Musica (sight singing tchr. 1993-95), Westminster Alumni Choir. Democrat. Home: 7475 Normans Bridge Rd Hanover VA 23069

ARP LOTTER, DONNA, investor, venture capitalist; b. Henrietta, Tex., Dec. 17, 1950; d. T.S. Jr. and Coy Lee (Howard) Grimsley; m. Bruce D. Lotter, Feb. 18, 1984; children: Brandon, Collin. BS, Midwestern State U., 1975, M in Counseling, 1979. Sales rep. Burroughs-Wellcome Co., Fort Worth, Tex., 1978-79; sales mgr. Procter & Gamble Co., Dallas, 1979-84; pres. Arp-Lotter Investments, Colleyville, Tex., 1984—; prin. DBL Investments, Inc.; sec., officer KCB Corp., Inc.; bd. dirs. Landmark Bank. Chmn., trustee Baylor Hosp., Grapevine, Tex., 1991; bd. dirs. Am. Cancer Soc.; bd. govs. N.E. Arts Coun.; bd. dirs. North Tex. Commn. Hardin scholar Midwestern State U., 1975; named Alumnus of Yr. Midwestern State U., 1995. Mem. Bus. Profl. Womens Club, Nat. Assn. Women Bus. Owners, Colleyville C. of C. (pres. 1995), Am. Heart Assn. (bd. dirs.). Republican. Methodist.

ARQUETTE, PATRICIA, actress; b. Apr. 8, 1968; d. Lewis and Mardi A.; m. Nicolas Cage, 1995. Actress: (films) A Nightmare on Elm Street 3: Dream Warriors, 1987, Far North, 1988, The Indian Runner, 1991, Prayer of the Rollerboys, 1991, Ethan Frome, 1993, Trouble Bound, 1993, Inside Monkey Zetterland, 1993, True Romance, 1993, Holy Matrimony, 1994, Ed Wood, 1994, Infinity, 1995, (TV movies) Daddy, 1987, Dillinger, 1991, Wildflower, 1991, Betrayed by Love, 1994. Office: UTA 9560 Wilshire Blvd 5th Fl Beverly Hills CA 90212

ARQUETTE, ROSANNA, actress; b. N.Y.C., Aug. 10, 1959; d. Lewis and Mardi A.; m. John Sidel, Dec. 1993. Actress: (TV films) Having Babies II, 1978, Dark Secret of Harvest Home, Zuma Beach, The Executioner's Song, 1982, In the Deep Woods, 1992 (films) S.O.B., 1981, Baby it's You, 1983, Desperately Seeking Susan, 1985, After Hours, 1985, Silverado, 1985, The Aviator, 1985, 8 Million Ways To Die, 1986, Nobody's Fool, 1986, The Big Blue, 1988, New York Stories, 1989, The Linguini Incident, 1992, Fathers and Sons, 1992, Nowhere to Run, 1993, Pulp Fiction, 1994, Search and Destroy, 1995. Office: Internat Creative Mgt 8942 Wilshire Blvd Beverly Hills CA 90211-1934*

ARQUIT, NORA HARRIS, writer; b. Brushton, N.Y., June 30, 1923; d. Samuel Elton George and Ester Cecelia (Gillen) Harris; m. Gordon James Arquit, Nov. 12, 1948; children: Christine Elaine Arquit, Kevin James Arquit, Candace Susan Arquit-Martel. BS in Music Edn., Ithaca Coll., 1945, MS, 1962; postgrad., St. Lawrence U., 1946-47, 74, Cornell U., 1970-71, N.Y. State Coll., Potsdam, 1973. Music dir., band dir., tchr. N.Y. State Schs., 1945-77; guest conductor U.S. Air Force Band, Washington, U.S. Navy Band, Washington, various massed bands in U.S.A., Canada, Europe. Author: Before My Own Time and Since, 1978, From Hamlet to Cold Harbor, 1989, Our Lyon Line, 1993, The History of the New York State, Society of the National Society of the Daughters of the American Colonists, 1994. Mem. AAUW, Summit N.J. Club, United School Band Dirs. Assn. (past state and nat. chmn.), N.Y. State United Retired Tchrs., Delta Omicron Internat. Music Fraternity, Ithaca Music Club, Nat. Soc. of Magna Charta Dames, Nat. Soc. U.S. Daughters 1812, Nat. Soc. Daughters of Founders & Patriots of Am., Nat. Soc. Sons and Daughters of Colonial Wars, Nat. Soc. New England Women, Daughters of Union Vets., Nat. Soc. Daughters of Am. Colonists, The Denison Soc. Home: 130 Christopher Circle Ithaca NY 14850

ARRASMITH, MARY ELLEN, secondary school educator; b. Wadsworth, Ohio, June 22, 1964; d. John Frederick and Anna Teresa (Wakim) deAguiar; m. Jerry Lee Arrasmith, Aug. 5, 1989; children: David Lee, Krista Marie. BS magna cum laude, Eastern Mich. U., 1987. Substitute tchr. Ann Arbor, Mich., 1987-88; spl. needs coord. Airport H.S., Carleton, Mich., 1988; tchr. Monroe (Mich.) Pub. Sch., 1988—; mem. Profl. Devel. Com. Monroe, 1988—, Social Studies Curriculum Com., Monroe, 1991. Youth counselor Hugh O'Brien Found., Mich., 1988; fundraiser Mich. Humane Soc., Monroe, 1993. Mem. Nat. Coun. Social Studies, Mich. Coun. Social Studies (mid. sch. com., renaissance com.). Office: Monroe High Sch 901 Herr Rd Monroe MI 48161-1318

ARRIETA, CELINA MARIA, foreign language educator, Spanish; b. Medellin, Antioquia, Colombia, Dec. 27, 1958; came to U.S., 1988; d. Eduardo and Ana Maria (Urrego) Vasco; m. Raul Emeterio Arrieta, Dec. 20, 1980; children: Andres Felipe, Juan Camilo, Jesse Alexander. B in Lang. Teaching, Pontifical Bolivarian U., Medellin, Colombia, 1981. Cert. Spanish educator, N.J. Tchr. Spanish La Inmaculada Sch., Itagui, Colombia, 1979; tchr. English La Presentacion Sch., La Estrella, Colombia, 1980; monitor English dept. Pontifical Bolivarian U., Medellin, Colombia, 1981; tchr. English La Inmaculada Sch., Sahagún, Colombia, 1982; tchr. French and English Los Cedros Sch., Medellin, 1983-88; tchr. Spanish Zarephath (N.J.) Christian Schs., 1989—; adviser yearbook The Torch, 1989—. Roman Catholic. Office: Zarephath Christian Schs Weston Canal Rd Zarephath NJ 08890

ARRINGTON, DOROTHY ANITA COLLINS, retired real estate broker; b. Laurel, Miss., Sept. 9, 1922; d. Jeff Clay and Maude Eula (Sudduth) Collins; m. Robert Newton Arrington, Oct. 27, 1956; children: Robert William, Cynthia Anne Arrington Morris. AA, Jones County Jr. Coll., 1941; student, U. Ala., 1942-43. Assoc. realtor Town & Country Village Realtors, Houston, 1970-72, McGuirt & Co., Realtors, Houston, 1974-77, 79-81, Duffy & LaRoe, Realtors, Houston, 1978-79; owner-broker Dotty Arrington, Realtors, Houston, 1972-74; asst. sales mgr. Realmco, Inc., Houston, 1977-78; pres. Dotty Arrington, Inc., Houston, 1981-89, ret., 1989; adult tchr. Bethel Bible Series. Mem. Daus of the King, Delphians. Republican. Episcopalian.

ARRINGTON, HARRIET ANN, historian, women's biographer, writer; b. Salt Lake City, June 22, 1924; d. Lyman Merrill and Myrtle (Swainston) Horne; m. Frederick C. Sorensen, Dec. 22, 1943 (div. Dec. 1954); children: Annette S. Rogers, Frederick Christian, Heidi S. Swinton; m. Gordon B. Moody, July 26, 1958 (div. Aug. 1963); 1 child, Stephen Horne; m. Leonard James Arrington, Nov. 19, 1983. BS in Edn., U. Utah, 1957. Cert. tchr., Utah, Ga. Supr. surg. secs. Latter-day Sts. Hosp., Salt Lake City, 1954-58; tchr. Salt Lake City Schs., 1954-57, Glynn County Schs., Brunswick, Ga., 1957-58; from med. sec. to office mgr. Dr. Horne, Salt Lake City, 1962-83; tchr. Carden Sch., Salt Lake City, 1973-74, women's history rschr., tchr.; mem. Utah Women's Legis. Coun.; co-establisher Arrington Archives, Utah State U. Author: Heritage of Faith, 1988; contbr. articles to profl. jours. and confs. Dist. chmn. Utah Rep. Com., 1972-76; mem. art com. Salt Lake City Bd. Edn.; chmn. art exhibit Senator Orrin Hatch's ann. Utah Women's Conf., 1987; past pres., cultural revinement and/or spiritual living tchr. LDS Women's Relief Soc.; chmn. Utah Women Artists' Exhbn., AAUW, Utah divsn., 1986-87. Recipient Vol. Action award Utah Women Artists' Exhbn., 1987, resolution of appreciation Utah Arts Coun., 1989. Mem. AAUW

(Utah state cultural refinement chmn., cert. of appreciation 1988), DAR (Utah Am. history chmn., editor state paper, Friends of Humanities, Arts, Scis. & Social Sci. award 1995), Old Main Soc. Utah State U., Chi Omega (past pres. alumni chpt.). Home and Office: 2236 S 2200 E Salt Lake City UT 84109-1135

ARRINGTON, KAREN KEMP, marketing executive; b. Salisbury, Md., Feb. 11, 1953; d. Robert George and Laverne (Briggs) Kemp; m. Daniel Richard Arrington III, Dec. 19, 1981; children: Daniel Richard IV, James William. BS, Iowa State U., 1975; MEd, Salisbury State U., 1979. Dir. horticultural project Chesapeake Rehab. Ctr., Easton, Md., 1975-76; mgr. greenhouses Bountiful Ridge Nurseries, Inc., Princess Anne, Md., 1976-77; instr. horticulture Dorchester Bd. Edn., Cambridge, Md., 1978-80, Fredrick (Md.) Bd. Edn., 1980-87; instr. agronomy Frederick Community Coll., 1985; treas. Kemp's Ltd., Inc., Martinsburg, W.Va., 1985-87; pres. Kemp's Ltd., Inc., Mt. Airy, Md., 1987-94; mgr. U.S. retail sales Kord Products, Ltd., Brampton, Ont., Can., 1995—; keynote speaker Vocat. Counseling Orgn., Md., 1980-88; cons. retail and comml. mktg. groups, 1977-91; dir. Russian-Georgian Rose Project, Tblissi, 1993. Editor newsletter The Spreader, 1990; featured narrator documentary Our Land, Our Future, 1980 (Gold award 1980); exhibitor Assn. Nurserymen, Balt. and King of Prussia, Pa., 1986-91. Coach 4-H, FFA, NJHA, and other youth orgns., Md., 1977-91; state chair Soil Conservation Poster Competition, Md., 1990-91; judge horticulture county fairs, state and nat. 4-H and FFA activities, 1977-91. Named Conservation Tchr. of Yr., State Soil and Water Conservation Svc., Annapolis, Md., 1984, Outstanding Young Co-Operator, Md. and Va. Coop., Lancaster, Pa., 1988. Mem. DAR, Md. Greenhouse Growers Assn., New Market Grange, Md. Hist. Soc., Hackers Creek Hist. Soc., Somerset Pa. Hist. Soc. Office: Kemp's Ltd Inc 44 E 3rd St Frederick MD 21701-5311

ARRON, JUDITH HAGERTY, concert hall executive; b. Seattle, Dec. 8, 1942; d. Richard Graydon and Bernice Sarah (Lund) Hagerty; m. Ronald David Arron, Aug. 31, 1968; children: Joseph Richard, Edward Daniel. MusB, U. Puget Sound, 1964. Mem. spl. projects staff Am. Symphony Orch. League, Washington, 1964-69; research specialist youth concert study U.S. Office Edn., Washington, 1967; dir. regional and edn. programs Cin. Symphony, 1969-76, mgr., 1976-86; exec. dir. Carnegie Hall, N.Y.C., 1986—; cons., panelist Ky. Arts Council, Frankfort, 1970—; panelist Ohio Arts Council, Columbus, 1970-80; career devel. council Wilmington (Ohio) Coll., 1980-85; mentoring council Coll. Mt. St. Joseph, Cin., 1985-87. chmn. Lay adv. com. U. Colo. Health Sci. Ctr. Bone Marrow Transplant program, 1992—; bd. dirs. Leukemia Soc. Southwest Ohio, Cin., 1985; vice chair Music for Life Benefit, N.Y.C., 1987, adv. com. 1990, 93. Recipient Arts Adminstr. of Yr. award Arts Mgmt. News Svc., 1992. Mem. Am. Symphony Orch. League, Internat. Soc. Performing Arts Adminstrs. Office: Carnegie Hall Corp 881 7th Ave New York NY 10019-3210

ARROTT, PATRICIA GRAHAM, artist, art instructor; b. Pitts., July 27, 1931; d. George Patterson and Helen (Gilleland) Graham; m. Anthony Schuyler Arrott, June 6, 1953; children: Anthony Patterson, Helen Graham, Matthew Ramsey, Elizabeth. BFA in Painting and Design, Carnegie-Mellon Univ., 1954; postgrad., Nat. Acad. Design, N.Y.C., 1985-87, Art Students League, N.Y.C., 1980-91. Cert. tchr. art, Pa., 1954. Instr. children's ceramics Handcraft House, Vancouver, B.C., Can., 1970-72; courtroom artist Vancouver, B.C., Can., 1972-73; pvt. portrait artist Vancouver, N.Y.C., 1975—; instr. Art Students League, N.Y.C., 1993—. One-woman shows include Pen & Brush Club, N.Y.C., 1992; group exhbns. include Nat. Acad. Design Ann. Exhbn., 1990, 92, 94, Cork Gallery, Lincoln Ctr., N.Y.C., 1991, Silver Point Etc. traveling exhbn., 1992-93, others. Recipient Helen M. Loggie Prize, 1990, and cert. of merit, 1994, Nat. Acad. Design; recipient Emily Nicholas Hatch award Pen & Brush Club, 1989-91, Elizabeth Morse Genius award, 1988, 90, 93, 95, others. Mem. Art Student's League (life; mem. bd. 1989-92, women's v.p. 1991-92), Am. Fine Arts Soc. (mem. bd. 1991-92), Mayflower Soc. (life), Kappa Kappa Gamma (life). United Presbyterian.

ARROYO, MERCEDES, elementary education educator, psychologist; b. Ponce, P.R., Mar. 6, 1954; came to the U.S., 1969; d. Anibal Arroyo and Mercedes Marrero; 1 child, Juan Daniel. AA, Touro Coll., 1980, BA in Psychology, 1982; MS in Edn., Hunter Coll., 1989; postgrad., Fordham U., 1993—. Human Svc. Counseling cert.; tchg. cert. Sr. counselor Hartley House, N.Y.C., 1980-82; cmty. coord. Bd. of Edn., N.Y.C., 1982-83, elem. sch. tchr., 1983-93; admissions asst. counselor Touro Coll., N.Y.C., 1981-82; cmty. liaison Child Devel. Inc., N.Y.C., 1982-83. Pres., treas. PTA, N.Y.C., 1978-82; instr., English tutor Hartley House, N.Y.C., 1979-84; treas. West 46 St. Block Assn., N.Y.C., 1986-87. Recipient Vol. Svcs. for Children award Vol. Svcs. for Children of N.Y., 1980, 84, Citations for Excellence and Leadership, Coun. Suprs. and Adminstrs., N.Y.C., 1980, 81; named Outstanding Young Women Am., 1982. Mem. APA (divsn. 16), Nat. Assn. Sch. Psychologists. Roman Catholic.

ARSENAULT, DEBRA ANN, physician; b. Seattle, Mar. 25, 1965; d. J. Paul and Ann (Bergstrom) A.; m. Ted Phillip Briski, May 25, 1996. BS, Whitworth Coll., 1987; DO, Coll. Osteo. Medicine, 1991. Commd. lt. USN, 1991; intern USN Naval Med. Ctr., San Diego, 1991-92, resident in ob-gyn., 1995—; gen. med. officer 1st Marine Air Wing, Fleet Marine Force, Okinawa, Japan, 1992-93; gen. med. officer emergency dept. Naval Hosp. Guam, 1993-95; mem. Exec. Com. Med. Staff, Agana, Guam, 1993-95; physician advisor Civic Action Team, 1994-95. Recipient cert. of appreciation Guam Police Dept., 1995. Fellow ACOG (jr.); mem. Am. Osteo. Assn. Home: 7 Antigua Ct Coronado CA 92118

ARSHT, ADRIENNE, lawyer, broadcasting company executive, banking executive; b. Wilmington, Del., Feb. 4, 1942; d. Samuel and Roxana (Cannon) Arsht; m. Myer Feldman, Sept. 28, 1980. BA, Mt. Holyoke Coll., 1963; JD, Villanova U., 1966. Bar: Del. 1966. Assoc. Morris, Nichols, Arsht and Tunnell, Wilmington, 1966-69, Bregman, Abel and Kay, Washington, 1979-84; dir. govt. affairs TWA, N.Y.C., 1969-79; pres., chmn. bd. Land Title & Escrow Corp., Washington, 1981-86; v.p. Ardman Broadcasting Corp., Washington, 1984—, also bd. dirs.; chmn. bd. Totalbank Corp. Fla., Miami, 1986—, also bd. dirs.; chmn. Eve Stillman Corp., N.Y.C., 1989—, also bd. dirs.; bd. dirs. Ardman, Inc., Washington, Capital Broadcasting, Inc., Kansas City, Mo., Trade Nat. Bank, Miami. Bd. dirs. Washington Opera Co., 1982-84, Am. Ballet Theatre, N.Y.C., 1984-90; founder, chmn. Van Guard Found., Washington, 1987-94, Fit and Fabulous, Washington, 1992-93; mem. exec. com. Lombardi Cancer Ctr., Washington, 1988-92; cons. Best Buddies, Washington, 1991—; mem. Com. of 200. Named Woman of Yr., Am. Ballet Theatre, 1989. Mem. Del. Bar Assn., Women's Internat. Forum, Miami C. of C., Rana Soc., Potomac Tennis Club (Md.), Gov.'s Club (Palm Beach, Fla.). Office: Total Bank 2720 Coral Way Miami FL 33145

ARSHT, LESLYE ALENE, public relations executive; b. St. Louis, June 28, 1945; d. Raymond I. and Martorie (Meyer) A. BA, U. Houston, 1968. With pres. news summary The White House, Washington, 1968-72; pub. affairs officer U.S. EPA, Washington, 1972-75; mgr. pub. rels. Union Carbide Corp., Washington, 1975-79; mgr. corp. communications Cabot Corp., Boston, 1979-83, dir. pub. affairs, 1983-86; deputy asst. to the pres., deputy press sec. The White House, 1987-89; assoc. vice chancellor news and pub. affairs Vanderbilt U., Nashville, 1989-91; counselor to the sec. of edn., dir. communications U.S. Dept. Edn., Washington, 1991-92; pres. Coalition for Goals 2000, Washington, 1992—; cons. Arsht & Co., Boston, 1986. Class mem. Leadership Nashville, 1990-91. Recipient 1990 Gold Key award Pub. Rels. News, 1990, TWIN award YWCA, Boston, 1986, Matrix award Women in Communications, Yankee chpt., 1982; named Communication of Yr. IABC, Yankee chpt., 1981. Republican. Jewish. Office: Coalition for Goals 2000 Sch Edn Human Devel George Washington U Washington DC 20052

ARTELT, LOUISA LINETTE, fundraiser, fundraising consultant; b. Beatrice, Neb., Mar. 7, 1961; d. Emory Joseph and Linette Josephine (Olson) Giannangelo; m. Robert George Artelt, Apr. 8, 1989. Bs in Edn., U. Nebr., 1984. Area rep. Am. Cancer Soc., Lincoln, Neb., 1985-87; assoc. dir. cmty. camp. Nat. Multiple Sclerosis, Chgo., 1987-89; devel. cons. LA Devel. Cons., Chgo., 1989, 92-93; asst. to CEO Joseph Weil & Sons, Inc., LaGrange Park, Ill., 1989-92; devel. dir. Nat. Multiple Sclerosis Soc., Norwalk, Conn., 1993-95; fund devel. dir. Girl Scouts, Bridgeport, Conn., 1995—. Soloist St. Paul Luth. Ch., Westport, Conn., 1993—, choir mem., 1993—. Mem. Conn. Yankees for Neb., Jr. League of Eastern Fairfield (project chair 1994-96), Welcome Club of Fairfield/Easton (gourmet chair 1993-95), Scandinavian Club, Wednesday Afternoon Musical Club, Sigma Alpha Iota (life). Republican. Lutheran. Office: Girl Scouts 87 Washington Ave Bridgeport CT 06604

ARTESANI, MARYANN, elementary education educator; b. Providence, Sept. 13, 1950; d. Frederick F. and Marrietta (DiSandro) Lanni; m. William A. Artesani III, Sept. 10, 1972; 1 child, Aubrie Anne. AA, R.I. Jr. Coll., 1970; BA, Mt. St. Joseph Coll., 1972; MA, R.I. Coll., 1974. Cert. tchr., R.I., paralegal. Tchr. Warwick (R.I.) Sch. Dept., 1972—; pub. speaker N.Eng. Reading Conf., Newport, R.I., 1992. Editor, columnist Teaching Pre K-8 mag., 1991—; contbr. poetry to anthologies. Pres. Western Hills Elem. Sch. PTG, Cranston, R.I., 1991-92, 94-95; v.p. Western Hills Jr. High Sch. PTG, Cranston, 1992-93; bd. dirs. Robertson Sch. PRG, Warwick, 1992-93, 93-95. Recipient Key to the City, Mayor of Warwick, 1976, citation, Mayor of Warwick, 1976, 92, Citation for Excellence in Teaching, R.I. Ho. Reps., Providence, 1991, 93, Cert. Poetic Achievement, Amherst Soc., 1991, Key to City, Mayor of Cranston, 1995, Citation, Warwick Sch. Com., 1995, Share the Gold award Elfun Soc. G.E., 1995. Mem. RITAWL (guest pub. speaker 1991), Am. Fedn. Tchrs., Assn. Early Childhood Internat. (pub. speaker R.I. chpt. 1991), New Eng. Reading Assn., R.I. Fedn. Tchrs., Nat. Authors Registry, Warwick Tchrs. Union, Bus. and Profl. Womens Club, Providence Bus. and Profl. Womens Club (1st v.p.), Western Hills Jr. High Sch. PTG (pres. 1993-94), Assn. Supervision and Curriculum. Home: 67 Kimberly Ln Cranston RI 02921-2625 Office: Robertson Sch 70 Nausauket Rd Warwick RI 02886-7505

ARTHUR, BEATRICE, actress; b. N.Y.C., May 13, 1926; d. Philip and Rebecca Frankel; m. Gene Saks, May 28, 1950 (div.); 2 sons. Student, Blackstone Coll., also Franklin Inst. Sci. and Arts; student acting with, Erwin Piscator, Dramatic Workshop, New Sch. Social Research. Theatrical appearances include: Lysistrata, 1947, Dog Beneath the Skin, 1947, Gas, 1947, Yerma, 1947, No Exit, 1948, The Taming of the Shrew, 1948, Six Characters in Search of An Author, 1948, The Owl and the Pussycat, 1948, Le Bourgeois Gentilhomme, 1949, Yes Is for a Very Young Man, 1949, Creditors, 1949, Heartbreak House, 1949, Three Penny Opera, 1954, 55, Shoestring Revue, 1955, Seventh Heaven, 1955, The Ziegfeld Follies, 1956, What's The Rush?, summer 1956, Mistress of the Inn, 1957, Nature's Way, 1957, Ulysses in Nightown, 1958, Chic, 1959, Gay Divorcee, 1960, A Matter of Position, 1962, Mame, 1966 (Tony award best supporting mus. actress), Fiddler on the Roof, 1964; stock appearances with Fiddler on the Roof, Circle Theatre, Atlantic City, summer 1951, State Fair Music Hall, Dallas, 1953, Music Circus, Lambertville, N.J., 1953, resident commedienne, Tamiment (Pa.) Theatre, 1953; numerous TV and nightclub appearances, 1948—; motion picture appearances That Kind of Woman, 1959; Lovers and Other Strangers, 1970, Mame, 1974, History of the World Part I, 1981, Stranger Things, 1995; TV movie: My First Love, 1988; TV appearances include All in the Family, 1971, leading role in TV series Maude, 1972-78 (Emmy award for Best Actress in a Comedy Series 1977), The Golden Girls, 1985-92 (Emmy award for Best Actress in a Comedy Series 1988), The Beatrice Arthur Spl., TV series 30 Years of TV Comedy's Greatest Hits. Mem. Artists Equity Assn., Screen Actors Guild, AFTRA. *

ARTHUR, DIANE BUSH, recreational facility executive; b. Brattleboro, Vt., Dec. 6, 1940; d. George Barrett Bush and Eleanor Frances (Wood) Bush Anderson; m. James Hurley Harris, June 22, 1962 (div. Mar. 1968); children: Luke Patrick Harris, Mark Scott Harris; m. Kenneth Eugene Arthur, July 16, 1983. Diploma in nursing, Franklin County Pub. Hosp., 1963. RN. Supervisor obstetrics Brattleboro Hosp., 1968-74; head nurse Kessler Hosp., Hammonton, N.J., 1975; utilization review nurse Atlantic City (N.J.) Med. Ctr., 1975-77; asst. dir. nursing, maternal and child health Newcomb Hosp., Vineland, N.J., 1977-78; dealer, pres. dealer's coun. Caesars Boardwalk Regency, Atlantic City, 1979-81; pit supervisor Playboy Casino/Hotel, Atlantic City, 1981-88, Trop World, Atlantic City, 1989-90; casino exec., pit ops. Peppermill Casino/Hotel, Mesquite, Nev., 1990; games mgr., asst. dir. tng. Dubuque (Iowa) Casino Belle, 1992; shift mgr., casino mgr. Mississippi Belle II, Clinton, Iowa, 1991-92; keno coord., asst. casino shift mgr. Casino Magic, Bay St. Louis, Miss., 1993-95; games mgr. Dakota Magic Casino, Hankinson, N.D., 1995-96, games cons., 1996—; dir. Miss Vt. Scholarship Pageant, 1970-73. Mem. NAFE. Home: 1418 Ave A Wahpeton ND 58075

ARTHUR, ELIZABETH JEAN, human resources professional; b. Charleston, S.C., Nov. 22, 1951; d. Paul Worthen and Emily Mildred (Sheldon) A.; m. Andrew Harry Mansfield, Aug. 30, 1980. BA, Conn. Coll., 1973. Pharmaceutical buyer Bangor Drug Co., Portland, Maine, 1973-79; location coord. Ernst & Young, Portland, 1980-92; dir. human resources and adminstrn. Maine Employers' Mutual Ins. Co., Portland, 1993—. Bd. dirs. Greater Portland YMCA, 1994—, Maine Health Mgmt. Coalition, Portland, 1994—, Cumberland County Pvt. Industry Coun., Portland, 1995—. Mem. Maine Employee Benefit Coun., Human Resource Assn. So. Maine, Maine Human Resource Mgmt. Assn. Home: 18 Prout Pl Cape Elizabeth ME 04107 Office: Maine Employers Mutual Ins 261 Commercial St Portland ME 04101

ARTHUR, JEWELL KATHLEEN, dental hygienist; b. Bloomington, Ind., Apr. 12, 1947; d. Gerald E. and Wilma Kathleen (McDonald) Beyers; m. Leland Stanley Arthur, Sept. 21, 1968; children: Sherri Kay, Brian Lee. AS in Dental Hygiene, Ind. U., 1968. Lic./registered dental hygienist. Infection control mgr., dental hygienist Office Dr. Thomas Watkins, DDS, Bloomington, Ind., 1990—; speaker and presenter in field. Vice-chmn. precinct Rep. Com., Batholomew, 1987—; chmn. Batholomew Consolidated Sch. Aids Com., Columbus, 1988—; vice chair City of Columbus Bd. Zoning Appeals, 1989-93, Bartholomew County Pers. Adminstrn. Com., 1993—; councilwoman Batholomew County Coun., Columbus, Ind., 1993—. Mem. Am. Assn. Ret. Persons, Am. Dental Hygienists Assn. (liaison 1989—, Disting. Svc. award 1994), Ind. Dental Hygienists Assn. (pres. 1986-87, del. 1991—, Comty. Svc. award 1991, Outstanding Dental Hygienists of Yr. award 1991), Ind. Pub. Health Assn. (chair legislation 1986-89), Driftwood Valley Dental Hygienists Assn. (trustee 1989-91), Assn. Ind. Counties, DAR-Joseph Hart, Order Eastern Star. Republican. Methodist. Home: 1800 Clover Ct Columbus IN 47203-3615

ARTL, KAREN ANN, business owner; b. Bainbridge, N.Y., July 4, 1950; d. Douglas Robert and Beverly Florence (Schofell) Moore; m. Robert Edward Gurney, June 15, 1969 (div. June 1981); children: Douglas Albert Gurney, Rebecca Susan Gurney; m. Jeffrey Joseph Artl, Nov. 8, 1986; 1 child, Grace Beverly. BA in Edn., SUNY Coll. at Oneonta, 1972; MA in Reading and Edn., Cleve. State U., 1981. Tchr. reading Independence (Ohio) Mid. Sch., 1979-81; sr. editor Am. Greetings Corp., Cleve., 1981-87; mem. adj. faculty Lorain Community Coll., Cleve., 1987-89; owner WordsWorth Studio, Inc., Rocky River, Ohio, 1989-93; owner, pres. WordsWorth Studio, Inc.; conf. speaker, trainer, cons. Social Expression Industry. Author: (biog. textbook) M. Washington, etc., 1991, (children's book) I'm Me and You're Not, 1991; concept developer Guy Gilchrist Prodns., 1992, inspirational plaque line for Christian market; editor CR Gibson/Gift Books, 1993, Gibson Greetings, 1993. Vol. Am. Cancer Soc., Cleve., 1991. Mem. AAUW, NAFE, Greeting Card Assn., Greeting Card Creative Network, Soc. Children's Book Writers. Lutheran. Home and Office: WordsWorth Studio Inc 7260 Capri Way Apt 9 Maineville OH 45039-9490

ARUJ, ESTRELLA, fashion designer, artist; b. Cordoba, Argentina, Oct. 23, 1934; came to U.S., 1963; d. Alberto and Regina (Gaguine) A.; m. Moises Aruj, Apr. 5, 1952; children: Hector Ricardo, Alberto Silvio. Degree in fashion design, Fashion Inst. Tech., 1968, degree in buying and merchandising, 1970. Designer Herman Gowns Pvt. Collection, N.Y.C., 1963-64; fashion coord. Bonwit Teller, Westchester, N.Y., 1964-68; head designer, master patternmaker Aaron Kahmi-Kamhi Group, N.Y.C., 1968-87, Dorothea of Palm Beach, Fla., 1993-94; costume designer, prodr. Fla., 1990—. One-woman shows at Carimor Gallery, N.Y., 1985; exhibited in group shows at Argentinean Consulate, N.Y.C., 1985, Jewells Fine Art Gallery, N.J., 1985, 86, Art in Public Places Program, Palm Beach, 1990, Palm Beach C.C., 1991. Mem. Argentina Arts Orgn. (pres. 1995-96, exec. dir. bd. 1995—), Palm Beach Cultural Coun. of Arts, Orgn. Cultural Argentina (head, bd. dirs. 1992—), Ctr. for Creative Edn. (exec. com. 1994—). Jewish. Home: 7752 Forestay Dr Lake Worth FL 33467 Office: Argentina Arts Orgn 7752 Forestay Dr Lake Worth FL 33467

ARUTYUNYAN, EMMA, radio-broadcaster; b. Yerevan, Armenia, Aug. 14, 1946; came to U.S., 1988; d. Hambartsum and Vartanush (Babayan) A.; m. Sako Mkrtchyan, Feb. 17, 1971; 1 child, Aram. MS, State U. Yerevan, 1969. Radioastrophysicist, rsch. scientist Byurakan Astrophys. Observatory, Armenia, 1969-78; teaching asst., physicist Polytech Inst. Yerevan, Armenia, 1978-87; internat. radio-broadcaster Voice of Am., Washington, 1992—. Contbr. scientific articles to profl. jours. Assoc. mem. Am. Mus. Natural History, 1995—. Recipient award Cen. Com. Dosaaf USSR, Moscow, 1967, Pres. Cen. Com. Dosaaf USSR, 1967. Mem. Smithsonian Instn. (nat. assoc. mem.).

ARVIN, LINDA LEE, counselor; b. York, Pa., May 12, 1952; d. Paul Henry and Mary Elizabeth (Stein) Horsermyer; m. Michael Eugene Arvin, Dec. 16, 1978 (div.); children: Melissa Elizabeth, Michael Alexis. BA, George Washington U., 1981; postgrad., Johns Hopkins U. Sr. staff Cmty. Ministry, Rockville, Md., 1989-92; sr. counselor Arlington (Va.) Cmty. Residences, 1992-93; program dir. Montgomery County Coalition for the Homeless, Rockville, 1993—. Mem. ACA, AAUW, Md. Assn. for Counseling and Devel. Democrat. Methodist. Home: 2733 Jennings Rd Kensington MD 20895 Office: Laytonsville Havens 5834 Riggs Rd Laytonsville MD 20882

ARVIZU, CHARLENE SUTTER, elementary education educator; b. San Jose, Calif., Mar. 1, 1947; d. Joseph Carl and Marjorie Loreen (Nylin) Sutter; m. Ambrose Emanuel Arvizu, Apr. 7, 1980; children: Joseph Todd Nottingham, Matthew Sutter. BA in Art, San Jose State U., 1964, lifetime tchg. credential grades K-9, 1969, lifetime spl. edn. grades K-14, 1969, specialist/learning handicapped, 1969. Tchr. edn. mentally retarded class grades K-12 Berryessa Union Sch. Dist., 1969-71, resource ctr. dir. grades K-5, 1971-73, kindergarten tchr. Ruskin Sch., 1974—; instr. Ohlone Coll., Fremont, Calif., 1980-89, Chapman Coll., 1985-88, San Jose County Office Edn., 1985-94; nat. lectr., cons. and presenter in field. Author: Read It Again, 1990, Whole Language Strategies in the Classroom, 1991, Strengthening Your Kindergarten Using Thrmatic, Integrate Literature Based Strategies, 1993, Kindergarten 5 Day Institute Book, 1994. Recipient Disting. Sch. award Office of Mayor of San Jose, Calif., 1987. Mem. Internat. Reading Assn., Calif. Reading Assn., Internat. Book Assn. for Young Readers, Children's Book Coun. Inc., Calif. Sch. Age Consortium, Planetary Citizens-One World-One People, Soc. Children's Book Writers, Delta Kappa Gamma. Home: 3010 Daurine Ct Gilroy CA 95020-9552 Office: Ruskin Sch 1401 Turlock Ln San Jose CA 95132-2347

ARZOUMANIAN, LINDA LEE, early childhood educator; b. Madison, Wis., Apr. 29, 1942; d. James Arthur Luck and Rosemary M. (Peacock) Engstrom; m. Youri Feridoon Arzoumanian, Oct. 7, 1967; children: Stephan, Aaron. BS, Stout State U., Menomonie, Wis., 1964; MEd, Ohio U., Athens, 1969; EdD, Nova U., 1994. Cert. tchr. vocat., secondary, community coll., Ariz. Residence hall asst. Ohio U., Athens, 1965-67; quality control supr. Advalloy, Inc., Palo Alto, Calif., 1967; tchr. adult edn. Eau Claire (Wis.) Pub. Sch., 1964-65; patient svc. dietitian Camden Clark Meml. Hosp., Parkersburg, W.Va., 1970; adminstr. pre-sch. Fishkill (N.Y.) Meth. Nursery Sch., 1976-84; substitute tchr. Tucson Unified Sch. Dist., 1987; tchr. pre-sch. Tanque Verde Luth. Presch., Tucson, 1988-89; cons., early childhood edn. curriculum specialist Tucson Unified Sch. Dist., 1988-93; instr. Ctrl. Ariz. Coll., 1990—, Prescott Coll., 1991-92; dist. moderator Sch. Community Partnership Coun., Tucson, 1988-90; dir. child and family svcs. in prevention and early intervention treatment Children's Managed Behavioral Health Care Svcs. of Pima County, Inc., Tucson, 1990—; mem. supts. adv. cabinet Tucson Unified Sch. Dist., 1988-89, mem. curriculum and instrn. coun., 1989-90, spl. edn. pre-sch. adv. com., 1989-91, info. tech. bond rev. com., 1989—, sex edn. curriculum adv. com., core curriculum com., 1988-90, 2000 com., 1988-89, and various others; nat. child devel. assoc. adv./field adv., nat. child devel. assoc. rep. Nat. Assn. for Edn. of Young Children; grant-swriter Comstock Found.; validator early childhood programs for Nat. Acad. Early Childhood Programs. Mem. Dutchess County Child Devel. Com., Poughkeepsie, N.Y., 1979-81; advancement chmn. troop 1968 Boy Scouts Am., Tucson, 1986, com. person troop 194, 1986-89; mem. joint com. on site based decision making Tucson Unified Sch. Dist./Tucson Edn. Assn., 1989—; active Armenian Cultural Soc.; early childhood edn. adv. com. Cen. Ariz. Coll.; life mem. Ariz. PTA; mem. Pima County Children's Coord. Coun., Pima County Youth Svcs. Team, Children's Adv. Coun., Prevention Design Team, Prevention Coun., Ariz. Dept. Health Svcs. Coun., Children's Treatment and Prevention com., Tucson Unified Sch. Dist. Ind. Citizens Com., Early Childhood Edn. Coun. Consortium. Mem. AAUW, ASCD, NAFE, Assn. Childhood Edn. Internat., World Future Soc., Nat. Assn. Edn. Young Children, So. Ariz. Child Care Assn. Family Resource Coalition, Tucson Assn. Edn. Young Children (pres.). Home: 8230 E Ridgebrook Dr Tucson AZ 85750-2442 Office: 333 W Fort Lowell Rd Ste 219 Tucson AZ 85705-5920

ARZT, DONNA ELAINE, law educator; b. Phila., Dec. 9, 1954; d. Alvin H. and Lois (Silver) A.; m. Stephen J. Whitfield, Aug. 21, 1977 (div. Sept. 1982). BA, Brandeis Univ., 1976; JD, Harvard Univ., 1979; LLM, Columbia Univ., 1988. Bar: Mass. 1979, N.Y. 1988. Assoc. Rosenfeld, Botsford & Krokidas, Boston, 1980-82; asst. atty. gen. Dept. Atty. Gen., Boston, 1982-85; cons. Assn. for Civil Rights, Jerusalem, Israel, 1986; asst. prof. Syracuse (N.Y.) Univ., 1988-91, assoc. prof., 1992-96, prof., 1996—; adj. prof. Touro Law Ctr., Huntington, N.Y., 1987-88; gen. coun. Soviet Jewry Logal Adv. Ctr., Waltham, Mass., 1979-88; Eng. editor Israel Yearbook on Human Rights, Tel Aviv, 1986-87. Author: Refugees into Citizens, 1996; co-author: Religious Human Rights, 1995, Beyond Confrontation, 1995, Der Einflus deutscher Emigranten, 1993. Bd. adv., mem. Refugee Resettlement Com., Ithaca, N.Y., 1995—; exec. com. Program on Analysis & Resolution of Conflicts, 1993; project dir. Coun. on Fgn. Rels., 1994—; exec. com. Union of Countries for Soviet Jews, 1980-87. Recipient Tyson award for Excellence in Human Rights Advocacy Union of Coun. for. Soviet Jews, 1990; travel grant Internat. Com. of the Red Cross, Geneva, Switzerland, 1993; rsch. grant. Jacob Blaustein Inst. for Human Rights, 1987-88. Mem. ABA, Am. Soc. Internat. Law, Assn. of Am. Law Sch. Democrat. Jewish. Office: Syracuse Univ Coll Law E I White Hall Syracuse NY 13244

ASAAD, KOLLEEN JOYCE, special education educator; b. West Union, Iowa, July 13, 1941; d. Leonard Henry and Catherine Adelade (Bishop) Anfinson; children: Todd, Robin, Tara, Jason. BA in Elem. Edn., Upper Iowa U., 1961; MA in Spl. Edn. and Adminstrn., U. Cin., 1973. Elem. tchr. Fredericksburg (Iowa) Elem. Sch., 1961-62, Tyler Sch., Cedar Rapids, Iowa, 1962-64, Oasis Sch., 29 Palms, Calif., 1964-69, Longfellow Sch., Waterloo, Iowa, 1969-70; spl. edn. tchr. Fairview Sch., Cin., 1970-77; learning disabilities tchr. Lincoln Sch., Portsmouth, Ohio, 1977-78; dir. spl. edn. Vermilion Assn. for Spl. Edn., Danville, Ill., 1978-94; dir. edn. Swann Spl. Care Ctr., Champaign, Ill., 1994—; mem. Govtl. Rels. Com., Ill. Coun. for Exceptional Children, Jacksonville, Ill., 1992. Bd. mem. Crosspoints, Danville, Catlin Music Boosters, pres.; active Catlin Athletic Boosters. Named Best Adminstr., Regional Supt. of Schs., 1991. Mem. Coun. for Exceptional Children, Coun. for Adminstrs. of Spl. Edn., Ill. Adminstrs. of Spl. Edn., Assn. for Persons with Severe Handicaps, Exec. Club. Lutheran. Home: 122 Mapleleaf St Catlin IL 61817-9646 Office: Swann Spl Care Ctr 109 Kenwood Rd Champaign IL 61821-2905

ASAKAWA, TAKAKO, dancer, dance teacher, director; b. Toyko, Feb. 23, 1939; came to U.S., 1962; d. Kamenosuke and Chiaki Asakawa. Student, Tokyo schs., 1962-91. Pron. dancer Martha Graham Dance Co., N.Y.C., 1962-76, 81—; dancer Alvin Ailey, 1968-69, Pearl Lang, 1967, Lar Lubovitch, 1974-80; guest tchr. at Martha Graham Sch., Juilliard Sch.; co-founder Asakawalker Dance Co. Performer Bell Telephone Hours, L.A., 1970; performed as Eliza, The King and I. Named Legendary Woman of Am., St. Vincent's Hosp. Mem. Am. Guild Musical Artists. Home and Office: 257 Central Park W New York NY 10024-4103

ASANO, HISAKO, fine arts educator; b. Osaka City, Japan, Jan. 5, 1944; came to the U.S., 1960; d. Denzo and Matsuko Asano; m. Michael B. Gould,

Feb. 12, 1972 (div. 1981). BFA, U. So. Calif., 1966, MFA, 1971. Educator U. So. Calif., L.A., 1970—; educator Loyola Marymount U., L.A., 1971-72, L.A. County High Sch., 1986, South Bay Adult Sch., Manhattan Beach, Calif., 1977-88, L.A. County Mus. Art, 1989, Palos Verdes (Calif.) Art Ctr., 1989-90, Torrance (Calif.) Art Ctr., 1990—, So. Coast Botanic Garden, Rolling Hills, Calif., 1987—, L.A. Harbor Coll., 1976—. Exhibited works in numerous shows including U. So. Calif., 1971, Malone Gallery, L.A., 1975, L.A. Mus., 1974-75, So. Coast Botanic Garden, 1989. Mem. Printmaking Soc., Women Archtl. League, L.A. Jr. Chamber Com., Friends of Fine Arts. Home: 27838 Palos Verdes Dr E Rancho Palos CA 90275-5151 Office: U So Calif University Park Los Angeles CA 90089-0292

ASBJORNSON, ELIZABETH ERICA, real estate executive; b. Omaha, Nebr., Sept. 25, 1964; d. Norman Harold and Helen Elizabeth (Longstreth) A. BA in Econ./Polit. Sci., St. Olaf Coll., 1986; MBA in Fin./Real Estate, U. Denver, 1990. Securities acct. Bellamah, Neuhauser & Barrett, Washington, 1986-88; property acct. The John Akridge Co., Washington, 1988; asst. property mgr. The RREEF Funds, Sunnyvale, Calif., 1990-91; real estate analyst Kemper Real Estate Mgmt. Co. Bedford Properties, Lafayette, Calif., 1991-93; asset mgr., real estate mgr. Kemper Corp., Chgo., 1993-96; portfolio mgr. Heitman Fin., Chgo., 1996—. Mem. Jr. League of Chgo. Mem. Chgo. Real Estate Coun., Inst. of Real Estate Mgmt., Comml. Real Estate Exec. Women, Urban Land Inst. Republican. Presbyterian. Home: 1730 N Clark St #2311 Chicago IL 60614 Office: Heitman Financial 180 N LaSalle St Chicago IL 60601

ASBURY, JUDY VALBRACHT, artist, educator; b. Defiance, Ohio, Dec. 28, 1942; d. Edward Luther and Mildred June (Musgrave) Valbracht; m. Ralph Lee Asbury, May 12, 1979; 1 child, Nora Elizabeth. Student, UCLA, 1961-63; cert. in nursing, City Coll. San Francisco, 1968; BA, Marlboro Coll., 1972; postgrad., U. Vt., 1972-74. RN, Calif., N.Mex., Vt., N.Y.; cert. tchr., libr., N.Mex. Arts instr. Art Explorations, Albuquerque, 1991—; adult instr. Jemez Pueblo, N.Mex., 1992—; libr. Jemez Pueblo Libr., 1994—; illustrator Kahawai, Honolulu, 1983-84; writer Pulsar, IAAA, N.Y.C., 1989-90; ceramicist Ralph Asbury, Ponderosa, 1985-88. One-woman show at Hayden Planetarium, N.Y.C., 1993, Mus. N.Mex.; exhibited in group shows at Basel Art 20, 1989, Moscow, 1988. Mem. Buddhist Peace Fellowship, Berkeley, Calif., 1995—; founder Friends of the Jemez, Jemez Pueblo, 1985—. Ashoka Stupa painting fellow, 1985; Sumi-e painting scholar Jemez Bodhi Mondala, 1980, painting scholar Gandy Brodie Sch. Find Arts, 1974. Mem. Internat. Assn. Astron. Artists, OURS Found., Soc. Layerists in Multi Media, Greenpeace. Buddhist. Home: PO Box 170 Jemez Pueblo NM 87024 Office: Jemez Pueblo Cmty Libr PO Box 9 Jemez Pueblo NM 87024

ASCH, SANDRA L., investment banker; b. Chgo., July 3, 1967; d. Morton J. and Charlotte E. (Endres) A. BS in Mech. Engring., U. Tex., 1990; MBA in Fin., Columbia U., 1994. Assoc. engr. IBM, Austin, Tex., 1990-92; investment banking assoc. Kidder, Peabody, N.Y.C., 1994-95, Cowen & Co., San Francisco, 1995—.

ASCHENBRENER, CAROL ANN, pathologist, educator; b. Dubuque, Iowa, Dec. 22, 1944; d. Lester Bernard and Marian Barbara (Wiehl) Kemp; m. Thomas D. Aschenbrener, June 10, 1968 (div. Oct. 1972); 1 child, Erin Jean. BA, Clarke Coll., 1966; MS in Anatomy, U. Iowa, 1968; MD, U. N.C., 1971. Diplomate Am. Bd. Pathology. Intern in pathology U. Iowa Hosps., 1971-72, resident in anatomic pathology, neuropathology, 1972-74; instr. pathology Coll. Medicine U. Iowa, Iowa City, 1974; asst. prof. Coll. Medicine U. Iowa, Iowa City, 1974-79, assoc. prof., 1979-87, prof., 1987—, assoc. dean, 1983-88, sr. assoc. dean, 1988-90, exec. assoc. dean, 1990—; bd. dirs. 1st Nat. Bank, Iowa City. Contbr. articles to profl. jours., chpts. to med. texts. Bd. dirs. alumni bd. Clarke Coll., Dubuque, 1983-87. Nat. Merit scholar, 1962-66; Am. Cancer Soc. fellow, 1972-73. Fellow Coll. Am. Pathologists, Am. Assn. Neuropathologists; mem. AMA (sect. del.), Assn. Am. Med. Colls. (chmn. student affairs nat. com. 1987-89), Iowa Med Soc. (sec., treas. bd. trustees 1985—), Liaison Com. on Med. Edn., Nat. Bd. of Med. Examiners, Nat. Cancer Inst. (edn. adv. com.), Alpha Omega Alpha. Democrat. Roman Catholic. Home: 603 N 62nd St Omaha NE 68132-1958 Office: Univ Nebr Med Ctr Office of Chancellor 42nd And Dewey St Omaha NE 68198-0001

ASCHOFF, MAUREEN JANE, librarian; b. Jersey City, N.J., June 12, 1945; d. Antohny J. and Catherine (Scudder) Salese; children: Jerry, Shamane, Max. BA, N.J. State Coll., 1967; MS, Calif. State Coll., 1975. Libr. County of Orange, Villa Park, Calif., 1984-96, Orange (Calif.) Unified Sch. Bd., 1991—. Pres. Orange Bd. Edn., 1993-95; founder Orange Unified Ednl. Found., 1996; rsch. dir. Taxpayer Action Network, Orange County, 1989-92; mem. Ednl. Task Force, Orange, 1993-95; mem. Fiscal Adv. Coun., Orange, 1993—; pres. Orange Fin. Authority, 1993-95; mem. PTA, Orange, 1975—; mem. Orange Rep. Women, Calif. Rep. Assembly, YMCA. Recipient PTA Honorary Svc. award, 1987; named Woman of the Yr., Calif. State Assembly (71st Dist.), 1995. Mem. AAUW, Nat. Coun. Women Advs. to Congress.

ASCONE, TERESA PALMER, artist, educator; b. Cortland, N.Y., Nov. 1, 1945; d. Lawrence Henry and Bernice Rosella (Holcomb) Palmer; m. Michael Wayne Ascone, Oct. 15, 1965 (div. Jan. 1995); 1 child, Michael Palmer. Student, Alaska Meth. U., Alaska Pacific U., U. Alaska. Painter/tchr. Alaska Pacific U., Anchorage, 1989-91, U. Alaska, 1992; pvt. tchr. watercolor Anchorage, 1992—; owner Alaskan Portfolio, 1981—; tchr. U. Alaska, Anchorage, 1992—. Juried shows include Alaska State Fair, 1979-80, Fur Rendezvous Juried Show, 1979, 80, All Alaska Juried Show, 1981, 84, 85, 90, Alaska Watercolor Soc. juried show, 1981, 83, 85, 86, 87, 88, 89, 90, 91, April in Paris juried exhibit at Capt. Cook Hotel, 1982, 83, 84, 87, Featured Artist, 1986, Watercolor Fairbanks, 1989, Women Artist of West 1st Ann. Internat. Show, 1990; one women shows include Anchorage Mcpl. Librs., 1980, 82, NBA Heritage Libr., 1986, Alaska Pacific U., 1989, Chitose City Hall, Chitose, Hokkaido, Japan, 1990; represented in permanent collection Alaska Pacific U.; cover artist Arctic Horizons Mag., 1986, Alaska Horizons Mag., 1986; subject of TV spl., 1988; developer original design, manufacture & mktg. The Ultimate Palette, 1993; author: We're All Artists: Watercolor for Everyone, 1994; editor, publisher Hot Press Mag., 1994. Mcpl. commr. Anchorage Sister Cities Commn., 1991-93. Recipient Vol. of Yr. Caverly Sr. Ctr., 1986, various art show awards to date; works chosen as ofcl. gifts to cities of Inchon, Korea and Magadan, Russia and Whitby, Eng. from city of Anchorage. Mem. Alaska Watercolor Soc. (v.p. 1983), Alaska Artists Guild, N.W. Watercolor Soc.

ASCUENA, VIKKI PEPPER, secondary school educator; b. Jerome, Idaho, Oct. 13, 1953; d. Rex and Oneita P.; 1 child, Whitney. BA, Boise State U., 1975, MA, 1980. Tchr. Meridian (Idaho) Jr. H.S., 1975-87; tchr. Meridian (Idaho) H.S., 1987—, chairperson English dept., 1993—; curriculum writer Meridian Schs., 1980—; mem. adj. faculty Boise State U., 1988-90; presenter in field. Grantee NEH Victorian Seminar, 1987; named Meridian Jr. H.S. Tchr. of Yr., 1987, Meridian H.S. Tchr. of Yr., 1994, Meridian Dist. Tchr. of Yr., 1994. Mem. NEA, Idaho Edn. Assn., Meridian Edn. Assn., Idaho Coun. Tchrs. English (treas. 1988-91, v.p. 1991-92, pres. 1992-93, past pres. 1993-94), Support for Learning and Tchg. English (newsletter editor 1993-94, developer Micron project rep. 1994—). Office: Meridian HS 1900 W Pine Ave Meridian ID 83642-1961

ASH, CYNTHIA ANNETTE, business educator, tax consultant; b. Chgo., Feb. 6, 1956; d. James C. and Celia Ann (Green) Jackson; 1 child, Caprice Lenard Jackson; m. Dennis Wayne Ash, Apr. 25, 1991; 1 child, Celia Ann. BBA, Western Mich. U., 1979, MBA, 1987. Enrolled agt. IRS. Tax specialist Grant Thornton CPA, Kalamazoo, Mich., 1979-85; acad. advisor Western Mich. U., Kalamazoo, Mich., 1986-89; instr. Davenport Coll., Kalamazoo, Mich., 1990—. Treas. Village Vandalia, Mich., 1995-96; fin. advisor Underground Railroad Found., Vandalia, 1995—. Mem. Inst. Mgmt. Accts. (faculty adv. student chpt. 1991—). Pentecostal. Office: Davenport Coll 4123 W Main St Kalamazoo MI 49006

ASH, DOROTHY MATTHEWS, civic worker; b. Dresden, Germany, Nov. 10, 1918; came to U.S., 1924; d. Kurt Horst and Ana (Sekes) Matthesius; m. Harry A. Ash, Apr. 13, 1941 (dec. June 1981); children: Fredrick Curtis, Dorothea Ash Linklater. Dancer, 1933-40; treas. Inheritance Abstractors Inc., Chgo., 1949-70; reporter Miami (Fla.) Sun Post, 1983; reporter, columnist Social Mag., Miami, 1984—; chmn. Miss Universe Pageant, 1983-85; cruise chmn. Miami U., 1984, mem. Pres.'s Club, 1983. Pres. Big Bros. and Big Sisters, 1982-83; founding mem. World Sch. of Arts, 1985—; founding Notable Douglas Gardens 1988: Pres.'s Club U. of Miami, 1989; founding and bd. mem. Cancer Link Rsch., 1990; mem. Bd. Animal Welfare; active Project: Newborn, Am. Cancer Soc., March of Dimes, chmn. quest for the best, 1988-92, winner gourmet gala, 1988, Children's Resource, Erase Diabetes, founding and bd. mem. 1990, Cerebral Palsy Found., Theatre Arts League, Linda Ray Infant Ctr., Miami City Ballet, Am. Ballet; bd. dirs. Greater Miami Opera, 1975—; pub. rels. vol. Miami Heart Inst., 1988—; com. mem. Miami Beach (Fla.) Beautification Program, 1984; mem. bd. Miami Mayor's Ad Hoc Com., 1984; mem. com. Challenger Seven Meml., 1988; active Cousteou Coun.; numerous others. Named Woman of Yr., Big Bros. and Big Sisters, Miami, 1981, Best Dressed, Am. Cancer Soc., 1981, Outstanding Humanitarian and Civic Leader, Mayor City of Miami, 1985, Woman of the Yr., Project: New Born, 1985, Miss Charity, Biscayne Bay Hosp., 1986, Queen of Hearts, Miami Children's Hosp., 1988; recipient Shining Star award Bon Secours Hosp., 1993, Patron Recognition award Mia Heart Rsch. Inst., 1993, Goddess of Love award Villa Maria Hosp., 1995. Mem. Miami Internat. Press Club. Home: 10245 Collins Ave Bal Harbour FL 33154-1406 also (summer): 330 W Diversey Pky Chicago IL 60657-6229

ASH, JENNIFER GERTRUDE, writer, editor; b. Jan. 16, 1963; d. Clarke and Agnes Ash; m. D.A. Joseph Rudick, Apr. 7, 1990; children: Clark Albert, Amelia, Eleanor. BA, Kenyon Coll., 1985; postgrad., New Sch. Social Rsch. Assoc. editor Women's Wear Daily, 1986-87; contbg. editor Town and Country, New York, 1992-95. Author: Private Palm Beach, 1992, The Expectant Father: Facts, Tips, and Advice for Dads-to-Be, 1995. Fellow Frick Collection. Democrat. Roman Catholic. Home: 901 Lexington Ave New York NY 10021 Office: Pam Bernstein Inc 7901 Madison Ave New York NY 10021*

ASH, MARY KAY WAGNER, cosmetics company executive; b. Hot Wells, Tex., May 12; d. Edward Alexander and Lula Vember (Hastings) Wagner; m. Melville Jerome Ash, Jan. 6, 1966 (dec.); children: Marylyn Theard (dec.), Ben Rogers, Richard Rogers. Student, U. Houston, 1942-43. Mgr. Stanley Home Products, Houston, 1939-52; nat. tng. dir. World Gift Co., Dallas, 1952-63; founder, chmn. emeritus Mary Kay Cosmetics, Dallas, 1963—; speaker to various orgns. Bd. dirs. Horatio Alger Assn.; chmn. bldg. fund. Prestonwood Bapt. Ch., Dallas; hon. chmn. Tex. Breast Screening Project, Am. Cancer Soc. Office: Mary Kay Cosmetics Inc 16251 N Dallas Pkwy Dallas TX 75248-2696*

ASH, SHARON KAYE, real estate company executive; b. Altus, Ark., July 21, 1943; d. William Clyde and Odus Marie (Drew) Cline; m. J.W. Ash, June 1, 1966 (div. Oct. 1978); 1 child, Brian Edward. B.S., S.W. Mo. State U., 1985; grad. Realtor Inst.; cert. residential specialist. Lic. real estate broker, Mo. Personal lines asst. Squibb Ins., Springfield, Mo., 1967-69; bookkeeper Hood-Rich, Architects and Engrs., Springfield, 1969-89; owner Ash Computer Service, Springfield, 1985—; owner, broker Ash Real Estate, Springfield, 1985—;dir. Multilist Svc. Featured in Home Gym and Fitness mag., 1995. Mem. Womens Coun. Realtors (past pres. Springfield chpt., Member of Yr. 1993), Mo. Assn. Realtors, Nat. Assn. Realtors, Springfield Area C. of C., Million Dollar Sales Club (life mem.), Multi Million Dollar Club. Democrat. Episcopalian. Avocations: golf, boating, reading, collecting clowns, jogging. Home: PO Box 10585 Springfield MO 65808-0585 Office: Ash Real Estate 1340 W Battlefield St Ste 114 Springfield MO 65807-4102

ASHBY, CATHERINE VIRGINIA, county government official; b. Winchester, Va., Apr. 10, 1948; d. Edward Francis and Alice Osborn (Coleman) Brown; m. Robert Nelson Ashby Jr., July 1, 1967; children: Robert Nelson III, Bartley David. Grad. high sch., Purcellville, Va. With County of Loudoun, Leesburg, Va., 1968—; tax tech., dep. County of Loudoun, 1980-85, commr. revenue, 1985—. Treas., Loudoun 4-H Assocs., Inc., Leesburg, 1985—. Mem. Commrs. of Revenue Assn. Va., Internat. Assn. Assessing Officers, No. Va. League Commrs. of Revenue (pres. 1988-89), Va. Assn. Assessing Officers, Va. Assn. Local Execs. Constl. Officers. Democrat. Methodist. Office: Loudoun Commr Revenue PO Box 7000 1 Harrison St SE Fl 1 Leesburg VA 20177-7000

ASHBY, NORMA RAE BEATTY, journalist, beauty consultant, Mont., Dec. 27, 1935; d. Raymond Wesley Beatty and Ella Mae (Lamb) Beatty Watson Mehmke; m. Shirley Carter Ashby, Sept. 5, 1964; children: Ann, Tony. BA, U. Mont., Missoula, 1957. Reporter, Helena Ind. Record, 1953-56; picture dept. Life mag., N.Y.C., 1957-58; picture researcher MD Med. Newsmag., N.Y.C., 1959-61; producer, hostess TV Show Today in Mont., Sta. KRTV, Great Falls, 1962-85; editor Noon News, Sta. KRTV, 1985-88, beauty cons. Mary Kay Cosmetics, Inc., 1988—; freelance journalist, 1988—. Author: What Is A Montanan?, 1971, Montana Woman, 1977, Montanans, 1982, scriptwriter: Last Chance Gulch, 1964, Gentle Giants, 1969, Our Latchstring is Out, 1979, Paris Gibson, 1983, Martha, Pioneer Woman, 1984, Great Falls Centennial, 1984, First Ladies of Montana, 1986, Anuka, Montana's Island Home, 1986, North American Indian Days, 1987, Missiles of October, 1987, First Ladies of Montana with Norma Ashby, 1996; (co-author) Symbols of Montana, 1989. Mem. First Presbyn. Ch.; co-chmn. Cascade County Bicentennial Com., Great Falls, 1974-76; founder, chmn. C.M. Russell Auction, Great Falls, 1979; bd. dirs. Mont. Physicians Service, Helena, 1980-87; co-chmn. Great Falls Centennial Com., 1982-84; Festivals chmn. Cascade Coounty 89ers, 1987-89; coord. Mont. Statewide BellRinging Project, 1989; chair Mont. Jefferson awards; pres. Cascade County Mental Health Assn., 1980-82; elder First Presbyn. Ch.; bd. dirs. Cascade County Hist. Soc., 1987-91, Mental Health Assn. Mont., also editor; coord. Mont. Statehood Centennial Bell Award, 1990—. Co-host Children's Miracle Network Telethon, 1989-94. Recipient TV Program of Yr. award Greater Mont. Found. 1982—, Communication and Leadership award Mont. Toastmasters Internat., 1983, Preservation award Cascade County Hist. Soc., 1994; named Tribune Most Influential Woman in Great Falls, 1984, hon. mem. Blackfeet Tribe Blackfeet Reservation, Browning, Mont., 1981, Mont. TV Broadcaster Yr., 1985. Mem. Women in Communications (founder, pres. Great Falls, Mont. chpt. 1988-90), Great Falls Advt. Fedn. (dir., Silver medal 1980, Scriver Bronze medal 1993), AWRT (founder, pres. Mt. Big Sky chpt. 1967, recipient cert. of commendation 1982). Club: PEO, Broadcast Pioneers.

ASHBY, ROSEMARY GILLESPY, college president; b. Farnham, Surrey, Eng., May 16, 1940; came to U.S. 1967; d. Robert Dymock and Margaret Lois (Gillespy) Watson; m. John Hallam Ashby, June 17, 1967. B.A., U. Capetown, S. Africa, 1960; B.A., Cambridge U., 1963, M.A., 1967, M.Litt., 1972. Head resident Radcliffe Coll., Cambridge, Mass., 1968-70, asst. dir. career planning, 1969-70; dir. residence, instr. French Pine Manor Coll., Chestnut Hill, Mass., 1970-71, dean students, 1971-75, acting pres., 1975-76, pres., 1976—; pvt. tutor Sao Paulo, Brazil, 1963-65; teaching asst. U. Capetown, 1959-60; panelist N.E. Assn. Schs. and Colls., Boston, 1983, Nat. Assn. Ind. Schs., Boston, 1985. Author chpt. in book. Adv. bd. Keimei Fund for Internat. Edn., N.Y.C., 1978—. Nat. Endowment of Humanities fellow, 1984. Mem. Mass. Commn. on Post-secondary Edn., Assn. Am. Colls. (exec. com. 1977-78), Assn. Ind. Colls. and Univs. in Mass. (exec. com. 1977-80, 89-92), Women's Coll. Coalition (exec. com. 1985-88), Am. Inst. Fgn. Study (bd. acad. advisors 1986—), New England Bd. Higher Edn. (Mass. delegate 1993—), Rassias Found. (bd. overseers 1993—). Home: 41 Crafts Rd Chestnut Hill MA 02167-1823 Office: Pine Manor Coll Office of the President 400 Heath St Chestnut Hill MA 02167-2332

ASHDOWN, MARIE MATRANGA (MRS. CECIL SPANTON ASHDOWN, JR.), writer, lecturer; b. Mobile, Ala.; d. Dominic and Ave (Mallon) Matranga; m. Cecil Spanton Ashdown Jr., Feb. 8, 1958; children: Cecil Spanton III, Charles Coster; children by previous marriage: John Stephen Gartman, Vivian Marie Gartman. Student, Maryville Coll. Sacred Heart; student, Springhill Coll. Feature artist, women's program dir. daily program Sta. WALA, WALA-TV, Mobile, 1953-58; v.p., dir. Met. Opera Guild, N.Y.C., 1970-78, opera instr. in-svc. program, 1970-80; opera instr. in-svc. program Marymount Coll., N.Y.C., 1979-85; exec. dir. Musicians Emergency Fund, Inc., N.Y.C., 1985—; cons. No. Ill. U. Coll. of Visual and Performing Arts, 1985—; lectr. in field. Author: Opera Collectables, 1979, contbr. articles to profl. jours. Recipient Extraordinary Service award March of Dimes, 1958, Medal of Appreciation award Harvard Bus. Sch. Club N.Y.C., 1974, Cert. Appreciation, Kiwanis Internat., 1975, Arts Excellence award N.J. State Opera, 1986. Mem. AAUW, Successful Meetings Directory, Nat. Inst. Social Scis., Com. for U.S.-China Rels. Home: 25 Sutton Pl S Apt 16K New York NY 10022-2456 Office: Musicians Emergency Fund Inc 820 2nd Ave Ste 203 New York NY 10017-4504

ASHE, KATHY RAE, special education educator; b. Bismarck, N.D., Oct. 24, 1950; d. Raymond Charles and Virginia Ann (Mason) Lynch; m. Barth Eugene Olson, Aug. 11, 1973; 1 child, William Raymond; m. Fredrick A. Ashe, Aug. 5, 1994. B.S., U. N.D., 1972; MS in Spl. Edn., U. N.D., 1987. Cert. elem. tchr. with spl. edn. credential, N.D. Instr., Grafton State Sch., N.D., 1972-74; tchr. spl. edn. Grand Forks Sch. Dist., N.D., 1974—; bd. dirs. Agassiz Enterprises; mem. RAD com. Valley Jr. High; mem. transition governing bd., Region IV. Bd. dirs. Assn. Retarded Citizens, Devel. Homes, Inc., N.D. Sch. Blind Found.; spl. needs recreation program Grand Forks Park Bd., 1973-76; mem. Spl. Olympics Area Mgmt. Team, 1984—. Named N.D. Tchr. of Yr., Coun. of Chief State Sch. Officers, 1981. Mem. AAUW, Delta Kappa Gamma (sec. 1984-86, pres. 1990-94), Alpha Phi (alumni pres. 1984-86, 90-91, alumni treas. 1995—), Pi Lambda Theta, Phi Delta Kappa. Republican. Roman Catholic. Avocations: sporting events, civic work, cross stitch, bowling. Home: 3208 Walnut St Grand Forks ND 58201-7665

ASHE, MAUDE LLEWELLYN, home economics educator; b. Bakersfield, Calif., Feb. 9, 1908; d. Richard Samuel and Marguerite J. (Loudon) A. AB, U. Calif., 1928; MS, Oreg. State U., Corvallis, 1944; postgrad., San Jose (Calif.) State Coll., 1936-38, Stanford U., 1948. Cert. tchr., Calif. Instr. in home econs. Oreg. State U., 1943; assoc. prof. home econs. San Jose State U., 1944-73, emeritus prof. home econs., 1973—. Author: Finding West Country Ancestors, 1939. Mem. Santa Clara County Fair Assn., San Jose, 1968; v.p. Kern Genealogy Soc., Bakersfield, Calif., 1986. Mem. AAUW (sec., chmn. San Jose chpt. 1978), Calif. Ret. Tchr.'s Assn., Calif. Ret. State Employees, Emeritus Faculty Assn., Nat. Trust for Hist. Preservation, Family Assn. of Austin, Geer Family Assn., Calif. Home Econs. Assn. (chmn. com. San Francisco chpt. 1965, state advisor to student clubs No. Calif. area 1966), Imperial Valley Gem and Mineral Soc. (charter), Phi Upsilon Omicron. Democrat. Home: 9100 Park # 509C Lenexa KS 66215

ASHENBRENNER, DAWN MARIE, physical therapist; b. Wautoma, Wis., Nov. 4, 1969; d. David Lee and Dorothy Louise (Malolepsy) A. BS in Phys. Therapy, U. Wis., 1991; postgrad., St. Joseph's U., Phila., 1996—. Lic. phys. therapist, Pa. Phys. therapist Sioux Valley Hosp., Sioux Falls, S.D., 1991-94, Crozer-Chester Med. Ctr., Upland, Pa., 1995—; phys. therapist Premier Rehab., Dillon, S.C., 1994, Able Rehab., Coos Bay, Oreg., 1994, Wausau (Wis.) Hosp., 1994-95. Vol. Dem. Party, Sioux Falls, 1992, Big Bros./Big Sisters, Sioux Falls, 1993-94. Mem. Am. Phys. Therapy Assn. Office: Crozer Chester Med Ctr Cmty Divsn 1 Medical Ctr Blvd Upland PA 19013

ASHENFELTER, VIRGINIA EVELYN, sales executive; b. Orange, N.J., May 23, 1943; d. Charles Milton and Evelyn (Piccot) Wilson; m. Orley Ashenfelter, Dec. 22, 1965; children: Theresa Sydney, Bevin Meredith, Gillian Mairead. BA, Scripps Coll., 1965. Tchr. Stuart County Day Sch., Princeton, N.J., 1968-72; sales assoc. Randall Cook, Princeton, N.J., 1982-89, Peyton Assoc., Princeton, N.J., 1990—. Episcopalian. Office: Peyton Assoc 343 Nassau St Princeton NJ 08540

ASHFORD, BENITA LYNN, reading, language and speech educator; b. Marshall, Tex., Sept. 15, 1955; d. President and Carrie Bell (Smith) Noiel; m. Lorenzo Ashford, Jr., Aug. 27, 1983; children: Elizabeth, Shay. BS in All-Level Speech/Drama, East Tex. State U., Commerce, 1978, MEd in Ednl. Adminstrn., 1993. Cert. tchr., instrnl. leadership, mid-mgmt. Tchr. reading, coach Lincoln H.S., Dallas, 1986-92; tchr. reading/lang. Pearl C. Anderson Mid. Sch., Dallas, 1992—; tchr. English II, speech Skyline H.S. Evening Acad., Dallas, 1994—; staff devel. assoc. Tng. and Devel., Dallas, 1993—; presenter Nat. Edn. Book Co., Birmingham, Ala., 1994; del. African Am. Child Placed in Crisis, Detroit, Mich. Named Miss Texarkana Ark., 1981, Miss Galaxy Internat. Youth Together Inc., Las Vegas, Nev., 1983, Miss Oak Cliff, City of Dallas, 1980; recipient Grad. Minortiy Scholarship East Tex. State U., Commerce, 1993. Mem. NAACP, ASCD, PTA, Internat. Reading Assn., Nat. Staff Devel. Coun., Classroom Tchrs. Dallas, Phi Delta Kappa, Alpha Kappa Alpha. Democrat. Baptist. Home: 6102 Waterway Dr Garland TX 75043

ASHFORD, EVELYN, former track and field athlete; m. Ray Washington; 1 child, Rana. Student, UCLA. Track and field athlete, 1976—. Competed in 1976 Olympics; winner 2 Gold medals, 1984 Olympics (Women's 100 Meters, Women's 4x100-Meter); winner Gold medal, 1988 Olympics (Women's 4x100-Meter); recipient Flo Hyman award Women's Sport Found., 1989; winner Gold medal, 1992 Olympics, Barcelona, Spain (4x100-Meter). Address: 818 N Plantation Ln Walnut CA 91789-1282*

ASHKIN, ROBERTA ELLEN, lawyer; b. N.Y.C., July 1, 1953; d. Sidney and Beverly Ashkin. BA magna cum laude, Hofstra U., 1975; JD, St. John's U., N.Y.C., 1978. Bar: N.Y., 1979, U.S. Dist. Ct. (ea. and so. dists.), 1980. Program dir. Sta. WVHC-FM, N.Y.C., 1974-75; assoc. editor Matthew Bender, N.Y.C., 1975-79; assoc. Morris & Duffy, N.Y.C., 1979-81, Lipsig, Sullivan & Liapakis, N.Y.C., 1981-84, Julien & Schlesinger, P.C., N.Y.C., 1984-89; adminstrv. law judge N.Y.C. Dept. Transp., 1988-92; ptnr. Trolman & Glaser, P.C., N.Y.C., 1991—. Chmn. bd. Actor's Classical Troupe, 1987-89. Mem. N.Y. State Bar Assn., Assn. Trial Lawyers Am., N.Y. Trial Lawyers Assn., Phi Beta Kappa.

ASHLEIGH, CAROLINE, art and antiques appraiser. BA, Worcester (Mass.) Coll., 1973; cert. in appraisal studies, NYU, 1994. Profl. lectr. The Community House, Birmingham, Mich., Village Club, Bloomfield Hills, Mich., Franklin (Mich.) Hist. Soc.; collectibles expert WJBK-TV2, Southfield, Mich.; columnist Detroit Monthly Mag.; edn. dept. staff Detroit Inst. Arts, 1988—; appraiser Frank H. Boos Appraisers & Auctioneers, Bloomfield Hills, 1993-96; regional rep. Leslie Hindman Auctioneers, Chgo., 1996—; appraiser Chubbs Antique Roadshow, WGBH-TV, Boston, 1996—; lectr. in field. Columnist Detroit Monthly, 1995-96. Mem. Detroit Inst. of Arts (mem. docent com. 1988—), Appraisers Assn. of Am., Nat. Mus. of Women in the Arts, Cranbrook Art Mus. Home: 344 W Brown St Birmingham MI 48009

ASHLEY, DARLENE JOY, psychologist; b. N.Y.C., Oct. 29, 1945; d. George Geiger and Ann Debra (Bernstein) Munzer; m. Joseph Michael O'Brien, Sept. 23, 1974 (div. June 1981); 1 child, Sundara Amber; m. Roy William Fagan, Aug. 16, 1991. BA with honors, Antioch Coll., 1966; MA, NYU, 1973; PhD, Calif. Grad. Sch. Family Psychology, San Rafael, 1987. Lic. clin. psychologist, Hawaii, Calif.; diplomate Am. Bd. Med. Psychotherapists; lic. marriage, family and child counselor, Calif.; cert. Calif. Community Coll. instr., biofeedback therapist, Biofeedback Cert. Inst. of Am. Psychology instr. Coll. of the Redwoods, 1977-82; instr. psychology North Am. Coll., San Rafael, 1980; cons., psychol. examiner Hawaii Bd. Edn., Hilo, 1982; lectr. U. Hawaii, Hilo and Manoa (Honolulu), 1982—; predoctoral clin. psychology intern Redwood Ctr., Berkeley, Calif., 1983-85; pvt. practice psychotherapy, San Rafael and Berkeley, 1985-87; pvt. practice psychology, Darlene Ashley, PhD and Assocs., Kailua Kona, Hawaii, 1988—; workshop presenter, 1977—; instr. psychology Coll. of Redwoods, Ft. Bragg, Calif., 1978-82; presenter AM-FM Sta. KMPO, Caspar, Calif., AMú-FM Sta. KKON, Kealakekua, Hawaii. Author: Voluntary Controls Training Handbook, 1982; author: (cassette) Deep Relaxation, 1983. Bd. dirs. Friends of Child Advocacy Ctr., 1995—; mem. Task Force on Worker's Compensation Reform for Hawaii, 1994-95; proponent Ho. bill pertaining to psychologists, 1988; mem. com. Rep. Virginia Isbell's Fundraiser, Kailua-Kona, 1988—. Recipient rsch. grant NSF, Mus. Natural History, N.Y.C., 1965, NIMH, NYU, 1968-70, fellowship NIMH, 1969, Outstanding Rsch. award Biofeedback Soc. Calif., 1987. Mem. APA, NAFE, Assn. Applied Psychophysiology and Biofeedback, Hawaii Psychol. Assn., Biofeedback/Behavioral Medicine Soc. Hawaii. Office: 75-5744 Alii Dr Ste 237 Kailua Kona HI 96740-1740

ASHLEY, ELIZABETH, actress; b. Ocala, Fla., Aug. 30, 1941; d. Arthur Kingman and Lucille (Ayer) Cole; m. George Peppard (div.); 1 son, Christian Moore; m. James Michael McCarthy. Student ballet with, Tatiana Semenova; student, La. State U., 1957-58; grad., Neighborhood Playhouse, N.Y.C., 1961. Apptd. Pres.'s council 1st Nat. Council on the Arts, 1965-69; dir. Am. Film Inst., 1968-72. Appeared on Broadway in The Highest Tree, 1961, Take Her, She's Mine, 1962, Barefoot in the Park, 1963; motion pictures include The Carpet Baggers, 1963, Ship of Fools, 1964, The Third Day, 1965, Marriage of a Young Stockbroker, 1971, Paperback Hero, 1974, Golden Needles, 1974, Rancho Deluxe, 1975, 92 in the Shade, 1976, The Great Scout and Cathouse Thursday, 1976, Coma, 1978, Windows, 1980, Paternity, 1981, Lookin' to Get Out, 1982, Split Image, 1982, Dragnet, 1987, Dangerous Curves, 1987, A Man of Passion, 1988, Vampire's Kiss, 1989, Mallrats, 1995; TV work includes (series) Evening Shade, CBS, 1990-94; TV movies include When Michael Calls, 1972, Second Chance, 1972, The Heist, 1972, Your Money or Your Wife, 1972, One of My Wives is Missing, 1976, The War Between the Tates, 1977, A Fire in the Sky, 1978, Svengali, 1983, Stage Coach, 1986, He's Fired, She's Hired, 1984, Warm Hearts, Cold Feet, 1987, The Two Mrs. Grenvilles, 1987, Orleans (series), The Rope, Blue Bayou, 1990, Reason for Living: The Jill Ireland Story, 1991, In the Best Interest of the Children, 1992, (mini series) The Buccaneers, 1995; stage appearances include The Enchanted, Washington, 1973, The Skin of Our Teeth, Washington, Broadway, 1975, Cat on a Hot Tin Roof, Stratford, Conn. and Broadway, 1974, Agnes of God; author: Postcards from the Road, 1978. Recipient Antoinette Perry award, 1962. Mem. Actors Equity, Screen Actors Guild, AFTRA. Office: Writers and Artists Agy 19 W 44th St Ste 1000 New York NY 10036*

ASHLEY, ELLA JANE (ELLA JANE RADER), medical technologist; b. Dewitt, Ark., Mar. 6, 1941; d. Clayton Ervin and Emma Mae (Coleman) Funderburk; m. Albert Ashley, Sept. 27, 1957 (div. Nov. 1962); 1 child, Cynthia Gayle. Student, Westark Community Coll. Cert. clin. lab. technologist, clin. lab. scientist. Lab. asst. U. Ark. Med. Ctr., Little Rock, 1966-67; lab. technician II Ark. State Hosp., Little Rock, 1967-68; staff technologist Cooper Clinic, Ft. Smith, Ark., 1969-71; asst. chief technologist Lab. of America (Labcorp), Ft. Smith, 1972—; mem. profl. adv. panel Med. Lab. Observer, 1976—. research in lithium carbonate. Mem. Am. Soc. Med. Technology. Lutheran. Home: 1310 S Houston St Fort Smith AR 72901-7271 Office: Labcorp 500 Lexington Ave Fort Smith AR 72901-4641

ASHLEY, LADELL CAROL, transportation executive; b. Monterey Park, Calif., Aug. 27, 1962; d. Bernard Eugene and Barbara Marie (Roksa) A. Diploma, Rosemead (Calif.) H.S., 1980. Firefighter Calif. Conservation Corps, Klamath, 1980-81; foreperson, deckhand Sterling Seafoods, Sitka, Alaska, 1982-84; deckhand Glacier Bay Lodge, Seattle, 1984; relief capt., chief mate Exploration Cruise lines, Seattle, 1985-88; relief capt. Pacific N.W. Explorer, Prince William Sound, Alaska, 1989; capt. Yachts Around, Seattle, 1990, YachtShip CruiseLines, Seattle, 1991-94; capt. Americas Cup Races, San Diego, 1992, Alaska Sea Charters, Valdez, Alaska, 1989. Democrat. Roman Catholic.

ASHLEY, LYNN, educator, consultant, administrator; b. Rock Island, Ill., Nov. 18, 1920; d. Francis Ford and Cleo Marguerite (Monahan) Haynes; m. Edward Messenger Ashley, Aug. 16, 1946; children: Edward Jr., Ann Rice, Rebecca Pocisk, William. BS in Social Psychology, Union Inst., Cin., 1978; MEd., U. Cin., 1979, EdD, 1985. Clk. Lumberman's Mutual Casualty Co., Chgo., 1940-41; account asst. Quaker Oats Co., Chgo., 1941-43; riveter Douglas Aircraft Co., Chgo., 1943-44; organizer, dir. Forest Park Youth Ctr., Forest Park, Ohio, 1967-73; staffing coord. Presbytery of Cin., 1973-78; grad. teaching asst. U. Cin., 1978-84; pres. Nat. Corrective Tng. Inst., Cin., 1979—; adj. faculty, mem. undergrad. studies bd. Union Inst., 1986—; cons. Hamilton County Probation Dept., Warren County Juvenile Ct., 1987—; field rep. Women in Mil. Svc. for Am.; trainer, cons. Allen County Juvenile Ct. Councilwoman City of Forest Park, 1981-85, organizer cmty. rels. coun., 1983; mem. Cin.-Harare, Zimbabwe Sister Cities Assn., 1989—; mem. Ohio Gov.'s Adv. Com. on Women Vets., 1993—. With WAC, 1944-46. Recipient in Recognition award Forest Park City Coun., 1985, In Appreciation award Union Inst., 1987, Recognition award AMVETS, U. Cin., 1993, award Commonwealth of Ky., 1989. Mem. Am. Corrections Assn., Nat. Assn. Corrective Tng. Affiliates (pres. 1987—), Women's Army Corp Vet. Assn., Assn. Family and Conciliation Cts., Am. Probation and Parole Assn. Office: Nat Corrective Tng Inst 811 Hanson Dr Forest Park OH 45240-1921

ASHLEY, RENEE, creative writing instructor, consultant; b. Palo Alto, Calif., Aug. 10, 1949. BA in English with spl. honors, San Francisco State U., 1979, BA in French, 1979, BA in World and Comparative Lit., 1979, MA, 1981. Instr. creative writing West Milford (N.J.) Cmty. Sch., 1983-85; creative writing instructor, cons. artist residencies Rockland Ctr. for Arts, West Nyack, N.Y., 1985—; adj. prof. English divsn. William Paterson Coll., comm. arts divsn. Ramapo Coll., Mahwah, N.J., 1989-93; vis. poet Geraldine R. Dodge Found., 1987—, Morris Area Coun. on Arts, 1989-91; on site evaluator N.J. State Coun. on Arts, 1989—, Bergen County (N.J.) Dept. Cultural and Hist. Affairs, 1990—; lectr. in field. Author: Salt, 1991 (Brittingham prize in Poetry 1991, Pushcart prize XVII spl. mention 1992-93); contbr. to anthologies including Touching Fire: Erotic Writings by Women, 1989, What's a Nice Girl Like You?, 1992, Breaking Up Is Hard to Do, 1994; contbr. to American Voice, Antioch Review, Harvard Review, others. Fellow N.J. State Coun. Arts, 1985, 89, 94, Yaddo, Saratoga Springs, N.Y., 1990, McDowell Colony, Peterborogh, N.H., 1993, 94; grantee Poets and Writers, Inc., 1986, N.Y. State Coun. Arts, 1986; recipient Washington prize in poetry Word Works, Inc., 1986, Lit. Excellence award, Kenyon Review, 1990, 92. Mem. MLA, Acad. Am. Poets, Poetry Soc. Am. (Ruth Lake Meml. award 1987, Robert H. Winner award 1989), Nat. Coun. Tchrs. English. Office: c/o Publicity Dir U Wis U Wis Press 114 N Murray Madison WI 53715*

ASHLEY, SHARON ANITA, pediatric anesthesiologist; b. Goulds, Fla., Dec. 28, 1948; d. John H. Ashley and Johnnie Mae (Everett) Ashley-Mitchell; m. Clifford K. Sessions, Sept. 1977 (div. 1985); children: Cecili, Nicole, Erika. BA, Lincoln U., 1970; postgrad., Pomona Coll., 1971; MD, Hahnemann Med. Sch., Phila., 1976. Diplomate Am. Bd. Pain Mgmt., Am. Bd. Anesthesiologists. Intern pediatrics Martin Luther King Hosp., L.A., 1976-77, resident pediatrics, 1977-78, resident anesthesiology, 1978-81, mem. staff, 1981—. Named Outstanding Tchr. of Yr., King Drew Med. Ctr., Dept. Anesthesia, 1989, Outstanding Faculty of Yr., 1991. Mem. Am. Soc. Anesthesiologists, Calif. Med. Assn., L.A. County Med. Soc., Soc. Regional Anesthesia, Soc. Pediatric Anesthesia. Democrat. Baptist. Office: Martin Luther King Hosp 12021 Wilmington Ave Los Angeles CA 90059-3019

ASHLEY-GILBERT, ANN AVA, gynecologist; b. Kendall, Fla., Dec. 28, 1948; d. John Henry Ashley and Johnnie Mae (Everett) Mitchell; m. George Gilbert, July 6, 1979 (div. June 1991); 1 child, Reyna; m. Pierre Eugene Biry, Sept. 28, 1991. BA, Lincoln U., Pa., 1970; MD, Jefferson Med. Coll., 1976. Diplomate Am. Bd. Ob-Gyn. Intern ob-gyn. Mt. Sinai Med. Ctr., Milw., 1976-77; resident ob-gyn. Martin Luther King Jr. Gen. Hosp., L.A., 1977-80; pvt. practice, Altamonte Springs, Fla., 1982—; mem. spkrs. bur. NIH, Washington, 1995. Bd. dirs. Am. Cancer Soc., Orlando, Fla., 1994—, Healthy Start, Seminole County, Fla., 1994—. Lt. (j.g.) USPHS, 1980-82. Recipient outstanding leadership award African Am. Student Union, U. Ctrl. Fla., 1991. Fellow ACOG; mem. Am. Assn. Gynecologic Laparoscopists, Fla. Med. Assn. (membership com. 1993, pres. 1993-95), Ctrl. Fla. Med. Soc. (pres. 1990). Democrat. Baptist. Office: Altamonte Women's Ctr 707 Ballard St Ste 1000 Altamonte Springs FL 32701

ASHLEY-LINDER, ANNETTE, dental consultant, educator; b. N.Y.C., May 2, 1942; d. Michael and Lee (Gorin) Ashley; m. Fredric Linder, Sept. 1, 1963; children: Elise, Joanna. A in Dental Hygiene, West Liberty State Coll., 1962; BS in Human Resources & Mgmt., Va. Commonwealth U., 1987. Registered dental hygienist. Dental hygienist N.Y., Fla., Va., 1963-94; pres., founder, CEO Capital Assocs. Dental Consulting, Richmond, Va., 1987—; internat. cons. for various dental practices in U.S. and Can.; internat. lectr., clinician ADA, Internat. World Dental Congress, others. Contbr. articles to profl. jours. Mem. Am. Acad. Dental Practice Adminstrn., Va. Dental Hygienists Assn., Dental Hygienists Assn.

ASHTON, BARBARA GRANT, system engineer; b. N.Y.C.. Student, SUNY, Stony Brook, 1965-67; BA in Math. and Philosophy, N.Mex. Highlands U., 1970, MA in Math., 1971; MBA, Golden Gate U., 1986. Sys. engr./programmer Deering-Milliken, Inc., Spartanburg, S.C., 1973-76; project leader/programmer USA Info. Processing Levi Strauss & Co., San Francisco, 1976-80, womenswear divsn. sys. mgr. USA Info. Processing, 1980-82; ops. sys. mgr. USA Info. Processing Levi Strauss & Co., San Francisco and Dallas, 1982-86; dir. USA Info. Processing Levi Strauss & Co., San Francisco, 1986-89; dir. Info. Resources, European divsn. Levi Strauss & Co., Brussels, 1989-94, project mgr. USA Customer Svc. Supply Chain, 1994-95; mem., educator Common and Guide, 1980-83; founding mem., mem. steering com. Textile Apparel Linkage Coun., 1986-89. Contbr. articles to profl. jours. Chair social action com. First Unitarian Ch., San Francisco, 1983-86; mem. Nat. Ovarian Cancer Coalition, 1996. Mem. Project Mgmt. Inst. Home: Rue du Charme 79, Brussels Belgium 1190

ASHTON, BETSY FINLEY, broadcast journalist, author, lecturer; b. Wilkes-Barre, Pa., May 13, 1944; d. Charles Leonard Hancock Jones and Margaretta Betty (Hart) Jones Layton; m. Arthur Benner Ashton, Nov. 5, 1966 (div. 1972); m. Robert Clarke Freed, May 18, 1974 (div. 1981); m. Jacob B. Underhill III, Oct. 17, 1987. BA, Am. U., 1966, postgrad. in fine arts, 1969-71; student in painting, Corcoran Sch. Art, 1968. Tchr. art Fairfax County (Va.) Pub. Schs., 1967-70; reporter, anchor Sta. WWDC, Washington, 1972-73, Sta. WMAL-AM-FM, Washington, 1973-75; corr. Sta. WTTG-TV, Washington, 1975-76, Sta. WJLA-TV, Washington, 1976-82; consumer corr. CBS News and Sta. WCBS-TV, N.Y.C., 1982-86; sr. corr. Today's Bus., 1986-87; personal fin. contbr. CBS Morning Program, 1987, Lifetime Cable TV, 1988—; anchor FNN Money Talk, 1989; bd. dirs. Lowell E. Mellett Fund for a Free and Responsible Press, Washington, 1979-82; courtroom artist numerous trials, Washington, 1978-81. Reporter TV news report Caffeine, 1981 (AAUW award 1982); reporter spot news 6 P.M. News, 1979 (Emmy award); author: Betsy Ashton's Guide to Living on Your Own, 1988. Concert master of ceremonies Beethoven Soc., Washington, 1979-82. Recipient Laurel award Columbia Journalism Rev., 1984, Outstanding Alumna award Am. U., 1985, Outstanding Media award Am. U., 1986, Best Consumer Journalism citation Nat. Press Club, 1983. Mem. Soc. Profl. Journalists (nat. bd. dirs. 1996—, pres. N.Y. chpt. 1994, Washington chpt. 1980-81, bd. dirs. N.Y. chpt. 1989—), Friends of Thirteen (bd. dirs. 1995—), Alpha Chi Omega (v.p. chpt. 1964-66). Episcopalian.

ASHTON, ELIZABETH ANN, information industry manager; b. Washington, Jan. 16, 1947; d. Robert H. Snedeker and Harriett Leeds (DePriest) Miller; m. Terry E. Naylor, May 11, 1985. BA, UCLA, 1968; spl. cert., Keio U., Tokyo, 1970; MA, U. So. Calif., 1972, PhD, 1977. Japanese market mgr. System Devel. Corp., Santa Monica, Calif., 1977-81; sales mgr. Lexis-Nexis, Dayton, Ohio, 1981-90; product mgr. Lexis-Nexis, N.Y.C., 1991—. Mem. NAFE, NOW, UCLA Alumni Assn. Democrat. Congregationalist. Home: 9643 Bridlewood Trl Dayton OH 45458 Office: Lexis-Nexis PO Box 933 Dayton OH 45401-0933

ASHTON, JEAN WILLOUGHBY, library director; b. Detroit, Mar. 1, 1938; d. Gerald Woodrow and Dorothy (McEwen) Willoughby; m. Robert William Ashton, Mar. 30, 1960; children: Katherine, Susanna, Emily, Isabel. BA, U. Mich., 1959; MA, Radcliffe Coll., 1961; PhD, Columbia U., 1970; MLS, Rutgers U., 1985. Lectr. Fisk U., Nashville, 1962-64; asst. prof. English L.I. U., Bklyn., 1969-73; reference libr. N.Y. Hist. Soc., N.Y.C., 1984-87, assoc. libr. pub. svcs., 1987-89, acting libr., 1989-90, dir. libr., 1990-93; dir. rare books and manuscripts libr. Columbia U., N.Y.C., 1993—; vis. lectr. N.Y. area Colls., 1976-80; lectr. N.Y. Coun. for the Humanities, 1988-92; coord. Comm. for Resources in N.Y. History, 1987-90. Author: (book) Harriet Beecher Stowe: A Reference Guide, 1976; contbr. articles to N.Y. Times, Am. Lit. Realism, Prospects, Magill's Lit. Ann., New Bklyn., Imprint, Biblion, RQ. Vol. BAM Theater Co., Bklyn., 1980-81; mem. bd. govs. Rsch. Librs. Group, 1989-91.; mem. Metro Adminstrv. Svcs. Com., 1990-92. Recipient Avery Hopwood Writing award U. Mich., 1959; Woodrow Wilson fellow Woodrow Wilson Found., 1959; faculty scholar Columbia U., 1966-67. Mem. ALA, Am. Printing History Assn., Bibliog. Soc. Am., Soc. History Authorship, Readership and Pub. Librs., The Grolier Club. Home: 300 W 108th St Apt 14 B New York NY 10025 Office: Rare Book and Manuscript Libr Columbia U 535 W 114th St New York NY 10027-7029

ASHTON, SISTER MARY MADONNA, healthcare administrator; b. St. Paul; d. Avon B. and Ruth (Fehring) A. BA, Coll. St. Catherine, St. Paul, 1944; LHD (hon.), Coll. St. Catherine, 1996; MSW, St. Louis U., 1946; MHA, U. Minn., 1958. Joined Congregation Sisters of St. Joseph of Carondelet, Roman Cath. Ch., 1946. Dir. med. social service dept. St. Joseph's Hosp., St. Paul, 1949-56; dir. out-patient dept. St. Mary's Hosp., Mpls., 1958-59; asst. adminstr. St. Mary's Hosp., 1959-62, adminstr., 1962-68, exec. v.p., 1968-72, pres., 1972-82; commr. health State of Minn., 1983-91; pres. Carondelet LifeCare Ministries, St. Paul, 1991—; dir. Client Security Bd. of Minn. Supreme Ct., 1993—, St. Catherine's Coll., St. Paul; mem. bd. sci. counselors Nat. Cancer Inst. Recipient Sabra Hamilton award Program in Hosp. Adminstrn. U. Minn., 1958; Minn. Health Citizen of Yr. award, 1977, Gaylord Anderson Leadership award, 1988; Bush summer fellow Harvard Sch. Bus., 1976. Fellow Am. Coll. Healthcare Execs.; mem. Nat. Cath. Health Assn. (sec.). Home: 5101 W 70th St Apt 120 Minneapolis MN 55439-2105 Office: Carondelet LifeCare 1884 Randolph Ave Saint Paul MN 55105-1747

ASHTON, RITA L., retired manufacturing company professional; b. Shelbyville, Ky.; d. Edward and Bernice (Simpson) Clark; children: Lee Ann Butler, Eddie Burton; stepchildren: Mike Butler, Steve Butler; m. Herbert Ashton; stepchildren: David, Herbie. With Cricketeer Mfg., Harrodsburg, Ky., Jonothan Logan, Harrodsburg; substitution clk. Am. Greeting Corp., 1968-73; with Corning Glass, Harrodsburg, 1978-92. Author, pub.: Lumix Finds Calley a Home (Golden Poet award Eddie Lou Cole Poetry, Pres.'s award for excellence in lit. works Nat. Authors Registry 1994); contbr. poetry to pubs.

ASHTON, ROSE MARY, elementary school educator; b. Washington, May 9, 1959; d. Clarence Nelson and Rose Marie (Sansalone) Beck; m. James Douglas Ashton, Nov. 28, 1980; children: Joshua David, Zachary Daniel, Rebekah Rose, Michael Thomas. BA, Mary Baldwin Coll., 1994. Tchrs. aide St. Johns Child Devel. Ctr., Washington, 1978-79, Farrell Montessori Sch., Bethesda, Md., 1979-80, Brookmont Learning Tree, Bethesda, 1979-80; substitute tchr. Bedford (Va.) County Pub. Schs., 1992—; tchr. 2d grade Huddleston (Va.) Elem. Sch., 1995—; advisor Supts. Parent Adv. Coun., Bedford, 1994—; tutor elem. lang. arts, Moneta, Va., 1994; curriculum devel. com. mem. Huddleston Elem. Sch., 1995, tchr. rep. PTA, 1995. Treas. Parent Involvement Com., Huddleston, Va., 1993—; coach Odyssey of the Mind, Huddleston, 1994; Sunday sch. tchr. Mentow Bapt. Ch., Huddleston, 1992—; mem. hospitality com. PTA. Mem. ASCD, Nat. Coun. of Tchrs. of English, Psi Chi. Home: RR 1 Box 43 Moneta VA 24121-9707

ASHTON-BAGSHAW, MARIA CHRISTINE, law librarian; b. St. Paul, Nov. 14, 1968; d. Frank A. and Dorothy A. (Lee) Ashton; m. Troy Daniel Bagshaw, Aug. 17, 1991. BA, Bowling Green State U., 1991; postgrad., Kent State U. Dep. clk. Painesville (Ohio) Mcpl. Ct., 1991-94; asst. law libr. Lake County Libr. Assn., Painesville, 1994—. Vol. Madison (Ohio) Thanksgiving Cmty. Dinner, 1989-94, Madison Christmas Basket Program, 1993—; active Nat. Trust Hist. Preservation, 1992-94. Mem. Ohio Regional Assn. Law Librs, Bowling Green State U. Alumni Assn., Phi Kappa Phi, Phi Alpha Theta, Phi Beta Kappa (XI chpt.). Democrat. Roman Catholic. Home: 6882 S Ridge Rd Unionville OH 44088 Office: Lake County Law Libr Assn 47 N Park Pl Painesville OH 44077

ASKEW, PAMELA, art history educator, retired; b. Poughkeepsie, N.Y., Feb. 2, 1925; d. Ralph Kirk and Constance (Atwood) A. BA, Vassar Coll., 1946; MA, NYU, 1951; PhD, U. London, 1954. Instr. Vassar Coll., Poughkeepsie, N.Y., 1950-51, 54-57, curator, art gallery, 1956-59, asst. prof., 1957-62, assoc. prof., 1962-69, prof., 1969-85, prof. emeritus, 1985—. Author: Caravaggio's Death of the Virgin, 1990. Mem. Coll. Art Assn. (bd. dirs. 1970s, Disting. Tchg. of Art History award 1988), Am. Soc. for Sixteenth Century Studies, Renaissance Soc. of Am., others. Home: Valley Farm Rd Rte 3 Box 422 Millbrook NY 12545

ASKEY, THELMA J., legislative staff member; b. Lakehurst, N.J.. BA, Tenn. Tech. U., 1970; postgrad., George Washington U., Am. U. Press asst. Rep. John Duncan, 1972-74; editor The Nat. Rsch. Coun. Marine Bd., 1974-76; asst. minority trade counsel Ho. Com. Ways and Means, 1976-79, minority trade counsel, 1979—. Office: 1106 Longworth House Office Bldg Washington DC 20515

ASKIN, MARILYN, lawyer; b. N.Y.C.; d. Simon and Lena (Merker) Klein; m. Frank Askin, Aug. 6, 1960; children: Andrea, Jonathan, Daniel. B.S. in Edn., CCNY, 1954; postgrad. Russian Inst., Columbia U., 1958-60; J.D., Rutgers U., 1970. Bar: N.J. 1970. U.S. Dist. Ct. N.J. 1970, U.S. Supreme Ct. 1977, N.Y. 1983; cert. in elder law, 1995. Journalist The Record, Hackensck, N.J., 1956-62; tchr. high sch. English, Newark, 1964-67; regional dir. Am. Jewish Congress, Newark, 1971-76; counsel Pub. Documents Com., Washington, 1976-77; sr. atty. Essex Newark Legal Services, Orange, N.J., 1978-93; of counsel, Fein, Such, Kahn & Shepard, Parsippany, N.J., 1993-95; lectr. Inst. Continuing Legal Edn., 1983, 87—; adj. faculty Rutgers Law Sch., 1984—; mem. ethics com. Supreme Ct. Dist., 1985—, adj. faculty Seton Hall U. Law Sch., 1992—; mem. Supreme Ct. Com. on Rels. with Media, 1990—, Supreme Ct. Com. on Women in the Cts., 1994—; Editl. bd. N.J. Lawyer Mag., 1987—. Rev. bd. Children in Placement, Essex County, 1980—; bd. trustees Chr-Ill. (home health non-profit), 1983—. Author: ABC's of Elder Law, 1990, Elder Law, 1993, Elder Law Made Easy!, 1995, Long-Term Care Insurance, 1995, Reverse Mortgages, 1993, Nursing Home Residents As Clients, 1994. Mem. Nat. Acad. Elder Law Attys.Essex County Bar Assn. (chair com. on rights of elderly 1981—), N.J. State Bar Assn. (chair aging and the law com. 1985-89), N.J. Women Lawyers, Essex County Women Lawyers (pres. 1989-91), Nat. Legal Aid and Defender Assn. (chair sr. citizen sect. 1986-89), Rutgers Law Sch. Alumni Assn. (pres. 1993-94). Office: 193 Zeppi Ln West Orange NJ 07052-4129

ASKOV, EUNICE MAY, education educator; b. St. Louis, Nov. 20, 1940; d. David Hull and Marjorie Jane (Gutgsell) Nicholson; m. Warren Hopkins Askov, Jan. 22, 1967; children: David, Karen. BA in English, Denison U., 1962; MA in English, U. Wis., 1966, PhD in Curriculum and Instrn., 1969. English and reading tchr. Rich Twp. High Sch., Park Forest, Ill., 1962-64; reading svc. reading specialist U. Wis., Madison, 1965-66, project asst. Wis. R & D Ctr. for Cognitive Learning, 1966-67, rsch. assoc., 1969-72, lectr. dept. curriculum and instrn., 1968-69; coord. adult basic edn. programs U. Wis. Extension, 1966-67; remedial reading specialist Lincoln Jr. High Sch., Madison, 1966; adult basic edn. tchr. Madison Vocat., Tech. and Adult Schs., 1967-68; asst. prof. elem. edn. Minn. State U., Bemidji, 1972-74; assoc. prof. Pa. State U., University Park, 1974-79, prof., 1980—; presenter seminars on adult edn., Germany, 1986, 93; cons., speaker in field; mem. editorial bd. Jour. Ednl. Rsch., Adult Basic Edn., Am. Reading Forum Yearbook; mem. steering com. Adult Literacy and Tech.; memory and cognitive processes program reviewer NSF; mem. panel nat. work group on cancer and literacy Nat. Cancer Inst.; workshop leader Pa. Right to Read; organizer, coord. Pa. State Coalition for Adult Literacy; mem. adv. coun. Pa. State Libr. Workplace. Contbr. articles to profl. publs. Mem. celebration com. Pa., Yes!, 1990; mem. Pa. task force Project Literacy U.S.; adv. mem. goal 5 task force Pa. 2000. Fulbright sr. scholar, 1983; Literacy Leader fellow Nat. Inst. for Literacy, 1994-95. Mem. ASCD, Am. Assn. Adult and Continuing Edn. (chair, mem. various coms., bd. dirs.), Am. Edn. Rsch. Assn., Nat. Reading Conf. (chair, organizer symposia), Nat. Clearinghouse Literary Edn. (adv. bd.), Internat. Reading Assn. (chair, mem. various coms.), Keystone State Reading Assn. (mem. adult lit. com., chair rsch. com., pres. disabled reader spl. interest coun. Pa.), Mid-State Literacy Coun. (bd. dirs., pers. com., long range planning com.), Mid-State Reading Coun. (pres.), Nat. Coun. Tchrs. English, Pa. Assn. Adult and Continuing Edn., Phi Beta Kappa, Phi Delta Kappa. Democrat. Methodist. Office: Pa State U Inst for Study Adult Lit 204 E Calder Way Ste 209 State College PA 16801-4756

ASPERÍLLA, PURITA FALGUI, retired nursing administrator; b. Manila, Aug. 21; came to U.S., 1968; d. Cirilo and Casimira (Falgui) A. Grad. nurse, U. Philippines, 1941, BSN, 1952; MSN, Case Western Res. U., 1956; MEd, Columbia U., 1970, EdD, 1971. RN, N.Y. Head nurse Philippine Gen. Hosp., Manila, 1941-45; coord. clin. Coll. Nursing Manila Cen. U., Caloocan City, The Philippines, 1951-53; dean, prof. Manila Cen. U., Caloocan City, 1954-59; dean, prof. U. of the East/Ramon Magsaysay Meml. Med. Ctr. Coll. Nursing, Quezon City, Philippines, 1959-70, DON,, 1959-64; asst. dean Phillips-Beth Israel Sch. Nursing, N.Y.C., 1971-86. Mem. Ladies of Charity, N.Y. Archdiocese, 1991—; vol. Immaculate Conception Parish, N.Y.C., 1979—. Internat. Coop. Adminstrn. fellow Dept. Health and Human Svcs., 1955-56; fellowship grantee China Med. Bd., 1965-66, study grantee, 1969-70. Mem. ANA, Nat. League Nursing, Nursing Edn. Alumni Assn. Columbia U., Philippine Nurses Assn. N.Y. (adviser 1971—), Philippine Nurses Assn. Am. (founding adviser 1979—), Philippine Nurses Assn. (Philippines; exec. v.p. 1966-68), Philippine Nurses Assn. N.J. (adviser 1974—), U. of East Nursing Alumni Assn. U.S. (adviser 1984—). Democrat. Roman Catholic. Home: 333 E 14th St Apt 3A New York NY 10003-4209

ASPINALL, MARA GLICKMAN, marketing and general management professional; b. N.Y.C., Aug. 14; d. Alvin and Betty Glickman. BA, Tufts U., 1983; MBA, Harvard U., 1987. Assoc. First Boston Corp., N.Y.C., 1986; cons. Bain & Co., Inc., Boston, 1987-90; dir. mktg., client svcs. Hale and Dorr, Boston, 1990—. Mem. editorial bd. Rainmaker's Quar. Chmn. Am. Cancer Soc., Mass., 1996—; bd. assocs. Arts Boston; mem. corp. exec. coun. WGBH. Mem. Nat. Assn. Law Firm Mktg. (pres. New Eng.), Assn. Tufts Alumnae (pres. 1988-90, 92-94, alumni trustee rep. bd. trustees), Harvard Bus. Sch. Assn. (chairperson reunion com.). Office: Hale and Dorr 60 State St Boston MA 02109-1801

ASTAIRE, CAROL ANNE TAYLOR, artist, educator; b. Long Beach, Calif., Aug. 26, 1947; d. John Clinton and Carolyn Sophie (Wright) Taylor; m. Frederic Astaire, Jr., Feb. 14, 1971; children: John Carroll, Johanna Carolyn. BFA, UCLA, 1969; grad. summer studies, Salzburg Summer Sch., Klessheim, Austria, 1969; cert. secondary sch. tchr., Calif. State U., Long Beach, 1971; postgrad., Calif. Polytechnic State U., San Luis Obispo, 1986-87. Cert. secondary sch. tchr. life, Calif. Tchr., tutor, cons. art edn. San Luis Coastal Unified Sch. Dist., San Luis Obispo, 1980-89. Author: (book) Left Handed Poetry from the Heart, 1993; artist: work in permanent collections. Yergeau Musée Internat. Art, Montreal, Can., 1991, Travis (Calif.) AFB Mus., 1990. Founder, trustee, San Luis Coastal Unified Sch. Dist./Found. Arts Art Core, 1988-92; mem. adv. coun. Coastal Comty. Edn. and Svcs., San Luis Obsipo, 1989-92, screening com. UCLA Alumni scholarship, 1993-95. Nat. finalist Kodak Internat. Newspaper Snapshot award, 1993. Mem. Nat. Mus. of Women in Arts (charter), Fine Arts Coun., San Luis Obispo Art Ctr., San Luis Obispo Art Coun., Oil Pastel Acrylic Group Brushstrokes (hon. mention 1994), Ctrl. Coast Watercolor Soc., Ctrl. Coast Photo. Soc. Republican. Episcopalian.

ASTER, RUTH MARIE RHYDDERCH, business owner; b. Cleve., Aug. 15, 1939; d. Roy William and Ruth Marie (Teckmeyer) Rhydderch; m. Ferdinand Aster, Nov. 23, 1963; children: Anneliese Ruth Aster Wilt, Christian Josef Roy. Student, Cooper Sch. Art, 1956-57; BS, Kent State U., 1962. Art tchr. North Olmsted (Ohio) Jr. and High Sch., 1962; art dept. chmn. Andrews Sch. for Girls, Willoughby, Ohio, 1963-64; co-owner, treas. Aster Cabinet Shop, Chesterland, Ohio, 1963—; co-owner, v.p., treas. Ferdl Aster Ski Sch., Chesterland, 1964—; owner, v.p., sec., treas. Ferdl Aster Ski Shop, Chesterland, 1972—; owner, v.p., advt. designer, fashion buyer, tour advisor Ferdl Aster Sport Ctr., Chesterland, 1985—; chmn. region IV U.S. Ski Assn., Colorado Springs, Colo., 1980-84, Alpine ofcl., 1983-88; ski racing coach U.S. Ski Coaches Assn., Park City, Utah, 1980-89; adv. bd. First County Bank, Chesterland, 1992—; adv. coun. U.S. Postal Svc., Chesterland, 1993—. Exhibited paintings and photographs to various shows, 1963-93. Creator blind ski program Cleve. (Ohio) Sight Ctr., 1969; pres., trustee Chesterland (Ohio) Hist. Found., 1986—; chair, vice chair, commr. Chester Twp. Zoning Com., Chesterland, 1987—; life friend Friends of Geauga West Libr., 1989—; mem. Rep. Ctrl. Com., 1996. Mem. Internat. Platform Assn., Chesterland C. of C. (pres., v.p., treas., trustee, Bus. Person of Yr. 1993), Cmty. Improvement Corp. Geauga County (re-organ. com., nominating com., trustee), North Ea. Ohio Ski Retailers Assn. (bd. mem. 1987—), Kent State U. (life mem.), Silver Reunion Com. (bd. mem., v.p.), Chi Omega, Alpha Psi Omega, Gamma Delta. Lutheran. Office: Ferdl Aster Ski Shop 8330 Mayfield Rd Chesterland OH 44026-2520

ASTONE, ANNETTE MARIE, secondary education educator; b. Sharon, Pa., Nov. 12, 1960; d. Joseph Louis and Helen Katherine (Janosko) A. Student, Pa. State U., 1983-85; BE, Edinboro (Pa.) U., 1989; MS in Edn., Youngstown (Ohio) U., 1996. Math. tchr. Farrell (Pa.) Area Sch. Dist., 1990—; advisor student coun., head math. dept., 1992—. Mem. NEA, Pa. State Edn. Assn. Home: 919 Park Ave Farrell PA 16121 Office: Farrell Area Sch Dist 1660 Roemer Blvd Farrell PA 16121

ASTOR, BROOKE, foundation administrator, philanthropist, writer; b. Portsmouth, N.H.; d. John Henry and Mabel (Howard) Russell; m. Vincent Astor. LLD (hon.), Columbia U., 1971, Brown U., 1980; LHD (hon.), Fordham U., 1980, NYU, 1986; PhD in Biomed. Sci. (honoris causa), Rockefeller U., 1986. Pres., trustee Astor Home for Children; trustee Hist. Hudson Valley, Marconi Internat. Fellowship; trustee and hon. chmn., mem. devel. com., mem. exec. com. N.Y. Pub. Libr., N.Y.C.; life trustee, mem. conservation com. N.Y. Zool. Soc.; trustee emeritus, mem. coun. of fellows Pierpont Morgan Libr.; trustee emeritus, chmn. vis. com. dept. Asian art, mem. acquisitions com., exec. com. ex officio Met. Mus. Art, N.Y.C.; life trustee Rockefeller U. Author: Patchwork Child, 1962, rev. edit., 1993, The Bluebird Is at Home, 1965, Footprints, 1980, The Last Blossom on the Plum Tree, 1986; feature editor: House and Garden, 1946-56, cons. editor, 1956-93. Mem. N.Y. State Pk. Commn., 1967-69. Decorated dame Venerable Order of St. John of Jerusalem; recipient Anniversary medal Astor, Lenox and Tilden Founds. of N.Y. Pub. Libr., 1961, award Sisters of Good Shepherd and Children of Madonna Heights Sch. for Girls, 1963, Client Award cert. N.Y. State Assn. Architects, 1964, award Pk. Assn. N.Y.C. Inc., 1965, Honor award HUD, 1966, cert. of appreciation City of N.Y., 1967, Albert S. Bard Merit award City Club N.Y., 1967, Award of Honor, Women's Aux. N.Y. chpt. AIA, 1968, Rector's award St. Phillip's Ch., 1968, Michael Friedsam medal Archtl. League N.Y., 1968, award Brotherhood-In-Action, Inc., 1968, Outstanding Contbn. award Am. Soc. Landscape Architects, 1968, Spirit of Achievement award Albert Einstein Coll. Medicine, Yeshiva U., 1969, Good Samaritan award P. Ballentine & Sons, 1969, Good Samaritan award Prospect Block Civic Assn., 1969, Disting. Svc. award N.Y. region Rotary, 1970, YWCA honor, 1970, Housing award N.Y. Met. chpt. Nat. Assn. Housing and Redevel. Officials, 1971, $24 award Mus. City of N.Y., award N.Y. Pub. Libr., 1972, Albert Gallatin medal NYU, 1972, spl. citation AIA, 1973, Medal of Merit award Lotos Club, 1973, commendation Neighborhood Com. for the Asphalt Green, 1975, commendation ARCS Found., 1976, Pres.'s medal Mcpl. Art Soc. N.Y., 1976, Gold Medal award N.Y. Zool. Soc., 1978, Elizabeth Seton Humanitarian award N.Y. Foundling Hosp., 1978, Little Apple award Met. Mus. Art, Little Apple award Morgan Library, Little Apple award N.Y. Public Library, Little Apple award N.Y. Zool. Soc., Little Apple award Rockefeller U., Little Apple award South St. Seaport and Sta. WNET-TV/Channel 13, 1978, New Yorker for N.Y. award Citizens Com. for N.Y.C., 1980, 1st Myer Myers Cultural award City of N.Y., award Citizens Housing and Planning Coun., 1980, Bishop's Cross, Diocese of N.Y., 1980, Forsythia award Bklyn. Bot. Garden, 1981, award Pks. Coun., 1981, Woman of Conscience award Appeal of Conscience Found., 1981, commendation Lower Manhattan Cultural Coun., 1984, Disting. New Yorkers award Bowery Savs. Bank, 1984, Gov.'s Arts award State of N.Y., 1985, Am. Acad. and Inst. Arts and Letters award, 1986, Marconi Internat. Fellowship Coun. award, 1986, landmark plaque and medallion N.Y. Landmarks Preservation Found., 1987, Gold medal St. Nicholas Soc., N.Y.C., 1987, Fashion Industry award Coun. of Fashion Designers Am., 1988, Presdl. Citizen's medal Pres. Reagan, 1988, Nat. Medal of Arts, Nat. Endowment for the Arts, 1988, World Monuments Fund The Hadrian award, 1991, annual humanitarian award ARC of Greater N.Y., 1993, Eleanor Roosevelt medallion City of N.Y., 1993, 8th Annual Town & Country Most Generous American award, The Hearst Corp. and Hearst Mags., 1993, The Mayor's award of Honor and Culture, City of N.Y., 1993, 10th Annual Humanitarian award N.Y., 1993, Richard Rodgers award for Disting. Svc., Profl. Children's Sch., 1994, Scroll of Honor, N.Y. coun. Navy League of U.S., 1994; Brooke Astor Day proclaimed by Mayor of N.Y.C., March 5, 1992. Fellow Am. Acad. Arts and Scis.; mem. Mcpl. Art Soc. N.Y., Pilgrims U.S., Venerable Order St. John of Jerusalem (dame), The Century Assn., Colony Club, Knickerbocker Club, N.Y. Yacht Club, Sleepy Hollow Country Club. Office: The Vincent Astor Found 405 Park Ave New York NY 10022-4405

ASTUCCIO, SHEILA MARGARET, educational administrator; b. Biddeford, Maine, Apr. 24, 1943; d. James T. III and Margaret H. (Cameron) Rollinson; m. Joseph Kevin Astuccio, Aug. 22, 1976 (dec. Apr. 1992); children: James M., Sheila E. BS in Edn., Salem (Mass.) State Coll., 1968, MEd, 1975; cert. advanced grad. studies, Lesley Coll., Cambridge, Mass., 1983. Cert. elem. tchr. and prin., supr., dir., Mass. Elem. educator Hood Elem. Sch., Lynn, Mass., 1968-79; tchr. grades 3 and 4 Lynn (Mass.) Pub. Schs., comp. coord., facilitator, 1981-84, tchr. academically talented, 1979-81, 84-85, computer program specialist, 1986-87, computer implementation team leader, MIS dir., 1987—; owner operator Pilot Imaging Computer Imaging, Lynn, Mass., 1991-92; tchr. adult edn. North Shore C.C., 1982-87; part-time real estate broker, 1979—; part-time mktg. cons. IDN, 1993-95. Mem. Chpt. II adv. coun., 1979-83; nat. grad. alumni rep. Lesley Coll., 1984-85; chair Mayor's Computer Adv. Com., 1985-86; participant Educators in Industry GE/Salem State Coll., 1983. Recipient Educators in Industry cert., 1983, Novell Netware Adminstr. and Sys. Installation/Configuration certs., 1994-95; Chpt. II grantee, 1984. Mem. ASCD, AAUW, NAFE, NSBA, DECUS, PEI Nat. Users Group, New Eng. Pentamation Users Group, Boston Computer Soc. Office: Data Center LVTI 80 Neptune Blvd Lynn MA 01902 also: PO Box 2613 South Hamilton MA 01982-0613

ASWAD, BARBARA, anthropology educator; b. Kalamazoo, Mich., Jan. 5, 1937; d. Robert Theodore and Helen Hoffman (Going) Black; m. Ahmed Adnan Aswad, Sept. 15, 1962; 1 child, Samir. PhD, U. Mich., 1968. Prof. anthropology Wayne State U., Detroit, 1966—. Co-editor: Family & Gender Among Muslims in America, 1996; editor: Arabic Speaking Communities in America, 1974; contbr. articles to profl. jours. Bd. dirs. Arab Cmty. Ctr. Econ. & Social Svcs., Dearborn, Mich., 1972-96. Fulbright grantee, 1965; recipient Alumni Svc. award Wayne State U., 1994, Arab of Yr. Svc. award Arab Cmty. Ctr. Econ. & Social Svcs., 1996. Fellow Am. Anthrop. Assn., Middle East Studies Assn. (pres. 1991-92). Office: Wayne State U Dept Anthropology Detroit MI 48202

ASWAD, BETSY (BETSY BECKER), writer; b. Binghamton, N.Y., Feb. 10, 1939; d. George Marrinan and Jane (Sprout) Becker; m. Richard N. Aswad, Sept. 22, 1962; children: Jem, Kristin. B.A.in English with honors, Harpur Coll., Binghamton; M.A., SUNY, Binghamton, 1965, Ph.D. with distinction, 1973. Mem. film editing staff Sta. WNBF-TV, Binghamton, 1957; apprentice So. Tier Playhouse, summers 1957, 58; asst. editor Link Log, 1962-63; from teaching asst. to instr. English SUNY, Binghamton, 1963-74, mem. adj. faculty, 1974-83, fellow Coll.-in-the Woods, 1973. Author: Winds of the Old Days (Edgar Allan Poe spl. award Mystery Writers Am.), 1980, paperback edit., 1983; Family Passions, 1985. Sec., Friends of Binghamton Pub. Libr., 1977-78; vol. Probe, Binghamton Gen. Hosp., 1978-79, Meals on Wheels, 1979-82, St. Mary's Soup Kitchen, 1983—, Binghamton Downtown Forum, 1986—. Mem. Women's Nat. Book Assn. (hon. 1986). Home: 201 Deyo Hill Rd Johnson City NY 13790-5109

ATAMIAN, SUSAN, nurse; b. Cambridge, Mass., Sept. 14, 1950; d. Raymond H. and Alice (Chakerian) A. BA, Simmons Coll., 1972, MS, 1995. RN, Mass.; cert. infection control. Staff nurse Mass. Gen. Hosp., Boston, 1972-74, pvt. duty nurse, 1975-76, staff nurse, 1976-77; rsch. asst. III U. Cinn. Hosp., 1980-81; rsch. study nurse Mass. Gen. Hosp., Boston, 1977-80, instr. nursing, 1982-84, sr. rsch. study nurse, 1984-87, dir. clin. rsch. nurse group, 1985-90, infection control nurse, 1988-90; infection control nurse clinician Mass. Gen. Hosp., Boston, 1990-92; staff nurse Kimberly Nurses, Orange, Calif., 1982; coord., clin. rsch., vascular surg. div. Mass. Gen. Hosp., 1992—; cons. nutrition and liver diseases, McGaw Labs., Santa Ana, Calif., 1980-81; chmn. faculty devel. libr. com. Shepard Gill Sch., Boston, 1983-84; mem. rsch. nurses forum, Mass. Gen. Hosp., 1992—. Class agt. 1972 Simmons Coll., 1972, 86—, mem. com. alumnae fund, 1987-89, reunion com., 1990—, com. on classes, 1991-92, class of 1972 reunion fund chair, 1991-92. Mem. ANA, Am. Nurses Fund. Century Club, Assn. Practitioners Infection Control, Soc. for Vascular Nursing, Mass. Nurses Assn., Rsch. Nurses Forum Mass. Gen. Hosp., Simmons Coll. Nursing Honor Soc., Simmons Club Boston (bd. dirs. 1988-90, v.p. 1990-92, co-chmn. boutique 1992-94, mem. nominating com. 1994-95), Coun. Armenian Am. Nurses (chair resource com.), Sigma Theta Tau. Mem. Armenian Apostolic Ch. Office: Mass Gen Hosp Wang Acc Ste 458 Boston MA 02114

ATCHINSON, JUDY FITZNER, composer; b. Schenectady, N.Y., Sept. 28, 1941; d. Eugene Adolf and Wanda (Nowicki) F.; m. Robert Alan Atchinson, May 15, 1971 (May 1978); m. Brian Michael O'Neil, May 11, 1990; children: Dawn Elizabeth, Beth Robin. B.Mus., Hartt Coll. Music, Hartford, Conn., 1964, MFA, 1970. adj. faculty Union Coll., Schenectady, 1979-86, Russell Sage Coll., Troy, N.Y., 1979-86; artist-in-residence Hudson Valley C.C., Troy, 1980-93, Barnard Coll., N.Y.C., 1995—, Skidmore Coll., Saratoga, N.Y.; guest artist Temple U., Phila., 1991, New Paltz (N.Y.) Coll., N.Y. State Theater Program, Albany, N.Y., 1981-89, N.Y. State Dance Mus., Saratoga, N.Y., 1992-95, Carlisle Project, Carlisle, Pa., 1992-95; artistic dir. Am. Composers Forum, Albany, 1986—. Composer: Electronic Music for Peter Pucci & Co., 1995, violin and cello piece, 1990, 2 pcs. for Barnard Coll., 1995, Diary, electronic and vocal piece/Smithsonian Mus., 1988, WomanSong/cello pieces, 1990, others. Bd. dirs. Saratoga City Ballet, Simons Rock Dance Festival, Poughkeepsie, N.Y., Internat. Assn. Dance Musicians; founder, dir. Quest-Inner City Arts Found., Schenectady, 1993-96, Dance Plus Dance Festival, Saratoga, 1990-96; advisor Law Order Justice, Schenectady, 1993-96; bd. dirs. Schenectady 2000, 1995-96. N.Y. Found. for Arts grantee, 1992-94, Meet the Composer grantee, 1980-96, Lila Wallace Reader's Digest grantee, 1993. Democrat. Home: 1131 Van Antwerp Rd Schenectady NY 12309

ATHANSON, MARY CATHERYNE, elementary school principal. Prin. Marjorie Kinnan Rawlings Elem. Sch., Pinellas Park, Fla. Office: Marjorie Kinnan Rawlings Elem Sch 6505 68th St Pinellas Park FL 34665-4946

ATKEISON, BARBARA JEAN, university director; b. Moscow, May 19, 1938; d. Samuel Garrison and Mavis Marie (Hoskins) Jones; m. Ernest Chevis Atkeison, Sept. 29, 1956 (dec. Jan. 1992); children: Ernest Chevis Jr., Edwin Spencer. BA in Bus. Adminstrn. and Acctg., Antioch Coll., 1982; MS in Edn. Adminstrn. and Supervision, U. Memphis, 1991. Lic. affiliate real estate broker, Tenn. Chief acct. Fayette County Pub. Sch. Sys., Somerville, Tenn., 1969-76, bus. mgr., 1976-86; coop. edn. coord., coll. placement dir. State Tech. Inst., Memphis, 1986-90, asst. dir. bus., industry and govt. tng. divsn., 1990-92, asst. dir. instnl. devel., 1992-95, dir. devel., 1995—; interim assessor of property Fayette County Govt., Somerville, 1992-95; mem. adv. coun. to develop uniform fin. acctg. and resporting structure for pub. elem. and secondary schs. State of Tenn. Dept. Edn., 1979. Planner, orgn. 5 county-wide polit. campaigns. Recipient Disting. Svc. award Fayette County Governing Body Commrs., 1979. Mem. Nat. Coun. for Resource Devel. (mem. legis. com. 1989-90, fed. funding task force coms. 1994, 95, 96, presenter ann. conf. 1995), Tenn. Coun. for Resource Devel. (presenter ann. conf. 1995), Tenn. Coop. Edn. Assn. (sec. 1989-90, liaison person to Southeastern Coop. Edn. Assn. 1988-90), Nat. Soc. Fund Raising Execs., Women in Higher Edn. Assn., Fayette County C. of C. (chair West Fayette chpt. livabilit com. 1995, exec. bd. 1995, past pres. West Fayette chpt. 1995, Woman of Yr. 1983). Home: 1780 Wilbourne Rd Oakland TN 38060

ATKERSON, TERESA SUSAN, newspaper editor; b. McAlester, Okla., Dec. 30, 1955; d. Virgil Riley and Joanne Ruth (Gill) A. BA, U. Sci. and Arts Okla., Chickasha, 1976, postgrad., 1980-83. Social worker I, Dept Human Svcs., McAlester, 1978-80; co-owner Sooner Constrn., McAlester, 1984-89; family, ch. and entertainment editor McAlester News Capital & Dem., 1987—. Bd. dirs. March of Dimes, McAlester Pub. Sch. Found., Adult and Cmty. Edn., Friends of Libr. of McAlester, Women in Safe Homes, Kiamichi Actors Studio Theatre; mem. Teenage Pregnancy Prevention Task Force; mem. planning com. Red Ribbon Week; mem. awareness com. Dist. III Okla. Cultural Coalition; active United Way McAlester, Soc. for Creative Anachronism, McAlester Pub. Schs. Parent U., MPS Learn and Serve, Parent's Club's Parents as Tchrs. adv. com. Recipient young careerist award Noon Bus. and Profl. Women's Club, 1990, McAlester Bus. and Profl. Women's Club, 1991, 3d place awrd for internat. pressbook competition Epsilon Sigma Alpha, 1990, Outstanding Media Person for Okla., Am. Heart Assn., 1991, 92; Actress of Yr. awrd Kiamichi Actors Studio Theatre, 1991, 94, Prodn. Mgr. of Yr. award 1994, 96, Supporting Actress of Yr. award, 1995, 96. Republican. Baptist. Office: McAlester News Capital & Dem 500 S 2d St McAlester OK 74501

ATKINS, APRIL DAWN, kindergarten educator; b. Burlington, N.C., Nov. 16, 1970; d. Joseph Louis and Patricia Lynn (Joynt) Williams; m. Mark Allen Atkins, June 25, 1994. BA in Elem. Edn., U. N.C., Wilmington, 1993. Tutor Crossroads, Wilmington, 1992-93, U. N.C., Wilmington, 1992; dir. child care Antian Cmty. Ch., Burlington, N.C., 1992; sales auditor Byrd's Food Stores, Burlington, N.C., 1989-93 summers; kindergarten tchr. Burlington City Schs., 1993—. Mem. Profl. Educators N.C. (sch. rep. 1994—). Republican. Home: 1901D Malone Rd Burlington NC 27215

ATKINS, HANNAH DIGGS, retired state official; b. Winston-Salem, N.C., Nov. 1, 1923; d. James Thackeray and Mabel (Kennedy) Diggs; m. Charles Nathaniel Atkins, May 24, 1943 (dec. Dec. 1988); children: Edmund E., Charles N., Valerie Atkins Alexander; m. Everett Patton O'Neal, June 12, 1993 (div. Jan. 1996). BS, St. Augustine's Coll., 1943; BLS, U. Chgo., 1949; LHD (hon.), Benedict Coll., Columbia, S.C.; MPA, U. Okla., 1987; cert., Harvard U., 1987. Law libr. Okla. State Libr., Oklahoma City, 1959-68; mem. Okla. State Legislature, Oklahoma City, 1968-80, U.S. Commn. to UNESCO, 1979-82; del. UN Gen. Assembly, 1980; asst. dir. Okla. Dept. Human Svcs., 1983-87; Okla. sec. of state, cabinet sec. human resources Oklahoma City, 1987-91; adj. prof. polit. sci. U. Ctrl. Okla., Edmond, 1991-92, U. Okla., Norman, 1991-93, Okla. State U., Stillwater, 1991-93; former nat. committeewoman Dem. Nat. Com.; pres., Okla. chpt. Am. Soc. Pub. Adminstrn.; bd. dirs. Women Execs. in State Govt., ACLU; former chmn. Okla. adv. com. U.S. Commn. on Civil Rights; bd. dirs. Nat. Women's Edn. Fund, Washington. Mem. AAUW (Kate Barnard award), Am. Soc. Pub. Adminstrn. (pres. Okla. chpt., Advancing Excellence in Pub. Svc. 1989), Phi Beta Kappa, Alpha Kappa Alpha. Democrat. Episcopalian.

ATKINS, HONEY JEAN, retired business executive; b. Chgo., Mar. 6, 1932; d. Anthony Theophane and Mary Jean (Barrett) Shelvis; m. Robert Claremore Atkins, Aug. 30, 1975. Grad., Rome City H.S., Rome City, Ind., 1948. Mgr. Pacific Telesis, Santa Ana, Calif., 1956-82. Commr. cultural commn. City of La Quinta (Calif.), 1994—; mem. adv. com. Riverside County Free Libr., La Quinta, 1995—; mem. adv. bd. CVC Concert Assn., 1995—; bd. dirs. Friends of Libr., v.p., 1993—. Named Citizen of Yr., La Quinta C. of C., 1996, Woman of Distinction, Soroptimists, 1995. Mem. La Quinta Arts League (pres.), La Quinta Arts Found. (bd. dirs., vol. chair), La Qinta Hist. Soc. (fundraising chair 1994-95), Round Table West (founder Desert chpt., chair), La Quinta Prpductions (pres.).

ATKINS, JOANNA PANG (JOANNA PANG), dancer, actress, choreographer, director; b. Berkeley, Calif., Feb. 9; d. Joseph H. Panganiban Sr. and Lynette Stevens DeFazio; m. Richard Atkins, 1982; 1 child, Davy Steven Atkins. Student, San Francisco State Coll., 1964-65. Child performer, dancer with ptnr. and brother Joey; with San Francisco Ballet and San Francisco Opera Co., 1952-63; prin. dancer nat. and internat. tours Toy-Wing Oriental Dance Co., 1965-70; mem. faculty Ballet Arts, Oakland, 1963-64; instr., prin. performer Robicheau Ballet, Boston, 1969-72; cons., guest lectr., artist-in-residence N.J. State Coun. on Arts, 1994—. Appeared on The Ted Randall Dance Party, San Francisco, 1959-61, Dick Stewart Dance Party, San Francisco, 1961-62, Art Laboe Show, and Earl McDaniel Show, L.A., 1959, Lawrence Welk show, 1961; appeared with U.S. Govt. Mil. Shows, 1954-56, N.Y.C. Ballet, 1955; appeared on stage in South Pacific, West Side Story, Music Man, Song of Norway, numerous others; appeared on TV shows Saturday Night Live, CBS Daytime 90, Edge of Night, The Doctors, All My Children; in films Voices, Once A Thief, Stardust Memories, others; appeared in TV commls.; dir., choreographer Getting to Know You, 1994, In the Mirror, 1995, Independence, 1996; dir., choreographer multicultural folk dance program St. Vincent Martyr Sch., Madison, N.J., 1995, Briarwood Sch., Florham Park, N.J., 1996. Mem. SAG, AFTRA, Actors Equity Assn. Home and Office: 149 Ridgedale Ave Florham Park NJ 07932-1708

ATKINS HOGGATT, SARAH BETH, small business owner; b. Stillwater, Minn., Jan. 23, 1965; d. Robert Donald and Phyllis Jeanette (Nelson) Atkins; m. John George Hoggatt, Sept. 17, 1994; 1 stepchild, Sara Ann Hoggatt. BS in Math., U. Wis., 1989. Dir. opers. Diversified Comm., Madison, Wis., 1987-91; exec. asst. Meriter Health Svcs., Madison, 1991-95; owner Archovations Inc., Hudson, Wis., 1995—. Mem. friends of kids steering com. Big Bros./Big Sisters, Madison, 1991-93; treas. bd. dirs. Wil-Mar Neighborhood Ctr., Madison, 1992-93. Mem. NAFE, Toastmaster's Internat. (v.p. edn., 1994—). Democrat. Office: Archovations Inc 1205 Saint Croix St Hudson WI 54016

ATKINSON, BARBARA FRAJOLA, pathologist; b. Mpls., Oct. 19, 1942. BA, Coll. of Wooster, Ohio, 1964; MD, Thomas Jefferson U., 1974. Diplomate Am. Bd. Pathology in clin. and anatomic pathology and cytopathology; lic. physician, Pa. Intern in clin. and anatomic pathology U. Pa., Phila., 1974-75, resident, 1975-78, NIH pulmonary tng. fellow in pulmonary pathology, 1976-77, NIH rsch. fellow in pulmonary pathology, 1977-78; asst. instr. pathology dept. pathology U. Pa. Sch. Medicine, Phila., 1974-78, asst. prof. dept. pathology and lab. medicine, 1978-84, assoc. prof., 1985-87; mem. pathology grad. group U. Pa. Sch. Medicine, 1985-87; prof., chair dept. pathology and lab. medicine Med. Coll. of Pa. and Hahnemann U., Phila., 1987-94; sr. mem. Ctr. for Gerontol. Rsch. Med. Coll. Pa., Phila., 1994-96; Annenberg dean Med. Coll. Pa. and Hahnemann U. Sch. Medicine, 1996—; assoc. scientist Wistar Inst. Anatomy and Biology, 1983-87; mem. staff dept. pathology Hosp. of U. Pa., 1978-87, dir. cytopathology, 1978-87, med. program dir. Sch. Cytotech., 1978-86; chair dept. pathology and lab. medicine Med. Coll. Pa., 1987-94; dir. Delaware Valley Regional Lab. Svcs., Med. Coll. Hosps. and St. Christopher's Hosp. for Children, 1991-96; chair dept. pathology and lab. medicine Med. Coll. Pa. and Hahnemann U., 1994-96; trustee Am. Bd. Pathology, 1992-95. Mem. editl. bd. Lab. Investigation, 1988-94, Modern Pathology, 1990-94, Human Pathology, 1992—; manuscript reviewer Cancer, Diagnostic Cytopathology, Modern Pathology, 1988-94; abstract rev. bd. U.S. and Can. Acad. Pathology, 1989-92; rev. panel Am. Soc. Clin. Pathology Abstract, 1991-96; contbr. articles to profl. jours., chpts. to books. Bd. dirs., treas. Laennec Soc. Phila., 1979-81; bd. dirs. Thyroid Soc. Phila., 1982-84; exec. com., bd. dirs. Med. Coll. Pa., 1994-96; bd. trustees Hahnemann U., 1994-96. Recipient Golden Apple Teaching award for excellent sci. teaching, 1994; grantee NIH, 1985-88, Takeda-Abbott R&D, 1989-94, NIA, 1991-94. Mem. AMA, Am. Soc. Cytology, Coll. Am. Assn. Exptl. Biologists, Am. Med. Women's Assn. (Janet M. Glasgow Meml. Scholarship 1974), Am. Soc. Clin. Pathologists (coun. on cytopathology 1989-94), Assn. Pathology Chmn. (v.p. 1992-94), Am. Assn. Cancer Rsch., Internat. Acad. Cytopathology, Phila. Pathology Soc., Pa. Assn. Pathologists, Coll. Physicians Phila., Phila. Cancer Rsch. Assn., Phila. County Med. Soc., Papanicolaou Soc. Cytopathology, Coun. of Deans of AAMC. Home: 715 St Georges Rd Philadelphia PA 19119 Office: Office of the Dean Med Coll Pa and Hahnemann U 2900 Queen Lane Philadelphia PA 19129

ATKINSON, CHRISTINE ANNE, curator; b. Kansas City, Kans., May 26, 1965; d. John Patterson and Andrea Janet (Gresser) A. BA in Humanities, U. Colo., 1987. Lobby supr. Dept. of Visitor Svcs., Mus. of Modern Art, N.Y.C., 1988-89; pub. programs asst. Dept. of Edn., Mus. of Modern Art, N.Y.C., 1989-90; artist, educator Minn., 1994—; comic book artist asst. DC Comics/Peter Gross, 1992—; comic book artist instr. Minn. Mus. of Am. Art, Mpls., 1995—; curatorial dir., visual curator No Name Exhbns., Mpls., 1993—, also bd. dirs.; tour guide Walker Art Ctr., Mpls., 1992—, teen programs cons., 1996—; adv. panel Mpls. Arts Commn., 1994—. Neighborhood arts program Mpls. Arts Commn., 1994. Mem. Phi Beta Kappa. Home: 3240 10th Ave S Minneapolis MN 55407 Office: No Name Exhbns PO Box 581696 Minneapolis MN 55459-1698

ATKINSON, HOLLY GAIL, physician, journalist, author, lecturer, human rights activist; b. Detroit, Oct. 20, 1952. BA in Biology magna cum laude, Colgate U., 1974; MD, U. Rochester, 1978; MS in Journalism, Columbia U., 1981. Diplomate Nat. Med. Bds. Intern in internal medicine Strong Meml. Hosp., Rochester, N.Y., 1978-79; rschr. Walter Cronkite's Universe show CBS News, N.Y.C., 1981-82; med. reporter CBS Morning News, N.Y.C., 1982-83; on-air co-host Bodywatch health show PBS, 1983-88; contbg. editor and health columnist New Woman mag., 1983-88; on-air corr., med. editor Lifetime Med. TV, 1985-89, sr. v.p. programming and med. affairs, 1989-93; assoc. editor Journal Watch, 1986-90; med. corr. Today Show NBC News, N.Y.C., 1991-94; exec. v.p. Reuters Health, N.Y.C., 1994—; editor HealthNews, 1994—; mem. trustee's com. U. Rochester, 1983-90. Author: Women and Fatigue, 1986. Vol. nat. and local level Am. Heart Assn., 1984-91, bd. dirs., chmn. nat. comms. com. Am. Heart Assn., 1987-91; bd. dirs. Phys. Human Rights, 1994—, NOW LDEF, 1996—. Recipient Young Achievers award Nat. Coun. Women, 1986, Achievement award Soc. Advancement Women's Health Rsch., 1995. Mem. Phi Beta Kappa. Office: Reuters Health Info Svc 825 8th Ave New York NY 10019-7416

ATKINSON, REGINA ELIZABETH, medical social worker; b. New Haven, May 13, 1952; d. Samuel and Virginia Louise Griffin. BA, U. Conn., Storrs, 1974; MSW, Atlanta U., 1978. Social work intern Atlanta Residential Manpower Center, 1976-77, Grady Meml. Hosp., Atlanta, 1977-78; med. social worker, hosp. coordinator USPHS, Atlanta, Palm Beach County (Fla.) Health Dept., West Palm Beach, 1978-81; dir. social services Glades Gen. Hosp., Belle Glade, Fla., 1981-95; case mgr. divsn. sr. svcs. Palm Beach County Cmty. Svcs., West Palm Beach, Fla., 1996—; instr. Palm Beach Jr. Coll.; participant various work shops, task forces. Vice pres. Community Action Council South Bay, 1978-79. Whitney Young fellow, 1977; USPHS scholar, 1977. Mem. NAFE, NAACP, Am. Hosp. Assn. (soc. for social work adminstrn. in health care), Soc. Hosp. Social Work Dirs., Assn. State and Territorial Pub. Health Social Workers, Nat. Assn. Black Social Workers, Nat. Assn. Social Workers, Fla. Soc. for Hosp. Social Work Dirs. (adminstrn. in health care), Glades Area Assn. for Retarded Citizens. Home: 525 1/2 SW 10th St Belle Glade FL 33430-3712 Office: 810 Datura St Ste 100 West Palm Beach FL 33401-3128

ATKINSON, SUSAN D., producing artistic director, theatrical consultant; b. Phila., May 23, 1944; d. Joseph A. and Josephine (Mierley) Davis; m. Robert Atkinson, 1971 (div. 1986). BA, Juniata Coll., 1966; postgrad., San Francisco State Coll., 1968-69, U. Calif., Berkeley, 1968-69. Dir. Am. Conservatory Theatre, San Francisco, 1967-72; guest dir. Berkeley Repertory Theatre Co., 1968-69; dir. Marin Shakespeare Festival, Marin County, Calif., 1968-69; producing artistic dir. Repertory Theatre Co. Bucks County, Doyleston, Pa., 1980-86, Bristol (Pa.) Riverside Theatre, 1986—; guest dir. Grove Shakespeare Festival, 1992. Bd. dirs. Pa. Coun. on the Arts, Harrisburg, Pa., 1989—. Mem. Soc. Stage Dirs. and Choreographers (cert.). Office: Bristol Riverside Theatre PO Box 1250 Bristol PA 19007-1250

ATKINSON, VALERIE J., writer, legal administrator; b. Austin, Tex., Mar. 3, 1959; d. Vernon T. and Mildred K. (Heaton) A. BA, U. Tex., 1981; postgrad., Universidad de Salamanca, Spain, 1983, City U., London, 1987. Assoc. exec. State Bar of Tex./Mead Data, Austin, 1988-93; sys. adminstr. First Tex. Lawyer's Bull. Bd. Svc., Austin, 1993—. Author: Paralegal Guide to Intellectual Property, 1994; editor newsletter Legal Asst. News, 1989-90; writer Tex. Pocket Part to Accompany The Law of Real Property, 1993; commentator, interviewer: (radio program) Inside the Internet, KOOP 91.7, Austin, 1995. Mem. Austin Authors for the First Amendment. Office: First Tex Lawyers Bulletin Bd Svc 13 Sunrise Acres Kyle TX 78640

ATLAGOVICH, RITA MARIE, communications executive; b. Cleve., Mar. 6, 1960; d. John and Rita Jane (Martin) A. BSBA in Acct. & Computer Sci., Ohio State U., 1984, MA in Slavic & East European Studies, 1993. Internal auditor GTE, Marion, Ohio, 1984-86; deregulated acct. GTE, Fort Wayne, Ind., 1986, revenue acct., 1986-87; mgr. facility cost audits LCI Internat., Columbus, Ohio, 1987-90; dir. Ohio Mus. Assn., Columbus, Ohio, 1992-94; internat. mktg. mgr. ConQuest Telecomm. Svcs. Corp., Columbus, Ohio, 1994-95, facilities planning mgr., 1995—. Bd. pres. Nat. Abortion and Reproductive Rights Action League, Ohio Edn. Found., Columbus, 1994—; bd. dirs. Greater Columbus Cmty. Shares, Columbus, 1994—. Home: 337 Iswald Rd Columbus OH 43202 Office: ConQuest Telecomm Svcs Corp 5500 Frantz Rd Dublin OH 43017

ATLAS, NANCY FRIEDMAN, judge; b. N.Y.C., May 20, 1949. BS, Tufts U., 1971; JD, NYU, 1974. Bar: N.Y. 1975, U.S. Dist. Ct. (so. and ea. dists.) N.Y. 1975, U.S. Ct. Appeals (2nd cir.) 1975, U.S. Dist. Ct. (so. dist.) Tex.

1982, U.S. Ct. Appeals (5th cir.) 1982, U.S. Dist. Ct. (no. dist.) Tex. 1989. Law clerk to Hon. Dudley B. Bonsal U.S. Dist Ct. (so. dist.) N.Y., 1974-76; assoc. Webster & Sheffield, 1977-78; asst. U.S. atty. So. Dist. N.Y., 1979-82; shareholder Sheinfeld, Maley & Kay, P.C., Houston, 1982-95, dir., 1994-95; judge U.S. Dist. Ct. Tex., Houston, 1995—; lectr. numerous programs CLE. Mng. editor NYU Annual Survey Am. Law, 1973-74; contbr. numerous articles to profl. jours. Chair Tex. Higher Edn. coord. Bd., 1992-95; mem. Tex. Coun. Workforce and Econ. Competitiveness, 1993-95. Fellow ABA Found., State Bar Tex., Houston Bar Assn.; mem. ABA (co-chair ADR com. litigation sect. 1994-95, bus. and litigation joint task force on bankruptcy practice 1994-95), Fed. Bar Assn. (trustee), Houston Bar Found., Phi Beta Kappa. Office: US Courthouse 515 Rusk St Houston TX 77002*

ATSUMI, IKUKO, management school administrator, educator; b. Nagoya, Japan, May 28, 1940; came to U.S., 1980; d. Zenzo Kato and Kaoru Atsumi. BA, Aoyama-Gakuin U., Tokyo, 1964, MA, 1970, PhD equivalent, 1976. Tenured assoc. prof. Aoyama-Gakuin U., Tokyo, 1970-82; founder, pres. Feminist Mag., Tokyo, 1977-80; rsch. fellow Radcliffe and Harvard U., Cambridge, Mass., 1982-83; founder, pres. Intercultural Bus. Ctr., Inc., Framingham, Mass., 1983—; guest writer U.S. State Dept./Internat. Writers' Workshop, Iowa City, 1975. Author, editor: Sales Success in Asia, 10 vols., 1995; author, co-editor (with Kenneth Rexroth, anthology): Women Poets of Japan, 1977; author essay. Bd. advisor Worcester (Mass.) Poly. Inst. Sch. Mgmt., 1991—; founder Pacific Rim Bus. Coun., 1994. Fellow Am. Coun. Learned Socs., 1980-81; rsch. grantee Ella Lyman Cabot Trust, 1983. Office: Intercultural Bus Ctr Inc Framingham Office Park Ste 103 1661 Worcester Rd Framingham MA 01701-5401

ATTEBURY, JANICE MARIE, accountant; b. Sterling, Ill., Sept. 8, 1954; d. Carl Edwin and Eileen Marie (Gilley) McDonald; m. Rudy Joe Attebury, July 8, 1972 (div. 1977); 1 child, Nicole Marie. Student, Okaloosa Walton Jr. Coll., Fort Walton Beach, Fla., Sauk Valley Coll., Dixon, Ill., Houston Community Coll.; BSBA in Acctg., Calif. U. for Advanced Studies, 1990; grad., Rhema Bible Tng. Ctr., 1992. Office mgr. Diamond Jim Enterprises, 1973-74; mgr. data processing dept. Sterling High Sch., 1974-75; bookkeeper 3-G Care Mgmt., Inc., 1977-78, office mgr., 1978-81; staff acct. Jerry T. Paul, CPA, 1982-84; staff acct. Lindgren, Callihan, Van Osdol and Co., Ltd., 1984-85, jr. acct., 1985-89; mgr. Riverside Cemetery, Sterling, 1989-90; pvt. practice J.M. Attebury Acctg. & Bookkeeping Svc., 1989-90, A & E Acctg., Sterling, Ill., 1990—; mgr. tng. dept., mgr. cons. dept. Omega C.G. Ltd., Lombard, Ill., 1993—. Mem. corp. bd. dirs., CEO Abiding Word Christian Ctr., Sterling, 1985-94, fin. adminstr., 1985-94; tng. coord. Omega C.G. Ltd., 1994—; mem. corp. bd. Twin City Crists Pregnancy Ctr., Sterling, 1988-90. Mem. NAFE, Nat. Soc. Pub. Accts., Nat. Soc. of Tax Profls. Republican. Mem. Charismatic Ch. Office: 409 4th Ave Sterling IL 61081-3750

ATTEE, JOYCE VALERIE JUNGCLAS, artist; b. Cin., Apr. 4, 1926; d. LeRoy Francis and Clara Marie (Becker) Jungclas; B.A., Rollins Coll., 1948; postgrad. U. Cin., 1952, 54, Art Acad. Cin., 1962-64, Edgecliff Coll., 1967; m. William Robert Attee III, Oct. 25, 1952; children: Robin Wilson, Wendy Ann. One-man shows include Loring Andrews Rattermann Gallery, 1964, Town Club, 1966, 69, 72, 75, 78, 81, 82, 83, 84, 90, Jr. League Office, 1975, Court Gallery, 1969, Bissingers', 1970, 76, Cin. Nature Ctr., 1974, 78, Cin. Country Day Sch., 1974; group shows include Town Club Cin., 1984, Bissinger's, 1984, Cin. Art Mus., 1962, Zoo Arts Festival, 1961, 62, 66, Town Club Cin., 1973-75, 77-79, 80-84, 85, Palm Beach (Fla.) Galleries, 1974, Showcase of Arts, 1976, Ursuline Ctr., 1976, Court Galleries, 1977, Indian Hill Artists, 1957-76, 82, 83, regional and local shows Nat. League Am. Pen Women, 77, 78, also nat. biennial art exhibit, 1970, Nat. Bicentennial Show, Washington, 1976, James H. Barker Gallery, Palm Beach, Fla., 1979, 80, 81, 82, Nantucket, 1982, Cin. Women's Club Show, 1979, Cin. Nature Ctr., 1983, Kimberton (Pa.) Gallery, 1988-89, Town Club, 1995; represented in permanent collections: Bissingers, Cin. Recipient 1st prize in still life or flowers Cin. Womans Art Club, 1965, 69; Marjorie Ewell Meml. award, 1975. Mem. Nat. League Am. Pen Women (past pres. Cin. br., past state art chmn. 1st prize graphics 1975), Women's Art Club Cin. (past v.p.), Jr. League Cin., Jr. League Garden Circle (pres. 1974-75, speaker on flower paintings 1990). Episcopalian. Clubs: Town, University, Indian Hill, Cin. Woman's. Author: Elbey Jay, 1964. Home: 8050 Indian Hill Rd Cincinnati OH 45243-3908

ATTERBURY, BETTY WILSON, music educator, researcher; b. L.A., Apr. 29, 1937; d. Jack Wilson and Viola Narrow; m. Robert Malcolm Atterbury, June 21, 1958; children: Christine, Carolyn, Robert. BS, SUNY, Potsdam, 1959; MS, CUNY, 1970; PhD, Northwestern U., 1982. Instr. Canon Lawrence Tchr. Tng. Coll., Lira, Uganda, 1966-68; tchr. elem. music Babylon (N.Y.) Pub. Schs., 1968-71, Mid. Country Schs., Centereach, N.Y., 1971-80; grad. asst. Northwestern U., Evanston, Ill., 1980-81; asst. prof. music Appalachian State U., Boone, N.C., 1981-85; prof. U. So. Maine, Gorham, 1985—. Author: Mainstreaming Exceptional Children in Music, 1990; co-author: Experience of Teaching General Music, 1995; editor: Elementary Music-The Best of MEJ, 1991; contbr. articles to profl. jours. Mem. Music Educators Nat. Conf., Maine Music Educators Assn. (rsch. chmn. 1985—, pres. 1992-94, exec. v.p. 1994-96), Coll. Music Soc., Coun. for Rsch. in Music Edn. (adv. com. Bull. 1989—), Pi Kappa Lambda, Sigma Alpha Iota. Office: U So Maine Dept Music 37 College Ave Gorham ME 04038

ATTIAS-YON, ELIZABETH YOUNG, medical administrator; b. Balt., May 22, 1962; d. Arthur and Patricia Ann (Young) Beneckson; m. Andre-Philippe Yon, May 7, 1994. BS with honors, St. Mary's Coll., 1984; M of Med. Sci., Emory U., 1987; DSc, Johns Hopkins U., 1992. Rsch. asst. Ctr. to Prevent Childhood Malnutrition, Bethesda, Md., 1992; territory mgr. Parke-Davis Pharms., Balt., 1992-95; dir. med. rsch., assoc. dir. med. and sci. affairs Parke-Davis S.E., Atlanta, 1995—. Author: (book chpt.) The Art and Mystery of Historical Archaeology, 1994. Nat. MCH tng. grantee U.S./Hopkins, 1987-92. Mem. APHA, AAUW, Perinatal Health and Fitness Network, Nat. Mus. for Women in Arts. Democrat. Presbyterian. Office: Parke-Davis SE CBU 1050 Crown Pointe Pkwy Atlanta GA 30338

ATTINGER, JOËLLE MARIE EMANUELLE, journalist; b. Davos, Switzerland, June 9, 1951; came to U.S., 1953; d. Ernst Otto and Françoise Marie (Daubige) A.; m. Bernard Ellis Cohen, May 8, 1982; children: Celia, Abigail. CEP, Inst. Politics, 1972; BA, Wellesley Coll., 1973. Reporter Time Mag., Paris, 1973-77; corr. Time Mag., Washington, 1977-80, Boston, 1980-88; bur. chief Time Mag., N.Y.C., 1988-90, dep. chief corrs., 1990-93, chief corrs., asst. mng. editor, 1993—; fellow Inst. Politics Harvard U., Cambridge, Mass., 1985. Staffer Georges Berard-Quelin Senatorial Campaign, Dordogne, France, 1972. Office: Time Mag 1271 Ave of Americas New York NY 10020

ATTKISSON, SHARYL T., newscaster, correspondent, writer; b. St. Petersburg, Fla.; d. Robert F. Thompson and Judith Jon (Starr) Crist; m. James H. Attkisson, Feb. 18, 1984; 1 child, Sarah Judith Starr Attkisson. BS in Broadcast Journalism, U. Fla., 1982. Reporter, prodr. Sta. WTVX-TV, Ft. Pierce, Fla., 1982-85; reporter Sta. WBNS-TV, Columbus, Ohio, 1985-86, Sta. WTVT-TV, Tampa, Fla., 1986-90; anchor, corr. Cable News Network, Atlanta, 1990-93, CBS News, N.Y.C., 1993-94, CBS News Washington, 1995—; mem. adv. bd. Coll. Journalism U. Fla., Gainesville, 1994-96, chmn. telecomm. adv. bd., 1996—. Author: Unreliable Sources, 1993. Recipient First Pl. TV Reporting Communicator's award Fla. Agribusiness Inst., 1983, 1st Place award Mature Media Nat. Awards, 1993, Bronze Medal award, Mature Media Nat. awards, 1994, First Place Sports Reporting award Sigma Delta Chi, 1990. Office: CBS News Washington 2020 M St NW Washington DC 20036-3368

ATWATER, MARY MONROE, science educator; b. Roswell, N.Mex., July 26, 1947; d. John C. and Helen (Wallace) Monroe; children: Helena A., Jonathen A. BS magna cum laude, Meth. Coll., 1969; MA, U. N.C., 1972; PhD, N.C. State U., 1980. Nat. sci. coord. Fayetteville (N.C.) State U., 1975-77; teaching asst. dept. maths. and sci. N.C. State U., Raleigh, 1977-79, rsch. asst., 1977-79; assoc. dir. N.Mex. State U., Las Cruces, 1980-83; asst. prof., program dir. sci., maths., tech. edn. Atlanta U., 1984-87, assoc. prof. and program dir. sci., math., tech. edn., 1987; asst. prof. dept. sci. edn. U. Ga., 1987-92, assoc. prof. dept. sci. edn., 1993—; vis. assoc. prof. Cornell U., 1993; adj. prof. Atlanta U., 1987-88; mem. rev. com. NSF, 1993, cons., 1994, Harvard-Smithsonian Ctr. Astrophysics, 1993, N.Y. Biology Network Workship, 1993, ABT Assocs., Inc., 1993; mem. adv. com. World Book Publ., 1993; presenter at numerous convs., speaker in field. Co-editor Multicultural Edn.: Inclusion of All, 1994; contbr. chpts. to books; contbr. numerous articles to profl. jours. Cons. Sci. Edn. in Mich. Schs., 1990-91; elem. sci. curriculum guide project Ga. Dept. Edn., 1988-90; judge numerous internat., state, local sci. fairs, 1978-96. Recipient Herbert Lehman Edn. Fund award, 1965, NSTA OHAUS award for innovations in four-yr. coll. tchg., 1990, Coll. Edn. & Psychology Disting. Alumnus award N.C. State U., 1996; numerous rsch. grants; Lily Tchg. fellow, 1989. Fellow AAAS; mem. ASCD, Am. Chem. Soc., Am. Edn. Rsch. Assn., Assn. Edn. Tchrs. in Sci., Assn. Tchr. Edn., Ga. Sci. Tchrs. Assn., Nat. Assn. Multicultural Edn., Nat. Assn. Rsch. in Sci. Tchg., Southeastern Assn. Edn. Tchrs. in Sci., Phi Delta Kappa (Warren Finley Rsch. award 1996). Home: 2035 Timothy Rd Athens GA 30606-3295 Office: U Ga 212 Alderhold Hall Athens GA 30602-7126

ATWELL, SHIRL JAE, composer; b. Kansas City, Mo., Oct. 8, 1949; d. Norman Jerome and Mary Louella (O'Bleness) A. MusB in Edn., Kans. State Tchrs. Coll., 1972; MusM, U. Louisville, 1976. Music educator Jefferson County Pub. Schs., Louisville, 1974-84, 88—; freelance composer, arranger, performer Louisville, 1984-88; music dir., conductor various prodns., Louisville, 1976-89. bassist SBTS Orchestra, Louisville, 1993—. Composer: (folk opera) Sagegrass, 1983 (Premiere award 1986), (contemporary opera) Esta Hargis, 1986 (Premiere award 1991), (ballet) Lucy, 1991 (Recording award 1996), (orch. suite) Movements Four South, 1986 (Premiere award 1993). Recipient Clifford Shaw Meml. award McDowell Music Club, 1984, Cert. of Appreciation, County Judge, Jefferson County, 1988. Mem. ASCAP, Am. Music Ctr., Music Educators Nat. Conf., Nat. Sch. Orchestra Assn., Am. String Tchrs. Assn. Office: Lassiter Middle Sch 8200 Candleworth Dr Louisville KY 40214

ATWOOD, COLLEEN, costume designer. Films include: Firstborn, 1984, (TV movie) Out of the Darkness, 1985, Bring on the Night, 1985, Manhunter, 1986, Critical Condition, 1987, Someone to Watch Over Me, 1987, The Pick-Up Artist, 1987, Torch Song Trilogy, 1988, Married to the Mob, 1988, Fresh Horses, 1988, For Keeps, 1988, Hider in the House, 1989, The Handmaid's Tale, 1989, Joe Verses the Volcano, 1990, Edward Scissorhands, 1990, Silence of the Lambs, 1991, Rush, 1991, Lorenzo's Oil, 1992, Love Field, 1992, Philadelphia, 1993, Born Yesterday, 1993, Cabin Boy, 1994, Wyatt Earp, 1994, Ed Wood, 1994, Little Women, 1994 (Acad. award nominee for best costume design 1994), Mars Attack That Thing You Do, 1994. Office: IATSE 13949 Ventura Blvd Ste 309 Sherman Oaks CA 91423-3570*

ATWOOD, DIANA FIELD, business owner, innkeeper; b. Rochester, N.Y., Nov. 3, 1946; d. Edwin Havens and Barbara (Field) A.; m. Kenneth Durant Milne, June 10, 1967 (div. Apr. 1982); m. Howard Samuel Tooker, May 5, 1985 (div. Aug. 1994). BA, Skidmore Coll., 1968. Owner, innkeeper Old Lyme (Conn.) Inn, 1976—; vice-chmn., bd. dirs. Maritime Bank & Trust, Essex, Conn., 1995—; incorporator Lawrence Meml. Hosp., New London, Conn., 1990-95. Trustee Conn. River Mus., Essex, 1976—, pres., 1989-94, chmn., 1994—; trustee Lyme Hist. Soc., Old Lyme, 1985-87, Lyme Acad. Fine Arts, Old Lyme, 1982—, treas., 1992—; vice chmn. Mystic Coast Travel and Leisure Coun., 1992-94, chmn. 1994—; dir. The Nature Conservancy (Conn. Chpt.1994—); adv. bd. Norwich Navigators, 1995—; dir. Corp. for Regional Econ. Devel., 1995—. Mem. Nat. Restaurant Assn., Conn. Restaurant Assn. (bd. dirs. 1991-93), Prof. Assn. Innkeepers, Master Chef's Inst., Gray Gables Croquet Club (founder), U.S. Croquet Assn. (chmn. mktg. com.). Republican. Presbyterian. Home: 12 Tantummaheag Rd Old Lyme CT 06371-1137 Office: Old Lyme Inn Inc 85 Lyme St # 787 Old Lyme CT 06371-2336

ATWOOD, HOLLYE STOLZ, lawyer; b. St. Louis, Dec. 25, 1945; d. Robert George and Elise (Sauselle) Stolz; m. Frederick Howard Atwood III, Aug. 12, 1978; children: Katherine Stolz, Jonathan Robert. BA, Washington U., St. Louis, 1968; JD, Washington U., 1973. Bar: Mo. 1973. Jr. ptnr. Bryan Cave, St. Louis, 1973-82, ptnr., 1983—, exec. com., 1995—. Bd. dirs. St. Louis council Girl Scouts U.S., 1976-86; trustee John Burroughs Sch., St. Louis, 1983-86. Mem. ABA, Met. St. Louis Bar Assn., Washington U. Law Sch. Alumni Assn. (pres. 1983-84). Club: Noonday (St. Louis) (bd. govs. 1983-86). Office: Bryan Cave 1 Metropolitan Sq 211 N Broadway Saint Louis MO 63102-2750

ATWOOD, JOYCE CHARLENE, curriculum and instruction administrator, consultant; b. Chillicothe, Ohio, Apr. 29, 1943; d. Pearl and Blanche (Martindill) Workman. BS in Edn., Ohio U., 1965, MEd, 1969; postgrad., Ohio State U., 1976-88, Ashland U., 1992-94. Cert. tchr., supr., adminstr. 4th-6th grade tchr. Chillicothe (Ohio) City Schs., 1965-73, K-3d grade reading tchr., 1973-86, tchr. leader reading recovery, 1986-88, asst. prin. mid. sch., 1988-89, adminstrv. asst., 1989-93, asst. supt. for curriculum and instrn., 1993—; cons. study skills for mgmt. in industry Pickaway-Ross Joint Vocat. Sch., Chillicothe, 1984-88; mem. Child Care Adv. Bd., Portsmouth (Ohio), 1993—. Sec., v.p. Big Bros. and Sisters, Ross County, 1989-93; mem. Walnut St. Ch. Staff Parish, Chillicothe, 1991-94; coord. Area Artist Series, Ross County, 1989—; edn. chairperson Ross County Area Labor Mgmt., 1990—. Named to Ross County Women's Hall of Fame, Ross County C. of C., 1993. Mem. ASCD, Internat. Reading Assn., Buckeye Assn. Sch. Adminstrs., Altrusa, Kiwanis, Phi Delta Kappa. Methodist. Home: 10 Overlook Dr Chillicothe OH 45601-1456

ATWOOD, MARGARET ELEANOR, author; b. Ottawa, Ont., Can., Nov. 18, 1939; d. Carl Edmund and Margaret Dorothy (Killam) A. BA, U. Toronto, 1961; AM, Radcliffe Coll., 1962; postgrad., Harvard U., 1962-63, 65-67; LittD (hon.), Trent U., 1973, Concordia U., 1980, Smith Coll., Northampton, Mass., 1982, U. Toronto, 1983, U. Waterloo, 1985, U. Guelph, 1985, Mt. Holyoke Coll., 1985, Victoria Coll., 1987, Univ. de Montréal, 1991, McMaster U., 1996; LLD (hon.), Queen's U., 1974. Lectr. in English U. B.C., 1964-65, Sir George Williams U., 1967-68, U. Alta., 1969-70; asst. prof. English York U., Toronto, 1971-72; writer-in-residence U. Toronto, 1972-73, U. Ala., Tuscaloosa, 1985; Berg Chair NYU, 1986; writer-in-residence Macquarie U., Australia, 1987, Trinity U., San Antonio, 1989. Author: (poetry) Double Persephone, 1961, The Circle Game, 1967, The Animals in That Country, 1968, The Journals of Susanna Moodie, 1970, Procedures for Underground, 1970, Power Politics, 1973, Poems for Voices, 1970, You Are Happy, 1975, Selected Poems, 1976 (Am. edit. 1978), Selected Poems, 1966-84, Margaret Atwood Poems, 1965-75, 1991, Two-Headed Poems, 1978, True Stories, 1981, Interlunar, 1984, Selected Poems II, 1986, Morning in The Burned House, 1995; (novels) The Edible Woman, 1969 (Am. edit. 1970), Surfacing, 1972 (Am. edit. 1973), Lady Oracle, 1976, Life Before Man, 1979, Bodily Harm, 1981, The Handmaid's Tale, 1985, Cat's Eye, 1988 (City Toronto Book award 1989, Coles Book of the Yr. 1989, Can. Booksellers Assn. Author of Yr. 1989, Book of Yr. award Found. for Advancement of Can. Letters, Periodical Marketers Can., 1989, Torgi Talking Book award 1989), The Robber Bride, 1993 (award for Fiction Can. Authors Assn. 1993, Trillium award for Excellence in Ont. Writing 1993, Regional Commonwealth Lit. award); (short stories) Dancing Girls, 1977, Bluebeard's Egg, 1983, Murder in the Dark, 1983, Wilderness Tips, 1991 (Trillium award 1992, Book of Yr. award Periodical Marketers of Can., 1992), Good Bones, 1992; (juvenile) Up in the Tree, 1978, Anna'a Pet, 1980, For the Birds, 1990, Princess Prunella & the Purple Peanut, 1995; (non-fiction) Survival: A Thematic Guide to Canadian Literature, 1972, Second Words: Selected Critical Prose, 1982, Strange Things: The Malevolent North in Canadian Literature, 1995; (TV scripts) The Servant Girl, Can. Broadcasting Co., 1974—, (with Peter Pearson) Heaven on Earth, Can. Broadcasting Co., 1986; editor: (with Shannon Ravenal) The Best American Short Stories 1989; (with Robert Weaver) The New Oxford Book of Canadian Short Stories in English, 1995; contbr. poems, short stories, revs. and articles to scholarly jours. and consumer mags. Recipient E.J. Pratt medal, 1961, Pres.'s medal U. Western Ont., 1965, YWCA Women of Distinction award, Gov. Gen.'s award, 1966, 1st pl. Centennial Commn. Poetry Competition, 1967, Union Poetry prize Chicago, 1969, Bess Hoskins prize of Poetry Chicago, 1974, City of Toronto Book award, 1977, Can. Booksellers Assn. award, 1977, award for short fiction Periodical Distbr. Can., 1977, St. Lawrence award for Fiction, 1978, Radcliffe Grad. medal, 1980, Molson award, 1981, Internat. Writer's prize Welsh Arts Council, 1982, Book of Yr. award Periodical Distbrs. of Can. and Found. for Advancement Can. Letters, 1983, Los Angeles Times Fiction award, 1986, Gov. Gen.'s Lit. award, 1986, Ida Nudel Humanitarian award, 1986, Toronto Arts award, 1986, Arthur C. Clarke award for Best Sci. Fiction, 1987, shortlisted for Ritz Hemingway prize, Paris, 1987, Commonwealth Lit. Prize regional award, 1987, 94, Silver medal for Best Article of Yr. Council for Advancement and Support of Edn., 1987, Nat. Mag. award 1st prize, 1988, Sunday Times award for literary excellence, YWCA Women of Distinction award 1988, Centennial medal Harvard U., 1990, John Hughes prize Welsh Devel. Bd., 1992, Commemorative medal 125th Anniversary of Can. Confedn., 1992, Trillium award for excellence in Ont. writing, 1995; Guggenheim fellow, 1981; decorated companion Order of Can., 1981, Order of Ont., 1990; named Woman of Yr. Ms. Mag., 1986, Humanist of Yr., 1987, Chevalier de l'Ordre des Arts et des Lettres, 1994. Fellow Royal Soc. of Can., Am. Acad. Arts and Scis. (fgn. hon. lit. mem. 1988). Address: care Oxford U Press, 70 Wynford Dr, Don Mills, ON Canada M3C 1J9

ATWOOD, MARY SANFORD, writer; b. Mt. Pleasant, Mich., Jan. 27, 1935; d. Burton Jay and Lillian Belle (Sampson) Sanford; B.S., U. Miami, 1957; m. John C. Atwood, III, Mar. 23, 1957. Author: A Taste of India, 1969. Mem. San Francisco/N. Peninsula Opera Action, Hillsborough-Burlingame Newcomers, Suicide Prevention and Crisis Center, DeYoung Art Mus., Internat. Hospitality Center, Peninsula Symphony, San Francisco Art Mus., World Affairs Council, Mills Hosp. Assos. Mem. AAUW, Suicide Prevention Aux. Republican. Club: St. Francis Yacht. Office: 40 Knightwood Ln Hillsborough CA 94010-6132

AU, CAROL LEE, publisher, artist; b. Mansfield, Ohio, Dec. 3; d. Ernest C. McGinty and Beulah M. (McKinley) Burton; m. Gunther Sagel Meisse, 1962 (div. 1981); children: Marka Lyle, Melinda Lane, Gunther Meisse II, Robert Meisse; m. Charles H. Au, Mar. 9, 1982. BA in Comm. cum laude, Chatham Coll., 1988; MA, Duquesne U., 1994. Mktg. dir. Johnny Appleseed Broadcasting Corp., Mansfield, 1962-81; CEO Au Comm., Inc., Mansfield, 1981—; dir. Rexall/Showcase, Internat. Guest artist Harmarville Rehab., Pitts., 1994. Coord. Fox Chapel Presbyn. Ch., Pitts., 1992, active cmty. missions, 1995; civil projects coord. Guyasuta Garden Club, Pitts., 1994-96; founder Mansfield Rotary Anns., 1972—. Recipient FM Radio Pioneer award Nat. Assn. FM Broadcasters, 1972. Mem. AAUW, Nat. Mus. women in the Arts, Nat. Libr. of Poetry Semi-Finalists. Republican.

AU, KATHRYN HU-PEI, educational psychologist; b. Honolulu, May 8, 1947; d. Harold Kwock Ung and Mun Kyau (Hew) A. AB, Brown U., 1969; MA, U. Hawaii, 1976; PhD, U. Ill., 1980. Ednl. specialist Kamehameha Schs., Honolulu, 1971-80, ednl. psychologist, 1980-95; assoc. prof. U. Hawaii, Honolulu, 1995—. Author: Literacy Instruction in Multicultural Settings, 1993. Nat. scholar Nat. Assn. for Asian and Pacific Am. Edn., 1980. Mem. Nat. Reading Conf. (pres. elect 1994-95), Am. Ednl. Rsch. Assn. (v.p. 1992-94). Office: U Hawaii Coll Edn 1776 University Ave Honolulu HI 96822

AUBERJONOIS, JUDITH MIHALYI, theatrical producer and writer; b. N.Y.C., Feb. 22, 1944; d. Dave and Elsa (Perlmutter) Mihalyi; m. Rene Murat Auberjonois, Oct. 19, 1963; children: Tessa, Remy-Luc. BFA, Carnegie-Mellon U., 1965. Actor Am. Conservatory Theater, San Francisco, 1965-69, Lincoln Ctr. Rep., N.Y.C., 1969; founder L.A. Classic Theatre Works, 1984-89; spl. project coord. Mark Taper Forum, L.A., 1990; devel. dir. Dave Bell Assocs., L.A., 1991-93; freelance writer and prodr. L.A., 1993—; theatre critic L.A. Weekly, New West mag., L.A. 1980's. Playwright: Seen Better Days, 1996.

AUBI, EILEEN, artist, educator; b. N.Y.C., Jan. 27, 1933; d. Jack Gurstein and Shirley (Seltzer). Student, Skowhegan Sch Paintg/Sculpture, Maine, 1958, Bklyn. Museum Art Sch., 1959-61, Art Students League, Woodstock, 1961, Museum of Modern Art, N.Y.C., 1964-66. Jewelry designer Aubi Designs, Inc., 1971-90; instr. Sch. of Visual Arts, N.Y.C., 1987—, New Sch. for Social Rsch., 1987—; guest spkr. sculpture SUNY, New Paltz, 1976. Work included in shows at Va. Museum of Fine Art, Richmond, 1987, Mari Gallery of Westchester (N.Y.), 1976, Asset Gallery, London, England, 1975, Puerto Banus Gallery, Marbella, Spain, 1974, Fabian Gallery, Madison Ave., N.Y., 1973, MADE IN NEW YORK campaign, 1983, Metropolitan Museum of Art Manchu Dragon Show, 1980, Am. Crafts Museum, N.Y., 1965; prin. works include sculpture in Prudential Securities collection, San Antonio, Tex., 1993, R.S. Reynolds Meml. award sculpture, 1981. Prix de Cachet award nominee, 1981. Mem. Citizens Union, Artists Equity. Home: 300 W 55th St New York NY 10019

AUBIN, BARBARA JEAN, artist; b. Chgo., Jan. 12, 1928; d. Philip Theodore and Dorothy May (Chapman) A. BA, Carleton Coll., 1949; B Art Edn., Sch. Art Inst. Chgo., 1954, M Art Edn., 1955. Lectr. Centre D'Art & Haitian Am. Inst., Port-Au-Prince, Haiti, 1958-60; asst. prof. Sch. Art Inst. Chgo., 1960-67, Loyola U., Chgo., 1968-71; lectr. Calumet Coll., Hammond, Ind., 1971-75; prof. art Chgo. State U., 1971-91; ret., 1991; vis. prof. art Wayne State U., Detroit, Mich., 1965; vis. artist St. Louis C.C., Forest Park, Mo., 1980, 81, U. Wis., Green Bay, 1981. One-woman shows include Coutryside Arts Ctr., Arlington Heights, Ill., 1954, Avant Arts Gallery, Chgo., 1954, Riccardo's Restaurant and Gallery, Chgo., 1956, Evanston (Ill.) Twp. H.S., 1958, Centre d'Art, Port-au-Prince, Haiti, 1960, Chgo. Pub. Libr., 1960, Chgo. Acad. Fine Arts, 1965, Oxbow Summer Acad. Fine Arts, 1965, Lewis Towers Gallery, Loyola U., Chgo., 1970, Chgo. State U., 1971, 74, 85, North River Cmty. Gallery, Northeastern Ill. U., Chgo., 1974, Ill. Arts Coun., Chgo., Crossroads-Jr. Mus., Art Inst. Chgo., 1976, Fairweather Hardin Gallery, Chgo., 1978, 80, 85, 90, U. Wis., 1981, Illini Union Gallery, U. Ill., Urbana, 1986, Countryside Art Ctr., Arlington Heights, 1987, Artemisia Gallery, Chgo.; exhibited in group shows at I Woman Exhbn., Chgo., 1960, 78, 80, 85, 89, Vanderpoel Art Assn., Beverly Art Ctr., Chgo., 1992, Ancient Echoes, Chgo., 1992, Renaissance Ct., Chgo. Cultural Ctr., 1993, Artemisia Gallery, Chgo., 1994, Art Place Gallery, Chgo, 1994, Chgo. State U., 1994, Chgo. Women's Caucus for Art, 1994, Eastern Ill. U., Charleston, 1994, ARC Gallery, Chgo., 1995, N.Mex. Art League, Albuquerque, 1996; represented in permanent collections at Art Inst. Chgo., Ill. State Mus., Ball State Mus., Calumet Coll., Hammond, Ind., Shimer Coll., Waukegan, Ill., Kemper Group Collection, Long Grove, Ill., State of Ill. Bldg., Chgo., Seyfarth, Shaw, Fairweather & Geraldson, Washington, Ernst & Ernst, Chgo., Foote, Cone & Belding, Chgo., U.S. League of Savs. and Loans, Chgo., Northside Industries, Chgo., Keck, Cushman, Mahin & Cate, Chgo., Gould, Inc., Rolling Meadows, Ill., First Nat. Bank Chgo., Ill. Tool Works, Chgo., Internat. Mineral and Chem., Skokie, Ill.; reporter Women Artists News, 1977, 80, 83-86. V.p. Midwest region Womens Caucus for Art, Chgo., 1982-88; founder local chpt. Chgo. Women's Caucus for Art, 1973; bd. dirs. Chgo. Artists Coalition, 1992-94. Recipient George D. Brown Fgn. Travel fellowship Sch. Art Inst. Chgo., 1955-56, Art grant Fulbright Found., 1958-60, grant Huntington Hartford Fedn., 1963, Project Completion grant Ill. Arts Coun., 1978, 79. Mem. Arts Club Chgo., Chgo. Artists Coalition, Chgo. Womens Caucus for Art, Albuquerque United Artists, N.Mex. Art League. Home: 5101 Glenwood Pointe NE Albuquerque NM 87111

AUCHINCLOSS, PAMELA PRATT, art dealer, arts management executive; b. Okla. City, Apr. 11, 1956; d. Bayard Cutting Auchincloss and Mary Christy (Pratt) Williams; m. Garner Handy Tullis, Nov. 10, 1984 (div. June, 1993); m. Steven Henry Madoff, Aug. 11, 1993; children: Lucian Auchincloss Madoff, Sloan Pratt Madoff. Student, U. of the Pacific, Stockton, Calif., 1974-76. Dir. Winter Park (Colo.) Forum, 1977-79; dir. Pamela Auchincloss Gallery, Santa Barbara, Calif., 1979-87, N.Y.C., 1987—; bd. dirs. Santa Barbara Contemporary Arts Forum, 1983-87; bd. trustees U. Calif., Santa Barbara, 1983-87. Editor, publisher (mag.) Artline, 1982-84. Bd. trustees, chmn. student affairs Pratt Inst., 1989—; bd. dirs., chmn. devel. com. Housing Works, Inc., 1990—. Office: Arts Mgmt Svcs 601 W 26th St New York NY 10001

AUDIA, CHRISTINA, librarian; b. Carolina, W.Va., July 6, 1941; d. John and Roze (Horvath) A. B.S. in Edn., Wayne State U., 1967, M.S. in L.S., 1969. Cert. librarian, Mich. Chief libr. original cataloging dept. Detroit Pub. Libr., 1980-89, bibliographic database mgr., 1989—; specialist for monograph cataloging Mich. Libr. Consortium, 1987-89; mem. Dalnet

Database Standards Com., 1989—. Mem. ALA. Office: Detroit Pub Libr Database Mgmt Dept 5201 Woodward Ave Detroit MI 48202-4093

AUEL, JEAN MARIE, author; b. Chgo., Feb. 18, 1936; d. Neil Solomon and Martha Amelia (Wirtanen) Untinen; m. Ray Bernard Auel, Mar. 19, 1954; children: RaeAnn Marie, Karen Jean, Lenore Jerica, Kendall Poul, Marshall Philip. MBA, U. Portland, 1976, LittD (hon.), 1984; HHD (hon.), U. Maine, 1986; LHD (hon.), Mt. Vernon Coll., 1986; HHD (hon.), Pacific U., 1995. Office and tech. positions, then tech. writer, credit mgr. Tektronix, Inc., Beaverton, Oreg., 1964-76. Author: The Clan of the Cave Bear, 1980 (Friends of Lit. award 1980, finalist Best First Novel Nat. Book Awards 1980), The Valley of Horses, 1982, The Mammoth Hunters, 1985, The Plains of Passage, 1990 (Waldo award Waldenbooks 1990, Persie award WIN/WIN 1990). Bd. dirs. Oreg. Mus. Sci. and Industry, 1993—; hon. campaign chair Oreg. Coun. for Humanities, 1991; speaker, fund raiser various charitable and ednl. orgns. Recipient Excellence in Writing award Pacific N.W. Booksellers Assn., 1980, award Scandinavian Kaleidoscope of Art and Life, 1982, Bronze Sculpture award Publieksprijs voor het Nederlandse Boek, 1990, Silver Trowel award Sacramento Archeol. Soc., 1990, contbn. award Dept. Interior/Soc. for Am. Archaeology, 1990, Nat. Zoo award, Centennial medal Smithsonian Instn., 1990, Golden Plate award Am. Acad. Achievement, 1986. Mem. PEN, Authors Guild, Willamette Writers (life), Oreg. Writers Colony (charter mem.), Internat. Women's Forum (bd. dirs. 1985-93), Mensa (hon. v.p. 1990—). Office: Jean V Naggar Lit Agy 217 E 75th St New York NY 10021-2902

AUERBACH, ELISE, archaeologist, art historian; b. N.Y.C., Feb. 22, 1960; d. Herbert and Adell (Sherman) A.; m. Guillermo Algaze, June 30, 1985 (div. June 1994). BA, U. Pa., 1981; PhD, U. Chgo., 1994. Archaeologist Lachish Excavations, Israel, 1980-81; ceramicist Lidar Höyük Excavations, Turkey, 1983; archaeologist Sheikh Hamad Excavations, Syria, 1984-85; history instr. Columbia Coll., Chgo., 1986-87; archaeologist Abu Hamad Excavations, 1987, Ashqelon (Israel) Excavations, 1988-89, Tigris-Euphrates Reconnaissance Project, Turkey, 1988-89, Titris Höyük Excavations, Turkey, 1991-92; postdoctoral fellow Getty Grant Program, Santa Monica, Calif., 1995—. Contbr. articles to scholarly jours. Ryerson travel grantee, U. Chgo., 1985. Mem. Am. Hist. Assn., Am. Schs. Oriental Rsch. (ASOR/ZION travel grantee 1983), Amnesty Internat. (coord. local group 113 1994—, mem. Mid. East coord. group 1995—, mem. planning com. for 1994 ann. gen. meeting 1994), Coll. Art Assn., Sierra Club, Greenpeace. Democrat. Jewish.

AUERBACK, SANDRA JEAN, social worker; b. San Francisco, Feb. 21, 1946; d. Alfred and Molly Loy (Friedman) A. BA, U. Calif., Berkeley, 1967; MSW, Hunter Sch. Social Work, 1972. Diplomate clin. social work. Clin. social worker Jewish Family Services, Bklyn., 1972-73; clin. social worker Jewish Family Services, Hackensack, N.J., 1973-78; pvt. practice psychotherapy San Francisco, 1978—; dir. intake adult day care Jewish Home for the Aged, San Francisco, 1979-91. Mem. NASW (cert., bd. dirs. Bay Area Referral Svc. 1983-87, chmn. referral svc. 1984-87, state practice com. 1987-91, regional treas. 1989-91, rep. to Calif. Coun. Psychiatry, Psychology, Social Work and Nursing, 1987—, chmn. 1989, 93, v.p. cmty. svcs. 1991-93, chair Calif. polit. action com. 1993-95), Am. Group Psychotherapy Assn., Mental Health Assn. San Francisco (trustee 1987—). Home: 1100 Gough St Apt 8C San Francisco CA 94109-6638 Office: 450 Sutter St San Francisco CA 94108-4206

AUFDENKAMP, JO ANN, retired librarian; b. Springfield, Ill, Mar. 22, 1926; d. Erwin C. and Johanna (Ostermeier) A.; B.A., MacMurray Coll. for Women, 1945; B.L.S., U. Ill., 1946; postgrad. U. Chgo., 1964-66; J.D., John Marshall Law Sch., 1976. Asst. libr. Commerce Libr. U. Ill., 1946-48; libr. Fed. Res. Bank of Chgo., 1948-80; adminstr. info. services legal dept. Lincoln Nat. Life Ins. Co., Ft. Wayne, Ind., 1980-81; asst. trust officer Central Trust and Savs. Bank, Geneseo, Ill., 1981-83; practice law, 1983-84; cons. Ill. Valley Libr. System, 1984-87, Harvey (Ill.) Pub. Libr., 1987-89; libr. Bus. and Econs. Libr. No. Ill. U., De Kalb, 1989-95; ret., 1995; with Office Nat. Planning, Liberia, 1963. Mem. ALA, Spl. Libraries Assn. (Disting. Mem. award bus. and fin. divsn. 1995), Ill. Library Assn. Republican. Lutheran. Home: 350 Miller Ave De Kalb IL 60115-2310

AUGER, DIANNE LESLIE, university admissions counselor; b. Sioux Falls, S.D., Apr. 2, 1965; d. Kenneth Edward and Sandra Sue (Glaser) Bickett; m. Richard Wendell Auger, July 24, 1993. BA, Augustana Coll., 1989; MS, Mankato State U., 1994. Fin. coord. A Christian Ministry in the Nat. Parks, N.Y.C., 1986-87; dir. youth First United Meth. Ch., New Ulm, Minn., 1989-91; guidance counselor St. Paul Pub. Schs., 1994-95; admission counselor U. Iowa, Iowa City, 1995—; mem. steering com. Parents Communication Network, New Ulm, 1989-90. Democrat. Office: U Iowa Admissions Office John G Bowman House 230 N Clinton Iowa City IA 52242-1703

AUGUR, MARILYN HUSSMAN, distribution executive; b. Texarkana, Ark., Aug. 23, 1938; d. Walter E. and Betty (Palmer) H.; m. James M. Augur, Dec. 29, 1962; children: Margaret M. Hancock, Elizabeth H. Taylor, Ann Louise. BA, U. N.C., 1960; MBA, So. Meth. U., 1989. Pres. North Tex. Mountain Valley Water, Dallas, 1989—; bd. dirs. Camden News Pub. Co., Little Rock. Trustee Hussman Found., Little Rock, 1991—, U. Tex. Southwestern Med. Found., 1993—, Nat. Jewish Hosp., 1993—, Marilyn Augur Found., Dallas, 1991—; bd. dirs. Baylor Health Sys. Found., 1992—, chmn., 1995; bd. dirs. Dallas Summer Musicals, 1992-95, mem. exec. com., 1992-94; bd. dirs. Tate Lectr. Series, 1994—, Salvation Army, 1996, adv. bd.; mem. Tex. Bus. Hall of Fame, 1992—, exec. com., 1994; exec. com. Dallas Citizens Coun., 1994-95, Dallas County C.C., Dist. Found., 1995, Dallas Helps, 1995, Charter 100. Mem. Dallas Country Club, Crescent Club, Dallas Women's Club, Beta Gamma Sigma. Episcopalian. Office: North Tex Mountain Valley Water 3131 Turtle Creek Blvd Dallas TX 75219

AUGUST, JUDITH L., cosmetics consultant, distributor, developer, creator, and marketer; b. L.A., May 10, 1941; d. Victor and Florance (Herman) Liebman; m. Laurence ugust, 1962 (div. 1975); children: Melissa August-Levin, Scott David. Student, Art Ctr. Sch., 1959-60, UCLA, 1960-62. Fashion model, 1961-73; developer parfumerie Let's Face It, New Orleans, 1973-79; founder August Co., L.A., 1980—; beauty advisor Bon Reisette Health Spa, Lancaster, Calif., 1985-92, Two Bunch Palms Spa, Palm Desert, Calif., 1984-86; tng. dir. Aida Grey Cosmetics, Beverly Hills, Calif., 1980-84; appearance cons. Western Airlines, L.A., 1984-87. Author: How to Be Chic, Gorgeous & Sexy-though Pregnant, 1970; creator Judith August Corrective Cosmetics; contbr. articles to profl. jours. Recipient Achievement award YWCA, 1973-79.

AUGUSTINE, KATHY MARIE, state legislator, primary school educator; b. L.A., Calif., May 29, 1956; d. Philip Blase and Katherine Alice (Thompson) A.; m. Charles Francis Augustine, July 22, 1988; children: Andrea, Greg, Larry, Dallas. AB, Occidental Coll., 1977; MPA, Calif. State U., Long Beach, 1983. Flight attendant Continental Airlines, Houston, 1978-83; crew scheduler Delta Airlines, L.A., 1983-88; tchr. Diocese of Reno/Las Vegas, 1990-92; mem. Nev. Legislature, 1992-94, Nev. Senate, 1995—. Mem. Active Rep. Women's Club, Las Vegas, Nev., 1992-93. Recipient Achievement award Bank of Am., Calif., 1974, Achievement Medallion Am. Legion, 1974, Congressional Internship grantee, Washington, 1975. Mem. AAUP (v.p. programs), Am. Legislative Exchg. Coun. (transportation com.), Nat. Conf. of State Legislators (arts & tourism com.), Nev. Dance Theater Guild, Jr. League of Las Vegas (sr. legis. rep.), Clark County Panhellenic Assn. (treas.), Italian-Am. Club of Las Vegas, Women Legislator's Lobby. Republican. Roman Catholic. Home: 1400 Maria Elena Dr Las Vegas NV 89104-1846*

AUGUSTINOVICZ, AUDREY ANNE, trauma nurse, critical care nurse; b. Anderson, Ind., Oct. 24, 1968; d. Richard T. and Dianne Marie (Swartz) A. BSN, Ball State U., 1991. RN Ind., Va., Fla., Conn., Hawaii, Mich., Wash., Vt., D.C.; Cert. BSN, Trauma Nursing Core Class, Advanced Cardiac Life Support, BLS. Trauma nurse Methodist Hosp., Indpls., 1989-91; travel emergency room RN St Mary's Hosp., Richmond, Va., 1992; travel trauma nurse Brandon Hosp., Brandon, Fla., 1993, Yale-New Haven Hosp., New Haven, Conn., 1993; home healthcare nurse Interim Healthcare, Muncie, Ind., 1993—, Kimberly Quality Care, Muncie, Ind., 1993-94; travel trauma nurse Kona Hosp., Kealakeukua, Hawaii, 1993-94, Northeastern Vermont Regional, St. Johnsbury, Vt., 1994; med. surg. nurse Community Hosp., Anderson, Ind., 1990—; staff RN AIDS Task Force, Anderson, Ind.; speaker Student Nurse Assn., Community Hosp., Anderson; emergency med. tech. DIA. Vol. EMT Pendleton Emergency Ambulance Fire Dept. Republican. Roman Catholic.

AUMACK, SHIRLEY JEAN, financial planner, tax consultant; b. Newark, May 17, 1949; d. Herbert O. and Edythe V. (England) Marlatt; m. Kenneth J. Aumack, Oct. 25, 1969; children: Douglas, Steven. BA in Econs., Wilson Coll., 1971. Cert. fin. planner, enrolled agt.; registered investment advisor. Account exec. N.J. Bell Telephone, Scotch Plains, N.J., 1972-76; ptnr., ind. contr. Personal Mgmt. and Planning Inc., Matawan, N.J., 1982-90; pvt. practice fin. planner Fair Haven, 1990—; instr. fin. planning Momouth County Park System, Lincroft, N.J., 1991, Rutgers U., 1993, 94, Rumson Cmty. Edn., 1995—. Pres. Performing Arts Soc., Rumson Fair-Haven Regional High Sch., 1992-94. Mem. Internat. Assn. for Fin. Planning (seminar speaker 1990), Inst. Cert. Fin. Planners, Nat. Assn. Enrolled Agts., Accreditation Coun. for Accountancy and Taxation (tax advisor). Office: 21 Cedar Ave # E Fair Haven NJ 07704-3264 also: 2 Ethel Rd Bldg 201A Edison NJ 08817-2839

AUNE, DEBRA BJURQUIST, lawyer; b. Rochester, Minn., June 13, 1956; d. Alton Herbert and Violet Lucille (Dutcher) Bjurquist; m. Gary ReMine, June 6, 1981 (div. June 1993); children: Jessica Bjurquist ReMine, Melissa Bjurquist ReMine; m. David Aune, Jan. 1, 1995. BA, Augsburg Coll., 1978; JD, Hamline U., 1981. Bar: Minn. 1981. Assoc. Hvistendahl & Moersch, Northfield, Minn., 1981-82; adjuster Federated Ins. Cos., Owatonna, 1982-84; advanced life markets advisor Federated Life Ins. Co., Owatonna, 1984-87; mktg. svcs. advisor Federated Ins. Cos., 1987-89, 2d v.p., corp. legal counsel, 1989-92, v.p. gen. counsel, 1992—. Mem. Hamline Law Rev., 1979-80. Pres. Owatonna Ins. Women, 1983-84; charter commr. City of Owatonna, 1992—. Mem. ABA, Minn. State Bar Assn., 5th Dist. Bar Assn., Steele County Bar Assn. (sec. 1986-87, v.p. 1987-88, pres. 1988-89), Assn. Life Ins. Counsel, Alliance Am. Insurers (legal com. 1989—). Lutheran. Office: Federated Ins Cos 121 E Park Sq Owatonna MN 55060-3046*

AURETTO, CHRISTINE MARIE, reading specialist; b. Pitts., Nov. 11, 1953; d. Anthony and Eleanor Lilian Auretto; 1 child, Luke. BA, So. Calif. Coll., 1983; MA, Calif. State U., Long Beach, 1989. Cert. tchr., Calif., Wash. K-1st grade tchr. Marantha Acad., Costa Mesa, Calif., 1977-81, 5th grade tchr., 1984-85; tchr. gifted program Vancouver (Wash.)/Cornerstone Sch., 1985-86; 1st grade Cambodian bilingual tchr. Long Beach Unified Sch. Dist., 1986-92; 2d grade tchr. Battleground (Wash.) Sch. Dist., 1992-93; 1st grade tchr. Vancouver Sch. Dist., 1993-94, reading tchr., specialist, 1994—. Pres. Neighborhood Group/Citizens Adv. Com., Clark County, Vancouver, 1994—. Hanake Edn. scholar, 1982. Mem. ASCD, Phi Delta Kappa. Office: Martin Luther King Elem Sch 4801 Idaho St Vancouver WA 98661-6327

AURIN, NIKKI-DAWN, marketing professional; b. Oceanside, Calif., May 18, 1963; d. Austin and Ina Harriet (Gayer) A. Cert. in mktg. comm., U. Calif., Irvine, 1992. Mktg. coord. Computer Software Design, Anaheim, Calif., 1983-86; product devel. mgr. United Ad Label Co., Inc., Brea, Calif., 1987-95; mktg. dir. Gateway Bus. Forms, South Gate, Calif., 1995—. Active Downey (Calif.) Civic Light Opera, 1987, Fullerton (Calif.) Civic Light Opera, 1993. Mem. Am. Guild Patient Account Mgrs., Postal Consortium. Republican. Home: 1681 W Tedmar Ave # 15 Anaheim CA 92802

AUSBURN, LYNNA JOYCE, vocational and technical curriculum developer, consultant; b. Austin, Tex., July 18, 1944; d. Richard F. and Mary Joyce (Aab) Burt; m. Floyd B. Ausburn, July 30, 1966. BS, U. Tulsa, 1966, MA, 1970; PhD, U. Okla., 1976. English and drama tchr. John Marshall High Sch., Oklahoma City, 1966-67; English and speech tchr. West Jr. High Sch., Muskogee, Okla., 1967-70; lang. arts tchr. Muskogee High Sch., 1970-73; grad. teaching asst. clin. instrnl. media and devel. Coll. Edn., U. Okla., 1974-76; edn. svcs. coord. Swinburne Coll. of Tech. and Further Edn., Melbourne, Australia, 1976-84; head planning and rsch. Frankston Coll. Tech. and Further Edn., Melbourne, 1984-89; curriculum devel. coord. Okla. Dept. Vocat. and Tech. Edn., Stillwater, 1990—; sessional lectr. Monash U., Melbourne, 1976-83, external PhD thesis examiner, 1980-84; sessional lectr. State Coll. Victoria, Melbourne, 1980-91; rsch. cons. Vocat. Orientaion Ctr., Royal Melbourne Inst. Tech., 1979; vis. rschr. Pauua New Guinea U. Tech., Lae, 1980; cons., instr. Colombo Plan Staff Coll., Singapore, 1983, Australian Devel. Assistance Bur., Dept. Fgn. Affairs, Bangladesh, 1985, Regional Edn. Ctr. Sci. and Math., Penang, Malaysia, 1986, 88; resource speaker UNESCO Workshop on Tech. Edn. and Nat. Productivity, Colombo, Sri Lanka, 1995; sr. rschr. USAF, 1977-79, Nat. Ctr. R & D, Adelaide, 1983-84; speaker in field. Co-author Evaluation Basics for Instructional Methods and Materials, 1981, Instructional Development Skills for Teaching, 1985; contbr. articles to profl. publs., chpt. to book. Recipient Hon. Mention article award Writer's Digest Nat. Competition, 1991, 92; award-winning photographer, 1990-95; named Bus. Assoc. of Yr., Am. Bus. Women's Assn., 1995. Mem. Australian Coll. Edn., Okla. Vocat. Assn., Am. Vocat. Assn., Okla. Vocat. Instrnl. Materials (state advisor 1992—), Soc. for Tech. Comms., Phi Delta Kappa. Republican. Home: RR 3 Box 47 Cleveland OK 74020-9505 Office: Okla Dept Vocat & Tech Edn 1500 W 7th Ave Stillwater OK 74074-4398

AUSTER, CAROL JEAN, sociology educator; b. Bloomington, Ind., Mar. 2, 1954; d. Donald and Nancy Eileen (Ross) A.; m. Neil George Gussman, Aug. 23, 1986; children: Lauren Jean, Lisa Amy. AB in Social Rels., Colgate U., 1976; MA in Sociology, Princeton U., 1979, PhD in Sociology, 1984. Instr. sociology Franklin and Marshall Coll., Lancaster, Pa., 1981-84, asst. prof., 1984-88, assoc. prof., 1988-96, prof., 1996—, acting chair dept., 1982-83, chair dept., 1988-91; NSF rsch. assoc. N.H. Coll., Manchester, 1974, Hampshire Coll., Amherst, Mass., 1975; cons. dept. planning Lancaster (Pa.) Gen. Hosp., 1984—. Author: The Sociology of Work: Concepts and Cases, 1996; contbr. articles, revs. to profl. jours. N.Y. State Regents scholar Colgate U., 1976; Princeton U. fellow, 1977-80; Rockefeller Found. grantee U. Ill., 1979-80, Alfred P. Sloan Found. grantee, 1993-96. Mem. AAUP (dist. VII rep. to nat. coun. 1986-89, com. F. on confs. 1986-92, memberships grants com. 1987-89, 2d v.p. 1990-92, chair com. B. on ethics 1994—), Am. Sociol. Assn. (com. on employment 1994—), Soc. for Study Social Problems, Sociologists for Women in Society, Ea. Sociol. Soc., So. Sociol. Soc. Office: Franklin and Marshall Coll Dept Sociology Lancaster PA 17604

AUSTER, NANCY EILEEN ROSS, economics educator; b. N.Y.C., Aug. 19, 1926; d. Norman L. and Edith Cornelia (Jacobson) Ross; m. Donald Auster, Aug. 18, 1946; children: Carol J., Ellen R. AB, Barnard Coll., 1948; MBA, Ind. U., 1954. Rsch. assoc. The Conf. Bd., N.Y.C., 1948-51; editor publs. Bur. Bus. Rsch. Ind. U., Bloomington, 1954-56; lectr. St. Lawrence U., Canton, N.Y., 1962-66; from asst. prof. to prof. Canton Coll. Tech., SUNY, 1966-82, disting. svc. prof. econs., 1982-91, disting. svc. prof. econs. emeritus, 1991—; pres. univ. faculty senate SUNY, 1973-75; mem. chancellor's adv. com. disting. tchg. prof. SUNY, 1983-86, chair, 1986-87. Author: (with Donald Auster) Men Who Enter Nursing: A Sociological Analysis, 1970; contbr. articles to profl. jours. Chair adv. coun. St. Lawrence County CETA, Canton, 1977-82. Recipient Professions Excellence award N.Y. State/United U., 1991; USPHS grantee, 1966-70. Unitarian-Universalist. Home: 21 Craig Dr Canton NY 13617

AUSTERMAN, DONNA LYNNE, Spanish language educator; b. Colorado Springs, Colo., Aug. 5, 1947; d. Herman Raymond Ogg and Shirley (Cooper) Price; m. Thomas Lanham Brown, Jan. 26, 1966 (div. Jan. 1972); 1 child, Thomas Roy; m. Randy Lynn Austerman, Nov. 25, 1972; 1 child, Michael Neil. Student, Washburn U., 1965-67; BS, Pittsburg State U., 1970, MS, 1971; postgrad., U. Kans., 1980, U. Okla., 1983, Okla. State U., 1990. Cert. tchr. (life), Mo., std. tchr., Okla. Tchr. Spanish, English Liberal (Mo.) R-2 Schs., 1970-72, Unified Sch. Dist. 346, Mound City, Kans., 1972-74, Nowata (Okla.) Pub. Schs., 1983-86; tchr. Spanish Bartlesville (Okla.) Sch. Dist. # 30, 1986—. Steering com. mem. North Ctrl. Assn., 1993—. Mem. NEA, ASCD, Am. Assn. Tchrs. Spanish and Portuguese, Nat. Staff Devel. Coun., Okla. Edn. Assn., Okla. Fgn. Lang. Tchrs. Assn., Bartlesville Edn. Assn., Bartlesville Fgn. Lang. Coun., Bartlesville Profl. Improvement Com. (chmn. mid-h.s. staff devel. com.). Home: 5648 Steeper Dr Bartlesville OK 74006-9116 Office: Bartlesville Mid/HS 5900 Baylor Dr Bartlesville OK 74006-8909

AUSTIN, ANN SHEREE, lawyer; b. Tyler, Tex., Aug. 25, 1960; d. George Patrick and Mary Jean (Brookshire) A. BA cum laude, U. Houston, 1983; JD, South Tex. Coll., 1987. Bar: Tex. 1987, U.S. Dist. Ct. (no. dist.) Tex. 1988, U.S. Ct. Appeals (5th cir.) 1989, U.S. Dist. Ct. (we. dist.) Tex. 1990, U.S. Ct. Appeals (D.C. cir.) 1992, U.S. Supreme Ct. 1992, U.S. Dist Ct. (ea. dist.) Tex. 1993. With First City Ops. Ctr., Houston, 1980-85; law clk. Lipstet, Singer, Hirsch & Wagner, Houston, 1985-86, Pizzitola, Hinton & Sussman, Houston, 1986-87; briefing atty. Hon. Hal M. Lattimore Ct. Appeals, 2d Jud. Dist., Ft. Worth, 1987-88; assoc. Cantey & Hanger, Ft. Worth and Dallas, 1988-93, Smith, Ralston & Russell, Dallas, 1993-94, Russell, Austin & Henschel, Dallas, 1994-95; prin. Ann S. Austin, Atty. at Law, Arlington, 1995—; tchr. Project Outreach State Bar of Tex., 1992. Chpt. editor: Cases and Materials on Civil Procedure, 1987. Mem. Ft. Worth Hist. Preservation Soc., com. mem., 1992; fundraiser Nat. Com. Prevention Child Abuse, 1988—, Women's Haven. Mem. Tex. Young Lawyers Assn. (women in the profession com. 1992-94, profl. ethics and grievance awareness com. 1992-94, jud. rev. com. 1990), Dallas Bar Assn. (jud. com. 1993-94), Dallas Assn. Young Lawyers, Dallas Women's Bar Assn., Ft. Worth Tarrant County Young Lawyers Assn. (treas. 1989-90, dir. 1989, judge Teen Ct., co-chair Adopt-A-Sch. program), Tarrant County Women's Bar Assn., 5th Cir. Fed. Bar Assn., Am. Inns. of Ct. Methodist. Office: Ann S Austin Atty at Law St James Place Ste 102 2115 St Michaels Dr Arlington TX 76011-9131

AUSTIN, BERIT SYNNOVE, small business owner, warehouse assistant; b. Oslo, Norway, July 22, 1938; came to U.S., 1957; d. Johan Andreas and Astrid (Bjerke) Irgens; m. William Paul Austin, Dec. 22, 1961 (div. 1978); children: Lisa Christine, Paul Erik, Ivar Jon. AA, Saddleback Coll., 1984, AS, 1988. Accounts payable clk. Dynatech Corp., Santa Ana, Calif., 1976-78; accounts payable acct., jr. buyer/Kardex Brunswick Corp., Costa Mesa, Calif., 1978-81; fin. clk. Fluor Corp., Irvine, Calif., 1981-84; warehouse asst. Saddleback Coll., Mission Viejo, Calif., 1984—; owner, cons. Home Prescription, Lake Elsinore, Calif., Mission Viejo, 1984—. Mem. Sierra Country Club, Sons of Norway Fraternal Internat. Soc. (historian 1972, publicity dir. 1973, asst. soc. dir. 1974, social dir. 1992, cultural dir. 1994, pres. 1996). Republican. Lutheran. Home: PO Box 4013 Mission Viejo CA 92690-4013 Office: Home Prescription PO Box 4013 Mission Viejo CA 92690

AUSTIN, JUDY ESSARY, scriptwriter; b. Jackson, Tenn., Apr. 7, 1948; d. Hershel Dee and Elizabeth Sue (Rhodes) Essary; m. James Michael Austin, July 4, 1965; children: James Allan Austin, Julia Ann Austin Patterson. AS, DeKalb Coll., 1988; BA in Communications and Journalism, Mercer U., 1989. Retail mgr. Bankers Note, Atlanta, 1980-84, Le Chocolat Elegant, Atlanta, 1984-85; student asst. student affairs DeKalb Coll., Dunwoody, Ga., 1987-88; asst. art dir. Sportime, Atlanta, 1990-92; writer, prodr. CAMA, Atlanta, 1993-94; freelance scriptwriter Atlanta, 1994-96; bd. dirs. Second Wind Orgn., Dekalb Coll., Dunwoody, 1987-88. Scholar Am. Bus. Womens Assn., 1987. Mem. Women in Communications, NAFE, Phi Kappa Phi. Home: 3133 Raymond Dr Atlanta GA 30340-1826

AUSTIN, MARGARET CULLY, school administrator; b. St. Louis, July 18, 1930; d. Ben Allen and Rosalie Ada (Mersman) Cully; m. June 19, 1954; children: Steven W., Katherine E., Andrea C. AA in Music, Motlow State C.C., Tullahoma, Tenn., 1973; BS in Elem. Edn., Mid. Tenn. State U., 1975, MEd in Reading, 1979; Cert. in Adminstrn., Trevecca Coll., Nashville, 1989. Elem. music tchr. St. Paul the Apostle Sch., Tullahoma, Tenn., 1969-73; teaching prin. Normandy Sch., Bedford County, Tenn., 1975-76; reading specialist Bedford County Schs., 1976-88, Chpt. I cons. tchr., 1989-94, supr. title I/fed. projects, 1994—, testing coord., 1994—, reading cons. spl. edn., 1994—; supe Mem. NEA, Tenn. Edn. Assn., Bedford County Edn. Assn., Internat. Reading Assn., Tenn. Supr. of Edn. Assn. Home: 601 Crestwood Dr Tullahoma TN 37388-2929 Office: Bedford County Bd of Edn 500 Madison St Shelbyville TN 37160-3341

AUSTIN, MARY JANE, small business owner; b. Autauga, Ala., Aug. 17, 1955; d. Henry and Janie Ella (Lewis) A.; 1 child, Keith Roderick. Student, San Diego State U., 1990—. Ptnr. Bobbie's & Marcie's, Prattville, Ala., 1982-85; office asst. Montgomery (Ala.) Area Skills, 1987-88; clk. Am. Svc. Life, Montgomery, 1986-89; ptnr. Say What? Distbrs., Chula Vista, Calif., 1994; owner M.J. Austin Distbg. Co., Chula Vista, 1994—. Author: Secret of Our Ancestors, 1993, Black Men Are Their Own Worst Enemies, 1996; contbr. articles to popular publs. Fundraiser Day of the Young Child, Chula Vista, 1996; co-chair Carol Bower Organ Transplant, Chula Vista, 1996, Hillcrest Home for Abused Children, Chula Vista, 1996; docent Old Town State Hist. Park, San Diego, 1996; vol. Bob Filner for Congress, National City, Calif., 1996. Mem. NOW, NAFE, Chi Epsilon. Democrat. Home: 272 Kennedy St #56 Chula Vista CA 91911 Office: MJ Austin Distbg Co PO Box 121671 Chula Vista CA 91912

AUSTIN, PAGE INSLEY, lawyer; b. Balt., May 1, 1942; d. John Webb and Sallie Byrd (Massey) Insley. BA in Philosophy, Valparaiso U., 1962; MA in Philosophy, Washington U., St. Louis, 1963; postgrad., Yale U., 1963-66; JD, U. Tex., 1977. Bar: Tex. 1977, U.S. Dist. Ct. (so. dist.) Tex. 1978, U.S. Ct. Appeals (10th cir.) 1980, U.S. Ct. Appeals (5th cir.) 1981, U.S. Supreme Ct. 1986. Instr. Yale U., New Haven, 1966-67, U. Houston, 1967-73; assoc. Vinson & Elkins, Houston, 1977-84, ptnr., 1984—; adj. prof. U. Tex., 1986-87. Mem. ABA, Tex. Bar Assn., Houston Bar Assn., Am. Law Inst., Order of Coif, Chancellors. Home: 2706 Glen Haven Blvd Houston TX 77025-2102 Office: Vinson & Elkins 2500 First City Tower 1001 Fannin St Houston TX 77002

AUSTIN, SIGRID LINNEVOLD, counselor; b. Madison, Wis., Aug. 15, 1939; d. Bernhard Olaf Johann and Agnes Elizabeth (Spiva) Linnevold; m. William Jerome Austin, May 16, 1962; children: Christopher Peter, Douglas Patrick, Colin Michael. BA, Barnard Coll., 1961; MS, Va. Commonwealth U., 1986. Lic. profl. counselor. Sr. counselor Peninsula Hosp., Hampton, Va., 1986-88; counselor Williamsburg (Va.) Ctr. for Therapy, 1988—; counselor outreach program Williamsburg Hosp., 1988—; counselor eating disorder program Williamsburg Hosp. Outreach, 1993; crisis counselor William & Mary Police Dept., 1993—; adj. faculty Va. Commonwealth U., Richmond, 1988-90. Asst. editor: (newsletter) The Addiction Letter, 1986-89; contbr. articles to profl. jours. Bd. dirs. Surry County Soc. Prevention of Cruelty to Animals, Surry, Va., 1993; active Nat. Trust Hist. Preservation, Washington, 1992-93, Nat. Conservancy, 1992-93. Scholar Sch. Pub. Affairs, Va. Commonwealth U., 1986. Mem. Internat. Assn. Eating Disorders, Nat. Assn. Alcohol and Drug Abuse, Va. Assn. Alcohol and Drug Abuse, Va. Mental Health Assn., Va. Assn. Clin. Counselors, Obsessive Compulsive Found., Phi Kappa Phi. Democrat. Lutheran. Office: Williamsburg Ctr Therapy 217 Mclaws Cir Ste 2 Williamsburg VA 23185-5649

AUTH, JUDITH, library director. BA in English Lit., U. Calif., Riverside, 1968, grad. advanced mgmt. program, 1990; MLS, UCLA, 1971. Children's libr. Marcy br. Riverside City & County Pub. Libr., 1971-73, ctrl. libr. children's rm., 1973-75, coord. children's svcs., 1975-80, area br. supr., 1980-85, head ctrl. libr., 1985-87, acting head tech. svcs., 1987-88, asst. libr. dir., 1988-91, libr. dir., 1991—; asst. to city mgr. in charge of entrepreneurial mgmt. program City of Riverside, 1988-91. Mem. ALA, Am. Soc. Pub. Adminstrn., Calif. Libr. Assn. (leadership inst. task force 1992-93, mem. assembly 1994), Calif. County Librs. Assn. (sec. 1992-94), So. Calif. Coun. Lit. for Children and Young People (bd. dirs. 1975-90). Office: Riverside City & County Libr 3021 Franklin Ave Riverside CA 92507

AUTOLITANO, ASTRID, consumer products executive; b. Havana, Cuba, Aug. 25, 1938; came to U.S., 1966; d. Manuel and Efigenia (Giquel) Rodriguez; m. Dominick Autolitano, July 23, 1977; children: Astrid Martinez, Manuel Martinez. Student, U. Havana, 1962-64, El Camino Coll., Torrance, Calif., 1968-71, UCLA, Westwood, 1973-75, Columbia U., 1983. Multi-lingual sec. Mattel Toys, Hawthorne, Calif., 1966-69, coord. internat. sales, 1969-73, mgr. Pan Am. sales, 1973-78, dir. export sales and licensees, 1978-83, v.p. Latin Am., 1983-89; sr. v.p. Latin Am. Mattel Toys, El Segundo, Calif., 1989-95, exec. v.p. Latin Am., 1995-96, exec. v.p. Ams., 1996—. Office: Mattel Toys 333 Continental Blvd El Segundo CA 90245-5032

AUTON, LINDA MAY EISENSCHMIDT, lawyer, nurse; b. Alexandria, Va., Sept. 14, 1952; d. Clyde Raymond and Katherine Mae (Flewelling) Eisenschmidt; m. William G. Auton, May 26, 1973. ADN, Laramie County C.C., Cheyenne, Wyo., 1979; BS magna cum laude, Bridgewater State Coll., 1983; JD, Suffolk U., 1988. Bar: Mass. 1988, Ga. 1990, U.S. Supreme Ct. 1994; RN, Mass. Staff and charge nurse VA Med. Ctr., Boston, 1979-80, Cardinal Cushing Gen. Hosp., Brockton, Mass., 1980-85; paralegal Powers & Hall, Boston, 1985-88, assoc., 1988-89; ptnr. Dunn & Auton, Boston, 1989-91; pvt. practice, Abington, Mass., 1991—; developer innovative geropsychiat. unit, unit mgr. Provident Nursing Home, Boston, 1983-84; created AdvoGuard charitable guardianship orgn., 1996; mem. Cranberry Spl. Ethics, Middleboro, Mass., 1993—. Author: Legal, Ethical and Political Issues in Nursing, 1994. Mem. Am. Assn. Nurse Attys. (bd. dirs., exec. com. 1984—, pres. 1994), Am. Psychiat. Nurses Assn., Mass. Nurses Assn. (legis. com. dist. III, entrepreneur coun. 1994), Rockland C. of C., Phi Delta Phi. Office: 231 Centre Ave Abington MA 02351-2207

AUTUMN, CHRISTINE, art educator; b. Bklyn., Jan. 27, 1962; d. Frances Pauline (Everette) Gütter; 1 child, Yaneis Brii. BFA, Pratt Inst., 1984-87. Lic. educator. Art instr. The Puppet Loft, N.Y.C., summer 1986; intern Bklyn. Childrens Mus., 1987-88; bd. of edn. tchr. Ind. Sch. 232 Winthrop Jr. H.S., Bklyn., 1988-89; art tchr. The Studio in a Sch., N.Y.C., 1989-90; instr. N.Y.C. Housing Authority Art Camp, 1990; freelance programs Saturday Art Sch., Taos, N.Mex., 1991; owner pottery bus. Taos, 1992—; mentor Somos, Taos, 1994—; tchr. masters and apprentices, N.Y.C., 1989. Contbr. poetry to anthologies; exhibited in group shows Little Bomb Big Bomb, 1995, Write to Write, 1995, Folk Art at the TCA Iconography, 1991, 92. Home: PO Box 2098 Taos NM 87571

AUYONG, JAN, biologist; b. Honolulu, May 20, 1951; d. Clarence Kwai Fong and Janet Kam Yee (Lum) Auyong; m. Richard Holt Titgen. BA in Psychology, BS in Biol. Scis., U. Hawaii, 1974; MA in Biol. Scis., U. Calif., Santa Barbara, 1981; PhD Resources Devel., Tex. A&M U., 1983. Grad. rsch. asst. U. Calif., Santa Barbara, 1975-76; prin. investigator Marine Rec. Com., Solana Beach, Calif., 1976-78; grad. rsch. asst. Tex. A&M U., College Station, 1979-79, 81-83; policy analyst Dept. of Interior, Washington, 1980; specialist Sea Grant Ext. Svc., Honolulu, 1983-89, asst. dir., 1985-89; dep. dir. Nat. Coastal Resources R&D Inst., Newport, Oreg., 1989-92; prin. Mar Res Assocs., South Beach, Oreg., 1992—; asst. dir. programs Oreg. Sea Grant, Corvallis, 1995—; faculty Marine Resource Mgmt. Program, Oreg. State U., Corvallis, 1992—; cons. Mar Res Assocs., 1992-95. Contbr. articles to profl. jours., chpts. to books. Vice pres. Lincoln County ARC, Newport, Oreg., 1992-95; advisor Ocean Recreation Coun. of Hawaii, 1985-89; chmn. organizing com. Congress on Coastal/Marine Tourism, 1989-91, 94—. Recipient Svc. award Pacon Internat., Honolulu, 1996, Marine Option Program, Honolulu, 1989. Mem. Marine Tech. Soc. (recreation and tourism chair 1996—), Hawaii Assn. Women in Sci. (treas. 1986-89), Hawaiian Acad. Sci. (sec.-treas. 1988-89), The Coastal Soc., Human Dimensions in Wildlife. Home: 434 SE 95th Ct South Beach OR 97366-9713

AVAKIAN, ARLENE VOSKI, women's studies educator; b. New York, Apr. 4, 1939; d. Vaghinak and Berjouhe (Tutuian) A.; single; children: Neal Christopher Ryan, Leah Ryan. BS in Art History, Columbia U., 1961; MA in Social History, U. Mass., 1975, EdD, 1985. Exec. dir. female studies program Cornell U., Ithaca, N.Y., 1970-71; staff asst. women's studies U. Mass., Amherst, 1975-86, lectr. women's studies, 1986-93, assoc. prof. women's studies, 1993—; staff assoc. black studies, women's studies, faculty devel. project U. Mass./Smith Coll., Amherst, Mass., 1981-83; faculty Sch. Social Work Smith Coll., Northampton, Mass., 1990-93. Author: Lion Woman's Legacy: An Armenian American Memoir, 1992; editor: Through the Kitchen Window: Feminists and Food, 1997; co-editor: Afro-American Women and the Vote, 1997. Pres. Amherst (Mass.) Based Organization to Develop Equitable Shelter, 1989—; bd. dirs. Civil Liberties Union of We. Mass., Northampton, Mass., 1990—, Zoryan Inst. for Contemporary Documentation and Rsch., Cambridge, Mass., 1995—; exec. bd. Project SAVE photographic archive of Armenian people, 1990-95. Scholar Rites and Reason program Brown U., Providence, 1982-84; recipient Commonwealth award for Outstanding Svc., State of Mass., Boston, 1985, David Burres award Civil Liberties Union of We. Mass., Northampton, 1993. Mem. Armenian Femisists (founding mem.). Home: 333 Strong St Amherst MA 01002 Office: U Mass Women's Studies 208 Bartlett Amherst MA 01003

AVALLONE, SUSAN BUTTERFIELD, oncological nurse; b. Gardner, Mass., Apr. 5, 1953; d. Richard Waldo and Margaret Allen (Shevis) Butterfield; m. John Avallone, Oct. 21, 1988 (dec.); children: Kristin Rose, Megan Jean. Diploma, Leominster Hosp. Sch. Nursing, 1974; BSN magna cum laude, Salem State Coll., 1988. RN, Colo. Head nurse laminar air flow unit M.D. Anderson Hosp. and Tumor Inst., Houston; staff nurse Dana Farber Cancer Ctr., Boston; sr. staff nurse bone marrow transplant unit Brigham and Women's Hosp., Boston; supr. home health care Physicians Home HealthCare Ltd., Colorado Springs, Pueblo, Colo.; now with Gardner Vis. Nursing Assn. Mem. Sigma Theta Tau. Home: 46 Conant St Gardner MA 01440

AVENI, BEVERLY A., executive aide; b. Stamford, Conn., Sept. 2, 1959; d. Anthony B. Sr. and Lucille F. (Ferretti) A.; m. Jon T. Gallup, Sept. 17, 1989. BA in Polit. Sci., U. Conn., 1981. Legal asst. Cummings and Lockwood, Stamford, 1981-86; family law paralegal Piazza, Melmed and Ackerly, P.C., Stamford, 1986-88; litigation paralegal Abate and Fox, Stamford, 1988-95; exec. aide to mayor City of Stamford, 1995—; pres. Conn. Assn. Paralegals, Bridgeport, 1989-91; mem. seminar faculty, co-author seminar skills book for paralegal Conn. Discovery Skills, 1995. Vol. counselor Rape and Sexual Abuse Crisis Ctr., Stamford, 1983-87; dist. rep. Dem. City Com., Stamford, 1992-96, sec., 1994-96; local coord. Sen. Christopher Dodd's 1992 Reelection Campaign, 1994-96; mem. congl. dist. adv. coun. Conn. Permanent Commn. on Status of Women, 1996; mem. commn. City of Stamford's XV Charter Revision Commn., 1994-95; mem. Mayor's cabinet; Mayor's rep. on various civic coms. and bds. Home: 21 Dartley St Stamford CT 06905 Office: City of Stamford 888 Washington Blvd Stamford CT 06904-2152

AVERETT-SHORT, GENEVA EVELYN, college administrator; b. Boston, Mar. 12, 1938; d. William Pinkney and Geneva Zepplyn (Stepp) A.; m. Roger Inman Blackwell, Dec. 19, 1959 (div. 1975); children: Thomas, LaVerne, Constance; m. Floyd J. Short Jr., July 3, 1984. BA in Social Sci., Bennett Coll., Greensboro, N.C., 1958; EdM, SUNY, Buffalo, 1972; paralegal cert., Prince George's C.C., Largo, Md., 1994. Social caseworker Erie County Dept. Pub. Welfare, Buffalo, 1958-59; substitute tchr. Buffalo Bd. Edn., 1959-60; employment inteviewer N.Y. Dept. Labor, Div. Employment, Buffalo, 1967-69; admissions counselor SUNY, Buffalo, 1969-72; assoc. dean students U. Utah, Salt Lake City, 1972-74; coordinator counseling svcs. Ednl. Devel. Prog., SUNY, Fredonia, 1974-77; acting dir. Ednl. Devel. Prog., SUNY, 1976-77; substitute tchr. Greensboro (N.C.) pub. schs., 1977-78; prog. asst. D.C. Dept. Human Svcs. Commn. on Pub. Health, 1978-89; assessment counselor, coord. Prince George's Community Coll., Largo, Md., 1989-94; cons. in field. Active in past various charitable orgns. Mem. Nat. Alumnae Assn. Bennett Coll., S. Fla. Alumnae Assn. (sec. Bennett Coll. chpt., 1996—), Pierians, Inc. (pres. D.C. chpt. 1992-94). Democrat. Episcopalian. Address: 21621 Altamira Ave Boca Raton FL 33433

AVERSA, DOLORES SEJDA, educational administrator; b. Phila., Mar. 26, 1932; d. Martin Benjamin and Mary Elizabeth (Esposito) Sejda; BA, Chestnut Hill Coll., 1953; m. Zefferino A. Aversa, May 3, 1958; children: Dolores Elizabeth, Jeffrey Martin, Linda Maria. Owner, Personal Rep. and Pub. Rels., Phila., 1965-68; ednl. cons. Franklin Sch. Sci. and Arts, Phila., 1968-72; pres., owner, dir. Martin Sch. of Bus., Inc., Phila., 1972—; file reader, cons. for ct. reporting and travel tng. Southwestern Pub. Co., 1990; mem. ednl. planning com. Ravenhill Acad., Phila., 1975-76. Active Phila. Mus. of Art, Phila. Drama Guild. Mem. Nat. Bus. Edn. Assn., Pa. Bus. Edn. Assn., Am. Bus. Law Assn., Pa. Sch. Counselors Assn., Am.-Italy Soc., Am. Soc. Travel Agts. (sec. Del. Valley chpt., edn. chmn. Del. Valley chpt., nat. travel educators com.), Phila. Hist. Soc., World Affairs Coun. Phila., Hist. Soc. Pa., Phila. Orch. Mem. ASTA (sch. div., nat. educators com.), Chestnut Hill Coll. Alumnae Assn. Roman Catholic. Home: 2111 Locust St Philadelphia PA 19103-4802 Office: 2417 Welsh Rd Philadelphia PA 19114-2213

AVERY, BYLLYE YVONNE, health association administrator. BA in Psychology, Talladega Coll., 1959; MEd in Spl. Edn., U. Fla., 1969; LHD (hon.), Thomas Jefferson U., 1990, SUNY, Binghamton, 1990, Bowdoin Coll., 1993; LLD (hon.), Bates Coll., 1995. Occupl. and recreational therapy aide N.E. Fla. State Hosp., 1959-65; resource tchr. for emotionally disturbed Richard L. Brown Elem. Sch., Jacksonville, Fla., 1966-68; learning disabilities resource tchr. Waldo (Fla.) Cmty. Sch., 1969-70; head tchr. children's mental health unit U. Fla., Gainesville, 1970-76, instr. dept. psychiatry, 1970-76; co-founder, dir. edn. Gainesville, 1976-78; co-founder, dir. pub. rels. Birthplace: An Alternative Birth Environment, Gainesville, 1978-80; dir. CETA Santa Fe C.C., Gainesville, 1980-82; exec. dir., founder Nat. Black Women's Health Project, Atlanta, 1982-90, founding pres., 1990—; vis. fellow dept. health and social behavior Sch. Pub. Health Harvard U., 1991-93; cons. in field. Contbr. articles to profl. publs.; prodr. films: It's Up To Us (PBS documentary), 1985, On Becoming A Woman: Mothers and Daughters Talking Together, 1987. Bd. dirs. Nat Women's Health Network, 1976-81, New World Found., 1986-91, W.K. Kellogg Internat. Friendship Program, 1989-94, Boston Women's Health Book Collective, 1990-92, Global Fund for Women, 1989—, Internat. Women's Health Coalition, 1989—; bd. visitors Tucker Found. Dartmouth Coll., 1990—; mem. women's cancer adv. bd. Dana Farber Cancer Ctr., Boston; mem. adv. com. on rsch. on women's health Office Rsch. on Women's Health, NIH, Bethesda, Md. Recipient Outstanding Woman of Color award Nat. Inst. Women of Color, 1987, NOW, 1987, Svc. award Religious Coalition for Abortion Rights, 1988, Outstanding Svc. to Women and Children award Children's Def. Fund, 1988, award for cmty. svc. in sci., health and tech. award Essence mag., 1989, John D. and Catherine T. MacArthur Found. Fellowship award, 1989, Women of Achievement award YWCA, Atlanta, 1990, Orthro Woman of 21st Century award Orthro Pharm., 1991, Cmty. Svc. award Spelman Coll., 1991, Trends Setters award Nat. Health Coun., 1993, Woman of Achievement award Ms. Found., 1993, Grassroots Realist award Ga. Legis. Black Caucus, 1994, Gustav O. Lienhard award Inst. of Medicine, 1994, Dorothy I. Height Lifetime Achievement award, 1995, Pres.' citation Am. Pub. Health Assn., 1995. Office: Nat Black Women's Health Fund 1237 Ralph D Abernathy Blvd Atlanta GA 30310

AVERY, CHRISTINE ANN, pediatrician; b. Bklyn., Mar. 30, 1951; d. Basil Steven and Mary P. Goerner; m. Henry Jakob Wachtendorf, June 7, 1973; 1 child, James. BS summa cum laude, U. Houston, 1972; MD, U. Tex. Health Sci. Ctr., 1976. Resident in pediatrics U. Tex. Health Sci. Ctr., San Antonio, 1976-79, asst. clin. prof. pediatrics and otorhinolaryngology; dir. Otitis Media Study Ctr., NIH, San Antonio, 1980-87, asst. prof. pediatrics Cornell Med. Ctr., 1987-89; assoc. dir. anti-inflammatory/pulmonary clin. rsch. pharm. div. Ciba-Geigy Corp., Summit, N.J., 1989-93, assoc. dir. cardiovascular clin. rsch. pharm. divsn., 1994-95, assoc. dir. med. affairs, 1995—. Contbr. articles to profl. jours. Recipient Physician Recognition award, 1979, 82, 85. Republican. Roman Catholic. Office: Ciba-Geigy Corp Pharm Div 556 Morris Ave # 3081 Summit NJ 07901-1330

AVERY, JEANNE, writer, astrologer; b. Pinehurst, Ga., Oct. 24, 1931; d. Bolin Ivey Leaptrot and Lucy Mae Hawkins; m. Thomas Joseph Henesy (div. June 1964); children: Sharon Andrews, Diane Erdman, David Henesy. BA, George Washington U., Washington, 1952. Author: The Rising Sign, 1982, Astrological Aspects, 1985, Astrology and Your Past Lives, 1987, Astrology and Your Health, 1989, A Soul's Journey, 1996. Bd. dirs. Internat. Transpersonal Psychology. Mem. Am. Fedn. Astrologers (tchr., lectr. 1972-90), Nat. Assn. Transpersonal Psychology (bd. dirs.). Democrat. Presbyterian.

AVERY, LAURA J., fund raising consultant; b. Norwood, Mass.; d. Lyman Carew and Edith (Henry) A. BA, Wells Coll., 1973. Admissions officer Bennett Jr. Coll., Millbrook, N.Y., 1973-74; devel. officer Scripps Coll., Claremont, Calif., 1974-77; mgr. Quincy Howe Photography, N.Y.C., 1977-78; campaign dir. Riverdale Country Sch., Bronx, N.Y., 1978-81; v.p. Marts and Lundy, Inc., Lyndhurst, N.J., 1981—, also bd. dirs. Trustee Wells Coll., Aurora, N.Y., 1994—; adv. bd. Women's Sports Found., East Meadow, N.Y., 1993—; bd. dirs. SHR Habitat for Humanity, Norfolk, Va., 1995—. Democrat. Home: PO Box 1305 Chesapeake VA 23327

AVERY, MARGARET, make-up artist, singer; b. Lorain, Ohio, July 20, 1951; d. Joseph Raymond and Margaret Mae (Meszes) Nagy; m. Jim Avery; (div. 1981). Makeup artist Cinandre Salon, N.Y.C., 1975-77, freelance mags., commls., video, N.Y.C., 1977-90; freelance make-up artist, 1977-94; singer N.Y.C., 1985-94, Jan Wallmans, Trocadero, Angry Squire, Eighty Eights, Duplex, The Supper Club, N.Y.C.; spokesperson Complex 15 (moisturizer) Nat'l 1989, Schering Lab. Media (TV-Radio Press); cons. Mary Kay Cosmetics; vol. worker for Diana Vreeland, Met. Mus. Art, N.Y.C., 1980-83. Makeup work for various mags. including Vogue, Self, Glamour, Mademoiselle, Harper's Bazaar, Elle, Bride's, Cosmopolitan, New Woman, Mirabella, New York, New York Times Mag., German Vogue, French Vogue, Italian Vogue, Harper's Queen, Brit. Vogue, Lears; makeup work for various notables including Goldie Hawn, Isabella Rosellini, Brooke Shields, Shari Belafonte, Paulina, Tracy Pollan, Nicolette Sheridan, Donna Dixon, Virginia Madsen, Dustin Hoffman, Victoria Principal, Lori Singer, Twyla Tharpe, Joanna Pacula, Barbara Bush, (photographers) Helmut Newton, Richard Avedon, Irving Penn, Denis Piel, Eric Boman, Deborah Turbeville, Andrea Blanche, Susan Shacter, Lord Snowdon, Al Pacino. Democrat. Roman Catholic. Office: Streeters 568 Broadway Rm 504A New York NY 10012

AVERY, MARY ELLEN, pediatrician, educator; b. Camden, N.J., May 6, 1927; d. William Clarence and Mary (Miller) A. AB, Wheaton Coll., Norton, Mass., 1948, DSc (hon.), 1974; MD, Johns Hopkins U., 1952; DSc (hon.), Trinity Coll., 1976, U. Mich., 1975, Med. Coll. Pa., 1976, Albany Med. Coll., 1977, Med. Coll. Wis., 1978, Radcliffe Coll., 1978; MA (hon.), Harvard U., 1974; LHD (hon.), Emmanuel Coll., 1979, Northeastern U., 1981, Russell Sage Coll., 1983, Meml. U., Newfoundland, 1993. Intern Johns Hopkins Hosp., 1953-54, resident, 1954-57; research fellow in pediatrics Boston, 1957-59, Balt., 1959-69; assoc. prof. pediatrics Johns Hopkins U., 1964-69; prof., chmn. dept. pediatrics McGill U. Med. Sch., 1969-74; prof. pediatrics Harvard U., 1974—; physician-in-chief Montreal Children's Hosp., 1969-74, Children's Hosp. Med. Center, Boston, 1974-85; mem. Med. Rsch. Coun. Can.; mem. study sect. NIH, 1968-71, 84-88. Author: The Lung and Its Disorders in the Newborn Infant, 4th edit., 1981, (with A. Schaffer) Diseases of the Newborn, 1971, 6th edit. (with H.W. Taeusch and R. Ballard), 1991; (with G. Litwack) Born Early, 1984; author, editor: (with L. First) Pediatric Medicine, 1988, 2nd edit., 1994; also articles; mem. editorial bd. Pediatrics, 1965-71, Am. Rev. Respiratory Diseases, 1969-73, Am. Jour. Physiology, 1967-73, Jour. Pediatrics, 1974-84, Medicine, 1985, Johns Hopkins Med. Jour., 1978-82, Clin. and Investigative Critical Care Medicine, 1990, New Eng. Jour. Medicine, 1990-95. Trustee Wheaton Coll. (1965-85), Radcliffe Coll., Johns Hopkins U., 1982-88. Recipient Mead Johnson award in pediatric rsch., 1968, Trudeau medal Am. Thoracic Soc., 1984, Nat. Medal of Sci. NSF, 1991; Markle scholar in med. scis., 1961-66. Fellow AAAS (dir. 1989), NAS, Internat. Pediatric Assn. (standing com. 1986-89), Am. Acad. Pediatrics, Am. Acad. Arts and Scis., Royal Coll. Physicians and Surgeons Can.; mem. Can. Pediatric Soc., Am. Physiol. Soc., Soc. Pediatric Rsch. (pres. 1972-73), Brit. Pediatric Assn. (hon.), Inst. Medicine (coun. 1987), Am. Pediatric Soc. (pres. 1990), Phi Beta Kappa, Alpha Omega Alpha. Office: 221 Longwood Ave Boston MA 02115-5817

AVERY, MAURINE ANN, health record administrator; b. St. Paul, Aug. 19, 1929; d. Myron Rosenow and Myrtle Charlotte (Bladholm) Grant; m. Eugene Vernon Avery, June 29, 1951; children: Susan, Cathlin, James, William, Anne. BA cum laude, Coll. St. Scholastica, 1976; BA, U. Minn., 1951. Registered record adminstr. Health info. system analyst St. Louis Park Med. Ctr., Mpls., 1976-81; med. data specialist Found. for Health Care Evaluation, Mpls., 1981; instr. Seattle U., 1984-85; health record adminstr. Fircrest Sch., Seattle, 1986-88; med. records coord. Group Health, Inc., Mpls., 1988-91; health record cons. Good Samaritan of Minn., St. Paul, 1992-94; retired; cons. in field. Co-author: Medical Records in Ambulatory Care, 1984; contbr. articles to profl. publs. Mem. NOW, Am. Health Info. Mgmt. Assn., Minn. Health Info. Mgmt. Assn. (numerous coms. 1975—), Am. Med. Record Assn. (Literary award 1984), Zeta Tau Alpha. Mem. United Ch. of Christ. Home: 9505 Woodbridge Rd Bloomington MN 55438

AVERY, VIDA LETITIA, accountant, secondary education educator; b. Nashville, Sept. 6, 1962; d. Parnell Napolean and Gloria Magdalene (Reid) Avery. B.A. in Econs., Spelman Coll., 1984, MA in Edn. Brenau U., 1995. Cert. tchr. Ga. Mgr. trainee United Labs. Am., Marietta, Ga., 1984-85; fin. coordinator Tempa Temporaries, Atlanta, 1985-86; staff acct. Turner Assocs., Atlanta, 1986-88; asst. acct. TBS Turner Program Svcs., 1988-89, jr. acct., 1989-90; sr. acct. The Atlanta Journal/Constitution, 1990-92; English tchr. DeKalb County Sch. System, Doraville, Ga., 1992—. Democrat. Mem. Ch. Christ.

AVILES, YVETTE MARIE, human resources specialist; b. N.Y.C., Oct. 29, 1966; d. Gilbert Anthony and Zaida Luz (Alers) A. BA in Psychology, LaSalle U., 1988; postgrad., Fairleigh Dickson Univ., 1992—. Asst. mgr. Consumer Value Stores, Teaneck, N.J., 1988-89; sr. unit supr. Covenant House, N.Y.C., 1989; human resource recruiter Republic Nat. Bank, N.Y.C., 1990-93; nat. recruiter Butler TG/G Com., Montvale, N.J., 1993-94; recruiter Am. Cyanamid, Wayne, N.J., 1994—. Mem. Soc. Human Resources Mgmt., NAFE. Home: 164 Ft Lee Rd Teaneck NJ 07666-3901 Office: Am Cyanimid 1 Cyanamid Plz Wayne NJ 07470-1712

AVIN, DOROTHY ELIZABETH CLARK, retired educator, artist; b. Gt. Barrington, Mass., Sept. 30, 1948; d. Frederick Holley and Catharine Annette (Lippincott) Clark; m. Brian Howard Avin, June 28, 1968 (div. Dec. 1986; children: Jacquelyn Estelle, Lori Catharine Avin Meringolo. Student, SUNY, Buffalo, 1966-68; BA in Art Edn., Roosevelt U., 1971. Cert. advanced 5-12 profl. math. tchr., 7-12 art tchr., Md. Substitute tchr. Chgo. Pub. Schs., 1971-72, Miami (Fla.) Jackson Sr. H.S., 1972-73, Montgomery County (Md.) Pub. Schs., 1977-79; office mgr. BH Aim, Pa., 1980-84; substitute tchr. Sherwood H.S., Sandy Spring, Md., 1985-86; office mgr. Brian H. Avin, M.D., P.A., 1980-84; tchr. math. Magruder H.S., Rockville, Md., 1986-87, Blair H.S., Silver Spring, Md., summer 1987; tchr. math. Bethesda (Md.)-Chevy Chase H.S., 1987-88, 90, tchr. art, 1987, 88-90; ret., 1990; curriculum developer, textbook evaluator Montgomery County Pub. Schs., Rockville, 1985-89. Exhibited in group show Albright Knox Mus. Contemporary Art, Buffalo, 1966, Caraitas Soc. of St. John's Coll., Annapolis, Md., 1990-96, Agora Galalery, N.Y.C., 1992; represented in permanent collection Mus. Without Wall, Bemus Point, N.Y. Active various charitble orgns., Montgomery County, 1977-80, Anne Arundel County, Md., 1995—; fundraiser Wolf Trap Ctr. for Performing Arts, Va., 1986, Sherwood H.S., 1985-86. Recipient achivement in arts award Washington Performing Arts, 1987, art award Nat. Renaissance Alive in Am., 1991, 92, letter of recognition Barker Found., Washington, 1993; named Soho Internat. Competition winner, 1992. Mem. NEA, Md. Fedn. Art, Mus. in Arts Mus. (charter). Episcopalian. Home and Studio: 1084 Broadwater Point Rd Churchton MD 20733

AVINGER, SHARI RAE, accountant; b. Rantoul, Ill., Nov. 23, 1960; d. Ronald Quentin and Rachael Anne (Addicott) A.; m. Michael Allen Westerbuhr, Oct. 26, 1981 (div. Apr., 1985). AAS in Acctg., So. Nev. C.C., Las Vegas, 1996. Mgr. Texaco Refining & Mktg., Inc., Colo. Springs, Colo., 1989; food & beverage auditor MGM Marina, Las Vegas, 1989-90, Hacienda Hotel, Casino, Las Vegas, 1990-94; fin. and systems analyst Sahara Hotel, Casino, Las Vegas, 1994-95, POS supr. and systems analyst, 1995—. Mem. Inst. Mgmt. Accts., Phi Theta Kappa. Office: Sahara Hotel & Casino 2535 Las Vegas Blvd S Las Vegas NV 89109

AVOLIO, ANITA, state official; b. Trenton, N.J., Nov. 14, 1958; d. Pat and Rose (Volpe) A. BA, Boston U., 1980. Lic. real estate sales assoc., Pa., N.J. Employee rels. asst. Mobil R & D Corp., Paulsboro, N.J., 1980-82; labor rels. coord. State N.J. Dept. Human Svcs., Trenton, 1982—. Mediator Mcpl. Ct., Hamilton Twp., 1994—. Home: 112 Summit Trace Rd Langhorne PA 19047

AVRAHAM, REGINA, retired secondary education educator; b. Ludenscheid, Germany, Aug. 15, 1935; Came to U.S., 1937.; d. Joseph and Feiga (Press) Artman; m. Josef Esa Abraham, Mar. 12, 1962; children: Randi Beth, Jesse Richard. BS, City Coll., N.Y.C., 1955. Elem. tchr. N.Y. Bd. Edn., 1955-63; tchr. N.Y. Bd. Edn., Bklyn., 1963-91; sci. cons., contbg. writer N.Y.C. Bd. Edn. Sci. Curriculum, 1996—; sci. and health magnet tchr. Bd. Edn., N.Y., 1987-91; presenter in field. Author: Our Founding Sisters, 1976, Readings in Life Science, 1986, Readings in Physical Science, 1986, The Downside of Drugs, 1988, Substance Abuse Treatment and Prevention, 1988, The Circulation System, 1989, The Digestive System, 1989, The Reproductive System, 1989; contbg. editor Tchr. Ctrs. Consortium, 1989. Woodrow Wilson fellow, 1989; named Tchr. of Yr., Bklyn. Sch. Bd., 1987. Mem. United Fed. Tchrs. Democratic. Home: 2218 Avenue P Brooklyn NY 11229-1508

AVRAM, HENRIETTE DAVIDSON, librarian, government official; b. N.Y.C., Oct. 7, 1919; d. Joseph and Rhea (Olsho) Davidson; m. Herbert Mois Avram, Aug. 23, 1941; children: Lloyd, Marcie, Jay. Student, Hunter Coll., N.Y.C., George Washington U.; ScD (hon.), So. Ill. U., 1977; DLitt (hon.), Rochester Inst. Tech., 1991; DSc (hon.), U. Ill., 1993. Systems analyst, methods analyst, programmer Nat. Security Agy., 1952-59; systems analyst Am. Rsch. Bur., 1959-61, Datatrol Corp., 1961-65; supervisory info. systems specialist Libr. of Congress, Washington, 1965-67, asst. coord. info. systems, 1967-70, chief MARC Devel. Office, 1970-76, dir. Network Devel. Office, 1976-80, dir. processing systems, network and automation planning, 1980-83, asst. libr. for processing svcs., 1983-89, assoc. libr. Collection Svcs., 1989-92; ret. Libr. Congress, 1992; chmn. network adv. com. Libr. of Congress, Washington, 1981-92, chmn. emerita network adv. com., 1992—; chair subcom. 2 sectional com. Z39 Am. Nat. Standards Inst., 1966-80, RECON Working Task F, 1968-73, Internat. Rels. Round Table, 1986=87, subcom. 4 working group 1 on character sets Internat. Orgn. for Standardization, 1971-80; lectr. sch. of info. and libr. sci. Cath. U. Am., Washington, 1973—, com. mem. strategies for 80's, 1980-81; bd. visitors libr. and learning resources com., 1980; mem. internat. standards coord. com. Info. Sys. Standards Bd., 1983-86; del. to U.S. nat. com. UNESCO/Gen. Info. Program, 1983; chair internat. rels. com. Nat. Info. Standards Orgn., 1983-92. Bd. editors: Jour. Library Automation, 1970-72; contbr. articles to profl. jours. Recipient Superior Svc. award Libr. of Congress, 1968, Margaret Mann citation, 1971, Fed. Woman's award, 1974, Achievement award ALA/Libr. Info. Tech. Assn., 1980, Meritorious Svc. award ANSI, 1992, Disting. Exec. Svc. award Fed. Govt., 1990; co-recipient Rsch. Libr. of Yr. award Assn. Coll. and Rsch. Libr. Acad., 1979. Fellow Internat. Fedn. Libr. Assns. and Instns. (chair working group on content designators 1972-77, chair profl. bd. 1979-81, mem. program mgmt. com. 1983-90, mem. exec. bd. 1983-87, 1st v.p. 1985-87); mem. ALA (bd. dirs., past pres. info sci. and automation div., John Ames Humphrey Forest Press award 1990, Melvil Dewey award 1981, Lippincott award 1988), Am. Soc. Info. Sci. (spl. interest group on libr. automation and networks 1965), Spl. Librs. Assn. (Recognition award 1990), Assn. Libr. and Info. Sci. Edn., Assn. Bibliog. Agys. Gt. Britain, Australia, Can. and U.S. (del. 1977—). Home: 1776 Elton Rd Silver Spring MD 20903-1701

AVRECH, GLORIA MAY, psychotherapist; b. San Jose, Calif., Oct. 17, 1944; d. Benjamin and Lillian (Yudelowitz) A.; life ptnr. William Woodruff. BA, U. Calif., Berkeley, 1966; MSW, U. Md., 1969; PhD, Inst. Clin. Social Work, Calif., 1987. Bd. cert. social worker. Sch. social worker Balt. City Pub. Schs., 1969-70; psychiatric social worker Calif. Dept. Social Welfare Cmty. Svcs. Br., L.A., 1970-72; clin. social worker Pasadena (Calif.) Child Guidance Clinic, 1972-82; pvt. practice psychotherapist Pasadena, 1976—; field instr. U. So. Calif. Sch. Social Work, L.A., 1978-82. Contbr. book and movie revs., Jour. Psychological Perspectives, 1989-95. VISTA fellow, Balt., 1967-68, Children's Bur. fellow, Balt., 1968-69. Mem. NASW, Soc. Clin. Social Work, Assn. Humanistic Psychology, Assn. Transpersonal Psychology, Analytical Psychology Club. Democrat. Office: 130 S Euclid Ave Ste 6 Pasadena CA 91101

AWE, CLARA, academic administrator; b. Lagos, Nigeria, Nov. 25; came to U.S., 1978; d. Michael and Philomena (Ekeocha) Okorie; m. Yinka Awe, June 24, 1978; children: Abiola, Bola. BS, Roosevelt U., 1981, MS, 1983; D Ednl. Adminstrn., No. Ill. U., 1995. Tng. specialist Truman Coll., Chgo.,

1986-87; admissions counselor Chgo. State U., 1986-87; sr. admissions counselor Coll. of Pharmacy/U. Ill., Chgo., 1991-92, asst. to the dean, 1993, dir. of urban health, 1993—; adj. prof. Chgo. State U., 1986-87, Northeastern U., Evanston, Ill., 1986-88, Coll. of Pharmacy, U. Ill., 1995—. Vol. Meals on Wheels, Chgo., 1994—; mentor Urban H.S. Students, Chgo., 1991—. Mem. AAUW, Ill. Concerned Blacks in Higher Edn., Assn. of Black Women in Higher Edn., Am. Coun. on Ednl. Nat. Identification, Am. Ednl. Rsch. Assn., Assn. for Study of Higher Edn., Beta Gamma Sigma. Home: 18058 Tarpon Ct Homewood IL 60430

AWIAKTA, MARILOU, poet, writer, lecturer; b. Knoxville, Tenn., Jan. 24, 1936; m. Paul Thompson, Dec. 22, 1957; children: Alix, Audrey, Andrew. BA, U. Tenn., 1958. Lectr. Brandeis U., Tufts U., N. Mex.; cons. Aaron Copeland Festival. Author: Abiding Appalachia: Where Mountain and Atom Meet, 1978, 8th edit., 1995 (selected by U.S. Info. Agy. for Women in Contemporary World tour 1986), Rising Fawn and the Fire Mistery-A Story of Heritage, Family and Courage, 1833, 1983 (selected by U.S. Info. Agy. for Women in Contemporary World tour 1986), anniv. edit., 1992; Selu: Seeking the Corn-Mother's Wisdom, 1993, abridged version on audiocassettte, 1995 (Grammy award nomination 1995), monographs; contbr. to anthologies, periodicals including MS mag., Parabola, Greenfield Review, others; performed works on TV including Telling Tales, 1990; cons. to film The Good Mind, 1982; Tell It on the Mountain produced for Nat. Pub. Radio. civilian liaison officer and translator USAF, Laon AFB, France, 1964-67; mem. literary panel Tenn. Arts Commn., 1982-89, chair, 1987-89; bd. dirs. Nat. Conf. Christians and Jews, 1984-90, Women's Found. Greater Memphis, 1995—; commr. Mayor's Internat. Heritage Commn., 1987-90; mem. Leadership Memphis, 1984—, Network Girl Scouts Am., 1986, Women's Com. Against Crime, 1988-90.; bd. dirs. Tenn. Humanities Coun., 1994—, chair grants com., 1995-96. Recipient Woman of Vision award Women of Achievemnt, 1988, Disting. Tenn. Writer award Smoky Mountain Writer's Conf., 1989, Outstanding Contbrn. to Appalachian Lit. Appalachian Writers Assn. 1991, Leadership award Nat. Conf. Christians and Jews, Person of Quality award NOW. Mem. Native Am. Inter Tribal Assn. (cofounder 1982, amb. at large 1986-90), Wordcraft Cir. of Native Am. Writers and Storytellers (coord. Tenn. 1994-95, mem. bd. nat. caucus 1995—). Agent: c/o Fulcrum Pub Ste 350 350 Indiana St Golden CO 80401*

AXELROD, BERNADETTE BONNER, television director, producer; b. Honolulu, Mar. 7, 1963; d. Horace Teddlie and Florence Ayson (Suyat) B. Student, Loyola Marymount U., 1981-82; BS in Broadcast Journalism, U. Ill., 1985. Prodn. asst. Sta. KITV-TV (ABC), Honolulu, 1984; studio technician Sta. WCIA-TV (CBS), Champaign, Ill., 1984; teaching asst. U. Ill., Champaign, 1984-85; programming coord. People's Choice TV, Rantoul, Ill., 1985; dir., tech. dir. Sta. WICS-TV (NBC), Springfield, Ill., 1985-89; producer, dir. Sta. KPLR-TV, St. Louis, 1989-90, Sta. WFLD-TV (Fox), Chgo., 1990-95, Sta., WLS (ABC), Chgo., 1995—; prodr. Children's Miracle Network Telethon, Springfield, 1988-89, dir., St. Louis, 1990; speaker St. Louis Sch. Partnership Program, 1990, U. Ill., Champaign, 1994; dir. Fox News Chgo., 1990; prodr., dir. A Sleek Preview, 1993, Bumper to Bumper, 1994. Recipient 3 Midwest Emmy award nominations, 1993, 2 nominations, 1994. Mem. NATAS, Dirs. Guild Am. (mem. East/Midwest coun. 1994—, Chgo. coordinating com. 1994—), Kappa Tau Alpha, Phi Kappa Phi. Roman Catholic. Office: WLS-ABC 190 N State St Chicago IL 60601

AXELROD, LEAH JOY, tour company executive; b. Milw., Sept. 7, 1929; d. Harry J. and Helen Janet (Ackerman) Mandelker; m. Leslie Robert Axelrod, Mar. 10, 1951; children: David Jay, Craig Lewis, Harry Besser, Garrick Paul, Bradley Neal, Nell Anne. BS, U. Wis., 1951. Creative drama specialist Highland Park Parks & Recreation Dept., Ill., 1962-82; program specialist Pub. Libr., Highland Park, 1972-82; ednl. cons. Bd. Jewish Edn., Chgo., 1973-80; children's edn. specialist Jewish Community Ctr., Chgo., 1975-82; tour cons. My Kind of Town Tours, Highland Park, 1975-79, pres., 1979—. Editor: Highland Park: All American City, 1976. Co-author: Highland Park By Foot or By Frame, 1980; Highland Park: American Suburb, 1982. Bd. dirs. Midwest Fedn. Temple Sisterhoods, 1975-79, Midwest Zionist Youth Commn.; pres. B'nai Torah Sisterhood, 1982-84; founding mem., v.p. Highland Park Hist. Soc., pres. 1987-94, past pres., 1994—, bd. dirs., 1996—; bd. dirs. Ill. State Hist. Soc., 1989—, Friends Jens Jenson, 1995—; founder, bd. dirs. Chgo. Jewish Hist. Soc.; mem. exec. com. Apple Tree Theatre Co., mem. at large, mem. adv. bd.; active Highland Park Historic Preservation Commn. Mem. Nat. Assn. Women Bus. Owners, Am. Theatre Assn., Ill. Theatre Assn. (dir. creative dramatics 1977-79), Hadassah Club (Highland Park chpt.), Chgo. Area Women's History Conf. Bd., Coun. for Ill. History, North Shore Sr. Ctr. (assoc. bd. mem.) Home: 2100 Linden Ave Highland Park IL 60035-2516 Office: My Kind of Town Tours Inc PO Box 924 Highland Park IL 60035-0924

AXTHELM, NANCY, advertising executive. Exec. v.p. Grey Advt. Inc. Office: Grey Advt Inc 777 Third Ave New York NY 10017*

AYALA, ROWENA WINIFRED, principal; b. Detroit; d. Reginald Peter Ayala, Sept. 17, 1955; children: Kevin, Terrence, Peter, Kathryn, Gail, Gladys. BS, Mich. State U., 1955; MEd, Marygrove Coll., 1972; EdD, Wayne State U., 1977. Tchr. Cass Tech. High Sch., Detroit, 1967-75; jr. adminstrv. asst. Detroit Pub. Schs., 1975-80; prin. Crockett Adult Edn. & Career Ctr., Detroit, 1980—; bd. dirs. Crockett Tech. High Sch., Detroit, 1980—. Mem. Jack and Jill Am., Detroit, Great Lakes chpt. of the Links, Inc.; bd. dirs. Barat Human Svcs., Detroit. Recipient Disting. Svc. award Mich. Black Coll. Alumni Assn., 1987, Achievement award Booker T. Washington Assn., 1990. Mem. NAACP (life), Am. Vocat. Assn., Mich. Assn. Secondary Sch. Prins., Mich. Assn. Health Occupation (hon. life), Orgn. Sch. Adminstrs. and Suprs., Met. Area Svc. Orgn., Alpha Kappa Alpha, Phi Delta Kappa. Roman Catholic. Home: 19444 Parkside St Detroit MI 48221-1834 Office: Crockett Tech High Sch 571 Mack Ave Detroit MI 48201-2137

AYCOCK, PAMELA GAYLE, insurance account manager; b. Kenansville, N.C., July 22, 1961; d. Herbert Carol and Judith Ann (Thigpen) A. Assoc. Bus. Adminstrn., James Sprunt Community Coll., 1990; student, N.C. State U., 1979-80. Cert. ins. svc. rep., profl. ins. woman; lic. ins. agt. Adminstrv. specialist Brown & Root, Inc., Bay City, Tex., 1980-81, Houston, 1981-83; litigation supr. Brown & Root, U.S.A., Houston, 1983-85; underwriting asst. Interstate Casualty Ins., Kinston, N.C., 1985-89; account exec. SIA Group, Jacksonville, N.C., 1989-95; acct. mgr. Alexander & Alexander of the Carolinas, Inc., Raleigh, N.C., 1995—. Author: East Duplin Boosters Club Athletic Program, 1987, 88. Mem. com. Wallace (N.C.) Area Cancer Fund, 1990. Recipient CISR award Ind. Ins. Agts. of N.C., 1995. Mem. NAFE, DAR (award 1979), Am. Soc. Quality Control (charter Gulf Coast sect., sec. 1980-81, chmn. publicity 1980-82), Onslow Assn. Ins. Profls. (membership com. 1991-93, Cystic Fibrosis chmn. 1991-92), N.C. Assn. Ins. Women (bd. dirs. 1990-96, publicity chmn. 1991-92, membership chmn. 1992-93, by-laws chmn. 1993-94, state v.p. 1992-93, state pres.-elect 1993-94, state pres. 1994-95, chmn. of the bd. 1995-96). Democrat. Baptist. Home: 44 Penwood Rd Willow Spring NC 27592

AYDELOTTE, MYRTLE KITCHELL, nursing administrator, educator, consultant; b. Van Meter, Iowa, May 31, 1917; d. John J. and Larava Josephine (Gutshall) Kitchell; m. William O. Aydelotte, June 22, 1956; children—Marie Elizabeth, Jeannette Farley. B.S., U. Minn., 1939, M.A., 1947, Ph.D., 1955; postgrad., Columbia U. Tchrs. Coll., summer 1948. Head nurse Charles T. Miller Hosp., St. Paul, 1939-41; surg. teaching St. Mary's Hosp. Sch. Nursing, Mpls., 1941-42; instr. U. Minn., 1945-49; dir., dean State U. Iowa Coll. Nursing, 1949-57, prof., 1957-62; assoc. chief nurse VA Hosp. Rsch. for Nursing, Iowa City, 1963-64, chief nursing rsch., 1964-65; prof. U. Iowa Coll. Nursing, 1964-76, 82-88; exec. dir. Am. Nurses Assn., 1977-81; dir. nursing U. Iowa Hosps. and Clinics, 1968-76; mem. sci. adv. bd. Ctr. for Health Rsch. Wayne State U., 1972-76, Inst. Medicine, 1973—; cons. U. Minn., 1970, 82, 90, U. Rochester, 1971, U. Mich., 1970, 73, U. Colo., 1970-71, U. Hawaii, 1972-73, Ariz. State U., 1972, U. Nebr., 1972-73. Contbr. articles to profl. jours.; editorial bd.: Nursing Forum, 1969-72, Jour. Nursing Adminstrn, 1971. Mem., v.p. Iowa City Library Bd., 1961-67; mem. Johnson County Bd. Health, 1967-70; mem. adv. com. on family living courses Iowa City Bd. Edn., 1970-72. Served with Army Nurse Corps, 1942-46. Mem. Am. Nurses Assn., Am. Hosp. Assn., Am. Acad. Nursing, Sigma Theta Tau (research com. 1968-72). Home: 201 N 1st Ave Apt 308 Iowa City IA 52245-3614

AYLIN, ELIZABETH TWIST PABST, real estate broker, developer; b. Pueblo, Colo., Aug. 22, 1917; d. Earl Joshua and Mabel Prudence (Benning) Twist; m. Julius Frohne Pabst, Apr. 16, 1944 (dec. Mar. 1984); children: Rachel Pabst Mrvichin, Jane Selkirk Pabst; m. Robert Norman Aylin, May 5, 1990. AB, U. No. Colo., 1939. English lang. teacher high sch., Holyoke, Colo., 1939-40; sec. to chancellor U. Denver, 1940-41; sec. to regional dir. Civil Svc., Denver, 1941-42; pers. dir. Denver Med. Depot, U.S. Quartermaster Corps, 1942; bus. adminstr. Pabst Home Builders and Lumber Co., Houston, 1945-84; owner, pres. Selkirk Island Corp., Houston, 1984—, Selkirk Island Utilities Corp., Houston, 1984—, Pabst Corp., Houston, 1984—. Wave ensign USN, 1942-44. Recipient Alumni Contbn. to Bus. award U. No. Colo., 1991. Mem. Houston Area Ret. Officers Assn. (v.p. 1986-90, 92-93). Home: 3835 Olympia Dr Houston TX 77019-3031 Office: 1 Selkirk Rd Bay City TX 77414-9341

AYLON, HELENE, artist; b. Bklyn., Feb. 4, 1931; d. Anshel Greenfield and Etta (Scheinberg) Greenfield Bodoff; m. Mandel Fisch, Nov. 24,1949 (dec. Feb. 1961); children: Nathaniel, Renee Emunah. BA cum laude, Bklyn. Coll., 1960; MA in Women's Studies, Antioch West U., San Francisco, 1981. Exhibited in group shows Berenson Gallery, Fla., 1970, Aldrich Mus., Conn., 1970, 94, Whitney Mus., 1970, Skidmore Coll., Saratoga Springs, N.Y., 1971, Storm King Art Ctr., Mountainville, N.Y., 1972, Oakland Mus., 1975, Dart Gallery, Chgo., 1976, U. Calif., Irvine, Oberlin Coll., U. Wis., 1978-80, Mus. Contemporary Hispanic Art, 1987, Harn Mus., Gainesville, Fla., 1994, Mus. Modern Art, 1993-94, also others; process painting includes Max Hutchinson Gallery, N.Y.C., 1970, 72, Betty Parsons Gallery, 1975, 79, Susan Caldwell Gallery, N.Y.C., 1975; installation art includes Cleve. Ctr. for Contemporary Art, 1989, Knoxville Mus., 1993, U. Art Mus., Berkeley, 1996, N.Y. Jewish Mus., 1996; represented in permanent collections Mus. Modern Art, Univ. Art Mus., Berkeley, Calif., San Francisco Mus. Modern Art, Richmond Art Mus., Mus. Contemporary Art, Haifa, Israel, Oakland Mus., Whitney Mus.; commns. include works for Starett City, San Francisco Airport, NYU Med. Ctr., chapel, John F. Kennedy Airport. Grantee N.Y. Found. for Arts, 1994, N.Y. State Coun. on Arts, 1995, Pollock/Krasner grantee, 1995. Home and Studio: 55 Bethune St Apt 808 New York NY 10014

AYLWARD, MARCIA EILEEN, artist, educator; b. Kansas City, Mo., Jan. 27, 1956; d. Charles Livingston and Rosemary Anita (Hughes) Aylward; m. John Davis Carroll, Oct. 9, 1993. BFA, Kansas City Art Inst., 1988; MFA, Parsons Sch. Design, 1991. Art instr. Kansas City Art Inst., Maplewood Woods C.C., Kansas City, Mo., Kansas City Acad. Home: 6010 Oak St Kansas City MO 64113

AYRAULT, EVELYN WEST, psychologist, writer; b. Buffalo, Mar. 3, 1922; d. John and Evelyn (West) A.; BS, Fla. State Coll. for Women, 1945; MA, U. Chgo., 1947. Chief psychologist, asst. prin. Crippled Children's Sch., Jamestown, N.D., 1947-48; psychologist, tchr. spl. edn. dept. Sharon (Pa.) Public Schs., 1948-50; chief psychologist, instr. Med. Coll. Va., Richmond, 1950-52; pvt. practice, psychology N.Y.C., 1952-68; clin. psychologist, Erie, Pa., 1968—; dir. psychol. services United Cerebral Palsy Assn., Miami, Fla., 1952-54, Erie County (Pa.) Crippled Children's Soc., 1968-78; mem. med. staff HealthSouth Great Lakes Rehab. Hosp., Erie, Pa., 1986—; psychol. cons. Shriners Hosp. for Crippled Children, Erie. Mem. Am., Pa. psychol. assns., Council for Exceptional Children, Psi Chi. Author: Take Step, 1963; You Can Raise Your Handicapped Child, 1964; Helping the Handicapped Teenager Mature, 1971; Growing Up Handicapped, 1978; Sex, Love, and the Physically Handicapped, 1981. Home: 10054 Law Rd North East PA 16428-3750

AYRES, JANICE RUTH, social service executive; b. Idaho Falls, Idaho, Jan. 23, 1930; d. Low Ray and Frances Mae (Salem) Mason; m. Thomas Woodrow Ayres, Nov. 27, 1953 (dec. 1966); 1 child, Thomas Woodrow Jr. (dec.). MBA, U. So. Calif., 1952, M in Mass Comms., 1953. Asst. mktg. dir. Disneyland, Inc., Anaheim, Calif., 1954-59; gen. mgr. Tamasha Town & Country Club, Anaheim, Calif., 1959-65; dir. mktg. Am. Heart Assn., Santa Ana, Calif., 1966-69; state exec. dir. Nev. Assn. Mental Health, Las Vegas, 1969-71; exec. dir. Clark Co. Easter Seal Treatment Ctr., Las Vegas, 1971-73, mktg. dir., fin devel. officer So. Nev. Drug Abuse Coun., Las Vegas, 1973-74; exec. dir. Nev. Assn. Retarded Citizens, Las Vegas, 1974-75; assoc., cons. Don Luke & Assocs., Phoenix, 1976-77; program dir. Inter-Tribal Coun. Nev., Reno, 1977-79; exec. dir. Ret. Sr. Vol. Program, Carson City, Nev., 1979—; chair sr. citizen summit State of Nev., 1996; conductor workshops in field. Bd. suprs. Carson City, Nev., 1992—; commr. Carson City Parks and Recreation, 1993—; obligation bond com., legis. chair Carson City; bd. dirs. Nev. Dept. Transp., 1993; active No. Corp. for Nat. and Cmty. Svc. by Gov., 1994, V&TRR Commn., 1993, chair, 1995, vice-chmn., chmn. pub. rels. com., bd. dirs. Hist. V&TRR Bd., chair PR Cmty./V&RR Commn., vice-chair Carson City Gen. Obligation Bond Commn., Nev. Home Health Assn.; appointed liaison Carson City Sr. Citizens Bd., 1995; chmn. 1st ann. summit Rural Nev. Sr. Citizens, Carson City; pres. No. Nev. R.R. Found., 1996—; chair Tri-Co-R.R. Commn., 1995. Named Woman of Distinction, Soroptimist Club, 1988, Outstanding Dir. of Excellence, Gov. State of Nev., 1989, Outstanding Dir., Vol. Action Ctr., J.C. Penney Co.; named to Western Fairs Assn. Hall of Fame for outstanding contbns. to the fair industry, 1995. Mem. AAUW, Am. Mgmt. Assn. (bd. dirs.), Am. Mktg. Assn., Internat. Platform Assn., Nat. Pub. Rels. Soc. Am. (chpt. pres.), Women Radio and TV, Nat. Soc. Fund Raising Execs., Nev. Fair and Rodeo Assn. (pres.), Nev. Assn. Transit Svcs. (bd. dirs., legis. chmn.), Nev. Women's Polit. Caucus, Nat. Women's Polit. Caucus, Am. Soc. Assn. Execs. Home: 1624 Karin Dr Carson City NV 89706-2626 Office: Ret Sr Vol Program 801 N Division St Carson City NV 89703-3925

AYRES, JAYNE LYNN ANKRUM, community health nurse; b. Reed City, Mich., Oct. 12, 1944; d. Quinten Wayne and Marshia Agetha (Crum) Ankrum; m. Ronald Francis Ayres, Apr. 16, 1977; children: Linda, Michele, Julie. ADN, Manatee C.C., Bradenton, Fla., 1975. RN, Fla., Ga. Staff nurse med.-surg., cardiac, oncology and float team Sarasota (Fla.) Meml. Hosp., 1975-77; nursing supr. Upjohn Healthcare Svcs., Sarasota, 1981-85; staff nurse Devereux Found., Kennesaw, Ga., 1986-89; staff nurse, supr. Vis. Nurse Health Sys., Metro, Atlanta, 1989—. Vol. ARC, M.U.S.T. Ministries Health Clinic for Homeless, Summer Olympics Games, 1996. Mem. Am. Legion (hon.), Fla. Nurses Assn. (hon.), Beta Sigma Phi.

AYRES, MARY ELLEN, government official; b. Spokane, Wash., June 23, 1924; d. Frank H. and Marion (Kellogg) A. Student, U. Wash., 1942-43; B.A., Stanford U., 1946; postgrad., Am. U., 1960. With Henry von Morpurgo, Advt., 1946-47; reporter Wenatchee Daily World, Wash., 1947-50, Washington Post, 1951-52; with U.S. Fgn. Service, Dept. State, 1950-51; mem. editorial staff Changing Times, 1952-61; editor Family Guide, Kiplinger Washington Editors, 1958-61, Bur. Labor Stats., Manpower Adminstrn., U.S. Dept. Labor, 1962-67; pub. info. specialist Bur. Indian Affairs, U.S. Dept. Interior, 1967-75; writer-editor Bur. Labor Stats., 1975—; tchr. newsletter class Dept. Agriculture Grad. Sch., 1975-89, editing style and technique class, 1987-89; past treas. Govt. Info. Orgn. Mem. publicity com. Nat. Capitol YWCA, 1982-83; dir. Wenatchee High Sch. Scholarship Found., 1988—. Mem. Nat. Assn. Govt. Communicators (founding treas., dir. 1975-80, 89-91, chmn. Blue Pencil Contest 1987, nat. capital chpt. treas. 1989), Am. News Women's Club, Am. Econ. Assn., Stanford U. Alumnae Assn., Kappa Kappa Gamma. Episcopalian. Club: Nat. Press (Washington). Home: 2400 Virginia Ave NW Apt C802 Washington DC 20037-2612 Office: Bur Labor Stats 2 Massachusetts Ave NE Washington DC 20212

AZARIAN, ROSANNE MARIE, writer, consultant; b. Boston, Nov. 19, 1946; d. Harutune and Barbara (Juliano) A.; m. Daniel W. Edwards, May 8, 1970 (div. 1975); m. Robert M. Lester III, July 21, 1977 (div. Feb. 1995). BA, U. Md., 1983. Federal women's program mgr. U.S. Army, Shape, Belgium, 1983-85; mktg. dir. Psychemedics, Santa Monica, Calif., 1978-88; regional sales mgr. Ctr. for Corp. Health, L.A., 1990-92, Healthtrac, L.A., 1992-94; self-employed writer, cons. Long Beach, Calif., 1994—; cons. Atman Internat., Pacific Palisades, Calif., 1995—. Author: Anais Nin: A Book of Mirrors, 1996. Mem. Nat. Mus. Women in the Arts, AAUW, Soc. Muse of the Southwest, ACLU. Office: Studio 2 643 W Broadway Long Beach CA 90802

AZARPAY, GUITTY, education educator; b. Teheran, Iran, Oct. 28, 1939; came to U.S., 1953; d. Rahim and Shekar (Dowlatshahi) A.; m. Ralph Werner Alexander, Dec. 18, 1963; 1 child, Vesa Alexander. PhD, U. Calif., Berkeley, 1964. Prof. U. Calif., Berkeley, 1963-94, U. Calif. Grad. Sch., Berkeley, 1994—. Author: Urartian Art & Artifacts, 1969, Sogdian Painting, 1981; mem. editl. bd. Enclopaedia Iranica, 1994—. Mem. AIA, AOS, Bulletin Asia Inst. Home: PO Box 908 Mill Valley CA 94942 Office: Univ Calif Near Ea Studies Berkeley CA 94720

AZCUENAGA, MARY LAURIE, government official; b. Council, Idaho, July 25, 1945. AB, Stanford U., 1967; JD, U. Chgo., 1973. Atty. FTC, Washington, 1973-75, asst. to gen. counsel, 1975-76, staff atty. San Francisco regional office, 1977-80, asst. regional dir., 1980-81, asst. to exec. dir., 1981-82, litigation atty. Office of Gen. Counsel, 1982, asst. gen. counsel for legal counsel, 1983-84, commr., Washington, 1984—; mem. Adminstrv. Conf. of the U.S., 1990-95. Trustee Food and Drug Law Inst., 1990—. Office: FTC 6th & Pennsylvania Ave NW Washington DC 20580-0002

AZEVEDO, CLARA MARGARET, secondary school counselor; b. Ripon, Calif., June 10, 1926; d. Urbano and Matea (Inda) Ruiz; m. Ernest Martin Azevedo, Aug. 27, 1949 (dec. Oct. 1980); children: Alan, Loren, Stephen, Ann, Lynn. BA, U. of Pacific, Stockton, Calif., 1947; MA, Calif. State U. Stanislaus, Turlock, 1972. Gen. secondary life credential, gen. sch. svcs. credential, pupil pers. credential. Tchr. Davis (Calif.) Joint Union H.S., 1948-49, Escalon (Calif.) H.S., 1949-50; tchr. adult evening program Ripon (Calif.) H.S., 1951-58; tchr. Spanish Ripon, River, Four Tree Elem. Schs., Ripon, 1961-66; tchr. Grace Davis H.S., Modesto, Calif., 1967-73, Fred Beyer H.S., Modesto, 1973-75; bilingual counselor Thomas Downey H.S., Modesto, 1975—; Hispanic liaison Modesto City Schs., 1966—. Author: Family Genealogy, 1990. Lectr., eucharist min. Our Lady of Fatima, Modesto, 1980—; instr. swimming ARC, Modesto, 1955-72; dir. recreation Ripon Recreation Commn., 1958-64; mem. Leadership Modesto, 1985; pres. Soroptimist Internat., Modesto, 1990. Honoree Leadership Modesto, 1985-86. Mem. Nat. Tchrs. Assn., Calif. Sch. Counselor Assn., Calif. Assn. Health, Phys. Edn., Recreation, Network of Modesto, Modesto Tchrs. Assn., Modesto Counselor Assn. (pres., sec. 1978-80), Delta Kappa Gamma (pres.). Democrat. Roman Catholic. Home: 280A W Rumble Rd Modesto CA 95350

AZICRI, NICOLETTE MALY, artist, educator; b. Erie, Pa., Dec. 10, 1950; d. Nicholas and Sophie Agnes (Maciulewicz) Maly; m. Max Azicri, Apr. 14, 1973; children: David, Danielle (twins). BS in Edn., Edinboro U., 1971, BFA in Ceramics, 1985, MA in Painting and Ceramics, 1988; MA in Counseling, Gannon U., 1976. Cert. elem. edn., spl. edn., 1971, elem. counseling 1976. Tchr. spl. edn. and grades K-12 Sch. Dist. of City of Erie, 1972-95; faculty mem. Pa. State, Erie. Exhbns. include: Three Rivers Art Festival, Pitts., 1990, 93, 95 (award), Westmoreland C.C. Nat. Exhbn., Youngwood, Pa., 1990, 93, 95, Carnegie Art Mus., Pitts., 1993, Am. Facism Nat. Exhbn., Artsquad Contemporary Gallery, Easton, Pa., 1993, 66th Ann. Nat. Juried Exhbn., Art Assn. Harrisburg, Pa., 1994, Resurgam 2d Ann. Nat. Exhbn., Resurgam Gallery, Balt., 1994, Nat. Art League's 63d Art Exhbn., Douglaston-N.Y.C., 1994, Mari Galleries Nat. Exhbn., N.Y.C., 1994, No. Nat. Art Competition Nicolet Coll. Gallery, Rhineland, Wis., 1995 (award), Internat. Exhbn. Antiquarium Gallery, Omaha, 1995-96, 41st Artists Nat. Coastal Ctr. for the Arts, St. Simon Island, Ga., 1994 (award 1996), Art Ctr. of No. N.J., New Milford, 1995, 10th Ann. Greater Midwest Internat. Ctrl. Mo. State U. Art Ctr. Gallery, 1995 (award), Personal Visions III Nat. Exhbn., An Art Place Inc. Gallery, Chgo., 1995, Impact Women's Gallery 3d Nat. Exhbn., Buffalo, 1996, State of Arts Gallery, Itchaca, N.Y., 1996. Vol. Gertrude Barber Ctr., Erie, 1970, Hospitality House for Women, Erie, 1973-76, Spl. Olympics, Erie, 1973-76, 1st Night Erie Com., 1991-96, AAUW Holly Trail, Erie, 1994-96. Mem. AAUW, Erie Art Mus., Meadville Coun. of the Arts, Chautuaqua Art Assn., Nothwest Pa. Artists Assn., Twins Mother Club. Home: 1152 W 6th St Erie PA 16507

AZÍOS, BLANCA STELLA, pediatrician, medical administrator, educator; b. Laredo, Tex., July 3, 1940; d. Enrique Luis and Blanca Stella (Zuniga) A. BA, U. St. Thomas, 1961; MD, U. Tex., 1965. Diplomate Am. Bd. Pediats. Intern in pediats. John Sealy Hosp., Galveston, Tex., 1965-66, resident in pediats., 1966-68; pediatrician Clinic of the Southwest, Houston, 1968-72, Southwest Pediat. Assn., Houston, 1972-94; asst. prof. Baylor Coll. Medicine, Houston, 1994—; med. dir. Harris County Cmty. Health Clinic, Houston, 1994—; attending pediatrician Harris County Hosp. Dist., Houston, 1994—; chief pediats. Meml. Hosp. Southwest, Houston, 1970-72, 84-91; pres., med. dir. Southwest Pediat. Assocs., Houston, 1979-94; attending physician Tex. Children's Hosp., Meth. Hosp., Hermann Hosp., Women's Hosp., Meml. Hosp., St. Luke's Hosp., Park Plz. Hosp. Fellow Am. Acad. Pediats.; mem. Tex. Pediatrician Soc., Harris County Med. Soc., Houston Pediat. Soc. Roman Catholic. Home: 10802 Vickijohn Ct Houston TX 77071-1824 Office: Baylor College of Medicine One Baylor Plz Rm 650E Houston TX 77030 also: People's Health Ctr 6630 De Moss Houston TX 77074

AZRACK, JOAN M., judge; b. 1951. BS, Rutgers Univ., N.J., 1974; JD, N.Y. Law Sch., 1979. With U.S. Dept. of Justice, 1979-81, U.S. Attorney's Office (N.Y. ea. dist.), 1982-90; magistrate judge U.S. Dist. Ct. (N.Y. ea. dist.), 2nd circuit, Brooklyn, 1991—. Office: US District Court 225 Cadman Plz E Rm 333 Brooklyn NY 11201-1818*

AZZARONE, CAROL ANN, advertising executive; b. Jersey City, Aug. 1, 1946; d. Paul Buglione and Catherine (DellaFave) LicCalsi; m. Dominick L. Azzarone, May 13, 1967 (div. 1989); children: Anthony Paul, Kathryn Ann. AA, Bergen Community Coll., 1982; BA, Ramapo Coll., 1984. Editorial asst. McGraw-Hill, Inc., N.Y.C., 1964-69; real estate agt. Auburn Realty, Inc., Bergenfield, N.J., 1975-80, Weichert Realty, Morris Plains, N.J., 1975—; pub. rels. coord. Ridgefield (N.J.) Bd. Edn., 1982-84; mktg. dir. Spa Lady Corp., Fairfax, Va., 1984-86, Newson Fitness, Morristown, N.J., 1986-88; creative dir. Publ. Corp., Morristown, 1988-90; advt. dir. RonTon Advt., Union, N.J., 1990—; advt. cons. Gianni Disegnatore, West Caldwell, N.J., 1991-92. Editor (newsletters) Ridgefield Sch. News, 1982-84, Cliffside Park Sch. News, 1984-85, The Grapevine, 1985-86. Mem. NOW, 1989—. N.J. Bell scholar N.J. Bell Corp., 1980, Bergen Community Coll. Alumni scholar, 1981. Mem. NOW, NAFE (First Place Award of Excellence 1996, Jersey award for web-site adv.), Advt./Pub. Rels. Assn., N.J. Advt. Club, Phi Theta Kappa. Democrat. Roman Catholic. Office: Ronton Advt 2285 Rte 22 W Union NJ 07083

AZZI, DONNA M., English language educator; b. Martins Ferry, Ohio; d. Aldo R. and Mary V. (Bartok) Dolfi; m. James R. Azzi; children: Susanne T. Azzi Kramer, Jennifer L. BS in Edn., Ohio U.; JD, U. Tenn.; MS, Lincoln Meml. U. Co-owner Spectrum Interiors, Oak Ridge, Tenn., 1978-86; owner The Cloth Shop, Oak Ridge, 1984-86; tchr. English Buckeye Local Schs., Rayland, Ohio, 1986-88; tchr. English Newark (Calif.) Meml. H.S., 1988, chair English dept.; sr. tchr. English Knox County Schs., Knoxville, Tenn., 1988—; mem. ethics com. Bearden H.S., Knoxville, 1993-95, curriculum com., 1995—. Named Caring, Committed, Concerned Tchr., Knoxville News Sentinel, 1991. Mem. Phi Delta Kappa. Office: Bearden H S 8352 Kingston Pike Knoxville TN 37919-5449

AZZI, JENNIFER, basketball player; b. Oak Ridge, Tenn., Aug. 31, 1968; d. James and Donna Azzi. Diploma, Stanford U., 1990. Basketball player Arvika Basket, Sweden, 1995-96; basketball player Viterbo, Italy, Orchies, France; mem. Nat. Women's Basketball Team. Recipient gold medal Goodwill Games, 1994, World Championship Qualifying team, 1993, U.S. Olympic Festival West Team, 1987; 2 gold medals World Championship and Goodwill Games, 1990, bronze medal Pan Am. Games, 1991, World Championship team, 1994, Wade Trophy, 1990; named Al-Pac 10 1st team, 1988, 89, 90, MVP NCAA Final Four, 1990, NCAA West Region, 1990, Naismith Nat. Player Yr., 1990, Kodak All-Am. 1st team, 1989, 90. Office: USA Basketball 5465 Mark Dabling Blvd Colorado Springs CO 80918-3842

AZZONI, MARGARET WICKER, architect, painter; b. N.Y.C., May 26, 1959; d. Alfred Arthur and Janet Sage (Elderkin) A. BA, Princeton U., 1981; M in Arch., Princeton Grad. Sch. Arch., 1984. Registered architect N.Y. Draftsman Terence R. Williams, N.Y.C., 1981, Voorsanger & Mills, N.Y.C., 1982; sr. designer James Stewart Polshek & Ptnrs., N.Y.C., 1985, Voorsanger & Mills, 1986; architect Charles T. Young Architects, N.Y.C., 1987-94; solo practice architecture N.Y.C., 1989—. Solo exhbn. Gold/Smith Gallery, Boothbay Harbor, Maine, 1996, Martha Lincoln Gallery, Vero Beach, Fla., 1996, Carspecken-Scott Gallery, Wilmington, Del., 1996; group exhbns. include Amos Eno Gallery, Soho, N.Y.C., 1994, Brownstone Gallery, N.Y.C., 1993, 94, Nexus: Columbia U., N.Y.C., 1984. Fundraiser South St. Seaport Mus., N.Y.C., 1988-91. Mem. AIA. Democrat. Episcopal.

BAAS, JACQUELYNN, art historian, museum administrator; b. Grand Rapids, Mich., Feb. 14, 1948. BA in History of Art, Mich. State U.; Ph.D. in History of Art, U. Mich. Registrar U. Mich. Mus. Art, Ann Arbor, 1974-78, asst. dir., 1978-82; editor Bull. Museums of Art and Archaeology, U. Mich., 1976-82; chief curator Hood Mus. Art, Dartmouth Coll., Hanover, N.H., 1982-84, dir., 1985-89; dir. U. Calif. Berkeley Art Mus. and Pacific Film Archive, Calif., 1989—; organizer exhbns. Contbr. articles to jours. and catalogues. NEH fellow, 1972-73; Nat. Endowment Arts fellow, 1973-74, 87-88. Mem. Coll. Art Assn. Am., Print Council Am., Am. Assn. Museums, Assn. Art Mus. Dirs.. Office: U Calif Berkeley Art Mus and Pacific Film Archive 2625 Durant Ave Berkeley CA 94720-2250

BABA, MARIETTA LYNN, business anthropologist, b. Flint, Mich., Nov. 9, 1949; d. David and Lillian (Joseph) Baba; m. David Smokler, Feb. 14, 1977 (div. 1982); 1 child, Alexia Baba Smokler; m. Ronald Delon Glotta, June 23, 1990. BA with highest distinction, Wayne State U., 1971, MA in Anthropology, 1973, PhD in Phys. Anthropology, 1975; MBA Mich. State U., 1994. Asst. prof. sci. and tech. Wayne State U., Detroit, Mich., 1975-80, assoc. prof. anthropology, 1980-88, prof., 1988—, spl. asst. to pres., 1980-82, econ. devel. officer, 1982-83, asst. provost, 1983-85; assoc. provost, 1985-89, dir. Internat. Programs and Interim Assoc. Dean of Grad. Sch., 1988-89, assoc. dean grad. sch., 1989-90, acting chair Dept. Anthropology, 1990-92; program dir. transformations to quality orgns., dir. social, behav. and econ. scis. NSF, 1994—; founder, corp. officer Applied Rsch. Teams Mich., Inc., Detroit, Intelligent Techs., Inc., Detroit; evolution researcher Wayne State U., 1975-82; cons. GM Rsch. Labs., 1988-92, Electronic Data Systems, 1990-93, McKinsey Global Inst., 1991; rsch. contractor GM/EDS, 1990—. With USAF, SBIR, 1992-94; lectr. nat. and internat. symposia, profl. confs. Contbr. numerous papers and abstracts to tech. jours; patentee in field. Bd. dirs. City-Univ. Consortium, Detroit, 1980-83; v.p. Neighborhood Svc. Orgn., Detroit, 1980-85; mem. State Rsch. Fund Feasibility Rev. Panel, 1982-94; mem. adv. panel on tech., innovation and U.S. trade U.S. Congl. Office Tech. Assessment, 1990-91, mem. panel on electronic enterprise, 1993-94; active Leadership Detroit Class IV, 1982-83; dir. Mich. Tech. Coun. (SE div.), 1984-85. Job Partnership Tng. Act grantee, 1981-90; NSF grantee, 1982, 84-85. Adv. editor for orgnl. anthropology American Anthropologist, 1990-93; Issued letters patent for method to map joint ventures and maps produced thereby. Fellow Am. Anthrop. Assn. (bd. dirs. 1986-88, exec. com. 1986-88, del. to the Internat. Union Anthrop. and Ethnol. Sci. 1990-94, chair global commn. anthropology, 1993—), Nat. Assn. Practice Anthropology (pres. 1986-88), Soc. Applied Anthropology, Phi Beta Kappa, Sigma Xi (Morton Fried award, 1991), Beta Gamma Sigma. Office: Wayne State U 137 MacKenzie Hall Detroit MI 48202

BABAO, DONNA MARIE, community health, psychiatric nurse, educator; b. St. Louis, May 6, 1945; d. Wilbert C. and Cecelia (Hogan) Bremer; widowed; 1 child, Tonya J. Diploma, Henry Ford Hosp. Sch. Nursing, Detroit, 1966; BSN, Calif. State U., Sacramento, 1978, MS in Nursing, 1989; MA in Edn., Calif. State U., Chico, 1985. Cert. pub. health nurse; master tchr. cert. Staff nurse U. Calif. Med. Ctr., San Franicsco, 1968-72; staff and charge CCU nurse Children's Hosp. of San Francisco, 1972-78; pub. health nurse Sutter-Yuba Health Dept., Yuba City, Calif., 1979-81; instr. nursing Yuba Coll., Marysville, Calif., 1981—; psychiat. charge nurse Sunridge Hosp., Yuba City, 1994—. Writer health column, 1986-90; chpt. to textbooks; reviewer nursing textbooks. 1st lt. Nurse Corps, U.S. Army, 1966-68. Mem. Nat. League Nursing, Calif. Tchrs. Assn., Vietnam Vets. Am., Am. Holistic Nurses Assn.

BABB, MARGARET L., elementary school educator; b. Chgo., Ill., July 8, 1950; d. Charles Joseph and Marian Elaine (Andrews) Phelps; m. David Paul Babb, Jan. 5, 1985; children: Joseph Paul Ivacic, James Andrew Ivacic. BS in Edn., U. Ill., 1972; MS in Edn., No. Ill. U., 1976. Tchr. 1st, 2nd grade Clifford Carlson Sch., Rockford, Ill., 1972-77; primary cons. gifted program Martin Luther King Sch., Rockford, Ill., 1979-80, tchr. gifted edn. 2nd grade, 1980-81, tchr. gifted edn. 4th grade, 1983-86; tchr. gifted edn. 3rd grade John T. Haight Sch., Rockford, Ill., 1986-89, Martin Luther King Sch., Rockford, Ill., 1989-91; tchr. 3rd grade Marsh Sch., Rockford, Ill., 1991—; instr. Level II tng. for gifted edn. cert., Edn. Svc. Ctr. #1 and Rockford (Ill.) Coll., 1990—; presenter in field. Co-author: Creative Wordcard Projects, 1974. Mem. steering com. Beattie Is., Rockford, Ill., 1983-84; bd. dirs. Rockford Woman's Club, 1977-94. Mem. Internat. Reading Assn. (presenter), Delta Kappa Gamma (officer, initiation chair 1981-94, ways and means com.), Phi Delta Kappa. Lutheran. Home: 4390 Ruskin Rd Rockford IL 61101 Office: Marsh Elem Sch 2021 Hawthorne Dr Rockford IL 61107

BABB, PAMELA RUBY, fundraiser, opera singer; b. Bklyn., May 16, 1960; d. Prince Nathan and Bernita (Williams) B. BA in Music Performance, Hampton U., 1982; MPA, Columbia U., 1984. Sys. analyst N.Y.C. Office Payroll Adminstrn., 1985-90; coord. fin. resources Girl Scouts U.S.A., N.Y.C., 1989-90; mgr. Bus. Vols. for Arts, Arts and Bus. Coun., N.Y.C., 1990-93; coord. client svcs. Bklyn. In Touch, 1994; devel. mgr. Harlem Sch. Arts, N.Y.C., 1994—; cons. Abyssinian Devel. Corp., N.Y.C., 1995—; profl. singer Grace Bumbry Black Heritage Vocal Ensemble, 1994—. Bd. dirs. Talbot Perkins Children Svcs. Orgn., N.Y.C., 1993—. Mem. Delta Sigma Theta. Office: Harlem Sch Arts 645 St Nicholas Ave New York NY 10030

BABBAGE, JOAN DOROTHY, journalist; b. Montclair, N.J., Jan. 10, 1926; d. Laurence Washburn and Dorothy A. (Davenport) Babbage; m. Vernon H. Ellsworth, Mar. 6, 1971. B.A. in English, Mt. Holyoke Coll., 1948; postgrad. Art Students League, New Sch. for Social Research. Publicist Paramount Internat. Films, N.Y.C., 1952-58; reporter Newark News, 1960-67, food editor, 1967-72; feature writer, reporter Star-Ledger, Newark, 1972—. Author: (with others) Past and Present Lives of New Jersey Women, 1990; contbr. bus. articles to New Jersey Business mag., articles to Official Dog mag. Operator rescue orgn. SaintSaver, N.J., N.Y., Pa.; v.p. jr. group Women's Nat. Republican Club, N.Y.C., 1955. Recipient recommendation award N.J. br. Humane Soc. U.S., PICA Club N.J. award, 1980, Community Media award Assn. Retarded Citizens, Morris County Unit, N.J., 1987, Willard H. Allen Agrl. Communications Media award, N.J. Agrl. Soc., 1988, Communicator of Yr. award N.J. Dept. Agriculture, 1990. Appeared on NBC-TV to demonstrate dog tng. Office: Star-Ledger Court St Newark NJ 07101

BABBITT, KATHY JEAN, public relations executive, marketing executive, consultant; b. Westfield, N.Y., Oct. 9, 1950; d. Clarence Randy and Boots (Florence Porter) Johnson; m. David Clair Babbitt, Feb. 14, 1970; children: Jeannette, Kimberly, Dione. Student, Lancaster (Pa.) Coll. of Bible, 1968-69; grad., Moody Bible Inst. Evang. Sch., 1972-74, East Tenn. State U., 1975, Ecole de Commerce, Neuchatel, Switzerland, 1977, U. Neuchatel, 1978, Austin C. C., 1989. Missionary Mission Aviation Fellowship, Zaire, 1978-81; comml. artist Christian Printing Svc., Anaheim, Calif., 1981; newscaster Sta. KABN Radio, Big Lake, Ark., 1983-84; owner Babbitt and Assocs. Mktg. and Pub. Rels., Palmer, Alaska, 1984-86, Flowery Branch, Ga., 1986-88, Austin, Tex., 1988-91, Claypool, Ind., 1991—; cons. in field; lectr. in life mgmt.; instr. writing courses. Author: Habits of the Heart, 1990 (1st pl. award 1991); editor: Downscaling, 46510, 1993 (1st pl. Nat. award 1993), Downscaling; Simplify and Enrich Your Lifestyle, 1993 (1st pl. Nat. award 1993); host talk show, 1995. Missionary Mission Aviation Fellowship, Zaire, Africa, 1978-81; promotional designer Edna Devries for State Senate, Palmer, 1984; campaign mgr. Al Strawn for Borough Mayor, Palmer, 1984-85; organizer youth employment opportunities, 1985. Recipient 1st Pl. award for pub. affairs Pub. Rels. Soc. Am., 1985, 1st Pl. award for speaking Toastmasters, 1985, 15 awards plus Sweepstakes award Alaska Press Women, 1986, 7 1st Pl., 3 2nd, 1 3rd Pl. award Women's Press Club Ind., 1994; recipient over 50 state and nat. awards for writing. Mem. Tex. Press Women (1st pl. Gym brochure 1989, publrs. resource group brochure 1990), Nat. Fedn. Press Women. (3rd Pl. pub. affairs 1986, 4-color brochure 1994, 1st Pl. 2-color brochure, 1988, nat. award 1993). Republican. Evangelical. Home and Office: PO Box 1262 Buford GA 46510-9261

BABCOCK, BARBARA ALLEN, lawyer, educator; b. Washington, July 6, 1938; d. Henry Allen and Doris Lenore (Moses) B.; m. Thomas C. Grey, Aug. 19, 1979. AB, U. Pa., 1960; LLB, Yale U., 1963. Bar: Md. 1963, D.C. 1964, JD (hon.), U. San Diego 1983, U. Puget Sound, 1988. Law clk. U.S. Ct. Appeals D.C., 1963; assoc. Edward Bennett Williams, 1964-66; staff atty. Legal Aid Agy., Washington, 1966-68; dir. Pub. Defender Svc. (formerly Legal Aid Agy.), 1968-72; assoc. prof. Stanford U., 1972-77, prof., 1977—; asst. atty. gen. U.S. Dept. Justice, 1977-79. Ernest W. McFarland Prof. Law, 1986—. Democrat. Author: (with others) Sex Discrimination and The Law, 1975; (with Carrington) Civil Procedure, 1977; contbr. articles to profl. jours. Home: 835 Mayfield Ave Palo Alto CA 94305-1052 Office: Stanford U Sch Law Stanford CA 94305

BABCOCK, MARGUERITE LOCKWOOD, addictions treatment therapist, writer; b. Jacksonville, Fla., Jan. 1, 1944; d. Allen Seaman and Emilie (Lockwood) B. BA in Art History, Am. U., 1965; M Counselor Edn., U. Pitts., 1982. Cert. addictions counselor, Pa. Addictions therapist South Hills Health Sys., Pitts., 1978-81; addiction therapist, clin. supr., clin. dir. Alternatives- Turtle Creek Mental Health/Mental Retardation/D&A Ctr., Pitts., 1981-86; addictions therapist, coord. Ligonier Valley Treatment Ctr., Stahlstown, Pa., 1987-88; addictions clin. supr., unit dir. Ctr. for Substance Abuse Mon-Yough, McKeesport, Pa., 1988-96; utilization mgmt. and coordination Mon-Yough, McKeesport, 1996—; adj. instr. in addictions courses Seton Hill Coll., Greensburg, Pa., 1989-91, C.C. Allegheny County, West Mifflin, Pa., 1989-91, Pa. State U., McKeesport, 1993—; pvt. trainer, writer, Acme, Pa., 1985—; cons. in field. Co-author, co-editor: Challenging Codependency: Feminist Critiques, 1995; contbr. articles to profl. jours.; book reviewer Internat. Jour. Contemporary Sociology, Las Vegas, Nev., 1996—. Fellow Andrew Mellon Found., 1966-68, NSF, 1967. Mem. Pa. Assn. Alcoholism and Drug Abuse Counselors (bd. dirs. 1994—), Ligonier Valley Writers, Phi Kappa Phi, Alpha Lambda Delta. Home and Office: RD 1 Box 138 Acme PA 15610

BABCOCK, MICHELE E., banking executive; b. Gowanda, N.Y., 1971. BA in Psychology, SUNY, Buffalo, 1993, BA in Polit. Sci., 1993; postgrad., SUCNY, Buffalo, 1994. Legal sec. First Investors Corp., Manhattan, 1993; investment acctg. sec. Tchr.'s Retirement System, Manhattan, 1993; sr. legal sec. Magner, Love & Morris, Buffalo, 1993-94; customer svc. rep. Key Corp., Amherst, N.Y., 1995-96; grad. intern Career Devel. SUCNY, Buffalo, 1995-96, Ednl. Opportunity Program, 1996. Vol. educator Children's Mus. of Manhattan, 1993; campaign vol. Rep. Party, N.Y.C., 1993; religious edn. tchr. St. Joseph's Ch., Gowanda, 1995-96; vol. chair summer events Gowanda C. of C., 1996. Mem. NOW, Nat. Assn. Student Pers. Adminstrs., Coll. Student Pers. Assn. N.Y., Career Planning and Adult Devel. Network, Sierra Club. Mem. Independence Party. Roman Catholic. Office: Buffalo State Coll Career 306 Grover Cleveland Hall 1300 Elmwood Ave Buffalo NY 14222

BABEL, DEBORAH JEAN, social worker, accountant; b. Fulton, N.Y., Oct. 12, 1959; d. Sheldon Rowell and Mary Jane (Dimon) Ford; m. Charles Jacob Babel III, Sept. 7, 1984; children: Casandra Jane, Stefan Michael (dec.). BA in Acctg., Aurora (Colo.) C.C., 1985; BS in Social Work, U. Denver, 1989. Cert. respite care for abused children. Acct. Dale Conklin and Assocs. CPA Firm, Englewood, Colo., 1981-84, Beechcraft Aviation Inc., Denver, 1985-87; v.p. The Attachment Disorder Parents Network, Boulder, Colo., 1989—; pres. The Parents Help Network, Aurora, 1993—; adv. Adoptive Families of Am., Mpls., 1989—, Colo. Coalition for Children, Denver, 1989—, Fedn. of Families for Childrens Mental Health, Alexandria, Va., 1989—, The Attachment Ctr., Evergreen, Colo., 1989—. Contbr. articles to profl. jours. Mem. NAFE, NASW, Nat. Com. on the Prevention of Child Abuse, Attachment Disorder Parents Network (v.p. 1988—, Parent Advocacy award 1989), N.Am. Coun. on Adoptable Children (Warmline and Parent Advocate). Democrat. Roman Catholic. Home and Office: Parents Help Network 3235 S Parker Rd #1308 Aurora CO 80014

BABEL, RAYONIA ALLEEN, librarian, educator; b. Herrin, Ill., Sept. 5, 1935; d. Hubert Ray and Mabel Alleen (Manning) Vaughn; m. Jerald Lee Babel, Sept. 5, 1954 (div. 1973); children: Thomas, Carl, Penny, Heidi, Krista. Student, Milliken U., 1953-55; BA in Edn., No. Ill. U., 1970, MA in Libr. Sci., 1971. Cert. tchr., Ill. Head ref. svcs. Aurora (Ill.) U., 1971—. Precinct committeeman Dems. of Kane County, 1973-78; treas. Charlemagne on the Fox Questers, 1991-93; sec. Restorations of Kane County. Mem. Libras, Inc. (v.p. 1991-92, pres. 1992-93). Methodist. Home: 623 Katherine St Saint Charles IL 60174-3734 Office: Aurora U Libr 347 S Gladstone Ave Aurora IL 60506-4877

BABICH, CANDY KAYE, elementary school educator; b. Duluth, Minn., May 2, 1950; d. Frank Albert and Bernice Marion (Westerlund) Sandstedt; m. Boris Martin Babich, July 6, 1973; children: Jesse Stephen, Tiffany Bernice. BS, U. Minn., Duluth, 1973; postgrad., Bemidji State U., 1990-94. 4th grade tchr. James Madison Sch., Virginia, Minn., 1973-74; chpt. I tchr. Cotton (Minn.) Elem. Sch., 1974-75; 5th grade tchr. Franklin Elem. Sch., Eleveth, Minn., 1975-76; 3d grade tchr. Mountain View Elem. Sch., Colorado Springs, 1986-87; 4th grade tchr. Pine Valley Elem. Sch., Colorado Springs, Minn., 1988; spl. edn. tchr. Cherry (Minn.) H.S., Colorado Springs, 1989; chpt. I tchr. Cherry Elem. Sch., Hibbing, Minn., 1991—. Mem. ASCD, Internat. Reading Assn., Am. Fedn. Tchrs. Home: 2345 Suomi Rd Hibbing MN 55746-8526

BABIN, REGINA-CHAMPAGNE, artist, consultant; b. New Orleans, July 17, 1956; d. Eddie Anthony and Martha Ann (Bergeron) Champagne; m. Terry Lynn Babin, Apr. 25, 1981; children: Jonathan Paul, Michelle Elizabeth. BA, Nicholls State U., 1978, postgrad., 1992-96. Pvt. portraitist Houma, La., 1972—; freelance artist, musician, writer So. Portraits, Plus, Houma, 1981—; bank teller Raceland Bank and Trust, Larose, La., 1979-80; sch. tchr. Lockport (La.) Christian, 1979-80; bank teller Nat. Bank Commerce, Kenner, La., 1980-81; free-lance author Terrebonne Enhancement Commn., Houma, 1985—; artist-in-residence, tour guide Terrebonne Hist. and Cultural Soc., Houma, 1981-85; founding chairperson Houma (La.)-Terrebonne Community Band, 1984-85; gallery dir. Terrebonne Fine Arts Guild, Houma, 1985-86; founding bd. dirs. Houma (La.)-Terrebonne Arts & Humanities Coun., 1985-87. Author, composer: (books with music) Pistoche, 1985, Santa's Prayer, 1991, The J.A.M. Adventure, 1994, (anti-drug packet with music tape) Just Say No To Drugs, 1989 (Nat. Jr. Aux. award 1990, South La. Alcohol and Drug Abuse Coun. 1990). Art/music demonstrater Terrebonne Parish Libr., St. Charles Parish Libr., 1980's; art program designer, instr. Y.M.C.A., Houma, 1981-87; artist, docent musician Southdown Mus., Houma, 1981-87; hurricane aid vol. ARC, Houma, 1986. Recipient Cert. Honor/Svc. award South La. Alcohol and Drug Abuse Coun., Houma, 1989. Mem. ALA, Internat. Reading Assn., Nat. Mus. Women in Arts (charter mem., supporter), Terrebonne Fine Arts Guild, Terrebonne Hist. and Cultural Soc., Houma Jr. Aux. (life). Republican. Office: So Portraits Plus 107 Willard Ave Houma LA 70360-7554

BABIOR, ERICA, psychiatric clinical specialist; b. Bklyn., July 26, 1947; m. Anai Hernandez, 1995. Diploma, Beth Israel Sch. Nursing, N.Y.C., 1968; BA in Psychology, New Sch. Social Rsch., 1973; MA in Psychology, Northwestern Univ. Coll., Tulsa, 1981. RN cert., Calif. Staff nurse Beth Israel Med. Ctr., N.Y.C., 1968-71; nurse mgr. Odyssey House, N.Y.C., 1971-73; med. adminstr. Liberation House, Stamford, Conn., 1974-76; psychiat. clin. specialist Cedars-Sinai Med. Ctr., L.A., 1977-79; asst. DON, Kaiser Mental Health Ctr., L.A., 1979-81; coord. nursing care N.Y. Hosp.-Cornell Med. Ctr., White Plains, 1982-84; clin. nurse specialist Kaiser Permanente, L.A., 1985-88; mental health and chem. dependency specialist MCC/Cigna, L.A., 1990—; mem. clin. faculty UCLA Sch. Nursing, 1989—. Chmn. women's rights ACLU, Calif., 1995. Mem. NOW, ANA, Am. Assn. Suicidology, Calif. Nurses Assn., Feminist Minority, AIDS Project L.A. Democrat.

BACA, MARY FRANCES, mental health therapist; b. Sante Fe, N. Mex., Aug. 31, 1963; d. Alfred Cylde and Rita Martha (Padilla) B.; m. Leslie L. Lopez, Oct. 7, 1995. BA, U. N. Mex., 1986; MA, Webster U. St Louis, 1989. Lic. Profl. Clin. Counselor. Mental health worker Bernalillo City Mental Health Ctr., Albuquerque, 1984-86; child devel. spl. U. N. Mex., Albuquerque, 1986-87; mental health worker Heights Psychiat. Hosp., Albuquerque, 1986-87; soc. worker III, investigator Child Protective Svcs., Albuquerque, 1988-89; therapist, case mng. Genesis Womens Ctr., Albuquerque, 1989-90; residential dir. Teen Parent Residence, Albuquerque, 1990-92; instr. U. N. Mex., Albuquerque, 1993—, rsch. asst., 1995—; therapist, pvt. practice Odyssey Counseling Svcs., Albuquerque, 1990—. Mem. Assn. for Counseling & Devel. Office: Odyssey Counseling Svcs 120 Madeira NE #224 Albuquerque NM 87108

BACALL, LAUREN, actress; b. N.Y.C., Sept. 16, 1924; m. Humphrey Bogart, May 21, 1945 (dec. 1957); children: Stephen, Leslie; m. Jason Robards, July, 1961 (div.); 1 son, Sam. Student pub. schs., Am. Acad. Dramatic Art. Actress in Broadway plays Franklin Street, 1942, Goodbye Charlie, 1959; motion picture actress, 1944—, film appearances include To Have and Have Not, 1945, Confidential Agent, 1945, The Big Sleep, 1946, Dark Passage, 1947, Key Largo, 1948, Young Man With a Horn, 1949, Bright Leaf, 1950, How To Marry a Millionaire, 1953, Woman's World, 1954, The Cobweb, 1955, Blood Alley, 1955, Written on the Wind, 1956, Designing Woman, 1957, The Gift of Love, 1958, Flame Over India, 1959, Shock Treatment, 1964, Sex and the Single Girl, 1965, Harper, 1966, Murder on the Orient Express, 1974, The Shootist, 1976, Health, 1980, The Fan, 1981, Tree of Hands, 1987, Appointment With Death, 1987, Mr. North, 1988, Misery, 1990, A Star for Two, 1991, All I Want for Christmas, 1991, Ready to Wear (Prêt-à-Porter), 1994; appeared in Broadway play Cactus Flower, 1966-68, Applause, 1969-71 (Sarah Siddons award 1975); also road co., 1971-72, London co., 1972-73 (Tony award for best actress in a musical 1970); Broadway play Woman of the Year, 1981 (Tony award for best actress in a musical 1981, Sarah Siddons award 1983), Sweet Bird of Youth, 1983 (London, 1985, Australia, 1986, L.A., 1987; TV spl. The Paris Collections, 1968, Applause, 1973, A Commercial Break (Happy Endings), 1975; TV movies: Perfect Gentlemen, 1978, Dinner at Eight, 1989, The Portrait, 1992, A Foreign Field, 1993, From the Mixed Up Files of Mrs. Basil E. Frankweiler, 1995; author: Lauren Bacall By Myself, 1978, Lauren Bacall Now, 1994. Recipient Am. Acad. Dramatic Arts award for achievement, 1963, Standard award London Evening, 1973, Nat. Book award, 1979; decorated comdr. Order of Arts and Letters (France), 1995. Office: care Johnnie Planco William Morris Agy 1325 Ave Of The Americas New York NY 10019-4701

BACARELLA, FLAVIA, artist, educator; b. Bklyn.; d. Salvatore John and Angeline Mary B. MA, New Sch. for Social Rsch., N.Y.C., 1975; MFA, Bklyn. Coll./CUNY, 1983. Lectr. Herbert H. Lehman Coll., Bronx, N.Y., 1972—. Grantee N.Y. Found. Arts, 1986. Mem. Women's Caucus for Art. Coll. Art Assn. Office: Herbert H Lehman Coll Bedford Park Blvd W Bronx NY 10468

BACH, BETTY JEAN, health services educator; b. Jackson, Ky., Dec. 25, 1952; d. Eugene Parker and Celeste White B. AA, Ea. Ky. U., 1975, postgrad. student, 1989, BS, 1995; student, Ohio U., 1984, Morehead U., 1986. RN, Ky.; cert. ob-gyn. nurse practitioner, advanced RN practitioner. Staff nurse, nurse practitioner Breathitt County Health Dept., Jackson, Ky., 1975-80; sch. health nurse, health svcs. coord. Breathitt County Bd. Edn., Jackson, 1983-88; health svcs. instr. Breathitt Area Vocat. Edn. Ctr., Jackson, 1988—. Mem. NEA, Ky. Edn. Assn. Am. Vocat. Assn., Vocat. Assn. Kappa Delta Pi. Home: Highway 30 E Rousseau KY 41366

BACH, CYNTHIA, educational company executive, writer; b. N.Y.C., Oct. 28; m. Norman Namerow (div.); children: Laura Marie, Marc Adam. BA in Art Edn., UCLA, 1955; MPA, U. So. Calif., 1978; LDS, Calif. Luth., 1993. Cert. gen. elem., spl. seconary art, & gen. jr. h.s. tchr. Staff asst. L.A. Unified Sch. Dist., 1976; rainbow tchr., gifted coord. Trinity Elem. Sch., L.A., 1978-81; field worker/in-svc. for parents and staff educator Hubbard Elem. Sch., Sylmar, Calif., 1981-90; student observer Liggett Elem. Sch., Panorama City, Calif., 1990-92; tng. tchr. Vena Elem. Sch., Arleta, Calif., 1992-93; pres. Comprehensive Learning Systems. Author: Alternatives to Retail Marketing for Seniors (Bur. of Consumer Affairs). Lectr. Sr. Citizens Bur of Consumer Affairs, City Hall; past pres. local PTA. Nat. Art scholar, Chouinard Art Inst. scholar. Mem. NAFE, AAUW, 1st Century Soc. UCLA, Phi Alpha Alpha. Home: 5140 White Oak #214 Encino CA 91316

BACH, LINDA ANN, critical care nurse; b. S.I., N.Y., Sept. 3, 1964; d. Peter Vincent and Frances Mary (Galletta) B. AAS in Nursing, Coll. S.I., 1992. Cert. provider ACLS, PALS. Staff nurse med./surg. unit S.I. Univ. Hosp., 1992-93, staff nurse emergency dept., 1993-95, staff nurse neuro ICU/neuro unit, 1995—, nurse care coord. emergency dept., 1995—. Roman Catholic. Home: 128 Tallman St Staten Island NY 10312-4914

BACH, LINDA WALLINGA, special education educator; b. Rock Rapids, Iowa, Feb. 13, 1953; d. Warren Dale and Beverley (Gardner) Wallinga; m. Daniel Lee Beber, Nov. 2, 1974 (div. Nov. 1980); m. Daniel Louis Bach, June 10, 1981; children: Davin Lane, Thadeous Colin. BEd, U. Nebr., 1975; M Early Childhood Edn., U. S.C., 1989. Substitute tchr. Omaha Pub. Schs., 1975-76; drug mgr. Alan Eber Assocs., Denver, 1976-77; spl. edn. tchr. Winters (Tex.) Elem. Sch., 1978-81; substitute tchr. Dept. Def. Sch., Woodbridge, U.K., 1981-83; spl. edn. tchr. DeLaine Elem. Sch., Sumter, S.C., 1983-85; lead spl. edn. tchr. Oakland Elem. Sch., Sumter, 1985-94; tchr. spl. edn. Oakland Elem. Sch., 1994—; mem. project team to write presch. and kindergarten inclusion program for handicapped children and regular children, 1994; mem. action team for site-based 5 yr. planning Oakland Spl. Olympics Team Coach Elem. Sch., 1994. Chair Oakland Elem. Sch. PTA Haloween Carnival, Sumter, 1989, 90, 92. Basic skills multi-sensory curriculum mini-grantee S.C. Coun. Exceptional Children and Upgrade Systems, 1990, Edn. Improvement Act grantee for improving math. and reading skills, 1995. Mem. NEA, PTA, Coun. Exceptional Children (sec.-treas. 1988-90, membership chmn. 1990-93, pres. elect 1993-94, membership chmn. 1995—). Methodist. Office: Oakland Elem Sch Oakland St Oakland Plantation Sumter SC 29154

BACHAND, ALICE JEANNE, school library media specialist; b. Sayre, Pa., Sept. 21, 1957; d. Charles Edward and Donna Jeanne (Osborne) Merrick; m. James Joseph Bachand, July 17, 1982; children: Janelle Alison, Jodi Nicole. Student, Paul Valéry U., Montpellier, France, 1977-78; BA, Wartburg Coll., 1979; MLS, Emporia State U., 1985. French tchr. Dunlap (Iowa) H.S., 1979, Clifton-Clyde H.S., Clyde, Kans., 1980-85; sch. libr. media specialist Hillcrest H.S., Cuba, Kans., 1984-86, Linn (Kans.) H.S., 1986-92, Clay Center (Kans.) Cmty. Middle Sch., 1992—. V.P. WELCA, Concordia, Kans., 1989-91; sec. of edn., ALCW, Concordia, 1982-84; brownie helper Girl Scouts of Am., Clyde, 1995-96; ch. librarian, Concordia Lutheran Ch., 1984—. Mem. NEA (Kans. chpt. pres. 1991-92), Kans. Reading Assn., Kans. Assn. Sch. Librarians (nominating com. 1992), Thunderbird Reading Coun. Lutheran. Home: RR2 Box 158 Clyde KS 66938 Office: Clay Ctr Cmty Middle School 935 Prospect Clay Center KS 67432

BACHARACH, NANCY LOU, education educator; b. Eau Claire, Wis., Feb. 22, 1956; d. Elroy Donald and Agnes Marie (Erickson) Strand; m. David William Bacharach, June 19, 1982; children: Kimberly Jo, Megan Roxanne. BS, U. Wis., Eau Claire, 1978; MEd, Tex. A&M U., 1984, PhD, 1987. Cert. elem. tchr., Wis. Tchr. Durand (Wis.) pub. schs., 1978-80; tchr. Eau Claire area schs., 1980-82; grad. student, grad. asst. and instr. Tex. A&M U., College Station, 1983-86; prof. Syracuse (N.Y.) U., 1987-89, St. Cloud (Minn.) State U., 1989—. Author: Learning Together: A Manual for Multi-age Grouping, 1995; contbr. articles to profl. jours. Recipient Outstanding Faculty award St. Cloud State U., 1991, Prof. of Yr. award Kappa Delta Pi, 1995. Mem. Orgn. of Tchr. Educators in Reading (pres. 1993-94), Am. Ednl. Rsch. Assn., Internat. Reading Assn., Assn. Tchr. Educators, Nat. Coun. Tchrs. English. Home: 2251 26th Ave S Saint Cloud MN 56301-5063 Office: St Cloud State U 720 4th Ave S Saint Cloud MN 56301-4442

BACHER, JUDITH ST. GEORGE, executive search consultant; b. New Rochelle, N.Y., July 14, 1946; d. Thomas A. and Rose-Marie (Martocci) Baiocchi; B.S., Georgetown U., 1968; M.L.S., Columbia U., 1971; m. Albert Bacher, Jan. 2, 1972; 1 son, Alexander Michael. Researcher, Time mag., N.Y.C., 1968-71; librarian Mus. Modern Art, N.Y.C., 1971-72; cons. Informaco Inc., N.Y.C., 1972-74, Booz-Allen & Hamilton, N.Y.C., 1974-79; prin. Nordeman Grimm/MBA Resources, N.Y.C., 1979-96; assoc. dir. Spencer Stuart, 1996—; mem. White House Adv. Com. on Personnel, Exec. Office of Pres., 1979-81; co-founder Research Roundtable, pres. 1981-83. Mem. Assn. of Exec. Search Cons. (N.E. region chair 1994—), Internat. Assn. Corp. and Profl. Recruiters (bd. dirs. 1996—), Phi Beta Kappa. Office: Spencer Stuart 277 Park Ave New York NY 10172

BACHMAN, CAROL CHRISTINE, trust company executive; b. Buffalo, Jan. 20, 1959; d. Christian George and Joan Marie (Fincel) B. Student, Grad. Inst. Internat. Study, 1979-80; AB, Smith Coll., 1981; grad., New Eng. Sch. Banking, 1987. Trust asst. BayBank Middlesex, Burlington, Mass., 1984-85, sr. trust asst., 1985-87, trust adminstr., 1987, trust officer, 1987-88; estate settlement specialist Bank of Boston, 1988-90, system cons., 1990, mgr. adminstrv. support svcs., asst. v.p., 1990—. Roman Catholic. Home: 58 Circuit Ave Waterbury CT 06708-2160 Office: Bank of Boston 81 W Main St Waterbury CT 06702-2006

BACHNER, BARBARA LAVERDIERE, artist; b. Waterville, Maine, Sept. 14, 1934; d. Thaddeus Eugene and Bernadette Arthemise (Vashon) LaVerdiere; m. Robert Lawrence Bachner, Mar. 22, 1959; 1 child, Suzanne Jouvé. BA in Fine Arts magna cum laude, NYU, 1968; student, Nat. Acad. Sch. Design, 1975-78, Art Students League, 1977-80, 82-84; postgrad., Johnson State Coll., 1995—. Solo shows include Kleinert Arts Ctr., Woodstock, N.Y., 1992, TAI Gallery, Woodstock, 1994, Pen and Brush, N.Y.C., 1995, Fletcher Gallery, Woodstock, N.Y.; juried shows include Pastel Soc. Am., N.Y.C., 1978, 80, Five Towns Juried Show, Woodmere, N.Y., 1983, Woodstock Artists Assn., 1989—, Springfield (Mo.) Art Mus., 1990, U. Tex., Tyler, 1991, CUNY, Bayside, 1994, Nat. Arts Club, N.Y.C., 1984, 95, Nat. Assn. Women Artists, 1995-96, Krasdale Corp. Galleries, White Plains, N.Y., 1995-96; group shows include Artists of Ulster County, Kingston, N.Y., 1989, Woodstock (N.Y.) Artists Assn. Mems. Show, 1989—, Pen & Brush, N.Y.C., 1990—, SUNY, New Paltz, 1992, A.I.R. Gallery, N.Y.C., 1992, Gallery Korea, N.Y.C., 1993, Woodstock Sch. Art, 1994; permanent collections include Texaco Corp., Houston, Printmaking Workshop, N.Y.C., Kaatsbaan Internat. Dance Ctr., Woodstock, Tivoli, N.Y., numerous pvt. collections. Recipient Dan Gottschalk award, 1991. Mem. Nat. Assn. Women Artists, Women's Caucus Art, Coll. Art Assn., N.Y. Artists Equity Assn., Pen & Brush (Solo Show award 1993, 96), Woodstock Artists Assn. (Dan Gottschalk award 1991, Breth-Borkmann award 1995), Ulster Arts Alliance, Art Students League (Concours award 1978, 81, 84, Merit scholar 1979, 83). Home: 25 Sutton Pl S #19N New York NY 10022

BACHRACH, EVE ELIZABETH, lawyer; b. Oakland, Calif., July 3, 1951; d. Howard Lloyd and Shirley Faye (Lichterman) B. AB cum laude, Boston U., 1972; JD with honors, George Washington U., 1976. Bar: D.C. 1976, U.S. Dist. Ct. D.C. 1976, U.S. Ct. Appeals (D.C. cir.) 1976. Assoc. Stein, Mitchell & Mezines, Washington, 1976-79; assoc. gen. counsel Cosmetic, Toiletry, and Fragrance Assn., Washington, 1979-85; v.p., assoc. gen. counsel, corp. sec. Nonprescription Drug Mfrs. Assn., Washington, 1985—; guest lectr. Am. U., Washington, 1986—, George Washington Nat. Law Ctr., Washington, 1986—, Cath. U. Law Sch., 1988—. Vol. lawyer Legal Counsel for the Elderly, Washington, 1978—. Mem. ABA (food and drug com., antitrust sect., adminstrv. law sect.), D.C. Bar Assn., Fed. Bar Assn. (chmn. food and drug com. 1986-90), Food and Drug Law Inst. (chmn. writing awards com. 1982-88, vice chmn. 1987-89, chmn. 1990, editl. adv. bd. Food Drug Law Jour.). Office: Nonprescription Drug Mfrs Assn 1150 Connecticut Ave NW Washington DC 20036-4104

BACHRACH, LYNN S., pharmaceutical contract research organization executive; b. N.Y.C., Feb. 26, 1951; d. Jesse Silberstein and Nancy (Cohen) Sawyer. BA, Antioch Coll., 1973. Saleswoman Dunhill Greater Phila., 1974-76, Meloy Labs., Phila., 1976-78, Physio Control, Phila., 1978-80, Datamedix, Phila., 1980-82; sr. v.p. C.P. Rehab. Corp. Midlantic, Phila., 1982-87; sr. v.p. sales and mktg., pres. C.P. Rehab. Corp., N.Y.C., 1987-89; pres. The Cardiac Rehab. Co. and Clin. Rsch. Group, Phila., 1989—. Mem. Drug Info. Assn., Assn. Clin. Pharmacology, Tech. Coun. Greater Phila., Am. Assn. Cardiovascular and Pulmonary Rehab., Tri-State Soc. for Cardiovascular and Pulmonary Rehab. Jewish. Office: The Cardiac Rhab Co PO Box 127 Haverford PA 19041-0127

BACHRACH, NANCY, advertising executive; b. Providence, Jan. 29, 1948; d. David and Maida Horovitz. BA magna cum laude, Conn. Coll. for Women, 1969; MA with honors, Brandeis U., 1973, PhD, 1975. Assoc. dir. Grey France, Paris, 1980-84; sr. v.p., account mgmt. Grey Advt., N.Y.C., 1985-91, exec. v.p., 1992—. Author: The Irrefutability of Skepticism, 1975. Bd. dirs. Nat. Ctr. for Learning Disabilities, N.Y.C., 1992—. Named one of 100 Best and Brightest Women, Advt. Age, 1988; named to Acad. Women Achievers, 1992. Office: Grey Advt Inc 777 3rd Ave New York NY 10017

BACKALENICK, IRENE MARGOLIS, theater critic; b. Providence, Aug. 12, 1921; d. Max and Lydia (Silverman) Margolis; m. William Backalenick, Oct. 10, 1947; children: Paul, Lynn, Lisa, Kim. BA summa cum laude, Brown U., 1947; MA in Edn., U. Bridgeport, 1960; PhD in Theater, CUNY, 1988. Freelance writer for various publs. N.Y.C., 1960—; lectr. in field. Author: East Side Story, 1988 (award Nat. Fedn. Press Women). Recipient N.Y. Times Pubs. award, 1975. Mem. Am. Theatre Critics Assn., Nat. Fedn. Press Women (theater critism), Conn. Critics Circle (co-founder), Outer Critics Circle, Women in Comm. (co-founder Fairfield County chpt.), Drama Desk, Conn. Press Club (co-founder), Phi Beta Kappa. Democrat. Home and office: 373 Greens Farms Rd Westport CT 06880-5656

BACKER, GRACIA YANCEY, state legislator; b. Jefferson City, Mo., Jan. 25, 1950; m. F. Mike Backer; 1 child, Justin. Student, S.W. Mo. State Coll. Mem. Mo. Ho. of Reps., 1983—; now majority floor leader. Active NAACP. Democrat. Baptist. Home: RR 2 Box 281 New Bloomfield MO 65063-9584 Office: Mo Ho of Reps State Capitol Building Jefferson City MO 65101-1556*

BACKER, JOANNE ARLENE, case manager; b. St. Paul, Dec. 15, 1950; d. Clarence Frederick and Beatrice P. (Slavik) B. BA in Psychology, U. Minn., 1977, BA in German, 1979; MA in German, Northwestern U., 1981. Family caseworker Ramsey County Cmty. Human Svcs., St. Paul, 1983—; freelance writer; staff writer The Guitarist, 1990-93. Mem. Minn. Guitar Soc. (bd. dirs. 1990—, v.p. 1994—), Soroptimists of Greater Twin Cities (v.p. 1996), League Minn. Poets.

BACKES, LORA STEPHENS, speech/language pathologist; b. Baton Rouge, Nov. 21, 1959; d. Preston M. and Geraldine (Ducote) Stephens; m. Charles E. Backes, Dec. 15, 1979; children: Michelle, Katherine, Emily. BS, La. State U., 1983; MEd, Southeastern La. U., Hammond, 1989. Cert. speech./lang./hearing specialist, supr. student teaching. Speech/lang. pathologist Ascension Parish Sch. Bd., Gonzales, La., 1983-93; instr., clin. supr. Valdosta (Ga.) State U., 1993—. Mem. Am. Speech/Lang. Hearing Assn., Ga. Speech/Lang. Hearing Assn., La. Speech/Lang. Hearing Assn., St. John's Coun. Cath. Women, Delta Kappa Gamma, Phi Delta Kappa. Roman Catholic. Home: 1802 Englewood Dr Valdosta GA 31602-2280 Office: Valdosta State U Coll Edn Bldg Valdosta GA 31698

BACKSTROM, LORRAINE L., nursing administrator, geriatrics nurse; b. Glendive, Mont., Nov. 24, 1942; d. Raymond W. and Florence L. (Midboe) Leaf; m. Leslie G. Backstrom, Dec. 19, 1964; children: Kimberli, Allyson, Leslie Guy, Gretchen, Rebecca. BSN, Idaho State U., 1967. RN, Idaho. Charge nurse emergency room Parkview Hosp., Idaho Falls, Idaho; nursing supr., dir. quality assurance Good Samaritan Ctr., Idaho Falls, dir. nursing and health svcs. Home: 440 N Hanson Ave Shelley ID 83274-1004

BACKUS, JAN, state legislator; b. Norristown, Pa., July 30, 1947; m. Robert Backus; 3 children. Student, U. Vt., U. Adelaide, South Australia, Kilkenny Tech. Coll., South Australia. Mem. Vt. State Senate, 1989—. Home: 162 N St Winovski VT 05404 Office: Vt State Senate State Capitol Montpelier VT 05602*

BACKUS, THERESA ANN, marketing professional; b. Parkersburg, W.Va., Apr. 19, 1965; d. Richard Crandall and Eloise Mae (Stephens) B. BS in Communications, Ohio U., 1987; MA in Internat. Transactions, George Mason U., 1995. News anchor WOUB-TV, Athens, Ohio, 1985-87, WXIL-FM, Parkersburg, W.Va., 1986-87; mktg. asst. Grand Ctrl. Mall, Vienna, W.Va., 1986-87; publicist Pub. Affairs Satellite Sys., Washington, 1987-88; fgn. svc. communications officer Dept. of State, Washington, 1988-91, Athens, Greece, 1988-91; dir. mktg. Springfield (Va.) Mall, 1991—. Co-chmn. Springfield Days, 1995-96, pageant dir., 1995-96; bd. dirs. Mktg. Edn. Adv., Fairfax, Va., 1991—. Mem. Internat. Coun. Shopping Ctrs., Springfield C. of C. (bd. dirs. 1995), Ohio U. Alumni Assn. (social chmn. 1995-96). Democrat. Methodist. Home: 6002 C Curtier Dr Alexandria VA 22310 Office: Springfield Mall 6500 Springfield Mall Springfield VA 22150

BACON, A(DELAIDE) SMOKI, public relations consultant, radio and television host; b. Brookline, Mass., Jan. 29, 1928; d. Alfred Leon and Ruth Dorothy (Burns) Ginepra; m. Edwin Conant Bacon, May 11, 1957 (dec. July 1974); children: Brooks Conant, Hilary Conant; m. Richard Francis Concannon, Oct. 13, 1979. Student, Art Inst. Boston, 1947; grad., Jackson Von Ladau Sch. Design, Boston, 1951. Pub. rels. cons. Boston, 1968—; pres. Bacon-Concannon Assocs., Boston, 1979-95; dir. craftsmobiles Summerthing Program, Boston, 1968-73; dir. exhibits Citifair, Boston, 1974; dir. Victorian exhibits Bicentennial Boston 200, 1975, dir. spl. events, 1976; cons. spl. events. Inst. Contemporary Art, 1977-78, Boston Tea Party Ship, 1978-79; fundraiser Mass. Assn. Mental Health, 1979; dir. promotions Met. Ctr., 1979; coord. grand finale celebration Boston Jubilee 350, 1979-80; coord. Elliot Norton Awards, 1983; pub. rels. Dyansen Gallery, Boston, 1987-88, French Speaking League, 1987; cons. spl. events Jordan Marsh, 1987; fundraiser, pub. rels. Boston Philharmonic, 1988; coord. 30th anniversary celebration Charles Playhouse, 1988; fundraiser Elliot Norton Awards, 1989; coord. benefit New Eng. Premiere of film Glory Afro-Am. Mus., 1990; pub. rels. cons. Boston Chamber Music Soc., 1990; pub. rels. Paul Sorota Gallery of Fine Arts, 1990-91; fundraising cons. Internat. Inst., 1991; pub. rels., fundraiser Brookline H.S. Sesquicentennial Celebration, 1992-93; co-host radio show Celebrity Time, 1980—; co-host TV show On the Town; guest lectr. Boston U. Sch. Pub. Rels., 1979, ARC, 1987, Radcliffe Coll. 4'O'Clock Forums, 1989; contbg. editor Design Times Mag. Social calendar editor Boston Tab Newspaper, 1987-90; contbg. editor Design Times Mag.; columnist BeaconHill News. Candidate Dem. State Rep., Mass., 1980; Bastille Day chmn. French Libr. Boston, 1994—; local adv. com. Nat. Trust for Historic Preservation; bd. dirs. Boston Lit. Hour; host parents com. Harvard Coll.; bd. dirs. Mugar Libr., Spl. Collections, 1994—; vis. com. Mus. Fine Arts, Eqyptian Dept., 1994—; bd. trustees Boston Arts Festival, 1960-63; bd. dirs., treas. Samaritans, Boston, 1974-84; art auction chairperson WGBH-Pub. Radio-TV, Boston, 1969-70; bd. dirs. Urban League Ea. Mass., Boston, 1975-85; former mem. numerous civic coms. Recipient Woman of Great Achievement award Cambridge Young Women's Assn., 1991; named One of Boston's 100 Female Leaders, Boston Mag., 1980; Guest of Honor, Womens' City Club Ann. Dinner Dance, 1979. Democrat. Home: 9 Fairfield St Boston MA 02116-1601 Office: Bacon Concannon Assocs 9 Fairfield St Boston MA 02116-1601

BACON, BETTY J. NICHOLS, preschool educator and administrator; b. Erie, Pa., June 22, 1938; d. Andrew Jackson and Betty VanBuren (Crawford) Nichols; m. Robert Sargent Bacon, June 8, 1968; 1 child, Julie Sargent. BA, U. Colo., 1962, MA, 1967; postgrad., Miami U., Oxford, Ohio. Cert. secondary tchr., Mass., secondary and elem. tchr., Ohio. High sch. tchr. Rogers Hall, Lowell, Mass., 1963-66; elem. tchr. Broomfield (Colo.) Sch. Dist., 1967-68, Sacred Heart Sch., Boulder, Colo., 1968-71, Talawanda Sch. Dist., Oxford, 1971-75, 81-82; tchr., adminstr. City of Oxford Preschool, 1982—; leader workshops Butler County Tchrs. Assn., Hamilton, Ohio, 1972, 74, 85; v.p. Oxford Assn. Educationally Gifted, 1983-85. Neighborhood dir., troop leader Girls Scouts U.S., Oxford, 1982-91 (Key award 1988); mem. Butler County Mental Health Bd., Hamilton, 1985-87; chmn. membership drive McCullough-Hyde Hosp., Oxford, 1989; vol. asst. coach Talawanda Girls Tennis Team, Oxford, 1994—. Named Oxford Citizen of the Yr., City Coun. Com., 1987. Mem. Ohio Tchrs. Assn., Butler County Assn. Edn. Young Children (Outstanding Child Profl. 1994), Alpha Omicron Pi. Republican. Lutheran. Home: 411 Maxine Dr Oxford OH 45056

BACON, CAROLINE SHARFMAN, investor relations consultant; b. Ann Arbor, Mich., Aug. 27, 1942; d. Mahlon Samuel and Mary Patricia (Potter) Sharp; m. William Lee Sharfman, Sept. 5, 1964 (div. 1985); m. James Edmund Bacon, Nov. 4, 1989. BA with distinction, U. Mich., 1964; MBA, Columbia U., 1975. Assoc. Goldman, Sachs & Co., N.Y.C., 1975-80, v.p., 1980-83; v.p. Goldman Sachs Money Markets Inc., N.Y.C., 1983-90; sr. cons. investor rels. Burson-Marsteller, 1991; mng. dir. Johnnie D. Johnson & Co. Investor Rels., N.Y.C., 1992-95; investor rels. cons., Redding, Conn., 1996—; bd. dirs. Redding Open Lands, Inc. Mem. Phi Beta Kappa, Phi Sigma Iota, Beta Gamma Sigma. Episcopalian.

BACON, CYNTHIA THORNTON, nursing administrator; b. Balt., Sept. 15, 1964, d. Francis Kenneth and Carol (Dennis) T.; married. M Adminstrv. Sci., Johns Hopkins U., 1992, MA in Nursing, 1996, MSN, 1996. Clin. nurse Johns Hopkins Hosp., Balt., 1987-90, sr. clin. nurse, 1990-92, nurse mgr., 1992-96; staff nurse Riverside Regional Med. Ctr., Newport News, Va., 1996, float pool coord., mgr., 1996—. Mem. AACN (Nurse of Yr. Chesapeake Bay chpt. 1994). Office: Riverside Regional Med Ctr Nursing Adminstrn 500 J Clyde Morris Blvd Newport News VA 23601

BACON, ELIZABETH MORROW, librarian, writer, editor, educator; b. L.A., Sept. 15, 1914; d. James Edwin and Elizabeth Margaret (Hodenpyl) Morrow; m. George Richards Bacon, Sept. 7, 1939 (div. June 1963); children: David Nathaniel, Daniel Carl. BA, Bryn Mawr Coll., 1935; MLS, U. Calif., Berkeley, 1958. Children's book editor various publishing firms, N.Y.C., 1935-52; ctrl. children's svcs. librarian Contra Costa County Libr., Pleasant Hill, Calif., 1959-70; dir. children's svcs. Solano County Libr., Vallejo, Calif., 1970-78; lectr., Sch. of Libr. and Info. Studies U. Calif., Berkeley, 1978-84; lectr. extension classes Calif. State U. Sonoma, Solano Cmty. Coll., U. Calif. Berkeley, 1970-82. Author: See Through the Sea, 1955, See Up the Mountain, 1958, Jewish Holidays, 1967, A Great Miracle, 1968, People at the Edge of the World, 1991; editor: How Much Truth Do We Tell the Children?, 1988; contbr. articles and book revs. to profl. jours. Mem. exec. com. Friends Com. on Legis., Sacramento, Calif., 1974—; mem. adv. com. Criminal Justice Project, Am. Friends Svc. Com., Oakland, Calif., 1994—; vol. organizer Am. Fedn. Tchrs. AFL-CIO, Berkeley, 1979-86. Recipient spl. recognition Bay Area Storytelling Festival, Berkeley, 1994, Tribute of a Lifetime Com. of Correspondence, San Francisco, 1994. Mem. Assn. Children's Librarians (book rev. chair 1971), Soc. Children's Book Writers (spkr. 1977), Calif. Libr. Assn. (various coms. 1968-78). Mem. Soc. of Friends. Home: 1320 Addison C-232 Berkeley CA 94702

BACON, MARTHA BRANTLEY, small business owner; b. Wrightsville, Ga., Apr. 20, 1938; d. William Riley and Susie Mae (Colston) B.; m. Albert Sidney Bacon, Jr., Aug. 3, 1958; children: Albert Sidney, III, Gregory Riley. BS, Ga. So., Statesboro, 1959; grad., Realtors Inst., 1959; Post Grad., U. Va., Charlottesville, 1978-80, Adrian Hall Interior Design, Savannah, Ga., 1984. Lic. real estate broker, Ga., Va. Tchr. Chatham Bd. Edn., Savannah, Ga., 1961; co-owner mgr. Two Kentucky Fried Chicken Restaurants, Charlottesville, Va., 1967-80; real estate broker Real Estate III, Charlottesville, Va., 1978-83, Landmark Realty, Statesboro, Ga.; tree farmer Johnson Co., Ga., 1980—; mgr., co-owner Restaurant, 1987-92; co-owner Plunderosa Antiques and Collectibles, Statesboro, Ga., 1993—; v.p. Bd. Realtors Statesboro Ga. 1985; regional franchise agt., owner Ice Cream Churn of South Ga. Chmn. Jaycettes Gov. Columbus, Ga., 1962; vol. First Bapt. Ch. Pers. Com., Charlottesville, 1978, U. Va. Hosp., 1980-83; com. mem. Athletic Hall of Fame Ga. So. U.; mem. Ga. Forestry Stewardship, 1991—. Recipient Outstanding Sales award Real Estate III Co. Charlottesville 1980; named Outstanding Jaycette 1961, Jaycettes Gov. Columbus, 1962. Mem. AAUW, Charlottesville Restaurant Assn., Westchester Garden Club, Ga. Restaurant Assn., Ga. So. Univ. Alumni Bd., Ga. So. Symphony Guild, Ga. So. Univ. Athletic Boosters Club, Pilot Club, Evergeen Garden Club, Ga. (v.p.), Optimist (Stateboro essay chmn.),. Baptist. Home: 30 Golf Club Cir Statesboro GA 30458-9163

BACON, SYLVIA, retired judge; b. Watertown, S.D., July 9, 1931; d. Julius Franklin and Anne Rae (Hyde) B. AB, Vassar Coll., Poughkeepsie, N.Y., 1952; cert., London Sch. Econs., 1953; LLB, Harvard U., 1956; LLM, Georgetown Law Ctr., Washington, 1959. Bar: D.C. 1956, U.S. Supreme Ct. 1963. Law clk. to fed. judge, 1956-57; asst. U.S. Atty. Washington, 1957-65; assoc. dir. Pres. Commn. on Crime in D.C., 1965-67; trial atty. U.S. Dept. Justice, 1967-69; exec. asst. U.S. atty. Washington, 1969-70; judge D.C. Superior Ct., Washington, 1970-92; judge-in-residence Columbus Sch. Law Cath. U. Am., Washington, 1993-95, lectr., 1995—; adjudicator Office of Compliance, U.S. Congress, Washington, 1996—; adj. prof. Georgetown Law Ctr., 1968-70; mem. faculty Nat. Inst. Trial Advocacy, 1991—; bd. dirs. Nat. Ctr. State Cts., 1975-79, Nat. Coll. Criminal Def., 1978-86; mem. faculty Nat. Jud. Coll., 1974-79, bd. dirs., 1980-87; lectr. Am. Acad. Jud. Edn., 1972-82. Bd. dirs. Nat Home Libr. Found., 1968-70. Mem. AAUW, ABA (bd. dirs. 1988-91), Bar Assn. D.C. (bd. dirs. 1965-67), D.C. Women's Bar Assn., Am. Inns of Ct., Exec. Women in Govt., Bus. and Profl. Women's Assn., Nat. Assn. Women Judges, Supreme Ct. Hist. Soc. Home: 2500 Q St NW Washington DC 20007-4373 Office: Cath U Am Columbus Sch Law 3600 MacCormack Dr NE Washington DC 20064

BACON, VICTORIA LEE, psychologist, educator; b. Bellows Falls, Vt., Mar. 15, 1955; d. George William and Shirley Ann (Norris) Bacon. BA, Fitchburg State U., 1977; MA, Anna Maria Coll., 1979; cert. advanced grad. study, Northeastern U., 1988, EdD, 1992. Lic. psychologist, Mass.; cert. psychologist, N.H. Counselor Fitchburg (Mass.) H.S., 1978-81; dir. counseling svcs. Fitchburg State Coll., 1981-84; adj. faculty mem. U. Mass., Lowell, 1985-96; psychologist AGES, Worcester and Rockland, Mass., 1987-90, Counseling and Consultation Ctr., Chelsea, Mass., 1988-92; doctoral clin. psychology intern Worcester Youth Guidance Ctr., 1990-91; clin. psychology fellow Brookside Hosp., Nashua, N.H., 1992-93; cons. Collaborative for Women's Sports, Marlboro, Mass., 1992—; pvt. practice psychology Littleton, Mass., 1993—; asst. prof. counselor edn. Bridgewater (Mass.) State Coll., 1996—. Disaster response psychologist Mass. Psychol. Assn., Boston, 1995—. Mem. APA. Office: Brdgewater State Coll Dept Counselor Edn Bridgewater MA 02325

BADALUCO, NANCY L., elementary education educator; b. Terre Haute, Ind., Sept. 18, 1947; d. Marvin O. and Marie M. (Miller) Weddle; 1 child, James M. Badaluco. BS, Ind. State U., 1968; MA, Mich. State U., 1971, postgrad. in Reading, 1972—. Elem. tchr. Sibley Elem. Sch., Grand Rapids, Mich., 1968-74; elem. reading/math. tchr. Alger Park Elem., Grand Rapids, Mich., 1976-94; elem. tchr. Campus Sch. of Arts and Lit., Grand Rapids, Mich., 1994-96; tchr. Covell Elem. Sch., 1996—; presenter Classroom Assessment Conf., 1996. Mem. Women's Resource Ctr., Grand Rapids, 1985—. Recipient Outstanding Computer Lab. award Jostens Computer Systems, 1993-94. Mem. Mich. State Alumni Assn., Mich. Coun. Tchrs. Math. (Longevity award 1994-95), Mich. Reading Assn., Delta Gamma Alumni Assn., Delta Gamma. Democrat. Baptist. Home: 3707 Dawes Ave SE Grand Rapids MI 49508 Office: Covell Elem 1417 Covell Rd NW Grand Rapids MI 49504

BADDOUR, ANNE BRIDGE, aviatrix; b. Royal Oak, Mich.; d. William George and Esther Rose (Pfiester) Bridge; m. Raymond F. Baddour, Sept. 25, 1954; children: Cynthia Anne, Frederick Raymond, Jean Bridge. Student, Detroit Bus. Sch., 1948-50. Stewardess Eastern Airlines, Boston, 1952-54; instr. aero. Powers Sch., Boston, 1958; co-pilot, flight attendant Raytheon Co., Bedford, Mass., 1958-63; flight dispatcher, ferry Pilot Comerford Flight Sch., Bedford, 1974-76; adminstrv. asst., ferry pilot Jenney Beachcraft, Bedford, 1976; mgr., pilot Balt. Airways, Inc., Bedford, 1976-77; pilot Lincoln Lab. Flight Test Facility MIT, Lexington, 1977—; aviation cons., corp. pilot Energy Resources, Inc., Cambridge, Mass., 1974-84; holder World Class speed records for single-engine aircraft; Boston to Goose Bay, Labrador, 1985, Boston to Reykjavik, Iceland, 1985, Portland, Maine to Goose Bay, 1985, Portland to Reykjavik, 1985, Goose Bay to Reykjavik, 1985; records for twin-engine aircraft: Sept Isles to Goose Bay, 1988, Mont Joli to Goose Bay, 1988, Presque Isle to Goose Bay, 1988, Millinocket to Goose Bay, 1988, Bedford to Goose Bay, 1988, Goose Bay to Narssassrag, Greenland, 1988, Narssassrag to Klevelevic, Iceland, 1988, Narssassrag to Reykjavik, 1988, Bedford to Narssassrag, 1988, Millinochet to Narssassrag, 1988, Presque Isle to Narssassrag, 1988, Bedford to St. John, 1991, Bedford to Charlottetown, 1991, Charlottetown to Kennebunk, 1991, Charlottetown to Portsmouth, 1991, Muncton to Bedford, 1991, St. John, to Kennebunk, 1991, St. John to Bedford, 1991. Bd. dirs. Cambridge Opera, 1977-79; mem. campaign coun. Mus. Transp., Boston; mem. coun. assocs. French Libr. in Boston; commr. Commonwealth of Mass., Mass. Aero. Commn., 1979-83; chmn. regional adv. coun. FAA, 1984-88; trustee bd. adminstrn. Amelia Earhart Birthplace Mus., 1992-93; trustee Daniel Webster Coll., Nashua, N.H., 1995—. Winner trophy Phila. Transcontinental Air Race, 1954, New Eng. Air Race, 1957, Clifford B. Harmon trophy Internat. Aviatrix, 1988; recipient Spl. Recognition award FAA, 1990; honoree Internat. Aviation Forest of Friendship, Atchison, Kans., 1991; named Pilot of the Year, New Eng. sect. Internat. Women Pilots Orgn./The Ninety-Nines, Inc., 1992. Mem. Fedn. Aeronautique Internat., Nat. Aero. Assn., Ninety-Nines (New Eng. Safety trophy 1986), Aero Club New Eng. (v.p. 1978-80, dir. 1978—), Aircraft Owners Pilots Assn., Nat. Pilots Assn., U.S. Sea Plane Pilots Assn., Assn. Women Transcontinental Air Race, Bostonian Soc., English Speaking Union, Soc. Exptl. Test Pilots, Friends of Switzerland, French Ctr. Libr., Belmont Hill Club, St. Botolph Club, Chilton Club, Boston Women's Travel Club, Harvard Travellers Club. Republican. Episcopalian. Office: MIT Lincoln Lab 244 Wood St Lexington MA 02173-6426

BADEL, JULIE, lawyer; b. Chgo., Sept. 14, 1946; d. Charles and Saima (Hyrkas) B.; m. Craig B. Feldpausch, Feb. 3, 1968 (dec. Dec. 1986). Student, Knox Coll., 1963-65; BA, Columbia Coll., Chgo., 1967; JD, DePaul U., 1977. Bar: Ill. 1977, U.S. Dist. Ct. (no. dist.) Ill. 1977, U.S. Ct. Appeals (7th and D.C. cirs.) 1981, U.S. Supreme Ct. 1985, U.S. Dist. Ct. (ea. dist.) Mich. 1989. Hearings referee State of Ill., Chgo., 1974-78; assoc. Cohn, Lambert, Ryan & Schneider, Chgo., 1978-80; assoc. McDermott, Will & Emery, Chgo., 1980-84, ptnr., 1985—; legal counsel, mem. adv. bd. Health Evaluation Referral Svc. Chgo., 1980-89; bd. dirs. Alternatives, Inc., Chgo. chpt. Asthma and Allergy Found., 1993-94, Glenwood Sch. for Boys. Author: Hospital Restructuring: Employment Law Pitfalls, 1985; editor DePaul U. Law Rev., 1976-77. Mem. ABA, Columbia Coll. Alumni Assn. (1st v.p., bd. dirs. 1981-86), Pi Gamma Mu. Office: McDermott Will & Emery 227 W Monroe St Chicago IL 60606-5016

BADENHOP, SHARON LYNN, psychologist, educator, entrepreneur; b. Roswell, N.Mex., Feb. 21, 1946; d. Charles Theodore and Anna (Burke) B.; BA in Ednl. Psychology, SUNY-Oneonta, 1967, MS, 1969, MS in Counselor Edn., 1971. Cert. mental health adminstr. Tchr. Gilbertsville (N.Y.) Central Sch., 1968-70; guidance counselor Delaware Acad., Delhi, N.Y., 1970-71; instr. SUNY-Oneonta, 1971-75; prof. SUNY-Delhi, 1974-75; psychol. case worker United Cerebral Palsy Assn., 1977-78; psychologist in psychogeratrics Rochester (N.Y.) Psychiat. Center, 1979, dir. edn. and tng. dept., 1979-81, psychologist, 1981-90; instr. U. Rochester, 1978-91, Rochester Inst. Tech., 1981-83, 92—; psychologist Securecare, 1985-91; founder, pres. USA East Assocs., Inc., 1991—; founder, sec. Internat. Resource Group. Bd. dir. East House. Lic. guidance counselor, N.Y. State; cert. mental health adminstr.; cert. tchr. grades 1-6, N.Y. State, GEMS cons. Mem. NAFE, APA, Clin. Sociology Assn., Soc. Internat. Devel., Assn. Mental Health Adminstrs., Rochester Profl. Cons. Network, Coun. on Fgn. Rels. Home and Office: 18 Hollingham Rise Fairport NY 14450-1609

BADER, LORRAINE GREENBERG, textile designer, consultant; b. Bklyn., Sept. 5, 1930; d. Isidore and Sadie (Schreier) Greenberg; m. Martin Bader, June 24, 1950; children: Evan Ashley, Reid Scott, Wade. Student, Parsons Sch. Design, 1948-49. Textile stylist, dir. design, fashion and spl. creative projects, color coord. Cortley Fabrics Corp., N.Y.C., 1950-64, Avon Fabrics, N.Y.C., 1964-67, R.S.L. Fabrics Corp., N.Y.C., 1967-71; textile stylist, fashion dir. Shirley Fabrics Corp., N.Y.C., 1971-76; interior designer, decorator Lorraine Bader Interiors, Lawrence, N.Y., 1976-79; textile stylist, dir. design, fashion, and spl. projects, color coord. Lida Inc., N.Y.C., 1979-81; textile designer Fresh Paint, N.Y.C., 1981-87; textile designer for women's wear, children's wear, fabrics, sweaters, scarves, dinnerware, tablecloths, placemats and bedding for home furnishings Lorraine Bader Designs, Hackensack, N.J., 1987—. Scholar Parsons Sch. Design, 1948. Mem. The Fashion Group.

BADER, ROCHELLE LINDA (SHELLEY BADER), educational administrator. BA in Speech Arts, BA in Edn., Hofstra U., 1970; MLS, U. Md., 1973; EdD, George Washington U., 1993. Mgmt. intern Office Civil Pers., Dept. of the Army, Pentagon, Washington, 1971; circulation libr. George Washington U. Med. Libr., Washington, 1971-73; head reference libr. Himmelfarb Health Scis. Libr./George Washington U. Med. Ctr., Washington, 1973-75, head Audio Visual Study Ctr., 1975-78, chief Access and Facilities Svcs. Divsn., 1978-79, chief Reader Svcs. Divsn., 1979-80, assoc. dir., 1980, dir., 1980-90; dir. ednl. resources George Washington U. Med. Ctr., Washington, 1990—; audio visual cons. Regional Med. Libr. Program, D.C. Metro area, 1977-79; mem. nat. adv. com. U. Iowa, 1984-85; mem. Med. Ctr. Faculty Senate Com. on Health Scis. Programs, George Washington U., Washington, 1989, chmn. Health Scis. Programs Ednl. Evaluation Com., 1993—, many other coms.; adv. com. Found. for Health Svcs. Rsch., 1992-93; presenter in field. Consulting editor: Biomedical Comms., 1983-84; mem. editorial rev. bd.: The Jour. of Biocommunication, 1988-92, Annual Statistics of Medical School Libraries in the United States and Canada, 12th, 13th and 14th edits., 1989-93; contbr. articles to profl. jours. Grantee Coun. on Libr. Resource, 1989-90, Nat. Libr. Medicine, 1991, NSF, 1993-94; recipient Disting. Svc. award Health Scis. Comms. Assn., 1986. Mem. Am. Med. Informatics Assn. (exec. com. edn. workshop group 1991—, MLA rep. to adv. coun. 1992—), Assn. Am. Med. Colls. (group on med. edn., coun. on acad. scos. 1991—), Assn. Acad. Health Scis. Libr. Dirs. (pres. 1986-87, chmn. fin. com. 1987-88), Assn. Biomedical Comms. Dirs. (membership com. 1989-91, program com. 1991), Health Scis. Comms. Assn. (coord. interactive media festival 1990-91, chmn. awards com. 1992, pres. 1984-85), Med. Libr. Assn. (bd. dirs. 1995—), Beta Phi Mu. Home: 12225 Seline Way Potomac MD 20854 Office: George Washington U Med Ctr 2300 I St NW Washington DC 20037-2337

BADGER, SANDRA RAE, health and physical education educator; b. Pueblo, Colo., Nov. 2, 1946; d. William Harvey and Iva Alberta (Belveal) Allenbach; m. Graeme B. Badger, Oct. 9, 1972; 1 child, Jack Edward. BA in Phys. Edn., U. So. Colo., Pueblo, 1969; MA in Arts and Humanities, Colo. Coll., 1979; postgrad., Adams State U., Alamosa, Colo., 1980-91. Cert. tchr., secondary endorsement in health and phys. edn., Colo. Head women's swimming coach Mitchell High Sch., Doherty High Sch., Colorado Springs, Colo., 1969-90; head dept. Health Edn. Doherty High Sch., 1979—; trainer student asst. program CARE, Colorado Springs, 1983—; trainer drug edn. U.S. Swim Olympic Tng. Ctr., Colorado Springs, 1988-89; trainer in track and field, Colorado Springs, 1989, 91; cons. Assocs. in Recovery Therapy, 1989—; speaker in field. Author, editor: Student Assistant Training Manual, 1983-95. Bd. dirs. ARC, Colorado Springs, 1990-96, sec., 1991—, mem. health and safety com., 1990-95; reviewer ARC/Olympic Com. Sports Safety Tng. Manual Handbook Textbooks; mem. comprehensive health adv. com. Dept. Edn., State of Colo., Denver, 1991. Recipient Svc. award ARC, 1985, Coach of Yr. award Gazette Telegraph, 1979, 84, CARE award State of Colo., 1988, others; Gamesfield grantee, 1985; Nat. Coun. on Alcoholism grantee, 1990. Mem. NEA, Colorado Springs Edn. Assn. Office: Doherty High Sch 4515 Barnes Rd Colorado Springs CO 80917-1519

BADURA, LYNN MARIE, association executive; b. Loup City, Nebr., July 2, 1967; d. Roman Francis and Patricia Jo (Golus) B. BS in Bus. Adminstrn., U. Nebr., 1989. Telemktg. trainer Watts Mktg., Lincoln, Nebr., 1989-90; campaign coord. United Way, Lincoln, Nebr., 1989-90; devel. dir. Combined Health Agys., Lincoln, Nebr., 1990-93; corp. projects dir. Nat. Kidney Found., Kansas City, Mo., 1993—. Big sister YMCA, Lincoln, 1990-93, Kansas City, 1993—. Mem. Nat. Soc. Fundraising Execs., Greater Kansas City Coun. Philanthropy. Democrat. Roman Catholic. Home: 9419 W 88 St Overland Park KS 66212

BAEHNMAN, GRETA MAE, music educator; b. Plum City, Wis., Aug. 1, 1951; d. Rudolph C. and Lucille Helen (Hoffman) Swanson; m. Steven Charles Baehnman, June 16, 1979. B of Music Edn., U. Wis., 1974. K-12 vocal music Weyauwege (Wis.) Fremont Schs., 1974-77, elem. music tchr., 1974—; bd. dirs. Ctrl. Wis. Uniservice Coun., Wausau. Active children's ch. choir S.S. Peter and Paul Ch., Weyauwega, 1983-85. Mem. NEA, Weyauwega-Fremont and Edn. Assn. (v.p. 1991-93), Wis. Edn. Assn., Wis. Music Edn. Assn., Music Edn. Nat. Conf. Roman Catholic. Office: Weyauwega-Fremont Schs PO Box 580 Weyauwega WI 54983-0580

BAERMANN, DONNA LEE ROTH, property executive, retired insurance analyst; b. Carroll, Iowa, Apr. 28, 1939; d. Omer H. and Mae Lavina (Larson) Real; m. Edwin Ralph Baermann, Jr., July 8, 1961; children: Beth, Bryan, Cynthia. BS, Mt. Mercy Coll., 1973; student Iowa State U.-Ames, 1957-61. Cert. profl. ins. woman; fellow Life Mgmt. Inst. Ins. agt. Lutheran Mut. Ins. Co., Cedar Rapids, Iowa, 1973; home economist Iowa-Ill. Gas & Electric Co., Cedar Rapids, Iowa, 1973-77; supr. premium collection Life Investors Ins. Co. (now Aegon USA), Cedar Rapids, 1978-83, methods and procedures analyst, 1987-94, sr. supr. policy svc., 1987-84; v.p. bd. dirs. Roth & Assocs., Roth Farms, Roth Inc. & Readymix, Roth Apts. Inc., 1988-90; pres. bd. dirs. Roth & Assocs., Roth Farms, Roth, Inc., Roth Readymix, Roth Apts. Inc., 1990-96; pres., CEO Roth Apt. Corp., 1990—, Baermann Apts Inc., 1992-94; pres. Baermann Apts. Inc.; mem. telecom. study group com. 1982-83, mem. productivity task force, 1984-94. Mem. Internat. Platform Assn., Citizens Com. for Persons with Disabilities, Nat. Assn. Ins. Women, Nat. Mgmt. Assn. (bd. dirs. Cedar Rapids chpt.), DAR, Knights of Malta (named Damsel of Ancient Order of St. John, N.Y.C.), Chi Omega. Republican. Presbyterian. Home: 361 Willshire Ct NE Cedar Rapids IA 52402-6922

BAERNSTEIN, PRUDENCE RENEE, history educator; b. Bar Harbor, Maine, June 18, 1963; d. Albert II and Judith Priscilla (Haynes) B.; m. Wietse Thijs de Boer, June 17, 1993. AB, Cornell U., 1985; PhD, Harvard U., 1993. Asst. prof. history Miami U., Oxford, Ohio, 1993—. Mem. Friends of Libr. com. Am. Acad. in Rome, 1994—. Fulbright scholar, 1988-89; Mrs. Giles Whiting Found. fellow Harvard U., 1991-92, Friedrich Solmsen fellow Inst. for Rsch. in Humanities, U. Wis., 1995-96; recipient Rome prize in post-classical studies Am. Acad. in Rome, 1990-91. Mem. Am. Hist. Assn., Sixteenth Century Studies Conf., Soc. for Italian Hist. Studies, Renaissance Soc. Am. Home: 793 Yale Saint Louis MO 63130 Office: Miami U Dept History Oxford OH 45056

BAESSLER, CHRISTINA A., medical/surgical nurse; b. Phila., Feb. 10, 1948; d. Harry and Mary (Moreken) B. Diploma, St. Agnes Sch. Nursing, 1968; student, Neumann Coll., 1977-81; BSN, LaSalle U., 1987, MSN, 1993. RN, Pa.; cert. CPR, BCLS. Project coord., asst. adminstr. Nat. Cardiovascular Rsch. Ctr., Haddonfield, N.J.; cardiac arrhythmia suppression trial project coord. Hahnemann U. Hosp., Phila.; grad. hosp. nurse researcher in cardiology Hahneman U. Hosp., Phila.; gallstone lithotripsy nurse clin. coord. Hahnemann U. Hosp., Phila., coord. electrophysiology rsch. and quality assurance, 1990—, antiarrhythmics verses implantable defibrillators rsch. coord., 1993—, antihypertensives and lipid lowering agents for the prevention of heart attacks trial rsch. coord., 1995—. Contbr. articles to profl. publs. Recipient Vol. Recognition award S.E. Pa. chpt. Am. Heart Assn., 1982, Little Flower H.S. Disting. Alumnae award, 1996. Mem. AACN (life, pres. S.E. Pa. chpt. 1975-76), Sigma Theta Tau (v.p. Kappa Delta chpt. 1989-94, rsch. award, 1995). Home: 848 Windermere Ave Drexel Hill PA 19026-1534

BAEZ, JOAN CHANDOS, folk singer; b. S.I., N.Y., Jan. 9, 1941; d. Albert V. and Joan (Bridge) B.; m. David Victor Harris, Mar. 1968 (div. 1973); 1 son, Gabriel Earl. Appeared in coffeehouses, Gate of Horn, Chgo., 1958, Ballad Room, Club 47, 1958-68, Newport (R.I.) Folk Festival, 1959-69, 85, 87, 90, 92, 93, 95, extended tours to colls. and concert halls, 1960s, appeared Town Hall and Carnegie Hall, 1962, 67, 68, U.S. tours, 1970—, concert tours in Japan, 1966, 82, Europe, 1970-73, 80, 83-84, 87-90, 93—, Australia, 1985; rec. artist for Vanguard Records, 1960-72, A&M, 1973-76, Portrait Records, 1977-80, Gold Castle Records, 1986-89, Virgin Records, 1990-93, Grapevine Label Records (UK), 1995—, Guardian Records, 1995—, European record albums, 1981, 83, award 8 gold albums, 1 gold single; albums include Ring Them Bells, 1995, Rare, Live & Classic (box set), 1993; author: Joan Baez Songbook, 1964, (biography) Daybreak, 1968, (with David Harris) Coming Out, 1971, And a Voice to Sing With, 1987, (songbook) An Then I Wrote, 1979. Extensive TV appearances and speaking tours U.S. and Can. for anti-militarism, 1967-68; visit to Dem. Republic of Vietnam, 1972, visit to war torn Bosnia-Herzegovina, 1993; founder, v.p. Inst. for Study Nonviolence (now Resource Ctr. for Nonviolence, Santa Cruz, Calif.), Palo Alto, Calif., 1965; mem. nat. adv. coun. Amnesty Internat., 1974-92; founder, pres. Humanitas/Internat. Human Rights Com., 1979-92; condr. fact-finding mission to refugee camps, S.E. Asia, Oct. 1979; began refusing payment of war taxes, 1964; arrested for civil disobedience opposing draft, Oct., Dec., 1967. Office: Diamonds & Rust Productions PO Box 1026 Menlo Park CA 94026-1026

BAEZA, CHERYL ANNE, psychiatric social worker; b. Wichita, Kans., Aug. 6, 1946; d. Andrew and Verda Mae (Gilbreth) Washburn; m. Patrick W. Campbell, Sept. 6, 1964 (div. June 1976); 1 child, Patrick Daron; m. Hector Baeza, Oct. 26, 1980. BA in English and Edn., U. Colo., 1969; MSW, U. So. Calif., 1978. Lic. clin. social worker. Social worker Lanterman State Hosp., Pomona, Calif., 1978-79, L.A. County Dept. Adoptions, 1979-83, Children's Home Soc., Santa Ana, Calif., 1983-84, Psychol. Health Care, Orange, Calif., 1985-88, FHP, Fountain Valley, Calif., 1988—; project dir. Ct. Apptd. Spl. Advs., Orange, 1984-85, Western Youth Svcs., Garden Grove, Calif., 1985-88; field instr. U. So. Calif., L.A., 1986-95; adj. prof. Calif. State U., Long Beach, 1986-89; mem. Task Force, Child Sexual Abuse Network, Orange, 1987-88; conf. chair Alliance for Mentally Ill., Orange County, 1994-95. Joint Honor scholar State of Colo., 1964-69; recipient McConnell Found. stipend , 1977-78. Mem. NASW (program chair 1985-86), AAUW (EF chair/program chair 1992-94), AMIOC, CAMI, NAMI. Democrat.

BAEZA, VIRGINA, accoutant; b. El Paso, Tex., Dec. 29, 1968; d. Ramon and Maria Asuncion (Beltran) B. Attended, U. Tex., El Paso, 1987-89; BBA, U. Tex., San Antonio, 1991. Acctg. intern U. S. Acctg. Assn., San Antonio, 1991; acct. Acctg. Reporting Consolidation Ctr., San Antonio, 1992-93, Valero Energy Corp., San Antonio, 1993—. Mem. Inst. of Mgmt. Accts., Am. Soc. of Women Accts., Inst. Internal Auditors. Democrat. Roman Catholic. Home: 2818 Redland Creek San Antonio TX 78259 Office: 530 McCullough Ave San Antonio TX 78215-2198

BAGA, MARGARET FITZPATRICK, nurse, medical office manager; b. Mount Vernon, N.Y., Mar. 20, 1951; d. John James and Margaret Mary (Wade) F.; m. Victor Bonoan Baga, June 22, 1974; children: Jessica Margaret, Victoria Lynn, Kathryn Naomi. RN, Misericordia Hosp. Sch. Nursing, Bronx, N.Y., 1971. RN, N.Y., Fla. RN Fordham Hosp., Bronx, 1971-74, Coney Island Hosp., Bklyn., 1974-75; RN, office mgr. Victor B. Baga M.D., P.A., Venice, Fla., 1975—. Mem. women's bd. Venice (Fla.) Hosp. Found., nominating chair, project chair, patrons party chair, ann. gala chair, v.p., 1988-94, edn. grant making com. 1994—; bd. dirs. The Venice Cotillion, 1991-94; mem. Congrl. Club-Dan Miller, 1995—; mem. sch. bd. Cardinal Mooney H.S.; mem. parent network for admissions, mem. parents com. Phillips Exeter Acad.; cmty. adv. bd. PALS Sarasota County, 1996—; ballet amb. Sarasota Ballet of Fla., 1989-91; bd. dirs. Ballet Eddy Toussaint, Sarasota, 1992-94. Mem. Fla. Med. Assn. Alliance (fall conf. co-chair 1993-94, south west dist. v.p. 1994-95, state chair 1995-96, mem. com. physicians resource network 1995-96, apptd. state chmn. 1996—, mem. fin. com., nominating com., long range planning com.), AMA Alliance (del. ann. conv.), Sarasota County Med. Soc. Aux. (pres. county coun. 1992-93, corr. sec. south br. 1985-86, v.p. south br. 1989-90, recording sec. 1994-95), Venice Area Toastmasters. Republican. Roman Catholic. Home: 708 LaGuna Dr Venice FL 34285

BAGAN, DIANA LYNN, clinical mental health counselor; b. Jamestown, N.D., July 15, 1953; d. Louis J. and Kathlene A. (Wilmart) H.; div. 1983; children: Alissa Lynn, MIke, Joe. BS in Elem. Edn., Phys. Edn., U. N.D., 1974; MEd in Clin. Counseling, N.D. State U., 1990. Lic. profl. counselor, N.D.; cert. counselor Nat. Bd. Clin. counselor Discovery Counseling, Fargo, N.D., 1991-92; clin. counselor, dir. Choices Counseling & Edn. Ctr., Bismarck, N.D., 1992—; facilitator workshops Choices, Bismarck, 1992—. Contbr. articles to ARCA Woman Mag., 1991—. Mem. Am. Counseling Assn., Am. Mental Health Counselors Assn., N.D. Assn. for Counseling and Devel., N.D. Mental Health Counselors Assn. (bd. dirs. 1991-92). Office: Choices Coun & Edn Ctr 120 N 3rd St Ste 50 Bismarck ND 58501

BAGARIA, GAIL FARRELL, lawyer; b. Detroit, Oct 6, 1942; d. Vincent Benjamin and Inez Elizabeth (Coffey) Farrell; m. William James Bagaria, Nov. 28, 1964; children: Bridget Ann, William James, Benjamin George. B.A., U. Detroit, 1964; J.D., Cath. U. Am., 1980. Bar: Md. 1980, U.S. Dist. Ct. Md. 1982. Cons. Miller & Webster, Clinton, Md., 1980-82; pvt. practice law, Bowie, Md., 1982—. Mem. Prince George's Women Lawyers Caucus (sec. 1984, pres. 1986), Md. State Bar Assn., Women's Bar Assn. Md., Prince George's County Bar Assn., Soroptimist Internat. (Bowie-Crofton chpt., pres. 1988-89, 93-94), Greater Bowie C. of C. (bd. dirs. 1995—). Democrat. Roman Catholic. Office: PO Box 759 Bowie MD 20718-0759

BAGBY, ROSE MARY, pollution control administrator, chemist; b. Jackson, Miss., Feb. 18, 1947; d. Woodrow Lewis and Mary Alice (Wolverton) Holley; m. Barry Alan Bagby Sr., June 1, 1974 (div. Mar. 1978); 1 child, Barry Alan II. AA, Hinds Cmty. Coll., 1967; BS in Chemistry, Miss. Coll., 1970; Cert. in Med. Tech., St. Sch. Med. Tech., Vicksburg, Miss., 1970. Cert. class IV pollution control operator, Miss. Med. technologist Jeff Davis Meml. Hosp. Clin. Lab., Natchez, Miss., 1970-73, Vicksburg (Miss.) Hosp. Clin. Lab., 1973-74; lab. mgr. Vicksburg Water Pollution Control Ctr., 1973-92, plant mgr./lab. mgr., 1992—; mem. adv. bd. for certification Miss. Dept. Environ. Quality, Jackson, Miss., 1989-91, adv. bd. revolving fund, 1988-94. Mem. Miss. Rep. Party, Jackson, 1990—. Mem. Water Environ. Fedn. (dir. 1976—), Miss. Water Environ. Assn. (pres. 1976—, com. chmn., Past Pres. award 1989, Dir. award 1994, Arthur Sidney Bedell award 1995), Miss. Water and Pollution Control Ops. Assn. (dir. 1989-92, pres. 1992-93, Howard K. Williford Svc. award 1992, 94, Past Pres. award 1994, Pollution Control Operator of Yr. 1985), Vicksburg Warren C. of C. (Edn. 2000 com. 1993—), United Way Warren County (Vol. award 1986). Republican. Baptist. Home: 211 Kendra Dr Vicksburg MS 39180

BAGLEY, AMY L., state legislator; b. Portsmouth, N.H., Apr. 23, 1971; d. Paul David and Micheleen Gail (Mahoney) B. BA in Polit. Sci. cum laude, Emmanuel Coll., 1990-91; BA in Polit. Sci., Keene State Coll., 1991-94. Cons. Dick Swett for Congress, Bow, N.H., 1992; state representative N.H. State Ho. of Reps., Concord, 1993—. Vol. Clinton N.H. Primary Campaign, Manchester, N.H., 1991-92. Challenge scholar Keene State Coll., Keene, N.H., 1993-94. Mem. Nat. Order Women Legislators, 1993—. Democrat. Office: NH Ho of Reps State House Concord NH 03301

BAGLEY, CONSTANCE ELIZABETH, lawyer, educator; b. Tucson, Dec. 18, 1952; d. Robert Porter Smith and Joanne Snow-Smith. AB in Polit. Sci. with distinction, with honors, Stanford U., 1974; JD magna cum laude, Harvard U., 1977. Bar: Calif. 1978, N.Y. 1978. Tchg. fellow Harvard U., 1975-77; assoc. Webster & Sheffield, N.Y.C., 1977-78, Heller, Ehrman, White & McAuliffe, San Francisco, 1978-79; assoc. McCutchen, Doyle, Brown & Enersen, San Francisco, 1979-84, ptnr., 1984-90; lectr. bus. law Stanford (Calif.) U., 1988-90, lectr. mgmt., 1990-91, lectr. law and mgmt., 1991-95, sr. lectr. law and mgmt., 1995—; also lectr. Stanford Exec. Program; lectr. exec. program for growing cos. Stanford U.; lectr. Stanford Mktg. Mgmt. Exec. Program; bd. dirs. Alegre Enterprises, Inc., Latina Publ. LLC; corp. practice series adv. bd. Bur. Nat. Affairs, 1984—; faculty adv. bd. Stanford Jour. Law, Bus. and Fin., 1994—; lectr., planning com. Calif. Continuing Edn. Bar, L.A., San Francisco, 1983, 85-87; lectr. So. Area Conf., Silverado, 1988, Young Pres. Orgn. Internat. U. for Pres., Hong Kong, 1988. Author: Mergers, Acquisitions and Tender Offers, 1983, Managers and the Legal Environment: Strategies for the 21st Century, 1991, 2d edit., 1995; co-author: Negotiated Acquisitions, 1992, Cutting Edge Cases in the Legal Environment of Business, 1993, Proxy Contests and Corporate Control, 4th edit., 1996; contbr. editor: Calif. Bus. Law Reporter, 1984-95. Vestry mem. Trinity Episcopal Ch., San Francisco, 1984-85; vol. Moffit Hosp. U. Calif., San Francisco, 1983-84. Mem. ABA, Acad. Legal Studies in Bus., Stanford Faculty Club, Phi Beta Kappa. Republican. Office: Stanford U Grad Sch Bus Stanford CA 94305-5015

BAGLEY, EDYTHE SCOTT, theater educator; b. Marion, Ala.; d. Obie and Bernice (McMurry) Scott; m. Arthur Moten Bagley, June 5, 1954; 1 child, Arturo Scott. BEd, Ohio State U., 1949; MA in English, Columbia U., 1954; MFA in Theater Arts, Boston U., 1965. Instr. Elizabeth City (N.C.) State Coll., 1953-56; asst. prof. Albany (Ga.) State Coll., 1956-57, A&T U., Greensboro, N.C., 1957-58, Norfolk (Va.) State Coll., 1963-65; assoc. prof. theater Cheyney (Pa.) U., 1971—, also chair dept. theater arts; cons. in black theater Mich. State U., East Lansing, 1969-71; mem. speaker's bur. Martin Luther King Jr. Fed. Holiday Commn. Dir. numerous coll. prodns., 1968-71. Spl. asst. to Coretta Scott King. Mem. NAACP, AAUW, NAFE, Nat. Coun. Negro Women, Theater Assn. Pa., The Links Inc. (chair com. on arts 1972-80), Womens Internat. League for Peace and Freedom, Nat. Assn. Dramatic and Speech Arts, The Pa. Martin Luther King Jr. Assn. for Nonviolence (bd. dirs.), The Martin Luther King Jr. Ctr. for Nonviolent Soc. Change (bd. dirs.). Home: 2 Derry Dr Cheyney PA 19319 Office: Cheyney U Cheyney PA 19319

BAGLEY, MARY CAROL, literature educator, writer, broadcaster; b. St. Louis, Mar. 11, 1958; d. Robert Emmet and Harriet Elaine (Hohreiter) B.; children: Jerry Joseph, Sarah Elizabeth. BA, U. Mo., St. Louis, 1980; MA, U. Mo., 1982; PhD, St. Louis U., 1993. Feature editor Current Newspaper, Normandy, Mo., 1977-82; mng. editor Watermark Lit. Mag., St. Louis, 1982-85; vis. lectr. So. Ill. U., Edwardsville, 1985—; instr., head. bus. writing St. Louis U., 1985—; news broadcaster Am. Cablevision, Florissant, Ferguson, Mo., 1986—; assoc. prof. Mo. Bapt. Coll.; guest speaker Sta. KMOX-TV, KSDK-TV, St. Louis Writing Festival, St. Louis Community Coll., and others, chancellor's com. Sta. KWMU Radio Adv. Bd., 1980, participant McKendree Writer's Conf., 1986. Author: The Front Row: Missouri's Grand Theaters, 1984, Professional Writing Types, 1990, Willa Cather's Myths, 1994, The Politics of Realism, 1995, Selected Readings in 19th and 20th Century Literature, 1994, (with others) The Fabulous Fox Theater, 1985; freelance writer, 1976—; editor: A Guide to St. Louis Theaters, 1984; bd. editors (book) Business Writing Concepts, 1986, Handbook for Professional and Academic Writing, 1988 (recipient Cert. of Appreciation 1986); adv. bd. mem. Bus. Comm. Today, 1986. Co-chmn, Theater Hist. Soc. Conclave, St. Louis, 1984; pres., Ambassador Theater Trust, 1986. Recipient William Barnaby Faherty award, 1992. Mem. Writer's Guild, Theater Hist. Soc. (bd. dirs. 1986), Am. Assn. Univ. Instrs., Nat. Coun. Tchrs. English, U. Mo. English Alumni Assn. (v.p. 1985, senator rep. 1979), Pi Alpha Delta (hon.), Sigma Tau Delta (sponsor), Phi Beta Kappa. Home: 12539 Falling Leaves Ct Saint Louis MO 63141-7464 Office: Mo Bapt Coll 337 Field Hall Saint Louis MO 63141

BAGNARA, SUSAN DUDLEY, small business owner; b. Staten Island, N.Y., June 27, 1946; d. Alden Woodbury and Dorothy Helen (Newth) Dudley; m. Joseph Albert Bagnara, Aug. 21, 1971 (div.); children: Steven, Merrill, James. BS in Elem. Edn., Wagnar Coll., 1968; MS in Elem. Edn., CUNY, 1971. Elem. sch. tchr. N.Y.C. Bd. Edn., Staten Island, 1968-76; owner women's clothing store Josan Designs, ltd., Amherst, N.H., 1983—; gen. mgr. Ehrman Needlepoint, Amherst, 1993—; dist. sales mgr. The Carlisle Collection, Ltd., N.Y.C., 1991-92, trainer, coach, 1992-94; corp. field liaison Ltd. Editors for Her, Carlisle, 1989-90. Pres. Bus. and Profl. Women's Assn., Milford, N.H., 1993-94, Amherst Jr. Women's Club, 1983-84, Amherst PTA, 1982-83; chmn. Boy Scouts Am., Amherst, 1985-87. Mem. Bus. and Profl. Women's Club (advisor, past v.p., past pres.). Republican. Congregationalist. Home: 10 Storybrook Ln Amherst NJ 03031 Office: Ehrman Needlepoint 5 Northern Blvd Amherst NH 03031

BAHL, ANN BILLINGTON, educator, interpreter; b. Tulsa, May 19, 1951; d. Morris Randall Jr. and Doris Virginia (Gray) Putnam; children: Christopher Douglas Bahl, Kari Elizabeth Bahl. BA in English, Gallaudet U., 1974. Dir., coach for dance Minn. Sch. for the Deaf, Faribault, Minn., 1976-81; interpreter-trainer St. Paul Tech. Coll., 1975—; tchr. Faribault Sr. H.S., 1986-94, Lakeville (Minn.) Sr. H.S., 1994—; tchr. Mankato (Minn.) State U., 1982-91; team mem. State of Minn. ASL Comm. Proficiency Interview, St. Paul, 1990—. Dir. Nat. Assn. of the Deaf Miss Deaf Am. Pageant, Washington, 1988—; dir., co-founder Miss Deaf Minn. Pageant, St. Paul, 1976, 88-89. Named Minn. Woman of Yr. Minn. Assn. of the Deaf Citizens, Inc., 1989. Mem. Nat. Assn. of the Deaf (v.p. 1972—, 1st award Miss Deaf Am. 1972-74, Randall McClelland award 1992, Knights of the Flying Fingers award 1994), Minn. ASL Tchrs. (v.p. 1992—), Nat. ASL Tchrs. Assn. Republican. Office: Lakeville Sr High Sch 19600 Ipava Ave W Lakeville MN 55044

BAHL, JANICE MIRIAM, director religious education; b. Allentown, Pa., Apr. 13, 1937; d. Franklin Clayton and Emma (Kosarek) B. BA, Newmann Coll., 1976; MA in religious studies, St. Charles Borromeo Sem., 1985; diploma religious studies, Sacred Congregation Clergy, Vatican City, Rome, 1985. Joined Sisters of St. Francis of Phila., 1962. Tchr. St. Mary of the Assumption, Phila., 1965-71, St. Mary Sch., Schwenksville, Pa., 1971-73; elem. tchr. St. Benedict Sch., Phila., 1973-76; jr. high tchr. Resurrection Sch., Chester, Pa., 1976-79, SS Coleman Neumann Sch., Bryn Mawr, Pa., 1979-80; elem. tchr. St. Stanislaus Sch., Lansdale, Pa., 1980-84; dir. religious edn. St. Stanislaus Parish, Lansdale, Pa., 1984-90, St. Andrew Roman Cath. Ch., Catasauqua, Pa., 1991-93, Assumption BVM, Northampton, Pa., 1991-93, St. Paul Parish, Norristown, Pa., 1993—; religious cons. Silver Burdett Ginn, Morristown, N.J., 1987—. Scout leader, coord. Gt. Valley coun. Girl Scouts U.S., Allentown, Pa., 1945, mgr. Camp Woodhaven, Pine Grove, summer, 1995—; mem. Catasauqua Ministerium, 1992-93; mem. UN 50th anniversary com. Sister of St. Francis of Phila., 1994—; mem. Assn. Phila. PD/CARE Archdiocese of Phila., 1984-90, 94—; mem. Allentown Coord. Religious Edn. Diocese of Allentown, 1991-93; mem. religious curriculum Archdiocese of Phila., 1974-90, mem. planning com. Eastern Pa. DRE Gathering Planning CoCom., 1988-90, chair, 1990-94; mem. Coun. of Elem. Sch. Religion Leaders Archdiocese Phila., 1995—. Recipient Mother Katherine Drexel Assn. Phila. Parish Dirs., 1994—. Democrat. Roman Catholic. Home: St Paul Convent 353 E Johnson Hwy Norristown PA 19401-2020 Office: St Paul Religious Edn Office 351 E Johnson Hwy Norristown PA 19401

BAHNER, SUE (FLORENCE SUZANNA BAHNER), radio broadcasting executive; b. Phila.; d. William and Florence (Quinlivan) McElwee; m. David S. Bahner; children—Suzanna Elizabeth, Carol Aileen. Grad. Columbia Bus. Coll., 1950. Various exec. sec. positions, 1954-74; office mgr. Sta. WYRD, Syracuse, N.Y., 1974, gen. mgr., 1974-80; gen. mgr. Sta. WWWG-AM, Rochester, N.Y., 1980-93; gen. mgr. WDCW, Syracuse, N.Y., 1993—; pres. The Cornerstone Group, 1986—. Bd. dirs. Rescue Mission, Syracuse; active Eastern Hills Bible Ch. Mem. Greater Syracuse Assn. Evangelicals (treas. 1993—), Nat. Religious Broadcasters (pres. ea. chpt. 1984—, bd. dirs. 1983—, 2nd. v.p., 1992—). Office: Nat'l Religious Broadcasters 7839 Ashton Ave Manassas VA 22110

BAHORSKI, JUDY ANN WONG, computer specialist, learning strategist; b. Pueblo, Colo., Oct. 15, 1949; d. Yen Gim and Ngon (Mah) Wong. BA, So. Colo. State U., 1971; MEd, U. Nev., Las Vegas, 1976. Cert. tchr., Nev. 2d grade tchr. Sunrise Acres Elem. Sch., Las Vegas, 1971-77; 2d grade tchr. Myrtle Tate Elem. Sch., Las Vegas, 1977-84, 3d grade tchr., 1984-85; reading specialist Martin Luther King Jr. Elem. Sch., Las Vegas, 1988-90; reading specialist Charlotte Hill Elem. Sch., Las Vegas, 1990-91, computer specialist, 1991-93; learning specialist Mable Hoggard Math./Sci. Magnet Sch., Las Vegas, 1993—, mem. elem. tech. com., 1991-92, mem. supt. tech. study com., 1989-90; computer tchr. trainer Clark County Sch. Dist., Las Vegas, 1984—. Life mem. PTA, 1986—. Mem. Internat. Reading Assn., Reading Improvement Coun., Clark County Classroom Tchrs. Assn., Nev. Edn. Assn., Computer Using Educators (pres. 1991-92), Phi Delta Kappa. Democrat. Roman Catholic. Office: Mabel Hoggard Math/Sci Magnet Sch 950 N Tonopah Dr Las Vegas NV 89106-1902

BAHR, LAUREN S., publishing company executive; b. New Brunswick, N.J., July 3, 1944; d. Simon A. and Rosalind J. (Cabot) B. Student, U. Grenoble, France, 1964; B.A. (Branstrom scholar), MA, U. Mich., 1966. Asst. editor New Horizons Pubs., Inc., Chgo., 1967, Scholastic Mags., Inc., N.Y.C., 1968-71; supervising editor Houghton Mifflin Co., Boston, 1971;

product devel. editor Appleton-Century-Crofts, N.Y.C., 1972-74; sponsoring editor McGraw-Hill, Inc., N.Y.C., 1974-75; editor Today's Sec. mag., 1975-77; sr. editor Media Systems Corp., N.Y.C., 1978; sr. editor coll. dept. CBS Coll. Pub., N.Y.C., 1978-82, mktg. mgr. fgn. langs., dir. mktg. adminstrn., 1982-83; dir. devel. Coll. div. Harper & Row, N.Y.C., 1983-86, dir. mktg. coll. div., 1986-88, pub. cons., 1988-91; v.p., editorial dir. P.F. Collier, Inc., N.Y.C., 1991—. Democrat. Jewish. Home: 444 E 82nd St New York NY 10028-5903

BAHR, SHEILA KAY, physician; b. Highland Park, Mich., June 2, 1956; d. Thomas Joseph and Catherine Mary (McCrohan) Bernhardt; m. Wayne Edward Bahr, June 19, 1981. BS, U. Mich., Dearborn, 1978; DO, Mich. State U., 1982. Diplomate Am. Osteo. Bd. of Internal Medicine. Intern Botsford Gen. Hosp., 1982-83, resident in internal medicine, 1983-86; staff physician Health Alliance Plan, Livonia, Mich., 1986-87; pvt. practice Farmington, 1987-95; physician Henry Ford Health Sys., 1996—; asst. clin. prof. Coll. Osteo. Medicine Mich. State U., 1991—. Regent's scholar U. Mich., 1974; named Physician Trainer of Yr., Garden City (Mich.) Osteo. Hosp., 1990. Fellow Am. Coll. Osteo. Internists; mem. Am. Osteo. Assn., Mich. Assn. Osteo. Physicians and Surgeons, Oakland County Osteo. Assn. Office: 9327 Telegraph Redford MI 48239

BAHRANI, NEDA JEAN, programmer/analyst, consultant; b. Pontiac, Mich., June 3, 1956; d. Abdul Sattar Bahrani and Chrystine Margret (Whiting) McDaniel; m. Robert Currens (div. Sept. 1983). A Bus. in Computer Tech., U. Cin., 1984. Programmer Don Frey & Assocs., Ft. Thomas, Ky., 1985-87; programmer/analyst Directel, Inc., Westerville, Ohio, 1987-88; cons. Analyst Internat., Columbus, Ohio, 1988-89; MIS adminstr. Mettler Toledo divsn. Toledo Scale, Westerville, 1989-93; sr. programmer/analyst Hammacher Schlemmer, Fairfield, Ohio, 1993-94; owner, cons., technician Mac Visions, West Chester, Ohio, 1994—; programmer/analyst II Matrixx Mktg., Cin., 1995—. Editor newsletter Cinmug News, 1995—, PCHA News, 1995—. Trustee Princeton Crossing Home Owners Assn., Port Union and West Chester, 1995—. Mem. Cin. Met. Helwet Packard Users Group (publs. com. 1996, co-chair 1995), Cin. Met. Users Group (co-chair 1995, publs. contact 1996), Cin. Zool. Soc., Smithsonian Inst. Republican. Presbyterian. Home: 9165 Erie Cir West Chester OH 45069

BAILES, HELEN TUCKER, mathematics educator; b. Beaumont, Tex., Mar. 5, 1944; d. John Graham and Ida Eugenia (Chastain) Tucker; m. Howard Leon Bailes, July 12, 1966; children: Alma, Wendy. BA, Converse Coll., 1966; MS, Old Dominion U., 1985. Tchr. math. Oscar Smith High Sch., Chesapeake, Va., 1967-70; tchr. math., dept. chair Portsmouth (Va.) Cath. High Sch., 1972-85; tchr. math. Maury High Sch., Norfolk, Va., 1985-93, Salem (Va.) High Sch., 1993—. Mem. NEA, Va. Edn. Assn., Salem Edn. Assn., Nat. Coun. Tchrs. Math., Va. Coun. Tchrs. Math., Blue Ridge Coun. Tchrs. Math., Beta Sigma Phi (v.p., treas.). Episcopalian. Home: 4149 Twin Mountain Dr Vinton VA 24179-1023 Office: Salem High Sch 400 Spartan Dr Salem VA 24153-3202

BAILEY, ANN V., federal agency administrator. BA, Goucher Coll., 1959. Libr. USIA, 1959-61, staff asst., 1961-66; corr. asst. Office Edn. HEW, 1966-68, chief of commr.'s corr. staff, 1968-74; com. mgmt. officer Office Asst. Sec. Intergovtl. and Interagy. Affairs Dept. Edn., Washington, 1974—; acting dir. Goals 2000 Initiative Svc., 1993. Office: Office Asst Sec Intergovtl & Interagy Affairs 400 Maryland Ave SW Washington DC 20202-0001

BAILEY, DEENA TAMARA, health care administrator; b. Haifa, Israel, June 13, 1947; came to U.S., 1960; d. Fred Ephraim and Devora (Glaser) Mansbacher; m. Wayne W. Bailey, Apr. 4, 1970 (div. 1977); 1 child, Devora Elyse. BS in Health Sci., U. Redlands, 1989; MHA, U. So. Calif., 1995. Mgr. dept. surgery Cedars-Sinai Med. Ctr., L.A., 1980-87; mgr. cardiovascular intervention ctr. Cedars-Sinai Med. Ctr., 1988-93; dir. Cardiology Mgmt. Svcs., 1993-94; adminstrv. resident UniHealth, Burbank, Calif., 1994-95; adminstrv. dir. UniHealth-Arroyo Seco Med. Group/Mgmt. Svcs., 1995—. Mem. Health Care Execs. So. Calif., Women in Health Adminstrn. (pres. 1993), Am. Coll. Cardiovasc. Adminstrs. (regional dir. 1990-92), Am. Coll. Health Care Execs., (assoc.), U. So. Calif. Health Svcs. Adminstrs. Alumni Assn. (pres. 1996-97), Med. Group Mgmt. Assn., Calif. Med. Group Mgmt. Assn., L.A. Med. Group Mgmt. Assn. Democrat. Jewish.

BAILEY, EXINE MARGARET ANDERSON, soprano, educator; b. Cottonwood, Minn., Jan. 4, 1922; d. Joseph Leonard and Exine Pearl (Robertson) Anderson; m. Arthur Albert Bailey, May 5, 1956. B.S., U. Minn., 1944; M.A., Columbia U., 1945; profl. diploma, 1951. Instr. Columbia U., 1947-51; faculty U. Oreg., Eugene, 1951—, prof. voice, 1966-87, coordinator voice instrn., 1969-87, prof. emeritus, 1987—; faculty dir. Salzburg, Austria, summer 1968, Europe, summer 1976; vis prof., head vocal instrn. Columbia U., summers 1952, 59; condr. master classes for singers, developer summer program study for high sch. solo singers, U. Oreg. Sch. Music, 1988—. Profl. singer, N.Y.C.; appearances with NBC, ABC symphonies; solo artist appearing with Portland and Eugene (Oreg.) Symphonies, other groups in Wash., Calif., Mont., Idaho, also in concert; contbr. articles, book revs. to various mags. Del. fine arts program to Ea. Europe, People to People Internat. Mission to Russia for 1990. Recipient Young Artist award N.Y.C. Singing Tchrs., 1945, Music Fedn. Club (N.Y.C.) hon. award, 1951; Kathryn Long scholar Met. Opera, 1945. Mem. Nat. Assn. Tchrs. Singing (lt. gov. 1968-72), Oreg. Music Tchrs. Assn (pres. 1974-76), Music Tchrs. Nat. Assn. (nat. voice chmn. high sch. activities 1970-74, nat. chmn. voice 1973-75, 81-85, NW chmn. collegiate activities and artists competition 1978-80, editorial com. Am. Music Tchr. jour. 1987-89), AAUP, Internat. Platform Assn., Kappa Delta Pi, Sigma Alpha Iota, Pi Kappa Lambda. Home: 17 Westbrook Way Eugene OR 97405-2074 Office: U Oreg Sch Music Eugene OR 97403

BAILEY, GRACE DANIEL, retired secondary school educator; b. Wilson, N.C., Dec. 7, 1927; d. James Clenon and Ella Mae (West) Daniel; m. Hubert Jesse Bailey, Apr. 27, 1951; 1 child, Vicky Lynette Bailey Freeman. BS in Bus. Edn. and English, East Carolina U., 1950, MAE in Guidance and Counseling, 1966. Tchr. bus. edn., English Apex (N.C.) H.S., 1950-51; tchr. bus. edn. Atlantic Christian Coll., Wilson, N.C., summer 1951; tchr. bus. edn., English Lucama (N.C.) H.S., 1951-53, 1956-75, tchr. bus. edn., counselor, 1975-77, counselor, 1977-78; counselor Hunt H.S., Wilson, 1978-79, counselor, dept. chair, 1979-86, ret., 1986. Sec. adv. com. Cmty. Manpower and Tng., Wilson, 1973-74; organizer Wilson Cmty. Coun., 1973-74; sec. Wilson County Humane Soc., 1978; mem. edn. com. Am. Cancer Soc., Wilson, 1987-88. Recipient award Am. Legion, Wilson, 1986; grantee Wilson County Mental Health Assn., 1964. Mem. AAUW, N.C. Assn. Educators (treas. Wilson County chpt. 1974-75), Wilson County Guidance Pers. Assn. (organizer, 1st pres. 1966-67), Wilson Women's Club (co-chairperson comm. com. 1993-94), Delta Kappa Gamma (v.p. Gamma Mu chpt. 1986-88, pres. 1988-90). Methodist. Home: 4021 Us Highway 117 Wilson NC 27893-0916

BAILEY, JOSELYN ELIZABETH, physician; b. Pine Bluff, Ark.; d. Joseph Alexander and Angeline Elaine (Davis) B.; B.Mus., Manhattanville Coll., 1952; M.Music Edn., Manhattan Sch. Music, 1954; M.D., Howard U., 1971. Straight med. intern Huntington Meml. Hosp., Pasadena, Calif., 1971-72, resident, 1972-74; fell in nephrology Wadsworth VA Hosp., Los Angeles, 1975-77; practice medicine specializing in internal medicine and nephrology, Torrance, Calif.; assoc. staff Torrance Meml., South Bay; active Little Company of Mary hosps.; attending staff Harbor Gen. Hosp.; clin. faculty Dept. Medicine, UCLA; active staff Bay Harbor Hosp., trustee, 1982—.

BAILEY, JOY HAFNER, university program administrator, psychologist, educator; b. Weehawkin, N.J., Aug. 15, 1928; d. Elmar William and Fern (Williams) Hafner; children: Kerry, Jan, Leslie, Liza, Annie Laurie, Kristin. BA, Austin Coll., 1974; MS, East Tex. State U., 1975, EdD, 1977. Lic. marriage and family therapist, profl. counselor; nat. cert. counselor. Counselor, instr. East Tex. State U., 1976-80; dir. student support services acad./counseling program Ga. State U., 1980—, asst. prof. learning support programs, 1980—, asst. prof. counseling and psychol. svcs., 1988—; pvt. practice marriage and family therapy. Mem. APA, Am. Counseling Assn., Am. Assn. Marriage and Family Therapists (approved supr.), Ga. Assn. Marriage and Family Therapists (approved supr.), Atlanta Mallet Club (v.p. 1989-92), Psi Chi. Office: Ga State U 1 Park Place South SE Ste 701 Atlanta GA 30303-2911

BAILEY, KRISTEN, legal assistant; b. Davenport, Iowa, Jan. 5, 1952; d. Donald Ray and Alta Llewellyn (Mandler) B. AS, Mo. So. State Coll., 1974; cert. paralegal studies, Rockhurst Coll., 1978. Legal sec. Ralph E. Baird, Lawyer, Joplin, Mo., 1972-75; legal asst. Benny J. Harding, Atty. at Law, Kansas City, Mo., 1976-87, Polsinelli, White, Vardeman & Shalton, Kansas City, 1988—; speaker in field. Vol. Heartland's Sch. Riding, Overland Park, Kans., 1988—; mem. Friends of the Zoo, Kansas City Mus. Assn. Winner Ark. and Iowa state championships, 3-gaited Pleasure Horse, Am. Saddlebred Pleasure Horse Assn., 1981; named Kansas City Legal Sec. of Yr., 1979. Mem. ATLA (paralegal mem. 1993-95), Kansas City Assn. Legal Assts. (bd. dirs. 1993-94), Kansas City Legal Sec. Assn. (bd. dirs. 1977-89, 92-93, pres. 1979-81, life mem.), Mid-Am. Saddle Horse Club (sec. 1981-83). Republican. Methodist. Office: Polsinelli White Vardeman & Shalton 700 W 47th St Ste 1000 Kansas City MO 64112-1805

BAILEY, LINDA HAGER, natural resources consultant; b. Deposit, N.Y., Sept. 23, 1944; d. George and Eva Francis (Kellet) Hager; m. Richard M. Bailey, June 29, 1974; children: John Thomas, Jennifer Anne. BA, Coll. of Wooster, 1966; MPH, U. Calif., Berkeley, 1971, JD, 1976. Bar: Calif. 1980, Nev. 1981. Health planner NorCoa Health, Ukiah, Calif., 1971-72; dep. atty. gen. State of Nev., Carson City, 1981-83; pvt. practice Oakland, Calif., 1983-86; gen. counsel/mgr. Mendocino County Water Agy., Ukiah, 1986-90; exec. sec. Eel-Russian River Commn., Ukiah, 1989—; mem. Skunk County Railroad Task Force, Ukiah, 1987, Mendocino County Forest Adv. Com., Ukiah, 1987-90, Mendocino County Forest Adv. Com., Ukiah, 1989-92; forestry cons. Mendocino County, Ukiah, 1994-95. Vol. Peace Corps, Niger, 1966-68; conservation chair Peregrine Audubon Chpt., Ukiah, 1990—; dir. Econ. Devel. Financing Corp., Ukiah, 1994—; pres. Ukiah Valley Friends of Libr., Ukiah, 1992-94; mem. Creek Coalition, Ukiah, Nat. Women's Polit. Caucus, Sierra Club. Mem. Great Old Broads for the Wilderness, Phi Beta Kappa. Democrat. Presbyterian. Office: 308 S School St Ste 8 Ukiah CA 95482

BAILEY, LOIS MARIAN ADAMS, artist; b. Mahanoy City, Pa., Aug. 21, 1927; d. Raymond William and H. Marian (Jones) Adams; m. John Davis Bailey, Aug. 20, 1949 (div. 1966). Student, Frankford Hosp. Sch. Nursing, Phila., 1948, Art Students League, N.Y.C., 1969-70; AAS, Parsons Sch. Design, 1982; student, New Sch., N.Y.C. RN. Represented in numerous pvt. collections. Mem. Composers, Authors and Artists of Am., Nat. Mus. Women in Arts, Beaux Arts Soc. (sec. 1993). Buddhist. Home: 220 W 19th St Rm 2 A New York NY 10011-4035

BAILEY, MARIANNE THERESE, social service administrator; b. Evanston, Ill., Dec. 26, 1949; d. Eugene Thomas and Marguerite O'Brien B. Student, Sorbonne, Paris, 1970, San Francisco Coll. Women, 1967-69; BA, Barat Coll. of Sacred Heart, 1971; cert., U. Paris, Sorbonne, 1972; ancien élève, Ecole du Louvre, Paris, 1973-74. Cert. cmty. transp. mgr. Tchr. 2d and 3d grade Marymount Internat. Sch., Neuilly, France, 1971-72; dir. Ctr. Audio Visuel des Langues, Enghien, France, 1973-76; pre-sch. dir. P.L. Child Care Ctrs., Glenview, Ill., 1976-81; with dept. def. civilian Child Support Svcs., Ft. Sheridan, Ill., 1981-82; dir. tng. and spl. events N.W. Mcpl. Conf., Mt. Prospect, Ill., 1982-84; exec. dir. PRC Paratransit Svcs., Park Ridge, Ill., 1984—; mem. Nat. Transp. Cert. Coun., 1996—. Vice pres. N.W. Suburban chpt. Citizens with Disabilities; lobbyist disabled and sr. citizens State of Ill.; treas., exec. bd. Wheeling Twp. Rep. Org., 1988—, del. Rep. State Conv., Ill., 1994, 96; pres. N.W. Suburban Coun. for Cmty. Svcs., 1989-91; v.p. Twp. Ofcls. Ill. Disabled Advocacy, 1985-90, pres., 1990—; active Chgo. Area Transp. Study, 1984—, Gov.'s Task Force on Aging and Disability, 1987—, PACE-ADA Adv. Com., 1990—, Sage Sr. Advocacy Group, 1990—; mem. Twp. Ofcls. of Cook County, N.W. Suburban Regional Transp. Consortium, 1992—, Project Action Ill. steering com., 1995—. Mem. AAUW, ALTRUSA, Am. Pub. Transit Assn., Am. Pub. Works Assn., Cmty. Transp. Assn. Am. (state del. 1992—), Ill. Paratransit Assn. (bd. dirs., sec. 1987-91), Ill. Assn. for Cmty. Transp. (bd. dirs.), Ill. Alliance Info. and Referral, Cmty. Transp. Assn. Am. (state del. 1992—), Lions Club (v.p. 1990-92, pres. 1992-93, Lion of the Yr. 1991-92, mem. bd. dirs. 1988-94, dist. diabetes awareness chmn. 1991-93), Pi Delta Phi. Roman Catholic. Home: 740 Weidner Rd Buffalo Grove IL 60089 Office: PRC Paratransit Svcs 1700 Ballard Rd Park Ridge IL 60068-1006

BAILEY, MARY KATHERINE, sculptor, writer, video maker; b. N.Y.C., Jan. 1, 1960; d. John Turner and Katherine (Gerwig) B.; m. Toby Stephen Welles. BA with honors, Brown U., 1982. adj. prof. sculpture, Fairfield U., 1993—; bd. dirs. Silvermine Guild Art Ctr., New Canaan, Conn., vice chairman bd., 1994—. One person exhbns. include Art Place Gallery, Southport, Conn., 1987, Silvermine Guild Art Ctr., New Canaan, Conn., 1988, Anne Jaffe Gallery, Miami, 1989, Sound Shore Gallery, Stamford, Conn., 1991, Cast Iron Gallery, N.Y.C., 1992, Sacred Heart U., Fairfield, Conn., 1992, Housatonic Mus. Art, Bridgeport, Conn., 1993, Fairfield U., 1993.; in permanent collecions New Sch. Social Rsch., Housatonic Mus. Art, Zurich Reinsurance Ctr.; prodr., dir., writer: (video) The Surgery, 1994. Grantee New Eng. Found. Arts, 1993, Conn. Film and Video Competition Conn. Commn. on Arts and CPTV, 1995. Mem. Sculptors Guild, Silvermine Guild Art Ctr. Home: 240 Poverty Hollow Rd Redding CT 06896

BAILEY, MICKEY WILSON, elementary school educator; b. Amory, Miss., Feb. 5, 1949; d. Jesse Lyndon and Rivers (Mize) Wilson; m. Gregory Paul Bailey, June 18, 1971; children: Rebecca Lynn, Benjamin Mark. AA, Freed-Hardeman Coll., Henderson, Tenn., 1969; BS, Miss. State U., 1971. Cert. tchr., Ga. 2d grade tchr. Fulton County Schs., Palmetto, Ga., 1971-72, Monroe County Schs., Amory, 1972-73; 5th grade reading tchr. Coweta County Schs., Newnan, Ga., 1973-74, 2d grade tchr., 1983-88; 2d grade tchr. Greater Atlanta Christian Schs. now Arlington Christian Sch., Fairburn, Ga., 1988—. Mem. Newnan Ch. of Christ. Mem. Profl. Assn. Ga. Educators, Gold Wing Rd. Riders Assn. Home: 26 College St Newnan GA 30263-2021

BAILEY, NANCY JOYCE, educator; b. Detroit, May 9, 1942; d. Thomas Hill and Margaret (McGrath) Rainey; m. Carl John Bailey, June 12, 1963; 1 child, John. BA, Vanderbilt U., 1960; internat. exchange student, Stuttgart, Germany, 1960; postgrad., U. Mex., 1957, U. Santa Clara, 1975, George Washington U., 1979-80. Cert. early childhood edn. tchr., early childhood specialist. Hostess Brentwood (Tenn.) Country Club, 1960; adminstrv. aide U.S. Senate, Washington, 1966; sec. U.S. Ho. of Reps., Washington, 1971-74; tchr. D.C. Pub. Schs., 1961—; bd. dirs Cabvin Internat. Corp., 1985—; rep. Washington Tchrs. union, 1982-94; founder David Lipscomb U., Nashville, 1988; participant Internat. Tchr. Exch. Program, Korea, 1994. Keyperson United Way Campaign, Washington, 1974-93; docent The White House, Exec. Office of the Pres., Washington, 1987—; vol. First Lady's Corr., The White House, Washington, 1990—, Social Sec.'s Office, East Wing, 1993, Office of First Lady, 1993; coord. Presdl. Youth Vol. Day, 1993; mem. Nat. Trust for Historic Preservation, 1990—, Friendship Force of Nat. Capital Area, 1993—, People to People Internat. of Nat. Capital Area, 1993—; mem. adv. bd. New Visions for Child Care, Inc., 1993; chair Local Schs. Restructuring Team, 1992-93; participant Internat. Tchr. Exch. Program, Korea, 1994; mem. exec. com. YWCA Internat. Fair, Washington, 1994; del. Internat. Women's Friendship Conf. World Peace, Washington, 1995. Recipient Internat. Cooperation award Am. Fgn. Study Program, Am. Study Program, 1984-86, Am. Student Ednl. Travel. Mem. Delta Group (mem. coun. 1989-92), Am. Fedn. Tchrs., Internat. Reading Assn., World Affairs Coun. Home: 10729 Deborah Dr Potomac MD 20854-2714 Office: La Salle Sch Riggs Rd and Madison St NE Washington DC 20011

BAILEY, PATRICIA PRICE, lawyer, former government official; b. Ft. Smith, Ark., June 20, 1937; m. Douglas L. Bailey; 2 children. BA in History cum laude, Lindenwood Coll., 1959; MA in Internat. Affairs, Tufts U., 1960; JD summa cum laude, Am. U., 1976. Bar: D.C., U.S. Ct. Appeals (D.C. cir.), U.S. Ct. Appeals (8th cir.), U.S. Supreme Ct. Editor, rsch. analyst Bur. of Intelligence and Rsch., U.S. Dept. State, 1960-61; exec. asst. Bur. for Latin Am., then asst. to dep. coordinator Alliance for Progress, AID, 1961-66; advisor fgn. affairs Rep. F. Bradford Morse, 1967-68; legal asst. Office of Counsel to Pres. in White House, 1976; spl. asst. to asst. atty. gen. U.S. Dept. Justice, 1977-79; exec. asst. to gen. counsel U.S. Merit systems Protection Bd., 1979; commr. FTC, Washington, 1979-88; ptnr., Squire, Sanders & Dempsey, Washington, 1989—; bd. dirs. Arbella Mut. Ins. Co.; bd. dirs., trustee Avdel PLC; mem. adv. com. Impact of Women in Pub. Office Rutgers U. Eagleton Inst. Politics. Contbr. articles to profl. jours. Bd. dirs. The Washington Ctr., 1987-89, Women's Legal Def. Fund, 1982-83, Lindenwood Coll., Found. for Women's Resources; mem. Dean's Adv. Coun. Washington Coll. Law of Am. U.; mem. Spl. Commn. to Rev. Honor System and Honor Code at West Point, 1988. Recipient Spl. Recognition award Nat. Assn. Attys. Gen., 1987, Philip Hart Pub. Svc. award Consumer Fedn. Am., 1985. Mem. Women's Bar Assn. of D.C. (bd. dirs. 1981-83, bd. dirs. Women's Bar Assn. Found. 1981-85, named Woman Lawyer of Yr., 1988). Office: Squire Sanders & Dempsey PO Box 407 1201 Pennsylvania Ave NW Washington DC 20044*

BAILEY, RITA MARIA, investment advisor, psychologist; b. Frankfurt, Germany, June 10, 1949; came to U.S., 1957; d. Ludwig and Gertrude (Cierniak) Fleischmann; m. William W. Bailey, Feb. 17, 1974; children: Anne Christine, Cynthia Patricia. BS in Psychology, Austin Peay U., 1975, MA in Psychology, 1977, postgrad., 1977-79. Cert. counselor, Tenn. Editor U.S. Army Spl. Warfare Inst., Ft. Bragg, N.C., 1967-74, edn. officer, 1979-82; edn. officer Augsburg (Germany) Cmty. Ctr., 1982-85; pvt. practice counseling Leavenworth, Kans., 1985-90; pvt. practice investments, 1990—; sr. investment advisor pvt. orgns., Washington, 1991—. Author: Extroversion and Introversion, 1978, Special Warfare Training Plan, 1981; author, editor tng. manual Foreign Small Arms, 1982. Dir. Energy Conservation Campaign, Clarksville, 1976; founder, dir. Women's Support Ctr., Leavenworth, 1986. Mem. Nat. Assn. Investors, Alpha Mu Gamma. Roman Catholic.

BAILEY, SUSAN CAROL, commercial banking executive; b. Muskogee, Okla., Apr. 10, 1954; d. William E. and Lula M. (Holloway) Green; m. Wayne M. Bailey, Aug. 6, 1976; 1 child, Nathan W. BS in Fin., So. Ill. U., 1982, MBA, 1983. Tech. asst. ops. Marsh Stencil Machine Co., Belleville, Ill., 1973-85; loan officer Delmar Fin. Co., Belleville, 1985-86; asst. v.p., asst. br. mgr. Fidelity Fed. Savs. and Loan Assn., Fairview Heights, Ill., 1986; asst. v.p., br. mgr. Fidelity Fed. Savs. and Loan Assn., Belleville, 1986-87, v.p., br. mgr., 1987-89, v.p., br. mgr., Metro E. Deposit Acquisition & Fin. Svcs. officer, 1989-90; v.p., comml. loan officer, dir. mktg. Union Bank Ill., Swansea, 1991-96; v.p., comml. loan officer Bank of Alton, Ill., 1996—; fin. cons., Caseyville, Ill., 1985-86. Mem., treas. Belleville Welcome Wagon; mem. allocations bd. United Way Greater St. Louis; active leadership program Leadership Ctr. St. Louis, 1993-94, Civic Leader Tour, Scott AFB, 1994; chairperson telepathy St. Clair County Am. Heart Assn., 1995. Mem. St. Louis Fedn. Socs. for Coating Tech. (exec. com. 1980-85, chmn. edn. com. 1983-84), Belleville Bd. Realtors, Edwardsville-Collinsville Bd. Realtors, Women's Coun. Realtors, Homebuilders Assn., Belleville Econ. Progress (amb.), Belleville Postal Coun. (bd. dirs.), Ill. Bankers Assn., So. Ill. Network of Women (alliance rep., pres. 1991—), Fin. Women Internat., Noon Networking of Women, Fairview Hts. C. of C. (amb.), Swansea C. of C. (bd. dirs.), Rotary. Home: 710 Belleville Rd Caseyville IL 62232-1142 Office: Bank of Alton 1520 Washington Alton IL 62002

BAILEY, SUSAN MCGEE, educational administrator, researcher, educator; b. Boston, June 10, 1941; d. Hugh Paul and Florence Anna (Brockett) McGee; m. Jerald Elliott Bailey, June 25, 1966 (div. Mar. 1976); 1 child, Amy. BA, Wellesley Coll., 1963; postgrad., Boston U., 1965; MA, U. Mich., 1969, PhD, 1971; LittD (hon.), Pine Manor Coll., 1993. Tchr. elem. and mid. sch. Mich., Taiwan, Dominican Republic, 1963-67, tchg. fellow U. Mich. and Mich. State U., 1968-70; postdoctoral fellow Johns Hopkins U., Balt., 1972-73, 1972-73; bur. chief Conn. State Dept. Edn., Hartford, 1974-78; dir. Policy Rsch. Office Harvard U., Cambridge, Mass., 1978-80; dir. Resource Ctr. Ednl. Equity, Washington, 1980-85, exec. dir. Ctr. for Rsch. on Women Wellesley (Mass.) Coll., 1985—, exec. dir. Wellesley Ctrs. for Women, 1995—; adj. prof. Cen. Conn. State U., New Britain, 1976-78; prof. women's studies and edn. Wellesley Coll., 1996—; presenter in field. Author: How Schools Shortchange Girls, 1992; editor: Girls in School, 1992; co-author: Policies for the Future, 1982; mem. cons. bd. Jour. Ednl. Equity and Leadership, 1980-86; contbr. articles to profl. jours. Founding bd. dirs. Spl. Peace Corps, Sherborn, Mass., 1993—; mem. bd. visitors Brimmer and May Sch., Chestnut Hill, Mass., 1992—; bd. dirs. PATH, Natick, Mass., 1988-92, Elem. Extended Day, Bethesda, Md., 1984-86, Conn. Pub. TV, 1977-78; mem. adv. bd. Eureka Project, Girls Inc., 1993—, Nat. Women's History Project, 1994—; bd. dirs. Nat. Coun. Rsch. on Women, 1988-94, pres. bd., 1992-94; founding bd. dirs. N.E. Coalition of Ednl. Leaders, 1977-78; vol. tchr. YMCA, Bethesda, Md., 1980-93. Recipient Abigail Adams award Mass. Women's Polit. Caucus, 1992; state policy fellow Inst. for Ednl. Leadership-George Washington U., 1978-79, Social Sci. Ednl. Rsch. fellow U. Fellowship-U. Mich., 1968-70. Mem. Am. Ednl. Rsch. Assn. (chair spl. interest group rsch. on women in edn. 1986-87, Willystine Goodsell award 1989, Activist/Policy award 1992), Phi Lambda Theta, Phi Delta Kappa. Office: Wellesley Coll Wellesley Ctrs for Women 106 Central St Wellesley MA 02181

BAILEY, WENDY ANN, pediatric endocrinologist; b. Oak Park, Ill., Mar. 4, 1956; d. Robert Carl and Persis Etta (Warren) Roos; m. Dean Alan Bailey, June 20, 1981; children: Karen Lynne, Kathryn Nicole. BA, DePauw U., 1978; MD, Uniformed Svcs. U. Health Sci., 1982. Commd. ens. USN, 1978, advanced through grades to comdr., 1987; pediatric intern Naval Hosp. San Diego, 1982-83, pediatric resident, 1984-86, staff pediatrician, 1986-88, pediatric endocrinologist, 1991—; gen. med. officer Naval Air Sta. North Island, Coronado, Calif., 1983-84; fellow in pediatric endocrinology U. Calif.-San Diego Med. Ctr., 1988-91. Fellow Am. Acad. Pediatrics, Am. Coll. Endocrinology; mem. Assn. Mil. Surgeons U.S., Am. Diabetes Assn., Am. Assn. Clin. Endocrinologists. Office: Naval Medical Ctr Dept Pediatrics Portsmouth VA 23708

BAILEY-AUDETTE, GEORGIA ANNE, rehabilitation counselor; b. Florence, Ala., Aug. 14, 1948; d. Walter Roy and Mary Frances (Andrews) Bailey; m. William Ryan deGraffenried Jr., June 5, 1971 (div. Jan. 1986); children: Ryan III, Frances; m. Francis Henry Audette, Oct. 2, 1993. BS in Biology, U. Ala., 1970, MA in Rehab. Counseling, 1988. Cert. rehab. counselor; cert. case mgr. Biology tchr. Westlawn Jr. High, Tuscaloosa, Ala., 1970-72; sci. tchr. 7th grade Brookwood Forest Elem., Birmingham, Ala., 1972-75; human physiology tchr. Tuscaloosa (Ala.) Acad., 1976-77; relocation dir. Duckworth Morris Real Estate, 1985-86; advt. sales assoc. WZBQ-102.5 Radio, 1986-87; vocat. rehab. counselor State of Ala., 1989-90; rehab. counselor Gen. Rehab. Svcs., Tampa, Fla., 1990-92; sr. rehab. specialist Comprehensive Rehab. Assocs., Tampa, 1992—. Contbg. columnist Tuscaloosa (Ala.) News, 1979-86. Chmn. heritage week Tuscaloosa (Ala.) Preservation Soc., 1980-81; pres. Jr. League Tuscaloosa, 1982-83; area coun. rep. dist. V, Jr. League Am., N.Y.C., 1983-84. Named Outstanding Civic Vol., Tuscaloosa (Ala.) Preservation Soc., 1982. Mem. Am. Rehab. Counseling Assn., Fla. Assn. Rehab. Profls. in Pvt. Sector.

BAILEY-JONES, CARLA LYNN, nursing administrator; b. Balt., June 4, 1957; d. Carlton L. and Helen P. (Wales) B.; m. Dean C. Jones, Mar. 1988. BS in Nursing, U. Md., Balt., 1979; MS in Health Sci., Towson (Md.) State U., 1987. Nurse clinician I, charge nurse, clin. nurse U. Md. Med. Systems, Balt., 1981-87; maternal transport coord. U. Md. Med. Systems Hosp., Balt., 1979—; rsch. nurse Tokos Med. Corp., Balt., 1988-91; perinatal care coord. U. Md. Med. Systems/Hosp., 1993—; assoc. faculty U. Md. Sch. Nursing; mem. fetal and infant mortality rev. bd. Healthy Start; mem. State Commn. on Infant Mortality Prevention. Mem. Assn. Women's Health, Obstetric and Neonatal Nurses, State Commn. Infant Mortality Prevention, Md. Nurse's Assn., Nat. Perinatal Assn., Md. Perinatal Assn.

BAILEY-SCHMIEDIGEN, BETTY-JEAN, cultural organization administrator; b. Bluefield, W. Va., June 30, 1941; d. Harvey Lee and Virginia Mae Mary (Tuell) B.; m. George August Schmiedigen, Apr. 1963; 1 child, John-Adam Bailey Schmiedigen. AA, 1975; BS, U. Md., 1977, MEd, 1980; Cert. Completion, Sorbonne U., France, 1976, 87. Cert. paralegal, Md. Jr. acct., jrs. engr. The Chespeake and Potomac Telephone Co.; researcher Smithsonian Instn., Washington; paralegal Dept. Edn., Washington; staff asst. NEA, Washington; congl. liaison officer Dept. Commerce, Washington; program specialist Nat. Endowment for the Humanities, Washington; elem. sch. tchr. Prince George's County Pub. Sch. Editor: Festival Fall Cookbook,

1995. Vice mayor, coun. mem. Town of Brentwood, Md.; chairperson, rep. transp. com., cable com., cmty. com., events com., others; mem. Rte. 1 Corridor task group; tutor in lang. and computer, Oasis, 1995-96. Served in USNR, 1980-86. Mem. The Nat. Mus. Women Arts, Libr. Congress Assocs. (founder, charter), Washington Performing Arts Soc., U. Md. Alumni Assn., Kennedy Ctr. Stars. Presbyterian. Home: 3408 Upshur St Brentwood MD 20722 Office: Nat Endowment Humanities 1100 Pennsylvania Ave NW #511 Washington DC 20506

BAILLIE-DAVID, SONJA KIRSTEEN, controller; b. Lac Megantic, Quebec, Canada, Mar. 26, 1961; came to the U.S., 1964; d. Patrick Eugene and Erika (Bagdonowich) Baillie-David; m. Glenn Frank Skoff, Nov. 12, 1988; 1 child, Elaine Elise Skoff. AA, Joliet Jr. Coll., 1983; BBA, Coll. St. Francis, 1985; MBA in Entrepreneurship, DePaul U., 1992. CPA, Ill. Auditor Peat, Marwick Main, Chgo., 1985-87; auditor Ill. Tool Works, Chgo., 1987-88, fin. analyst, 1988-89; fin. systems project mgr. Ill. Tool Works, Glenview, Ill., 1989-94; controller U.S. Wire-Tie Systems, Woodridge, Ill., 1994-96, Pennysaver Publs., Inc., Tinley Pk., Ill., 1996—. Mem. Ill. CPA Soc., NAFE, Am. Mgmt. Assn. Roman Catholic. Office: Pennysaver Publs Inc 17746 Oak Park Ave Tinley Park IL 60477

BAILLOS, MARIANNE T., secondary education educator; b. Cleve., Aug. 8, 1938; d. Michael Tkach and Mary Bugosh; children: Paul Michael, Peter Emanuel, Philip Andrew. BS, Mich. State U., 1960. Cert. tchr., Mich., Iowa, Va. Tchr. Singer Sewing Machine Co., Cleve., 1954; English tchr. Greece, 1960-61; tchr. Baldwin (Mich.) Pub. Schs., 1961-62, Waverly Pub. Schs., Lansing, Mich., 1962-67; mgr. real estate property Mason City, Iowa, 1978-88; area dir. Am. Cancer Soc., Mason City, 1987-89; tchr. various schs., Va., 1990-95, Lancaster (Va.) H.S. Pres. AAUW, Mason City, 1980-82. Eastern Orthodox.

BAIMAN, GAIL, real estate broker; b. Bklyn., June 4, 1938; d. Joseph and Anita (Devon) Yalow; m. James F. Becker, Oct. 1970 (div. 1978); children: Steven, Susan, Barbara. Student Bklyn. Coll., 1955-57. Lic. real estate broker, N.Y., Pa., Fla. Personnel-pub. relations dir. I.M.C., Inc., N.Y.C., 1970-72; pres., broker Gayle Baiman Assocs., Inc., N.Y.C., 1972-74; v.p., broker Tuit Mktg. Corp., Mt. Pocono, Pa., 1974-83; pres., broker Ind. Timeshare Sales, Inc., St. Petersburg, Orlando, 1983—. Author: Vacation Timesharing, A Real Estate, 1992. Mem. Am. Resort Developers Assn., Better Bus. Arbitrator Assn., Internat. Resale Brokers Assn. (co-founder), Chmns. League, Better Bus. Bur. Arbitrators. Office: Ind Timeshare Sales Inc 10344 66th St Pinellas Park FL 34666-2305

BAIN, AMANDA KAY, revenue commissioner; b. Pell City, Ala., Oct. 14, 1941; d. Hughel and Mary Frances (Cooper) Goodgame; m. Terry Dale Bain; children: Greg, Stephanie, Cory. Grad. H.S., Pell City, Ala. Clk. St. Clair County, Pell City, 1970-72, chief clk., 1973-93, revenue commr., 1994—. Active St. Clair Dem. Club, 1990-96, St. Clair Hist. Com., 1993-96. Recipient cert. of appreciation Am. Cancer Soc., 1994. Mem. Assessing and Collecting Assn. (legis. com. 1994-96), Kiwanis, Greater Pell City C. of C. (pres. 1996), Bus. and Profl. Women (pres. 1995, 96, Woman of Yr. 1994). Baptist. Home: 5105 Cedar Ln Pell City AL 35125

BAIN, DIANE MARTHA D'ANDREA, clinical nurse specialist in critical care; b. Westfield, Mass., June 29, 1949; d. John Anthony and Eva Margaret (Gerulis) D'Andrea; m. John Kenneth, Sept. 24, 1972. AS with hons., Quinsigamond Community Coll., 1971; BS with high hons., Worcester State Coll., 1977; MS with highest honors, U. Mass., Worcester, 1987. Staff and asst. head nurse MICU and crit. care St. Vincent Hosp., Worcester, 1971-77; instr. St. Vincent Hosp. Sch. Nursing, 1977-79; nurse educator critical care U. Mass. Hosp., Worcester, 1979-87, clin. nurse specialist critical care, 1987-93; assoc. faculty U. Mass. Grad. Sch. Nursing, Worcester, 1987-93, Worcester State Coll., 1987-93; presenter, lectr., cons. for regional orgns., agencies, and hosps. Reviewer for Applied Rsch. nursing jour., 1988-89; contbr. articles to profl. jours. Mem. AACN, Sigma Theta Tau, Iota Phi.

BAIN, RENEE MARIE, academic program administrator; b. St. Louis, Aug. 7, 1959; d. Russell Quin and Nadine Elizabeth (Haynes) Dismuke; 1 child, Devin Marie. BS, Mo. Bapt. Coll., 1981; MS, So. Ill. U., 1988. Admissions counselor Mo. Bapt. Coll., St. Louis, 1981-84, fin. assistance dir., 1991—; admissions counselor So. Ill. U., Edwardsville, 1985-88; fin. assistance counselor St. Charles (Mo.) County C.C., 1988-91. Mem. Mo. Assn. Student Fin. Aid Pers., Nat. Assn. Student Fin. Aid Pers. Baptist. Office: Mo Bapt Coll One College Park Dr Saint Louis MO 63141

BAINBRIDGE, DONA BARDELLI, international marketing executive; b. Irvington, N.J., Feb. 27, 1953; d. Alfred and Dona Ellen (Self) B.; m. Harry M. Bainbridge, May 23, 1981 (dec.); 1 child, Harry Michael. Certificat de Langue, Sorbonne, U. Paris, 1974; BA, U. Ky., 1975; MA in Internat. Studies, Am. U., 1978; MSc in Econ. and Social Planning in Developing Countries , U. London, 1979. Research assoc. Woodrow Wilson Internat. Ctr. for Vis. Scholars, Washington, 1976-77, World Bank, Washington, 1977-79; legis. asst. to Congressman Marc Lincoln Marks, Washington, 1979-80; internat. trade analyst Internat. Trade Adminstrn., U.S. Dept. Commerce, Washington, 1980-82; internat. mgmt. cons. Coopers and Lybrand, 1982-86 ; v.p. Bankers Trust Co., Internat. Pvt. Banking, 1986-88; sr. mktg. dir. internat. services BDO Seidman, N.Y.C., 1988-90; founder, pres. D.H. Bainbridge Assocs., 1990—. Chair person nat. mem. Am. Friends of London Sch. Econs., 1981-83, nat. bd. dirs., 1982-84, 1994-96; chmn. mem. com.; mem. ops. com., bd. dirs. Camp Sloane YMCA. Lakeville, Conn.; endowment com. Women's Studies in Religion program Harvard Divinity Sch.; mem. bd. trustees The Washington Episcopal Sch., Bethesda, Md.; mem. adv. bd., chmn. White Plains Salvation Army, 1992-93. Mem. Soc. for Internat. Devel. D.C. Chpt., Bus. and Profl. Women's Clubs Am. (acad. scholar 1971), Nat. Press Club, Fin. Women's Assn. N.Y., Kiwanis. Democrat. Lutheran.

BAINS, LESLIE ELIZABETH, banker; b. Glen Ridge, N.J., July 28, 1943; d. Pliny Otto and Dorothy Ethel (Keeley) Tawney; m. Harrison Mackellar Bains Jr.; Harrison III, Tawney Elizabeth. BA, Am. U., 1965. Asst. treas. Citicorp, N.Y.C., 1965-73; v.p. Mfrs. Hanover, N.Y.C., 1973-80; v.p., div. exec. Chase Manhattan Bank, N.Y.C., 1980-86, v.p., group exec., 1986-87, sr. v.p. group exec., 1987-91; mng. dir. Citibank, N.Y.C., 1991-93; exec. v.p. Republic Nat. Bank, N.Y.C., 1993—; bd. dirs. Interplast, 1990—, Bankers Lawyers Com., 1983—. Chmn. Ednl. Cable Consortium, Summit, N.J., 1987-91; exec. com., bd. visitors Kogod Sch. Bus., Am. U., 1992—; trustee Am. U., 1994—; bd. dirs. Jr. Achievement, N.Y.C., 1996—, Duke U. Inst. for Pub. Policy; mem. Coun. Fgn. Rels., 1991—; mem. exec. com. bd. visitors Sch. Pub. Policy, Duke U. Named Achiever of Yr. YWCA, 1985, One of Top 100 Women in Corp. Am., Bus. Month., 1989. Mem. Am. Bankers Assn. (bd. dirs. pvt. banking coun.), Fin. Women Internat. (treas. 1981-83, v.p. 1983-84, pres. 1984-85, vice chmn. Edn. Found. 1980-81), Fin. Women's Assn., Women and Founds. Office: Republic Nat Bank 452 5th Ave New York NY 10018-2706

BAIR, MYRNA LYNN, state senator; b. Huntington, W.Va., Oct. 26, 1940; d. Charles Thomas and Velma Elvera (Schoenlein) North; B.S. in Chemistry, U. Cin., 1962; Ph.D., U. Wis., 1968; m. Thomas Irvin Bair, Mar. 12, 1966; children—Thomas Irvin, Catherine Lynn. Asst. prof. chemistry Beaver Coll., Glenside, Pa., 1966-70; instr. chemistry U. Del., 1974-76, asst. prof. edn., 1977-79; asst. dir. pub. info. Del. Energy Office, Wilmington, 1978-79; mem. Del. Senate, 1981—; vice chair women's network, assembly on states Nat. Conf. of State Legislatures, 1994-95; sr. mgmt. advisor Coll. Urban Affairs and Pub. Policy, dir. women's leadership tng. program, 1989—. Contbr. articles to sci. jours. Bd. dirs. Del. Lung Assn.; trustee Wesley Coll.; mem. Nat. Republican Com., Wilmington Rep. Women's Club. Recipient Freshman award Chem. Rubber Co., 1959; DuPont Co. Teaching award, 1963, Pres.'s award Jr. League, 1988; NSF fellow, 1964-66. Mem. AAUW, Phi Beta Kappa, Iota Sigma Pi, Alpha Lambda Delta. Methodist. Office: Legislative Hall State Capital Bldg Dover DE 19903*

BAIR, SUSANNE PAULETTE, university administrator; b. Rochester, Ind., Nov. 21, 1958; d. Richard Paul and M. Jeanette (Schluntz) B. BS, Ind. State U., 1981, MS, 1985; D of Phys. Edn., Ind. U., 1991. Athletic dir. Attica (Ind.) H.S., 1982-88; assoc. athletic dir. N.E. Mo. State U., Kirksville, 1991-93; dir. devel. and external affairs Sch. Health, Phys. Edn., Recreation, Ind. U., Bloomington, 1993—; mem. alumni bd. Sch. Health, Phys. Edn., Recreation, Ind. U., Bloomington, 1993—. Trustee Ind. U., Bloomington, 1989-91; bd. dirs. Luth. Campus Ministry, Bloomington, 1995—. Mem. Rotary. Home: 401 Sheffield Dr Bloomington IN 47408 Office: Ind U Sch Health Phys Ed Rec HPER 146 Bloomington IN 47405

BAIRD, ANN BRISBANE, art gallery director; b. Greenville, Miss., Aug. 3, 1948; d. Joseph Bedent and Nancy Merkel (Trigg) B.; m. Richard Robin Childers (div. 1979). BA, Rollins Coll., 1970; postgrad., North Tex. State U., 1974-78, U. Tex., 1979-80; MA, U. Fla., 1996. Instr. Cedar Valley Coll., Dallas, 1978-80; mgr., owner The Saint-Simons Café, St. Simons Island, Ga., 1980-84; curator U. Gallery, Gainesville, Fla., 1991-93; asst. curator Harn Mus. of Art, Gainesville, 1992-94; dir. Thomas Center Galleries, Gainesville, 1994-96, Bascom-Louise Gallery, Highlands, N.C., 1996—, Highlands Ctr. for Visual Art, 1996—. Mem. Fla. Assn. of Mus., Am. Assn. of Mus. Episcopalian. Home: Box 282 Highlands NC 28741 Office: Bascom-Louise Gallery Box 430 Highlands NC 28741

BAIRD, LOURDES G., federal judge; b. 1935. BA with highest honors, UCLA, 1973, JD with honors, 1976. Asst. U.S. atty. U.S. Dist. Ct. (ctrl. dist.) Calif., L.A., 1977-83, U.S. atty., 1990-92; ptnr. Baird & Quadros, 1983-84, Baird, Munger & Myers, 1984-86; judge East L.A. Mcpl. Ct., 1986-87; adj. prof. law Loyola U., L.A., 1986-90; judge L.A. Mcpl. Ct., 1987-88, L.A. Superior Ct., 1988-90; U.S. atty. ctrl. dist. Calif., 1990-92; judge U.S. Dist. Ct. (ctrl. dist.) Calif., L.A., 1992—; faculty civil RICO program Practicing Law Inst., San Francisco, 1984-85, western regional program Nat. Inst. Trial Advocacy, Berkeley, Calif., 1987-88; adj. prof. trial advocacy Loyola U., L.A., 1987-90. Recipient Silver Achievement award for the professions YWCA, 1994; named Woman of Promise, Hispanic Womens' Coun., 1991, Alumnus of Yr., UCLA Sch. Law, 1991. Mem. Mexican-Am. Bar Assn., Calif. Women Lawyers, Hispanic Nat. Bar Assn., UCLA Sch. Law alumni Assn. (pres. 1984). Office: US Dist Ct Ctrl Dist Calif Edward R. Roybal Bldg 255 E Temple St Ste 770 Los Angeles CA 90012-3334*

BAIRD, MARIANNE SAUNORUS, critical care clinical specialist; b. Chgo., Dec. 15, 1953; d. John and Irene (Lameka) Saunorus; m. Thomas W. Baird, Sept. 10, 1983; 1 child, Rachel. BSN, Loyola U., Chgo., 1975; MSN, Emory U., 1982. Critical care RN, cert. advanced cardiac life support affiliate faculty mem., Ga. Supr. surg. nursing Rush-Presbyn. St. Lukes Med. Ctr., Chgo.; staff nurse, clin. mgr. intensive care unit St. Joseph's Hosp., Atlanta, dir. meg.-surg. unit, clin. specialist, case mgr. Author several nursing textbooks; contbr. articles to profl. jours. Recipient Fed. traineeship Emory U., 1980-81; named one of Outstanding Young Women of Am., 1991. Mem. AACN (bd. dirs. Atlanta chpt. 1984-86), Blue Key Nat. Honor Fraternity, Kappa Gamma Pi, Sigma Theta Tau. Home: 3788 Glengarry Way Roswell GA 30075-2615

BAIRD, ZOË, insurance company executive, lawyer; b. Bklyn., June 20, 1952; d. Ralph Louis and Naomi (Allen) B.; m. Paul Gewirtz, June 8, 1986; 1 child, Julian Baird Gewirtz. AB, U. Calif., Berkeley, 1974, JD, 1977. Bar: Washington, 1979, Calif. 1977, Conn. 1989. Law clk. Hon. Albert Wollenberg, San Francisco, 1977-78; atty., advisor Office Legal Counsel U.S. Dept. Justice, Washington, 1979-80; assoc. counsel to the Pres. The White House, Washington, 1980-81; assoc., then ptnr. O'Melveny & Myers, Washington, 1981-86; counsellor, staff exec. GE, Fairfield, Conn., 1986-90; v.p., gen. counsel Aetna Life & Casualty, Hartford, 1990-93, sr. v.p. gen. coun., 1993—; bd. dirs. Sci. Pk. Devel. Corp., New Haven, So. New Eng. Telecom. Corp., mem. bd. contbrs. Mem. Am. Lawyer Media, N.Y.C. (bd. contbrs.). Office: Aetna Life & Casualty 151 Farmington Ave Hartford CT 06156-0001*

BAIRSTOW, FRANCES KANEVSKY, labor arbitrator, mediator, educator; b. Racine, Wis., Feb. 19, 1920; d. William and Minnie (DuBow) Kanevsky; m. Irving P. Kaufman, Nov. 14, 1942 (div. 1949); m. David Steele Bairstow, Dec. 17, 1954; children: Dale Owen, David Anthony. Student U. Wis., 1937-42; BS, U. Louisville, 1949; student Oxford U. (Eng.), 1953-54; postgrad. McGill U., Montreal, Que., 1958-59. Rsch. economist U.S. Senate Labor-Mgmt. Subcom., Washington, 1950-51; labor edn. specialist U. P.R., San Juan, 1951-52; chief wage data unit WSB, Washington, 1952-53; labor rsch. economist Canadian Pacific Ry. Co., Montreal, 1956-58; asst. dir. indsl. rels. ctr. McGill U., 1960-66, assoc. dir., 1966-71, dir., 1971-85, lectr., indsl. rels. dept. econs., 1960-72, asst. prof. faculty mgmt., 1972-74, assoc. prof. faculty mgmt., 1974-83, prof., 1983-85; lectr. Stetson Law Sch., Fla. spl. master Fla. Pub. Employees Rels. Commn., 1985—; dep. commr. essential svcs. Province of Que., 1976-81; mediator So. Bell Telephone, 1985—, AT&T and Comm. Workers Am., 1986—; cons. on collective bargaining arbitrator to OECD, Paris, 1979; cons. Nat. Film Bd. of Can., 1965-69; arbitrator Que. Consultative Coun. Panel of Arbitrators, 1968-83, Ministry Labour and Manpower, 1971-83, United Airlines and Assn. Flight Attendants, 1990-95, State U. System of Fla., 1990—; Orlando Utilities Commn., Orlando, 1994, FDA, 1996—, Social Security Adminstrn., 1996—; mediator Canadian Public Svc. Staff Rels. Bd., 1973-85; contbg. columnist Montreal Star, 1971-85. Chmn. Nat. Inquiry Commn. Wider-Based Collective Bargaining, 1978. Fulbright fellow, 1953-54. Mem. Canadian Indsl. Rels. Rsch. Inst. (exec. bd. 1965-68), Indsl. Rels. Rsch. Assn. Am. (mem. exec. bd. 1965-68, chmn. nominating com. 1977), Nat. Acad. Arbitrators (bd. govs. 1977-80, program chmn. 1982-83, v.p. 1986-88, nat. coord. 1987-90), Nat. Treasury Employees Assoc. Home and Office: 1430 Gulf Blvd Apt 507 Clearwater FL 34630-2856

BAISIER, MARIA DAVIS, English language educator, theater director; b. Louisville, Aug. 15, 1947; d. Alvin Joseph and Alice Josephine (Ostertag) Davis; m. Bernard Leon Baisier, May 23, 1970; children: Bernard Paul Leon, Aimée Louise Davis. BA, St. Mary's Dominican Coll., 1969; secondary cert. in English, Tulane U., 1992. Asst. mng. editor So. Ins. Mag., New Orleans, 1979-85; tchr. St. Catherine of Siena Sch., Metairie, La., 1969-75, 85—, chair English dept., 1985—, dir. theatre, 1991—. Creator, dir. Camp Big Foot Summer Camp, Metairie, 1974, 75; v.p. Sacred Heart Sch. PTA, Anniston, Ala., 1977; vol. worker Sta. WYES-TV Auction, New Orleans, 1978-83; mem. women's com. New Orleans Opera Assn., 1979—, chair Opera Ball, 1984; various com. positions Women's Guild, 1980-84; chair ann. fundraiser fair St. Francis Xavier Ch., 1982-84; mem. hospitality com. Rep. Nat. Conv., 1988. Mem. Nat. Coun. Tchrs. English, Kappa Delta Pi, Phi Beta. Home: 210 Hector Ave Metairie LA 70005-4118

BAIZA, MARY PESINA, social services administrator; b. Mission, Tex., May 28, 1944; d. Patricio and Maria Cuevas (Gutierrez) Pesina; m. Eusebio Molina Baiza, Jan. 8, 1966; children: Julie Suzanne, Elizabeth. Cert. in Nursing, South Plains Coll., 1966; BS, Tex. Tech. U., 1984. Cons. Eastfield Coll., Mesquite, Tex., 1972-76; coord. Heath Sci. Ctr. Tex. Tech U., Lubbock, 1977-83; interior designer J.C. Penney, Lubbock, 1984-85; dir. Guadalupe Econ. Svc. Inc., Lubbock, 1985-87; coord. Cmty. Resource Gruop, Inc., Lubbock, 1988—. Dir. South Plains Assn. Govts., Lubbock, 1992; v.p. Christ the King Sch. Bd., 1981-83; mem. health edn. bd. St. Mary's of the Plains Hosp., 1988. Recipient Marble plaque City of Roaring Spring, 1990, Leadership Tex. Found. for Women award, 1992. Mem. Am. Mktg. Assn. (sec. 1983-90). Democrat. Roman Catholic. Home: 7004 Wayne Ave Lubbock TX 79424 Office: CRG Inc 1901 University Ave Lubbock TX 79410

BAJOIE, DIANA E., state legislator; b. July 8, 1948. Former mem. La. State Ho. Reps. from 91st dist.; mem. La. State Senate. Alt. del. Dem. Nat. Party Conf., 1978. Office: La State Senate State Capitol PO Box 15168 New Orleans LA 70175*

BAK, DIANN LEE, accountant; b. Chgo., Oct. 10, 1949; d. Joseph Stanley and Stella Mary (Waclawek) B. AA in Bus. Adminstrn., Daley Coll., Chgo., 1987; BA in Acctg., DePaul U., Chgo., 1991. With HHS, Chgo., 1967-81, supr., 1981—. Mem. Am. Soc. Women Accts. (chair com. Chgo. chpt. 1990-93), Golden Key Club, Delta Mu Delta, Beta Gamma Sigma, Beta Alpha Psi. Roman Catholic. Office: Social Security Adminstrn 9730 S Western Ave Evergreen Park IL 60642-2814

BAK, SUNNY, photographer; b. N.Y.C., July 25, 1958; d. Chun Suk and Bie Liang (Kwik) B. AB, CCNY, 1976; postgrad., New Sch. for Social Rsch., N.Y.C., 1982-85, UCLA, 1987. Pres. Sunny Bak Photography, N.Y.C., 1976-83; staff photographer The Hamptons Newspaper Mag., Southampton, N.Y., 1978-84; sec., treas. Sunny Bak Studio, Inc., N.Y.C., 1983-87, pres., 1988—; pres. Sunny Bak Pub. Rels., N.Y.C., 1984-85; dir. pub. rels. H.H. Assocs., N.Y.C. and L.A., 1985-87; dir. west coast ops. KCG Prodns., N.Y.C., 1987-88; dir. photography The Secret, 1995. Photographer: Vamps, Sirens, Temptresses, 1984-85, 32 covers of Womans World mag., 1985-88, Lic. to Ill, 1987, Pupple, 1988, Detail's mag. cover, 1989. Best selling cover, Newsweek, 1994. Mem. Advt. Photographer's Am., Assn. Asian Pacific Am. Artists, Asian Pacific Women's Network. Democrat. Buddhist.

BAKEMAN, CAROL ANN, administrative services manager, singer; b. San Francisco, Oct. 27, 1934; d. Lars Hartvig and Gwendolyne Beatrice (Zimmer) Bergh; student UCLA, 1954-62; m. Delbert Clifton Bakeman, May 16, 1959; children: Laurie Ann, Deborah Ann. Singer, Roger Wagner Chorale, 1954-92, L.A. Master Chorale, 1964-86, The Wagner Ensemble, 1991—; libr. Hughes Aircraft Co., Culver City, Calif., 1954-61; head econs. libr. Planning Rsch. Corp., L.A., 1961-63; corporate libr. Econ. Cons., Inc., L.A., 1963-68; head econs. libr. Daniel, Mann, Johnson & Mendenhall, archs. and engrs., L.A., 1969-71, corporate libr., 1971-77, mgr. info. svcs., 1978-81, mgr. info. and office svcs., 1981-83, mgr. adminstrv. svcs., 1983—, sr. assoc., 1996—; travel mgr. AECOM Tech. Corp., 1996—; pres., Creative Libr. Sys., L.A., 1974-83; libr. cons. ArchiSystems, divsn. SUMMA Corp., L.A., 1972-81, Property Rehab. Corp., Bell Gardens, Calif., 1974-75, VTN Corp., Irvine, Calif., 1974, William Pereira & Assos., 1975; mem. office sys. and bus. edn. adv. bd. Calif. State U. Northridge, 1992—. Mem. Assistance League, So. Calif., 1956-86, mem. nat. auxilaries com. 1968-72, 75-78, mem. nat. by laws com. 1970-75, mem. assoc. bd. dirs., 1966-76. Mem. AFTRA, SAG, Am. Guild Musical Artists, Adminstrv. Mgmt. Soc. (v.p. L.A. chpt. 1984-86, pres. 1986-88, internat. conf. chmn. 1988-89, internat. bd. dirs. 1988-90, internat. v.p. mgmt. edn. 1990-92), L.A. Master Chorale Assn. (bd. dirs. 1978-83), L.A. Bus. Travel Assn. (bd. dirs. 1995), Nat. Bus. Travel Assn. (nat. conv. seminar com. 1994-95). Office: DMJM 3250 Wilshire Blvd Los Angeles CA 90010-1599

BAKER, AMANDA SIRMON, university dean, nursing educator; b. Daphne, Ala., Apr. 3, 1934; d. Joel Green and Edna Mae (Miller) Sirmon; m. Malcolm Davis Baker, Mar. 30, 1957; children: Leonard Eric, Michael Davis. BSN, U. Ala., Tuscaloosa, 1955; M in Nursing, U. Fla., Gainesville, 1972, PhD, 1974; cert., Bryn Mawr Coll., 1983. Office nurse R.P. Maxon, M.D., Ft. Walton Beach, Fla., 1955-58; pub. health nurse County Health Dept., Clovis, N.Mex., 1963-64; staff nurse, night supr. Pheobe Putney Hosp., Albany, Ga., 1964-67; developer, implementor home svc. nursing program for children and adults with cerebral palsy United Cerebral Palsy, Southwest Ga., 1967-68; instr. in child health, med./surg. and pharmacology Albany (Ga.) Jr. Coll., 1968-69; grad. teaching asst. child health nursing U. Fla., 1972-73, grad. teaching assoc. child health nursing, 1973-74, asst. dean continuing profl. edn. Coll. of Nursing, 1974-76, asst. dean. undergrad. studies, 1976-78, acting dean Coll. of Nursing, 1978-80, asst. dean. undergrad. studies Coll. of Nursing, 1980-81, assoc. dean Coll. of Nursing, 1981-85; dean Sch. of Nursing Troy State U., 1985-89; dean Coll. of Nursing U. South Ala., 1989—; mem. search com. Coll. Medicine, 1990-92, chair search com. VPAA, 1990-91, mem. fin. resources com., 1991-93, chair subcom.; speaker and presenter in field. Contbr. articles to profl. jours. Chair Ala. Nurses Polit. Action Com., 1986-89. Mem. ANA (coun. nurse rschr., S.E. region accrediting com., charter 1974-78), NLN (coun. baccalaureate and higher degree end. 1974-96), Ala. State Nurses Assn. (dist. 8 chpt.), Ala. League for Nursing, Soc. for Rsch. in Nursing Edn., Am. Assn. Colls. Nursing (semi-ann. meetings 1985—, program com. 1990-92, pub. rels. com. 1992-94, govtl. affairs com. 1994-96), So. Coun. on Collegiate Edn. in Nursing, Phi Kappa Phi, Pi Lambda Theta, Sigma Theta Tau. Presbyterian. Office: U South Ala Coll Nursing Springhill Campus Mobile AL 36688

BAKER, ANITA, singer; b. Toledo, Jan. 26, 1958; m. Walter Bridgeforth, Jr., Dec. 24, 1988; 1 child, Walter Baker Bridgeforth. Mem. funk band Chapter 8, Detroit, 1978-80; receptionist Quin & Budajh, Detroit, 1980-82; ind. singer, songwriter, 1982—. Rec. artist: (with Chapter 8) I Just Wanna Be Your Girl, 1980, (solo albums) The Songstress, 1983, Rapture, 1986 (Grammy award for best rhythm and blues vocal performance 1987), Giving You the Best That I Got, 1988 (Grammy awards for best rhythm and blues song, 1988, best rhythm and blues performance, female, single, 1988, best album, 1989), Compositions, 1990 (Grammy award for best rhythm and blues performance, 1990), Rhythm of Love, 1994 (Grammy award nominee for best album 1995, best female vocal 1995, best song 1995); songs include No More Tears, Angel, Caught Up in the Rapture, Sweet Love (Grammy award best rhythm and blues song 1987), Same Ol' Love, You Bring Me Joy, Been So Long, No One in the World. Recipient Grammy award gospel, soul, best performance, duo, group, choir or chorus, 1987, NAACP Image award, best female vocalist and best album of yr. Office: All Baker's Music 345 N Maple Dr Beverly Hills CA 90210-3827*

BAKER, ANITA DIANE, lawyer; b. Atlanta, Sept. 4, 1955; d. Byron Garnett and Anita (Swanson) B.; m. Thomas Johnstone Robison III, Sept. 26, 1995. BA summa cum laude, Oglethorpe U., 1977; JD with distinction, Emory U., 1980. Bar: Ga. 1980. Assoc. Hansell & Post, Atlanta, 1980-88, Kitchens, Kelley, Gaynes, Huprich & Shmerling, 1989-90; asst. gen. counsel NationsBank Corp., 1991—. Mem. ABA (com. on savs. and loan instns., com. on consumer fin. svcs.), Atlanta Bar Assn., Ga. Bar Assn., Atlanta Hist. Soc., Pace Acad. Alumni Assn. (bd. dirs.), Oglethorpe Univ. Alumni Assn. (bd. dirs.), Order of Coif, Phi Alpha Delta, Phi Alpha Theta, Alpha Chi, Omicron Delta Kappa. Office: NationsBank Corp 600 Peachtree St NE Fl 5 Atlanta GA 30308-2214

BAKER, BETTY LOUISE, retired mathematician, educator; b. Chgo., Oct. 17, 1937; d. Russell James and Lucille Juanita (Timmons) B.: BE, Chgo. State U., 1961, MA, 1964; PhD, Northwestern U., 1971. Tchr. math. Harper High Sch., Chgo., 1961-70; tchr. math. Hubbard High Sch., Chgo., 1970-85, also chmm. dept.; tchr. Bogan High Sch., 1985-94, ret., 1994; part-time instr. Moraine Valley C.C., 1982-83, 84-86. Cultural arts chmn. Hubbard Parents-Tchrs.-Student Assn., 1974-76, lst v.p., program chmn., 1977-79, 82-84, pres., 1979-81; organist Hope Luth. Ch., 1963—. Univ. fellow, 1969-70; cert. tchr. high sch. and elem. grades 3-8 math., Ill. Mem. Nat. Coun. Tchrs. Math., Ill. Coun. Tchrs. of Math., Math. Assn. Am., Chgo. Tchrs. Union, Nat. Coun. Parents and Tchrs. (life), Sch. Sci. and Math. Assn., Assn. for Supervision and Curriculum Devel., Am. Guild of Organists, Luth. Collegiate Assn., Walther League Hiking Club, Met. Math. Club Chgo., Kappa Mu Epislon, Rho Sigma Tau, Mu Alpha Theta (sponsor), Kappa Delta Pi, Pi Lambda Theta, Phi Delta Kappa. Contbr. articles to profl. jours. Home: 3214 W 85th St Chicago IL 60652-3727

BAKER, BONNIE BARBARA, mental health and school counselor, educator; b. Bklyn., Aug. 22, 1949; d. Irving Charles and Martha (Besner) B.; m. Thomas Andrew Ridgik, Aug. 4, 1990. BAE, U. Fla., 1971, PhD, 1985; MEd, U. N.C., 1972. Lic. mental health counselor, Fla. Sch. counselor Alachua County Schs., Gainesville, Fla., 1972—; mental health counselor Gainesville Counseling and Devel. Ctr., 1985—. Contbr. book chpt. to Managing Your School Counseling Program; editor (booklet) How to Choose a College: A Guide to Students with a Disability. Vol. counselor U. Fla. Student Svcs., 1991—. Recipient Joe Wittmer Leadership award Chi Sigma Iota, 1994. Mem. ACA (mem. ethics com. 1987-88), Am. Sch. Counselor Assn., Am. Mental Health Counselors Assn., Fla. Counseling Assn. (treas. 1979-82, chair govt. rels. 1988-89, Leadership award 1989), Fla. Sch. Counselor Assn. (treas. 1978-80, pres. 1983-84). Home: PO Box 14155 Gainesville FL 32604-2155 Office: Gainesville Counseling & Devel Ctr 2831 NW 41st St Ste F Gainesville FL 32606-6690

BAKER, C. B., retired day care director, organizer, communicator; b. Ft. Wayne, Ind.; d. James Edwin Sr. and Susie Mae (Nutter) Doelling; m. Gerald R. Baker, June, 1962 (div. 1966); 1 child, Erin Lee; m. Jeffrey E. Baker, June, 1967 (div. 1972); 1 child, Shannon Rae. Student, Internat. Bus. Coll., Ft. Wayne, 1961. Expeditor Wayne Fabricating, Ft. Wayne, 1971; county adminstr. Champaign (Ill.) County Bd., 1974-76; sec. WICD-TV, Champaign, 1976-77; ops. chmn. 40 Plus of Colo., Inc., Denver, 1983, v.p., 1984-85, pres., 1985-86; co-dir. St. Anne's Extended Day Program, Denver, 1986-88; self-employed organizer Denver, 1988—. Editor The Village Voice newsletter, Savoy, Ill., 1974. Chmn. Winfield Village Swimming Pool Com., Savoy, 1975; dir. Mich. Sugar Festival, Sebewaing, 1991. Mem. Am. Bus. Women's Assn., Colo. Women's C. of C.

BAKER, CHRISTINE MARIE, secondary education educator; b. Tucson, Sept. 19, 1951; d. Howard Harold and Dorothy (Rice) B.; m. Steven Edward Willhoite, Aug. 24, 1968 (div. Dec. 1995); children: Stacey Leigh Rubalcava, Michael Edward Willhoite. BA, U. Calif., Berkeley, 1990; tchg. credential, San Francisco State U., 1991. Cert. tchr. secondary social sci. and govt., Calif. Tchr. social sci. Franklin Jr. H.S., Vallejo, Calif., 1993—; dept. chair social sci. Franklin Jr. H.S., Vallejo, 1994—; mem. newspapers in edn. adv. bd. San Francisco Newspaper Agy., 1995-96; mem. instrnl. improvement coun. Franklin Jr. H.S., Vallejo, 1995—, mem. leadership coun., 1994-95. Vol. after-sch. homework club Franklin Jr. H.S., 1993—. Democrat. Office: Franklin Jr H S 501 Starr Ave Vallejo CA 94590

BAKER, CINDY LOU, mathematics educator; b. Hornell, N.Y., Jan. 18, 1953; d. Merton Laverne and Norma Dawn (Southworth) Preston; m. Robert Jay Baker, July 28, 1973; children: Jay Robert, Andrea Lee, Joshua Ethan. BA in Math., William Smith Coll., 1974; MS in Edn., Alfred U., 1981. Cert. tchr., N.Y. Tchr. H.S. math. Andover (N.Y.) Ctrl. Sch., 1975—; class advisor Andover Ctrl. Sch., 1984-88, 92-96, choir accompanist, 1965—, Nat. Honor Soc. advisor, 1989-94. Mem. Order of Ea. Star (musician 1986-90). Home: 3798 Baker St Ext Andover NY 14806-9660 Office: Andover Ctrl Sch 31-35 Elm St Andover NY 14806

BAKER, CORNELIA DRAVES, artist; b. Woodbury, N.J., Mar. 2, 1929; d. Carl Zeno and Cornelia (Powell) Draves.; m. Philip Douglas Baker, July 16, 1955; children: Brinton, Todd, Claudia, Samuel. Student, Ohio Wesleyan U., 1947-50, Goethe U., Frankfurt, Ger., 1950-52. Travel dir. Am. Youth Hostels, Inc., N.Y.C., 1953-57; artist Cornelia Gallery, Kumamoto, Japan, 1990—, L'Atelier Inc. Gallery, Piermont, N.Y., 1994—; gallery dir. Presbyn. Ch., Franklin Lakes, N.J., 1989—, Marcella Gettman Gallery, New Milford, N.J., 1993-96; bd. dirs. Bergen Mus. Art and Sci., N.J., 1996—. One woman shows include Ramapo Coll., 1986, Shimada Mus., Kumamoto, 1990, Sekaikan Gallery, Tokyo, 1990, Bergen Mus. Art and Sci., 1993, L'Atelier Inc. Gallery, 1994, N.Y. Theol. Sem., N.Y.C., 1996; represented in permanent collections Bergen Mus. Art and Sci., Paramus, N.J., Beekley Internat. Skiing Fine Art and Graphics. Chair social problems com. Borough of Franklin Lakes Coun., 1973-76. Recipient Best of Show award Ringwood Manor Assn. of the Arts, 1987, Bergen Mus. Art and Sci., 1989, Emeriti award for excellence N.J. Ctr. for Visual Arts, 1989, Excellence cert. Internat. Art Competition, 1988, Women Making History in Arts award Bergen County, N.J., 1993, Crabbie award Art Calendar, 1994. Mem. Nat. Assn. Women Artists (printmaking jury chmn. 1992-94), Salute to Women in the Arts (pres. 1988-90), Altrusa Club of Bergen County, N.J. Republican. Presbyterian. Home: 293 Greenridge Rd Franklin Lakes NJ 07417-2011

BAKER, DANETTE P., newspaper editor, reporter; b. Lubbock, Tex., Nov. 6, 1963; d. John W. and Velma (Daniell) Phillips; m. John W. Baker, Nov. 22, 1986; children: Brynna Danae, Clayton Daniell. AAS in Graphic Arts, South Plains Coll., Levelland, Tex., 1987; BS in Journalism, West Tex. State U., 1991. Lifestyles reporter Lubbock (Tex.) Avalanche-Journal, 1991-92, lifestyles editor, 1992—; adv. bd. Lubbock County Extension, 1994—. Recipient Howard Scripps Journalism award, Ind. U., 1991, award for gen. reporting, Rolling Stone mag., N.Y.C., 1991, award for gen. column writing, AP Mng. Editors, Tex., 1996. Mem. Women in Comm., Inc. (coord. student chpt. 1996—, FOI chair 1994-95). Baptist. Office: Lubbock Avalanche-Jour 710 Ave J Lubbock TX 79401

BAKER, DEBORAH ALYSANDE, poet; b. Bartlesville, Okla., Oct. 8, 1949; d. Curtis Lee and Alice Cathrine (Fears) B. BS in Speech, Tex. Woman's U., 1977. Contbr. anthologies Rainbows and Rhapsodies, 1988, Orchids and Daffodils, 1988, Living Jewels, 1993; contbr. to periodicals A Galaxy of Verse, 1988, 89, Gt. Plains Canal and Avalon Dispatch, 1994, Lines 'N Rhymes, 1994, The Apostolic Crusade, 1996. Initiator, leader Mineral Wells (Tex.) Singles, 1988, 90. Mem. Brazos Writers Group (co-founder 1988—). Home: Apt 33 2503 SE 7th St Mineral Wells TX 76067-5710

BAKER, DIANE R.H., dermatologist; b. Toledo, Nov. 17, 1945. BS, Ohio State U., 1967, MD cum laude, 1971. Diplomate Am. Bd. Dermatology. Intern U. Wis. Hosp., Madison, 1971-72, resident in dermatology, 1972-74; resident in dermatology Oreg. Health Sci. Ctr., Portland, 1974-76; pvt. practce, Portland, 1976—; clin. prof. dermatology Oreg. Health Sci. U., 1986—; mem. med. staff Meridian Park Hosp., Tualatin, Oreg., 1981—. Mem. Am. Acad. Dermatology, Am. Dermatol. Assn., Oreg. Med. Assn., Oreg. Derm. Soc., Alpha Omega Alpha. Office: Dermatol Assocs 9495 SW Locust St Portland OR 97223-6665

BAKER, DONNA MARIE, secondary school educator; b. Pitts., June 26, 1949; m. Gary L. Baker. BS in Edn., Edinboro U., 1971, cert. media specialist, 1981; MA in Edn., Allegheny Coll., 1974. Cert. tchr., Pa. English tchr. Conneaut Sch. Dist./Conneaut Valley H.S., Conneautville, Pa., 1973—; mem. various coms. Conneaut Sch. Dist./Conneaut Valley H.S., Conneautville; mem. com. Ctr. for Curricular Change Allegheny Coll., Meadville, Pa. Mem. NEA, Pa. Edn. Assn., Conneaut Edn. Assn., N.W. Pa. Tchrs. English, Nat. Coun. Tchrs. English. Home: 14092 Limber Rd Meadville PA 16335-9435 Office: Conneaut Valley HS 22154 State Hwy 18 Conneautville PA 16406-0330

BAKER, DOROTHY SWARTZ, small business owner; b. Harrisburg, Pa., Oct. 4, 1932; d. Fred and Mable Margaret (Bupp) Swartz; m. Lawrence E. Baker, May 8, 1954; children: Margaret B. Chrencik, Mark L. Baker, Mary B. Walters. AA, Harrisburg (Pa.) C.C., 1970; B.Humanities, Pa. State U., 1973, MA, 1981. Underwriter Pa. Nat. Ins., Harrisburg, 1973-76, supr. rating dept., 1976-79, methods, procedures analyst, 1979-84; self-employed Harrisburg, 1984—. Author: AVM (booklet), 1989, (short stories) Grandma and Her Sickness, 1992, Indian Beads, 1992. Bd. dirs. Penbrook Learning Ctr., Harrisburg, 1993—; mem. Internat. Gamma Support Group, Harrisburg, 1996; workshop leader Contact USA, Columbus, Ga., 1996. Democrat. Home and Office: 333 N Hoernerstown Rd Harrisburg PA 17111

BAKER, EDITH MADEAN, counselor; b. Greeley, Colo., Oct. 7, 1942; d. Richard Luther and Catherine Jane (John) Tatman; m. Richard Dennis Baker, Oct. 24, 1964; children: Kimberly Baker Parker, Gregory. Student, U. No. Colo., 1961; BA, U. Colo., 1964; postgrad., San Jose (Calif.) State U., 1969-70; EdM, Oreg. State U., 1978. Cert. counselor, Oreg. Tchr. Spaulding Sch. Dist., Waukegan, Ill., 1965-67, Alhambra Pvt. Sch., Phoenix, 1968-69; pvt. practice counseling Corvallis, Oreg., 1977-80; counselor Salem (Oreg.) Sch. Dist., 1978-79; testing specialist Corvallis Sch. Dist., 1980, counselor, 1980-88; counselor Springfield (Oreg.) Sch. Dist., 1988—; chair activity curriculum com. Corvallis Sch. Dist., 1984, chair prin. selection com., 1985. Member Symphony Guild, Eugene, Oreg., 1988—, PTA; bd. dirs. Boys and Girls Club, Corvallis, 1984-88, Assn. for Retarded Citizens, Eugene, 1989-90; chair Parent Graduation Celebration, Corvallis, 1985, 88. Mem. NEA, Oreg. Counseling Assn., Oreg. Edn. Assn., Mental Health Assn. of Oreg., Springfield Edn. Assn., Univ. Women's League, Delta Kappa Gamma, Kappa Delta Pi, Delta Delta Delta. Democrat. Home: 3336 Bardell Ave Eugene OR 97401-5801 Office: Thurston Mid Sch 6300 Thurston Rd Springfield OR 97478-7057

BAKER, FAITH MERO, elementary education educator; b. Pitts., May 9, 1941; d. Vincent G. and Georgetta (Rothwell) Mero; m. Gerald A. Baker, Dec. 22, 1968; children: Jeremy D., Kara L. BA, Carlow Coll., Pitts., 1963; MEd, U. Pitts., 1965, postgrad., 1966-68. Cert. elem. and spl. edn. tchr., Pa. Tchr. sci. Pitts. Pub. Schs., 1963-64, tchr. spl. edn., 1968-87, tchr., primary sci. specialist, 1987—; leader instrnl. team Fulton Acad., Pitts., 1988—; facilitator, tchr. Project Wild and project Aquatic Wild, Project Learning Tree, Pitts., 1988—; mem. leadership team Fulton Acad. for New Am. Schs.-area Sch. to Career. Leader Girl Scouts U.S.A., Monroeville, Pa., 1979-86; mem. Supts. Roundtable Gateway Schs., Monroeville, Pa., 1987-89. Mem. AAUW (scholarship chmn. Monroeville br. 1996—), Pitts. Fedn. Tchrs. (bldg. steward 1968—), Pa. Bus. and Profl. Women's Assn. (bd. dirs. dist. 3, 1991—, mem. polit. action com., pres. Monroeville 1987-88, 92-93), U. Pitts. Alumni Assn. (ast v.p. 1987-88, sec. 1989-91), Delta Kappa Gamma, Alpha Delta Kappa (treas. 1992—), Phi Delta Gamma (sec. Kappa chpt. 1986-90, pres. 1982-84, regional coord. 1984-86, nat. v.p. 1992-94, nat. pres. 1994-96). Democrat. Roman Catholic. Home: 102 Penn Lear Dr Monroeville PA 15146-4734 Office: Fulton Acad Hampton St Pittsburgh PA 15206

BAKER, FRANCES LOUISE, social work consultant; b. Rochelle, Ill., Dec. 3, 1947; d. Raymond Francis and Evelyn Louise (Weinreich) Saathoff; children: Michele Dawn, Kevin Allen. BA in Drawing and Painting, U. So. Miss., Hattiesburg, 1979, MSW, 1981. Facilitator, trainer, child advocate, 1981—; social work cons. Miss. State Dept. Health, Jackson, 1981—; trainer sudden infant death project Miss. State Dept. Health, Jacksonville, 1981-85, dir. Domestic Violence Shelter statewide, 1985-93, cons. sexual assault crisis, 1985-93, cons. addiction and pregnancy, 1993—; rsch. asst. Geriatric Edn. Ctr., Jackson, 1990-93; pres., co-founder Born Free of Miss., Inc., Jackson, 1993—; trainer Age Quake '21, 17 southeastern states, 1991-93; trainer, support worker, phone worker Contact Teleministry, 1985-95; trainer Magic of Conflict, 1989—; co-founder Miss. Advocates for Victims of Crime, 1985-87; conf. planner and experiential trainer on various topics; trainer Red Cross HIV/AIDS prevention statewide, 1989—. Mem. Nat. Mus. Women, Washington, 1989—, Nat. Resource Ctr. for Women, 1990—. Mem. ACLU, Miss. Conf. on Social Welfare (legis. chair 1990-92), Cert. Pub. Mgrs., Miss. Puppetry Guild (sec. 1989—). Home: 4517 Kings Hwy Jackson MS 39206

BAKER, GERALDINE E., artist; b. Ennis, Tex., May 17, 1925; d. Benjamin and Lorene Saylors; m. Daniel Arthur Baker; children: Rebecca Ann Rhoads, Daniel Arthur II. BA, U. Tex., 1946. 1st regional dir. Tex. Fine Arts, Austin, 1975-76; fine arts chairwoman Woman's Club Houston, 1976; assoc. mem. Nat. Mus. of Women in the Arts, Washington, 1994, Washington Watercolor Soc., 1994-95. Author of poems. tchr. of bible moderators Women of Grace Presbyn. Ch., Houston, 1974-76, life mem., 1976; organist Trinity (Tex.) Presbyn. Ch., 1982-88. Mem. AF-PEO (sec. 1996), Calligraphy Guild. Republican.

BAKER, GERRY LYNNE, public relations executive. BA, Calif. State U., Fullerton. Account mgr. Les Goldberg PR, sr. account mgr., 1990-91; founder, pres. Gerry Lynne Pub. Rels., Huntington Beach, Calif., 1992—. Office: Gerry Lynne Pub Rels 17888 Hawes Ln Huntington Beach CA 92647-7014*

BAKER, GINGER LEE, oncological/cardiac nurse; b. East Chicago, Ind., June 6, 1944; d. William Lester and Edith (Craig) Savitz; m. Ray Baker, Aug. 5, 1988; children: Darcey, Eric, Ronald, Donald, Scott, Angela, Cody, Casey. Assocs., Purdue U., 1983; BSN, U. Phoenix, 1994. Cert. oncology nurse. Staff nurse St. Catherine Hosp., East Chicago; staff coord. Riverside (Calif.) Community Hosp., now shift coord. Recipient Women of Achievement award YWCA, 1987, ACE award, 1994. Mem. Oncology Nursing Soc., ACLS.

BAKER, GWENDOLYN CALVERT, United Nations official; b. Ann Arbor, Mich., Dec. 31, 1931; m. James Baker; children: JoAnn, Claudia, James Jr. BA, U. Mich., 1964, MA, 1968, PhD, 1972. Tchr. Ann Arbor Pub. Schs., 1964-69; lectr. U. Mich., 1969-70, instr., 1970-72, assoc. prof., 1972-76, dir. affirmative action programs, 1976-78; chief minorities and women's programs Nat. Inst. Edn., Washington, 1978-84; v.p., dean, graduate and children's programs Bank St. Coll. Edn., N.Y.C., 1981-84; nat. exec. dir. YWCA of USA, N.Y.C., 1984-93; pres., CEO U.S. Com. for UNICEF, N.Y.C., 1993—. *

BAKER, HELEN DOYLE PEIL, realtor; b. Los Angeles, June 26, 1943; d. James Cyril and Jacqueline (White) Doyle; m. Gary Edward Peil, Aug. 5, 1967 (dec. May 6, 1969); children: Andrea Christine, Kevin Doyle; m. Nathaniel W. Baker, Jr., Jan. 1, 1971 (div. July 23, 1983). AA, Santa Monica Coll., 1963; postgrad., U. Wash., 1963-64. Licensed real estate agent; cert. domestic violence counselor. Sales, mgmt. trainee Saks Fifth Ave., Beverly Hills, Calif., 1958-63; flight attendant Am. Airlines, Los Angeles, 1964-67; realtor, assoc. Stapleton Assocs., Honolulu, 1978-80; realtor Dolman Assocs. Inc., Kailua, Hawaii, 1980-87; loan rep. Honolulu Mortgage Co., Kailua, 1986-87; pres., owner, realtor Helen Baker Properties, Inc., Honolulu, 1987-93; v.p. Internat. Property Investment, Inc., Honolulu, 1993-94; owner Property Investment Internat., 1994—; pres. Global Listing Svc. Hawaii Inc., 1990—. Dir. Kailua Community Coun., 1987-91; pres., v.p., sec. Aikahi Community Assn., Kailua, 1980-85; vol. Am. Cancer Soc., Heart Assn. Schs., Kailua, 1971-86; adv. spouse abuse shelter, 1995—. Mem. Nat. Assn. Realtors, Hawaii Assn. Realtors, Honolulu Bd. Realtors, Real Estate Brokerage Council, Realtors Nat. Mktg. Inst., Hist. Hawaii Found., C. of C., Rotary. Office: Property Investment Internat PO Box 37066 Honolulu HI 96837-0066

BAKER, HELEN MARIE, health services executive; b. Tulsa, Oct. 12, 1946; d. Joseph Donald and Caroline Emma (Nelson) Waldhelm; m. Lewis Edward Browder, 1964 (div. 1966); m. Lawrence Selden Baker, Nov. 23, 1978; children: Lawrence Nelson, Marjorie Lyn. Student, U. Tex., 1965-66. Staff asst. to pres. White House, Washington, 1970-73; v.p. Mgmt., Systems, Sales, Inc., Washington, 1973-74, Inter-Am. Svcs., Inc., Washington and Tex., 1974-83; v.p. Med. Diversified Svcs. Inc., San Antonio, 1983-90, exec. v.p., 1990-92, also bd. dirs., pres., CEO, 1992—. Editor newsletter Physician and Family, 1983-86. Elder St. Andrew Presbyn Ch., San Antonio, 1986-89; sponsor San Antonio Symphony. Mem. San Antonio Mus. Assn. (sponsor), Club of Sonterra. Republican. Office: Med Diversified Svcs 15600 San Pedro Ave Ste 107 San Antonio TX 78232-3738

BAKER, JOSEPHINE L. REDENIUS (MRS. MILTON G. BAKER), minister, civic leader, retired career officer, former public relations company executive; b. Oceanville, N.J., Aug. 31, 1920; d. Jacob and Josephine (Palmer) Redenius. Student, Columbia U., 1948-49, L.I. U., 1957-58, George Washington U., 1947-48; grad., U.S. Army Indsl. Coll., 1962; MA in Journalism, Am. U., 1963; LHD, Temple U., 1964; MA in Religious Studies, St. Charles Sem., 1981; MDiv., Eastern Baptist Theol. Sem., 1984; D Ministry, Ea. Bapt. Theol. Sem., 1990. Ordained Deacon Episcopal Ch. Enlisted as pvt. WAAC, 1943; advanced through grades to lt. col. U.S. Army, 1963; col. Pa. N.G., 1967; intelligence officer atomic installations throughout U.S. and Can., 1943-53; asst. office chief of staff Army Forces Far East, Japan, 1953-56; pub. info. officer Office Chief of Info., Washington, 1958-61; chief Women's Army Corps recruiting U.S. Army, 1962-66, U.S. Army Command info liaison officer, 1966-67, ret., 1967; dir. pub. rels. and devel. Valley Forge Mil. Acad. and Coll., Wayne, Pa., 1967-71, bd. trustees, 1970-79, 93—, chair pers. and benefits, 1993—; pres. St. Cornelius the Centurian Chapel Valley Forge Mil. Acad. and Jr. Coll., Wayne, Pa., 1976—; pres. Potential Inc., Ardmore, Pa., 1979-83, Intercounty Trading Co., Inc., Surfside, Fla., 1976-80; with missionary Women to Women Fedn. Mission to No. China, 1993. Deacon All Souls' Episcopal Ch., Miami Beach, Fla., 1987-93; bd. dirs. Valley Forge Freedom Valley dist. Girl Scouts Am., Republican Women of Pa., Opera Guild of Miami; dir. St. Anne's Home for Women, Phila.; v.p. Episcopal Ch. Women, Diocese of Pa., 1982-84; pres. Episcopal Women, Diocese of S.E. Fla., 1990-93, mem. exec. bd., 1990-93; bd. dirs. Duncan Conf. Ctr, 1990-93, Delray Beach, Fla.; dr. of ministry All Saints Episcopal Ch., Norristown, Pa., 1993—. Decorated Legion of Merit, Pa. Meritorious Service medal; U.S. Army Commendation medal with oak leaf cluster; recipient Order Golden Sword Valley Forge Mil. Acad., 1986, Martha Washington medal S.R., 1990; named Disting. Alumnus Am. U., 1969. Mem. AAUW, Pub. Rels. Soc. Am., Am. Personnel and Guidance Assn., Am. Coll. Personnel Assn., Nat. Vocat. Guidance Assn., Am. Sch. Counselors Assn., Pa. Med. Missionary Soc. (dir. 1983-89), Am. Legion Aux., Ret. Officers Assn. (v.p. Valley Forge chpt. 1993—), Assn. U.S. Army (Anthony J. Drexel Biddle medal 1968), Army-Navy Union, Assn. Measurement and Evaluation in Guidance, Am. Legion, La Boutique Des Hult Chapeaux et Quarante Femmes, Emergency Aid of Pa., Women in Communications, Soc. of St. Francis (3d order), Ret. Officers Assn. (dist. v.p., 1993—), Mil. Order World Wars, Miami Heart Inst. Aux., Miami Heart Instl. Rev. Bd., Surf Club, Bald Peak Colony Club, Miami Beach Women's Club, Miami Beach Garden Club (chaplain), St. David's Golf Club, Acorn Club.

BAKER, KANDRA See INGA, KANDRA JOYCE

BAKER, KATHERINE JUNE, elementary school educator, minister; b. Dallas, Feb. 3, 1932; d. Kirk Moses and Katherine Faye (Turner) Sherrill; m. George William Baker, Jan. 30, 1955; children: Kirk Garner, Kathleen Kay. BS, BA, Tex. Women's U., 1953, MEd, 1979; cert. in religious edn., Meadville Theol. U., 1970; postgrad., North Tex. State U., 1987—; DD (hon.), Am. Fellowship Ch., 1981. Cert. elem. and secondary tchr., adminstr., Tex.; lic. and ordained min. Kingsway Internat. Ministries, 1991. Mgr. prodn. Woolf Bros., Dallas, 1953-55; display mgr. J.M. Dyer and Co., Corsicana, Tex., 1954; advt. artist Fair Dept. Store, Ft. Worth, 1954-56; artist, instr. Dutch Art Gallery, Dallas, 1960-65; dir. religious edn. 1st Unitarian Ch., Dallas, 1967-69; dir. day care, tchr. Richardson (Tex.) Unitarian Ch., 1971-73; dir. camp Tres Rios YWCA, Glen Rose, Tex., 1975-76; dir. program of extended sch. instrn. Hamilton Park Elem. Sch. Richardson Ind. Sch. Dist., 1975-78, tchr. Dover Elem. Sch., 1979-92, tchr. Jess Harben Elem. Sch., 1979-92; founder ednl., editorial and arts/evang. assn. Submitted Ministries, Richardson, 1992—; dir. Flame Fellowship Internat., 1987—, state rep., 1994—. Contbr. articles to ch. newspaper, 1967-69; exhibited in group show at Tex. Art Assn., 1966; one-woman show Dutch Art Gallery - Northlake Ctr., Dallas, 1965. Advocate day care Unitarian Universalist Women's Fedn., Boston, 1975-76, mem. nominating com., 1976-77. Mem. NEA, ASCD, Nat. Coun. Social Studies, Tex. State Tchrs. Assn. (treas. Richardson chpt. 1984-85), Women's Ctr. Dallas, Sokol Athletic Ctr., Smithsonian Assn., Dallas Mus. Assn., Alpha Chi, Delta Phi Delta (pres. 1952-53), Phi Delta Kappa. Home: 2711 Sherrill Park Dr Richardson TX 75082-3217

BAKER, KATHY WHITTON, actress; b. Midland, Tex., June 8, 1950. Appearences include (theatre) Fool for Love, 1983 (Obie award 1983, Theatre World award 1984), Desire Under the Elms, 1984, Aunt Dan and Lemon, 1986, (films) The Right Stuff, 1983, Street Smart, 1987 (Nat. Soc. Film Critics Best Supporting Actress award 1987), Permanent Record, 1988, A Killing Affair, 1988, Clean and Sober, 1988, Jacknife, 1989, Dad, 1989, Mr. Frost, 1989, Edward Scissorhands, 1990, Article 99, 1992, Jennifer 8, 1992, Mad Dog and Glory, 1993, (TV movies) Nobody's Child, 1986, The Image, 1990, One Special Victory, 1991, (TV series) Picket Fences, 1992— (Emmy award Outstanding Lead Actress in a Drama Series, 1993, 1995, Golden Globe award, Best Actress in a TV Drama Series, 1994). Office: ICM Tracey Jacobs 8942 Wilshire Blvd Beverly Hills CA 90210*

BAKER, LILLIAN L., author, historian, artist, lecturer; b. Yonkers, N.Y., Dec. 12, 1921; m. Roscoe A. Baker; children: Wanda Georgia, George Riley. Student, El Camino (Calif.) Coll., 1952, UCLA, 1968, 77. Continuity writer Sta. WINS, N.Y.C., 1945-46; columnist, free-lance writer, reviewer Gardena (Calif.) Valley News, 1964-76; free-lance writer, editor Gardena, 1971—; lectr. in field; founder, editor Internat. Club for Collectors of Hatpins and Hatpin Holders, bi-monthly newsletter Points, ann. Pictorial Jour., 1977—, conv. and seminar coord., 1979, 82, 84, 87, 90, 92. Author: Collector's Encyclopedia of Hatpins and Hatpin Holders, 1976, third printing, 1993, 100 Years of Collectible Jewelry 1850-1950, 1978, rev. edit., 1986, 88, 89, 91, 92, 94, Art Nouveau and Art Deco Jewelry, 1980, rev. edit. 1985, 87, 88, 90, 91, The Concentration Camp Conspiracy: A Second Pearl Harbor, 1981 (Scholarship Category award of Merit, Conf. of Calif. Hist. Socs. 1983), Hatpins and Hatpin Holders: An Illustrated Value Guide, 1983, rev. edit. 1988, 90, 91, 94, Creative and Collectible Miniatures, 1984, rev., 1991, Fifty Years of Collectible Fashion Jewelry: 1925-1975, 1986, rev. edit., 1988, rev., 1991, 94, Dishonoring America: The Collective Guilt of American Japanese, 1988, American and Japanese Relocation in World War II: Fact Fiction and Fallacy, 1989 (Pulitzer prize nomination, George Washington Honor medal Freedom Found., 1991), rev. edit., 1991, The japanning of America: Redress and Reparations Demands by Japanese-Americans, 1991, 20th Century Fashionable Plastic Jewelry, 1992, revised 1994, 95, The Common Doom, 1992, Dishonoring America: The Falisfication of World War II History, 1995; established The Lillian Baker Collection Hoover Archives, 1989; author poetry; contbg. author Vol. VII Time-Life Encyclopedia of Collectibles, 1979; numerous radio and TV appearances. Co-founder Ams. for Hist. Accuracy, 1972, Com. for Equality for All Draftees, 1973; chair S. Bay election campaign S.I. Hayakawa, for U.S. Senator from Calif., 1976; witness U.S. Commn. Wartime Relocation, 1981, U.S. Senate Judiciary Com., 1983, U.S. Ho. Reps. Judiciary Com., 1986, U.S. Ho. Reps. Subcommittee on Appropriations, 1989; guest artist U.S. Olympics, 1984. Recipient award Freedoms Found., 1971, George Washington Honor medal, 1989, Ann. award Conf. Calif. Hist. Socs., 1983, monetary award Hoover Instn. Stanford (Calif.) U., 1985, award Pro-Am. Orgn., 1987, Golden Poet award Internat. Poets Soc., 1989, Editor's Choice award for outstanding achievement in poetry Nat. Libr. Poetry, 1994. Fellow Internat. Biog. Assn. (life); mem. Nat. League Am. Pen Women, Nat. Writers Network, Nat. Writers Club, Soc. Jewelry Historians U.S.A. (charter), Art Students League N.Y. (life), Nat. Historic Soc. (founding), Nat. Trust for Historic Preservation (founding), Ams. for Hist. Accuracy (co-founder), World War II Nat. Commemorative Assn. (adv. bd. 1993-95), The Ctr. for Civilian Internee Rights Inc. (hon.), other orgns. Home and Office: 15237 Chanera Ave Gardena CA 90249

BAKER, LINDA SUE, elementary foreign language educator; b. Poplar Bluff, Mo., June 3, 1960; d. Walter Vesper and Mary Jane (Weber) B. BA, Southwest Bapt. U., 1982; MA, Southwestern Bapt. Theol. Sem., 1985; MEd, U. Ctrl. Okla., 1995. Tchr. elem. fgn. lang. Bartlesville (Okla.) Ind. Sch. Dist. #30, 1992—. Acteens dir. Highland Park Bapt. Ch., Bartlesville, 1993—, vol. ESL tchr., 1993—. NEH/OSU grantee, Stillwater, Okla., 1993-94, Bartlesville Profl. Devel. grantee, 1993, 94. Mem. NEA, Am. Assn. Tchrs. Spanish and Portuguese, Okla. Edn. Assn., Okla. Elem. Fgn. Tchrs. Assn. (treas. 1993—), Okla. Fgn. Lang. Tchrs. Assn., Bartlesville Edn. Assn., Kappa Delta Pi. Home: PO Box 1464 Bartlesville OK 74005-1464 Office: Will Rogers 4620 E Frank Phillips Blvd Bartlesville OK 74006-8418

BAKER, LORI ANN, physical therapist; b. Detroit, July 16, 1957; d. Richard Gary and Mary Barbara (Vail) Griffith; m. Joseph Kurtyka, Nov. 22, 1980 (div. Sept. 1984); m. William Randall Baker, June 24, 1989; 1 child, Katherine Elisabeth Baker. BS, U. Mich., 1979; MBA, Kennesaw Coll., 1990. Phys. therapist Lansing Sch. Dist., Mich., 1979-81, Mich. Sch. for Blind, 1980-81, Ingham Med. Ctr., 1980-81; pediatric phys. therapist Toledo Hosp., 1981-84, Childrens Ortho Hosp. and Med. Ctr., Seattle, 1984-85; pediatric clin. specialist Kennestone Hosp., Marietta Ga., 1985-89, supr. acute care therapy, 1989-90; phys. therapist Am. Home Health Care, 1987-91; contract phys. therapist, 1990-91; clin. mgr. Atlanta Rehab. Inst., 1991-95; phys. therapist Grandview Health Care Ctr., Atlanta, 1995—, Lumpkin County Schs., Atlanta, 1995—, Global Rehab., 1996—. Mem. Am. Phys. Therapy Assn., Neurodevelopmental Treatment Assn. Avocations: stained glass; furniture refinishing, running, biking. Home: 402 Wild Hill Rd Woodstock GA 30188-1972 Office: 340 W Peachtree St NW Ste 250 Atlanta GA 30308-3517

BAKER, LUCY, artist; b. Wellesley, Mass., Feb. 24, 1955; m. Kenworth William Moffett, Apr. 15, 1983 (div. 1990); 1 child; 1 stepdaughter. BFA, Goddard Coll., 1975; cert. welding, Platt Tech., 1977. Represented by Galerie Gerald Piltzer, Paris. Contbr. to book New, New, Painting, 1992; one woman exhbns. include Waltham (Mass.) Studios, 1981-84, Babson Coll., Wellesley, Mass, 1983, Shippee Gallery, N.Y.C., 1987, Fine art 2000, Stamford, Conn., 1996; group exhbns. include Grand Palais, Paris, 1993, Chgo. Art Fair, 1993, 94, Musee des Beaux-Arts, Charleroi, Belgium, 1993, The Nice (France) Mus., 1993, Stadtische Galerie Goppingen, Ger., 1993, F.I.A.C. French Art Fair, Paris, 1993, N.Y. Art Fair, 1994, Espace Tour Eiffel, Paris, 1994, Salander-O'Reilly Gallery, N.Y.C., 1994 Gallery Gallery-ism, Seoul, South Korea, 1995, Robert Vanderleelei, Alberta, Can., 1996, Galerie Piltzer, Paris, 1996, Fine Art 2000, 1996. Mem. Boston Painters and Sculptors (pres.). Home and Studio: 98 Old Long Ridge Rd Stamford CT 06903

BAKER, LYNNE RUDDER, philosophy educator; b. Atlanta, Feb. 14, 1944; d. James Maclin and Virginia (Bennett) Rudder; m. Thomas B. Baker III, Feb. 1, 1969. BA, Vanderbilt U., 1966, MA, 1971, PhD, 1972; student, Johns Hopkins U., 1967-68. Asst. prof. philosophy Mary Baldwin Coll., Staunton, Va., 1972-76; asst. prof. philosophy Middlebury (Vt.) Coll., 1976-79, assoc. prof., 1979-84, prof., 1984-94, acting dean arts and humanities, 1982, chairperson humanities divsn., 1982-85, acting chairperson philosophy, 1986-87; prof. U. Mass., Amherst, 1989—, dir. philosophy grad. program,

1994—; mem. panel to select summer seminars NEH, Washington, 1982, mem. panel to select fellows, 1989-90. Author: Saving Belief: A Critique of Physicalism, 1988, Explaining Attitudes: A Practical Approach to the Mind, 1995; contbr. scholarly articles to profl. jours. Trustee Vanderbilt U., Nashville, 1969-70, mem. alumni bd. dirs., 1985-89. Mellon fellow, 1974, NEH fellow, 1983-84, Nat. Humanities Ctr. fellow, 1982-83, Woodrow Wilson Internat. Ctr. for Scholars fellow, 1988-89. Mem. Am. Philos. Assn. (program com. 1983, exec. com. 1992-95), Soc. for Philosophy and Psychology, Soc. Christian Philosophers (exec. com. 1992-95), Soc. Women in Philosophy, Phi Beta Kappa. Democrat. Episcopalian. Office: U Mass Dept Philosophy Amherst MA 01003

BAKER, MARY ALICE, communication educator, consultant; b. Stuart, Okla., Sept. 9, 1937; s. James Roy and Emma M. (Bird) B. BS, U. Okla., 1959, MA in Speech, 1966; PhD in Communication, Purdue U., 1983. Speech and debate tchr. SE High Sch., Oklahoma City, 1959-65; instr. Ea. Ill. U., Charleston, 1966-69; assoc. prof. Lamar U., Beaumont, Tex., 1966-75, 78—, dir. forensics, 1969-75, Regents' Merit prof., 1984, pres. faculty senate, 1986-88. Contbr. articles to profl. jours. David Ross fellow, 1977. Mem. Tex. Speech Communication Assn. (regional rep. 1978-88), Speech Communication Assn. Am., Tex. Assn. Coll. Tchrs. (regional v.p. 1985—, pres.-elect 1988-89, state pres. 1989-90), Tex. Forensics Assn. (pres. 1974), Internat. Communication Assn., Zeta Phi Eta, Alpha Delta Pi. Democrat. Episcopalian. Avocations: reading, politics, travel. Office: Lamar U Dept Communication Beaumont TX 77710

BAKER, MARY ANN, software project administrator; b. Coffeyville, Kans., Aug. 8, 1957; d. Earl D. and Lois L. (Benning) B. BS, St. Edward's U., Austin, Tex., 1979, MBA, 1994. Cert. project mgr. Software engr. Boeing Computer Svcs., Wichita, Kans., 1979-81, Martin Marietta, Denver, 1981-84, Tracor Aerospace, Austin, 1984-89; software project mgr. Wayne, Austin, 1989-93, Tracor Aerospace, Austin, 1993—. Treas. Hidden Valley Water Coop., Austin, 1994-95. Recipient Cert. of Leadership, Univ. YWCA, Austin, 1987-88; named to Outstanding Young Women of Am., 1988. Mem. LWV, Soc. Women Engrs. (sec. 1994-95), Assn. Old Crows, Delta Mu Delta. Roman Catholic. Office: Tracor Aerospace 6500 Tracor Ln Austin TX 78725

BAKER, MEGAN LOUISE, gifted education educator; b. West Covina, Calif., July 16, 1963; d. Byron Eugene and Margery Ann (Norcross) B.; m. Frederick Ernest Urben II, July 6, 1991. BA in History, U. Colo., 1985; MA in Polit. Sci., Purdue U., 1986; postgrad. cert., Colo. State U., 1988. Cert. tchr., Wash. Tchr. gifted humanities and social studies Sumner (Wash.) Jr. H.S., 1988-92; tchr. math. and social studies Nova Sch., Lacey, Wash., 1992—. Alto Tacoma Civic Chorus, 1992—. Mem. Nat. Coun. Tchrs. Math., Nat. Coun. Social Studies, Nat. Assn. Gifted Children, N.W. Gifted Child Assn. (sec. 1992-94), Wash. Assn. Educators Talented and Gifted (rep. to bd. 1993-94, Tchr. of Yr. 1994). Democrat. Presbyterian. Office: Nova Sch 5610 30th Ave SE Lacey WA 98503-3849

BAKER, PAMELLA BLYTHE, elementary education educator; b. Talladega, Ala., Sept. 28, 1950; d. Waldon Casey and Glenda (Horton) Blythe; m. Dale H. Baker, May 26, 1973; 1 child, Leslie Dale. BA, U. Montevallo, Ala., 1990, MEd, 1992. Cert. in elem. edn., Ala. Elem. tchr. Pinecrest Elem. Sch., Sylacauga, Ala., 1990—. Mem. Sylacauga Beautification Coun., 1985—; mem. Sylacauga Arts Coun., 1985—; active Girl Scouts, Sylacauga, 1982-84; vol. Leukemia Assn., Ala., 1980—; dir. youth choir Bapt. Ch. Mem. NEA, Ala. Edn. Assn., Sylacauga Tchrs. Assn., Nat. Sci. Tchrs. Assn., Phi Delta Kappa. Home: 2006 Arrowhead Dr Sylacauga AL 35150-1732 Office: Pinecrest Elem Sch 615 Coaling Rd Sylacauga AL 35150-8744

BAKER, REBECCA LOUISE, musician, music educator, consultant; b. Covina, Calif., Apr. 12, 1951; d. Allan Herman and Hazel Margaret (Maki) Flaten; m. Jerry Wayne Baker, Dec. 22, 1972; children: Jared Wesley, Rachelle LaDawn, Shannon Faith. Grad. high sch., Park River, N.D.; student, Trinity Bible Inst., 1968-69. Sec. Agrl. Stblzn. & Conservation Svc. Office, Park River, N.D., 1969; pianist, singer Paul Clark Singers & Vic Coburn Evangelistic Assn., Portland, Oreg., 1969-72; musician, singer Restoration Ministries Evangelistic Assn., Richland, Wash., 1972-80; musician, pvt. instr. Calvary Temple Ch., Shawnee, Okla., 1980-81; organist, choirmaster St. Francis Episcopal Ch., Tyler, 1984-87; co-founder, owner Psalmist Sch. of Music & Recording Studio, Whitehouse, 1983—; pianist/entertainer Willowbrook Country Club, Tyler, Tex., 1991—; pianist, vocalist Mario's Italian Restaurant, Tyler, 1994—; pianist Garner Ted Armstrong, Tyler, 1986—; pianist, dir. Children's Choir, Calvary Bapt. Ch., Tyler, 1987—; pianist, entertainer Ramada Hotel, Tyler, 1988-90; pianist Whitehouse (Tex.) Sch. Dist. choirs, 1988—; accompanist Tyler Area Children's Chorale, 1988-90, Univ. Interscholastic League; pvt. instr. keyboard and vocal. Composer: Religious Songs (12 on albums), 1979; pianist, arranger, prodr., rec. artist 6 albums; editor, arranger: Texas Women's Aglow Songbook, 1987; editor Shekinah Glory mag., 1989—; developer improvisational piano course; star, prodr. mus. religious spls. nat. syndicated for TV, 1995; played for receptions honoring Gov. George Bush and Congressman John Bryant. Performer, spkr. many charitable, civic and religious orgns., Tex. and U.S. including AAUW, Kiwanis Clubs; co-founder Psalmist Mins. Internat., 1988—; founder, pres. Christian Music Tchr.'s Assn., 1991; worship leader Mayor's Prayer Breakfast, Tyler, 1994. Mem. Women's Aglow Fellowship (music dir., spkr., performer at retreats and tng. seminars including reception honoring Tex. Gov. George W. Bush and Congressman John Bryant; starred in and produced two musical TV religious spls. aired on several Tex. channels 1995). Republican. Full Gospel. Home and Office: Psalmist Music & Recording PO Box 961 Whitehouse TX 75791-0961

BAKER, ROBIN MICHELE LESLIE, sales executive; b. Glendale, Calif., May 12, 1968; d. Robert and Bonnie Sue (Vold) B. BA in Polit. Sci., U. Calif., Berkeley, 1990. Exec. asst. Ronald Reagan Presdl. Found., Century City, Calif., 1988; on-air reporter Sta. KMIR-TV, Palm Desert, Calif., 1991; mktg. coord. Trimark Prodns., Santa Monica, Calif., 1991-92; dir. internat. sales & adminstrn. Rysher Entertainment, Burbank, Calif., 1992—; TV mktg. cons. Transp. Scis. Corp., L.A., 1991—. Vol. Children's Hosp., L.A., 1986; charter mem., organizer This Little Light Found., L.A., 1991—; mem. Jr. League, L.A., 1992—. Recipient Class I Gymnastics Champion award U.S. Gymnastics Found., 1980, Individual All Around Champion award Calif. Interscholastic Fedn., 1985, All Star award Women's Sports Found., 1986. Mem. Am. Film Market Assn. (sr.). Republican. Lutheran. Home: 8123 Tuscany Ave Playa Del Rey CA 90293 Office: Rysher Entertainment 3400 Riverside Dr #600 Burbank CA 91505

BAKER, ROSALYN, state legislator; b. El Campo, Tex., Sept. 20, 1946. BA, Southwest Tex. State U., 1968; student, U. Southwestern La., 1969. Lobbyist, asst. dir. Govt. Rels. Nat. Edn. Assn., Washington, 1969-80; owner, retail sporting goods store Maui, Hawaii, 1980-87; legis. aide to Hon. Karen Honita Hawaii Ho. of Reps., Honolulu, 1987, mem., 1989-93; Hawaii state senator, 1994—, majority leader, 1995—; vice-chair ways and means com.; mem. health, agrl. and labor com., comms. and pub. utilities; co-chair rules com. Hawaii State Dem. Conv., 1990, resolutions com. 1994. Del.-at-large Dem. Nat. Conv., 1984, 92; mem. exec. com. Maui County Dem. Com., 1986-88; vice chmn. Maui Svc. Area Bd. om Mental Health and Substance Abuse; active Am. Cancer Soc., Work Day Vol., Soroptimist Internat. Democrat. Home: PO Box 10394 Lahaina HI 96761-0394 Office: Hawaii State Senate State Capitol Honolulu HI 96813

BAKER, RUTH BAYTOP, music educator; b. Pittsfield, Mass., Nov. 6, 1908; d. Thomas Nelson and Lizzie (Baytop) B. BA, Oberlin (Ohio) Coll., 1933; BS in Music Edn., Oberlin Conservatory, 1934; MA, Columbia U., 1964, MEd, 1988. Cert. tchr., N.Y. Tchr. music Tillotson Coll., Austin, Tex., 1934-35, Winston-Salem (N.C.) Tchrs. Coll., 1935-37, Colonel Young Meml. Fedn., N.Y,.C., 1937-38, Livingstone Coll., Salisbury, N.C., 1938-39, Colonel Young Meml. Fedn., N.Y.C., 1939—. Sec.-treas. Colonel Young Meml. Found., N.Y.C., 1950—. Recipient Contbr. as Voice Tchr. award Mary Cardwell Dawson Art Guild, 1993, Cert. of Achievement, Afro Arts Cultureal Ctr., Inc., 1993. Mem. Nat. Assn. Tchrs. Singing, N.Y. Singing Tchrs. Assn., Associated Music Tchrs. League N.Y., Inc. Congregationalist. Office: Colonel Young Meml Found PO Box 475 301 W 125th St New York NY 10027

BAKER, RUTH HOLMES, retired secondary education educator; b. Tewksbury, Mass., July 8, 1922; d. William Angus and Anna Martha (Lynch) MacIntyre; m. William Otis Baker; children: Leigh Holmes Flannery, Bruce William, Christopher Doty, Douglas MacIntyre, Deborah Woodbury Black. BA, Tufts U., 1944; postgrad., U. Wyo., 1944-45, Union Theol. Sch., 1947-48, Columbia U., 1947-48. Cert. water safety instr. Instr. swimming ARC, Manchester-by-the-Sea, Mass., 1937-54, Wenham, Mass., 1954—; tchr., athletic dir. Shore Country Day Sch., Beverly, Mass., 1960-71, Gov. Dummer Acad., Byfield, Mass., 1972-79; tchr., coach Manchester-by-the-Sea H.S., Mass., 1980-83; bookstore and snack bar mgr. Pingree Sch., Hamilton, Mass., 1984—. Republican. Episcopalian. Home: 40 Cherry St Wenham MA 01984

BAKER, SARA ANN KONTOFF, environmental artist, art educator; b. Boston, Oct. 2, 1933; d. Julian and Rose (Kutnick) Kontoff; m. Elliot Baker, June 13, 1954; children: Andrea, Melanie, Jonathan. BA in English Lit., Boston U., 1954; MS in Visual Studies, MIT, 1986. Tchr. English, social studies high sch., Havre de Grace, Pt. Perry, Md., 1954-55; dir. recreation & art therapy Washingtonian Hosp., Jamaica Plain, Mass., 1968-69; founder, co-dir. Ctr. for Creative Living & Tuftonboro (N.H.) Playhouse, 1970-75; tchr. art Wellesley (Mass.) Jr. High Sch., 1973; asst. prof. art history Art Inst. Boston, 1984, 85—; sr. lectr. art Northeastern U., Boston, 1986—; lectr. art history Mt. Ida Coll., Newton, Mass. & Boston Archtl. Ctr., 1988, '89; cons. in field. One-woman shows include Painting, Galleria Sistina D'Arcie, Rome, Italy, 1978, Environ. Art, Gallery 355, Boston, 1981, Commn. for Neon Installation, Children's Mus., Boston, 1992, Matrix Gallery, Provincetown, 1993, Dean's Gallery, Sloan Sch., MIT, Boston, 1995. Apptd. by mayor to Planning & Advisory Com., Kenmore-Fenway, Boston, 1988; co-chair Kenmore Residents Assn., Boston, 1988—. Recipient Pres.'s prize in sculpture Cambridge (Mass.) Art Assn., 1972; finalistWestland Ave. Sculpture competition. Mem. Boston Visual Artists Union (fair practice com. 1973-85), Women Artists Boston (co-chair 1974-75), Boston Soc. Architecture (art & architecture com. 1988-96), Coll. Art Assn. Office: Boston Ctr for Arts 551 Tremont St Boston MA 02116

BAKER, SUSAN MARIE VICTORIA (ERDLEN), writer, artist; b. Phila., Pa., Aug. 30, 1961; d. John Joseph and Dorothy Phyllis (Dispensiere) Erdlen. BA in Liberal Arts/Comm., Rowan State Coll., 1983; postgrad., U. of Arts, Phila. Asst. editor Jersey Woman Mag., Marlton, 1983-85; advt. and editorial asst. Regal Communications, Moorestown, N.J., 1987-88; adminstrv. asst. Adams and Braverman Advt. Inc., Phila., 1989-90, Rosanio, Bailets & Talamo Inc., Cherry Hill, N.J., 1990-92; pub. rels. and publs. cons. Roger Williams U., Providence; art critic, columnist Newport/Providence/Boston Chronicle; jeweler-crafter and healing artist. Author 3 books; songwriter; art editor Avant mag., 1981; contbr. poetry to various publs.; composer numerous songs. Active animal rights and environ. activities; mem. Newport Cultural Arts Alliance. Recipient awards for poetry.

BAKER, TERRIE LEE, newspaper publisher; b. Clinton, Ill., Feb. 2, 1961; d. Richard Lynn and Connie Lee (Roethe) Smith; m. Bryan R. Baker, Sept, 5, 1981; 1 child, Alison Bryanne. From sales rep. to gen. mgr. Clinton Daily Jour., 1979-88; publisher News Media Corp./Clinton Daily Jour., 1988—. Bd. dirs. Clinton Unit Sch. Dist. #15, 1995—. Mem. Clinton C. of C. (pres. 1995, treas. 1987), Rotary. Home: 55 Hilltop Drive Clinton IL 61727 Office: Clinton Daily Jour Rt 54 W Clinton IL 61727

BAKER-HINTON, SANDRA JONES, artist, audio and video consultant; b. Kingsport, Tenn., Apr. 5, 1943; d. William Edgar and Lola Treva (Carr) Jones; m. Jimmy Harold Baker (div. 1986); children: Eric Christopher, David William; m. Bruce Collins Hinton. BS in Art Edn., East Tenn. State U., Johnson City, 1965. Tchr. Walker County Dept. Edn., Rossville, Ga., 1963-68; founding mem., treas. In-Town Gallery, Chattanooga, 1975—; co-owner Chattanooga valley Audio, Rossville, 1990—; artist-in residence Chattanooga Sch. Arts and Scis., 1990, Big Ridge Elem. Sch., Chattanooga, 1990, O.N. Jonas Found., Whitfield County (Ga.) Schs., 1991-95; Dalton (Ga.) Creative Arts Guild, 1990-95. One-person shows at Hunter Mus. Art, Chattanooga, Kennedy-Douglas Fine Arts Ctr., Florence, Ala., Raintree Fine Arts Gallery, Chattanooga, 1988, Blue Cross-Blue Shield, 1991, Greater Visions Gallery, Nashville, 1993, Carroll Reece Mus., East Tenn. State U., Johnson City, 1993—; exhibited in group shows at In-Town Gallery, Chattanooga, Dalton (Ga.) Creative Arts Guild, 1990, Dimensions Gallery Sch. of Arts and Scis., Chattanooga, 1990, Tenn. Watercolor Soc., 1980, 88, 89, 92, 93, 95, 96, Ga. Watercolor Soc., 1981, 92, 93, So. Watercolor Soc., 1982, Virginia Beach (Va.) Boardwalk Show, 1987-94, Artstravaganza, Chattanooga, 1985-86, 88-89, 93-94, Southdown Fine Arts Biennial, Houma, La., 1988, Creative Arts Guild Show, Dalton, 1986-95, Dekalb Coun. for Arts, Atlanta, 1988, ART Sta. First Ann. Invitational, 1993-95, Art in Autumn CAL-TVA Exhibit, 1990-95, Ga. Watercolor Mem. Show, 1990, 91, 92, Festival of the Masters, Walt Disney World, 1991, Assn. Visual Arts Airport Show, 1992, 94, 95; represented in corp. collections. Bd. dirs. Chattanooga Prison Ministries, 1985-90; bd. mem. Gov.'s Grassroots Grant Program, Dalton, 1994-95; treas. In-Town Gallery, 1980-95. Recipient Purchase award Ga. Art Collection, 1981, Merit award Creative Arts Guild, Dalton, 1983, 85, 95, 1st and 2nd pl. Ann. Blue Cross-Blue Shield Show, 1989, 91, 92, 93, 1st pl. CAL Airport, 1995, 3rd and Meirt award CAL-TVA Exhibit, 1989, 2nd Pl. and Merit award 1991, 3rd Pl., 1993, Corp. Purchase award Creative Arts Guild Show, Dalton, 1989, Riverbend Com. Purchase award, Chattanooga, 1991, 3rd Pl. award ART Sta. Show, 1992. Mem. Tenn. Watercolor Soc. (pres. 1994-95, bd. dirs. 1994-96), Ga. Watercolor Soc. (regional dir. 1993-96), Assn. Visual Artists. Baptist. Home: 40 Cora Ann Dr Rossville GA 30741 Office: Chattanooga Valley Audio & Video Cons 40 Cora Ann Dr Rossville GA 30741

BAKER KNOLL, CATHERINE, state treasurer; b. Pitts.; d. Nicholas James and Theresa Mary (May) Baker; m. Charles A. Knoll Sr. (dec.); children: Charles A. Jr., Mina B., Albert B., Kim Eric. BS in Edn., Duquesne U., 1952, MS in Edn., 1973. Dir. western Pa. region Safety Adminstrn. Dept. Transp., Pitts., 1971-79; exec. dir. community svc. Dept. of Adminstrn., Allegheny County, Pa., 1980-88; treas. Pa. Treasury Dept., Harrisburg, 1988—; owner, operator pvt. bus. firm, Pitts., 1952-70. Mem. Pa. Dem. State Com., Pa. Fedn. Dem. Women, YMCA Bd., Pitts., Harrisburg, Duquesne U. Alumni Bd., Mom's House, Zontas Inc. Bd. Mem. Nat. Assn. State Treas., Women Execs. in State Gov., Coun. State Gov. (exec. com. ea. region). Roman Catholic. Office: Treasury Dept 129 Fin Bldg Harrisburg PA 17120*

BAKER-LIEVANOS, NINA GILLSON, jewelry store executive; b. Boston, Dec. 19, 1950; d. Rev. John Robert and Patricia (Gillson) Baker; m. Jorge Alberto Lievanos, June 6, 1981; children: Jeremy John Baker, Wendy Mara Baker, Raoul Salvador Baker-Lievanos. Student, Mills Coll., 1969-70; grad. course in diamond grading, Gemology Inst. Am., 1983; student in diamondtology designation, Diamond Coun. Am., 1986—. Cert. store mgr., Jewelers Cert. Coun., Jewelers Am. Artist, tchr. Claremont, Calif., 1973-78; escrow officer Bank of Am., Claremont, 1978-81; retail salesman William Pitt Jewelers, Puente Hills, Montclair, Calif., 1981-83, asst. mgr., 1983; mgr. William Pitt Jewelers, Puente Hills, Santa Maria, Calif., 1983-91, corp. sales trainer, 1988-89; sales and design specialist Merksamer Jewelers, Santa Maria, 1991; mgr. Merksamer Jewelers, San Luis Obispo, Calif., 1991-92, Santa Maria, Calif., 1992-94; diamond specialist cons. Merksamer Jewelers, Santa Maria, 1994-96; pres., ops. mgr. Dancer House Designs, Santa Maria, Calif., 1996—. Artist tapestry hanging Laguna Beach Mus. Art, 1974. Mem. Cen. Coast Pla. Adv. Bd., 1992. Recipient Cert. Merit Art Bank Am., 1968. Mem. NAFE, Internat. Platform Assn., Speaker's Bur., Santa Maria C. of C., Compassion Internat. Republican. Roman Catholic. Office: Dancer House Designs PO Box 5783 Santa Maria CA 93455

BAKER-ROELOFS, MINA MARIE, retired home economics educator; b. Holland, Mich., Mar. 1, 1920; d. Thomas and Fannie (DeBoer) Baker; m. Harold Eugene Roelofs, Aug. 16, 1985; children: Howard, Donald, Ann. BS, Iowa State U., 1942, MS, 1946; postgrad., Ariz. State U., 1965, Ind. State U., 1968, 76. Dietitian Annville (Ky.) Inst., 1942-45; chmn., tchr. home econs. Cen. Coll., Pella, Iowa, 1946-85, ret., 1985; mem. dean's grad. adv. coun. Iowa State U., Ames, 1955-56, coord. coop. plan, 1967-85. Editor: Dandy Dutch Recipes, 1991; co-editor: Pella Collectors Cookbook, 1982, A Taste of the World, 1992. Mem. com. Pell Hist. Soc. Grantee Govt. Cross-Cultural, 1974, NEH, 1980. Mem. AAUW, Am. Home Econ. Assn. (life), Iowa Home Econ. Assn. (pres. 1953-55, sec. 1979-81, Disting. Svc. award 1985), Iowa Elder Hostel Tchr. Ctrl. Coll. Aux., PEO Sisterhood, Women's Social and Literary Club (pres. 1990-92). Republican. Mem. Reformed Ch. Home: 229 Main St Pella IA 50219-2024

BAKKILA, MARTHA LOUISE, secondary education educator; b. Bridgeport, Conn., Apr. 18, 1942; d. Frederic Carter and Rosabelle Martha (Maki) Warner; m. Frank E. Lattin, July 3, 1968 (dec. 1981); m. Jalmer Oscar Bakkila, Dec. 18, 1982. BA in History, Marietta Coll., 1964; MS in Edn., Western Conn. State U., 1968, postgrad., 1977. Social studies tchr. Redding (Conn.) Sch., 1964-65, Bethel (Conn.) High Sch., 1966-75; reading tchr. Gulf High Sch., New Port Richey, Fla., 1977-85, 92—, reading resource specialist, 1985-92; presenter 4th Nat. Secondary Reading Conf., Orlando, Fla., 1993; participant Sta. WEDU-TV Educating Florida Blueprint 2000, Tampa, 1993. Named Outstanding Advisor Fla. Future Educators Am., 1990-91. Mem. AAUW (newsletter editor West Pasco br. 1981-95), ASCD, Internat. Reading Assn., Fla. Reading Assn., Fla. Secondary Reading Assn., Pasco County Reading Coun. (treas. 1981-82, 91-92), Delta Kappa Gamma, Alpha Gamma Delta. Home: 4242 Chipmunk Dr New Port Richey FL 34653-6433 Office: Gulf High Sch 5355 School Rd New Port Richey FL 34652-4322

BALABAN, EILEEN, advertising executive. Sr. v.p., CFO Chapman Direct Advt., N.Y.C. Office: Young & Rubicam Inc 285 Madison Ave New York NY 10017-6401*

BALABAN-PERRY, ELEANOR, retired advertising executive; b. Chgo., Sept. 2, 1914; d. Abraham and Anna (Gorindar) Balaban; m. Paul Noble Sutton, Mar. 1935 (div. 1940); m. Charles Edson Rose, June 1940 (div. 1960); m. William Perry Feb. 16, 1967 (dec. Sept. 1979); 1 child, Sydney Rose. BA, U. Wis., 1935; postgrad., U. Chgo., 1943, Loyola U., Chgo., 1991-92, Columbia Coll., 1990. Founder, CEO Elron, Chgo., 1949-61; mktg. exec. Roth Bros., Chgo., 1962-67; advt. dir. Carsons, Chgo., 1971-82; retired, 1982; curriculum chair Inst. for Learning in Retirement, 1993, coord., presenter, 1993-95. Mem. editl. bd. Inst. for Learning in Retirement Jour., 1993-96; editor: Renaissance Court Anthology 1-2-3, 1994-96, Keeping Our Heads On Straight, Journal Writing in the Golden Years, 1996; author numerous poems and short stories. Fund raising vol. The Childrens Home, Peoria, Ill., 1982; citizens com. People for Am. Way, Washington, 1988; pres. Friends of Renaissance Ct., Chgo., 1995-96. Recipient Honor award Cook County (Ill.) Sheriff, 1995, Ill. Cert. Lifetime Achievement, Women History, 1995. Mem. Am. Narcolepsy Assn.

BALAKIAN, ANNA, foreign language educator, scholar, critic, writer; b. Constantinople, Turkey, July 14, 1916; came to U.S., 1926; d. Diran and Kohar (Panosian) B.; m. Stepan Nalbantian, Dec. 15, 1945; children: Suzanne, Haig. B.A., Hunter Coll., 1936; M.A., Columbia U., 1938, Ph.D., 1943; L.H.D. (hon.), New Haven U., 1977. Mem. faculty Syracuse U.; prof. French and comparative lit. N.Y. U., 1955—, chmn. comparative lit. dept., 1978-86; vis. prof. City U. N.Y., State U. N.Y., Stony Brook; lectr. in numerous univs., including U. Oxford, Eng., College de France, Paris; producer ednl. radio broadcasts. Author: Literary Origins of Surrealism, 1947 (transl. into Spanish and Portugese), Surrealism: the Road to the Absolute (transl. into Japanese), 1959, 1986, The Symbolist Movement: a critical appraisal, 1967 (transl. into Spanish), Andre Breton: Magus of Surrealism, 1971 (transl. into Spanish), The Fiction of the Poet: from Mallarmé to the Post-Symbolist Mode, 1992; (essays) The Snowflake on the Belfry: Dogma and Disquietude in the Academic Arena, 1994; editor, chief contbr.: The Symbolist Movement in the Literature of European Languages, 1983; editor: André Breton Today, 1989; editor, translator: Eva the Fugitive (Rosamel del Valle), 1990; reviewer Saturday Rev., 1960-73; contbr. numerous articles on 19th and 20th century lit. to French, Am. and English scholarly jours., most recent on the problematics of modernism. Recipient Distinguished Scholar award Hofstra Faculty, 1975; Guggenheim fellow, 1969-70; Nat. Endowment grantee and cons., 1970-79; Am. Council Learned Socs. grantee; Internat. Research Exchange grantee. Mem. Am. Comparative Lit. Assn. (pres. 1977-82), Internat. Comparative Lit. Assn. (v.p. 1982-85), Am. Assn. Tchrs. French (nat. v.p. 1968-71), Modern Lang. Assn., PEN Club, Phi Beta Kappa. Mem. Armenian Apostolic Ch. Home: 16 Linden Ln Old Westbury NY 11568-1610 Office: 19 University Pl New York NY 10003-4501

BALAS, EDITH, art historian, educator; b. Cluj, Romania, June 20, 1929; came to U.S., 1967; s. Alexander and Klara (Rooz) Lövy; m. Egon Balas, Dec. 21, 1948; children—Anna Balas Waldron, Vera Balas Koutsoyannis. Lic. in philosophy C.I. Parhon U., Bucharest, 1952, diploma in philosophy, 1952; M.A., U. Pitts., 1970, Ph.D., 1973. Editor, Pub. House of the Acad., Bucharest, 1952-55; instr., lectr. C.I. Parhon U., 1955-58; tchr. Matei Basarab High Sch., Bucharest, 1958-66; instr. U. Pitts., 1975-77, research assoc., 1978—; assoc. prof. art history Carnegie Mellon U., Pitts., 1978-91, prof., 1991—. Author: Brancusi and Rumanian Folk Tradition, 1987, Michelangelo's Medici Chapel: A New Interpretation, 1995; contbr. articles to profl. jours. Fellow Andrew Mellon Found., 1972-73, 73-74, AAUW, 1971-73. Mem. Coll. Art Assn. Am. Home: 136 Beechwood Ln Pittsburgh PA 15206-4526

BALCH, NELDA CAROLINE, humanities educator; b. Kelley's Island, Ohio, July 13, 1916; d. Robert John and Lydia Amelia (Schnittker) K.; m. Donald Arthur Balch, Aug. 8, 1948 (dec. 1969). BA, Albion (Mich.) Coll., 1937; MA, U. Minn., 1938; student, Yale U., 1941, Northwestern U., 1946, U. Mich., Mich. State U., U. Oregon. Asst. prof. Simpson Coll., Indianola, Iowa, 1939-43, West Liberty (W.Va.) State Coll., 1946, Linfield Coll., McMinnville, Oreg., 1946-52; prof., chair Kalamazoo (Mich.) Coll., 1954-81, prof. non-traditional classes, 1981-85, dir., reader Faculty Readers, 1960-92, dir., reader Noontime Tales, 1985—, emeritus prof., 1981—. Author: The Kalamazoo College Festival Playhouse, contbr. articles to Notable Women in American Theatre, 1989; dir., playwright Noel Coward, 1989, Camille and Rodin, Gertrude Stein, Paula M. Becker, Mabeland; actress; featured in Emancipated Spirits, 1983. Founder, mng. dir. Festival Playhouse, Kalamazoo, 1964-81; active Friends of Art Ctr., Venice, Fla., 1990—, Kalamazoo Arts Coun., 1987—; Aero Club dir. ARC, Eng. and France, 1943-45. Recipient Cmty. Arts. Medal, Kalamazoo Arts Coun., 1985; tchg. fellow U. Minn., 1938-39; Nelda K. Balch Playhouse dedicated in her honor, 1981. Mem. Am. Assn. Univ. Women (former v.p.), Kalamazoo Art Inst., Phi Beta Kappa. Democrat. Methodist. Home: 1708-B Lake Pl Venice FL 34293

BALCOMB, MARY NELSON, design studio owner; b. Mich., Apr. 29, 1928; d. Andrew and Selma (Martin) Nelson; m. Robert S. Balcomb, July 3, 1948; children: Stuart V., Amis. AA, Am. Acad. Art, 1948; BFA cum laude, U. N.Mex., 1968; MFA, U. Wash., 1971. Advt. mgr. Broome Furniture Co., Albuquerque, 1949-55; designer Custom Interiors, Albuquerque, 1956-66; art tchr. Sandra Girls' Sch., Albuquerque, 1966-68; co-owner Woolcot, Inc., Bellevue, Wash., 1975-80; owner Balcomb Design Studio, Silverdale, Wash., 1981—. Author: Nicolai Fechin, 1975 (Rounce and Coffin award), Les Perhacs, Sculptor, 1975, William F. Reese, 1984 (Rounce and Coffin award), Robin-Robin/A Journal, 1995; contbr. articles to periodic jours. Creator Children's Art Ctr. Found., Seattle, 1972, bd. dirs., 1972-80. Recipient Painting award Frye Art Mus., 1994, Honorarium Prix de West Nat. Cowboy Hall of Fame, 1995. Mem. Author's Guild, Phi Kappa Phi, Lambda Rho. Home: PO Box 1922 Silverdale WA 98383*

BALDASSANO, CORINNE LESLIE, radio executive; b. N.Y.C., May 16, 1950; d. Nicholas and Olga (Phillips) Baldassano. BA cum laude, Queens Coll., CUNY, 1970; MA in Theatre, Hunter Coll., CUNY, 1975; MBA in Fin., NYU, 1986. Program dir., ops. mgr. Sta. KAUM-FM, Houston, 1977-79; dir. programming Sta. WSAI-FM, Cin., 1979-81; dir. programming ABC Contemporary and FM Radio Networks, N.Y.C., 1981-84; regional mgr. affiliate relations United Stations Radio Networks, N.Y.C., 1985-87; dir. ABC Entertainment Radio Network, N.Y.C., 1987-90; v.p. programming ABC Radio Networks, 1990-94; v.p. programming Unistar Radio Networks, L.A., 1994; v.p. programming SW Networks, N.Y.C., 1994-95, sr. v.p. of programming SW Networks, 1995—; guest lectr. Wharton Sch. Bus., Phila., 1983, St. John's U., N.Y.C., 1983-84; bd. dirs. Country Radio Broadcasters, Inc., Nashville, 1990—, chmn. agenda com., 1990. Alumni mem. Govs. Com. Scholastic Achievement, N.Y.C., 1984-85. Mem. NYU Bus. Forum (bd. dirs. 1988-91, v.p., treas. 1990-91), Internat. Radio and TV Soc. (planning com., faculty/industry seminar 1986, 87, chmn. Summer Fellowship Program 1988), Nat. Music Found. (N.Y. bd. 1992-93, 94—). Democrat. Roman Catholic. Avocations: travel, theatre, dancing, running, music. Office: SW Networks 1370 6th Ave New York NY 10019-4602

BALDAUF, JILL CHRISTINE, advertising executive; b. San Diego, Nov. 1, 1957; d. Thomas William and Janet Marie (Baxter) B. BA, UCLA, 1979, MBA, 1981. Asst. account exec. Benton & Bowles, N.Y.C., 1981-82; account exec. Ogilvy & Gatner, Los Angeles, 1982-83; v.p. mgmt. supr. Grey Advt., L.A., 1983-92; exec. v.p., mng. ptnr. Griffin Bacal Inc., N.Y.C., 1992—. Founder Profls. Against Cancer, L.A., 1988; bd. dirs. Am. Cancer Soc., L.A., 1987—; mem. fundraising com. Anderson Grad. Sch. Mgmt. UCLA, 1987, 88, mem. bd. visitors; mem. Jr. League, L.A., 1987—. Republican. Episcopal. Office: Griffin Bacal Inc 130 Fifth Ave New York NY 10011 Office: Griffin Bacal Inc 130 Fifth Ave New York NY 10011

BALDRIGE, LETITIA, writer, management training consultant; b. Miami Beach, Fla.; d. Howard Malcolm and Regina (Connell) B.; m. Robert Hollensteiner; children: Clare, Malcolm. BA, Vassar Coll., 1946; postgrad., U. Geneva, 1946-48; D.H.L. (hon.), Creighton U., 1979, Mt. St. Mary's Coll., 1980, Bryant Coll., 1987, Kenyon Coll., 1990. Personal-social sec. to amb. Am. Embassy, Paris, 1948-51; intelligence officer Washington, 1951-53; asst. to amb. Am. Embassy, Rome, 1953-56; dir. pub. rels. Tiffany & Co., 1956-60; social sec. The White House, 1961-63; pres. Letitia Baldrige Enterprises, Chgo., 1964-69; dir. consumer affairs Burlington Industries, 1969-71; pres. Letitia Baldrige Enterprises, Inc., N.Y.C. and Washington, 1972—. Author: Roman Candle, 1956, Tiffany Table Settings, 1958, Of Diamonds and Diplomats, 1968, Home, 1972, Juggling, 1976, Amy Vanderbilt's Complete Book of Etiquette, 1978, Amy Vanderbilt's Everyday Etiquette, 1979, Entertainers, 1981, Letitia Baldrige's Complete Guide to Executive Manners, 1985, Letitia Baldrige's Complete Guide to a Great Social Life, 1987, Complete Guide to the New Manners for the '90s, 1990, New Complete Guide to the Executive Manners, 1993, (novel) Public Affairs Private Relations, 1990; columnist Copley News Syndicate, New Choices, Mag.; contbg. editor Town & Country Mag. Adv. bd. Folger Shakespear Libr., Washington, Mt. Vernon Ladies Assn., Washington, Reading Is Fundamental, ARC History and Edn. Ctr. Republican.

BALDWIN, BETTY JO, computer specialist; b. Fresno, Calif., May 28, 1925; d. Charles Monroe and Irma Blanche (Law) Inks; m. Barrett Stone Baldwin Jr.; two daughters. AB, U. Calif., Berkeley, 1945. With NASA Ames Rsch. Ctr., Moffett Field, Calif., 1951-53, math tech. 14' Wind Tunnel, 1954-55, math analyst 14' Wind Tunnel, 1956-63, supr. math analyst Structural Dynamics, 1963-68, supervisory computer programmer Structural Dynamics, 1968-71, computer programmer Theoretical Studies, 1971-82, adminstrv. specialist Astrophys. Experiments, 1982-85, computer specialist, resource mgr. Astrophysics br., 1985—; v.p. B&B Baldwin Farms, Bakersfield, Calif., 1978—. Mem. IEEE, Assn. for Computing Machinery, Am. Geophys. Union, Am. Bus. Womens Assn. (pres., v.p. 1967, one of Top 10 Women of Yr. 1971). Presbyterian. Office: NASA Ames Rsch Ctr Mail Stop 245-6 Moffett Field CA 94035-1000

BALDWIN, DOROTHY LEILA, secondary school educator; b. Irvington, N.J., Feb. 28, 1948; d. Daniel Thomas and Lillian Frances (Wainright) B. BA, Kean Coll., Union, N.J., 1969, MA in Edn. and Humanities, 1971; EdD in Adminstrn. and Supervision, Seton Hall U., 1987, cert. reading specialist, 1979, cert. bus. adminstr., 1985. Tchr., reading coord. St. Paul Apostle Sch. Irvington, 1969-74; tchr. Summit (N.J.) Jr. High Sch., 1975-79; social studies coord. K-9, chmn. dept. 7-9 Summit Pub. schs., 1979-87; social studies supr. Livingston (N.J.) Pub. Schs., 1987; prin. Point Road Sch, Little Silver, N.J., 1987-89; dir. gifted edn. K-12 Clifton, N.J., 1989-90; prin. Sch. Two, Clifton, N.J., 1989-90, Deerfield Sch., Mountainside, 1990-92, Eisenhower Sch., Bridgewater-Raritan, N.J., 1992—; adj. prof. Montclair (N.J.) State Coll.; tchr. adult and community schs.; cons. in field; workshop coord. Author books; contbr. articles to profl. jours. PTA scholar, 1965. Mem. ASCD, Nat. Assn. Elem. Sch. Prins., Nat. Coun. Social Studies, Am. Assn. Sch. Adminstrs., N.J. Assn. Elem. Sch. Prins., Somerset County Assn. Elem. Sch. Prins., Phi Delta Kappa, Kappa Delta Pi. Home: 737 River Rd Chatham NJ 07928-1136 Office: Eisenhower Sch Bridgewater NJ 08807

BALDWIN, IRENE S., corporate executive, real estate investor; b. Dodge City, Kans., Sept. 8, 1939; d. Albert A. McMichael and Eleanor L. (Johnson) McMichael McGrath; m. Miles Edward Baldwin, June 30, 1961. BS, Friends U., 1961. Dress designer, Wichita, 1959-61; social worker Sedgwick County, Kans., 1963-65; owner motel chain, Kans., 1965—; comml. and agrl. real estate investor, 1971—; corp. sec.-treas. Baldwin, Inc., Kans., 1970—, fin. advisor, 1970—; pvt. practice fin. cons., Colby, Kans., 1975—; founder, advisor Charitable Found., Kans., 1980—. Fundraiser various charitable orgns., 1982—; pvt. placement of homeless animals, Kans. and Nebr., 1965—. Helped develop 1st artificial front leg for canines, 1985. Avocations: horseback riding, hiking, travel, sewing, drawing. Home and Office: 2320 S Range Ave Colby KS 67701-9056

BALDWIN, JANET SUE, library media specialist; b. McPherson, Kans., Feb. 15, 1951; d. Gerald William and Eleanor Elizabeth (Markham) Jackson; m. Gregory Lee Baldwin, Aug. 11, 1972; children: Ryan Gregory, Chase Jackson. BS in Edn., U. Kans., 1973. Cert. elem. edn. educator, libr. sci. Tchr. Eskridge (Kans.) Grade Sch., 1973-76; elem. tchr. Dover (Kans.) Grade Sch., 1976-81, libr., 1981-89; libr. media specialist Hudson Elem. & Belvoir Elem. Sch., Topeka, 1989-92, Crestview Elem. Sch., Topeka, 1992-96, New Meadows Elem. Sch., Topeka, 1996—; chpt. 1 storyteller Chase Mid. Sch., Topeka, summer 1992; computer instr. to tchrs. Summer Acad., Topeka, 1993; tchr. computers Bishop Elem. Sch., Topeka, summers 1994, 95. Mem. NEA, Kans. Reading Assn. (hospitality conf. co-chair 1992, membership com. chair 1995-96, Outstanding Kans. Reading Educator Topeka nominee 1994), Kans. Nat. Edn. Assn., Kans. Assn. Sch. Librs. Home: 551 NE Edgewood Dr Topeka KS 66617

BALDWIN, JANICE MURPHY, lawyer; b. Bridgeport, Conn., July 16, 1926; d. William Henry and Josephine Gertrude (McKenna) Murphy; m. Robert Edward Baldwin, July 31, 1954; children: Jean Margaret, Robert William, Richard Edward, Nancy Josephine. AB, U. Conn., 1948; MA, Mt. Holyoke Coll., 1950; postgrad. U. Manchester, Eng., 1950-51; MA, Fletcher Sch., Tufts U., 1952; JD, U. Wis., 1971. Bar: Wis. 1971, U.S. Dist. Ct. (we. dist.) Wis. 1971. Staff atty. Legis. Coun., State of Wis., Madison, 1971-74, 75-78, sr. staff atty., 1979-94; pvt. practice, Madison, 1994—; atty. adviser HUD, Washington, 1974-75, 78-79. Mem. AAUW, NOW, LWV (sec. Dane County 1996-97), U.S. Women's Polit. Caucus, Legal Assn. for Women, Dane County Bar Assn. (legis. com. 1980-81, long range planning com. 1990—, law for the pub. 1993-94), Wis. Bar Assn. (pres. govt. lawyers divsn. 1985-87, bd. govs. 1985-89, treas. 1987-89, participation of women in the bar com. 1987—, professionalism com. 1990—, bd. bar examiners review 1990-94, law-related edn. com. 1992-95, govt. lawyers divsn. 1981—), Wis. Women's Network, Wis. Women's Polit. Caucus, U. Wis. Univ. League, Older Women's League. Home and Office: 125 Nautilus Dr Madison WI 53705-4329

BALDWIN, KRISTA MICHELLE, management analyst; b. Washington, Aug. 21, 1968; d. Grover Cleveland and Judith Ann (McAuliffe) B. AA in Bus. Adminstrn., Charles County C. C., LaPlata, Md., 1988; BS in Bus. Adminstrn., Towson State U., 1990. Program analyst U.S. Govt. Printing Office, Washington, 1990-92, mgmt. analyst, 1992—. Office: US GPO Supt of Documents 710 N Capitol St NW Washington DC 20401

BALDWIN, LEONA B. (NONI BALDWIN), insurance agent; b. Portland, Jan. 18, 1934; d. Abram Martilla and Ida (Sophia) Heiskari; m. Walter Lee Baldwin, Jan. 26, 1953; children: Cathy Baldwin-Johnson, Keith Baldwin, Julie Baldwin, Amy Clifford. Student, Clark Jr. Coll., 1952-53. CLU, Chartered Fin. Cons., Life Underwriter Tng. Fellow. Sec. Bill Pottle, CLU, Anchorage, 1972-75; office mgr. Wilson & Baldwin, Anchorage, 1976-79; life ins. agt. N.Y. Life, Anchorage, 1979—. Mem. Nat. Assn. Life Underwriters (bd. trustees 1993—), Women Life Underwriters Confedn. (nat. pres. 1987-88, nat. edn. chmn. 1988-90, Nat. Woman of Yr. award 1990), So. Alaska Life Underwriters (pres. 1986-87), Anchorage Estate Planning Coun. (sec. 1991-92, v.p. 1992-93, pres. 1993-94), Am. Bus. Women (pres. Arctic Nugget chpt. 1980-81), Alaska Life Underwriters (pres. 1987-88, nat. committeeman 1990-93, Man of Yr. award 1987). Lutheran. Office: Baldwin Fin Concepts 2525 Blueberry Rd Ste 107 Anchorage AK 99503-2647

BALDWIN, LISA R., critical care nurse; b. Silverton, Oreg., Aug. 17, 1960; d. Roger W. Baldwin and Udene L. Allen. BSN, Walla Walla Coll., 1982; MS in Nursing, Oreg. Health Scis. U., 1991, post Masters cert. Cmty. Health Nursing, 1993, postgrad., 1993—. RN, Oreg. Staff nurse Providence Med. Ctr., Portland, Oreg., 1982—; asst. clin. mgr. ICU VA Med. Ctr., Portland, 1991-93, nurse educator critical care, 1994—; nurse mgr. Providence Med. Ctr., 1996—; tchg. asst. Oreg. Health Scis. U., Portland, 1992-94, 95-96, rsch. asst., 1994-96; mem. logical job analysis panel Nat. Coun. State Bds., Chgo., 1993, item writer, Princeton, N.J., 1993. U. Club Found. fellow, Portland, 1994. Mem. ACCN, Oreg. Health Decisions.

BALDWIN, MARYANN POWELL, school counselor, educator; b. Waterbury, Conn., Apr. 22, 1947; d. Harvey A. and Gracemary (Cizek) Stackman; m. Timothy H. Powell, July 26, 1969 (div. June 1983); 1 child, Lisa Anne Powell; m. Dennis A. Baldwin, Nov. 21, 1991. BA in Elem. Edn., Clemson U., 1969, MA in Guidance/Counseling, 1971; PhD in Edn., U. South Fla., 1979. Lic. mental health counselor, Fla. 1st grade tchr. Walhalla (S.C.) Elem. Sch., 1969-70, Ravenel Elem. Sch., Seneca, S.C., 1970-72; guidance counselor Twin Lakes Elem., Tampa, Fla., 1972-80; coll. placement specialist Acad. of Holy Name, Tampa, 1982-84; resource tchr. Plant High Sch., Tampa, 1984-85, guidance counselor, 1985-88; guidance counselor Middleton Jr. High Sch., Tampa, 1988-93, Van Buren Jr. High Sch., Tampa, 1993—; adj. instr. U. South Fla., Tampa, 1977—, Hillsborough C.C., Tampa, 1993—; counselor for migrants Summer Migrant Inst., Tampa, 1993—; pvt. practice therapy, Tampa, 1975—. Co-author: (manual) How to Set Up a Volunteer Tutoring Program, 1990. U. South Fla. Grad. Coun. fellow, 1975, 76; Kappa Kappa Gamma rehab. scholar Clemson U., 1969. Mem. ACA, Fla. Counseling Assn. (conv. sec. 1989), Hillsborough Counseling Assn. (recognition chair 1988-91, mental health liaison chair 1994—), Phi Delta Kappa. Home: 3215 Taragrove Dr Tampa FL 33618-2544 Office: Van Buren Jr High Sch 8715 N 22nd St Tampa FL 33604-2105

BALDWIN, VELMA NEVILLE WILSON, personnel consultant; b. Meade, Kans., Aug. 31, 1918; d. Charles Chester and Anna Velma (Neville) Wilson; m. Claude David Baldwin, Jan. 31, 1942 (dec. Nov. 1976). AB, U. Kans., 1940. Placement working students U. Kans., 1940-41; with War Dept., Washington, 1942-45; rsch asst. Dr. A.C. Kinsey, Ind. U., 1946; with Carter Oil Co., Denver, 1948-50; with pers. Bur. Budget, Washington, 1951-55; asst. to dir. pers. Treasury Dept., 1955-59; pers. officer, dir. adminstrn. Office Mgmt. and Budget, 1959-79; cons. in field. Recipient Career Svc. award Nat. Civil Svc. League, 1975. Mem. Am. Soc. Pub. Adminstrn. (past exec. bd.), Soc. Pers. Adminstrn. (exec. bd.), Cosmos Club (Washington), Phi Beta Kappa. Home: 2234 49th St NW Washington DC 20007-1057

BALENTINE, VICKI EILEEN, education director; b. Phoenix, June 5, 1950; d. Neil Charles McLeod and LaRue (Nanny) Ralston; m. John Gavin Balentine, Aug. 16, 1969; children: Hallie Ellen, Jenna Anne. BA, U. Ariz., 1971, MEd, 1972, PhD, 1986. Cert. prin. grades K-12, supt. Tchr. grades K-4, curriculum specialist Tucson (Ariz.) Unified Sch. Dist., 1971—, reading resource tchr., 1971-86, ombudsperson, 1987-88, prin. Davidson Elem. Sch., 1988-91, prin. Sam Hughes Elem. Sch., 1991-93, dir. dropout prevention and spl. projects, 1993—. Author: (handbook) Dropout Prevention Planning Handbook, 1994. V.p. Tucson (Ariz.) Youth Ctr., 1993-95; pres. bd. trustees Northminster Presbyn. Ch., Tucson, 1993; mem. planning com. League L.Am. Citizen Student Leadership Conf., Tucson, 1994-96; mem. bd. dirs. Youth On Their Own, 1996. Recipient Cmty. Svc. award FBI, 1994, 95. Mem. ASCD, Internat. Reading Assn., Tucson Area Reading Coun (pres. 1988-89), Phi Delta Kappa. Democrat. Presbyterian. Office: Tucson Unified Sch Dist 1010 E 10th St Tucson AZ 85719-5813

BALES, RUBY JONES, retired special education facilitator; b. Fayetteville, Tenn., Aug. 17, 1933; d. Albin O. and Jenny Katharine (Pickett) Jones; m. Emory H. Bales, Nov. 25, 1954; children: N. Katharine (dec.), David Emory, Evelyn Ann, Patrick Lee. BS in Biology, Tenn. Technol. U., 1956; MA in Supervision, Human Rels., George Washington U., 1975; EdD in Curriculum Instrn. and Reading, U. Md., 1984. Cert. tchr. grades 1-6, prin., supr., elem., middle sch. reading tchr. K-12. Tchr. gen. sci., math. Niceville (Fla.) Elem. Sch., 1956-57, Ruckel Jr. H.S., Niceville, 1957-59; tchr. biology, physical sci. Leon H.S., Tallahassee, 1959-60; tchr. 5th grade Potomac Elem. Sch., Dahlgren, Va., 1960-61, Charles County Pub. Schs., La Plata, Md., 1965-73; acting adminstrv. asst. Charles County Middle Pub. Sch.s, La Plata, Md., 1973-74; program coord. Mitchell Elem. Sch., Charles County, La Plata, 1974-75, adminstrv. asst., 1975-77; prin. Dr. James Craik Elem. Sch., Pomfret, Md., 1977-84, Eva Turner Elem. Sch., Waldorf, Md., 1984-86; instrnl. supr. elem. schs. Charles County Sch. Dist., La Plata, 1986-94. Supt. Charles County Fair Sch. Exhibit, County Fair Bd., 1986-94. NSF scholar Fla. State U., 1958. Republican. Home: PO Box 373 Dahlgren VA 22448-0373

BALICK, HELEN SHAFFER, judge; b. Bloomsburg, Pa.; d. Walter W. and Clarissa K. (Bennett) Shaffer; J.D., Dickinson Sch. Law, 1966; m. Bernard Balick, June 29, 1967. Bar: Pa. 1967, Del. 1969. Probate adminstr. Girard Trust Bank, Phila., 1966-68; pvt. practice law, Wilmington, Del., 1969-74; staff atty. Legal Aid Soc. Del., Wilmington, 1969-71; master Family Ct. Del., New Castle County, 1971-74; bankruptcy judge, U.S. magistrate Dist. Del., Wilmington, 1974-80; bankruptcy judge Dist. Del., 1974-94, chief judge, 1994—. guest lectr. Dickinson Sch. Law, 1981-87; lectr. Dickinson Forum, 1982. Pres. bd. trustees Community Legal Aid Soc., Inc., 1972-74; trustee Dickinson Sch. Law; mem. Citizens Adv. Com. Wilmington, 1973-74, Wilmington Bd. Edn., 1974. Named to the Hall of Fame of Del. Women, 1994. Mem. ABA (judicial adminstrn. sect.), Del. Bar Assn., Fed. Bar Assn., Nat. Conf. Bankruptcy Judges (bd. govs. 1986), Nat. Assn. Women Lawyers, Del. Alliance Profl. Women (Trailblazer award 1984), Nat. Assn. Women Judges, Internat. Women's Forum (del. chpt.), Wilmington Women in Bus. (bd. dirs. 1980-83), Am. Judges Assn., Am. Coll. Bankruptcy, Forum of Exec. Women, Am. Bankruptcy Inst., Turnaround Mgmt. Assn. (bd. dirs.), Dickinson Sch. Law Gen. Alumni Assn. (exec. bd. 1977-80, 87—, v.p. 1981-84, pres. 1984-87, outstanding alumni award 1991), Internat. Women's Forum (Del. chpt.), Phi Alpha Delta. Office: US Bankruptcy Ct 824 Market St Wilmington DE 19801

BALIS, JENNIFER LYNN, career planning educator; b. Hamlin, W.Va., Nov. 23, 1946; d. Louis Byron Floyd and Brunilda (Guiterrez) Castillo; 1 child, Theodore Berndt. AA, Del Mar Coll., 1987; BA, U. Tex., 1989; BS, So. Ill. U., 1992. Nursing educator Driscoll Found. Children's Hosp., Corpus Christi, Tex., 1986-88; peer counselor U. Tex., Edinburg, 1989-90; tchr. Mission (Tex.) Ind. Sch. Dist., 1990; instr. San Diego Job Corps, 1992-95; cons. Fleet Feet Running Club, San Diego, 1990-91. Chairperson United Way, Corpus Christi, 1988. With USNR, 1984—. Mem. AAUW, Am. Vocat. Assn., Psi Chi (pres. 1989-90). Republican. Roman Catholic. Home: PO Box 390666 San Diego CA 92149-0666 Office: Bur Naval Pers Washington DC 20370-5000

BALK, MARY DALE, drug prevention specialist, elementary school educator; b. Nashville, July 30, 1939; d. Dale Ivan Knox and Mary Lucille (Clower) Cooke; children: Susan Lynne Kradel, Rebecca Lynne Demo, Melissa Lynne Balk. BS in Edn., Miami U., Oxford, Ohio, 1961, MEd, 1967. Cert. addictions prevention profl.; cert. elem. edn. English; cert. specific learning disabilities K-12; cert. guidance counselor. Tchr. Marion (Ind.) High Sch., 1971-73; guidance counselor Justice Jr. High Sch., Marion, 1973-74; tchr. of the emotionally handicapped Red Bug Elem. Sch., Maitland, Fla., 1974-76; English tchr. Teague Middle Sch., Altamonte Springs, Fla., 1976-78, Lake Brantley High Sch., 1978-88; guidance counselor Lake Mary (Fla.) Elem. Sch., 1978-88; drug prevention specialist Seminole Co. (Fla.) Schs., 1988—; county Red Ribbon chmn. Nat. Red Ribbon Campaign, Seminole County, 1989—; adj. tchr. Seminole C.C.; guest speaker educators convs. Vice chmn. sch. bd. Sweetwater Episcopal Acad., 1985-88; active HRS Community Task Force for Residential Placement for Dep. Children, 1979-80; chmn. Seminole County Red Ribbon Campaign for a Drug-Free Am., 1989—; exec. com. Seminole County Am. Heart Assn. Mem. Winter Park Univ. Club, Fla. Alcohol and Drug Abuse Assn., Fla. Student Assistance Program Network (sec.). Home: 111 Valley Cir Longwood FL 32779-3460 Office: Drug Prevention Office 1401 S Magnolia Ave Sanford FL 32771-3400

BALKCOM, CAROL ANN, insurance agent; b. Newport, R.I., June 20, 1952; d. Robert Terrence and Barbara Ruth (Hilton) Hannaway; m. Richard Roger Balkcom, Oct., 1981; children: Richard Robert, Geoffrey Adam. BA, R.I. Coll., 1974, MA in Teaching, 1981; Cert. Life Underwriter, Am. Coll., 1984, CHFC, 1986. CLU, ChFC. Tchr. Lincoln (R.I.) Jr. High Sch., 1974-78; sales agt. Met. Life Ins. Co., Pawtucket, R.I., 1978-80; mgr., agt. Phoenix Mut. Life Ins. Co., Providence, 1980-94; instr. R.I. Lic. Sch., Providence, 1986-93; dist. mgr. New Eng. Life, New Port Richey, 1994—. Mem. R.I. Life Underwriters (bd. dirs. 1981-84, 90—, 1st v.p. 1983-84). Office: New Eng Life 6313 Adams St New Port Richey FL 34652-2301

BALL, ARDELLA PATRICIA, library media educator; b. Nashville, Dec. 15, 1932; d. Otis Hugh and Mary Ellen (Staples) Boatright; m. Wesley James Ball, June 15, 1931; children: Wesley James, Roderic Lynn, Weselyn Lynette, Patrick Wayne. AB, Fisk U., Nashville, 1953; MSLS, Atlanta U., 1956; ScD, Nova U., 1991. Tchr., libr. Fayetteville (Tenn.) H.S., 1954-57; children's libr. N.Y. Pub. Libr., summer 1957; cataloger Ala. A&M U., Huntsville, 1957-59; sr. cataloger St. Louis U., 1960-65; cataloger G.E.L. Regional Libr., Savannah, Ga., 1965-68; cataloger Armstrong State Coll., Savannah, 1968-74, instrnl. devel. libr., 1974-77, libr. media educator, 1977—. Author course manuals for core media courses. Bd. mem. Greenbrier Children's Ctr., Savannah, 1985—; vol. Hospice Savannah, 1985—. Mem. ALA, Ga. Libr. Assn., Ga. Media Assn., Coastal Ga. Libr. Assn. Democrat. Mem. Ch. of Christ. Home: RR 3 Box 410 Savannah GA 31406-9801 Office: Armstrong State Coll 11935 Abercorn St Savannah GA 31419-1909

BALL, MARCIA, vocalist; b. Orange, Tex., Mar. 20, 1949; m. Gordon Fowler. Student, La. State U., 1967. Mem. band Freda and the Firedogs, Austin, Tex., 1972-74; founder, mem. band Marcia Ball Band (formerly Marcia and the Misery Bros.), 1975. Performer (solo recording) I Want to Be a Cowboy's Sweetheart, 1975, (album) Circuit Queen, 1978, Soulful Dress, 1983, Hot Tamale Baby, 1986, Gatorhythms, 1989, Dreams Come True, 1991, Blue House, 1994; appeared at New Orleans Jazz and Heritage Festival, 1978;. Office: Rounder One Camp St Cambridge MA 02140*

BALL, PATRICIA ANN, physician; b. Lockport, N.Y., Mar. 30, 1941; d. John Joseph and Katherine Elizabeth (Hoffmaster) B.; m. Robert E. Lee, May 18, 1973; children—Heather, Samantha. B.S., U. Mich., 1963; M.D., Wayne State U., 1969. Diplomate Am. Bd. Internal Medicine, Am. Bd. Hematology, Am. Bd. Med. Oncology. Intern, resident Detroit Gen. Hosp., 1969-71; resident Jackson Meml. Hosp., Miami, Fla., 1971-72; fellow Henry Ford Hosp., Detroit, 1972-74; staff physician VA Hosp., Allen Park, Mich., 1974-77; practice medicine specializing in hematology and oncology, Bloomfield Hills, Mich., 1977—; mem. faculty dept. medicine Wayne State U. Sch. Medicine, Detroit, 1974—. Mem. Founders Soc., Detroit Inst. Arts. Mem. ACP, AMA, Mich. State Med. Soc., Oakland County Med. Soc., Mich. Soc. Hematology and Oncology, Alpha Omega Alpha. Avocations: photography; skiing. Office: 1575 S Woodward Ave Ste 210 Bloomfield Hills MI 48302-0561

BALL, ROSAMUND ANN, secondary education educator; b. Charleston, W.Va., Jan. 30, 1945; d. James Andrew and Beatrice (Smith) B. BA in Secondary Edn., Shepherd Coll., 1968. Cert. secondary edn. in history, govt., English; cert. reading specialist, Pa. Tchr. secondary edn. Chambersburg (Pa.) Area Sch. Dist., 1969—. Editor: The Obstetrical Records of Dr. A.A. Biggs, 1994, Cemetery, Death, and Miscellaneous Records from Hagerstown, Md., 1994, The Records of Rev. John Alex Adams of Sharpsburg, Md., 1994, Antietam National Cemetery Payroll Book, 1866-1867, 1994, The Letters of Thomas A. Boult, 1995, The Records of Dr. Augustin A. Biggs, vol. 1-36, 1996; author: Index to the Records of the Lutheran Churches in the Sharpsburg, Md. Area, 1989, Index to the History of Boonsboro, Md., 1991, Index to the Letters of Jacob Miller, 1995, Index for Register of Persons Who Have Died in Sharpsburg, Md. and Surrounding Neighborhoods, 1995, Index to the Atlas of Washington County, Md., 1877, 1995, Washington County, Md. Jury List, 1877, 1996. Recipient 5-Yr. Vol. Svc. award Washington County Free Libr., 1995. Mem. Huguenot Soc. Md. Democrat.

BALLANFANT, KATHLEEN GAMBER, newspaper executive, public relations company executive; b. Horton, Kans., July 11, 1945; d. Ralph Hayes and Audrey Lavon (Heryford) G.; m. Sid Roberts; children: Andrea, Benjamin. BA, Trinity U., 1967; postgrad. NYU, 1976, Am. Mgmt. Inst., 1977, Belhaven Coll., 1985. Pub. info. dir. Tex. Dept. Community Affairs, Austin, 1972-74; pub. affairs mgr. Cameron Iron Works, Houston, 1975-77, Assoc. Builders and Contractors, Houston, 1982-84; pres. Ballanfant & Assoc., Houston, 1977-82, 84—; pres. Village Life Inc., 1985—; pres., chief exec. officer Village Life Publs.; owner Village Life newspaper, Southwest News newspaper, Houston Observer/Times newspaper, Village Life Printing & Typesetting, South Post Oak newspaper; mem. adv. council on Construction Edn., Tex. So. U., Houston, 1984—; mem. task force on ednl. excellence Houston Ind. Sch. Dist., 1983—; mem. devel. bd. Inter First Fannin Bank, 1986-88; bd. dirs. Bellaire Hosp., Westbury-Southwest Assn. Author: Something Special-You, 1972, Prevailing Wage History in Houston, 1983; editor newspaper Bellaire Texan, 1981-82, Austin Times, 1971. Vice pres. West Univ. Republic Women's Club, Houston, 1984—; fgn. vis. chmn. Internat. Inst. Edn., Houston, 1980—; docent Houston Zoo, 1982. Named Tex. Woman of Achievement Tex. Womans Hosp., 1986; recipient Apollo IX Medal of Honor Gov. Preston Smith, 1970, Child Abuse Prevention award Gov. Dolph Briscoe, 1974, Tex. Community Newspaper Assn. (pres. 1988—, bd. dirs. 1987—). Mem. Bellaire C. of C. (bd. dirs. 1987—, sec., treas. 1988), Rotary. Republican. Presbyterian. Avocations: traveling, racquetball, reading. Office: Village Life Inc 5160 Spruce St Bellaire TX 77401-3309

BALLANTINE, MORLEY COWLES (MRS. ARTHUR ATWOOD BALLANTINE), newspaper editor; b. Des Moines, May 21, 1925; d. John and Elizabeth (Bates) Cowles; m. Arthur Atwood Ballantine, July 26, 1947 (dec. 1975); children—Richard, Elizabeth Ballantine Leavitt, William, Helen Ballantine Healy. A.B., Ft. Lewis Coll., 1975; L.H.D. (hon.), Simpson Coll., Indianola, Iowa, 1980. Pub. Durango (Colo.) Herald, 1952-83, editor, pub., 1975-83, editor, chmn. bd., 1983—; dir. 1st Nat. Bank, Durango, 1976—, Des Moines Register & Tribune, 1977-85, Cowles Media Co., 1982-86. Mem. Colo. Land Use Commn., 1975-81, Supreme Ct. Nominating Commn., 1984-90; mem. Colo. Forum, 1985—, Blueprint for Colo., 1985-92; pres. S.W. Colo. Mental Health Ctr., 1964-65, Four Corners Opera Assn., 1983-86; bd. dirs. Colo. Nat. Hist. Preservation Act, 1968-78; trustee Choate/Rosemary Hall, Wallingford, Conn., 1973-81, Simpson Coll., Indianola, Iowa, 1981—, U. Denver, 1984—, Fountain Valley Sch., Colorado Springs, 1976-89, trustee emerita, 1993—; mem. exec. com. Ft. Lewis Coll. Found., 1991—. Recipient 1st place award for editorial writing Nat. Fedn. Press Women, 1955, Outstanding Alumna award Rosemary Hall, Greenwich, Conn., 1969, Outstanding Journalism award U. Colo. Sch. Journalism, 1967, Distinguished Service award Ft. Lewis Coll., Durango, 1970; named to Colo. Community Journalism Hall of Fame, 1987; named Citizen of Yr. Durango Area Chamber Resort Assn., 1990. Mem. Nat. Soc. Colonial Dames, Colo. Press Assn. (bd. dirs. 1978-79), Colo. AP Assn. (chmn. 1966-67), Federated Women's Club Durango, Mill Reef Club (Antigua, W.I.) (bd. govs. 1985-91). Episcopalian. Address: care Herald PO Drawer A Durango CO 81302

BALLANTYNE, MAREE ANNE CANINE, artist; b. Sydney, NSW, Australia, Oct. 22, 1945; came to U.S., 1946; d. Charles Venice and Yvonne Mavis (McSpeerin) Canine; m. Kent McFarlane Ballantyne, Apr. 22, 1967; children: Christopher Kent, Joel Sokson. AA, Del Mar Coll., 1966; BA in English, U. Tex., 1971; postgrad., U. South Ala., 1974, U. Houston, 1981, Sonoma State U., 1982, 84, 85. Exhibited paintings in Mass., Tex., Ala.; creator logo for Gulf Coast Area Childbirth Edn. Assn., 1972, logo for Calif. Health Resources, 1985; contbr. articles to profl. jours. Charter mem. Gulf Coast Area Childbirth Edn. Assn., Mobile, Ala., 1971-76; mem. Mus. Guild, Corpus Christi, 1978-80, Art Mus., Mobile, 1972-76, Nat. Trust for Hist. Preservation, 1977-80. Recipient Cert. Appreciation, USCG, 1993, Letter of Appreciation USCG, 1993. Mem. Nat. Mus. of Women in the Arts (charter 1987-97), Coast Guard Officers Wives Club. Home: 1920 SW 56th Ave Plantation FL 33317-5938

BALLARD, BARBARA W., state legislator; m. Albert L. Ballard. Rep. dist. 44 State of Kansas, 1993—; adminstr., dir. U. Kans. Democrat. Home: 1532 Alvamar Dr Lawrence KS 66047-1605 Office: U Kans Emily Taylor Women's Ctr 115 Strong Hall Lawrence KS 66045-7301

BALLARD, MARION SCATTERGOOD, software development professional; b. Montclair, N.J., Dec. 19, 1939; d. Alfred G. and Helen F. (Galey) Scattergood; m. Frederic L. Ballard Jr., Dec. 20, 1974; children: William, Robert; 1 stepchild, Anne A. Ballard. BA, Smith Coll., 1961; MA, U. Pa., 1963; MBA, American Univ., 1990. Lectr. Temple U., Phila.; mathematician UNIVAC, Blue Bell, Pa.; v.p. FINPAC Corp., Narberth, Pa.; pres. DataPlus, Inc, Washington. Chmn. bd. Sandy Spring Friends Sch.; sec. bd. Sidwell Friends Sch. Mem. Nat. Assn. Women Bus. Owners, Phi Beta Kappa, Sigma Xi.

BALLARD, MARY ANNE, musician; b. Louisville, Feb. 27, 1942; d. James Curtis and Mary Caroline (Green) Drye; m. Frederic Lyman Ballard (div. Oct. 1974); 1 child, Anne Adams; m. Belton Langdon Corson (dec. Apr. 1985); m. Alexander Blachly, Oct. 2, 1988. BA, Wellesley Coll., 1964; MA, U. Pa., 1974. Dir. early misuc activities U. Pa., Phila., 1971-91; dir. music arts Princeton (N.J.) U., 1982-91; faculty PEabody Conservatory, 1981-89; Bd. dirs. Early Music Am., Phila. Bach Festival. Performer New World Consort, 1973-80, Balt. Consort, 1980—. Home: 1515 N Lake George Dr Mishawaka IN 46545

BALLARD, MARY MELINDA, financial communications and investment banking firm executive; b. Sikeston, Mo., Apr. 21, 1958; d. Claude M. and Mary (Birnbach) B.; m. Emil Pena, Jan. 1, 1989 (div. July 1990); m. Ronald C. Allison, Oct. 1994; 1 child, Reese Colton Allison. BA, Monmouth Coll. 1976, MBA, NYU 1980, postgrad. Columbia U. V.p. corp. comm. United Brands Co., N.Y.C., 1976-79; v.p. mktg. Oscar de la Renta Ltd., 1979-81; pres., chief exec. officer Ficom Internat., Inc., N.Y.C., 1981—; exec. v.p. Ruder Finn Inc., N.Y.C., 1989—; dir., CEO MBP Interests Inc., 1989—; ptnr. Kamero Ptnrs., 1994—; officer/dir. Texas Interlock Corp., 1995—; bd. dirs. Nat. Coun. Real Estate Investment Fiduciaries, Tex. Interlock Corp.; cons. to fgn. govts. and major corps. Contbr. articles to profl. jours. Trustee Ballard Family Found., Children's Aid Soc.; exec. mem. Tex. Dem. Roundtable, 1994—. Recipient CLIO Ann. Report award Fin. World, 1984, 86. Mem. Internat. Assn. Bus. Communicators (Golden Quill 1984), Pub. Relations Soc. Am., Urban Land Inst., Nat. Investor Relations Inst. Methodist. Avocations: collecting art, thoroughbred race horses, ranching. Home: PO Box 746 Dripping Springs TX 78620-0746

BALLAS, NADIA S., writer, poet; b. Phila., Dec. 27, 1971; d. Samir K. and Nida (Abdo) B. BA in English Lit., Rosemont (Pa.) Coll., 1994; postgrad., Suffolk Univ., 1996—. Cons. image and writer cons. Cherry Hill, N.J., 1991-94. Author: (poetry anthologies/collections): Beyond the Stars, 1995, Best Poets of 1996, 1996. Congl. aide Congressman Andrews, Somerdale, N.J., 1995; intern Camden County Dem. Com., Cherry Hill, 1995; vol. West Jersey Hosp., Voorhees, 1988; friend John F. Kennedy Libr.; mem. N.J. Dem. Victory Fund, Dem. Nat. Com.; vol. Children's Def. Fund. Named Best Poet of 1996, Nat. Libr. of Poetry, Ohio. Mem. NOW. Office: 4 Longfellow Pl # 1104 Boston MA 02114

BALLESTEROS, PAULA M., nurse; b. Jonesport, Me., Oct. 18, 1950; d. Paul Frederick and Janice Madeline (Beal) Mitchell; m. Ernesto Gascon Ballesteros, Apr. 4, 1981; children: Christopher, Jonathan. BS in Profl. Arts, St. Joseph's Coll., 1984; BSN, Husson/Ea. Me. Med. Ctr. Baccalaureate Sch. Nursing, 1994. Cert. Nursing Adminstrn. Patient care mgr. Ea. Me. Med. Ctr., Bangor, 1974—, bd. trustees, 1993-95; chairperson adv. bd. Ea. Maine Tech. Coll., Bangor, Me., 1993-94; pres. Me. Coun. Nurse Mgrs., 1991-93, Ea. Me. Med. Ctr. auxiliary, Bangor, Me., 1993-95. Contbr. articles to profl. jours. Mem. St. Joseph Hosp. Auxiliary. Mem. Am. Orgn. Nurse Execs., Penobscot Med. Soc. Auxiliary, Me. Assn. Hosp. Auxiliaries (pres. 1994—). Democrat. Protestant. Home: 78 Packard Dr Bangor ME 04401 Office: Ea Maine Med Ctr 489 State St Bangor ME 04401-6616

BALLEW, DORIS EVELYN, accountant, company executive; b. Knox County, Tenn., Sept. 6, 1938; d. James Elmer and Grace Elizabeth (Wright) Dossett; m. George Thomas Reep, Feb. 4, 1955 (div. June 1969); children: Sherrie Lynn Akins, Kimberley Michelle Niles; m. David Woodward Ballew, Oct. 9, 1969 (div. Dec. 1989); 1 child, Melissa Marie. Student, U. P.R., 1957, U. Tenn., 1975-84, Draughon's Coll., 1982, Knoxville Bus. Coll., 1974. CPA, Tenn. Acct. Shoney's Restaurants, Knoxville, Tenn., 1961-64, Tinsley Tire Co., Knoxville, Tenn., 1964-65; chief acct. Kuhlman-Murphy Co., Knoxville, Tenn., 1965-77; v.p., contr., treas. Lawler Wood, Inc. and Wood Properties, Inc., Knoxville, Tenn., 1977—. Mem. Old Smoky Railway Mus. (treas. 1978-83). Mem. Nat. Assn. Accts., Knoxville Jaycettes, AICPA, Tenn. Soc. CPA's, Beta Sigma Phi (pres. 1982-83, 89). Home: 148 Country Walk Dr Powell TN 37849-3453 Office: 1600 Riverview Tower 900 S Gay St Knoxville TN 37902-1810

BALLING, LOUISE MARY, social worker; b. North Tonawanda, N.Y.; d. Leo and Mary Anna (Achatz) B. BA, D'Youville Coll., 1960; MSW, SUNY, Buffalo, 1970. Cert. social worker, N.Y. Med. social worker Deaconess Hosp. of Buffalo, N.Y., 1972-80; social worker N.Y. State Office of Mental Health, Helmuth, 1981-94, Buffalo, 1994—; developer high risk pregnancy index and rsch. study. Bd. dirs. Hist. Soc. of Tonawandas, 1985-92; vol. Albright Knox Art Gallery, Buffalo, 1978-91; docent Long Homestead, Tonawanda, 1982—. Mem. English Speaking Union. Home: 57 Park St Springville NY 14141-1116

BALLINGER, DEBRA ANN, physical education educator, consultant; b. Cleve., May 16, 1951; d. Ernest C. and Martha L. (Klein) Krauth; children: Justin, Lyndsey, Amanda. BA in Music and Phys. Edn., Elmhurst Coll., 1968-72; MA in Edn., U. South Fla., 1976; M in Counseling, Ariz. State U., 1987, PhD in Secondary Edn., 1987. Tchr., coach Air Acad. Jr. H.S., Colorado Springs, 1972-75; dir. youth activities 32 TFS, Camp New Amsterdam, The Netherlands, 1976-80; grad. asst. Ariz. State U., Tempe, 1980-81; music and phys. edn. tchr. Dhahran (Saudi Arabia) Acad. SAIS, 1981-83; faculty assoc. Ariz. State U., Tempe, 1984-87; asst. prof. Old Dominion U., Norfolk, Va., 1988-92; asst. prof., dept. chair Christopher Newport U., Newport News, Va., 1992-94; asst. prof. health, phys. edn., and recreation Va. Commonwealth U., Richmond, 1994—; cons. in sport performance and psychology, York County, 1987-94. Contbr. articles to profl. jours. Youth choir dir. Yorkminster Presbyn. Ch., Yorktown, Va., 1988-94; vol. instr. ARC, 1988-94. Mem. Va. Assn. Health, Phys. Edn., Recreation, and Dance (pres. 1993-96, Outstanding Tchr. of Yr. 1993, Pathfinder award 1994), Assn. for Advancement of Applied Psychologists (cert. sports psychology). Office: Va Commonwealth U/Dept HPER Box 842037 817 W Franklin St Richmond VA 23284-2037

BALLINGER, GAIL BETH, administrator; b. Lancaster, Calif., Aug. 10, 1950; d. Richard C. and June D. (Piercy) B.; m. James W. Rich, Aug. 22, 1984; 1 child, Jennifer. BS magna cum laude, Chapman U., 1993. Legal sec. Brobeck, Phleger & Harrison, San Francisco, 1970-76; lead sec., office mgr. Brobeck, Phleger & Harrison, L.A., 1976-79, adminstr., 1987—; paralegal, mgr. AMFAC, Inc., San Francisco, 1981-86; office adminstr. Brobeck, Phleger and Harrison LLP, Newport Beach and Denver, 1987—; spkr. Assns. of Legal Adminstrs./Regional, Costa Mesa, Calif., 1994. Mem. Order of the Amaranth, Lancaster, Calif., 1981—. Mem. Assn. of Legal Adminstrs. (spkrs. com. 1993-94, dir. com. 1994-96). Office: Brobeck Phleger & Harrison 4675 MacArthur Ct Newport Beach CA 92660

BALLOU, CLAUDIA ARCENEAUX, graphic designer, artist, calligrapher; b. Baton Rouge, Sept. 26, 1945; d. Claude Joseph and Barbara (Robin) Arceneaux; m. Teague Jackson, Dec., 1972 (div. 1974); m. Jack Wayne Ballou, Dec. 23, 1986. Student, U. Paris and Acad. Julian, 1965; grad., John McCrady Art Sch., New Orleans, 1966; postgrad., Temple U., 1977-78. Cert. ct. reporter. Tchr. fine art Shoeburyness (Eng.) H.S., 1967; graphic designer Kennesaw Press, Atlanta, 1968-77; graphics liaison Du Pont Co., Wilmington, Del., 1979-86; prodn. scheduler, with pub. rels. dept. Gregory & Assocs., Wilmington, 1987-88; v.p. graphic svcs. Peyton & Assocs., Inc., Wilmington, 1988-94; co-founder Chase Comms., Wilmington, 1994—; artist-in-residence Del. Arts Commn., Wilmington, 1993, 94. Designer book jacket, typography and layout The Soul of Economies, 1990; graphic designer numerous brochures. Mem. coun. Del. Art Mus., Wilmington, 1990—; mem. comm. com. Am. Heart Assn., Wilmington, 1995—; adminstrv. asst. Del. del. White House Conf. on Small Bus., 1994 ; tchr. arts and crafts, event planner Kiwanis Girls Club, Wilmington, 1995—. Named Mem. of Month Del. Art Mus. Coun., 1993. Mem. Del. Women's Networking Luncheons (steering com. 1995-96).

BALL-SARET, JAYNE ADAMS, business owner; b. East St. Louis, Ill., Apr. 10, 1956; d. H. Jay and Faye M. (Adams) Ball; m. Mitchell I. Saret. BA, Ea. Ill. U., 1977, MA, 1983. Interior designer Carter's Furniture, Charleston, Ill., 1977-85; from customer svc. advisor to dir. client svc. Consol. Comm., Mattoon, Charleston, Ill., 1985-94; owner, designer Grand Ball Costumes, Charleston, 1985—. Pres., dir. Charleston Cmty. Theatre, 1983-85. Mem. Phi Alpha Eta. Republican. Office: Grand Ball Costumes 609 6th St Charleston IL 61920

BALLWEBER, HETTIE LOU, archaeologist; b. Pitts., Dec. 27, 1944; d. Nicholas George and Harriett Elizabeth (Tucker) Beresh; m. Walter David Boyce, Aug. 24, 1963 (div. 1984); children: Michael David, Steven Todd; m. William Arterberry Ballweber, Nov. 8, 1986. BA summa cum laude, Calif. U., Pa., 1985; M. Applied Anthropology, U. Md., 1987. Cons. archaeologist Monongahela, Pa., 1980-85; archaeologist archeology div. Md. Geol. Survey, Balt., 1985-86; dir. Md. New Directions, Balt., 1987; cons. Columbia, Md., 1987—; prin. ACS Cons., Columbia, Md., 1987—; bd. dirs. Alternative Directions, Inc., Balt. Author: First People of Maryland, 1985, Archaeology!, 1996; contbr. articles to profl. jours. State publicity chmn. Pa. Congress Parents and Tchrs., Harrisburg, Pa., 1981-84, regional v.p., 1984. With USN, 1979-87. Fellow Soc. Applied Anthropology; mem. Mon-Yough Archaeol. Soc. (pres. 1983-84), Westmoreland Archaeol. Soc. (v.p. 1982-83), Coun. Md. Archeology (pres. 1990-91), Washington Assn. Profl. Anthropologists, Soc. Hist. Archaeology, Shriners, Order Eastern Star. Home and Office: 3212 Peddicoat Ct Woodstock MD 21163-1132

BALMASEDA, LIZ, columnist; b. Puerto Padre, Cuba, 1959. AA, Miami-Dade (Fla.) C.C., 1979; BS Comm., Fla. Internat. U., 1981. Intern Miami Herald, Fla., 1980, with Spanish lang. publ., 1981, gen. assignment reporter, feature writer, 1987, with Sunday Mag. tropic, 1990, local columnist, 1991; ctrl. Am. bur. chief Newsweek, El Salvador, 1985; field prodr. NBC News, Honduras. Appeared on NBC Today Show, Oprah show. Recipient 2d place Ernie Pyle award Scripps Howard Found, 1984, 3d place feature writing Fla. Soc. Newspaper Editors, 1st prize Guillermo Martinez-Marquez contest Nat. Assn. Hispanic Journalists., 1989, Pulitzer Prize for commentary, 1993, 1st prize commentary Fla. Soc. Newspaper editors. Office: The Miami Herald One Herald Plaza Miami FL 33101*

BALSTER-SMITH, LAURA CATHERINE, daycare provider; b. Atlanta, Aug. 22, 1957; d. Vernon Henry and Janet Cassandra (Hill) Balster; m. Sanford James Rixey, Feb. 10, 1978; m. Anthony Oliver Smith, Dec. 15, 1985; children: Robin May, Devin Vernon. BA in Lit., Wilmington Coll., 1980. Owner, operator Bean Sprout Day Care, Norman, Okla., 1988—; founder, minister Weddings Your Way, Norman, 1993—. Co-founder, pres. Norman (Okla.) Unitarian Universalist Fellowship, 1990, v.p., 1992-94, pres., 1994-96; facilitator Adult Religious Edn., Norman. Mem. ACLU, NOW, Norman Family Day Care Assn., Nature Conservancy, World Wildlife Fund. Democrat. Home: 526 E Comanche Norman OK 73071

BALTER, BERNICE, religious organization administrator. Exec. dir. Women's League for Conservative Judaism, N.Y.C. Office: 48 E 74th St New York NY 10021*

BALTER, FRANCES SUNSTEIN, civic worker; b. Pitts.; d. Elias and Gertrude (Kingsbacher) Sunstein. Student Sarah Lawrence Coll., 1939-41, New Sch. Social Rsch., 1941-43, Bennington Coll., 1941, 42; cert. Harvard Inst. Arts Adminstrn., 1973; m. James Stone Balter, May 15, 1948; children: Katherine (Mrs. Ross Anthony), Julia Frances, Constance (Mrs. Owen Cantor), Daniel Elias. Adminstrv. asst., assoc. producer Ednl. Television Sta. WQED-TV, Pitts., 1963-67; producer, mng. dir. Freedom Readers, 1964-67; co-founder, incorporator, sec. bd. dirs. Pitts. Coun. for Arts, 1967-70; cultural cons. Mayor's Office, Dir. of Office of Cultural Affairs, Pitts., 1968; initiator Three Rivers Arts Festival 1960; co-dir. Ohio and Miss. River Valley Art Festival, 1961-62; mem. Pa. Coun. on Arts, 1972-78; co-founder Pioneer Crafts Coun. Mill Run Pa., 1972; exec. dir. Poetry On The Buses, 1974—; bd. dirs. Coun. for Arts MIT, 1985-93, Palm Beach Festival, 1987-89. Named Woman of Yr. in Art Post-Gazette, 1969. Mem. Assoc. Councs. on Arts, Nat. Soc. Arts and Letters, Nat. League of Am. PEN Women (Pitts. chpt., assoc. 1990—). Home: 1603 Bayhouse Point Dr Sarasota FL 34231-6774 also: 1515 Pelican Point Dr Sarasota FL 34231

BALTIMORE, RUTH BETTY, social worker; b. Wilkes-Barre, Pa., Feb. 27, 1926; d. Samuel Jr. and Theresa (Bergsmann) Bloch; m. Martin Joseph Baltimore, Feb. 6, 1949; children: Francie, Sandy. BA in Psychology, Skidmore Coll., 1948; postgrad., U. Scranton, 1965, 70. Sch. social worker Wyoming Valley West Sch. Dist., Kingston, Pa., 1966-89; retired; cons. in field. Co-author: (booklet) Guide for Teachers on Reporting Child Abuse, 1970. Bd. dirs. Youth Svcs. Commn., Wilkes-Barre, 1986-87, Victims Resource Ctr., Wilkes-Barre, 1990—; bd. dirs. Luz County Adv. Bd. Children and Youth, Wilkes-Barre, 1988—, vice chairperson, 1991, chairperson, 1992-96. Recipient Connie Coun. Svc. award Nat. Coun. Jewish Women, Wilkes-Barre, 1959. Mem. Valley Tennis and Swim Club (pres.-elect 1994, pres. 1995-96). Home: 630 Newberry Estate Dallas PA 18612

BALTZER, PATRICIA GERMAINE, elementary education educator; b. Johnstown, Pa., May 16, 1951; d. Harry and Doris Mae Findley; m. Dennis Duane Baltzer, Jan. 5, 1985; 1 child, Kourtney Noelle. BS, U. Pitts., Johnstown, 1973; cert. prin., Ind. U. Pa., 1994. Cert. prin., Pa. Tchr. Windber (Pa.) Area Sch. Dist., 1973—, chairperson sci. com.; coord. Project Hugs and Kisses, Windber, 1993-96. Mem. Assn. for Childhood Edn. Internat. (Successful Teaching award 1993), Keystone State Reading Assn., Laurel Highlands Math. Alliance, Pa. Assn. Elem. Sch. Prins. (student), Bus. and Profl. Women's Orgn. (Young Careerist chairperson). Office: Windber Area Sch Dist Windber PA 15963

BALUKONIS, CHERYL ANN, cultural organization administrator; b. Cambridge, Mass.; d. William John and Georgianna Bernice (Antonelli) B. AS, Cardinal Cushing Coll., 1965; student, Boston Conservatory, 1973-83; cert. piano performance study, New Eng. Conservatory, 1987, 88; postgrad. theory and composition, Harvard U., 1978-81. Sr. program adminstr. Mass. Cultural Coun., Boston, 1982—; mem. adv. bd. Boston Globe Fedn., Boston, 1986; nat. task force mem. Nat. Endowment Arts, Ams. with Disabilities Act, Washington, 1993-94. Composer mus. compositions; contbg. author: Design for Accessibility: An Arts dministrator's Guide to Cultural Access, 1994. Mem. Greenpeace, Washington; active Big Sister Assn., Boston. Recipient Creative Leadership award Mass. Office of Affirmative Action, 1985, Big Sister Recognition award Big Sister Assn., 1994; fellow for arts policy Nat. Endowment Arts, 1983. Office: Mass Cultural Coun # 2 120 Boylston St Boston MA 02116-4600

BAMBER, LINDA SMITH, accounting educator; b. Columbus, Ohio, Jan. 4, 1954; d. Charles Randall and Martha Jo (Wise) Smith; m. Edward Michael Bamber, Mar. 13, 1981. BS summa cum laude, Wake Forest U, 1976; MBA, Ariz. State U., 1980; PhD, Ohio State U., 1983. Cost acct. RJ Reynolds, Winston-Salem, N.C., 1975-76, gen. acct., 1976-77; tutor, rsch. asst. Ariz. State U., Tempe, 1977-78; teaching asst. Ohio State U., Columbus, 1978-82; asst. prof. U. Fla., Gainesville, 1983-88, assoc. prof., 1988-90; assoc. prof. U. Ga., Athens, 1990-96, prof., 1996—; vis. assoc. prof. Ind. U., Bloomington, 1989-90. Author: Annotated Instructor's Edition of Cost Accounting: A Managerial Emphasis, 1990, 93, 96, assoc. editor: Acctg. Horizon, 1993—; mem. editl. bd. The Acctg. Rev., 1987-89, 93—, Advances in Acctg., 1992—; contbr. articles to profl. jours. Selig fellow U. Ga., 1991, Terry fellow U. Ga., 1994, 95; recipient Rsch. Devel. award U. Fla., 1985, Tchg. award Ohio State U., U. Fla., U. Ga., 1981-94. Mem. Am. Acctg. Assn. (S.E. dir. fin. reporting sect. 1993-94, group leader, panelist chmn. New Faculty Consortium 1991-94), Beta Gamma Sigma (mem. coun. 1995—, mgmt. acctg. sect. chmn. membership outreach com. 1995—), Phi Beta Kappa, Phi Kappa Phi. Office: U Ga JM Tull Sch Acctg Athens GA 30602

BANAS, C. LESLIE, lawyer; b. Swindon, Wiltshire, Eng., Oct. 29, 1951; came to U.S. 1957; d. Stanley M. and Helena Ann (Boryn) B.; m. Dale J. Buras, May 1, 1976; children: Eric, Andrea. BA honors program, U. Detroit, 1973; JD, Wayne State U., 1975. Bar: Mich. 1976, U.S. Supreme Ct. 1980. Atty. Hyman & Rice, Southfield, Mich., 1976-77; ptnr. Hyman, Gurwin, Nachman, Friedman & Winkelman, Southfield, 1982-87, Honigman Miller Schwartz and Cohn, Detroit, 1987—; mem. Mich. Housing Coun., Lansing. Contbr. articles to profl. jours. Bd. trustees Karmanos Cancer Inst. Mem. ABA, State Bar Mich., Fed. Bar Assn., Detroit Bar Assn., Oakland County Bar, Women's Econ. Club, Birmingham Athletic Club. Roman Catholic. Office: Honigman Miller Schwartz and Cohn 2290 1st National Bldg Detroit MI 48226

BANCEL, MARILYN, fund raising management consultant; b. Glen Ridge, N.J., June 15, 1947; d. Paul and Joan Marie (Spangler) B.; m. Rik Myslewski, Nov. 20, 1983; children: Carolyn, Roxanne. BA in English with distinction, Ind. U., 1969. Cert. fund raising exec. Ptnr. The Sultan's Shirt Tail, Gemlik, Turkey, 1969-72; prodn. mgr. High Country Co., San Francisco, 1973-74; pub. Bay Arts Rev., Berkeley, Calif., 1976-79; dir. devel. Oakland (Calif.) Symphony Orch., 1979-81; assoc. dir. devel. Exploratorium, San Francisco, 1981-86, dir. devel., 1986-91; prin. Fund Devel. Counsel, San Francisco, 1991-93; v.p. The Oram Group, Inc., San Francisco, 1993—; mem. fin. com. Synergy Sch., San Francisco, 1992—, co-chair endowment com., 1993—; adj. faculty U. San Francisco, 1993—. Fellow U. Strasberg, France, 1968. Mem. Nat. Soc. Fund Raising Execs. (bd. mem. Golden Gate chpt.), Am. Assn. Fund Raising Counsel, Devel. Execs. Roundtable, Phi Beta Kappa. Democrat. Office: The Oram Group 44 Page St Ste 604C San Francisco CA 94102-5986

BANCO, BARBARA ANN, banker; b. Highland Park, Mich., May 26, 1950; d. John Alexander and Betty Florence (Fletke) B. Student, Henry Ford C.C., Dearborn, Mich., 1968-70; BA, U. Mich., 1972. Cert. elem. tchr., Mich., mortgage broker/lender lic., Mich. Svc. rep. Mich. Bell Telephone Co., Southfield, 1972-84; billing rep. Mich. Bell Telephone Co., Oak Park, 1984-86; ICSC rep. Mich. Bell Telephone Co., Southfield, 1986-88; coin technician Mich. Bell Telephone Co., Clawson, 1988-94; sr. loan officer Pacific World Mortgage Banking, Bloomfield Hills, Mich., 1986-94; pres. Banco Mortgage Ctr., Birmingham, Mich., 1994—. Mem. BBB, Birmingham (Mich.) C. of C., Mich. Mortgage Brokers Assn., Southeastern Builders Assn. of Mich., Birmingham Power Squadron, U. Mich. Alumnae Club. Republican. Lutheran. Office: Banco Mortgage Ctr 1157 S Adams Rd Birmingham MI 48009

BANCROFT, ANN, polar explorer; b. 1956; d. Dick and Debbie B. Former tchr., coach, wilderness instr. St. Paul, Minn.; mem. Steger Internat. Polar Expedition, 1986 (first woman to reach the North Pole by dogsled); leader Am. Women's Trans-Antartic Expedition, 1993 (first women's team to reach the South Pole on skis). Named Ms. Mag. Woman of Yr., 1987; inductee Girls and Women in Sport Hall of Fame, 1992; recipient Women First award YWCA, 1993. Office: care Rhonda Grider 2110 Laurelwood Dr Thousand Oaks CA 91362-4635*

BANCROFT, ANNE (MRS. MEL BROOKS), actress; b. N.Y.C., Sept. 17, 1931; d. Michael and Mildred (DiNapoli) Italiano; m. Mel Brooks, 1964; 1 son. Broadway stage appearances include Two for the Seesaw, 1957 (Tony award 1957), The Miracle Worker, 1959-60 (Tony award 1960), Devils, 1977, Golda, 1977-78, Duet for One, 1981; stage appearances include Mystery of the Rose Bouquet, 1989; motion pictures include Treasure of the Golden Condor, 1952, Don't Bother to Knock, 1952, Tonight We Sing, 1953, The Kid from Left Field, 1953, Demetrius and the Gladiators, 1954, Gorilla at Large, 1954, The Raid, 1954, A Life in the Balance, 1954, The Brass Ring, 1954, Naked Street, 1955, New York Confidential, 1955, The Last Frontier, 1955, Girl in the Black Stockings, 1957, Restless Breed, 1957, The Pumpkin Eater, 1964, Seven Women, 1966, Slender Thread, 1966, The Graduate, 1967, Young Winston, 1972, The Prisoner of 2nd Avenue, 1975, The Hindenburg, 1975, Lipstick, 1976, Silent Movie, 1976, The Turning Point, 1977, Fatso, 1979, The Elephant Man, 1980, To Be or Not to Be, 1983, Garbo Talks, 1984, Agnes of God, 1985, 'Night, Mother, 1986, 84 Charing Cross Road (Brit. Acad. award 1987), Torch Song Trilogy, 1988, Bert Rigby You're a Fool, 1989, Honeymoon in Vegas, 1992, Love Potion #9, 1992, Point of No Return, 1993, Mr. Jones, 1993, Malice, 1993, How to Make an American Quilt, 1995, Home for the Holidays, 1995; TV appearances include Kraft Music Hall, Jesus of Nazareth, 1977, Marco Polo, 1982, Broadway Bound, 1992, Mrs. Cage, PBS, 1992, Oldest Living Confederate Widow Tells All, 1994 (Emmy nomination), The Homecoming, 1996; dir., writer, star: (TV spl.) Annie-The Woman in the Life of Men, 1970 (Emmy award 1970). Recipient Acad. award for performance in The Miracle Worker, 1962, Best Actress award Cannes Internat. Film Festival for performance in Pumpkin Eater, 1964, Lifetime Achievement in Comedy award Am. Comedy Awards, 1996. Address: c/o The Culver Studios 9336 W Washington Blvd Culver City CA 90232*

BANCROFT, AUDREY FRANCES PIERCE, librarian; b. Chgo., Nov. 9, 1957; d. Jack Allen and Margaret Patricia (Van Slobig) Sandefur; m. R. Christopher Pierce, May 4, 1996. BS, Colo. State U., 1980; MS of Info. Scis., U. Pitts., 1990, MLS, 1991; postgrad., Ind. U., 1991-94. Libr. asst., tutor Colo. State U., Ft. Collins, Colo., 1975-79; quotations, sales, customer svc. profl., 1975-81; substitute tchr. Oak Grove Sch. Dist., San Jose, Calif., 1985-86; libr. technician, sec. Oreg. State U., Corvallis, 1987-89; reference libr. sci. libr. Wash. State U., Pullman, 1994-95, acting head edn. libr., 1995—. Author: (rsch. bibliography) Ethics and Information, 1991; co-author: (presentation) Response Avoidance in the Treatment of Trichotillomania, 1994. Recipient Math. and Sci. Achievement award Soc. Women Engrs., 1975, Student Leadership award U. Pitts. Alumni Assn., 1991, Robert Wayne Smith Book awrd Oreg. State u., 1988; fellow psychology dept. Ind. U., 1991, 93. Mem. ALA, Am. Soc. Info. Scientists, Mensa. Office: Wash State U Brain Edn Libr 130 Cleveland Hall Pullman WA 99164-2112

BANCROFT, ELIZABETH ABERCROMBIE, publisher, analytical chemist; b. N.Y.C., Mar. 2, 1947; d. John Chandler and Ruth Abercrombie (Robinson) B. AB, Harvard U./Radcliffe Coll., 1979; postgrad. in forensic scis. John Jay Coll. Criminal Justice, 1982. Asst. dir. research Bagley Fordyce Research Labs., N.Y.C., 1979-83, dir. research and publs., Washington office, 1984-86; dir. Nat. Intelligence Book Ctr., 1986—; pub. Surveillant: Aquisitions and Commentary for Intelligence and Security Professionals. Mem. Assn. Fgn. Intelligence Officers, Naval Intelligence Profls., Nat. Mil. Intelligence Assn., Nat. Hist. Intelligence Mus., Nat. Intelligence Study Ctr., Washington Book Pubs. Assn., Am. Bookseller Assn. Republican. Episcopalian. Clubs: Harvard/Radcliffe of Washington; Chemists of N.Y. Office: Nat Intelligence Book Ctr 2020 Pennsylvania Ave NW Washington DC 20006-1846

BANCZAK, PEGGY J., lawyer. BA, U. Wis., 1978, JD, 1981. Atty. Delhi Gas Pipeline Corp.; from assoc. atty. to sr. atty. Lone Star Gas Co., 1985-93; v.p., gen. counsel Ensearch Devel. Corp., Dallas, 1993—. Mem. Tex. Bar Assn., Wis. Bar Assn., Dallas Bar Assn., Gulf Coast Cogeneration Assn., Fed. Energy Bar Assn., Natural Gas Soc. North Tex. Office: Enserch Devel Corp 1817 Wood St Ste 550W Dallas TX 75201-5605

BANDA, GERALDINE MARIE, chiropractic physician; b. Orange, N.J., Oct. 15, 1951; d. Albert Joseph and Maria Grace B.; 1 adopted child, Gabriele Grace. BA, Seton Hall U., 1974; D of Chiropractic, N.Y. Chiropractic Coll., 1984. Cert. scoliosis mgmt. specialist. Staff writer The Herald News, Passaic, N.J., 1974-77; tchr. St. Genevieve's Roman Cath. Sch., Elizabeth, N.J., 1977-80; chiropractic physician Banda Chiropractic Office, Cranford, N.J., 1984—. Contbr. articles to profl. jours. and newspapers. Activist community svc. projects and scoliosis screenings, Cranford, 1984—. Named Outstanding Young Woman of Am., 1981. Mem. Am. Chiropractic Assn. (mem. coun. on diagnostic imaging), N.J. Chiropractic Soc., Cranford C. of C., N.J. Women's Bus. Owners Assn. Office: Banda Chiropractic Office 347 Lincoln Ave E Cranford NJ 07016-3157

BANE, MARY JO, federal agency administrator; b. Princeville, Ill., Feb. 24, 1942; d. Fred W. and Helen (Callery) B.; m. Kenneth Winston, May 31, 1975. BS in Internat. Rels., Georgetown U., 1963; MAT, Harvard U., 1966, DEd, 1972. Tchr. English U.S. Peace Corps, Liberia, 1963-65; tchr. social studies Arlington (Mass.) Pub. Schs., 1966-67; tchr. English and social studies Brookline (Mass.) Pub. Schs., 1968-71; rsch. assoc. Ctr. Ednl. Policy Rsch. and Huron Inst. Harvard U., Cambridge, Mass., 1971-72, project co-dir. Ctr. Study of Pub. Policy, 1972-75, assoc. prof. edn., lectr. in sociology, 1977-80, assoc. prof. pub. policy, 1981-86, dir. Malcolm Wiener Ctr. for Social Policy, 1987-92, prof. pub. policy, 1986-90, Malcolm Wiener Prof. of Social Policy, 1990-92; lectr. in Sociology U. Mass., Boston, 1972-75; assoc. dir. Ctr. Rsch. on Women, asst. prof. edn., lectr. in sociology Wellesley (Mass.) Coll., 1975-77; dep. asst. sec. for program planning and budget analyst Office Planning and Budget U.S. Dept. Edn., Washington, 1980-81; exec. dep. commr. N.Y. State Dept. Social Svcs., 1984-86, commr., 1992-93; asst. sec. Adminstrn. for Children and Families Dept. Health and Human Svcs., Washington, 1993—; Ida Bean vis. prof. U. Iowa, 1980; chair bd. overseers panel study income dynamics Inst. Rsch. U. Mich., 1982-86; regents lectr. U. Calif., Berkeley, 1987; mem. adv. com. urban poverty NAS, 1986-90, chair com. child devel. rsch. and pub. policy, 1987-90; mem. pres. adv. coun. Columbia U. Tchrs. Coll., N.Y.C., 1988-92; mem. grants adv. coun. Smith Richardson Found., 1989-92; bd. dirs. Manpower Demonstration Rsch. Coun., 1989-92; active William T. Grant Found. Commn. on Work, Family and Citizenship, 1987-88. Author: (with others) Inequality: A Reassessment of the Effects of Family and Schooling in America, 1972, Here to Stay: American Families in the Twentieth Century, 1974, Japanese translation, 1981, (with George Masnick) The Nation's Families 1960-90, 1980; editor: (with Donald Levine) The Inequality Controversy, 1975, (with Manuel Carballo) The State and the Poor in the 1980s, 1984, (with Kenneth I. Winston) Gender and Public Policy: Cases and Comments, 1993, (with David Ellwood) Welfare Realities: From Rhetoric to Reform, 1994; contbr. articles to profl. jours. Fellow Nat. Acad. Pub. Adminstrn.; mem. Am. Sociol. Assn., Population Assn. Asm., Assn. Pub. Policy Analysis and Mgmt. Office: Dept Health and Human Svcs Adminstrn Children and Families 901 D St SW Washington DC 20447-0002

BANES, BETH PEAVY, elementary school educator; b. Columbia, Miss., Apr. 5, 1944; d. Colin and Ava H. Peavy; m. Stan E. Banes, Jan. 30, 1974; children: Robert, Scott, Matt, Micah. BA, Wm. Carey Coll., 1966; MS, East Tex. State U., 1986. Cert. tchr., Tex. Sci. tchr. Quitman (Miss.) Jr. H.S., 1966-74; piano tchr. Fairfax, Va., 1974-75, Greenville, Tex., 1975-80; sci. tchr. Greenville (Tex.) Intermediate Sch., 1980-86, Omniplex Sci. Mus., Oklahoma City, Okla., 1986-88; tchr. Wiley Post Elem. Sch. Putnam City Ind. Sch. Dist., Oklahoma City, Okla., 1988-89; sci. tchr. Hillside Acad. Garland (Tex.) Ind. Sch. Dist., 1989—. Pres. PTA, Greenville, 1980-81; mem. Dist.-wide Ednl. Improvement Com., Garland, 1994-95; chmn. Hunt County chpt. March of Dimes, Greenville, 1970s; pres. Hunt County Mothers of Twins, Greenville, 1976-79; chmn. block/st. Mothers March, Garland, 1994-95. Grantee Putnam City Schs. Found., 1988. Mem. Assn. Tex. Profl. Educators (past state rep.), Sci. Tchrs. Assn. Tex. Republican. Baptist. Office: Hillside Acad Excellence 2014 Dairy Rd Garland TX 75041-2001

BANK, MARJI D., actress; b. Dallas, Sept. 22, 1923; d. John and Rose (Kaufman) Doctoroff; m. Harvey Stuart Bank, Feb. 14, 1954 (dec. Dec. 1980); children: Roanne Veldhuizen-Bank, Heidi Sue Cairns. AA, U. Chgo., 1940; BS, Northwestern U., 1944. Appeared in Shear Madness, Chgo., 1982-88. Mem. SAG, AFTRA, Actor's Equity Assn., The Arts Club. Democrat. Jewish.

BANKARD, MICHELLE LYNN, counselor; b. Balt., July 13, 1970; d. Donald Wayne and Mary Jo (Malicki) B. BA in Psychology, Coll. of Notre Dame of Md., Balt., 1992; MA in Counseling, Beaver Coll., Glenside, Pa., 1995. Program instr. CHANGE, Inc., Westminster, Md., 1992; sch. counseling intern Wordsworth Acad., Fort Washington, Pa., 1994-95; drug and alcohol prevention counselor HARBEL, Balt., 1995—. Mem. ACA, Psi Chi. Democrat. Home: 3717 Belair Rd Baltimore MD 21213 Office: HARBEL Cmty Orgn Inc 5807 Harford Rd Baltimore MD 21214

BANKO, RUTH CAROLINE, library director; b. Phillipsburg, N.J., Mar. 28, 1931; d. Arthur William and Virginia Miller (Wilson) Osborn; m. Marvin Kenneth Banko (dec.); children: David, Sallie, Susan, Joseph, Elisabeth. Cert. libr. tech. asst., Northampton AreaC.C. Salesman Stanley Home Products, 1958-95; dir. Riegelsville (Pa.) Pub. Libr., 1974—. Social ambudsman County Agy. on Aging, Doylestown, Pa.; asst. dir. Pearl Buck Found., Dublin, Pa.; mem. Riegelsville Fire Aux., 1992—; councilman, Planning Commn., Riegelsville Borough Coun., 1972-89; mem. States Legis. Com., 1972-88; mayor Borough of Riegelsville, 1990—; disaster chmn., blood chmn., bd. mem. ARC, Doylestown, 1966-86; pres. jr. high and area coun. PTA, Easton, 1966-74; pres. Boro Coun., 1980-81. Recipient award for svc. ARC, Doylestown. Mem. Pa. Boroughs Assn. (legis. com. 1972—), Pa. Mayors Assn., Easton Area Coun. PTAs (life). Democrat. Lutheran. Home: 449 Easton Rd Riegelsville PA 18077-0223 Office: Riegelsville Pub Libr 615 Easton Rd Riegelsville PA 18077-0065

BANKS, ANNA DELCEINA, financial planner; b. Newark, Oct. 8, 1952; d. James William and Serena D. (Holland) B. BS, Rutgers U., 1975; grad., U.S. Postal Svcs. Mgmt. Acad., Potomac, Md., 1984; postgrad., NYU, 1988, 90—. Lic. life and health ins. agt., N.J., lic. securities series 6, N.Y., N.J. Clk. U.S. Postal Svc., Newark, 1974-78; acctg/specialist N.Y. Postal Data Ctr., N.Y.C., 1978-83, mgr. women's program, 1983-85, acct., 1985-90; fin. planner PC Tax Prep. Assocs., Newark, 1985—; trainer various personal devel. seminars, 1980-85; workshop leader Basic Fin. Planning, 1990; instr. Am. Assn. Retired Persons, 1991—; instr., promoter Successful Money Mgmt. Seminars, Newark, 1991—; adj. prof. personal fin. Essex County Coll. Sch. Continuing and Community Edn., 1991—; instr. High Sch. Fin. Planning Program, Coll. for Fin. Planning, Denver, 1991—; bus. cons. Jr. Achievement No. N.J., Newark, 1992—. Columnist City News, Newark, 1992—; fin. editor N.J. Perspectus News Mag., Newark, 1990—; fin. columnist Daily Challenge Pubs., N.Y.C., 1994—; contbr. articles to profl. jours. Lay minister Elmwood Presbyn. Ch., East Orange, N.J., 1992—. Named Businessperson of Yr., Future Bus. Leader Am. State Leadership Conf., 1994. Mem. Nat. Assn. Tax Practitioners (nat. bd. dirs. 1993—, corp. sec. 1994—), Nat. Soc. Pub. Accts., Nat. Soc. Notaries, Nat. Tax Practitioners (charter bd. dirs., sec. N.J. chpt. 1987—), Nat. Assn. Negro Bus. and Profl. Bus. Women's Clubs (bd. dirs., treas. N.J. chpt. 1990—), Inst. Cert. Fin. Planners (cert.), Internat. Tng. in Communication Coun. I (pres. 1984-85, 1st place speech contest award 1985). Republican. Office: 1st Choice Fin Svcs 60 Glenwood Ave East Orange NJ 07017

BANKS, BETTIE SHEPPARD, psychologist; b. Birmingham, Ala., June 8, 1933; d. Francis Wilkerson and Bettie Pollard (Woodson) Sheppard; B.A., Ga. State U., 1966, M.A., 1968, Ph.D., 1970; m. Frazer Banks, Jr., Mar. 22, 1952; children: Bettie Banks Daley, Lee Frazer Banks III. Clin. assoc. Lab. for Psychol. Svcs., Ga. State U., 1968-70; intern Ga. State U. Counseling Ctr., 1969-70, Ga. Mental Health Inst., Atlanta, 1970-71, psychologist, 1971-72, chief psychologist, 1973; pvt. practice, Atlanta, 1972—; adj. assoc. prof. clin. psychology Ga. State U.; adj. asst. prof. Dept. Psychiatry, Emory U., 1974-83, 94—; mem. peer rev. panel Ga. Med. Care Found., 1980-86, chmn., 1986-88. Diplomate in clin. psychology Am. Bd. Profl. Psychology; Nat. Register Health Svc. Psychology Providers, 1977—, Nat. Register Cert. Group Psychotherapists, 1994—. Fellow Ga. Psychol. Assn. (chmn. div. E 1980, program chair ann. meeting 1991, treas. divsn. F 1993-95, chair public divsn. F 1995—); mem. APA, Am. Acad. Psychotherapists (exec. com. 1980-82, sec. 1982-86, 94—, ann. workshop chair 1979, com. ann. Inst. and Conf. 1975, 86, com. ann. workshop 1984), Am. Group Psychotherapy Assn. (clin. mem., co-chair local host com. 1995 Ann. Inst. and Conf.), Atlanta Group Psychotherapy Soc. (bd. exec. com. 1982-83, 91-92, treas. 1995—), Southeastern Psychol. Assn. Episcopalian. Club: Jr. League. Cons. editor Voices, The Art and Science of Psychotherapy, 1978-84. Office: 18 Lenox Pointe NE Atlanta GA 30324-3171

BANKS, HELEN AUGUSTA, singer, actress; b. Petersburg, Va., Sept. 8, 1922; d. Robert Augustus and Helen (Fisher) B. Student, Victoria Sch. of Music, N.Y.C., 1940-43. Singer and actress. Mem. pub. safety com. Cmty. Bd. No. 9, 1983—. Recipient Svc. award The Bd. Christian Edn., St. John Bapt. Ch., N.Y.C., 1989. Mem. Am. Guild Variety Artists, Am. Assn. Ret. Persons, Sickle Cell Found., U.S. Ski Team Found., Internat. Skiing History Assn. Democrat. Baptist. Home: Apt 6 408 West 150 St New York NY 10031

BANKS, LISA JEAN, government official; b. Chelsea, Mass., Dec. 19, 1956; d. Bruce H. and Jean P. (Como) Banks. BS in Bus. Adminstrn., Northeastern U., 1979. Coop trainee IRS, Boston, 1975-79, revenue officer, Reno, 1979-81, spl. agt., Houston, 1981-84, Anchorage, 1984-90; spl. agt. DVA-OIG Procurement Fraud Task force, Boston, 1990-92, spl. agt. NASA Kennedy Space Ctr., 1992, NASA OIG-KSC, 1992—, fed. womens program mgr., 1980-81; pres. Make-A-Wish Found. of Cen. Fla., 1994—. Recipient Superior Performance award IRS, 1981, Spl. Achievement award, 1987, 89, Employee Suggestion award, 1990. Mem. Nat. Assn. Treasury Agts. Roman Catholic Office: NASA Office of Inspector Gen PO Box 21066 Kennedy Space Center FL 32815

BANKS, MARGARET AMELIA, retired law educator, librarian, author, consultant; b. Quebec City, Que., Can., July 3, 1928; d. Thomas Herbert and Bessey (Collins) B. BA, Bishop's U., Lennoxville, Que., 1949; MA, U. Toronto, 1950, PhD, 1953. Archivist Ont. Archives, Toronto, 1953-61; law librarian U. Western Ont., London, 1961-89, assoc. prof. faculty law, 1974-86, prof., 1986-89, prof. emeritus, 1989—. Mem. Can. Assn. Law Libraries, Am. Inst. Parliamentarians, Nat. Assn. Parliamentarians, Osgoode Soc. for Can. Legal History, Arts and Letters Club of Tor. Anglican. Author: Edward Blake, Irish Nationalist, 1957, Using a Law Library, 1971, (with Karen E.H. Foti) 6th edit., 1994, Law at Western, 1959-84, 1984, The Libraries at Western, 1989, Understanding Canada's Constitution, 1991. Home and Office: 231 Windsor Ave Unit 9, London, ON Canada N6C 2A5

BANKS, MELANIE ANNE, nutritionist, biochemist, educator; b. McKeesport, Pa., Oct. 27, 1956; d. Raymond Joseph and Emma Dea (Thomas) B. BA in Music, U. Pitts., 1976, BS in Biochemistry, 1977; MS in Chemistry, Duquesne U., 1980; PhD in Nutritional Biochemistry, W.Va. U., 1986. Cert. nutrition specialist. Clin. rsch. technician Children's Hosp., Pitts., 1979-82; rsch. asst. W.Va. U., Morgantown, 1982-86; rsch. assoc. dept. Pathology U. Pitts., Pitts., 1986-87; rsch. assoc. div. respiratory diseases Nat. Inst. of Occupational Safety and Health, Morgantown, 1987-89; rsch. assoc. dept. food sci. and human nutrition U. Fla., Gainesville, 1989-91; instr. div. health sci. Santa Fe C.C., Gainesville, 1989-92; rsch. chemist div. food chem. Am. Bacteriol. and Chem. Rsch. Corp., Gainesville, 1991-92; rsch. chemist lipid nutrition lab. USDA, Beltsville, Md., 1992-94; instr. Biology Prince George's C.C., Largo, Md., 1993-94; asst. prof. biochemistry Lecom, Erie, Pa., 1994—. Vol. entertainer Gainesville area nursing homes, 1989-92; mem. Big Bros./Big Sisters greater Gainesville, 1989-90. Capt. USAR, 1990—. USDA Post-doctoral fellow, 1992, Nat. Rsch. Coun. Post-doctoral fellow, 1986. Mem. Soc. Armed Forces Med. Lab. Scientists, Am. Inst. Nutrition, Am. Dietetic Assn., Sigma Xi. Home: 1203 W 36th St Erie PA 16508-2447

BANKS, RELA, sculptor; b. Yaroslav, Poland, Oct. 8, 1933; came to U.S., 1947; d. Jacob and Frieda (Weintraub) Heuberg; m. Stanley Frederic Banks, Aug. 9, 1953; children: Andrew Howard, J. Monica, Gary Mitchell. Student, Mus. Modern Art, 1957, Art Students League, N.Y.C. and Woodstock, N.Y., 1958-61, Summit (N.J.) Art Ctr., 1966-75. Chmn. nat. juried exhibit Summit Art Ctr., 1976, mem. adminstrv. com., 1977-79, chmn. standing com. spl. events, trustee; mem. exec. com. Phoenix Gallery, N.Y.C., 1983; chmn. membership com. Stone Sculpture Soc. N.Y., 1980-82. One-woman shows include Robins Art Gallery, South Orange, N.J., 1973, Montclair (N.J.) Coll., 1974, Caldwell (N.J.) Coll., 1974, 83, Summit Art Ctr., 1976, Newark Acad., Livingston, N.J., 1976, Douglas Coll., New Brunswick, N.J., 1978, First Women's Bank, N.Y.C., 1979, Phoenix Gallery, 1979, 81, 83, Morris Mus. Arts and Scis., Morristown, N.J., 1983, Ann Leonard Gallery, Woodstock, 1983, NECCA Mus., Bklyn., Conn., 1985, Schiller-Wapner Galleries, N.Y.C., 1985, 87, Ann Norton Sculpture Galleries, West Palm Beach, Fla., 1987, David Gary Ltd, Millburn, N.J., 1988; exhibited in group shows at Phoenix Gallery, 1979, 83, Morris Mus. Art, 1979, 83, Invitational Woodstock Artists Assn., 1980, 84, Eilaine Benson Gallery, Bridgehampton, N.Y., 1980, Searles Art Ctr., Great Barrington, Mass., 1980, Nabisco Art Gallery, 1981, Summit Art Ctr., 1981, First Womens Bank, 1981, Fairleigh Dickinson U., Madison, N.J., 1983, NYU Grad. Sch. Bus., 1983, AT&T Gallery, Basking Ridge, N.J., 1984, Shering Plough Gallery, N.J., 1984, New Orleans Mus. Art, 1986, Gallery Contemporary Art at U. Colorado Springs, Colo., 1986, Schiller-Wapner Galleries, 1986, Lever House, N.Y.C., 1986, Aldrich Mus. Contemporary Art, Ridgefield, Conn., 1986, Okla. Art Ctr., Oklahoma City, 1987, "After Henry Moore", Emily Lowe Mus., Hofstra U., Hempstead, N.Y., 1988, group exhibition , Poland; represented in permanent collections New Orleans Mus. Art, Everson Mus., Syracuse, N.Y., Morris Mus. Sci. and Art, Okla. Art Ctr., Vassar Coll. Gallery, Poughkeepsie, N.Y., Millburn (N.J.) Pub. Library, Minn. Mus. Art, Mpls., Woodstock Hist. Soc., Fordham U., Lincoln Ctr., N.Y.C., Aldrich Mus. Contemporary Art, Warsaw Mus., Poland, various pvt. and corp. collections. Mem. Woodstock Artists Assn. Office: Rela Banks Studio Mink Hollow Rd Woodstock NY 12498

BANKSON, MARJORY, religious association administrator; m. Peter Bankson. BA in Govt. and Econs., Radcliffe Coll., 1961; M in Am. History, U. Alaska, 1961, postgrad., Va. Episcopal Sem. H.S. history and English tchr.; counselor Dartmouth Coll., 1969-70; profl. potter, 1970-80; pres. Faith at Work, Falls Church, Va., 1985—. Author: Briaded Streams: Esther and a Woman's Way of Growing, Seasons of Friendship: Naomi and Ruth as a Pattern, This Is My Body...Clay, Creativity and Change, (videos) The Potter and Clay, With Tongues of Fire (Five Women from the Book of Acts). Mem. Ch. of the Saviour. Office: 150 S Washington St Ste 204 Falls Church VA 22046-2921

BANNAN, KATHRYN E., government relations specialist; b. Jackson, Mich., Apr. 4, 1960; d. Philip Eugene and Joan Kathleen (Jacob) B. BA in Spanish, Kalamazoo Coll., 1981; MA in Legis. Affairs, George Washington U., 1991. Tchr. Am. Sch. Guatemala, Guatemala City, 1981-84; cons. Arecibo (P.R.) Community Health Care Inc., 1984-85; fed. govt. affairs Assoc. Hoffmann-La Roche, Washington, 1985-92, regional mgr., state govt. affairs, 1992-95; Washington rep. Lawrence Berkeley Lab., 1995—. Elected mem. Arlington County Rep. Com., Arlington, Va., 1991—; elected del. Va. Rep. Conv., 1992-94, appd. mem. Arlington County Commn. on Status of Women, 1992—; vol. Kyle McSlarrow for Congress, Arlington, 1992, 94. Mem. Washington Area State Rels. Group (bd. dirs. 1992-94), Women in Govt. Rels., Arlington Young Reps., Potomac Pachyderms. Roman Catholic. Home: 4623 31st Rd S # 1 Arlington VA 22206-1618

BANNER-BACIN, LINDA LENORE, program analyst; b. Greenville, S.C., Jan. 7, 1956; d. John Lewis and Stella (Nidock) Banner; m. Mark Stephen Bacin, June 25, 1994. AAS in Horticulture, SUNY, Cobleskill, 1976; Ba in Humanities, SUNY, Stonybrook, 1979; MBA, Pepperdine U., 1995. Jr-sr. h.s. tchr. U.S. Peace Corps, Liberia, W. Africa, 1980-82; adaptive aquatics instr. City of Oxnard, Calif., 1983; flight coord. Air Camarillo, Calif., 1984-85; police dispatcher City of Oxnard, 1985-86; program analyst Naval Surface War Ctr., Port Hueneme, Calif., 1987—; chairperson Fed. Women's Program, Port Hueneme, 1990-94; mem. Equal Employment Opportunity Com., Port Hueneme, 1992-94. Vol. Focus on the Masters, 1996; mem. Carnegie Art Mus., 1994—, Banner Elk Hist. Soc., 1989—. Recipient Beyond War award Beyond War Award Found., 1987. Mem. Am. Soc. Mil. Comptrollers, Am. Rose Soc. Ventura, Ventura County Maritime Mus., Carnegie Art Mus. Home: 461 S F St Oxnard CA 93030

BANNISTER, DENISE H., publishing executive; b. 1950. Asst. contr. Gainesville (Ga.) Times Gannett, Pensacola, Fla., 1983-84; contr. Gannett, 1984, pres., pub., 1986; pres., pub. Gannett, Huntington, 1989; v.p., pub. Pensacola New Jour. Gannett East Regional Group, 1991—. Office: Pensacola News Jour 1 News Journal Plz Pensacola FL 32501-5607*

BANTEL, LINDA MAE, art museum director; b. King City, Calif., May 30, 1943; d. Clifford Burnett and Helen Vernelle (Mallicote) Bantel; m. David Hollenberg, June 15, 1980; 1 child, Matthew Bantel Hollenberg. M.A., NYU, 1973. Research cons. N.Y. Hist. Soc., N.Y.C., 1975-76; guest co-curator Art Mus. of South Tex., Corpus Christi, Tex., 1977-79; research assoc. Met. Mus. Art, N.Y.C., 1978-80; curator, dir. of mus. Pa. Acad. Fine Arts, Phila., 1980-95. Co-author: (with James Thomas Flexner) The Face of Liberty: Founders of the U.S., 1975; author: The Alice M. Kaplan Collection, 1980, William Rush, American Sculptor, 1982; (with Marcus Burke) Spain and New Spain: Mexican Colonial Arts in Their European Context, 1979; contbr. to American Paintings in the Metropolitan Museum of Art Vol. II: A Catalogue of Works by Artists Born Between 1816-1845, 1985, (with others) Searching Out the Best, 1988, Raphaelle Peale Still Lifes, 1988; contbr. to Antiques mag., 1989. Mem. Coll. Art Assn., Am. Assn. Mus., Assn. Art Mus. Dirs. Home: 703 W Phil Ellena St Philadelphia PA 19119-3513

BANUELOS, BETTY LOU, rehabilitation nurse; b. Vandergrift, Pa., Nov. 28, 1930; d. Archibald and Bella Irene (George) McKinney; m. Raul, Nov. 1, 1986; children: Patrice, Michael. Diploma, U. Pitts., 1951; cert., Loma Linda U., 1960. RN, Calif.; cert. chem. dependency nurse. Cons. occupational health svcs. Bd. Registered Nurses, 1984—; lectr., cons. in field. Recipient Scholarship U. Pitts. Mem. Dirs. of Nursing, Calif. Assn. Nurses in Substance Abuse. Home and Office: 15 Oak Spring Ln Laguna Beach CA 92656-2980

BAQIR, FARZANA ELIZABETH, box office manager, theatrical director; b. Washington, Nov. 22, 1966; d. Farsad Alex and Virginia Eve (Graybill) B. BA, U. Md., 1989, postgrad., 1996. Stage mgr. various theatres U. Md., College Park, 1984-90, house mgr. dept. theatre, 1986-89, pub. rels. asst. dept. theatre, summer 1989, box office mgr. dept. theatre, 1992—; asst. box office mgr. Arena Stage, Washington, 1989-92. Vol. Washington Area Clinic Defense Task Force, 1994—; co-founder, dir. feminist theatre workshop U. Md., College Park, 1993—. Theatre Patrons scholar U. Md., College Park, 1989. Mem. NOW, Box Office Mgmt. Internat. Democrat. Office: Dept Theatre U Md College Park MD 20742

BARAB, PATSY LEE, nutritionist, consultant, realtor; b. Indpls., Sept. 24, 1934; BS, Mich. State U., 1956, MA, 1970; 1 child, Gregory; m. John D. Barab Jr., April 8, 1995. Asst. prof. Med. Coll. Ga., Augusta, 1972-82; nutrition cons., 1982—; assoc. Meybohm Realty, Inc., Augusta, 1987—. Mem. program com. Gertrude Herbert Art Inst., 1992—; mem. promotion com. Imperial Theater. Mem. Am. Dietetic Assn., Ga. Dietetic Assn., Augusta Dietetic Assn., Am. Home Econ. Assn., Ga. Heart Assn., Ga. Nutrition Coun., Soc. Nutrition Edn., Nutrition Today Soc. (charter), Nutritionists in Nursing Edn. (nat. chmn. 1983-84), AAUP, AAUW, GRI, CRS, Augusta Opera Club, Ruth Newman Shapiro Guild, Houndslake Country Club, Racquet Club, Million Dollar Club (life), Omicron Nu, Pi Beta Phi (arrowmont chmn. Augusta Alumnae Club 1992—). Home: 8 S Dorset Ave Ventnor City NJ 08406-2832

BARAD, JILL ELIKANN, toy company executive; b. N.Y.C., May 23, 1951; d. Lawrence Stanley and Corinne (Schuman) Elikann; m. Thomas Kenneth Barad, Jan., 28, 1979; children: Alexander David, Justin Harris. BA English and Psychology, Queens Coll., 1973. Asst. prod. mgr. mktg. Coty Cosmetics, N.Y.C., 1976-77, prod. mgr. mktg., 1977; account exec. Wells Rich Greene Advt. Agy., L.A., 1978-79; product mgr. mktg. Mattel Toys, Inc., L.A., 1981-82, dir. mktg., 1982-83, v.p. mktg., 1983-85, sr. v.p. mktg., 1985-86, sr. v.p. product devel., from 1986, exec. v.p. product design and devel., exec. v.p. mktg. and worldwide product devel., 1988-89; pres. girls and activity toys div. Mattel Toys, Inc. (name now Mattel Inc.), L.A., 1989—; pres., bd. dirs. Mattel USA, El Segundo, Calif., 1990—; pres., COO Mattel, Inc., El Segundo, Calif., 1992—; bd. dirs. Bank of Am., Microsoft Corp., Claremont U. Ctr. Bd. dirs. Town Hall of Calif.; trustee Queens Coll.; chair exec. adv. bd. Children Affected by AIDS Found.; bd. govs. Childrens Miracle Network. Mem. Am. Film Inst. (charter). Office: Mattel Inc 333 Continental Blvd El Segundo CA 90245-5032*

BARADZI, AMELIA JANE, stained glass artist, restorationist; b. Bay Shore, N.Y., Mar. 26, 1947; d. Stephen A. and Frances (De Palma) B. BA, La. Technol. U., 1970. Cert. K-6 tchr., La. Tchr. St. John's Elem. Sch., Central Islip, N.Y., 1971-72; pres. Stained Glass Creations Ltd., Bay Shore, 1972-91; sec.-treas. Baradzi Glass Inc., Bay Shore, 1991-92; owner, mgr. Stained Glass by Amelia, Bay Shore, 1993—, L.I. Stained Glass Restoration and Conservation Studio, Bay Shore, 1995—. Designer, mfr., commissions art glass Poinsettia, 1985-87, Story of Creation, 1987, Peacock, 1989; designer, mfg. leaded glass Edwardian flowercases and sconces, 1994. Mem. Bus. Improvement Dist., Bay Shore, 1994-95. Roman Catholic. Home: 75 Ontario Dr Bay Shore NY 11706-3826 Office: Stained Glass by Amelia 50 Bay Ave Bay Shore NY 11706

BARAL, LILLIAN, artist, retired educator; b. Perehinsko, Carpathia, Poland; d. Leon and Esther (Ludmer) B. BA, Hunter Coll., 1939, MA in Art, 1969. Cert. fine arts, secondary English, elem. tchr., N.Y. Sec., publicity asst. Coun. for Democracy, N.Y.C.; translator, radio script writer, announcer U.S. Office of War Info., Voice of Am., N.Y.C.; writer, publicity specialist Citizens Com. on Displaced Persons, N.Y.C., Consulate Gen. of Israel, N.Y.C.; publicity specialist Madison Books, Pub. House, N.Y.C., Brandeis U., Waltham, Mass.; pub. rels. dir. Israel Govt. Tourist Office, N.Y.C.; publicity asst. Huntington Hartford Gallery of Modern Art, N.Y.C.; fine arts tchr. Parsons Jr. H.S., Queens, N.Y., 1962-82; painter, sculptor, 1956—; art tour leader 92d St YMHA, 1985, 86. Exhbns. include N.Y. Pub. Libr., Little Gallery, 1966, Whitehouse Gallery, N.Y.C., 1967, Am. House, N.Y.C., 1968, Lord & Taylor, N.Y.C., 1970, Center Art Gallery, N.Y.C., 1971, Marie Pellicone Gallery, N.Y.C., 1979, Womanart Gallery, N.Y.C., 1979, BFM Gallery, N.Y.C., 1980, Bennet Gallery, Fairfield, Conn., 1981, Queens Mus., 1981, New Sch. for Social Rsch., N.Y.C., 1982, Lever House, N.Y.C., 1983, W.C. Post Coll., L.I., N.Y., 1984, Southhampton Coll., L.I., 1984, Queensborough C.C. Art Gallery, N.Y.C., 1985, 86, UAHC Gallery, N.Y.C., 1988, Mari Galleries, Mamaroneck, N.Y., 1989; represented in permanent collections Yad Vashem Mus., Jerusalem, 1991; shows at B'nai B'rith Klutznick Nat., Jewish Mus., Washington, Libr. Gallery, U. Maine, Augusta, Chaffee Ctr. Visual Arts, Rutland, Vt., Holocaust Mus. and Resource Ctr. Jewish Fedn., Scranton, Pa., 1995; also numerous pvt. collections; subject newspaper, mag. articles, TV interview. Mem. N.Y. Artists Equity (exec. bd. 1985-86), United Fedn. Tchrs., Mus. Modern Art (N.Y.C.). Home: 98-50 67th Ave Forest Hills NY 11374-4965 Studio: 30 E 20th St New York City NY 10003-1310

BARALD, PATRICIA A., lawyer; b. St. Louis, Mo., June 26, 1948. BA, MA summa cum laude, Brown U., 1970; JD summa cum laude, Cornell U., 1973. Bar: N.Y. 1974, D.C. 1975. Asst. prof. law Cornell Law Sch., 1973-75; ptnr. Covington & Burling, Washington. Mem. Order of the Coif. Office: Covington & Burling PO Box 7566 1201 Pennsylvania Ave NW Washington DC 20044-7566*

BARAN, SHIRLEY WALTERS, artist, sculptor; b. New Orleans; d. Harmon Jesse and Willa Mae Walters; m. Helko Eli Baran; children: Steven Jesse, Lisa Jane, Paul Vinson. Student, Corcoran Mus. Sch. Art, 1943-45, U. Ark., 1945-48, Pratt Inst., 1945-48. Co-owner, illustrator Baran-Walters Advt., Tulsa, Okla., 1949-65; free lance illustrator, painter, sculptor Greenville, S.C., 1966-81; art coord. Her Majesty Industries, Greenville, S.C.; illustrator, layout artist Millbrae (Calif.) Sun, Boutique Villager, Burlingame, Calif., Foster City (Calif.) Progress, Millbrae Leader, San Carlos (Calif.) Inquirer, Belmont (Calif.) Courier Bull., 1981-93; freelance designer Clay Art Co., San Francisco, 1987—; doll designer Friends Forever, Windsor, Calif., 1987—. Asst. leader Girl Scout Troop 40, Greenville. Recipient Merit award S.C. Watercolor Soc., 1978, Best in Category Original Sculpture Doll award Doll Artisan Guild, 1987, 89, Internat. Doll Expo, 1995. Office: Friends Forever PO Box 691 Windsor CA 95492

BARANSKI, CHRISTINE, actress; b. May 2, 1952; d. Lucien and Virginia (Mazerowski) B.; m. Matthew Cowles, Oct. 15, 1983. BA, Juilliard Sch., 1974. Plays include 'Tis a Pity She's a Whore, The Real Thing (Antoinette Perry award 1984), Cat on a Hot Tin Roof, She Stoops to Conquer, Angel City, Blithe Spirit, Coming Attractions, The Undefeated Rumba Champ, Otherwise Engaged, A Midsummer Night's Dream (Obie award 1983), Rumors (Antoinette Perry award 1989), Nick and Nora, 1991, Lips Together Teeth Apart, 1992; (films) Soup for One, 1981, Lovesick, 1983, Crackers, 1985, 9 1/2 Weeks, 1986, Legal Eagles, 1986, The Pick-up Artist, 1987, Reversal of Fortune, 1990, Life with Mikey, 1993, Addams Family Values,

1993, The War, 1994, The Ref, 1994, The Birdcage, 1996; (TV series) Cybill, 1995— (Emmy award 1995, SAG award for Comedy Show); (TV movie) To Dance with the White Dog, 1993; (TV appearences) Playing for Time, Murder Ink, All My Children, Big Shots in America, Texas, Another World. *

BARANSKI, JOAN SULLIVAN, publisher; b. Andover, Mass., Apr. 6, 1933; d. Joseph Charles and Ruth G. (McCormack) Sullivan; m. Kenneth E. Baranski, Apr. 20, 1970. B.S., U. Mass., Lowell, 1955. Tchr. Andover Public Schs., 1955-61; assoc. editor sci. and reading sch. dept. Holt, Rinehart and Winston, N.Y.C., 1961-65; promotion coord. sch. dept. Harcourt Brace Jovanovich, N.Y.C., 1965-74; mgr. div. verifiability and testing Harcourt Brace Jovanovich, 1974-75; editor-in-chief Teacher mag., Macmillan Co., Stamford, Conn., 1975-81; editor-in-chief sch. dept. Harper & Row Pubs., N.Y.C., 1981-84; v.p., editor-in-chief Globe Book Co., Simon and Schuster Edn. Group, 1984-88; pub. Joint Coun. Econ. Edn., N.Y.C., 1989-92; pub. Econs. Am., Nat. Coun. on Econ. Edn., N.Y.C., 1992—. Contbg. author: Winston Basic Reading Series, 1963, Little Owl Program, 1964. Home: 250 E 87th St New York NY 10128-3115 Office: 1140 Avenue Of The Americas New York NY 10036-5803

BARBA, ROBERTA ASHBURN, retired social worker; b. Morgantown, W.Va., June 23, 1931; d. Robert Russell and Mary Belle (Rogers) Ashburn; m. Harry C. Barba, Jan. 28, 1956 (div. June 1963); 1 child, Gregory Robert; m. Robert Franklin Church, May 10, 1972. BSSW, W.Va. U., 1953; post-grad., U. Conn., Hartford, 1953-54; MSSW, NYU, 1957. Diplomate in Am. Bd. Examiners; lic. N.Y., W.Va. Pvt. practice W.Va., 1968—; evaluator P.A.C.E., Star City, W.Va., 1973-74; social worker Family Svc. Assn., Morgantown, W.Va., 1974-75, 85-87; human resources asst., social worker Sundale Rest Home, Morgantown, 1977-79; cons., residential svcs. specialist Coordinating Coun. for Ind. Living, Morgantown, 1983-88; provider W.Va. Dept. Welfare, Human Svcs., Morgantown, 1980-87; social worker maternity svcs. Monongalia County Health Dept., Morgantown, 1985-87; social worker Hospice of Preston County, Kingwood, W.Va., 1988-89; shelter worker, field work instr. Bartlett House W.Va. Sch. Social Work, Morgantown, 1986-90; case mgr. Region VI Area Agy. on Aging, Fairmont, W.Va., 1990-92; case mgr. geriatric program W.Va. U., Morgantown, 1992-95; ret., 1995. Author: (with others) Working with Terminally Ill, 1990, (short fiction) Kids Know, 1992; freedom writer Amnesty Internat., 1987—. George Davis Bivens Found. grantee, 1953-54. Mem. NASW (charter mem., cert. diplomate), ACLU, NOW, Acad. Cert. Social Workers, W.Va. Human Resources Assn., W.Va. Child Care Assn., Monongalia County Coun. Social Agys, Phi Beta Kappa. Home: 429 Fairmont Rd Morgantown WV 26505-4244

BARBE, BETTY CATHERINE, financial analyst; b. Chgo., Dec. 24, 1930; d. Norbert Lambert and Helen Weishaar; m. Edward William, Aug. 8, 1953; children: Leonard Walter, Roger Andrew. Student, U. Toledo, 1970, 85. Acct. Gorr Printing, Allstate Ins., Muntz TV, Chgo., 1947-53; hostess Welcome Wagon Internat., Maumee, Ohio, 1965-70; v.p. sec., cost acctg. Craftmaster, Toledo, 1970-72; sec., estimator Grinnell Fire Protection, Toledo, 1972-73; exec. sec., payroll Crow, Inc. Aviation, 1973-77; asst. city clk., payroll City of Perrysburg, 1977-83, tax adminstr., 1983—. Vol. George Bush campaign candidates, 1978—; v.p. bd. Zepf Comty. Mental Health, Toledo, 1986-87; reader for Sight Ctr.; mem. Women Alive! Coalition, 1987—, Nat. Women's Polit. Caucus, 1987—, MADD, 1987—, YWCA, Perrysburg Arts Coun.; mem. Lourdes Coll. Aux., 1990. Honoree Maumee Valley coun. Girl Scouts U.S., 1990; named Woman of Yr., Bus. and Profl. Women Black Swamp Region II. Mem. Internat. Inst., Nat. Fedn. Bds. and Profl. Women, Key to the Sea Bus. and Profl. Womens Orgn. (pres. 1982-83, 83-84), Maumee Bus. and Profl. Women (pres. 1995-96, 96—), Maumee Valley Toastmasters (pres. 1989—, area gov.), Toledo Opera Soc. Assn., Two Toledos (sec., 1st v.p.), Christ Child Soc., Maumee C. of C. (sec.), Samagama Club, Zonta II (treas.), Rotary (Paul Harris fellow). Republican. Roman Catholic. Home: 724 W Wayne St Maumee OH 43537-1923 Office: City of Perrysburg 201 W Indiana Ave Perrysburg OH 43551-1525

BARBER, JOAN MARIE, artist; b. Portland, Oreg., Mar. 11, 1941; d. Wesley John and Borghild (Hovde) Wachtman; m. Willson Benn Barber, Dec. 31, 1965; children: Katherine Rose, Olive Mae. Student, Portland Mus. Art Sch., 1959-63. Hoorn-Ashby Gallery, N.Y.C., Nantucket, Mass., 1996—, Uce Stebich Gallery, Lenox Mass., 1996—; One-Woman's shows at Hanna Gallery, Stockbridge Mass.,1995, 94. 93, Exhibited in numerous group shows Oreg., Calif., Va., Wash. D.C., N.J., Mass., 1964—. Democrat.

BARBER, MARSHA, company executive; b. Peoria, Ill., Dec. 7, 1946; d. Jack R. and Dorothy M. (Zeine) Hursey; m. Thomas L. Barber, June 15, 1968; 1 child, Brett A. BS, So. Ill. U., Carbondale, 1968; postgrad., So. Ill. U., Edwardsville. Ctr. mgr. Exec. Ctrs. Northeast Ohio/Hdqrs. Cos., Columbus; now pres. Plus 1 Exec. Stes, Columbus; instr. elem. edn., Alton, Ill.; regional coun. rep. Ill. Edn. Assn.; mem. So. Ill. U. Edn. Adv. Coun. Mem. Women's Bus. Bd., Columbus, Ohio. Mem. NEA, Columbus Area C. of C. (small bus. adv. coun., exec. com., chair N.W. Area Bus. Coun.), Sports Car Club Am.

BARBER, MICHELE A., special education educator; b. Titusville, Pa., Jan. 18, 1964; d. Robert R. Averill and Carol A. (Fish) Covell; m. Timothy M. Barber, July 12, 1986. BS in Elem. Edn., U. of Pa., Clarion, 1985; MEd in Reading, U. of Pa., Slippery Rock, 1990. Substitute tchr. Warren County Sch. Dist., 1985-86; head tchr. Happy Hours Children's Ctr., Vienna, Va., 1986; substitute tchr. Fairfax County Sch. Dist., Springfield, Va., 1987; substitute tchr. various suburban schs., New Castle, Pa., 1987-90, Pitts., 1990-91; ESL tchr. Allegheny Intermediate Unit, Pitts., 1991, 92-93; reading specialist Woodland Hills Sch. Dist., Pitts., 1991-92, 93-94, New Brighton (Pa.) Sch. Dist., 1993, Oil City (Pa.) Sch. Dist., 1994-95, Erie City (Pa.) Sch. Dist., 1995—; fed. programs monitor Pa. Dept. Edn., Harrisburg, 1993-94; mem. early childhood task force, Woodland Hills Sch. Dist., 1994. Recipient scholarship Dr. Barbara Barnes, Titusville, Pa., 1981. Mem. NEA, ASCD, Three Rivers Reading Coun., Internat. Reading Assn. Nat. Coun. Tchrs. Math., Pa. Assn. Fed. Programs Coords., Erie Reading Coun. Home: 2963 Holman Dr Erie PA 16509

BARBETTA, MARIA ANN, health records administrator, consultant; b. Bristol, Pa., Mar. 20, 1956; d. Eugene Charles and Anna Barbetta. AA, Bucks County Community Coll., 1976; BS, Coll. Allied Health Professions, Temple U., 1978. Dir. med. records Cumberland Regional Health Plan, Vineland, N.J., 1978; dir. med. record dept. St. Mary Hosp., Langhorne, Pa., 1978—; cons. med. records St. Joseph's Home for Aged, Holland, Pa., 1983-94; spkr. on med. record topics to various orgns., nationally, 1983—; cons. on health info. mgmt., optical imaging syss., 1990—. Mem. Am. Mgmt. Assn., Nat. Med. Records Imaging Users Group (sec. 1992-93, chairperson 1994-95, past chairperson 1995-96), Am. Health Info. Mgmt. Assn. (contbg. author jour. 1992, 93), Pa. Health Info. Mgmt. Assn. (edn. com. 1985-87, 91-92, project mgr. strategic plan 1987-89, sec. 1990-91, edn. com. 1991-92), RTAS Med. Record Users Group (co-chair 1993-94, 94-95), Southeastern Pa. Health Info. Mgmt. Assn. (chmn. membership com. 1987-88, membership com. 1988-89, chmn. program and edn. 1989-90, sec. 1992-93, pres.-elect 1996—). Avocations: cross-country skiing, volunteer work, reading, traveling. Home: 4707 Grandview Ave Bensalem PA 19020-1011 Office: St Mary Hosp Langhorne-Newtown Rd Langhorne PA 19047

BARBIERI, BARBARA CAROLYN, newspaper editor; b. Rockford, Ill., Oct. 18, 1929; d. John Edward and Eleanora Elvira (Nelson) Forsell; m. James Charles Barbieri, Apr. 28, 1951; children: Charles Edward, Cynthia Jean Barbieri Pastore. BA, DePauw U., 1951. 1st grade tchr. Bluffton (Ind.) Schs., 1953-54; photographer, arts editor News-Banner Publs., Bluffton, 1975—. Past pres. Bluffton-Wells County Pub. Libr. Bd.; elder Presbyn. Ch., Bluffton. Mem. Newspapers in Edn. (state pres. 1995-96), Northeastern Ind. Radio Readers (bd. dirs. 1995—), Kappa Kappa Kappa, Alpha Chi Omega, Bayview Reading Club. Office: News Banner Publs 125 N Johnson St Bluffton IN 46714

BARBIERI-MULEE, ALICE MARIE, retired secondary education educator; b. Chgo., Oct. 18, 1918; d. John and Josephine (Slezak) Zylowski; m. Victor Oscar Barbieri, June 18, 1944 (dec. May 1987); children: Ronald Francis Barbieri, Vicki Lynne Barbieri-Creager; m. Martin J. Mulee, Mar. 4, 1995. B of Music Edn., DePaul U., 1941. Cert. coll. tchr. Tchr. music K-6 Sch. Dist., Berwyn, Ill., 1941-44; tchr. music K-6 Calumet Twp., Gary, Ind., 1945-47, tchr. h.s. and jr. h.s., 1948-55; tchr. K-6 City of Gary, 1958-75; tchr. Mohave C.C., Lake Havasu, Ariz., 1975-96; substitute tchr. h.s. Sch. Dist., Lake Havasu, 1977-80. With choral group Filareci Dudiarz, Chgo., 1939-44; singer, soloist Chgo. Opera Co., 1939-44; choir dir. Our Lady of the Lake Cath. Ch., 1975-95. Scholar Tribune Music Festival, 1942. Mem. AAUW. Home: 2861 Indian Pipe Dr Lake Havasu City AZ 86406

BARBIS, JEAN W., counselor; b. Richlands, Va., Nov. 6, 1939; d. Verner E. and Edith M. (Hunt) Wyatt; m. Elio M. Barbis; children: Anthony, Susan, Margaret, Elizabeth. BA, Miami U., Ohio, 1961; MS, SUNY, 1979. Mental health coord. US Embassy, Caracas, 1983-91; faculty Unimet, Caracas, 1983-91; family outreach counselor No. Va. Family Svc., Falls Ch., 1992—; cons. Sexual Assault and Victims Advocacy Svc., Woodbridge, Va., 1992—; sec. Va. Alligned Against Sexual Assault, mem. bd., 1992—; presenter in field. Mem. Unitarian Ch. Fellow PEO; grantee Fairfax County, Va., 1992—, Prince William County, Va., 1993—. Mem. Am. Counseling Assn., Nat. Orgn. Male Survivors (charter). Office: No Va Family Svc #207 Falls Church VA 22041

BARBO, DOROTHY MARIE, obstetrician, gynecologist, educator; b. River Falls, Wis., May 28, 1932; d. George William and Marie Lillian (Stelsel) B. BA, Asbury Coll., 1954; MD, U. Wis., 1958; DSc (hon.), Asbury Coll., 1981. Diplomate Am. Bd. Ob-Gyn. Resident Luth. Hosp. Milw., 1958-62; instr. Sch. Medicine Marquette U., Milw., 1962-66, asst. prof., 1966-67; assoc. prof. Christian Med. Coll. Punjab U., Ludhiana, India, 1968-72; assoc. prof. Med. Coll. Pa., Phila., 1972-87, prof., 1988-91; prof. U. N.Mex., Albuquerque, 1991—; med. dir. Women's Health Ctr., 1991—; acting dept. chair Christian Med. Coll., Punjab U., 1970; dir. Ctr. for Mature Woman Med. Coll. Pa., 1983-91; examiner Am. Bd. Ob-Gyn, 1984—; bd. dirs. Ludhiana Christian Med. Coll., N.Y.C., Svc. Master Co. Ltd., Downers Grove, Ill., 1982-91. Co-author: Care of Post Menopausal Patient, 1985; editor: Medical Clinics of N.A., vol. 71, 1987; contbr. chpt. to book. Student chpt. sponsor Christian Med. and Dental Soc., Phila., 1973-93, trustee, 1991-95, pres.-elect Nat. Christian Med. and Dental Soc.; tchr., elder Leverington Presbyn. Ch., Phila., 1988-91; interviewer Reader's Digest Internat. fellowships, Brunswick, Ga., 1982—; bd. dirs. Phila. chpt. Am. Cancer Soc., 1980-86, vol., 1984. Named sr. clin. trainee USPHS, HEW, 1963-65, one of Best Woman Drs. in Am. Harper Bazaar, 1985. Fellow ACS (sec. Phila. chpt. 1990), ACOG, Am. Fertility Soc.; mem. Obstet. Soc. Phila. (pres. 1989-90), Phila. Colposcopy Soc. (pres. 1982-84), Philadelphia County Med. Soc. (com. chmn. 1989-90), Alpha Omega Alpha. Office: U N Mex Dept Ob-Gyn 2211 Lomas Blvd NE Albuquerque NM 87131-6285

BARBOUR, CLAUDE MARIE, minister; b. Brussels, Oct. 2, 1935; came to U.S., 1969; Diploma d'État d'Infirmières, Ècole d'Infirmières, Paris, 1956; diploma d'Ètudes Religieuses, Faculté Libre de Théolog, Paris, 1958; MST, N.Y. Theol. Sem., 1970; DST, Garrett Evang. Theol. Sem., 1973. Ordained to ministry Presbyn. Ch., 1974. Youth counselor Young Women's Christian Assn., Geneva, 1959-61, Edinburgh, 1965-67; missionary Paris Evang. Missionary Soc., So. Africa, 1962-64; deaconess Ch. of Scotland, Edinburgh, 1967-69; from asst. to assoc. pastor First United Presbyn. Ch., Gary, Ind., 1974-80; from asst. to assoc. prof. Cath. Theol. Union, Chgo., 1976-86, prof., 1986—; prof. McCormick Theol. Sem., Chgo., 1990-96; founder, dir. Shalom Ministries and Community, Chgo., 1975—; parish assoc. First Presbyn. Ch., Evanston, Ill., 1983—. World Coun. Chs. scholar, Geneva, 1969, United Presbyn. Ch. Commn. on Ecumenical Mission and Rels., N.Y., 1972; recipient Laskey award United Meth. Ch. Womens Div. the Bd. Global Ministries, N.Y., 1972, Civic award Ind. Women's Coun., 1976, Challenge of Peace award Chgo. Ctr. for Peace Studies, 1991, Martin P. Wolf O.F.M. award Justice, Peace and Integrity of Creation Coun. of the English-Speaking Conf. of the Order of Friars Minor, 1996. Mem. AAUW, Internat. Assn. for Mission Studies, Nat. Assn. Presbyn. Clergywomen, Am. Soc. Missiology, Assn. Prof. Mission, Midwest Fellowship Prof. Mission, Assn. Presbyn. in Cross-Cultural Mission. Home: 1649 E 50th St Apt 21A Chicago IL 60615-6109 Office: Catholic Theological Union 5401 S Cornell Ave Chicago IL 60615-5698

BARBOUR, PATRICIA ANNE, elementary education educator, flight attendant; b. N.Y.C., Oct. 5, 1961; d. Walter Edward and Marie Barbour. BS in Psychology, Loyola Marymount U., 1983; diploma, Assn. Montessori Internat., 1985; MEd in Adminstrn. and Supervision, George Mason U., 1993, MEd in Curriculum and Instrn., 1994. Tchr. Montessori Sch., L.A., 1984-85; kindergarten-4th grade tchr. St. Martin of Tours Sch., L.A. Archdiocese, Brentwood, Calif., 1985-86; customer svc. rep. Nordstrom, L.A., 1986-87; flight attendant Am. Airlines, L.A., Washington, 1987—; substitute tchr. Spotsylvania County Schs., Fredericksburg, Va., 1990-93; 1st grade tchr. Ben D. Quinn Sch., Craven County Schs., New Bern, N.C., 1994-95; 1st grade tchr. Courtland Elem. Sch., Spotsylvania, Va., 1995—, staff devel. com., 1995—; co-chmn. sch. climate com. So. Assn. Colls. and Schs., New Bern, 1994—. Author curriculum materials. Mem. ASCD, Assn. for Childhood Edn. Internat., Nat. Coun. Tchrs. Math., N.C. Coun. Tchrs. of Math., Phi Delta Kappa, Kappa Delta Pi (outstanding student award 1994). Roman Catholic. Home: 14213 Burlingame Ln Fredericksburg VA 22407-1585 Office: Courtland Elem Sch 6601 Smith Station Rd Spotsylvania VA 22553

BARCA, KATHLEEN, marketing executive; b. Burbank, Calif., July 26, 1946; d. Frank Allan and Blanch Irene (Griffith) Barnes; m. Gerald Albino Barca, Dec. 8, 1967 (dec. May 1993); children: Patrick Gerald, Stacia Kathleen. Student, Pierce Coll., 1964; B in Bus., Hancock Coll., 1984. Teller Security Pacific Bank, Pasadena, Calif., 1968-69, Bank Am., Santa Maria, Calif., 1972-74; operator Gen. Telephone Co., Santa Maria, Calif., 1974-83, supr. operator, 1983-84; account exec. Sta. KRQK/KLLB Radio, Lompoc, Calif., 1984-85; owner Advt. Unltd., Orcutt, Calif., 1986-88; regional mgr. A.L. Williams Mktg. Co., Los Alamos, Calif., 1988-89; supr. Matol Botanical Internat., 1989-91; account exec. Santa Maria Times, 1989—. Author: numerous local TV and radio commercials, print advt. Activist Citizens Against Dumps in Residential Environments, Polit. Action Com., Orcutt and Santa Maria; chmn. Community Action Com., Santa Maria, Workshop EPA, Calif. Div., Dept. Health Svcs. State of Calif.; vice coord. Toughlove, Santa Maria, 1988-89; parent coord., mem. steering com. ASAP and Friends, 1988-89. Mem. NAFE, Womens Network-Santa Maria, Ctrl. Coast Ad (recipient numerous awards), Santa Maria C. of C. (amb. representing Santa Maria Times 1990-94, asst. chief amb. 1993-94). Democrat. Home: 357 Saratoga Ave Grover Beach CA 93433

BARCLAY, DEBRA SUE, public relations professional, media consultant; b. Grand Rapids, Mich., Sept. 17, 1959. BFA in Comms., U. Cin., 1981. Reporter Energy Daily, Def. Week, 1981-82; editor, media cons. CleanWater Action Project, 1983; reporter Sta. WWWK, Sta. WAMU, Nat. Pub. Radio, Washington, 1982-84; pub. rels. Pollock and Fenton Comms., Washington, 1983-86; newsdesk MacNeil-Lehrer News Hour, Washington, 1984; comms. dir., editor, nat. spokesperson Ctr. for Auto Safety, Washington, 1986-95; owner Barclay Comms., Silver Spring, Md., 1996—; mem. pub. affairs adv. bd. Advocates for Auto and Hwy. Safety, Washington; cons. Ctr. for Sci. in Pub. Interest, Washington, AARP; appeared on nat. TV including ABC Good Morning Am., CNN, CNBC, CBC Can., Fox, NBC, 1986-95; quoted in nat. press including N.Y. Times, WallStreet Jour. Freelance writer for Am. Film, City Paper, Nuclear Times, LA Times, Newsday, Miami Herald, USA Today, Knight-Ridder, WHFS Press, Sentinel Newspapers, WWW Online Mags.; writer, photographer for Scene Mag.; writer for Clifton Mag., Cin. Mag. Pianist Takoma Metaphys. Ch., Takoma Park, Md., 1996—; vol., spkr., comms. cons. MADD, Md. and Fla., 1996. Mem. NAFE, Investigative Reporters and Editors, Nat. Assn. Self-Employed, Women in Comms., Washington Ind. Writers, Montgomery County TV Md. Democrat. Office: Barclay Comms # 33 9000 Manchester Rd Silver Spring MD 20901-4124

BARCUS, MARY EVELYN, primary school educator; b. Peru, Ind., Apr. 3, 1938; d. Arthur Gibson and Mildred (Neher) Shull; m. Robert Gene Barcus, Aug. 9, 1959; children: Jennifer Sue, Debra Lynn. BS, Manchester Coll., 1960; MA, Ball State U., 1964. Kindergarten tchr. Miami Elem. Sch., Wabash, Ind., 1960-64; elem. tchr. Crooked Creek Sch., Indpls., 1964-72; preschool tchr. Second Presbyn. Preschool, Indpls., 1980-85, Speedway Coop., Indpls., 1985-86; tchr. asst. St. Monica Cath. Sch., Indpls., 1990; preschool tchr., fun club tchr. Arthur Jordan YMCA, Indpls.; preschool tchr. Indpls. (Ind.) Children's Mus., 1979—; docent sch. tours Children's Mus., Indpls., 1987—; interpreter at Indpls. children's mus.; facilitator Systematic Tng. Effective Parenting, Indpls. Writer: (children's songs) Piggback Songs for Infants and Toddlers, 1985, Piggyback Songs in Praise of God, 1986; editor elem. sch. newspaper; producer (with others) weekly show for cable TV. Profl. vol., libr. helper in local sch. systems; office helper North Cen. High Sch.; served on PTOs in various capacities; mem. Crossroads Guild, Parents Day Out of St. Luke's Meth. Ch., mem. ch. bd., Two's Tchr. Early Childhood Ctr.; Sun. sch./vacation ch. sch. tchr.; bd. dirs. Manchester Coll. Parents Assn. Mem. AAUW (charter, sec.), NEA (life), Ind. Assn. Edn. Young Children (state conf. com.), Pi Lambda Theta. Democrat. Mem. Church of Brethren. Home: 2230 Brewster Rd Indianapolis IN 46260-1521

BARDACH, JOAN LUCILE, clinical psychologist; b. Albany, N.Y., Oct. 3, 1919; d. Monroe Lederer and Lucile May (Lowenberg) B. AB, Cornell U., 1940; AM in Psychology, NYU, 1951; PhD in Clin. Psychology, 1957; cert. in psychoanalysis and psychotherapy, NYU, 1970. Supr. clin. psychologist NYU Rusk Inst. Rehab. Medicine, 1959-61; asst. chief and acting chief psychologist Rusk Inst. Rehab. Medicine, 1962-65, dir. psychol. services, 1965-82; research psychologist, mem. faculty N.Y. Med. Coll., 1961-62; clin. prof. rehab. medicine (psychology) NYU, 1976—, supr. postdoctoral program psychoanalysis and psychotherapy, 1978—; pvt. practice clin. psychology and psychoanalysis N.Y.C., 1957—; non-govtl. orgn. rep. to UN Internat. Ctr. Sociol., Penal and Penitentiary Rsch. and Studies, Messina, Italy, 1985—; prin. investigator NIMH, 1976-81; mem. adv. bd. Coalition Sexuality and Disability, Planned Parenthood, 1983-89; cons. in field. Contbr. articles to profl. jours., chpt. to books. Recipient 3 awards for ednl. film, Choices: In Sexuality With Physical Disability, Internat. Film Festivals, Pioneer award for Sexual Attitude Reassessment Workshops The Coalition on Sexuality and Disability, 1989; NIMH fellow Inst. Sex Rsch., U. Ind., 1976. Fellow Am. Orthopsychiat. Assn.; mem. Am. Psychol. Assn., Am. Congress Rehab. Medicine, Sex Info. and Edn. Council U.S., Nat. Register Health Service Providers in Psychology, Eastern Psychol. Assn., N.Y. State Psychol. Assn. Home & Office: 50 E 10th St New York NY 10003-6223

BARDEEN-HENSCHEL, ANN, anesthesiology educator; b. Milw., Sept. 17, 1921; d. Charles Russell Bardeen and Ruth Hames; widowed; children: Kira, Ingrid, Rhonda (dec.). BS in Med. Sci., U. Wis., 1942, MD, 1945. Diplomate in anesthesiology, London, Am. Bd. Anesthesiologists. Instr. anesthesiology U. Wis. Med. Sch., Madison, 1953-54; instr. anesthesia U. Sask., Saskatoon, Can., 1954-60; from asst. prof. to assoc. prof. Med. Coll. Wis., Milw., 1960-68; assoc. clin. prof. Froedtert Meml. Luth. Hosp., Milw., 1978—; chair inst. rsch. com. Med. Coll. Wis., Milw., 1971-78, mem. tranfusion com., 1969—. Fellow Royal Coll. Physicians and Surgeons Can., Faculty Anesthesia Royal Coll. Surgery London; mem. AAUW (name grantee), Am. Med. Women's Assn. (Civic Svc. award), Alpha Omega Alpha. Home: 412 N Lake Rd Oconomowoc WI 53066

BARDEN, JANICE KINDLER, personnel company executive; b. Cleve.; d. Norman Allen and Bessie G. (Black) Kindler; m. Hal Barden, Nov. 12, 1944 (dec. Jan. 1985) 1 child, Sheryl Andrea Barden Coholan. BBA, Miami U., Oxford, Ohio, 1947; M in Indsl. Psychology, Kent State U., 1948. Asst. dir. admissions Fairleigh Dickinson U., Teaneck, N.J., 1950-53; gen. mgr. Pilots Employment Assocs., Teterboro, N.J., 1953-71; founder, pres. Aviation Pers. Internat., New Orleans, 1971—; commr. jury U.S. Dist. Ct. (ea. dist.) La., New Orleans, 1965—; lectr. in field. Chmn. History of Aviation Collection U. Tex., Dallas, 1980—; served on Pres. Com. Rehab. Vietnam POW Pilots; mem. FAA's Blue Ribbon Panel. Recipient Disting. Alumnus award Kent State U., 1986, Cuyahoga Falls H.S., 1988, Doswell award Nat. Bus. Aircraft Assn., 1994. Mem. AAUW, Nat. Bus. Aircraft Assn. (chmn. conf. 1975, 85, 87, 90, 94), Flight Safety Found. (chmn. corp. seminar), Profl. Aircraft Maint. Assn., Bus. and Profl. Women's Club, Kent State Alumni Assn. (bd. dirs. 1976-82), Order of Rainbow (grand coord. 1973-84), Psi Chi. Republican. Episcopalian. Office: Aviation Pers Internat PO Box 6846 New Orleans LA 70174-6846

BARDSLEY, KAY, historian, dance professional; b. Port Said, Egypt, Apr. 17, 1921; came to U.S., 1929; d. Chris and Helen (Jones) Lanitis; m. James Calvert Bardsley, May 30, 1947 (wid. Sept. 1978); children: Wendy Jane, Amy Kim; m. Donald Marshall Kuhn, Feb. 25, 1990. Student, Duncan Dance Tng./Carnegie, Hall, Steinway Hall Studios, N.Y.C., 1931-42; BA cum laude, Hunter Coll., 1942. Dance debut Maria-Theresa Duncan, N.Y.C., 1934; soloist Maria-Theresa Heliconiades, N.Y.C., 1936-42; Duncan tchr. Maria-Theresa Sch., N.Y.C., 1937-46; tchr. Creative Dance for Children, N.Y.C., 1960-66, Isadora Duncan-Maria-Theresa Heritage Group, N.Y.C., 1977-87; fashion editor Woman's Day, N.Y.C., 1943-45; TV work WPIX Gloria Swanson Hour, 1948-49; writer/producer ABC Network/Don Ameche Langfor Show, 1949-50; syndicated film series producer, 1950-60; producer video documentation of Duncan Repertory, 1976-80. Writer, lectr. in field; prodr.: (documentary) The Last Isadorable, 1988, Isadore Duncan and the Birth of Modern Dance, 1995; contbr. articles to profl. dance jours. and publs. including Dance Scope, 1977, Ballet Rev., 1991, 94; most recent works in field include ReAnimations of Duncan Masterworks, A Four-year Project, presented at Dance ReConstructed Conf., Rutgers U., 1992, numerous conf. presentations and documentation of Isadora Duncan's 1st sch.; pub. by Congress for Rsch. in Dance Ann., 1979. Trustee Coun. for the Arts in Westchester, n.Y., 1973-76; bd. dirs. Bicentennial Com., Chappaqua, N.Y., 1973-76; co-chmn. Community Day, 1973, 75. Grantee NEA, N.Y.C., 1980; pioneer NYU/Master Tchng. Dance Tng. Inst., 1987. Mem. Soc. for Dance History Scholars, Am. Dance Guild, World Dance Alliance, Dance Critics Assn. (assoc.), Isadora Duncan Internat. Inst. (pres., founder 1978-96). Office: IDII 6305 S Geneva Cir Englewood CO 80111-5437

BAREOFF, KATHY See ZOUBAREFF, OLGA KATARINA

BARGAR, ELLEN JUNE, music educator; b. Columbus, Ohio, Aug. 5, 1967; d. Philip Noel and Martha Evelyn (Early) Myers; m. John Reeder Bargar, Aug. 15, 1989. MusB in Piano summa cum laude, Ohio State U., 1990, BME cum laude, 1990. Cert. tchr. K-12, music, Ohio, Calif. Class piano tchr. Yamaha Music Sch., San Jose and Mountain View, Calif., 1990-91; tchr. vocal and instrumental New Haven Unified Sch. Dist., Union City, Calif., 1990—; telemarketer Toledo (Ohio) Symphony Orch., Summers, 1988, 89. Mem. Am. String Tchrs.' Assn. (string orch. asst. dir., counselor Summers1987-88), Calif. Music Tchrs.' Assn., Golden Key Honors Soc., Music Educators Nat. Conf., Delta Omicron (sec. 1987-88, treas. 1988-89), Phi Kappa Phi. Home: 310 Ventura Ave #3 Palo Alto CA 94306 Office: New Haven Unified Sch Dist Union City CA 94587

BARHAM, PATTE (MRS. HARRIS PETER BOYNE), publisher, author, columnist; b. L.A.; d. Frank Barham and Princess Jessica Meskhi Gleboff; student U. So. Calif., U. Ariz.; LittD, Trinity So. Bible Coll.; hon. doctorate, Cambridge, Eng., D Internat. Arts. War corr., Korea; syndicated columnist; cable TV show; acting sec. of state, State of Calif., 1980-81; Life mem. AAU, former v.p. pub. rels.; active House Ear Inst.; internat. com. L.A. Philharmonic. Author: Pin up Poems; Rasputin: The Man Behind the Myth, 1977; Peasant to Palace: Rasputin's Cookbook, 1990; Marilyn: The Last Take, 1992. Decorated dame Sovereign Order of Alfred the Great, Grand Cross, Patron of Honor; Campagnon de la Couronne d'Epines, Ancienne Abbaye-Principaute de San Luigi. Mem. DAR, Outrigger Canoe, Waikiki Yacht (Hawaii); Wilshire Country, Ebell, Balboa Bay; Met. (N.Y.C.); Delta Gamma.

BARIL, NANCY ANN, gerontological nurse practitioner, consultant; b. Paterson, N.J., May 10, 1952; d. Kenneth Gerald and Jeanette Elenore (Girodet) Keiser; m. Joel Mark Baril, Apr. 15, 1984; children: Jason Kenneth, Jennifer Jean. AA, Gulf Coast C.C., 1976; BS in Nursing, Fla. State U., 1978; M in Nursing, UCLA, 1983. Registered pub. health nurse, Calif.; ANA cert. gerontol. nurse practitioner. Charge nurse, nurse preceptor Cedar Sinai Med. Ctr., L.A., 1979-83; RN Nursing Svcs. Incorp., Sherman Oaks, Calif., 1980-83; nurse practitioner Santa Monica Peer Counseling Ctr., Santa Monica, Calif., 1983; nurse cons., gerontol. nurse practitioner Summit Health Ltd., Burbank, Calif., 1983-85; nurse cons. Geriatric Assocs., Granada Hills, Calif., 1983-85; nurse cons., gerontol. nurse practitioner Care Enterprises West, Burbank, 1985-86; patient svcs. coord., gerontol. nurse practitioner

ARA Living Ctrs., Glendale, Calif., 1986-87; DON, gerontol. nurse practitioner Astoria Convalescent Hosp. Sign of the Dove, Sylmar, Calif., 1988-91; gerontol. nurse practitioner Balboa Plz. Med. Group, 1991—. Mem. PTA, Granada Hills, 1985. Mem. ANA, Calif. Coalition of Nurse Practioners, Calif. Nursing Assn., Gerontol. Soc., Sigma Theta Tau (rec. sec. 1983-85). Democrat. Episcopalian. Avocations: reading, crossword puzzles, gardening, jet-skiing. Home: 17831 Tuscan Dr Granada Hills CA 91344-1094 Office: Balboa Med Group 10605 Balboa Blvd Ste 200 Granada Hills CA 91344

BARKER, BARBARA, real estate professional; b. Pulaski, Tenn., July 18, 1938; d. Dan and Anna (Butler) Ingram; m. Emmet Barker, Nov. 25, 1960; children: Melanie, Lynn, Harvey, Dan. BS, U. Tenn., 1960. Home economist Knoxville (Tenn.) Utilities Bd.; tchr. Arlington High Sch., Arlington Heights, Ill.; pres. Barbara Barker and Assocs., Brownsville, Tenn., Deerfield (Ill.) Ptnrs.; also owner, mgr. Re/Max Deerfield; Prundential preferred properties Deerfield, Ill. Exec. bd., treas. Arden Shore Sch.; elder Presbyn. Ch. Mem. Nat. Assn. Realtors, Ill. Assn. Realtors, Women's Coun. Realtors (pres. 1993-94, exec. bd.), North Shore Bd. Realtors, Tenn. Home Econs. Assn. (v.p.). Home: 1050 Meadowbrook Ln Deerfield IL 60015-3459 Office: 990 S Waukegan Rd Lake Forest IL 60045-2655

BARKER, BARBARA YVONNE, respiratory therapist; b. Whittier, Calif., Apr. 19, 1951; d. Donald Wayne and Ruth Berta (Hagen) Schutt; m. Jimmy D.W. McWilson, Feb. 23, 1974 (div. Sept. 1980); m. Richard Alexander Barker, Aug. 01, 1987; 1 child, Christina Nicole. AS in Respiratory Therapy, Mt. San Antonio Coll., Walnut, Calif., 1971; BS in Bus. Adminstrn., U. Redlands, 1989; MPA, Marist Coll., 1996. Lic. nursing home adminstr., Calif.; registered respiratory therapist; lic. respiratory care practitioner. Neonatal respiratory therapist U. Calif.-San Diego Med. Ctr., 1971-74; respiratory therapy supr. Hillside Hosp., 1974-75; asst. dir. ops. J.D.W. McWilson and Assocs., 1975-77; sales rep. Baxter-Travenol Home Respiratory Therapy, 1984-86; clin. application specialist Infrasonics, Inc., 1987-88; respiratory therapist/clin. coord., nursing home adminstr. Sharp Health Care, 1977-84, 88-90; nursing home adminstr. Care West Anza, 1990, Brighton Pl. Spring Valley, San Diego, 1990-91; dir. respiratory care No. Dutchess Hosp., Rhinebeck, N.Y., 1991—; cons. health care delivery systems various acute and long term care orgns., Dutchess County, N.Y., 1991—; developer quality assurance program long term care facility, San Diego, 1990; med. products researcher devel. neonatal ventilator device FDA, San Diego, 1988; coord. regional healthcare seminar, Dutchess County, Marist Coll. Author quality assurance protocol durable med. equipment cos., San Diego Am. Lung Assn., 1989; developer instrnl. manuals for patients with chronic lung disease and asthma, San Diego, 1990. Bd. mem. San Diego chpt. Calif. Assn. Health Facilities, 1990-91; participant Christmas in April civic rebldg. program, Poughkeepsie, N.Y., 1992-93. Mem. Am. Assn. Respiratory Therapy, Calif. Soc. Respiratory Therapy (treas., bd. mem., ednl. developer 1986-90), Calif. Assn. Health Facilities, Mid Hudson Repiratory Care Dirs. Assn. Democrat. Lutheran. Home: 2 Birch Hill Dr Poughkeepsie NY 12603-6132 Office: No Dutchess Hosp 10 Springbrook Ave Rhinebeck NY 12572-1115

BARKER, CELESTE ARLETTE, computer scientist; b. Redding, Calif., Apr. 19, 1947; d. Edwin Walter Squires and Rachel (Kinkead) Layton; m. Julius Jeep Chernak, Sept. 13, 1970, (div. 1980); children: Sean Matthew, Bret Allen; m. Jackson Lynn Barker, Oct. 8, 1988. BA in Art, San Francisco State U., 1970; AA in Engring. Tech., Coll. Marin, 1980; MBA in Mgmt., Golden Gate U., 1988. Cert. netware engr. Art tchr. San Rafael (Calif.) Schs., 1971-75; owner, photographer Julius Chernak Photography, Novato, Calif., 1970-76; draftsman Donald Foster Drafting, San Rafael, 1975-76; surveyor Parks Dept. State Calif., Inverness, 1976; electric draftsman Pacific Gas & Electric, San Rafael, 1976-78, electric engring. estimator, 1978-79; mktg. rep. Pacific Gas & Electric, Santa Rosa, 1980-85; valuation analyst Pacific Gas & Electric, San Francisco, 1985-86, budget analyst, 1986-88, budget system project mgr., 1988-89; fin. asset mgr. Pacific Gas & Electric, Vallejo, Calif., 1989-90; ops. mgr. San Francisco Mus. Modern Art, 1990-91; cons. CB Cons., Atlanta, 1991-93; computer local area network mgr. Ga. Inst. Tech., Atlanta, 1993-94; systems integrator Bank South, Atlanta, 1994-95; mgmt. info. sys. mgr. Dinwiddie Constr., San Francisco, Calif., 1995-96; process/project mgr. Sybase, Inc., Emeryville, Calif., 1996—. Dir. Mariner Green Townhomes Assn., treas. 1987-88. Mem. Network Profls. Assn., Sierra Club. Home: 29 Woodside Way San Rafael CA 94901

BARKER, GLORIA S., government and community affairs professional; b. Greensboro, N.C., Mar. 8, 1938; d. George Frederick and Emma Lenoir (Oliphant) Shaw; m. Rodney Dinsmore Steele, Jr., Dec. 21, 1958 (Nov. 30, 1974); children: Laura Kimberlea Steele Young, Michael Shawn, Karen Elizabeth; m. Jeter Olive Barker, Jr., June 25, 1991. Student, Guilford Coll., 1956-57, N.C. State U., 1984-86. Engring. sec. J.E. Sirrine, Raleigh, N.C., 1975-76; legal sec., paralegal Thorp & Anderson, Raleigh, N.C., 1976-78, Kalyvas & Assocs., Myrtle Beach, S.C., 1978-80; paralegal Golden Corral Corp., Raleigh, S.C., 1981-89, adminstr. labor and employment law, 1989-93; dir. govt. and cmty. affairs Golden Corral Corp., Raleigh, 1994—. Commr. Gov.'s Commn. on Workforce Preparedness, Raleigh, N.C., 1995-96; mem. State Govt. Affairs Coun. Mem. N.C. Restaurant Assn. (dir. 1994—), Nat. Restaurant Assn. (mem. com. chair 1993—), Assn. Execs. N.C., N.C. Free, Adult Student Orgn. N.C. State U. (pres. 1985-86). Republican. Methodist. Office: Golden Corral Corp PO Box 29502 5151 Glenwood Ave Raleigh NC 27626

BARKER, JUDY, foundation executive; b. Burlington, N.C., Feb. 5, 1941; d. Thelma Ferguson; children: Lesa, Lori. Student, Ohio State U., Franklin U.; HHD, Xavier U., 1986. Administrv. asst. children's Hosp., Columbus, Ohio, 1963-68, Mount Carmel Hosps., Inc., Columbus, 1969-72; adminstr. Borden Found., Borden, Inc., Columbus, 1973-75, exec. dir., 1975-83, dir. civic affairs, 1977-79, pres., 1983—, v.p. social responsibility, 1979—; Bd. dirs. Ohio State U. Hosps.; mem. Columbus Commn. on Ethics and Values; mem. adv. bd. Ohio State U. Sch. Home Econs.; mem. found. ctr. adv. nat. Nat. Directory Corp. Giving; active N.Y. Contbns. Adv. Group; mem. corp. adv. bd. Philanthropic Adv. Svc.; bd. dirs. Coun. Better Bus. Bur. Found., Greater Columbus Art Coun.; mem. Afro.-Am. adv. bd. Columbus Mus. Art. Bd. dirs. Pub./Pvt. Ventures, Ohio State U. Hosps., Columbus Commn. on Ethics and Values; mem. Sch. Home Econs. adv. bd. Ohio State U.; mem found. ctr. adv. bd. nat. Directory Corporate Giving; active N.Y. Contributions Adv. Group; mem. corp. adv. com. Philanthropic Adv. Svc.; mem., bd. dirs. Coun. Better Bus. Bur. Founds., Greater Columbus Arts Coun.; mem. Afro-Am. adv. bd. Columbus Mus. of Art; bd. dirs Columbus Airport Authority. Recipient award to women achievers YWCA, 1982, 84, 91, named Woman of Yr. YMCA Columbus, Ohio; recipient cmty. svc. award United Negro Coll. Fund, 1981. Office: Borden Inc 1620 E Broad St Columbus OH 43203

BARKER, KATE, film company executive. Sr. v.p. prodn. and feature animation Universal Pictures, Universal City, Calif. Office: Universal Pictures 100 Universal City Plz Universal City CA 91608*

BARKER, NANCY LEPARD, university official; b. Owosso, Mich., Jan. 22, 1936; d. Cecil L. and Mary Elizabeth (Stuart) Lepard; m. J. Daniel Cline, June 6, 1956 (div. 1971); m. R. William Barker, Nov. 18, 1972; children: Mary Georgia Harker, Mark L. Cline, Richard E., Daniel P., Melissa B. Van Arsdel, John C. Cline, Helen Grace Garrett, Wiley D., James G. BSc, U. Mich., Ann Arbor, 1957. Spl. edn. instr. Univ. Hosp. U. Mich., Ann Arbor, 1958-61; v.p. Med. Educator, Chgo., 1967-69; asst. to chmn., dir. careers for women Northwood U., Midland, Mich., 1970-77, asst. prof., chmn. dept. fashion mktg. and merchandising, 1972-77, dir. arts programs and external affairs, 1972-77, v.p., 1978—; cons. and lectr. in field; bd. dirs. First of Am. Bank Corp. Co-author: (children's books) Wendy Well Series, 1970-72; contbr. chpts. to books, articles to profl. jours. Advisor Mich. Child Study Assn., 1972—; chmn. Matrix: Midland Festival, 1978; bd. dirs. Nat. Coun. of Women, 1971—, pres., 1983-85, chmn. centennial com., 1988; bd. dirs. Concerned Citizens for the Arts, Mich., Family and Children's Svcs., Internat. Coun. Women, Paris. Recipient Hon. award Ukrainian Nat. Women's League, 1983, Disting. Woman award Northwood U., 1970, Outstanding Young Woman award Jr. C. of C., 1974; named one of Outstanding Young Women in U.S. and Mich., 1974; nominee (2) Mich. Women's Hall of Fame. Mem. Internat. Coun. Women (bd. dirs. Paris 1991—), The Fashion Group, Internat. Furnishings and Design Assn. (pres. Mich. chpt. 1974-77), Mich. Women's Studies Assn. (founding mem.), Midland Art Coun. (pres. 2 terms, 25th Anniversary award), Internat. Women's Forum, Mich. Women's Forum, Contemporary Rev. Club, Midland County Lawyers' Wives, Zonta, Phi Beta Kappa, Phi Kappa Phi, Alpha Lambda Delta, Phi Lambda Theta, Phi Gamma Nu, Delta Delta Delta. Republican. Episcopalian. Home: 209 Revere St Midland MI 48640-4255 Office: Northwood U Off of VP Midland MI 48640-2398

BARKER, RUBY FAYE, business education educator; b. Floydada, Tex., Jan. 12, 1945; d. John W. and Eddie M. (Caldwell) Cumbie; m. Tommy G. Barker, Aug. 28, 1965; children: Brian, Craig, Tametha. BBA, West Tex. A&M U., 1967; MEd, Tarleton State U., 1973; PhD, U. North Tex., 1982. Sec. Anderson, Clayton & Co., Plainview, Tex., 1967-68; H.S. tchr. Austin (Tex.) Ind. Sch. Dist., 1968-69; tchg. asst. Tarleton State U., Stephenville, Tex., 1972-74, instr., 1974-77, from asst. prof. to assoc. prof., 1977-95, prof., 1995—, dept. head, 1988—. Contbr. articles to profl. jours. Mem. adv. bd. Weatherford (Tex.) Coll., 1986—; co-treas. Harvey Bapt. Ch., Stephenville, 1994, Sunday sch. tchr., 1983—. Mem. Tex. Bus. Edn. Assn. (Bus. Tchr. of Yr. 1978, Collegiate Bus. Tchr. of Yr. 1989), Nat. Bus. Edn. Assn., S.W. Adminstrv. Svcs. Assn., Tex. Bus. Tchr. Edn. Coun. (pres. 1990-91). Home: RR 3 Box 94B Stephenville TX 76401-9511 Office: Tarleton State U Box T-0330 Stephenville TX 76401

BARKER, SARAH EVANS, judge; b. Mishawaka, Ind., June 10, 1943; d. James McCall and Sarah (Yarbrough) Evans; m. Kenneth R. Barker, Nov. 25, 1972. BS, Ind. U., 1965; JD, Am. U., 1969; LLD (hon.) U. Indpls., 1984; Doctor Pub. Svc. (hon.) Butler U., 1987; LLD (hon.) Marian Coll., 1991; LHD U. Evansville, 1993. Bar: Ind., 1969, U.S. Dist. Ct. (so. dist.) Ind., 1970, U.S. Ct. Appeals (7th cir.), 1973, U.S. Supreme Ct., 1978. Legal asst. to senator U.S. Senate, 1969-71, spl. counsel to minority, govt. ops. com., permanent investigations subcom., 1971-72; dir. rsch., scheduling and advance Senator Percy Re-election Campaign, 1972; asst. U.S. atty. So. Dist. Ind., 1972-76, 1st asst. U.S. atty., 1976-77, U.S. atty., 1981-84; judge U.S. Dist. Ct. (so. dist.) Ind., 1984-94, chief judge, 1994—; assoc., then ptnr. Bose, McKinney & Evans, Indpls., 1977-81; mem. long range planning com. Jud. Conf. U.S., 1991—, exec. com., standing com. fed. rules of practice and procedure, dist. judge rep., 1988-91; mem. jud. coun. 7th cir. Ct. Appeals, jud. fellows commn. U.S. Supreme Ct.; bd. advisors, Ind. U., Bloomington and Indpls., Valparaiso Law Sch.; bd. visitors Ind. U. Sch. of Law, Bloomington. Mem. Ind. Hist. Soc., Conner Prairie Bd. Dirs.; bd. dirs. Meth. Hosp. Ind.; bd. govs. Ind. Fiscal Policy Inst. Recipient Peck award Wabash Coll., 1989, Touchstone award Girls Club of Greater Indpls., 1989, Leach Centennial 1st Woman award Valparaiso Law Sch., 1993; named Ind. Woman of Yr., Women in Comm., 1986. Mem. ABA, Ind. Bar Assn., Indpls. Bar Assn. (Antoinette Dakin Leach award 1993), Fed. Judges Assn., Nat. Assn. Former U.S. Attys., Am. Judicature Soc. (bd. dirs.), Lawyers Club, Kiwanis. Republican. Methodist. Office: US Dist Ct 210 US Courthouse 46 E Ohio St Indianapolis IN 46204-1903*

BARKER, SARAH MEREDITH LEE ALLEGRA, artist; b. L.A., Oct. 15, 1961; d. William Kilmer and Geraldine Allegra (Mahaney) B. AA, Santa Monica Coll., 1982; BA, Calif. State U., Northridge, 1984; MFA, Otis/Parsons, 1988. Exhibited in 1 person show at ST Bar, N.Y.C., 1992, in 2 person show at West L.A. (Calif.) City Hall Gallery, 1990; group exhbns. include U. So. Calif. Fine Arts Gallery, L.A., 1988, Claremont (Calif.) Grad. Sch., 1988, Rico Gallery, L.A., 1988, Wegner Gallery, L.A., 1988, Epoche Gallery, Bklyn., 1990, Right Bank Gallery, Bklyn., 1991, 92, New Direction, 1991, Elston Gallery, N.Y.C., 1992, Prince St. Gallery, N.Y.C., 1992, Test Site Gallery, N.Y.C., 1992, Scream Gallery, N.Y.C., 1992, Williamsburg Art Festival, Bklyn., 1993, Rome (N.Y.) Art and Cmty. Ctr., 1993, Bklyn., 1994, NORMCA, New Orleans, 1994, Flamingo East, N.Y.C., 1995, Ronald Feldman Fine Arts, N.Y., 1995, Jack Tilton Gallery, 1995 (Dealers First Choice), Pierogi 2000, N.Y.C., 1996, Art Initiatives, N.Y.C., 1996, The Pier Show, Bklyn., 1996, Charas/El Bohio, N.Y.C., 1996; represented in various permanent collections. Mem. Bklyn. Waterfront Artist Coalition, Coll. Art Assn., Women's Caucus for Art, Art Initiatives. Studio: 14 Dunham Pl Brooklyn NY 11211

BARKETT, ROSEMARY, federal judge; b. Ciudad Victoria, Tamaulipas, Mex., Aug. 29, 1939; came to U.S., 1946, naturalized, 1958; BS summa cum laude, Spring Hill Coll., 1967; JD, U. Fla., 1970. Bar: Fla., U.S. Dist. Ct. (so. dist.) Fla., U.S. Ct. Appeals (5th cir.), U.S. Supreme Ct. Pvt. practice West Palm Beach, Fla., 1971-79; judge 15th Jud. Cir. Ct., Palm Beach County, Fla., 1979-84, 4th Dist. Ct. Appeal, West Palm Beach, Fla., 1984-85; assoc. justice Supreme Ct. Fla., Tallahassee, Fla., 1985-92, chief justice, 1992-94; judge U.S. Ct. of Appeals (11th cir.) Fla., Miami, 1994—; mem. faculty U. Nev., Reno, Fla. Jud. Coll. Mem. editorial bd. The Florida Judges Manual. Mem. vis. com. Miami U. Law Sch.; mem. bd. visitors St. Thomas U. Recipient Woman of Achievement award Palm Beach County Commn. on Status of Women, 1985; named to Fla. Women's Hall of Fame, 1986. Fellow Acad. Matrimonial Lawyers; mem. ABA, Fla. Bar Assn. (family law sect., chairperson ct. stats. and workload com. and study commn. on guardianship law, lectr. on matrimonial media and criminal law continuing legal edn.), Palm Beach County Bar Assn., Am. Acad. Matrimonial Lawyers (award 1984), Fla. Assn. Women Lawyers (Palm Beach chpt.), Nat. Assn. Women Judges, Palm Beach Marine Inst. (former chairperson, bd. trustees), Acad. Fla. Trial lawyers (Achievement award 1988), Assn. Trial Lawyers Am. (Achievement award 1986). Office: 99 NE 4th St Rm 1262 Miami FL 33132-2140*

BARKIN, ELLEN, actress; b. N.Y.C., Apr. 16, 1955; m. Gabriel Byrne, 1988; 1 son, Jack. Student, CUNY; grad., Hunter Coll. Ind. theatrical, film actress, 1980—. Theatrical prodns. include Shout Across the River, 1980, Killings on the Last Line, 1980, Extremities, 1982; appeared on TV soap Search for Tomorrow; TV films include Kent State, 1981, We're Fighting Back, 1981, Terrible Joe Moran starring James Cagney, 1984, Act of Vengence, 1986, Clinton and Nadine, 1988; film appearances include Diner, 1982, Daniel, 1983, Tender Mercies, 1983, Eddie and the Cruisers, 1983, The Adventures of Buckaroo Banzai, 1984, Harry and Son, 1984, Enormous Changes at the Last Minute, 1985, Down by Law, 1986, Desert Bloom, 1986, The Big Easy, 1987, Siesta, 1987, Made in Heaven, 1987, Sea of Love, 1989, Johnny Handsome, 1989, Switch, 1991, Man Trouble, 1992, Mac, 1993, This Boy's Life, 1993, Into the West, 1993, Bad Company, 1995, Wild Bill, 1995, Mad Dog Time, 1996, The Fan, 1996. *

BARKLEY, MARLENE A. NYHUIS, nursing administrator; b. Waupun, Wis., Aug. 31, 1934; d. Fred and Esther Elsie (Leu) Nyhuis; m. Peter Don Barkley, Sept. 1, 1956; children: Peter Scott, John Fredric. Dipl. nursing, Milw. County Hosp., 1955; cert. nurse practitioner, U. Miami, Fla., 1976; AA, Miami Dade C.C., Fla., 1983; BSN cum laude, U. Miami, 1985; MSN, Barry U., 1996. RN, Fla. Nurse Waupun (Wis.) Meml. Hosp., 1956-57; nurse coord. Courtland Med. Ctr., Milw., 1958-61, Planned Parenthood, Bloomington, Ind., 1971-74; nurse practitioner Miami VA Med. Ctr., 1976-83, program dir., 1983—. Mem. ANA (cert.), Advanced Practice Coun., Fla. Nurses Assn., So. Pain Soc., U. Miami Alumni Assn., Sigma Theta Tau. Presbyterian. Home: 14248 SW 97 Ter Miami FL 33186

BARKLEY, MONIKA JOHANNA, quality control professional; b. Lexington, Ky., Feb. 22, 1961; d. Ellis Leon McCollum and Doris Leni (vonderLippe) Hutson; m. Samuel Custer Barkley II, Feb. 14, 1986. Cert. in acctg., Fayette City Vocat.-Tech Coll., 1982. Claims processor Western Ins., Lexington, 1979-82; constrn. sec. Price, Inc.-Neal, Inc., Lexington, 1982-84; quality control adminstr. Jacobs Builders, Inc., Jacksonville, N.C., 1984-90; pres. Unicorn Constrn., Goldsboro, N.C., 1984—; quality control adminstr. Flynn Co., Inc., Dubuque, Iowa, 1988-89; sec. to pres. Wooten Oil Co., Goldsboro, N.C., 1990-91; contract adminstr. Colejon Corp., Cleve., 1991-95; office mgr.-adminstr. JC&B Constrn. Co., Goldsboro, N.C., 1995—; sec., treas. Vet.'s Contracting, Lexington, 1988-92. Rep. dist. chair, Lexington, 1979; county coord. Dole for Pres., Hayes for Gov., Jones for Congress, 1996; alt. del. to Rep. Nat. Conv., 1996; alt. del. Rep. Nat. Conv., 1996. Recipient Contractor Safety award U.S. Army Corp Engrs., Seymour Johnson AFB, N.C., 1988, Contractor of Yr. award, 1988. Fellow VFW Aux. (Outstanding Svc. award 1985), Order of Ea. Star; mem. Vets. United for Strong Am. (nat. sec. 1985-89), Pearl Harbor Commemorative Assn. (nat. sec. 1989—, Wayne County Rep. Women's Club (v.p. 1995), Wayne County Citizens For Better Tax Control (sec. 1995). Baptist. Home and Office: PO Box 10627 Goldsboro NC 27532-0627

BARKMAN, DEBRA RAE, nephrology nurse; b. Winfield, Kans., Aug. 18, 1954; d. Raymond O. and Gloria Mae (Stangle) B. Diploma, Wesley Sch. Nursing, Wichita, Kans., 1975; BS in Health Arts, Coll. St. Francis, Joliet, Ill., 1985. RN, Kans.; cert. nephrology nurse. Staff nurse, surg. gynecology Wesley Med. Ctr., Wichita, 1975-78, staff nurse, acute dialysis, 1978-79, head nurse, acute dialysis, 1979-86; head nurse, acute dialysis svcs. Wichita Dialysis Ctr., 1986-88, edn. and quality coord., 1988-92, quality, risk mgmt., satellite supr., 1992-94; ops. clin. mgr. Renal Mgmt. Applications, Inc., 1995—; mem. early intervention prevention steering com. Nat. Kidney Found., N.Y.C., 1993-95, mem. key person legis. com., 1992—; mem. Nat. Task Force on Technician Practice Del., 1995-96; elected mem. ESRD Network # 12 Med. Rev. Bd., 1994-97. Nursing editor Family Focus Patient Jour. of Nat. Kidney Found., 1995; author abstracts. Mem. quality of dialysis steering com. Nat. Kidney Found., 1995—, bd. dirs., 1995—. Recipient cert. for meritorious svc. Big. Bros.-Big Sisters, Sedgwick County, Kans., 1982, 83, NKF Disting. Svc. award, 1996; Am. Nephrology Nurses Assn. grantee, 1992. Mem. Am. Nephrology Nurses Assn. (chpt. pres.-elect 1992, chpt. chair 1993), Assn. Practitioners in Infection Control (chpt. legis. rep. 1992-95), Coun. Nephrology Nurses and Technicians (program chair ann. meeting 1992-93, Outstanding Contbn. award 1992, nat. coun. chair 1994-96, Delta Sigma Chi. Republican. Roman Catholic. Home: 6725 Shade Ln Apt 1301 Wichita KS 67212-3373 Office: Renal Mgmt Applications Inc Ste 900 600 S Cherry St Denver CO 80222

BARLEY, BARBARA ANN, accountant; b. Sewickley, Pa., June 19, 1954; d. William Stephen and Maude Adel (Wilt) B. BS in Math., BA in Bus. magna cum laude, Westminster Coll., 1976. CPA, Ohio, Wis. Staff acct. Price Waterhouse & Co., Pitts., 1976-78; internal auditor Federated Dept. Stores, Inc., Cin., 1978-79; gen. ledger mgr. Formica Corp., Cin., 1980-81; staff acct. Bethesda Hosp., Cin., 1981-82; acctg. mgr. Madison Area Assn. for Retarded Citizens Devel. Ctrs. Corp., Madison, Wis., 1982-88; dir. fin. Retardation Facilities Devel. Found., Inc., Madison, Wis., 1988—; treas. Integrated Community Work, Inc., Madison, 1989-90. Treas. Access to Cmty. Svcs., Inc., 1988—; mem. Environ. Def. Fund, 1986—; treas. Peace Project Inc., Madison, 1985-95; coms. Wis. Nuclear Weapons Freeze Campaign, Madison, 1985-86, Madison nuclear free zone com., Madison, 1986. Mem. AICPA, ACLU, Wis. Inst. CPAs, Amnesty Internat., Sierra Club, Kappa Mu Epsilon, Omicron Delta Epsilon, Delta Sigma Rho-Tau Kappa Alpha, Omicron Delta Kappa. Unitarian. Home: 101 Femrite Dr #107 Madison WI 53716 Office: Retardation Facilities Devel Found Inc 2875 Fish Hatchery Rd Madison WI 53713-3120

BARLOW, LINDA, social services administrator, trainer; b. Jamaica, N.Y.; d. Philip and Shirley (Simon) Kass; m. Steven Barlow, Aug. 20, 1972; children: Andrew, Gregory, Russell. BA, U. Bridgeport, 1969; MA, Boston U., 1970; profl. diploma, Fordham U., 1974. Cert. rehab. counselor. Counselor Manpower Devel. Tng. Program, Williamsburg, N.Y., 1970-75; vocat. rehab. counselor Elmhurst (N.Y.) Hosp., 1975-77; asst. dir. career planning & placement Stevens Inst. Tech., Hoboken, N.J., 1977-78; divsn. dir. EAC, Inc., Carle Place, N.Y., 1978—; cons., trainer NDRI, N.Y.C., 1983-94; Adv. mem. Hofstra U. Rehab. Counseling Program, NYU Rehab. Counseling Program. Author: (tng. manuals) Vocational Rehab in the Treatment Setting, 1990, Vocational Testing, 1990; contbr. articles to profl. jours. Vol. Queens Spl. Olympics, Make-A-Wish Found.; mem. Utopia Estate Civic Assn. Mem. Assn. Vocat. Rehab. Advocacy for Substance Abuse (Svc. award), Mental Health Assn., L.I. Coalition Full Employment. Office: EAC 1 Old Country Rd Carle Place NY 11514-1807

BARLOW, NADINE GAIL, planetary geoscientist; b. La Jolla, Calif., Nov. 9, 1958; d. Nathan Dale and Marcella Isabel (Menken) B.; divorced. BS, U. Ariz., 1980, PhD, 1987. Instr., planetarium lectr. Palomar Coll., San Marcos, Calif., 1982; grad. rsch. asst. U. Ariz., Tucson, 1982-87; postdoctoral fellow Lunar and Planetary Inst., Houston, 1987-89; NRC assoc. NASA/Johnson Space Ctr., Houston, 1989-91, vis. scientist, 1991-92, support scientist exploration programs office, 1992; vis. scientist Lunar and Planetary Inst., Houston, 1992-95; assoc. prof. U. Houston, Clear Lake, 1991-95; pres. Minerva Rsch. Enterprises, 1995—; instr. astronomy, dir. Robinson Obs. U. Ctrl. Fla., Orlando, 1996—; co-dir. intern program Lunar and Planetary Inst., 1988-89. Editor (slide set) A Guide to Martian Impact Craters, 1988; assoc. editor Encyclopedia of Earth Sciences, 1996; contbr. articles to profl. jours. Named among Outstanding Women and Ethnic Minorities Engaged in Sci. and Engring., Lawrence Livermore Nat. Lab., 1991. Mem. AAUW (pres. Clear Lake chpt. 1991-93, program v.p. 1993-95, v.p. interbr. coun. 1990-91, chmn. Tex. task force on women and girls in sci. and math. 1991-92, dir. state pub. policy 1991-94, Tex. Woman of Yr. 1992, mem. pub. policy com. 1994-95, chmn. steering com. Tex. ednl. equity 1994-95), Am. Astron. Soc. (com. on status of women in astronomy 1995—, pres. officer divsn. planetary scis. 1993—, status of women in astronomy com. 1987-90), Astron. Soc. of Pacific, Meteoritical Soc., Am. Geophys. Union, Geol. Soc. Am., Assn. Women in Sci. (Gulf Coast Houston chpt. councilor 1994-95, pres. 1995-96), Assn. Women Geoscientists. Office: U Ctrl Fla Dept Physics Dept of Physics Orlando FL 32816

BARNARD, ANN WATSON, retired academic administrator, educator, writer; b. Kansas City, Mo., Feb. 17, 1930; d. Howard Dale and Gladys (Conklin) Watson; (div. 1959); children: Faith, John. BA in English, U. Kansas City, 1950, MA in English, 1952; PhD in Humanities, U. Mo., Kansas City, 1963. Tchr. English Blackburn Coll., Carlinville, Ill., 1960-93, chair dept. English, 1964-93, prof. emerita, 1993—; chair humanities div. Blackburn Coll., 1979-85, coll. marshal, 1989-93. Author poetry; contbr. articles to profl. jours. Mme. Common Cause, Defenders of Wildlife. Blackburn Coll. grantee, 1987-90. Mem. Assn. for Can. Studies in the U.S., Am. Studies Assn., Modern Lang. Assn., Nat. Coun. Tchrs. of English, AAUW, NOW. Democrat. Episcopalian.

BARNARD, ARLENE, retired secondary education educator; b. Red Lion, Pa., Apr. 7, 1922; d. W. Collins and Nettie Ellen (Curran) Workinger; 1 child, Tiffany West. BS, Indiana U. of Pa., 1942; MA, San Diego State U., 1979; postgrad., Stanford U., 1983. Cert. secondary tchr., computer ctr. dir., Calif. Tchr. S.W. Jr. H.S., Sweetwater H.S. Dist., San Diego, 1968-76, tchr. 12th grade English and English lit., 1976-94; chair English dept.; gifted/talented edn. coord., 1979-83; microcomputer instr., summer 1983; Stanford U. intern, summer 1984. Recipient scholarship Stanford U. Mem. NEA, Calif. Tchrs. Assn., Sweetwater Edn. Assn., Calif. Scholarship Fedn. (advisor), Phi Delta Kappa. Home: 3334 Rio Vista Dr Bonita CA 91902-1039

BARNER, ANNABEL MONROE, pastoral counselor; b. Pitts., Nov. 30, 1925; d. Samuel North and Annabel (McKibben) Monroe; m. Charles Ray Barner, Aug. 14, 1948; children: Bruce Monroe, Craig McLean, Leslie Ann. BA, Ohio Wesleyan U., 1947; postgrad., Case Western Res. U., 1974-78; MA, Ashland Theol. Sem., 1979; MDiv (hon.), Pitts. Theol. Sem., 1984; postgrad., Gestalt Inst., 1988, Process Comm. Inst., 1992. Producing dir. WPGH and KDKA radio and TV stas., Pitts., 1943-47; comml. writer, traffic contr. Sta. WRFD and WMRN, Worthington and Marion, Ohio, 1947-50; tutor emotionally disturbed youth Rocky River (Ohio) Bd. Edn., 1967-83; pastoral counselor Rocky River Presbyn. Ch., 1972-82, Samaritan Counseling Ctr., Elyria, Ohio, 1983-88; chaplain Fairview (Ohio) Gen. Hosp., 1980-81; counselor-at-large Greater Cleve. Counseling Svc., Inter Ch. Coun., 1981—; instr. Ohio Wesleyan U., Delaware, 1947-50, teaching fellow, 1948-50; mem. steering com. West Side Extended Care Ctr., Cleve., 1978; field placement counselor emergency svcs. West Side Community Health, Cleve., 1978; psychol. counselor Welsh Home, Westlake, Ohio, 1980-82; pastoral counselor John Knox Presbyn. Ch., North Olmsted, Ohio, 1988—; trainer Kahler Comm., Little Rock, 1991. Author, editor explanations of laws and statutes, State of Miss., 1953-55; author radio scripts and documentaries, 1950; contbr. articles to profl. publs. Media spokesperson Clergy for Choice, Lorain County, Ohio, 1990—, Friends of the Libr., Rocky River, 1972—; organizer Linden Sch., Lorain, 1988; mem. Open Door West, Cleve., 1990—. Gestalt Inst. scholar, 1985, 86. Mem. NOW, Nat. Trust for Historic Preservation, Am. Assn. Pastoral Counselors, Greenpeace, World Wildlife Fund, Habitat for Humanity, Sierra Club, Cleve. Art Mus., Spring

Valley Country Club, Delta Gamma, Theta Alpha Phi. Home: 2694 Goldwood Dr Cleveland OH 44116-3013 Office: John Knox Presbyn Ch 25200 Lorain Rd North Olmsted OH 44070-2057

BARNES, ALETA WILLIS, communication and drama educator; b. Lake Charles, La., Aug. 6, 1950; d. Earl William and Iva Eloise (Hatsfelt) Willis; divorced; 1 child, Jason Andrew. BA, McNeese U., 1972, MEd, 1978. Cert. educator. Tchr. St. Louis H.S., Lake Charles, 1977-78, Sulphur H.S., Lake Charles, 1984—; tchr. Upward Bound, McNeese U., Lake Charles, Sowela Tech. Inst., Lake Charles Am. Banking Inst.; motivational/mgmt. spkr., workshop dir. Author curriculum guides and dramatic prodns. Pres., organizer Youth Soccer League, Lake Charles, 1980—; dir., author, organizer Spring Drama Prodn., Sulphur; coach, dir. Dance Line/soccer/speech team, Sulphur. Recipient Class Act award Sta. KPLC-TV, Lake Charles, 1993. Mem. NEA, La. Assn. Educators, Calcasieu Educators Assn. Democrat. Home: 408 Fairfield Lake Charles LA 70605 Office: Sulphur H S 100 Sycamore Sulphur LA 70663

BARNES, CANDACE ECCLES, quality control professional; b. Quincy, Mass., Nov. 24, 1949; d. Alton and Pauline (Regnier) Eccles; children: Kimberly Spaulding, Jeremy. BS in Biology, Rensselaer Poly. Inst., 1972. Rsch. asst. Albany (N.Y.) Med. Coll., 1972-73; chemist Beiersdorf, Inc., South Norwalk, Conn., 1979-81, quality control supr., 1981-86; quality control mgr. Inline Plastics, Corp., Milford, Conn., 1986-94, Cuno, Inc., Meriden, Conn., 1994—. Republican. Office: Cuno Inc 400 Research Pky Meriden CT 06450-7172

BARNES, CONSTANCE INGALLS (MRS. RUSSELL C. BARNES), retired librarian; b. Atchison, Kans., July 30, 1903; d. Sheffield and Lucy (Van Hoesen) Ingalls; B.A., U. Kans., 1925; M.A., U. Mich., 1950, M.A. in L.S., 1955; postgrad. Ecole du Louvre, France, 1960, Vergilian Soc., Cumae, Italy, summer 1963; m. Russell C. Barnes, Oct. 1, 1927; children: Lucie-Jeanne (Mrs. Todd Seymour), John J.I. Librarian, Cranbrook Acad. Art, Bloomfield Hills, Mich., 1955-74, 80-81. Mem. LWV, AAUW, Internat. Arthurian Soc., Alliance Francaise, Founders Soc. Detroit Inst. Arts, Village Woman's Club (Bloomfield Hills), Kappa Alpha Theta. Home: Canterbury-On-The-Lake 5601 Hatchery Rd Waterford MI 48329

BARNES, CYNTHIA LOU, gifted education educator; b. Yale, Okla., Jan. 14, 1934; d. Ira and Billie (Reed) Canfield; m. Edward M. Barnes, Jr., June 1, 1954; children: Edis, Barbara, Warren, Adrienne. BS, U. Tulsa, 1970; MS, Okla. State U., 1981. Substitute tchr. Tulsa Pub. Schs., 1970-73, kindergarten tchr., 1981-94, gifted edn. tchr., 1994—; pre-sch. tchr. Meml. Drive Meth., Tulsa, 1976-81; curriculum coord. Barnard Elem. Sch., Tulsa, 1992—, site-base co-chmn., 1992-93; bd. dirs. Great Expectations Educators, Inc., Tulsa, 1985—; cons. kindergarten guide Tulsa Pub. Schs., 1985 Curriculum Writing Team for gifted Edn. Tulsa Public Schs., 1996; presenter Elem. Educators Conv., 1994. Confirmation class coord. Meml. Drive United Meth., Tulsa, 1988-94. Grantee Tulsa Edn. Fund, 1994. Mem. Okla. Assn. for Gifted, Creative and Talented, Tulsa Classroom Tchrs. Math. (conf. presider 1994). Home: 7824 E 22nd Pl Tulsa OK 74129-2416

BARNES, DENISE MELLOTT, elementary education educator; b. Bridgeport, Conn., Sept. 9, 1956; d. James Joseph and Margaret Mary (Relihan) Mellott; m. Charles Franklin Barnes, Oct. 4, 1986. BS, Ea. Conn. State U., Willimantic, 1978; MS, So. Conn. State U., New Haven, 1988, postgrad., 1990. Tchr. Assumption Sch., Fairfield, Conn., 1978-81; tech. ibr. ConDiesel, Waterbury, Conn., 1981-87; tchr. 2d grade Blackham Elem. Sch., Bridgeport, 1988—. Democrat. Roman Catholic. Home: 29 Flora St Milford CT 06460 Office: Blackham Elem Sch 425 Thorme St Bridgeport CT 06606

BARNES, INA JEAN, retired elementary educator; b. Albuquerque, Mar. 18, 1947; d. Frederick Joseph and Mary Jo (Jones) Ponzer; m. William Anderson Barnes, June 8, 1968; 1 child, William Joseph. BS, U. N.Mex., 1969, MA, 1975. Elem. sch. tchr. Grants/Cibola County Schs., Grants, N.Mex., 1969-94, ret., 1994. Recipient Literacy award Internat. Reading Assn., 1995. Mem. AAUW (Woman of Yr. 1994-95), Retired Tchrs. Assn., Magna Charta Dames, Delta Kappa Gamma (pres. Psi chpt. 1980-82, 94-96, 2d v.p. 1995-97). Democrat. United Methodist. Home: 209 Washington Grants NM 87020

BARNES, JHANE ELIZABETH, fashion design company executive, designer; b. Balt., Mar. 4, 1954; d. Richard Amos and Muriel Florence (Chase) B.; m. Howard Ralph Feinberg, Dec. 12, 1981 (div.); m. 2d, Katsuhiko Kawasaki, Feb. 12, 1988. A.S., Fashion Inst. Tech., 1975. Pres., designer Jhane Barnes for ME, N.Y.C., 1976-78, Jhane Barnes Inc., N.Y.C., 1978—. Recipient Coty award Menswear Am. Fashion Critics, 1980, 1984, Contract Textile award Am. Soc. Interior Designers, 1983, 84, Product Design awards Inst. Bus. Designers and Contract Mag., 1983-86, 94, Outstanding Am. Menswear Designer award Woolmark, 1990, Dalmore, 1990; named Most Promising Designer Cutty Sark, 1980, Outstanding Designer, 1982; Outstanding Menswear Designer, Coun. of Fashion Designers Am., 1982, Design Resources Coun., 1989, 94. Office: Jhane Barnes Inc 24 W 40th St Fl 14 New York NY 10018-3904

BARNES, JOANNA, author, actress; b. Boston, Nov. 15, 1934; d. John Pindar and Alice Weston (Mutch) B. BA, Smith Coll., 1956. Actress appearing in motion pictures: Auntie Mame, 1958, B.S. I Love You, 1971, Spartacus, 1963, The Parent Trap, 1966, The War Wagon, 1971; TV appearances include What's My Line, The Tonight Show with Johnny Carson, Merv Griffin Show, Trials of O'Brien, Dateline: Hollywood, Murder She Wrote; book reviewer L. A. Times, syndicated columnist Chgo. Tribune, N.Y. News Syndicate, 1963-65; author: Starting from Scratch, 1968, The Deceivers, 1970, Who Is Carla Hart, 1973, Pastora, 1980, Silverwood, 1985. Mem. Phi Beta Kappa.

BARNES, LAHNA HARRIS, water treatment company owner; b. New Albany, Ind., May 23, 1947; d. Robert and Catherine (Edwards) H. AA, U. Louisville, Louisville, Ky., 1969. Cert. real estate broker, accredited crisis counselor, paralegal. Property mgr. various cos., Jeffersonville, Ind. and Louisville, 1966-76, 78-80, 81-83; sales agt. Century 21, Clarksville, Ind., 1978-80; sales broker Bass & Weisberg Realtors, Jeffersonville, Ind., 1980-81; owner Superior Typing Svc., Jeffersonville, Ind., 1983-89, 91-93, Barnes Realty Mgt., Jeffersonville, Ind., 1983-85; corp. sec. Water Energizers Inc., Jeffersonville, Ind., 1987-90; v.p. Water Energizers Inc., Jeffersonville, 1991-92, 94—, co-owner, bd. dirs., 1992—; property mgr. Gardenside Terrace Coop., 1992-93. Author numerous poems; contbr. articles to local newspapers. Active Right To Life, New Albany, 1990—, Realtors Polit. Action Com., 1980-83, NFIB, 1986—, Equal Housing Commn., 1980-83; counselor Ctr. for Lay Ministries, New Albany, Ind., 1972-75; coord. Perot Petition Com. for Clark County, 1992; presdl. elector, Ind., 1992; mem. Rainforest Action Network, 1996—; coord. USA Make A Difference Day, 1995; vol. ARC, 1995—; mem. Kentuckiana Ozone Prevention Coalition, 1996—. Mem. SCLC (charter mem. So. Ind. chpt., bd. dirs. 1992-94, social justice com. 1992-93, editor The Voice of Freedom newsletter 1992-94), Assn. Water Technologies. Office: Water Energizers Inc 3008 Middle Rd Jeffersonville IN 47130-5500

BARNES, LESLIE DIANE, secondary education educator; b. Subic Bay, The Philippines, Sept. 23, 1968; (parents Am. citizens); d. William Davis and Bonnie Lynn (Weber) Glod; m. Bobby Wayne Barnes, May 31, 1998; children: MacKenzie Aryn, Kelsey Taylor. Student, Tex. Christian U., 1987-88; BS in Biology, secondary edn. cert., U. North Tex., 1992. Tchr. sci., tchr. Saturday sch. Hedrick Mid. Sch., Lewisville, Tex., 1992-93, Palms Mid. Sch., L.A., 1993-94.

BARNES, MAGGIE LUE SHIFFLETT (MRS. LAWRENCE BARNES), nurse; b. nr. Spur, Tex., Mar. 29, 1931; d. Howard Eldridge and Sadie Adilene (Dunlap) Shifflett; m. T.C. Fagan, Jan. 1950 (dec. Feb. 1952); 1 child, Lawayne; m. Lawrence Barnes, Sept. 2, 1960. Student, Cogdell Sch. Nursing, 1959-60, Western Tex. Coll., 1972-76; postgrad. Meth. Hosp. Sch. Nursing, Lubbock, Tex., 1975; BSN, W. Tex. State U., 1977. RN, Tex.; cert. gerontol. nurse, Am. Nurses Credentialing Ctr. Fl. nurse D.M. Cogdell Meml. Hosp., Snyder, Tex., 1960-64, medication nurse, 1964-76, asst. evening supr., 1976-78, charge nurse, after 1978, evening nursing supr., 1980; nursing supr. Scurry, Borden, Mitchel, Fisher, Howard Counties, West Cen. Home Health Agy., Snyder, 1980-83; emergency rm. evening supr. Root-Meml. Hosp., 1983-89; dir. of nurses Snyder Oak Core Ctr., 1989-91, Mountain View Lodge, Big Spring, Tex., 1991-92, Med. Arts. Hosp. Home Health, 1992-93, Metplex Home Health Svcs., Snyder, 1993-94, ret. 1994; part time nurse 1994—; regional coord. home health svcs. Beverly Enterprises, 1983. Den mother Cub Scouts, Boy Scouts Am., Holliday, Tex., 1960-61; mem. PTA, Snyder, Tex., 1960-69; adv. Sr. Citizens Assn.; mem. Tri-Region Health Systems Agy., 1979—; mem. adv. bd. Scurry County Diabetes Assn., 1982—. Mem. Vocat. Nurses Assn. Tex. (mem. bd. 1963-65, div. pres. 1967-69), Emergency Dept. Nursing Assn. Apostolic Faith Ch. (sec., treas. 1956-58). Home: 8239 CR 473 Hermleigh TX 79526-9704

BARNES, MARGARET ANDERSON, business consultant; b. Johnston County, N.C.; m. Benjamin Barnes, Dec. 26, 1959. BS, N.C. Ctrl. U., 1958; MA, U. Md., 1975; PhD, Columbia Pacific U., 1986. Lic. ins. agt.; ordained Christian elder in World Evangelism, 1992. Math. tchr. Tarboro (N.C.) Sch. Sys., 1959-61; math. statistician Bur. of Census, Suitland, Md., 1962-67, 69-70, Govt. of D.C., 1967-68; cons. NIH, Bethesda, Md., 1970-72; chief of data stds. Nat. Insts. of Health, Bethesda, Md., 1972-73; with exec. clearance office HEW, Rockville, Md., 1973-77; founder, pres. MABarnes Cons. Assoc., Lanham, Md., 1978-95; commr. State of Md. Accident Fund, Balt., 1979-89; mem. adv. bd. Universal Bank, Lanham, 1980-83, Interstate Gen. Corp., St. Charles, Md., 1981-83; founder Christian Ministries, 1983—, Christ Centered Ministries Esprit, 1995—; profiled for First Record: "Women of Achievement in Prince George's County History", 1994. Chairwoman Glenwood Park Civic Assn., Lanham, 1967-80. Democrat. Home: PO Box 586 Lanham Seabrook MD 20703-0586 Office: Christ Centered Ministries Esprit PO Box 802 Lanham Seabrook MD 20703-0802

BARNES, NANCY, international development specialist, consultant; b. Hartford, Conn., Oct. 21, 1946; d. E. Bartlett and Alice Beatrice (Cook) B.; m. Fernando Lima; 1 child, Maya Luciana Barnes de Lima. BA, Goucher Coll., 1968; MPA, Harvard U., 1987. Project coord./ednl. planner Policy Tng. Ctr., Cambridge, Mass., 1977-80; cmty. devel. field coord. Commonwealth of Mass., Boston, 1980-81; ednl. planner Ministry of Edn., Maputo, Mozambique, 1981-86; sr. emergency officer UNDP, Maputo, Mozambique, 1987-92; chief, assessment planning UNOHAC, Maputo, Mozambique, 1992-94; cons. UNOPS, Luanda, Angola, 1995-96; rsch. and writing grant MacArthur Found., Chgo., 1995—; court-apptd. mem. to CDAC-monitoring, Sch. Desegregation, Boston, 1977-81, mem. bd. City-Wide Ednl. Coalition, Boston, 1975-79, mem. bd. Haymarket Found., Boston, 1975-77. Editor, author: Race to Power: Struggle for Southern Africa, 1974, From Common School to Magnet School: Selected Essays in the History of Boston Schools, 1979. Bd. govs. Maputo Internat. Sch., 1995-96, parents com. chair 1991-94; founding mem. parent coop. and governing bd. Piu-Piu Day Care Ctr., Maputo, 1987-91. Mem. AAUW, Acad. Coun. on UN Sys. Home: Box 4484, Maputo Mozambique

BARNES, PATIENCE PLUMMER, writer, editor; b. Mt. Vernon, N.Y., Sept. 28, 1932; d. Charles Sumner and Elinor Agnes (Keaney) Plummer; m. James John Barnes, July 9, 1955; children: Jennifer Chase Barnes Wilson, Geoffrey Prescott. BA, Smith Coll., 1954. With J. Walter Thompson Co., N.Y.C., 1950-55; freelance writer, editor, 1955—; rsch. assoc. wabash Coll., 1988—. Author: (with J.J. Barnes) Hitler's Mein Kampf in Britain and America, 1930-39, 1980, James Vincent Murphy, Translator and Interpreter of Fascist Europe, 1880-1946, 1987, Private and Confidential: Letters from British Ministers in Washington to Their Foreign Secretaries in London, 1845-67, 1993: editor: Free Trade in Books; A Study of the London Book Trade Since 1800, 1964 (J.J. Barnes), Authors, Publishers and Politicians: The Quest for an Anglo-American Copyright Agreement, 1815-54, 1974 (J.J. Barnes); contbr. articles to profl. jours. Active Meals on Wheels, 1964—; jr. choir dir. St. John's Episcopal Ch., Crawfordsville, 1965-71; bd. dirs. Sugar Creek Swim Club, 1971-72, Cmty. Chorus, 1972-74, LWV, Montgomery County, 1981—, Crawfordsville unit Indpls. Symphony Orch., 1985-88, Mecklenburgh Festival Opera, London, 1985; del. Dem. State Conv., Indpls., 1988; mem. Feminist Reading Group, Wabash Coll., 1993-94. Home: 7 Locust Hill Crawfordsville IN 47933

BARNES, REBECCA MARIE, assistant principal; b. Jackson, Tenn., Nov. 5, 1942; d. Hewitt C. and Willette (Atwater) Johnson; m. Timothy Barnes; children: Mark, Michael, Matthew. BA in Edn., Harris Tchrs. Coll., 1965; MA, Webster U., 1983. Cert. tchr. elem. and mid. sch., reading, gifted/talented. Tchr. St. Louis Pub. Schs., 1965—; asst. prin. Compton-Drew ILC Middle Sch. at the Sci. Ctr., 1996—. Vol. Habitat for Humanity, St. Louis, 1993, Berea House, Black Repertory Theater. Named Tchr. of Yr. Iota Phi Lambda, 1983; recipient Outstanding Svc. award United Negro Coll. Fund, 1991. Mem. ASCD, Internat. Reading Assn., Nat. Mid. Schs. Assn., Gifted Assn. Mo., Mo. Botanical Gardens, St. Louis Sci. Ctr., Delta Sigma Theta (treas., exec. bd.). Home: 2655 Wedgwood Dr Florissant MO 63033-1429

BARNES, SALLY ANDERSON, organization effectiveness and employee involvement facilitator; b. Sioux City, Iowa, Feb. 9, 1955; d. William David and Betty Ruth (Smith) Anderson; m. Barney B. Barnes, Oct. 22, 1986. BS in Journalism, U. Houston, 1979. Asst. tng. specialist U. Tex., Austin, 1975-77; client coord. Bus. Internat. Corp., NY, Houston, 1978-79; employment counselor John L. Cloud Placement Svc., Houston, 1979; sr. employment recruiter Tex. Commerce Bank, Houston, 1979-81; dir., pers. officer Post Oak Bank, Houston, 1981-82; pers. rep. Austin divsn. Lockheed Corp., 1982-90, TQM/employee involvement facilitator, 1991-94, mgr. Career Transition Ctr., 1994-95; v.p. The Right People, Inc., 1995—; exec. dir. Lockheed's Bucks of the Month Club, 1983-84; dir. Lockheed Employee Recreation Assn., 1982-84. Mem. Nat. Employee Recreation Assn., Nat. Mgmt. Assn. Republican. Methodist. Home: 3611 Black Mesa Holw Austin TX 78739-7534

BARNES, SANDRA HENLEY, publishing company executive; b. Seymour, Ind., Jan. 15, 1943; d. Ray C. and Barbara (Cockerham) Henley; m. Ronald D. Barnes, Sept. 3, 1961; children: Laura Winkler, Barrett and Garrett (twins). Student, Ind. State U., 1962-63. Asst. sales mgr. Marquis Who's Who, Indpls., 1973-79, sales, svc. mgr., 1979-82, mktg. ops. mgr., 1982-84; mktg. mgr. Marquis Who's Who, Chgo., 1984-86; dir. mktg. Marquis Who's Who, Wilmette, Ill., 1986-87; v.p. mktg. Macmillan Directory Div., Wilmette, 1987-88; group v.p. product mgmt. Marquis Who's Who, Wilmette, 1988-89; pres. Marquis Who's Who, 1989-92; v.p. Reed Reference Pub., New Providence, N.J., 1992—. Republican. Office: Reed Elsevier New Providence 121 Chanlon Rd New Providence NJ 07974-1541*

BARNES, SARA LYNN, school system administrator; b. Lampasas, Tex., Jan. 9, 1940; d. Wesley Homer and Wilma Chlotide (Robertson) Scott; m. Rodney Roy Barnes, Jan. 26, 1980; children: Rodney Roy Jr., Cathie Darlene Jackson Elder, Nikki Marie Jackson Seimears, Robin Lou Barnes Groskurth. BS, U. Mary Hardin-Baylor, 19960; MEd, Tarleton State U., 1985. Cert. tchr., vocat. tchr., supt., adminstr., Tex. Tchr., chmn. bus. dept. Copperas Cove (Tex.) H.S., 1969-70, vocat. tchr., 1970-74; adminstrv. asst. for bus. Copperas Cove Sch. Dist., 1974-81; dir. bus. svcs. Copperas Cove Ind. Sch. Dist., 1981-88, bus. mgr., 1988-90, exec. dir. bus. svcs., 1990-92, asst. supt. ops., 1992—, interim supt., 1994; instr. evening coll. Ctrl. Tex. Coll., Killeen, Tex., 1973-80, mem. budget task force, 1989; mem. First Vocat. Office Edn. Adv. Bd., 1971-72. Bd. dirs. Copperas Cove United Way, 1984-87, Copperas Cove Econ. Devel. Corp., 1990, Greater Ft. Hood United Way, Copperas Cove, 1992-95. Fannie Breedlove Davis scholar, 1958-60; recipient cert. of achievement in excellence Govt. Fin. Officers Assn., 1991-94. Mem. Tex. Assn. Sch. Bus. Ofcls., Am. Assn. Sch. Bus. Ofcls. (internat. panel rev. mem. 1991—, cert. of excellence 1991-94), Tex. Assn. Impacted Schs. (treas. 1990—), Copperas Cove Exch. Club (treas. 1996, bd. dirs. 1991-93, Exchangite of Yr. 1992), Delta Kappa Gamma (v.p. 1988-90, State scholar 1995). Home: 2960 Grimes Crossing Rd Copperas Cove TX 76522 Office: Copperas Cove Ind Sch Dist PO Box 580 Copperas Cove TX 76522

BARNES, SHARON BENDER, radiologic technology educator; b. Birmingham, Ala., Aug. 13, 1954; d. Maxie B. Jr. and Audrey (Webb) Bender; m. Guy Montgomery Barnes, Apr. 13, 1984; children: Travis, Chad. AAS, Jefferson State Jr. Coll., 1975; BS, U. Ala., Birmingham, 1979, MPH, 1989. Cert. radiologic technologist Am. Registry Radiologic Technologists. Radiologic technologist East End Meml. Hosp., Birmingham, 1974-77; clin. coord., mem. faculty Jefferson State C.C., 1977— Author: Clinican Competency Forms, 1992. Mem. Religious Coalition for Reproductive Rights, Dem. Nat. Com. Mem. Assn. Educators in Radiol. Scis., Am. Soc. Radiologic Technologists, Ala. Soc. Radiologic Technologists (del. 1973—), Am. Assn. Women in C.C.s (pres. local chpt. 1996), Birmingham Regional Soc. Radiologic Technologists, Ala. Assn. Radiol. Sci. Educators (chair by-laws com. 1996). Methodist. Home: 214 Cahaba Ridge Dr PO Box 432 Trussville AL 35173 Office: Jefferson State CC 2601 Carson Rd Birmingham AL 35215

BARNES, SHIRLEY MOORE, psychiatric social worker, genealogist; b. Bedminster, N.J., Jan. 13, 1931; d. George and Marian (Van Nuys) Moore; m. William E. Barnes, Sept. 13, 1952; children: John Leighton, Ellen Leigh, Kimberley Jean. Student, Tusculum Coll., 1948-50; BA, Rutgers U., 1952; MSW, U. Pa., 1954. Lic. clin. social worker, Vt. Caseworker Children's Aid Soc., Phila., 1952-55; psychiat. social worker West Jersey Hosp. and Psychiat. Clinic, Camden, N.J., 1960-61, VA Hosp., Brockton, Mass., 1972; psychiat. social worker Mental Health Svcs. Vt., Springfield, 1973-77, adminstr., coord. aftercare and rehab., 1977-82, psychiat. social worker, supr., 1982-96; developer psycho-rehab. for retarded and mentally ill Mental Health Svcs. Vt., Proctorsville, 1980-82, founder Beekman House, 1979; ret., 1996. Author: Thomas Edward Currin, Sr., Margaret Jane Cubbon, 1993, The Kindred Venturers, 1994; contbr. articles to various publs. Bd. dirs. J.F. Tatum Sch. PTA, Haddonfield, N.J., 1966-68, High Rock Sch. PTA, Needham, Mass., 1971-72. Recipient 1d place for best all around work in art dept. N.J. Federated Women's Clubs, 1966. Mem. NASW, Acad. Cert. Social Workers, Nat. Geneal. Soc., New Eng. Hist. and Geneal. Soc. Home: 3 Walnut Way Springfield VT 05156-9142 Office: Mental Health Svcs SE Vt 107 Park St Springfield VT 05156-3028

BARNES, ZELMA JO, social worker; b. Coweta County, Ga., Aug. 29, 1938; d. William Hamp and Annie Opal (Duncan) Hyatt; m. Jack Raymond Barnes, Sept. 15, 1955; 1 child, John Hamp. AA in Criminal Justice, LaGrange Coll., 1979, BA in Social Work, 1983; MS, Columbus (Ga.) Coll., 1991; grad. police inst., U. Louisville, 1985. Patrol officer La Grange (Ga.) Police Dept., 1974-79, sgt. internal affairs, 1979-81, lt. watch comdr., 1981-94; social svcs. dir., admissions dir. Brian Ctr. Nursing Care, LaGrange, 1994—. Mem. Troup County Rep. Women, LaGrange, 1989—; advisor explorer post Boy Scouts Am., LaGrange, 1978-82; instr. ARC, LaGrange, 1980—. Mem. AAUW, Peace Officers Assn. Ga., Columbus Coll. Alumni Assn., LaGrange Coll. Alumni Assn., So. Police Inst. Alumni Assn., Ret. Enlisted Assn. Presbyterian. Home: 473 Camelot Ct LaGrange GA 30240 Office: Brian Ctr Nursing Care 2111 West Point Rd La Grange GA 30241

BARNETT, CHERYL LEE, sculptor, educator; b. Calif., Feb. 24, 1956; d. Charles A. and Neville Rae Barnett. BA in Art, U. Calif., Santa Cruz, 1977, postgrad., 1983; postgrad., Western Mich. U., Oahu, Hawaii, 1981, Western Mich. U., Innsbruck, Austria, 1982; MA in Art, Calif. State U., Fresno, 1985. Art therapist Merced (Calif.) Manor Psychiat. Hosp., also others, 1979-81, 83; dir. art gallery Merced Coll., 1981-83, instr. art Summer Coll. for Kids, 1983-84, instr. art, 1981-86, 88—; instr. Fresno Art Ctr., 1985; patina specialist Artworks Foundry & Gallery, Berkeley, Calif., 1986-88; lectr. AAUW, Merced, 1979, U. Calif., 1979. One-woman shows include Merced Coll. Art Gallery, 1982, 84, 89, 94, Fresno Art Mus., 1984, Phebe Conley Art Gallery, Calif. State U., Fresno, 1985, The Art Ctr., Visalia, Calif., 1986, Erika Meyerovich Gallery, San Francisco, 1986-87, Banaker Gallery, Walnut Creek, Calif., 1988, Eleonore Austerer Gallery, San Francisco, 1993; group exhbns. include Kamaehameha Libr., Honolulu, 1981, Sparkasse Bank, Innsbruck, Austria, 1982, Merced Coll. Art Gallery, 1982-83, Calif. State U., Stanislaus Art Gallery, Turlock, Calif, 1984, Fig Tree Gallery, Fresno, 1985, Coll. of the Sequoias, Visalia, Calif., 1986, Fresno City Coll., 1986, Artworks Gallery, Berkeley, Calif., 1986-87, Civic Arts Gallery, Walnut Creek, Calif., 1988, 3 COM Corp., Santa Clara, Calif., 1988, Berkeley Art Ctr., 1988, Artworks Foundry Gallery, Berkeley, 1986-93, Carnegie Ctr. for the Arts, Turlock, 1989, Pro Arts Gallery, Oakland, Calif., 1989, The Arts Commn. of San Francisco, 1989, Merced Civic Ctr., 1989, Humboldt Cultural Ctr., Eureka, Calif., 1989, Herbert Palmer Gallery, L.A., 1990, One Market Plz., San Francisco, 1990, Hitachi Corp., Santa Clara, 1991, Napa Art Ctr., 1991, Artifacts, San Francisco, 1991-92, A Garden Gallery, Berkeley, 1992, Merced County Arts Ctr., 1992, Ops Art, San Francisco, 1993, Cadence Design Ctr., San Jose, 1993, Network Gen., Menlo Park, 1994, Synopsys Inc., Mountain View, 1994, Contract Design Ctr., San Francisco, 1995, 96, Mendocino Art Ctr., 1995, Eleonore Austerer Gallery, 1990-96, Bradford Gallery, 1996, The Vault, 1996, Sonora & Murphy, Calif., 1996. Recipient Achievement award Bank Am., 1974, award for tchg. Nat. Inst. for Staff and Orgnl. Devel., 1996; Cyril E. Smith scholar, 1974-78. Mem. Internat. Sculpture Ctr., Pacific Rim Scupture Group, Nat. Mus. of Women in the Arts (charter), Women's Caucus for Art. Office: Merced Coll Art Dept 3600 M St Merced CA 95348 Studio: 729 Heinz Ave Ste 3 Berkeley CA 94710

BARNETT, ELIZABETH HALE, organizational consultant; b. Nashville, Mar. 17, 1940; d. Robert Baker and Dorothy (McCarthy) Hale; m. Crawford F. Barnett Jr., June 6, 1964; children: Crawford F. III, Robert H. BA, Vanderbilt U., 1962. Receptionist, sec. U.S. Atty. Gen. Robert F. Kennedy, Washington, 1962-64; free-lance cons. Atlanta, 1973-76; pres. E.H. Barnett & Assocs. orgnl. cons., trainers, Atlanta, 1976-86; trustee The Ga. Conservancy, Atlanta, 1978-92, chmn. bd. trustees, 1986-88, chmn. adv. bd., 1994—; legis. asst. to Senator Michael J. Egan Ga. State Senate, Atlanta, 1990-93. Bd. dirs. Jr. League Atlanta, 1973-75, High Mus. Art, Atlanta, 1977—, v.p. bd. adminstrn. & support, 1994—, sec. bd. and exec. com., 1977—, v.p. adminstrn. bd. dirs., United Way Met. Atlanta, 1981-84, ARCS Found., Atlanta chpt.; active Leadership Atlanta, 1976—, White House Fellows Selection Panel, 1995-96; chmn., pres. bd. dirs. Vol. Coms. Art Mus. U.S. and Can., 1976-79; chmn. bd. dirs. Met. Atlanta chpt. ARC, 1978-80, hon. bd. dirs., 1980—; cmty. adv. com. NW Ga. Coun. Girl Scouts Am., 1979-83; coun. mem. USO Ga., 1981—; bd. sponsors Atlanta Women's Network; apptd. to Ga. Clean and Beautiful Citizens Adv. Com., 1990, Ga. Solid Waste Mgmt. Commn., 1990; appt. sec. to Gov.'s Environ. Edn. Coun., 1992—; sci. coun. Ga. Coalition for Sci. Tech. and Math. Edn., 1993—. Named one of Ten Outstanding Young Women of Am., 1977, Outstanding Young Woman of Ga., 1977; honored by Ga. State Legis., Atlanta, 1978. Mem. LWV. Episcopalian. Office: 3250 Howell Mill Rd NW Ste 205 Atlanta GA 30327-4108

BARNETT, JAHNAE HARPER, academic administrator; b. Dec. 9, 1946; m. Eddie L. Barnett, Jan. 27, 1968. BSE in Bus., Ark. State U., 1966; M in Bus. Edn., U. Miss., 1967, PhD in Higher Edn. and Student Pers. Svcs., 1972; post doctoral, U. Mo., 1984. Grad. asst. U. Miss., 1966-67; instr. bus. and econs. N.W. Miss. Jr. Coll., Senatobia, 1967-71; spl. cons. planning and evaluation Dept. Edn. State of Mo., Jefferson City, 1972-73; asst. prof. William Woods U., Fulton, Mo., 1973-79, chmn. dept. bus. and econs., 1974-83, coord. adminstrv. and consumer svcs., 1979, assoc. prof., 1979-83, prof., v.p. admissions, retention, and devel., 1983-90, pres., 1990—. Mem., chair exec. bd. Fulton Area Devel. Corp., Mo. Colls. Fund; 1st vice chair Ind. Colls. and Univs. Mo.; mem. Women's Coll. Coalition; bd. regents St. Mary's Health Ctr. Home: 1810 Westminster Ave Fulton MO 65251-1068 Office: William Woods Univ Office of President Fulton MO 65251

BARNETT, LINDA KAY SMITH, vocational guidance counselor; b. Booneville, Miss., Nov. 20, 1955; d. John Thomas and Clara Vernell (Brown) Smith; m. William Wayne Barnett, June 26, 1982; 1 child, John William. AA, N.E. Miss. C.C., Booneville, 1975; BS, Miss. State U., 1977, MEd, 1978, EdS, 1982. Vocat. guidance counselor, dist. test coord. Iuka (Miss.) City Schs., 1979-91; vocat. guidance counselor Tishomingo County Schs., Iuka, 1991—. Treas. Iuka High Sch. PTA, 1984-85. Mem. Miss. Sch. Counselors Assn. (state v.p. secondary divsn. 1992-94), N.E. Counseling Assn. (pres. 1989-90, pres.-elect 1987-88, 88-89, sec.-treas. 1982-83), Nat. Bd. for Cert. Counselors (nat. cert. counselor, nat. cert. sch. counselor). Ch. of Christ.

BARNETT, MARY LOUISE, elementary education educator; b. Exeter, Calif., May 1, 1941; d. Raymond Edgar Noble and Nena Lavere (Huckaby) Hope; m. Gary Allen Barnett, Aug. 9, 1969; children: Alice Marie, Virginia Lynn. BA, U. of Pacific, 1963; postgrad., U. Mont., 1979-82, U. Idaho,

1984—. Cert. life elem. tchr., Calif.; standard elem. credential, Idaho; elem. tchr., Mont. Tchr. Colegio Americano de Torrean, Torreon, Coahuila, Mexico, 1962-63, Summer Sch. Primary Grades South San Francisco, 1963-66, Visalia (Calif.) Unified Sch. Dist., 1966-69, Sch. Dist. # 1, Missoula, Mont., 1969-73, Fort Shaw-Simms Sch. Dist., Fort Shaw, Mont., 1976-83, Sch. Dist. #25, Pocatello, Idaho, 1983-93, Greenacres Elem., Pocatello, 1993-94; tchr. 2d grade Bonneville Elem., Pocatello, 1994-95; tchr. Windsong Presch., Missoula, Mont., 1995—. Foster mom Ednl. Found. Fgn. Students, Pocatello, Idaho, 1986-89; vol. Am. Heart Assn., Am. Cancer Soc., Pocatello, 1986-88, Bannock March of Dimes, Pocatello, 1988, Pocatello Laubach Lit. Tutoring, 1989; state v.p. membership, del. to P.W. Australian Mission Study; vice moderator Kendall Presbyn. Women, moderator, 1991—; moderator Kendall P.W. 1990-92. Recipient scholarship Mont. Delta Kappa Gamma Edn. Soc., Great Falls, Mont., 1976, Great Falls AAUW, 1980, Great Falls Scottish Rite, 1981, Five Valleys Reading Assn., Missoula, Mont., 1982. Mem. AAUW (v.p., mem. com. Idaho divsn. 1990-92, book chair 1995—), ASCD, NEA, Nat. Coun. Tchrs. English, Internat. Reading Assn., Assn. Childhood Edn. Internat., Laubach Literacy Tutors (sec. 1993—), Bus. and Profl. Women Pocatello (sec. 1993—), Mortar Bd., Alpha Lambda Delta, Delta Kappa Gamma (state fellowship chmn., corr. sec. Pocatello chpt. 1986-88, 2d v.p. 1994-96), Moose (musician 1981-82), Order Eastern Star (musician 1984-85), Gamma Phi Beta (sec. Laubach Tutors 1993-95), Delta Kappa Gamma (2d v.p. Phi chpt. 1996—). Democrat. Presbyterian. Home: 103 E Crestline Dr Missoula MT 59803-2412 Office: Windsong Presch 303 Pattee Canyon Dr Missoula MT 59803-2912

BARNETT, PATRICIA ANN, public relations professional; b. Culver City, Calif., Jan. 25; d. Howard Taft and Sarah (Ross) B. BJ, U. Tex., 1978. Program specialist Dallas C. of C., 1978-79, comm. specialist, 1979-81; mgr. pub. rels. Trailways Corp., Dallas, 1981-82, dir. pub. rels., 1982-85; sr. account exec. Keller-Crescent Co., Dallas, 1985-87; dir. comm. Office of Pvt. Sector Initiatives The White House, Washington, 1987-89; dir. pub. affairs United Way Am., Alexandria, Va., 1989-91; dir. pub. rels. Dally Advt., Ft. Worth, 1992-94; dir. corp. and found. rels. So. Meth. U., Dallas, 1994-96, dir. major gifts, 1996—. Mem. Pub. Rels. Soc. Am. (accredited, Silver Anvil award 1985), Women in Comm., Inc. (bd. dirs. Dallas chpt. 1981-82, Matrix 1985), Nat. Press Club, Jr. League Dallas. Republican. Office: So Meth U PO Box 750402 Dallas TX 75275-0402

BARNETTE, JEANNE HOLMAN, retired administrative assistant, educator; b. Balt., Feb. 15, 1924; d. George Willis and Martha Annette (Alrich) Holman; m. Arthur Rudolph Ridgeway, Jr., June 12, 1942 (div. Dec. 1971); children: Sally Jeanne, Blair Holman, Alice Annette; m. Newton Hall Barnette, Dec. 31, 1987 (dec. Feb. 1995). Cert. Sectl. Sci., U. S.C., 1942. Clk. Ration Bd., Columbia, S.C., 1942-43; sec. Hartsville (S.C.) Chem. Co., 1950-52; libr. sec. Queens Coll., Charlotte, N.C., 1959-61; adminstrv. asst. edn. Myers Park Bapt. Ch., Charlotte, 1962-79; adminstrv. asst. pers. Charlotte-Mecklenburg Schs., 1979-89; tchr. presch. St. John's Bapt. Ch., Charlotte, 1989-90, Covenant Presbyn. Ch., Charlotte, 1990-92, Myers Park Bapt. Ch., Charlotte, 1992—. Mem. Nat. Assn. for Edn. Young Children, N.C. Assn. for Edn. of Young Children (governing bd. me., historian, conf. planning com.), Charlotte-Mecklenburg Assn. for Edn. Young Children (bd. dirs. 1978-88), Charlotte-Mecklenburg Assn. Ednl. Office Profls. (bd. dirs. 1982-88).

BARNEY, CHRISTINE ANNE, psychiatrist, educator; b. Rochester, N.Y., July 11, 1959. BS with honors and distinction, Cornell U., 1980, MS, 1985; MD, U. Rochester, 1986. Diplomate Am. Bd. Psychiatry and Neurology; cert. psychiatrist; lic. medicine, N.H. Resident in psychiatry Dartmouth Med. Sch., 1986-90; co-leader med. intern's support group Dartmouth Hitchcock Med. Sch., 1987-88.; on-call psychiatrist Nashua Brookside Hosp., 1988-90; chief resident, instr. clin. psychiatry Dartmouth Med. Sch., 1989-90; pvt. practice outpatient psychiatrist, 1990—; group leader yr. 1 interviewing course Dartmouth Med. Sch., 1987-88, sect. co-leader 4th yr. course, 1992, adj. asst. prof. psychiatry, 1992—; lectr. med. aspects of AIDS, Vt. Law Sch., 1987; presenter, orgnl. com. mem. ann. seminar Psychobiology of Women, 1990—; supr. to psychiat. residents, 1991—; co-leader incest survivors support group West Control Svcs., Lebanon & Newport, N.H., 1989-90; adj. prof. psychiatry Dartmouth Med. Sch., 1992—. Trustee, 2d co-chair Fairlee Libr. Mem. AMA, Am. Psychiat. Assn., Assn. Gay & Lesbian Psychiatrists, N.H. Psychiat. Assn. (councillor on N.H. psychiat. soc. exec. coun. 1992—, sec.-treas. 1995—, del. from N.H. to carrier adv. 1992), N.H. Med. Soc., N.Y. State Coll. Agricultures Honor Soc., Alpha Zeta, Alpha Omega Alpha. Office: The Carriage House 6 S Park St Lebanon NH 03766-2613

BARNEY, DEBORAH DABROWSKI, merchandising executive; b. Summit, N.J., June 19, 1955; d. Henry L. and Florence V. (Bauder) Dabrowski. BA, Lehigh U., 1977. Retail buyer L.L. Bean, Inc., Freeport, Maine, 1981-83, inventory buyer, 1983-84, asst. mgr. product devel., 1984-86, mgr. product devel., 1986-91, dir. product devel., 1991-94; v.p. merchandising Norm Thompson, Beaverton, Oreg., 1994—. Vol. Greater Portland (Oreg.) United Way, 1992, 93. Recipient Tribute to Women in Bus., Twin, Portland, 1992. Office: Norm Thompson 19545 NW Von Neuman Dr #200 Beaverton OR 97006

BARNHART, CYNTHIA ANN, editor; b. Bronxville, N.Y., Aug. 29, 1934; d. Arthur Howard and Doris Helen (Kraeger) Rogers; m. Robert Knox Barnhart, Sept. 16, 1955; children: Michael G., John R., David F., Katherine E., Rebecca L. BA, Bryn Mawr Coll., 1957; guest sr., Barnard Coll., 1956-57. From gen. editor. to asst. mng. editor Clarence L. Barnhart, Inc., Bronxville, 1976-92; asst. mng. editor Rogers Knox & Barnhart, Inc., Brewster, N.Y., 1992—. Co-author: Let's Read, 1970. Sec. S.E. Dem. Com., Brewster, 1995—; dir. Girl Scouts Am., Briarcliff Manor, N.Y., 1969-70; pres. Bryn Mawr Club Westchester, N.Y., 1972-74; dir. Christian edn. Briarcliff Congl. Ch., 1974-76. Democrat. Office: Rogers Knox & Barnhart Inc PO Box 479 Brewster NY 10509

BARNHART, ELIZABETH ANNE, data processing specialist; b. Daytona Beach, Fla., Oct. 14, 1955; d. David Richards and Elizabeth Frances (Frederick) B. AS in Computer Scis., Daytona Beach C.C., 1975. Cert. data processor; cert. systems profl. Computer programmer Melweb Signs, Daytona Beach, Fla., 1976; supr. data processing Bunnell (Fla.) Gen. Hosp., 1976-77; computer programmer, operator Daytona Budweiser, Port Orange, Fla., 1977-80; data processing mgr. City of Port Orange, 1980—; cons. Volusia-Lake-Flagler Pvt. Industry Corp., Daytona Beach, 1984-86. Mem. Data Processing Mgmt. Assn. (exec. v.p. Halifax Area chpt. 1983-84, pres. 1985, bylaws dir. 1986, awards dir. 1987, several awards). Democrat. Roman Catholic. Office: City of Port Orange 1000 City Center Cir Port Orange FL 32119-4144

BARNHART, JO ANNE B., government official; b. Memphis, Aug. 26, 1950; d. Nelson Alexander and Betty Jane (Fitzpatrick) Bryant; m. David Lee Ross, Feb. 14, 1976 (div. June 1983); m. David Ray Barnhart, May 24, 1986. Student U. Tenn., 1968-70; B.A., U. Del., 1975. Space and time buyer deMartin-Marona & Assocs., Wilmington, Del., 1970-73; adminstrv. asst. Mental Health Assn. Wilmington, 1973-75; dir. SERVE nutrition program Wilmington Sr. Ctr., 1975-77; legis. asst. to Senator William V Roth, Jr., Washington, 1977-81; dep. assoc. commr. Office Family Assistance, HHS, Washington, 1981-83, assoc. commr., 1983-86; Rep. staff dir. U.S. Senate Govt. Affairs Com., 1987-90; asst. sec. family support HHS, Washington, 1990-91, asst. sec. for children and families, 1991-92; staff U.S. Sen. William V. Roth, 1993—. Campaign mgr. U.S. Senator William V. Roth, 1988, 1994; polit. dir. Nat. Rep. Senatorial Com., 1995—. Republican. Methodist.

BARNHILL, CYNTHIA DIANE, accountant; b. Wilmington, N.C., Oct. 15, 1958; d. James Randolph Barnhill and Mildred Butler Nobles. AAS, Cape Fear C.C., Wilmington, N.C., 1979; BS, N.C. Wesleyan Coll., Rocky Mount, 1991; cert. nonprofit mgmt., Duke U., 1994; AAS in Acctg., Durham Tech. Coll., 1996; MBA, City U., Durham, 1996; postgrad., Pa. State U. Cert. employee benefit specialist. Site supr. New Hanover Summer Feeding Program, Wilmington, 1977; clk. III, nursing svc. New Hanover Regional Hosp., Wilmington, 1979-84; prodn. tech. Amkost, Wilmington, 1985-86; account rep. V U. N.C. Hosps., Chapel Hill, 1987-88; personnel specialists U.N.C., Chapel Hill, 1988-89; acct. Piedmont Health Svcs. Inc., Chapel Hill, N.C., 1989—. Vol. N.C. Rep. Com. Mem. Nat. Assn. Accts., Am. Coll. Healthcare Execs., Carolinas Chpt. CEBS, Phi Beta Lambda. Baptist. Home: 2701 Homestead Rd Apt 1205 Chapel Hill NC 27516 Office: Piedmont Health Svcs Inc PO Box 17179 Chapel Hill NC 27514

BARNHOUSE, LILLIAN MAY PALMER, retired medical surgical nurse, researcher, civic worker; b. Canton, Ohio, Sept. 26, 1918; d. Frank Barnard and Jenny Mildred (Leggett) Shear; m. Arnold Barnhouse, June 26, 1940; 1 child, James Wilson. Diploma, Aultman Hosp. Sch. Nursing, Canton, 1939. RN, Ohio, obstetrics specialty. Supr., 1943-44; nurse physician's office Canton, Ohio, 1943-49; ind. critical care nursing local hosps., 1953-68. Instr., blood bank worker ARC, 1940-70; mem. Rep. Nat Com., 1980—; vol. genetic researcher, 1972—; vol. in community. Mem. Ohio Nurses Assn. (past v.p., past chmn. dist. legis. com.), First Families of Ohio, Ladies Oriental Shrine.

BARNHOUSE, RUTH TIFFANY, priest, psychiatrist; b. La Mur, Isere, France; d. Donald Grey Barnhouse and Ruth W. Tiffany; m. Francis C. Edmonds Jr. (div.); children: Francis, Ruth; m. William F. Beuscher (div. 1968); children: Robert, Wiliam, Christopher, Thomas, John. Student, Vassar Coll.; BA, Barnard Coll., Columbia U.; MD, Columbia U., 1950; postgrad., Boston Psychoanalytic Inst., 1966-67, Episcopal Theological Sch., 1969-70; ThM, Weston Coll. Sch. Theology, 1974. Diplomate Am. Bd. Psychiatry and Neurology; ordained priest Episcopal Ch., 1980. Intern Monmouth Meml. Hosp., Long Branch, N.J., 1950-51; resident in psychiatry McLean Hosp., Waverly, Mass., 1953-55, staff psychiatrist, 1958-78; fellow in psychiatry Mass. Gen. Hosp., Boston, 1955-56; pvt. practice, 1956—; prof. psychiatry and pastoral care Perkins Sch. Theology So. Meth. U., Dallas, 1980-89, prof. emerita, 1989—; staff psychiatrist Mass. Mental Health Ctr., 1958-59; clin. asst. Harvard U., 1959-78; vis. lectr. in pastoral theology Weston Coll. Theology, 1973-75; adj. prof. pastoral theology Va. Theol. Sem., 1978-80, Loyola Coll., Columbia, Md., 1978-80; with courtesy staff Sibley Hosp., 1979-80; lectr., workshop leader in field. Author: Identity, 1984, Clergy and the Sexual Revolution, 1987, A Woman's Identity, 1994; asst. editor Anglican Theol. Rev.; co-editor: Male and Female: Christian Approaches to Sexuality; contbr. numerous articles to profl. jours. Pres. Peacemakers, Inc., 1989-90, Isthmus Inst., 1989-91. Recipient Maura award Women's Ctr. of Dallas, 1987. Fellow Am. Psychiat. Assn. (life, vice chmn. com. on religion 1989-93), Royal Soc. Medicine; mem. AAS, AAUP, Am. Med. Women's Assn., Am. Acad. Psychoanalysis (sci. assoc.), Am. Acad. Religion, Cong. Anglican Theologians (past pres.), Dallas Area Women Psychiatrists, Hermetic Acad., Internat. Physicians for Prevention of Nuclesar War, Mass. Med. Soc., North Tex. Psychiat. Soc., Physicians for Social Responsibility. Office: Ste 350 100B Turtle Creek Village Dallas TX 75219

BARNHURST, CHRISTINE LOUISE, broadcast executive; b. Salt Lake City, Sept. 3, 1949; d. Joseph Samuel and Luana Jean (Jackson) B. BS, U. Utah, 1971. From account exec. to mktg. specialist Bonneville Internat. Corp. KSL TV, Salt Lake City, 1972-84; mgr. corp. media funding U. Utah, Salt Lake City, 1985-86; dir. advt. Larry H. Miller Group, Salt Lake City, 1986-89; dir. mktg. and promotion Sta. KXIV TV Am. TV of Utah, Salt Lake City, 1989-92; gen. sales, mktg. and promotion mgr. Sta. KJZZ TV Larry H. Miller Comms., Salt Lake City, 1993-96; freelance producer of corp. sales and tng. videos. Bd. dirs., telethon producer March of Dimes; bd. dirs. YWCA, Relief Soc. LDS Ch. Gen. Bd. Recipient Nat. Print Ad award Athena, 1990, Walt Disney Top Mktg. and Promotion award, 1992, INTV Indy award, 1991, BPME Gold/Silver/Bronze awards, 1989-93, Telly awards, 1992, 93, 94, 95, 96, Gold/Silver/Bronze Addy award Utah Advt. Fedn., Emmy award, 1992, 94, March of Dimes Recognition Svc. award, 1982. Mem. Am. Mktg. Assn. (exec. mem.), Promax.

BARNICK, HELEN, retired judicial clerk; b. Max, N.D., Mar. 24, 1925; d. John K. and Stacy (Kankovsky) B. BS in Music Edn. cum laude, Minot State Coll., 1954; postgrad., Am. Conservatory of Music, Chgo., 1975-76. With Epton, Bohling & Druth, Chgo., 1968-69; sec. Wildman, Harrold, Allen & Dixon, Chgo., 1969-75; part-time assignments for temporary agy. Chgo., 1975-77; sec. Friedman & Koven, Chgo., 1977-78; with Lawrence, Lawrence, Kamin & Saunders, Chgo., 1978-81; sec. Hinshaw, Culbertson et al., Chgo., 1982; sec. to magistrate judge U.S. Dist. Ct. (we. dist.) Wis., Madison, 1985-91; dep. clk., case adminstr. U.S. Bankruptcy Ct. (we. dist.) Wis., Madison, 1992-94; ret., 1994. Mem. chancel choir 1st Bapt. Ch., Mpls.; mem. choir, dir. sr. high choir Moody Ch., Chgo.; mem. chancel choir Fourth Presbyn. Ch., Chgo., Covenant Presbyn. Ch., Madison; dir. chancel choir 1st Bapt. Ch., Minot, N.D.; bd. dirs., sec.-treas. Peppertree at Tamarack Owners Assn., Inc., Wisconsin Dells, Wis.; mem. Festival Choir, Madison. Mem. Christian Bus. and Profl. Women (chmn.), Bus. and Profl. Women Assn., Sigma Sigma Sigma. Home: 7364 Old Sauk Rd Madison WI 53717-1213

BARNS, DORETHA MAE CLAYTON, librarian, organization executive; b. Fairmont, W.Va., Nov. 28, 1917; Sylvester Richard and Della Pearl (Morgan) Clayton; m. William Derrick Barns, Sept. 3, 1947. AB, Fairmont State Coll., 1939; MA, W.Va. U., 1940; BS in L.S., Western Res. U., 1947. Tchr., librarian Wetzel County (W.Va.) Schs., 1940-41; Preston County Schs., 1944-46; teaching fellow dept. English W.Va. U., 1941-43; sec. to dean grad. sch., 1942-44, cataloguer library, 1947-48; dir., Internat. relations chmn. LWV, W.Va., 1969-89, 2d v.p., 1981-83, 87-89; bd. dirs. W.Va. affiliate Coun. of Internat. Programs, 1975-87. Author: An Outline of the West Virginia Merit System, 1957; West Virginia's Interest in Foreign Trade, 1971; International Services Available to West Virginia Businesses, 1980. Mem. Kappa Delta Pi, Nu Alpha Phi. Republican. Mem. Soc. Friends. Home: 512 Beverly Ave Morgantown WV 26505-4920

BARNUM, BARBARA STEVENS, nursing educator; b. Johnstown, Pa., Sept. 2, 1937; d. William C. and Freda Inzes (Claycomb) Burkett; m. H. James Barnum (dec.); children: Lauren, Elizabeth, Catherine, Anne, Shauna, Sallee, David. AA in Nursing, St. Petersburg Jr. Coll., 1958; BPh, Northwestern U., 1967; MA, DePaul U., 1971; PhD, U. Chgo., 1976. RN, Ill., N.Y. Dir. nursing svcs. Augustana Hosp. and Health Care Ctr., Chgo., 1970-71; dir. staff edn. U. Chgo. Hosps. and Clinics, 1971-73; prof. U. Ill., Chgo., 1973-79; dir. div. health svcs., sci. and edn. Columbia U. Tchrs. Coll., N.Y.C., 1979-87; editor Nursing & Health Care Nat. League for Nursing, N.Y.C., 1989-91; editor div. nursing Columbia-Presbyn. Med. Ctr., Columbia U., N.Y.C., 1991-95; prof. Sch. Nursing Columbia U., N.Y.C., 1995—; chmn. bd. Barnum & Souza, N.Y.C., 1989-92; civilian cons. to surgeon gen. USAF, 1980-87. Author: Nursing Theory, Analysis, Application and Evaluation, 4th edit., 1994, Writing for Publication: A Primer for Nurses, 1995, (with K. Kerfoot) The Nurse as Executive, 4th edit., 1995, Spirituality and Nursing: From Traditional to New Age, 1996; editor: Nursing Leadership Forum, 1994—. Mem. governing bd. Nurses House, 1979-86, Nat. Health Coun., 1981-90, others. Fellow Am. Acad. Nursing (governing bd. 1982-84); mem. Sigma Theta Tau (Founders' award 1979). Home: 80 Park Ave Apt 15G New York NY 10016-2537 Office: Columbia U Sch Nursing 630 W 168th St New York NY 10032

BAROLINI, HELEN, writer, translator, educator; b. Syracuse, N.Y., Nov. 18, 1925; m. Antonio Barolini, Nov. 8, 1950 (dec.); children: Teodolinda, Susanna, Nicoletta. AB magna cum laude, Syracuse U., 1947; MLS, Columbia U., 1959. Lectr. Pace U., Pleasantville, N.Y., 1990—; lectr. Padua, Italy and Westchester C.C., Valhalla, N.Y., 1988; writer-in-residence Quarry Farm, Elmira Coll., 1989; resident scholar Rockefeller Found.'s Bellagio Study Ctr., Lake Como, Italy, 1991. Creative works include Umbertina, 1979, The Dream Book, 1985, Love in the Middle Ages, 1986, Festa, 1988, Aldus and His Dream Book, 1991, Chiaroscuro, 1996, ; stories in Literary Olympian II, Love Stories by New Women, and numerous jours.; translated 7 books from Italian; scholar-cons., advisor to film Tarantella. Recipient Susan Koppelman award Am. Culture Assn., 1987, Am. Book award 1986, Ams. of Italian Heritage Literary award, 1984, Marina-Velca Journalism prize, Italy, 1970; Nat. Endowment for Arts grantee, 1976; fellow MacDowell Colony, 1974, Yaddo fellow, 1965. Mem. PEN Am. Ctr., Nat. Writers Union, Hudson River Writers Assn., Phi Beta Kappa. Home and Office: 86 Maple Ave Hastings On Hudson NY 10706

BARON, LINDA, psychotherapist, consultant; b. N.Y.C., Feb. 12; d. Jack and Sylvia (Paff) B. BEd in Elem. Edn., U. Miami, MEd in Learning Disabilities, 1973, MEd in Counseling Psychology, 1974. Lic. mental health counselor, Fla., marriage and family therapist, Fla.; cert. addictions profl., Fla., mental health counselor, Wash.; lic. profl. counselor, Ga.; nat. cert. counselor; internat. cert. alcohol and drug counselor; cert./ clin. hypnotherapist, master practitioner neuro-linguistic programming; biofeedback practitioner. Tchr. elem. sch. Dept. Def. Overseas Sch. System, Japan, The Philippines, Eng.; rehab. counselor Office Vocat. Rehab., Miami, Fla.; acting supr., clin. counselor Metro-Dade Alcohol and Drug Abuse Counselor, Miami, 1978-80, dir. community and media rels., 1980-87; pvt. practice North Miami, Fla., 1980—; psychotherapist and cons. in pvt. practice, Atlanta, 1995—; adj. prof. psychology St. Thomas U., Miami, 1977-80; cons. Miami Vice and Crime Story TV shows, 1984-91; cons., seminar leader in stress mgmt. and women's issues various orgns., bus., media, 1990—; founder, pres. P.R.I.S.M.-Program Relaxation, Imagery and Stress Mgmt., 1994—. Prodr. Alcohol and Drug Abuse pub. svc. announcement, 1985 (Emmy nomination). Organizing vol. various Dem. candidates, 1971—; vol. ARC, Dade County, Fla., 1992; activist Am. Rights Found. Fla.; founding bd. dirs. Informed Families Dade County, 1981-85; bd. dirs. MADD, 1984-91; mem. Women's Career ORT, 1996—. Recipient Citation of Appreciation, Am. Bus. Woman's Assn., 1991. Mem. NATAS, ACA, Am. Assn. Marriage and Family Therapy (clin. mem.), Fla. Alcohol and Drug Abuse Assn., Assn. Advance Ethical Hypnosis, Atlanta Women's Network, Women's Health Care Execs., Ga. Marriage and Family Therapy Assn., Lic. Profl. Counselors of Ga., Vegetarian Soc. Ga., Inst. Noetic Scis., PETA, Animal Rights Found. Fla. Democrat. Address: 3232 Cobb Pky # 275 Atlanta GA 30339

BARON, SONDRA WINTHROP, educator, writer; b. Bklyn., June 29, 1934; d. Samuel and Ann (Bernard) Winthrop; m. Harold Baron, Sept. 26, 1954; children: Pamela Jean, Ellen Cecile Baron Johnson. BS cum laude, Adelphi U., 1970, MA, 1976. Cert. secondary tchr., N.Y. Actress Provincetown Playhouse, N.Y.C., 1951-53; script cons. WOR Mutual Broadcasting, 1953-54; tchr. E. Islip (N.Y.) H.S., 1972-94; curriculum writer hon. English East Islip Schs., 1980-85, curriculum writer sociology, 1991-94, cons. N.Y. Regents Soc. Studies Dept., Albany, 1988. Grantee Nat. Endowment For Humanities, 1988. Mem. Am. Assn. U. Women. Home: 91 Fawn Dr East Islip NY 11730

BARON, SUSAN R., lawyer; b. St. Louis, Jan. 9, 1952; d. Charles B. B. and Betty D. Leventhal; m. Ralph J. Ibson, Sept. 18, 1994; 1 child, Zoe Kaitlyn. BA, Washington U., 1973; JD, Georgetown U., 1978. Bar: DC 1978. Law clk. to sec. US Dept. Housing and Urban Devel., Washington, 1975-76; ptnr. Dunnells, Duvall & Porter, Washington, 1978-93; dir. Nat. Corp. Housing Partnerships, Washington, 1994—; mem. steering com. Washington Legal Clinic for the Homeless, 1989-92. Mem. adv. bd. Seeds of Peace, Washington, 1993—. Mem. Nat. Leased Housing Assn. (pres. 1992-93, dir. 1979-93), Phi Beta Kappa. Democrat. Home: 4810 Chevy Chase Bld Chevy Chase MD 20815

BARONDESS, LINDA HIDDEMEN, professional society executive; b. Phila., Aug. 25, 1945; d. William and Audrey (Roan) Hiddemen; m. Jeremiah A. Barondess, Dec. 10, 1982. Dir. med. edn. ACP, Phila., 1978-83; exec. v.p. Am. Geriatrics Soc., N.Y.C., 1983—. Contbr. articles to profl. jours. Mem. Cosmopolitan Club. Office: Am Geriatrics Soc 770 Lexington Ave New York NY 10021-8165

BARONE, ANGELA MARIA, artist, researcher; b. Concesio, Brescia, Italy, June 29, 1957; came to U.S., 1983; d. Giuseppe and Adelmina (D'Ercole) B. Laurea cum laude in geol. scis., U. Bologna, Italy, 1981; PhD in Marine Geology, Columbia U., 1989. Cert. in profl. photography, N.Y. Inst. Photography, N.Y.C., 1992; cert. in the fine art of painting and drawing North Light Art Sch., Cin., 1993. Collaborative asst. Marine Geology Inst., Bologna, 1981-83, Inst. Geology and Paleontology, Florence, Italy, 1982-83, Sta. de Geodynamique, Villefranche, France, 1982; grad. rsch. asst. Lamont-Doherty Geol. Obs., Palisades, N.Y., 1983-89; postdoctoral rsch. asst. Lamont-Doherty Geol. Obs., Palisades, 1989; postgrad. rschr. Scripps Instn. of Oceanography, La Jolla, Calif., 1990-92; artist San Diego, 1993—. Contbr. articles to profl. jours. Mem. Am. Geophysical Union (co-pres. meeting session 1990), Nat. Assn. Fine Artists, Nat. Mus. Women in Arts (assoc.), Internat. Platform Assn. Home: 7540 Charmant Dr Apt 1222 San Diego CA 92122-5044

BARONE, ROSE MARIE PACE, writer, former educator; b. Buffalo, Apr. 26, 1920; d. Dominic and Jennie (Zagara) Pace; m. John Barone, Aug. 23, 1947. BA, U. Buffalo, 1943; MS, U. So. Cal., 1950; cert. advanced study, Fairfield (Conn.) U., 1963. Tchr. Angola (N.Y.) High Sch., 1943-46, Puente (Calif.) High Sch., 1946-47, Jefferson High Sch., Lafayette, Ind., 1947-50; dir. Warren Inst., Bridgeport, Conn., 1951-53; instr. U. Bridgeport, 1953-54; tchr. bus. subjects Bassick H.S., Bridgeport, 1954-74, Harding H.S., Bridgeport, 1974-80; instr. Fairfield U., Conn., 1969; freelance writer, 1980—; chair State Poetry Festival, 1987. Founder Pet Rescue; chmn. comty. affairs com. Area Coun. Cath. Women, 1988-90, sec., 1990-91, chmn. family affairs com., 1991, v.p., 1992-93; chmn. comty. affairs Ch. Women United, 1992—, state area chmn., 1995—. Pace-Barone Minority scholar Fairfield U., Auerbach Found. scholar, 1956; recipient Playwriting prize Conn. Federated Women's Clubs, 1955, 1st prize for poetry, 1985, Short Story award Federated Women Conn., 1987, 88, 90, Citizen award Bridgeport Dental Assn., 1982, State/Town Hero award, 1986, Anniversary medal and marble statuette Fairfield U., Cmty. Care Successful Aging award, 1992, Salute to Women award YWCA, 1993, Woman of Substance award, 1994, craft and flower awards. Mem. NEA, AAUW (treas. 1957-58, named gift grant 1989, cultural and poetry chair 1992—, rec. sec. 1992-93, internat. rels. 1993-94, v.p. program 1995—, contest chair 1995—), Am. Assn. Ret. People (v.p. 1987-88, pres. 1988-89, 94-95, instr. 55 Alive, cmty. affairs chair 1990-94, 95—), Owl (sec. 1987-89, pres. 1989-90), Nat. League Am. PEN Women (Bridgeport historian 1966-84, state historian 1983—, treas. br. 1985-88, state pres. 1986-88, state lit. chair 1988—, br. membership chair 1990, Nat. Historian award 1976, 88), Fairfield Area Poets (founder, pres. 1990—, editor 4 vols. Conn. poets), UN Assn. USA (pres. Bridgeport 1964-66, 68-70, v.p. 1988—, chmn. area UN Days 1960—, pres. Conn. chpt. 1971—, state chmn. UNICEF to 1984, area UNICEF Ctr. 1984—, state historian 1984—), Conn. Bus. Tchrs., Bridgeport Edn. Assn. (sec. 1966-68), VFW (aus. 1989), Am. Legion (aux. contest chair 1989—, historian 1993-95, Aux. Nat. Cmty. Svc. award 1993), Fairfield Philatelic Soc. (sec. 1971-78, founder advisor Philatelic Jrs. 1972-80), Fairfield U. Women's Club (founder, pres. 1950, 74—, v.p. 1973-74), Southport Women's Club (garden dept. sec. 1981-85, chmn. 1985-87), Pi Omega Pi. Home: 1283 Round Hill Rd Fairfield CT 06430-7329

BARONE, SANDRA M., state legislator; b. Providence, Oct. 31, 1946; d. Henry and Esther Segal Factoroff; m. John Barone Jr., 1973; 1 child, Raechel. BA, R.I. Coll., 1968; postgrad., U. R.I. Vol. Peace Corps, Liberia, 1969-70; realtor T.R. Little Realtors, 1985—; mem. R.I. Ho. of Reps., 1990—; mem. HEW com., 1990—; vice chmn. adoption registry com.; mem. internship com.; mem. com. to study state scholarships and dept. environ. mgmt. Active ACLU, Common Cause, Coalition to Preserve Choice, Barrington Dem. Town Commn., East Providence Dem. City Com. Mem. R.I. Assn. Realtors, R.I. Women's Legis. Caucus, R.I. Women's Polit. Caucus. Democrat. Jewish. Home: 19 Rustwood Dr Barrington RI 02806-3214 Office: RI Ho of Reps State House Providence RI 02903

BAROSS, JAN, artist; b. Oaklawn, Calif., Feb. 5, 1943; d. Nathan and Estelle (Kaplan) Meadoff. BA, San Francisco State U., 1966; MA, Oreg. State U., 1976. Mem. Northwest Playwrights Guild (bd. dirs. 1989—), Artist Repertory Theatre, Northwest Writers Inc. (artistic coun. 1990—).

BARR, DONNA, author, artist; b. Everett, Wash., Aug. 13, 1952; d. Donald Martin and Dorothy Cecilia (Krahmer) Colbert; m. Daniel E. Barr, Aug. 9, 1974. BA in German Lang. and Lit., Ohio State U., 1978. Janitor U. Wash. Hosp., Seattle, 1978; clk. U. Wash., Seattle, 1979; author, artist Seattle, Bremerton, 1986—. Author, artist: (continuing series) The Desert Peach, 1986—, Stinz, 1986—. With U.S. Army, 1970-73. Recipient Best Ongoing Title award Comics Creators Guild, 1992, The Inkpot award, 1996. Mem. Nat. Writers Union, Cartoonists Northwest, Friends of Lulu, Pacific Northwest Booksellers Assn. Home and Office: A Fine Line 1318 N Montgomery Bremerton WA 98312-3056

BARR, IRENE N., artist representative; b. Boston, Feb. 4, 1942; d. Myer David and Mary (Harmon) Karas; m. Martin Marcus, May, 1961; children: Lori Beth, Lawrence Scott Marcus. Student, Mt. Ida Jr. Coll., 1959-61. Night auditor, front desk assoc. Logan Airport Hotel, E. Boston, 1965-79; mng. dir. E. Coast Music Prodn., W. Hyannisport, Mass., 1983—; pres. Youth Adv. Bd., Medfield, Mass., 1981-82.

BARR, JANE KAY, investment advisor; b. Wichita Falls, Tex., June 18, 1947; d. William Marshall and Jane (Marriott) Kay; m. Oliver James Barr IV, Apr. 30, 1968 (div. Feb. 1980); children: Oliver James V, William Bolt. BA in Anthropology, U. Colo., 1977. Product devel. mgr. JHB Internat., Denver, 1975-80; exec. v.p. David Wendell Assocs., Inc., Portsmouth, N.H., 1981—, also bd. dirs. Mem. St. Andrew's Soc. of Maine (treas. 1992-93), Pi Beta Phi. Roman Catholic. Home: 38 Beechstone St Apt 4 Portsmouth NH 03801-6338 Office: David Wendell Assocs Inc 1000 Market St Portsmouth NH 03801-3358

BARR, MARLENE JOY, volunteer; b. Grosse Pointe Farms, Mich., Feb. 25, 1935; d. Max John and Viola Christina (Funke) Bielenberg; m. John Monte Barr, Dec. 17, 1954; children: John Monte Jr., Karl Alexander, Elizabeth Marie Letter. Student, Mex. City Coll., 1955; BA, Mich. State U., 1956; MA, Ea. Mich. U., 1959. Cert. elem. edn. Tchr. A.G. Erickson Sch., Ypsilanti, Mich., 1956-66; chair 5th grade tchrs., sec. curriculum coun. Ypsilanti Pub. Schs., 1961-66; receptionist Barr, Anhut, and Assoc., P.C., Ann Arbor, Mich., 1989-95; vol. Thrift Shop Assn. of Ypsilanti, 1969—; block coord. Ypsilanti Recycling, 1990—. Mem. Fletcher Sch. Adv. Coun., 1980-81, Ann Arbor Power Squadron, 1965—; mem. chancel choir Emmanuel Luth. Ch., 1980—, youth coord., 1983-89, sec. youth standing com., 1983-89, ch. coun. 1986-90, endowment com. sec. 1995—; v.p. Thrift Shop Assn. Ypsilanti, 1979-81, pres. 1981-83, scheduling chmn. 1993—; bd. dirs. Ypsilanti Cmty. Choir, 1984—; asst. leader Girl Scouts U.S., 1978-81; sec. troop 290 Boy Scouts Am., 1989-95; rm. mother Fletcher Elem. Sch. Ypsilanti, 1982-83, High/Scope Ednl. Rsch. Found. Endowment Bd., 1993-96. Mem. AAUW (life), chmn. gourmet arts study group 1968—), Ann Arbor Women's City Club (chmn. ways and means com. 1995—), Friends of the Ypsilanti Dist. Libr., Depot Town Assn., Law Wives of Washtenaw County (editor 1970-72), Ladies Lit. Club (corr. sec. 1976-78), sec. bd. trustees 1982-86, v.p. 1986-90, pres. 1990-92, treas., bd. trustees 1992—), Chandler Birthday Club (treas. 1990), Ypsilanti Hist. Soc. (life) (P.E.O., chaplain 1991-93), Ann Arbor Power Squadron of U.S. Power Squadron, Ann Arbor Bike Touring Soc. (co-chair One Hell of a Ride 1995), Alpha Delta Kappa (pres. Beta Zeta chpt. 1965-68, historian 1986-88, pres. area X pres. coun. Mich. ADK chpt. 1966-68). Lutheran. Home: 1200 Whittier Rd Ypsilanti MI 48197-2152

BARR, MARY JEANETTE, art educator; b. Chgo., Dec. 30, 1928; d. George Leonard and Leonore Loretto (Marsicano) Tompkins; m. David Harper Barr, Aug. 28, 1954; children: Michael, Nadine, Thomas, Ellen. BS, Ill. State U., 1971, MS, 1981, EdD, 1988. Art specialist teaching cert. K-12, Ill. Art specialist K-8 Chester-East Lincoln Sch. Dist. #61, Lincoln, Ill., 1971-74, Lincoln Elem. Sch. Dist. #27, 1974-80; instr. art edn. Ill. State U., Normal, 1980-85; prin. Carroll Elem. Sch., Lincoln, 1985-87; prof. art edn. Wichita (Kans.) State U., 1988-90, West Ga. Coll., Carrollton, 1990—; art tchr. Lincoln Recreation Dept., summers, 1975-79; writer grant Arts in Gen. Edn. program Lincoln Elem. Sch. Dist. 27, 1979-80; presenter tchr. inst. workshops Ill. State Bd. Edn., 1980-83; mem. Ill. Curriculum Coun., Ill. State Bd. Edn., 1982-88, sec., 1987; panelist gen. meeting Ill. Assn. Art Educators State Conf., Peoria, 1984; workshop participant Getty Ctr. Edn. in the Arts, Cin., 1993; judge numerous profl. and amateur art shows. Author: (with Michael Youngblood) Illinois Art Education Association Position Paper on Art Education, 1987; The Illinois Curriculum Council: Visions and Directions, 1988; contbr.: Art Activities for the Handicapped, 1982. Float designer/parade Jr. Women's Club, Lincoln, 1974-80; chmn. mural C. of C., Lincoln, 1980; festival presenter Carrollton Elem. Schs., 1993, 94; judge H.S. art show U.S. Rep. Darden, Carrollton, 1993, Dallas, Ga., 1994. Recipient Ada Bell Clark Welsh Scholarship Ill. State U., 1984, Exemplary Svc. award Ill. State U. Student Elem. Edn. Bd., Ill. State U., 1985. Mem. ASCD, AAUP, Nat. Art Edn. Assn. (Tchr. of Yr. 1984), Assn. Tchr. Educators, Found. Internat. Cooperation (chpt. chair 1963—), Ga. Art Edn. Assn. (bd. mem. student chpts. 1990—, Higher Edn. Tchr. of Yr. 1994). Roman Catholic. Home: 110 Frances Pl Carrollton GA 30117-4332 Office: West Ga Coll 1600 Maple St Carrollton GA 30117-4116

BARR, PAMELA S., public relations executive. BA in Journalism cum laude, W.Va. U. Promotion and sales mgr. WKSU, Akron; mktg. and pub. rels mgr. Ohio Ballet; acct. exec. Watt, Roop & Co., Cleve., 1984-86, sr. acct. mgr., 1986-88, v.p., 1988-91, sr. v.p., 1991—. Mem. Pub. Rels. Soc. Am. (past pres.). Office: Watt Roop & Co 1100 Superior Ave E Cleveland OH 44114-2518*

BARR, SARAH LOUISE, television anchor, reporter; b. Wethersfield, Conn., Dec. 14, 1963; d. Allan Ferguson and Ursula (Wolf) B. BA, Temple U., 1986. News writer Sta. WPVI-TV, Phila., 1985-86; writer, producer Sta. KYW-TV, Phila., 1986-88; news reporter, anchor Sta. WHYY-TV, Wilmington, Del., 1988-92; anchor, reporter, writer, field producer WDIV TV, Detroit, 1992-94; anchor, reporter WGAL-TV, Lancaster, Harrisburg, 1994—. Mem. AFTRA, Radio, TV, News Dir. Assn., Women Communications, Nat. Assn. Exec. Women. Democrat. Lutheran. Office: Sta WGAL-TV 1300 Columbia Ave Lancaster PA 17604

BARR, SHIRLEY, public relations executive; b. Wilson, Okla., Nov. 24, 1936. BS in Journalism, U. North Tex., 1958. Sr. v.p., media rels. group Churchill Group, 1975-91; founder, chmn. Shirley Barr Pub. Rels., Houston, 1991—. Recipient Excalibur awards Pub. Rels. Soc. Am., 1989-92. Mem. Food and Beverage Soc., Pub. Rels. Counselors Acad. Office: Shirleybarr Pub Rels Ste 750 5177 Richmond Ave Houston TX 77056-6736

BARRACA, LYNDA ANN, secondary education educator; b. San Diego, July 14, 1953; d. Eric Eugene and Ann Dela (Harlow) Roberts; m. Joseph William Barraca, Mar. 22, 1975; children: Jessica Leigh Barraca, Jayme Lyn Barraca;. BS in Zoology, Ohio State U., 1975; MA in Environ. Edn., Governor's State U., University Park, Ill., 1976. Cert. tchr. K-12, Ill. Sci. tchr. Crete-Monee Sch. Dist., Crete, Ill., 1976—; cadre leader, presenter staff devel. in coop. learning Crete-Monee H.S., 1991—, mem. sch. improvement team, 1993—. Recipient NSF grant Argonne Nat. Lab., 1988, Impact II Disseminator award Ill. Math. & Sci. Acad., Aurora, 1990; Howard Hughes Inst. fellow U. Chgo., summer 1996. Mem. ASCD, Ill. Sci. Tchrs. Assn. (presenter 1991 conf.), World Wildlife Found., Nat. Assn. Biology Tchrs. Office: Crete Monee H S 760 W Exchange St Crete IL 60417-2049

BARRANGER, MILLY SLATER, performing arts company executive, writer; b. Birmingham, Ala., Feb. 12, 1937; d. C. C. Slater and Mildred (Hilliard) Hinson; m. G. K. Barranger, 1961 (div. 1984); 1 child, Heather Dalton Barranger Case. BA, U. Montevallo, 1958; MA, Tulane U., 1959, PhD, 1964. Lectr. La. State U., New Orleans, 1964-69; asst. to assoc. prof. Tulane U., New Orleans, 1969-82, chmn. dept. theatre, 1971-82; prof., chmn. dramatic art U. N.C., Chapel Hill, 1982—; producing dir. PlayMakers Repertory Co., Chapel Hill, 1982—; pres. Am. Theatre Assn., 1978-79; disting. vis. assoc. prof. U. Tulsa, 1981; vis. young prof. in humanities U. Tenn., Knoxville, 1981-82; scholar-in-residence Yale Sch. Drama, New Haven, Conn., 1982. Author: Theatre: A Way of Seeing, 1980, 86, 91, 95, Theatre: Past and Present, 1984, Understanding Plays, 1990, 94, Jessica Tandy, 1991, Margaret Webster, 1994; co-editor: Generations: An Introduction to Drama, 1971, Notable Women in American Theatre, 1989; contbr. articles to profl. jours. Trustee The Paul Green Found., 1982—. Recipient New Orleans Bicentennial award for achievement in the arts, 1976, award for profl. achievement S.W. Theatre Conf., 1978, Pres.'s award U. Montevallo, 1979. Fellow Coll. of Fellows of the Am. Theatre; mem. Nat. Theatre Conf. (pres. 1978-79, bd. dirs. 1991-93), Assn. Theatre in Higher Edn., League Profl. Theatre Women N.Y. Office: U NC CB # 3230 Chapel Hill NC 27599-3230

BARRAS, BARBARA, psychologist, educator, consultant, small business owner; b. Piqua, Ohio, Mar. 7, 1938; d. Howard and Anna B. (Elzea) Mabbitt; m. Alfred P. Barras; children: Deborah Seifert, Tony, Bryan. BS, Long Beach (Calif.) State U., 1980. Model Florence Smales, Santa Ana, Calif., 1968-76; salesperson, bookkeeper Pacific Mfg. Engring. Co., Los Alamitos, Calif., 1972-74; program coord. Quaker Gardens, Stanton, Calif., 1968-72; tchr. Garden Grove (Calif.) Unified Sch. Dist., 1972—; prof. psychology Coastline Coll., Fountain Valley, Calif., 1976 ; cons. in pvt. practice, Westminster, Calif., 1976—. Sr. advisor 4 documentaries To Hear, PBS, 1981. Mem. NAFE. Republican. Home: 9941 Westhaven Cir Westminster CA 92683-7552 Office: Coastline CC 11460 Warner Ave Fountain Valley CA 92708

BARRASI, SUSAN, artist; b. Bronx, N.Y., Jan. 16, 1963; d. Vincent Peter Barrasi and Donata Cardona; m. Joseph Peter Badalamente, Apr. 7, 1990. BFA, Sch. Visual Arts, 1986; student, Art Students League, 1992-95. Sculptor U. California, Pa., 1995-96; artist Racz & Dessimoz Advt. Agy, N.Y.C., 1985-95, Fusion Graphics, Flushing, N.Y., 1992-94; artist Simplicity Patterns, N.Y.C., 1988-87, Am. Kennel Club, N.Y.C., 1987, Alfred Hitchcock Mag., N.Y.C., 1987, McCalls Mag., N.Y.C., 1986; exhbns. include Springfield (Mass.) Mus. Arts, 1995, Lincoln Ctr., N.Y.C., 1992, Oil Painters Am., Chgo., 1992, Catharine Lorillard Wolf Club, N.Y.C., 1992, 95, Nat. Arts Club, N.Y.C., 1993, Salmagundi Club, N.Y.C., 1991-92, 95; artist for postage stamps, men's ties and garments; commd. portraits and landscapes. Recipient Excellence award Manhattan Arts Internat., 1993; Merit scholar Art Student League, 1993. Mem. Oil Painters Am., Art Students League N.Y., Art Soc. Old Greenich (First prize, honorable mention 1993), Artist Equity, Valley Artist Assn. (2d prize 1993). Home and Office: 666 West End Ave Apt 5M New York NY 10025

BARRATT, CYNTHIA LOUISE, pharmaceutical company executive; b. El Paso, Tex., Feb. 13, 1953; d. John Edward and Louise Joy (Lacy) B.; m. Nat G. Adkins, Jr., Oct. 5, 1980. BJ, U. Tex., 1975. Buyer Joske's of Tex., San Antonio, 1975-80, Craigs of Tex., Houston, 1981-83; v.p. sales ops. Akorn, Inc., Abita Springs, La., 1980-86; CEO, chmn. bd. dirs. NGLC Corp., Richmond, Tex., 1983—; pres., CEO, bd. dirs. CynaCon/Ocusoft, Richmond, 1986—. Mem. NAFE, Rosenberg/Richmond C. of C., DAR, Ft. Bend County Mus. Assn. Office: OcuSoft Inc PO Box 429 Richmond TX 77406-0429

BARRAZA-KEIM, MONICA, designer, apparel. BFA, Parsons Sch. Design. Pres., designer Three-Fifty Fifth, Ltd., N.Y.C. Recipient Latina Excellence Fashion award, 1995. *

BARREDO, RITA M., auditor; b. Torrington, Conn., June 24, 1953; d. Avelino and Josephine (DiNoia) B. BA, U. Conn., 1975; BS, Post Coll., 1981; MS in Acctg., U. Hartford, 1984, MBA, 1990. CPA, Conn.; cert. info. sys. auditor, cert. internal auditor. Timekeeper Timex Corp., Waterbury, Conn., 1976-85; auditor Def. Contract Audit Agy., Lexington, Mass., 1985—. Mem. AICPA, Am. Womens Soc. CPAs, Conn. Soc. CPA (continuing profl. edn. com. 1989-95, social and recreation com. 1996—), Inst. Mgmt. Accts. (sec. Waterbury chpt. 1994—), Inst. Internal Auditors, Info. Sys. Audit and Control Assn. Home: 130 Dawes Ave Torrington CT 06790-3627 Office: Def Contract Audit Agy 400 Main St East Hartford CT 06108

BARRELL, SUSAN, performing company administrator; b. Mt. Pleasant, Pa.. Co. mgr. Ballet West, Salt Lake City, 1983-90, from gen. mgr. to exec. dir., 1990—. Office: Ballet West 50 W 200 S Salt Lake City UT 84101-1642

BARRERA, ELVIRA PUIG, counselor, therapist, educator; b. Alice, Tex., Dec. 11, 1943; d. Carlos Rogers and Delia Rebecca (Puig) B.; 1 child, Dennis Lee Jr. BA, Incarnate Word Coll., 1971; M of Counseling and Guidance, St. Mary's U., San Antonio, 1978; specialist degree in marriage and family therapy, St. Mary's U., 1989. Lic. profl. counselor; lic. marriage & family therapist; lic. chem. dependency counselor. Tchr. Edgewood Ind. Sch. Dist., San Antonio, 1965-74, Dallas Ind. Sch. Dist., 1971-72, Northside Ind. Sch. Dist., San Antonio, 1974; ednl. cons. Region 20-Edn. Service Ctr., San Antonio, 1974-79; career edn. coordinator San Antonio Ind. Sch. Dist., 1979-84, counselor, 1984-91; family coord. C.A.T.C.H. Project, U. Tex. Health Sci. Ctr., Houston and Austin, 1991—; cons. Small Bus. Adminstrn., 1981, U.S. Office Edn., Washington, 1981-82, Tex. Edn. Agy., Austin, 1979-80; cons., writer San Antonio Ind. Sch. Dist. and Tex. Edn. Agy., 1985; cons. to various edn. publs. Chairperson career awareness exploring div. Boy Scouts Am., 1982-87. Named Disting. Alumna, Incarnate Word Coll., 1983; recipient Spurgeon award Boy Scouts Am., 1985, Merit award, 1986, Growth award, 1986, Internat. Profl. and Bus. Women's Hall of Fame, 1995. Mem. So. Tex. Pers. and Guidance Assn. (bd. dirs. 1981-82), San Antonio Area Women Deans, Adminstrs. and Counselors Assn. (treas. 1984-86), Austin Assn. for Marriage and Family Therapy, Incarnate Word Coll. Aumni Assn. (mem. adv. bd. 1990—), St. Mary's U. Alumni Assn., San Antonio Hash House Harriers (treas. 1990-91), Ctrl. Tex. Counseling Assn., Mex. Am. Bus. and Profl. Women's Assn., Delta Kappa Gamma (2d v.p. 1982-84, 1st v.p. 1986-88), Chi Sigma Iota. Roman Catholic. Home: 907 Aurora Cir Austin TX 78757-3415 Office: U Tex Edn Annex 3 # 203 Austin TX 78712

BARRETT, BEATRICE HELENE, psychologist; b. Cin., Dec. 8, 1928; d. Oscar Slack and Helen (Kaiper) B.; m. Harold Sheffield Van Buren, Oct. 6, 1966 (div. Oct. 1985). BA, U. Ariz., 1950; MA, U. Ky., 1952; PhD, Purdue U., 1957. Lic. psychologist, Mass. Grad. tchg. asst. in psychology U. Ky., Lexington, 1950-52; psychology asst. Longview State Hosp., Cin., 1951, staff psychologist, 1952; staff psychologist Children's Outpatient and Cons. Svcs. Ind. U. Med. Ctr., Indpls., 1954-57, chief psychologist, 1957-59; instr. psychology Ind. U. Med. Sch., Indpls., 1956-60; rsch. assoc. dept. psychiatry Ind. U. Med. Ctr., Indpls., 1959-60; pvt. practice clin. psychology Indpls., 1957-60; research fellow in psychology Sch. of Medicine Harvard U., Boston, 1960-62; lectr. in spl. edn. Grad. Sch. Edn., Boston U., 1962-63; dir. psychol. rsch. Walter E. Fernald State Sch., Belmont, Mass., 1962-69; dir. behavior prosthesis lab. Walter E. Fernald State Sch., Belmont, 1963-92; chief psychologist, 1969-92; assoc. psychologist Eunice Kennedy Shriver Ctr. for Mental Retardation, Inc., Waltham, Mass., 1982—; instr. Mass. Psychol. Ctr., 1972; lectr. in spl. edn. Lesley Coll. Grad. Sch., 1974-76; adj. assoc. prof. Northeastern U., 1983-92; psychology cons. Carter Meml. Hosp., Indpls., 1959-60; mem. exec. com. Boston Behavior Therapy Interest Group, 1973-74. Cons. editor, mem. adv. bds. various profl. jours.; contbr. numerous articles to profl. jours. Mem. Ind. Gov.'s Youth Coun., 1959-61; mem. spl. adv. com. on mental retardation Ind. Dept. Pub. Instrn., 1959-61; mem. task force Mass. Mental Retardation Planning Project, 1965-66; mem. adv. bd. Cambridge Ctr. for Behavioral Studies, 1981-87, 93-94, trustee, 1987-93, 94—, chair devel. com., 1987-89, mem. subcom. on planned giving, 1992-95, chmn. nominating com., 1992-93, mem., 1993—, exec. com., 1993, 94—, mem. subcom. on acad. and sci. programs, 1992—; treas. B.F. Skinner Found., 1996—; mem. com. on dance edn. Spl. Commn. on Performing Arts, 1976-77; mem. art acquisition com. DeCordova Mus., 1978-80, mem. contemporary arts coun., 1985-87; trustee Boston Repertory Ballet, 1977-79, Boston Ballet Co., 1970-76, sec. bd., 1974-75, exec. com., 1974-76. Grantee Nat. Assn. for Retarded Citizens, 1963, NIHM, 1963-76. Fellow APA, Mass. Psychol. Assn. (Ezra Saul Psychol. Svc. award 1979), Behavior Therapy and Rsch. Soc. (charter clin.); mem. Assn. for Mentally Ill Children (human rights com. 1979-81), Am. Acad. on Mental Retardation (v.p. 1969-74, at-large exec. com. 1975-77), Ea. Psychol. Assn., Assn. for Advancement Behavior Therapy, Assn. Behavior Analysis (jour. adv. bd. 1983-87, chair task force on right to effective edn. 1986-91, presdl. adv. group on edn. and pub. policy 1994-95), Stage Harbor Yacht Club (Chatham, Mass., race com. 1984-86), Sigma Xi, Phi Kappa Phi. Home: RFD 5 Box 236A Winter St Lincoln MA 01773

BARRETT, CAROLYN HERNLY, paralegal; b. Geneva, Ill., Jan. 17, 1954; d. Wayne Francis and Genevieve (Moyer) Hernly; m. Bradley Clayton Barrett, June 20, 1976; children: Heather Hernly, Lance Clayton, Colin Courtney. Grad., Moser Bus. Coll., 1975; BS in Bus. Mgmt., Nat.-Louis U., 1996. Legal sec. Rathje, Woodward, Dyer & Burt, Wheaton, Ill., 1975-77; paralegal Chadwell, Kayser, Ruggles, McGee & Hastings, Chgo., 1978-80, Patrick James Perretti, Glen Ellyn, Ill., 1992-94, 96—. Pres. Forest Glen PTA, Glen Ellyn, 1988-90; mem. Rep. Senatorial Innter Cir., Washington, 1991—, Nat. Trust for Hist. Preservation; chair ways and means com. Glen Ellyn Hist. Soc., 3d v.p., 1992—. Recipient Medal of Freedom, Rep. Senatorial Inner Cir., 1994. Mem. DAR, Nat. Fedn. Rep. Women, Women in Arts (charter). Presbyterian. Home: 675 N Main St Glen Ellyn IL 60137-4045

BARRETT, COLLEEN CROTTY, airline executive; b. Bellows Falls, Vt., Sept. 14, 1944; d. Richard Crotty and Barbara (Hennessey) Blanchard; 1 child, Patrick Allen Barrett. A.A. with highest honors, Becker Jr. Coll., 1964. Legal sec. Oppenheimer Rosenberg Kelleher & Wheatley, San Antonio, 1968-72, adminstrv. asst., paralegal, 1972-78; corp. sec. Southwest Airlines, Dallas, 1978—, exec. asst. to pres. and chmn., 1980-85, v.p. adminstrn., corp. sec., 1985-90, exec. v.p. customs, 1990—. Mem. Leadership Tex. Democrat. Roman Catholic. Office: SW Airlines Co PO Box 37611 Dallas TX 75235-1600

BARRETT, DOROTHY, performing arts administrator; b. L.A., Feb. 28, 1917; d. Lester Arnold and Kathryn (Halverson) Silvera; m. Robert A.H. Cochrane, May 20, 1949 (div. Feb. 1965); 1 stepchild, Michele Cochrane Shaw. Student, LA C.C., 1937-38. Adminstrv. dir. Am. Nat. Acad. of Performing Arts, 1964—; founder, dir. Acad. Children's Workshop, 1964—; produced, choreographed 30 Christmas shows, 1964—; tchr. of dance Barrett Sch. of the Arts, North Hollywood, 1948, Am. Nat. Acad., Studio City, 1964—, tchr. of acting, 1964—; tchr. of speech UCLA Extension, West Hollywood, 1972. Actress, dancer: (motion pictures) A Damsel in Distress, 1937, The Great Waltz, 1938, Gone with the Wind, 1939, Frisco Sal, Wizard of Oz, 1939, Juke Box Soundies, 1942, Hot Money, 1944, Monsieur Beaucaire, 1945, The Imperfect Lady, 1947, Perils of Pauline, 1945, The Stork Club, 1945, Mildred Pierce, 1945, A Bell for Adano, 1945, Weekend at the Waldorf, 1945, Blue Skies, 1946, Connecticut Yankee in King Arthur's Court, 1947, California, 1947, Samson and Deliliah, 1948, The Babe Ruth Story, 1948; (Broadway stage productions) Earl Carroll's Vanities, 1939, Buddy De Sylva's Louisiana Purchase, 1940, Billy Rose's Diamond Horseshoe, 1943, George Abbott's Beat the Band, 1942, others; (TV) co-star KTLA's Secrets of Gourmet, 1946; author: (poetry) Between the Bookends, 1942, The Tolucan, The Legal Journal, 1959, Valley Green Sheet & Van Nuys News; contbr. articles to jours. Active Am. Women's Vol. Svc., 1942. Named Miss Culver City, 1937; recipient award ARC, 1943, Humanitarian award for work with children City of L.A., 1994. Office: Am Nat Acad Performing Arts 10944 Ventura Blvd Studio City CA 91604-3340

BARRETT, ELIZABETH ANN MANHART, nursing educator, psychotherapist, consultant; b. Hume, Ill., July 11, 1934; d. Francis J. and Grace C. (Manhart) Fridy; children: Joseph B., Jeffrey F., Paula G. Brown, Pamela M. Shetler Carpino, Scott D. BS in Nursing summa cum laude, U. Evansville, 1970, MA, 1973, MS in Nursing, 1976; grad. Gestalt Assocs. for Psychotherapy, 1982; PhD in Nursing, NYU, 1983; grad. Am. Inst. for Mental Imagery, 1995. Instr. nursing U. Evansville, Ind., 1970-73, asst. prof., 1973-76; staff nurse Welborn Bapt. Hosp., Evansville, 1975-76; staff nurse Bellevue Psychiat. Hosp., N.Y.C., 1976-79; clin. tchr. CUNY, 1977-82; asst. prof. Adelphi U., 1979-80; group practice Nurse Healers, 1979-82; pvt. practice psychotherapy, 1980—; nurse researcher Mt. Sinai Med. Ctr., N.Y.C., 1982-86, asst. dir. nursing, 1983-86; assoc. prof. Hunter Coll., N.Y.C., 1986-89, prof., 1994—, dir. grad. studies, 1989-92, coord. Ctr. for Nursing Rsch., 1993—; cons. Internat. Soc. Univ. Nurses; co-chair adv. com. Martha E. Rogers Ctr. for Study of Nursing Svc., 1994-96. Mem. com. Regional Health Planning Council, Evansville, 1974-77. Mem. editl. bd. Alt. Therapies in Health and Medicine, 1995—. Recipient Disting. Nursing Alumnus award NYU, 1994, Disting Nurse Rschr. award Found. N.Y. State Nurses Assn., 1995. Fellow Am. Acad. Nursing; mem. Am. Nurses Assn. (cert. psychiat.-mental health, coun. nurse rschrs.), Nat. League Nursing, Ea. Nursing Rsch. Assn. (charter), Soc. Rogerian Scholars (co-founder, 1st pres. 1988-90), NOW, Phi Kappa Phi, Sigma Theta Tau (Upsilon chpt. pres. 1986-88), Alpha Tau Delta, Sigma Xi. Home: 415 E 85th St Apt 9E New York NY 10028-6358 Office: Hunter Coll 425 E 25th St New York NY 10010-2547

BARRETT, GLENDA FAYE, family nurse practitioner; b. Fla., June 5, 1957; d. Bernard T. and Kate (Lavendar) Rigdon; m. Joseph W. Barrett, Oct. 21, 1982; children: Lauren Nichole, Joseph Kyle. ADN, Meridian (Miss.) Jr. Coll., 1977; BSN, U. So. Miss., 1986; MSN, U. Miss. Cert. CPR instr., ACLS, TNCC. Staff nurse Rush Hosp., Newton, Miss.; dir. nursing Hilltop Manor Nursing Home, Union, Miss.; home health nurse Lairds Home Health, Newton; dir. nursing Rush Hosp., Newton; family nurse practitioner Decatur Med. Clinic. Mem. ANA, AANP, Miss. Nurses Assn., MNAPA. Home: PO Box 131 Decatur MS 39327-0131

BARRETT, JANE HAYES, lawyer; b. Dayton, Ohio, Dec. 13, 1947; d. Walter J. and Jane H. Barrett. BA, Calif. State U.-Long Beach, 1969; JD, U. So. Calif., 1972. Bar: Calif. 1972, U.S. Dist. Ct. (cen. dist.) Calif. 1972, U.S. Ct. Appeals (9th cir.) 1982, U.S. Supreme Ct. Assoc. Arter, Hadden, Lawler, Felix & Hall, L.A., 1972-79, ptnr., 1979-94, mng. ptnr., 1984-93; ptnr. Preston, Gates & Ellis, 1994—; mng. ptnr. Preston, Gates & Ellis, L.A., 1994—; lectr. bus. law Calif. State U., 1973-75. Mem. adv. bd. Harriet Buhai Legal Aid Ctr., 1991—, mem. bd. pub. counsel; pres. Pilgrim Parents Orgn. 1990-91. Named Outstanding Grad. Calif. State U., Long Beach, 1988, Outstanding Alumnae Polit. Sci., 1993. Fellow Am. Bar Found.; mem. ABA (bd. govs. 1980-84, chmn. young lawyes div. 1980-81, com. on delivery of legal svcs. 1985-89, exec. coun. legal edn. and admissions sects. 1985-89, fin. sec. torts and ins. practice 1982-83, adv. mem. fed. judiciary com. 1994—, treas. Am. Bar Endowment 1984-90, bd. dirs. 1990—, sec. 1993—, bd. fellows young lawyers div. 1992—), Calif. State Bar (com. adminstrn. of justice, editl. bd. Calif. Lawyers 1981-84), Legion Lex (bd. dirs. 1990-93). Democrat.

BARRETT, JANET TIDD, academic administrator; b. Crystal City, Mo., Nov. 29, 1939; d. Lewis Samuel and Mamie Lou (Hulvey) Tidd; m. David Clark Barrett, June 3, 1961; children: Barbara, Pam. Diploma in nursing, St. Lukes Hosp. Sch. Nursing, 1960; BSN with honors, Washington U., St. Louis, 1964, MS in Nursing, 1979; PhD, St. Louis U., St. Louis, 1987. Assoc. prof. Maryville Coll., St. Louis, 1979-89; academic dean Barnes Coll., St. Louis, 1989-91; dir. BSN program Deaconess Coll. of Nursing, 1991—. Contbr. author to Beare and Meyers: Principles of Medical-Surgical Nursing. St. Lukes Hosp. scholar; recipient Sister Agnita Claire Day Rsch. award St. Louis U. Mem. Nat League Nursing, Mo. League Nursing, St. Luke's Alumni Assn., N. Am. Nursing Diagnosis Assn., Sigma Theta Tau, Pi Lambda Theta, Phi Delta Kappa.

BARRETT, JESSICA (DONNA ANN NIPERT), psychotherapist; b. Paterson, N.J., July 25, 1952; d. Donald Alfred and Gloria Emma (Lustica) Nipert; m. John David Barrett, Sept. 9, 1977 (div. June 1982); 1 child, Ashley Elizabeth. BA, UCLA, 1975; MA, Azusa Pacific U., 1981. Lic. marriage, family, child counselor; cert. hypnosis profl. With employee relations Engrs. and Architects Exec. Assn., L.A., 1975-79; practicing psychotherapy Toluca Lake and Burbank, Calif., 1983—; instr., supr. Phillips Grad. Inst., Encino, Calif., 1986—; psychotherapist Pasadena (Calif.) Outpatient Eating Disorders Program, 1987-88; cons. Texaco Employee Assistance Program, Studio City, 1985-86, NBC Employee Assistance Program, Burbank, 1986-87, 93—; lectr. various groups, Burbank, San Fernando Valley, 1983-87; spl. therapist Am. Psych-Mgmt. Inc., Value Behavioral Health, Vista Health Mgmt., Managed Health Networks, MCC/EAP and Provider, Calnet, Options, Wellness Network, Health Mgmt. Resource Svcs., 1985—; assessment and referral liaison Nat. Resource Cons., San Diego, 1983-93, Employee Support Sys. Corp., Orange, Calif., 1985—, Health and Human Resource Ctr., 1984-92. Mem. AAUW, Employee Assistance Profls. Assn. (bd. dirs. 1983-86), Am. Assn. Marriage and Family Therapists (clin.), Stepfamily Assn. Am., Calif. Family Study Ct. Alumni Assn. (sec.-treas. 1987-88, v.p. programs 1988-89), Eye Movement Desensitization Reprocessing Internat. Assn. (charter mem.), Glendale Area Mental Health Profls.

BARRETT, JUDITH ANN, salon owner; b. N.Y.C., Dec. 15, 1940; d. William Patrick and Eleanor Margaret (McClaurey) B. Grad., Aquinas H.S., 1958. Sec. Avon Products, N.Y.C., 1960-73; owner The Girl's Beauty Shop, Port Richey, Fla., 1974—. CEO, founder Enraged People Against Rape, Pasco, Fla., 1990-93. Recipient Outstanding Contbrn. and Dedication to Fla Residents, U.S. Congress M. Bilirakis, Washington, 1992, Cmty. Svc. Pres. award Cmty. Svc. Coun. of W. Pasco, 1992, Humanitarian award Pasco Co. Sheriffs Dept., 1991-92. Mem. West Pasco Rep. Club, Waves Nat., Am. Legion. Republican. Roman Catholic.

BARRETT, LIDA KITTRELL, mathematics educator; b. Houston, May 21, 1927; d. Pleasant Williams and Maidel (Baker) Kittrell; m. John Herbert

Barrett, June 2, 1950 (dec. Jan. 1969); children: John Kittrell, Maidel Horn, Mary Louise. BA, Rice U., 1946; MA, U. Tex., Austin, 1949; PhD, U. Pa., 1954. Instr. math. U. Conn., Waterbury, 1955-56; vis. appointment U. Wis., Madison, 1959-60; lectr. U. Utah, Salt Lake City, 1956-61; assoc. prof. U. Tenn., Knoxville, 1961-70, prof., 1970-80, head math. dept., 1973-80; assoc. provost No. Ill. U., DeKalb, 1980-87; dean, arts and scis. Miss. State U., Mississippi State, 1987-91; sr. assoc. Edn. and Human Resources Directorate NSF, Washington, 1991-95; prof. math. U.S. Mil. Acad., West Point, N.Y., 1995—; ind. math. cons., Knoxville, Tenn., 1964-80. Contbr. articles on topology and math. edn. to profl. jours. Mem. Math. Assn. Am. (pres. 1989, 90), Am. Math. Soc., Soc. Indsl. and Applied Math., Nat. Coun. Tchrs. Math., Am. Assn. Higher Edn., Phi Kappa Phi, Sigma Xi. Episcopalian. Office: US Mil Acad Math Sci Dept West Point NY 10996

BARRETT, LINDA L., real estate executive; b. Hudson, Mich., Aug. 16, 1948; d. David John and Georgia Elizabeth (Spengler) B.; 1 dau., Toni. Student, U. Mich., 1970-73. Cert. residential brokerage mgr. Sales mgr. Collins Real Estate, Hudson, Mich., 1973-79; owner, broker Homeland Real Estate, Lake Leann, Mich., 1979-82; mgr. broker Mid-Mich. Real Estate, Jackson, Mich., 1982-85; exec. v.p. Michael Saunders & Co., Sarasota, Fla., 1986-95, cons., 1995—; mem. adv. bd. Sotheby's Internat. Mem. AAUW, NAFE, Internat. Real Estate Fedn., Nat. Mktg. Inst., Nat. Assn. Realtors, Fla. Assn. Realtors, Sarasota C. of C., Bradenton C. of C., Com. of 100, 2000 Notable Am. Women (profl. stds. com. woman's coun.), Econ. Devel. Coun., CRB, Estates Club.

BARRETT, LOIS YVONNE, minister; b. Enid, Okla., Nov. 9, 1947; d. Hugh Preston and Audrey Lucille (Wilson) B.; m. Thomas Bruce Mierau, June 26, 1977; children: Barbara, Susanna, John. BA, U. Okla., 1969; MDiv, Mennonite Bibl. Sem., 1983; PhD, Union Grad. Sch., 1992. Ordained to Christian ministry, 1985. Assoc. editor The Mennonite, Newton, Kans., 1971-77; editor The House Ch. newsletter, Wichita, Kans., 1978-80, 83-85; instr. Great Plains Sem. Edn. Prog., North Newton, Kans., 1985, 90, 92; co-pastor Mennonite Ch. of the Servant, Wichita, Kans., 1983-92; exec. sec. Commn. Home Ministries Gen. Conf. Mennonite Ch., Newton, 1992—; mem. exec. coun. Inst. Mennonite Studies, Elkhart, Ind., 1983—; mem. ecumenical peace theology working group Mennonite Cen. Com., Akron, Pa., 1988-92; writer Inter-Mennonite Confession of Faith com., 1988-95; editorial com. Mennonite Ency. V, 1985-87. Author: The Vision and the Reality, 1983, Building the House Church, 1986, The Way God Fights, 1987, Doing What is Right, 1989. Convener Chs. United for Peacemaking, Wichita, 1986, 88-89, bd. dirs., 1983-90; pres. Midtown Citizens Assn., 1977-78; mem. Citizens Participation Orgn., 1977-80. Recipient Am. Bible Soc. award, 1983. Mem. Am. Acad. Religion, Am. Soc. Ch. History, Phi Beta Kappa. Home: 1508 Fairview St Wichita KS 67203-2634 Office: Gen Conf Mennonite Ch Commn Home Ministries 722 N Main St Newton KS 67114-1819

BARRETT, LORETTA ANNE, publishing executive; b. Mt. Vernon, N.Y., July 1, 1941; d. Edward Vincent and Irene Marie (Wynne) B. Student, Rosemont (Pa.) Coll., 1958-60; BA cum laude, U. Pa., 1962, MAT, 1965. Editor Doubleday & Co. Anchor Press, N.Y.C., 1965-67; editorial dir. Doubleday & Co. Special Projects, N.Y.C., 1967-72; exec. editor, publisher Anchor Press, Doubleday & Co., N.Y.C., 1972-83; exec. editorial v.p. Doubleday & Co., N.Y.C., 1983-90; pres. Loretta Barrett Books, Lit. Agy., 1990—; bd. dirs. Reading is Fundamental, Washington, 1967—, Through the Flower, Santa Fe, N.Mex., 1986—. Assoc., trustee Coun. Pa. Women U. Pa., 1989; bd. dirs. Athena Inst., Haverford, Pa., 1987—, Grandparenting Found., Lake Placid, N.Y., 1987. Mem. Women in the Media, Assn. of Author's Reps., Inc. Democrat. Roman Catholic. Office: Loretta Barrett Books 101 5th Ave New York NY 10003-1008

BARRETT, PAULETTE SINGER, public relations executive; b. Paris, Dec. 20, 1937; came to U.S., 1947; d. Andrew M. and Agatha (Kinsbrunner) Singer; m. Laurence I. Barrett, Mar. 9, 1957 (div. 1983); children: Paul Meyer, David Allen, Adam Singer. BA, NYU, 1957; MS in Journalism, Columbia U., 1958. News dir. Yardney Electric Corp., N.Y.C., 1958-61; freelance writer newspapers and pub. relations orgns., N.Y.C. and Washington, 1961-73; assoc. dir. pub. info. Columbia U., N.Y.C., 1973-77; from account exec. to v.p., then sr. v.p. Edelman Pub. Rels. Worldwide, N.Y.C., 1977-80, sr. v.p. and gen. mgr., 1980, exec. v.p., gen. mgr., 1986-88, exec. v.p., dir. corp. affairs div., 1988-89; exec. v.p. Rowland Co., N.Y.C., 1980-82; exec. dir. communications UJA-Fedn./N.Y., N.Y.C., 1982-86; sr. v.p., mng. dir. Hill and Knowlton, Chgo., 1989-90; pres. Barrett Comm., Chgo., 1990—. Bus. and mktg. coms. Ill. Arts Alliance Found.; internat. adv. bd. Elmhurst Coll. Holocaust Edn. Project; bd. dirs. Temple Sholom. Office: Barrett Comms 1555 N Astor St Ste 23 Chicago IL 60610-1673

BARRETTA-KEYSER, JOLIE, professional athletics coach, author; b. Phila., Aug. 17, 1954; d. Philip Francis and Norma Roberta (Podoszek) Barretta; m. Joel D. Keyser; children: Evan Barrett, Kyra Lani. Student, U. Calif., Long Beach, 1972-76, U. Florence, Italy, 1974-75. Tchr. gymnastics Los Angeles City Sch. Dist., 1973-77, judge, 1976-82; coach, choregrapher Kips Gymnastic Club, Long Beach, Calif., 1976-78, So. Calif. Acrobatics Team, Huntington Beach, Calif., 1979-81, UCLA, 1980-82; pres. West Coast Waves Rhythmic Gymnastics, Rolling Hills Estates, Calif., 1980—; mem. coaching staff U.S. Nat. Rhythmic Gymnastics Team, 1983—; coach Centro Olimpico Nazionale Italia, Rome, 1974-76; lectr. dance, phys. edn. Calif. State U., Dominguez Hills, Carson, 1981-92; French lang. mistress of ceremonies rhythmic gymnastics event U.S. Olympic Games, L.A., 1984; invited observer Inst. Phys. Culture, Bejing, 1985, Bulgarian Gymnastics Fedn., Sophia, 1982-90; meet dir. state and regional championships, L.A. County, 1984, '86; internat. lectr. body alignment; pres. Rhythymic Gymnasts Devel. Program, 1984—; developer RIGOR (Rhythmic Gymnastics Outreach) for U.S.A. recreation programs; mem. rhythmic gymnastics adv. com. & bd. Internat. Spl. Olympics, 1990—. Author: Body Alignment, 1985; columnist Internat. Gymnast Mag., 1987-90. Tour leader Acad. Tours Inc. U.S./Bulgaria Friendship Through Sports Ann. Tour, N.Y. and Bulgaria, 1987. Recipient recognition plaque U.S. Womens Sports Awards Banquet, 1984-89. Mem. U.S. Rhythmic Gymnastics Coaches Assn. (pres. 1984—), U.S. Gymnastics Fedn. (bd. dirs. 1985—, nat. team coach 1984—, mem. del., coach internat. competitions U.S., Mex., Hungary, Bulgaria, Belgium, Can. 1984—, choreographer age group devel. compulsory div. 1987, staff Olympic Tng. Ctr. 1984—), Inst. Noetic Scis., Internat. Spl. Olympics (adv. bd. rhythmic gymnastics). Republican. Office: West Coast Waves 11661 San Vicente Blvd Ste 609 Los Angeles CA 90049-5114

BARRETT-CONNOR, ELIZABETH LOUISE, epidemiologist, educator; b. Evanston, Ill., Apr. 8, 1935; m. James D. Connor. BA, Mt. Holyoke Coll., 1956, DSc (hon.), 1985; MD, Cornell U., 1960; MD (hon.), U. Utrecht, The Netherlands, 1996, U. Bergen, Norway, 1996. Diplomate Am. Bd. Internal Medicine, Nat. Bd. Med. Examiners. Instr. medicine U. Miami, Fla., 1965-68, asst. prof. medicine, 1968-70; asst. prof. community and family medicine U. Calif., San Diego, 1970-74, assoc. prof. community and family medicine, 1974-81, prof. community and family medicine, 1981—, acting chair dept. community and family medicine, 1981-82, chmn. dept. family and preventative medicine, 1982—; vis. prof. Royal Soc. Medicine, London, 1989; mem. hosp. infection control com. VA Med. Ctr., San Diego, 1971—. Contbr. articles to profl. jours. NIH grantee, 1970-95, Am. Heart Assn. grantee, 1980-81. Mem. Am. Heart Assn. (chmn. budget com. coun. on epidemiology 1987-88, chmn. coun. on epidemiology 1988-89), Am. Pub. Health Assn. (chmn. epidemiology sect. 1989—), Assn. Tchrs. Preventive Medicine (bd. dirs. 1987—), Inst. Medicine. Office: U Calif #0628 La Jolla CA 92093

BARRIE, BARBARA ANN, actress; b. Chgo., May 23, 1931; d. Louis and Frances Rose (Boruszak) Berman; m. Jay Malcolm Harnick, July 23, 1964; children: Jane Caroline Harnick, Aaron Louis Harnick. BFA, U. Tex., 1953. Appeared with N.Y. Shakespeare Festival, 1960, 65, 69, Am. Shakespeare Festival, 1958-59; appeared on Broadway in: Wooden Dish, 1955, Beaux Stratagem, 1959, Company, 1970, Prisoner of Second Ave., 1972, Selling of the President, 1971, California Suite, 1976, The Killdeer, 1974 (Obie award, Drama Desk award 1974), Big and Little Phoenix Theatre, N.Y.C., 1979, Isn't it Romantic, 1984, Fugue, Long Wharf Playhouse, 1986, After-Play, 1995; numerous TV appearances including Barney Miller, Two of a Kind, 1982, Barefoot in the Park, 1982, Double Trouble (series), 1984-85, as Mamie Eisenhower in Backstairs at the White House, Family Ties, 1987, Mr. President, 1987, TV movies include: The Execution, My Breast; appeared in films One Potato, Two Potato, 1964 (Cannes Festival Acting award 1964), The Caretakers, 1963, Breaking Away, 1979 (Oscar nomination), Private Benjamin, 1980, Real Men, 1986, The Passage, End of the Line, 1986. Active ERA. Mem. AFTRA, SAG, Actors Equity Assn., Acad. Motion Picture Arts and Scis. Office: care The Gersh Agency 232 N Canon Dr Beverly Hills CA 90210*

BARRINGER, MARGARET CHEW, poet; b. Bryn Mawr, Pa., Apr. 16, 1946; d. Richard Wethered Drew and Anne Sophia Penn (Chew) B.; 1 child, Elizabeth Sandwith Saltonstall. Student, U. Pa., 1977-79, Bryn Mawr Coll., 1980-82. Founder, pres. Community Workshops Inc., Phila., 1971-76, Intown E. Corp., Phila., 1975-77, Am. Poetry Ctr., Phila., 1983-92; chmn., 1992—; v.p. Barringer Crater Co., Winslow, Ariz., 1982-92; with community devel. Walnut St. Theatre, Phila., 1974-76; lit. panelist Pa. Coun. on Arts, Md. State Arts Coun., Del. State Arts Coun. Mem. adv. bd. Am. Poetry Rev. Mem. Mayor's Cultural Adv. Coun., Phila., 1987-91. Mem. Franklin Inn Club (bd. dirs. 1988-91, pres. 1990-91). Home: 315 S 18th St Philadelphia PA 19103

BARRIOS, MARY ELIZABETH HECK, lawyer; b. Thibodaux, La., July 23, 1960; d. Herman Andrew and Barbara Mary (Sanchez) Heck; m. Michael C. Barrios. BA, Nicholls State U., 1980; JD, La. State U., 1983; LLM, Tulane U., 1993. Bar: La. 1963, Fla. 1990, U.S. Dist. Ct. (mid. dist.) La. 1984, U.S. Ct. Appeals (5th cir.) 1984. Pvt. practice Baton Rouge, 1991—; assoc. Ungelsby & Brown, Baton Rouge, 1985-88; ptnr. Unglesby & Barrios, Baton Rouge, 1988-89. Mem. steering com. John Breaux Campaign, Baton Rouge, 1986; active Citizens for a Clean Environment; mem. Capital Area Ct. Apptd. Special Advocate Assn. Mem. ABA, ATLA, La. Trial Lawyers Assn. (chmn. criminal law com. 1988), La. Bar Assn. (young lawyers sect. rep. 1988-90, criminal sect.), La. Assn. Criminal Def. Lawyers, Baton Rouge Bar Assn. (pub. rels. com. 1984—), Baton Rouge Assn. Women Attys. (legis. com. 1984—), La. Law Inst. (adv. com. 1989—). Democrat. Roman Catholic. Lodge: Sertoma. Office: PO Box 880 Denham Springs LA 70727-0880

BARRIS, MARY BETH NICHOLS, assistant principal secondary school; b. Wilson, N.C., May 26, 1939; d. Hoyt Battle and Ruby Ethel (Boykin) Nichols; m. John Charles Barris, Aug. 19, 1967. BS, E. Carolina U., 1962; MS in Edn., No. Ill. U., 1977, Cert. advanced studies (Type 75), 1987. Cert. tchr., ednl. adminstrn., strategic planning facilitator. Tchr. Meadow Sch., Benson, N.C., 1961-63; libr. Tarboro (N.C.) H.S., 1963-68; media specialist DeKalb (Ill.) H.S., 1968-86, dean of students, 1986-93, asst. prin., 1994-95; prin. Malta (Ill.) H.S., 1996—; dir. theater Meadow Sch., Benson, 1964, Tarboro H.S., summer 1966; sponsor cheerleaders Tarboro H.S. 1965-66; bowling coach, DeKalb H.S., 1973; coach pom pom squad, DeKalb H.S., 1976-84; facilitator strategic planning, DeKalb H.S., 1991-96, Stockton H.S., 1993-94; panel mem. Tri County Adminstrs., St. Charles, Ill., 1991. Actress Stagecoach Comty. Theatre, 1973-78; speaker, presenter ednl. groups. Mem. ASCD, Nat. Assn. Sch. Strategic Planners, Order of Ea. Star, Phi Delta Kappa. Baptist. Home: 322 S Main St Sycamore IL 60178

BARRISKILL, MAUDANNE KIDD, primary school educator; b. Balt., Apr. 2, 1932; d. John Graydon and Maudine (Adams) Kidd; m. Peter Herbert Barriskill, Nov. 30, 1957; children: John, Michael. BA, So. Meth. U., 1954; student early childhood edn., Old Dominion U., 1970; student, Katharine Gibbs Sch., N.Y.C., 1954-55, Juilliard Sch. Music, N.Y.C., 1948-50. Exec. sec., copywriter trainee J. Walter Thompson Advt. Agy., N.Y.C., 1955-59; founder Maude Barry Interior Design, Virginia Beach, 1970-73; founder, dir. The Home Sch., Virginia Beach, 1975—; tchr. Ea. Shore Chapel Presch., Virginia Beach, 1970-75, Montessori Child Devel. Ctr., Virginia Beach. Author children's books and workbooks. Tchr. Sunday sch. Home: 4721 Newgate Ct Virginia Beach VA 23455-4033

BARRON, GRETTA LOUISE, accountant; b. Massillon, Ohio, May 17, 1958; d. Lloyd William and Shirley ruth (Carver) Smail; m. James Daniel Lindsay, Aug. 25, 1976 (div. June 1980); 1 child, Jessica Bernice Lindsay (dec.); m. Donald Alan Barron, Aug. 15, 1987; children: Shaley Nicole, Shane Alan. BS in Acctg., U. Akron, 1996. Bookkeeper Evergreen (Colo.) Bank, 1980-82; benefits adminstr. Prudential Ins. Co., Akron, 1982-91; co-owner Canal Fulton (Ohio) Cafe, 1993-94. Roush Meml. scholar U. Akron, 1995-96. Mem. Inst. Mgmt. Accts. (v.p. comms. U. Akron chpt. 1995-96). Methodist. Home: PO Box 48 North Lawrence OH 44666

BARRON, PEGGY PENNISI, management consultant; b. Chgo., Jan. 27, 1958; d. Louis Legendre and Jane Harriet (Peters) Pennisi; m. Stan Barron, May 3, 1986; children: Brian Alexander, Christine Deanna. BS with honors, U. Ill., Chgo., 1979. Data processing mgr. Oasis Aviation, Inc., L.A., 1980-87; pres. Millennium Enterprises, Marina Del Rey, Calif., 1987—. Mem. NAFE, Phi Beta Kappa, Phi Kappa Phi. Home and Office: 3008 Yale Ave Marina Del Rey CA 90292

BARRON, ROBERTA, human resources management consultant; b. N.Y.C., May 11, 1940; d. Irv and Roslyn (Engerow) Yellin; m. Harold S. Barron, Nov. 17, 1963; children: Lawrence Ira, Jean Louise. Student, UCLA, 1960-61; BA, Conn. Coll., 1962; MSIR, Loyola U., Chgo., 1987. Corp. pub. dept. staff Time Inc., N.Y.C., 1962-64; pub. relations cons., 1965-87; cons. Exec. Assets, Chgo., 1987-88, Barron Assocs., Chgo., 1988—. Mem. IAOP, Women's Athletic Club. Office: 180 E Pearson St Chicago IL 60611-2130

BARRON, TIANA LUISA, foundation developer, fundraiser, educator; b. Omaha, Mar. 26, 1952; d. James Patrick Barron and Maria Isabel (Pasos) McAdoo; m. Jerry Peter Mastora (div.); children: Peter Uriah Mastora, Travis Burnell Thom, Taylor Morgan Lewis. Pres., founder S.A.V.E., Sherman Oaks, Calif., 1987—; producer, writer, dir. S.A.V.E., L.A., 1992—. Author: Mommy Was I Adopted, 1992. Adv. bd. The Family Hispanic Ins., L.A., 1990; vol., counselor San Fernando Valley Juvenile Hall, Slymar, Calif., 1990, Sojourn. Recipient Honor for S.A.V.E. Day George Bush, George Deukmejian, Mayor Bradley, Bd. Suprs., L.A., 1989. Home and Office: 4375 Ventura Canyon Ave # 1 Sherman Oaks CA 91601-5105

BARROW, MARIE ANTONETTE, elementary education educator; b. Jamaica, Nov. 2, 1952; d. Edward Emmanuel and Mildred Pancheta (Brown) Rerrie; m. Michael Andre Barrow; children: Melissa Alicia, Matthew Andre. BA, Coll. of New Rochelle, 1976; MA, Bank St. Coll. Edn., 1982. Tchr. spl. edn. Ossining (N.Y.) Pub. Schs., 1978-91, tchr. 2d grade, 1991—; presenter Brookside Sch., Ossining, 1994, Staff Devel. Ctr., White Plains, N.Y , 1992; mem. study group to examine elem. sch. gifted/talented programs, Ossining Union Free Sch. Dist., 1993-94. Mem. Assn. for Supervision and Curriculum Devel., Tchr.s for Child Centered Learning, Brookside Sch. Behavior Com. (chmn. 1990-92). Home: 38 Manitou Trl White Plains NY 10603-3020

BARROW, MARY, public relations executive. Publicist Universal Studios Tour; newswriter, prodr. Sta. KABC-TV, L.A.; publicist Sta. KTLA-TV, L.A., 1975-80; dir. publicity GWB TV divsn., 1980-81; dir. corporate comm. Golden West Broadcasters, 1981-83; founder, owner Barrow/Hoffman PR, Duarte, Calif., 1983—. Office: Barrow Hoffman PR 2998 Hacienda Dr Duarte CA 91010-2310

BARRS, JENNIFER ANNE, journalist; b. Baton Rouge, Apr. 10, 1958; d. J.J. and Gladys Lucille (Geldard) W.; m. Charles Kent Tucker, May 19, 1979 (div. Dec. 1986); m. William J. Barrs, Apr. 21, 1993. BFA, So. Methodist U., Dallas, 1980. Staff writer consumer column The Dallas Morning News, 1980; editor and staff writer Longview Morning Jour., 1980-83; staff writer The Dallas Downtown News, 1984-85; assoc. editor Dallas City Mag. The Dallas Times Herald, 1985-86, gen. assignment reporter, 1986-87; columnist, critic and staff writer The Tampa (Fla.) Tribune, 1987—. Recipient Mng. Editors award Associated Press, 1982, Paul R. Ellis award Am. Heart Assn., 1982, Citation of Merit-Anson Jones award Tex. Med. Assn., 1983, 84, Katie award Newspaper Press Club of Dallas, 1985, Gen Excellence in Feature Writing award Fla. Press Club, 1993. Mem. Soc. Profl. Journalists (Tampa Bay chpt., bd. dirs. 1993-95, Excellence award 1993, Outstanding Achievement award 1995). Office: The Tampa Tribune 202 S Parker St Tampa FL 33606

BARRY, BONNIE B., trade association executive; b. Pocatello, Idaho, July 17, 1940; d. Kyle and Lael Corrine (Smith) Bettilyon; 1 child, Robyn Matthies Randall. Student, Mills Coll., 1958-59; BA, U. Utah, 1962; cert., ITCA, 1976. CCIM. Spl. svcs. mgr. Sperry Rand Missile Div., Salt Lake City, 1962-64; mgr. travel dept. Utah Motor Club, Salt Lake City, 1965-67; owner Aggie Travel Svc., Davis, Calif., 1968-77, also bd. dirs.; founding ptnr. SECRET Travel Svc., Maui, Hawaii, 1979—; exec. v.p. Assn. Retail Travel Agts., 1979—; pres., CEO Bettilyon Investment Co., Salt Lake City, 1990—; tng. dir. ednl. work-study programs for mem. travel agys., U.S. and Can.; mem. faculty U. Calif. Extension, Davis, 1974-77. Mem. Nat. Travel Agts. (adv. bd. to Pan Am. World Airways 1973-77), Assn. Retail Travel Agts. (nat. bd. dirs. 1974-78), Giants Travel Coop. (v.p. Western chpt. 1972-74), Am. Assn. Retail Travel Agts., Soroptomists. Republican. Morman. Home: 3 Nail Driver Ct # 1388 Park City UT 84060-6707 Office: Bettilyon Investment Co 333 2nd Ave # D Salt Lake City UT 84103-2626

BARRY, JANET CECILIA, retired elementary school educator; b. Jersey City, May 12, 1944; d. John Aloysius and Mary Elizabeth (Hart) B.; BA, Paterson State Coll., 1966; MA, Georgian Ct. Coll., 1978. Tchr., Paterson (N.J.) Pub. Sch. No. 12, 1966-68; tchr. Walnut St. Elem. Sch., Toms River (N.J.) Regional Sch. System, 1968-88; supr. instrn. Cedar Grove Elem. Sch., Toms River Regional Sch. System, 1988-90; supr. instrn. North Dover Elem. Sch., 1990-94, Hooper Ave. Elem. Sch., 1994-95, ret., 1995; supr. instruction Toms River Regional Schs. Mem. Aviation Space Edn. Found. Recipient N.J. Gov.'s Excellence in Teaching award, 1987. Mem. NEA, Nat. Coun. Tchrs. English, Nat. Sci. Tchrs. Assn., N.J. Edn. Assn., Ocean County Edn. Assn., Toms River Edn. Assn., Assn. for Supervision and Curriculum Devel., N.J. Reading Assn., N.J. Assn. for Supervision and Curriculum Devel., Internat. Reading Assn., Ocean County Reading Coun. (rec. sec., 1st v.p., pres.), Georgian Ct. Coll. Grad. Sch. Alumni Assn. (sec.), N.J. Prins. and Suprs. Assn., Challenger Ctr. for Space Edn. Educator's Network, Coun. for Elem. Sci. Internat., Delta Kappa Gamma (chmn. programs, ednl. svcs., communications, Zeta chpt.).

BARRY, JOYCE ALICE, dietitian; b. Chgo., Apr. 27, 1932; d. Walter Stephen and Ethel Myrtle (Paetow) Barry; student Iowa State Coll., 1950-52, Loyola U., 1952-58; B.S., Mundelein Coll., 1955; postgrad. Simmons Coll., 1963-64, U. Ga., 1979, Calif. Western U., 1980—. Reg. dietician. Prodn. supr. Marshall Field & Co., Chgo., 1955-59; dir. food services Women's Ednl. and Indsl. Union, Boston, 1959-62; dir. food services Wellesley Public Schs., Mass., 1962-70; cons. Stokes Food Services, Newton, Mass., 1960-70; regional dietitian Canteen Corp., Chgo., 1970-83; gen. mgr. bus. devel. Plantation-Sysco, Orlando, Fla., 1983-87; dir. product devel. corp., quality assurance, procurement Mariott Internat. Hdqrs., Washington, 1987-95; owner food svc. consulting svc., 1995—; vis. lectr.; research adv. council Restaurant Bus. Mag.; career adv. council, Am. Dietetics Assn.; treas. Dietitians in Bus. Mem. Am. Home Econs. Assn., Internat. Fedn. Home Economists, Home Economists in Bus., Am. Dietetics Assn., Nat. Assn. Female Execs., Dietitians in Bus., Tex.-Mex. Frozen Food Coun., Internat. Food Technologists, Nat. Frozen Food Coun. Republican. Roman Catholic. Club: La Chaine des Rotisseurs. Home and Office: 175 Heron Bay Cir Lake Mary FL 32746-3423

BARRY, LEI, medical equipment manufacturing executive; b. Fitchburg, Mass., May 27, 1941; d. Leo Isaacson and Irene Helen (Melanson) Isaacson Godbout; m. Delbert M. Berry (div.); children: David M., Susan L.; m. Frank H. Mahan III, June 25, 1976; stepchildren: Jodi L., Sarah C., Amy S., Frank H. IV. Grad. high sch., Waltham, Mass. Advt. salesperson, broadcaster various radio and TV stas., N.C. and Tex., 1961-67; New Eng. sales rep. Hollister, Inc., Chgo., 1967-71, Northeastern sales mgr., 1971-76; v.p., ptnr. Mahan Assocs., Blue Bell, Pa., 1976—; pres. Blue Bell Bio-Med., Inc., 1982—. Bd. mgrs. YMCA, Ambler, 1989-95. Mem. Whitpain Twp. Planning Commn., 1986-91; pres., bd. dirs. Interfaith of Ambler; mem. affordable housing adv. coun. Fed. Home Loan Bank, Pitts. Mem. Healthcare Mfrs. Mktg. Coun. (bd. dirs.), Blue Bell Rotary, Wissahickon Valley C. of C. (bd. dirs. 1987-92), Wissahickon Valley Hist. Soc. (past bd. dirs.), Health Industry Reps. Assn. Republican. Avocations: tennis, skiing, gourmet cooking. Office: Blue Bell Bio-Med Inc PO Box 455 Blue Bell PA 19422-0455

BARRY, LOUISE MCCANTS, retired college official; b. Appleton, Ark., Apr. 22, 1924; d. Jesse Blaine and Piety Ethel (Griffin) Spears; m. Robert Orville McCants, Aug. 22, 1947 (div. 1982); children: Blaine, Janice, Robert; m. William Burnett Barry, Feb. 16, 1993. BS, Okla. State U., 1944, MS, 1948; PhD, Ohio State U., 1974. Statistician Stanolind Oil & Gas Co., Tulsa, 1944-46; instr. Okla. State U., Stillwater, 1946-49; analytical statistician U.S. Air Force, Wright-Patterson AFB, Ohio, 1949-52; prof. math. Sinclair Community Coll., Dayton, Ohio, 1966-78; dir. rsch. U. Mid-Am., Lincoln, Nebr., 1978-79; acad. dean Kirkwood Community Coll., Cedar Rapids, Iowa, 1979-83; dir. instrn. Met. Community Colls., Kansas City, Mo., 1983-88; cons. numerous colls. in U.S. and Gt. Britain, 1974—. Author: Womanchange!, 1986, Retire to Fun and Freedom, 1988, A Price Beyond Rubies, 1996; contbr. articles to profl. jours. Mem. Iowa Humanities Bd., 1980-83; bd. dirs. Cedar Rapids Symphony, 1980-83, United Way Fund Drive, Cedar Rapids, 1982, Mo. Humanities Coun., 1984—, Mo. Bio-Ethics Coun., 1987—; del. Iowa Rep. Conv., 1982. Mem. Am. Assn. Cmty. Jr. Colls., Nat. Speakers Assn., Kansas City Women's C. of C. (edn. com. 1986—), Friends of Art, AAUW, Civil War Roundtable, Western Posse, Phi Mu Epsilon, Kappa Delta Pi. Roman Catholic. Home and Office: 121 W 48th St Kansas City MO 64112

BARRY, MARIAN THERESE, nurse; b. Camden, N.J., Sept. 19, 1934; d. Joseph Adam and Frances Irene (Grula) Plavcan; m. John Francis Barry, Jr., May 10, 1962 (dec. Feb. 1991); children: Jacqueline, John, Therese, Danielle, Joseph, Michelle. Diploma in nursing, Misericordia Hosp., Phila., 1955; BSN, Villanova U., 1959. RN, N.J., Pa. Charge nurse emergency room Our Lady of Lourdes Hosp., Camden, 1955-56, instr. nursing, 1960-62; instr. nursing Cooper Med. Ctr., Camden, 1959-60; case mgr. Vis. Nurse Assn. So. N.J., Kennemede, N.J., 1980—. Roman Catholic. Home: 125 E Williams Ave Barrington NJ 08007

BARRY, MARILYN WHITE, dean, educator; b. Weymouth, Mass., Sept. 12, 1936; d. Harland Russell and Alice Louise (Dwyer) White; m. Dennis Edward Barry, July 11, 1959; children—Dennis Edward, Christopher Gerard. BS in Edn. Bridgewater State Coll., 1958; Ed.M. in Spl. Edn., Boston U., 1969, Ed.D. in Spl. Edn., 1974. Tchr. Weymouth pub. schs. (Mass.), 1958-60; spl. edn. instr. Boston U., 1972-74; asst. prof. in spl. edn. Bridgewater State Coll., (Mass.), 1974-79, assoc. prof., 1979-83, prof., 1983-87, chmn. spl. edn. dept., 1979-87, coordinator dept. grad. programs, 1979-87, adminstr. bilingual spl. edn., 1983-86, dean grad. sch., 1987—. Co-author human service workers curriculum materials. Boston U. fellow, 1967-74; 3 Disting. Service awards, Bridgewater State Coll., 1980, 82, 85; Bilingual Spl. Edn. grantee, 1980, 83. Mem. Council Exceptional Children (Mass. chpt. founder, past pres., learning disabilities chpt.), Mass. Assn. Children With Learning Disabilities (past v.p.), Phi Delta Kappa, Pi Lambda Theta. Democrat. Roman Catholic. Home: 138 Bedford St Lakeville MA 02347-1351 Office: Bridgewater State Coll Grad Sch Conant Sci Bldg Bridgewater MA 02324

BARRY, MARYANNE TRUMP, federal judge; b. N.Y.C., Apr. 5, 1937; d. Fred C. and Mary Trump; m. John J. Barry, Dec. 26, 1982; 1 child, David W. Desmond. BA, Mt. Holyoke Coll., 1958; MA, Columbia U., 1962; JD, Hofstra U., 1974, LLD (hon.); LLD (hon.), Seton Hall U., Caldwell Coll. Bar: N.J. 1974, N.Y. 1975, U.S. Ct. Appeals (3d cir.), U.S. Supreme Ct. Asst. U.S. Atty., 1974-75, dep. chief appeals div., 1976-77, chief appeals div., 1977-82, exec. asst. U.S. Atty., 1981-82, 1st asst., 1981-83; judge U.S. Dist. Ct., N.J., 1983—; chmn. Com. on Criminal Law Jud. Conf. of U.S. Fellow Am. Bar Found.; mem. ABA, N.J. Bar Assn., Am. Judicature Soc. (bd. dirs.), Assn. Fed. Bar State of N.Y. (pres. 1982-83). Office: US Dist Ct PO & Courthouse Bldg Fed Square PO Box 999 Newark NJ 07101-0999

BARRY, MILDRED CASTILLE, artist; b. Sunset, La., Feb. 23, 1924; d. Joseph Hippoman and Beatrice Victoria (Tinney) Castille; m. Francis Xavier Barry, Aug. 16, 1947; children: Christopher, Kevin, Maureen, Robin, Shane,

Kim. BA in Edn., Sam Houston U., 1958. Cert. tchr., Tex. Tchr. Sacred Heart Elem., Conroe, Tex., 1959-67, Conroe Sam Houston Elem., 1967-68, Houston Ind. Sch. Dist. Elem., 1968-69; tchr., stuent of Ernest Gaives, author-in-residence U. So. La., Lafayette, 1985-87, instr. memoir writing classes, 1995-96. Exhibited in group shows Opelonsas, La., 1973 (1st pl.). With WAC, 1944-45. Mem. Writers Guild. Roman Catholic. Home: 309 Beverly Dr Lafayette LA 70503

BARRY, NADA DAVIES, retail business owner; b. London, Dec. 2, 1930; d. Ernest Albert J. and Natalie Emma (Rossin) Davies; m. Jacob J. Ebeling-Koning, Aug. 1952 (div. 1962); m. Robert I Barry, 1963 (div. 1976); children: Natasha E.-K. Sigmund, Derek B. Ebeling-Koning, Gwen E.-K. Waddington, Trebor C. Barry. Student, Mills Coll., 1948-50; BA, Barnard Coll., 1952. Owner The Wharf Shop, Sag Harbor, N.Y., 1968—; founder Sag Harbor Youth Com. Bd. dirs. The Hampton Day Sch., Bridgehampton, N.Y., 1966-74; active Noyac Civic Coun., Ladies Village Improvement Soc., Sag Harbor, LWV of The Hamptons; founder Sag Harbor Youth Com. Mem. AAUW, Sag Harbor C. of C. (bd. dirs.), Nat. Trust Historic Preservation, Nature Conservancy, Sanibel-Captiva Conservation Found., Bailey-Matthews Shell Mus., Barnard Coll. Club. Office: The Wharf Shop PO Box 922 Sag Harbor NY 11963-0025

BARRY, PAULA JEAN, artist; b. Elmhurst, Ill., June 20, 1962; d. Jon David and Grace Elizabeth (Bergendorff) Schneider; m. Daniel James Barry, July 18, 1980; children: Dustin Michael, Eric Jon, Danielle Marie. Basic Art Certificate, Art Instrn. Schs., 1993. Works published in Illustrator mag., 1994, The Drawing Board, 1995; art piece displayed, Mpls., 1993. Tchr. Hearts at Home home sch., Manteca, Calif., 1991-93; contbr. Moore Found. home sch., 1991—. Mem. Smithsonian Inst. (assoc.), 700 Club.

BARRY, SUSAN BROWN, writer, manufacturer; b. San Antonio, Tex., Sept. 14, 1944; d. Earl A. Jr. and Betty (Galt) Brown; m. Richard Hanley Barry, June 25, 1966 (div. 1973); children: Andrew Earl, Brice Galt. AB, Sweet Briar (Va.) Coll., 1966. Scriptwriter Stas. KUHT-TV, KDOG-TV, KEYT Radio, Houston, 1972-77; originator, adminstr., cons. publ. program Rice U., Houston, 1977-79; liaison book promotion Dell. Publs., Viking Publs., and others, Houston, 1979-85; pres. Savage Designs, Houston, 1985-88; cons. U. Calif., Santa Barbara, 1985; rare book, manuscript cataloguer, writer Randall House Rare Books. Producer hospice-related tng. video and articles; book critic Houston Post; designer greeting cards Neiman-Marcus Dept. Stores; writer Bicentennial Play Houston Pub. Schs. (now in Nat. Archives). Founding coord. Reach to Recovery program Am. Cancer Soc.; rep. Choice in Dying, 1994-96; mem. adv. bd. Hearts for AIDS Found., 1992-94; mem. hospice team Hospice Austin; bd. dirs., com. chair Austin Parks Found., 1995—. Mem. Assn. for Death Edn. and Counseling (chmn. pub. rels. 1992-94), Jr. League (numerous coms. and chairmanships), Asia Soc. (adv. com., fin. chmn. Houston chpt. 1984-85), Austin Coun. on Fgn. Affairs. Republican. Unitarian. Home and Office: 114 W 7th St Ste 8 Austin TX 78703

BARRY(-BRANKS), DIANE DOLORES, podiatrist; b. Cornwall, Ont., Can., Apr. 3, 1958; d. George Henry and Dolores Angeline (Latulippe) Barry; m. Paul Lloyd Branks, Sept. 19, 1987; children: Katherine Ann Branks, Andrew Joseph Branks, Annemarie Elizabeth Branks. BS, U. San Diego, 1980; BMed. Sci., Calif. Coll. Podiatric Medicine, 1983, D Podiatric Medicine, 1985. Lab technician Scripps Rsch. Inst., La Jolla, Calif., 1980, Salk Inst., La Jolla, Calif., 1981, Quidel Labs., La Jolla, Calif., 1982; dry waller Barry Drywall, San Diego, 1985; med. office mgr. Bay Harbor Podiatry Group, Harbor City, Calif., 1985; podiatry resident VA West L.A., 1986; podiatrist Bay Harbor Podiatry Group, 1987-88, Southeast Med. Ctr., Huntington Park, Calif., 1987-88, Kaiser Permanente, Fontana, Calif., 1988—. Fellow Am. Coll. Foot & Ankle Surgeons, Am. Coll. Foot & Ankle Orthopedics; mem. Am. Podiatric Med. Soc., Am. Diabetic Assn., Calif. Podiatric Med. Soc. (alt. 1994, 96, del. 1995), So. Calif. HMO Podiatric Med. Soc. (founder, pres. 1989-91). Republican. Roman Catholic. Office: Kaiser Permanente Med Ctr 9985 Sierra Ave Fontana CA 92335

BARRYMORE, DREW, actress; b. L.A., Feb. 22, 1975; d. John Jr. and Jaid Barrymore. Appearences include (films) Altered States, 1980, E.T.: The Extra-Terrestrial, 1982, Irreconcilable Differences, 1984, Firestarter, 1984, Cat's Eye, 1985, Poison Ivy, 1992, Bad Girls, 1994, Boys on the Side, 1995, Batman Forever, 1995, Mad Love, 1995; (TV episodes) Amazing Stories, 1985, Con Sawyer and Hucklemary Finn, 1985, 2000 Malibu Road, 1992; (host) Hansel and Gretel, 1986; (TV movies) Suddenly Love, 1978, Bogie, 1980, The Screaming Woman, 1986, Babes in Toyland, 1986, Conspiracy of Love, 1987, Beyond Control: The Amy Fisher Story, 1993; (TV spls.) Screen Actors Guild 50th Anniversary, 1984, Night of 100 Stars II, 1985, Happy Birthday, Hollywood, 1987, Disney's 30th Anniversary, 1987. Office: care UTAMorris Agy 9560 Wilshire Blvd/5th Fl Beverly Hills CA 90212*

BARSHEFSKY, CHARLENE, diplomat. BA with honors, U. Wis.; JD, Catholic U. Ptnr. Steptoe & Johnson, Washington, 1975-93; deputy U.S. Trade Rep. Exec. Office of the Pres. of the U.S., Washington, 1993-96, U.S. Trade Rep., 1996—; bd. dirs. Internat. Legal Studies Program Am. U. Sch. of Law. Editorial adv. bds. European Business Law Review, Internat. Trade Corp, International Trade Corporate Counsel Advisor; assoc. editor: Catholic U. Law Review. Mem. ABA (vice chair internat. law sect., chair publications com., co-chaired internat. litigation com.). Office: Exec Office of the President US Trade Rep 600 17th St NW Washington DC 20508-4801*

BARSHOP, CELIA J., theatre administrator; b. Dallas, Feb. 3, 1962; d. Jerry M. and Wauscel (Larue) B. BA, So. Meth. U., 1984, MA, 1995. Mem. staff Rep. Nat. Conv., Dallas, 1984; on-site coord. Soc. Petroleum Engrs., Dallas, 1985-86; conv. svcs. mgr. Sheraton Hotel, Dallas, 1987; acting dir. Mktg. Ticketmaster, Dallas, 1987-95; account exec. PCA Health Plans of Tex., Inc., Dallas, 1995; mng. dir. Majestic Theatre, Dallas, 1995—. Event Chair AIDS Resource Ctr., Dallas, 1992-94; bd. dirs. Zero Tolerance for Violence 1993-94; bd. dirs. USA Film Festival, Dallas, 1993—; mem. adv. coun. Oak Lawn Cmty. Svcs./Lifewalk, 1996—.

BARSOM, VALERIE, state legislator. BA, Clark U., 1982; JD, New Eng. Sch. Law, 1991. Sales asst. KVR Inc., Springfield, Mass., 1982-84; clk. Kamberg, Berman, Gold & West, Springfield, 1984-85; legis. asst. to Hon. Robert Howarth Mass. Ho. of Reps., Boston, 1985-92, mem., 1993—. Republican. Home: 667 Tinkham Rd Wilbraham MA 01095-2436 Office: Mass Ho of Reps State Capitol Boston MA 02133*

BART, GEORGIANA CRAY, artist, educator; b. Wilkes-Barre, Pa., Oct. 30, 1948; d. William Getamyne and Jean Marie (Milisaukas) Cray; m. Michael Douglas Bart, Dec. 2, 1972; children: Jean Michelle, Marjorie Alison, Michael Douglas William Jr. BA in Fine Arts and Art Edn., Wilkes Coll., 1970; MEd in Art Edn., U. Pitts., 1972; pvt. studies in painting. Tchr. art Wyoming Valley West Sch. Dist., Kingston, Pa., 1971-72; substitute tchr., adult art instr. Pub. Sch. Price Georges County, Md., 1972-76; instr. early childhood edn. dept., tchr. adult art Luzerne County C.C., Nanticoke, Pa., 1976-78; tchr. elem. art Wyoming Valley Montessori Sch., Kingston, 1991-92; subsitute tchr. Wyoming Sem. Lower Sch., Forty Fort, Pa., 1984-94; tchr. studio arts U. Scranton, Pa., 1995—; represented by Laura Craig Galleries, Scranton, Bixler Gallery, Stroudsburg, Pa., Perry House Galleries, Alexandria, Va., William Ris Galleries, Camp Hill, Pa.; mem. Art Jury, Wilkes-Barre, 1977-78. One-woman shows include Sheehy Gallery, Kings Coll., Wilkes-Barre, 1993, Hanover Bank, West Pittston, Pa., 1993, Am. Savs. Bank, Hazelton, Pa., 1994, Doshi Ctr. Contemporary Art, Harrisburg, Pa., 1995, Wilkes U., 1995, AFA Gallery, Scranton, Pa., Art Assn. Harrisburg, 1996, Hazleton Art League, 1996; exhibited in group and juried shows at Wyoming Valley Art League galleries and off-site exhbns., 1989-95 (2nd pl. painting award 1990, Purchase award 1991, Grumbacher gold medallion 1993, 2nd pl. pastel 1994, 96, 3rd pl. painting 1994, 1st pl. pastel 1995, 2nd pl. graphics 1996), Lackawanna Arts Coun., Scranton, Pa., 1989, 90, 91, 92, 93 (2nd pl. painting award 1992, 2nd pl. graphics award 1993), 36th Ann. Nat. Juried Exhbn. of Mamaroneck Artists Guild Westbeth Gallery, N.Y.C., 1994, Nat. Arts Club, N.Y.C., 1994 (Catharine Lorillard Wolf Pres.'s award 1994, Still Life Painting award 1994), Baum Sch. Art, Allentown, Pa., 1994, Susquehanna Art Soc., Selinsgrove, Pa., 1994, AFA Gallery, Scranton, 1995, Salmagundi Club, N.Y.C., 1995-96, Perry House Galleries, Alexandria, 1995, Audubon Artists, N.Y.C., 1995, 96, Everhart Mus., Scranton (3d pl. award 1995), Ctrl. Pa. Festival Arts, 1995, Monroe County Arts Coun., Stroudsburg, 1995, Phila. Internat. Contemporary Art Competition, Old City, 1996, Broome St. Gallery summer exhbn., Soho, N.Y.C., 1996, several others; represented in permanent pvt. and pub. collections; author: The Best of Oil, 1996, The Best of Pastel, 1996, Manhattan Arts International, 1996. Set designer pvt. sch. theatrical prodn., Forty Fort, 1993; vol. Am. Heart Assn., 1992-96, Am. Cancer Soc., 1992-93, 94, 95; mem. area Rep. com., Wilkes-Barre, Pa., 1983-85; mem. Everhart Mus., Scranton, Pa. Recipient 1st pl. painting award Moscow County Fair, 1990, 92, 3rd pl. painting award, 1991, 1st pl. painting award, 1992, 3rd pl. drawing award, 1993, Purchase award Hazleton (Pa.) Art League, 1991, 2nd pl. graphics award Wilkes-Barre Fine Arts Fiesta, 1993, honorable mention award Contemporary Gallery, Marywood Coll., Scranton, 1993, Artist Showcase award Manhattan Arts Internat. Mag., 1996; Pastel Study scholar Pastel Soc. Am., N.Y.C., 1996. Mem. Nat. Assn. Women Artists, Wyo. Valley Art League, Artists for Art of AFA Gallery, MacDonald Art Gallery, Sordoni Art Gallery, Contemporary Arts Corridor, Doshi Ctr. Contemporary Art, Art Assn. Harrisburg, Salmagundi Club (N.Y.C.), N.Y. Artists Equity Assoc., Inc. Roman Catholic. Home: 123 Brader Dr Wilkes Barre PA 18705-3704

BART, POLLY TURNER, commercial real estate developer; b. Peterborough, N.H., Feb. 28, 1944; d. Benjamin Franklin and Catherine (James) B.; m. Harry Nelson Pharr II, Oct. 27, 1969 (div. May 1972); 1 child, Greta Rose Bart. BA, Radcliffe Coll., 1965; M in City Planning, U. Calif., Berkeley, 1974, PhD, 1979. Cons. city planning Marshall Kaplan, Gans & Kahn, San Francisco, 1967; city planner County of Napa, Calif., 1968-69; asst. instr. U. Tex., Austin, 1971-72; cons. Dept. HUD, Washington, 1979-81; asst. prof. U. Md., College Park, 1981-84; real estate salesperson Coldwell Banker Comml. Real Estate Services, Balt., 1984-87; pres. Investment Properties Brokerage, Inc., Balt., 1988—; faculty Johns Hopkins U., Berman Real Estate Inst., 1993—; bd. dirs. assoc. Columbia Forum, Md., 1981-85; contbr. Nat. Urban Policy Report to Congress, 1980. Fellow Radcliffe Coll., 1962-64, Danforth Found., 1975-79, Ford Found., 1981. Mem. Comml. Real Estate Women (co-founder). Home and Office: Investment Properties Brokerage Inc 12280 Howard's Lodge Rd Sykesville MD 21784

BARTELL, SANDRA JEAN, librarian; b. Wausau, Wis., Dec. 3, 1963; d. Jean L. Bartell. BA in History, U. Wis., Milw., 1988, MA in History, 1995, MS in Libr. & Info. Sci., 1995. Libr. tech. Milw. Area Tech. Coll., 1991-95; libr. asst. U. Wis., Milw., 1992-95; libr. New Haven (Conn.) Free Pub. Libr., 1995—. Vol. West Allis (Wis.) Hist. Soc., 1991-94. Mem. ALA, NOW, Internat. Women's Writing Guild, Nature Conservancy. Democrat. Office: New Haven Free Pub Libr 133 Elm St New Haven CT 06510

BARTELLI, ALICE HILL, librarian, secondary education educator; b. Greenfield, Ill., Dec. 26, 1951; d. Byron Mitchell Hill Jr. and Mary (Valentine) Downard; m. Stephen Rhoades, Aug. 13, 1973. BA, Pitts. State U., Kansas, 1974; MLS, U. Hawaii, Honolulu, 1975. Cert. tchr. Ill. Librarian Library For the Blind & Physically Handicapped, Honolulu, 1975-76, Office of Library Svcs., Honolulu, 1976-77; audiovisual librarian Hawaii State Library, Honolulu, 1977-79, children's librarian, 1979-85; library cons. City Council, Greenfield, Ill., 1987-94; substitute tchr. Greene County Sch. Dists., Ill., 1990—; coord. photography contest Com. for Hawaii, Nat. Library Week, Honolulu, 1982; story teller Honolulu Zoo, 1983, Bishop Mus., Honolulu, 1984, Greenfield Pub. Library, Ill., 1986—. Author: (guide book) Greene County Days, 1994, (profl. jour.) Illinois Libraries, 1991; compiler: (guide book) Greene County Days, 1995, (directory) A Directory of 16MM Film Services in Hawaii, 1979. Broadcaster Hawaii Pub. TV, Honolulu, 1982-84; historian Civic Hist. Display Commn., Greenfield, 1986; building cons. Greenfield Pub. Library, 1987-94.

BARTELS, BETTY J., nurse; b. Cin., Mar. 7, 1925; d. William Charles and Irene Agnes (McLean) Roth; m. Donald Arthur Bartels Sr.; children: Donald A. Jr., Virginia, Frederick, Bernadette. Nursing diploma RN, Good Samaritan Hosp., 1946; postgrad. libr. sci., Barry Coll., 1966-70. RN Sun Ray Health Resort, Miami, Fla., 1949-51; vol. libr. St. James Cath. Sch., Miami, 1966-70; RN North Shore Med. Ctr., Miami, 1970-72; charge RN Villa Maria Rehab. Ctr., Miami, 1972-76; pvt. duty RN Miami, 1976-80; staff RN North Shore Med. Ctr., Miami, 1979-91. Author: Amotrophic Lateral Sclerosis: Helping the Patient with Lou Gehrigs Disease, 1979, RN Mag., 1979. Vol. Bon Secours Hosp./Villa Marla Nursing Ctr., 1990—. Mem. Third Order of St. Dominic (pres., prioress 1974-80, 92—). Democrat. Roman Catholic.

BARTELS, JOANIE, children's entertainer; b. Dorchester, Mass., May 21, 1953. Children's singer, 1985—; contbr. backup vocals to Gino Vanelli and others. Recs. include Happy Feet and a Silly Beat, 1993, Beep Beep and Splish Splash, 1993, Bringing Up Baby, Vol. 1, Vol. 2, Vol. 3, 1993, (video) Simply Magic, Episode 1: The Rainy Day Adventure, 1993. Office: 419 N Larchmont Ste 13 Los Angeles CA 90004 also: BMG Kidz Times Square 1540 Broadway New York NY 10036*

BARTELS, SUSAN HERDMAN, art educator, artist; b. Yonkers, N.Y., May 29, 1941; d. Raymond Charles and Ellen (Saunders) Herdman; m. John C. Barker, June 12, 1965 (div. July 1984); children: Jennifer, Carrie, John; m. Robert John Bartels, Apr. 7, 1990. BFA, Alfred U., 1963; MA, U. Iowa, 1965. Art educator Muscatine (Iowa) Pub. Schs., 1965-66, Iowa City Pub. Schs., 1966-67, Regina High Sch., Iowa City, 1967-68; artist, owner Custom Stained Glass, Bettendorf, Iowa, 1979-84, Herdman Photographic Archive (formerly Native Images), Bettendorf, Iowa, 1992—; art educator Davenport (Iowa) Cmty. Schs., 1985—. Group shows include Drake U., Des Moines, 1984, U. Iowa, Iowa City, 1987, 91, Davenport Mus. Art, 1987, Quad City Arts Coun., Rock Island, Ill., 1987, Whispering Winds Gallery, Iowa City, 1991, Quincy (Ill.) Art Ctr., 1992, Walton Art Ctr., Fayetteville, Ark., 1992, 93, Alias Gallery, Atlanta, 1992, Ga. Tech., Atlanta, 1992, Lincoln (Colo.) Art Ctr., 1992, 93, Davenport Mus. Art, 1992, Mus. Anthropology U. Calif., Chico, 1992, Red Mesa Art Gallery, Gallup, N.Mex., 1992, Putnam County Arts Coun., Mahopac, N.Y., 1992, Near Northwest Arts Coun., Chgo., 1993, North Platte Valley Art Guild, Scottsbluff, Nebr., 1993, U. Iowa, 1993, Chautaugua Art Assn. Galleries, 1993, Greater Harrisburg (Pa.) Arts Coun., 1993, 94, Fla. Soc. Fine Arts, Miami, Fla., 1993, Columbia Arts Ctr., Vancouver, Wash., 1993, Eiteljorg Mus. Am. Indian and Western Art, Indpls., 1994, Maude Kerns Art Center, Eugene, Oreg., 1994, Soc. Contemporary Photography, Kansas City, 1994, Mus. Northwest Colo., Craig, 1994, Fuller Mus. Art, Brockton, Mass., 1994, Perry House Galleries (Silver medal), Alexandria, Va., 1995, No. Colo. Artists Assn., Fort Collins, Colo., 1996, Photo Nat. 96 (2nd place award), Mo., 1996, Oscar Howe Art Ctr., S. Dakota, 1996; permanent collections include Am. Indian Art Ctr., Chgo., Mus. Anthropology U. Calif., Chico, Deere and Co., Moline, Ill, Eiteljorg Mus. Native Am. & Western Art, EverColor Corp., El Dorado Hills, Calif., Heard Mus. Libr. & Archives, Phoenix. Mem. Nat. Mus. Am. Indian, Nat. Mus. Women in Arts, Davenport Indian Parent Adv. Com., 1991-95. Recipient Best of Show award Quad City Arts Coun., 1987, Best of Photography Ann. Photographers Forum Mag., 1993, others; grantee Iowa Arts Coun., 1995. Mem. Iowa Alliance for Arts Edn., Quad City League of Native Ams. Home: 3303 Oxford Dr Bettendorf IA 52722-2667

BARTELSTONE, RONA SUE, gerontologist; b. Bklyn., Jan. 10, 1951; d. Herbert and Hazel (Mittman) Canarick; m. Alan Joel Markowitz. BS in Social Welfare, SUNY, Buffalo, 1972; MSW, Ind. U., 1974. Licensed Clin. Social Worker, Fla. Diplomate of Social Work. Social worker YM-YWHA of Greater N.Y., 1974-75; dist. supr. N.Y.C. Housing Authority, Bklyn., 1975-77; field instr. Barry U. Sch. Social Work, 1980-81; project dir. United Family & Children's Svcs., 1977-81; faculty Miami Dade Community Coll., 1981-82; adult educator Sch. Bd. Dade County, 1981-82; med. social worker Mederi Home Health Agy., 1979-82; mem. adj. faculty Nova U., 1986-88; pvt. practice Rona Bartelstone Assocs., Inc., Ft. Lauderdale, Fla., 1981—; adj. faculty Fla. Internat. U., S.E. Ctr. on Aging, 1996; cons. and trainer in field. Contbr. articles to various mags. d. dirs. Jewish Vocat. Svcs., Miami, 1985-92; mem. funding panel Area Agy. on Aging, Miami, 1985-89; active Friends of the Family Counseling Svcs., Miami, 1983-88; adv. bd., chair internship subcom. Lynn U., 1993—; exec. bd. Fla. Geriatric CAre Mgrs., 1993—; chair tng. com., exec. v.p. Alzheimer's Assn., Miami, 1994-96; co-chair Nat. Acad. Cert. Care Mgrs., 1994—. Recipient Dade County Citizen of the Yr. award, 1982, NASW Social Worker of the Yr. award, 1982-83, Trail Blazer award, 1984, Up & Comers award in health care Price Waterhouse and So. Fla. Bus. Jour., 1990. Mem. NASW (treas. 1987-89), Gerontology Soc. Am., Am. Soc. on Aging, Nat. Coun. on Aging, Assn. Profl. Geriatric Care Mgrs. (pres. 1988-94, chmn. credential com. 1993—), Nat. Acad. Cert. Care Mgrs. (co-chmn. 1994—), Fla. Geriatric Care Mgrs. Assn. (exec. bd. 1993—). Democrat. Jewish. Home: 2365 N 37th Ave Hollywood FL 33021-3645 Office: 2699 Stirling Rd Ste 304C Fort Lauderdale FL 33312-6517

BARTER, ELIZABETH CATHERINE, accountant; b. Mobile, Ala., Sept. 26, 1960; d. Charles James and Mary Catherine (McDowell) B. BS, U. South Ala., 1983. Securities/sales rep. A.L. Williams, Mobile, 1984-85; acctg. clk. Mexalloy Internat., Mobile, 1985-86; acctg. mgr. Agromex, Inc., Mobile, 1986-90, Browning-Ferris Industries, Atlanta, 1990—. Mem. Inst. Mgmt. Accts. Home: 245 Blue Heron Ln Alpharetta GA 30201 Office: Browning-Ferris Industries 3045 Bankhead Hwy Atlanta GA 30318

BARTER, JUDITH ANN, museum director; b. Chgo., May 21, 1951; d. Frederick Joseph and Emily Mary (Bate) B. BA in Art History, Ind. U., 1973; MA in Art History, U. Ill., 1975; PhD in Cultural History, U. Mass., 1991. Curatorial asst. Krannert Art Mus., Univ. Ill., Urbana, 1974-75; asst. curator St. Louis (Mo.) Art Mus., 1975-78; curator of collections Mead Art Mus., Amherst (Mass.) Coll., 1978-86, assoc. dir., 1986-92; Field-McCormick curator Am. Arts Art Inst. of Chgo., 1992—; vis. fellow Smithsonian Instn., summer 1992; Mass. state rep. Assn. Coll. and Univ. Mus. Author: Currents of Expansion, 1978, American Watercolors and Drawings, 1986, American Watercolors and Drawings at the Wadsworth Atheneum, 1988, Representing Revolution, 1989, Porkopolis: Sue Coe's Jungle, 1993, The Prairie School: Decorative Arts, 1996; mem. editl. bd.: Mass Rev., Amherst, 1986-91; reviewer Choice Mag., Middletown, Conn., 1980—. Trustee Williamstown (Mass.) Conservation Lab. Travel fellow NEH, Washington, 1989; recipient Chmn.'s award Art Inst. Chgo., 1994. Office: Art Inst Chgo 111 South Michigan Ave Chicago IL 60603

BARTH, DIANA, actress, playwright, journalist, editor; b. L.A., May 31, 1929; d. Harry and Sarah (Pressman) Newman; m. Leslie Klein, Nov. 21, 1951 (div. Oct. 1974); 1 child, Randall. BA in Social Scis. summa cum laude, Fordham U., 1979. Prof. actress N.Y.C., 1950—; theatre adminstr. Bklyn. Acad. Music, 1970-72, N.Y. State Coun. on the Arts, 1972-75; assoc. editor Simon & Schuster, N.Y.C., 1968-70; pvt. practice Knopf, Doubleday, McGraw-Hill, N.Y.C., 1970—; assoc. dir., pub. rels. Internat. Ctr. for Women Playwrights, N.Y.C., 1995—; critic, feature writer various pubs., N.Y.C. Playwright: Tides, Legacy, Struggles of Stefania; prodr. plays including The Lion Theatre, Adelaide, Australia, Alice's Fourth Floor, N.Y.C., 1988—, Pen & Brush Club, N.Y.C., 1990—. Playwrights fellow Ctr. for Creative Arts and Scis., Hambidge, Ga., 1992; recipient Sussman/Stevenson/Davis 2d prize prose award, 1994, 3rd prize prose award, 1995. Mem. AFTRA, SAG, Am. Theatre Critics Assn., Actors Equity Assn., Drama Desk, Outer Critics Cir., Pen & Brush Club, The 42nd St. Workshop. Home and Office: 535 W 51st St 3A New York NY 10019

BARTH, KATRINE, chemical company executive; b. N.Y.C., Mar. 27, 1947; d. Frank and Gertrude (Flamm) B.; 1 child, Ariana. Certificat d'Etudes Politiques, Institut d'Etudes Politiques, Paris, 1967; BA, Sarah Lawrence Coll., Bronxville, N.Y., 1968; MA, Brandeis U., 1969, PhD, 1970. Prof. advanced degree program Goddard Coll., Plainfield, Vt., 1972-74; asst. account exec. Frank Barth Advt., Inc., N.Y.C., 1976-77, account exec., 1977-79, gen. mgr., 1979-81, creative dir., exec. v.p., 1981-84, pres., 1984—; COO Richard James Specialty Chems. Corp., 1993—. Pres.: (documentary films) The Link Between Us, (Cine Bronze award 1980), Parade (Cine Gold award 1986). Jewish. Office: Richard James Specialty Chem Co Frank Barth Inc 9 Washington Ave Hastings On Hudson NY 10706

BARTH, M. JANE, secondary school educator; b. Hutchinson, Minn., Mar. 23, 1950; d. Albert Leo and Margaret Janice (Ditmore) B. BS, Winona State U., 1972; BA, Humboldt State U., 1981; MA, George Mason U., 1989. Lic. postgrad. profl., Va. State Bd. Edn. Tchr. English and history Greene Vocat. H.S., Xenia, Ohio, 1983; tchr. adult edn. Prince William County Schs., Independent Hill, Va., 1983-84; tchr. lang. arts Woodbridge (Va.) Mid. Sch., 1984-89; tchr. English and history Stonewall Jackson H.S., Manassas, Va., 1989—. Mem. adv. bd. Oak Cares, Burke, Va., 1996—. Lt. (j.g.) USNR, 1975-79. NEH fellow, Sarah Lawrence Coll., 1995. Mem. AAUW, Nat. Coun. Tchrs. of English, Orgn. Am. Historians. Unitarian Universalist. Office: Stonewall Jackson HS 8820 Rixlew Ln Manassas VA 22110

BARTH, SHARON LYNN, nurse; b. Stamford, Conn., Oct. 27, 1948; d. Donald Eric and Jane Dolores (Fabrizio) Walker; m. James Leander Barth Jr., June 8, 1967; children: Kristen Lynne, Jennifer Leigh, Shannon Lynlee. AA, Coll. of Albermarle, Elizabeth City, N.C., 1974; BSN, Calif. State U., Sacramento, 1991. RN, Calif.; Neonatal Advanced Life Support, Calif.; cert. lactation educator. Staff nurse Kaiser Permanente, Sacramento, 1991-93, charge nurse, 1993—; guest lectr. Teen Parenting classes, Maternal-Child classes CSUS. Mem. Assn. Women's Health, Assn. Obstetric and Neonatal Nurses, Phi Kappa Phi, Sigma Theta Tau, Golden Key. Home: 8142 Bonnie Oak Way Citrus Heights CA 95610

BARTHOLD, CLEMENTINE B., retired judge; b. Odessa, Russia, Jan. 11, 1921; came to U.S., 1925; d. Joseph Anton and Magdalene (Richter) Schwan; m. Edward Brendel Barthold, July 5, 1941 (dec.); children: Judith Anne Barthold DeSimone, John Edward. Student Aberdeen Bus. Coll., 1940; BGS, Ind. U. Southeast, 1978; JD, Ind. U.-Indpls., 1980. Bar: Ind. 1980, U.S. Dist. Ct. (so. dist.) Ind., 1980. Sec. and asst. to mgr. Clark County C. of C. (Ind.), 1959-60; chief probation officer Clark Circuit Ct. and Superior Cts., Jeffersonville, 1960-72; rsch. cons. Pub. Action Correctional Effort, Clark and Floyd Counties, 1972-75; instl. parole officer Ind. Women's Prison, Indpls., 1975-80; atty. State of Ind., 1980-83; judge Clark Superior Ct. No. 1, Jeffersonville, 1983-95, ret., 1995. Active in developing and implementing juvenile delinquency prevention and alternative programs, group counseling for juvenile delinquents and restitution programs. Recipient Good Govt. award Jeffersonville Jaycees, 1966, Good Citizenship award, 1967; Wonder Woman award, 1984, Robert J. Kinsey award, 1986, Sagamore of Wabash award, 1986, Outstanding Cmty. Svc. award Social Concerns League, Jeffersonville, 1966, Disting. Svc. award, Outstanding Contbn. to Field of Correction award, Women of Achievement award, Jeff BPW Appreciation award, Juvenile Justice award, Disting. Contemporary Women in History award, Disting. Leadership award, Women of Achievement award 1982-83, Appreciation award VIPO, 1983, Children and Youth Recognition award 1984, Gov's Exemplary award, 1985, 88, 89, 92, Commitment to Youth award 1987, Warren W. Martin award, 1973, 87, Outstanding Child Advocacy in Ind. award, 1987, Community Svc. award, 1988, Orgnl. Renewal award, 1988, Parents Without Ptnrs. award, 1989, Ind. Youth Investment award, 1992, Excellence in Pub. Info. & Edn. award, 1992. Mem. Ind. Bar Assn., Clark County Bar Assn., Ind. Correctional Assn. (pres. 1971, Disting. Service award 1967, 85), Ind. Judges Assn., Nat. and Ind. Juvenile and Family Ct. Judges (bd. dirs.), Ind. Juvenile Justice Task Force, Ind. U. Alumni Assn., Howard Steamboat Mus., LWV, Bus. and Profl. Women's Club, Ladies Elks Aux. Democrat. Roman Catholic. Home: 948 E 7th St Jeffersonville IN 47130-4106

BARTHOLOMEW, ANITA, freelance writer; b. Bay Shore, N.Y., Jan. 14, 1949; d. Guido and Elizabeth (Ornato) Del Giudice m. Frank J. Tomaino, Oct. 5, 1968 (div.); 1 child, Alexander G. Tomaino. Student, SUNY, Purchase, 1981-83, Sch. Visual Arts, N.Y.C., 1984. Copywriter Ventura Assocs., N.Y.C., 1982-83, Equity Advt., N.Y.C., 1983-84, Pace Advt., N.Y.C., 1984-85; prin. Bartholomew & Co., Tarrytown, N.Y., 1985—; dir. mktg. Chacma Inc., N.Y.C., 1991-92; sr acct. supr. Tech. Solutions Inc., 1992-93; freelance copywriter, IBM, RAM Mobile Data, Dictaphone Corp., Sharp Electronics, numerous others; cons. NBC-TV movie "A Secret Between Friends." Contbr. articles to Woman's Day mag., YM mag., Longevity mag., Reader's Digest, Good Housekeeping, many others. Mem. Am. Soc. Journalists and Authors, Nat. Assn. Sci. Writers, Mensa.

BARTLE, ANNETTE GRUBER (MRS. THOMAS R. BARTLE), artist, writer, photographer; Came to U.S., 1940; d. Henry and Maria (Harczyk) Gruber; m. Thomas R. Bartle, Dec. 5, 1957 (dec. 1964); 1 child, Eve

Marie. Bacheliere, U. Sorbonne, Paris, 1940; BA, Elmira Coll., N.Y., 1943; student, Ecole des Beaux Arts, Paris, 1940, Art Student League (scholar 1949), 1947-50. One-woman shows include: Midtown Galleries, N.Y.C., 1957, 60, 63, 66, Feingarten, Chgo., 1957, Wickersham Gallery, 1970; exhibited in group shows: AAAL, 1963, Detroit Art Inst., 1958, 62, 65, 67, Pa. Acad., 1959, 60, 66, Butler Art Inst., 1960, 64, 65, Cin. Art Mus., 1960, 62, 67; represented in permanent collections: Am. Internat. Underwriters, Union Carbide, Conn. Mut. Life, Mural Port Authority Heliport, N.Y. Worlds Fair; author: African Enchantment, 1980; contbr. articles and photographs to mags., newspapers, jours. including: N.Y. Times, Christian Sci. Monitor, Phila. Inquirer, L.A. Times, Palm Beach Life, Travel Weekly, Diverson, American Way, Senior World, Good Housekeeping since 1991, numerous others. Trustee Morris Animal Found.; active various community drives. Pan Am. Travelling fellow, 1950; recipient citation for outstanding achievements 90th U.S. Congress, 1968. Fellow Mcpl. Art Soc.; mem. Am. Fedn. Arts, Artists Equity, Soc. Profl. Journalists, Women's Nat. Rep. Club. Address: 231 E 76th St New York NY 10021-2134

BARTLETT, ALICE BRAND, psychotherapist, educator, dean, researcher; b. Carrollton, Mo., Oct. 27, 1950; d. Daniel Arthur and Nellie May (Farmer) Brand; m. Thomas Sidney Bartlett, Aug. 12, 1989. BA, U. Mo., 1972, MLS, 1973; postgrad., Topeka Inst. Psychoanalysis, 1979-96. Dir. libr. Mo. Inst. Psychiatry, St. Louis, 1973-74; chief libr. Menninger Clinic, Topeka, 1975—, psychotherapist, 1984—, assoc. dean info./media Karl Menninger Sch. Psychiatry, 1988—, E. Greenwood prof., 1990—; prin. investigator Child and Family Ctr. Menninger Clinic, 1995—; cons. C.F. Menninger Meml. Hosp., Topeka, 1987—; bd. dirs., asst. treas. Psychoanalytic Rsch. Consortium, N.Y.C. and Topeka, 1989-95. Contbr. articles to profl. pubis. Interfuture scholar, 1971-72. Mem. Am. Psychoanalytic Assn. (chair libr. com. 1991—, Liddle grantee 1985), Med. Libr. Assn. (co-chair ethics com. 1985-87), Topeka Psychoanalytic Soc. (recorder 1983-86, program chair 1993—). Office: Menninger Clinic 5800 SW 6th Ave Topeka KS 66606-9604

BARTLETT, DIANE SUE, clinical mental health counselor; b. Laconia, N.H., Dec. 6, 1947; d. Fred Elmer and Dorothy Pearl (Wakefield) Davis; m. Josiah Henry Bartlett, Aug. 23, 1980; 1 child by previous marriage, Fred Louis Hacker; 1 step child, Juliet. AA, Plymouth State Coll., 1982; B in Gen. Studies summa cum laude, U. N.H. Sch. for Lifelong Learning, 1984; MEd., Plymouth State Coll., 1988. Cert. clin. mental health counselor. Police comms. specialist Divsn. Motore Vehicles, Concord, N.H., 1970-76, br. office mgr., 1976-83, coord. motor vehicles registrations, 1983-84; tax collector City of Dover, N.H., 1984; intern Lakes Region Mental Health Divsn., Laconia, N.H., 1985; counselor Latchkey Pastoral Counseling, Laconia, 1984-87; family therapist, Children's Best Interest, Laconia, 1988—; mental health counselor Carroll County Mental Health Svcs., Wolfeboro, N.H., 1988-95; mental health counselor, pvt. practice, Ossipee, N.H., 1995—. Mem. Town of Moultonboro Sch. Feasibility Study Commn., 1978; adminstrv. bd. mem., chmn. pastor-parish rels. com. United Meth. Ch., Moultonboro, N.H., 1983—, N.H. annual conf., 1986-88, participant N.H. Ann. Conf. on Status and Role of Women, Concord, 1985—; mem. Friends of Families in Carroll County, 1995—. N.H. Charitable Found. grantee, 1985. Mem. Internat. Soc. for Study of Dissociation, Am. Counseling Assn., Am. Mental Health Counselors Assn. Avocations: skiing, swimming, reading, writing. Home: PO Box 14 Moultonborough NH 03254-0014 Office: Mountainside Bus Ctr 127 Rte 28 Ossipee NH 03864

BARTLETT, ELIZABETH SUSAN, audio-visual specialist; b. Bloomington, Ind., Sept. 11, 1927; d. Cecil Vernon and Nell (Helfrich) Bartlett; m. Frederick E. Sherman, July 8, 1955 (div. 1978). Student, Ind. U., 1946-48. Traffic-continuity dir. WTTS-Radio, Bloomington, Ind., 1947-48; program dir. WTTV-TV, Indpls., 1949-59; creative dir. Venus Advt. Agy., Indpls., 1960-68; prodn. mgr. Nat. TV News, Detroit, 1968-71; owner, producer Susan Sherman Prodns., Greenwich, Conn., 1971-73; audiovisual officer NSF, Washington, 1973—; lectr. in field. Concept writer/prodr. film: The Observatories, 1981; prodr.: Science: Woman's Work, 1982, Keyhole of Eternity, 1975, What About Tomorrow?, 1978, The American Island, 1970, The New Engineers, 1986, Discover Science, 1988, A Brain, Books and a Curiosity, 1992, others. Recipient Silver award Internat. Film and TV Festival of N.Y., 1970, 74, Gold medal Nat. Ednl. Film Festival, 1982, 89, Chris Bronze plaque Columbus Film Festival, 1982, Bronze award Internat. Film & TV Festival of N.Y., 1982, Gold award 1976, Gold Camera award U.S. Indsl. Film Festival, 1982, Silver Cindy award, Info. Film Producers Assn., 1982, award for creative excellence U.S. Indsl. Film Festival, 1975, Techfilm Festival award, 1979, 80, 88, Gold award Houston Internat. Film Festival, 1987, Art Direction Mag. Creativity award, 1988; named Outstanding Woman for Contbn. in Arts, Federally Employed Women, 1984. Mem. Am. Women in Radio and TV (chpt. pres. 1953-56, 69-70), Washington Film and Video Coun. (pres. 1978-79), Coun. on Internat. Non-Theatrical Events (adv. bd., Golden Eagle award 1970, 74, 76-79, 82, 87), Women in Film and Video. Home: 809 S Columbus St Alexandria VA 22314-4206 Office: NSF Audiovisual 4201 Wilson Blvd Arlington VA 22230-0001

BARTLETT, JANE SUSAN, elementary education educator; b. St. Paul, Apr. 2, 1956; d. Henry Charles and Delores Madelyn (Johnson) Hammer; m. Gary V. Bartlett, Nov. 7, 1990. BA in Elem. Edn., Augsburg Coll., Mpls., 1990; MA, U. St. Thomas, 1993. Cert. elem. tchr., Minn. Substitute tchr. Mpls. Pub. Schs., 1989 90; substitute tchr. Anoka-Hennipen Schs., Anoka, Minn., 1989-90, Benson, Glenwood, Starbuck, Alexandria, Brandon Schs., 1990-91; kindergarten tchr. Starbuck (Minn.) Elem. Sch., 1991—; student rep. for Minn. Edn. Assn. at Augsburg Coll., 1988-89; bldg. rep. for Minnewaska Area Tchrs., Glenwood, 1993-94; mem. Tchrs. Senate Minnewaska Area Tchrs., Glenwood, 1992-95. Mem. Parkers Prairie (Minn.) Study Club, 1994. Mem. Minn. Kindergarten Assn. (video libr., mem. exec. bd. 1992—), Assn. for Childhood Edn. Internat. Home: RR 1 Box 185 Parkers Prairie MN 56361-9750

BARTLETT, JANET SANFORD WALZ, school nurse; b. Bryn Mawr, Pa., Aug. 13, 1930; d. Edward Joseph Walz and Anna Downing (Little) Walz Tomlin; m. Joseph Richard Bartlett, May 6, 1952 (div. April 1972); children: Cheryl, Elaine, Karen, Lee, Patrick, Michael. Diploma nursing, Meml. Mission Sch. Nursing, 1953; EMT-I cert., El Paso C.C., 1983. RN, N.C., Tex. Office nurse William F. Hillier M.D., Asheville, N.C., 1953-55; school nurse Ysleta Ind. Sch. Dist., El Paso, 1973-93. Author: (manual) Sch. Nurse Manual, 1979, Volunteer's Handbook, 1979, (cookbook) Bartlett Heritage Cookbook; editor: (newsletter) Nurses Notes Newsletter, 1983-88; co-creator, copyrighter D.K. Buster, 1989. Mem. El Paso Health Issues Forum, 1985-88; co-chair El Paso Oral Health Commn., 1987—; life mem. PTA; pres. El Paso Coun. bd. dirs. Campfire Girls, Inc., 1971-74, also Blue Bird leader, Camp Fire guardian; active Boy Scouts Am., Girl Scouts Am.; com. chair El Paso chpt. Am. Cancer Soc.; co-chair Ysleta Sch. Dist. Employee Wellness, 1989-90, compiler manual; sec. United El Paso Birth Packet Com., 1993-96, chmn., 1996—. Recipient Luther Halsey Gulick award, 1972, Outstanding Staff Support award Ysleta Vol. Svcs., 1988-89, Stand Up for El Paso award KDBC TV, 1991, REACH award YWCA/El Paso Healthcare System, 1992, El Paso Pks. and Recreation Woman of Yr. award, 1995. Mem. Nat. Assn. Sch. Nurses, Tex. Assn. Sch. Nurses (region 19 v.p. 1982-83, Sch. Nurse of Yr. 1990, state Pres.'s award 1990, Sch. Nurse of Yr. award 1991), Ysleta Sch. Nurses Assn. (pres. 1988, Sch. Nurse of Yr. 1987, World Healer award 1995), Assistance League of El Paso (yearbook chmn. 1994, 95, Sch. Bell. com. 1994—). Home: 10249 Bayo Ave El Paso TX 79925-4347

BARTLETT, MAURINE R., lawyer; b. Ironwood, Mich.. AB magna cum laude, U. Mich.; JD magna cum laude, Georgetown U., 1979. Bar: D.C. 1979, N.Y. 1988. Ptnr. Cadwalader, Wickersham & Taft, N.Y.C. Editor Georgetown Law Jour., 1979; contbr. articles and reports to profl. jours. Mem. ABA (mem. com. on fed. regulation of securities 1985-86, subcom. on fin. futures and options 1985-86), Bar Assn. of D.C., Phi Beta Kappa, Phi Kappa Phi. Office: Cadwalader Wickersham & Taft 100 Maiden Ln New York NY 10006*

BARTLETT, SHIRLEY ANNE, accountant; b. Gladwin, Mich., Mar. 28, 1933; d. Dewey J. and Ruth Elizabeth (Wright) Frye; m. Charles Duane Bartlett, Aug. 16, 1952 (div. Sept. 1982); children: Jeanne, Michelle, John, Yvonne. Student, Mich. State U., 1952-53, Rutgers U., 1972-74. Auditor State of Mich., Lansing, 1951-66; cost acct. Templar Co., South River, N.J., 1968-75; staff acct. Franco Mfg. Co., Metuchen, N.J., 1975-78; controller Thomas Creative Apparel, New London, Ohio, 1978-80; mgr. gen. acctg. Ideal Electric Co., Mansfield, Ohio, 1980-85; staff acct. Logangate Homes, Inc., Girard, Ohio, 1985-88; pvt. practice acctg. Youngstown, 1985—; acct. Universal Devel. Enterprises, Liberty Twp., Ohio, 1987-88; v.p. Lang Industries, Inc., Youngstown, 1984-93. Author: (play) Our Bicentennial-A Celebration, 1976. Soloist various orchestras, Mich., Va.; mem. Human Relations Commn., Franklin Township, 1971-77, Friends of Am. Art; treas. Heritage Found., New Brunswick, N.J., 1973-74, New London Proceeds Corp., 1979-83; commr. Huron Park Commn., Ohio, 1979-83; elected Dem. com. mem., N.J., Ohio, 1970-82; vol. IRS for small bus., 1988-94; mem. planning com. Youngstown State U. Tax Insts., 1990-95, presenter, 1990—; bd. dirs., treas. Discovery Place, Inc., 1991-95. Mem. NAFE, NOW (treas. Youngstown chpt. 1986-93), Am. Soc. Women Accts. (bd. dirs. 1986-88, 96—, v.p. 1988-89, pres. 1989-91, bd. dirs., 1996—, scholarship com. 1991—, chair chpt. devel. 1995-96, chair program com. 1996), Nat. Women's Polit. Caucus, Bus. and Profl. Women (v.p. 1980—), Am. Soc. Notaries, Women's Jour. Network, Citizen's League of Greater Youngstown, Internat. Platform Assn., Friends of Am. Art, Youngstown Opera Guild. Democrat. Unitarian. Club: Franklin JFK (treas. 1970-72, v.p. 1973-78), Chataqua Literary, Scientific Circle (pres. 1979—). Home and Office: Bartlett Acctg Svcs 370 Goldie Rd Liberty Township OH 44505-1950

BARTLING, DIANA KAY, counselor, mediator; b. Fairfield, Ill., Aug. 29, 1954; d. Milo E. and Nina M. (Moreland) Wadsworth; m. Dean M. Bartling, Feb. 9, 1974; children: Jonathan D., Jaime L. AA in Liberal Arts, Joliet Jr. Coll., 1991; BA in Psychology, Governor's State U., 1992, MA in Counseling, 1995. Counselor Luth. Family Svcs., Joliet, Ill., 1994-96, Rock Creek Ctr., Lemont, Ill., 1995-96, Counseling Offices, New Lenox, Ill., 1995—; group facilitator, program coord. Cancer Support Ctr., Homewood, Ill., 1995—; dir. counseling lab. Governor's State U., 1994-95. Mem. discipline adv. bd. New Lenox Sch. Dist., 1985; bd. dirs. New Lenox PTO, 1985-86. Mem. ACA, Mediation Coun. Ill., Chi Sigma Iota. Office: Counseling Offices 114 Church St Ste 201 New Lenox IL 60451

BARTLING, PHYLLIS MCGINNESS, oil company executive; b. Chillicothe, Ohio, Jan. 3, 1927; d. Francis A. McGinness and Gladys A. (Henkelman) Bane; m. Theodore Charles Bartling; children: Pamela, Theodore, Eric C. Student, Ohio State U., 1944-47. Bookkeeper, Bartling & Assocs., Bartling Oil Co., Houston 1974-80; sec.-treas., dir. both cos., 1980—. Co-chmn. ticket sales Tulsa Opera, 1956-61; bd. dirs. Tex. Speech and Hearing Ctr., Houston, 1967-70. Republican. Episcopalian. Avocations: gardening, bicycling, cooking, golf. Home and Office: 11 Inwood Oaks Dr Houston TX 77024-6803

BARTNOFF, JUDITH, judge; b. Boston, Apr. 14, 1949; d. Shepard and Irene F. (Tennenbaum) B.; m. Eugene F. Sofer, Sept. 10, 1978; 1 child, Nelson Bartnoff Sofer. B.A. magna cum laude, Radcliffe Coll., 1971; J.D. (Harlan Fiske Stone scholar), Columbia U., 1974; LL.M., Georgetown U., 1975. Bar: D.C. 1975, U.S. Dist. Ct. D.C. 1975, U.S. Ct. Appeals (D.C. cir.) 1980, U.S. Ct. Appeals (fed. cir.) 1985, U.S. Ct. Appeals (11th cir.) 1988, U.S. Ct. Appeals (3d cir.) 1989, U.S. Claims Ct. 1991. Fellow Inst. Pub. Interest Representation, Georgetown Law Ctr., Washington, 1974-75; staff atty. Council Pub. Interest Law, Washington, 1975-77; spl. asst. to asst. atty. gen. criminal div. Dept. Justice, Washington, 1977-78; assoc. dep. atty. gen. Dept. Justice, 1978-80; spl. asst. U.S. atty. Office of U.S. Atty., Washington, 1980-81, asst. U.S. atty., 1982-85; assoc. firm Patton, Boggs & Blow, 1985-87, ptnr., 1988-94, assoc. ind. counsel, 1993-94; assoc. judge Superior Ct. of D.C., Washington, 1994—; mediator U.S. Dist. Ct. D.C., 1991-94; mem. com. on pro se litigation U.S Dist. Ct., 1991-94. Fellow Am. Bar Found.; mem. Am. Judicature Soc., Nat. Assn. of Women Judges. Office: 500 Indiana Ave NW Washington DC 20001-2131

BARTO, DEBORAH ANN, physician; b. West Chester, Pa., July 27, 1948; d. Charles Guy and Jeannette Victoria (Golder) B. BA, Oberlin Coll., 1970; MD, Hahnemann U., 1974. Intern, resident Kaiser Permanente Hosp., San Francisco, 1974-77; dir. med. oncology Evergreen Hosp., Kirkland, Wash., 1980-85, head oncology quality assurance, 1992-94; med. dir. Cmty. Home Health Care Hospice, Seattle, 1981-84; hosp. ethics com. Evergreen Hosp., 1995-96. Mem. Evergreen Women's Physicians. Democrat. Buddhist. Office: Evergreen Profl Plz 12911 120th Ave NE Ste E-60 Kirkland WA 98034-3027

BARTOLACCI, SUSAN, public relations officer; b. Dobbs Ferry, N.Y., Aug. 18, 1965; d. A. Ralph and Valerie Anne (Wissler) B. BS in Bus. Adminstrn., Bucknell U., 1987. Tchr. English Japan Nat. Broadcasting Co., Tokyo, 1988-89; asst. account exec. Commons Co., Ltd., Tokyo, 1989-90; account exec. Leo Burnett-Kyodo Co., Ltd., Tokyo, 1990-93; account supr. Campbell Mithun Esty, Inc., N.Y.C., 1993-94; assoc. pub. affairs officer UN Devel. Fund Women, N.Y.C., 1994—. Ambassadorial fellow Rotary Found., 1987-89. Mem. Rotaract Club UN (founder, v.p. 1995-96, pres. 1996—). Home: 315 E 65th St 4J New York NY 10021

BARTOLI, JILL SUNDAY, reading and language arts researcher and educator; b. Carlisle, May 17, 1945; d. Harvey Preston and Helen Elizabeth (Hershey) Sunday; m. James Carl Bartoli, June 26, 1971; children: David Carl, Daniel Joseph, Stephen Mario, Catherine Elizabeth, Patrick Preston. BA in English and Speech, U. Ky., 1966, MA in English, 1967; MEd in Reading, Shippensburg U., 1977; PhD in Lang. Arts and Family Literacy, U. Pa., 1986. Cert. supr. comm., cert. reading specialist, Pa. Tchr. English and speech Cumberland Valley H.S., Mechanicsburg, Pa., 1969-73; lectr. English Pa. State U., York, 1968-69; rsch. assoc. U. Pa., Phila., 1988-89, lectr., 1987-89; assoc. prof. Elizabethtown (Pa.) Coll., 1990—; coll.-sch. partnership dir. Elizabethtown and Steelton Sch. Dist., 1989—, rsch. grant dir., writer, 1992—. Author: Unequal Opportunity, 1995; co-author: Reading/Learning Disability, 1988; contbr. articles to profl. jours. Organizer, mem. Social Justice Coalition, Carlisle, Pa., 1990—; mem. cmty. svc. com. Elizabethtown Coll., 1992—. Mem. Nat. Coun. Tchrs. of English (mem. nominating com. 1980-92, presenter), Nat. Assn. for Edn. of Young Children, Am. Ednl. Rsch. Assn. (session chairperson 1985-96), Internat. Reading Assn., Kappa Delta Pi (counselor 1992—), Phi Delta Kappa. Home: 316 Garland Dr Carlisle PA 17013 Office: Elizabethtown Coll 1 Alpha Dr Elizabethtown PA 17022

BARTOLO, DONNA MARIE, hospital administrator, nurse; b. Springfield, Ill., Mar. 21, 1941; d. Elmer Ralph Bartolomucci and Zoe (Rose) Cavatorta. Diploma in nursing, St. John's Sch. Nursing, Springfield, Ill., 1962; BS, Milliken U., 1976; MA, Sangamon State U., 1978. Pediatric nurse Springfield Clin., 1962-64, physician's asst., 1972-74; gynecol. nurse Watson Clin., Lakeland, Fla., 1964-66; cons. state sch. nurses Office of Edn. State of Ill., Springfield, 1974-78; assoc. dir. operating rm. svcs. Cedars-Sinai Med. Ctr., L.A., 1978-82; co-dir. div. nursing, 1981-82; surg. nurse Emory U. Hosp., Atlanta, 1966-70, asst. dir. nursing, surg. svcs., 1982-94, dir. surg. svcs., dir. nursing, 1994—, dir. nursing for surg. scis., 1995—; adj. prof. Nell Hodgson Woodruff Sch. Nursing Emory U. Mem. editorial bd. Perioperative Nursing Quarterly; contbr. articles to nursing jours. Mem. Org. Nurse Execs., Ga. Assn. Nurse Exec. (pres. elect, pres. 1992), Assn. Operating Rm. Nurses, Sigma Theta Tau (sec. 1990—). Home: 1328 Mill Glen Dr Dunwoody GA 30338-2720

BARTON, ANN ELIZABETH, financial executive; b. Long Lake, Mich., Sept. 8, 1923; d. John and Inez Mabel (Morse) Seaton; m. H. Kenneth Barton, Apr. 3, 1948; children: Michael, John, Nancy. Student Mt. San Antonio Coll., 1969-71, Adrian Coll., 1943, Citrus Coll., 1967, Golden Gate U., 1976, Coll. Fin. Planning, 1980-82. CFP. Tax cons., real estate broker, Claremont, Calif., 1967-72, Newport Beach, Calif., 1972-74; v.p., officer Putney, Barton, Assocs., Inc., Walnut Creek, Calif., 1975-94; bd. dir. Fin. Svc. Corp. Cert. fin. planner. Mem. Internat. Assn. Fin. Planners (registered investment advisor), Calif. Soc. Enrolled Agts., Nat. Assn. Enrolled Agts., Nat. Soc. Public Accts., Inst. CFP. Office: Putney Barton Assocs Inc 1243 Alpine Rd Ste 219 Walnut Creek CA 94596-4431

BARTON, ELIZABETH SPINDLER, psychologist, fiber artist; b. York, Eng., Apr. 27, 1943; came to the U.S., 1976; d. George Richard and Norah (Richardson) Spindler; m. John Laing Barton, Dec. 28, 1966; children: Alexandra Clare, Felicity Jane. BA, Hull (U.K.) U., 1965; MSc, Leeds (U.K.) U., 1967, PhD, 1975. Lic. psychologist, Ga. Clin. psychologist Claypenny Hosp., Easingwold, U.K., 1962-65, St. James Hosp., Leeds, U.K., 1965-66, Scalebor Park Hosp., Burley in Wharfedale, U.K., 1966-67, Kans. Neurol. Inst., Topeka, Kans., 1968-69, Meanwood Park Hosp., Leeds, 1969-76, St. Louis Devel. Disability Treatment Ctr., St. Louis, 1977-79; asst. prof. S.E. Mo. State U., Cape Girardeau, 1979-86; clin. psychologist U. Ga., Athens, 1987—. Exhibited works in shows at Lyndon House Art Show, Athens, 1986, 87, 88, 93, 94, 95, Quilt Nat. 1995, San Diego Art Mus., 1996, Mobile (Ala.) Mus. Art, 1996, Halsey Gallery, Charleston, S.C., others; individual artist commn. Hartsfield Internat. Airport, 1995-96; contbr. articles to profl. jours. Individual Artist grantee State of Ga., 1994; Individual Artist grantee SAF/NEA, 1995. Mem. Ga. Psychol. Assn. Office: Univ Health Svc Univ of Ga Athens GA 30605

BARTON, JACQUELINE K., chemistry educator; b. N.Y.C., May 7, 1952; d. William and Claudine (Gutchen) Kapelman; m. Peter Brendan Dervan, Mar. 3, 1990. AB summa cum laude, Columbia U., 1974, PhD, 1978; postdoctoral, Yale U., 1979-80. Asst. prof. Hunter Coll, N.Y.C., 1980-82; asst. prof. Columbia U., N.Y.C., 1983-85, assoc. prof., 1985-86, prof. chemistry and biology, 1986-89; prof. Calif. Inst. Tech., Pasadena, 1989—; vis. rsch. assoc. dept. biophysics Bell Labs., 1979; mem. chemistry adv. com. NSF, 1985-88; mem. metallobiochemistry study sect. NIH, 1986-90, chmn., 1988-90; bd. dirs. Dow Chem. Co. NSF predoctoral fellow, 1975-78, NIH postdoctoral fellow, 1979-80, Alfred P. Sloan fellow, 1984, MacArthur Found. fellow, 1991—; Camille and Henry Dreyfus Tchr. scholar, 1986-91; recipient Harold Lamport award N.Y. Acad. Scis., 1984, Alan T. Waterman award NSF, 1985, Fresenius award Phi Lambda Upsilon, 1986, Eli Lilly Biochemistry award, 1987, Pure Chemistry award Am. Chem. Soc., 1988, Sci. and Tech. award Mayor of N.Y., 1990, Baekeland medal Am. Chem. Soc., 1991, Garven medal Am. Chem. Soc., 1992, Am. Acad. Arts and Scis. medal 1991. Office: Calif Inst Tech Divsn Chemistry 127 # 72 Pasadena CA 91125

BARTON, JANICE SWEENY, chemistry educator; b. Trenton, N.J., Mar. 22, 1939; d. Laurence U. and Lillian Mae (Fletcher) S.; m. Keith M. Barton, Dec. 20, 1967. BS, Butler U., 1962; PhD, Fla. State U., 1970. Postdoctoral fellow Johns Hopkins U., Balt., 1970-72; asst. prof. chemistry East Tex. State U., Commerce, 1972-78, Tex. Woman's U., Denton, 1978-81; assoc. prof. Washburn U., Topeka, 1982-88, prof., 1988—, chair chemistry dept., 1992—; mem. undergrad. faculty enhancement panel NSF, Washington, 1990; mem. NSF instr. lab. improvement panel, 1992, 96. Contbr. articles to profl. jours. Active Household Hazardous Waste Collection, Topeka, 1991, Solid Waste Task Force, Shawnee County, Kans., 1990; mem. vol. com. YWCA, Topeka, 1984-87. Rsch. grantee Petroleum Rsch. Fund, Topeka, 1984-86, NIH, Topeka, 1985-88; instrument grantee NSF, Topeka, 1986, 95. Mem. Am. Chem. Soc. (sec. Dallas-Ft. Worth sect. 1981-82), Kans. Acad. Sci. (pres.-elect 1991, pres. 1992), Biophys. Soc., Sigma Xi (pres. TWU club 1980-81), Iota Sigma Pi (mem.-at-large coord. 1987-93). Home: 3401 SW Oak Pky Topeka KS 66614-3218 Office: Washburn U Dept Chemistry Topeka KS 66621

BARTON, JUDITH HAWKINS, nurse; b. Fredericksburg, Va., Feb. 26, 1939; d. Aubrey Benjamin and Constance Elizabeth (Roach) Hawkins; m. Cline Dwight Barton Jr., Apr. 19, 1961; children: Elizabeth, Kathryn, Anne Carey, Dwight III. BSN, Med. Coll. Va., 1961; BLS in Hist. Preservation, Mary Washington Coll., 1996. RN, Va. Staff nurse U. Va., Charlottesville, 1961-63, Richmond (Va.) Meml. Hosp., 1963-66, Princeton (N.J.) Hosp., 1966-67, Zurbrugg Meml. Hosp., Riverside, N.J., 1967-74, Med. Pers. Pool, Alexandria, Va., 1974-75, Fredericksburg Nursing Home, 1975-77, Mary Washington Hosp., Fredericksburg, 1978—; office nurse Office of Dr. William Butzner, Fredericksburg, 1977-78; resource nurse preceptor Mary Washington Hosp. Mem. Old Stone Warehouse com. City of Fredericksburg, 1992—. Mem. DAR (vice regent Overwharton Parish chpt. 1993—). Episcopalian. Office: Mary Washington Hosp Sam Perry Blvd Fredericksburg VA 22401

BARTON, MARIE ANITA, computer-aided design and drafting technician; b. Portland, Jan. 29, 1948; d. Richard Paul Barton and Irene (Webb) Lamme. BS, Portland State U., 1970. Draftsman City of Portland, 1977-88, Computer-Aided Design and Drafting technician, 1989—; mem. women's adv. com. Dept. Transp., Portland, 1983-84, mem. employee adv. team, 1994-96. Author: A Woman's Touch, 1979; spkr. in field. Presenter, spkr. Expanding Your Horizons, Portland, 1981, 83, 84, 86, 87; panel mem. Steps to Success, Portland, 1992, 93; mentor, spkr. Teen Parent Mentorship program pub. schs., Portland, 1993, 94, 95; vol. spkr. Women's Advocates in Sci. Engring. & Maths., 1995—. Mem. City of Portland Planning and Engring. Employees Assn. (v.p. 1979), Seth Network Internat. (charter). Office: City of Portland 1120 SW 5th Ave Portland OR 97204

BARTON, PAULINE, writer; b. Hollister, Mo., Apr. 13, 1923; d. Clinton Ben and Rosa Victoria (Kaneaster) Layton; m. Benjamin Lee Barton, Dec. 22, 1945; children Ben Lee, John Paul. BS in Edn., S.W. Mo. State U., 1960; MS in Edn., Drury Coll., 1967. Wartime assembly line GM, Anderson, Ind., 1942-44; tchr. Hollister (Mo.) Schs., 1945-46, 49-51, 56-59; bus. tchr. Branson (Mo.) Schs., 1959-77, adult edn., 1981-83, home bound educator, 1983-84; freelance writer Mo., 1984—; Chmn. Taney County Bus. Tchrs., 1960-61, Southwest Mo. Bus. Tchrs., 1976-77; historian, White River Valley Hist. Soc., Mo., 1987-90, sec., treas., 1994—. contbr. articles to profl. jours., books. Leader Boy Scouts of Am., Branson, Mo., 1954-62; counselor Am. Field Service Exchange student, Branson, Mo., 1972-80; Bd. and aide Christian Action Ministry, Branson, Mo., 1986--. mem. AAUW, Ozark Writer's League, Tri-Lakes Community theatre, LWV, Am. Cancer Soc., Women of the Ch., Am. Legion Aux., VFW Aux. Republican. Presbyterian. Home: 1159 Bee Creek Rd Branson MO 65616-9144

BARTON-COLLINGS, NELDA ANN, political activist, newspaper, bank and nursing home executive; b. Providence, Ky., May 12, 1929; m. Harold Bryan Barton, May 11, 1951 (dec. Nov. 1977); children: William Grant (dec.), Barbara Lynn, Harold Bryan, Stephen Lambert, Suzanne; m. Jack C. Collings, Mar. 28, 1992. Student, Western Ky. U., 1947-49; grad., Norton Meml. Infirmary Sch. Med. Tech., 1950; student, Cumberland Coll., 1978, LLD (hon.), 1991. Lic. nursing home adminstr.; registered med. technician. Pres., chmn. bd. Barton & Assocs. Inc., Corbin, Ky., 1977—, Hazard Nursing Home Inc., Ky., 1977—, Health Systems Inc., Corbin, 1978—, Corbin Nursing Home Inc., 1980—, Williamsburg Nursing Home, Inc., 1978—, Key Distbg. Inc., 1980—, Barbourville Nursing Home Inc., 1981—, The Whitley Whiz Inc., Williamsburg, 1983—; chmn. bd. dirs. Tri-County Nat. Bank., 1985—; pres., chmn. bd. dirs. Harlan Nursing Home, Inc., 1986—, Knott Co. Nursing Home, Inc., 1986—; pres. Tri-County Bancorp, Inc., 1987—; pres., chmn. bd. Instl. Pharmacy, Corbin, Ky., 1990—, Wolfe County Health Care Ctr., 1990—; mem. exec. com. Corbin Deposit Bank, 1982-84; bd. dirs. Greensburg (Ky.) Deposit Bank, Williamsburg (Ky.) Nat. Bank, Campbellsville Nat. Bank, McCreary Nat. Bank, Laurel Nat. Bank, 1994—. Pres.'s Coun. on Rural Am., 1990-92; chmn. Greene County Bancorp Inc.; organizer, dir. Laurel Nat. Bank, 1996—; mem. nat. adv. com. SBA, 1990-92; active Nat. Policy Forum, 1994—. Mem. Fed. Coun. on Aging, 1982-87; bd. dirs. Leadership Ky., 1984-88, adv. com., 1987—; v.p. Southeastern Ky. Rehab. Com., 1981-93; mem. devel. bd. Cumberland Coll., 1981—, Fair Housing Task Force, Corbin, 1981-84, Ky. Mansions Preservation Found. Inc., Corbin Community Devel. Com., 1970-83; cub scout den mother, 1965-67; pres. Corbin Cen. Elem. PTA, 1963-65; vice chmn. 9th dist. PTA, 1958-59; Rep. nat. committeewoman for Ky., 1968-96, sec., 1993-96; vice-chmn. Rep. Nat. Com., 1984-93; sec.-treas. Nat. Rep. Inst. Internat. Affairs, 1984-86; active numerous other polit. orgns. Recipient Ky. Woman of Achievement award Ky. Bus. and Profl. Women, 1983, Recognition award Joint Rep. Leadership, U.S. Congress, Dwight David Eisenhower award, 1970, John Sherman Cooper Disting. Service award Ky. Young Reps. Fedn., 1987, Outstanding Layperson award Ky. Med. Assn., 1992, Nelda Barton Community Svc. award Ky. Assn. Health Care Facilities, 1992; named Ky. Col., 1968; Nelda Barton Day proclaimed by Mayor of Corbin, 1973; named Ky. Rep. Woman of Yr., Ky. Fedn. Rep. Women, 1969; Western Ky. U. Acad. scholar, 1947-49. Mem. Am. Coll. Nursing Home Adminstrs., Ky. Assn. Health Care Facilities (legis. com. 1980—), Ky. Assn. Nursing Home Adminstrs. (bd. dirs., polit. action com. 1979—), Ky. Med. Aux. (chmn. health edn. com. 1975-77), Am. Health Care Assn., Ky. Commn. on Women, Women's Aux. So. Med. Assn. (Ky. counselor), Whitley County Med. Aux.

(pres. 1959-60), Aux. Ky. Med. Assn., Ky. Mothers Assn. (parliamentarian 1970—, hon. Mother of Ky. award 1983), Ky. C. of C. (bd. dirs. 1983—, v.p. Region 5 1985—, 1st vice chmn. 1989, chmn. 1990-91). Home: 1311 7th Street Rd Corbin KY 40701-2207 Office: Health Systems Inc PO Box 1450 Corbin KY 40702-1450

BARTOSZ, KIM A., secondary school educator; b. Balt., Sept. 9, 1964; d. Norbert P. and Lynn B. (Shipp) B. Student, Temple U., 1982-83; AA, Catonsville (Md.) C.C., 1985; BS cum laude, Pfeiffer Coll., Messenheimer, N.C., 1987; MS, U. Wis., La Crosse, 1988; postgrad., Towson State U., 1990-91, Loyola Coll., Md., 1994-95. Cert. in phys. edn. K-12, health edn., Md. Program coord. U.S. Health and Tennis Corp. Am., Towson, Md., 1989-90; tchr. phys. edn. Good Shepherd Ctr., Halethorpe, Md., 1991-92, Baltimore County Pub. Schs., Towson, 1992—; PACE instr. Catonsville (Md.) C.C., 1991-92; comty. first aid and safety instr. Red Cross of Md., Balt., 1989—; ofcl. Balt. Bd. Ofcls. of Women's Sports, Phoenix, Md., 1990—; coach Baltimore County Pub. Schs., 1992—; instr. YMCA, Balt., 1983-94; cons., instr. Positive Health-Howard County Hosp., Ellicott City, Md., 1989-91. Contbg. author: (manual) Level III of Principle of Exercise Programs, 1990. Vol. Hoop It Up, Cystic Fibrosis Found., Balt., 1991-93; co-coord. Swimathon, Am. Heart Assn., Messenheimer, 1986, Hoops, 1996, Project Adventure, 1996—. Mem. NEA, AAHPERD, Md. Assn. for Health, Phys. Edn., Recreation and Dance, IDEA, Md. State Tchrs. Assn., Nat. Fedn. Interscholastic Ofcls. Assn., Phi Delta Sigma. Home: 208 Sanford Ave Baltimore MD 21228-5149

BARTOW, DIANE GRACE, marketing and sales executive; b. Maspeth, N.Y., Apr. 20, 1948; d. Alfred Otto and Charlotte Florence (Bronnenkant) Bruggeman; m. Eugene A. Bartow, Aug. 29, 1992; children: Jason, Trudi. AAS, Queensborough C.C., 1967; BS, Nova Southeastern U., 1979. Jr. acct. Exxon, N.Y.C., 1967-69; acct. BRM Assos., N.Y.C., 1969, Texaco, N.Y.C., 1969-74; supr. Eutectic, Flushing, N.Y., 1974-76; regional industry dir. Am. Express, N.Y.C., 1976-83; v.p. Eastern Exclusives, Boston, 1983-85; pres. The Mktg. Dept., 1985-86, sr. v.p., gen. mgr. Rogers Merchandising Inc., 1986-92; exec. v.p., COO Bartow Ins. Agy., Inc., 1992—; seminars Marketing to Win. Author tng. manual, Travel newsletter, 1982, Ins. Update, 1992. Trustee, v.p. Murray Hill Neighborhood Assn., 1982, 7 E. 35th Corp., 1983; chmn. judging Promotion and Advt. Awards, 1990. Recipient VISTA award Am. Express, 1983. Mem. Nat. Assn. Advt. and Promotional Allowances (judging chair 1996), Am. Soc. Travel Agts (tour relations com. 1983), Am. Hotel and Motel Assn., Am. Film Assn., Am. Mgmt. Assn., Sigma Mu Omega (pres. Bayside, N.Y. 1966-67). Home: 7 E 35th St New York NY 10016-3810

BARTTER, KATHRYN SUE, state official; b. Dearborn, Mich., Apr. 19, 1965; d. Neale G. Bartter and Elaine B. Baker. BS, Ohio U., 1987. Legis. intern Ohio Legis. Svc. Commn., Columbus, 1988-89; legis. aide Ohio Senate, Columbus, 1989-91; legis. liaison Ohio EPA, Columbus, 1991-93, dep. dir., 1993—. Mem. Ohio Rep. Women's Campaign Fund, Columbus, 1994—. Office: Ohio EPA 1800 Water Mark Dr Columbus OH 43216-0149

BARTUCCI, JANET EVELYN, marketing communications executive; b. Flushing, N.Y., Jan. 14, 1952; d. Louis Joseph and Evelyn Doris (Montleon) B.; m. Reuben Samuel, Oct. 18, 1981; children: Alexandra Elizabeth, David Lawrence. AAS in Communications, Fashion Inst. Tech., N.Y.C., 1972. Asst. account exec. Saul Krieg, N.Y.C., 1972-74; publicity mgr. Grosset & Dunlap, N.Y.C., 1974-76; account exec. Burson Marsteller, N.Y.C., 1976-79; v.p. Myers CommuniCounsel, N.Y.C., 1979-85; pres. Bartucci-Samuel, Inc., N.Y.C., 1985-91; sr. v.p., dir. consumer products M Booth & Assocs., N.Y., 1991—. Mem. Women in Communications, Am. Inst. Wine and Food, James Beard Found. Office: M Booth & Assocs Inc 470 Park Ave S New York NY 10016-6819

BARTZ, CAROL, software company executive; b. Alma, Wis., Aug. 29, 1948; m. William Marr; 1 child. BS in Computer Sci. with honors, U. Wis., 1971; DSc (hon.), Worcester Poly. Inst.; LittD (hon.), William Woods U. With sales mgmt. dept. 3M Corp., Digital Equipment Corp., 1976-83; mgr. customer mktg. Sun Microsys., 1983-84, v.p. mktg., 1984-87, v.p. customer svc., 1987-90, v.p. worldwide field ops., exec. officer, 1990-92; chmn. bd., CEO, pres. Autodesk, Inc., San Rafael, Calif., 1992—; pres. Sun Fed., from 1987; bd. dirs. AirTouch Comm., Cadence Design Sys., Cisco Sys., Inc.; mem. President's Export Coun., 1994; mem. corp. adv. bd. Nat. Assn. Securities Dealers. Bd. dirs. U. Wis. Sch. Bus., Nat. Breast Cancer Rsch. Found., Found. for Nat. Medals Sci. and Tech.; mem. adv. coun. Stanford U. Bus. Sch.; mem. Com. of 200; adv. for women's health issues; former mem. Ark. of Gov.'s Econ. Summit, Little Rock. Recipient Donald C. Burnham Mfg. Mgmt. award Soc. Mfg. Engrs., 1994. Mem. Calif. C. of C. (bd. dirs.). Office: Autodesk Inc 111 Mcinnis Pky San Rafael CA 94903-2773*

BARTZ, JUDITH ANDERSON, nurse; b. Bay City, Mich., July 28, 1954; d. Clifford Roy and Alice May (Mead) Anderson. AAS, Delta Coll., 1975; ADN, Coll. Lake County, 1980; BSN, U. Mich., 1995. RN, Mich.; cert. gerontol. nurse ANCC. Dir. rehab. Carestoel of McHenry, Ill., 1980-81; charge nurse Haven Park Nursing Ctr., Zeeland, Mich., 1982-87; staff nurse Pocono Med. Ctr., Stroudsberg, Pa., 1987-89, Bronson Meth. Hosp., Kalamazoo, Mich., 1989-95; charge nurse Bronson Vicksburg (Mich.) Hosp., 1995—; item writer for cert. exam Assn. Rehab. Nurses, Skokie, Ill., 1984, book reviewer, 1987-93. Mem. domestic violence task force Bronson Meth. Hosp., Kalamazoo, 1993—. Mem. ACCN, Emergency Nurses Assn. Home: 110 Lanark Ct Kalamazoo MI 49006

BARUCH, MONICA LOBO-FILHO, psychological counselor; b. Rio de Janeiro, Jan. 11, 1954; d. Max and Margot Lobo-Filho; m. Robert Karl Baruch, Dec. 30, 1973 (div. May 1985). BA in Psychology, U. Rochester, 1975; MA in Counseling Edn., U. Mo., Kansas City, 1978. Cert. Nat. Bd. Cert. Counselors. Tchr. curriculum devel. St. Patrick's Sch., Rio de Janeiro, 1974-76; tchr., soccer coach Pembroke Country Day Sch., Kansas City, Mo., 1977-78; tchr., trainer Berlitz Sch. Langs., Kansas City and Washington, 1976-79; counselor, cons. Youth Understanding, Washington, 1979-81; pvt. practice, 1981—; academic faculty counselor Georgetown U., Washington, 1982-90; newsletter editor, mem. exec. bd. Greater Washington Coalition of Mental Health Profls. and Consumers, 1996—. Co-author: Weight Control: A Guide for Counselors and Therapists, 1987. Named one of Outstanding Young Women in Am., 1981. Mem. ACA, Am. Mental Health Counselors Assn., Multiple Personality Study Group, Md. Mental Health Counselors Assn. (program chmn. 1989, exec. bd. 1993), Md. Assn. Counseling and Devel. (ethics com. 1990, chairperson profl. practice devel. 1996-97).

BASEMAN, SANDRA LIBBIE, editor; b. Detroit, Nov. 22, 1949; d. Jerome Sylvan and Mildred (Zaff) B.; m. Carl A. Keene, May 23, 1971; children: Jerome, Rachel. AB, U. Mich., 1971, AM, 1976. Admitted Registry of Fin. Planning Practitioners; CFP. Asst. editor Great Lakes Basin Commn., Ann Arbor, Mich., 1974-76; grad. student tchg. asst. U. Mich., Ann Arbor, 1976-78; mktg. asst. Caz Co., Santa Clara, Calif., 1978-79; pvt. pracitce fin. advisor San Jose, Calif., 1979-93; fin. advisor, mktg. coord. Reinhardt Werba Bowen, San Jose, 1993-94, dir. corp. comm., 1994—; bd. mem., membership dir. Inst. CFP, Silicon Valley Chpt., 1984-87; bd. mem. Internat. Assn. for Fin. Planning, Santa Clara County Chpt., San Jose, 1986-87. Phone counselor, trainer Women's Crisis Ctr., Ann Arbor, 1973-76; precinct leader Dem. Party, San Jose, 1992; bd. mem. pub. rels. East Hills Elem. Sch., San Jose, 1992-94; vol. clinic def. Planned Parenthood, San Jose, 1993. Office: Reinhardt Werba Bowen 1190 Saratoga Ave #200 San Jose CA 95129

BASHAM, DEBRA ANN, archivist; b. Hattiesburg, Miss., Mar. 18, 1960; d. John Crosby and Barbara May (Dunn) B.; m. Ernest Richard Fauss, Apr. 26, 1986; children: Ernest James Fauss, John Richard Fauss. BA in History, Millsaps Coll., 1982; MA in History, U. Del., 1984. Archivist W.Va. State Archives, Charleston, 1984—. Mem. Mid-Atlantic Regional Archives Conf. (former state rep.), Soc. Am. Archives Conf. Democrat. Methodist. Office: Culture & History Div W Va State Archives 1900 Kanawha Blvd E Charleston WV 25305-0300

BASHAM-TOOKER, JANET BROOKS, retired geropsychologist, educator; b. Hampton, Va., Sept. 27, 1919; d. Thomas Westmore and Cora Evelyn Brooks; m. Linwood Cecil Basham (div. 1968); m. Frederick Fitch Tooker. BA cum laude, U. N.C., Greensboro, 1948; ABD in Psychology, Calif. State U., L.A., 1981; MA in Human Devel., Pacific Oaks Coll., 1984. Tchr., Calif. Grad. asst. psychology Duke U., Durham, N.C., 1948-49; tchr. Albuquerque City Schs., 1950-51; tchr. L.A. City Schs., 1953-54, counselor, 1981; lectr. L.A., 1988—; now ret.; docent Las Angelitas del Pueblo, L.A., 1971-74; active project with autistic children, through Pepperdine Univ., UCLA Neuropsychiatric Inst., L.A., 1974. Author numerous poems. Mem. planning com., women's conf. Commn. on Status of Women, Pasadena, Calif., 1982-85, sr. com. Task Force on Aging, San Marino, Calif., 1986-89, bd. dirs. United Way, Arcadia, Calif., 1984-88, Symphony Guild, Fayetteville, 1990; adv. mem. San Gabriel Presbytery Commn. on Aging, 1984-88; mem. grad. studies subcom. Calif. State U., L.A., 1975-78; v.p. San Marino Aux. Meth. Hosp., Arcadia, Calif., 1985-86; docent Duarte Hist. Soc., Calif., 1986-89; moderator sr. adults 1st United Presbyn. Ch., Fayetteville, 1990; facilitator fin. info. program for women AARP, Fayetteville, 1990; vol. in gerontology Fayetteville (Ark.) City Hosp., 1991, Health Care Unit, Butterfield Trail Village, Fayetteville, 1993; adv. com. Single Parent Scholarship Fund, Fayetteville, 1992. Recipient Margaret Noffsinger award Va. Intermont Coll., 1937. Mem. AAUW, Am. Soc. Aging, Mental Health Assn., Older Women's League, LWV, Phi Beta Kappa, Phi Theta Kappa. Republican. Presbyterian.

BASHFORD, PATRICIA ANN, communications educator; b. Columbus, Ohio, June 23, 1929; d. Carey McCune and Mary Josephine (Kent) Young; m. Ralph Leroy Burt, May 1, 1956 (dec. Nov. 1958); 1 child, Rob Carey Burt; m. Bernard Dean Bashford, June 10, 1964 (dec. Sept. 1984); 1 child, Ronald Dean. B in Lit. Interpretation, Emerson Coll., 1952; MA in Speech, U. Colo., 1960. Instr. Bridgewater (Mass.) State Coll., 1960-62; asst. prof. Iowa State U., Ames, 1962-64; part-time instr. U. Colo., Boulder, 1964-68, Rivers Country Day Sch., Weston, Mass., 1968-70; asst. prof. Grahm Jr. Coll., Boston, 1971-79; adj. prof. Mass. State Coll. Sys., Bedford, Haverhill, 1979-81, Emerson Coll., Boston, 1980; asst. prof. Boston U., 1981-83; prof. Middlesex C.C., Bedford, Mass., 1984—; media cons. Root Bashford Corp., Reading, Wakefield, Mass., 1979-83. Contbg. author: Organizational Behavior: Cases, Exercises, Readings, 1989; prodr., dir., writer: (videos) The Place of Seeing, 1989, Seeing Design, 1989, The Spirits Are Crying, 1993; prodr., dir. Bashford Multimedia, Reading, Mass., 1984—; actor Vox Novus Ind. Film Co., Hollywood, Calif., 1952-56; writer: (children's TV series) Barry Enterprizes, 1957-58. Bd. dirs. New Eng. Theatre Conf., Waltham, Mass., 1982-86, hostess, 1983-86; cmty. assn., trainer Effectiveness Tng. Assn., Weston, 1970-75; dir., lighting designer Cmty. Theatre, Reading and Concord, Mass., 1973-87. Recipient award Am. Found. Blind, N.Y.C., 1963; named Best Actress, New Eng. Theatre Conf., Brandeis U., Waltham, 1987. Mem. Univ. Film and Video Assn. Home: 128 Salem St Reading PA 01867 Office: Middlesex C C Springs Rd Bedford MA 01730

BASHORE, IRENE SARAS, research institute administrator; b. San Jose, Calif.; d. John and Eva (Lionudakis) Saras; m. Vincent Bashore (div.); 1 child, Juliet Ann. BA, Pepperdine U., 1950; MA in Theatre Arts, Calif. State U., Fullerton, 1977. Founder, exec. dir. Inst. for Dramatic Rsch., Fullerton, Calif., 1967—.

BASINGER, KAREN LYNN, renal dietitian; b. Mechanicsville, Md., July 4, 1955; d. Leonard Marcus and Mary Jane (Harding) Brookbank; m. Joseph Andrew Basinger, Nov. 17, 1984; 1 child, James Marcus. BS, U. Md., 1977; MS, Hood Coll., 1987. Lic. nutritionist. Libr. technician Bowie (Md.) State Coll., 1973-79; instr. St. Mary's County Adult Edn., Leonardtown, Md., 1979-80; home economist Zamoiski Co., Balt., 1977-83; nutritionist/WIC coord. South County Health Plan, Prince Frederick, Md., 1979-80; nutritionist Walter Reed Army Med. Ctr., Washington, 1980-82; renal dietitian Mid Atlantic/BMA, Camp Springs, Md., 1982-87, Kidney Care Ctr., Landover, Md., 1987—; instr. dietary intern program Andrews AFB, 1988-91; lectr. in field. Mem. profl. adv. bd. Nat. Kidney Found./NCA, 1989-94; chair coun. on renal nutrition Nat. Kidney Found., 1993-94, program chair, 1990-92. Recipient Spl. Recognition Nat. Kidney Found./NCA, 1990, 92, Recognized Renal Dietitian/NCA, 1991, 94. Mem. Am. Nutritionists Assn., Am. Home Econs. Assn., Md. Home Econs. Assn. (bylaws chair 1982-94), Am. Dietetic Assn., Washington Metro. Coun. on Renal Nutrition (chair 1986-91, nutrition symposium chair 1989), U. Md. Alumni Assn. Democrat. Lutheran. Office: Kidney Care Ctr 1300 Mercantile Ln Ste 194 Landover MD 20785-5339

BASINGER, KIM, actress; b. Athens, Ga., Dec. 8, 1953; d. Don Basinger; m. Ron Britton, 1980 (div. Feb. 1990); m. Alec Baldwin, August 19, 1993. Student, Neighborhood Playhouse, N.Y.C. Model Eileen Ford Agy., N.Y.C., 1972-77; ind. actress, 1977—. Starring role (TV series) Dog and Cat, 1977; TV films include Katie-Portrait of a Centerfold, 1978, The Ghost of Flight 401, 1978, Killjoy, 1981, (TV miniseries) From Here to Eternity, 1979; (feature films) Hard Country, 1981, Mother Lode, 1982, Never Say Never Again, 1983, The Man Who Loved Women, 1983, The Natural, 1984, Fool for Love, 1985, 9 1/2 Weeks, 1986, No Mercy, 1986, Blind Date, 1987, Nadine, 1987, My Stepmother is an Alien, 1988, Batman, 1989, The Marrying Man, 1991, Final Analysis, 1992, Cool World, 1992, The Real McCoy, 1993, The Getaway, 1994, Ready to Wear (Prêt-à-Porter), 1994. *

BASKETT, CHRISTINA ST. CLAIR, fund raising executive; b. Cheyenne, Wyo., Feb. 17, 1960; d. William Warren and Christina Addison (Dann) St. Clair; m. Douglas Helm Baskett, Sept. 5, 1987; children: David Anderson, Robert William. BA, Wellesley Coll., 1982; MBA, MA, So. Methodist U., 1987. Cert. fund raising exec.. From asst. to dir. bldg. ops. to asst. dir. fin. aid New England Conservatory, Boston, 1982-85; asst. dir. devel. Dallas Symphony Assn., 1987-89; dir. devel. Dallas Mus. Natural History, 1989-92; dir. major gifts KERA/KDTN, Dallas, 1993-96, dir. devel., 1996—. Active Jr. League Dallas, 1995—; sec. bd. dirs. Wellesley Coll. Club, 1992 ; bd. dirs., chair fundraising com. First Presbyn. Day Sch., Dallas, 1994; singer Dallas Symphony Chorus, 1986-91. Mem. Nat. Soc. Fund Raising Execs. (treas., bd. dirs. 1995—). Republican. Office: KERA/KDTN 3000 Harry Hines Blvd Dallas TX 75201

BASKIN, ROBERTA, television correspondent; b. Atlanta, Jan. 16, 1952; d. Alan Baskin and Suzanne Pallister; m. James Albert Trengrove, Sept. 19, 1987; children: Chelsea, Vanessa. Student, Elmira Coll., 1969-70. Dir. Consumer Affairs Office, Syracuse, N.Y., 1974-77; consumer reporter Sta. WMAQ-TV, Chgo., 1977-79; investigative reporter Sta. WLS-TV, Chgo., 1979-84; consumer editor Sta. WJLA-TV, Washington, 1984-91; corr. CBS News, Washington, N.Y.C., 1992—; bd. mem. Fund for Investigative Journalism, Washington, 1992-94. Telethon host Sta. WETA-TV, Washington, 1987-94. Recipient Peabody awards U. Ga., 1982, 86, Edward R. Murrow award Radio-TV News Dirs. Assn., 1983, 90, duPont-Columbia awards Columbia U. Sch. of Journalism, 1987, 90, Ohio State awards. Mem. NATAS (16 local Emmy awards Chgo., Washington chpts.), Am. Fedn. TV and Radio Artists (bd. dirs. 1993-94). Office: CBS News Washington Bureau 2020 M St NW Washington DC 20036-3368

BASQUIN, MARY SMYTH (KIT BASQUIN), museum curator; b. N.Y.C., July 3, 1941; d. Joseph Percy and Virginia Sandford (Gibbs) Smyth; m. Maurice Hanson Basquin, Feb. 4, 1967 (div. Feb. 1984); children: Susan, Peter Lee, William. BA, Goucher Coll., Balt., 1963; MA, Ind. U., 1970. Asst. dir. pub. rels. Indpls. Mus. Art, 1971-72; dir. Kit Basquin Gallery, Frankfort, Ind., 1972-79, Indpls., 1977-79, Milw., 1981-83; curator edn. Haggerty Mus. Marquette U., Milw., 1988-95; dir. outreach Milw. Wis. Humanities Coun., Madison, 1995—; instr. art history Concordia U., Mequon, Wis., 1991, instr. Marquette U., Gaza, 1992-96; pres. contemporary art soc. Milw. Art Mus., 1986-87, prints and drawings subcom., 1991—, pres. Print Forum, 1996—; mem. program com. Midwest Mus. conf., Milw., 1992. Editor New Art Examiner, Chgo., 1980-81; contbr. articles to profl. jours. Bd. dirs. Am. Inside Teatre, Genesee Depot, Wis., 1994-95. Mem. Univ. Club N.Y., Univ. Club Milw., Oconomowoc Lake Club. Episcopalian. Home & Office: 925 East Wells St Apt 225 Milwaukee WI 53202

BASS, JANN T., artist, consultant, educator; b. Hobbs, N. Mex., June 10, 1941; d. Leonard Orlean and V. Elizabeth (Harris) Thomas; div. Student, Corcoran Sch. Art, 1963; BFA, U. Colo., 1965. Instr. Art Students' League, Denver, 1985-88; artist, instr. plain air workshops Art Students' League, Marble, Colo., 1989; artist, instr. Bass Studio Workshops, Denver, 1990-95. Featured in books, Artists' mag., Defenders of Wildlife mag., Southwest Art; has exhibited in N.Y., Mass., Ohio, N. Mex., Calif. including Saks Galleries, Denver, 1986—, Lagerquist Galleries, Atlanta, 1993—, Taos Traditions Gallery, 1992-96. Asst. to Senator Gordon Allott, Washington, 1963; artist, illustrator Rocky Mountain Tchr. Corps., Washington, 1979-90; artist, donor KRMA Channel 6 pub. t.v., Denver, 1984—. Recipient Artist of Merit award Audubon Soc. Grasslands Inst., 1980, Snyder award Gilpin County Arts Assn. , 1982, Award of Merit Works on Paper, 1983. Mem. Nat. Mus. Women Artists. Office: Bass Studios 2700 Walnut Studio B Denver CO 80205

BASS, LYNDA D., medical/surgical nurse, educator; b. Suffolk, Va.; d. H.M. and Katie Lea Bass. BSN, N.C. Agrl. and Tech. State U., Greensboro, 1968; MS in Nursing, Cath. U. Am., 1974; Gen. Surgery Clin. Specialist, George Washington U. Hosp., Washington. Cert. BCLS instr. Clin. instr. Suburban Hosp., Bethesda, Md.; edn./tng. quality assurance coord. Howard U. Hosp., Washington; clin. educator Providence Hosp., Washington; nursing instr. VA Md. Healthcare Sys., Balt.; coord. clin. staff Devel. Mount Vernon Hosp., Alexandria, Va. Capt. U.S. Army, 1968-71, Vietnam. Mem. Nat. Nursing Staff Devel. Assn., Chi Eta Phi.

BASS, MARTHA POSTLETHWAITE, high school principal; b. Wichita, Kans., Dec. 6, 1942; d. John Emmett and Norma Louise (Lanning) Postlethwaite; m. Elmer Lee Bass, July 22, 1981; step children: Sheryl, Terry. BA in Edn., U. N.Mex., 1964, MA, 1966. Endl. lic. adminstr., supt., English tchr., drama speech tchr., counselor. Asst. dean women, instr. Hanover (Ind.) Coll., 1966-68; asst. dean women U. N.Mex., Alburquerque, 1969-69; elem. counselor Alburquerque Pub. Schs., 1969-74, guidance coord., 1974-77, high sch. asst. prin., 1977-87; high sch. prin. Del Norte High Sch. Alburquerque Pub. Schs., 1987—; bd. dirs. Albuquerque Child Guidance Ctr.; pres., cons. Acad. Ednl. Leadership, Alburquerque, 1986-90. Title VII Fed. grantee Child Encouragement Project, Alburquerque, 1977; named Woman on the Move YWCA, Alburquerque, 1990. Mem. Nat. Assn. Secondary Sch. Prins., Alburquerque Assn. Secondary Sch. Prins. (past bd. dirs., treas. 1986-87), Rotary Club of Albuquerque (RYLA chair 1990-93). Office: Del Norte High Sch 5323 Montgomery Blvd NE Albuquerque NM 87109-1302

BASS, RUTH MARY HASKINS, journalist; b. Springfield, Mass., July 18, 1934; d. Ralph Warner and Hilda Marie (Allen) Haskins; m. Milton R. Bass, May 27, 1960; children: Michael Jon, Elissa Allen, Amy Brunell. AB in English, Bates Coll., 1955; MS in Journalism, Columbia U., 1956. Police and ct. reporter The Berkshire Eagle, Pittsfield, Mass., 1956-61; freelance writer, editor Berkshire Week mag., Pittsfield, Mass., 1963-68; editor Berkshire Sampler, Pittsfield, Mass., 1977-87; assoc. sunday editor Berkshire Eagle, Pittsfield, Mass., 1987-90; Sunday editor Pittsfield, Mass., 1990-96; columnist Berkshire Eagle, Richmond, Mass., 1996—. Author: (book series) Herbal Sweets, Herbal Salads, Herbal Bread, Herbal Soups, Tomatoes Love Herbs, Peppers Love Herbs, Onions Love Herbs, Mushrooms Love Herbs, 1996; co-author: Tech. Career Guide, 1962. Selectman Town of Richmond, 1972-77, mem. fin. com., 1990—, chmn., 1993—; mem. bd. health, 1972-90; leader Girl Scouts US, Richmond, 1982—. Recipient Best Column in New Eng. award UPI, 1988, Charles and Mary Kusik Citizenship award, Richmond, 1994.

BASSETT, ANGELA, actress; b. N.Y.C., Aug. 16, 1958. Appeared in (plays) Colored People's Time, 1982, The Mystery Plays, 1984-85, The Painful Adventures of Pericles, Prince of Tyre, 1986-87, Joe Turner's Come and Gone, 1986-87, (Broadway) Ma Rainey's Black Bottom, (Broadway) Joe Turner's Come and Gone, 1988, King Henry IV Part I, 1987; (TV movies) Line of Fire: The Morris Dees Story, 1991, The Jacksons: An American Dream, 1992, A Century of Women, 1994; (films) F/X, 1986, Kindergarten Cop, 1990, Boyz N the Hood, 1991, City of Hope, 1991, Innocent Blood, 1992, Malcolm X, 1992, Passion Fish, 1992, What's Love Got to Do with It, 1993 (Acad. award nominee for best actress 1993, Golden Globe award best actress in a musical or comedy 1994), Strange Days, 1995, Panther, 1995, Waiting to Exhale, 1995, A Vampire in Brooklyn, 1995. Office: care Krost/Chapin 9911 W Pico Blvd Ph I Los Angeles CA 90035-2718*

BASSETT, BARBARA WIES, editor, publisher; b. Dec. 5, 1939; m. Norman W. Bassett. BA, U. Conn., 1961; student, New Sch. for Social Rsch., 1961-62. Product devel. Fearn Soya, Melrose Park, Ill., 1973-75; product devel. Modern Products, Milw., 1973-75; editor, pub. Bestways Mag., Carson City, Nev., 1977-89; pub. The Healthy Gourmet Newsletter, 1989-91, Fine Wine-Good Food Newsletter, 1991—; publicity dir. Nev. Artists Assn., 1994—; owner Gualala (Calif.) Galleries, 1989-90; owner, operator cooking sch. Greensboro N.C. 1969-73. Author: Natural Cooking, 1968, Wok and Tempura, 1969, Japanese Home Cooking, 1970, The Wok, 1971, Super Soy, 1973, The Health Gourmet, 1981, International Healthy Gourmet, 1982; one-woman show paintings Dolphin Gallery, Gualala, Calif., 1990, River Gallery, Reno, 1994; 2 women show 1992, 94, 96, Dolphin Gallery, Calif., 1994, solo exhbn. Nev. Artists Assn. Gallery, 1993, 95, 96; featured artist Nev. State Libr., 1996, West Nev. C.C., 1996; restaurant critic Reno Gazette Jour., 1995—. Recipient First Place adult fiction Nev. State Lit. Co., 1995. Mem. Nat. League Am. Pen Women, Inst. Food Technologists, Pastel Soc. of the West Coast, Inst. Am. Culinary Profls.

BASSETT, CAROL ANN, magazine, video, and radio documentary writer, producer, journalism educator; b. Langley AFB, Va., Mar. 2, 1953; d. William Brainard and Genevieve (Rivaldo) B. BA summa cum laude in Humanities, Ariz. State U., 1977; MA in Journalism, U. Ariz., 1982. Ptnr. Desert West News, Tucson, 1985-90; freelance writer Tucson, 1980-95, Missoula, Mont., 1995—; mem. faculty U. Mont. Sch. Journalism, Missoula, 1996—. Editor Tucson Weekly, 1989-90; contbr. numerous articles to nat. and internat. mags. including N.Y. Times. Recipient 2d Place Gen. Reporting award Ariz. Press Club, 1987, Gold medal for best environ. documentary Houston Internat. Film Festival, 1990, 1st Place Gen. Reporting award Ariz. Press Club, 1992, Silver Medal for Energy Issues documentary, Houston Internat. Film Festival, 1992; co-recipient Alfred I. duPont Columbia award, 1984-85, First Place award Investigative Reporting, 1986, 1st Place Polit. Reporting, 1989, First Amendment Journalism award, 1986; grantee Fund for Investigative Journalism, 1985, 87, Corp. for Pub. Broadcasting, 1988, Oxfam Am., 1991.

BASSETT, TINA, communications executive; b. Detroit; m. Leland Kinsey Bassett; children: Joshua, Robert. Student, U. Mich., 1974, 76-78, 81, Wayne State U., 1979-80. Advt. dir. Greenfield's Restaurant, Mich. and Ohio, 1972-73; dir. advt. and pub. relations Kresco, Inc., Detroit, 1973-74; pub's. rep. The Detroiter mag., 1974-75; pub. relations dir. Detroit Bicentennial Commn., 1975-77; prin. Leland K. Bassett & Assocs., Detroit, 1976-86; intermediate job devel. specialist Detroit Council of the Arts, 1977; project dir. Detroit image campaign Dept. Pub. Info., City of Detroit, 1975, spl. events dir., 1978; dep. dir. Dept. Pub. Info. City of Detroit, 1978-83, dir., 1983-86; pres., prin. Bassett & Bassett, Inc., Detroit, 1986—. Publicity chmn. Under the Stars IV, V, VI, VII, VIII, IX and X, Benefit Balls, Detroit Inst. of Arts Founders Soc., 1983-88, Detroit Inst. of Arts Founders Centennial Ball, 1985, publicity chmn. Mich. Opera Theater, Opera Ball, 1987; program lectr. Wayne County Close-Up Program, 1984; mem. ctrl. planning com. Am. Assn. Mus.; mem. Founders Soc., Detroit Inst. Arts, 1988—; mem., publicity chair Grand Prix Ball, 1989; co-chair, producer Mus. Ball Ctr. for Performing Arts; bd. dirs. arts coun. Detroit Inst. Arts, 1996. Named Outstanding Woman in Agy. Top Mgmt., Detroit chpt. Am. Women in Radio and TV, 1989. Mem. AIA (hon., pub. dir. 1990-91, Richard Upjohn fellowship 1991), Detroit Hist. Soc., Music Hall Assn., Pub. Rels. Soc. Am. (Advt. Woman of Yr. 1989), Woman's Advt. Club Detroit. Home: 30751 Cedar Creek Dr Farmington Hl MI 48336-4989 Office: Bassett & Bassett Inc 672 Woodbridge St Detroit MI 48226-4302

BASSMAN, ALICE JANE, psychotherapist, jewelry and sculpture designer; b. Bklyn., May 2, 1951; d. Herbert Murray and Edith (Weiner) Bierman; m. Mitchell Jay Bassman, Jan. 3, 1971; children: Damien Adam, Nili Tamara. BA in French, Duke U., 1973; MA in Psychol. Svcs., Marymount Coll., 1994; postgrad. studies in Psychology, Am. Sch. Profl. Psychology, Rosslyn, Va., 1995—. Intern therapist Friendship House, Loudoun, Va.,

1993-94; residential counselor (homeless shelter) Mondloch House Rte 1 Corridor, Alexandria, Va., 1994—; mental health/mental retardation residential therapist Rock Hill Home, Fairfax, Va., 1995—; designer, mfr., proprietor, My Designs, Burke, Va., 1990—. Author, composer: (booksongs) The Nili and Gold Star Rainbow Series; clock designer. Bd. dirs., soccer coach Fairfax Police Youth Club, 1981-86; bd. dirs. artist, fund raiser, The Arlington (Va.) Ballet, 1986-87; organizer, vol. in pub. rels. The Women's Ctr. of No. Va.; 1990—; listener, interviewer No. Va. Hotline, 1994—. Recipient Hon. Mention in Kloc Kit nat. contest, 1992. Mem. ACA, NAFE, APA, Kappa Delta Pi, Delta Epsilon Sigma, Psi Chi.

BASSO, ANN MARIE, teacher of dance; b. Silver Spring, Md., Aug. 24, 1963; d. Frank Joseph and Andrea Mae (Gooding) B.; m. Nicolas Tsabiras, Mar. 13, 1992. H.s. grad., Silver Spring, Md.; student, Montgomery Coll. Sec. Embassy of Tunisia, Washington, 1986-87, Carriage Hill Nursing Ctr., Silver Spring, Md., 1987-91; adminstrv. asst. Fox Chase Rehab., Silver Spring, 1991-93; asst. to state dir. Rehab. Works, Rockville, Md., 1993-95; tchr. ball room dancing Tom Woll and Assocs., Fairfax, Va., 1987—. Mem. Phi Theta Kappa. Home and Office: 5010 Adrian St Rockville MD 20853

BASSO, KATHLEEN ALYSSA, lawyer; b. Allenhurst, N.J., Jan. 29, 1964; d. Michael Joseph and Marianne (Neapolitan) B. Student, U. Manchester, 1984-85; BS, Tulane U., 1986; JD, Boston Coll., 1989. Assoc. Parker, Chapin, Flattau & Klimpl, N.Y.C., 1989-93; corp. counsel Automatic Data Processing, Inc., 1993-95; 2d v.p. Chase Manhattan Bank, 1995-96; vice pres., asst. gen. counsel Goldman, Sachs & Co., N.Y.C., 1996—. Vol. Presdl. Election Campaign, Boston, 1988, Vols. of Legal Svcs., Inc., N.Y.C., 1991, Lawyers for Arts, N.Y.C., 1994. Mem. Beta Gamma Sigma. Democrat. Roman Catholic. Home: 125 W 85th St # 2R New York NY 10024-4415 Office: Goldman Sachs & Co 85 Broad St New York NY 10004

BASS-RUBENSTEIN, DEBORAH SUE, social worker, educator, consultant; b. Springfield, Ill., Jan. 21, 1951; d. Ralph and Dorothy Bernice (Feuer) Bass; m. Jeffrey Rubenstein, Oct. 12, 1975; children: Jonathan, Benjamin. BA, MSW, U. Ill., 1973. Social worker Dept. Human Resources, Washington, 1974-75; analyst Asst. Sec. for Planning and Evaluation, Washington, 1975-76, Adminstrn. for Pub. Svcs., Washington, 1976-79, Health Care Financing Adminstrn., Washington, 1979; sr. analyst OHDS, Washington, 1979-83, 84-87, Adminstrn. on Aging, Washington, 1983-84; dir. Office Human Devel. Svcs., Exec. Secretariat, HHS, Washington, 1987-90; cons. and pres. Deborah Bass Assocs., Manassas, Va., 1990—; assoc. faculty Johns Hopkins Sch. Continuing Studies, 1993; sec. U.S. com. Internat. Coun. on Social Welfare, Washington, 1991-93, bd. dirs., 1987-90; convenor Fed. Social Workers Consortium, Washington, 1986-90; participant Dartmouth-Hitchcock Med. Ctr. Project on Family Support, 1993; co-facilitator Unity in the Community, 1995—, chair, 1996—; mem. multi-cultural com. Prince William County Sch. Divsn., 1993—; chair civic affairs com., Congregation Ner Shalom Sisterhood, 1996—; mem. polit. affairs com. Jewish Cmty. Ctr. of No. Va. Author: Caring Families, 1990, Helping Vulnerable Youths, 1992; contbr. Ency. Social Work, 1995. Chmn. Congregation Nev Shalom Sisterhood civic affairs com., 1996—; co-pres. Coles Sch. PTO, Manassas, 1987-88; bd. dirs. Mid-County Coalition, Prince William County, Va., 1986; mem. multi-cultural com. Prince William County Sch. Divsn., 1993—; co-facilitator Citizens of Faith/Citizens Concerned About Discrimination in Prince William County, 1994-95, Unity in the Cmty., 1995—. James scholar U. Ill., 1969-73. Mem. NASW (poetry com. 1988-90). Home and Office: 7092 Kings Arms Dr Manassas VA 22111-3237

BASU, SUNANDA, scientific administrator, researcher in space physics; b. Calcutta, West Bengal, India, Dec. 9, 1940; d. Chunilal and Amita Chatterjee Ganguli; m. Santimay Basu, Apr. 5, 1961; 1 child, Susanto. BSc in Physics, Calcutta (India) U., 1960, PhD in Radio Physics, 1972; AM in Physics, Boston U., 1963. Rsch. assoc. Inst. Radio Physics, U. Calcutta, India, 1973-75; NAS resident rsch. assoc. Air Force Geophysics Lab., Hanscom AFB, Mass., 1975-78; sr. physicist Emmanuel Coll., Boston, 1978-89; sr. rsch. physicist Inst. Space Rsch., Boston Coll., 1989-92; program dir. aeronomy, atmospheric scis. divsn. NSF, Arlington, Va., 1992—; mem. com. Solar Terrestrial Rsch. Panel on Jicamarca Radio Obs., Peru, 1980-83; chairperson CEDAR Working Group on High Latitude Plasma Structure, 1987-92, STEP WG3 Project on Global Aspects of Plasma Structures, 1990—, USNC/URSI Commn. G, 1994—, mem. exec. com., 1988-90, vice chairperson, 1991-93; mem. adv. com. atmospheric scis. NSF, 1988-92; organizer CEDAR/HLPS & STEP/GAPS Workshop, Peaceful Valley, Colo., 1992; cons. Ctr. Space Rsch. MIT, Cambridge, Mass., 1991-92; active U.S. Nat. Delegation to Internat. Sci. Radio Union Gen. Assemblies, 1981, 84, 87, 90, 93. Author chpts. to books; contbr. over 60 papers, articles to profl. jours. Mem. AAAS, Am. Geophy. Union, Internat. Sci. Radio Union (mem. commns. G and H), Sigma Xi (pres. Hanscom chpt. 1986-87). Office: NSF 4201 Wilson Blvd Rm 775 Arlington VA 22230-0001

BATCH, MARY LOU, guidance counselor, educator; b. McKeesport, Pa.. BS in Edn., Cen. State U., Wilberforce, Ohio, 1970; MS in Spl. Edn., Syracuse U., 1971; PhD in Counselor Edn., U. Pitts., 1982. Cert. in spl. and elem. edn., Ohio; cert. in elem. and mid. sch. edn., secondary guidance, Va.; cert. in NK-8 edn., edn. of mentally retarded, Va. Various edn. and counseling positions Va. schs., military and other insts., 1965-72; tchr. adult edn. Big Bend C.C., Germany. Am. Coll. System Overseas, 1973-75; counselor, coord. U. Pitts., 1976-79; asst. prof. spl. edn. Ind. U. of Pa., 1979-85; testing specialist C.C. of Allegheny County, Braddock Ctr., Pa., 1985-86; guidance counselor Henrico H.S., Henrico County Schs., Richmond, Va., 1987—, John Rolfe Middle Sch., Richmod, 1991-96, Maude Trevett Elem. Sch., 1996—; edn. specialist U.S. Govt. in Germany, 1974-75; cons., workshop conductor, in Pa., N.J., Va. at ednl. facilities, civic orgns. and with parent groups, 1978—; mem. So. States Evaluation Team, Manassas Va., 1988; mem. peer advisor steering com. and student peer advisor supr. Henrico High Sch., 1987-90; extended del. position Citizen Ambassador Program of People to People Internat. to Soviet Union and Hungary, Am. Sch. Counselor Assn., 1991, U.S./China Joint Conf. on Edn., 1992. Bd. dirs. Richmond Residential Svcs., 1989—, sec., 1990-91, chmn. program and planning com., 1991-92, vice chmn., 1992—; group facilitator Henrico County Ct. Alternative; mem. Henrico County Edn. 2000 Commn., mem. action team; active in Head Start movement and teen parenting counseling; mem. Statewide Mid. Sch. Coun., 1994—; mem. tech. pres. steering com. Henrico County Pub. Schs., 1994—; active Nat. Multiple Sclerosis Soc., inductee leadership cir., 1995; mem. steering com. Tech Prep Henrico County, Richmond, Va., 1994-95; mid. sch. state rep. coun. mem., 1995. Inductee, Nat. Leadership Circle. Mem. LWV, ASCD, Am. Fedn. Tchrs., Nat. Coun. of Negro Women, Va. Personnel and Guidance Assn., Va. Sch. Counselors Assn., Richmond Personnel and Guidance Assn., Henrico County Guidance Assn. (pres. 1989-91), Va. Assn. Multicultural Devel., Greater Richmond Involved Parents, Nat. Coun. for Self Esteem, Nat. Coun. Sr. Citizens, Alpha Kappa Mu, Zeta Phi Beta. Home: 5022 W Seminary Ave Richmond VA 23227-3408 Office: John Rolfe Mid Sch 6901 Messer Rd Richmond VA 23231-5507

BATCHELDER, ALICE M., federal judge; b. 1944; m. William G. Batchelder III; children: William G. IV, Elisabeth. BA, Ohio Wesleyan U., 1964; JD, Akron U., 1971; LLM, U. Va., 1988. Tchr. Plain Local Sch. Dist., Franklin County, Ohio, 1965-66, Jones Jr. High Sch., 1966-67, Buckeye High Sch., Medina County, 1967-68; assoc. Williams & Batchelder, Medina, Ohio, 1971-83; judge U.S. Bankruptcy Ct., Ohio, 1983-85, U.S. Dist. Ct. (no. dist.) Ohio, Cleve., 1985-91, U.S. Ct. of Appeals (6th cir.), Cleveland, 1991—. Mem. ABA, Fed. Judge's Assn., Medina County Bar Assn. Office: 807 E Washington St Ste 200 Medina OH 44256-3330

BATCHELDER, ANNE STUART, former publisher, political party official; b. Lake Forest, Ill., Jan. 11, 1920; d. Robert Douglas and Harriet (McClure) Stuart; m. Clifton Brooks Batchelder, May 26, 1945; children: Edward, Anne Stuart, Mary Clifton, Lucia Brooks. Student Lake Forest Coll., 1941-43. Clubmobile driver ARC, Eng., Belgium, France, Holland and Germany, 1943-45; pub., editor Douglas County Gazette, 1970-75, 79-90; bd. dirs. Firstier Bank Omaha; dir., treas. U.S. Checkbook Com. Mem. Rep. Ctrl. Com. Nebr., 1955-62, 70-83, vice chmn. Ctrl. Com., 1959-64, chmn., 1975-79, mem. fin. com., 1957-64; chmn. women's sect. Douglas County Rep. Fin. Com., 1995, vice chmn. com., 1958-60; v.p. Omaha Woman's Rep. Club, 1957-58, pres., 1959-60; alt. del. Nat. Conv., 1956, 72, del., 1980, 84, 88; mem. Rep. Nat. Com. for Nebr., 1964-70; asst. chmn. Douglas County Rep. Ctrl. Com., 1971-74; 1st v.p. Nebr. Fedn. Rep. Women, 1971-72, pres., 1972-74; chmn. Nebr. Rep. Com., 1975-79; chmn. fundraising com. Nat. Fedn. Rep. Women, 1981-93, vice chmn., 1994-96, chmn., 1996—; mem. Nebr. State Bldg. Commn., 1979-83; Rep. candidate for lt. gov., 1974. Sr. v.p. Nebr. Founders Day, 1958; bd. dirs. YWCA, 1983-89, Omaha Libr. Found., 1991—; past trustee Brownell Hall, Vis. Nurse Assn., Omaha Libr. Found.; past pres. Nebr. chpt. Freedoms Found. at Valley Forge; chmn. fin. George Bush for Pres., Nebr., 1987-88; apptd. Kennedy Ctr. Performing Arts, 1989, 94, Pres.' Adv. Com. on the Arts, 1990—; mem. Nebr. Rep. State Fin. Com., 1990, Nat. Fin. Com. Bush-Quayle, 1992; active Omaha Meth. Hosp. Found., Brownell-Talbot Sch. Found. Elected to Nebr. Rep. Hall of Fame, 1984. Mayflower Soc., Colonial Dames, P.E.O., Nat. League Pen Women Omaha Country, Omaha. Presbyterian. Home: 6875 State St Omaha NE 68152-1633

BATCHELOR, KAREN LEE, English language educator; b. Oregon City, Oreg., June 17, 1948; d. Jewel Elaine Durham; m. Luis Armando, Mar. 17, 1978 (div. Aug. 1988); children: Virginia, Travis. BA in English, San Francisco State U., 1971, MA in English, 1980. Vol. U.S. Peace Corps, Andong, South Korea, 1972-74; tchr. English as second lang. City Coll. San Francisco, 1975—; tchr. trainer U. Calif., Berkeley, 1986—; acad. specialist USIA, 1991—; speaker in field. Co-author: (textbooks) Discovering English, 1981, In Plain English, 1985, More Plain English, 1986, The Writing Challenge, 1990; contbr. articles to profl. jorus. Mem. Tchrs. English to Speakers of Other Langs., Calif. Tchrs. English to Speakers of Other Langs. Office: City Coll San Francisco 50 Phelan Box L 168 San Francisco CA 94112

BATCHELOR, RUBY STEPHENS, retired nurse; b. Rocky Mount, N.C., Sept. 27, 1931; d. Paul Madison and Ruby Leigh (Coggins) Stephens; m. Sherwood H. Batchelor, Nov. 1, 1952; children: Paula S. Liggon, G. Brooks. Diploma, Wilson Sch. Nursing, 1953; student, Atlantic Christian Coll. Cert. med./surg. nurse. Assessment nurse Wilson (N.C.) Meml. Hosp., head nurse pediatrics, primary care nurse ob./gyn. unit, primary care nurse med./surg. unit, primary care nurse psychiat. unit, 1991-93, ret., 1993; organizer Al-A-Non, Wilson, N.C., 1973. Deacon Westview Christian Ch., 1995, 96, 97. cjmn. membership com., 1996. Mem. N.C. Nurse's Assn. (past dist. pres.), Am. Nurses' Assn. Home: 1300 Dogwood Ln NW Wilson NC 27896-1420

BATCHO, DONNA M., trade association executive; b. Hackensack, N.J., Feb. 12, 1956; d. Edward S. and Anna (Koroly) B. BA, Ramapo Coll. N.J., 1982; MPA, Columbia U., 1993. Sec. UN, N.Y.C., 1975-78; outreach worker Cmty. Action, Littleton, N.H., 1982-84; spl. projects coord. UN Environ. Program, N.Y.C., 1988-89; exec. asst. Ford Found., N.Y.C., 1989-95; exec. dir. N.E. Organic Farming Assn.-N.J., Pennington, 1995—; sustainable agr. cons. Czech and Slovak Ministries of Agr., 1990-95. Convenor sustainable agr. U.S. Citizen's Network on UN Commn. on Environment and Devel., N.Y.C., 1990-92; UN nongovt. orgn. working group rep. Internat. Fedn. of Organic Agrl. Movements, 1990—. Grantee German Marshall Fund, Slovak Republic, 1991, Rockefeller Bros. Fund, Czech and Slovak Republics, 1991, Trust for Mutual Understanding, Slovak Republic, 1994. Office: NOFA-NJ 33 Titus Mill Rd Pennington NJ 08534

BATEMAN, IRIS HENDRIX, merchandise coordinator; b. Greer, S.C., Oct. 6, 1940; d. Walter Lee and Rosa Bell (Quinn) Hendrix; m. Robert B. Bateman, May 20, 1961. Diploma in bus., Doughn's Bus. Coll., 1959; cert. in bus., Greenville Tech., 1961. Sec. Springs Industries, Lyman, S.C., 1958-90, from sec. to merch. coord., 1990—. Bapt. Women's dir. Greer Bapt. Assn. Named Woman of Yr., Am. Bus. Woman, 1980, Heritage World, 1981. Mem. NAFE, Am. Bus. Women's Assn. (sec. inner circle 1975, v.p. 1976), Nat. Notary Assn., Greer Jaycettes (sec. 1970, pres. 1971). Home: 9 Cottage Ln Taylors SC 29687-5827 Office: Springs Industries Pacific St Lyman SC 29365-1707

BATEMAN, JEAN BUDINGTON, writer, poet, home furnishings consultant; b. Springfield, Mass., Oct. 24, 1923; d. Harold Fairchild and Josephine Elizabeth (Eckel) Budington; m. John Travis Lisenby Jr., Nov. 9, 1944 (div. Aug. 1961); children: Jo, John Travis III; m. E. Wallace Bateman, Mar. 11, 1967 (dec.). Student, Syracuse U., 1941-45. Supr., textile designer M. Lowenstein, N.Y.C., 1961-67; color coord. Celanese Corp., N.Y.C., 1967-68; outside saleswoman Jens Risom Design, N.Y.C., 1968-70, Jack Lenor Larsen, N.Y.C., 1970-78, Design Solution, Phoenix, 1985-89; sales rep. Judy Wilson & Assocs., Phoenix, 1989-91; owner, rep. Jean Bateman Assocs., Phoenix, 1991-94; home furnishings cons. Phoenix, 1994—. Author: (poetry) Healing Legacies, 1996; contbr. poetry to Nat. Libr. Poetry, Latino Stuff Rev., Ilian Press (hon. mention 1996). Fellow Internat. Furnishings and Design Assn. (pres. Ariz. chpt. 1986-87, chmn. Nat. Ednl. Found. 1993). Home and Office: 16621 N 34th Ave Phoenix AZ 85023

BATEMAN, SHARON LOUISE, public relations executive; b. St. Louis, Oct. 18, 1949; d. Frank Hamilton and Charlotte Elizabeth (Hogan) B. Student, Drury Coll., 1967-69; BJ, U. Mo., 1971. Asst. dir. pub. relations Cardinal Glennon Hosp. for Children, St. Louis, 1971-76; staff asst. pub. relations Ozark Air Lines, St. Louis, 1976-80; mgr. corp. relations Kellwood Co., St. Louis, 1980-83; mgr. corp. communications May Dept. Stores Co., St. Louis, 1983-86, dir. corp. communications, 1986-94; mgr. comm. Arthur Andersen, St. Louis, 1995 . Bd. dirs. St. Michael's Houses, 1996—. Recipient Best Regional Airline Employee Publ. award Editor's Assn. Am. Transp. Assn., 1978. Mem. Internat. Assn. Bus. Communications (pres. St. Louis chpt. 1977), Pub. Rels. Soc. Am. (sec. St. Louis chpt. 1983, bd. dirs. 1988-90, v.p. 1991). Republican. Office: 1010 Market St Saint Louis MO 63101

BATES, BARBARA J. NEUNER, retired municipal official; b. Mt. Vernon, N.Y., Apr. 8, 1927; d. John Joseph William and Elsie May (Flint) Neuner; m. Herman Martin Bates, Jr., Mar. 25, 1950; children: Roberta Jean Bates Jamin, Herman Martin III, Jon Neuner. BA, Barnard Coll., 1947. Confidential clk. to supr. Town of Ossining, N.Y., 1960-63, receiver of taxes, 1971-90; ret.; pres. BNB Assocs., Briarcliff Manor, N.Y., 1963-83, Upper Nyack Realty Co., Inc., Briarcliff Manor, 1966-71. V.p. Ossining (N.Y.) Young Rep. Club, 1958; pres. Young Womens Rep. Club Westchester County (N.Y.), 1959-61; regional committeewoman N.Y. State Assn. Young Rep. Clubs, 1960-62; mem. Westchester County Rep. Com., 1963-95; mem. Ossining Women's Rep. Club, 1960-92, pres., 1984-85; mem. Westchester County Women's Rep. Club, 1957-92. Mem. DAR, Jr. League Westchester-on-Hudson, Receivers Taxes Assn. Westchester County (legis. liaison, v.p., pres. 1984-85), Hackley Sch. Mothers Assn. (pres. 1968), R.I. Hist. Soc., Ossining Hist. Soc., Westchester County Hist. Soc., Briarcliff-Scarborough Hist. Soc., Ossining Woman's Club. Congregationalist. Home: 78 Holbrook Ln Briarcliff Manor NY 10510-1122 also: 663 Reynolds Rd Chepachet RI 02814-1629

BATES, BETH (MARY E. BATES), lawyer; b. Savannah, Tenn., June 25, 1957; d. J.B. and Billie (Price) Stricklin; m. Glenn Richard Bates, Mar. 29, 1986; 1 child, Virginia Elizabeth. BS, Miss. U. for Women, 1979; JD, U. Tenn., 1982. Bar: Tenn. 1982. Law clk. to Judge Mark Walker Ct. Criminal Appeals, Covington, Tenn., 1982-83; assoc. Law Offices of Dwight Hawkes, Humboldt, Tenn., 1983-87; atty. West Tenn. Legal Svcs., Inc., Jackson, Tenn., 1987—, also bd. dirs. Author: History of Cherry's Chapel Church, 1983 (dist. 3rd place 1983). Mem. ABA, Ten. Bar Assn., Tenn. Lawyers' Assn. for Women, Cir. VII United Meth. Women (pres. 1995—), Lawyers Assn. for Women (sec. 1994), Tenn. Bus. and Profl. Women (area coord. 1993-94, regional dir. 1995-96), Jackson Bus. and Profl. Women (sec. 1989-90, 2d v.p. 1990-91, 1st v.p. 1991-92, pres. 1992-93, Young Careerist 1990). Democrat. Methodist. Home: 221 Campbell St Jackson TN 38301 Office: West Tenn Legal Svcs Inc 210 W Main Jackson TN 38302

BATES, BEVERLY JOYCE, retired educator and computer professional; b. San Francisco, Sept. 5, 1930; d. Ezra John Hughes and Lois Ruth (Barr) Bates; m. Truman Winfield Massee, Sept. 8, 1953 (div. Mar. 1978); children: Rebecca Lynn and Rachel Dorian (twins), Daniel L. BS in Home Econs., Oreg. State U., 1952; postgrad., Idaho State U., 1965-66; AA in Interior Design, Cañada Coll., 1982; computer cert., Caňada Coll., 1985. Tchr., substitute tchr. Sch. Dist. 411, Twin Falls, Idaho, 1965-70; rancher Jerome, Idaho, 1970-78; interior designer Menlo Park, Calif., 1978-83; bookkeeper Redwood City, Calif., 1980-85; computer specialist Stanford Linear Accelerator Ctr., Menlo Park, 1985-89; ret., 1989. Author: Gertrude's Story, 1995; designer, creator Tawanka Indian crafts. Vol. Eugene (Oreg.) Free Network, 1996. Mem. Oreg. Geneal. Soc. Democrat.

BATES, CAROL ANN, education educator; b. Jackson, Mich., Dec. 9, 1948; d. George Wallace and Nedra Lorraine (O'Neil) Wilcox; m. Dallas Kelvin Bates, June 19, 1971; 1 child, Caleb Allan. AA, Jackson C.C., 1969; BS in Elem. Edn. and Spl. Edn., U. Idaho, 1973; MA, Columbia U., 1990. Resource rm. spl. edn. tchr. Elem. Sch.-West Park, Moscow, Idaho, 1974-75; spl. edn. tchr. co-op presch. Copper Country Intermediate Sch. Dist., Hancock, Mich., 1976-77, spl. edn. tchr., 1977-90; prof. learning disabilities program Suomi Coll., Hancock, 1990—, dir. acad. computing, 1991—; bd. dirs. Oak House, Inc., Hancock; bd. dirs. Copper Country Workshop, Inc., Hancock, 1991-92, pres. bd., 1992-94. Mem. Coun. for Exceptional Children, Mich. Assn. Distance Learning, Learning Disabilities Assn., Internat. Soc. for Tech. in Edn., Mich. Assn. for Computer Users in Learning, Assn. for Retarded Citizens, Alpha Delta Kappa. Office: Suomi Coll 601 Quincy St Hancock MI 49930-1832

BATES, KATHY, actress; b. Memphis, June 28, 1948. BFA, So. Meth. U., 1969. Film appearances include Taking Off, 1971, Straight Time, Come Back to the Five and Dime, Jimmy Dean, Jimmy Dean, Summer Heat, Arthur 2: On the Rocks, Signs of Life, High Stakes, Men Don't Leave, Dick Tracy, White Palace, Misery (Acad. award for Best Actress 1990, Golden Globe award), At Play in the Fields of the Lord, 1991, The Road to Mecca, Prelude to a Kiss, Fried Green Tomatoes (Golden Globe nomination, BAFTA nomination), Used People, A Home of Our Own, North, Curse of the Starving Class, Dolores Claiborne, 1994; stage appearances include Vanities, 1976, Semmelweiss, Crimes of the Heart, The Art of Dining, Goodbye Fidel, 1980, Chocolate Cake and Final Placement, 1981, 5th of July, Come Back to the 5 & Dime, Jimmy Dean, Jimmy Dean, 'night, Mother, 1983 (Tony nomination, Outer Critics Circle award), Two Masters: The Rain of Terror, 1985, Curse of the Starving Class, Frankie and Johnny in the Clair de Lune (OBIE award 1988), The Road to Mecca; TV appearances include (series) The Love Boat, St. Elsewhere, Cagney & Lacey, L.A. Law, China Beach, (miniseries) Murder Ordained, (movies of the week) Johnny Bull, No Place Like Home, Roe vs. Wade, Hostages, The Stand; dir. Talking With, PBS Great Performances. Office: Susan Smith & Assocs 121 N San Vicente Blvd Beverly Hills CA 90211-2303*

BATES, LURA WHEELER, trade association executive; b. Inboden, Ark., Aug. 28, 1932; d. Carl Clifton and Hester Ray (Pace) Wheeler; m. Allen Carl Bates, Sept. 12, 1954; 1 child, Carla Allene. BSBA, U. Ark., 1954. Cert. constrn. assoc. Sec.-bookkeeper, then officer mgr. Assoc. Gen. Contractors Miss., Inc., Jackson, 1958-77, dir. adminstrv. svcs., 1977—, asst. exec. dir., 1980—; owner, Ditty Bag Supply Co., 1987—; adminstr. Miss. Constrn. Found., 1977—; sec. AIA-Assoc. Gen. Contractors Liaisonship Coms., 1977—; sec. Carpenters Joint Apprenticeship Coms., Jackson and Vicksburg, 1977—. Sec. Marshall Elem. Sch. PTA, Jackson, 1962-64, v.p., 1965; sec.-treas. Inter-Club Coun. Jackson, 1963-64; tchr. adult Sunday sch. dept. Hillcrest Bapt. Ch., Jackson, 1975-82; dir. Bapt. Women WMU, 1987—, sec., 1992—; tchr. adult Sunday sch. dept. 1st Bapt. Ch., Crystal Springs, Miss., 1989—; mem. exec. com. Jackson Christian Bus. and Profl. Women's Coun., 1976-80, sec., 1978-79, pres., 1979-80. Named Outstanding Woman in Constrn. Miss., 1962-63, Outstanding Mem. Nat. Assn. Women in Constrn. Fellow Internat. Platform Assn.; mem. AAUW, NAFE, Nat. Assn. Women in Constrn. (life, chpt. pres. 1963-64, 76-77, 92-93, nat. v.p. 1965-66, 77-78, nat. dir. Region 5, 1967-68, nat. sec. 1970-71, 71-72, pres. 1980-81, coord. cert. constrn. assoc. program 1973-78, 83-84 guardian-contr. Edn. Found. 1981-82, chmn. nat. bylaws com. 1982-83, 85-88, nat. parliamentarian 1983-92), Nat. Assn. Parliamentarians, U. Ark. Alumni Assn. (life, pres. ctrl. Miss. chpt. 1992-93, 93-94, 94-95), Delta Delta Delta. Editor NAWIC Image, 1968-69, Procedures Manual, 1965-66, Public Relations Handbook, 1967-68, Profl. Edn. Guide, 1972-73, Guidelines & Procedures Handbook, 1987-88; author digests in field. Home: 1007 Lee Ave Crystal Springs MS 39059-2546 Office: 2093 Lakeland Dr Jackson MS 39216-5010

BATES, MARGARET HABECKER, secondary education educator; b. Seattle, June 23, 1951; d. Jack Norman and Catherine Lenard (Hamilton) Bigford; m. Thomas Benjamin Habecker, Mar. 30, 1985 (div.); m. Jerry L. Bates, Apr. 1, 1992. BA in Anthropology, Ctrl. Wash. U., 1973; MA in Anthropology and Demography, U. Ill., 1977. Cert. tchr., Wash.; nat. cert. in early adolescent lang. arts Nat. Bd. Profl. Tchg. Stds. Teaching fellow U. Ill., Urbana, 1975-76; with theme reader program Kent (Wash.) Sch. Dist., 1977-81; tchr. Ridgefield (Wash.) Sch. Dist., 1981-92, Vancouver (Wash.) Sch. Dist., 1992—; curriculum cons., Vancouver, 1991—; mem. sci. cadre Vancouver Sch. Dist., 1992—; field test candidate Nat. Bd. for Profl. Teaching Standards, Detroit, 1993—; student tchr. mentor E.S.D. # 112, Vancouver, 1988-91. Mem. steering com. Sci. Math. Advancement Reachout for Tchrs., Vancouver, 1992—; active Citizens for Schs., Ridgefield, 1985-91, Shumway Site Coun., co-chair, 1992—; active Shumway Bldg. Leadership Team, 1992-93, Middle Sch. Vision Task Force, 1993-94. Rsch. fellow NSF, 1993, Harvard Sch. Edn., 1992, Nat. Endowment for Humanities, 1990-91, 84. Mem. Ridgefield Edn. Assn. (pres.-elect, pres.), Wash. Edn. Assn. (chair PAC), S.W. Wash. FOund. (Clark County Tchr. of Yr. 1990). Episcopalian. Office: Discovery Mid Sch 800 W 40th St Vancouver WA 98663

BATES, MARGARET HELENA, special education educator; b. Irvington, N.J., Jan. 27, 1943; d. Marcel Bogstahl and Helena Christina (Yarosczynsky) Bogstahl; divorced; children: Robert Crew, Diane Carlyle. BA, Coll. Steubenville, 1966; MS, St. Cloud State U., 1982. Cert. tchr. English, spl. edn., emotionally/behaviorally disorders and learning disabilities, Minn. Tchr. Ind. Sch. Dist. # 742, St. Cloud, 1976—. Adv. bd. Minn. Acad. Excellence Found., St. Paul., 1993-94; state coun. chair Minn. Edn. Assn., 1993—; co-chair. St. Cloud Edn. Assn., 1979-84; sec. Audubon Soc., 1992—; historian Stearns County Theatrical Co., 1992, 93, 94; bd. dirs. The New Tradition Theatre Co., 1988-89. Grantee Bremer Found., 1991, incentive grantee Ind. Sch. Dist. 742. Mem. Coun. for Exceptional Children, Minn. Coun. Children with Behavior Disorders, Minn. Educators of Children with Emotional Disorders, Delta Kappa Gamma (1st v.p. 1994—). Home: 825 17th Ave S Saint Cloud MN 56301-5234 Office: Area Learning Ctr 809 12th St N Saint Cloud MN 56303-2847

BATES, MARGARET LEWIS, communications executive; b. Seattle, Jan. 13, 1942; d. David Arthur and Anne L. (Karns) Lewis; divorced; 1 child, David Charles Bates. BA in English, U. Wash., 1964; MA in Comm., Columbia U., 1977, EdM in Comm., 1979, EdD in Comm., 1981. H.S. tchr. Washington and, Mass., 1964-73; instr. Columbia U. Tchrs. Coll., N.Y.C., 1978, adminstr., 1979; lectr. NYU, N.Y.C., 1982; scriptwriter, interactive designer Exhibit Tech., Inc., N.Y.C., 1982-83; dir. tng. and edn. Videodisc Pub. Inc., N.Y.C., 1983-88, v.p., 1989; v.p. Humanware/Citibank, N.Y.C., 1989-91; dir. prodn. Downtown Digital/AT&T, N.Y.C., 1991-95, dir. new bus. devel., 1995—; adj. prof. Marymount Manhattan Coll., 1978-83, NYU, 1987—; cons., instr. Hunter Coll., 1986-87; mem. adv. bd. Morgan Evan and Co., N.Y.C., 1996; spkr. and panelist in field. Prodr. (16mm film) David Wagoner: My Ways to Go, 1970, (video disc) The Helga Pictures, 1988 (Bronze award). Mem. Internat. Interactive Comm. Soc., N.Y. New Media Assn. (program com. 1995-96). Home: 106 Morningside Dr #93 New York NY 10027 Office: Downtown Digital 32 Avenue of Americas New York NY 10013

BATES, RAMONA LEE, plastic surgeon; b. Ft. Leonard Wood, Mo., July 29, 1957; d. Theo Steve Bates and Theda Ann (Keathley) Sowell; m. Brett S. Herndon, Oct. 6, 1990. BA in Physics with high honors, U. Ark., 1978; MD, U. Ark., Little Rock, 1982. Flexible internship Earl K. Long Hosp., Baton Rouge, La., 1982-83; gen. surgery resident Ohio Valley Med. Ctr., Wheeling, W.Va., 1983-86; gen. practice Calico Rock (Ark.) Med. Ctr., 1986; head and neck fellow Mercy Hosp., Pitts., 1987; plastic surgery resident Boston U. Hosp., 1987-89; hand surgery fellow Ark. Hand Surgery, Little Rock, 1989-90; pvt. practice plastic surgery Little Rock, 1990—; presenter in field. Fellow ACS (assoc.); mem. AMA, Ark. Med. Soc., Ark. Plastic Surgeons, Ark. Hand Club, Physicians for Human Rights, Pulaski County Humane Soc., Am. Quilt Study Group, Am. Quilters Soc., Ark. Quilter's Guild, Phi Beta Kappa, Mortar Bd. Office: Ste 701 500 S University Little Rock AR 72205

BATES STOKLOSA, EVELYNNE (EVE BATES STOKLOSA), educational consultant, educator; b. Camden, N.J., Mar. 13, 1946; d. Linwood T. and Eve Mary (Widzenas) Bates; m. Leslie E. Stoklosa, Apr. 15, 1968; children: Phillip J., Kristine L. BS in Home Econs. Edn., Buffalo State U Coll., 1968, MS in Home Econs. Edn., 1971, Cert. Advanced Studies, 1994. Cert. sch. dist. adminstr. Tchr. Parkside Elem. Sch., Kenmore, N.Y., 1968-69, Kenmore West High Sch., 1968-71, 73-75, Kenmore Jr. High Sch., 1977-80, Ken-Ton Continuing Edn., Kenmore, 1980-87, Kenmore Mid. Sch., 1981—; owner, pres. EBS Decors, Tonawanda, N.Y., 1986-87; edn. cons. Villa Maria Coll., Buffalo, N.Y., 1980—, adv. bd. interior design dept., 1980—; facilitator student of the month award program Kenmore Mid. Sch., 1982—, active mem. sch. planning team, 1984—, facilitator design team, 1990-93; participant Buffalo Summit, 1994. Editor parent informational pamphlet, 1992, faculty informational newsletter, 1992-94. Erie County Nutrition Assn. grantee. Mem. AAUW (bd. dirs. 1992-94), ASCD, Am. Vocat. Assn., Am. Fedn. Tchrs., N.Y. State Home Econs. Tchrs. Assn. (Tchr. of Yr. 1992-93, Most Outstanding Leadership and Creativity award 1987), N.Y. State United Tchrs., Western N.Y. Women in Adminstrn., Kenmore Tchrs. Assn. (bldg. rep.), Phi Delta Kappa, Phi Upsilon Omicron. Home: 165 Greentree Rd Tonawanda NY 14150-6409 Office: Kenmore-Town of Tonawanda 1500 Colvin Blvd Kenmore NY 14223-1118

BATORSKI, JUDITH ANN, art association administrator; b. Eden, N.Y., Oct. 8, 1949; d. John Michael and Ethel (Owens) B.; m. Michael J. Rocco (div. Oct. 1980); 1 child, Flora. Student retail mgmt., Colo. Springs Coll. Bus., 1981; AS in Fine Arts, Suffolk Community Coll., 1983; BA, SUNY, Stonybrook, 1985, MA, 1987; postgrad., Columbia Coll. Chgo. Film Sch., 1985. Caretaker, asst. mgr. Farmer's Shared Home, Danbury, N.H., 1979-80; cert. educator Assn. for Childbirth at Home, Internat., L.A., 1980; accts. payable clk. Pikes Peak Community Coll., Colorado Springs, Colo., 1981-82; office mgr. Three Village Meals-on-Wheels, Stonybrook, 1984; grad. sec. art dept. SUNY, 1986-87, art gallery intern Fine Arts Ctr., 1987; dir. ops., dir. master classes and free concerts Islip Arts Coun., East Islip, N.Y., 1987-89; cons. N.Y. State Coun. on the Arts, N.Y.C., 1989—; participant Arts in Bus. Mgmt. seminar Citibank/ABC, N.Y.C., 1987, cmty. leaders luncheon Fox Channel 5, N.Y.C., 1987; asst. to dir. Newsday's L.I. Summer Arts Festival Cmty. Affairs Dept., 1989, Suffolk County Motion Picture and TV Commn., Hauppauge, N.Y., 1988, 89, 90—, Summer Film Festival, 1988-90; cons. N.Y. State Coun. Arts, 1989-90, cons., 1990-91; interior decorator Trans-Designs, 1992; ind. contractor KM-Matol Corp, Que., Can., 1993; intern Nat. Inst. Inner Healing, Rich in Mercy Inst. Photographs included in Photography Forum's Coll. Photography Ann., 1985. Campaign dir. Food for Poland, Colorado Springs, 1982; organizer Granite State Alliance, Portsmouth, N.H., 1979, Safe 'n' Sound anti-nuclear campaign, Shoreham, N.Y., 1979; grad. rep. Sch. Continuing Edn. SUNY Stonybrook, judicial com. on acad. standing, SUNY Stonybrook, 1986-87; vol. Vietnam Vets. Theatre Ensemble, 1988, New Community Cinema, Huntington, N.Y., 1988; active exec. com. Dowling Coll. Spring Tribute Concert, Oakdale, N.Y., 1989; asst. to dir. Newsday Community Rels. Dept. L.I. Arts 89, 1989; founding mem. com. corr. L.I. Green Party, Brookhaven Twp., 1990—; participant Life in the Spirit seminar Cath. Charismatic Renewal, N.Y., 1992; tchr. Our Lady of Mt. Carmel Ch., N.Y., 1991—; active Pastoral Coun., 1992—. Mem. Internat. Platform Soc., Contemporary Hispanic Artists of L.I. (advisor to bd. dirs. Ctrl. Islip 1988-89). Roman Catholic. Home: 40-74 W 4th St Patchogue NY 11772

BATT, ALYSE SCHWARTZ, programmer, analyst; b. Bronx, N.Y., Aug. 8, 1960; d. Irwin Aaron and Beryl (Leff) Schwartz; m. David Charles Batt, Feb. 14, 1993; children: Shannon Paige, Megan Brooke. AAS, SUNY, Farmingdale, 1980; BBA, Hofstra U., 1987; MS in Mgmt. Engring., Long Island U., 1995. Programmer trainee State Ins. Fund, N.Y.C., 1980; programmer analyst cons. Bradford Nat. Corp., N.Y.C., 1981-83; programmer E.F. Hutton, N.Y.C., 1983; programmer analyst Chase Manhattan Bank, N.Y.C., 1983-87; sr. systems analyst Met. Life Ins. Co., N.Y.C., 1987-89; sr. programmer analyst Orion Pictures Corp., N.Y.C., 1989-91, Chase Manhattan Bank, N.Y.C., 1991—. Mem. Bayshore Skating Club, Commack Skating Club, Massapequa Road Runners Club, N.Y. Road Runners Club, Plainview-Old Bethpage Road Runners Club, Ladies Aux. Massapequa Fire Dept. Republican. Jewish. Home: 153 Massachusetts Ave Massapequa NY 11758-4111

BATTAGLINI, LINDA JACKSON, strategic planner; b. Bridgeport, Conn., May 18, 1950; d. James Richard and Jean Eleanor (Power) Jackson; m. Richard Anthony Battaglini Jr., May 30, 1971 (div. May 1992); children: Cara Lillian, Adam Richard. AAS, Broome Community Coll., Binghamton, N.Y., 1969; BA in Maths., SUNY, Binghamton, 1971, MS in Acctg., 1977. Staff acct. Wilson Hosp., Johnson City, N.Y., 1977-78, mgr. gen. acctg., 1978-79, planner, 1979-81; planner United Health Svcs., Binghamton, 1981-84, dir. planning, 1984-86, corp. planner, 1986-94; sr. strategis planning cons. The Burlington (Mass.) Group, 1994-96; prin. Battaglini Consulting, Burlington, 1996—. Bd. dirs. Planned Parenthood, Binghamton, 1989-91, SUNY Binghamton Found., 1989-94; treas. local polit. campaign, 1985. John A. Hartford Found. N.Y.C. grantee, 1982-83, 1993-96. Mem. Health Care Forum, Healthcare Fin. Mgmt. Assn., Futurist Soc., The Planning Forum, SUNY Binghamton Alumni Assn. (treas. 1983-85, v.p. 1986-87, pres. 1987-91, past pres. 1991-95). Unitarian Universalist. Office: 1111 Arboretum Way Burlington MA 01803

BATTEN, JANE KIMBERLY, Olympic athlete; b. McRae, Ga., Mar. 29, 1969. Winner 2d place NCAA 400 meter hurdles, 1990, 3rd place 400 meter hurdles, 1991, 1st place 400 meter hurdles Mobil/USA Championships, 1991, 5th place World Championships, 1991, 4th place, 1992, Silver medal 400 meter hurdles Atlanta Olympics, 1996. Office: c/o USA Track & Field PO Box 120 Indianapolis IN 46206*

BATTILLO, KATHRYN, director foundation relations; b. Boston, Sept. 22, 1952; d. Robert W. and Mary (Mulkern) Lent; m. Thomas Alan Battillo, Dec. 15, 1977; 1 child, Michael. BS, Bridgewater State Coll., 1976; MLS, Simmons Coll., 1979. Libr. Plymouth (Mass.) Pub. Libr., 1976-80; assoc. dir. Simmons Coll., Boston, 1980-85, U. Vt., Burlington, 1985-87; dir. alumni ann. fund Babson Coll., Wellesley, Mass., 1987-90; dir. grad. alumni MIT, Cambridge, Mass., 1990-95, assoc. dir. found. rels., 1995—; adj. faculty Lesley Coll., Cambridge, 1995-96. Contbr. articles to profl. jours. Mem. ASAE, CASA (various positions). Democrat. Roman Catholic. Office: MIT 77 Mass Ave 10-277 Cambridge MA 02139

BATTLE, LUCY TROXELL (MRS. J. A. BATTLE), retired middle school dean; b. Bridgeport, Ala., June 28, 1916; d. John Price and Emily Florence (Williams) Troxell; student U. Ala., Montevallo, 1934-35; B.S. Fla. So. Coll., 1951; postgrad. U. Fla., 1954, Fla. State U., 1963, Oxford (Eng.) U., 1979, 80, 81; M.A., U. South Fla., 1970; m. Jean Allen Battle, Aug. 25, 1940; 1 dau., Helen Carol. Asst. postmaster, Bridgeport, Ala., 1936-40; asst. dir. personnel office Sebring (Fla.) AFB, 1942-44; tchr. Cleveland Court Sch., Lakeland, Fla., also Forest Hill Sch., Carrollwood Sch., Tampa, Fla., 1949-64; dean of girls Greco Jr. High Sch., Tampa, 1964-68. Bd. dirs. Tampa Oral Sch. for Deaf. Recipient Outstanding Service award Fla. So. Coll. Woman's Club, 1942. Mem. NEA, Am. Childhood Edn. Internat., AAUW, Delta Kappa Gamma, Kappa Delta Pi, Phi Mu. Methodist. Club: Carrollwood Village Golf and Tennis. Author: (with J.A. Battle) The New Idea in Education, 1968. Home and Office: 11011 Carrollwood Dr Tampa FL 33618-3905

BATTLE, ROMONA ANITA, educational administrator, consultant; b. N.Y.C., Dec. 31, 1950; d. Conley Napoleon and Annie Laurie (Simmons) B.; 1 child, Dinah Cianci Washington. BA in History and Secondary Edn., Morris Brown Coll., 1973; MEd in Elem. Edn., Ala. State U., 1976, cert. edn. specialist in elem. edn., 1985. Cert. in adminstrn. and supervision, Ga. History tchr. Waycross (Ga.) H.S., 1974-75; 4th grade tchr. Crawford St. Elem. Sch., Waycross, 1976-80, 5th grade tchr., 1981-84; k-5 lead tchr. McDonald St. Elem. Sch., Waycross, 1984-88; 7th grade lang. arts tchr. Charles T. Walker Magnet Sch., Augusta, Ga., 1989; asst. prin. Willis Foreman Elem. Sch., Augusta, 1989-92; lead tchr., counselor Mcdonald Street Elem. Sch., Waycross, 1992-93; child serve coord., cons. GLR5/Okefenokee RESA, Waycross, 1993—; participant Gov.'s Sch. Leadership Inst., Ga. Edn. Leadership Acad., Atlanta, 1993-94. Developer instnl. game, 1981. Mem. Family & Children Svcs. Adoption Adv. Bd., Waycross, 1987. Mem. Phi Delta Kappa, Inc. (Delta Zeta chpt., chair Teach-A-Rama 1984-86, chair human rights and edn. com. 1988-89, chair asst.-youth guidance program 1986-87, Achievement in Edn. award 1983-84, 85-86, 88-89, Nat. Citation 1984-85). Home: 1204 Riverside Ave Waycross GA 31501-6349

BATTLES, ROXY EDITH, novelist, consultant, educator; b. Spokane, Wash., Mar. 29, 1921; d. Rosco Jirah and Lucile Zilpha (Jacques) Baker; m. Willis Ralph Dawe Battles, May 2, 1941; children: Margaret Battles Holmes, Ralph, Lara. AA, Bakersfield (Calif.) Coll., 1940; BA, Calif. State U., Long Beach, 1959; MA, Pepperdine U., 1976. Cert. tchr. English, adult basic edn. and elem. edn., Calif. Free-lance writer 50 nat. and regional mags., 1940—; tchr. elem. Torrance (Calif.) Unified Schs., 1959-85; tchr. adult edn. Pepperdine U., Torrance, 1969-79, 88-89; free-lance children's author, 1966—; mystery novelist Pinnacle Publs., N.Y.C., 1980; with Tex. A&M U., 1988; instr. Mary Mount Coll., Harbor Coll., 1995; author-in-residence Young Authors Festival, Am. Sch. Madrid, 1991; lectr. in field. Author: Over the Rickety Fence, 1967, The Terrible Trick of Treat, 1970, 501 Balloons Sail East, 1971, The Terrible Terrier, 1972, One to Teeter-Totter, 1973, 2d edit., 1975, Eddie Couldn't Find the Elephants, 1974, repints, 1982, 84, 88, What Does the Rooster Say, Yoshio?, 1978, The Secret of Castle Drai, 1980, The Witch on Room 6, 1987, 3d edit., 1989 (nominee Garden State, Nene, and Hoosier awards), The Chemistry of Whispering Caves, 1988. Active So. Calif. Coun. on Lit. for Children and Young People, 1973-80, 87—. Recipient Commendation UN, 1979; Hoosier award nominee, 1990; Garden State award nominee, 1990, Nene award nominee, 1992, 93. Mem. S.W. Manuscripters (founder), Surfwriters. Home: 560 S Helberta Ave Redondo Beach CA 90277-4353

BATTS, BARBARA A., obstetrician and gynecologist; b. St. Louis, Nov. 19, 1951; d. Robert H. and Betty L. (Mauer) B. BA, Stanford U., 1974; MD, St. Louis U., 1978. Diplomate Am. Bd. Ob/Gyn. Residency in ob/gyn. U. Kans., Kans. City, 1978-82; pvt. practice Kans. City, Mo., 1982—; asst. clin. prof. U. Kans. Med. Ctr., Kans. City, 1982—; chmn. dept. ob/gyn. St. Joseph's Health Ctr., Kans. City, Mo., 1995—, mem. exec. com.; adv. bd. Centerpoint. Fellow Am. Coll. Ob/Gyn.; mem. AMA, ACLU (contbg. mem.), Amnesty Internat. (contbg. mem.), Mo. State Med. Soc., Met. Med. Soc., Kans. City Gynecological Soc. (organizer seminars). Office: Assocs in Ob/Gyn Ltd 1010 Carodelet # 328 Kansas City MO 64114

BATTS, DEBORAH A., judge; b. Phila., Apr. 13, 1947; d. James Alexander Emmanuel, Jr. and Ruth Violet (Silas) Batts; 2 children. BA, Radcliffe Coll., 1969; JD, Harvard U., 1972. Summer atty. Foley, Hoag & Eliot, Boston, Mass., 1970, Kaye, Scholer, Fierman, Hays & Handler, N.Y.C., 1971; law clerk to Hon. Lawrence W. Pierce U.S. Dist. Ct. (so. dist.) N.Y., N.Y.C., 1972-73; assoc. atty. Cravath, Swaine & Moore, N.Y.C., 1973-79; asst. U.S. atty. criminal divsn. U.S. Dist. Ct. (so. dist.) N.Y., N.Y.C., 1979-84; assoc. prof. law Fordham U., 1984-94, adj. prof. law, 1994—; spl. assoc. counsel dept. investigation N.Y.C., 1990-91; commr. law revision com. State of N.Y., 1990-94; judge U.S. Dist. Ct. (so. dist.) N.Y., N.Y.C., 1994—; Bd. trustees Cathedral Sch., N.Y.C., 1990—; mem. faculty Corp. Counsel Trial Advocacy Program, 1988-94. Contbr. articles to legal jours. Trustee Spence Sch., 1987-95. Mem. Second Cir. Fed. Bar Coun., Assn. Bar. City N.Y. (lesbians and gay men in the profession 1991-95), Lesbian and Gay Law Assn. Greater N.Y., Met. Black Bar Assn. Office: US Courthouse 500 Pearl St Rm 2510 New York NY 10007

BATY, PEGGY JUNE, museum administrator; b. San Diego, Apr. 2, 1956; d. Thomas Russell and Margaret June (Czykoski) Cox; m. Bruce W. Baty, Mar. 22, 1980. BS, MS, Mid. Tenn. State U., 1980; PhD, U. Tenn., 1985. Chmn. dept. aviation Ga. State U., Atlanta, 1985-86; dir. Ctr. Excellence for Aviation and Space Edn., Embry-Riddle Aero. U., Daytona Beach, Fla., 1986-88; dean acad. support Embry-Riddle Aero. U., Prescott, Ariz., 1988-90; assoc. v.p., acad. dean Parks Coll. St. Louis U., Cakokia, Ill., 1990—; mem. cons. staff Nat. Congress on Aviation and Space Edn., Maxwell, Ala., 1986—. Contbg. author: Emergency Management Handbook, 1991; contbr. articles on avication edn., women in aviation and air disasters to profl. jours. Recipient nat. championship award for excellence in aviation edn. FAA, 1989. Mem. Univ. Aviation Assn. (trustee 1988-91, pres. 1992-93), Exptl. Aircraft Assn. (bd. dirs. found. 1991-96), Coun. Aviation Accreditation, Women in Aviation Internat. (pres., founder). Home: 101 Maple #F Dayton OH 45459 Office: Internat Women's Air and Space Mus One Chamber Plz Ste A Dayton OH 45402

BAUER, BARBARA ANN, marketing consultant; b. Fairfield, Ohio, Dec. 4, 1944; d. Charles P. and Grace J. (Peteka) B.; m. Joseph J. Strojnowski. AA, So. Sem. Jr. Coll., Buena Vista, Va., 1964; BA, Am. U., 1966. Pub. relations, advt. specialist Sta. WOR-AM-FM-TV, N.Y.C., 1966-67; pub. relations mgr. Continental Corp., N.Y.C., 1967-68; dir. corp. communications Am. Internat. Group, N.Y.C., 1968-80; dir. mktg. mgmt. infos. CIGNA Corp., Phila., N.Y.C., 1980-83; asst. v.p. Citicorp Credit Services Inc., N.Y.C., 1983-87; v.p., dir. mktg. Skandia Am. Group, N.Y.C., 1987-88, v.p. corp. communications, 1988-89; pres. Bauer Mktg. and Communications, Goshen, N.Y., 1989—. Lifetime mem. Girl Scouts U.S. Mem. Pub. Relations Soc. Am. (accredited, counselors' acad.), Women Execs. Pub. Relations (dir. 1986—), Assn. Ind. Reins. Cons., Assn. Profl Ins. Women (chair pub. rels., advisor bd. dirs.).

BAUER, BARBARA GAE, literary executive; b. Bklyn., Sept. 1, 1948; d. James Vincent and Gaetanina Antoinette (Palumbo) Mangano; m. Clinton Bonaventure Bauer, 1975 (div. 1994); children: Guy, Lucy. BA, Hunter Coll., 1970; MA, St. John's U., 1971, PhD, 1979. Pres., founder Barbara Bauer Lit. Agy., Matawan, N.J., 1984—. Mem. jazz vocal group Nuage. Spkr. 125th Birthday Luncheon, Hunter Coll., N.Y.C., 1995. Democrat. Roman Catholic. Office: Barbara Bauer Lit Agy 179 Washington Ave Matawan NJ 07747-2944

BAUER, BETH E., insurance appeals manager; b. Terre Haute, Ind., May 4, 1960. BSBA, St. Mary of the Woods Coll., 1982. Unit mgr. Reuben H. Donnelley Corp., Terre Haute, Ind., 1983-87; directory processing mgr. Reuben H. Donnelley Corp., Terre Haute, 1987-93, mgr. composition support, 1993-95; appeals mgr. AdminaStar Fed., Indpls., 1995—. Mem. Inst. of Mgmt. Accts., Indpls. Zool. Soc., Alumnae Assn. of St. Mary of the Woods Coll. Office: AdminaStar Fed 8115 Knue Rd Indianapolis IN 46250

BAUER, DEBORAH SCHLUTER, psychotherapist; b. Ames, Iowa, Nov. 15, 1968; d. Gerald Emil and Carolyn Jean (Finnell) Schluter; m. Keith Alan Bauer, July 17, 1993. BS, Mary Washington Coll., 1991; MSW, Va. Commonwealth U., 1993. Lic. clin. social worker, Tenn. Psychotherapist Turtle Creek (Pa.) Valley Mental Health/Mental Retardation, 1993-95, Child and Family Svcs., Inc., Knoxville, Tenn., 1995-96, Family Practice Assocs., Madisonville, Tenn., 1996—. Vol. disaster relief com. Turtle Creek Mental Health/Mental Retardation, 1994-95; vol. advocate Rappahannock Area Coun. Against Sexual Assault, Fredericksburg, Va., 1990-91. Minnie Rob Phaup scholar Mary Washington Coll., 1990. Mem. NASW, Phi Beta Kappa. Lutheran. Home: 546 Hiwassee Rd Madisonville TN 37354

BAUER, ELAINE LOUISE, ballet dancer; b. Indpls., July 18, 1949; d. Thomas Bryant and Elenita Mae (Bodwell) B.; m. D. David Brown, June 5, 1971. BA in Dance magna cum laude, Butler U., 1971, DFA (hon.), 1989. Registered fine arts craft artist. Mem. corps. de Ballet Boston Ballet Co., 1971; soloist Boston Ballet Co., Boston, 1972, principal ballerina, 1974-89; ret., 1989; ballet mistress Boston Ballet Co., 1990—; artistic dir. Boston Ballet Sch.'s Children's Summer Workshop, 1986-90. Starred (with Rudolf Nureyev in) N.Y.C. debut of La Sylphide., 1980. Com. mem. Task Force on Future of Butler U. Fine Arts Coll., Indpls., 1986; co-organizer Glasnost Dance Medicine Conf., 1990; mem. bd. visitors Walnut Hill Sch. Fine Arts, 1991—, Butler U. Fine Arts Sch., 1996—. Recipient Alumni Achievement award, Butler U., 1987, Eliot Norton award for lifetime achievement in dance Boston Theater Dist. Orgn., 1990; named to North Cen. High Sch. Alumni Hall of Fame, 1991. Office: Boston Ballet 19 Clarendon St Boston MA 02116-6107

BAUER, ELIZABETH KELLEY (MRS. FREDERICK WILLIAM BAUER), consulting energy economist; b. Berkeley, Calif., Aug. 7, 1920; d. Leslie Constant and Elizabeth Jeanette (Worley) Kelley; A.B., U. Calif. at Berkeley, 1941, M.A., 1943; Ph.D. (fellow), Columbia U., 1947; m. Frederick William Bauer, July 5, 1944; children: Elizabeth Katherine Bauer Keenan, Frederick Nicholas. Instr. U.S. history and studies Barnard Coll., N.Y.C., 1944-45; lectr. history U. Calif. at Berkeley, 1949-50, 56-57; rsch. asst. Giannini Found., 1946-49, asst. rsch. agrl. economist, 1957-60; exec. sec. Internat. Conf. on Agrl. and Coop. Credit, U. Calif. at Berkeley, 1952-53, exec. sec. South Asia Project, 1955-56; registrar Holy Names Coll., Oakland, Calif., 1971-72; rsch. assoc. Brookings Instn. and Nat. Acad. Pub. Adminstrn., Washington, 1973; fgn. affairs officer Internat. Energy Affairs, Fed. Energy Adminstrn. Washington, 1974-77; fgn. affairs officer Office of Current Reporting, Internat. Affairs, Dept. Energy, Washington, 1977-81; dir. policy analysis and evaluation Nat. Coal Assn., Washington, 1981-83. Mem. Calif. Com. to Revise the Tchrs. Credential, 1961; trustee Grad. Theol. Union, Berkeley, 1972-74; bd. dirs. St. Paul's Towers and Episcopal Homes Found, Oakland, 1971-72. Recipient Superior Achievement award Dept. Energy, 1980; U. Calif. Alumni citation, 1983, 93. Mem. AAUW (Calif. chmn. for higher edn. 1960-62), Prytanean Honor Soc., AAAS, P.E.O., Mortar Bd., Phi Beta Kappa, Pi Lambda Theta, Sigma Kappa Alpha, Phi Alpha Theta, Pi Sigma Alpha. Democrat. Episcopalian. Author: Commentaries on the Constitution, 1790-1860, 1952; (with Murray R. Benedict) Farm Surpluses: U.S Burden or World Asset?, 1960; (with Florence Noyce Wertz) The Graduate Theological Union, 1970. Co-author, editor: The Role of Foreign Governments in the Energy Industries, 1977. Home: 708 Montclair Dr Santa Rosa CA 95409-2822

BAUER, JEAN MARIE, accountant; b. Morristown, N.J., Sept. 10, 1958; d. Earl F. and Patricia A. (O'Brien) W.; m. Ronald F. Bauer, Sr. AA in Acctg., County Coll. of Morris, 1978; BSBA, Coll. of St. Elizabeth, Convent Station, N.J., 1986. Sec. to payroll supr. Monroe Calculator, Morris Plains, N.J., 1979-80; clk. typist Stewart Title, Morris Plains, 1980-81; with BASF Corp., Mount Olive, N.J., 1981—; credit rep. chems. div. BASF Corp., Parsippany, N.J., 1986-88; property acct. II BASF Corp., Mount Olive, N.J., 1988—. Co-leader folk group Sacred Heart Ch. of Dover, N.J., 1981, adult leader youth group, 1982, eucharistic minister, 1986-93; eucharistic minister, vol., religious edn. chr. St. Jude Ch., Budd Lake, N.J., 1993; spl. dep. registrar boro Mountain Lakes, N.J., 1976. Named one of Outstanding Young Women in Am., U.S. Jaycees, 1985. Mem. Cath. Daughters Am. (treas. Dover chpt. 1987-89, regent 1989-91). Republican. Home: 18 Indian Ln Hackettstown NJ 07840-2608 Office: BASF Corp Property Acctg 3000 Continental Dr N Budd Lake NJ 07828

BAUER, JUDY MARIE, minister; b. South Bend, Ind., Aug. 24, 1947; d. Ernest Camiel and Marjorie Ann (Williams) Derho; m. Gary Dwane Bauer, Apr. 28, 1966; children: Christine Ann, Steven Dwane. Ordained to ministry Christian Ch., 1979. Sec. adminstrv. asst. Bethel Christian Ctr., Riverside, Calif., 1975-79; founder, pres. Kingdom Advancement Ministry, San Diego, 1979—, trainer, mgr. cons., Tex., Ariz., Calif., Oreg., Washington, Ala., Okla., Idaho and Republic of South Africa, Guam, Egypt, The Philippines, Australia, Can., Mozambique, Malarwie, Mex., Zimbabwe, Poland, Guatemala, Israel, Scotland, Ireland, Japan, Eng., Zambia, Botheswana, Holland, 1979—; pres. Witty Outerwear Distbrs. Internat., Inc., 1993-96 ; founder, co-pastor Bernardo Christian Ctr., San Diego, 1981-91; evangelism dir. Bethel Christian Ctr., 1978-81, undershepherd minister, 1975-79, adult tchr., 1973-81; pres., founder Bethel Christian Ctr. of Rancho Bernardo, Calif., 1991—; condr. leadership tng. clinics, internat. speaker, lectr. in field. Author syllabus, booklet, tng. material packets. Pres., Bernardo Christian Ctr., San Diego, 1981-91. Mem. Internat. Conv. Faith Ministries, Inc. (area bd. dirs. 1983-88).

BAUER, KAREN MARY, accountant, consultant; b. Balt., Nov. 25, 1956; d. Bernard Thomas and Mary Szmajda Sporney; m. Michael Joseph Bauer, Aug. 29, 1987; children: John Henry, Anna Marie. BA, Loyola Coll., 1978; MS, U. Balt., 1983; exec. internat. bus. cert., Georgetown U., 1994. CPA, Md. Corp. sec. Allied Rsch. Corp., Vienna, Va., 1991—, chief acctg. officer, 1994—; prin., sec.-treas. Anchor Loan Co., Ltd., Balt., 1992—; sec.-treas. ARC Svcs., Inc., Vienna, 1993—; prin., pres. Ark Roofing & Sheet Metal, Inc., Gaithersburg, Md., 1994—. Mem. AICPA, Md. Assn. CPAs, Am. Soc. Corp. Secs. Home: 17818 Stoneridge Dr Gaithersburg MD 20878-1020 Office: Allied Rsch Corp 8000 Towers Crescent Dr Ste 750 Vienna VA 22182-2700

BAUER, KATHARINE PERKINS, lawyer, environmental analyst; b. Portland, Oreg., Mar. 14, 1949; d. Norris Humphrey II and Katharine (Heath) Perkins; m. J. Mark Bauer, May 29, 1971; children: Jacob, Ian M., Liesl M. BA in English, U. Oreg., 1971; BA in Med. Tech., Sacred Heart Gen. Hosp., Eugene, Oreg., 1971; M Environ. Studies, Evergreen State Coll., Olympia, Wash., 1986; JD cum laude, U. Puget Sound, 1992. Bar: Wash. 1993. Med. technologist, Portland, 1971-73; mem. rsch. staff VA Hosp., Portland, 1973-75, ARC Blood Bank, Portland, 1974; environ. analyst, lobbyist Wash. Environ. Coun., Seattle, 1986-90, bd. dirs., v.p. for liaison, mem. exec. com., 1987-89; rsch. asst. U. Puget Sound Sch. Law, Tacoma, 1991-93; rsch. analyst, clk. Office Wash. State Atty. Gen., Olympia, 1991-92; ind. contractor Lane Powell Spears Lubersky, Olympia, 1992-93; ptnr. Meeks Morgan Bauer, PLLC, Olympia, 1994—; lectr. CLE, U. Puget Sound/Seattle U. Sch. Law, 1994, mem. adj. faculty law clinic, 1994-95. Asst. editor Internat. Aspects Environ. Edn., 1986; columnist Sr. News, Ret. Tchrs. Assn., 1994—. Active Thurston Mason County Med. Aux., 1979—, chmn. Thurston-Mason Counties organ donation campaign, 1982; vol. tchr. Pioneer Elem. Sch., 1980-91, Lincoln Grade Sch., 1983-87; coach Olympia Youth Soccer Club, 1985—, pres., 1987-89; subcom. co-chmn. long range planning North Thurston Ground Water Adv. Com., 1987-89; mem. McNeil Island rev. panel Wash. Dept. Corrections, 1988; mem. Centennial Clear Water Fund adv. com. Wash. Dept. Ecology, 1987-88, mem. tech. subcom. on global warming 2010 Commn., 1989; mem. project evaluation com. Wash. Dept. Natural Resources, 1987, mem. aquatic lands enhancement account adv. com., 1989; mem. subcoms. land use and transp. transp. goals, steering com. Wash. Dept. Transp., 1988-89; mem. Olympia Planning Commn., 1988-89. Mem. Wash. State Bar Assn. (gift and estate tax com. 1994-96, program chair ethics com. CLE), Thurston County Bar Assn. (South Puget Sound estate planning coun. 1993-96), LWV, Am. Soc. Clin. Pathologists, N.W. Assn. for Environ. Studies. Office: 1235 4th Ave E Ste 200 Olympia WA 98506

BAUER, LYN, special education educator; b. June 25, 1953; d. George Joseph and Madeline Helen (Jacobs) B.; children: Peter, Tip (dec. 1993), Emily, Kate. BS in Edn., Psychology, SUNY, New Paltz, 1989, MS in Spl. Edn./Correctional Edn., 1990. Spl. edn. tchr. Ulster County BOCES, N.Y. Vice-chair Town of Shawangunk Dem. Club, 1990—; mem. Dem. Nat. Com., 1991—; vice-chair Town of Shawangunk Dem. Com., 1992—; del. 3d Jud. Dist., 1992—; legislator Ulster County, 1992-93, 96—; treas. com. to Elect Judge Mary Work, 1990, 94; mem. Hist. Soc. Shawangunk and Gardiner, LWV, Mohonk Preserve, NOW, Phillies Bridge Farm Project, Stewart Park and Res. Coalition, Ulster Arts Alliance, Ulster County Mental Health Assn., Ulster County YWCA, Ulster Performing Arts Ctr., Wallkill Valley Rail Trail; bd. dirs. So. Ulster adv. coun. Am. Heart Assn. Democrat. Home: 1201 Rt 208 Wallkill NY 12589

BAUER, MARION DANE, writer; b. Oglesby, Ill., Nov. 20, 1938; d. Chester and Elsie (Hempstead) Dane; m. Ronald C. Bauer, June 25, 1959 (div. Dec. 1988); children: Peter Dane, Elisabeth Alison. AA, LaSalle-Peru-Oglesby Jr. Coll., 1958; student, U. Mo., 1958-59; BA in Lang. Arts, U. Okla., 1961, postgrad., 1961-62. Author: Shelter from the Wind, 1976 (Notable Children's Book ALA, 1976), Foster Child (Golden Kite Honor Book award Soc. Children's Book Writers 1977), Tangled Butterfly, 1980, Rain of Fire, 1983 (Tchrs.' Choices award Nat. Coun. Tchrs. of English 1984, Revs. Choice award ALA Booklist 1983, Children's Book award Jane Addams Peace Assn. 1984), Like Mother, Like Daughter, 1985, On My Honor, 1986 (Newbery Honor Book 1987, Notable Children's Book ALA 1986, Best Books of 1986 Sch. Libr. Jour., Editors' Choice Booklist 1986, Pub.'s Weekly Choice The Yr.'s Best Books 1986, Flicker Tale Children's Book award, N.D., 1989, Golden Archer award, Wis. 1989, William Allen White Children's Book award, Kans., 1989, BBY, IRA selection for Janusc Korczak Lit. Competition Poland 1990), Touch the Moon, 1987, A Dream of Queens and Castles, 1990; (drama) God's Tears: A Woman's Journey, Face to Face, 1991 (Children's Book of Distinction, Hungry Mind Review, 1992), What's Your Story? A Young Person's Guide to Writing Fiction, 1992 (Notable Children's Book ALA 1992), Ghost Eye, 1992, A Taste of Smoke,

1993, A Question of Trust, 1994; editor: Am I Blue? Coming Out from the Silence, 1994, When I Go Camping With Grandma, 1995, A Writer's Story, From Life to Fiction, 1995, Alison's Wings, 1996, Our Stories, A Fiction Workshop for Young Authors, 1996; contbr. articles, short stories to mags. and books in field. Mem. Authors Guild, Authors League Am., Soc. Children's Book Writers and Illustrators. Democrat. Home: 8861 Basswood Rd Eden Prairie MN 55344-7407 Office: Clarion 215 Park Ave S New York NY 10003-1603

BAUGH, VANESSA SOLOMON, elementary and middle school counselor; b. New Kensington, Pa., Mar. 29, 1953; d. Albert Joseph and Rosemont G. (Thomas) Solomon; m. Richard A. Baugh, June 25, 1978; children: Maria Elaine, Timothy Allen. BA in Sociology, Pa. State U., 1975, MEd in Counselor Edn., 1976. Cert. ednl. specialist. Elem. and mid. sch. counselor Pa.-Trafford Sch. Dist., Harrison City, Pa., 1976—; leader in small group and elem. counseling activities emphasizing self-esteem, decision-making, responsibility and coping skills; sponsor Trafford Mid. Sch. Student Coun., 1991-96, sponsor student yearbook, 1984—. Mem. adv. panel: (books) Child Abuse and Neglect, 1984, Counseling and Guidance in the Schools, 1992. Explorer post leader Boy Scouts Am., 1989—; mem. Penn-Trafford Drug and Alcohol Prevention Coun., 1993; past chair Penn-Trafford Chem. People Task Force, 1982. Recipient Status Achievement award Westmoreland County Federated Women's Club, 1995. Mem. NEA (mem. adv. panel publs.), Pa. State Edn. Assn., Pa-Trafford Edn. Assn., Westmoreland Sch. Counselors Assn. (v.p., program chair 1993-95, corr. sec. 1991-93, pres. 1995—). Home: 708 Scott St Penn PA 15675-9709 Office: Trafford Schs 100 Brinton Ave Trafford PA 15085-1034

BAUGHMAN, JENNIFER JANE, automotive executive; b. Youngstown, Ohio, Dec. 14, 1967; d. Gail William and Mary Linda (McCoy) B. B Bus./Mgmt., Temple U., 1990, MBA, 1994. Tng. mgr. environ. scis. Marriott Corp., Phila., 1990-94; zone mgr. Ford Motor Co., Detroit, 1994—. Mem. NAFE, Temple Owl Club, Pi Sigma Epsilon. Presbyterian. Home: 5040 Heather Dr Dearborn MI 48126-2878

BAUGHMAN, LEONORA KNOBLOCK, lawyer; b. Bad Axe, Mich., Mar. 21, 1956; d. Lewie L. and Jannette A. (Krajenka) K.; m. Jene W. Baughman, Dec. 5, 1981; children: Wesley J. and Adrianne J. Student, Cen. Mich. U., 1973-75; AB, U. Mich., 1977; JD, U. Notre Dame, 1981. Bar: Mich. 1981, U.S. Dist. Ct. (ea. dist.) Mich. 1982. Assoc. Foster, Swift, Collins & Coey, P.C., Lansing, Mich., 1981-86; staff atty. Chrysler Fin. Corp., Troy, Mich., 1987—. Mem. ABA, Mich. Bar Assn., Nat. Assn. Women Lawyers, Am. Bankruptcy Inst., State Bar Mich. (sec. bus. law sect., speaker 4th ann. comml. law seminar). Office: Chrysler Financial Corp 27777 Franklin Rd Southfield MI 48034

BAUKNECHT, BARBARA BELLE, educator; b. Gleason, Wis., Apr. 21, 1933; d. William John and Jessie Marie (Fox) Beyer; m. Ross Eugene Bauknecht, Aug. 11, 1956; children: JoDee Ann Moran, Shelley Marie Courter, Wanda Jean Pace, Todd Randall. Tchr. cert., Lincoln County Normal, Merrill, Wis., 1953; BS, U. Wis., Stevens Point, 1964, M, 1974. Lic. tchr. grades 1-8, reading tchr. K-12, reading specialist K-12. Tchr. grades 5 and 6 Crandon, Wis., 1953-57; tchr. grades 7 and 8 Elcho, Wis., 1957-59; pub. libr. Three Lakes, Wis., 1963-66; tchr. Title 1, reading tchr. Three Lakes, 1966-74, tchr., reading specialist, 1974—; retired, 1995; tchr., founder Story Hour - Presch. Program, Three Lakes and Sugar Camp, Wis., 1964—; reading coord. Three Lakes Sch. Dist., Three Lakes and Sugar Camp, 1978—; tchr. grades 4, 5, 6, 7, 8 Sch. Dist., Crandon and Elcho, Wis., 1957-59; mem., chmn. Read Com. Three Lakes Dist., 1978—. Co-founder Ecumenical Vaction Bible Sch., 1978—; chmn. bd. Ed U. Demmer Meml. Libr., Three Lakes, 1989—; Sunday sch. supt. Union Congl. Ch., Three Lakes, 1977—, moderator, 1988—; local organizer, leader Campfire Girls, 1970-75. Recipient Ind. Celebrate Lit. award Headwaters Reading Coun., Rhinelander, Wis., 1990; Kohl Scholarship/Fellowhip CESA Dist. Winner, 1992. Congregationalist. Mem. Ch. of Christ. Home: 6653 Schoenfeldt Rd Three Lakes WI 54562-9703 Office: Sch Dist Three Lakes PO Box 280 Three Lakes WI 54562-0280

BAUM, CAROL GROSSMAN, physician; b. N.Y.C., June 14, 1958; d. Jacob Joseph and Anita Pearl (Serbrinsky) Grossman; m. Michael Seth Baum, June 16, 1985; 1 child, Daniel Joseph. BS, CCNY, 1979; MD, NYU, 1983. Diplomate Nat. Bd. Med. Examiners, Am. Bd. Internal Medicine, Am. Bd. Allergy & Immunology. Resident in internal medicine St. Luke's Hosp., N.Y.C., 1983-86; fellow in allergy & clin. immunology Cornell U. Med. Coll., N.Y.C., 1986-88; pvt. practice internal medicine, allergy-clin. immunology N.Y.C., 1988-90; asst. attending allergy clinic N.Y. Hosp., N.Y.C., 1988—; dir. allergy clinic St. Luke's Hosp., N.Y.C., 1989-90, William F. Ryan Community Health Ctr., 1990; dir. dept. allergy and clin. immunology N.E. Permanente Med. Group, White Plains, N.Y., Stamford, Conn., 1990—; clin. instr. medicine, Cornell U. Med. Coll., N.Y.C.; asst. attending N.Y. Hosp., White Plains Hosp. Ctr., St. Agnes Hosp.; lectr., presenter in field. Contbr. articles to profl. jours. Fellow ACP, Am. Acad. Allergy, Asthma and Immunology; mem. AMA, Am. Med. Women's Assn., Westchester Med. Soc., N.Y. Acad. Scis., Am. Coll. Physician Execs., Phi Beta Kappa, Sigma Xi. Office: N E Permanente Med Group 210 Westchester Ave White Plains NY 10604-2914 also: NE Permanente Med Group 1266 E Main St Stamford CT 06901

BAUM, CYNTHIA DENISE, artist; b. York, S.C., Feb. 6, 1965; d. James Nelson Bechtler and Janet Arleen (Bechtler) Stoud; m. Geoffrey Carlton Baum Jr.; children: Geoffrey Carlton III, Jason. Cert. completion, Art Instrn. Sch., 1992. Exhbns. include Art Instrn. Sch. Gallery, 1990, La. Art and Artist Guild Gallery, 1991, 13th Ann. Lesbian and Gay Pride Parade and Festival, Long Beach, 1996. Home: 2220 E Whittier Blvd La Habra CA 90631

BAUM, ELEANOR, electrical engineering educator, academic administrator; b. Poland, Feb. 10, 1940; came to U.S., 1942; d. Sol and Anna (Berkman) Kushel; m. Paul Martin Baum, Sept. 2, 1962; children: Elizabeth, Jennifer. B.S.E.E., CUNY, 1959; M.E.E., Poly Inst. N.Y., 1961, Ph.D., 1964; DS (hon.), Union Coll., 1993, Notre Dame, 1995. Engr. Sperry Gyroscope Co., N.Y.C., 1960-61; instr. Poly. Inst. N.Y., N.Y.C., 1961-64; asst. prof. elec. engring. Pratt Inst., N.Y.C., 1964-67, assoc. prof., 1967-71, prof., chmn. dept. elec. engring., 1971-84, dean Sch. Engring., 1984-87; dean Sch. Engring., Cooper Union for Advancement Sci. and Art, N.Y.C., 1987—; exec. dir. Cooper Union Rsch. Found., N.Y.C., 1987—; cons. engring. to various corps.; accreditation visitor Accreditation Bd. Engring. and Tech., 1983—, bd. dirs., fellow, 1994; organizer career confs. for careers in engring., careers for women, N.Y.C., 1970—; chair bd. examiners Grad. Record Exam., 1984-90; bd. dirs. Alleghany Powers Systems, U.S. Trust Co., Avnet, Inc.; commr. Engring. Workforce Commn., 1990—; mem. engring. adv. bd. NSF, 1989-94; mem. adv. bd. Duke U., Rice U., U.S. Mcht. Marine Acad., 1992—; mem. U.S./Japan Engring. Edn. Task Force, 1994—. Contbr. tech. articles and articles on engring. careers and edn. to profl. jours. Recipient Disting. Alumnus award Poly. Inst. N.Y., 1986, Alumni Achievement award CCNY, 1986, Emily Warren Roebling award Womens' Hall of Fame, 1988, Achievement award Mich. State U., 1992, Outstanding Woman Scientist award, 1992 Assn. Women Sci. Fellow IEEE (Steinmetz award 1990), Soc. Women Engrs. (Upward Mobility award 1990, Achievement award engrs. joint com. L.I. 1995); mem. Am. Soc. Engring. Edn. (bd. dirs. 1989—, v.p. 1992-93, pres. 1995—, various nat. task forces), Nat. Engring. Deans Coun. (bd. dirs. 1987—, chair 1990-93), N.Y. Met. Deans Assn. (chmn. 1985-90), N.Y. Acad. Scis. (bd. govs. 1994—), Order of Engr. (bd. govs. 1985-92, competitiveness policy coun. subcom. critical techs. 1992—, nat. rsch. coun. bd. engring. edn. 1991-95), Eta Kappa Nu, Tau Beta Pi (Achievement award Mich. Tech. U. 1995). Office: Cooper Union Advancement Sci & Art Office of Dean 51 Astor Pl New York NY 10003-7139

BAUM, HENRIETTE, retired real estate manager; b. Rotterdam, The Netherlands, Apr. 13, 1906; came to U.S., 1939; d. Herman and Maria (Cohen) Hertzberger; m. Morton Baum (dec. Feb. 1968). Grad. h.s., Rotterdam. Mem. Secret Svc., 1941-43; real estate owner and mgr. N.Y., 1945-63; advisor artists and singers, 1950—. Bd. dirs. Harlem Sch. Arts, N.Y.C., Manhattan Sch. Music, N.Y.C., N.Y.C. Opera, N.Y.C. Ctr., numerous others. Mem. Santa Fe Opera (chmn. nat. bd. 1970—), Curtis Inst. Music (bd. dirs. 1995—), St. Louis Nat. Bd. Opera, Santa Fe Chamber Music Soc., Hunter Coll. Opera (pres.), East Hampton Music Festival.

BAUM, HOLLY, lawyer; b. N.Y.C., Aug. 25, 1956; d. Nathan and Bella (Raphael) B.; m. James W. Taylor; 1 child, Esther. BA, SUNY, Binghamton, 1978; MA, SUNY, Buffalo, 1984, JD cum laude, 1988. Bar: N.Y. 1989. Assoc. Hogdson, Russ, Andrews, Woods & Goodyear, Buffalo, 1988-92; spl. counsel Humphrey & Assocs., Buffalo, 1992-95; pvt. practice Buffalo, 1995—; instr. CEBS Program, Buffalo, 1993; mem. faculty Inst. for Tax Studies SUNY, Buffalo, 1992. Assoc. Buffalo Law Review, 1986-87. Pres. Lawyers for Choice, Buffalo, 1995—; bd. dirs. Precious Jewels Day Care Ctr., Buffalo, 1990—, treas., 1990-94; pres. El Museo Francisco Oller y Diego Rivera, Inc., Buffalo, 1994—. Recipient Cert. of Appreciation Women's Studies Coll., 1985, Herman Badillo Sch., 1996, award Adolf Homberger Law Alumni Assn., 1988; Sephardic Jewish Brotherhood of Am. meml. scholar, 1974-78. Mem. ABA, N.Y. Bar Assn., Erie County Bar Assn., N.Y. Women's Bar Assn. (Western N.Y. chpt., chair parental leave com. 1991-96, state dir. 1995-96, pres.-elect 1996-97, co-chair long range planning com. 1996—). Democrat. Jewish. Home: 62 Colonial Cir Buffalo NY 14213 Office: 120 Delaware Ave Ste 426 Buffalo NY 14202

BAUM, INGEBORG RUTH, librarian; b. Berlin, Sept. 20; d. Ella Koch; Oberlyceum (scholar), Kassel, Germany, 1926-33; postgrad. Georgetown U., 1963-70; m. Albert Baum, Feb. 16, 1938 (div. 1960); children: Harro Siegward, Helma Sigrun (Mrs. George Meadows). Came to U.S., 1951, naturalized, 1957. Export corr. Bitter-Polar, Germany, 1933-35, Henschel Locs, Germany, 1936; exec. sec. Fieseler Airplane Mfrs., Germany, 1936-38; interpreter, sec. UNRRA, Germany, 1946-48; payroll supr., civilian dept. U.S. Army, Wetzlar PX, Germany, 1948-51; asst. librarian Supreme Council, Ancient and Accepted Scottish Rite, Washington, 1951-70, librarian and museums curator, 1970—; appraiser rare books and documents; v.p. Merical Elec. Contractors, Inc., Forestville, Md., 1974-83. Mem. Am. Soc. Appraisers, Calligraphers Guild. Mem. Ch. Jesus Christ of Latter-day Saints. Free-lance contbr. to Pabelverlag, Rastatt, Germany, Harle, Ofcl. Publs., Inc., others. Avocations: travel, art. Home: 2480 16th St NW Apt 416 Washington DC 20009-6702 Office: 1733 16th St NW Washington DC 20009-3103

BAUM, SELMA, customer relations consultant; b. Bklyn., Jan. 15, 1924; d. Samuel and Tillie (Bayer) Goldman; m. Milton W. Baum, Jan. 19, 1947; children: Victor C., Cynthia Baum-Baicker. Student, NYU New Sch. for Social Rsch. Communications mgr. Sobel & Goldman, Inc., N.Y.C., 1941-48; pub. rels. cons., 1948-65; comparison shopper Gimbels, Valley Stream, N.Y., 1965-67, mgr. comparison shopping office N.Y. div., N.Y.C., 1967-75, dir. consumer affairs East div., 1975-84; dir. corp. customer rels. Saks Fifth Ave., N.Y.C., 1984-89; cons. customer rels., Palm Beach, Fla., 1989—; lectr., writer in field. Arbitrator Met. N.Y. Better Bus. Bur. Mem. NAFE, Am. Mgmt. Assn. (industry panelist), N.Y. & N.J. Retail Mchts. Coun. (v.p.), Women in Communication (award N.Y. chpt. 1984), Nat. Retail Mchts. Assn. (consumer affairs com.), Fashion Group, Am. Coun. on Consumer Interests, Soc. Consumer Affairs Profls. in Bus. (chpt. pres. 1981-82, nat. dir. 1983-86, bd. dir. Found. 1985-89; nat. treas., fin. chmn., v.p. 1986-87, award N.Y. chpt. 1983), Greater N.Y. WINS (regional affairs com.), Direct Mktg. Assn. (customer rels. count. 1987-88). Home and Office: 3460 S Ocean Blvd Apt 715 Palm Beach FL 33480-5944

BAUM, SUSAN JEAN, theatre, film and television professional; b. Miami, July 12, 1950; d. Frederick Gilbert and Irma Jean Baum. BA, U. Fla., Gainesville, 1972. Mem. staff Direct Theatre, N.Y.C., 1974-76, Children's Television Workshop, N.Y.C., 1976-77, Time-Life Films, N.Y.C., 1977-79, British Broadcasting Corp., N.Y.C., 1984—; mgr. Actors Connection, N.Y.C., 1990—, Actors Information Project, N.Y.C., 1985-89; mem. adv. bd. Cinewomen NY, N.Y.C., 1995. Actress: various films, TV commercials and theatre, 1975—; dir. Julius Caesar, 1995; co-writer: (with James Harter) Under the Stone, 1989, What Goes Around..., 1990, Buried Treasure, 1991, Heart of the Nation, 1992; bus. mgr. and prodn. office coord. The Middletown Film Project, 1979-82, Pumping Iron II: The Women, 1983-84, Eugene Smith: Through A Glass Darkly, 1989; asst. prodn. mgr.: 3-2-1-Contact Season II, 1984; rschr., editl. asst. Hometown, 1982, The Great Getty, 1985, Where is Nicaragua, 1987. Mem. SAG, AFTRA, Actor's Equity Assn., Am. Shakespeare Project., Rogue Repertory Co.

BAUMANN, CAROL EDLER, political science educator; b. Plymouth, Wis., Aug. 11, 1932; d. Clarence Henry and Beulah Hanetta (Weinhold) E.; m. Richard Joseph Baumann, Feb. 28, 1959; children: Dawn Carol, Wendy Katherine. BA in Internat. Rels., U. Wis., 1954; PhD in Internat. Rels., London Sch. Econs./Polit. Sci., 1957. Chmn. Internat. Rels. Major U. Wis., Milw., 1962-79; dep. asst. sec. Bur. of Intelligence and Rsch./Dept. of State, Washington, 1979-81; prof. U. Wis., Milw., 1972-95, dir. internat. studies and programs, 1982-88, emeritus, 1995—; dir. Inst. of World Affairs, Milw., 1964—. Author: Program Planning About World Affairs, 1991, The Diplomatic Kidnappings, 1973; editor: Europe in NATO: Deterrence, Defense, and Arms Control, 1987, Western Europe: What Path to Integration?, 1967. Active Gov.'s Commn. on the UN, 1964-79, 82-89; dem. candidate 9th Congl. Dist., 1968; mem. World Affairs Coun. of Milw., 1964-75. Named Marshall scholar, 1954-57; recipient Pub. Svc. Achievement award Common Cause in Wis., 1991. Mem. Atlantic Coun. of U.S. (edn. com., bd. dirs.), China Coun. of Asia Soc., Coun. on Fgn. Rels., Fgn. Policy Assn. (bd. dirs. 1990—, editl. adv. com. 1977-79, 82-88), Nat. Coun. World Affairs Orgns. (pres. 1977-79, bd. dirs. 1992-96), UN Assn. of USA (bd. dirs. 1977-79, 82-89), Soc. for Citizen Edn. in world Affairs (pres. 1977-79), Com. on Atlantic Studies, Internat. Studies Assn., Phi Kappa Phi, Phi Beta Kappa. Democrat. Lutheran. Home: W 6248 Lake Ellen Dr Cascade WI 53011 Office: U Wis Milw Inst of World Affairs PO Box 413 Milwaukee WI 53201

BAUMANN, PRISCILLA, medieval art history educator, researcher; b. Bklyn., May 12, 1937; d. William Ambrose and Julia Frances (Morris) Fitz Gerald; m. Roger-Henri Baumann, Jan. 28, 1961; children: Robert C., Philippe G., Caroline. BA in French Lit., Manhattanville Coll., 1958; MA in French Lit., Middlebury Coll., 1959; MSLS, Peabody Libr. Sch., 1960; PhD in Medieval Studies, Boston U., 1992. Reference libr. N.Y. Pub. Libr., N.Y.C., 1960-61; vis. lectr. Tufts U., Medford, Mass., 1989-90; instr. medieval art history Radcliffe Seminars, Radcliffe Coll., Cambridge, Mass., 1990—, coord., lectr. Seminars Study Tour, 1995; docent, lectr. Fogg Art Mus., Harvard U., 1982—; lectr. Mediterranean cruise Harvard U. Alumni Assn., 1994. Contbr. articles to profl. jours. Fulbright scholar, Paris, 1958-59. Mem. Coll. Art Assn., Medieval Acad., Am. Soc. Ch. History, Soc. Medieval and Renaissance Philosophy, Internat. Ctr. Medieval Art. Home: 26 Everett Ave Winchester MA 01890

BAUMEL, JOAN PATRICIA FRENCH, educator, writer, lecturer; b. Winona, Minn., Mar. 12, 1930; d. William Oswald and Gertrude Marie (Fitzgerald) French; m. Herbert Baumel, July 11, 1971. Student, l'Ecole du Louvre, France, 1950-51; student with high honors, Inst. Phonétique Sorbonne, Paris, 1950-51; BA magna cum laude, Douglass Coll., 1952; postgrad., U. Detroit, 1952-55, Case Western Reserve U., 1960, U. Akron, 1962, U. Notre Dame, 1963, Manhattanville Coll., 1971; MA in French, Rutgers U., 1965; PhD in Modern Langs., Fordham U., 1985. Tchr. French lang. and culture, elem. and coll. levels various schs. including Mother House of Religious of the Sacred Heart, Kenwood, Albany, N.Y., Ohio, Mich., 1955-66; tchr. French White Plains (N.Y.) Pub. High Sch., 1966-86; curricula creator Akron (Ohio) Pub. Schs., 1962-63; co-dir. Baumel Assocs., Yonkers, N.Y., 1984—, Concerts and Lectures with Herbert Baumel, 1991—, Words and Music Programs with Herbert Baumel, 1991—, Waverly Heights, Gladwyne, Pa., 1993-95, Workmen's Circle Lodge, Sylvan Lake, N.Y., 1994, Thomas Paine/Huguenot Hist. Soc., New Rochelle, N.Y., 1995—; lectr. French lang. and culture Yonkers (N.Y.) Pub. Libr., 1992, Greenburgh (N.Y.) Pub. Libr., 1992, anti-semitism CUNY Grad. Ctr., B'nai B'rith Internat. Mus., Washington, 1st Unitarian Soc., Westchester, N.Y., Rockland (NY.) Ctr. for Holocaust Studies, Unitarian Ch. of All Souls, N.Y.C., Temple Beth Israel, Port Washington, N.Y., Holocaust Resource Ctr. and Archives, Queensborough C.C., CUNY, 1991, Women's Am. ORT, Midchester Jewish Ctr., Yonkers, 1992, Ctrl. Queens YM & YWCA, N.Y.C., 1992. Author: Paul Claudel and the Jews: A Study in Ambivalence, 1985; lectr. topics include French Anti-Semitism; The Gallic Road to the Concentration Camp; Klaus Barbie and the Children of Izieu, numerous others. Mem. adv. bd. Mark Brent Dolinsky Meml. Found. Recipient Woodrow Wilson fellowship, 1958-59, Yearbook Dedication award White Plains (N.Y.) Pub. H.S., 1980. Mem. Am. Assn. Tchrs. French, Nat. Writers Union, White Plains Tchrs. Assn., N.Y. State Assn. Fgn. Lang. Tchrs., French Inst./Alliance Francaise, Alliance Francaise Westchester, Phi Beta Kappa. Home and Office: Baumel Assocs 86 Rosedale Rd Yonkers NY 10710-3033

BAUMGARDNER, BARBARA BORKE, publishing consultant; b. Harrisburg, Pa., Nov. 8, 1937; d. Otto Lockhart Borke and Margaretta Mildred (Feigley) Borke Traugh; m. E. Wayne Baumgardner, July 12, 1958; children: Brian Wayne, Bruce Edward. AB, Gettysburg (Pa.) Coll., 1959; MLA, Western Md. Coll., 1976, MEd, 1982. Cert. secondary tchr., Md. Sales promoter Scott, Foresman & Co., Chgo., 1959-60; tchr. Carroll County Pub. Schs., Westminster, Md., 1964-84; cons. McDougall, Littell & Co., Evanston, Ill., 1984-91; adj. prof. Western Md. Coll., Westminster, 1975. Mem. Savannah Symphony Women's Guild. Mem. AAUW, Women's Assn. Hilton Head, Mensa, Fed. Garden Clubs of Md., Phi Mu. Republican. Presbyterian. Home: 9 Man O War Hilton Head Island SC 29928-5248 also: 6635 Silver Lake Dr Park City UT 84060

BAUMGARTNER, EILEEN MARY, government official; b. St. Cloud, Minn.; d. Florian H. and Kathleen (Keefe) B.B.A., Coll. St. Catherine, St. Paul, 1964; M.P.A., U. Minn., Mpls., 1970. Tchr., U.S. Peace Corps, Ethiopia, 1964-66; researcher N.Y. Med. Coll., N.Y.C., 1967-68, Minn. State Planning Agy., St. Paul, 1970-73; legis. analyst tax com. Minn. Ho. of Reps., St. Paul, 1973-78; legis. dir. to Congressman Sabo, U.S. Ho. of Reps., Washington, 1979-90, adminstrv. asst., 1991-93; chief staff Ho. Budget Com., 1993-94, minority staff dir. Ho. Budget Com., 1995—. Mem. Am. Soc. Pub. Adminstrn. Democrat. Roman Catholic. Office: 222 O'Neil House Office Bldg Washington DC 20515

BAUMGARTNER, MARY S., graphic designer; b. St. Cloud, Minn., Dec. 12, 1957; d. Florian Herman and Kathleen (Keefe) B. BA in Studio Arts, U. Minn., Mpls., 1981; BFA in Graphic Design, Acad. Art Coll., San Francisco, 1987. Agrl. ext. agt. U.S. Peace Corps, Manticao, Misamis, Oriental, Philippines, 1982-84; computer artist Chartmasters, San Francisco, 1988-90; pres., owner MSB Design, San Francisco, 1990—. Recipient award Art Dirs. Club Gallery, N.Y.C., 1990. Mem. Internat. Interactive Comm. Soc., Computer Human Interaction.

BAUMOL, HILDA, management consultant; b. New Haven, Jan. 6, 1923; d. Aaron and Sophie (Horowitz) Missel; m. William J. Baumol, Dec. 27, 1941; children: Ellen, Daniel. BA, Hunter Coll., 1942. Exec. dir. Twentieth Century Fund Performing Arts Study, Princeton, N.J., 1960-64; cons. Mathematica, Princeton, N.J., 1965-72; pres. Consultants in Industry Econs., Princeton, N.J., 1972-90. Co-editor: Inflation and the Performing Arts, 1984; contbr. chpts. to books, articles to profl. jours.

BAUNER, RUTH ELIZABETH, library administrator, reference librarian; b. Quincy, Ill.; d. John Carl and M. Irene (Nutt) B. BS in Edn., Western Ill. U., 1950; MS, U. Ill., 1956; postgrad., So. Ill. U., 1974, PhD, 1978. Asst. res. libr. Western Ill. U., Macomb, 1950; tchr., libr. Sandwich (Ill.) Twp. High Sch., 1950-54; circulation dept. asst. U. Ill. Libr., Urbana, 1955; asst. edn. libr. So. Ill. U., Carbondale, 1956-63, acting edn. libr., 1963-64, edn. and psychology libr., 1965-93, assoc. prof. curriculum and instrn. dept., 1971-93; coord. freshman yr. experience program, vis. assoc. prof. Coll. of Liberal Arts, Carbondale, 1994—; dir. Grad. Residence Ctr. Librs., So. Ill. U., 1973-79; cons. in field; subject matter expert Learning Resources Svc. Interactive Video, Carbondale, 1990-91, also scriptwriter. Co-author: The Teacher's Library, 1966; contbr. articles to profl. jours. Pres. alumni constituency bd. Coll. Edn., Carbondale, 1988-89; bd. dirs. So. Ill. U. chpt. UN, 1985-86, 94—; mem. Carbondale Bd. Ethics, 1989—. Recipient Luck Has Nothing To Do With It award Oryx Press, 1993. Mem. ALA, AAUP (v.p. So. Ill. U. chpt. 1972-73), AAUW (univ. rep. Carbondale br. 1988-89), Assn. Coll. and Rsch. Librs. (chmn. edn. and behavioral scis. sect. 1976-77, Most Active Mem. award 1968-93), Ill. Libr. Assn., Phi Delta Kappa, Phi Kappa Phi, Delta Kappa Gamma. Office: So Ill U Faner Hall 2427 Carbondale IL 62901-4522

BAUR, ISOLDE NACKE, translator, freelance writer, public speaker; b. Dresden, Saxonia, Germany, May 27, 1923; came to U.S., 1954; d. Otto Ernst and Anna Louise (Liebscher) Nacke; m. Karl Baur, Oct. 23, 1943 (dec. Oct. 1963); children: Ulrich, Marieluise Baur-Kailing. Student, Draughton's Bus. Coll., Dallas, 1964, U. Tex., Arlington, 1974. Milliner Cohn Co., Dresden, Fed. Republic Germany, 1937-39; drill press operator Zeiss-Ikon Corp., Dresden, 1939-41; engring. aid Messerschmitt Aircraft Corp., Augsburg, Fed. Republic Germany, 1941-43; blue print collaborator Ling-Temco-Vought Aerospace Corp., Dallas, 1963-64; office clk. Barnes Group Inc., Grand Prairie, Tex., 1964-69; freelance translator, writer, pub. speaker, 1969-71; manpower analyst Xerox Corp., Dallas and Ft. Worth, 1971-76; owner Baur Translation Svc., 1972—. Contbr. articles to jours. Mem. coun. German Day in Tex. Coun., Dallas, 1964—, awards chmn., 1978-88, hon. chmn., 1981; bd. dirs. Dallas Goethe Ctr., 1964-74, 2d v.p., membership chmn., 1970-72, 1st v.p./program chmn., 1973-75; sec. Unitarian Universalist Ch. Arlington, 1968-70; vol. guardian Tarrant County, Ft. Worth, 1988—; co-leader Girl Scouts Am., 1955-63. Mem. Soaring Soc. Am., Am. Translators Assn. (exec. com. conv. 1981), Tex. Soaring Assn. (hon. life, treas. 1964-66, sec. 1976-78, editor Spirals newsletter 1978-80), Acad. Flying Club U. Tech./Stuttgart (hon. sr.).

BAUTISTA, CAROL STONEY, electric power industry administrator; b. South El Monte, Calif., Nov. 3, 1949; d. Floyd Oakland and Madge V. (Roberts) Stoney; m. Ben Benito Makahanohano Bautista; children: Patty Kawohikukapulani, Oakland N. Kaululaau. AA, Rio Hondo Coll., 1969; BA, Calif. State U., L.A., 1977. Cert. ESL and adult edn. tchr., Calif. Various positions So. Calif. Edison Co., Rosemead, 1972-88, project administr., 1988—; seminar chairperson Women and Minority Bus. Enterprises, Rosemead; mem. adv. L.A. County Office of Emergency Mgmt., assistance to fire victims. Author feminist poetry and short stories; contbr. articles to profl. jours.; cartoonist and letterer newspapers and mags. Activist United Farmworkers Union, 1960's, 70's; local organizer Neighborhood Watch Program, 1982—; guest AM L.A. TV Program, 1988—, Channel 7 News, 1988—; instr. Coalition for Literacy, 1987; counselor Amnesty; instr. ESL Program, 1987; bd. dirs., mgr. Bobby Sox Softball, 1979-85; bd. dirs. Hui O'Hana Waialua, 1984—, Team USA Women's Softball, 1985; chair reunion com. Rosemead High Sch. Class 1967, 1986—; racewalker/marathoner L.A. Marathon, others, 1994—; mem. L.A. Roadrunners, 1994—, LAPD Policettes, 1994—, SCE/G.O. #3 Bible Study, 1994—, Rowland Heights Ch. of the Nazarene, 1993—. Recipient Women in Leadership award Calif. State Senate, Cmty. Svc. award Vietnam Vets. Vols., Mgmt. awards YWCA of L.A.. Mem. NAFE, NOW, Women's History Project, Edison Roundtable (steering com., com. chair). Democrat. Home: 2296 S Oldridge Dr Hacienda Hgts CA 91745-5637 Office: So Calif Edison Co PO Box 800 Rosemead CA 91770-0800

BAUTISTA-MYERS, LILIAN, writer, editor; b. San Diego; d. Jose Delos Angeles and Juanita (Perez) Bautista; m. Jimmy Clarence Brinkley, June 6, 1959 (div. 1964) 2 children; m. Donald Allen Myers, Oct. 28, 1966 (div. 1990); children: Sherri Lynn, Johnny Martin, David Allen. BA in English, Calif. State U., Northridge, 1970; MS in Edn., SUNY, Albany, 1972; EdD in Ednl. Adminstrn., Okla. State U., 1980. Adminstrv. officer, writer Capitol Hill Educator, Albany, 1972-73; asst. to dir., tech. editor/writer, coordinator grant and contract activities, contracts and grants mgmt. officer Okla. State U., 1973-79; co-owner/writer The Last Word, writing and graphic arts, Omaha, 1979-81; freelance writer, copywriter, editor, 1972—; speaker, fundraiser; coordinator grants mgmt. and devel. Met. Tech. C.C., Omaha, 1981-83; devel. officer Cath. Dept. Edn., Archdiocese of Omaha, 1984-85; exec. dir. Cooperating Hampton Rds. Orgns. for Minorities in Engring. CHROME, Inc., Norfolk, Va., 1985-90; dir. Ctr. Indsl. Engring. Tech., Conn. State U., 1990-91; dir. grants and contracts Coll. Edn. U. South Fla., Tampa, 1992—. Author, editor in field. Democrat. Home: 15401 Plantation Oaks Dr Tampa FL 33647-2161

BAUTZ, LAURA PATRICIA, astronomer; b. Washington, Sept. 3, 1940; d. Charles Kothe and Laura (Stauverman) B. BA in Physics, Vanderbilt U., 1961; PhD in Astronomy, U. Wis., Madison, 1967. From instr. to assoc.

prof. astronomy Northwestern U., Evanston, Ill., 1965-75; program dir. astronomy sect. NSF, Washington, 1972-73, sr. staff assoc. NSF, 1975-79, dep. dir. physics divsn., 1979-81, dir. astronomy divsn., 1982-90; vis. researcher Lawrence Berkeley Lab., 1990-92, dep. dir. physics divsn. NSF, 1992-93, internat. programs divsn., 1994—. Fellow AAAS; mem. Internat. Astron. Union, Am. Phys. Soc., Phi Beta Kappa. Home: 1325 18th St NW Apt 506 Washington DC 20036-6510 Office: 4201 Wilson Blvd Arlington VA 22230-0001

BAXTER, BETTY CARPENTER, educational administrator; b. Sherman, Tex., 1937; d. Granville E. and Elizabeth (Caston) Carpenter; m. Cash Baxter; children: Stephen Barrington, Catherine Elaine. AA in Music, Christian Coll., Columbia, Mo., 1957; MusB in Voice and Piano, So. Meth. U., Dallas, 1959; MA in Early Childhood Edn., Tchrs. Coll., Columbia, 1972, MEd, 1979, EdD, 1988. Tchr. Riverside Ch. Day Sch., N.Y.C., 1966-71; headmistress Episcopal Sch., N.Y.C., 1972-87, headmistress emeritus, 1987—; founding head Presbyn. Sch., Houston, 1988-94; dir. Chadwick Village Sch., Palos Verdes Peninsula, Calif. Author: The Relationship of Early Tested Intelligence on the WPPSI to Later Tested Aptitude on the SAT. Mem. ASCD, Nat. Assn. Episcopal Schs. (former gov. bd., editor Network publ.), Nat. Assn. Elem. Sch. Prins., Ind. Schs. Assn. Admissions Greater N.Y. (former exec. bd.), Nat. Assn. for Edn. of Young Children, L.A. Assn. Sch. Heads, Nat. Assn. Elem. Sch. Prins., Assn. Supervision and Curriculum Devel., Kappa Delta Pi, Delta Kappa Gamma. Republican. Presbyterian. Home and Office: 26800 S Acamedy Dr Palos Verdes Peninsula CA 90274

BAXTER, CARLA LOUISE CHANEY, insurance product specialist; b. Indpls., Nov. 4, 1955; d. Carlton S. and Jennie B. (Yates) Chaney; m. Andrew Louis Baxter, Sept. 20, 1980; 1 child, Andranise Louise. BA in Mktg., Ball State U., 1979. Lic. realtor, Ind.; CPCU (bd. dirs., instr. Ind. chpt.); cert. profl. ins. woman; assoc. risk mgmt.; assoc. mgmt. Zoning technician Dept. Met. Devel., Indpls., 1975; dir. mktg. Urban Tng. and Devel. Systems Inc., Indpls., 1979-80; casualty underwriter Wausau Ins. Cos., Indpls., 1980-84; sr. casualty underwriter CNA Ins. Cos., Indpls., 1984-85; nat. accounts underwriter Nationwide Ins. Cos., Columbus, Ohio, 1985-87; sr. casualty underwriter Home Ins. Co., Indpls., 1987-90; product specialist Am. States Ins. Cos., 1990-94, field sales mgr., 1994—; instr. Profl. Ins. Agts. of Ind. Speaker various chs. and civic groups; dir. choir Trinity Ch., Indpls., 1983—; mem. Consortium African-Am. Christian Women. Statonian scholar, 1975-76; N.G. Gilbert scholar Ball State U., 1978. Mem. Cert. Profl. Ins. Women, Indpls. Assn. Ins. Women, Indpls. Underwriters Assn., Ins. Inst. Am. (cert.), Urban League, Alpha Kappa Alpha (Career Day group leader 1984, scholar 1974-75, 75-76). Baptist. Avocations: roller skating, aerobics, singing. Office: Am States Ins Co 500 N Meridian St Indianapolis IN 46204-1213

BAXTER, CYNTHIA, primary school educator, music educator; b. Big Spring, Tex., Apr. 18, 1947; d. Joseph Eugene and Nell Harper (Greene) Pond; m. Kenneth Leon Baxter, June 28, 1969; children: Joe Kenneth, Michael Andrew, Michelle Diane. B in Music Edn., Baylor U., 1969. Cert. vocal music tchr. all level, Tex. Music tchr. Robinson (Tex.) Elem. Sch., 1969-74, McCord Elem. Sch., Vernon, Tex., 1978—; elem. music coord. Vernon Ind. Sch. Dist., 1978-89; piano tchr. pvt. practice, 1962—. Mem. Tex. Music Educators Assn., Tex. Choral Dirs. Assn., Assn. Tex. Profl. Educators, Am. Coll. Musicians. Baptist. Office: McCord Elem Sch 2915 Sand Rd Vernon TX 76384

BAXTER, DUBY YVONNE, government official; b. El Campo, Tex., July 21, 1953; d. Ray Eugene and Hazel Evelyn (Roades) Allenson; m. Loran Richard Baxter, April 7, 1979. Student, Alvin Jr. Coll., 1971, Tex. Tech U., 1972; cert. legal sec., Alaska Bus. Coll., 1974; student, Alaska Pacific U., 1981, Anchorage Community Coll., 1981-85, U. Santa Clara, 1982-83; BBA in Mgmt. cum laude, U. Alaska, Anchorage, 1985. Sr. office assoc., legal sec. Municipality of Anchorage, 1975-78; exec. sec. Security Nat. Bank, Anchorage, 1978-80, Alaska Renewable Resources Corp., Anchorage, 1980-82; pers. mgmt. specialist Dept. of Army, Ft. Richardson, Alaska, 1986-87; pers. mgmt. specialist, position classification specialist 10th Mtn. Div. (Light) Civilian Pers. Office, Ft. Drum, N.Y., 1987-89; pers. mgmt. specialist Civilian Pers. Office Alaska Dist. U.S. Army C.E., Anchorage, 1989-90; position classification specialist Civilian Pers. Office, 6th Inf. Divsn. (Light)-USA Garrison, Ft. Richardson, Alaska, 1990-91, 11th AF Cen. Civilian Personnel Office, Elmendorf AFB, Alaska, 1991-93; position classification specialist U.S. Army C.E., Anchorage, 1994-96, spl. project advisor, 1996—; small bus. owner, 1994—; by-laws com. mem. spl. emphasis program Fed. Women's Program, Ft. Richardson, 1986-87; instr. Prevention of Sexual Harassment, Ft. Richardson, 1986-87. Contbr. Alaska Repertoire Theater, Anchorage, 1982-87; leader Awana Christian Youth Orgn., Anchorage, 1985-87; ch. treas. Watertown (N.Y.) Bible Brethren Ch., 1988-89; mission bd. mem. Anchorage Grace Brethren Ch., 1991-92. Mem. NAFE, Classification and Compensation Soc., Missions Bd., U. Alaska Alumni Assn., Bernese Mountain Dog Club, Concerned Women for Am. Office: USACE CENPA-HR PO Box 898 Anchorage AK 99506-0898

BAXTER, MEREDITH, actress; b. Los Angeles, June 21, 1947; d. Tom and Whitney (Blake) Baxter; m. David Birney, Apr. 10, 1974 (div. 1989); children: Ted, Eva, Kate, Peter and Mollie (twins). Student, Interlochen Arts Acad., Mich. Actress (films) including Ben, 1972, Stand Up and Be Counted, 1972, Bittersweet Love, 1976, All the President's Men, 1976, The November Plan, 1976, (TV movies) The Cat Creature, 1973, The Stranger Who Looks Like Me, 1974, The Imposter, 1975, The Night That Panicked America, 1975, Target Risk, 1975, Little Women, 1978, The Family Man, 1979, Beulah Land, 1980, The Two Lives of Carol Letner, 1981, Take Your Best Shot, 1982, Family Ties Vacation, 1985, The Rape of Richard Beck, 1985, Kate's Secret, 1986, The Long Journey Home, 1987, Winnie, 1988, She Knows Too Much, 1989, Jezebel's Kiss, 1990, The Kissing Place, 1990, Burning Bridges, 1990, A Bump in the Night, 1991, A Mother's Justice, 1991, A Woman Scorned: The Betty Broderick Story, 1992, The Betty Broderick Story: Part 2, 1992, (also exec. prodr.) Darkness Before Dawn, 1993, My Breast, 1994, One More Mountain, 1994, For the Love of Aaron, 1994; (plays) Guys and Dolls, Talley's Folley, Butterflies are Free, Varieties; star (TV series) Bridget Loves Bernie, 1972-73, Family, 1976-80, Family Ties, 1982-89; (TV spls.) Vanities, 1981, Missing...Have You Seen This Person?, 1985, Diabetes Update, 1986, Other Mothers, 1993, TV's Funniest Families, 1994; other TV appearances include The Interns, Police Woman, Medical Story, City of Angels, McMillan and Wife, The Streets of San Francisco. Mem. Am. Diabetes Assn. Office: care William Morris Agency 151 S El Camino Dr Beverly Hills CA 90212-2704*

BAXTER, MILLIE MCLEAN, business owner, educator; b. Denver, Mar. 14, 1926; d. Stanley Allan and Jessie (Brown) McL.; m. Glenn A. Hettler, Dec. 28, 1949 (div. Mar. 1969); children: Douglass Kent, Linda Horn, Joni Birdsall; m. Jack Stanley Baxter, Feb. 4, 1977; children: David, Fred. Grad., Dickenson Bus. Sch., 1944; student, U. Colo., 1944-46; grad., McConnell Modeling Sch., 1946, Jones Real Estate Coll., 1971. With sales and mktg. The Arnold Corp., Denver, 1973-84; broker, mgr. Evergreen (Colo.) Properties, 1984-87; broker, owner Century 21 Evergreen Real Estate, 1987-92; ind. mgr. Real Estate Tng. Ctr., Evergreen, 1987-91; personal life history tchr. Sr. Resource Ctr., Evergreen, 1992—; distbr. Bay Formula D Products, Evergreen, 1993—; vol. computer instr. for srs., 1991—. Author: How to Write Your Life History for a Family Legacy, 1994. Mem. Denver Bd. Realtors (Salesperson of Yr. 1978), Denver Brokers Council, Evergreen Bd. Realtors, Jefferson County Bd. Realtors, Sales and Mktg. Council (Salesperson of Yr. 1979, Golden Medallion award 1978, 79, 80, 81, 82, 83). Republican. Office: Bax Products Inc PO Box 733 Evergreen CO 80439-0733

BAXTER, NANCY, medical writer; b. Grand Rapids, Mich., Oct. 3, 1950; d. Robert Emerson and Mary (Knoblauch) B. BA in Journalism, Am. U., 1972. Asst. dir. publs. Am. Speech, Lang. and Hearing Assn., Washington, D.C., 1973-77; mng. editor Biomedia, Inc., Princeton, N.J., 1977-79; editor A.M. Best Co., Oldwick, N.J., 1979-81; mng. editor Continuing Profl. Edn. Ctr., Inc., Princeton, N.J., 1981-82; med. writer/editor Biomed. Info. Corp., N.Y.C., 1982-83; pres. Baxter Med. Communications, Co., Warren, N.J., 1983—. Mem. Am. Med. Writers Assn. Home and Office: 18 Stiles Rd Warren NJ 07059-5413

BAY, LIBBY, college administrator, English language educator; b. N.Y.C., Dec. 22, 1932; d. Abraham and Faye (Orkofsky) Goldstein; m. Morris Bay, Nov. 24, 1965; children: Robin Bay Gilenson, Beth. BA, Hunter Coll., 1954; MA, U. Chgo., 1955; postgrad., NYU, 1955-57. Lectr. Bklyn. Coll., 1957-61, Hunter Coll., 1961-65; prof. SUNY/Rockland, Suffern, N.Y., 1965—; English chair SUNY/Rockland, Suffern, 1975-93, humanities divsn. chair, 1993—; liberal arts faculty Regents Coll., Albany, N.Y., 1985—; guest lectr. local librs., Rockland and Orange Counties, 1990—; grant dir. NEH, Washington, 1970-72, Am. Assn. C.C., Washington, 1991-93; lay mem. 9th Jud. Grievance Com., N.Y., 1985-93. contbr. chpts. to books and articles to mags. and jours. Commn. mem. Women's Commn. Rockland County Legis., 1988—; exec. bd. dirs. Hunter Coll. Alumni, Rockland Coll., 1975—, newsletter editor, 1978-90. Named Outstanding Adminstr. in Higher Edn., Nat. C.C. Charter Assn., 1994; Mellon fellow CUNY Grad. Ctr., 1986; summer study grants NEH, 1992, Ams. Communities grant, 1995-96; (2) Mellon fellowships CUNY, fellowship East-West Inst. Hawaii, 1996. Mem. Nat. Two-Yr. Coll. Assn. (assoc. chair 1992—), Assn. Depts. of English (exec. bd. dirs. 1993—), N.E. Regional English Assn. (exec. bd. dirs. 1980—). Home: 1 Danville Rd Spring Valley NY 10977 Office: SUNY/Rockland 145 College Rd Suffern NY 10901

BAYARD, SUSAN SHAPIRO, educator, small business owner; b. Boston, Dec. 26, 1942; d. Morris Arnold and Hester Muriel (Blatt) Shapiro; m. Edward Quint Bayard, Jan. 4, 1969; children: Jeffrey David, Lucy Quint. BA, Syracuse U., 1964; MA, U. Calif., Berkeley, 1966; Cert. Advanced Grad. Study, Boston U., 1984. Rsch. chemist Harvard Med. Sch., Boston, 1966; asst. scientist Polaroid Corp., Cambridge, Mass., 1966-67; instr. Boston U., 1968-70, Wheelock Coll., Boston, 1978-81; chmn. sci. dept. Tower Sch., Marblehead, Mass., 1981-85; dir., owner Bayard Learning Ctr., Marblehead, 1985—; coord. Instructional Design Lab. Salem State Coll., 1995—; vis. lectr. Salem State Coll., 1994—; ednl. cons./workshop facilitator Swampscott (Mass.) Pub. Schs., Lynn (Mass.) Pub. Schs., Salem (Mass.) State Coll., 1986-91; instr./cons. N.E. Consortium, North Andover, Mass., 1986—. Mem. Town Mtg., Swampscott, 1988—, Supt. Screening Com., Swampscott, 1987, Mass. Ednl. TV Prog. Selection Com., 1979-87, Sch. Improvement Coun., Swampscott, 1988-89, Curriculum Evaluation Com., Swampscott, 1978-80. Grantee NSF, Syracuse U., 1962, 64; named Outstanding Woman Grad. Student, Boston U. Women's Guild, 1977. Mem. Nat. Sci. Tchrs.'s Assn., Pi Lambda Theta. Jewish. Office: Bayard Learning Ctr PO Box 604 Swampscott MA 01907-3604

BAYER, ADA-HELEN, industrial and organizational psychologist, educator; b. Hamburg, Germany, Sept. 26, 1961; came to U.S., 1962; d. Manfred E. and Margret H. (Janssen) B.; m. Steven L. Patrick, Aug. 20, 1994. BA, BS magna cum laude, Brock U., Ont., Can., 1984; MS, Rensselaer Polytech. Inst., 1987; MA, PhD, George Mason U., 1992. Adj. prof. George Mason U., Fairfax, Va., 1989-93; rsch. psychologist Aerospace Scis. Inc., Fairfax, Va., 1991-93; cons. The Coe Group, Burke, Va., 1992—; sr. rsch. psychologist HADRON/EISI, Balt., Va., 1993—; adj. asst. prof. Va. Tech., Falls Church, 1994—, Johns Hopkins U., Balt., 1994—; bd. dirs. PMO, Alexandria, Va. Contbr. articles to profl. jours. Recipient merit fellowship Rensselaer Polytech. Inst., Troy, N.Y., 1984-86, George Mason U., Fairfax, Va., 1989-92. Mem. APA, NAFE, Soc. for Indsl./Orgnl. Psychology. Home: 10864 Burr Oak Way Burke VA 22015 Office: HADRON/EISI Ste 401 6810 Deerpath Rd Baltimore MD 21227

BAYLEY, SUZANNE LUDEY, civic volunteer; b. Vienna, W.Va., Apr. 14, 1920; d. Charles Addison and Patty (Spence) Ludey; m. Thomas Way Bayley, Feb. 7, 1942; children: Patty Ruth Bayley Dhondt, Thomas Way Bayley III, Charlotte Ann Bayley Schindelholz. Attended, Rollins Studio of Acting, 1938-1939; BA, Finch Coll., 1940. founder Children's Theatre Bur., Parkersburg, W.Va., 1946-48; actress, dir., adminstr. Actor's Guild of Parkersburg, 1956-57; pres. At Theatre group, 1962, play reading chair 1963-65, bldg. chair 1975-76; mem. founding com. Artsbridge Fine Arts coun., Parkersburg, 1977— (Visionary of Yr., 1978). Prodr. Eden on the River, Blennerhassett Drama Assn., 1987. Mem. Jr. League, Parkersburg, 1942-62; v.p. Friends of Blennerhassett, 1975; commr. Blennerhassett Island project, 1988-91, docent, 1988-95. Recipient Lifetime Achievement award Altrusa Club and YWCA, 1992; Cmty. Svc. award named in her honor Actors Guild, 1976. Republican. Roman Catholic.

BAYLIS, KATHLEEN DONNA, project manager; b. Cin., Oct. 8, 1947; d. Merritt Don and Mary Lee (Atkisson) B. BA in Psychology, Hillsdale Coll., 1969; MS in Edn., Ind. U., 1971; MBA, Nova Southeastern U., 1996. Property mgr. Peppertree Bay Condominium, Sarasota, Fla., 1975-79; club mgr. Ramar Group Cos., Inc., Venice, Fla., 1979-88; v.p. adminstrn. Plantation Assocs., Venice, 1988-91; gen. mgr. club ops. Plantation Golf and Country Club, Venice, 1991-95; project mgr. Sarasota County Com. of 100, Sarasota, 1995—; vice chmn. Sarasota County Tourism Adv. Coun., Sarasota, 1989-92. Pres. South County Resource Ctr., Venice, 1994—. Mem. Club Mgrs. Assn. Am. (cert. club mgr., bylaws com. chair 1994-95), S.W. Fla. Regional Planning Coun., Cmty. Found. Sarasota County (sec. 1990—), Plantation Cmty. Found. (hon. life mem.), Venice Area C. of C. (pres. 1992-93), Leadership Sarasota Alumni Assn., Manatee/Sarasota Internat. Trade Club (bd. dirs. 1995-96), Pilot Club Venice (pres. 1989-90). Republican. Home: 148 DaVinci Dr Nokomis FL 34275

BAYNE, KATHRYN ANN LOUISE, veterinarian; b. Santa Monica, Calif., Feb. 4, 1959; d. Richard Harry and Loretta Mary (Kennedy) B.; m. Mark Cofer Haines, May 19, 1990. BS cum laude, Calif. State Poly. U., 1979; MS, Wash. State U., 1982, PhD, 1986, DVM, 1987. Vet. behaviorist NIH, Bethesda, Md., 1987-94; assoc. dir Assn. for the Assessment & Accreditation of Lab. Animal Care, Rockville, Md., 1994—; Diplomate Am. Coll. Lab. Animal Medicine. Inventor in field; author publs. in field. Comdr. USPHS. Recipient Foster award, USPHS commendaton and achievement awards; named Alumnus of Yr. award Westlake Sch. Mem. AVMA, Animal Behavior Soc., Am. Soc. Lab. Animal Practitioners, Assn. Primate Vets. (pres.), D.C. Vet. Med. Assn. (pres.), Scientists Ctr. for Animal Welfare (v.p. bd. dirs.). Office: AAALAC International 11300 Rockville Pike Ste 1211 Rockville MD 20852

BAYNE, MELBA LOIS, mechanical engineer; b. Nov. 4, 1930; d. Louis Rudolph and Lucille Pauline (Schuman) Beckmeyer; children: Melanie Lee Bayne Williams, Melissa Ann Bayne. Student, U. Ill., 1948-51, Detroit Inst. Tech., 1955-56. Mech. sys. dir. Smith, Hinchman & Grylls, Detroit, 1951-53; mech. sys. designer Johnson & McGaughan, Washington, 1954-55, Smithi, Hinchman & Grylls, 1955-61; mech. engring. cons. Houston and Boston, 1961-78; asst. mech. dept. head Bernard Johnson Assocs., Washington, 1978-81; sr. mech. engr. Washington Met. Area Transit Authority, 1981—. Author, co-author, presenter numerous technical documents on elevators, escalators, safety devices, sys. safety mapping and ventilation at nat. transit confs., fire protection assn. confs., and internat. ventilation symposiums. Mem. ASHRAE (chair 1985-87), Nat. Fire Protection (chair ventilation guidelines task group 1994—), Transportation Rsch. Bd., Am. Pub. Transit Assn. (chair ventilation com. 1993—, escalator/elevator com., steering com.). Home: Walking H Farm 16360 Bradford Rd Culpeper VA 22701 Office: Washington Metro Area Transit Authority 600 5th St NW Washington DC 20001

BAYS, MICKY ANN, medical technologist; b. Casper, Wyo., Mar. 27, 1956; d. Jerome Richard and Marjorie Alice (Williamson) Galles; m. William Fredrick Bays, Sept. 15, 1979 (div. Aug. 1993). BS, U. Wyo., 1979. Med. technologist Am. Soc. Clin. Pathologists, Casper, 1979—. Bd. dirs. Make A Wish Found., Casper, 1993-94. Republican. Roman Catholic. Home: 2312 Linda Vista Casper WY 82609 Office: Wyoming Med Ctr 1233 E 2nd St Casper WY 82601

BAYSINGER, JANE ANN, elementary school music educator; b. Tell City, Ind., Oct. 16, 1951; d. James William and Alice Ellen (Connor) B. BS, Ind. State U., 1973, MS, 1978. Cert. K-12 music tchr., Ind. Music tchr. Pine Village Elem. and Williamsport Elem. Met. Sch. Dist. Warren County, Williamsport, Ind., 1973—. organist St. Patrick Cath. Ch., 1973—; mem., substitute accompanist Benton County Ext. Homemakers Chorus, 1984—. Mem. Ind. Gen. Music Edn. Assn. (adv. bd. 1989—), Warren County Edn. Assn. (treas. 1970's, scholarship com. 1980's), Music Educator's Nat. Conf., Ind. State Tchrs.' Assn. Home: 307 E Lafayette St # 223 Pine Village IN 47975-8000 Office: Williamsport Elem Sch 206 E Monroe St Williamsport IN 47993-1242

BAZIN, NANCY TOPPING, English language educator; b. Pitts., Nov. 5, 1934; d. Frank Williamson Topping and Helen Luther Arnold Wilson; m. Maurice Jacques Bazin, Dec. 21, 1958 (div. 1978); children: Michel Francois, Christine Nicole; m. Robert Eliot Reardon, Jan. 4, 1992. BA, Ohio Wesleyan U., 1956; MA, Middlebury Grad. Sch. French, 1958; PhD, Stanford U., 1969; postgrad., Inst. Higher Edn. Adminstrn., 1977. Asst. prof. English Rutgers U., New Brunswick, N.J., 1970-77; dir. women's studies U. Pitts., 1977-78; assoc. prof. English and women's studies Old Dominion U., Norfolk, Va., 1978-84, dir. women's studies, 1978-85, chair dept. English, 1985-89, prof. English and women's studies, 1984—; manuscript reader for various publs.; exch. faculty lectr. U. Rabat, Morocco; vis. scholar Inst. for Advanced Studies, Ind. U., Bloomington, 1994. Author: Virginia Woolf and the Androgynous Vision, 1973; co-editor: Conversations with Nadine Gordimer, 1990; contbr. articles to various jours., essays to books in field. Recipient Outstanding Faculty award State Coun. for Higher Edn. in Va., 1994; Ball Bros. Rsch. Found. fellow, 1994; Resident fellowship Va. Ctr. for the Humanities, 1995. Mem. MLA (v.p. women's caucus 1978-81), South Atlantic MLA, Nat. Women Studies Assn., African Lit. Assn., Nat. Coun. Tchrs. English, Phi Beta Kappa, Phi Kappa Phi, Sigma Tau Delta, Kappa Delta Pi (mortar bd.). Democrat. Home: 4005 Gosnold Ave Norfolk VA 23508-2917 Office: Old Dominion U Dept English Norfolk VA 23529-0078

BEACH, LINDA MARIE, total quality management professional; b. Washington, May 5, 1949; d. Robert L. and Agnes I. (O'Brien) B.; m. Robert L. Riley; 1 child, Grace. AAS in Bus. and Mktg. cum laude, No. Va. Community Coll., 1973; BA cum laude, Luther Rice Coll., 1975; MBPA, Southeastern U., 1977; DBA, Pacific Western U., 1988. Computer systems adminstr. Def. Mapping Agy., Brookmont, Md., 1967-80; mgr. methods and procedures Bur. Nat. Affairs, Inc., Washington, 1980-82; quality and reliability engr. Gen. Electric, Arlington, Va., 1982; sr. product assurance engr. Fairchild Industries, Germantown, Md., 1982-84, CIT-ALCATEL, Reston, Va., 1984-86; software product assurance mgr. Contel, Fairfax, Va., 1986-87; group leader quality engring. Software Productivity Consortium, Reston, 1987-89; dir. quality assurance NYMA, Inc., Greenbelt, Md., 1989—; product mgr. P4, Inc., Sterling, Va., 1989-92; instr. Learning Tress Internat., Vienna, Va., 1988-96; assoc. prof. No. Va. C.C., Sterling, 1984-89; instr. Anne Arundel C.C., 1993—; adj. faculty Potomac Coll., 1996—. Contbg. editor Info. Mgmt., 1983-85. Mem. IEEE, Am. Soc. for Quality Control, Assn. for Computing Machinery, Internat. Test and Evaluation. Home: 1704 Plane Tree Way Bowie MD 20721-3019 Office: NYMA Inc 7501 Greenway Center Dr Greenbelt MD 20770-3514

BEACH, LISA (ELIZABETH) FORSTER, artist, educator; b. Ypsilanti, Mich., Feb. 3, 1937; d. Ralph Dale and Mildred E. (Drake) Bruce; m. Donald M. Forster, Apr. 19, 1962 (div. June 1988); children: Alan, Kenneth, Susan; m. David E. Beach, Feb. 14, 1989. BS in Art Edn., Edinboro U. of Pa., 1959; MFA, Rochester Inst. Tech., 1987. Art instr. Mercer (Pa.) Sch. Sys., 1959-60, Irondequoit (N.Y.) Pub. Schs., 1961-62; painting instr. Meml. Art Gallery of U. of Rochester, Rochester, N.Y., 1983-85; tchg. asst. Edgar Whitney Painting Tours, 1983-84; art instr., dir. Topnotch Resport and Spa, Stowe, Vt., 1989-95; painting instr. Stowe Hollow Studio, 1989—; drawing and painting instr. Vt. Inst. Life Long Learning Elder Hostel, Stowe, 1992—; ski instr. Stowe Mt. Resort, 1990—; mem. visual arts com. Helen Day Art Ctr., Stowe, 1988—; membership campaign chmn. Meml. Art Gallery of U. of Rochester, Rochester, 1971; chmn. art divsn. PBS Channel 21 Auction, Rochester, 1972. Mem. Nat. Watercolor Soc. (signature mem.), No. Vt. Artists, Profl. Ski Instrs. Am. (cert. level II). Office: Stowe Hollow Studio 288 Upper Pinnacle Rd Stowe VT 05672

BEACH, MILDRED A., state legislator; b. Wolfeboro, Mar. 2, 1924. Student, U. N.H. Mem. Air Resources Coun., 1979-96, vice chair 1984-96; mem. Wolfeboro Bd. of Adjustment, 1980-92, vice-chair 1984-90; pres. N.H. Travel Coun., 1986-88; dir. N.H. Hospitality Assn., 1987-90, N.H. Vocat. Tech. Coll., 1986-90; mem. N.H. Joint Promotion Program Matching Grants, 1985-96. Home: PO Box 696 Wolfeboro NH 03894-0696 Office: NH Ho of Reps State Capitol Concord NH 03301

BEADERSTADT, ANDREA ANGLIN, community relations manager; b. Detroit, Feb. 11, 1949; d. Hartley Raymond and Margaret Mary (Ward) Anglin; m. John Henry Beaderstadt, Dec. 22, 1977; children: Matthew Geoffrey, Christopher Erik. BA in Journalism magna cum laude, Wayne State U., 1970; MA in Print Communications, Am. U., Washington, 1971. Legis. asst. Rep. Martha W. Griffiths, Mich., 1971-74; legis. specialist LWV, Washington, 1974-75; legis. asst. Rep. James V. Stanton, Ohio, 1976-77; instr. Ferris State Coll., Big Rapids, Mich., 1977-78; dir. Small World, Inc., Kodiak, Alaska, 1980-81; personnel asst. USCG, Kodiak, 1981-82; copy editor The Anchorage Times, 1982-83; asst. prof. St. Michael's Coll., Winooski, Vt., 1983-89; asst. prof. English dept. SUNY, Plattsburgh, 1989—; cmty. rels. mgr. WPI, Inc., 1995—; reporter The Alaska Fisherman mag., Juneau, 1980; del. Ctr. for Study Can., Northeast and Mid. Atlantic Conf. Can. Studies. Bd. dirs. Vt. Woman, 1988-90. Research fellow St. Michael's Coll. Ctr. for Advancement of Pvt. Higher Edn., Japan, 1987. Mem. Nat. Fedn. Press Women, Nat. Newspaper Assn., Am. Coun. Que. Studies, New Eng. Press Assn. (writing coach), New Eng. Newspaper Assn., Vt. Press Assn. (sec. 1984-89), Women in Communication. Lutheran. Home: RR 2 Box 153E Alburg VT 05440-9625 Office: Plattsburgh AFB 426 US Oval Plattsburgh NY 12903

BEAL, ILENE, bank executive. BA, Wellesley Coll., 1967. Mgmt. trainee Nat. Shawmut Bank, Boston, 1967-71; from asst. sec. to exec. v.p. BayBanks, Inc., Boston, 1972—; successively asst. v.p., v.p., sr. v.p. BayBanks, Inc., now exec. v.p., sec., clk. Office: BayBanks Inc 175 Federal St Boston MA 02110-2210

BEAL, WINONA ROARK, retired church administrator; b. Birchwood, Tenn., Aug. 11, 1924; d. Thomas Jefferson and Minnie Belle (Price) Roark; m. Charles Hugh Beal, Aug. 6, 1949; children: Jeremy Lawrence, Eric David. BSBA, Tenn. Tech. U., 1948; postgrad., So. Bapt. Theol. Sem., 1950-54, U. Louisville, 1951-53, Manatee C.C., 1958-60. Tchr. Washington (Ga.) H.S., 1948-50; asst. to treas. So. Bapt. Theol. Sem., Louisville, Ky., 1951-54; asst. to bus. mgr. Agnes Scott Coll., Decatur, Ga., 1968-71; religious edn. dir. Bay Haven Bapt. Ch., Sarasota, Fla., 1976-84, office program dir., 1985-89; ret., 1989; spiritual guide, dir. Bay Haven Elem. Sch., Sarasota, 1965-68; mem. Sapphire Stores-Indian Beach Assn., Sarasota, 1985-96, State Bd. Missions, Fla. Bapt. Conv., 1993-95, re-elected 96-99, mem. program com., 1993-94. 94-95. loans com. 1995-98. Mem. S.W. Fla. Bapt. Assn. (exec. com. 1976-96, dir. Vacation Bible Sch. 1976-89, student work 1976-80, clerk 1994—), S.W. Manatee Assn. (pres. of Metochai), Pastors Wives of S.W. Fla. Assn. (pres. 1972, 80, 84-89), Fla. Pastors' Wives Conf. (v.p. 1975, program chair 1979, sec.-treas. 1983, conf. historian 1983). Democrat. Home: 638 Beverly Dr Sarasota FL 34234-2706

BEALE, BETTY (MRS. GEORGE K. GRAEBER), columnist, writer; b. Washington; d. William Lewis and Edna (Sims) B.; m. George Kenneth Graeber, Feb. 15, 1969. A.B., Smith Coll. Columnist, Washington Post, 1937-40; reporter and columnist Washington Evening Star, 1945-81; weekly columnist North Am. Syndicate (formerly Field Newspaper Syndicate), 1953-89; ret., 1989; lectr. in field. Author: Power at Play: A Memoir of Parties, Politicians and The Presidents in My Bedroom, 1993. Recipient Freedom Found. award, 1969, named Woman of Distinction, 1987. Address: 2926 Garfield St NW Washington DC 20008-3536

BEALE, GEORGIA ROBISON, historian, educator; b. Chgo., Mar. 14, 1905; d. Henry Barton and Dora Belle (Sledd) Robison; m. Howard Kennedy Beale, Jan. 2, 1942; children: Howard Kennedy, Henry Barton Robison, Thomas Wight. AB, U. Chgo., 1926, AM, 1928; PhD, Columbia U., 1938; student Sorbonne and Coll. de France, 1930-34. Reader in history U. Chgo., 1927-29; lectr. Barnard Coll., 1937-38; instr. Bklyn. Coll., 1937-39; asst. prof. Hollins (Va.) Coll., 1939-41, Wellesley Coll., 1941-42, Castleton (Vt.) State Coll., 1968-70; vis. assoc. prof. U. Ky., Lexington, 1970-72; professorial lectr. George Washington U., 1983-84. Author: Revellière-lépeaux, Citizen Director, 1938, 72, Academies to Institut, 1973, Bosc and the Exequatur, 1978, The Botnophiles of Angers, 1996; contbg. author Historical Dictionary of the French Revolution, 1985; also articles. Mem. Madison (Wis.) Civic Music Assn. and Madison Symphony Orch. League, 1958—; hon. trustee Culver-Stockton Coll., 1974—. Univ. fellow Columbia U., 1929-30. Mem. AAUW (European fellow 1930-31), Am., So. Hist. Assns., Soc. French Hist. Studies, Western Soc. French History (hon. mem. exec. council), Am., Brit. socs. 18th century studies, Phi Beta Kappa, Pi Lambda Theta, Phi Alpha Theta, Pi Kappa Delta. Clubs: Reid Hall (Paris); Brit. Univ. Women's (London). Office: The Ridge Orford NH 03777 also: 2816 Columbia Rd Madison WI 53705-2259

BEALE, JANE, advertising executive. Exec. v.p., dir. human resources N.W. Ayers & Ptnrs., N.Y.C. Office: NW Ayers & Ptnrs Worldwide Plz 825 Eighth Ave New York NY 10019-7498*

BEALE, SUSAN YATES, social worker; b. Saginaw, Mich., Nov. 17, 1943; d. William Miller and Dorothy LaVerne (Langdon) Yates; m. Henry B.R. Beale, Aug. 27, 1966; children: Andrew, Nathaniel. AB cum laude, Oberlin Coll., 1966; MA, U. Chgo., 1969. Lic. ind. clin. social worker; lic. cert. social worker; bd. cert. in clin. social work ABE. Social worker West Side VA Hosp., Chgo., 1969-70, D.C. Dept. Human Resources, Washington, 1970-72, D.C. Pub. Schs., Washington, 1972-73; pvt. practice Washington, 1973-74; dir. social svc. Capitol Hill Hosp., Washington, 1974-80; social worker No. Va. Dialysis Ctr., Alexandria, 1982-87, Vis. Nurse Assn., Rockville, Md., 1987-89; sr. social worker Hospice of Washington, 1989-95; sr. social svcs. analyst Microeconomic Applications, 1982—; pres. Coping Ptnrs., Washington, 1996—. Tchr. Royal Scottish Country Dance Soc. Mem. Nat. Assn. Social Workers (diplomate in clin. social work), Greater Washington Soc. Clin. Social Workers, Nat. Assn. Profl. Geriatric Care Mgrs. (advanced profl.). Office: Coping Ptnrs 4354 Warren St NW Washington DC 20016-2438

BEALL, GRACE CARTER, business educator; b. Birmingham, Ala., Sept. 12, 1928; d. Edgar T. and Kate (Eubank) Carter; m. Vernon D. Beall, Aug. 27, 1948; children: Robert, Timothy. BS, La. Coll., 1949; MEd, La. State U., 1955; postgrad., U. Wis., East Tex. State U., Temple U., Southwestern Bapt. Theol. Sem., U. Ga. Tchr., asst. prin. Franklin Parish Sch. Bd., Crowville, La., 1949-54; tchr. Grant Parish Sch. Bd., Dry Prong, La., 1954-55; tchr., coord. Rapides Parish Sch. Bd., Pineville, La., 1955-73; assoc. prof. La. Coll., Pineville, 1974-93; past vice chair of faculty, prof. emeritus, 1993—; cons. in field; sec.-treas. Gulf Coast Athletic Conf., 1983—, Nat. Assn. Intercollegiate Athletics Dist. 30, 1983—. Vice chair Civil Svc. Bd., Pineville, 1975--. Recipient Outstanding Svc. award La. Vocat. Assn., 1971, Outstanding Secondary Educators Am., 1973. Mem. AAUP (past sec.), La. Bapt. Hist. Assn. (pres., bd. dirs.), Phi Delta Kappa (historian), Delta Kappa Gamma (past pres.), Kappa Kappa Iota. Republican. Baptist. Home: 3232 Crestview Dr Pineville LA 71360-5804

BEALL, JOANNA MAY, painter; b. Chgo., Aug. 17, 1935; d. Lester Thomas and Dorothy Welles (Miller) B.; student Yale U. Sch. Fine Arts, 1953-57, Art Inst. Chgo., 1957; m. H.C. Westermann, Mar. 31, 1959. One-man shows include: Great Bldg. Crack-Up Gallery, N.Y.C., 1973, James Corcoran Gallery, Los Angeles, 1974, Gallery Rebecca Cooper, Washington, 1975; group shows: Allan Frumkin, Chgo., 1960, 61, Whitney Mus., N.Y.C., 1973, Art Inst. Chgo., 1976, Univ. Galleries, Los Angeles, 1979, Xavier Fourcade, N.Y.C., 1980, 85; vis. artist U. Colo., Boulder, 1979, 84. Mem. Artists Equity Assn., Visual Artists and Galleries Assn. Article The World of Joanna Beall (Melinda Wortz) appeared in Art Week mag., 1974. Home: PO Box 5028 Brookfield CT 06804-5028

BEALS, NANCY FARWELL, state legislator; b. El Paso, July 21, 1938; d. Fred Whitcomb and Katharine Doane (Pier) Farwell; m. Richard William Beals, June 30, 1962; children: Katharine, Robert, Susannah. BA in Polit. Sci., Bryn Mawr Coll., 1960; MA in Teaching, Harvard U., 1961. Gropu leader Exptl. Internat. Living, Putney, Vt.; jr. high sch. tchr. Winceshter (Mass.) Pub. Schs., 1961-62; high sch. tchr. Hamden (Conn.) Pub. Schs., 1962-64; state rep. Conn. Gen. Assembly, Hartford, 1993—; Flemming fellow Ctr. for Policy Alternatives, 1995. Mem. various local and regional offices PTA, Chgo. and Hamden, 1970-83; local pres., state bd. dirs. LWV, Conn., 1979-82; mem., sec., chmn. Hamden Bd. Edn., 1983-92. Recipient Citizenship award for Conn. Philip Morris Corp., 1992, Hamden Notable award Friends of Hamden Libr., 1986, Children's Hero award Children's Trust Fund, 1995; named Legislator of Yr. Conn. Libr. Assn., 1994. Democrat.

BEAMAN, JOYCE PROCTOR, retired secondary and elementary school educator, writer; b. Wilson, N.C., Apr. 27, 1931; d. Jesse David and Martha Pauline (Owens) Proctor; m. Robert Hines Beaman; 1 child, Robert David. BS, East Carolina Coll., 1951, MA, 1952. English and French tchr. Stantonsburg (N.C.) H.S., 1952-53, Snow Hill (N.C.) H.S., 1953-60; English and French tchr. Saratoga (N.C.) Ctrl., 1968-78, French tchr., libr., 1968-72, libr., 1972-78; libr. Elm City (N.C.) Mid. Sch., 1978-82, Spaulding Elem. Sch., Spring Hope, N.C., 1987-92; mem. Competency Test Commn. N.C., Raleigh, 1983-84. Author: Broken Acres, 1971, All for the Love of Cassie, 1973, Bloom Where You Are Planted, 1975, You Are Beautiful: You Really Are, 1981. Recipient Terry Sanford Creativity and Innovation in Edn. state award, 1977. Mem. Kappa Delta Pi, Delta Kappa Gamma (state chmn. 1978-80). Home: 8427 Piney Grove Church Rd Walstonburg NC 27888

BEAMAN, MARGARINE GAYNELL, scrap metal broker; b. Feb. 26; d. Margaret Lena Geisweidt; m. Robert W. Beaman; children: Richard Beaman, Ronald Beaman, Lorene Barrera, Jessica Barrera. Student, U. Houston, U. Mich. V.p. Beaman Metal Co., Inc., Austin, 1972—; pres. Beaman Acctg. and Cons., Austin, 1975—. Chair Capital Area Workforce Devel. Bd., 1996; vol. RIF; mem. bd. Austin Crime Stoppers Edn., Austin C. of C., Homeless Com., Cmty. Action Network; vice chair Trans County Hist. Commn.; chair Capital Area Workforce Devel. Bd. Recipient Gov.'s Vol. of Yr. award, 1982, Mayor's Meritorious award, 1982, Svc. awards Sertoma Club, N.Y. Am. Coun. of Blind, Nat. Community Schs. award, Citizen Leadership award Freedom Found. at Valley Forge, 1986, Migel Medal award Am. Found. for Blind N.Y.C., 1992, Outstanding Contrbn. award Blinded Vets. Assn., 1995; inducted into Tex. Assn. Pvt. Colls. Hall of Fame, Austin Women's Hall of Fame; named Outstanding Blind Worker of Tex., 1982, Most Worthy Citizen of Austin, 1989, Austin's Most Worthy Citizen, 1989. Mem. Tex. Fedn. Bus. and Profl. Women's Clubs (Outstanding Dist. Businesswoman 1996), Exec. Women Internat. (past state pres.), Internat. Cert. Consumer Credit Execs., Nat. Assn. Fin. Aid Adminstrs., Austin C. of C., Austin Women's C. of C., Gen. Fedn. Women's Club, Pvt. Industry Coun., Am. Coun. of Blind, Zonta Internat., Rotary (pres. East Austin chpt. 1995-96). Home: 1406 Wilshire Blvd Austin TX 78722-1129 Office: 3409 E 5th St Austin TX 78702-4911

BEAMER, BETSY DAVIS, state official; b. Charleston, W.Va., Feb. 6, 1959; d. Donald Dallas and Laura (Steward) Davis; m. James William Beamer; Aug. 1, 1992. BA in Journalism, Radford U., 1981. News reporter Va. Leader, Pearlsburg, 1980-81, News Gazette, Lexington, Va., 1982; program coord. Muscular Dystrophy Assn., Roanoke, Va., 1983; fin. dir. Stafford for Congress, Pearlsburg, 1984, Chichester for Lt. Gov., Richmond, 1985, Nat. Rep. Congress Commn., Washington, 1985, Epperson for Congress, Winston-Salem, N.C., 1986-90, Rep. Party Va., Richmond, 1990-92; sec. of commonwealth State of Va., Richmond, 1992—. Mem. Nat. Assn. Secs. State, Herrico GOP Women. Republican. Baptist. Home: 1503 Old Compton Rd Richmond VA 23233-4055 Office: Old Finance Bldg Capitol Sq Richmond VA 23219*

BEAN, DEANA SAFFORD, artist, travel consultant; b. Springfield, Mass., June 18, 1946; d. Dean Wilbur and Merle Watkins (Woodard) Safford; m. Richard Peter Bean, Oct. 17, 1968; children: Duane Matthew (dec.) and David Andrew (twins), Dana Robert, Matthew Adams. Student, W.Va. Wesleyan Co., 1966. Co-owner Gallery Six, Rocky Neck, Mass., 1996—; travel cons. Magic World travel, Springfield, Mass., 1991-94, The Cruise and Vacation Store, East Longmeadow, Mass., 1994—; vol. U.S. Peace Corps, Iran, 1968; distbr. Seamless Internat., Inc., 1996. Author: East and Me; A Personal Encounter With the Mid East, 1992. mem. coun. Springfield Art League, 1992-95. Recipient Watercolor awards Longmeadow Shops Art Exhibit, 1991, 94, Pastel awards, 1989, 93. Mem. N.Am. Marine Arts Soc., Acad. Artists Assn. (membership chmn. 1993-96, Watson-Guptill award 1991), Nat. Mus. Women in the arts (charter), Am. Artist Profl. League, Rocky Neck Art Colony, Nat. Safety Assocs. (sales coord. 1995-96, Bronze medal 1995).

BEAN, JANET RICHARDS, civic and arts center executive; b. Youngstown, Ohio; d. Howard J. and Henrietta (Menning) Richards; m. Philip G. Bean. Student, Miami U., Oxford, Ohio; BA summa cum laude, Youngstown U.; MS in LS, U. Ill., Champaign; cert. in bus. adminstrn., U. Ill., Chgo. Head Info. Ctr., Chgo. Pub. Libr., 1971-74, chief gen. info. svcs., 1975-78, dir. Cultural Ctr., 1978-84; libr. dir. Mercy Ctr. Hosp., Aurora, Ill., 1985-88; dir. devel. Paramount Arts Ctr., Aurora, 1988-92, exec. dir., 1992—; exec. dir. Aurora Civic Ctr. Authority, 1992—; mem. exec. bd. Fox Valley Arts Coun., Geneva, Ill., 1992—, pres., 1992-94. Contbr. to Funk and Wagnalls Ency., 1974. Founder Friends of the Paramount, 1988; bd. dirs. Aurora Conv. and Tourism Bur., 1992—; mem. awards com. YWCA, Aurora, 1996; com. mem. Aurora Econ. Devel. Commn., 1996—. Named Woman of Distinction, YWCAA, 1993; recipient Crystal award Citibank, Naperville, Ill., 1994. Mem. Nat. Soc. Fundraising Execs., Assn. Performing Arts Presenters, Women in Mgmt. (exec. bd. Aurora, chmn. awards com. 1996, Achievement award 1993, Nat. Charlotte Danstrom award 1993), Aurora C. of C. (ctrl. devel. com. 1992—), Rotary (exec. bd. Aurora, co-chmn. program com. 1995-96). Office: Aurora Civic Ctr Authority 8 E Galena Blvd Ste 230 Aurora IL 60506

BEAN, JESSIE HICKS, charitable organization volunteer; b. Villa Rica, Ga., 1933; d. Walter and Elsie (Matthew) Hicks; married and divorced; four children; m. Stuart Bean, 1972; nine stepchildren. Student, Sch. Nursing, St. Joseph Infirmary, Atlanta, 1954. Dir. nurses Jefferson Tuberculosis Sanitarium, Lakeshore Rehabilitation Hosp., Birmingham, Ala., 1971-72. Extensive civic activities, including pres. Birmingham (Ala.) Humane Soc. Aux., 1996-97, pres. Med. Aux. State Med. Soc., 1991-92, pres. Birmingham Dist. Kidney Found., 1991-94, v.p. 1993-94, pres. Salvation Army Women's Aux., 1992-93, bd. dirs. 1996-97; pres. Birmingham Area Coun. of Clubs, 1992-93, bd. dirs., 1996-97; adv. bd. Salvation Army, 1992-93, Ala. Symphony, 1992-93; pres. Friends of Hoover (Ala.) Libr., 1996-97; and many others; active mem. Shades Valley Lutheran Ch. Birmingham, 1963—, pres. social ministry com., 1972—, mem. bd. Evangelical Lutheran Ch. in Am., Southeastern Synod, 1987-89, ch. coun. mem. 1986-88, conv. parliamentarian; bd. dirs. Ballet Women of Birmingham, 1996-97, Birmingham Opera Guild, 1996-97, Ala. Kidney Found., Starlake Garden Club. Nominated for Woman of Yr., Birmingham, 1987, 88; recipient Cmty. Svc. award Jefferson County Med. Aux., 1978. Mem. Nat. Assn. Parliamentarians (various offices), Ala. Assn. Parliamentarians (various offices), Ala. Symphonic Assn. (mem. bd.), Southern Med. Assn. (mem. bd. doctor's day councilor for aux. 1996-97), Am. Cancer Soc. (bd. dirs.), Met. Dinner Club (bd. dirs.), Hoover Hist. Soc. (pres. 1996-97) and many other assns. Home: 1777 Deo Dara Dr Birmingham AL 35226-2743

BEAN, PAMELA B., state legislator; b. Rutland, Vt., Apr. 25, 1942; m. Linwood H. Jr.; 3 children. Mem. Lebanon City Coun.; mayor City of Lebanon, 1978; asst. majority leader N.H. Ho. of Reps., 1995—. mem. Lebanon Planning Bd.; mem. bd. dirs. Lebanon Indsl. Assn., Valley Health Care Coalition. Home: 9 Grandview Ave Lebanon NH 03766-9805 Office: NH State House State Capital Concord NH 03301*

BEAN, WENDY JEANNE, accountant; b. Allston, Mass., Sept. 8, 1960; d. Gene Wendell and Bette Lois (Bartlett) Iwans; m. Thomas Lafferty Bean, July 25, 1981; children: Adam Scott, Corey Thomas. AS, Thomas Coll., 1980, BS in Acctg., 1988. CPA, Maine, N.H. Supervising sr. tax specialist KPMG Peat Marwick, Portland, Maine, 1980-88, sr. mgr., 1992-94; v.p., tax mgr. Amos Keag Bank, Manchester, N.H., 1988-92; sr. mgr., mktg. dir., head tax dept. Runyon Kersteen Ouellette, South Portland, Maine, 1994—. Treas. Citizens for Portland Baseball, 1993-95; bd. dirs. Maine Estate Planning Coun., Portland, 1995—; treas. Maine Estate Planning Coun., 1996—; vol. Maine Retirement Com., 1996—; mem. fin. resource com. Unite Way, 1996—. Mem. AICPA, Maine Soc. CPAs, Maine Estate Planning Coun. Office: PO Box 428 42 Main St Kennebunk ME 94943-9428

BEANE, CYNTHIA ANN, gerontology nurse, educator; b. New Albany, Ind., Nov. 4, 1959; d. Walter Maxwell and Lois Velleda (Dreher) B.; divorced; children: Christopher, David, Deborah, Micheal, Crystal. Cert. in journalism, Newspaper Inst., 1985; cert. in med. assisting, Barton Sch., 1984; LPN, Summers County Sch. Nursing, 1988; ASN, SUNY, Albany, 1990. Staff nurse, educator Andrew S. Rowan Meml. Home, Sweet Springs, W.Va., 1988-90; med./surg. nurse Humana Hosp. Greenbrier valley, Fairlea, W.Va., 1990; staff nurse Greenbrier Manor Nursing Home, Fairlea, W.Va., 1991-92; med./surg. nurse Greenbrier Valley Med. Ctr., Ronceverte, W.Va., 1992-94; geriatric nurse Riverview Nursing Home, Rich Creek, Va., 1994-96; nurse supr. The Springs Nursing Ctr., Hot Springs, Va., 1996—; ARC instr. County of Monroe, W.Va. Vol. Monroe County Coun. on Aging. Democrat. Home: PO Box 11 Gap Mills WV 24941-9801 Office: The Springs Nursing Ctr PO Drawer I Hot Springs VA 24445

BEANE, JUDITH MAE, psychologist; b. Durham, N.C., Mar. 28, 1944; d. Joseph William Sr. and Antoinette Gwathmey (Dew) Sr. BA, Campbell U., 1967; MRE, Golden Gate Bapt. Theol. Sem., Mill Valley, Calif., 1972; PhD, Profl. Sch. of Psychology, San Francisco, 1988. Lic. psychologist, Calif.; mental health therapist II, Northern Neck-Middle Peninsula Cmty. Svcs. Bd.; cert. rehab. provider. Home missionary So. Bapt. Home Mission Bd., Atlanta, 1967-69; loan officer Coop Credit Union, Corte Madera, Calif., 1969-70; emergency svcs. specialist Community Action Marin, San Rafael, 1976-78; program coord. Marin Treatment Ctr., San Rafael, Calif., 1980-85; church sec. St. Paul's Episcopal Church, San Rafael, 1979-81; psychol. intern Raleigh Hills Hops., Redwood City, Calif., 1984; psychol. asst. Lic. Psychologisis, San Anselmo, Calif., 1985-96; bd. dirs. The Open Door Ministries, Inc., Sausalito, Calif., 1971—; psychologist Mill Valley, Calif., 1992-93; cons. Ross (Calif.) Hosp., 1991. Guest speaker for Turn on Marin, San Rafael, Calif., 1985. Recipient award Marin County People Speaking, 1985. Mem. Am. Psychol. Assn. (assoc.), Calif. State Psychol. Assn., Marin County Psychol. Assn., Am. Counseling Assn. Baptist. Home: PO Box 172 Lancaster VA 22503-0172

BEARCE, JEANA DALE, artist, educator; b. St. Louis; d. Clarence Russell and Maria Emily Dale; m. Lawrence F. Rakovan, June 7, 1969; children: Barbara Emily, Luke, Francesca. B.F.A., Washington U., St. Louis, 1951; M.A., N.Mex. Highlands U., 1954. Vis. artist, various lectureships India, Pakistan, 1961-62, 93; founder art dept. U. Maine, Portland, 1965, chmn. and dept. rep., 1965-70, asst. prof. art, 1967-70; assoc. prof. U. Maine, 1970-81, prof., 1982—; Reflections South India sabbatical, 1992-93. Exhibited one-woman shows, Portland Mus. Art, Maine, 1958, U. Maine, Orono, 1958, 65, 69, 77, 80, Madras Govt. Mus., India, 1962, Gallery 65, Paris, 1964, Bristol Mus. Art, R.I., 1965, Center Gallery, N.Y.C., 1974, Benbow Gallery, Newport, R.I., 1979, Ctr. for the Arts, Chocolate Ch., Bath, Maine, 1988, USM Gallery, 1991, Main Gallery U. So. Maine, 1991, others, group show, Boston Mus. Art, Library of Congress, Phila. Print Club, Springfield Mus., Mo., Birmingham Mus. Art, Ala., others; represented permanent collection, St. Louis Art Mus., U.S. Edn. Found. in India, New Delhi, U. Maine, Orono and Portland, Bklyn. Mus. Art, Cornell U. Mus. Art, Calif. Coll. Arts and Crafts, Sarasota Art Assn., Fla., Bowdoin Coll., Brunswick, Maine; executed murals, N.Mex. Highlands U., Bowdoin Longfellow-Hawthorn Library, Brunswick, sculpture reliefs, St. Bartholomew, Cape Elizabeth, Maine, St. Charles Ch. Brunswick; retrospective, Maine Ctr. for the Arts, 1988. Mem. artist's com. Maine Art Gallery, 1957-75, 80-87; mem. Maine com. Skowhegan Sch. Painting and Sculpture, 1972—. Recipient various awards; recipient Fannie Cook award People's Competition, 1958, 59; sabbaticals to India: Return to India-Creative Paintings and Printmaking, 1987, South India-Painting and Printmaking, 1993, The Maine to India Series USM Environ. Studies Ctr., 1996. Mem. Bowdoin Coll. Mus. Assocs. Home: 327 Maine St Brunswick ME 04011-3310 Office: U So Maine College Ave Gorham ME 04038-1004

BEARD, AMANDA, swimmer, Olympic athlete; b. Irvine, Calif., Oct. 29, 1981. Mem. Pan Pac Team, 1995; swimmer U.S. Olympic Team, Atlanta, 1996. Recipient 2 silver medals in 100 meter breaststroke and 200 meter breaststroke Olympic Games, Atlanta, 1996, gold medal in 4x100 medley relay Olympic Games, Atlanta, 1996; holder Am. record for 100 meter breastroke, 1996. Office: US Swimming Inc One Olympic Plz Colorado Springs CO 80909*

BEARD, ANN SOUTHARD, government official, travel company executive, art framing company executive; b. Denver, Jan. 13, 1948; d. William Harvey and Cora Alice Cornelia (Caldwell) Southard; m. Terrill Leon Beard, Dec. 20, 1970 (div. Oct. 1980); 1 son, Jeffery Leon; m. Rainer G. Froehlich, Feb. 12, 1988 (div. 1992). BA, Willamette U., 1970; postgrad U. Calif.-San Diego, 1981-82. Exec. asst. Kidder Peabody & Co., San Francisco, 1970-72; adminstrv. aide Arthur Anderson & Co., Portland, Oreg., 1972-73; owner, mgr. Beard's Frame Shoppes, Inc., Portland, 1973-80; dir. mktg. Multnomah County Fair, Portland, 1979; owner, CEO Ann Beard Spl. Events, San Diego, 1980-82; pres. Frame Affair, Inc., San Diego, 1982-86, Jack Oil Co., Inc., Greeley, 1982—; co-owner, v.p. Froehlich Internat. Travel, La Jolla, Calif., 1987-92; chief of protocol Mayor Susan Golding's Office, City of San Diego, 1993—; v.p. 146 Co., Inc., Greeley, pres., 1970-88; lectr., cons. SBA, San Diego, 1980-85. Mem. Civic Light Opera, Old Globe Theatre; bd. dirs. San Diego Master Chorale, 1981-92; mem. state bd. Miss Calif. Pageant/Miss Am., 1982-87; mem. citizens adv. bd. Drug Abuse Task Force/Crime Prevention Task Force, San Diego, 1983-87; campaign coord. Bill Mitchell for City Coun., 1985; candidate for Congress; staff aide to dep. mayor, 1987; mem. Lead San Diego Alumni, 1988, Scripps Hosp. Aux., 1992—, Internat. Visitors Coun., 1993—, San Diego County Commn. on the Status of Women, 1993—; mem. Internat. Affairs Bd., San Diego, 1993—; bd. dirs. La Jolla Rep. Women Fedn., 1992—. Mem. Am. Mktg. Assn., World Affairs Coun., San Diego C. of C., Save Our Heritage Orgn., Charter 100 San Diego, San Diego 1988 Alumna Willamette U., 1909 Univ. Club (bd. dirs. 1992—, pres. 1996—), Univ. Club San Diego (mktg., devel. and social dir. 1987-88), Delta Gamma. Office: 6671 S La Jolla Scenic Dr La Jolla CA 92037-5735

BEARD, BERNICE TALBOTT, writer; b. New Windsor, Md., Sept. 1, 1927; d. Edwin Warfield and Henrietta Alice (Snader) Talbott; m. Paul William Beard, Oct. 9, 1948; 1 child, Jeffrey Paul. BA cum laude, Western Md. Coll., 1974, M of Liberal Arts, 1981. Stenographer, sec. Balt. Gas. and Elec. Co., 1944-51; feature writer Carroll County Times, Westminster, Md., 1956-57; asst. dir. admissions, counselor Western Md. Coll., Westminster, 1963-72, exec. asst. to pres. and elected sec. bd. trustees, 1972-89; freelance writer Westminster, 1989—; campus rep. Am. Coun. Edn. Advancement of Women in Higher Edn., Western Md. Coll., 1979-85, sec. coll. corp., 1985-89. Contbr. articles to mags. and newspapers. Mem. AAUW (v.p. membership 1978-82, Carroll county br. meml. com. 1993—), Nat. Mus. Women in Arts (charter mem.). Republican. Mem. Ch. of Brethren.

BEARD, CAROL ELAINE, art educator; b. Boston, May 26, 1945; d. William John and Madolyn Ruth (Johnson) Beard; children: John C. Zajac, Matthew D. Zajac. BSE, Mass. Coll. Art, 1967; student, U. Mass., Dartmouth, 1986, Stonehill Coll., Stoughton, Mass., 1989. Cert. art tchr., art supr., Mass. Art tchr. Framingham (Mass.) Sch. Dept., 1967-71; art dir. Norfolk (Mass.) Recreation Dept., 1974-83; instr. art Franklin (Mass.) High Sch. Adult Edn., 1986-87; dir. art Norfolk Sch. Dept., 1980—, student coun. advisor, 1993—; freelance artist graphic designs for various town bds. and orgns, 1967—; collaborator Step-Outside: Cmty.-Based Art Edn., 1994. Author: (poetry) Fallen Requiem, 1964; designer soft sculptures. Mem. Norfolk Ins. Com., 1989—, Norfolk Sch. Com., 1990—; chair Collective Bargaining Com., Norfolk, 1988—; invited exch. tchr. Wash. Ambassadorship Program, 1994. Mem. ASCD, NEA, Mass. Tchrs. Assn., Norfolk Tchrs. Assn. (pres. 1988—, Tchr. of Yr. 1992), Nat. Art Edn. Assn., Mass. Art Edn. Assn., Norfolk County Tchrs. Assn. Home: 26 Farrington St Franklin MA 02038-2003 Office: Centennial Sch 70 Boardman St Norfolk MA 02056-1006

BEARD, DEBORAH FAYE, accounting and finance educator; b. Caruthersville, Mo., Mar. 20, 1951; d. Roy Howard Jones and Alice Jewel (Chism) Brock; m. Daniel Howard Beard, May 24, 1975; children: Brian Daniel, Laura Elizabeth. BS in Sec. Edn., Southeast Mo. State, Cape Girardeau, Mo., 1973, MA in Tchg., 1974; PhD in Bus. Adminstrn., U. Ark., Fayetteville, 1987. CMA, 1989. Instr. Shawnee Coll., Ill., 1975-76; grad. asst. U. Ark., Fayetteville, 1981-82; instr., asst. prof. Southeast Mo. State U., Cape Girardeau, 1976-91, assoc. prof., 1991-96, chairperson, 1991-96; dir. Alumni Assn. Bus. Profls., Capr Girardeau, 1993-96, Golf Adv. Bd., 1996. Contbr. articles to profl. jours. Recipient Faculty Mem. of Yr. award Acctg. & Fin. Club, 1994, Hometown Hero award Hardees/KGMO, 1994. Mem. Mo. Assn. Acctg. Educators (sec.-treas. 1994-96), Inst. Mgmt. Accts. (faculty adv. 1995-96), Phi Delta Kappa (v.p. mem. 1992-94, pres. 1994-95). Baptist.

BEARD, JENNIFER JANE, marketing executive; b. Rockford, Ill., May 7, 1971; d. James Sheridan and Nancy Jane (Johnson) B. BA in Journalism & Mass Comm., Drake U., Des Moines, 1993. Account exec. Telecom USA Pub. Co., Cedar Rapids, Iowa, 1993-94; mktg. dir. Midwest Title & Surety Agy., Rockford, Ill., 1994; sales rep. Hub Printing, Inc., Rochelle, Ill., 1994-95; territory mgr. Heartland Comm., Pleasant Hill, Calif., 1995; pres., dir. Answer USA, Rockford, Ill., 1995—; pres., cons. Creative Mktg. Solutions, Rockford, 1991-95. Big Sister vol. Big Bros. Big Sisters, Rockford, 1995-96. Mem. YMCA (amb. 1995-96), Rotary Internat. (dir. 1994-96, sec. 1996—). Republican. Roman Catholic. Office: Answer USA 3022 Wallin Ave Rockford IL 61101

BEARD, LILLIAN B. MCLEAN, physician, consultant; b. N.Y.; d. John Wilson and Woodie (Durden) McLean; m. Delawrence Beard, Aug. 20, 1967. BS, Howard U., 1965, DM, 1970. MD, 1970. Pvt. practice pediatrics Lillian M. Beard, Washington, D.C., 1973—; assoc. prof. pediatrics George Washington U., 1983—; asst. prof. community medicine Howard U., 1983—; contbg. editor Good Housekeeping Mag., N.Y., 1989-95; health adv. WUSA-TV, Washington, 1992-95; communications cons. to industry including: Carnation Nutritional Products; mem. bd. dirs. Nat. Women's Econ. Alliance, 1993—; Children's Hosp., 1993—. Recipient Disting. Leadership award Nat. Assn. Equal Opportunity in Higher Edn., 1993, Disting. Svc. award Nat. Med. Assn., 1990, Hall of Fame in Medicine award, 1994, Healthy Babies Project "Making a Difference" award, 1995, Howard U. Alumni Achievement award, 1996. Fellow Am. Acad. Pediatrics; mem. Nat. Med. Assn., Am. Acad. Pediatrics (physician recognition awards 1993—). Home: 10517 Alloway Dr Potomac MD 20854-1662 Office: 5505 5th St NW Washington DC 20011-6513

BEARDMORE, DOROTHY, state education official; b. Chgo.; m. William Beardmore; 2 children. BA, Cornell U. Cert. due process spl. edn. hearing officer Mich. Dept. Edn. Mem. bd. edn. Rochester Cmty. Schs., 1967-75; mem. Bd. Edn. Oakland Schs., Oakland County Intermediate Sch. Dist., 1974-84; treas., v.p., sec. State Bd. Edn., Lansing, Mich., 1984—, pres., 1990-92, sec., 1994-96; mem. profl. devel. adv. coms. State Bd., Dept. Edn., Mich. Legis., Mich. Assn. Sch. Bds.; chair study Nat. Assn. State Bds. Edn., 1988, bd. dirs. representing 12 midwestern states, chair by-laws com.; apptd. by gov. Midwestern Higher Edn. Com.; at-large del. Southeast Mich. Coun. Govts. Dir. Rep. Women's Forum. Recipient Disting. Svc. award Mich. Assn. Career Edn., 1989, Svc. award Phi Delta Kappa, 1989, Can Doer award Sci. and Tech. Quest Honor Roll, 1991, Spirit of Independence award Oakland-Macomb Counties Ctr. for Ind. Living, 1991, Paul Harris fellow Rotary Internat., 1989, Edn. Leadership award Mich. Elem. and Mid. Sch. Prins. Assn., 1995. Mem. Delta Kappa Gamma (hon.). Office: Edn Bd PO Box 30008 Lansing MI 48909-7508

BEARDSLEY, KATHLEEN MARY, accountant; b. Jackson, Mich., May 1, 1955; d. Eugene Joseph and Alberta Marie (Dzikowicz) Ziepiela; m. Christopher William Macklin, Aug. 10, 1974 (div. Dec. 1980); children: Nicole Christine, David William; m. Richard Warren Beardsley, Apr. 29, 1982. BA in Bus. and Econs., Spring Arbor Coll., 1988. Acctg. asst. Wacker Silicones Co., Adrian, Mich., 1988-89; gen. acctg. analyst Consumers Power Co., Jackson, Mich., 1989—. Mem. Inst. Mgmt. Accts. (cert. mgmt. acct., dir. Lansing/Jackson chpt. 1995—). Roman Catholic. Office: Consumers Power Co 212 W Michigan Jackson MI 49201

BEARE, MURIEL ANITA NIKKI, public relations executive, author; b. Detroit, Mar. 7, 1928; d. Elbert Stanley and Dorothy Margaret (Welch) Brink; m. Richard Austin Beare, June 15, 1946; 1 child, Sandra Lee. AA, Miami Dade Community Coll., 1974; BA, Skidmore Coll., 1979. Writer, Key

West Citizen (Fla.), 1959, Miami News (Fla.), 1967; field dir. Fla. Project HOPE, 1967-68, southeastern area dir., 1968 69; asst. v.p. pub. relations I/D Assocs., Inc., Miami, 1969-70; pres. Nikki Beare & Assocs., Miami, 1971—; v.p. South Fla. office Cherenson, Carroll & Holzer, Livingston, N.J., 1973; sr. v.p. D.J. Edelman, Inc., 1981-83; moderator, producer Women's Powerline, Sta. WIOD, Miami, 1972-77; co-owner South Miami Travel Service, South Miami, 1976-78; pres. Gov.'s Sq. Travel, Inc., Tallahassee, 1979-85, Travel Is Fun, Miami, 1985-90; bd. dirs, corp. sec. Imperial Bank. Author: Pirates, Pineapples and People: Tales and Legends of the Florida Keys, 1961; From Turtle Soup to Coconuts, 1964; Bottle Bonanza, A Handbook for Antique Bottle Collectors, 1965; producer cable TV program Traveler's Digest, 1986-92. Chmn. adv. bd. Met. Dade County Library, 1964; active Greater Miami Host Com.; former chair Met. Dade County Com. Status Women, 1971-76, City of Miami Commn. Status Women, 1985-92; active Met. Gen. Land Use Master Planning Com., 1973-74; Gov.'s Com. Employment Handicapped, 1970-72; chmn. Met. Dade Fair Housing and Employment Appeals Bd., 1975-78; active Miami YWCA's; chmn. Handicapped and Elderly subcom. Met. Dade Transit Devel. Com.; mem. Fla. Ins. Commn. Task Force, 1975, Dade County Democratic Exec. com., 1972-76, South Fla. Health Planning Council, 1972-74; founding mem. Nat. Women's Polit. Caucus, 1971—; pres. Capitol Women's Polit. Caucus; v.p. Fla. Women's Polit. Caucus; v.p. Herstory, 1971—; candidate Fla. Senate, 1974, Fla. Ho. of Reps., 1976; past pres. adv. bd. Inst. for Women, Fla. Internat. U.; pres. Fla. Feminist Credit Union, 1975-78; bd. dirs. Community Health Inst. South Dade County, 1975-77; mem. Jobs for Miami, 1980-88; chmn. Fla. Gov.'s Small Bus. Adv. Council, 1981-83, Greater Miami Tourism Coalition, 1983-85; del. White House Conf. on Small Bus., 1980, 86; chmn. publicity com. Asta World Congress, 1989; co-chmn. FIU Sch. Journalism and Mass Communications Adv. Bd. Recipient Silver Image award Pub. Relations Assn., 1967-68; named to Fla. Women's Hall of Fame, 1994. Mem. AAUW, LWV, NOW, Hist. Assn. So. Fla., Friends of Everglades, Women's C. of C. So. Fla., Am. Soc. Travel Agts., Women in Communications, Nat. Assn. Women Bus. Owners, Pub. Rels. Soc. Am., Fla. Pub. Rels. Soc., Women's Inst. for Freedom of the Press, Antique Bottle Collectors Assn. Fla., Caribean Tourism Orgn., YWCA, Miami Internat. Press Club, South by Southeast Profl. Women In Travel. Democrat. Office: Nikki Beare & Assocs Inc RR 3 Box 786 Havana FL 32333-9594

BEARMAN, TONI CARBO See CARBO, TONI

BEARWALD, JEAN HAYNES, company executive; b. San Francisco, Aug. 31, 1924; d. Joseph Robert and Edna Haynes (Goudey) Bearwald; m. William Henry Sherburn, Apr. 12, 1969 (dec. 1970); 1 child by previous marriage, David Richard Cross. BA, Stephens Coll., Columbia, Mo., 1945. Adminstrv. asst. Bearwald & Assocs., Sacramento, 1966-78; acct. Truck Parts Co., Sand City, Calif., 1979-80; pres., chief exec. officer Bearwald and Assocs., Fresno, Calif., 1980-89, Las Vegas, N.Mex., 1989-91; owner Traditions D'Elegance, Santa Fe, 1991—; program dir. hosp. and institution State of Calif. Ann. Conf., Carmel, 1980-82. Chmn. Sunset Serenade Gala, Santa Fe Opera Guild, 1993-94. Republican. Episcopalian. Home and Office: 941 Calle Mejia Apt 1604 Santa Fe NM 87501-1470

BEARY, SHIRLEY LORRAINE, retired music educator; b. New Albany, Kans., Feb. 4, 1928; d. Howard Warren and Bertha Adelia (Wilcox) Fogelsanger; children: Stephanie Beary Johnson, Susan Beary Maloney. BA, Andrews U., 1949; MusM, U. Redlands, 1967; D Mus. Arts, Southwestern Bapt. Theol. Sem., 1977. Tchr. music Nevada, Iowa, 1949-50; prof. music Southwestern Adventist Coll., Keene, Tex., 1959-84, lectr. Christian ethics, 1978-84; prof. music Oakwood Coll., Huntsville, Ala., 1984-94; ret., 1994; ch. organist Seventh-day Adventist Ch., Kalamazoo, 1951-59, Keene, 1959-80, min. music, 1980-82. Mem. bd. advisors Am. Biog. Inst., Raleigh, N.C. Mem. Coll. Music Soc., Am. Hymn Soc., Internat. Adventist Music Assn. Democrat. Home: 2615 Oak Valley Dr Yreka CA 96097-9744

BEASLEY, MARY CATHERINE, home economics educator, administrator, researcher; b. Portersville, Ala., Nov. 29, 1922; d. Albert Otis and Beulah Green (Killian) Reed; m. Percy Wells Beasley, Dec. 15, 1956 (dec. Dec. 1958). BS in Home Econs., Bob Jones U., 1944; MS, Pa. State U., State College, 1954, EdD, 1968. Tchr. Geraldine and Collinsville (Ala.) High Sch., 1944-45; vocat. home econs. tchr. Glencoe (Ala.) High Sch., 1945-48, Washington County High Sch., Chatom, Ala., 1948-51; home econs. tchr. Homewood Jr. High Sch., Birmingham, Ala., 1958-60; asst. supr. and subject matter specialist Ala. Dept. Edn., Montgomery, 1951-57; asst. prof. Samford U., Birmingham, 1960-62; instr. U. Ala., Tuscaloosa, 1951, asst. prof. then assoc. prof., 1962-68, dir. continuing edn. in home econs., 1968-84, prof., 1984-87, prof. emeritus consumer sci. Coll. Human Environ. Sci., 1988—. Author: (with others) Human Ecological Studies, 1986. Pres. Joint Legis. Coun. of Ala., 1973-75; dir. On Your Own Program, 1970-80. Recipient Creative Programming award Nat. U. Extension Assn., 1979. Mem. Am. Home Econs. Assn. (chmn. rehab. com. 1973, 75, leader 1986), Southeastern Coun. on Family Rels. (pres. 1982-84, Disting. Svc. award 1988), Ala. Home Econs. Assn. (pres. 1961-63, leader 1985), Ala. Coun. on Family Rels. (pres. 1981-83, Disting. Svc. award 1987), Altrusa Club of Tuscaloosa (pres. 1988-89, exec. bd. Ft. Payne/DeKalb 1989-93, corr. sec. 1995-96), Collinsville Study Club (v.p. 1992-93, pres. 1996-98), Alpha Delta Kappa (treas. Tuscaloosa chpt. 1973-75), Phi Upsilon Omicron, Kappa Omicron Nu. Republican. Baptist. Home: 12860 US Hwy 11 Collinsville AL 35961-9171

BEASLEY, MAURINE HOFFMAN, journalism educator, historian; b. Sedalia, Mo., Jan. 28, 1936; d. Dimmitt Heard and Maurine (Hieronymous) Hoffman; m. William C. McLaughlin, May 20, 1966 (div. 1969); m. Henry R. Beasley, Dec. 24, 1970; 1 child, Susan Sook. BJ, BA in History, U. Mo., 1958; MS in Journalism, Columbia U., 1963; PhD in Am. Civilization, George Washington U., 1974; Cert. in Brit. History, U. Edinburgh, Scotland, 1964. Edn. editor Kansas City (Mo.) Star, 1959-62; staff writer Washington Post, 1963-73; asst. prof. journalism U. Md., College Park, 1975-80, assoc. prof., 1980-86, prof. 1987—. Author: Eleanor Roosevelt and the Media: A Public Quest for Self-Fulfillment, 1987; (with others) Women in Media, 1977, The New Majority, 1988, Taking Their Place! Documentary History of Women and Journalism, 1993 (One of Outstanding Acad. Books, Choice 1994); editor: (with others) Voices of Change: Southern Pulitzer Winners, 1978, One Third of a Nation (hon. mention Washington Monthly Book Award 1982), 1981; editor: White House Press Conferences of Eleanor Roosevelt, 1983; mem. adv. bd. Am. Journalism, 1983—, Jour. of Mass Media Ethics, Mass Com. Rev.; corr. editor Journalism History, 1995—; contbr. articles to acad. jours. Violinist, Montgomery Coll. Symphony Orch., 1975—; pres., Little Falls Swimming Club, Inc., 1988-89. Gannett Teaching Fellowships Program fellow, 1977; Pulitzer traveling fellow Columbia U., 1963; Eleanor Roosevelt studies grantee Eleanor Roosevelt Inst., 1979-80; named one of nation's outstanding tchrs. of writing and editing Modern Media Inst. and Am. Soc. Newspaper Editors, 1981, most outstanding woman U. Md., Coll. Park Pres. Commn. on Women's Affairs, 1993, Haiman award for disting. scholarship in freedom of expression Speech Comm. Assn., 1995. Mem. Assn. Edn. in Journalism and Mass Communications (exec. com. 1990-91, 94-95, standing com. on profl. freedom and responsibility 1985, vice chair 1987-89, chair 1990-91, sec. history div. 1986-87, vice-head 1987-88, head 1988-89, pres. elect 1992, pres. 1993-94, leader People-to-People delegation to China and Hong Kong 1994, Outstanding Contbn. to Journalism Edn. award 1994), Am. Journalism Historians Assn. (pres.-elect 1988-89, pres. 1989-90), Am. News Women's Club (bd. govs. 1986-87), Women in Communications (bd. dirs. Washington chpt. 1985-87), Nat. Fedn. Press Women, Soc. Profl. Journalists (chair nat. hist. site com. 1986-87, bd. dirs. Washington chpt. 1988-90, pres. Washington chpt. 1990-91, dir. region 2 and mem. nat. bd. 1991-92, award for disting. svc. to local journalism Washington chpt. 1994), Internat. Assn. Mass Comm. Rsch., Orgn. Am. Historians, Am. Hist. Assn., Phi Beta Kappa, Omicron Delta Kappa. Democrat. Unitarian. Home: 4920 Flint Dr Bethesda MD 20816-1746 Office: U Md Coll Journalism College Park MD 20742

BEATH, PAULA MARIE RUARK, education educator, consultant; b. Cambridge, Md., Dec. 1, 1950; d. Paul Kenneth and Ellen Marie (Parks) Ruark; 1 child, Ernest Ballard Beath. BS in Elem. Edn., Salisbury State Coll., 1972, MS in Elem. Edn., 1975; PhD in Reading and Early Childhood Edn., U. Md., 1979. Cert. elem./mid. sch. supr., prin., reading specialist grades K-12, elem. grades 1-6 and mid. sch. supt. Elem. tchr. Dorchester County Bd. Edn., Cambridge, Md., 1972-78, sch. prin., 1979-94, reading specialist, 1995—; specialist Md. State Dept. Edn., Balt., 1994-95; vis. prof., coord. Reading Ctr., and liaison with Montgomery and Prince George's Counties, U. Md., College Park, 1978-79; adj. prof. Salisbury (Md.) State U., 1994—. Author: Survival Reading Task Cards, 1976, Teacher's Survival Guide-Dimensions of Learning and Its Role in Maryland's Educational Initiatives, 1996. Choir dir. Hoopers Meml. Ch., Hoopersville, Md., 1970-80, cert. lay leader, 1975-80, mem. adminstrv. bd., 1979-84, Sunday sch. tchr., 1972-81; collaborate with YMCA to implement programs for county youths; designer vol. program in collaboration with Dorchester County Commn. on Aging; mem. Dorchester County Mus. Com. Named Md. Tchr. of Yr., 1978; recipient award Dorchester Ret. Tchrs. Assn., 1978; named to Outstanding Young Women of Am., 1980. Mem. ASCD, Md. Assn. Elem. Sch. Prins., Nat. Staff Devel. Coun., Delta Kappa Gamma, Phi Delta Kappa. Home: 2216 Horn Point Rd Cambridge MD 21613-3379

BEATTIE, ANN, author; b. Washington, Sept. 8, 1947; d. James and Charlotte (Crosby) B.; m. Lincoln Perry. B.A., Am. U., 1969; M.A., U. Conn., 1970; L.H.D. (hon.), Am. U., 1983. Vis. asst. prof. U. Va., Charlottesville, 1976-77, vis. writer, 1980; Briggs Copeland lectr. English Harvard U., Cambridge, Mass., 1977. Author: Chilly Scenes of Winter, 1976, Distortions, 1976, Secrets and Suprises, 1979, Falling In Place, 1980, Jacklighting, 1981, The Burning House, 1982, Love Always, 1985, Where You'll Find Me, 1986, Alex Katz, 1987, Picturing Will, 1990, What Was Mine, 1991. Recipient Disting. Alumnae award Am. U., 1980, award in lit. Am. Acad. and Inst. Arts and Letters, 1980; Guggenheim fellow, 1977. Mem. Am. Acad. and Inst. of Arts and Letters, 1992, PEN, Authors Guild. Office: care Janklow and Nesbit 598 Madison Ave New York NY 10022-1614*

BEATTY, BETTY JOY, library educator; b. Columbus, Ohio, Mar. 25, 1926; d. Lee E. and Gladys (Heffner) Howard; m. James Auerhan Hecht, May 6, 1950 (dec. July 9, 1974); children: James Auerhan (dec.), Timothy Lee, David Arthur; m. Benjamin M. Beatty, Dec. 19, 1975. BFA, Ohio State U., Columbus, 1947, MA, 1948. Branch librarian Warder Public Library (now Clark County Library), Springfield, Ohio, 1957-59; librarian, teacher Shawnee H.S., Springfield, 1959-66; acquisition librarian Wittenberg U., Springfield, 1966-72, head, technical svcs., 1972-84, acting dir. univ. libraries, 1983-84, assoc. prof. emerita, 1992—; mem. bd. dirs. Faculty Devel. Orgn., Springfield, 1975-78 pres. Wittenberg U. Fed. Credit Union, Springfield, 1979-81, sec. 1984-87; pres. AAUP, Springfield, 1980. Treas. Springfield Symphony Women's Assn., 1974-76; sec. bd. dirs. Touch of Love AIDS Support, Springfield, 1988-95. Mem. Alpha Chi Omega Sorority (pres. 1964-66, sec. 1985-87, 94-96). Democrat. Roman Catholic. Home: 615 Piney Branch Springfield OH 45503

BEATTY, CONNY DAVINROY, lawyer; b. Belleville, Ill., July 28, 1959; d. William Thomas and Kay (Schuck) Davinroy; m. Daniel Patrick Beatty, Aug. 23, 1986; children: Robert Daniel, Alexandria Marie. BA cum laude, Monmouth Coll., 1981; JD cum laude, St. Louis U., 1987, MBA, 1987. Bar: Mo. 1987, U.S. Dist. Ct. (ea. dist.) 1987, Ill. 1988, U.S. Dist. Ct. (so. dist.) 1988. Assoc. Thompson Coburn (formerly Thompson & Mitchell), St. Louis, 1987-95, ptnr., 1996—. Mem. vol. lawyer program Legal Svcs. Ea. Mo.; bd. dirs. Belleville Area unit Ill. divsn. Am. Cancer Soc.; alumni bd. dirs. Monmouth Coll.; mem. Millstadt Cmty. Band. Recipient Disting. Young Alumni award Monmouth Coll., 1995. Mem. ABA, Mo. Bar Assn., Ill. Bar Assn., Bar Assn. Met. St. Louis, Healthcare Fin. Mgmt. Assn. (advanced mem.), St. Louis Health Lawers Assn., Pi Beta Phi. Home: 11 Coronation Dr Millstadt IL 62260-1809 Office: Thompson Coburn 1 Mercantile Ctr Saint Louis MO 63101

BEATTY, FRANCES, civic worker; b. Chgo., Apr. 17, 1940; d. Pasquale and Rose (Brunetti) Calomeni; m. Robert Alfred Beatty, Aug. 24, 1963; children: Bradford, Roxanna. BA, Northwestern U., 196l; MA, U. Chgo., l967. Tchr. math. Proviso West High Sch., Hillside, Ill., 196l-66. Active Oak Brook Dist. 53 Sch. Bd., 1979-85; mem. women's bd. Field Mus. Natural History, Chgo., 1985—, mem. founders coun., 1988—, treas. women's bd., 1991-93; mem. governing bd. Chgo. Symphony, 1985-92; trustee Chgo. Symphony Orch., 1992—; mem. women's bd. Ravinia Festival, Highland Park, Ill., 1987—, Northwestern U., Evanston, Ill., U. Chgo.; mem. coun. Wellness House, Hinsdale, Ill., 1994. Mem. Alumnae of Northwestern U. (pres. 1996—), Woman's Athletic Club Chgo. (3d v.p. 1985-87, 1st v.p. 1992-94, pres. 1994-96), John Evans Club.

BEATTY, FRANCES FIELDING LEWIS, art dealer; b. N.Y.C., Nov. 23, 1948; d. John Robert Anthony and Anne (Kidder) B.; m. Allen A. Adler; children: Alexander H.L., Anthony B. BA, Vassar Coll., 1970; MA, Columbia U., 1973, PhD, 1980. Instr. Ramapo Coll., Mahwah, N.Y., 1972-74, Columbia U., N.Y.C., 1974-76; editor Art World Mag., N.Y.C., 1976; v.p. Richard L. Feigen & Co., N.Y.C., 1978—; bd. dirs. The Drawing Ctr. Co-author: Louise Nevelson Catalogue, 1977; contbr. Andre Masson Catalogue, 1977. Mem. contemporary council Mus. Modern Art, N.Y.C., 1978—; bd. dirs. Checkerboard Found., N.Y.C., 1980—. Grantee Columbia U., 1977; Noble Found. fellow Columbia U., 1972, Vassar Coll., 1975. Mem. Nat. Soc. Colonial Dames. Office: Richard L Feigen & Co 49 E 68th St New York NY 10021-5012

BEATY, LINDA J., customer picture framer; b. Glendale, Calif., Nov. 27, 1942; d. Clayton F. and Betty J. (Templeman) Hinze; m. Larry D. Dodge, Aug. 14, 1960 (div. 1982); children: Laurie Jane, Loren D.; m. Milton E. Beaty, Oct. 21, 1984. Student, U. Wyo., 1960; AA, Ea. Wyo. Coll., 1966; postgrad., Rocky Mountain (Colo.) Sch. of Art, 1982. Art instr. Ea. Wyo. Coll., Torrington, 1977-81; owner Books and Things, Torrington, 1976-81; dir. El Prado Gallery, Santa Fe, N. Mex., 1983-84; real estate salesperson Santa Fe, 1986—; owner Acres Estates Frame Shop, Sante Fe, 1986-95. Various solo and group shows, Wyo., Colo., Ariz., N.Mex., Carribean. Mem. C. of C. Wyo. Mem. Art Assn., Jay Cees. Mem. Christian Ch. Home: MHP SP 195 Country Club Gardens Santa Fe NM 87505 Office: 751 Airport Rd Santa Fe NM 87505

BEAUBIEN, ANNE KATHLEEN, librarian; b. Detroit, Sept. 15, 1947; d. Richard Parker and Edith Mildred Beaubien. Student, Western Mich. U., 1965-67; BA, Mich. State U., 1969; AM in Libr. Sci., U. Mich., 1970. Reference libr., bibliographic instr. U. Mich. Libr., Ann Arbor, 1971-80, dir. MITS, 1980-85, head coop. access svcs., 1985—; head Business & Cooperative Access Svcs., 1995—. Author: (booklet) Psychology Bibliography, 1980; co-author: Learning the Library, 1982; contbr. articles to profl. jours., editor, conf. proc., 1987. Pres. Ann Arbor Ski Club, 1978-79; mem. vestry St. Clare's Episcopal Ch., Ann Arbor, 1986-89. Recipient Woman of Yr. award Ann Arbor Bus. and Profl. Women's Club, 1982, Disting. Alumnus award Sch. Info. and Libr. Studies, U. Mich., 1987. Mem. ALA, Assn. Coll. and Rsch. Librs. (pres. 1991-92). Office: U Mich Libr 106 Hatcher Grad Libr Ann Arbor MI 48109

BEAUDET, PATRICIA SUZANNE, photography editor; b. Chgo., Aug. 6, 1951; d. André Marcel and Helen Gertrude (Joiner) B. Assoc. photography editor Playboy Enterprises Inc., Chgo., 1970—. Contbg. photographer Rolling Stone Illustrated History of Rock and Roll, 1992; rschr., photo editor: The Playboy Book: Forty Years, 1994. Democrat. Roman Catholic. Home: PO Box 31351 Chicago IL 60631-0351

BEAUDET, SUSAN LEIGH, information specialist, city councilor at large; b. Manchester, N.H., Oct. 6, 1971; d. Armand Emile and Constance Aurore (Knittel) B. BS, Boston U., 1993. Sec. New Eng. Towing, Manchester, N.H., 1986-88; sec., receptionist Somersworth (N.H.) Housing Authority, 1989; sr. peer counselor Boston U. Office of Fin. Assistance, Boston, 1989-93; info. specialist Ctr. for Resource Mgmt., South Hampton, N.H., 1993—. Jr./sr. class advisor Somersworth H.S. Class of 1996, 1994-96; councilor at large City of Somersworth, 1993—; campaign mgr. state rep. Dana Hilliard, Somersworth, 1994; dist. coord. Clinton/ Gore 96, Somersworth, 1996—. Mem. Somersworth Jaycees. Democrat. Home: 272 Green St. Somersworth NH 03878 Office: Ctr for Resource Mgmt 2 Highland Rd South Hampton NH 03827

BEAUDOIN, CAROL ANN, psychologist; b. Lowell, Mass., Mar. 30, 1949; d. Adrien P. and Rita J. (LeBlanc) B.; B.A. with honors, U. Fla., 1971; M.Ed. in Counseling, Boston U., 1973, Ed.D. in Counseling Psychology, 1979. Psychiat. aide U. Fla.-Shands Teaching Hosp., Gainesville, 1970-71; trainee VA Hosp., Gainesville, 1971-72; attendant Boston State Hosp., 1972, intern, 1973; intern Univ. Hosp., also Counseling Center, Northeastern U., Boston, 1973-74, Dorchester Mental Health Center, also Carney Hosp., 1974-75; staff psychologist Human Resource Inst., Boston, 1974-80, treatment team leader, 1975-80; pvt. practice psychology, Brookline, Mass., 1980—. Mem. Am. Psychol. Assn. Office: 1101 Beacon St Brookline MA 02146-5502

BEAUDRY, DIANE FAY PUTA, medical staff services director; b. Manitowoc, Wis., Mar. 6, 1947; d. Ruben William and Gertrude Katherine (Novak) Puta. BSN, Alverno Coll., 1971; MS in Ednl. Adminstrn., U. Wis., Milw., 1979, PhD in Urban Edn., 1991. Staff nurse St. Mary's Hosp., Milw., 1971-72, St. Anthony's Hosp., Milw., 1972-74; nurse coord. Pvt. Initiative in PSRO, Wis., 1974-75; insvc. instr. Deaconess Hosp., Milw., 1975-77, insvc. coord., 1977-81; dir. nursing staff devel./quality assurance Good Samaritan Med. Ctr., Milw., 1981-84, dir. quality assurance, 1984-85, dir. utilization mgmt., 1985-88; mgr. quality mgmt. Sinai Samaritan Med. Ctr., Milw., 1988-89, dir. med. staff svcs. and quality mgmt., 1989—. Author: (with others) Interdisciplinary QA: Issues in Collaboration, 1991; author poem. mem. Nat. Assn. for Healthcare Quality, Alverno Coll. Alumnae Assn., U. Wis. Alumni Assn., Delta Epsilon Sigma, Kappa Gamma Pi. Home: 11047 N Riverland Ct 36W Mequon WI 53092-4900 Office: Sinai Samaritan Med Ctr PO Box 342 Milwaukee WI 53201-0342

BEAUMONT, JEANNE MARIE, writer; b. Darby, Pa., June 15, 1954; d. John J. and Josephine Mary (Krajcik) B. BA in English, Eastern Coll., 1979; MFA, Columbia U., 1989. Copywriter, editor Wyeth Labs., Radnor, Pa., 1980-83; copywriter William Douglas McAdams, N.Y.C., 1983-84; copy supr. Rolf Werner Rosenthal Inc., N.Y.C., 1984-87; freelance editor, writer N.Y.C., 1987—; editor, pub. American Letters & Commentary, N.Y.C., 1992—; resident faculty Frost Place Ann. Festival of Poetry, Franconia, N.H., 1990, 91, 94, 96; guest poet Poets House, Isle Magee, No. Ireland, 1992; reader Women's Poet Series Douglass Coll. of Rutgers U., New Brunswick, N.J., 1996. Contbr. poems to more than 60 nat. jours. and mags. Recipient Thyra Ferre Bjorn Creative Writing award Eastern Coll., 1979, Billee Murray Denny Poetry hon. mention awards Lincoln Coll., 1992, 93, 1st Pl. in Dimensional Mail Series Mail Works Achievement award Fisher-Stevens, 1985; winner Nat. Poetry Series 1996. Democrat. Home and Office: 120 W 70th St New York NY 10023

BEAUMONT, MONA, artist; b. Paris; d. Jacques Hippolyte and Elsie M. (Didisheim) Marx. m. William G. Beaumont; children: Garrett, Kevin. Postgrad., Harvard U., Fogg Mus., Cambridge, Mass. One-woman shows include Galeria Proteo, Mexico City, Gumps Gallery, San Francisco, Palace of Legion of Honor, San Francisco, L'Armitiere Gallery, Rouen, France, Hoover Gallery, San Francisco, San Francisco Mus. Modern Art, Galeria Van der Voort, San Francisco, William Sawyer Gallery, San Francisco, Palo Alto (Calif.) Cultural Ctr., Galerie Alexandre Monnet, Brussels, Honolulu Acad. Arts; group shows include San Francisco Mus. Modern Art, San Francisco Art Inst., DeYoung Meml. Mus., San Francisco, Grey Found. Tour of Asia, Bell Telephone Invitational, Chgo., Richmond Art Ctr., L.A. County Mus. Art, Galerie Zodiaque, Geneva, Galerie Le Manoir, La Chaux de Fonds, Switzerland, William Sawyer Meml. Exhibit, San Francisco, others; represented in permanent collections Oakland (Calif.) Mus. Art, City and County of San Francisco, Hoover Found., San Francisco, Grey Found., Washington, Bulart Found., San Francisco; also numerous pvt. collections. Mem. Soc. for Encouragement of Contemporary Art, Bay Area Graphic Art Coun., San Francisco Art Inst., San Francisco Mus. Modern Art, Capp Street Project, San Diego Mus. Contemporary Art, L.A. Mus. Contemporary Art. Recipient ann. painting award Jack London Square, 2 ann. awards San Francisco Women Artists, One-man Show award San Francisco Art Festival; purchase award Grey Found., San Francisco Women Artists (2), San Francisco Art Festival; included in Printworld Internat., Internat. Art Diary, Am. Artists, N.Y. Art Rev., Calif. Art Rev., Art in San Francisco Bay Area. Address: 1087 Upper Happy Valley Rd Lafayette CA 94549-2805

BEAUPAIN, ELAINE SHAPIRO, psychiatric social worker; b. Boston, Nov. 1, 1949; d. Abraham and Anna Marilyn (Gass) S.; m. Dean A. Beaupain, Feb. 14, 1987; 1 child, Andrew. BA, McGill U., Montreal, Que., 1971, MSW, 1974. Ind. clin. social worker, Mass.; cert. social worker, Maine; cert. social worker with ind. practice lic., Maine; lic. ind. clin. social worker, Mass. Psychiat. social worker Bangor (Maine) Mental Health Inst., 1974-75; outpatient therapist The Counseling Ctr., Bangor, 1975-76, The Counseling Ctr., Millinocket, Maine, 1979-86; asst. core group leader adolescent unit Jackson Brook Inst., Portland, Maine, 1986-87; area dir. Community Health and Counseling Svcs., 1981-86; pvt. practice social work, 1987—, psychotherapy with individuals, couples and families Millinocket and Bangor, 1987—. Mem. AAUW, Nat. Assn. Social Workers, Acad. Cert. Social Workers (diplomate 1992). Republican. Office: 122 Pine St Bangor ME 04401-5216

BEAUSOLEIL, DORIS MAE, federal agency administrator, housing specialist; b. Chelmsford, Mass., Jan. 9, 1932; d. Joseph Honorius and Beatrice Pearl (Smith) B.; student State Tchrs. Coll., Lowell, Mass., 1949-51; BA in Sociology and Psychology, Goddard Coll., Plainfield, Vt., 1954; MA in Human Relations, N.Y.U., 1957; postgrad. CUNY, N.Y.C., 1988—. With div. human rights N.Y. State, N.Y.C., 1960-69, housing dir., 1966-68; housing cons. Nat. Com. Against Discrimination in Housing, N.Y.C., 1969-70; housing cons. Edwin Gould Found., N.Y.C., 1970-71; human resources cons. interfaith housing strategy com., housing cons. Fedn. Prot. Welfare Agencies, Inc., N.Y.C., 1971-72; self-employed housing cons., 1972-74; equal opportunity compliance specialist N.Y./N.J. HUD, N.Y.C., 1975—, Fed. women's program coordinator, 1975-79; br. chief Title VI Sect. 109 Compliance div. fair housing and equal opportunity Region II, HUD, N.Y.C., 1979-84; founding mem. N.Y. State HUD Com.; adv. panel Housing Mag., 1979; cons., examiner N.Y. State Civil Svc. Commn., 1970-93. Mem. Nat. Assn. Human Rights Workers (Outstanding Service award 1974), Citizens Housing and Planning Coun., Nat. Assn. Housing and Devel. Ofcls., Goddard Coll. Alumni Assn. (sec. 1988-90), Rep. Bus. Women's Club (pres. 1985-88, bd. dirs. 1989-91). Republican. Unitarian. Home: 392 Central Park W New York NY 10025-5868 Office: 26 Federal Plz Rm 3532 New York NY 10278

BECHERER, DEBORAH ZORN, banker; b. Youngstown, Ohio, Feb. 9, 1958; d. Robert L. and Joan M. (Wilkos) Zorn; m. William B. Becherer Jr., May 22, 1983. BS in Bus. Edn. magna cum laude, Youngstown State U., 1980; MBA, Coll. of William and Mary, 1983; cert., Grad. Sch. Banking, Madison, Wis., 1989. Trainee advanced mgmt. Bank One of Ea. Ohio, Youngstown, 1983-84, officer comml. loans, 1984-86, asst. v.p., 1986—. Mem. allocation com. United Way Planning, Youngstown, 1984-86; pres. Lake to River coun. Girl Scouts U.S., 1987-91; liaison bd. dirs. Mahoning County Red Cross, Youngstown, Cen. Christian Day Care Ctr., Youngstown. Mem. NAFE, Am. Inst. Banking, Jr. League of Youngstown, Alumni Assn. Coll. of Wm. and Mary, Delta Zeta Alumni Assn. Republican. Methodist. Home: 7099 Oak Dr Youngstown OH 44514-3763 Office: Bank One of Ea Ohio 6 Federal Plz W Youngstown OH 44503-1410

BECHTEL, SHERRELL JEAN, psychotherapist; b. Birmingham, Ala., Sept. 23, 1961; d. Lewis Eugene and Sarah Rozelle (Sherrell) B. BS in Social Work, U. Ala., Birmingham, 1989; MSW, U. Ala., Tuscaloosa, 1990. Cert. addiction specialist; cert. group psychotherapist; lic. clin. social worker, Tenn., Ga. Vol. counselor Planned Parenthood, Birmingham, 1986-88; intern Bradford Adult Chem. Dependency, Birmingham, 1989; rsch. staff asst. U. Ala., Tuscaloosa, 1989-90; intern counselor Bradford Adolescent Chem. Dependency, Birmingham, 1990; primary counselor The Crossroads, Chattanooga, 1990-92; owner S. J. Bechtel LCSW, CAS, Chattanooga, 1991—; rschr. Ala. Comm. Youth, Montgomery, 1989-90; trainer Legal and Jud. Aspects Child Welfare, Decatur, Ala., 1989; presenter Ala. Victim Compensation, Mobile, 1990; speaker Limestone Correctional Facility, Huntsville, 1990; lectr. Grad. Sch. Social Wk., Tuscaloosa, 1990, U. Tenn., Chattanooga. Subcom. mem. Atty. Gen. Alliance Against Drug Abuse, Birmingham, 1989; speaker Victims of Crime and Leniency, Tuscaloosa, 1990; planning com. Holistic Health Retreat, Birmingham, 1988; mem. Tenn. Coun. on

Children and Youth-Legis./Policy. Mem. NASW (pres. student orgn. 1986-89), Tenn. Alcohol Drug Assn., Jewish Community Ctr., Phi Kappa Phi. Office: 7405 Shallowford Rd Ste 280 Chattanooga TN 37421-2662

BECK, DONNA LOUISE, business educator, English educator; b. Winston-Salem, N.C., Feb. 14, 1959; d. Cecil Warren and Anna May (Galloway) N.; m. David Bradley Sullivan, Oct. 8, 1994; 1 child, Mariah Wynne; 1 stepchild, Christopher Lucas. B in Bus. Adminstrn., Gonzaga U., 1984; MA, Ball State U., 1994, MAE, 1996. Adminstr. rep. Assocs. Fin. Svcs., Durham, N.C., 1985-86; asst. dean admissions High Point (N.C.) U., 1986-89; adv. admissions Crl. Oregon C. C., Bend, 1989-92; tchr. English Berlitz, Kobe, Japan, 1992-93; grad. asst. bus. edn. Ball State U., Muncie, Ind., 1993-96, instr., 1995; organizer, moderator panel discussion Pacific N.W. Assn. Coll. Admissions Counselors, 1991; presenter in field. Mentor Wings, Bend, Oreg., 1991. Mem. Assn. Bus. Commn. (manuscript reviewer for The Procs.), Delta Pi Epsilon. Democrat. Home: 13605 Eagle Ridge Dr # 1725 Fort Myers FL 33912 Office: Bus Edn/Office Adminstrn Ball State Univ Muncie IN 47306

BECK, DORIS OLSON, library media director; b. Kingsville, Tex., June 4, 1930; d. Thomas Leon and Estelle (Fosselman) Olson; m. John Roland Beck, Feb. 9, 1951; children: Elizabeth Joan, Thomas Roland, Patricia Lind, John William. BS in Chemistry, Tex. A & I Coll., 1949, BSChemE, 1950; MLS, Wayne State U., 1975. Cert. secondary educator with libr. endorsement, Ariz. Chemist Patterson's Lab., Harlingen, Tex., 1950-51; asst. libr. Tex. A & I Coll., Kingsville, Tex., 1951; chemist U.S. Geol. Svc., Stillwater, Okla., 1951-53; bookkeeper, nurse's aide McKenzie Co. Hosp., Watford City, N.D., 1953-54; math. tchr. Prescott Jr. High, Corpus Christi, Tex., 1954; chemist U.S. Geol. Svc., Columbus, Ohio, 1957-58; math. tchr. Christiansberg (Va.) High Sch., 1967-69; sci. tchr. East Jr. High Sch., Farmington, Mich., 1969-70; sci./math. tchr. Jane Addams Jr. High Sch., Royal Oak, Mich., 1970-78; math support Oakland Vocat. Sch., Royal Oak, 1978-79; head libr. S.W. Bapt. Coll., Pontiac, Mich., 1977-79; libr. media dir. Humboldt (Ariz.) Jr. High, 1979-87, Bradshaw Mt. Jr. High, Dewey, Ariz., 1987—; site based com. Bradshaw Mt. Jr. High Sch., Dewey, Ariz., 1992—. Ch. libr., cons., 1993—. Mem. Ariz. Libr. Assn., Ariz. Ednl. Media Assn., Delta Kappa Gamma, Alpha Delta Kappa. Republican. Baptist. Home: PO Box 25824 3829 Valorie Prescott Valley AZ 86312 Office: Bradshaw Mt Jr High Sch Humboldt Unified Sch Dist Dewey AZ 86327

BECK, DOROTHY FAHS, social researcher; b. N.Y.C.; d. Charles Harvey and Sophia (Lyon) Fahs; m. Hubert Park Beck, Aug. 20, 1930 (dec. Jan. 1989); 1 child, Brenda E.F. AB, U. N.C., 1928; MA, U. Chgo., 1932; PhD (Gilder fellow), Columbia U., 1944, postdoctoral study, 1955-56. Am.-German Student Exch. fellow, Fed. Republic Germany, 1928-29. Dir. econ. rsch. ADA, 1929-32; social worker Emergency Relief Adminstrn. N.J., 1933-34, statistician, 1934-35; statistician U.S. Office Edn., 1935-36; assoc. social economist U.S. Cen. Statis. Bd., 1936-38; rsch. supr., author Am. Coll. Dentists, 1940-42; statistician Am. Heart Assn., 1947-53, Cornell U. Med. Coll., 1951-53; asst. prof. biostats. Am. U. Beirut, 1954: dir. rsch. Family Svc. Am., N.Y.C., 1956-81, dir. study counselor attitudes and feelings, 1982-87, evaluation rsch. cons., 1982-87. Co-founder, Fahs-Beck Fund for Rsch. and Experimentation; donor-adviser The N.Y. Community Trust, 1986—. Fellow Am. Sociol. Assn.; mem. Acad. Cert. Social Workers, Am. Assn. Marriage and Family Therapy (affiliate), Nat. Coun. Family Rels., Groves Conf., Am. Statis. Assn., Nat. Assn. Social Workers, Soc. Study Social Problems, Am. Pub. Health Assn., Phi Beta Kappa. Unitarian-Universalist. Author: Patterns in Use of Family Agency Service, 1962, Marriage and the Family Under Challenge, 1976, New Treatment Modalities, 1978, Counselor Characteristics: How They Affect Outcomes, 1988; co-author: Costs of Dental Care Under Specific Clinical Conditions, 1943, Myocardial Infarction, 1954, Clients' Progress within Five Interviews, 1970, How to Conduct a Client Follow-Up Study, 1974, 2d enlarged edit., 1980, Progress on Family Problems, 1973. Home: 50 Crosslands Dr Kennett Square PA 19348

BECK, ELLEN, public relations executive; b. N.Y.C., May 22, 1961. BA, Am. U., 1984. Dir. sta. rels. PubSat, 1985-86; v.p. Britt-Vasarely and Assocs., 1986-87; sr. account exec. Fleishman-Hillard, 1987-90; account exec. Richardson, Myers and Donofri, 1990, Porter/Novelli, 1990-92; founder, pres. Beck Comm., Ellicott City, Md., 1992-93; dir. mktg. Avtek Assocs., Inc., 1993—. Office: Avtek Assocs Inc 1703 Underwood Rd Sykesville MD 21784-5730

BECK, FRANCES JOSEPHINE MOTTEY (MRS. JOHN MATTHEW BECK), secondary education educator; b. Eleanora, Pa., July 12, 1918; d. George F. and Mary (Wisnieski) Mottey; B.S., Ind. State Tchrs. Coll., 1939; M.A., U. Chgo., 1955, Ph.D., 1980; m. John Matthew Beck, Aug. 23, 1941. Jr. visitor Pa. Dept. Pub. Assistance, 1940-41; asst. to the sec. dept. edn. U. Chgo., 1952-58, asst. sec., 1958, asst. dean of students Grad. Sch. Edn., 1958-75; asst. to dean Sch. Edn., De Paul U., Chgo., 1975-79, asst. prof., 1979-82; reading tchr. Bontemps Pub. Sch., Chgo., 1982-85, Chgo. Pub. Sch., 1982—; reading instr. Central YMCA, Chgo., 1958-61. Bd. dirs. Reading is Fundamental, Chgo., 1979—. Recipient Aquin Guild award, 1990, Educator of Yr. award Phi Delta Kappa, 1993. Mem. Internat. Reading Assn., Chgo. Area Reading Assn. (dir. 1980-85), Delta Kappa Gamma. Pi Lambda Theta (nat. v.p. 1966-70, 1st v.p. 1971-74, pres. Chgo. area chpt. 1987-91), Sigma Sigma Sigma. Co-author: Extending Reading Skills, 1976; contbr. articles to profl. jours. Home and Office: 5832 S Stony Island Ave Chicago IL 60637-2025

BECK, HELEN FRANCES SUMMER, architectural artist; b. Richmond, Va., Apr. 16, 1948; d. Hugh Harrison and Mary Elizabeth (Cates) Summer; children: Timothy, Jeremy, Susan. BVA, Ga. State U., 1970, MFA, 1991. Designer architectural Helen S. Beck, Atlanta, 1972-81, 83-84, Am. Bell, Somerset, N.J., 1981-82; drafter structural Benneth & Pless Cons. Engrs., Atlanta, 1984-86; designer architectural Alan Salzman & Assocs., Atlanta, 1987-88; operator computer Starzer & Ritchie Engrs., Atlanta, 1988-94; designer self employed, Atlanta, 1994—; design licensing agreement Inter-continental Greetings, Ltd., N.Y.C., 1987—; represented by Novus Gallery, Atlanta, 1991-92, Fay Gold Gallery, Atlanta, 1987-88. Exhibited in group shows at Decatur Arts Alliance Visual Arts Exhbn., Atlanta, 1993, Dogwood Festival Invitational Show, Atlanta, 1992, Quinlay Art Ctr., Gainesville, Ga., 1991, Ga. State U. Art Gallery, 1989; designs for Paces Papers by Jackie, Atlanta, 1987, Ritz Carlton Hotels, 1987. Home and Office: 2697 Skyland Dr NE Atlanta GA 30319

BECK, ISABEL HOLDERMAN, psychologist, consultant; b. Boise, Idaho, Mar. 17, 1916; d. Frank John Holderman and Beulah Beatrice Dennis; m. Lester Fred Beck, Dec. 22, 1956 (div. July 1969). AA in Journalism, L.A. Jr. Coll., 1939; BA in Psychology, Occidental Coll., 1941, MA in Psychology, 1949; PhD in Psychology, U. So. Calif., 1959. Cert. psychologist, Calif.; lic. psychologist, Calif. Pers. technician Lockheed Aircraft, Burbank, Calif., 1943; psychologist L.A. City Schs., 1949-52; counselor, curriculum coord. L.A. Jr. Colls., 1953-66; sr. mem. profl. staff S.W. Regional Lab., Inglewood, Calif., 1966-68; pvt. cons. Inglewood, 1968-70; prof. psychology Santa Barbara (Calif.) City Coll., 1970-73; pvt. practice, 1973-94; cons. Wexler Films, L.A., 1957-70, KCET-TV, L.A., 1967-69, Calif. State Colls. TV Project, Sonoma, 1974-75, L.A. C.C., 1969. Author: (monograph) Occupational Education: Foundation for a Master Plan, 1969; co-author: (jour.) Ednl. Tech. IX, 1969. Mem. grand jury Santa Barbara County, 1980-81, arts commn., 1985-91; mem. arts adv. com. Santa Barbara City, 1985-89, TV adv. com., 1983-85. Lt. USN, 1943-46. Named Arts Advocate of Yr., Santa Barbara Arts Coun., 1986. Home: 2327 Edgewater Way Santa Barbara CA 93109

BECK, JOAN WAGNER, journalist; b. Clinton, Iowa, Sept. 5, 1923; d. Roscoe Charles and Mildred (Noel) Wagner; m. Ernest William Beck, Sept. 9, 1945; children—Christopher, Melinda. B.J. cum laude, Northwestern U., 1945, M.S. in Journalism, 1947. Radio script writer O.W.I. Voice of Am., 1945-46; copy writer Marshall Field & Co., 1947-50; feature writer Chgo. Tribune, 1950-61, writer syndicated column about young people, 1956-61, syndicated column about children, 1961-72, editor daily features sect., 1972-75, mem. editorial bd., 1975-92; syndicated editorial page columnist, 1974—. Author: How to Raise a Brighter Child, 1967, (with Dr. Virginia Apgar) Is My Baby All Right?, 1973, Effective Parenting, 1976, Best Beginnings, 1983. Hon. chmn. Mother's March of Met. Chgo. chpt. Nat. Found. March of Dimes, 1970-75; trustee Ill. Children's Home and Aid Soc., 1971-92, life trustee, 1992—; mem. Women's Bd. Northwestern U. Coun. of 100, 1993—. Recipient AP award for best newspaper feature series award Ill., 1964, best feature, 1966, best columns, 1983, 84, Alumni Merit award Northwestern U., 1965, Alumnae award, 1977, Nat. award of Achievement Alpha Chi Omega, 1966, 1st pl. award Penny-U. Mo., 1973, Lisagor award dor editorials, 1982, 88, 91, and commentary, 1994, UPI Ill. award for editorial writing, 1984, commentary award Am. Soc. Newspaper Editors, 1994; named to Chgo. Journalism Hall of Fame, 1994. Mem. Chgo. Network, Chgo. Headline Club, Alpha Chi Omega. Methodist. Office: Chicago Tribune 435 N Michigan Ave Chicago IL 60611-4001

BECK, KAREN SUE, physical education educator; b. Dayton, Ohio, June 9, 1953; d. James Stewart and Carolyn Jo (Dorman) B. BS in Phys. Edn., Ohio State U., 1977; MS in Exercise Physiology, U. Dayton, 1983, tchg. cert. in spl. edn., 1988, tchg. cert. in health, 1990. Phys. edn. tchr. Incarnation Elem. Sch., Centerville, Ohio, 1977-87; athletic trainer Centerville H.S., 1981-83; spl. edn. tchr. Northmont H.S., Clayton, Ohio, 1987-94, athletic trainer, 1990, phys. edn. tchr., 1990-92, 94—, strength and conditioning coach, 1993—; adult edn. weight trainer, 1995; bodybuilding club coach Nat. Physique Com. U.S. Weightlifting Fedn., 1988—; mem. women's swim team Ohio State U., Columbus, 1973-77. First aid and CPR instr. ARC, Dayton, 1992—. Mem. AAHPERD, Nat. Strength and Conditioning Assn. Roman Catholic. Home: 6942 Salem Ave Clayton OH 45315 Office: Northmont Sr HS 4916 National Rd Clayton OH 45315

BECK, LOIS GRANT, anthropologist, educator; b. Bogota, Colombia, Nov. 5, 1944; d. Martin Lawrence and Dorothy (Sweet) Grant; m. Henry Huang; 1 dau., Julia. BA, Portland State U., 1967; MA, U. Chgo., 1969, PhD, 1977. Asst. prof. Amherst (Mass.) Coll., 1973-76, Univ. Utah, Salt Lake City, 1976-80; from asst. to assoc. prof. Washington U., St. Louis, 1980-92, prof., 1992—. Author: Qashqa'i of Iran, 1986, Nomad, 1991; co-editor Women in the Muslim World, 1978. Grantee Social Scis. Rsch. Coun., 1990, NEH, 1990-92. Mem. Middle East Studies Assn. (bd. dirs. 1981-84), Soc. Iranian Studies (exec. sec. 1979-82, edit. bd. 1982-91). Office: Washington U Dept Anthropology 1 Brookings Dr Saint Louis MO 63130-4862

BECK, MARY VIRGINIA, lawyer, public official; b. Ford City, Pa., Feb. 29, 1908; BA, U. Pitts., 1929, LLB, 1932, JD, 1968. Bar: Mich. 1944. Elected to Common Coun. City of Detroit, 1950-70; bd. suprs. County of Wayne, Mich., 1950-69; exec. dir. Ukrainian Info. Bur., Detroit; ret., 1995. Chmn. Policemen & Retirement Fund Commn., Detroit, 1958-62; chmn. Wayne County Port Commn., 1962-68; mem. Gov.s Commn. on Status of Women, 1962, Gov.'s Commn. on Econ. Devel., 1962, World Fedn. Ukrainian Women (hon.), Ukrainian Nat. League of Women Am. (hon.). Recipient Cert. of Merit Fashion Group of Detroit, 1955; Ruth Houston Whipple award Plymouth Bus. and Profl. Woman's Club, 1956; Sport Guild award Sprots Guild Detroit, 1956; award Detroit Dental Soc., 1957; citation Detroit Cancer Fighters, 1959; Ukrainian Community Service award Ukrainians of the Free World, 1960; Ukrainian of Yr. award Ukrainian Grad. Club of Detroit and Windsor, 1963; award Amvets of World War II, 1967; Woman of the Yr. award Soroptimist Club, 1968, inducted into Detroit's Bowling Hall of Fame, 1974, inducted into Mich.'s Women Hall of Fame, 1992, others. Mem. Mich. State Bar, Detroit Bar Assn., Women Lawyers Assn. Mich., Nat. Assn. Women Lawyers, Detroit Bus. Womans Club, Nat. Fedn. Profl. and Bus. Women, Internat. Platform Assn., World Fedn. Ukranian Women's Orgns. (hon.), Ukranian Nat. Women's League Am. (hon.).

BECK, PAMELA SUE SMAZENKA, accountant; b. Toledo, May 11, 1957; d. Robert J. and Wilma M. (Layman) Smazenka; m. Carl W. Beck, Sept. 30, 1978; children: Maureen E., Sylvia A. BA, Western Mich. U., 1978, BBA, Eastern Mich. U., 1984; MBA, U. Toledo, 1995. Substitute tchr. Monroe County, Mich., 1978-82; adult edn. tchr. Bedford Pub. Schs., Temperance, Mich., 1981-84, Mason Consolidated Schs., Erie, Mich., 1984-85; staff acct. Transvc. Sys., Toledo, 1985-87; acct. U. Toledo, 1986-93, supr. gen. acctg., 1993—; mem. supr. bd. UT/MCO Fed. Credit Union, Toledo, 1995—. Mem. Ladies aux. VFW, Petersburg, Mich., 1975—. Mem. Inst. Mgmt. Accts. Office: U Toledo 2801 W Bancroft Toledo OH 43606

BECK, TERESA, retail executive. BS in Fin., U. Utah, MS in Acctg. V.p., contr. Alpha Beta Co. Am. Stores Subsidiarty, Salt Lake City; v.p., contr. Am. Stores Co., Salt Lake City, exec. v.p. fin., CFO. Office: Am Stores Co 709 E South Temple Salt Lake City UT 84102-1205

BECK, WENDY ANN, treasurer; b. Norwalk, Conn., Oct. 21, 1964; d. Walter Rudolph Jr. and Lois Ann (Brahm) Gartner; m. Basil K. Beck, Jr., Dec. 23, 1989. CPA, Fla. Sr. tax acct. Lincare Holdings, Inc., Clearwater, Fla., 1987-93; treas., sr. dir. of treasury and tax Checkers Drive-In Restaurants, Inc., Clearwater, 1993—. Mem. AICPA, Fla. Inst. of CPA, Inst. of Mgmt. Accts. (spl. activities dir. 1992-93), Am. Mgmt. Assn. Republican. Home: 19315 Eastbrook Dr Odessa FL 33556 Office: Checkers Drive-In Restaurants Inc 600 Cleveland St 8th Fl Clearwater FL 34615

BECKER, BARBARA L., lawyer; b. Nov. 27, 1963. BA, Wesleyan U., 1985; JD, NYU, 1988. Bar: N.Y. 1989. Ptnr. Chadbourne & Parke LLP. Mng. editor Rev. of Law and Social Change, 1984-85. Mem. Phi Beta Kappa. Office: Chadbourne & Parke LLP 30 Rockefeller Plz New York NY 10112*

BECKER, BETSY See ASWAD, BETSY

BECKER, BETTIE GERALDINE, artist; b. Peoria, Ill., Sept. 22, 1918; d. Harry Seymour and Magdalene Matilda (Hiller) B.; m. Lionel William Wathall, Nov. 10, 1945; children: Heather Lynn (dec.), Jeffrey Lee. BFA cum laude, U. Ill., Urbana, 1940; postgrad. Art Inst. Chgo., 1942-45, Art Student's League, 1946, Ill. Inst. tech., 1948. Dept. artist Liberty Mut. Ins. Co., Chgo., 1941-43; with Palenskie-Young Studio, 1943-46; free lance illustrator N.Y. Times, Chgo. Tribune, Saturday Rev. Lit., 1948-50; co-owner, operator Pangaea Gallery/Studio, Fish Creek, Wis.; pvt. tutor, tchr. studio classes. Exhibited one-man show Crossroads Gallery, Art Inst. Chgo., 1973; exhibited group shows including Critics' Choice show Art Rental Sales Gallery Art Inst. Chgo., 1972, Evanston-North Shore exhbns., 1964, 65, Chgo. Soc. Artists, 1967, 71, Union League, 1967, 72, Women in Art, Appleton (Wis.) Gallery Art, Milw. Art Mus., 1986, Neville Pub. Mus., Green Bay, Wis., 1987, Valperine Gallery, Madison, Wis. 1989, 92, Wis. Arts Gallery, Allouez, 1990, 94, North Cen. Coll., Naperville, Ill., 1991, Neville Mus., Green Bay, Wis., 1990, 91, 95-96, Art Works Gallery, Green Bay, 1992, 94, Tria II Gallery, Fish Creek, Wis., Oesterle Gallery, N. Ctrl. Coll., Naperville, 1993, Neville Mus., Green Bay, 1993-94, Rabbi Joseph L. Baron Mus., Milw., 1994, Beacon St. Gallery, Chgo., 1995, Paint Box Gallery, Ephraiph, Wis., 1995—, Oldtown Gallery, Chgo., 1995, William Bonifas Fine Arts Ctr., Escanaba, Mich., 1996; represented in permanent collection Witte Meml. Mus., San Antonio, Miller Art Ctr., Stugeon Bay, Wis., Neville Mus., Green Bay, Wis.; executed mural (with F. Wiater) Talbot Lab. U. Ill., Urbana, 1940; contbr. articles and illustrations to mags. and newspapers. Active Campfire Girls, Chgo., 1968, 70; art chmn., mem. exec. bd. local PTA, 1959-60; active various art festivals, 1967—. Mem. Chgo. Soc. Artists (rec. sec. 1968-77, print and drawing show), Wis. Arts Coun., N.E. Wis. Arts Coun. (bd. dir.), Alumni Assn. Art Inst. Chgo., Door County Art League, Wis. Women in the Arts, Soc. Exptl. Artists. Republican. Mem. Unity Ch. Home: 46 E Pine St Sturgeon Bay WI 54235-2726

BECKER, DEBORA JEAN, research marketing consultant, artist; b. Mt. Vernon, N.Y., Dec. 19, 1953; d. Joseph Anthony and Jean Helen (Riley) B. Assoc. dir. Import/Export Mktg. Svc., Tampa, 1981-83; mgr. Door Store Fla., Inc., Tampa, 1983-85; exec. sec. payables and receivables Am. Phone Ctrs., Inc., 1986-87; collector medicaid liason S.T. Childers DDS, Tampa, 1988-91; owner Rsch. Mktg. Cons., Tampa, 1991—; proprietor Crystalline Designs, Tampa, 1983—. Home and Office: Rsch Mktg Cons Crystalline Designs 3314 Iowa Ave W Tampa FL 33611-4616

BECKER, GAIL ROSELYN, museum director; b. Long Branch, N.J., Oct. 22, 1942; d. Joseph and Adele (Michelsohn) B. BA, Vassar Coll., 1964. Exhibit project officer U.S. Info. Agy., Washington, 1967-87, chief devel. and prodn. exhibits, 1987-91; exec. dir. Louisville Sci. Ctr. (formerly Mus. History and Sci.), 1991—; mem. Ky. Sci. and Tech. Coun., bd. dirs., 1993—. Bd. dirs. Louisville Advanced Tech. Coun., 1993—, Louisville Com. Fgn. Rels.; active Leadership Loisuville. Recipient Presdl. Design awards Nat. Endowment for the Arts, Washington, 1984, 88, 92, Special Achievement award U.S. Info. Agy., Washington, 1988. Mem. Am. Assn. Mus. (bd. dirs. 1994—), Louisville Com. Fgn. Rels. (bd. dirs.), Assn. Sci.-Tech. Ctrs. (bd. dirs. 1992—), Vassar Coll. Alumnae Assn., Rotary. Office: Louisville Sci Ctr 727 W Main St Louisville KY 40202-2633

BECKER, JILL MARGARET, dancer, educator; b. Buffalo, Dec. 31, 1949; d. Richard William and June (Hurst) B.; m. Ira Beryl Brukner, Aug. 29, 1988; 1 child, Raphael Walsh. BA in dance, SUNY, Brockport, 1969-72; MA in performing arts, Am. U., Washington, 1975-77. Dance instr. N.Y.U., N.Y.C., 1980, Jersey City (N.J.) State Coll., 1978-86; artistic dir. Jill Becker & Dancers, Inc., N.Y.C., 1980-86; pvt. practice dancer, tchr., choreographer Amsterdam, Holland, 1986-88; artist in residence Middlebury (Vt.) Coll., 1989-93; pvt. practice dancer, tchr., choreographer Ithaca, N.Y., 1993-96; tchr. Cornell U., 1995-96, Conn. Coll., 1996—. Choreographer, performer in several full evening dances. Recipient individual artists grant The Arts of the Southern Finger Lakes, Corning, N.Y., 1996, spl. opportunities stipend Catskills Art Coun., Ithaca, 1995, Cornell Coun. on the Arts grant Cornell U., Ithaca, 1995, choreographers fellow Nat. Endowment for Arts, 1983.

BECKER, JO, peace activist; b. Elkhart, Ind., Mar. 31, 1964; d. Palmer J. and Ardys (Preheim) B.; m. Jan S. Hesbon, Oct. 8, 1988. Cert., Beijing Langs. Inst., 1983; BA, Goshen Coll., 1985; MA in Polit. Sci., Syracuse U., 1996. Interim program coord. Fellowship of Reconciliation, Nyack, N.Y., 1986-87, mem. program staff, 1987-92, exec. dir., 1993—. Contbr. articles to profl. jours. Organizer Rocklanders for Peace in C.Am., Nyack, 1985-88; mem. exec. com. War Registers League, N.Y.C., 1989-93. Mem. Mennonite Ch. Office: Fellowship of Reconciliation Box 271 Nyack NY 10960

BECKER, JOANN ELIZABETH, insurance company executive; b. Chester, Pa., Oct. 29, 1948; d. James Thomas and Elizabeth Theresa (Barnett) Clark; m. David Norbert Becker, June 7, 1969. BA, Washington U., St. Louis, 1970, MA, 1971. CLU; FLMI/M. Tchr. Kirkwood (Mo.) Sch. Dist., 1971-73; devel. and sr. devel. analyst Lincoln Nat. Life Ins. Co., Ft. Wayne, Ind., 1973-77, systems programming specialist, 1977-79, sr. project mgr., 1979-81, asst. v.p., 1981-85, 2d v.p., 1985-88, v.p., 1988-91; pres., CEO The Richard Leahy Corp., Ft. Wayne, 1991-93; pres. Lincoln Nat. Corp. Equity Sales Corp, Ft. Wayne, 1993-94; v.p. portfolio mgmt. group Lincoln Nat. Investment Mgmt. Co., Ft. Wayne, 1994—. Contbr. articles to profl. jours. Bd. dirs. Ind. Humanities Coun., Indpls., 1991—, treas., mem. exec. com., 1994-95, mem. devel. com. 1995—; bd. dirs. Auburn (Ind.) Cord Duesenberg Mus., 1995—, mem. devel. com., 1995—. Named Women of Achievement, YWCA, Ft. Wayne, 1986, Sagamore of Wabash, Gov. State of Ind., 1990. Fellow Life Mgmt. Inst. Soc. Ft. Wayne (pres. 1983-84, honors designation 1980); mem. Life Ins. Mktg. Rsch. Assn. (Leadership Inst. fellow, mem. exec. com. 1993-94, mem. fin. svcs. com. 1993-94), Am. Mgmt. Assn., Ft. Wayne C. of C. (mem., chmn. audit-fin. com. 1989—).

BECKER, JUDITH SAVAGE, human resources specialist; b. East Grand Rapids, Mich., Nov. 27, 1938; d. Byron Bonham and Irene M. (Poscik) Savage; m. Donald Conrad Becker, Aug. 12, 1961; children: Jeffrey C., Wendy R., Jill E. BS in Design, U. Mich., 1960; MS in Edn., Monmouth U., 1994. Supr. human resources Macy's, Toledo, 1981-82; mgr. Macy's, Newark, 1982-85; mgr. Citibank, Shrewsbury, N.J., 1985-87, asst. v.p. human resources, 1987-93; v.p. human resources Citibank, Long Island City, N.Y., 1993-95; pres., owner HR Solutions, Gerrardstown, W.Va., 1996; chair Citibank Charitable Contbns., N.J., 1989-92; founder, dir. Asbury Park (N.J.) H.S. mentor-protege program, 1990-93. Bd. dirs. Clean Ocean Action, Sandy Hook, N.J., 1989-93; trustee Brookdale C.C., Lincroft, N.J., 1989-90. Mem. ASTD, ACA, Soc. for Human Resources Mgmt., Profl. Bus. Women's Assn. Home and Office: HR Solutions Virginia Line Rd PO Box 214 Gerrardstown WV 25420

BECKER, JULIETTE, psychologist, marriage and family therapist; b. L.A., Sept. 22, 1938; d. Louis Joseph and Elissa Cecelia (Bevacqua) Cevola; m. Richard Charles Sprenger, Aug. 13, 1960 (div. Dec. 1984); children: Lisa Anne, Stephen Louis, Gina Marie, Paul Joseph, Gretchen Lynette; m. Vance Benjiman Becker, Nov. 7, 1986. BA in Psychology, Calif. State U., Fullerton, 1983; M in Marriage and Family Therapy, U.S. Internat. U., 1985; PhD in Clin. Psychology, William Lyon U., 1988. Therapist Villa Park (Calif.) Psychol. Svcs., 1985-88, psychologist, 1988—. Mem. APA, Am. Assn. Marriage, Family and Child Therapists, Calif. Assn. Marriage, Family and Child Therapists. Office: Villa Park Psychol Svcs 17871 Santiago Blvd Ste 206 Orange CA 92667-4131

BECKER, MAGDALENE NEUENSCHWANDER, educator; b. Beaverdam, Ohio, Sept. 5, 1915; d. Walter and Viola Etta (Gratz) Neuenschwander; m. Homer Gerald Becker, Aug. 18, 1935; 1 child, Rachel Etta. BA, Westminster Coll., New Wilmington, Pa., 1954, MEd in Guidance and Counseling, 1971; postgrad. in English, U. Pitts., 1962-65. Cert. tchr. Tchr. pub. speaking New Castle (Pa.) Sr. High Sch., 1954-61; tchr. advanced English Butler (Pa.) Area Sr. High Sch., 1961-77; with Learning Ctr. Sheldon Jackson Coll., Sitka, Alaska, 1977-79; cataloger, reference librarian Lees Coll., Jackson, Ky., 1979-83; coordinator conf. ctr. Cook Christian Tng. Sch., Tempe, Ariz., 1983-85; tutor Armstrong-Ind. County Intermediate Unit, Indiana, Pa., 1985-92; tutor ESL Lakeland, Fla., 1992-94; evaluator Mid-Atlantic Sch. Examiners, 1966; examiner Nat. Coun. Tchrs. of English, 1964-76. Author 11 computer discs of GED programs, 1987-88. Tchr. Sunday Sch., Presbyn. Ch., 1940—, deacon, elder, 1985—, vice moderator women's gathering, 1993-95; bd. dirs. Group Homes, Indiana, 1986-89; vol. in nursing home, 1985-92; sec. Lake Hunter Fellowship. Mem. NEA, Pa. State Edn. Assn., Indiana County Edn. Assn., AAUW (pres. Indiana br. 1988-90, exec. v.p. 1986-88). Republican. Home: A303 16 Lake Hunter Dr Lakeland FL 33803-1280

BECKER, MARY LOUISE, political scientist; b. St. Louis; d. W. R. and Evelyn (Thompson) Becker; divorced; children: James, John. BS, Washington U., St. Louis, 1949, MA, 1951; PhD, Radcliffe Coll., 1957; postgrad., U. Karachi (Pakistan), 1953-54. Intelligence rsch. analyst Dept. State, Washington, 1957-59; internat. rels. officer AID, Washington, 1959-64, community rels. officer, 1964-66, sci. rsch. officer, 1966-71, UN rels. officer, 1971-91; pres. Internat. Devel. Enterprises, Washington, 1992—; adviser U.S. dels. 19th, 21st, 23d, 24th, 26th, 28th, 30th, 32d, 34th Governing Coun. sessions UN Devel. Program; adv. U.S. del. 3d prep. com. meeting World Conf. UN Decade for Women; adviser U.S. dels. UNICEF exec. bd. sessions, 1987-91; lectr. internat. rels. civic orgns., student groups, 1954—; mem. U.S. Com. for UN Fund for Women. Author: Muhammed Iqbal, 1965; contbg. editor: Concise Ency. of Middle East, 1973; contbr. articles to govt. publs. Mem. adv. bd. chmn. internat. student placement Washington Citizenship Seminar, Nat. YMCA-YWCA, Washington, 1961-71. Blewett fellow Washington U., 1951, Resident fellow Radcliffe Coll., 1952-56; Fulbright scholar U. Karachi, 1953-54. Mem. AAUW, Am. Polit. Sci. Assn., Soc. Internat. Devel., Assn. Asian Studies, Asia Soc., Middle East Inst., UN Assn. (bd. dirs. Nat. Capital area 1991—), South Asian Muslim Studies Assn. (v.p. 1992—), Mo. Soc. Washington (sec. 1959-60), Mortar Bd., Chimes, Internat. Club, Harvard Club (Washington), Alpha Lambda Delta, Beta Gamma Sigma, Eta Mu Phi, Pi Sigma Alpha. Presbyterian. Office: North Bldg Ste 700 601 Pennsylvania Ave NW Washington DC 20004-2601

BECKER, SUSAN D., history educator; b. Cleve., Apr. 30, 1938; d. Kenneth George and Laura Jane (Biddlingmyer) Deubel; m. Edmund Heinz Becker, Dec. 1969 (div. Mar. 1972). AB, Ohio U., 1960; MA, John Carroll U., 1971; PhD, Case Western Res. U., 1975. Tchr. St. Joseph's Acad., Cleve., 1962-64, John Marshall High Sch., Cleve., 1964-69; from asst. to assoc. prof. history U. Tenn., Knoxville, 1974—; part time tchr. John Carroll U., Cleve., 1975—, Cleve. State U., 1975—. Author: The Origins of The Equal Rights Amendment, 1980, (with others) Decades of Discontent, 1983; co-author: (2 vols.) Discovering the American Past, 3rd edit., 1994. Mem. Am. Hist. Assn., Am. Studies Assn., Orgn. Am. Historians, Coordinating Coun. Women in History, Phi Beta Kappa, Phi Alpha Theta. Office: U Tenn Dept History 1101 McClung Tower Knoxville TN 37996

BECKER, SUSAN KAPLAN, management consultant, educator; b. Newark, Jan. 4, 1948; d. Charles and Janet Kaplan; m. William Paul Becker, 1969 (div. 1977). BA in English cum laude, with distinction, U. Pa., 1968, MA, 1969, PhD, 1973, MBA in Fin., 1979. Instr. English Bryn Mawr (Pa.) Coll., 1972-74; assoc. editor U. Pa., Phila., 1975, asst. dir., lectr. urban studies, 1975-77; fin. analyst Phila. Nat. Bank, 1979-82; asst. v.p. Chem. Bank, N.Y.C., 1982-84; v.p. Bankers Trust Co., N.Y.C., 1984-85; prin. Becker Cons. Svcs., N.Y.C., 1985—; adj. assoc. prof. mgmt. comm. Stern Sch. Bus. N.Y.U., 1990—; cons./evaluator Pa. Humanities Council, Phila., 1977-78; mem. editorial bd. Mgmt. Comm. Quar., 1993—. Author: How to Develop Profitable Financial Products for the Institutional Marketplace, 1988; contbr. articles and revs. to profl. jours. Vol. N.Y. Cares, 1989-92, N.Y.C. affiliate Am. Heart Assn., 1995—. U. Pa. fellow, 1968-72; E.I. DuPont de Nemours fellow, 1979, N.Y. Regents Coll. Teaching fellow, 1968-70. Mem. Am. Mktg. Assn. (leadership coun. N.Y. chpt. 1988-91, EFFIE judge 1990-92), Internat. Comm. Assn. (reviewer tech. and comm. divsn. 1991), Fin. Women's Assn. N.Y. (profl. devel. com. 1995—). Democrat. Office: 155 E 29th St New York NY 10016-8101

BECKERMAN-RODAU, RUTH, non-profit association administrator; b. N.Y., 1957; married; two children. BA in Fine Arts, SUNY, Stony Brook, 1978; JD, Western New Eng. Coll., 1981. Cmty. devel. mgr. Anne Grady Corp., Holland, Ohio, 1990-94; exec. dir. Alzheimer's Assn. N.W. Ohio, Toledo, 1994—; adv. bd. mem. N.W. Ohio Devel. Ctr., Toledo, 1995—. Office: Alzheimers Assn NW Ohio 2500 N Reynolds Rd Toledo OH 43615

BECKER-ROUKAS, HELANE RENÉE, securities analyst, financial executive; b. N.Y.C., May 7, 1957; m. Arnold and Ella Florence (Feldman) Becker; m. George Paul Roukas, Sept. 6, 1980; children: Samuel Matthew, Hannah Beth. BA, Montclair State U., 1979; MBA in Fin., NYU, 1984. Options coord. Donaldson Lufkin & Jenrette, N.Y.C., 1979-81; mktg. coord. E.F. Hutton & Co., N.Y.C., 1981-82; securities analyst Prudential-Bache Securities, N.Y.C., 1982-86; v.p., analyst Drexel Burnham Lambert, N.Y.C., 1986-87; mng. dir., analyst Lehman Bros., N.Y.C., 1987-94; v.p., analyst Smith Barney, N.Y.C., 1995—; speaker various airline industry confs. and panels; senate commn. on civil titrotor. Columnist Corp. Travel Mag., 1990. Mem. Senate Commn. on Civil Tilt Rotor. Named to Internat. Investor All-Am. Rsch. Team, 1985-94. Mem. Soc. Airline Analysts (pres. 1996—), Profl. Women in Bus., Wings Club, Short Hills Assn., NYU Alumni Assn. N.J. Office: Smith Barney 388 Greenwich St New York NY 10013

BECKHAM, JANETTE HALES, religious organization administrator; b. Springville, Utah; m. Robert H. Hales, June, 1955 (dec. March, 1988); 5 children; m. Ray E. Beckham, Apr. 7, 1995. BS, Brigham Young U. Instr. Missionary Tng. Ctr., LDS Ch., Salt Lake City; mem. Utah State Legislature, Salt Lake City; pres. Relief Soc., LDS Ch., Salt Lake City; young women gen. pres. LDS Ch., Salt Lake City. Vol. many health and edn. projects; bd. dirs. Nat. Cougar Club. Home: 2125 N 1400 E Provo UT 84604-2104

BECKLEY, JEANINE SUSAN, nuclear medicine technologist; b. Rome, N.Y., Jan. 31, 1964; d. Jerry Slater and Glada Ruth (Kingsbury) B. AA, Prince George's C.C., Largo, Md., 1989. Cert. nuclear medicine technologist. Nuc. medicine technologist Nuc. Cardiology Lab., Silver Spring, Md., 1989-93; chief nuc. medicine technologist So. Md. Nuc. Cardiology, Clinton, 1993-95; asst. chief nuc. medicine tech. Cardio Diagnostic Ctr., Chevy Chase, Md., 1995—; mem. rsch. apprentice program Naval Rsch. Lab., Washington, 1982; student rep. med. isotope tech. program Prince George's C.C., 1987-89. Acad. scholar Findlay (Ohio) U., 1982, music scholar, 1982, senatorial scholar Prince George's C.C., 1987-89. Mem. Soc. Nuclear Medicine, Am. Soc. Nuclear Cardiology (assoc.), Am. Soc. Radiologic Technologists. Republican. Methodist. Office: Cardio Diagnostic Ctr 5530 Wisconsin Ave # 740 Chevy Chase MD 20815 also: Laurel Park Animal Hosp 7401 Van Dusen Rd Laurel MD 20707

BECKMAN, JUDITH KALB, financial counselor and planner, educator, writer; b. Bklyn., June 27, 1940; d. Harry and Frances (Cohen) Kalb; m. Richard Martin Beckman, Dec. 16, 1961; children: Barry Andrew, David Mark. BA, Hofstra U., 1962; MA, Adelphi U., 1984. Cert. fin. planner; registered investment adviser, stockbroker. English tchr. Long Beach High Sch., 1962-65; Promotion coordination pub. rels. Mandel Sch. for Med. Assts., Hempstead, N.Y., 1973-74; exec. dir. Nassau Easter Seals, Albertson, N.Y., 1974-76; dir. pub. info. Long Beach (N.Y.) Meml. Hosp., Long Beach, 1976-77; account rep. First Investors, Hicksville, N.Y., 1977-78; sales asst., then account exec. Josephthal & Co. Inc., Great Neck, N.Y., 1978-81; v.p., cert. fin. planner Arthur Gould Inc., Great Neck, N.Y., 1981-88; pres. Fin. Solutions (affiliated with Seco West Ltd., Goldner Siegfried Assocs. Inc.), Westbury, N.Y., 1988—; adj. instr. Adelphi U., Garden City N.Y., 1981-83, Molloy Coll., Rockville Ctr., N.Y., 1982-84; lectr. SUNY-Farmingdale, 1984-85; creater, presenter seminars, workshops on fin., investing, 1981—. Fin. columnist The Women's Record, 1985-93; writer quar. newspaper The Reporter, 1987. Coord. meat boycott, L.I., 1973; mentor SUNY Old Westbury, 1989-93; co-founder, chair L.I. del. High Profile Men and Women, Colonie Hill, Hauppauque, N.Y., 1985; treas. L.I. Alzheimer's Found., 1989-93, trustee, 1993-95; apptd. to Nassau County Women's Adv. Coun. by County Exec., 1990; chief adv. coun. Ctr. for Family Resources. Recipient citation for leadership Town of Hempstead, N.Y., 1986, 89, L.I. Press Club award, 1987, 92, Mentor award SBA, 1989, Fin. Svcs. award SBA, 1991, L.I. Assn. Fin. Svc. Advocate award, 1991, Woman of Distinction in Bus. award Women on the Job, 1989, Bus. Leadership citation Nassau County, N.Y., 1989, Supr. award Town of Hempstead, 1989. Mem. Nat. Assn. Women Bus. Owners L.I. (bd. dirs. 1987-89, membership chair 1996, v.p. membership 1996), Women's Econ. Developers of L.I. (bd. dirs. 1985-92), Internat. Assn. Fin. Planners, Inst. Cert. Fin. Planners, L.I. Ctr. Bus. and Profl. Women (pres. 1984-86, Pres.' award 1992), NALU, Kiwanis (bd. dirs. 1994—, chair fund raising 1994, chair cmty. svcs. 1995—, v.p. membership 1996). Republican. Jewish. Home: 2084 Beverly Way Merrick NY 11566-5418 Office: Fin Solutions Fin Planning Office 2084 Beverly Way Merrick NY 11566-5418 also: 400 Post Ave Ste 200 Westbury NY 11590-2226

BECKMAN, KAREN, advertising executive. Sr. v.p., acct. dir. Deutsch, Inc., N.Y.C. Office: Deutsch Inc 215 Park Ave S New York NY 10003*

BECKMANN, MICHELE LILLIAN, secretary; b. Bklyn., Feb. 15, 1957; d. Anton and Alice Naomi (Williams) Prudich; m. Robert Westcott Beckmann, Apr. 18, 1981; children: Andrew Isaac, Walter Ian (twins). BA, Ea. Wash. U., 1978. Cert. profl. sec. Lead sec. New Way Homes, Spokane, 1980-81; libr. asst. Spokane Pub. Librs., 1981-82; office asst. Spokane County Assesor's Office, 1982; data processing clk. Aztech-Comstock, Spokane, 1983-84; finishing opr. Hollister-Stier Labs., Spokane, 1984; pvt. sec. Danial Kallestad, CLU, ChFC, Spokane, 1985; office asst. Wash. State U., Pullman, 1986-87, sec. III, 1987-89, project sec., 1989-92; owner Bhunkey Bros. Ink, Colfax, 1992—. Mem. Pullman Fair Housing Commn., 1989—, vice chmn., 1989-90; mem. local coun. Camp Fire, Inc., 1989-90; precinct officer Whitman County Dems., Colfax, Wash., 1988-90. Recipient WO-HE-LO Medallion Camp Fire Ind., 1975; cert. appreciation Pullman Fair Housing Commn., 1989, 91. Democrat. Home and Office: 1702 N Riverside Ln Colfax WA 99111-9755

BECKWITH, BARBARA JEAN, journalist; b. Chgo., Dec. 11, 1948; d. Charles Barnes and Elizabeth Ann (Nolan) B. BA in Journalism, Marquette U., 1970. News editor Lake Geneva (Wis.) Regional News, 1972-74; asst. editor St. Anthony Messenger, Cin., 1974-82, mng. editor, 1982—; mem. U.S. Cath. Conf. Communications Com., 1990-92. Mem. Cath. Press Assn. (bd. dirs. 1986-96, v.p. 1988-90, pres. 1990-92, best interview 1982, best photo story 1985), Women in Comms., Cin. Editors Assn., Fedn. Ch. Press Assns. of Internat. Cath. Union of the Press (3d v.p. 1989-92, pres. 1992—), Nat. Cath. Assn. for Broadcasters and Communicators (bd. dirs. 1989-96). Office: St Anthony Messenger 1615 Republic St Cincinnati OH 45210-1219

BECKWITH, SANDRA SHANK, judge; b. Norfolk, Va., Dec. 4, 1943; d. Charles Langdale and Loraine (Sterneberg) Shank; m. James Beckwith, Mar. 31, 1965 (div. June 1978); m. Thomas R. Ammann, Mar. 3, 1979. BA, U. Cin., 1965, JD, 1968. Bar: Ohio 1969, Ind. 1976, Fla. 1979, U.S. Dist. Ct. (so. dist.) Ohio 1971, U.S. Dist. Ct. Ind. 1976, U.S. Supreme Ct. 1977. Sole practice, Harrison, Ohio, 1969-77, 79-81; judge Hamilton County Mcpl. Ct., Cin., 1977-79, 81-86; judge Ct. Common Pleas, Hamilton County Div. Domestic Rels., 1987-89; assoc. Graydon, Head and Ritchey, 1989-91; judge U.S. Dist. Ct. (so. dist.) Ohio, 1992—; mem. Ohio Chief Justice's Code of Profl. Responsibility Commn., 1984, Ohio Gov.'s Com. on Prison Crowding, 1984-90, State Fed. Com. on Death Penalty Habeas Corpus, 1995—. Methodist. Office: Potter Stewart US Courthouse Ste 810 Cincinnati OH 45202

BEDELIA, BONNIE, actress; b. N.Y.C., Mar. 25, 1948; d. Philip and Marian (Wagner) Culkin; m. Kenneth Luber, Apr. 15, 1969; children: Yuri, Jonah. Student, Hunter Coll., N.Y.C.; studied with Uta Hager, Herbert Berghof studios; studied with Lee Strasberg, Actors Studio. Stage appearances include The Glass Menagerie, 1970, The Sea Gull, 1970, As You Like It, 1970, Midsummer Night's Dream, 1970; Broadway appearances include Isle of Children, 1960, Enter Laughing, 1963, The Playroom, 1965, Happily Never After, 1966, My Sweet Charlie, 1967 (Theatre World award 1967); film appearances include Gypsy Moths, 1969, They Shoot Horses, Don't They?, 1969, Lovers and Other Strangers, 1970, Rosalie, 1972, Between Friends, 1973, The Big Fix, 1978, Heart Like a Wheel, 1983, Death of an Angel, 1986, The Boy Who Could Fly, 1986, Violets are Blue, 1986, The Stranger, 1987, Die Hard, 1988, Prince of Pennsylvania, 1988, Fat Man & Little Boy, 1989, Presumed Innocent, 1990, Die Hard II, 1990, Needful Things, 1993, Speechless, 1994; TV series Love of Live, 1961-67, The New Land, 1974, mini-series Salem's Lot, 1979; TV films Then Came Bronson, 1969, Sandcastles, 1972, Hawkins on Murder, 1973, A Message to My Daughter, 1973, A Time for Love, 1973, Heatwave, 1974, A Question of Love, 1978, Walking Through the Fire, 1979, Fighting Back, 1980, Million Dollar Infield, 1982, Memorial Day, 1983, The Lady from Yesterday, 1985, Alex, The Life of a Child, 1986, When the Time Comes, 1987, Somebody Has to Shoot the Picture, 1990, Switched At Birth, 1991, A Mother's Right: The Elizabeth Morgan Story, 1993, The Fire Next Time, 1993, Fallen Angels (The Quiet Room), 1993 (Emmy nomination, Guest Actress - Drama, 1994). Recipient Golden Globe award, 1983. Office: care ICM c/o Michael Black 8942 Wilshire Blvd Beverly Hills CA 90211*

BEDENBAUGH, ANGELA LEA OWEN, chemistry educator, researcher; b. Seguin, Tex., Oct. 6, 1939; d. Wintford Henry and Nelia Melanie (Fischer) Owen; m. John Holcombe Bedenbaugh, Dec. 27, 1961; 1 child, Melanie Celeste. BS cum laude, U. Tex., 1961; PhD in Organic Chemistry, U. S.C., 1967. Geol. mapping asst. Roland Blumberg Assocs., Seguin, summer 1958, 59; chemistry lab. instr. U. Tex., Austin, 1960-61; rsch. assoc. chemistry U. So. Miss., Hattiesburg, 1966-80, rsch. assoc. prof. chemistry, 1980—. Author: (with John H. Bedenbaugh) Handbook for High School Chemistry Teachers, 1985, (with John H. Bedenbaugh) Teaching First Year Chemistry, 1988, 3d rev. edition, 1990. Mem. adminstrv. bd. Parkway Heights United Meth. Ch., 1974-75, women's unit leader, 1973-75, women's unit treas., 1977, Wesleyan Svc. Guild v.p., 1970, Sunday Sch. tchr., 1973-74; bd. dirs. Forrest Stone Area Opportunity Inc., 1970-72, bd. dirs. exec. com., 1972, mem. com. to rewrite pers. policies and procedures, 1971, mem. Headstart monitoring com., 1971-72, mem. pers. screening com., 1971; mem. nat. Women's Polit. Caucus, 1976—; mem. Toastmasters Internat., 1986—, club. pres., 1993, area gov., 1994. Prin. investigator rsch. grant U.S. Dept. Energy, U. So. Miss., 1980; co-prin. investigator rsch. grant NSF, U. So. Miss., 1985, adminstrv. dir. rsch. grant, 1988-92, 93—, others. Mem. NSTA (mem. nat. resource rev. panel for rev. of instrnl. materials), Am. Chem. Soc. (chairperson 1984-85, program chairperson 1983-84, Chemist of Yr. 1991), Miss. Sci. Tchrs. Assn. (Disting. Sci. Tchr. award 1994, exec. bd. 1994—), Delta Kappa Gamma (pres. Miss. state br. 1989-91, chairperson internat. rsch. com. 1980-82, chairperson internat. computer share fair at internat. conv. 1994), Sigma Xi (charter, sec.-treas. 1967-69, treas. 1970, pres. 1973-74, program chairperson 1972-73). Democrat. Methodist. Home: 63 Suggs Rd Hattiesburg MS 39402-9642 Office: Univ So Miss PO Box 8466 Hattiesburg MS 39406-8466

BEDFORD, AMY ALDRICH, public relations executive, corporation secretary; b. Pendleton, Oreg., July 13, 1912; d. Edwin Burton and Elsie (Conklin) Aldrich; m. J.M. Bedford (wid.); 1 child, Jacqueline Bedford Brown. BS, Oreg. State U., 1933. Mgr. comml. dept. East Oregonian, Pendleton, 1950-75, mgr. pub. rels., 1975—; corp. sec. East Oregonian Pub. Co., Pendleton, 1950—. Bd. dirs. Oreg. Status of Women Com., 1972-75, Oreg. Law Enforcement Commn., 1975-82, Arts Coun. Pendleton. Recipient Pendleton First Citizen award C. of C., 1962, Gov.'s award for the Arts, 1988. Mem. Women in Communications, Oreg. Press Women, AAUW (pres. 1956-58, grantee 1965), LWV, Pendleton River Parkway Found., World Affairs Coun. Oreg., Altrusa. Home: PO Box 1456 Pendleton OR 97801-0365 Office: East Oregonian Pub Co PO Box 1089 Pendleton OR 97801-1089

BEDICS, LYNN FAY, nurse; b. Scranton, Pa., May 13, 1947; d. Gerald Joseph and Esther Naomi (Sachse) O'Malley; m. Francis J. Bedics, Jr., Mar. 11, 1989. Grad., St. Luke's Hosp. Sch. Nursing, N.Y.C., 1968; BSN cum laude, Cedar Crest Coll., 1982. RN, Pa.; cert. comty. health nurse ANA Credentiality Ctr. Staff nurse emergency room Allentown Gen. Hosp., 1971; part-time charge nurse Phila. VA Hosp., 1971-72; critical care nurse St. John's Hosp., Tulsa, 1972-74; ICU nurse Allentown Osteo. Hosp., 1975-79; staff nurse VA Outpatient Clinic, Allentown, 1979-86; nurse mgr. Dept. Vets. Affairs, Outpatient Clinic, Allentown, 1986—; instr.-trainer CPR, Am. Heart Assn., Allentown, 1980-89. Mem. coord. com. Combined Fed. Campaign, Lehigh Valley, Pa., 1984-86; bd. dirs. YWCA, Allentown, 1986-88, Korea-Vietnam Meml. Inc., Lehigh Valley, 1987—, sec., 1991-94; mem. Vietnam Vets. Health Initiative Commn., 1995—. 1st lt. Nurse Corps, U.S. Army, 1967-70, Vietnam. Decorated Bronze Star medal; recipient excellence in Nursing award Dept. Vets. Affairs, 1989, VA Adminstr.'s Hands and Heart award Dept. Vets. Affairs Med. Ctr., Wilkes-Barre, Pa., 1989, Legion of Honor award Chapel of Four Chaplains, 1994. Mem. Assn. for Ambulatory Care Providers Ea. Pa. (v.p. 1987-89, pres. 1989-90, bd. dirs., chairperson edn. com. 1994—), United Women Vets. Pa. VFW, Sigma Theta Tau, Beta Sigma Phi (internat. honr.). Republican. Home: 1118 N 27th St Allentown PA 18104-2904 Office: Dept Vets Affairs Outpatient Clinic 2937 Hamilton Blvd Allentown PA 18103-2819

BEDNARZ, SHIRLEY DIANE, publishing company executive; b. Wis. Rapids, Wis., Sept. 15, 1946; d. Stewart Fausch and Marge (Lyons) Peterson; m. Timothy F. Bednarz, Aug. 14, 1989. B in Edn., U. Wis., Stevens Point, 1974, M in Profl. Devel. magna cum laude, 1981; PhD in Bus. Adminstrn., Pacific Western U., 1994. Tchr. Wis. Rapids Pub. Schs., 1974-90; ret., 1990; CEO Bednarz Bus. Strategies, Stevens Point, Wis., 1990—; pres., owner Menagerie Pet Ctr., Wis. Rapids, 1977-90. Author books; contbr. articles to profl. publs. Mem. NAFE, Nat. Assn. Univ. Women. Home and Office: Bednarz Bus Strategies 2025 Main St Stevens Point WI 54481-3019

BEDNARZYK, MICHELE SMITH, family nurse practitioner, educator; b. Alton, Ill., Dec. 9, 1958; d. William H.C. and Rosalie Anne (Low) Smith; m. Paul Anthony Bednarzyk, Aug. 18, 1990. BSN, Avila Coll., 1980; MN, U. S.C., 1991. Cert. FNP, ANCC. Commd. 2d lt. USAF, 1980, advanced through grades to capt., 1983; staff nurse USAF, Alamogordo, N.Mex., 1980-83; staff nurse, asst. charge nurse USAF, Upper Heyford, Eng., 1983-86; adminstrv. family clinic nurse Shaw AFB USAF, Sumter, S.C., 1986-90; FNP Family Medicine Assocs., Augusta, Ga., 1991-94; asst. prof. U. S.C., Aiken, 1991-94; vis. faculty U. North Fla., Jacksonville, 1994—; nurse practitioner Orange Park Pediatrics, Orange Park, Fla., 1995—; mem. adv. bd. Nat. Health Care, North Augusta, S.C., 1992-94, Keysville (Ga.) Convalescent Health Ctr., 1992-94. Vol. Am. Heart Assn., Augusta, 1992, 93, Am. Cancer Assn., Augusta, 1992, 93. Mem. ANA, AAUP, Am. Assn. Nurse Practitioners. Republican. Roman Catholic. Office: Orange Park Pediatrics 2140 South St Orange Park FL 32073

BEDRICK, BERNICE, retired science educator, consultant; b. Jersey City, Sept. 29, 1916; d. Abraham Lewis and Esther (Cowan) Grodjesk; m. Emanuel Arthur Bedrick, Dec. 25, 1938 (dec. 1967); children: Allen Paul, Jane Bedrick Abels; m. Samuel Milberger, Sept. 23, 1984 (dec. 1984); stepchildren: Susan Milberger Rafael, Stanford. BS, U. Md., 1938; MA, NYU, 1952. Cert. tchr., N.J. Tchr. Linden (N.J.) Pub. Sch. System, 1950-69, supr. sci. curriculum, 1969-79, sch. prin., 1979-87; ret., 1987. Co-author: A Universe to Explore, 1969; developer program of safety and survival N.J. Dept. Edn., 1975. Founder, mem., bd. dirs. Temple Mekor Chayim, Linden; pres. bd. trustees Linden Pub. Libr., 1989-90, v.p., 1991; pres. Friends of Linden Libr., 1987-92, 95—. Recipient Cmty. Vol. Svc. award B'Nai B'Rith, 1993, Outstanding Sr. Citizen of Yr., City of Linden, 1996. Mem. NEA (life), N.J. Edn. Assn. (life), Am. Fedn. Sch. Adminstrs. (chpt. pres. 1984-86), Linden Edn. Found. (bd. dirs.), N.Y. Acad. Scis., N.J. Prins. and Suprs. Assn., N.J. Sci. tchrs. Assn., Nat. Sci. Tchrs. Assn., Alumni Assn. U. Md. (life), N.J. PTA (life), Hadassah (life), Linden Ceramics Club (sec. 1991-92, 95—), Nat. Coun. Jewish Women (life), Alpha Lambda Delta, Phi kappa Phi. Home: 2016 Orchard Ter Linden NJ 07036-3719

BEDROSSIAN, URSULA KAY KENNEDY, editor; b. Austin, Tex., Dec. 8, 1948; d. Richard Arch and Ursula Marie (Jones) Kennedy; m. Carlos Wanes Bedrossian, Aug. 8, 1970; children: Vanessa, Richard, Robert. BS, Jacksonville U., 1972; MEd, Vanderbilt U., 1984; PhD, St. Louis U., 1991. Registered med. technologist and cytotechnologist Am. Soc. Clin. Pathologists. Med. technologist Del Oro Med. Lab., Houston, 1977-78; edn. coord., lab. supr. dept. family practice U. Tex. Med. Sch., Houston, 1978-81; rsch. asst. VA Med. Ctr., Nashville, 1981-84; clin. instr. dept. pathology St. Louis U., 1985-89; dir. edn. and quality I DMC Univ. Labs., Detroit, 1991—; mng. edtor Wiley-Liss, N.Y.C., 1989—. Mng. editor Diagnostic Cytopathology, 1984—; asst. editor The Prostate, 1992-95; contbr. articles to sci. jours. Dir. med. relief Armenian Gen. Benevolent Union, 1993—. Recipient commendation U.S. Army 101st Workhorse Bn., Badhersfeld, Germany, 1985. Mem. Clin. Lab. Mgmt. Assn., Am. Soc. Cytotech. (faculty continuing med. edn. 1991—, liaison to Papunivolaou Ssoc. Cytopathology 1993—), Armenian Am. Bus. Coun., Brazilian Cultural Club. Office: DMC Univ Labs 4201 St Antoine Detroit MI 48201

BEDSOLE, ANN SMITH, former state senator; b. Selma, Ala., Jan. 7, 1930; d. Malcolm White and Sybil (Huey) Smith; m. Massey Palmer Bedsole, 1958; children: Mary Martin Bedsole Riser, John Henry Martin, Loraine Bedsole Demmas. Student, U. Ala., 1948, U. Denver, 1955-56; LLD (hon.), Mobile Coll., 1984, Huntingdon Coll., 1985. Mem. Ala. Rep. Exec. Com., 1966-74; del. seconded nomination Nixon for Pres. Rep. Nat. Conv., 1972; Rep. Presdl. Elector, 1972; Ala. state rep., 1978-82; Ala. state senator, 1982-94. Trustee Huntington Coll., Spring Hill Coll.; founder, bd. dirs. Ala. Sch. Math. and Sci.; bd. dirs. Voices for Alabama's Children, Mobile Mental Health Ctr.; mem. Jr. League of Mobile; bd. dirs. Vol. Mobile, Inc.; mem. steering com. Mobile United. Recipient M.O. Beale Scroll of Merit award Mobile Press Register, 1971-72, award for outstanding contbn. to forestry in Ala. Soc. Am. Foresters, 1986, Legislative Conservationist of Yr. award Ala. Wildlife Fedn., 1987; named 1st Lady of Mobile, 1972, Mobilian of Yr., 1993; inducted into Women's Acad. of Honor, 1987. Methodist. Office: PO Box 16642 Mobile AL 36616

BEDSWORTH, O. DIANE, retail executive; b. Detroit, Nov. 30, 1942; d. William H. and Olive Emily (Ludwig) Goodson; m. Gary J. Bedsworth, Apr. 4, 1964 (div. Feb. 1983); children: Jay William, Pamela Diane. Student, Mich. State U., 1961-64. Interior designer Dayton-Hudson Corp., Mpls., 1973-85; pres. Bedsworth Design Internat., Blackhawk, Calif., 1985—; owner Bedsworth Style, Danville, Calif., 1989—; cons. San Souci Hotel, Taipei, Taiwan, 1980—, Hotel Group, Inc., 1982-83, Corp. Homes, Damman, Saudi Arabia, residential homes, Hawaii, Calif., Ariz., 1986—. Mktg. dir. Sta. KTCA-TV Pub. Auction, Mpls., 1979-83, chairwoman, 1983, 84. Mem. Am. Soc. Interior Designers (profl.). Republican. Episcopalian. Office: Bedsworth Style 1822 Whitecliff Way Walnut Creek CA 94596

BEE, ANNA COWDEN, dance educator; b. Birmingham, Ala., Feb. 17, 1922; d. Porter Guthrie and Marion Irene (McCurry) Cowden; A.B., Samford U., 1944; student Chalif Sch. Dance, N.Y.C., 1950-54; m. Alon Wilton Bee, Oct. 21, 1942; children—Anna Margaret Bee Foote, Alon Wilton. Mem. faculty Byram High Sch., Jackson, 1945-52; mem. faculty Hinds Jr. Coll., Raymond, Miss., 1952—, dir. Hi-Steppers, girls' precision dance group; chaperone Miss Mississippi to Miss Am. Pageant; condr. charm clinics for teenagers; judge beauty pageants. Bd. dirs. Multiple Sclerosis Soc., Jackson, 1966-72; state chmn. Miss. Easter Seal Soc. campaign, 1966, 79; chmn. women's div. United Way, Jackson, 1973. Recipient Hinds C.C. svc. award, 1993, Miss Miss. Vol. of Yr. award, 1995, Miss Am. Vol. of Yr. award, 1995, Dance Tchrs. Unlimited Lifetime Achievement award, 1996; named Woman of Achievement, Jackson Bus. and Profl. Women's Club, 1967-78., Miss. Legislature commendation for contbn. to youth, 1981; Anna Cowden Bee Hall named in her honor Hinds C.C. Bd. Trustees, 1993. Mem. Nat. Faculty Dance Educators Am., Dance Masters Am., Miss. Edn. Assn., Miss. Assn. Health and Phys. Edn., Beta Sigma Omicron. Baptist. Producer halftime shows Gator Bowl, 1958, 64, 81, Sugar Bowl, 1960, Hall of Fame Bowl, 1977, 79, Mid-America Bowl, 1988, Senior Bowl, 1988. Home: 304 Alta Woods Blvd Jackson MS 39204-4906 Office: Hinds Jr Coll Raymond MS 39154

BEEBE, CORA PRIFOLD, government official; b. San Francisco, Nov. 3, 1937; d. George and Beatrice (Ehni) Prifold; m. Ronald Beebe, Jan., 1959 (div.). Student, Hollins Coll., Va., 1955-57, Am. U., 1957-58; BA, U. Mich., 1959, MA, 1961; LHD (hon.), Southeastern U., 1993. Adminstrv. asst. Am. Polit. Sci. Assn., 1962-64; research assoc. Inst. Comparative Studies of Polit. Systems, Washington, 1963-65; program planning and evaluation specialist U.S. Office Edn., Washington, 1965-68, planning coordinator, 1968-73, dir. planning and budget div., 1973-80; prin. dep. asst. sec. for elem. and sec. edn. Dept. Edn., Washington, 1980-81; asst. sec. adminstrn. U.S. Treasury Dept., Washington, 1981-84; dir. office of policy, budget and program mgmt. OSWER, EPA, Washington, 1984-86; dir. office of planning, budget and evaluation Dept. Commerce, Washington, 1986-87; commerce & justice br. chief Office of Mgmt. and Budget, 1987-94, advisor to assoc. dir. gen. govt. and fin., 1994; exec. dir. adminstrn. Office of Thrift Supervision, Washington, 1994—. Mem. women's com. Washington Performing Arts Soc., 1983-87. Recipient HEW Superior Svc. award, Presdl. Rank award, 1989; Inst. World Affairs fellow, 1956, Am. Edn. Abroad fellow, 1960. Mem. Exec. Women in Govt. Program and Budget Analysis. Home: 540 N St SW Apt S 304 Washington DC 20024-2903 Office: Office Thrift Supervision 1700 G St NW Washington DC 20552

BEEBE, GRACE ANN, special education educator; b. Wyandotte, Mich., Feb. 16, 1945; d. Cecil Vern and Elizabeth Lucille (Tamblyn) B. BA, Ea. Mich. U., 1967; MEd, Wayne State U., 1970; postgrad., U. Mich., 1973-78. Cert. spl. edn. tchr., Mich. Tchr. POHI 1st grade Grand Rapids (Mich.) Pub. Schs., 1967-69; tchr. title VI Taylor (Mich.) Pub. Schs., 1970-73, tchr. Physically or Otherwise Health Impaired pre-kindergarten, 1973-79, tchr. POHI 1st-3rd grades, 1979-81, tchr. POHI pre-kindergarten, 1981-84, tchr., cons. POHI, 1984—. Area coord. Indian Trails Camp, Grand Rapids, 1979—. Recipient Recognition award 4-H Wayne County Handicapped Riding, 1986, Indian Trails Camp, 1990; Ronald McDonald Children's Charities grantee, 1990; State of Mich. Spl. Edn. scholar, 1966-67, Vocat. Rehab. scholar, 1969-70. Mem. SCADS (alt. rep.), N.Am. Riding for the Handicapped Assn., Mich. Fedn. Tchrs., Physically Impaired Assn. Mich., Taylor Fedn. Tchrs. (ancillary v.p. 1990-92), Taylor Handicapped Assn., Allen Park Assn. for Handicapped, Trenton Hist. Soc. (exec. bd. 1988—), Coun. for Exceptional Children, Phi Delta Kappa, Alpha Delta Kappa. Republican. Methodist. Home: 2225 Emeline St Trenton MI 48183-3653 Office: Taylor Spl Edn Dept 11010 Janet St Taylor MI 48180-4079

BEEBE, MARY LIVINGSTONE, curator; b. Portland, Oreg., Nov. 5, 1940; d. Robert and Alice Beebe. B.A., Bryn Mawr Coll., 1962; postgrad. Sorbonne, U. Paris, 1962-63. Curatorial asst. Fogg Art Mus., Harvard U., Cambridge, Mass., 1966-68; Apprentice Portland Art Mus., 1963-64, Boston Mus. Art, 1964-65; exec. dir. Portland Ctr. for Visual Arts, 1973-81; dir. Stuart Collection U. Calif.-San Diego, La Jolla, 1981—; cons. in field. Mem. art steering com. Portland Devel. Commn., 1977-80; bd. dirs. Henry Gallery, U. Wash., Seattle, 1977-80; project cons. Nat. Rsch. Ctr. for Arts, N.Y.C., 1978-79; bd. dirs. Art Mus. Assn. San Francisco, 1978-84; bd. dirs., trustee Art Matters Inc., 1985—; trustee Russell Found., 1982-94; hon. mem. bd. dirs. Portland Ctr. for Visual Arts, 1984-91; mem. arts adv. bd. Centre City Devel. Corp., San Diego, 1982-94; arts adv. bd. Port of San Diego; panel mem., cons. Nat. Endowment Arts; juror numerous art shows and exhbns. Nat. Endowment Arts fellow, 1979. Recipient Allied Professions award AIA, 1992. Contbr. articles to profl. jours. Office: The Stuart Collection U Calif San Diego 9500 Gilman Dr La Jolla CA 92093-0010

BEEBE, NAOMI MARIE, financial consultant, accountant; b. Schenectady, N.Y.; m. William Lloyd Beebe, Nov. 5, 1983. AA in Bus. Adminstrn., Schenectady C.C., 1979; postgrad., Union Coll., 1983, U. Phoenix, San Jose, Calif., 1989-90. Lic. tax preparer, Calif. Sr. cost acctg. clk., cost specialist, labor analyst GE, Schenectady, N.Y., 1973-83; acct. Accts. Inc., 1986-89; owner, fin. cons. Real-Time Consulting, Bookkeeping & Tax Svc., Santa Clara, Calif., 1989—; named del. to Fin. Mgmt. and Auditing Delegation to Russia People to People Internat.; authorized reseller, software cons. State of the Art (Mas90) Accounting Software, 1994—. Creator: (software enhancement) Financial Analysis, 1983 (Merit award 1983). Ch. youth advisor Fisher United Meth. Ch., Schenectady, 1983; treas. Sunnyvale (Calif.) Homeowners Assn., 1990. Mem. Nat. Soc. Pub. Accts., Inst. Mgmt. Accts., Calif. Assn. Ind. Accts. (chpt. pres. 1991-92), Inland Soc. Tax Cons. (chpt. sec. 1993-94). Office: Real-Time Consulting 1556 Halford Ave # 103 Santa Clara CA 95051-2661

BEEBE, SANDRA E., retired English language educator, artist, writer; b. March AFB, Calif., Nov. 10, 1934; d. Eugene H. and Margaret (Fox) B.; m. Donald C. Thompson. AB in English and Speech, UCLA, 1956; MA in Secondary Edn., Calif. State U., Long Beach, 1957. Tchr. English, Garden Grove (Calif.) High Sch., 1957-93, attendance supr., 1976-83, ret., 1993. Contbr. articles to English Jour., chpts. to books; watercolor artist; exhbns. include AWS, NWS, Okla. Watercolor Soc., Watercolor West, La. Watercolor Soc., Knickerbocker Artists N.Y., Montana WCS, Midwest Watercolor Soc., Butler Inst. Am. Art, Youngstown, Ohio, Kings Art Ctr., Audubon Artists N.Y.; cover artist Exploring Painting, 1990, title page Understanding Watercolor, American Artist, 1991. Named one of the Top Ten Watercolorists The Artists Mag., 1994; recipient Best Watercolors award Rockport Press, 1995; chosen for Design Poster selection, 1995. Mem. Am. Watercolor Soc., Nat. Watercolor Soc., Midwest Watercolor Soc., Watercolor West, Allied Artists N.Y., Knickerbocker Artists N.Y., Audobon Artists N.Y., West Coast Watercolor Soc., Rocky Mountain Nat. Watermedia Honor Soc., Jr. League Long Beach, Kappa Kappa Gamma. Republican. Home: 7241 Marina Pacifica Dr S Long Beach CA 90803-3899 Studio: B-Q Gallery 3920 E 4th St Long Beach CA 90814-1656 also: 239 Mira Mar Ave Long Beach CA 90803-6153 also: Beacon Hill West Gallery Carmel CA 93921

BEECHY, MARIA, bank executive, merchant banker. Exec. v.p. merchant banking Chase Manhattan, N.Y.C. Office: Chase Manhattan 1 Chase Main Plz New York NY 10081*

BEELER, B. DIANE, writer, executive; b. Maryville, Tenn., Mar. 10, 1953; d. Peggy Ann (DeHart) B.; m. James McRay Cormani, June 12, 1975 (div. Sept. 1985); children: Julie Ann Cormani, Valerie Marie Cormani. BA in Music, Agnes Scott Coll., 1974; postgrad., U. Tenn., 1974-75; MS in Bus., U. Tex. at Dallas, Richardson, 1984. Grad. teaching asst. U. Tex. at Dallas, Richardson, 1983-84; knowledge engr., tech. spokesperson Texas Instruments, Austin, 1985-86, product mktg. engr., 1987-88; sr. product mgr. Novell, Austin, 1988-90, mgr. mktg. programs, 1990-91; pvt. cons. Austin, 1992; pres. Beeler Enterprises, Oak Ridge, Tenn., 1993—; gen. mgr. Oak Ridge Civic Music Assn., 1995—; affiliate Speakers USA, Pigeon Forge, Tenn., 1993; gen. mgr. Oak Ridge Civic Music Assn., 1995-96. Columnist: (bus. column) The Oak Ridger, 1993-94; contbr. articles to profl. jours. Mem. Class Leadership, Austin, 1990-91, Leadership Oak Ridge, 1994; mem. steering com. Employees Support Parenting Program, Austin, 1990-92; music dir. Unity Ch., Knoxville, Tenn., 1993-95; bd. dirs. Oak Ridge Civic Music Assn., 1993-94. Mem. Am. Mktg. Assn. (exec. mem.), Nat. Assn. for Self-Employed, Ridge C. of C. Office: 145 Highpoint Ln Oak Ridge TN 37830

BEEMAN, BARBARA, social work supervisor; b. Bayonne, N.J., Sept. 29, 1949; d. David and Jeanette (Agaman) B.; life companion Bill Bannon. BA, Jersey City State Coll., 1971. Lic. social worker, N.J. Reporter The Dispatch, Union City, N.J., 1971-73; social worker Hudson County Welfare, Jersey City, 1973-83, supr. social work, 1983—; mem. steering com. Food and Shelter Coalition, Jersey City, 1990—. Singer, musician, bandleader: (with Barbara Beeman Band) Moving Day, 1986, So the Story goes, 1989; performer coffeehouses, bookstores. Performer Let's Celebrate "Race Against Hunger," Jersey City, 1985-93, Bayonne (N.J.) Hometown Fair, 1993, 94, 95, N.J. Seafood Festival, Belmar, N.J., 1991, 92, M.S. Race, Liberty Park, Jersey City, 1992-93, "Standdown" N.J. Homeless Vets. Conf., 1994. Democrat. Roman Catholic. Home: 25 W 35 St Bayonne NJ 07002 Office: Hudson Co Dept Social Svcs 100 Newkirk St Jersey City NJ 07306

BEER, ALICE STEWART (MRS. JACK ENGEMAN), retired musician, educator; b. Redwood Falls, Minn., Sept. 29, 1912; d. Robert and Isabel (Montgomery) Stewart; m. Jack Engeman, Dec. 14, 1974; children by previous marriage: W. Robert, Jane K. Beer Mosher, Elizabeth S. Beer-Shilling. MusB, Northwestern U., 1934, MusM, 1952; postgrad., Johns Hopkins U., 1954, 60, Mexico City Coll., 1956, U. Md., 1957. Tchr. pub. schs., Lawton, Mich., 1934-39, Battle Creek, Mich., 1949-51; tchr. Balt. Pub. Schs., 1951-53, supr. music, 1953-77; tchr. summer sessions various colls. and univs., 1957-85; adj. faculty Peabody Inst., John's Hopkins U., Balt., 1981-85; cons. Alliance for Arts in Edn., Balt. County Pub. Schs., 1982-90, cons. curriculum, 1984-91; pres. Pickersgill Apt. Retirement Assn. Author: Teaching Suggestions, Birchard Music Series II and III, 1962, Teaching Music: What, How and Why, 1973, Teaching Music to the Exceptional Child. A Handbook for Mainstreaming, 1980, Teaching Music, 1982, Patriotic Color Sound Filmstrips/Videos, 1967-69; mem. editorial bd. Maryland Music Educator Jour., 1990—; contbr. articles to profl. jours. Mem. bd. lady mgrs. Balt. Street Clinic, 1986—; ordained elder Towson Presbyn. Ch., chmn. nominating comm. Prebyterian women. Recipient Director's Recognition award for commitment to music edn. and extraordinary contbn. to art of teaching, 1986; inductee Md. Music Educators Hall of Fame, 1989. Mem. AAUW (mem. Towson br.), Nat. Conf. Music Educators, Md. Music Educators Assn., Pres.'s Club Cir. U. Md., Officers and Faculty Club of U.S. Naval Acad., Pres.'s Club Circle, Phi Beta. Republican. Home: 615 Chestnut Ave # 1401 Baltimore MD 21204-3742

BEER, CLARA LOUISE JOHNSON, retired electronics executive; b. Bisbee, Ariz., Jan. 14, 1918; d. Franklin Fayette and Marie (Sturm) Johnson; m. Philip James McElmurry, May 15, 1937 (div. July 1944); children—Leonard Franklin, Philip James Jr.; m. William Sigvard Beer, July 15, 1945 (dec. Aug. 31, 1977); 1 son, Douglas Lee; m. Kenneth Christy Huntwork, May 1, 1982. Student, Merritt Bus. Sch., Oakland, Calif., 1935, Bus. Instrn. Sch., Palo Alto, Calif., 1955. Sec., artist M.R. Fisher Studios, Oakland, 1936-40; piano, organ instr. Anna May Studios, Palo Alto, 1948-50; pvt. piano, organ instr. Palo Alto, 1949-56; sec. Stanford Electronics Labs., Stanford U., 1955-58; corporate sec. and exec. sec. to chmn. bd. Watkins-Johnson Co., Palo Alto, 1958-88; dir., sec. Watkins-Johnson Internat., 1968-88, Watkins-Johnson Ltd., 1971-88, Watkins-Johnson Assocs., 1977-88. Mem. Nat. Secs. Assn., Christian Bus. and Profl. Women's Coun. (sec. 1966-67, adviser 1968). Home: 24157 Hillview Dr Los Altos CA 94024

BEERBOHM, ELISA NEWELL, advertising professional; b. Palo Alto, Calif., May 15, 1960; d. Harry S. and Dorothy L. (Perkins) B. BA, UCLA, 1984; MBA, U. So. Calif., 1994. Sr. account mgr. Tribune Newspapers, L.A., 1987-96; western regional mgr. Std. Rate and Data Svc., L.A., 1996—. Bd. dirs. Advt. Industry Emergency Fund, 1996—. Mem. Am. Mktg. Assn., L.A. Advt. Club, Women in Comm. Office: Std Rate and Data Svc 11500 Olympic Blvd #385 Los Angeles CA 90064-1527

BEERBOWER, CYNTHIA GIBSON, lawyer; b. Dayton, Ohio, June 25, 1949; d. Charles Augustus and Sarah (Rittenhouse) Gibson; m. John Edwin Beerbower, Aug. 28, 1971; children: John Eliot, Sarah Rittenhouse. BA, Mt. Holyoke Coll., 1971; JD, Boston U., 1974; LLB, Cambridge U., Eng., 1976. Bar: N.Y. 1975. Assoc., Cadwalader, Wickersham & Taft, N.Y.C., 1975-76; assoc. Simpson, Thacher & Bartlett, N.Y.C., 1977-81, ptnr., 1981-93; internat. tax counsel U.S. Dept. Treasury, Washington, 1993-94, dep. asst. sec. tax policy, 1994—. Mem. ABA, Assn. Bar City N.Y., N.Y. State Bar Assn. (com. co-chmn. 1987-93). Presbyterian. Home: 720 Park Ave New York NY 10021 Office: US Dept Treasury 1500 Pennsylvania Ave NW Washington DC 20005-1007

BEERS, CHARLOTTE LENORE, advertising agency executive; b. Beaumont, Tex., July 26, 1935; d. Glen and Frances (Bolt) Rice; m. Donald C. Beers, 1971; 1 dau., Lisa. B.S. in Math. and Physics, Baylor U., Waco, Tex., 1958. Group product mgr. Uncle Ben's Inc., 1959-69; sr. v.p., dir. client services J. Walter Thompson, 1969-79; chief operating officer Tatham-Laird & Kudner, Chgo., from 1979, mng. ptnr., chmn. and chief exec officer; vice chmn. RSCG Group Roux Seguela, Cayzac & Goudard, France; chmn., CEO Ogilvy & Mather Worldwide, N.Y.C., Ogilvy Group Inc., N.Y.C. Named Nat. Advt. Woman of Yr. Am. Advt. Fedn., 1975. Mem. Am. Assn. Advt. Agencies (chmn. from 1987), Women's Advt. Club Chgo., Chgo. Network. Republican. Episcopalian. Office: Ogilvy & Mather Worldwide Group Inc 309 W 49th St #12 New York NY 10019*

BEERS, ROSANNE TESDELL, consultant; b. Polk County, Iowa, July 10, 1947; d. Edward Seton Jr. and Merna Belle (Opp) Tesdell; m. Dennis Dean Beers, Aug. 31, 1974; children: Michael Tesdell, Cory Brandon. BA in Journalism, Drake U., 1976, MS in Counseling, 1990. Cert. disability mgmt. specialist. Freelance bus. writer Des Moines, 1976-83, freelance career and small bus. cons., 1983-91; rehab. specialist Gen. Rehab. Svc., Des Moines, 1991; mktg. rep., rehab. specialist Career Design, Des Moines, 1991-92; cons., coach career, small bus., rehab. Beers Consulting, Des Moines, 1992—; Jefferies scholarship and ednl. mentoring adv. com. Young Women's Resource Ctr., Des Moines, 1995—; edn. and career advisor House of Mercy, Des Moines, 1995—. Co-author: West Des Moines From Railroads to Crossroads 1893-1993, 1993. Fellow Coach Univ. (various vol. roles 1995—); mem. ACA, NAFE, Internat. Coach Fedn., Nat. Rehab. Assn., Iowa Assn. Svc. Providers in Pvt. Rehab. (treas. 1994—).

BEERS, SUSAN ALICE, dean; b. Tucson, July 21, 1946; d. Laverne G. and Claire M. (Liles) B. BA, Chapman U., 1968; MA, Calif. State U., Long Beach, 1972; postgrad. in Edn., Pepperdine U. Cert. tchr., Calif. Tchr. Norwalk (Calif.) H.S., 1969-74; realtor assoc. Nolan Real Estate, Laguna Beach, Calif., 1988-90; prof. Fullerton (Calif.) Coll., 1974-89, athletic dir., dept. chair, 1989-92, dean phys. edn./athletics, 1992—, interim dean counseling/student devel., 1995—; mem. dist. mgmt. negotiation team Fullerton Coll., 1994-95, pres. Orange Empire Conf. Com., 1995—, Title IX officer, 1994—; presenter in field. Editor Scope newsletter, 1992—. Mem. Dept. Social Svc., Orange, Calif., 1992; Scope rep./presenter State Legis. Conf., 1994; prsenter Calif. Assn. Health, Sacramento, 1995. Mem. AAHPERD, State Commn. on Athletics, State Cmty. Coll. Orgn. of Phys. Educators (pres. 1993-95, spkr. 1995). Democrat. Home: 607 Fontana Way Laguna Beach CA 92632 Office: Fullerton Coll 321 E Chapman Fullerton CA 92632-2011

BEESON, VIRGINIA REED, naval officer, nurse; b. Franklin, N.J., Mar. 14, 1951; d. Colin Reed and Marion (Dailey) B. BSN magna cum laude, U. Vt., Burlington, 1973; MS in Nursing Adminstrn., Boston U., 1987. RN, Vt.; cert. in nursing adminstrn.; cert. ATLS. Commd. ensign USN, 19, advanced through grades to capt., 1994; staff and charge nurse various locations, 1973-85; charge nurse gen. surgery ward Nat. Naval Med. Ctr., Bethesda, Md., 1987-89; Nurse Corps assignment officer U.S. Navy Annex, Washington, 1989-91; head leadership tng. div. Naval Sch. Health Scis., Bethesda, 1991; dir. Nursing Svcs. Naval Hosp., Jacksonville, Fla.; speaker in field. Decorated Naval Commendation medal (3), Navy Achievement medal, Meritorious Svc. medal. Mem. ANA, Fla. Nurses Assn., Women Officers Profl. Assn., Am. Coll. Healthcare Exec., Am. Orgn. of Nurse Exec., Sigma Theta Tau. Home: 91 San Juan Dr F-4 Ponte Vedra Beach FL 32082 Office: Naval Hosp Jacksonville FL 32214

BEETON, BEVERLY, academic administrator; b. Brigham City, Utah, Feb. 18, 1939; d. Thain Joseph and Florence (Hatch) B. PhD, U. Utah, 1976. Asst. to v.p. acad. affairs U. Utah, Salt Lake City, 1972-78; assoc. provost/v.p. acad. affairs Govs. State U., University Park, Ill., 1981-83; vice chancellor acad. affairs U. Alaska Southeast, Juneau, 1983-88; provost/vice chancellor acad. affairs U. Alaska, Anchorage, 1988-95; cons. Time-Life Books, N.Y.C., 1977, Calif. State U., Long Beach, 1983; commr. Commn. on Colls. of Northwest Assn. Schs. and Colls., Seattle, 1986-93; mem. nat. adv. bd. Women of the West Mus., Boulder, Colo., 1994—. Author: Letters of Elizabeth Wells Cumming, 1977, Women Vote in the West, 1986, (with others) One Woman, One Vote, 1995. Bd. dirs. YMCA, Chgo., 1972-82; chair com. Commonwealth North, Anchorage, 1996.

BEETS, HUGHLA FAE, retired secondary school educator; b. Eustace, Tex., Aug. 1, 1929; d. Hubert Edgar and Beatrice (Roark) Bonsal; m. Anneel Randolph Beets, Sept. 14, 1946. BA, North Tex. State U., 1958, MA, 1960; postgrad., U. Mass., 1967. Cert. tchr., Tex. Tchr. Seagoville (Tex.) Ind. Sch. Dist., 1958-65, Dallas Ind. Sch. Dist., 1965-70; owner, mgr. Mabank (Tex.) Ins. Agy., 1970-77, Beets Interiors, Mabank, 1970—; ptnr., mgr. Cedar Creek Title Co., Mabank, 1977-80; tchr. govt. and econs. Athens (Tex.) Ind. Sch. Dist., 1981-91; cons. U.S. Office Edn., Washington, 1968-69; mem. devel. com. Edn. Profl. Devel. Act Tex. Edn. Agy., 1969. Cons. edn. com. Goals for Dallas, 1969; vice chairperson Kaufman (Tex.) County Improvement Council, 1975. Chmn. beautification com. Keep Tex. Beautiful, Mabank, 1990-91; grant adminstr. Avanti Cmty. Theater, 1993-95, bd. dirs., 1993-96, v.p., 1995-96; co-chair United Way Campaign, 1991-92, dir. Henderson County, 1992—; mem. Planning and Zoning Commn., City of Mabank, 1992—; sec. Indsl. Found., 1971-75. Recipient Outstanding Ex-Student award Trinity Valley C.C., Athens, 1974; Cert. of Recognition, Internat. Thespian Soc., 1994, Lifetime Achievement award Cedar Creek C. of C., 1996. Mem. NEA, Athens Edn. Assn. (pres. 1982-83), Tex. State Tchrs. Assn. (pres.-elect dist. X 1970), Tex. Classroom Tchrs. Assn. (state bd. dirs. 1969-70), Classroom Tchrs. Dallas (pres. 1968-69), Mabank C. of C. (bd. dirs. 1978-80, 91-92, Citizen of Yr. 1977). Democrat. Methodist. Home: 112 N Canton St PO Box 318 Mabank TX 75147

BEGIN, JACQUELINE SUE, college administrator; b. Urbana, Ohio, Oct. 20, 1951; d. Gerald L. Sr. and Norma M. (Bezold) B. AA, Clark State c.C., 1991; BA, Antioch Coll., 1993, MA, 1996. Rschr., organizer Holywell Trust, Derry, No. Ireland, 1992; rsch. asst. peace studies dept. Antioch Coll., Yellow Springs, Ohio, 1993; adminstrv. asst. Comty. Action Commn. Fayette County, Washington Court House, Ohio, 1994-95; admissions assoc. Admissions Office Antioch Coll., Yellow Springs, 1995—; student presenter Boulding Libr. dedication Antioch Coll. and McGregor Sch. of Antioch U., Yellow Springs, 1995; rschr. on women in No. Ireland, McGregor Sch., Yellow Springs, 1996; chair, organizer Beyond Hate: Living with Our Deepest Difference Conf., Holywell Trust, Derry, 1992. Founder, activist for environment Students Against Violation of Earth (S.A.V.E.), Springfield, Ohio, 1989-91; activist for animal rights People for Ethical Treatment of Animals (PETA), Springfield, 1987-93; peace activist Clark State Peace Activists, Yellow Springs, 1991—; activist for women specific issues The McGregor Sch. of Antioch U., Yellow Springs, 1994—. Comty. scholar Clark State C.C., 1990, News-Sun scholar, 1991, Chatterjee scholar Antioch Coll., 1992. Mem. Ohio Assn. Coll. Admissions Counselors. Office: Antioch Coll Admissions Off 795 Livermore St Yellow Springs OH 45387

BEGLARIAN, EVE, composer; b. Ann Arbor, MI, July 22, 1958; d. Grant and Joyce Ellyn (Heeney) B. BA magna cum laude, Princeton U., 1980; MA, Columbia U., 1983. Freelance composer, 1978—, freelance audio producer, 1983—. Composer: FlamingO for Chamber Orchestra, 1995, TypOpera - Music Theater, 1994, Machaut in the Machine Age I-IV, 1986-95, Overstepping, Inc., 1991. Grantee Meet the Composer, 1995-96, Cary Trust, 1995, Music in Motion, 1994, Rockefeller Found., Bellagio, Italy, 1995. Mem. Am. Soc. Composers, Authors, Pub., League of Composers Internat. Soc. of Contemporary Music (pres. 1983-86), Am. Music Ctr., Am. Composing Forum, N.Y. New Music Ensemble (bd. dirs. 1983—).

BEGOS, JANE DU PREE, museum professional, independent scholar; b. Athens, Tenn., Dec. 14, 1930; d. Crawford and Edna Imogene (Neil) Du Pree; m. Kevin Paul Begos, Sept. 7, 1957 (div. Mar. 1995); children: Kevin Paul Jr., Cassandra Jane; m. William N. Richardson, June 30, 1995. AB, U. Ga., 1951; MA, Columbia U., 1965. Programs dir. John Jay Homestead State Hist. Site, Katonah, N.Y., 1976-86; cons. editor READEX Micropublication Corp., Am. Women's Diaries Series, New Canaan, Conn.; records clk. collections mgmt. unit Bur. Hist. Sites, Waterford, N.Y., 1988-90; curator Dutchess County Hist. Soc., 1990-92; dir. Northumberland County Hist. Soc., 1992—; cons. Pa. Humanities Coun. project Raising Our Sites: Women's History in Pa. Editor: A Women's Diaries Miscellany, 1989; editor, pub. (newsletter) Women's Diaries, 1983-86; columnist Diarist's Jour., 1988—; contbr. articles to profl. jours.; complier of many women's diaries bibliographies, 1977—. Lt. (j.g.) USNR, 1952-57. Mem. So. Assn. of Women's Historians, Berkshire Conf. of Women's Historians, Nat. Women's Studies Assn., Communal Socs. Assn., Costume Soc. Am., Columbia Univ. Grad. Faculties Assn., Nat. Soc. DAR. Democrat. Roman Catholic.

BEHAR, DIANE SOLOMON, marketing and public relations professional, freelance writer, consultant; b. N.Y.C., May 17, 1952; d. Solomon and Frieda Behar. Spanish language cert., La Universidad Internacional, 1969; BA, Cornell U., 1974; MBA, U. Pa., 1983. Legis. analyst Com. on the Budget U.S. Ho. of Reps., Washington, 1975-77, legis. asst. and speechwriter Office of Congressman Oberstar, 1977-81; account exec. Doyle Dane Bernbach Advt., N.Y.C., 1983-85; dir. of pub. affairs and speechwriter Mayor's Office of Bus. Devel., N.Y.C., 1985-88; dir. of mktg. Mayor's Offfice of Bus. Devel., N.Y.C., 1988-91; sr. mktg. analyst Dep. Mayor's Office for Econ. Policy and Mktg., N.Y.C., 1991-95; sr. bus. analyst & grants mgr. Mayor's Dept. Bus. Svcs., N.Y.C., 1995—; mktg. cons. Work Late/Eat Right Gourmet Food Delivery Svcs., N.Y.C., 1985-87; lectr. in field. Contbr. articles to profl. jours. Mem. coun., fundraiser Fresh Air Fund, 1987—; bd. dirs., fundraiser Pentacle Danceworks, 1984—; v.p. bd. dirs. Children's Orch. Soc., 1990—. Morgenthau fellow, 1981-83, Dupont fellow, 1981-83, fellow Nat. Endowment for Arts, 1983. Mem. NAFE, Am. Mgmt. Assn., Am. Mktg. Assn., Women Execs. in Pub. Rels., Global Bus. Assn N.Y., Musicians Soc. N.Y., Cornell Club. Home: 201 E 69th St New York NY 10021-5770 Office: NYC Dept of Bus Svcs 110 William St New York NY 10038-3901

BEHBEHANIAN, MAHIN FAZELI, surgeon; b. Kermanshah region, Iran; d. M Jaafar and Ozra (A.) B.; m. Abolfath H. Fazeli, Sept, 4, 1969; children: Pouneh, Pontea. BS, Wilmington (Ohio) Coll., 1961; MD, Med. Coll. of Pa., Phila., 1965; general surgeon, Lankenan Hosp., Phila., 1970. Diplomate Am. Bd. Surgery. Chief surgery, pres. med. staff Imperial Ct. Hosp., Teheran, Iran, 1971-79; gen. surgery Riddle Meml. Hosp., Media, Pa., 1980—; pvt. practice Chester, Media, Phila., Pa., 1984—; Mem. operating room com. Riddle Meml. Hosp., Media, 1988—, also Emergency room com., utilization com. Editor-in-chief Behkoosh Jour. of Medicine, Teheran, 1976-79. Recipient Gilson Colby Engel award, 1966. Fellow Am. Coll. Surgeons; mem. AMA, Am. Women Surgical Soc., Pa. Med. Soc., Del. County Med. Soc. Office: Riddle Meml Health Care Ctr 1088 W Baltimore Pike Media PA 19063-5136

BEHLAR, PATRICIA ANN, political science educator; b. New Orleans, Jan. 16, 1939; d. James Edward and Maude Albertine (Davis) B. BA, U. New Orleans, 1966; MA, La. State U., 1968, PhD, 1974. Instr. Northwestern State U. of La., Natchitoches, 1971-72; instr. Pan Am. U., Edinburg, Tex., 1974-76; asst. prof. Pan Am. U., Edinburg, 1976-77, U. Ark., Pine Bluff, 1977-84; asst. prof. Pittsburg (Kans.) State U., 1986-92, assoc. prof., 1992—; mem. U. Ark. Pine Bluff Winthrop Rockefeller lectures steering com., 1980-82; referee Ark. Polit. Sci. Jour., 1983-84; alt., edit. com. Univ. Press of Kans., 1991-93; mem., edit. com. Univ. Press of Kans., 1993-95; book rev. editor, The Midwest Quarterly, 1994—. Audio reader for the blind, Pittsburg, 1992. Recipient La. State U. fellowship, 1970-71. Mem. Am. Polit. Sci. Assn., Sou. Polit. Sci. Assn., Kans. Polit. Sci. Assn., Southwestern Social Sci. Assn., Phi Kappa Phi. Democrat. Roman Catholic. Home: 508 Hobson Dr Pittsburg KS 66762-6315 Office: Pittsburg State U Dept Social Sci Pittsburg KS 66762

BEHLER, DIANA IPSEN, Germanic language and literature educator; b. N.Y.C.; d. Walter F. and Marie M. (Kroger) Ipsen; m. Ernst Behler, Nov. 24, 1967; children: Sophia, Caroline. B.A., U. Wash., 1965, M.A., 1966, Ph.D., 1970. Asst. prof. Germanics Germanics U. Wash., Seattle, 1971-74; assoc. prof. Germanics and comparative lit. U. Wash., Seattle, 1974-81, prof., 1981—; chmn. dept Germanics U. Wash., 1978-88, 1990. Author: The Theory of tne Novel in Early German Romaniticism, 1978; translations: Hegel, Jacobi, Fichte; contbr. articles to profl. jours. Younger Humanist fellow NEH, 1972-73. Mem. Am. Assn. Tchrs. German, N.Am. Nietzsche Soc. Home: 5525 NE Penrith Rd Seattle WA 98105-2844 Office: U Wash Dept Germanics Box 353130 Seattle WA 98195

BEHLMAR, CINDY LEE, business manager, consultant; b. Smyrna, Tenn., July 4, 1959; d. James Wallace and Barbara Ann (Behlmar) Gribble. BBA, Coll. William and Mary, 1981; MBA, Old Dominion U., 1995. Adminstrv. extern Hampton (Va.) Gen. Hosp., 1981-82; mktg. rep., then supr. mktg. svcs. PruCare of Richmond, Va., 1983-85; exec. dir. PhysicianCare, Inc., Newport News, Va., 1986-89; provider rels. cons. Va. Health Network, Richmond, 1989-91; ind. cons. Tidewater Health Care, Virginia Beach, Va., 1991-92; chief ops. officer Tidewater Phys. Therapy, Inc., Newport News, 1993-95; ind. cons. Yorktown, Va., 1996—; sec., bd. dirs. Greater Peninsula Area Med.-Bus. Coalition, Newport News, 1987-89; symposium faculty mem. Am. Hosp. Assn., Orlando, Fla., 1987, Washington, 1988. Mem. ch. coun. St. Mark Luth. Ch., Yorktown, Va., 1988-91. Fin. Exec. Inst. scholar, 1993. Mem. Inst. Mgmt. Accts., Peninsula Toastmasters, Phi Kappa Phi, Beta Gamma Sigma. Home: 103 Jean Pl Yorktown VA 23693-3007

BEHNKE, DOLEEN, computer and environmental specialist, consultant; b. Alameda, Calif., Sept. 23, 1950; d. Charles Joseph Ziegler and Dola Faye (Cushing) Peterson; m. Glen Allwin Pellett, June 26, 1971 (div. 1986); children: mark D., Michael J.; m. Danny Lynn Carr, Dec. 29, 1986 (div. 1996); m. Jon T. Behnke, June 28, 1996. BA, U. Wis., Madison, 1973. Notary Pub., Mich. Budget analyst Ednl. Testing Svc., Princeton, N.J., 1979-80; tech. recruiter Uniforce Svcs., Inc., Rock Hill, S.C., 1983-84; mgr. tng. and documentation Electronic Data Systems Corp., Troy, Mich., 1985-87; tech. writer, trainer, analyst cons. CES, Inc., Troy, 1989-92; pres. D'Carr Co., Inc., Roseville, Mich., 1988-93; tech. writer, trainer, cons. Eaton Corp., Southfield, Mich., 1988-93; pres., CEO Carr-Ben Tech Ltd., Whitmore Lake, Mich., 1996—; installer Gt. Plains Acctg., Fargo, N.D., 1990—; cons. Hazardous Materials Info. Exch., Washington, 1989—; cons., tech. writer Saturn Corp., 1991-92, Blue Cross Blue Shield, Southfield, Mich., 1992-93, 95—; tech. wrtier FANUC Robotics, N.A., Inc., Auburn Hills, Mich., 1993-95. Co-author: CIW-Weld Monitor, 1990, 93. Mem. AAUP, ASTD, NAFE, Internat. Platform Assn., Greater Trenton Musicians Union, Profl. Bus. Women's Assn., Macom County Dems., Mich. Dems., Roseville Kiwanis (pres., lt. gov.-elect 1996—, clown 1994—). Democrat. Roman Catholic. Office: 133 Belmont Ln Whitmore Lake MI 48189

BEHNKE, MARYLOU, neonatologist, educator; b. Orlando, Fla., Sept. 1, 1950; d. Ernest Edmund and Elizabeth (Kolb) B. BS in Chemistry, U. Fla., 1972, MD, 1976. Diplomate Am. Bd. Pediatrics, Am. Bd. Neonatology-Perinatology. Intern dept. pediatrics Coll. Medicine, U. Fla., Gainesville, 1976-77, resident, 1977-79, chief resident, 1979-80, fellow in neonatology, 1981-83, asst. prof., 1979-81, 83-89, assoc. prof., 1989—; adj. asst. prof. Coll. Nursing, Gainesville, 1988-89, adj. assoc. prof., 1989—, mem. senate-at-large, 1984-89, mem. grad. studies faculty, 1988—; med. dir. neonatology ICU Shands Hosp., Gainesville, 1983-89, neonatal developmental follow-up program, 1989—; presenter at nat. and internat. meetings, 1981—; ad hoc mem. spl. rev. com. on human devel. rsch. NIH, 1991—, chair, 1993, 94. Mem. editl. bd. Death Studies, 1983-94; contbr. articles to med. jours., chpts. to books. Grantee NIH, 1984-87, 91—, Nat. Inst. on Drug Abuse, 1991—, Ctr. for Substance abuse Treatment, 1993—. Fellow Am. Acad. Pediatrics; mem. Fla. Med. Assn., Alachua County Med. Soc., Nat. Perinatal Assn., So. Soc. for Pediatric Rsch., Fla. Interagy. Coord. Coun. for Infants and Toddlers, Fla. Soc. Neonatal Perinatologists. Republican. Mem. Ch. of Christ. Home: 426 SW 40th St Gainesville FL 32607-2749 Office: J Hillis Miller Health Ctr Dept Pediatrics Box 100296 Gainesville FL 32610

BEHRENS, BEREL LYN, physician, academic administrator; b. New South Wales, Australia, 1940. MB, BS, Sydney (Australia) U., 1964. Cert. pediatrics, allergy and immunology. Pediatric pulmonary intern Royal Prince Alfred Hosp., Australia, 1964; resident Loma Linda (Calif.) U. Med. Ctr., 1966-68; with Henrietta Egleston Hosp. for Children, Atlanta, 1968-69, T.C. Thompson Children's Hosp., Chattanooga, 1969-70; instr. pediatrics Loma Linda U., 1970-72, with dept. pediatrics, 1972—, dean Sch. Medicine, 1986-91, pres., 1990—. Office: Loma Linda U Office of the President Loma Linda CA 92350

BEHRENS, ELLEN ELIZABETH COX, writer, counselor, educator; b. Fremont, Ohio, July 25, 1957; d. William Luther and Dorothy Cox. BA in English, Denison U., 1979; MFA in Creative Writing, Bowling Green State U., 1990. Writer in residence Ohio Arts Coun., 1991-94; ednl. devel. counselor Sch. Social Work Delphi Chassis Sys. facility U. Mich., Sandusky, Ohio, 1994—; adj. faculty Firelands Coll., Terra Tech. Coll., 1988-94; cons. Bowling Green State U., 1991-94. Author: None But the Dead and Dying, 1996; asst. editor: Mid-American Review, 1988-90, fiction editor, 1990-94, advisory editor, 1994—; contbr. short stories to anthologies, Descant, Fiction, Echoes, Paragraph, other literary mags. Individual Artist fellow Ohio Arts Coun., 1992. Mem. Bowling Green State U. Creative Writing Alumni Assn. (bd. dirs. 1990—), Associated Writing Programs, Tchrs. and Writers Collaborative, Ohioana Lib. Assn. Home: P O Box 1643 Sandusky OH 44871-1643 Office: Delphi Chassis Syss 2509 Hayes Ave Sandusky OH 44870

BEHRENS, UTA MONIQUE, investment company owner, writer; b. Solingen, Germany, Aug. 6, 1941; came to U.S., 1965; d. Alfred and Margarete Scharlotte (Muhs) Melsbach; m. William Fredrick Behrens, Dec. 16, 1966; children: Nicole-Margarete, William Fredrick Jr., Simone-Monique. Student, U. Cambridge, Eng., 1960-61, Alliance Francaise, Paris, 1963, Berlitz Sch. of Lang., Munich, 1965; AA in German, Phoenix Coll., 1971; BA in German, Ariz. State U., 1985. Lic. real estate cons., Ariz. Exec. sec. fgn. affairs NORAFILM GmbH, Munich, 1963-65; flight attendant Am. Airlines, L.A., 1966-67; real estate mgmt./acquisitions Behrens Properties, Phoenix, 1970-92; owner UMB Enterprises, Phoenix, 1995—; dir. Home Owners' Assn., Phoenix, 1995; hostess TV shows Ednl. Mgmt. Group, Scottsdale, Ariz., 1994-95. Contbr. stories to anthologies and popular publs., poetry to anthologies. Pres. Kiwis (Am. Airlines F/A), Phoenix, 1969-70; charity chmn. Maricopa County Bar Aux., Phoenix, 1970-71, vol., 1968-94; docent, interpreter, vol. Ariz. Hist. League, Phoenix, 1993-96. Mem. Jaguar Club Cen. Ariz. (v.p., sec. 1993-96), Kiwi Club (pres., parliamentarian, charity chair, Kiwi with Heart 1994), Phi Beta Kappa, Phi Kappa Phi. Home: 5328 E Lafayette Blvd Phoenix AZ 85018

BEIDLEMAN, LINDA HAVIGHURST, biologist; b. Lakewood, Ohio, Apr. 23, 1948; d. John Graham and Mary Jane (Sagen) Havighurst; m. Jeffrey Stuart Price, Dec. 23, 1970 (div. Apr. 1983); adopted children: Joshua J., S. Benjamin; m. Richard Gooch Beidleman, June 3, 1991; stepchildren: Kirk, Janet B. Robson, Carol B. Tiemeyer. BA in Biology, Colo. Coll., 1970; MA in Biology, Rice U., 1975. Tchr. asst. Colo. Coll., Colorado Springs, 1969-70, instr., summer 1993; tchr. asst. No. Ariz. U., Flagstaff, 1970-71; self-employed profl. biologist El Cerrito, Calif., 1975—; instr. Rocky Mountain Nature Assn., Estes Park, Colo., summer 1995, 96, Aspen (Colo.) Ctr. for Environ. Studies, summer 1996. Collaborator: (book) Marine Invertebrates of the Pacific Northwest, 1987;l co-author: Plants of the San Francisco Bay Region, 1994; contbr. articles to profl. jours. Soccer coach El Cerrito Soccer Club and H.S., 1977-88; soccer referee Alameda-Contra Costa (Calif.) Youth Soccer, 1978—. Mem. Calif. Bot. Soc., Colo. Native Plant Soc. (v.p. plant sales 1985-92, mem.-at-large 1992-95), Calif. Native Plant Soc., Western Soc. Naturalists. Home and Office: 766 Bayview Ave Pacific Grove CA 93950

BEIL, KAREN MAGNUSON, editor, writer, educator; b. Boston, Feb. 15, 1950; d. Victor Berger and Dorothy (Hall) Magnuson; m. James A. Beil, Feb. 24, 1973; children: Kimberly Erika, Kirsten Annika. Student, Upsala Coll., 1967-68; BA cum laude, Syracuse U., 1971. Reporter City News Bur. of Chgo., 1971-72; research editor N.Y. State Dept. Environ. Conservation, Albany, 1973-75, asst. editor, 1975-76, editor, 1976-78, assoc. dir. info. services The Conservationist Mag., N.Y. State Environ. Notice Bull., 1978-81; freelance editor and writer, 1981—; exec. bd. dirs., co-founder Children's Lit. Connection; cons. in field. Author: Grandma According to Me, 1992; contbr. articles to profl. jours. Mem. Nat. Audubon Soc., The Children's Lit. Connection (v.p., treas.), Soc. Children's Book Writers and Illustrators.

BEINECKE, CANDACE KRUGMAN, lawyer; b. Paterson, N.J., Nov. 26, 1946; d. Martin and Sylvia (Altshuler) Krugman; m. Frederick W. Beinecke II, Oct. 2, 1976; children: Jacob Sperry, Benjamin Barrett. BA, NYU, 1967; JD, Rutgers U., 1970. Bar: N.Y. 1971. Assoc., then ptnr. Hughes, Hubbard & Reed, N.Y.C., 1970—; lectr., chmn. Practising Law Inst., N.Y.C. Bd. dirs. Merce Cunningham Found., N.Y.C., Jacob's Pillow Dance Festival, Lee, Mass., First Eagle Fund of Am.; mem. vis. com. Met. Mus. Art Watson Libr. Mem. ABA, Assn. Bar City of N.Y., River Club, Women's Forum. Office: Hughes Hubbard & Reed One Battery Park Plaza New York NY 10004-1466

BEIRNE, DANIELLE ULULANI, state legislator; m. David Haili Keawe; 4 children. AA, Windward C.C., 1988; BA, U. Hawaii, 1988, postgrad., 1988-92. Rep. dist. 46 State of Hawaii; with Outrigger Hotels; mem. bd. dirs. Hui Na'auao; v.p. Kahana 'Ohana Unity Coun. Mem. Ko'olauloa Hawaiian Civic Club (v.p.), Ka'a'awa, Kahana, Punaiu'u, Hauula, Laie, Kahalu'u & Ko'olauloa Cmty. Assns. Democrat. Home: PO Box 653 Kaneohe HI 96744-0653 Office: Hawaii House Reps State House Honolulu HI 96813*

BEISWENGER, ELEANOR HAVEN, literature educator; b. Detroit, June 24, 1926; d. Irving Elbert and Grace Ellen (Weimeister) Hutchins; m. John DeWitt Nothstine, Aug. 16, 1947 (dec. Nov. 1958); children: David John Nothstine, Mark Robert Nothstine Beiswenger, Jill Ellen Nothstine Beiswenger; m. Hugo Andreas Beiswenger, Mar. 21, 1964. AA, Henry Ford C.C., Dearborn, Mich., 1962; AB with honors, U. Mich., Dearborn, 1964; AM in English, U. Mich., Ann Arbor, 1966, PhD in Am. Culture, 1969. Asst. prof. English Clarkson Coll., Potsdam, N.Y., 1969-74; English/reading specialist U. Tenn., Nashville, 1975-76; asst. prof. English Austin Peay State U., Clarksville, Tenn., 1977-83, assoc. prof. English, 1983-86, prof. English, 1986-94, disting. prof. emeritus, 1994 ; chair student affairs com. Clarkson Coll., 1970-73; senator, mem. exec. com., v.p. Austin Peay State U., 1982-85, 88-91; bd. dirs. Coop. Ctr. for Study in Britain, 1990-94; internat. del. People to People/Citizen Ambassador Program, Russia and Lithuania, 1993. Guest editor jour. So. Quar., 1990, 93; contbr. articles to profl. publs. Essay contest coord. for area high schs., Clarksville, 1982-93; essay contest judge for area elem. schs., Montgomery County, Tenn., 1985-93; spkr. in field. Cmty. scholar Henry Ford C.C., 1958-62; James Angell scholar U. Mich., 1964-66; Rackham prize fellow U. Mich., 1966-69; grantee Tenn. Com. for Humanities, Austin Peay State U. Tower Fund, 1985, 87-89, 91-93. Mem. AAUW, Jane Austen Soc. N.Am. (bd. dirs.), Elizabeth Gaskell Soc., Brontë Soc., Edith Wharton Soc., Phi Kappa Phi. Mem. Ethical Soc. St. Louis. Home: 871 Newport Ave Webster Groves MO 63119

BEITZ, ALEXANDRA GRIGG, political activist; b. Cin., Oct. 15, 1960; d. Kenneth Andrew and Betty Ann (Carpenter) Grigg; m. Charles Arthur Beitz III, Oct. 17, 1987; 1 child, Madeleine Grigg Beitz. BA, Vassar Coll., 1982; MBA, Wake Forest U., 1985. Asst. buyer Bloomingdale's, N.Y.C., 1982-83; dept. mgr. Bloomingdale's, Stamford, Conn., 1983; intern Ciba-Geigy Corp., Greensboro, N.C., 1984; retail sales promotion mgr. Hanes Hosiery, N.Y.C., 1985-86; market rep. May Co., N.Y.C., 1986-87; freelance polit. cons. Winston-Salem, N.C., 1990—. Vol. Planned Parenthood, Winston-Salem, N.C., 1988—, Southeastern Ctr. for Contemporary Art, Winston-Salem, 1992—, exec. bd. dirs. Friends, 1983, v.p.-pres. elect, 1994, pres., 1995; vol. Am. Cancer Soc., Winston-Salem, 1992-94; bd. dirs. Planned Parenthood of the Triad, Winston-Salem, 1995—.

BEKELMAN, JUDITH WELLES, public affairs executive; b. N.Y.C., Jan. 15, 1946; d. John and Millicent (Richman) Welles; m. Alan M. Bekelman, June 26, 1966 (div. Sept. 1994); children: David B., Justin E. BA, Vassar Coll., 1963. Speechwriter, editor U.S. Dept. Interior, Washington, 1965-66; asst. to dir. VISTA, Washington, 1967-70; speechwriter to sec. HHS, Washington, 1971-76, mgr. pub. affairs, 1977-86; dir. comm. and pub. affairs Pension Benefit Guaranty Corp., Washington, 1987—. Commr. County Health Planning Commn., Md., 1986-88. Recipient 1st place ann. report competition Fin. World, 1991, 92. Mem. Nat. Assn. Govt. Communicators (Gold Screen award 1992, award of Excellence 1994). Office: Pension Benefit Guaranty Corp 1200 K St NW Washington DC 20005-4025

BEKEY, SHIRLEY WHITE, psychotherapist; b. L.A.; d. Lawrence Francis and Alice (King) White; m. George Albert Bekey, June 10, 1951; children: Ronald S., Michelle E. BA in Psychology, Occidental Coll., L.A., 1949; MSW in Psychiat. Social Work, UCLA, 1954; PhD in Edn. Psychology, U. So. Calif., 1980. Lic. clin. social worker, Calif.; cert. in pupil pers., parent-child edn. Caseworker outpatient svcs. Calif. State Dept. Mental Health, Montebello; caseworker Lowman Sch. for Handicapped, L.A. Unified Sch. Dist., North Hollywood, Calif., 1971-72; psychotherapist Hofmann Psychiat. Clinic, Glendale (Calif.) Adventist Hosp., 1973-75; pvt. practice psychotherapy Encino, Calif., 1980—; speaker nat. radio, TV expert on children's emotional problems. Mem. World Affairs Coun., L.A., 1960—. Fellow Soc. for Clin. Social Work; mem. NASW, APA, Am. Ednl. Rsch. Assn., Nat. Assn. Gifted Children, Assn. Transpersonal Psychology, Inst. Noetic Sci., Assn. Ednl. Therapists, Calif. Soc. Clin. Hypnosis, Analytical Psychology Club L.A., Nat. Assn. Poetry Therapy, Calif. Assn. Gifted. Office: 4924 Balboa Blvd #199 Encino CA 91316

BELANGER, MICHELLE CONSTANCE, rehabilitation counselor; b. Woonsocket, R. I., Nov. 14, 1968; d. Donald C. and Suzanne L. (Beaulieu) Bibeault; m. Paul Emile Belanger Jr., Apr. 3, 1993; 1 child, Jacob Paul Belanger. BS, Springfield Coll., 1990; MA, Assumption Coll., 1993. Cert. Rehab. counselor. Youth vocat. specialist No. R.I. Cmty. Mental Health Ctr., Woonsocket, 1990-91; employment specialist Project With Industry, Inc., Providence, R.I., 1991-96; rehab. specialist Paul Revere Ins. Group, Worcester, Mass., 1996—. Mem. Nat. Rehab. Assn., Am. Counseling Assn., R.I. Rehab. Assn., R.I. Placement Coalition. Democrat. Roman Catholic. Home: 2415 Mendon Rd Woonsocket RI 02895 Office: Paul Revere Ins Group Worcester MA 01608

BELCASTRO, BONITA ROWAN, social work educator; b. Youngstown, OH, Oct. 18, 1948; d. Albert Steven and Helen Rebecca (Brenner) Rowan; m. James Anthony Belcastro, Aug. 13, 1971; children: Rebecca Lucia, Jesse Rowan. BA, Ohio U., 1970; MSW, W.Va. U., 1973; postgrad., U. Pitts. Lic. social worker, Pa. Supr. Children Svcs., Erie, Pa., 1973-75; asst. dir. Resources for Prevention, Erie, 1975-79; asst. prof. Gannon U., Erie, 1980-88; program coord. Family Svcs., Erie, 1988-89; asst. prof. social work Edinboro (Pa.) U., 1988—; adj. instr. Mercyhurst Coll., Erie, 1975-79, Pa. State U., State College, 1975-79; mem. adv. bd. Office of Children and Youth, Erie, 1982-96. Mem. divsn. com. United Way of Erie County, Erie, 1988—, mem. allocations panel, 1988—. State Sys. of Faculty Devel. grantee, 1994. Mem. NASW, Pa. Assn. Undergrad. Educators, Coun. Social Work Edn. Democrat. Office: Edinboro U 120 Hendricks Hall Edinboro PA 16444

BELCHER, JULIANNA, lawyer; b. Ft. Lauderdale, Fla., Nov. 5, 1963; d. Frederic Hoberg and Bette Lynn (Stewart) Burrall; m. John Michael Belcher, Sept. 8, 1991; 1 child, Brenna Lynn. BA in English, U. Fla., 1984; MBA in Finance, Fla. State U., 1988, JD, 1991. Bar: Ga., Fla. Assoc. atty. Tinkler & Groff, Decatur, Ga., 1992-93; atty.-at-law pvt. practice, Marietta, Ga., 1993; so. mgr. and counsel Nat. Automatic Merchandising Assn., Marietta, 1993—. Office: Nat Automatic Merchandising Assn # 24-250 1640 Powers Ferry Rd Marietta GA 30067-5485

BELCHER, LA JEUNE, automotive parts company executive; b. Chgo., Nov. 16, 1960; d. Lewis Albert and Dorthy (Brandon) B. BA, Northwestern U., 1982; postgrad., Am. Inst. of Banking, 1983-84. Notary pub.; securities lic.; ins. lic., Ill. Securities processor Am. Nat. Bank, Chgo., 1983, divisional asst., 1983-84; mgmt. trainee Toyota Motor Distbrs., Carol Stream, Ill., 1984-85, dist. parts mgr., 1985-90, sr. customer rels. adminstr., 1990—; fin. rep. Waddell and Reed, 1992; founder Crystal Clear Concepts; fin. rep. Waddell and Reed, 1992; rep. to Japan-U.S. Toyota Dealer Meeting, Tokyo, 1985; owner Crystal Clear Concepts. Author: (booklet) The Cutting Edge: 127 Tips to Improve Your Professional Image. Mem. alumni admissions coun. Northwestern U., Evanston, Ill.; bd. dirs. Boys and Girls Club; comty. docent Art Inst. Chgo. Mem. NAFE, NAACP, Northwestern Club Chgo., Toastmasters (edn. v.p. 1988, 94, 95, advt. v.p. 1989, pres. 1990-93), Delta Sigma Theta. Office: Toyota Motor Distbrs 2350 Sequoia Dr Aurora IL 60506-6211

BELCHER-REDEBAUGH-LEVI, CAROLINE LOUISE, nursing home administrator, nurse; b. Dixon, Ill., May 23, 1910; d. Charles R. and May Caroline (Barnes) Kreger; m. Richard E. Belcher, Nov. 24, 1934 (dec. 1964); children: Richard Charles (dec.), Mary; m. Charles H. Redebaugh, Dec. 3, 1966 (dec. 1979); m. Paul Levi, July 20, 1985 (dec. Sept. 1993). R.N., Katherine Shaw Bethea Sch. Nursing, 1930. Nurse, various hosps., 1930-49; adminstr. Orchard Glen Nursing Home, Dixon, Ill., 1949-76; coordinator Sr. Action Ctr., Springfield, Ill., 1977-87; charter mem. Ill. Nursing Home Adminstrs. Licensure Bd., 1970-76; mem. Sauk Valley Community Coll. Found., Dixon, Ill., 1988, adv. com. for sr. programs, 1988, chmn. ball com., 1989-90, Co Coun. on Aging, 1988, various adv. coms. advocating for srs. Contbr. articles to profl. jours. Mem. nat. adv. com., del. White House Conf. on Aging, 1961-81; v.p. Ill. Joint Council to Improve Health Care for Aged, 1953, pres., 1954; chair Sec. State George Ryan Adv. Com. Health Maintenance, 1991; charter mem. bd. dirs. Lee County Vol. Care Ctr., 1994, Free Health Clinic. Mem. Capitol City Rep. Women (v.p. 1983-90), Lee County Rep. Women, State Council on Aging, Am. Coll. Nursing Home Adminstrs. (charter, edn. com., pres.), Am. Nursing Home Assn. (v.p. 1953), Ill. Nurses Assn. (bd. dirs.), Ill. Nursing Home Adminstrs (charter), Sr. Illinoisian's Hall of Fame (charter). Home: 1420 Eustace Dr Dixon IL 61021-1742

BELETZ, ELAINE ETHEL, nurse, educator; b. N.Y.C., Jan. 5, 1944; d. Harry and Rose (Friedman) B. RN, Mt. Sinai Hosp., N.Y.C., 1968; BS in Nursing, Fairleigh Dickinson U., 1970; MA, NYU, 1974; MEd, Columbia U., 1978, EdD, 1979. Staff nurse ICU Mt. Sinai Hosp., 1968-70, asst. head nurse, 1970; adminstrv. supervisory relief nurse, 1973-74, 77-78; clin. instr. Roosevelt Hosp. Sch. Nursing, N.Y.C., 1970-73; nurse gerontologist St. Luke's Hosp. Ctr., N.Y.C., 1974; asst. dir. nursing Bklyn. Hosp., N.Y.C., 1975-77; asst. prof. nursing Hunter Coll., CUNY, 1978-81; v.p. nursing Mt. Sinai Hosp., Med. Ctr., Chgo., 1982-83; assoc. prof. nursing Villanova (Pa.) U., 1983—; lectr.; cons. nursing adminstrn., labor relations in health care; mem. task force on block grants. Ill. Dept. Health. Contbr. articles to profl. jours.; internat. cons. and lectr. Bd. dirs. Hadassah Nurses Coun., Phila., 1993-94; pres.-elect, 1994-96, pres. 96—. Recipient Disting. Achievement award Columbia U. Nursing Edn. Alumni Assn., 1989. Fellow Am. Acad. Nursing; mem. Am. Nurses Assn. (bd. dirs. 1982-87, mem. polit. action com. 1982-86), N.Y. State Nurses Assn. (treas. 1977-78, pres.-elect 1978-79, pres. 1979-81, bd. trustees, cert. of appreciation 1981, hon. recognition award 1987), Pa. Nurses Assn. (nominating com. 1985-86, chair polit. action com. 1990-92), N.Y. Counties Registered Nurses Assn. (nominating com. 1973, dir. 1975-78, Amanda Silvers award 1981), Shershower Benevolent Assn., Nursing Edn. Alumni Assn. (Leadership award 1989), Sigma Theta Tau, Phi Kappa Phi. Jewish. Office: Villanova U Grad Program Nursing Health Care Adminstrn Coll Nursing Villanova PA 19085

BELFER, NANCY B., design educator; b. Buffalo; d. Albert and Helen (S.) Barback; m. Bernard Belfer, Sept. 1, 1951; 1 child, Lauren Belfer Church. Diploma, Albright Art Sch., Buffalo, 1950; BS, SUNY, Buffalo, 1951; MFA, Rochester Inst. Tech., 1963. Prof. design SUNY, Buffalo, 1960—. Author: Designing in Batik and Tie Dye, 1972, Designing in Stitching and Applique, 1972, Weaving: Design & Expression, 1974, Batik and Tie Dye Techniques, 1993; contbr articles to profl. jours.; solo exhbns. include Daemen Coll., Buffalo, 1994, Adams Art Gallery, Dunkirk, N.Y., 1995-96; also represented in nat. and regional group shows. NEA fellow, 1981. Mem. Am. Craft Coun., Friends of Fiber Art Internat., Buffalo Soc. Artists. Office: SUNY Coll 1300 Elmwood Ave Buffalo NY 14222

BELFER, SHIRA GOLDRING, cantor; b. Detroit, Oct. 12, 1955; d. Judah Goldring and Florence (Weintraub) B. MusB, Syracuse U., 1977, EdB, 1977; M in Sacred Music, Hebrew Union Coll., 1993. Cert. music tchr., Ny., Fla., Mass. Coord. dept. edn. United Synagogue Am., 1982-86; cons. Jewish edn. and programming Am. Jewish Congress and Ednl. Alliance, N.Y.C., 1989-90; bar mitzvah tutor Temple Israel, N.Y.C., 1991-93; cantor various temples, 1986-96, Congregation Tifereth Israel, New Bedford, Mass., 1994—; substitute cantor, 1986—; recreational therapist Hebrew Rehab. Ctr. for Aged, Roslindale, Mass.; tutor, tchr. Temple Israel, Boston, Concord (Mass.) Area Jewish Group, Temple Emeth Religious Sch., Brookline, Mass.; music tchr. St. Anne's Home-Sch. for Emotionally Disturbed Children, Methuen, Mass., Temple Soc. of Concord Religious Sch., Syracuse, N.Y., Oceanside (N.Y.) Jewish Ctr.; music dir. Cejwin Camps, Port Jervis, N.Y., Grossman Camp, Westwood, Mass.; music program dir. Solomon Schecter Day Sch., Newton, Mass., Miamonides Sch., Brookline, Temple Beth Shalom Religious Sch., Needham, Mass.; guitar tchr. Syracuse Instn. Enabling Edn., pvt. students. Rec. artist The Feast of Freedom Haggadah, 1984; contbg. author Bar/Bat Mitzvah Education Source Book, 1993. Dir. The Jewish Lifecycle. Mem. Am. Conf. Cantors, Cantors Assembly Am., Women Cantors Network, Music Educators Nat. Conf.

BEL GEDDES, JOAN, writer; b. Los Angeles; d. Norman and Helen (Sneider) Bel G.; m. Barry Ulanov, Dec. 16, 1939 (div. 1968); children: Anne, Nicholas, Katherine. B.A., Barnard Coll. Columbia U., 1937. Researcher and theatrical asst. to Norman Bel Geddes, Inc., N.Y.C., 1937-41; publicity dir. Compton Advt., Inc., N.Y.C., 1942; new program mgr. Compton Advt., Inc., 1943-47; pub. info. officer UNICEF, N.Y.C., 1970-76, chief editorial and publs. services, 1976-79, cons. devel. edn., Universal Children's Day (over 100 countries), 1979-85, editor Almanac World's Children, 1985-90; editor Pate Inst. Bull., 1988-94; tchr. drama Birch Wathen Sch., N.Y.C., 1950; mem. faculty Inst. Man and Sci., Rensellaerville, N.Y., 1969. Interviewer-hostess: weekly radio program Religion and the Arts, NBC, 1968; author: Small World: A History of Baby Care from the Stone Age to the Spock Age, 1964, How to Parent Alone: A Guide for Single Parents, 1974, To Barbara With Love--Prayers and Reflections by a Believer for a Skeptic (Catholic Press Assn. award 1974), Are You Listening, God?, 1994, (with others) Art, Obscenity and Your Children, 1969, American Catholics and Vietnam, 1970, The Future of the Family, 1971, Holiness and Mental Health, 1972, The Children's Rights Movement, 1977, And You, Who Do You Say I Am?, 1981; translator: (with Barry Ulanov) Last Essays of Georges Bernanos, 1955; editor: Magic Motorways (Norman B. Geddes), 1940, Earth: Our Crowded Spaceship (Isaac Asimov), 1974; editor in chief: My Baby mag, 1954-56, Congratulations mag, 1954-56. Rep. to UN Balkan-Ji-Bar Internat. Orgn. for Child and Youth Welfare of the World. Mem. Authors League Am., Assn. Former Internat. Civil Servants, The Coffee House, World Future Soc., Theilard de Chardin Assn., Mcpl. Arts Soc. N.Y., Am. Film Inst., Internat. Inst. Rural Reconstrn. (mem. internat. coun.), Thomas More Soc. (pres. 1966), Barnard Coll. Alumnae Assn. (class v.p. 1972-76, 92—, pres. 1976-82), N.Y. City Mission Soc., Guilford Friends of Music, Pate Inst. Human Survival (bd. dirs. 1989-95), The Charles A. and Anne Morrow Lindbergh Fund, Citizens Against Govt. Waste. Roman Catholic. Home and Office: 60 E 8th St New York NY 10003-6514

BELISSARY, KAREN, interior designer; b. Columbia, S.C., May 20, 1959; d. James Charles and Linda Gail (Bouknight) B. BFA in Design, N.Y. Sch. Interior Design, 1989; grad., Nat. Ctr. Paralegal Studies, Atlanta, 1991. Pvt. practice interior design, Florence, S.C., 1989—; dir. Pee Dee region Am. Intercultural Exch., Florence, 1989—. Sec. Soc. for Autistic Children, Florence, 1983; v.p. Florence County Dem. Com., 1985; group leader Friends Florence Mus., 1986; bd. dirs. Heart Fund, Florence, 1987, Internat. Women's Club Florence, 1988-89, Florence Area Arts Coun., 1986-87; mem. Friends of Libr., Florence. Named Outstanding Mem., Soc. for Autistic Children, 1983; grantee Young Adult League, 1987. Mem. NOW, Am. Soc. Interior Designers, Amnesty Internat., Greenpeace, Cosmoplitan Book Club (pres.), The Door (pres.), Colonial Heights Garden Club. Greek Orthodox. Home: 3719 Gentry Dr Florence SC 29501-7717 Office: Am Intercultural Exch 804 Loop Rd # 2D Florence SC 29501

BELKIN, JANET EHRENREICH, lawyer; b. N.Y.C., Feb. 17, 1938; d. Irving and Pauline (Hamburger) Ehrenreich; m. Myron D. Belkin, June 29, 1958; children: Lisa Belkin Gelb, Gary, Kira. AB, Vassar Coll., 1958; PhD, St. John's U., 1975; JD, Hofstra U., 1978; LLM, NYU, 1983. Bar: N.Y. 1979, U.S. Dist. Ct. (so. dist.) N.Y. 1979. Vice pres., counsel Equitable Life Assurance Soc., N.Y.C., 1978-91; with Coll. of Ins., N.Y.C., 1991-92; exec. dir. Ctr. Internat. Ins. Studies Coll. of Ins., 1992—; counsel Sutherland, Asbill & Brennan; cons. Reg. of Fin. Svcs.; exec. dir. Ctr. Internat. Ins. Studies. Mem. ABA (coun. mem. adminstrv. law sect. 1985-88, chair sect. 1994-95). Home: 3014 Hewlett Ave S Merrick NY 11566-5313 Office: Coll of Ins 101 Murray St New York NY 10007-2132

BELKNAP, BARBARA, graphic designer, artist; b. St. Paul, Apr. 23, 1963; d. Rowan Curtis and Karen Ann (Hermanson) B.; m. Saleh J.S. Hamshari, Feb. 22, 1986. BA in Art, St. Olaf Coll., 1985; postgrad., Md. Inst. Coll. Art, 1990-95. Art dir. Health Risk Mgmt., Mpls., 1986-87; freelance designer Washington, 1987-88; sr. designer Loyola Coll. in Md., Balt., 1988-93; design dir. mktg. dept. USF&G, Balt., 1993—. Prints exhibited in shows, 1993, 95, 96. Literacy tutor The Learning Bank, Balt., 1991-96. Mem. Am. Inst. Graphic Artists (bd. dirs. 1995-96), Md. Printmakers, Nat. Mus. Women in Arts, Balt. Mus. Art. Democrat. Presbyterian. Home: 907 Stubblefield Ln Baltimore MD 21202 Office: USF&G Mktg Dept 100 Light St 31st Fl Baltimore MD 21202

BELKNAP, JODI PARRY, graphic designer, business owner, writer; b. New Canaan, Conn., June 4, 1939; d. Corliss Lloyd and Joan (Pike) Parry; m. William Belknap III, Feb. 20, 1970 (div. Nov. 1982). AB in English and Writing, Barnard Coll., 1962; MA in Drama and Theater, U. Hawaii at Manoa, Honolulu, 1988. Life elem. tchr. credential, Calif. Tchr. grade 6 Ruth Fyfe Sch., Las Vegas, Nev., 1963-64; tchr. grades. 2,3 Schilling Sch., Hayward, Calif., 1964-69; master tchr. U. Calif., Hayward, 1967-69; editor Island Heritage Ltd., Honolulu, 1970-73; Pacific bur. chief OAG Publs. (Dun and Bradstreet), Honolulu, 1972-82; freelance writer, columnist various mags. and publs., 1976-88; owner Belknap Pub. and Design, Honolulu, 1987—. Author: (books) Majesty, The Exceptional Trees of Hawaii, 1982, Kaanapali, 1981, Halekulani, 1982, (children's book) Felisa and the Magic Tikling Bird, 1973; prin. design projects for Gray Line Hawaii, 1993-95, Sheraton Moana Surfrider, 1988-96, others. Pro bono pub. Friends of Honolulu Bot. Gardens, 1996. Recipient Gold award Hospitality Mktg. Assn. Internat., 1995, award Hawaii chpt. Pub. Rels. Soc. Am., 1993, 94, Ilima award of excellence Internat. Assn. Bus. Communicators, 1989, 90. Mem. Soc. Children's Book Writers, Pacific Printing and Imaging Assn., Small Bus. Hawaii. Office: Belknap Pub PO Box 22387 Ste 604 770 Kapiolani Honolulu HI 96813

BELL, DELORIS WILEY, physician; b. Solomon, Kans., Sept. 30, 1942; d. Harry A. and Mildren H. (Watt) Wiley; children—Leslie and John. B.A., Kans. Wesleyan U., 1964; M.D., U. Kans., 1968. Diplomate Am. Bd. Ophthalmology. Intern St. Luke's Hosp., Kansas City, Mo., 1968-69; resident U. Kans. Med. Ctr., Kansas City, 1969-72; practice medicine specializing in ophthalmology, Overland Park, Kans., 1973—. Mem. AMA, Kans. Med. Soc. (pres. sect. ophthalmology 1985-86, speaker of the house 94—), Am. Acad. Ophthalmology (counciller 1988-93, chair state govtl. affairs 1993—), Kans. Soc. Ophthalmology (pres. 1985-86), Kansas City Soc. Ophthalmology and Otolaryngology (sec. 1984-86, pres.-elect 1988, pres. 1989). Avocations: photography; travel. Office: 7000 W 121st St Ste 100 Shawnee Mission KS 66209-2010

BELL, ERZSEBET, critical care nurse; b. Seattle, Wash., Sept. 26, 1962; d. Gyula Toppanto and Louise (Walker) Hailey; m. Kenneth Rayford Bell, Feb. 21, 1980; children: Carmon Danae, Brittany LeAnn. ADN, La. State U., 1982; postgrad., Troy State U., 1991—. RN, CCRN, Ga.; BLS, ACLS, ACLS instr. Staff nurse, charge nurse, relief supr. LaSalle Gen. Hosp., Jena, La., 1983-86; staff nurse, charge nurse Med. Ctr., Columbus, Ga., 1986-88, Drs. Hosp., Columbus, 1988—; head nurse ICU, relief supr. Hughston Sports Medicine Hosp., Columbus, 1990-91; part time staff nurse Columbus Cardiac Catheterization Lab., Columbus, 1993—. Mem. AACN. Baptist.

BELL, FRANCES LOUISE, medical technologist; b. Milton, Pa., Apr. 28, 1926; d. George Earl and Kathryn Robbins (Fairchild) Reichard; m. Edwin Lewis Bell II, Dec. 27, 1950; children: Ernest Michael, Stephen Thomas, Eric Leslie. BS in Biology cum laude, Bucknell U., 1948; MT, Geisinger Meml. Hosp., 1949. Registered med. technologist. Med. technologist Burlington County Hosp., Mt. Holly, N.J., 1949-50, Robert Packer Hosp., Sayre, Pa., 1950, Carle Hosp./Clinic, Urbana, Ill., 1951-52, St. Joseph Hosp., Reading, Pa., 1972-83. Vol. Crime Watch, City Hall, Reading, 1985-90, Am. Heart Assn., Reading, 1956—, March of Dimes, Reading, 1956-72, Am. Cancer Soc., Reading, 1956-71, Multiple Sclerosis, Reading, 1956-72, Reading Musical Found., 1985-90, Hist. Soc. Berks County; corr. sec. women's aux.,

1986-90; fin. sec. aux. Albright Coll., 1988-95; hospitality co-chmn. women's com. Reading Symphony Orch., 1985-90, editor yearbook women's com., 1992-96; editor yearbook Reading Symphony Orch. League, 1996—; chmn. hospitality Reading-Berks Pub. Librs., 1988-91; mem. Friends Reading Mus., Berks County Conservancy. Mem. AAUW (assoc. editor bull. 1961-63, cultural interests rep. 1967-68), Woman's Club of Reading (treas. 1986-88, fin. sec. 1991—), United Meth. Women, World Affairs Coun. Berks County, Libr. Soc. Albright Coll., Phi Beta Kappa. Republican. Methodist. Home: 1454 Oak Ln Reading PA 19604-1865

BELL, GLORIA MARJORIE, property owner/manager; b. Inglewood, Calif., July 12, 1928; d. Oran Moffet and Gertrude (Ogden) B.; m. Lacy Clark, July 3, 1949 (div. June 1964); children: Scott Clark, Valli Clark, Vicki Clark, Vanett C. Walters. BA, San Diego State U., 1949. Postal clk. U.S. Post Office, San Diego, Calif., 1945; bd. marker N.Y. Stock Index J.A. Hogle and Co. Stock Exch., San Diego, 1948; inventory sales clk. Woolworth Dept. Store, San Diego, 1949; salesperson Del Mar (Calif.) Caterers, 1947-49; inventory sales mgr. U.S. Naval Ships Store, North island, Calif., 1949-50, Atsugi, Japan, 1951; kindergarten tchr. U.S. Naval Air Sta., Sangley Point, Philippines, 1957-58; tchr. piano lessons Sangley Point, 1957-58; mgr. personal income properties San Diego; ptnr. Dyna-Med, Inc., San Diego, 1967-68; trustee/cons. Bell Family Trust, San Diego, 1982-87, 87-95; agt. Bell Estate, 1982—. Exhibitor paintings, sculptures, archtl. designs, wood block prints, San Diego State U., 1948-49. Mem. Nat. Trust for Hist. Preservation, Am. Mus. of Natural History, Nat. Space Soc., Consumers Union, Smithsonian Assocs., Gamma Phi Beta. Republican.

BELL, JEANNE VINER, public relations counselor; b. Los Angeles, Feb. 27, 1923; d. Herman and Mary (Kaufman) Spitzel; m. Melvin A. Viner, Feb. 1, 1942 (dec.); children: Michael, Karen Viner Fawcett; m. 2d, J. Raymond Bell, Dec. 15, 1974 (dec.). Student UCLA, Am. U., George Washington U. Prin. Jeanne Viner Spl. Svcs., Washington, 1958-61; prin. Jeanne Viner Assocs., Washington, 1961-82; pub. rels. counselor, 1982—; bd. dirs. Independence Fed. Bank, Washington, Independence Fed. Fin. Corp., Washington. Contbr. articles to profl. jours., mags., books. Presdl. appointee to adv. coun. SBA, 1983—, Pres.'s Com. on People with Disabilities, 1982-96; bd. dirs. Arthritis Found. of Met. D.C., 1982—; bd. dirs. Arthritis Found. Met. D.C., 1982-95; mayoral appointee to D.C. Adv. Com. on Resources and Budget, 1981-90, D.C. Pvt. Industries Coun., 1983—; bd. visitors U. Md. Coll. Journalism, 1989—; bd. trustees U. Bridgeport (Conn.). Recipient Outstanding Leadership and Achievement award State Bus. and Profl. Women's Clubs, Washington, 1981, Met. Washington Women Bus. Advocate of Yr. Fellow Pub. Rels. Soc. Am.; mem. Capital Press Women (pres. 1980-82, Woman of Achievement 1982, Communicator of Achievement 1983), Am. News Women's Club (bd. govs. 1969-70, pres. 1988-90). Club: Nat. Press (Washington). Address: 3506 Winfield Ln NW Washington DC 20007-2344 also: 9460 Hidden Valley Pl Beverly Hills CA 90210-1310

BELL, JOAN LEE, director, theater; b. Chehalis, Wash., Nov. 25, 1951; d. Alfonse John and Mary Margaret (Sterns) Kuder; m. Richard Orville Bell, Mar. 5, 1977; 1 child, Alexis Teresa. AA, Centralia Coll., 1972; BFA, U. Mont., 1974; MA, U. Colo., 1976. Artistic & producing dir. Evergreen Playhouse, Centralia, Wash., 1975; bd. dirs. Nomad Players, Boulder, Colo., 1977-79; ptnr., publisher Armado and Moth, Boulder, Colo., 1979-96; pres. Boulder (Colo.) Theatre Producers Guild, 1987-96; dir., actor The Upstart Crow Theatre Co., Boulder, 1980-96, bus. mgr., 1985-96. Co-editor: Auditions and Scenes From Shakespeare, 1979, Actors' Editions of Shakespeare, 1993-96. Democrat. Roman Catholic. Home: 2131 Arapahoe Ave Unit A Boulder CO 80302-6601

BELL, KAREN JUNE, critical care nurse; b. Forsyth County, N.C., Aug. 28, 1954; d. James Cecil and Margaret (Vaughn) B. Student, Rex Hosp. Sch. Nursing, Raleigh, N.C.; BSN, East Carolina U., 1983. Cert. BCLS, ACLS; instr. Am. Heart Assn.; cert. CCRN. Asst. clin. mgr., staff RN med. ICU Rex Hosp., Raleigh, 1977-91; staff nurse ICU Western Wake Med. Ctr., Cary, 1992-93; nurse cons. Divsn. of Facility Svc., State of N.C., 1993-94; staff RN ICU Moses H. Cone Meml. Hosp., 1994-95; med. policy analyst, Medicare adminstr. CIGNA Healthcare, 1995—. Recipient Great 100 Nurse Excellence award, N.C., 1990. Mem. AACN (past treas., speaker, com. mem. Raleigh chpt.).

BELL, MARIA ANTOINETTE, music educator; b. Jackson, Tenn., July 20, 1970; d. Nathaniel and Climatene (Freeman) B. BS, Lambuth U., 1992; MA, Freed-Hardeman U., 1994. Music tchr. Polk Clark Sch., Jackson, 1993—; site dir. Polk Clark Sch., Milan, Tenn.; substitute tchr. Jackson Sch. System, 1993; ednl. asst. West Tenn. Cerebral Palsy, Jackson, 1991-92; tchr.'s asst. Lambuth Presch., Jackson, 1988-94; min. of music Cumberland Ch., Jackson, 1989-92. Cert. music tchr., Tenn. Mem. Tenn. Edn. Assn., Milan Edn. Assn., NEA, Alpha Kappa Alpha. Home: 56 D Garland Dr Jackson TN 38305

BELL, MARTHA ALICE, architect; b. Parkston, S.D., July 14, 1953; d. Jay Quentin and Dorothy Rose (Topping) B.; m. Glen O. Reeser, May 31, 1975. BA in Architecture, Iowa State U., 1975. Lic. arch. Wis., Ill., Ohio. Arch. Tilton & Lewis Assocs., Chgo., 1978-82, project mgr., 1982-85; prin., owner Martha Bell & Assocs., Palatine, Ill., 1986—; chair Downtown Palatine (Ill.) Revitalization Commn., 1991—. Bd. mem. William Rainey Harper C.C. Found. Bd., Palatine, 1991—. Mem. AIA, Rotary Club Palatine (past sec., youth exch. chair). Office: Martha Bell & Assocs 241 N Bothwell St Palatine IL 60067

BELL, M(ARY) KATHLEEN, retired government official, civic leader; b. Washington, July 7, 1922; d. Daniel W. and Sadie (Killeen) B. AB, Smith Coll., 1943, MA (hon.), 1959. With Dept. of State, Washington, 1944-73; fgn. affairs officer Office Internat. Econ. and Social Affairs Bur. Internat. Orgn. Affairs, Washington, 1950-56, officer in charge, 1964-66, chief div. instnl. devel. and coordination, 1966-71, dir. system coordinations staff, 1971-73, cons., 1973-75, retired, 1975; asst. to exec. sec. U.S. del. San Francisco Conf. UN, 1945; mem. staff UNESCO, London, 1945-46; asst. to U.S. rep. to 2nd, 3rd, 4th, 5th sessions Econ. and Social Coun., 1946-47; advisor to U.S. rep. Econ. and Social Council, 1948-70; alt. rep. Econ. and Social Coun., N.Y.C. and Geneva, 1971-73; U.S. mem. on com. on non-govt. orgns. Econ. and Social Coun., 1955-65, U.S. mem. interim com. program meetings, 1950-67, chmn. interim com. program meetings, 1952-54; adviser to U.S. del. prep. commn. Internat. Atomic Energy Agy., Vienna, 1957; advisor to U.S. del. Internat. Atomic Energy Agy., 1957-61; adviser to U.S. del. 1st Assembly Inter-govtl. Maritime Consultative Orgn., London, 1959; advisor U.S. Rep. to Coun., London, 1959; del. ad hoc com. rules procedures 1st Assembly Inter-govtl. Maritime Comsultative Orgn., London, 1960; adviser to U.S. del. 16th Gen. Assembly of UN, N.Y.C., 1961; mem. spl. com. on coordination 16th Gen. Assembly of UN, 1964; advisor to U.S. rep. Tech. Assistance Com., 1964; advisor U.S. del. 9th, 10th and spl. session governing council UN Devel. Program, N.Y.C. and Geneva, 1970; dep. U.S. rep. to governing council UN Devel. Program, Geneva, 1973; alt. U.S. rep. Joint Meeting Adminstrv. Com. Coordination and Spl. Com. Coordination, N.Y.C., 1971-72; alt. U.S. rep. 1st session Rev. and Appraisal Com., N.Y.C. and Geneva, 1972; trustee Washington Theol. Consortium, also v.p. bd., chmn. bd., 1972-79; trustee Smith Coll., 1976-82, chmn. bd., 1979-82; mem. Carnegie Coun. Ethics and Internat. Affairs, 1983-89; bd. dirs. Chs. Ctr. for Theology and Pub. Policy, 1985-95, v.p., 1987-95; mem. exec. com. Assn. Theol. Schs., 1984-88; bd. dirs. Capitol Area div. UN Assn., 1986-89, UN Assn. Am., 1988-90. Recipient Outstanding Svc. award Dept. of State, 1959; decorated Lady Comdr. with star, Order of Holy Sepulchre. Home: 3816 Gramercy St NW Washington DC 20016-4226 also: 1043 Hillsboro Mile Pompano Beach FL 33062-2153

BELL, MARY SUTTON, school counselor; b. Wilmington, N.C., Jan. 24, 1932; d. Ivey J. and Annie May (Hobbs) Sutton; m. Guy W. Rawls, Jr., Feb. 2, 1952 (div. Oct. 1976); children: Guy W. III, Jane Rawls Simon, Charles R.; m. Herbert Patterson Bell, Jr., Oct. 22, 1976. MEd in Sch. Counseling, N.C. State U., 1970; EdD, Nova U., 1985. Adminstrv. cert. East Carolina U., 1987. Counselor Ravenscroft Sch., Raleigh, N.C., 1959-62; tchr. Ravenscroft Sch., Raleigh, 1962-76; sch. counselor New Hanover Pub. Schs., Wilmington, N.C., 1976—; Teaching Fellows group leader, Raleigh, N.C., 1993-94. Trustee Cape Fear Cmty. Coll., Wilmington, 1980—, S.E. Ctr. for Mental Health, 1978—; Pender Dem. Precinct and County v.p. and sec., Burgaw, N.C., 1985—. Recipient Best Educator award, Channel 3 TV, Wilmington, 1990. Mem. Phi Delta Kappa, Delta Kappa Gamma-Theta (v.p., pres., 1980—). Democrat. Episcopalian. Home: 6440 Bell & Williams Rd PO Box 36 Currie NC 28435-0036 Office: Mary C. Williams School 801 Silver Lake Wilmington NC 28412 also: 3707C Reston Ct Wilmington NC 28402

BELL, MAXINE TOOLSON, state legislator, librarian; b. Logan, Utah, Aug. 6, 1931; d. John Max and Norma (Watson) Toolson; m. H. Jack Bell, Oct. 26, 1949; children: Randy J. (dec.), Jeff M., Scott Alan (dec.). Assocs. in Libr. Sci., Coll. So. Idaho; CSI, Idaho State U., 1975. Librarian Sch. Dist. 261, Jerome, Idaho, 1975-88; mem. Idaho Ho. of Reps., 1988-. Bd. dirs. Idaho Farm Bur., 1976-77; rep. western states Am. Farm Bur. Women, 1990-93, vice chmn., 1993—; vice chmn. Am. Farm Bur., 1992—; mem. Jerome County Rep. PRecinct Com., 1980-88. Home: 194 S 300 E Jerome ID 83338-6532

BELL, MICHELLE DODRILL, development researcher; b. Ft. Hood, Tex., Dec. 18, 1962; d. James Paul and Judith Anne (Campbell) Dodrill; m. Michael William Bell, June 27, 1992. BA, U. Louisville, 1985. Exhibits rschr. Mus. of History and Sci., Louisville, 1985-89; editor UMI/Data Courier, Louisville, 1989-90; devel. rschr. Vanderbilt U., Nashville, 1990—; rep. Vanderbilt U. Staff Adv. Coun., Nashville, 1994-96. Mem. Assn. Profl. Rschrs. for Advancement (mem. Tenn. chpt.).

BELL, MILDRED BAILEY, lawyer, educator; b. Sanford, Fla., June 28, 1928; d. William F. and Frances E. (Williford) Bailey; m. J. Thomas Bell, Jr., Sept. 18, 1948 (div.); children: Tom, Elizabeth, Ansley. AB, U. Ga., 1950, JD cum laude, 1969; LLM in Taxation, N.Y. U., 1977. Bar: Ga. 1969. Law clk. U.S. Dist. Ct. No. Dist. Ga., 1969-70; prof. law Mercer U., Macon, Ga., 1970-94, prof. emeritus, 1994—; mem. Ga. Com. Constl. Revision, 1978-79; bd. dirs. Arrowhead Travel, Inc. Bd. editors Ga. State Bar Jour., 1974-76; contbr. articles to profl. jours., chpts. in books. Mem. ABA, Ga. Bar Assn., Phi Beta Kappa, Phi Kappa Phi. Republican. Episcopalian. Home: 14226 Foliage Ct Midlothian VA 23112

BELL, REGINA JEAN, corporate consulting company executive; b. Lebanon, Mo.; d. Stephen S. and Ida M. (Reaves) B. BA, Draughens U.; postgrad., Butler U., Ind.-Purdue U., Indpls., 1968. Prodn. mgr. Howe Mfg. Co., Inc., Indpls., 1958-64; v.p. budgetary control Howe Engring. Co., Inc., Indpls., 1964-67; mgr. material control Nat. Aluminum Div., Indpls., 1968-84; owner Brown County Letter Shop, Nashville, Ind., 1985-89; pres. Trend 90's Corp. Cons. Co., Venice, Fla., 1993—.

BELL, SHARON KAYE, small business owner; b. Lincoln, Nebr., Sept. 14, 1943; d. Edwin B. and Evelyn F. (Young) Czachurski; m. James P. Kittrell (div. Sept. 1974); children: Nathan James, Nona Kaye; m. Joseph S. Bell, June 5, 1976; stepchildren: Eugene, Patricia, Bobbie, Linda. Continuing edn./active tax preparer/interviewer assoc., H&R Block, Laguna Hills, 1987—. Various positions mgmt., bookkeeping, 1961-71; bookkeeper Internat. Harvester, Chesapeake, Va., 1971-73, Cheat'AH Engring., Santa Ana, Calif., 1973-74, Fre Del Engring., Santa Ana, Calif., 1974-75; bookkeeper/mgr. Tek Sheet Metal Co., Santa Ana, Calif., 1975-79; owner, bookkeeper Bell's Bookkeeping, Huntington Beach, Calif., 1979-86, Fountain Valley, Calif., 1986—, Laguna Hills, Calif., 1986—; tax preparer H.R. Block, 1989—. Mem. Inst. Mgmt. Accts. (bd. dirs. 1985-86, sec. 1986-87, v.p. 1987-90, dir. manuscripts 1990-91), Nat. Notary Assn., NAFE, Wives of Submarine Vets. World War II (v.p. L.A. chpt. 1986-87, treas. 1990-92), Nat. Soc. Pub. Accts., Internat. Platform Assn. Republican. Office: Bells Bookkeeping PO Box 2713 Laguna Hills CA 92654-2713

BELL, SUSAN JANE, nurse; b. Columbus, Ohio, July 24, 1946; d. Donald Richard Bell and Martha Jane (McDowell) Nichols; m. Robert Earlin Ward, Oct. 24, 1964 (div. 1984); children: Duane Allen Ward, Melissa Jane Ward, Bryan Thomas Ward. Degree in nursing, Columbus Sch. Practical Nursing, 1986; ADRN, Columbus State C.C., 1989; student, Franklin U., 1993—. RN, Ohio; cert. CPR; notary pub., Ohio. Nurse's asst. Riverside Meth. Hosp., Columbus, 1970-80, Norworth Convalescent Ctr., Columbus, 1980-86; lic. practical nurse, charge nurse Heartland Thurber Care Ctr., Columbus, 1986-89; staff nurse Am. Nursing Care, Columbus, 1989—; medicare home visitation, staffing and pvt. duty nurse Telemed, Columbus, 1989—; asst. head nurse Northland Terr., Columbus, 1989; supr. Elmington Manor, Columbus, 1989; staff nurse cardiac step down unit Grant Hosp., Columbus, 1989-92; nurse med. ICU, CCU and pediatric ICU, 1992-93; charge nurse critical/skilled unit First Cmty. Village Health Care Ctr., Columbus, 1992-95; pres. Bell Mktg. Distbrs., pvt. duty ALS ventilator patients Med. Pers. Poole; regional claims rep. Fed. Resources Group. Rev. Am. Fellowship Ch. Mem. NAFE, ASPCA, YMCA, Internat. Clergy Assn., World Wildlife Fund., Nature Conservancy, Ohio Hist. Found. (archives/libr. divsn.), Nat. Audubon Soc., Environ. Def. Fund, Nat. Wildlife Fedn., Nature Conservancy, Humane Soc. U.S., AASPCA, Ohio Hist. Soc. Archives Libr.

BELL (JARRATT), CORINNE, psychologist; b. Holly Springs, Miss., July 6, 1943; d. Robert Norris and Laura Kathleen (Robinson) Reed; m. John Baker Jarratt; children: Jeffrey Kenneth Bell, Jennifer Bell Monroe, Joshua Brown Jarratt. BA with highest honors, U. Tenn., 1976, MA, 1978, PhD, 1985. Lic. psychologist, Tenn. Rsch. asst. Lakeshore Mental Health Inst., Knoxville, 1976; instr. psychology dept. Roane State C.C., Harriman, Tenn., 1978; cons., sch. psychologist dept. spl. edn. U. Tenn., Knoxville, 1979-80; pvt. practice psychology Knoxville, 1979—; founder, psychologist, ptnr. Clin. & Sch. Assocs., Knoxville, 1985-96; v.p. mktg. Lark Industries, Inc., Knoxville, 1994-95, also bd. dirs.; founder, adminstr., psychologist Behavioral Health Ctr. Child & Adult Svcs., Knoxville, 1996—; cons. social svcs. Dept. Human Svcs., Tenn., 1985—. Contbr. articles to profl. jours. Mem. adv. bd. John Tarleton Children's Home, Knoxville, 1987-93, Florence Crittendon Agy., 1994—; bd. dirs. Sexual Assault Crisis Ctr., Knoxville, 1987-94, Children's Ctr. Knoxville, 1995—; mem., cons. Knox County Child Abuse Rev. Team, Knoxville, 1982—; vol. Knox County Mental Health Assn. and Interfaith Health Clinic. Acad. scholar U. Tenn., 1974; rsch. grantee Knox County Children's Found., 1979. Mem. APA, Tenn. Psychol. Assn. (pub. rels. chair 1992-94), Knoxville Area Psychol. Assn. (treas. 1986-88, pub. rels. chair 1989-90, pres. 1990-91), Unified Psychology Coalition (co-founder, legis. chair/spokesperson 1989-92), Tenn. Assn. Sch. Psychologists, Mortar Bd., Phi Kappa Phi, Phi Beta Kappa. Episcopalian. Office: Behavioral Health Ctr Child & Adult Svcs 3624 Vandeventer Ave Knoxville TN 37919

BELL/JACKSON, MARIANNE JEANNE, elementary education educator; b. Chgo., Feb. 13, 1944; d. David Vincent and Jeanne Elizabeth Bell; m. Michael Ross Jackson, Aug. 12, 1989; m. Roscoe Edward Mitchell; 1 child, Atala-Nicole; m. Jerry Alan Levy. B Art History, U. Chgo., 1967; M Elem. Edn., U. Wis., Platteville, 1985. Lic. tchr. 1st - 8th grades. Sec. The Filter People, Chgo., 1960-66; office mgr. U. Chgo. Maroon, 1966-68; asst. program dir. Emerson & Taylor House Community Ctrs., Chgo., 1968-71; child advocate Lawndale Day Care Ctr., Chgo., 1971-73; potter, owner Burnt Earth Pottery, Hollandale, Wis., 1973-85; tchr. Madison (Wis.) Met. Sch. Dist., 1985—; cons. Ednl. Devel. Ctr., Newton, Mass., 1991-92; Search for Extra Terrestrial Intelligence pilot program tchr., 1993-94; resource agt. Am. Astron. Soc., 1994—. Author: Model for a 4th Grade Curriculum, 1990 (with Larry Johns) Proposal for Construction of an Effigy Mound, 1990, The Swan Twins, ColoranDraw 1, 1995; contbr. to Poetry Out of Wisconsin, 1982; inventor ColoranDraw Books, 1995. Recipient 1st pl. for pottery, 1st pl. for hand painted ceramics Cambridge (Wis.) Art Fair, 1979; named to Golden Apple Club Madison Met. Sch. Dist., 1993. Mem. Madison Tchrs. Inc., Wis. Earth Sci. Tchrs., Greenpeace, Amnesty Internat., People for Ethical Treatment of Animals. Lutheran Buddhist. Home: 6251 Portage Rd De Forest WI 53532-2900 Office: Madison Met Sch Dist Lake View Elem 1802 Tennyson Ln Madison WI 53704-2323

BELLAH, LINDA RUTH, design consultant; b. Dallas, Nov. 8, 1944; d. Glover Bee and Ola Moss (Rogers) B.; m. Larry Hurtado, 1965 (div. 1975); 1 child, Tiffany Lynn Hurtado Cerasoli; m. Theodore Buder, 1980 (div. 1988); m. Bob Cote, 1990 (div. 1992). BA in Edn., Ctrl. Bible Coll., 1966. Min. Assemblies of God, Lewisville, Tex., 1959-63; youth pastor Assemblies of God Ch., Akron, Ohio, 1967-68; youth pastor, tchr. Assemblies of God Ch., Cleve., 1968-69; activities coord. Assemblies of God Ch., Glenview, Ill., 1970-74; sales rep. King & Leslie, Denver, 1976-78; pres. Bellah Enterprises, Canon City, Colo., 1978-96. Founder Women's Retreats (Nat.) Assemblies of God, Chgo., 1974; pres. No. Ill. Assemblies of God Women's Missionary Coun., Chgo., 1974-75; co-founder Rocky Mt. Singles, Denver, 1978-81; coord. Cancun (Mex.) Disaster Relief, 1987; mem. Valley Bible Ch., 1990-96; co-tchr. Bible Study Group, 1996. Named Vol. of Yr. Step 13, 1990, Pres. Bush 1000 Points of Lights, 1991. Mem. Nat. Assn. Bus. Women, Christian Bus. Women, Colo. Hist. Soc., Great Books Discussion Program, Rotary Internat. (fund raiser 1995). Republican. Home: 1226 Elm Ave Canon City CO 81212 Office: Deweese Lodge Bed & Breakfast 1226 Elm Canon City CO 81212

BELLAMY, CAROL, international organization executive; b. Plainfield, N.J., 1942. BA with honors, Gettysburg Coll., 1963; JD, NYU, 1968. Asst. commr. Dept. Mental Health and Mental Health Retardation Svc., N.Y.C.; with Peace Corps., Guatemala, Ctrl. Am.; assoc. Cravath, Swaine & Moore, N.Y.C.; mem. N.Y. State Senate; prin. Morgan Stanley & Co., N.Y.C.; mng. dir. Bear Stearns, N.Y.C.; dir. Peace Corps., Washington, 1993-95; exec. dir. UNICEF, 1995—. Office: UNICEF Office of Exec Director 3 United Nations Plz New York NY 10017*

BELLAMY, JENNIFER RACHELLE, artist; b. Clio, S.C., Aug. 9, 1944; d. Leland and Myrtle Lee (Wise) Wiggins; m. Marvin James Bellamy, May 19, 1963; 1 child, Audrey Katherine Rollins. BA in Art & Performance magna cum laude, U. Tex., 1989, postgrad., 1992-93, 95—. Dist. sec. Corning Glass Works, Richardson, Tex., 1977-80; adminstrv. asst. The Chase Manhatten Bank, Dallas, 1981-85; owner The Bellamy Studio, Richardson, Tex., 1990-93, 95—. Recipient tchg. assistantships U. Tex., Dallas, 1993. Mem. AAUW, Coll. Art Assn., Richardson Civic Art Soc., Phi Theta Kappa. Lutheran. Office: The Bellamy Studio 404 Summit Dr Richardson TX 75081

BELLANGER, BARBARA DORIS HOYSAK, biomedical research technologist; b. Syracuse, N.Y., Oct. 24, 1936; d. Edward George and Bernardine Elizabeth (Blaney) Hoysak; m. Ronald Patrick Bellanger, July 1, 1961; children: Laura Jeanne, Andrea Lynne, Janis Anne. BS, Syracuse U., 1958. Cert. lab. animal technician. Tech. asst. Bur. of Labs., Syracuse, 1958; rsch. scientist Bristol Labs., Syracuse, 1958-63; rsch. assoc. Syracuse Cancer Rsch. Inst., 1973—. Pres. CNS Northstars Band Parents, Inc., Cicero-North Syracuse, N.Y., 1986-87. Mem. Am. Assn. Lab. Animal Sci. (cert. lab. animal technician, sec. Upstate N.Y. br. 1990—, Technician of Yr. award 1992), N.Y. Acad. Scis., Alpha Gamma Delta (pres. Alpha alumnae chpt. 1959-60, treas. 1989—). Home: 410 David Dr North Syracuse NY 13212-1929 Office: Syracuse Cancer Rsch Inst Presdl Plz 600 E Genesee St Syracuse NY 13202-3111

BELLANTONI, MAUREEN BLANCHFIELD, manufacturing executive; b. Warren, Pa., Mar. 18, 1949; d. John Joseph and Patricia Anne (Southard) Blanchfield; m. Michael Charles Bellantoni, Aug. 12, 1972; children: Mark Christopher, Melissa Catherine. BS in Fin., U. Bridgeport, 1976; MBA, U. Conn., Stamford, 1979. Fin. analyst Dictaphone Corp., Rye, N.Y., 1970-73, Gen. Telephone & Electronics, Stamford, 1973-74, Smith Kline Ultrasonic Products, now Branson, Danbury, Conn., 1974-77; fin. mgr. Gen. Foods, White Plains, N.Y., 1977-80; contr. Branson Ultrasonics Corp. div. Emerson Electric, Danbury, Conn., 1980-88; v.p. fin. Branson Ultrasonics Corp. div. Emerson Electric, Danbury, 1988-90; v.p. fin., CFO Automatic Switch Co. divsn. Emerson Electric, Florham Park, N.J., 1990-93, PYA/Monarch, Inc. divsn. Sara Lee Corp., Greenville, S.C., 1993-94; v.p. fin. CFO Meat Group Sara Lee Corp., Cordova, Tenn., 1994—; bd. dirs. Michael Foods, Inc. Vice chair Nat. Legacy Campaign Cancer Fund, Franciscan Sister of Poor Found. Mem. Fin. Execs. Inst., S.C. C. of C., Danbury C. of C. (leadership program 1989), Beta Gamma Sigma. Home: 3407 Lake Pointe Cove Memphis TN 38125-8842 Office: 8000 Centerview Pky Ste 300 Cordova TN 38018

BELLEAU, CLAUDIA LOUISE NICOLE See ROBITAILLE, CLAUDIA LOUISE NICOLE

BELLER, LUANNE EVELYN, accountant; b. Ft. Dodge, Iowa, Feb. 5, 1950; d. Gerald L. and Evelyn E. (Liston) Heyl; m. Stephen M. Beller, June 28, 1970; children: Clancy D., Corby L. BA, Oreg. State U., 1977; MBA, Rochester Inst. Tech., 1981. CPA, Ill. Plant acct. DuBois Plastic Products, Avon, N.Y., 1977-79, coll. acct. SUNY, Geneseo, 1979-81; gen. acctg. supr. M&M/Mars, Inc., Cleveland, Tenn., 1981-83, Hackettstown, N.J., 1983-84; sales rep. M&M/Mars, Inc., Jacksonville, Ill., 1984-86, terr. sales supr., 1986-88; gen. acctg. coord. Kal Kan Foods, Inc., Columbus, Ohio, 1988-90, fin. info. coord., 1990-92, gen. acctg. supr., 1992—. Vol. Girl Scouts Am., Jacksonville, 1985-88, Bexley, Ohio, 1988—; mem. edn. com., mem. sound control com. Bexley United Meth. Ch., 1989—. Mem. Phi Kappa Phi, Beta Gamma Sigma, Beta Alpha Psi. Democrat.

BELLES, ANITA LOUISE, health care researcher, consultant; b. San Angelo, Tex., Aug. 30, 1948; d. Curtis Lee and Margaret Louise (Perry) B.; m. John Arvel Willey, Jul. 13, 1969 (div. Aug. 1978); children: Suzan Heather, Kenneth Alan; m. John W. Portfield, Dec. 22, 1992. BA, U. Tex., 1972; MS in Health Care Adminstrn., Trinity U., 1984. dir. family planning Bexar County Hosp. Dist., Tex., 1987; mgmt. engr. Inpatient Support Applications, 1987-88, instr. grad. sch. health care adminstrn. S.W. Tex. State U.; researcher on cardiovascular rsch. on artificial heart and heart transplantation, San Antonio Regional Heart Inst., 1993. Regional emergency med. service tng. coordinator Bur. Emergency Med. Service, Lake Charles, La., 1978-79; exec. dir. Southwest La. Emergency Med. Service Council, Lake Charles, 1979-83; project coordinator Tulane U. Med. Sch., New Orleans, 1982-83; dir. La. Bur. of Emergency Med. Service, Baton Rouge, 1982; pres. Computype, Inc., San Antonio, 1983-86, Emergency Med. and Safety Assocs., La. and Tex., 1982—; dir. family planning Bexar County Hosp. Dist., Tex., 1987; mgmt. engr. Inpatient Support Applications, 1987-88; instr. grad. sch. health care adminstrn. S.W. Tex. State U. Editor A.L.E.R.T., 1980-83, San Antonio Executive News, 1987—, Family Living, 1987-88; feature writer Bright Scrawl, 1985-86; contbr. numerous articles on emergency med. services to profl. jours. Bd. dirs. Thousand Oaks Homeowner's Assn., sec., treas., 1985; active Trinity U. Health Care Alumni Assn., Jr. League San Antonio, The Parenting Ctr., Baton Rouge, 1982-83, Jr. League Lake Charles, 1982, Campfire Council Pub. Relations Com., Lake Charles, 1982; newsletter editor Community Food Co-Op, Newsletter Editor, 1979; vol. Lake Charles Mental Health Ctr., 1974. Recipient Outstanding Service award La. Assn Registered Emergency Med. Technicians, 1983, Southwest La. Assn. Emergency Med. Technicians, 1983; named Community Leader KPLC TV, Lake Charles, 1981, regional winner Assn U. Programs in Health Adminstrn., HHS Sec's. Competitions for Innovations in Health, 1982. Mem. Nat. Assn. Emergency Med. Technicians., Tex. Assn. Emergency Med. Technicians, Am. Coll. Health Care Execs., Am. Assn. Automotive Medicine, Southwest La. Assn. Emergency Med. Technicians (founding mem., v.p. 1979-80, CPR com. chmn. 1980-81, pub. relations com. chmn. 1981-82, bd. dirs. 1980-82), Am. Mgmt. Assn., Nat. Soc. Emergency Med. Service Adminstrs., Nat. Coalition Emergency Med. Services, Am. Composition Assn. Methodist.

BELLES, CAROL JEAN, customer service representative; b. Newark, Aug. 19, 1965; d. Joseph Elmer and Jennie Mae (Ferguson) B.; children: Heather Nicole, Charles Edward. BBA in Acctg., Athens State Coll., 1996. Head teller 1st Ala. Bank, Huntsville, 1985-90; recreation dir. Wyndham Park, Huntsville, 1990-95; customer svc. rep. Fluid Controls, Inc., Huntsville, 1995—. Mem. AICPA, Inst. Mgmt. Accts. Republican. Mem. Ch. of Christ. Home: 611 Naugher Rd Huntsville AL 35811

BELLINGER, GRETCHEN, artist; b. Hartford, Conn., Apr. 22, 1946; d. Kenneth Philip Bellinger and Elizabeth Schaffer. Student, Sophia U., Tokyo, 1967; BS, Skidmore Coll, 1968; MFA, Cranbrook Acad. of Art, Bloomfield Hills, Mich., 1970. Dir. Matl. Resource Ctr. Skidmore, Owings & Merrill, Chgo., 1970-73; mgr. textile devel. Knoll Internat., N.Y.C., 1973-74; promotion dir. V'Soske, Inc., N.Y.C., 1974-76; pres. Gretchen Bellinger, Inc, Cohoes, N.Y., 1976—; cons. for Concorde refurbishings, Brit. Airways, Heathrow Airport, Eng., 1984. Acad. exhbns. include: Oneonta State U., N.Y., 1969, Lawrence Stevens Gallery, Detroit, 1970, Thirty-Fifth Ann. Exhibit/Conn. Craftsmen, Hartford, 1970, Fine Arts Gallery, Birmingham, Mich., 1970, Art in Other Media, Rockford, Ill., 1970-71, Fur and Feathers/

Sheboygan, Mich., 1971, Master Weavers and Proteges, Birmingham, 1971, others; mus. collections include Met. Mus. Art, N.Y.C., 1985, Montreal Mus. of Decorative Arts, Can., 1985, Cranbrook Acad. of Art, 1986, The Art Inst. of Chgo., 1989, Smithsonian Instn.'s Mus. of Design, Cooper-Hewitt Mus., N.Y.C., 1990, others; media events Women of Design Traveling Trunk Exhbn., N.Y., 1992, Washington, 1993, Chgo., 1993, San Francisco, 1993-94, Miami, 1994, Charlotte, 1994, L.A., 1994; featured on CNN Style with Elsa Klensch, 1987, 94; contbr. articles to numerous profl. jours. Recipient Merit award Conn. Craftsmen, 1970, Harold Bartlett award/Art in Other Media, 1970, various other art awards. Mem. The Arts Club/Chgo., Decorative Fabrics assn., The Decorator's Club, Adirondack Mus./N.Y. Office: Gretchen Bellinger Inc PO Box 64 31 Ontario St Cohoes NY 12047

BELLM, JOAN, civic worker; b. Alton, Ill., June 20, 1934; d. Harvey Jacob and Alma Lorene (Roberts) Goldsby; m. Earl David Bellm, Oct. 1, 1955; children: David, Lori, Michael. Editor Best of IDEA newsletter, 1991-96. Organist, dir. jr. choir St. Mary's Cath. Ch., 1958-78; mem. adv. bd. Carlinville (Ill.) Area Hosp., 1981-86; trustee Blackburn Coll., Carlinville, 1983-86; bd. dirs. Cath. Children's Home, Diocese of Springfield, Ill., 1986—; founder, bd. dirs., state networker Ill. Drug Edn. Alliance, 1982-86, pres., 1987-89; bd. dirs., nat. networker Nat. Fedn. Parents for Drug-Free Youth, Washington, 1984-86; mem. Ill. Gov.'s Adv. Coun. on Alcoholism and Substance Abuse, 1989-93; founder Drug Watch Internat., 1991, Internat. Drug Strategy Inst., 1993, invited participant Internat. Private Sector Conf. on Drugs, Seville, 1993, advisor U.N. Internat. Drug Ctrl. Program, 1994 ; numerous others. Recipient letter of endorsement Pres. of U.S., 1981, citation of recognition Ill. Dept., Am. Legion, 1981, Meritorious Svc. award, 1982, award Ill. Drug Edn. Alliance award, 1984, Southwestern Ill. Law Enforcement Commn., 1984, Carlinville Sch. Bd., 1985, Outstanding Svc. award Nat. Fedn. Parents, 1986, award Ill. Alcohol and Drug Dependence Assn., 1986, Optimist Internat., 1987, Ill. Drug Edn. Alliance, 1988, Outstanding Citizen award Blackburn U., 1989, Citizen of Yr. award, Carlinville, 1990. Home: PO Box 227 Carlinville IL 62626-0227

BELLO, SHERE CAPPARELLA, foreign language educator; b. Norristown, Pa., Sept. 4, 1956; d. Anthony and Patsy (Robbins) Capparella. BA in Spanish and French, Rosemont (Pa.) Coll., 1978; BA in Mktg., Ursinus Coll., 1991; student, Institut Internat. D'Enseignement de la Langue Française, France, 1992, Escuela de Idiomas, Spain, 1992; MEd in Multicultural Edn., Eastern Coll., 1993; ballet student, Novak and Kovalska; Spanish flamenco/castenet student, José Greco. Cert. in French/Spanish. Salesperson Spectrum Communications Corp., Norristown, 1977-79, sales and mktg. mgr., 1986-87; asst. sales and adminstrv. asst. Tettex Instruments, Inc., Fairview Village, Pa., 1979-83; owner, instr. Shere's World of Dance and Fine Arts, Jeffersonville, Pa., 1982-88; multilingual exec. sec. Syntex Dental Products, Inc., Valley Forge, 1984-86; v.p. Captrium Devel. Corp., Exton, Pa., 1987-89; cons. Mary Kay Cosmetics, 1988-96; sales mgr. Spectrum Communications, 1989-92; tchr. Spanish and French Middletown (Pa.) Area Sch. Dist., 1992-94; adj. prof. Spanish Messiah Coll., Grantham, Pa., 1996—; market rsch. analyst Capital Health Sys., Harrisburg, Pa., 1995; Spanish and French tchr. Elizabethtown (Pa.) Area Sch. Dist., 1996—; v.p. La Bella Modeling Agy., Collegeville, Pa., 1979-82; choreographer and dance instr. La Bella Sch. Performance, Collegeville, 1979-82. Judge state and nat. pageants Miss Am. Scholarship, Jr. Miss. Nat. Teen and Pre-Teen, All-Am. Talent, Ofcl. Little Miss Am., Little Miss Diamond, Talent Olympics, Talent Unltd., 1979—; producer, choreographer Miss Montgomery County Pageant, Plymouth Meeting, Pa., 1985; co-producer, choreographer Miss Del. Valley Pageant, Horsham, Pa., 1983-84; confraternity Christian Doctrine kindergarten tchr. Visitation Parish, 1987-88. Recipient award Internat. Leaders in Achievement, 1989, Community Leaders of Am., 1989. Mem. Am. Coun. Tchrs. Fgn. Langs., Am. Assn. Tchrs. French, Pa. State MLA, Pa. State Edn. Assn., Christian Children's Fund, Am. Assn. Tchrs. Spanish, Kappa Delta Pi. Roman Catholic. Home: 4700 Cumberland St Harrisburg PA 17111-2725

BELLOCK, PATRICIA RIGNEY, county government official; b. Chgo., Oct. 14, 1946; d. John Dungan and Dorothy (Comiskey) Rigney; m. Charles Joseph Bellock, Nov. 8, 1969; children: Colleen, Dorothy. BA, St. Norbert Coll., 1968. With customer rels. 3M Corp., Chgo., 1968-69; tchr. jr. h.s. Milw. and Fairbanks, Alaska, 1970-72; v.p. sports corps. Dor-Mor-Pat Corp., River Forest, Ill., 1976-84; mem. DuPage County (Ill.) Bd. from Dist. #3, 1992—; asst. treas. DuPage County Forest Preserve Dist. Mem. sch. bd. St. Isaac Jogues Sch., Hinsdale, Ill., 1989-91; bd. dirs. Hinsdale Cmty. House, 1987-89, U. Ill. Gerontology Rsch., 1988-91, Hinsdale Youth Ctr., 1987-90, DuPage County Bd. Health, Wheaton, 1990—, Care and Counseling Ctr., Downers Grove, 1977—, pres., 1986-89. Recipient Health Dept. award State of Ill., 1992. Roman Catholic. Home: 138 E 6th St Hinsdale IL 60521-4650 Office: Office County Board DuPage County Ctr 421 N County Farm Rd Wheaton IL 60187-3978

BELLONI, ALESSANDRA, artistic director; b. Rome, July 24, 1954; came to U.S., 1971; d. Eugenio and Elvira (Rossetti) B.; m. Dario Bollini, June 22, 1991; 1 stepchild, Daphne. Student, Internat. Lyceum of Langs., Rome, NYU, Fiesole-Urbino, Italy. Artist in residence NYU, N.Y.C., 1981-91; artistic dir., co-founder I Giullari di Piazza, N.Y.C., 1982—; singer Carnegie Recital Hall, N.Y.C., 1985; dir., singer, actress Carnegie Hall, Pitts., 1986; dir., prodr. Walt Disney World, Orlando, Fla., 1985-86; dir., singer Lincoln Ctr.- Alice Tully, N.Y.C., 1985-88, 92-96; tchr., performer, dir. Caramoor Mus., Katonah, N.Y.; artist in residence Cathedral St. John the Divine, N.Y.C., 1993—; tchr., spkr., lectr. N.Y. State Pub. Schs., N.Y.C., 1990—; performer adv. bd. Meditations on the Dark Mother, Santa Fe, 1993.dir. N.Y. State Dept. Cultural Affairs, 1985—, N.Y. State Coun. on the Arts, 1986—. Author, dir., singer (opera) 1492-1992: Earth, Sun and Moon, 1992, Stabat Mater: Donna de Paradiso, 1995-96, (concert) Dance of Ancient Spider, 1996; singer, percussionist (compact disk) Earth, Sun and Moon, 1995. Performing Arts grantee N.Y. State Coun. on the Arts, 1982—; recipient cert. appreciation Mayor of L.A., 1983; named Woman of Yr. Italian-Am. Women Orgn., 1996. Mem. Percussive Arts Soc. Roman Catholic. Home: 500 W 111 St # 2G New York NY 10025 Office: I Giullari Di Piazza c/o St John the Divine 1047 Amsterdam Ave New York NY 10025

BELLO-REUSS, ELSA NOEMI, physician, educator; b. Buenos Aires, Argentina, May 1, 1939; came to U.S., 1972; naturalized, 1989; d. Jose F. and Julia M. (Hiriart) Bello; B.S., U. Chile, 1957, M.D., 1964; m. Luis Reuss, Apr. 15, 1965; children: Luis F., Alejandro E. Intern J.J. Aguirre Hosp., Chile, 1963-64; intern, then resident in internal medicine U. Chile, Santiago, 1964-66; pvt. practice medicine specializing in nephrology Santiago, 1967-72; prof. pathophysiology Sch. Nutrition U. Chile, 1970-72; Internat. NIH fellow U. N.C., Chapel Hill, 1972-74; vis. asst. prof. physiology U. N.C., Chapel Hill, 1974-75; Louis Welt fellow U. N.C.-Duke U. Med. Ctr., 1975-76; mem. faculty Jewish Hosp. St. Louis, 1976-83, asst. prof. medicine, physiology and biophysics Washington U. Sch. Medicine, St. Louis, 1976-86, assoc. prof. physiology dept. cell biology and physiology, 1986; assoc. prof. medicine U. Tex. Med. Br., Galveston, 1986-94, prof. dept. internal medicine and dept. phys. and biophys. medicine, 1994—, dir. Renal Clin, 1995—; mem. reviewers res. study sect. NIH, 1991-95; chair Women's Coun. Internat. Medicine U. Tex. Med. Bd. chpt., 1993—, mem. rsch. coun. Author: (with others) The Kidney and Body Fluids in Health and Disease, 1983; contbr. articles on nephrology and epithelial electrophysiology to med. and physiology jours. Mem. Internat., Am. Socs. Nephrology, Royal Soc. Medicine, Nat. Kidney Found. of S.E. Tex. (med. adv. bd., chairperson med. adv. bd., bd. dirs. 1994-95), Coun. of Women in Nephrology, Tex. Med. Assn., Am. Fedn. Clin. Rsch., Am. Soc. Renal Biochemistry and Metabolism, Internat. Soc. Renal Nutrition and Metabolism, Am. Physiology Soc., Am. Heart Assn., Kidney Coun., Soc. Gen. Physiologists, Math. Assn. Am., Gt. Houston and Gulf Coast Nephrology Assn., NIH Gen. Medicine B Study Sect. (mem. 1987-91), Reserve reviewer 1991-95, VA grant reviewer, Sigma Xi. Office: U Tex Med Br Dept Medicine Nephrology OJS 4 200 Galveston TX 77555-0562

BELLOSPIRITO, ROBYN SUZANNE, artist, publisher, editor; b. Glen Cove, N.Y., Sept. 11, 1964. BA, L.I. U., 1986. Receptionist EAC Gallery, Albertson, N.Y., 1986; asst. Slide Libr. The Met. Mus. Art, N.Y.C., 1987-88, The Frick Art Reference Libr., N.Y.C., 1988-89; adminstrv. asst. L.I. U. Libr., Greenvale, N.Y., 1989-93; pub., editor The Exhibitioner Art Mag., Old Brookville, N.Y., 1993—, curator exhbns., 1994—; guest dir. Sea Cliff (N.Y.) Gallery, 1994. Exhbns. include Crystal Art Gallery, N.Y.C., 1988, Hutchins Gallery, Greenvale, N.Y., 1990, 91, Nassau County Mus. Art, Roslyn, N.Y., 1990, Orgn. Ind. Artists Salon, N.Y.C., 1991, Time Factor Delirium, Glen Head, N.Y., 1992, Sakura Gallery, Kennedy Airport, N.Y.C., 1992, PAAS Gallery, N.Y.C., 1992, Ward-Nasse Gallery, N.Y.C., 1992, 94, Outrlimits Art Gallery, Franklin Square, N.Y., 1993, Space Lab Gallery, Huntington, N.Y., 1993, Sea Cliff (N.Y.) Gallery, 1993, 94, Prince St. Gallery, N.Y.C., 1994, Meridian Gallery, Sea Cliff, N.Y., 1994, Foster Freeman Gallery, San Antonio, 1994, UN 4th Conf. on Women, Beijing, 1995, The Foot Sq. Space, Sea Cliff, 1995, and others; permanent collections include Nat. Mus. Women in Arts, 1-800-Flowers, Inc., and pvt. homes. Mem. Nat. Mus. Women in Arts, Women's Caucus for Art. Address: PO Box 302 Locust Valley NY 11560

BELL WILSON, CARLOTTA A., state official, consultant; b. Detroit, Dec. 7, 1944; d. Albert Powell and Elfrieda (Bertram) Bell; divorced; children: Lizette C. Wilson, SaMia M. Wilson, Shira M. Ingram. AA, Wayne County C.C., Detroit, 1975; BS, Wayne State U., 1979; MEd, Bowling Green State U., 1983. Dental asst. Fred Colvard, DDS, Detroit, 1968-73; edn. coord. Merrill Palmer Inst., Detroit, 1979-81; head start evaluator Cmty. Devel. Inst., Wayne County, 1981; grad. asst. Bowling Green (Ohio) State U., 1981-83; child care worker Meth. Children's Village, Detroit, 1984-85; tchr. New Calvary Head Start, Detroit, 1985; child welfare specialist Mich. Dept. Social Svcs., Detroit, 1985-93; resource program analyst teen parent program Mich. Independence Family Agy., Lansing, 1993—; conf. presenter U. Mich., Ann Arbor, 1995, Mich. Assn. Cmty. and Adult Edn., Bellaire, 1995. Mem. Toastmasters. Roman Catholic. Home: 2110 Chene St Detroit MI 48207 Office: Mich Family Independence Agy 235 S Grand Ste 510 Lansing MI 48909

BELMONT-RIVERA, PORTIA JANE, secondary art educator, English language educator; b. Bristol, Eng., Feb. 14, 1957; came to the U.S., 1984; d. William George and Hylda May (Rook) Hobbs; m. Robert Lerma, June 14, 1986 (div. June 1989); 1 child, Erica Portia Lerma; m. Dann Rivera, July 4, 1993; 1 child, Dann Diego. Student, U. Regina, Can., 1983; BA, U. Tex., Brownsville, 1986. Secondary English tchr. Brownsville (Tex.) Ind. Sch. Dist., 1986—, secondary art tchr., 1991—. Mem. Nat. Art Edn. Assn., Tex. Art Edn. Assn. (regional dir. 1993-95), Rio Art Edn. Assn. (media dir. 1993-94), Tex. Art Edn. (regional dir.). Home: 74 Mcfadden Hut Dr Brownsville TX 78520-8909 Office: Simon Rivera High 6955 FM 802 Brownsville TX 78521

BELOBRAIDICH, SHARON LYNN GOUL, elementary education educator; b. Detroit, Oct. 21, 1940; d. William A. and Lillian Mae (Atkinson) Goul; m. Frank Glen Belobraidich, Mar. 24, 1962 (dec. May 1987); children: Caryn Lyn, Ellyn Elizabeth. BA, Mich. State U., 1962; MA, Ea. Mich. U., 1968. Tchr. Waverly Schs., Lansing, Mich., 1962-63, Plymouth (Mich.) - Canton Schs., 1963—; bldg. rep. Plymouth Canton Edn. Assn., 1963-94, sec., 1974-90, v.p., 1990—; del. to rep. assembly NEA, Mich. Edn. Assn., 1990—. Experienced Tchr. fellow U.S. Govt., 1967-68. Mem. AAUW, Mich. Diabetes Assn. (bd. dirs. 1971-87), Beacon Hollow Condo Assn. (pres. 1994—), Alpha Delta Kappa (sec. 1968-70, pres. 1972-74, 76-78). Home: 12498 Pinecrest Dr Plymouth MI 48170-3061

BELOVANOFF, OLGA, retired health care facility administrator; b. Buchanan, Sask., Can., July 1, 1932; d. Frederick Alexander and Dora (Konkin) B. Grad. high sch., Kamsack, Sask., Can. From clk. to adminstrv. officer Sask. Health Dept. Cancer Clinic, Saskatoon, 1951-78; bus. mgr. Sask. Cancer Found. Saskatoon Clinic, Saskatoon, 1979-90, ret., 1990. Dir. Sask. Br. Can. Tenpin Fedn., Inc. Home: 420 3d Ave N, Saskatoon, SK Canada S7K 2J3

BELSTERLING, JEAN INNES, retired medical librarian; b. Phila., Feb. 2, 1928; d. George McNeely Belsterling and Mary Thornton (Innes) Bowman. Grad., Bryn Mawr Hosp. Sch. Nursing, 1948; BA, U. Pa., 1974; MS, Drexel U., 1976. RN, Pa. Nurse Bryn Mawr (Pa.) Hosp., 1948-51; commd. ensign USN, 1951, advanced through grades to lt. comdr., 1961; ret., 1971; med. libr. West Jersey Health System, Voorhees, N.J., 1976-90, ret., 1990; coord. S.W. N.J. Libr. Consortium, 1985-90. Deacon Trinity Presbyn. Ch., Cherry Hill, N.J., 1976-79, trustee, elder, 1984-87. Mem. AAUW, DAR, USN League. Home: 214 Shady Ln Marlton NJ 08053-2716

BELT, AUDREY E(VON), social worker, consultant; b. New Orleans, June 23, 1948. BS in Social Work, Grambling State U., 1970; MSW in Social Work Adminstrn., U. Mich., 1972. Adult probation officer City/County San Francisco Hall of Justice, 1973-74; child welfare worker dept. social svcs. City/County San Francisco, 1974-79; rsch. and planning specialist City of Ann Arbor (Mich.) Model Cities Interdisciplinary Agy; cons. in field. Grambling State U. scholar, 1966-70, U. Mich. scholar, 1971-72. Mem. ABA, NASW (edn. task force), Am. Orthopsychiat. Assn., Am. Humane Soc. (exec. asst. dir., sec. exec. bd.), Child Welfare League Am., N.Y. Acad. Scis., Smithsonian Rsch. Instn., Alpha Kappa Delta. Democrat. Roman Catholic. Home and Office: PO Box 424288 610 Polk St Apt 217 San Francisco CA 94103

BELT, JEAN RAINER, art gallery owner; b. Selma, Ala., Sept. 12, 1942; d. Sterling Price and Saidee (Crook) Rainer; m. Kemplin C. Belt, Aug. 31, 1963; children: Keven Curtis, Kelly B. Jones. BS in Math., U. Ala., 1964. Founder, ptnr. Corp. Art Source, Montgomery, Ala., 1983-92, owner, 1992—; owner CAS Gallery & Frames, Montgomery, Ala., 1994; juror Jubilee Galleria Art Show, Montgomery, 1987, Riofest, Harlingen, Tex., 1989-90, BCA on My Own Time, Montgomery, 1990; guest lectr. Riofest, 1990; dir. Armory Gallery Arts Coun. Montgomery, 1989-91; advisor Montgomery Bus. Com. Arts, 1990-94 (Bus. in Arts award 1989); curator Armory Gallery, Montgomery, 1989. Bd. dirs Arts Coun. Montgomery, 1980-94, pres., 1985-87, 92-93; mem. adv. bd. Montgomery Symphony Assn., 1993—; pres. Jr. League Montgomery, 1984, treas., 1981; Stephen min. 1st United Meth. Ch., Montgomery, 1992-94. Named Vol. Action Ctr. Vol. of Yr., 1989; recipient Bus. in the Arts award Montgomery Bus. Com. for the Arts, 1989, Disting. Vol. in the Arts award Art Coun. Montgomery, 1996. Mem. Nat. Assn. Corp. Art Mgrs., Montgomery C. of C., U. Ala. Alumni Assn. Office: Corp Art Source 2960 Zelda Rd # F Montgomery AL 36106-2649

BELTAIRE, BEVERLY ANN, public relations executive; b. Detroit, Aug. 21, 1926; d. Charles H. and Henrietta (Lucker) Strauss; m. Mark A. Beltaire, Nov. 7, 1947; children: Mark IV, Jeffrey, Barbara, Suzanne. Student, Highland Community Coll., Highland Park, Mich., 1944-45, Wayne State U., 1946-47; HHD (hon.), Siena Heights Coll., 1990. Writer Detroit Free Press, 1945-47; pub. The Skyline mag., Detroit, 1947-55; v.p. Gille Beltaire, Inc., Detroit, 1956-59; women's editor Sta. WXYZ-TV, Detroit, 1956-59; pres. Beltaire, Vincent & Hull, Detroit, 1959-61; pres. and chief exec. officer PR Assocs., Inc., Detroit, 1961—; bd. dirs. Fed. Res. Bank Chgo., Detroit., Standard Fed. Bank. Mem. Pvt. Industry Coun., Gov.'s Commn. Future for Higher Edn.; sec. Mich. Bus. Ptnrship., Detroit Com. of 200; chmn. Leadership Detroit; bd. govs. Greater Mich. Found., Lansing; bd. dirs. Econ. Alliance for Mich., Met. Detroit Conv. and Visitors Bur., Detroit Econ. Growth Corp. Named Advt. Woman of the Yr., Women's Ad Club, 1978, Mich. Woman of the Yr., Am. Lung Assn. Southeastern Mich., 1985; recipient Nat. Clarion award Women in Communications, Inc., 1978, Disting. Community Svc. award Anti-Defamation League B'nai B'rith, 1990, Humanitarian of the Yr. award March of Dimes, 1991, Silver awards (4) Pub. Rels. Soc. of Am., 1972, 83, 88, 92. Mem. Pub. Rels. Soc. Am. (Silver Anvil award 1972, 83, 88, 92), Women in Communications, Inc. (Headliner award 1982), Greater Detroit C. of C. (chmn. bd. dirs. 1982-83), Adcraft Detroit Club, Econ. Detroit Club (exec. bd. dirs.), Detroit Club, Renaissance Club, Hunt Club. Office: PR Assocs Inc Ford Bldg 615 Griswold Ste 418 Detroit MI 48226

BELTON, BETTY KEPKA, art educator, artist; b. Wilson, Kans., Mar. 11, 1934; d. Frank and Rose Betty (Kepka) Hochman; m. Glen S. Belton, 1969 (div. 1974); 1 child, Risa-Marie. BS in Art Edn., Emporia State U., 1956; MS in Art Edn., Ft. Hays State U. Cert. art tchr., Kans. Jewelry apprentice Ursula Letovsky, Omaha, 1957-60; designer Hallmark Cards, Kansas City, Mo., 1960-62; art tchr. Linn (Kans.) Unified Sch. Dist. 223, 1966-69; murals, design Parsons (Kans.) Jr. High Sch., 1974-75; freelance writer, designer, artist Better Homes and Garden, 1975-77; inspector El Kan, Ellsworth, Kans., 1977-79; dist. coord., art tchr. Unified Sch. Dist. 328, Wilson, Kans., 1979—; adv. bd. Wilson C. of C., 1980-84, Kans. Scholastic Art Awards, 1991-94; mem. Inst. for Improving Visual Arts in Edn., The Getty Ctr., Cin. Art Mus.; participant, cultural contbr. Smithsonian Instn., Nat. Park Svc., Washington, 1976; workshop leader Kans. State U., Manhattan, 1983; nat. folk art contbr. Kans. Future Homemakers, Reston, Va., 1988; panelist Southwest Regional Rural Arts Conf., Garden City, Kans., 1989, Arts in Edn., Kans. Arts Commn., Salina, 1991; cons. DeCordova Mus. Art, Lincoln, Mass., 1990. Author: Egg Lap Studio and Batiking Method for Making Czechoslovakian Kraslice, 1984; contbr. Crafts in America, 1988, American Folk Masters, 1992; patentee lap studio for Czech Kraslice, 1984. Recipient Nat. Heritage fellowship Nat. Endowment Arts, Washington, 1988, Gov.'s award Kans. Gov. Joan Finney, Topeka, 1992, Master Folk Artist Apprenticeship Program, Kans. State Hist. Soc., 1985-86, 87-88, 91-92. Mem. NEA, Kans. Art Edn. Assn. (Art Enhancer award 1985), Czech Soc. Arts and Scis., Ellsworth Area Arts Coun. (v.p. 1992-94, adv. bd.). Home: 1007 N Grand PO 445 Ellsworth KS 67439 Office: Wilson HS Wilson KS 67490

BELTON, SHARON SAYLES, mayor; b. St. Paul, Minn., May 13, 1951; m. Steve Belton, Aug. 29, 1981; children: Coleman, Jordan, Kilayna. Student, Macalester Coll. Asst. dir. Minn. Program for Victims of Sexual Assault; parole officer Minn. Dept. Corrections; mayor City of Mpls., 1994—. Pres. Nat. Coalition Against Sexual Assault; co-founder, pres. Harriet Tubman Shelter for Battered Women; mem. Mpls. City Coun. 8th Ward, 1983-93, pres. 1989-93; bd. dirs. Bush Found., Macalester Coll., Children's Theater, Neighborhood Revitalization Policy Bd., United Way, Greater Mpls. Food Bank, Affordable Housing Coalition, Youth Coord. Bd., Turning Point, Affordable Day Care Coalition, Mpls. Initiative Against Racism, Met. Task Force on Devel. Disabilities, econ. devel. strategy steering com. Mpls. C. of C. Office: Office of the Mayor 350 S 5th St Minneapolis MN 55415-1316

BELTZNER, GAIL ANN, music educator; b. Palmerton, Pa., July 20, 1950; d. Conon Nelson and Lorraine Ann (Carey) Beltzner. BS in Music Edn. summa cum laude, West Chester State U., 1972; postgrad., Kean State Coll., 1972, Temple U., 1972, Westminster Choir Coll., 1972, Lehigh U., 1972. Tchr. music Drexel Hill Jr. High Sch., 1972-73; music specialist Allentown (Pa.) Sch. Dist., 1973—; tchr. Corps Sch. and Cmty. Devel. Lab., 1978-80, Corps Cmty. Resource Festival, 1979-81, Corps Cultural Fair, 1980, 81. Mem. aux. Allentown Art Mus., aux. Allentown Hosp.; mem. woman's com. Allentown Symphony, The Lyric Soc. of the Allentown Orch.; mem. Allentown 2d and 9th Civilian Police Acads.; bd. dirs. Allentown Area Ecumenical Food Bank. Decorated Dame Comdr., Ordre Souverain et Militaire de la Milice du St. Sepulcre; recipient Cert. of Appreciation, Lehigh Valley Sertoma Club; Excellence in the Classroom grantee Rider-Pool Found., 1988, 91-92. Mem. AAUW, NAFE, ASCD, Am. String Tchrs. Assn., Am. Viola Soc., Internat. Platform Assn., Allentown Edn. Assn., Music Educators Nat. Conf., Pa. Music Educators Assn., Am. Orff-Schulwerk Assn., Phila. Area Orff-Schulwerk Assn., Soc. Gen. Music, Am. Assn. Music Therapy, Internat. Soc. Music Edn., Internat. Tech. Edn. Assn., Assn. for Tech. in Music Instrn., Choristers Guild, Lenni Lenape Hist. Soc., Lehigh Valley Arts Coun., Allentown Symphony Assn., Midi Users Group, Nat. Sch. Orch. Assn., Lehigh County Hist. Soc., Confedn. Chivalry, Maison Internat. des Intellectuels Akademie, Order White Cross Internat. (apptd. dist. comdr. for Pa./U.S.A. dist., nobless of humanity), Airedale Terrier Club of Greater Phila., Kappa Delta Pi, Phi Delta Kappa, Alpha Lambda. Republican. Lutheran. Home: PO Box 4427 Allentown PA 18105-4427

BELYEA, CASSANDRA JEAN, paralegal, legal researcher, social worker; b. Rochester, N.Y., July 17, 1957; d. Raymond Howard Belyea and Corinne Frances (O'Kelley) Lee; m. Raul Rodriguez, June 2, 1980 (div. 1989); children: Anastasia, Tatiana, Raul II. Student, U. Md., Germany, 1979-80, U.S. Army Tng. Support Ctr., 1981-83, St. Mary of Woods, 1989-95; BSW, U. Indpls., 1991. Cert. legal asst., med. records clk., social svc. designee. Vol. activist VISTA, Kansas City, Mo., 1976-77; counselor Shares, Shelbyville, Ind., 1977; self employed paralegal San Antonio, 1982-85, Orlando, Fla., 1985-88; adminstrv. asst. Orlando Airport Marriott, 1985-88; paralegal Forgey & Forgey Attys. at Law, Shelbyville, 1988-95; dir. med. records/quality assurance Sheffield Manor, Franklin, Ind., 1990-92; with social svcs. Coburn Pl., Indpls., 1992-93; br. mgr. Work Force, Indpls., 1993-95; with social svcs. Parkview Pl., Indpls., 1994-95; tchr. Headstart, Kansas City, 1976-77, Shelbyville, 1988-89. Pres. parent coun. Headstart, Shelbyville, 1988-89; vol. Habitat for Humanity, Orlando, 1988. With U.S. Army, 1979-85. Decorated Good Conduct medal, Overseas medal; Cert. recipient Headstart, 1989, Ind. Sports Games, 1990. Mem. NAFE, Am. Legion, Young Reps., Ind. Assn. Paralegals (bankruptcy div.), Ind. Legal Assts., Inds. Assn. Quality Assurance Profls. Republican. Methodist. Home: 540 N Wickham Rd # 128 Melbourne FL 32935

BELZER, ELLEN J., negotiations and communications consultant; b. Kansas City, Mo., May 22, 1951; d. Meyer Simmon and Fay (Weinstein) B. Student, U. Okla., 1969-70, U. Ibero-Americana, Mexico City, 1971; BA, Northwestern U., 1973; MPA, U. Mo., Kansas City, 1976. Rsch. asst. dept. polit. sci. Northwestern U., Evanston, Ill., 1970-73; adminstrv. asst. Ctrs. for Regional Progress Midwest Rsch. Inst., Kansas City, 1974; various positions to dir. socioecons. div. Am. Acad. Family Physicians, Kansas City, 1974-86; pres. Belzer Seminars and Cons., Kansas City, 1986—; instr. communication Avila Coll., Kansas City, 1987-92, dept. continuing edn. U. Kans., Lawrence, 1989-92; speaker on negotiation strategies, conflict resolution techniques, communication skills, 1986—; mediator for hosps., physician groups, state health depts., community health ctrs., others. Contbr. articles to profl. publs., also monographs. Campaign vol. for local candidate, Kansas City, 1970, 82. Democrat. Home: 21 W Bannister Rd Kansas City MO 64114-4009 Office: 7140 Wornall Rd Ste 203 Kansas City MO 64114-1300

BEMIS, MARY FERGUSON, magazine editor; b. N.Y.C., Dec. 28, 1961; d. Edmund Augustus and Anne Adoian (Nalbandian) B. BFA in Writing, Johnson State Coll., 1983. Co-editor, co-pub. Ave. Literary Rev. Ave. Publs. Inc., Burlington, Vt., 1983-85; editor Unique Hair and Beauty Mag., 1994; editor Lady's Circle Mag. Lopez Publs., N.Y.C., 1987-94, editor, 1989-94; freelance editor, writer Mus. Sci., Boston, 1991-93; freelance editor Woman's Day Spl. Interest Publs., 1995—. Co-editor: The Green Mountain Rev., 1982-83, Nature Through Her Eyes; Art and Literature by Women, 1994, Journey Into the Wilderness, 1994. Mem. Women in Comm., Inc. Democrat. Mem. Unitarian Ch. Home and Office: 5th Fl 36 East 20 St New York NY 10003

BEMKER, MARY, counselor; b. Louisville, Ky., Feb. 18, 1958; d. Norbert James and Hattie (Hagan) Boemker; divorced, 1979; 1 child, Victoria Leigh. BS, Spalding U., Ind. U.; MS, Ind. U.; Specialist Degree in Counseling Psych., Spalding U.; MSN, U. Ala.; D (hon.), London Inst. Applied Rsch. Cert. tchr., Ind., Ky., sch. psychologist, Ind., counselor and edni. tester, Ky.; registered nurse, Ky., Ind.; cert. family life edn., CD nurse, CD mgr. Ednl. psychologist Ky. Bapt. Hosp., Louisville, 1976-77; substance abuse counselor River Region, Louisville, 1977-78; nurse cons. Changing Patterns, Inc., Louisville, 1981-84; academic counselor, lectr. Ind. U. Sch. Nursing, 1985-88; ednl. prevention intervention coord., rsch. coord. youth/family activity, cons. Choice, Inc., Louisville, 1988—; counselr substance abuse Morton Ctr.; advisor in field. Contbr. articles to profl. jours. Panel mem. Gatorade Sports Medicine; mem. Ky. Women's Substance Abuse Network. Named to Honorable Order of Ky. Colonels. Mem. Ky. Women's Substance Abuse Network, Am. Assn. Counseling and Devel., Am. Assn. Profl. Hypnotherapists, Ky. Nurses Assn. (mem. coun.), Am. Assn. Social Psychiatry, Internat. Coun. Nurses, Assn. for Humanistic Orthopsychiatry, Gatorade Panel Sports Medicine, Nat. Wildlife Fedn., Sierra Club, Sigma Theta Tau, Kappa Delta Phi, Pi Lambda Theta. Roman Catholic. Home: 1209 Curlew Ave Louisville KY 40213-1209

BENACH, SHARON ANN, physician assistant; b. New Orleans, Aug. 28, 1944; d. Wilbur G. and Freda Helen (Klaas) Cherry; m. Richard Benach, Dec. 6, 1969 (div. Oct. 1976); children: Craig, Rachel. Degree, St. Louis U.,

1978. Physician asst. VA Hosp., St. Louis, 1982-84, Maricopa County Health Svcs., Phoenix, 1984—. Served with USPHS, 1978-82. Recipient Outstanding Performance award HHS. Mem. Maricopa Faculty Assn. (div. internal medicine), Mensa. Jewish. Home: 5726 N 10th St No 5 Phoenix AZ 85014-2273

BENARIO, JANICE MARTIN, classics educator; b. Feb. 19, 1923; m. Herbert W. Benario, Dec. 23, 1957; children: Frederick M., John H. AB in Latin, Goucher Coll., 1943; AM in Classical Lit., Johns Hopkin's U., 1949, PhD in Classical Lit., 1952. Teaching intern St. John's Coll., 1953-54; from instr. to asst. prof. Sweet Briar Coll., 1954-60; asst. prof. English and classics Ga. State U., 1960-62, assoc. prof., 1962-84; co-prof. in charge Intercollegiate Ctr. for Classical Studies, Rome, 1984-85; assoc. prof. Emory U., 1989-94. Editor: Vergilius, 1960-63, 73-79, mem. editorial bd., 1963-73; book rev. editor: Arch, 1964-69; editor: Ga. Classicist, 1981-83. Ford Found. grantee 1953-54, Fulbright grantee, 1957. Mem. Classical Soc. of Am. Acad. in Rome (treas., v.p., pres. 1963-69), Classical and Modern Fgn. Lang. Assn. (pres. 1969-71), Atlanta Soc. Archaeol. Inst. Am. (pres. 1979-80), Ga. Classical Assn. (pres. 1985-87), Vergilian Soc. Am. (co-exec. sec. 1992-93). Home: 430 Chelsea Cir NE Atlanta GA 30307-1269

BENBERRY, CUESTA RAY, historian; b. Cin., Sept. 8, 1923; d. Walter and Marie (Jones) Ray; m. George Lynn Benberry, Mar. 25, 1951; 1 child, George Valdez Benberry. BA, Stowe Tchrs. Coll., St. Louis, 1945; postgrad., St. Louis U., 1954-56; Cert. Library Sci., Harris-Stowe Coll., St. Louis, 1968; MEd, U. Mo., St. Louis, 1974. Reading specialist St. Louis pub. schs., 1945-85; ind. scholar and lectr. quilt history St. Louis, 1969—; cons. Calif. Afro-Am. Mus., L.A., 1985, Ferrero Films, San Francisco, 1985-86, Williams Coll. Mus. Art, Williamstown, Mass., 1988-89, Met. Mus. Art, N.Y.C., 1990; curated quilt exhbn. St. Louis Art Mus., 1992-93. Author: Always There: The African-American Presence in American Quilts, 1991; co-author: A Patchwork of Pieces: An Anthology of Early Quilt Stories, 1845-1940, 1993; rsch. editor Nimble Needle mag., 1972-76, Nat. African-Am. Craft Exhibition and Symposium, Wilberforce U., Ohio, 1992—; contbr. articles to profl. jours. Established African-Am. Quilt Archive, Vaughn Cultural Ctr., Urban League, St. Louis, 1984; bd. dirs. African-Am. Arts and Crafts Conf., Wilberforce U., 1992—. Named to Quilters Hall of Fame, Continental Quilting Congress, Vienna, Va., 1983; First Place in the Arts, African Meth. Episcopal Ch., Tucson, 1989, award for Leadership in the Arts, YWCA, St. Louis, 1989, for contbn. to arts, Sigma Gamma Rho, St. Louis, 1981. Mem. Am. Quilt Study Group (bd. dirs. 1983-86), Elder Craftsmen of N.Y.C. (adv. com. 1990—), Nat. Quilting Assn., Quilters Guild London, Afro-Am. Hist. Genealogical Soc. AME Ch. Home and Office: 5150 Terry Ave Saint Louis MO 63115-1051

BENCH, LINDA PARRIS, business manager; b. Wilmington, Del., Mar. 15, 1959; d. Benjamin Joseph and Norma Lee (Hutchison) Miller; m. Joseph Thomas Bench, June 10, 1978; children: Joseph Wayne, Shawn Parris. G-rad. h.s., Middletown, Del. Adminstrv. asst. Windfields Farm, Chesapeake City, Md., 1978-81, 86-88; bus. mgr. Northview Stallion Sta., Chesapeake City, 1988—. Mem. Nat. Mus. Women in Arts, Nat. Trust Hist. Preservation, Nature Conservancy, Lighthouse Preservation Soc. Mem. Rep. Club. Methodist. Home: 24 Yellowfield Blvd Elkton MD 21921 Office: Northview Stallion Sta Inc 55 No Dancer Dr Chesapeake City MD 21915

BENCINI, SARA HALTIWANGER, concert pianist; b. Winston Salem, N.C., Sept. 2, 1926; d. Robert Sydney and Janie Love (Couch) Haltiwanger; m. Robert Emery Bencini, June 26, 1954; children: Robert Emery, III, Constance Bencini Waller, John McGregor. Mus. B., Salem Coll., 1947; postgrad. grad. Juilliard Sch. Music, 1948-50; M.A., Smith Coll., 1951; D In Mus. Arts, U. N.C., Greensboro, 1989. Head piano dept. Mary Burnham Sch. for Girls, Northampton, Mass., 1949-51; pianist, composer dance and drama dept. Smith Coll., 1951-52; head music dept. Walnut Hill Sch. for Girls, Natick, Mass., 1952-54; pvt. piano tchr., High Point, N.C., 1954-66; concert pianist appearing in Am. and Europe, 1948—; duo-piano performances with PBS-TV, Columbia, S.C., 1967, Winston Salem Symphony, N.C., 1964-68, Ea. Mus. Festival, Greensboro, N.C., 1969. Democrat. Presbyterian.

BENDELL, MARILYN, artist, educator; b. Grand Ledge, Mich., Sept. 19, 1921; d. Roy Edgar and Ruth Elizabeth (Foote) B; m. Joseph Henry Hyams, May 20, 1944 (dec. Jan. 1960); children: Deborah, David; m. George E. Burrows, Aug. 19, 1973. Grad., Am. Acad. Art, 1942; studied with, Pierre Nuyttens, Arnold E. Turtle. Exhibitions include Marilyn Bendell Gallery, Bradenton, Fla., 1967-81, Wadle Galleries Ltd., Santa Fe, 1979-86, Joe Wade Fine Arts, Santa Fe, 1986-93, Chgo. Galleries, 1951-54, Brown County Art Galleries Assn., Nashville, Ind., 1959-80, Frank Oehlschlaeger Galleries, Chgo., Sarasota, Fla., 1963-68, Art League Manatee County, Bradenton, 1971, Sedgwick's Magellan House, Tampa, Fla., Mountain Trails Gallery, Santa Fe, 1993, Huntsman Gallery, Aspen, 1993, Rice & Falkenberg, Palm Beach, 1995, others; represented in permanent collections at Saginaw (Mich.) Mus., Principia Coll. St. Louis, pvt. collections. Recipient First Place oil award Chgo. North Shore Art Guild, 1952, First Place award All Ill., 1954, Best of Show award Longboat Key Art Ctr., 1968, others. Fellow Royal Soc. Encouragement Arts; mem. Internat. Platform Assn., Western Acad. Women Artists. Home: Rt 1 Box 92MN Santa Fe NM 87501

BENDER, BETTY BARBEE, food service professional; b. Lexington, Ky., Apr. 29, 1932; d. Richard Carroll and Sarah Elizabeth (Rodes) Barbee; m. David H. Bender, Dec. 14, 1957; children: Bruce, Carroll. BA in Home Econs., Mont. State U., 1954; MS in Food Service Mgmt., Miami U., Oxford, Ohio, 1980. Adminstrv. dietitan Mass. Gen. Hosp., Boston, 1955-56; asst. chief dietitan Meth. Hosp., Indpls., 1957-61; chief dietitan Community Hosp., Indpls., 1961-63; supervising dietitian Chgo. Area ARA, 1963-67; asst. food service supr. Dayton (Ohio) Bd. Edn., 1969, mgr. food service, 1969—; cons. Nat. Frozen Food Assn., Washington, 1983, Crescent Metal Products Co., Cleve., 1985. Contbr. articles to profl. jours. Recipient 26th Ann. Foodsvc. Facilities Design award Instrs. Mag. for Commissary Design, 1972, Silver and Gold Plate awards Internat. Foodsvc. Mfrs. Assn., 1985, Pres.'s award Ohio Sch. Food Svc. Assn., 1987, FAME Golden Star award, 1992; recognized for outstanding contbns. to child nutrition program Ohio Ho. of Reps., 1972, 84. Mem. Am. Sch. Food Svc. Assn. (nat. pres. 1983, chmn. 1978-80, maj. city sect.), Ohio Sch. Food Svc. (pres. 1977), Dayton Sch. Adminstr. Assn., Dayton Sch. Mgmt. Assn. (pres. 1993-94), Am. Dietetic Assn. (cert., chair dietary practice group 1990-91, award for Excellence in Mgmt. Practice 1992, Food Svc. Dir. Yr. 1994), Ohio Dietetic Assn., Dayton Dietetic Assn., Soc. Nutrition Edn. (panel 1983). Democrat. Home: 7217 Tarryton Rd Dayton OH 45459-3450 Office: Dayton Bd Edn Food Svc Dept 125 Heid Ave Dayton OH 45404-1217

BENDER, BETTY WION, librarian; b. Mt. Ayer, Iowa, Feb. 26, 1925; d. John F. and Sadie A. (Guess) Wion; m. Robert F. Bender, Aug. 24, 1946. B.S., N.Tex. State U., Denton, 1946; M.A., U. Denver, 1957. Asst. cataloger N. Tex. State U. Library, 1946-49; from cataloger to head acquisitions So. Meth. U., Dallas, 1949-56; reference asst. Ind. State Library, Indpls., 1951-52; librarian Ark. State Coll., 1958-59, Eastern Wash. Hist. Soc., Spokane, 1960-67; reference librarian, then head circulation dept. Spokane (Wash.) Public Library, 1968-73, library dir., 1973-88; vis. instr. U. Denver, summers 1957-60, 63, fall 1959; instr. Whitworth Coll., Spokane, 1962-64; mem. Gov. Wash. Regional Conf. Libraries, 1968, Wash. Statewide Library Devel. Council, 1970-71. Bd. dirs. N.W. Regional Found., 1973-75, Inland Empire Goodwill Industries, 1975-77, Wash. State Library Commn., 1979-87, Future Spokane, 1983-88, vice chmn., 1986-87, pres., 1987-88. Recipient YWCA Outstanding Achievement award in Govt., 1985. Mem. ALA (mem. library adminstrn. and mgmt. assn. com. on orgn. 1982-83, chmn. nominating com. 1983-85, v.p./pres.-elect. 1985-86, pres. 1986-87), Pacific N.W. Library Assn. (chmn. circulation div. 1972-75, conv. chmn. 1977), Wash. Library Assn. (v.p./pres.-elect 1975-77, pres. 1977-78), AAUW (pres. Spokane br. 1969-71, rec. sec. Wash. br. 1971-73, fellowship named in honor 1972), Spokane and Inland Empire Librarians (dir. 1967-68), Am. Soc. Pub. Adminstrn. Republican. Lutheran. Club: Zonta (pres. Spokane chpt. 1976-77, dist. conf. treas. 1972). Home: E221 Rockwood Blvd # 504 Spokane WA 99202

BENDER, JANET PINES, artist; b. Chgo., June 14, 1934; d. Nathan and Hana (Leff) Pines; m. Irwin Robert Bender, Feb. 25, 1966. BS, U. Wis., 1955; MA, Northwestern U., 1956; postgrad., U. Ill./Loyola U., Chgo., 1955-56, Tyler Sch. Fine Arts, Phila., 1957. One-woman shows include One Ill. Ctr., Chgo., 1979, 87, Olive Hyde Gallery, Fremont, Calif., 1980, 81, N.A.M.E. Gallery, Chgo., 1982, W.A.R.M. Gallery, Mpls., 1984, A.R.C. Gallery, Chgo., 1985, 87, 89, 94, 96, R.H. Love Galleries, Chgo., 1989, 92, Soho 20 Gallery, N.Y.C., 1990, Galerie Thea Fischer-Reinhardt, West Berlin, Germany, 1990. R.H. Love Contemporary Gallery, Chgo., 1992, 96, Artemisia Gallery, Chgo., 1996; exhibited in group shows at Mus. Sci. and Industry, Chgo., 1995, 96, Artimesia Gallery, Chgo., 1996, Gallery 750, Sacramento, 1996, Women's Nat. Art Gallery, Washington, 1995, Rockford (Ill.) Art Mus., 1994, U. Wis. Art Gallery, Madison, Amos Enos Gallery, N.Y.C., 1993, Tonali Gallery, Mexico City, 1992, Renaissance Soc., Chgo., 1986, Ill. State Mus., 1983, 72nd Newport (R.I.) Nat. Exhbn., 1983, Chauttaqua Nat. Exhbn., 1981, Zolla Leiberman Gallery, Chgo., 1980; represented in permanent collections at Young & Rubicam, Chgo., Brown-Forman Corp., Louisville, Nugent Wenckus Corp., Chgo., Louis Zahn Drug Co., Melrose Park, Ill, Fuller Comml. Brokerage Co., Chgo., Dynamark Inc., Chgo., Aabott Distbn., Miami, Art Beasley Inc., San Diego, Siegel, Denberg, Vanasco, Shivkovsky, Moses and Shoenstadt, Chgo., Altschuler, Melvoin & Glassner, Chgo., Shafer, Meltzer & Lewis Assocs., Wilmette, Ill., Schiff, Hardin & Waite, Chgo. Bd. dirs. A.R.C. Gallery, Chgo., 1984—; juror IAFA Awards, 1993. Recipient Ill. Arts Coun. Project Completion grants, 1979, 81-82, Visual Arts Fellowship grant Ill. Arts Coun., 1983; fellow Northwestern U., 1955-56. Mem. NAFE, Women's Caucus for Art, Nat. Woman's Mus., Mus. Contemporary Art, Art Inst. Chgo., Chgo. Artist Coalition, Ill. Arts Alliance, Mus. Modern Art (N.Y.), Met. Mus. Art (N.Y.), Coll. Art Assn., Peace Mus., Ill. State Gallery, Com. for Artist Rights (organizing com. 1988), Oriental Art Soc., Siam House, Pi Lambda. Studio: 2001 N Elston Ave Chicago IL 60614-3901

BENDER, JESSICA DEE, speech language pathologist; b. Bklyn., Jan. 3, 1943; d. Benjamin and Mildred (Feldman) Waldbaum; m. Carl M. Bender, June 18, 1966; children: Michael, Daniel. AB, Cornell U., 1964; MAT, Harvard U., 1965; MA, St. Louis U., 1981. Cert. clin. competence speech pathology. Editor of textbooks Ginn and Co., Pubs., Boston, 1965-69; freelance editor, 1969—; speech lang. pathologist Spl. Sch. Dist. of St. Louis (Mo.) County, 1981—. Mem. Spl. Dist. NEA (bd. dirs. 1992-96, speech-lang. rep. 1992-94, corr. sec. 1994096), Am. Speech Lang. Hearing Assn., Mo. Speech Lang. Hearing Assn. Office: Spl Sch Dist St Louis County 12110 Clayton Rd Saint Louis MO 63131

BENDER, KRISTIN LYNN LAPPE, optometrist; b. Emmetsburg, Iowa, Sept. 25, 1964; d. Robert Hermann and Betty Jane (Ehrich) Lappe; m. Alan Henry Bender, Apr. 3, 1993. BA in Music Performance, Iowa State U., 1988; OD, U. of Ala., Birmingham, 1992. Bd. cert. optometrist. Optomentric asst. Drs. Erickson and Schuchert, Algona, Iowa, 1988; optometric technician Dr. James Skoney, O.D., Birmingham, 1991-1992; extern St. Lukes Eye Inst., Tarpon Srings, Fla., 1992, optometrist, 1992-93; optometrist Vision 21, Tampa and Largo, Fla., 1993—; clarinet and golf instr., Algona, 1984-87; mem. St. Luke's Eye Care Network, Tarpon Springs, 1993—. Vol. Vets. Hosp., Birmingham, 1991. Recipient Borish award for Optometric Rsch., U. Ala.-Birmingham Sch. of Optometry, 1992, Citizenship award Algona, 1983; named Miss Congeniality, Emmetsburg, Iowa, 1983; Heart of Am. Contact Lens Soc. grantee , 1991; Karl King Music scholar, Fort Dodge, Iowa, 1983, State of Iowa scholar, 1983. Mem. Gold Key Internat. Optometric Honor Soc., UAB Sch. of Optometry, Am. Optometric Assn., Ctrl. Suncoast Optometric Soc., So. Edn. Coun. for Optometry, Fla. Optometric Assn., Pinellas Soc. of Optometrists, Mortar Bd., Ia. State U. Home: 2761 Countryside Blvd #102 Clearwater FL 34621

BENDER, LINDA ARLENE, bank officer; b. Ft. Wayne, Ind., Sept. 4, 1951; d. Edward Walter and Lois C.L. (Bender) Dinkel; m. Dale Alan, June 12, 1971; children: Jennifer, Emily, Andrew. Student, U. Hawaii, 1969-73; BA in Sociology, Ind. U., Ft. Wayne, 1975; postgrad., St. Francis Coll., 1994—. Media dir. HPN, Inc., Ft. Wayne, 1981-84; media mgr. North Am. Van Lines, Ft. Wayne, 1984-88, mgr. advt. and pub. rels., 1988-92; mgr. mktg. NBD Bank, Ft. Wayne, 1992-94, trust officer, 1994—; bd. dirs. Ft. Wayne Advt. Assn. Editor: Ft. Wayne Ad Assn., 1984-85. actress Ft. Wayne Civic Theater, 1988—, Purdue-Ind. Theatre. Home: 8826 Village Grove Dr Fort Wayne IN 46804-2645 Office: NBD Bank 1 Summit Sq PO Box 2345 Fort Wayne IN 46801-2345

BENDER, PINKY TILL, minister; b. Charleston, S.C., Apr. 21, 1937; d. Wallace Conrad and Erna Louise (von Postel) T.; m. Michael Swift Bender; children: Louise, Katherine, David. BA in Journalism, Winthrop U., 1960; MDiv, Erskinel Theol. Sem., 1984; D in Ministry, Columbia Sem., 1993. Writer Presbyn. Ch. (USA), Louisville, 1983—; prof. Queens Coll., Charlotte, N.C., 1985-93; pastor McQuay Meml. Presbyn. Ch., Charlotte, 1986—; chair ARC Blood Svcs., Charlotte, 1991-95, Clergy Assn. Bd., Charlotte, 1995-96. Author (curriculum) Bible Discovery, 1983-93; editor (study books) Presbyterian Women, 1990-92. Mem. AAUW (life, Ednl. Found. Program grantee 1983), Presbyn. Writers Guild. Home: 5001 Belford Ct Charlotte NC 28226-7801

BENDER, RANDI LAINE, occupational therapist; b. Omaha, July 17, 1947; d. Kenneth Norman and Lois (Harmon) Anderson; m. Howard Jeffrey Bender, May 22, 1971; children: Rebecca Jennifer, Heidi Julia (dec. March 1990). BS, U. Ill., 1970; MS, Calif. Coll. for Health Scis., 1996. Registered occupational therapist. Occupational therapist Westchester County Med. Ctr., Valhalla, N.Y., 1970-76, UCP Therapeutic Nursery, Washington, 1987-89, Edward Mazique Parent Child Ctr., Washington, 1989, Great Oak Ctr., Silver Spring, Md., 1989-92, Montgomery Primary Achievement Ctr., Silver Spring, 1993—; co-monitor Riverdale Presbyn. Ch.; actress Riverdale Players. Mem. Coun. for Exceptional Children, Am. Occupational Therapy Assn., DAR, Riverdale Presbyn. Ch. Democrat. Home: 4200 Sheridan St Hyattsville MD 20782-2137

BENDER, VIRGINIA BEST, computer science educator; b. Rockford, Ill., Feb. 10, 1945; d. Oscar Sheldon and Genevieve Best; m. Robert Keith Bender, July 19, 1969; children: Victoria Ruth, Christopher Keith. BS in Chemistry, Math., No. Ill. U., 1967; postgrad., U. of Ill. Coll. of Med., 1967-69; MBA, Loyola U., Chgo., 1973. Cert. computer profl. Sr. systems rep. Burroughs Corp., Chgo., 1969-73; systems analyst Marshall Field & Co., Chgo., 1973-74; project leader Fed. Home Loan Bank, Chgo., 1974-76; sr. systems analyst United Air Lines, Elk Grove Village, Ill., 1976-78; supr. Kemper Group, Long Grove, Ill., 1978-82; prof. computer info. sys., coord. computer info. sys. William Rainey Harper Coll., Palatine, Ill., 1982—; spkr. Midwest Computer Conf., DeKalb, Ill., 1988, moderator, 1991; exch. prof. Maricopa C.C., Mesa, Ariz., 1990, rsch. sabbatical, 1993; spkr. conf. info. tech. League for Innovation, Kansas City, Mo., 1995; steering com. Midwest Computer Conf., 1995—. Nation chief YMCA mother-dau. group Indian Maidens, Des Plaines, 1982-83. Named Tchr. of the Month Burroughs Corp., Chgo, 1972. Mem. Inst. Certification Computer Profls. (life), Ill. Assn. of Data Processing Instrs., No. Ill. Computer Soc., Bay Area Multimedia Coll. Consortium, No. Ill. Alumni Assn. (life). Methodist. Home: 411 W Hackberry Dr Arlington Heights IL 60004-1938 Office: William Rainey Harper Coll 1200 W Algonquin Rd Palatine IL 60067-7373

BENDICK, JEANNE LOUIS, author, illustrator; b. N.Y.C., Feb. 25, 1919; d. Louis Xerxes and Amelia Maurice (Hess) Garfunkel; m. Robert Louis Bendick, Nov. 24, 1940; children—Robert Louis, Jr., Karen Bendick Watson Holton. B.A., Parsons/New Sch., 1939. Author: (children's sci. books): Mathematics Illustrated Dictionary, How Much and How Many Egyptian Tombs (Tombs of the Ancient Americas), Eureka Series; Caves; Markets; (with Glenn Blough) Nature Sci. Series; author Sci. Experiences series, The First Books of series (space travel; satellites; automobiles, also others); author, co-author edn. materials: textbooks Ginn Sci. Program, multimedia programs, Starting Points, Learning Experiences, You and Me and Our World; author filmstrips: The Seasons; story editor, writer NBC children's series The First Look for TV. Recipient several Best Sci. Books of Yr. awards. Mem. Nat. Sci. Tchrs. Assn., ALA, Authors League, Authors Guild, Writers Guild of Am. East. Jewish.

BEN-DOR, GISÉLE, conductor; b. Montevideo, Uruguay; married; 2 children. Student, Acad. of Music, Tel Aviv, Yale Sch. of Music. Music dir. Annapolis Symphony, Md., Pro Arte Chamber Orch. of Boston, Santa Barbara Symphony, Calif.; resident condr. Houston Symphony; guest condr. N.Y. Philharm., 1993, 95, Israel Philharm., 1991. Recs. with London Symphony, Israel Chamber Orch. Office: Santa Barbara Symphony Orch Arlington Theatre 1900 State St Ste G Santa Barbara CA 93101-2429

BENEDICT, CATHLEEN MARY, elementary school educator; b. Jersey City, Oct. 7, 1960; d. James Lawrence and Margret Mary (Cullen) B. BA, Coll. of St. Elizabeth, 1983. Cert. tchr. pre. sch., elem., spl. edn.; cert. lang. proficiency in Spanish., N.J. Tchr. Our Lady of Mercy Sch., Whippany, N.J., 1983-89, Riverview Elem. Sch., Denville, N.J., 1989—; tchr. rep. pupil assistance com., Riverview Sch., Denville, N.J., 1993—, Denville Curriculum Coun., 1993-94. Recipient Gov.'s Tchr. Recognition award, N.J. State Dept. of Edn., Princeton, 1994; cert. accomplishment Nat. Assn. Elem. Sch. Prins., Trenton, 1994. Mem. NEA, N.J. Edn. Assn., Denville Edn. Assn. Home: 52 Oakwood Vlg Apt 6 Flanders NJ 07836-8921 Office: Riverview Elem Sch 33 Saint Marys Pl Denville NJ 07834-2122

BENEDICT, LINDA SHERK, insurance company executive; b. Hartford, Conn., Jan. 25, 1945; d. Robert William and Marjorie Joan (Drysdale) Sherk; m. Geoffrey Clinton Benedict, Sept. 13, 1969 (div. 1981). AB in Social Psychology magna cum laude, Harvard U., 1967; MBA in Fin., U. Conn., 1980; postgrad., Harvard Bus. Sch., 1991. CLU, 1981. Analyst market rsch. Polaroid Corp., Cambridge, Mass., 1967-70, Transaction Tech., Cambridge, 1970-72; mgr. market rsch. Ocean Spray Cranberries, Hanson, Mass., 1972-76; with Conn. Gen. Life, Bloomfield, 1976-86, regional v.p. claims, 1983-86; with Blue Cross Blue Shield of Md., Balt., 1986-93, v.p., gen. mgr. individual market divsn., 1986-92; chair Sterling Health Svcs., Inc., 1988-93, v.p. consumer svcs. medicare and individual market, 1992, sr. v.p. ins. bus., 1992-93; v.p., gen. mgr. sr. markets Trigon Blue Cross Blue Shield, Roanoke, Va., 1994—. Campaign chmn. Blue Cross United Way, Balt., 1987, Roanoke, 1995; bd. dirs. S.W. Va. Health Sys. Agy., 1995—, Columbia Freestate Health Sys., Balt., 1987-93; fin. com., exec. com., treas., 1st v.p., chmn. fin. com. Meals on Wheels, 1987-94; active Lit. Vols., Hartford, 1985-86, bd. dirs., 1984-86; participant The Leadership Greater Balt. Com., 1990. NSF grantee, 1966-67; Disting. scholar Wall St. Jour. U. Conn., 1980. Mem. Am. Mgmt. Assn., C. of C. Bloomfield (pres. 1977-79). Home: 5936 Saddleridge Rd Roanoke VA 24018-4628

BENEDICT, MARGARET ROSE (PEGGY BENEDICT), English language and speech educator; b. Sheridan, Wyo., Jan. 4, 1948; d. Francis William and Carlotta Hamilton (Whitney) B.; m. Robert Morrell Dorsey, June 26, 1994. BA, U. No. Colo., 1970; Masters, U. Colo., 1978. Master cert. tchr., Colo. Comms. specialist Union Oil of Calif., L.A., 1970-72; tchr. English and drama Pacific Palisades (Calif.) Sch., 1972-74; tchr. English John Dewy Jr. H.S., Thornton, Colo., 1974-75, Highland H.S., Thornton, 1975-79; tchr. speech/debate, asst. coach speech team Cherry Creek H.S., Englewood, Colo., 1980-90, head coach debate team and forensics team, 1992—. Sec., bd. dirs. Nat. Abortion Rights Action League, 1991—; head coach state champion debate team, Colo., 1982—; asst. forensics coach nat. champion team, 1992. Head coach state champion debate team, Colo., 1982—; asst. forensics coach nat. champion team, 1992. Mem. NOW, NEA, Nat. Coun. Tchrs. English, Nat. Forensics League (One Diamond Coach award 1993), Colo. Edn. Assn. (state rep. 1972—), Colo. Lang. Arts Soc., Mapleton Edn. Assn. (pres. 1974-76), Cherry Creek Tchrs. Assn. (faculty rep. 1979—), Phi Delta Kappa. Democrat. Episcopalian. Home: 730 Humboldt St Denver CO 80218-3512 Office: Cherry Creek Schs 9300 E Union Ave Englewood CO 80111-1306

BENEDICT, MARY ELLEN, economics educator; b. Pitts., Jan. 31, 1953; d. Raymond D. Burchill and Gertrude B. Walzer; m. Louis M. Benedict, Sept. 16, 1978. BA, Waynesburg Coll., 1974; MS, Carnegie Mellon U., 1985, PhD, 1991. Asst. apt. mgr. Highland House, Pitts., 1975-76; employment svc. interviewer Pa. Dept. of Employment Svc., Pitts., 1976-82; instr. Heinz Sch. Pub. Policy & Mgmt., Carnegie Mellon U., Pitts., 1985-87, coord. teaching asst. program, 1987-89, adj. prof., 1990-91; asst. prof. dept. econs. Bowling Green (Ohio) State U., 1991—; instr. Heinz Sch. Pub. Policy & Mgmt., Carnegie-Mellon U., Pitts., summers 1984-85, adj. prof., summers 1993-95, alumni exec. bd., 1988—, vice-chair, 1994—; presenter in field. Contbr. articles to profl. jours. Active Neighborhood Assn., Etna, Pa., 1990-91, Wood County Humane Soc., Bowling Green, 1994—, Animal Friends, Pitts. Faculty Rsch. grantee Bowling Green State U., 1992-93, Gibs grantee, 1995, Coll. Summer Rsch. grantee, 1992, 95; Mellon U. fellow, 1985-86; recipient Quantitative Skills Summer Inst. Tchg. Excellence award, 1984, Alumni Clan Svc. award, 1994. Mem. Am. Econ. Assn., Midwestern Econ. Assn., Western Econ. Assn., Com. on Status of Women in Econ. Professions. Office: Bowling Green State U Dept of Econs Bowling Green OH 43403

BENEDICT, THERESA MARIE, secondary education mathematics educator; b. East Rutherford, N.J., Feb. 6, 1939; d. Michael and Rosaria Trivigno; m. Willliam F. Benedict, Oct. 3, 1964' children: Gerard Michael, Willliam Francis. BS in Edn., Seton Hall U., 1978; MA in Adminstrn., Jersey City State Coll., 1989. Math tchr. Wayne (N.J.) Hills High Sch., 1978-79, Ramsey (N.J.) High Sch., 1980, Lakeland Regional High Sch., Wanaque, N.J., 1980—; advisor Vol. in Edn., Passaic County, N.J., 1986-89, Student Asst. Team, Lakeland High Sch., Wanaque, N.J., 1990—; coord. student/tchr. lunch program for at-risk students, 1991—. Leader 4-H Clubs, Wayne, N.J., 1975-88; advisor Parish Ch. Coun., Wayne, n.J., 1989—; church eucharistic minister, 1986—. Mem. Assn. Math. Tchrs. N.J., Nat. Tchrs. of Math., ASCD. Roman Catholic. Home: 45 Brandywine Rd Wayne NJ 07470

BENEDIS, SHEILA MEYER, sculptor; b. Norwich, Conn., June 5, 1936; d. Maurice William and Tessie Y. Meyer; m. Howard Benedis, Sept. 1969; 1 child, Greg. BA, Mt. Holyoke Coll., 1958; MS, Pace U., 1987. judge Westchester County Womens Clubs, Pocantico, N.Y., 1996; lectr. in field. One-woman shows include Interchurch Ctr., N.Y.C., 1996; exhibited in group shows at Castle Gallery, 1993, 95, Gallery of Hastings, N.Y., 1993, 95, Corvallis (Orreg.) Ctr., 1994, Paramount Ctr., Peekskill, N.Y., 1994, Arka Gallery, Vilnius, Lithuania, 1994, Interchurch Ctr., 1994, Neuberger Mus., Purchase, N.Y., 1994, 95, Pace U., Pleasantville, N.Y., 1995; represented in permanent collections at Neuberger Mus., 1995, Mus. Applied Arts, 1994. Recipient Internat. award Women in Design, 1983, Purchase award Channel 13 Art Auction, 1984; program on her work TCI Cable, 1996. Home and Office: 22 Forest Ave Hastings On Hudson NY 10706

BENENSON, ESTHER SIEV (MRS. WILLIAM BENENSON), nursing home administrator, gerontologist; b. Jerusalem (parents Am. citizens); d. Joshua and Anna (Sanders) Siev; B.S., Hunter Coll., 1972, M.S., 1974; M.Ed., Tchrs. Coll., Columbia U., 1976, Ed.D. in Gerontology, 1981; m. William Benenson, Sept. 15, 1957; children: Michael J., Sharon G., Amy L., Blanche S. Exec. dir. Flushing (N.Y.) Manor Nursing Home, 1959—, Flushing Manor Care Center, 1974—. Registered nurse. Adj. assoc. prof. C.W. Post Coll., L.I. U., 1972-77, also mem. adv. bd., dept. health care and public adminstrn.; mem. Bd. Examiners Licensing Nursing Home Adminstrs. N.Y. State, 1970-74; adv. council N.Y. State Health Planning Commn., 1974; bd. dirs. Health Systems Agy. of N.Y.C., 1994-96, 1st v.p. Queensboro Council Social Welfare. Fellow Am. Coll. Health Care Adminstrs., Am. Acad. Med. Adminstrs., Royal Soc. Health; mem. APHA, Soc. Public Health Educators, Gerontol. Soc., Soc. N.Y. State Health Facilities Assn. Inc., Greater N.Y. Health Care Facilities Assn.

BENÉT, CARMEN RENEE, chemical engineer; b. Jackson, Miss., Feb. 16, 1968; d. Richard Ward and Helen Vail (Curry) B.; m. Douglas Nelson Andree Jr., Jan. 18, 1985 (div. Jan. 1987); 1 child, Rebecca Renee. BSChemE, U. Md., Balt., 1992. Assoc. quality control supr. Davison divsn. W. R. Grace, Balt., 1990-92; engr. Hershey (Pa.) Chocolate, N.A., 1992—. Mem. AIChE (sec. 1993-96). Republican. Office: Hershey Chocolate NA 1025 Reese Ave Hershey PA 17033

BENGTSON, BETTY GRIMES, library administrator; b. Milledgeville, Ga., June 22, 1940; d. Lodrick Livingston and Nancy Rachel (Clack) G.; m. Peter Yeager Bengtson, Aug. 4, 1962; 1 child, David Eric. BA, Duke U., 1962; MLS, Cath. U., 1967; M Gen. Adminstrn., U. Md., 1986. Asst. catalog libr. Macalester Coll. Libr., St. Paul, 1967-68; cataloger Notre Dame Coll. Libr., Belmont, Calif., 1968-72; cataloger Georgetown U. Libr., Washington, 1972-74, asst. acquisitions libr., 1974-75, head cataloging dept., 1975-82; assoc. dir. tech. svcs. U. Tenn. Libr., Knoxville, 1982-88; assoc. dir. bibliog. control U. Wash. Libr., Seattle, 1988-90; dir. librs. U. Wash., Seattle, 1990—. Editor: Classification of Library Materials, 1990. Mem. ALA, Assn. for Coll. and Rsch. Librs., Libr. and Info. Tech. Assn. (bd. dirs. 1994—), Commn. Preservation and Access (bd. dirs. 1993—), Online Computer Libr. Ctr. Users Coun. (pres. 1990-91), Wash. Libr. Assn., Seminars on Acad. Computing (bd. dirs. 1993—), Assn. Rsch. Libs. (bd. dirs. 1995—). Office: U Wash Allen Libr Box 352900 Seattle WA 98195

BENHAM, LELIA, small business owner, social/political activist; b. Cartersville, Ga., July 15, 1945; d. Emory and Nellie Pearl (Carson) Benham; m. Larry L. Mabins, Jan. 15, 1966 (div. 1970); children: Gary K., Margo L., Berrie E. Student, North Cen. Tech. Coll., Mansfield, Ohio, 1981-83, 91—, Mansfield Bus. Coll., 1964-66, 84-85. Bookkeeper/sec. M-R-M Cmty. Action Program, 1970-72; with The Tappan Co., 1972-81; sec./bookkeeper daycare ctr. Mansfield Opportunities Industrialization Ctr., 1983-84; office svcs. contractor FSC Ednl., Inc., Mansfield, 1988-89; sales asst. Hill's Dept. Store, Mansfield, 1988-90; pres./dir. Benham & Co., Mansfield, 1988—; ind. sales distbr. Shaklee Products, 1985-86; home health habilitation aide, waiver/supportive living provider Ohio Dept. Mental Retardation and Developmentally Disabled, 1992—, Richland Newhope Ctr., Mansfield, 1992—; nurse asst. Mansfield Meml. Geriatric Ctr., 1994; nat. and internat. cons. in field. Editor Richland NOW News, 1985-87, 91-92. Cand. Mansfield Sch. Bd. and City Coun., 1987, 89, 91; founding mem. adv. bd., bd. dirs. Litter Prevention and Recycling/KAB (Mid-Ohio Clean Scene), 1982-96; v.p., founding treas. Sister Cities Assn., Mansfield, 1986-94; active various charitable orgns.; mem. Ohio Women Inc.; bd. dirs. Canton Regional Transit Authority, 1989-96, Cleve. Sch. Bd., 1989-93, Ohio Dept. Adminstrv. Svcs. Minority Bus. Enterprise, 1989-96, others; adv. bd. mem. Keep Yourself Alive, 1992, 93. Recipient 10 billboard advt. awards Cleve. Regional Transit Authority Community Minority Taskforce, 1991, Keeper of the Flame Proclamation award Ohio Sec. of State, 1990, award AFrican Am. Women Agenda of Ohio,. 1991, others. Mem. NOW (Richland County founder, pres. 1985-96, Scholarship award 1987, task force chair state bd. racial and ethnic diversity 1993—), NAACP (Ohio rep. to state orgns. 1989—, Pres.'s award 1982, Cmty. award 1988). Democrat. Ch. of God in Christ. Home and Office: Benham & Co 166 Western Ave Mansfield OH 44906

BENHAM, PRISCILLA CARLA, religion educator, college president; b. Berkeley, Calif., Jan. 30, 1950; d. Carl Thomas and Bebe (Harrison) Patten; m. Donald W. Benham, Mar. 30, 1986; 1 child, Charmaine P. Benham. BS summa cum laude, Patten Coll., 1969; BA in Psychology, Coll. Holy Names, 1971; MA in New Testament with honors, Wheaton Coll., 1972; PhD in New Testament, Drew U., 1976. Prof. New Testament Patten Coll., Oakland, Calif., 1975—, pres., 1983—; v.p. Christian Evang. Chs. Am., Oakland, 1989—; co-pastor Christian Cathedral, Oakland, 1964—; co-founder Christian Cathedral Chorale, Oakland, 1975—; tree planting participant David Ben Gurion Forest, Israel, 1975. Co-author: Before the Times, 1989, The World of the Early Church, 1991; mem. editorial bd. Pentecostal Theology; contbr. articles to profl. jours. Violinist Redwood Symphony. Mem. AAUP, Am. Assn. Higher Edn., Am. Assn. Pres. Ind. Colls. and Univs. (bd. dirs.), Am. Coun. Edn., Assn. Ind. Calif. Colls. and Univs., Soc. Bibl. Lit., Am. Acad. Religion, Bar-Ilan Assn. of the Greater Bay Area, Western Coll. Assn. Pres. Small Ind. Colls., Regional Assn. East Bay Colls. and Univs. (mem. at-large exec. com.), Oakland C. of C., Nat. Assn. Intercollegiate Athletics, Rotary of Oakland, Phi Delta Kappa. Office: Patten Coll 2433 Coolidge Ave Oakland CA 94601-2630

BENING, ANNETTE, actress; b. Topeka, May 29, 1958; m. Steven White (div.); m. Warren Beatty, 1992; children: Kathlyn Bening Beatty, Benjamin Beatty. Student, Mesa Coll.; theatre degree, San Francisco State U.; studied at, Am. Conservatory Theatre. Films include The Great Outdoors, 1988, Valmont, 1989, The Grifters, 1990 (Acad. award nomination best supporting actress 1990), Postcards from the Edge, 1990, Guilty by Suspicion, 1991, Regarding Henry, 1991, Bugsy, 1991, Love Affair, 1994, Richard III, 1995, The American President, 1995, Mars Attacks!, 1996; stage appearances Coastal Disturbances, 1986, (Tony award nomination 1986, Clarence Derwin award 1987, Theatre World award 1987), Spoils of War, 1988; TV movies Manhunt for Claude Dallas, 1986, Hostage, 1988. Office: care CAA 9830 Wilshire Blvd Beverly Hills CA 90212-1804*

BENITEZ, SYLVIA MARIA, artist; b. Balt., June 27, 1957; d. Eugene E. Benitez and Betty Stewart. BFA, U. Md., 1979; postgrad., Manhattan Graphics Ctr., 1992, Greenwich House Pottery, 1994-95. sculpture workshop leader, 1992. One-woman exhbns. include Tompkins Squ. Libr., N.Y.C., 1982, Johns Hopkins U., 1986, Howard County C.C. Gallery, 1987, Madeira Sch. Gallery, Mc Lean, Va., 1987, Columbia (Md.) Assn. Arts, 1988, Cardinal Gallery, Annapolis, Md., 1990, Villa Julie Coll., Balt., 1991; group exhbns. include Kentler Internat. Drawing Ctr., Bklyn., 1993, Artist Talk on Art, N.Y.C., 1993, Kingsborough C.C., Bklyn., 1993, 96, One Main, Bklyn., 1993, Socrates Sculpture Pk., Long Island City, N.Y., 1993, Empire Fulton Ferry Sculpture Pk., 1993, Deutche Bank, N.Y.C., Look Out Sculpture Pk., Damascus, 1994, Embarcadero Ctr., San Francisco, 1994, Metro Regional Ctr., Portland, Oreg., 1994, Transmission Gallery, Scotland, 1994, Gallery One Twenty Eight, N.Y.C., 1995, Howard County Ctr. Arts Gallery, 1995, Pier Show, Bklyn., 1995, Alternative Authoring Strategies, N.Y.C., 1996; murals painted at Pocomoke (Md.) H.S., 1988, Rock Creek Elem. Sch., Silver Spring, Md., 1991, Howard Career Ctr., Wilmington, Del., 1993, Steven Decatur Sch., Clinton, Md., 1993, St. Catherines of Siena Sch., Wilmington, 1994, Lefferts Homestead, Bklyn., 1994, Thurmont Mid. Sch., 1996. Home: 165 Hicks St Brooklyn NY 11201

BENJAMIN, ADELAIDE WISDOM, community volunteer and activist; b. New Orleans, Aug. 23, 1932; d. William Bell and Mary (Freeman) Wisdom; m. Edward Bernard Benjamin Jr., May 11, 1957; children: Edward Wisdom, Mary Dabney, Ann Leith, Stuart Minor. Student, Hollins Coll., 1950-52; BA in English, Newcomb Coll., 1954; JD, Tulane U., 1956; student, Loyola U., New Orleans, 1980-81; grad. extension program Sewanee Theol. Sch., U. South, 1982. Assoc. Wisdom, Stone, Pigman and Benjamin, New Orleans, 1956-58; tchr. ext. courses Tulane U., 1984—; postgrad.; speaker, panelist on school issues various local and nat. groups. Mem. Tulane Law Rev., 1954-56. Pres. bd. New Orleans Symphony, 1984-89; trustee, Mary Freeman Wisdom Charitable Found., sec., 1987-92, pres., 1990-94, treas., 1994—; pres. E&A Charitable Found., New Orleans, 1983—; bd. dirs. Nat. Symphony Orch., Washington, 1992—, RosaMary Charitable Found., New Orleans, 1978—, Loyola Univ., New Orleans, 1989—, mem. exec. com., 1996—, La. Mus. Found. Bd., New Orleans, 1989—, exec. com., 1991—, Children's Hosp., New Orleans, 1976-79, Southeast La. Girl Scouts Coun., New Orleans, 1989—, Louise S. McGehee Sch., New Orleans, 1990—, v.p., 1991—, La. Nature and Sci. Ctr., New Orleans, 1992—, Newcomb Children's Ctr., New Orleans, 1991-94, New Orleans Mus. Art Fellows Forum, 1991—; mem. adv. bd. dept. psychiatry LSU Med. Ctr., 1992—; active Trinity Episc. Ch., New Orleans, sec. parish coun., 1973-75, sec. vestry, 1975-79, leader Trinity Quartet, 1979-84; local YWCA, 1967-75, 76-79, sec. bd. dirs., 1967-68, 1st v.p., 1968-69; trustee Metairie Park Country Day Sch., 1971-79, sec., 1976-79, pres. PTA, 1975-76; mem. Loving Cup selection com. New Orleans Times Picayune, 1985, Bur. Govtl. Rsch.; adv. bd. Pub. Radio Sta. WWNO, 1980—; bd. dirs Parenting Ctr., 1981—, chmn. by-laws com., 1983-84, chmn. pers. com., 1982-83; adv. bd Tulane Summer Lyric Theatre, Tulane U., 1972—, pres. adv. bd., 1977-79. Recipient Weiss Brotherhood award Nat. Conf. Christians and Jews, 1986, Outstanding Philanthropist, Nat. Soc. Fundraising Execs., 1986, Volunteer Activist Award, St. Elizabeth Guild, 1986, Jr. League Sustainer award, 1987, Disting. Alumna award McGehee Sch., 1987, George Washington Honor Medal for Individual Achievement, Freedom Found. at Valley Forge, 1988, Living and Giving award Juvenile Diabetes Found. 1991, Outstanding Citizen New Orleans award La. Colonials, 1994, Jacques Yenni award Outstanding Community Svc. Sch. Bus. Adminstrn. Loyola Univ., 1994, Integritas Vita award for outstanding cmty. svc. Loyola U., 1994; named Goodwill Ambassador for Louisiana Gov.'s Commn. Internat. Trade, Industry and Tourism, 1987, Sweet Art, Contemporary Arts Ctr., 1988, Significant Role Model, Young Leadership Coun., 1988, Woman of Distinction S.E. La. Girl Scout Coun., 1992. Mem. ABA, LWV, La. Bar Assn., New Orleans Bar Assn., Jr. League New Orléans (exec. com. 1971-72, bd. dirs. 1967-72), Ind. Women's Orgn., Com. 21, Am. Symphony Orch. League, Quarante Club (2d v.p. 1978-79), Sybarites Club, Debutante Club, Le Debut des Jeunes Filles Club, New Orleans Town Gardners (pres. 1979-80), Thomas Wolfe Soc. (life mem.). Home: 1837 Palmer Ave New Orleans LA 70118-6215

BENJAMIN, DEBORAH ANN, English language educator; b. New Britain, Conn., Jan. 10, 1953; d. William Newton and Barbara Jane (Tuttle) B. BA in Secondary Edn.-English, U. Conn., 1975; MS in Counseling, Ctrl. Conn. State Coll., New Britain, 1981. Cert. tchr. English 7-12. Tchr. Southington (Conn.) Bd. Edn., Southington H.S., 1976—; yearbook advisor Southington H.S., 1977-88; advisor Writers' Club/Lit. Mag., Southington, 1985—; corrective action team leader Quality Plus, Southington H.S., 1992—. Author: (booklet) My Backyard Kingdom, 1988. Music leader/dir. Southington Ward/Primary, 1989-92, pres., 1992-94; pres. Hartford Conn. Stake Primary, Bloomfield, 1994—; mem. Friends of New Britain Mus. Am. Art, 1982—. Recipient Cert. of Appreciation Conn. State Assembly, 1979. Mem. Nat. Coun. Tchrs. English, Conn. Coun. Tchrs. English, Conn. Poetry Soc. Mem. Latter-day Saints Ch. Office: Southington HS 720 Pleasant St Southington CT 06489-2713

BENJAMIN, EILEEN H., photographer; b. San Francisco, Nov. 18, 1945; d. Oswald and Helen (Torres) Basora; m. Norman L. Benjamin, Jan. 20, 1979; 1 child, Victor E. Elliot III. AA, Foothill Coll., 1966; BSBA, Coll. Notre Dame, 1978. Statistician Lockheed, Sunnyvale, Calif., 1970-72, adminstrv. asst., 1972-76, project coord. environ. test, 1976-78, project analyst, coord., 1978-81; freelance photographer Calabasas, Calif., 1983-85; pvt. practice photography Telluride, Colo., 1987—. Exhbns. include Durango Termar Gallery, 1988, Telluride Art Festival, 1988, 89, 90, Aspen Mus., 1989, Cheyenne Old West Mus., 1989, Aspen Hill Gallery Photography, 1990, Cherry Creek Art Festival, U.S. Embassy, Spain, 1991-92, Vail Art Festival, 1992, Dallas 500 Art Festival, 1993-96, Telluride Golden West Gallery, 1993, Denver Mus. Natural History, 1994, Chicago Old Town Art Festival, 1994-96, Main St. Art Festival, Ft. Worth, 1995, Columbus Art Festival, 1995, Sedona Art Festival and Photograpjy, 1995-96, and many others; contbr. photographs to profl. jours. County coord. Perot Campaign, Telluride, 1992. Mem. Nat. Mus. Women in Arts, Telluride Coun. for Arts & Humanities, Nat. Mus. Am. Indians, Telluride Hist. Mus., Buffalo Bill Histr. Ctr., Friends of Photography. Republican. Roman Catholic. Home and Office: PO Box 1445 Telluride CO 81435

BENJAMIN, KATHRYN MARY, mathematics educator; b. Newport News, Va., June 2, 1954; d. John Riley and Caryl (Smadbeck) Phillips; m. William Warren Holden, July 9, 1972 (div. Nov. 1978); 1 child, William J. T. Holden; m. Franklin Ross Benjamin, July 12, 1985; 1 child, Laura K. Benjamin. AA with distinction, Suffolk County C.C., 1983; BA magna cum laude, Hofstra U., 1984, MA with distinction, 1989. Tech. asst., math. ctr. Nassau C.C., Garden City, N.Y., 1984-88; adj. instr. math. Hofstra U., Hempstead, N.Y., 1985-88; asst. prof. math. Suffolk County C.C., Brentwood, N.Y., 1989—; sec. exec. com. Acad. Assembly of Suffolk County C.C. West, 1993—, adv. Western Student Press, 1994—. Recipient Chancellor's award for excellence in tchg., SUNY, 1995, Cert. of Merit, Suffolk County Legislature, 1995. fem. NOW, AAUW, Math. Assn. of Am., Planned Parenthood Fedn., N.Y. State Math. Assn. of Two Yr. Colls., Phi Beta Kappa, Phi Theta Kappa (v.p. 1982). Democrat. Office: Suffolk County Cmty Coll Crooked Hill Rd Brentwood NY 11717

BENJAMIN, MAIRA MERCEDES, software engineer; b. Bklyn., Aug. 27, 1959; d. Reynaldo Mario and Gloria (Moronta) B. BA in Stats., U. Calif., Berkeley, 1983. Reliability engr. Xerox/DiabloSystems, Inc., Fremont, Calif., 1983-84; software engr. Ask Computer Systems, Inc., Los Altos, Calif., 1984-89, Sybase, Inc., Emeryville, Calif., 1989-93, Computerware Corp., Alameda, Calif., 1993-95, Sybase Inc., Emeryville, Calif., 1995—. Vol. Project Literacy, Oakland, 1986, Jesse Jackson for Pres. campaign, Berkeley, 1984. Mem. Nat. Assn. Female Execs., Am. Statis. Assn., Am. Prodn. Inventory and Control Soc., Am. Soc. for Quality Control. Democrat. Clubs: Toastmasters (charter pres. 1985-86) (Los Altos, Calif.); Commonwealth (San Francisco). Office: Sybase Inc 6475 Christie Ave Emeryville CA 94608-1010

BENJAMIN, ROSEMARY, real estate broker; b. N.Y.C., Jan. 1, 1947; d. Bracy and Emma Louise (Aultman) Wills; m. Eugene W. Benjamin, Apr. 11, 1971; children: Kandy, Tia L., Genélle. BS in orgnl. mgmt., Nyack Coll., 1996. Lic. real estate saleswoman nd broker, N.Y.; commd. notary; cert. real estate appraiser. Paralegal law firm, Suffern, N.Y., 1988-95; broker, owner Campagne Lifesstyle Realty, Suffern, 1991—; asst. to dir. Abbott House Therapeutic, foster boarding home program, Irvington, N.Y., 1995—. Mem. Coalition for Battered Women, N.Y.C., 1978-80; bd. dirs. L.I.V.E. (Let Incest Victims Emerge), Rockland, N.Y., 1980-85, Queens County Mental Health Soc., 1982-85; sec. Rockland County Legislature's Office, New City, N.Y., 1993-94. Democrat. Roman Catholic. Home: 48 Springbrook Rd Nanuet NY 10954 Office: Campagne Lifestyle Realty 2 Executive Blvd Ste 201 Suffern NY 10901

BENJAMIN, SHEILA PAULETTA, secondary education educator; b. Sept. 28, 1948. AA, Montreat-Anderson Coll., 1966; BA in History, Belhaven Coll., 1968; MEd in History, U. Tampa, 1979. Cert. gifted, social studies and bible tchr. Tchr. Hillsborough H.S., Tampa, Fla., 1980-93; now tchr. Bloomingdale H.S., Valrico, Fla.; clinician tchr. Suncoast Area Tchr. Tng. Honors Program; supervising tchr. Fla. Beginning Tchr. Program; dir. workshops in field. Aviation educator USAF-CAP; vol. Nat. Pks. Svc. 99s-Internat. Women's Pilot Assn. Recipient Photography awards Fla. Strawberry Festival and Hillsborough County Fair; Latin Am. Studies grantee NEH, 1983, African Studies, 1985; Fulbright-Hays scholar in Egypt, 1986, Honduras, 1993. Mem. ASCD, DAR, Nat. Space Soc., Nat. Coun. Social Studies, World Aerospace Edn. Orgn. (U.S. del., Amman, Jordan), Gulf Coast Archeol. Soc., Fla. Alliance for Geography, Fla. Aerospace Edn. Assn. (founding pres.), Fla. Anthrop. Soc. (bd. dirs., Appreciation award, Preservation award), Men of Menendez (Historic Fla. Militia Inc.), Mid. East Educators Network, Hillsborough Classroom Tchr. Assn. (NEA), Hillsborough County/Fla. Social Studies Coun., Young Astronauts, Bibl. Archeol. Soc., Challenger Ctr. Found. (founding sponsor), Fulbright Alumni Asns., Sun-N-Fun EAA, Phi Delta Kappa. Home: 605 Fieldstone Dr Brandon FL 33511-7936 Office: Bloomingdale High Sch 1700 E Bloomingdale Ave Valarico FL 38594

BENJAMIN, SUSAN SELTON, elementary school educator; b. N.Y.C., June 3, 1946; m. Robert F. Benjamin, Nov. 30, 1968; children: Joshua, Alana. BS, Cornell U., 1968; MEd, Tufts U., 1969. Tchr. Wakefield (Mass.) Schs., 1969-73, Los Alamos (N.Mex.) Schs., 1973—; resource tchr. Montessori Sch. House, San Diego, 1986; tchr. U. N.Mex., Los Alamos, 1989, 90; cons. Activities Integrating Math. and Sci. (AIMS) Nat. Leadership, Fresno, Calif., 1992—. Chair leadership Hadassah, Los Alamos, 1991—. Named Outstanding Women of N.Mex., 1980; recipient Presdl. award for excellence in math. tchg. N.Mex. State, 1990, 92, Leadership award Hadassah, 1996. Mem. Nat. Coun. Math. Tchrs. Home: 315 Rover Blvd Los Alamos NM 87544

BENKERT-MILLER, STACEY ANN, elementary school educator; b. St. Louis, Mar. 28, 1964; d. Oliver Frank and Margaret Hildegard (Brabec) Benkert. BS in Elem. Edn., U. Mo., St Louis, 1993; M in Elem. Edn., Nat.-Louis U., 1995. Savings supr. Comty. Fed. Savings & Loan, St. Louis, Mo., 1982-90; office sec. Amusement Concepts, Inc., Arnold, Mo., 1990-92; cheerleading sponsor Melville Sch. Dist. Oakville H.S., St. Louis, 1991-93; 2nd grade tchr. Fox C-6 Sch. Dist., Arnold, 1993—; student tchr. Melville Sch. Dist., St Louis, Fox C-6 Sch. Dist., Arnold, Mo., 1992; tchr. U. Mo. Sat. Acad., St. Louis, 1992. Mem. NEA. Home: 841 Barnsley Dr Saint Louis MO 63125 Address: 921 Reed Ave Saint Louis MO 63125

BENLON, LISA L., state legislator; b. July 9, 1953; m. Randal, July 9, 1953; 2 children. Student, Johnson County C.C. Councilman City of Shawnee, 1988-91; rep. dist. 17 State of Kans., 1991—; mgr. acctg. office. Home: 7303 Earnshaw St Shawnee KS 66216-3505 Office: Kans Ho of Reps State Capitol Topeka KS 66612

BENNATON, CATHERINE GENEVIEVE, graphic designer, fine artist; b. Burbank, Calif., Feb. 19, 1952; d. Carlos Alberto and Anna Kathleen (Spencer) B.; m. Cory Sewelson, May 30, 1985. AA in Fine Art, L.A. Valley Calif., 1972; BA in Fine Art, Calif. State U., Northridge, 1975. Clerk Valley News and Greensheet, Van Nuys, Calif., 1974-75; sr. designer Daily News, Van Nuys, 1976-87; design coord. L.A. Times, 1987-93; artist representation Fresh Paint and Lonny Gans and Assocs., L.A., 1983-84. Exhbns. include Double Rocking "G" Gallery, 1982, Antelope Valley Coll. Gallery, Lancaster, Calif., 1983, L.A. Artcore, 1983, Calif. State U. at Northridge, 1984, Gallery West, L.A., 1985, El Camino Coll. Art Gallery, Torrance, Calif., 1985, Orlando Gallery, Sherman Oaks, Calif., 1986, Carnegie Art Mus., Ventura, Calif., 1987, Christopher/John Gallery, Santa Monica, 1990, Long Beach (Calif.) Arts Gallery, 1995, The Park Ave. Armory, N.Y.C., 1995. Recipient Nat. Co-op Adv. award, Calif. Newspaper Assn., 1992. Mem. L.A. County Mus. of Art, Mus. of Contemporary Art. Democrat.

BENNER, MARY WRIGHT, marketing professional; b. Chgo., Aug. 4, 1956; d. Robert V.L. and Sara Helen (Beeler) W.; m. Thomas G. Benner, Aug. 8, 1987; children: Sara Eleanor, Robert Fox. BA, Conn. Coll., 1979; MBA, Columbia U., 1983. Rsch. assoc. Acad. for Contemporary Problems, Washington, 1979-81; rating specialist Standard & Poor's, N.Y.C., 1983-84; asst. adminstr. Twp. of Princeton, N.J., 1984-86; v.p. Fin. Guaranty Ins. Co., N.Y.C., 1986—. Mem. Pub. Works Forum (bd. dirs. 1986-88), Assn. for Govtl. Leasing and Fin. (bd. dirs. 1991-95, treas. 1994-95). Methodist. Home: 33 Sommer Ave Maplewood NJ 07040-3127 Office: Fin Guaranty Ins Co 115 Broadway New York NY 10006-1604

BENNETT, ALMA JEAN, theater educator; b. Iaeger, W.Va., July 30, 1941; d. Charles Henry and Retha Alma (Shrewsbury) Muncy; m. Paul Andrew Bennett, June 15, 1963; 1 child, Jason Andrew. BS in Edn., W.Va. U., 1963, MA in Drama, 1969; PhD in Theater, Kent State U., 1992. Tchr. pub. schs. W.Va. and Ohio, 1963-69; instr. speech dept. W.Va. U., Morgantown, 1970-72; instr., costume designer speech/drama dept. Ea. Ky. U., Richmond, 1969-70; tchr. h.s. Barbour County Bd. of Edn., Philippi, W.Va., 1977-81; prof. speech/theater Alderson-Broaddus Coll., Philippi, 1981—; adjudicator Am. Coll. Theater Festival, Buckhannon, W.Va., 1991, W.Va. Comty. Theater Festival, Morgantown, 1995; advisor Peer Assistance Network, W.Va. Dept. Culture and History, Charleston, W.Va., 1995—; pres. W.Va. U. Theater Alumni Bd., Morgantown, 1995—. Contbr. book revs., articles, essays to profl. publs. Univ. fellow for rsch. Kent State U., 1991; faculty devel. grantee Appalachian Coll. Assn. Inc., 1996. Mem. Popular Culture Assn. (nat. chair 1992—), Assn. for Theater in Higher Edn., W.Va. Theater Conf., Barbour County Arts and Humanities Coun. (past pres., v.p. 1976—), Delta Kappa Gamma. Methodist. Office: Alderson-Broaddus Coll Box 2158 Philippi WV 26416

BENNETT, BOBBIE JEAN, state official; b. Gwinnett County, Ga., July 13, 1940; d. William Claude and Clara Maude (Nichols) Holcome; BBA magna cum laude, Ga. State U., 1973; 1 child, Terri Lynne. With Ga. State Merit System, Atlanta, 1960—, sr. acct., 1967, asst. div. dir., 1968-70, fiscal officer, 1970-74, div. dir., 1975-78, asst. dep. commr., 1978—, asst. commr., 1985—, dep. commr., 1992, commr. 1992. Mem. Ga. Fiscal Mgmt. Coun., Ga. Coun. Pers. Adminstrn., Employers Coun. Flexible Compensation (bd. dirs.), Nat. Assn. Deferred Compensation Adminstrs. (sec., past pres.), Nat. Assn. State Pers. Execs. (pres.), Ga. Govt. Benefit Assn., Atlanta Govt. Benefit Assn., Atlanta Health Care Alliance, State and Local Govt. Benefit Assn. (past pres.), Internat. Pers. Mgmt. Assn. (past pres. Atlanta chpt.), Internat. Found. on Employee Benefits (com. mem.), Beta Gamma Sigma, Phi Kappa Phi, Beta Alpha Psi. Democrat. Home: 2072 Malabar Dr NE Atlanta GA 30345-1624 Office: State Merit System 200 Piedmont Ave SE Atlanta GA 30334-9010

BENNETT, CAROL(INE) ELISE, reporter, actress; b. New Orleans, Dec. 27, 1938; d. Gerald Clifford Graham and Edna Doris (Toennies) Kerr; m. Ralph Decker Bennett Jr., Feb. 27, 1966; children: Ralph Decker III, Katherine Elise. BA, U. B.C., Vancouver, Can., 1960; BLS, McGill U., Montreal, Que., Can., 1962. Libr. various locations, 1962-76; reporter TV/radio Washington-Ala. News Reports, Washington, 1981—. Appeared on stage Girl in My Soup, 1978; in film Prime Risk, 1984; host weekly TV program Modern Maturity, 1986-88. Vol. reader Recording for the Blind, Washington, 1985—. Mem. SAG, AFTRA, Actor's Equity, Soc. Profl. Journalists. Home: 115 Southwood Ave Silver Spring MD 20901-1918

BENNETT, CATHERINE JUNE, data processing manager, educator, consultant; b. Augusta, Ga., June 19, 1950; d. Robert Stogner and Catherine Sue (Jordan) Robinson; m. Danny Marvin Bennett, Sept. 5, 1971; children: Timothy Jordan, Robert Daniel. BS in Stats., U. Ga., 1971, MA in Bus., 1973. Programmer William M. Shenkel & Assocs., Athens, Ga., 1971-73; sys. analyst U. Ga., Athens, 1973-76; product cons. ISA/SUNGARD, Atlanta, 1976-78, project leader, 1978-80, mgr. product support, 1980-85, hotline mgr., sr. fin. specialist, 1986-88; mem. edn. staff Investment Client Support, 1988-90, mgr. investment reporting, 1990-91, mgr. reporting, 1991-93, mgr. devel., 1993-95, dir. acctg. products svcs., 1996—. Den leader pack # 419 Cub Scouts, 1989-90, treas., 1990-95; head ofcl. Duluth Thunderbolts, 1994; mem. Gwinnett Swim League (sec. 1995—). Avocations: bridge, swimming, travel. Home: 3604 Berkeley Lake Rd Duluth GA 30136-3008 Office: ISA/SUNGARD 500 Northridge Rd Atlanta GA 30350-3315

BENNETT, CATHLEEN DEMARCO, lawyer, consultant; b. N.Y.C., July 7, 1965; d. Edward James and Grace Jean (Bailey) DeMarco; m. Scott Harold Bennett, June 10, 1995. BA, Villanova (Pa.) U., 1987; JD, Dickinson Sch. Law, 1990; MGA, U. Pa., 1995. Bar: N.J. 1990, Pa. 1990. Law clk. to chief judge Appellate divsn. Superior Ct. N.J., 1990-91; assoc. Dillon, Bitar & Luther, Morristown, N.J., 1991-95; cons. Policy Studies, Inc., Denver, 1995—; cons. Delaware River Port Authority, Camden, N.J., 1995, Phila. Health Dept., 1994-95. Bd. dirs. ARC, Morristown, 1994-95; chair Young Friends of the ARC, Summit, N.J., 1992-95. Recipient Nat. Comm. award ARC, 1994; Fels scholar, U. Pa., 1994-95. Mem. ABA, N.J. Bar Assn., Nat. Child Support Enforcement Assn., N.J. Child Support Enforcement Assn., Assn. of Mgmt. Analysts in State and Local Govt. Democrat. Office: Policy Studies Inc Ste 900 999 18th St Denver CO 80202

BENNETT, DOROTHY JEAN, art educator; b. Detroit, June 10, 1950; d. George Leonard and Shirley Isabell (Heston) Dunkirk; m. James Morgan Bennett, Nov. 6, 1976; children: Alex James, Brett Dunkirk, Kelly Anne. BA, Ea. Ill. U., 1974, MA, 1980, Tchr. Cert., 1988. Draftsperson Moore Bus. Forms, Charleston, Ill., 1973-86; art tchr. Lakeland Coll., Mattoon, Ill., 1989, Crestwood Sch., Paris, Ill., 1989-94, Jefferson Sch., Charleston, Ill., 1994—; visual arts dir. Coles County Arts Coun., Charleston, 1988—; regional inst. com. Regional Supt. of Schs., Charleston, 1991-94; tchr. Ill. Art Edn. Conf. Workshops, Charleston, 1988, 91, 93, 95, 96; lectr. Nat. Art Edn. Conf., Phoenix, 1992, Houston, 1995, San Francisco, 1996; tchr. sculpture summer art sch. Ea. Ill. U., 1994, 95, 96, tchr. adult art sch., 1996, tchr. minority sch., 1995, 96. Mem. NEA, Ill. Art Edn. Assn. (Ill. Art Tchr. of 1994 award in conjunction with Ea. Ill. U.), Nat. Art Edn. Assn., Ill. Edn. Assn. Methodist.

BENNETT, EILEEN PATRICIA, copy editor, reporter; b. Garfield, N.J., July 12, 1954; d. Jerry Ralph and Marie Ann (Mangano) Tedesco; m. Charles Corson Bennett, Sr., May 26, 1979; stepchildren: Charles Jr., Wendy; adopted daughter, Unity. AA, Cumberland County Coll., 1974; BA, Glassboro State Coll., 1976. Reporter Today's Sunbeam, Salem, N.J., 1975; reporter Bridgeton (N.J.) Evening News, 1976-81, city editor, 1981-86, mng. editor, 1986-90, editor, 1990-93; editor Millville (N.J.) News, 1991-93; reporter, stringer Phila. Bull., 1979, Phila. Inquirer, 1979; copy editor, staff writer Press of Atlantic City, 1993-95, 96—; editor The Current Newspapers, Pleasantville, 1995—, asst. editor, 1995-96; staff writer Press of Atlantic City, 1996—. Recipient Voice of Am. award VFW, Bridgeton, Best Column award Am. Pub. Co., 1992. Mem. Soc. Profl. Journalists, Nat. Hist. PreservationTrust, Mauricetown Hist. Soc. Roman Catholic. Home: 2 D St Mauricetown NJ 08329 Office: Press Atlantic City Devins Ln Pleasantville NJ 08232

BENNETT, ELSIE MARGARET, music school administrator; b. Detroit, Mar. 30, 1919; d. Sy and Ida (Carp) Blum; m. Morton Bennett, June 20, 1937 (dec.); children: Ronald, Kenneth. Cert., Ganapal Conservatory Detroit, 1941; B.Mus. in Theory, Wayne State U., 1945; M.A. in Music Edn., Columbia U., 1946; postgrad. Columbia U., Manhattan Sch. Music. Music studio mgr., tchr. Bennett Music Sch., Bklyn., 1946—, dir. 1946—; music arranger, 1946—; tchr. Schiff Sch. Music, 1972-80, owner, 1972—; tchr. Robotti Accordion Acad. and Pkwy. Music Sch., 1945-46; owner Margolies Sch. Music, Acad. of Music Sch.; editor Accordion World Mag., 1945-56; works include: Easy Solos for Accordion, 1946; Bass Solo Primer, 1948; Hebrew and Jewish Songs and Dances for Accordion, 1959, Vol. 1, 1951, Vol. 2, 1953; Hanon for Accordion, 1953; Accordion Music in the Home, 1953; Folk Melodies for Accordion, 1954; Five Finger Melodies for Accordion, 1954; First Steps in Scaleland for Accordion, 1956; First Steps in Chordland for Accordion, Vol. 1, 1961, Vol. II, 1961. Mem. Bklyn. Community Council. Mem. Am. Accordionists Assn. (governing bd., pres. 1973-74, plaque, 1962, service to governing bd. award 1942-60, Silver Cup 1974-75), Bklyn. Music Tchrs. Guild (dir., past sec.), Accordion Tchrs. Guild, L.I. Music Tchrs. Assn.

BENNETT, ERICA RUND, flight control administrator; b. Seattle, July 3, 1955; d. John Charles and Shirley Mae (Knobel) Rund; m. Robert MacKenzie Bennett, Mar. 19, 1978 (div. Dec. 1993); children: Kristin MacKenzie, Audrey Anne. Student, U. Colo., 1973-75; BA, U. Wash., 1977. Lic. aircraft dispatcher FAA. Gen. agt. Western Airlines, Anchorage, 1978-79; flight attendant Wien Air Alaska, Anchorage, 1979-84; aircraft dispatcher Horizon Air, Portland, Oreg., 1989-93, flight control adminstr., 1993—. Patroller Nat. Ski Patrol, Alyska, Alaska, 1984-88, Heavenly Valley, Calif., 1988-89; vis. authors com. Friends of Libr., Anchorage, 1984-88; mem. exec. bd. PTA Rogers Park, Anchorage, 1984-88. Mem. AAUW, NOW, Aircraft Dispatchers Fedn.

BENNETT, FRANCES, artist; b. Urbana, Ark., Dec. 1, 1934; d. William J. and Thula M. (Stegall) Flynn; m. Billy T. Bennett, June 27, 1952; children: Kent, Joye Anderson, Tommy, Paul. Represented by Country Scenes and Wild Things; tchr. art classes. One-woman shows include Oil and Brine Mus., Smackover, Ark., 1992, South Ark. Arts Ctr., El Dorado, 1992, Am. Art Gallery, Hot Springs, Ark., 1994, Snyder Mus., Bastrop, La., 1995; group shows include Hudson River Valley Wildlife Art Show, Kingston, N.Y., 1995, So. Wildlife Festival, Decatur, Ala., 1995, 96, Operation Wildlife Art Show and Sale, Leavenworth, Kans., 1996, bi-annual art shows League of Women Voters, Camden, Ark., 1992-96. Mem. Nat. Mus. Women in Arts, So. Ark. Arts Ctr. Home: Rt 2 Box 96 Spearsville LA 71277

BENNETT, GEORGIA CADWALADER, educational consultant; b. Phila., May 25, 1949; d. Henry and Caroline (Seelye) Cadwalader; m. Minshall Godfrey Strater (div. May 1976); 1 child, Charles Godfrey Strater III; m. Stephen Huston Bennett, Jan. 1, 1989. AA, U. N.H., 1984. Admissions assoc. Brewster Acad., Wolfeboro, N.H., 1981-84; assoc. Group Ednl. Planners, Spring House, Pa., 1984-89, Ednl. Adv. Svcs., Phila., 1989-91; pres. Bennett Ednl. Resources, West Chester, Pa., 1991—. Bd. mem. Planned Parenthood Chester County, Pa., 1992—; chalice bearer St. Peter's Ch. in the Great Valley, Malvern, Pa., 1992—; mem. Women's Referral Network, Exton, Pa., 1994—. Named Phila. 100 1995, Wharton Small Bus. Devel. Ctr., Phila., 1995. Mem. NAFE, Soc. for Human Resource Mgmt., World Affairs Coun., Employee Relocation Coun. Republican. Episcopalian. Office: Bennett Ednl Resources 310 N High St West Chester PA 19380

BENNETT, GERALDINE MAE PAULETTE, publisher, author; b. Kingston, Ont., Can., May 22, 1943; came to U.S., 1986; d. George MacKenzie and Thelma Geraldine (Carl) Wartman; m. Walter James Rider, Aug. 12, 1960 (div. 1986, dec. 1988); children: Terry Lynn, Caren, Debra, Tracy Drum, Paul; m. Clifford Lyle Bennett, Jr., 1986; 1 adopted child, Conrad Alexander. Ordained minister, 1971. Minister First Ch. of Spiritual Guidance, Huntsville, Ont., 1973-76; family ct. counselor Family Ct., Kingston, 1976-78; editor/owner The New Dawn Pub. Co., Dexter, N.Y., 1991—; counselor First Ch. of Spiritual Guidance, 1973-82. Author: Mickey and Honor, Conrad's Dilemma, Who Am I-Getting a Jump on Life, 1996, Opening the Door to Your Inner Self, 1996; (book series) The Katrina Tells series, 1994; (videos) Synchronizing Your Self—Getting It Together, 1996, Gaining Equilibrium and Keeping It, 1996; editor The Heart Beat mag., 1991—. Leader 4-H, Holeford, Ont., Can., 1964-69, cub scouts/Boy Scouts Am., Yarker, Ont., 1969-71, Girl Guides of Can., Yarker, 1969-71.

BENNETT, JANET SANDHOFF, physical education educator; b. Goodrich, Mich., Apr. 19, 1951; d. William John and Lucille Marie (Bates) Sandhoff; m. Gerald Alan Bennett; children: Richard Jay Permuy, Julie Lauren Huber, Kaycee Lynn Huber. AA, Manatee Jr. Coll., Bradenton, Fla., 1971; BA in Phys. Edn., U. South Fla., 1973, MA in Adaptive Phys. Edn., 1986. Dir. presch., tchr. Bayshore Reform Ch., Bradenton, 1983-86; tchr. gifted Bradenton Christian Sch., 1985-86; tchr. phys. edn. Harlee Mid. Sch., Bradenton, 1986-87; perceptual motor specialist Snitz Products, Bradenton, 1875-89; owner, dir., tchr. Jungle Gym, Mt. Pleasant, S.C., 1987-90; instr. Parent Workshops, Charleston, S.C., 1987—; owner, tchr. Jumpnastics, Charleston, 1987—, also bd. dirs., 1990—. Author: (book and tape) 5 and 10 You Can Do It Again, 1986; producer movement edn. movie, 1974. Mem. Nat. Phys. Edn. Assn., Nat. Assn. Parents and Tchrs. Children Under Six. Republican. Home: 2047 Hallahan Ct Mount Pleasant SC 29464-6250

BENNETT, JOAN HIERHOLZER, artist; b. Grand Rapids, Mich.; d. Frank R. and Bernice H. (Cooper) Hierholzer; m. John Pine Bennett (div.); children: David Pine, Charles Cooper. BFA, U. Tex., 1952; MFA, Rutgers U., 1969. Solo shows include Phoenix Gallery, N.Y.C., Rutgers Art Gallery, New Brunswick, N.J., Drew Chem. Corp., Boonton, N.J., Ednl. Testing Svc., Princeton, N.J., AT&T, Basking Ridge, N.J.; group shows include Arc Gallery, Chgo., Montclair (N.J.) Art Mus., Mus. of S.W., Midland, Tex., N.J. State Mus., Trenton, Witte Mus., San Antonio, Dallas Mus. Fine Arts, Bodley Gallery, N.Y.C., Richmond (Ind.) Art Mus., Nat. Acad., N.Y.C., Kimball Art Ctr., Park City, Utah, Goddard Ctr. for Visual Arts, Ardmore, Okla., many others; permanent collections include Exxon, N.J., Schering-Plough, N.J., Deloitte, Haskin & Sells, N.J., NASA Gallery, Kennedy Space Ctr., Fla., Johnson & Johnson, N.J., Bristol-Meyers Squibb, N.J., many others. Trustee, mem. arts adv. coun. Hunterdon Art Ctr., 1980—. Fellow MacDowell Colony. Mem. Nat. Assn. Women Artists, Women's Caucus for Arts, Nat. Arts Club, Artists Equity, Artshowcase, Hunterdon Art Ctr. Home: 760 County Rd 513 Pittstown NJ 08867

BENNETT, LISA, artist; b. Eng., Aug. 3, 1922; came to U.S., 1927; d. Reuben and Hannah Dora (Hacker) Bernstein. BA, Goddard Coll., MA, 1976. Instrl. coord. Walnut Creek (Calif.) Civic Arts, 1964-76; critic, art reviewer, essayist, reporter West Art, 1964-79, San Francisco Territorial News, 1962, 63; freelance writer Washington, 1980-81; adminstrn. coord. Gesell Inst., New Haven, 1982-84; owner, lectr. bur. Bennett Programs, San Francisco, 1985-86, freelance bus. writer, 1987-89; arts lectr. Oxford U., 1990-93; spl. editor Oxford U. Press, 1990-91; adj. lectr. Hunter Coll., N.Y.C., 1992; freelance lectr. San Francisco State U., 1974-79, U. Calif., Dominican Coll., St. Mary's Coll., San Quentin Prison (Coll. of Marin), Hayward State Coll. One-woman shows include Lincoln Gallery, 1960, Firehouse Gallery, Cowell, Calif., 1966, Womens Resource Ctr., Sarasota, 1995, Sheraton Hotel, Boston, 1995, U.S. Garage, Sarasota, 1996; exhibited in group shows at Art Students League, 1955, Golden Gate Gallery, San Francisco, 1961, Civic Arts, Walnut Creek, 1966, St. Edwards Art Gallery, Oxford, 1991, U.S. Garage, Sarasota, 1993, Sarasota Visual Art Ctr., 1994, Sur-la-Mer Gallery, Sarasota, 1995, Francesca Armijo Presents Gallery, 1996. Mem. Nat. Mus. for Women in the Arts. Home: 401 Palm Ave Sarasota FL 34236

BENNETT, LOIS, real estate broker; b. N.Y.C., Dec. 23, 1933; d. Richard and Fern (Steinberg) B.; m. Barry Silverstein, June 8, 1958 (div. May 1978); children: Mark Shale, Susan Beth, Thomas Benjamin. BA, Smith Coll., 1955. Cert. residential specialist, broker/salesman, Fla. Counselor Women's Health Ctr., Sarasota, Fla., 1977-78; investment counselor, stockbroker Pvt. Bourse Inc., Sarasota, 1978-79; realtor-assoc. Harrison Properties, Inc., Sarasota, 1984-86; broker/salesman Mt. Vernon Realty Co., Inc., Sarasota, 1986-91; broker-salesman Re/Max Properties, Sarasota, 1991-96. Bd. dirs. Planned Parenthood S.W. Fla., Sarasota, 1978-84, fundraising chmn., 1982-84; bd. dirs. Family Counseling Ctr., Sarasota, 1978-81, 90, Sarasota County Arts Coun.; mem. exec. com., bd. dirs. Fla. West Coast Symphony, Sarasota, 1982-88; chmn. spl. events 1st ann. Sarasota French Film Festival, 1989, co-chmn. spl. events, 1990; bd. dirs. Asolo Performing Arts Ctr., Sarasota, 1990-95; bd. dirs. Sarasota French Film Festival, 1989-94; mem. film commn. Com. of 100, 1989-92; chmn. Sarasota County Arts Day, 1994-95. Mem. Women's Coun. Realtors, Realtors Inst. (grad.), Re/Max 100% Club, Sarasota C. of C. Office: Michael Saunders & Co 1801 Main St Sarasota FL 34236

BENNETT, M. DEE, state legislator; b. Little Rock, Ark., Aug. 20, 1935. Rep. dist. 59 State of Ark., 1993—; cons. Greater Friendship, Inc. Democrat. Office: Ark State Reps State Capitol Little Rock AR 72201

BENNETT, MARGARET AIROLA, lawyer; b. San Francisco, July 20, 1950; d. Virgil Raymond and Caroline (Maccoun) Airola; m. Eugene Le Brun Bennett, Mar. 1, 1980; children: Scott, Brad, Elizabeth. AB cum laude, U. Calif., Berkeley, 1972; JD, U. San Francisco and Loyola U., 1976. Bar: Ill.1976, U.S. Dist. Ct. (no. dist.) Ill. 1977, U.S. Ct. Appeals (7th cir.) 1983. Intern Cook County State's Atty.'s Office, Chgo., 1975-76; assoc. Dunlap, Thompson & Boyd, Ltd., Libertyville, Ill., 1977-79; ptnr. Bennett & Bennett, Ltd., Oak Brook, Ill., 1980—; atty. rep. McDonald's Corp., Oak Brook, 1982—, County of DuPage, Wheaton, Ill., 1990-95. Counsel fo DuPage Ill. Fair and Exposition Authority, County of DuPage, 1991-95, co-chmn. next generation com.; mem. devel. coun. Good Samaritan Hosp., 1988-92. Mem. DuPage County Bar Assn. (chmn. real estate law com. 1994-95, Cert. of Appreciation 1989, chmn. profl. responsibility com. 1996—), Ill. State Bar Assn. (cert. of Appreciation 1990), Womens Bar Assn. DuPage County, Evang. Health Found. (bd. sponsors 1988-92). Republican. Roman Catholic. Home: 11 Lochinvar Ln Oak Brook IL 60521-1612 Office: Bennett and Bennett Ltd 720 Enterprise Dr Hinsdale IL 60521

BENNETT, MARY See THOMPSON, DIDI CASTLE

BENNETT, MICHELE MARGULIS, women's health nurse; b. Oakland, Calif., Mar. 16, 1962; d. Frank and Rosalyn Barbara (Danneman) Margulis; m. Dennis Kerry Bennett, Jan. 1, 1991 (div. Jan. 12, 1995); 1 child, Caitlyn Anne. BA, U. Fla., 1984; BSN, Fla. Internat. U., 1990. Cert. childbirth educator. Staff nurse maternity Lyster Army Cmty. Hosp., Ft. Rucker, Ala., 1991-94; clin. staff nurse maternity Darnall Army Cmty. Hosp., Ft. Hood, Tex., 1994-96; head nurse postpartum ward WOMACK Med. Ctr., Ft. Bragg, N.C., 1996—; mem. jr. officer coun. Ft. Hood, 1994-96. Capt. U.S. Army, 1984—. Mem. AWHONN. Republican. Jewish.

BENNETT, MILDRED LORLINE, elementary school educator; b. Pierce, W.Va., Jan. 17, 1931; d. Pete L. and Lectie Lorline (Lipscomb) Bava; m. William Von Bennett, 1951; 1 child, William Albert. BS, Davis & Elkins Coll., 1978; MA, W.Va. U., 1983, postgrad. Cert. elem. edn. tchr. Title I reading aide Tucker County Bd. Edn., Parsons, W.Va., 1963-78, elem. tchr., 1978-96; mem. book com. Tucker County Bd. Edn., Blue Ribbon Math. com.; mem. curriculum com. Parsons Elem./Mid. Sch., 1991-95. V.p. Tucker County chpt. Am. Cancer Soc., Parsons, 1982-90, PTO, Parsons; primary tchr. Sunday Sch., 1987-95; mem. Tucker County Chorus, 1990-92. Mem. AAUW, Nat. Presveta, W.Va. Edn. Assn., Slovene Lodge, Foresters. Democrat. Home: 302 Pennsylvania Ave Parsons WV 26287-1151 Office: WVa U PO Box 6009 Morgantown WV 26506-6009

BENNETT, MONA BLEIBERG, psychiatrist, clinical services director; b. Newark, Aug. 22, 1941; d. Jacob and Claire (Barban) Bleiberg; m. Michael Isaiah Bennett, Apr. 11, 1975; children: Rebecca Leah, Sarah Bleiberg. BA, U. Chgo., 1959-63; MD, Harvard U., 1967. Diplomate Am. Bd. Psychiatry. Resident in medicine Beth Israel Hosp., Boston, 1967-69; resident in psychiatry Mass. Mental Health Ctr., Boston, 1969-71, resident in child psychiatry, 1971-73, psychiatrist, 1973-84, dir. outpatient and emergency svcs., 1978-84; dir. mental health Brookside Park Family Life Ctr., Boston, 1973-78; dep. commr. Mass. Dept. Mental Health, Boston, 1984-91; adminstr. McLean Hosp., Belmont, Mass., 1991—; dir. office clin. svcs. dept. psychiatry Harvard Med. Sch., Belmont, 1991—; asst. prof. Harvard Med. Sch., Boston, 1993—; assoc. prof. U. Mass. Med. Sch., Worcester, 1986-93. Fellow Am. Psychiat. Assn.; mem. Am. Coll. Psychiatrists, Acad. Child and Adolescent Psychiatry, Phi Beta Kappa, Alpha Omega Alpha. Jewish. Office: McLean Hosp 115 Mill St Belmont MA 02178-1041

BENNETT, OLGA SALOWICH, civic worker, graphic arts researcher, consultant; b. Detroit, June 30, 1925; d. Nicholas Stefanovich and Maria Elarionovna (Mikuliak) Salowich; m. Robert William Bennett, Dec. 20, 1947; 1 child, Susan Roberta. Student, U. Mich., 1943-45, Parsons Sch. Design, 1948, U. Md., Nagoya, Japan, 1959; BA, NYU, 1975. Graphic artist Silver & Co., N.Y.C., 1948-50; editor, pub. Bull., organizer radio series LWV, Pitts., 1950-55; instr. Nanzan U., Nagoya, 1959; aide, cons. to U.S. hon. consul, Safi, Casablanca, Morocco, 1962-65; chmn. internat. affairs LWV, Montclair, N.J., 1966-73; conf. coord. UN Assn., Madison, N.J., 1974; weekly broadcaster LWV, San Juan, P.R., 1979-81; lectr. color theory Cunard, Ltd., London, Miami, Fla., 1985-88; bd. dirs., docent Ctr. Fine Arts, Miami, 1990-92; docent Bass Mus. Art, Miami Beach, Fla., 1990-92, Vizcaya Mus. Art, Miami, 1983—; cons. on corp. overseas placement. Author artist brochures, ednl. pamphlets; translator Russian-Am. Conf., Miami, 1990. Mem. panel theater award com. New Theater, Miami, 1991. Mem. AAUW, LWV, UN Assn., NYU Alumni Assn., New Sch. Alumni Assn., Fgn. Policy Assn., Great Decisions Program. Democrat. Russian Orthodox. Home: Kings Creek S Apt A1-402 7727 SW 86th St Miami FL 33143-7283

BENNETT, PEGGY ELIZABETH, librarian, library director, educator; b. Columbus, Ga., Aug. 22, 1935; d. William Osborne and Ola Lee (McMahan) B. BA in Chemistry, So. Coll., 1956; cert. med. technologist, Glendale Sch. Med. Tech., Glendale, 1957; MS in Libr. Sci., Fla. State U., 1971. Med. technologist Glendale (Calif.) Hosp., 1957-59, Columbus (Ga.) Med. Ctr., 1960-61; sec. Seventh-Day Adventists Ch. Orgns., various, 1961-67; med. technologists Warm Springs (Ga.) Found., 1967-69, Thrash Labs., Columbus, Ga., 1969-70; libr. So. Coll. Seventh-Day Adventist, Collegedale, Tenn., 1971—; dir. librs. So. Coll. of Seventh-Day Adventist, Collegedale, 1986—; presenter in field, 1979-87; developer Processing Ctr. for Southeastern Adventist Sch. Librs., 1981; cons. Adventist Network of Gen. Ednl. Librs., Collegedale, 1981—, Girl's Preparatory Sch., Chattanooga, 1984-85. Author: Library Pathfinder for MIT, 1972; contbr. articles to profl. jours. Mem. ALA, Assn. of Seventh-Day Adventists Librs. (v.p. 1981-82, pres. 1982-83), Southeastern Libr. Assn., Chattanooga Area Libr. Assn., Solinet Lambda Users' Group (exec. com. 1984, steering com.), Beta Phi Mu. Seventh Day Adventist. Home: 4640 Pierson Dr Collegedale TN 37315 Office: So Coll of SDA Industrial Dr Collegedale TN 37315

BENNETT, REBECCA EATON, artist; b. Decatur, Ala., Sept. 27, 1957; d. Herbert Jess and Eleanor Alice (Cross) Eaton; divorced; 1 child, Rachel Katherine. AS, Calhoun Coll., 1991; BA in Art and Bus. Adminstrn., Athens State Coll., 1993. Owner Ye Ole Abode Studio, Decatur, 1993—; instr. UAW-Chrysler Huntsville (Ala.) Tng., 1994-95, O/E Learning, Inc., Troy, Mich., 1995—; project dir. Walter Jackson Elem., Decatur, 1995—. Cultural arts chairperson, key communicator Westlawy Elem. PTA, Decatur, 1993-94; cultural arts chairperson Walter Jackson Elem. PTA, 1994—. Mem. Am. Craft Assn., Ala. Alliance for Arts Edn., Huntsville Arts League. Republican. Baptist. Office: Ye Ole Abode Studio PO Box 843 Decatur AL 35602

BENNETT, SHARON KAY, music educator; b. West Jefferson, Ohio; d. Harold Stewart and Dorothy Eleanor (McKinley) B. BMus, Eastman Sch. Music, 1960, MMus, 1962. Asst. prof. Univ. Iowa, Iowa City, 1980-84, Capital U., Columbus, Ohio, 1992—; adj. lectr. Otterbein Coll., Westerville, Ohio, 1986-87, Capital U., 1985-92; resident coloratura Nurnberg (Germany) Opera, 1970-73, Hamburg (Germany) State Opera, 1973-76; resident guest artist Scottish Opera, Glasgow, 1976-77; presenter symposium. Author: 40 Vocalises, 1993, Class Voice Simplified, 1994. Recipient 1st place award Iowa Symphony competition, 1981; named to Women of Achievement, YWCA, 1986; Rockefeller Found. grantee, N.Y.C., 1966-68; Old Gold fellow U. Iowa, Iowa City, N.Y. and Paris; Capital U. faculty devel. grantee, 1995. Mem. Nat. Assn. Tchrs. of Singing, Opera Am., Coll. Music Soc. (mem. nat. com. women, music, and gender), Sigma Alpha Iota (sec. 1985-87). Home: 2877 Astor Ave Columbus OH 43209-2626

BENNETT, SHIRLEY ANN, maintenance executive, business technologist educator; b. Buffalo, Nov. 5, 1952; d. Edward Stoklosa and Florence (Ulanowski) Valin; m. Jeffrey Michael Bennett, July 3, 1975; children: Tara, Shauna, Shira, Brett, Eric. BS in Edn., SUNY Coll. at Buffalo, Buffalo, 1974; MBA, SUNY, Buffalo, 1982. Cert. tchr., N.Y. Tchr. Niagara Falls (N.Y.) Bd. Edn., 1974-75, Kensington Bus. Inst., Buffalo, 1976-80; asst. prof. SUNY, Buffalo, 1980—; v.p. Bennett Janitorial Svc., Williamsville, N.Y., 1976—. Active Jewish Ctr. of Greater Buffalo, Amherst, 1983—, Girl Scouts U.S., Buffalo, 1985—. Mem. Epsilon Delta Epsilon, Iota Lambda Sigma (Alpha Lambda chpt.). Home: 76 Alran Dr Williamsville NY 14221-1409 Office: SUNY at Buffalo EOC 465 Washington St Buffalo NY 14203-1707

BENNETT, VERNA GREEN, employee relations executive; b. Memphis, Oct. 4, 1942; d. Agee and Philistine Louvenia (Jackson) Green; m. John Paul Bennett, Sept. 24, 1966 (div. Dec. 3, 1978). BS in Bus. Edn., Knoxville Coll., 1965. Tchr. Stevens Lee High Sch., Asheville, N.C., 1965-66; adminstr. external affairs Youth in Action, Bklyn., 1966-67; adminstr. cmty. rels., pub. rels. Pepsi Cola Co., N.Y.C., 1967-70; staff asst., coll. rels. coord., hdqrs. recruiter Mobil Corp., N.Y.C., 1970-80; western region recruiter Mobil Corp., L.A., 1980-87; EEO rels. mgr. Mobil Corp., Fairfax, Va., 1987—; mem. corp. adv. bd. Nat. Assn. Minority Engr. Adminstrs., Fla., 1980-96, Am. Indian Sci. and Engring., Boulder, 1990-96, NAACP ACTSO, Balt., 1989-96; motivational spkr., lectr. on recruitment. Pres. New Dominion chpt. Nat. Coalition of 100 Black Women, 1992-96, chmn. chpt. devel. com., nat. bd. dirs., 1993-96; commr. Nat. Com. Working Women, Washington, 1990-94; chmn. bd. Coun. on Career Devel. for Minorities, Dallas, 1986-96, exec. dir. elect, 1997—; mem. No. Va. Urban League, Alexandria, 1990-96. Recipient Presdl. Achievement and Nat. Amigo of Yr. awards SER-Jobs for Progress, Dallas, 1988, 89, 90, 94, Donald H. McGannon award Nat. Urban League, N.Y.C., 1992, youth award Delta Sigma Theta, 1992. Mem. NAACP (life), Bus. and Profl. Women (corp. adv. resource devel. 1992-96). Home: 1600 N Oak St Apt 1425 Arlington VA 22209-2768 Office: Mobil Corp Ste 2C917 2335 Gallows Rd Fairfax VA 22037

BENNETT MINNERLY, DENISE PATRICIA, artist, art educator; b. Cleve., Sept. 24, 1960; d. Gordon W. and Yvonne L. (Debegasa) Bennett; m. Barry H. Minnerly, May 9, 1987; children: Sarah Anne, Gillian Catherine. BS, BA cum laude, U. Vt., Burlington, 1984. Cert. tchr. K-12. Pub. rels. profl. Royal Copenhagen, N.Y., 1985-87; art tchr. Stamford (Conn.) Schs., 1987-88; art tchr. After Sch. Art Program, Darien, Conn., 1988-92, Rowayton, Conn., 1988-95; art dir. Rowayton Civic Assn., 1987—, Darien Arts Coun., 1988. Author, illustrator: (children's book) Color Tree, 1991. Vol. Women's Crisis Ctr., Norwalk, Conn., 1982—. Home: 183 Highland Ave Norwalk CT 06853

BENNIN, HOPE ELIZABETH, communication educator; b. Columbus, Wis., Jan. 23, 1959; d. Eugene Donald and Sally Ann (Virchow) B. BS in English, U. Wis., Stevens Point, 1982, BS in Communication, 1982, MA in Communication, 1987. Adminstrv. asst. C.Y. Allen/Profl. Comm. Svcs., Stevens Point, 1982-84; LTE office asst. U. Wis., Stevens Point, 1984-87, lectr. divsn. comms., 1984-86; tchr. summer sch. Stevens Point Sch. Dist., 1984-87; tchr. lang. arts St. Paul Luth. Sch., Stevens Point, 1983-87; instr. Prestonsburg (Ky.) C.C., 1987-90, asst. prof., 1990-92, assoc. prof. comm., 1992—; tchr. summer sch. Stevens Point Sch. Dist., 1984-87. Author poetry pub. in N.Y. Poetry Anthology, Disting. Poets of Am., Whispers in the Wind, Best Poets of 1995. Corres. sec. Jenny Wiley Festival Bd., Prestonsburg, 1992—; judge KCTE Writing Competition, Ky., 1987—, Young Authors Competition, Prestonsburg, 1987—; presenter Candlelight Vigil/Desert Storm, Prestonsburg. Recipient Excellence Award for Tchg. Nat. Inst. Staff and Orgnl. Devel., 1993; U. Ky. C.C. Sys. grantee, 1990, 91, 95, Great Tchr. grantee, 1988, AACC Svc. Learning grantee, 1995. Mem. ASCD, Speech Comm. Assn., Ky. Comm. Assn., Nat. Coun. Tchrs. English, Ky. Coun. Tchrs. English, Ky. ASCD. Office: Prestonsburg Cmty College One Bert T Combs Dr Prestonsburg KY 41653

BENNING, LESLIE CECILE, management consultant, marketing strategist; b. Morristown, Tenn., Apr. 3, 1957; d. Thomas Cobb and Harriet Anne (Floyd) B.; m. Rafael Bejarano-Narbona, Nov. 9, 1991. Student, U. Seville, Spain, 1977-78; BA with honors, U. N.C., 1979; MBA, Columbia U., 1982. Sr. product mgr. Gen. Foods Corp., White Plains, N.Y., 1982-88; prin. Booz, Allen & Hamilton, Inc., N.Y.C., 1988-93; ptnr. The Cambridge Group, Greenwich, Conn., 1994—. Recipient Pres.'s Mktg. Innovation award, Gen. Foods Corp., 1988. Mem. Profl. Women Singers Assn. (bd. dirs. 1992-95), Chi Omega (panhellenic coun. 1976-79). Office: The Cambridge Group 10 Glenville St Greenwich CT 06831

BENO-CLARK, CANDICE LYNN, chemical company executive; b. New Brunswick, N.J., Mar. 25, 1951; d. Andrew Jule and Claire May (Blanchard) Beno; m. John W. Clark, Sr., Dec. 8, 1990. BA magna cum laude, U. Conn., 1973, MS in Biochemistry, 1974, postgrad., 1974-75. Grad. asst. U. Conn., 1973-75; lab. technician Linde div. Union Carbide Corp., Keasbey, N.J., 1976-78, sr. lab. technician Linde div., 1978-79; regional tech. supr. Linde div. Union Carbide Corp., South Plainfield, N.J., 1979; asst. staff engr. Linde div. Union Carbide Corp., Springfield, N.J., 1979-82, staff engr. Linde div., 1982-84; tech. bus. cons. Linde div. Union Carbide Corp., Danbury, Conn., 1984-85; staff engr. Linde div. Union Carbide Corp., Somerset, N.J., 1985-87; mgr. Linde div. Union Carbide Corp., Springfield, 1987-89; mgr. Linde div. Union Carbide Indsl. Gases, Inc., Danbury, Conn., 1989-91, internat. mgr., 1991—; internat. mgr. Praxair, Inc., Danbury; supr. Landmark Edn., Edison, N.J., 1984-87; guest seminar leader, 1985—, course mgr., 1984-86. Mem. Am. Soc. Quality Control, Compressed Gas Assn. (chmn. 1984-91, vice chmn. 1982-88, Svc. award 1991), Semicondr. Equipment and Material Inst. (co-chmn. 1987-91, editor jour. 1982-88, Outstanding Svc. award 1884-89, Leadership award 1988, Mortar Board, Phi Beta Kappa, Phi Kappa Phi. Democrat. Home: 405 Newark Ave Point Pleasant Beach NJ 08742-4143 Office: Praxair Inc 39 Old Ridgebury Rd # 1524 Danbury CT 06810

BENOIT, NANCY LOUISE, state legislator, educator; b. New Haven, Conn., Jan. 25, 1944; d. James Michael and Florence Louise (Bray) Wynne; m. Raymond George Benoit, Aug. 8, 1970; children: Michael, Patrick. BA, Albertus Magnus Coll., 1965; MEd, Wayne State U., 1969. Tchr. St. Vincent de Paul High Sch., Detroit, 1965-69; community organizer Social Progress Action Corp., Woonsocket, R.I., 1969-71; dir. Little Shares Day Care Ctr., Woonsocket, 1971-73; edn. coordinator Northwest Head Start, North Providence, R.I., 1978-84; mem. R.I. Ho. of Reps., 1985—, chair joint legis. commn. on child care, 1985—, mem. adult edn. commn., 1985-88, mem. health, edn. and welfare com., 1986-88, mem. fin. com., 1989-92; dep. majority whip, 1991-92; chair permanent legis. oversight commn. Dept. for Children, Youth and Families; chair House com. on Health, Edn. and Welfare, 1993—. Bd. dirs. Woonsocket Head Start and Day Care, R.I. affiliate Literacy Vols. of Am., 1985-88; commr. Blackstone River Valley Nat. Corridor Commn.; bd. mgrs. Woonsocket Family and Child Care Svcs., 1973-87; v.p., bd. dirs. Health Svcs., Inc., Woonsocket, 1974—; founder Women for Women, 1983—; vol. coord. Vols. in Action, Providence, 1984-86; grant coord. C.C. R.I., Lincoln, 1986-87. Named one of Outstanding Young Women in Am., Woonsocket and E.I. Jaycees, 1980, Legislator of Yr. United Way of Southeastern New England; recipient Francesco Cannistra Svc. award Health Svcs., Inc., 1986, Outstanding Svc. award R.I. Day Care Dirs. Assn., 1986. Mem. Common Cause, Sierra Club, Audubon Soc. Democrat. Roman Catholic. Office: RI Gen Assembly Providence RI 02903*

BENSEL, CAROLYN KIRKBRIDE, psychologist; b. Orange, N.J., Sept. 21, 1941; d. William Everitt and Margaret Mary (McGlynn) B.; A.B. with honors in Psychology, Chestnut Hill Coll., 1963; M.S., U. Mass., 1964, Ph.D. (Univ. fellow), 1967. Teaching asst. U. Mass., Amherst, 1963-64, research asst., 1964-66; human factors psychologist Grumman Aerospace Corp., Bethpage, N.Y., 1967-71; chief human factors group U.S. Army Natick (Mass.) Research, Devel. and Engring. Ctr., 1971—. Lic. psychologist, Mass. Fellow Human Factors Soc., APA; mem. Ergonomics Soc., Soc. Engring. Psychologists, Internat. Ergonomics Assn., AAAS, Sigma Xi. Editor: Proc. 23d Ann. Meeting of Human Factors Soc., 1979. Office: Sci & Advanced Tech Directorate Army Natick Research Devel Engring Ctr Kansas St Natick MA 01760

BENSEN, PAMELA PARKE, emergency medicine physician, educator; b. Plainfield, N.J., Dec. 27, 1944; m. C. (Kork) Bensen III; children: Jeannie McKay, C. (Neil) W. Bensen IV. Student, Northwestern U., 1964; BS in Biology and Chemistry, Upsala Coll., 1966; MD, Med. Coll. Pa.; postgrad., Dartmouth Koop Inst. Diplomate Am. Bd. Emergency Medicine; cert. ACLS, BLS, Advanced Trauma Life Support, Advanced Pedit. Trauma Life Support. Intern in emergency medicine Med. Coll. Pa., resident in emergency medicine; mem. emergency medicine staff St. Mary's Gen. Hosp.-St. Mary's Regional Med. Ctr., Lewiston, Maine, 1973—, chief emergency svcs., 1974-78, dir. Ctrl. Maine Vocat. Inst. Paramedic Tng. Program, 1978-79; dir. emergency svcs. St. Mary's Gen. Hosp.-St. Mary's Regional Med. Ctr., Lewsiton, Maine, 1982-87; mem. staff Bath (Maine) Meml. Hosp., 1986—, dir. emergency svcs., 1989-90; mem. staff Miles Meml. Hosp., Damariscotta, Maine, 1989—, dir. emergency svcs., 1989-91; mem. staff St. Andrews Hosp., Boothbay Harbor, Maine, 1990-93, dir. emergency svcs., 1990-91; adj. asst. prof. clin. medicine Dartmouth Med. Sch., Hanover, N.H., 1990—; mem. med. adv. com. Region I Medicare, Maine Medicaid, Maine Blue Shield; instr. ACLS, ATLS, Pediat. Advanced Life Support, EMT to schs., gen. public, medical pers.; med. dir. New Eng. Med. Svcs., 1987—; co-founder Dictate, Inc., 1987—, pres., 1991—, med. advisor, 1922—; mem. med. adv. bd. Virutal Physician, 1994—; spkr. TV, radio, confs., programs, assemblies in field; med. advisor Lost Valley Ski Patrol, 1974-79; bd. dirs. Androscoggin Valley Red Cross, 1975; co-dir. Lewiston-Auburn Rape Crisis Intervention Team, 1977-79; dir. Alert Ambulance, Lewiston, Maine, 1978-79; bd. dirs. Tri-County Regional EMS Coun., med. control com., edn. standards and evaluation com.; mem. physician adv. bd. Maine EMS Med. Dir., 1982-85; mem. Nat. Bd. Med. Examiners, 1986-87; mem. So. Maine Med. Control Com., 1988-92, EMS Coun., 1990-92, v.p. 1990-92; EMS dir. Regional Meml. Hosp., 1988-90; mem. Mid Coast Maine Med. Control Com., 1989-91; chair Coastal Edn. and Evaluation Com., 1989-90; pres. Maine Emergency Physicians, P.A., 1979-82, 83-89, sec., 1989—; pres., CEO Emergency Medicine Assocs., 1985—; med. advisor Poland Rescue, 1973-88; part-time Ctrl. Maine Med. Ctr., Lewiston, Kennebec Valley Med. Ctr., Augusta, Maine, Sebasticook Valley Hosp., Pittsfield, Maine, Stephens Meml. Hosp., Norway, Maine, Waldo County Hosp., Belfast, Maine; instr. various paramedic courses, 1973—. Editor Maine Emergency Physicians Interim Comm., 1979-84, 88-93; mem. editl. bd. Maine EMS Jour., 1990-93, ED Mgmt., 1989—; co-editor Women in Emergency Medicine, 1986-89. Recipient Disting. Alumnae award Upsala Coll., 1985, Cmty. Svc. award Am. Woman's Med. Assn., 1991, Appreciation award Bath/Brunswick EMS, 1992; grantee Emergency Medicine Found., 1993. Fellow Am. Coll. Emergency Physicians (grad. edn. com. resident rep. 1971-73, continuing med. edn. com. 1973-79, ACEP-Chubb malpractice ins. claims rev. bd. N.E. sect. 1973-75, pub. rels. com. 1981-82, spkrs. bur. 1983, bd. nominating com. 1988-89, profl. liability com. 1988-90, medico-legal com. 1990-92, ED design resources list 1992—, liaison to Physician Insurers Assn. Am. 1992-94, emergency medicine practice com. 1994—, councilor State of Maine 1973-82, 89-92, coun. awards com. 1990, coun. steering com. 1978-80, chair coun. nominating com. 1979-81, pres. Maine chpt. 1974-79, nat. bd. dirs.-numerous coms., sects., Coun. Meritorious Svc. award 1989, editor newsletter 1989-92); mem. AMA, Am. Coll. Physician Execs., Maine Med. Assn., Med. Transcription Svc. Owners, Med. Transcription Industry Alliance (bd. dirs. 1993—). Office: 11 Mechanic Falls Rd Oxford ME 04270-9713

BENSHOOF, JANET L., lawyer, association executive; b. Detroit Lakes, Minn., May 10, 1947; m. Richard Klein; children: David, Eli. BA summa cum laude, U. Minn., 1969; JD, Harvard U., 1972. Dir. law reform South Bklyn. Legal Svcs., 1972-77; dir. reproductive freedom project ACLU, N.Y.C., 1977-92; founder, pres. Ctr. Reproductive Law & Policy, N.Y.C., 1992—; guest lectr. Yale U., Columbia U., Rutgers U., Case Western Reserve U. Contbr. articles to profl. jours. Recipient Margaret Sanger award, 1986, Christopher Tietze Humanitarian award Nat. Abortion Fedn., 1988, Gloria Steinem award Ms. Found. Women, N.Y.C., 1989, 10 for 10 award Ctr. Population Optiums, 1990; named one of 100 Most Influential Lawyers in Am. Nat. Law Jour., 1991, 94; MacArthur Found. Fellowship grantee, 1992—. Mem. ABA, Am. Pub. Health Assn., N.Y.C. Bar Assn. Office: Ctr Reproductive Law & Policy 120 Wall St New York NY 10005-3904*

BENSINGER, VALERIE VIDA, special education educator; b. Fredericksburg, Va., Oct. 3, 1969; d. Michael Ronald Vida and Audrey Vida Stanley. BS in Psychology, Longwood Coll., Farmville, Va., 1991, MS in Spl. Edn., 1992. Cert. tchr., Va. Tchr. non-categorical class Riverview Elem. Sch., Spotsylvania County Schs., Spotsylvania, Va., 1992—. Mem. NEA, Coun. for Exceptional Children, Va. Edn. Assn., Spotsylvania Edn. Assn. Baptist.

BENSON, A. LEGRACE GUPTON, humanities educator, researcher; b. Richmond, Va., Feb. 23, 1930; d. Herbert Lee and Frances Lillian W. (Covalt) Gupton; m. Thomas Fawcett Benson, Aug. 9, 1952 (dec. Feb. 1976);children: Thomas Lawck, Lawrence Thane, Theodore Lloyd. BA, Meredith Coll., 1951; MFA, U. Ga., 1956; PhD, Cornell U., 1974. Asst. prof. Cornell U., Ithaca, N.Y., 1968-72; asst. prof. Wells Coll., Aurora, N.Y., 1972-75, assoc. dean, 1975-77; assoc. dean Empire State Coll. SUNY, Albany, 1977-80; coord. arts, humanities, comms. Ctr. Distance Learning SUNY, Saratoga Springs, N.Y., 1981-83, prof. Ctr. Distance Learning, 1985-93; prof. emerita Ctr. Distance Learning SUNY, Saratoga Springs, 1993—; ind. scholar Haitian studies, Ithaca, N.Y., 1994—. Author: (textbook) Understanding the Visible World, 1984; co-author: (textbook) Educational Planning: A Guide for Adult Distance Learners, 1985; mem. editl. bd. Prologue, Golden Hill literary mags., Jour. Caribbean Assn. Profls. & Scholars, 1981-93; contbr. articles to mags. Chair, vice chair so. tier regional plan City of Ithaca (N.Y.) Planning Bd., rep. ward IV Tompkins County Bd. Reps., N.Y., 1973-77; vol. tchr. Literary Vols. Am., Ithaca, N.Y., 1994—. vis. scholar NEH Cornell U., 1985. Mem. Coll. Art Assn., African Studies Assn., Arts Coun. African Studies, Haitian Studies Assn., Canadian Assn. for Lat. Am. and Caribbean Studies. Democrat. Roman Catholic. Home and Office: 314 E Buffalo Ithaca NY 14850

BENSON, BARBARA ELLEN, state agency administrator; b. Rockford, Ill., June 5, 1943; d. Olander Anton and Eleanor Margaret (Lydon) B. BA, Beloit Coll., 1965; MA, Ind. U., 1969, PhD, 1976. Editor Eleutherian Mills-Hagley Found., Wilmington, Del., 1973-80; dir. libr. Hist. Soc. Del., Wilmington, 1980-90, exec. dir., 1990—. Author: Logs and Lumber, 1989, (with Michael Biggs) Wilmington: the City and Beyond, 1990; contbr. articles to jours., chpts. to books. Vice chairperson Del. Humanities Forum, 1987-92, chairperson, 1992-94; bd. dirs. Sister Cities, Wilmington, 1985-89, ofcl. visitor to Kalmar, Sweden, 1985; bd. dirs. State Records Commn. Del., 1987—; mem. rev. bd. Del. Hist. Preservation, 1990-96; bd. dirs. Hist. Red Clay Valley, 1994-96; mem. adv. com. Del Hist. Records, 1987—. Mem. Nat. Soc. of Fund Raising Execs., Am. Assn. of Mus., Am. Assn. State and Local History (state awards chmn. 1987-94, state membership com. 1996—), Mid Atlantic Regional Archivists (bd. dirs. 1983-87). Office: Hist Soc Delaware 505 N Market St Wilmington DE 19801-3004

BENSON, BERNICE LAVINA, elementary education educator; b. Wolford, N.D., Sept. 30; d. Therman George and Annie Catherine (Hittle) Ritzman; m. Benjamin Melvin Benson, June 11, 1941 (dec.); 1 child, Beverly Ann. Student, Jamestown Coll.; BS in Edn., No. State Coll., 1964, MA equivalent. Cert. elem. tchr., S.D.; commd. Stephen's min., 1995. Tchr. 1st-6th grade Southam (N.D.) Sch. System, 1935-41; tchr. 1st grade Pierre (S.D.) Sch. System, 1953-84; tchr. Title I Fed. Devel. Reading Program, Pierre, 1984-87; tchr.-tutor Title IV Fed. Tutorials for Native Americans, Pierre; supr. student tchrs. No. State Coll., Pierre. Past officer, past mem. various state coms. Delta Kappa Gamma; charter mem. Capital U., Pierre; sponsor Discovery Ctr., Pierre; mem. YMCA, Pierre; spl. events worker VFW Aux., Pierre; mem. Fine ARts Coun., Pierre; actress Never Too Late, Pierre Players Drama Assn.; mem. planning com. for new bldg., mem. meml. com. Luth. Meml. Ch. Mem. NEA (state exec. uni-serve com.), Pierre Edn. Assn., S.D. Edn. Assn., Pierre Tchrs. Assn. (pres.), Internat. Reading Assn., Assn. for Childhood Edn., AAUW, DAR (past offices), PEO (past pres., all offices), Annie D. Tallent Club. Home: 324 Mary Ln Pierre SD 57501-2213

BENSON, BETTY G., state legislator; b. Pioneer, Tenn., Mar. 29, 1943; M. Jim A. Benson; children: Timothy, James, Krisila. BS, U. Idaho, 1987, MS, 1994. Senator Idaho State Senate, Boise, 1990-92. Mem. Gamma Theta Upsilon, Sigma Xi. Democrat. Home: 2305 Wallen Rd Moscow ID 83843-8497

BENSON, BETTY JONES, school system administrator; b. Barrow County, Ga., Jan. 11, 1928; d. George C. and Bertha (Mobley) Jones; m. George T. Benson; children: George Steven, Elizabeth Gayle, James Claud, Robert Benjamin. BS in Edn., N. Ga. U., Dahlonega, 1958; MEd in Curriculum and Supervision, U. Ga., Athens, 1968, edn. specialist in Curriculum and Supervision, 1970. Tchr. Forsyth County (Ga.) Bd. Edn., Cumming, 1956-66, curriculum dir., 1966—; asst. supt. for instrn. Forsyth County Schs., 1981—. Active Alpine Ctr. for Disturbed Children; chmn. Ga. Lake Lanier Island Authority; mem. North Ga. Coll. Edn. Adv. Com., Ga. Textbook Com.; adv. Boy Scouts; Sunday sch. tchr. 1st Baptist Ch. Cumming; active Forsyth County Substance Abuse Commn., Forsyth County Drug Task Force, Forsyth County Vision 20/20 Com., Forsyth County Drug Commn., Forsyth County Interagency Council for Children and Youth, Forsyth County Health Bd., local coord. council Family and Children Svcs., Blue Ridge Cir. Ct.-Cherokee/Forsyth County Domestic Violence Task Force. Mem. NEA, Ga. Assn. Educators (bd. dir.), ASCD, Ga. Assn. Supervision and Curriculum Devel. (pres.), Assn. Childhood Edn. Internat., Bus. and Profl. Women's Club, Internat. Platform Assn., Ga. Future Tchrs. Adv. Assn. (pres.), Profl. Assn. Ga. Educators, Ga. Assn. Ednl. Leaders (dir.), HeadStart Dirs. Assn., Forsyth County Hist. Soc., Sawnee Mountain Community Ctr. Assn., Ga. Cumming/Forsyth County C. of C. (mem. edn. com.), Mountain Local Coord. Coun. Home: 1235 Dahlonega Hwy Cumming GA 30130-4525 Office: 101 School St Cumming GA 30130-2427

BENSON, CONSTANCE LOUISE, religious educator; b. Geneva, Ill., Mar. 22, 1950; d. Donald E. and Alice M. (MacPherson) Benson; m. Brian D'Agostino, Oct. 16, 1982. BA in English Lit. magna cum laude, Wheaton (Ill.) Coll., 1972; MDiv in Bibl. Studies, Harvard Div. Sch., 1980; MPhil in Religion and Christian Ethics, Columbia U., 1986, postgrad. Teaching asst. Gordon-Conwell Sem., spring 1975; interim pastor West Delhi (N.Y.) Presbyn. Ch., summer 1980; adj. asst. prof. religious studies Manhattan Coll., Riverdale, N.Y., 1990, Fordham U., N.Y.C., 1991-94; lectr. in field. Contbr. articles to profl. jours. Rsch. assoc. Ctr. on Violence and Human Survival, CUNY. Columbia U. acad. merit scholar, 1991; Ernst Troeltsch Gesellschaft travel grantee, 1988; Union Theol. Sem. fellow, 1981-82. Mem. Am. Acad. Religion, Soc. of Bibl. Lit., Soc. of Christian Ethics. Democrat. Unitarian-Universalist. Home: 360 Riverside Dr Apt 4D New York NY 10025-2750

BENSON, ELAINE KLEBANOFF GOFF, journalist, art gallery owner; b. Phila., Apr. 30, 1924; d. Benjamin P. and Elizabeth (Miller) Klebanoff; m. Warren Goff, July 3, 1943 (div. 1964); children: William M., Virginia L., Neal M., Kimberly Goff Kay; m. Emanuel M. Benson, Dec. 26, 1964 (dec. 1971); m. Joseph F.X. Kaufman, Jan. 21, 1974. BA, U. Pa., 1944; LHD (hon.), L.I. U., 1987, 89, L.I. U., Southampton, 1988. Dir. pub. rels. Phila. Mus. Coll. Art, 1957-62; free lance journalist, 1960—; dir. Elaine Benson Gallery, Bridgehampton, N.Y., 1965—; dir. of community rels. Southampton (N.Y) Hosp., 1968-89; dir. Elaine Benson Gallery, Bridgehampton, N.Y., 1964—; editor The Hampton Mag., Bridgehampton, 1983-84, Dan's Papers, 1989. Author: Coffee and Brazil, 1962, Unmentionables: A Brief History of Underwear, 1996. Bd. dirs. Hampton Classic Horse Show, Bridgehampton, 1980—, Cultural Ctr. Southampton, 1988—; coun. overseers Southampton Coll., 1991—; cons. Southampton Hosp. Home: PO Box 3034 Montauk Hwy Bridgehampton NY 11932

BENSON, ELIZABETH POLK, Pre-Columbian art specialist; b. Washington, May 13, 1924; d. Theodore Booton and Rebecca Dean (Albin) B. BA, Wellesley Coll., 1945; MA, Cath. U. Am., 1956. Mus. aide, curator Nat. Gallery of Art, Washington, 1946-60; curator Pre-Columbian Collection, Dumbarton Oaks, Washington, 1962-79, dir. Ctr. for Pre-Columbian Studies, 1971-79; rsch. assoc. Inst. Andean Studies, Berkeley, Calif., 1980—; lectr. Cath. U. Am., Washington, 1968, 69; adj. prof. Columbia U., N.Y.C., 1973; sr. lectr. U. Tex., Austin, 1985; Andrew S. Keck disting. vis. prof. Am. U., Washington, 1987; cons. Montreal Mus. Fine Arts, 1980-84, 90-92, Princeton U. Art Mus., 1980, 82, 87; mem. adv. bd. L.Am. Indian Lits. Jour., Pitts., 1989—; mem. adv. com. Found. for Advancement of Mesoamerican Studies, Crystal River, Fla., 1994—; mem. pres.'s adv. coun. Bowers Mus. Cultural Art, Santa Ana, Calif., 1995—; co-curator traveling exhbn. Birds and Beasts of Ancient L.Am., 1995—. Author: The Maya World, 1967, 72, 77, The Mochica, 1972; co-author: Museums of the Andes, 1981, Atlas of Ancient America, 1986; co-editor: Olmec Art of Ancient Mexico, 1996. Mem. Soc. Woman Geographers, The Lit. Soc., Latin Am. Indian Lits. Assn. (v.p. 1989—, co-chair mus. com. 1994—). Home and Office: 8314 Old Seven Locks Rd Bethesda MD 20817-2005

BENSON, JOANNE E., lieutenant governor of Minnesota; b. Jan. 4, 1943; m. Robert Benson; 2 children. BS, St. Cloud State U. Mem. Minn. Senate, St. Paul, 1991-94; lt. gov. State of Minn., St. Paul, 1994—. Office: State Capitol Rm 130 Saint Paul MN 55155

BENSON, KAREN A., nursing educator; b. Havre, Mont., Sept. 10, 1946; d. William Duncan and Norma Evelyn (Erickson) Ross; children: Alice, Evan, David, Marc. BSN, Mont. State U., 1968; MS in Biology, Wash. State U., 1978, PhD in Vet. Sci., 1983; MS in Nursing, Oreg. Health Scis. U., 1986. Lectr. Seattle U. Contbr. articles to profl. publs. Dr. Lynn A. George scholar; Sigma Xi rsch. grantee. Mem. ANA, Wash. State Nurses Assn., Am. Holistic Nurses Assn., Sigma Theta Tau, Phi Kappa Phi. Home: 17103 25th Ave NE Seattle WA 98155-6124

BENSON, LILLIAN, film and videotape editor; b. N.Y.C., June 12, 1949. BFA, Pratt Inst., 1970. Film/videotape editor various orgns., 1973—, Film Roos, L.A.; guest spkr. in field. Recipient Emmy award nomination for Eyes on the Prize, 1990. Mem. Am. Cinema Editors. Democrat.

BENSON, LUCY PETERS WILSON, political and diplomatic consultant; b. N.Y.C., Aug. 25, 1927; d. Willard Oliver and Helen (Peters) Wilson; m. Bruce Buzzell Benson, Mar. 30, 1950 (dec. Mar. 1990). B.A., Smith Coll., 1949, M.A., 1955; L.H.D. (hon.), Wheaton Coll., Norton, Mass., 1965; LL.D. (hon.), U. Mass., 1969; L.H.D. (hon.), Bucknell U., 1972; LL.D. (hon.), U. Md., 1972; L.H.D. (hon.), Carleton Coll., 1973; LL.D. (hon.), Amherst Coll., 1974, Clark U., 1975; H.H.D., Springfield Coll., 1981; L.H.D. (hon.), Bates Coll., 1982. Mem. jr. exec. tng. program Bloomingdale's, N.Y.C., 1949-50; asst. dir. pub. rels. Smith Coll., 1950-53; rsch. asst. dept. Am. studies Amherst Coll., 1956-57; pres. Amherst LWV, Mass., 1957-61; pres. Mass. LWV, 1961-65, nat. pres., 1968-74; mem. Gov.'s cabinet and sec. human svcs. Commonwealth of Mass., 1975; mem. spl. commn. on adminstrv. rev. U.S. Ho. of Reps., Washington, 1976-77; under sec. State Security Assistance, Sci. and Tech. U.S. Dept. State, Washington, 1977-80; cons. U.S. Dept. State and SRI Internat., Washington, 1980-81; pres. Benson and Assocs., Amherst and Washington, 1981—; vice chmn. Citizen Network for Fgn. Affairs; trustee N.E. Utilities, 1971-74, 76-77; bd. dirs. Continental Group, Inc., Dreyfus Fund, Dreyfus Liquid Assets, Dreyfus Asset Allocation Fund, Dreyfus 401K Fund, Dreyfus Third Century Fund, Inc., Grumman Corp., Comms. Satellite Corp., Gen. Reins. Corp., Dreyfus Worldwide Dollar Money Market Fund, Inc., Logistics Mgmt. Inst. Mem. steering com. Urban Coalition, 1968, exec. com., 1970-75, 80-84, co-chmn., 1973-75; mem. Gov. Mass. Spl. Com. Rev. Sunday Closing Laws, 1961; mem. spl. commn. Mass. Legislature to Study Budgetary Powers of Trustees U. Mass., 1961-62; mem. Gov. Mass. Com. Rev. Salaries State Employees, 1963, Mass. Adv. Bd. Higher Ednl. Policy, 1962-65, Mass. Bd. Edn. Adv. Com. Racial Imbalance and Edn., 1964-65, Mass. adv. com. U.S. Commn. Civil Rights, 1964-73; vice chmn. Mass. Adv. Council Edn., 1965-68; mem. Mass. Com. Children and Youth Com. to Study Report by U.S. Children's Bur., Mass. Youth Svc. Div., 1967; mem. pub. adv. com. U.S. Trade Policy, 1968; mem. vis. com. John F. Kennedy Sch. Govt.; mem. Trilateral Commn., Coun. Fgn. Rels. Mem. town meeting, Amherst, 1957-74, finance com., 1960-66; trustee Edn. Devel. Center, Newton, Mass., 1967-72, Nat. Urban League, 1974-77, Smith Coll., 1975-80, Brookings Instn., 1974-77, Alfred P. Sloan Found., 1975-77, 81—, Bur. Social Sci. Rsch., Inc., 1985-87; bd. dirs. Catalyst, 1972-90, Internat. Exec. Svc. Corps, Atlantic Coun. of U.S., 1988—, vice chmn., 1993—; former bd. govs. Am. Nat. Red Cross, Common Cause, Women's Action Alliance; bd. govs. Internat. Ctr. on Election Law and Adminstrn., 1985-87; trustee Lafayette Coll., 1985—, vice chmn., 1990—. Recipient Achievement award Bur. Govt. Research, U. Mass., 1963; Distinguished Service award Boston Coll., 1965; Smith Coll. medal, 1969; Distinguished Civil Leadership award Tufts U., 1965; Distinguished Service award Northfield Mount Hermon Sch., 1976; Radcliffe fellow Radcliffe Inst., 1965-66, 66-67. Mem. NAACP, ACLU, Nat. Acad. Pub. Adminstrn., UN Assn., Urban League, Assn. Am. Indian Affairs, East African Wildlife Soc., Jersey Wildlife Preservation Trust Channel Islands, Internat. Inst. Strategic Studies. Home and Office: 46 Sunset Ave Amherst MA 01002-2018

BENSON, MARIE FRANCES, counselor; b. Chgo., July 14, 1952; d. Emil J. and Frances M. (Sawicki) Guidice; m. Robert Lee Benson, June 8, 1974; children: James R., Paul J. BS in Edn., No. Ill. U., 1974, MS in Edn., 1994. Registered counselor, Ill.; cert. tchr., Ill. Tchr. Hiawatha Sch. Dist. 426, Kirkland, Ill., 1979-95; counselor Rochelle (Ill.) Sch. Dist. 231, 1995—; trainer of trainers Here's Looking At You, 2000 drug curriculum, 1991—. Mem. DeKalb County Partnership for Substance Abuse Free Environ., 1991. Recipient bronze award Scholastic Coach mag., 1989. Mem. Am. Sch. Counselors Assn., Ill. Assn. Student Assistance Profls., Ill. Edn. Assn., Rochelle Elem. Edn. Assn. Home: 110 River Dr DeKalb IL 60115 Office: Rochelle Sch Dist 231 1050 N 9th St Rochelle IL 60168

BENSON, SANDRA JEAN, media specialist; b. Winona, Minn., Apr. 13, 1949; d. Artha B.O. and Virginia H. (McNamer) Thompson. BS, U. Wis., River Falls, 1975, MAT in Elem. Edn., 1982. Libr. Cen. High Sch., Paddock Lake, Wis., 1974-76; media specialist Hudson (Wis.) Pub. Schs., 1976—; instr. U. Wis., River Falls, 1991—; cons. tech. several ednl. and bus. orgns., River Falls, 1990—. Mem. ALA, Wis. Ednl. Media Assn., Soc. Sch. Librs. Internat., Assn. for Ednl. Communications and Tech. (div. sch. media specialist). Office: Hudson Mid Sch 1300 Carmichael Rd Hudson WI 54016-7711

BENSON, SARA ELIZABETH, real estate broker, real estate appraiser; b. Columbia, S.C., Nov. 29, 1960; d. Herbert Lankford Benson and Anna Marian (Stanley) Tucker; m. Donald Edward O'Connor, Apr. 29, 1984 (div. Oct. 1993); m. Donald Joseph DeBat, Aug. 20, 1994; children from previous marriage: D. Edward, Herbert L. Benson IV. Student, U. S.C., 1977, Am. Conservatory Music, Chgo., 1978-81. Lic. real estate broker, Ill., S.C.; designated cert. real estate brokerage mgr.; approved ind. fee appraiser; cert. real estate appraiser, Ill. V.p. O'Connor & Assocs., Chgo., 1982-92; pres., owner Benson Stanley Realty, Chgo., 1990—; owner Sara Benson Cons., Inc., Chgo., 1992—; fee appraiser FHA, HUD, Chgo., 1986—; speaker, author in field. Mem. NAFE, Nat. Assn. Realtors, Assn. Fed. Appraisers, Real Estate Buyer's Agt. Coun., Ill. Assn. Realtors, Chgo. Assn. Realtors (chair profl. standards com.), North Shore Bd. Realtors, Real Estate Brokerage Mgrs. Coun., MLS No. Ill., Nat. Assn. Ind. Fee Appraisers, Bus. Execs. Assn. Chgo. Office: Benson Stanley Realty 1708 N Wells St Chicago IL 60614-5806

BENSON, SARAH D., rehabilitation services professional; b. Charleston, May 27, 1961; d. Harold and Sarah Jane (Burch) Dayse; m. Larry Benard Benson, Aug. 11, 1984. AA, U. S.C., 1980, BA, 1981; MA, Webster U., 1991. Clin. counselor S.C. Dept. Mental Health, Columbia, 1982-85, dir. adult svcs., 1988-93; exec. dir. Aiken County Help One, Aiken, S.C., 1984-88; state dir. program svc. Easter Seals of S.C., Columbia, 1993-95; dir. The Rose M. Lowe Easter Seals Rehab. Ctr., 1993-95; program dir. Rehab Care Group, Orangburg, S.C., 1995—; co-owner SPOT Therapy Svcs., Columbia, S.C., 1995. Mem. S.C. Developmental Disability Coun., Columbia, 1993-94, United Way ot the Midlands, 1993—. 1st lt. USAFR, 1996—. Named Profl. of the Yr. S.C. Autistic Soc., 1991. Mem. Nat. Assn. Female Execs., S.C. Assn. Med. Mgrs., Exec. Dirs.' Assn. Home: 124 Westport Dr Columbia SC 29223 Office: Rehab Care Group Regional Med Ctr 3000 St Matthew Rd Orangeburg SC 29115

BENSON, SHARON JOAN, mathematics educator; b. Glendale, Calif., Aug. 23, 1964; d. Paul John and Arleen Camille (Green) B. BS in Math., Calif. Poly. State U., 1987; MST in Math., U. N.H., 1992. Cert. single subject clear math., Calif. Tchr. math. Victor Valley Union High Sch. Dist., Victorville, Calif., 1988—; part-time instr. Victor Valley C.C., Victorville, 1993—. Mem. Nat. Coun. Tchrs. Math., Calif. Math. Coun., Oreg. Coun. Tchrs. of Math., Assn. Women in Math. Republican. Roman Catholic. Office: Victor Valley High Sch 16500 Mojave Dr Victorville CA 92392-3822

BENT, MARY JANE, photographer; b. Allentown, Pa., Jan. 12, 1945; d. William Edward and Jean Louise (Moore) Fowler; m. George Bent, Aug. 20, 1966 (div. Mar. 1988); children: Colin William, Geoffrey Fowler. BA, Mt. Holyoke Coll., 1966; women-in-sci. cert., Chatham Coll., 1983. Rsch. assoc. Yale U., New Haven, 1966-68; rsch. asst. Coll. Physicians and Surgeons Columbia U., N.Y.C., 1968-72; instr. in photography Pitts. Ctr. for Arts, 1980-89; staff photographer Allegheny Gen. Hosp., Pitts., 1983-89, sr. photographer, 1989-94; dir. photography Allegheny Health, Edn. and Rsch. Found., Pitts. and Phila., 1994—; part-time photographer Allegheny Gen. Hosp., 1980-83. Coordinator, editor: Portrait of an Urban Medical Center, 1991 (Addy award 1992, PRA Print Mag. award 1992); contbr. numerous photographs to profl. publs. Bd. dirs. Silver Eye Ctr. for Photography, Pitts., 1992—; sec. Photoimagers Guild, Pitts., 1984-87. Presbyterian. Home: 750 S Linden Ave Pittsburgh PA 15208 Office: Allegheny Health Edn & Rsch 320 E North Ave Pittsburgh PA 15212

BENTEL, MARIA-LUISE RAMONA AZZARONE (MRS. FREDERICK R. BENTEL), architect, educator; b. N.Y.C., June 15, 1928; d. Louis and Maria-Teresa (Massaro) Azzarone; m. Frederick R. Bentel, Aug. 16, 1952; children: Paul Louis, Peter Andreas, Maria Elisabeth. BArch, MIT, 1951; Fulbright scholar, Scuola d'Architettura, Venice, Italy, 1952-53. Registered profl. architect, Conn., N.Y., N.J., Va., Vt. registered profl. planner, N.J. Partner Bentel & Bentel (Architects), Locust Valley, N.Y., 1955—; pres. Tesstoria Realty Corp., N.Y.C., 1961—; v.p., sec.-treas. Correlated Designs, Inc., Locust Valley, 1961—; partner Cobblestone Enterprises, 1967; founding mem. Locust Valley Bus. Dist. Planning Commn., 1968—; regional vice chair MIT Ednl. Coun.; adv. mem. MIT Coun. for the Arts; assoc. prof. architecture Sch. Architecture and Fine Arts N.Y. Inst. Tech.; mem. APD panel N.Y. State Coun. for Arts, 1985-89. Archtl. works include C.W. Post Coll. L.I. U (N.Y. State Assn. Architects award 1975, Gold Archi award L.I. Assn. Architects 1974), Hempstead Bank, Nassau Centre Office Bldg., North Shore Unitarian Sch., Plandome, N.Y., Shelter Rock Library, Searingtown, N.Y., St. Anthony's Ch., Nanuet, N.Y., Kinloch Farm, Va., Steinberg Learning Center-Woodmere (N.Y.) Acad., St. Francis de Sales Ch., Bennington, Vt., Neitlich residence, Oyster Bay Cove, N.Y., Amityville (N.Y.) Pub. Library, Jericho (N.Y.) Pub. Library, John B. Gambling residence, Lattingtown, N.Y., Glen Cove (N.Y.) Boys' Club at Lincoln House, Salten Hall, N.Y. Inst. Tech., N.Y. Coll. Osteo. Med. at N.Y. Inst. Tech., Old Westbury, Commack (N.Y.) Pub. Library, St. Mary Star of the Sea Ch., Far Rockaway, Oberlin Residence, St. Hyacinth's Ch.; Museums at Stony Brook, St. Joseph's Coll. Libr., N.Y. Inst. Tech. Libr., 1989, Simpson residence, St. Stephen's Ch., Warwick, N.Y., 1991, Pavilion Old Westbury (N.Y.); contbr. religious architecture chpt. to Time Saver Standards (De Chiara and Callender), 1973. Mem. comml. panel Am. Arbitration Assn.; bd. dirs. L.I. Soc. AIA; chmn. adv. panel on govt. bldg. projects GSA, 1976; chmn. Inst. Internat. Edn.; mem. nat. adv.-selection com. Fulbright-Hays awards, 1976-78, 80, 82; chair Locust Valley Libr. Adv. Bd., 1973-80. Named Woman Architect of Year Nassau-Suffolk County, 1976. Fellow AIA (corp. mem., chmn. design com., dir. L.I. chpt.); mem. N.Y. State Assn. Architects (chmn. design awards com.), Nat. Coun. Archtl. Registration Bds., MIT Alumnae Assn., MIT Alumni L.I. Home: 23 Frost Creek Dr Locust Valley NY 11560-1029 Office: 22 Buckram Rd Locust Valley NY 11560-1928

BENTLEY, ELLEN JANE, physician; b. Marion, Ind., Apr. 7, 1954; d. Alfred Dodds and Henriette (Hillenius) B.; m. Charles Patrick Fikes, Oct. 11, 1986; 1 child, Kathryn. BA, Wheaton Coll., 1975; MD, St. Louis U., 1983. Diplomate Am. Bd. Ob/Gyn. Physician Carver Cmty. Health Ctr., Schenectady, N.Y., 1987-91; pvt. practice Bangor, Maine, 1991—. Mem. Am. Coll. Ob/Gyn. Office: 417 State St Bangor ME 04401

BENTLEY, LISSA FRANCES, elementary education educator; b. N.Y.C., June 30, 1963; d. George Albert III and Nancy Ann (McNamara) B. AB, Smith Coll., 1985; MA, Columbia U., 1988. Legal asst. Davis Polk &

Wardwell, N.Y.C., 1985-87; presch. tchr. Episcopal Sch., N.Y.C., 1988-89; elem. tchr. Greenwich (Conn.) Pub. Schs., 1989—. Lector, eucharistic min. St. Mary Ch., Greenwich, 1991—. Mem. Greenwich Edn. Assn. (rep. profl. rights and responsibilities com. 1994—), Greenwich-Stamford Smith Club (alumnae admissions coord. 1989—), Kappa Delta Pi. Office: North Street Sch 381 North St Greenwich CT 06830

BENTLEY, MARGARET ANN, librarian; b. Tawas City, Mich., June 13, 1956; d. Rupert A. and Joy A. (Bills) B. AB in English, Gordon Coll., 1978; MA in Libr. Sci., U. Mich., 1979. Cert. libr., Mich. Adult svcs. libr., asst. dir. Shiawassee Dist. Libr. (formerly Owosso Pub. Libr.), Owosso, Mich., 1979—. Author: 75 Years of Service, 1989. Mem. AAUW (treas. 1984—), Mich. Libr. Assn., Beta Phi Mu, Lambda Iota Tau, Phi Alpha Chi. Office: Shiawassee Dist Libr 502 W Main Owosso MI 48867

BENTLEY, SARA, newspaper publishing executive. Pres. Gannett Northwest Newspaper Group, Salem, Oreg., 1988—. Office: Statesman-Journal Co Inc PO Box 13009 280 Church St NE Salem OR 97301*

BENTLEY-MIXON, CHARMAINE CLARK, secondary education educator; b. Austin, Dec. 15, 1954; d. Harold Ray and Charmaine Bentley; m. Charles Oliver Mixon, May 4, 1980; 1 child, Charlotte Farrar Mixon. BA in Anthropology, U. Tex., 1977, BS in Geological Sci., 1977; BS in Computer Sci., SW Okla. State U., 1984, MEd in Math., 1988. DATA engr. Dresser Industries, Magcobar DATA, Oklahoma City, 1972-82; tchr. Dallas Ind. Sch. Dist., 1988—, tchr., technologist F.D. Roosevelt H.S., 1992—. Asst. troop leader Girl Scout U.S., Farmers Branch, Tex., 1992-95, Sunshine Literacy Project Coord., 1989-91; v.p. IB Parent Booster Com., Plano, Tex., 1995-96; troop chmn. Boy Scout Am., Elk City, Okla., 1986-87. Recipient Award of Appreciation, City of Farmers Branch, 1990; Tandy Tech. scholar, Fort Worth, 1994. Mem. Am. Assn. Petroleum Geologists, Nat. Coun. Tchrs. Math., Internat. Soc. Tech. Edn., Tex. Coun. Tchrs. Math., Tex. Computer Edn. Assn., Assn. Tex. Profl. Educators. Episcopalian.

BENTON-BORGHI, BEATRICE HOPE, educational consultant, author, publisher; b. San Antonio, Nov. 7, 1946; d. Donald Francis and Beatrice Hope (Peche) Benton; BA in Chemistry, North Adams State Coll., 1968; MEd, Boston U., 1972; m. Peter T. Borghi, Aug. 12, 1980; children: Kathryn Benton Borghi, Sarah Benton Borghi. Tchr. chemistry Cathedral H.S., Springfield, Mass., 1968-69; tchr. sci. and history Munich (W.Ger.) Am. H.S., 1969-70; tchr. English, Tokyo, Japan, 1970-71; tchr. chemistry and sci. Marlborough (Mass.) H.S., 1971-80; project dir., adminstr. ESEA, Marlborough Pub. Schs., 1976-77; CEO, pres., chmn. bd. dirs. Open Minds, Inc., 1996—; project dir., proposal writer Title III, Title IX, U.S. Dept. Edn., 1975-76, 76-77; evaluation team New Eng. Assn. Schs. and Colls., 1974, 78; mem. regional dept. edn. com., 1977-78; ednl. cons., lectr., 1978—. Author: Project ABC (Access By Computer), 1991, Alternative Funding/Recycling Project, 1991, Down the Aisle, 1996, Best Friends, 1996, A Thousand Lights, 1996, Whoa, Nellie!, 1996. Energy conservation rep. Marlborough's Overall Econ. Devel. Com., 1976; mem. strategic planning com. Upper Arlington Sch., Ohio, 1994; chmn. Marlborough's Energy Conservation Task Force, 1975; dir. Walk for Mankind, 1972; sec. Group Action for Marlborough Environment, 1975-76; bd. dirs. Girls Club, Marlborough, 1979; pres. Sisters, Inc., 1979-83, dba Open Minds, 1995. Mem. AAUW, Council for Exceptional Children, Nat. Women's Health Network. Home: 2449 Edington Rd Columbus OH 43221-3047 Office: Open Minds Inc PO Box 21325 Columbus OH 43221-0325

BENTZ, PENNY LENNEA, special education educator; b. Fremont, Nebr., Nov. 29, 1949; d. Edward Earl and June Lorraine (Larson) B.; 1 child, Nikole Lorraine. BA in Edn., Wayne State Coll., 1972. Cert. tchr., Wash., Nebr. Tchr. grades K-2 Sch. Dist. 23, Valley, Nebr., 1972-74; tchr. Sch. Dist. 90, Scribner, Nebr., 1976-77; substitute tchr. Westside Sch. Dist., Millard Pub. Schs., Omaha, 1974-88; spl. edn. tchr. Lake Washington Sch. Dist., Kirkland, 1988-89, 91—, Renton (Wash.) Schs., 1989-90, CHILD Inst., Bellevue, Wash., 1990-91; mem. adv. com. Comprehensive Sys. of Pers. Devel., Olympia, Wash., 1993-95; mem. Lake Washington Sch. Dist. Leadership Com. Severe Behavior Disabled Edn. grantee Seattle U., 1993. Mem. NEA, Wash. Edn. Assn. spl. edn. commn. 1992-95, spl. edn. cert. prarprofl. task force), Lake Washington Edn. Assn. (bldg. rep. 1991-95), Delta Kappa Gamma (pres. 1994—). Methodist. Home: 8501 Willows Rd NE Apt 246 Redmond WA 98052

BENVENISTE, DEBRA HENRIETTE, clinical social worker; b. N.Y.C., July 7, 1956; d. Jacques and Sheila Ann (Kraus) B. BA in Sociology and French, SUNY, Binghamton, 1978; MA in Criminal Justice, Clark U., 1982; MSW, Smith Coll., 1987. Lic. clin. social worker, Conn. Drug and alcohol counselor Chandler Street Ctr., Worcester, Mass., 1980-85; clin. social worker Dept. Correction, Somers, Conn., 1987-94, Youth Svc. Bur., Mansfield, Conn., 1989-95; pvt. practice Canterbury (Conn.) Psychotherapy Assocs., 1995—; clin. cons. Brooklyn (Conn.) House, 1993—, Gilead House, Middletown, Conn., 1994—; condr. workshops, Mass., Conn., 1982—; MSW field supr. Smith Coll. Sch. for Social Work, Northampton, Mass., 1991-94, Fordham U., Bronx, N.Y., 1995—. Author: Diagnosis and Treatment of Sociopaths and Clients with Sociopathic Traits, 1996. Clk. Holland (Mass.) Econ. Devel. Bd., 1995—. Mem. NASW, Acad. Cert. Social Workers, Conn. Soc. Clin. Social Work, Phi Beta Kappa. Office: Canterbury Psychotherapy Assocs PO Box 266 39 S Canterbury RD Canterbury CT 06331

BENVENUTO, VIRGINIA A., journalist, magazine mananging editor; b. Montivideo, Uruguay, Mar. 26, 1959; d. Albert J. and Lidia E. (Nichele) B. BS in Journalism, U. Md., 1988. Mng. editor Telecomm. Alert, United Comm. Group, Bethesda, Md., 1988-90; staff writer Ill. Politics, CNC Pub., Chgo., 1991-92; assoc. editor Control Ambiential, Advanstar Comm., Glen Ellyn, Ill., 1992-93; mng. editor Alimentos Procesados, Cahners Publishing Co., Des Plaines, Ill., 1993-95, Environ. Solutions, Environ. Product News, Santa Ana, Calif., 1995—. Mem. Soc. Profl. Journalists. Office: Avanstar Comm Ste 600 201 E Sandpointe Ave Santa Ana CA 92707

BENZ, RACHEL BERMAN, dancer; b. Berkeley, Calif., Nov. 14, 1963; d. Ronald Berman and Judith Ellen Harding; m. Eric Charles Benz, Nov. 20, 1988. BFA, SUNY, Purchase, 1985. Dancer Ballet Hispanico of N.Y., N.Y.C., 1985-87, Joyce Trisler Danscompany, N.Y.C., 1987-89, May O'Donnel Concert Dance Co., N.Y.C., 1988, Paul Taylor Dance Co., N.Y.C., 1989—. Dancer benefit for Paul Newman's Hole in Wall Gang Camp for Children, 1995, Paul Taylor: Speaking in Tongues, PBS Dance in Am. TV program, 1991, Paul Taylor: The Wrecker's Ball, PBS Dance in Am. TV program, 1996. Active Dancers Responding to AIDS. Office: Paul Taylor Dance Co 552 Broadway Fl 2D New York NY 10012-3947

BENZIES, BONNIE JEANNE, clinical and industrial psychologist; b. Chgo., May 3, 1943; d. Roy Benzies and Margaret Lucille (Hernly) Benzies-Sorensen. BS, MacMurray Coll., 1965; MS, Ill. Inst. Tech., 1971, PhD, 1980. Lic. clin. psychologist; cert. nat./internat. cert. alcohol and other drug abuse counselor; cert. alcohol, tobacco and other drug abuse preventionist; diplomate, bd. cert. forensic examiner. Statistician, psychologist State of Ill., Chgo., 1966-73; psychologist State of Ill., Manteno, 1976-82; pub. svc. adminstr. State of Ill., Elgin, 1988—; psychologist Ingalls Meml. Hosp., Harvey, Ill., 1982-84, Cook County Juvenile Ct., Chgo., 1987-88; pvt. practice Chgo., Hanover Park, Palatine, Ill., 1984—; cons., trainer PREVENTION PLUS of Palatine, 1994—; grad. tchg. asst. Ill. Inst. Tech., Chgo., 1973-74; mem. staff Hoffman Estates Med. Ctr., Woodland Hosp., Hoffman Estates. Co-author psychol. test: Time Questionnaire, 1979. Mem. Nat. Task Force on Depressive Disorders, 1991—; mem. Statewide Subcom. on Mentally Ill Substance Abuser, 1991-93. MacMurray scholar, 1961-65, Am. Legion scholar, 1963-64; recipient Achievement award in addictions counseling Loop Coll., 1986. Mem. APA, Am. Assn. Christian Counselors, Am. Bd. Forensic Examiners, Chgo. Assn. for Psychoanalytic Psychology, Employee Assistance Profls. Assn., Christian Assn. Psychol. Studies, Internat. Critical Incident Stress Found., Inc., Palatine C. of C. Home and Office: Prevention Plus of Palatine 1531 E Anderson Dr Palatine IL 60067-4101

BENZIO, DONNA MARIE, cardiopulmonary rehabilitation nurse; b. Connellsville, Pa., June 5, 1955; d. John Robert and Ewaldina Marie (Kosisko) Bartholomai; m. Benjamin Arthur Benzio, Nov. 18, 1978; children: Benjamin, Ashley, Zachary. Diploma in nursing, Mercy Hosp., Pitts., 1978; student, Pa. State U., Fayette. RN, Pa.; BLS, Am. Heart Assn.; cert. outpatient cardiac rehab. nursing Nursing Cons., Inc. Med. staff nurse Uniontown Hosp., 1976-77, staff nurse ICU, 1977-80, cardiac rehab. nurse, 1980-87, dir. cardiac diagnostics, 1987-91, cardiopulmonary rehab. nurse, 1991—; leader cardiac club Uniontown Hosp.; bd. dirs. Am. Heart Assn., Uniontown. Recipient Appreciation award Am. Heart Assn., 1990-92, Walk-A-Thon cert., 1992. Mem. Am. Assn. Cardiovascular and Pulmonary Rehab. Roman Catholic. Home: RD 1 Box 304 Connellsville PA 15425-9201

BENZO-BONACCI, ROSEMARY ANNE, health facility administrator; b. Utica, N.Y., Apr. 28, 1955; d. Rocco Anthony and Grace Lillian (Maggi) B.; m. Michael V. AAS, Mohawk Valley C.C., 1988; BS, New Sch. for Social Rsch., 1992, postgrad., 1994—. With Mohawk Valley C.C., Utica, 1977-89, alumni asst., 1989-93; dir. vol. svcs., pub. rels. and devel. Charles T. Sitrin Health Care Ctr., New Hartford, N.Y., 1993—; program dir. Youth Mentorship Activities Program in Health Care Svcs. Dept. Health N.Y. Pres. Vol. Horizons, 1993—, Coalition for Tobacco Control, 1994; bd. dirs., mem. task force pub. edn. sector Utica Coalition for a Smoke-Free Cmty., 1989-93, chair ann. coalition meeting, 1990-91; chair search com. for tech. asst. Mohawk Valley C.C., 1990. Mem. Mohawk Valley C.C. Alumni Assn. (bd. dirs. 1991-93). Democrat. Roman Catholic. Home: 16 Symphony Pl Whitesboro NY 13492-2227 Office: Charles T Sitrin Health Care Ctr Box 2050 Tilden Ave New Hartford NY 13413

BERARD, MARIA DOLORES, clothing designer; b. Havana, Cuba, June 10, 1960; came to U.S., 1960; d. Pedro and Maria Luisa (Olagorta) Barquin; m. Roger Ernest Berard, Apr. 23, 1983; children: Jason Anthony, Roger August, Lucas Adrian, Sophia Anastasia. Student, U. Vt., 1979-83. Part owner Aimee's Children's Clothing, Shelburne, Vt., 1984-85; tchr. Ch. St. Ctr. for Cmty. Edn., Burlington, Vt., 1986; custom designer, seamstress Pietz-Barquin, Burlington, 1986; quilter Country Linens from Vt., Burlington, 1986-87; designer, pres. Loli of Vt., Inc., St. Albans, 1987—. Lifetime mem. PTA, City Elem., St. Albans, 1992—; religious educator St. Mary's Cath. Ch., St. Albans, 1993. Recipient award as Woman of Achievement, Bus. and Profl. Women Franklin County, 1994. Democrat. Roman Catholic.

BERARDELLI, CATHERINE MARIE, women's health nurse, nurse educator; b. Portland, Oreg., Aug. 22, 1949; d. Francis Lawrence and Jean Carolyn (Petersen) Ison; m. Victor Francis Berardelli Jr., May 28, 1988. BSN, U. Oreg., 1972; MSN, U. So. Maine, Portland, 1985; PhD, Adelphi U., 1994, FNP, 1995. RN; cert. in inpatient obstetrics, family nurse practitioner. Night staff nurse Dornbecker Childrens Hosp., Portland, Oreg., 1972-73; night charge nurse Maine Med. Ctr., Portland, 1973-78; evening supr. St. Andrews Hosp., Boothbay Harbor, Maine, 1978-82, DON, 1982-85; instr. nursing Cen. Maine Med. Ctr. Sch. Nursing, Lewiston, 1985-88, U. So. Maine Sch. Nursing, Portland, 1986-90; clin. nurse specialist Long Island Jewish Med. Ctr., New Hyde Park, N.Y., 1990-92; clin. learning lab. coord. Adelphi U., Garden City, N.Y., 1991-94; dir. nursing programs Westbrook Coll., 1995—; adj. assoc. prof. Simmons Coll., 1995—; expert witness Kelly Remmel & Zimmerman, Portland, 1989-92; test item writer Nat. League Nursing, N.Y.C., 1991; vis. prof. Sch. Nursing Adelphi U., 1993-95. Co-author patient edn. brochure. Mem. Maine People's Alliance, Portland, 1985-90; mem. New Eng. Women's Studies Assn., 1987; bd. dirs. Kaler Vaill Home for Older Women, 1996. U. So. Maine rsch. grantee, 1989. Mem. ANA, Assn. Women's Health Obstetrics and Neonatal Nurses, Nat. League Nursing, Maine Nursing Honor Soc. (charter), Maine Nurse Practitioners Assn., Sigma Theta Tau. Home: 149 Pine Point Rd Scarborough ME 04074-8855

BERARDINI, JACQUELINE HERNANDEZ, lawyer; b. Pueblo, Colo., Sept. 16, 1949; d. Basilio Hernandez and Lorenza (Huerta) Zamarripa; stepfather John E. Zamarripa; m. Jose A. Soliz, Aug. 1971 (div. 1980); 1 child, Christopher A.; m. Brian J. Berardini, Oct. 17, 1981; 1 child, Michael J. BA in Psychology, U. Colo., 1971; MA in Counseling, U. No. Colo., 1973; JD, U. Denver, 1980. Bar: Colo. 1980, U.S. Dist. Ct. Colo. 1980, U.S. Ct. Appeals (10th cir.) 1990, U.S. Supreme Ct. 1991. Sr. rehab. counselor divsn. rehab. Colo. Dept. Social Svcs., 1974-77; assoc. Jeffrey A. Springer, P.C. law firm, 1980-85; dep. atty. gen. Office of Colo. Atty. Gen., 1985-91; asst. to dir., dir. multi-media focal group Office of Environment, Colo. Dept. of Health, Denver, 1991-93, dir. environ integration group Colo. Dept. Health and Environment, Denver, 1993—; apptd. to superfund rev. subcom. Nat. Adv. Com. on Environ. and Policy and Tech., EPA; apptd. to subcom. on transport and opening of waste isolation pilot plant Western Govs.' Assn.; mem. subcom. on federal facilities compliance Nat. Govs.' Assn.; apptd. Pueblo Army Depot Chem. Demilitarization Citizen Rev. Com.; alt. mem. high-level radioactive waste com. Western Interstate Energy Bd.; presenter in field; lead negotiator Colo. Rocky Flats cleanup, 1996. Contbr. articles to profl. jours. Mem. Colo. Bar Assn., Denver Bar Assn., Colo. Hispanic Bar Assn., Colo. Hispanic League. Office: Colo Dept Health and Environment 0E/EIG B2 4300 Cherry Creek Dr S Denver CO 80222-1530

BERASI, MARION THERESA, nurse; b. Sewickley, Pa., July 20, 1953; d. Michael Edward and Helen Eleanor (Pollack) Dzurko; m. Santo C. Berasi, July 10, 1982. BSN, Alderson Broaddus Coll., 1975; MBA, U. Steubenville, 1988; postgrad., U. Pitts., 1994. RN, Pa. Staff nurse U. Pitts. Med. Ctr., 1975-80, sr. staff nurse, 1980—. Co-writer, chair med. presentation A Detour on the Road to Recovery, 1994. V.p. condo. coun. Kentley House, Pitts., 1990-92, treas., 1992-94, sec., 1994—. Mem. ANA, NAFE, Pa. Nurses Assn., Am. Nurses Found. Roman Catholic. Home: 5619 Kentucky Ave Pittsburgh PA 15232

BERBERIAN, SUE, information systems specialist; b. Plainfield, N.J., Nov. 25, 1959; m. Lance V. Berberian, Apr. 20, 1991. BA in English Lit., Rutgers U., 1986. Dist. syss. engring. mgr. Businessland Corp., N.Y.C., 1989-92; northeast regional tech. advisor Compucom Syss., N.Y.C., 1992; mgr. network & PC svcs. Ernst & Young, N.Y.C., 1993; sys. cons. EDS, Bedminster, N.J., 1993-95; dist. sys. mgr. Telxon Corp., Woodbridge, N.J., 1995-96; dir. info. tech. MCS, Somerset, N.J., 1996—. Home: 303 Top Ave Green Brook NJ 08812

BERCH, BETTINA EILEEN, writer; b. Washington, May 25, 1950; d. Julian and Mollie (Lewis) B.; 1 child, Seferina. BA, Barnard Coll., N.Y.C., 1971; MA, U. Wisc., Madison, 1973, PhD, 1975. Asst. prof. econs. Williams Coll., Williamstown, Mass., 1976-77, Barnard Coll., N.Y.C., 1977-85; columnist, contbg. editor Belles Lettres Mag., North Potomac, Md., 1993—. Author: The Endless Day: The Political Economy of Women & Work, 1982, Radical By Design: The Life & Style of Elizabeth Hawes, 1988. Home and Office: 878 W End Ave 4A New York NY 10025

BERCOVITCH, HANNA MARGARETA, editor; b. Chgo., Il., Sept. 5, 1934; d. Sven Victor and Elizabeth (Rubin) Malmquist; m. Sacvan Bercovitch, July 29, 1956 (div. Mar. 1987); 1 son, Eytan. Student, St. Thomas More Coll., 1960, Sir George Williams Coll., Montreal, 1960-61. Acquisition librarian Honnold Library, Claremont, Calif., 1961-62, acting rare book librarian, 1962-63, spl. project staff, 1963-64; asst. editing Partisan Rev., Rutgers U. Congress Monthly, N.Y.C., 1974-75, 78-80; free lance research assoc. Columbia U., N.Y.C., 1965-80; sr. editor Library of Am. Literary Classics, N.Y.C., 1980-86, editor-in-chief, 1986—; guest curator Melville Whitman Exhibit, N.Y. Pub. Libr., 1982. Environ. commr. City of Leonia, N.J., 1971-73. Mem. Grolier Club (N.Y.C.). Office: Libr Am Lit Classics US 14 E 60th St New York NY 10022-1006

BERENS, BETTY KATHRYN MCADAM, community program administrator; b. Wheeling, W.Va., Dec. 17, 1927; d. Will and Elizabeth Margaret (Wickham) McAdam; m. Alan Robert Berens, June 18, 1949; children: Robert Seton, Kathryn Elizabeth. BA cum laude, We. Res. U., 1949; postgrad., Kent State U., 1967. Vol. various cities, Ohio, 1963-88; founder Western Res. Human Svcs., Akron, Ohio, 1975-84; cons. Hudson (Ohio) Local Schs., Addison County, Vt., 1968-88, coord. cmty./sch. vol. program (VIP); pres. aux. bd. Porter Med. Ctr., Middlebury, Vt., 1990-92; vol. Hawthornden State Hosp., Cleve., 1963-65; vol. probation officer Mcpl. Ct., Cuyahoga Falls, Ohio, 1973-74; comm. chmn. Elderly Svcs. Inc., Middlebury, 1990-95; cmty. sch. vol. cons. Ohio Dept. Edn., Columbus, 1984-88; bd. dirs. Addison County Home Health Care Agy., Champlain Valley Agy. on Aging. Bd. dirs. Porter Med. Ctr., 1990-92; bd. dirs. Internat. Inst., Akron, 1983-88, pres., 1986-87; mem. Summit County Bd. Edn., Akron, 1977-88, pres., 1981, 86; chmn. Hudson Cares, 1974-76; comm. chmn. Addison County United Way. Recipient Cmty. Svc. award Hudson Jaycees, 1984, Commendation for Outstanding Svc. in Edn., Pres. Ronald Reagan, 1988. Mem. Phi Delta Kappa (Leader in Edn. 1977, 88). Home: RR 2 Box 3510 Middlebury VT 05753-8904

BERESFORD, MADELEINE ROSAMOND SYLVIA, theater director, puppeteer; b. N.Y.C., Jan. 28, 1959; d. John Spencer Beresford and Myriam Ruth (Cohn) Hartog; m. Jeffrey Allen Burger, May 1, 1994; 1 child, Andre Beresford Burger. Mime student, Etienne Decroux, Paris, 1977; BA in Theater Arts, Oberlin Coll., 1981; apprentice, Salzburg Marionette Theater, Austria, 1980; student of Lee Tien-lu, Taipei, 1989. Sound technician Ridiculous Theatrical Co., N.Y.C., 1978; puppeteer, puppetmaker Ragabash Puppet Theater, N.Y.C., 1981-87; performer, workshop leader Shadowbox Theater, N.Y.C., 1985-92; puppetry tchr. Columbia Grammar Sch., N.Y.C., 1986-88; writer, dir., performer, puppetmaker Nassau County Puppetry Program, Mineola, N.Y., 1990-91; dir. Chinese Hand-Puppetry Project, N.Y.C., 1992; artistic dir., co-founder Galapagos Puppet Theater, Ridgewood, N.J., 1987—. Prodr.: (film) Theater of the Palms: The World of Puppet Master Lee Tien-lu, 1989; performer, writer puppet shows, 1987—. Grantee Henson Found., 1991. Jewish. Home and Office: 158 Hope St Ridgewood NJ 07450-4505

BERESFORD, MARY JO THERESA, theatre educator; b. Cin., July 13, 1949; d. William Dale and Coletta Josephine (Megrew) B. BA, Edgecliff Coll., 1971; MFA, U. Cin. Conservatory of Music, 1977. Teaching asst. U. Cin., 1975-77; lectr. Edgecliff Coll., Cin., 1978-80; choreographer Xavier U. Singers, Cin., 1973-86; lectr. U. Cin., 1980-84, No. Ky. Univ., Highland Heights, Ky., 1982—; chair Golden Galazy Awards Speech/Drama Com., Cin., 1992-96; critic Ohio Cmty. Theatre Assn., Cin., 1987-96. Dir. plays Assassins, 1994, Biloxi Blues, 1994, Tintypes, 1992, The Pajama Game, 1996. Poll worker Hamilton County Bd. Elections, Norwood, Ohio, 1990-93. Mem. AAUW, S.E. Theatre Conf., Ky. Theatre Assn. Democrat. Roman Catholic. Home: 5413 Carthage Ave Norwood OH 45212-1023 Office: No Ky Univ Nunn Dr Highland Heights KY 41099-1007

BERETS, EILEEN TOLKOWSKY, artist; b. Antwerp, Belgium, July 15, 1930; came to U.S., 1940; d. Marcel and Marthe Germaine (Kleinberg) Tolkowsky; m. Donald J. Berets, June 24, 1956; children: James Carl, Susan Lee. BA in Economics, Wellesley Coll., 1952; student, Art Student's League, N.Y.C., 1953-56; studied with Ethel Todd George, Stamford, Conn., 1983, 84, studied with Diane Faxon, 1984-92; student, Silvermine Guild, 1984-87. Cons. Stone Studio, Stamford, Conn., Our World Gallery, 1991—. Solo and duo exhbns. include U. Conn., Stamford, 1984, Stamford Art Assn. Landmark Tower, 1986, New Canaan (Conn.) Art Assn. Waveny Carriage Barn, 1988, Greenwich (Conn.) Art Soc. Marsh & McLennan, 1989, Conn. Commn. Arts Legis. Bldg., Hartford, 1990, Our World Gallery, Stamford, 1991, Darien (Conn.) Libr., 1992, Art in the Garden, 1995; exhibited in group shows at (juried) Nat. Arts Club, N.Y.C., 1984, Stamford Art Assn., 1984-95, Art Soc. of Old Greenwich, 1984-93, Conn. Art Ann. Competition Stamford Mus., 1985, 88, 91, Greenwich Art Soc., 1985-95, New Canaan Soc. Arts, 1992-95, (invitational) AAUW Salute to Conn. Artists, 1983-88, Stamford Cmty. Arts Coun. Eight Watercolorists, 1985, Conn. Pub. TV Preview Exhbn., Hartford, New Haven, Stamford, 1990, 91, Hartford Architecture Conservancy, 1991, Wellesley Coll., 1992, Stamford Art Assn. Lucas Industries, 1992, 93, Faber Birren Nat. Color Award show, 1996; represented in permanent collections Stamford Art in Pub. Places Program, 1990-95, Lending Art Collection Greenwich Pub. Libr., Pres.'s Office Turner Entertainment Co., L.A., Pres.'s Office Conservation Mgmt. Inc., Washington, various private collections; commissions include Fellowship for Jewish Learning, Conservation Mgmt., Inc., Washington, individual collectors. Dir., v.p., pres. LWV, Stamford; sec., dir. Family and Children's Svcs.; Stamford rep. South Western Regional Planning Agy.; chair task force mass transp. Stamford Area Commerce and Industry Assn.; dir. Stamford Art Assn., 1994, 95, 96. Recipient Best Watercolor award Greenwich Art Soc., 1989, 2d prize Stamford Art Assn., 1991, Allan Bernard award Greenwich Art Soc., 1996. Mem. Nat. League Am. Pen Women. Home: 47 East Ridge Rd Stamford CT 06903

BEREZIN, TANYA, artistic director, actress; b. Phila., Mar. 25, 1941; d. Maurice and Bettye (Shifrin) Berezin; m. Robert Leeming Thirkield, June 29, 1969 (div. June 1977); children: Lila Joy, Jonathon Schuyler; m. Mark Beers Wilson, Oct. 18, 1987. Student, Boston U., 1959-63. Co-founder Circle Repertory Co., N.Y.C., 1969, artistic dir., 1986-94; resident acting coach All My Children (ABC Daytime), 1994—. Appeared in (TV shows) St. Elsewhere, 1984, Law and Order, 1992, 93, 94, (play) Angels Fall, 1983, Moundbuilders, 1975 (Obie award), (film) Awakenings, 1993; producer Prelude to a Kiss, Destiny of Me, Three Hotels.

BERG, BARBARA KIRSNER, health education specialist; b. Cin., Dec. 6, 1954; d. Robert and Mildred Dorothy (Warshofsky) Kirsner; m. Howard Keith Berg, Apr. 8, 1984; children: Arielle, Allison, Stacy. BA, Brandeis U., 1976; MEd, U. Cin., 1977. Cert. health edn. specialist Nat. Commn. for Health Edn. Credentialing, Inc., Mass. Health educator S.W. Ohio Living Assn., Cin., 1977-79; coord. adminstrv. edn. N.E. Regional Med. Edn. Ctr., Northport, N.Y., 1979-81; patient health edn. coord. VA Med. Ctr., Buffalo, 1981-87; clin. asst. prof. SUNY, Buffalo, 1982-87; dir. comty. health edn. N.W. Hosp. Ctr., Balt., 1987-89; coord. law and health care program U. Md. Sch. Law, Balt., 1989-90; med. mgmt. cons. Dr. Howard K. Berg, Owings Mills, Md., 1990—; cons. health edn. Edward Bartlett, Assoc., Rockville, Md., 1987-88; mem. adult edn. com. Chizuk Amuno Congregation, Balt., 1993—, mem. bd. dirs., 1996—, chair cultural arts com., 1996—. Bd. dirs., mem. Am. Lung Assn. Western N.Y., Buffalo, 1983-86, Pumpkin Theater, Balt., 1990-91; chair domestic concerns com. Balt. Jewish Coun., 1994—, sec., bd. dirs., 1996—; sec. women's dept. Associated Jewish Charities, Balt., 1994—; mem. sch. bd. nominating conv. Baltimore County, 1995—. Mem. APHA, Soc. for Pub. Health Edn., Am. Jewish Com., Phi Delta Kappa. Jewish. Home and Office: 12116 Heneson Garth Owings Mills MD 21117

BERG, HELEN MACDUFFEE, retired university program director, statistician; b. Columbus, Ohio, July 15, 1932; d. Cyrus Colton and Mary Augusta (Bean) MacD.; m. Alan Ben Berg, June 6, 1981 (dec. July 1989); children: Christopher Clayton Ward, Ellen Elizabeth Ward Valachovic. BA, U. Wis., 1953; MS, Oreg. State U., 1973. Mathematician U.S. Naval Rsch. Lab., Madison, Wis., 1953-56; rsch. asst. Oreg. State U., Corvallis, 1963-72, project coord., 1975-86, dir. survery rsch. ctr., 1986-93, ret., 1993; rsch. assoc. U. Ill., Urbana, 1973-75. Contbr. articles to profl. jours. Mayor City of Corvallis, 1995—. Mem. Corvallis City Coun., 1991-94, pres., 1993-94. Democrat. Office: Corvallis City Hall 501 SW Madison Ave Corvallis OR 97333

BERG, JANET ELAINE, fashion retailer, journalist; b. Buffalo; d. Louis and Fannie Ruth (Greenwald) Gelb; m. Vernon Berg, Oct. 21, 1945 (dec. Oct. 1985); children; Peter, Richard. BA in English/Econs., Adelphi U., 1942; postgrad., NYU, 1943-44. Writer radio specifications Signal Corps, Red Bank, N.J., 1942-44; rschr. Celanese Corp, N.Y.C., 1944-46; owner retail chain The Mart/Fashion Page, Ohio, 1948-60; buyer, merchandiser WRENS/Allied Stores Pogues/Assn. Dry Goods, Ohio, 1960-72; sr. editor Retail Week, N.Y.C., 1972-83; owner retail store The Dutchman, Rhinebeck, N.Y., 1977-93; visitor svcs. asst. Wave Hill, Riverdale, N.Y., 1994—; freelance writer N.Y. Apparel News, Accessories Mag., Pret Fashions, Stores Mag., Hosiery/Body Fashions, Sportswear/Jeans Internat.; instr. Lab. Inst. Merchandising, Dutchess C.C.; spkr. in field. Counselor Svc. Corps of Ret. Execs., White Plains, N.Y., Nat. Exec. Svc. Corps, N.Y.C. Mem. Trends N.Y. (past v.p.). Home and Office: 5700 Arlington Ave 2V Riverdale NY 10471

BERG, LILLIAN DOUGLAS, retired chemistry educator; b. Birmingham, Ala., July 9, 1925; d. Gilbert Franklin and Mary Rachel (Griffin) Douglas; m. Joseph Wilbur Berg, June 26, 1950; children: Anne Berg Jenkins, Joseph Wilbur III, Frederick Douglas. BS in Chemistry, Birmingham So. Coll., 1946; MS in Chemistry, Emory U., 1948. Instr. chemistry Armstrong Jr. Coll., Savannah, Ga., 1948-50; rsch. asst. chemistry Pa. State U., University

Park, 1950-54; instr. chemistry U. Utah, Salt Lake City, 1955-56; prof. chemistry No. Va. C.C., Annandale, 1974-96. Mem. Am. Chem. Soc., Am. Women in Sci., Mortar Bd. Soc., Iota Sigma Pi, Sigma Delta Epsilon, Phi Beta Kappa. Home: 3319 Dauphine Dr Falls Church VA 22042-3724

BERG, LINDA THOMS, real estate broker; b. Englewood, N.J., May 27, 1948; d. Arthur W. and Lois A. (Sommerhalter) Thoms; m. Max R. Berg, May 14, 1967; children: Lisa, Darren. BS, Ariz. State U., 1992; M. in Counseling, U. Phoenix, 1995. Grad. Realtor Inst.; cert. residential specialist; cert. residential broker; cert. real estate appraiser, N.J. Founder, CEO Triton Ho. Sr. Citizens Residential Living, 1972-78; pres., ptnr., broker Berg, Brown & Lewis Real Estate, Point Pleasant Beach, N.J., 1984-86; mgr. Diane Turton Realtors, Sea Girt, N.J., 1986-89, Coldwell Banker Success Realty, Tempe, Ariz., 1992—. Editor/pub. Point Pleasant Beach Guidebook, 1976-79. Commr. Dept. Law and Pub. Safety, N.J., 1986-89; v.p., chmn. fundraising Ariz. State U. Adult re-Entry Connection, 1990-92; v.p. Point Pleasant Beach C. of C., 1978-81; mem. profl. stds. com. South Monmouth Bd. Realtors, Manasquan, N.J., 1984-86; vol. counselor Salvation Army ARC. Mem. ACA, AAUW, NAFE, Tempe C. of C., Ariz. State U. Alumni Assn., S.E. Valley Regional Assn. Realtors, Golden Key, Gamma Beta Phi. Home: 601 E Citation Ln Tempe AZ 85284 Office: Coldwell Banker Success 655 W Warner Rd Ste 101 Tempe AZ 85284

BERG, LISA BRESSLER, cultural consultant; b. Morristown, N.J., Mar. 17, 1955; d. Bernard and Teresa Stern Bressler; m. Michael Berg, June 27, 1976; children: Adam Matthew, Joshua Martin. B Music Edn., Hartt Coll. Music, 1976; MSW, Rutgers U., 1995. Asst. dir. program devel. Internat. Comm. Inc., Tokyo, 1990-91; cross-cultural trainer Diversity Mgmt. Inst., Tokyo, 1991-93; tng. cons. Anti-Defamation League, West Orange, N.J., 1993-95; intercultural cons. Internat. Profl. Rels., Inc., West Orange, N.J., 1995—; mem. planning com. Rutgers Social Group Work Symposium, New Brunswick, N.J., 1994-95. Auction chair B'nai Shalom, West Orange, 1995; telephone counselor Tokyo English Lifeline, 1992-93; fundraising chair Japan Israel Women's Welfare, 1989-91. Mem. Internat. Soc. Intercultural Edn., Tng. & Rsch. Office: Internat Profl Rels Inc 5 Murphy Ct West Orange NJ 07052

BERG, LORINE MCCOMIS, retired guidance counselor; b. Ashland, Ky., Mar. 28, 1919; d. Oliver Botner and Emma Elizabeth (Eastham) McComis; m. Leslie Thomas Berg, Apr. 27, 1946; children: James Michael, Leslie Jane. BA in Edn., U. Ky., 1965; MA, Xavier U., 1969. Tchr. A.D. Owens Elem. Sch., Newport, Ky., 1963-64, 6th dist. Elementary Schs., Covington, Ky., 1965-69; guidance counselor Twenhofel Jr. H.S., Independence, Ky., 1969-78, Scott H.S., Taylor Mill, Ky., 1978-84. Bd. dirs. Mental Health Assn., Covington, Ky, 1970-76, v.p., 1973 (valuable svc. award 1973); mem. Lakeside Christian Ch., Ft. Mitchell, Ky. Named to Honorable Order of Ky. Colonels, Hon. Admissions Counselor U.S. Naval Acad.; cited by USN Recruiting Command for Valuable Assistance to USN, 1981. Mem. Am. Assn. of Univ. Women, Covington Art Club, Retired Tchrs. Assn., Kappa Delta Pi, Delta Kappa Gamma, Phi Delta Kappa. Democrat. Home: 11 Idaho Ave Covington KY 41017-2925

BERG, MARGARETE CLAIRE, banker; b. Seattle, Feb. 21, 1948; d. Orville Clarence and Margaretha Katharina (Hanz) B. BA in Edn., Western State U., Bellingham, Wash., 1970, BA in French/German, 1972; MA in Germanics, U. Wash., 1979, PhD in Comparative Lit., 1994. Banker Seattle First Nat. Bank, 1972—. Mem. MLA, Western State U. Alumni Assn., U. Wash. Alumni Assn. Democrat. Lutheran. Home: 129 NE 161st St Seattle WA 98155

BERG, SISTER MARIE MAJELLA, university chancellor; b. Bklyn., July 7, 1916; d. Peter Gustav and Mary Josephine (McAuliff) B. BA, Marymount Coll., 1938; MA, Fordham U., 1948; DHL (hon.), Georgetown U., 1970, Marymount Manhattan Coll., 1983. Registrar Marymount Sch., N.Y.C., 1943-48; prof. classics, registrar Marymount Coll., N.Y.C., 1949-57; registrar Marymount Coll. of Va., Arlington, 1957-58, Marymount Coll., Tarrytown, N.Y., 1958-60; pres. Marymount U., Arlington, Va., 1960-93, chancellor, 1993—; pres. Consortium for Continuing Higher Edn. in Va., 1987-88; mem. com. Consortium of Univs. in Washington Met. Area, 1987-93, chmn., 1992-93. Contbr. five biographies to One Hundred Great Thinkers, 1965; editor Otherwords column of N.Va. Sun newspaper, Arlington. Bd. dirs. Internat. Hospice, 1984—, HOPE, 1983—, SOAR, 1993—, 10th Dist. Congl. Award Coun., No. Va.; vice chmn. bd. Va. Found. Ind. Colls., 1992-93; cmty. advisor Jr. League No. Va., 1992—; mem. Friends of TACTS, 1994—. Recipient commendation Va. Gen. Assembly, Richmond, 1990, 93, Elizabeth Ann Seton award, 1991, Arlington Notable Women award Arlington Commn. on Status of Women, 1992, Voice and Vision award Arlington Cmty. TV Channel 33, 1993, Pro Ecclesia et Pontifice medal Holy See, 1993; elected to Va. Women's Hall of Fame, 1992; named Washingtonian of Yr., Washingtonian mag., 1990. Roman Catholic. Home and Office: Marymount U Office of Chancellor 2807 N Glebe Rd Arlington VA 22207-4224

BERG, MARY JAYLENE, pharmacy educator, researcher; b. Fargo, N.D., Nov. 7, 1950; d. Ordean Kenneth and Anna Margaret (Skramstad) B. BS in Pharmacy, N.D. State U., 1974; PharmD, U. Ky., 1978. Lic. pharmacist, N.D., Ky., Iowa. Fellow in pharmacokinetics Millard Fillmore Hosp./ SUNY, Buffalo, 1978-79; asst. prof. U. Iowa, Iowa City, 1980-85, assoc. prof., 1985-95, prof., 1995—; with dept. clin. rsch., clin. pharmacology/ pharmacokinetics F. Hoffmann-La Roche, Ltd., Basel, Switzerland, 1992; mem. adv. com. rsch. on women's health NIH, 1995—. Reviewer Cin. Pharmacy, 1984—, Epilepsia, 1987—; editor: Internat. Leadership Symposium, The Role of Women in Pharmacy, 1990, Pharmacy World Congress '91; Women-A Force in Pharmacy Symposium, 1992, Gender-Related Health Issues, 1996; contbr. articles to Drug Intelligence & Clin. Pharmacy, New Eng. Jour. of Medicine, Jour. Forensic Scis., Therapeutic Drug Monitoring, Epilepsia. Advisor Kappa Epsilon, Iowa City, 1980-94; pres. Mortar Bd. Alumnae, Iowa City, 1986-88. NIH grantee, 1984, Nat. Insts. on Drug Abuse grantee, 1986; recipient Career Achievement award Kappa Epsilon, 1985. Mem. Am. Assn. Pharm. Scientists, Am. Soc. Hosp. Phrmacists (chair spl. interest group of clin. pharmacokinetics 1987-89), Am. Epilepsy Soc., Am. Pharm. Assn., Internat. Forum of Women for Pharmacy (U.S. contact), Fedn. Internat. Pharmaceutique (del. World Health Assembly 1992), Leadership Internat., Women in Pharmacy (bd. dirs. 1991—), Sigma Xi, Rho Chi, Kappa Epsilon, Phi Beta Delta. Lutheran. Office: U Iowa Coll of Pharmacy Iowa City IA 52242

BERG, SHMUELA, painter, sculptor; b. Ithaca, N.Y., Dec. 8, 1963; d. William Otto Keegan and Beverly Jean Eifer. BFA, New Paltz State U., 1983; postgrad., Tulane U.; student, Art Acad., Urbino, Italy, Art Acad., Neve Yeshiva, Jerusalem. artist-in-residence Betzal El Sch. of Art and Design, Jerusalem, Nat. Endowment Arts, 1992, 93, 94. One person shows include Glass Impressions, Stuart, Fla., 1989, Fifth Ave. Gallery, Melborne, Fla., 1990, Ctr. for Arts Mus., Stuart, 1993, Hanson Gallery, 1994, Barristers Gallery, 1994; exhibited in group shows Hist. Sunrise Theatre, 1988, Ariel Gallery Greene St., Soho, N.Y., 1990, Jaffe Baker Gallery, Boca Raton, Fla., 1992, Gov.'s Mansion Benefit for La. County on Child Abuse, Baton Rouge, 1994, Gallier Hall Mayors Art Exhbn., 1995, La Mieux Gallery Group, 1995; works exhibited in residences Betzel Al Sch. Art and Design, Jerusalem, 1992; commd. works include Harbor Fed. Bank, Ft. Pierce, Fla., 1993, Maurices Bistro, French Boy, 1994; prodr.: (TV series) Sam's World. Recipient Excellence awards Ctr. for Arts Mus., 1989, 93. Mem. Nat. Gallery for Women in Arts (registry mem.), Arts Coun., Ctr. for Arts Mus., Contemporary Mus. Art. Jewish. Home: 621 Nashville New Orleans LA 70115

BERGÉ, CAROL, author; b. N.Y.C., 1928; d. Albert and Molly Peppis; m. Jack Bergé, June 1955; 1 child, Peter. Asst. to pres. Pendray Public Relations, N.Y.C., 1955; disting. prof. lit. Thomas Jefferson Coll., Allendale, Mich., 1975-76; instr. adult degree program Goddard Coll. at Asilomar, 1976; tchr. fiction and poetry U. Calif. Extension Program, Berkeley, 1976-77; assoc. prof. U. So. Miss., Hattiesburg, 1977-78; vis. prof. Honors Ctr. and English dept. U. N.Mex., 1978-79, 87; vis. lectr. Wright State U., 1979, SUNY, Albany, 1980-81; tchr. Poets and Writers, Poets in the Schs. (N.Y. State Council on Arts), 1970-72, Poets in the Schs. (Conn. Commn. Arts); proprietor Blue Gate Gallery of Art and Antiques, 1988-96. Author: (fiction) The Unfolding, 1969, A Couple Called Moebius, 1972, Acts of Love: An American Novel, 1973 (N.Y. State Coun. on Arts CAPS award 1974), Timepieces, 1977, The Doppler Effect, 1979, Fierce Meltronome, 1981, Secrets, Gossip and Slander, 1984, Zebras or Contour Lines, 1991; (poetry) The Vulnerable Island, 1964, Poems Made of Skin, 1968, The Chambers, 1969, Circles, as in the Eye, 1969, An American Romance, 1969, From a Soft Angle: Poems About Women, 1972, The Inexpected, 1976, Rituals and Gargoyles, 1976, A Song, A Chant, 1978, Alba Genesis, 1979, Alba Nemesis, 1979; editor Ctr. Mag., 1970-84, pub., 1991—; editor Miss. Rev., 1977-78, Subterraneans, 1975-76, Paper Branches, 1987, Light Yrs.: The N.Y.C. Coffeehouse Poets of the 1960's, 1996; contbg. editor Woodstock Rev., 1977-81, Shearsman mag., 1980-82, S.W. Profile, 1981; editor, pub. CENTER Press, 1991-93; pub.: Medicine Journeys (Carl Ginsburg), Coastal Lives (Miriam Sagan), 1991; co-pub.: Zebras (Carol Berge). Nat. Endowment Arts fellow, 1979-80. Mem. Authors' League, Poets and Writers, MacDowell Fellows Assn., Nat. Press Women. Home: 562 Onate Pl Santa Fe NM 87501-3674

BERGEMAN, CLARISSA HELLMAN, special education educator; b. Davenport, Iowa, Feb. 28, 1947; d. Karl Herman and Virginia Clara (Morgan) Hellman; m. George William Bergeman, Oct. 24, 1968; 1 child, Jessica Ann. BA, U. Iowa, 1970. Cert. spl. edn. kindergarten-12th grade, mentally retarded, Va. Spl. edn. tchr. Iowa City Schs., 1970-72; elem. tchr. Peace Corps, Liberia, West Africa, 1972-75; English as second lang. tchr. Loudoun County Pub. Schs., Lessburg, Va., 1975-76; spl. edn. tchr. Loudoun County Pub. Shs., Leesburg, Va., 1976—; curriculum developer in field, 1970-92. Cmty. organizer Vols. in Svc. to Am., Ctrl. Fla., 1968-69; bd. dirs. Every Citizen Has Opportunities Sheltered Workshop, Purcellville, Va., 1987-90. Named Spl. Educ. Tchr. of Yr., Assn. Retarded Citizens Va., 1990. Mem. NEA, Va. Edn. Assn., Alpha Delta Kappa (chaplain 1991-94, sgt. at arms 1994—). Home: 35441 Williams Gap Rd Round Hill VA 22141

BERGEN, CANDICE, actress, writer, photojournalist; b. Beverly Hills, Calif., May 9, 1946; d. Edgar and Frances (Westerman) B.; m. Louis Malle, Sept. 27, 1980 (dec. 1995); 1 dau., Chloe. Ed., U. Pa. Model during coll. Films include The Group, The Sand Pebbles, The Day the Fish Came Out, Live for Life, The Magus, Soldier Blue, Getting Straight, The Hunting Party, Carnal Knowledge, T.R. Baskin, The Adventurers, 11 Harrowhouse, Bite the Bullet, The Wind and the Lion, The Domino Principle, The End of the World in Our Usual Bed in a Night Full of Rain, Oliver's Story, Starting Over, Rich and Famous, Gandhi, 1982, Stick, 1985; TV series: Murphy Brown, 1988— (Emmy award, Leading Actress in a Comedy Series, 1988-89, 89-90, 91-92, 93-94, 94-95); TV films Arthur the King, 1985, Murder by Reason of Insanity, 1985, Mayflower Madam, 1987, Tim, 1996; TV miniseries Hollywood Wives, 1985, Trying Times, Moving Day; author Knockwood; photojournalist credits include articles for Life, Playboy; dramatist: (play) The Freezer (included in Best Short Plays of 1968). Recipient Emmy awards for lead actress in a comedy series, 1989, 90, 92, 94, 95.

BERGEN, NANCY A., marketing professional; b. Detroit, Aug. 16, 1948; d. Joseph T. and Helen E. (Schrier) B. BA, U. Hartford, West Hartford, Conn., 1970. CPCU. Acctg./media mgr. Lowengard & Brotherhood, Hartford, Conn., 1970-79; project mgr. Roncari Industries, East Granby, Conn., 1979-82; mktg. mgr. Arthur Noll Agy., Bloomfield, Conn., 1982—.

BERGEN, POLLY, actress; b. Knoxville, Tenn.; d. William and Lucy (Lawhorn) Burgin; m. Freddie Fields, Feb. 13, 1956 (div. 1976); children: Kathy, Pamela, Peter. Pres. Polly Bergen Cosmetics, Polly Bergen Jewelry, Polly Bergen Shoes. Author: Fashion and Charm, 1960, Polly's Principles, 1974, I'd Love To, But What'll I Wear, 1977; author, producer for TV: Leave of Absence, 1994; Broadway plays include Champagne Complex, John Murray Andersons' Almanac, First Impression, Plaza Suite, Love Letters; films include Cape Fear, Move Over Darling, Kisses for My President, At War with the Army, The Stooge, That's My Boy, The Caretakers, A Guide for the Married Man, Making Mr. Right, Cry-Baby, 1990, Dr. Jekyll and Ms. Hyde, When We Were Colored, 1994; performed in one woman shows in Las Vegas, Nev., and Reno; albums: Bergen Sings Morgan, The Party's Over, All Alone By The Telephone, Polly and Her Pop, The Four Seasons of Love, Annie Get Your Gun and Do Re Mi, My Heart Sings, Act One Sing Too; numerous TV appearances including star of The Polly Bergen Show, NBC-TV; other TV appearances include The Helen Morgan Story, 1957 (Emmy award as best actress), To Tell the Truth, Death Cruise, Murder on Flight 502, How to Pick Up Girls!, Born Beautiful, The Lightning Field, The Surrogate, For Hope; miniseries include The Winds of War (Emmy nomination), 79 Park Ave, War and Remembrance, 1988 (Emmy nomination); writer, prodr. NBC movie Leave of Absence, 1994. Bd. dirs. Martha Graham Dance Ctr., The Singer Co., Soc. Singers, Calif. Abortion and Reproductive Rights Action League, Show Coalition; hon. canister campaign chairperson Cancer Care, Inc., Nat. Cancer Found.; founder Nat. Bus. Coun. for ERA; mem. Planned Parenthood Fedn., Am. Bd. Advs.; mem. nat. adv. com. NARAL, Hollywood Women's Polit. Com. Recipient Fame award Top Ten in TV, 1957-58, Troupers award Sterling Publs., 1957, Editors and Critics award Radio and TV Daily, 1958, Outstanding Working Woman award Downtown St. Louis, Inc., Golden Plate award Am. Acad. Achievement, 1969, Outstanding Mother's award Nat. Mothers' Day Com., 1984, Best Achievement in New Jewelry Design award, 1986, Cancer Care award, 1989, Woman of Achievement award LWV, 1990, Extraordinary Achievement award Nat. Women's Law Ctr., 1991, Freedom of Choice award Calif. Abortion and Reproductive Rights Action League, 1992; Polly Bergen Cardio-Pulmonary Rsch. Lab., Children's Rsch. Inst. and Hosp., Denver dedicated, 1970. Mem. AFTRA, AGVA, SAG, Actors Equity. Office: care Jan McCormack 11342 Dona Lisa Dr Studio City CA 91604-4315

BERGEN, VIRGINIA LOUISE, principal, language arts educator; b. St. Louis, Apr. 5, 1945; d. Roland Daniel Paton and Gladys (Crawford) Gibson; m. Robert Elwood Bergen, July 11, 1964; children: Robert Brandon, Jennifer Lynn. BA, So. Ill. U., 1971, MS, 1973, EdS, 1975; Ednl. Adminstrn. Cert., U. Oreg., 1981. Cert. K-12 Ed. Ad., K-9 tchr., K-12 spl. edn., speech corr., reading specialist, Colo., Oreg., Ill, Mo., N.Mex. Speech therapist Dist. #175, Belleville, Ill., 1971-73; K-12 clin. tchr. Collinsville (Ill.) Dist. #10, 1973-74, jr. high sch. LD tchr., 1974-78; edn. resource cons. Douglas Edn. Svc. Dist., Roseburg, Oreg., 1978-80; child devel. specialist Roseburg Dist. #4, 1980-82; asst. prin. Mesa County Valley Dist. #51, Grand Junction, Colo., 1982-85, prin., 1985—; vis. lectr. So. Ill. U., 1976-78; instr. Met. State Coll., Denver, 1989-91; lectr. Mesa State Coll., Grand Junction, 1991-92; in-svc. provider Mesa County Valley Sch. Dist. #51, 1982—, mem. standards and assessment steering com.; founding mem. governance bd. Basil T. Knight Staff Devel. Ctr., Dist. #51, Grand Junction, 1986-89. Mem. Colo. Assn. Sch. Execs., Phi Delta Kappa. Office: Fruitvale Elem Sch 585 30 Rd Grand Junction CO 81504-5658

BERGER, BARBARA PAULL, social worker, marriage and family therapist; b. St. Louis, June 18, 1955; d. Ted and Florence Ann (Vines) Paull; m. Allan Berger, Dec. 27, 1980; children: Melissa Dawn, Tammi Alyse, Jessica Lauren. BS, U. Tex., 1977; MSSW, U. Wis., 1978. Diplomate Am. Bd. Clin. Social Work; lic. social worker, Tex., Miss., Ky.; cert. marriage and family therapist. Clin. social worker Child and Family Svcs., Buffalo, 1980-81, United Cerebral Palsy Assn., St. Louis, 1982-83; clin. social worker/ coord. Jewish Family Life Edn. Jewish Family Svc., Dallas, 1984-85, 88-90; instr. Miss. Delta C. C., Greenville, 1991; child and adolescent therapist United Behavioral Systems, Louisville, 1993-94; therapist CMG Health-Inpsych, Louisville, 1994—. Mem. NASW, Acad. Cert. Social Workers, Am. Assn. Marriage and Family Therapy, Phi Kappa Phi, Pi Lambda Theta, Omicron Nu. Home: 2719 Avenue Of The Woods Louisville KY 40241-6281

BERGER, CAROLYN, judge; b. N.Y.C., Dec. 20, 1948; d. Melvin and Elaine Joyce (Ritter) B.; m. Fred S. Silverman, Feb. 15, 1981; children: Danielle Alexis, Michael Louis. BA, U. Rochester, 1969; MEd, Boston U., 1971, JD, 1976. Bar: Del. 1976, U.S. Dist. Ct. Del. 1976, U.S. Ct. Appeals (3d cir.) 1981, U.S. Supreme Ct. 1981. Dep. atty. gen. Del. Dept. Justice, Wilmington, 1976-79; assoc. Prickett, Ward, Burt & Sanders, Wilmington, 1979, Skadden, Arps, Slate, Meagher & Flom, Wilmington, 1979-84; vice-chancellor Ct. of Chancery, Wilmington, 1984—; justice Del. Supreme Ct., 1994—. Mem. ABA, Del. Bar Assn., Bd. Bar Examiners (assoc.). Office: Carvel State Bldg 11th Fl 820 N French St Wilmington DE 19801*

BERGER, DIANNE GWYNNE, educator; b. N.Y.C., Mar. 10, 1950; d. Harold and Mary Bell (Mott) Gwynne; m. Robert Milton Berger, Aug. 25, 1974; children: Matthew Robert Gwynne, Daniel Alan Gwynne. BS, Cornell U., 1971; MS, Drexel U., 1974; PhD, U. Pa., 1992. Cert. sexuality educator, family and consumer sci. educator and family life educator, Pa. Tchr. family and consumer scis., sexuality edn. Wallingford-Swarthmore Sch. Dist., 1972—; cons., Swarthmore, 1986—, Swarthmore Presbyn. Ch., 1995, Elwyn Insts., Media, Pa., 1989-91, Phila. Task Force on Sex Edn., 1991-93. Cons. Trinity Coop. Day Nursery, Swarthmore, 1980-93, Renaissance Edn. Assn., Valley Forge, Pa., 1987-94, A Better Chance, Inc., Swarthmore, 1990-91. Grantee Impact, Inc., 1990. Mem. NEA, Am. Assn. Family and Consumer Scis., Soc. for Sci. Study of Sex (sec. Ea. Region), Nat. Coun. on Famly Rels., Am. Assn. Sex Educators, Counselors and Therapists (chair Delaware Valley sect.). Home: 304 Dickinson Ave Swarthmore PA 19081-2001

BERGER, GISELA PORSCH, psychotherapist; b. Milw., Mar. 3, 1962; d. Kurt Wilhelm Bernhard and Gudrun Margaret (Wolf) Berger; m. Phillip James Townsend, May 20, 1984 (div. June 1993). BA, Purdue U., 1984; MEd, The Citadel, Charleston, S.C., 1992. Lic. profl. counselor, S.C., 1996, Master Addictions Counselor, 1996, Nat. Cert. Counselor, 1996. Exec. officer USAF 41st Mil. Airlift Squadron, Charleston, 1984-86; sect. comdr. USAF 437th Orgnl. Maintenance, Charleston, 1986-87; protocol officer USAF, Andrews AFB, 1987-88; sect. comdr. USAF 1776 Supply Squadron, Washington, 1988-90; clin. counselor Berkeley County Commn. Alcohol and Drug Abuse, Moncks Corner, S.C., 1993-94, Cmty. Control Ctr., Charleston, 1995—; pres. Company Grade Officers' Coun., Charleston AFB, 1986-87. Capt. USAF, 1984-90. Mem. ACA, Nat. Assn. Alcoholism and Drug Addiction, Mensa (program chair 1995-96), Alpha Tau Chi (pres. 1991-93). Presbyterian. Office: Community Control Ctr 2462 Leeds Ave Bldg B North Charleston SC 29405

BERGER, JOYCE MURIEL, foundation executive, author, editor; b. N.Y.C., Oct. 20, 1924; d. Samuel and Daisy (Lichtenstein) Zeitlin; m. Arthur Seymour Berger, Feb. 11, 1946. BA magna cum laude, N.Y. U., 1944, MA, 1946. Editor Theta Psychical Rsch. Found., Durham, N.C., 1978-80; sec.-treas., libr. Survival Rsch. Found., administr. Internat. Inst. for Study of Death, Miami, Fla., 1980—; convener confs. Internat. Inst. Study of Death, Miami, 1985, 87, Survival Rsch. Found., Miami, 1986. Co-author: Reincarnation Fact or Fable, 1991, Encyclopedia of Parapsychology, 1991, Fear of the Unknown, 1995; co-editor: To Die or Not to Die, 1990, Perspectives on Death and Dying, 1989; lectr. and seminar coord. in field. Right to Die conf. grantee Fla. Endowment of the Humanities, Tampa, 1987. Mem. Am. Soc. for Psychical Rsch., Soc. for Psychical Rsch., The Book Group of South Fla., Phi Beta Kappa. Office: Survival Rsch Found PO Box 630026 Miami FL 33163-0026

BERGER, MIRIAM ROSKIN, creative arts therapy director, educator, therapist; b. N.Y.C., Dec. 9, 1934; d. Israel and Florence (Frankel) Roskin; m. Meir Berger, July 16, 1967 (div. June 1981); children: Jonathan Israel. Student, Barnard Coll., 1952-53; BA, Bard Coll., 1956; postgrad., CCNY, 1956-58, NYU. Alumni dir. Bard Coll., Annandale-on-Hudson, N.Y., 1958-59; dance therapist Manhattan Psychiatric Ctr., N.Y.C., 1959-60; performer, educator Jean Erdman Theater of Dance, N.Y.C., 1959-62; dir. adult program Hebrew Arts Sch., N.Y.C., 1964-68; faculty Dance Notation Bur., N.Y.C., 1974-75, 77; asst. prof. dance therapy program NYU, 1975—, acting dir. dance therapy program, 1991, dir. dance edn. program, 1993—; dir. creative arts therapies Bronx Psychiatric Ctr., N.Y.C., 1970-90; leader internat. workshops on dance/movement therapy, Gt. Britain, France, Sweden, Brazil, Italy, Yugoslavia, Germany, Holland, Russia, Czech Republic; mem. editl. bd. The Arts in Psychotherapy; keynote spkr. Internat. Congress on Dance Therapy, Berlin, 1994; bd. dirs. Dance Libr. of Israel. Prodr. off-Broadway The Coach with the Six Insides, 1962-63; author, prodr. Non-Verbal Group Process, 1978; co-editor Am. Jour. Dance Therapy, 1991-94; led dance therapy session Senate hearing on Aging, 1992; contbr. articles to profl. jours. Bd. dirs. Theater Open Eye, 1978-82, v.p. bd. trustees, 1982-89, pres., 1989-94; bd. Dance Libr. Israel, 1996; bd. dirs. Internat. Cmty. Dance Libr. of Israel. Recipient NYU scholarship, 1981, Best Paper award Med Art World congress on Arts and Medicine, 1992. Mem. Am. Dance Therapy Assn. (founder, bd. dirs. 1967-76, v.p. 1974-76, 92, credential com. 1976, 82, keynote speaker at nat. conf. 1991, pres. 1994), Acad. Registered Dance Therapists, Dance Libr. Israel (bd. dirs.). Home: 2 Horizon Rd Fort Lee NJ 07024-6525 Office: NYU 35 W 4th St New York NY 10012-1120

BERGER, NANCY SUE, nursing researcher; b. N.Y.C., Apr. 22, 1957; d. Morris H. and Marilyn (Resnick) B.; m. Jonathon Andrew Leff (div. 1990). BSN, U. Colo., 1988. RN 1977. Staff nurse intensive care Hosp. U. Pa., Phila., 1981-84; clin. rsch. nurse U. Colo. Health Sci. Ctr., Denver, 1985-90, VA Med. Ctr., Denver, 1989-90; dir. clin. rsch. U. Colo. Health Sci. Ctr., 1990-94; clin. rsch. assoc. Bayer Corp., Berkeley, Calif., 1994—. Contbr. articles to profl. jours. Vol. Planned Parenthood, Denver, 1992, Walnut Creek, Calif., 1994—, Calif. Coastal Clean-Up, 1994-95, Colo. Nat. Abortion Rights Action League, 1993. Mem. Am. Assn. Urological Assocs., Assocs. Clin. Pharm., Sigma Theta Tau. Democrat. Jewish. Office: Bayer Corp 800 Dwight Way Berkeley CA 94701

BERGER, PATRICIA WILSON, retired librarian; b. Washington, May 1, 1926; d. Thomas Decatur Wood and Nina Hughes; m. George Hamilton Combs Berger, May 20, 1970. BA, George Washington U., 1965; MSLS, Cath. U. Am., 1974. Asst. librarian, ops. rsch. office Johns Hopkins U., Chevy Chase, Md., 1949-51; asst. ops. rsch. analyst Johns Hopkins U., 1951-54; head librarian CEIR, Washington, 1954-55; chief, tech. info. and library services Human Relations Area Files, Yale U., 1955-57; tech. info. officer, chief librarian Inst. for Def. Analyses, Washington, Arlington, Va., 1957-67; dir. tech. info. and security programs Lambda Corp., Arlington, 1967-71; chief librarian U.S. Commn. on Govt. Procurement, Washington, 1971-72; head gen. reference br., later dep. chief librarian U.S. Patent and Trademark Office, Arlington, 1972-76; chief library div. U.S. Nat. Bur. Standards, Gaithersburg, Md., 1976-78; dir. info. resources and services U.S. EPA, Washington, 1978-79; chief library and info. services U.S. Nat. Bur. Standards, 1979-83, chief info. resources and services, 1983-91; dir. Office Info. Svcs. Nat. Inst. Standards and Tech., 1990-92; ret., 1992; cons. libr., info. and security matters, 1965—; del. White House Conf. on Librs. and Info. Svc., 1979; bd. dirs. Universal Serial and Book Exch., 1983-84; chmn. Nat. Info. Standard Orgn., Am. Nat. Standard Inst., 1981-83, elected Nat. Info. Standard Orgn. fellow, 1989. Mem. editl. bd. Sci. and Tech. Librs., 1979-92; contbr. articles to profl. jours. Appointed by Govs. of Va. to State Library Bd., 1986-90, 90-95, vice chair, 1992-93, chair, 1993-94; bd. dirs. Va. Commn. for Reenactment of Battle First Bull Run, 1960-61; bd. dirs. Freedom to Read Found., 1988-90, 92-94; appointed U.S. Postmaster Gen's. Commn. Lit., 1990-92. Recipient Internat. Women's Yr. award Dept. Commerce, 1976, Bronze medal, 1980, Silver medal, 1984, Outstanding Adminstrv. Mgr. award, 1985, H.W. Wilson Pub. Co. award, 1980, Disting. Svc. award U. Richmond Librs., 1989, Cert. of Recognition, Gov. State of Va., 1989, Resolution of Esteem, Va. State Libr. Bd., 1988, award Coun. Libr. and Media Technicians, 1989; named Outstanding Alumnus in Libr. and Info. Sci., Cath. U. Am., 1988. Mem AAAS (elected assn. fellow 1992), Spl. Librs. Assn. (exec. bd. Washington chpt. 1970-71, pres. Washington chpt. 1977, elected assn. fellow 1987), ALA (coun. 1984-88, exec. bd. 1986-90, v.p./pres.-elect 1988-89, pres. 1989-90, immediate past pres. 1990-91), Va. Libr. Assn., D.C. Libr. Assn., Fed. Librs. Roundtable (pres. 1982-83, Achievement award 1985), Cosmos Club, Chi Omega, Beta Phi Mu. Democrat. Episcopalian. Home: 105 Queen St Alexandria VA 22314-2610

BERGER, PEARL, library director; b. N.Y.C., Nov. 30, 1943; d. Baruch Mayer and Tova (Brandwein) Rabinowitz; m. David Berger, June 14, 1965; children: Miriam Esther, Yitzhak, Gedalyah Aaron. B in Religious Edn., Yeshiva U.; BA, Bklyn. Coll., 1965; MLS, Columbia U., 1974. Diploma tchr. Hebrew. Tchr. Hebrew & Jewish studies Yeshiva of Crown Heights, Bklyn., 1963-65; asst. libr. YIVO Inst. Jewish Rsch., N.Y.C., 1976-80; head tech. svcs. Librs. Yeshiva U., N.Y.C., 1980-81, head libr. Pollack Libr., 1981-83, head libr. main ctr. librs., 1983-85, dean librs., 1985—; v.p. Coun. Archives & Rsch. Librs. in Jewish Studies, 1984-86, pres. 1986-89. Assoc. editor: Jour. Judaica Librarianship, 1983; contbr. articles to profl. jours.; compiler catalog Guide to Yiddish Classics on Microfiche, 1980. Recipient Benjamin Gottesman Libr. Chair Yeshiva U. Me. Am. Libr. Assn., Metro.

Ref. Rsch. Libr. Agency (trustee 1991—, sec. 1993—), Assn. Jewish Librs. (rsch., spl. librs. divsn., v.p. 1982-84, pres. 1984-86), Beta Phi Mu. Office: Yeshiva U Dean of Libraries 500 W 185th St New York NY 10033-3201

BERGER, VIVIAN OLIVIA, lawyer, educator; b. N.Y.C., July 22, 1944; d. Jacob and Rita (Both) Berger; m. Curtis Jay Berger, June 17, 1973. BA, Harvard U., 1966; JD, Columbia U., 1973. Bar: N.Y. 1974, U.S. Dist. Ct. (so. and ea. dist.) N.Y. 1974, U.S. Ct. Appeals (2d cir.) 1974, U.S. Supreme Ct. 1979, U.S. Dist. Ct. (no. dist.) N.Y. 1980, U.S. Ct. Appeals (10th cir.) 1986. Law clk. to judge U.S. Ct. Appeals (2d cir.), N.Y.C., 1973-74; asst. prof. law Columbia U., N.Y.C., 1975-77, assoc. prof. law, 1977-80, prof. law, 1983—; vice dean Columbia U., 1989-93, Nash prof. law, 1993—; asst. dist. atty. N.Y. County, N.Y.C., 1977-83; of counsel Hoffinger Friedland Dobrish Bernfeld & Stern, P.C., N.Y.C., 1994—; mem. adv. commn. 1st dept. N.Y. Appellate Div., N.Y.C., 1984—; asst. counsel Legal Def. Fund NAACP, N.Y.C., 1986—. Contbr. articles to profl. jours. Vol. mediator Queens Mediation Ctr., 1985-86; arbitrator small claims N.Y.C. Civil Ct., 1986—; nat. bd. dirs. ACLU, N.Y.C., 1980—, gen. counsel, 1986—; bd. dirs. First Dept. Assigned Counsel Corp., 1991—, So. Ctr. for Human Rights, 1990—. Mem. ABA, Assn. of Bar of City of N.Y. (civil rights com. 1979-82, criminal cts. com. 1983-86, 91-94, criminal advocacy com. 1986-89, coun. on criminal justice 1991—, spl. com. on capital representation 1994—, com. on jud. adminstrn. 1989-91), N.Y. Women's Bar Assn., N.Y. State Dist. Atty.'s Assn., Am. Law Inst., N.Y. Lawyers Against the Death Penalty. Office: Columbia Law Sch 435 W 116th St New York NY 10027-7201 also: Hoffinger Friedland Dobrish Bernfeld & Stern 100 E 59th St New York NY 10022

BERGER-KRAEMER, NANCY, speech and language pathologist, artist; b. N.Y.C., Aug. 15, 1941; d. George G. and Ruth (Kirsch) Berger; m. Aaron Kraemer, July 10, 1966; children: Lea, Steven. BA, Adelphi U., 1963; MS in Edn., Queens Coll., 1968; cert. clin. competency in speech pathology. Lic. and cert. speech and lang. pathologist, N.Y., N.J.; permanent cert. speech and hearing for handicapped, N.Y. Speech therapist Dist. # 24 Sch. Sys., Valley Stream, L.I., 1962-64; dir. speech and lang., hearing/speech pathologist Port Chester Sch. Dist., Rye, N.Y., 1965-66; speech and lang. pathologist Roselle Park (N.J.) Sch. Sys., 1966-67, Willis Sch. for Educationally Handicapped, Plainfield, N.J., 1967-68, St. Barnabas Med. Ctr., West Orange, N.J., 1971-73; pvt. practice Maplewood, N.J., 1968—; lectr., spkr., spl. edn. cons. in field. Numerous one-woman shows in N.J., N.Y., N.Y.C.; group exhbns. include N.J. Ctr. Visual Arts, Summit, N.J., City Without Walls, Newark, Bergen Mus., Jersey City Mus., Trenton City Mus., N.J. State Mus., Montclair Art Mus., Noyes Mus., Phoenix Gallery, Veridian Gallery, Pendar Gallery, Gallerie Ambiente, Germany, William Carlos Williams Ctr. for Arts, San Diego Art Inst., Stedman Art Gallery, New Brunswick, N.J., Fordham U.-Lowenstein Libr., N.Y.C., SUNY Gallery, Stony Brook, N.Y., Johnson & Johnson, Cali Assocs., Bellemead Devel. Corp., AT&T, Nabisco Brands, Beneficial Ins. Co., Prudential Ins. Co., Pleiades Gallery, N.Y.C., Art Ctr. No. N.J., Art Assn. Harrisburg, Stamford Art Assn., Princeton (N.J.) Art Assn., Bucknell U. Ctr. Gallery, NYU/Washington Sq. East Galleries, Newark (N.J.) Mus., The Waterloo Found. for the Arts, Inc., Stamford, others. Mem. Am. Speech Lang. Hearing Assn., Auditory Verbal Internat. (charter, lectr. 1975—), Alexander Graham Bell Assn., N.J. Speech and Hearing Assn.

BERGERON, TRACEY ANNE, mental health nurse, educator; b. Concord, N.H., Mar. 17, 1952; d. Ernest George and Yvette Sylvia (Hunneyman) Caldwell; m. Scott Martin Bergeron, Aug. 5, 1980. BA in Elem. Edn., Plymouth (N.H.) State Coll., 1974; diploma, Concord Hosp. Sch. Nursing, 1981; M in Edn. and Human Svcs., New Eng. Coll., Henniker, N.H., 1988; BSN, Graceland Coll., 1996. Lic. elem. tchr.; RN, N.H.; cert. psychiat.-mental health nurse. Sch. nurse Barrington (N.H.) Sch., 1984-89; charge nurse Wentworth Douglass Hosp., Dover, N.H., 1981-90, Seaborne Hosp., Dover, 1984-86; nurse reviewer W.B. Saunders Pub. Co., Phila., 1992—; nurse trainer, cons. Div. Devel. Svcs., Dover, 1995—; maternal/child nurse Portsmouth Pre Natal Clinic, 1989-95, Portsmouth Regional Hosp., 1989-95; psychiat. nurse Portsmouth Pavillion, 1987—; clin. instr. McIntosh Coll., Dover, N.H., 1990 . Contbr. articles to profl. jours.; co-author nursing newsletter The GrapeVine. Mem. Intercultural Nursing Assn., Devel. Disabilities Nurses Assn., Kappa Delta Phi. Home: 732 Route 153 Middleton NH 03887-6102 Office: McIntosh Coll 23 Cataract Ave Dover NH 03820-3908

BERGESON, DONNA POTTIS, lawyer; b. Warwick, N.Y., Aug. 21, 1960. BA magna cum laude, U. S.C., 1981, JD, 1984. Bar: Ga. 1984. Ptnr. Alston & Bird, Atlanta. Mem. ABA, Atlanta Bar Assn., Gwinnett County Bar Assn., State Bar of Ga., Ga. Acad. Hosp. Attys., Phi Beta Kapa, Phi Eta Sigma. Office: Alston & Bird 1 Atlantic Ctr 1201 W Peachtree St Atlanta GA 30309-3424*

BERGIN, BARBARA DAWN, adult education educator; b. Elmira, N.Y., May 29, 1935; d. Leon Bert and Leah M. (Kniffin) Corey; m. Jack Henry Lindquist, Apr. 5, 1957 (wid. Mar. 1959); 1 child, Kai Lindquist Enenbach; m. John Joseph Bergin, June 29, 1968; 1 child, Amy Louise. Student, SUNY, Fredonia, 1954-57; BS TV/Radio, Ithaca Coll., 1961; MA Reading, Ea. Mich. U., 1986. Cert. tchr. K-8, Mich., reading K-12. Pub. rels. prodn. asst. WGBH-TV Pub. Broadcasting, Boston, 1961-63; promotions asst. WKBD-TV, Southfield, Mich., 1965-67; tchr. Detroit Pub. Schs., 1967-69, 83-84; lang. arts/computer instr. Dearborn (Mich.) Adult and Community Edn., 1987-92, faculty, coord., 1992—; part-time faculty schoolcraft Coll.; cons. Brooks Correctinal Facility, Muskegon, Mich., 1991; steering com. Livonia Sch. Bd. Adv. Coun., Mich., 1975-78. Co-editor: Lines: An Autoworkers' Anthology, 1990; presenter in field. Vol. Livonia Pub. Schs., 1971-83. Mini-grantee Mich. Dept. Edn., Lansing, 1988; named Mich. Region 1 Adult Edn. Tchr. of Yr., Mich. Coun. on Learning for Adults/Mich. Dept. Edn., Owosso, 1994. Mem. Internat. Reading Assn. (newsletter co-editor adult literacy spl. interest group 1990-96, Mich. Coun. on Learning for Adults (mem. chmn. 1991—), Adult Lit. and Tech., Mich. Reading Assn., Mich. Assn. for Computer Users for Learning. Home: 35310 West Chicago Livonia MI 48150 Office: UAW/Ford Rouge Acad Dearborn Assembly Plant 3001 Miller Rd Dearborn MI 48121

BERG-JOHNSON, KAREN ANN, photographer, art educator; b. Mpls., Sept. 25, 1959; d. Wallace Edgar and sylvia June (Schyman) Berg; m. Jay Timothy Johnson, May 20, 1983; children: Christina Berg, Caroline Paige. BFA, U. Minn., 1981, MFA, 1984. Instr., chair photography dept. Art Ctr. of Minn., Crystal Bay, 1982-84; teaching asst. studio art dept. U. Minn., Mpls., 1983; instr. of art Bethel Coll., St. Paul, 1984-87, asst. prof., 1988-92, assoc. prof., 1992—, chairperson art dept., 1994—; juror mus. workers show Katherine Nash Gallery, U. Minn., 1989, chair adv. com., 1981-83. One woman show include Honors Gallery, U. Minn., 1981, Art Ctr. of Minn., Crystal Bay, 1983, Katherine Nash Gallery, 1983, Jewish Community Ctr., Mpls., 1984; exhibited in group shows at Studio Arts Gallery U. Minn., Mpls., 1980, 84, Katherine Nash Gallery, 1981, 88, Coffman Gallery 1, 1982-83, U. Art Mus., 1987, NA Gallery, Northfield, Minn., 1983, Art Ctr. of Minn., Crystal Bay, 1984, Daedalus Gallery, Mpls., 1984, 310 Arts Gallery, Mpls., 1984, Wall St. Gallery, St. Paul, 1984, B Square One Gallery, Mpls., 1984, Eugene Johnson Gallery of Art Bethel Coll., St. Paul, 1984-87, Minn. State Fair, St. Paul, 1986, Mpls. Inst. of Arts, 1986, Sioux City (Iowa) Art Ctr., 1987, Pinder Gallery, N.Y.C., 1987, Foundry Gallery Washington, 1987, San Diego Art Inst., 1987, Mpls. Coll. Arts and Design Gallery, 1988, Mid Hudson Arts and Sci. Ctr., Poughkeepsie, N.Y., 1988, N.J. Ctr. for Visual Arts, Summitt, 1989, Forum Gallery, Mpls., 1989, Miami Expo '89, Fla., 1989, Cen. Mo. State U. Art Ctr. Gallery, Warrensburg, 1990, Jewish Community Ctr. of Houston, 1990, W.A.R.M. Gallery, Mpls., 1990, Phipps Ctr. for Arts, Hudson, Wis., 1990, Laguna Gloria Art Mus., Austin, Tex., 1991, Barrett House Galleries, Poughkeepsie, N.Y., 1991, ARC Gallery, Chgo., 1991, Pleiades Gallery, N.Y.C., 1991, Univ. Gallery U. Del., 1992, Downey Mus. Art, Calif., 1992, Mus. Without Walls, Internat., Bemus Point, N.Y., 1993, New England Fine Art Inst., Boston, 1993, The Phipps Ctr. for Arts, Hudson, Wis., 1993, 94, New Gallery S.D. Sch. Mines and Tech., Rapid City; numerous others. U. Minn. grantee, 1981-83; recipient Juror's award Leedy Voulkos Art Ctr., 1991, Artist's Choice award Phipps Ctr. for Arts, 1990, Juror's award N.J. Ctr. for Visual Arts, 1989, NA Gallery, 1983, Purchase award Univ. Art Mus., 1987. Mem. Soc. for Photographic Edn. Home: 3688 Woodland Trl Saint Paul MN 55123-2406 Office: Bethel Coll Art Dept 3900 Bethel Dr Saint Paul MN 55112-6902

BERGMAN, ANNE NEWBERRY, foundation administrator, civic activist; b. Weatherford, Tex., Mar. 12, 1925; d. William Douglas and Mary (Hunter) Newberry; m. Robert David Bergman, Aug. 17, 1947; children: Elizabeth Anne Bozzell, John David, William Robert. BA, Trinity U., San Antonio, 1945; postgrad., UCLA, 1946-47. Councilperson City Weatherford (Tex.), 1986-91, mayor pro tem, 1990-91; pres. Weatherford Libr. Found., 1989—; mem. Heritage Gallery Com., Weatherford Pub. Libr. (Mary Martin Collection), 1993—; bd. dirs. Manna Store House, Inc., 1990—. Founder Hist. Home Tour, Weatherford, 1972; co-chairperson Spring Festival Bd., 1976, Weatherford Planning and Zoning Commn., 1980-85; fundraising chairperson Weatherford Libr. Found., 1985-86; chairperson Tex. State Rev. Com. Cmty. Devel. Block Grants, 1987-91; pres. Tex. Fedn. Rep. Women, 1975-77; regional coord. George Bush for Pres. campaign, 1980, 88; co-chairperson Congl. Dist. 12 Bush-Quayle campaign, 1992, Tex. Women Support Pres., 1983-84; del. Nat. Rep. Conv., 1988; mem. Episcopal Churchwomen's Cabinet, Diocese of Ft. Worth, sec., 1995, 96, del. ECW Triennial, Episcopal Ch. U.S.A., 1997. Named Outstanding Rep. Woman, Tex. Fedn. Rep. Women, 1981. Mem. Parker County Rep. Women, DAR (Weatherford chpt.), Weatherford C. of C. (Outstanding Citizen of the Yr. 1988), Friends of Weatherford Pub. Libr. (life, charter pres. 1959-61, pres. 1973-74). Home: 609 W Josephine St Weatherford TX 76086-4055

BERGMAN, CIEL OLSEN (CHERYL BOWERS), artist, educator; b. Berkeley, Calif., Sept. 11, 1938; d. George Olaf Olsen and Evelyn Ruth (Melbin) Givant; m. Lynn Franklin Bowers, Aug. 29, 1959; children: Bridgit Lynne, Erik George. RN, Santa Rosa (Calif.) Nursing Sch., 1959; MFA with honors, San Francisco Art Inst., 1973. Lectr. in art Calif. State U., Hayward, 1974-75; asst. prof. U. Oreg., Eugene, 1975-76; asst. prof. U. Calif., Berkeley, 1976-77; asst. prof. U. Calif., Santa Barbara, 1977-79, assoc. prof., 1979-84, prof., 1984-94, prof. emerita, 1994—; spkr. in field. One-woman exhbns. include Ian Birksted Gallery, London, 1980, 82, Ivory/Kinpton Gallery, San Francisco, 1980, 82, 85, Kirk deGooyer Gallery, L.A., 1981, 83, Pamela Auchincloss Gallery, Santa Barbara, 1986, Santa Barbara Contemporary Art Forum, 1987, Dorothy Goldeen Gallery, L.A., Jaffe Baker Gallery, Boca Raton, Fla., 1990, others; group exhbns. include N.Y.C. Mcpl. Art Soc., 1990, On Paper Gallery II, Tokyo, 1990, Artemisia Gallery, Chgo., 1990, Masaki Takahashi Tokoro Gallery, L.A., 1990, Warwick Gallery, Seattle, 1991, Donna Beam Gallery, 1992, 93, Berkely (Calif.) Art Ctr., 1994, Ro Snell Gallery, Santa Barbara, 1994, Leigh Yawkey Woodson Mus., 1995, numerous others; collections include The Whitney Mus., N.Y.C., San Diego Mus., The Newport (Calif.) Harbor Mus., San Francisco Mus. Modern Art, Nat. Gallery, Washington, Met. Mus. Art, N.Y.C. Recipient SECA award Soc. for Encouragement of Creative Arts, 1975, Tiffany award, 1980. Mem. Artists' Equity, Nat. Mus. Women Painters, Santa Fe Mus. Art. Studio: PO Box 95 Coyote NM 87012

BERGMAN, NANCY PALM, real estate investment company executive; b. McKeesport, Pa., Dec. 3, 1938; d. Walter Vaughn and Nellie (Sullivan) Leech; 1 child, Tiffany Palm Taylor. Student, Mt. San Antonio Coll., 1970, UCLA, 1989-93. Corporate sec. U.S. Filter Corp., Newport Beach, Calif., 1965—; pres. Jaguar Research Corp., Los Angeles and Atlanta, 1971—; owner Environ. Designs, Los Angeles, 1976—; pres. Prosher Corp., Los Angeles., 1978-83; now pres., dir. Futura Investments, Beverly Hills; chief exec. officer Rescor, Inc. Author: Resident Managers Handbook. Home: 8 Fincher Way Rancho Mirage CA 92270-3036 Office: 144 S Beverly Dr Ste 500 Beverly Hills CA 90212-3023

BERGMANN, MALENA NAOMI, artist, art educator; b. Miami, Fla., Oct. 25, 1967; d. Randall William Bergmann and Nancy June (Call) Bryant; m. William Graydon Miller, May 27, 1993. Cert. of completion, Russian Sch Norwich U., 1987; BFA, U. N.C., 1985-89; MFA, U. Fla., 1989-92. GTA instr. U. Fla., Gainesville, 1989-92; prof. Laredo (Tex.) C.C., 1993-94; adj. prof. art Miami (Fla.) Dade C.C., 1994-96; asst. prof. Johnson C. Smith U., Charlotte, N.C., 1996—; adj prof Winthrop U., Rock Hill, S.C., 1996—; vis. artist lectr. U. Ctrl. Fla., Orlando, 1994; instructor Monroe County Adult Edn. ESL, Key Largo, Fla., 1995. Artist: solo exhibitions include Secret Spaces Elliot Ctr. Gallery, Greensboro, N.C., 1990, Guilt Most Fowl: MFA thesis Exhibition, U. Gallery, Gainesville, Fla., 1992, Sprockets, Breasts etc.; LJC Art Gallery, Laredo, Tex.; group shows include (invitational) Two by Four: Focus Gallery, 1990, The Raw and Refined: A Show of Sculpture, Vincent's Ear Gallery, Tampa, Fla., 1990, Dialogue, Five Women Artists, Women's Studies Gallery, Gainesville, 1991, Faculty Invitational Drawing Exhibition, Art Barn Gallery, Middle Tenn. State U., Murfreesboro, Tenn., 1992, Overhang: Three Contemporary Painters, Dedicated Space Gallery, Bklyn., 1994, Urgency of Touch, Works Gallery, San Jose, Calif., 1996; (juried exhibitions) Artists of Fla. Exhbition, Sarasota Art Assn., 1991, McNeese Nat. Works on Paper, McNeese State U., Abercromie Gallery, Lake Charles, La., 1993, Halpert Biennial, Catherine Smith Gallery, Appalachian State U., Boone, N.C., 1993, Scene and Unseen, 2d Nat. Art Exhibition Ea. New Mex. U., Portales, 1993, Abstraction: Nat. Juried Show, Doshi Ctr. for Contemporary Art, Harrisburg, Pa., 1995, 9th Coastal Nat., Glynn Art Assn., St. Simons Island, Ga., 1995, Nat. Works on Paper: Artists Listen to the Earth, Marsh Art Gallery, Richmond, Va., 1996, Abstraction II: Nat. Juried Exhibit Doshi Ctr. Contemporary Art, Harrisburg, Pa., 1996, Imaginings: Stage Gallery, Merrick, N.Y., 1996, Art from Detritus: Recycling with Imagination, Artists Talk on Art, Pitts., 1996, others. Recipient Posey Found. grant, Southeast Bank, Sarasota, Fla., 1991; named to vis. artist roster N.C. Arts Coun., roster of approved artists, S.C. Arts Commn., 1994—. Mem. Sierra Club, Nature Conservancy. Home: 2920 Enfield Rd Charlotte NC 28205

BERGMANN, MERRIE, computer science educator; b. Morristown, N.J., Dec. 23, 1950; d. Arnold Oliver and Alfreda (Jazwinski) B. BA in Math. and Philosophy, Douglass Coll., 1972; MA in Philosophy, U. Toronto, 1973, PhD in Philosophy, 1976; MS in Computer Sci., Wright State U., 1985. Asst. prof. philosophy Dartmouth Coll., Hanover, N.H., 1976-83; asst. prof. computer sci. Wright State U., Dayton, Ohio, 1983-85; asst. prof. computer sci. Smith Coll., Northampton, Mass., 1985-92, assoc. prof. computer sci., 1992—. Co-author: The Logic Book, 3d edit., 1996. Chairperson Cummington (Mass.) Hist. Commn., 1989—. Mem. Am. Philos. Assn., Assn. for Computational Linguistics, Cognitive Sci. Soc., Sigma Xi. Office: Smith Coll Dept Computer Sci Northampton MA 01063

BERGQUIST, SANDRA LEE, medical and legal consultant, nurse; b. Carlton, Minn., Oct. 13, 1944; d. Arthur Vincent and Avis Lorene Portz; m. David Edward Bergquist, June 11, 1966; children: Rion Eric, Taun Erin. BS in Nursing, Barry U., 1966; MA in Mgmt., Central Mich. U., 1975; student U. So. Calif., 1980-82. R.N., registered advanced nurse practitioner; cert. physician asst. Commd. 2d lt. U.S. Air Force, 1968, advanced through grades to lt. col., 1985; staff and charge nurse U.S. Air Force, 1968-76, primary care nurse practitioner, McConnell AFB, Kans., 1976-79, officer in charge Wheeler Med. Facility, Wheeler AFB, Hawaii, 1979-83, supr. ambulatory care services, Elgin AFB, Fla., 1983-84; med.-legal cons., Pensacola, Fla., 1985—; risk mgr., quality assurance coordinator HCA-Twin Cities Hosp., Niceville, 1986-88. Bd. dirs. Okaloosa County (Fla.) Coun. on Aging, 1984—; adv. bd. Advanced Home Health, 1990—; chairperson Niceville/Valparaiso Task Force on Child Abuse Prevention, Fla., 1985-88; chmn. home and family life com. Twin Cities Women's Club, Niceville, 1985-88; chmn. advancement com. Gulf Coast coun. Boy Scouts Am., 1985-87; instr. advanced and basic cardiac life support Hawaii Heart Assn. and Tripler Armaii Heart Assn. and Tripler Army Med. Ctr., 1981-83. Decorated Commendation medal with 1 oak leaf cluster, USAF Meritorious Service medal, Air Force Commendation medal. Mem. Am. Assn. Critical-Care Nurses, Am. Assn. Physician Assts., Assn. Mil. Surgeons U.S., Soc. Ret. Air Force Nurses, Soc. Air Force Physician Assts., Twin Cities Women's Club. Lutheran. Avocations: computer programming, reading, handicrafts.

BERGSTROM, BETTY HOWARD, consulting executive; b. Chgo., Mar. 15, 1931; d. Seward Haise and Agnes Eleanor (Uek) Guinter; BS in Speech, Northwestern U., 1952, postgrad., 1983; postgrad U. Nev., Reno, 1974; m. Robert William Bergstrom, Apr. 21, 1979; children: Bryan Scott, Cheryl Lee, Jeffrey Alan, Mark Robert, Philip Alan. Dir. sales promotion and pub. relations WLS-AM, Chgo., 1952-56; account exec. E.H. Brown Advt. Agy., Chgo., 1956-59; v.p. Richard Crabb Assocs., Chgo., 1959-61; pres., owner Howard Assocs., Calif. and Chgo., 1961-76; v.p. Chgo. Hort. Soc., 1976-90; pres. Bergstrom Assocs., Chgo., Carefree, Ariz., 1990—. Del., Ill. Constl. Conv., 1969-70, mem. com. legis. reform, 1973-74, cts. and justice com., 1971-74; apptd. mem. Ill. Hist. Library Bd., 1970, Ill. Bd. Edn., 1971-74. AAUW fellowship grant named in her honor; recipient Communicator of Yr. award Women in Communication, 1983. Mem. Nat. Soc. Fund Raising Execs. (cert. fund raising executive, bd. dirs. 1983-92, sec. 1986, v.p. 1990-92, nat. bd. dirs., 1990-92, Pres's. award, 1988), Fortnightly Club (bd. dirs. 1994-96), Am. Assn. of Museums, Am. Assn. Bot. Garden and Arboreta, Garden Writers Am., AAUW, Northwestern U. Alumni, U. So. Calif. Alumni Assn., LWV. Mem. editorial bd. Garden mag. Glenview Community Ch., 1977-89, Fourth Presbyn. Ch., 1990—, trustee, 1994—; editor Garden Talk, 1976-86; contbr. articles on fund devel., horticulture, edn. advt. and agr. to profl. jours.; editor Ill. AAUW Jour., 1966-67. Office: 111 E Chestnut Ste 42H Chicago IL 60611-2051 also: 100 Easy St PO Box 5253 Carefree AZ 85377

BERGSTROM, ELAINE, novelist; b. Cleve., Dec. 13, 1946; d. Howard and Eleanor Schmieler; m. Carl J. Bergstrom, 1974 (div.); children: Lenore Marie, Kriista. BA, Marquette U., 1970. Novelist Red Bird Studios; writing coach. Author: Shattered Glass, 1989, Blood Alone, 1990, Blood Rites, 1991, Daughter of the Night, 1992, Tapestry of Dark Souls, 1993, Baroness of Blood, 1995, (using psuedomym Marie Kiraly) Mina, 1994, Leanna, 1996; work represented in Women Who Walk Through Fire, Daughters of Darkness, 1993, Tales of Ravenloft, 1994. Office: Donald Maas Lit Agy 157 W 57th St New York NY 10019*

BERHOW, MARY KATHRYN, genealogy researcher; b. Madison, Wis., July 29, 1943; d. William George and Vera Eileen (Jacoby) Broome; m. Bennett Francis Berhow, Aug. 17, 1966; children: Jana Dannemiller, Jodi. Tchr. cert., Barron County Tchrs. Coll., Rice Lake, Wis., 1963; BS in Edn., U. Wis., Whitewater, 1991. Tchr. St. Bridget's Sch., Omaha, 1963-64, Elroy (Wis.)-Kendall-Wilton Joint Sch. Dist., 1964-66, Mauston (Wis.) Sch. Dist., 1966-67; cons., sales assoc. Stitch 'N Time, Ft. Atkinson, Wis., 1985-88; archives vol. Lancaster County Hist. Soc., Lancaster, Pa., 1992-96, geneal. rsch. asst., 1994—, mem. outreach com., 1994-96, mem. collections com., 1996—. Mem. Leadership Lancaster, 1993—; staff rep. Friends of Tanger Arboretum, Lancaster, 1994—. Mem. Nat. Geneal. Soc., Assn. Profl. Genealogists, Libr. of Congress, Golden Key, Kappa Delta Pi. Democrat. Roman Catholic. Home: 1713 St Philips Dr Lancaster PA 17603 Office: Lancaster County Hist Soc 230 N President Ave Lancaster PA 17603-3125

BERK, KERRY MACCARTNEY, telecommunications industry executive; b. Mt. Holly, N.J., Jan. 25, 1953; d. William H. and Marilyn (Raisner) Mac Cartney; m. Michael Alan Berk, Jan. 3, 1981; children: Kelly Lynn, Karen Ann. BA summa cum laude, Gettysburg Coll., 1975; MS with honors, Drexel U., 1981; EdD, Nova Southeastern U., 1996. Mgmt. asst. pub. rels. dept. Bell of Pa./Bell Atlantic, Phila., 1975-76, account exec. mktg. dept., 1976-78, promotions mgr. mktg. dept., 1978-79, assessor and assessment ctr. leader pers. dept., 1979-80, staff mgr. strategic planning/witness support, 1980-84, staff mgr. sales delivery and regulatory dept., 1984-85, project mgr. tng. and devel., 1985-86, mng. editor employee communications, 1986-87, dir. employee communications, 1987-95, regional mgr. mktg. compensation, 1995-96, regional mgr. strategic initiatives, 1996—; cons. pub. rels.; leader seminars and workshops. Officer bd. fellows Gettysburg (Pa.) Coll., 1979-83, bd. trustees, 1984-88, chair student affairs com., 1987-88; exec. bd. PTA Lynnewood Sch.; mem. adv. bd. Pa. State U., Great Valley, Del. County. Named Outstanding Young Leader, Gettysburg Coll., 1979, one of mems. Outstanding Com. of Yr., Phila. Jaycees, 1980, VIP, RVRHS, 1994. Mem. NAFE, Internat. Assn. Bus. Communicators (cert., accrediteed bus. communicator), Pub. Rels. Soc. Am., Nat. Assn. for Edn. of Young Children, Phi Beta Kappa. Office: Bell Atlantic One Parkway 9C 1717 Arch St Philadelphia PA 19102

BERKA, MARIANNE GUTHRIE, health and physical education educator; b. Queens, N.Y., Dec. 25, 1944; d. Frank Joseph and Mary (DePaul) Guthrie; m. Jerry George Berka, June 1, 1968; children: Katie, Keri. BS, Ithaca Coll., 1966, MS, 1968; EdD, NYU, 1990. High sch. tchr. Northport High Sch., 1966-67; full prof. health, phys. edn. and recreation Nassau Community Coll., Garden City, N.Y., 1968—. Mem. AAHPERD, AAHPER, Assn. Women Phys. Educators N.Y. State (chpt. chmn. 1973-74, chpt. treas. 1980-84), N.Y. State Assn. Health, Phys. Edn. and Recreation (J.B. Nash scholarship com. 1983—), Am. Assn. Sex Educators, Counselors and Therapists (cert. sex educator), Am. Coll. Sports Medicine (cert. health/fitness instr.). Roman Catholic. Home: 90 Bay Way Ave Brightwaters NY 11718-2008 Office: Nassau Community Coll P226 HPER Garden City NY 11530

BERKE, JUDIE, publisher, editor; b. Mpls., Apr. 15, 1938; d. Maurice M. and Sue (Supak) Kleyman; student U. Minn., 1956-60, Mpls. Sch. Art, 1945-59. Free lance illustrator and designer, 1959—; pres. Berke-Wood, Inc., N.Y.C., 1971-80, Manhattan Rainbow & Lollipop Co. subs. Berke-Wood, Inc., 1971-80; pres. Get Your Act Together, club act staging, N.Y.C., 1971-80; pres. Coordinator Pubs.,Inc., 1982-87; pres., chief exec. officer, Health Market Communications, 1987—; pres. Pub. and Media Services, Burbank, 1987—; pub., editor Continuing Care Coordinator, Health Watch mags.; pres. Continuing Care Coordinator Convs. and Seminars; pres. Rainbow and Lillipop Prodns., 1994—; cons. to film and ednl. cos.; guest lectr. various colls. and univs. in Calif. and N.Y., 1973—; cons., designer Healthy Lifestyles mag.; writer, illustrator, dir. numerous ednl. filmstrips, 1972—, latest being Focus on Professions, 1974, Focus on the Performing Arts, 1974, Focus on the Creative Arts, 1974, Workstyles, 1976, Wonderworm, 1976, Supernut, 1977; author, illustrator film Fat Black Mack (San Francisco Ednl. Film Festival award, part of permanent collection Mus. Modern Art, N.Y.C.), 1970; designer posters and brochures for various entertainment groups, 1963—; composer numerous songs, latest being Time is Relative, 1976, Love Will Live On in My Mind, 1976, My Blue Walk, 1976, You Make Me a Baby, 1982, Let's Go Around Once More, 1983, Anytime Anyplace Anywhere, 1987, Bittersweet, 1987, Sometimes It Pays, 1987, Gimme Back My Money Blues, Everybody Wants Me But the One I Love, Skin to Skin, It's Your Turn to Sing the Blues, Deny Till You Die, Men Just Call It Woman Talk, Poor Me, Women's Work is Never Done, 1993; composer/author off-Broadway musical Street Corner Time, 1978; producer: The Real Estate TV Shows 1988-89; contbr. children's short stories to various publs., also articles. Trustee The Happy Spot Sch., N.Y.C., 1972-75. Mem. Nat. Fedn. Bus. and Profl. Women, NAFE, Am. Acad. Polit. and Social Sci., Women in Animation.

BERKELEY, BETTY LIFE, educator; b. St. Louis, May 25, 1924; d. James Alfred and Anna Laura (Voltmer) Life; m. Marvin Harold Berkeley, Feb. 7, 1947; children: Kathryn Elizabeth, Barbara Ellen, Brian Harrison, Janet Lynn. AB, Harris Tchrs. Coll., 1947; MA in Ednl. Adminstrn., Washington U., St. Louis, 1951; PhD, U. North Tex. , 1980. Tchr. St. Louis pub. schs., 1946-48, Clayton pub. schs., Mo., 1948-49, Lamplighter Pvt. Sch., Dallas, 1964-67; program devel. specialist Richland Coll., Dallas, 1980-84, instr., 1981—; adj. prof. U. North Tex., Denton, 1981—, cons. Sch. Cmty. Svcs. Ctr. for Studies on Aging, 1981—; pres. Retirement Planning Svcs., Dallas, 1984—. Contbr. articles to profl. jours. Named Outstanding Alumna Coll. of Edn. U. of North Tex., 1992. Mem. Dallas Commn. on Status of Women, 1975-79; bd. dirs. Dallas Municipal Library, 1979-83, Sr. Citizen Greater Dallas, 1986-92, Council on Adult Ministry Lovers Lane United Meth. Ch., 1982; charter mem. bd. dirs., life mem. Friends of U. North Tex. Libr.; mem. Pres.'s Coun. U. North Tex., mem. vol. mgmt. edn. task force, 1978-82. Mem. AAUW (pres. 1973-75; Outstanding Woman of Tex. 1981). Club: Women's Council of Dallas County (v.p. 1977-79). Avocations: travel, cooking, gardening, needlework. Home and Office: 13958 Hughes Ln Dallas TX 75240-3510

BERKEY, JUDITH OSTERHOUDT, computer science consultant; b. Kingston, N.Y., Jan. 15, 1943; d. Edmund Francis and Margaret Elizabeth (Lachmann) Osterhoudt; m. Walter Harry Berkey, June 26, 1965; children: Edmund Osterhoudt, Judson Lawrence. BS, Syracuse U., 1964; MS, George Mason U., 1986, PhD, 1990. Programmer IBM Corp., Endicott, N.Y., 1964-67; systems engineer IBM Corp., Charleston, S.C., 1967-68; lectr. George

Mason U., Fairfax, Va., 1987-90; pvt. practice Manassas, Va., 1990—; systems analyst EG&G Analytical Svcs. Ctr., Inc., Manassas, 1991—; lectr. George Washington U., 1992; cons. Booz-Allen & Hamilton, 1993-94. Contbr. articles to profl. jours. Recipient Woman of Yr. award Manassas Jour. Messenger, 1978, Keep Am. Beautiful award, 1979. Mem. IEEE, AAUW (div. bd. 1982-83), Assn. of Computing Machinery. Home and Office: 1307 Sawbridge Way Reston VA 20194

BERKHEMER-CREDAIRE, BETSY, public relations executive; b. Washington, Jan. 31, 1947; d. Robert Walter and Claire (Myers) Berkhemer; m. Criston Credaire, Mar. 23, 1985. B.S. in History, UCLA, 1968. Reporter Ventura (Calif.) Star Free Press, 1965-68; editor Gardena (Calif.) Valley News, 1968-70; writer Sta. KTTV Metromedia News, Los Angeles, 1970-71; publicist Disney Studios, NBC, Burbank, Calif., 1971-73; pres., owner Berkhemer & Kline Inc., Pub. Rels., Los Angeles, 1973-88; pres. Berkhemer, Kline, Golin, Harris Communications, 1988-93, exec. v.p. western region bus. devel., 1993—. Chmn. bd. dirs. March of Dimes So. Calif., Alliance Bus. for Childcare Devel., L.A. Edn. Ptnrship. Mem. UCLA Alumni Assn. (chmn. bd. dirs.). Office: Berkhemer Kline Golin/Harris One Bunker Hill 601 W 5th St Fl 4 Los Angeles CA 90071-2004*

BERKLEY, EMILY CAROLAN, lawyer; b. Richmond, Va., Mar. 2, 1950; d. Charles Garvice and Edna Gray (Berkley) Broom; m. Richard E. Bird, Sept. 6, 1969 (div. Mar. 1988); children: Jessica A. Bird, Martel J. Bird. Student, Coll. of William and Mary, 1968-70; BS in Psychology cum laude, Tufts U., 1972; JD magna cum laude, Temple U., 1977. Ptnr. Ballard, Spahr, Andrews & Ingersoll, Phila., 1977—; seminar panelist Pa. Bar Inst., 1992, Practicing Law Inst., 1993, 94, 95, 96. Mem. long range planning com. Performing Arts for Tredyffrin-Easttown Sch. Dist., Berwyn, Pa., 1989, chair subcom. on creativity, futures com., 1990; active United Way, 1989-91; bd. dirs. Devon-Strafford Little League, 1992-95. Fellow Am. Bar Found.; mem. ABA (mem. com. on legal opinions, mem. Uniform Comml. Code com., chair task force on exportation of Uniform Comml. Code 1995—, mem. comml. fin. svcs. com., vice chmn. interest and usury subcom. 1989-93, panelist satellite seminar fundamentals of asset based financing 1990, instr. Ctrl. and Ea. European law initiative 1993, internat. law sect.), Am. Coll. Comml. Fin. Lawyers (mem. bd. regents 1993—), Pa. Bar Assn. (mem. steering com., legal options drafting group, mem. real estate opinion project), Phila. Bar Assn. Office: Ballard Spahr Andrews et al 1735 Market St Philadelphia PA 19103-7501

BERKLEY, MARY CORNER, neurologist; b. Balt., Apr. 6, 1926; d. Henry Evans and Eleanor (Diggs) Corner; m. Kelly McKenzie Berkley, Sept. 3, 1955 (dec. Oct. 1984); children: Henry Evans, Robert Bruce; m. Warren Frederick Gorman, May 31, 1986. AB, Bryn Mawr Coll., 1946; MD, Johns Hopkins U., 1950. Diplomate Am. Bd. Psychiatry and Neurology. Intern, resident Cin. Gen. Hosp., 1950-52; resident in medicine Strong Meml. Hosp., Rochester, N.Y., 1952-53, fellow in neurology, 1953-56; pvt. practice Rochester, 1956-58, Janesville, Wis., 1958-60; resident in neurology U. Mich. Med. Ctr., Ann Arbor, 1960-64; sr. instr. Hahnemann Med. Coll., Phila., 1965-68; pvt. practice neurology Gallipolis, Ohio, 1968-70, Mt. Vernon, Ill., 1970-76; staff neurologist VA Med. Ctr., Phoenix, 1976-95, ret., 1995. Fellow Am. Acad. Neurology; mem. Alpha Omega Alpha.

BERKMAN, CLAIRE FLEET, psychologist; b. New Orleans, Dec. 5, 1942; d. Joel and Margaret Grace (Fishler) Fleet; m. Arnold Stephen Berkman, Apr. 27, 1975; children: Janna Samantha, Micah Seth Siegel. BA, Boston U., 1964; EdM, Harvard U., 1966; EdD, Boston U., 1970. Asst. prof. Counseling Ctr., Mich. State U., East Lansing, 1971-75, assoc. prof., 1975-78, assoc. prof. dept. psychiatry, 1975-82, clin. assoc. prof., 1986-87; pvt. clin. practice, 1975—; cons. Cath. Family Social Service, Lansing, 1979-83; mem. adv. bd. Cir. Ct. Family Counseling Program, 1982-88. V.p. Kehillat Israel Synagogue, 1975-76, pres. 1992-94; bd. dirs. Jewish Welfare Fedn., Lansing, 1974-75, 84-87; mem. children's task force State Bar Mich., 1993-95. NDEA fellow, 1968-70. Mem. Am. Psychol. Assn., Mich. Psychol. Assn., Mich. Soc. Forensic Psychologists. Office: 4084 Okemos Rd Okemos MI 48864-3258

BERKMAN, LILLIAN, foundation executive, corporation executive, art collector; b. N.Y.C.. B.A. summa cum laude, NYU, 1942, M.A. summa cum laude, 1943, H.H.D. (hon.), 1976; DFA (hon.), Marquette U., 1996. Dir. pub. relations J.I. Case Co., 1957-60; pres. Gen. Alarm Corp., N.Y.C., 1965—; corp. dir., head advt. and pub. relations Am. Tractor Corp., 1948-56; dir. Allied Stores Corp., 1974-86, Mich. Nat. Corp., 1977-86, Mich. Nat. Bank, Detroit, 1977-87, Mich. Nat. Investment Corp., 1978-87, MNC-Western Leasing, 1980-87, Capital Corp., 1980—; pres. Rojtman Found., Inc., 1967—; cultural advisor Coca Cola Co., 1978—; bd. dirs. Sterling Nat. Bank N.Y., Sterling Nat. Corp., Sterling Bancorp.; v.p., asst. to chmn. for corp. planning and devel. Associated Comm. Corp., 1988-94, vice chmn., 1990-94; v.p., asst. to chmn. long range planning Associated Group, Inc., 1995—. Fellow in perpetuity Met. Mus. Art, N.Y.C., 1964—; donor Rojtman Medieval Sculpture Gallery, 1964, trustee medieval art com., 1974—; mem. exec. council Inst. Fine Arts, N.Y. U., 1972—; trustee Am. Wing, 1976—, Poly. Inst. N.Y., 1977—; nat. adv. coun. St. Petersburg (Fla.) Mus. Fine Arts, 1990—; fellow Pierpont Morgan Library, 1969—, Frick Mus., N.Y., 1980—, Nat. Council San Francisco Museums, 1985—; bd. dirs. United Cerebral Palsy Research and Ednl. Found., Inc., 1973—, Inner City Scholarship Fund, 1980—, Salvation Army, 1986—; mem. Met. Opera Nat. Council, 1973—; overseer U. Pa. Mus., 1982—; dir. Latin Am. Arts Council, 1988—; chmn. Theban expdn. to Valley of the Kings, Egypt, 1977—; cultural advisor to Costa Rica, 1978—; chmn., bd. dirs. Associated American Artists, Inc., 1983—. Recipient Highest Honor award Nat. Indsl. Advertisers Assn., 1956, Pere Marquette award Marquette U., 1966, Philippine Golden Heart Presdl. award for cultural interchange, 1976, Kairos award Marquette U., 1992, Friends of Inner-City Scholarship Fund award, 1996. Mem. Nat. Assn. Corp. Dirs., Economic Club of N.Y., Lotos Club, Univ. Club of N.Y., Phi Beta Kappa Assocs. (bd. dirs., v.p. Middle Atlantic dist. awards com.). Home: 22 E 64th St New York NY 10021-7212

BERKOWITZ, ALICE ORLANDER, management consultant, hearing and speech educator; b. N.Y.C.. BA, MA, PhD, NYU, 1970; MBA, CUNY, 1986. Lic. in audiology and speech pathology, N.Y. Audiologist, speech pathologist Manhattan Eye, Ear and Throat Hosp., N.Y.C., 1959-61; acting dir. Hearing and Speech Ctr., chief audiologist NYU Coll. Dentistry, N.Y.C., 1961-66; dir. audiological and speech svcs. Manhattan Eye, Ear and Throat Hosp., N.Y.C., 1966-77; regional dir. profl. and ednl. svcs. Audiotone, Inc., N.Y.C. and Phoenix, Ariz., 1977-88; regional mgr. Frye Electronics, Inc., N.Y.C. and Tigard, Oreg., 1987-92; N.E. regional mgr. hearing instruments group Telex Comms., Inc., N.Y.C. and Mpls., 1988-90; exec. dir. Practice Mgmt. Cons. Co., N.Y.C., 1986—; adj. instr. speech dept. NYU Sch. Edn., N.Y.C., 1961-66; adj. prof. hearing and speech St. John's U., N.Y.C., 1993-94; lectr., panel participant various profl. meetings, univs. and hosps. Contbr. to numerous profl. publs. Mem. Am. Speech-Lang.-Hearing Assn. (dual cert. in audiology and speech pathology), Am. Auditory Soc., Alliance for Healthcare Strategy and Mktg., Acad. Dispensing Audiologists, Acad. Rehab. Audiology, Acoustical Soc. Am., Am. Acad. Audiology, Audiology Study Group N.Y., N.Y. State Speech Lang. Hearing Assn., N.Y. Soc. Health Planning. Office: Practice Mgmt Cons Co 39 Gramercy Park N New York NY 10010-6302

BERLAGE, GAI INGHAM, sociologist, educator; b. Washington, Feb. 9, 1943; d. Paul Bowen and Grace (Artz) Ingham; m. Jan Coxe Berlage, Aug. 7, 1965; children: Jan Ingham, Cari Coxe. BA, Smith Coll., 1965; MA, So. Meth. U., 1968; PhD, NYU, 1979. Tchr. math. Piner Jr. High Sch., Sherman, Tex., 1968-69; asst. prof. sociology Iona Coll., New Rochelle, N.Y., 1971-83, assoc. prof., 1983-88, chmn. dept., 1981-90, 96—, prof., 1988—; coord. urban studies program, 1984-90, gerontology program, 1984-90, NCAA faculty athletic rep., 1996—. Author: Experience with Sociology: Social Issues in American Society, 1983, Understanding Social Issues: Sociological Fact Finding, 1987, 2d edit., 1990, Women in Baseball: The Forgotten History, 1994, Understanding Social Issues: Critical Thinking and Analysis, 1993, 96; mem. editl. bd. Jour. Sport and Social Issues, 1990-94; contbr. articles to profl. jours. Commr. Wilton Commn. on Aging and Social Svcs., 1980-88, chmn., 1982-88; co-chmn. Wilton Task Force on Youth Coun., 1988; chmn. Wilton Task Force Com. for Outreach Program, 1981-82, Wilton Task Force on Day Care, 1983-88; mem. Wilton Task Force for Pub. Health Nursing Assn., 1981-82, Wilton Sport Coun., 1985-88; bd. dirs. Wilton Meals on Wheels, 1983-88; fellow N.Am. Faculty Network of Northeastern Univs. Ctr. for Study of Sport in Soc. Recipient Best Profl. Paper award Third Annual Cooperstown Symposium on Baseball and the Am. Cultre; named to Iona Coll. Women of Achievement, 1993. Mem. Am. Sociol. Assn., N.Am. Soc. Sociology of Sport, Wilton Assn. for Gifted Edn. (pres. 1980-81), N.Am. Soc. for Sports History (treas. 1992-93), Soc. for Am. Baseball Rsch., Women's Sport Found. (resources coun.). Office: Iona Coll Dept Sociology New Rochelle NY 10801

BERLAM, ANN ELMORE, legislative administrator; b. Lincolnton, N.C., Oct. 30, 1947; d. Lee and Madeline (Sain) Elmore; m. Robert A. Berlam, May 26, 1984. BA, Rollins Coll., 1969; MEd, Duke U., 1970; postgrad., George Washington U., 1971-72. Cert. tchr., adminstr., N.C. Policy asst. Learning Inst. of N.C., Durham, 1969-71; congl. staff asst. U.S. Ho. Reps., Washington, 1971-74; congl. liaison N.C. Dept. Pub. Instrn., Raleigh, 1974-84, divsn. dir., 1984-89, legis. dir., 1989—; chmn. steering com. Nat. Chpt. 2 Dirs., Raleigh, 1988-89; fed. liaison rep. steering com. Coun. Chief State Sch. Officers, Washington,, 1974-89. Author: Report on Education Legislation, 1990, 6th edit., 1995. Mem. Dem. Women of Wake County, Raleigh, 1989—. Mem. State Employees Assn. of N.C., Duke U. Alumni Assn., Rollins Coll. Alumni Assn., Phi Delta Kappa, Kappa Delta Pi. Lutheran. Office: NC State Bd Edn 301 Wilmington St Raleigh NC 27601

BERLAND, KAREN INA, psychologist; b. N.Y.C., Nov. 14, 1947; d. Max and Lillian (Graf) B. BA in Psychology, SUNY, Buffalo, 1969; MEd in Ednl. Psychology, U. Ill., 1971; D. Psychology, U. Denver, 1984. Cert. sch. psychologist, clin. psychologist. Sch. psychologist City Sch. Dist. Rochester (N.Y.), 1971-73, Denver Pub. Sch., 1973—; psychology intern Vets. Hosp., West Haven, Conn., 1983-84; psychologist Aurora (Colo.) Community Mental Health Ctr., 1985-92; expert witness Denver County Ct. Mem. APA, Colo. Soc. Sch. Psychologists (pres. 1986-87, leadership award 1987), Colo. Psychol. Assn. (PAC chair, treas.), Colo. Women's Psychologists (western regional dir. and Colo. rep. 1976-83), Assn. Advancement of Behavior Therapy, Mensa. Democrat. Jewish. Home: 1171 Forest St Denver CO 80220-4450

BERLIN, BEATRICE WINN, visual artist, printmaker; b. Phila., May 27, 1922; d. Benjamin and Pauline (Neubauer) Winn; m. Herbert Edward Berlin, Oct. 21, 1945; m. 2d., Warren Joseph Sturmer, Aug. 21, 1971; children—Arlene (dec.), Janice. Student Moore Coll. Art, Phila., Phila. Coll. Art; student Samuel Maitin, Hitoshi Nakazato, Kenjilo Nanao. Lectr. Phila. Print Club, Phila., 1964-68; instr. Intaglio techniques Long Beach Island Ctr. Arts and Sci., N.J., 1970; freelance artist, Pa., 1963-76, Calif., 1976—; represented in pub. collections including Phila. Mus. Art., Bklyn. Art. Mus., N.Y. Public Library, Phila. Main Library, De Cordova Mus., Mass., U. So. Calif., N.J. State Mus., Temple U., Phila., U. Pa., Phila., Lebanon Valley Coll., Pa., Ocean City Cultural Ctr., N.J., San Francisco Art Mus., Achenback Coll. Recipient Phila. Water Color Club drawing prize, 1976, 82, Ocean City (N.J.) Boardwalk best in show prize, 1973. Lebanon Valley (Pa.) Coll. purchase prize, 1973, Hazelton (Pa.) Art League purchase prize, 1972, Cheltenham (Pa.) Art Ctr. Nat. Print Exhbn. first prize, 1970. Mem. Calif. Soc. Printmakers, Artists Equity Assn.

BERLIN, DORIS ADA, psychiatrist; b. Newark, May 23, 1919; d. Samuel and Fanny (Lippman) B.; m. Saul R. Kelson; children: Joel, Tamar. BS in Pharmacy, Columbia U., 1940; MD, Med. Coll. Va., 1948; MPH in Community Mental Health, U. Mich., 1966. Cert. Am. Bd. Psychiatry and Neurology; lic. psychiatrist N.Y., Va., Ohio, Mich., Tex., Calif. Intern Beth Israel Hosp., N.Y.C., 1948-49; resident in psychiatry Bellevue Hosp., N.Y.C., 1949-52; pvt. practice N.Y.C., 1952-57, Toledo, 1957-66, Fishkill and Poughkeepsie, N.Y., 1984—; clin. asst. in psychiatry NYU Coll. Medicine, 1952-57; asst. in psychiatry U. Hosp., N.Y., 1952-53; clin. asst. vis. neuropsychiatrist Bellevue Hosp., N.Y., 1954-57; lectr. mental health Sch. Pub. Health U. Mich., 1966-68; dir. profl. edn. Toledo State Hosp., 1969-70; clin. assoc. prof. N.Y. Sch. Psychiatry, 1970-81; dir. residency program Hudson River Psychiat. Ctr., Poughkeepsie, 1970-83, others. Mem. citizen's adv. bd. Lucas County (Ohio) Welfare Dept., 1963-67, chair, 1965-66; bd. dirs. Jewish Family Svc., Toledo, 1969-70; mem. policy coun., rehab. com. Toledo Area Program on Drug Abuse, 1970; bd. dirs. Dutchess County Assn. for Sr. Citizens, 1993-96. Grantee NEH, 1979. Fellow Am. Psychiat. Assn. (chair editl. bd. Hosp. and Cmty. Psychiatric Jour., 1979-80, task force on cmty. mental health ctrs., 1983-88, com. on advertisers and exhibitors 1989-92, vice-chair lifers caucus, 1990-91, chair lifers orgn. 1992), Am. Coll. Psychiatrists (Laughlin fellowship com. 1976-79); mem. Am. Acad. Psychoanalysis (com. on psychoanalysis and cmty. mental health 1967-68), Dutchess County Med. Soc. (psychiatrists' rep. to coun. 1985—, treas. 1987). Home and Office: 66 Mitchell Ave Poughkeepsie NY 12603-3423

BERLIN, MEREDITH RISE, editor; b. Bronxville, N.Y., Nov. 22, 1955; d. Marvin and Seena (Goldsmith) Brown; m. Jordan Stuart Berlin, Aug. 13, 1988; children: Gregory Samuel, Lauren Julia, Connor David. BS, Emerson Coll., 1976. With circulation-subscription World Bus. Weekly, N.Y.C., 1978-79; feature editor Soap Opera Digest, N.Y.C., 1979-82, editor-in-chief, 1982-91; editor-at-large, 1991—, Soap Opera Digest, N.Y.C.; exec. producer Soap Opera Awards NBC-TV, L.A., 1988-91; commentator WCBS-TV Noon News, 1987—; commentator NBC's House Party; producer, journalist Afternoon TV Show, 1982. Columnist N.Y. Post, 1994—. Recipient 3 Emmy nominations, 1988, 89; named N.Y. Alumni of Yr. Emerson Coll. Mem. NOW, AFTRA, Am. Soc. Mag. Editors.

BERLINER, BARBARA, librarian, consultant; b. Bklyn., July 14, 1947; d. Robert and Mildred M. (Sklar) Morris; 1 child, Stefanie Lauren. BA in Anthropology, NYU, 1969; MLS, Columbia U., 1970. Libr. N.Y. Pub. Libr., N.Y.C., 1970-81, sr. libr., telephone reference, 1981-86, supervising libr., telephone reference, 1986-92, head libr., Mid-Manhattan sci. and bus., 1992-93; coord. NYPL Express, N.Y.C., 1993—; cons. John Wright, N.Y.C., 1991; bibliographer Collier's Encyclopedia. Author: The Book of Answers, 1990. Mem. ALA, Spl. Librs. Assn., N.Y. Libr. Assn., Planetary Soc. Home: 74 W Columbia Ave Palisades Park NJ 07650-1004 Office: NYPL Express 188 Madison Ave New York NY 10016

BERLINER, RUTH SHIRLEY, real estate company executive; b. N.Y.C., June 20, 1928; d. Irving William and Florence (Tomback) Blum; m. Arthur Ivan Berliner, Sept. 23, 1948; children: Daniel Scott, Michael Robert, Eric Lance. BA, Empire State Coll., Westbury, N.Y., 1974; diploma, Wilsey Sch. Interior Design, Hempstead, N.Y., 1975; MBA, Adelphi U., 1980. Lic. real estate broker, N.Y. Sec. to dir. librs. NYU, N.Y.C., 1948-50; sec. Paragon Mut. Syndicates Inc., N.Y.C., 1958-72; v.p. Paragon Mut. Investors Svcs., N.Y.C., 1972-78; pres. Ruth S. Berliner, Inc., N.Y.C., 1978—; pres. Irmed Corp., 1983—; cons. E. 59th St. Assocs., N.Y.C., 1962-70, Amrep Corp., N.Y.C., 1968-75, FKBA Assocs., N.Y.C., 1974-78; mem. stores com. Real Estate Bd. N.Y., 1984-94. Vice pres. NYU Dental Sch. Parents Assn., 1974-76; bd. dirs. Hadassah, Hewlett, N.Y., 1978-87; advisor Citizens for Charter Change, N.Y.C., 1987—. Mem. Nat. Assn. Realtors, Real Estate Bd. N.Y. (store com. 1984-95, 96, econ. devel. com. 1994-96), Inwood Club. Office: 450 7th Ave Rm 2309 New York NY 10001

BERLOWE, PHYLLIS HARRIETTE, public relations counselor; b. N.Y.C.; d. Louis and Rose (Jachez) Berlowe. Student, Hunter Coll., 1950-52. Account exec. Ted Sills & Co., N.Y.C., 1959-63, Harshe-Rotman & Druck, N.Y.C., 1963-65; exec. v.p. Edward Gottlieb & Assocs, N.Y.C., 1965-78; v.p. Hill & Knowlton, Inc., N.Y.C., 1972-79; v.p., group supr. Doremus & Co., N.Y.C., 1980-83, Marketshare divsn. Doremus & Co., N.Y.C., 1983-86; pres. The Berlowe Group, N.Y.C., 1986—. Named to founding roster Nat. Honor Roll of Women in Pub. Rels., No. Ill. U., 1993. Fellow Pub. Rels. Soc. Am. (citations 1976-78, 80-83, Silver Anvil 1977); mem. Counselors Acad. (chmn. 1981), Women Execs. in Pub. Rels. (pres. 1982), N.Y. Pub. Rels. Soc. (pres. 1990-91, citations 1993-95, John W. Hill award 1992). Office: The Berlowe Group 201 W 77th St New York NY 10024-6606

BERLY, ALICE ANNE, financial administrator; b. Portland, Oreg., Aug. 18, 1935; d. John Joseph and Curtiss Roxanne (Hottel) Pearl; m. Tommy Joe Pressley, Dec. 12, 1954 (div. June 1963); 1 child, Diana Lynn Pressley Covington; m. Arthur Raymond Woods, Oct. 26, 1974 (dec. Dec. 1975); m. Thomas Edward Berly, Sept. 16, 1979. AASA, Clark County C.C., North Las Vegas, Nev., 1983; BSBA, U. Nev., Las Vegas, 1985, MBA, 1987. Fin. adminstr. U.S. Dist. Ct., Las Vegas, 1987—; ptnr. Rich Ms I, 1993—. Instr. 55 Alive Mature Driving, Las Vegas, 1987-93. Mem. Inst. Mgmt. Acctg., Phi Kappa Phi. Home: 1111 N Lamb #238 Las Vegas NV 89110

BERMAN, BARBARA, educational consultant; b. N.Y.C., Oct. 15, 1938; d. Nathan and Regina (Pasternak) Kopp; children: Adrienne, David. BS, Bklyn. Coll., 1959, MS, 1961; adminstrv./supervision cert., Coll. S.I., 1971; EdD, Rutgers U., 1981. Tchr. N.Y.C. Pub. Schs., 1959-70; project coord., dir. fed. projects Rutgers U., New Brunswick, N.J., 1976-80; math. cons. B & F Ednl. Cons., Inc., S.I., N.Y., 1978—; dir. fed. math. project Ednl. Support Systems, Inc., S.I., 1981—; adminstrv. dir. Foresight Sch., S.I., 1985—; dir. Great Beginnings Infant and Toddler Ctr., 1989—. Co-author: (books) Fractions and Decimals for Junior High School: A Model Integrating Process and Content Skills, 1980, Metric Mini-Course, 1981, Mathematics: Getting in Touch, Books I and II, 1985, Color Tiles, 1986, Mathematics Through Measurement, 1983, Mathematics Institute for the Elementary School Tchr., 1980, Math Corners: Probability, 1993. Mem. Nat. Coun. Tchrs. Math., Nat. Staff Devel. Coun., N.Y. Acad. Scis., Nat. Coun. Suprs. Math. (ea. regional dir.). Home: 512 Valleyview Pl Staten Island NY 10314-5535 Office: Ednl Support Systems Inc 446 Travis Ave Staten Island NY 10314-6149

BERMAN, CAROL, commissioner; b. Bklyn., Sept. 21, 1923; d. Hyman and Sarah (Levy) B.; m. Seymour Jerome Berman, May 19, 1944; children: Elizabeth, Charles. BA, U. Mich., 1943. Trustee Bd. Edn., Lawrence, N.Y., 1973-77; senator State of N.Y., Albany, 1978-84; spl. rep. State Divsn. for Housing, Hempstead, N.Y., 1985-86; commr. N.Y. State Commn. on Lobbying, Albany, 1988-92, N.Y. State Commn. of Elections, Albany, 1992—. N.Y. co-chair Nat. Jewish Dem. Coun., 1988—, Met. Airport Noise Mitigation Rev. Commn., 1992—; del. Dem. Nat. Conv., N.Y., 1992; vice-chair Nassau Dem. County Com., Mineola, N.Y., 1970-72. Mem. Phi Beta Kappa, Phi Kappa Phi. Jewish. Home: 42 Lord Ave Lawrence NY 11559 Office: NY State Bd Elections Empire State Plz Swan St Bldg Core 1 Albany NY 12223

BERMAN, CAROL WENDY, psychiatrist; b. N.Y.C., Sept. 14, 1951; d. Irving and Dora (Adler) B.; m. Martin Farber, Feb. 5, 1994. BA, U. Calif., Berkeley, 1972; MD, NYU, 1981. Diplomate Am. Bd. Psychiatry and Neurology. Intern, resident in psychiatry St. Lukes-Roosevelt Hosp., N.Y.C., 1982-85; rsch. fellow in psychiatry NYU Med. Ctr., N.Y.C., 1986-87, mem. attending staff, 1987—; pvt. practice, N.Y.C., 1988—. Contbr. numerous articles to med. jours.; patentee device to prevent drunk driving. Active legal problems of mentally ill, Bar Assn. City N.Y., 1993—. Recipient writing prize Psychiat. Annals, 1987. Mem. Am. Psychiat. Assn. Office: 866 UN Plz Rm 473 New York NY 10017

BERMAN, CONSTANCE HOFFMAN, medieval historian, educator. BA, Carleton Coll., 1970; MA, U. Wis., 1972, PhD, 1978. Prof. history U. Iowa, Iowa City, 1988—. Author: Medieval Agriculture, The Southern-French Countryside and the Early Cistencious, 1986. Office: W 616 Seashore Hall Iowa City IA 52242

BERMAN, ELEANORE, artist; b. N.Y.C., Sept. 2, 1928; d. Isidor and Elsie (Goldstein) Berman; children: Deborah Nicholas, Jan Nicholas, Anthony Nicholas, David Lazarof. BA, UCLA, 1950. One-woman shows include: Kirk De Gooyer Gallery, L.A., 1982, Kouros Gallery, N.Y.C., 1982, L.A. City Hall, 1984, Gallery Xt, Brussels, 1985, New Eng. Ctr. for Contemporary Art, Mass., 1985, Mcpl. Gallery, Kampen, The Netherlands, 1986, Mcpl. Gallery, Amstelveen, The Netherlands, 1986, Rose Cafe, Venice, Calif., 1988, Lisa Kurts Gallery, Memphis, 1989, Boritzer/Gray Gallery, Santa Monica, Calif., 1991, San Bernardino County Mus., Calif., 1994, Wichita Falls (Tex.) Mus., 1995, L.A. Art Core, 1996; exhibited in group shows: LAART, N.Y.C., 1986, U. Hawaii, Hilo, 1986, L.A. County Mus. Art, 1981, Boston Ctr. for the Arts, 1981, Wesleyan Coll., Conn., 1980, Newport (R.I.) Harbor Mus., 1977, Nat. Acad. Western Art Traveling Exhbn., 1988, L.A.-U.K. Print Connection, 1989, Bonnie Fridholm Gallery, Asheville, N.C., 1989; represented in permanent collections: L.A. County Mus. Art, Bklyn. Mus., Milw. Art Ctr., Grunwald Graphic Art Ctr., UCLA, others. Mem. Nat. Assn. of Women Artists, So. Calif. Women's Caucus for the Arts, L.A. Printmaking Assn., Nat. Watercolor Soc., Artists Equity Assn. (adv. bd. 1980-84).

BERMAN, JANICE SANDRA, psychologist; b. Charleston, W. Va., Sept. 3, 1966; d. Donald and Marcia (Samuels) B. BA and MA, Johns Hopkins U., 1988; PhD, U. Vt., 1993. Predoctoral intern Mass. Mental Health Ctr./Harvard Med. Sch., Boston, 1992-93; postdoctoral fellow Children's Hosp./Harvard Med. Sch., Boston, 1993-94, Harvard Cmty. Health Plan, Boston, 1993-94; therapist sexual abuse treatment team Children's Hosp., Boston, 1995; assoc. clin. dir. Childrens and Family Ctr. of NSMC, Salem, Mass., 1994—; mem. Women's Mental Health Collective, Somerville, Mass., 1994—; child coord. The Trauma Ctr., Brookline, Mass., 1996—. Asst. editor (periodical) Women and Therapy, 1991-92; contbr. articles to profl. jours. Mem. APA, Am. Profl. Soc. on the Abuse of Children, Mass. Psychol. Assn., Assn. Women in Psychology, Sigma Xi. Office: Women's Mental Health Collective 61 Roseland St Somerville MA 02143

BERMAN, LAURA, journalist; b. Detroit, Dec. 8, 1953; d. Seymour Donald and Rose (Mendelson) B.; m. Christopher M.F. Norris, Feb. 24, 1985. AB, U. Mich., 1975. Writer, reporter Detroit Free Press, 1976-86; columnist The Detroit News, 1986-93; freelance writer, 1994—; sr. writer The Detroit News, 1995—. Mem. Am. Soc. Journalists and Authors, Inc. Office: The Detroit News 615 W Lafayette Detroit MI 48226

BERMAN, LORI BETH, lawyer; b. N.Y.C., June 27, 1958; d. George Gilbert and Sara Ann (Abrams) B.; m. Jeffrey Ganeles, Nov. 26, 1983; children: Caryn Elissa, Steven Aaron. BA magna cum laude, Tufts U., 1980; JD, George Washington U., 1983. Assoc. Margolies, Edelstein & Scherlis, Phila., 1983-84, White and Williams, Phila., 1984-87, Brownstein Zeidman & Schomer, Washington, 1987-89; v.p. legal & compliance Pointe Savs. Bank, Boca Raton, Fla., 1990-95. Mem., Jour. Internat. Law and Econs. Mem. exec. coun. United Jewish Appeal Fedn., Washington, 1987-89, Boca Raton, 1990—, Leadership Boca, 1992. Mem. ABA, D.C. Bar Assn., Fla. Bar Assn., Boca Raton C. of C. Democrat. Jewish.

BERMAN, MIRA, advertising agency executive; b. Danzig, June 1, 1928; d. Max and Riva (Gutman) B.; m. Richard D. Freedman, Jan. 23, 1972. Student, Profl. Children's Sch., Berkshire Music Sch. and Festival, Juilliard Sch. Music, David Mannes Coll. Music, NYU, Columbia U. Chief copywriter Girl Scouts U.S., 1948-50; sr. copywriter Bamberger's, 1950-52; advt. dir., head women fashions Bond Stores, 1952-55; copy dir. Robert Hall, 1955-56; advt. copy dir. Gimbel's, N.Y.C., 1956-57; dir. pub. rels., fashion Snellenburg's, 1957-59; sr. v.p. pub. rels. and advt. Lavenson Bur. Advt., 1959-66; pres. Allerton, Berman & Dean, 1966-76; chairperson, chief exec. officer Gemini Images, Inc., 1976-86; pres. The Bradford Group, 1986—; mem. faculty master's degree program in tourism and travel adminstrn. New Sch. for Social Research, N.Y.C.; Co-chmn. 1st ann. Internat. Symposium Travel and Tourism, Am. Mgmt. Assn.; co-chmn. 1st ann. Marketing Through Retailers Symposium, 1966-67, staff lectr., 1967-70; condr. Modern Bank Practices Seminars; Am. Assn. Advt. Agencies rep. to Nat. Advt. Rev. Bd. Author: Marketing Through Retailers, 1967, also Spanish and Japanese edits; Travel editor: Woman's Life Mag. Exec. dir. Am. Friends of Ezrath Nashim Hosp., Jerusalem Geriatric and Mental Health Ctr., 1986-91, The Africa Travel Assn., 1990—, Assembly of Nat. Tourist Office Reps., 1991—, Nat. Coun. of Women U.S.A., 1988-90, Am. Israel Opera Found., 1986-89; dir. devel. PROMESA Found., Inc. Recipient Israel Ministry Tourism award; Fashion Gold medal; Carl V. Cesery award Tile Contractors Assn. Am.; silver award; bronze award; AMITA Sister award; winner Gold medal Internat. Film and TV Festival N.Y., Grand award. Mem. Am. Advt. Fedn. (named one of Ten Top Women in Advt.), Fin. Publicist Assn. Am., The Fashion Group, Pub. Rels. Soc. Am. (bd. govs.), Phila. Pub. Rels. Assn., Am. Soc. Travel Agts., Soc. Advancement Travel for Handicapped (dir. travellers with disabilities awareness week), International Tourism Assn., Nat. Coun. Women., Women Execs. Internat. (exec. dir.). Home: 116 Central Park S New York NY 10019-1559 Office: 347 5th Ave Ste 610 New York NY 10016-5010

BERMAN, MONA S., actress, playwright, theatrical director and producer; b. Jersey City; d. Edward and Mary (Auster) Solomon; m. Carroll Z. Berman; children: Marcie S. Berman Ries, Laura Jane. BA, Beaver Coll., postgrad. Columbia U., MFA, Boston U. Tchr. English, drama Jersey City High Schs.; actress indsl., stage, TV, Valley Players, Holyoke, Mass., The Millbrook Playhouse, Mill Hall, Pa., 1991; owner, dir. The Theatre Sch. and Producing Co., Maplewood, N.J.; chmn. drama edn. YM-YWHA of Met. N.J. Cons., Clark Ctr. for Performing Arts, N.Y.C., 1965-66; instr. South Orange, Maplewood Adult Sch., 1967; artistic dir. Children's Theatre Co. Inc., Maplewood, 1968-70; cons. The Whole Theater Co.; dir. pub. relations Co. 3 by 2. Playwright: Hello Joe, That Ring in the Center, The Big Show, Interim, Who Can Belong?, Sudden Changes, Without Malice, Interim 2; producer, dir. A Night of Stars; guest theatre reviewer El Paso Herald Post, 1980-82. Active Boston United Fund, 1955-59, chmn. Boston residential area, 1957; bd. dirs. Greater Boston Girl Scouts Am., 1956-58, Tufts Med. Faculty Wives, 1956-58; active S. Fla. Theatre League. Mem. Am. Theater Assn., Playwrights Unit 42d St. Theater Ctr. N.Y.C., Dramatists Guild, Actors Equity Assn., Profl. Actor's Assn. Fla., Waterfront Ensemble N.J. Address: 8925 Collins Ave Surfside FL 33154

BERMAN, MURIEL MALLIN, optometrist, humanities lecturer; b. Pitts.; d. Samuel and Dora (Coopersman) Mallin; m. Philip I. Berman, Oct. 23, 1942; children: Nancy, Nina, Steven. Student, U. Pitts., 1943, Carnegie Tech. U., 1944-45; BS, Pa. State Coll. Optometry, 1948; postgrad., U. Pitts., 1950, Muhlenberg Coll., 1954, Cedar Crest Coll., 1953; DFA (hon.), Cedar Crest Coll., 1972; hon. degree, Hebrew U., Israel, 1982; DHL (hon.), Ursinus Coll., 1987, Lehigh U., 1991. Lic. Pa., N.J. Practice optometry Pitts.; sec.-treas., dir. Philip and Muriel Berman Found.; underwriting mem. Lloyd's of London, 1974-87; lectr. on travels, art, UN activities, women's status and affairs. Producer: weekly TV show College Speak-Out, 1967—; producer, moderator: TV show Guest Spot. Active in UNICEF, 1959—, ofcl. non-govtl. orgns., 1964, 74; U.S. State Dept. del. UN Internat. Women's Yr. Conf., Mexico City, 1975; mem. State Dept. Arts and Humanities Com. Nat. Commn. on Observance of Women's Yr., 1975; adv. com. U.S. Ctr. for Internat. Womens Yr., Washington; founder, donor Carnegie-Berman Coll. Art Slide Library Exchange; mem. Aspen (Colo.) Inst. Humanistic Studies, 1965, Tokyo, 1966; chmn. exhibits Great Valley council Girl Scouts U.S.A., 1966; adminstrv. head, chmn. various events Allentown Bicentennial, 1962; vice-chmn. Women for Pa. Bicentennial, 1976; co-chmn. Lehigh County Bicentennial Bell-Trek, 1976; patron Art in Embassies Program, Washington, 1965—; chmn. Lehigh Valley Ednl. TV, 1966—; program chmn. Fgn. Policy Assn. Lehigh County, 1965-67; treas. ann. ball Allentown Symphony, 1955—; mem. art adv. com. Dieruff High Sch., Allentown, 1966—; co-chmn. art. com. Episcopal Diocese Centennial Celebration, 1971; mem. Pa. Council on Status of Women, 1968-73; reappointed Pa. Gov.'s Commn. on Women, 1984; chmn. numerous art shows; mem. Art Collectors Club Am., Am. Fedn. Art, Friends of Whitney Mus., Mus. Modern Art, Mus. Primitive Art, Jewish Mus., Kemmerer Mus., Bethlehem, Pa., Univ. Mus., Phila., Archives of Am. Art, Met. Opera Guild, others; ofcl. del. Dem. Nat. Conv., 1972, 76, mem. Democratic Platform Com., 1972; mem. Pa. Humanities Coun., 1979—; bd. dirs. Heart Assn. Pa., Allentown Art Mus. Aux., Phila. Chamber Symphony, Baum Art Sch., Lehigh County Cultural Ctr., Heart Assn. Pa., Baum Art Sch., Young Audiences, Israel Mus., Hadassah Womens Orgn.; bd. govs. Pa. State System of Higher Edn., 1986—; trustee Kutztown State Coll., 1960-66, vice-chmn. bd., 1965; trustee, sec. bd. Lehigh Community Coll.; mem. nat. bd. UN-U.S.A., 1977—; trustee Pa. Council on Arts, Pa. Ballet, Smithsonian Art Council, Bonds for Israel, Hadassah (nat. bd. with portfolio), Am. Friends Hebrew U., 1984; bd. regents Internat. Ctr. for Univ. Teaching of Jewish Civilization, Israel, 1982—; fine arts chmn. Women's Club; mem. com. on Prints, Drawings, & Photography Pa. Mus. Art, 1984; hon. chmn. Bucks County Coillectors Art Show. Named Woman of Valor State of Israel, 1965; recipient Centenial Yr. hon. citation Wilson Coll., 1969; Henrietta Szold award Allentown chpt. Hadassah; Outstanding Woman award Allentown YWCA, 1973; George Washington Honor medal Freedoms Found. at Valley Forge, 1985; Hazlett award Outstanding Service to Arts Pa.; Outstanding Citizen award Boy Scouts Am., 1982, Myrtle Wreath award Pa. Region Hadassah, Mt. Scopus award State of Israel Bonds, 1984, Woman of Yr. award Am. Friends Hebrew U., Phila., 1984, others; hon. fellow Hebrew U., 1975; Centennial citation Wilson Coll., 1969. Mem. LWV, YWCA, Hist. Soc. Lehigh County, Lehigh Art Alliance, Phila. Art Alliance, UN We Believe, Am. Fedn. of Art., Pa. Hist. Soc. (life), Jewish Publ. Soc. Am. (former pres., chmn. bd. 1984), Disting. Daughters of Pa. Jewish. Club: Wellesley. Address: 1150 S Cedar Crest Blvd Ste 203 Allentown PA 18103-7900

BERMAN, SARA JANE, library director; b. Bklyn., Apr. 29, 1936; d. Max and Mary Louise (Pellegrino) Witkin; m. Norman Noel Berman, Nov. 18, 1938; children: Leslie Collins, Suzanne Berman. BA in Edn., Queens Coll., 1958; postgrad., C.W. Post Coll., 1989. Cert. tchr., N.Y. Tchr. of gifted Pub. Sch. Dist. #24, Queens, N.Y., 1975-87; tchr. of libr. Pub. Sch. Dist. #14, Queens, N.Y., 1987-91; sci. workshop tchr. Clark Botanic Garden, Albertson, N.Y., 1992; dir. of libr. East Williston (N.Y.) Pub. Libr., 1994—. Sec. Libr. Bd. of Trustees, East Williston, 1989-94; mem. L.I. Storytelling, Nassau County, N.Y., 1994-95; workshop leader N.Y.C. Tchrs. Consortium, N.Y.C., 1987-90; campaign mgr. Doreen Banks for Clk., North Hempstead, 1991; com. person Dem. Party, Nassau County, 1989—; mem. U.F.T. Women's Rights Com., N.Y.C., 1988-89; vol. Project Frail, Nassau County, 1992—. Recipient Impact II Developer Grant, 1989, 91. Mem. ALA, United Fedn. of Tchrs., Edith Stein Guild, The Betsy-Tacy Soc. Home: 10 Donald St East Williston NY 11596 Office: The East Williston Pub Libr 2 Prospect St East Williston NY 11596

BERMAN-HAMMER, SUSAN, public relations executive; b. Buffalo, Sept. 12, 1950; d. Leonard and Judith H. (Goldenberg) Berman; m. Tony Hammer, Aug. 17, 1975; 1 child, Erik Jason. BA, Northwestern U., 1972, MS in Journalism, 1975. Pub. info. asst. Sta. WBBM-TV, Chgo., 1972; news asst. exec. trailer Dem. Nat. Conv. ABC-TV News, Miami, Fla., 1972; writer Chgo. Conv. and Visitors Bur., 1973-75; Washington corr. Sta. WYEN, Des Plaines, Ill., 1975; sr. v.p. Herbert H. Rozoff Assocs., Inc., Chgo., 1976-82; pres., owner Susan L. Berman Assocs., Inc., Deerfield, Ill., 1982—; v.p. corp. communications Sheldon Good & Co., Chgo., 1988-89; chairperson Chgo. Communications/10, a consortium in field, 1982-83. Asst. regional dir. Nat. Movement for Student Vote, Chgo., 1972; bd. dirs. Chgo. Women in Broadcasting, 1972-76, Younger Set Jewish Fedn., Dallas, 1985-87; trustee North Shore Sch. Dist. 112 Found., 1995—; mem. North Shore Sch. Dist. 112 Caucus, 1995; sec., mem. exec. bd. Edgewood Sch. PTO; liaison to North Shore Sch. Dist. 112, 1995-96, also safety co-chair; founder, chair steering com. Safe Home Program North Shore Sch. Dists. 112 & 109, 1994—; Sherwood Sch. PTO liaison to North Shore Sch. Dist. 112 & CIC Legis. Com., Highland Park, Ill., 1994-95; mem. young women's exec. bd., v.p. cmty. devel., co-chair Trendsetter luncheon, co-chair Insights com., nominating com. Shalom Chgo. com., mem. campaign cabinet Jewish United Fund Chgo., 1991-96; bd. dirs. nat. women's com. North Shore chpt. Brandeis U., 1991-93; exec. bd., v.p. programming, reenrollment and membership, nominating com. Tamarisk chpt. ORT, Deerfield, Ill., 1990-95; chair comm. com. North Shore Congregation Israel, Glencoe, Ill., 1993-94; spokesperson and co-leader Parents Against Proposed Annexation of Deerfield subdivsns. from North Shore Sch. Dist. 112 into Deerfield Sch. Dist. 109, 1993-94. Recipient Recognition award City Coun. of Highland Park, Ill. Mem. North Shore Congregation Israel, Northwestern U. Alumni Club, Alpha Lambda Delta, Multiplex, Chgo. Soc. Clubs. Office: 9 Tamarisk Ln Deerfield IL 60015-5075

BERMEL, KATHY LEE, financial executive; b. Sigourney, Iowa, Mar. 26, 1970; d. Leon J. and Rose M. Leinen; m. Jodi A. Bermel, Aug. 8, 1993. Student, Am. Inst. Bus., 1988-89; BA, U. No. Iowa, 1993. Staff acct. Carney, Alexander, Marnold & Co., Waterloo, Iowa, 1993-94; ops. supr. Iowa Cmty. Credit Union, Waterloo, 1994—. Bd. dirs. Grundy Center (Iowa) Presch., 1996—; v.p. Black Hawk Credit Union, Waterloo, 1994-96. Mem. AAUW (sec. Grundy Center chpt. 1993—). Home: 1405 Windsor Dr Grundy Center IA 50638

BERMUDEZ, CHERIE PHYLLIS, social studies educator; b. Bklyn., Mar. 18, 1946; d. Hyman and Lily (Cohen) Brozen; m. Joseph A. Bermudez, Oct. 15, 1966. BA, Queens Coll., 1966, MS in Edn.-Social Studies, 1969, MS in Edn.-ESL, 1992. Tchr. social studies and ESL N.Y.C. Bd. Edn. IS 292, Bklyn., 1967—; yearbook adviser, photographer IS 292, Bklyn., 1991—, student coun. adviser, 1985-87; mem. bd. examiners licensing test devel. N.Y.C. Bd. Edn., 1985-88; part-time assoc. mgr. R.H. Macy's, 1968-92. Recipient fellowships Am. Gathering of Jewish Holocaust Survivors, 1988, Internat. Edn. Ctr., 1991. Mem. United Fedn. Tchrs., Nat. Coun. Social Studies, TESOL. Office: IS 292 300 Wyona St Brooklyn NY 11207-3522

BERN, PAULA RUTH, columnist; b. Pitts., July 27, 1934; m. Joseph Bern, Dec. 21, 1954; children: Bruce, Caryn, Marshall, Samuel, Rona. BA, Pa. State U., 1956; MA, U. Pitts., 1978, PhD, 1980. Editor-in-chief Jaffe Pub. Co., Los Angeles, 1958-63; on-air producer Sta. WQED-TV, Pitts., 1963-65; dir. univ. relations and devel. Robert Morris Coll., Pitts. and Coraopolis, 1965-69, Point Park Coll., Pitts., 1969-72; pres. Bern Assocs., Inc., 1972—; CEO The Exec. TV Workshop, Pitts., 1987—; tchr. sr. exec. seminars Grad. Sch. Urban and Pub. Affairs, Carnegie Mellon U., 1985-90; contbg. editor New Women mag., 1988—; syndicated columnist Scripps Howard News Svc., Washington, 1994—. Author: Point Park College: A History, 1980; How to Work for a Woman Boss (Even if You'd Rather Not), 1987, Keep Your Feet Off the Desk, 1994. Trustee Pitts. Ballet Theatre, Inc., 1973—; bd. dirs. Council for Internat. Visitors, 1975-91, Exec. Women's Council, 1980—; mem. adv. council Internat. Poetry Forum, 1979—, Pa. Commn. for Women; bd. dirs. Nat. Assn. Commns. Women. Recipient Am. Coun. on Edn. award, 1982. Mem. Women in Communications, Pub. Relations Soc. Am., Delta Sigma Rho, Phi Beta Kappa. Office: Scripps Howard News Svc 1090 Vermont Ave NW Washington DC 20005-4905

BERNAL, IDALIA, artist; b. Mexico City, Sept. 12, 1957; came to the U.S., 1986; d. Rafael and Idalia (Villarreal) Bernal; m. Warren C. Wills, Jr., Dec. 3, 1977 (dec. 1978); m. John Robert Pankratz, 1985; 1 child, Julia Beatrice. M in Internat. Rels., U. Nacional Autonoma de Mexico, 1982. Cultural attache Dakar, Senegal, 1982-86, Phila., 1986-90; artist Reading, Pa., 1990—; exhibit City Hall, Phila., 1990, Freedman Gallery, Reading, Pa., 1995, judge S. Street Art Show, Phila. 1991-95. Mem., advisor Mexican Soc., Phila., 1987-95, adv. Women of the World, Reading, 1994-95. Home and Studio: 1616 Olive St Reading PA 19604

BERNARD, BESS MARY, interior designer, consultant; b. Bklyn.; d. Hyman and Fannie Bernard. Formerly, with Melanie Kahane Assoc.; pres. Bernard Design Internat., Ltd., N.Y.C., 1960—; internat. cons. in field; lectr. in field. Prin. works include dining room for kindergarten children Marymount Sch., boutique for East Park Cultural Ctr., various projects for Waldorf Astoria hotel, apt. for pres. of Mitsubishi, numerous corp., hosp. and internat. projects. Chmn. Bklyn. Jewish Hosp.; lectr. interior design Sloan-Kettering Meml. Hosp. working with recuperating patients. Recipient various vol. awards Bklyn. Jewish Hosp., United Hosp. Fund. Office: Waldorf Astoria 301 Park Ave New York NY 10022-6806

BERNARD, CATHY S., management corporation executive; b. Bronx, N.Y., Nov. 13, 1949; d Burton and Norma (Ebb) B. BBA, George Washington U., 1971, M of Pub. Adminstrn., 1978; MA, U. Miami, 1972. Cert. property mgr. Staff asst. HEW, Washington, 1970-74; evaluation specialist OEO, Washington, 1974; tchr. St. Patrick's Acad., Washington, 1975; asst. prof. No. Va. C.C., Woodbridge, 1976-78; staff dir. Dem. Nat. Conv., N.Y.C., 1976; pres., chief exec. officer CSB Assocs. Mgmt. Corp., Riverdale, Md., 1977—; mem. Housing Opportunities Commn., Kensington, Md., 1979-93, chmn., 1988, vice chair, 1980, 87, chair pro tem, 1986, chair housing honor roll, 1985-88, Moderate Priced Dwelling Unit Commn.; mem. exec. coun. Inst. Real Estate Mgmt., Washington, 1982-87, cert. property mgr. Mem. adv. coun. Suburban Hosp., Bethesda, Md., 1984-89; bd. dirs. Ivymount Sch. for Handicapped, Potomac, Md., 1987—; treas. Jewish Coun. on Aging, 1988; treas., bd. dirs. Jewish Found. for Group Homes, Rockville, Md., 1989-91; trustee Roundhouse Theater, 1992—, treas., 1994—; bd. trustees Temple Emanuel, Kensington, Md., 1994—; candidate Md. State Legislature, 1986; pres. Cmty. Housing Res. Bd., 1985. Recipient Hughes award for property mgmt., 1980, Jewish Coun. award, 1989. Mem. Montgomery County C. of C. (bd. dirs., v.p. housing com. 1981-82), Apt. and Office Bldg. Assn. (bd. dirs., chmn. affordable housing com. 1990—). Office: CSB Assocs Mgmt Corp PO Box 647 Riverdale MD 20738-0647

BERNARD, RUTH FAYE, artist, educator; b. New Haven, Conn., May 5, 1951; d. Edward Robert and Naomi (Rudnick) Bernard; m. Peter Jermain Moore, Oct. 14, 1973 (div. 1980); m. Henry White Welch, Jr., July 24, 1991. Cert. in Fine Art, Sch. of Worcester Art Mus., Mass., 1973; BFA, Mass. Coll. of Art, 1987; MFA, Queens Coll./CCNY, 1989. Vis. instr. Queens Coll. CUNY, 1989; instr. painting Pa. Govs. Sch. of Excellence in Art, Erie, Pa., 1989, 90; assoc. prof. Pa. Sch. of Art and Design, Lancaster, 1989—. Artist: selected exhibitions include: (solo and two person) Syracuse Women's Ctr., The Modern Times Cafe, Cambridge, Mass., 1983, Mass. Coll. of Art Exit Show, Boston, 1986, Queens Coll. Thesis, Flushing, N.Y., 1989, Ward Lawrence Gallery N.Y.C, 1989, Pa. Sch. of Art & Design, Lanacaster, 1991, Cultural Coun. of Lancaster County, 1994, Here to Timbuktu, Lancaster, 1991, 95, Gettysburg (Pa.) Coll., 1995, Pa. State, Harrisburg; group shows: Sch. of Worcester Art Mus., 1973, Modern Times Cafe, 1983, Copley Soc., Boston, 1981-85, Kingston Gallery, Boston, 1986, North Hall Gallery, Boston, 1985, 86, Pa. Govs. Sch. for Arts, Bloomsburg U., 1989, Mercyhurst Coll., Pa. 1990, Bowery Gallery, N.Y., 1992, 93, Nittany Lion Competitive Show, Reading, Pa., others; represented in corp. and pvt. collections. Dir., designer Art Enrichment Program for Children with Learning Disabilities, 1992, 93; judge local art shows: WITF Children's Art Contest, 1991, 92, 93, Mount Gretna Art and Craft Show, 1993, Art Assn. of Lancaster County, 1994, Lancaster Outdoor Show, 1995. Recipient Liquitex award for excellence, 1989; scholar Profl. and Bus. Women's Assn. Orange, Conn., 1987; fellow Vt. Studio Ctr., Johnson, 1991. Mem. Coll. Art Assn., Am. Assn. Coll. Art Profs., Berks County Art Alliance. Home: 539 W King St Lancaster PA 17603 Office: Pa Sch Art and Design 204 N Prince St Lancaster PA 17603

BERNARD, SUZANNE M., lawyer; b. Albany, N.Y., Jan. 23, 1967. BA, Syracuse U., 1989; JD, Albany Law Sch., 1992; LLM, NYU, 1993. Bar: N.Y., 1993. Assoc. atty. N.Y.C., 1993-95; asst. corp. counsel City of N.Y., Bklyn., 1995—. Office: City of NY Law Dept 175 Remsen St Brooklyn NY 11201

BERNARD, VIOLA WERTHEIM, psychiatrist; b. N.Y.C., Feb. 22, 1907; d. Jacob and Emma (Stern) Wertheim; m. T.C. Bernard, Aug. 1, 1934 (div. June 1938). BS, NYU, 1933; MD, cornell U., 1936. Diplomate Am. Bd. Psychiatry and Neurology. Intern Jersey City Med. Ctr., 1937-38; resident in psychiatry Grasslands Hosp., Valhalla, N.Y., 1938-39, N.Y. State Psychiat. Inst. and Hosp., 1939-40; mem. staff Harlem Bur. Child Guidance N.Y. Bd. Edn., 1940-42; practice medicine specializing in psychiatry and psychoanalysis N.Y.C., 1940—; assoc. in psychiatry Columbia, 1948-55; asst. clin. prof., 1955-57, assoc. clin. prof., 1957-61, clin. prof., 1961-72; founder, dir. div. community and social psychiatry, dept. psychiatry Sch. Pub. Health and Adminstrv. Medicine, 1956-69; attending psychiatrist Presbyn. Hosp., 1963-72; cons. psychiat. svcs., 1972-82; tng. analyst Columbia Psychoanalytic Ctr., 1946—; faculty N.Y. Sch. Social Work, Columbia, 1947-58; psychiat. cons. Ethical Culture Schs., 1947-56; rsch. cons. Bank St. Coll. Edn., 1950-61; chief psychiat. cons. Louise Wise Svcs., 1942-81; sr. psychiat. cons. 1981—; chair, mental health sect. Citizens Com. for Childrenof N.Y., Inc., 1945-65, charter mem., 1945-71; mem. N.Y. State Dept. of Health, Bd. for Profl. Med. Conduct, 1975-77; sci. program cons. to chief mental health study ctr., div. mental health svc. programs, NIMH, 1978-79. Co-editor: Urban Challenges to Psychiatry, 1969, Crises of Family Disorganization, 1971; contbr. chpt. to Am. Handbook of Psychiatry, 1974; contbr. articles to profl. jours. Co-chair, com. psychiat. svcs. for children City of N.Y. Dept. of Hosps., 1961-63; mem. N.Y.C. Mayor's Com. on Cts., 1956-57; spl. cons. to tng. com. NIMH, USPHS, 1950-54; mem. State of N.Y. Com. for Children, 1971; bd. dirs. Wiltwyck Sch. for Boys, 1942-69, chair com. on treatment program, 1950-69. Fellow Am. Coll. Psychoanalysts, Am. Pub. Health Assn., Am. Psychiat. Assn. (life, v.p. 1971-72, chair commn. on childhood and adolesence, 1973-76, coun. on children, adolescents and their families, 1976-77, cons., com. on psychol. effects of nuclear arms devel., 1987-88, mem. counc. on nat. affairs, 1983-87, cons. 1988-93), Am. Orthopsychiat. Assn., Am. Psychoanalytic Assn. (life, chair com. community psychiatry, 1968-77, cons. 1988-93), N.Y. Acad. Medicine; mem. AMA, AAAS, N.Y. State Med. Soc., N.Y. County Med. Soc., Am. Acad. Child Psychiatry, Group for Advancement of Psychiatry (life, mem. com. social issues, dir. 1961-63, 73-77, com. on psychiatry and politics, 1977-80, com. on preventive psychiatry, 1981-94), N.Y. Coun. on Child Psychiatry, N.Y. Acad. Scis., World Fedn. Mental Health. Home and Office: 930 Fifth Ave New York NY 10021-2651

BERNAY, BETTI, artist; b. 1926; d. David Michael and Anna Gaynia (Bernay) Woolin; m. J. Bernard Goldfarb, Apr. 19, 1947; children: Manette Deitsch, Karen Lynn. Grad. costume design, Pratt Inst., 1946; student, Nat. Acad. Design, N.Y.C., 1947-49, Art Students League, N.Y.C., 1950-51. Exhibited one man shows at Galerie Raymond Duncan, Paris, France, Salas Municipales, San Sebastian, Spain, Circulo de Bellas Artes, Madrid, Spain, Bacardi Gallery, Miami, Fla., Columbia (S.C.) Mus., Columbus (Ga.) Mus., Galerie Andre Weil, Paris, Galerie Hermitage, Monte Carlo, Monaco, Casino de San Remo, Italy, Galerie de Arte de la Caja de Ahorros de Ronda, Malaga, Spain, Centro Artistico, Granada, Spain, Circulo de la Amistad, Cordoba, Spain, Studio H Gallery, N.Y.C., Walter Wallace Gallery, Palm Beach, Fla., Mus. Bellas Artes, Malaga, Harbor House Gallery, Crystal House Gallery, Internat. Gallery, Jordan Marsh, Fontainebleau Gallery, Miami Beach, Carriage House Gallery, Galerie 99, Pageant Gallery, Carriage House, Miami Beach, Rosenbaum Galleries, Palm Beach; exhibited group shows at Painters and Sculptors Soc., Jersey City Mus., Salon de Invierno, Mus. Malaga, Salon des Beaux Arts, Cannes, France, Guggenheim Gallery, Nat. Acad. Gallery, Salmagundi Club, Lever House, Lord & Taylor Art Gallery, Nat. Arts Gallery, Knickerbocker Artists, N.Y.C., Salon des Artistes Independants, Salon des Artistes Francais, Salon Populiste, Paris, Salon de Otono, Nat. Assn. Painters and Sculptors Spain, Madrid, Phipps Gallery, Palm Beach, Artists Equity, Hollywood (Fla.) Mus., Gault Gallery Cheltenham, Phila., Springfield (Mass.) Mus., Met. Mus. and Art Center, Miami, Fla., Planet Ocean Mus., Charter Club, Trade Fair Ams., Guggenheim Gallery, N.Y.C.; represented in permanent collections including Jockey Club Art Gallery, Miami, Mus. Malaga, Circulo de la Amistad, I.O.S. Found., Geneva, Switzerland, others. Bd. dirs. Men's Opera Guild; mem. adv. bd. Jackson Meml. Hosp. Project Newborn; mem. women's com. Bascom Palmer Eye Inst.; mem. working com. Greater Miami Heart Assn., Am. Heart Assn., Am. Cancer Soc., Alzheimer Grand Notable, 2d Generation Miami Heart Inst., Sunrisers Mentally Retarded, Orchid Ball Com., Newborn Neonatal Intensive Care Unit, U. Miami, Jackson Meml. Hosp. Recipient medal City N.Y., medal Sch. Art Leagues, N.Y.C., Prix de Paris Raymond Duncan, 1958, others. Mem. Nat. Assn. Painters and Sculptors Spain, Nat. Assn. Women Artists, Société des Artistes Français, Société des Artistes Independants, Fedn. Francais des Sociétés d'Art Graphique et Plastique, Artists Equity, Am. Artists Profl. League, Am. Fedn. Art, Nat. Soc. Lit. and Arts, Met. Mus. and Arts Center Miami, Pres.'s Club U. Miami. Clubs: Palm Bay, Jockey, Turnberry, Club of Clubs Internat., Miami Shores Country. Address: 10155 Collins Ave Apt 1705 Bal Harbour FL 33154-1629

BERNER, CYNTHIA KAY, librarian; b. Concordia, Kans, Aug. 31, 1958; d. William Clifford and Donna Darlene (Brown) B. AA, Cottey Coll., 1978; BA, U. Kans., 1980; MALS, U. Denver, 1981. System cons. Panhandle Libr. Network, Scottsbluff, Nebr., 1981-82; dir. Winfield (Kans.) Pub. Libr., 1982-84; from Westlink br. mgr. to coord. ext. svcs. Wichita (Kans.) Pub. Libr., 1984-95, coord. adminstrv. svcs., 1995—. Editor Propeller mag., 1995-96 (Comm. award Assn. Jr. Leagues Internat. 1995); editor (newsletter) LWV, Wichita Met., 1993. Chair pub. libr. sect. Kans. Libr. Assn., 1988-89; pres. Philanthropic Ednl. Orgn. (chpt. IM), Wichita, 1989-90; active Jr. League Wichita. Mem. ALA, Pub. Libr. Assn. (dir. pub. libr. systems sect. 1995—), Mountain Plains Libr. Assn. (chair pub. libr. sect. 1988-89, intellectual freedom com. 1988-90, sec. 1996—). Methodist. Home: 6418 O'Neil St Wichita KS 67212 Office: Wichita Pub Libr 223 Main St Wichita KS 67202

BERNER, JUDITH, mental health nurse; b. Tamaqua, Pa., June 19, 1938; d. Ralph Edgar and Ethel Mary (Williams) B. Diploma in nursing, Temple U. Hosp., 1959; AS, Coll. of Ganado, 1975, MS in Community Health, D of Med. Adminstrn. (hon.); BA, Stephens Coll., 1977; MEd, U. Ariz., 1980; LD (hon.), U. Iceland. RN, Ariz., N.Mex., Pa. Nursing adminstr. Project HOPE Internat. Office & Hosp. Ship, Washington, 1970-72; assoc. adminstr. Navajo Nation Health Found., Ganado, Ariz., 1972-79; clin. instr. psychiat. nursing Mo. So. State Coll., Joplin, 1986; nurse/therapist Presbyn. Kaseman Hosp., Albuquerque, 1986-93; emergency svcs. clinician for mental health svcs. Presbyn. Healthcare Systems, also Hts. Psychiat. Hosp., Albuquerque, 1994—; regional clin. coord. Mental Health Svcs., Inc., 1995—. Mem. ANA (cert. in psychiat. and mental health nursing), AACD, Internat. Acad. Behavioral Medicine, Counseling and Psychotherapy, Inc.

BERNER, MARY, publisher. Publisher Glamour Mag. Office: Conde Nast Publications 350 Madison Ave New York NY 10017*

BERNER, NANCY JANE, biology educator and researcher; b. Hackensack, N.J., Sept. 20, 1962; d. William Gilbert Jr. and Joan Helen (McCullough) B.; m. David Bartels Coe, May 26, 1991; 1 child, Alexis Jordan Berner-Coe. BS, U. Idaho, 1986, MS, 1988; PhD, Stanford U., 1992. Asst. prof. biology U. of the South, Sewanee, Tenn., 1992—. Contbr. articles to Jour. Exptl. Biology. NSF grantee, 1995. Mem. AAAS, Am. Physiol. Soc., Am. Soc. for Integrative and Comp Bio, Am. Soc. Mammalogists, Am. Assn. Women in Sci. Office: U of the South 735 University Ave Sewanee TN 37383-0001

BERNER, SALLY MUTCHOW, artist; b. Madison, Wis., Oct. 25, 1945; d. Paul John and Helen Hudson (Leyse) Mutchow; m. John Paul Berner, Aug. 1, 1970 (div. Aug. 1980). Student, U. Wis., 1964-67, Madison Bus. Coll., 1968, N.E. Wis. Tech. Coll., 1987, John Gordon Sch. Art, Green Bay, Wis., 1986—. Asst. co. sec., sales mgr. advt. specialty divsn. Leyse Aluminum Co., Kewaunee, Wis., 1971-79; pet portrait and wildlife artist Green Bay, Wis., 1986—. Solo shows include Georgia-Pacific Corp. Hdqrs., Port Edwards, Wis.; exhibited in group shows at Miller Art Ctr. Juried Ann. Shows, Sturgeon Bay, Wis., 1989-94, Invitational "Wildlife Biennial VII, Sturgeon Bay, 1995, Art Show at the Dog Show, Wichita, Kans., 1991, 93, 94, 96, Dog Days Dog Art Show, Kathleen Ewing Gallery, Washington, 1991, Artworks Gallery, Green Bay, Wis., 1992, 96, William Bonifas Fine Arts Ctr., Escanaba, Mich., 1993, Anderson Arts Ctr. "Fire & Ice" show, Kenosha, Wis., 1994, Hardy Gallery, Ephraim, Wis., 1995; works in permanent collections at Neville Pub. Mus., Green Bay, Wayland Acad., Beaver Dam, Wis., Kit Hammond Collection, Savannah, Ga., John C. Towers Collection, McLean, Va., many pvt. collections. Recipient Merit award Miller Art Ctr., 1992, Purchase award Neville Pub. Mus., 1993, Purchase awards Appleton Art Ctr. and Secura Ins., 1994. Mem. Green Bay Arts Unltd. (membership dir. 1991-92, People's Choice award 1990, 1st place award 1992, Merit award and People's Choice 1995), Door County Art League (treas. 1994-95, Award of Excellence 1993), Wis. Women in the Arts, Wis. Painters and Sculptors, Naples (Fla.) Art Assn., Sedona (Ariz.) Art Ctr. Congregationalist. Home and Office: 180 W Briar Ln Green Bay WI 54301

BERNFELD, CATHERINE ELLEN, elementary special education educator; b. Kingston, N.Y., July 8, 1950; d. Raymond Charles and Josephine (Marsico) Lindhurst; m. William Steven Bernfeld, June 28, 1974; children: Rebecca Lynn, Jennifer Lynn, Adam Steven. BS in History and Sociology, Russell Sage Coll., Troy, N.Y., 1972; MS in Spl. Edn., L.I. U., 1996. Cert. tchr., N.Y. Tchr. Ctrl. Elem. Sch., Port Jervis, N.Y., 1972-74, Our Lady of Lourdes Sch., Bethesda, Md., 1974-77; head tchr. Open Day Schs., Shrub Oak, N.Y., 1989-95; tchr. Putnam-Westchester BOCES Pre-Sch., Yorktown Heights, N.Y., 1995-96, Pub. Sch. 86, Bronx, N.Y., 1996—. Asst. troop leader Girl Scouts U.S., Yorktown Heights, 1985-88; den leader Cub Scouts, Boy Scouts Am., 1990-95, merit badge counselor, 1995, mem. com. Boy Scout Troop. Linda Frazier Latimer Profl. scholar, 1994. Mem. Westchester Assn. for Edn. of Young Children, Yorktown Sch. Dist. PTA (former pres.). Republican. Roman Catholic. Home: 1371 Edcris Rd Yorktown Heights NY 10598-3613

BERNFIELD, LYNNE, psychotherapist; b. N.Y.C., Mar. 16, 1943; d. Meyer and Lilian Claire (Pastel) B.; m. Arthur Dawson Richards, June 16, 1982. BA, Hofstra U., 1964; MA, Asuza Pacific U., 1981. Lic. marriage, family, and child therapist, Calif., Fla. Founder, dir. Writers & Artists Inst., L.A., 1984—. Author: When You Can You Will, 1993. Mem. ASCAP, Calif. Assn. Marriage and Family Therapists, Am. Assn. Marriage and Family Therapists.

BERNHAGEN, LILLIAN FLICKINGER, school health consultant; b. Cleve., Oct. 1, 1916; d. Norman Henry and Bertha May (Rogers) Flickinger; m. Ralph John Bernhagen, Sept. 2, 1940; children: Ralph, Janet Elizabeth Darling, Penelope Anne Braat. Student, Ohio Wesleyan U., 1934-37; B.S., R.N., Ohio State U., 1940, M.A., 1958; postgrad., LaVerne Coll., 1972-73. Cert. health edn. specialist. Asst. dir. Kiwanis Health Camp for Underprivileged Children, Steubenville, Ohio, summer 1940; asst. dir. nurses Jefferson Davis Hosp., Houston, 1940-41; ARC instr. Ohio State U., 1943, 63, elem. edn. lectr., 1970; dir. health services Worthington (Ohio) City Schs., 1951-76; health edn. instr. Ohio State U., 1976-77; spl. cons. venereal disease and sex edn. Ohio Dept. Health, 1976-82; sch. health cons., 1976—; vice chmn. medicine/edn. com. on sch. and coll. health AMA, 1976-78, chmn., 1978-80. Author: Sex Education: Understanding Growth and Social Development, 1968, What A Miracle You Are-Boys, 1968, 3d rev. edit., 1986, What A Miracle You Are-Girls, 1968, 3d rev. edit., 1986, Toward a Reverence for Life, 1971, Personality, Sexuality and Stereotyping, 1974, (with others) Growth Patterns and Sex Education: A Suggested Curriculum Guide K-12, 1967; contbr. articles to profl. jours., mags. Bd. dirs. Hearing and Speech Ctr. of Columbus and Franklin County, 1954-57, sec., 1957; mem. nat. adv. com. Nat. Ctr. for Health Edn., 1978-82; sec.-tres. Ohio Wesleyan U. Class of 38, 1968-78, 83-88; bd. dirs. V.D. Hotline Columbus and Franklin County, 1974-87, bd. expansion chmn., 1978-85, pres., 1985-86; mem. profl. adv. com. Ptnrs. Home Health Inc., 1991—; mem. Worthington Hist. Soc., Doll Docent, 1982—; mem King Ave. United Meth. Ch., 1938—; mem. choir, 1950—, pres., 1961-63, pastor/parish rels. com., 1985-88, bd. trustees, 1989-92, adminstrv. coun., 1992—, edn. commn., 1982-85, nominations and pers., 1992-94; treas. Franklin County Women's Golf Tournament, 1992. Recipient Centennial award Ohio State U., 1970, Outstanding Alumna award Ohio State U. Sch. Nursing, 1964, Disting. Service award Mich. Sch. Nurses Assn., 1972, hon. mention La Sertoma Internat. Woman of Yr., 1972. Fellow Am. Sch. Health Assn. (v.p. 1974, pres. 1976, governing coun. 1973-88, chmn. health guidance in sex edn. com. 1963-67, 71-77, chmn. sr. adv. coun. 1983-89, Disting. Service award 1969, Howe award 1979, cert. of merit, 1985, mem. awards com. 1986-89, mem. hist. com. 1989—), Am. Pub. Health Assn. (chmn. com. on urban health problems 1972); mem. NEA (life, ret.), Sex Edn. and Info. Coun. of U.S., Worthington Edn. Assn. (v.p. 1961-62, Tchr. of Year 1972-73), Cen. Ohio Tchrs. Assn. (chmn. sch. health svcs. sect. 1963), Ohio State U. Women's Golf Assn. (chmn. 1973, parliamentarian 1988—), Ohio Wesleyan U. Alumni Assn. (chmn. alumni recognition com. 1994-95, bd. dirs. 1989-95, chmn. bylaws revision com. 1991—, mem. orgn. com. 1994-95), Columbus Women's Dist. Golf Assn. (treas. 1985, sec. 1987, v.p. 1989, pres. 1990, adv. bd. 1991-95, parliamentarian 1996—), Columbus Computer Soc., Chi Omega (pres. Columbus Alumnae chpt. 1947-49, fin. adv. Ohio Wesleyan U. 1964-76, Outstanding Alumna of Yr. State of Ohio 1986), Pi Lambda Theta (citation award 1971, mem. program com. 1986-89, chmn. by laws revision com. 1990—, parliamentarian), Sigma Theta Tau, Phi Delta Kappa. Clubs: Monnett, Worthington Women's. Home and Office: 5916 Linworth Rd Worthington OH 43085-3357

BERNHARD, SANDRA, actress, comedienne, singer; b. Flint, Mich., June 6, 1955; d. Jerome and Jeanette B. Stand-up comedienne nightclubs, Beverly Hills, Calif., 1974-78; films include Cheech and Chong's Nice Dreams, 1981, The King of Comedy, 1983 (Nat. Soc. Film Critics award), Sesame Street Presents: Follow That Bird, 1985, Track 29, 1988, Without You I'm Nothing, 1990, Hudson Hawk, 1991, Truth or Dare, 1991, Inside Monkey Zetterland, 1993; also appears in Heavy Petting, 1988, Perfect, 1985, The Whoopee Boys, 1986, Casual Sex?, 1988; stage appearances (solo) Without You I'm Nothing, 1988, Giving Till It Hurts, 1992; TV appearances (host) Living in America, 1990; regular guest The Richard Pryor Show, Late Night with David Letterman; TV series Roseanne; albums (co-author 8 songs) I'm Your Woman, 1985, Without You I'm Nothing, 1989; books include Confessions of a Pretty Lady, 1988, Love Love and Love, 1993. Home: care Susan DuBow 9171 Wilshire Penthouse Beverly Hills CA 90210*

BERNHARDSON, IVY SCHUTZ, lawyer; b. Fargo, N.D., Aug. 22, 1951; d. James Newell and Phyllis Harriet (Iverson) Schutz; m. Mark Elvin Bernhardson, Sept. 1, 1973; children: Andrew Schutz, Jenna Clare. BA, Gustavus Adolphus Coll., 1973; JD, U. Minn., 1978. Bar: Minn. 1978, U.S. Dist. Ct. Minn. 1978. Staff atty. Gen. Mills, Inc., Mpls., 1978-83, asst. sec. to bd. dirs., 1982—, assoc. counsel, 1983-85, sr. assoc. counsel, 1985—, v.p., 1988—. Trustee Gustavus Adolphus Coll., 1989—, vice chair bd. dirs., 1992-95, chair, 1995—; trustee Fairview Southdale Hosp., 1993—; dir. Fairview Hosp. and Healthcare Svcs., 1996—. Mem. ABA, Am. Soc. Corp. Secs. (dir.), Minn. Bar Assn., Hennepin County Bar Assn. Lutheran. Office: Gen Mills Inc 1 General Mills Blvd Minneapolis MN 55426-1347

BERNHEIM, HEATHER STANCHFIELD PETERSON (MRS. CHARLES BERNHEIM), civic worker; b. Houston; d. Weed and Mylla (Stanchfield) Peterson; student U. Tex., 1938-42; m. Charles A. Bernheim, July 18, 1973. Docent chmn. Harris County Heritage Soc., 1969-70, v.p., after 1970; vol. worker Hermann Hosp., 1968-69; team capt. Mus. Fine Arts Ball, Houston, 1969; maintenance fund drive worker Mus. Fine Arts, 1970, trustee, chmn. costume council, 1986-88; docent Costume Inst., Met. Mus. Art, N.Y.C., 1978, co-chmn. Costume Inst., 1980-81, chmn., 1981-82, mus. guide, 1978—; chmn. Costume Inst. Mus. Fine Arts, Houston, chmn. Grand Gala Ball, 1989; trustee Mus. Fine Arts, Houston; auction chmn. Bluebonnet Ball, Harris County Heritage Soc., 1984; bd. dirs. Planned Parenthood N.Y.C. Mem. N.Y. Jr. League, Kappa Alpha Theta Alumni Assn. Club: Houston. Home: 173 Sage Rd Houston TX 77056-1417

BERNICK, CAROL L., corporate executive; m. Howard Bernick; children: Craig, Peter, Lizzy. Grad., Tulane U. Mem. mktg. staff Alberto-Culver Co., Melrose Park, Ill., 1974-79, dir. new products, 1979-81, dir. new bus. devel. group, 1981-84, v.p., 1984-88, group v.p., 1988-90, exec. v.p. worldwide mktg., 1990-92, exec. v.p., 1992—; pres. Alberto-Culver USA, Melrose Park, Ill., 1994—. Founder Firends of Prentice; bd. dirs. Northwestern Meml. Hosp. Corp.; active women's bd. Five Hosps. Elderly Program, women's bd. Boy's and Girls Clubs of Chgo.; gen. trustee Lincoln Acad. Ill. Recipient Leadership in Bus. award YWCA Met. Chgo., 1992. Mem. Young Pres. Orgn., Econ. Club Chgo. Office: Alberto-Culver Co 2525 Armitage Ave Melrose Park IL 60160-1125

BERNING, LOUISE JUSTINE, bank executive; b. Scott City, Kans., Nov. 16, 1949; d. Paul William and Leona Mae (Macy) Numrich; m. Terrence A. Berning, June 21, 1969 (div. Oct. 1983); children: Christopher Justin, Jonathan Tate, Nicholas Brandon, Elizabeth Brooke. BS in Econs., Tex. Women's U., 1971. Asst. cashier Security State Bank, Scott City, Kans., asst. v.p., 1985-89, v.p., 1989—, asst. trust officer, 1989—. Bd. dirs. United Sch. Dist. #466 Bd. Edn., Scott City, 1991-95, v.p., 1993-94, pres., 1994-95; treas. Scott County Hist. Soc., Scott County Health Care Found. Mem. AAUW, KANZA Soc. of High Plains Pub. Radio (chmn.). Home: 902 Crescent Ave Scott City KS 67871 Office: Security State Bank PO Box 188 Scott City KS 67871

BERNSON, MARCELLA SHELLEY, psychiatrist; b. N.Y.C., Aug. 24, 1952; d. Maxwell Isaac and Priscilla Edith (Zuckerman) Bernson; m. Richard A. Sherman, Apr. 3, 1974; children: Eric Z., Gregory I. BA in Biology summa cum laude, Hofstra U., 1973; MD, Albert Einstein Coll. Medicine, 1976. Diplomate Am. Bd. Psychiatry and Neurology. Resident in psychiatry Bronx (N.Y.) Mcpl. Hosp. Ctr., 1976-79; assoc. dir. med. student edn. in psychiatry U. Medicine and Dentistry of N.J.-N.J. Med. Sch., Newark, 1979-81; pvt. practice psychiatry Westfield, N.J., 1981-86; cons. psychiatrist Healthwise EAP, Elizabeth, N.J., 1985-86; med. chief adult ambulatory svcs. dept. psychiatry Elizabeth Gen. Med. Ctr., 1986-87, asst. dir. dept. psychiatry, 1987-88; dir. tng. psychiat. svc. VA Med. Ctr., E. Orange, N.J., 1988-89; med. dir. partial care Occupl. Ctr. Union County, Roselle, N.J., 1989-92; cons. psychiatrist Union County Ednl. Svcs. Commn., Westfield, 1992-95; med. dir. Richard Hall CMHC, Bridgewater, N.J., 1995—; instr. U. Medicine and Dentistry of N.J.-N.J. Med. Sch., Newark, 1979-81, asst. prof. clin. psychiatry, 1988-89, staff psychiatrist Elizabeth Gen. Med. Ctr., 1985-88, 92-95; profl. adv. com. Somerset County Mental Health Bd. Mem. Am. Psychiat. Assn., N.J. Psychiat. Assn. (tri-county chpt., Union County rep. 1989-90), Assn. Women Psychiatrists. Office: Richard Hall CMHC 500 North Bridge St PO Box 6877 Bridgewater NJ 08807

BERNSTEIN, ADRIANA BENNETT, library and information consultant; b. Jersey City, Nov. 21, 1960; d. William Bradley and Frances Ann (Pagano) Bennett; m. Bernard Bernstein, Dec. 30, 1989. BA in English, Rutgers U., 1982; MA in Liberal/Women's Studies, CUNY, 1985, MLS in Children and Youth Svcs., 1987. Mgr. The Book Stop, Bergenfield, N.J., 1984-86; coord. community libr. program Irvington (N.J.) Pub. Libr., 1986-87; childrens' svcs. libr. Tenafly (N.J.) Pub. Libr., 1987-89, coord. of computerized tech. svcs., 1988-89; dir. Kenilworth (N.J.) Pub. Libr., 1989-96; libr. and info. cons. New Brunswick, N.J., 1996—. Founder and pres. Livingston Coll. Women's Collective Alumni Assn., New Brunswick, N.J., 1982-92, Nat. Feminist Alliance, New Brunswick, 1992—. Mem. ALA, N.J. Libr. Assn. (chair honors, awards and resolutions com. 1989-92, mem. ways and means com., scholarship com., others), Librs. of Union County Consortium (v.p. 1990-91, exec. bd. 1992-93), Livingston Coll. Alumni Assn., Sch. of Comm., Info. and Libr. Studies Alumni Assn., Voices in Action Inc. (treas. 1995-96). Office: 4 Delavan St New Brunswick NJ 08901

BERNSTEIN, CAROLE ROBIN, poet, copywriter; b. Bklyn., May 27, 1960; d. Jack and Barbara L. (Zemen) B.; m. John T. Prendergast, May 5, 1990. BA in English, U. Pa., 1981; MA in Creative Writing, Johns Hopkins U., 188. Tchg. asst. Johns Hopkins U., Balt., 1987-88; mktg. mgr. Oxford U. Press, N.Y.C., 1988-89; coll. promotion mgr. Paragon House, N.Y.C., 1989-90; mktg. mgr. Harper Collins, N.Y.C., 1990-91; self-employed promotional copywriter Bklyn., 1992—. Author (poetry chapbook) And Stepped Away from the Circle, 1995 (winner Sow's Ear Poetry Chapbook Contest, 1994); contbr. poems to lit. mags. Recipient honorable mention Allen Ginsberg Poetry Awards, Passaic (N.J.) Cmty. Coll., 1994, Soc. of Alumni Poetry 2d prize, U. Pa., 1980.

BERNSTEIN, CARYL SALOMON, lawyer; b. N.Y.C., Dec. 22, 1933; d. Gustav and Rosalind (Aron) Salomon; m. William D. Terry, June 12, 1955 (div. 1967); children: Ellen Deborah, Mark David; m. Robert L. Cole, Jr., Oct. 25, 1970 (div. 1975); m. George K. Bernstein, June 17, 1979. B.A. with honors, Cornell U., 1955; J.D., Georgetown U., 1967. Bar: D.C. 1968, U.S. Dist. Ct. D.C. 1968, U.S. Ct. Appeals (D.C. cir.) 1968, U.S. Supreme Ct. 1971. Atty. Covington & Burling, Washington, 1967-73; staff atty. Overseas Pvt. Investment Corp., Washington, 1973-74, asst. gen. counsel, 1974-77, v.p. for ins., 1977-81; sr. v.p., gen. counsel, sec. Fed. Nat. Mortgage Assn., Washington, 1981-82, exec. v.p., gen. counsel, sec., 1982-93; sr. counsel Shaw, Pittman, Potts & Trowbridge, Washington, 1993—. Contbr. articles to profl. jours., chpt. to book; mem. bd. editors Georgetown Law Jour., 1966-67; mem. editorial adv. bd. Housing and Devel. Reporter, 1986-87; mem. bd. dirs. Nat. Housing Conf., 1983-93, 94-96. Bd. dirs. Citizens Bank Md., 1989-92, Marine Spill Response Corp., Nat. Symphony Orch. Assn., Georgetown U. N.Y. Regents scholar, 1951-55. Mem. ABA, Fed. Bar Assn. D.C. Bar Assn., Am. LAw Inst., Adminstrv. Conf. U.S. Office: Shaw Pittman et al 2300 N St NW Washington DC 20037

BERNSTEIN, CONSTANCE RUTH, trial consultant; b. Charlotte, N.C., Jan. 12, 1938; d. Lewis and Miriam (Lewith) B. BS, U. Wis., 1959, MS, 1962. Lectr. Mundelein Coll., Chgo., 1965-68, U. New South Wales, Sydney, Australia, 1969; producer TV documentaries Australian Broadcasting Commn., 1970-74; dir. Constance Bernstein Tng. Inst., Copenhagen, Denmark, 1974-81; pres. The Synchronics Group, San Francisco, 1981—; adj. faculty Stanford U. and U. of San Francisco Law Schs., 1991—, U. Calif. Berkeley, 1995; cons. in field. Author: Techniques in Non Verbal Persuasion, 1988; contbr articls to profl. jours. Activist Clergy Concerned, Chgo., 1965-68. Nat. Defense scholar 1960, Rockefeller scholar, 1961, Fulbright scholar, 1962. Mem. Am. Soc. Trial Cons. Home and office: 19 Divisadero St San Francisco CA 94117

BERNSTEIN, GERDA MEYER, artist; b. Hagen, Westphalia, Germany; d. Arthur Meyer and Claire Hartmann; m. Saul Bernstein; children: David, Carolyn, Marc, Jeffrey. Student, Art Inst. Chgo., MFA, 1978. founder Artists, Residents of Chgo., 1973. One woman shows include Angeleski Gallery, N.Y.C., 1960, Artists, Residents of Chgo. Gallery, 1974, 75, 78, Elmhurst (Ill.) Coll., 1979, Karl Ernst Osthaus Mus., Hagen, West Germany, 1982, A.I.R. Gallery, N.Y.C., 1985, 89, Neuer Berliner Kunstverein, 1987, Bochum (Germany) Mus., 1987, Badischer Kunstverein, Karlsruhe, Germany, 1987, Rockford (Ill.) Coll., 1991, Beacon St. Gallery, Chgo., 1993Fassbender Gallery, Chgo., 1994, Robert F. DeCaprio Art Gallery, Moraine Valley Coll., Palos Hills, Ill., 1994, Alt. Mus., N.Y.C., 1995; exhibited in group shows at Art Inst. Chgo., 1954, 55, 56, 77, 82, 89, 92, 94, Isaac Delgado Mus., New Orleans, 1954, San Francisco Mus. Art, 1955, U. Chgo., 1961, U. Wis., Madison, 1962, 93, Whitney Mus. Am. Art, N.Y.C., 1973, Carleton Coll., Northfield, Minn., 1974, Sangamon State U., Springfield, Ill., 1974, Ill. State Mus. Art, Springfield, 1976, A.I.R. Gallery, 1977, 84, 88, 1134 Gallery, Chgo., 1977, U. Mo., St. Louis, 1977, U. Ill., Urbana and Chgo., 1977, Cultural Ctr., Chgo., 1978, 81, 89, Rutgers U., New Brunswick, N.J., 1979, Columba Coll., Chgo., 1981, Print Club Phila., 1981, Midwest Mus. Am. Art, Elkhart, Ind., 1981, Purdue (Ind.) U., 1981, Mus. Contemporary Art, Chgo., 1984, No. Ill. U., DeKalb, 1984, 90, Neuer Berliner Kunstverein, 1984, Women's Interart Ctr., N.Y.C., 1985, U.N. Conf. Women, Nairobi, Kenya, 1985, Ministerio de Cultura, Madrid, 1986, Chgo. Office Fine Arts, 1989, Franklin Furnace Gallery, N.Y.C., 1991, Peace Mus., Chgo., 1993, Spertus Mus., Chgo., 1994, Minn. Mus. Am. Art, St. Paul, 1995, Southeastern Ctr. Contemporary Art, Winston-Salem, N.C., 1995-96, Ellis Island, N.Y., 1996. Active Feminist Majority, Planned Parenthood, So. Poverty Law Ctr., Amnesty Internat., Holocaust Mus. Mem. NOW. Democrat. Home: 1441 Waverly Highland Park IL 60035 Office: Artspace 95 4 West Washington Chicago IL 60607

BERNSTEIN, JANNA S. BERNHEIM, art educator; b. Memphis, July 21, 1951; d. Berthol Moise and Aline Joy (Kahn) Bernheim; m. Eugene Bernstein Jr., Aug. 12, 1978 (div. Apr. 1992); children: Rachel, Claire, Ruth. BFA, Washington U., 1973; MFA, Memphis State U., 1979, MAT, 1991. Graphic artist Cleo Wrap, Inc., Memphis, 1978-80, Memphis Bd. of Edn., 1980-81; art instr. Memphis Arts Coun., 1983-86, Memphis Brooks Mus., 1985-88; art tchr. St. Agnes Acad./St. Dominic Sch. for Boys, Memphis, 1991—; chmn. cultural arts Richland Elem. Sch., Memphis, 1988-90. Co-author: (lesson packets) Ancient Egypt: An Educator's Guide, 1991, Imprint on the World, 1993; exhibited in group shows at Memphis Brooks Mus., 1976, Memphis May Banner Competition, 1981. Curator docent edn. Temple Israel Judaica Mus., Memphis, 1994; mem. gifts and arts com. Temple Israel, Memphis, 1994—; docent Wonders Internat. Cultural Svcs., Memphis, 1986, 92, 93; worker Temple Israel Habitat for Humanity, Memphis. Shakespeare Festival grantee Tenn. Arts Commn., 1994. Mem. Tenn. Art Edn. Assn., West Tenn. Art Edn. Assn. (exhbn. coord. 1993-95), Memphis Artists Crafts Mem. Assn. (bd. dirs. 1993-95). Home: 319 Fernway Cv Memphis TN 38117-2012 Office: St Dominic Sch for Boys 30 Avon Rd Memphis TN 38117-2502

BERNSTEIN, JONINE LISA, biometry researcher, epidemiologist, educator; b. San Francisco, Aug. 4, 1958; d. Cal and Roz (Kasden) B.; m. Randy M. Mastro; 1 child, Arianna Clara. AB, Brown U., 1981; MS in Applied Biometry, U. So. Calif., 1983; PhD in Epidemiology, Yale U., 1992. Indsl. hygienist divsn. occupational health and radiation control R.I. Dept. Health, Providence, 1978; project dir. Policy Rsch. Inc., Balt., 1980; biostatis. cons. dept. biometry, project coord. dept. ophthalmology U. So. Calif., L.A., 1981-83, biostatistician, project coord. divsn. occupational medicine, 1983; rsch. asst. environ. scis. lab. Mt. Sinai Sch. Medicine, N.Y.C., 1978-79, 80, biostatistician dept. biomath. scis., 1983-86, instr. biostats. and epidemiology, 1983-87, rsch. assoc., 1986-87, biostatis. cons. dept. cardiology, 1987-92; rsch. asst. prof. lab. epidemiology and biostats. Kaplan Ctr. and Inst. Environ. Med./NYU Med. Ctr., N.Y.C., 1992-94; asst. prof. dept. cmty. medicine Mt. Sinai Sch. Medicine, 1994—; student project coord. Brown U., Providence, 1979-80, student instr. occupational safety and health, 1980; project coord. L.A. Com. on Occupational Safety and Health, 1981-83; rsch. assoc. Sch. Epidemiology and Pub. Health, Yale U., New Haven, 1991-92; teaching asst. dept. biometry U. So. Calif., 1982; presenter profl. confs. Contbr. articles to sci. jours. Vol. coord. R.I. Com. on Occupational Safety and Health, Providence, 1977-81. Nat. Rsch. Svc. tng. grantee Yale U., 1987-89, 89-91, rsch. grantee dept. med. affairs Conn. divsn. Am. Cancer Soc., 1991. Mem. AAAS, Am. Soc. Preventive Oncology (Best Poster award 1995), Soc. Epidemiologic Rsch. (Abraham M. Lilienfeld Student Prize Competition award 1992), N.Y. Acad. Scis., N.Y.C. Epidemiology Group. Democratic. Jewish. Home: 50 W 9th St Apt 4B New York NY 10011-8910 Office: Mt Sinai Sch Medicine Divsn Epidemiology 1 Gustave Leury Pl Box 1043 New York NY 10029

BERNSTEIN, PATRICIA ROBIN, podiatrist; b. Jacksonville, Fla., Sept. 20, 1956; d. Sol and Artelia (Moorman) B. Student, Jacksonville U., 1974-75; BA in Biology, Hofstra U., 1978; MS in Med. Biology, L.I. U., 1988; DPM, Pa. Coll. Podiatric Medicine, 1993. Cert. chemistry supr., N.Y., med. technologist in chemistry, hematology, microbiology, blood bank, and urinalysis. Fla., supr. for chemistry, hematology and microbiology, Fla. Med. technologist St. Clare's Hosp. & Health Ctr., N.Y.C., 1982-89; med. technologist Meml. Sloan-Kettering-Cancer Ctr., N.Y.C., 1984-89, S.E. Ga. Regional Med. Ctr., Brunswick, 1994—; lab. rep. pub. relations com. St. Clare's Hosp. & Health Ctr., N.Y.C., 1983-84; chairperson for Nat. Med. Lab. week, 1984; chemistry chairperson Nat. Med. Lab. week Meml. Sloan Kettering Cancer Ctr., N.Y.C., 1988. Mem. NAFE, Am. Soc. Clin. Pathologists (assoc.), Am. Soc. for Microbiology, Am. Assn. Women Podiatrists, Pa. Podiatric Med. Students Assn., Iota Sigma Pi. Home: 653 Monument Rd #305 Jacksonville FL 32225

BERNSTEIN, PHYLISS LOUISE, psychologist; b. Balt., Nov. 27, 1940; d. Samuel Wilfred and Helen Dorothy (Gerson) Wilke; m. Robert Bernstein, June 7, 1964; children: Steve, Susan, David. BA in Psychology summa cum laude, Avila Coll., 1980, MS in Psychology summa cum laude, 1981; PhD in Couseling Psychology with high honors, U. Mo., Kansas City, 1986. Lic. psychologist, Mo. Psychotherapist Community Counseling Ctr., Kansas City, Mo., 1983-85; assoc. psychologist Counseling and Human Devel. Svcs., Kansas City, Mo., 1985-86; ptnr., psychologist Counseling Psychologists and Assocs., Kansas City, Mo., 1987—; staff priviliges Bapt. Med. Ctr., Menorah Med. Ctr.; dir. Jewish Vocat. Svcs., Kansas City, 1988-91, U. Mo. Edn. Dept., Kansas City, 1991—, Jewish Family and Children Svcs., 1992—. Contbr. articles to profl. jours. Life mem. Nat. Coun. Jewish Women. Kansas City; bd. dirs. Avila Coll. Mem. APA, Nat. Register Health Svc. Providers in Psychology, Greater Kansas City Psychol. Assn., Phi Kappa Phi, Pi Lambda Theta, Psi Chi. Office: Counseling Psychologists 4901 Main St Ste 302 Kansas City MO 64112-2674

BERNSTEIN, VIVIAN D., special education author, educational consultant; b. Bklyn., Mar. 14, 1948; d. Irving J. and Nettie (Tambor) Bernstein; m. Neil H. Bernstein, June 23, 1974; children: Aliza, Rachel. BA cum laude, Bklyn. Coll., 1969; MA in Ednl. Psychology, NYU, 1970. Cert. tchr. spl. edn., deaf edn., common brs., N.Y. Tchr. hearing and lang. impaired N.Y.C. Pub. Schs., Bklyn. and Queens, 1970-80; spl. edn. author Steck Vaughn Pub. Co., Austin, Tex., 1978—; edn. cons., workshop leader Schs. in N.Y. State, 1990—. Author: American Government: Freedom, Rights, Responsibilities, 1992, Decisions for Health, 1993, Life Skills for Today's World, 1994, America's Story, 1995, World History and You, 1997, America's History: Land of Liberty, 1997, World Geography and You, 1993.

BERON, GAIL LASKEY, real estate analyst, consultant, appraiser; b. Detroit, Nov. 13, 1943; d. Charles Jack Laskey and Florence B. (Rosenthal) Eisenberg; divorced; children: Monty Charles, Bryan David. Cert. real estate analyst, Mich. Chief/staff appraiser Ft. Wayne Mortgage Co., Birmingham, Mich., 1973-75; pvt. practice fee appraiser S.C., Iowa, Mich., 1976-80; pres. The Beron Co., Southfield, Mich., 1980—; cons. ptnr. Real Estate Counseling Group Conn., Storrs, 1983—, Real Estate Counseling Group Am., prin., 1984—; lectr. real estate confs. Recipient M. William Donnally award Mortgage Bankers Assn. Am., 1975. Mem. Appraisal Inst. (nat. faculty 1991—), Soc. Real Estate Appraisers (bd. dirs. Detroit chpt. 1980-82, nat. faculty 1983-91), Am. Inst. Real Estate Appraisers (bd. dirs. Detroit chpt. 1982-86, nat. faculty 1984-91), Nat. Assn. Realtors, Detroit Bd. Realtors, Southfield Bd. Realtors, Women Brokers Assn. (treas. Southfield chpt. 1981-83), Young Mortgage Bankers (bd. dirs. 1974-75), B'nai B'rith. Home: 7008 Bridge Way West Bloomfield MI 48322-3527 Office: Beron Co 17228 Westhampton Rd Southfield MI 48075-4351

BERRESFORD, SUSAN VAIL, philanthropic foundation executive; b. N.Y.C., Jan. 8, 1943; d. Richard Case and Katherine Vail (Marsters) Berresford Hurd; m. David F. Stein (div.); 1 son, Jeremy Vail Stein. Student, Vassar Coll., 1961-63; B.A. cum laude in Am. History, Radcliffe Coll., 1965. Vol. UN Vol. Services, N.Y.C., summer 1962; sec. to Theodore H. White, summer 1964; program officer Neighborhood Youth Corps, N.Y.C., 1965-67; program specialist Manpower Career Devel. Agy., N.Y.C., 1967; human resources adminstrn. specialist Manpower Career Devel. Agy., 1968; freelance cons., writer Europe and U.S., 1968-70; program officer nat. affairs div. Ford Found., N.Y.C., 1970-80; program officer in charge Ford Found., 1980-81, v.p., 1981-95, exec. v.p., COO, 1995-96, pres., 1996—. Office: Ford Found 320 E 43rd St New York NY 10017-4816

BERRIGAN, HELEN GINGER, federal judge; b. 1948. BA, U. Wis., 1969; MA, Am. U., 1971; JD, La. State U., 1977. Staff rschr. Senator Harold E. Hughes, 1971-72; legis. aide Senator Joseph E. Biden, 1972-73; asst. to mayor City of Fayette, Miss., 1973-74; law clk. La. Dept. Corrections, 1975-77; staff atty. Gov. Pardon, Parole and Rehab. Commn., 1977-78; prin. Gravel Brady & Berrigan, New Orleans, 1978-94, Berrigan, Litchfield, Schonekas, Mann & Clement, New Orleans, 1984-94; judge U.S. Dist. Ct. (ea. dist.) La., New Orleans, 1994—; active La. Sentencing Commn., 1987. Active Com. of 21, 1989, pres., 1990-92, ACLU of La., 1989—, v.p., 1993—, Forum for Equality, 1990—, chmn., 1993—, Amistad Rsch. Ctr. Tulane U., 1990—. Mem. La. State Bar Assn. (mem. fed. 5th cir. 1986—), La. Assn. Criminal Def. Lawyers, New Orleans Assn. Women Attys. Office: US Dist Ct 500 Camp St Rm 556 New Orleans LA 70130-3313

BERRY, BARBARA TORRES, marketing consultant; b. San Diego, July 24, 1954; d. Leonard and Barbara Jane (Walker) Torres; m. Randal Lynn Berry, May 20, 1989. AA in Business, Grossmont Coll., 1974; BS in Foods and Nutrition, San Diego State U., 1978; MS in Nutrition Comms., Boston U., 1982. Registered dietitian; cert. home economist. Editl. publicist Sunkist Growers, Inc., Sherman Oaks, Calif., 1982-85; dir. consumer svcs. Con Agra, Inc., Omaha, 1985-87; mktg. cons. Global Food Mktg., Omaha, 1987-90; dir. of sales/mktg. Shade Pasta, Inc., Fremont, Nebr., 1990-93; pres. Excel Mktg., Arlington, Nebr., 1993—. Recipient New Achievers award, Nebr. Home Economics Assn., 1990. Mem. Am. Dietetic Assn. (recognized Young Dietitian in Calif. 1980), Am. Assn. Family and Consumer Scis., Pioneer Amateur Radio Club (treas. 1994—), Toastmasters (Competent Toastmaster 1987).

BERRY, CAROL A., insurance executive; b. Walla Walla, Wash., Sept. 8, 1950; d. Alan R. and Elizabeth A. (Davenport) B. BA, Wash. State U., 1972. Asst. mgr. L.A. reg. claims CIGNA, Santa Monica, Calif., 1981-83; reg. adminstr. Equicor, Sherman Oaks, Calif., 1983-89; dir. sys. for managed care Blue Cross of Calif., Woodland Hills, Calif., 1989-90; dir. field account svcs. Managed Health Network, L.A., 1990-94; v.p. VertiHealth Adminstrv. Svcs., Chatsworth, Calif., 1994—; lectr. in field. Mem. Pres.'s Commn. on Status of Women. Mem. NAFE, Assn. Info. Mgrs. Healthcare Industry, HFMA, Wash. State U. Alumni Assn. Home: 6155 Lockhurst Dr Woodland Hills CA 91367-1203

BERRY, CECILIA ANNE, nephrology nurse practitioner; b. Brighton, Sussex, Eng., Nov. 14, 1945; came to U.S., 1969; d. Dominic and Vera Denise (Lewry) Marini; children: Anne Da-Silva, Tuan Samahon, Yasmin Samahon, Rohan Samahon; m. Robert H. Berry, July 28, 1990. Diploma, Brighton and Hove Sch. Nursing, 1967; BSN, U. Rochester, N.Y., 1989, MS, 1995. RN, N.Y.; cert. nephrology nurse. Surg. staff nurse U. Rochester Med. Ctr., 1969-72, float staff nurse, pvt. duty nurse, 1972-77; staff nurse in dialysis Monroe Comty. Hosp., Rochester, 1977-82; from staff nurse dialysis level II to level IV, leader U. Rochester (N.Y.) Med. Ctr., 1982-91; dialysis clinician Park Ridge Health Care Sys., Rochester, 1991-96; nurse practitioner dialysis unit Medina (N.Y.) Meml. Hosp., 1996—; dialysis nurse educator St. Mary's Hosp., Rochester, 1994. Contbr. articles to profl. jours. Pres. Young Women's Orgn.-Brockport Ward. Mem. Am. Nephrology Nurses Assn. (pres. Gt. Lakes chpt. 1991-93), Nat. Kidney Found. (coun. for nephrology nurses and technicians), Brockport Ward Young Women's Orgn. (pres.). Mormon. Home: 102 Hollybrook Rd Brockport NY 14420-2504 Office: Medina Meml Hosp 1555 Long Pond Rd Medina NY 14103

BERRY, CHARLENE HELEN, librarian, musician; b. Highland Pk., Mich., Jan. 4, 1947; d. Harold Terry and Mattie Lou (Colvin) B. BSE, Wayne U., 1964-68, MA, 1969-70, MLS, 1971-74; postgrad., Howard Sch. Broadcast Arts, 1992. Ordained music minister. Libr. asst. Wayne State U., Detroit, 1970-74; libr. serials cataloger SUNY, Stony Brook, 1975-79; cataloger Madonna U., Livonia, Mich., 1980—; organist various area chs., Detroit, 1981—, 1st Ch. of Christ, Wyandotte, Mich., 1986—; music min. Gospel Light House Ministries, Detroit, 1991—; scholar, performer, tchr. hammer dulcimer, 1986—; libr. cons. Superior Twp. (Mich.) Libr. Bd., 1989-91; host Charlene Berry's Dulcimer World, Sta. WCAR, Garden City, Mich., WALE, Providence, R.I. Composer: Dulcimer Delights, 1991, marches, waltzes, free compositions and solo symphony, 1993, Dulcimer Praise, 1993, Fruits of the Spirit, 1993; solo recs.: Traditional Dulcimer, 1989, Christmas Dulcimer, 1989, Sacred Dulcimer, 1990, Dulcimer Fun, 1991, Dulcimer Praise, 1993, Fruits of the Spirit, 1993, Dulcimer Americana, 1995; (video) Hammering the Hammer Dulcimer, 1994. Pres. Libr. Staff Assn., SUNY, 1978-79; ch. libr. Ch. Bds. Coms., Long Island, Detroit, 1975—; bd. dirs. Livonia Symphony Soc.; performing artist Mich. Touring Arts Agy., 1994-96. Recipient Performance award Silver Springs Dulciner Soc., 1988, 89, 90, Interat. Order of Merit, ASCAP; named Internat. Woman of Yr., 1992-93, Most Admired Woman of Decade. Fellow Internat. Biographical Assn. (life). Am. Biographical Inst. (Woman of Yr. 1993); mem. AAUW, ALA, NAFE, Am. Biographical Rsch. Assn. (hon. dep. gov.), Bus. and Profl. Women, Am. Soc. of Notaries, Am. Fedn. Musicians, Am. Guild Organists (bd. dirs. 1985-88), Plymouth C. of C., Luth. Ch. Musicians Guild, Order Ea. Star, Kappa Delta Pi. Home and Office: Dulcimer Evente 49614 Oak Dr Lot 67 Plymouth MI 48170-2353

BERRY, CORA SUE, counselor, banker; b. Sidney, Nebr., May 19, 1954; d. Sidney James and Myrtle Marie (Mueller) Simmerman; m. Dennis Gene Berry, Aug. 17, 1974; 1 child, Susan. BS, Chadron (Nebr.) State Coll., 1975, M. in Counseling, 1981. Lic. mental health practitioner; cert. profl. counselor. Acad. and personal counselor Lourdes H.S., Nebraska City, Nebr., 1977-82, Lyman (Nebr.) Pub. Schs., 1982-83, St. Francis H.S., Humphrey, Nebr., 1983-84; psychotherapist Cath. Family Social Svcs., Columbus, Nebr., 1983-87; psychotherapist in pvt. practice Columbus, 1985-87, McCook, Nebr., 1987—; featured presenter Divorce Recovery Seminar, McCook, 1990—, Mng. Depression, McCook, 1994, DayCo Corp., McCook, 1990; spl. guest presenter Alcoholism-The Family Disease, Columbus, 1987; bd. dirs. State Bank of Trent, Trenton. Peer rev. bd. Nebr. Dept. Pub. Instns., Lincoln, 1995; cons. State of Nebr. Foster Care Rev. Bd., Norfolk/North Platte, 1983—. Named Disting. Young Alumnus, Chadron State Coll., 1989, Wman of the Yr., McCook Bus. and Profl. Women, 1989. Mem. ACA, Nebr. Assn. Alcoholism and Drug Abuse Counselors, Nebr. Coalition for Domestic Violence and Sexual Abuse. Republican. Roman Catholic. Home and Office: 812 W 13th St Mc Cook NE 69001

BERRY, DAWN BRADLEY, lawyer, writer; b. Peoria, Ill., Mar. 11, 1957; d. Raymond Coke and Clarette (Williams) Bradley; m. William Lars Berry, July 12, 1980. BS, Ill. State U., 1979, MS, 1982; JD, U. Ill., 1988. Bar: N.Mex. 1988, U.S. Dist. Ct. N.Mex. 1988, U.S. Ct. Appeals (10th cir.) 1993. Assoc. Modrall, Sperling, Roehl, Harris and Sisk, Albuquerque, 1988-90; pvt. practice Tijeras and Albuquerque, 1990—; assoc. Hinkle Law Offices, Albuquerque, 1995-96. Author: Equal Compensation for Women, 1994, The Domestic Violence Sourcebook, 1995, The Divorce Sourcebook, 1995, The Fifty Most Influential Women in American Law, 1996. Pres., bd. dirs. Talking Talons Youth Leadership, Inc., Tijeras, 1993—. Recipient Outstanding Young Alumni award Ill. State U., 1996; Rickert scholar for pub. svc. U. Ill., 1988. Mem. NAFE, N.Mex. Women's Bar Assn., S.W. Writer's Workshop. Home: 222 Raven Rd Tijeras NM 87059-8016 Office: 222 Raven Rd Tijeras NM 87059-8016

BERRY, HALLE, actress; b. Cleve., Aug. 14, 1968; d. Jerome and Judith (Hawkins) B.; m. David Christopher Justice, Jan. 1, 1993. Appeared in films Jungle Fever, 1991, The Last Boy Scout, 1991, Strictly Business, 1991, Boomerang, 1992 (Image award nominee 1992), Fatherhood, 1993, The Program, 1993, The Flintstones, 1994, Losing Isaiah, 1995, The Rich Man's Wife, 1996; TV mini-series Queen, 1992, Solomon & Sheba, 1995; TV series include Living Dolls, 1989, Knots Landing, 1992; also appeared in episodes of Amen, A Different World, They Came From Outer Space. Named Miss Teen All-Am., 1985, Miss U.S.A., 1987. Office: William Morris Agy 151 S El Camino Dr Beverly Hills CA 90212-2704*

BERRY, JANET CLAIRE, librarian; b. Jonesboro, Ark., Dec. 1, 1948; d. Troy Berry and Olivia Rosetta (Irwin) Thompson; m. Julius Jerome Mitcham, Mar. 27, 1970 (div. 1981); m. Gary Neville Hays, Nov. 10, 1987 (div. 1989). BSE, U. Cen. Ark., 1970; MLS, Vanderbilt/Peabody U., 1981. Libr./tchr. Greenbrier (Ark.) High Sch., 1970-72; employment counselor Dixie Employment Agy., Little Rock, 1973-76; sr. libr. asst. U. Ark. for Med. Sci., Little Rock, 1976-85; coord. cataloging svc. Ark. State Libr., Little Rock, 1985—; Instr. U. Ark., Little Rock, 1986-88. Editor La Docere for Am. Bus. Women's Assn. newsletter (regional top 5 award 1991, 92). Mem. ALA, Ark. Libr. Assn. (pres. 1983-84), Ark. Region Sports Car Club of Am. (editor 1988—), Am. Bus. Women's Assn. (La Petite Roche chpt., editor 1990-92, 1992 Woman of Yr.). Democrat. Methodist. Office: Ark State Libr One Capitol Mall Little Rock AR 72201

BERRY, JANIS MARIE, lawyer; b. Everett, Mass., Dec. 20, 1949; d. Joseph and Dorothy I. (Barbato) Sordillo; m. Richard G. Berry, Dec. 27, 1970; children: Alexis, Ashley, Lindsey. BA magna cum laude, Boston U., 1971, JD cum laude, 1974. Bar: Mass. 1974, U.S. Dist. Ct. Mass. 1975, U.S. Ct. Appeals (1st cir.), 1980, U.S. Supreme Ct. 1982. Law clk. Mass. Supreme Jud. Ct., Boston, 1974-75; assoc. Bingham, Dana & Gould, Boston, 1975-80; asst. U.S. atty. Boston, 1980-81; spl. atty. dept. justice N.E. Organized Crime Strike Force, Boston, 1981-84; chief atty. dept. justice N.E. Organized Crime Drug Task Force, Boston, 1984-86; ptnr. Ropes & Gray, Boston, 1986-94; founding ptnr. Berry, Ottenberg, Dunkless & Parker, Boston, 1995-96; ptnr. Roche, Carens & DeGiacomo, 1996—; instr. Harvard Law Sch., 1983-86, Inst. Trial Advocacy, Boston, 1984-87; lectr. Dept. Justice Advocacy Inst., 1986; mem. Mass. Bd. of Bar Overseers, 1989-93; bd. mem. Mass. Housing Fin. Agy., 1995—; chmn. merit selection panel U.S. Magistrate, 1989, Mass. Jud. Nominating Coun., 1991-92. Author: Defending Corporations Public Contracts Jour., (with others) Federal Criminal Practice, 1987. Candidate Mass. Atty. Gen., 1994; mem. Mass. Com. for Pub. Counsel Svcs., Boston, 1986-91; v.p. Boston Inn of Ct., 1990-91; trustee Atlanticare Hosp., 1990-94. Spl. Commendation award Dept. of Justice, Washington, 1983. Mem. Mass. Bar Assn., Boston Bar Assn., Am. Law Inst., Women's Bar Assn., Phi Beta Kappa. Office: Roche Carens & DeGiacomo One Post Office Sq Boston MA 02110

BERRY, JONI INGRAM, hospice pharmacist, educator; b. Charlotte, N.C., June 6, 1953; d. James Clifford and Patricia Ann (Ebener) Ingram; m. William Rosser Berry, May 29, 1976; children: Erin Blair, Rachel Anne, James Rosser. BS in Pharmacy, U. N.C., 1976, MS in Pharmacy, 1979. Lic. pharmacist, N.C. Resident in pharmacy Sch. Pharmacy, U. N.C., Chapel Hill, 1977-79, adj. asst. prof., 1985—; pharmacist Durham County Gen. Hosp., Durham, N.C., 1977-79; coord. clin. pharm. Wake Med. Ctr., Raleigh, N.C., 1979-80; co-dir. pharmacy edn. Wake Area Health Edn. Ctr., Raleigh, 1980-85; pharmacist cons. Hospice of Wake County, Raleigh, 1980—; co-owner Integrated Pharm. Care Systems, Inc., 1995—. Mem. editorial adv. bd. Hospice Jour., 1985-91, 94—, Jour. Pharm. Care in Pain and Symptom Mgmt., 1992—; reviewer Am. Jour. Hospice Care, 1986—; editor pharmacy sect. notes NHO Coun. Hospice Profls.; contbr. articles to profl. jours. Troop leader Girl Scouts U.S.A., Raleigh, 1987—, trainer, 1989-91, mgr. svc. unit, 1990-94; Sunday sch. tchr. St. Phillips Luth. Ch., Raleigh, 1990-92, 94-95, asst. min., 1995—. Recipient Silver Pinecone award Girl Scouts U.S., 1991, Golden Rule award J.C. Penney Co., 1991. Mem. Am. Pharm. Assn. (hospice pharmacist steering com. 1990—), Acad. of Pharmacy Practice and Mgmt. (mem.-at-large 1996—), Am. Soc. Hosp. Pharmacists, Nat. Hospice Orgn., Am. Pain Soc., N.C. Pharm. Assn. (Don Blanton award 1985, mem. continuing edn. com. 1986-87, com. chair 1981-84), N.C. Soc. Hosp. Pharmacists (bd. dirs. 1984-86, program com. 1988-91), Wake County Pharm. Assn. (sec. 1982-85), Rho Chi. Democrat. Office: Hospice Wake County 4513 Creedmoor Rd Fl 4 Raleigh NC 27612-3815

BERRY, LEORA MARY, school nurse; b. Peoria, Ill.; d. William Henry and Harrietta Estella (Booker) Wilson; div. ADN, Ill. Ctrl. Coll., 1971; BSN, Wright State U., 1984; MS, Ohio State U. Cert. sch. nurse, Ohio. Staff nurse U. Ill. Hosp., Chgo., 1971-72; burn unit head nurse Childrens Med. Ctr., Dayton, Ohio, 1973-80, recovery rm. nurse, 1980-86; grad. tchg. asst. Ohio State U., Columbus, 1987-88; staff nurse VA Med. Ctr., Dayton, 1988-89; clin. instr. Dayton Sch. Practical Nursing, 1990-91; sch. nurse Dayton Pub. Schs., 1991—; mem. adv. bd. Horizons in Nursing, Wright State U., 1989-90. Vol. health screening Delta Sigma Theta, Health Fair, 1985. Mem. Ohio Nurses Assn. (polit. action com. 1988-90, dist. 10 pres. 1992-94, dist. 10 bd. dirs. 1988—, Nurse of Yr. 1994), Dayton Black Nurses Assn., Sigma Theta Tau. Methodist.

BERRY, MARY FRANCES, federal agency administrator, history and law educator; b. Nashville, Feb. 17, 1938; d. George Ford and Frances Southall (Wiggins) B. B.A., Howard U., 1961, M.A., 1962; Ph.D., U. Mich., 1966, J.D., 1970; hon. degree, Cen. Mich. U., Howard U., U. Akron, 1977, Benedict Coll., U. Md., Grambling State U., 1979, Bethune-Cookman Coll., Clark Coll., Del. State Coll., 1980, Oberlin Coll., Langston U., 1983, Marian Coll., Haverfod Coll., 1984, Colby Coll., CUNY, 1986, DePaul U., 1987. Bar: D.C. 1972. Asst. prof. history Central Mich. U., Mt. Pleasant, 1966-68; asst. prof. Eastern Mich. U., Ypsilanti, 1968-69; assoc. prof. Eastern Mich. U., 1969-70, U. Md., College Park, 1969-76; acting dir. Afro-Am. studies, 1970-72, dir., 1972-74, acting chmn. div. behavioral and social scis., 1973-74, provost div. behavioral and social scis., 1973-76; prof. history, prof. law U Colo. at Boulder, 1976-80, chancellor, 1976-77; prof. history and law Howard U., Washington, 1980—; Geraldine R. Segal prof. Am. Social Thought U. Pa., 1987—; asst. sec. for edn. HEW, Washington, 1977-80; mem., now chmn U.S. Commn. on Civil Rights, 1980—, now chmn.; adj. assoc. prof. U. Mich., 1970-71; mem. com. visitors U. Mich. Law Sch., 1976-80; mem. nat. adv. panel on minority concerns Coll. Bd., 1980-84; mem. adv. bd. Feminist Press, 1980—; mem. research adv. com. Joint Ctr. for Polit. Studies, 1981—; mem. editorial adv. com. Marcus Garvey Papers, 1981—; mem. adv. bd. Inst. for Higher Edn. Law and Governance, U. Houston, 1983—; Geraldine R. Segal prof. of am. social thought U. Pa., 1987—. Author: Black Resistance/White Law, 1971, Military Necessity and Civil Rights Policy, 1977, Stability, Security and Continuity, Mr. Justice Burton and Decision-Making in the Supreme Court, 1945-58, 1978, (with John Blassingame) Long Memory: The Black Experience in America, 1982; Why ERA Failed, 1986; asso. editor Jour. Negro History, 1974-78; contbr. articles, revs. to profl. jours. Bd. dirs. ARC, Washington, 1980—; trustee Tuskegee U., 1980—; mem. adv. bd. Project '87, 1978—; mem. council UN U., 1986—. Recipient Athena (disting. alumni) award U. Mich., 1977, Roy Wilkins Civil Rights award NAACP, 1983, Image award, 1983, Allard Lowenstein award, 1984, President's award Congl. Black Caucus Found., 1985, Woman of Yr. award Nat. Capital Area YWCA, 1985, Hubert H. Humphrey Civil Rights award Leadership Conf. on Civil Rights, 1986, Rosa Parks award SCLC, Black Achievement award Ebony Mag., Woman of Yr. award Ms. Mag., 1986. Mem. ABA, Nat. Bar Assn., D.C. Bar Assn., Nat. Acad. Public Adminstrn., Orgn. Am. Historians (exec. bd. 1974-77), Assn. Study of Afro-Am. Life and History (exec. bd. 1973-76), Am. Hist. Assn. (v.p. for profession 1980-83), Am. Soc. Legal History, Coalition 100 Black Women (hon.), Delta Sigma Theta (hon.). Office: Commn on Civil Rights Office of Chmn 624 9th St NW Washington DC 20425-0001*

BERRY, MELANIE ELIZABETH, marketing and public relations executive; b. Norman, Okla., June 14, 1962; d. Larry Howard Phipps and Nancy Carol (Sprague) Haberland; m. John Charles Berry, May 5, 1984; children: Aubrey Kate, Heath Gresham. BA, Furman U., 1984. Sr. sales rep. IBM, Rochester, N.Y., 1985-86; br. mgr. Eczel Corp., Rochester, 1986-88; from nat. accts. mgr. to market devel. specialist Epson Am., Inc., Rockville, Md., 1988-93; dir. mktg. Phipps Group, Olney, Md., 1993-94; pres., owner Berry Bylines, Silver Spring, Md., 1994—. Author: The Interior Designer's Marketing Workbook, 1995; author, editor: (newsletter) Executive Baby, 1995—. Dir. music program New Life Cmty. Ch., 1992—. Mem. NAFE, Women in Comms., Mother's Access to Careers at Home, Delta Delta Delta. Republican. Home: 17425 St Theresa Dr Olney MD 30832 Office: Berry Bylines PO Box 12117 3802 Internat Dr Silver Spring MD 20908

BERRY, NANCY WESTPHAL, art educator; b. San Angelo, Tex., Aug. 22, 1935; d. William H. and Lillian (Womble) Westphal; m. Thomas R. Berry, Sept. 12, 1957; children: Ann-Leslie, Blair Bardwell. BS in Interior Design, U. Tex., 1957; MFA in Art Edn., So. Meth. U., 1976, MA in Art History, 1983. Art specialist The Trinity Sch., Midland, Tex., 1965-71; art educator Dallas Mus. Art, 1974-78; cons. art The Winston Sch., Dallas, 1974-75; instr. art edn. So. Meth. U., Dallas, 1976-81; curator of edn. Meadows Mus., Dallas, 1976-85; asst. prof. art So. Meth. U., Dallas, 1981-86; dir. edn. Dallas Mus. Art, 1989-91; asst. prof. art U. N. Tex., Denton, 1991—; mem. faculty North Tex. Inst. for Educators in the Arts, Dallas, 1992—; program dir. Nat. Ctr. for Art Mus./Sch. Collaborations, Dallas, 1994—; cons. Amon Carter mus., Ft. Worth, 1983-91, Museo Del Prado, Madrid, 1983. Editor: Museum Education: History, Theory, Practice, 1990; author, editor: Art Links, 1993. Mem. Dallas Bus. Com. for the Arts, 1991; spkr., cons. Jr. League of Dallas, 1978, 80, 83. Mem. Nat. Art Edn. Assn. (dir. mus. divsn., 1987-89, mem. devel. com.), Tex. Art Edn. Assn. (dir. mus. divsn. 1979-81), Am. Assn. Mus. (mem. edn. com.), Tex. Assn. Mus. Episcopalian. Office: U of N Tex PO Box 5098 Denton TX 76203-0098

BERRY, NORMA JEAN, social worker; b. Charleston, W.Va., Jan. 7, 1946; d. Carl E. and Dora Lee (Hamm) Inman; m. Julian, July 5, 1974, (div. 1980); m. Vincent L. Swadis, Sept. 12, 1985. BS, Morris Harvey Coll., 1967; MSW, W.Va. U., 1975. Social Worker. Social worker Fla. State Dept. of Welfare, Crestview, 1968-69; asst. adminstr. Hilltop Home for the Elderly, Charleston, 1970-71; social worker W.Va. Dept. of Welfare, Charleston, 1971-74; social worker VA Hosp., Huntington, W.Va., 1974-82, Temple, Tex., 1982-1990; psychotherapist Minirth-Meier, Tunnell & Wilson Psychiat. Clinic, Belton, Tex., 1990-91; social worker Vets. Affairs Med. Ctr., Temple, Tex., 1991—; real estate agt. Bruzzese Realty Co., Huntington, 1980-81; salesperson Mary Kay Cosmetics, Temple, 1983-84. Recipient Outstanding Svc. award DAV, 1981. Home: 8920 Trailridge Dr Temple TX 76502-5210 Office: Olin E Teague Veteran Ctr Temple TX 76504

BERRY, VERONICA ANNE, non-profit organization administrator; b. Washington, June 10, 1953; m. William Berry, Nov. 2, 1985; 1 child, Malcolm Douglas. BA in Psychology, George Washington U., 1975; MPA, Xavier U., Cin., 1986. Program dir. Student Nat. Med. Assn., Washington, 1975-78; dep. dir. Avondale Redevel. Corp., Cin., 1982-94; dir. Adoption Awareness Alliance, Cin., 1994—. Editor/writer newsletter All About Adoption. Mem. field svc. bd. United Way, Cin., 1993—; sec. Nat. Coun. Negro Women, Cin., 1988-90. Mem. Nat. Assn. Fund Raising Execs. (com.). Office: Adoption Awareness Alliance 11370 Springfield Pl Cincinnati OH 45246

BERRYHILL, MARY FINLEY, emergency nurse; b. Miami Beach, Fla., Dec. 11, 1944; d. Clyde A. and Alice J. (White) Finley; m. Michael W. Berryhill (div. Nov. 1977); children: Jennifer Ann, John Michael; m. Robert L. Snyder, July 18, 1996. BSN, U. Fla., 1967. RN; cert. emergency nurse, emergency nursing pediatric course instr., trauma nurse core course instr. Staff nurse, nurse clinician Shand's Teaching Hosp. U. Fla., Gainesville, 1967-68; rsch. assoc. Coll. Nursing U. Fla., Gainesville, 1968-70; childbirth educator Ocala, Fla., 1970-78; outpatient obstetrics nurse Heith H. Knorr, Ocala, 1970-72; state coord. Am. Soc. Psychoprophylaxis, Ocala, 1974-78; student health svc. nurse Berkshire Sch., Sheffield, Mass., 1978-90; nurse emergency dept. Fairview Hosp., Great Barrington, Mass., 1984—, shift dir., 1992—. Emergency childbirth instr. South Berkshire Vol. Ambulance Squad, Great Barrington, Mass., 1983-93, mem., v.p., 1984-85. Mem. Emergency Nurses Assn. (treas. Berkshire chpt. 1993, pres.-elect 1996, trauma nurse core curriculum instr. 1992—, emergency nurse pediat. curriculum instr. 1993—, Mass. state pediat. com. 1994—). Home: PO Box 587 Great Barrington MA 01230-0587 Office: Fairview Hosp 29 Lewis Ave Great Barrington MA 01230-1713

BERSIN, RUTH HARGRAVE, priest, social services administrator; b. LaPorte, Ind., Sept. 16, 1939; d. Jacob Harold and Rowena Adeline (Hullett) Hargrave; m. Richard Lewis Bersin; children: Jacob David Antonio, Rebekah Adeline Juana. BS in Edn., Ind. U., 1962; MA in Religion, Colgate Rochester Div. Sch., 1965; MDiv, Yale Div. Sch., 1982; D of Ministry, Grad. Theol. Found., 1993. Ordained priest, 1984. Dir. ednl. devel. ctr. Commodore, Japan, 1972-75; dir. spl. projects, refugees svcs. coord. Episcopal Social Svcs., Bridgeport, Conn., 1982-89; asst. dir. Interfaith Conf. Met. Washington, 1992-93; exec. dir. Tokyo English Lifeline, 1989-92; asst. priest Good Shepherd Episcopal Ch., Burke, Va., 1994; exec. dir. Phoenix Comty. Svcs., Washington, 1995-96; assoc. priest Grace Episcopal Church, Lawrence, Mass., 1996—; dir. Devel. Trauma Ctr., Brookline, Mass., 1996—; mem. Ecumenical commn. Diocese of Washington, 1995, Diocese of Conn., 1984-89; bd. dirs. My Sister's Pl., 1996; priest St. Monica's Capitol Hill, Washington, 1995-96; interim asst. priest Episc. Congregation, U.S. Naval Base, Yokosuka, Japan, 1989-92. Leader NOVA Trauma Team, Oklahoma City, 1995, Refugee Adv. Coun., State of Conn., 1984-89, Refugee Welfare Com. Nat. Ch. World Svc., 1986; bd. dirs. Women's Crisis Ctr., Norwalk, Conn., 1980-83; mem. Nat. Coalition Against Sexual Assault. Mem. NAFE, Nat. Coalition Against Sexual Assault, Am. Assn. Pastoral Counseling (counselor in tng.), Jungian Soc. Washington, Internat. Assn. Trauma Counselors, Internat. Soc. Traumatic Stress Studies, Nat. Soc. Fund Raising Execs., Assembly of Episcopal Hosps. and Chaplains. Democrat.

BERSIN, SUSAN JOYCE-HEATHER (REIGNBEAUX JOYCE-HEATHER BERSIN), critical care nurse, police officer; b. Lakewood, Ohio, July 11, 1945; d. Richard George Sr. and Ireene Rose (Brenner) Bersin; m. Robert Joseph Okragley, Dec. 23, 1972 (div. Apr. 1993); 1 child, MaryRose Reignbeaux. BS in Zoology, Kent State U., 1975, BSN, 1976, BS in Chemistry, 1976; MS in Med.-Surg Nursing, Case Western Res. U., 1979. RN, Ohio; cert. critical care nurse. Driver Waite Transport, Akron, Ohio, 1967-68, Cleve. Transit System, 1968-70; CEO, chief technician Corvair Repair & Mobile Svc., Berea, Ohio, 1970—; critical care nurse Deaconess Hosp., Cleve., 1976-79, St. Luke's Hosp., Cleve., 1979-81, St. John Hosp., Cleve., 1981—; police officer Cleve. Police Dept., 1971—. Served with USN, 1963-67, Viet Nam. Mem. Sigma theta Tau (charter mem. Delta Xi chpt.). Roman Catholic. Home: 412 Waverly St Berea OH 44017-2145

BERSON, ROBIN KADISON, librarian; b. Mount Vernon, N.Y., May 29, 1945; d. Richard Joseph and Beryl Constance (Schleicher) Kadison; m. Robert J. Berson, May 20, 1967; children: Jessica, William. BA, Bryn Mawr Coll., 1967; MA, NYU, 1968; MLS, Columbia U., 1972. Tchr. history Fieldston Sch./Upward Bound, N.Y.C., 1968, Calhoun Sch., N.Y.C., 1969-70, Columbia Prep. Sch., N.Y.C., 1970-71; crafts therapist Morningside Heights Neighborhood Assn., N.Y.C., 1975-76; mng. editor History of Edn. Quar., N.Y.C., 1978-85; freelance editor various acad. presses N.Y.C., 1985-89; dir. upper sch. libr. Riverdale Country Sch., N.Y.C., 1991—; nat. libr. adv. bd. dirs. Greenwood Pub., Westport, Conn., 1995—. Author: Marching to a Different Drummer, 1994; contbr. book revs. Sch. Libr. Jour., bimonthly column Wilson Libr. Bull., revs. New Press. rschr., editor Coalition for the Homeless, N.Y.C., 1988-89; bd. dirs. Encampment for Citizenship, Phila., 1995-96. Senatorial scholar State of Pa., 1963-67; Grad. fellow Woodrow Wilson Nat. Fellows, 1967-68; Coun. for Basic Edn./NEH grantee, 1994. Mem. ACLU (rschr. 1973-74), AAUW, NOW, Common Cause, Pub. Citizen, Greenpeace. Home: 80 La Salle St 20F New York NY 10027 Office: Riverdale Country Sch Upper Sch Libr 5250 Fieldston Rd Bronx NY 10471

BERT, CAROL LOIS, educational assistant; b. Bakersfield, Calif., Oct. 15, 1938; d. Edwin Vernon and Shirley Helen (Craig) Phelps; m. John Davison Bert, Sept. 26, 1964; children: Mary Ellen, John Edwin, Craig Eric, Douglas Ethan. BS in Nursing, U. Colo., 1960. Med. surg. nurse U.S. Army, Washington, 1960-62, Ascom City, Korea, 1962-63, San Antonio, 1963, Albuquerque, 1964-65; ednl. asst. Jefferson County Schs., Arvada, Colo., 1979—. Sec. Parent, Tchr., Student Assn. Arvada West High Sch., 1987-88. Club: Colo. Quilting Coun. (1st v.p. 1988, 89, inducted into Hall of Fame, 1992). Avocations: reading, quilting, camping, fishing, tennis. Home: 5844 Oak St Arvada CO 80004-4739 Office: Allendale Elem Sch 5900 Oak St Arvada CO 80004-4741

BERT, CLARA VIRGINIA, home economics educator, administrator; b. Quincy, Fla., Jan. 29, 1929; d. Harold C. and Ella J. (McDavid) B. BS, Fla. State U., 1950, MS, 1963, PhD, 1967. Cert. tchr., Fla.; cert. home economist; cert. pub. mgr. Tchr. Union County High Sch., Lake Butler, Fla., 1950-53, Havana High Sch., Fla., 1953-65; cons. rsch. and devel. Fla. Dept. Edn., Tallahassee, 1967-75, sect. dir. rsch. and devel., 1975-85, program dir. home econs. edn., 1985-92, program specialist resource devel., 1992—; cons. Nat. Ctr. Rsch. in Vocat. Edn., Ohio State U., 1978; field reader U.S. Dept. Edn., 1974-75. Author, editor booklets. Mem. devel. bd., adv. bd. Family Inst., 1994—. U.S. Office Edn. grantee, 1976, 77, 78; recipient Dean's award Coll. Human Scis., Fla. State U., 1995; named Disting Alumna Coll. Human Scis., Fla. State U., 1994. Mem. Am. Home Econs. Assn. (state treas. 1969-71), Am. Vocat. Assn., Fla. Vocat. Assn., Fla. Vocat. Home Econs., Fla. Home Econs., Am. Vocat. Edn. Rsch. Assn. (nat. treas. 1970-71), Nat. Coun. Family Rels., Am. Ednl. Rsch. Assn., Fla. State U. Alumni Assn. (bd. dirs. home econs. sect.), Havana Golf and Country Club, Kappa Delta Pi, Kappa Omicron Nu (chpt. pres. 1965-66), Delta Kappa Gamma (pres. 1974-76), Sigma Kappa (pres. corp. bd. 1985-91), Phi Delta Kappa. Office: Fla Dept Edn FEC Tallahassee FL 32399

BERTAGNOLLI, LESLIE A., lawyer; b. Bloomington, Ill., Nov. 11, 1948. BA, Ill. State U., 1970, MA, 1971; PhD, U. Ill., 1975, JD, 1979. Bar: Ill. 1979. Ptnr. Baker & McKenzie, Chgo. Office: Baker & McKenzie 130 E Randolph Dr Chicago IL 60601*

BERTELL, MARY KATHERINE, retired art educator, executive secretary; b. Buffalo, July 13, 1925; d. Paul George and Helen Josephine (Twohey) B. BS in Edn., SUNY, Buffalo, 1946, postgrad., 1947-65. Tchr. art grades 1-12 Skaneateles, N.Y., 1946-48; tchr. art grades 9-12 Buffalo, 1949-82; exec. sec. Ministry of Concern for Pub. Health, Buffalo, 1988—. Roman Catholic. Office: Ministry of Concern for Pub Health PO Box 1487 Buffalo NY 14231-1487

BERTELLE, JEANNE T., publishing company executive, human resources director; b. Bklyn., Oct. 14, 1947; d. John A. and Florence (Bellitti) B.; m. Silvio Rosato. BA in English, Bklyn. Coll., 1968; postgrad. in Drama, Hunter Coll., 1975-77. Pers. adminstr. Chem. Bank, N.Y.C., 1968-70; employment interviewer L.I. Coll. Hosp., Bklyn., 1970-71; sr. job analyst health svcs. mobility study, Rsch. Found. CUNY, N.Y.C., 1971-76; pers. mgr. Doubleday & Co., N.Y.C., 1976-88; dir. human resources McGraw-Hill Inc., N.Y.C., 1988—; com. mem. Direct Mail Assn., N.Y.C., 1984; cons., editor Health Svcs. Mobility Study, N.Y.C., 1976-77. N.Y. State Regents scholar, 1964-68. Mem. Am. Soc. Pers. Adminstrs., Assn. Am. Pubs. (chair industry salary survey 1987—). Roman Catholic. Club: Scott House (Bklyn.) (v.p.). Home: 1104 Hunters Run Dobbs Ferry NY 10522-3419 Office: McGraw-Hill Inc 1221 Ave Of The Americas New York NY 10020-1001

BERTELSEN, DELORA PEARL, human resources professional, mayor; b. Provo, Utah, Apr. 7, 1936; d. Lave and Nellie (Evans) B. BA, Brigham Young U., 1958, MPA, 1985. Tchr. Las Palmas Jr. High, North Sacramento, Calif., 1958-60; ch. rep. LDS Ch., Paris, France, 1960-62; dept. sec. polit. sci. Brigham Young U., Provo, 1963-66; sec., legal aide Litton Industries, Washington, 1966-69; office mgr., rsch. asst. Inst. Pub. Adminstrn., Washington, 1969-72; exec. sec. Supreme Ct. U.S., Washington, 1972-76; asst. to dean Marriott Sch. Mgmt. Brigham Young U., Provo, 1976-95, equality opportunity mgr., 1995—. Founding bd. mem. Springville (Utah) World Folkfest, 1985-90, bd. mem. Ctrl. Utah Water Conservancy Dist., Orem, Utah, 1988-89, Springville (Utah) Mus. Art, 1990—; mem. city coun. Springville City, 1980-87, mayor, 1990—; chair So. County Mayors, 1995—; mem. Coun. Govts., 1990—. Mem. Mountainland Assn. Govts. (chair steering com. 1995, chair regional planning 1996—), Kiwanis Club (membership com. 1990—). Mem. LDS Ch. Office: Office of the Mayor 50 S Main Springville UT 84663

BERTENSHAW, BOBBI CHERRELLE, producer; b. Bklyn., Oct. 22, 1961; d. Eli and Marcia Janet (Forman) Slachofsky; m. William H. Bertenshaw III, Dec. 16, 1984. Diploma, Nat. Broadcast Sch., Phila., 1982, Health Maintenance Inst., Flushing, N.Y., 1985. Radio, TV producer Coun. of Chs., N.Y.C., 1981-84, Radio and TV Roundup Prodns., N.Y.C., 1982—; producer, dir. WOR Radio, N.Y.C., 1982—; dir. communications Delfon Rec. Soc., 1987—; chief exec. officer Radio & TV Roundup Prodns., 1991—; programming cons. N.J. NetworkPublic TV, 1992—; communications dir. Delfon Recording Soc., 1987—; producer-dir. Stat. WOR Radio N.Y., 1983—; co-producer People Working for People, Sta. WWOR TV N.Y. and Cable TV Network of N.J., 1988—. Recipient Cape TV award Cable TV Network N.J., 1987, N.J. State Fair awards, 1990, 91, 92, 93, 94, 95, 96; named Miss Lima Bean Nat. Lima Bean Assn., 1986-87. Mem. Women in Communications, Internat. Platform Assn., Am. Symphony Orch. League, N.J. Coun. of Chs. (dept. communications 1983—), Feathered Fanciers Soc. (sec. 1992—), Nat. Lima Bean Assn. (co-chmn. 1988—). Home: 653 Sunhaven Dr Clayton NJ 08312 Office: Delfon Rec Soc PO Box 1700 Livingston NJ 07039-1700

BERTHOLD-ROSEN, BONNIE MADELINE, elementary school educator, consultant; b. Sellersville, Pa., Nov. 23, 1950; d. Willard Miller and Anna Agnes (Dugard) Berthold; m. Robert G. Rosen. BS in Elem. Edn. with high honors, Kutztown State U., Pa., 1972; MS in Edn. with disting. recognition, Temple U., 1975; Prin.'s cert., U. Pa., 1978. Elem. sch. tchr. Reading Sch. Dist., Pa., 1972-79, summer sch. instr., 1972-79, workshop presenter, 1972—, curriculum developer, 1974-79, adminstv. inter, 1977-79; owner, adminstr. Wooly Bear Day Care Sch., Lansdale, Pa., 1979-94; asst. prof. Montgomery County C.C., Blue Bell, Pa., 1985—; 1st grade tchr. No. Penn Sch. Dist., 1995—; instr. Montgomery County Intermediate Unit, 1995—; cons. in field; presenter coll. and cmty. workshops. Contbr. articles to mags. Bd. dir. No. Penn Boy's and Girl's Club. Recipient Outstanding Tchrs. Am. award Bd. of Advisors, 1975; named Tchr. of Yr. Reading/Berks County C. of C., 1976; George B. Hancher scholar Kutztown State U., 1971. Mem. Montgomery/Bucks Assn. for Edn. of Young Children (pres. 1982-84, bd. dirs. 1993—), Nat. Assn. for Edn. of Young Children, Pa. Assn. for Edn. of Young Children, Pa. Assn. Child Care Adminstrs., Small Bus. Coun. (presenter), Del. Valley Child Care Coun. (sec.), North Penn C. of C. (small bus. coun.). Republican. Lutheran. Avocations: piano, water sports, reading, constructing and designing learning materials. Home: 106 Holly Dr Lansdale PA 19446-1617 Office: Inglewood Elem Sch 1313 Allentown Rd Lansdale PA 19446

BERTI, MARGARET ANN, early childhood education educator; b. Jersey City, Oct. 1, 1961; d. John Albert and Jane Matilda (McNair) Condon; m. Douglas Anthony Berti, Aug. 4, 1990; children: Matthew Douglas, Allison Nicole. BA, William Paterson Coll., Wayne, N.J., 1983, MEd, 1985. Tchr. 1st grade Paterson (N.J.) Pub. Schs., 1984-85; tchr pre-kindergarten and ESL Dallas Ind. Sch. Dist., 1985-92; tchr. kindergarten Pearland (Tex.) Ind. Sch. Dist., 1992—. Named Tchr. of Yr., George W. Truett Elem. Sch., 1988, Rustic Oak Elem. Sch., Pearland, 1994; named to Outstanding Young Women of Am., 1991; Title VII grantee Tex. Woman's U., 1987. Mem. Nat. Assn. Edn. Young Children, Classroom Tchrs. Dallas (bldg. rep. 1991), Dallas-Internat. Reading Assn. (corr. sec. 1992), Pearland Edn. Assn. (bldg. rep. 1993-95), Delta Kappa Gamma (Delta Rho chpt.). Roman Catholic. Home: 1526 Saxony Ln Houston TX 77058-3442

BERTINI, CATHERINE ANN, United Nations world food program administrator; b. Syracuse, N.Y., Mar. 30, 1950; d. Fulvio and Ann (Vino) B.; m. Thomas Haskell, 1988. Degree, SUNY. Youth dir. N.Y. Rep. State Com., 1971-74; with Rep. Nat. Com., 1975-76; mgr. pub. policy Container Corp. Am., 1977-87; dir. Office Family Assistance, U.S. Dept. Health and Human Svcs., 1987-89; acting asst. sec. U.S. Dept. Health and Human Svcs., 1989; asst. sec. U.S. Dept. Agrl., 1989-92; exec. dir. UN World Food Programme, Rome, 1992—; UN panel mem. sec. gen.'s High Level Personalities on African Devel., UN, 1992—. Commr. Ill. State Scholarship Comm., 1979-84; mem. Ill. Human Rights Comm., 1985-87. Recipient Leadership in Human Svcs. award Am. Pub. Welfare Assn., 1990, Pub. Svc. award Am. Acad. Pediatrics, 1991, Leadership award Nat. Assn. WIC Dirs., 1992, Quality of Life award Auburn U., 1994. Fellow Harvard U., 1986. Office: UN World Food Program, Via Cristoforo Colombo 426, 00145 Rome Italy

BERTINI, JUDITH EMERLINE, government agency administrator; b. Phila., Feb. 25, 1944; d. John C. and Mildred A. Emerline; m. Francis A. Bertini. BA, Syracuse U., 1966; MA, U. Cin., 1967; MLS, Cath. U., 1977; postgrad., George Washington U., 1987, Harvard U., 1990. Archivist asst. Fed. Records Ctr. Nat. Archives, Washington, 1968; intelligence rsch. specialist CIA, Washington, 1968-71, Dept. Army, Washington, 1971-73; intelligence rsch. specialist dangerous drugs unit, Asian heroin unit, spl. analysis unit, estimates unit, organized crime unit Drug Enforcement Adminstrn., Washington, 1975-81, supervisory intelligence rsch. specialist, organized crime and terrorism unit, operational intelligence sect., 1981-84, supervisory intelligence rsch. specialist, operational intelligence sect., 1984-89, assoc. dep., asst. adminstr. for intelligence, 1989-92, dept. asst. adminstr. intelligence divsn. Office of Intelligence Liaison and Policy, 1992—. Office: Drug Enforcement Adminstrn Washington DC 20537

BERTOLOZZI, VICTORIA MARGARET, management analyst; b. Chgo., May 14, 1948; d. Charles Victor and Olga (Giachetti) Bertolozzi. AA, U. Md., 1975, BA in Bus. and Mgmt., 1977; MBA, Savannah State Coll., 1986; postgrad. in bus. adminstrn., Nova Southeastern U., 1991—. Job developer New Visions for Newport County, Newport, R.I., 1978, adminstrv. asst. to dir., 1978-80, program dir., 1980-82; mktg. dir. Charter Broad Oaks Hosp., Savannah, Ga., 1982-86; mgmt. analyst City of Savannah, 1987-91, program analyst, 1991-93, sr. program analyst, 1994—. Mem. ASPA, Aca. Internat. Bus. Home: 213 Executive Park Dr Savannah GA 31406 Office: City of Savannah PO Box 1027 Savannah GA 31402-1027

BERTRAND, ANNABEL HODGES, civic worker, artist, calligrapher; b. Birmingham, Ala., Jan. 4, 1915; d. Thomas Edmund and Mae (Crawford) Hodges; m. John Raney Bertrand, Oct. 23, 1942; children: John Thomas, Diana Bertrand Williams, Karen Bertrand Wilson, J'May Bertrand Rivara. BS, Tex. Woman's U., 1935, MA, 1936; postgrad., Columbia U., 1938. Tchr. White Deer (Tex.) Consol. Sch., 1936-37, Tyler (Tex.) Pub. Sch. System, 1938-39; instr. Sam Houston State U., Huntsville, Tex., 1939-42; interim tchr. Portsmouth (N.H.) Pub. Sch., 1943. Bd. dirs. Rome Area Coun. for the Arts, 1980—, Ga. Coun. for Arts and Humanities, Atlanta, 1979-83, Mental Health Assn. Floyd County, Rome, Ga., 1980—; active High Mus. Art, Atlanta, 1979—, Rome Symphony Guild, 1980—, Friends of Rome/Floyd County Libr., 1985—, Christian Personhood Book Discussion Group of First United Meth. Ch., 1980—. Mem. AAUW, United Meth. Women, Rome Music Lovers Club, Sigma Alpha Iota (patroness). Republican. Home: 18 Rosewood Rd Rome GA 30165-4269

BERTRAND, CATHERINE, religious organization administrator. Mem. Sch. Sisters of Notre Dame, Cath. Ch. Vocat. dir. Sch. Sisters of Notre Dame, Mankato, Minn.; assoc. vocat. dir. Archdiocese of St. Paul/Mpls.; exec. dir. Nat. Religious Vocat. Conf., Chgo.; tchr., pastoral min., prison min., vocat. min.; presenter workshops, retreats, programs in field. Developer various brochures, study guides and video projects. Office: 1603 S Michigan Ave Ste 400 Chicago IL 60616

BERTRAND, LYNNE, freelance journalist, writer; b. Exeter, N.H., Oct. 30, 1963; d. George and Shirley (Hatch) B.; m. Hans Tennsma, Aug. 14, 1988; children: Nicholaas, Goergia Rae. BA, Gordon Coll.; MA, NYU. Newspaper reporter, freelance journalist, writer, 1987—. Author: One Day, Two Dragons, 1991, Good Night, Teddy Bear, 1992. Let's Go! Teddy Bear, 1992, Who Sleeps in the City?, 1994; humor columnist, Working Mother. Chair Williamsburg Sch. Com., 1993—. Democrat. Home: PO Box 761 Williamsburg MA 01096*

BERTSCHE, LINDA LOU, psychiatric clinical nurse specialist; b. Wauseon, Ohio, Oct. 21, 1952; d. James Edwin and Genevieve (Shuppert) B.; m. James R. Yoder, Sept. 24, 1977; children: Rachael Erin, Timothy Luke. BSN, Goshen (Ind.) Coll., 1974; MSN, Ind. U.-Purdue U., Indpls., 1990. Cert. clin. nurse specialist in psychiat. mental health nursing care of adults, ANCC; prescriptive authority, Ind. Psychiat. nurse Elkhart (Ind.) Gen. Hosp., 1974-76, staff nurse High Park Physicians, Goshen, 1976-78; psychiat. nurse Otis Bowen Ctr., Warsaw, Ind., 1978-80, cons., 1986-87; staff nurse Borgess Hosp., Kalamazoo, 1980-82; houseparent Africa Inter Mennonite Mission, Kinshasa, Zaire, 1982-85; staff nurse Oaklawn Hosp., Goshen, 1987-90; cons. Elkhart County Spl. Edn., Goshen, 1991-93; psychiat. nurse specialist North Eastern Ctr., Kendallville, Ind., 1991—. Recipient Miller-Erb Nursing Devel. award Mennonite Bd. Missions, 1988-89, Elmer Ediger Meml. scholarship, 1989-90. Profl. Nurse Traineeship awardee, 1989-90. Mem. Ind. State Nurses Assn. (bd. dirs. Dist. 12, 1991-94, psychiat.-mental health coun. 1990—), Advocates for Child Psychiat. Nursing, North Ctrl. Ind. Hon. Nursing Soc., Sigma Theta Tau. Home: 2106 Independence Dr Goshen IN 46526-1420 Office: North Eastern Ctr Kendallville IN 46755

BERUBE, GEORGETTE B., senator; State senator 16th dist., Maine, 1985—. Democrat. Office: Maine State Senate 3 State House Station Augusta ME 04333 also: 195 Webster St Lewiston ME 04240-5546*

BERUBE, MARGERY STANWOOD, publishing executive; b. Middleborough, Mass., Nov. 18, 1943; d. John Peter and Dorothy Cole (Stanwood) Wholan; m. Edgar Roger Berube, Sept. 12, 1967. BA in English, Wilkes Coll., 1965. Creative and prodn. mgr., dir. editorial ops. Med. div. Houghton Mifflin Co., Boston, 1978-81, dir. editorial ops. Reference div., 1982-85, v.p., dir. editorial ops. Trade and Reference div., 1986-87, v.p., dir. editorial art prodn. and mfg. services, 1987-91, v.p., dir. lexical pub., prodn. and mfg. svcs., 1991—. Mem. Bookbuilders (bd. dirs. 1976-80). Office: Hougton Mifflin Co 222 Berkeley St Boston MA 02116-3748

BESCH, LORRAINE W., special education educator; b. Orange, N.J., June 27, 1948; d. Robert Woodruff and Minnie (Wrightson) B.; m. William Lee Gibson, July 10, 1982. AA in Liberal Arts, Mt. Vernon Coll., 1968; BA in Sociology, U. Colo., 1970; MA in Spl. Edn., U. Denver, 1973. Cert. handicapped thcr., N.J. Elem. resource rm. tchr. Beeville (Tex.) Ind. Sch. Dist., 1973-75; trainable mentally retarded tchr. Kings County Supt. Schs., Hanford, Calif., 1975-78; h.s. resource rm. tchr. Summit (N.J.) Bd. Edn., 1980-81; h.s. resource rm. tchr. Westfield (N.J.) Bd. Edn., 1981—, head coach field hockey, 1981-83, mem. crisis mgmt. team, 1982-87; N.J. del. 23d IBC/ABI Internat. Congress on Arts and Comm., San Francisco, 1996. Del. N.J. 23rd IBC/ABI Internat. Congress on Arts and Comm., San Francisco, 1996. Mem. AAUW, NEA, Coun. Exceptional Children (Learning Disabilities divsn.), N.J. Edn. Assn., Westfield Edn. Assn. (del. 1983-90, tech. com. 1993-94, conf. funds com. 1994—), Hartford Family Found. (v.p., sec. 1991—), Wrightson-Besch Found. (sec.-treas. 1994—). Home: 8 Lone Oak Rd Basking Ridge NJ 07920-1613 Office: Westfield HS 550 Dorian Rd Westfield NJ 07090-3302

BESCHORNER, SHARON ANNE, financial analyst; b. Omaha, Nov. 25, 1953; d. Alphonse Joseph and Cleopha Magdelena (Krumm) Grohmann; m. Fred John Beschorner, Oct. 5, 1979; children: John, Laura. BS in BA, U. Nebr., Omaha, 1976, MBA, 1988. CPA, Nebr.; CMA. Corp. auditor Union Pacific Corp., Omaha, 1976-79; sr. analyst facility costing Union Pacific R.R., Omaha, 1979-80, asst. mgr. applied cost, 1980-85, asst. mgr., rsch. analyst, 1985-86, asst. mgr. contract compliance, 1986-88, mgr. fin. assess, 1988-90, mgr. comml. investment, 1990-91, dir. state taxes, 1991-95, dir. fin. planning, 1996—. Bd. dirs. Nebr. Tax Rsch. Coun., Lincoln, 1992-96. Mem. AICPAs, Am. Cancer Soc. (bd. dirs. 1996—), Nebr. Soc. CPAs (com. on state taxation 1991-95), U. Nebr.-Omaha Alumni Assn. (bd. dirs. 1996—). Republican. Roman Catholic. Home: 7032 Northland Dr Omaha NE 68152 Office: Union Pacific Railroad 1416 Dodge St Rm 738 Omaha NE 68179-0001

BESHAR, CHRISTINE, lawyer; b. Paetzig, Germany, Nov. 6, 1929; came to U.S., 1952, naturalized, 1957; d. Hans and Ruth (vonKleist-Retzow) von Wedemeyer; m. Robert P. Beshar, Dec. 20, 1953; children: Cornelia, Jacqueline, Frederica, Peter. Student, U. Hamburg, 1950-51, U. Tuebingen, 1951-52; B.A., Smith Coll., 1953. Bar: N.Y. 1960, U.S. Supreme Ct. 1971. Assoc. firm Cravath, Swaine & Moore, N.Y.C., 1964-70; ptnr. Cravath, Swaine & Moore, 1971—. Bd. dirs. Catalyst for Women Inc., 1977—; trustee Colgate U., 1978-84, Smith Coll., 1987—; mem. state bd. Nature Conservancy, N.Y., 1993—. Inst. Internat. Edn. fellow, 1952-53; recipient Disting. Alumnae medal Smith Coll., 1974. Fellow Am. Coll. Probate Counsel, Am. Bar Found.; mem. Assn. Bar City N.Y. (exec. com. 1973-75, v.p. 1985-86), N.Y. State Bar Assn. (ho. of dels. 1971-80, v.p. 1979-80), N.Y. Bar Found. (bd. dirs. 1977—), UN Assn. (bd. dirs. 1975-89), Fgn. Policy Assn. (bd. dirs. 1978-87), Cosmopolitan Club, Gipsy Trail Club. Presbyterian. Home: 120 E End Ave New York NY 10028-7552 Office: Cravath Swaine & Moore 825 8th Ave New York NY 10019-7416 also: Stone House Farm PO Box 533 Somers NY 10589-0533

BESHEARS, BETTY WILLIAMS, nurse; b. Lenoir, N.C., Aug. 21, 1954; d. Milton Franklin and Irene Mantha (Mask) Williams; m. Robert Ross Beshears, Sept. 2, 1986. ADN, Western Piedmont Coll., 1979; BSN, Lenoir Rhyne Coll., 1995. RN, N.C.; cert. EMT, BLS, ACLS, advanced trauma life support, mobile intensive care nurse, cert. emergency nurse preceptor, laser operator, cell saver operator/coord., PALS. Health care tech. Broughton Hosp., Morganton, N.C., 1972-79, deaf interpretor, rsch. tech., 1978-79, staff nurse, 1979-80; RN, staff nurse Caldwell Meml. Hosp., Lenoir, 1979-89, asst. supr. emergency dept., 1981-89, EMT, 1980-89, mobile intensive care nurse, cert. emergency room nurse, 1982-89; BLS nurse Caldwell Meml. Hosp. and Catawba Meml. Hosp., Lenoir and Hickory, N.C., 1979—; preceptor Catawba Meml. Hosp., Hickory, 1991-95, coord. autotransfusion, 1991-94, team leader vascular surgery, laser operator, 1992—. Active Mt. Hermon Meth. Ch., Hudson, N.C., 1954—. Western Piedmont/N.C. Bd. Nursing grantee, 1978-79. Mem. Assn. Operating Rm. Nurses (capt. 1989-90), Mu Sigma Epsilon, Sigma Theta Tau. Home: 6204 Vandresser Point Hickory NC 28601

BESHUR, JACQUELINE E., pet training consultant, writer; b. Portland, Oreg., May 8, 1948; d. Charles Daniel and Mildred (Domreis) Beshears. BA, UCLA, 1970; MBA, Claremont Grad. Sch., 1980; postgrad., City U., Seattle, 1989-90. Dir. and founder L.A. Ctr. for Photog. Studies, 1972-76; precious gem distbr. Douglas Group Holdings, Australia, 1976-78; small bus. owner BeSure Cleaning, 1981-90; animal trainer, exotic livestock farmer, 1990—. Author: Good Intentions Are Not Good Enough, 1992. Dir. County Citizens Against Incineration, 1987—, Ames Lake Protection Com., 1989—. Mem. Bridges for Peace, Nature Conservancy, Wash. Wilderness Coalition, Issaquah Alps Club, Inland Empire Pub. Lands Coun. Republican. Fundamentalist. Office: BeSure Tng PO Box 225 Carnation WA 98014-0225

BESNETTE, CARRIE ANNA, academic administrator; b. Flagstaff, Ariz., Apr. 5, 1968; d. Frank H. and Linda S. (Curton) B. BA, U. Ariz., 1990; MA, UCLA, 1993, PhD, 1995. Rsch. asst. Arizona State Senate, Phoenix, 1990; regional dir./asst. dir. admissions U. Ariz., L.A., 1990—; rsch. assoc. UCLA, 1992—, grad. teaching asst., 1992-93, lectr., instr., 1996—; congressional intern U.S. Ho. Reps., Washington, Tucson, Ariz., 1989; cons. Acad. Insights, Fort Collins, Colo., 1990. Co-founder, chairperson Big Sisters L.A., 1990—. Recipient Newcomers award Western Assn. Coll. Admissions Counselors, 1994; Grad. Rsch. & Teaching fellow, 1992-95. Mem. AAUW, Assn. Study Higher Edn., Am. Ednl. Rsch. Assn. Office: U Ariz Western Region Office 10573 W Pico Blvd #183 Los Angeles CA 90064

BEST, ALYNDA KAY, conflict resolution service administrator; b. Amarillo, Tex., June 20, 1947; d. William Otho and Ruby Jewel (Hamby) Mauldin; m. Paul Wesley Best, Mar. 31, 1978; children: Brett Allison, Trevor William. BA, Tex. Tech. U., 1969; MBA, U. Tex. of Perian Basin, Odessa, 1983. Asst. bus. mgr. Med. Arts Clinic, Lubbock, Tex., 1969-72; fin. supr. Tex. Dept. Human Resources, Lubbock, 1972-79; pvt. practice bus. dir. Odessa, 1979-87; corp. mgr. Midland (Tex.) Emergency Physicians, 1987-95; pres. Conflict Resolution Ctr., Inc., Midland, 1995—. Co-author: (pamphlet) Midland Municipal Water Supply, 1992. Treas. LWV, Odessa/Midland, 1980-82, chmn. nat. res. Midland 1990-93; treas. Hospice of Odessa, 1983-85, Santa Rita PTA, Midland, 1990-92; dir. outreach First Christian Ch., Midland, 1991-93; mem. yearbook com. Midland/Odessa Symphony, 1994; leader Girl Scouts/Boy Scouts, 1986-94; active Midland Cmty. Theatre. Mem. AAUW, Am. Med. Soc., Midland Med. Assn. (excursion coord. 1994-95), Tex. Med. Assn. Aux. (state dist. rep.). Office: Conflict Resolution Ctr Inc 200 N Loraine Ste 514 Midland TX 79701

BEST, LISA ELINE, elementary education educator; b. Wilmington, Del., Jan. 9, 1958; d. Robert Kenneth and Shirley Mae (Tressler) Eline; m. Brian David Best, Apr. 18, 1987 (div. Dec. 5, 1994). BE, U. Del., 1980, BS in Spl. Edn., 1980, MS in Early Childhood Edn., 1983. Cert. primary, spl. edn., early childhood tchr., Md., Del. Spl. edn. resource room Cecil County Sch. Dist., Bainbridge, Md., 1980-83; kindergarten tchr. Cecil City Sch. Dist., Calvert, 1983-86; all day kindergarten, spl. edn. tchr. Milford (Del.) Sch. Dist., 1986-87; 1st grade tchr. Red Clay Sch. Dist., Wilmington, Del., 1987-91, Milford Sch. Dist., 1991—; adj. prof. Coll. Edn. undergrad. program Wilmington Coll., 1993—; mem. English, lang. arts commn., Dept. Pub. Instrn., Dover, Del., 1991—; cons., workshop conductor, sch. dists. in Del., statewide confs., 1990—. Contbr. articles to state and local newspapers, 1995—. Named Student Tchr. of Yr. U. Del. Edn. Dept., 1980, Heritage Elem. Tchr. of Yr., Wilmington, 1990, Red Clay Tchr. of Yr., 1990, Del. Tchr. of Yr. Dept. Pub. Instrn., 1990-91. Mem. NEA, Internat. Reading Assn. (Hall of Excellence 1993, 94), Del. Assn. Chilhood Edn. Internat., Assn. Childhood Edn. Internat. (Elizabeth Breathwalte award 1993), Del. Edn. Assn., Diamond State Reading Assn. (chairperson), Delta Kappa Gamma (Beta chpt.). Home: 38 Bryan Dr Rehoboth Beach DE 19971-9733

BEST, MARY LANI, university program coordinator; b. Hilo, Hawaii, June 3, 1944; d. Stanley Clark and Emma Holokahiki (Martinson) Brooks; m. Leningrad Elarionoff, Aug. 14, 1965 (div. 1981); children: Kimberly Kehaunani, Grad. Ikaika; m. Gary Dean Best, Dec. 7, 1984 (div. 1996). BA, U. Hawaii, Hilo, 1988; MS, Creighton U., 1991. Substitute tchr. Hilo High Sch., 1990; counselor secondary alternative program Westside High Sch., Omaha, 1991; coord. Ctr. for Gifted & Talented Native Hawaiian Children U. Hawaii, Hilo, 1991—. Contbr.: (book) Sociology of Hawaii, 1992; co-editor: Glimpses of Hawaiian Daily Life and Culture, 1994. Active Hale O Na Alii, Hilo, 1988—. Mem. AACD. Republican. Home: 84 Pukihae St Apt # 304 Hilo HI 96720 Office: U Hawaii 200 W Kawili St Hilo HI 96720-4075

BESTEHORN, UTE WILTRUD, retired librarian; b. Cologne, Germany, Nov. 6, 1930; came to U.S., 1930; d. Henry Hugo and Wiltrud Lucie (Vincentz) B. BA, U. Cin., 1954, BEd, 1955, MEd, 1958; MS in Library Sci., Western Res. U. (now Case-Western Res. U.), 1961. Tchr. Cutter Jr. High Sch., Cin., 1955-57; tchr., supr. libr. Felicity (Ohio) Franklin Sr. High Sch., 1959-60; with libr. sci. dept. Pub. Libr. Cin. and Hamilton County, 1961-78, with libr. info. desk, 1978-91; ret., 1991; textbook selection com., Felicity-Franklin Sr. High Sch., 1959-60; supr. Health Alcove Sci. Dept. and annual health lectures, Cin. Pub. Library, 1972-77. Book reviewer Library Jour., 1972-77; author and inventor Rainbow 40 marble game, 1971, Condominium game, 1976; patentee indexed packaging and stacking device, 1973, mobile packaging and stacking device, 1974. Mem. Clifton Town Meeting, 1988—; mem. Bookfest 90 com. Pub. Libr. Cin. and Hamilton County. Recipient Cert. of Merit and Appreciation Pub. Library of Cin., 1986. Mem. Cin. Chpt. Spl. Libraries Assn. (archivist 1963-64, 65-70, editor Queen City Gazette bull. 1964-69), Pub. Library Staff Assn. (exec. bd., activities com. 1965, welfare com. 1966, recipient Golden Book 25 yr. service pin, 1986), Friends of the Library, Greater Cin. Calligraphers Guild (reviewer New Letters pub. 1986-88), Delta Phi Alpha (nat. German hon. 1951). Republican. Mem. United Ch. of Christ. Home: 3330 Morrison Ave Cincinnati OH 45220-1440

BESTER, MARGOT FRANCES, lawyer, telecommunications consultant; b. Buffalo, May 7, 1954; d. Eugene and Halina (Herbe) B.; children: Brian Lawrence Markowitz, Eric Robert Markowitz. BA, SUNY, Binghamton, 1976; JD, Albany Law Sch., 1979. Bar: D.C. 1979. Atty., advisor FCC, Washington, 1979-86; dir. regulatory rels. U.S. Telephone Assn., Washington, 1986-87; prin. Murphy & Demory Ltd., Washington, 1987-94; sr. assoc. Booz-Allen & Hamilton, McLean, Va., 1994—. Mem. Fed.. Comm. Bar Assn. Office: Booz Allen & Hamilton 14800 Conference Center Dr Chantilly VA 22021

BEST-GORING, CYNTHIA LOVALE, elementary school principal; b. Washington, Aug. 24, 1950; d. Alexander Henry and Annie Belle (Spruill) Best; m. Anthony Trevor Goring, Apr. 27, 1975; children: Alexis, Trevor. BA in Elem. ELdn., Columbia Union Coll., 1972; MEd, U. Md., 1975, M.Reading, 1981. Cert. std. profl. cert., advanced profl. cert., Md. Tchr. Prince George's County Pub. Sch. Sys., 1972-82; reading specialist Bladensburg (Md.) Elem. Sch., 1983-88; vice prin. Beltsville (Md.) Acad. Ctr., 1988-89; tchr. specialist Area Asst. Supt.s Office, 1989-92; prin. Berkshire Elem. Sch., Forestville, Md., 1992-94, Adelphi ATLAS Communities Elem. Sch., Adlephi, Md., 1994—; staff devel. cons. Prince George's County, Md., 1989—; spkr. in field. Pianist Pennsylvania Ave. SDA Ch., Capital Hts., Md., 1984-94, Sligo SDA Ch., Takoma Park, Md., 1994—. Targeted Poverty grantee, 1994-95, Sch.-Wide Improvement grantee, 1995-96. Mem. ASCD, New Am. schs. Devel. Corp. Democrat. Home: 7208 Wingate Dr Glenndale MD 20769 Office: Adelphi Elem Sch 8820 Riggs Rd Adelphi MD 20783

BESTON, ROSE MARIE, college president; b. South Portland, Maine, Sept. 27, 1937; d. George Louis and Edith Mae (Archibald) Beattie; m. John Bernard Beston, Feb. 1, 1970. B.A., St. Joseph's Coll., 1961; M.A., Boston Coll., 1963; Ph.D., U. Pitts., 1967; Cert. of Advanced Study, Harvard U., 1978. Mem. faculty St. Joseph's Coll., Maine, 1967-68, SUNY, Oneonta, 1968-69, Southeast Mo. State Coll., 1969-70, U. Queensland and Western Australian Inst. Tech., 1970-76, U. Hawaii, Manoa, 1976-77; assoc. acad. dean Worcester (Maine) State Coll., 1978-80; dean for acad. affairs Castleton (Vt.) State Coll., 1980-84; pres. Nazareth Coll. Rochester, N.Y., 1984—; mem. Neylan Commn., Assn. Cath. Colls. and Univs.; mem. Pres.'s Network of Campus Compact. Contbr. articles to profl. jours. Bd. govs. Genesee Hosp., Rochester; bd. dirs. Greater Rochester Visitors Bur. Mem. AAUW, Mediaeval Acad. Am., Nat. Assn. Ind. Colls. and Univs., Assn. Commonwealth Lang. and Lit. Studies, Greater Rochester C. of C. (bd. dirs.), Oak Hill Country Club, Genesee Valley Club, Phi Delta Kappa.

BETENBAUGH, HELEN RECKENZAUN, Episcopal priest, writer; b. Morristown, N.J., Feb. 10, 1943; d. Paul Frederick and Norma Kathryn (Held) Reckenzaun; m. Gordon Murray Betenbaugh, June 5, 1965 (div. Oct. 1987); children: Melanie, Jennifer. MusB, Westminster Choir Coll., Princeton, N.J., 1964; MusM, Peabody Conservatory, Balt., 1968; MDiv with honors, So. Meth. U., Dallas, 1993, postgrad. Cert. church musician. Min. of music First United Methodist Ch., El Dorado, Ark., 1968-75; min. of music and fine arts Westminster Presbyn. Ch., Lincoln, 1975-82; mem. faculty Union Coll., Lincoln, Nebr., 1976-79; music critic Lincoln Jour., 1977-80; staff U. Nebr., Lincoln, 1982-85; organist, choirmaster St. Paul's Episcopal Ch., Orange, Tex., 1987-89; dir. Christian Edn. Ministries, Episcopal Ch. of the Transfiguration, Dallas, 1990-96; asst. to rector Episc. Ch. of the Good Shepherd, Dallas, 1996—; profl. accompanist, 1965-89; organ and harpsichord recitalist, 1964-85; faculty, clinician, conductor, keynote speaker, presenter, facilitator for conventions, workshops, confs., profl. assns. and festivals in field. Contbr. articles to profl. jours. Sec. bd. dirs. League of Human Dignity, Lincoln, 1982-85; mem. steering com. A World of Difference, Beaumont, Tex., 1988-89; mem. pres's. adv. com. on the needs of disabled persons So. Methodist U., Dallas, 1990-93. Recipient Harold M. Kaufman Meml. Social Ethics award B'nai Brith, 1993. Mem. AAUW, Am. Guild Organists (newsletter editor 1962, dir., editor nat. conv. book, preacher nat. conv. 1994), Assn. Physically Challenged Mins. (charter 1990, sem. rels. officer 1990-93, program dir. 1993, nat. co-chair 1994-95), Assn. Anglican Musicians, Episcopal Womens Caucus, Mensa. Home: 2302 18th St Plano TX 75074-4924

BETHIN, CHRISTINA Y., linguist, language educator; b. Rochester, N.Y., Aug. 12, 1950. BA in Russian and Spanish, U. Rochester, 1972; MA in Slavic Langs. and Lit., U. Ill., 1974, PhD in Slavic Linguistics, 1978. Cert. secondary lang. tchr., N.Y. Lectr. U. Va., Charlottesville, 1978-79; asst. prof. SUNY, Stony Brook, 1979-85, assoc. prof., 1985-95, prof., 1995—, dir. Dr. Arts program in fgn. langs., 1992-94, dept. chair, 1994—. Author: Polish Syllables: The Role of Prosody in Phonology and Morphology, 1992; assoc. editor Slavic and East European Jour., 1995—; mem. editorial bd.

Jour. Slavic Linguistics, 1993—. NEH fellow, 1988-89, 93-94; IREX grantee for summer exch. of lang. tchrs., Moscow, 1990. Fellow Ukrainian Acad. Arts and Scis. in U.S.; mem. Am. Assn. Tchrs. of Slavic and East European Langs., Am. Assn. for Advancement of Slavic Studies, Am. Assn. for Ukrainian Studies, Linguistic Soc. Am., Phi Beta Kappa (v.p. Stony Brook chpt. 1987-88). Office: SUNY Germanic and Slavic Langs Stony Brook NY 11794-3367

BETLACH, MARY CAROLYN, biochemist, molecular biologist; b. Madison, Wis., June 12, 1945; d. William Thompson Stafford and Carolyn Jesse Gillette McCormick; m. Charles J. Betlach, Nov. 14, 1970 (div. 1978); children: John F., Melanie Carolyn. Student, U. Wis., 1963-68; PhD, U. Calif., San Francisco, 1992. Staff rsch. assoc. dept. pediatrics U. Calif., San Francisco, 1970-72, staff rsch. assoc. dept. microbiology/biochemistry, 1972-83, rsch. specialist dept. biochemistry, 1983-93; sr. scientist Parnassus Pharms., Alameda, Calif., 1993-94; dir. molecular biology Kosan Bioscis., Burlingame, Calif., 1995—; adj. asst. prof. dept. pharm. chemistry, U. Calif., San Francisco, 1993—; mem. various grant rev. panels. Contbr. chpts. to books, articles to Gene, Microbiology, Nucleic Acids Rsch., Biochemistry, Jour. Bacteriology, others. Mem. AAAS, Am. Soc. for Microbiology.

BETSINGER, PEGGY ANN, oncological nurse; b. St. Charles, Mo., Dec. 11, 1939; d. Edward and Dorothy (Brockgrietens) Oelklaus; m. Richard Betsinger, Mar. 17, 1964 (div. Mar. 1986); children: Bryon, Alicia. Diploma, St. John's Hosp. Sch. Nursing, St. Louis U., St. Louis, 1960; student, U. Colo., Colorado Springs, 1973, St. Joseph Coll., 1985. RN, Ohio, Mo.; cert. oncology-chemotherapy nurse. Charge nurse oncology unit Grandview Hosp., Dayton, 1976-81; asst. dir. nurses Alta Nursing Home, Dayton, Ohio, 1982-86; nurse oncology unit De Paul Hosp., St. Louis, 1986—. Vol. nurse ARC, 1971-74. Capt. Nurse Corps, USAF, 1961-64. Mem. Oncology Nursing Soc.

BETTERIDGE, FRANCES CARPENTER, retired lawyer, mediator; b. Rutherford, N.J., Aug. 25, 1921; d. James Dunton and Emily (Atkinson) Carpenter; m. Albert Edwin Betteridge, Feb. 5, 1949 (div. 1975); children: Anne, Albert Edwin, James, Peter. A.B., Mt. Holyoke Coll., 1942; J.D., N.Y. Law Sch., 1978. Bar: Conn. 1979, Ariz. 1982. Technician in charge blood banks Roosevelt Hosp., N.Y.C. and Mountainside Hosp., Montclair, N.J., 1943-49; substitute tchr. Greenwich High Sch. (Conn.), 1978-79; intern and asst. to labor contracts office Town of Greenwich, 1979-80; vol. referee Pima County Juvenile Ct., Tucson, 1981-85, judge Pro Tempore Pima County Justice Cts., 1988-91; sole practice immigration law, Tucson, 1982-87; commr. Juvenile Ct., Pima County Superior Ct., Tucson, 1985-87; hearing officer Small Claims Ct., Pima County Justice Cts., Tucson, 1982; mediator Family Crisis Svc., Tucson, 1982-85. Pres. High Sch. PTA, Greenwich, 1970, PTA Council, 1971; mem. Greenwich Bd. Edn., 1971-76, sec., 1973-76; com. chmn. LWV Tucson, 1981, bd. dirs., 1984-85; bd. dirs., sec. Let The Sun Shine Inc., Tucson, 1981—; vol. referee Pima County Superior Ct., 1981-85; lectr. Tucson Mus. Art, 1994—; part time site coord. Elderhostel, Oaxaca, Mex., 1995. Mem. ABA, Conn. Bar Assn., Ariz. Bar Assn., Pima County Bar Assn., Ariz. Women Lawyers Assn., Point o'Woods Club. Republican. Congregationalist. Avocation: imports folk art from Oaxaca, Mex. Home and Office: 5320 N Campbell Ave Tucson AZ 85718-4908

BETTIN, JANENE EDNA, real estate broker; b. Schaller, Iowa, Nov. 11, 1943; d. Robert A. and Edna (Harris) Bath; m. Thomas L. Bettin, June 20, 1964; 1 child, Christopher. Student U. No. Iowa, 1961; BS, Tex. A&I U., 1965. Grad. Realtors Inst.; cert. residential specialist, residential brokerage mgr. Tchr. high sch., Corpus Christi, Tex., 1965-70; tchr. Village Acad., Mt. Lebanon, Pa., 1973-76; broker, assoc. Re/Max Metro Properties, Inc., Denver, 1977-86; broker, br. mgr. Perry & Butler, Littleton, Colo., 1986-89; broker Van Schaack Residential Realty, Inc., 1989; broker, owner Prime Properties, Englewood, Colo., 1989-94, Moore & Co., Denver, 1994—. Chmn. Blood Bank, South Suburban Bd. Realtors, 1980, chmn. Schs. Com., 1980; pres. South Suburban Bd. Realtors, 1985-86. Bd. dirs., officer Bristol Cove Homeowners Assn., Littleton, Colo., 1983; officer, treas. Arapahoe Youth League-Warriors, 1981. Mem. Realtors Nat. Mktg. Inst., Womens Coun. Realtors (pres. 1982-83), Colo. Assn. Realtors (instr. 1981—, dir. 1984, v.p. 1987), Cert. Residential Specialists (pres. Colo. chpt. 1984, nat. instr. 1985-86), Cert. Residential Brokerage Mgrs. (instr. 1986-92), Omega Tau Rho. Republican. Methodist. Club: Mt. Lebanon Newcomers (pres. 1973-74). Home: 7540 S Cove Cir Littleton CO 80122-3332

BETTS, BARBARA LANG (MRS. BERT A. BETTS), lawyer, rancher, realtor; b. Anaheim, Calif., Apr. 28, 1926; d. W. Harold and Helen (Thompson) Lang. BA magna cum laude, Stanford U., 1948; LLB, Balboa U., 1951; m. Roby F. Hayes, July 22, 1948 (dec.); children: John Chauncey IV, Frederick Prescott, Roby Francis II; m. Bert A. Betts, July 11, 1962; 1 child, Bruce Harold; stepchildren: Bert Alan, Randy W., Sally Betts Joynt, Terry Betts Marsteller, Linda Betts Hansen, LeAnn Betts Wilson. Bar: Calif. 1952, U.S. Supreme Ct. 1978; pvt. practice law, Oceanside, Calif., 1952-68, San Diego, 1960—, Sacramento, 1962—; ptnr. Roby F. Hayes & Barbara Lang Hayes, 1952-60; city atty., Carlsbad, Calif., 1959-63; v.p. Isle & Oceans Marinas, Inc., 1970-80, W. H. Lang Corp., 1964-69; sec. Internat. Prodn. Assos., 1968—, Margaret M. McCabe, M.D., Inc., 1977-88 . Chmn. Traveler's Aid, 1952-53; pres. Oceanside-Carlsbad Jr. Chambrettes, 1955-56; vice chmn. Carlsbad Planning Commn., 1959; mem. San Diego Planning Congress, 1959; v.p. Oceanside Diamond Jubilee Com., 1958. Candidate Calif. State Legislature, 77th Dist., 1954; mem. Calif. Dem. State Central Com., 1958-66; co-chmn. 28th Congl. Dist., Dem. State Central Com., 1960-62; alt. del. Dem. Nat. Conv., 1960; co-sponsor All Am. B-24 Liberator Collings Found. Named to Fullerton Union High Sch. Wall of Fame, 1986. Mem. Am. Judicature Soc., Nat. Inst. Mcpl. Officers, ABA, Calif. Bar Assn., San Diego County Bar Assn., Oceanside C. of C. (sec. 1957, v.p. 1958, dir. 1953-54, 57-59), AAUW (legis. com. 1958-59); local pres. 1959-60; asst. state legis. chmn. 1958-59), Heritage League (2d div. 8th Air Force), No. San Diego County Assn. Cs. of C. (sec.-treas.), Bus. and Profl. Women's Club (So. dist. legislation chmn. 1958-59), DAR (regent Oceanside chpt. 1960-61), San Diego C. of C., San Diego Hist. Soc., Fullerton Jr. Assistance League, Calif. Scholarship Fedn. (life), Loyola Guild of Jesuit High Sch., Phi Beta Kappa. Clubs: Soroptimist Internat. (pres. Oceanside-Carlsbad 1958-59, sec. pub. affairs San Diego, Imperial Counties 1954; pres. of pres.'s council San Diego and Imperial counties and Mexico 1958-59), Barristers, Stanford (Sacramento), Stanford Mothers, Heritage League (2nd air divsn. USAAF). Author: (with Bert A. Betts) A Citizen Answers. Home: 441 Sandburg Dr Sacramento CA 95819-2559 Office: Betts Ranch PO Box 306 Elverta CA 95626-0306 also: 1830 Avenida del Mundo #1608 Coronado CA 92118

BETTS, BARBARA STOKE, artist, educator; b. Arlington, Mass., Apr. 19, 1924; d. Stuart and Barbara Lillian (Johnstone) Stoke; m. James William Betts, July 28, 1951; 1 child, Barbara Susan (dec.). BA, Mt. Holyoke Coll., 1946; MA, Columbia U., 1948. Cert. tchr., N.Y., Calif., Hawaii. Art tchr. Walton (N.Y.) Union Schs., 1947-48, Presidio Hill Sch., San Francisco, 1949-51; free-lance artist San Francisco, 1951; art tchr. Honolulu Acad. Arts, summer 1952, 59, 63, 85, spring 61, 64; libr. aide art rm. Libr. of Hawaii, Honolulu, 1959; art tchr. Hanahauoli Sch., Honolulu, 1961-62, Hawaii State Dept. Edn., Honolulu, 1958-59, 64-84; owner Ho'olaule'a Designs, Honolulu, 1973—. Illustrator: Cathedral Cooks, 1964, In Due Season, 1986; exhibited in Hawaii Pavilion Expo '90, Osaka, Japan, State Found. of Culture and Arts, group shows since 1964, one person shows 1991, 96; represented in Arts of Paradise Gallery, Waikiki, 1990—; traveling exhbns. include Pacific Prints, 1991, Printmaking East/West, 1993-95, Hawaii/Wis. Watercolor Show, 1993-94. Mem. Hawaii Watercolor Soc. (newsletter editor 1986-90), Nat. League Am. Pen Women (art chmn. 1990-92, sec. 1992-94, nat. miniature art shows 1991, 92, 93, 95), Honolulu Printmakers (dir. 1986, 87), Assn. Hawaii Artists. Republican. Episcopalian. Home: 1520 Ward Ave Apt 203 Honolulu HI 96822-3550

BETTS, DIANNE CONNALLY, economist, educator; b. Tyler, Tex., Sept. 23, 1948; d. William Isaac and Martine (Underwood) Connally; m. Floyd Galloway Betts Jr., Feb. 14, 1973. BA in History, So. Meth. U., 1976, MA in History, 1980; MA in Econ., U. Chgo., 1986; PhD in Econ., U. Tex., 1991. Affiliated scholar Inst. for Rsch. on Women and Gender/Stanford U., 1993—; economist, tech. analyst, fin. cons. Smith Barney, Dallas, 1994—; mem. women studies coun. So. Meth. U., 1993-94, Fulbright campus interviewing com. mem. 1992-93, pub. rels. and devel. liaison dept. econ., 1990-92, faculty mentor U. honors first year mentoring program,adj. asst. prof. dept. econ. and history So. Meth. U., 1992—, vis. asst. prof. 1990-92, faculty, Oxford, summer 1991-93, adj. instr. dept. history, 1989-90, adj. instr. dept. econ., 1985-89, teaching asst. dept. history, spring 1980; lectr. dept. polit. economy U. Tex., Dallas, summer 1988. Author: Crisis on the Rio Grande: Poverty, Unemployment, and Economic Development on the Texas-Mexico Border, 1994, Historical Perspectives on the American Economy: Selected Reading, 1995; contbr. articles to profl. jours. Rsch. Planning grant NSF, 1992; recipient Marguereta Deschner Teaching award, 1991; Humanities and Scis. Merit scholar, 1978. Mem. Am. Econ. Assn., Am. History Assn., Econ. History Assn., Cliometric Soc., Social Sci. History Assn., N.Am. Conf. on British Studies, Nat. Coun. for Rsch. on Women (affiliate), Omicron Delta Epsilon, Phi Alpha Theta. Home: 6267 Revere Pl Dallas TX 75214-3099 Office: Smith Barney 500 N Akard St Ste 3900 Dallas TX 75201-6604

BETTS, NORA LINDEN, kennel owner; b. Toledo, July 31, 1961; d. Bryan Jesse and Patricia Lynn (Sullivan) Wilkerson; m. Jeffrey Allen Betts, Mar. 15, 1985; 1 child, Bryan Jeffrey. Student, Davis Bus. Coll., 1980-81, 81-83, Cornell U., 1991. Cert. small animal dietitian/nutritionist, cert. animal behaviorist/psychologist. Kennel supr. Karnik Inn of Toledo, Holland, Ohio, 1989-90; vet. technician Trilby Animal Hosp., Toledo, 1989-90; kennel mgr. Pampered Pet Petel, Erie, Mich., 1983-89, kennel owner, 1990—. Contbr. articles to profl. newsletters. Speaker in field Bedford Pub. Schs., Lambertville, Mich., 1989, 90, 91, 92, Monroe (Mich.) County Libr. System, 1992; active Nat. Audubon Soc., 1993—, Defenders of Wildlife, 1991—, World Wildlife Fund, 1992—, Maumee Valley Save-A-Pet, 1992—. Mem. ASPCA, Nat. Humane Edn. Assn., People for the Ethical Treatment of Animals, Am. Boarding Kennels Assn. (cert. kennel technician, cons. 1990—), Nat. Fedn. Ind. Bus., Nat. Dog Groomers Assn., Toledo Vet. Med. Assn., Humane Soc. Monroe. Methodist. Office: Pampered Pet Petel 7190 Dixie Hwy Erie MI 48133-9660

BETTS, WENDY H., operations administrator, research consultant; b. Niles, N.Y., June 27, 1963; d. John Ralph Sr. and Patricia Joan (Hayes) B.; m. Derek Stephen Bessey, July 18, 1987. B in Sociology, U. Maine, 1985; M of Pub. Policy and Mgmt., U. So. Maine, 1994. Rsch. asst. Edmund S. Muskie Inst. of Pub. Affairs Univ. So. Maine, Portland, 1987-95; dir. ops. Youth Alternatives, Inc., Portland, 1995—; bd. dirs. Maine Women's Lobby, Augusta; ind. beauty cons. Mary Kay Cosmetics, Portland, 1995—. Author/contbr.: Maine KIDS COUNT Data Book, 1994, 95; co-author: Conducting Family Focused Community Events, 1994, Conducting Community Assessments, 1994; author: (chpt.) Working with Rural Youth, 1994. Mem. NOW, Pub. Policy and Mgmt. Alumni Assn. (pres. 1995—), Phi Kappa Phi. Home: PO Box 3861 Portland ME 04104 Office: Youth Alternatives Inc One Post Office Square PO Box 596 Portland ME 04112

BETZ, BETTY, nutritionist, program coordinator; b. N.Y.C., Feb. 14, 1936; d. Frank and Kathleen Hogan; m. James A. Betz, Jan. 22, 1955; children: James, Stephen, Mary, Peter, Matthew, Elizabeth, Andrew. BS, Lehman Coll., 1984. Dietitian Riverdale Neighborhood House, Bronx, N.Y., 1976-85; Women/Infants/Children nutritionist Bronx Lebanon Hosp. Ctr., 1985-90; Women/Infants/Children coord. Comprehensive Family Care Ctr. Montefiore Med. Ctr., Bronx, 1990—. Mem. Riverdale (N.Y.) Run, 1994—. Mem. Am. Home Econs. Assn., Women/Infants/Children Assn. of N.Y. State (treas. 1990—), Women/Infants/Children Assn. N.Y.C. (sec. 1991-93), Maternal Child Health Network. Home: 5848 Tyndall Ave Bronx NY 10471-2108 Office: Comprehensive Family Care Montefiore Med Ctr 1175 Morris Park Ave Bronx NY 10461-1915

BETZER, SUSAN ELIZABETH BEERS, family physician, geriatrician; b. Evanston, Ill., Aug. 24, 1943; d. Thomas Moulding and Mary Ella (Waidner) Beers; m. Peter Robin Betzer, June 18, 1965; children: Sarah Elizabeth, Katherine Hannah. AB in Biol. Scis. magna cum, Mount Holyoke Coll., 1965; PhD in Oceanography, U. R.I., 1972; MD, U. Miami, 1978. Diplomate Am. Bd. Family Practice, Am. Bd. Geriatrics. Rsch. assoc. dept. marine sci. U. South Fla., St. Petersburg, 1973-74, rsch. scholar, scientist, 1975-76; resident in family practice Bayfront Med. Ctr., St. Petersburg, 1978-81; pvt. practice St. Petersburg, 1982—; clin. asst. prof. dept. family medicine U. South Fla., Tampa, 1982—; consulting physician Fed. Employee Health Clinic, Honolulu, 1981-82. Contbr. articles to profl. jours. Mem. sch. adv. com. St. Petersburg H.S., 1996—; bd. dirs. Fla. Orch., Tampa, 1983-86, 88—, pres., 1985-86, mem. exec. com., 1988—, v.p. bd. trustees 1996—, founder, chair audience devel. com., St. Petersburg, 1990-94; bd. dirs. Suncoast Ctr. Cmty. Mental Health, St. Petersburg, 1992-93; trustee Bayfront Med. Ctr., Bayfront Health Svcs., 1992—, vice chair, 1993-96; vol. physician St. Petersburg Free Clinic, 1979—. Recipient Golden Baton award St. Petersburg Fla. Orch. Guild, 1994; named Woman of Distinction, Suncoast coun. Girl Scouts U.S., 1994. Mem. Am. Acad. Family Physicians (Mead Johnson award 1980), Am. Med. Women's Assn., Fla. Acad. Family Physicians (Dr. of the Day, Fla. Legislature 1995, 96), Mount Holyoke Alumnae Assn. (vol. fund raiser, mem. alumnae honors rsch. com. 1988-91, mem. alumnae devel. com. 1996—), Phi Beta Kappa. Home: 1830 7th St N Saint Petersburg FL 33704-3322 Office: 461 7th Ave S Saint Petersburg FL 33701-4818

BEU, MARJORIE JANET, music director; b. Elgin, Ill., Nov. 22, 1921; d. Herman Henry and Hattie Belle (Beverly) B. MusB, Am. Conservatory Music, 1949; B Musical Ed, 1949, M in Musical Ed., 1953; advanced cert. No. Ill. U., 1969; DEd, U. Sarasota, 1979. Music tchr. Sch. Dist. 21, Wheeling, Ill., 1961-64; music and fine arts coord., 1964-68, asst. supt. instrn., 1968-79; min. of music United Meth. Ch., Sun City Center, Fla., 1980—; dir. Sun City Ctr. Kings Point Community Chorus, 1984-89; pres. Council Study and Devel. Ednl. Resources, 1971-79. Pres., Wheeling Community Concerts Assn.; dir. Community Chorus; pres. Sun City Center Concert Series. Mem. NEA, Am. Guild Organists and Choir Dirs., Music Educators Nat. Conf., Assn. Supervision and Curriculum Devel., Ill. Edn. Assn., Ill. Council Gifted, No. Ill. Assn. Ednl. Research, Evaluation and Devel. (pres.), Mu Phi Epsilon, Phi Delta Kappa (sec. N.W. Suburban Cook County chpt.), Kappa Delta Pi (pres. also counselor alumni com.). Home: 610 Fort Duquesna Dr Sun City Center FL 33573-5156

BEUERLEIN, SISTER JULIANA, hospital administrator; b. Lawrenceburg, Tenn., June 19, 1921; d. John Adolph and Sophia (Held) B. R.N., St. Joseph's Sch. Nursing, Chgo., 1945; BS in Edn., DePaul U., 1947; MS in Nursing Edn., Marquette U., 1954; postgrad., St. Louis U., 1966-69. Operating room supr. St. Joseph's Hosp., Alton, Ill., 1945-48; dir. sch. of nursing and nursing svc. Providence Hosp., Waco, Tex., 1948-56, St. Joseph's Hosp., Chgo., 1956-62; asst. adminstr. St. Joseph's Hosp., 1962-63; adminstrv. asst. St. Mary's Hosp., Evansville, Ind., 1963-65; adminstr. St. Mary's Hosp., 1965-73, pres. governing bd., 1965-73; adminstr. St. Joseph Hosp., Chgo., 1973-81; pres. governing bd. St. Joseph Hosp., 1973-75; adminstr. St. Thomas Hosp., Nashville, 1981-89; dir. spl. devel. programs Providence Hosp., Southfield, Mich., 1989—; Mem. governing bd. St. Vincent's Hosp., Indpls., 1969-73; mem. governing bd. St. Mary's Hosp., Milw., 1974-75, chmn., 1978-79; mem. governing bd. Providence Hosp., Southfield, Mich., 1975-78, chmn. governing bd., 1977-78; mem. Chgo. Health Systems Agy., 1976-79; mem. gov. bd. St. Thomas Hosp., Nashville, Hubbard Hosp., Nashville; pres. gov. bd. St. Vincent Hosp., Birmingham, Ala.; mem. Am. Hosp. Assn. Commn. on Nursing, 1980-89. Mem. bd. dirs. St. Mary's Med. Ctr., Evansville, Ind., Middle Tenn. Med. Ctr., Murfreesboro. Fellow Am. Coll. Hosp. Adminstrs. (com. on elections); mem. Cath. Tenn. Hosp. Assns., Nasville C. of C. (bd. dirs.). Office: Providence Hosp Devel Dept 22255 Greenfield Rd Ste 228 Southfield MI 48075-4818

BEUGEN, JOAN BETH, communications company executive; b. Chgo., Mar. 9, 1943; d. Leslie and Janet (Glick) Caplan; B.S. in Speech, Northwestern U., 1965; m. Sheldon Howard Beugen, July 16, 1967. Founder, prin., pres. The Creative Establishment, Inc., Chgo., N.Y.C., San Francisco and Los Angeles, 1969-87, founder, pres. Cresta Communications Inc., Chgo. 1988—; speaker on entrepreneurship for women. Del., White House Conf. on Small Bus., 1979; vice-chmn. Ill. Del. to White House Conf., 1979; trustee Mt. Sinai Hosp. Med. Ctr.; bd. dirs. Chgo. Network; bd. dirs. Chgoland. Enterprise Ctr. Recipient YWCA Leadership award, 1985; named Entrepreneur of Yr., Women in Bus. Mem. Nat. Assn. Women Bus. Owners (pres. Chgo. chpt. 1979), Ill. Women's Agenda, Chgo. Assn. Commerce and Industry, Midwest Soc. Profl. Cons., Chgo. Audio-Visual Producers Assn., Chgo. Film Council, Women in Film, Com. of 200, Nat. Women's Forum, Overseas Edn. Fund Women in Bus. Com. Contbr. articles in field to profl. jours. Office: The Cresta Group 1050 N State St Chicago IL 60610-2855

BEVERLY, LAURA ELIZABETH, special education educator; b. Glen Jean, W.Va., Nov. 26; d. Sidney and Alma Logan. BA in Elem. Edn., W.Va. State Coll., 1960; MS in Spl. Edn., Bklyn. Coll., 1969; postgrad., Oxford (Eng.) U., 1974, N.Y.U., 1982. Cert. elem./spl. edn. tchr., N.Y. Tchr. Bd. Coop. Ednl. Svcs., Westbury, N.Y., 1966—; mem. adv. bd. Am. Biographical Inst. Inc., Raliegh, N.C., 1985—. Mem. ASCD, Am. Inst. of Parliamentarians, Royal Soc. Health, Phi Delta Kappa. Home: PO Box 346 Glen Jean WV 25846

BEVERSDORF, ANNE ELIZABETH, astrologer, author, educator; b. Houston, Tex., Aug. 14, 1949; d. S. Thomas and Norma (Beeson) B. BA, U. Tex., 1972; MLS, Ind. U., 1974. Founding librarian Social Studies Devel. Ctr. Ind. U., Bloomington, 1975-79, info. specialist Vocat. Edn. Services, 1982-83, info. dissemination specialist Devel. Tng. Ctr., 1983; librarian Agy. for Instructional TV, Bloomington, 1980-82; info. specialist Ind. Clearinghouse for Computer Edn., Indpls., 1983-86; Calif. mktg. rep. Minn. Ednl. Computing Corp., San Marcos, Calif., 1986-88; pres., chief exec. officer Beversdorf Assocs., Ltd., Vista, Calif., 1988-93; freelance writer, lectr. Astrology, Vista, Calif., 1993—; conf. planner Ind. Council for the Social Studies, Bloomington, 1976-79; cons. Procter & Gamble Ednl. Services, Cin., 1981-85, Brazil Office of Tech. Edn., Rio de Janeiro, Porto Alegre, 1986; instr. Ind. U., Indpls., 1986; mem. faculty San Diego State U., 1988-91. Contbr. over 30 articles to U.S. and internat. profl. jours. Mem. Nat. Coun. for Geocognic Rsch., Am. Fedn. Astrologers, San Diego Astrol. Soc., So. Calif. Astrol. Network. Home and Office: 1119 Anza Ave Vista CA 92084-4517

BEYER, CHARLOTTE BISHOP, investment management marketing executive; b. N.Y.C., Oct. 16, 1947; d. Edward Morton and Charlotte Reid (Handy) Beyer; BA, Hunter Coll., 1969; m. Warren P. Weitman, Jr., July 28, 1967; children: Catherine Scott, Michael Benjamin. With Bankers Trust Co., N.Y.C., 1970-81, v.p. trust svcs. and securities ops., 1979-81; v.p. prin. client svc. and mktg. Wood Struthers and Winthrop Mgmt. Corp. subs. Donaldson Lufkin and Jenrette, N.Y.C., 1985-89, sr. v.p., 1987-89; v.p. Lazard Freres Asset Mgmt., N.Y.C., 1989-90; founder, cons., researcher Charlotte Beyer Assocs., 1990—; founder Inst. Pvt. Investors Rsch. and Ednl. Forum, 1992. Trustee Westover Sch., Middlebury, Conn., 1987—. Episcopalian. Office: Inst Pvt Investors 469 Morris Ave Summit NJ 07901-1568

BEYER, KAREN HAYNES, social worker; b. Cleve. BA, Ohio State U., 1965; MSW, Loyola U., Chgo., 1969; postgrad. Family Inst., Northwestern U., 1979; MPA, Roosevelt U., 1992; CBA U. Ill. Chgo., 1995. Lic. clin. social worker Ill. With Cuyahoga County Div. Child Welfare, Cleve., 1965, Dallas County Child Welfare Unit, Dallas, 1966; with Luth. Social Svcs. Ill., Chgo., 1967-73; pvt. practice psychotherapy, family mediation, Schaumburg, Ill., 1975-93; therapist Family Svcs. Assn. Greater Elgin (Ill.), 1973-77, dir. profl. svcs., 1977-83; dir. HHS Village of Hoffman Estates, Ill., 1983-93; exec. dir. Larkin Ctr., Elgin, Ill., 1993—. Mem. NASW, Rotary. Unitarian. Office: Larkin Ctr 1212 Larkin Ave Elgin IL 60123-6042

BEYER, SUZANNE, advertising agency executive; b. N.Y.C., Dec. 28, 1928; d. Harry and Jennie Hillman; student Nassau Community Coll., 1963-65; grad. Conservatory of Musical Art, N.Y.C., 1947; m. Isadore Beyer, Oct. 19, 1947; children—Pamela Claire, Hillary Jay. Singer, tchr. piano, N.Y.C., 1947-66; asst. to v.p. media dir. Robert E. Wilson, Advt., N.Y.C., 1967-72; media planner, media buyer Frank J. Corbett div. BBDO Internat., N.Y.C., 1972-77; media planner, media buyer Lavey/Wolff/Swift div. BBDO Advt., N.Y.C., 1977-80, sr. media planner, 1980-83, media supr., 1983-94; media supr. Lyons, Lavey, Nichel, Swift, N.Y.C., 1995-96; pharm. advt. med. media cons., 1996—; soprano Opera Assn. Nassau, 1976—; soprano United Choral Soc., Woodmere, L.I., 1970—, Armand Sodero Chorale, Baldwin, L.I., 1980-86, Rockville Centre Choral Soc, 1986—. Mem. Pharm. Advt. Council, L.I. Advt. Club, Healthcare Bus. Women's Assn. Home: 66 Fonda Rd Rockville Centre NY 11570-2751

BEYER-MEARS, ANNETTE, physiologist; b. Madison, Wis., May 26, 1941; d. Karl and Annette (Weiss) Beyer. B.A., Vassar Coll., 1963; M.S., Fairleigh Dickinson U., 1973; Ph.D., Coll. Medicine and Dentistry N.J., 1977. NIH fellow Cornell U. Med. Sch., 1963-65; instr. physiology Springside Sch., Phila., 1967-71; teaching asst. dept. physiology Coll. Medicine & Dentistry N.J., N.J. Med. Sch., 1974-77, NIH fellow dept. ophthalmology, 1978-80; asst. prof. dept. ophthalmology U. Medicine and Dentistry N.J., N.J. Med. Sch., Newark, 1979-85, asst. prof. dept. physiology, 1980-85, assoc. prof. dept. physiology, 1986—, assoc. prof. dept. ophthalmology, 1986—; vis. assoc. prof. dept. ophthalmology and vision sci. U. Wis., Madison, 1995—; cons. Alcon Labs. Contbr. articles in field of diabetic lens and kidney therapy to profl. jours. Chmn. admissions No. N.J., Vassar Coll., 1974-79; mem. minister search com. St. Bartholomew Episcopal Ch., N.J., 1978, fund-raising chmn., 1978, 79; del. Episc. Diocesan Conv., 1977, 78; long range planning com. Christ Ch., Ridgewood, N.J., 1985-87, vestry, 1994-95. Recipient NIH Nat. Rsch. Svc. award, 1978-80, Found. CMDNJ Rsch. award, 1980; grantee Juvenile Diabetes Found., 1985-87, NIH, NEI grantee, 1980-95, Pfizer, Inc. grantee, 1985-89, 93—. Mem. Am. Physiol. Soc., N.Y. Acad. Scis., Soc. for Neurosci., Am. Soc. Pharmacology and Exptl. Therapeutics, Assn. for Rsch. Vision & Ophthalmology, Internat. Soc. for Eye Research, AAAS, The Royal Soc. Medicine, Internat. Diabetes Found., Am. Diabetes Assn., European Assn. Study of Diabetes, Aircraft Owners and Pilots Assn., Sigma Xi. Home: 120 Ely Pl Madison WI 53705-9999

BEYERSDORF, MARGUERITE MULLOY, educator; b. Terry, Mont., Apr. 20, 1922; d. John William and Laura Agnes (Mahar) Mulloy; m. Curtis Alexander Beyersdorf, 1946; 1 child, Mary Jo Wright. Kindergarten-Primary Cert., Coll. St. Catherine, St. Paul, 1942; PhB, Marquette U., 1945; postgrad., Gonzaga U., Spokane, Wash., 1957-62, Ea. Wash. State U., 1977-79. Tchr. grade 3 Sacred Heart Sch., Oelwein, Iowa, 1942-43; tchr. grades 1 and 2 Jr. Mil. Acad., Chgo., 1943-44; tchr. history, English Fairfield (Wash.) High Sch., 1945-46; substitute tchr. Riverside High Sch., 1957; tchr. Mead (Wash.) Sch. Dist., 1958-75; owner/mgr. First Ave. Parking Lot, Spokane, Wash., 1957—. Vol. Spokane N.W. Communities Found., 1982—; active United Way Spokane, 1950, ARC, Am. Cancer Soc., Multiple Sclerosis Soc., others; vol. coord. Dominican Outreach Found. to Domicile Single Parent Families; canteen vol. Spokane Blood Bank, 1981—; vol. Miryam's House of Transition, 1989—. Recipient Vol. of Yr. Golden Rule award J.C. Penney Co., 1993; grantee NSF, Whitworth Coll., 1967. Mem. NEA, APGA, AAUW (bd. dirs. Spokane br., chmn. scholarship com.), Wash. Edn. Assn.-Retired (del. rep. assembly, mem. comm. com 1993—, chmn. comm. commn. 1993—), Mead Edn. Assn. (sec., exec. bd., former bldg. rep., mem. curriculum com.).

BEY-POWELL, DIANE, consumer advocate, housing specialist; b. Pitts., Mar. 29, 1952; d. Christopher and Ruth Sproul Bey; m. Charles M. Powell. BA, Chatham Coll., 1974; MPA, U. Pitts, 1980. Cert. credit counselor Nat. Found. for Consumer Credit. Employment supr. Alcoa, Pitts., 1981-84; program dir. Opportunities Industrialization Ctr., Pitts., 1986-88; employment specialist Port Authority, Pitts., 1988-90; comty. housing specialist and instr. Consumer Credit, Pitts., 1990—; mem. Internat. Assn. Bus. Communicators, 1988-90. Inventor: The Money Game (fin. edn. resource program for middle sch. students), 1993. Mem. adv. bd. YWCA, Pitts., 1993—. Recipient Urban Youth Action award, Pitts., 1981, Black Achievers award Opinion Mag., Pitts., 1993. Mem. Nat. Housing Counseling Fedn., Nat. Assn. Housing and Devel. Officials.

BHANDARI, RAJIKA, psychologist; b. New Delhi, Sept. 10, 1970; came to U.S., 1992; d. Arvind Bhandari and Sudha Anand. BA in Psychology with honors, U. Delhi, New Delhi, 1991; MS in Psychology, N.C. State U., 1994, postgrad., 1994—. Sr. social rep. Social Aid, New Delhi, 1989-90; rsch. asst. Nat. Ctr. for Human Settlements and Environment, Bhopal, India, 1990-92; tchg. asst. dept. psychology N.C. State U., Raleigh, 1993-95, rsch. asst. dept. psychology, 1995—; instr. IBM, Research Triangle Park, N.C., 1994, 95;

presenter, rschr. in field. contbr. articles to profl. jours. Vol. Nat. Svc. Scheme, Indraprastha Coll., New Delhi, 1988-89, pres. Women's Devel. Ctr., 1990-91. Internat. Grad. fellow N.C. State U. Alumni Assn., 1994, Kenan fellow Kenan Inst. for Sci., Engring. and Tech., 1995; Human Resource Devel. Fund Rsch. grantee Coll. of Edn. and Psychology Found., 1993; Bhagwanti Kapoor Meml. scholar, 1990, Nat. Merit scholar U. Delhi, 1991. Mem. AAUW (internat. grad. fellow 1995), Soc. for Cmty. Action and Rsch. (student affiliate), Human Rights Com., UN Assn.-U.S.A., Sigma Iota Rho, Psi Chi. Office: NC State U Dept Psychology Box 7801 Raleigh NC 27606

BIAGI, SHIRLEY ANNE, journalism educator; b. San Francisco, June 21, 1944; d. Herbert Hamilton Rickey and Gerbina Mary (Biagi) Rickey; m. Victor J. Biondi, May 2, 1964; children: Paul and Tom (twins), David. BA, Calif. State U., Sacramento, 1967, MA, 1975. Prof. Calif. State U., Sacramento, 1975—, chmn. dept., 1987-92. Author: How to Write and Sell Magazine Articles, 1981, 2d rev. edit., 1989, Interviews That Work, 1986, 2d rev. edit., 1992, Media/Impact, 1988, 3d rev. edit., 1996, Media/Reader, 1990, 3d rev. edit., 1996. Recipient teaching award Poynter Inst., 1983; Danforth fellow, 1981-86. Mem. Assn. for Edn. in Journalism and Mass Comm. (exec. bd. 1990-94), Am. Journalism History Assn. (bd. dirs. 1994—). Office: Calif State Univ 6000 J St Sacramento CA 95819-2605

BIALAS, GAIL TOMLINSON, marketing and public relations executive; b. Jacksboro, Tex., Oct. 5, 1948; d. Luther Glenn and Dorothy (Dodson) Prunty; m. Warren N. Tomlinson, Aug. 29, 1969 (div. Jan. 1986); 1 child, Elizabeth; m. Michael George Bialas, Apr. 25, 1987. BJ, U. Tex., 1970. Pub. rels. asst. Dallas Pub. Libr., 1970-72, pub. rels. dir., 1972-94, mktg. mgr., 1994—; pres. Women in Comm., Dallas, 1976-78. Editor Petals and Thorns newsletter, 1994—; columnist Downtown Bus. News, 1994. Bd. dirs. Partnership-Arts Culture Edn., Dallas, 1991-93, Greater Dallas Cmty. Chs., Dallas, 1985-87, Dallas Teenage Newspaper, 1994—, Pastoral Counciling Ctr., Dallas, 1996—, Tex. Democratic Women, 1993-95. Named Most Valuable Mem. Women in Comm., 1974-75. Mem. Zonta Club Dallas North (pres. 1994-95), Collin County Rose Soc. (v.p., newsletter editor 1994—), Tex. Reelers, North Tex. Traditional Dance Soc., Southwest Celtic Music Assn. Methodist. Office: Dallas Pub Libr 1515 Young Dallas TX 75201

BIANCHI, MARIA, critical care nurse, adult nurse practitioner. Diploma, Catherine Laboure Sch. Nursing, 1979; Grad., Fitchburg (Mass.) State Coll., 1985; postgrad., Russell Sage Coll., Troy, N.Y.; adult nurse practitioner, Mass. Gen. Hosp., Boston. Cert. post-anesthesia care nurse; critical care specialist 1993. Recovery as mgmt. educator, mktg. and recruitment cons., cons. in critical care nursing; nurse mgr. ICU and pediatric ICU Baystate Med. Ctr., Springfield, Mass., 1980-89; recruitment and staff St. Francis Med. Ctr., 1989-92; advanced practice nurse U. Mass. Med. Ctr., Worcester, 1995—; critical care nurse Mass. Gen. Hosp., 1992-93, adult nurse practitioner, 1995-96; rsch. in pain, burn trauma, stress reduction, holistic methods for high risk individuals in maximum penitentiary. Mem. AACN, Am. Soc. Post-Anesthesia Nursing (Boston chpt. editl. cons.), Sigma Theta Tau. Office: 33 Duclos Dr Feeding Hills MA 01030-1409

BIBBY, REGINA NANETTE, manufacturing company executive; b. Jacksonville, Fla., Sept. 20, 1960; d. Allan Harvey and Dorothy Jennette (Munster) B.; 1 child, Christal Shantu Bibby. BS, Brenau Coll., Gainesville, Ga. Customer svc. staff Tandem Computer Co., Marietta, Ga., 1982-83; office mgr. Am. Indsl. Design, Atlanta, 1983-84; dir. Kato Spring of Ga. Inc., Duluth, 1984—. Co-membership chair Nat. Congress of Parents and Tchrs., Ga. Dist. 13, 1990—; local sch. adv. com., 1993, 94. Mem. Am. Prodn. and Inventory Control Soc., Am. Mgmt. Assn., Gwinnette Safety Profl. Assn., Atlanta C. of C., Gwinnett C. of C. Republican. Roman Catholic. Office: Kato Spring of Ga Inc 2590 Breckinridge Blvd Duluth GA 30136-4968

BIBLE, FRANCES LILLIAN, mezzo-soprano, educator; b. Sackets Harbor, N.Y.; d. Arthur and Lillian (Cooke) B. Student, Juilliard Sch. Music, 1939-47. Artist-in-residence Shepherd Sch. of Music Rice U., Houston, 1975-91. Appeared throughout U.S., Australia, Europe including Vienna Staatsoper, Karlsruhe Staatsoper, Dublin Opera Co., N.Y.C. Opera, NBC-TV Opera, San Francisco Opera, Glyndebourne Opera, San Antonio Opera Festival, New Orleans Opera, Houston Grand Opera, Miami Opera, Dallas Opera; appeared in concer with major symphonies; world premiers (opera): The Ballad of Baby Doe, The Crucible, The Troubled Island, The Dybuk. Named Woman of the Yr. in Opera, Mademoiselle, 1949. Mem. Am. Guild Mus. Artists (past 3d v.p., bd. dirs. 1989-91), Sigma Alpha Iota (hon.), Beta Sigma Pi (hon.). Republican. Episcopalian. Home: 2377 Thata Way Hemet CA 92544-7009

BIBLIOWICZ, JESSICA M., financial analyst; b. 1959. Formerly with assesment mgmt. divsn. Shearson Lehman Bros.; past dir. sales and mktg. Prudential Mutual Funds; now exec. v.p., oversees mutual funds and insured investor group Smith Barney, N.Y.C. Office: Smith Barney Inc 388 Greenwich St New York NY 10013*

BICK, KATHERINE LIVINGSTONE, scientist, international liaison, consultant; b. Charlottetown, Can., May 3, 1932; came to U.S., 1954; d. Spurgeon Arthur and Flora Hazel (Murray) Livingstone; m. James Harry Bick, Aug. 20, 1955 (div.); children: James A., Charles L. (dec.); m. Ernst Freese, 1986 (dec. 1990). BS with honors, Acadia U., Can., 1951, MS, 1952; PhD, Brown U., 1957; DSc (hon.), Acadia U., 1990. Research pathologist UCLA Med. Sch., 1959-61; asst. prof. Calif. State U., Northridge, 1961-66; lab. instr. Georgetown U., Washington, 1970-72, asst. prof., 1972-76; dep. dir. neurol. disorder program Nat. Inst. Neurol. and Communicative Disorders and Stroke, NIH, Bethesda, Md., 1976-81, acting dep. dir., 1981-83, dep. dir., 1983-87; dep. dir. extramural research Office of Dir. NIH, 1987-90; sci. liaison Centro Studio Multicentrico Internazionale Sulla Demenza, Washington, 1990-95; cons. Nat. Rsch. Coun., Italy, 1991—, The Charles A. Dana Found., N.Y.C., 1993—. Editor: Alzheimer's Disease: Senile Dementia and Related Disorders, 1978, Neurosecretion and Brain Peptides, Implications for Brain Functions and Neurol. Disease, 1981, The Early Story of Alzheimer's Disease, 1987, Alzheimer Disease, 1994; contbr. articles to profl. jours. Pres. Woman's Club, McLean, Va., 1968-69; bd. dirs. Fairfax County (Va.) YWCA, 1979-80; pres. Emerson Unitarian Ch., 1964-66; mem. Bethesda Pl. Cmty. Coun., 1992—, pres., 1993-94. Recipient Can. NRC award Acadia U., 1951-52, NIH Dir.'s award, 1978, Spl. Achievement award NIH, 1981, 83, Superior Svc. award USPHS, 1986, Presdl. Rank award meritorious sr. exec., 1989; Universal Match Found. fellow Brown U., 1956-57, Fed. Exec. Inst. Leadership fellow, 1980. Fellow AAAS; mem. Am. Neurol. Assn., Am. Acad. Neurology, Assn. for Rsch. in Nervous and Mental Disease, Internat. Brain Rsch. Orgn., World Fedn. Neurology Rsch. Group on Dementias (exec. sec. Am. region 1984-86, chmn. 1986-93), Soc. for Neurosci., Acad. of Medicine (Washington).

BICKERSTAFF, MINA MARCH CLARK, university administrator; b. Crowley, Tex., Sept. 27, 1936; d. Winifred Perry and Clara Mae (Jarrett) Clark; m. Billy Frank Bickerstaff, June 12, 1954 (div. 1960); children: Billy Mark, Mina Gayle Bickerstaff Basaldu. AA, Tarrant County Jr. Coll., 1982; BBA, Dallas Bapt. U., 1991. Dir. pers. svcs. Southwestern Bapt. Theol. Sem., Ft. Worth, 1976—. Mem. Coll. and Univ. Pers. Assn., Seminary Woman's Club (past treas.), Alpha Chi. Baptist. Office: Southwestern Bapt Theol Sem PO Box 22000 Fort Worth TX 76122

BICKERTON, JANE ELIZABETH, university research coordinator; b. Shrewsbury, Shropshire, Eng., Apr. 16, 1949; came to U.S., 1978; d. Donald Samuel George and Lucy Mary (Hill) B.; m. Anthony Andrew Hudgins, Mar. 18, 1978 (div. Feb. 1995); children: Alexis Kathryn, Samantha Lucy. Grad. health visitor, North London U., 1977; BA, Oglethorpe U., 1980; MA, Ga. State U., 1991. RN, Ga.; grad. RN, U.K.; cert. family planning nurse, U.K. Nurse St. Bartholomews Hosp., London, 1967-72; housing advisor Shelter Housing Aid Ctr., London, 1973-76; owner, dir. Jane Bickerton Fine Arts, Atlanta, 1978-85; curator Ga. State U. Gallery, 1985; co-curator Arts Festival of Atlanta, 1995; coord. rsch. study Emory U., Atlanta, 1995—; co-presenter More Prodns., Ga. State U. Gallery; bd. dirs. Art Papers Inc., chmn., 1982-84, acting chmn., 1990—, art reviewer, 1993—; co-curator bathhouse, billboards, art-in transit Arts Festival Ga., 1995; co-prodr. grant Ga. Humanities Coun.; adj. instr. Atlanta Coll. Art, 1993—; panelist NEA, 1993; part-time nurse Feminist Women's Health Ctr., 1980-90; pers. mgr., asst. mgr. Brit. Pavilion Shop, Expo '92, Spain; visual arts panelist Bur. Cultural Affairs, 1987; juror Arts Festival, Atlanta, 1989. Author: (with John Fletcher) Guide to First-Time House Buyers, 1975; contbg. editor Art Papers, 1981-85; writer: "Suns" parts/pieces/fragments, 1996. Vol. comty. worker, Guatemala, 1976; mem. adv. com. Arts Festival Atlanta, 1991-93; com. mem. Grady H.S. Parents, Tchrs. and Students Assn.; chmn. com. fine arts Inman Mid. Sch. PTA, 1990-92, Morningside Elem. Sch. PTA, 1986-88; bd. dirs. Pub. Domain, 1992—. Mem. 20th Century Art Soc. at High Mus. (programming com. mem. 1993, bd. dirs. 1993—, v.p. 1994—, pres. 1996—). Home: 1036 High Point Dr Atlanta GA 30306

BICKFORD, JEWELLE WOOTEN, investment banker; b. Evanston, Ill., Dec. 12, 1941; d. James A. Wooten and Phyllis (Taber) Kades; m. Nathaniel J. Bickford, Feb. 1, 1962; children: Laura C., Emily A. BA, Sarah Lawrence Coll., 1977. Trustee, chair com. on gen. programs and issues Community Svc. Soc., N.Y.C., 1973-77; dir. community bd. assistance unit Office of the Mayor, N.Y.C., 1977-80; v.p. Citibank, N.A., N.Y.C., 1980-84; v.p. Dillon, Read & Co., Inc., N.Y.C., 1984-85, sr. v.p., 1985-88; pres. Trepp, Bickford Fin. Svcs. Inc., 1988-90, Bickford & Ptnrs., Inc., N.Y.C., 1991-94, Bickford Capital Advisors, L.P., 1991-94; mng. dir., head capital markets Rothschild, Inc., N.Y.C., 1994—; mem. adv. bd. First Womens Bank, 1975-78. Trustee South St. Seaport Theater, chmn. bd., 1978-83; trustee Coro Found., 1982-89; mem. Citizens Com. for Children; bd. dirs. Phoenix House Found.; trustee, v.p. bd. trustees Fountain House; mem. bus. com. Met. Mus. Art. Mem. Fin. Women's Assn., Women's Forum (bd. dirs.). Democrat. Episcopalian. Club: River (N.Y.C.). Home: 969 5th Ave New York NY 10021-1742 Office: Rothschild Inc 1251 Ave of the Americas New York NY 10020

BICKHART, KATHLEEN FOLK, journalist; b. Reading, Pa., Apr. 11, 1960; d. David Thomas and Janice Patricia (Battle) Folk; m. Terry Alan Bickhart, June 15, 1985; children: Jordan, Alexa. BA, Duquesne U., 1982. Sportswriter Reading Eagle Co., 1982-85, sports copy editor, 1985-89, dep. sports editor, 1989-95, editor "Voices", 1995—. Mem. Phi Kappa Phi. Democrat. Office: Reading Eagle Co PO Box 582 Reading PA 19603

BICOUVARIS, MARY VASSILICOU, education educator; b. Tripolis, Greece, June 4, 1939; came to U.S., 1960; d. Nickolas George and Georgia (Lymberopoulos) Vassilicos; m. James Gregory Bicouvaris; children: Greg, Valerie. Elem. edn. diploma, Pedagogical Acad. Tripolis, Greece, 1958; BS in Secondary Edn., Ohio State U., 1963; LHD (hon.), Hampton U., 1989; MA in Edn., The Coll. William and Mary, 1970; PhD in Urban Svcs., Old Dominion U., 1994. History tchr. grades 7-9 Jefferson Davis Jr. High, Hampton, Va., 1963-66, 68-76; history and govt. tchr. Bethel H.S., Hampton, Va., 1976-91; govt. and internat. politics tchr. Hampton Roads Acad., Newport News, Va., 1991-95; assoc. prof. edn. Christopher Newport U., Newport News, Va., 1995—; trustee Nat. Coun. for History Edn., 1990—, Christopher Newport U., 1989-95, adj. faculty; edn. advisory panel New Am. Sch. Devel. Corp., 1990—; coun. mem. Nat. Coun. for History Stds., 1991-95; adj. faculty George Washington U., bd. advisors scholar program, 1995-96; presenter in field. Contbr. articles to profl. jours. Bd. dirs., v.p., 1st v.p. UN Assn., Peninsula chpt., 1983-88; bd. dirs., 1st v.p. Peninsula Literacy Coun., 1983-86; active Greek Orthodox Ch., Newport News, PTA. Fulbright Hays scholar, Israel, Egypt, 1984, Delta Kappa Gamma Internat. scholar, 1990; recipient Disting. Educator award Am. Hellenic Ednl. and Progressive Assn., 1989, Disting. Alumni award Ohio State U. Coll. Edn., 1989, Mary Hatwood Futrell award Va. Edn. Assn., 1989; scholarships named in her honor by Hampton Lions Club, Greek Orthodox Ch. Newport News. Mem. ASCD, Nat. Coun. for History Edn. (founding mem.), Nat. Coun. for the Social Studies, coun. for Basic Edn., Am. Ednl. Rsch. Assn., Assn. Tchr. Educators, Va. Assn. Tchr. Educators, Hellenic Womans Penelope Soc. (past. pres., v.p., treas., 1st v.p. 1995-96), Phi Delta Phi. Office: Christopher Newport U Newport News VA 23606-2998

BIEBER-ROBERTS, PEGGY EILENE, communications editor, journalist, researcher; b. Mobridge, S.D., Jan. 8, 1943; d. John J. and Lenora (Schlepp) B. BS, No. State U., Aberdeen, S.D., 1966; MA, U. Wyo., 1984; PhD, U. Wash., 1990. Vol. Peace Corps, Turkey, 1966-68; tchr. secondary pub. schs., Idaho, 1968-69, Pine Ridge (S.D.) Reservation, 1969-71; co-founder Medicine Bow Post weekly newspaper, 1977; legis. reporter various weekly newspapers, Wyo., 1980-82; co-founder Medicine Bow Post weekly newspaper, Wyo., 1977; owner, pub. Capitol Times mag., Cheyenne, Wyo., 1982-84; publisher Skyline West Press, 1983; lectr. pub. rels. and advt. U. Wash., Seattle, 1986-88; rsch. analyst Elway Rsch./Jay Rockey Co., Seattle, 1989-90; asst. prof. mass media U. Wyo., Laramie, 1990—; indexer McGraw/Hill, Bedford Books, also others, 1988—. Author, editor hist. almanacs for various states, 1984-87; contbr. articles to profl. jours., chpts. to books. Publicity chmn. Laramie County Dem. Com., Cheyenne, 1982; mem. Wind River Indian Reservation Comm. com. of the No. Arapaho Tribe. Recipient 1st Place award for feature writing, Co-1st Place award for editorials Wyo. Press Assn., 1982, Alumni Assn. Faculty Growth award U. Wyo., 1994; named Stout fellow U. Wash., 1990. Mem. Turkish Studies Assn., Internat. Assn. Mass Comm. Rsch., Assn. Ednl. Journalism and Mass Comm., Internat. Comm. Assn., Mid East Studies Assn. Office: Dubai Women's Coll Higher Colls of Tech, Dept Mass Media, Dubai United Arab Emirates

BIEDERMAN, JOHANNA MONTEFUSCO, professional society administrator, nurse; b. Jamaica, N.Y., Feb. 28, 1941; d. Nicholas and Rose (Mucci) Montefusco; m. Harry Biederman, Feb. 11, 1961; children: Diane, David, Deborah. AAS in Nursing, Suffolk County C.C., Selden, N.Y., 1984; BS in Health Adminstrn., St. Joseph's Coll., 1987; MS in Health Care Adminstrn., SUNY, Stony Brook, 1995. RN, N.Y. RN Brookhaven Meml. Hosp., Patchogue, N.Y., 1984-87; rehab. specialist Cost Containment, Braintree, Mass., 1987-88; dir. chpt. svc. Nat. Multiple Sclerosis Soc., Hauppauge, N.Y., 1988-91, pres., 1991—, mem. nat. mgmt. team, 1994—. Dir. Soundview Acres Civic Assn., Shorham, N.Y., 1985-90. Mem. N.Y. State Nurses Assn., L.I. Profl. Women's Assn. Home: 10 Salty Way Shoreham NY 11786 Office: 200 Parkway Dr South Hauppauge NY 11788

BIEGEL, EILEEN MAE, hospital executive; b. Eau Claire, Wis., Nov. 13, 1937; d. Ewald Frederic and Emma Antonia (Conrad) Weggen; student Dist. One Tech. Inst., 1974, also part time, corr. student U. Wis., Madison; grad. mgmt. seminars; student Upper Iowa U., 1984—; m. James O. Biegel, Oct. 6, 1956; children: Jeffrey Alan, John William. Exec. sec. to pres. Broadcaster Services, Inc., Eau Claire, Wis., 1969-74; exec. sec. to exec. v.p. Am. Nat. Bank, Eau Claire, 1975-77; exec. asst. to pres. Luther Hosp., Eau Claire, 1977—, asst. corporate sec., 1984—; mem. exec. staff, 1985—; asst. corp. sec. Luther Health Care Corp., 1984—; mem. secretarial adv. council Dist. One Tech. Sch. 1975—; corp. sec. Northwest Health Ventures, 1988-92, bd. dirs. State pres. Future Homemakers Am., 1955; mem. governance com. Wis. Hosp. Assn. Cert. profl. sec., 1980; sec. bd. dirs. Chestnut Properties. Mem. Eau Claire Womens Network (founder, mem. steering com.), Profl. Secs. Internat. (chmn. goals and priorities com., pres. Eau Claire chpt. 1982-83), Wis. Hosp. Assn. (gov. com.). Home: 4707 Tower Dr Eau Claire WI 54703-8717 Office: 310 Chestnut St Eau Claire WI 54703-5230

BIEGELSEN, ANNIE M., human services specialist; b. St. Louis, July 3, 1969; d. Paul S. and Elaine L. Biegelsen. BA with honors, U. Chgo., 1991; cert., World Union Jewish Students, Arad, Israel, 1992. Legal asst. Taft, Stettinius & Hollister, cin., 1993-94; office svcs. vol. coord. AIDS Action Com., Boston, 1994—; health and safety instr. ARC, Boston, 1994—; youth advocacy program coord. Women's State-Wide Legis. Network, Boston, 1995-96; WALK office mgr. AIDS Action Com., Boston, 1994. Vol. Kibbutz Sde Boker, HaNegev, Israel, 1992; mem. Mass. Women's Polit. Caucus, Boston, 1996. Home: 338 Summer St Somerville MA 02144 Office: AIDS Action Com 131 Clarendon St Boston MA 02116

BIEHL, JANE M., rehabilitation services professional; b. Canton, Ohio, Oct. 24, 1950; d. George Henry and Katherine Elizabeth (Holl) B. BA, Heidelberg Coll., 1972; MLS, Emory U., 1974; MEd, Kent State U., 1991. Cert. Rehab. Counselor. Children libr. Akron (Ohio) Summit County Pub. Libr., 1974-78; children's cons. Mideastern Ohio Libr. Organ., 1978-81, dir., 1988-91; children coord. Stark Dist. Libr., Canton, Ohio, 1981-86; intern Nat. Tech. Inst. for the Deaf, Rochester, N.Y., 1991; asst. dir. Massillon (Ohio) Pub. Libr., 1986-88; grad. asst. Kent State U., 1992-93; rehab. counselor Rehab. Svcs. Comm., Youngstown, Ohio, 1993—; adj. faculty Walsh U., Canton, 1986—; workshop presenter Kent State U., 1992-93. Contbr. articles to profl. jours. Active Self Help-Hard of Hearing People, Youngstown, Canton, 1986—, Ea. Ohio Rehab. Organ., 1994—. Named Deaf Woman of Yr., Quota Club, 1984. Mem. Am. Counseling Assn., Self Help for Hard of Hearing, Assn. for Edn. of Blind, Nat. Assn. of the Deaf. Protestant. Office: Bur of Svcs for Visually Impaired 1350 5th Ave Ste 204 Youngstown OH 44504

BIEHL, JULIANNE, art educator; b. Pitts., Sept. 25; d. James Newton and Julia Eva (Freeauf) Addis; m. Edward Robert Biehl, June 11, 1955; children: Kathy Anne, Kimberly Anne, Kurt Edward, Karen Nancy. BS in Art Edn., Indiana U. Pa., 1952; MA in Art, So. Meth. U., 1972; postgrad., U. North Tex., 1974-75. Art tchr. Titusville (Pa.) Jr. H.S., 1952-53, Langley Jr.-Sr. H.S., Pitts., 1953-55, U. Pitts. Lab. Sch., Richardson (Tex.) North Jr. H.S., 1972-78, J.J. Pearce H.S., Richardson, 1978-84; artist, painter, printmaker Evelyn Siegel Gallery, Fort Worth, 1990—, Edith Baker Gallery, Dallas, 1995—; art tchr. Sch. of Continuing Edn., So. Meth. U., Dallas, 1992-93; lectr. to staff Timberlawn Psychiat. Hosp., Grand Rounds Meeting, 1989. Solo shows include So. Meth. U. Women's Ctr., 1992, U. Tex., Arlington, 1994; group shows at Bradford Coll., Mass., Dartmouth St. Gallery, Albuquerque, El Dorado Gallery, Colorado Springs, Grand Prairie Visual Arts Ctr., Fine Arts Ctrn., Taos, N.Mex., Soc. Internat. Des Beaux-Arts Salon, Paris, 1993, Evelyn Siegel Gallery, Ft. Worth, 1995, Jansen-Perez Gallery, San Antonio, 1995, Salon SIBA, 1996, numerous others; contbr. articles to profl. jours. Recipient Florence Art Gallery award Tex. Visual Art Assn., 1995, 2d pl. award Grand Prairie Visual Art Assn., 1990, 1st pl., 1990, Kimmel award Soc. of Watercolor Artists, Awards Fine Arts Ctr. En TAOS, 1984, 85, Nasher award Southwestern Watercolor Soc., 1991, others; Painting scholar Carnegie Tech. Mem. Dallas Womens Caucus for Art (treas. 1991, bd. dirs. 1990-92), Southwestern Watercolor Soc., Soc. of Layerists in Multi-Media, Tex. Visual Art Assn., So. Meth. U. Women's Club, So. Graphics Coun. Home and Studio: 2925 Rosedale Ave Dallas TX 75205 also: 3805 Dollar Lake Dr Estes Park CO 80517

BIEHLE, KAREN JEAN, pharmacist; b. Festus, Mo., July 18, 1959; d. Warren Day and Wilma Georgenia (Hedrick) Hargus; m. Scott Joseph Biehle, Aug. 22, 1981; children: Lauren Rachel, Heather Michelle. Student of pre-pharmacy, U. Mo., Columbia, Mo., 1977-79; BS in Pharmacy, U. Mo., Kans. City, Mo., 1982. Reg. Pharmicist. Pharmacy res. U. Iowa Hosp. & Clinics, Iowa City, Iowa, 1982-83; pharmacist Jewish Hosp. of St. Louis, St. Louis, 1983-86; pharmacy mgr. Foster Infusion Care, St. Louis, 1986-88; staff pharmacist Cardinal Glennon Children's Hosp., St. Louis, 1988-90; pres. Lauren's Specialty Foods, Inc., St. Louis, 1988-89; pharmacy mgr. Curaflex Health Svcs., St. Louis, 1989-91; asst. dir. Cobb Hosp. and Med. Ctr., Austell, Ga., 1991-94; asst. dir. pharmacy Publix Supermarkets, Marietta, Ga., 1994-96; acct. exec. Nats. Healthcare, Inc., Marietta, Ga., 1996—; preceptor St. Louis Coll. Pharmacy, 1984-91, U. Ga. Sch. Pharmacy, 1992. Vol. March of Dimes Walk-a-thon, 1985-90. Recipient Roche Pharmacy Communications Award, Roche Pharmaceuticals, Kans. City, 1982, I Dare You Award, 4-H Club, Nevada, Mo., 1976. Mem. Am. Soc. Hosp. Pharmacists, Kappa Epsilon, Alpha Delta Pi (St. Louis Alumnae pres. 1989-90). Republican. Baptist. Home: 2431 Westport Cir Marietta GA 30064-5707

BIELEFELDT, CATHERINE C., sales executive; b. Bellwood, Ill.; d. William Anton and Linda (Buchert) B. MusB in Piano Performance, Chgo. Conservatory Coll.; student El Conservatorio de Mex., Mexico City; postgrad. Northwestern U., CBS Sch. Mgmt., 1980. Dept. mgr. Fair Store, Oak Park, Ill., 1950-62; piano sales cons. Lyon & Healy Co., Oak Park and Oak Brook, Ill., 1963-77; dir. Steinway Hall, dir. nat. sales tng. Steinway & Sons, Long Island City, N.Y., 1978-82; v.p. sales, pub. rels. and advt. Hendricks Music Co., Downers Grove, Ill., 1983—; sales seminar instr. Jordan-Kitt's Music, Wells Music, Washington and Denver, 1983-85, Lauzon Music, Ottawa, Can., 1986—, Meridian Music, Indpls., 1989. Author: The Wonders of the Piano, The Anatomy of the Instrument, 1984, 3d edit., 1996; editor The Keynote Newsletter; contbr. articles to profl. jours. Mem. Evanston Music Club, Sigma Alpha Iota (past pres. alumnae chpt., recipient numerous awards). Republican. Lutheran. Home: 190 S Wood Dale Rd Apt 1101 Wood Dale IL 60191-2246 Office: Hendricks Music 421 Maple Ave Downers Grove IL 60515-3806

BIERI, BARBARA NORMILE, systems analyst, consultant; b. Trenton, N.J., Jan. 4, 1951; d. William Donald and Beatrice Marie (Noon) Normile; m. Paul Daniel Bieri, Apr. 13, 1991. BS in Edn., St. Francis Coll., 1972; postgrad., Pa. State U., 1976, Mercer County C.C., 1983, 85-86. Cert. tchr. elem. and secondary math., N.J., Pa. Tchr. math. and sci. St. Anthony Sch., Trenton, N.J., 1972-77; tchr. math. Cumberland Regional H.S., Seabrook, N.J., 1977-82; programmer N.J. Dept. Human Svcs., Trenton, 1982-84; programmer, analyst Computer Svcs. Group, Trenton, 1984; sr. computer sys. designer Martin Marietta Data Sys., Princeton, N.J., 1984-86; sr. sys. mgr. Storey/Ross/Barker, Inc., Lambertville, N.J., 1987-90; cons. BPN Cons., Hamilton, N.J., 1990-93, MIACO Corp., Landover, Md., 1993-94; sr. sys. analyst Data Based Sys. Internat., Flemington, N.J., 1994—; union rep., negotiating team Cumberland Regional Edn. Assn., Seabrook, N.J., 1980-81; computer tchr. adult edn. West Windsor (N.J.) Plainsboro Adult Edn. Program, 1983-86. Committeewoman Dem. Party, Bridgeton, N.J., 1980. Mem. NAFE, N.J. Novell Users Group, MDBS Users Group, Oracle Users Group, Gamma Sigma Sigma (v.p. 1971-72). Home: 249 Hobart Ave Hamilton NJ 08629-1622 Office: Data Based Sys 31 Highway 12 Flemington NJ 08822

BIERLEIN, STACY LYNNE, writer; b. Saginaw, Mich., Jan. 21, 1968; d. Gary Robert and Patricia Wells (Foster) B. BS, Syracuse U., 1990; pub. cert., U. Chgo., 1992; MFA, Columbia Coll., 1994. Fiction writing tutor Columbia Coll., Chgo., 1992-94; assoc. for design/sales M.C. Hoffmann Design, Chgo., 1993-95; dir. devel. Workshirts Writing Ctr., Chgo., 1995—; literary coord. Eclectic Junction for Art, Chgo., 1994—; founding dir. Art in New Places, Chgo. and L.A., 1995—. Editor of fiction and poetry (literary jour.) Fish Stories, 1994-96; author (manual) Moon Crossing Bridge Poetry Workshop Manual, 1996; contbr. to mag. Vol. NOW, Chgo., 1993—, New Group for Contemporary Art, Chgo., 1993—. Recipient New Writing award Santa Barbara Writer's Com., Santa Barbara, Calif., 1994. Mem. Am. Acad. Poetry, Nat. Assn. for Poetry Therapy, Chgo. Coun. on Fgn. Rels.

BIERLY, SHIRLEY ADELAIDE, communications executive; b. Waterbury, Conn., Jan. 19, 1924; d. Samuel and Frances Ada (Bogorad) Brown; m. Leroy Elwood Bierly, Jan. 19, 1946 (div. 1951); children: Lee Jr., Dennis Ray, David Lincoln. Student, Orange Coast Coll., 1963-66, L.A. City Coll., 1967-69. Mgr. Pacific Telephone, San Francisco, Calif., 1953-82; exec. dir. Sr. Power Office, San Francisco, 1982—. Convener Calif. Legis. Coun. for Older Am., San Francisco, 1984—, treas. Calif. Assn. of Older Am., 1984—, mem. Sr. Action Network, San Francisco, 1991—, Congress of Calif. Sr., Sacramento, 1994—; bd. trustees Agape Found. Mem. Am. Civil Liberties Union, Older Women's League, Gray Panthers. Office: Calif Assn for Older Ams 805 Howard St San Francisco CA 94103-3009

BIERY, EVELYN HUDSON, lawyer; b. Lawton, Okla., Oct. 12, 1946; d. William Ray and Nellie Iris (Nunley) Hudson. BA in English and Latin summa cum laude, Abilene (Tex.) Christian U., 1968; JD, So. Meth. U., 1973. Bar: Tex. 1973, U.S. Dist. Ct. (we. dist.) Tex. 1975, U.S. Dist. Ct. (so. dist.) Tex. 1977, U.S. Dist. Ct. (no. dist.) Tex. 1979, U.S. Ct. Appeals (5th cir.) 1979, U.S. Ct. Appeals (11th cir.) 1981, U.S. Supreme Ct. 1981. Atty. Law Offices of Bruce Waitz, San Antonio, 1973-76; mem. LeLaurin & Adams, P.C., San Antonio, 1976-81; ptnr., head bankruptcy, reorganization and creditors' rights sect. Fulbright & Jaworski, San Antonio, 1981—, mem. policy com., 1996—; speaker on creditors' rights, bankruptcy and reorganization law at numerous seminars; lectr. Southwestern Grad. Sch. Banking, Dallas, 1980, La. State U. Sch. Banking, 1994; presiding officer, U. Tex. Sch. of Law Bankruptcy Conf., 1976, 94, State Bar Tex. Creditors' Rights Inst., 1985, State Bar Tex. Advanced Bus. Bankruptcy Law Inst., 1985, State Bar Tex. Inst. on Advising Officers, Dirs. and Ptnrs. in Troubled Bus., 1987, State Bar Tex. Advanced Creditors Rights Inst., 1988; pres. San Antonio Young Lawyers Assn., 1979-80; mem. bankruptcy adv. com. fifth cir. jud. coun., 1979-80; vice-chmn. bankruptcy com. Comml. Law League Am., 1981-83; mem. exec. bd. So. Meth. U. Sch. Law, 1983-91. Editor: Texas Collections Manual, 1978, Creditor's Rights in Texas, 2d edit., 1981;

author: (with others) Collier Bankruptcy Practice Guide, 1993. Del. to U.S./ Republic of China joint session on trade, investment and econ. law , Beijing, 1987; designated mem. Bankruptcy Judge Merit Screening Com. State of Tex. by Tex. State Bar Pres., 1979-82; patron McNay Mus., San Antonio; rsch. ptnr. Mind Sci. Found., San Antonio; diplomat World Affairs Coun., San Antonio. Recipient Outstanding Young Lawyer award San Antonio Young Lawyers Assn., 1979. Fellow Soc. of Internat. Bus. Fellow, Am. Coll. Bankruptcy Attys., Tex. Bar Found. (life), San Antonio Bar Found.; mem. Tex. Bar Assn. (chair bankruptcy com. 1982-83, chair corp., banking and bus. law sect. 1989-90), Tex. Assn. Bank Counsel (bd. dirs. 1988-90), San Antonio Young Lawyers Assn. (pres. 1979-80), Plaza Club San Antonio (bd. dirs. 1982—), Zonta (Chair Z club com. 1989-90), Order of Coif. Office: Fulbright & Jaworski 300 Convent St Ste 2200 San Antonio TX 78205-3723

BIESEL, DIANE JANE, librarian; b. N.Y.C., Feb. 15, 1934; d. Douglas and Runa (Patterson) Stevens; m. Donald W. de Cordova, June 24, 1956 (div. July 1971); m. David Barrie Biesel, Sept. 25, 1982. BS, Trenton State Coll., 1956; MLS, Rutgers U., 1969; MA in Edn., Seton Hall U., 1974, cert. in supervision, 1976. Tchr., librarian Arlington (Va.)) Bd. Edn., 1956-58; media specialist elem. schs., librs. River Edge (N.J.) Bd. Edn., 1958-91; lectr., instr. children's lit. Alphonsus Coll., Woodcliff Lake, N.J., 1969-72; field svc. cons. N.J. Dept. Edn., 1969-71; cons. New Books Preview Baker and Taylor Co., 1972-76; adj. prof. Seton Hall U., 1978-79; mem. award com. Rutgers U. Grad. Sch. Libr. Svc., 1978-79; series editor Scarecrow Press, Metuchen, N.J., 1992—. Editor: School Library Media Series, Sch. Librarianship Series. Mem. com. academically gifted River Edge Bd. Edn., 1977-83, mem. study skills com., 1988-90, mem. affirmative action com., 1988-90; mem. River Dell Librs. Coop., 1988-91; mem. choir All Saints Ch., Bergenfield, 1971—, lay reader, 1973—, vestrywoman, 1980-83, del. Diocesan Conv., 1978—; mem. ecumenical commn. Diocese of Newark, 1992, mem. Child Devel. Ctr. Bd., 1994—. Mem. ALA, Am. Assn. Sch. Librs. (ret., mem. com. instrnl. media 1971-76, affiliate assembly by-laws com. 1977-78, program com. 1992-93, rep. kid diversity programming com. 1993—, ABC Clio award com. 1994—, legis. com. 1994—, ret. mems. internat. group 1993—, membership com. 1994—), Ednl. Media Assn. N.J. (state chmn. recruitment 1968-69, state chmn. hospitality 1972-73, state chmn. county liaison 1973-74, co-pres. 1977-78), Bergen County Sch. Librs. Assn. (pres. 1966-68), River Edge Tchrs. Assn. (pres. 1964-66), Assn. Ednl. Comm. Tech. (nat. nominating com. 1978-79, coun. 1978-79, steering com. 1979-80, evaluation com. 1979, co-chmn. liaison com. with Am. Assn. Sch. Librs. 1979-83, nat. nominating com. 1980-82, awards com. 1981-89), Sch. Media Specialists (program com. 1982-84, bd. dirs. region II 1983-84, pres. 1986, mem. task force on librs. and info. sci., White House, writing com., co-author: Information Power, 1988), Nat. Button Soc., N.J. Button Soc., Bergen Button Buffs (founding grandmother 1993). Home: 315 Schraalenburgh Rd Haworth NJ 07641-1200

BIFANO, LINDA CELESTE, nursing administrator; b. Detroit, July 26, 1953; d. Daniel Frank and Roberta (Hudson) B. ADN, Henry Ford C.C., Dearborn, Mich., 1975; BSN, Madonna U., 1982; MSN, Oreg. Health Scis. U., 1992; MPA, Portland State U., 1992. RN, Mich., 1975. Nurse mgr. Vis. Nurses Assn., Portland, Oreg., 1983-86; sales and mktg. exec. Foster Med. Corp., Portland, 1986-89; exec. dir. Northwest Neighborhood Nurses, Inc., Portland, 1992-94; health policy specialist State of Oreg., Portland, 1994-95; dir. patient care svcs. Suburgan Med., Portland, 1995—. Inventor in field; contbr. articles to profl. jours. Citizens adv. bd. mem. Housing Authority Portland, 1992—; chair pub. policy com. Am. Lung Assn., Portland, 1995. Recipient Gov.'s Cert. Appreciation, 1989, Outstanding Customer Svc. award Pacificare of Oreg., 1990. Mem. ANA, Oreg. Nurses Found. (bd. dirs.), Oreg. Nurses Assn. (better health steering com. 1993-96, nurses polit. action com. 1994-96, cabinet on health polity chair 1989-92, Polit. Involvement award 1992, Meritorious Svc. award 1987), Sigma Theta Tau Beta Psi chpt. Home: 4210 SW View Point Ter #5 Portland OR 97201 Office: Healthfirst Med Group Inc 10535 NE Glisan Portland OR 97220

BIGAR, NICOLE MICHELINE, painter, sculptor; b. Paris, Nov. 24, 1926; came to U.S., 1940; d. Alfred and Madeleine (Weill) Weil; m. Raymond Bigar, Apr. 28, 1946; children: Philippe, Dominique. Student, Barnard Coll., 1945-49, Art Student's League, Mus. Modern Art. Tchr. Art Student's League, N.Y.C., Pub. Sch. 92, N.Y.C. One-woman shows at Phyllis Radcliff Gallery, N.Y.C., 1972, Randall Gallery, N.Y.C., 1977, Benson Gallery, Bridgehampton, N.Y., 1980, 81, 85, 86, 96, Benton Gallery, Southampton, N.Y., 1987, 88, 89, 90, 92, Athena Fine Arts Gallery, N.Y.C., 1993, 94, Pharos Gallery, N.Y.C., 1995; exhibited in group show at Benton Gallery, 1994, 95, 96; represented in permanent collections at Guild Hall Mus., East Hampton, N.Y., Hecksher Mus., Huntington, N.Y., Lees Jr. Coll., Jackson, Ky., Scandinavian-Am. Found., N.Y.C., Vogue Publ., London. V.p. Victor D'Amico Inst. Art, 1980—. Recipient Best Abstract Painting award Guild Hall. Home: 1107 5th Ave New York NY 10128

BIGELOW, BARBARA WINSOR, county official; b. Detroit, Nov. 9, 1946; d. Albert Edson and Helen Mary (Winsor) B. BA, Ohio State U., 1968. Computer programmer Ohio State U., Columbus, 1971-77; programmer analyst Carlson Cos., Plymouth, Minn., 1977-80; mgr. data processing Mpls. Cmty. Devel. Agy., 1980-83; mgr. data processing North Slope Borough, Barrow, Alaska, 1984-87, dep. dir. adminstrn. and fin., 1987-90; dir. adminstrn. and fin. City of Allentown, Pa., 1990-94; dir. fiscal affairs County of Northampton, Easton, Pa., 1994—, cons. Mpls. Voter Registration, 1980-83; peer cons. Pa. Dept. Cmty. Affairs, Harrisburg, 1992-94. Bd. dirs. Pa. Mcpl. Retirement Sys., Harrisburg, 1990-94, Great Valley coun. Girl Scouts U.S.A., 1990-95; bd. dirs., treas. Pa. Sinfonia Orch., Allentown, 1991-96; mem. fin. com. ARC of Lehigh Valley, Allentown, 1995-96; mem. Great Valley Girl Scout Found., 1996—. Mem. Rotary. Democrat. Presbyterian. Office: County of Northampton 669 Washington St Easton PA 18042

BIGELOW, JO P. D., foundation administrator; b. Macon, Ga., Jan. 30, 1915; d. Zollie F. and Sara Alice (Neuner) Pritchett; m. R.L. Daughtrey, May 7, 1933 (dec. May 1965); children: James Arthur (dec.), Sara Josette Daughtrey Powell. Grad. high sch. State news editor Ft. Myers (Fla.) News-Press, 1952-73, woman's editor, 1952-73; v.p., pres., bd. dirs. and sec. Koreshan Unity & Pioneer Ednl. Found., Estero, Fla., 1982—. Editor The American Eagle. Office: Koreshan Unity Foundation Inc PO Box 97 8661 Corkscrew Rd Estero FL 33928

BIGELOW, KATHRYN, film director; b. 1951. Student, San Francisco Art Inst., Whitney Mus. Ind. Study Program, Columbi U. Sch. Film. Director: (films) The Loveless, 1982, Near Dark, 1987, Blue Steel, 1990, Point Break, 1991; script supr. Union City, 1980; author: (screenplays) (with Monty Montgomery) The Loveless, (with Eric Red) Near Dark. Office: care CAA 9830 Wilshire Blvd Beverly Hills CA 90212-1804*

BIGELOW, MARTHA MITCHELL, retired historian; b. Talladega Springs, Ala., Sept. 19, 1921; divorced; children: Martha Frances, Carolyn Letitia. B.A., Montevallo U., 1943; M.A. (tuition fellow, Julius Rosenwald scholar 1943-44, Cleo Hearson scholar, summer 1944, Ency. Brit. fellow 1944-45), U. Chgo., 1944, Ph.D., 1946. Assoc. prof. history Miss. Coll., Clinton, 1946-48, Memphis State U., 1948-49; Assoc. prof. history U. Miss., 1949-50; assoc. curator manuscripts Mich. Hist. Collections, U. Mich., Ann Arbor, 1954-57; prof. history Miss. Coll., 1957-71, chmn. dept. history and polit. sci., 1964-71; dir. Bur. of History, Mich. Dept. State, 1971-90; sec. Mich. Hist. Commn., Mich. Dept. State, state historic preservation officer, 1971-90; coord. for Mich., Nat. Hist. Publs. and Recs. Commn., 1974-90. Contbr. articles profl. publns. Mem. Am. Assn. State and Local History (v.p. 1979-80, pres. 1980-81, fellow summers 1958, 59), Orgn. Am. Historians, Nat. Assn. State Archives and Recs. Assn., So. Hist. Assn., Mich. Hist. Soc., Miss. Hist. Soc. Home: 201 N Jefferson St Clinton MS 39056-4237

BIGELOW, PAGE ELIZABETH, public policy professional; b. Louisville, Feb. 9, 1948; d. William Simpson and Page Elizabeth (Smith) B. BA, Wells Coll., 1970; postgrad., NYU, 1971-72, Gen. Theol. Sem., 1971-72. Rsch. asst., libr. Nat. Mcpl. League, N.Y.C., 1970-75, rsch. dir. ethics in govt. project, 1975-80, dir. representation project, 1981-84; sr. assoc. Nat. Civic League (formerly Nat. Mcpl. League), N.Y.C., 1983-87; staff cons. state-city commn. on integrity in govt. N.Y., N.Y.C., 1986-87; mem. sr. staff Inst. Pub. Adminstrn., N.Y.C., 1987-95, cons., 1995—. Author: From Norms of Rules, Regulating the Outside Interests of Public Officials, 1989, Annotated Bibliography on Citizenship and Ethics, 2d edit., 1993, Money, Politics and the Public Trust: Gifts, Illegal Gratuities, Bribery, Extortion and Campaign Contributions, 1995; editor: Proceedings of the International Conference on Ethics in Government, 1995. Mem. citizens adv. panel to joint legis. com. on revision and simplification of tax code, N.Y., 1982-86; del. Ednl. Priorities Panel, N.Y.C., 1984-94; mem. Citywide Sch. Bd. Elections Com., N.Y.C., 1985—. Mem. Coun. on Govtl. Ethics Laws, Jr. League N.Y.C. (corp. sec. 1986-88, 90, Honored Vol. 1990). Episcopalian. Home: 5 Berkeley Rd Maplewood NJ 07040-2511

BIGGERS, KATHLEEN HANCOCK, elementary education educator; b. South Boston, Va., May 18, 1967; d. Charlie Pierman and Gladys Sue (Parsons) Hancock; m. Robert W. Biggers Jr., June 30, 1990; 1 child, Chadwick Wayne. BS in PK-4 edn., Longwood Coll., Farmville, Va., 1988, endorsement to teach mentally disturbed, 1993, M in Learning Disabled, 1993. Tchr. Charlotte (Va.) County Sch. Sys., 1988-90, Prince Edward County Sch. Sys., Farmville, 1991—; mem. curriculum and design team, Farmville, 1992—; mem. parent outreach com., Farmville, 1992-93; chmn. kindergarten and design team, Farmville, 1992—. Leader Girl Scouts, Charlotte County, 1989-91, cookie rep., 1990-91; leader Acteens, Worsham Bapt. Ch., 1993-94; mem. Bacon Litter Com., Charlotte County, 1987-89. Recipient award of excellence-Leader Against Litter, Charlotte County Litter Com., 1987-89. Mem. ASCD, Women Missionary Union. Home: Rt 3 Box 315-E Rd 665 Farmville VA 23901

BIGGERSTAFF, MYRA, artist, designer, educator; b. Logensport, Ind., Feb. 6, 1905; d. Oliver Benjamin and Blanche (Berry) B.; m. Roland Kvistberg, 1933 (div. 1946); m. William Burroughs Holliday, 1951. BFA, Bethany Coll., 1932, Columbia U., 1953; MFA, Swedish Royal Acad., 1953. Assoc. prof. fine arts Trinity U., San Antonio, Tex., 1948-50; assoc. prof., chmn. textile design dept. Fashion Inst. Tech., N.Y.C., 1960-72; ret. One-woman shows Joslyn Mus., Omaha, Mus. Nebr. Art, Kearney, Sheldon Galleries, Lincoln, Nebr., Alebys, Stockholm, Grand Hotel Royal, Stockholm, Agora Gallery, N.Y.C., 1992; numerous group shows in U.S. and fgn. countries, most recent being Nemaha Valley Mus., Auburn, Nebr., Mus. Nebr. Art, Kearney, Birger Sandzen Meml. Gallery, Bethany Coll., Lindsborg, Kans.; work profiled in N.Y. Art Rev., Ency. Living Am. Artists, Mus. Women in Arts, Washington, Manhattan Arts mag., Nat. Mus. Am. Art; represented in permanent collections at JFK Meml. Mus., Boston, Sheldon Meml. Mus., Lincoln, Nebr., Mus. of Nebr. Art, Kearney, Nemaha Valley Mus., Auburn. Instr. Riverside Ch. Arts and Crafts Cmty. Svc., N.Y.C., 1954-60; mem. Nemaha Valley Mus., 1985—, Mus. Nebr. Arts. Recipient painting award Audubon Artists Inc., 1960, 61, 67, 79, Internat. Soc. Artists, 1978, Catherine Lorillard Wolfe Club, 1971, 73, 80, Nat. Art Club, 1972. Fellow Internat. Acad. Arts and Letters (life); mem. Pastel Soc. Am., Nat. Assn. Women Artists (painting award 1960, 76, 77, 79, 80), Artists Equity, Nat. Artists Profl. League, Audubon Artists, Internat. Soc. Artists. Address: RR 1 Box 4 Rm 109 Auburn NE 68305-1722

BIGGS, ANTOINETTE BAILEY, real estate broker; b. Rhinebeck, N.Y., May 24, 1936; d. Donald Cheney and Felicita Mercedes (Rivera) Bailey; m. Robert Laney Bush, June 5, 1955 (div. Mar. 1971); children: Denise Lee Bailey McLeod, Lisa Anne Mooney, Amy Suzanne Curry, Patrick Laney Bush; m. Hubbard Kavanaugh Biggs, June 27, 1973. AA with honors, Polk C.C., Winter Haven, Fla., 1992; BA in Interpersonal Comm. cum laude, U. Ctrl. Fla., 1994; matriculated, Thomas M. Cooley Law Sch., 1995—. Cert. real estate brokerage mgr., real estate specialist. Legal sec. Fagan & Crouch, Attys., Gainesville, Fla., 1953-61; real estate salesperson Huskey Realty, Realtors, Maitland, Fla., 1968-70, Roberts & Gilman, Realtors, Maitland, 1970-73; real estate broker Hubbard K. Biggs, Realtor, Lake Wales, Fla., 1973-74; pres. Biggs Appraisal & Realty, Inc., Winter Haven, 1974-95, Biggs & Biggs, Inc., Winter Haven, fla., 1974—; pres. Lake Wales Bd. of Realtors, 1983, 84, also multiple chairmanships; edn. chmn. Winter Haven Bd. of Realtors, 1974, 81. mem. real estate adv. com. Polk C. C., 1980-93. Recipient Excellence in Ed. awards Winter Haven Bd. Realtors, 1974, 75, 76, 77, 81, 82, Realtor of Yr. award, 1984. Mem. DAR, Nat. Assn. Realtors, Lake Wales Bd. Realtors, Women's Coun. Realtors (v.p. 1980-81), Winter Haven Bd. Realtors, Phi Theta Kappa, Phi Kappa Phi, Golden Key Nat. Honor Soc. (pres. U. Ctrl. Fla. chpt. 1993-94). Republican. Roman Catholic. Home: 241 Volusia Dr Winter Haven FL 33884-1405 Office: Biggs & Biggs Inc Realtors 241 Volusia Drive Winter Haven FL 33884

BIGHAM, CECILIA BETH, communications and marketing professional; b. Harrisburg, Ark., May 13, 1956; d. Jimmy and Patsy Jean (Collins) B.; m. Jeffrey Stephen Yallope, Aug. 31, 1993. BA in Speech Comms., U. Ark., 1978. Editor, staff writer Holiday Inns, Memphis, 1981-84; project analyst Hi-Net Comm., Inc., Memphis, 1984-85; sr. tech. writer ground ops. worldwide policies/procedures Fed. Express Corp., Memphis, 1985—; freelance video prodr., talent scout Vin Di Bona Prodns., Inc., L.A., 1990-92; cons., joint founding mem. Milpara Computer Sys. Corp., Memphis, 1993—, also bd.dirs. Vol. Memphis-in-May, 1984-89; vol. fundraiser Am. Cancer Soc., 1988-91. Recipient Cert. of Appreciation, Am. Cancer Soc., 1990. Mem. NAFE, Soc. for Tech. Comm., Phi Kappa Phi. Republican. Methodist.

BIGHAM, WANDA RUTH, college president; b. Barlow, Ky., June 19, 1935; d. Herbert Martin and Ada Florene (Baker) Durrett; m. William M. Bigham, Jr., June 7, 1958; children: William M. III, Janet Kaye, Julia Lynn. BME, Murray State U., 1956; MM, Morehead State U., 1971, MHE, 1973; EdD, U. Ky., 1978; cert., Inst. For Ednl. Mgmt. -Harvard U., 1982; LittD (hon.), Loras Coll., 1989. Dir. TRIO programs Morehead (Ky.) State U., 1972-85, assoc. dean acad. affairs, dir. instructional sys., 1982-85, acting dean grad. and spl. acad. programs, 1984-85; exec. asst. to pres. Emerson Coll., Boston, 1985, v.p. for devel., 1986; pres. Marycrest Coll., Davenport, Iowa, 1986-92, Huntingdon Coll., Montgomery, Ala., 1993—. Bd. dirs. Ala. World Affairs Coun., Montgomery, 1994—, Montgomery Symphony Orch., 1993—, Ala. Shakespeare Festival, 1996—, NASCUMC, 1996—; exec. com. Ctrl. Ala. chpt. ARC, Montgomery, 1995; mem. Leadership Ala., 1994—; co-chair Quad Cities Vision for the Future, Davenport, 1987-92. Recipient Pres.'s award Davenport C. of C., 1988, Women of Spirit and Note award Cmty. Com. of Davenport, 1991, Hope for Humanity award Jewish Fedn. of Q1, Rock Island, Ill., 1993; named to Alumni Hall of Fame, Morehead Stae U., 1988, Disting. Alumna, Murray State Coll., 1988. Mem. Am. Coun. on Edn. (mem. coun. of fellows, bd. dirs. 1994—, fellow in higher edn. adminstrn. 1983-84), Internat. Assn. Univ. Pres., Montgomery C. of C., Sigma Alpha Iota (Sword of Honor 1956), Phi Kappa Phi, Kappa Delta Pi. Home: 1393 Woodley Rd Montgomery AL 36106 Office: Huntingdon College 1500 E Fairview Ave Montgomery AL 36106

BILANIUK, LARISSA TETIANA, neuroradiologist, educator; b. Ukraine, July 15, 1941; came to U.S., 1951; d. Yaroslav and Myroslava (Hryculak) Zubal; m. Oleksa-Myron Bilaniuk, Nov. 14, 1964; children: Larissa Indira, Laada Myroslava. BA, Wayne State U., 1961, MD, 1965. Diplomate Am. Bd. Radiology (cert. neuroradiology 1996). Resident in radiology Hosp. of U. Pa., Phila., 1966-70; fellow Fondation Ophtalmologique, Paris, 1972; assoc. in radiology U. Pa. Sch. Medicine, Phila., 1973-74, asst. prof., 1974-79, assoc. prof., 1979-82, prof., 1982—; with Children's Hosp. of Phila., 1992—; reviewer grants rsch. NIH, Washington, 1983-86, St. Goran lectr. Karolinska Inst., Stockholm, 1984; vis. prof. Grosshadern Clinics, U. Munich, 1988, Inst. Med. Radiology, Kharkiv, Ukraine, 1996; invited lectr. USSR, 1976, 90, People's Republic China, 1977, France, 1980, 82, 89, 94, 96, Japan, 1984, 90, Swden, 1984, 92, Eng., 1985, The Netherlands, 1985, Italy, 1986, 87, 90, 92, Germany, 1987, 95, Chile, 1993, Australia, 1995. Co-editor 3 radiology books; contbr. over 200 articles on radiology to med. jours. and chpts. to books. Rsch. fellow Cancer Rsch. Ctr., Heidelberg, Fed. Republic Germany, 1967-68. Fellow Am. Coll. Radiology; mem. Radiol. Soc. N.Am., Am. Soc. Neuroradiology, European Soc. Neuroradiology, Soc. for Pediatric Radiology, Soc. Magnetic Resonance in Medicine, Ukrainian Med. Assn. N.Am., Sigma Xi. Office: Childrens Hosp of Phila 324 S 34th St Philadelphia PA 19104-4345

BILBO, LINDA SUE HOLSTON, home health nurse; b. Poplarville, Miss., Mar. 20, 1955; d. Theo Gilmore Sr. and Dimple Bernice (Loveless) Holston; divorced; 1 child, Emily LeNore. Diploma, St. Dominic Sch. Nursing, 1976; postgrad., William Carey Coll., 1993—. RN, Miss., La. RN staff nurse med.-surg. Bogalusa (La.) Med. Ctr., 1976-78, Lakeside Hosp., Metairie, La., 1978-80; RN staff nurse ICU/CCU Jo Ellen Smith Hosp., New Orleans, 1980-81; RN staff nurse surgery West Jefferson Hosp., Marrero, La., 1981-82; RN staff nurse home health South Miss. Home Health, Hattiesburg, 1982—; instr. BLS Am. Heart, Miss. Children's Sun. Sch. tchr. 1st Bapt. Ch., 1990-95; active PTA, Poplarville, Miss. 1985-95, Poplarville Band Booster, 1991-95. Named Nat. Essay Contest winner Am. Jour. Nursing, 1993, 94. Mem. Miss. Nurses Assn. Home: PO Box 294 Poplarville MS 39470-0294 Office: South Miss Home Health PO Box 16929 Hattiesburg MS 39404-6929

BILDER, DOROTHEA, artist, educator; b. Dayton, Ohio, Oct. 4, 1940; d. Angelo Konstantine and Lelica Joannides Bilder. BFA, Ill. Wesleyan U., Bloomington, 1962; MFA, So. Ill. U., Carbondale, 1964; student, Sch. of Art Inst. Chgo., 1963, Sch. Art, Terni, Italy, 1967. Grad. teaching asst. So. Ill. U., 1962-64; instr. painting Adult Evening Sch., Oak Park, Ill., 1965-68; tchr. J.S. Morton West H.S. and Jr. Coll., 1964-68; prof. art No. Ill. U., DeKalb, 1968—; artist-in-residence, vis. artist various locales. Exhibited in numerous shows including Foster Gallery, Fine Arts Ctr., U. Wis., Eau Claire, 1995, Tarleton State U. Gallery of Art, Stephenville, Tex., 1995, Freeport Art Mus. and Cultural Ctr., 1995, 4th World Conf. on Women, Beijing, 1995, Nat. Mus. of Women in the Arts, Washington, 1995, George A. Spiva Ctr. for the Arts, Joplin, Mo., 1995, Trenton (Ill.) State Coll., 1995; works included in permanent collections of State of Ill., Citibank, Winnetka, Ill., Columbia Coll./Mo. Arts Coun., Valdosta State Coll., Ctrl. Queensland U., Rockhampton, Queensland, Australia, Quincy (Ill.) Art Ctr., U. Wis., Eau Claire. Mem. AAUW, Fla. Artists Alliance, So. Graphics Coun., The Print Consortium. Internat. Monoprinters Guild, Chgo. Women's Caucus for Art, Alpha, Coll. Art Assn., Arts club of Chgo., Ptnrs. of the Ams., The Print Club, Coll. Art Assn. Am., Mid Am. Coll. Art Assn., Graphics Soc., Delta Phi Delta, others. Home: 2707 Greenwood Acres Dr De Kalb IL 60115

BILDERBACK, CAROLYN, choreographer, performer, dance educator; b. Portland, Oreg., May 11, 1915; d. Joseph Brown and Carolyn (Leete) B. BA, Reed Coll., 1938; postgrad., San Francisco State Coll., 1939-41. Performing mem. Katherine Litz Dance Co., N.Y.C., 1950-53; dir. Carolyn Bilderback Dance Theaater, N.Y.C., 1967—; mem. faculty Manhattan Sch. Music, N.Y.C., 1965-82; workshop leader Am. Dance Festival, Duke U., Durham, N.C., 1974, Internat. Women's Writing Guild, N.Y.C., 1987; resident The Strong Dance Fund, Emma Willard Sch., Troy, N.Y., 1978; resident centennial edn. program U. Nebr., Lincoln, winter 1979; co-designer, tchr. workshop Hollyhock Holistic Learning Ctr., Cortes Island, B.C., Can., 1994; adj. prof. movement and dance Union Theol. Sem., N.Y.C., 1960—, guest instr. fantasy and religious experience, 1988; choreographer operas Aspen (Colo.) Music Festival, summers 1956-58; choreographer, dancer Cauldron Prodns., N.Y.C., 1992. Author: Gatherings from a Dancer's Journal, 1992; choreographer Fragments and Observaations, 1969; choreographer, prodr. solo dance concert, 1990, 95; dir., prodr. film From the Inside Out, 1969. Grantee Mary Reynolds Babcock Found., 1969. Fellow Am. Dance Guild; mem. NOW. Home: 26 Grove St Apt 5C New York NY 10014

BILES, MARILYN MARTA, painter; b. Wilmington, Del., Oct. 3, 1935; d. Albert Humbert and Anne Marie (DeRogatis) Marta; m. George Ronald Bower, June 30, 1956 (div. May 1970); children: Michele Bower Alvarado, Nancy Bower Guthrie, Randall William. Student Moore Coll. Art, 1953-54, St. Mary's Coll., 1959-61, Mus. Fine Arts, Houston, 1972-74. Art tchr. Contemporary Arts Mus., Houston, 1969-73, 80-81; head art dept. pre-primary div. Duchesne Acad., Houston, 1970-72; project coord. Nan Fisher, Inc., Houston, 1983-84; one-woman shows include Brown & Scurlock Galleries, Beaumont, Tex., 1st Nat. City Bank, Houston, 1980, Christ Ch. Cathedral, 1981-82, Toni Jones Gallery, 1981, U. Houston, 1982, Station Gallery, Greenville, Del., 1984, Boyar Norton & Blair, 1986, Martha Turner Properties, 1986, Cancerfighters of Houston, 1991, R.S.V.P. Collection, Miami, Fla., 1993, Chateaux Piada, Bordeaux, France, 1993, Musée de la Commanderie d'Unet, Bordeaux, 1993, 1994, San Felipe Plz., Houston, 1996; group shows include: U. Houston, 1977, 79, Nat. Cape Coral Exhbn., Fla., 1979, Toni Jones Gallery, 1979, Assistance League of Houston, 1979, 80, Golden Crescent Gallery, Houston, 1984, Conrad Gallery, Galveston, Tex. 1991, Pima Coll. Tucson, La Sorbonne, Paris, 1992, Musée de la Commanderie d'Unet, Bordeaux, 1992, Spirit Echoes Gallery Invitational, Austin Tex., 1992, 2nd anniversary show, 1994, Hotel de Ville, Paris, 1993, Wirtz Gallery, Miami, Fla., 1993, New England Fine Arts Inst., Boston, 1993, Spirit Echoes Gallery, Austin, Tex., 1994; coord., designer art programs Spring Branch Schs., Houston, 1968-70; coord. art exhibits St. John the Divine Episcopal Ch., Houston. Bd. dirs. Spring Branch YWCA, Houston, 1973-74; docent Harris County Heritage Soc., Houston, 1970-72; mem. bd., v.p. Arcs Found., Inc., Houston, 1983; bd. dirs., gala chmn. Houston Grand Opera Guild, 1983-84, governing bd. assn., 1984-85, co-chmn. gala, 1985; founder, pres. Mus. Med. Sci. Assn., Houston, 1986-87; mem. com. Can-Do-It Charity Fundraiser, Peter W. Guenther Art History Scholarship Fund at U. Houston. Mem. Artists Equity (dir. Houston chpt. 1980), Art League Houston, Tex. Fine Arts Assn., Univ. Club Houston, Houston Racquet Club, World Trade Club (v.p. women's assn. 1974-75). Republican. Episcopalian. Home: 9337 Katy Fwy Ste 171 Houston TX 77024-1515

BILITER, EVELYN ROSE, elementary education educator; b. Williamson, W.Va., Mar. 18, 1956; d. Marvin Rascoe Sr. and Matilda (Lambert) B. BS, Pikeville (Ky.) Coll., 1981; postgrad., Morehead State U., 1984—. Cert. elem. tchr., Ky. Tchr.'s aide Pike County Bd. of Edn., Majestic, Ky., 1974-81; tchr. Pike County Sch Sys., Majestic, 1981—. Mem. NEA, Ky. Edn. Assn. Republican. Presbyterian. Office: Majestic Knox Creek Sch PO Box 199 Majestic KY 41547-0199

BILL, SUSAN, violist; b. Portland, Maine, Oct. 15, 1954; d. Charles Rufus and Muriel Jean (Quinn) Brown; m. Robert George Bill, July 13, 1985; children: Samuel Charles, George Arthur, Timothy Winston. BS, U. Maine, 1976; MusM, Boston Conservatory, 1993. Violist Nat. Orchestral Assn., N.Y.C., 1985; prin. violist Cape Cod Symphony, Hyannis, Mass., 1986-93; violist numerous orchs., Mass., 1986-93; music tchr. Sacred Heart Sch., Quincy, Mass., 1990-93. Music dir. St. Chrysostom's Ch., Quincy, 1992—. Mem. Am. String Tchrs. Assn., Pi Beta Phi, Pi Kappa Lambda. Democrat. Episcopalian.

BILLAU, ROBIN LOUISE, engineering and consulting executive; b. Denver, Sept. 19, 1951; d. Emerson Roy and Catherine Louise (Brewster) Billau; m. Edward E. Adams. BA, Western State Coll., 1973; MS, Colo. State U., 1977. Cert. indsl. hygienist. Life sci., indsl. hygienist Mont. Energy Devel. & Rsch. Inst., Butte, 1977-79; indsl. hygiene supr. Mountain States Energy, Butte, 1979-81; asst. prof. Mont. Coll. Mineral Sci. Tech., Butte, 1981-83; indsl. hygiene supr. EG & G Idaho, Idaho Falls, 1983-85, unit mgr., 1985-87, group mgr., 1987-88, sr. tech. adv., 1988-90; cons. environ. mgmt., indsl. hygiene RLB Cons., Inc., Houghton, Mich., 1990-92; mgr. Jason Assocs. Corp., Idaho Falls, Idaho, 1992-94, Lockheed Martin Environ. Systems, Pocatello, Idaho, 1994-95; cons. environ. health and safety Bozeman, Mont., 1996—. Mem. Am. Indsl. Hygiene Assns., Am. Bd. Indsl. Hygiene Idaho Am. Indstl. Democrat. Home and Office: 174 Quinn Creek Rd Bozeman MT 59715-9635

BILLAUER, BARBARA PFEFFER, lawyer, educator; b. Aug. 9, 1951; d. Harry George and Evelyn (Newman) Pfeffer; BS with honors, Cornell U., 1972; JD, Hofstra U., 1975; MA, NYU, 1982. Bar: N.Y. 1976, Fed. Dist. Ct. N.Y., 1977, U.S. Ct. Appeals (2d cir.) 1978, U.S. Supreme Ct. 1984; assoc. firm Bower & Gardner, N.Y.C., 1974-78; sr. trial atty. Joseph W. Conklin, N.Y.C., 1978-80; assoc. dept. head Curtis, Mallet-Prevost, Colt & Mosle, N.Y.C., 1980-82; ptnr. Anderson, Russell, Kill & Olick, N.Y.C., 1982-86, Stroock & Stroock & Lavan, N.Y.C., 1986-90; ptnr., chair environ. and toxic tort practice Keck, Mahin, Cate & Koether, 1990-93; prin. Barbara P. Billauer & Assocs., Lido Beach, N.Y., 1993—; adj. assoc. prof. NYU Grad. Sch., 1982-88; lectr. Rutger's U. Med. Sch.; adminstrv. law judge N.Y.C. Dept. Transp., 1981-84; mem. jud. screening com. Coordinated Bar Assn., 1983-86; mem. Bronx County jud. screening panel, spl panel Citywide Ct. Adminstrn. 1982-85, Hebrew Acad. Nassau County, 1990—, Am. Com. for Shenkar Coll.; bd. dirs. Weizmann Inst., Am. Com. 1987—. Co-author: The Lender's Guide to Environmental Law: Risk and Liability, 1993. Fellow Am. Bar Found. (indoor air polution, comml. leasing sect. 1990-93); mem.

ABA, L.I. Bar Assn. (mem. environ. energy com. 1994—), Met. Women's Bar Assn. (v.p. 1981-83, pres. 1983-85, chmn. bd. 1985-87), Nat. Conf. Womens Bar Assn. (bd. dirs., v.p. 1989—), Internat. Coun. Shopping Ctrs. (mem. environ. com.), N.Y. State Bar Assn., Nat. Assn. Bar Pres., Am. Soc. Law and Medicine, Network of Bar Leaders State of N.Y. and City of N.Y., Assn. of Bar of City of N.Y. (products liability com. 1983-86, sex and the law com. 1986-89), Am. Soc. Microbiology, Am. Arbitration Assn., Brit. Occupational Hygiene Soc., N.Y. Acad. Scis., AAUW, AAAS, Am. Soc. Safety Engrs. Office: Barbara P Billauer & Assocs 146 Eva Dr Lido Beach NY 11561-4818

BILLER, GERALDINE POLLACK, curator; b. Milw., Apr. 4, 1933; d. Sidney Samuel and Frieda (Eisenberg) Pollack; m. Joel Wilson Biller, May 1, 1955; children: Sydney Ellen, Andrew John, Charles Benjamin. BS, Northwestern U., 1955; MA, U. Wis., 1991. Tchr. art Va. Sch. System, 1955-56, Internat. Sch., The Hague, The Netherlands, 1959-62; adminstr. internat. rels. program Georgetown U., Washington, 1973-75; freelance graphic designer Washington, Milw., 1978-86; art historian, curator Milw. Art Mus., 1988—. Mem. Wis. State Dem. Adminstrv. Com., 1992-93; v.p. women's divsn. cmty. planning com. Milw. Jewish Fedn., 1986-90; pres. bd. dirs. Jewish Family Svcs., Milw., 1991-94. Home: 4716 N Wilshire Rd Milwaukee WI 53211-1262

BILLETER, BEVERLY J., elementary education educator; b. Corpus Christi, Tex., June 3, 1947; d. Bob D. and Elvera Florence (Pica) Hoover; m. Keith R. Billeter, Febr. 7, 1970; children: Brian, Todd. BA, Calif. State U., Chico, 1969. Cert. tchr., 1970. Tchr. Santa Ana (Calif.) Unified Sch. Dist., 1970-71, New Haven Unified Sch. Dist., Union City, Calif., 1972-75, San Jose (Calif.) Unified Sch. Dist., 1985—; mem. Leadership Team A. Darling Sch., San Jose, 1991-92; rep. San Jose Tchrs. Assn., 1992-94. Co-author: children's liturgies, 1981-84. Mem. AAUW (legis. chair 1991-92). Republican. Roman Catholic. Office: San Jose Unified Sch Dist Lenzan Ave San Jose CA 95118

BILLETER, MARIANNE, pharmacy educator; b. Durham, N.C., Feb. 28, 1963; d. Ralph Leonard and Nancy Jane (Chambers) B. BS in Pharmacy, Purdue U., 1986, PharmD, 1987. Cert. pharmacotherapy specialist. Pharmacy extern Commd. Officer Student Tng. and Extern Program, USPHS-FDA, Rockville, Md., 1983; radiopharmacy extern Commd. Officer Student Tng. and Extern Program, USPHS-NIH, Bethesda, Md., 1984; pharmacy extern Indian Health Svc. Commd. Officer Student Tng. and Extern Program, USPHS, Tahlequah, Okla., 1985; pharmacist Beaumont Hosp., Royal Oak, Mich., 1986; pharmacy resident U. Ky., Lexington, 1987-89, fellow in infectious diseases, 1989-90; asst. prof. Xavier Univ. of L.A., New Orleans, 1990—; relief pharmacist Ochsner Med. Instns., New Orleans, 1991-96; cons. Abbott Labs., Abbott Park, Ill., 1991—. Contbr. chpts. to books and articles to profl. jours. Mem. Am. Assn. Colls. Pharmacy, Am. Coll. Clin. Pharmacy, Am. Soc. Health-Sys. Pharmacists, La. Soc. Pharmacists, Soc. Infectious Diseases Pharmacists (bd. dirs.), Am. Soc. Microbiology. Office: Xavier Coll Pharmacy 7325 Palmetto St New Orleans LA 70125-1056

BILLINGS, BECKY LEIGH, nurse; b. Provo, Utah, Aug. 19, 1964; d. Laird Dean and Helen Virginia (Jack) B. Orem high sch., Utah, 1982; Cert. Lic. Practical Nurs, Utah Tech. Coll., Provo, 1985. Lic. practical nurse, Nebr., Utah. On call-practical nurse Utah Valley regional Med. Ctr., Provo, 1985-86, staff nurse, 1986; head nurse Westside Care Home, Lexington, Nebr., 1987; case coord. Universal Home Care, Lexington, Nebr., 1988; staff nurse chem. dependancy unit Richard Young Hosp., Kearney, Nebr., 1989-91; staff nurse cardiac unit Good Samaritan Hosp., Kearney, Nebr., 1991, North Suburban Med. Ctr., Denver, 1992-93; office nurse, pediatrics, 1994—. Vol. Co-Therapeutic Riding Ctr. Handicapped Children. Home: PO Box 576 Louisville CO 80027

BILLINGS, JUDITH A., state education official. Supt. public instrn. State of Washington, 1988—. Office: Public Instruction Dept PO Box 47200 Olympia WA 98504-7200*

BILLINGS, LETHA MARGUERITE, nurse; b. Navina, Okla., June 27, 1909; d. Edgar Hubert and Blanche Edith (Hubbard) Ladner; m. Carroll Humphrey, Aug. 15, 1928 (div. 1931); m. Ralph Melvin Billings, May 19, 1935 (dec. 1981); children: William Edgar, Betty Luella (dec.). Diploma, Okla. Meth. Hosp., Guthrie, Okla., 1929; student, Chgo. Lying-in Hosp., 1931-32, Cook County Hosp., Chgo., 1932. RN, Okla., Calif. Pvt. duty nurse Guthrie Hosp., Wesley Hosp., Oklahoma City, 1930-31; sch. nurse Logan County Schs. and Guthrie Schs., 1932-33; FERA adminstr. Logan County FERA, 1933-35; sch. nurse Guthrie Schs., 1936-38; night supr., mem. obstet. staff Mercy Hosp., Bakersfield, Calif., 1941-44; instr., trainer Home Care, ARC, Woodward, Okla., 1949-55; co-owner Billings Advt. Assn., Woodward, 1950-75; cons. Woodard Nursing Ctr., 1989-91; supr. Woodward Meml. Hosp. and Health Ctr., 1952-84; local coord., long term care Am. Assn. Ret. Persons, Woodward, 1991—. Chmn. Christian Women's Fellowship, First Christian Ch., 1952. del., 1995; del. Rep. County Assn. Wooodward, 1991, White House Conf. on Aging, 1995; mem. Silver Haired Legislature form Dist. 11, Oklahoma City, 1988-92, mem. exec. com., 1990-92; mem. Okla. Health Planning Com., 1969-70; pres. adv. bd. Nutrition Coun.; health advocate, local coord. and long term care State Am. Assn. Retired Persons; mem. Okla. nursing com. ARC; mem. adv. coun. Area Agy. on Aging; vol. Sr. Ctr. Woodward. Named Outstanding Older Oklahoman State Conf. on Aging, 1993. Mem. ANA (econ. and gen. welfare com. 1958-61, study of functions com. 1962-64, chmn. nominating com. 1972, exec. com. pvt. duty sect. 1988-92), Okla. Nurses Assn. (pres. 1958, Nurse of Yr. 1959), Okla. Dist. 18 Nurses Assn., Okla. Fedn. Women's Clubs (past pres. 3rd dist., edn. chmn., health chmn. 1994), Okla. Congress Parents and Tchrs. (pres. 1964-67), PTA (nat., state life mem.), Order Ea. Star (treas., past matron), PEO (chpt. sec.), Ladies Elks. Home and Office: 1419 Hillcrest Dr Woodward OK 73801-4339

BILLINGS, PATRICIA ANN COLLINS, nurse practitioner; b. San Diego, Jan. 31, 1946; d. Normon Clyde and Mary Asunda (Fantoni) Collins; m. George M. Whitehead, June 12, 1966 (div. Mar. 1975); children: Garrett Grafton Rayne, Sharna Raynel, Adrianna Megan, Autumn Leigh; m. Russell F. Billings II, Aug. 19, 1989. BS in Nursing, Loma Linda (Calif.) U., 1967, MPH, 1971; cert. Pediatric Nurse Practitioner, U. Calif, San Diego, 1979. RN, Calif., Idaho; cert. nurse practitioner, Idaho, Calif. Pub. health nurse San Bernadino County, Calif., 1967-72, San Diego County, 1974; sch. nurse, pediatric nurse practitioner Vista (Calif.) Unified Sch. Dist., 1974-85; pediatric nurse practitioner Sharp Rees-Stealy Med. Group, San Diego, 1985-94; pediatric nurse practitioners Pediatric Ctr., Twin Falls, Idaho, 1994—. Contbg. editor Pediatric Nursing, 1994—. mem. Pres.'s Coun., San Diego, 1984-85; bd. dirs. Idahoans Concerned With Adolescent Pregnancy, 1995—. Recipient USPHS scholarship, 1971. Fellow Nat. Assn. Pediatric Nurse Practitioners (cert. chmn. 1987-93); mem. Am. Acad. Pediats. (mem. Idaho chpt.), San Diego Assn. Pediatric Nurse Practitioners (legis. chair 1993-94, editor pedits. nursing assessment 1995—, 1993 Pediatric Nurse Practitioner of Yr.). Republican. Office: Pediatric Ctr 388 Martin St Twin Falls ID 83301-4544

BILLINGSLEY, FLORENCE ILONA, nurse, case manager; b. Detroit, Dec. 27, 1943; d. John and Doris Fannie (Crieghton) B. LPN, Detroit Practical Nursing Ctr., 1963; ADN, Highland Pk. Cmty. Coll., 1973; BSN, Wayne State U., 1983. RN, Mich.; diplomate Am. Bd. Quality Assurance and Utilization Rev. Physicians; cert. case mgr. Nurse preceptor, staff nurse, charge nurse Harper Hosp., Detroit, 1964-76; pub. health nurse Detroit Health Dept., 1976-86; discharge planning coord. Detroit Receiving Hosp., 1985-86; clin. svcs. mgr. Med. Ctr. Healthcare, Detroit, 1985-88; spl. instr. JTPA Sch. Practical Nursing, Detroit, 1988-89; case mgr. AIDS Consortium of S.E. Mich., Detroit, 1989-90; liaison nurse Renaissance Home Health Care, Oak Park, Mich., 1990-91; alternative health svcs. case mgr. United Am. Healthcare Corp., Detroit, 1991-95; disability mgr. Aetna Ins. Co., Warren, Mich., 1995—. Vol. for breast and prostate screening programs Mich. Cancer Found., Detroit, 1992—; hospice vol. Hospice of Mich., Detroit, 1993—. Recipient Minority Nurse grant for Grad. Studies in Cmty. Health Nursing, State of Mich., 1989-90. Mem. Mich. Nurses Assn. (del. to conv. 1994-95), Citizens for Better Care, Breast Cancer Resource Task Force, Wayne State U. Alumni Assn., Chi Eta Phi Lambda Chi. Office: Aetna Ins Co 6565 E Eight Mile Rd Warren MI 48091

BILLITER, FREDA DELOROUS, elementary education educator; b. McAndrews, Ky., Oct. 15, 1937; d. David Wilson and Evalyn May (Puckett) Kendrick; m. William Jefferson Billiter, Sept. 12, 1954; 1 child, Cynthia Delorous. BS in Edn., Ohio U., 1969, MEd, 1987. Cert. elem. tchr., media specialist, reading specialist. Departmental tchr. Ironton (Ohio) City Schs., 1965-66, 3d grade tchr., 1966-67; 2d grade tchr. Portsmouth (Ohio) City Schs., 1969—. Coord. sec. Scioto County Hist. Soc., Portsmouth, 1980-82; choir mem. Shawnee State U. and Cmty. Choir, Portsmouth, 1973—, Wesley United Meth. Ch. Chancel Choir, Portsmouth, 1985—, Portsmouth Cmty. Chorale, 1993—; mem. Scioto County Hist. Soc. and Nat. Trust. Martha Holden Jennings scholar Ohio U., 1988-89; recipient Cert. of Participation, Portsmouth Area Arts Coun., 1990. Mem. NEA, AAUW, Ohio Edn. Assn., Internat. Reading Assn., S.E. Ohio Coun. Tchrs. English, Scioto County Mus. and Cultural Ctr., Ohio Hist. Soc., Order Ea. Star, Phi Delta Kappa (awards chmn. 1990-91, 94-95), Delta Kappa Gamma (1st v.p. 1990-92, pres. 1992-94), Ohio Bus. and Profl. Women, Kappa Delta Pi (svc. award 1986). Republican. Home: 2890 Circle Dr Portsmouth OH 45662-2445 Office: Wilson Elem Sch 613 Campbell Ave Portsmouth OH 45662-4468

BINDER, AMY FINN, public relations company executive; b. N.Y.C., June 13, 1955; d. David and Laura (Zeisler) Finn; children: Ethan Max, Adam Finn, Rebecca Eve. BA with honors, Brown U., 1977. Freelance photographer N.Y.C., 1977-78; account exec. Newton & Nicolazza, Boston, 1978-79, Agnew, Carter, McCarthy, Boston, 1979-80; dir. pub. relations City of New Rochelle, N.Y., 1980-82; dir. urban communications Ruder-Finn, N.Y.C., 1982-85, v.p., 1985-86, exec. v.p., 1986-87, pres., 1987—. Photographer: Museum without Walls, 1975, The Spirit of Man: Sculpture of Kaare Nygaard, 1975, Knife Life and Bronzes, 1977, St. Louis: Sculpture City, 1988, The Triumph of the American Spirit: Johnstown, Pennsylvania, 1989. Mem. Internat. Ctr. of Photography (mem. pres. coun.), Pres. Assn. of Am. Mgmt. Assn. Democrat. Jewish. *

BINDER, ELAINE KOTELL, consultant to associations; b. Boston, Oct. 12, 1938; d. Maxwell and Florence (Blumsack) Kotell; m. Richard A. Binder, Aug. 28, 1960; children: Mark Stephen, Jonathan Stuart. AB, Radcliffe Coll., 1960; MA, U. Md., 1975. Tchr. City of Medford, Mass., 1960-62; project dir. Wider Opportunities for Women, Washington, 1971-75, Women's Equity Action League Fund, Washington, 1976-78; mng. ptnr. Binder, Elster, Mendelson, Wheeler, Bethesda, Md., 1978-80; adminstrn. dir. AAUW, Washington, 1980-85; exec. dir. B'nai B'rith Women, Washington, 1985-94; pres. Binder Assocs., Bethesda, 1994—; sr. ptnr. Tecker Consultants, Trenton, N.J., 1994—; cons. Bethesda, 1975-76. Co-author: Careers for Peers, 1973; contbr. articles to profl. jours. Trustee Temple Shalom, Silver Spring, Md., 1974-76; pres., v.p. Montgomery County Commn. for Women, Rockville, Md., 1978-80; commr. Anti-Defamation League, N.Y., 1985—; bd. dirs. Jewish Coun. for the Aging, 1996—. Fellow Am. Soc. Assn. Execs. (bd. dirs. 1990-93, vice chmn. 1994), Greater Washington Soc. Assn. Execs. (com. chair 1989—). Democrat. Jewish. Office: Tecker Consultants 427 River View Exec Park Trenton NJ 08611 Office: Binder Assocs 6704 Bradley Blvd Bethesda MD 20817

BINDER, ELLEN, photographer; b. N.Y.C., Jan. 2, 1960; d. David and Muriel (Reinitz) B. BA cum laude, Smith Coll., 1982. Mem. profl. adv. bd. Harriman Inst., Columbia U., N.Y.C., 1996, vis. scholar, 1993; guest lectr. NYU Internat. Ctr. Photography, Sch. Visual Arts, New Sch. for Social Rsch. Photographer numerous publs. including N.Y. Times Mag., N.Y. Mag., L.A. Times Mag., Elle Mag. (Eng. and Japan), Harper's Bazaar, Stern Mag. (Germany), Observer Sunday Mag. (Eng.), Mirabella Mag., Mother Jones Mag., Metropolis, Guardian Mag. (Eng.); book illustration for Penguin Group; photographer various newspapers including N.Y. Times-Weekly in Rev., Village Voice, Dallas Morning News, Times, Guardian, Observer (London), El Pais (Spain), John Fairfax Ltd. (Australia); group exhbns. include Fotofest, Houston, 1990, Gallery at Hastings-on-Hudson, N.Y.C., 1992, Fotofestival Naarden, The Netherlands, 1995. Recipient 1st place Mag. Picture Story Pictures of Yr., Nat. Press Photographer's Assn., 1993, grant W. Eugene Smith Meml. Fund, 1994; photographer profile Photo Dist. News, 1995. Mem. Profl. Adv. Bd., Harriman Inst., Columbia U., N.Y.C., 1996.

BINDER, MADELINE DOTTI, counselor; b. Chgo., Oct. 7, 1942; d. Martin and Anne (Sweet) Binder; children: Mark Nathan, Marla Susan. BEd, Nat. Coll. Edn., 1964, MS, 1972, MS in Human Svcs.-Counseling, 1993. Tchr., Rochester Schs. (Minn.), 1963-64, Orange County Schs., Orlando, Fla., 1967-68; reading cons. Palatine Schs. (Ill.), 1972-73; instr. Parent Effective Tng., Wilmette, Ill., 1974-76, tchr. Effectiveness Tng., 1974-76; pres. Profls. Diversified, Wilmette, Ill., 1976-89; remedial and enrichment reading tchr. Waukegan (Ill.) Pub. Schs., 1986; pres. Lifeline, 1989-90; mgmt. cons. World Wide Diamonds Assn., Schaumburg, Ill., 1979-89, Artistic Color, Dallas, 1983-87; Pearl direct distbr. Amway Corp., Ada, Mich., 1976-94; exec. distbr. NU Skin, 1992; distbr. Emerald-Starlight Internat., 1994—; psychotherapist, 1993—. Author: Organic Gardening, 1975, The Go-Getters Planner, 1986, Singles Guide to Chicagoland, 1995. Leader, Camp Fire Girls, Evanston, Ill., 1963, 75. Recipient Ednl. Scholarship, Nat. Coll. Edn., 1971. Mem. Phi Delta Kappa, Alpha Delta Omega. Jewish.

BINDER, MILDRED KATHERINE, retired county public welfare agency executive; b. York, Pa., Jan. 5, 1918; d. Jemie Irving and Emma Jane (Billet) Binder. BA magna cum laude in Sociology, Hood Coll., 1940. Sec., mgr. Stock's Appliances, York, 1940-42; caseworker York County Bd. Assistance, Pa. Dept. Public Welfare, 1942-49, 1953-58, supr., 1949-53, 1958-59, exec. dir., 1959-83. Past mem. exec. com. York County Employment and Tng. Com.; past mem. dept. task forces state Social Service Delivery to Client Info. System, also mem. state ops. rev. bd.; past mem. bd. York County Coun. Alcoholism, 1959-62, Cmty. Progress Coun., 1965-67; co-chmn. Cmty. Dialogue Com., 1968-69; mem. bd. Pre-Paid Health York, Inc., 1979; mem. human svcs. planning coalition United Way, 1978-83, chmn. coun. agy. execs., 1967-71, 1976-78; past mem. consumer adv. couns. Gen. Telephone, Met. Edison; bd. dirs. Literacy Council of York County, 1985-86; mem. York County Human Svcs. Adv. Com., 1983-87; mem. York County Area Agy. on Aging Adv. Com., 1989-95. Named Boss of Yr., Am. Bus. Women, 1973; named in commendations Pa. gov., Pa. Ho. of Reps. Mem. Am. Public Welfare Assn., AAUW (bd. dirs. York br. 1984-96), York County Hist. Soc. (bd. dirs. 1989—), York Transp. Club (bd. dirs. 1987-91), Coll. Club York (bd. dirs. 1994—), Hood Coll. Club (pres. 1993—). Home: 1611 W Market St York PA 17404-5416

BINGAMAN, ANNE K., lawyer; b. Jerome, Ariz., July 3, 1943; d. William Emil and Anne Ellen (Baker) Kovacovich; m. Jeff F. Bingaman, Sept. 14, 1968; 1 child, John. BA in History, Stanford U., 1965; gen. course cert. with honors, London Sch. of Econs., England, 1964-65; LLB, Stanford U., 1968. Bar: Calif. 1969, N.Mex. 1969, Ariz. 1969, U.S. Dist. Ct. D.C. 1983. Atty. Brown & Bain, Phoenix, 1968-69, N.Mex. Bur. Revenue, Santa Fe, 1969-70, Modrall, Sperling, Roehl, Harris & Sisk, Albuquerque, 1970, N.Mex. Atty. Gen's. Office, Santa Fe, 1970-72; asst. prof. to assoc. prof. U. N.Mex. Sch. Law, Santa Fe, 1972-76; founding ptnr. Bingaman & Davenport, Santa Fe, 1977-82; ptnr. Brown, Bain & Bingaman, Santa Fe and Washington, 1982-84, Onek, Klein & Farr, Washington, 1984-85, Powell, Goldstein, Frazer & Murphy, Washington, 1985-93; asst. atty. gen. Anti-Trust Div. U.S. Dept. Justice, Washington, D.C., 1993—. Contbr. articles to profl. jours. Mem. exec. com. Stanford Law Sch. Bd. Visitors, 1978-80, 88-90; mem. for N.Mex. of 10th Cir. Jud. Nominating Panel, 1977-80. Ford Found. fellow 1975; recipient Nat. Vol. award Stanford Assocs., 1989. Fellow Am. Bar Found.; mem. ABA, N.Mex. Bar (founder, vice-chair antitrust sect. 1982-85, chair com. to rewrite comm. property & other state laws to conform to ERA), Am. Law Inst. Democrat. Episcopalian. Office: US Dept Justice Antitrust Div 10th & Constitution Ave NW Washington DC 20530

BINGHAM, JINSIE SCOTT, broadcast company executive; b. Greencastle, Ind., Dec. 28, 1935; d. Roscoe Gibson and Alpha Edith (Robinson) Scott; m. Frank William Wokoun, Jr. (dec.); children: Douglas Scott, Richard Frank; m. Richard Innes Bingham, June 24, 1964. Student, DePauw U., Greencastle, 1952-53, Northwestern U., 1953, Coe Coll., 1953-54. Exec. sec. Ind. Young Dems., 1958-60; receptionist Ind. House of Reps., Indpls., 1959; saleslady Avon Products, Greencastle, 1961-64; sales mgr. Sta. WJNZ (formerly WXTA), Greencastle, 1969-77, owner, pres., gen. mgr., 1977-94; owner Radio Greencastle, 1997—; former ptnr. Sta. WVTL, Monticello, Ill., Sta. KBIB, Monette, Ark.; speaker DePauw U. Comm. Seminar, 1981, 85; vis. lectr., 1986—. Com. chair Legis. Awareness Seminar, 1978-86; co-chair Greencastle Gaelic Festival, 1983-84; charter mem. Greencastle 2001, 1985—, Greencastle Civic League, 1984—, Greencastle Merchant's Assn., 1983—, Cmty. Resources Coun., 1982—; charter mem., corp. sec. Main St. Greencastle, 1983-87, v.p., 1987-88, pres., 1989-90, chmn., 1990-91; charter mem., bd. dirs. Greencastle Vol. Fire Dept., 1986, Greencastle Devel. Ctr., 1988-89, Greencastle Cmty. Child Care Ctr., 1983—, Putman County United Way, 1992—, campaign chair 1996; bd. dirs. Putnam County Comprehensive Ctr., 1994—; mem. Greencastle Zoning Bd. Appeals, 1984—, v.p., 1985-88, pres., 1988—; announcer Putnam County Fair Parade, 1977—; cmty. host Hoosier Hospitality Days, 1981-84; active Putnam County Com. for Econ. Strength, 1979-83; mem. Gov.'s Commn. for Drug Free Ind., 1992—, Putnam County Visions, 1992—, Greencastle Jaycees, 1981, Putnam County Found., 1992—, pres., 1996; v.p. Putnam County Hist. Soc. (pres. 1996); founding chmn. Greencastle Cmty. Schs. Scholarship Fund Drive, 1995—. Named Outstanding Citizen, Jaycees, 1981, Sagamore of the Wabash, Ind. Gov. Evan Bayh, 1995. Mem. Broadcast Pioneers (life), Putnam County Bd. Realtors, Am. Women in Radio and TV (pres. Ind. chpt. 1979-82), Indpls. Network Women in Bus. (charter), Women in Comm., Inc. (bd. dirs. 1983-84, MATRIX co-chair 1984, Frances Wright award, 1993), Am. Legion Aux., Nat. Assn. Broadcasters, Ind. Broadcasters Assn. (v.p. FM 1982), Greencastle Bus. and Profl. Women's Club (pres. 1976-77, 79-80, Woman of Yr. 1994), Indpls. Ad Club, Women's Press Club Ind., Indpls. Press Club, Nat. Fedn. Press Women, Ind. Dem. Editorial Assn. (sec. 1987, v.p. 1988, pres. 1990), Ind. C. of C., Greencastle C. of C. (bd. dirs. 1979-83, pres. 1982), VFW (pres. ladies aux. 1966-68), Ind. Geneal. Soc., Milestone Car Soc., Packard Club Ind., Ind. Soc. Pioneers, Daus. of 1812 (pres. Tippecanoe chpt. 1981, state v.p. 1982), DAR, Daughters of the Union, Soc. Descendants of Valley Forge, Rotary (bd. dirs., pres. 1994-95), Delta Theta Tau, Sigma Delta Chi, Soc. Profl. Journalist. Mem. Christian Ch. (Disciples of Christ). Club: Windy Hill Country. Lodges: Order Eastern Star, Internat. Order Job's Daus. (life), Women of Moose.

BINGHAM, JUNE, writer, playwright; b. White Plains, N.Y., June 20, 1919; d. Max J.H. and Mabel (Limburg) Rossbach; m. Jonathan B. Bingham, Sept. 20, 1939 (dec. July 1986); children: Sherry B. Downes, Micki B. Esselstyn, Timothy, Claudia B. Meyers; m. Robert B. Birge, Mar. 28, 1987; 1 stepchild, Robert R. Student, Vassar Coll., 1936-38; BA, Barnard Coll., 1940. Writer, editor U.S. Treasury, Washington, 1943-45; editorial asst. Washington Post, 1945-46; writer Tarrytown (N.Y.) Daily News, 1946. Author: Do Cows Have Neuroses?, Do Babies Have Worries?, Do Teenagers Have Wisdom?, Courage to Change: An Introduction to Life and Thought of Reinhold Niebuhr, 1961, paperback, 1992, U Thant: The Search for Peace, 1970, (play) Triangles, 1986, You and the I.C.U., 1990, Eleanor and Alice, 1996, (with others) The Inside Story: Psychiatry and Everyday Life, 1953, The Pursuit of Health, 1985, (musical) Squanto and Love, 1992, Young Roosevelts, 1993, The Other Lincoln, 1995; contbr. articles to nat. mags., newspapers and profl. jours. Bd. dirs. Barnard Coll., 1970-76, African-Am. Inst., N.Y.C., 1973-90, Riverdale Mental Health Assn., 1983—, Woodrow Wilson Found., Princeton, N.J., 1959-64, 83-89, Lehman Coll. Found., 1983-90, Ittleson Ctr. for Childhood Rsch., 1958-90; founder T.L.C.; trained liaison comforter Vol. Program of Presbyn. Hosp., N.Y.C. Named Alumna of the Yr., Rosemary Hall, 1976. Mem. Authors Guild (nominating com. 1987-90), Dramatists Guild, PEN, Cosmopolitan Club. Democrat. Home: 5000 Independence Ave Bronx NY 10471-2804

BINGHAM, SYLVIA JONES, fund raising professional; b. Northampton, Mass., Oct. 21, 1929; d. John Paul and Mildred (Woodward) Jones; m. George M. Rynick, June 7, 1949 (div. Aug. 1975); children: Stephen, David, Ellen Solt, Janet DePooter; m. Harry Souder Bingham, Jan. 1, 1980; children: Ronald, Gary, Timothy, Tamara. BA, Fairleigh Dickinson U., 1981. Devel. rschr., assoc. dir. instl. advancement George Sch., Newtown, Pa., 1975-80; dir. donor rels. Fairleigh Dickinson U., Rutherford, N.J., 1982-87; dir. planned giving Rider U., Lawrenceville, N.J., 1987-96. Founder, coord. Yardley (Pa.) Area Chronic Fatigue Syndrome Support Group. Mem. Princeton Area Planned Giving Group. Presbyterian.

BINION, GAYLE, political science educator; b. N.Y.C., Sept. 20, 1946; d. Samuel and Ruth (Brovich) B. BA, CCNY, 1967; MA, UCLA, 1969, PhD, 1977. Prof. polit. sci. U. Calif., Santa Barbara, 1976—, dir. Washington Ctr., 1994-96; exec. dir. ACLU of So. Calif., L.A., 1986-87; vis. asst. prof. San Diego State U., 1974-76; ethics hearing officer APA, Washignton, 1993—; USIA Internat. lectr., Bangladesh, Pakistan, Nepal, Sri Lanka, 1993. Contbr. chpt. to biog. dictionary, articles to profl. jours. Founding pres. Santa Barbara Women's Polit. Com., 1987-89. U. Calif. Humanities Faculty fellow, 1990, Interdisciplinary Humanities Ctr. grantee, 1991. Mem. Law and Society Assn. (trustee 1993-96), Am. Polit. Sci. Assn. (chair ethics com. 1989-92), Western Polit. Sci. Assn. (exec. com. 1981-83). Office: U Calif Dept Polit Sci Santa Barbara CA 93106

BINKLEY, YILDIZ BARLAS, library director; b. Istanbul, Turkey, Nov. 16, 1943; came to the U.S., 1967; d. Riza and Belkis (Balin) Barlas; m. Donald Hugh Binkley, Dec. 28, 1942. BLS, U. Ankara, Turkey, 1966; MLS, Vanderbilt U., 1971; EdD, Tenn. State U., 1994. Libr. Tenn. Mcpl. League, Nashville, 1970-71; REF, ACQ, SER libr., asst. dir. Tenn. State U., Nashville, 1971-89, dir. librs. MCS, 1989—. Recipient grant Nat. Sec. Ag., Nashville, 1992-94. Mem. Tenn. Libr. Assn. (chairperson membership com. 1984, chairperson nominations com. 1986), Southeastern Libr. Assn., Phi Delta Kappa (chpt. rschr.). Office: Tenn State Univ 3500 John A Merritt Blvd Nashville TN 37209-1561

BINKOWSKI, SYLVIA JULIA, executive assistant, consultant; b. Dearborn, Mich.; d. Steve S. and Cecelia Maria (Kwiatkowski) B. BS in Psychology and Comms., Ea. Mich. U., 1978. Sr. project coord. U.S. Treas. Dept., Detroit, 1979-83; sr. legis. asst. Congressman William D. Ford, Washington, 1983-91; head purchasing Decision Support Sys., McLean, Va., 1991-93; cons. The Eagle Cos., Annandale, Va., 1993-95; exex. asst., office mgr. Nat. Ports & Waterways Inst., Rosslyn, Va., 1995—; coord. U.S. Congress/German Bundestag Staff Exch. Program, 1989; cons. STC, London, 1992-93. Fund raiser Senatorial Campaign Com., 1984—, Congl. Campaign Com., 1984—; vol. Alexandria (Va.) Jaycees, 1988. Mem. Desiree Club/Four Seasons Hotel (membership com. 1994-96), House Legis. Asst. Assn. (founder, pres. emeritus, award 1989). Roman Catholic. Home: 6493 Frenchmens' Dr Ste 202 Alexandria VA 22312 Office: Nat Ports & Waterways Inst 1300 N 17th St Ste 310 Rosslyn VA 22209

BINKS, REBECCA ANNE, communications executive; b. Oak Park, Ill., July 23, 1955; d. Donald Melvin and Elizabeth June (Lobdell) B.; m. Cary Emmett Donham, June 22, 1980; 1 child, Samuel Joseph Donham. Student, Goodman Sch. Drama, Chgo., 1973-76; BA in Liberal Arts, Columbia Coll., Chgo., 1983; MS in Mktg. Comm., Roosevelt U., 1993. Freelance lighting designer, theater tech. Chgo., N.Y.C., 1975-80; retail mgr. Coffee and Tea Exch., Chgo., 1981-84; sales assoc. K&S Photographies, Chgo., 1984-87; supr. client services AGS&R Communications, Chgo., 1987-88; mgr. Meeting Express Systems, Chgo., 1988-90; pres. Binks & Assocs. Inc., Chgo., 1990-95; co-dir. Northside Parents Network, 1996—; mem. faculty mktg. comm. Columbia Coll., Chgo., 1992—; mem. faculty English Chgo. State U., 1995; tchr. travel photography, Chgo., 1987. Designer: (cookbook) Kitchen Angst, 1993; exhibited in group and one-woman shows. Mem. internal communications com. Girl Scouts, Chgo., 1989-91. Mem. NAFE, Chgo. Coun. on Fgn. Rels., Am. Mktg. Assn., Internat. Assn. Bus. Communications.

BINNICKER, MARGARET DUNCAN, history educator, editor; b. Nashville, Nov. 13, 1951; d. Thomas Edgar and Edith Rebecca (Hatchett) Duncan; m. Charles Mathews Binnicker Jr., Aug. 25, 1973. BA in History, U. of South, 1973; MA in Liberal Studies, Dartmouth Coll., 1989; postgrad., Mid. Tenn. State U., 1994—. Subscription mgr. The Sewanee (Tenn.) Rev., 1976-77; tchr., chair history faculty St. Andrew's (Tenn.)-Sewanee Sch., 1977-94, dir. coll. counseling, 1982-90; editl. asst. Tenn. Hist. Soc., 1995—; mem. curriculum task force for nat. history stds. in world history Nat. Ctr. for History in the Schs., L.A., 1993-94. Vol. in univ. archives U. of South,

Sewanee, 1994-95. DeWitt Wallace fellow in world history Woodrow Wilson Nat. Fellowship Found., 1991, TORCH tchr./fellow, 1992-95. Mem. Am. Hist. Assn., World History Assn., Am. Assn. State and Local History, Nat. Trust Hist. Preservation, Tenn. Classical Assn., Phi Alpha Theta, Kappa Alpha Theta (Beta Omega chpt.). Home: 82 Abbott Martin Ln Sewanee TN 37375 Office: Tenn Ency Project Mid Tenn State U PO Box 80 Murfreesboro TN 37132

BINNIE, NANCY CATHERINE, nurse, educator; b. Sioux Falls, S.D., Jan. 28, 1937; d. Edward Grant and Jessie May (Martini) Larkin; m. Charles H. Binnie. Diploma, St. Joseph's Hosp. Sch. Nursing, Phoenix, 1965; BS in Nursing, Ariz. State U., 1970, MA, 1974. Intensive care charge nurse Scottsdale (Ariz.) Meml. Hosp., 1968-70, coordinator critical care, 1970-71; coordinator critical care John C. Lincoln Hosp., Phoenix, 1971-73; prof. nursing GateWay Community Coll., Phoenix, 1974—; coord. part-time evening nursing programs Gateway Community Coll., 1984—, interim dir. nursing, 1989, 91. Mem. Orgn. Advancement of Assoc. Degree Nursing, Practical and Assoc. Coun. Nursing Educators, Ariz. Coun. Nurse Educators. Office: Gateway C C 104 N 40th St Phoenix AZ 85034-1704

BINSFELD, CONNIE BERUBE, lieutenant governor; b. Munising, Mich., Apr. 18, 1924; d. Omer J. and Elsie (Constance) Berube; B.S., Siena Heights Coll., 1945, D.H.L. (hon.), 1977; postgrad. Wayne State U., 1966-67; m. John E. Binsfeld, July 19, 1947; children—John T., Gregory, Susan, Paul, Michael. County commr., Leelanau County, Mich., 1970-74; mem. Mich. Ho. of Reps., 1974-82, asst. rep. leader, 1979-81; del. Nat. Conv., 1980, 88, 92; mem. Mich. Senate, 1982-90, asst. rep. leader, 1979, 81; lt. gov. State of Mich., 1990—. Mem. adv. bd. Nat. Park System. Named Mich. Mother of Year, Mich. Mothers Com., 1977; Northwestern Mich. Coll. fellow. Mem. Nat. Council State Legislators, LWV, Siena Heights Coll. Alumnae Assn. Republican. Roman Catholic. Home: RR 2 Maple City MI 49664-9802 Office: Office of Lt Gov State Capitol Bldg PO Box 30026 Lansing MI 48909*

BINTLIFF, BARBARA ANN, law librarian, educator; b. Houston, Jan. 14, 1953; d. Donald Richard and Frances Arlene (Appling) Hay; m. Byron A. Boville, Aug. 20, 1977 (div. 1992); children: Bradley, Bruce. BA, Cen. Wash. U., 1975; JD, U. Wash., 1978, MLL, 1979. Bar: Wash. 1979, U.S. Dist. Ct. (ea. dist.) Wash. 1980, Colo. 1983, U.S. Dist. Ct. Colo. 1983. Libr. Gaddis and Fox, Seattle, 1978-79; reference libr. U. Denver Law Sch., 1979-84; assoc. libr., sr. instr. Sch. Law U. Colo., Boulder, 1984-88, assoc. prof., libr. dir., 1989—; legal cons. Nat. Ctr. Atmospheric Rsch., Environ. and Societal Impacts Group, Boulder, 1980. Editor: A Representative Sample of Tenure Documents for Law Librarians, 1988, 2nd edit., 1994, Chapter Presidents' Handbook, 1989, Representatives Handbook, 1990; mem. editorial bd. Legal Reference Svcs. Quarterly, Perspectives: Teaching Legal Research and Writing; contbr. articles to profl. jours. Mem. Am. Assn. Law Librs., Colo. Bar Assn., Colo. Assn. Law Librs. (pres. 1982), Southwestern Assn. Law Librs. (pres. 1987-88, 91-92). Episcopalian. Office: U Colo Law Libr Campus Box 402 Boulder CO 80309

BIR, MICHELLE MARIE, sales executive; b. Canandaigua, N.Y., June 29, 1965; d. Thomas A. and Carol A. (Genecco) B. BS in Econs., Wells Coll., 1987. Merchandiser Bratt-Foster, Syracuse, N.Y., 1988-89; sales exec. 110 Winner Eastman-Kodak Co., Cape Girardeau, Mo., 1989-95; retail rep. Hallmark Cards, Inc., St. Louis, 1995—. Mem., starter Make-A-Wish Found., Cape Girardeau, 1989. Mem. Am. Women's Econ. Devel. Assn., Cape Girardeau Jaycees. Democrat. Roman Catholic. Home: 518 N Sprigg St Cape Girardeau MO 63701 Office: Eastman Kodak Co 5609 K Hunters Valley Ct Saint Louis MO 63129

BIRCH, GRACE MORGAN, library administrator, educator; b. N.Y.C., June 3, 1925; d. Milton Melville and Adeline Ellsdale (Springer) Morgan; m. Kenneth Francis Birch, Oct. 26, 1947; children: Shari R., Timothy F. B.A., U. Bridgeport, 1963; M.L.S., Pratt Inst., 1968. With Bridgeport Pub. Library, Conn., 1949-66; asst. town librarian Fairfield Pub. Library, Conn., 1966-69, dir. Trumbull Library System, Conn., 1969—, lectr. Housatonic Community Coll., Bridgeport, 1970—; lectr. self-motivation, 1989—. Judge, Barnum Festival Soc. Bridgeport, 1971-73; mem. Trumbull Multi-Arts Com., Trumbul Prevention Coun. Mem. ALA, New Eng. Library Assn., Conn. Library Assn. (pres. 1972), Southwestern Conn. Library Council (pres. 1975-77), Fairfield Library Adminstrs. Group (pres. 1976-77). Democrat. Episcopalian. Avocations: sketching, dancing, traveling. Home: 175 Brooklawn Ave Bridgeport CT 06604-2011 Office: The Trumbull Libr 33 Quality St Trumbull CT 06611-3140

BIRCH, VERA, retired physician; b. Lugansk, Ukraine, June 15, 1930; d. Alexander and Raissa (Djumuk) Ritter; m. Eckard O. Foelsch, Oct. 22, 1955 (div. Nov. 1977); children: Karin, Brunhild, Ortwin, Silke, Boris; m. James B. Birch, Aug. 18, 1979 (div. Jul. 1983). MD, U. Freiburg, Germany, 1956. Rotating intern hosps. in Lübeck, Goslar and Berlin, 1957-60; resident in internal medicine Free U., Berlin, 1963-64; gen. practice Heidelberg, Germany, 1965-68; sr. resident in internal medicine U. Bonn, Germany, 1965-68; internist N.E. Health Ctr., Rochester, N.Y., 1973-74; resident fellow in oncology Genessee Hosp., Rochester, N.Y., 1975; physician St. John's Home, Rochester, 1975-77, Westside Health Ctr., Rochester, 1977-79; gen. practice medicine Geneseo, N.Y., 1980-94; ret., 1994. Paintings and photographs exhibited in shows at Rochester Inst. Tech., 1990, SUNY-Geneseo, 1992, Livonia, N.Y., 1993, minigalleries, 1995. Recipient Physician's Recognition award AMA, 1994—. Home: 20 Rorbach Ln Geneseo NY 14454

BIRCHMORE, CAROLINE BOWERS, nurse practitioner, consultant; b. Memphis, July 14, 1963; d. Shirley (Sanders) Eason; m. Mark Vaughn Birchmore, Nov. 13, 1993. ASN cum laude, Shelby State Coll., 1983; BSN cum laude, U. Memphis, 1988; MSN magna cum laude, Emory U., 1992. RN, Tenn., Ga., S.C.; ACLS; FNP. Staff nurse St. Francis Hosp., Memphis, 1983-85, head nurse, 1985-86, pain mgmt. coord., 1986-88; flight attendant Delta Airlines, Atlanta, 1988; clin. IV nurse ICU Emory U. Hosp., Atlanta, 1989-92; nurse practitioner VA Hosp., Atlanta, 1993-94; family nurse practitioner Lexington Med. Ctr., Columbia, S.C., 1994—; pres. Nurse Practitioners Assn., Inc., Lexington, S.C., 1995—. Mem. Womens Coun. Columbia Running Club, 1996—. Mem. ANA, Am. Coll. Nurse Practitioners, S.C. Nurses Assn. (com. mem. 1996—, polit. action com. 1996, advance practice coun. 1996), Ga. Nurses Assn. (del. 1992-96, award 1996), Advance Practice Coun., Golden Key Nat. Honor Soc., Phi Theta Kappa, Sigma Theta Tau, Alpha Epsilon Delta, Gamma Beta Phi. Presbyterian. Office: Nurse Practitioner Assocs Inc 205J Columbia Ave Ste 145 Lexington SC 29072

BIRD, CHLOE EDWARDS, sociologist; b. Clinton, N.C., Aug. 18, 1964; d. Christopher Park Bird and Carole Elaine (Edwards) Smith; m. Allen Martin Fremont, Oct. 17, 1993. BA in Sociology, Oberlin Coll., 1986; MA in Sociology, U. Ill., 1988, PhD in Sociology, 1992. Instr. dept. health and social behavior Harvard U. Sch. Pub. Health, Boston, 1994—; postdoctoral fellow New Eng. Med. Ctr. and Harvard Sch. Pub. Health, Boston, 1992-94; sr. project dir. Health Inst., New Eng. Med. Ctr., Boston, 1994-96; asst. prof. cmty. health and sociology Brown U., Providence, 1996—. Mem. editl. bd. Women's Health Issues; contbr. articles to profl. jours. Mem. APHA, Am. Sociol. Assn. (co-recipient Elliot Freidsen Outstanding Publ. award Med. Sociology sect. 1995), Sociologists for Women in Soc., Sigma Xi, Phi Kappa Phi. Office: Ctr Gerontol / Health Care Rsch Brown U Box G-B223B Providence RI 02912

BIRD, KAREN DIANA STUMP, special education educator; b. Great Lakes Naval Base, Ill., Sept. 11, 1954; d. Edison Robert and Helen Anne (Larson) Stump; m. Kerry R. Bird, July 29, 1978; children: Alicia Deanne, Jennifer Nicole. BS, Northwestern State U., Natchitoches, La., 1975, postgrad., 1977-83; MEd, La. State U., Shreveport, 1994; MA, La. State U., 1994. Rehab. tchr. La. Assn. for the Blind, Shreveport, 1976-81, dir. rehab., 1981-83; rehab. tchr. New Outlook on Life, Shreveport, 1984-85; tchr. homebound pre-sch. handicapped Goldman Sch. C-BARC, Shreveport, 1986-89; spl. edn. tchr. Westwood Elem. Sch., Caddo Parish Schs., Shreveport, 1989-92, Walnut Hill Elem./Mid. Sch., Caddo Parish Schs., Shreveport, 1992—. Vol., Walnut Hill PTA, 1986—, Capt. Shreve High PTA, 1995—. Grantee Caddo Pub. Edn. Found., 1996—. Mem. Caddo Assn. Educators (rep.), Coun. for Exceptional Children, Caddo-Bossier Zoo Founders, La. State U. Shreveport Alumni Assn., Kappa Delta Pi. Baptist. Office: Walnut Hill Elem/Mid Sch Woolworth Rd Shreveport LA 71129

BIRD, SARAH ANN, writer; b. Ann Arbor, Mich., Dec. 26, 1949; d. John Aaron and Colista Marie (McCabe) B.; m. George Roger Jones, Nov. 15, 1980; 1 child, Gabriel Bird-Jones. Bachelor's degree, U. N.Mex., 1973; Master's degree, U. Tex., 1976. Author: (novels) Alamo House, 1986, Boyfriend School, 1989 (Book to Remember N.Y. Pub. Libr.), Mommy Club, 1992 (Best Work of Fiction Tex. Inst. Letters), Virgin of the Rodeo, 1993. Mem. Tex. Inst. Letters (councilor 1995—), Writer's Guild West. Office: care Kris Dahl ICM 40 W 57th St New York NY 10019

BIRD, SHARLENE, clinical psychologist; b. N.Y.C., Sept. 3, 1957; d. Rubin and Dina Bird. BA in Psychology & Hispanic Studies, Vassar Coll., 1979; MA in Applied Psychology, Adelphi U., 1986; MA in Human Resources Mgmt., New Sch. for Social Rsch., N.Y.C., 1987; PsyD in Clin. Psychology, Yeshiva U., 1992. Lic. psychologist, N.Y. Clin. extern St. Mary's Children & Family Svcs., Syosset, N.Y., 1980-81; behavior modifier Flower Hosp./Terence Cardinal Cooke, N.Y.C., 1981-82; clin. psychology extern Met. Ctr. for Mental Health, N.Y.C., 1986-87; clin. psychology intern NYU Med. Ctr./Bellevue Hosp., N.Y.C., 1989-90; postdoctoral fellow in human sexuality N.Y. Hosp./Cornell Med. Ctr., 1990-93, 96—; family therapist Roberto Clemente Family Guidance Ctr., N.Y.C., 1991-93, 96—; healthcare planning analyst Inst. for Family & Community Care, N.Y.C., 1993-96; pvt. practice N.Y.C., 1994—; supr. NYU Med. Ctr./Bellevue Hosp., N.Y.C., 1992—; part-time clin. instr. dept. psychiatry NYU Med. Ctr., 1995—; tng. cons. Inst. for Family and Comty. Care, N.Y.C., 1993; weekly permanent radio talk show co-host Siempre a Tu Lado, Sta. WADO 1280-AM, 1992-95. Chair bd. dirs. Mothers of Childrens with AIDS, N.Y.C., 1991-93. Mem. APA, N.Y. State Psychol. Assn., Am. Orthopsychiat. Assn., Assn. Hispanic Health Profls. (bd. dirs., mem. at large 1995—), Am. Assn. Sex Educators, Counselors and Therapists, Am. Group Psychotherapy Assn., Assn. for Advancement of Behavior Therapy, Sigma Delta Phi. Office: 112 W 56th St Ste 15-S Rm C New York NY 10019-3834

BIRD-PORTO, PATRICIA ANNE, personnel director; b. N.Y.C., June 16, 1952; d. Jacques Robert and Muriel (Cooper) Bird; m. Joseph Porto, May 5, 1984; 1 child, Jennifer Ashley. BA, U. So. Calif., 1975; cert. in legal assistantship, U. Calif., Irvine, 1987. Cert. in transp. demand mgmt. Orange County Transit Dist., 1988. Mgr. Bullock's Westwood, West L.A., 1976-78; mgr. ops. Lane Bryant, L.A., 1978-79; supr. employment, dir. personnel May Co. Dept. Stores, 1979-81; adminstr. personnel, dir. benefits Zoetrope Studios, Hollywood, Calif., 1981-82; personnel and ops. analyst Auntie Barbara's, Beverly Hills, Calif., 1982-86; dir. personnel Baylylop, Santa Ana, Calif., 1986-88; pres. Creative Pers. Assocs., 1986-89; owner Flowerman Corona, Del Mar, Calif., 1987—; U.S. dir. human resources UIS, Inc., 1988-93. Co-chair Pro-Wilson Orange County. Home: 7 Stardust Irvine CA 92715-3769 Office: 3100 E Coast Hwy Corona Del Mar CA 92625

BIRDSEY, ANNA CAMPAS, civil engineer, architect; b. Balt., Nov. 21, 1949; d. William and Katy (Hondros) Campas; m. Tom D. Birdsey, June 3, 1973; children: Thomas William, Scott Stratton. BArch, Rensselaer Polytech. Inst., 1972; BSCE, Union Coll., 1977. Registered profl. engr., architect, N.Y. Staff architect-engr. GE Co., Schenectady, N.Y., 1972-73; architectural designer Fay Evans, P.C., Troy, N.Y., 1974-75, Golub Corp., Schenectady, 1975-77, Einhorn, Yaffee, Prescott, P.C., Albany, N.Y., 1979-80; jr. engr. N.Y. State Office Gen. Svc., Design and Constrn. Group, Albany, 1980-82, asst. bldg. structural engr., 1982-87, sr. bldg. structural engr., 1987—; bd. dirs. Montessori Sch. of Albany, 1990-92. Mem. Bethlehem Music Assn. (treas.), Rensselaer Alumni Assn. (class corr. alumni news). Home: 41 Darroch Rd Delmar NY 12054-3916

BIRDSONG, ALTA MARIE, volunteer; b. Ft. Worth, July 18, 1934; d. Alton Roy and Artie Marguerite (Bentley) Flowers; m. Kenneth Layne Birdsong, Oct. 18, 1958; children: Suzanne Denise, Jeffrey Layne. BBA in Acctg. magna cum laude, U. North Tex., 1955. Cost engr. Tex. Instruments, Inc., Dallas, 1955-62; self-employed part-time acct. Atlanta, 1972—. Mem. DeKalb County Cmty. Rels. Com., 1981-93, chair, 1984-87; mem. Atlanta Regional Com. Adv. Group, 1981-88, Met. Atlanta United Way, 1985—; resource investment vol. sch. age children; chair Sch. Age Child Care Coun., 1987-90; mem. DeKalb County Task Force on Personal Care Homes, DeKalb County Task Force on Personal Care Homes, DeKalb County Task Force on Domestic Violence; mem. steering com. for bond referendum DeKalb Bd. Edn.; mem. Vision 2020 Governance Stakeholders ARC, 1994-95. Recipient John H. Collier award for Camp Fire, 1991, Luther Halsey Gulick award for Camp Fire, 1993, Frederic E. Ruccius award for Camp Fire, 1993, Mortar Bd. Alumni Achievement award, 1991, Woman of Yr. award Atlanta Alumnae Panhellenic, 1983, Women Who Have Made a Difference award DeKalb YWCA, 1985. Mem. AAUW (divsn. pres. 1987-89, pres. elect 1987-89, mem. v.p. 1984-86, recording sec. 1982-84, nominating com. 1993-97, chair 1995-97), Atlanta Coun. Camp Fire (pres. 1992-94, v.p. 1990-92, region fin. officer 1989-90, region nominating com. chair 1991-92), Atlanta Alumnae Panhellenic (pres. 1978-79, v.p. 1977-78), Freedoms Found. at Valley Force (Atlanta chpt. pres. 1991-92, v.p. 1990-91, v.p. publicity 1988-89, treas. 1985-87, sec. 1983-85, ea.-so. region adv. 1994—), Nat. Women's Conf., Delta Gamma Alumnae (Atlanta chpt. 1st. v.p. 1985-87, treas. 1972-74, Oxford award 1992). Home: 5241 Manhasset Cv Atlanta GA 30338-3413

BIRGE, ESTHER BONITA, middle school educator; b. Greenville, S.C., Nov. 29, 1961; d. Robert Wayne and Ruth Evelyn (Bush) Koenig; m. Hubert Lamar Birge, Aug. 2, 1985; 1 child, Travis Lamar. BS in Elem. Edn., Bob Jones U., 1983; MEd in Early Childhood Edn., Mercer U. Atlanta, 1990. Cert. tchr. Ga. Tchr. 2d grade Cornerstone Bapt. Sch., Stone Mountain, Ga., 1983-90, tchr. 7th grade, 1992—. Recipient Tchr. of the Year Dekalb (Ga.) County Private Sch., 1994-95. Mem. Ga. Assn. Christian Schs. (cert.). Republican. Home: 3803 Palisade Ct Lithonia GA 30058-7128 Office: Cornerstone Bapt Sch 1400 Grayson Hwy Lawrenceville GA 30245

BIRKENSTOCK, JOYCE ANN, artist; b. Kansas City, Oct. 6, 1943; d. James Warren and Jean Lois (Hale) B.; m. Galen Richard Durkin, Sept. 6, 1969; 1 child, Lee Ann Durkin. Portrait artist Portraits South, Raleigh, N.C., 1982-85, Stellers Gallery, Jacksonville, Fla., 1988-96; pub. Arts Uniq, Cookville, Tenn., 1995—; artist Leanin' Tree Pub., Boulder, Colo., 1990—. Represented in permanent collections at Disney Prodns., Macon, Ga. Hist. Soc., Cornell Mus., Fla. Nat. Bank, Diocese of Palm Beach, Fla., Diocese of Miami, Harid Conservatory, Latner Found., Fairfield U. Recipient Purchase award Disney Prodns., First in Oil Boynton Festival of Arts, Disting. Achievement in Portrait Painting Nat. Portrait Sem., N.Y., Merit award, Best of Show Boca Raton Ctr. for the Arts, M. Grumbacher Silver Medallion Catherine Lorillard Wolfe 85th Ann. N.Y., People's Choice award Human Images Broward Art Guild, Honoarable Mention Lighthouse Gallery, Merit award, Best of Show Human Images Exhbn. Broward Art Guild. Mem. Am. Soc. of Portrait Artists, Nat. Assn. Women Artists. Home: 11692 North Lake Dr Boynton Beach FL 33436

BIRKETT, CYNTHIA ANNE, theater company executive; b. Kansas City, Mo., Oct. 31, 1960; d. Alan Kendal and Barbara Jean (Burnett) B. Student, Baker U., 1979-80. Dance instr., receptionist, office mgr., sales rep. Nina Molleson Overland Park (Kans.) Sch. of Dance, 1972-80; mgr., instr. Kinetics Fitness Ctr., Evanston and Chgo., 1980-85; asst. to Lea Darwin Giordano Dance Ctr., Evanston, 1980-82; ptnr., owner Kinetic's Fitness/Portess Med. Ctr., Chgo., 1984-85; ops. dir. Ctr. Theater Ensemble & Tng. Ctr. Actors, Dirs., Playwrights, Chgo., 1985—; works with numerous actors, Chgo., 1990-92. Fundraiser UNICEF, Kansas City and Chgo., 1969-91, Salvation Army, Chgo., 1980-85; mem. Overland Park Christian Ch., 1969-80. Recipient Oli award Artists/Peers and Colleagues Theater Adminstrs., 1991. Mem. DAR, Nat. Geographic Soc., Smithsonian Inst.

BIRKHOLZ, LIZ, artist; b. Phoenix, Nov. 28, 1967; d. Harlo LaGarr Birkholz and Maureen Webb; m. Richard Lawrence Larson, Oct. 9, 1993. BFA, U. Utah, 1990; MFA, Ariz. State U., 1993. panelist Artist Trust GAP awards, Seattle, 1995; exhbn. program juror Commencement Art Gallery, Tacoma, Wash., 1995; guest artist Cornish Coll. of Arts, Seattle, 1995, Oreg. Sch. Arts and Crafts, Portland, 1996; artist in residence Light Work, Syracuse, N.Y., 1996. Exhibited in group shows at Contemporary Artists Ctr., North Adams, Mas., 1992, Scottsdale (Ariz.) Ctr. for Arts, 1993, Alternative Mus., N.Y.C., 1993, San Francisco Camerawork, 1993, Works/San Jose, Calif., 1994, Bellevue (Wash.) Art Mus., 1995, Assn. Internat. Photography Art Dealers, N.Y.C., 1994-96, S.E. Mus. Photography, Daytona Beach, Fla., 1996, Seattle Art Mus., 1996. Recipient 2d award Nat. Soc. Arts and Letters, 1991, Purchase award U. Del. Biennial, 1992. Office: PO Box 4803 Seattle WA 98104-0803

BIRMAN, JOAN S., mathematician, educator; b. N.Y.C., May 30, 1927; d. George and Lilian (Siegel) Lyttle; m. Joseph Leon Birman, Feb. 22, 1950; children: Kenneth, Deborah, David. Student, Swarthmore Coll., 1944-46; BA, Barnard Coll., 1948; MA in Physics, Columbia U., 1950; PhD in Math., NYU, 1968; DSc (honoris causa), Israel Inst. Tech., 1995. Systems analyst Gen. Precision Equipment, 1950-53, W. L. Maxson Corp., 1953-55; staff mem. Tech. Rsch. Group, 1955-60; asst. prof. math. Stevens Inst., N.Y.C., 1968-71; assoc. prof. math. Stevens Inst. Tech., 1972-73; prof. math. Barnard Coll., N.Y.C., 1973—, chmn. dept. math., 1973-87, 89-91; vis. asst. prof. Princeton (N.J.) U., 1971-72; assoc. prof. U. Paris Sud, fall 1980, U. Paris VII, fall 1987; Lady Davis vis. prof. Technion, spring 1981; vis. prof. Hebrew U. Jerusalem, 1988, Inst. Advanced Study, spring 1988; rev. com. Fulbright Scholars, 1983-86; conf. bd. Math. Scis. Rev. Panel, 1984-85; topology panel Internat. Cong. Mathematicians, 1990; mem. U.S. Nat. Com. for Math., 1991-94; conf. organizer; internat. invited lectr. in field various univs., rsch. ctrs. and profl. confs. Author, editor chpts. to books; mem. editorial bd. Math. Rsch. Letters, 1993—, Topology and its Applications, 1993—; contbr. numerous rsch. articles, revs. to profl. jours. Sloan Found. fellow, 1974-76, Sr. Sci. Faculty fellow, Great Britain, spring 1981, Japan Soc. Promotion of Sci. fellow, Sept. 1980, Guggenheim fellow, 1994-95; NSF summer rsch. grantee, 1973—, U.S.-Israel Binational Sci. Found. grantee, 1990-93, Inst. Sci. Exch. grantee, Torino, Italy, summer 1986, Institut des Hautes Etudes Scientifiques grantee, Bures-sur-Yvette, France, summer 1991; recipient Chauvenet prize Mathematical Assn. of Am., 1996. Mem. Am. Math. Soc. (nominating com. 1989-91, mem.-at-large 1978-80, 90-93, human rights com. 1989-91, exec. com. 1992-96, long range planning com. 1993-95, chair 1994-95), N.Y. Acad. Scis. (women in sci. com. 1983-84), Math. Assn. Am. (Chauvenet prize 19950. Home: 100 Wellington Rd New Rochelle NY 10804-3708 Office: Columbia U Dept Math New York NY 10027

BIRMINGHAM, KATHLEEN CHRISTINA, secondary school educator; b. Newark, July 29, 1950; d. Charles J. and Mary D. (DiZio) B. BA in History, Montclair State Coll., 1972; postgrad., Syracuse U., 1978-80. Cert. tchr., N.Y., N.J. Social studies tchr. Cath. Diocese of Syracuse (N.Y.), 1977-88, Sherburne-Earlville Mid. Sch., Sherburne, N.Y., 1989—; coord. standardized testing Blessed Sacrament Sch., Syracuse, 1978-86; mem. policy bd. Cen. N.Y. Teaching Ctr., Syracuse, 1987-88. Tutor Literacy Vols., Syracuse, 1977-78; vol. Everson Mus., Syracuse, 1988-89. Mem. Nat. Coun. of the Social Studies, N.Y. State Coun. of the Social Studies, Ctrl. N.Y. Coun. of the Social Studies, Pi Gamma Mu. Home: 108 Wheeler Ave Norwich NY 13815 Office: Sherburne-Earlville Mid Sch Sherburne NY 13460

BIRNBAUM, LUCIA CHIAVOLA, historian, educator; b. Kansas City, Mo., Jan. 3, 1924; d. Salvatore and Kate (Cipolla) Chiavola; m. Wallace Birnbaum, Feb. 3, 1946; children—Naury, Marc, Stefan. AB, U. Calif., Berkeley, 1948, MA, 1950, PhD, 1964. Lectr., U. Calif., Berkeley, 1963-64, rsch. assoc., 1982-83, 86, 90-96; asst. prof. history San Francisco State U., 1964-69; mem. faculty Feminist Inst., Berkeley, 1981—; assoc. prof. doctoral program feminist spirituality Calif. Inst. Integral Studies, San Francisco, 1994—; vis. scholar Grad. Theol. Union, 1983-94, 95-96. Soroptimist fellow, 1955; affiliated scholar Inst. for Research on Women and Gender, Stanford U., 1987-94; Disting. woman scholar U. Calif., Davis, 1987; guest lectr. U. Sydney, Australia, 1989, U. Melbourne, Australia, 1989, U. di Padua, 1990; adj. prof. Calif. Coll. Arts and Crafts, Oakland, 1991-92. Recipient Anniversary award San Francisco State U., 1988; named to African Am. Multicultural Educators Hall of Fame, 1996. Mem. PEN Am. Ctr., Orgn. Am. Historians, Am. Italian Hist. Assn. (pres. Western Regional Chpt. 1978-82), Nat. Women's Studies Assn., Center for Women and Religion of Grad. Theol. Union, Women's Party for Survival. Author: La Religione e le Donne Siculo Americane, 1981, Liberazione della Donna: Feminism in Italy, 1986 (Am. Book award 1987), Black Madonnas, Feminism, Religion and Politics in Italy, 1993, also articles. Home: 349 Gravatt Dr Berkeley CA 94705-1503

BIRNBAUM, S. ELIZABETH, lawyer; b. Ft. Belvoir, Va., Jan. 20, 1958; d. Myron Lionel and Emma Jane (Steiner) Birnbaum. AB, Brown U., 1979; JD, Harvard U., 1984. Bar: Colo. 1984, D.C. 1985, U.S. Dist. Ct. D.C. 1987, U.S. Ct. Appeals (D.C. cir.) 1988, U.S. Ct. Appeals (10th cir.) 1988, U.S. Ct. Appeals (4th cir.) 1990, U.S. Supreme Ct. 1990. Clk. to Justice Dubofsky Supreme Ct. Colo., Denver, 1984-85; assoc. Dickstein, Shapiro & Morin, Washington, 1985-87; counsel to water resources program Nat. Wildlife Fedn., Washington, 1987-91; counsel com. resources U.S. Ho. Reps., Washington, 1991—. Editor-in-chief Harvard Environ. Law Rev., 1984. Mem. Am. Water Resources Assn., D.C. Bar (steering com., sect. environment, energy and natural resource law). Office: 1329 Longworth House Office Bldg Washington DC 20515

BIRNKRANT, JEANNE ANN, artist, actress, social worker; b. N.Y.C.; d. William Benjamen and Dorothy Leona (Solow) B. BA, Barnard Coll.; MSW, Columbia U.; postgrad., New Sch. Social Research, 1968-70, Arts Students League, 1970-75, Berghoff Acting Studios, 1975-80, 88-89. Chief psychiat. social worker N.Y. Psychoanalytic Inst., 1970-76; children's psychotherapist Bellevue Hosp., N.Y.C., 1976-78; psychotherapist, dir. social work Met. Hosp., N.Y.C., 1978-84; actress various cos.; chief psychiatric social worker N.Y.C. Madison Ave. Med. Ctr., 1991—; dir. Park Ave Psychotherapy Ctr., N.Y.C., 1988-89; psychotherapist Creedmore Psychiat. Ctr., Queens, N.Y., 1993-95. Prin. sculpture works include (bronze) Strident Man (1st prize) South Park Artist Group, N.Y.C. 1984), Winged Bird Fantasy (1st prize Nantucket Contemporary Callery, Mass., 1985), Screaming Motherland and Child (1st prize 1989), Nat. Contemporary Juried Art Show, 1989, Fifth Ave. Contemporary Gallery, N.Y.C., 1989, Whyte Gallery Sculpture Show, N.Y.C., 1992; appeared in movies Ransom, 1996, Turk 182, Cotton Club, Nuts, Radio Days, Ghostbusters, Ghostbusters II, Go Beverly, Round Midnight, Prizzi's Honor, Fatal Attraction, Last Exit to Brooklyn, See No Evil, Hear No Evil, Mortal Thoughts, 1990, Frankie and Johnnie, 1991, Boomerang, 1992, The Concierge, 1992, Batman Returns, 1992, Malcom X, 1993, City Hall, 1994, Smoke, 1994, Dead Presidents, 1994, Batman Forever, 1995, Dead Man Walking, 1995; theater includes On Golden Pond, 1991; appeared in TV shows Superman Anniversary Spl., 1988, Dreamstreet, Coach, 1994, The Cosby Mysteries, 1995, N.Y. Undercover, 1995. County Com. woman Village Ind. Dems., N.Y.C.; patron Mus. Modern Art. Nat. Mental Health fellow, Jewish Guild for Blind fellow. Mem. Screen Actors Guild, Actors Equity Assn., Nat. Assn Social Workers (cert.), AFTRA. Home and Office: PO Box 20953 New York NY 10023-1497

BIRO, MARI RELI, sculptor, painter, educator; b. Medias, Romania, July 19, 1948; came to U.S., 1965; d. Josef and Agnes (Csato) Marmarosch; m. Alexander Schlesinger, 1972 (div. 1979); 1 child, Julian; m. Tibor Berkovits, Sept. 23, 1982; children: Michael, Diana. BFA with honors, Pratt Inst., 1972. English tchr. Yeshiva Ohel Moshe, Bklyn., 1978-79, Yeshiva R'tzahd, Bklyn., 1979-81, Bd. Edn., Bklyn., 1990-92; art tchr. Shashelet, Bklyn., 1992-93. Fellow Nat. Assn. Women Artists (Jeffrey Childs Willis Meml. Sculpture award 1995), Orgn. Ind. Artists, Bklyn. Waterfront Artists Coalition, Art Iniatives, Artists Talk On Art.

BIRON, CHRISTINE ANNE, medical science educator, researcher; b. Woonsocket, R.I., Aug. 8, 1951; d. R. Bernard and Theresa Priscilla (Sauvageau) B. BS, U. Mass., 1973; PhD, U. N.C., 1980. Rsch. technician U. Mass., Amherst, 1973-75; grad. researcher U. N.C., Chapel Hill, 1975-80; postdoctoral fellow Scripps Clinic and Rsch., La Jolla, Calif., 1980; fellow U. Mass. Med. Sch., Worcester, 1981-82, instr., 1983, asst. prof., 1984-87; vis. scientist Karolinska Inst., Stockholm, 1984; asst. prof. Sch. Medicine Brown U., Providence, 1988-90, assoc. prof., 1990-96, prof., 1996—; mem. AIDS and related rsch. study sect. 3 NIH, 1991-93; mem. exptl. immunology study sect. NIH, 1993—. Assoc. editor Jour. Immunology, 1990-94; bd. editors Proceedings of Soc. for Exptl. Biology and Medicine, 1993—; contbr. articles, revs. to sci. jours.; sect. editor Jour. Immunology, 1995—; editor Jour. Nat. Immunity, 1994—. Leukemia Soc. Am. fellow, 1981, Spl. fellow, 1983, scholar, 1987; grantee NIH, 1985—; rsch. grantee MacArthur Found., 1991—. Mem. AAAS, Am. Assn. Immunologists (co-chmn. symposium 1990, 94, 95, 96), Am. Soc. Virology, Sigma Xi. Office: Brown U Biomed Ctr Box G-B618 Providence RI 02912

BIRSTEIN, ANN, writer, educator; b. N.Y.C., May 27, 1927; d. Bernard and Clara (Gordon) B.; m. Alfred Kazin, June 26, 1952 (div. 1982); 1 child, Cathrael. BA, Queens Coll., 1948. Lectr. The New Sch. Queens Coll., N.Y.C., 1953-54; writer-in-residence CCNY, 1960; lectr. The Writers Workshop, Iowa City, 1966, 72; lectr. Sch. Gen. Studies Columbia U., N.Y.C., 1985-87; dir., founder Writers on Writing Barnard Coll., N.Y.C., 1988—; adj. prof. English Hofstra U., L.I., 1980, Barnard Coll., N.Y.C., 1981-93; film critic Vogue mag. Author: Star of Glass, 1950, The Troublemaker, 1955, The Sweet Birds of Gorham, 1966, Summer Situations, 1972, Dickie's List, 1973, American Children, 1980, The Rabbi on Forty-Seventh Street, 1982, The Last of the True Believers, 1988; co-editor: The Works of Anne Frank; past contbg. editor Inside mag.; contbr. to Book World, Confrontation, Connoisseur, Geo, Inside, Mademoiselle, McCall's, N.Y. Times Book Rev., N.Y. Times Travel Sect., The New Yorker, The Reporter, Vogue, Washington Post, among others. Nat. Endowment of Arts grantee, 1983; Fulbright fellow, 1951-52. Mem. PEN (former mem. exec. bd., former chair admissions com.), Authors Guild (former mem. coun.), Phi Beta Kappa (hon.). Democrat. Jewish. Home: 1623 3rd Ave # 27jw New York NY 10128-3638

BISCHEL, MARGARET DEMERITT, physician, managed care consultant; b. Moorhead, N.D., Nov. 8, 1933; d. Connie Magnus Nystrom and Harriett Grace (Petersen) Zorner; m. Raymon DeMeritt, 1953 (div. 1958); 1 child, Gregory Raymon; m. John Bischel, 1961 (div. 1964); m. Kenneth Dean Serkes, June 7, 1974. BS, U. Oreg., Eugene, 1962; MD, U. Oreg., Portland, 1965. Diplomate Am. Bd. Internal Medicine, Nat. Bd. Med. Examiners. Resident, straight med. intern Los Angeles County/U. So. Calif. Med. Ctr., 1965-68, NIH fellow nephrology, 1968-70, asst. prof. renal medicine, 1970-74; asst. prof., instr. medicine U. So. Calif., 1968-74; instr. nephrology East L.A. City Coll., 1971-74; dir. med. edn. Luth. Gen. Hosp., Park Ridge, Ill., 1974-78, dir. nephrology sect., 1977-80, pres. med. staff, 1974-88; founding mem., med. dir., dir. med. svcs. Luth. Health Plan, Park Ridge, 1983-87; clin. assoc. prof. medicine Abraham Lincoln Sch. Medicine U. Ill., 1975-80; sr. cons. Parkside Assocs., Inc., Park Ridge, 1986-88; pvt. practice Chgo., 1974-88; physician Buenaventura Med. Clinic, Ventura, Calif., 1989-94, med. dir., 1992-94; prin. Apollo Managed Care Cons., Santa Barbara, Calif., 1988—; trustee Luth. Health Care System, Park Ridge, 1986-90, Unified Med. Group Assn., Seal Beach, Calif., 1993-94; hon. lifetime staff mem. Luth. Gen. Hosp., Park Ridge; mem. formulary com. HealthNet, 1992-94, med. adv. com. TakeCare, 1993-94, quality assurance com. PacifiCare, 1993-94; mem. doctor's adv. network AMA, 1994—. Mem. editl. adv. bd. Managed Behavioral Health Care Man., Credentials and Privileging Manual, Capitation Mgmt. Report; contbr. articles to profl. jours., chpts. to books; editor: Med. Mgmt. Manual, Managed Care Bull. Fellow Am. Coll. Physicians (Calif. Gov.'s advisor 1993—); mem. Am. Coll. Physicians Execs., Am. Coll. Med. Quality, Nat. Assn. Physician Hosp. Orgns., Nat. Assn. Managed Care Physicians, Sigma Xi. Office: Apollo Consulting Group 860 Ladera Ln Santa Barbara CA 93108-1626

BISCHOFF, JOYCE ARLENE, information systems consultant, lecturer; b. Chgo., Apr. 1, 1938; d. Carl Henry and Gertrude Alma (Lohn) Winterberg; m. Kenneth B. Bischoff, June 6, 1959; children: Kathryn Ann, James Eric. BS in Math., Ill. Inst. Tech., 1959; cert. computer tech., U. Del., 1979. Programmer, analyst Inst. of Gas Tech., Chgo., 1959-60, U. Ghent, Belgium, 1960-61; database adminstr. Med. Ctr. Del., Wilmington, 1979-84; sr. database analyst ICI Ams., Wilmington, 1984-87; sr. cons. CSC Ptnrs., Malvern, Pa., 1987-90; pres. Bischoff Cons., Inc., Hockessin, Del., 1990—; chairperson, founder Del. Valley DB2-SQL/DS Users Group, Phila., 1986-90; task force leader DB2 performance task force Guide Internat., Chgo., 1987-90; speaker, mem. conf. planning com. Internat. DB2 Users Group. Author: (with others) Handbook of Data Management, 1993, Data Warehouse: Practical Advice From the Experts, 1997; contbr. articles to profl. jours. Recipient McGrath award Del. Valley DB2-SQL/DS Users Group, 1990, Quality award Guide Internat., 1989. Mem. Internat. Platform Assn., N.Y. Acad. Scis., Assn. for Computing Machinery (Del. Valley chpt. pres. 1986-87, program chair 1985-86), Data Processing Mgmt. Assn. (Wilmington chpt.), Network of Women in Computer Tech., Sigma Kappa (pres. 1958-59). Home and Office: Bischoff Cons Inc 1007 Benge Rd Hockessin DE 19707-9242

BISCHOFF, SUSAN ANN, newspaper editor; b. Indpls., July 31, 1951; d. Thomas Anthony and Betty Jean (Coons) B.; m. Jim B. Barlow, June 20, 1975; 1 child, Samantha Lynn. BA, Ind. U., 1973. Rschr.-reporter Congl. Quar., Washington, 1973-74; city desk reporter Houston Chronicle, 1974-75, bus. reporter, 1975-79, asst. bus. editor, 1979-84, bus. editor, 1984-86, asst. mng. editor, 1986—; Houston corr. Kiplinger, Tex. Letter, Washington, 1980-85. Bd. dirs. Houston Chronicle Employees Fed. Credit Union, 1980-87, House Mus. Natural Scis.; mem. exec. com. U.S. Olympic Festival VII, Houston, 1985-86; mem. exec. com. Gulf Coast March of Dimes Birth Defects Found.; mem. class policy Leadership Houston, 1992-94; founding bd. dirs. Greater Houston Women's Found.; mem. nom. com., bd. dirs. Gulf Coast affiliate United Way; adv. bds. Child Advocates, Houston Food Bank, San Jacinto Girl Scouts. Named Outstanding Woman in Houston Journalism YWCA, 1989, Fabulous Femme Greater Houston Women's Found., 1994, Woman of Distinction Crohn's & Colitis Found., 1996; recipient Outstanding Vol. Achievement award Gulf Coast United Way, 1995. Mem. Soc. Profl. Journalists, Am. Assn. Sunday and Feature Editors (dir.), Press Club of Houston Ednl. Found. (founding bd. dirs.). Home: 6407 Schuler St Houston TX 77007-2064 Office: Houston Chronicle 801 Texas St Houston TX 77002-2906

BISCHOFF, THERESA, medical center executive; b. Rockville Center, N.Y., Nov. 6, 1953; d. Robert and Collette (Burke) Peters; m. Paul Bischoff, May 19, 1984; 1 child, Craig. BS in Acctg. cum laude, U. Conn., 1975; MBA, NYU, 1991. Auditor Arthur Andersen, Stamford, Conn., 1975-79; mgr. corp. acctg. Great No. Nekoosa, Stamford, Conn., 1979-81; mgr. external reporting Squibb Corp., Princeton, N.J., 1981-83; dir. acctg. practices Squibb Corp., Princeton, 1981-84; sr. dir. acctg. svcs. NYU Med. Ctr., 1984-87; v.p. finance N.Y.U. Med. Ctr., 1987-93; clin. prof. health care mgmt. NYU Sch. Medicine, 1993—; dep. provost, exec. v.p. NYU Med. Ctr., 1993—; bd. dirs. First Option Health Plan of N.Y., Combined Coord. Coun., 1984—, VHA-Metro N.Y., 1993—; mem. curriculum rev. com. Robert F. Wagner Grad. Sch. Pub. Svc., NYU, 1993-94; mem. beneficiary hosp. adv. com. United Hosp. Fund, 1994—; mem. adminstrv. bd. Coun. of Teaching Hosps., 1995—. Mem. AAMC (mem. group instnl. planning 1989-93, group on bus. affairs 1984-94, mem. project subcom. publishing: Space Planning and Mgmt. in Acad. Med. Ctrs. 1991, north-east regional sec.-treas. 1994), Greater N.Y. Hosp. Assn. (mem. bd. dirs. 1994—, mem. fiscal policy com. 1987-93, mem. health care exec. forum 1987—, sec. 1990-92), Hosp. Fin. Mgmt. Assn., Hosp. Assn. N.Y. State (trustee 1994). Office: NYU Med Ctr 550 1st Ave New York NY 10016-6481

BISHKOFF, CHERYL PRIEBE, oboist; b. Bethlehem, Pa., Apr. 23, 1953; d. John Louis and Ernestine (Barton) Priebe; m. Joseph Andrew Bishkoff, May 16, 1981; 1 child, David Andrew. Student, New Eng. Conservatory, 1971-73; MusB, Va. Commonwealth U., 1974, MusM, 1977. Prin. oboe Fredonia (N.Y.) Chamber Players, 1985—, Albany (N.Y.) Symphony Orch., 1991-93, R.I. Philharm., Providence, 1995—; acting prin. oboe Binghamton (N.Y.) Symphony Orch., 1993-94, Buffalo Philharm. Orch., 1994-95; co-prin. oboe Bethlehem (Pa.) Bach Festival Orch., 1995—. Coord. Sunday lunch program Ch. of the Good Shepherd, Newburgh, N.Y., 1995—. Mem. Internat. Double Reed Soc. Home: 73 Clinton St Newburgh NY 12550

BISHOP, ANN SHOREY, mental health nurse; b. N.Y.C., Jan. 4, 1947; d. George Heaysman and Clara Bessie (Garrison) Shorey; married; 1 child, George John. Diploma in nursing, Montgomery Hosp. Sch. Nursing, 1967; BSN, U. Pa., 1971; postgrad., Med. Coll. Va., 1976-77. RN, Pa. Staff nurse med.-psychiatry Montgomery Hosp., Norristown, Pa., 1967-69; staff nurse psychiat. med.-surg. Mercer Med. Ctr., Trenton, N.J., 1972-76, Rancocas Valley Hosp., Rancocas, N.J., 1977-79; med., psychiat. mental health and chem. dependency staff nurse Helene Fuld Med. Ctr., Trenton, N.J., 1980—. Mem. Nat. League for Nursing. Mem. Soc. of Friends. Office: Helene Fuld Med Ctr 750 Brunswick Ave Trenton NJ 08638-4143

BISHOP, C. DIANE, state agency administrator, educator; b. Elmhurst, Ill., Nov. 23, 1943; d. Louis William and Constance Oleta (Mears) B. BS in Maths., U. Ariz., 1965, MS in Maths., MEd in Secondary Edn., 1972. Lic. secondary educator. Tchr. math. Tucson Unified Sch. Dist., 1966-86, mem. curriculum council, 1985-86, mem. maths. curriculum task teams, 1983-86; state supt. of pub. instrn. State of Ariz., 1987-95, gov. policy advisor for edn., 1995—; mem. assoc. faculty Pima C.C., Tucson, 1974-84; adj. lectr. U. Ariz., 1983, 85; mem. math. scis. edn. bd. NRC, 1987-90, mem. new standards project governing bd., 1991; dir. adv. bd. sci. and engrng. ednl. panel, NSF; mem. adv. bd. for arts edn. Nat. Endowment for Arts. Active Ariz. State Bd. Edn., 1984-95, chmn. quality edn. commn., 1986-87, chmn. tchr. crt. subcom., 1984-95, mem. outcomes based edn. adv. com., 1986-87, liaison bd. dirs. essential skills subcom., 1985-87, gifted edn. com. liaison, 1985-87; mem. Ariz. State Bd. Regents, 1987-95, mem. com. on preparing for U. Ariz., 1983, mem. high sch. task force, 1984-85; mem. bd. Ariz. State Community Coll., 1987-95; mem. Ariz. Joint Legis. Com. on Revenues and Expenditures, 1989, Ariz. Joint Legis. Com. on Goals for Ednl. Excellence, 1987-89, Gov.'s Task Force on Ednl. Reform, 1991, Ariz. Bd. Regents Commn. on Higher Edn., 1992. Woodrow Wilson fellow Princeton U., summer 1984; recipient Presdl. Award for Excellence in Teaching of Maths., 1983, Ariz. Citation of Merit, 1984, Maths. Teaching award Nat. Sci. Research Soc., 1984, Distinction in Edn. award Flinn Found., 1986; named Maths. Tchr. of Yr. Ariz. Council of Engrng. and Sci. Assns., 1984. Mem. AAUW, NEA, Nat. Coun. Tchrs. Math., Coun. Chief State Sch. Officers, Women Execs. in State Govt. (bd. dirs. 1993), Ariz. Assn. Tchrs. Math., Women Maths. Edn., Math. Assn. Am., Ednl. Commn. of the States (steering com.), Nat. Endowment Arts (adv. bd. for arts edn.), Nat. Forum Excellence Edn., Nat. Honors Workshop, Phi Delta Kappa. Republican. Episcopalian. Office: Ariz Gov's Office 1700 W Washington Phoenix AZ 85007-3209

BISHOP, CAROLYN BENKERT, public relations counselor; b. Monroe, Wis., Aug. 28, 1939; d. Arthur C. and Delphine (Heston) Benkert; m. Lloyd F. Bishop, June 15, 1963. BS, U. Wis., 1961; grad., Tobe-Coburn Sch., N.Y.C., 1962. Merchandising editor Co-Ed Mag., N.Y.C., 1962-63; advt. copywriter Woodward & Lothrop, Washington, 1963-65; home furnishings editor Co-Ed Mag., N.Y.C., 1965-68; editor Budget Decorating Mag., N.Y.C., 1968-69; home furnishings editor Family Cir. Mag., N.Y.C., 1969-75; v.p., pub., editorial dir. Scholastic, Inc., N.Y.C., 1975-80; owner Mesa Store Home Furnishings Co., Aspen, Colo., 1980-83; dir. pub. rels. Snowmass Resort Assn., Snowmass Village, Colo., 1983-86; pres. Bishop & Bishop Mktg. Communications, Aspen, 1986—; mem. media rels. com. Colo. Tourism Bd., Denver, 1987-90. Author: 25 Decorating Ideas Under $100, 1969; editor: Family Circle Special Home Decorating Guide, 1973. Bd. dirs. Aspen Camp Sch. for the Deaf, 1987-90. Recipient Dallas Market Editorial award Dallas Market Ctr., 1973, Dorothy Dawe award Chgo. Furniture Market, 1973, Guardian of Freedom award, Anti-Defamation League Appeal, 1974. Mem. Rocky Mountain Pub. Rels. Group (chmn. 1991-93), Pub. Rels. Soc. Am. (accredited, small firms co-chair counselors acad. 1992-93), Aspen Writers' Found. (bd. dirs. 1991-93), Tobe-Coburn Alumni Assn., U. Wis. Alumni Assn. Democrat.

BISHOP, CLAIRE DEARMENT, engineering librarian; b. Youngstown, Ohio, Oct. 12, 1937; d. Eugene Howard and Ruth (Bright) DeA.; m. Carl R. Meinstereifel, 1956 (div. 1964); children: Paul, Dawn; m. Olin Jerry Dewberry, Jr., 1974 (div. 1979); m. J. Bruce Bishop, May 6, 1992. B.S., Clarion State U., 1967; M.L.S., Ga. State U., 1977. Cert. libr. media specialist, Ga. Libr. Henry County, Stockbridge, Ga., 1967-69; head libr. Russell High Sch., East Point, Ga., 1969-84; engrng. libr. Rockwell Internat., Duluth, Ga., 1984-88; rep. GIDEP, Corona, Calif., 1984-88; libr. Raytheon Co., 1990, MSD, Bristol, Tenn., 1988-90; owner rubber stamp store Claire's Collectables, St. Augustine. Author newsletter: Blueline. Mem. Mensa. Democrat. Avocations: computers, writing, information broker. Home: 238 Ravenswood Dr Saint Augustine FL 32095-3027

BISHOP, ETHEL MAE See GULLETTE, ETHEL MAE BISHOP

BISHOP, FAIRA LEE, library educator; b. Hinds County, Miss., Dec. 15, 1942; d. Ansel Bruce and Dora Alma (Langley) Lee; m. Billy M. Bishop, July 11, 1965. BA with distinction, Miss. Coll., 1964; MLS, U. Miss., 1972; PhD, U. So. Miss., 1989. Cert. tchr., sch., libr., sch. adminstr., Miss. Tchr. secondary English pub. schs., Greenville and Jackson, Miss., 1964-68; acad. libr. Miss. Delta C.C., Moorhead, 1969-71; tchr. Latin and English pub. sch., Oxford, Miss., 1971-73; libr. ssecondary and elem. schs., Clinton, Miss., 1977-94; instr. U. So. Miss. Sch. Libr. and Info. Sci., Hattiesburg, 1990—. Trustee Clinton Libr., 1976. Mem. AAUW (treas. 1996-97), Miss. Libr. Assn. (ad hoc com. 1984-85), U. Miss. Med. Ctr. Women's Club (rec. sec. 1995-96), Friends Rowland Med. Libr., U. Miss. Alumni Assn., Maids and Matrons Club (v.p. 1996-98), Phi Kappa Phi, Beta Phi Mu, Phi Delta Kappa. Baptist. Home: 340 Cascades Cir E Clinton MS 39056

BISHOP, JENNIFER ANN, photographer; b. Cleve., May 1, 1957; d. Warner Bader Bishop and Katharine Sue (White) McLennan; m. Daniel Mark Epstein, Dec. 20, 1994; 1 child, Theodore John Epstein. BA, Johns Hopkins U., 1979. Staff photographer The Balt. News Am., 1980-81; freelance photographer, 1981—; contbg. photographer City Paper, Balt., 1977-94; mem. Actuality Picture Agy., N.Y.C., 1992—; workshop tchr. Internat. Ctr. for Photography, N.Y.C., 1993-95. Recipient 3 City Arts grants Balt. City Arts Coun., 1987, 89, 91, 2 Photography fellowship grants Md. State Arts Coun., 1989, 93, award of excellence Soc. Publ. Designers, 1990, 96, award of excellence Comm. Arts mag., 1991, Cert. of Excellence award 11th Annual Am. Photography Competition, 1995. Office: 843 W University Pkwy Baltimore MD 21210

BISHOP, LINDA DILENE, lawyer, small business owner; b. La Grange, Ill., Dec. 21, 1961; d. James William and Margaret Ann Bishop. BA, U. Colo., 1985, JD, 1987. Bar: Colo., 1988, Ill., 1989, Fla., 1990, Fed. Ct. (no. dist. Ill.) 1992, (cen. dist. Ill.) 1994; cert. travel cons., real estate broker, mediator. Dep. dist. atty. Colorado Springs (Colo.) Dist. Atty., 1987-89, Jefferson County Dist. Atty., Golden, Colo., 1989-91; owner, pres. Bishop and Bishop, Oak Brook, Ill., 1991—, Great Lakes Installation Co., Oak Brook, 1991—, Bishop Travel Ctr., Oak Brook, 1992—; analyst draft codes for ea. Europe Ctrl. & East European Law Initiative, Washington, 1993, 94, 95. Mem. Colo. Bar Assn., Ill. Bar Assn., Fla. Bar Assn., Assn. Retail Travel Agts., Pacific Assn. Travel Agts., Internat. Forum Travel and Tourism. Republican. Home: 716 S Stough Hinsdale IL 60521-4412 Office: Bishop and Bishop 1111 W 22d St Ste C-40 Oak Brook IL 60521-1940

BISHOP, LORAINE KELLY, middle school educator; b. Pocahontas, Miss., Jan. 16, 1945; d. Eddie and Elee (Cooper) Kelley; children: Stephanie, Thomas. BA in History, Jackson State U., 1966, MS, 1967, MS in Guidance, 1968, AA in Social Studies Edn., 1972. Tchr. Hinds County Schs., Utica, Miss., 1966-68; tchr. Jackson (Miss.) Pub. Schs., 1968—, chair dept. social studies, 1980-94, ednl. specialist social studies; sponsor student coun. N.W. Mid. Sch., Jackson, 1989, sponsor hist. soc., 1990, sponsor active citizenship, 1990, team acad. arts, 1989; student counselor 1985—. Contbr. to book: Africa and Its People, 1971. Mem. AAUP, NEA, Nat. Assn. of Student Activity Advisors, Hist. Soc., Alpha Kappa Alpha. Democrat. Baptist. Home: 820 Rutherford Dr Jackson MS 39206 Office: NW Jackson Mid Sch 7020 Hwy 49N Jackson MS 39213

BISHOP, LOUISE WILLIAMS, state legislator; b. Cairo, Ga., June 27, 1933; d. Elijah and Sarah (Hines) Williams; m. James Alburn Bishop (div.); children: Todd James, Tabb Jody, Tamika Joy, James Alburn Jr. B in Communications and Radio Broadcasting, Am. Found. Dramatic Arts. Ordained min. Baptist Evangelist Ch., 1978. With Sta. WHAT; program host Sta. WDAS; mem. Pa. Ho. of Reps., Harrisburg, 1988—. Recipient numerous awards including Richard Allen award African Meth. Episc.Ch., Community Svc. award Missionary Baptist Pastors Conf., Outstanding Citizen award Phila. Mayor's Coun. on Youth Opportunity. Mem. Pa. Legis. Black Caucus (sec.), NAACP, Nat. Assn. Women Legislators, Nat. Polit. Congress Black Women, Nat. Assn. Women's Clergy, Bapt. Min.'s Conf., Afro-Am. Hist. and Cultural Mus. Democrat. Home: 2460 N 59th St Philadelphia PA 19131-1208 Office: Pa Ho of Reps State Capitol Harrisburg PA 17120*

BISHOP, PATRICIA HOOVER, reading specialist; b. Hanover, Pa., July 28, 1935; d. Aaron Jones and Edith (Leichliter) Hoover; m. William Alexander Bishop, June 29, 1957; children: Tamilyn Sue, Philip Alan. BS, Maryville Coll., 1957; cert. reading specialist, Pa. State U., 1978. Elem. tchr. Ridgway (Pa.) Area Sch. Dist., 1957-60; tchr. reading Clearfield (Pa.) Area Sch. Dist., 1970-80, coord. reading and fed. programs, 1981—. Mem. Cen. Pa. Dist. Libr. Bd., 1985—, pres. 1993, 96; bd. dirs. Joseph and Elizabeth Shaw Pub. Libr., 1984—, pres.; elder Presbyn. Ch. Mem. AAUW (pres. 1970-72, v.p. program 1991-93, Woman of the Yr. 1972), Pa. Assn. Fed. Program Coords. Republican. Home: 220 Charles Rd Clearfield PA 16830-1019

BISHOP, RUTH ANN, coloratura soprano, voice educator; b. Homewood, Ill., Feb. 21, 1942; d. George Bernard and Grace Mildred (Hoke) Riddle; m. John Allen Reinhardt, June 9, 1962 (div. 1975); children: Laura, Jonathon; m. Merrill Edward Bishop, Aug. 16, 1975; stepchildren: Mark, Lynn. BS in Music Edn., U. Ill., 1962; M of Music in Voice, Cath. U. Am., 1972; postgrad., U. Md., 1975. Music tchr. Prince Georges County (Md.) Schs., 1963-71, Yamaha Music Co., College Park, Md., 1971-73; voice tchr. Prince Georges Community Coll., Largo, Md., 1972-75, U. Md., College Park, 1975; profl. lectr. voice Chgo. Mus. Coll. Roosevelt U., 1977-82; tchr. voice McHenry County Coll., Crystal Lake, Ill., 1978—, Elgin (Ill.) Community Coll., 1981—; pvt. voice tchr. Crystal Lake, 1975—; dir. music Epworth United Meth. Ch., Elgin, 1984-86, Cherub choir 1st Congl. Ch., Crystal Lake, 1986-88; mem. Camerata Singers, Lake Forest, 1988, Arts Chorale of Elgin Choral Union; performer, vocal dir. Woodstock (Ill.) Mus. Theatre Co., 1983—; soprano soloist Internat. Band Festival, Besana Brianza, Italy, 1993. soprano soloist, Oratorio- The Psalms of David, 1986, opera, The Light of the Eye, 1985-86, Children's Day at the Opera, Washington, 1972, U.S. Navy Band, The White House, 1969; soloist with Crystal Lake Community Choir and Band, 1987—, First Congl. Ch., 1975—, others. Ill. State scholar, 1959. Mem. Nat. Assn. Tchrs. Singing (chpt. rec. sec. 1984-86, bd. mem. Chgo. chpt. 1995-97), Sigma Alpha Iota, Pi Kappa Lambda, Kappa Delta. Republican. United Ch. of Christ. Home: 951 Cambridge Ln Crystal Lake IL 60014-7608 Office: Elgin Community Coll Dept Music 1700 Spartan Dr Elgin IL 60123-7189

BISHOP, VIRGINIA WAKEMAN, retired librarian and humanities educator; b. Portland, Oreg., Dec. 28, 1927; d. Andrew Virgil and Letha Evangeline (Ward) Wakeman; m. Clarence Edmund Bishop, Aug. 23, 1953; children: Jean Marie Bishop Johnson, Marilyn Joyce. BA, Bapt. Missionary Tng. Sch., Chgo., 1949, Linfield Coll., McMinnville, Oreg., 1952; MEd, Linfield Coll., McMinnville, Oreg., 1953; MA in Librarianship, U. Wash., 1968. Ch. worker Univ. Bapt. Ch., Seattle, 1954-56, 59-61, pre-sch. tchr. parent coop presch., 1965-66; libr. N.W. Coll., Kirkland, Wash., 1968-69; undergrad. libr. U. Wash., Seattle, 1970; libr., instr. Seattle Cen. Community Coll., 1970-91. Leader Totem coun. Girl Scouts U.S., 1962-65; pres. Wedgwood Sch. PTA, Seattle, 1964-65; chair 46th Dist. Dem. Orgn., Seattle, 1972-73; candidate Wash. State Legislature, Seattle, 1974, 80; bd. dirs. Univ. Bapt. Children's Ctr., 1989-95, chair, 1990-95; vol. Ptnrs. in Pub. Edn., 1992-96. Recipient Golden Acorn award Wedgwood Elem. Sch., 1966. Mem. LWV of Seattle (2d v.p. 1994-96), U. Wash. Grad. Sch. Libr. and Info. Sci. Alumni Assn. (1st v.p. 1986-87, pres. 1987-88). Baptist. Home: 3032 NE 87th St Seattle WA 98115-3529

BISHOPRIC, SUSAN EHRLICH, public relations executive; b. N.Y.C.. AAS, Fashion Inst. Tech., 1965; student, N.Y. Sch. Interior Design, New Sch. Social Rsch. Exec.-in-tng. Bloomingdales, Abraham & Strauss; merchandise coord. Seventeen mag.; publicity dir. Germaine Monteil Cosmetiques; account exec. Rowland Co., 1968-69, account supr., 1969-73, v.p., 1973-75, sr. v.p., creative dir., 1975-78, exec. v.p., 1979-81; pub. rels. dir. Susan Gilbert & Co., 1984-86; head pub. rels. divsn. Beber Silverstein & Ptnrs., 1986-89; founder, pres. Bishopric Agy., Coral Gables, Fla., 1989—. Office: Bishopric Agy 400 Viscaya Ave Coral Gables FL 33134-7160

BISIENERE, JOANNE MARIE, accountant; b. Falmouth, Mass., Aug. 23, 1968; d. Harold Francis and Mary Jean (Chucka) B. BA in Acctg., U. South Fla., 1989, M Accountancy, 1994. CPA, Fla.; cert. mgmt. acct. Asst. contr. Wenczel Tile Co., Tampa, Fla., 1992-93; acctg. mgr. Breed Techs., Inc., Lakeland, Fla., 1993—. Mem. AICPA, Fla. Inst. CPAs, Inst. Mgmt. Accts., Golden Key.

BISSET CARPENTER, SUZANNE See FOX, SELENA MARIE

BISSETT, BARBARA ANNE, steel distribution company executive; b. Cleve., Sept. 27, 1950; d. George Jr. and Helen (Kirkwood) B.; m. Kerry Mark Kitchen, Oct. 6, 1979; children: Mark Jeffrey, Lauren Brooke. BFA, U. Denver, 1974. Inside sales rep. Bissett Steel Co., Cleve., 1977-78, inside sales mgr., 1978-80, v.p., 1980-88, pres., 1988—; mentor strategic planning course Greater Cleve. Growth Assn., 1987-95. Bd. dirs. Greater Cleve. Growth Assn. Govt. Affairs, 1994—; trustee Enterprise Devel., Inc., 1994—. Mem. Am. Soc. Metals, Steel Svc. Ctr. Inst. (v.p. programming young leadership forum 1989, pres. 1991-93, bd. dirs. No. ohio chpt., v.p. 1994, pres. north Ohio chpt. 1995-97), Coun. Smaller Enterprises (leadership coun. 1989—, bd. dirs. 1990—, first vice chair 1996), Assn. Women in Metals Industries, Cleve. Yacht Club, Women's City Club. Republican. Presbyterian. Home: 1994 Coes Post Run Cleveland OH 44145-2059 Office: 9005 Bank St Cleveland OH 44125-3425

BISSONNETTE, SHEILA ROSE, professional society administrator; b. Lincoln, Maine, Aug. 5, 1953; d. George Joseph and Evangeline Marie (Blanchette) B. BS, U. Maine, 1976; MS, Boston Coll., 1983. Cert. assn. exec. Counselor St. Andre Group Homes, Bangor, Maine, 1977-78; program coord. Diocesan Human Rels. Svcs., Orono, Maine, 1978-81; assoc. dir. Heart and Hand House, Philippi, W.Va., 1983-88; exec. dir. St. Vincent de Paul Soc., Atlanta, 1988—. Mem. sec. Hunger Walk, Atlanta, 1988-95; treas. Ga. Vol. Orgn. Active in Disaster, Atlanta, 1990—; bd. dirs., com. chair Atlanta chpt., ARC, 1988—; mem. Christian Emergency Help Ctrs., Atlanta, 1988-92. Recipient Alan R. Johnson Leadership award, 1996. Mem. Ga. Soc. of Assn. Execs. (v.p. 1995-96), Ga. Soc. of Assn. Execs. Found. (chair 1991-95). Democrat. Roman Catholic. Office: St Vincent de Paul Soc 26 Third St NW Atlanta GA 30308

BISWAS, LINDA JOYCE, midwife; b. Lancaster, Pa., June 12, 1951; d. John Millhouse and Julia Louise (Moore) Kilheffer; m. Harold Biswas, Feb. 27, 1987 (div. Aug. 1994); children: Adina Bornini, John Abram. RN, St. Josephs Hosp. Sch. Nursing, 1972; cert. nurse midwife, Frontier Sch. of Midwifery, 1978. RN, Pa., N.J.; cert. family nurse practitioner, Pa.; cert. nurse midwife, Pa., N.J. Staff RN in ICU/CCU St. Joseph's Hosp., Lancaster, Pa., 1972-74; missionary nurse, midwife/RN/family nurse practitioner Churches of God Mission, Bangladesh, 1974-90; staff nurse midwife Tricenter Midwifery Svcs., Huntingdon, Pa., 1990-92, Rhoades Family Health Svcs., Quarryville, Pa., 1984, 92-93, Shore Meml. Hosp., Somers Point, N.J., 1993—. Author, translator: Training Manual for Village Health Promoters, 1983. Mem. Am. Coll. of Nurse Midwives. Republican. Mem. Chs. of God. Home: 6 Woodlot Ct Somers Point NJ 08244 Office: Shore Meml Hosp Prenatal Clinic 1 E New York Ave Somers Point NJ 08244

BITNER, JERRI LYNNE, information systems professional; b. York, Pa., May 11, 1951; d. Ernest Maclellan and Gertrude Pauline (Beck) B. BS, Pa. State U., 1974. Procurement agt. Def. Indsl. Supply Ctr., Phila., 1975-77; contracts specialist Navy Ships Parts Control Ctr., Mechanicsburg, 1977-81; procurement analyst, then supr. Navy Fleet Material Support Office, Ctrl. Design Agy., 1981-87, dir. procurement systems div., 1987-94, dir. APADE/C2/Reengineering divsn., 1994-96, tandem rapid rehost project mgr., 1996—. Methodist. Office: USN Fleet Material Support Office Fleet Material Support Office PO Box 2010 Mechanicsburg PA 17055-0792

BITTEL, MURIEL HELENE, managing editor; b. N.Y.C., Mar. 22; d. Ernest Henry and Helen Minnie (Seibel) Albers; m. Robert Gifford Walcutt,

June 15, 1946; children—Lynn Lowell Walcutt, Mark James Walcutt, Judith Anne Walcutt; m. Lester Robert Bittel, May 8, 1973. B.A., Douglass Coll. Feature writer Daily Home News, New Brunswick, N.J.; editor Fawcett Pubs., N.Y.C., 1940-46; pub. relations dir. Electrovox/Walco Inc., East Orange, N.J., 1946-62; mng. editor Acad. Hall Pubs., Bridgewater, Va., 1974—. Mng. editor: Ency. Profl. Mgmt., 1978; Handbook Profl. Mgrs., 1985, A Surprise in Every Corner, 1994, Island Adventures, 1995. Home: 106 Breezewood Ter Bridgewater VA 22812-1433

BITTEN, MARY JOSEPHINE, municipal official; b. Brighton, Mich., May 20, 1942; d. William Frederick and Josephine Grace (Wright) Belz; m. Gerald A. Bitten, (div. Dec. 1982); children: Joann, Mark, Scott. Student, Howell High Sch., 1960. Bookkeeper Bitten Brothers, Brighton, Mich., 1963-67; v.p. Holiday Of Hartland (Mich.), 1977-88; acct. Taylor Bldg., Detroit, 1978-79; pres. Mar-Bar Ins., Brighton, Mich.; real estate mgr. C-21, Howell, Mich., 1979-86; township clk. Township of Brighton (Mich.), 1987—; self-employed builder Brighton, Mich., 1986—. Mem. Republican Women, dir. Livingston County Clks., treas. Livingston County Township Assn., 1988, chmn. Brighton Township Recycling, 1988, Mich. Township Assn., Brighton Area C. of C. Mem. Merry Maids 707, Inc. (pres. 1990—). Lutheran.

BITTENCE, MARY M., lawyer; b. Houghton, Mich., Jan. 10, 1952. BA summa cum laude, Cleve. State U., 1976, JD summa cum laude, 1982. Bar: Ohio 1982. Ptnr. Baker & Hostetler, Cleve. Bus. editor: Cleve. State Law Review, 1981-82. Mem. ABA, Ohio State Bar Assn., Cleve. Bar Assn. Office: Baker & Hostetler 3200 Nat City Ctr 1900 E 9th St Cleveland OH 44114-3401*

BITTLE, DONNA LEE TREADWAY, library/media specialist; b. Trenton, N.J., June 5, 1957; d. Richard G. Sr. and MaryLou Treadway; m. Roland S. Bittle Jr.; children: Steven, Andrew. BS, Trenton State Coll., 1979, MEd, 1983. Librarian Freehold Twp. H.S., 1979-89; M.S. librarian Hamilton Twp., 1989-90, Moorestown, 1990-93, Lumberton, 1995—. Mem. AAUW, BCSMA, Ednl. Media Assn. N.J., West Jersey Reading Coun., West Jersey Rose Soc. Republican. Home: 69 Sherwood Lane Mount Holly NJ 08060

BITTLER, SANDI ELAINE, sports association administrator; b. Pitts., Apr. 24, 1968; d. Ronald Paul and Meredith Lee B. AB in Biology, Princeton Univ., 1990. Fan svcs. asst. Nat. Basketball Assn., N.Y.C., 1990-91, coord. ops., 1991-93, mgr., business affairs, 1993-96; adminstr. Women's Nat. Basketball League, N.Y.C., 1996—. NCAA scholar, 1990. Mem. Women in Sports and Entertainment (wise mem.). Office: WNBA 645 5th Ave New York NY 10022

BIVENS, CONSTANCE ANN, elementary school educator; b. Madison, Ind., June 26, 1938; d. Nelson and Virginia (Cole) B. BS, George Peabody Coll. for Tchrs., now Vanderbilt U., 1960, MA, 1966; EdD, Nova U., Ft. Lauderdale, Fla., 1982. Cert. educator. Tchr. Broward County Schs., Ft. Lauderdale, Fla., 1960-61, 65—, Jefferson County Schs., Louisville, Ky., 1961-62, Ft. Knox (Ky.) Schs., 1962-64, Madison (Ind.) Consol. Schs., 1964-65; chmn. K-Adult Coun., Nova Schs., Ft. Lauderdale, 1976-78; cons. 1978-80. Author: Boots, Butterflies, and Dragons, 1982. Mem. Hollywood Hills United Meth. Ch., 1966—, mem. adminstrv. bd. Sing in Chancel Choir, pres. Sunday Sch. class, 1991-94, Walk to Emmaus, 1990, 91-92; active Children's Cancer Caring Ctr. Inc., Broward County chpt., 1986—, Hollywood Hist. Soc., Zool. Soc. Fla., Nat. Audubon Soc. Mem. AAUW, NEA, Fla. Reading Assn., Hist. Madison, Inc., Jefferson County Hist. Soc., Internat. Order King's Daus. and Sons, Irish Cultural Inst., Delta Kappa Gamma (internat. expansion com. 1986-88, chmn. internat. program of work com. 1988-90, internat. rep. World Confedn. Orgns. of Teaching profession 1989, chmn. S.E. regional conf. 1991, internat. nominations com. 1992—, chmn. 1994—, 1st v.p. Mu state 1993-95, Mu state pres. 1995-97, Sara Ferguson Achievement award 1990). Republican. Methodist. Home: 5516 Arthur St Hollywood FL 33021-4608 Office: Nova Blanche Forman Elem Sch 3521 Davie Rd Fort Lauderdale FL 33314-1604

BIVONA, VIRGINIA SIENA, graphic products manufacturing company executive; b. Cleve., May 16, 1931; d. Vincent James Sr. and Virginia Catherine (Johnson) Siena; divorced; children: Mark, Lawrence, Stephanie, Matthew, Elizabeth. Student, Western Res. U., 1950-53. Advt. dir. Am. Direct Mail Mktg., Dallas, 1981-78; pres. Tex. Grid Systems, Inc., Richardson, 1982-93; gen. mgr. Tex. Grid Systems (div. Visu-Com Inc.), Balt., 1993—; pres. G&G Distributing Inc., 1996—. Author: Notes from a Chameleon, 1984, Dirty Dining, A Cookbook for Lovers, 1991, For My Daughters, A History of Women the History Forgot, 1994, Ida Mae Tuftweiler & The Traveling Tea Party, 1996. Vol. Hist. Preservation League, Dallas, 1987—. Mem. Noetic Sci. Inst., Dallas Ft. Worth Writers Workshop, Nat. Mus. Women in Arts, Philosophers Forum, Internat. Platform Assn. Home and Office: 9750 Forest Lane No 208 Dallas TX 75243

BIXENSTINE, KIM FENTON, lawyer; b. Providence, Feb. 26, 1958; d. Barry Jay Fenton and Gail Louise (Traverse) Weinstein; m. Barton Aaron Bixenstine, June 25, 1983; children: Paul Jay, Nathan Alexis. BA, Middlebury Coll., 1979; JD, U. Chgo., 1982. Bar: Ohio 1982, U.S. Dist. Ct. (no. and so. dists.) Ohio 1983, U.S. Ct. Appeals (6th cir.) 1983. Law clk. to presiding judge U.S. Dist. Ct. (so. dist.) Ohio, Cin., 1982-83; assoc. Jones, Day, Reavis & Pogue, Cleve., 1983-90, ptnr., 1991—. Bd. dirs. Planned Parenthood Greater Cleve., 1991—, sec. 1992-93, v.p. 1994—. Mem. Ohio Bar Assn. (bd. govs. litigation sect.), Ohio Women's Bar Assn. (trustee 1995-96, chair legis. com., trustee 1994-95), Cleve. Bar Assn. (bd. dirs. 1993-96, chair standing com. on lawyer professionalism 1994-96, bd. liaison to jud. selection com. 1996—, minority outreach com. 1993—, commn. on women in the law 1988—), chair commn. on women in the law 1992-93). Office: Jones Day Reavis & Pogue N Point 901 Lakeside Ave Cleveland OH 44114

BIXLER, MARGARET TRIPLETT, former manufacturing executive; b. Bluffton, Ohio, Sept. 15, 1917; d. Ray Leon and Etta Mabel (Lantz) Triplett; m. Roland M. Bixler, July 1, 1939; children: Katharine, David. AB, U. Mich., 1939; MA, U. New Haven, 1982. Sec. of bd. J-B-T Instruments, Inc., New Haven, 1940-76, chmn. of bd., 1976-91; ret., 1992. Author: Winds of Freedom, 1991, 2d edit., 1995.

BIZUB, JOHANNA CATHERINE, library director; b. Denville, N.J., Apr. 13, 1957; d. Stephen Bernard and Elizabeth Mary (Grizzle) B.; m. Scott Jeffrey Smith, 1992. BS in Criminal Justice, U. Dayton, 1979; MLS, Rutgers U., 1984. Law libr. Morris County Law Libr., 1981-83, Clapp & Eisenberg, Newark, 1984-86; dir. libr. Sills Cummis, 1986-94; libr. dir. Montville (N.J.) Twp. Pub. Libr., N.J., 1994—. Mem. ALA, N.J. Law Librs. Assn. (treas. 1987-89, v.p./pres.-elect 1989-90, pres. 1990-91), Am. Assn. Law Librs. (pvt. law librs. SIS, vice chair 1992-93, chair 1993-94, past chair 1994-95), N.J. Libr. Assn., Assoc. Libr. of Morris county (v.p. 1995, pres. 1996), Spl. Libr. Assn. N.J. (treas. 1990-92), Am. Legion Aux. (treas. Rockden unit 175 1983-93). Democrat. Roman Catholic. Home: 11 Elm St Rockaway NJ 07866-3108 Office: Montville Twp Pub Libr 90 Horseneck Rd Montville NJ 07045-9626

BIZZELL YARBROUGH, CINDY LEE, school counselor; b. Griffin, Ga., June 20, 1951; d. William Emerson and Senora Elizabeth (Henderson) B.; m. Gary Keith Phillips, Nov. 6, 1980 (div. Nov. 1990); m. Randy Yarbrough; 1 child, Delana Michelle. Student, North Ga. Coll., 1969-70; BA in Elem. Edn., West Ga. Coll., 1993, MS in Behavior Disorders, 1993; MS in Learning Disabilities, 1993, MS in Counseling and Ednl. Psychology, 1993. K-12 reading, math., sci. and elem. edn. tchr. Pike County Schs., Zebulon, Ga., 1972—; tchr., counselor of emotionally disturbed Pike County Elem. Sch., 1973—; tchr. of emotionally disturbed and behavior disorders Pike County H.S., 1993—; crisis counselor McIntosh Trail Mental Health Mental Retardation, 1994; cons. Alcoholics Anonymous, Griffin, 1982—, Pike County Coun. on Child Abuse, 1990—; lectr., presenter in field. Author: Hippotherapy for the Emotionally Disturbed, 1988; contbr. articles to profl. pubs. Leader, instr. Girl Scouts U.S., Meansville, Ga., 1969-90; co-coord. Ga. Spl. Olympics, Pike County, 1980—; pres. Internat. Reading Assn., Griffin, 1978; asst. leader 4H, 1992-93; substitute Sunday sch. tchr. local Meth. Ch. Recipient Sci. award Ford Found., 1966; named Res. Champion Open Jumper, Dixieland Show Cir., 1989. Mem. N.Am. Handicapped Riders Assn. (presenter), Profl. Assn. Ga. Educators. Democrat. Home: 734 Buck Creek Rd Griffin GA 30223-7915 Office: Pike County Schs Hwy 19 Zebulon GA 30295

BJERKNES, INGER, nurse; b. Copenhagen, Nov. 8, 1937; came to the U.S., 1962; d. Oluf Reinholt and Dagny Mundberg (Pedersen) Poulsen; m. Vilhelm Bjerknes, Feb. 9, 1963 (dec. Feb. 1995); children: Torbjorn, Christian. AA in Mental Health with high honors, Prince George's C.C., Largo, Md., 1976, AA in Nursing with high honors, 1980; BSN magna cum laude, Georgetown U., 1988, MSN, 1991. Aftercare coord., family and youth counselor So. Area Youth Svcs., Forrestville, Md., 1976-78; staff nurse Georgetown U. Med. Ctr., Washington, 1980-90, asst. nurse coord. surg. unit, 1990-92, asst. nurse coord. med. unit, 1992—; clin. educator Prince George's C.C., Largo, 1991-92. Mem. Sigma Theta Tau. Home: 12205 Wheeling Ave Upper Marlboro MD 20772

BJORKLUND, JANET VINSEN, speech pathologist; b. Seattle, July 31, 1947; d. Vernon Edward and Virginia Lea (Rogers) B.; m. Dan Robert Young, Dec. 04, 1971; children: Emery Allen, Alanna Vinsen, Marisa Rogers. Student, U. Vienna, Austria, 1966-67; BA, Pacific U., 1969; student, U. Wash., 1970-71; MA, San Francisco State U., 1977. Cert. clin. speech pathologist, audiologist. Speech pathologist, audiological cons. USN Hosp., Rota, Spain, 1972-75; traineeship in audiology VA Hosp., San Francisco, 1976; speech pathologist San Lorenzo (Calif.) Unified Schs., 1975-77, 78-81; dir. speech pathology St. Lukes Speech and Hearing Clinic, San Francisco, 1977-78; audiologist X.O. Barrios, M.D., San Francisco, 1977-81; cons. Visually Impaired Infant Program, Seattle, 1981-82; speech pathologist Everett (Wash.) Schs., 1982-94; speech-lang. pathologist, supr. Sultan (Wash.) Schs., 1995—; supr. pediat. programs speech pathology Group Health Coop. Puget Sound, Seattle, 1994; cons. Providence Hosp. Childrens Ctr., Everett, 1985-93, Pacific Hearing and Speech, 1988-93; rep. audiology adv. com. Ednl. Staff Assocs. Speech-Lang. Pathology, Wash., 1995—. Author: (with others) Screening for Bilingual Preschoolers, 1977, (TV script), Clinical Services in San Francisco, 1978, Developing Better Communication Skills, 1982. Chair Washington Mid. Sch. Site Coun., 1995—. Mem. Am. Speech-Lang. and Hearing Assn., Wash. Speech and Hearing Assn. (regional rep. 1985-86, chair licensure task force 1986-88, rep. Birth to Six Project 1988-91, pres. 1993), Pub. Edn. Adv. Com. (rep. 1995—), Phi Lambda Omicron (pres. Pacific U. chpt. 1968). Congregationalist.

BJORNCRANTZ, LESLIE BENTON, librarian; b. Jersey City, Mar. 1, 1945; d. David and Jeanne (Proctor) Benton; m. Carl Eduard Bjorncrantz, Aug. 31, 1968; 1 child, William. BA, Wellesley Coll., 1967; MLS, Columbia U., 1968. Rsch. libr. Alderman Libr. U. Va., Charlottesville, 1968-70; reference libr. Northwestern U. Libr., Evanston, Ill., 1974-78, curriculum libr., 1970—, edn. bibliographer, 1974—, psychology bibliographer, 1989—, core libr., 1989—; nat. adv. bd. ERIC Clearinghouse on Info. Resources, Syracuse, N.Y., 1988—. Co-editor: (book) Curriculum Material Center Collection Policy, 1984, Guide for the Development & Management of Test Collections, 1985. Bd. dirs. Internat. Visitors Ctr., Chgo., 1973-76; class rep., fund raiser class of 1967, Wellesley (Mass.) Coll., 1987-92. Scholar Wellesley Coll., 1967. Mem. ALA, ASCD, Assn. Coll. & Rsch. Librs. (sec. 1977-79, 85-87, chair curriculum materials com. 1984-85), Am. Ednl. Rsch. Assn., Am. Soc. for Info. Sci., Spl. Libr. Assn., Phi Delta Kappa (historian NU chpt. 1982—). Home: 2146 Forestview Rd Evanston IL 60201-2057 Office: Northwestern U Libr 1935 Sheridan Rd Evanston IL 60208-0821

BJORNSON, MARIA, theatrical designer. Theatrical designer London, 1971—. Designer (mus.) over one hundred prodns. including: The Phantom of the Opera (Antoinette Perry awards for best scenic design and best costume design 1988, Drama Desk award for Best Set and Costume 1988), Follies (Drama Mag. Designer of Yr.), Aspects of Love (Drama Mag. Designer of Yr.), (operas) Janacek Cycle (Prague Silver medal design), Cosi Fan Tutte, Mahagonny, Figaro, Carmen, Valkyrie, Toussaint L'Ouverture, Donnerstag Aus Licht, Tales of Hoffmann, Rosenkavalier (theatre) Blue Angel, Measure for Measure, Lulu, Camille, A Midsummer's Night Dream, Hamlet, The Tempest, Hedda Gabler, Katya Kasanova, 1994, Sleeping Beauty, 1994, The Rise and Fall of the City of Mahagonny, 1995. recipient Designer's Designer Great Britain Observer Mag., 1989.

BLACHOR, EVELYN, organization administrator; m. Isaac Blachor; 3 children. Grad., Stern Coll.; M in English, Adelphi U. Chmn. English dept. Yeshiva H.S., Queens, N.Y.; nat. v.p., mem. fin. com. AMIT Women, N.Y.C., chmn. pub. rels., pres., mem. exec. bd., bd. dirs. Mem. editl. bd. AMIT Woman mag. V.p. Young Israel of West Hempstead; orricer Nassau County Holocaust Meml. and Edn. Ctr. Office: 817 Broadway New York NY 10003

BLACK, BARBARA ARONSTEIN, legal history educator; b. Bklyn., May 6, 1933; d. Robert and Minnie (Polenberg) A.; m. Charles L. Black, Jr., Apr. 11, 1954; children—Gavin B., David A., Robin E. BA, Bklyn. Coll., 1953; LLB, Columbia U., 1955; MPhil, Yale U., 1970, PhD, 1975; LLD (hon.), N.Y. Law Sch., 1986, Marymount Manhattan Coll., 1986, Vt. Law Sch., 1987, Coll. of New Rochelle, 1987, Smith Coll., 1988, Bklyn. Coll., 1988, York U., Toronto, Can., 1990, Georgetown U., 1991. Assoc. in law Columbia U. Law Sch., N.Y.C., 1955-56; lectr. history Yale U., New Haven, 1974-76, asst. prof. history, 1976-79, assoc. prof. law, 1979-84; George Welwood Murray prof. legal history Columbia U. Law Sch., N.Y.C., 1984—, dean faculty of law, 1986-91. Editor Columbia Law Rev., 1953-55. Active N.Y. State Ethics Commn., 1992-95. Recipient Fed. Bar Assn. prize Columbia Law Sch., 1955. Mem. Am. Soc. Legal History (pres. 1986-90), Am. Acad. Arts and Scis., Am. Philos. Soc., Mass. Hist. Soc., Supreme Ct. Hist. Soc., Selden Soc., Century Assn. Office: Columbia U Sch Law 435 W 116th St New York NY 10027-7201

BLACK, BARBARA CROWDER, educational consultant; b. Woodbine, Iowa, Feb. 11, 1922; d. John Hershel and Elsie May (Jenkins) Crowder; m. (Estel) Eugene Black, Sept. 1, 1944; 1 child, (Estel) Eugene Jr. (dec. 1993). AB, N.Mex. Western U., 1946; teaching credential, UCLA, 1964; cert. in reading, math., Calif. State U., 1969, 72; postgrad., Sacramento State U., 1977-89. Cert. tchr., Calif. Tchr. Chavez County Schs., Roswell, N.Mex., 1942-44; tchr. ESL 6th St. Elem. Sch., Silver City, N. Mex., 1946-47; girls athletic coach Silver City Jr. High Sch., Silver City, N. Mex., 1946-47; tchr. Lovington (N.Mex.) Pub. Schs., 1950-51, Long Beach (Calif.) Unified Sch. Dist., 1951-58, Santa Maria (Calif.) Elem. Sch. Dist., 1958-59; tchr. spl. edn. Bellflower (Calif.) Unified Sch. Dist., 1959-67; instr. Sacramento Unified Sch. Dist., 1968-79; co-owner, v.p. El Paso Southwestern R.R. Ednl. Consultants, Sacramento, 1985—; demonstration tchr. Long Beach Unified Sch. Dist., 1952-59; master tchr. to student tchrs. Calif. State U., Long Beach, 1954-59, Sacramento, 1972-73; supr. tchr. aides Sacramento Unified Sch. Dist., 1969-79; co-editor revision of math. testing materials, 1977; English instr. Jian Ping Mid. Sch., Shanghai, China, 1992; pvt. tutor in computers, math. and reading elem. sch. children, 1994—; seminar coord. China New Renaissance Soc, U. Calif., Sacramento, historian, 1996—. Co-author tchr. manuals in sci. and arithmetic, tchrs. guide for social studies; cons., editor: Barking at Shadows (Gene Black, Jr.), 1994, Effing the Ineffible (Gene Black, Jr.), 1995. Elder Westminster Presbyn. Ch., Sacramento, 1973—; Bd. dirs. Calif. State R.R. Mus. Docents, Sacramento, 1981-89; vol. Jed Smith Sch. Computer Class, Sacramento, 1989, Habitat for Humanity, 1994. Grantee Sacramento County Office Edn., 1969, Calif. Dept. Edn., 1972-73, Study-Miller Math Specialists; recipient cert. spl. commendation Calif. Dept. Parks, 1988. Mem. Calif. Tchrs. Assn., Calif. Ret. Tchrs. Assn., Calif. State Libr. Found., Sacramento State Parks Docent Assn. (membership chair 1981-87, Outstanding Svc. award 1983, 86, 87, 89, Silver cert. for 15 yrs. Vol. Svc. Calif. State Railroad Mus.), Renaissance Soc. (Calif. State U. Sacramento), Sigma Tau Delta (pres. 1944-46). Office: El Paso Southwestern R R Capitol Towers Ste 14M 1500 7th St Sacramento CA 95814-5444

BLACK, BEVERLY HOLSTUN, psychiatric social worker; b. Thomaston, Ga., Sept. 27, 1942; d. Gordon Robinson and Louise (Hooten) Holstun; m. Frank Anderson Black, Dec. 27, 1963 (div. 1988); children: Sereina Louise, Margot Elisabeth; m. Michael Summers Lynch, Dec. 31, 1992. BA in English, U. Denver, 1963; MSW, U. S.C., 1979. Diplomate in social work. Tchr. Sumter County, S.C., 1975-77; clin. social worker Santee-Wateree Mental Health Ctr., Sumter, S.C., 1979-81; psychiat. social worker Ctr. for Personal and Family Growth, Valdosta, Ga., 1981-83; dir. Anxiety Disorders Ctr., Round House Psychiat. Ctr., Alexandria, Va., 1983—; speaker, lectr. on anxiety disorders, 1985—. Editor, expert videos for United Way, 1986, 87; appearances on TV as expert on anxiety disorders. Mem. adv. bd. No. Va. Women's Ctr., Vienna, 1985—; advisor 1st Family Support Ctr. in Air Force, Moody AFB, Valdosta, 1982, YMCA Women's Shelter, Sumter, 1980; mem. adv. bd. CIA, Washington, 1995—. Mem. AAUW, Nat. Assn. Social Workers. Republican. Baptist. Home: 6313 Mori St Mc Lean VA 22101-3153 Office: Round House Sq Psychiat Ctr 1444 Duke St Alexandria VA 22314-3403

BLACK, BONNIE JEAN, art education educator; b. Springfield, Mo., Oct. 1, 1946; d. Lilburn F. and Irene (Burns) Blankenship; m. David Eric Black, Dec. 18, 1971; 1 child, Steven Loren. BFA, S.W. Mo. State U., 1969; MEd, U. Mo., 1987, PhD, 1991. Grad. asst. U. Mo., Columbia, 1988-91; asst. prof. art edn. Ark. State U., Jonesboro, 1991—. Recipient Packwood Art Edn. scholarship U. Mo., 1990. Office: Ark State Univ PO Box 1920 State University AR 72467

BLACK, CATHLEEN PRUNTY, publishing executive; b. Chgo., Apr. 26, 1944; d. James Hamilton and Margaret (Harrington) B. BA, Trinity Coll., 1966. Advt. sales rep. Holiday mag., N.Y.C., 1966-69, Travel & Leisure mag., N.Y.C., 1969-70, New York mag., 1970-72; advt. dir. Ms. mag., 1972-75, assoc. pub., 1975-77; assoc. pub. New York mag., 1977-79, pub., 1979-83; pres. USA Today, 1983, pub., 1984-91; exec. v.p. mktg. Gannett Co., Inc., from 1985, also bd. dirs.; pres., CEO Newspaper Assn. Am., Reston, Va., 1992-95; pres. Hearst Mags., N.Y.C., NY, 1996—. Office: Hearst Mags 959 8th Ave New York NY 10019

BLACK, CORA JEAN, evangelist, wedding consultant; b. Mt. Pleasant, Pa., July 30, 1941; d. Alfred John and Ruby Isabel (Waugaman) B.; m. Arthur Byron Everett, Mar. 27, 1974. Student, Greensberg Bus. Coll., 1962, Moody Bible Inst., 1966; DD, Internat. Bible Inst., 1972; postgrad., Seton Hill Coll., 1986. Ordained evangelist; notary public. Advt. display silk-screen artist West Penn Power Co., Greensburg, Pa., 1962-63; missionary to W.I. Gospel Light Ministry, New Stanton, Pa., 1964; pers. dir., Pa. state chair Assn. Internat. Gospel Assemblies of DeSota, Mo., 1970-80; founder, pres. America for Christ Ministry, New Stanton, 1974—; owner, founder Sea-Jay's All Faith Wedding Chapel, New Stanton, 1979—; coord. Holy Land tours, 1971-83; mem. Kathryn Kuhlam Concert Choir, Pitts., 1955-62; owner Sea-Jay All Pet Hotel, New Stanton. Composer religious music; author: I Received Christ; weekly radio broadcasts on 11 stas., 1967—. Mem. Ctrl. Westmoreland C. of C., Westmoreland Hist. Soc., New Stanton Hist. Soc. (sec.-treas. 1995—), Am. Assn. Christian Counselors (charter mem., counselor), Pa. Assn. Notaries, Am. Biog. Inst. Assn. (dep. gov. 1995—), DAR. Republican. Home: 440 N Center Ave PO Box 192 New Stanton PA 15672 Office: Sea-Jays 440 N Center Ave New Stanton PA 15672

BLACK, EILEEN MARY, elementary school educator; b. Bklyn., Sept. 20, 1944; d. Marvin Mize and Anne Joan (Salvia) B. Student, Grossmont Coll., El Cajon, Calif., 1964; BA, San Diego State U., 1967; postgrad., U. Calif., San Diego, Syracuse U. Cert. tchr., Calif. Tchr. La Mesa (Calif.)-Spring Valley Sch. Dist., 1967—. NDEA grantee Syracuse U., 1968; recipient 25 Yrs. Svc. award La Mesa-Spring Valley Sch. Dist., 1992. Mem. Calif. Tchrs. Assn., Calif. Young Reps. Roman Catholic. Home: 9320 Earl St Apt 15 La Mesa CA 91942-3846 Office: Northmont Elem Sch 9405 Gregory St La Mesa CA 91942-3811

BLACK, FRANCES PATTERSON, library administrator; b. Huntsville, Ala., July 27, 1949; d. Fred C. and Mary Jane (Baird) Patterson; m. Larry David Black, Aug. 29, 1970; 1 child, Amy Susan. BA, U. Ala., 1971, MLS, 1972. Dir. Fairhope (Ala.) Pub. Library, 1972-77; rsch. asst. State Libr. Ohio, Columbus, Ohio, 1977-78; head tech. and extension svcs. Southwest Pub. Librs., Grove City, Ohio, 1978-86, asst. dir. pub. svcs., 1986-88, dir., 1988—; mem. libr. adv. bd. Orient (Ohio) Correctional Instn., 1988-91; mem. adult basic edn. adv. bd. Southwestern City Schs., 1991-94. Mem. planning Grove City Arts in the Alley, 1988—; bd. dirs. OHIONET, 1991—, pres., 1992-95; mem. Blue Ribbon Commn. for Ohio Pub. Libr. Info. Network, 1994-95; mem. OPLIN Bd., 1995—. Mem. ALA, AAUW, Pub. Libr. Assn., Libr. Adminstrn. and Mgmt. Assn., Ohio Libr. Coun., Grove City Area C. of C., Westland Area Bus. Assn., Rotary Club. Office: SW Pub Librs 3359 Park St Grove City OH 43123-2631

BLACK, JANET VERONICA, social services administrator; b. Warren, Ohio, Nov. 6, 1957; d. James Leebrent and Jimmie Mae (Bell) Thomas; 1 child, Lashara H. Black. Counselor Portage County Juvenile Ctr., Ravenna, Ohio, 1980-83; child care worker Marycrest Sch. Girls, Independence, Ohio, 1983-85, Youth Residential Svcs., Akron, Ohio, 1985-86; counselor, cmty. liaison New Horizons Youth Shelter, Medina, Ohio, 1986-87; vol. dir. Battered Women's Shelter, Akron, 1987-89; membership devel. mgr. Western Res. Girl Scout Coun., Akron, 1989-92; tng. & lesbian rights dir. NOW, Washington, 1992-94; cmty. educator Planned Parenthood Stark County, Canton, Ohio, 1994—. Recipient Black Woman of Excellence award YWCA, 1991. Mem. NOW (chair women of color issues Akron Area chpt. 1987-89, chair lesbian issues Ohio chpt. 1988-92, mem. lesbian rights com. 1990-92, mem. affirmative action com. 1990-92, Woman of Yr. award Akron chpt. 1989). Democrat. Roman Catholic. Office: Planned Parenthood Stark County 2663 Cleveland Ave NW Canton OH 44709

BLACK, LORI ANNETTE, secondary school educator; b. Tiffin, Ohio, Feb. 11, 1967; d. Marlin Jacob and Mary Jane (Gosche) B. BS, Ohio State U., 1989. English, speech tchr. Calvert H.S., Tiffin, 1989—; advisor Sr. Class Calvert H.S., Tiffin, 1989-90, cheerleaders, 1989-91, Nat. Honor Soc., 1994—; volleyball coach, 1989—, musical and play dir. 1990-94. Named Tchr. of Month, Student Coun., Calvert H.S., 1992, 94. Mem. Nat. Fedn. Interscholastic Coaches Assn., Ohio H.S. Volleyball Coaches Assn., Nat. Cath. Ednl. Assn., Calvert Athletic Boosters, Ohio State U. Alumni Assn. Roman Catholic. Home: 106 1/2 Benner St Tiffin OH 44883-2215 Office: Calvert HS 152 Madison St Tiffin OH 44883-2825

BLACK, LYNNE MARIE, financial director; b. Manistee, Mich., July 6, 1956; d. Frank Raymond and Margaret Mary (Thompson) Moser; m. Don Richard Black, Sept. 11, 1982; 1 child, Marissa Lynn. Assoc. degree, Ferris State U., 1976. Sec. Glen of Mich., Manistee, 1976-77; print media buyer, sec. Norman-Navan Advt., Grand Rapids, Mich., 1977-79; purchasing sec. Keeler Brass Co., Grand Rapids, 1979-82; pers. sec. Life Savers, Inc., Holland, Mich., 1982-84; adminstrv. asst. United Way of Kent County, Grand Rapids, 1984-88; fin. dir. The Grand Rapids Found., 1988—; cons. Black-Nicewander, P.C., Jenison, Mich., 1989-94. Mem. Grand Rapids Jaycees, asst. sec., dir., asst. treas., project chair, treas. Mem. Elks, Phi Gamma Nu. Republican. Roman Catholic. Home: 3536 Cascade Rd SE Grand Rapids MI 49546-2141

BLACK, MARGARET LOUISE, job placement coordinator; b. Houston, Apr. 28, 1954; d. Laurence N. and Wilma (Mowery) B. BBA magna cum laude, Sam Houston State U., 1974; MDiv, So. Meth. U., 1981. CPA, Tex. Auditor State of Tex., 1975-78; bookkeeper Green, Gilmore, et al, Dallas, 1978-80; min. United Meth. Ch., Houston, 1980-87; employment interviewer Tex. Employment Commn., Houston, 1987-91; job placement coord. San Jacinto Coll., Houston, 1991—. Squadron commdr. CAP, Liberty, Tex., 1986-89, Baytown, Tex., 1996. Mem. S.W. Assn. Colls. and Employers, North Channel C. of C. Home: 107 Oak Creek Dayton TX 77535 Office: San Jacinto Coll N 5800 Uvalde Houston TX 77049

BLACK, MAUREEN, realty company executive; b. Manchester, Eng., Feb. 4, 1937; came to U.S., 1957, naturalized, 1962; d. William Henry and Kathleen Mary (Cleaver) Jackson; grad. Felt and Tarrant Comptometer Sch., Eng., 1953; student Alamogordo br. N.Mex. State U., 1959-60, 62-63; m. Charles J. Dugan, Nov. 1979; 1 dau., Karen Elizabeth Black. Office mgr., personnel dir. J.C. Penney Co., Alamogordo, 1958-66; exec. sec. to project mgr. Re-entry System div. Gen. Electric Co., Holloman AFB, 1967-68; soc. editor, columnist Alamogordo Daily News, 1968-73; regional corr. El Paso (Tex.) Times, 1968-75; free lance writer and photographer; script writer Film Unit 505, Alamogordo, 1971; realtor asso. Shyne Realty, Alamogordo, 1975-77, West Source Realtors, 1977-80; owner, broker Hyde Park West Realty Co., 1980—. Pres., Alamogordo Music Theatre, 1971-72. Mem. planning com. tourism, recreation, convs. Gov. of N.Mex., 1965; mem. N.Mex. State Film Commn., 1973-74; life mem. Aux. of Zia Sch. for Handicapped Children, pres. Aux., 1975-76, 80-82; mem. Zia Sch. Bd., 1988-89, v.p., 1991-92; pres. Zia Found., 1988-89, 91-92, v.p. Zia Found. 1994-96. Recipient service award Nat. Found., March of Dimes, 1971; Americanism medal DAR, 1972; named Career Woman of Yr., Alamogordo chpt. Am. Bus. Women's Assn., 1971. Mem. Alamogordo C. of C. (chmn. convs. and motion picture com. 1965—), Nat. Assn. Realtors, Realtors Assn. N.Mex., Internat. Realtors Assn. Alamogordo Bd. Realtors (chmn. public relations com., v.p. 1981-82, pres. 1983-84), N.Mex. Opera Guild. Home: 1206 Desert Eve Dr Alamogordo NM 88310-5503 Office: PO Box 2021 Alamogordo NM 88311-2021

BLACK, NAOMI RUTH, writer, editor; b. Springfield, Mass., Oct. 19, 1957; d. Henry Arnold and Zelda Edith (Hodosh) B.; m. John Ian Bralower, July 22, 1990; 1 child Thomas Hart Bralower. BA in Anthropology, Beloit Coll., 1979; student, Radcliffe Pub. Procedures. Project coordinator, editor Woodward-Clyde Cons., San Francisco, 1978-80; asst. editor, travel editor William Morrow Co., N.Y.C., 1980-83; mng. editor Quarto Mktg. Ltd., N.Y.C., 1983-85; freelance writer N.Y.C., 1985—; assoc. editor Colors mag., N.Y.C., 1991, sr. editor, 1992-93. Author: Seashore Entertaining, 1987, Dude Ranches of the American West, 1988, Ten Terrific Parties, 1990, (as N.R. Gordon) Seashells, 1990, The Ghost Town Storyteller, 1992; co-author: The American Mail-Order Gourmet, 1986, East Coast Bread and Breakfast Guide, 1989, The New England Companion, 1990; editor Appie News, N.Y.C., 1992; contbr. articles to profl. jours. Bd. dirs. Writers and Pubs. Alliance for Nuclear Disarmament, N.Y.C., 1987-88. Mem. Appalachian Mountain Club (Appie News editor 1992).

BLACK, PAGE MORTON, civic worker; b. Chgo.; d. Alexander and Rose Morton; m. William Black, Mar. 27, 1962. Student, Chgo. Mus. Coll. Singer, pianist, Pierre Hotel, N.Y.C., Warwick Hotel, One Fifth Ave. Sherry Netherland Hotel; singer radio show and comml. Chock Full o' Nuts Corp.; rec. artist Atlantic Records, Den Records; co-founder Page and William Black Post-Grad. Sch. Medicine, Mt. Sinai Med. Sch., 1965—; chmn., mem. exec. bd. Parkinsons' Disease Found., Columbia U. Med. Ctr. (mem. adv. coun.); mem. nat. vis. coun. Columbia U. Health Scis. Faculties; hon. chmn. Chock Full O' Nuts Corp., 1983-90; founding mem. ASPCA. Recipient Ann. award Parkinsons' Disease Found., 1987, Police Athletic League, 1992, Mahattan Mag. award, 1992. Home: Premium Pt New Rochelle NY 10801

BLACK, PATRICIA ANNE, special education educator; b. Detroit, Mar. 21, 1959; d. William C. and Eileen A. (Droste) B. BS, Wayne State U., 1982; MEd, Ariz. State U., 1989. Cert. in spl. edn. K-12, elem. edn. K-8, Ariz., Mich. Tchr. spl. edn./severely handicapped Chandler (Ariz.) Sch. Dist., 1983-88, tchr. 2d grade, 1988-91, tchr. 3d grade, 1991-92; tchr. trainable mentally impaired Lake Shore Sch. Dist., St. Clair Shores, Mich., 1993—. Office: Rodgers Elem Sch 21601 L'anse Saint Clair Shores MI 48081

BLACK, PATRICIA JEAN, medical technologist; b. Milw., Oct. 22, 1954; d. Dale B. and Geraldine L. (Milligan) Heywood; m. Robert S. Black, Oct. 14, 1978. BS, Millikin U., 1978; degree in med. tech., St. Mary's Hosp., 1978. Med. technologist Mercy Hosp., Urbana, Ill., 1978-85; biol. lab. technician No. Regional Rsch. Ctr., USDA Agrl. Rsch. Svc., Peoria, Ill., 1985-88; lab. mgr. Chapman Cancer Ctr., Joplin, Mo., 1989—. Patentee in field. Mem. AAUW, Am. Soc. Clin. Pathologists (cert., assoc.), Clin. Lab. Mgmt. Assn., Zeta Tau Alpha (scholar chmn. 1976, house mgr. 1977), Sigma Zeta.

BLACK, REBECCA HARDY, student; b. Athens, Ala., Nov. 20, 1967; d. Douglas Buford and Betty Sue (Shumarker) Hardy. BS, Athens State Coll., 1963; postgrad., A & M U., Normal, Ala. Asst. editor The Athenian, Athens, 1992-93. Mem. NOW, ACLU, AAUW, Order Ea. Star. Democrat. Islamic.

BLACK, RITA ANN, communications executive; b. Newark, Sept. 2, 1950; d. Henry and Mary (Solomon) Black; m. David Joseph Franus, Dec. 30, 1973. B.A. in English, U. Rochester, 1972; M.S. in Journalism, Columbia U., 1975. Accredited bus. communicator. Sr. editor Book Prodn. Industry, mag., New Canaan, Conn., 1972-74, 75-76; mgr. publs. AAUP, N.Y.C., 1976-78; sr. communication specialist Ciba-Geigy Corp., Ardsley, N.Y., 1978-80, mgr. internal communication, 1980-84; exec. speechwriter IBM Corp., Armonk, N.Y., 1984-86, sr. info. rep., 1986-88; program adminstr. U.S. media rels., 1988-90; program mgr. corp. media rels., 1990-91; sr. program adminstr. corp. image advt., 1991-92; nat. mktg. mgr. Deloitte & Touche LLP, Wilton, Conn., 1993—. Mem. Pub. Relations Soc. Am. (Bronze Anvil award 1996), Internat. Assn. Bus. Communicators (dir. 1982-84, Gold Quill 1983, 84, Dist. I award of excellence 1982), Phi Beta Kappa. Office: Deloitte & Touche LLP 10 Westport Rd Wilton CT 06897-4522

BLACK, ROSA LEE, health systems administrator; b. Phoenix, Ariz., Apr. 7, 1940; d. John D. and Dessie R. (Hammond) B.; m. Millard Joseph Votteri, June 17, 1989; 1 child, Karen Ann. BA, Whittier Coll., 1962; MSW, U. Calif., Berkeley, 1964. Vol. U.S. Peace Corps, Senegal, 1964-66; med. soc. worker Mobilization For Youth, N.Y.C., 1967; tng. specialist Child Study Assn., N.Y.C., 1968-69; adolescent svcs. dir. Planned Parenthood Mt. Zion Hosp., San Francisco, 1970-80; policy assoc. Calif. Dept. Health Svcs., Sacramento, 1981-85, health sys. adminstr., 1990—; soc. svc. specialist Calif. Dept. Soc. Svcs., Sacramento, 1986-89; instr. U. Calif., San Francisco, 1971-76; lectr. U.S. Agy. for Internat. Devel., San Francisco, 1974; cons. CDC Ctrl. and Prevention, Atlanta, 1991—; instr. Calif. State U., Sacramento, 1992-94; cons. Substance Abuse & Mental Health Svcs. Adminstrn., Rockville, Md., 1993—. Co-author: Adolescent Health Services Systems, 1974, HIV-Related Tuberculosis Program Analysis, 1990, Approaches to Public Health Interagency Collaboration, 1993, Legal & Ethical Issues Posed by the Tuberculosis Epidemic as it Affects Alcohol and Other Drug Treatment Providers, 1995. Mem. Nat. Assn. of Soc. Workers, Nat. Peace Corps. Assn., Am. Assn. of U. Women. Office: Calif Dept Health Svcs PO Box 942732 Sacramento CA 94234-7320

BLACK, ROSA VIDA, writer, educator; b. Lovell, Wyo., Sept. 18, 1903; d. Robert John Bischoff and Rose Ann Jensen; m. Clinton Melford Black, June 4, 1925 (dec. May 1989); children: Harvey, Jean, Homer, John, Evelyn, Merrill, Francis, Carol. Student, U. Wyo., 1922-24, U. Utah, 1946. Tchr. Converse Sch. Dist., Douglas, Wyo., 1922-23, Granite Sch. Dist., Salt Lake City, 1946, Granger Camp Daus. of Utah Pioneers, Salt Lake City, 1950—; speech dir. Kearns 13th ward L.D.S. Ch. Young Women Mut. Improvement Assn., 1968, pres., 1924-25; writer, narrator script Kearns North Stake Relief Soc. Singing Mothers Concert, 1967, 68; lectr. on womanhood and patriotic subjects to girls' groups; writer, presenter tribute to builders of Lovell Canal, 1993; program chmn. Basin (Wyo.) Woman's Club, 1942. Author: Mother of the Year, 1969, Mother Stood Tall, 1971, Open Door to the Heart, 1986, Meet My Wonderful Family, 1993, (essays) I Believe, 1996, (histories) Under Granger Skies, 1963 (award), Proud of Kearns, 1979 (award), Lovell, Our Pioneer Heritage, 1986; co-author: Living Testimonies, Personal Histories, 1967. Panel advisor PTA, Salt Lake City, 1950; judge of election Rep. Party, Lovell, 1924; reader Relief Soc., Granger, Utah, 1953, pres., 1934-41, organist, 1957-60, social sci. tchr., 1952-54, theology tchr., 1954; mem. Young Women Orgn., pres., 1944; missionary, Australia, 1971-73, Nauvoo, Ill., 1975-77; asst., planner children's parade, Laramie, Wyo., 1932; counselor Stake Relief Soc., Laramie, 1931; pres. Children's Primary Orgn., Basin, Wyo., 1941-42. Recipient Cert. of Merit, Am. Mothers com., 1969. Mem. Daus. of the Utah Pioneers (capt. 1968—, pres. 1988-89, tchr. 1992—). Democrat. Mormon. Office: Daus of Utah Pioneers 330 N Main St Salt Lake City UT 84103

BLACK, SHARON SUE GIBBONS, veterinary pathologist, educator; b. Jackson, Miss., Aug. 8, 1959; d. Mack Graham and Carolyn Sue (Bland) Gibbons; m. John Gaston Black, May 25, 1985; 1 child, John Casey. BS, U. So. Miss., 1981; DVM, Miss. State U., 1985, PhD, 1994; postgrad., U. Ga., 1989-91. Diplomate Am. Coll. Vet. Pathologists. Small animal practitioner Animal Clinic Oxford, Miss., 1985-86; diagnostic lab. veterinarian U. Ga., Tifton, 1987-88, Athens, 1990-91; asst. prof. Coll. Vet. Medicine Miss. State U., 1994—; presenter in field. Contbr. articles to profl. jours. Mem. AAUW (Starkville br.), Assn. Women Veterinarians, Am. Vet. Med. Assn., Phi Zeta (Omega chpt.). Office: Miss State U Coll Vet Medicine Box 9825 Mississippi State MS 39762

BLACK, SHAWN MORGADO, dancer; b. Tuscaloosa, Ala., Sept. 29, 1964; d. Hank Scott Jr. and Olivia Jane (Matthews) B.; m. Jeffrey R. Bornemann, July 7, 1988. Grad., Ala. Sch. Fine Arts, 1982. Prin. dancer Alabama Ballet, Birmingham, 1981-83; dancer Atlanta Ballet, 1983-84; mem. corps de ballet Am. Ballet Theatre, N.Y.C., 1984-91, soloist, 1991—; dancer Twyla Tharpe Dance Co., N.Y.C., 1993—. Performances with ABT include La Bayadere, Bruch Violin Concerto No. 1, Fall River Legend, The Rite of Spring, Rodeo, The Sleeping Beauty, Swan Lake, Symphonic Variations. Democrat. Lutheran. Office: Am Ballet Theatre 890 Broadway New York NY 10003-1211

BLACK, SHERYL ELAINE HALE, author; b. Covington, Ky., Sept. 18, 1947; d. Letcher Talmadge and Mary Nell (Quinn) Hale; children: Shawna Lee Futrelle Aiken, Lawrence Kelly Aiken; m. Caroll Don Black, Sept. 7, 1991. Student, St. Paul Hosp., Dallas, 1970, Amherst Careet Ct., Greenville, Tex., 1990. Respiratory therapist St. Paul Hosp, Dallas, 1969-71; exec. sec., receptionist D.P.A., Inc., Dallas, 1971-73; asst. mgr. Am. Condominium Corp., Dallas, 1973-75; head credit investigation dept. Triangle Pacific Cabinet, Dallas, 1975-77; head merchandiser Am. Greeting Card Corp., Dallas, 1979-80; owner, operator Midlakes Grocery, Royce City, Tex., 1980-81; exec. sec., receptionist Amherst Career Ctr., Greenville, 1990-91. Author: Is Christ Come?. . .In the Flesh?, 1993, Forgotten Lady, 1994, As She Lived...Who I Am!, 1994, Deceived by Default, 1994, Escape From Flesh, 1994, Proverbs for Success, 1995, (children's books) Buttons and Lacey, The Good Manners Bears, 1987, Pennelope Jones, 1993. Recipient Honor Soc. award Amherst Career Ctr., 1990. Democrat. : 509 Franklin Ave Indialantic FL 32903 Home: 509 Franklyn Ave Indialantic FL 32903

BLACK, SHIRLEY TEMPLE (MRS. CHARLES A. BLACK), former ambassador, former actress; b. Santa Monica, Calif., Apr. 23, 1928; d. George Francis and Gertrude Temple; m. John Agar, Jr., Sept. 19, 1945 (div. 1949); 1 dau., Linda Susan; m. Charles A. Black, Dec. 16, 1950; children: Charles Alden, Lori Alden. Ed. under pvt. tutelage; grad., Westlake Sch. Girls, 1945. Rep. to 24th Gen. Assembly UN, N.Y.C., 1969-70; amb. to Ghana Accra, 1974-76; chief of protocol White House, Washington, 1976-77; amb. to Czechoslovakia Prague, 1989-92; mem. U.S. Delegation on African Refugee Problems, Geneva, 1981; mem. public adv. com. UN Conf. on Law of the Sea; dep. chmn. U.S. del. UN Conf. on Human Environment, Stockholm, 1970-72; spl. asst. to chmn. Pres.'s Council on Environ. Quality, 1972-74; del. treaty on environment USSR-USA Joint Commn., Moscow, 1972; mem. U.S. Commn. for UNESCO, 1973—. Began film career at age 3 1/2; first full-length film was Stand Up and Cheer; other films included Little Miss Marker, Baby Take a Bow, Bright Eyes, Our Little Girl, The Little Colonel, Curly Top, The Littlest Rebel, Captain January, Poor Little Rich Girl, Dimples, Stowaway, Wee Willie Winkie, Heidi, Rebecca of Sunnybrook Farm, Little Miss Broadway, Just Around the Corner, The Little Princess, Susannah of the Mounties, The Blue Bird, Kathleen, Miss Annie Rooney, Since You Went Away, Kiss and Tell, 1945, That Hagen Girl, War Party, The Bachelor and the Bobby-Soxer, Honeymoon, 1947; narrator, actress: TV series Shirley Temple Storybook, NBC, 1958, Shirley Temple Show, NBC, 1960; author: Child Star: An Autobiography, 1988. Dir. Bank of Calif.; dir. Fireman's Fund Ins. Co., BANCAL Tri-State Corp., Del Monte Corp.; Mem. Calif. Adv. Hosp. Council, 1969, San Francisco Health Facilities Planning Assn., 1965-69; Republican candidate for U.S. Ho. of Reps. from Calif., 1967; bd. dirs. Nat. Wildlife Fedn., Nat. Multiple Sclerosis Soc., UN Assn. U.S.A.; bd. dirs. exec. com. Internat. Fedn. Multiple Sclerosis Socs. Appointed col. on staff of Gov. Ross of Idaho, 1935; commd. col. Hawaiian N.G.; hon. col. 108th Rgt. N.G. Ill.; dame Order Knights Malta, Paris, 1968; recipient Ceres medal FAO, Rome, 1975, numerous other state decorations. Mem. World Affairs Council No. Calif. (dir.), Council Fgn. Relations, Nat. Com. for U.S./China Relations. Club: Commonwealth of Calif. *

BLACK, SUSAN, public relations executive; b. N.Y.C., Feb. 24, 1953; d. Owen Joseph and Joan Anne (Gorman) B.; m. John Berard, May 23, 1992; 1 child, Alexander Black Mitchell. BA, Conn. Coll., 1974. Asst. editor Continental Ins., N.Y.C., 1975-76; pub. affairs officer Citibank, N.Y.C., 1976-78; mgr. Gen. Signal, Stamford, Conn., 1978-81; account exec., v.p., sr. v.p. Hill and Knowlton, N.Y.C., 1981-91; prin. Dilenschneider Group Inc., N.Y.C., 1991—. Office: Dilenschneider Group Inc 200 Park Ave Fl 26 New York NY 10166-0005

BLACK, SUSAN HARRELL, federal judge; b. Valdosta, Ga., Oct. 20, 1943; d. William H. and Ruth Elizabeth (Phillips) Harrell; m. Louis Eckert Black, Dec. 28, 1966. BA, Fla. State U., 1965; JD, U. Fla., 1967; LLM, U. Va., 1984. Bar: Fla. 1967. Atty. U.S. Army Corps of Engrs., Jacksonville, Fla., 1968-69; asst. state atty. Gen. Counsel's Office, Jacksonville, 1969-72; judge County Ct. of Duval County, Fla., 1973-75; judge 4th Jud. Cir. Ct. of Fla., 1975-79; judge U.S. Dist. Ct. (mid. dist.) Fla., Jacksonville, 1979-90, chief judge, 1990-92; judge U.S. Ct. Appeals (11th cir.) Fla., Jacksonville, 1992—; faculty Fed. Jud. Ctr.; mem. U.S. Judicial Conf. Com. on Judicial Improvements; bd. trustees Am. Inns. Ct. Found. Trustee emeritus Law Sch. U. Fla.; past pres. Chester Bedell Inn of Ct. Mem. Am. Bar Assn., Fla. Bar Assn., Jacksonville Bar Assn. Episcopalian. Office: US Dist Ct PO Box 53135 Jacksonville FL 32201-3137*

BLACKBURN, CHRISTINE LOUISE, minister; b. Chgo., Nov. 29, 1948; d. Andrew Francis and Lois Evelyn (Kennedy) B. BA with honors & distinction in religion, Hamline U., 1970; MDiv cum laude, Andover Newton Theol. Sch., 1974. Ordained United Meth. Ch. Campus minister United Ministries in Higher Edn., River Falls, Wis., 1974-77; dir. The Univ. Christian Movement in New Eng., Cambridge, Mass., 1978-94; field edn. supr. United Theol. Sem., New Brighton, Minn., 1975-77, Episcopal Div. Sch., Cambridge, 1981—; cons., 1994—. Treas. ACLU, River Falls, 1975-76; tour leader Students/Tchrs. Organized for the Prevention of Nuclear War, USSR, 1986. Mem. NOW, Internat. Assn. Women Ministers, Nat. Campus Ministry Assn., Affirmation, Mobilization for Survival, Campus Ministry Women (NCMA rep. 1975-77). Home: 39 Harvey St Cambridge MA 02140-1735

BLACKBURN, SADIE GWIN ALLEN, executive; b. San Angelo, Tex., Oct. 14, 1924; d. Harvey Hicks Allen and Helen (Harris) Weaver; m. Edward Albert Blackburn Jr., Feb. 25, 1946; children: Edward III, Catherine Ledyard, Robert Allen. BA, Rice U., 1945, MA, 1975. Bookkeeper, trust dept. State Nat. Bank, Houston; tchr. elem. sch. Galveston, Tex.; mng. ptnr. Storey Creek Partnership, Houston, 1989—; spl. projects dir. San Jacinto; dir. master plan State Historial Park; lectr. in landscape design history. Co-author: Houston's Forgotten Heritage, 1822-1914, 1991; contbr. articles to gardening publs. Newsheet chmn. Jr. League, Galveston, 1950-53, art chmn., Houston Jr. League, 1957-58, mental health study com., 1959-61, 2d v.p., 1962-63, provisional chmn., 1962-63, interview chmn., 1963-64; adv. bd. Bayou Bend Gardens chmn. Mus. Fine Arts, 1973-74, Bayou Bend adv. com., 1987-89; v.p. Mental HEalth Assn., 1957-62; asst. treas. Child Guidance Assn., 1962-65; mem. Rice U. Hist. Commn., 1974-75. Recipient Sweet Briar Disting. Alumna award, 1991. Mem. Garden Club Am. (zone chmn. 1977-79, founders fund vice chmn. 1979-80, dir. 1980-82, rec. sec. 1982-84, v.p. 1984-86, archive co-chmn. 1986-87, 1st v.p. 1987-89, pres. 1989-91), Nat. Wildflower Rsch. Ctr., Nat. Parks and Conservation Assn., San Jacinto Mus. History (pres. bd. 1975-77). Republican. Episcopalian.

BLACKBURN, SHARON LOVELACE, federal judge; b. 1950. BA, U. Ala., 1973; JD, Samford U., 1977. Law clk. to Hon. Robert Varner U.S. Dist. Ct. Ala., 1977-78; staff atty. Birmingham Area Legal Svcs., 1979; asst. U.S. atty. U.S. Atty's. Office, 1979-91; judge U.S. Dist. Ct. (no. dist.) Ala., Birmingham, 1991—. Mem. Birmingham Bar Assn. Office: US Dist Ct 140 US Courthouse 1729 5th Ave N Birmingham AL 35203-2049*

BLACKER, HARRIET, public relations executive; b. N.Y.C., July 23, 1940; d. Louis and Rebecca (Siegel) B.; m. Roland Algrant, Aug. 6, 1970 (div. Jan. 1981); m. Matthew E. Harlib, Aug. 25, 1988. B.A., U. Mich., 1962. Exec. dir. publicity Random House, N.Y.C., 1974-79; East Coast v.p. Pickwick Maslansky Koenigsberg, N.Y.C., 1980-81; v.p. pub. relations Putnam Pub. Group, N.Y.C, 1981-85; pres. Harriet Blacker, Inc., N.Y.C., 1986-90; ptnr. Blacker Hunter Pub. Rels. Inc., N.Y.C., 1990-93; pres. Blacker Communications, N.Y.C., 1993—. Mem. Publishers Publicity Assn. (sec. 1973-75, treas. 1982-83, pres. 1983-85), Women's Media Group.

BLACKERBY, BETTY MULLINS, insurance company executive; b. S.C., July 28, 1941; d. Gary Mullins and Ruth Finley; m. William Ivy Blackerby. AB, Coker Coll., 1962; SS, U. Guadalajara; MA, U. Madrid, 1966. Cert. in ins. S.C., Ga., Va., W.Va., N.C. Tchr. Wade Hampton High Sch., Greenville, S.C., 1962-63, 68-72, Annandale (Va.) High Sch., 1963-65; tchr., adminstr. Edn. Ctr. U.S. Army, Germany, 1965-67, 72-75; tchr. Heidelburg (Germany) High, 1975-79, Spartanburg (S.C.) Meth. Coll., 1980-82, Anderson (S.C.) County, 1983-86; ins. sales mgr. AFLAC, Anderson, 1988-91, 94—; tng. coord. AFLAC, 1992, 93; mktg. coord. Am. Family Life Assurance Co., Columbus, Ga., 1988—. Vol. Meals on Wheels, Anderson, 1984-86; sponsor cancer support group, Anderson, 1985—; co-founder Hospice of Upstate, Anderson, 1988—; core mem. Anderson Leadership Alliance, 1996—. Office: AFLAC PO Box 4111 Anderson SC 29622

BLACKHAM, ANN ROSEMARY (MRS. J. W. BLACKHAM), realtor; b. N.Y.C., June 16, 1927; d. Frederick Alfred and Letitia L. (Stolfe) DeCain; m. James W. Blackham Jr., Aug. 18, 1951; children: Ann C., James W. III. AB, Ohio Dominican Coll., 1949; postgrad., Ohio State U., 1950. Mgr. br. store Filene & Sons, Winchester, 1950-52; broker Porter Co. Real Estate, Winchester, 1961-66; sales mgr. James T. Trefrey, Inc., Winchester, 1966-68; pres., founder Ann Blackham & Co. Inc., Realtors, Winchester, Mass., 1968—. Mem. bd. econ. advisors to Gov., 1969-74; participant White House Conf. on Internat. Cooperation, 1965; mem. Presdl. Task Force on Women's Rights and Responsibilities, 1969; mem. exec. coun. Mass. Civil Def., 1965-69; chmn. Gov.'s Commn. on Status of Women, 1971-75; regional dir. Interstate Assn. Commn. on Status of Women, 1971-74; mem. Gov. Task Force on Mass. Economy, 1972; mem. Gov.'s Jud. Selection Com., 1972, Mass. Emergency Fin. Bd., 1974-75; mem. bd. registration Real Estate Brokers & Salesman Commonwealth of Mass., 1991-94, chmn. 1994—; bd. visitors Ohio Dominican Coll., 1995—; corporator, trustee Charlestown Savs. Bank, 1974-84; corporator Winchester Hosp., 1983—; mem. Winchester 350th Anniversary Commn.; mem. design rev. commn. Town of Winchester; bd. dirs. Phoenix Found., Bay State Health Care, Mass. Taxpayers Found., Speech and Hearing Found., Baystate Health Mgmt., Realty Guild Inc., (v.p. 1995—, bd. dirs.); mem. regional selection panel White House Fellows, 1973-74; mem. com. on women in svc. U.S. Dept. Def., 1977-80; 2d v.p. Doric Dames, 1971-74, bd. dirs., 1974—; dep. chmn. Mass. Rep. State Com., 1965-66, 96—; sec. Mass. Rep. State Conv., 1970, del., 1960, 62, 64, 66, 70, 72, 74, 78, 90; state vice chmn. Mass. Rep. Fin. Com., 1970; alt. del.-at-large Rep. Nat. Conv., 1968, 72, del., 1984; Rep. State Committeewoman, 1996—; pres. Mass. Fedn. Rep. Women, 1964-69; v.p. Nat. Fedn. Rep. Women, 1965-79; pres. Scholarship Found., 1976-78, Mass. Fedn. Women's Clubs; dir., v.p. Realty Guild, Inc.; mem. Mass. Rep. State Com., 1996—; alumnae liaison The Beaumont Sch. for Girls. Recipient Pub. Svc. award Commonwealth of Mass., 1978, Merit award Rep. Party, 1969, Pub. Affairs award Mass. Fedn. Women's Clubs, 1975; named Civic Leader of Yr., Mass. Broadcasters, 1962; recipient Bus. Owner of Yr. award New England Women Bus. Owners, 1995. Mem. Greater Boston Real Estate Bd. (bd. dirs.), Eastern Middlesex Bd. Realtors (life mem. multi million dollar club), Mass. Assn. Real Estate Bds. (bd. dirs.), Nat. Assn. Real Estate Bd. (women's coun.). Brokers Inst., Coun. Realtors (pres. 1983-84), Winchester C. of C. (bd. dirs.), Greater Boston C. of C., Nat. Assn. Women Bus. Owners, ENKA Soc., Rotary Internat., Tequesta Fla. Country Club, Capitol Hill Club, Ponte Vedra Club, Winchester Boat Club, Winchester Country Club, Wychemere Harbor Club, Womens City Boston Club, Winton Club (sec., bd. dir.). Home: 60 Swan Rd Winchester MA 01890-3747 Office: Ann Blackham & Co Inc 9 Thompson St Winchester MA 01890-2903

BLACKMAN, CINDY, musician, composer; b. Yellow Springs, Ohio, Nov. 18, 1959. BA, U. Hartford; MA, Berklee Coll. Music. Represented by Muse Records, 1987—; performer jazz clubs, N.Y., 1982—. Contbr. recording to (album) Verses; performed and recorded albums with Jackie McLean, Lenny Dravitz, Jacky Terrasson, others; albums include Arcane, 1988, Code Red, 1992, Trio+ two, 1992, Telepathy, 1994. Office: Muse Records 106 W 71st St New York NY 10023*

BLACKMAN, JEANNE A., policy advisor; b. Decatur, Ill., Sept. 23, 1943; d. Robert Russell and Elizabeth Irene (DeWolfe) Shulke; m. Gary L. Blackman, Apr. 16, 1963 (div. Aug. 1983); children: Jeffrey Lynn, Stephanie Sue; m. Bill Weitekamp, Nov. 21, 1995. BS Elem. Edn., Ind. U., 1965; MS in Edn. Adminstrn., Eastern Ill. U., 1979. Cert. tchr. and adminstr.; lic. real estate salesperson. Elem. tchr. Taylorville (Ill.) Community Sch. Dist., 1965-86; real estate salesperson Craggs-Adams Realtors, Taylorville, 1985-87; adminstrv. asst. to chief of staff Ill. Dept. of Aging, Springfield, 1986-87, consumer adv., 1987-89; lobbyist Ill. Guardianship and Advocacy Commn., Springfield, 1989-95; policy advisor Office of the Atty. Gen., Springfield, Ill., 1995—; pres. Taylorville Edn. Assn., 1983-85; mem. adv. coun. Gov.'s Rehab., Springfield, 1987—; chmn. Springfield Civil Svc. Commn., 1995—. Co-founder, treas. Ill. Vol. Optometry Svcs. to Humanity, Taylorville, 1976—; pres. Capitol City Rep. Women's Club, 1988—; pres. Women in Mgmt., 1989—, pres.-elect, 1990; fundraiser, chairperson Ill. Women's Polit. Caucus, Springfield, 1985—; pres. Am. Field Svc. Student Exch. Program, Taylorville, 1985-87; bd. dirs. LWV Springfield chpt., 1984—; pres. bd. dirs. Mental Health Ctrs. Ctrl. Ill., 1994—; trustee Lincolnland C.C., 1989, vice chair 1992-93, chmn. 93-94; pres. Ill. C.C. Trustees Assn., 1992; mem. Mayor's Commn. Internat. Visitors; chmn. Springfield (Ill.) Civil Svc. Commn., 1995—. Mem. AAUW (edn. chairperson Taylorville chpt. 1985—), DAR, Sister Cities Assn. Springfield, Ill. Women in Govt. (bd. dirs. 1988—, v.p. 1990—), Women's Legis. Network, Ill. Fedn. Rep. Women (v.p., bd. dirs. 1988—, ways and means com. 1987—, world affairs coun. 1990—), Greater Springfield C. of C., Rotary, Delta Delta Delta. Presbyterian. Home: 19 Washington Pl Springfield IL 62702-4634 Office: Office of the Atty Gen 500 S 2nd St Springfield IL 62706

BLACKMAN, MARY DAVE, music educator; b. Dunn, N.C., Dec. 7, 1955; d. John Edwin and Mary Lou (Core) B. BA, U. S.C., 1978, M Music Edn., 1984; PhD, U. Tex., 1989. Cert. tchr., S.C. Asst. instr. U. Tex., Austin, 1985-89; assoc. prof. music Weber State U., Ogden, Utah, 1989—, chmn. dept. performing arts, 1995—; cons. Davis County Schs., Farmington, Utah, 1990—; mem. textbook adv. com. Utah Office Edn., Salt Lake City, 1994-97. Author: Music Essentials Handbook, 1989; editor interFACE, 1992—. Mem. Austin Cmty. Band, 1986-89, New Am. Symphony, Ogden, 1989—, Salt Lake Symphonic Winds, Salt Lake City, 1994—; bd. dirs. Utah Mus. Theatre, Ogden, 1995—; coord. children's choirs Washington Heights Bapt. Ch., Ogden, 1990-95. Fellow U. Tex., 1984, grantee, 1988; scholar Weber State U., 1990, 92. Mem. Music Educators Nat. Conf. (chmn. spl. rsch. interest group western divsn. 1994—), Utah Music Educators Conf. (editor 1992—), Phi Kappa Phi, Pi Kappa Lambda. Office: Weber State U 1905 University Cir Ogden UT 84408-1905

BLACKMER, CORINNE ELISE, English educator; b. L.A., May 12, 1955; d. Arthur Ezra and Elizabeth Gloria (Pylypchuk) B. BA, UCLA, 1986, MA, 1988, PhD, 1992. Tchg. fellow UCLA, 1989-92, vis. asst. prof., 1992-93; asst. prof. So. Conn. State U., New Haven, 1993—; vis. Mellon fellow Yale U., New Haven, 1996—. Editor, contbr.: En Travesti: Women, Gender, Subversion, Opera, 1995. Mem. MLA (mem. gay and lesbian issues com. 1994-96), AAUW, NOW, ACLU. Democrat. Episcopalian. Home: 43 Highland Ave Branford CT 06405 Office: So Conn State U 501 Crescent St New Haven CT 06515

BLACKSTOCK, VIRGINIA LEE LOWMAN (MRS. LEROY BLACKSTOCK), civic worker; b. Bixby, Okla., July 2, 1917; d. Joseph Arthur and Winifred (Lundy) Lowman; student Tulsa Coll. Bus., 1935-37; m. Leroy Blackstock, Dec. 29, 1939; children—Vincent Craig, Priscilla Gay (Mrs. Richard S. Kurz), Burch Lee, Lore Anne (Mrs. Dwight Mitchell), Trena Jan (Mrs. Frank Dale). Legal sec. law firm, Tulsa, 1937-41. Chmn. program Internat. Students in Tulsa, 1955-65; mem. Tulsa Council Camp Fire Girls, 1963-66; mem. youth com. Tulsa Philharmonic Soc., 1969-70; now mem. women's assn.; pres. Eliot Elementary P.T.A., 1961-62, Edison High Sch. P.T.A., 1971-72; mem. Tulsa Opera Guild. Co-chmn. Democratic precinct No. 132, 1960-67. Mem. Tulsa County Bar Aux. (pres. 1954-55, sec. 1962-63, chaplain 1966-67). Baptist. Clubs: Petroleum. Home: 7213 S Atlanta St Tulsa OK 74136-5508

BLACKSTON, BARBARA JEAN, dean biblical institute; b. Camden, N.J., Jan. 11, 1944; d. Allen Maxie and Phyllis Irene (Armstrong) Kee; m. Claude Anthony Kellam, Feb. 2, 1963 (div. June 1972); children: Claude Anthony Jr., Derrick Laeon, Debra Lynn Kellam Elshaikh; m. Harry Henry Blackston, Aug. 23, 1986. BA in Theology, United Christian Coll., Wilmington, Del.., 1987; AA in Christian Ministry, Geneva Coll., Beaver Falls, Pa., 1992, BS in Urban Ministry Mgmt., 1994. Ordained to ministry, 1994. Clerk-typist II New Castle County Prothonotary's Office, Wilmington, Del., 1969-80; dep. sheriff New Castle County Sheriffs Dept., Wilmington, Del., 1980-90; substitute tchr. Smyrna (Del.) Sch. Dist., 1994—, Appoquinimink Sch. Dist., Middletown, 1994—; Bible class tchr. Faith Unity Fellowship Ministries, Millington, Md., 1994—, ministerial and adminstrv. bd., 1994—. Author: (book) Developing A Bible Institute, 1992. Mem. cmty. group Say No To Drugs, Middletown, 1988; coord. seminars Neighborhood House, Middletown, 1993-94. Recipient award for outstanding achievements with Sunday sch. Trinity A.M.E. Ch., 1993. Home: PO Box 386 Middletown DE 19709 Office: Fellowship Bibl Theol Inst Box 31850 Millington MD 21651

BLACKWELL, DOROTHY PATTON, artist; b. Columbia, S.C., May 6, 1949; d. Charles Shannon and Dorothy Mitchell (Kelly) B. BA in Cultural Geography, Macalester Coll., St. Paul, 1974; Cert. Moyen, French Lang./Lit., Sorbonne, Paris, 1977; postgrad., Escola de Artes Visuais, Rio de Janeiro, 1984-86. Owner Blackwell Studios, Camden, S.C., 1993—; onwer Blackwell Studios, Rio de Janeiro, 1993—; Dorland Mountain Arts Colony residency, Temecula, Calif., 1994; art columnist Rio Life, 1987-89. One woman shows include: Sao Jose dos Campos, Brazil, 1987, Sao Paulo, Brazil, 1987, N.Y.C., 1988, Museu de Arte Contemporaneo, Goiania, Goias, Brazil, 1993, Brasilia, Brazil, 1993, Recife, Pernambuco, Brazil, 1993, Louisville, 1995, Camden, 1996; group shows in cities including Rio de Janeiro, Brasilia, Sao Paulo, Asheville, N.C., Salvador, Bahia, Brazil, Cairo, Camden, Burlingame, Calif., Boca Raton, Fla., Greenville, S.C., Charleston, S.C., Washington. Mem. Am. Coun. of the Arts, Nat. Mus. of Women in the Arts, Nat. Artists Equity Assn. Episcopalian. Office: Blackwell Studios 1202 Broad St PO Box 399 Camden SC 29020

BLACKWELL, JEANNINE, foreign language educator; b. Tyron, N.C., July 26, 1949; d. Benjamin and Lois (Turner) B.; m. Michael Taylor Jones, Dec. 18, 1987; 1 child, Bettina. BA, Duke U., 1971, MA, 1975; PhD, Ind. U., 1982. Asst. prof. German Mich. State U., East Lansing, 1983-85; asst. prof. German U. Ky., Lexington, 1985-89, assoc. prof. German, 1989—; assoc. dean arts & scis. U. Ky., 1992-94. Assoc. editor Colloguia Germanica jour., 1994—; co-editor (spl. issue) Cultural Contentions in Early Modern Germany, 1996. Fulbright fellow, 1989-90. Mem. Modern Lang. Assn. (discipline exec. com. 1995—), Coalition Women in German (steerimg com. 1985-88). Office: U Ky German Dept 1055 Patterson Tower Lexington KY 40506

BLACKWOOD, LOIS ANNE, elementary education educator; b. Denver, Sept. 18, 1949; d. Randolph William and Eloise Anne (Green) Burchett; m. Clark Burnett Blackwood, June 26, 1971; children: Anna Colleen, Courtney Brooke. BA, Pacific U., 1971. Tchr. Forest Grove (Oreg.) Pub. Schs., 1971-72, Clarksville (Tenn.) Pub. Schs., 1972-73, Dept. of Defense Schs., Frankfurt, Germany, 1973-76; tchr. St. Vrain Valley Schs., Longmont, Colo., 1977—, presenter insvcs. and symposia, 1977-93, also tchr. of tchrs.; cons. Brush Pub. Schs., 1985; presenter U. No. Colo. Symposium, 1987, Greater San Diego Math. Conf., 1992-95, rural math. connections project U. Colo., 1992-94, So. sect. Calif. Coun. Math. Tchrs., 1992-95. Recipient sustained superior svc. award U.S. Army, Frankfurt, 1975, outstanding performance award, 1976; Presdl. award for excellence in math. tchg. State of Colo., 1991, 94, Outstanding Elem. Math. Tchr. award Colo. Coun. Tchrs. Math., 1993; named Outstanding Tchr. of Yr., Longmont Area C. of C., 1992. Mem. NEA, Colo. Edn. Assn., St. Vrain Valley Tchrs. Assn., Phi Delta Kappa. Republican. Home: 1175 Winslow Cir Longmont CO 80501-5225 Office: Cen Elem Sch 1020 4th Ave Longmont CO 80501-5356

BLADE, MELINDA KIM, archaeologist, educator, researcher; b. San Diego, Jan. 12, 1952; d. George A. and Arline A. M. (MacLeod) B. BA, U. San Diego, 1974, MA in Teaching, 1975, MA, 1975, EdD, 1986. Cert. secondary tchr., Calif., cert. community coll. instr., Calif., registered profl. historian, Calif. Instr. Coronado Unified Sch. Dist., Calif., 1975-76; head coach women's basketball U. San Diego, 1976-78; instr. Acad. of Our Lady of Peace, San Diego, 1976—, chmn. social studies dept., 1983—, counselor, 1984-92, co-dir. student activities, 1984-87, coord. advanced placement program, 1986-95, dir. athletics, 1990; mem. archaeol. excavation team U. San Diego, 1975—, hist. researcher, 1975—; lectr., 1981—. Author hist. reports and research papers. Editor U. San Diego pubs. Vol. Am. Diabetes Assn., San Diego, 1975—; coord. McDonald's Diabetes Bike-a-thon, San Diego, 1977, 78; bd. dirs. U. San Diego Sch. Edn. Mem. Nat. Council Social Studies, Calif. Council Social Studies, Soc. Bibl. Archeology, Assn. Supervision and Curriculum Devel., Assn. Scientists and Scholars Internat. for Shroud of Turin, Medieval Acad. Am., Medieval Assn. Pacific, Am. Hist. Assn., Western Assn. Women Historians, Renaissance Soc. Am., San Diego Hist. Soc., Phi Alpha Theta (sec.-treas. 1975-77), Phi Delta Kappa. Office: Acad Our Lady of Peace 4860 Oregon St San Diego CA 92116-1340

BLADEN, LAURIE ANN, women's health nurse; b. Van Wert, Ohio, June 28, 1962; d. Arnold Hugh and Evelyn Martha (Woods) Kirchenbauer; m. David C. Bladen, Apr. 24, 1982; children: Maureen, Nathan, Olivia. ADS in Nursing, Lima Tech. Coll., 1981; BSN, N.Y. Regents Coll., 1983. Staff nurse pediatrics Mercer Cmty. Hosp., Coldwater, Ohio, 1981-85, coord. pediatric unit, 1985-87, house supr., 1987-90, staff nurse obs-gyn., 1990-93, coord. JACHO, 1992—; ind. nurse evaluator Ohio Nurse Testing Svc., Columbus, 1993-95; chair retention com. Mercer City Hosp., 1993-94. Author: CNOR Handbook for Success, 1994. Home: 3085 Slavik Rd Coldwater OH 45828 Office: Mercer Cmty Hosp 800 W Main St Coldwater OH 45828-1613

BLADES, CAROL BRADY, public relations executive; b. Providence, R.I., Dec. 10, 1947; d. James Joseph and Alice Mary (Hartigan) Brady; children: Matthew Blades, Elizabeth Blades. Student, Trinity Coll., 1965-67, George Washington U., 1967-68; BA in Journalism, NYU, 1969. Exec. v.p. The Softness Group, Inc., N.Y.C., 1979-87, pres., 1987-93, pres., CEO, 1993—. Mem. Women Execs. in Pub. Rels. (bd. dirs. 1990-93, v.p. 1993—). Roman Catholic. Office: The Softness Group Inc 381 Park Ave S New York NY 10016-8806

BLAEDEL, JOAN ROSS, artist, art educator; b. Boston, Sept. 21, 1942; d. John Stuart and Lulu Margery (Nelson) Ross; m. David S. Blaedel, Aug. 25, 1969 (div. 1996). BA, Conn. Coll., 1964; postgrad., Yale U., 1964-65; MA, U. Iowa, 1967, MFA, 1968; Advanced Cert. in Poetry, U. Wash., 1996. Cert. tchr., Wash. Instr. painting, printmaking Seattle Art Mus., 1992, Edmonds (Wash.) C.C., 1992—, Pratt Fine Arts Ctr., Seattle, 1992—; active Artist in the City program Seattle Arts Commn., 1979-81, New Proposals program King County Arts Commn., 1977, 80. One-person shows include Karl Bornstein Gallery, Santa Monica, 1982, Surrey (B.C., Can.) Art Gallery, 1982, Seattle Art Mus., 1981, 82, Lawrence Gallery, Portland, Oreg., 1987, 88, Foster/White Gallery, Seattle, 1981, 83, 85, 87, 89, 90, Skagit Valley Coll., Mt. Vernon, Wash., 1990, Green River C.C., Auburn, Wash., 1985, 90, 1004 Gallery, Port Townsend, Wash., 1993, Grover/Thurston Gallery, Seattle, 1991, 93, 95, others; exhibited in more than 200 group and juried shows. Mem. Bumbershoot Festival Commn., Seattle, 1985-91; mem. Seattle Arts Commn., 1981-85. Mem. N.W. Print Coun. (charter), Book Arts Guild, N.W. Inst. for Architecture and Urban Studies in Italy.

BLAGDON, JANET CLAIRE, elementary school art educator; b. Medford, Mass., Dec. 13, 1939; d. Harry Mainwaring and Anstias Marian (Considine) B. BS in Edn., State Coll. Boston, 1961; MS in Art Edn., Mass. Coll. Art, 1973. Cert. tchr. elem., art, English, Mass. Elem. tchr. Jenkins Sch., Scituate, Mass., 1961-63, Hatherly Sch., 1963-66; tchr. art Scituate Jr. H.S., 1966-69; elem. tchr. Obregon Sch., Pico Rivera, Calif., 1969-70, Kingsbury, Phillips, Bates Schs., Wellesley, Mass., 1970—. Artist: many paintings entered in juried shows, published prints, Classic Collection of Fine Arts, 1992. Recipient numerous art awards from various groups including Bristol Art Mus., South Shore Art Ctr., Plymouth Art Guild, Duxbury Art Ctr. Mem. NEA, Mass. Tchrs. Assn., Wellesley Tchrs. Assn., Copely Soc. (John Singleton Copley award 1984), South Shore Art Ctr., North River Arts Assn. Home: 54 Emerson Rd Needham MA 02192

BLAIN, CHARLOTTE MARIE, physician, educator; b. Meadeville, Pa., July 18, 1941; d. Frank Andrew and Valerie Marie (Serafin) B.; student Coll. St. Francis, 1958-60, DePaul U., 1960-61; M.D., U. Ill., 1965; m. John G. Hamby, June 12, 1971 (dec. May 1976); 1 son, Charles J. Hamby. Intern, resident U. Ill. Hosps., Chgo., 1967-70; practice medicine specializing in internal medicine, Elmhurst, Ill., 1969—; instr. medicine U. Ill. Hosp., 1969-70; asst. prof. medicine Loyola U., 1970-71; mem. staff Elmhurst Meml. Hosp., 1970—; clin. asst. prof. Chgo. Med. Sch., 1978-95, U. Ill. Med. Sch., 1995—. U. Ill. fellow in infectious diseases, 1968-69. Bd. dirs. Classical Symphony. Diplomate Am. Bd. Family Practice, Am. Bd. Internal Medicine. Fellow A.C.P., Am. Acad. Family Practice; mem. AMA, Am. Soc. Internal Medicine, Am. Profl. Practice Assn., Am. Profl. Practice Assn., AAAS, Royal Soc. Medicine, DuPage Med. Soc. Roman Catholic. Club: Univ. (Chgo.). Contbr. articles and chpts. to med. jours. and texts. Home: 320 Cottage Hill Ave Elmhurst IL 60126-3302 Office: 135 Cottage Hill Ave Elmhurst IL 60126-3330

BLAINE, DOROTHEA CONSTANCE RAGETTÉ, lawyer; b. N.Y.C., Sept. 23, 1930; d. Robert Raymond and Dorothea Ottilie Ragetté; BA, Barnard Coll., 1952; MA, Calif. State U., 1968; EdD, UCLA, 1978; JD, Western State U., 1981; postgrad. in taxation Golden Gate U. Bar: Calif. 1982, U.S. Dist. Ct. (ea., so. and cen. dists.) Calif., 1982. Mem. tech. staff Planning Rsch. Corp., L.A., 1964-67; assoc. scientist Holy Cross Hosp., Mission Hills, Calif., 1967-70; career devel. officer and affirmative action officer County of Orange, Santa Ana, Calif., 1970-74, sr. adminstrv. analyst, budget and program coord., 1974-78; spl. projects asst. CAO/Spl. Programs Office, 1978-80, sr. adminstrv. analyst, 1980-83; pvt. practice, 1982—; instr. Am. Coll. Law, Brea, Calif., 1987; judge pro tem Orange County Mcpl. Ct., 1988—. Bd. dirs. Deerfield Community Assn., 1975-78, Orange YMCA, 1975-77. Mem. ABA, ACLU, Trial Lawyers Am., Calif. Trial Lawyers Assn., Orange County Trial Lawyers Assn., Calif. Women Lawyers, Nat. Women's Polit. Caucus, Calif. Bar Assn., Orange County Bar Assn. (Orange County del. to Calif. State Bar Conv. 1985-96, bd. dirs. Orange County lawyers referral svc. 1988-92, mandatory fee arbitration com. 1996), Delta Theta Phi, Phi Delta Kappa. Office: 3 Imperial Promenade Fl 4 Santa Ana CA 92707-5908

BLAINE, GLORIA BECKWITH, volunteer; b. Mpls., Nov. 21, 1924; d. Ralph Monroe and Edna Cathryn (Christenson) Beckwith; m. Charles Gillespie Blaine, Dec. 16, 1944 (div. 1985); children: Cathryn Blaine Muzzy, Susan Blaine Nesbitt, Charles Gillespie Jr. Student, Smith Coll., 1942-45. Mem. jr. bd. Buffalo Gen. Hosp., 1953-61, pres. jr. bd., 1958, patient rep., 1981—, chmn. patient rep. program, 1985-91. Bd. dirs. Psychiat. Clin. for Children and Adolescents, Buffalo, 1952-58, 67-73, United Way, Buffalo and Erie County, 1960-66, Planned Parenthood, Buffalo and Erie County, 1962-68; trustee Buffalo Sem., 1967-73; bd. dirs. United Way of Buffalo and Erie County, 1960-66, chmn. women's div., 1961; mem. Buffalo Fine Arts Acad., Buffalo Philharm Soc., Buffalo Zool. Soc., Buffalo Women for Downtown. Mem. Garret Club. Republican. Episcopalian. Home: 751 W Ferry St Buffalo NY 14222-1619

BLAINE, JANE ELAINE MICHAUD, counselor; b. San Antonio, May 20, 1945; d. John Leon and Minnie Lee (Carter) B.; m. Leo C. Michaud, June 30 (div. Nov. 1985); 1 child, Laura Lynn Michaud. BS, East Tex. State U., 1967, MEd, 1971, MS, 1984, EdD, 1989. Lic. prof. counselor; cert. tchr. Tchr. for dyslexic children Dallas Ind. Sch. Dist., 1968-91; assoc. neurocognitive assessor, therapist Dallas Neuropsychological Inst., Dallas, 1992-93; founder, dir. The Living Child Found., Dallas, 1993—; cons. Lakeview Neurorehabilitative Ctr., West Ossipee, N.H., 1995. Vol. Children's Med., Dallas, 1995—. Mem. ACA, Tex. Profl. Counselors, Tex. Assn. of Mental Health Counselors, Tex. Assn. of Assessment Counselors, Delta Kappa Pi, Delta Kappa Gamma (Epsilon chpt.), Phi Delta Kappa. Republican. Jewish. Office: The Living Child Found 6301 Gaston Ave 813 Dallas TX 75214

BLAIR, BONNIE, former professional speedskater, former Olympic athlete; b. Cornwall, N.Y., Mar. 18, 1964; d. Charlie and Eleanor B. Student, Mont. Tech. Univ. Mem. U.S. Olympic Team, Sarajevo, Yugoslavia, 1984; Gold medalist, 500m Speedskating, Bronze medalist 1,000m Calgary Olympic Games, 1988; Gold medalist, 500m Speedskating Albertville Olympic Games, 1992, Gold medalist, 1000m Speedskating, 1992; Gold medalist, 500m Speedskating Lillehammer Olympic Games, 1994, Gold medalist, 1000m Speedskating, 1994; pro tour speedskater, 1994-95. Recipient James E. Sullivan award for Outstanding U.S. amateur athlete, 1993, Sportswoman of the Year, Sports Illustrated, 1994. *

BLAIR, CAROL, social worker, therapist; b. South Ozone Pk., N.Y., Apr. 27, 1946; d. Harold Arthur Mac Pherson and Muriel Dorothy Page; (div. Aug. 1985); children: Karen, Laura. BA in Psychology, SUNY, Old Westbury, 1978; MSW, Adelphi U., 1989. Cert. social worker; credentialed alcoholism counselor. Welfare examiner Dept. Social Svc., Nassau County, N.Y., 1980-90; staff social worker People Outpatient Clinic, Bethpage, N.Y., 1990-92, Care Ctr. Children's Alcohol Resource Edn., Freeport, N.Y., 1992—. Mem. Dem. Nat. Com., Washington, 1995; mem. screening com. for psychotherapy NOW, Hempstead, N.Y., 1995—. Mem. NASW. Home: 92 E Lake Ave Massapequa Park NY 11762

BLAIR, ELEANOR SLIM, owner preschool; b. Phila., Feb. 17, 1939; d. William and Eleanor Hardy (Van Tine) Slim; m. Bryce Dixon Blair, Oct. 1, 1960; children: Bryce D. Jr., Barbara Jean, Susan Eleanor. BA, Coll. Mt. St. Joseph, 1975. Substitute tchr. Medina (Ohio) City and County Sch. Dists., 1975-77; presch. tchr., adminstr. Medina County YMCA, 1977-83; owner Hobby Horse Presch., Medina, 1983—. Vol. ARC, Medina, 1975-79; Sunday sch. tchr. St. Paul's Episcopal Ch., Medina, 1977-84. Mem. AAUW, Akron Area Assn. Edn. Young Children, DAR. Home: 726 Falling Oaks Dr Medina OH 44256

BLAIR, KATHIE LYNN, social services worker; b. Oakland, Calif., Sept. 29, 1951; d. Robert Leon Webb and Patricia Jean (Taylor) Peterson; m. Terry Wayne Blair, Dec. 29, 1970 (div. 1972); 1 child, Anthony Wayne. Eligibility worker Dept. Social Services, San Jose, Calif., 1974-76; adult and family services worker State of Oreg., Portland, 1977-90; guest speaker welfare advocacy groups, Portland, 1987. Translator: Diary of Fannie Burkhart, 1991; contbr. articles to profl. jours.; developer word game for children. Mem. Nat. Geog. Soc., A Brotherhood Against Totalitarian Enactments, Oreg. State Pub. Interest Rsch. Group, Clan Chattan Assn., Portland Highland Games Assn., Harley Owners Group, Ladies of Harley. Democrat.

BLAIR, MARIE LENORE, retired elementary school educator; b. Maramec, Okla., Jan. 9, 1931; d. Virgil Clement and Ella Catherine (Leen) Strode; m. Freeman Joe Blair, Aug. 26, 1950; children: Elizabeth Ann Blair Crump, Roger Joe. BS, Okla. A&M Coll., 1956; MS, Okla. State U., 1961, postgrad., 1965-68. Reading specialist Pub. Schs. Stillwater (Okla.), 1966-88. Past bd. dirs. Okla. Reading Council. Mem. Internat., Okla., Cimarron (past pres.) reading assns., NEA, Okla. Edn. Assn., Stillwater Edn. Assn., Kappa Kappa Iota. Democrat. Mem. Disciples of Christ. Lodges: Demoley Mothers, Rainbow Mothers, Lahoma, White Shrine Jerusalem (past worthy high priestess). Order White Shrine Jerusalem (past supreme queen's attendant), Internat. Order of Rainbow for Girls (Okla. exec. com.), Order Eastern Star (past grand Martha, past grand rep. of Nebr. in Okla.). Home: RR 1 Maramec OK 74045-9801

BLAIR, PATRICIA WOHLGEMUTH, economics writer; b. N.Y.C., Nov. 30, 1929; m. James P. Blair, Aug. 13, 1964; children: David A., Matthew W. BA with honors, Wellesley Coll., 1950; MA, Haverford Coll., 1952. Officer U.S. Agy. Internat. Devel., New Delhi, 1953-55, 63-64; editor Carnegie Endowment for Internat. Peace, N.Y.C., 1956-63, Devel. Digest, Nat. Planning Assn., Washington, 1965-68; staff assoc. Commn. on Internat. Devel., World Bank, Washington, 1969-70; ind. cons., writer, editor, 1970—. Editor: Health Needs of the World's Poor Women, 1980; contbr. articles to profl. publs. Mem. adv. com. Unitarian-Universalist Holdeen India Fund, Washington, 1984—; bd. dirs. Equity Policy Ctr., Washington, 1980-85. Mem. Soc. Internat. Devel. (internat. governing coun. 1975-79), Assn. Women in Devel., Asia Soc., UN Assn. Home and Office: 1411 30th St NW Washington DC 20007-3141

BLAIR, ROBIN ELISE FARBMAN, financial and management consultant, accountant; b. Detroit, Jan. 22, 1951; d. Aaron A. and Marie A. (Prager) Farbman; m. Charles E. Manley, 1996. B.A., Mich. State U., 1974; post-grad. Wayne State U., 1976, Pace U., 1985, New Sch. for Social Rsch., 1992-93. Drama critic Lansing State Jour., Mich., 1974; asst. editor Gale Research Co., Detroit, 1974-77; copy chief Ballantine Books, Random House, N.Y.C., 1977-79; fin. mgr. and adminstr. Ark Restaurants Corp., N.Y.C., 1980-83; owner, pres., acct., cons., Robin Blair Acctg. Services, N.Y.C., 1984—. Mem. Nat. Assn. Female Execs., N.Y. SBA. Democrat. Unitarian. Avocations: writing; piano. Address: 59 W 76th St New York NY 10023-1543

BLAIR, VIRGINIA ANN, public relations executive; b. Kansas City, Mo., Dec. 20, 1925; d. Paul Lowe and Lou Etta (Cooley) Smith; m. James Leon Grant, Sept. 3, 1943 (dec. July 1944); m. Warden Tannahill Blair, Jr., Nov. 7, 1947; children: Janet, Warden Tannahill, III. BS in Speech, Northwestern U., 1948. Free-lance writer, Chgo., 1959-69; writer, editor Smith, Bucklin & Assocs., Inc., Chgo., 1969-72, account mgr., 1972-79, account supr., 1979-80, dir. pub. relations, 1980-85; pres. GB Pub. Rels., 1985—; judge U.S. Indsl. Film Festival, 1974, 75; instr. Writer's Workshop, Evanston, Ill., 1978; dir. Northwestern U. Libr. Coun., 1978-91, dir. alumnae bd., 1986—, John Evans Club bd., 1990—. Emmy nominee Nat. Acad. TV Arts & Scis., 1963; recipient Service award Northwestern U., 1978, Creative Excellence award U.S. Indsl. Film Festival, 1976, Gold Leaf merit cert. Family Circle mag. and Food Coun. Am., 1977. Mem. Pub. Rels. Soc. Am. (counselors acad.), Am. Advt. Fedn. (lt. gov. Ill. 6th dist.), Women's Advt. Club Chgo. (pres.), Publicity Club Chgo., Nat. Acad. TV Arts & Scis., John Evans Club (bd. dirs.), Woman's Club Evanston (pres.), Zeta Phi Eta (Svc. award 1978, 93), Alpha Gamma Delta, Philanthropic and Ednl. Orgn. (Ill. chpt. pres.. dist. pres.). Author dramas (produced on CBS): Jeanne D'Arc: The Trial, 1961; Cordon of Fear, 1961; Reflection, 1961; If I Should Die, 1963; 3-act children's play: Children of Courage, 1967. Home and Office: 463 Highcrest Dr Wilmette IL 60091-2357

BLAIR-LARSEN, SUSAN MARGARET, educator; b. Plainfield, N.J., May 28, 1950; d. Adam Craig and Edith Elizabeth Blair; m. Bruce Osborn Larsen, July 15, 1989. BS, Castleton (Vt.) State Coll., 1972; MS, U. Scranton, Pa., 1974; EdD, U. Pa., 1984. Tchr. Palisades Sch. Dist., Kintnersville, Pa., 1973-75; reading specialist Lakewood (N.J.) Sch. Dist., 1975-84; prof. U. Minn., Morris, 1984-85, Rutgers U., Newark, 1985-88, Trenton (N.J.) State Coll., 1988-96, Coll. of N.J., Trenton, 1996—. Author: An Integrative Approach to Language Instruction, 1993; co-author: Joining the Forces to Guide the New Teacher, 1993. Mem. Mantoloking and Bay Head (N.J.) Women's Rep. Club. Mem. Internat. Reading Assn., Ea. Ednl. Rsch. Assn., Phi Delta Kappa (10 Yr. award 1990), Pi Lambda Theta, Kappa Delta Pi. Roman Catholic.

BLAKE, BRETT ELIZABETH, English language educator; b. Chicopee, Mass., Dec. 13, 1956; d. Robert W. and Carol C. (Clark) B.; 1 child, Robbie Clark Moe. BA, SUNY, Stony Brook, 1978; MA, Northwestern U., 1989; PhD, U. Ill., Chgo., 1994. Cert. ESL tchr., N.Y. Part-time adj. faculty Nat. Louis U., Chgo., 1991-94; asst. prof., dir. grad. TESOL Nazareth Coll., Rochester, N.Y., 1994—; mem. adv. bd. Children's Ctr., Chgo., 1991-93. Contbr. articles to profl. jours. Recipient Bilingual fellowship U.S. Dept. Edn., 1990. Mem. Am. Edn. Rsch. Assn., Nat. Coun. Tchrs. of English (chair panel session nat. conf. 1995), N.Y. State Reading Assn. (reviewer, editl. bd. 1995—), N.Y. State TESOL, Phi Sigma Iota. Office: Nazareth Coll 4245 East Ave Rochester NY 14618

BLAKE, CATHERINE C., judge; b. Boston, July 27, 1950; d. John Ballard and Jean Place (Adams) B.; m. Frank Eisenberg, June 22, 1974, 3 children. BA magna cum laude, Radcliffe Coll., 1972; JD cum laude, Harvard Law Sch., 1975. Bar: Mass. 1975, Md. Ct. Appeals 1977, U.S. Ct. Appeals (4th cir.) 1977, U.S. Dist. Ct. Md. 1977, D.C. 1979. Assoc. Palmer & Dodge, Boston, 1975-77; asst. U.S. atty. Dist. of Md., Balt., 1977-83, first asst. U.S. atty., 1983-85, 86-87, U.S. atty. (court-appointed), 1985-86; U.S. magistrate judge U.S. Dist. Ct. Md., Balt., 1987-95, U.S. dist. ct. judge, 1995—. Mem. Fed. Bar Assn., Md. Bar Assn., Nat. Assn. of Women Judges, Fed. Judges' Assn. Office: US Courthouse 101 W Lombard St Rm 110 Baltimore MD 21201-2626

BLAKE, DARLENE EVELYN, political worker, consultant, educator, author; b. Rockford, Iowa, Feb. 26, 1947; d. Forest Kenneth and Violet Evelyn (Fisher) Kuhlemeier; m. Joel Franklin Blake, May 1, 1975 (dec. Jan. 1989); 1 child, Alexander Joel. AA, North Iowa Area Community Coll., Mason City, 1967; BS, Mankato (Minn.) State Coll., 1969; MS, Mankato (Minn.) State U., 1975. Cert. profl. tchr., Iowa; registered art therapist. Tchr. Bishop Whipple Sch., Faribault, Minn., 1970-72; art therapist C.B. Wilson Ctr., Faribault, 1972-76, Sedgwick County Dept. Mental Health, Wichita, Kans., 1976-79; cons. Batten, Batten, Hudson & Swab, Des Moines, 1979-81; pres. J.F. Blake Co., Inc., Des Moines, 1990—; polit. cons. to Alexander Haig for Pres., 1987-88; mgmt. tng. specialist Comms. Data Svcs., Inc., Des Moines, 1988-90, exec. mgr. customer svc. spl. interest fulfillment div., 1990-92; mem. nat. adv. bd. Alexander Haig for Pres., 1987-88; cert. cons. assoc. Drake, Beam, Morin, Inc., Des Moines, 1993—. Exhibited in one-woman show at local libr., 1970. Mem. U.S. Selective Svc. Bd. 26 and 27, Polk County, Iowa, 1981—; sustaining mem. Rep. Nat. Com.; Rep. cand. Polk County Treas., Des Moines, 1982; chmn. Polk County Rep. Party, 1985-88; commr. Des Moines Commn. Human Rights and Job Discrimination, 1984-89; mem. Martin Luther King Scholarship Com., 1986-88; mem. Iowa State Bd. Psychology Examiners, 1983-90; mem. 5th Dist. Jud. Nominating Commn., 1990-96. Mem. Am. Art Therapy Assn., Iowa Art Therapy Assn. (pres. elect 1984-85, founder), Des Moines Garden Club (pres. 1984-85), Polk County Rep. Women (pres. elect 1983-85). Lutheran. Home and Office: 3815 SW 30th St Des Moines IA 50321-2050

BLAKE, DONNA JO, community relations professional; b. San Antonio, Dec. 17, 1954; d. Earl Le Roy and Eleanor JoAnne (Peterson) Lahm; m. Robert Walter Blake, Aug. 13, 1977; children: Bret, Jenna. BSBA, Nebr. Wesleyan U., 1993. Sec. Dorsey Labs., Sandoz Pharms. Corp., Lincoln, Nebr., 1973-75, adminstrv. sec., 1975-81, adminstrv. asst. II, 1981-95, adminstr. cmty. affairs, 1995—. Vol. Rape Crisis Line, Lincoln, 1980-82; bd. dirs. YWCA, Lincoln, 1990-91, Child Devel. Venture, Lincoln, 1995—, Lancaster County chpt. ARC, 1996—; Sunday sch. tchr. St. Mark's United Meth. Ch., Lincoln, 1993—. Democrat. Home: 2327 N 76th St Lincoln NE 68507 Office: Sandoz Pharms Corp 10401 Hwy 6 Lincoln NE 68517

BLAKE, LAURA, architect; b. Berkeley, Calif., Dec. 26, 1959; d. Igor Robert and Elizabeth (Denton) B. BA in Art History, Brown U., 1982; MArch, UCLA, 1985. Architect The Ratcliff Architects, Berkeley, 1986-90, IDG Architects, Oakland, Calif., 1990-92, ELS Architects, Berkeley, 1992—. Organizer charity ball Spinsters San Francisco, 1988, sec., 1988-89, mem. adv. bd., 1989-92; mem. San Francisco Jr. League. Recipient Alpha Rho Chi bronze medal, 1985. Mem. AIA. Republican. Episcopalian. Office: ELS Architects 2040 Addison St Berkeley CA 94704-1104

BLAKELEY, KELLIE ELDER, accountant, small business owner; b. Galveston, Tex., Nov. 16, 1962; d. Jack Donald Elder Jr. and Donna Roxanne Hardwick; m. Matthew Grant Blakeley, May 18, 1985; 1 child, Robert Preston. AA, Kilgore Coll., 1983; BBA, U. Tex., Tyler, 1987. Fiscal asst. Dallas Ser-Jobs for Progress, Dallas, 1987-89; contr. Casey's Ltd. (doing bus. as The Dog House), Dallas, 1989; adminstrv. asst. Carlisle Outdoor, Dallas, 1989; acct. Accts. On Call, Dallas, 1990; asst. contr. Lebco, Inc. (doing bus. as LA-Z-Boy), Dallas, 1990-91, customer svc. rep., 1991-94, acctg., MIS asst., 1991-95; pres. KEB Svcs., Inc., Dallas, 1995—; acct. Lincoln Property Co., Dallas, 1995—. Vol. Vol. Income Tax Assistance, Tyler and Dallas, 1985, 87; mem. Vickery Place Neighborhood Assn., Dallas, 1991—, Gloria Dei Handbell Choir, Dallas, 1995—; dean leader Boy Scouts Am., 1996. Mem. Inst. Mgmt. Accts., Greater Dallas C. of C., St. Thomas Aquinas Parents Assn. Republican. Roman Catholic. Home: 5310 Vickery Blvd

Dallas TX 75206 Office: KEB Svcs Inc PO Box 35586 Dallas TX 75235-0586

BLAKELEY, LINDA, writer, producer, psychologist, television host; b. Bklyn., July 26, 1941; d. Charles and Blanche (Josephson) Berkow; m. Dec. 17, 1961 (div. 1983); children: Stacey, Scott. BA, UCLA, 1964; MA, Calif. State U., Northridge, 1977; PhD, Calif. Grad. Inst., 1985. Founder, dir. Parents Sharing Custody, Beverly Hills, Calif., 1984-87; pvt. practice specializing in treatment of eating disorders Beverly Hills, 1984—; trainer Calif. Assn. Marriage and Family Therapists, 1988, 89; producer, host Positive Self Images interview/talk show. Author: ABC's of Stress Management, 1989, Do It with Love-Positive Parenting After Divorce, 1988, (audio tape) Success Strategies, 1992, The Magic Dress, 1996. Mem. adv. bd. Nat. Coun. Alcoholism and Drug Abuse, 1991-92. Mem. Calif. Psychol. Assn. (state bd. dirs. media com. 1989-92, chair-elect media divsn.), Calif. Assn. Marriage and Family Therapists (chmn. ethics com. L.A. chpt.), Beverly Hills C. of C. (pres. women's network 1989-90, chmn. health care com. 1989), Women in Film, Nat. Assn. Anorexia, Bulimia Assn. Disorders. Office: 420 S Beverly Dr Ste 100 Beverly Hills CA 90212-4410

BLAKELY, CAROLYN FRAZIER, university dean; b. Mangolia, Ark., Feb. 13, 1936; d. James D. and Mary E. (Brewer) Frazier; m. Neal Nathanial Blakely, June 7, 1959; children: Karen Joy, Earl Kevin. BA in English, Ark. AM&N Coll., 1957; MA in English, Atlanta U., 1964; PhD, Okla. State U., 1984. Tchr. various schs., Magnolia, 1957-62; asst. prof. English Grambling (La.) State U., 1963-66; asst. prof. English U. Ark., Pine Bluff, 1968-86, asst. to chancellor, 1986-90, interim vice chancellor academic affairs, 1990-91, interim chancellor, 1991, dean honors coll., 1992—; instr. writing lab Okla. State U., 1978-79. Contbr. articles to profl. jours. Bd. dirs. Delta Cultural Ctr., Helena, Ark., 1986—, Knox Nelson State Literacy Bd., Little Rock, 1985—, United Way Arts & Scis. Ctr., Pine Bluff, 1986—, vice chmn.; Worthen's Women's Adv., 1986—; past pres. Sister Cities, Pine Bluff; sec. Ark. Inst. Bd., Ark. Humanities Coun. Mem. Nat. Coun. Tchrs. English, So. Regional Honors Coun. (pres. 1991-92), Nat. Collegiate Honor Soc., Leadership Pine Bluff (pres. 1989-90), Sigma Tau Delta Nat. English Honor Soc., Alpha Kappa Alpha Sorority (pres. 1985-86, 95—). Democrat. Baptist. Home: 1101 W 23rd Ave Pine Bluff AR 71603-4201 Office: U of Ark Honors Coll 1200 University Dr Pine Bluff AR 71601-2799

BLAKELY, DELORES PHINELLA, financial consultant, business advisor; b. Manning, S.C., May 4, 1960; d. Aaron Jr. and Daisy (Kennedy) McF.; m. Lenard Jerome Blakely, Nov. 7, 1989; children: Seneca Duwayne McFadden, Crystal, Lynnette. BA in Bus. Mgmt., U. S.C., 1985; MBA in Fin. Mgmt., Morgan State U., 1988. Cert. fin. coord. Learning mgr. Sumter (S.C.) Area Tech., 1981-85; sales assoc. Fed. Machine Corp., Des Moines, 1985-87; pres. McFadden and Assocs., Sumter, 1987-90; CEO Blakely and Assocs., Sumter, 1990—, bus. advisor, 1993—. Vol. Mental Health Assn., Sumter, 1994-95; mentor Salvation Army Boys and Girls Club, 1993. Mem. NAFE, NOW, Acad. Polit. Sci., Nat. Assn. Fin. Cons., Internat. Alliance of Fin. Cons., S.C. Sheriff Assn. Democrat. Baptist. Home: 35 Pathfinder Dr Sumter SC 29153 Office: Blakely and Assocs Fin Svcs PO Box 2910 Sumter SC 29151

BLAKELY, INA YVETTE, company official; b. Little Rock, Jan. 20, 1964; d. Everett Jordan and Wanda Carolyn (Beulah) B. BS, U. Ark., Pine Bluff, 1987; MS in Adminstrn., Ctrl. Mich. U., 1996. Sec. Alternatives for Children and Families, 1986-89; adminstrv. asst. Market Opinion Rsch., Detroit, 1989-90; sales assoc. Paul Harris Stores, Southfield, Mich., 1990-91; account analyst Sycron Corp., Grand Blanc, Mich., 1990-92; office mgr. Ennis Ctr. for Children, Flint, Mich., 1993-94; admissions rep. Ross Med. Edn. Ctr., Flint, 1994-95; employee benefits clk. City of Flint, 1996—. Treas., bd. dirs. Dort-Oak Park Neighborhood House, Flint, 1992. Mem. NAFE, Alpha Kappa Alpha. Methodist.

BLAKELY, REGINA HOPPER, lawyer; b. Albuquerque, Apr. 21, 1959; d. Bobby Gene and Lois Marie (Oels) H.; m. Mark Kevin Blakely, Aug. 3, 1985. BA in Polit. Sci., U. Ark., 1981, JD, 1985. Bar: Ark. 1985, U.S. Dist. Ct. (ea. and we. dists.) Ark. 1986, U.S. Ct. Appeals (8th cir.) 1986. Entertainer Dept. of Def., Washington, 1983-84, Miss Ark. Miss Am. Pageant, Atlantic City, 1983-84; assoc. Arnold, Grobmyer and Haley, Little Rock, 1985-87; reporter Sta. KTHV-TV, Little Rock, 1987; news reporter, anchor Sta. KATV-TV, Little Rock, 1987-91; corr. CBS News, N.Y.C., 1991-92, CBS News/Newspath, Washington, 1992—. Fundraiser Easter Seals, Little Rock, 1988; mistress of ceremonies Miss Ark. Pageant, Hot Springs, 1984—; bd. dirs. Washington chpt. Child Help, 1995-96. Recipient Emmy award, 1992. Mem. ABA (securities com. 1985-92), Ark. Bar Assn. (securities com. 1985-92), Ark. Assn. Securities Dealers (exec. sec. 1985-92), Zeta Tau Alpha. Methodist. Office: CBS News 2020 M St NW Washington DC 20036-3368

BLAKESLEE-STEIS, CAROLYN, artist; b. Washington, Dec. 5, 1957; d. R.D. and Elaine Blakeslee; m. Drew F. Steis, Aug. 10, 1985; children: Dexter, Alex, Sheila, Timothy. Student, Mary Washington Coll., Corcoran Sch. of Arts, Washington. Pianist Hyatt Regency/Capitol Hill, Washington, 1980-86; editor-in-chief Art Calendar, Westover, Md., 1986—. Editor: Making a Living as an Artist, 1992, Getting the Word Out: The Artist's Guide to Self-Promotion, 1995, Getting Exposure: The Artist's Guide to Exhibiting the Work, 1995. Republican. Office: Art Calendar 25742 Frenchtown Rd Westover MD 21871

BLAKESLEY, SHEILA, real estate officer; b. Forsyth, Mont., Apr. 14, 1932; d. Robert E. and Eleanor E. (Borer) McKeever; m. Bruce L. Blakesley, Oct. 4, 1954. Student, Mt. St. Clare Coll., Clinton, Iowa. Sec. 1st State Bank Forsyth, 1951-56, bookkeeper, 1965, asst. cashier, real estate loan officer. Mem. Forsyth Womans Bowling Assn., Immaculate Conception Altar Soc., Forsyth Country Club. Roman Catholic. Office: 1st State Bank Forsyth 880 Main St Forsyth MT 59327

BLALOCK, ANN BONAR, policy analyst, evaluation researcher; b. Parkersburg, W.Va., Apr. 16, 1928; d. Harry and Fay (Conley) Bonar; m. Hubert Blalock, Jr., 1951; children: Susan Blalock Lyon, Kathleen Blalock McCarrell, James W. AB, Oberlin Coll., 1950; MA, U. N.C., 1954; MSW, U. Wash., 1978. Pvt. cons. Admiralty Inlet Consulting, Hansville, Wash. Co-author: Introduction to Social Research; co-editor: Methodology in Social Research; editor Evaluation Forum, Evaluating Social Programs. Recipient research award Partnership for Employment and Tng. Careers. Mem. NASW (past pres. Wash. State chpt.), Am. Eval. Assn. (past com. chair), Assn. Pub. Policy Analysis and Mgmt. Home: PO Box 409 Hansville WA 98340-0409

BLALOCK, SHERRILL, investment advisor; b. Newport News, Va., June 9, 1945; d. David Graham and Martha Lee (Bennett) B.; m. Jonathan L. Smith, Oct. 27, 1985; 1 child, Graham C.G. BA, Smith Coll., 1967. Chartered fin. analyst. Investment broker Legg Mason & Co., Washington, 1968-77, Blyth Eastman Dillon, Washington, 1977-80; portfolio mgr., mng. dir. Mitchell Hutchins, N.Y.C., 1980-88; gen. ptnr., portfolio mgr. Weiss Peck & Greer, N.Y.C., 1988-95; gen. ptnr. Delphi Asset Mgmt., N.Y.C., 1995—. Mem. investment com. Diocese of N.Y. of Episcopal Ch., 1992—, trustee Estate and Property of Diocesan Conv. of N.Y., 1996—. Mem. Washington Soc. Investment Analysts, Inst. Chartered Fin. Analysts. Office: Delphi Asset Mgmt 20th Fl 485 Madison Ave New York NY 10022

BLANC, CARYN, retail executive. Sr. v.p. distbr. and store adminstrn. Kohl's Corp., Menomonee Falls, Wis. Office: Kohl's Corp N 54 W 13600 Woodale Dr Menomonee Falls WI 53051*

BLANCHARD, BETHANY ANNE, art educator; b. Watertown, N.Y., Oct. 22, 1961; d. Orin Lewis and Lena Cassie (Lytle) Rogers; m. Steven Irving Blanchard, June 28, 1991; 1 child, Cassie Malena. Student, Brockport State Coll., 1980; BA, Potsdam State Coll., 1983; MA in Edn., St. Lawrence Coll., 1989. Permanent tchrs. cert. Art tchr. Indian River Sch. Dist., Phila., 1984—; mem. ednl. adv. com. IRMS, Phila., 1993; active N.Y. State United Tchrs., Albany. Writer of three pub. songs. Active Citizens Against Violent Acts, Canton, N.Y., 1983-84.

BLANCHARD, COLLEEN DIANA, trade association administrator; b. Madison, S.D., May 7, 1945; d. Dale Roland Coates and Clair B. (Frewaldt) Kubik; m. Rodney James Blanchard, Mar. 9, 1966 (div. Apr. 1985); children: Brent Alan, Darin Layne. BS, Dakota State Coll., 1968; postgrad., N.E. Mo. State U., 1972, Pers. Dynamics Inst., 1973, Laverne U., 1973-74. Cert. tchr., Iowa. Tchr. Laverne (Calif.) U., 1973-74, Oskaloosa (Iowa) Community Schs., 1968-85; owner C. J.'s Hallmark Shop, Oskaloosa, 1985-89; south cen. states dist. mgr. Jerry Elsner Co., N.Y.C., 1989-91; mgr., spl. regional trainer Nat. Fedn. Ind. Bus., Omaha, 1991; presenter at seminars and workshops in field, Oskaloosa, 1973-75. Diplomat Oskaloosa C. of C., 1986-89; project dir. Community Devel. Found., Oskaloosa, 1984; vol. United Community Svcs., Oskaloosa, 1980-85; campaign worker Rep. Party, Oskaloosa. U.S. Dept. Edn. grantee, 1976; recipient Outstanding Educator award Oskaloosa Edn. Assn., 1974, Summit award Nat. Fedn. Ind. Bus. for Achievement, 1994. Roman Catholic. Home: 11905 Wakeley Plz # 5 Omaha NE 68154-2431

BLANCHARD, KAREN MARIE, development professional; b. Holyoke, Mass., Sept. 30, 1965; d. Ralph Joseph and Nancy Louise (Lecnar) B. AS in Bus. Adminstrn., Holyoke (Mass.) C.C., 1985; BS in Human Svcs., Springfield (Mass.) Coll., 1995. Adminstrv. asst. United Way, Holyoke, 1987-89; devel. assoc. Providence Ministries, Holyoke, 1989—. Mem. Women in Devel. of Western Mass. (treas. 1995-96). Roman Catholic. Office: Providence Ministries Box 6269 476 Appleton St Holyoke MA 01040

BLANCHARD, MARGARET MOORE, educator; b. Columbus, Ga., Dec. 29, 1938; d. Robert Moore and Ann (Keller) B. BA, Incarnate Word Coll., 1960; MA, St. Louis U., 1962; PhD, Union Inst., 1990. Instr. St. Louis U., 1960-62, Grailville C.C., Cin., 1962-64, LeMoyne Coll., Syracuse, N.Y, 1964-66, U. Wis., Madison, 1967-69; asst. prof. Morgan State U., Balt., 1969-71; adminstr. Women's Growth Ctr., Balt., 1972-74; asst. prof. Towson State U., Balt., 1975-90; assoc. prof. Vt. Coll., Montpelier, 1990—; dir. The Grad. Program, Montpelier, 1995—. Author: Ten Irish-American Women Poets, 1987, The Rest of the Deer, 1993; co-author: Restoring the Orchard, 1994, Duet, 1995; author of poems; contbr. articles to profl. jours. Mem. Nat. Assn. Poetry Therapy, Nat. Women's Studies Assn. (cmty. coord. 1993), Nat. Coun. Tchrs. English, Internat. Women's Writers Guild, LVW. Office: The Grad Program Vt Coll Montpelier VT 05602

BLANCHETTE, JEANNE ELLENE MAXANT, artist, educator, performer; b. Chgo., Sept. 25, 1944; d. William H. and L. Barbara (Martin) Maxant; m. Yasuo Shimizu, Apr. 28, 1969 (div. 1973); m. William B. Blanchet, Aug. 21, 1981 (dec. May 1993). BA summa cum laude, Northwestern U., 1966; MFA, Tokyo U., 1971; MA, Ariz. State U., 1978; postgrad., Ill. State U., 1979-80; PhD, Greenwich U., 1991. Instr. Tsuda U., Kodaira, Japan, 1970-71; free-lance visual, performing artist various cities, U.S., 1973—; artist in residence YMCA of the Rockies, Estes Park, Colo., 1976-81 summers; prof. fine arts Rio Salado Coll., Surprise, Ariz., 1976-91; lectr. Ariz. State U. West, Sun City, 1985-93; lectr., evaluator several arts cons. including Ariz. Humanities Coun., 1993; Prescott Melodrama ragtime pianist, 1993, 94; artist with Performing Arts for Youth, 1994—. Selected for regional, state, nat. juried art shows, 1975—, mus. and gallery one-woman shows of computer art, 1988—; author: Original Songs and Verse of the Old (And New) West, 1987, A Song in My Heart, 1988, Reflections, 1989, The Mummy Story, 1990; contbr. articles to newspapers, profl. jours. Founding mem. Del Webb Hosp. Woodrow Wilson fellow, 1966; ADA B.C. Welsh scholar, 1980; recipient numerous art, music awards, 1970—, major computer art awards in regional, nat., and internat. shows, 1990—. Mem. Nat. League Am. Pen Women (sec. chpt. 1987, v.p. 1988, pres. 1990-92, pres. Colo. chpt. 1996—), Ariz. Press Women (numerous awards in original graphics and writing 1980s, 90s), Nat. Fedn. Press Women, Northwestern U.'s John Evans Club, Henry W. Rogers Soc., P.E.O., Phi Beta Kappa. Home and Office: 411 Lakewood Cir # C-907 Colorado Springs CO 80910-2617

BLANCHFIELD, SYLVIA LOUISE, nursing educator; b. Walla Walla, Wash., Nov. 10, 1947; d. Meade N. and Mary Frances (Nelson) Kinzer; m. Roger L. Blanchfield, July 12, 1970; children: Loralee N., Brett J. BS, Walla Walla Coll., 1969; MS, Drake U., 1991; postgrad., Iowa State U. RN, Iowa. Staff nurse, health educator Iowa Women's Reformatory, Rockwell City, 1981-83; ICU nurse Stewart Meml. Cmty. Hosp., Lake City, Iowa, 1983-88; nursing instr. Des Moines Area C.C., Boone, Iowa, 1988—; summer honorarium Iowa State U., Ames, 1996; mem. accreditation com. Des Moines Area C.C., 1993-96, faculty fellow, 1994; guest prof. Union Coll., Lincoln, Nebr., 1993 (summer). Author publs. in field. Vol. various chs., Lions Club, Mothers Clubs, hospice/bereavement group, SMCH, Lake City, 1976-81; mem. Farm Bur., Jefferson, Iowa; chair program platform com. Iowa-Mo. Women's Retreats, Des Moines, 1988-95; mem. Gov.'s Vol. of Yr. Com., Greene County. Psychiatric nursing trainee U.S. Dept. Health Edn., 1968. Mem. Nat. League for Nursng, Iowa League for Nursing, Nursing Faculty Assn. (staff devel. coord. 1992-94), Federated Women's Club (past pres., v.p., sec.), Sigma Theta Tau (Zeta Chi chpt.). Republican. Home: 767 110th St Churdan IA 50050-8538 Office: Des Moines Area CC 1125 Hancock Dr Boone IA 50036-5326

BLANCO, CAROL ELLEN KUCHLER, choreographer, educator; b. Marin County, Calif., Oct. 9, 1961. BA in Theater, U. Calif., Berkeley, 1984; attending, Bklyn. Coll. Asst. company mgr. Murray Louis Dance, N.Y.C., 1988, ISO Dance, N.Y.C., 1989; company mgr. Robert Kovich Co., N.Y.C., 1990-92, Douglas Dunn & Dancers, N.Y.C., 1992-95; artistic dir. The Blanco Dances, N.Y.C., 1992—; performer Off-Off Broadway, N.Y.C., 1990-96; choreographer Off Broadway, N.Y.C., 1996; tchr. dance, staff UN, N.Y.C., 1993—; Pres. Kovich Dance Found., N.Y.C., 1990—. Artistic assoc. Spin Theater, 1994—. Recipient Scholarship/Merit award Nikolais/Louis Found., 1988, 89, Cunningham Dance Found., 1990. Mem. AAUW, Soc. Stage Dirs. & Choreographers. Home: PO Box 985 New York NY 10011

BLANCO, KATHLEEN BABINEAUX, lieutenant governor; m. Raymond; 6 children. With La. State Legis. Dist. 45, 1984-88, mem. house edn. com., mem. house transp., hwys., and pub. works com.; mem. house edn. com., mem. house transp., hwys. and pub. works com. Pub. Svc. Commn., La., 1988-94, chair, 1993, 94; lt. gov. La. State Govt., 1995—. Address: PO Box 44243 Baton Rouge LA 70804*

BLANCO, LAURA, film producer; b. Havana, Cuba, July 3, 1956; came to U.S., 1960; d. Lauro and Marina (Mardones) B.; m. Robert F. Shainheit, June 30, 1988. Asst. box office treas., press agt. Zev Bufman Entertainment, Inc., Orlando, St. Petersburg, Fla., 1978-83; press agt. Kool Jazz Festival and Heritage Fair, Orlando, 1982; producer La. World Exposition Inc., New Orleans, 1983-84, Festival Ventures, Inc., Miami, Fla., 1985-86; producer/dir. hispanic events Festival Prodns., Inc., N.Y.C., 1986-87; pres. Blanco Shainheit Prodns., Blanco Shainheit Music, N.Y.C., 1988—; ptnr. unanimo, 1992—; ASCAP Pop Songwriters' Workshop, 1992. Prodr. film The Summer of My Dreams, 1994, Bricks, 1995. Bd. dirs. Artists Community Fed. Credit Union, 1988-90. Mem. ASCAP, Am. Latin Music Assn. Democrat. Jewish.

BLAND, ANNIE RUTH (ANN BLAND), nursing educator; b. Bennett, N.C., Oct. 14, 1949; d. John Wesley and Mary Ida (Caviness) Brown; m. Chester Wayne Bland; 1 child, John Wayne; stepchildren: Jason Tyler, Adam Mathew. BS in Nursing, East Carolina U., Greenville, N.C., 1971; MS in Nursing, U. N.C., 1978; postgrad., U. S.C., 1996—. RN, N.C.; cert. clin. specialist in adult psychiat./mental health nursing; cert. BLS instr. Staff nurse VA Med. Ctr., Durham, N.C., 1974-75, 77-80; psychiat. clin. instr. Duke U. Med. Ctr., Durham, 1980-82, asst. head nurse, 1982-90, staff nurse, 1993—; psychiat. clin. nurse specialist John Umstead Hosp., Butner, N.C., 1990-93; psychiat. head nursing instr. Alamance C.C., Graham, N.C., 1994-96. Asst. Sunday sch. tchr. Mt. Hermon Bapt. Ch., Durham, 1994, 96—. With USN, 1971-74, capt. USNR, 1974—. Recipient award for nursing excellence Great 100 Orgn., Raleigh, N.C., 1991, Letter of Appreciation Am. Heart Assn., Chapel Hill, 1992. Mem. ANA, N.C. Nurses Assn. (sec. dist. 11, 1981), Naval Res. Assn., Assn. Mil. Surgeons U.S., U. N.C. Alumni Assn. and Sch. Nursing, East Carolina U. Alumni Assn. and Sch. Nursing, Nat. Alliance for Mentally Ill, Epilepsy Found. Baptist. Home: 3226 Carriage Trl Hillsborough NC 27278-9554 Office: U South Carolina Coll of Nursing Columbia SC 29208

BLAND, DOROTHY M., newspaper publishing executive; b. Little Rock, Aug. 27, 1958; d. Lee Jr. and Dorothy G. (Freeman) B. BS in Journalism, Ark. State U., 1980; MBA in Mktg., George Washington U., 1988. Reporter to asst. city editor Rockford (Ill.) Register Star, 1980-83; reporter to mng. editor libr. U.S.A. Today, Arlington, Tex., 1983-90; asst. to regional pres. Gannett/Rockford Register Star, 1990-92; pres., pub. Chillicothe (Ohio) Gazette, 1992-94, Ft. Collins (Colo.) Coloradoan, 1994—. Participant Vols. in Pub. Schs., Ft. Collins, 1995—; bd. dirs. area United Way, Ft. Collins, 1995—. Mem. Nat. Assn. Black Journalists, Am. Soc. Newspaper Editors, Nat. Assn. Minority Media Execs., Soc. Profl. Journalists, Ft. Collins C. of C., Rotary (Ft. Collins club). Office: Ft Collins Coloradoan 1212 Riverside Fort Collins CO 80525

BLAND, ERLENA CHISOLM, artist, sculptor; b. Washington; d. Charles Sumner and Erlena Viola (Holmes) Chisolm; m. Charles Neal Bland; children: Charles Neal Bland Jr., Lisa Frances Bland Malone. BA, Howard U., 1944; BLS, U. Md., MLS, 1968. Subject cataloguer, acquisition searcher Libr. of Congress, Washington, 1944-55; cataloguer Howard U., Washington, 1959; libr., media specialist D.C. Pub. Schs., Washington, 1969-84; sculptor, painter, 1972—; curator Health Collection Meharry Med. Coll., Nashville, 1949-50. Individual Artist grantee D.C. Commn. Arts and Humanities, 1994. Mem. Internat. Sculpture Ctr., Washington Sculpture Group. Home: 1711 Kalmia Rd NW Washington DC 20012 Office: Chisolm Bland Studio 52 O St NW Washington DC 20001

BLANEY, DOROTHY GULBENKIAN, academic administrator. BA in Comparative Lit. with high hons., Cornell U., 1962; Woodrow Wilson Fellow Comparative Lit., U. Calif., Berkeley, 1963; PhD in English, SUNY, Albany, 1971. Asst. prof. English SUNY, Albany, 1968-71; coord. N.Y. State Doctoral Rev. Program, Albany, 1971-73; asst. commr. higher edn. planning and policy analysis N.Y. State Edn. Dept., Albany, 1973-78, dep. commr. higher edn. and professions, 1978-81; cons. Internat. Labor Office, Internat. Mgmt. Inst., Geneva, N.Y.C., Switzerland, U.S., 1981-82; exec. v.p. Pace U., N.Y.C., 1982-88; pres. Cedar Crest Coll., Allentown, Pa., 1989—. Co-author (with Ernst R. May): (book) Careers for Humanists, 1981; columnist for Times Mirrors, Morning Call, and, occasionally, U.S.A. Today, Phila. Inquirer, Atlanta Constitution; contbr. articles to mags. and jours. Office: Cedar Crest Coll Office of the President 100 College Dr Allentown PA 18104-6132

BLANFORD, MICHELLE MARIE, sales professional; b. Chgo., July 1, 1970; d. J. William and Nancy Elizabeth (Kleine) B. BS in Mktg., Boston Coll., 1992. Front desk supr. Chgo. Marriott Downtown, 1992-93, conv. fl. mgr., 1993-94, exec. meeting coord., 1994-95, catering sales mgr., 1995; exec. meeting mgr. Marriott, Irvine, Calif., 1996—. Vol. maintenance and upkeep of retirement home Chgo. Housing Authority, 1994. Mem. NOW, Boston Coll. Alumni Club Chgo.

BLANK, FLORENCE WEISS, literacy educator, editor; b. Bridgeport, Conn.; d. Maurice Herbert and Henrietta Helen (Shapiro) Weiss; m. Bernard Blank, Apr. 10, 1965 (dec. Aug., 1989). Student Journalism, English, Psychology, Richmond Profl. Inst.; student, U. Richmond, Northwestern U., Va. Union U., 1967, 73, 74, U. Wis., Milw., 1971, Va. Commonwealth U., 1973, D.C. Tchrs. Coll., 1975. Tchr. adult edn. dept. Richmond (Va.) Pub. Sch. System, 1952-77; project dir., tchr. tng. and edn. dir., tchr. Right to Read Fed. Grant, D.C., 1976-79; in-svc. tchr. tng. U. D.C., Washington, 1975-87; cons.-tchr. in-svc. tchr. tng. program Durham (N.C.) City Schs., 1983-87; tchr. adult edn. dept. Henrico County (Va.) Pub. Schs., 1987—; dir., condr. numerous in-svc. tng. seminars, classes for elem. and secondary sch. and adult edn. tchrs. in Va., D.C., Md.; tchr. of ESL classes in evening sch.; tchr., spl. com. tng. program for Chesapeake and Ohio Ry., Richmond, 1955-59; tchr. spl. class for postal and fed. employees at Phyllis Wheatley YWCA, Richmond, 1968; dir., tchr. Weiss Reading Inst., Richmond, 1960-76. Co-author: (with Carolyn W. Guertin) Sound Skill Builder, 1976; editor-in-chief: Sure Steps to Reading and Spelling, 1976, The Science of Reading and Spelling. Mem. Am. Assn. for Adult and Continuing Edn., Learning Disabilities Assn., The Learning Disabilites Coun. of Richmond, Altrusa Internat. Inc. of Capital City of Va.

BLANK, JOAN GILL, journalist, illustrator; b. Buffalo, Apr. 3, 1928; d. Ralph C. and Miriam A. Epstein; m. Harvey Blank, Sept. 14, 1975; children: Robin, Susan, Prudence. AB, Sarah Lawrence Coll., 1949. Editor, art dir. Investment Sales Monthly, Coral Gables, Fla., 1964-68, Fla. Commentary, Hollywood, 1973-75, Communique, Miami, Fla., 1974-75; editor, designer Born of The Sun, 1975-76; freelance writer, 1950—; cons. in field, 1963—; pres. Grapetree Prodns., Inc., 1981—. Author: Give Your Whole Self, 1981, Key Biscayne, A History of Miami's Tropical Island & The Cape Florida Lighthouse, 1996; author, illustrator: Laugh Lines, 1982; contbr. articles and photo-features to mags. and newspapers. Mem. Nat. Press Club, Phi Theta Kappa, Chi Delta Phi. Democrat. Address: 600 Grapetree Dr Apt 10cn Key Biscayne FL 33149-2704

BLANK, JULIE LYNN, secondary education educator; b. Bloomington, Ind., Nov. 23, 1960; d. Logan Fink and Shirley (Remaley) B.; m. Jean-Luc Roger Patrice Marcais, Mar. 28, 1980 (div. Feb. 1985); m. James Morris Southall, Dec. 27, 1993 (sep.); 1 child from previous marriage, Jamie Southall. AB in French Lang. and Lit., U. Calif., Berkeley, 1984; single subject tchg. credential, San Francisco State U., 1994. Longterm substitute French tchr. Terra Nova H.S., Pacifica, Calif., 1993-94; longterm substitute CLAD/ELD Havenscourt Jr. H.S., Oakland, Calif., 1995; computer tchr. Calaveras Hills H.S., Milpitas, Calif., 1995—; consumer math tchr. Calaveras Hills H.S., Milpitas, 1996—. Vol. for polit. campaign Boxer for Senate, San Francisco, 1992. Grantee Crumpton/Baxter/Bonham, San Francisco State U., 1993. mem. AAUW, Am. Fedn. Tchrs. French. Democrat. Episcopalian. Home: 3639 Crow Canyonland San Ramon CA 94583 Office: Milpitas Unified Sch Dist Bldg 300 1331 E Calaveras Blvd Milpitas CA 95035

BLANKEN, SARAH STUBER, retired foundation administrator; b. Clay, Pa., Jan. 18, 1928; d. Harry Miles and Mamie (Stauffer) Stuber; m. Edmund M. Blanken Jr., Sept. 6, 1947 (div. 1993); children: Lynne Einhaus, Ed III, Susan Sellmeyer, Barbara Amato. V.p. Nat. Coalition for Protection Children and Families, Cin., 1989-93; ret., 1993. Pres. Boone County Rep. Women, Exec. Svc. Corps. Cin., Federated Women's Club and St. Luke Aux.; co-founder No. Ky. Women's Forum; bd. dirs. Enough is Enough!, 1996—, Citizens for Cmty. Values, Cin., 1983-96, Religious Alliance Against Poronography, Cin., 1986—. Presbyterian. Office: Enough is Enough! Campaign PO Box 888 Fairfax VA 22030

BLANKENBURG, JULIE J., librarian; b. Madison, Wis., Dec. 22, 1956; d. Henry A. and Marjorie L. Blankenburg; m. Wayne I. Zimmerman, July 16, 1991; 1 child, Troy Anthony. BA in Theatre, U. Wis., 1979, MA in LS, 1980. Libr. asst. 3 and 4, then libr. assoc. II, Wis. Reference and Loan Libr., Madison, 1980-82; libr. asst. Dane County Bookmobile, Madison, 1983; libr. asst. 2 Meml. Libr., U. Wis., Madison, 1983-84, libr. svcs. asst. 3 Law Libr., 1984-88; asst. libr. USDA Forest Products Lab. Libr., Madison, 1988-93, libr., 1994—. Mem. ALA, Spl. Librs. Assn., Wis. Libr. Assn., Theatre Libr. Assn. Office: USDA Forest Svc Forest Products Lab Libr One Gifford Pinchot Dr Madison WI 53705-2398

BLANKENSHIP, JUANITA CHAPMAN, court administrator; b. Miles City, Mont., Feb. 25, 1935; d. Terry Stilson Chapman and June Harriet (Brown) Shelden; m. Thomas Hall Blankenship, June 5, 1956 (div. July 1974). BA, U. Mont., 1956; postgrad., U. Hawaii, 1966-67; MA, U. Nev., Las Vegas, 1970. Mgmt. asst nuc. propulsion office U.S. AEC/NASA, Jackass Flats, Nev., 1962-65; adminstrv. analyst Clark County, Las Vegas, 1970-73, staff dir., criminal justice planner So. Dist. Allocation com., 1973-80; asst. dir. juror svcs. L.A. Superior Ct., 1981-88, dir. juror svcs., 1988-92, adminstr. litigation support, 1992—; mem. adv. com. Voir Dire Calif. Jud. Coun., 1992-93, Am. Bar Assn. Making Jury Svc. Accessible, Washington, 1994; mem. planning com. workshop jury mgrs., 1985; mem., vice chair adv. com. Criminal Justice Tng. Ctr. U. So. Calif., L.A., 1977-81. Co-author: Handbook for Court Specialists, 1976. Bd. dirs., pres. Andalucia Townhomes Com. Assn., Covina, 1989—; charter mem. L.A. Mus. Contemporary Art, 1985—. Recipient Cmty. Svc. award Covina Coord. Coun., 1990, Achievement award Jury Edn. & Mgmt. Forum, 1992. Mem. AAUW (br. treas. 1992-93, membership treas. 1995—, grant honoree 1986), ASPA (chpt. pres. 1972-73, nat. coun. 1974-77, sect. chair 1978-79, exec. com. 1974-80, 96—, criminal justice sect., Pub. Adminstr. of Yr. award Las Vegas br. 1978), Nat. Assn. State Cts., Phi Kappa Phi. Democrat. Office: LA Superior Ct 111 N Hill St Los Angeles CA 90012

BLANKENSHIP, VIRGINIA RADER, psychology educator; b. Washington, Ind., Jan. 2, 1945; d. Owen Richard and Kathleen Virginia Rader; m. Timothy Sims, Feb. 8, 1963; 1 son, Mark Alan; m. 2d, Bruce Blankenship, May 25, 1974. BS, Ind. State U., 1974, PhD, U. Mich., 1979. Asst. prof. sch. edn. Ind. U., Bloomington, 1979-81; asst. prof. psychology, 1981-88; coord. women's studies, 1984-89, assoc. prof. psychology, 1988-90; assoc. prof. psychology No. Ariz. U., 1990—, chair dept. psychology, 1990-95. Recipient Spencer Found. award, 1980, Rsch. Experience for Undergraduates Site award NSF, 1996. Mem. Am. Psychol. Assn., Sigma Xi. Democrat. Contbr. articles to profl. jours. Home: 5130 Hickory Dr Flagstaff AZ 86004 Office: Northern Ariz U 345 5BS/PO Box 15106 Flagstaff AZ 86011

BLANKS, NAOMI MAI, retired English language educator; b. Trezevant, Tenn., June 22, 1917; d. Hubbard Tazewell and Clara Clyde (Smith) Williamson; m. Jeff J. Blanks Jr., June 19, 1936 (dec.); children: Barbara, Jeff III, George (dec.). Student, Lambuth Coll., Jackson, Tenn., 1934-35; BA, Bethel Coll., McKenzie, Tenn., 1961; MA, George Peabody Coll., Nashville, 1966. Tchr. lang. arts Trezevant (Tenn.) Jr. High Sch., 1957-60; tchr. English McKenzie (Tenn.) High Sch., 1961-68; assoc. prof. English Bethel Coll., McKenzie, 1968-85; ret.; cons. lang. arts Harcourt Brace Jovanovich. Reviewer biography: T.S. Eliot: A Life, 1986, Waldo Emerson, 1982. Bd. dirs. Carroll County Devel. Ctr., Huntingdon, Tenn., 1976-88. NEH seminar grantee, 1980; NDEA fellow, 1965; recipient Alumni Svc. award, Bethel Coll., 1984, Tchr. of the Yr., 1975, 84. Mem. AAUP, So. Assn. Sec. Schs. and Colls. (evaluation com.), Delta Kappa Gamma (chpt. pres. 1970-72). Democrat. Methodist. Home: PO Box 186 Trezevant TN 38258-0186

BLANTON, LINDA GAYLE, counselor, former educator; b. Rockford, Ill., Mar. 15, 1940; d. Clyde Martin and Agatha (Happe) Christiansen; m. Paul Edward Blanton, Aug. 6, 1972; 1 child, Diane Renee Hayes; 1 stepchild, Linda Jean DeLawder. BS in Edn./Music Supervision, Wittenberg U., Springfield, Ohio, 1962; MEd, Wright State U., 1968, MS in Mental Health Counseling, 1990, Cert. in Gerontology, 1994. Lic. social worker, Ohio; lic. profl. counselor, Ohio; cert. tchr. elem. music, Ohio; cert. in reading supervision, Ohio; cert. elem. prin., Ohio; cert. counselor Nat. Bd. Cert. Counselors. Tchr. elem. music Northmont Schs., Englewood, Ohio, 1962-63; elem. tchr. New Carlisle (Ohio) Bethel Local Schs., 1963-69; instr. continuing edn. dept., music dept. Wittenberg U., 1968-80; instr. edn. dept. summer and Saturday programs Wright State U., Dayton, Ohio, 1968-80; supr. fed. edn., tchr. Ohio Vets. Children's Home, Xenia, 1969-86; psychology asst., cognitive specialist Rehab Continuum, Cin., 1990—. Developer elem. materials. Youth leader, fin. sec. First Luth. Ch., Xenia, 1979-89; vol. Greene Meml. Hosp., Xenia, 1986—, Children's Med. Ctr., Dayton, 1990—; Christian relief overseas project for hunger organizer Xenia Area Assn. Chs., 1990; active Greater Xenia Habitat for Humanity, 1991—. Recipient Outstanding Paper on Alzheimers Disease, Profl. and Sci. Ohio Conf. on Aging, Ohio Network Ednl. Cons. in the Field of Aging, Ohio Rsch. Coun. on Aging, 1995. Mem. ASCD, ACA, Ohio Mental Health Counselors Assn., Ohio Ret. Tchrs. Assn., Greene County Ret. Tchrs. Assn., Internat. Soc. for Study of Multiple Personality and Dissociation, Ohio Wander Freunde and Xenia Peg Legs (corr. sec. 1989-92, membership chairperson 1991—, v.p. 1992-96, pres. 1996), Ohio Rsch. Coun. on Aging, Miami Valley Counseling Assn., Sigma Alpha Iota (v.p. 1966-67), Delta Kappa Gamma (v.p. 1976-78, pres. 1978-80, sec. 1988-90), Phi Delta Kappa. Lutheran. Home: 92 Kinsey Rd Xenia OH 45385-1537

BLANTON, PATRICIA LOUISE, periodontal surgeon; b. Clarksville, Tex., July 9, 1941; d. Ben E. and Mildred L. (Russell) B. MS, Baylor U., 1964, PhD, 1967, DDS, 1974, cert., 1975. Diplomate Am. Coll. Bd. Oral Medicine. Teaching asst. Baylor Coll. of Dentistry, Dallas, 1963-67, asst. prof., 1967-70, spl. instr., 1970-73, assoc. prof., 1974-76; resident periodontics VA Hosp., Dallas, 1975; prof. Baylor Coll. of Dentistry, Dallas, 1976-85, Baylor U. Grad. Sch., Dallas, 1976—; prof., chmn. Baylor Coll. of Dentistry, Dallas, 1983-85; cons. VA Hosp., Dallas, 1979-82; adj. prof. Baylor Coll. of Dentistry, Dallas, 1985—; cons. Commn. on Dental Accreditation and Coun. of Dental Edn., 1981—; v.p. State Anatomical Bd., Tex., 1983-85; mem. ADA-AADS Liaison Com., 1983—; chmn. Nat. Insts. Health, Oral Biology and Medicine Study Sect. II, 1985-86. Author: Periodontics for the G.P., 1977, Current Therapy in Dentistry, 1980, An Atlas of the Human Skull, 1980 (1st place honors 1981). Invited participant Am. Coun. on Edn., Austin, 1984; mem. liaison com. Dallas County Dental Soc.-Am. Cancer Soc., Dallas, 1976-78; bd. dirs. Dallas Dental Health Programs, 1992-93, S.W. Med. Found., 1992-93; bd. devel. Hardin-Simmons U., 1995—. Named one of Outstanding Young Women in Am., 1976. Fellow Am. Coll. Dentists, Internat. Coll. Dentists; mem. ADA (alt. del.), Tex. Dental Assn. (bd. dirs. 1995—), Am. Assn. Anatomists, Am. Acad. Periodontology, Am. Acad. Oral Medicine, Am. Acad. Osseointegration, S.W. Soc. Periodontology, Dallas County Dental Soc. (pres. 1992-93), Xi Psi Phi, Omicron Kappa Upsilon (pres. 1992-93). Office: 4514 Cole Ave Ste 902 Dallas TX 75205-4176

BLANTYRE, ALEXANDRA, artist, poet; b. L.A., Mar. 28, 1968; children: Shammy, Mocheri. Student, Fashion Inst. Tech., N.Y.C., 1993-94, Polimoda U., Florence, Italy, 1994. Talent coord. Joe Franklin Show, N.Y.C., 1987-90. Prodr. play: The Damnation of Theron Ware, 1993; co-prodr.: (animation project) The Littlest Christmas Tree, 1992, (play) Hide Your Love Away, 1992; author: (poems) And Then We Kissed, 1994; compiler, editor: From Muse to Goddess, 1994.

BLASCHKE, RENEE DHOSSCHE, alderman; b. San Antonio, Oct. 4, 1938; d. Raoul Albert Emil and Lillian Lenore (Parker) Dhossche; m. Kenneth Blaschke; children: Kenneth, Rex, Rochelle. Office mgr. Smithville (Tex.) Hosp., 1958-68; tax assessor, collector City of Smithville, 1968-76; mgr., buyer Ken's Rexall Pharmacy, Smithville, 1976-92, ret., 1992; alderman City of Smithville, 1977-82, 94—. Alderman City of Smithville, 1977-82, 94—; past pres. region X, bd. dirs. Tex. Mcpl. League; trustee, chmn. fin., chmn. adminstrv. bd. 1st United Meth. Ch., Smithville; active Boy Scouts Am., Girl Scouts U.S.; chmn. Smithville Bicentennial Commn., Smithville Sesquicentennial Commn., Smithville Centennial Com., bd. dirs. Keep Tex. Beautiful, Tex. Urban Forestry Coun., Smithville CFC, 1994—, Smithville Econ. Devel. Bd., 1994—; Smithville Tree Bd., Smithville Tree City USA, Keep Smithville Beautiful; sec.-treas. Trees for Tex. Gov.'s Task Force-Earth Day, 1990; devel. bd. Seton Hosp., 1979—. Named Garden Club Woman of Yr., State Fair Tex., 1993. Mem. Am. Pharm. Assn. Aux., Tex. Pharm. Assn. Aux., Tex. Garden Clubs (pres. 1991-93, life mem.), Nat. Coun. State Garden Clubs (master flower show judge, landscape design critic, presenter seminars, design cons.), U. Tex. Ex-Students (past pres.), Smithville Garden Club (pres.), Smithville C. of C. (city hostess, bd. dirs., chmn. econ. devel. bd. 1994—, pres. 1996—).

BLATT, SYLVIA, chemist; b. N.Y.C., July 10, 1918; d. Armand and May (Krauss) B. BA, Hunter Coll., 1938; MS in Edn., CCNY, 1940. Asst. chemist Morrisania City Hosp., N.Y.C., 1948-51; chemist Bd. Water Supply, N.Y.C., 1951-54; sr. chemist N.Y.C. Dept. Health, 1954-62, prin. chemist, 1961-71, prin. rsch. scientist, 1971-85; cons. N.Y.C. Dept. Health and pvt. physicians, 1985-88. Mem. Am. Assn. Clin. Chemistry (bd. dirs. 1980-84, mem. coun. 1980-844, award for outstanding contbn. through svc. to clin. chemistry), Phi Beta Kappa, Phi Sigma. Home: 200 E 15th St New York NY 10003

BLATTNER, MEERA MCCUAIG, computer science educator; b. Chgo., Aug. 14, 1930; d. William D. McCuaig and Nina (Spertus) Klevs; m. Minao Kamegai, June 22 1985; children: Douglas, Robert, William. BA, U. Chgo., 1952; MS, U. So. Calif., 1966; PhD, UCLA, 1973 . Rsch. fellow in computer sci. Harvard U., 1973-74; asst. prof. Rice U., 1974-80; assoc. prof. applied sci. U. Calif. at Davis, Livermore, 1980-91, prof. applied sci., 1991—; adj. prof. U. Tex., Houston, 1977—; vis. prof. U. Paris, 1980; program dir. theoretical computer sci. NSF, Washington, 1979-80. Co-editor: (with R. Dannenberg) Multimedia Interface Design, 1992. NSF grantee, 1977-81, 93—. Mem. Soc. Women Engrs., Assn. Computing Machinery, IEEE Computer Soc. Contbr. articles to profl. jours. Office: U Calif Davis/Livermore Dept Applied Sci Livermore CA 94550

BLATZ, LINDA JEANNE, marketing professional; b. N.Y.C., Dec. 8, 1950; d. William Edmund and Jeanne Grace (Hyman) B. BS, U. Md., 1972. Mgr. sales Milliken & Co., N.Y.C., 1972-81; retail market mgr. Greenwood Mills Mktg. Co., N.Y.C., 1981-89; dist. mgr. Steelcase Inc., N.Y.C., 1989-94, tng. cons., 1994-95, team leader, 1995—. Contbr. articles to profl. jours. Mem. N.Y.C. Ballet Guild, PEO; mem. jr. com. N.Y.C. Ballet; v.p. membership, bd. mgrs. exec. com. N.Y. Jr. League (Outstanding Vol. award 1991-92). Recipient Outstanding Vol. of the Yr. award N.Y. Jr. League, 1992. Mem. AAUW, U. Md. Alumni Assn., Am. Woman's Econ. Devel. Corp., East River Rowing Club, Sandbar Beach Club (membership bd.), Alpha Gamma Delta. Congregationalist. Home: 2 Tudor City Pl New York NY 10017-6800 Office: 510 5th Ave New York NY 10036-7507

BLAUNSTEIN, PHYLLIS REID, communications and marketing executive; b. N.Y.C., July 4, 1940; d. Alex and Elsie (Rothstein) Lepler; m. Robert Philip Blaunstein, June 17, 1962; children: Eric Reid, Mar Reid. BA in English, SUNY, Albany, 1962; MA in Speech Pathology and Audiology, U. Tenn., 1967. English tchr. Knox County Bd. Edn., East Cleveland Bd. Edn., Cleve., 1962-66; instr. speech pathology and audiology U. Tenn., Knoxville, 1968-73; dir. Hearing and Speech Clinic U. Tenn. Meml. Rsch. Hosp., Knoxville, 1972-73; program mgr., coord. for ethical practice affairs Am. Speech, Hearing and Lang. Assn., Washington, 1973-75; spl. asst. to dep. commr. Bur. Edn. for the Handicapped U.S. Dept. Edn., Washington, 1976-77; dir. spl. projects Nat. Assn. State Bds. Edn., Washington, 1977-78, assoc. exec. dir., 1978-79, dep. exec. dir., 1979-80, exec. dir., 1981-87; sr. counsel The Widmeyer Group, Washington, 1988—; cons. Ford Found., U.S. Edn. Dept., USPHS, Md. State Dept. Edn., Ednl. Comm., Inc., Nat. Assn. State Dirs. Spl. Edn.

BLAXALL, MARTHA OSSOFF, economist; b. Haverhill, Mass., Feb. 2, 1942; d. Michael M. and Eve Joan (Kladky) Ossoff; BA, Wellesley Coll., 1963; PhD, Fletcher Sch., Tufts U., 1971; m. John Blaxall, May 15, 1970 (div. 1989); children: Jenifer, Johanna. Economist, Abt Assocs. Inc., Cambridge, Mass., 1965-68; budget examiner Office Mgmt. and Budget, 1969-72; sr. profl. asso. Inst. Medicine, Nat. Acad. Scis., 1972-76; dir. rsch. Health Care Fin. Adminstrn., U.S. Dept. Health and Human Svcs., 1976-79; dir. Office Utilization and Devel., Nat. Marine Fisheries Svc., Dept. Commerce, 1979-82; assoc. prof. dept. community and family medicine Georgetown U. Med. Sch., 1982; pres. BBH Corp., 1982-87; prin. Chase, Brown & Blaxall, Inc., 1983-87; v.p. ICF Inc., Washington, 1987-89; Hill and Knowlton Econs. Group, Washington, 1990-91; dir. agribusiness trade and investment group, Devel. Alternatives Inc., Bethesda, Md., 1991-93, dir. mktg. devel. group, 1993-95, bd. dirs., 1994—, v.p. 1995—; treas. Fedn. Orgns. Profl. Women, 1974-76, 83-84, exec. coun., 1982. Trustee Sheridan Sch., Washington, 1978-86, Coun. for Excellence in Govt., 1991—, Washington-Moscow Exchange, 1991-92, bd. dirs., 1990-93, Children's Health and Environ. Ctr.; active Inst. Women's Policy Studies, 1993—, Devel. Alternatives Inc., 1994—. NDEA fellow, 1964-65. Mem. Am. Econ. Assn., Nat. Economists Club (v.p. 1990-91). Co-editor: Women in the Workplace: The Implications of Occupational Segregation, 1976. Home: 3516 Winfield Ln NW Washington DC 20007-2344

BLAYDES, STEPHANIE ANNE, policy analyst; b. East Lansing, Mich., Aug. 6, 1963; d. David Fairchild and Sophia (Boyatzies) B. BA in Philosophy, Gettysburg Coll., 1985. Staff asst. to Majority Whip Tom Foley U.S. House Reps., Washington, 1986-87, staff asst. to Majority Whip Tony Coelho, 1987-89, spl. asst. to Hon. Robert E. Wise Jr., 1989-93, mem. svcs. advisor House info. sys., 1993-94; sr. health program analyst health svcs. financing Dept. Def., Washington, 1995; sr. program analyst Dept. Def. Policy & Planning Coord. Of Health Affairs, Washington, 1996—; program analyst policy & planning coordination Dept. Def., Washington, 1996—. Vol. Bob Wise for Congress, Washington, 1989-93; mem. host com. Kids County dinner Stewart B. McKinney House, Washington, 1993—; vol. cons. Doug Costle for U.S. Senate, Washington, 1994. Democrat. Greek Orthodox. Home: 1403 Sharps Point Rd # 4 Annapolis MD 21401-6139 Office: Dept Defense Policy & Planning Coord Health Affairs 2E265 The Pentagon Washington DC 20301

BLAZEK, JANET MARIE, financial executive, research analyst; b. Ennis, Tex., Apr. 2, 1971; d. Frank J. and Cecilia M. (Zhanel) B. AB in Sociology cum laude, Harvard U. Intern Jones Day Reavis & Pogue, Dallas, summer 1989, BBC/Midland Bank, London, summer 1990, Media Point Advtg., Dallas, summer 1991, Kidder Peabody, Boston, summer 1992; fin. analyst Goldman Sachs, N.Y.C., 1993-95; CFO, rsch. analyst Corbin & Co. Capital Mgmt., Ft. Worth, 1995—. Interviewer Harvard Schs. Com. Mem. Harvard Club. Home: Stonegate Villas Apt 1028 2501 Oak Hill Cir Fort Worth TX 76109 Office: Corbin & Co University Centre II 1320 S University Dr # 406 Fort Worth TX 76107

BLAZEK-WHITE, DORIS, lawyer; b. Easton, Md., Nov. 17, 1943; d. George W. and Nola M. (Buterbaugh) Defibaugh; children: Christine T., Judson M.; m. Thacher W. White. BA, Goucher Coll., 1965; JD, Georgetown U., 1968. Bar: D.C. 1969, Virgin Islands 1969, U.S. Ct. Appeals (3d cir.) 1969, U.S. Ct. Appeals (D.C. cir.) 1971, Md. 1979. Gen. practice with Judge Warren H. Young, U.S. Virgin Islands, 1968-70; assoc. Covington & Burling, Washington, 1970-76, ptnr., 1976—. Mem. Am. Coll. Trust and Estate Counsel. Office: Covington & Burling PO Box 7566 1201 Pennsylvania Ave NW Washington DC 20044

BLAZINA, JANICE FAY, transfusion medicine physician; b. Youngstown, Ohio, Apr. 20, 1953; d. Joseph and Cordelia Evelyn (Mitchell) B. BS, Youngstown State U., 1975; MD, Ohio State U., 1978. Diplomate Am. Bd. Pathology. Resident in anat. and clin. pathology U. Ala. Med. Ctr., Birmingham, 1978-82; assoc. pathologist various hosps., Bryan, Tex., 1982-83, High Plains Bapt. Hosp., Amarillo, Tex., 1983-84; fellow in blood banking Baylor U. Med. Ctr., Dallas, 1984-85; asst. prof. dept. pathology Ohio State U., Columbus, 1985-93, asst. prof. Sch. Allied Med. Professions, 1987-93; asst. dir. transfusion svc. Ohio State U. Hosp., 1985-89, assoc. dir., 1989-90, dir., 1990-93, med. dir. histocompatibility, paternity, apheresis and phlebotomy svcs., 1987-93, divsn. med. tech., 1987-93; asst. med. dir. Carter Blood Ctr., Ft. Worth, 1993-95, med. dir., 1995-96. Contbr. articles to profl. publs. Grantee: Bremer Found., 1987. Mem. AMA, Am. Soc. Apheresis, Am. Soc. Histocompatibility and Immunogenetics, Am. Assn. Blood Banks (insp. 1987—), Am. Med. Womens Assn., Ohio Assn. Blood Banks (trustee 1990-93, sec. 1992-93), Ohio Acad. Sci., Grad. Women Sci., Assn. Women Sci. Cen. Ohio (v.p. 1989-90, pres. 1990-91). Mem. Church of Christ.

BLECK, PHYLLIS CLAIRE, surgeon, musician; b. Oak Park, Ill., Mar. 10, 1936; d. William Fred and Mildred A. (Jones) B. BS, U. Ill., 1958; MM, Northwestern U., 1968; DMA, U. So. Calif., 1970; postgrad., Autonoma U., Guadalajara, Mex., 1973-76; MD, Rush Med. Coll., 1979; MS in Surgery, U. Ill., 1983. Diplomate Am. Bd. Surgery, Am. Bd. Thoracic Surgery. Prin. trumpet Fla. Symphony Orch., 1960-66, Orch. Sinfonica Nat. de Peru, 1965; instr. Thornton Jr. Coll., 1966-68; lectr. U. So. Calif., 1969-73; asst. prof. Whittier Coll., 1973; intern Rush Presbyn. St. Luke's Med. Ctr., Chgo., 1979-80, resident, asst. in gen. surgery, 1980-82, instr. gen. surgery, 1982-84; resident in cardiothoracic surgery U. Medicine and Dentistry N.J., 1984-87; pvt. practice medicine specializing in cardiothoracic surgery, Aurora, Ill., 1987—; asst. prof. Rush U., 1996. Editor: Mozart Divertimento for Winds; research on vascular ischemia. Fellow ACS, Am. Coll. Chest Physicians, Ill. Thoracic Surg. Soc., Ill. Surg. Soc.; mem. AAAS, Soc. Thoracic Surgeons, Kappa Delta Pi, Pi Kappa Lambda, Sigma Alpha Iota. Office: 1315 N Highland Ave Aurora IL 60506-1400

BLECKER, NAOMI PERLE, credit manager; b. N.Y.C., Mar. 3, 1956; d. Sidney and Zelda (Pologe) B. Student, CUNY, 1973-77. Credit mgr. new accounts Gimbel's Dept. Store, N.Y.C., 1975-78; credit mgr. Eue/Screen Gems div. Columbia Pictures Corp., N.Y.C., 1977-82; credit mgr. Trans Am. Video, Svcs. AME, Inc., N.Y.C., 1982-92; credit mgr. Editel divsn. of Unitel Video, N.Y.C., 1992—. Mem. Nat. Assn. Credit Mgmt. (chmn. motion picture and t.v. group 1982—), Nat. Assn. Female Execs., Am. Jewish Congress. Democrat. Home: Briarwood 14130 Pershing Cres Jamaica NY 11435-1952

BLEDSOE, MARY LOUISE, medical, surgical nurse; b. Sylacauga, Ala., May 21, 1935; d. Thomas Franklin and Beulah Mae (Vines) Borden; m. Ralph Johnson Bledsoe, June 28, 1958; children: Lynn, Steve, Johnny. LPN, N.F. Nunnelley Tech. Sch., Childersburg, Ala., 1971; AA, Alexander City (Ala.) Jr. Coll, 1989; BSN, Jacksonville (Ala.) State U., 1991. RN, Ala. Pediatric nurse Sylacauga Hosp., 1971-90; med./surg. staff nurse Coosa Valley Med. Ctr., Sylacauga, 1991-92, med./surg. chg. nurse, 1993-94; med./surg. staff nurse Coosa Valley Bapt. Med. Ctr., Sylacauga, 1994-96, charge nurse, 1996—. Musician/choir dir. Rising Star Bapt. Ch., Sylacauga, 1985-93, Mt. Olive Bapt. Ch., Childersburg, 1993-96. 1Mem. ANA, Ala. State Nurses Assn., Phi Theta Kappa. Baptist. Home: 980 Coaling Rd Sylacauga AL 35150-8743

BLEIBERG, GERTRUDE TIEFENBRUN, artist; b. N.Y.C., Mar. 11, 1921; d. Samuel and Anna (Gross) T.; m. Donald Joseph Bleiberg (wid.); children: Diana Jacobson, Deborah Jacobson, Victoria Zatkin, Wendy Maybaum. BE, UCLA, 1941; Gen. Secondary Tchg. Credential, U. So. Calif., L.A., 1942; BFA, San Francisco Art Inst., 1975, MFA, 1977. Tchr. Quincy (Calif.) H.S., 1942-44; substitute tchr. Palo Alto Unified Sch. Dist., 1966-75; co-owner Pluma Indsl. Hosp., Quincy, 1944-59; artist Palo Alto, 1977—. One-woman shows include Bridge Gallery, San Francisco, 1980, Monterey Peninsula Mus. of Art, Calif., 1982, San Jose Mus. of Art, Calif., 1983, Print Club, Phila., 1986, City of Palo Alto, Calif., 1986, Wenninger Gallery, Boston, 1988, Elizabeth S. Fine Mus., San Francisco, 1988, Branner Spangenberg Gallery, Palo Alto, 1989, Jennifer Pauls Gallery, Sacramento, 1986, 90, Richard Sumner Gallery, Palo Alto, 1994, San Francisco Mus. of Art Rental Gallery, 1996; retrospective San Francisco Mus. of Art Rental Gallery, 1996, Palo Alto Cultural Ctr., 1996, Koret Gallery, Palo Alto, 1996, Stanford Faculty Club, Stanford (Calif.), U., 1996; group exhbns. include Richard Hansen Fine Arts Gallery, Fresno, 1988, Pajaro Valley Art Coun., Art Mus. of Santa Cruz, 1988, Stanford U. Faculty Club, 1989, 96, Palo Alto Cultural Ctr., 1989, 96, Bank of Am., Raychem; numerous others; pub. collections include Rutgers Archives Coll., N.J., San Jose Mus. of Art; work pub. in numerous catalogues and publs. Mem. AAUW, Women's Caucus of Art (Lifetime Achievement award 1992-93), Soroptimist. Democrat. Home: 275 Southwood Dr Palo Alto CA

BLEIER, CAROL STEIN, writer, researcher; b. N.Y., Jan. 31, 1942; d. Shelley and Ruth (Brown) Stein; m. Michael Bleier, Oct. 9, 1966; children: Thomas, Lisa, Mark. BA in English Lit., Syracuse U., 1963; MLS, U. Pitts, 1986. Pub. info. specialist IRS, Washington, 1964-68; columnist Springfield (Va.) Ind., 1977-78; mktg. cons. Greater Pitts. Mus. Coun., 1986-88; pub. rels. dir. Greater Pitts. Literacy Coun., 1988-89; writer, 1985—. Author: (periodicals) Wilson Libr. Bulletin, 1985, 87, 88; co-author: (corp. history book) The Ketchum Spirit: A History of Ketchum Communications Inc., 1992; contrib. (ency.) Encyclopedia of Library History, 1994. Mem. ALA, Beta Phi Mu. Democrat. Jewish. Home: 214 Lynn Haven Dr Pittsburgh PA 15228-1821

BLESCH, K(ATHY) SUZANN, small business owner; b. Evansville, Ind., Dec. 14, 1951; d. Robert Lee McBride and E. Jean (Oliver) Schumacher; m. Larry J. Blesch, Aug. 17, 1974; children: Nicholas R., Spencer A., Clayton W. Grad. Grad. Realtors Inst., Ind. U., 1979; cert. residential specialist, Nat. Assn. Realtors, 1980. Waitress, hostess Skyway & Pete's, Evansville, Ind., 1971-73; operator, asst. mgr. Stecklers T.A.S., Evansville, 1969-71; salesperson, broker Midwest Realty, Evansville, 1973-78; broker, owner Blesch Realty, Evansville, 1978-80; broker, salesperson Brand Realty, Evansville, 1980-83; owner, operator Nick Nackery Pl., Evansville, 1985—. Bd. dirs. Hope of Evansville, 1976-79. Mem. Nat. Costumers Assn. Home and Office: 201 E Virginia St Evansville IN 47711-5529

BLESSEN, KAREN ALYCE, free-lance illustrator, designer; b. Columbus, Nebr.. BFA, U. Nebr., 1973. Freelance illustrator, 1973-86; designer Dallas Morning News, 1986-89, freelance illustrator, designer, 1989—; owner, illustrator Karen Blessen Illustration, Dallas, 1989—. Rep. Tex. in Absolut Statehood series, Absolut; illustrator: Be An Angel, 1994. Recipient Pulitzer Prize for explanatory journalism, 1989; awards from N.Y. Art Dirs. Club, Soc. Newspaper Design, Dallas Press Club; commd. by Absolut to represent Tex. in Absolut Statehood series. Home and office: Karen Blessen Illustration 6327 Vickery Blvd Dallas TX 75214-3348

BLETHEN, SANDRA LEE, pediatric endocrinologist; b. San Mateo, Calif., May 16, 1942; d. Howard Albion and Laura Katherine (Wolf) B.; m. Fred I. Chasalow, Nov. 26, 1966. SB in Biochemistry, U. Chgo., 1961; PhD in Biochemistry, U. Calif., Berkeley, 1965; MD, Yeshiva U., 1975. Diplomate Am. Bd. Pediatrics. Fellow biochemistry Brandeis U., Waltham, Mass., 1965-68; instr. biochemistry U. Calif., San Diego, 1968-69; asst. prof. San Francisco State U., 1969-71; resident in pediatrics Columbia Presbyn. Med. Ctr., N.Y.C., 1975-77; fellow pediatric endocrinology U. N.C., Chapel Hill, 1977-79; asst. prof. pediatrics Washington U., St. Louis, 1979-84; assoc. prof. pediatrics SUNY, Stony Brook, 1985-96; assoc. attending pediatrician L.I. Jewish Med. Ctr., New Hyde Park, N.Y., 1984-90; attending pediatrician Univ. Hosp., Stony Brook, 1991-96; cons. Genentech, Inc., South San Francisco, Calif., 1985-96, Diagnostic Systems Labs., Webster, Tex., 1989-96. Mem. editorial bd. Steroids, 1990—, Jour. of Endocrinology and Metabolism, 1995—; contbr. 65 articles to profl. jours. Predoctoral fellow NSF, 1961-63, Postdoctoral fellow USPHS, 1965-67. Mem. Am. Pediatric Soc. (program com. 1994), Endocrine Soc., Lawson Wilkens Pediatric Endocrine Soc. (membership chair 1994-95), Soc. for Pediatric Rsch., Phi Beta Kappa, Alpha Omega Alpha. Office: Med Affairs Genentech Inc 460 Point San Bruno Blvd South San Francisco CA 94080

BLEVINS, DONNA CATON, writer; b. Naha City, Okinawa, Japan, Jan. 13, 1965; came to U.S., 1967; d. Donald Herbert Jr. and Setsuko (Ukuda) Caton; m. Gary Lee Blevins, Feb. 29, 1992. BA in English, Ga. State U., 1991. Prin. dancer Ruth Mitchell Dance Co., Atlanta, 1976-83; paper distbr. U.S. A. Today newspaper, Roswell, Ga., 1983-84, Atlanta Jour./Constitution, 1986-88; optical technician Dr. John W. Hollier, O.D., Roswell, 1983-85; fitness instr. Am. Fitness Ctr., Roswell, Ga., 1984-86; waitress Kobe Steaks, Atlanta, 1988; air import specialist Nippon Express U.S.A., Inc., Atlanta, 1988-92; writer's asst., editor Laurie Lee Dovey, Alpharetta, Ga., 1992-93; freelance writer, photographer, 1993—; model for artist Lisa Iris, Atlanta, 1989; dancer TV comml. Ruth Mitchell Dance Co., 1980, Mr. Jr. Am. Contest, Atlanta, 1980; cons., Atlanta, 1993—, Plano, Tex., 1993-94, L.A., 1995—. Founder The Momo Newsletter, 1996; contbr. articles to mags. and newspapers. Pell grantee, 1984-85. Mem. Nat. Orgn. Outdoor Women, Dog Writers Assn. Am., Cat Writers Assn. (Excellence cert. for best cat photo 1994, Muse medallion 1994). Office: PO Box 135 Zachary LA 70791-0135

BLEVINS, PATRICIA M., state legislator. Mem. Del. State Sen., 1992—. Office: 209 Linden Ave Wilmington DE 19805-2515 Office: Del State Senate Legislative Hall Dover DE 19903*

BLEY, CARLA BORG, jazz composer; b. Oakland, Calif., May 11, 1938; d. Emil Carl and Arlene (Anderson) Borg; m. Paul Bley, Jan. 27, 1959 (div. Sept. 1967); m. Michael Mantler, Sept. 29, 1967 (div. 1992); 1 dau., Karen. Student public schs., Oakland. mem. adv. bd. Jazz Composers Orch. Assn. Freelance jazz composer, 1956—, pianist, Jazz Composers Orch., N.Y.C., 1964—, European concert tours, Jazz Realities, 1965-66; founder, WATT, 1973—, toured Europe with Jack Bruce Band, 1975; leader, Carla Bley Band, touring, U.S. and Europe, 1977—; composed, recorded: A Genuine Tong Funeral, 1967, (with Charlie Haden) Liberation Music Orch., 1969; opera Escalator Over the Hill, 1970-71 (Oscar du Disque de Jazz 1973), Tropic Appetites, 1973; composed: chamber orch. 3/4, 1974-75; film score Mortelle Randonnée, 1983; recorded: Dinner Music, 1976, The Carla Bley Band: European Tour, 1977, Musique Mecanique, 1979, (with Nick Mason) Fictitious Sports, 1980, Social Studies, 1980, Carla Bley Live!, 1981, Heavy Heart, 1984, I Hate to Sing, 1985, Night Glo, 1985, Sextet, 1987, Duets, 1988, Fleur Carnivore, 1989, The Very Big Carla Bley Band, 1991, Go Together, 1993, Big Band Theory, 1993, Songs With Legs, 1995. Named winner internat. jazz critics poll Down Beat mag., 1966, 71, 72, 78, 79, 80, 83, 84; Best Composer of Yr., Down Beat Readers' Poll, 1984, composer/

arranger of yr., 1985-92; Guggenheim fellow, 1972; Cultural Coun. Found. grantee, 1971, 79; Nat. Endowment for the Arts grantee, 1973, Oscar du Disque de Jazz (for Escalator Over the Hill) 1973; named Best in Field Jazz Times critics poll, 1990, Best Arranger, Downbeat Critics Poll, 1993, 94, Best Arranger, Downbeat Readers' Poll, 1994; recipient Prix Jazz Moderne from Academie du Jazz for The very Big Carla Bley Band album, 1992. Office: care Watt Works PO Box 67 Willow NY 12495

BLICKENSTAFF, KATHLEEN MARY, mental health nurse, nursing educator; b. Greenville, Ohio, Oct. 24, 1950; d. Donald Edward and Mary Ann (Subler) Berger; m. Daniel E. Blickenstaff, June 10, 1972 (div. Mar. 1988); children: Benjamin Arin, Amanda Marie, Kathryn Megan. BS, Ohio State U., 1972, MS, 1973, sch. nurse cert., 1990; postgrad., Capital U. Law Sch., 1994—. Cert. sch. nurse grades K-12. Cons. cmty. educator S.W. Cmty. Mental Health Ctr., Columbus, 1973-77; patient and cmty. educator Daniel E. Blickenstaff, DDS, Inc., Columbus, 1977-86; staff nurse Riverside Meth. Hosp., Columbus, 1986-90; clin. instr. Columbus (Ohio) State C.C., 1989; asst. prof. Capital U., Columbus, 1989-96; assoc. prof. Capital U., 1996—; mem. cmty. svcs. com. Mid Ohio Dist. Nurses Assn., Columbus, 1990—, bd. dirs., 1991-94. Leader Girl Scouts, Grandview Heights, Ohio, 1989-93; bd. dirs. H.S. PTO, Grandview Heights (Ohio) City Schs., 1990-93, treas. H.S. PTO, 1990-92, co-chair oper. levy, 1991. Mem. ABA, ANA, Ohio Nurses Assn., Am. Psychiat. Nurses Assn., Nat. Assn. Sch. Nurses, Ohio State Bar Assn., Columbus Bar Assn., Sigma Theta Tau. Republican. Roman Catholic. Home: 1138 Westwood Ave Columbus OH 43212-3240 Office: Capital Univ 2199 E Main St Columbus OH 43209-3913

BLIEBERG, HELENE ANDREA, communications executive; b. N.Y.C., Aug. 13, 1955; d. Seymour and Esther (Kaplan) B. BA in Broadcast Mktg., English, SUNY, Buffalo, 1977; postgrad., Polytechnic of Cen. London, 1977. Account exec. The Softness Group, Inc., N.Y.C., 1977-78; dir. pub. relations The Grossinger (N.Y.) Hotel, 1978-79, mgr. sales, 1979-80, dir. mktg., 1980-82; mgr. press. info. CBS Radio Networks, N.Y.C., 1982-83; mgr. sales devel. and promotion CBS Nat. Sales, N.Y.C., 1983-84; dir. media rels. CBS Radio div. CBS Inc., N.Y.C., 1984-89, dir. communications, 1989-94, v.p. communications, 1994—. Mem. Internat. Radio and TV Soc., Internat. Assn. Bus. Communicators, Pub. Relations Soc. of America, Promotion and Mktg. Execs. in the Elec. Media (mem. bd. dirs.). Office: CBS Inc 51 W 52nd St New York NY 10019-6119

BLIGE, MARY JANE, recording artist; b. Yonkers, N.Y., Nov. 1, 1971; d. Cora Blige. Albums include: What's the 411?, 1992, (double platinum award), My Life, 1994 (debuted at top of Billboard's R&B album chart); recordings include I'll Do For You, 1991, (duet) Changes, One Night Stand. Recipient Soul Train Music award, 1993, N.Y. Music award, NAACP Image award. Office: Uptown Records 729 7th Ave 12 th Fl New York NY 10019*

BLISSITT, PATRICIA ANN, nurse; b. Knoxville, Tenn., Sept. 23, 1953; d. Dewitt Talmadge and Imogene (Bailey) B. BSN with high honors, U. Tenn., 1976, MSN, 1985; postgrad., U. Wash., 1996—. RN; cert. in case mgmt.; cert. trauma nurse core course, ACLS, pediat. advanced life support. Staff nurse neurosci. unit City of Memphis Hosp., 1976-78, head nurse neurosci. unit, 1978-79; physician's asst. Dr. John D. Wilson, Columbus, Miss., 1979-81; staff nurse med.-surg.-trauma ICU U. Tenn. Meml. Hosp., Knoxville, 1982-83; staff nurse neurosci. ICU Bapt. Meml. Hosp., Memphis, 1985-86, clin. nurse specialist neurosci., 1986-94, trauma coord., 1991-93, neuro case mgr., 1993-94; staff nurse neurosurg. ICU Harborview Med. Ctr., Seattle, 1994—; nurse cons. neurosci. VA Hosp., Memphis, 1986; mem. adv. com. Tenn. Bd. Nursing Practice. Author: (with others) Critical Care Nursing in Clinics of North America, 1990, Jour. Neurosci. Nursing, 1986, 92, Guidelines for Critical Care Nursing; abstractor: Nursing SCAN in Critical Care, 1995—; contbr. articles to sci. jour., chpt. to book; mem. editl. cons. bd. Focus on Critical Care, 1990-92. Mem. ANA (mem. coun. med.-surg. nurses, mem. coun. clin. nurse specialists), Am. Assn. Neurosci. Nurses (cert. neurosci. nurse, pres. local chpt. 1989-90, treas. local chpt. 1987-89, mem. neurosci. nursing test devel. com. Am. Bd. Neurosci. Nursing 1996—, nat. lectr., mem. resource devel. com., mem. continuing edn./ann. sci. program com., program/seminar chairperson local chpt. 1990-93, mem. nurse practice com., chairperson patient edn. project 1991-92, mem. program/seminar com., program/seminar chairperson mid-South chpt. 1990-93, chairperson nat. resource devel. com. 1992-94, pres. local chpt. 1995—), AACN (life, cert. critical care nurse, lectr., mem. CCRN corp. exam. devel. com. 1989-92, NTI spkr. 1992, editl. cons. bd. 1990-92, pres.-elect Greater Memphis area chpt. 1989-90, pres. 1990-91, immediate past pres., chairperson nat. critical care awareness week 1990-93, chpt. cons. region II 1991-93, chpt of yr. com. chairperson 1992-94, chairperson-elect Puget Sound chpt. program 1995-96, chairperson program com. 1996-97), Am. Assn. Spinal Cord Injury Nurses, Wash. Nurses Assn., Tenn. Nurses Assn. (mem. com. on practice 1992-93), Tenn. Nursing Congress (pres. 1990-94), Sigma Theta Tau. Methodist. Avocation: music. Home: 1105 Spring St Apt 405 Seattle WA 98104-3513

BLITT, RITA LEA, artist; b. Kansas City, Mo., Sept. 7, 1931; d. Herman Stanley and Dorothy Edith (Sofnas) Copaken; m. Irwin Joseph Blitt, Apr. 18, 1951; 1 child, Chela Connie. Student, U. Ill., 1948-50; BA, Kansas City U., 1952; postgrad., Kansas City Art Inst., 1952-54. Freelance painter, sculptor Leawood, Kans., 1958—. One-woman exhbns. include Unitarian Gallery, Kansas City, Mo., 1965, Spectrum Gallery, N.Y.C., 1969, Angerer Gallery, Kansas City, Mo., 1974, Battle Creek (Mich.) Civic Art Ctr., 1975, Harkness Gallery, N.Y.C., 1977, Martin Schweig Gallery, St. Louis, 1977, Gargoyle Gallery, Aspen, Colo., 1978, Tumbling Waters Mus., Montgomery, Ala., 1978, St. Louis U., 1980, Leedy-Voulkos Gallery, Kansas City, Mo., 1987, Joy Horwich Gallery, Chgo., 1987, Goldman Gallery, Haifa, Israel, 1989, Bet Shmuel, Jerusalem, 1989, Goldman Kraft Gallery, Chgo., 1990, Singapore Nat. Mus., 1991, Albrecht-Kemper Mus., St. Joseph, Mo., 1991, Aspen (Colo.) Inst., 1992, Foothills Art Ctr., Golden, Colo., 1992, Mackey Gallery, Denver, 1992, U. Ill., Urbana, 1994, Kennedy Mus.-U. Ohio, Athens, 1994, Krasl Art Ctr., St. Joseph, Mich., 1994, Baker U., Baldwin, Kans., 1995, Ctrl. Exch., Kansas City, Mo., 1995, Atchison (Kans.) Muchnik Gallery, 1996; group exhbns. include Kansas City (Mo.) Mus., 1959, Ringling Mus., Sarasota, Fla., 1967, Springfield (Mo.) Mus., 1967, Joslyn Mus., Omaha, 1972, Doug Drake Gallery, Kansas City, 1975, Conry Gallery, Kansas City, Mo., 1976, Cyvia Gallery, New Haven, 1977, Gargoyle Gallery, Aspen, Colo., 1979, Putney Gallery, Aspen, 1979, Carrefour Gallery, N.Y.C., 1979, Elaine Benson Gallery, Bridgehampton, N.Y., 1980, Tall Grass Fine Arts Gallery, Kansas City, Mo., 1980, 81, Art and Design Gallery, N.Y.C., 1982, Winter Manhattan (Kans.), Streker, Gallery, 1983, Joanne Lyons Gallery, Aspen, 1984, Banaker Gallery, 1987, 88, Andrea Ross Gallery, Santa Monica, Calif., 1990, LA 90, L.A., 1990, Eva Cohon, Chgo., 1995, Obere Galerie, Berlin, 1995, Din Deutsches Inst., Berlin, 1995, many others; permanent collections include Albrecht-Kemper Mus., St. Joseph, Mo., Ga. Inst. Tech., JFK Libr., Cambridge, Mass., Kennedy Mus. Ohio U., Athens, Nat. Mus. Singapore, Skirball Mus., L.A., Spertus Mus., Chgo., Kansas City (Mo.) Children's Mus., Kennedy Mus., Ohio U., Ga. Tech. Ctr. for the Arts, and other numerous pvt. and pub. collections; sculptures in numerous pub. places. Mem. Soc. Fellow The Nelson Gallery Found., The Aspen Inst.; bd. dirs. Trio Found.; mem. The Stop Violence Coalition. Mem. Internat. Sculpture Ctr., Kansas City Artists Coalition. Office: 8900 State Line Rd Ste 333 Leawood KS 66206-1936

BLITZ, PEGGY SANDERFUR, corporate travel management company official; b. Pitts., Apr. 12, 1940; d. Charles I. and Rebecca Polk (McBride) Wallace; m. Clark L. Blitz, Aug. 25, 1962 (div. Apr. 1974); children: Danette L., Jonathan D. BS, Ball State U., 1962; postgrad., No. Ill. U., 1976-77. Cert. speech therapist, spl. edn. tchr. Tchr. mentally retarded Anderson (Ind.) Pub. Schs., 1962-64; speech therapist Elgin (Ill.) Pub. Schs., 1964-66; pvt. practice speech therapy Elgin, 1966-68; tchr. mentally retarded Easter Seal Rehab. Ctr., Elgin, 1968-77; account exec. Whitehall Hotel, Chgo., 1977-79; regional mgr. IVI Travel Inc., Milw., 1979-85; sr. v.p. IVI Travel Inc., Dallas, 1985-88; pres. Travelmasters, Inc., Chgo., 1988-91; staff devel. Kemper Securities, Inc., Chgo., 1991-92; pres. Travel Mgmt. Cons., St. John, V.I., 1991—; property mgr. Short-Term Vacation Rentals, 1992—. Presbyterian. Home and Office: PO Box 8333 Cruz Bay VI 00831-8333

BLIZNAKOV, MILKA TCHERNEVA, architect; b. Varna, Bulgaria, Sept. 20, 1927; came to U.S., 1961, naturalized, 1966; d. Ivan Dimitrov and Maria Kesarova (Khorozova) Tchernev; m. Emile G. Bliznakov, Oct. 23, 1954 (div. Apr., 1974). Architect-engr. diploma, State Tech. U., Sofia, 1951; Ph.D., Engring.-Structural Inst., Sofia, 1959; Ph.D. in Architecture, Columbia U., 1971. Sr. researcher Ministry Heavy Industry, Sofia, 1950-53; pvt. practice architecture Sofia, 1954-59; assoc. architect Noel Combrisson, Paris, 1959-61; designer Perkins & Will Partnership, White Plains, N.Y., 1963-67; project architect Lathrop Douglass, N.Y.C., 1967-71; assoc. prof. architecture and planning Sch. Architecture, U. Tex., Austin, 1972-74; prof. Coll. Architecture, Va. Poly. Inst. and State U., Blacksburg, 1974—; prin. Blacksburg, 1975—; bd. dirs. founder Internat. Archives Women in Architecture, Va. Poly. Inst. and State U., The Parthena award, 1994. Prin. works include Speedwell Ave. Urban Renewal, Morristown, N.J., 1967-69, Wilmington (Del.) Urban Renewal, 1968-70, Springfield (Ill.) Ctrl. Area Devel., 1969-71, Arlington County (Va.) Redevel., 1975-77; author: (with others) Utopia e Modernitá, 1989, Reshaping Russian Architecture, 1990, Russian Housing in the Modern Age, 1993, Nietzsche and Soviet Culture, 1994, New Perspectives on Russian and Soviet Artistic Culture, 1994. William Kinne scholar, summer 1970, vis. scholar Inst. Advanced Russian Studies, The Wilson Ctr. of Smithsonian Instn., 1988; NEA grantee, 1973-74, Am. Beautiful Found. grantee, 1973, Internat. Rsch. and Exch. Bd. grantee, 1984-93; Fulbright Hays rsch. fellow, 1983-84, 91; recipient Parthend award, 1994. Mem. Internat. Archive Women in Architecture (founder, chair bd. dirs.), Am. Assn. Tchrs. Slavic and East European Langs., Soc. Archtl. Historians, Nat. Trust Hist. Preservation, Am. Assn. Advancement of Slavic Studies, Assn. Collegiate Schs. of Planning, Inst. Modern Russian Culture (chairperson architecture, co-founder, dir.), Assn. Collegiate Schs. of Architecture. Home: 2813 Tall Oaks Dr Blacksburg VA 24060-8109 Office: Coll Architecture Va Poly Inst And State Blacksburg VA 24061

BLOCH, ANDREA LYNN, physical therapist; b. Cleve., Nov. 25, 1952; d. Sanford and Nadalane Lee (Benchell) B. BA in Zoology, Miami U., Oxford, Ohio, 1974; MA in Allied Health Scis., Kent State U., 1975; Cert. in Phys. Therapy, Ohio State U., 1977. Lic. phys. therapist, Ohio; bd. cert. orthopedic clin. specialist. Asst. dir. phys. therapy The Mt. Sinai Med. Ctr., Cleve., 1977-86; dir. rehab. therapy svcs. Marymount Hosp., Garfield Heights, Ohio, 1986-88; pres., owner Bloch Phys. Therapy, Inc., University Heights, Ohio, 1988—; speaker Arthritis Found.; speaker in field; mem. Ohio Occupl. Therapy, Phys. Therapy and Athletic Trainers Bd., 1994—. Editor newsletter Cleve. Phys. Therapy Orthopedic Study Group, 1989-91; contbr. articles to profl. jours. Chmn. essay-poster contest University Heights Meml. Day Parade, 1985-91; mem. coun.-at-large City of University Heights. Mem. AAPHERD, NAFE, Am. Phys. Therapy Assn. (reimbursement chmn. N.E. dist. Ohio 1992—), Am. Back Soc., Am. Soc. Profl. and Exec. Women, Ohio Phys. Therapy Assn., Delta Zeta Eastside Alumnae (program chmn. 1985-87, ways and means com. 1987-88, v.p. 1988-90, pres. 1990-92), Delta Zeta Province Alumnae (bd. dirs. Ohio V-N 1991-94, Outstanding Province V Alumna award 1992), Eta Sigma Gamma. Office: 2195 Warrensville Center Rd University Heights OH 44118-3155

BLOCH, BARBARA JOYCE, writer, editor; b. N.Y.C., May 26, 1925; d. Emil William and Dorothy (Lowengrund) B.; m. Joseph B. Sanders, Aug. 3, 1944 (div. 1961); children: Elizabeth Sanders, Ellen Janice Benjamin; m. Theodore S. Benjamin, Sept. 20, 1964. Student, NYU, 1943-45, New Sch. Social Rsch., 1966. Office mgr. Writers War Bd., N.Y.C., 1943-45, Westchester Dem. Com., White Plains, N.Y., 1955-56; mgr. Westchester Symphony Orch., 1957-62; mng. editor Cooking Ency., Rutledge Books, N.Y.C., 1970-71; pres. Internat. Cookbook Services, White Plains, 1978—; columnist House Beautiful, 1984-87; cookbook editor Benjamin Co., 1990—; cons. in field; tchr. cooking classes White Plains, 1975-80; lectr. in field. Author: Anyone Can Quilt, 1975; Meat Board Meat Book, 1977; If It Doesn't Pan Out, 1981; Garnishing Made Easy, 1983, Microwave Party Cooking, 1988, A Little Jewish Cookbook, 1989, A Little New England Cookbook, 1990, A Little Southern Cookbook, 1990, A Little New York Cookbook, 1990; editor/author: All Beef Cookbook, 1973; In Glass Naturally, 1974; Fresh Ideas with Mushrooms, 1977; Holly Farms Complete Chicken Cookbook, 1984; Gulden's Cookbook, 1985, A Centennial Celebration of Recipes from Solo, 1988, Salute to the Great American Chefs, 1988, TCBY and More, 1989, GoldStar Micro-Convection Cookbook, 1991, Healthy Cooking with Amway Queen Cookware, 1993, McCormick/Schilling's New Spice Cookbook, 1994; Am. adapter The Cuisine of Olympe, 1983, Baking Easy and Elegant, 1984, series of 3 English cookbook mags., 1984-87, Best of Cold Foods, 1985, Cakes and Pastries, 1985, series of 12 Creative Cuisine books, 1985, The Art of Cooking, 1986, The Art of Baking, 1987, Perfect Pasta, 1992, Rocky Food, 1994; editor contbr. various books; contbr. articles to profl. jours. Nat. bd. dirs. Emcampment for Citizenship, N.Y.C., 1966-72; bd. dirs. YWCA Central Westchester, 1965-71, Westchester Ethical Humanist Soc., 1968—; exec. com., pres. Internat. Student Exchange of White Plains, 1955-70; bd. dirs. Westchester Chamber Music Soc., 1986—. Jewish. Home and Office: Internat Cookbook Svcs 21 Dupont Ave White Plains NY 10605-3537

BLOCH, JULIA CHANG, foundation administrator, former government official; b. Chefoo, Peoples Republic of China, Mar. 2, 1942; came to U.S., 1951, naturalized, 1962; d. Fu-yun and Eva (Yeh) Chang; m. Stuart Marshall Bloch, Dec. 21, 1968. BA, U. Calif., Berkeley, 1964; MA, Harvard U., 1967, postgrad. in mgmt., 1987; DHL (hon.), Northeastern U., Boston, 1986. Vol. Peace Corps, Sabah, Malaysia, 1964-66, tng. officer East Asia and Pacific region, Washington, 1967-68, evaluation officer, 1968-70; mem. minority staff U.S. Senate Select Com. on Nutrition and Human Needs, Washington, 1971-76, chief minority counsel, 1976-77; dep. dir. Office of African Affairs, U.S. Internat. Comm. Agy., Washington, 1977-80; fellow Inst. Politics, Harvard U., Cambridge, Mass., 1980-81; asst. adminstr. Bur. for Food for Peace and Voluntary Assistance, AID, Washington, 1981-87, asst. adminstr. Bur. for Asia and Near East, 1987-88; assoc. U.S.-Japan Rels. Program, Ctr. for Internat. Affairs, Harvard U., Cambridge, Mass., 1988-89; ambassador to Kingdom of Nepal, 1989-93; group exec., v.p. Bank Am., San Francisco, 1993-96; pres. The U.S.-Japan Found., 1996—; dir. Am. West Airlines, 1994—; trustee Eisenhower Exchange Fellowship, 1995—; U.S. Senate rep. World Conf. on Internat. Women's Yr., Mex., 1975; advisor U.S. Del. to Food and Agr. Orgn. Conf., Rome, 1975; rep. Am. Council Young Polit. Leaders, Peoples Republic China, 1977; charter mem. Sr. Exec. Svc., 1979; head U.S. del. Biennial Session World Food Programme, Rome, 1981-86, Devel. Assistance Com. Meeting on Non-Govtl. Orgns., Paris, 1985, Intergovtl. Group on Indonesia, The Hague, The Netherlands, 1987, World Bank Consultative Group Meeting, Paris, 1987, mem. exec. women in govt., 1988-93, mem. coun. fgn. rels., 1991—; mem. com. to visit art mus. Harvard U., 1989—; mem. U.S. Nat. Com. for Pacific Econ. Cooperation, 1984—; mem. adv. bd. Women's Campaign Fund, 1976-78, trustee, bus. leadership circle, 1994—; exec. bd. mem. Internat. Ctr. for Rsch. on Women, 1974-81; mem. presdl. adv. coun. Peace Corps, 1988-89; mem. Am. Himalayan Found. Bd., 1994, Am. Refugee Com. Bd., 1993—. Author: A U.S.-Japan Aid Alliance, 1991; co-author: Chinese Home Cooking, 1986; mem. Nat. Presdl. Debate Forum, 1987-92; mem. nat. adv. coun. Experiment in Internat. Living, 1981-83; commr. Asian Art Mus., San Francisco, 1994. Recipient Hubert Humphrey award for internat. svc., 1979, Humanitarian Svc. award AID, 1987, Leader for Peace award Peace Corps, 1987, Asian Am. Leadership award, 1989, Brotherhood/Sisterhood award Nat. Conf. on Christians and Jews, 1996; named Outstanding Woman of Color, Nat. Inst. for Women of Color, 1982, Woman of Distinction, Nat. Conf. for Coll. Women Student Leaders and Women of Achievement, 1987, Disting. Pub. Svc. award Nat. Assn. Profl. Asian Pacific Am. Women, 1989; Ford Found. Study fellow for internat. devel. Harvard U., 1966, Paul Harris award Rotary, 1992, Award of Honor Narcotic Enforcement Assn., 1992. Mem. Orgn. Chinese Am. Women (founder, chair 1977—, bd. dirs., Woman of Yr. 1987), Asia Soc. (pres. coun. 1989, trustee 1994), Prytannean Honor Soc., Coun. Fgn. Rels., Mortar Bd. Republican. Avocations: ceramics, gourmet cooking, collecting art. Office: US-Japan Found 145 E 32d St 12th Flr New York NY 10016

BLOCK, ANN LEE, legislative assistant; b. Akron, Ohio, Oct. 21, 1929; d. Joseph and Hinda (Freishtat) Dante; m. Samuel N. Block, May 2, 1954; children: Deborah Block Temin, Arleen Root, Jeffrey, Joni, Marci. BS in Business, U. Akron, 1951. Office mgr. Israel Bond Orgn., Akron, 1951-53; sec. Israel Embassy, Washington, 1953-54; legis. aide Md. House of Delegates, Annapolis, 1978-86; legis. asst. Md. Senate, Annapolis, 1986-94, case worker, legis. asst., 1994—. Pres. Pioneer Women (now Na'amat USA), 1968-72, Am. affairs chmn., membership chmn., 1983-95, bd. dirs. 1965—, Woman of the Yr. award, 1974, vocat. tng. scholar, 1987, seminarist to Israel, 1966, soviet jewry chmn. Jewish Cmty. Coun., 1986. Democrat. Jewish. Home: 11704 Fulham St Silver Spring MD 20902

BLOCK, BONNIE, organization executive, lawyer. Adoption and foster care caseworker AFDC; pvt. practice law; chmn. Nat. Coun. Fellowship of Reconciliation, Nyack, N.Y. NC chmn. LU, past chmn. interfaith com.; former nat. coord. Luth. Peace Fellowship, editor newsletter PeaceNotes; vol. cmty. organizer; active numerous nonviolent struggles for peace and justice. Office: Nat Coun Fellowship of Reconciliation Box 271 Nyack NY 10960

BLOCK, ELIZABETH H., medical facility researcher; b. Chgo., Apr. 18, 1939; d. Edward V. and Elizabeth H. (Leavitt) Platt; m. Peter C. Block, Dec. 28, 1963; children: Lisa, David, Christopher. AA, Bradford Jr. Coll., 1958; BS in Edn., Wheelock Coll., 1960. Elem. sch. tchr. Walpole (Mass.) Sch. Dist., 1960-61, Redwood City (Calif.) Sch. Dist., 1961-62, Wayland (Mass.) Pub. Schs., 1962-65; rsch. coord. Mass. Gen. Hosp., Boston, 1984-90, Providence St. Vincent Hosp., Portland, Oreg., 1991—. Home: 3510 SW Sherwood Pl Portland OR 97201 Office: Providence St Vincent Hosp 9205 SW Barnes Rd Portland OR 97225

BLOCK, JANET LEVEN (MRS. JOSEPH E. ROSEN), public relations consultant; b. Chgo.; d. Benjamin J. and Rosebud (Goldsmith) Leven; student Brenau Coll. for Women, Gainesville, Ga., Northwestern U.; m. Albert William Block, Sept. 27, 1947 (div.); m. Joseph E. Rosen, Dec. 5, 1985; children: Mitchell Block, Stephanie Block McEwen. Reporter, Chgo. Am. Newspaper, 1939-40; catalog advt. Alden's Chgo. Mail Order Co., N.Y.C., Chgo., 1940-42; stylist and public relations dir. Fashion Advt. Co., N.Y.C., 1942-44; asst. account exec., stylist Buchanan & Co., Advt. Agy., N.Y.C., 1944-46; advt. agy account exec. Abbott Kimball Co., Chgo., 1946-47; free-lance merchandising and public relations rep., Cin., 1960-64; v.p. public relations, spl. events Lazarus (previously Shillito's), Cin., 1964-87; cons. pub. relations and advt. Cin., 1987—. Vice chair adv. bd. Hoxworth Blood Ctr., 1986-88; bd. dirs. Children's Heart Assn., 1975—; Friends of Hamilton County Parks, 1979-80 (treas., 1982); ARC, 1984-86, Salvation Army, 1983-85, Friends of U. Cin. Conservatory of Music, 1994—, Great Rivers council Girl Scouts U.S.A., 1980-83, Family Service, 1985-88; Cin. Commn. on the Arts, Cin. Ballet 1985-91; mem. licensing com. Cin. Bicentennial Com., 1985-87; trustee Wood Hudson Cancer Rsch. Lab., 1988—; mem. adv. bd. Sch. Nursing U. Cin., 1992—; mem. founder's bd. Abrahamson Pediatric Eye Inst. of Children's Hosp., 1995—. Recipient Silver Medal award Advertisers' Club Cin., 1976; named YWCA Career Woman of Achievement, 1982, Woman of Yr. Cin. Enquirer, 1991. Mem. Fashion Group Cin. (past regional dir.), Downtown Council (promotion chmn. 1975-76, 80-81), Public Relations Soc. Am. (dir. 1974-75, sec. 1976, treas. 1977), TV Soc. Am., Bus. and Profl. Women's Club, Advt. Club. Cin. (dir. 1967-87, v.p. 1972, Advt. Woman of Yr. 1972, mem. Speakers Bur. 1973—, pres. 1973-74, AAF Silver medal 1976), Women in Communications. Home: 2324 Madison Rd Apt 1107 Cincinnati OH 45208-2640

BLOCK, NADINE L., school psychologist; b. Medford, Wis., Oct. 7, 1936; d. Franklin and Sara (Milles) Ludwig; divorced. BS in Edn., U. Wis., 1958; postgrad., Ohio State U., 1974. Cert. sch. psychologist; lic. sch. pscyhologist. Sch. psychologist Franklin County Bd. Edn., 1975-83; founder, exec. dir. Ctr. for Effective Discipline, Columbus, Ohio, 1987—; co-founder, coord. Nat. Coalition to Abolish Corporal Punishment in Schs., 1987—; govtl. liaison Ohio Sch. Psychologists, Westerville, Ohio, 1981-92; Founding bd. mem. Support for Talented Students, Inc., 1983—, regional dir., 1988-90; co-founder Ohio Pupil Svcs. Orgn., Columbus, 1987; co-chmn. End Physical Punishment of Children, 1995—; mem. adv. bd. child abuse prevention com. Childrens Hosp., Columbus, 1995—. Contbr. articles to profl. jours.; co-editor: Law Relevant to Psycholog. Practice, 1988; prodr. of various videotapes; speaker for several groups. Trustee Syntaxis Group Homes, Columbus, 1994—, pres., 1988-90; pres. Special Edn. PAC, Columbus, 1994—; treas. Voices for Children & Youth, Columbus, 1995. Recipient Oak Tree award Ohio PTA, 1991, Broken Paddle award Am. Acad. Pediatrics, 1992, M. Burley Disting. Svc. award Ohio Coalition, 1993. Mem. Nat. Assn. Sch. Psychologists (gov. rels. chmn. 1984-90). Republican. Roman Catholic. Office: Ctr for Effective Discipline 155 W Main St # 100-B Columbus OH 43215

BLOCK, RUTH, retired insurance company executive; b. N.Y.C., Nov. 7, 1930; d. Albert and Celia (Shapiro) Smolensky; BA, Adelphi U., 1952; m. Norman Block, April 5, 1952. With Equitable Life Assurance Soc. of U.S., 1952-87, v.p., planning officer, 1973-77, sr. v.p. in charge individual life ins. bus., 1977-80, exec. v.p. individual ins. bus.'s, 1980-87, duties expanded to include group life and health bus.'s, chief ins. officer, 1984-87; chmn., chief exec. officer Equitable Variable Life Ins. Co., 1980-84; bd. dirs. Amoco Corp., Ecolab Inc., (40) ACM Mut. Funds; trustee Life Underwriter Tng. Coun., 1983-85; vis. exec. Mobil Co. U. Iowa, 1978. Bd. dirs. Stamford (Conn.) YWCA, 1977-80, Donaldson, Lufkin & Jenrette, 1983-86, Avon Products, 1985-91, St Lukes Cmty. Svcs., 1991-94; nat. chmn. Equitable United Way, 1978. Recipient Disting. Alumni award Adelphi U. Sch. of Bus., 1979, Catalyst award 1983, WEAL award, 1983, N.Y.C. YMCA award. Mem. Nat. Assn. Securities Dealers (gov. at large 1982-84), Com. of 200, Womens Econ. Round Table, Rsch. Bd.(emeritus), Bus. Execs for Nat. Security, Women's Forum N.Y. and Conn. Office: PO Box 4653 Stamford CT 06907-0653

BLOCKUS, KATHLEEN ANN MARY, accountant; b. Somerville, N.J., Dec. 12, 1955; d. Kasmier Henry Blockus and Theresa Mary Kaczanowski. AAS in Acctg., Raritan Valley C.C., North Branch, N.J., 1990. Word processor Am. Cyanamid, Bound Brook, N.J., 1973-82; statistical typist Ortho Diagnostic Sys., Raritan, N.J., 1983-85, acctg. clk., 1985-87, sales coord., 1987-92, acctg. asst., 1992—. Typist St. Mary's Roman Cath. Ch., Bound Brook, N.J.; cheerleading advisor St. Mary's Grammar Sch., Bound Brook, 1980-83. Mem. Inst. Mgmt. Accts. Home: 39 Van Keuren Ave Bound Brook NJ 08805

BLODGETT, LYNDA DANYELLE, fashion design and manufacturing specialist; b. Woburn, Mass., Apr. 12, 1957; d. William Edward III and Elizabeth Kathren (Hoag) B.; m. Gregory Ronald Duff, Aug. 6, 1977 (div. Sept. 1989); children: Rebecca Julieanne, Christine Elizabeth. BFA, Art Inst. Chgo., 1979; postgrad., Tex. Woman's U., 1985-95, U. Dallas, 1995—. Owner stores, fashion designer, pattern prodn. mgr., 1979-85; instr. fashion pattern making Bauder Coll., Arlington, Tex., 1984-85; instr. fashion design, textiles, history, dept. chairperson Miss Wade's Fashion and Merchandising Coll., Dallas, 1985-90; owner Danyelle Gowns, Arlington, 1990-95; video coord. fashion shows Miss Wade's Fashion and Merchandising Coll., 1985-89, fashion group sponsor, coord. group fashion show, 1988-89. Writer ednl. courses in field. Craft vol. Girl Scouts U.S., Kennedale, Tex., 1992; cookie mom Girl Scouts U.S., Ft. Worth, 1992-94; tutor, vol., coord. Christmas party and Easter egg hunt Trinity River Mission, Dallas, 1995-96; mem. Roaring Singles class Lovers Ln. United Meth. Ch., 1988—, mem. United Meth. Women, 1994—, mem. sew and sew group, adult charity work officer, 1995-96, mem. Mary sharing group, 1996—. Mem. AAUW, NAFE. Home: 1007 Mapleview Dr Arlington TX 76018

BLOEMER, ROSEMARY CELESTE, bookkeeper; b. St. Louis, Jan. 26, 1930; d. Edward J. and Leslie F. (McCreary) Walsh; m. Edward H. Bloemer, Sept. 4, 1948; children: Stephen, Diane, Janet. Cert. in court reporting, Bayside Coll., San Francisco, 1948; student, U. Mo., St. Louis, 1949-51, 83. Teller Roosevelt Savs. & Loan, 1967; income tax sec. Boatmen's Nat. Bank, St. Louis, 1968-73; sec. psychology dept. Washington U., St. Louis, 1978; beverages contr. Chase-Park Plaza Hotel, St. Louis, 1977-81; owner Bloemer Tax Svc., St. Louis, 1975—; legal sec. Lickhalter Law Office, St. Louis, 1970-88, Law Office of James K. Steitz, St. Louis, 1981-83; bookkeeper, tax advisor Mo. Hwy. Patrol Assn., Inc., St. Louis, 1981-83; bookkeeper, tax acct. Mo. State Hwy. Patrol Civilian Employees Assn., St. Louis, 1983-92; acct. Clarion Hotel, St. Louis, 1986, Bel-Air Hilton Inn, St. Louis, 1984-85; consignment standard stock machine screws, contr. accounts receivable Consol. Aluminum Co., 1973-75; sec. to 5 fin. specialists Cmty. Devel. Agy., St. Louis, 1980-81; tax preparer H&R Block, 1991-95; mem. team of reporters Price Waterhouse, 1990-96. Arbitrator, shopper, speaker Better Bus. Bur. St. Louis, 1980—; sec. to pres. Bd. Higher Edn., Christian Ch., 1975-77; vol. in choir Shrine of St. Joseph, St. Louis. Mem. Nat. Soc. Tax Profls., Nat. Assn. Tax Practitioners, Am. Soc. Notaries; Internat. Platform Assn.

Roman Catholic. Home and Office: 1435 Trampe Ave Saint Louis MO 63138-2541

BLOG, GLORIA DELOSH, property administrator; b. Norfolk, N.Y., May 13, 1931; d. Leo George and Bernice Fredricka (Gooshaw) DeLosh; m. Orville Allen Bush, July 26, 1948 (dec. 1955); m. Lawrence Blog, Apr. 20, 1970. Attended, Syracuse U., 1956-60, Syracuse Beauty Sch., 1961, New Haven Tech. Sch., 1963-65. Bus. contr. Mega Engring., Lancaster, Calif., 1964-84; property adminstr. Bayco Fin. Corp., Sherman Oaks, Calif., 1984-88, Rodin-Lawson Mgmt. Co., Inc., Sherman Oaks, 1988—. Sec. Pacific Art Guild, 1989-90. Office: Property Mgmt 4635 Stoner Ave # 1 Culver City CA 90230

BLOMQUIST, ROBIN ALICE, artist, elementary education educator; b. Dinuba, Calif., May 14, 1913; d. Joseph Samuel and Lotta D. (Kennedy) Johnson; m. Carl Leonard Blomquist, Aug. 28, 1937; children: Robin John C., Carla May, Victoria, Alson, Mary, Joseph, Valanne. Student, San Diego Acad. Fine Arts, 1932-37, San Diego State Coll., 1936-37; BA, Chico State Coll., 1962, postgrad., 1963—; student, Calif. Sch. Arts Craft, Oakland, Calif., 1967. Cert. (life) elem., secondary tchr., Calif.; spl. cert. reading, Calif. State Dept. Edn., 1963-68. Artist, demonstrator Fed. Art Project, San Diego, 1936-37; adult edn. tchr. San Joaquin County Schs., Escalon, Calif., 1949-50, Kern County Schs., Taft, Shafter, Calif., 1950-52; adult edn. tchr. Shasta Coll., Redding, Calif., 1953-58, adult art tchr., 1973-81; art, mech. drawing tchr. Corning (Calif.) H.S., 1953-62; art tchr. Corning (Calif.) Elem. Sch., 1953-54; spl. reading, math tchr. Gerber (Calif.) Elem., 1963-74; substitute, home tchr. Tehama Schs., Red Bluff, Calif., 1973-93; ptnr., conservator, restorer Selected Arts Gallery, Chico, Calif., 1963-72; conservator Los Molinos (Calif.) Antiques, 1963-90; mem. Internat. Reading Conf., Eng., 1969, Alaska, 1970, Scotland, 1971. Troop leader Girl Scouts U.S., 1945-50, Camp Fire Girls, 1928-36, 4-H, 1938-41, Cub Scouts, 1953-55; mem. Tehama County (Calif.) Gen. & Hist. Soc., Hist. Commn., 1976-96, Arts Coun., 1982-85; pres. Tehama County Tchrs. Orgn., 1954-55, pres. Bus. Profl. Women, Corning, Calif., 1962-63, pres. United Meth. Women, Corning, 1964, 90; host Exch. Student Program, Sweden, Morocco, 1958-59, 74-75, Internat. Christian Youth Exch.; mem. (life) PTA, Calif. Recipient 2nd Internat. Art Schs. award Internat. Latham Found., 1934, scholar San Diego Acad. Fine Arts, 1932-35. Mem. Am. Assn. Ret. Persons (scholarship chmn., citizen of the year, 1995), AAUW, Women in the Arts, Calif. Ret. Tchrs., No. Calif. Doll Club, United Fedn. of Doll Clubs, Corning Friends of Libr., Delta Kappa Gamma (v.p. 1980-81, pres. 1981-82). Democrat. Methodist. Home: 1417 Colusa St Corning CA 96021

BLOMQUIST-STANBERY, RUTH ELLEN, computer services company owner, elementary education educator; b. Chgo., Feb. 12, 1949; d. Roy Theodore Sr. and Ruth Theresa (Johnson) Blomquist; m. Donald Loran Stanbery, Aug. 16, 1985; children: Elyn Nicole Blomquist, Dena Terese Blomquist, Lukas Brock Theodor Stanbery. BA, Elmhurst (Ill.) Coll., 1979; MA, No. Ill. U.; postgrad., Nat. Coll. Edn., Evanston, Ill. Sec., real estate and comml. mortgage First Nat. Bank of Chgo., 1972-73; substitute tchr. DuPage County (Ill.) Schs., 1979-82; tchr., adminstr. DuPage Alt. Elem. Sch., Downers Grove, Ill., 1979-82; with Jewel Foods, Lombard, Ill., 1982-83; office and factory worker Frank's Office Svcs., St. Charles, Ill., 1984-85; in sales and distbn. Homes Mag., Downers Grove, 1987-88; youth counselor Job Tng. Partnership Act, Ogle County, Rochelle, Ill., 1990; in prodn. Del Monte Corp., DeKalb, Ill., 1985-91; on-line prodn. coord. and facilitator The Suter Co., Sycamore, Ill., 1991-93; owner, CEO Stanbery Computer Svcs., Rochelle, Ill., 1994—. Contbr. articles to profl. jours. Mem. AAUW, ASCD, Ill. Edn. Assn., Nat. Coun. Tchrs. English, Order Ea. Star, Job's Daus., Phi Delta Kappa, Omicron Delta Kappa, Kappa Delta Epsilon. Congregationalist. Home: PO Box 55 Malta IL 60150-0055 Office: Stanbery Computer Svcs 508 N 2d St Box 546 Rochelle IL 61068

BLON, BERNADETTE SCARCI, accountant; b. Canonsburg, Pa., Jan. 26, 1959; d. Joseph Anthony and Mary Ann Elizabeth (Churray) Scarci; m. Howard Henry Blon, Aug. 14, 1993. BA, Washington and Jefferson Coll., 1990. Brokerage analyst Equibank, Pitts., 1982-85, acct. Consol Inc., Pitts., 1985—. Roman Catholic. Home: 533 E McMurray Rd McMurray PA 15317 Office: Consol Inc 1800 Washington Rd Pittsburgh PA 15241

BLONSHINE, SHEENA KAY, medical, surgical nurse; b. Traverse City, Mich., Oct. 15, 1945; d. LeRoy H. and Arta M. (Terry) Blonshine. Diploma, Orange Meml. Sch. Nursing, 1966; BSN cum laude, Boise State U., 1994. RN, Idaho, Fla. Staff nurse Tampa (Fla.) Gen. Hosp., 1966-72; pvt. scrub nurse Blank, Pupello, Bessone, M.D., Tampa, 1972-82; staff nurse St. Luke's Regional Med. Ctr., Boise, 1982-84, asst. head nurse, 1984-86, dir. cardiovasc. surgery, 1986—; Bd. dirs. Heart Inst. St. Luke's Regional Med. Ctr. Nagel scholar Boise State U. Mem. NAFE, Assn. Nurses Execs., Assn. Oper. Rm. Nurses (CNOR nat. cert. bd., ednl. lectr. nat. meeting 1988, bd. dirs. Treasure Valley chpt. 1990, 94,), Sigma Theta Tau (Mu Gamma chpt.). Home: 12184 W Hickory Dr Boise ID 83713-2465 Office: Saint Luke's Regional Med Ctr 190 E Bannock St Boise ID 83712-6241

BLOOD, PEGGY A., college administrator; b. Pine Bluff, Ark., Feb. 8, 1947; d. Roscoe C. and Zelphia (Mayo) B.; m. Lawrence A. Davis, May 31, 1975; children: Lauren A., Pawnee A., Zelana P. BS, U. Ark., Pine Bluff, 1969; MFA, U. Ark., 1971; PhD, Union Inst., Cin., 1986; MA, Holy Names Coll., 1987. Art dir. Office Econ. Opportunity, Altheimer, Ark., 1969; acting. dept. chair, asst. prof. art Univ. Ark., Pine Bluff, 1971-74; activity coord. Good Samaritan Home, Oakland, Calif., 1978-80; art instr. Chabot Community Coll., Hayward, Calif., 1980-81, Solano Community Coll., Suisun, Calif., 1980-90; prin. Palma Ceia Christian Elem. Sch., Hayward, Calif., 1983-84; curriculum chmn., instr. Calif. IMPACT, Oakland, 1985-87; ctr. dir. Chapman U., Fairfield, Calif., 1988—; art cons. Sch. bd. trustee Benicia (Calif.) Unified Sch. Dist., 1989-93; bd. mem. Nat. Inst. Art & Disabilities, Richmond, Calif., 1988-90, Girl Scouts Am., Solano County, Calif., 1995-96. Recipient Ledalle Morehead scholarship, U. Ark., Pine Bluff, 1968; named first Afro-Am. grad. MFA in Art, U. Ark., Fayetteville, 1971, Outstanding Bay Area Artist, Oakland (Calif.) Arts, 1985. Mem. AAUW, Nat. Art Edn. Assn., Coll. Art Assn., Calif. Sch. Bd. Assn., C. of C., LWV (bd. mem. 1980-82), Rotary, Alpha Kappa Alpha (first prize art award 1982-83). Roman Catholic. Office: Chapman U 230 Link Rd Suisun City CA 94585-1672

BLOOM, GLENNA RAE, radiologic technologist; b. Clearfield, Pa., Aug. 13, 1956; d. Galen Foster and Helen Marie (Wise) B. AAS, Middlesex C.C., 1986; BS, Clarion U. of Pa., 1978. Remedial reading tchr. Mullins (S.C.) Jr. H.S., 1978-80, jr. high libr., 1980-84; radiologic technologist John F. Kennedy Med. Ctr., Edison, N.J., 1986-88; computerized temography technologist John F. Kennedy Med. Ctr., Edison, 1988-94; radiologic/mammography technologist DuBois (Pa.) Regional Med. Ctr., 1994—. Mem. DAR, Am. Soc. of Radiologic Technologists, Clarion U. Alumni Assn., Phi Theta Kappa. Mem. Ch. Brethren. Home: 844 State St Curwensville PA 16833

BLOOM, IRIS MARIE, self-defense instructor, writer; b. El Paso, Tex., Apr. 30, 1960; d. John Porter and Eva Louise (Platt) B.; life ptnr. Denis Doyon, Mar. 4, 1989. BA, Wellesley Coll., 1984; cert. massage therapist, Massage Arts and Scis. Ctr., Phila., 1996. Cert. women's self-defense instr. Organizer War Resisters League, N.Y.C., 1985-88; writer internat. divsn. Am. Friends Svc. Ctr., Phila., 1992-95; founder, mem. coord. com. Women Act for Peace, Phila., 1990-92; founder Global Action to Help End Rape (GATHER), Phila., 1993—; instr., comty. liaison Amulis Women's Self-Def., Phila., 1991-95; instr., dir., founder AWARE: Mind/Body/Spirit Self-Def., Phila., 1995—. Contbr. poetry to mags. Comty. organizer various orgns., Boston, N.Y.C., Phila. and Washington. Mem. Nat. Coalition Against Domestic Violence, Nat. Coalition Against Sexual Assault, Seven Mountains Spirit First Kung Fu. Home: 4808 Windsor Ave Philadelphia PA 19143

BLOOM, JANE IRA, saxophonist, composer; b. Boston, Jan. 12, 1955; d. Joel Warren and Evelyn (Kerner) B.; m. Joseph Giro Grifasi. BA magna cum laude, Yale U., 1976, MusM, 1977. Rec. artist, saxophonist, producer Outline Records, N.Y.C., 1978-82, Enja Records, N.Y.C., 1983, JMT Records, N.Y.C., 1985, CBS Records, N.Y.C., 1986-89, Arabesque Records, 1992—; saxophonist, composer Town Hall, N.Y.C., 1991, Carnegie Hall, 1994. Performer, composer, producer Symphony Space, 1986. Named winner Downbeat Internat. Critics Poll, 1979-87; Nat. Endowment for the Arts grantee 1977, 86, 95. Mem. Am. Fedn. Musicians, Nat. Space Inst.

BLOOM, JUDITH, lawyer; b. Mobile, Ala., Dec. 4, 1960; d. P. Irving and Patricia F. (Frankel) B.; m. Jonathan Marc Minnen, Apr. 2, 1960; children: Michael Bloom Minnen, Molly Eleanor Minnen. BA, Bryn Mawr Coll., 1983; JD, Emory U., 1988. Bar: Ga. 1988, Tenn. 1988. Asst. dir. Anti Defamation League B'nai Brith, N.Y.C., 1983-85; assoc. Grant, Konvalinka & Grubbs, Chattanooga, Tenn., 1987, Dale Buchanan & Assocs., Chattanooga, Tenn., 1988-90; staff atty., pro-bono coord., fundraiser Southeast Tenn. Legal Svcs., Chattanooga, Tenn., 1990—. Contbr. article to profl. jour. Mem. Vol. Atty. Task Force, Tenn., 1991—. Mem. Chattanooga Bar Assn. (pro bono liaison 1990—, appreciation award 1994), State Bar of Ga., Tenn. Bar Assn. Democrat. Jewish. Home: 1102 Signal Rd Signal Mountain TN 37377 Office: Southeast Tenn Legal Svcs 737 Market St Chattanooga TN 37405

BLOOM, KATHRYN RUTH, public relations executive; d. Morris and Frances Sondra (Siegel) B. BA, Douglass Coll.; MA, U. Toronto, Can. Dir. spl. projects United Jewish Appeal, N.Y.C., 1973-78; mgr. pub. affairs Bristol-Myers-Squibb Co., N.Y.C., 1978-86; mgr. pub. rels. pharm. and nutritional Bristol-Myers Squibb Co., N.Y.C., 1986-90, dir. pharm. and rsch. communications, 1990-91; dir. communications Biogen, Inc., Cambridge, 1992—. Mem. N.Y.C. com. Women's Campaign Fund, 1984-91; v.p., bd. dirs. N.Am. Conf. on Ethiopian Jewry, N.Y.C., 1985-93; overseer Boston Lyric Opera; dir. Jewish Vocat. Svc. of Boston. Mem. Women Execs. in Pub. Relations, The Boston Club, Phi Beta Kappa. Office: Biogen Inc 14 Cambridge Ctr Cambridge MA 02142-1401

BLOOM, MICHELLE, foreign language educator; b. Bklyn., Feb. 28, 1947; d. Seymour and Zena (Bayuk) M.; m. Michael Robert Bloom, Aug. 20, 1967; children: Marc, Deborah. BA, SUNY, Albany, 1967, MA, 1982. Cert. tchr., adminstr., N.Y. Tchr. Guilderland Jr. H.S., Guilderland Ctr., N.Y., 1967-70, Acad. of the Holy Names, Albany, 1979-81, Ravena (N.Y.)-Coeymans-Selkirk Ctrl. Sch. Dist., 1981-85; dept. chair Ravena (N.Y.)-Coeymans-Selkirk Ctrl. Sch. Dist., 1985-87; supr. fgn. langs. Shenendehowa Ctrl. Sch. Dist., Clifton Park, N.Y., 1987-93; fgn. langs. supr. Guilderland Ctrl. Sch. Dist., 1993—; mem. curriculum assessment com. (langs. other than English) N.Y. State Edn. Dept., Albany, 1992—. Mem. Am. Coun. Teaching Fgn. Langs., N.Y. State Assn. Fgn. Lang. Tchrs. (bd. dirs. 1989-91, sec. 1993-94, v.p. 1995, exec. com. 1993—, Service award 1991, Anthony Papalia award 1991, pres.-elect 1996). Office: Guilderland H S School Rd Guilderland Center NY 12085

BLOOM, NANCY MARIE, educator; b. Boston, Oct. 24, 1948; m. John Howard Bloom, June 30, 1972; 1 child, Jeffrey Howard. BS in Bus. Edn., Husson Coll., 1971; MS in Bus. Edn., Suffolk U., 1978. Tchr. Franklin (Mass.) High Sch., 1971—; dean Fitchburg (Mass.) State Coll., 1976-88; tchr. Fitchburg (Mass.) State Coll., Franklin, 1995—, 1994-95; mem. tech. com. Franklin Pub. Sch. System, 1993-95. Author: Oceanview Associate: A Word Processing Textbook, 1986. Mem. Nat. Desktop Publishing Assn., R.I. Bus. Edn. Assn., Mass. Bus. Edn. Assn. (dir.), Mass. Computer Using Educators, Boston Computer Soc. Home: 371 Village St Medway MA 02053 Office: Franklin High Sch 218 Oak St Franklin MA 02038

BLOOM, PHYLLIS, Spanish language educator. BA in Spanish Lang. and Lit., George Washington Univ., 1968; student, Univ. Madrid, Spain, 1966; cert. in Advanced Study of Spanish, Centro De Documentacion Cultural, Mexico, 1972, Jaimes Balmes, Mexico, 1974; postgrad., Univ. Calif., L.A., 1977, Univ. Calif., L.A., 1992-93. Instr. Spanish lang., culture and lit. Wellesley H.S., Mass., 1968-69; coord. Spanish lang. program, instr. Spanish and English Yavneh Hebrew Acad., L.A., 1969-71; instr. Spanish lang., culture and lit. Westlake Sch. for Girls, L.A., 1971-78; bilingual sales rep. Empress Pearls, Hollywood, Calif., 1975-76; sr. area sales rep. Pitney Bowes, L.A., 1979-82; founder, instr. The Spanish Teacher, Encino, Calif., 1979—; instr. ESL Garfield Cmty. Adult Sch., L.A., 1975-76. NDEA fellow Spanish Inst. Knox Coll., Ill., 1969. Mem. Calif. Fgn. Lang. Tchrs. Assn., Am. Assn. Tchrs. of Spanish and Portuguese, Am. Coun. Teaching Fgn. Langs., Computer Assisted Learning and Instruction Consortium, Computer Assisted Lang. Learning. Office: The Spanish Teacher 17066 Empanada Pl Encino CA 91436

BLOOMBERG, IRMA F. See **STEINBERG, IRMA FRANCES**

BLOOMER, PATRICIA BOSWELL, therapist; b. Balt., Dec. 6, 1957; d. William Patterson and Lois Eleanor (Wintermute) Boswell; m. Peter Lawrence Bloomer, Oct. 3, 1981; children: Landon Lawrence, Jena Elizabeth. BS, U. Del., Newark, 1980; MA, W.Va. U., 1984. Cert. addictions counselor. Treatment specialist Fayette County Drug and Alcohol Commn., Uniontown, Pa., 1981-87; therapist in pvt. practice Uniontown, 1986—, cons., educator in pvt. practice, 1986—; presenter Office of Drug & Alcohol Programming, Harrisburg, Pa., 1986—; cons. Crime Victim Ctr., Uniontown, 1994-95. Designer, presenter (workshop) A Womens Knowing, 1994. Mem. Am. Assn. Counseling and Devel. Office: 355 McClellandtown Rd Uniontown PA 15401

BLOOMFIELD, INGRID LEA, cardiology nurse; b. Fairfax, Mo., Dec. 5, 1965; d. Arthur John and Rosalee Elaine (Frazee) B.; m. Arthur Krieger. BSN, Molloy Coll., Rockville Centre, N.Y., 1989, MSN, 1992; Post Masters Cert., SUNY, Stone Brook, 1994. CCRN, ANP; cert. ACLS; RN-C, N.Y. Nurse's asst. South Nassau Communities Hosp., Oceanside, N.Y., 1985, LPN, 1985-89, staff nurse, 1989—; critical care nurse CCU St. Francis Hosp., Roslyn, N.Y., 1989—; adult nurse practitioner in cardiology North Shore Univ. Hosp., Manhasset, N.Y., 1994—. Mem. AACN, ANA, Am. Heart Assn., N.Y. State Nurses Assn., Nat. League Nursing, N.Y. State Coalition Nurse Practitioners, Am. Acad. Nurse Practitioners, L.I. Coalition of Nurse Practitioners, Sigma Theta Tau, Psi Chi. Independent. Presbyterian. Office: North Shore Univ Hosp Dept Cardiology Community Dr Manhasset NY 11030

BLOOMGARDEN, KATHY FINN, public relations executive; b. N.Y.C., June 9, 1949; d. David and Laura (Zeisler) Finn; m. Zachary Bloomgarden; children: Rachel, Keith, Matthew. BA, Brown U., 1970; MA, Columbia U., PhD. Pres. Rsch. & Forecasts, N.Y.C.; pres., dir. Ruder-Finn, Inc., N.Y.C., 1988—. Bd. dirs. CARE, Women's Forum, N.Y. Arthritis Found. Mem. Pub. Rels. Soc. Am., Nat. Investor Rels. Inst., Swedish-Am. C. of C. Jewish. Home: 1084 North Ave New Rochelle NY 10804-3618 Office: Ruder Finn 301 E 57th St New York NY 10022-2900*

BLOS, JOAN W., author, critic, lecturer; b. N.Y.C., Dec. 9, 1928; m. Peter Blos, Jr., 1953; 2 children, 1 deceased. B.A., Vassar Coll., 1950; M.A., CCNY, 1956. Asso. publs. div., mem. tchr. edn. faculty Bank St. Coll. Edn., N.Y.C., 1958-70; lectr. Sch. Edn., U. Mich., Ann Arbor, 1972-80; U.S. editor Children's Literature in Education, 1976-81. Author: "It's Spring!" She Said, 1968, (with Betty Miles) Just Think!, 1971, A Gathering of Days: A New England Girl's Journal, 1930-32, 1979 (Newbery medal ALA, Am. Book award 1980), Martin's Hats, 1984, Brothers of the Heart: A Story of the Old Northwest, 1837-38, 1985, Old Henry, 1987, Lottie's Circus, 1989, The Grandpa Days, 1989, One Very Best Valentine's Day, 1990, The Heroine of the Titanic, 1991, A Seed, A Flower, A Minute, An Hour, 1992, Brooklyn Doesn't Rhyme, 1994, The Days Before Now, 1994, Hungry Little Boy, 1995.

BLOSSER, PAMELA ELIZABETH, metaphysics educator, counselor, minister; b. Norman, Okla., Dec. 12, 1946; d. William Bernard and Emma Elizabeth (Armbrister) Carpenter; m. William Richard Stewart, June 10, 1969 (div. Apr. 1979); m. Paul Gerald Blosser Jr., Sept. 24, 1994. BA, Tex. Christian U., 1969; DDiv, Interfaith Ch. Metaphysics, Windyville, Mo., 1992; DMetaphysics, Sch. Metaphysics, Windyville, 1994. Ordained to ministry Interfaith Ch. of Metaphysics, 1992; cert. in counseling. Dir. metaphysics ctrs. Sch. Metaphysics, various locations, 1979-89; directress Golden Moments Montessori, Columbia, Mo., 1987-89; instr. metaphysics Sch. Metaphysics, various locations, 1977-89; readings coord. Sch. Metaphysics, Windyville, 1989—, dir. printing, 1989—, instr. metaphysics, 1991—; min. of music Interfaith Ch. Metaphysics, Windyville, 1990—, min., 1995—; dir. Coll. Prep. Camp for Children, Sch. Metaphysics, Windyville, 1990—; mem. ordination bd. Interfaith Ch. of Metaphysics, 1993—. Author: (books of essays) Power of Structure, 1988, Total Recall, 1993; contbr. articles to profl. jours. Mem. Dallas County Ministerial Alliance, Dallas County Homemakers (sec.-treas. 1995-96), Homemaker Club Windyville (v.p. 1995, pres. 1996). Republican. Home: HCR 1 Box 15 Windyville MO 65783 Office: Sch of Metaphysics HCR 1 Box 15 Windyville MO 65783

BLOUNT, JACKIE MARIE, educator; b. Tullahoma, Tenn., Dec. 19, 1959; d. Edward Buck and Gwendolyn Maude (Merritt) B. B.Music Edn., U. N.C., 1983, MAT in Physics Tchg., 1989, PhD in Social Found. of Edn., 1993. Cert. tchr. music, physics, N.C. Tchr. physics Lexington (N.C.) H.S., 1985-90; grad. asst. U. N.C., 1990-93; asst. prof. Iowa State U., Ames, 1993—. Contbr. articles to profl. jours. Mem. N.C. Human Rels. Commn., Raleigh, 1987-90. Woodrow Wilson Found. Spencer Dissertation fellow, 1992-93, Dean Smith Scholarship Found. scholar, 1991-92, John Motley Morehead Found. scholar, 1978-82. Mem. Am. Ednl. Studies Assn., Am. Ednl. Rsch. Assn., History of Edn. Soc., Midwest History of End. Soc. Democrat. Office: Iowa State U Dept Curriculum and Instrn N157 Lagomarcino Hall Ames IA 50011

BLOXOM, MARGUERITE DORIS, bibliographer; b. Denver, Sept. 24, 1932; d. Rex and Helen Marguerite (Deibler) B. BA, U. Colo., 1954; MA, Ohio State U., 1956, U. Md., 1963; PhD, U. Md., 1970. Rsch. asst. Bell Telephone Labs., Murray Hill, N.J., 1956-57; advt. rschr. AT&T, N.Y.C., 1957-59; testing asst. USN Pers. Rsch. Field Activity, Washington, 1959; rsch. asst. HumRRo, Washington, 1960-64; instr. U. Md., College Park, 1964-70; bibliographer Libr. of Congress, Washington, 1971-91, sr. bibliographic specialist, 1992-95. Author: Pickaxe and Pencil: References for the Study of WPA. Mem. Cmty. Tennis Assn. Chincoteague Va. (sec. 1991—).

BLUE, CATHERINE ANNE, lawyer; b. Boston, Feb. 17, 1957; d. James Daniel and Angela Devina (Savini) Mahoney; m. Donald Sherwood Blue, Oct. 4, 1980; children: Mairead Catherine, Edward Pierce. BA, Stonehill Coll., North Easton, Mass., 1977; JD, Coll. William and Mary, 1980. Bar: Pa. 1980. Atty., Aluminum Co. Am., Pitts., 1980-83, Pa. Dept. Revenue, Harrisburg, 1983-85, State Workmen's Ins. Fund, Pitts., 1985-87, Met. Pitts. Pub. Broadcasting (name now QED Communications Inc.), 1987-91, gen. counsel, 1991-95; regional gen. counsel Ctrl. region AT&T Wireless Svcs., 1995—. Mem. Pa. Bar Assn., Allegheny County Bar Assn. Democrat. Home: 118 Washington St Pittsburgh PA 15218-1352 Office: AT&T Wireless Svcs 2630 Liberty Ave Pittsburgh PA 15222

BLUE, ROSE, writer, educator; b. N.Y.C.; d. Irving and Frieda (Rosenberg) Bluestone. BA, Bklyn. Coll.; postgrad. Bank St. Coll. Edn., 1967. Tchr., N.Y.C. Public Schs., 1967—; writing cons. Bklyn. Coll. Sch. Edn., 1981-83. Author: A Quiet Place, 1969; Black, Black Beautiful Black, 1969, How Many Blocks Is The World, 1970, Bed-Stuy Beat, 1970, I Am Here (Yo Estoy Aqui), 1971, A Month of Sundays, 1972, Grandma Didn't Wave Back, 1972 (teleplay 1983), Nikki 108, 1973, We are Chicano, 1973, The Preacher's Kid, 1975, Seven Years from Home, 1976, The Yo Yo Kid, 1976, The Thirteenth Year, 1977, Cold Rain on the Water, 1979, My Mother The Witch, 1981 (teleplay 1984), Everybody's Evy, 1985, Heart to Heart, 1986, Goodbye Forever Tree, 1987, The Secret Papers of Camp Get Around, 1988, Barbara Bush First Lady, 1990, Colin Powell Straight To The Top, 1991, Barbara Jordan-Politician, 1992, Defending Our Country, 1993, Working Together Against Hate Groups, 1993, People of Peace, 1994, The White House Kids, 1995, Whoopi Goldberg Entertainer, 1995, Bring Me A Memory, 1996; lyricist: Drama of Love, 1964, Let's Face It, 1961, Give Me a Break, 1962, My Heartstrings Keep Me Tied To You, 1963, Homecoming Party, 1966. Contbg. editor: Teacher mag., Day Care mag. Mem. Authors Guild Am., Authors League Am., PEN, Mensa, Profl. Women's Caucus, Broadcast Music, Inc. Home and Office: 1320 51st St Brooklyn NY 11219-3552

BLUESTEIN, LYNDA SHANNON, medical administration/management professional; b. San Marcos, Tex., Apr. 26, 1947; d. Louis Timothy and Jewel Lillian (Binkley) Shannon; m. Peter Hill Holmstrom, Sept. 21, 1968 (div. Dec. 1980); children: Aimee, Jacob; m. Paul Alan Bluestein, Nov. 6, 1982. BA, Calif. State U., Long Beach, 1971; MPH, UCLA, 1977. With VISTA, Altus, Okla., 1971-72; health educator No. Ky. Dist. Health Dept., Covington, 1972-74; dir. health edn. HMO Concepts, Inc., Anaheim, Calif., 1977-80; dir. pub. rels. Am. Med. Internat., Anaheim, 1980; dir. mktg. and pub. rels. Charter Med. Corp., Hawaiian Gardens, Calif., 1981; dir. profl. rels. Humana, Norwalk, Conn., 1982-83; dir. med. group U. Calif. Med. Sch., Irvine, 1983-88; product line mgr. Long Beach (Calif.) Heart Inst., 1988-89; dir. primary care network St. Joseph Hosp., Orange, Calif., 1989-91; v.p. for practice integration and devel. Physician's Choice Health Care Orgn., Ridgefield, Conn., 1995—. Founder, pres. C/Birth, Inc., Orange County, Calif., 1978—; founding bd. mem. Conn. Coalition Against Gun Violence, Fairfield, 1993—, IMPACT, Fairfield County, 1993—; mem. Dem. Town Com., Fairfield, 1993—; bd. mem., v.p. Greater Bridgeport Interfaith Action, 1994—; singer, mem. Serendipity Chorale, 1994—. Mem. APHA, AAUW, LWV, Am. Coll. Med. Practice Execs., Conn. Women in Healthcare Mgmt., Med. Group Mgmt. Assn. Unitarian-Universalist. Office: Physicians Choice Inc 650 Danbury Rd Ridgefield CT 06877

BLUHM, BARBARA JEAN, communications agency executive; b. Chgo., Mar. 5, 1925; d. Maurice L. and Clara (Miller) B. Student Coll. William and Mary, 1943-45; BS, U. Wis., 1947. Exec. tng. program Carson Pirie Scott & Co., Chgo., 1947-52; home economist Lever Bros. Co., Chgo., 1952-57; field rep. The Merchandising Group, N.Y.C., 1957-62; v.p. The Merchandising Group, N.Y.C., 1962-82, pres., 1982-87, chmn., 1987-90. Publicity chmn. James Lenox House Assn., N.Y.C., 1980-90; vol. Venice Hosp., Venice Little Theatre; mem. Coll. Club of Venice, Friends of the Venice Art League, Venice Symphony. Mem. Venice Yacht Club. Republican. Presbyterian. Home: 1470 Colony Pl Venice FL 34292-1550

BLUITT, KAREN, technical manager, software engineer; b. N.Y.C., Oct. 25, 1957; d. James Bertrand and Beatrice (Kaufman) B.; m. Kenneth Mark Curry, Nov. 24, 1979 (div. Dec. 1991). BS, Fordham U., 1979; MBA, Calif. State Poly. U., 1982; postgrad., George Mason U. Software engr. Hughes Aircraft Co., Fullerton, Calif., 1979-81; microprocessor engr. Beckman Instruments Co., Fullerton, 1981-82, Singer Co., Glendale, Calif., 1982-83; sr. software engr. Sanders Assoc., Nashua, N.H., 1983-85; software project mgr. GTE Corp., Billerica, Mass., 1985-86; sr. software engr. Wang Labs, Lowell, Mass., 1986-87; project task leader Vanguard Rsch., Lexington, Mass., 1987-88; program mgr. Applied Rsch. & Engring., Bedford, Mass., 1989-91; program mgr. Sparta, McLean, Va., 1992-93; prin. software engr. Sci. Applications Internat., Arlington, Va., 1993-94; tech. mgr. CACI, Arlington, 1994-94, Booz-Allen & Hamilton, Vienna, Va., 1995, MRJ, Inc., Fairfax, Va., 1996—. 1st lt. USAR, 1979-88. Scholar Gov. N.Y. Scholarship Com., 1975-79; Beta Gamma Sigma scholar, 1978—. Mem. IEEE, AAUW, Am. Brokers Network, Assn. Computing Machinery, Data Processing Mgmt. Assn., Soc. Women Engrs. Office: MRJ Inc 10560 Arrowhead Dr Fairfax VA 22030

BLUM, BARBARA DAVIS, banker; b. Hutchinson, Kans.; d. Roy C. and Jo (McKinnon) Davis; children: Devin, Hunter, Ragan, Davis. Student, U. Kans.; BA, Fla. State U., MSW, 1959. Mem. faculty Pediat. Psychiatry Clinic, U. Kans. Med. Ctr., Lawrence; acting adminstr. Suffolk County (N.Y.) Mental Health Clinic, Huntington, L.I.; founder, ptnr. Mid-Suffolk Ctr. for Psychotherapy, Hauppage, L.I., N.Y.; v.p. Restaurant Assocs. Ga., Inc., Atlanta; dep. adminstr. U.S. EPA, Washington, 1977-81; mem. Pres.'s Interagy. Coordinating Coun.; chmn., pres., CEO Abigail Adams Nat. Bancorp and Adams Nat. Bank; chairperson U.S./Japan Environ. Agreement, 1977; head 1st U.S. Environ. Del. to China, 1978; chmn. Environ. Policy Inst., 1981-84; sr. advisor UN Environ. Program, 1981-84; bd. dirs. Washington Bd. Trade; chairperson Ctr. for Policy Alternatives; trustee Fed. City Coun.; mem. nat. adv. coun. U.S. SBA. Chmn. D.C. Econ. Devel. Fin. Corp.; founder Leadership Washington; del. UN Mid Decade Conf. on Women, 1980; bd. dirs. Kaiser Permanente Mid Atlantic; dep. dir. Carter-Mondale U.S. presdl. campaign, 1976, Carter/Mondale Transition Team, Washington, 1976-77; panelist Clinton-Gore Econ. Conf., Little Rock and Atlanta; presdl. appointee bd. dirs. Inst. for Am. Indian Art. Decorated comdr.'s cross Order of Merit W. Ger.; recipient Disting. Service award

Federally Employed Women, 1978, Spl. Conservation award Nat. Wildlife Fedn., 1976, Orgn. of Yr. award Ga. Wildlife Fedn., 1974, Disting. Service award Americans for Indian Opportunity, 1978. Mem. Washington Women's Forum, Internat. Women's Forum, Cosmos Club, Econs. Club. Democrat.

BLUM, BARBARA MEDDOCK, retired association executive; b. Oil City, Pa., Nov. 8, 1938; d. Marvin Lee and Hazel Genevieve (Jackson) Meddock.; m. Stuart Hollander Blum, Sept. 21, 1963. BA in Psychology, Allegheny Coll., 1960. Psychometrist, researcher Hofstra U., Hempstead, N.Y., 1960-62; adminstrv. asst., editor The Asia Soc., N.Y.C., 1962-66, exec. asst., 1966-72, adminstrv. officer, 1972-85, dir. adminstrn., 1985-88, ret. 1988.

BLUM, DEBORAH, reporter. Sr. writer The Sacramento (Calif.) Bee; sci. writer in residence U. Wis., Madison, 1993. Author: The Monkey Wars, 1994. Recipient Pulitzer Prize for beat reporting, 1992. Mem. Nat. Assn. Sci. Writers (bd. dirs.), Sigma Xi. Office: Sacramento Bee PO Box 15779 Sacramento CA 95852-0779*

BLUM, EVA TANSKY, lawyer; b. Pitts., July 29, 1949; d. Harry and Jeanette N. Tansky; 1 child. BA, U. Pitts., 1970, JD, 1973. Bar: Pa. 1973. Atty. U.S. Dept. Commerce, Washington, 1973-76, U.S. Air, Washington, 1976-77; sr. v.p., dir. corp. risk mgmt. and compliance PNC Bank Corp., Pitts., 1990—. Mem. com. Pitts. Health and Welfare Planning Assn., 1985-89; bd. dirs. Family Health Coun., Pitts., 1987-94, Forbes Health Found., 1992—, WQED, Pitts., U. Pitts. Alumni Assn.; bd. dirs., sec. ARC Western Pa. chpt.. 1992-94; trustee Am. Jewish Com., Pitts., 1977—. Mem. ABA, Pa. Bar Assn., Allegheny County Bar Assn. Office: PNC Bank Corp One PNC Plaza 249 Fifth Ave Pittsburgh PA 15222-2707

BLUM, JOAN KURLEY, fundraising executive; b. Palm Beach, Fla., July 27, 1926; d. Nenad Daniel and Eva (Milos) Kurley; m. Robert C. Blum, Apr. 15, 1967; children: Christopher Alexander, Martha Jane, Louisa Joan, Paul Helmuth, Sherifa. BA, U. Wash., 1948. Cert. fund raising exec. U.S. dir. Inst. Mediterranean Studies, Berkeley, Calif., 1962-65; devel. officer U. Calif. at Berkeley, 1965-67; pres. Blum Assocs., Fund-Raising Cons., San Anselmo, Calif., 1967-92, The Blums of San Francisco, 1992—; mem. faculty U. Calif. Extension, Inst. Fund Raising, SW Inst. Fund-Raising U. Tex., U. San Francisco, U.K. Vol. Movement Group, London, Australasian Inst. Fund Raising. Contbr. numerous articles to profl. jours. Recipient Golden Addy award Am. Advt. Fedn.; Silver Mailbox award Direct Mail Mktg. Assn., Best Ann. Giving Time-Life award, others; decorated commdr. Sovereign Order St. Stanislas. Mem. Nat. Soc. Fund-Raising Execs. (dir.), Nat. Assn. of Hosp. Devel., Women Emerging., Rotary (San Francisco), Fund Raising Inst. (Australia), Tahoe Yacht Club. Office: 202 Evergreen Dr Kentfield CA 94904-2708 also: 73 Albert Ave Ste 8, Chatswood Sydney NSW 2067, Australia

BLUM, LORI GAY, elementary school educator; b. Lincoln, Nebr., Aug. 21, 1958; d. James G. and LaVonne F. (Habenicht) Orr; m. Gary L. Blum, Dec. 21, 1979; children: Joshua, Jessica. BS in Edn., Concordia Tchrs. Coll., Seward, Nebr., 1980; MEd, U. Nebr., 1986. Tchr. grades 4-8 Saunders County Dist. 20, Ashland, Nebr., 1981-84; reading specialist K-6 Raymond Ctrl. Schs., Valparaiso, Nebr., 1984-90; reading specialist 7-9 Goodrich Mid. Sch./Lincoln Pub. Schs., 1990-95; tchr. grade 6 Campbell Elem. Sch./Lincoln Pub. Schs., 1995—; co-presenter/owner Reading All the Way, Malcolm, Nebr., 1990-93. Sunday sch. tchr. St. Paul's Luth. Ch., Malcolm, 1993—, vacation Bible sch. dir., 1992—; pres. Malcolm PTO, 1988-90. Recipient Nebr. Tchr. Achievement award Kiewit Found., Omaha, 1989, Award for Excellence in Teaching, Cooper Found., Lincoln, 1990; Vaughn Found. grantee, 1991. Mem. Internat. Reading Assn. Democrat. Home: 8401 NW 112th St Malcolm NE 68402-9521 Office: Campbell Elem Sch 2200 Dodge St Lincoln NE 68521

BLUM, SARAH LEE, nurse psychotherapist; b. Atlantic City, N.J., Dec. 5, 1939; d. David and Diana (Fedner) B.; m. Joseph J. McGoran, Aug. 24, 1970 (div. 1986); children: Lorna Hope Marie, Sean-David Justin. BSN, Seattle U., 1971; M in Nursing, U. Wash., 1976. Cert. clin. specialist. Nurse Atlantic City Hosp., 1960-62, Kaiser Found. Hosp., L.A., 1963-66; instr. nursing North Idaho Coll., Coeur D'Alene, 1972-74; pvt. practice Federal Way, Wash., 1977-85, Auburn, Wash., 1985—; nurse psychotherapist Christian Counselling Svc., Tacoma, 1977-83; founder The Found. for Planetary Healing; creator Drums, Dreams & Re-Membering; cons. in field; presenter workshops. Contbr. articles to profl. jours. Creator Healing Day, 1985. Capt. Nurse Corps, U.S. Army, 1966-71, Vietnam. Fellow Am. Orthopsychiatric Assn.; mem. ANA, Nat. Nursing Hon. Soc., Internat. Transactional Analysis Assn., Inst. Developmental Edn. and Psychotherapy (bd. dirs. 1989-93, chair profl. membership com. 1991-94), Vietnam Veterans of Am. (bd. dirs. 1983-85, 1st woman mem.). Home and Office: 303 O St NE Auburn WA 98002-4645

BLUMBERG, BARBARA SALMANSON (MRS. ARNOLD G. BLUMBERG), retired state housing official, housing consultant; b. Bklyn., Oct. 2, 1927; d. Sam and Mollie (Greenberg) Salmanson; m. Arnold G. Blumberg, June 19, 1949 (dec. June 1989); children: Florence Ellen Schwartz, Martin Jay, Emily Anne. BA, De Pauw U., 1948; postgrad., New Sch. for Social Rsch., N.Y.C. Mem. pub. rels. dept. Nate Fein & Co., N.Y.C., 1948-51; freelance pub. rels. cons., 1960—; councilwoman North Hempstead, N.Y., 1975-82; adviser to energy com. N.Y. State Assembly, N.Y.C., 1982-84; dir. spl. needs housing Divsn. Housing and Cmty. Renewal, State of N.Y., 1984-89, ret., 1989; mem. bd. visitors Pilgrim State Hosp. Pres. UN Assn. Great Neck, N.Y., 1967-69, chmn. China Study Workshop, 1966-67; pres. Shalom chpt. Hadassah, 1955-57; exec. v.p. Lakeville PTA, Great Neck, 1963-65, Great Neck South Jr. H.S., 1965-66; co-chair UNICEF, Great Neck, 1968-70, spkrs. bur., 1971—; v.p. Herricks Cmty. Life Ctr., 1976-77, B'nai B'rith, Lake Success, N.Y.; coord. 6th Congl. Dist., N.Y. McGovern for Pres.; bd. dirs. New Dem. Coalition Nassau, Am. Jewish Congress, Day Care Coun. Nassau County, Citizens Sch. Com., Great Neck; active Reform Dem. Assn. Great Neck; platform com. Nassau Dem. Com.; del. Dem. Nat. Conv., 1992; adv. com. to spkr. N.Y. State Assembly; resource coun., housing devel. com. Cmty. Advocates; chair North Hempstead Housing Authority; trustee L.I. Power Authority, 1994-96. Recipient award Anti-Defamation League, New Hyde Park, N.Y., 1975, Alumni award DePauw U., 1977, Hadassah New Life award, 1980, Women's Pole of Honor, North Hempstead, 1994. Mem. North Shore Archeol. Assn. (chmn. study group), Women in Comm., Internat. Platform Assn., L.I. Womens Network (co-convenor), Interfaith Nutrition Network (v.p.), Cmty. Advocates (bd. dirs.), Mental Health Assn. Nassau County (bd. dirs.), North Shore NAACP, N.Y. Alumni Club DePauw U. (trustee), Alpha Lambda Delta. Home: 12 Birch Hill Rd Great Neck NY 11020-1309

BLUMBERG, BETTY LOU, secondary education educator; b. New Haven, July 20, 1936; d. Adolph and Sylvia (Levine) Perlroth; m. Joseph Richard Blumberg, Dec. 20, 1956; children: Nancy Mae, Debra Lee. BA, Vassar Coll., 1957; MS, So. Conn. State Coll., 1967; CAS, Wesleyan U., 1981, M.Humanities, 1995. Tchr. English Hillhouse H.S., New Haven, 1957-59; lectr. English Albertus Magnus Coll., New Haven, 1965-71; tchr. English Hamden Hall County Day Sch., Hamden, Conn., 1971—, dept. chair English, coord. 7-12, 1982-92; tchr. docent com. Yale U./Brit. Art Mus., 1992—; student tchr. supr. Albertus Magnus/Hamden Hall, Yale U./Hamden Hall, 1973, 86; book reviewer Hadassah, Tower One, B'nai Jacob Synagogue, Hamden Libr. Bd. dirs. Ezra Acad., Woodbridge, Conn., 1986; mem. bd. edn. B'nai Jacob Synagogue, 1990-91. Shakespeare Studies fellow Yale U., summer 1958; recipient citation Women in Leadership, YWCA, 1991. Mem. New Haven Vassar Club (bd. dirs., alumni rep. to coun. 1986—), Cum Laude Soc. Hamden Hall (sec. 1986—). Democrat. Jewish. Office: Hamden Hall County Day 1108 Whitney Ave Hamden CT 06517

BLUME, JUDY SUSSMAN, author; b. Elizabeth, N.J., Feb. 12, 1938; d. Rudolph and Esther (Rosenfeld) Sussman; m. John M. Blume, Aug. 15, 1959 (div. Jan. 1975); children: Randy Lee, Lawrence Andrew; m. George Cooper, June 6, 1987; 1 stepchild, Amanda. B.A. in Edn., NYU, 1960; LHD (hon.), Kean Coll., 1987, Endicott Coll., 1995. Author: (fiction) including The One in the Middle is the Green Kangaroo, 1969, Iggie's House, 1970, Are You There God? It's Me, Margaret (selected as outstanding children's book 1970), Freckle Juice, 1971, Then Again, Maybe I Won't, 1971, It's Not the End of the World, 1972, Tales of a 4th Grade Nothing, 1972, Otherwise Known as Sheila the Great, 1972, Deenie, 1973, Blubber, 1974, Forever, 1975, Tales of a Fourth Grade Nothing, 1976, Starring Sally J. Freedman as Herself, 1977, Superfudge, 1980, Tiger Eyes, 1981, The Pain and the Great One, 1984, Just As Long As We're Together, 1987, Fudge-A-Mania, 1990, Here's to You, Rachel Robinson, 1993, others; (adult novels) Wifey, 1977, Smart Women, 1984; (other writings) The Judy Blume Diary, 1981, Letters to Judy: What Kids Wish They Could Tell You, 1986, The Judy Blume Memory Book, 1988; exec. producer (25 min. film) Otherwise Known As Sheila The Great, Barr Films, 1988. Founder, trustee The Kids Fund, 1981. Recipient Carl Sandburg Freedom to Read award Chgo. Pub. Libr., 1984, The Civil Liberties award ACLU, 1986, John Rock award Ctr. for Population Options, 1986, Margaret A. Edwards for lifetime achievement ALA, 1996; contbr. numerous Children's Choice award, U.S.A., Europe, Australia. Mem. PEN, Authors Guild, Nat. Coalition Against Censorship, Soc. Children's Book Writers (bd. dirs.). Jewish. Office: care Harold Ober Assocs 425 Madison Ave New York NY 10017-1110*

BLUMENFELD, SUE DEBORAH, lawyer; b. N.Y.C., Nov. 5, 1952; d. Abraham H. and Judith (Solomon) B.; m. William Charles Rapp, Jan. 1, 1982; children: Adam, Nicholas, David. BA, SUNY, 1974; JD, Rutgers U., Camden, N.J., 1977. Bar: N.J. 1977, D.C. 1981, U.S. Dist Ct. N.J. 1977, U.S. Dist. Ct. D.C. 1981, U.S. Superior Ct. D.C. 1981, U.S. Ct. Appeals (D.C. cir.) 1984. Atty. Bur. Competition FTC, Washington, 1977-79, spl. asst. to chief Common Carrier Bur., 1979-81; assoc. Pierson, Ball & Dowd, Washington, 1981-83; assoc. Willkie, Farr & Gallagher, Washington, 1983-86, ptnr., 1986—. Office: Willkie Farr & Gallagher 1155 21st St NW Ste 600 Washington DC 20036-3308

BLUMENTHAL, BEVERLY RENEE, social worker; b. Tulsa, Sept. 20, 1931; d. Abe and Zola Claire (Milsten) Brand; m. Robert Louis Blumenthal, Aug. 30, 1953; children: Pamela (dec.), Karen, Brad. BA in Psychology, U. Tex., 1953, MSW, 1972. Lic. clin. social worker-advanced clin. practitioner, Tex.; lic. marriage and family therapist. Vis. tchr. (sch. social worker) Dallas Ind. Sch. Dist., 1972-74; adminstr., therapist Dallas County Mental Health-Mental Retardation Ctr., 1975-78; pvt. practice Dallas, 1978—; part time therapist, group leader, student supr. Cmty. Psychotherapy Ctr., Dallas, 1978-85; cons. in field. Bd. dirs., chmn. various coms. The Family Place, Temple Shalom; bd. dirs., pres. Victims Outreach, 1988-91; active Mayor's Adv. Com. on Crime, 1989-91, Dallas Commn. Children and Youth, 1993-96, Dallas Jewish Coalition for the Homeless; bd. dirs. Multiple Sclerosis, North Tex. chpt., 1989—, Golden Acres, 1989-96, Cmty. Homes for Adults, Inc., 1990-96, Dallas Psychoanalytic Found., 1995—; team leader Disaster Svcs. Mental Health Com., 1990—, co-chair, 1996—. Recipient Prism award Mental Health Assn. Greater Dallas, 1995, Hope award Multiple Sclerosis Soc., North Tex. chpt. Mem. Nat. Assn. Social Workers (chmn. Dallas unit, state bd., chmn. state bd. rev. com., clin. case conf. com., steering com. Dallas unit, Social Worker of Yr. Dallas unit 1984), Am. Assn. Marriage and Family Therapy, Am. Soc. Clin. Hypnosis, Mental Health Assn. (bd. dirs. 1990-96), Internat. Soc. for Traumatic Stress Studies, Mental Health Assn. Tex. (bd. dirs. 1995—), Tex. Assn. Marriage and Family Therapy, Tex. Assn. Social Workers, Dallas Soc. Psychoanalytic Psychology, Dallas Assn. Marriage and Family Therapy (treas.). Jewish. Office: 8226 Douglas Ave Ste 521 Dallas TX 75225

BLUMENTHAL, IRIS ROVEN, retired editor; b. N.Y.C., Sept. 1, 1929; d. Max Ira Roven and Etta Bochner; m. Stanley Alvin Blumenthal, Oct. 30, 1960; children: Daniel, Jonathan, Elana. BA, Barnard Coll., 1950; MA in English Lit., Columbia U., 1954; MS in Pub. Comm., Syracuse U., 1983. Assoc. tech. editor McGraw-Hill Book Co., N.Y.C., 1957-68; mng. editor Syracuse (N.Y.) U., 1979-83; project editor GE, Syracuse, 1983-87; dir. comm. Cazenovia (N.Y.) Coll., 1987-88; sr. editor Cornell U., Ithaca, N.Y., 1988-91. Bd. dirs. Ctrl. N.Y. Assn. Learning Disabilities, Syracuse, 1985-88, Congregation Am Echad, Park Forest, Ill., 1994—; docent Chgo. Architecture Found., 1994—; vol. tutor Adult Literacy Inst., Chicago Heights, Ill., 1996—. Home: 1321 Brassie Ave Flossmoor IL 60422

BLUMENTHAL, SUSAN JANE, physician; b. N.Y.C., June 29, 1952; d. Stanley Robert and Eloyse Shirlee (Levine) B.; m. Edward John Markey, June 26, 1988. BA, Reed Coll., 1971; MD, U. Tenn., 1976; MPA, Harvard U., 1982; D (hon.), Trinity Coll., 1996. Diplomate Am. Bd. Psychiatry and Neurology. Intern. Stanford U. Sch. of Medicine, 1976-77, residency and fellowship, 1977-80; fellow NIMH, 1980-81, assoc. dir. Psychiatry Tng. Rev., head suicide rsch. unit and coord. of project depression, 1982-85, chief behavioral medicine program, 1985-93; clin. asst. prof. Tufts Med. Ctr., 1981-82; clin. asst. prof. psychiatry George Washington Sch. Medicine, 1982-86; clin. assoc. prof. psychiatry Georgetown Sch. Med., 1986-91; clin. prof. psychiatry Georgetown Sch. Medicine, Washington, 1991—; chief behavioral medicine Rsch. Br., NIMH, 1993-94; clin. prof. psychiatry Tufts Sch. Med., 1995—; chair NIH Coordinating Com. on Health and Behavior, 1991-94; co-chair NIH Reunion Task Force, 1992-94; dep. asst. sec. health, asst. surgeon gen. HHS, 1994—, chair fed. coordinating com. breast cancer, fed. coordinating com. women's health and the environ., co-chair nat. breast cancer action plan, coordinating com. women's health issues U.S. Public Health Svc.; mem. Pres.'s Interagy. Coun. on Women. Editor: Suicide Over the Life Cycle, 1989, Premenstrual Syndrome, 1985; mem. editl. bds. Jour. Women's Health, Depression; health columnist Elle Mag.; contbr. articles to sci. jours. Mem. Nat. Commn. on Sleep Disorders Rsch., workgroup on mental health Pres. Task Force on Health Care Reform, global commn. on Women's Health WHO. Capt. USPHS, 1992-94, rear adm., 1994—. Decorated Outstanding Svc. medal, Commendation medal, Meritorious Svc. medal USPHS. Mem. AMA, Nat. Women's Health Resource Ctr. (bd. dirs.), Am. Psychiat. Assn. (cons. Joint Coun. on Pub. Affairs), Am. Coll. Psychiatrists, Group for Advancement of Psychiatry, Am. Med. Women's Assn. (past chair com. on publicity and pub. rels., Pres.'s citation, 1996), Congl. Club, Internat. Club, Soc. Advancement Women's Health Rsch. (bd. dirs., v.p., scientific dir.), Am. Suicide Found. (bd. dirs. Washington divsn., pres.), Starlight Found. (chmn. sci. adv. bd.). Office: HHS Rm 712 E 200 Independence Ave SW Washington DC 20201-0004

BLUMKIN, LINDA RUTH, lawyer; b. N.Y.C., Aug. 25, 1944; d. Louis and Edith (Fortus) Blumkin. A.B. cum laude, Barnard Coll., 1964; LL.B. cum laude, Harvard U., 1967, LL.M., 1973. Bar: N.Y. 1968, U.S. dist. ct. (so. dist.) N.Y. 1969, U.S. Ct. Apls. (2nd cir.) 1969, U.S. Supreme Ct. 1982. Assoc. Fried, Frank, Harris, Shriver & Jacobson, N.Y.C., 1967-71, ptnr., 1979—; lectr. Boston U., 1971, asst. prof. mgmt., 1972-73; assoc. Breed, Abbott & Morgan, N.Y.C., 1973-77; asst. dir. Bur. Competition FTC, 1977-79. Mem. ABA, N.Y.C. Bar Assn. Office: Fried Frank Harris Shriver & Jacobson 1 New York Plz Fl 24 New York NY 10004

BLUMSTEIN, RENEÉ J., research and statistical consultant; b. Bklyn., Apr. 1, 1957; d. Robert and Rosalie (Burak) B. BA, Queens Coll., N.Y., 1978; MA, Columbia U., 1980, MEd, 1982, MPhil, 1984, PhD, 1986. Rsch. psychologist CCNY, 1980-85; rsch. cons. AT&T, N.Y.C., 1986; rsch. analyst Citibank, N.Y.C., 1986-87, rsch. and statis. cons., 1987—; rsch. and statis. cons. Informed Decision Svcs., Inc., N.Y.C., N.J.; adj. prof. rsch. methods CUNY, 1990—. Scholar Columbia U., 1981. Mem. Am. Psychol. Assn., Nat. Assn. Women Bus. Owners, Am. Edn. Rsch. Assn. Home and Office: 14 Ingold Dr Dix Hills NY 11746

BLUM-VEGLIA, CHERYL ANN, accountant; b. Elizabeth, N.J., Jan. 5, 1966; d. Kenneth Peter and Mary Jo (Faccone) B. BA in Acctg. and Fin., Muhlenberg Coll., 1988. CPA, Pa. Auditor Deloitte & Touche, Parsippany, N.J., 1988-91; internal auditor N.J. Hwy. Authority, Woodbridge, 1991—. vol. Inst. for Children with Cancer and Blood Disorders. Mem. N.J. Soc. CPA's. Pa. Inst. CPAs, Muhlenberg Coll. Alumni Amb. Assn. Roman Catholic.

BLUNDEN, JERALDYNE, performing company executive. Artistic dir. Dayton (Ohio) Contemporary Dance Co. Office: Dayton Contemporary Dance Co 126 N Main St Ste 200 Dayton OH 45402-1214*

BLUTH, B. J. (ELIZABETH JEAN CATHERINE BLUTH), sociologist, aerospace educator; b. Phila., Dec. 5, 1934; d. Robert Thomas and Catherine Cecelia (Boxman) Gowl; m. Thomas Del Bluth, Aug. 20, 1960 (dec. Aug. 6, 1980); children: Robert Thomas, Richard Del. B.A. in Sociology (Washington semster fellow), Bucknell U., 1953; M.A., Fordham U., 1960; Ph.D., UCLA, 1970. Teaching fellow in methods of social research Fordham U., 1957-58; reading instr. St. Margaret's High Sch., Tappahannock, Va., 1958-59; instr. history, civics and English, Rosary High Sch., San Diego, 1959-60; successively instr., asst. prof. sociology Immaculate Heart Coll., Los Angeles, 1960-65; prof. sociology Calif. State U., Northridge, 1965-87; grantee NASA Ames Research Ctr., Moffett Field, Calif., 1982-83; grantee space sta. program NASA, Washington, 1983-87; aerospace technologist system engrng. div. space sta. program office NASA, Reston, Va., 1987-90, spl. asst. to dep. program dir. space sta. freedom program and ops., 1990-94; spl. tech. asst. to dir. Edn. Div. NASA, Washington, 1994—; cons. Immaculate Heart Cmty., L.A., 1967-69; engrng. rsch. NASA Space Sta. design Boeing Aerospace Co., 1982-83; mem. Presdl. Citizens Adv. com. on Space, Coun. Nat. Space Policy, Nat. Tech. Com. on Soc. & Tech., UN team on relevance of space activities to econ. and social devel.; professor emeritus Calif. State U., 1987—; computational scis. and informatics inst. dir.'s search com. George Mason U., 1992-93. Editor: (with others) Search for Identity Reader, vol. I and II, 1973, (with S.R. McNeal) Update on Space, vol. I, 1961, Parson's General Theory of Action, 1982, Space Station Habitability Report, 1983, Soviet Space Station Analog, 1983, Space Station Human Productivity Study NASA, 1986, Russian Mir Space Station Analog, 1993; contbr. articles to profl. jours. Recipient Alpha Omega faculty awards, 1966, 74, disting. teaching award Calif. State U., Northridge, 1968, NASA superior accomplishment award, 1990, NASA, performance awards 1991-94; Inst. Advancement in Teaching and Learning fellow, Calif. State U., 1974. Fellow Am. Astronautical Soc.; mem. AIAA (chpt. award for outstanding program 1980), Am. Sociol. Assn., L5 Soc., Brit. Interplanetary Soc., Inst. Social Sci. Study of Space (acad. adv. bd.), Space Studies Inst., Internat. Acad. Astronautics (com. on space econs. and benefits), Phi Beta Kappa. Republican. Office: NASA Code FE Edn Div 300 East St SW Washington DC 20546

BLYTH, ANN MARIE, secondary education educator; b. Sharon, Pa., June 18, 1949; d. Chester Stanley and Mary Clara (Romian) Kacerski; m. Lynn Allan Blyth, June 26, 1976 (dec. June 1983); 1 stepchild, Breton Alan Blyth; 1 child, Amanda Lynn. BS in Edn., Kent (Ohio) State U., 1971; postgrad., Loyola U., New Orleans, 1973-74; MS in Teaching, John Carroll U., 1978. Cert. comprehensive sci., maths. and physics tchr., Ohio. Jr. high math. tchr. New Philadelphia ((Ohio) Bd. of Edn., 1971-72; high sch. sci. and math. tchr. Hubbard (Ohio) Exempted Village Bd. of Edn., 1972-76, Painesville (Ohio) City Local Bd. Edn., 1976—; instr. math. Morton Salt, Painesville, 1979-80; part-time faculty Lake Erie Coll., 1992. Mem. Adv. Bd. Western Res. br. Am. Lung Assn. of Ohio, Painesville, 1986-89, sec, 1988-89, Northeastern br., Youngstown, Ohio, 1989—; judge state level Nat. Pre-teen and Pre-Teen Petite Pageants, 1990. Martha Holden Jennings Found. scholar, 1984-85; named Tchr. of the Yr., Harvey High Sch. Key Club, 1981-82. Mem. NEA, Ohio Edn. Assn., Northeastern Ohio Edn. Assn., Painesville City Tchrs. Assn., Am. Assn. Physics Tchrs., Nat. Sci. Tchrs. Assn., Cleve. Regional Coun. of Sci. Tchrs., Sci. Edn. Coun. of Ohio. Democrat. Episcopalian. Home: 8545 Willow Ln Chardon OH 44024-9231 Office: Thomas W Harvey High Sch 167 W Washington St Painesville OH 44077-3328

BLYTH, MYRNA GREENSTEIN, publishing executive, editor, author; b. N.Y.C., Mar. 22, 1939; d. Benjamin and Betty (Austin) Greenstein; m. Jeffrey Blyth, Nov. 25, 1962; children: Jonathan, Graham. B.A., Bennington (Vt.) Coll., 1960. Sr. editor Datebook mag., N.Y.C., 1960-62, Ingenue mag., N.Y.C., 1963-68; book editor Family Health mag., 1968-71; book and fiction editor, then assoc. editor Family Circle mag., N.Y.C., 1972-78; exec. editor Family Circle mag., 1978-81; editor-in-chief Ladies' Home Jour., 1981—, pub. dir., sr. v.p., 1987—; freelance writer, contbr. mags. Author: (novels) Cousin Suzanne, 1975, For Better and For Worse, 1978; contbr. articles to New Yorker mag., New York mag., Redbook mag., Cosmopolitan mag., Reader's Digest. Bd. dirs. Child Care Action Campaign, N.Y.C., 1989—; mem. nat. adv. bd. Susan G. Komen Breast Cancer Found.; active The Communitarians, Nat. Commn. on Am. Jewish Women. Mem. Am. Soc. Mag. Editors (exec. com. 1989—), N.Y. Women in Comm., Inc. (Amb. of Excellence), Women's Media Group, Authors League, Overseas Press Club (bd. govs.). Office: Ladies' Home Jour 125 Park Ave20th Fl New York NY 10017-5516*

BLYTHE, CHRISTINA JOSEPHINE, financial analyst, consultant; b. Orange, N.J., Apr. 5, 1963; d. Winthrop Augustus and Ilse B. (Niessner) B. B in Acctg., Seton Hall U., 1985. Staff acct. E. F. Hutton, Inc., N.Y.C., 1985-88; acctg. mgr. Outback Clothing, Berkeley, Calif., 1988-90, Crescent Jewelers, Oakland, Calif., 1990-91; asst. controller Crescent Jewelers, Oakland, 1991-93, fin. analyst, 1993-95; cons. Acctg. Solutions, San Francisco, 1995—. Democrat. Roman Catholic. Home: 4433 Brookdale Ave Oakland CA 94619

BOAL, LYNDALL ELIZABETH, social worker; b. London, England, Feb. 19, 1936; came to U.S., 1953; d. George Woodall and Mary Barbara (Pearce) Cadbury; m. R. Bradlee Boal Aug. 29, 1959 (div. Sept. 1983); children: Jennifer, Peter. BA (hon.), Swarthmore (Pa.) Coll., 1957; MS, Simmons Coll. Sch. Social Work, Boston, 1959. Cert. sch. social worker, N.Y.; lic. social worker, Mass. Social worker Beth Israel Hosp., Boston, 1959-60, Mt. Sinai Hosp., N.Y.C., 1960-61, Meml. Sloan-Kettering Hosp, N.Y.C., 1961-63; cons. Dist. Nursing Svc., Mt. Kisco, N.Y., 1964-65; exec. dir. Planned Parenthood, Mt. Kisco, N.Y., 1965-68; dir. social worker No. Westchester Hosp., Mt. Kisco, N.Y., 1968-78; social worker Fox lane High Sch., Bedford Schs, 1978-81; chmn. com. on handicapped Bedford (N.Y.) Schs., 1981-86; social worker Chappaqua (N.Y.) Sch., 1988—; instr. Fordham U. Sch. Social Svcs., 1994—; bd. dirs. No. Westchester Guidance Ctr., Mt. Kisco; pres. Soc. Hosp. Social Work Dirs., Westchester, N.Y., 1976-78. Chmn. Narcotics Guidance Coun., Bedford, 1972-75; No. Westchester Coun. Equality pres., Bedford, 1984-86; bd. dirs. Sherrill House, Boston, 1986-88; Dem. Committeeman, Bedford, 1983-86. Mem. NASW (sec. N.Y. state chpt. 1993—, pres.-elect 1995-96, chair state pers. com. 1993-94, pres. Westchester divsn. 1969-71, 91-92, Merit Svc. award Westchester divsn. 1993, sch. social work sect. steering com. 1994-96), Am. Orthopsychiat. Assn., N.Y. State Sch. Social Workers Assn., Kappa Delta Pi. Democrat. Mem. Soc. of Friends. Home: 508 Millwood Rd Mount Kisco NY 10549-3700 Office: Chappaqua Schs Off of Sch Social Worker Chappaqua NY 10514

BOAL, MARCIA ANNE RILEY, clinical social worker, administrator; b. Carthage, Mo., Sept. 29, 1944; d. William Joseph and Thelma P. (Simpson) Riley; m. David W. Boal, Aug. 12, 1967; children: Adam J. W., Aaron D. Boal. BA, U. Kans., 1966, MSW, 1981. Lic. clin. social worker. Child therapist Gillis Home for Children, Kansas City, Mo., 1981; social worker Leavenworth (Kans.) County Spl. Edn. Cooperative, 1981-84; sch. social worker, dir. health and social svcs. Kans. State Sch. for the Blind, Kansas City, Kans., 1984—; pvt. practice adoption counseling and workshops, 1981—; field instr. Sch. of Social Welfare, Kans. U., 1986—. Author: Surviving Kids, 1983, Teaching Social Skills to Blind and Visually Impaired Children, 1987. Nat. networking chmn. Jr. League Kansas City, 1977-81; bd. dirs. Wyandotte House Ind, 1973-81, Kans. Action For Children, Topeka, 1981, Gov.'s Commn. on Parent Edn., Topeka, 1984—, Lake of the Forest, 1994— (sec.). Named Kans. Sch. Social Worker of Yr., 1989. Mem. Council Exceptional Children, Nat. Assn. Social Workers, Kans. Assn. Sch. Social Workers, Am. Orthopsychiat. Assn., Kans. Conf. Social Welfare, R.P. Found., Phi Kappa Phi. Home: Lake Of The Forest Bonner Springs KS 66012 Office: Kans St Sch for Blind 1100 State Ave Kansas City KS 66102-4411

BOARDMAN, EDNA, library media specialist, educator; b. Frazer, Mont., Jan. 22, 1935; d. Karl and Christina (Zweigle) Schieve; foster parents Emil and Ella Berg; m. Harold D. Boardman, June 1, 1959 (dec. 1985); children: Chase H., Mary E. BS, Minot State U., 1958. Cert. media specialist. English tchr. Garrison (N.D.) H.S., 1958-60; English tchr. Rugby (N.D.) H.S., 1968-70, libr. media specialist, 1970-76; libr. media specialist Magic City Campus Minot (N.D.) H.S., 1976—. Author: Censorship: The Problem that Won't Go Away, 1992; contbr. articles to profl. jours. Bd. dirs. Germans from Russia Heritage Soc., Bismarck, N.D., 1990—; active Vincent United Meth. Ch., Minot, 1976—, Minot Commn. on Status of Women, 1980-82. Mem. NEA, N.D. Libr. Assn. (sect. pres. 1986-89), Sch. Libr. Media Assn. Home: 515 16th St SW Minot ND 58701

BOARDMAN, MAUREEN BELL, community health nurse; b. Hartford, Conn., June 11, 1966; d. Jack Russell and Mary Elizabeth (Brumm) Bell; m. Byron Earl Boardman, June 4, 1988. BSN, U. Maine, Orono, 1988; MSN, U. Tenn., 1991. ACLS; cert. family nurse practitioner. Charge nurse med.-surg. divsn. Scott County Hosp., Oneida, Tenn., 1988-89, employee health nurse, 1989-92; RN team leader Oneida Home Health, 1989, Quality Home Health, Oneida, 1989-90; family nurse practitioner Straightfork Family Care Clinic, Pioneer, Tenn., 1992—; mem. child abuse rev. team Dept. Human Svcs., Huntsville, Tenn., 1993—. Med. advisor, liaison Scott County (Tenn.) Sch. Systems Sci. Fair Com., 1992—; bd. dirs., editor newsletter, 1993—, v.p., 1995-96 Appalachian Arts Coun., Oneida. Mem. Tenn. Nurses Assn. (del. to conv. 1994, 95, 96), Sigma Theta Tau (sec. Gamma Chi chpt. 1996-98). Roman Catholic. Home: RR 3 Box 213 Oneida TN 37841-9532 Office: Straightfork Family Care Clinic Rt 1 Box 320 Hwy 63 Pioneer TN 37847

BOARMAN, MARJORIE RUTH, manufacturing company executive, consultant; b. Lakeland, Fla., Apr. 14, 1953; d. Hugh Francis and Nancy Addair (McCracken) Roberts; m. Edward F. Moore, June 28, 1975 (div. 1986); children: Kulani Anne, Brittany Elizabeth; m. James Louis Boarman, Feb. 5, 1987; 1 child, Joshua; stepchildren: Steven, Christina, Paulette. BS in Edn., Fla. State U., 1975; MEd, U. Hawaii/Manoa, 1978. Cert. tchr., Fla., Mo. Substitute tchr. KCCA Preschs., Honolulu, 1975; tchr. Hickam Day Care Ctr., Hickam AFB, Hawaii, 1975-77; tchr., sales rep. Grolier Interstate Inc., Honolulu, 1977; tchr. Kiddie Kollege Presch., Hickam AFB, 1977-79, Our Lady of Sorrows Schs., St. Louis, 1979-80; program dir. Clayton (Mo.) YWCA, 1981-82; cons. Parent Talk Svcs., Phoenix, 1983-85; tchr. Polk County Schs., Polk City, Fla., 1986-89; co-owner Boarman Built Inc., Green Ridge, Mo., 1989—. Co-creator: Bon Voyage board game, 1992. V.p. Green Ridge 2000 Team, 1995—; leader, coord. Camp Fire Boys and Girls, Lakeland, 1988—; bd. dirs. Boswell PTA, Auburndale, 1991-92. Mem. NAFE, Auburndale C. of C. (bd. dirs. 1991-92), Green Ridge C. of C. (bd. dirs. 1994-96), Sedalia Bus. and Profl. Women (2nd v.p. membership chmn. 1994-95, 1st v.p. issues mgmt. chmn. 1995-96, pres.-elect 1996-97, State Individual Devel. award), Kappa Delta Pi. Republican. Pentecostal. Home and Office: Boarman Built Inc PO Box 145 Green Ridge MO 65332-0145

BOATWRIGHT, CHARLOTTE JEANNE, hospital marketing and public relations executive; b. Chattanooga, Dec. 12, 1937; d. Clifton Gentry and Veltina Novella (Braden) Blevins; m. Robert W. Boatwright; children: Lynn Kay, Janis Ann, Karen Jean, Mary Ruth, Melody Susan, April Celeste. Diploma, Erlanger Sch. Nursing, Chattanooga, 1963; BS, U. Tenn., Chattanooga, 1976, MEd, 1981; PhD, Columbia Pacific U., San Rafael, Calif., 1987. RN, Tenn. Surgeon's asst. William Robert Fowler, M.D., Chattanooga, 1963-64; instr. med.-surg. nursing Baroness Erlanger Hosp. Sch. Nursing, 1964-67, instr. fundamentals nursing, 1971-74, chmn. dept. mental health-psychiat. nursing, 1977-81; staff nurse Meml. Hosp., Chattanooga, 1967-68, nursing supr., 1968-70; dir. inservice edn. Hutcheson Med. Ctr., Ft. Oglethorpe, Ga., 1970-71; youth work cons. Sewanee Dist. Episcopal Chs., Chattanooga, 1975-76; dir. spl. projects North Park Hosp., Chattanooga, 1984-87, dir. mktg. and pub. rels., 1987—; pres. CBB Comms.; freelance writer. mem. dept. youth work Episcopal Diocese Tenn., 1975-77, mem. violence in soc. resource team; condr. adult ch. sch. groups St. Martin's Episcopal Ch., Chattanooga; vice chmn. Brynewood Park Cmty. Assn., 1985, 86; founder, chairperson Domestic Violence Coalition of Greater Chattanooga, 1994. Mem. Am. Coll. Healthcare Execs. (nominee), Tenn. Hosp. Assn., Tenn. Soc. for Hosp. Mktg. and Pub. Rels., Chattanooga C. of C., U. Tenn. Alumnae Assn., Columbia Pacific U. Alumnae Assn., Chi Sigma Iota. Republican.

BOATWRIGHT, JANICE ELLEN WILLIS, school system administrator; b. Bremen, Ga., Apr. 15, 1939; d. Wilson Matthew and Sue Winifred (Pope) Willis; m. James Bolden Boatwright, Sr., Feb. 11, 1961; children: James B. Jr., Jamee Ellen. BS in Edn., West Ga. Coll., 1960, MEd, 1974; EdD, Nova Southeastern U., 1991. Tchr. Haralson County Bd. of Edn., Buchanan, Ga., 1961-63; media specialist Haralson County Bd. of Edn., Buchanan, 1970-71, tchr., asst. prin., 1974-76, curriculum dir., 1977—; media specialist Tallapoosa (Ga.) Bd. of Edn., 1963-67; adv. bd. Haralson County Media Assn., Buchanan, 1988—, Haralson Libr. Bd., Tallapoosa, 1990—, Haralson Edn. Collaborative, Buchanan, 1992—. Editor: Haralson County Georgia A Resource Guide for the Teaching of Social Studies, 1991. Dir. Haralson County Adult Edn., Tallapoosa, 1991—; program chmn. Delta Kappa Gamma, Cedartown, Ga., 1992-94; ednl. chmn. Buchanan Women's Club, 1993—; bd. dirs. Ga. Youth Sci. and Tech. Ctr., Inc., 1992—. Recipient Mother of Yr. award Buchanan Women's Club, 1993, Disting. Svc. award Ga. Assn. Curriculum and Instructional Supervision, 1994. Mem. ASCD, Nat. Assn. Edn. Young Children, Nat. Assn. Pupil Svcs. Adminstrs., Nat. Staff Devel. Coun., Ga. Staff Devel. Coun., Ga. Assn. Supervision and Curriculum Devel., Nat. Assn. for Supervision and Curriculum Devel., Ga. Assn. Ednl. Leaders, Ga. Coun. Econ. Devel., Ga. Assn. Cmty. Edn., Haralson 2000 (chair goal one), Ga. Assn. Sch. Superintendents. Methodist. Home: 735 Seabreeze Lake Rd Buchanan GA 30113-4474 Office: Haralson County Bd Edn 10 Van Wert St Buchanan GA 30113-4879

BOAZ, DONIELLA CHAVES, psychotherapist, consultant; b. Grand Junction, Colo., Apr. 8, 1934; d. Leon T. and Marian (Fonder) Hutton; m. Richard Boas, Apr. 7, 1956 (div. 1983); children: Roxanne, Annika, Becca; m. Jack J. Chaves, Mar. 11, 1995. Cert. pastoral ministry Seattle U., 1978; cert. clin. pastoral edn. Va. Mason Hosp., 1979; BA, Antioch West, 1980; postgrad. Lan Ting Inst. cross-cultural studies PROC, 1986, 92, 94, C.G. Jung Inst., Zurich, 1986, 87, 89. Cert. neuro-linguistic programmer, 1983. Owner Donalee's Studio of Dance, Kirkland, Wash., 1952-63; adminstrv. asst. Ch. of Redeemer, Kenmore, Wash., 1974-76; counselor Eastside Mental Health, Bothell, Wash., 1976-79; psychotherapist, Seattle, 1979—; owner, cons. Optimum Options, Seattle, 1979-94, founder DISCOVERIES Seminars, various other govt., bus., non-profit orgns., nat. and internat. trainer, cons.; mem. adj. faculty Seattle U., Northwest Coll. Holistic Studies and Huston Sch. Theology, 1980-87; mem. Wash. State Dept. Health Adv. Com. for Cert. Mental Health Counselors, 1994—. Author: Embrace Your Child-Self: Change Your Life, 1993. V.p. Episcopal Ch. standing com. on stewardship, 1979-81; active in local politics., 1968-80; mem. Clin. Pastoral Edn. Mem. Seattle Counselors Assn. (pres.), Wash. Mental Health Coun. Assoc., Coalition of Mental Helath Profls. Avocations: philosophy, carpentry, bridge, entertaining, traveling. Office: Counseling Assoc Grosvenor House 500 Wall St Ste 309 Seattle WA 98121-1534

BOBENHOUSE, NELLIE YATES, insurance company executive; b. Spickard, Mo., May 3, 1936; d. Joseph Howard and Nellie Elizabeth (Tuttle) Yates; m. Lewis L. Griffin, Apr. 22, 1956 (div. Jan. 1964); 1 child, Elizabeth Anne Griffin Schafer; m. Robert A. Bobenhouse, Aug. 28, 1965. Student, St. Joseph (Mo.) Jr. Coll., 1955, Grandview Coll., 1980. Sec. News-Press & Gazette, St. Joseph, 1954-56; sec., bookkeeper Wilson's Locker & Ins., Spickard, Mo., 1956-60, Oyler's Locker, Spickard, 1960-64; sec. Equitable of Iowa Agy., Des Moines, 1964-68, agy. office supr., 1968-94. City clk. City of Spickard, 1959-60; support group leader, co-founder Chronic Fatigue Syndrome Soc., Des Moines, 1988—; bd. dirs. Iowa Chronic Fatigue Syndrome/CFIDS Assn., Cedar Rapids, 1991; mem. Des Moines Women's Club, 1994—, Urbandale Garden Club, 1994—. Fellow Life Mgmt. Inst.; mem. Ins. Women Des Moines (com. chmn. 1975), P. Buckley Moss Soc., Beta Sigma Phi (sec.-treas. 1958-60, Woman of Yr. 1959). Republican. Disciple of Christ. Home: 905 59th St West Des Moines IA 50266-7516

BOBO, GENELLE TANT (NELL BOBO), office administrator; b. Paulding County, Ga., Oct. 31, 1927; d. Richard Adolph and Mary Etta (Prance) Tant; m. William Ralph Bobo, May 1, 1948; children: William Richard, Thomas David (dec.). AS, Berry Coll., Mt. Berry, Ga., 1947. Exec. sec. Macon (Ga.) Kraft Co., 1951-54; med. sec. Drs. Loveman & Fleigleman, Louisville, 1954-55; tchr. Fulton County Schs., Palmetto, Ga., 1960-68; exec. sec. Rayloc, Atlanta, 1968-70; adminstrv. coord. U. Ga., Athens, 1970-77; assoc. to dir. Mission Svc. Corps, Home Mission Bd. So. Bapt. Conv., Atlanta, 1977-94; rschr., writer Sta. 11-TV, Atlanta, 1989. Author: Driven by a Dream, 1992. Philanthropy chmn. Exec. Women, Inc., Atlanta, 1968-69; mem. adv. coun. Baylor U., Waco, Tex., 1993—. Mem. NAFE. Baptist. Home: 87 Vickers Rd Fairburn GA 30213-1139 Office: 4200 N Point Pky Alpharetta GA 30202-4174

BOBROW, SUSAN LUKIN, lawyer; b. Cleve., Jan. 18, 1941; d. Adolph and Yetta (Babkow) Lukin; m. Martin J. Bolhower, Nov. 28, 1986 (div. Dec. 1988); children from previous marriage: Elizabeth Bobrow Pressler, Erica, David. Student, Antioch Coll., Yellow Springs, Ohio, 1958-61; BA, Antioch Coll., L.A., 1975; JD, Southwestern U., L.A., 1979. Bar: Calif., 1980. Owner, ptnr. Mediation Assocs., Beverly Hills, Calif., 1982; atty. Law Offices of Susan Bobrow, Beverly Hills, Calif., 1983-88; assoc. Schulman & Miller, Beverly Hills, 1988-89; staff counsel Fair Polit. Practices Commn., Sacramento, Calif., 1990-96; sr. counsel Calif. State Lottery, 1996—; mem. panel for paternity defense L.A. Superior Ct., 1984. Exhibited paintings at Death and Trasnfiguration Show, Phantom Galleries, Sacramento, 1994. Bd. dirs. San Fernando Valley Friends of Homeless Women and Children, North Hollywood, Calif., 1985-88; mem. adv. bd. Project Home, Sacramento Interfaith Svc. Coun., 1990-91; v.p. cmty. affairs B'nai Israel Sisterhood, Sacramento, 1991-93. Recipient commendation Bd. Govs. State Bar of Calif., 1984. Mem. Inst. Noetic Scis., Sacramento Inst. Noetic Scis. (steering coun. 1994), Los Angeles County Bar Assn. (Barristers com. on adminstrn. of justice 1985), Sacramento County Bar Assn. (barristers' com. on profl. responsibility 1993-94, alt. del. to state bar conv. 1991). Democrat. Office: Calif State Lottery Commn 600 N 10th St Sacramento CA 95814

BOBRUFF, CAROLE MARKS, radio show producer, personality; b. N.Y.C., Nov. 11, 1935; d. Morris Frank and Harriet (Lehman) Marks; m. Jerome Bobruff, June 20, 1954 (div. 1986); children: Ellen, Neal, Paul, Mark. Student, Quinnipac Coll., 1954-55, U. N.C., 1955-56; AS, U. New Haven, 1981; BS in Human Services, N.H. Coll., 1982. Founder, dir. Tyndall Air Force Daycare Ctr., Panama City, Fla., 1957-60; med. asst. Digestive Disease Assocs., New London, Conn., 1974-82; program coord. Pre-Trial Release Program, Norwich, New London, Conn., 1982-84; case mgr., counselor residential criminal justice program Cochegan House, Montville, Conn., 1984-85; exec. dir. Ret. Sr. Vol. Program So. New London County, 1984-91; producer, host radio program Senior Focus Sta. WSUB, Groton, Conn., 1991—; treas. Dir. Vols. in Agys., New London, 1986—, Conn. RSVP Dirs., 1987; bd. dirs. Cochegan House, Widowed Persons Service, Waterford, Conn. Editor: Senior Citizens Guide to Discounts and Services, 1988; editor, author: RSVP Newsletter, 1984—; columnist: The Day, 1987. Pres. women's aux. New London County Med. Assn., 1986-87; bd. dirs. League Women Voters, New London, HOSPICE, New London, Am. Cancer Soc. New London County. Recipient Proclamation Community award Town of Waterford, 1989, Community Service award The Connection, Inc., 1987. Mem. Women's Network New London County, Children and Family Services, Pub. Relations Network, Nat. Assn. Female Execs., Brandeis U. Jewish. Home: 223 Flanders Rd Unit 10 Niantic CT 06357-1223

BOCCHINO, FRANCES LUCIA, oil company official; b. Bronx, N.Y., July 5, 1944; d. Pasquale and Mary Ruth (Lacerenza) B. Grad. high sch., Bklyn., 1962. Various positions Texaco Inc., N.Y.C., 1965-86; sr. analyst exec. dept. Texaco Inc., Harrison, N.Y., 1987-90, transfer agt., 1990-95; comms., 1995—. Active Whitestone (N.Y.) Taxpayers Assn. Mem. Corp. Transfer Agts. Assn. Republican. Roman Catholic. Home: 15-15 150th St Whitestone NY 11357-2530 Office: Texaco Inc 2000 Westchester Ave White Plains NY 10604-3613

BOCCHINO, SERENA MARIA, artist; b. Englewood, N.J., Mar. 22, 1960; d. William Anthony and Lucia Maria (Cowfalone) B.; m. Stephen Henry; 1 child, Ezra Zachary Keough. Student, Wroxton Coll., Oxfordshire, Eng., 1980; BA, Fairleigh Dickinson U., 1982; MA, NYU, 1985. art specialist Stephens Cooperative Sch., Hoboken, N.J. and YWCA of Ridgewood, 1985-86; lectr. Fairleigh Dickinson U., Madison, 1985-86; dir. art edn. YM-YWCA Summer Program, Ridgewood, 1987; lectr., studio instr. PS1 Mus., L.I., 1987-88, SUNY, Plattsburgh, 1988; adj. prof. Raritan Valley C.C., Somerville, N.J., 1991—; instr. Somerset Art Assn., Far Hills, N.J., 1991—, art camp dir., 1994. One-woman shows include Penine Hart Gallery, N.Y.C., 1988, 90, Elliot Smith Gallery, St. Louis, 1989, Phyllis Rothman Gallery, Fairleigh Dickinson U., Madison, N.J., 1990, Stuio Bocchi, Rome, 1990, Sylvia Schmidt Gallery, New Orleans, 1991, Johnson & Johnson, Skillman, N.J., 1992, Rabbet Gallery, New Brunswick, N.J., 1994, Raritan Valley C.C., Somerville, N.J., 1995-96, Princeton (N.J.) U., 1995-96, Trenton (N.J.) City Mus., 1995-96, Bergen Mus. Art and Sci., Paramus, N.J., 1995-96, Spl. Projects Internat., N.Y.C., 1995-96, numerous others; group exhbns. include OIA Exhbn., N.Y.C., 1993, Rammarine Gallery, L.I., N.Y., 1994, Women's Studies Gallery, Princeton U., 1994, Trenton City Mus., 1994, Madelyn Jordan Gallery, N.Y.C., 1994, Seton Hall U., Sch. Law, Newark, 1994, A Ctr. for Contemporary Art, Newark, 1994, The Garage, Hoboken, N.J., 1994, Trans Hudson Gallery, Jersey City, 1994, Cathedral Arts Gallery, Jersey City, 1995, Watchung (N.J.) Arts Ctr., 1995, The Bergen Mus. Art and Sci., Paramus, 1995, Eighth Floor Gallery, N.Y.C., 1995, numerous others; represented in permanent collections Art in Embassies Program, Washington, Noyes Mus., Oceanville, N.J., Trenton State Mus., Trenton City Mus., Bergen Mus. Arts and Scis., Paramus, The Paterson (N.J.) Art Mus., Johnson and Johnson, New Brunswick, Duff & Phelps, Chgo., others. Home: 600 Hudson St 3C Hoboken NJ 07030-2843

BOCCIA, JUDY ELAINE, home health agency executive, consultant; b. San Diego, Aug. 29, 1955; d. Robert Garrett and Jerry Athalee (Carruth) Stacy; 1 child, Jennifer Lynn. BSN, Calif. State U., San Diego, 1978. RN, Calif.; lic. pub. health nurse, Calif. Staff nurse Univ. Hosp., U. Calif., San Diego, 1978-80, 81-82, Moffitt Hosp., San Francisco, 1980-81, Humana Huntington, Huntington Beach, Calif., 1982-84; intravenous and hospice vis. nurse Town & Country Nursing, Garden Grove, Calif., 1984-85; vis. nurse Vis. Nurse Assn., Orange, Calif., 1985-86; v.p. Doctors and Nurse Med. Mgmt., Newport Beach, Calif., 1986-89; dir. nursing HMSS, So. Calif., 1989-90; pres. Premier Care, Irvine, 1990-91, Homelife Nursing & Staffbuilders, Lake Forest, Calif., 1991—; cons., Calif., 1987—; pres. Homelife Nursing-Staff Builders, O.C., 1991—; AIDS educator; presenter in field. Mem. Oncology Nursing Soc., Intravenous Nurse Soc. Democrat. Methodist. Home: 28232 Festivo Mission Viejo CA 92692-2617 Office: Homelife Nursing Inc 23832 Rockfield Blvd Ste 280 Lake Forest CA 92630-2820

BOCK, CAROLYN ANN, author, consultant, trainer, small business owner; b. New Bavaria, Ohio, Jan. 25, 1942; d. Wilfred Ignatius and Marcella Mary (Birkemeier) Gerschutz; m. Donald Charles Bock, Sept. 7, 1974; 1 son, Jonathon Edward. Student Notre Dame Coll., 1960-62, John Carroll U., 1962-66. With sales and promotions dept. Schaffer Diversified Corp. and other cos., Cleve., 1962-74; columnist, writer West Life Newspaper, Westlake, Ohio, 1980-83, Westlaker Times, Lorain, Ohio, 1983-84; owner Dynamic Living Assocs., Westlake, 1986—. Feature writer, bus., arts, families, health. Author: Authors, Artists and Auras, 1988, Gerschutz family history, 1989. Co-founder, trustee Community Action Team, Westlake, 1980-85, Westlake Arts Coun., co-founder, 1983-84, pres., 1984-85; chmn. Morning Sem., Rocky River, Ohio, 1981-85; pres. Westlake PTA Council, 1980-82, Parkside Jr. High PTA, Westlake, 1983-84; active Boy Scouts, Cub Scouts, Clagie Playhouse, Westlake Hist. Soc., 1985—. Recipient Outstanding Svc. award Cub Scouts, 1980; hon. life mem. Ohio PTA, 1982; Ohio Arts Coun. grantee 1984, 85. Mem. Westlake C. of C., Soc. Profl. Journalists, Acad. Profl. Cons. and Adminstrns. Republican. Mem. Untarian Universalist Ch. Avocations: traveling, reading, cooking, gardening. Home and Office: 23553 Belmont Dr Cleveland OH 44145-2712

BOCKIAN, DONNA MARIE, data processing executive; b. N.Y.C., June 4, 1946; d. Forrest Mager and Mary C. (Lovelace) Hastings; m. James Bernard Bockian, Sept. 16, 1984; children: Vivian Shifra, Adrian Adena, Lillian Tova. BA in Psychology, Vassar Coll., 1968; diploma in systems analysis NYU, 1978. Computer programmer RCA, N.Y.C., 1968-71; systems analyst United Artists Corp., N.Y.C., 1971-78; project leader Bradford Nat. Corp., N.Y.C., 1978-81; project mgr. Mfrs. Hanover Trust, N.Y.C., 1981-83; project mgr. Chem. Bank, N.Y.C., 1983-86; mgr. fin. systems Salomon Bros., N.Y.C., 1986-87; v.p. James B. Bockian and Assocs., 1987-93; mgr. systems quality assurance GAB Bus. Svcs., Inc., Parsippany, N.J., 1989-91; mgr. bus. systems GAB Bus. Svcs., Inc., Parsippany, N.J., 1991-93; mgmt. cons. ADIA Info. Techs., Inc., Piscataway, N.J., 1994; assoc. Data Mgmt. and Integration Svcs., Merrill Lynch & Co., Inc., 1995—. Mem. Assn. Women in Computing (exec. com. 1982-83), Data Adminstrn. Mgmt. Assn. N.J., Vassar Club. Avocation: photography. Home: 26 Farmhouse Ln Morristown NJ 07960-3019

BOCKRATH, LISSA ANN, gallery owner, artist; b. Warren, Ohio, Nov. 22, 1971; d. Mike James and Margaret (Flick) B. BFA with honors, Cleve. Inst. Art, 1995. Mem. staff studio tutoring svcs. Cleve. Inst. Art, 1991-95; instr. in watercolors Regency Towers, Parma, Ohio, 1992-93; owner, dir. Bockrath Gallery, Cleve., 1995—. Merit scholar Cleve. Inst. Art, 1990-95. Mem. Murray Hill Arts Assn. (publicity com.), Spales Nonprofit Arts, Nova. Office: Bockrath Gallery 2026 Murray Hill Rd Cleveland OH 44106

BOCK-TOBOLSKI, MARILYN ROSE, artist, art educator; b. South Bend, Ind., Jan. 21, 1941; d. Francis John and Mildred Irene (Moser) Bock; m. James Joseph Tobolski, Sept. 1, 1962; children: Erica Francis, Jessica Moser, Melina Jamie. BS in Fine Arts, Ind. U., 1964; postgrad. in Painting, Mich. State U., 1965-66; MS in Fine Arts, St. Francis Coll., 1975. Art instr. Ft. Wayne (Ind.) Cmty. Schs., Northwest Allen County Sch. Sys., South Bend (Ind.) Cmty. Sch. Corp.; assoc. faculty drawing and painting dept. continuing edn. Ind. U.-Purdue U., Ft. Wayne, Ind., 1975-85, Sch. Fine and Performing Arts, 1978-89, 91-92, Sch. Edn., 1983-85, 89-90, women's art history course Dept. Women's Studies and Ind. U., Purdue U. Sch. Fine & Performing Arts IUPU, 1996; drawing instr. Dept. Parks and Recreation, Ft. Wayne, 1989-96; guest artist gifted and talented visual art programs, mentor program Ft. Wayne Cmty. Schs., 1991, art dept. Northwest Allen Schs., Fort Wayne, 1986, 87, 88, 89, 90, Metro Sch. Sys., Wabash, Ind., 1986, 87, Bunche Elem. Sch., Ft. Wayne, 1994, 95, 96. One woman exhbns. include Del. Cmty. Coll., Media, Pa., 1970, Tri-State Coll.. Angola, Ind., 1971, Ft. Wayne (Ind.) Mus. Art, 1972, Manchester (Ind.) Coll., 1973, Watsons-Crick Gallery Purdue U., West Lafayette, Ind., 1975, Lakeview Gallery St. Francis Coll., Ft. Wayne, 1975, 83, Artlink Contemporary Artspace, Ft. Wayne, 1979, St. Mary's Coll., Notre Dame, Ind., 1982, Thomas Smith Fine Art Gallery, Ft. Wayne, 1985, Canterbury Art Ctr. Gallery, Ft. Wayne, 1988, Allen County Pub. Lib. Galleries, Ft. Wayne, 1993; group exhbns. include South Bend (Ind.) Art Ctr., 1961, 76, 91, Lansing (Mich.) Cmty. Gallery, Ball State U., Muncie, Ind., 1973, 74, 76, 82, Ind. U.-Purdue U., Ft. Wayne, 1974, 75, 77, 78, 81, 88, Ft. Wayne Mus. Art, 1975, 77, 78, 79, 83, 86, 87, Linker Gallery, Ft. Wayne, 1977, Ind. State Mus., Indpls., 1978, 80, Artlink Contemporary Artspace, Ft. Wayne, 1978, 79, 80, 81, 83, 85, 86, 87, 88, 95, 1st Presbyn. Ch. Gallery, Ft. Wayne, 1977, 81, Lakeview Gallery St. Francis Coll., Ft. Wayne, 1978, 89, Unitarian Gallery, Ft. Wayne, 1979, Anderson (Ind.) Coll., 1980, A. Montgomery Ward Gallery U. Ill., Chgo., Indpls. Art League, 1991, J. Barrett Galleries, Toledo, 1982, Ft. Wayne Pub. Lib., 1983, 86, Indpls. Mus. Art, 1983, Radsdall Gallery U. Ky., Lexington, 1984, Liturgical Visual Art Exhibit, Chgo., 1984, Cryna Internat. Gallery, Chgo., 1984, Wehrle Art Gallery Ohio Dominican Coll., Columbus, 1986, Thomas Smith Fine Art Gallery, Ft. Wayne, 1986, 87, Indpls. Press Club,1986, Artemisia Gallery, Chgo., 1986, Canterbury Art Ctr., Ft. Wayne, 1987, Schumacher Gallery, Columbus, 1987, Johnson Humrickhouse Mus., Coshocton, Ohio, 1989, J. Beck Gallery, Ft. Wayne, 1989, Rapp Gallery, Louisville, Ky., 1990, Vincennes (Ind.) U., 1992, Allen County Pub. Lib., Ft. Wayne, 1983-86, 92, 94, 95, 96, Reynolds-Heller Gallery, Columbus, 95, Lakeland Art Assn., Warsaw, Ind., 1996; represented in numerous private and pub. collections Ft. Wayne Mus. Art; executed paintings for St. Vincent De Paul Ch., Ft. Wayne, Ind., Crosier Ctr., Ft. Wayne, Downtown on the Landing, Ft. Wayne, others; featured in Art Insight, The Communicator, News-Sentine, Arts Ind., The Indianapolis NE, NUVO and others. Recipient award of Excellence Schumacher Gallery, 1987. Mem. Soc. Layerists in Multi Media, Artlink Contemporary Gallery (panel mem. 1979-82, 84-88), Chgo. Artists' Coalition. Roman Catholic. Home: 11534 Cherrywood Dr Fort Wayne IN 46845 Studio: Quelle Arts 2000 N Wells St Fort Wayne IN 46807

BOCKWITZ, CYNTHIA LEE, psychologist, psychology/women's studies educator; b. Hallock, Minn., Apr. 11, 1954; d. Rodney Lee and Jeanette Yvonne (Vilen) B. AA in Arts and Scis., Richland Coll., 1983; BA in Psychology, U. Tex., Dallas, 1985; MA in Counseling Psychology, Tex. Woman's U., 1992. Lic. profl. counselor, Ga. Pers. adminstr. Automatic Data Processing, Miami, Fla., 1974-77; office mgr. G.A. Dexter Co., Atlanta, 1977-79; human resources mgr. No. Telecom, Atlanta and Dallas, 1979-84; mental health worker Timberlawn Psychiat. Hosp., Dallas, 1984-85; acct. NEC Am., Dallas, 1986-87; asst. program dir. Arbor Creek Hosp., Sherman, Tex., 1989; lic. profl. counselor Trinity Counseling Ctr., Carrollton, Tex., 1989-93, Atlanta, 1993—; adj. instr. psychology Tex. Woman's U., Denton, 1988-92; instr. psychology DeKalb Coll., Atlanta, 1993—; cons. The Resource Ctr., Atlanta, 1993-94, Laurel Heights Hosp., 1994—; mem. exec. com. Women Clinicians Network, Atlanta, 1994, 95. Mem. NOW (fin. contbr.), APA (assoc.), Am. Assn. for Marriage and Family Therapy (assoc.), Assn. for Women in Psychology, Ga. Marriage and Family Therapy Assn. (legis. com. 1993-94), Assn. for Play Therapy, Ga. Assn. for Play Therapy, Nat. Assn. of Masters in Psychology. Democrat. Home: 711 Tuxworth Cir Decatur GA 30033-5620 Office: Laurel Heights Hosp 934 Briarcliff Rd NE Atlanta GA 30306-2618

BODA, VERONICA CONSTANCE, lawyer; b. Phila., Oct. 8, 1952; d. Louis Paul and Helen Ann (Zwigaitis) B. AB, Wilson Coll., 1974; JD, Vermont Law Sch., 1978; LLM in Taxation, Villanova U., 1989. Bar: Pa. 1978, U.S. Dist. Ct. (ea. dist.) Pa. 1982, U.S. Tax Ct. 1984. Staff atty. Cape-Atlantic Legal Services, Atlantic City, 1978-79; sole practice Phila., 1980—; tchr. Am. Inst. for Paralegal Studies, Phila., 1982-86; instr. bus. adminstrn. program Pa. State U., Media, Pa., 1987-88; ins. agt. Prudential Ins. Co., Wayne, Pa., 1985-86; ins. broker V C Boda & Co., Phila., 1986—. Author: (with others) Newberg on Class Actions, 1985; editor Women Lawyers Jour., 1993—; contbr. articles to profl. jours. Bd. dirs. Emergency Aid of Pa. Found., 1994—; bd. dirs. Colonial Phila. Hist. Soc., 1983, pres., 1984-89; rec. sec. Martin S. Wilson Jr. Ctr. for Arts. Mem. Nat. Assn. Women Lawyers (treas., pres.), Phila. Bar Assn. (chair com. real estate sect. 1984-86). Democrat. Roman Catholic. Office: PO Box 1587 Philadelphia PA 19105-1587

BODE, BARBARA, foundation executive; b. Evanston, Ill.; d. Carl and Margaret Emilie (Lutze) B. B.A. magna cum laude, U. Md., MA; scholar, Ludwig-Maximillians-Universitat, Munich; English Speaking Union scholar, U. London; Bundesrepublik scholar, Goethe Institut, Lubeck, W. Ger.; postgrad. NDEA fellow, UCLA. Woodrow Wilson teaching fellow N.C. Central U., Durham; pres. Children's Found., Washington, 1970-86, Council on Founds., 1986-89; v.p. Coun. Better Bus. Bur., 1990-95; exec. dir. Coun. Bettter Bus. Bur. Found., 1990-95. Bd. dirs. Children's Found., Rainbow TV Works, Nat. Com. for Responsive Philanthropy, Disability Rights, Edn. and Def. Fund Partnership, Women's Campaign Fund, 1984-88; founding mem. Women of Washington, 1992—, Leadership Washington, class of 1994, 94—. Woodrow Wilson Nat. Found. fellow, 1963-64. Mem. Women and Founds. Corp. Philanthropy, Washington Regional Assn. Grantmakers. Episcopalian. Home: 1661 Crescent Pl NW Washington DC 20009-4074 Office: DREDF Partnership Ste 220 1633 Q St NW Washington DC 20009

BODE, GERTRUDE BETH, artist, educator; b. Porto Rico, W.Va., Oct. 6, 1949; d. Harlin James and Alcindia Arizanna (Perine) B. BA, Salem-Teikyo U., 1972. Cert. elem. and secondary tchr., W.Va. Tchr. Morgan Elem. Sch., Clarksburg, W.Va., 1972, Lost Creek Elem. Sch., W.Va., 1973-76, Ziesing Elem. Sch., Spelter, W.Va., 1976-77, Adamston Elem. Sch., Clarksburg, W.Va., 1977-96. Group shows include Clarksburg Pub. Libr.; represented in pvt. collections. Treas. Harrison County Watercolor Soc., Clarksburg, W.Va., 1974—. Mem. NEA, W.Va. Edn. Assn., Harrison County Reading Coun. Democrat. Roman Catholic. Home: 1234 N 15th St Clarksburg WV 26301 Office: Adamston Elem Sch 1636 W Pike St Clarksburg WV 26301

BODI, SONIA ELLEN, academic librarian; b. Chgo., June 24, 1940; d. Franz Frithiof and Elsa (Noren) Bergquist; m. Peter Phillip Bodi, July 30, 1966; 1 child, Eric Christopher; stepchildren: Glenn Peter, John Jeffrey. Student, U. Edinburgh (Scotland), 1960-61; BA, Augustana Coll., Rock Island, Ill., 1962; MA Libr. Sci., Rosary Coll., 1977; MA, Northwestern U., 1986. English and history tchr. Gemini Jr. High Sch., Niles, Ill., 1962-64, Nagoya (Japan) Internat. Sch., 1964-65; English tchr. Old Orchard Jr. High Sch., Skokie, Ill., 1965-67; reference libr. Wilmette (Ill.) Pub. Library, 1976-79, Kendall Coll., Evanston, Ill., 1979-81; head reference and instructional libr. North Park Coll., Chgo., 1981—, asst. prof. bibliography, 1985-87, assoc. prof. bibliography, 1988—, chair divsn. humanities, 1988—, prof. bibliography, 1992—, interim libr. dir., 1996—. Contbr. articles to profl. jours. Pres. PTA, Lincolnwood, Ill., 1977-79; mem. Bd. Edn.,

Lincolnwood, 1980-91, sec., 1981-84, pres., 1984-87; mem. 1st Presbyn. Ch. of Evanston, elder, 1989—, Stephen ministry leader, 1992—. Mem. Ill. Libr. Assn., ALA, Am. Assn. Coll. & Rsch. Librs., Lincolnwood Friends of the Libr., Beta Phi Mu. Democrat. Home: 6710 N Trumbull Ave Lincolnwood IL 60645-3740 Office: North Park Coll 3225 W Foster Ave Chicago IL 60625-4810

BODIAN, MIRIAM, history educator; b. Balt., Aug. 14, 1948; d. David and Elinor (Widmont) B. BA in History & Lit., Harvard U., 1969; MA in Jewish History, Hebrew U., Jerusalem, 1981, PhD in Jewish History, 1988. Asst. prof. Judaic Studies Yeshiva U., N.Y.C., 1988-90; asst. prof. Judaic Studies & History U. Mich., Ann Arbor, 1990—. Office: U Mich Dept History 3609 Haven Hall Ann Arbor MI 48109

BODINSON, NANCY SUE, art educator; b. Kansas City, Mo., May 5, 1948; d. Herbert Van Dyke and Julia Antonette (Omerzu) Davis; m. Larry Gordon Moore, June 3, 1973 (div. Sept. 1985); children: Scott Gordon, Carrie Anne; m. Larry Joseph Bodinson, Dec. 24, 1989. BA, Baker U., Baldwin, Kans., 1970; MEd, Lesley Coll., 1990. Cert. art tchr. grades K-12, Mo. Art instr. grades K-6 Mary Harmon Weeks Sch., Kansas City, Mo., 1970-73, 74-75, Doty Elem. Sch., Detroit, 1973-74, Notre Dame de Sion, Kansas City, Mo., 1975-87; Montessori pre-sch. art instr. grades K-8 Mt. Washington German Magnet, Kansas City, 1987-95; art instr. Harold Holliday Montessori, Kansas City, 1995—; curriculum writer Kansas City Sch. Dist., 1992-94; presenter in field. mentor Baker U. Alumni Profl., 1995; mem. visual & perf. arts curriculum and assesment devel. Kansas City, Mo. Sch. Dist., 1995—; selected to participate in the Mo. Assessment Project (MAP 2000). Named Elem. Art Tchr. of Yr. for State of Mo., Mo. Art Edn. Assn., 1991. Mem. Am. Fedn. of Tchrs., Nat. Art Edn. Assn., Mo. State Tchrs. Assn., Delta Delta Delta. Home: 4921 Parish Dr Roeland Park KS 66205-1371 Office: Harold Holiday Montessori Sch 7227 Jackson Kansas City MO 64132

BODKIN, RUBY PATE, corporate executive, real estate broker, educator; b. Frostproof, Fla., Mar. 11, 1926; d. James Henry and Lucy Beatrice (Latham) P.; m. Lawrence Edward Bodkin Sr., Jan. 15, 1949; children: Karen Bodkin Snead, Cinda, Lawrence Jr. BA, Fla. State U., 1948; MA, U. Fla., 1972. Lic. real estate broker. Banker Barnett Bank, Avon Park, Fla., 1943-44, Lewis State Bank, Tallahassee, 1944-49; ins. underwriter Hunt Ins. Agy., Tallahassee, 1949-51; tchr. Duval County Sch. Bd., Jacksonville, Fla., 1952-77; pvt. practice realty Jacksonville, 1976—; tchr. Nassau County Sch. Bd., Jacksonville, 1978-83; sec., treas., v.p. Bodkin Corp., R&D/Inventions, Jacksonville, 1983—; assoc. Brooke Shields Innovative Designer Products, Inc., Kendall Park, N.J., 1988—. Author: Bodkin Bridge Course for Beginners, 1996; patentee in field including immersion detection cir., 1992, pushbutton clasp, 1996. Mem. Jacksonville Symphony Guild, 1985—, Southside Jr. Woman's Club, Jacksonville, 1957—, Garden Club Jacksonville, 1976—; bd. dirs. (fin. dir.) Riverside Woman's Club of Jacksonville, 1991-92. Recipient 25 Yr. Service award Duval County Sch. Bd., 1976, Tchr. of Yr. award Bryceville Sch., 1981. Mem. UDC, Am. Contract Bridge League, Fla. Edn. Assn. (pers. problems com. 1958), Duval County Classroom Tchrs. (v.p. membership 1957), Woman's Club Jacksonville Bridge Group. Home: 1149 Molokai Rd Jacksonville FL 32216-3273 Office: Bodkin Jewelers & Appraisers PO Box 16482 Jacksonville FL 32245-6482

BODNER, SUSAN R., marketing and communications executive; b. N.Y.C., Apr. 20, 1949; d. Milton Meyer and Muriel Ruby (Walash) Swersky; m. Lawrence Bodner, Oct. 25, 1970 (div. June 1975); children: Jennifer Lynn Bodner, Jason Ross Bodner. BA in Edn., U. Md., 1970; BA in English, 1971; paralegal cert., Barry Coll., 1980; MBA, Ga. State U., 1980. Tchr. devel. curriculum Solomon Shecter Hillel Community Day Sch., North Miami Beach, Fla., 1974-77; English tchr. Hebrew Acad. Atlanta, 1977-78; life underwriter, estate planner Life Va. Ins., Atlanta, 1978-79; paralegal, probate and estate mgmt. Abrams, Anton Robbins, Resnick, Schneider & Mager, Hollywood, Fla., 1980-81; svc. cons. mktg. dept. Southern Bell, Ft. Lauderdale, Fla., 1981-83; dir. community rels. The Jewish Home, Atlanta, 1984-87; dir. mktg. and comm. svcs. The United Jewish Fedn. Metrowest, Whippany, N.J., 1988-95; exec. dir. mktg. and comm. Jewish Fedn. Greater Phila., 1995—; pub.'s rep. The Jewish Pub. Group-The Jewish Exponent, 1995—; pubs. rep., adminstr. The Metrowest Jewish News, Whippany, 1988-95; cons. strategic mktg., comms. and pub. rels. for philanthropic orgn. and beneficiary agys., Whippany, 1988-95; pub. Metrosource, community resource book, 1990—, Inside Quar., lifestyle mag., 1994. Life mem. Nat. Coun. Jewish Women, Millburn-Shorthills, 1984—. Mem. NAFE, N.J. Press Women (state and nat. comm. award 1990, 91, 92, 93, 94), N.J. Exec. Women, Pub. Rels. Soc. Am., Am. Mktg. Assn. Office: Jewish Fedn Greater Phila 226 S 16th St Philadelphia PA 19102

BOE, LYNN FRANCES, elementary education educator; b. Bronx, N.Y., Sept. 20, 1949; d. Matthew and Frances Elizabeth (Hutchinson) Gaska; m. Robert Boe, Apr. 7, 1968; children: Robert Craig, Jonathan Thor, Sarah Elizabeth. BS with honors, Western N.Mex. U., 1989, M Tchg., 1993. Cert. master tchr., N.Mex. Tchr. reading Silver City Sch., 1989; substitute tchr., Silver City and Bayard, N.Mex., 1989-90; elem. tchr. Quemado (N.Mex.) Schs., 1990—, head tchr., 1995—. Leader San Juan 4-H Club, Mimbres, N.Mex., 1985-89; young mother's rep. Apple Valley Ext. Club, Mimbres, 1988; leader Girls in Action, Quemado Bapt. Ch., 1991—. Mem. Cardinal Key, Sigma Tau Delta. Office: Quemado Sch PO Box 128 Quemado NM 87829-0128

BOEHM, CAROL GENE, adult health nurse practitioner; b. Richland, Wash., Nov. 13, 1954; d. Gene Connor and Eleanor Betty (Pester) Loud; children: Jennifer Ann, Edward Gene. ADN, Ind. U., 1978; BSN, East Carolina U., 1991; MSN, The Cath. U. of America, 1995, FNP cert., 1996. RN, Md., N.C.; CRNP, CEN; cert. ACLS instr., BLS instr. Staff, charge nurse ICU Meth. Hosp. of Ind., Indpls., 1978-80; supr. Noxubee Gen. Hosp., Macon, Miss., 1980-84; nurse clinician I U. Md. Med. Ctr., Balt., 1984-88; asst. nurse mgr. Craven Regional Med. Ctr., New Bern, N.C., 1989-91; quality assurance, infection control Britthaven of Jacksonville, N.C., 1991-92; edn. specialist critical care Washington Adventist Hosp., Takoma Park, Md., 1988-89, 92-95; nurse practitioner family practice office, Prince Frederick, Md., 1995-96; cardiovascular nurse practitioner Cheverly, Md., 1996—; ACLS coord. Adventist Health Care Mid-Atlantic, Montgomery County, Md., 1992-95; clin. cons. Baxter/Edwards Critical Care, 1995—. Recipient Grad. Scholarship award Cath. U. of America, 1993-95. Mem. ANA, AACN, Nat. Assn. Pediat. Nurse Assocs. & Practitioners, Emergency Nurses Assn., Md. Nurses Assn., Golden Key, Sigma Theta Tau, Phi Kappa Phi. Republican. Baptist. Home: 10812 Winston Churchill Ct Upper Marlboro MD 20772

BOEHM, KATHRYN ELAINE, pediatrician, educator; b. Zanesville, Ohio, Dec. 22, 1959; d. Kester Bernell and Lola Irene (Seem) B. BA, Capital U., 1981, Cert. Tchr., 1982; MD, Med. Coll. Ohio, 1986. Resident in pediats. Med. Coll. Ohio, Toledo, 1986-89; staff physician Toledo Family Health Ctr., 1989-90; adolescent medicine fellow Johns Hopkins, Balt., 1990-92; contract physician Greater Dundack Pediats., Balt., 1990-92; asst. prof. pediats., gen. acad. pediats. divsn., sect. chief adolescent medicine Med. Coll. Ohio, 1992—; bd. dirs. Teen Line, Maumee, Ohio. Mem. Ambulatory Pediat. Assn., Soc. for Adolescent Medicine, Am. Acad. Pediats., Midwest Soc. for Pediat. Rsch. Lutheran.

BOEHM, P. DIANN, elementary education educator; b. Tulsa, Apr. 13, 1954; d. George Mural and Mabel Adella (Harris) Floyd; m. John Charles Boehm, Jr., June 2, 1979; children: Rachel Rebbecca, John Patrick, Katherine Louise. BS in Edn., George Mason U., 1981. Cert. elem. tchr., Tex. Tchr. 4th grade Internat. Sch., Manila, Philippines, 1981-82; tchr. prekindergarten Resurrection Episc. Ch., Austin, Tex., 1982-83; tchr. 9th grade St. Louis Cath. Sch., Austin, 1983-84; tchr. 4th grade St. John's Sch., Houston, 1984-85; tchr. kindergarten St. Thomas Cath. Sch., Austin, 1986-87; tchr., tech. coord. St. Andrew's Episc. Sch., Austin, 1989—; prin., coord. High Tech Schoolhouse, Tex.; tchr. HHC, Austin, 1991—; keynote speaker Fla. State Computer Conf.,1991—; cons. Scholastic pubs. Author: (book) The Internet Schoolhouse, A Teacher's Best Friend; contbr. articles on tech. in edn. to various pubs. Chair person bd, Episc. Ch. Women, St. David's Episc. Ch., 1989—, chair person United Thank Offering, 1991—. Named Tex. Tchr. of Yr. in Tech., Tex. Dept. Edn., 1992, Apple Disting. Educator. Mem. Tex. Ctr. Edn. Technology (hon. mention 1991, '92), VITAL (Leadership in Tech. award 1992). Republican. Office: Internet Schoolhouse 58 St Stephens Sch Rd Austin TX 78746

BOEHM, TONI GEORGENE, seminary dean, nurse; b. New Kensington, Pa., Dec. 28, 1946; d. Sylvio Chipoletti and Eula Gene (Smittle) Fox; m. Raymond Stawinski, Dec. 11, 1965 (div. Sept. 1978); 1 child, Michelle Stawinski Ivy; m. Jay Thomas Boehm, Apr. 28, 1983; children: Jonathon, Kimberly, Allison Cole, Amanda. Diploma, Allegheny Valley Sch. Nursing, Natrona Heights, Pa., 1967; family nurse practitioner cert., U. Kans., 1976; BA in Edn., Ottawa (Kans.) U., 1978; MSN, U. Mo., Kansas City, 1981; grad., Unity Sch. of Christianity, Unity Village, Mo., 1989. Ordained to ministry Assn. of Unity Chs.; cert. occupl. health nurse. Nurse Allegheny Valley Hosp., Natrona Heights, 1967-74; head nurse, dir. nursing Truman Med. Ctr., Kansas City, Mo., 1974-78; mgr. med. Hallmark Card Inc., Kansas City, Mo., 1978-85; sr. staff specialist ANA, Kansas City, Mo., 1985-87; dean of adminstrn. Unity Sch. Christianity, 1987—; nat. spkr. and freelance writer for ministry and self-unfoldment. Author: The Spiritual Intrapreneur, 1996. Mem. nat. steering com. for fundraising Unity Sch. of Christianity; mem. women's coun. U. Mo. Recipient scholarships. Mem. ANA, NCCJ, Mo. Nurses Assn. (bd. dirs. 1975-85), U. Mo. Sch. Nursing Alumni Assn., Assn. Unity Chs. (urban curriculum com. 1987—, ministerial edn. com. 1987—, field licensing com. 1990). Republican. Home: 430 N Winnebago Dr Lake Winnebago MO 64034-9321 Office: Unity Sch Christianity Lees Summit MO 64065

BOEHME, SARAH ELIZABETH, museum curator; b. Orange, Tex., Aug. 3, 1948; d. Lawrence Herbert and Gwendolyn (Dixon) B. BA, Sarah Lawrence Coll., 1970; MA, Bryn Mawr Coll., 1973, PhD, 1994. Curator, instr. St. Lawrence U., Canton, N.Y., 1973-77; curator Stark Mus. Art, Orange, 1978-82; John S. Bugas curator Whitney Gallery Western Art, Buffalo Bill Hist. Ctr., Cody, Wyo., 1986—; guest curator U. Wyo., Laramie, 1987, 88. Author: Rendezvous to Roundup: The First 100 Years of Art in Wyoming, 1990, Absarokee Hut: The Joseph Henry Sharp Cabin, 1992, Buckeye Blake: Art on the Western Front, 1993; co-author: Frontier America: Art and Treasures of the Old West, 1988, Seth Eastman: A Portfolio of North American Indians; contbr. articles to profl. publs. Bd. dirs. Park County (Wyo.) Arts Coun., 1989—, Wyo. Arts Coun., 1992-95; v.p. Wyo. Church Coalition. Smithsonian predoctoral fellow, 1983-86; Whiting fellow, 1984-85, Samuel H. Kress fellow. Mem. AAUW (state membership v.p.), Coll. Art Assn., Am. Assn. Mus. Methodist. Home: 2013 Newton Ave Cody WY 82414-4428 Office: Buffalo Bill Hist Ctr 720 Sheridan Ave Cody WY 82414-3428

BOEHMER, RAQUEL DAVENPORT, television producer, newsletter editor; b. Bklyn., Feb. 24, 1938; d. John Joralemon Davenport and Fanny (Barberis) Allison; m. Peter Joseph Boehmer; children: Kristian Ludwig, Louisa, Timothy Joralemon. BA, Wells Coll., 1959. Radio producer Maine Pub. Broadcasting Network, Bangor, 1977—; developer, editor consumer newsletter Seafood Soundings, Monhegan, Maine, 1986-92; columnist, editor newsletter New Monhegan Press, Monhegan, Maine, 1989—, chief editor, 1995—; speaker Seafare, L.A., 1986; keynote speaker Beyond Wells Day, Wells Coll., Aurora, N.Y., 1988; pres. bd. dirs. Monhegan Artists' Residency Corp. Writer, prodr. (radio commentary) Whole Foods for All People, 1977—; prodr., host (TV cooking program) Different Kettle of Fish, 1984; prodr. on-camera talent TV cooking program Great Tastes of Maine, Maine Pub. TV, 1996; author: A Foraging Vacation, 1982, Raquel's Maine Guide to New England Seafoods, 1988, Raquel's Maine Guide to Northeast Winter Vegetables. Writer legislation, Maine legis., 1985, 87, 91; treas. Monhegan Plantation, 1970-72, chair bicentennial com., 1976; chair Monhegan Sch. Bd., 1973-74; co-chair Monhegan Solid Waste Com., 1988—; commr. Maine State Liquor and Lottery Commn., 1996—. Recipient Pub. Svc. award Maine Nutrition Coun., Alumnae award Wells Coll., 1992; named Gt. New Eng. Cook, Yankee mag., 1986. Mem. Women's Fisheries Network (bd. dirs. N.E. chpt. 1992-94, sec. to nat. bd. dirs. 1994—), Colonial Dames Am., Women's Strike for Peace, Yankee Exch. Home and Office: Lobster Cove Rd #10 Monhegan ME 04852-0365

BOEHR, DIANE LINDA, librarian, consultant; b. N.Y.C., Oct. 8, 1950; d. Alvin and Elsie (Glickstein) Plotkin; m. Danny Arthur Boehr, Aug. 22, 1970; children: Michelle Beth, Joshua David. BS, CCNY, 1971; MLS, U. Md., 1983. Libr. svcs. cons. Costabile Assocs., Bethesda, Md., 1983—; instr. AJ Seminars, Rockville, Md., 1993—; adj. prof. U. Md., College Park, 1994—; chair cataloging policy com. Online Audiovisual Catalogers, 1995—. Active B'nai Israel Congregation, Rockville, 1979—; pres. Washington chpt. Asthma and Allergy Found. Am., 1978-80. Mem. ALA, Beta Phi Mu. Office: Costabile Assocs 4800 Montgomery Ln Bethesda MD 20814

BOELENS, PATRICIA ANN, accountant, nurse; b. Grinnell, Iowa, May 21, 1943; d. Harold Willis and Mary Louise (Phipps) Andes; m. William Carl Laubengayer, Aug. 15, 1963; children: Karl E., Kevin E.; m. Francis Raymond Boelens, Sept. 19, 1992; stepchildren: Kristina M., Kirk M. Diploma in nursing, St. Lukes Hosp., Cedar Rapids, Iowa, 1965; BSN, Coe Coll., 1976; AAS in Acctg. Tech., Kirkwood C.C., Cedar Rapids, 1987. Staff nurse Cedar Rapids, 1974-77; dir. nursing North Brook Manor Care Ctr., Cedar Rapids, 1977-78; staff nurse Linn County Pub. Health, Cedar Rapids, 1979-81; staff acct. Jean E. Kruse, CPA, Cedar Rapids, 1987-88; office mgr. Gordon Mollman, PA, Cedar Rapids, 1988-89; staff acct. Cindy Davis & Assocs., Moline, Ill., 1990-93, Watts & Assocs., Moline, Ill., 1993-94, AAA Iowa, Bettendorf, 1994-95, On With Life, Inc., Ankeny, Iowa, 1996—; spkr. continuing edn. workshops for various orgns., 1977-79; Iowa Nurses Assn. rep. Iowa Health Sys. Agy., Iowa City, 1979-83. Chair vol. adv. com. Linn County Coun. on Aging, Cedar Rapids, 1978-81. Nominee Nurse of Yr., Jour. Gerontol. Nursing, 1978. Mem. ANA (Iowa del. 1982), Iowa Nurses Assn. (continuing edn. rev. panel 1976-78, 3d v.p. 1978-80), Inst. Mgmt. Accts. (treas. Illowa chpt. 1992-94), Nat. Assn. Tax Practitioners, Kiwanis (com. chair Moline chpt. 1991-94), Phi Theta Kappa, Sigma Theta Tau. Home: 209 13th St SW Altoona IA 50009-2403 Office: On With Life Inc 715 SW Ankeny Rd Ankeny IA 50021

BOESE, LILLIAN R., performing company executive. Exec. dir. Milw. Ballet. Office: 504 W National Ave Milwaukee WI 43204*

BOESE, SANDRA JEAN, publishing executive; b. Ely, Minn., July 31, 1940; d. John Frank and Millie Jean (Prebeg) Simonick; m. Lee Robert Boese Sr., June 15, 1963; children: Lee Robert Jr., Joy Karin. BA in Speech and Elem. Edn., Marquette U., 1962. Elem. tchr., 1962-67; pub., editor Classroom Connections, Inc., Merced and Sacramento, 1988—, also chmn. bd.; pres. Calif. State Bd. Edn., Sacramento, 1984-86; exec. dir. Teen Talk Radio Show, 1994—. Trustee Merced City Sch. Dist., 1975-83; commr. Calif. Post-Secondary Edn. Commn., Sacramento, 1983; bd. dirs. Far-West Lab., San Francisco, 1984, The Achievement Coun., San Francisco, 1985. Recipient Commendation of Exempary Svc. award Calif. State Senate, 1983, Cert. of Appreciation, Calif. State Dept. Edn., 1983; named Woman of Distinction Soroptimist Internat., 1987. Mem. AAUW (Woman of Distinction 1986), Calif. Sch. Bds. Assn. (bd. dirs. del. assembly, 1978-81, chmn. conf. 1979-80, founder chmn. polit. action com. 1982-83, Outstanding Svc. award 1982, Spl. Recognition 1986), Merced City C. of C. (pres. 1985-86, Athena award 1988), Nat. Assn. State Bds. Edn. (bd. dirs. 1984-86), Assn. Marquette U. Women (Mary Neville Bielefeld award 1986). Republican. Roman Catholic. Office: Classroom Connections Inc 2824 Park Ave Ste C Merced CA 95348-3375

BOESZ, CHRISTINE, statistician; b. Bridgeton, N.J., May 26, 1944; d. Stanley Marion and Cecilia Marie (Cantinlon) Clark; m. Daniel Lester Boesz, June 26, 1965. AB, Douglass Coll., New Brunswick, N.J., 1966; MS, Rutgers U., 1967; postgrad., U. Mich. Asst. prof. Math. Valdosta (Ga.) State Coll., 1967-69; statistical analyst Alamo Area Coun. Govts., San Antonio, 1969-71, Bexar County Med. Found., San Antonio, 1971-74; exec. dir. Bexar County Med. Found., 1974-78; dep. dir. compliance office HMO U.S. Govt., Rockville, Md., 1978-86; sr. program and policy analyst Prepaid Health Care Health Care Financing Adminstrn., Washington, 1986-87, dir. compliance divsn. Prepaid Health Care, 1987-92, dir. ops. Office of Managed Care, 1992-95; v.p. govt. programs NYLCare Health Plans, N.Y.C., 1995—; faculty preceptor George Washington U., 1995. Contrb. chpts. to books, articles to profl. jours. Pres. Scientists Cliffs Assn., Pt. Republic, Md., 1985-86. Recipient Pew Meml. Trust fellowship U. Mich., 1990-92. Mem. AAUW, APHA, Am. Statis. Assn., Nat. Assn. Managed Care Regulators (pres. 1985-86, sec. 1981-84, Lifetime Achievement award 1994), Zonta. Office: NYLCare Health Plans 1 Liberty Pla New York NY 10006

BOETTCHER, NORBE BIROSEL, chemist; b. Manila, June 6, 1932; d. Dionisio Martinez and Filomena (Cuaresma) Birosel; m. Robert Arnold Boettcher, June 6, 1961; 1 child, Heidi Noriko. BS in Chemistry, Philippine Women's U., 1953; postgrad., U. Iowa, 1955-57. Chemist, rsch. and devel. Lawry's Foods, Inc., L.A., 1957-61; chemist, quality control, rsch. and devel. Sunsweet Products, San Jose, Calif., 1964-68; teaching asst., rsch. chemist Coe Coll., Cedar Rapids, Iowa, 1969-77; chemist, rsch. and devel. Penford Products Co., Cedar Rapids, 1977-92, analytical chemist customer lab. svc., 1992—. Mem. Brucemore, Inc., Cedar Rapids, Met. Opera Guild, N.Y.C. Mem. AAAS, AAUW, Cedar Rapids Art Mus., Philippine-Am. Club (social chmn. 1987-89, pres. Linn County, Iowa 1989-91, bd. dirs. 1992—), Iowa Poetry Assn. Republican. Roman Catholic. Home: 348 7th St Marion IA 52302-3325 Office: Penford Products Co 1st St SW Cedar Rapids IA 52406

BOGACZYK, KATHRYN, defined contribution plan conversion specialist; b. Warsaw, N.Y., Aug. 29, 1963; d. Charles Frederick and Mary Jane (Garbo) B.; m. Charles Marc Vernet, May 28, 1988. BA/BS in History of Art Am. Civilization, U. Pa., 1985. With William M. Mercer, Phila., 1982-86, recordkeeper, 1988-91; gallery asst. Helen Drutt Gallery, Phila., 1986-87; conversion specialist Corestates Bank NA, Phila., 1991-95, Bisys, Ambler, Pa., 1995-96; cons. SunGard, Phila., 1996—. Tutor Ctr. for Literacy, Phila., 1990—. Office: SunGard Centre Philadelphia PA 19102

BOGAD, CAROLYN MCWILLIAMS, educational administrator, educator; b. Montebello, Calif., June 22, 1947; d. Carroll Weldon and Opal Fayetta (Jacobs) McW.; m. Steven R. Bogad; children: Lesley Meredith, Molly Elizabeth, Neely Kathleen. BA in Anthropology, U. Calif., Santa Barbara, 1969, MA in Ednl. Adminstrn., 1981, postgrad. Cert. adminstrv. svcs., K-12 multiple subjects and single subject, social scis., English, humanities tchr., Calif. Tchr. Goleta (Calif.)) Union Sch. Dist., 1970-75, Sherman Oaks (Calif.) Elem. Sch., 1991-93; supr. tchr. edn., instr. U. Calif. Grad. Sch. Edn., 1975-82; asst. head Adat Ari El Daya Sch., North Hollywood, Calif., 1982-87; head Sinai Aakiba Acad., Westwood, Calif., 1982-87; lectr. edn. Calif. State U., Northridge, 1986-88; gen. studies cons., dir. presch. through grade 8, Sephardic Hebrew Acad., L.A., 1988-91; sch. dir., ednl. cons. and therapist Bridges Acad., L.A., 1993—; tchr. writing under consultation Johns Hopkins U. Ctr. for Academically Talented Youth, Calif. Inst. for Talented Youth, UCLA, summers 1991, 92; workshop leader in field; conf. presenter in field; mem. accreditation team Western Assn. Schs. and Colls.; cons. in field, 1980—. Author curriculum materials on lng. arts, social studies, math., computers, ESL, multi-cultural edn. for adults and children. Named One of Top 10 Educators in L.A., L. Times. Mem. ASCD, AAUW (v.p. membership L.A. 1992-93), Nat. Coun. Tchrs. English, Nat. Coun. Tchrs. Math., Calif. ASCD, Assn. Calif. Sch. Adminstrs., Calif. Reading Assn., Calif. Assn. for Gifted, San Fernando Valley Assn. for Gifted, Kappa Delta Pi. Home: 4842 Gaynor Ave Encino CA 91436 Office: Bridges Acad 15223 Burbank Blvd Sherman Oaks CA 91006

BOGAN, ELIZABETH CHAPIN, economist, educator; b. Morristown, N.J., Aug. 22, 1944; d. Daryl Muscott and Tirzah (Walker) Chapin; m. Thomas Rockwood Bogan, June 5, 1965; children: Nathaniel Rockwood, Andrew Allerton. AB, Wellesley Coll., 1966; MA, U. N.H., 1967; PhD, Columbia U., 1971. Mem. faculty Fairleigh Dickinson U., Madison, N.J., 1971-92, prof. econs., 1982-92; chmn. merit scholarship com. Farleigh Dickinson U., Madison, N.J., 1981-82, chmn. dept. econs. and fin., 1981-84, 87-91, reviewer univ. press; mem. faculty Princeton (N.J.) U., mem. faculty, sr. lectr. in econs., 1992—; vis. prof. Princeton U., 1991. Reviewer: Fin. Analyst Jour.; author articles and macroecons. text. Recipient Outstanding Tchr. award Fairleigh Dickinson U., 1979, 86, 87; NSF fellow, Pres'. fellow, Earhart fellow Columbia U., 1968-71. Mem. AAUP, Am. Econ. Assn., Ea. Econ. Assn., Atlantic Econ. Soc. Congregationalist. Clubs: Wellesley, Beacon Hill. Home: 41 Windermere Ter Short Hills NJ 07078-2254 Office: Princeton U 109 Fisher Hall Princeton NJ 08540

BOGAN, MARY FLAIR, stockbroker; b. Providence, July 9, 1948; d. Ralph A.L. and Mary (Dyer) B.; B.A., Vassar Coll., 1969. Actress, Trinity Sq. Repertory Co., R.I., Gretna Playhouse, Pa., Skylight Comic Opera, Milw., Cin. Playhouse, Playmakers' Repertory, N.C.; mem. nat. co. No Sex, Please, We're British; also TV commls., 1970-77; account exec. E.F. Hutton & Co., Inc., Providence, 1977-86; account v.p. Paine Webber, 1986—; econ. reporter Sta. WPRI-TV, 1982-85, Sta. WJAR-TV, 1987—. Treas. Red Bridge Council Rep. Women; chmn. new mems. com. R.I. Fedn. Rep. Women. Recipient Century Club award, 1980, 81, 82, 83, 85; Blue Chip Sales award, 1983, 85, Pacesetter Sales Award, 1986-90. Named. Woman of the Yr. Profl. Bus. and Rep. Women's Assn. Mem. Women's Assn., Barker Players, Univ. Club, Brown Faculty, Barker Players. Home: 18 Cooke St Providence RI 02906-2023 Office: PaineWebber One Citizens Plz Ste 900 Providence RI 02903

BOGARD, CAROLE CHRISTINE, lyric soprano; b. Cin.; d. Harold and Helen Christina (Whittlesey) Geistweit; m. Charles Paine Fisher, Dec. 30, 1966; children: Christine, Pamela. Student, San Francisco State U. Debuts include: Despina in Cosi fan Tutte (Mozart), San Francisco, 1965, Poppea in Coronation of Poppea (Monteverdi), Netherlands Opera, 1971; other appearances include, Boston Opera, N.E.T., orchs. Boston, Madrid, Minn., Phila., Pitts., San Francisco, summer festivals, Mostly Mozart, N.Y., Tanglewood, Carmel, Aston Magna, Gt. Barrington, Mass., appeared in concerts throughout Europe and with Smithsonian Chamber Players, 1976—; recorded numerous albums including 1st rec. of songs of John Duke for his 80th birthday, 1979, recital of Groupe des Six; premiered songs of Dominic Argento in, Holland, 1978, songs of Richard Cumming (in collaboration with Donald Gramm); regular participant rec. and scholarly projects, Smithsonian Instn.; judge regional auditions, Boston; tchr., with emphasis on technique as taught in last Century. Mem. Sigma Alpha Iota. Home: 161 Belknap Rd Framingham MA 01701-3803

BOGART, CAROL LYNN, small business owner, freelance reporter, video producer, radio personality; b. Lakewood, Ohio, Mar. 9, 1949; d. Lloyd William and Evelyn Mary (Overmyer) B.; 1 child, Michael Lloyd. BLS, Bowling Green State U., 1973; grad., Nat. Theater Conservatory, Denver, 1992. Reporter, anchor WNEP-TV, Scranton, Pa., 1975-76; reporter WXIA-TV, Atlanta, 1976-79; reporter, fill-in morning anchor WLS-TV, Chgo., 1979-82; anchor, reporter KMGH-TV, Denver, 1982-89; media cons., video producer, voice-over and on-camera talent Bogart Inc., Denver, 1989-93; reporter, field prodr., writer WOTO-WUAB-TV, Cleve., 1995-96; radio host WTTF Radio, Tiffin, Ohio, 1996—; field producer, writer WUAB and WOIO-TV, Cleve., 1996; guest speaker various schs. and univs., Denver, 1982-93, Cleve. 1994-96. Voiceover talent. Mem. Greater Cleve. Growth Assn., Coun. of Sml. Enterprises; vol. Odyssey of the Mind coach, pet therapy, grief counseling. Mem. AFTRA, SAG, Nat. Assn. Broadcast Engrs. and Techs. Presbyterian.

BOGART, JANE, set decorator; b. N.Y.C., Mar. 19, 1919; d. Stephen and Florence Mathilde (Lowe) Gitnick; m. Paul Bogart Mar. 22, 1941 (div. 1988); children: peter, Tracy, Jennifer. Actor, puppeteer Berkley Marionettes, N.Y.C., 1940-45; apprentice Paramount Pictures, L.A., 1973-74; set decorator The Fortune, L.A., 1975-76, 20th Century Fox, L.A., 1977-79, TV Movies & TV Series, 1978-80, I.T.C. On Golden Pond, 1980-81; set decorator for Irreconcilable Differences, 1983, The River, 1984, Violets Are Blue, 1985, Down & Out in Beverly Hills, 1985, Nothing in Common, 1986, Planes, Trains, Automobiles, 1987, Broadcast News, 1987, Scenes From a Mall, 1990, Fifty, 1991.

BOGART, JUDITH SAUNDERS, public relations executive; b. Batesville, Ind., Nov. 16, 1936; d. David Rodman and Anne Eva (Kohles) Saunders; m. William Robert Bogart, Oct. 22, 1971. BA, Baldwin-Wallace Coll., 1958. Dir. pub. rels. Greater Cin. Girl Scout Coun., 1958-61, Nation's Capital Girl Scout Coun., Washington, 1963-65, Gt. Rivers Girl Scout Coun., Washington, 1965-68; account rep. Edn. Funds Inc., Providence, 1967-68; dir. cmty. rels. Cin. Human Rels. Commn., 1968-76; cmty. rels. cons. Cin., 1976-77; v.p. pub. rels. Jewish Hosp. Cin., 1977-85; exec. v.p. Diversified Communicatons Inc., Cin., 1985-88; pres. Judith Bogart Assocs., Cin., 1989-91; dir. pub. rels. Sive/Young & Rubicam, Cin., 1991-96. Pres. Gt. Rivers coun. Girl Scouts U.S., 1984-87, bd. dirs., 1987—; bd. dirs. Nat. Coun. Internat. Visitors, Washington, 1988-95, chmn., 1991-93; trustee Cin. Internat. Visitors Ctr., 1981-87; co-chmn. pub. rels. Greater Cin. Bicentennial, 1985-88; mem. planning bd. United Way, Cin., 1987—; mem. cmty. rels. bd. Xavier U., Cin., 1983—, chmn., 1991—; bd. dirs. Family Svc. Cin. Area, 1995—; mem. pub. rels. com. ARC Hamilton County, 1995—, Mayor's Commn. Children, 1996—; pub. rels. chair Kids Voting Southwest Ohio, 1996—. Named Career Woman of Achievement, YWCA, 1983. Fellow Pub. Rels. Soc. Am. (accredited, nat. pres. 1983, pres. Cin. chpt. 1976, Outstanding Mem. 1977); mem. Women in Comms., Inc. (nat. headliner 1982, nat. pub. rels. com., Outstanding Woman in Comms. 1976), N.Am. Pub. Rels. Coun. (pres. 1989), Bankers Club (bd. govs. 1995—, bd. dirs. 1995—).

BOGART, WANDA LEE, interior designer; b. Ashville, N.C., Feb. 26, 1939; d. Bob West and Virginia Elizbeth (Worley) McLemore-Snyder; m. Sterling X. Bogart, Feb. 12, 1962; children: Kevin Sterling, Kathleen Elizabeth. BA, San Jose (Calif.) State U., 1961. Cert. interior designer. Tchr. Redondo Beach (Calif.) Sch. Dist., 1962-65; free-lance interior designer Ladera, Calif., 1970-75; designer MG Interior Design, Orange, Calif., 1975-80; prin., pres. Wanda Bogart Interior Design Inc., Orange, 1980—. Contbr. articles to profl. jours. Named one of Top 20 Interior Designers in So. Calif. Ranch and Coast Mag., 1987. Mem. Internat. Interior Design Assn. (profl. mem., cert.), Am. Soc. Interior Design (profl. mem., cert.), Orange C. of C. Office: Wanda Bogart Interior Design Inc 1440 E Chapman Ave Orange CA 92666-2229

BOGDAN, CAROLYN LOUETTA, financial specialist; b. Wilkes-Barre, Pa., Apr. 15, 1941; d. Walter Cecil and Ethna Louetta (Kendig) Carpenter; m. James Thomas Bogdan, May 5, 1961; 1 child, Thomas James. Grad. high sch., Kingston, Pa. Head bookkeeper Forty Ft. (Pa.) State Bank, 1959-63, U.S. Nat. Bank, Long Beach, Calif., 1963-65; office mgr. United Parts Exchange, Long Beach, 1976-81; contract adminstr. Johnson Controls, Inc., Rancho Dominguez, Calif., 1981-88, credit coord., 1989—; co-owner, acct. Bogdan Elec. R & D, Lakewood, Calif., 1981—. Mem. Radio Amateur Civil Emergency Svc., Los Angeles County Sheriff Dept., 1974—, records keeper, 1988-93, radio comms. officer, 1994—. Mem. NAFE, Nat. Notary Assn., Am. Inst. Profl. Bookkeepers, Tournament of Roses Radio Amateurs (pin chmn. 1975—), Calif. State Sheriff's Assn. (assoc.). Republican. Home: 3713 Capetown St Lakewood CA 90712-1437 Office: Johnson Controls Inc 19118 S Reyes Ave Rancho Dominguez CA 90221-5898

BOGGS, CORINNE CLAIBORNE (LINDY BOGGS), former congresswoman; b. Brunswick Plantation, La., Mar. 13, 1916; d. Roland Philomen and Martha Corinne (Morrison) Claiborne; m. Thomas Hale Boggs, Jan. 22, 1938 (dec.); children: Barbara Boggs Sigmund (dec.), Thomas Hale Jr., Corinne Boggs Roberts, William Robertson (dec.). BA, Sophie Newcomb Coll., Tulane U., 1935, LLD (hon.); LittD, U. St. Thomas; DPub Svc. (hon.), Trinity Coll., Washington, 1975; hon. degree, St. Mary of Woods; LLD, Loyola U., Notre Dame U., Wesleyan U., Cath. U. Law Sch., Xavier U., St. Mary's Coll., St. Thomas Aquinas Coll., Univ. New Orleans, Our Lady of Holy Cross Coll., Notre Dame Sem., Coll. of St. Elizabeth. Tchr. history and English St. James Parish, La., 1936-37; elected to 93d Congress to fill vacancy caused by death of husband, 1973; re-elected to 94th-101st Congresses from 2d La. Dist., 1973-91; ret., 1991; mem. appropriations com. majority mem. from Ho. of Reps., Am. Revolution Bicentennial Adminstrn. Bd., chmn. Commn. Ho. of Reps. Bicentenary; mem. campaign com. Dem. Nat. Com., 1974; first chairwoman Dem. Nat. Conv., 1976; mem. com. on Bicentennial of U.S. Constn. Pres., Dem. Congl. Wives Forum, 1954, Womans Nat. Democratic Club, 1958-59, Congl. Club, 1971-72; co-chmn. Inaugural Balls for Presidents John F. Kennedy, 1961, Lyndon Johnson, 1965; mem. Nat. Hist. Publs. and Records Com.; bd. dirs. La. Council for Music and Performing Arts; hon. bd. dirs. Met. New Orleans chpt. Nat. Found. March of Dimes; bd. advisers. CLOSE-UP and Presdl. Classroom; regent emeritus Smithsonian Instn.; mem. president's council Tulane U. Recipient Weiss Meml. award NCCJ, 1974; Nat. Oak award La. Assn. Ind. Colls. and Univs., Disting. Service medal Saint Mary's Dominican Coll., 1976, Humanitarian award AMVETS Nat. Aux., Torch of Liberty award B'nai B'rith, 1976, Gala IV award Birmingham So. U., 1976, Eleanor Roosevelt Humanitarian award, 1977, E. Roosevelt Centennial award, 1984, 1st woman recipient Disting. Alumna award Tulane U., 1986; 1st woman recipient VFW Congl. award, 1986; bldg., rm. in U.S. Capitol bldg., energy bldg. Tulane U., U.S. Vets. Hosp. Unit, New Orleans, Challenger Space Ctr. and Mission Control Ctr., Baton Rouge, and dam named in her honor. Mem. Nat. Soc. Colonial Dames, LWV, Internat. Fedn. Cath. Alumni, Internat. Women's Forum. Mailing Address: 6823 Saint Charles Ave New Orleans LA 70118-5665

BOGGS, FRANCES SKELTON, elementary school level adminstrator; b. Chattaanooga, Tenn., Aug. 30, 1942; d. Thomas Asa and Shara Janicé Skelton; m. Richard Ray Boggs, June 28, 1969; children: Christopher Richard, Carolyn Janese. BS in Early Childhood Edn., Ga. So. Coll., 1964; MEd, Ga. Southwestern Coll., 1987; EdS, Mercer U., 1991. Tchr. 1st grade Griffin (Ga.) Spalding County Bd. Edn., 1964-65, 66-69, Chatham County Bd. Edn., Savananah, Ga., 1965-66; tchr. 2d grade Jackson County Bd. Edn., Jefferson, Ga., 1974-75, Lamar County Bd. Edn., Barnesville, Ga., 1977-89; adminstr., lead tchr. Lamar County Bd. Edn., Barnesville, 1989-94, adminstr., instrnl. coord., 1994-96; cons. Ga., 1993-94; adj. instr. Mercer U. Coll., Macon, 1992—. Past pres., mem. Am. Cancer Soc., Barnesville, 1987—; instr., presenter The Ga. Child Care Tng. Program, Athens, Ga., 1990—; mem., ednl. dir. Clearn Cmty. Commn. Mem. AAUW (past pres.), ASCD (assoc.), Profl. Assn. Ga. Educators (bldg. rep.). Presbyterian. Office: Lamar County Elem Sch 154 Burnette Rd Barnesville GA 30204

BOGGS, NORENE RUTH, visual artist; b. Albany, N.Y., July 1, 1935; d. Norman Anthony Swasey and Helena Ruth Emerick; m. Edward William Boggs, June 23, 1956; children: Jeffrey E., Linda Boggs Yeomans. BS in Graphic Arts, Simmons Coll., 1956. tchr. of art therapy Cumberland County Nursing Home, Carlisle, Pa., 1970-73; art tchr. Messiah Village Retirement Cmty., Mechanicsburg, Pa., 1987-90. Exhibited in group shows at William Penn Meml. Mus., Harrisburg, Pa., 1975-81, 83-91, 93, Washington County Mus. Fine Art, Hagerstown, Md., 1975-77, Pa. Watercolor Soc., 1980, 82, 87, Allentown Art Mus., 1980, Lebanon Valley Coll., Annville, Pa., 1978-81, State Capitol, Harrisburg, Pa., 1985, Messiah Coll., Grantham, Pa., 1987, 91, Art Assn. Harrisburg, Pa., 1987, Gov.'s Home, Harrisburg, 1988, 91, Pa. State U., Harrisburg, 1989, Temple U., Harrisburg, 1990, Harrisburg Area C.C., 1992; represented in permanent collections at Messiah Coll., Grantham, Pa., Art Assn. of Harrisburg. Mem. Pa. Watercolor Soc. Home: 17 Broadmoor Dr Mechanicsburg PA 17055

BOGGS, WILLENE GRAYTHEN, abstractor, oil and gas broker, consultant; b. Vancouver, Wash., Mar. 10, 1939; d. William Louis and Zorah (Williams) Graythen; m. Ray Buck Glasgow, Feb. 8, 1964 (div. June 1969); m. Harry Maurice Boggs, May 23, 1993. BA in History, Centenary Coll., 1975; postgrad., La. State Law Sch., 1984, S.E. La. U., 1989. Tchr., educator St. Tam Parish Sch. Bd., Lacombe, La., 1964-65; abstractor St. Tam Parish Legal News, Covington, La., 1965-66, Kansas City Title Ins. Co., New Orleans, 1966-69, Lawyers Title Ins. Corp., New Orleans, 1975-77, Frawley, Wogan, Miller & Co., New Orleans, 1977-79; owner, mgr. Idea House and Sweet Home Antiques, Metairie, La., 1973-76; owner, mgr., abstractor, oil and gas broker Willene Glasgow & Assocs., Metairie, 1969-73; owner, mgr., abstractor Willene Glasgow & Assocs., Covington, La., 1979-93; pres. WCV Mgmt., Inc., Nashville, 1993-94; asst. to art dir. Bascom-Louise Gallery, Highlands, N.C., 1996. Author: Decoupage and Related Crafts, 1972; contbg. writer Times-Picayune, New Orleans, 1989. Bd. dirs. Air, Water and Earth Inst., Covington, 1989; bd. dirs., pres. Pontchartrain Area Recycling Coun., Inc., Covington, 1989, 90, 91, 92, 93; mem. Citizens Adv. Com. on Solid Waste, 1988, 89, 90, 91, 92; coord. Pontchartrain Area Recycling Conv., 1988; fund raiser March of Dimes, Am. Cancer Soc., Arthritis Found., others, 1986—. Named hon. sec. state State of La., 1987. Mem. AAUW (conf. chmn. 1988-89, 92-93, chmn. Ednl. Found. 1989-91, Mem. of Yr. award Covington-Mandeville br. 1989, v.p. membership 1991-93), Petroleum Landman's Assn., Covington C. of C. (legis. chmn. 1988—, Mem. of Yr. award 1988), Art League of Highlands (membership chmn. 1996), Highlands-Cashiers Garden Club. Home and Office: 145 Mt Lori Dr Highlands NC 28741

BOGHOSIAN, PAULA DER, computer business consultant; b. Watervliet, N.Y., Nov. 19, 1933; d. Harry and Osgi (Piligian) der B. BS magna cum laude, Syracuse U., 1964, MS, 1967; postgrad., SUNY, Oswego, 1972, SUNY, Albany, 1974. Cert. profl. sec. Asst. prof. Cazenovia (N.Y.) Coll., 1964-73; instr. Bd. of Coop., Syracuse, N.Y., 1973-76, dir. bus. careers, 1976-92; cons. computer bus., prin. Syracuse, 1984—. Zonta scholar, 1964; Jessie Smith Noyes grantee Syracuse U., 1965. Mem. Assn. Info. Systems Profl. (com. chmn.), Bus. Tchrs. Assn. of N.Y. State, Adminstrv. Mgmt. Soc., Eastern Bus. Tchrs. Assn., Assn. for Supervision and Curriculum Devel., Assn. of Am. Jr. Colls., Assn. of Am. U. Profs., Nat. Assn. for Armenian Studies and Rsch. Harvard U., Internat. Tng. Communications (v.p. 1985-86), Delta Pi Epsilon, Beta Gamma Sigma, Phi Kappa Phi, Pi Lambda Theta, Sigma Lamda Delta. Republican. Mem. Armenian Apostolic. Home: 3181 Bellevue Ave Apt B6 Syracuse NY 13219-3156

BOGHOSSIAN, JOAN THOMPSON, artist; b. Newport, R.I., Mar. 6, 1932; d. Joseph and Hope (Bliss) Thompson; m. Paul O. Boghossian Jr., 1952 (dec. July 1995); children: Carol Boghossian Spencer, Paul O. III, David M., Nancy Boghossian Staples. BS, U. R.I., 1953. One person shows at Attletoro Mus., Newton Libr. Gallery; two-person shows at Providence Art Club (J. Banigan Sullivan prize 1984), Dodge House Gallery; group exhbns. at R.I. Watercolor Soc. (1st in watercolor 1988, 91, Block Artists Merchandise award 1989, Grumbacher Gold Medallion 1990, 93, 94), Mystic Art Assn. (1st in watercolor 1990, 92, 93, 95, Mystic Manor spl. award for aquatint 1992), Wickford Art Assn. (1st in watercolor 1986, 1st in all-media 1993, 2d in oil 1995), South County Art Assn. (award 1987, Florence B. Kane award 1989, Herbert Richard Cross award 1992, C. Gordon Harris award 1993), Peel Gallery-Danby, Vt., New Eng. South Shore Artists (Best in Show 1986), Cape Cod Art Assn. (1st in watercolor 1987, 90, 1st in graphics 1987, 2d in watercolor 1988, 92, Juror's award of merit 1994), Warwick Arts Found. (1st in watercolor 1985), others. Home: 640 East Ave Pawtucket RI 02860 Studio: 7 Thomas St Providence RI 02903

BOGOLUB, ELLEN BETH, social work educator; b. Chgo., Oct. 28, 1948; d. William and Lillian (Kletnick) B.; m. Neil Friedman, June 14, 1992. BA cum laude, U. Chgo., 1970; MSW, NYU, 1973; PhD, Rutgers U., 1986. Social worker Jewish Bd. of Family and Children's Svcs., N.Y.C., 1973-80; psychotherapist Lincoln Inst. for Psychotherapy, N.Y.C., 1980-86; asst. prof. sch. of social welfare SUNY, Stony Brook, 1986-91; asst. prof. sch. of social work Adelphi Univ., Garden City, N.Y., 1991—. Author: Helping Families Through Divorce, 1995; contbr. articles to profl. publs. Pub. spkr. on divorce; interviewer of Holocaust survivors Survivors of the Shoah Visual History Found., 1995. Mem. NASW (Award for Outstanding Contbn. 1991), Phi Beta Kappa. Home: 524 Pond Path Setauket NY 11733 Office: Sch of Social Work Adelphi Univ Garden City NY 11530

BOGOMOLNY, ABBY, elementary educator; b. Bklyn., Feb. 17, 1953; d. Samuel and Frances B. BA, Bklyn. Coll., 1974; MA, San Francisco State U., 1990. Cert. hypnotherapist, Calif. Instr. Cabrillo Coll., Aptos, Calif., 1990—, DeAnza Coll., Cupertino, Calif., 1990—; bd. dirs. Hillel Found., Santa Cruz, Calif. Author: Nauseous in Paradise, 1986, Black of Moonlit Sea, 1991, People Who Do Not Exist, 1996; editor: The World Between Women, 1986. Talk show host KUSP (FM), Santa Cruz, 1995—. Cabrillo Coll. Faculty grant, 1994-95, Spectra Artist grant, So. Calif. Cultural Commn., 1995-96. Mem. MLA. Office: PO Box 7361 Santa Cruz CA 95061

BOGSTAHL, DEBORAH MARCELLE, market research consultant; b. Irvington, N.J., June 5, 1950; d. Marcel and Helena Christina (de Jaroszynsky) Bogstahl; m. Richard Neil Press, Mar. 20, 1976; children: Alexandra Boman, Michelle Boman. BA in English Edn., Trenton State Coll., 1972. Cert. tchr., N.J. Project dir. U.S. Testing Co., Hoboken, N.J., 1973-75; project dir. J. Walter Thompson Co., N.Y.C., 1975-77; rsch. account exec. Dancer Fitzgerald Sample, N.Y.C., 1977-80; group rsch. mgr. Bristol-Myers Co., N.Y.C., 1980-87; dir. rsch. Med. Econs. Co., Inc., Oradell, N.J., 1987-90; market rsch. mgr. The Mennen Co., 1991-92, Reckitt & Colman, Inc., Montvale, N.J., 1992—; Contbr. poetry to anthology. Mem. Am. Mktg. Assn., Product Devel. and Mgmt. Assn., Healthcare Bus. Women's Assn. Democrat. Roman Catholic. Avocations: sailing, reading, writing, music.

BOGUE, LUCILE, retired private school educator, author; b. Salt Lake City, Apr. 21, 1911; d. Roy D. and Maude E. (Callicotte) Maxfield; m. Arthur E. Bogue, Dec. 25, 1935 (dec. 1979); children: Sharon Bogue Young, Bonnie. AA, Colo. Coll., 1932; BA, U. No. Colo., 1934; MA, San Francisco State U., 1973. Tchr. Creede (Colo.) Pub. Sch., 1934-36, Steamboat Springs (Colo.) Pub. Sch., 1946-62, Whiteman Sch., Steamboat Springs, 1957-59; founder, pres. Yampa Valley Coll., Steamboat Springs, 1962-66; dir. guidance Am. Sch. in Japan, Tokyo, 1966-68; dean Anna Head Sch., Oakland, Calif., 1968-72; ret. Author: (poetry) Typhoon! Typhoon!, 1969; (novel) Salt Lake, 1980; (non-fiction) Dancers on Horseback, 1984, I Dare You! How to Stay Young Forever, 1990; (plays) Bon Voyage and I. . .As in Identity, 1996. Mem. Nat. League Am. PEN Women (pres. 1987-91, Women of '94), Calif. Writers Club (pres. 1981-87), Dramatists Guild. Democrat. Unitarian. Home: 2611 Brooks El Cerrito CA 94530

BOHANAN, YVETTE MARIE, information systems manager; b. Clayton, Mo., Mar. 3, 1964; d. Joseph Mario and Dorothy Mae (Darst) Barera; m. Montgomery Allan Bohanan, Oct. 17, 1996; children: Rebecca Kaye, Mitchell Allan. BS in Math., Maryville U. Network engr. Meridian Tech. Corp., St. Louis, 1986-89; pres. Binary Systems, Inc., St. Louis, 1989-91; sr. programmer, analyst Mallinckrodt Med., St. Louis, 1991-93; mgr. Talx Corp., St. Louis, 1993; chief tech. officer Tapestry Computing, St. Louis, 1993-96; sr. mgr. Sequent Computer Systems, Beaverton, Oreg., 1996—. Vol. Mo. Jr. Acad. Sci., St. Louis, 1983-96, Monshanto/Post-Dispatch Sci. Fair, St. Louis, 1983-84. Recipient Golden Eagle award Am. Acad. Achievement, 1982.

BOHANNON, SARAH VIRGINIA, personnel operations technician; b. Roanoke, Va., Mar. 1, 1947; d. Laurence S. and Sarah Elizabeth (Smith) B. AA in Bus. Adminstrn. Mgmt., Nat. Bus. Coll., 1983. Pers. appointment clk. IRS, Richmond, Va., 1983-84; pers. ops. technician Commonwealth of Va., Richmond, 1985—. Mem. NAFE, Am. Biog. Inst. (life, dep. gov. 1991, hon. mem. rsch. bd. advisors 1991, mem. women's inner circle of achievement 1991), Va. Pub. Health Assn. Home: 2220 Clarke St Richmond VA 23228-6049 Office: Commonwealth of Va Richmond VA 23219-2110

BOHANON, KATHLEEN SUE, neonatologist, educator; b. Mpls., 1951. BA summa cum laude, U. Minn., 1973, MD, 1977. Diplomate Am. Bd. Pediats., Am. Bd. Neonatal-Perinatal Medicine. Commd. 2d lt. USAF, 1973, advanced through grades to col., 1995; resident in pediats. Case Western Res. U., Cleve., 1977-80; gen. pediatrician USAF, 1980-85; fellow in neonatology Wilford Hall Med. Ctr., San Antonio, 1985-87; neonatologist, dir. neonatal ICU USAF Med. Ctr., Wright-Patterson AFB, Ohio, 1987-95, chmn. dept. pediat., 1995—; asst. clin. prof. pediats. U. N.D. Sch. Medicine, Grand Forks, 1981-82, Wright State U. Sch. Medicine, Dayton, Ohio, 1987—, Uniformed Svc. U. Health Scis., Washington, 1988—; mem. com. Infant Bio-Ethics Com., Dayton, 1990—. Mem. Am. Acad. Pediats. Office: 74th MDOS/SGOC 5030 Pearson Rd Dayton OH 45433-5515

BOHLE, SUE, public relations executive; b. Austin, Minn., June 23, 1943; d. Harold Raymond and Mary Theresa (Swanson) Hastings; m. John Bernard Bohle, June 22, 1974; children: Jason John, Christine K. BS in Journalism, Northwestern U., 1965, MS in Journalism, 1969. Tchr. pub. high schs Englewood, Colo., 1965-68; account exec. Burson-Marsteller Pub. Relations, Los Angeles, 1969-73; v.p., mgr. pub. relations J. Walter Thompson Co., Los Angeles, 1973-79; founder, pres. The Bohle Company, L.A., 1979—; former exec. v.p. Ketchum Pub. Rels., L.A.; free-lance writer, instr. communications Calif. State U. at Fullerton, 1972-73; instr. writing Los Angeles City Coll., 1975-76; lectr. U. So. Calif., 1979—. Contbr. articles to profl. jours. Dir. pub. rels. L.A. Jr. Ballet, 1971-72; pres. Panhellenic Advisers Coun., UCLA, 1972-73; mem. adv. bd. L.A. Valley Coll., 1974-75, Coll. Communications Pepperdine U., 1981-85, Sch. Journalism U. So. Calif., 1987—, Calif. State U., Long Beach, 1988-93; bd. visitors Medill Sch. Journalism Northwestern U., 1984—. Recipient Alumni Svc. award Northwestern U., 1995; Univ. scholar, 1961-64, Panhellenic scholar, 1964-65. Fellow Pub. Rels. Soc. Am. (bd. dirs. L.A. chpt. 1981-90, v.p. 1983, pres. 1989, del. nat. assembly 1980, co-chmn. long-range strategic com. 1990, pres.'s adv. coun. 1991, exec. com. Counselors Acad. 1984-86, sec.-treas. 1990, chmn. 1992, sec. Coll. Fellows 1993, chmn. 1995); mem. Pub. Rels. Orgn. Internat. (U.S. founder, bd. dirs. 1994—), Women in Comm., Shi-ai, Delta Zeta (editor The Lamb 1966-68, Woman of Yr. award 1993), Kappa Alpha Tau. Office: Ste 550 1999 Avenue of the Stars Los Angeles CA 90067-6022

BOHLKEN, DEBORAH KAY, banking executive, government consultant, lobbyist; b. Anchorage, Nov. 16, 1952; d. Darrell Richard and Gertrude Ann (Merkel) B. BA, U. Ark., 1975, MSW, 1977. Specialist community devel. State of Ark., Little Rock, 1976-77, supr. community area, 1977-78, mgr. evaluation and data processing, 1978-80; corp. analyst Systematics, Inc., Little Rock, 1980-83, mgr. corp. planning and rsch., 1983-85, group mgr. planning, rsch., Washington Congl. liasion, 1985-89, 91—, corp. mgr. legis. and regulatory, legal dept., 1990-91; mktg., planning and devel. mgr. Systematics, Inc., 1992-95; mgr. legis. and regulatory govt. svcs. Systematics Info. Svcs., Inc., Little Rock, 1992-95; v.p. ALLTEL Info. Svcs., Little Rock, 1994-95; pres. BCA, Inc., Little Rock, 1995—; pres. BCA, Inc., Little Rock, 1996. Contbr. articles and papers to profl. publs. Bd. dirs. Cen. Ark. Radiation Therapy Inst. Hotline, Little Rock, 1980-82, Cancer Soc., Little Rock, 1986-89; state chair Cansurmount, Little Rock, 1985-89. Nat. Juvenile Justice Law Enforcement Adminstrn. explimary data processing grantee, 1976-78. Mem. NAFE, Nat. Assn. Bank Svcs., Fin. Mgrs. Assn., Am. Mgmt. Assn. Methodist. Office: BCA Inc 1817 Foreman Dr Little Rock AR 72212

BOHM, SHERRY E(LLEN), preschool director; b. Phila., May 11, 1954; d. Eddie Benjamin and Anne Kate (Press) Press; m. Michael N. Bohm, May 30, 1976; children: Mendel, Ariella, Joseph, Elan. BS in Early Childhood, Temple U., 1975, MA in Elem. Edn., 1977; postgrad., Gratz Coll., 1982. Cert. elem., early childhood tchr., Pa. Tchr. Harry B. Kellman Acad., Cherry Hill, N.J., 1975-81; tchr. Adath Jeshurun Pre-Sch. and Kindergarten, Elkins Park, Pa., 1982-86, pre-sch. coord., 1986—, pre-sch. dir., 1989—. Sisterhood pres. cong. B'nai Israel Ohev Zidek, Phila., 1992-94. Grantee Auerbach Ctrl. Agy. for Jewish Edn., 1989-90, 93-94, 94-95, Winner of Tchr. initiated project, 1989; recipient Jewish Heritage award Assn. of Orthodox Jewish Tchrs., 1995. Mem. Early Childhood Coun. of Auerbach Ctrl. Agy. for Jewish Educators, Nat. Assn. for the Edn. of Young Children, Del. Valley Assn. for the Edn. of Young Children. Jewish. Home: 2103 Emerson St Philadelphia PA 19152-2406 Office: Adath Jeshurun Presch & Kindergarten 7763 Old York Rd Elkins Park PA 19027

BOHN, CHARLOTTE GALITZ, real estate executive; b. Chgo., Aug. 7, 1930; d. Chester Charles and Sarah Madelyn (McCarthy) B; m. Robert Allan Galitz, Nov. 25, 1955; children: Charles Robert, Thomas Allan, Madelyn Clare, (div. Sept. 1965). Student, Northwestern U., 1955, City Coll., Chgo., 1989. Lic. real estate salesperson, N.C. Lab. tech. Kraft Foods Rsch. Lab., Glenview, Ill., 1950-56; researcher data processing control Kemper Ins. Co., Chgo., 1967-70; jr. acct. Tractor Supply Co., Chgo., 1970-75; real estate salesman MGM Realty Co., Chgo., 1975-81, 85-88, Prime Realty, 1989—; broker Bohn Real Estate Agy, Raleigh, N.C., 1981-85; founder, pres. Pvt. Rsch., Chgo., 1985—; researcher zoning map City of Raleigh, 1980-81; bd. dirs. Off-Campus Writers Workshop. Contbr. various rsch. projects and sci. proposals. Vol. Chgo. Boys' Club; treas. churchwomen of St. Mary's, Crystal Lake, Ill.; vol. lifeguard Easter Seal Soc.-Multiple Sclerosis, Raleigh, 1983-84, PTA, 1967-77; bd. dirs. Off-Campus Writer's Workshop; chair grammar sch. 50th reunion, 1994; scholarship judge Mensa, Chgo., 1995, 96. Recipient Adviser Emblem of Merit award Jr. Achievement, 1955. Mem. AAAS, Smithsonian Inst. (assoc.), Nat. Trust Hist. Preservation, Raleigh C. of C., Jaycee Aux. (restaurant mgr.), Chgo. N. Side Realty Bd., Nat. Geog. Soc., Wilson Ctr. Assn., Mensa (nominating), Am. Assn. Ret. Persons, Irish Am. Heritage Ctr., Libr. Congress (assoc. charter). Roman Catholic. Home: 6126 W Roscoe St Chicago IL 60634 Office: Private Rsch 6126 W Roscoe St Chicago IL 60634-4145

BOHN, DONNA SCHUHMANN, accountant; b. Louisville, Feb. 5, 1959; d. George Nicholas and Helen Rachel (Flood) Schuhmann; m. Bruce Allen Bohn, Oct. 8, 1983; 1 child, Geoffrey Allen. BS in Acctg., U. Ky., 1981; MBA, Bellarmine Coll., 1986. Acct. Brown & Williamson Tobacco Corp., Louisville, 1982-84, supr., 1984-91, analyst market rsch., 1991-94, sr. fin. analyst, 1994—; Bd. dirs., treas. B & W Fed. Credit Union, Louisville, 1993-95. Vol. Vols. Am., Louisville, 1992-94. Mem. Inst. Mgmt. Accts. (bd. dirs. 1981-96), Toastmasters Internat. (pres., v.p., sec./treas.). Democrat. Roman Catholic. Home: 8099 Regency Woods Way Louisville KY 40220 Office: Brown & Williamson Tobacco Corp PO Box 35090 Louisville KY 40232

BOHN, SUSAN B., bank executive; b. Pitts., 1945. Grad., U. Pitts., 1983. Exec. v.p. corp. devel. and comms. PNC Bank Corp., Pitts., 1994—. Office: PNC Bank Corp One PNC Plaza Fifth Ave and Wood St Pittsburgh PA 15265*

BOHNE, CORAL L., public relations specialist; b. Anchorage, Alaska, June 2, 1958; d. Dwight Dean and Jacqueline Marie (Day) Robinson; m. Scott Allen Bohne, Aug. 27, 1983; children: Tavis Lee, Nicole Marie. BBA, Pacific Luth. U., 1980; MBA, Alaska Pacific U., 1991. Front desk mgr. Sheffield Anchorage/Travelodge, Alaska, 1980-81; adminstrv. asst. to v.p. marketing Sheffield Hotels/Westmark, Anchorage, 1981-86; owner Adminstrv. Assistance, Anchorage, 1986-88; adminstrv. asst. to pres. Alaska Pacific U., Anchorage, 1988-91; asst. v.p. pub. rels. Key Bank of Alaska, Anchorage, 1991—. Comm. chair March of Dimes Walk Am., 1993-95; organizer Key Bank Alaska Neighbors Make the Difference, 1992-95; mem. coordinating com. United Way Day of Caring, 1994, 96; mem. vol. com. Kids Vote, 1993-96; mem. dinner of champiions com. Multiple Sclerosis Soc. Alaska, 1994-96. Mem. Am. Mktg. Assn. (treas. 1991-96, AMI award 1993), Pub. Rels. Soc. Am. (Aurora award 1992, Excellence award 1993-95). Lutheran. Home: 13931 Venus Way Anchorage AK 99515 Office: Key Bank Alaska 101 W Benson Blvd Anchorage AK 99503

BOHNE, JEANETTE KATHRYN, mathematics and science educator; b. Quincy, Ill., June 7, 1936; d. Anton Henry and Hilda Wilhelminia (Ohnemus) B. BA, Ursuline Coll., Louisville, 1961; MA, St. Louis U., 1962. Cert. math. and chemistry tchr., N.D., Ill., Mo. Math. tchr. Ryan High Sch., Minot, N.D., 1962-66, Althoff Cath. High Sch., Belleville, Ill., 1966-72, St. Francis Borgia High Sch., Washington, Mo., 1974-77; math. tchr. St. Louis Pub. Schs., 1977—, head dept. math., 1977-85; speaker in field. Treas. Welcome Wagon Club, Washington, 1974-76; pres. Bus. and Profl. Women's Club, Washington, 1978-79; active Animal Protective Assn., Zoo Friends of St. Louis Zoo, S.W. Garden Neighborhood Assn., S.W. Garden Neighborhood Assn. Mobile Patrol. Mem. AAUW, NEA, Mo. State Tchrs. Assn., St. Louis Tchrs. Union, Nat. Coun. Tchrs. Math., Math. Educators Group St. Louis, Mo. Coun. Tchrs. Math., St. Louis Sci. Ctr., Urban Math. Collaborative St. Louis, Math. Assn. Am. Home: PO Box 2252 Saint Louis MO 63109-0252 Office: St Louis Pub Schs 911 Locust St Saint Louis MO 63101-1401

BOHNEN, MOLLYN VILLAREAL, nurse, educator; b. Balete, Aklan, Philippines, Nov. 1, 1941; came to the U.S., 1964; d. Wenceslao and Amparo Villareal; m. Robert Frank Bohnen, MD, June 20, 1965; children: Sharon Kay Taylor, Scott Owen David, Paul Alan. BSN, U. Philippines, 1962; MSN, U. Utah, 1971; EdD, U. San Francisco, 1984. Staff nurse U. Philippines Med. Ctr., Manila, 1962-64, St. Lukes Hosp., N.Y.C., 1964-65, Greystone Park Hosp., Morristown, N.J., 1965, Buffalo (N.Y.) Children's Hosp., 1965-66; vol. staff nurse Peace Corps, Cebu City, Philippines, 1966-68; asst. prof. Calif. State U., Sacramento, 1973-76, 82-84, lectr., 1979-82, assoc. prof., 1984-87, prof., 1987—; instr. Am. River Coll., Sacramento, 1977-78; medico-legal cons. Calif. law firms, 1975—; internat. nursing edn. cons. B/B Creation, Rancho Cordova, Calif., 1988—. Contbr. various articles in national and international profl. jours. Recipient J.V. Sotejo Medallion of Honor for national and international innovation and leadership in Nursing, U. Philippines, 1994. Mem. NAFE, ANA Calif., Golden Key, U. Philippines Nursing Alumni Assn. Internat., Sigma Theta Tau (treas. Zeta Eta chpt. 1982-84, rsch. award 1984), Phi Delta Kappa. Democrat. Roman Catholic. Home: 1441 Wild Plum Ct Klamath Falls OR 97601-1983 Office: Calif State U 6000 J St Sacramento CA 95819-6069

BOILEAU, NANETTE ERIKA, curator; b. Seattle, Mar. 9, 1965; d. Oliver Clark and Nan Elze (Halen) B. BFA, So. Meth. U., 1988; MFA, Pasadena Art Ctr. Coll. Design, 1994. Sales clk. Function Junction, St. Louis, 1987-88, Famous Barr, St. Louis, 1989; asst. mgr. Gourmet to Go, St. Louis, 1988-89; front desk clk. South Seas Plantation, Captiva, Fla., 1989-90; rm. reservationist Hotel Queen Mary, Long Beach, Calif., 1990-92; tchg. asst. Art Ctr., Pasadena, Calif., 1992-94; sec. OCB Inc., St. Louis, 1995; curator St. Louis U., 1996—. Office: MacLennan Gallery of Asian Art Busch Meml Ctr 20 N Grand Blvd Saint Louis MO 63103

BOIMAN, DONNA RAE, artist, art academy executive; b. Columbus, Ohio, Jan. 13, 1946; d. George Brandle and Donna Rae (Rockwell) Hall; m. David Charles Boiman, Dec. 8, 1973 (div. Aug. 1990). BS in Pharmacy, Ohio State U., 1969; student, Columbus Coll. Art & Design, 1979-83. Registered pharmacist, Ohio. Pharmacist, mgr. various retail stores, Cleve., 1970-73, Columbus, 1973-77; owner L'Artiste, Reynoldsburg, Ohio, 1977-81; pres. Cen. Ohio Art Acad., Reynoldsburg, 1981-90, Art Acad. Ctrl. Ohio, Reynoldsburg, 1990—; owner Big Red Designs, Reynoldsburg, 1989—; pub. rels. mgr. Freedom Farm Equestrian Ctr., Pataskala, Ohio, 1991—; cons. to Mayor City of Reynoldsburg, 1986-87; owner Ctrl. Ohio Art Graphics/Design/Website Design. Represented in permanent collections including Collector's Gallery Columbus Mus. Art, Gallery 200, Columbus Art Exch., The Huntington Collection, Dean Witter Reynolds Collection, Zanesville Art Ctr., Mt. Carmel East Hosp., Columbus, Corp. 2005, Radisson Hotels, Mich. and Ohio, Fifth 3d Bank, Bexley, Ohio, On Line Computer Libr., Dublin, Ohio; author: Anatomy Made Easy: Draw, Color and Learn, Anatomy and Structure: A Guide for Young Artists, 1988. Recipient John Lennon Meml. Award for the Arts, Internat. Art Challenge com., 1987. Mem. Pa. Soc. Watercolorists, Nat. Soc. Layerists in Multimedia, Columbus Art League, Cen. Ohio Watercolor Soc. (pres. 1983-84), Am. Quarter Horse Assn., Ohio Quarter Horse Assn., Allied Artists of Am. (assoc.), Licking County Art Assn., Nat. Wildlife Fedn., Ohio State U. Alumni Assn., Ohio State U. Pharmacy Alumni Assn. (charter), Mid-Ohio Dressage Assn., U.S. Dressage Fedn., Ohio Arabian Horse Assn., Internat. Arabian Horse Assn., Arabian Sport Assn., Inc. Office: Art Acad of Cen Ohio 7297 E Main St Reynoldsburg OH 43068-2105

BOISE, AUDREY LORRAINE, education educator; b. Hackensack, N.J., Feb. 12, 1933; d. Paul George and Lillian Rose (Goedecker) B. BA, Wellesley (Mass.) Coll., 1955; MA, Fairleigh Dickinson U., 1977. Cert. tchr. K-8, learning disabilities, supervision. Tchr. Township of Berkeley Heights (N.J.), 1958-67; learning cons. Borough of New Providence (N.J.), 1978-82, 1986—, Scotch Plains/Fanwood (N.J.), 1984-86; instr. Fairleigh Dickinson U., Madison, N.J., 1983, 1975-76; several other short-term teaching positions; supr. student tchrs., 1975-78; lectr. on fgn. countries and U.S. History, N.J., 1967—; travel agt. (part-time) 1972—. Mem. Rep. Nat. Com. Campaign Coun., Nat. Rep. Senatorial Com., Washington, Rep. Presdl. Task Force, Washington, Rep. Presdl. Legion of Merit, N.J. State Rep. Com., Trenton, Nat. Fedn. Rep. Women, Washington. Mem. NEA, AAUW, N.J. Assn. Learning Cons., Assn. for Children with Learning Disabilities, N.J. Edn. Assn., Internat. Platform Assn., Fortnightly Club, Hist. Soc. Summit. Methodist. Office: New Providence Bd Edn Dept Spl Svcs 360 Elkwood Ave New Providence NJ 07974

BOK, JOAN TOLAND, utility executive; b. Grand Rapids, Mich., Dec. 31, 1929; d. Don Prentiss Weaver and Mary Emily (Anderson) T.; m. John Fairfield Bok, July 15, 1955; children: Alexander Toland, Geoffrey Robbins. AB, Radcliffe Coll., 1951; JD, Harvard U., 1955. Bar: Mass. 1955. Assoc. Ropes & Gray, Boston, 1955-61; pvt. practice Boston, 1961-68; atty. New England Electric Sys., Westborough, Mass., 1968-73, asst. to pres., 1973-77, v.p., sec., 1977-79, vice chmn., 1979-84, chmn., 1984—, pres., CEO, 1988-89; bd. dirs. New England Power Co., Avery Denison Corp., Monsanto Co., John Hancock Mut. Life Ins. Co. Bd. dirs. Nat. Osteoporosis Found., Pine St. Inn; trustee Libr. of Boston Athenaeum, Urban Inst., Worcester Found. for Biomed. Rsch., Woods Hole (Mass.) Oceanog. Instn.; past pres. bd. overseers Harvard U.; mem. corp. Mass. Gen. Hosp. Fellow Am. Bar Found.; mem. ABA, Boston Bar Assn., Am. Acad. Arts and Scis., Phi Beta Kappa. Unitarian. Home: 53 Pinckney St Boston MA 02114-4801 Office: New England Electric System 25 Research Dr Westborough MA 01582-0001

BOK, SISSELA, philosopher, writer; b. Stockholm, Dec. 2, 1934; d. Gunnar and Alva (Reimer) Myrdal; m. Derek Bok, May 7, 1955; children—Hilary, Victoria, Tomas. BA, George Washington U., 1957, MA, 1958, LHD (hon.), 1986; PhD, Harvard U., 1970; LLD (hon.), Mt. Holyoke Coll., 1985; LHD (hon.), Clark U., 1988, U. Mass., 1991, Georgetown U., 1992. Lectr. Simmons Coll., Boston, 1971-72; lectr. Harvard-MIT Div. Health Scis. and Tech., Cambridge, 1975-82, Harvard U., Cambridge, 1982-84; assoc. prof. philosophy Brandeis U., Waltham, Mass., 1985-89, prof. philosophy, 1989-92; fellow Ctr. for Advanced Study, Stanford, Calif., 1991-92; Disting. fellow Harvard Ctr. Population and Devel. Studies, Cambridge, Mass., 1993—; mem. ethics adv. bd. HEW, 1977-80; bd. dirs. Population Coun., 1971-77; mem. Pulitzer Prize Bd., 1988-97, chmn., 1996-97. Author: Lying: Moral Choice in Public and Private Life, 1978 (Melcher award, George Orwell award), Secrets: On the Ethics of Concealment and Revelation, 1982, Alva: Ett kvinnoliv, 1987, A Strategy for Peace, 1989, Alva Myrdal: A Daughter's Memoir, 1991 (Melcher award), Common Values, 1995; mem. editl. bd. Ethics, 1980-85, Criminal Justice Ethics, 1980—, Contention, 1990—, Common Knowledge, 1991—. Bd. dirs. Inst. for Philosophy and Religion, Boston U.; mem. Pulitzer Prize Bd., 1989—. Recipient Abram L. Sachar Silver medallion Brandeis U., 1985, Radcliffe Coll. Grad. Soc. medal, 1993, Barnard Coll. medal of distinction, 1995. Fellow Hastings Ctr. (dir. 1976-84, 94—); mem. Am. Philos. Assn.

BOK, VICTORIA, community developer; b. Boston, Sept. 18, 1961; d. Derek Curtis and Sissela Ann (Myrdal) B. BA, Yale U., 1983; M of Pub. Policy, Harvard U., 1987. Mgmt. analyst Mass. Housing Fin. Agy., Boston, 1987-89; exec. dir. Salem (Mass.) Harbor Cmty. Devel. Corp., 1989-94; dir. City of New Haven (Conn.) Office Housing, 1994-95; mem. local adv. com. Local Initiatives Support Corp., New Haven, 1994—; bd. dirs. Elm Terr. Devel. Corp., New Haven; mem. exec. com. Mass. Assn. Cmty. Devel. Corps., Boston, 1989-94; mem. Partnership Enhance Neighborhoods, New Haven, 1994—; cons. The Cmty. Builders, 1996—. Mem. steering com. Habitat for Humanity Women's Build, New Haven, 1995. Recipient Yale U. Tyler award, New Haven, 1981, Salem Harbor Cmty. Devel. Corp. Appreciation award, 1994. Democrat.

BOKUNIEWICZ, MARY ANTOINETTE, fundraising executive; b. Detroit, Sept. 20, 1948; d. Leonard Anthony and Josephine (Juszczyk) B. B.Bus., U. N.Mex., 1988. Devel. dir. KUNM-FM Pub. Radio, Albuquerque, 1989—. Host, prodr. weekly freeform music program KUNM-FM, 1983—. Recipient Local Radio Devel. award for excellence in individual support Corp. for Pub. Broadcasting, 1991, Carol Burnett/U. Hawaii/AEJMC Ethics prize 2d place Assn. for Edn. in Journalism and Mass. Comm., 1987. Mem. Pub. Radio Assn. of Devel. Officers, Alliance for Pub. Broadcasting (v.p. 1995—). Office: Univ of New Mexico KUNM-FM Public Radio Albuquerque NM 87131-1011

BOLAND, PATRICIA ANN, museum director; b. Rochester, N.Y., Aug. 24, 1935; d. James Patrick and Florence Elva (Miller) Neary; m. Gerald Patrick Boland, June 30, 1956 (wid. June 1989); children: Patrick, Matthew, Daniel, Timothy, Sheila, Catherine. Student, Nazareth Coll., Rochester, N.Y., 1952-54. Tchr. St. Michael's Sch., Rochester, 1954-56, St. Peter and Paul Sch., Rochester, 1956-57; edn. dir. Ontario County Hist. Soc., Canandaigua, N.Y., 1972-81; city coun. mem. City of Canandaigua, 1975-79, mayor, 1979-85; owner Gourmet Deli, Canandaigua, 1983-84; dir. Granger Homestead Soc., Canandaigua, 1989—; bd. dirs. Canandaigua Nat. Bank; lectr. Irish history and culture. Author articles on various aspects of Irish history and culture. Mem. Canandaigua Dem. Com., 1975—, Ontario County Dem. Com., 1975—; elected to Ontario County Bd. Suprs., 1991-93; bd. dirs. Bristol Valley Playhouse, Naples, N.Y., 1980-87, Neighbor-to-Neighbor, Canandaigua, 1985—. Recipient William Mitchell award Canandaigua C. of C., 1989, Main St. award N.Y. State, HUD award, 1984. Office: Granger Homestead Soc 295 N Main St Canandaigua NY 14424-1228

BOLAÑOS, MARITZA F., lawyer, musician; d. Andres and Delia (Pereira) B. BM, U. Mich., 1974; MM, Juilliard Sch., N.Y.C., 1976; JD, Fordham U., 1992. Cert. in law Univ. Complutense, Madrid, 1990; bar: N.J., 1993, N.Y., 1994. Prin. harpist Symphony Orch. Mavacaito, Venezuela, 1977-80; law clk. U.S. Dist. Cts. (ea. and so. dists.) N.Y., 1992-94; associate Epstein Becker & Green, P.C., N.Y.C., 1994-95; articles editor Fordham Internat. Law Jour., N.Y.C., 1990-92. Bd. dirs. Thalia Spanish Theatre, N.Y.C., 1995—. Mem. ABA, World Harp Congress (com. mem. 1985—), Hispanic Nat. Bar Assn. (pres. N.Y. region 1995—), Assn. Bar of City of N.Y. (inter-Am. affairs com. 1992—), Juilliard Sch. Alumni Assn., Fordham Law L.Am. Alumni Assn. (pres. 1993-96). Office: Ste 5H 241 Ave of the Americas New York NY 10014-7500

BOLEJACK, SHELLY BESS, secondary education educator; b. Topeka, Mar. 22, 1967; d. Gary Robert and Shirley Sue (Goodwin) Evans; m. Richard Jay Bolejack, Dec. 21, 1991. BA, Washburn U., 1989. English tchr. Robinson Middle Sch., Topeka, 1989—; drug and alcohol intervention specialist Unified Sch. Dist. #501, Topeka, 1990-91; drug and alcohol group leader Robinson Middle Sch., Topeka, 1990-91. Recipient Women Educator Hon. Sorority award Alpha Delta Kappa, Topeka, 1994. Mem. Alpha Phi Sorority (alumni). Republican. Baptist. Office: Robinson Middle Sch 1125 SW 14th St Topeka KS 66604-2906

BOLENE, MARGARET ROSALIE STEELE, bacteriologist, civic worker; b. Kingfisher, Okla., July 11, 1923; d. Clarence R. and Harriet (White) Steele; student Oreg. State U., 1943-44; B.S., U. Okla., 1946; m. Robert V. Bolene, Feb. 6, 1948; children: Judith Kay, John Eric, Sally Sue, Janice Lynn, Daniel William. Technician bacteriology dept. Okla. Dept. Health, Oklahoma City, 1946-48; asst. bacteriologist Henry Ford Hosp., Detroit, 1948-49; bacteriol. cons., also asst. bus. mgr. Ponca Gynecology and Obstetrics, Inc., 1956-92, retired. Organizing dir. Bi-Racial Council, 1963; lay adviser Home Nursing Service, 1967-68; mem. exec. bd. PTA, 1956-71; active various community drives; sponsor Am. Field Service; patron Ponca Playhouse; bloodmobile vol. ARC; vol. Helpline. Republican precinct organizer, 1960. Mem. AAUW (treas. 1964-66), DAR (life, sec.-treas. 1961-67, 1st vice regent 1972-73, chpt. treas. 1974-84, chpt. chaplain 1991—, state schs. chmn. 1990-94), Kay-Noble County Med. Aux. (treas. 1957-58, 66-67), Ponca City Art Assn., Pioneer Hist. Soc., Okla. Heritage Assn., Okla. Hist. Soc., Daus. Founders and Patriots (life, state pres. 1980-84, registrar 1993—), Nat. Huguenot Soc., Hereditary Order First Families Mass. Daus. Am. Colonists (chpt. regent 1982-84, state flag chmn. 1990-92), Magna Charta Dames (treas. Okla. chpt. 1984), Order Colonial Physicians and Chirurgiens (life), Ancient and Honorable Arty. Co. Women Descs. Okla. Ct. (life, treas. 1983-84, registrar 1986—), Dames of Ct. of Honor, Colonial Dames of 17th Century, Daus. of Colonial Wars, Colonial Daus. 17th Century, U. Okla. Assn. (life), Lambda Tau, Phi Sigma, Alpha Lambda Delta. Presbyterian (elder 1983-86). Clubs: Ponca City Country, Ponca City Music, Red Rose Garden (pres. 1983-84, treas. 1993-95), Twentieth Century (rec. sec. 1992-94). Home: 2116 Juanito Ave Ponca City OK 74604-3813

BOLES, LENORE UTAL, nurse psychotherapist, educator; b. N.Y.C., July 3, 1929; d. Joseph Leo and Dorothy (Grosby) Utal; m. Morton Schloss, Dec. 17, 1955 (div. May 1961); 1 child, Howard Alan Schloss; m. Sam Boles, May 24, 1962; children: Anne Leslie, Laurence Utal; stepchildren: Harlan Arnold, Robert Gerald. Diploma in nursing, Beth Israel Hosp. Sch. Nursing, 1951; BSN, Columbia U., 1964; MSN, U. Conn., 1977. Lic. clin. specialist in adult psychiatry/ mental health nursing, advanced practice registered nurse. Staff nurse Beth Israel Hosp., N.Y.C., 1951, Kingsbridge VA Hosp., Bronx, N.Y., 1951-55; night supr. Gracie Square Hosp., N.Y.C., 1959-60; head nurse Elmhurst City Hosp., Queens, N.Y., 1960-62; nursing instr. Norwalk (Conn.) Hosp., 1966-74; asst. prof. U. Bridgeport, Conn., 1976-78; nurse psychotherapist Nurse Counseling Group, Norwalk, 1979—; nursing faculty Western Conn. State U., Danbury, 1978-80; adj. asst. prof Sacred Heart U., Bridgeport, Conn., 1983-89; adj. faculty Western Conn. State U., Danbury, 1994; nurse cons. Bradley Meml. Hosp., Southington, Conn., 1982, Lea Manor Nursing Home, Norwalk, 1982, St. Vincent's Hosp., Bridgeport, 1982-92; staff devel. nurse Silver Hill Hosp., New Canaan, Conn., 1980-86, 94; cons. in field, 1980—. Author: (book chpt.) Nursing Diagnoses for Psychiatric Nursing Practice, 1994. V.p. Sisterhood Beth El, Norwalk, 1969-71; bd. dirs. religious sch. Congregation Beth El, Norwalk, 1971-75, 79-80, rec. sec. bd. trustees, 1975-77, v.p. congregation, 1977-80, bd. trustees, 1980-83. Named Speaker of Yr., So. Fairfield County chpt. Am. Cancer Soc., 1976. Mem. ANA, Northeastern Nursing Diagnosis Assn. (chair N.E. region conf. 1985, chair planning com. 1984-85, chair nominating com. 1989-91), N.Am. Nursing Diagnosis Assn., Coun. Psychiat./Mental Health Clin. Specialists, Conn. Nurses Assn. (Del. to convs. 1977—, legis. com. dist. 3 1984-86, nominating com. 1988-90, Florence Wald award 1984, Conn. Nursing Diagnosis Conf. Group 1980-87), Conn. Soc. Nurse Psychotherapists (founding mem.). Democrat. Jewish. Home: 173 E Rocks Rd Norwalk CT 06851-1715 Office: Nurse Counseling Group 150 East Ave Norwalk CT 06851-5717

BOLEY, DONNA JEAN, state legislator; b. Bens Run, W.Va., Dec. 9, 1935; d. Glen A. and Grace (Jones) Northcraft; m. Jack Edward Boley, 1956; children: Kari Lynn, Brian Lee. Student, W.Va. U., Parkersburg. Chmn. Pleasant County Rep. Exec. Com., 1978—; mem. W.Va. Senate, 1986—; chmn. Rep. Platform. Com., W.Va.; 1st woman minority leader State Senate, 1991, 92, 93, 94, 95, 96. Mem. Nat. Rep. Platform Com. from W.Va., Houston, 1992; exec. com. Nat. Rep. Com., 1992, W. Va. nat. committeewoman, 1992, 93, 94, 95, 96. Mem. St. Marys Women's Club (pres. 1972-74, 80-81). Republican. Methodist. Office: Sen Minority Office Rm 245-M State Capitol Complex Charleston WV 25305

BOLGER, MARY PHYLLIS JUDGE, special education educator; b. Newark, Aug. 19, 1926; d. Michael Francis and Loretta Margaret (Reinhardt) Judge; m. William Patrick Bolger, Nov. 27, 1948 (dec. May 1973); children: Loretta, Francis, Christopher, Michael. BA, Montclair State U., 1946; MA in Reading Specialist, Seton Hall U., 1973. Cert. reading specialist, tchr. English, social studies, Spanish, and reading; cert. learning disabilites tchr., cons. Tchr. English Bd. Edn., Irvington, N.J., 1946-49; tchr. West Side H.S., Newark, 1963-69; reading specialist Roosevelt Jr. H.S., West Orange, N.J., 1969-77; LDT-C West Orange H.S. and Hazel Ave., 1977-91; tchr. English for fgn. born South Orange (N.J.) -Maplewood Adult Schs., 1949-64; adj. prof. edn. Seton Hall U., South Orange, 1974—; cons. dept. curriculum West Orange Bd. Edn., 1987-94; adv. bd. mem. Prospect House, East Orange, N.J., 1994. Editor: Beyond Common Sense: The Art of Intelligent Living, 1992; editor doctoral dissertations Seton Hall U., 1993—. Eucharistic min. St. Barnabas Hosp., Livingston, N.J., 1991—; pastoral care min. Our Lady of Sorrows, South Orange, 1989—, Rosary Altar Soc. mem., 1955—. Mem. N.J. Reading Assn. (co-chairperson Reading/Learning Disabilities com.), Seton-Essex Reading Coun. (pres., v.p.). Roman Catholic. Home and Office: 258 Audley St South Orange NJ 07079

BOLING, JEWELL, retired government official; b. Randleman, N.C., Sept. 26, 1907; d. John Emmitt and Carrie (Ballard) B. Student, Women's Coll., U. N.C., 1926, Am. U., 1942, 51-52. Interviewer N.C. Employment Service, Winston-Salem, Asheboro, 1937-41; occupational analyst U.S. Dept. Labor, Washington, 1943-57, placement officer, 1957-58, employment service adviser, 1959-61, occupational analyst, 1962, employment service specialist counseling and testing, 1963-69, manpower devel. specialist, 1969-74, ret., 1974. Author: Counselor's Handbook, 1967; Counselor's Desk Aid, Eighteen Basic Vocational Directions, 1967; Handbook for New Careerists in Employment Security, 1971; contbr. articles to profl. publs. Recipient Meritorious Achievement award U.S. Dept. Labor, 1972. Mem. AAAS, ACA, ASCD, AAUW, Am. Rehab. Counseling Assn. (archivist 1964-68), Nat. Capital Astronomers (editor Star Dust 1949-58), Nat. Career Devel. Assn., Internat. Platform Assn., N.Y. Acad. Scis., Assn. Measurement in Counseling and Devel., Assn. Humanistic Psychology, Planetary Soc., Smithsonians, Sierra Club, Nature Conservancy, Audubon Naturalist Soc., Wilderness Soc. Address: 5071 Us Highway 220 Bus N Randleman NC 27317-7655

BOLING, JUDY ATWOOD, civic worker; b. Madras, India, June 19, 1921 (parents Am. citizens); d. Carroll Eugene and Marion Frances (Ayrer) Atwood; m. Jack Leroy Boling, Apr. 8, 1941 (dec. July 1988); children: Joseph Edward, Jean Ann, James Michael, John Charles. AA, San Antonio Jr. Coll., 1940; student Rogue Community Coll., Grants Pass, Oreg., 1978-79, So. Oreg. State Coll., Ashland, 1982—. Contbr. articles to profl. jours. First aid instr. ARC, various locations, 1940-65, chmn. vols., Calif., 1961-62, Eng., 1964-65; den mother cub scouts Boy Scouts Am., Monterey, Calif., 1951-52; active Girl Scouts U.S., 1953—, coun. pres., Winema (Oreg.) Coun., 1971-73, 79-82, historian, 1990—, del. to nat. coun., 1966, 72, 81, cons. for nat. pubs., 1971, 79; Sunday sch. tchr. Base Chapel, Pyote, Tex., 1949-51, choir dir., 1951; Sunday sch. adminstr. Base Chapel, Morocco, 1954-55; Sunday sch. tchr. Hermon Free Meth. Ch., L.A., 1956-57; active United Way campaign, 1967-84, Childrens Festival, 1974-88; former liaison with local people in Japanese-Am., Franco-Am., Anglo-Am. orgns.; mem., patron Rogue Craftsmen Bd., Grants Pass, 1972-85, sec., 1972-78, v.p., 1978-85; bd. dirs. Rogue Valley Opera Assn., 1978-85, sponsor/mem., 1978—; bd. dirs. Community Concert, 1979-88, 92—, mem. Grants Pass Friends of the Symphony, 1989— (bd. dirs. 1992—); vol. RSVP, 1982—; historian Josephine County Rep. Women, 1982-86, treas., 1986-94, sec., 1994—; elected Rep. precinct committeeperson, 1991—; sustaining mem. Sta. KSYS pub. TV; mem. Sta. KSOR pub. radio; frequent pub. speaker. Recipient Thanks badge Girl Scouts U.S., 1957, 60, 73, Girl Scouts Japan, 1959, U.K. Girl Guides, 1982; others; cert. of appreciation USAF, 1959, City of Hagi, City of Fukuoka (Japan), Gov. of Fukuoka Prefecture; 2 citations Internat. Book Project; Oreg. Vol. award Sen. Packwood, 1983; Community Woman of Year award Bus. and Profl. Women, 1984, Nat. award Juliette Gordon Low World Friendship medal Girl Scouts Am., 1995. Mem. Josephine County Hist. Soc. (bd. dirs. 1991—), So. Oreg. Resources Alliance, Am. Host Found., Friends of Libr., Grants Pass Art Mus., Knife and Fork Club (bd. dirs. 1994—), Phi Theta Kappa. Address: 3016 Jumpoff Joe Creek Rd Grants Pass OR 97526-8778

BOLITHO, LOUISE GREER, educational administrator, consultant; b. Wenatchee, Wash., Aug. 13, 1927; d. Lon Glenn and Edna Gertrude (Dunlap) Greer; m. Douglas Stuart, June 17, 1950 (div. Dec. 1975); children: Rebecca Louise, Brian Douglas. BA, Wash. State U., 1949. With Stanford (Calif.) U., 1967-91, adminstrv. asst. physics labs., 1974-77, mgr. ctr. for research in internat. studies, 1977-84, law sch. fin. and adminstrv. services dir., 1984-86; computer cons., Palo Alto, Calif., 1984—; acting mgr. Inst. for Internat. Studies, 1987-88, fin. analyst, 1988-91. Mem. Peninsula vols., Menlo Park, Calif., 1986-94; budget com. chmn., bd. dirs. Mid-Peninsula Support Network, Mountain View, Calif., 1984-86; chairperson active older adults com. YMCA; pres. 410 Sheridan Ave. Homeowners Assn., 1989-93, treas., 1993—. Mem. AAUW (bd. dirs. 1987-88). Home and Office: 410 Sheridan Ave Apt 445 Palo Alto CA 94306-2020

BOLLING, VALERIE DIANE, elementary education educator; b. Aug. 25, 1965; d. Kathleen Curry. BA in English, Tufts U., 1987; MA in Elem. and Mid. Sch. Edn., Columbia U., 1993. Cert. tchr., Conn., N.Y. Writer, editor Mass. Dept. of Revenue, Boston, 1987-90; vol. Cmty. Svc. Vols., London, 1990-91; counselor Youth Shelter, Greenwich, Conn., 1991-92; tchr. Greenwich (Conn.) Pub. Schs., 1993—; tutor in field. Appeared in plays Am. Justice, 1993, Wine in the Wilderness, 1995, The Art of Dining, 1996, One Monkey Don't Stop No Show, 1996. Named Outstanding Young Woman in Am., 1988; faculty scholar Columbia U., 1992-93. Mem. Tufts U. Alumni Assn. (interviewer 1991—), Kappa Delta Pi.

BOLLINGER, MICHELE ANN, graphic designer, educator; b. Indpls., Dec. 13, 1962; d. Garry Lee and Bernice Ann (Beatty) B. BFA, Herron Sch. of Art, 1988; MFA, Cornell U., 1992. Asst. prof. U. Evansville, Ind., 1992-94; vis. asst. prof. Ill. Wesleyan U., Bloomington, 1994; graphic designer Schenle Hampton, Evansville, 1994-95; pres. Graphic Solutions, Inc., Evansville, Ind., 1996—; mem. continuing edn. faculty, U. So. Ind., Evansville, 1995—. Artist: Pan Am. Games Mural, Indpls., 1986 (Pan Am. XI award 1986); photographer Illustrator) Excavation in Murlo, Italy, 1993 (award for illustration and photography 1993). Office: Graphic Solutions 111 Main St Evansville IN 47734

BOLLINGER, PAMELA BEEMER, health facilities administrator; b. Chgo., Apr. 7, 1947; d. Eldred Harlan and Shirley Pearl (Olsen) Beemer; m. Gary Allen Bollinger, Aug. 23, 1969. BS, Millikin U., 1969. Med. technologist Rush-Presbyt. St. Luke's Med. Ctr., Chgo., 1969-70, exec. technologist, 1975-77; hematology supr. Meml. Hosp. DuPage County, Elmhurst, Ill., 1970-75; chief med. technologist U. Tex.-M.D. Anderson Hosp., Houston, 1977-88; lab. dir. Northeast Med. Ctr. Hosp., Humble, Tex., 1988-93; regional field svc. mgr. Corning Clin. Lab., Irving, Tex., 1994—; cons. Technicon Instruments Corp., Tarrytown, N.Y., 1984-88, Coulter Electronics, Inc., Hialeah, Fla., 1978-83. Contbg. author: Clinical Laboratory Annual, 1984, Phlebotomy Handbook, 1984, Clinical Hematology: Principles, Procedures, Correlations, 1988. Vol. Ponderosa Forest Civic Assn., Houston, 1985, Muscular Dystrophy Assn., Houston, 1980-81. Mem. Am. Soc. Clin. Pathology (cert.), Am. Soc. Med. Tech. (Joseph J. Kleiner meml. award 1985), Tex. Soc. Med. Tech. Home: 5037 Albany Dr Plano TX 75093-5076 Office: Baylor Univ Med Ctr 3600 Gaston Dallas TX 75246

BOLLINGER, SHARON MOORE, psychotherapist; b. Cape Girardeau, Mo., May 27, 1949; d. Raymond V. and Lucille (Broshuis) Moore; m. Skip Bollinger, Aug. 30, 1968; children: Kristell, Amber. AA, St. Louis C.C., 1988; BA in Psychology, Lindenwood Coll., St. Charles, Mo., 1990, MA in Profl. Counseling, 1992; postgrad., St. Louis U., 1996. Computer operator Clothworld/Brown Group, St. Louis, 1986-88; grad. asst. Lindenwood Coll., St. Charles, 1990-92; dir. social svcs. Wentzville (Mo.) Park Care Ctr., 1993—. Author and presenter in field. Vol. counselor St. Joseph's Health Ctr.-Hospice, St. Charles, 1991, All Saints Ch., St. Peters, Mo., 1992. Mem. ACA, Mo. Counseling Assn., St. Louis Counseling Assn., Alzheimers Assn., Phi Theta Kappa, Alpha Sigma Tau.

BOLLS, IMOGENE LAMB, English language educator; b. Manhattan, Kans., Sept. 25, 1938; d. Don Q. and Helen Letson (Keithley) Lamb; Nathan J. Bolls., Jr., Nov. 24, 1962; 1 child, Laurel Helen. BA, Kans. State U., 1960; MA, U. Utah, 1962. Instr. French Kans. State U., Manhattan, 1959-60; instr. English U. Utah, Salt Lake City, 1960-62; instr. to assoc. prof. Wittenberg U., Springfield, Ohio, 1963—; poet in residence, dir. journalism program Wittenberg U.; tchg. poet Antioch Writers' Workshop Antioch Coll., summers 1992-93, intensive seminar poet, summer 1994; poetry tchr. Ohio Poet-in-the-Schs. program, 1972-82; poetry instr. acad. camp. Author: (poetry) Glass Walker, 1983, Earthbound; work represented in anthologies including Ohio Women: Poems, 1989; contbr. more than 500 poems to mags. Recipient Individual Artist award Ohio Arts Coun., 1982, 90, Poetry prize S.D. Rev., 1983, Poetry award Kans. Quarterly, 1985, Ohioana Poetry award Ohioana Libr. Assn., 1995; finalist Vassar Miller Prize in Poetry, 1994; grantee Ireland, 1986, France, 1990, Am. Southwest. Mem. Acad. Am. Poets (assoc.), Poetry Soc. Am., Women in Comm. Office: Wittenberg U Dept English PO Box 720 Springfield OH 45501*

BOLOGNIA, JEAN LYNN, academic dermatologist; b. Hammond, Ind., July 1, 1954; d. John Paul and Jo Ann (Dill) B.; m. Dennis Lawrence Cooper, Aug. 25, 1985. BA summa cum laude, Rutgers U., 1976; MD cum laude, Yale U., 1980. Diplomate Nat. Bd. Med. Examiners, Am. Bd. Dermatology. Intern, resident in internal medicine Yale-New Haven Hosp., 1980-82, resident in dermatology, 1982-85; rsch. fellow dermatology Yale U. Sch. Medicine, New Haven, 1985-87, asst. prof. dermatology, 1987-93, assoc. prof. dermatology, 1993—; mem. coalition for dermatol. care women Am. Acad. Dermatology/Soc. Investigative Dermatology, Schaumburg, Ill., 1994—; med. coun. Skin Cancer Found., N.Y.C., 1995—; lectr. more than 20 univs. and internat. meetings. Author: (book chpt.) Harrison's Principles Internal Medicine, 1990, 94, 96; contbr. articles to profl. jours. including Nature, Jour. Investigative Dermatology, Archives Dermatology; mem. editl. bd. Jour. Women's Health, Pigment Cell Rsch., Current Opinion in Dermatology. Recipient Individual Nat. Rsch. award Nat. Inst. Cancer, 1987-89; rsch. fellow Dermatology Found., 1985. Mem. Am. Acad. Dermatology (melanoma/skin cancer com. 1995—, regulatory guidelines 1994-96, interdisciplinary edn. com. 1996—), Am. Fedn. for Clin. Rsch., Soc. for Investigative Dermatology (resident/fellow program com. 1996—), Am.

Bd. Dermatology (in-house tng. exam com. 1996—), Women's Dermatol. Soc. (chair networking com. 1996—), Alpha Omega Alpha. Office: Yale U Sch Medicine 500 LCI 333 Cedar St New Haven CT 06520

BOLOTIN, LORA M., business owner, electronics executive; b. Dallas; d. Joseph and Bertha Marshall; m. M. L. Bolotin, June 21, 1953; children: Linda Susan, Scott Evan, Kent Carter. BA in Edn., Roosevelt U., 1952; postgrad., UCLA, 1980, Calif. State U., Northridge, 1988. Cert. tchr., Ill. Tchr. Chgo. Bd. Edn., 1952-55; v.p. Bolotin Assocs., Inc., Woodland Hills, Calif., 1973-83, pres., 1984-96. Art Inst. of Chgo. scholar, 1946; recipient 2 Sterling Silver Art medals, Am. Legion, 1946, 47. Home: 16663 Calneva Dr Encino CA 91436-4167 Office: Bolotin Assocs Inc 21241 Ventura Blvd Ste 268 Woodland Hills CA 91364-2108

BOLSTAD, ROSE IRENE, singer, songwriter; b. Ayrshire, Iowa, Sept. 6, 1927; d. Grover Cleveland and Myrtle Irene (Dannewitz) Maiden; m. Bernard Austin Bolstad, June 17, 1950; children: Gordon Bernard, Margot Rose. BA, U. No. Iowa, 1948; MA, Ctrl. Wash. U., 1972. Elem. instr. music, sub. music tchr. Bremerton (Wash.) Sch. Dist., 1948-64; kindergarten, second grade tchr. Port Orchard (Wash.) Sch. Dist., 1964-67; sub. tchr. Bremerton Sch. Dist., 1967-80, Port Orchard Sch. Dist., 1983-84; pvt. voice and piano tchr., Bremerton, 1969-74. Choir dir. Navy Chapel, Bremerton, 1972-74, First Meth. Ch., Bremerton, 1950-52; dir. orch. First Bapt. Ch., Bremerton, 1969-74; organist Navy Chapel, 1979-83. Mem. ASCAP, Women in the Arts. Democrat. Baptist. Home: PO Box 4197 West Hills Sta Bremerton WA 98312

BOLSTER, JACQUELINE NEBEN (MRS. JOHN A. BOLSTER), communications consultant; b. Woodhaven, N.Y.; d. Ernest William Benedict and Emily Claire (Guck) Neben; student Pratt Inst., Columbia U.; m. John A. Bolster, May 8, 1954. Promotion mgr. Photoplay mag., 1949-53; merchandising mgr. McCall's, N.Y.C., 1953-64; dir. promotion and merchandising Harper's Bazaar, N.Y.C., 1964-71; dir. advt. and promotion Elizabeth Arden Salons, N.Y.C., 1971-76; dir. creative services Elizabeth Arden, Inc., 1976-78, dir. communications Elizabeth Arden Salons, 1978-87, communication cons., 1987—. Recipient Art Director's award 1961, 66. Mem. Fashion Group, Fashion Execs. Roundtable, Inner Circle, Advt. Women N.Y. (life), Women's Nat. Rep. Club (life). Episcopalian. Home and Office: 8531 88th St Woodhaven NY 11421-1308 also: Halsey Neck Ln Southampton NY 11968

BOLT, BRENDA ANNE, nurse; b. West Point, Ga., July 6, 1944; d. Wallace Berry and Burnie Sue (Mitchell) B. RN, St. Margaret Hosp., Montgomery, Ala., 1965. Commd. 2d lt. U.S. Army, 1967, advanced through grades to capt., 1971; mem. operating room staff George H. Lanier Hosp., Valley, Ala., 1965-67; asst. operating room supr., 1969-70, operating room, recovery room supr., 1984-85; operating room supr. U.S. Army 17th Field Hosp., Viet Nam, 1968-69; instr. Fort Leonard Wood Army Hosp., Mo., 1970-72; mem. operating room staff 2d Gen. Hosp., Landstuhl, Fed. Republic Germany, 1972-74; supr. infection control central material service, Martin Army Hosp., Fort Benning, Ga., 1974-77; oper. rm. supr. Keller Army Hosp., West Point, N.Y., 1977-79; oper. rm. central material svc. supr. Wurzburg Army Hosp., Fed. Republic Germany, 1979-82; head nurse, same day surgery Madigan Army Med. Ctr., Tacoma, Wash., 1982-84; supr. oper. and emergency rms. Chamber County Hosp., Lafayette, Ala., 1986-88; head nurse oper. rm./PACU George H. Lanier Meml. Hsop., Valley, Ala., 1988-93; unit mgr. OR/PAR/Amb. Svc. Ketchikan (Alaska) Gen. Hosp., 1993—. Decorated Nat. Def. medal, Army Commendation medal with three oak leaf clusters. Mem. Operating Room Nurses Assn. Democrat. Roman Catholic. Avocations: softball; skiing; camping; reading; gardening. Home: PO Box 1261 Ward Cove AK 99928-1261 Office: Ketchikan Gen Hosp Ketchikan AK 99901

BOLT, EUNICE MILDRED DEVRIES, artist; b. Clifton, N.J., Oct. 31, 1926; d. Lambert H. and Cora (Martin) DeVries; m. Maurice L. Bolt (dec. Nov. 1989); children: Macyn Bolt, Tamsen Bolt Clark, Valerie Martin Bolt Wegner. Grad., Pratt Inst. Art & Design, Bklyn., 1949; BA, Calvin Coll., 1952; MA, Western Mich. U., 1973. Book illustrator Fideler Pubs., Grand Rapids, Mich., 1952-53, Zondervan Pub. Co., Grand Rapids, Mich., 1953-56; prof. Calvin Coll., Grand Rapids, Mich., 1962-67, Grand Rapids C.C., 1968-91; represented by Corporate Portfolios and Bergsma Gallery, Grand Rapids, Rental/Sales Gallery of Grand Rapids Art Mus.; internat. art study tours coord. and guide, 1978—; fine art exhbn. juror, 1987—; lectr. art history, 1991—, presenter watercolor workshops, 1991—. Exhibited in group shows at Grand Rapids Art Mus., Kalamazoo Inst. Art, U. Mich. Schlusser Gallery, Pitts. Ctr. for the Arts, Westmoreland Mus. Art, Detroit Inst. Art. Home and Studio: 2421 Breton Rd SE Grand Rapids MI 49546-5627

BOLTON, (MARGARET) ELIZABETH, artist, poet; b. Cranston, R.I., Sept. 7, 1919; d. James Ewart and Pamela (White) Hill; m. Archer Leroy Bolton Jr., Nov. 29, 1941; children: Wendy, Daria, Pamela, James. Student, Colby Sawyer Coll., 1936-39. Sec. Dr. Augustus Thorndike, Boston, 1939-41; sec. rehab. orgn. Mass. Gen. Hosp., Boston, 1950-51; sec. Nat. Acad. Scis., Washington, 1957-60, Mitre Corp. Electronics, Burlington, Mass., 1961-62; exec. sec. Manpower, Burlington, 1961-69; sec. RCA, Burlington, 1962-63; substitute tchr. art pub. high schs., various cities, Mass., 1970-81. Exhibited in various group shows (1st prize 1979, 80); poetry pub. in New Voices, 1981, Golden Treasury of Great Poems, 1989, Vol. II, 1989, Summer Treasury of Poems of America, 1992, Fall Treasury of Poems of America, 1992. Mem. Friends of the Libr., 1986—. Recipient 2d prize Newburyport Art Assn., 1977, 1st prize Nashua Art Assn., 1986, Award of Merit Certs. (2) World of Poetry, 1988, Golden Poet award, 1989, Golden Poet award World of Poetry, 1992. Mem. Haverhill Art Assn., Seacoast Art Assn. Mem. Christian Ch. Home: 12 Glen Dr Hampstead NH 03841-2242

BOLTON, MARTHA O., writer; b. Searcy, Ark., Sept. 1, 1951; d. Lonnie Leon and Eunice Dolores Ferren; m. Russell Norman Bolton, Apr. 17, 1970; children: Russell Norman II, Matthew David, Anthony Shane. Grad. high sch., Reseda, Calif. Freelance writer for various comedians, 1975-86; newspaper columnist Simi Valley Enterprise, Simi, Calif., 1979-87; staff writer Bob Hope, 1986—, The Mark and Kathy Show, 1995—. Author: A Funny Thing Happened to Me on My Way Through the Bible, 1985, A View from the Pew, 1986, What's Growing Under Your Bed?, 1986, Tangled in the Tinsel, 1987, So. How'd I Get To Be in Charge of the Program?, 1988, Humorous Monologues, 1989, Let My People Laugh, 1989, If Mr. Clean Calls Tell Him I'm Not In, 1989, Journey to the Center of the Stage, 1990, If You Can't Stand the Smoke, Get Out of My Kitchen, 1990, Home, Home on the Stage, 1991, TV Jokes and Riddles, 1991, These Truths Were Made for Walking, 1991, When the Meatloaf Explodes It's Done, 1993, Childhood Is a Stage, 1993, Honey, It's Time To Weed the Carpets Again, 1994, Walke A Mile in His Truths, 1994, The Cafeteria Lady on the Loose, 1994, On the Loose, 1994, If the Pasta Wiggles, Don't Eat It, 1995, Bethlehem's Big Night, 1995, Club Family, 1995, When the Going Gets Tough, The Tough Start Laughing, 1995, (lyrics) Mouth in Motion. Pres. Vista Elem. Sch. PTA, Simi, 1980-81. Recipient Emmy nomination for outstanding achievement in music and lyrics, 1988, Internat. Angel award, 1991, Amb. award Media Fellowship Internat., 1995. Mem. ASCAP, NATAS, Nat. League Am. Pen Women (pres. Simi Valley br. 1984-86, 96—, Woman of Achievement award 1984, Pen Woman of Yr. award 1995), Writers Guild Am. West, Soc. Children's Book Writers. Office: PO Box 1212 Simi Valley CA 93062-1212

BOLTON, RUTHIE, basketball player; b. McClain, Miss.; d. Linwood and Leola Bolton; m. Mark Holifield. Diploma, Auburn U., 1989. Basketball player C.A. Fainizia, Italy, 1993, Erreti Faentza, Italy, 1994-95; mem. U.S.A. Women's Nat. Basketball Team. Lead singer Antidum Tarantula, Italy. 1st lt. USAR. Recipient gold medal 1994 Goodwill Games, 1994, World Championship Qualifying Team FIBA World Championship, 1993, World Univ. Games, 1991, U.S. Olympic Fesitval, 1986; bronze medal World Championship, 1994; named USA Basketball's Female Athelete of Yr., 1991, 1st Am. woman to play profl. basketball in Hungary and Sweden, 1990-91; named to NCAA 1989 Mideast Region All-Tournament Team, 1988, 89, NCAA Final Four All Tournament Team, 1988, SEC All-Academic Team, 1988, 89, All-SEC second team, 1989; earned SEc All-Tournament Team honors, 1988. Office: USA Basketball 5465 Mark Dabling Blvd Colorado Springs CO 80918-3842

BOLTZ, MARY ANN, aerospace materials company executive, travel agency executive; b. Far Rockaway, N.Y., Jan. 12, 1923; d. Thomas and Theresa (Domanico) Caparelli; m. William Emmett Boltz; children: Valerie Ann Boltz Austin, Beverly Theresa, Cynthia Marie Boltz O'Rourke. Grad. high sch., Lawrence, N.Y., 1941. Publicist CBS, N.Y.C., 1943-48; mgr. Coast-Line Internat. Distbrs. Ltd., Lindenhurst, N.Y., 1961-80, v.p., 1980-86, pres., 1987-90, CEO, 1990—; chief exec. officer Air Ship 'N Shore Travel, Woodmere, N.Y. and Marco Island, Fla., 1978—; pres. Bangor Realty, 1975. Formerly radio and TV editor local publs., writer Gotham Guide mag. Sec. Inwood Civic & Businessmen's Assn., 1952-64, pres., 1964-66, chmn. bd., 1967-68; pres. Lawrence Pub. Schs. System PTA, 1956-58; pres., life mem. Cen. Coun. PTA, 1958-60; founder Inwood Civic Scholarship Fund, 1964; v.p. Econ. Opportunity Coun., Inwood; mem. fundraising bd. yearly ball St. Joachim Ch., Cedarhurst, N.Y.; gift chmn. L.I. Bd. Boys Town of Italy; bd. dirs. Marco Island Cancer Fund Dr.; dir., promoter Marco Island Philharmonic Symphony; dir. polit. campaign William Sieffert, Oceanside, N.Y.; chmn. 30 yr. reunion Class of 41, 1971, 50 yr. reunion, 1991; asst. chmn. 50 yr. reunion Class of 42, 1991; fundraiser Stecker and Horowitz Sch. Music Dinner Com., 1978, Am. Bus. Women's Assn., Long Island charter chptr., Rockville Centre, N.Y., 1990-92, United fund, Red Feather Ball, 1992. Recipient award Nassau Herald Newspaper, Cedarhurst, Inwood Civic Assn., PTA Life Membership award, 25 Yr. Silver Medallion Boys Town of Italy, gold medal, 1995, Citizen of Yr. Bronze Plaque award Inwood Civic Assn., 1996. Mem. Am. Bus. Women's Assn. (L.I. charter chpt.), Nissoquogue Golf Club, Sun 'N Surf Beach Club, Island Country Club (Marco Island, Fla.), Desert Mountain Country Club. Republican. Roman Catholic. Home: 149 Hempstead Ave Rockville Centre NY 11570-2904 Office: Coast-Line Internat Distbrs 274 Bangor St Lindenhurst NY 11757-3633

BOMBA, ANNE KILLINGSWORTH, family relations and child development educator; b. Port Lavaca, Tex., Sept. 12, 1959; d. John Gilbert and Jane (Killingsworth) B. BS, Okla. State U., Stillwater, 1981, MS, 1987, PhD, 1989. Cert. in family and consumer scis.; cert. tchr., Okla. Kindergarten tchr. Tulsa Pub. Schs., 1981-85; asst. to editor Home Econs. Rsch. Jour., Stillwater, 1986; grad. asst., grad. assoc. in family rels. and child devel. Okla. State U., 1987-89; asst. prof. home econs. U. Miss., Oxford, 1989-95, assoc. prof. family and consumer scis., 1995—. Contbr. articles to profl. jours. Mem. AAUP, AAUW, Am. Assn. Family and Consumer Scis., Soc. for Rsch. in Child Devel., Nat. Assn. for Edn. Young Children, Nat. Coun. on Family Rels., So. Early Childhood Assn., Kappa Omicron Nu. Home: PO Box 1345 University MS 38677 Office: U Miss Dept Family and Consumer Scis 110 Meek Hall University MS 38677

BOMBA, MARGARET ANN, lawyer; b. Bklyn., July 1, 1947; d. Fred S. and Mary (Alban) Bomba; B.S., St. Francis Coll., 1975; postgrad. Columbia U., 1977; J.D., Bklyn. Law Sch., 1982; m. John N. Pizzuto, May 27, 1978. Sec., adminstrv. asst. Fieldcrest Mills, Inc., N.Y.C., 1966-71, product mgr. textiles for the home 1973-84; pvt. practice, N.Y.C., 1984—; sales and product mgmt. Wamsutta Mills Inc., N.Y.C., 1972-73; prof. law Parsons Sch. Design, 1985—; arbitrator N.Y. Stock Exchange, 1987—; pvt. practice, N.Y.C., Newark, 1984—; mem. faculty Practising Law Inst., 1993—; mem. faculty mental hygiene law N.Y. State Office Ct. Adminstrn., 1993—. Named to Catherine McAuley High Sch. Hall of Fame, 1995; recipient citation Office of Pres. of Borough of Bklyn., 1995. Mem. N.Y. County Lawyers Assn. (trade regulation com. 1985, real property com. 1986), ABA, Assn. Bar City of N.Y., Assn. Trial Lawyers Am., N.Y. State Bar Assn. (elder law sect., ethics and practice com. 1991—, mem. exec. com. elder law sect. 1994—, chair fraud and abuse com. 1994—, mem. faculty continuing legal edn. divsn. 1994—, spl. com. fin. abuse of the elderly, 1995—). Office: 14 Wall St New York NY 10005-2101 also: 430 Springfield Ave Berkeley Heights NJ 07922-1165

BOMBARDIERI, MERLE ANN, psychotherapist; b. Atlanta, Mar. 16, 1949; d. Sol and Sadie (Drucker) Malkoff; m. Rocco Anthony Bombardieri, Jr., Aug. 22, 1971; children: Marcella, Vanessa. B.A. in Psychology, Mich. State U., 1971; M.S.W., San Diego State U., 1976. Cert. clin. social workers, Mass., clin. hypnosis Am. Soc. Clin. Hypnosis; Diplomate Nat. Assn. Social Workers, Am. Bd. Examiners in Clin. Social Work. Crisis intervention worker and trainer Listening Ear, East Lansing, Mich., 1969-71; tchr. English as 2d lang. Instituto Brasil Estados Unidos, Rio de Janeiro, 1971-73; supr. infant unit Married Student Day Care Ctr., Mich. State U., East Lansing, 1973-74; psychotherapist/family life educator Family Svc. Assocs., San Diego, 1975-77; psychotherapist Dade Wallace Mental Health Ctr., Nashville, 1977-78; psychotherpist/workshop leader Met. Beaverbrook Mental Health Ctr., Waltham, Mass., 1980-81; pvt. practice psychotherapy, Acton-Belmont, Mass., 1982—; clin. dir. Resolve, Inc., infertility orgn., Belmont, 1982-84; clin. cons., 1984—; cons. HealthData Internat., Westport, Conn., 1983—, Open Door Soc., Newton, Mass., 1983—, First Day Film Corp., 1985—, Mass. Dept. Social Svcs., 1987; sec. Boston Fertility Soc., 1995, others; psychology seminar leader; radio and TV appearances. Author: The Baby Decision, 1981; founder, editor, pub. Wellspring newsletter; contbr. articles to profl. and med. jours. N.Y. State Regents scholar, 1967; NIMH trainee, 1970. Mem. Acad. Cert. Social Workers, Phi Beta Kappa, Phi Kappa Phi. Home: 4 Broadview Rd Acton MA 01720-4202 Office: 33 Bedford St Lexington MA 02173-4430

BOMBERGER, AUDREY SHELLEY, nursing administrator and educator; b. Lebanon, Pa., June 12, 1942; d. Allen Aunspach and Ruth Mae (Arnold) Shelley; m. Edward K. Bomberger, Sept. 29, 1963; children: Beth Ann, Gary Allen. Diploma in nursing, Reading (Pa.) Med. Ctr., 1963; BS in Edn., Millersburg U. Pa., 1975; MS in Edn., Temple U., 1979; PhD in Health Adminstrn., Columbia-Pacific U., San Rafael, Calif., 1983. RN, Pa., Calif. Staff nurse gen. med. unit Good Samaritan Hosp., Lebanon, 1963-65; charge nurse maximum security units VA Med. Ctr., Lebanon, 1965-70; charge nurse CCU, Lebanon Valley Gen. Hosp., Lebanon, 1970-75, dir. nursing edn., 1975-79; dir. hosp. edn. St. Mary's Hosp., Reno, 1979-84; dir. hosp. edn. and rsch. McKay-Dee Hosp.-IHC, Ogden, Utah, 1984-87; dir. edn. and staff devel. Salinas (Calif.) Valley Meml. Hosp., 1987-91; pres. Creative Health Svcs., Inc., Salinas, 1987-92; owner Bomberger & Assocs., Salinas, 1992—; adminstr. profl. svcs. Al Hada Hosp., Tiaf, Saudi Arabia, 1994-95; dir. nursing svc. Casa Serena Healthcare Ctr., Salinas, 1995-96, Cypress Rehab., Santa Cruz, Calif., 1996—; presenter on various nursing and mgmt. topics, 1989—; mem. adj. clin. faculty dept. nursing San Jose State U., 1990—; mem. nursing curriculum com., mem. affiliate faculty Weber State Coll., Ogden, 1985-87; mem. affiliate faculty, mem. curriculum com. Orvis Sch. Nursing, U. Nev., Reno, 1982-84; mem. Congl. Task Force to Implement Fed. Coll. Nursing, 1989-90. Author: Radiation and Health: Principles and Practices in Therapy and Disaster Preparedness, 1984; contbr. articles profl. jours., chpts. to books. Col. Nurse Corps, U.S. Army. Mem. ANA (cert. advanced nurse adminstr.), Am. Orgn. Nurse Execs., Am. Coll. Healtcare Execs., Am. Soc. Healthcare Edn. and Tng. (Nat. Edn. award 1981), Calif. Nurses Assn., Assn. Mil. Surgeons U.S., Res. Officers Assn. Home: 124-3 Nissen Rd Salinas CA 93901-2246

BONAHOOM, BARBARA JEAN, retired physical education educator; b. Raton, N.Mex., Sept. 4, 1943; d. Richard Joseph and Emily Adele (Haddad) B. BS, U. No. Colo., 1965; MS, U. N.Mex., 1971. Cert. edn., phys. edn. grades K-12, bus. edn. Secondary edn. phys. edn. and typing Fountain (Colo.)-Ft. Carson H.S., 1965-67; tchr. grade 7th history and 9th grade bus. Raton (N.Mex.) Pub. Schs., 1967-70; secondary phys. edn. tchr. St. Pius X H.S., Albuquerque, 1971-73, secondary phys. edn. and bus. tchr., 1974-75; elem. and secondary phys. edn. tchr. Raton (N.Mex.) Pub. Schs., 1976-93; ret., 1993. Pres. Raton (N.Mex.) Humane Soc., 1979—; city commr., police commr., pers. bd. mem. City of Raton, 1980-84; bd. dirs. NRA, Washington, 1989-95. Recipient Commendation for Watershed Project, Asst. Sec. Edn. and U.S. Commr. Edn., Washington, 1970, Outstanding Leadership in Conservation Edn. award N.Mex. Assn. Soil and Water Conservation Dist., 1970, N.Mex. Shooting Sports award, Raton, 1991; named Outstanding Young Woman in Am., 1971; Lay Person award N.Mex. Parks and Recreation Assn., 1980. Mem. AAHPERD, N.Mex. Health, Phys. Edn., Recreation and Dance. Republican. Roman Catholic. Home: 1108 S 5th St Raton NM 87740-4311

BONASSI, JODI, artist, marketing consultant; b. L.A., Aug. 22, 1953; d. Julian and Sara (DeNorber) Feldman; m. Raymond Gene Bonassi, June 7, 1986; 1 child, Spencer. Student, Otis Art Inst., L.A., 1972, Calif. State U., L.A., 1983-85, Calif. State U., Northridge, 1985-86. participating artist Concern Found. and World Cup Soccer Gala Event for Cancer Rsch., Beverly Hills, Calif., 1994. Artist: Creative With Words Publications, 1987; artist, pub. various greeting cards, 1994—; one-woman shows include Anastasia's Asylum, Santa Monica, Calif., 1993, Follow Your Heart, Canoga Park, Calif., 1994, Szechwan Inn, Canoga Park, 1994, Cobalt Cafe, Woodland Hills, Calif., 1995, Amore Restorante, Encino, 1995, Nicola's Kitchen, Woodland Hills, 1995, Spumante Restaurant, Studio City, Calif., 1995—, Le Petit Moulin, Santa Monica, 1996 Pt. Adesa, Rancho Mirage, Calif., 1996; exhibited in group shows at Bowles-Sorokko Gallery, Beverly Hills, 1994, ChaChaCha, Encino, Calif., 1994—, Lyn/Bassett Gallery, L.A., 1994, Topanga (Calif.) Canyon Gallery, 1994, Hartog Fine Art Gallery, L.A., 1995, Charles Hecht Gallery, Tarzana, Calif., 1995, New Canyon Gallery, Topanga, 1995, Truly Yours Restaurant, Tarzana, 1995, Made With Kare, West Hills, Calif., 1995, Gail Michael Collection, Northridge, 1995, Mythos Gallery, Burbank, 1995-96, Nicole Brown Simpson Found., 1996; represented in pvt. collections. Fellow Calif. Women Bus. Owners, L.A. Mcpl. Art Gallery Registry. Studio: Ste 160 22647 Ventura Blvd Woodland Hills CA 91364

BONAZZI, ELAINE CLAIRE, mezzo-soprano; b. Endicott, N.Y.; d. John Dante and Zina (Rossi) B.; m. Jerome Ashe Carrington, Sept. 21, 1963; 1 step-son, Christopher. B.M. (George Eastman scholar), Eastman Sch. Music. Artist-in-residence SUNY, Stonybrook; former mem. faculty Peabody Conservatory; vis. prof. Eastman Sch. Music, Rochester, N.Y., 1979. Debuts, Santa Fe Opera, 1958, Opera Soc. Washington, 1960, N.Y.C. Opera, 1965, Opera Internacional, Mexico City, Mexico, 1966, Mini-Met, 1973, Europe, West Berlin Festival opera, 1961, Spoleto (Italy) Festival, 1974, Castel Franco Festival Venetian Music, Venice, Italy, 1975, Berlin Bach Festival, 1976, Netherlands Opera, 1978, Minn. Opera, 1985, Artpark Festival, 1987, Opera Theater of St. Louis, 1988, New Orleans Opera, 1988, Paris, 1979, Spoleto-Charleston Festival, 1981, Edmonton Opera Can., 1990, New Orleans Opera, 1990, Winnipeg Opera, 1993; frequent Libr. of Congress concerts; title role in Pique Dance, Washington Opera, Rostropovich conducting, 1989, in Vanessa, Opera Theatre of St. Louis, 1988, Carlson's Midnight Angel, Opera Theatre of St. Louis, 1993; currently leading roles with N.Y.C. Opera; soloist, with most major Am. orchs., Canadian Broadcasting Corp., NET Opera Theatre, NBC, ABC, CBS TV networks, recs. on, Candide, Columbia, Vanguard, CRI, Folkways, Vox, Grenadilla, Pro Arte and Nonesuch Records; over 40 world premiers of major works by leading composers with major orchs. and opera cos. Named 1 of 6 honored alumni 50th Anniversary Year, Eastman Sch. Music, 1971, Trustees Council U. Rochester, 1976; formerly William Matheus Sullivan grantee. Mem. Mu Phi Epsilon. Home: 650 W End Ave New York NY 10025-7355 Office: care Trawick Artists 1926 Broadway New York NY 10023-6915

BONCHER, MARY, talent agent; b. Green Bay, Wis., Jan. 19, 1946; d. Anthony Peter and Bernice Mary (Lannoye) Williams; m. Joseph Phillip Boncher, Jan. 7, 1967; children: Yvette, Noelle. Diploma, Rosemary Bischoff Sch. Modeling, Milw., 1965. Dir. Mary Boncher Model Agy. & Sch. Ltd., Bloomington and St. Charles, Ill., 1970-80, Mary Boncher Model Agy. Ltd., St. Charles, 1980-84, Mary Boncher Model Mgmt. Ltd., Chgo., 1985-91; ptnr. ARIA Model & Talent Mgmt. Ltd., Chgo., 1992—, sec., treas.; fashion reporter TV and radio Men's Fashion Assn., N.Y.C., 1975-80, Eleanor Lambert's Am. Designer, N.Y. Fashion Press, N.Y.C., 1975-80; fashion corr. Green Bay Daily News, 1975-76. Lector Cath. mass, 1983-90, 92—; registered lobbyist, Ill. Mem. Am. Security Coun. (nat. adv. bd.), Ams. for Responsible TV and Radio, Ill. Creative Cmty. (pres.). Republican. Roman Catholic. Office: ARIA Model & Talent Mgmt Ltd 1017 W Washington St Ste 2A Chicago IL 60607

BONCHER, MARY KATHERINE, psychotherapist; b. Green Bay, Wis., Aug. 24, 1948; d. William John Jr. and Mildred (Slye) B.; m. Diogenes Ballester, Jan. 9, 1987; 1 child, Yajaira. BS in Theology History, Beloit Coll., 1970; MS in Counseling, U. Wis., 1979; postgrad., NYU, 1993—. Child and family therapist Dane County Advocates for Battered Women, Madison, Wis., 1980-82; children's therapist, alternatives to aggression Family Svcs., Madison, Wis., 1982-86; children helping children coord. Parental Stress Ctr., Madison, Wis., 1987—, child sexual abuse clin. coord. N.Y. Foundling Hosp., N.Y.C., 1993—. Mem. APA (student affiliate), NY State Coalition Against Rape. Office: NY Foundling Hospital 18 W 18th St 8th fl New York NY 10011

BOND, ANNE WAINSTEIN, museum curator, archaeologist; b. Washington, July 2, 1954; d. Leonard and Eleanor (Sullivan) Wainstein; m. Brooks L. Bond, Oct. 12, 1986. BA in Anthropology, Coll. of William and Mary, 1976; MA in Am. Civilization, U. Pa., 1977; postgrad., U. Colo., 1989—. Guide, info. aide, vol. Smithsonian Instn., Washington, 1968-70; archaeology evaluator, lab. aide Southside Hist. Sites, Williamsburg, Va., 1973-75; rsch. asst., anthropologist Coll. of William and Mary, Williamsburg, 1974-75; curator, archivist Bicentennial Dept. Health, Edn. and Welfare, Washington, 1976; curatorial asst. Phila. Mus. Art, 1976-77; archaeology asst. Alexandria (Va.) Archaeology, 1977; archaeologist Nat. Pk. Svc., Great Falls, Va., 1977; chief curator, state archaeologist W.Va. State Mus., Charleston, 1977-84; curator of material culture Colo. Hist. Soc., Denver, 1984—; cons. curator, scholar Women of West Mus., Boulder, Colo., 1995-96; cons. curator Aspen (Colo.) Hist. Mus., 1995; scholar faculty U. Denver/Metro State Coll., Denver, 1989-94; mem. grant/peer rev. panel Nat. Endowment Humanities, Washington, 1988-96. Author: The Georgetown Loop-A Guide, 1986; co-author: Guide to Historic Preservation Survey, 1983; reviewer: Nebraska History/Journal of West, 1993-95; contbr. articles to profl. jours. V.p., bd. dirs. W.Va. Opera Theater, Charleston, 1978-84; elder, nat. del. Presbyn. Ch. USA, Charleston and Denver, 1978-96; mem. vol. Jr. League Charleston, 1980-84; bd. dirs., singer, performer Charleston Symphony Orch./Chorus, 1978-84. Grantee Nat. Endowment Humanities, 1984-86, 87, Colo. Endowment for Humanities, 1993, Nat. Pk. Svc., 1994-98. Mem. Am. Assn. for State and Local History (spkr., award of merit 1995), Am. Assn. Mus., Colo. Coun. Profl. Archaeologists (bd. dirs.), Colo./Wyo. Assn. Mus. (spkr.), Soc. for Hist. Archaeology, Mountain Plains Mus. Assn. (spkr.). Office: Colo Hist Soc 1300 Broadway Denver CO 80203

BOND, FRANCES TORINO, academic administrator, consultant; b. Balt., Jan. 8, 1934; d. Michael Torino and Josephine Baccacchione; separated; children: William, Michael, Geoffrey, James. BS, Towson State U., 1955, MEd, 1963; PhD, U. Md., 1973. Faculty Towson (Md.) State U., 1962-74, chairperson early childhood, 1975-81, assoc. dean, 1982-94; assoc. dir. Fellows Program Peace Corps, Washington, 1995—. Creator, host, writer (video series) First Steps, 1987—; co-author (booklet) Reading to Your Child, 1985. Democrat. Roman Catholic. Home: 6901 Avondale Rd Baltimore MD 21212 Office: Peace Corps 1990 K St NW Rm 9500 Washington DC 20526

BOND, KARLA JO, educator; b. Abilene, Tex., Oct. 11, 1951; d. David Lipscomb and Elizabeth Rosalie (Henthorn) Kennamer; m. Lawrence Quinn Robinson, Apr. 1971 (div. June 1979); m. Dennis Earl Bond, July 28, 1979; children: Ryan Jeffrey, Blake Justin. BS in Edn., Abilene Christian U., 1972; MA, Maryville U., 1994. Tchr. Abilene (Tex.) Christian Campus Sch., 1972-73, LaMarque (Tex.) Pub. Schs., 1973-78, Kansas City (Kans.) Unified Sch. Dist. 500, 1979-90; tchr. Ft. Zumwalt Pub. Schs., O'Fallon, Mo., 1990—, coord. elem. sch. math., 1993—; instr. math. Math. Learning Ctr., Portland, 1990-92; leader math. insvc. Ft. Zumwalt Pub. Schs., 1990-94. Mem. NEA, ASCD, Nat. Coun. Tchrs. Math., Mo. Coun. Tchrs. Math., Math. Educators Greater St. Louis. Republican. Mem. Ch. of Christ. Office: Forest Park Elem Sch 501 Sunflower O'Fallon MO 63366

BOND, MELISSA ELAINE, school counselor; b. Evansville, Ind., Jan. 23, 1956; d. Dale Wellman and Mary Louise (Bain) Sauer; m. Ronald William Bond, July 1, 1977; children: Ross William, Hannah Elaine. BS, Ind. State U., 1977; MA, U. Evansville, 1980. Cert. school counselor, Ind. Tchr. phys. edn., health Evansville Pub. Schs., 1977-84, tchr. English, 1984-95, coord. English, 1990-94, counselor, 1995—. Active Jr. League of Evansville, Blue Grass United Meth. Ch. Recipient Nat. Middle Sch. award Dept. Edn., 1986; Eli Lilly Middle Sch. grantee Evansville, 1988, Youth Resources grantee, Evansville, 1992, 93. Mem. NEA, Am. Sch. Counseling Assn., Ind. State Tchrs. Assn., Ind. Sch. Counselor's Assn., Evansville Tchrs. Assn. Office: Thompkins Middle Sch 1300 W Mill Rd Evansville IN 47710

BOND, VICTORIA ELLEN, conductor, composer; b. L.A., May 6, 1945; d. Philip and Jane (Courtl) B.; m. Stephan Peskin, Jan. 27, 1974. B Mus. Arts, U. So. Calif., L.A., 1968; M Mus. Arts, Juilliard Sch. Music, 1975, D Mus. Arts, 1977; DFA (hon.), Washington and Lee U., 1992, Hollins Coll., 1995, Roanoke Coll., 1995. Condr., composer; mem. N.Y. State Coun. Arts Music Panel, 1987-90; bd. dirs. Am. Music Ctr., 1987—, N.Y. Women Composers, 1992—. Guest condr. Cabrillo Music Festival, Calif., 1974, White Mountains Music Festival, N.H., 1975, Aspen (Colo.) Music Festival, 1976, Shenandoah Music Festival, W.Va., 1977, Colo. Philharm., 1978, Houston Symphony, 1979, 86, Buffalo Philharm., 1979, Pitts. Symphony, 1980, N.W. Chamber Orch., Seattle, 1980, Anchorage Symphony, 1980, 82, Ark. Symphony, 1981, Hudson Valley Philharm., N.Y., 1981, Newton Symphony, Boston, 1982, Hartford Symphony, 1982, RTE Symphony, Dublin, Ireland, 1983, Albany Symphony Orch., 1984-85, Houston Symphony Orch., 1986, Richmond Symphony Orch., 1987, Williamsburg Symphony Orch., Greenville Symphony Orch., Des Moines Symphony Orch., Utah Symphony Orch., Cape Cod Symphony Orch., Tallahassee Symphony Orch., Va. Symphony Orch, 1988-90, Shanghai Symphony, 1993, 94; music dir. New Amsterdam Symphony Orch., N.Y.C., 1978-80, Pitts. Youth Symphony Orch., 1978-80, Empire State Youth Orch., 1982-86, Southeastern Music Ctr., 1983-84, Bel Canto Opera, 1983-86, Roanoke (Va.) Symphony Orch., 1986-95; artistic dir. Bel Canto Opera Co., 1986-88, Opera Roanoke, 1989-95; Exxon/Arts Endowment condr., Pitts. Symphony, 1978-80; recs. include Twentieth Century Cello, Two American Contemporaries, The Frog Prince, An American Collage, Live from Shanghai, Victoria Bond: Compositions; commd. by Pa. Ballet, 1978, Jacob's Pillow Dance Festival, 1979, Am. Ballet Theater, 1981, Empire State Inst. Performing Arts, 1983, 84, Stage One, Louisville, 1986, Ga. State U., 1986, L'Ensemble, 1990, Renaissance City Winds, 1990, Audubon String Quartet, 1990, Women's Philharm., San Francisco, 1993, Va. Explore Park and The Shanghai Symphony, 1994, D Day Found., 1994, Linda Plaut, 1994, The Billings (Mont.) Symphony, The Elgin (Ill.) Symphony. Bd. dirs. Am. Music Ctr. Recipient Victor Herbert award 1977, Perry F. Kendig award, 1988, ASCAP Composition award 1973—; Nat. Inst. for Music Theater grantee in opera conducting N.Y.C. Opera, 1985, Martha Baird Rockefeller grantee, 1978-79, Meet-The-Composer grantee in Composition, 1973—; Juilliard scholar, 1972-77; Juilliard fellow, 1975-77, Aspen Music Festival fellow, 1973-76; named Exxon/Arts Endowment Conductor, 1978-80, Woman of Yr. in Va., 1990, 91; featured on NBC Today show, 1990, profiled in C.S. Monitor, 1987, Wall Street Jour., 1987, other mags. and shows. Mem. ASCAP (recipient awards 1975—), Am. Symphony Orch. League, Am. Fedn. Musicians, N.Y. Women Composers, Mu Phi Epsilon.

BOND, WANDA WILSON, public relations and fund development professional; b. Durham, N.C., Oct. 7, 1954; d. Frontis Lee and Esther Ruth (Kelly) Wilson; 1 child, Kelly Katherine. BA, U. N.C., 1977. News reporter WGBG Radio, Greensboro, N.C., 1978; news anchor, reporter WBBB-WPCM Radio, Burlington, N.C., 1987-79; news anchor, producer, reporter WWBT-TV, Richmond, Va., 1979-85; nat. media rels. specialist Va. Commonwealth U., Richmond, 1985-86; dir. pub. affairs St. Mary's Hosp., Richmond, 1986-88; v.p. pub. rels. St. Barnabus Med. Ctr., Livingston, N.J., 1988; dir. corp. comm. United Network Organ Sharing, Richmond, 1988-95; spl. asst. to dir. Nat. White Collar Crime Ctr., Richmond, 1995-96; comm. cons. Richmond, 1996—. Exec. editor UNOS Update, 1988-95. Mem. NAFE, Nat. Assn. Fund-Raising Execs., Pub. Rels. Soc. Am., Internat. Assn. Bus. Communicators, Computer Profls. Soc. Responsibility. Home and Office: 1712 Windingridge Dr Richmond VA 23233

BONDAR, ROBERTA LYNN, Canadian astronaut; b. Sault Sainte Marie, Ont., Can., Dec. 4, 1945. BS in Zoology and Agr., U. Guelph, 1968; MS in Exptl. Pathology, U. Western Ont., 1971; PhD in Neurobiology, U. Toronto, 1974; MD, McMaster U., 1977; D.Hum.L. (hon.), Mt. St. Vincent U., 1990; DSc (hon.), Mt. Allison U., 1989, U. Guelph, 1990, Lakehead U., 1991, Laurentian U., 1991, McMaster U., 1992, U. Toronto, 1992, McGill U., 1992, York U., 1992, Royal Roads Military Coll., 1993, Meml. U., 1993, Laval U., 1993, Carleton U., 1993; LLD (hon.), U. Regina, 1992, U. Calgary, 1992; DU (hon.), U. Otawa, 1992; DSL (hon.), U. Toronto, 1993; DSc (hon.), U. Montreal, 1994, U. P.E.I., 1994, U. Western Ont., 1995. Postdoctorate fellow Nat. Rsch. Coun. Can., 1974; intern Toronto Gen. Hosp., 1977-78; resident U. Western Ont., 1978-80; neuro-ophthalmology fellow Tufts's New England Med. Ctr., Boston, 1981, Toronto Western Hosp., 1981-82; asst. prof. medicine, dir. Multiple Sclerosis Clinic McMaster U., 1982-84; asst. prof. dept. medicine divsn. neurology Ottawa Gen. Hosp., Ont., 1985-88; Canadian astronaut Govt. of Can., Ottawa, 1983-92, chairwoman Canadian Lifescis. Subcom. for Space Sta., 1985; payload specialist candidate 1st Internat. Microgravity Lab. Shuttle Flight, 1989-90, prime payload specialist, 1990-92; disting. prof. Ryerson Poly. U., 1992—; rsch. asst. Dept. Fisheries and Forestry, 1963-68; coach archery team, lectr. phys. edn. U. Guelph, 1966-67, histology tech. dept. zoology, 1967-68; teaching asst. U. Toronto, 1970-74; lectr. dept. nursing U. Ottawa, 1985-88; chmn. Can. life scis. com. for space sta. Nat. Rsch. Coun. Can., 1985-89; life scis. rep. Can. Adv. Coun. on Sci. Utilization Space Sta., 1986-88; lectr. dept. nat. def. flight surgeon course Biomed. Aspects Space Flight, 1986-92; civil aviation med. examiner Health and Welfare, Can., 1986-93; mem. sci. adv. panel Premier's Coun. on Sci. and Tech., 1988-89; mem. sci. staff Sunnybrook Med. Ctr., 1988-93; rsch. fellow Playfair Inst. Oculomotor Lab. Toronto Western Hosp., 1989; bd. trustees Nat. Mus. Sci. and Tech., 1990-93; bd. regents Can. Mobile Athlete and Sport Hosp., 1992-93; mem. pub. adv. com. State of Environment Reporting, 1992-95; mem. adv. bd. Order of Can., 1993; sr. advisor Royal Commn. on Edn., Ont., 1993-95; adj. prof. dept. biology U. N.Mex., Albuquerque, 1991-93, vis. rsch. scholar dept. neurology, 1993-95; vis. disting. fellow Faculty Health Scis. McMaster U., 1993-94; vis. rsch. scholar Univs. Space Rsch. Assn. Johnson Space Ctr., Houston, 1993-94; vis. disting. prof. U. Western Ont., London, 1994-96; CIBC disting. prof. U. Western Ont., 1996—; lectr. in field. Recipient Career Scientist award Ont. Ministry Health, 1982, Vanier award Jaycess of Can., 1985, William A. Vanderburgh Sr. Travel award, 1976, Presdl. Citation of Honor, Ala. Agrl. and Mech. U., 1990, Paul Harris Recognition award Rotary Club Ancaster, 1992, Space medal NASA, 1992, Merit award U. Western Ont. Alumni, 1992, La Personalité de l'Année, La Presse, 1992, Medaille de L'Excellence, L'Assn. des. Médecins de Langue Française du Can., 1992, Pres.'s award Coll. Physicians and Surgeons Ont., 1992, Alumnus of Yr. award U. Western Ont., 1992, Can. 125 medal, 1992, Kurt Hahn award Outward Bound, 1993, Woman of Distinction award YWCA, 1993, Outstanding Can. award Armenian Cmty. Ctr. Toronto, 1993, Alumnus of Yr. award U. Guelph, 1993, Communication and Leadership award Toastmasters Dist. 60, 1994, Spl. Recognition award Canadian Breast Cancer Found., Women's Intercultural Network Internat. Women's Day award, 1995, Canadian Unity award Thornhill Sec. Sch., 1995; fellow U. Western Ont., 1971, Ont. Ministry Health, 1981, Ryerson Poly. Inst., 1990; Nat. Rsch. Coun. Canada scholar, 1971-74; officer Order of Can., 1992, Order of Ont., 1993; inductee Hamilton Gallery Distinction, 1993; first Canadian woman to travel in space. Fellow Royal Coll. Physicians and Surgeons Can.; mem. Am. Acad. Neurology (Presdl. citation 1992), Am. Soc. Gravitational and Space Biology, Canadian Neurol. Soc., Canadian Aeros. and Space Inst., Canadian Soc. Aerospace Medicine (William R. Franks award 1990), Can. Soc. Aviation Medicine (treas. 1983-84, sec. 1984-85), Can. Med. Protective Assn., Can. Assn. Sports Medicine, Fedn. Med. Women in Can., Albuquerque Aerostat Ascension Assn., Coll. Physicians and Surgeons Ont., Flying Ninety-Nines Internat. Women Pilots Assn., Canadian Stroke Soc., Aerospace Med. Assn. (Hubertus Strughold award Space Medicine Br. 1992), Royal Astron. Soc. Can., The Lung Assn. (exec. coun.), Assn. Space Explorers, Canadian Fedn. Univ. Women (hon.), Zonta (hon.). Office: U Western Ont Faculty Kinesiology, Thames Hall, London, ON Canada N6A 3K7

BONDINELL, STEPHANIE, counselor, former educational administrator; b. Passaic, N.J., Nov. 22, 1948; d. Peter Jr. and Gloria Lucille (Burden) Honcharuk; m. Paul Swanstrom Bondinell, July 31, 1971; 1 child, Paul Emil. BA, William Paterson Coll., 1970; MEd, Stetson U., 1983. Cert. elem. educator, Fla.; guidance counselor grades K-12, Fla. Tchr. Bloomingdale (N.J.) Bd. Edn., 1971-80; edn. dir. Fla. United Meth. Children's Home, Enterprise, 1982-89; guidance counselor Volusia County Sch. Bd., Deltona, Fla., 1989—. Sec. adv. com. Deltona Jr. High Sch., 1984-88; sec. Deltona Jr. PTA, 1982; vice-chmn. adv. com. Deltona Mid. Sch., 1988, chmn., 1989-91, chmn., 1991-92; mem. Deltona High Adv. Com., 1995-96; mem. secondary sch. task force Volusia County Sch. Bd., 1986—; mem. Volusia County Rep. Exec. Com., Rep. Presdl. Task Force; mem. state adv. bd. Fla. Future Educators Am., 1991-92. Acad. scholar Becton, Dickinson & Co., N.J., 1966; N.J. State scholar, 1966-70; named girls state rep. Am. Legion, N.J., 1966, Tchr. of Yr. Deltona Lakes, 1991, 95; recipient Vol. Svc. award Volusia County Sch. Bd., Deland, 1985. Mem. ASCD, AAUW, Coun. Exceptional Children, Divsn. for Learning Disabilities, Fla. Assn. Counseling and Devel., N.J. Edn. Assn., Volusia Tchrs. Orgn., Internat. Platform Assn., Deltona Civic Assn., Deltona Rep. Club (v.p. 1991), 4 Townes Federated Rep. Women's Club (sec., v.p.), Stetson Univ. Alumni Assn. Home: 1810 W Cooper Dr Deltona FL 32725-3623 Office: Volusia County Sch Bd 2022 Adelia Blvd Deltona FL 32725-3976

BONDS, GEORGIA ANNA, writer, lecturer; b. N.Y.C., Dec. 30, 1917; d. Alex Matthews and Mattie Ethel (Stephens) Arnett; m. Alfred Bryan Bonds Jr., Feb. 23, 1939; children: Anna Belle, Alfred Bryan III, Alexandra Burke, Stephen Arnett. BA, U. N.C., Greensboro, 1938; MA, La. State U., 1940; postgrad., U. N.C., 1940-42, Baldwin-Wallace Coll., 1960s. Editl. asst. The So. Rev., Baton Rouge, 1938-39; editor Abstracts of Theses La. State U., Baton Rouge, 1940; editl. asst. pub. sch. curricula State of La., 1941; free-lance writer, lectr., 1943—; editor dist. newspaper United Meth. Ch., Cleve., 1979-91; lectr. on Egyptian days and ways, 1956-70, internat. concerns, 1970-85, Cherokee Indian heritage, 1985—. Editor: (English transl.) Wheat Growing in Egypt, 1954; author: The Lake Erie Girl Scout Council, the First Seventy-five Years, 1976; contbr. articles to popular mags. Active Girl Scouts USA, 1928—, leader, organizer troop 1, Cairo, 1953-55, mem. Lake Erie coun., Cleve., 1956—, leader, organizer Mounted troop, 1957-80, coun. bd. dirs., 1966-70, 79-87, coun. pres., 1979-84, mem. nat. coun., 1966-72, 78-83, troop leader internat. encampment, 1968, condr. world tour nat. and internat. ctrs., 1972, world conf. asst., 1984, organizer troops, Volgograd, Russia, 1991—; mem. Dist. United Meth. Women, Cleve., 1956—, bd. dirs., 1965-78, pres., 1974-78, com. on dist. superintendency, 1977-81, chair, 1978-81, mem. World Meth. coun., London, 1966; mem. Ch. Women United in Ohio, 1960—, state bd. dirs., 1966-72; active YWCA, Little Rock, 1950—, bd. dirs., 1950-53, bd. dirs. Cleve. chpt., 1977-79; active Philanthropic Ednl. Orgn., 1950—, bd. dirs. Ohio state chpt., 1965-71, pres., 1971. Recipient Outstanding and Dedicated Svc. award Girl Scouts of Lake Erie Coun., 1979, World Friendship and Understanding Through Girl Scouting award Girl Scouts of Lake Erie Coun., 1984, award of honor for fund raising S.W. Gen. Hosp. Found., 1996. Mem. AAUW (bd. dirs. 1984-89), Baldwin-Wallace Coll. Women's Club (hon. life mem.), Order of Ea. Star, Delta Zeta, Kappa Phi, Phi Beta Kappa (Cleve. assn. bd. dirs. 1964-69, pres. 1968). Home: PO Box 768 Berea OH 44017

BONDY, KATHLEEN NOWAK, nursing educator; b. South Bend, Ind., Apr. 1, 1942; d. Edward Frank and Helen Isabel (Kaminski) Nowak; m. Warren H. Bondy, Aug. 17, 1973 (dec. Dec. 1977). Diploma in Nursing, Holy Cross Ctrl. Sch. Nursing, South Bend, 1963; BSN, St. Louis U., 1966; MS, Boston U., 1970; PhD, NYU, 1976. Cert. rehab. nurse. Instr. Peter Bent Brigham Sch. Nursing, Boston, 1967-68; rehab. clin. specialist Newton Wellesley Hosp., Newton Lower Falls, Mass., 1970-72; asst. prof. Adelphi U., Garden City, N.Y., 1975-78; assoc. prof. U. Wis., Madison, 1978-93; postdoctoral rsch. fellow U. Pitts., 1991-93; prof. nursing U. Ctrl. Ark., Conway, 1993—. Editl. bd. Rehab. Nursing Jour., 1981-86; author/prodr. videotapes: Evaluation of Clinical Performance, 1981; contbr. articles to profl. jours. Spencer Found. grantee, 1979-80. Mem. Assn. Rehab. Nurses (bd. dirs. 1981-85, Outstanding Svc. award 1981, 85, Recognition for Editl. Bd. work 1992). Roman Catholic. Office: Univ of Central Arkansas 201 Donaghey Ave Conway AR 72035-5001

BONE, JANET WITMEYER (JAN BONE), author; b. Shamokin, Pa., Dec. 19, 1930; d. Paul Eugene and Kathryn (Bender) Witmeyer; BA, Cornell U., 1951; MBA, Roosevelt U., 1987; m. David P. Bone, Oct. 27, 1951; children: Jonathan, Christopher, Robert, Daniel. Newspaper and trade mag. writer, freelance writer, 1962—; sr. writer spl. advt. sects. Chgo. Tribune, 1986-93; writer newsletter Rand McNally, 1988-90; writer articles Nat. Safety Coun., 1989-93; tchr. creative writing adult edn. Sch. Dist. 211, Palatine, Ill., 1974-92; instr. English composition Roosevelt U., 1992—. Co-author: Understanding the Film, 5th edit., 1996; author: Opportunities in Film Production, 2d edit., 1990, Opportunities in Cable Television, 1983, 2d edit., 1990, Opportunities in Telecommunications, 1984, 3d edit., 1995, Opportunities in Computer-Aided Design and Computer-Aided Manufacturing (CAD/CAM), 1986, 2nd edit. 1993, Opportunities in Robotics, 1987, 2nd rev. edit., 1993, Opportunities in Laser Technology, 1988, Opportunities in Plastics Careers, 1991. Trustee William Rainey Harper Community Coll., Palatine, 1977-85, sec. bd. trustees, 1979-85. Recipient Chgo. Working Newsman's award, 1968, Sch. Bell award Ill. Edn. Assn., 1968, Am. Polit. Sci. Assn. award disting. reporting pub. affairs, 1970. Mem. Ind. Writers of Chgo. (bd. dirs. IWOCCORP 1991-93, publicity chair, 1994), Nat. Coun. Tchrs. of English (internat. consortiom chair, publicity and mktg. com. 1994), Phi Theta Kappa, Alpha Omicron Pi. Address: 353 N Morris Dr Palatine IL 60067-5646

BONE, ROSEMARY COOK, elementary education educator; b. Columbia, Tenn., Apr. 26, 1944; m. Thomas D. Bone Jr., Mar. 4, 1983; 1 child, Bryan D. BS, Mid. Tenn. State U., 1971. Tchr. 4th grade Mt. Pleasant (Tenn.) Elem. Sch., 1971-90, J.E. Woodard Elem. Sch., Columbia, 1990—. Mem. Nat. Tchrs. Assn., Tenn. Edn. Assn., Maury County Edn. Assn. (ednl. minigrantee 1992-93). Baptist. Home: 3005 Mcintire Dr Columbia TN 38401-5016 Office: J E Woodard Elem Sch 207 Rutherford Ln Columbia TN 38401

BONESTEEL, MARGARET DAVIDSON, university administrator, educator; b. Beaver Falls, Pa., Oct. 2, 1946; d. Howard Clement and Helen Emma (Leigh) Davidson; m. Robert Edwin Bonesteel, Aug. 23, 1969; children: Matthew Michael, Elizabeth Leigh. AB in English, Wittenberg U., 1968; MS in Higher Edn., Syracuse U., 1986, EdD in Higher Edn., 1994. Tchr. Liverpool (N.Y.) Ctrl. Schs., 1968-73; info. coord. Sch. of Edn., Syracuse (N.Y.) U., 1984-88, dir. field placement, 1990-92; instr. writing program Syracuse U., 1990—, assoc. dir. project advance, 1992—; cons. Marywood Coll., Scranton, Pa., 1992. Contbr. chpt. to book. Mem. AAUP, Nat. Coun. Tchrs. of English, Conf. on Coll. Composition and Comm. Home: 100 Cherry Tree Cir Liverpool NY 13090 Office: Project Advance 111 Waverly St Ste 200 Syracuse NY 13244

BONFANTE, LARISSA, classics educator; b. Naples, Italy; came to U.S., 1939, naturalized, 1951; d. Giuliano and Vittoria (Dompé) B.; m. Leo Ferrero Raditsa, May 2, 1973; children: Sebastian, Alexandra Bonfante-Warren. Student, Radcliffe Coll., 1950, U. Rome, 1951; BA, Barnard Coll., 1954; MA, U. Cin., 1957; PhD, Columbia U., 1966. Mem. faculty NYU, 1963—, prof., 1978—, chmn. dept. classics, 1978-84, 87-90; cons. in field. Author: Etruscan Dress, 1975, Reading the Past, Etruscan, 1990, (with Giuliano Bonfante) Out of Etruria, 1981, The Etruscan Language, 1983 (transl. into Italian 1985, into Romanian 1995); editor: Etruscan Life and Afterlife: Handbook of Etruscan Studies, 1986 (transl. into Romanian 1996), (with Francesco Roncalli) Antichità dall'Umbria a New York, 1991, (with Judith Sebesta, ed.) The World of Roman Dress, 1994; translator: Chronology of the Ancient World (E.J. Bickerman) 1986, The Plays of Hrotswitha of Gandersheim, 1979; also articles. Mem. Archaeol. Inst. Am. (gov. bd. 1982-88), Istituto di Studi Etruschi (fgn.), German Archaeol. Inst. (corres. mem.). Home: 50 Morningside Dr New York NY 10025 Office: NYU Classics Dept 25 Waverly Pl New York NY 10003-6759

BONHAM-HONTZ, NANCY LYNNE, art educator; b. Nanticoke, Pa., May 15, 1939; d. Russel George and Mildred Elizabeth (Symons) B.; m. Arthur Dean Hontz, Aug. 19, 1961. BS in Art Edn., Wilkes Coll., 1961; postgrad., Bloomsburg (Pa.) State Coll., 1962, Kutztown (Pa.) State Coll., 1963, Coll. Misericordia, 1973-75. Cert. art instr., supr., Pa. Art supr. Hanover (Pa.) Area Schs., 1961-62; jr. high sch.-mid. sch., art educator Dallas (Pa.) Area Schs., 1962-91, retired, 1991—. Illustrator (book) Verses & Visions, 1984. Mem. State PASR, Luzerne/Wyo. PASR, Cider Painters of Am., Sordoni Art Gallery, MacDonald Art Gallery (life). Home: Box 2117 Sunny Slope Farm RR#2 Shickshinny PA 18655

BONHAM-YEAMAN, DORIA, law educator; b. Los Angeles, June 10, 1932; d. Carl Herschel and Edna Mae (Jones) Bonham; widowed; children: Carl Q., Doria Valerie-Constance. BA, U. Tenn., 1953, JD, 1957, MA, 1958; EdS in Computer Edn., Barry U., 1984. Instr. bus. law Palm Beach Jr. Coll., Lake Worth, Fla., 1960-69; instr. legal environment Fla. Atlantic U., Boca Raton, 1969-73; lectr. bus. law Fla. Internat. U., North Miami, 1973-83, assoc. prof. bus. law, 1983—. Editor: Anglo-Am. Law Conf., 1980; Developing Global Corporate Strategies, 1981; editorial bd. Attys. Computer Report, 1984-85, Jour. Legal Studies Edn., 1985—. Contbr. articles to profl. jours. Bd. dirs. Palm Beach County Assn. for Deaf Children, 1960-63; mem. Fla. Commn. on Status of Women, Tallahassee, 1969-70; mem. Broward County Democratic Exec. Com., 1982—; pres. Dem. Women's Club Broward County, 1981; mem. Marine Coun. of Greater Miami, 1978—, Svc. award, 1979. Recipient Faculty Devel. award Fla. Internat. U., Miami, 1980; grantee Notre Dame Law Sch., London, summer 1980. Mem. AAUW (pres. Palm Beach county chpt. 1965-66), U.S. Coun. for Internat. Bus., No. Dade C. of C., Acad. Legal Studies in Bus., Alpha Chi Omega (alumnae club pres. 1968-71), Tau Kappa Alpha. Episcopalian. Office: Fla Internat U North Miami FL 33181

BONHIVER, BARBARA WARREN, mental health professional; b. Eugene, Oreg., Aug. 27, 1957; d. Arthur Hugh Warren, Jr. and Charlotte Ruth (Olson) Warren; m. Gary August Bonhiver, Febr. 21, 1982; 1 child, Emma Catherine Warren Bonhiver. AB in English, U. Calif., Berkeley, 1979; MS in Counseling, San Francisco State U., 1986. Co-dir. The Horizon, Northborough, Mass., 1972-75; phone counselor parental stress Family Svc. Agy., San Francisco, 1981-82, clinical intern, 1981-82; dir. vol. svcs. Marin Abused Women's Svcs., San Rafael, Calif., 1983-86, clinical intern, 1983-86; vol. program mgr. Sexual Assault Counseling Svcs., San Rafael, 1987-88, clinical intern, 1987-88; program coord. Newtown (Conn.) Youth Svcs., 1995—. Editor: (lit. mag.) Chimera, 1978-79. Social work mentor Newtown H.S., Newtown, COnn., 1995—. Recipient Disting. Svc. award Newtown High Sch. Mentorship Program. Mem. AAUW, Am. Assn. Marriage and Family Therapists, Nat. Trust for Historic Preservation, Wellesley Ctr. for Rsch. on Women, Soc. Northern Fairfield County. Democrat. Mem. Unitarian Universalist Ch. Home: PO Box 1328 Redding CT 06875

BONI, MIKI, artist; b. Bklyn., Nov. 10, 1938. BA, U. Guanajuato, 1974; children: Andrew, Viki. Dir. advt. and pub. rels. Kebo, Inc., Natick, Mass., 1965-74; tchr. painting and drawing U. Guanajuato (Mex.), 1974-76; exec. dir. Kreativ Assos., Watertown, Mass., 1976-82; prin. Miki Boni Assocs., 1982-86; editor, designer publ. Interface Found., Watertown, 1987-89, program dir., 1989-91; founder, propr. Silk Road, 1991-94. Exhbns. include Russian-Am. Cultural Ctr., Boston, Art on the Mountain, 1995-96. Recipient spl. painting award Lincoln Center, 1978. Mem. Nat. Assn. Neurolinguistic Programming (master practitioner), Women Art Profls. (co-founder, v.p.).

BONIFER, SHERYL LYNN, congressional aide; b. Alexandria, Va., Sept. 22, 1955; d. Robert R. and Marjorie A. (Davis) Price; m. Arthur J. Bonifer, Jr., Oct. 16, 1976 (div. 1992); children: Melissa, Justin. Student, No. Va. C.C.; student, Washington Bus. Sch. Various positions U.S. Ho. of Reps., Washington, 1975-79; asst. to pres. Bailey/Deardourff & Assocs., McLean, Va., 1980; office mgr. Office of Rep. Stan Parris, Washington, 1981-85; assoc. staff, legis. dir. Office of Rep. James H. Quillen, Washington, 1985—; with minority counsel, subcom. on legis. process Com. on Rules, Ho. of Reps., Washington, 1993-94. Republican. Office: Rules Subcom on Legis Process 101 Cannon House Office Bldg Washington DC 20515

BONINO, FERNANDA, art dealer; b. Torino, Italy, Jan. 5, 1927; came to U.S., 1963; d. Francesco Pogliani and Marina Collino; m. Alfredo Bonino, July 29, 1925 (dec. Jan. 1981). M in Art, U. Italy, Torino, 1942. Dir. Galeria Bonino Ltd., N.Y.C., 1963-90, dir., pres., 1981—. Mem. Art Dealers Assn. Am. Office: Galeria Bonino Ltd 48 Great Jones St New York NY 10012-1133

BONNELL, PAMELA GAY, library administrator; b. Monterey, Calif., Feb. 2, 1948; d. Dewey L. and Marlyce I. (Hansen) Scoggins; m. Chrisman E. Bonnell, Mar. 2, 1974 (div. 1983); m. Verneil S. Henerson, June 18, 1966 (div. 1971), 1 child, V. Samuel Henderson III; m. Hugh R. McElroy, Nov. 10, 1990. BA, Cameron U., Lawton, Okla., 1972; MLS, U. Okla., 1972-73. Libr. Met. Libr. System, Oklahoma City, 1974-75, Office of the City Mgr., Dallas, 1977-80; dir. audience devel. Dallas Symphony Orch., 1980-81; libr. Dallas Morning News, 1981-83; libr. mgr. Plano (Tex.) Pub. Libr. System, 1983-91; dir. libr. svcs. Waco-McLennan County Libr. System, Waco, Tex., 1992—. Author: Fund Raising for Small Libraries, 1983; contbr. chpt. to book, articles to profl. jours. Gala chmn. Easter Seal Soc., Dallas, 1988; bd dirs. Women's Shelter, Plano, Tex., 1991; pres. Townbluff Homeowners Assn., Plano, 1984-90; trustee Dallas Symphony Orch., 1981. Recipient SIRS Intellectual Freedom award Tex. Libr. Assn., 1990. Mem. ALA (councilor-at-large 1990-94, pres. Intellectual Freedom Round Table 1993-94, Shirley Olofson Meml. award 1974, Cert. of Spl. Thanks 1986, John Phillip Immroth award 1990), Ctrl. Tex. Women's Alliance (bd. dirs. 1992—), Leadership Waco Alumni Assn., Rotary, Jr. League. Home: 2334 Melissa Dr Waco TX 76708 Office: Waco-McLennan County Libr Sys 1717 Austin Ave Waco TX 76701-1741

BONNER, BESTER DAVIS, school system administrator; b. Mobile, Ala., June 9, 1938; d. Samuel Matthew and Alma (Davis) Davis; m. Wardell Bonner, Nov. 28, 1964; children: Shawn Patrick, Matthew Wardell. BS, Ala. State Coll., 1959; MS in Library Sci., Syracuse U., 1966; PhD, U. Ala., 1982. Cert. tchr. Librarian Westside High Sch., Talladega, Ala., 1959-64; librarian, tchr. lit. Lane Elem. Sch., Birmingham, Ala., 1964-65; head librarian Jacksonville (Ala.) Elem. Lab. Sch., 1965-70; asst. prof. library media Ala. A&M U., Huntsville, 1970-74; adminstv. asst. to pres. Miles Coll., Birmingham, 1974-78, chmn. div. edn., 1978-85; specialist media Montgomery County Pub. Schs., Md., 1987-88; dir. libr. and media svcs. div. curriculum and ednl. tech. Dist. of Columbia Pub. Schs., 1988—; forum leader Nat. Issues Forum, Domestic Policy Assn. U. Ala., Birmingham, 1983-84; mem. Libr. Svcs. Construction Act Adv. Com. Contbr. writer The Developing Black Family, 1975. Chmn. ethics commn. St. Ala., Montgomery 1977-81; radiothon sire coordinator United Negro Coll. Fund, Birmingham 1981. Mem. ALA, Ala. Instructional Media Assn. (pres. dist. II 1971-72), Assn. Women Deans and Adminstrs., Com. 100, D.C. Assn. Sch. Librs., D.C. Libr. Com., Am. Assn. Sch. Librs., Nat. Assn. State Ednl. Profls. Democrat. Methodist. Home: 9601 Burgess Ln Silver Spring MD 20901-4701

BONNER, KRISTINE ANNE, accountant; b. Bryn Mawr, Pa., Aug. 2, 1969; d. Francis Joseph and Marguerite Anne (Landau) B. BS in Acctg., Villanova U., 1991. Fund acct. Oppenheimer Capital, N.Y.C., 1991-94, Dubin & Swieca, N.Y.C., 1994—.

BONNER, SHIRLEY HARROLD, business communications educator; b. Pitts., July 22, 1929; d. William DeWitt Jr. and Erma Dorothy (Ruppert) Harrold; m. Joseph A. Bonner, Apr. 21, 1956; children: Margaret Leslie, Joseph Edward. BS in Edn., U. Pitts., 1951, MEd, 1971, PhD, 1981. With Gulf Oil Corp., Pitts.; tchr. Three Rivers Bus. Sch., Pitts., Antwerp (Belgium) Internat. Sch., Duff's Bus. Sch., Pitts., C.C. of Allegheny County, Pitts., Learning Ctr. Chatham Coll., 1994—. Author: Margaret of Austria, Governess of the Low Countries, 1507-1530, 2 vols.; contbr. articles to The Balance Sheet. Past bd. dirs. Am. Protestant Ch. of Antwerp. Mem. AAUW (pres. DuBois area br. 1967-69), Assn. for Bus. Communication, World Affairs Coun Pitts. (consul), Delta Zeta. Republican. Home: 403 Denniston Ave Pittsburgh PA 15206-4411

BONOSARO, CAROL ALESSANDRA, professional association executive, former government official; b. New Brunswick, N.J., Feb. 16, 1940; d. Rudolph William and Elizabeth Ann (Betsko) B.; m. Donald D. Kummerfeld, Sept. 8, 1962 (div. Jan. 1970); m. Athanasios Chalkiopoulos, Nov. 21, 1976 (separated Dec. 1990); 1 dau., Melissa. B.A., Cornell U., 1961; postgrad., George Washington U., 1961-62. Analytical statistician Office Mgmt. and Budget, Exec. Office of Pres., Washington, 1961-66; asst. dir. fed. programs div. U.S. Commn. on Civil Rights, Washington, 1966-68; dir. Office Fed. Programs U.S. Commn. on Civil Rights, 1968-69, dir. tech. assistance div., 1969-71, spl. asst. to staff dir., 1972, dir. women's rights program, 1972-79, asst. staff dir. for program planning and evaluation, 1979-80, asst. staff dir. congressional and public affairs, 1980-86; pres. Sr. Execs. Assn., Washington, 1986—. Vice chmn. Nat. Com. on Asian Wives of U.S. Servicemen, 1975-85; pres. Catholics for a Free Choice, 1980-83. Mem. Exec. Women in Govt., Sr. Exec. Assn. (dir. 1981-86, chmn. bd. dirs. 1983-86). Democrat. Home: 5504 Jordan Rd Bethesda MD 20816-1366 Office: Sr Execs Assn PO Box 7610 Washington DC 20044-7610

BONSACK, ROSE MARY HATEM, state legislator, physician; b. Havre de Grace, Md., Oct. 24, 1933; d. Joseph Thomas and Nasma (Joseph) Hatem; m. James P. Bonsack, Aug. 24, 1957; children: Jeanette, Karen, Thomas, David, James J. BS in Chemistry cum laude, Washington Coll., 1955; MD, Med. Coll. Pa., 1960. Intern Easton (Pa.) Hosp., 1961; physician outpatient clinic Kirk Army Hosp., Aberdeen Proving Ground, Md., 1962-74; chief outpatient clinic Kirk Army Hosp., Aberdeen Proving Group, Md., 1968-72, chief dept. hosp. clinics, 1972-74; contract physician Harford County Dept. Health, Md., 1975-78; utilization rev. officer Harford Meml. Hosp., Havre de Grace, 1981-82; pvt. practice Aberdeen, Md., 1981—; mem. Md. Gen. Assembly, 1991, chmn. house rules and exec. nominations com., 1991-94; coord. clinics Hypertensive Coun. Md., 1977-81; reviewer quality assurance for nursing homes in Harford County, Md. Licensing Div., 1977-81; utilization rev. officer Harford Meml. Hosp., Havre de Grace, 1981-82; med. dir. Ashley Alcoholic Rehab., Havre de Grace, 1983-84; mem. Bd. Med. Examiners Md.; mem., exec. sec. Commn. on Med. Discipline, 1985-88. V.p. St. Joan of Arc Home-Sch. Assn., 1968, pres., 1969, mem., 1968-85; v.p. No. Md. Heart Assn., 1969, pres., 1970, bd. dirs., 1973; bd. dirs. Mann House, Bel Air, Md., 1973-82, Harford County Cancer Soc., 1973-86; mem. John Carroll Home-Sch. Assn., 1974—, 1st v.p., 1975, pres., 1975; bd. dirs. John Carroll H.S., 1975—, pres. bd. dirs., 1979-85; mem. Harford County Dem. Cen. Com., 1987-90; mem. chief exec.'s coun. Harford C.C., 1990. Recipient Outstanding Contbn. to Md. Traffic Safety citation State of Md., 1969, Cert. of Merit for svc. Md. Cancer Soc., 1977, Women Helping Women award Soroptomists Harford and Cecil Counties, 1983-84. Mem. Am. Acad. Family Physicians (alt. del. 1990-94, del. from Md. 1994-96, chmn. chpt. affairs com. 1992—, commn. on regulation 1993-96), Med. Chirurgical Faculty Md., Hartford County Med. Soc. (sec. 1967, pres. 1968, v.p. 1978, 78, Outstanding Comty. Svc. citation 1979), Md. Acad. Family Physicians (v.p. 1987, pres. 1988). Office: Md Gen Assembly 118 W Bel Air Ave Aberdeen MD 21001-3238

BONTRAGER, JUDITH RUTH, educator; b. Youngstown, Ohio, June 17, 1939; d. Dwight Burr and Ruth Ida (Stand) Hoffman; m. G. DeWayne Bontrager, Aug. 20, 1960; children: Mark DeWayne, Todd David, Amy Sue. BS, Taylor U., 1960; MS, Nova U., 1981. Plantation cmty. presch., adminstr. Plantation, Fla., 1974-84; early intervention specialist Crossroads, Davie, Fla., 1984-85; instructional educator Broward County Schs., Fort Lauderdale, Fla., 1986-96; curriculum coord. Boward County Schs., Fort Lauderdale, 1988-94, tech. coord., 1991—; adminstrv. sec. The Ctr. for Counseling and Devel., Plantation, 1985—. Mem. AAUW (chmn. edn. com. 1988-92). Home: 817 S University Dr Plantation FL 33324 Office: The Ctr for Counseling and Devel 817 S University Dr Plantation FL 33324

BOOCHEVER, ANN PAULA, music educator; b. Juneau, Alaska, Sept. 3, 1950; d. Robert and Colleen (Maddox) B.; m. Richard L. Stenson, Aug. 22, 1973 (div. 1977); children: Heidi Liorah, Zachary F.; m. Scott H. Miller, Sept. 1987; 1 child, Spencer Miller. BE, Western State Coll. of Colo., 1972. Cert. type A tchr., Alaska; provisional cert. educator, Conn. Tchr. Juneau (Alaska) Sch. Dist., 1972-74, tchr. classroom music, 1982-83, 88-89; music tchr. pvt.music Juneau, Anchorage, 1974-80; pres. sch. tchr. Valley Pre-Sch. Coop., Juneau, 1986-87; co-founder, edn. dir. Alaska Children's Theatre, Juneau, 1985-89; instr. music edn. U. Alaska Southeast, Juneau, 1986-90; tchr. classroom music Newtown (Conn.) Bd. Edn., 1990—; dir. S.E. Alaska Native Fine Arts Camp, Alaska Children's Theatre, Juneau, 1989; presenter Music Educator's Nat. Conf., Waterbury, Conn., 1995, Alaska Staff Devel. Network, 1996, Southcentral Alaska Instrnl. Improvement Acad., Anchorage, Alaska. Producer, host, founder: (KTOO Pub. Broadcasting Sta.) "That's Kids", 1985-90, Rain Country, 1985-89; author: (play) Dealing With It, 1990, Adaptation of King Island Christmas, 1991; author: (book) My Dad and the Pear Tree, 1994; author, dir. musical stage adaptations of children's books, 1985-94. Delegation leader Creative Response, Saransk, Russia, 1992. Recipient Talent scholarship Boeing Sch. of Excellence, U. Wash., 1984, Spl. Recognition, Alaska Native Studies Program, 1989; named Outstanding Tchr. of Yr., Weller Found., 1993. Mem. Music Educators Nat. Conf., Am. Orff Schulwerk Assn. (Conn. chpt. Barbara Potter award 1992). Democrat. Office: Head O'Meadow Sch Bogg's Hill Rd Newtown CT 06482

BOOHER, ALICE ANN, lawyer; b. Indpls., Oct. 6, 1941; d. Norman Rogers and Olga (Bonke) B. BA in Polit. Sci., Butler U., 1963; LLB, Ind. U., 1966, JD, 1967. Bar: Ind. 1966, U.S. Dist. Ct. (so. dist.) Ind. 1966, U.S. Tax Ct. 1970, U.S. Ct. Customs and Patent Appeals 1969, U.S. Ct. Mil. Appeals 1969, U.S. Ct. Appeals (D.C. cir.) 1969, U.S. Supreme Ct. 1969; cert. tchr., Ind. Rsch. asst., law clk. Supreme and Appellate Cts. Ind., Indpls., 1966; legal intern, atty., staff legal advisor Dept. State, Washington, 1966-69; staff legal adviser Bd. Vets. Appeals, Washington, 1969-78, sr. atty., 1978—, counsel, 1991—; former counselor D.C. Penal Facilities and Shelters. Author: The Nuclear Test Ban Treaty and the Third Party Non-Nuclear States, also children's books; contbr. articles to various publs., chpts. to Whiteman Digest of International Law; exhibited crafts, needlepoint in juried artisan fairs. Bd. dirs. numerous community groups, including D.C. Women's Commn. for Crime Prevention, 1980-81; pres., legal adviser VA employees Assn. Recipient various awards; named Ky. Col., 1988. Mem. DAV, VFW Aux., LWV, Women's Bar Assn. D.C., D.C. Sexual Assault Coalition (chmn. legal com.), Butler U. Alumni Assn., Nat. Mus. Women in Arts, Bus. and Profl. Women (pres. D.C. 1980-81, nat. UN fellow 1974, nat. bd. dirs. 1980-82, 87—, Woman of Yr. award D.C. 1975, Marguerite Rawalt award D.C. 1986), USO, Women Officers Profl. Assns., Navy League U.S.A., Am. Legion Aux., Vietnam Vets. Am., Nat. Task Force on Women of the Mil. and Women Mil. POWS (chair Ester Peterson Tribute 1995).

BOOKER, BETTY MAE, writer; b. Allentown, Pa., Nov. 26, 1948; d. Harold George and Bessie (Bealer-Miller) Bartholomew; m. Samuel Efford Booker III, June 27, 1970; children, Liesel Tamarah, Dacey Justin, Jaeson Bartholomew. BA in English, Millersville State Coll., 1970. Contbr. poetry to jours. and lit. mags. including Plainsong, America, The Christian Century, Poetry Now. Home: 27826 Island Dr Salisbury MD 21801-2350

BOOKER, BRENDA LYNN, elementary school educator; b. Phila., Sept. 25, 1963. BS in Clin. Dietetics, Indiana (Pa.) U., 1985; cert. in Mid. Grades, Armstrong State Coll., 1993. Tchr. 7th grade math. and science Liberty County Mid./H.S., Hinesville, Ga., 1993; tchr. 5th grade Taylors Creek Elem. Sch., 1993—; poetry coord. Taylors Creek Elem. Sch., Hinesville, 1993—. Capt. U.S. Army, 1985-92. Methodist. Office: Taylors Creek Elem Sch 378 Airport Rd Hinesville GA 31313

BOOKER, DOROTHY OELRICH, educator; b. Hull, IA, Sept. 1, 1913; d. Charles David and Grace (Van Wyke) Oelrich; m. James Oakley Booker, Dec. 29, 1946; children: Paul, David, Philip, John. BS in music, Iowa State Tchrs. Coll., 1936; M in music, Northwestern Sch. of Music, 1940. Tchr. One Rm. Rural Sch., Sioux County, Iowa, 1930-32, Geneseo Consol. Sch., Buckingham, Iowa, 1936-39, Redlands H.S., Redlands, Calif., 1940-42, Reedley H.S. and Jr. Coll., Reedley, Calif., 1942-47; piano tchr., Sacramento, Calif., 1949-89, choir dir. Centennial U. Meth. Sacramento, 1952-62, organist, 1978-80. Mem. P.T.A. Hollywood Park Sch., 1954-65, founder Silver Friendship Club, 1964—, vol., dir. Clothes Closet for Needy, 1973-93. Recipient Faith and Svc. award South Sacramenta Ecumenical Parish, 1980, 93, Gold Cow award for vols. Heifer Project Internat., 1990. Mem. Sigma Alpha Iota. Home: 2315 Hooke Way Sacramento CA 95822-2821

BOOKER, NANA LAUREL, public relations executive; b. Waco, Tex., Aug. 5, 1946; d. Karl and Helen Dorothy (Keene) B. BA, Baylor U., 1968; MA, U. Fla., 1970; MBA, Pepperdine U., 1980. Asst. prof. comm. U. New Orleans, 1970-74, 1977-78; pub. rels. cons. New Orleans, 1974-78; dir. pub. rels. Touro Infirmary, New Orleans, 1976-78; dir. comm. Lifemark Corp., Houston, 1978-81; pres. Comm. Alliance, Houston, 1981-82; dir. internat. rels., comm. Mayor's Office, City of Houston, 1982-84; pres. Nana Booker & Assocs. (now Booker/Hancock & Assocs.), Houston, 1984—. Co-author: Introduction to Theatrical Arts, 1972. Mem. South Tex. Dist. Export Coun., Houston, 1988-92; press aide campaign K. Whitmire for Mayor, Houston, 1982; mem. exec. adv. bd. coll. bus. adminstrn. U. Houston, 1990—; bd. dirs. Escape Ctr., 1990-93, YWCA, Houston, 1991-92. Recipient Internat. Assn. Bus. Communicators award, Women in Comms. awards, Crystal award Am. Mktg. Assn., Outstanding Pub. Rels. Practitioner award Tex. Pub. Rels. Assn., 1996. Mem. Pub. Rels. Soc. Am. (accredited, chairperson internat. sect. 1993—, Excalibur award 1988, Cert. of Appreciation 1993, 94, 95, mem. U.S. coun.), Internat. Assn. Bus. Communicators, Internat. Pub. Rels. Assn., Houston World Trade Assn. (bd. dirs. 1986—), Houston-Shenzhen Sister City Assn. (bd. dirs. 1987-94), Swiss-Am. C. of C. (bd. dirs. 1987-90), River Oaks Breakfast Club.

BOOKER, SHIRLEY RUTH, entertainment specialist; b. Center, Tex., Oct. 15, 1947; d. Preston and Elminer Brittian; m. Charles Seach, Jan. 3, 1967 (div.); 1 child, Charles Seach Jr.; m. Patrick Henry Booker, Dec. 31, 1975; 1 child, Roshon Booker. BS in Social Work, U. Ctrl. Tex., 1992. Recreation specialist Community Recreation Divsn., Ft. Hood, Tex., 1974-88; comml. entertainment specialist Community Recreation Divsn., Ft. Hood, 1988—; cons. in field; rest and recuperation coord. S.W. Asia Theatre during Operation Desert Storm. Author: (jour.) Desert Storm/A Time to Love, 1992. Recipient Desert shield, Desert Storm medal Dept. of Def., 1992, Dept. of Army Comdr.'s award, 1985, Cert. of achievement, 1991, Superior Civilian Svc. award, 1991. Democrat. Mem. Assembly of God Ch. Home: 1310 Hammond Dr Killeen TX 76543-5220 Office: Hdqs and III Corps Bldg 1001 Rm 217 W/DPCA Fort Hood TX 76544

BOOKER, VALERIE SCOTT, tennis player; b. Raleigh, N.C.; d. James Frank and Helen (Blood) Scott; m. William J. Booker Jr., Mar. 3, 1990; children: Cameron Wells, William Rayworth. BA, Hollins COll. Sales asst. Merrill Lynch, Chgo., 1986-88; sales Caldwell Real Estate, South Boston, Va., 1988-90; Meyers-Boggs adminstr. Wellspring & Assocs., South Boston, Va., 1993—; tennis pro Halifax (Va.) Country Club, 1995—; bd. dirs. Halifax Country Club. Mem. NOW. Democrat. Methodist. Home: 15119 River Rd Sutherlin VA 24594

BOONE, ALICIA KAY LANIER, marketing communications consultant, writer; b. Ft. Worth, Sept. 3, 1941; d. John David and Reba Louise (Smith) Lanier; m. William T. Boone, July 22, 1967 (div. June 1988); children: Katherine, Suzanne, Lisa, Norma, Matthew. Student, Abilene (Tex.) Christian U., 1959-60, North Tex. State U., 1960-64; BA in Sociology cum laude, U. Tex., Dallas, 1993. Reporter Daily Oklahoman/Oklahoma City Times, 1964-66; feature writer Houston Post, 1967; info. rep. Okla. Dept. Inst., Social and Rehab. Services, Oklahoma City, 1967-73; dir. pub. info. United Way Mecklenburg-Union, Charlotte, N.C., 1974-76; account mgr., sr. writer Epley Assocs./Pub. Relations, Charlotte, 1977-78; account mgr. Yarbrough Co./Advt., Pub. Relations, Dallas, 1979-82; owner Boone & Assoc./Pub. Relations and Advt., Richardson, Tex., 1982-88; v.p. Yarbrough Co./Advt., Dallas, 1988-90; owner The Creative Solution, Dallas, 1990—; bd. dirs Hope Cottage, 1993-95; pub. Adoption Triad Forum, 1993—. Author, editor History of Child Welfare In Oklahoma, 1976. Mem. SBA (region VI adv. coun. 1990-94), Pub. Rels. Soc. Am., Assn. Women Entrepreneurs of Dallas (pres. 1987-88), Richardson C. of C. (editor newsletter 1986-87), Dallas Women in Bus. (Advt. of Yr. 1988), Small Bus. Congress in Dallas (co-chair 1988).

BOONE, CELIA TRIMBLE, lawyer; b. Clovis, N.Mex., Mar. 3, 1953; d. George Harold and Barbara Ruth (Foster) T.; m. Billy W. Boone, Apr. 21, 1990. BS, Ea. N.Mex. U., 1976, MA, 1977; JD, St. Mary's U., San Antonio, 1982. Bar: Tex. 1982, U.S. Dist. Ct. (no. dist.) Tex. 1983, U.S. Ct. Appeals (5th cir.) 1985, U.S. Supreme Ct. 1986. Instr. English, Eastern N.Mex. U., Portales, 1977-78; editor Curry County Times, Clovis, 1978-79; assoc. Schulz & Robertson, Abilene, Tex., 1982-85, Scarborough, Black, Tarpley & Scarborough, 1985-87; ptnr. Scarborough, Black, Tarpley & Trimble, Abilene, Tex., 1988-90, Scarborough, Black, Tarpley & Boone, 1990-94, of counsel Scarborough, Tarpley, Boone & Fouts, 1994-96; prin. Law Office of Celia Trimble Boone, , Abilene, 1996—; instr. legal rsch. and writing St. Mary's Sch. Law, 1981-82. Legal adv. to bd. dirs. Abilene Kennel Club, 1983-85; mem. landmarks commn. City of Abilene, 1989-90. Recipient Outstanding Young Lawyer of Abilene, 1988. Mem. ABA, State Bar Tex. (mem. disciplinary rev. com. 1989-93), Am. Trial Lawyers Assn., Tex. Trial Lawyers Assn., Tex. Criminal Def. Lawyers Assn., Tex. Acad. Family Law Specialists, Tex. Bd. Legal Specialization (cert. 1987), Abilene Bar Assn. (bd. dirs. 1985-86, 87-88, sec./treas. 1985-86), Abilene Young Lawyers Assn. (bd. dirs. 1985-86, 87-89, treas. 1985-86, pres.-elect 1987-88, pres. 1988-89), NOW, ACLU, Phi Alpha Delta. Democrat. Avocations: needlework, gardening. Office: 104 Pine St Ste 705 Abilene TX 79601

BOONE, DOROTHY MAE, county official; b. Gordon, Nebr., May 29, 1919; d. C.H. and Ethel Mae (Lewis) Perkins; m. M.H. Boone Oct. 2, 1943 (dec. Sept. 1954). AA, Iowa Western Community Coll., Council Bluffs, 1977; grad., Am. Legion Officers Sch., Indpls., 1973. Notary pub., Iowa. Nat. VA accredited svc. rep. Office Gen. Counsel, Washington, 1976—; exec. sec., adminstrv. asst., adminstrv. sec. Pottawattamie County Veterans' Affairs Commn., Council Bluffs, Iowa; dir. Veteran Affairs Commn., Pottawattamie County, 1987-92; profl. svc. officer DAV, 1989—; mem. local bd. SSS, Washington, 1980—; mem., chair Harrison, Shelby and Pottawattamie counties Shelby and Pottawattamie counties SSS, 1981—. Recipient Cert. of Appreciation Kiwanis, 1985, VA Nat. Svc. Officers award, 1960, SSS, 1991, commendation DAV, 1987, County Svc. award Nat. VA, 1986, 92, Woman of Yr. award Am. Biol. Inst., 1993, Rep. Congl. Order Liberty, 1993, Internat. Order Merit award, 1994, Rep. Nat. Congl. Order of Freedom, 1995, Internat. Order Merit award Bd. Internat. Biog. Ctr., Cambridge, Eng., 1994, Citizen of Yr. award His Royal Highness Kevin Prince Regent Hutt River Province Principality, 1995, Rep. Congl. Order of Freedom award Newt Gingrich, Spkr. of House, 1995, Cert. of Appreciation Ams. for Sr. Citizens in U.S.A., 1995 ; named Most Admired Woman of Decade Am. Biog. Inst., 1993, Citizen of Yr. Prince Kevin Prince Regent, 1995, Citizen of Royal Proclamation Prince Kevin Prince Regent, 1995. Home: 1320 N 21st St Council Bluffs IA 51501-0909

BOONSHAFT, HOPE JUDITH, public relations executive; b. Phila., May 3, 1949; d. Barry and Lorelei Gail (Rienzi) B. BA, Pa. State U., 1972; postgrad. Del. Law Sch., Kellogg Inst. Mgmt. Tng. Program writer Youth Edn., N.Y.C., 1972; legal aide to judge, Phila., 1973; dir. spl. projects Guiffre Med. Center, Phila., 1975; Arlen Specter senatorial campaign fin. dir., Phila., 1975; fin. dir. Jimmy Carter Presdl. Campaign, Atlanta, 1976; nat. fin. dir. Dem. Nat. Com., 1977-78; dir. devel. World Jewish Congress, N.Y.C., 1978; dir. devel. Yeshiva U., L.A., 1979; dir. communications Nat. Easter Seal Soc., Chgo., 1979-83; CEO Boonshaft-Lewis & Savitch Pub. Rels. and Govt. Affairs, L.A., 1983-93; sr. v.p. Edelman Worldwide, 1993-95, Sony Pictures Entertainment, L.A., 1995—; spl. adv. community rels. The White House, 1977-80; guest lectr. U. Ill., 1982, May Co.'s Calif. Women in Bus. Bd. dirs. L.A. Arts Coun., Hollywood Heritage Coun., Show Coalition, Jewish TV Network. Named 1 of 6 Non Stop Achievers, GermaineMonteil. Mem. Nat. Soc. Fundraisers, Am. Inst. Wine and Food (bd. dirs.), Am. Jewish Com. (exec. com.), Nat. Conf. Christians & Jews (bd. dirs.), Show Coalition, Jewish TV Network (bd. dirs.), Women's Nat. Dem. Club, Alpha Chi Omega. Home: 13168 Boca De Canon Ln Los Angeles CA 90049-2220 Office: Sony Pictures Entertainment 10202 W Washington Blvd Culver City CA 90232

BOORAS, HEATHER, creative director, graphic designer; b. Grosse Pointe, Mich., Jan. 19, 1970; d. Nickolas Pericles and Margaret (Ferguson) B. BA in English, U. Iowa, 1992. Sr. designer Trader Publishing, Farmington, Mich., 1992; owner, editor Zooom, Inc. Entertainment Mag., Troy, Mich., 1992-94; sr. designer Mich. Renaissance Festival, Birmingham, 1994; sr. designer, creative director Village Green Comms., Farmington Hills, Mich., 1994—. Head coach synchro Troy (Mich.) H.S. Athletics, 1993—; instr. synchro Troy Cont. Edn., 1993—. Recipient Best of the Best VG Entertainment, 1996k Intergenerational award State of Mich., 1996. Mem. AAUW, NOW, NAFE, Adcrafter Club Detroit, Alpha Chi Omega (v.p.). Greek Orthodox. Office: Village Green Comms 30833 Northwestern Hwy Farmington MI 48334

BOORD, PATRICIA MARIE, adult education educator; b. Johnstown, Pa., Mar. 2, 1955; d. Walter John and Lois Jean (Murnin) Czyrnik; m. Rodney Harvard Boord, Apr. 14, 1984; 1 child, Adam Michael. BS in Music Edn., Edinboro U. of Pa., 1977; MS in Tng. and Learning, Nova Southeastern U., Ft. Lauderdale, Fla., 1992. With FBI, Washington, 1979-82, document classification specialist, 1982-85; writer/editor FBI, Quantico, Va., 1985-88, instructional sys. specialist, 1988—; solo/1st cornet Nat. Concert Band Am., Alexandria, Va., 1981-85; prin. trumpet Constellation Dance Band, Alexandria, 1982-86, Concordia Tricentennial German Band, Washington, 1983-86, Middleburg (Va.) Players, 1985-86; music dir. Alexandria Citizens Band, 1985-86; mem. distance learning com. FBI Acad., Quantico, 1994—. Contbr. articles to profl. jours. Music dir. Vienna (Va.) Cmty. Band, 1981-85, Fredericksburg (Va.) United Meth. Ch. Instrumental Ensemble, 1989-91; instrumental music advisor Fairfax County (Va.) Coun. of Arts Adv. Panel, 1982-83. Named to Outstanding Young Women of Am., 1983. Mem. Assn. for Devel. of Computer-Based Instructional Sys. Office: FBI Academy Quantico VA 22135

BOOSE, SUE ANN, health facility administrator; b. Sandusky, Ohio, Aug. 23, 1955; d. William P. and Barbara A. (Biechele) Tuemler; m. Frederick J. Boose, Jan. 7, 1993. Owner/mgr. Ann-Sir Employment Svc., Sandusky, Ohio, 1975-91; paralegal/workers' compensation adminstr. Robert Zelvy, Atty., Sandusky, 1986-89; bus. mgr. Livingston Chiropractic Office, Norwalk, Ohio, 1993—. Named Woman of Yr. Providence Hosp. Women's Ctr., 1989. Mem. NOW, Chiropractic Assts. Support Team, Sandusky Bus. and Profl. Women (treas. 1996-97, Young Careerist 1979). Democrat. Roman Catholic. Home: 1101 State Rd 61 E Norwalk OH 44857

BOOTH, ANNA BELLE, accountant; b. Homesville, Ohio, Jan. 15, 1912; d. John Wilson and M. Pearl (Toomey) B.; m. Guy DiAmbrosio, Apr. 29, 1930; 1 child, Guy Booth. BA, Taylor Coll., 1930. Office mgr. in charge of mfg. Jacobs Tailored Clothes, Inc., Phila., 1931-41; acct., corp. cashier Lehigh Coal and Navigation Co., Phila., 1941-55; acct. Bishop & Hedberg, Phila., 1955-57; acct., office mgr. The Camax Co., Phila., 1957-60; office mgr., cashier New Eng. Mutual Life Ins. Co., Phila., 1960-67; acct. Wall & Ochs, Inc., Phila., 1967-71; comptr. Bisler Packaging Div./Pet, Inc., Phila., 1971-82; ret. Mem. Am. Soc. Women Accts. (Phila. pres. 1956-58, dir. 1952-54, 62-64, 73-75), LWV (Phila.). Home: 2122 Sansom St Philadelphia PA 19103-4429

BOOTH, BARBARA RIBMAN, civic worker; b. N.Y.C., May 2, 1928; d. Benjamin C. and Ceclia (Lowe) Ribman; m. Mitchell B. Booth, July 13, 1952; 1 child, Brian S. AA, Centenary Jr. Coll., Hackettstown, N.Y., 1948; BA, Barnard Coll., 1950. Pres. women's alliance, chmn., Christmas fair 1st Congl. Ch. of City of N.Y., 1959-63; mem. vol. com. Sheltering Arms Children's Svc., N.Y.C.; vol., coord. high sch. visits, pres. aux. N.Y. Hosp., 1989-91, co-chmn., 1995—; trustee Florence K. Griswold Meml. Fund. Com., All Souls Unitarian Ch., N.Y.C., United Hosp. Funds Auxiliary for N.Y. Hosp., 1996; bd. dir. women's div. Jefferson Dem. Club. N.Y.C.; committeewoman N.Y. County Dem. Com.; bd. govs., v.p. N.Y. Fruit and Flower Mission, Inc.; del. city conv., chmn. East Manhattan br. LWV. Recipient Auxilian of N.Y. Hosp. award, 1996. Home: 75 E End Ave New York NY 10028-7909

BOOTH, DIANNE WYATT, real estate broker; b. Birmingham, Ala., July 13, 1949; d. Lester C. and Mary (Brown) Wyatt; m. Marc A. Booth, June 28, 1969; children: Robin Elizabeth, Michael Anderson. Student, U. Ga., 1967-68, U. Ala., 1968-69. Adminstrn./admissions staff Bapt. Hosp./Montclair, Birmingham, 1968-69, Presbyn. Hosp., Dallas, 1969-72; opthalmic asst. Dixon, Lawaczeck & McKinnon, Birmingham, 1972-74; resident mgr. Windcliffe Apts. Trust, Birmingham, 1974-77; real estate agt. Strickland Realty, Birmingham, 1981-83; real estate broker Wyatt Realty, Inc., Birmingham, 1983—; pres. Wyatt Cos., Inc., Birmingham, 1988—; mgr. Wyatt Constrn. Co., Inc., Birmingham, 1980—; residential sales coun. Nat. Assn. Realtors, Washington, 1985, real estate brokerage coun., 1987; Ala. rep. womens coun. Nat. Assn. Home Builders, Washington, 1990; bd. dirs. Greater Birmingham Assn. Home Builders, 1991. Leader Girl Scout Cahaba Coun., Birmingham, 1980-86; appointee beautification bd. City of Hoover, Ala., 1981-84, chmn. Mayor's breakfast, 1984; Festival of Trees bd. mem. The Children's Hosp. Ala., Birmingham, 1993-94. Named Outstanding Mem. of the Yr., Magic City Frogmen, Birmingham, 1978. Mem. Greater Birmingham Assn. Homebuilders (pres., bd. mem., Mem. of Yr. 1991), The Charity League of Birmingham, Inc. (sr. sustainer, sec., exec. bd. mem.), Country Club Highlands Garden Club (pres., bd. dirs.), Sports Car Club Am. Ala. Region (officer), Hoover Svc. Club. Republican. Baptist. Office: Wyatt Cos Inc 227 Lorna Sq Birmingham AL 35216

BOOTH, JANE SCHUELE, real estate broker, executive; b. Cleve.; d. Norman Andrew and Frances Ruth (Hankey) Schuele; m. George Warren Booth, Dec. 6, 1968. AA, Stephens Coll., 1946; student, U. Mo., 1946-47. Lic. real estate broker, Fla. Assoc. J.M. Mathes Inc., N.Y.C., 1947-48; dept. supr. Lord and Taylor, Scarsdale, N.Y., 1948-50; art coord. J. Walter Thompson, Inc., N.Y.C., 1953-58; art buyer SSC&B Inc. Advt., N.Y.C., 1959-80; pres. Jane Schuele Booth Realty, Ocala, Fla., 1982—. Mem. Fla. Thoroughbred Fillies, Ocala, 1980—; charter mem., trustee Royal Dames for Cancer Rsch., Inc., Ocala, 1986—; treas. Ladies Aux. Fla. H.C.H. Inc., Ocala, 1986-90; bd. visitors Fla. Horsemen's Children's Home, Inc., 1983-90. Mem. Ocala/Marion County Assn. Realtors, Ocala/Marion County C. of C. (agribus./equine com.), Nat. Assn. Realtors, Fla. Assn. Realtors, Estates Club. Home: 1771 SW 55th Street Rd Ocala FL 34474-5933 Office: PO Box 5538 Ocala FL 34478-5538

BOOTH, JODY SHELTON, educational executive director; b. Norton, Kans., Aug. 4, 1944; d. James Pratt and Rita Merle (Thompson) Shelton. BA, Ottawa U., 1967; MEd, Emporia State U., 1977; EdD, Kans. U., 1991. Tchr. Belvoir Elem. Sch., Topeka, 1967-68, Ctrl. Elem. Sch., Olathe, Kans., 1968-77; prin. Westview Elem. Sch., Olathe, Kans., 1977-80, Tomahawk Elem. Sch., Olathe, Kans., 1980-88; exec. dir. human resources Olathe Dist. Schs., 1988—; cons. Master Tchr., Manhattan, Kans., 1981-86; adj. prof. Emporia (Kans.) State U., 1990—; chair North Ctrl. Edn. Team, 1984; mem. adv. coun. Sch. Edn., Kans. U., Lawrence, 1992—; mem. com. Five Yr. Tech. Plan, Olathe, 1991—. Contbr. articles to profl. jours. Recipient Outstanding Jayne award Jaycees, 1972, Outstanding Young Woman Kans., 1980. Mem. NAESP (Nat. Disting. Prin. award 1987-88), AASPA (affiliate), Kans. Career Devel. and Placement Assn., Kans. Assn. Elem. Sch. Prins. (pres., Nat. Disting. Prin. award 1987-88, Olathe C. of C., United Sch. Adminstrs. (bd. dirs.), Optimist. Home: 11546 S Brentwood Dr Olathe KS 66061-9388 Office: Olathe Dist Schs 1005 S Pitt St Olathe KS 66061-5242

BOOTH, LINDA LEIGH, vocational educator; b. Dallas, May 12, 1953; d. Federico Rose and Gladys Ruth (Petty) Buenrostro; m. Joe Henry Booth Jr., May 24, 1985; children: Kathryn Leigh, Elizabeth Rose. BS in Home Econs., Abilene Christian U., 1985. Instr. Abilene (Tex.) Ind. Sch. Dist., 1988—; mem. edn. vocat. adv. bd. Abilene Ind. Sch. Dist., Abilene, 1991—, mem. textbook selection com., 1990-91. Judge Future Homemakers of Am., Abilene, 1987-88; mem. children's ministries com. Univ. Ch. of Christ, 1993. Mem. Am. Vocat. Assn., Tex. Vocat. Spl. Needs Assn., Vocat. Home Econs. Tchrs. Assn. of Tex. (alt. dir. 1996—), Tex. Restaurant Assn., Abilene Restaurant Assn., Tex. Classroom Tchrs. Assn., Assn. Tex. Profl. Educators, Hospitality Educators Assn. Tex., Future Homemakers Am. Home: 709 Deborah Dr Abilene TX 79601-5535 Office: Abilene HS 2800 N 6th St Abilene TX 79603-7125

BOOTH, MARGARET A(NN), communications company executive; b. N.Y.C., Dec. 25, 1946; d. Herbert and Alice (Traum) B.; m. Marvin E. Schechter, Jan. 22, 1984. BS, U. Wis., 1968. Editl. asst. Bantam Books, N.Y.C., 1968-70; publicity asst. Ruder & Finn Inc., N.Y.C., 1970-71, dir. radio and TV, 1971-76, v.p., 1974-76; pres. Pub. Interest Pub. Rels., N.Y.C., 1976—, M. Booth & Assocs., Inc., N.Y.C., 1983—. Author: Promoting Issues and Ideas, 1987; contbr. articles to profl. jours. Bd. dirs. Task Force on Permanancy Planning for Foster Children, 1994. Recipient YWCA Salute to Women Achievers, City of N.Y., 1985. Mem. Pub. Rels. Soc. Am., Women in Comm. (Matrix award for Pub. Rels. 1987), Women Execs. in Pub. Rels. Office: M Booth & Assocs Inc 470 Park Ave S # 10N New York NY 10016-6819

BOOTH, RACHEL ZONELLE, nursing educator; b. Seneca, S.C., Feb. 10, 1936; m. Richard B. Booth, Feb. 13, 1957; 1 child, Kevin M. Student, Furman U., 1953-54; diploma in nursing, Greenville (S.C.) Gen. Hosp., 1956; student, U. Alaska, 1964-66; BS in Nursing, U. Md., Balt., 1968; MS in Nursing, U. Md., 1970, PhD in Adminstrn. Higher Edn., 1978. RN. Staff nurse VA Hosp., Murfreesboro, Tenn., 1957-58, U. Colo. Med. Ctr., Denver, 1957-58; nurse psychiatry dept. Patton State Hosp., Calif., 1958-59; staff nurse USAF Dispensary, Iraklion, Greece, 1959-60; charge nurse psychiatry Santa Rose Med. Ctr., San Antonio, 1961; staff nurse Shannon S.W. Tex. Meml. Hosp., San Angelo, 1962; supervisory clin. nurse, head nurse U.S. Dept. Health, Edn., and Welfare/USPHS/Indian Health Service, Anchorage, 1962-66; staff nurse U.S. Dept. Health, Edn., and Welfare/USPHS, Balt., 1966, 68; assoc. dir. dept. nursing U. Md. Hosp., 1970-76, dir. primary care nursing svc., 1976-81; asst. prof. Sch. Nursing U. Md., 1972-76, asst. prof. Sch. Pharmacy, 1972-80, acting assoc. dean Sch. Nursing, 1979-81, assoc. prof. Sch. Nursing, 1979, assoc. prof. clin. pharmacy, 1980-83, assoc. dean for undergrad. studies Sch. Nursing, 1981-83, co-dir. nurse practitioner program Sch. Nursing, 1972-76, chairperson grad. program dept. primary care, 1974-79; dean, Sch. of Nursing and asst. v.p. for health affairs Duke U., Durham, N.C., 1984-87; dean Sch. Nursing U. Ala. at Birmingham, University Station, 1987—; instr. Sch. Medicine U. Md., 1972-83, program dir. primary care nurse practitioner program continuing edn., 1976-82, project dir. Robert Wood Johnson Nurse Faculty Fellowship program, 1977-82; mem. joint practice com. Med. and Chirurg. Faculty Md., 1974-77, mem. tech. adv. com. for physician's assts. Bd. Med. Examiners Md., 1975-80; mem. adv. com. nursing program Community Coll. Balt., 1976-79; mem. Joint Commn. on Accreditation of Hosps., pres. Md. Council Dirs. of Assoc. Degree, Diploma, and Baccalaureate Programs, 1982-83; mem. adv. bd. nursing Essex Community Coll., 1983; mem. peer rev. panel advanced nurse edn. nursing div. U.S. Dept. Health and Human Services, 1987—. Editor (with others) Hospital Pharmacy, 1971-72; asst. editor Jour. Profl. Nursing, 1984-87; contbr. articles on nursing to prof. jours. Bd. dirs. Health and Welfare Coun. Ctrl. Md., Inc., 1974-78, v.p., 1975-78; mem. health adv. com. to Pres. of Pakistan, 1981—. Recipient numerous grants for nursing adminstrn., 1972—. Mem. ANA (mem. nat. rev. com. 1975-78, v.p. 1977, chair 1978), Internat. Coun. Nurses (observer conf. 1981), Nat. Acad. Practice for Nursing (vice chairperson 1984-89), Nat. Orgn. for Nurse Execs., Nat. League for Nursing, Coun. Nat. Acad. Practice, Am. Assn. Colls. in Nursing (dean's summer seminar com. 1984-85, edn. and credentialing com. 1985-86, nominating com. 1986-87, bd. dirs. 1989-96, pres.-elect 1992-94, pres. 1994-96), N.C. Orgn. Nurse Execs. (bd. dirs. 1986-87), So. Coun. Collegiate Edn. for Nursing (exec. com. 1986-91, v.p., bd. dirs. 1991-94), Sigma Theta Tau (chairperson nominating com. 1974, mem. 1975, rec. sec. 1980-83). Home: 3112 Bradford Pl Birmingham AL 35242-4602

BOOTH, ROSEMARY, management educator; b. New Rochelle, N.Y., Mar. 23, 1941; d. Robert Roche and Margaret Mary (Hogan) B. BA, Marquette U., 1962; MBA, Iona Coll., 1971; PhD, U. Ky., 1991. Sec. IBM, White Plains, N.Y., 1965-69; word processing mgr. IBM, N.Y.C., 1969-71; communications profl. IBM, Franklin Lakes, N.J., 1971-79; info. mgr. IBM, Lexington, Ky., 1979-89; IBM faculty loan Midway Coll., Lexington, Ky., 1988-89; asst. prof. U. N.C., Charlotte, 1991—; instr. United Way Leadership Devel. Program, Lexington, 1985-87. Bd. dirs. YWCA, Lexington, 1981-87, Vol. Ctr. Blue Grass, Lexington, 1986-90; adv. bd. Charlotte Vol. Ctr., 1994-95. Mem. Acad. Mgmt., Speech Comm. Assn., Assn. Bus. Comm. Home: 9503 Marsena Ct Charlotte NC 28213-3760 Office: U NC Dept Mgmt Charlotte NC 28223

BOOTHE, CHERRI WORSTELL, librarian; b. Clarksburg, W.Va., July 16, 1950; d. Carl Denton and Rosalie Iris (Law) Worstell; m. Frederick Dale Boothe, Aug. 12, 1972; 1 child, Meredith Lanay. AB in Edn., Glenville State Coll., 1972; MA in Speech Comm., W.Va. U., 1977. Cert. permanent libr. grades kindergarten through 12, W.Va.; cert. tchr. social studies and lang. arts grades 7 through 9, W.Va. Libr. Paden City (W.Va.) H.S., 1972-85, Big Chimney Elem. Sch., Charleston, W.Va., 1985-86, Sissonville (W.Va.) Elem. Sch., 1986—; writer program of studies Kanawha County Bd. Edn., Charleston, 1986, rep. to selection com., 1989, computer specialist, 1988—, rep. to tchrs. acad., 1994; attendant Josten's Sys., W.Va. State Dept. Edn., Charleston, 1988—. Editor: Kanawha County Program of Studies for Libraries, 1986. Mem. Sissonville H.S. Band Boosters, 1992—; opera actor W.Va. Symphony, 1987, 88; alto W.Va. Symphony Chorus, 1986—; mem. Aldersgate Choir, 1986—. Weather grantee W.Va. Edn. Fund, 1986, Traveling Stories grantee, 1989. Mem. NEA, W.Va. Edn. Assn., Kanawha Libs. Assn. (treas. 1988-94). Democrat. Methodist. Home: 1904 Demra St Sissonville WV 25320-9629 Office: Sissonville Elem Sch 8324 Sissonville Dr Sissonville WV 25320-9606

BOOTHS, RENEE GABRIELLE, upholstery textile designer; b. Dedham, Mass., Aug. 23, 1964; d. Bernard Michael and Brooke Ann (Trudell) Reagan; 1 child, Regan Ann Booths. AA in Art/Studio, Lasell Jr. Coll., 1984; BFA in Weaving & Textile Design, Rochester Inst. Technol., 1987. Art leader Camp Tara, Mallets Bay, Vt., 1983-84; painting supr. Rochester Inst. Tech. Phys. Plant, 1985-86; asst. to designer Harrisville (N.H.) Designs, 1986-87; sign artist Rochester Inst. Technol. Coll. Union Cafeteria, 1984-87; costumer Nat. Tech. Inst. of Deaf Performing Arts Theatre, Rochester, 1986-87, Hope Summer Repertory Theatre, Holland, Mich., 1987; dressmaker alterations Marge's Bridal Shop, Wyoming, Pa., 1990-91; design technician Chromatex, Inc., Hazleton, Pa., 1987-92, designer, 1992—. Exhibited in group shows including The Show, 1987, Rochester Inst. Technol., 1987, Lasell Jr. Coll., 1984. Named to Dean's List, Lasell Jr. Coll., 1982-84. Home: 509 E Diamond Ave Hazleton PA 18201

BOOZ, GRETCHEN ARLENE, marketing executive; b. Boone, Iowa, Nov. 24, 1933; d. David Gerald and Katherine Bevridge (Hardie) Berg; m. Donald Rollett Booz, Sept. 3, 1960; children: Kendra Sue (dec.), Joseph David, Katherine Sue. AA, Graceland Coll., 1955. Med. asst. Robert A. Hayne M.D., Des Moines, 1955-61; mktg. dir. Herald Pub. House, Independence, Mo., 1975—. Author: (book) Kendra, 1979. Mem. Citizens Adv. Bd., Blue Springs, Mo., 1979-91, Independence Mayor's Christmas Concert Com., 1987-91; bd. dirs. Comprehensive Mental Health, 1981-83, Child Placement Svcs., Independence, 1987-94, Hope House, Inc., Independence, 1987-91, Ctr. for Profl. Devel. and Life-long Learning, Inc., 1995-96; trustee Graceland Coll., Lamoni, Iowa, 1984-96. Mem. Leadership Edn. Action Devel. (L.E.A.D.), Independence C. of C. (diplomat, Outstanding Mem. award 1981). Republican. Mem. Reorganized Ch. Jesus Christ Latter Day Saints. Home: 1200 Crestview Dr Blue Springs MO 64014-2312 Office: Herald Pub House 3225 S Noland Rd Independence MO 64055-1317

BOOZER, SANDRA THOMAS, elementary school educator; b. Birmingham, Ala., June 30, 1957; d. Howard Proctor Thomas and Ellen Christine (Guthrie) Ray; step-father: Charles Lee Ray. BS in Early Childhood Edn., Elem. Edn., Samford U., 1979; MA in Early Childhood Edn., U. Ala., 1982. Tchr. kindergarten Gordo Elem. Sch., Pickens County, Ala., 1979-83, Roy Webb Elem. Sch., Calhoun County, Piedmont, Ala., 1983-87; tchr. kindergarten/T-1 Pleasant Valley Sch. Calhoun County, Jacksonville, Ala., 1987—; presenter Math. and Lang. Arts programs Calhoun County Bd. Edn., Anniston, Ala., 1992-94; mem. Profl. Devel. Com., Calhoun County Bd. Edn., Anniston, 1992-93. Vol. Lt. Gov. Election Campaign, Ala., 1979, Gov. Election Campaign, 1983, Jacksonville City Coun. Campaign, 1984, chmn. campaign, 1988; neighborhood vol. Gov. Election, 1990; mem. Creative Vision Federated, Jacksonville, 1990—; chmn. craft show Women's Club, 1991—, rec. sec., 1992—. Named to Outstanding Young Women of Am., 1979, 91. Mem. NEA, UDC (registrar Gen. John H. Forney chpt. 1991—, pub. rels. chmn. Ala. divsn. 1992-94, preservation of confed. records com. Ala. divsn. 1994-96), DAR (registrar Chinnabee chpt. 1990—, jr. membership com. chair 1990-92, Am. heritage com. chair 1990—), Magna Charta Dames, Ala. Edn. Assn. (legis. contact team 1987—), Internat. Reading Assn., Assn. Childhood Edn. Internat., Calhoun County Edn. Assn. (mem. exec. bd. 1988—, v.p. 1987-88, pres. 1988-89, rep. to del. assn. 1988—), Delta Kappa Gamma (rsch. chmn. Beta Phi chpt. 1991-92, v.p. 1992-94). Home: 903 12th Ave NE Jacksonville AL 36265

BORCHERS, KAREN LILY, child welfare administrator; b. Detroit, Apr. 4, 1940; d. Albert Oscar and Lily Louise (Denzler) B. BA in Psychology and Sociology, Mich. State U., 1961; AM in Social Svc. Adminstrn., U. Chgo., 1964; MS in Spl. Edn. Adminstrn., No. Ill. U., 1976; EdD in Early Childhood Edn./Adminstrn., Nova U., 1982. Cert. social worker. Child welfare worker Ill. Dept. Children & Family Svcs., Rockford, 1962-65; sch. social worker Komarek Schs., N. Riverside, Ill., 1965-67; exec. dir. Seguin Sch., Berwyn, Ill., 1967-72, Seguin Tng. Ctr., Cicero, Ill., 1967-72; adminstr. Orchard Hill, Madison, Wis., 1972-76; exec. dir. Children's Home Soc. Fla., West Palm Beach, 1976—; pres. Pathways to Growth, Inc., West Palm Beach, 1986—. Pres., founder Masterworks Chorus of the Palm Beaches, West Palm Beach, 1978—, Teen Musical Theatre, Inc., West Palm Beach, 1984—, Internat. Children's Chorus of the Palm Beaches, West Palm Beach, 1988-90; pres. Palm Beach Regional Achievement Ctr., West Palm Beach, 1979-84. Recipient Excellence in Health and Social Svcs. award Palm Beach County Commn., 1979. Mem. NASW, Civitan, Mensa. Home: 11984 Suellen Cir West Palm Beach FL 33414-6274 Office: Childrens Home Soc Fla 3600 Broadway West Palm Beach FL 33407-4844

BORDA, DEBORAH, symphony orchestra executive; b. N.Y.C., July 15, 1949; d. William and Helene (Malloy) B. BA, Bennington Coll., 1971; postgrad., Royal Coll. Music, London, 1972-73. Program dir. Mass. Coun. Arts and Humanities, Boston, 1974-76; mgr. Boston Musica Viva, Boston, 1976-77; gen. mgr. Handel and Haydn Soc., Boston, 1977-79, San Francisco Symphony, 1979-86; pres. St. Paul Chamber Orch., 1986-88; exec. dir. Detroit Symphony Orch., 1988-90; pres. Minn. Orch., Mpls., 1990-91; exec. dir. N.Y. Philharm., N.Y.C., 1991—. Office: NY Philharm Avery Fisher Hall 10 Lincoln Center Plz New York NY 10023-6912

BORDALLO, MADELEINE MARY (MRS. RICARDO JEROME BORDALLO), lieutenant governor of Guam, wife of former governor of Guam; b. Graceville, Minn., May 31, 1933; d. Christian Peter and Mary Evelyn (Roth) Zeien; m. Ricardo Jerome Bordallo, June 20, 1953; 1 dau., Deborah Josephine. Student, St Mary's Coll., South Bend, Ind., 1952; A.A., St. Katherines Coll., St. Paul, 1953; A.A. hon. degree for community service, U. Guam, 1968. Presented in voice recital Guam Acad. Music, Agana., 1951, 62; mem. Civic Opera Co., St. Paul, 1952-53; mem. staff KUAM Radio-TV sta., Agana, 1954-63; freelance writer local newspaper, fashion show commentator, coordinator, civic leader, 1963, nat. Dem. committeewoman for Guam, 1964-94, 1st lady of Guam, 1974-78, 81-85; senator 16th Guam Legislature, 1981-82, 19th Guam Legislature, 1987-88, 20th Guam Legislature, 1989-90, 21st Guam Legislature, 1991-92, 22nd Guam Legislature, 1993-94; Dem. Party candidate for Gov. of Guam, 1990, Lt. Gov. of Guam, 1994; Lt. Gov. of Guam, 1995—; del. Nat. Dem. Conv., 1964, 68, 72, 76, 80, 84, 88-92, pres. Women's Dem. Party Guam, 1967-69; rep. Presdl. Inauguration, Washington, 1965, 77, 85; del. Dem. Western States Conf., Reno, 1965, L.A., 1967, Phoenix, 1968, conf. sec., 1967-69; del. Dem. Women's Campaign Conf., Wash., 1965, Dem. Inauguration, 1992. Pres. Guam Women's Club, 1958-59; del Gen. Fedn. Women's Clubs Convs., Miami Beach, Fla., 1961, New Orleans, 1965, Boston, 1968; v.p. Fedn. Asian Women's Assn., 1964-67, pres., 1967-69; pres. Guam Symphony Soc., 1967-73, del. convs., Manila, Philippines, 1959, Taipei, Formosa, 1960, Hong Kong, 1963, Guam, 1964, Japan, 1968, Taipei, 1973; chmn. Guam Christmas Seal Drive, 1961; bd. dirs. Guam chpt. ARC, 1963, sec., 1963-67; pres. Marianas Assn. For Retarded Children, 1968-69, 73-74, 84—; bd. dirs. Guam Theatre Guild, Am. Cancer Soc.; mem. Guam Meml. Hosp. Vols. Assn., 1966—, v.p., 1966-67, pres., 1970-71; chmn. Hosp. Charity Ball, 1966; pres. Women for Service, 1974—, Beauty World Guam Ltd., 1981—, First Lady's Beautification Task Force of Guam, 1983—; pres. Palace Restoration Assn., 1983—; nominee Dem. party for Gov. of Guam, 1990. Mem. Internat. Platform Assn., Guam Rehab. Assn. (assoc.), Guam Lytico and Bodig Assn. (pres. 1983—), Spanish Club of Guam, Inetnon Famalaoan Club (pres. 1983-86), Guam Coun. of Women's Club (pres. 1993—). Home: PO Box 1458 Agana GU 96910-1458 Office: PO Box 2950 Agana GU 96910-2950

BORDAS, CAROL IRENE, patent lawyer; b. Pitts., Mar. 26, 1966; d. John and Irene Olga (Budul) B. BS in Mech. Engring., U. Pitts., 1988; JD, Duquesne U., 1995. Bar: Pa. 1993, U.S. Patent and Trademark Office 1993. Patent examiner U.S. Patent and Trademark Office, Washington, 1988-91; patent agt. Buchanan Ingersoll, Pitts., 1991-94; patent atty. Thorp, Reed & Armstrong, Pitts., 1994—. Author: Engineering Handbook, 1995. Mem. fin. com. Holy Ghost Byzantine Ch., McKees Rocks, Pa., 1995. Mem. Pitts. Intellectual Property Assn. Byzantine Catholic.

BORDELEAU, LISA MARIE, human services professional, consultant; b. Providence, Mar. 28, 1960; d. Roland John and Nancy Vivien (McIntosh) B.; m. John Theodore Endler, Sept. 8, 1991; children: Ian Endler Bordeleau, Meaghan Endler Bordeleau. BA cum laude, R.I. Coll., 1987; M in Liberal Arts, Harvard U., 1995. Devel. activities instr. Northern R.I.A.R.C., Woonsocket, R.I., 1980-82; residential counselor Live In a Freer Environ., Mansfield, Mass., 1981-82; staff advocate, asst. program coord. Beta Hostel Corp., Attleboro, Mass., 1983-85; program mgr., residential dir. Alternatives Unlimited, Inc., Whitinsville, Mass., 1985-86; mental health worker Butler Hosp., Providence, 1986-87; program mgr. Work Inc., North Quincy, Mass., 1987-89; dir. residential svcs. Beta Cmty. Svcs., Attleboro, Mass., 1989-94, dir. devel., 1995—; facilitator Eunice Kennedy Shriver Ctr., Waltham, Mass., 1993—, cons., 1995—; cons. Cooperative for Human Svcs., Malden, Mass., 1989-91, Optima Cons., Inc., Cranston, R.I., 1991—. Mem. North Attleborough Teen Ctr. Com., Mass., 1995. Mem. AAUW, NOW, The Feminist Majority. Home: 11 Greco Cir North Attleboro MA 02760

BORDELON, BARBARA JO, lawyer; b. Orange, Tex., May 6, 1948; d. Percy J. and Dorothy R. (White) B.; m. Phillip L. Fry (div.). BA in Govt., U. Tex., 1970, JD, 1973. Bar: Tex. 1974, Pa. 1990. Staff atty. Gen. Land Office, Austin, 1973-77; landman Chevron USA, New Orleans, 1977-80; sr. landman Transco Exploration, Houston, 1980-88; gen. counsel The Eastern Group, Inc., Washington, 1987—. Mem. ABA, Fed. Energy Bar Assn., Tex. Bar Assn., Pa. Bar Assn. Democrat. Roman Catholic. Home: 609 S Saint Asaph St Alexandria VA 22314-4118 Office: The Eastern Group Inc 2900 Eisenhower Ave Ste 300 Alexandria VA 22314-5223

BORDELON, CAROLYN THEW, elementary school educator; b. shelby, Ohio, Dec. 28, 1942; d. Burton Carl and Opal Mae (Harris) VanAsdale; m. Clifford Charles Spohn, Aug. 28, 1965 (div. Feb. 1982); m. Al Ramon Bordelon, Oct. 26, 1985. BA in History and Polit. Sci., Otterbein Coll., 1966; MA in Edn., Bowling Green State U., 1972; postgrad., Ohio State U., 1986—. Cert. tchr. grades 1-8, Ohio. Elem. tchr. Allen East Schs., Harrod, Ohio, 1966-68; elem. tchr. Marion (Ohio) City Schs., 1968-78, chpt. I reading tchr., 1978-86, reading recovery tchr., 1986-88; reading recovery tchr. Dublin (Ohio) City Schs., 1988—; adj. instr. reading dept.grad. studies Ashland (Ohio) U., 1996. Author: The Parent Workshop, 1992, Octopus Goes to School, 1995. Vol. Am. Heart Assn., Worthington, Ohio, 1991; mem. Rep. Nat. Com., Washington, 1994-95; mem. Royal Scots Highlanders, Mansfield, Ohio, 1976—. Recipient Excellence in Edn. award Dublin City C. of C., 1991-93, 96; Dublin City Schs./Ohio Dept. Edn. Tchr. Award grantee, 1993; Martha Holden Jennings Found. scholar, 1978. Mem. Archaeol. Inst. Am., Ohio Edn. Assn., Reading Recovery Coun. N.Am., Opera/Columbus, Phi Delta Kappa, Phi Alpha Theta. Presbyterian. Home: 3958 Fairlington Dr Upper Arlington OH 43220 Office: Griffith Thomas Elem Sch 4671 Tuttle Crossing Blvd Dublin OH 43017

BORDEN, AMANDA, gymnast, Olympic athlete; b. Cin., May 10, 1977. Student, U. Ga., 1996—. Mem. Nat. Team, 1990, 92-93, 93-94, 94-95, 95-96, 96—, Pan Am. Games Team, U.S. Olympic Gymnastics Team, Atlanta, 1996. Recipient Silver medal Team World Championships, 1994, Gold medal team competition Olympic Games, Atlanta, 1996; placed 1st in the floor exercise and 2d in the balance beam jr. divsn. Am. Classic, Salt Lake City, 1991, 1st in the floor exercise U.S. Classic, Knoxville, 1992, 2d for team Pacific Alliance Championships, Seoul, Korea, 1992, 3rd in all around and balance beam, 3rd for team in vault Am. Classic-World Championships Trials, Salt Lake City, 1993, 1st for team Hilton Challenge, L.A., 1993, 94, 3rd in uneven bars Tokyo Cup, 1993, 2d in all around Am. Classic-World Championships Trials, Oakland, Calif., 1994, 2d for team Team World Championships, Dortmund, Germany, 1994, 1st in the all around U.S. Classic, Palm Springs, Calif., 1994,, 3rd in all around, uneven bars and floor exercise Coca-Cola Nat. Championships, Nashville, 1994, 3rd in all around NationsBank World Team Trials, Richmond, Va., 1994, 2d for team in all around, 3rd for team in uneven bars, 2d in balance beam and floor exercise Am. Classic-Pan Am. Games Trials, Oakland, Calif., 1995, 1st in floor exercise, 2d in uneven bars Reese's Internat. Gymnastics Cup, Portland, 1995, 3rd in all around, 1st in balance beam and floor exercise McDonald's Am. Cup, 1995, 2d in all around Pan Am. Games, Mar del Plata, Argentina, 1995, 2d in all around and balance beam, 3rd for team in vault, 1st for team in uneven bars U.S. Classic, Colorado Springs, Colo., 1996, 1st for team and balance beam, 1st for team Budget Rent-a-Car Gymnastics Invitational USA vs. France, Miami, 1996. Office: care USA Gymnastics Pan Am Plz 201 S Capitol Ave Ste 300 Indianapolis IN 46225*

BORDEN, MARY JANE, designer, artist, consultant; b. Wheeling, W.Va., Dec. 11, 1952; d. Thomas John Jones and Pollye Richards Diehl; m. Charles Robert Borden, June 5, 1976; 1 child, Matthew Charles. BA, Otterbein Coll., 1975; MBA, U. Dayton, 1981. Customer info. rep. Columbus (Ohio) & So. Electric Co., 1977-82; market rsch. analyst Adria Labs., Dublin, Ohio, 1982-84, info. svcs. mgr., 1984-86, sr. info. analyst, 1986-91; owner, founder Borden Bus. Pubs., Westerville, Ohio, 1991—; intenet trainer Tng. Edge. Greater Columbus Free-Net, 1996. Co-founder LeadNet, Columbus, 1994. Mem. Am. Mktg. Assn. (dir. comm. 1984-86, Spl. Merit award 1985), Women in Comm. (coord. ind. comm. forum 1992-93, pres. Columbus chpt. 1995-96). Office: Borden Bus Pubs PO Box 1306 Westerville OH 43086

BORDOGNA, PAULA MESITE, communications executive; b. Framingham, Mass., July 15, 1958; d. Joseph George and Rose Mary (Pedulla) Mesite; m. Mark Aldo Bordogna, Aug. 29, 1992. BS, Worcester Poly. Inst., 1980; SMEE, MIT, 1984; MBA, Boston U., 1994. Programmer analyst Ensco, Springfield, Va., 1980-82; rsch. asst. MIT, Cambridge, Mass., 1982-83; sys. analyst GTE, Research Triangle Park, N.C., 1984-85; mem. tech. staff AT&T Bell Labs., North Andover, Mass., 1985-93, mgr. consumer broadband bus. devel., 1994-95. Co-author: (chpt.) Communications Handbook, 1996; contbr. articles to profl. jours. Mem. Sigma Xi, Tau Beta Pi. Office: Lucent Techs 1600 Osgood St North Andover MA 01845-1022

BOREK, JENNIFER ANN, English language educator; b. Belleville, Ill., Oct. 27, 1965; d. John Floyd and Jerrie Ruth (Tally) G.; m. Kenneth Dale Hall, Feb. 14, 1987 (div. Nov. 1993); children: Blake Hogendobler, Veronica Homyer, Floyd Harrison, Herbert Tomasiewicz; m. Thomas J. Borek, Dec. 11, 1994. BA, So. Ill. U., 1986, MS, 1993; PhD, St. Louis U., 1996. Reading tchr. Literacy Coun., Carbondale, Ill., 1984-90; pers. sec. So. Ill. U., Edwardsville, 1991-93; rsch. asst. St. Louis U., 1993-96; tchr. English Belleville (Ill.) Area Coll., 1993—; mem. steering com. Gateway Leadership Inst., St. Louis, 1993—; spkr. AIR, 1995, IATE, 1996. Author: (poetry anthology) Grass Roots, 1985, The Double Reed, 1995. Leadership scholar Blackburn Coll., 1983. Mem. ASCD, MLA, Nat. Coun. Tchrs. English, Phi Delta Kappa. Democrat. Roman Catholic. Home: 8 Pine Lake Dr Collinsville IL 62234-4918 Office: St Louis U Dept Edn 3750 Lindell Blvd Saint Louis MO 63108-3412

BORELL, LUDMILA IVANOVNA, ballerina, educator; b. Saratov, Russia, Aug. 4, 1928; came to U.S., 1993; d. Ivan and Taisia (Yulpatova) Borell; m. Vladimir Levinovsky, July 29, 1956; 1 child, Konstantin. Grad., Nat. Choreographic Sch., Saratov, 1946; M Degree, Russian Acad. of Theater Art, Moscow, 1961. Prin. dancer Nat. Opera and Ballet Theater, Saratov, 1946-66, M. Gorky's Mus. Theater, Magadan, USSR, 1966-74; ballet mistress in chief Nat. Light Music Theater, Saratov, 1976-80; artistic dir. Children's Ballet Studio, Moscow, 1980-92; prin. tchr. Russian Sch. Classical Dance, N.Y.C., 1994—. Contbr. articles to Soviet Ballet Mag., Internat. Ballet Ency. Mem. All-Russian Theater Socs., Saratov, 1954-93. Home: 9 Nixon Ct Apt C4 Brooklyn NY 11223

BORELLA, MARY DOROTHY, volunteer; b. Detroit, May 21, 1919; d. Gustave Adam Luka and Mary Amanda Suta; m. Arthur A. Borella, Aug. 11, 1942; children: Patricia, Arthur Jr., Peter, Joanna, Edwin, Eugenie, Richard. AB in Basic Scis., Wayne State U., 1939; postgrad., Bob Jones U., 1939-40. Various positions U.S. Postal Svc., Detroit, 1965-83; receptionist, typist ARC Office Vols., Detroit, 1985-91. Active ARC, Detroit, 1985—, Founders Soc. of Detroit Inst. Art, 1985-91, Girl Scouts U.S.A., Detroit; trustee Rep. Presdl. Task Force, Washington, 1989-91. Mem. Internat. Cultural Inst., Smithsonian Instn., Toastmasters Internat. Roman Catholic. Home: 11750 Wilshire Dr Detroit MI 48213-1619 Office: American Red Cross 100 Mack Ave Detroit MI 48201-2416

BOREN, LYNDA SUE, gifted education educator; b. Leesville, La., Apr. 1, 1941; d. Leonard and Doris (Ford) Schoenberger; m. James Lewis Boren, Sept. 1, 1961; 1 child, Lynda Carolyn. BA, U. New Orleans, 1971, MA, 1973; PhD, Tulane U., 1979. Prof. Northwestern State U., Natchitoches, La., 1987-89; propr. Colony Country House, New Llano, La., 1992-94; tchr. of gifted Leesville (La.) H.S., 1992—; vis. prof. Newcomb Coll., Tulane U., New Orleans, 1979-83, U. Erlangen-Nuremburg, Germany, 1981-82, Middlebury (Vt.) Coll., 1983-84, Ga. Inst. Tech., Atlanta, 1985-87, Srinakharinwirot U., Bangkok, 1989-90; mem. planning com. 1st Kate Chopin Internat. Conf., Natchitoches, La., 1987-89; Fulbright lectr. USIA and Bd. Fgn. Scholars, 1981-82, 89-90. Author: Eurydice Reclaimed: Language, Gender and Voice in Henry James, 1989; co-editor, author: Kate Chopin Reconsidered, 1992; contbr. numerous articles to profl. jours. Founding mem. John F. Kennedy libr. Recipient awards for watercolors; Mellon fellow Tulane U., 1977-78; NEH seminar fellow Princeton U., 1986. Mem. MLA, AAUW, DAR, IPA, Fulbright Alumni Assn., Women in the Arts, Art Guild, Audubon Soc. Democrat. Home: 1492 Ford's Dairy Rd New Llano LA 71461

BORETZ, NAOMI MESSINGER, artist, educator; b. Bklyn., June 9, 1935; d. Joseph and Sarah (Lesser) Messinger; m. Benjamin A. Boretz, Sept. 1, 1954; 1 child, Avron Albert. BA, Bklyn. Coll., 1957; MFA, CUNY, 1971; MA, Rutgers U., 1976; postgrad., Art Students League N.Y. Assoc. prof. fine arts, chair fine arts dept. Wilson Coll., Chambersburg, Pa., 1985—. Exhbns. include Westminster Arts Coun. Arts Ctr., London, 1971, Hudson River Mus., N.Y.C., 1975, Katonah Gallery, N.Y., 1976, Condeso-Lawler Gallery, N.Y.C., 1987, Carnegie-Mellon Art Gallery, Pitts., 1989, The Nelson Atkins Mus. of Art, St. Louis, 1994, Westbeth Gallery, N.Y., 1996, others; represented in pub. collections Met. Mus. Art, N.Y.C., Solomon R. Guggenheim Mus., N.Y.C., Brit. Mus., London, Nat. Mus. Am. Art, Washington, Yale U. Art Gallery, Joslyn Art Mus., Omaha, Walker Art Ctr., Mpls., Miami U. Art Mus., Oxford, Ohio, Fogg Art Mus. Harvard U., Cambridge, Mass., Glasgow (Scotland) Mus., San Jose (Calif.) Art Mus., Asheville (N.C.) Art Mus., others; contbr. to arts publs. Artist-fellow Va. Ctr. Creative Arts, 1973, 86, Ossabaw Found., 1975, Tyrone Guthrie Arts Ctr., Ireland, 1987, Writers-Artists Guild Can., 1988; grantee N.J. State Coun. on Arts, 1985-86. Home: 15 Southern Way Princeton NJ 08540-5318 Office: Wilson Coll Art Dept Chambersburg PA 17201

BORG, RUTH I., home nursing care provider; b. Chgo., Mar. 29, 1934; d. Axel Gunner and Charlotte (Benston) B. Diploma, West Suburban Sch. Nursing, 1956; tchr.'s degree, Chgo. Conservatory, 1958; BSN, Alverno Coll., 1981. Staff nurse Boath Meml. Hosp., Chgo.; head nurse psychiatry, head nurse long-term medicine VA North Chgo. Med. Ctr.; staff nurse, night supr. intermediate care VA Clement Zabiocki Med. Ctr., Milw.; pool nurse, in-home nursing care provider Milw. County Mental Health Complex; in-home nursing care provider. Contbr. 2 articles to profl. jours.

BORGEN, JULIE MARIE, banking executive; b. Wichita, Kans., Sept. 12, 1963; d. Claude Neil and Geraldine (Graber) C.; divorced; 1 child, Daniel Scott. BS, Kansas State U., 1986. Loan officer Lyons (Kans.) Federal Savings Assn., 1987—. Notary public, Kans., 1987—. Methodist. Office: Lyons Federal Savings Assn 200 E Ave S Lyons KS 67554

BORIGHT, LUCINDA LEWIS, counselor; b. Huntington, W.Va., Nov. 17, 1948; d. James O. and Elizabeth (McKee) Lewis; m. John M. Boright, June 23, 1972; children: Karl Lewis, John Matthew. BS, U. Ky., 1971; MEd, Ohio U., 1989, postgrad. Tchr. 1st grade South Point (Ohio) Schs., 1972-80; clin. counselor Pathways, Inc., Ashland, Ky., 1990-93; slin. supr. Ohio U., Athens, 1993—. Mem. Am. Counselors Assn., Am. Mental Health Counselors Assn., Ohio Counselors Assn. (treas. 1995—, exec. bd.), Ohi Mental Health Counselors Assn. (treas. 1988-92, 94—, bd. dirs.), Ohio Assn. Counselor Educators, Chi Simga Iota. Home: 2317 County Rd 15 South Point OH 45680

BORMAN, AMY J., lawyer; b. Detroit; d. Milton J. and Joanne (Kanelos) Costopolous; m. Robert D. Borman, Apr. 8, 1979; children: Dena, Gabe, Ethan. MusB, Wittenberg U., 1976; MusM, U. Mich., 1977; UD, U. Toledo, 1989. Bar: Mich., Ohio. Assoc. prof. Simon's Rock of Bard Coll., Great Barrington, Mass., 1980-85; performing musician N.Y.C., 1977-85; law clk. Cooper, Walinski & Cramer, Toledo, 1986-89, assoc., 1989-94, shareholder, 1994—. Editor U. Toledo Law Rev., 1988; author manuals Lorman Bus. Inst., 1994, 96. mem. Women's Law Assn. Mich., Washtenaw County Bar Assn., Toledo Bar Assn., Order of Coif. Office: Cooper Walinski & Cramer 900 Adams St Toledo OH 43624

BORN, BROOKSLEY ELIZABETH, lawyer; b. San Francisco, Aug. 27, 1940; d. Ronald Henry and Mary Ellen (Bortner) B.; m. Alexander Elliot Bennett, Oct. 9, 1982; children: Nicholas Jacob Landau, Ariel Elizabeth Landau, Andrew E. Bennett, Laura F. Bennett, Peter J. Bennett. AB, Stanford U., 1961, JD, 1964. Bar: D.C. 1966. Law clk. U.S. Ct. Appeals, Washington, 1964-65; legal rschr. Harvard Law Sch., 1967-68; assoc. Arnold and Porter, Washington, 1965-67, 68-73, ptnr., 1974-96; lectr. law Columbus Sch. Law, Cath. U. Am., 1972-74; adj. prof. Georgetown U. Law Center, Washington, 1972-73; chair U.S. Commodity Futures Trading Commn., 1996—. Pres. Stanford Law Rev, 1963-64. Chairperson bd. visitors Stanford U. Law Sch., 1987; bd. dirs. Nat. Legal Aid and Defenders Assn., 1972-79, Washington Legal Clinic for Homeless, 1993-96, Lawyers Com. for Civil Rights Under Law, 1993-96, Am. Bar Found., 1989—, Washington Lawyers Com. for Civil Rights and Urban Affairs, 1992-96; chairperson, bd. dirs. Nat. Women's Law Ctr., 1981—; trustee Ctr. for Law and Social Policy, Washington, 1977-96, Women's Bar Found., 1981-86. Mem. ABA (chair sect. ind. rights and responsibilities 1977-78, chair fed. judciary com. 1980-83, chair consortium on legal svcs. and the pub. 1987-90, bd. govs. 1990-93, chair resource devel. coun. 1993-95, chair coun. Fund for Justice and Edn. 1995-96, state del. from D.C. 1994—), D.C. Bar (sec. 1975-76, mem. bd. govs. 1976-79), Am. Law Inst., Southwestern Legal Found. (trustee 1993-96), Order of Coif. Office: Commodity Futures Trading Commn 1155 21st St NW Washington DC 20581

BORN, ETHEL WOLFE, church worker; b. Kasson, W.Va., Jan. 6, 1924; d. Otto Guy and Nancy Grace (Nestor) Wolfe; m. Harry Edward Born, Apr. 4, 1944 (dec. Aug. 1992); children: Rosemary Ellen (dec.), Barbara Anne Born Craig. Student, Ecumenical Inst., Geneva, 1983; BA, Mary Baldwin Coll., 1991. Author: A Tangled Web--A Search for Answers to the Question of Palestine, 1989, By My Spirit, Methodist Protestant Women in Mission, 1879-1939, 1990; contbr. articles to religious publs. Va. pres. United Meth. Women, 1972-76; bd. dirs. United Meth. Gen. Bd. Global Ministries, N.Y.C., 1976-84, v.p. women's divsn., 1980-84, v.p. com. on relief, 1980-84, Mid. East cons. women's divsn., 1984-88; chmn. N.Am. Coordinating Com. for Non-govtl. Orgns. UN Symposium, N.Y.C., 1986, 87; pres. N.Am. area, asst. world treas. World Fedn. Meth. Women, 1986-91, archivist, 1992—; mem. United Meth. Gen. Comm. Christian Unity and Inter-Religious Concerns, N.Y.C., 1988-96; mem. interfaith commn. Nat. Coun. Chs. of Christ, 1996-2001. Mem. Nat. LEague Am. Pen Women, Nat. Assn. Parliamentarians. Home: 3789 Knollridge Rd Salem VA 24153-1938

BORNEMAN, ALICE GREGORY, educator; b. Wilkes-Barre, Pa., June 15, 1940; d. Dwight Lewis and Margaret Elizabeth (Wolfe) Gregory; m. Edward Leo Borneman, Dec. 29, 1962; children: Margaret Ann, Linda Marie, Edward Gregory, Clayton Gregory. BS in Edn., Rider Coll., Lawrenceville, N.J., 1962; MA in Edn., Rider Coll., 1989. Bus. edn. tchr. Woodstown (N.J.) High Sch., 1962-64, Interboro High Sch., Glenolden, Pa., 1966-67, Parkland High Sch., El Paso, Tex., 1967-69, Lower Cape May (N.J.) High Sch., 1972-73; bus. edn. tchr. Wildwood (N.J.) High Sch., 1979—, chmn. dept. computer and bus., 1990—, ret., 1995; adj. prof. Atlantic Community Coll., 1990—. Exec. bd. mem. N.J. Bus. Edn. Assn., 1994-96; sec. Wildwood Civic Club, 1983-88; adv. coun. Cape May County Vocat. Sch., 1989—; mem. mastectomy support group Burdette Tomlin Meml. Hosp.; vol. Reach for Recovery; co-facilitator cancer support group Burdette-Tomlin Meml. Hosp. Recipient Walter A. Brower award for devotion to excellence in field of bus. edn. Rider Coll., 1989, Career Achievement award Wildwood Bd. Edn., 1994, Reach for Recovery Vol. of Yr. award Am. Cancer Soc., 1995. Mem. AAUW, Delta Pi Epsilon, Delta Kappa Gamma. Republican. Roman Catholic. Home: 8504 Seaview Ave Wildwood NJ 08260-3544

BORNSTEIN, RITA, academic administrator; b. N.Y.C., Jan. 2, 1936; d. Carl and Florence (Gates) Kropf; children: Rachel, Mark, Per; m. Harland G. Bloland. BA in English, Fla. Atlantic U., 1970, MA in English, 1971; PhD in Ednl. Leadership and Instrn., U. Miami, 1975. Tchr., adminstr. Dade County Pub. Schs. (Fla.), 1971-75; adminstr. dept. edn. U. Miami, Coral Gables, 1975-81, adminstr. divsn. of devel., 1981-85, v.p., 1985-90; pres. Rollins Coll., Winter Park, Fla., 1990—; dir. Barnett Bank Ctrl. Fla., Barnett Banks, Inc. Author: Freedom or Order: Must We Choose?, 1976; Title IX Compliance and Sex Equity: Definitions, Distinctions, Costs and Benefits, 1981; contbr. articles to profl. jours. Mem. Am. Coun. on Edn. (mem. com. leadership devel. 1991-93, bd. dirs. 1995—), Nat. Assn. Ind. Colls. and Univs. (bd. dirs. 1992-95, chair govt. rels. com. 1994-95), Fla. Coun. of 100. Office: Rollins Coll Office of Pres 1000 Holt Ave # 2711 Winter Park FL 32789-4499

BORODKIN, CLARICE, administrative assistant to federal judges; b. Bklyn., Nov. 26, 1924; d. Joseph and Rebecca (Blumenfeld) Haberman; m. Joshua Borodkin Feb. 22, 1948 (dec. Dec., 1968). Student, St. John's U., 1945-48. Sec. to ptnr. Davis, Polk & Wardell, N.Y.C., 1968-73; confidential asst. Justice State Supreme Ct., N.Y.C., 1974-75; sec., adminstrv. asst. U.S. Dist. Judges, N.Y.C., 1975-87; adj. lectr. NYU, 1974-85; archivist Jewish Archives of Fedn. of Jewish Philantrophies, Milw., 1992—. Reviewer (book) Volkell Legal Terminology, 1978; co-author: (with Douglas Finney) (student work manual) Legal Word Processing, 1984. Mem. Hadassah (group pres. N.Y. 1966-68, Presdl. award 1968, region recording sec. Milw. 1994—, chapter co-v.p. membership Milw. 1995—, group pres. Milw. 1995, Woman of Yr. Milw. 1994). Mem. NOW, Nat. Assn. Retired Fed. Employees, Planned Parenthood, U. Wis. Guild for Learning in Retirement. Jewish. Home: 3909 N Murray Ave Milwaukee WI 53211

BOROWSKI, JENNIFER LUCILE, corporate administrator; b. Jersey City, Oct. 23, 1934; d. Peter Anthony and Ludwika (Zapolska) B. BS, St. Peter's Coll., 1968; postgrad., Pace Coll., 1976-77. Mgr. benefits Amerada Petroleum Corp., N.Y.C., 1951-66, Mt. Sinai Hosp., N.Y.C., 1966-67; mgr. payroll and payroll taxes Haskins & Sells, N.Y.C., 1967-74; mgr. payroll and payroll tax Cushman & Wakefield, Inc., N.Y.C., 1975-89. Mem. Am. Payroll Assn. (bd. dirs. 1979-81, cert.), Am. Mgmt. Assn., Am. Soc. Payroll Mgrs., Internat. Platform Assn. (hon.), Am. Soc. Profl. Exec. Women, NAFE. Home: 36 Front St North Arlington NJ 07031-5822

BORRE, JOSEFINA BAUTISTA, secondary education educator; b. Maygnaway, San Andres, The Philippines, June 14, 1945; arrived in Saipan, 1990.; d. Francisco and Lociana (Bautista) B. BS in Elem. Edn., U. of The Philippines, The Philippines, 1967; cert. spl. edn., U. The Philippines, 1974, MEd, 1979; LLB, Lyceum of The Philippines, 1985. Comm. arts tchr. Pub. Sch., Catanduanes, The Philippines, 1967-72, spl. edn. tchr., 1975-76; govt. scholar in spl. edn. U. The Philippines, 1973-74; spl. edn. tchr. Manila City Schs., 1977-78, master tchr. I, spl. edn. tchr., 1979-84, master tchr. II, chairperson Silahis Ng Diwa Spl. Edn. Ctr., 1985-89; spl. edn. tchr. Pub. Sch. Sys., No. Mariana Islands, 1990-92, dept. chair Marianas H.S. Transition Program, 1993—; lectr. U. The Philippines, 1988; chairperson nat. capital region's study group on improvement of instrnl. materials for gifted Philippine Dept. Edn., 1989, chairperson nat. seminar workshop for revision of enrichment materials and handbook for gifted, 1990. Editor-in-chief San Andreas Ednl. Forum, Catanduanes, The Philippines, 1969-70; mem. editl. bd. Asian Conf. on Mental Retardation, Manila, 1973. Coord. Youth Civic Action Program, San Andreas Catanduanes, 1970-72; sec. Tchrs. Bliss Condominium Homeowners Assn., Philippines, 1984-85; pres. Tchrs. Welfare Fund, 1985-89; vol. worker outreach program for street children of Manila YWCA, 1987-89; facilitator First Nat. Conf. on Gifted, U. The Philippines, 1989; ofcl. Philippine del. Ptnrs. in Play Workshop, 1989, 9th Asian Conf. on Mental Retardation, Bangkok, 1989; ofcl. del. No. Mariana Islands 8th Ann. Pacific Rim 3d Internat. Coun. Exceptional Children, U. Hawaii, Honolulu, 1991; eucharistic min. Mt. Carmel Cathedral, Saipan, Mariana Islands, 1994—; sec. Marianas H.S. PTA, Saipan, 1993-94. Recipient Appreciation plaque Virac Pilot Sch., 1977, Presdl. award, 1984, Appreciation cert. YWCA, 1990, Appreciation cert. Philippine Consulate Mariana Islands, 1995. Mem. NAFE (MHS accreditation com.), Marianas Assn. Filipino Educators (sec. 1991-92, v.p. 1992-93, pres. 1993-95). Home: PO Box 3723 Ck Saipan MP 96950 Office: Marianas HS Susupe Saipan MP 96950

BORRESEN, MARY MARGARET, accountant; b. St. Croix Falls, Wis., Oct. 18, 1964; d. Robert Burdett and Arlene Delpha (Onsted) Patterson; m. Arlen Duane Borresen, Apr. 5, 1982; children: Adam, Nicholas, Patrick. BS in Acctg., U. Wis., River Falls, 1995. Telemarketer Classic Motorbooks, Osceola, Wis., 1986-90; acctg. officer Dept. Human Svcs., St. Paul, 1995—; ptnr. Borresen Flooring, St. Croix Falls, 1987-96. Leader Cub Scouts Am., treas., 1993—. Mem. Inst. Mgmt. Accts. Democrat. Office: Minn Dept Human Svcs 444 Lafayette Rd Saint Paul MN 55155

BORSOI, LOUISE CARTER, Spanish language educator; b. Orlando, Fla., Nov. 17, 1943; d. Julian Hubert and Eleanor Louise (Sheetz) Carter; m. Edward Eros Borsoi, Mar. 6, 1967; children: Carla Renée, Alexander Justin. BA, Fla. State U., 1964; MA, U. Ill., 1967. Cert. Spanish, French, Portuguese tchr., Fla. Spanish, English tchr. Edgewater H.S., Orlando, 1964-66; Portuguese tchg. asst. U. Ill., Urbana, 1966-67; Spanish, French tchr. Center Line (Mich.) H.S., 1967-69; adj. Spanish tchr. Valencia C.C., Orlando, 1973-75; adj. Spanish instr. Rollins Coll., Winter Park, Fla., 1976-81; English as 2d lang. tchr. Adult Cuban Project, Orlando, 1982-83; Spanish, French tchr. Lake Brantley H.S., Altamonte Springs, Fla., 1983-93; Spanish tchr. Trinity Prep. Sch., Winter Park, 1993—, reader Spanish advanced placement exams., 1995—; reader/evaluator NEH, Washington, 1994; preliminary reviewer NEH Fellowships/Fgn. Langs., Washington, 1991-92; evaluator of candidates NEH Seminar, Rollins Coll., Winter Park, 1989-90. Co-author (performance guide) Ana Maria Matute, 1989, Gabriel Garcia Marquez, 1989, Miguel de Unamuno, 1989. Mem. Jr. League of Orlando-Winter Park, 1976—; mem. Kappa Kappa Gamma Alumnae, Winter Park, 1964—, chair adv. bd., 1990-96. Rockefeller Found. fellow, 1987; recipient award NEH, 1988, 89, 96, Tchr./scholar for Fla. Reader's Digest/NEH, 1991-92. Mem. Am. Assn. Tchrs. of Spanish and Portuguese, Am. Assn. Tchrs. of French, Am. Coun. Tchrs. of Fgn. Langs. Democrat. Episcopalian. Office: Trinity Prep Sch 5700 Trinity Prep Ln Winter Park FL 32792-9414

BORSOS, ERIKA, cardiac care, medical/surgical nurse; b. Bakonycsernye, Hungary, May 8, 1952; d. John and Elizabeth (Nyevrikel) B. ADN, Thornton Community Coll., 1974, AS, 1979; BSN cum laude, U. S. Fla., 1984; candidate MSN, Andrews U., Berrien Springs, Mich., 1996—. RN Fla., Ind., Ill.;cert. BLS, ACLS Am. Heart Assn. Staff nurse, relief charge nurse, float nurse Ingalls Meml. Hosp., Harvey, Ill., 1974-79; staff nurse, team leader, float nurse Sarasota (Fla.) Meml. Hosp., 1979-84; staff nurse, clin. nurse I, cardiac catheter recovery nurse, preceptor Bon Secours Venice (Fla.) Hosp., 1985—. Editor, writer Cardiac Courier. Vol. pub. edn. Am. Cancer Soc., Sarasota Fla., 1983-90. Ill. State scholar, 1970. Mem. AACN, NLN (advocacy), Inst. Noetic Sci., Venice Hosp. Found., Folk Dance Coun., Sigma Theta Tau, Phi Theta Kappa (scholar). Home: 7416 Bounty Dr Sarasota FL 34231-7920

BORST-MANNING, DIANE GAIL, management consultant; b. Rochester, N.Y., Nov. 5, 1937; d. Howard Louis and Emily Kathleen (Crew) Borst; m. Steven Manning, Sept. 11, 1979 (dec. May 1991); m. Norman Edward Berg, Apr. 4, 1992. B.A. cum laude, Wagner Coll., 1959; M.B.A., N.Y.U., 1966. Planner N.Y.U. Med. Ctr., N.Y.C., 1962-76, assoc. dir. planning, 1976-78, dir. mgmt. services, 1978-80; dir. human resources Mt. Sinai Med. Ctr., N.Y.C., 1980-85, dir. planning, 1985-86; sr. v.p. The Manning Orgn., Inc., 1986—; pres. Diane Borst Manning Assocs., Inc., 1986—; instr. dept. health care mgmt. CUNY, 1982-92; adj. faculty Orange County Community Coll., 1986-88, Sarah lawrence Coll., New Sch. Social Research, 1986—, St. Joseph's Coll., 1992—. Editor: Managing Non-Profit Organizations, 1979. Author: (cassette) Managers and Secretaries—How to Achieve Teamwork, 1980. Chairperson grants Port Jervis Council for Arts; mem. Health Systems Agy. Bd., N.Y.C., 1976-79; trustee Helene Fuld Sch. Nursing, N.Y.C., 1989—; mem. planning com. of bd. Mercy Community Hosp., Port Jervis, N.Y.; mem. adv. bd. Inst. Bus. Industry & Govt. Orange County Community Coll. Fulbright fellow, 1959. Mem. N.Y. Personnel Mgmt. Assn. (bd. dirs. 1974-76), Greater N.Y. Hosp. Assn., Am. Compensation Assn., Bur. Nat. Affairs (personnel policy forum 1983-84), Am. Assn. Hosp. Planners, Assn. Am. Med. Colls. Group on Instrl. Planning. Club: City (N.Y.) Avocations: gardening; auto mechanics; carpentry, real estate. Office: 40 W 55th St Ste 9D New York NY 10019-5316

BORTON, MARY KEALEY, speech pathologist; b. Davenport, Iowa, Dec. 4, 1947; d. James Arnold and Catherine (Keane) Kealey; children: Thomas, James. BS, U. Iowa, 1968; MA, No. Ill. U., 1970. Lic. speech/lang. pathologist, Ala.; cert. adminstr., Ala. Hearing cons. Ill. Dept. Pub. Health, Champaign, Ill., 1970-73; speech pathologist Shelby County Bd. Edn., Columbiana, Ala., 1987-96; asst. prin. Oak Mountain Elem. Sch., 1996—. Pres. Pelham (Ala.) High Sch. PTO, 1994-96. Mem. Am. Speech Lang. Hearing Assn., Speech Hearing Assn. Ala. (presenter spring conv. 1994). Office: Oak Mountain Elem Sch 5640 Cahaba Valley Rd Birmingham AL 35242-4902

BORUT, JOSEPHINE, insurance executive; b. Bridgeport, Conn., Aug. 3, 1942; d. Frank and Catherine (Russo) Occhipinti; m. Arthur Lee Borut, Nov. 22, 1963; 1 child, Adam Seth. BS in Art, Hofstra U., 1964, MA in Humanities, 1971; cert. in mgmt., Adelphi U., 1984. Cert. art tchr., N.Y.; cert. mtgs. profl. Art tchr. Cen. Islip (N.Y.) Elem., 1964-65; coord. art dept. Mineola (N.Y.) Jr. High, 1965-70; art tchr., coord. Brandeis Sch., Lawrence, N.Y., 1979-81; mgr. community rels. Empire Blue Cross/Blue Shield, N.Y.C., 1984-85, mgr. conf. planning, 1985—; freelance artist, East Meadow, 1978-79; lectr. meeting planning. Contbr. articles to profl. jours. Recipient hon. mention L.I. Art Tchrs. Assn. Art Show,1966, 3d pl. art show Hofstra U., 1966, 2d pl. East Meadow Pub. Libr. Juried Art Show, 1979; Inst. II scholar, 1991, Profl. Edn. Conf. scholar, 1990. Mem. NAFE, NOW, Am. Soc. Assn. Execs., Meeting Planners Internat. Greater N.Y. (bd. dirs., com. chmn., pres. 1992-93, Meeting Planner of Yr. 1991), Am. Soc. Profl. and Exec. Women, Ins. Conf. Planners. Home: 1823 Kent St Westbury NY 11590-5305 Office: Empire Blue Cross/Blue Shield 622 3rd Ave New York NY 10017-6707

BORYSEWICZ, MARY LOUISE, editor; b. Chgo.; d. Thomas J. and Mabel E. (Zeien) O'Farrell m. Daniel S. Borysewicz, June 11, 1955; children: Mary Adele, Stephen Francis, Paul Barnabas. BA, Mundelein Coll., 1970; postgrad. in English lit., U. Ill, 1970-71; grad. exec. program, U. Chgo., 1981-82. Editor sci. publs. AMA, Chgo., 1971-73; exec. mng. editor Am. Jour. Ophthalmology, Chgo., 1973-95; asst. sec., treas Ophthalmic Pub. Co., 1985-95; guest lectr. U. Chgo. Med. Sch., 1979, Harvard U. Med. Sch., 1978, Northwestern U. Med. Sch., 1979, Am. Acad. Ophthalmology, 1976, 81. Editor: Ophthalmology Principles and Concepts, 7th and 8th edits., 1996; contbr. articles to sci. publs. Active vol. svcs. Art Inst. Chgo. Mem. Am. Soc. Profl. and Exec. Women, Coun. Biol. Editors (bd. dirs. 1988-91, mem. fin. com. 1985-88, mem. teller com. 1992-95), Internat. Fedn. Sci. Editors.

BOSAK, ROSELLA ANN, secondary education educator; b. Glen Cove, N.Y., Feb. 24, 1951; d. Daniel and Margaret (Sheridan) Mizvesky; m. Alan Edward Bosak, Sept. 15, 1979; children: Jim, David. BA in French, Doane Coll., 1973; student, Inst. for Am. U., Avignon, France, 1971, Monterey Inst. Fgn. Studies, 1978; postgrad. in French and Spanish, Pacific Luth. U., 1980-89; MS with honors, Kansas State U., 1992. Cert. tchr., Wash. Tchr. French Pius X H.S., East H.S., Lincoln, Nebr., 1973-76, South Huntington (N.Y.) Pub. Schs., 1977-78; tchr. French and Spanish Camden Cath. H.S., Cherry Hill, N.J., 1978-79, North Thurston Sch. Dist., Olympia, Wash., 1979-82, 85-89; reading specialist, ESL tchr. North Thurston Sch. Dist., Olympia, 1992—; guest spkr. Kans. State Advanced Fgn. Lng. Methods, Manhattan, 1990. Vol. Huntington (N.Y.) Hosp., 1977-78. Mem. Internat. Reading Assn., Wash. Edn. Assn., North Thurston Edn. Assn., Phi Delta Kappa, Phi Kappa Phi, Alpha Pi. Office: North Thurston Sch Dist 300 College St NE Olympia WA 98516-5338

BOSHIER, MAUREEN LOUISE, health facilities administrator; b. Elizabeth, N.J., Oct. 1, 1946; d. John Henry and Mary Hanora (McGarry) B.; m. Robert Hall Rea, May 23, 1987. BSN, Coll. Misericordia, Dallas, Pa., 1968; MS in Psychiat. Nursing, U. Colo., 1973; MBA, U. Phoenix, 1987. Clin. specialist psychiat. nursing Denver Gen. Hosp., 1973-74; dir. rehab. services N.Mex. Cancer Control, Albuquerque, 1976-80; exec. dir. N.Mex. State Bd. Nursing, Albuquerque, 1980-84; exec. v.p. N.Mex. Hosp. Assn., Albuquerque, 1984-88; adminstr. surg. services, sr. nursing adminstr. U. N.Mex. Hosp., Albuquerque, 1988-94; CEO, pres. N.Mex. Hosps. and Health Systems Assn., Albuquerque, 1995—; dir. Profl. Seminar Cons., Inc., Albuquerque, 1982—; v.p. exec. bd. N.Mex. Health Resources, Albuquerque, 1981—, pres., 1989; vice chmn., bd. dirs. Hosp. Home Health Care, Albuquerque, 1978—; dir. Acad. Seminars, Inc., 1982—. Contbr. articles to profl. jours. Sec. N.Mex. Ballet Co., Albuquerque, 1982-87; vice chmn. Gov.'s Task Force on Nursing Issues, Albuquerque, 1982-88; adv. bd. Subarea Coun. Health Systems, Albuquerque, 1980-84. Capt. U.S. Army, 1967-71. Recipient Woman on the Move award YWCA, 1992, Wharton Sch. of Bus. fellowship for health care execs., 1993. Mem. Am. Orgn. Nurse Execs. (vice chmn. legis. advocacy com. 1992-94, chmn. 1993-94), N.Mex. Orgn. Nurse Execs. (treas. 1988-89, pres. 1990), N.Mex. League for Nursing, N.Mex. Nurses Assn. (Nurse Adminstr. award 1984), Rotary, Albuquerque C. of C. (quality of life com. 1994—), Sigma Theta Tau (pres.-elect 1994, pres. 1995—, Mentor award Gamma Sigma chpt. 1994). Democrat. Home: 9520 Kandace Dr NW Albuquerque NM 87114 Office: N Mex Hosps and Health Sys Assn 2121 Osuna Rd NE Albuquerque NM 87113-1001

BOSLEY, KAREN LEE, English and journalism educator; b. Beech Grove, Ind., Sept. 23, 1942; d. Lowell Holmes and Kathryn Gertrude (Drake) Foley; AB in Lang. Arts summa cum laude, U. Indpls., 1965; MA in English, Northwestern U., 1967; MA in Journalism, Ball State U., 1984; postgrad. (Newspaper Fund fellow), U. Mo., 1973, Ohio U., 1977; m. Norman Keith Bosley, Dec. 21, 1964; children: Mark Harold, Rachael Kathryn, Keith Lowell, Sidney Clark. Copy editor, reporter Indpls. News, 1963-65; English tchr., yearbook adviser Beech Grove (Ind.) Jr. H.S., 1965-66; English tchr. So. Regional H.S., Manahawkin, N.J., 1967-68; prof. humanities, journalism and English, student newspaper adviser Ocean County Coll., Toms River, N.J., 1971—; part time reporter Daily Times-Observer, Toms River, 1972-77, part-time copy editor, 1993. Trustee Long Beach Island Hist. Assn., Friends of Island Library, 1975-79; pres. Long Beach I. PTA; chmn. Long Beach Twp. Dem. Mcpl. Com., 1971-78; Dem. committeeman Long Beach Twp. Dist. 2, 1971-78, 85—; mem. Long Beach Twp. Recreation Commn., 1972-77, chmn., 1972-75; bd. dirs. Ocean County Red Cross, 1972-78, Ocean County Family Planning, Inc., 1972-78, Student Press Law Ctr., 1989—; chmn. Cub Scout pack 32, Ocean County Council Boy Scouts Am.; founder, bd. dirs. Long Beach I. Hist. Assn., Island Democrats, Inc.; adminstrv. bd. First United Meth. Ch. Beach Haven Terrace (N.J.); sec. regional H.S. Band Parent Orgn., 1995—. Mem. AAUW (pres., dir. Barnegat Light Area br.), NEA, N.J. Edn. Assn., Ocean County Edn. Assn., Faculty Assn. Ocean County Coll. (v.p. 1984-85), Coll. Media Advisers, Inc. (disting. newspaper adviser for U.S. 2-yr. colls. 1978, dir., sec.), Assn. Edn. in Journalism and Mass Communications, Community Coll. Journalism Assn. (dir., v.p.), Soc. Profl. Journalists, Band Parents Orgn. (pres., corr. sec.), Sigma Delta Chi. Contbr. article to publ. in field. Home: 9 E Old Whaling Ln Long Beach Township NJ 08008-2930 Office: Ocean CC PO Box 2001 College Dr Toms River NJ 08754-2001

BOSSARD, CAROLYN DIANE, librarian; b. Schenectady, N.Y., Aug. 25, 1945; d. Howard Franklyn and Mabel Agnes (Fogg) Zink; m. Harold Dale Bossard, Aug. 12, 1973. BA in Econs., SUNY, Albany, 1967, MLS, 1970. Cert. pub. libr., N.Y. Libr. asst. SUNY, Albany, 1967-70; asst. libr. N.Y. State Dept. Motor Vehicles, Albany, 1970-73, sr. libr., 1973; interlibr. loan libr. Steele Meml. Libr., Elmira, N.Y., 1974-81, adult svcs. coord., 1981-91, adult svcs. coord., computer sys. mgr., 1991—. Mem. ALA, N.Y. Libr. Assn. Episcopalian. Home: 766 Spruce St Elmira NY 14904 Office: Steele Meml Libr 101 E Church St Elmira NY 14901

BOSTED, DOROTHY STACK, public relations executive; b. Newark, Apr. 6, 1953; d. Richard Joseph and Dorothy Marie (Irvin) Stack; m. Kenneth James Bosted, Aug. 22, 1976; 1 child, Danielle Whitney. Student, Lyndon State Coll., 1971-73; BA, NYU, 1975. Reporter The Daily Advance, Succasunna, N.J., 1974-75; producer, tech. intern Manhattan Cable TV, N.Y.C., 1975; editorial asst. Calif. Sch. Employees Assn., San Jose, 1975-76; news dir., anchor UA-Columbia Cablevision, Oakland, N.J., 1977-79, dir. pub. relations Overlook Hosp., Summit, N.J., 1981-84; pres. Dorothy Bosted Pub. Relations, Harding Twp., N.J., 1984-86; dir. pub. relations, communications Middlesex County Coll., Edison, N.J., 1986-88; mgr. corp. communications Hoechst Celanese Corp., Bridgewater, N.J., 1988-89; ptnr. Bosted-Burton Assocs., Coral Springs, Fla., 1986—; cons. Coral Springs, 1986—. Co-author: Writing with Impact, 1986; contbr. articles to N.Y. Times, various mags. Seminar leader Kinnelon (N.J.) Enrichment Program, 1978; trustee Middlesex County Coll. Found., Edison, 1986-88; bd. dirs. Middlesex County Coll. Alumni Assn., 1986-88. Recipient News Program ACE award Nat. Cable TV Assn., 1979, Spectrum of Talent merit award Internat. Assn. Bus. Communicators, 1982, Percy award N.J. Hosp. Mktg. and Pub. Relations Assn., 1982, 84, Tribute to Women and Industry award YWCA, Ridgewood, N.J., 1979; Mennen Co. scholar, 1971, Neighborhood House scholar, 1971, KP scholar, 1971. Mem. Tribute to Women and Industry Mgmt. Forum (v.p. pub. rels. Ridgewood chpt. 1986-87, bd. dirs. cen. N.J. chpt. 1989-91), Pub. Rels. Soc. Am. (editor N.J. chpt. newsletter 1987-89, bd. dirs. N.J. chpt. 1989-91). Home: 8738 NW 19th Dr Coral Springs FL 33071-6155

BOSTEK-BRADY, EVA MARIA, veterinarian; b. Passaic, N.J., June 21, 1961; d. Charles and Stella (Stepien) Bostek; m. Thomas Michael Brady Jr., May 23, 1992; 1 child, Ethan Thomas. BS with distinction, Cornell U., 1983; DVM summa cum laude, Ohio State U., 1987. Lic. N.J., N.Y., Mass., N.H., Vt., Pa. Veterinarian Anchor Animal Hosp., North Dartmouth, Mass., 1987-89, Madison (N.J.) Vet. Hosp., 1989—; cons. vet. The Seeing Eye, Inc., Morristown, N.J., 1989-91, St. Hubert's Giralda, Madison, N.J., 1989—; vet. coll. tutor Ohio State U., Columbus, 1985; coll. teaching asst. Cornell U., Ithaca, N.Y., 1981-83. Team capt. Ohio State U. Fund Raising Campaign, Mass., 1989; mem. exec. com. student chpt. Am. Vet. Med. Assn., Columbus, 1983-87; fin. aid com. grad. profl. coun., Columbus, 1983-85. Scholarship Am. Soc. of Animal Sci., 1983; named Presdl. Scholars finalist U.S. Office Edn., 1979. Mem. Am. Vet. Med. Assn., Am. Animal Hosp. Assn., Met. N.J. Vet. Med. Assn., Ohio State Vet. Medicine Alumni Assn., Cornell Agrl. and Life Scis. Alumni Assn., Cornell Clubs, Phi Kappa Phi, Phi Zeta, Omega Tau Sigma (class rep. 1983-86). Democrat. Roman Catholic. Home: 17 Old Army Rd Bernardsville NJ 07924-1808 Office: Madison Vet Hosp 262 Main St Madison NJ 07940-2210

BOSTER, CONSTANZA HELENA GAMERO, marketing and product development executive; b. San Salvador, Apr. 18, 1944; came to U.S. 1959; d. Raul and Alice (Interiano) Gamero; m. Davis E. Boster, May 25, 1978 (div. 1985); 1 child, Valerie Anne. BA cum laude, Dunbarton Coll., Washington, 1964. Owner Co. Centro Americana Computacion, Guatemala, 1969-78; mgr. Traulsen & Co., Inc., Fort Worth, Tex., 1983; v.p. Traulsen & Co., Inc., Whitestone, N.Y., 1985-89, exec. v.p., 1989—, also bd. dirs. Mem. NAFE, Nat. Restaurant Assn., Am. Mgmt. Assn., Round Table Women in Food Svc. Industry, James Beard Found., Network Exec Women in Hospitality, Inc., Met. Club. Republican. Roman Catholic. Office: Traulsen & Co Inc Mktg Dept PO Box 560169 College Point NY 11356-0169

BOSTIC, JACQUELINE WHITING, management consultant, retired postmaster, association executive; b. Houston, Jan. 3, 1938; d. Samuel and Martha (Countee) Whiting; m. Joseph W. Bostic, July 15, 1960 (dec. 1991); children: Shelby Lance, Ursula Jimmison, Kirksten Sinclair, Jacqueline F. Student, Fisk U., Hofstra Coll.; BA in Psychology, Tex. So. U., Houston. Libr. asst. N.Y. Pub. Libr., 1958-59; edn. specialist U.S. Postal Svc., 1967-74, investigator so. region, 1974-86; officer-in-charge U.S. Postal Svc., Highlands, Tex., 1980; postmaster U.S. Postal Svc., Porter, Tex., 1986-92; officer-in-charge U.S. Postal Svc., Pearland, Tex., 1988; comms. mgr. U.S. Postal Svc., 1990; pres. Mgmt.-Orgn. Cons., 1992—; substitute tchr. Houston Ind. Sch. Dist., 1968-70; chmn. bd. dirs. Houston Postal Credit Union, 1990-92; lectr. mgmt. seminars, 1968—; chmn. bd. dirs. Antioch Project Reach, 1996—. Editor Intercom, Jack & Jill Am. Found. Nat. v.p. Jack & Jill

Am., Inc., 1982-86; bd. dirs. Jack & Jill Am. Found.; nat. bd. dirs. YWCA of U.S.A., 1987-94, vol. mgmt. trainer, 1981—; pres. and chmn. bd. dirs. Houston Met. YWCA, 1982-86; active A-PLUS, UNCF, Telethon Gala; trustee Antioch Missionary Bapt. Ch., YWCA Retirement Fund; commnr. Clean Houston Commn.; legis. rep. Tex. Postal Workers. Recipient Black Houstonians Making History award, 1986, Dist. Achievement award Nat. Coun. Negro Women, Civic award Houston chpt. YWCA, Outstanding Svc. award United Negro Coll. Fund; named Vol. of Yr., Houston chpt. YWCA, Outstanding Vol., United Way/YWCA, Outstanding Jiller, Jack & Jill Am., Inc.; named to Pres.'s Cir., Houston C. of C. Mem. AFL-CIO (pres. Clerk Craft, Am. Postal Workers Union 1980-82, mem. ctrl. labor coun., bd. dirs. Tex. chpt.), NAACP, HMAC (bd. dirs.), NAFE, Nat. League Postmasters, Nat. Assn. Postmasters, Am. Bus. and Profl. Women, Network, United Negro Coll. Fund (Outstanding Svc. award), Rotary, Booker T. Washington Alumni Assn., Fisk Univ. Alumni Club, East Montgomery County C. of C., Delta Sigma Theta (bd. dirs., pres. Houston met. chpt. 1982-86, v.p. Delta Edn. and Charitable Found. 1992—). Home: 4410 Roseneath Dr Houston TX 77021-1617

BOSTON, BETTY LEE, investment broker, financial planner; b. Agana, Guam, Dec. 21, 1935; d. Homer Laurence and Bessie Margarete (Leech) Litzenberg; m. Filibert Roth Boston, Aug. 12, 1956; children: William Litzenberg, Beth Boston Tedesco, Brent Litzenberg. BA, U. Mich., 1958. Cert. Fin. Planner. Stockbroker I.M. Simon & Co., Murray, Ky., 1976-78, 1st of Mich. Corp., Murray, 1978-86; investment broker J.J.B. Hilliard, W.L. Lyons, Inc., Murray, 1986—; instr. adult edn. investment classes Murray State U., 1977—; investment commentator Sta. WKMS, Murray, 1987—. Investment columnist Purchase Area Bus. Jour., 1989-90. Chmn. Inter-Faith Coalition Congregations, Ann Arbor, 1971-73; pres. Need Line Ch. and Community Ministry, Murray, 1981-83; mem. Murray regional bd. Ky. Coun. on Econ. Edn., 1987—. Recipient Woman of Yr. award Murray Bus. and Profl. Women, 1988. Mem. AAUW (treas. Murray br. 1982-87, pres. 1991—), Rotary (sec. Murray chpt. 1990-95). Methodist. Home: 917 N 16th St Murray KY 42071-1523 Office: JJB Hilliard WL Lyons Inc 414 Main St Murray KY 42071

BOSTON, BILLIE, costume designer, costume history educator; b. Oklahoma City, Sept. 22, 1939; d. William Barrett and Margaret Emeline (Townsend) Long; m. William Clayton Boston, Jr., Jan. 20, 1962; children: Kathryn Gray, William Clayton III. BFA, U. Okla., 1961, MFA, 1962. Asst. to designer Karinski of N.Y., N.Y.C., 1966-67; prof. costume history Oklahoma City U., 1987—; rep. Arts Coun., Oklahoma City, 1987-90, Arts Festival, Oklahoma City, 1972-80; dir. ETC Theater, Oklahoma City SW Coll., 1979-83; actress Lyric Theatre, Oklahoma City, 1979-81. Exhibited in group shows at Taos, N.Mex., Santa Fe; represented in permanent collections in Dallas, Taos, Santa Fe, Tulsa, N.Y.C., La Jolla; costume designer Ballet Okla., Oklahoma City, 1979-84, Agnes DeMillie's Rodeo Ballet Okla., 1982, Royal Ballet Flanders, 1983, Pitts. Ballet, 1983, BBC's Childrens Prodn., 1984, 86, Lyric Theatre, Oklahoma City, 1987-95, Red Oak Music Theatre, Lakewood, N.J., 1988, Winter Olympics, 1988, Miss Am. Pageant, 1988, for JoAnne Worley in Hello Dolly, San Francisco Opera Circus, 1991, Jupiter (Fla.) Theatre, 1991—, Mame prodn. Conn. Broadway Theatre, 1991-92, Mobile (Ala.) Light Opera, 1992, The Boy Friend, Temple U., Japan, 1995, The Sound of Music, Lyric Stage, Dallas, 1995, Annie Get Your Gun, Guys and Dolls with Vic Damone, 1995, Westbury Flash Valley Forge Music Fair. Rep. Speakers Bur. Oklahoma City for Ballet, 1979-85; judge State Hist. Speech Tournament, Oklahoma City, 1985-87; chmn. State of Okla. Conf. on Tchr./Student Relationships, Oklahoma City, 1981. Recipient Gov.'s Achievement award, 1988, Lady in the News award, 1987. Mem. Alpha Chi Omega (house corp. bd. 1986-90). Methodist. Home: 1701 Camden Way Oklahoma City OK 73116-5121

BOSTON, GRETHA, mezzo-soprano, actress; b. Crossett, AK. B of Music, N Tex. State U., Denton; vocal study, with coaches Ruth Falcon, Maestro Franco Iglesias, Dr. William Riley, Virginia Botkin, Harold Geiberg, and John Wustman. Carnegie Hall debut, Mozart's Coronation Mass, 1991; concert performances include Beethoven's Ninth Symphony (Carnegie Hall), Handel's Messiah (Madison, WI & Arlington, TX), Bach's Magnificat & Vivaldi's Gloria (Dallas, TX), Durufle's Requiem (Champaign, IL) and appearances at the Cathedral of the Divine in Santa Barbara and the St. Louis Conservatory of Music; operatic roles include: Carmen in Bizet's Carmen, Lola in Mascagni's Cavalleria Rusticana (Westchester Lyric Fest), Charlotte in Massenet's Werther, The Mother in Menotti's The Consul, Ciesca in Puccini's Gianni Schicchi, Delilah in Saint-Saens's Samson et Delilah, Maddalena in Verdi's Rigoletto (N.Y. Grand Opera), Amneris in Verdi's Aida (N.Y. Grand Opera), Azucena in Verdi's Il Trovatore, Queenie in Kern & Hammerstein's Show Boat (Tony award Best Supporting Actress in a Musical 1995), Maria & Strawberry Woman in Gershwin's Porgy and Bess, 1993. 3rd place D'Angelo Young Artist Internat. Competition. *

BOSTON, LEONA, organization executive; b. Joliet, Ill., Aug. 4, 1914; d. Dorie Philip and Margaret (Mitchell) B. Student LaSalle Extension U., 1936-37, 46, Moody Bible Inst., 1939-40, U. Chgo., 1944-45. Tchr., Nat. Stenotype Sch., Chgo., 1937; stenotypist Rotary Internat., Evanston, Ill., 1937-44, sec. to comptroller, 1944-50, head personnel dept., 1950-65, exec. asst. to gen. sec., 1965-77; mem. exec. com. North Shore Festival of Faith, Northfield, Ill., 1978. Bd. dirs. YWCA, Evanston, 1961-63. Mem. Bus. Profl. Women's Club Evanston, 1965-80, chmn. fin. com., 1977-78. Evangelical (fin. sec. Bible Ch., Winnetka 1965-68, treas. 1979-80). Club: Zonta (Evanston, v.p., chmn. program com. 1969-70, pres. 1970-71, mem. membership com. 1976-78, 93-94, chmn. membership com. 1976-78, historian 1979-84, mem. past pres.' com. 1972—, mem. fin. com. 1985-89, 93—, chmn. fin. com. 1987-89, 94-97, mem. club history and archives com. 1989-91, 95-96, parliamentarian 1991-92, mem. intercity/internat. rels. com. 1993-94). Home and Office: 350 W Schaumburg Rd Schaumburg IL 60194-3450 also: 2025 San Marcos Dr SE Winter Haven FL 33880-6632

BOSWELL, TOMMIE C., middle school educator; b. Gainesboro, Tenn., Nov. 8, 1942; d. Tommy and Ethel (Draper) Cassetty; m. Neal Stanley Boswell, Aug. 28, 1965; children: Brian Andrew, James Travis. AA, Cumberland U., Lebanon, Tenn., 1962; BS, Tenn. Technol. U., 1965; MAT, Rollins Coll., Winter Park, Fla., 1980, EdS, 1984. Cert. tchr. English, social studies; cert. adminstrv. supr. Tchr. English and social studies Beaumont Middle Sch., Kissimmee, Fla., 1965-72, tchr. social studies, 1978-89; tchr. social studies Neptune Middle sch., Kissimmee, 1989—; team leader 8th Grade Acad. Team "Challengers", Kissimmee, 1994—. Founding pres. Canterbury Lane Neighborhood Assn., Kissimmee, 1988; mem. N.M.S. Program Improvement Coun., Kissimmee, 1994—. Named Social Studies Tchr. of the Yr., Fla. Coun. for Social Studies, 1984, 86, 89, Outstanding Tchr. of Am. History, Joshua Stevens chpt. DAR, Kissimmee, 1982; Delta Kappa Gamma scholar, 1980. Mem. Upper Cumberland Geneal. Soc. Republican. Methodist. Office: Neptune Middle Sch 2727 Neptune Rd Kissimmee FL 34744-6237

BOSWELL, WINTHROP PALMER, writer; b. Bklyn., Dec. 17, 1922; d. Carleton Humphries and Winthrop (Bushnell) Palmer; BA, Smith Coll., 1943; postgrad. U. S.C., 1956-58; MA, San Francisco State Coll., 1969; m. James Orr Boswell, Oct. 26, 1946; children: James Lowell, Rosalind Palmer, John Winthrop. Rsch. asst. G-2 Spl. Br., U.S. Army, 1943-46; rsch. asst. Hoover Instn., Stanford, Calif., 1976; docent Filoli, 1979-80; books include The Roots of Irish Monasticism, 1970; Irish Wizards in the Woods of Ethiopia, 1971; The Snake in the Grove, 1972; The Killing of the Snake King in Abyssinia, 1973; Hisperica Famina or The Garden of God, 1974; Bruce and the Question of Geomancy at Axum: The Evidence from the Norman Bayeux Tapestry, 1986, Abyssinian Elements in the Life of Saint Patrick, 1991. Mem. Soc. History of Discoveries, Peninsula Country Club (San Mateo, Calif.), Francisca Club (San Francisco), Ross Mountain Club.

BOTELHO, JOYCE MAY, university administrator, historian; b. Newport, R.I., July 7, 1957; d. George Manuel and Muriel Josephine (Gleason) B.; m. J. Stephen Grimes, May 23, 1992. AB, Bard Coll., 1979; MA, Brown U., 1986. Cert. archivist, Acad. Cert. Archivists. Interpreter, archivist Senate House State Hist. Site, Kingston, N.Y., 1979-80; asst. curator, graphics R.I. Hist. Soc., Providence, 1980-84, curator, graphics dept., 1984-87; archivist R.I. Supreme Ct. Judicial Records Sect., Pawtucket, R.I., 1990-91; asst. dir. John Nicholas Brown Ctr., Brown U., Providence, R.I., 1991-94; dir. John Nicholas Brown Ctr., Brown U., Providence, 1995—; mem. R.I. Coun. for the Preservation of Rsch. Resources, Providence, 1991-94; publs. com. R.I. Hist. Soc., Providence, 1994—; consulting archivist St. George's Sch., Newport, R.I., 1993—; mem. fellowship com. Ingenuity & Enterprise Ctr., Providence, 1995—. Author: (exhibit catalog) The Dorr Rebellion and R.I.'s Struggle for Equal Rights, 1992. Sec. Citizen's Adv. Com., Newport, R.I., 1989—, vice chair Planning Bd., Newport, R.I., 1991—. Mem. Orgn. Am. Historians, Am. Hist. Assn., Soc. Am. Archivists, New Eng. Archivists. Democrat. Roman Catholic. Office: Brown Univ John Nicholas Brown Ctr Box 1880 Providence RI 02912

BOTHWELL, DORR, artist; b. San Francisco, May 3, 1902; d. John Stuart and Florence Isabel (Hodgson) B. Student, Calif. Sch. Fine Arts, Rudolph Schaeffer Sch. Design, U. Oreg. Painter Tau, Manu'a, Am. Samoa, 1928-29, France, 1930-31, 49-51, 89, Eng., 1960-61, 89, West Africa and North Africa, 1966-67, Indonesia, 1974, People's Republic China, 1982, Japan, 1985, Mex., 1987; instr. Calif. Sch. Fine Arts, San Francisco, 1945-58, San Francisco Art Inst., 1959-60, Rudolph Schaeffer Sch. Design, 1960-61, Mendocino (Calif.) Art Ctr., 1962-93, San Francisco Art Inst., 1961; instr. Sonoma State Coll., summer 1964, U. Calif. Ext., Mendocino Art Ctr., 1965-71, 90; faculty Ansel Adams Yosemite Workshop, 1964-77, Victor (Colo.) Sch. Photography, 1979. Exhibitor, West Coast exhbns., 1927—, 3d biennial São Paulo, Brazil, Pitts. Internat., 1952, 55, Art: U.S.A., 1958, Bklyn. Mus., 1976, Mendocino (Calif.) Art Ctr., 1992; one-man shows include De Young Meml. Mus., San Francisco, 1957, 63; retrospective exhbn. Bay Window Gallery, Mendocino, 1985, Spl. Anniversary exhbn. 1986-87, Tobey Moss Gallery, L.A., 1989, 91, 93, Bothwell Studio, Mendocino, Calif., 1989, Mendocino Art Ctr., 1992, Gallery Mendocino, 1994-95; travelling exhbn. Oakland (Calif.) Mus., 1995, UCLA Mus., Westwood, 1995, Logan (Utah) Art Mus., 1995; works in permanent collection, San Diego Gallery Fine Art, Crocker Gallery, Sacramento, San Francisco Mus. Art, Whitney Mus. Am. Art, Bklyn. Mus., Mus. Modern Art, Fogg Mus., Met. Mus., Victoria and Albert Mus., London, Brit. Mus., London, Bibliothèque Nationale, Paris, France, Worcester (Mass.) Art Mus., Cleve. Mus. Art, Boston Mus. Art, Oakland (Calif.) Mus., DeYoung Mus., San Francisco, L.A. County Mus., 1994, Oakland Mus., 1995, Gene Autry Mus., L.A., 1995, Palms (Calif.) Art Guild, 1996; author: Notan: The Principle of Dark-Light Design, 1968, 2d edit., 1976, Danish edit., 1977, 3d edit., 1991. Recipient 1st prize, 4th ann. exhbn. San Francisco Soc. Women Artists, 1929; Pres.'s purchase prize, 1941; Leisser-Farnham award 7th ann. exhbn. San Diego Art Guild, 1932; hon. mention 7th ann. exhbn. So. Calif. Artists, 1933; spl. prize 9th ann. exhbn., 1937; Artists Fund prize ann. exhbn. drawings and prints San Francisco Art Assn., 1943; hon. mention 2d spring ann. Calif. Palace Legion of Honor, San Francisco, 1947; purchase prize 2d nat. print ann. Bklyn. Mus., 1948; 1st prize 9th ann. Nat. Serigraph Soc., N.Y.C., 1948. Home: 925 N Plaza Dr SP93 Apache Junction AZ 85220 also: HC1 Box 1055 Joshua Tree CA 92252 Office: Tobey Moss Gallery 7321 Beverly Blvd Los Angeles CA 90036-2503

BOTOE, CARLOTTA See CARLCANO, CARLOTTA MIGUELINA

BOTSFORD, BETH, swimmer, Olympic athlete; b. May 21, 1981. Swimmer Pan Am. Pacific Team, 1995, U.S. Olympic Team, Atlanta, 1996. Named Spring Nationals Rookie of the Meet, 1994; 1st place 200 meter backstroke, 100 meter backstroke Spring Nationals, 1995, 200 meter backstroke Summer Nationals, 1995; recipient Gold medal 100 meter backstroke Olympic Games, Atlanta, 1996. Mem. North Balt. Aquatic Club. Office: US Swimming Inc 1 Olympic Plaza Colorado Springs CO 80909*

BOTSFORD, MARY HENRICH, retired ophthalmologist; b. Buffalo, , Aug. 22, 1915; d. John William and Margarethe Ingeborg (Kähler) Henrich; m. Daniel Ray Botsford, Feb. 11, 1943 (dec. Dec. 1970); children: Daniel Jr., Janet B. Thrush, William H., Thomas H. BA, Mount Holyoke Coll., 1937; MD, U. Buffalo, 1941. Diplomate Am. Bd. Ophthalmology. Assoc. Ivan J. Koenig M.D., Buffalo, 1943-46, 56-60; pvt. practice Buffalo, 1960-84; retired, 1984; staff St. Francis Hosp., Buffalo, 1962-72, Vets. Hosp., Buffalo, 1962-72, Gowanda State Hosp., Helmuth, N.Y., 1962-80, Buffalo Children's Hosp., 1943-96, Buffalo Gen. Hosp., 1943-96. Founding bd. dirs., vol. Habitat for Humanity, Buffalo, 1985-96; vol. Meals on Wheels, Buffalo, 1985-96, Am. Cancer Soc., Buffalo, 1985-96. Recipient Outstanding Achievement in Medicine citation, SUNY, Buffalo, 1984. Mem. Am. Acad. Ophthalmology, Buffalo Ophthal. Club, N.Y. State Ophthal. Soc., Common Cause. Democrat. Lutheran.

BOTSFORD, TERESE MARIE, reading educator; b. SEattle, Aug. 31, 1950; d. Clare George and Dorothy Loretta (Noser) Costello; m. Allen Truman Hughes, July 9, 1971 (div. Mar. 1992); m. James Lloyd Botsford, June 18, 1994; children: Stephanie, Carrie, Jeffrey. BA, Ctrl. Wash. U., 1972; MA in Edn., Western Wash. U., 1992. Tchr. 4thgrade St. Joseph's Sch., Kennewick, Wash., 1972-75, tchr. 2d grade, 1975-76; tchr. 4th grade Kennewick Sch. Dist., 1977-78; tchr. kindergarten Shelton (Wash.) Sch. Dist., 1978-81, Grapeview (Wash.) Sch. Dist., 1981-86; tchr. grades 1-6 reading and math. South Kitsap Sch. Dist., Port Orchard, Wash., 1986-92, tchr. Reading Recovery, 1991—; insvc. presenter, instr. throughout northwestern Wash., 1985—; tchr. trainer South Kitsap Sch. Dist., 1988—, presenter parent tng., 1989—, developer math tutor program, 1988-91. Dir. religious edn. St. Joseph's Ch., Kennewick, 1976-78; chair various coms. Children's Hosp. Guild, Shelton, 1979-83; cantor St. Gabriel Ch., Port Orchard, 1988—. Mem. ASCD, NEA, N.Am. Coun. Reading Recovery, Wash. Edn. Assn., Internat. Reading Assn. Roman Catholic. Home: 7313 E Center St Port Orchard WA 98366-8469 Office: East Port Orchard Elem Sch 1964 Hoover Ave SE Port Orchard WA 98366-3034

BOTSIS, BETH ANN, administrative assistant, freelance musician, singer; b. Holland, Mich., May 4, 1958; d. Robert Constantine and Joan Dorian (Van Dyke) B. Student, Western Mich. U., 1976-77; MusB, Hope Coll., 1980; MusM, U. Md., 1985. Records mgr. Am. Mining Congress, Washington, 1983-88; asst. to dir. Interstate Mining Compact Commn., Herndon, Va., 1988—. Singer opera chorus The Washington Opera, 1984-88, The Wolf Trap Opera, Vienna, Va., 1985, 86; sang role of Geraldine in A Hand of Bridge, 1987; solo recitalist Washington met. area and Holland, Mich., 1985—. Mem. Am. Guild Musical Artists (bd. govs. 1989-94), Nat. Assn. Tchrs. Singing, Am. Assn. Christian Counselors. Republican. Presbyterian. Office: Interstate Mining Compact Commn 459B Carlisle Dr Herndon VA 22070

BOTTEL, HELEN ALFEA, columnist, writer; b. Beaumont, Calif.; d. Alpheus Russell and Mary Ellen (Alexander) Brigden; m. Robert E. Bottel; children: Robert Dennis, Rodger M., R. Kathryn Bottel Bernhardt, Suzanne V. Bottel Peppers. AA, Riverside Coll. Calif.; student, Oreg. State U., 1958-59, So. Oreg. Coll., 1959. Writer, editor Illinois Valley News, Cave Junction, Oreg., 1950-56; writer Grants Pass (Oreg.) Courier, Portland Oregonian, Medford (Oreg.) Mail Tribune, 1952-58; daily columnist Helen Help Us and Generation Rap King Features Syndicate, N.Y.C., 1958-83, columnist (with Sue Bottel), 1969-83; adv. bd. Internat. Affairs Inst., N.Y.C., Tokyo, 1986—; freelance mag. writer, author, lectr., 1956—. Author: To Teens with Love, 1969, Helen Help Us, 1970, Parents Survival Kit, 1979; contbg. editor, columnist Real World mag., 1978-84; weekly columnist Yomiuri Shimbun, Tokyo, 1982-90; thrice weekly columnist Sacramento Union, 1986-88; newspaper and mag. columnist Look Who's Aging (with dau. Kathy Bernhardt), 1992—; contbr. nonfiction to books and nat. mags. Staff mem. ACT Handicapped Children Games, Sacramento, 1986—; bd. dirs. Ill. Valley Med. Ctr., 1958-62, Childrens Ctr., Sacramento, 1969, Family Support Programs, Sacramento, 1991—; active Grants Pass Br. Oreg. Juvenile Adv. Com., 1960-62, Nat. Spina Bifida Assn.; charter patron Cosumnes River Coll., Sacramento, 1972—; nat. adv. bd. Nat. Anorexic Aid Soc., 1977-83; scholarship com. judge Exec. Women Internat., 1985. Recipient Women's Svc. Cup Riverside Coll., citation for aid to U.s. servicemen in Vietnam Gov. Ga., 1967, Disting. Merit citation NCCJ, 1970, 1st place award for books Calif. Press Women, 1970, Sacramento Regional Arts Coun. Lit. Achievement award, 1974, Alumna of Yr. award Riverside Coll., 1987, Gold and Silver medals Calif. Sr. Games (tennis), 1990-91. Mem. Am. Soc. Journalists and Authors, Internat. Affairs Inst. Presbyterian. Clubs: Calif. Writers, Southgate Tennis. Home: 2060 56th Ave Sacramento CA 95822-4112

BOTTINICK, DEBRA ANNE, health educator; b. New Rochelle, N.Y., June 26, 1954; d. Marvin and Rose (Magilnick) B. Student, Rutgers U., 1972-74; BS, U. Mass., 1976; postgrad., Bergen C.C., Paramus, N.J., summer 1981, Columbia U., 1981-82; MPH, U. Medicine & Dentistry N.J., 1986, postgrad., 1992—. Grad. teaching asst. Rutgers U., New Brunswick, N.J., 1985-86; field adminstr. The Travelers Cos., East Meadow, N.Y., 1987-88; owner Healthsharing, Mendham, 1987—; med. rschr. Mendham, 1989-92; AIDS edn. program mgr. Acad. Medicine N.J., Lawrenceville, 1989-90; supervising program devel. specialist Ctr. Continung Edn. U. Medicine and Dentistry N.J., Newark, 1990-94; program dir. edn. and tng. N.J. Med. Sch. TB Ctr., Newark, 1995—. Contbr. articles to profl. jours. Mem. APHA, Nat. Ctr. Environ. Health Strategies, Nat. Coalition Against Misuse of Pesticides. Office: U Medicine & Dentistry NJ NJ Med Sch Nat TB Ctr 65 Bergen St Ste GB1 Newark NJ 07107-3001

BOTTONE, JOANN, health services executive; b. Bklyn., June 20, 1943; d. Anthony and Claire (Bisesti) B.; m. William Recevuto, Feb. 12, 1989; children: Matthew, Sandra. RN, Kings County Hosp. Ctr., Bklyn., 1963; BS, St. Francis Coll., Bklyn., 1980; MPA, Russell Sage Coll., Albany, N.Y., 1986; PhD in Pub. Adminstrn. magna cum laude, Kensington U., 1995. From staff nurse, head nurse, quality assurance coord. Victory Meml. Hosp., Bklyn., 1961-81; instr. infection control Community Hosp. Bklyn., 1981-82; dir. quality assurance Profl. Stds. Rev. Orgn., Bklyn., 1982-85; devel. and coord. HIV post-test counseling program Greater N.Y. Blood Ctr., N.Y.C., 1985-88; dir. HIV/AIDS programs Health Sci. Ctr. SUNY, Bklyn., 1988—; tchr. SUNY Coll. Health Related Professions; mem. working group to develop statewide policies and procedures for health care workers involved in potential HIV exposures N.Y. State Health Commr., 1990; mem. tech. adv. group to develop guidelines for OSHA's bloodborne pathogen standard Greater N.Y. Hosp. Assn., 1992; lectr. in field. Contbr. articles to profl. jours. Mem. Am. Coll. Health Care Execs. (assoc.), Greater N.Y. Hosp. Assn. (tech. adv. group).

BOTTONE, MARIA ELENA, physical education educator, riding instructor; b. Hornell, N.Y., Dec. 14, 1967; d. Anthony John Bottone and Lois Elaine Dorey. BS in Phys. Edn., SUNY, Brockport, 1990; M in Elem. Edn., Elmira Coll., 1994. Head riding instr. Dun-Roamin Stable, Hornell, 1987-94; therapeutic riding instr. Look-Up Riders, Hornell, 1989-94; phys. educator Steuben-Allegany BOCES, Hornell, 1990-95; athlete U.S. Modern Pentathalon, San Antonio, 1994-95, U.S. Fencing Assn., Colorado Springs, Colo., 1994-95; phys. edn. tchr. grades K-5 Manitou Elem. Sch.; coach Spl. Olympics, Hornell, 1989-94, Games Physically Challenged, 1988-92, 4-H, Hornell, 1988-91, U.S. Pony clubs, 1987-94; horseback riding tchr. Pikes Peak Riding Acad., Colorado Springs. Named Riding Instr. of Yr. Am. Riding Inst. Cert. Program, 1991, Nat. champion U.S. Fencing Assn., 1995; named to World Team U.S. Modern Pentathlon, 1995. Mem. DAR, U.S. Modern Pantathlon Assn., U.S. Fencing Assn., Am. Horse Show Assn., N.Am. Riding Handicapped. Home: 2169 Giltshire Dr Colorado Springs CO 80904

BOUCHER, MADELEINE I., theology educator. BA in English Lang. & Literature, Mount St. Mary Coll., Hooksett, N.H., 1957; MA in English Lang. & Literature, Cath. U. Am., 1964; PhD in Religious Studies, Brown U., 1973. Instr. St. Anselm's Coll. Dept. Religious Studies, Manchester, N.H., 1969-72, asst. prof., 1972-74; asst. prof. Fordham U. Dept. Theology and Women's Studies Program, Bronx, N.Y., 1974-78, coord. biblical studies, 1974-79, asst. chmn., 1976-78, acting chmn., 1978-79, assoc. prof., 1978-84, dir. women's studies, 1994-95, 96—, prof., 1984—; lectr. Union Theolog. Sem. Dept. New Testament, N.Y.C., 1982; rsch. assoc., vis. lectr. Harvard Divinity Sch. Dept. New Testament and Women's Studies in Religion Program, Cambridge, Mass., 1983-84. Author: The Mysterious Parable: A Literary Study, 1977, The Parables, 1981, 2d edit., 1983; assoc. editor Cath. Biblical Quar., 1984-89; contbr. articles to profl. jours.; presenter in field. Bd. trustees St. Alphonsus Coll., Suffield, Conn., 1986-89. Mem. Cath. Biblical Assn. Am. (mem. exec. bd. 1976-78, mem. task force on role of women in early christianity 1976-80), Soc. Biblical Literature. Office: Fordham U Dept Theology 111 Collins Hall Bronx NY 10458

BOUCHER, MILDRED EILEEN, state agency administrator; b. Chelsea, Mass., Dec. 8, 1928; d. William Brennan and Lillian Beatrice (Baggs) Hudson; m. Lawrence Clifford Boucher, Oct. 4, 1947 (dec. 1980); children: Katherine, Lawrence, Deborah, Jayne, Lyle, Constance. AA with honors, Indian River Community Coll., Fort Pierce, Fla., 1982, AS, 1983; BS in Applied Tech. magna cum laude, Fla. Inst. Tech., 1984. Tchr., head sci. dept. Peace Corps, Republic of Kiribati, 1984-85; environ. health specialist State of Fla., Port St. Lucie, 1989—; chmn. St. Lucie County Environ. Control. Hearing Bd., Fort Pierce, 1985-89. Editor: The Electrolyte, 1982. Active diabetic screening, Fort Pierce, Port St. Lucie, 1982, 83; mem. village coun. Rongorongo Maneaba, Beru Island, Republic of Kiribati, 1985. Mem. Am. Soc. Clin. Pathologists (registrant), Fla. Pub. Health Assn., Alpha Epsilon Soc. Republican. Methodist. Home: 1879 SE Vesthaven Ct Port Saint Lucie FL 34952-8814 Office: HRS-Saint Lucie County Health Unit 714 Avenue C Fort Pierce FL 34950-4189

BOUDREAU, SHARON KAY, special education educator; b. Norfolk, Va., Oct. 26, 1956; d. Henry Crawford and Ida Ruth (Fantone) Roberson; m. James Anthony Boudreau, Aug. 2, 1980; children: Allison Leigh, Ethan Gray. BS in Edn., Old Dominion U., 1978, MS in Edn., 1985. Cert. tchr., Va. Elem. tchr. Norfolk City Schs., 1978-83, spl. edn. tchr., 1983-90; tchr., curriculum devel. specialist Chance program Old Dominion U., Norfolk, 1983-86; spl. edn. tchr. Va. Beach City Schs., 1990—, mem. Planning for Future steering com., 1993-94, coord. at-risk program Kempsville Mid. Sch., 1993-96, coord. child study team Kempsville Mid. Sch., 1994—, coord. spl. edn. dept. Kempsville Mid. Sch., 1994—, mem. faculty coun. Kempsville Mid. Sch., 1993—. Mem. Va. Reading Coun., Delta Kappa Gamma (Beta chpt.). Roman Catholic. Home: 533 Ingram Rd Virginia Beach VA 23452-7142 Office: Kempsville Mid Sch 860 Churchill Dr Virginia Beach VA 23464-2905

BOUDREAUX, GLORIA MARIE, nurse, educator; b. Lafayette, La., May 2, 1935; d. Simon Zepherin and Orta Marie (Pierret) B. Diploma, Charity Hosp. Sch. Nursing, 1962; BA maxima cum laude, St. Edward's U., 1974; MS in Psychiatric-Mental Health Nursing, Tex. Women's U., 1976. Head surg., med. nurse Lafayette (La.) Charity Hosp., 1962-65; commd. 1st lt. U.S. Army, 1965; advanced through grades to col. Nurse Corps, U.S. Army, 1983; ret. U.S. Army, 1995; psychiat. staff nurse VA Hosp., New Orleans, 1968-72; psychiatric nurse U.S. Army Nurse Corp., San Francisco and Augusta, Ga., 1966-67; instr. Tex. Woman's Univ. Sch. of Nursing, Houston, 1976-80; clin. specialist VA Med. Ctr., Houston, 1980-87; psychiat. nursing coord. Spring Shadows Glen, Houston, 1987-88; instr. assoc. degree nursing program Houston Community Coll., 1988-91; asst. prof. nursing La. State U., Eunice, 1992-96; with Circle of Support Home Health, 1996—; clin. specialist, cons. in psychiat.-mental health nursing. Recipient Nat. Def. Svc. medal, 1968, Army Res. Component medal, 1972, Armed Forces Res. medal, 1977 (10-yr. device 1988), Army Commendation medal, 1978, Army Meritorious Svc. medal, 1990, Presdl. Sports award, 1989, 90, 91. Mem. Am. Psychiatric Nurses Assn., Am. Orthopsychiatric Assn., Soc. for Edn. and Rsch. in Psychiatric-Mental Health Nursing, Res. Officers Assn. (chpt. pres. 1981-83), Assn. Mil. Surgeons of U.S., ANA (cert. in psychiat. mental health nursing), Vietnam Vets. Assn., Sigma Theta Tau, Retired Army Nurse Corps Assn., The Retired Officers Assn. Home: 307 Meadow Ln Lafayette LA 70506

BOUGHMAN, JOANN ASHLEY, dean; b. Kokomo, Ind., May 4, 1949; d. Robert George and Lydia Ann (Ashley) B. BS in Med. Tech., Ind. U., Indpls., 1972, PhD in Med. Genetics, 1978. Diplomate Am. Bd. Med. Genetics. Asst. prof. Med. Coll. Va., Richmond, 1979-82; assoc. prof. U. Md. Med. Sch., Balt., 1983-90, prof., 1990—; assoc. v.p. for rsch. U. Md. Balt. County, Balt., 1992-95, dean grad. sch., 1992—; v.p. for acad. affairs U. Md., Balt., 1995—; sec. Am. Bd. Med. Genetics, 1992-94, v.p., 1995-96; cons. NIH, Bethesda, Md., 1982—, Gallaudet U., Washington, 1977—. Contbr. articles to profl. jours., chpts. to 19 books; author ednl. materials. Bd. dirs., officer Har Sinai Congregation, Balt., 1987—; mem. exec. com. High Tech Coun., Balt., 1992—; com. chair Info. Tech. Bd., Balt., 1994—; mem. speaker bur. Jewish Family Svcs., Balt., 1987—. Grantee RP Genetics Registry Ctr., 1978-82, NIH, 1985-94, 90-94; Edwards fellow, 1976. Fellow

Am. Coll. Med. Genetics; mem. Am. Soc. Human Genetics (cert., com. chair 1994), Am. Assn. Dental Rsch., Am. soc. Clin. Pathologists, Exec. Women's Network. Office: U Md Balt 520 W Lombard St Baltimore MD 21201

BOUGIE, JACQUELINE DORIS, chiropractor; b. San Bernardino, Calif., Apr. 1, 1964; d. Edward John and Marie Blanche (Bishop) B. BS, Calif. State U., Fullerton, 1987, postgrad.; D Chiropractic, L.A. Coll. Chiropractic, 1991. Diplomate Am. Bd. Chiropractic Orthopedists. Clin. scis. resident L.A. Coll. Chiropractic, Whittier, Calif., 1992-94, asst. prof., 1995—; pvt. practice Rehab. Health-Care Network, L.A., 1994-95; utilization and quality mgmt. specialist Am. Chiropractic Network, San Diego, 1995—; lectr. post-grad. divsn. L.A. Coll. Chiropractic, 1993—. Contbr. articles to profl. publs. Grad. fellow Found. for Chiropractic Edn. and Rsch., 1994-96. Mem. AAUW, Am. Chiropractic Assn. Home: 11255 Tierrasanta Blvd Apt 82 San Diego CA 92124 Office: Am Chiropractic Network 8989 Rio San Diego Dr San Diego CA 92108

BOULDEN, JUDITH ANN, federal judge; b. Salt Lake City, Dec. 28, 1948; d. Douglas Lester and Emma Ruth (Robertson) Boulden; m. Alan Walter Barnes, Nov. 7, 1982; 1 child, Dorian Lisa. BA, U. Utah, 1971, JD, 1974. Bar: Utah 1974, U.S. Dist. Ct. Utah 1974. Law clk. to A. Sherman Christianson U.S. Cts., Salt Lake City, 1974; assoc. Roe & Fowler, Salt Lake City, 1975-81, McKay Burton Thurman & Condie, Salt Lake City, 1982-83; trustee Chpt. 7, Salt Lake City, 1976-82, Standing Chpt. 12, Salt Lake City, 1987-88, Standing Chpt. 13, Salt Lake City, 1979-88; sr. ptnr. Boulden & Gillman, Salt Lake City, 1983-88; U.S. Bankruptcy judge U.S. Cts., Salt Lake City, 1988—. Mem. Utah Bar Assn.

BOULDING, ELISE MARIE, sociologist, educator; b. Oslo, Norway, July 6, 1920; came to U.S., 1923, naturalized, 1929; d. Joseph and Birgit (Johnsen) Biorn-Hansen; m. Kenneth Boulding; Aug. 31, 1941; children: John Russell, Mark David, Christine Ann, Philip Daniel, William Frederic. B.A., Douglass Coll., 1940; M.S., Iowa State Coll., 1949; Ph.D., U. Mich., 1969. Research asso. Survey Research Inst., U. Mich., 1957-58, Mental Health Research Inst., 1959-60; research devel. sec. Center for Research on Conflict Resolution, 1960-63; prof. sociology, project dir. Inst. Behavioral Sci., U. Colo., Boulder, 1967-78; Montgomery vis. prof. Dartmouth Coll., 1978-79, chmn. dept. sociology, 1979-85; prof. emerita, 1985; sec. gen. Internat. Peace Rsch. Assoc., 1989-91; pres. IPRA Found., 1992—; mem. program adv. council Human and Social Devel. Program, UN Univ., 1977-80; mem. governing council, 1980-86. Author: (with others) Handbook of International Data on Women, 1976, Bibliography on World Conflict and Peace, 1979, Social System of Planet Earth, 1980, Women and the Social Costs of Economic Development, 1981; author: The Underside of History: A View of Women Through Time, 1975, rev. edit., 1992, Women in Twentieth Century World, 1977, Children's Rights and the Wheel of Life, 1979, Building a Global Civic Culture: Education for an Interdependent World, 1988, 90, One Small Plot of Heaven, 1990, (with Kenneth Boulding) The Future: Images and Processes, 1994; editor: Peace Culture and Society: Transnational Research and Dialogue with Clovis Brigagao and Kevin Clements (eds.), 1990; New Agendas for Peace Research: Conflict and Security Reexamined (ed.), 1992; Building Peace in the Middle East: Challenges for States and Civil Society, (ed.), 1993. Internat. chair Womens Internat. League for Peace and Freedom, 1967-70; mem. Exploratory Project on Conditions for Peace, 1984-90; mem. U.S. Commn. for UNESCO, 1978-84; mem. UNESCO Peace Prize jury, 1980-87; chair bd. Boulder Cmty. Parenting Ctr., 1988-92; bd. dirs. Am. Friends Svc. Com., 1990-94. Recipient Disting. Achievement award Douglass Coll., 1973, Ted. Lentz Peace award, 1980, Athena award, 1983, Nat. Women's Forum award, 1985, Inst. of Def., Disarmament, Peace and Democracy award, 1990—, Global Citizen award Boston Rsch. Ctr., 1995; named to Rutgers Hall of Disting. Alumni, 1994; Danforth fellow, 1965-67. Mem. Am. Sociol. Assn. (Jessie Bernard award 1982, Peace and War sect. award 1994), Internat. Sociol. Assn., Internat. Peace Rsch. Assn. (newsletter editor 1983-87), World Future Studies Fedn., Internat. Studies Assn., World Future Soc., Colo. Women's Forum, U. Mich. Alumni Assn. (Athena award 1983). Quaker. Home: 44 E Plain St Wayland MA 01778

BOULTINGHOUSE, (DANNIE) CAROL, business development specialist; b. Dallas, Sept. 11, 1954; d. Daniel Calvin and Mary Bennette (Temple) Wilkinson; m. Steven Ed Boultinghouse, Feb. 21, 1981 (div. June 1986); 1 child, Brian Steven. AD in Liberal Arts, Eastfield C.C., Mesquite, Tex., 1975; student, Abilene Christian Coll., Garland, Tex., 1976-77. Various secretarial positions Dallas, 1974-80; sec. CIGNA Internat., Dallas, 1980-83, underwriting asst., 1983-85, assoc. underwriter, 1985-87, account rep., 1987-92, bus. devel. specialist, 1992—. Mem. Marine Corps League Aux. Roman Catholic. Home: 3039 Sharpview Ln Dallas TX 75228-6084 Office: CIGNA Internat 600 Las Colinas Blvd E Ste 950 Irving TX 75039-5633

BOULTINGHOUSE, MARION CRAIG BETTINGER, editor; b. New Albany, Ind., Oct. 7, 1930; d. Losson Edward and Marion Craig (Klarer) Bettinger; m. Ray Allen Boultinghouse, Jan. 1, 1973. Student, Hanover Coll., 1948-50; BS, Fla. So. Coll., 1952; M.Ed., U. Louisville, 1960. Tchr. pub. schs. Lakeland, Fla., 1952, New Albany, 1953-55, 58-60, New Haven, 1955-58; editor Am. Edn. Publs., Middletown, Conn., 1960-63, Holt, Rinehart & Winston, N.Y.C., 1963-64, 69-72, Macmillan, Inc., N.Y.C., 1964-69, 72-75; editorial dir., v.p. sch. div. Macmillan, Inc., 1975-79; pres. Boultinghouse & Boultinghouse Inc.; pub. consultants Boultinghouse & Boultinghouse Inc., N.Y.C., 1976—. Author: Follow Me, Everybody, 1968. Office: 153 E 30th St New York NY 10016-7340

BOUNDS, NANCY, modeling and talent company executive; b. Rodney, Ark.; d. William Thomas and Mary Jane (Fields) Southard; m. Robert S. Bounds, 1960 (div. 1965); 1 child, Ronnie Jean; m. Mark Curtis Sconce, Nov. 28, 1972. Exec. dir. Internat. Fashion/Modeling Assn., N.Y.C., 1978; founding pres. Internat. Talent and Model Schs. Assn., N.Y.C., 1979-80; pres. Nancy Bounds Internat., Omaha, 1959—. Contbr. articles to profl. jours. Producer TV Heart Fund Auction, 1965; dir., choreographer fashion show N.Y. fashion editors, 1989, Czechoslovakian Model Search, Prague, 1991. Chairperson Douglas/Sarpy County Heart Assn., Omaha, 1966, 73-74. Recipient Nat. Tchr.'s award MiLady Pub. Co., 1965, Outstanding Service award Mayor of Omaha, 1984, Uta Halee Girls Village, 1983-87, March of Dimes service award, 1977, 84, Toys for Tots service award, 1986, Muscular Dystrophy citation of merit, 1982; named Best of Omaha, 1988-92, Woman of Distinction YWCA, 1992, 93, 94, 95; Nancy Bounds Day proclaimed by City of Omaha, 1994. Avocations: reading, painting, travel, golf, tournament bridge. Home: 4803 Davenport St Omaha NE 68132-3108 Office: 11915 Pierce Plz Omaha NE 68144

BOUNDS, SARAH ETHELINE, historian; b. Huntsville, Ala., Nov. 5, 1942; d. Leo Deltis and Alice Etheline (Boone) Bounds; AB, Birmingham-So. Coll., 1963; MA, U. Ala., Tuscaloosa, 1965, Ed.S. in History, 1971, PhD, 1977. Tchr. social studies Huntsville City Schs., 1963, 65-66, 71-74; residence hall adv., dir. univ. housing U. Ala., Tuscaloosa, 1963-65, 68-71; instr. history N.E. State Jr. Coll., Rainsville, Ala., 1966-68; instr. history U. Ala., Huntsville, 1975, 78-80, 85—, dir. Weeden House Mus., 1981-83; asst. prof. edn., supr. student tchrs. U. North Ala., Florence, 1978. Mem. AAUW, Assn. Tchrs. Educators, Nat. Council Tchrs. Social Studies, NEA, Ala. Hist. Assn., Ala. Assn. Historians, Ala. Assn. Tchrs. Educators, Huntsville Hist. Soc., Historic Huntsville Found., Alpha Delta Kappa (state pres. Ala. 1990-92, regional sec. 1991-93, internat. mem. com. 1993—), Kappa Delta Pi, Phi Alpha Theta. Methodist. Club: Huntsville Pilot (pres. 1990-91, club builder 1991-93, Ala. dist. lt. gov. 1995-96, Ala. dist. gov.-elect 1996—). Home: 1100 Bob Wallace Ave SE Huntsville AL 35801-2807

BOUNDS-SEEMANS, PAMELLA J., artist; b. Milton, Del., Nov. 5, 1948; d. James Wilson Bounds and Marguerite Edna (Rickards) Bounds Carey; m. Jeffrey Wayne Seemans, Mar. 20, 1984; children: Misty Autumn, Sterling Hunter, Jordan Windsor. BA, N.Mex. Highlands U., 1971, MA, 1972. Tchr. elem. art Indian River Sch. Dist., Frankford, Del., 1973-79; lectr. U. Md., 1981, U. Del., 1986, Del. Tech. and C.C., 1988, 75th Del. Womens Day Conf. at U. Del. Exhibited in group shows including Rehoboth (Del.) Art League, 1980, 89, 90, 92, 93, Tideline Gallery, Rehoboth Beach, Del., 1980—, Greenville, Del., 1993, Wicomico Art League, 1980, Del. Tech. and C.C., Georgetown, 1981, U. Md., 1981, Meth. Ch. Gallery, Milford, Del., 1981, Bluestreak Gallery, Wilmington, Del., 1989—, Blue Streak Art Gallery, Wilmington, 1993, Jamison Gallery, Santa Fe, 1993—, Del. Art Mus., 1996, Biennal 96 Del. Art Mus., numerous others; represented in permanent collections Sussex County Courthouse, also numerous pvt. collections. Donated art work to oncology ctr. Beebe Hosp. Found., 1995, Multiple Sclerosis Found. Del., Ronald McDonald House Del. Recipient award for outstanding body of work Torpedo Factory, Alexandria, Va., 1982; fellow State of Del. Divsn. of the Arts, 1995. Mem. Nat. Mus. of Women in the Arts, Del. Art Mus., Rehoboth Art League (2d prize 1981, Tunnel 2d place award for most outstanding work in exhibit 1990, Popular Vote award 1992, 1st place award 1993), Del. Ctr. for Contemporary Arts, Del. Ctr. for Creative Arts, Newark Arts Alliance, Del. Nature Soc., Mothers Multiple Births (v.p. 1987), Wicomo Art League (hon. mention 1981). Episcopalian. Home and Studio: 1203 Greenbank Rd Wilmington DE 19808-5842

BOURDEAUX, NORMA SANDERS, state legislator; b. Birmingham, Ala., June 10, 1930; d. Hanson Earle and Ethelyn Lou (Milton) Sanders; m. Thomas DeVane Bourdeaux Jr., Oct. 11, 1952 (dec.); children: Lisa B. Percy, Marian B. Barksdale, Ellen D., Thomas D. III. AA, Stephen's Coll., 1950; BA, U. Ala., 1952. Cert. picture framer. Tchr. art Meridian (Miss.) Separate Sch. Dist., 1961-63, 71-73; instr. art U. So. Miss., Meridian, 1966-72; owner Bourdeaux Frame & Gallery, Meridan, 1981-92; mem. Miss. House Reps., Jackson, 1992—. Chmn. Govs. Commn. for Children & Youth, Jackson, 1982-88, Govs. Adv. Human & Health Svcs., Jackson, 1984-88; bd. dirs. Hilltop House for Boys, Meridian, 1980—, Greater Meridian C. of C., 1980-85. Democrat. Episcopalian. Home: PO Box 3686 Meridian MS 39303-3686 Office: Miss Ho of Reps State Capitol Jackson MS 39201

BOURG, PAMELA WILKINSON, emergency nurse; b. New Orleans, Sept. 17, 1949; d. John Stephen and Melonie Louise (Costello) Wilkinson; m. Wilson Charles Bourg III, Dec. 17, 1971; children: Wilson Charles IV, Dominique, Noel. BSN, La. State U., New Orleans, 1971; MS, Boston U., 1975. RN; cert. adult nurse practitioner; cert. emergency nurse; cert. ACLS. Staff nurse emergency rm. Charity Hosp., New Orleans, 1971-73, Boston City Hosp., 1973-74, Univ. Hosp., Denver, 1976-77; head nurse-emergency U Colo. Med. Sch., Denver, 1977-78; asst. dir. nursing Denver Gen. Hosp., 1978-88, nursing supr., 1988-89; asst. clin. prof. U. Colo. Health Sci. Ctr., Denver, 1979—; med. office adminstr. Kaiser Permanente Health Plan, Denver, 1989-91, area adminstr., med. ctr. adminstr., 1991—; nurse host Copper Mountain (Colo.) Ski Patrol, 1990—; emergency nurse cons. to pvt. attys. Mem. Fitness Fair Bd., Our Lady of Fatima Sch., Lakewood, Colo., 1990—. Mem. Emergency Nurses Assn., Sigma Theta Tau. Home: 10909 W 30th Ave Lakewood CO 80215-7300 Office: Kaiser Permanente 2045 Franklin St Denver CO 80205-5437

BOURGAIZE, LINDA HARPER, educational administrator; b. Tacoma, Wash., May 1, 1947; d. Donald William and Helen (Harper) Bourgaize; 1 child, Matthew Harris. BA, San Jose State U., 1971, MS, 1973. Psychologist Whisman Sch. Dist., Mountain View, Calif., 1972; psychologist, coord., dir. pupil pers. svcs. Mt. Pleasant Sch. Dist., San Jose, 1972-81; dir. San Benito/Santa Cruz Counties Spl. Edn. Local Plan Area, Aptos, Calif., 1981-91; pvt. ednl. cons. La Selva Beach, Calif., 1991—; dir. Washington Twp. spl. edn. local plan area, dir. spl. svcs. Fremont (Calif.) Unified Sch. Dist., 1993—; cons. Calif. Dept. Edn., Sacramento, 1977—, cons., lobbyist, 1994-95; pvt. practice psychology and edn. cons., Calif., 1975—. Mem. steering com. Coalition for Adequate Funding for Disabled Children, Sacramento, 1987-93; chair Spl. Edn. Coalition, 1991-93. Mem. ASCD, LWV, PEO, Coun. Exceptional Children, Calif. Spl. Edn. Local Plan Area Adminstrs. (chmn. 1989-90, legis. chairperson 1990—), Assn. Calif. Sch. Adminstrs., Phi Delta Kappa. Democrat. Home: 27 Altivo Ave La Selva Beach CA 95076-1601

BOURNE, CAROL ELIZABETH MULLIGAN, biology educator, phycologist; b. Rochester, N.Y., May 4, 1948; d. William Thomas and Ruth Townsend (Stevens) Mulligan; m. Godfrey Roderick Bourne, Dec. 21, 1968. BA in Botany/Bacteriology, Ohio Wesleyan U., 1970; MS in Botany, Miami University, Oxford, Ohio, 1978; PhD in Natural Resources, U. Mich., 1992. Lab. asst. Ohio Wesleyan U., Delaware, 1968-70; biol. lab. tech. USDA-Forest Svc., Delaware, 1970-73; grad. rsch. asst. botany dept. Miami U., Oxford, 1973-75; electron microscopist coll. medicine U. Cin., 1975-76; rsch. asst. sch. pub. health U. Mich., Ann Arbor, 1978-80, rsch. assoc. coll. medicine, 1981-83, grad. rsch. asst. sch. natural resources, 1983-86, grad. teaching asst. dept. biology, 1987; postdoctoral scientist U. Fla., Ft. Lauderdale, 1990-92; adj. instr. ecology Fla. Atlantic U. Coll. Liberal Arts, Davie, 1992-93; adj. asst. prof. dept. biology U. Mo., St. Louis, 1994—; adj. asst. prof. biology, Washington U., St. Louis, 1994—. Contbr. articles to scholarly jours. Grantee NSF, 1987-89. Mem. Am. Inst. Biolog. Scis., Am. Soc. Plant Taxonomists, Phycological Soc. Am., Internat. Soc. for Diatom Rsch., Internat. Soc. for Plant Molecular Biology, Brit. Phycological Soc., Soc. for Study of Evolution. Office: U Mo at St Louis Dept Biology 8001 Natural Bridge Rd Saint Louis MO 63121-4499

BOURNE, KATHERINE KAY, journalist, educator; b. Lynn, Mass., Sept. 11, 1938; d. Schuyler Vandervort and Elsie Marie (Moyo) Day; m. William Nettleton Bourne; children: William Alexander, Katherine Loring. BS in Edn., Keene Tchrs. Coll., 1960; MEd, Harvard U., 1984. Tchr. Wachusett Regional High Sch., Holden, Mass., 1960-61; arts editor Bay State Banner, Boston, 1966—; dir. edn. Suffolk County House of Correction, Boston, 1979-84; edn. coord. Dept. Transitional Asst., Mass., 1984—. Contbr. music revs. to Christian Sci. Monitor. Dir. rels. Crime-out, Boston, 1983; mem. Gov.'s Commn. on Status of Women, 1970-74; co-founder, dir. Harvard-Radcliffe Forum Theatre, Cambridge, 1964-68; bd. dirs., mem. ARC Greater Boston, 1987-95, NAACP Boston, 1978-81. NEH journalism fellow, 1978; recipient Melnea A. Cass award Greater Boston YMCA, 1984. Mem. NAACP (life). Home: 52 High St Brookline MA 02146-7707 Office: Bay State Banner The Fargo Bldg 68 Fargo St Boston MA 02210-2122

BOURNE, LOUISE TABER, artist, educator; b. Stamford, Conn., Apr. 4, 1959; d. Russell and Miriam Anne (Young) Bourne; m. Edward Dennison Cheney, Sept. 17, 1994; 1 child, Mariner Taber Cheney. BFA, Maine Coll. Art, Portland, 1988; MFA, U. Mich., 1992. Adj. faculty U. Maine, Augusta, 1993-95; vis. asst. prof. U. Mich., Ann Arbor, 1993; vis. artist Youth Arts, Camden, Maine, 1994, 95. Exhibited works in shows at Ctrl. Maine Power Co., Augusta, 1990, Ellsworth (Maine) Libr. Gallery, 1991, Ctr. for Edn. of Women, Ann Arbor, 1992, Slusser Gallery, U. Mich., 1993, Frick Gallery, Belfast, Maine, 1995, Colby Coll., Waterville, Maine, 1995, McGrath Dunham Gallery, Castine, Maine, 1996; exhibits annually at the Leighton Gallery, Blue Hill, Maine, 1985—; executed murals for various pvt. homes and schs., including large 3D piece for U. Maine, Orono. Recipient Redstone award U. Mich. Sch. Art, 1991; U. Mich. fellow, 1990-92, Rackham Sch. Grad. Studies grantee, 1992. Mem. Coll. Art Assn., Union of Maine Visual Artists, Maine Craft Assn. Office: York Rd Gen Delivery East Blue Hill ME 04629

BOURQUE, MARY PHYLLIS, utility executive; b. El Paso, Tex., July 17, 1947. BS in Physics, U. Tex., El Paso, 1969; MBA in Fin., U. Chgo., 1975. Petroleum engr. Shell Oil Co.; asst. v.p., comml. lending officer First Nat. Bank Chgo.; v.p. gas supply, v.p. mktg. United Gas Pipeline Co.; asst. v.p. gas acquisition and contract mgmt. MidCon Corp.; v.p. gas supply Gas Co. N.Mex. divsn. Pub. Svc. Co. N.Mex., Albuquerque, 1987-90, sr. v.p. gas mgmt. svcs., 1990-95, sr. v.p. energy mgmt., mktg. and customer svc., 1995-96, sr. v.p. energy svcs., 1996—; mem. exec. com., bd. dirs. Assn. Commerce and Industry. Past pres., past treas. Hogres, Inc., now mem. exec. com.; treas., exec. com., bd. dirs. Albuquerque Econ. Devel.; bd. dirs. St. Joseph Healthcare Found. Mem. Pacific Coast Gas Assn. (gas mgmt. com.), Am. Gas Assn., Elec. Power Rsch. Inst. (bus. coun. on retail market bus. tools). Office: Pub Svc Co NMex Alvarado Sq Albuquerque NM 87158

BOURRET, MARJORIE ANN, educational advocate, consultant; b. Denver, Sept. 9, 1925; d. Walter Brewster and Grace Helen (Thompson) Leaf; m. Raymond Roland Bourret, May 28, 1955; children: Robert B., Ronald P. BSEE, BS in Engring. Physics, U. Colo., 1947. Cons. for child advocacy and interagy. coordination San Benito-Santa Cruz Spl. Edn. Local Plan Agy., Aptos, Calif., 1991; project coord. for Linkup to Learning Valley Resource Ctr., Ben Lomond, Calif., 1992-95. Contbg. author: Board/Superintendent Roles, Responsibilities and relationships, 1980; prin. author: Citizens Guide to Scotts Valley, 1984; also articles. Trustee, pres. Scotts Valley (Calif.) Union Sch. Dist., 1970-81, mem. bond oversight com., 1995—; mem., chmn. policy devel. com. San Benito-Santa Cruz Spl. Edn. Coord. Agy., 1980-81; cons. on code sect. 7579, 1990; mem. Calif. Adv. Commn. on Spl. Edn., Sacramento, 1984-89, chmn. legis. com., 1984, chmn. policy rev. com., 1987-89; mem. chmn. Hazardous Materials Adv. Commn., Santa Cruz, 1984-87; organizer, bd. dirs. Friends Long Marine Lab., U. Calif., Santa Cruz, 1979-84; bd. dirs. Group Home Soc., Santa Cruz, 1984-86; others. Recipient Disting. Engring. Alumna award Coll. Engring. & Applied Sci. U. Colo., 1994. Mem. Nat. Sch. Bds. Assn. (fed. rels. network 1977-81), Calif. Sch. Bds. Assn. (bd. dirs., com. chmn. 1977-81, mem. del. assembly 1974-81), LWV (pres. Santa Cruz County chpt. 1967-69). Home: 1160 Whispering Pines Dr Scotts Valley CA 95066-4627

BOUTELLE, JANE CRONIN, fitness consultant; b. Arlington, Mass., Nov. 3, 1926; s. William Francis and Sara (Gillis) Cronin; m. G. William Boutelle, 1953 (dec. 1973); children—Jeanne E., William R., James G. B.S., Boston U., 1948; M.A., Columbia U., 1953. Cert. tchr., Mass. Tchr. dance and health edn. Newton High Sch., Mass., 1948-51, Scarsdale High Sch., N.Y., 1951-55, Marymount Coll., Tarrytown, N.Y., 1955-58, Manhattanville Coll., Purchase, N.Y., 1958-59; pres., fitness cons. The Boutelle Method, Inc., Greenwich, Conn., 1973—. Author: Lifetime Fitness for Women, 1978. Contbr. articles to mags. Pres Westchester Dance Council, Westchester County, N.Y., 1956-57; mem. Nat. Alumni Bd. Boston U., 1981— (chmn. 40th reunion); mem. woman's com. Lighthouse, Westchester County, N.Y., 1983. Recipient Bravo award Greenwich YWCA, 1978. Mem. AAUW (chmn. edn. 1963-68), Soroptimists Internat. (chmn. scholarship com.) , Greenwich Woman's Club Gardeners (chmn. scholarship com.) Assn. Women in Phys. Edn. (chmn. 1954-55), Greenwich Assn. Pub. Schs. (chmn. 1968-73). Home: # 6 Huckleberry Ln Greenwich CT 06831 Office: The Boutelle Method Inc #6 Huckleberry Ln Greenwich CT 06831

BOUTZARELOS, IRENE MEHILOS, visual arts educator; b. Chgo., Feb. 17, 1951; d. William Gus and Helen (Petenes) Mehilos; m. John Peter Boutzarelos, Jan. 8, 1977. BS in Art Edn., No. Ill. U., 1973; M Sch. Counseling, Concordia U., 1994. Cert. art edn./spl. K-12, lang. arts edn., sch. counselor, Ill. Elem. art tchr. Elem. Sch. Dist. 88, Bellwood, Ill., 1974-79, 7th grade art tchr., 1979-80; K-6 art tchr. Elem. Sch. Dist. 4, Addison, Ill., 1981-86; 7th and 8th grade lang. arts and art tchr. Jr. H.S. Dist. 4, Addison, 1986-88, 7th and 8th grade art tchr., 1988-93; art tchr. H.S. Dist. 88, Addison, 1993-96; acad. counselor H.S. Dist. 88, Addison Learning Support Ctr., 1995; guidance counselor Addison Trail H.S., 1996—; elem. art cons., Cook and DuPage Counties, 1980-81. Exhibited in group shows at Addison Art Guild, 1987 (1st Place award), 88 (2d Place award), 90 (2d Place award). Bd. dirs., treas. Addison Ctr. for Arts; mem. Addison Cultural Arts Commn., 1987-89; educator, art instr. Holy Apostles Greek Orthodox Ch., Westchester, Ill., 1991—; citizens adv. coun. Ill. Alliance Arts Edn. Named Outstanding Educator of Yr., Indian Trail PTA, 1993; grantee Dist. 4 Bd. Edn., 1991, 92. Mem. Am. Counseling Assn., Am. Sch. Counseling Assn., Nat. Arts Edn. Assn., Ill. Arts Edn. Assn., Ill. Counseling Assn., Addison Art Guild (pres., sec. 1986—), Art Inst. Chgo., Ill. Sch. Counselor Assn., Ill. Mental Health Counselors Assn., Ill. Assn. Multi-Cultural Counseling. Home: 1221 Hickory Trl Addison IL 60101-1119 Office: Addison Trail H S 213 N Lombard Addison IL 60101

BOUVRIE, ALICE DUNGAN, scriptwriter; b. Santa Monica, Calif., Aug. 21, 1948; d. Co-prodr. documentary Living Under the Cloud: Chernobyl Today, 1994 (Spl. Jurors award 1994); scriptwriter Faces of Fortunes, 1984-85, A Taste of the Earth, 1994-95. Mem. Women in Film (membership chair 1994—), Women in Film Video (bd. dirs. 1994—), Dirs. Guild Am., Inst. Fgn. Studies (workshop leader 1996, Counselor of Yr. 1995-96). Democrat. Home and Office: 143 Woodside Ln Arlington MA 02174

BOVIS, BETH ANN, management consultant; b. Elmhurst, Ill., May 2, 1969; d. George and Betty Bovis. BS in Econs., U. Pa., 1991. Bus. analyst AT Kearney, Chgo., 1991-93, assoc., 1993-96; mgr. AT Kearney, N.Y.C., 1996—. Mem. NAFE. Office: AT Kearney 153 E 53d St New York NY 10010

BOVITZ, CAROLE JONES, psychotherapist; b. Tulsa, July 9, 1936; d. John Wesley Jones and Vada L. (Dailey) Friesen; m. Richard Stanley Bovitz, May 28, 1959; children: J. Scott, Jennifer Jean. BA in Psychology, Calif. State U., Northridge, 1969; MA in Psychology, Pepperdine U., 1982. Lic. marriage, family, child therapist; cert. employee assistance profl. Ptnr. Personnel Research Assocs., Chatsworth, Calif., 1979-82; pres. Carole Bovitz & Assocs., Huntington Beach and Torrance, Calif., 1982-88; provider rels. mgr. Personal Performance Consultants Inc., Irvine, Calif., 1988-92; pvt. practice Long Beach and Cerritos, Calif., 1992—; dir. presenting services Am. Bus. Concepts, Torrance, 1986-87; seminar cons., trainer Children's Hosp., Orange, Calif., 1986-87; cons. mgmt. seminars C. of C., Riviera Village Assocs., Redondo Beach, Calif., 1988. Pres. Calif. Legis. Roundtable, Sacramento, 1985-86; trustee governing bd. Sch. Dist., Goleta, Calif., 1976; bd. dirs. Calif. Ednl. Congress, Sacramento, 1984-86, Calif. Coalition Fair Sch. Fin., 1984-86. Mem. AAUW (vol. community leadership trainer 1985-88, state pres. 1984-86, state rep. to nat. bd. dirs. 1978-82, state dir. leadership 1988-89, pres. Orange County interbr. council pres.'s 1987-88, Calif. state fellowship endowment named in her honor 1986 in perpetuity, research grant named in her honor 1986 in perpetuity, gift honoree local chpts. 1976, 86, 94), Calif. Assn. Marriage and Family Therapists, Zonta. Democrat. Office: 11558 South St Ste 47 Cerritos CA 90703-6612

BOWDEN, ANN, bibliographer, educator; b. East Orange, N.J., Feb. 7, 1924; d. William and Anna Elisabeth (Herrstrom) Haddon; m. Edwin Turner Bowden, June 12, 1948; children: Elisabeth Bowden Ward, Susan Turner, Edwin Eric; m. William Burton Todd, Nov. 23, 1969. BA, Radcliffe Coll., 1948; MS in Library Services, Columbia U., 1951; PhD, U. Tex., 1975. Cataloger, reference asst. Yale U., 1948-53; manuscript cataloger, rare book librarian, librarian Humanities Research Ctr., librarian Acad. Ctr., U. Tex., Austin, 1958-63, lectr., sr. lectr. Grad. Sch. Library and Info. Sci., 1964-85, 88-89; coordinator adult services Austin Pub. Library, 1963-67, asst. dir., 1967-71, dep. dir., 1971-77, assoc. dir., 1977-86; bd. dirs. Tex. Info. Exchange, Houston, 1977-78; bd. dirs. AMIGOS Bibliog. Council, Dallas, 1978-82, chmn. bd., 1980-81, trustee emeritus, 1986—; chmn. AMIGOS '85 Plan, 1984-86; scholar in residence Rockefeller Found. Villa Serbelloni, Bellagio, Italy, 1986, Ransom Ctr. scholar U. Tex., Austin, 1990—; Zachariah Polson fellow Libr. Co. of Phila., 1990. Author (with W.B. Todd) Tauchnitz International Editions in English, 1988; editor: T.E. Lawrence Fifty Letters: 1921-1935, 1962; Maps and Atlases, 1978; assoc. editor Papers of the Bibliographical Soc. Am., 1967-82; contbr. articles to profl. jours. Served as cpl. USMC Women's Res., 1944-46. Mem. ALA (council 1975-79), Assn. Coll. and Research Libraries (chmn. rare book and manuscript sect. 1975-76), Tex. Library Assn. (chmn. publs. com. 1965-71), Bibliog. Soc. Am., Phi Kappa Phi, Kappa Tau Alpha. Club: Grolier (N.Y.C.).

BOWDEN, DOROTHY JACKSON, mathematics, art educator, artist; b. Pandora, Tex., Oct. 25, 1931; d. William Frederick and Ella Lee (Varnon) Jackson; m. Claude Byron White, Jan. 28, 1950 (dec. Sept. 19, 1963); children: Byronelle White Bly, Claudia White Hawn; m. Herbert Horton Bowden, Apr. 9, 1966; stepchildren: Mary Vesta Mellard, Herbert H. Jr., Cherie L. BS, S.W. Tex. State Coll., 1952, MEd, 1961. Lic. realtor, Tex. Tchr. Dickinson (Tex.) Ind. Sch. Dist., 1955-58; tchr. math. Comal County Rural Sch. Dist., New Braunfels, Tex., 1959-61, Goose Creek Ind. Sch. Dist., Baytown, Tex., 1961-66; tchr. math. Deer Park (Tex.) Ind. Sch. Dist., 1966-76, alternative sch. tchr., 1977-85; real estate math. tchr. Spencer Sch. Real Estate, Houston, 1976; tchr. art Stockdale, Tex., 1985-95; owner/mgr. Family Affair Tea Room and Antiques, Stockdale, 1987-91, Main St. Emporium, Stockdale, 1991-95, Oil Originals by Dottie B., Stockdale, 1995—. Author: Family Affair Cook Book, 1982. Bd. dirs. Deer Park Art League, 1976-85; adminstrv. coun. mem. Christ United Meth. Ch., Stockdale, 1985-96; vol. Stockdale Nursing Ctr., 1986—; mem. United Meth. Women; charter mem. Cultural Arts Coun., Deer Park. Named Girl of the Yr. Beta Sigma Phi, 1979. Mem. Nat. Bd. Realtors, Ex-Students Assn. of Stockdale Ind. Sch. Dist., Tex. Tchrs. Assn. (life), Ret. Tchrs. Assn. (pres., sec.), Am. Legion Aux. (sec.). Home and Office: Rt 2 Box 150 Stockdale TX 78160

BOWDEN, JODY LYNN, gerontological and pediatric nurse; b. Euclid, Ohio, July 14, 1961; d. Merle M. and Sarah Lynn (Korosy) Jackman; m. David R. Bowden, July 20, 1985 (dec. Feb. 1989); children: Chasity Baker,

David, Elijah, Andrew. Diploma, Tri-Rivers Marion (Ohio) Gen. Hosp. Sch. Practical Nursing, 1985. Lic. practical nurse, Ohio; cert. OOPNES Pharmacology. Relief nurse, occupational safety and health technician PPG, Crestline, Ohio, 1988; charge nurse Sunny Villa Care Ctr., Upper Sandusky, Ohio, 1987-89; staff nurse, med. pers. Marion; relief nurse Am. Nursing Care Inc., Marion, Ohio, 1987-93; LPN staff nurse Calcutta (Ohio) Health Care Ctr., 1995—. Mem. LPNs of Ohio. Home: 3 Pine Grove Rdg NE Salineville OH 43945-9479

BOWDEN, SALLY ANN, choreographer, teacher, dancer; b. Dallas, Feb. 27, 1943; d. Cloyd MacAnally and Sally Estelle. Student, Boston U., 1960-62. Mem. Paul Sanasardo Dance Co., N.Y.C., 1963-67; pvt. tchr., choreographer N.Y.C., 1968-70; faculty Merce Cunningham Dance Studio, N.Y.C., 1971-76; faculty, co-dir. Constrn. Co. Dance Studio, N.Y.C., 1972-77; choreographer Constrn. Co. Theater/Dance Assocs., N.Y.C., 1972—; artist-in-residence U. Wis., Madison, fall, 1975, N.C. Sch. of Arts, winter, 1978, U. Minn., Duluth, 1979, 1981-82, Kenyon (Ohio) Coll., fall 1980. Choreographer: Three Dances, 1969, Sally Bowden Dances and Talks at the New School, 1972, The Ice Palace, 1973, White River Junction, 1975, The Wonderful World of Modern Dance or The Amazing Story of the Plie, (1976) Wheat, 1976-77, Kite, 1978, Voyages, 1978, Morningdance, 1979, Crescent, 1980, Diverted Suite, 1983, Baby Dance, 1984. Recipient Creative Artists Public Service award for choreography, 1976-77; Nat. Endowment for the Arts Choreography fellow, 1975. Office: Theater/Dance Assocs 41 E 1st St New York NY 10003-9307

BOWEN, CLOTILDE DENT, retired army officer, psychiatrist; b. Chgo., Mar. 20, 1923; d. William Marion Dent and Clotilde (Tynes) D.; m. William N. Bowen, Dec. 29, 1945 (dec.). BA, Ohio State U., 1943, MD, 1947. Intern, Harlem Hosp., N.Y.C., 1947-48; resident and fellow in pulmonary diseases, Triboro Hosp., Jamaica, L.I., N.Y., 1948-50; resident in psychiatry VA Hosp., Albany, N.Y., 1959-62; pvt. practice, N.Y.C. 1950-55; chief pulmonary disease clinic, N.Y.C. 1950-55; asst. chief pulmonary disease svc., Valley Forge Army Hosp., Pa., 1956-59; chief psychiatry VA Hosp., Roseburg, Oreg., 1962-66, acting chief of staff, 1964-66; asst. chief neurology and psychiatry Tripler Gen. Hosp., Hawaii, 1966-68; psychiatr. cons. and dir. Rev. Br., Office Civil Health and Med. Program, Uniform Svcs., 1968-70; commd. capt. U.S. Army, 1955, advanced through ranks to col., 1968; neuropsychiat. cons. U.S. Army Vietnam, 1970-71; chief dept. psychiatry Fitzsimons Army Med. Ctr., 1971-74; chief dept. psychiatry. Tripler Army Med. Ctr., 1974-75; comdr. Hawley Army Clinic, Ft. Benjamin, Harrison, Ind., 1977-78, chief dept. primary care and cmty. medicine, 1978-83, chief psychiat. consultation svc., Fitzsimons Army Med. Ctr., 1983-85; chief psychiatry svc. med./regional office ctr. VA, Cheyenne, Wyo., 1987-90; staff psychiatrist Denver VA Satellite Clinic, Colorado Springs, Colo., 1990-96, ret., 1996; vol. staff physician, 1996—; Locum Tenums practice psychiatry, 1996—; surveyor, Joint Commn. on Accreditation Healthcare Orgns., 1985-92; assoc. prof. psychiatry U. Colo. Med. Ctr., Denver, 1970-83. Decorated Legion of Merit, several other medals; recipient Colo. Disabled Am. Vets. award, 1994-95. Fellow Am. Psychiat. Assn. (life), Acad. Psychosomatic Medicine; mem. AMA, Nat. Med. Assn., Menninger Found. (charter). Home: 1020 Tari Dr Colorado Springs CO 80921-2257

BOWEN, DEBRA LYNN, lawyer, state legislator; b. Rockford, Ill., Oct. 27, 1955; d. Robert Calvin and Marcia Ann (Crittenden) Bowen. B.A., Mich. State U., 1976; Rotary Internat. fellow Internat. Christian U., Tokyo, 1975; J.D., U. Va., 1979. Bar: Ill. 1979, Calif. 1983. Assoc., Winston & Strawn, Chgo., 1979-82, Washington, 1985-86, Hughes Hubbard & Reed, Los Angeles, 1982-84; sole practice, Los Angeles, 1984-93; mem. Calif. State Assembly, 1992—; gen. counsel, State Employee's Retirement System Ill., Springfield, 1980-82; adj. prof. Watterson Coll. Sch. Paralegal Studies, 1985. Exec. editor Va. Jour. Internat. Law, 1977-78; contbr. articles to profl. jours. Mem. mental health law com. Chgo. Council Lawyers, 1980-82. Wigmore scholar Northwestern U. Sch. Law, Chgo., 1976; recipient James Madison Freedom of Information award No. Calif. chpt. Soc. Profl. Journalists, 1995. Mem. Calif. Bar Assn. (exec. com. pub. law sect. 1990-94), Mortar Bd., Phi Kappa Phi. Office: Calif Assembly State Capitol Sacramento CA 95814-4906 Office: Dist Office 18411 Crenshaw Blvd Ste 280 Torrance CA 90504-5043

BOWEN, JEAN, music librarian, consultant; b. Albany, N.Y., Mar. 23, 1927; d. John W. and Grace Lester (Quier) B.; m. Henry F. Bloch, June 26, 1962; 1 child, Pamela A. Bloch. AB, Smith Coll., 1948, AM, 1956; MS, Columbia U., 1957. Curator Rodgers & Hammerstein Archives of Recorded Sound, N.Y.C., 1962-67; asst. chief music divsn. N.Y. Pub. Libr., N.Y.C., 1967-85, chief music divsn., 1985—; cons. Rockefeller Bros. Found., N.Y.C., 1963, 67, N.Y. Philharm., N.Y.C., 1984, Schubert Archives, N.Y.C., 1982; mem. faculty Rare Book Sch. Columbia U., N.Y.C., 1984, 87, 91; bd. dirs. Composers Recs. Inc., N.Y.C., Amphion Found., N.Y.C. Contbr. articles to High Fidelity, Opera News, Am. Record Guide, Saturday Rev., MLA Notes, New Grove Dictionary of Am. Music. Mem. Music Libr. Assn. Office: NY Pub Libr Music Divsn 40 Lincoln Center Plz New York NY 10023-7486

BOWEN, MARCIA KAY, customs house broker; b. Bradford, Pa., July 20, 1957; d. George W. Allen Jr. and Katherine (Jema) Allen; m. Glenn Edward Rollins, June 26, 1975 (div. 1979); m. Michael James Bowen, Dec. 27, 1983; children: James Derek, Kodie Ann. Student Houston Community Coll., 1978-81, Am. Mgmt. Assn., 1984-85. Lic. customs house broker. Asst. mgr. W.R. Zanes & Co. of La., Inc., Houston, 1975-76; sec. Westchester Corp., Houston, 1973-75; import br. mgr. Schenkers Internat., Inc., Houston, 1976-85; br. mgr. F.W. Myers & Co., Inc., El Paso, 1985-88, regional mgr., 1989-91; v.p. Southwest region The Myers Group (US) Inc., 1992—. Mem. NAFE, Houston Customs House Brokers Assn. (sec. 1977-79, mem. U.S. customs com. 1979-83), El Paso Customs House Brokers Assn. (v.p. 1994), Houston Freight Forwarders Assn., El Paso Fgn. Trade Zone Assn., Soc. Global Trade Execs., El Paso/Juarez Transp. and Distbn. Assn., Inc., El Paso Custon Brokers Assn. (v.p. 1994) Roman Catholic. Office: The Myers Group (US) Inc 34 Spur Dr El Paso TX 79906-5308

BOWEN, NANCY, sculptor, educator; b. Providence, May 25, 1955; d. Richard Le Baron and Phyllis Sewall (Brown) Bowen; m. John Francis Obuck, Sept. 15, 1984 (div. 1990). Student, Stanford U., 1975-78; BFA, Sch. Art Inst. Chgo., 1978; MFA, Hunter Coll., 1990. Asst. prof. Columbia U., N.Y.C., 1994—; vis. asst. prof. Bard Coll., Annandale-on-Hudson, N.Y., 1990, 92; vis. faculty Sarah Lawrence Coll., Bronxville, N.Y., 1990-94. Exhibited in solo shows at Galerie Farideh Cadot, Paris, 1981, Susan Caldwell Gallery, N.Y.C., 1983, Betsy Rosenfield Gallery, Chgo., 1991, Annina Nosei Gallery, N.Y.C., 1990, 91, 93, Chidlaw Gallery, Art Acad. Cin., 1994, Emison Art Ctr., DePauw U., 1992, others. Bd. dirs. Lyn Blumenthal Meml. Fund, Chgo., 1990—. N.Y. Found. for Arts fellow, 1989, Nat. Endowment for Arts fellow, 1994; European Ceramic Work Ctr. resident, Netherlands, 1995, Yaddo Art Colony resident, 1990, 92. Mem. Coll. Art Assn., Women's Caucus for Art. Office: Columbia U 617 Dodge Hall 116th St and Broadway New York NY 10027

BOWEN, PATRICIA LEDERER, dental educator; b. Evanston, Ill., July 5, 1943; d. John Arthur and Edna Virginia (Gerdl) Lederer; m. Clarence Henry Metzner Jr., June 1, 1963 (div. Feb. 1972); children: Donald Frederick, John Henry; m. Steven Casto Bowen, Mar. 1, 1973. Dental Hygienist, U. Louisville, 1972; B.Health Edn., U. Ky., 1982; MPA, Western Ky. U., 1985. Pvt. practice dental hygienist various locations, 1972-75; pub. health dental hygienist U.S. Army, Berlin, 1975-78; cmty. health dental hygienist U.S. Army Dental Activity, Ft. Knox, Ky., 1978-95, U.S. Army Health Svcs. Command, Ft. Knox, Ky., 1981-95; pub. health dental hygienist Meade County (Ky.) Sch. Sys., 1995—, LaRue County (Ky.) Sch. Sys., 1995—; instr. pub. dental health Elizabethtown (Ky.) C.C., 1996—; lectr. in field. Contbr. articles to profl. jours. Pub. health dental hygienist Lebanon (Ohio) Sch. Sys., 1974-75; pub. health dental program presenter Grand Junction, Colo., 1973-74; CPR instr./instr.-trainer Am. Heart Assn., Ft. Knox, 1985—, ARC, Ft. Knox, 1978-87. Decorated Order of Mil. Med. Merit, U.S. Army Health Svcs. Command, 1993, Patriotic Civilian Svc. award Dept. of Army, 1986, Award for Excellence, Delta Dental Ins. Co., 1991, 94. Mem. Am. Dental Hygiene Assn. (pub. health cons. for Ky. 1979-80), Am. Assn. Pub. Health Dentistry, Louisville Dental Hygiene Assn. (chair legislation 1982), Assn. of U.S. Army (v.p. publicity 1994—), Ky. Dental Hygiene Assn. (chair pub. health dental hygiene 1980-84), Ky. Oral Health Consortium (exec. sec.-treas. 1991—, chair 1995—). Home: 348 Greenbriar Ct Brandenburg KY 40108

BOWER, ANNE LIEBERMAN, English educator; b. N.Y.C., May 8, 1941; d. Frank J. Lieberman and Maxine (Scheuer) Donahue; m. Roger L. Bower, Dec. 1962 (div. Dec. 1987); children, Rachael, Aviva, Issac. BS in English, Columbia U., 1963; MA in English, W.Va. U., 1985, PhD in English, 1990. Exec. sec. Pitts. Psychoanalytic Inst., 1975-77; project mgr. Greene County Indsl. Devel., Waynesburg, Pa., 1977-79, Greene County Planning Ctr., Waynesburg, 1979-81; exec. dir. Wheeling (W.Va.) Creek Watershed Commn., Wheeling and Waynesburg, 1981-86; tchg. asst. English W.Va. U., Morgantown, 1983-85, 87-90; instr. in English Waynesburg Coll., 1985-87; assoc. prof. English Ohio State U., Marion, 1990—; spkr. Ohio Humanities Coun., Columbus, 1994-96. Author: Epistolary Responses: The Letter in 20th Century American Fiction and Criticism, 1996; contbr. chpts. to books. Vol. Turning Point, Marion, 1994—. Rsch. grantee Ohio State U., 1991-92, Schlesinger Libr., Radcliffe Coll., 1992, Ohio State U., 1994, Ohio Humanities Coun., 1996. Mem. MLA, Midwest MLA, Nat. Coun. Tchrs. English. Office: Ohio State U - Marion 1465 Mt Vernon Ave Marion OH 43302

BOWER, CATHERINE DOWNES, communications and public relations executive; b. Balt., Dec. 29, 1947; m. Réjean Pierre Proulx, Apr. 28, 1990. BA, Kent State U., 1969. Editor East Ohio Gas Co., Cleve., 1971-74; editor Personnel Administrator mag., Berea, Ohio, 1974-79, dir. communications, 1979-84; v.p. communications, pub. Am. Soc. Pers. Adminstrn. (name Soc. Human Resource Mgmt.), Alexandria, 1984-86; v.p. communications and pub. relations Am. Soc. Pers. Adminstrn. (name Soc. Human Resource Mgmt.), Alexandria, Va., 1986-91; sr. ptnr. Tecker Cons., Trenton, N.J., 1991—; pres. Cate Bower Communications, Alexandria and West River, Md., 1991—; project dir. Work in the 21st Century, 1984. Editor: Work Life Visions, 1987. Pres. Oak Cluster Community Council, Alexandria, 1985-89. Fellow Am. Soc. Assn. Execs. (cert.; vice chmn. comms. sect. coun. 1986-87, chmn. 1987-88, planning com. 1989-91, bd. dirs. Found. 1989-93, chair rsch. com. 1995-96, Best Pub. Rels. Program award 1984); mem. Internat. Assn. Bus. Communicators (pres. Cleve. chpt. 1974), Greater Washington Soc. Assn. Execs. (chair visibility task force 1994-95), West River Sailing Club. Office: Cate Bower Comms 5109 Holly Dr West River MD 20778-9744

BOWER, FAY LOUISE, academic administrator, nursing educator; b. San Francisco, Sept. 10, 1929; d. James Joseph and Emily Clare (Andrews) Saitta; BS with honors, San Jose State Coll., 1965; MSN, U. Calif., 1966, DNSc, 1978; children: R. David, Carol Bower Tomei, Dennis James, Thomas John. Office nurse Dr. William Grannis, Palo Alto, Calif., 1950-55; staff nurse Stanford Hosp., 1964-72; asst. prof. San Jose State U., 1966-70, assoc. prof., 1970-74, prof., 1974-82, coord. grad. program in nursing, 1977-78, chairperson dept. nursing, 1978-82; dean U. San Francisco, 1982-89, v.p. acad. affairs, 1988-89, dir. univ. planning and instl. rsch., 1989-91, pres. Clarkson Coll., 1991—; speaker; cons. univs.; vis. prof. Harding Coll., 1977, U. Miss., 1976; lectr. U. Calif., San Francisco, 1975. Cert. pub. health nurse, sch. nurse, Calif. Fellow Am. Acad. Nursing; mem. Nebr. Nurses Assn., Am. Pub. Health Assn. Calif., Nat. League Nursing (bd. dirs. 1993-95), Calif. League for Nursing (pres. 1989-92), Western Gerontol. Assn., Sigma Theta Tau (internat. pres. 1993-95), Jesuit Deans in Nursing (chair 1982-85). Democrat. Roman Catholic. Club: Rotary (Omaha). Author: (with Em O. Bevis) Fundamentals of Nursing Practice: Concepts, Roles and Functions, 1978; (with Margaret Jacobson) Community Health Nursing, 1978; The Process of Planning Nursing Care, 3d edit., 1982; author: Approaches to Teaching Primary Care, 1981, The Newman Systems Model: Application to Nursing Education and Practice, 1982, Managing a Nursing Shortage: A Guide to Recruitment and Retention, 1989, Cracking the Wall: Women in Higher Education Administration, 1993, (with Mae Timmons) Medical Surgical Nursing, 1995. Home: 1349 S 101st St # 303 Omaha NE 68124 Office: Clarkson Coll Office of Pres 101 S 42nd St Omaha NE 68131-2715

BOWER, JEAN RAMSAY, court administrator, lawyer; b. N.Y.C., Nov. 25, 1935; d. Claude Barnett and Myrtle Marie (Scott) Ramsay; m. Ward Swift Just, Jan. 31, 1957 (div. 1966); children: Jennifer Ramsay, Julia Barnett; m. Robert Turrell Bower, June 12, 1971 (dec. June 1990). AB, Vassar Coll., 1957; JD, Georgetown U., 1970. Bar: D.C. 1970. Exec. dir. D.C. Dem. Cen. Com., Washington, 1969-71; pvt. practice, Washington, 1971-78, 94—; dir. Counsel for Child Abuse and Neglect Office, D.C. Superior Ct., 1978-94. Mem. Mayor's Com. on Child Abuse and Neglect, 1973—, vice chmn., 1975-79; mem. Family Div. Rules Adv. Com., 1977-94; pres., bd. dirs. C.B. Ramsay Found., 1984—; cons. child welfare issues. Active D.C. Child Fatality Rev. Com., 1992—; bd. dirs. Friends D.C. Superior Ct., 1994—. Named Washingtonian of the Yr. Washing. Mag., 1978; recipient Beatrice Rosenberg award D.C. Bar, 1994. Mem. Women's Bar Assn. (bd. dirs. 1993-96, found. 1986-91, Woman Lawyer of Yr. 1986), D.C. Bar Assn. (election bd. 1994—, Beatrice Rosenberg award, 1994), Women's Bar Assn. Found (bd. dirs. 1986-91).

BOWERMAN-DUNKEL, ANN LOUISE, author, genealogist, educator; b. Branch County, Mich., June 4, 1933; d. George Allen and Mary (Thomas) Hubbard; m. Virgil Lee Bowerman, June 4, 1954 (div. 1977); children: William Lee, Sally Ann; m. Virgil Wayne Dunkel, Jr., May 23, 1987. BA, Western Mich. U., 1966, MSLS, 1971, MA, 1976. Cert. tchr. K-8, Mich., libr. sci. Tchr. Bethel #6 Sch. Dist., Coldwater, Mich., 1951-53; tchr. kindergarten Union City (Mich.) Schs., 1963-64; children's libr. Sturgis (Mich.) Pub. Libr., 1971-72; libr./media specialist Coldwater H.S., 1972-91; substitute tchr. Union City Schs., 1964-71, 91—. Author: The Bater Book, 1987, A Bowerman Family History, 1996; co-author: Mame Guide to School Libraries, 1980 (booklet); contbr. articles to profl. jours. Mem., chair governing bd. Woodlands Libr. Coop., Albion, Mich., 1973-74, 83-86; adv. coun. Calhoun and Branch Counties Regional Ednl. Media Ctr., Marshall, Mich., 1972-91; com. mem. So. Mich. Region of Coop., Albion, 1989-91; leader All Around 4-H Club, Union City, 1954-74; mem. Sullivan Lady's Aid Soc., Union City, 1955-74; chair winter program com. Tibbits Arts Found., Coldwater, 1980-90; mem. Coldwater Historic Preservation Assn., 1978-86; del. Mich. Rep. State Conv., Detroit, 1986; candidate for Branch County Commr., Coldwater, 1988; mem. Mich. Assn. for Computer Users in Learning, 1975-91; mem., pres., v.p., sec., program chmn. AAUW Coldwater Br., 1972-92. Recipient Cert. of Appreciation, Mich. Assn. for Media in Edn., 1980, 91, Golden Apple Retirement award Coldwater H.S., 1991. Mem. U.S. Tennis Assn., Am. Assn. Ret. People, Soc. of Genealogists (London), New Eng. Hist. Geneal. Soc., Descendants of Founders of Ancient Windsor, Ctrl. N.Y. Geneal. Soc., Nat. Soc. DAR (good citizen selection com.), Schenectady County Hist. Soc., Old Brutus Hist. Soc., Union City Geneal. Soc., St. Joseph County Hist. Soc., Crawford County Geneal. Soc., Beta Phi Mu. Home: 1820W 600N Howe IN 46746-9406

BOWERS, BEGE K., English educator; b. Nashville, Tenn., Aug. 19, 1949; d. John and Yvonne (Howell) B. BA in English cum laude, Vanderbilt U., 1971; student, U. Mich., 1985; MACT, U. Tenn., 1973, PhD, 1984. Asst. loan officer Ctr. for Fin. Aid and Placement, Baylor U., Waco, Tex., 1975-76; editorial asst. Wassily Leontief, NYU, N.Y.C., 1976-78; instr. bus. English Florence-Darlington Tech. Coll., Florence, S.C., 1979-80; tchr. English and French St. John's High Sch., Darlington, S.C., 1980-82; teaching asst. dept English U. Tenn., Knoxville, 1982-84; asst. prof. English Youngstown (Ohio) State U., 1984-88, assoc. prof., 1988-92, prof., 1992—, composition coord. dept. English, 1985-94, acting chmn. dept., 1989, asst. to dean Coll. Arts and Scis., 1992-93; part-time freelance editor MLA, N.Y.C., 1978-80; cons. Project Arete, Youngstown and Mahoning County Pub. Schs., 1984-87, Youngstown Pub. Schs., 1986, 87-88, 90-91, Macmillan Pub. Co., 1986, Trumbull (Ohio) County Schs., 1988, Akron Beacon Jour., 1994-95. Co-editor: CEA Critic, CEA Forum 1988—, (with Barbara Brothers) Reading and Writing Women's Lives: A Study of the Novel of Manners, 1991, (with Chuck Nelson) Internships in Technical Communication, 1991; editorial bd. South Atlantic Review, 1987-89; editor: of more than 40 pamphlets, 7 children's books, and 1 videoscript. Recipient John C. Hodges award U. Tenn., 1973, Disting. Professorship award for Teaching, 1987, Disting. Professorship award for Pub. Sci., 1996; Alumni Found. Rsch. fellow U. Tenn., 1978, Dissertation fellow U. Tenn., 1983, Davis Editorial fellow U. Tenn., 1984; Grad. Rsch. Coun. grantee Youngstown State U.; named Disting. Grad. Faculty Youngstown State U., 1988—. Mem. MLA, Coll. English Assn. (exec. bd., Disting. Svc. award 1996), Coll. English Assn. Ohio, Nat. Coun. Tchrs. English, Conf. on Coll. Composition and Comm., New Chaucer Soc. (asst. bibliographer 1986—), Assn. Tchrs. Tech. Writing, Soc. for Tech. Commn., No. Ohio Soc. for Tech. Commn., Gould Soc. (faculty com. pres. 1991-93), Phi Beta Kappa, Phi Kappa Phi (pres. 1991-92, sec. 1994—). Office: Youngstown State U Dept English Youngstown OH 44555

BOWERS, CAROLYN POWERS, business and office education educator; b. Clarksville, Tenn., Dec. 11, 1945; d. Carl Liberty and Margaret Eudora (Poyner) Powers; m. William Michael Bowers, June 27, 1963; chlidren: Laurie Lynn Bowers Swift, Margaret Alice Bowers Hooper. BS, Austin Peay State U., 1967, MA in Edn., 1975; postgrad., U. Tenn. Cert. tchr., Tenn. Tchr. bus. and office edn. Clarksville (Tenn.) High Sch., 1969-74, 94—, tchr. stenography lab, compuerized acctg. software tools, 1974-84; tchr. data processing Clarksville Vo-Tech Ctr., 1984-94, liason staff, 1990-93; mem. state steering com. Tenn. Tchrs. Study Coun., 1980-82; pres., v.p., sec. Curriculum Coordinating Com., 1983-89; advisor Bus. Profls. Am., Clarksville High Sch. and Vocat. Tech. Ctr. chpt., 1984-94. Tchr. CCD Immaculate Conception Ch., Clarksville, 1971-72, mem., 1964—; sponsor Future Tchrs. Am., 1994-95. Mem. NEA, Nat. Bus. Edn. Assn., Am. Vocat. Assn., Tenn. Bus. Edn. Assn., Tenn. Edn. Assn., Tenn. Vocat. Assn. (bd. dirs. bus. edn. 1992-94), Tenn. Office Edn. Tchrs. Assn. (pres. 1995-96), Clarksville Montgomery County Edn. Assn. (v.p., sec., treas., editor newsletter, Adopt-A-Sch. Coun. 1990—). Home: 2210 Springlot Rd Clarksville TN 37043-2205 Office: Clarksville High Sch 151 Richview Rd Clarksville TN 37043-4799

BOWERS, CHERYL See BERGMAN, CIEL OLSEN

BOWERS, ELIZABETH JANE, educational administrator; b. O'Neill, Nebr., Jan. 11, 1943; d. Leo Clement and Bridget Elizabeth (Boyle) Schneider; m. Robert S. Bowers, June 6, 1970; 1 child, Frank Leo. BA in Elem. Edn., Wayne State Coll., 1964; MEd in Guidance and Counseling, S.D. State U., 1973; postgrad., U. S.D., 1986—. Tchr. Bellevue (Nebr.) Pub. Schs., 1964-68, Ralston (Nebr.) Pub. Schs., 1968-70, Rapid City (S.D.) Area Sch., 1970-72; prin. staff devel. dir., curriculum coord. Douglas Schs., Ellsworth AFB, S.D., 1974-93; dir. tchr. edn. and cert. S.D. Dept. Edn., Pierre, 1993—; owner ceramic shop; apptd. Gov.'s Profl. Practices and Standards Commn., 1987-93. Editor newsletter The Caller, 1976-79. CCD coord. Cofraternity of Christine Doctrine, EAFB, 1983-89; bd. dirs. Juvenile Detention Ctr., Rapid City, 1991—, Dahl Fine Arts, Rapid City, 1986-92, Sch. Adminstrs. of S.D., Pierre, 1973-80; mem. liturgical com. EAFB Chaple; chmn. liturgical com. Our Lady of Perpetual Help Ch., 1990-92; pres. Rushmore Soccer League, 1989-90. Named Outstanding Prin., S.D. Assn. Elem. Sch. Prins., 1983; named to Nat. Assn. Sch. of Excellence, 1988; recipient Svc. award Rushmore Soccer League, 1990. Mem. Internat. Reading Assn., S.D. Reading Assn. (pres. 1989-92, coord. 1993—), Black Hills Reading Assn. (pres. 1988-89, Literacy award 1990, 91), Cadre, Phi Delta Kappa, Delta Kappa Gamma, Kappa Kappa Iota (pres.). Republican. Home: 5380 Saturn Dr Rapid City SD 57701-6768 Office: State Dept Edn 700 Governors Dr Pierre SD 57501-2291

BOWERS, ELIZABETH LEIGH, nurse midwife; b. Balt., Dec. 14, 1956; d. David Lee Bowers and Jane (Richmond) Lynn. BSN, Syracuse U., 1978, BS, 1982; MS, U. Utah, 1986. RNC, NCC. 3-11 charge nurse Loretto Geriatric Ctr., Syracuse, N.Y., 1978-79; nurse intern USAF Med. Ctr., Keesler AFB, Miss., 1979-80; staff nurse USAF Hosp., Reese AFB, Tex., 1980-82, Scott Med. Ctr., Scott AFB, Ill., 1983-84; nurse midwife 363d Med. Group, Shaw AFB, Ark., 1988-90, Elmendorf Regional Hosp., Elmendorf AFB, Ark., 1990-92; nurse midwife instr. Georgetown U./Malcolm Grow Med. Ctr., Andrews AFB, Md., 1990-92; nurse midwife 374th Med. Group, Yokota Air Base, Japan, 1992-94, 375th Med. Group, Scott AFB, 1994—. Lt. col. USAF, 1979—. Mem. ACOG (chpt. advisor 1982-83, 85-86), Am. Coll. Nurse Midwives (CNM, continuing edn. com. 1990-96, author poster session 1986), Alpha Chi Omega, Sigma Theta Tau. Office: 375th Med Group 310 W Losey Dr Scott AFB IL 62225

BOWERS, JANE MEREDITH, music educator; b. Mpls., Sept. 17, 1936. B in Music, Wellesley Coll., 1958; MA in Music History, U. Calif., Berkeley, 1962, PhD in Music History, 1971. Instr. U. N.C., Chapel Hill, 1968-72; asst. prof. dept. music history and musicology Eastman Sch. Music, Rochester, N.Y., 1972-73, 74-75; lectr., instr. women's studies, music and continuing edn. Portland (Oreg.) State U., 1976-80; instr. flute Reed Coll., Portlnt, 1979-81; asst. prof. dept. music U. Wis., Milw., 1981-84, assoc. prof., 1984-93, prof., 1993—, chmn. music history and lit. area, 1983-87, mem. faculty senate, 1983-86; lectr. women's studies program Cornell U., Ithaca, N.Y., spring 1979; vis. asst. prof. dept. music Oreg. State U., 1980-81; lectr. in field, 1969—; flutist Am. Wind Symphony, summer 1958, Cabrillo Music Festival, 1963-64; asst. prin. flutist Oakland Symphony Orch., 1962-65; free-lance Baroque flutist, N.Y.C., 1975-77; numerous recitals and chamber music concerts on modern and Baroque flute, 1964-85. Editor: Michel de La Barre: Pieces pour la Flute Traversiere, 1978, Joseph Boden de Boismor-tier: Petites Sonatres pour 2 Flutes Traversieres, 1993, (with Judith Tick) Women Making Music: The Western Art Tradition, 1150-1950, 1986, paperback edit., 1987 (Deems Taylor award ASCAP 1987, Pauline Alderman prize 1987); contbr. articles and revs. to profl. jours. and anthologies. Bd. dirs. Early Music Guild Oreg., 1981, Early Music Now, Milw., 1989-92. Alfred Hertz meml. travel scholar, 1965-66; postdoctoral fellow AAUW, 1973-74, 78-79, fellow Ctr. for 20th Century Studies, U. Wis.- Milw., 1982-83, Humanities Inst., 1988-89; grantee NEH, summers 1980, 84. Mem. Am. Mus. Instrument Soc. (rev. editor Jour. 1976-81, bd. govs. 1988-91), Am. Musicological Soc. (coun. 1982-84, mem., chmn. Noah Greenberg awrd com. 1987-89), Coll. Music Soc. (sec. com. on status of women 1972-74, mem. com. 1992—, tchr. Summer Inst. 1993), Soc. for Ethnomusicology (coun. 1995—, chmn. constn. revision com. 1996—), Am. Women Composers (editl. bd. 1992-94), Internat. Assn. Women in Music (editl. bd. 1995—), Assn. Women in Edn. (vice chmn., chmn. U. Wis.- Milw. 1985-87). Home: 2516 E Stratford Ct Shorewood WI 53211 Office: U Wis Sch Fine Arts Dept Music PO Box 413 Milwaukee WI 53201

BOWERS, KATHRYN INEZ, state representative; b. Memphis, May 2, 1943; d. James E. Haralson and Harriet (Thomas) Swanagan; m. Maurice Bowers, Oct. 7, 1961 (dec.); children: Desaree, Montrice. AA, Griggs Bus. Coll., 1962; student, Memphis State U., 1970-72. Employment counselor Allied Employment Agy., 1969-70; dir. publs. LeMoyne-Owen Coll., 1970-77; ins. agt. Equitable Life Assurance Co., 1977-79; area mgr. Nat. Revenue Corp., 1979-81; pres., owner Ask-Us, Inc., 1981-84; job developer supervisor Remodelers Constrn., Inc., 1984-89; contract inspector State of Tenn. Bd. Licensing Contractors, 1989-94; state rep. Tenn. Dist. 87, 1994—; exec. dir. Memphis Area Minority Contractors Assn., 1994—. Roman Catholic. Home: 1307 Swallow Ln Memphis TN 38116 Office: 209 War Memorial Dr Nashville TN 37243-1087

BOWERS, PATRICIA ELEANOR FRITZ, economist; b. N.Y.C., Mar. 21, 1928; d. Eduard and Eleanor (Ring) Fritz. Student scholar, Goucher Coll., 1946-48; BA, Cornell U., 1950; MA, NYU, 1953, PhD, 1965. Statis. asst. Fed. Res. Bank N.Y., N.Y.C., 1950-53; lectr. Upsala Coll., East Orange, N.J., 1953-59; researcher Fortune mag., N.Y.C., 1959-60; teaching fellow NYU, N.Y.C., 1960-62, instr., 1962-64; mem. faculty Bklyn. Coll., CUNY, 1964—, prof. econs., 1974—, chair dept. econs., 1996—. Author: Private Choice and Public Welfare, 1974. Sec. Friends of the Johnson Mus., Cornell U., 1989-91. Mem. Am. Econ. Assn., Econometric Soc., N.Y. Acad. Scis., Fgn. Policy Assn., Women's Econ. Round Table, Met. Econ. Assn. (sec. 1963-68, pres. 1974-75), Am. Statis. Assn. (univs. chmn. ann. forecasting confs. 1970-71, 71-72), Cornell Club N.Y., Kappa Alpha Theta. Home: 145 E 16th St New York NY 10003-3405 Office: CUNY Bklyn Coll Dept Econs Brooklyn NY 11210

BOWERS, PATRICIA NEWSOME, communications executive; b. Baton Rouge, June 21, 1944; d. Carl Allen and Sue Mayre (Powell) Newsome; m. Robert Lloyd Bowers Jr., Aug. 19, 1967 (div. Nov. 1979); children: Paige Ivy, Katherine Elizabeth. BJ, La. State U., 1967. Sr. writer, editor Litton Industries, Pascagoula, Miss., 1978-80; sr. presentations supr. Martin Marietta Aerospace, Orlando, Fla., 1980-81; mgr. presentations Martin Marietta Aerospace, Balt., 1981-85, mgr. pub. rels., 1985-90; dir. pub. rels. and corp. comm. Contraves USA, Pitts., 1990-92; sr. mgr. sector comms. Harris Electronic sys. sector Harris Corp., Melbourne, Fla., 1992-95; dir.

mktg. and pub. rels. Intracoastal Health Systems, Inc., West Palm Beach, Fla., 1995—. Coach Parkville Recreation Council, Balt., 1985-87; bd. dirs. Salvation Army, Human Resources Devel. Agy. Balt. County, Brevard Symphony Youth Orch.; adv. bd. Nat. Aquarium in Balt.; active Brevard Leadership. Mem. Pub. Rels. Soc. Am. (bd. dirs. Chesapeake conf. 1987, Silver Anvil Judge, 1991, 92), Nat. Press Club, Navy League (bd. dirs. Balt. council 1986-87), Balt. County C. of C. (leadership program 1986-87), Pitts. Press Club. Republican. Episcopalian. Office: Intracoastal Health Systems Inc 1309 N Flagler Dr West Palm Beach FL 33401

BOWERS, SABRA ELAINE, business manager, community activist; b. Toccoa, Ga., May 7, 1948; d. Sidney Johnson Slater and Betty Sue (Clark) Slater; m. Dana Lorraine Bowers. Student, Forrest Coll., Anderson, S.C., 1968, Dekalb Coll., Clarkston, Ga., 1972-77, Ga. State U., Atlanta, 1982. Unit leader Gen. Electric Credit Corp., Atlanta, 1968-70; accounts receivable mgr. So. Detectives, Atlanta, 1970-76; office mgr. for physicians Atlanta, 1976-80; real estate agt. Crest Realtors/Better Homes and Gardens, Norcross, Ga., 1980-82; owner Efficiency Plus, Duluth, 1991-94; market rschr. Compass Mktg. Rsch., 1993-95; gen. mgr. Studio Solutions Inc., 1995—. Author booklet; editor booklet and syllabus Dancecamp Tap, Jazz and Modern. Legis. chairperson Chattahoochee Elem. PTA, Duluth, 1989-90, mem. sch. adv. com., 1989—; legis. chairperson Duluth Mid. Sch. PTA, 1996—; mem. Leadership Gwinnett, 1990—; mem. Econ. Devel. Coun. Gwinnett County, 1991—; mem. steering com. Land Use Plan Update, Gwinnett County, 1991—; mem. Citizens Water Resources Coun., Gwinnett County, 1991—; mem. orgns. com. Gwinnett Clean and Beautiful, 1989—. Mem. LWV (mem.Vote '90 com. with Ga. Sec. of State 1989-90, pres. Gwinnett County league 1987-89, treas. 1996—, growth mgmt. chairperson 1991—, bd. dirs., chairperson nominating com., v.p. Ga. state 1989-90, water resources chairperson and lobbyist 1991—, Voter Svc. award 1988). Home: 3514 Debbie Ct Duluth GA 30155-9999 Office: Studio Solutions Inc 3116 Buford Hwy Duluth GA 30136

BOWERS, ZELLA ZANE, real estate broker; b. Liberal, Kans., May 24, 1929; d. Rex and Esther (Neff) Powelson; m. James Clarence Bowers, Aug. 12, 1949; (div. 1977); 1 child: Dara Zane. BA, Colo. Coll., 1951. Cert. real estate brokerage mgr. Sec. Bowers Ins. Agy., Colorado Springs, Colo., 1955-59, Cen. Colo. Claims Svc., Colorado Springs, 1959-63; pres. Premium Budgeting Co., Colorado Springs, 1962-67; pres., owner Monument Valley Realty, Inc., Colorado Springs, 1981-89; mng. broker The Buick Co. Buyer's Market; broker Haley Realty, Inc., Colorado Springs, 1990—; pres. Realtor Svcs. Corp., 1989. Hon. trustee The Palmer Found., Colorado Springs, 1980—, pres., 1983-84; trustee Pikes Peak United Way, 1988-91; pres. Vis. Nurse Assn., Colorado Springs, 1966-67, 74; dir. Colo. League Nurses, Denver, 1968; steering com. The Kennedy Ctr. Imagination Celebration, Colorado Springs, 1989-93, chmn., 1990-92; sec. Care & Share, Colorado Springs, 1984; chmn. McAllister House Mus., Colorado Springs, 1973-74; docent chmn. Colorado Springs Fine Arts Ctr., 1969-70; mem. historic preservation bd. City of Colorado Springs, 1989-94, chmn. 1989-92, mem. Compreshnsive Plan Task Force City of Colo., 1990-91; charter rev. commn. City of Colorado Springs, 1991-92; commr. Colo. Springs City Planning, 1995—; pres. Friends of the Libr., 1971-72; pres. Woman's Ednl. Soc. Colo. Coll., 1974-77; civil adminstrv. staff asst. Air Def. Filter Ctr., 1956-57, ground observer, 1956, others. Recipient Women's Trade Fair Recognition award, 1987. Mem. Nat. Assn. Realtors, Colo. Assn. Realtors (dir. 1987-91, 96—, v.p. S.E. dist. 1992, trustee edn. found. 1988-92, dir. housing opportunity found. 1991-93, Disting. Svc. award 1991, Polit. Svc. award 1992), Colorado Springs Bd. Realtors (pres. 1987-88, named Realtor of Yr. 1989), Pikes Peak Assn. Realtors, Children of the Am. Revolution (pres. 1956-57), Gamma Phi Beta. Avocations: genealogy, travel. Home: 128 W Rockrimmon Blvd # 104 Colorado Springs CO 80919-1876 Office: Haley Realty Inc 109 E Fontanero St Colorado Springs CO 80907-7452

BOWKER, SARAH SWANSON, artist, visual resources librarian; b. Harvey, Ill., July 4, 1945; d. Victor Ernest and Gustava Agnes (Howarth) Swanson; m. Jerry E. Bowker, Feb. 20, 1965; 1 child, Jeffrey Paul (dec.). BS, U. Wis., Stevens Point, 1967, U. Wis., Stout, 1983; MA, U. Iowa, 1986, MFA, 1987. Pvt. artist, 1987—; lectr. U. Wis.-Stout, Menomonie, 1988-92, visual resources libr., 1994—; asst. prof. St. Olaf Coll., Northfield, Minn., 1993-94; guest artist lectr. Carthage Coll., Kenosha, Wis., 1989, Concordia Coll., Moorhead, Minn., 1990, St. Olaf Coll., 1994, Moorhead (Minn.) State U., 1995, Bemidji (Minn.) State U., 1995. One-woman shows include Carthage Coll., Kenosha, 1990, Carleton Coll., Northfield, 1992, A.R.C. Gallery, Chgo., 1993, St. Olaf Coll., Northfield, 1994, Moorhead State U., 1995, Bemidji State U., 1995, Duluth (Minn.) Art Inst., 1995-96, Groveland Gallery, Mpls., 1995; group exhbns. include Kansas City (Mo.) Art Inst., 1985, 86, Columbia (Mo.) Coll., 1988, Milw. Art Mus. Cudahy Gallery, 1989, Northwestern U., Evanston, Ill., 1990, Milw. Art Mus., 1991, Madison (Wis.) Art Ctr., 1993. Bush Artist fellow Bush Found., 1992; grantee Wis. Arts Bd., 1988, 89. Office: U Wis Stout Dept Art and Design Visual Resources Ctr 323A Applied Arts Menomonie WI 54751

BOWLAN, NANCY LYNN, elementary and middle school educator; b. Walla Walla, Wash., Jan. 16, 1946; d. Ralph Reighard and Irene Elizabeth (Fisher) Nowlen; m. Buel Nathan Bowlan; children: Ronald, Sarah, Sandra, Michelle, John. BA, Ariz. State U., 1968. Tchr. Seligman (Ariz.) Schs., 1968-71, Page (Ariz.) Schs., 1976-87; tchr., ESL coord. Gila Bend (Ariz.) Schs., 1988-94; tchr. Hohokam Middle Sch., Tucson, 1994—. Leader Girl Scouts Am., Page, Ariz., 1974-75. Mem. Delta Kappa Gamma (chmn. state fin. com. Ariz. 1986-96, Alpha Zeta chpt. Casa Grande, Ariz. 1993, treas. Tau chpt., Flagstaff, Ariz. 1992, Lambda chpt. 1995-96), Ea. Star (Worthy Matron 1990). Republican. Home: 112 N Players Club Dr Tucson AZ 85745

BOWLER, MARIANNE BIANCA, judge; b. Boston, Feb. 15, 1947; d. Richard A. and Ann C. (Daly) B. BA, Regis Coll., 1967; JD cum laude, Suffolk U., 1976, LLD (hon.), 1994. Bar: Mass. 1978. Rsch. asst. Harvard Med. Sch., Boston, 1967-69; med. editor Mass. Dept. of Pub. Health, Boston, 1969-76; law clk. Mass. Superior Ct., Boston, 1976-77, dep. chief law clk., 1977-78; asst. dist. atty. Middlesex Dist. Atty.'s Office, Cambridge, Mass., 1978; asst. U.S. atty. U.S. Dept. of Justice, Boston, 1978-90, exec. asst. U.S. atty., 1988-89, sr. litigation counsel, 1989-90; U.S. magistrate judge U.S. Dist. Ct. Mass., Boston, 1990—; chmn. bd. trustees New England Bapt. Hosp., Boston, 1990—. Mng. editor This Week in Pub. Health, 1969-75. Trustee Suffolk U., Boston, 1994—; bd. dirs. The Boston Found., 1995—; dir. South Cove Nursing Facilities Found., Inc. Mem. Jr. League Boston, Suffolk Law Sch. Alumni Assn. (pres. 1979-80), Vincent Club. Democrat. Roman Catholic. Office: US Dist Ct 908 McCormack Post Office Boston MA 02109

BOWLER, MARY E., lawyer; b. White Plains, N.Y., Aug. 24, 1956; d. Garrett Francis and Constance Marie (Stiles) B.; m. Kenneth Alan Jones, Jun. 28, 1986; children: Matthew Garrett Jones, Daniel Adam Jones. BS, Cornell U., 1978; JD, Boston U., 1981. Lawyer E.I. du Pont de Nemours & Co., Wilmington, Del., 1981-85; counsel E.I. du Pont de Nemours & Co., Wilmington, 1985-91, sr. counsel, 1991—, asst. sec., 1994. Mng. editor Am. Jour. of Law and Medicine, 1980-81. Leader Girl Scouts of USA, Wilmington, 1982—; auction fin. chair Emmanuel Homeless Dining Room, Wilmington, 1984—; bd. dirs. Jr. League of Wilmington, 1995-96. Mem. Del. Bar Assn., Mass. Bar Assn., Cornell Alimni Assn. (Class 78 pres. 1988—). Roman Catholic. Home: 718 Hertford Rd Wilmington DE 19803-1618 Office: Du Pont De Nemours & Co 1007 Market St Wilmington DE 19898

BOWLES, BARBARA LANDERS, investment company executive; b. Nashville, Sept. 17, 1947; d. Corris Raemone Landers and Rebecca Aima (Bonham) Jennings; m. Earl Stanley Bowles, Nov. 27, 1971; 1 son, Terrence Earl. B.A., Fisk U., 1968; M.B.A., U. Chgo., 1971. Chartered fin. analyst, 1977. Banker to v.p. First Nat. Bank of Chgo., 1968-81; asst. v.p. Beatrice Cos., Chgo., 1981-84; v.p. investor relations Kraft Inc., Chgo., 1984-89; pres., founder The Kenwood Group Inc., Chgo., 1989—; bd. dirs. Black & Decker Corp., Hyde Pk. Bank, Children's Meml. Hosp, The Chgo. Urban League. United Negro Coll. Fund scholar, 1989. Mem. NAACP (life), Assn. for Investment Mgmt. and Rsch., Chicago Fisk Alumni Assn. (pres. 1983-85). Mem. United Ch. of Christ. Club: University (Chgo.). Avocations: tennis, bridge.

BOWLES, BETTY JONES, business education educator; b. Richmond, Va., June 10, 1947; d. Robert Lee and Blanche (Williamson) Jones; m. Norman Lee Bowles Sr., Feb. 14, 1970; children: Ruth Anne, Lee, Danny. BS, Va. Commonwealth U., 1969; M Humanities, U. Richmond, 1989. Cert. postgrad. profl., Va. Tchr. Lee Davis H.S., Mechanicsville, Va., 1969-72, 73-74, 84-87; sec. Battlefield Park Elem. Sch., Mechanicsville, 1972-73; sec. Stonewall Jackson Jr. H.S., Mechanicsville, 1982-84, tchr., 1987-91; tchr., dept. chair Atlee H.S., Mechanicsville, 1991—; mem. adv. bd. Commonwealth Coll., Richmond, Va., 1993—; presenter staff devel. workshop, activities on block scheduling pub. schs. in Va., 1993-94;, Walled Lake, Mich., 1994; Fayetteville, N.C., 1995; mem. Va.-Russia Tchr. Exchange in Moscow, 1995. Lit. sec. Cool Spring Bapt. Ch., Mechanicsville, 1988—. Named Vocat. Tchr. of Yr. Mechanicsville Rotary Club, 1994. Mem. Nat. Bus. Edn. Assn., So. Bus. Edn. Assn., Va. Bus. Edn. Assn., Va. Vocat. Assn. Baptist. Office: Atlee HS 9414 Atlee Station Rd Mechanicsville VA 23111-2600

BOWLES, LIZA K., construction executive. Pres. NAHB Rsch. Ctr., Upper Marlboro, Md. Office: NAHB Rsch Ctr 400 Prince Georges Blvd Upper Marlboro MD 20774-8731

BOWLING, JOYCE BLANKENCHIP, retired critical care nurse; b. White Deer, Tex., Nov. 17, 1932; d. Roy Lee and Myrtle Dove (Milhoan) Blankenchip; m. J.C. Bowling, July 24, 1952. Diploma, Northwest Tex. Sch. Nursing, 1953; AS, Amarillo Coll., 1953; BSN, West Tex. State U., 1983. RN, Tex.; cert. med.-surg. nursing, gerontology, nursing adminstrn. AACN; cert. emergency nurse. Staff nurse emergency rm. Parkland Hosp., Dallas, 1960-62; staff nurse Meth. Hosp., Dallas, 1962-68; staff nurse medicine, then head nurse CCU St. Paul Hosp., Dallas, 1969-73; charge nurse, supr. Southwestern Dialysis Ctr., Dallas, 1973-74; dir. nurses Caruth Rehab. Inst., Dallas, 1974-75; staff nurse VA Med. Ctr., Dallas, 1976-79; staff nurse VA Med. Ctr., Amarillo, Tex., 1979-85, head nurse surg. unit, 1985-88, clin. coord., 1988-96, ret., 1996. Mem. AACN (cert.), Emergency Nurses Assn. (cert.), Tex. Nurses Assn., Am. Heart Assn., Nat. Kidney Found., Am. Cancer Soc., Sigma Theta Tau. Home: RR 1 Box 556A-10 Amarillo TX 79121-9754

BOWMAN, BARBARA MAY, hotel owner; b. Pittsfield, Mass., July 30, 1933; d. Archibald and Elizabeth (Williamson) Sharkey; m. Robert B. Bowman, June 4, 1955; children: Glenn Sharkey, Scott Daniel, Jean Elizabeth. Diploma in Nursing, Hartford (Conn.) Hosp., 1954. RN, Mass. Staff nurse Mass. Gen. Hosp., Boston, 1955-56; staff nurse Vis. Nurse Assn., Natick, Mass., 1957-58, Salem, Mass., 1959-63; owner Henry Farm Inn, Chester, Vt., 1983—, Folger Hotel, Nantucket, Mass., 1963—. Past bd. dirs. Vis. Nurse Assn., Salem; bd. dirs. Salem Hosp., 1980s; active Mass. Conf. United Ch. of Christ, 1985—. Named Mass. Conf. Woman of the Yr. Synod of United Ch. of Christ, 1990. Mem. New Eng. Innkeepers Assn., New Eng. Women's Fellowship. Home: Green Mountain Turnpike PO Box 646 Chester VT 05143

BOWMAN, CYNTHIA ANN, state education official; b. Newark, May 7, 1959; d. James Robert and Anita R. (Petorella) B. BS, Trenton State Coll., 1981, MEd, 1982. Tchr. mktg. edn. Keansburg (N.J.) Bd. Edn., 1982-85, Middlesex County Vocat. Sch., Piscataway, N.J., 1985-86, Sayreville (N.J.) Bd. Edn., 1986-89; edn. planner N.J. Dept. Edn., Trenton, 1989-92, edn. devel. program specialist, 1992-96; tng. mgr. ShopRite Supermarket, Inc., Edison, N.J., 1996—; program mgr. Supermarket Career Tng. Programs, 1993. Vol. N.J. Spl. Olympics, Robbinsville, 1992—. Recipient Exemplary Program award, 1993. Mem. N.J. Mktg. Edn. Assn. (pres. 1983-89, sec., v.p., Ctrl. Region Tchr. of Yr. 1986, 87). Office: ShopRite Supermarket Inc 244 Raritan Ctr Pkwy Edison NJ 08818

BOWMAN, DOROTHY LOUISE, artist; b. Hollywood, Calif., Jan. 20, 1927; d. Bruce L. and Dorothy L. (Kalkman) B; m. Howard Hugh Bradford, Dec. 30, 1949 (div. 1965); children: Brock, Cyndra, Tal Scott, Heather, Delia, Callia. Student, Chouinard Art Inst., Calif., 1945-48, Jepson Art Inst., L.A., 1948-49; BA, Webster U., 1979. Serigrapher, printmaker, painter; represented in permanent collections: Immaculate Heart Coll., L.A. County Mus., Bklyn. Mus., Long Beach Mus., Crocker Art Gallery, Mus. Modern Art, Phila., Mus. Fine Arts, San Jose State Coll., De Cordova and Danna Mus., Boston Pub. Libr., Boston Mus. Fine Arts, N.Y. Pub. Libr., Rochester Meml. Gallery, U. Wis., U. Hawaii, U. Ill., U. Kans., Santa Barbara Mus., Achenbach Found. Legion of Honor, Mus. Modern Art, Monterey, Calif., Libr. Congress, Calif. State Libr. Archives, Arquivos Historicos De Arte Contemporanea Museu De Arte Moderna, San Paulo, Brazil, Ch. of Latter Day Saints History Mus., Salt Lake City; twice juried internat. show 27 countries, 1987. Address: 824 Lyndon St Apt C Monterey CA 93940-1976

BOWMAN, FAY LOUISE, artist; b. L.A., Feb. 8, 1936; d. Winfield John and Dorothy Ethel (Lane) Michalsky; m. George Arthur Bowman; children: John Winfield, David Lawrence. BA, UCLA, 1958; BFA, Art Inst. So. Calif., 1987. Elem. tchr. Alhambra, Calif., 1958-63, Costa Mesa, Calif., 1958-63. One-woman show includes Art Inst. So. Calif., 1987; exhibited in group show at Irvine Valley Coll., 1991; numerous pvt. collections. Sec. President's Club Art Inst., Laguna Beach, Calif., 1990; discussion leader of worldwide Bible Study Fellowship Laguna Beach Presbyn. Ch., 1994-95; active Ebell Club, 1973—. Mem. Designing Women of Art Inst., Assn. Art Inst. So. Calif. (pres. 1988—).

BOWMAN, HAZEL LOIS, retired English language educator; b. Plant City, Fla., Feb. 18, 1917; d. Joseph Monroe and Annie (Thoman) B.; AB, Fla. State Coll. for Women, 1937; MA, U. Fla., 1948; postgrad. U. Md., 1961-65. Tchr., Lakeview H.S., Winter Garden, Fla., 1939-40, Eagle Lake Sch., Fla., 1940-41; welfare visitor Fla. Welfare Bd., 1941-42; specialist U.S. Army Signal Corps, Arlington Hall, Va., 1942-43; recreation worker, asst. procurement officer ARC, CBI Theater, 1943-46; lab. technician Am. Cyanamid Corp., Brewster, Fla., 1946-47; instr., asst. prof. gen. extension div. U. Fla., Fla. State U., 1948-51; free-lance writer, editor, indexer, N.Y., Fla., 1951-55; staff writer Tampa (Fla.) Morning Tribune, 1956; staff writer, telegraph editor Winter Haven (Fla.) News-Chief, 1956-57; registrar/admissions officer U. Tampa, 1957-59; coll. counselor, Atlantic states, 1959-60; registrar/freshman adviser Towson State Tchrs. Coll., Balt., 1960-62; dir. student personnel, guidance, admissions Harford Jr. Coll., Bel Air, Md., 1962-64; instr. York (Pa.) Coll., 1965-66, asst. prof. English, journalism, 1966-69; tchr. S.W. Jr. H.S., Lakeland, Fla., 1969-70; tchr. learning disabled Vanguard Sch., Lake Wales, Fla., 1970-82; libr. asst. Polk County Hist. and Geneal. Libr., Bartow, Fla., 1986-91. Editor Tampa Altrusan, 1958-60, Polk County Hist. Calendar, 1986-90. Recipient Mayhall Music medal, 1933, Excellence in Cmty. Svc. award Nat. Soc. DAR, 1994. Mem. AAUW, NOW, Nat. Geneal. Soc., Mortar Bd., Polk County Hist. Assn. (editor Newsletter, 1990-94), Polk County Hist. Commn., 1992—, Alpha Chi Alpha, Chi Delta Phi. Home: 511 NE 9th Ave Mulberry FL 33860-2620

BOWMAN, JULIETTE JOSEPH, interior decorator, gourmet food consultant; b. Albany, Ga., Aug. 9, 1923; d. Solomon and Asma (Metrie) Joseph; m. David Stroud Bowman, Jan. 18, 1948; children: David, Steven, Denise. Student, Miss. State Coll. for Women, 1960. Buyer, bookkeeper Manhattan Fruit Co. and Deli, Albany, 1945-48; purchasing agent various German and English antique dealers, 1954-58, 61-64; buyer Atlanta Mdse. Mart. and Apparel Mart, 1974—, Atlanta Decorative Arts Ctr., 1974—, Atlanta Gift Mart, 1974—; interior decorator, personal shopper, Atlanta, 1974—; society editor Comml. Dispatch, Columbus, Mass., 1960; decorator The Party Ctr., Atlanta, 1984-86; gourmet food cons. Atlanta, 1983, 84, Sta. WPBA-TV, Atlanta, 1986; owner Juliette's Gourmet Pantry, Buckhead Design Ctr., Atlanta, 1995—. Bd. dirs. Freedom Found. Valley Forge, Alliance Theater Guild, High Mus. Art Affiliates, Atlanta Coun., Better Films Guild, Pro-Mozart Soc., Repertory Opera Co.; mem. Rabun Gap-Nacoochee Guild Atlanta, Atlanta Ballet Guild, Atlanta Symphony Guild, Salvation Army Guild, Ga. Trust for Hist. Preservation, Atlanta Hist. Soc., 100 Club Atlanta, Atlanta Music Club. Named hon. Lt. Col. for contbns. to arts in Atlanta, State of Ga. Mem. Frog Club (pres., founder). Home: 30 Karland Dr NW Atlanta GA 30305-1124

BOWMAN, MARGARET COON, retired public official, environmental educator; b. Rhinebeck, N.Y., Mar. 13, 1914; d. Ethan Allen and Alice Amelia (Traver) Coon; widowed. BA, Elmira Coll., 1936; cert., Clarke Sch. for Deaf, 1940. Tchr. Iowa Sch. for the Deaf, Council Bluffs, 1940-42, Alexander Graham Bell, Cleve., 1942-44; jr. exec. B. Altman & Co., N.Y.C., 1948-52; mgr. E. A. Coon & Co., Rhinebeck, N.Y., 1952-65; county commr. Indian River County, Vero Beach, Fla., 1982-92; mem. Hutchinson Island Study Com., 1984-85, Treasure Coast Regional Planning Coun., Stuart, Fla., 1988-92, Ind. R. County Transp. Com., Vero Beach, 1986-92. Author: Where to Find Birds in Florida, 1977; contbr. articles to profl. jours. Mem. Coun. on Aging, McKee Gardens, Vero Beach Civic Assn., Jackson House Preservation; bd. dirs., editor Marine Resources Coun., 1990-96; bd. dirs. LWV of Ind. River County, chmn. natural resources, 1992—. Staff sgt. WAC U.S. Army, 1944-46; ETO. Mem. Fla. Audubon Soc. (bd. dirs., spl. commendation 1980, chpt. pres. of yr. award 1990), Pelican Island Audubon Soc. (charter mem., pres., bd. dirs., sec. 1964—), friends of St. Sebastian River (bd. dirs. 1992—). Office: Pelican Island Audubon Soc Inc 1931 14th Ave Vero Beach FL 32960

BOWMAN, MARJORIE ANN, physician, academic administrator; b. Grove City, Pa., Aug. 18, 1953; d. Ross David and Freda Louise (Smith) Williamson; m. Robert Choplin; children: Bridget Williamson Foley, Skyler Weston Williamson Choplin. BS, Pa. State U., 1974; MD, Jefferson Med. Coll., 1976; MPA, U. So. Calif., L.A., 1983. Intern, then resident in family practice Duke U., Durham, N.C., 1976-79; med officer USPHS, Hyattsville, Md., 1979-82; clin. instr. uniformed svcs. U. of the Health Scis., Bethesda, Md., 1980-83; dir. family practice residency Sch. Medicine Georgetown U., Washington, 1983-86; prof., chair dept. family and community medicine Wake Forest U., Winston-Salem, N.C., 1986—; Author: Stress and Women Physicians, 1985; contbr. articles to profl. jours. Editor Archives Family Medicine, 1992—. Fellow Am. Acad. Family Physicians; mem. AMA, Soc. Tchrs. Family Medicine (bd. dirs. 1984-88, bd. dirs. Found. 1984—, v.p.1988-91, pres. 1991-92), Am. Pub. Health Assn. Republican. Unitarian. Office: Bowman Gray Sch Medicine Family & Cmty Medicine Medical Center Blvd Winston Salem NC 27157-1084

BOWMAN, MARY LOU, architect; b. Lynn, Mass., Oct. 7, 1960; d. John F. and Mary Irene (McLean) B. BArch, U. Fla., 1982; MArch, Calif. Polytechnic State U., 1984. Registered profl. arch., Fla. Project mgr. Goldenholz-Fischer, Ft. Lauderdale, Fla., 1987-90; project coord. Archtl. Design Group, Ft. Lauderdale, 1990-91; prin. Mary Lou Bowman Arch., Ft. Lauderdale, 1991-92, 95—; project arch. Goldenholz & Assocs., Ft. Lauderdale, 1992-94; sr. assoc. Merriman Assocs., Boca Raton, Fla., 1994-95; guest spkr. Barry U., Miami, Fla., 1988, Nat. Soc. Women in Constrn., Ft. Lauderdale, 1995; archtl. cons. in field. Chair site selection com. Habitat for Humanity of Broward County, Pompano Beach, Fla., 1992-93, chair archtl. com., 1993—, vice chmn. bd., 1993-95, chmn. bd. dirs., 1995—. Rensselaer scholar United Techs., 1978-82, AIA Found. scholar, 1982, Henry Adams medal, 1984. Home and Office: 1749 NE 15th St Fort Lauderdale FL 33304

BOWMAN, NANCY ELIZABETH, elementary school educator; b. Troy, Ohio, Apr. 11, 1951; d. Marland Jackson and Polly Ann (Weaver) Kingsbury; m. Gary Lynn Bowmann, June 4, 1976; children: Andrew Scott, Emily Lynn. BS in Elem. Edn., Ohio State U., 1973, MA in Reading Edn., 1976. Cert. Elem. Educator, Reading Educator, Reading Recovery. Elem. tchr. Fairbanks Local Schs., Milford Ctr., Ohio, 1973-79, sub. tchr., 1985-90, reading tchr., 1990-91, kindergarten and reading recovery tchr., 1991-95; Title I reading tchr., reading recovery tchr. Fairbanks Local Schs., 1995—; summer reading tutor Fairbanks Local Schs., 1991, literacy links site coord., 1994-96, strategic planning com., 1994-95; literacy intervention Madison Local Schs., London, Ohio, 1990-91. Author: Venture Capital Grant, 1994-95, N.E.T. Nutrition Grant, 1994-95. Libr. First Presbyn. Ch., Marysville, Ohio, 1982-90, bldg. com. mem., 1985-94, deacon, 1985-88, elder, 1990-93; v.p. Fairbanks Music Booster, 1991—; mem. Ohio Child Conservation League Devotions, 1992, program planner, 1994. Martha Holden Jennings Found. scholar, 1995-96; named Outstanding Young Educator, Milford Ctr. Jaycees, 1974-75. Mem. Ohio State U. Alumni Assn., Reading Recovery Coun. North Am., Internat. Reading Assn., The Literary Connection, Am. Vet. Med. Assn. Aux., Reading Recovery Adv. Coun. (Marion site), Phi Kappa Phi. Presbyterian. Home: 15303 Maple Ridge Rd Milford Center OH 43045-9746 Office: Fairbanks Elem Sch 153 E State St Milford Center OH 43045

BOWMAN, PATRICIA LYNN, lawyer; b. Mpls., July 5, 1956; d. Robert Lee and Delores Helen (Roberts) B. BA in History with distinction, Stanford U., 1978; JD cum laude, Harvard U., 1981. Assoc. Perkins Coie, Seattle, 1981-84, Foster, Pepper & Shefelman, Seattle, 1984-89; v.p., assoc. counsel Washington Mut. Bank, Seattle, 1989—. Bd. dirs., vice chair Common Ground, Seattle, 1987-93; bd. dirs. Elderhealth Northwest, Seattle, 1994—. Mem. ABA, Wash. State Bar Assn., Seattle-King County Bar Assn., Seattle Mortgage Bankers Assn. (mem. legal com.), Phi Beta Kappa. Office: Washington Mut Bank 1201 3rd Ave Seattle WA 98101-3000

BOWMAN-DALTON, BURDENE KATHRYN, education testing coordinator, computer consultant; b. Magnolia, Ohio, July 13, 1937; d. Ernest Mowles and Mary Kathryn (Long) Bowman; BME, Capital U., 1959; MA in Edn., Akron U., 1967, postgrad. 1976-87; m. Louis W. Dalton, Mar. 13, 1979. Profl. vocalist, various clubs in the East, 1959-60; music tchr. East Liverpool (Ohio) City Schs., 1959-62; music tchr. Revere Local Schs., Akron, Ohio, 1962-75, elem. tchr., 1975-80, elem. team leader/computer cons., 1979-85, tchr. middle sch. math., gifted-talented, computer literacy, 1981-92, dist. computer specialist, 1987-93, dist. statis. for standardize local testing, 1987-91, dist. tech. coord., 1993—; local and regional dir., Olympics of the Mind, also World Problem Captain for computer problem, 1984-86; cons., workshop presenter State of Ohio, 1987-91, dist. test coord., 1991—. Mem. Citizen Com., Akron, 1975-76; profl. rep. Bath Assn. to Help, 1978-80; mem. Revere Levy Com. 1986, Revere Bond Issue Com., 1991; audit com. BATH, 1977-79; vol. chmn. Antique Car Show, Akron, 1972-81; dist. advisor MidWest Talent Search, 1987-93; dist. statistician of standardized rech. test results. Martha Holden Jennings Found. grantee, 1977-78; Title IV ESEA grantee, 1977-81. Mem. Assn. for Devel. of Computer-Based Instructional Systems(dir. 1992-94), Ednl. Mgmt. Info. System (coord. for Revere Schs. 1992—), Assn. Supervision and Curriculum Devel., Phi Beta. Republican. Lutheran. Home: 353 Retreat Dr Akron OH 44333-1623 Office: 3195 Spring Valley Rd Bath OH 44210-0339

BOWMAN-RANDALL, GAYLE DARLENE, equal employment specialist, writer; b. Tallahassee, Mar. 5, 1964; d. Ollie Monroe and Gaynelle Annette (Sharpe) Bowman; m. David Keith Randall, Feb. 14, 1992; 1 child, Sterling Noelle. BS in Mktg., Hampton U., 1986. Admissions counselor Hampton U., 1984-87; equal employment specialist U.S. Dept. Def., Warren, Mich., 1987—; owner Diversified Writing and Bus. Svcs., Oak Park, Mich., 1989—. Author poetry and children's books. Mem. NAFE, Internat. Women's Writing Guild, Nat. Writers Assn., Alpha Kappa Alpha. Democrat. Presbyterian.

BOWNE, SHIRLEE PEARSON, credit union executive, real estate executive; b. High Shoals Twp., N.C., Mar. 11, 1936; d. Lloyd E. Pearson and Parnell (James) Garland; divorced; 1 child, Gregory Charles. Grad. high sch., Gaffney, S.C. Various secretarial positions, 1955-64; sales repr., pres. Real Estate Marketers, Inc., Tallahassee, FL, 1964-80; chief exec. officer Shirlee Bowne Mktg. & Devel. Inc., Tallahassee, 1980-91; vice chmn. Nat. Credit Union Adminstrn., Washington, 1991—; Consult. in field. Treas. Rep. Party Fla., 1988-91. Episcopalian.

BOWYER, JOAN ELIZABETH, medical technologist, realtor; b. Ellensburg, Wash., July 11, 1944; d. Chester Joseph and Rita Geneva (Newell) Howarth; 1 child, Suzanne Elise. BA, Ft. Wright Coll. of Holy Names, 1966; grad., Real Estate Sch. Oreg., 1982. Lic. med. technologist. Med. technologist Lab. of Clin. Medicine, Seattle, 1967-69, Sacred Heart Gen. Hosp., Eugene, Oreg., 1969-73, 74-76, McKenzie Willamette Hosp., Springfield, Oreg., 1976-77, Mid-Columbia Hosp., The Dalles, Oreg., 1977-82; realtor Red Carpet/Rick Hall Realty, Hillsboro, Oreg., 1982-85, Century 21 Columbia Realty, Portland, 1985—; med. technologist ARC, Portland, 1982-89, Corning Nicholas Inst. formerly Physicians Med. Lab., 1989-95, East Moreland Hosp., 1995—. Co-editor: The Dalles Gen. Hosp. Newspaper, 1980-82. Pres. Wasco County Edn. Service Dist. Parents Group, The

Dalles, 1978-82; founder, pres. Mid-Columbia Parents of Deaf, 1978-82; parental spokesperson Spl. Edn. Adv. Com., Salem, Oreg., 1980-82, activist parent for deaf/hearing impaired, 1977—. Mem. Med. Technologists of Am. Soc. Pathologists, Nat. Assn. Realtors, NAFE, Century 21 Investment Soc., Million Dollar Club. Democrat. Avocations: photography, dancing, hiking, travel. Home: 704 SE 38th Ave Portland OR 97214-3206 Office: Century 21 Columbia 2208 SE 182nd Ave Portland OR 97233-5608

BOXER, BARBARA, senator; b. Bklyn., Nov. 11, 1940; d. Ira and Sophie (Silvershein) Levy; m. Stewart Boxer, 1962; children: Doug, Nicole. BA in Econ., Bklyn. Coll., 1962. Stockbroker, econ. rschr. N.Y. Securities Firm, N.Y.C., 1962-65; journalist, assoc. editor Pacific Sun, 1972-74; congl. aide to rep. 5th Congl. Dist. San Francisco, 1974-76; mem. Marin County Bd. Suprs., San Rafael, Calif., 1976-82; mem. 98th-102d Congresses from 6th Calif. dist., mem. armed services com., select com. children, youth and families; majority whip at large, co-chair Mil. Reform Caucus, chair subcom. on govt. activities and transp. of house govt. ops. com., 1990-93, U.S. senator from Calif., 1993—, mem. banking, housing and urban affairs com., mem. budget com., mem. environ. and pub. works com. Pres. Marin County Bd. Suprs., 1980-81; mem. Bay Area Air Quality Mgmt. Bd., San Francisco, 1977-82, pres., 1979-81; bd. dirs. Golden Gate Bridge Hwy. and Transport Dist., San Francisco, 1978-82; founding mem. Marin Nat. Women's Polit. Caucus; pres. Dem. New Mems. Caucus, 1983. Recipient Open Govt. award Common Cause, 1980, Rep. of Yr. award Nat. Multiple Sclerosis Soc., 1990, Margaret Sanger award Planned Parenthood, 1990, Women of Achievement award Anti-defamation League, 1990. Jewish. Office: US Senate 112 Hart Senate Office Bldg Washington DC 20510-0505*

BOYAJIAN, CAROLE L., interior designer, graphic designer; b. Fresno, Calif., Jan. 6, 1948; d. Armon K. and Louise (Josephine) B.; BFA cum laude, The Art Ctr. Coll. Design, L.A., 1969. ASID, CID. Typographical liaison Doyle Dane Bernbach Advt., N.Y.C., 1969-70; prin. The Enchanted Nook Co., Pasadena, Calif., 1972-78; cons., pvt. practice pub. relations developer Ajijic, Jalisco, Mex., 1978-80; sales assoc. Forbes Monselle Inc., Los Angeles, 1980-84; prin. Carol Boyajian & Assocs., Beverly Hills, Calif., 1980—; co-owner ZERO Gallery, L.A., 1968-69; owner's rep./interior designer Robert Evans Co.; interior designer Internat. Mgmt. and Pub. Rels. div. of The Gordy Co., medical offices of Dr. Zion Yu and George Harrison; with West Coast Industries, Inc. Cons. Los Angeles Theater Ctr., 1985. Recipient Cert. Merit, Nat. Fedn. Music Tchrs., Fresno, Calif., 1965. Mem. AIA (profl. affiliate L.A. chpt., curator 100/100 exhbn.), Am. Soc. Interior Designers (cert.), Nat. Fedn. Music, Network Exec. Women in Hospitality. Republican. Home: 365 W Alameda Ave Apt 308 Burbank CA 91506-3340 Office: PO Box 663 Beverly Hills CA 90213-0663

BOYCE, EMILY STEWART, retired library and information science educator; b. Raleigh, N.C., Aug. 18, 1933; d. Harry and May (Fallon) B. BS, East Carolina U., 1955, MA, 1961; MS in Library Sci., U. N.C., 1968; postgrad., Cath. U. Am., 1977. Librarian Tileston Jr. High Sch., Wilmington, N.C., 1955-57; children's librarian Wilmington Pub. Library, 1957-58; asst. librarian Joyner Library East Carolina U., Greenville, N.C., 1959-61, librarian III, 1962-63; ednl. supr. II ednl. media div. N.C. State Dept. Pub. Instrn., Raleigh, 1961-62; assoc. prof. dept. library and info. scis. East Carolina U., Raleigh, 1964-76, prof., 1976-92, chmn. dept., 1982-89; retired, 1992; cons. So. Assn. Colls. and Schs., Raleigh, 1975—. Mem. Pitt County Hist. Preservation Soc., Greenville, Pitt County Mental Health Assn. Mem. ALA, AAUW, N.C. Library Assn., Southeastern Library Assn., Assn. Library and Info. Sci. Educators, Spl. Libraries Assn., LWV, NOW. Democrat. Home: 99 Moody Cove Rd Weaverville NC 28787-9746

BOYD, BARBARA H., state legislator; m. Robert Boyd, Jr.; 1 child, Janine. BS in Edn., St. Paul's Coll., Va. Former tchr. Cleve. Pub. Schs.; mem. coun. City of Cleveland Heights, Ohio, 1983-91, vice mayor, 1991, former mayor; current mem. dist. 9 Ohio Ho. Reps., Columbus. Former vol. coord. Cuyahoga County Juvenile Ct.; Dem. vice chair Cuyahoga County; past pres. Black Woman's Polit. Action Com.; former mem. youth violence com. Task Force on Violent Crimes; African-Am. adv. com. Notre Dame Coll. Ohio; ARTS Ednl. Theatre Co.; formerly active Monticello Field Supporters; active St. Andrew's Episc. Ch., Cleveland Heights. Mem. LWV (Cleveland Heights-University Heights chpt.), Cleveland Heights Dems., East Cleveland Dem. Club, Kiwanis, Delta Sigma Theta. Home: 3418 Washington Blvd Cleveland Heights OH 44118 Office: Ohio Ho Reps 77 S High St Columbus OH 43266-0603*

BOYD, DEBORAH ANN, pediatrician; b. Urbana, Ohio, Jan. 30, 1955; d. John A. Sr. and Juanita Jean (Routt) B. BA cum laude, Wittenberg U., 1977; MD, U. Cin., 1982. Diplomate Am. Bd. Pediatrics, Nat. Bd. Med. Examiners. Intern Children's Hosp. Med. Ctr., Cin., 1982-83, pediatric resident, 1982-85; pediatrician Nat. Health Svc. Corps, Springfield, Ohio, 1985-89, Community Hosp. Health Care Ctr., Springfield, 1989—; mem. Continuing med. edn. com. Mercy Med. Ctr., Springfield, 1989—, infection control com., 1987—. Adv. com. Miami Valley Child Devl. Ctr., Springfield, 1985—, New Parents as Tchrs., 1986—. Democratic. Home: 2310 N Limestone St Apt 118 Springfield OH 45503-1144 Office: Community Hosp Health Care 144 W Pleasant St Springfield OH 45506-2206

BOYD, JULIA MARGARET (MRS. SHELTON B. BOYD), lay church worker; b. Newton Grove, N.C., Mar. 7, 1921; d. Isaiah and Mary Lela (Blackman) Tart; m. Shelton Bickett Boyd, Feb. 21, 1944; children: Mary (Mrs. Edward Southerland III), Deborah (Mrs. John Wayne Pearson). BS, East Carolina U., 1942. V.p. WSCS, Lillington (N.C.) U. Meth. Ch., 1948-49; pres. Woman's Soc. Christian Svc., Mt. Olive, N.C., 1951-55, 59-61; sec. various coms. WSCS, 1st United Meth. Ch., Mt. Olive, N.C., from 1950, mem., sec. adminstrv. bd. and coun. ministries, from 1955, mem. local work area on edn., 1960-82, chmn., 1971-75, chmn. spiritual growth, 1971-75, mem. fin. com., 1985-87, 90-96; counselor United Meth. Youth Fellowship, 1960-67; adult del. Nat. Convocation Meth. Youth, 1964; pres. Goldsboro dist. United Meth. Women, 1955-59; mem. N.C. Conf. Bd. Edn., 1964-72; mem. N.C. Coun. on Youth Ministries, 1964-82, chmn., 1972-76; mem. adult staff youth, sr. high mins., 1972-92; mem. N.C. Conf. Coun. on Ministries, 1972-82; mem. Goldsboro dist. Coun. on Ministries, 1970—, sec., 1971—; also coord. youth ministries Goldsboro dist., 1964-82; del. SEJ Youth Conf., Arlington, Va., 1976, SEJ Leadership Devel. Workshop, Lake Junaluska, 1977; lay rep. Goldsboro dist. Conf. Coun. on Ministries, 1982-92, ann. conf. United Meth. Ch., 1985, 87, 90, 96, dist. trustee, 1993—; rep. N.C. Christian Advocate, 1985—; bd. dirs. Meth. Home for Children, 1993-96; mem., sec. dist. adv. com. Fremont Youth Home, 1988-96. Editor Meth. Messenger, 1965-68. Pres. PTA, Mt. Olive, 1955-56, Mt. Olive High Sch. and So. Wayne High Sch. Band Patron's Club, 1964-66; leader Girl Scouts U.S.A., 1956-57; active Community Chest. Named Lay Person of Yr. N.C. Conf. United Meth. Ch., 1979, (with husband) Outstanding Sr. Citizens of Mt. Olive, 1990; recipient cert. appreciation United Meth. Youth Fellowship, 1980, 83. Mem. Women's Aux. of N.C. Pharm. Assn. (corr. sec. 1976-77, rec. sec. 1977-78, 2d v.p. 1978-79, 1st v.p. 1979-80, pres. 1980-81, mem. nominating com. 1988-95, mins. com. 1988-89, hospitality com. 1989), United Meth. Women (mem. hist. com. Goldsboro dist. 1984, chairperson 1989, 94, v.p. local chpt. 1988-89), So. Wayne Country Club. Home: 400 W Main St Mount Olive NC 28365-2018

BOYD, KAREN JOHNSON, art dealer; b. Racine, Wis., May 16, 1924; d. Herbert Fisk and Gertrude Nikoline (Brauner) Johnson; m. Willard Hampton Keland, Mar. 19, 1945 (div. 1965); children: K. Nikoline, Karen H., Andrea K., William H.; m. William Beaty Boyd, June 26, 1982. BA, Bennington Coll., 1946. Pres. Perimeter Press, Inc., Racine, Wis., 1978-82, Perimeter Gallery, Inc., Chgo., 1982—. Trustee Bennington (Vt.) Coll., 1969—; bd. advisors Cooper-Hewitt Smithsonian Mus. Design, N.Y.C., 1980—; bd. dirs. Milw. Art Mus., 1981-92. Mem. Am. Craft Coun. (bd. dirs. 1981-92), Chgo. Art Dealers Assn., Arts Club Chgo. Office: Perimeter Gallery 210 W Superior St Chicago IL 60610

BOYD, LAURA WOOLDRIDGE, state legislator; b. Charlottesville, Va., June 5, 1949; d. Oscar Bailey Wooldridge and Martha Jane (Clarke) Jordan; m. Harry Sterling Boyd, July 31, 1979 (div. Apr. 1984); m. Joseph David Rambo, May 1, 1986; children: Susan Rebecca, Brooke Caitlin. BA in German, Duke U., 1970; MS in Huamnistic Edn., Marywood Coll., 1978; PhD in Counseling Psychology, Internat. Coll., 1982. Nat. cert. clin. mental health counselor. Pvt. practice Doylestown, Pa., 1975-78; project dir. Ct. Appointed Advocate Program for Cleve. County, 1984-85; owner, adminstr. The Family Ctr., Norman, Okla., 1978—; mem. Okla. Ho. Reps., Oklahoma City, 1992—; adj. faculty Mary Coll., Scranton, 1976-79. Reviewer Jour. on Traumatic Stress, 1990—, Trasactional Analysis Jour., 1984—; contbr. articles to profl. jours. Mem. Cleve. County Citizen's Adv. Bd.; bd. dirs. Alternative Support Edn. Progra; asst. coach Optimist League Girls Basketball; chair Norman Pub. Sch. Crisis Intervention Team; mem. St. John's Episcopal Ch.; parent vol. McKinley Elem. Sch. and Whittier Middle Sch.; kettle ringer Salvation Army; solicitor United Way; frequent leader Norman Regional Hosp. Breast Cancer Support Group; affiliate staff Norman Regional Hosp.; adv. com. Moore-Norman Vo-Tech Options Program. Mem. ACA, Am. Assn. for Marriage and Family Therapy (supr., chairperson profl. practice com. 1990-92), Am. Psychol. Assn. (Okla. state liaison to divsn. 43 family psychology 1987-90), Internat. Transactional Analysis Assn., Assn. of Family and Conciliation Cts., Profl. Assn. of Custody Evaluations (diplomate), Nat. Coun. on Family Rels., Okla. Psychol. Assn., Acad. Family Mediators (sr.), Am. Assn. Family Counselors and Mediators, Inc. (cert. supr.), Okla. Assn. for Marriage and Family Therapy, Norman Bus. Assn., Norman C. of C., Rotary Clubs Internat. Democrat. Episcopalian. Office: Okla Ho of Reps State Capitol Oklahoma City OK 73105

BOYD, LEONA POTTER, retired social worker; b. Creekside, Pa., Aug. 31, 1907; d. Joseph M. and Belle (McHenry) Johnston. Grad. Ind. (Pa.) State Normal Sch., 1927, student Las Vegas Normal U., N.Mex., 1933, Carnegie Inst. Tech. Sch. Social Work, 1945, U. Pitts. Sch. Social Work, 1956-57; m. Edgar D. Potter, July 16, 1932 (div.); m. Harold Lee Boyd, Oct. 1972. Tchr. Creekside (Pa.) Pub. Schs., 1927-30, Papago Indian Reservation, Sells, Ariz., 1931-33; caseworker, supr. Indiana County (Pa.) Bd. Assistance, 1934-54, exec. dir., 1954-68, ret. Bd. dirs. Indiana County Tourist Promotion, hon. life mem.; former bd. dirs. Indiana County United Fund, Salvation Army, Indiana County Guidance Ctr., Armstrong-Indiana Mental Health Bd.; cons. assoc. Community Rsch. Assocs., Inc.; mem. Counseling Ctr. Aux., Lake Havasu City, Ariz., 1978-80; former mem. Western Welcome Club, Lake Havasu City, Sierra Vista Hosp. Aux., Truth or Consequences, N.Mex. Recipient Jr. C. of C. Disting. Svc. award, Indiana, Pa., 1966, Bus. and Profl. Women's Club award, Indiana, 1965. Mem. Am. Assn. Ret. Persons, Daus. Am. Colonists, Concord Coalition. Lutheran. Home: 444 S Higley Rd Apt 219 Mesa AZ 85206-2186

BOYD, MARGARET, elementary education educator; b. Ardmore, Okla., Sept. 7; d. John Henry and Geneva (Brown) Smith; m. Donald G. Boyd, May 5, 1959; 1 child, Gilbert L. BS, Langston U., 1959; MS, Va. Poly. and State U., 1975; postgrad., George Mason U. Cert. tchr., Va.; ESL endorsement, Va. Mgr. pvt. kindergarten, Ardmore, 1959; tchr. Fairfax County Schs., Reston, Va., 1971—; travel agt. Mark Moseley Travel, Reston, 1982; receptionist Reston Cmty. Ctr., 1984; instr. Fairfax County Adult Edn., Herndon, Va., 1991, George Mason U., Reston, 1993; mgr., owner Spl. Occasions, Reston, 1992—; staff co-dir. Internat. Lodging Conf., Osipee, N.H., 1989—. Mem. No. Va. Juvenile Detention Commn., Alexandria, 1990-92; mem. ethics com. Reston Hosp., 1993—; exec. dir. Fairfax County Youth Lodging, Fairfax, Va., 1994—; mem. Reston Town Coun., 1989—; mem. exec. bd. Fairfax County 4-H, Fairfax, 1992—, Fairfax County Youth Violence Task Force, 1994—; mem. No. Va. chpt. Coalition 100 Black Women; mem. planning com. task force YMCA; exec. dir. Fairfax County Youth Leadership. Recipient Fairfax vol. award No. Va. Youth Svc. Coalition, 1993, Golden Eagle award Fairfax County Minority Achievement, 1994, Coun. of Chiefs award Am. Youth Found., 1994, Best of Reston award City of Reston, 1995, 96. Mem. Nat. Coun. Negro Women, Phi Delta Kappa, Delta Kappa Gamma, Alpha Kappa Alpha. Home: 1634 Chimney House Rd Reston VA 22090-4301

BOYD, MARY SIMON, pediatrician, educator; b. Huntington, W.Va., Oct. 18, 1952; d. Thomas Wesley and Ruth Amelia (Simon) B.; m. John Loren Henning, July 20, 1985; children: Caitlin Marie Henning, Colin Thomas Henning. BS in Math., W.Va. Wesleyan Coll., 1974; MD, W.Va. U., 1979. Instr. pediatrics Sch. Pediatrics W.Va. U., Morgantown, 1982-83, clin. asst. prof., 1993—; staff pediatrician Meml. Gen. Hosp., Elkins, W.Va., 1983-86, Davis Meml. Hosp., Elkins, W.Va., 1986—. Bd. dirs. Women's Aid in Crisis, Elkins, 1983-91; vestry mem. Grace Episcopal Ch., 1989-96. Fellow Am. Acad. Pediat. (breastfeeding coord. W.Va. 1991—). Democrat. Home: 306 Buffalo St Elkins WV 26241 Office: 911 Gorman Ave Ste 302 Elkins WV 26241

BOYD, PATRICIA ARLENE, real estate finance educator, time management consultant; b. Ft. Hood, Tex., Oct. 8, 1956; d. Grady Edward and Evelyn Warren (Baker) Watson; m. Michael Dennis Boyd, Oct. 7, 1989; 1 child, Zachary Taylor. Brokers Lic., U. Tex., Arlington, 1985. Cert. real estate and mortgage broker, Tex. Realtor Century 21 Tarver & Eppes, Arlington, 1980-83; loan officer Waterfield Mortgage, Bedford, Tex., 1988; br. mgr. WestAmerica Mortgage, Bedford, Tex., 1988-89; instr./loan officer Tartan Mortgage, Bellevue, Wash., 1990; dir. sales agt. tng. Century 21 N.W. Region, SeaTac, Wash., 1990-92; pres. Patricia Boyd Seminars, Inc., Arlington, 1992—; ind. cons. Franklin Quest, Salt Lake City, 1993—. Author: "Real" Finance: The Key to Listing and Selling Real Estate, 1992, "Real" Stuff You Need to Know about Buying and Selling Your Home, 1996; author (seminar) "Real" Accountability in Your Real Estate Team, 1995. Mem. Nat. Assn. Realtors, Ft. Worth Mortgage Bankers Assn. (agy. com. 1995—), Arlington Bd. Realtors (Rookie of Yr. 1981). Home: 3508 Corinthian Ct Arlington TX 76016 Office: Patricia Boyd Seminars Inc 430-M E Lamar Blvd Arlington TX 76011

BOYD, SUSAN CONE, chemical company executive; b. Nashville, Tenn., May 1, 1967; d. Thomas Fite and Charlotte Ladell (Huskey) Cone; m. Par Boyd. BA in English Lit., U. Tampa, 1990; postgrad studies, Vanderbilt U., 1992—. Office staff Cone Solvents, Inc., Nashville, 1990, sales rep., 1990-91; gen. mgr., v.p. Tennessee Adhesives Co., Mt. Juliet, Tenn., 1991-92; exec. v.p. Cone Solvents, Cone Oil Co., B & C Aviation, Nashville, 1992—, Tenn. Adhesives, Inc., Mt. Juliet, 1992—; new generation com., bd. dirs. Tenn. Oil Marketers Assn., Nashville, 1993-95; mem., chair membership com. Region IV Nat. Assn. Chem. Distributors, Washington, 1993-95. Fin. chair Ronnie Steine for Coun.-at-Large; commr. Nashville Conv. Ctr.; bd. dirs. Tenn. Repertory Theatre, Boys and Girls Club Mid. Tenn.; mem. citizen adv. coun. Davidson County Planning Commn.; bd. alumni Battle Ground Acad. 1992-95, bd. visitors, 1993—. Mem. Tenn. Leadership, Jr. League of Nashville (life), Nashville Rotary Club (life). Home: 107 Chatsworth Dr Nashville TN 37215-2432 Office: Cone Solvents Inc 240 Great Circle Rd Ste 320 Nashville TN 37228-1707

BOYD, VIRGINIA LEONA, accountant; b. Fairfax, Okla., Sept. 6, 1948; d. Samuel Edmund and Leona Margaret (Hall) Davis; m. James Robert Boyd, Aug. 23, 1969; children: James Christopher, Jessalyn Christine. BA in Acctg., Augustana Coll., Sioux Falls, S.D., 1978; MBA in Acctg., Ft. Hays State U., Hays, Kans., 1983. CPA, Kans. Office mgr., contr. Smith Jewelry, Inc., Sioux Falls, 1977-79; staff acct. Morris & Brock Pub. Accts., Russell, Kans., 1979-82; pres., owner Virginia Boyd, Pub. Acct., Russell, 1982-87; tax mgr., corp. sec. Restaurant Mgmt. Co. Wichita (Kans.), Inc., 1988—. Mem. Unified Sch. Dist. 262 Sch. Bd., Valley Center, Kans., 1995—. Mem. AICPA, Kans. Soc. CPA's, Ft. Hays State U. Alumni Assn. (life). Democrat. Home: 515 E Clay Valley Center KS 67147 Office: Restaurant Mgmt Co WichitaInc 555 N Woodlawn St Ste 3102 Wichita KS 66208

BOYD-BROWN, LENA ERNESTINE, history educator, education consultant; b. New Orleans, July 3, 1937; d. Eugene A. and Rosemary (Lewis) Boyd. BA, Xavier U., 1958; MA, Howard U., 1960; EdD, Rutgers U., 1979. History instr. So. U., New Orleans, 1960-61; tchr. Washington Pub. Schs., 1961-62; history instr. So. U., Baton Rouge, 1962-63; residence counselor N.C. Cen. U., Durham, 1963-64; counselor, instr. Howard U., Washington, 1964-65; asst. prof. history Grambling (La.) State U., 1965-68, Tuskegee (Ala.) U., 1968-70; assoc. examiner history Ednl. Testing Svc., Princeton, N.J., 1970-79; assoc. prof. history, edn. Dillard U., New Orleans, 1979-88; dir. testing, assoc. prof. history Hampton (Va.) U., 1988-89, assoc. prof. history, dept. history chairperson, 1989-91; assoc. prof. history div. social and polit. sci. Tex. A&M U., Prarie View, 1991—; testing cons. Lincoln (Pa.) U., 1974, So. U., Baton Rouge, 1979, New Orleans, 1986-89, Hampton U., 1988. Contbg. author, editor profl. jours. Martin L. King Jr. fellow, Rutgers U., 1977-78; fellow Howard U., 1958-60, Carnegie-Mellon U., Pitts., 1966-67. Mem. Assn. for Study Negro Life and History, Nat. Coalition of 100 Black Women (New Orleans chpt.), Orgn. Am. Historians, So. Hist. Soc., Southwestern Soc. Sci. Assn., Phi Alpha Theta, Phi Delta Kappa, Kappa Delta Pi, Alpha Kappa Alpha (Alpha Beta Omega chpt.). Office: Prairie View A & M Univ Div Social and Sci Prairie View TX 77446

BOYER, ANGELA, elementary school educator; b. Detroit, Sept. 9, 1948; d. William and Gertrude (Cosby) B. BS in Elem. Edn., Wayne State U., 1971, MS in Gen. Elem. Edn., 1978. Cert. tchr. K-9 sci., K-9 social studies, K-8 all subjects, Mich. Tchr. math. and sci. Detroit Bd. of Edn., 1973—. Named Tchr. of the Yr., Columbus Mid. Sch., 1995; U.S. Found. (NASA) fellow. Mem. Detroit ARea Coun. Math. Tchrs. Democrat. Home: 16957 Addison Southfield MI 48075

BOYER, KAYE KITTLE, association management executive; b. Peoria, Ill., July 5, 1942; d. Keith Howard and Evelyn Pearl (Benson) Kittle; m. Jon Frederick Boyer, Mar. 20, 1965; children: Tristan Donna, Kristine Monique Hitchens. Student, Merrill Palmer Inst., Detroit, 1964; BS in Home Econs., Pa. State U., University Park, 1964; MA in Sociology, Rutgers State U., New Brunswick, 1967. Cert. assn. exec.; cert. in family and consumer scis. Creative rschr. Nat. Inst. Drycleaning, Silver Spring, Md., 1963; extension home economist Md. Coop. Extension Svc., Westminster, 1964-65; coord. human resources N.J. Coop. Extension Svc., New Brunswick, 1966-67; instr. Douglass Coll., Rutgers U., New Brunswick, 1967-70; coord., instr. pilot project Urban Coalition of Met. Wilmington Inc., Wilmington, Delaware, 1972; asst. to chmn. 4-H Youth Devel. Dept., Cook Coll., 1973-74; feasibility study dir. Ocean County Coll., Toms River, N.J., 1975; exec. dir. N.J. Home Economics Assn., Manalapan, 1975-86; pres. Boyer Mgmt. Svcs., Manalapan, N.J. and Earleville, Md., 1984—; mgr. Costume Soc. Am., Earleville, 1984—; cons. Plumpton Pk. Zool. Gardens Rising Sun, 1988-89, bd. dirs., 1990-92; cons. N.J. White House Conf., Trenton, 1980, Baltimore County Med. Assn., 1995-96. Editor Exchs. Newsletter; resource dir., N.J. Programs and Svcs. Related to Adolescent Pregnancy. Mem. adv. com. dept. cmty. edn. Rutgers U., 1979-84; vol. Soroptimist Internat. of Elkton, Md., 1987-94; mem. Com. Libr. of Cecilton, pres., bd. dirs., 1986-92; player U.S. Pub. Links Amateur. Mem. AAUW (v.p. program devel. N.J. divsn. 1984-86), Am. Assn. of Family and Consumer Scis. (cert., Ruth O'Brien project grantee), Am. Soc. Assn. Execs. (cert.), Prof. Conv. Mgmt. Assn., Internat. Assn. of Facilitators, Md. Assn. of Nonprofit Orgns., Md. Soc. Assn. Execs. (bd. dirs. 1989-90, sec. 1990-92, v.p. 1992-93, pres. 1994-95, immediate past pres. 1995-96), Md. Assn. of Family and Consumer Scis., Kappa Omicron Nu (v.p. fin. 1992-93, chair constitution and bylaws com. 1994-97). Democrat. Home: PO Box 73 55 Edgewater Dr Earleville MD 21919

BOYER, LILLIAN BUCKLEY, artist, educator; b. Paterson, N.J., Mar. 1, 1916; d. George and Adele (Roomy) Buckley; m. Floyd E. Boyer, Jr., Sept. 7, 1935; 1 child, Karen Boyer Lloyd. BA in Art Edn., U. Ky., 1975. Field interviewer Survey Rsch. Ctr., U. Mich., 1963-68; 20 regional one-woman shows; instr. art U. Ky., Lexington; Ky. reporter for Sunshine Artists mag., 1976-85. Crusade chmn. Am. Cancer Soc., Anaheim, Calif., 1958, Orange County, Calif., 1959; active, hon. life mem. PTA, 1950-62; mem. Lexington Arts & Cultural Coun., Ky. Citizens for the Arts, Friends of Ky. Ednl. TV, JB. Speed Art Mus., Headley Whitney Mus., Friends of Lexington Pub. Libr.; pres., dir., life mem. Lexington Art League, 1976-80, 82-83, 84-86. Recipient 56 awards for print-making, painting and sculpture. Mem. U. Ky. Alumni Assn., Living Arts and Sci. Ctr., Friends of U.K. Art Mus., Nat. Mus. Women in Arts. Methodist. Address: 969 Holly Springs Dr Lexington KY 40504-3119

BOYES, PATRICE FLINCHBAUGH, lawyer, environmental executive; b. York, Pa., Aug. 1, 1957; d. Glenn Dale Flinchbaugh and Patricia Ann (Frey) Shultz; m. Stephen Richard Boyes, June 23, 1984. BA, Dickinson Coll., 1978; MA, U. Mich., 1980; JD, U. Fla., 1991. Bar: Fla. 1991, Fed. 1994. Law clk. Rakusin & Ivey, Gainesville, Fla., 1989; summer assoc. Hopping, Boyd, Green & Sams, Tallahassee, Fla., 1990; gen. counsel GeoSolutions, Inc., Gainesville/Tallahassee, Fla., 1986—; pres. Boyes & Assocs., P.A., Gainesville, Fla., 1991—, Wildcat Tech. Svc., Inc., 1995—; vice-chmn. City's Hist. Preservation Adv. Bd.; vol. Kanapaha Bot. Gardens; counsel Duckpond Neighborhood Assn.; pres. Wildcat Tech. Svcs., Inc., Gainesville, 1995—. Pres. Hist. Gainesville, Inc.; vice chair City's Hist. Preservation Adv. Bd.; vol. Kanapha Bot. Gardens; counsel Duckpond Neighborhood Assn., Inc. Recipient Keystone Press award Pa. Soc. Newspaper Editors and Pubs., 1981, City Beautification award, 1994, Hist. Preservation award, 1994, Fla. Trust for Hist. Preservation award, 1996; grad. fellow Modern Media Inst., St. Petersburg, Fla. Mem. ABA, Fla. Bar Assn. (pub. interest com. for environ. and land use sect.), Fla. Trial Lawyers Assn., 8th Jud. Cir. Bar Assn., Fla. Assn. Women Lawyers, Pi Delta Epsilon. Office: GeoSolutions Inc 602 S Main St Gainesville FL 32601-6718

BOYETT, JOAN REYNOLDS, arts administrator; b. L.A., May 2, 1936; d. Clifton Faris Reynolds and Jean Margaret (Howard) Hauck; m. Harry William Boyett, Oct. 5, 1956; children: Keven William, Suzanne Marie Boyett Liebherr. Student, Occidental Coll., 1954-55, Pasadena Playhouse, 1955-57. Mgr. youth activities L.A. Philharm. Orch., 1970-79; dir., founder edn. divsn. Music Ctr. Los Angeles County, 1979—, v.p. edn., 1988—; cons. NEA, Washington; chmn. arts edn. task force Calif. Arts Coun., Sacramento, 1993-95; arts edn. mem. Nat. Working Group, Washington, 1992-95. Active various coms. and task forces, L.A., Sacramento. Named Woman of Yr. L.A. Times, 1976; recipient Labor's award of honor County Fedn. Labor, L.A., 1984, Susan B. Anthony award Bus. and Profl. Women, 1986, Gov.'s award Calif. Arts Coun. and Gov., 1989. Mem. Calif. Art Edn. Assn. (Behind the Scenes award 1985), Calif. Dance Educators Assn. (Svc. award 1985), Calif. Ednl. Theatre Assn. (Outstanding Contbn. award 1990). Republican. Presbyterian. Home: PO Box 1805 Studio City CA 91614-0805 Office: The Music Ctr 717 W Temple St Ste 400 Los Angeles CA 90012

BOYKIN, BETTY RUTH CARROLL, mortgage loan officer, bank executive; b. Mobile, Ala., Dec. 14, 1943; d. John Calvin Sr. and Zimmie Mae (Burdette) Carroll; m. William Henry Boykin Jr., Sept. 9, 1961; children: Helen Carroll Boykin Ferris, John William. Student, Auburn U., 1961-62, U. Fla., 1969-72, Santa Fe C.C., 1972-90; BSBA, U. Mo., St. Louis, 1992. Asst. v.p., loan officer Guaranty Fed. Savs. and Loan, Gainesville, Fla., 1973-80; mortgage loan officer Fortune Mortgage Corp., Gainesville, 1980-86; mgr. Svc. Title Corp., Gainesville, 1986-87; account exec. Fla. Fed. Savs. Bank, Gainesville, 1987-88; banking officer 1st Union Nat. Bank (merger Fla. Nat. Bank), Gainesville, 1988-90; br. mgr., mortgage loan officer 1st Fed. Bank Mortgage Lending, Huntsville, Ala., 1993—; dir. Sys. Dynamics, Inc., 1980-89, AMJ, Inc., 1980-83; instr. mortgage lending Inst. Fin. Edn., Gainesville, 1986. Amb. PBS, Gainesville, 1989-90; chmn. loan com. Neighborhood Housing Svcs., Inc., Gainesville, 1985-90; dir. Gainesville Homebuilder's Homeowners Warranty Coun., 1984-86. Recipient Outstanding Svc. award Neighborhood Housing Svcs., Inc., 1985-90. Mem. Am. Mgmt. Assn., Am. Mktg. Assn., Mortgage Bankers Assn. North Ctrl. Fla. (v.p., pres.-elect 1989-90), Mortgage Officers Soc. (pres. Dist. IV 1980-81), Mortgage Bankers Assn. Huntsville (co-chair program com. 1994—), Women's Coun. Realtors, Huntsville/Madison County Builders Assn. (assocs. coun. mem., mem. women's coun.), Huntsville Bd. Realtors (affiliate), Huntsville C. of C., Gainesville C. of C., Delta Sigma Pi. Home: 35 Revere Way Huntsville AL 35801-2847 Office: First Fed Mortgage 2310 Market Pl SW Ste B Huntsville AL 35801-5250

BOYKIN, CATHERINE MARIE, health care administrator; b. Phila., Dec. 25, 1944; d. William Lee (dec.) and Marie Eleanor (Hewson) B.; m. Walter Miller Morris Jr., Sept. 3, 1977; 1 child, William Martin Boykin-Morris. BSN, Villanova U., 1966; cert. PNP, U. Conn., 1973; postgrad., U. Vt. Cert. PNP, Vt. Pub. health nurse U.S. Peace Corps, Osorno, Chile, 1967-68; coronary care specialist Queen of the Angels Hosp., L.A., 1969-70; pub. health nurse Orthopaedic Hosp., L.A., 1970-72; PNP N.E. Kingdom Mental Health Svcs., Newport, Vt., 1973-75, The Child Health Ctr., St. Johnsbury, Vt., 1975-81; pvt. practice nurse practitioner New Directions in Health, St. Johnsbury, 1981-84; PNP The Burke Schs., Burke Hollow, Vt., 1983-84; dir. health Lyndon Inst., Lyndon Center, Vt., 1984—; chair Vt. Joint Practice Com.: Vt. State Nurses Assn., Vt. State Med. Soc., 1981-83; coord. Drug-Free Schs., Lyndon Inst., Lyndon Center, 1984—; bd. mem. Heart Healthy

Vermonter Adv. Bd., St. Johnsbury, 1985-90; pediatric rep. Vt. State Bd. Nursing Nurse Practitioner Adv. Com., 1985—. Vice chairperson Caledonia County Dem. Com., St. Johnsbury, 1990-95, treas., 1995—; Justice of the Peace, Lyndonville, 1990—; chairperson Lyndon Town Dem. Com., Lyndonville, 1991—, Lyndonville Bd. Civil Authority, 1990—; mem. Lyndon Bd. Civil Authority, 1990—. Recipient Founding Assoc. award Club de Abstemios Nuevo Amanecer, Osorno, 1968. Mem. ANA, Vt. State Nurses Assn. (chairperson coun. of nursing practice 1975-77), Vt. State Sch. Nurses Assn., Vt. Pediatric Nurse Practitioners (treas. 1987-89, co-chair 1990—), Vt. Nurse Practitioners Inc., Am. Sch. Health Assn., Nat. Assn. Sch. Nurses, Nat. Family Life Edn. Network. Roman Catholic. Home: RR 2 Diamond Hill Lyndonville VT 05851-9802 Office: Lyndon Institute Lyndon Center VT 05850

BOYLAN, DONNA JEAN, school superintendent; b. Lancaster, Ohio, June 21, 1948; d. Leonard R. and Clara M. (Danner) Krile; m. Charles E. Boylan, Dec. 27, 1969; 1 child, Jason Charles. BS in Edn., Ohio U., 1969; MS in Edn., Kent (Ohio) State U., 1976, MLS, 1980. Lic. supt. Tchr. English, sociology Oletangy H.S., Delaware, Ohio, 1969-70; tchr. English East Holmes Schs., Berlin, Ohio, 1970-74, coord. libr. media, 1974-79; dir. East Ctrl. Ohio Edn. Resource Ctr., New Philadelphia, 1979-83; secondary supr. Holmes County Schs., Millersburg, Ohio, 1983-84, dir. curriculum and instrn., 1984-85, asst. supt., 1985-88; adj. prof. Ashland (Ohio) U., 1987-89; supt. Berne Union Schs., Sugar Grove, Ohio, 1991—; asst. dir. Ohio Dept. Edn., Columbus, 1989-91. Mem. Am. Assn. Sch. Adminstrs., Ohio Ednl. Libr. Media Assn. (pres. 1985), Ohio Assn. Supervision and Curriculum, Buckey Assn. Sch. Adminstrs., Kiwanis (mem. bd. 1991), Phi Delta Kappa. Office: Berne Union Local Sch Dist 506 N Main St Sugar Grove OH 43155-9500

BOYLAN, MICHELLE MARIE OBIE, medical surgical nurse; b. St. Louis, Jan. 22, 1962; d. James Martin and Yvonne Marie (DeLoof) Obie; m. Steven Arthur Boylan, June 5, 1962; children: Paige Brittany, Courtney Marie, Brandon James. BSN, Marquette U., 1984; MA, Webster U., 1996. RN. Commd. 2d lt. U.S. Army, 1984, advanced through grades to maj., 1994; pediatrics charge nurse William Beaumont Army Med. Ctr., El Paso, 1984-86, neonatal ICU charge nurse, 1986-87; asst. head nurse pediatrics 98th Gen. Hosp., Neurenberg, Germany, 1987-88; head nurse 98th Gen.Hosp., Neurenberg, Germany, 1987-90, U.S. Army Ft. Huachuca, Sierra Vista, Ariz., 1990-92; head nurse Winn Army Cmty. Hosp., Ft. Stewart, Ga., 1992—, infection control/quality improvement nurse, 1994—; lectr. in field. Decorated Army Commendation medal with 3 oak leaf clusters, Meritorious Svc. medal with 1 oak leaf cluster. Mem. Am. Profls. in Infection Control. Roman Catholic. Home: 870 Piros Dr Colorado Springs CO 80922 Office: Evans Army Cmty Hosp Fort Carson CO 80913

BOYLE, ANNE WICKHAM, investment advisor; b. Bronxville, N.Y., Sept. 26, 1950; d. William James and Elizabeth (Piccirilli) B.; m. Zachary Minor, May 27, 1995; children: Henry Sherwin, Sarah Sherwin. BA, NYU, 1972; M Pub. and Pvt. Mgmt., Yale U., 1981. Author: On the Streets, 1976, Pleasures, 1984, Dreams, 1995. Organizer Dem. Downtown, Tribeca, N.Y., 1979—, Nat. Coun. on Founds., Washington, 1995—. Fellow Nat. Endowment for Arts, 1976, 90-92, HEW, 1979-81. Mem. PTA Downtown Parents (Outstanding Achievement award), Elizabethian Club Yale, Tribeca Tennis Club. Democrat. Home: 38 N Moore St New York NY 10013 Office: Wizards Ste 60 E 42d St 1434 New York NY 10165

BOYLE, ANTONIA BARNES, audio producer, writer; b. Detroit, May 21, 1939; d. James Merriam and Florence (Maiullo) B.; 1 child, Caitlin Merriam. BS in Speech, Northwestern U., 1962; postgrad., U. San Francisco, 1996—. Staff announcer WEFM-FM, Chgo., 1975-78; pres. Boyle Communications, Chgo., 1978-85; exec. producer Nightingale-Conant Corp., Chgo., 1985-90, Cassette Prodns. Unltd., Irwindale, Calif., 1990-92; pres. Antonia Boyle & Co., 1992—. Author: The Optimal You, 1990, Taping Yourself Seriously, 1991; co-author: (with Jay Gordon) Good Food Today, Great Kids Tomorrow, 1994 (with Scott McKain) Just Say Yes, 1994. Chmn., bd. dirs. Horizons for the Blind, Chgo., 1984. Mem. Am. Fedn. Radio, TV Artists, Com.100 Northwestern U., NU Club, San Francisco. Home: 2526 39th Ave San Francisco CA 94116-2751 Office: Antonia Boyle & Co 236 W Portal Ave San Francisco CA 94127-1423

BOYLE, BARBARA JANE, insurance company executive; b. Shenandoah, Iowa, Mar. 1, 1936; d. Thomas Henry and Hazel Ingred (Gell) Hill; m. Richard F. Smith, Jan. 6, 1990; children: Jill, Chris Richardson. BA, Iowa State Tchrs. Coll., Cedar Falls, 1960. Tchr. elem. United Community Schs., Boone, Iowa, 1975-79; mgr. dist. sales World Book Ency., St. Paul, 1980-83; ins. agt. Allstate Ins. Co., St. Paul, 1983-84; mgr. market sales Allstate Ins. Co., Eden Prairie, Minn., 1985-88, market mgr. ind. agts., 1989-94, mgr. agy., 1995—. Fellow Life Underwriting Tng. Coun.; mem. Nat. Assn. Life Underwriters, Minn. Ind. Agt. Assn. Methodist.

BOYLE, BARBARA PRINCELAU, retired intelligence officer; b. Oakland, Calif., Sept. 21, 1923; d. Paul and Mary Emilie (Rueger) Princelau; m. John Joseph Boyle, Oct. 21, 1950 (dec.). BA, U. Calif., Berkeley, 1948. Intelligence officer CIA, Langley, Va., 1954-82. Bd. dirs. The Thrift Shop, Washington, 1988-92; mem. Women's Bd. Columbia Hosp. for Women Med. Ctr., Washington, 1986—, mem. exec. com., 1989-91; mem. com. Washington Antiques Show, 1989—; active Rep. Womens Fed. Forum, Washington, League of Rep. Women of D.C., Inc. Recipient Cert. of Distinction CIA, 1982. Mem. Ctrl. Intelligence Retiree Assn., Assn. Former Intelligence Officers (bd. dirs. 1993—), Sulgrave Club, U. Calif. Berkeley Alumni Club of Washington (rec. sec. 1976-77, v.p. 1984-86), Sigma Kappa (v.p. No. Va. alumnae 1992-95, devel. com. Sigma Kappa Found., Inc., 1993-95). Episcopalian. Home: 5101 River Rd Bethesda MD 20816-1512

BOYLE, BETSY H., educational administrator; b. Cleve., Feb. 18, 1946; d. John J. Jr. and Lois Frances (Hale) B. BA, Loretto Heights Coll., Denver, 1968; MA, U. No. Colo., 1978, postgrad. Cert. adminstr., Colo. Tchr. Archdiocese of Denver; prin. Presentation of Our Lady Sch., Denver; dir. instrnl. programs Office Cath. Schs., Denver, now assoc. supt. Contbr. articles to profl. jours. Mem. ASCD, Nat. Cath. Edn. Assn. (profl. presenter), Cath. Urban Educators, Schs. in Urban Neighborhoods.

BOYLE, GERTRUDE, sportswear company executive; b. Augsberg, Germany, 1924; came to U.S., 1938; d. Paul and Marie Lanfrom; m. Neil Boyle, 1948; children: Tim, Kathy, Sally. BA in Sociology, Univ. Ariz., 1947. Pres., CEO Columbia Sportswear Co., Portland, Oreg., 1970-88, CEO, 1988-94, chair, 1994—. Named one of Best Mgrs. Bus. Week Mag., 1994, Am.'s Top 50 Women Bus. Owners Working Woman mag., Woman of Yr. Oreg. chpt. Women's Forum, 1987. Office: Columbia Sportswear Co 6600 N Baltimore Portland OR 97203*

BOYLE, MARY, county commissioner; m. John J. Boyle; four children. Grad., St. Mary's Coll. Pres. Cuyahoga County Commrs., Cleve.; Bd. dirs. Nat. Assn. Counties (Ohio rep.); founding mem., former chair County Com. on Pub. Works; chair Criminal Justice Svcs. Supervisory Bd., Cleve., Brownfields Working Group, Cleve. Recipient award Ohio Environ. Coun., 1992, disting. pub. svc. award Cleve. State U. Nat. Honor Soc., 1995; named pub. servant of year 1992 Greater Cleve. Nurses Assn., pub. ofcl. of year 1995 Nat. Assn. Social Workers; inducted into Ohio Woen's Hall of Fame, 1983. Office: Cuyahoga County Commr 1219 Ontario St Rm 453 Cleveland OH 44113

BOYLE, PATRICIA DILYS, editor; b. Englewood, N.J., Jan. 5, 1962; d. Ambrose Purcell and Adelaide Dilys (Hawkins) B. BA in English Lit., Smith Coll., 1984; grande diplome, La Varenne Ecole de Cuisine, Paris, 1987. Assoc. editor Good Housekeeping Mag., N.Y.C., 1989-90; freelance food stylist, recipe cons. N.Y.C., 1990-92; food editor Chocolatier Mag., N.Y.C., 1992—, Pastry Art and Design Mag., N.Y.C., 1994—. Mem. N.Y. Women's Culinary Alliance. Home: # L-5 275 Engle St Englewood NJ 07631 Office: Chocolatier Mag 45 W 34th St #600 New York NY 10001

BOYLE, PATRICIA JEAN, judge; b. Detroit, Mar. 31, 1937. Student, U. Mich., 1955-57; B.A., Wayne State U., 1963, J.D., 1963. Bar: Mich. Practice law with Kenneth Davies, Detroit, 1963; law clk. to U.S. Dist. judge, 1963-64; asst. U.S. atty., Detroit, 1964-68; asst. pros. atty. Wayne County; dir. research, tng. and appeals Wayne County, Detroit, 1969-74; Recorders Ct. judge City of Detroit, 1976-78; U.S. dist. judge Eastern Dist. Mich., Detroit, 1978-83; assoc. justice Mich. Supreme Ct., Detroit, 1983—. Active Women's Rape Crisis Task Force, Vols. of Am. Named Feminist of Year Detroit chpt. NOW, 1978; recipient Outstanding Achievement award Pros. Attys. Assn. Mich., 1978, Spirit of Detroit award Detroit City Council, 1978, Mich. Women's Hall of Fame award, 1986. Mem. Women Lawyers Assn. Mich., Fed. Bar Assn., Mich. Bar Assn., Detroit Bar Assn., Wayne State U. Law Alumni Assn. (Disting. Alumni award 1979). Office: Mich Supreme Ct PO Box 30052 2d Fl Law Bldg Lansing MI 48909*

BOYLE, RENÉE KENT, cultural organization executive, translator, editor; b. Cairo, July 4, 1926; came to U.S., 1946; d. Maurice Colin and Victoria Smith; m. John E. Whiteford Boyle, Feb. 2, 1950; children: Vanessa Whiteford Wayne, Christopher, Andrea Heller, Mara Holloway. Diploma, St. Clare's Coll., Heliopolis, Egypt, 1944; postgrad., Rice U., 1947-48, Santa Monica Coll., 1950-51. Dep. dir. Am. Friends of Mid. East, Tehran, Iran, 1959-62, Les Amis Americains du Maghreb, Tunis, Tunisia, 1962-64; v.p. Fgn. Services Research Inst., Washington, 1964—; v.p. Whiteford Internat. Enterprise, Villars sur Ollon, Switzerland, 1967-74; vice dir. Essentialist Philosophical Soc., 1992—; pres. Wheat/Forders Press. Editor: Primers for the Age of Inner Space series, Beyond the Present Prospect, 1978, The Indra Web, 1982, Graffiti on the Wall of Time, 1982, Of the Same Root: Heaven, Earth & I, 1990, The Way of the Essentialist: Contra Sartre's Existentialism. Mem. Dem. Nat. Com., Washington, 1982—. Mem. Acad. Ind. Scholars (exec. dir.), Ams. for Dem. Action, People for Ethical Treatment of Animals, Sierra Club. Unitarian. Avocation: cordon bleu cooking. Home: 2718 Unicorn Ln NW Washington DC 20015-2234 Office: Fgn Svcs Rsch Inst PO Box 6317 Washington DC 20015-0317

BOYLES, CAROL ANN PATTERSON, career development educator; b. Waverly, N.Y., Aug. 26, 1932; d. Paul Bryan and Ruth Marion (Wilbur) Patterson; widowed 1981; 1 child, Scott Patterson. BA, Keuka Coll., 1953; MEd, U. Fla., 1957. Cert. tchr., Fla. Admissions officer Keuka Coll., Keuka Park, N.Y., 1953-56; residence counselor Fla. State U., Tallahassee, 1957-59; dir. guidance and counseling, assoc. dean student affairs Cen. Fla. Community Coll., Ocala, 1959-67; asst. dean student activities, orgns., asst. dean women Fla. State U., Tallahassee, 1967-69; dir. guidance Fla. Community Coll., Jacksonville, 1970-72; dir. coop. edn., placement U. North Fla., Jacksonville, 1972-83; dir. Career Devel. Ctr. U. North Fla., 1983-88, dir. Ctr. Exptl. Learning/Testing, 1988—; chmn. Career Expo, Jacksonville, 1977-91; chmn., mem. interuniv. sys. com. on career devel., 1972—; cons. coop. edn. programs; field reader U.S. Dept. Edn. Chmn. bd. dirs. Southside Christian Counseling Ctr., 1992-94, mem. 1988-94. Mem. ASTD, So. Coll. Placement Assn. (v.p. 1972—), Fla. Coop. Placement Assn. (pres. 1976-77, John Brownlee Leadership award 1991), Coop. Edn. Assn., Nat. Soc. Exptl. Edn., Jacksonville C. of C. (workforce preparation bd. bus. sch. partnership com., State of Fla. Coll. Acad. Skills Test adv. com. 1994—, Fla. Dept. Edn. ad hoc com. on placement testing 1995—), Keuka Coll. Alumni Assn., Kappa Delta Pi. Baptist. Home: 7804 Catawba Dr Jacksonville FL 32217-3642 Office: Univ N Fla 4567 Saint Johns Bluff Rd S Jacksonville FL 32224-2646

BOYSEN, MELICENT PEARL, finance company executive; b. Houston, Dec. 1, 1943; d. William Thomas and Mildred Pearl (Walker) Richardson; m. Stephen M. Boysen, Sept. 10, 1961 (dec. 1973); children: Marshella, Stephanie, Stephen. Student, Cen. Mo. State, 1973-75. Owner, pres. Boysen Enterprises, Kansas City, Mo., 1973-93; fin. cons., underwriter New Eng. Life Ins. Co., Kansas City, 1978-81; owner, pres. Boysen Agri-Svcs., Kansas City, 1984-94; pres. Boysen & Assocs., Inc., Kansas City, 1987—; stockholder, pres. Am. Crumb Rubber, Inc., Kansas City, 1996—; cons. San Luis Rey (Calif.) Tribal Water Authority, Wind River (Wyo.) Reservation, Cheyenne River (S.D.) Sioux, Iroquois Nations (N.Y.), 1983—; founding bd. dirs. , pres. Am. Indian Youth Orgn., Visible Horizons, 1987—. Founding bd. dirs. Rose Brooks Ctr. Battered Women, Kansas City, 1979-87, treas., 1979-81; exec. dir. The Flame Spirit Run, 1992; citationist, 1993; pres. Vol. Action Awards Program. Recipient Women of Conscience award Panel Am. Women of Greater Kansas City. Mem. Internat. Fin. Planners Assn., Internat. Agri-Bus. Assn., DAR, Kans. C. of C. and Industry, Kansas City C. of C. Methodist. Office: Boysen & Assocs 1130 Westport Rd Kansas City MO 64111

BOZA, CLARA BRIZEIDA, marketing and communications executive; b. Havana, Cuba, Apr. 18, 1952; came to U.S., 1957; d. Eduardo Otmaro and Hubedia Marta (Garcia) B. BA in English summa cum laude, Barry Coll., 1973, MA in Communication Media, 1988. Legal asst. supr. Steel Hector & Davis, Miami, Fla., 1978-80; program adminstr. Dade County Council Arts & Scis., Miami, 1980-82; dir. program devel. Nat. Found. for Advancement in Arts, Miami, 1982-85; exec. dir. Bus. Vols. for Arts/Miami, 1985-86; dir. mktg. Steel Hector & Davis, Miami, 1986-96; dir. practice devel. Arnold & Porter, Washington, 1996—; S.E. regional cons. Arts and Bus. Coun., N.Y.C., 1986-88; panelist So. Arts Fedn., Atlanta, 1983-84; panelist and spkr. various local, state, and nat. orgns. and assns. Recipient ednl. scholarship Barry Coll., Miami, 1969-73, Fla. Bd. Regents, 1969-73. Mem. ABA (commn. on advt. 1994—), Nat. Law Firm Mktg. Assn. (bd. dirs. and officer 1993, 94, 96), Am. Mktg. Assn. (bd. dirs. Miami chpt. 1992-96), Fla. Bar (standing com. on advt. 1993-96). Office: Arnold & Porter 4000 First Union Fin Ctr 555 Twelfth St Washington DC 20008

BOZONE, BILLIE RAE, librarian, consultant; b. Norphlet, Ark., Oct. 7, 1935; d. Guy Samuel and Vera (Jones) B. B.S. in Library Sci, Miss. State Coll. for Women, 1957; M.A., George Peabody Coll. for Tchrs., 1958. Asst. ref. librarian Miss. State U., State College, 1958-61, serials librarian, 1961-63; asst. ref. librarian U. Ill. at Urbana, 1963-65; asst. librarian New Eng. Mut. Life Ins. Co., Boston, 1965-67; sr. ref. librarian U. Mass., Amherst, 1967-68; head circulation dept. Smith Coll., Northampton, Mass., 1968-69; asst. librarian Smith Coll., 1969-71, coll. librarian, 1971-91; libr. cons., 1991—; bd. dirs. Hampshire Inter-library Center, Amherst, 1971-91; mem. exec. com. NELINET, 1977-79; chmn. Five Coll. Librarians Council, 1980-82, 90-91. Mem. ALA, Assn. Coll. and Research Libraries, Alpha Beta Alpha, Alpha Psi Omega. Home: 164 Red Gate Ln Amherst MA 01002-1845

BOZORTH, SHERRY CARLSON, music educator; b. Coos Bay, Oreg., Aug. 23, 1954; d. Edward Claud and Edythe Irene (Mohler) Carlson; m. David Lynn Bozorth, Dec. 18, 1983; children: Sarah, Joseph, Amy. BS in Edn. and Mus. Edn., Oreg. Coll. Edn., 1976; MA Interdisciplinary Studies, Oreg. State U., 1983. Cert. tchr. elem. K-8, music K-12. Music specialist grades 5-8 Molalla (Oreg.) Sch. Dist., 1976-77; music specialist grades 1-8 Oreg. Conf. of S.D.A., Portland, 1977-80; music specialist grades K-6 Evergreen Sch. Dist., Vancouver, Wash., 1980-90; music specialist grades K-5 Woodland (Wash.) Sch. Dist., 1990—; pvt. instr. piano, clarinet, flute, folk guitar; instrs. music edn. workshop, Evergreen Sch. Dist., Vancouver, 1984-89, mem. music curriculum com., 1982, 87. Instr. folk guitar Ridgefield (Wash.) Community Edn., 1981-82, Woodland Comm. Edn., 1982-83, Evergreen Comm. Edn., Vancouver, 1984-85; mem. Woodland Presbyn. Ch., choir dir., 1992—. Mem. Mu Phi Epsilon. Republican. Home: 808 Goerig Woodland WA 98674 Office: Woodland Elem Sch PO Box 370 Woodland WA 98674

BRAASCH, BARBARA LYNN, banker; b. Santa Monica, Calif., Apr. 14, 1958; d. C. Duane and René Barbara (Siegel) B. Student, Golden Gate U., 1989-91. Asst. v.p., sr. fin. analyst Wells Fargo Bank, San Francisco, 1976-94, asst. v.p., mgr., 1994—; mentor Jr. Achievement, L.A., 1980-83. 1st class scout Girl Scouts Am., 1976, leader, asst. leader, 1976-79, 84-87; vol. Open Hand, San Francisco, 1991-92, San Francisco AIDS Found., various women's groups, 1989—. Mem. Am. Compensation Assn. Democrat. Jewish. Office: Wells Fargo Bank 525 Market St Fl 18 San Francisco CA 94105-2708

BRABANT, LORI ANN, nursing administrator; b. Lynn, Mass., Sept. 28, 1960; d. Richard Woodruff and Nancy Joan (Higgins) Amidon; m. Timothy Cecil Brabant, Sept. 1, 1984; children: Timothy Jr., Daniel, Jillian. AD in Secretarial Sci. cum laude, No. Essex C.C., 1980; diploma LPN, Whittier Regional Vocat., 1983; ADN cum laude, St. Clair County C.C., 1993; student, U. Mich., 1995—. Cert. BCLS instr., ACLS; RN, Mich. LPN staff nurse Whitter Rehab. Hosp., Haverhill, Mass., 1983-84; LPN charge nurse Amesbury (Mass.) Nursing and Retirement, 1984-85; LPN staff nurse River Dist. Hosp., East China, Mich., 1990-93, RN critical care, 1993-95, RN hosp. supr., 1994—; RN relief staff nurse McKenzie Meml. Hosp., Sandusky, Mich., 1994—; continuous quality improvement mem. River Dist. Hosp., 1994-95. Mem. St. Mary Ch. Port Sanilac, 1988-94; chairperson Port Sanilac Summer Festival com., 1990-94. Recipient Outstanding Achievement award Jerry Lewis Telethon, 1989. Mem. United States Jaycees. Roman Catholic. Home: 7023 Palis Verdis Dr Port Sanilac MI 48469-9735 Office: River Dist Hosp 4100 River Rd East China MI 48054-2909

BRABEC, ROSEMARY JEAN, retail executive; b. St. Paul, Apr. 5, 1951; d. Peter Michael and Mary Jane (Nigro) Jacovitch; m. Loren W. Brabec, Sept. 16, 1972; children: Brenda Marie, Daniel Joseph. BS in Elem. Edn., St. Cloud State U., 1973. Tchr. Ind. Sch. Dist. 314, Braham, Minn., 1975-78; owner, mgr. Rosemary's Quilts and Baskets, Braham, 1988—; dir. Community Edn. Adv. Coun., Braham, 1978-95, chmn., 1992-95. Designer quilt block representing Minn. div. AAUW for display at Internat. Fedn. Univ. Women conv., Calif. Chmn. P.I.C.K. Immunization Clinic, Braham, 1978-85; vol. driver coord. Home Delivered Meals, Braham, 1984—; vol. coord. Com. to Build Robert Leathers Playground, Braham, 1985. Mem. AAUW (Minn. sec. 1985-87, v.p. 1987-89), Minn. Quilters, Braham Civic and Commerce Assn. Office: Rosemary Quilts and Baskets 103 W Central Dr Braham MN 55006-3033

BRABY, CAROL VIRGINIA, church official; b. Independence, Mo., Dec. 19, 1932; d. Frank L. and Mildred S. (Henson) Freeman; m. Thomas Richard Braby, June 21, 1953; children: Janice L. Braby Lotz, Joseph R. AA, Graceland Coll., Lamoni, Iowa, 1952; BA, U. Hawaii, 1956. Pub. rels. advt. asst. Herald House, Independence, 1952-53; mem. pub. rels. staff to Rep. Fred Schwengel, U.S. Ho. of Reps., Washington, 1955; freelance writer, 1956-80; dir. program svcs. Citrus coun. Girl Scouts U.S.A., Winter Park, Fla., 1980-85; coord. Elderhostel, Deerhaven, Paisley, Fla., 1989-92; coord. Elderhostel, Ref. LDS Ch., Independence, 1994—, mem. Women's Ministry Commn., 1975-83; mgmt. cons. Girl Scouts U.S.A., N.Y.C., 1986—; assoc. pastor Orlando congregation Ref. LDS Ch., 1986-89. Author: Heritage and Hope, 1982, also ch. edn. manuals for child and counselor, Christian edn. study courses, 1956-76. Bd. dirs. Citrus coun. Girl Scouts U.S.A., 1972-75, pres., 1977-80, nat. vol., 1986—; pres. Second Harvest Food Bank Ctrl. Fla., Orlando, 1988-90. Recipient Thanks Badge, Citrus coun. Girl Scouts U.S.A., 1976, World Cmty. award for youth leadership Ref. LDS Ch., 1982. Mem. Viewpax Mondiale (treas. 1987—). Democrat. Home: 47070 Central Ave Paisley FL 32767 also: 510 High Ridge Rd Franklin NC 28734

BRACKBILL, NANCY LAFFERTY, elementary education educator; b. Lancaster, Pa., Sept. 7, 1938; d. Jacob Martin and Erma Irene (Moser) Lafferty; m. Albert Landis Brackbill Jr., Aug. 6, 1960; children: Lynn Elizabeth, Lisa Ann. BS in Elem. Edn., Millersville U., 1960, cert. reading specialist, 1981. Tchr. kindergarten Hempfield Sch. Dist., Landisville, Pa., 1960-63; tchr. nursery sch. Zion U.C.C. Nursery Sch., Millersville, Pa., 1971-72; tchr. elem., reading Annville (Pa.)-Cleona Sch. Dist., 1978-79; tchr. reading Palmyra (Pa.) H.S., 1980-81; elem. tchr., reading specialist East Stroudsburg (Pa.) Area Sch. Dist., 1981—, chmn. elem. reading, 1991—. Mem. ASCD, Internat. Reading Assn., Nat. Coun. Tchrs. English, Colonial Area Reading Educators (legis. chair 1992, rec. sec. 1994), Pa. State Edn. Assn., Keystone State Reading Assn., Keystone State Leaders, East Stroudsburg Edn. Assn. Mem. Ch. of Christ. Home: 188 Brookside Ln Nazareth PA 18064-9109 Office: East Stroudsburg Area Schs 321 N Courtland St East Stroudsburg PA 18301

BRACKEN, CAROLYN JEAN, artist, children's book illustrator, actress; b. Santa Monica, Calif., Nov. 21, 1944; d. Edward Vincent and Constance (Nickerson) B.; m. Henry J. Franzoni, Mar. 3, 1996. BFA, Wash. U., St. Louis, 1966. Artist Norcross Greeting Cards, N.Y.C., 1967-75; ptnr., art dept. head White, Bracken, Noonan Advt. Agy., N.Y.C., 1975; freelance artist, illustrator N.Y.C., 1975 . Illustrator over 150 children's books including Noah's Ark, 1973, Animal Crackers, 1979, Here Comes the Fire Engines, 1981, Martha's House, 1982, The Care Bear and the Terrible Twos, 1983, Fast Rolling Fire Trucks, 1984, Follow the Zookeeper, 1984, Some Busy Hospital, 1985, You Can Say No, 1985, The Busy Schoolbus, 1986, Look At My Town, 1986, New Day, 1986, Jenny's New Baby Sister, 1987, Mother Goose, All Aboard, 1988, My Trike, 1989, Gingerbread House-Easy To Make, 1989, The Story of Santa Claus, 1989, Where Is Grandma Rabbit, 1989, The Haunted House, 1991, Scary Masks, 1992, Chutes and Ladders, 1994, Tales From the Cabbage Patch (4 book set), 1995, We Like To Do Things, 1995, The Ghost Who Was Afraid Of the Dark, 1996, numerous others; actress various playhouses. Mem. AEA, Soc. Children's Book Writers & Illustrators. Home and Office: P8-5 Panther Valley Hackettstown NJ 07840

BRACKEN, KATHLEEN, broadcasting professional. Story editor, analyst The James Komack Co./Warner Bros., Burbank, Calif., 1980-81; mgr. creative svcs. Columbia Pictures TV, Burbank, 1981-83; dir. advt. and promotion Telepictures Corp., L.A., 1983-87; v.p. spl. projects, advt. and promotion Lorimar-Telepictures Corp., Culver City, Calif., 1987-88; broadcast prodr., writer Jacobs & Gerber, Inc., L.A., 1988-89, line prodr. Odyssey Filmakers/Praxis Filmworks, L.A., 1989-91; promotion mgr. WWOR-TV, Secaucus, N.J., 1993-94; creative svcs. dir. KCOP-TV, L.A., 1994—; freelance broadcast prodr. for numerous clients, including CBS News, WNBC-TV, Lee Hunt Assocs., Showtime, Lifetime, Ha! TV, CNBC, others. Recipient two L.A. Emmys for broadcast prodns., 1994. Office: UPN 13 KCOP 915 N La Brea Ave Los Angeles CA 90038

BRACKEN, KATHLEEN ANN, nurse; b. Chgo., Mar. 14, 1947; d. Thomas James and Catherine Anastasia (Cowal) B.; RN, CNA, Little Company of Mary Hosp., Evergreen Park, Ill., 1968; BSN, Lewis U., 1984, MBA, 1989. Mem. staff Little Company of Mary Hosp., Evergreen Park, 1968-69, 71-73, supr. ICUs, 1976-79, dir. ICUs, 1979-91; v.p. patient care svcs. South Chgo. Community Hosp., 1991-93; staff nurse coronary care unit Little Co. of Mary Hosp., Torrence, Calif., 1969-70; staff nurse Chgo. Lying-In Clinic, U. Chgo., 1970-71; nurse mgr. VA Westside Med. Ctr., Chgo., 1994—; bd. dirs., chmn. nursing cardiovascular com. South Cook Heart Assn., 1977-83, recipient Meritorious Service award, 1979, 81, 82, 83, 84, 85, 86. Mem. NAFE, Chgo. Heart Assn., Assn. Critical Care Nurses (pres. Southside Chgo., Area chpt. 1983-84, rec. sec. 1984-85), Am. Heart Assn. (cardiovascular nursing coun., Ill. Orgn. Nursing Execs., Brain Injury Assn. Ill., Inc. (facilitator family support group), Chgo. Healthcare Exec. Forum, Delta Epsilon Sigma, Sigma Theta Tau. Home: 10321 S Campbell Ave Chicago IL 60655-1016 Office: VA Westside Med Ctr 820 S Damen Ave Chicago IL 60612-3728

BRACKEN, PEG, author; b. Filer, Idaho, Feb. 25, 1918; d. John Lewis and Ruth (McQuesten) B.; m. John Hamilton Ohman, June 15, 1991; 1 child from previous marriage, Johanna Kathleen Edwards. A.B., Antioch Coll., 1940. Author: The I Hate to Cook Book, 1960, The I Hate to Housekeep Book, 1962, I Try to Behave Myself, 1963, Peg Bracken's Appendix to The I Hate to Cook Book, 1966, I Didn't Come Here to Argue, 1969, But I Wouldn't Have Missed It for the World, 1973, The I Hate to Cook Almanack - A Book of Days, 1976, A Window Over the Sink, 1981, The Complete I Hate to Cookbook, 1986.

BRACKENRIDGE, N. LYNN, public relations and development specialist; b. Youngstown, Ohio, Sept. 9, 1957; d. John Bruce Brackenridge and Mary Ann Rossi; m. Harry Lee Carrico, July 1, 1994. BA, Lawrence U., 1978; MS, Georgetown U., 1980. Tchg. asst. Georgetown U., Washington, 1979-81, admissions officer, 1984-85, editor, writer devel., 1985-87, asst. dir. devel., 1987-89; dir. devel. Cath. Charities U.S.A., Washington, 1989-91, Johns Hopkins U. Bologna (Italy) Ctr., 1991-92; dir. devel. and pub. rels. Nat. Ctr. for State Cts., Williamsburg, Va., 1993—. Vol. Richmond (Va.) Ballet, 1993-95, Leukemia Soc. of Am., Hampton, Va., 1996—. Georgetown U. fellow, 1979-81; recipient diplome d'etudes Inst. d'Etudes Francaises de Touraine, 1976. Mem. Nat. Soc. Fund Raising Execs. (chmn. program com., pres.-elect 1996). Democrat. Home: 9303 Cragmont Dr Richmond VA 23229 Office: Nat Ctr for State Cts 300 Newport Ave Williamsburg VA 23185

BRACKETT, PRILLA SMITH, artist, educator; b. New Orleans, Nov. 8, 1942; d. Wilson Fitch and Hannah Balch (Coffin) Smith; m. George Conrad Brackett, Sept. 28, 1968; children: Ethan Samuel, Matthew Aaron. BA in Psychology and Sociology, Sarah Lawrence Coll., 1964, MA in Sociology, U. Calif., Berkeley, 1967; MFA in Painting and Drawing, U. Nebr., 1981. Grad. tchg. asst. U. Nebr., Lincoln, 1979-81; adj. prof. Simmons Coll., Boston, 1989; instr. DeCordova Mus. Sch., Lincoln, 1992-93; adj. prof. U. Mass. Harbor Campus, Boston, 1993, Salem (Mass.) State Coll., 1993; instr. landscape workshops Arts Pro Tem, Hancock, N.H., 1993-95, West Yellowstone, Mont., 1993-95; panel coord., moderator Nat. Women's Caucus for Art, San Francisco, 1989, Boston, 1996; panelist Coll. Art Assn. Nat. Conf., Chgo., 1992; guest lectr. and spkr. in field. One-woman shows include Winfisky Gallery, Salem (Mass.) State Coll., 1989, Cambridge (Mass.) Pub. Libr., 1989, Gallery 57, Cambridge, 1989, The Bunting Inst., Radcliffe Rsch. and Study Ctr., Cambridge, 1990, Soho 20 Invitational Space, N.Y.C., 1990, Wessell Libr., Tufts U., Medford, Mass., 1990, DeCordova Mus. and Sculpture Park, Lincoln, Mass., 1993, Gallery 57, Cambridge, Mass., 1994, others; group exhbns. include Lamont Gallery, Phillips Exeter (N.H.) Acad., 1994, The Art Complex Mus., Duxbury, Mass., 1995, Schlesinger Libr., Radcliffe Coll., Cambridge, 1995, World's Women On-Line! 1995-96: Computing Commons Gallery, Ariz. State U., Tempe, UN Fourth World Conf. on Women, Beijing, Artemesia Gallery, Chgo., Global Focus 1995-96: UN Fourth World Conf. on Women, Beijing, Nat. Mus. Women in the Arts, Washington, Rotenberg Gallery, Boston, 1996, others. Co-pres. Boston Chpt. of Amigos de las Americas, Boston, 1993-95. Recipient fellowship in painting Bunting Inst., Radcliffe Rsch. and Study Ctr., Cambridge, 1989-90, Travel grant John Anson Kittredge Ednl. Fund, Augusta, Maine, 1990, Earthwatch Artist award Earthwatch Watertown, Madagascar, 1990-92, The Francine Frank fellow residency Millay Colony of the Arts, Austerlitz, N.Y., 1994. Mem. Coll. Art Assn., Women's Caucus for Art (coord. for exhbns. nat. conf. 1986, co-chair Boston chpt. 1987-88). Home: 171 Lakeview Ave Cambridge MA 02138 Office: 75 Richdale Ave #11 Cambridge MA 02140

BRACY, TINA DENNELL, nursing home administrator, health care consultant; b. Phila., July 15, 1959; d. William T. and Jeanette C. (Green) B.; 1 child, Nicole J. BA in Health Sci. and Policy, U. Md., Catonsville, 1981; MBA, Howard U., 1987. Certp. nursing home adminstr. Asst. adminstr. Health Care Inst., Washington, 1987-90, adminstr., 1990-92; dep. dir. D.C. Village, Washington, 1992-93; adminstr. Lorien Nursing and Rehab. Ctr., Balt., 1993—; owner, operator Legacy Living for Srs., Balt.; internat. cons. Dominica, 1990-92; nursing home cons. Greater S.E. Cmty. Ctr. for Aging, Washington, 1990. Bd. dirs. D.C. Cmty. Svcs., Takoma Park, Md., 1994-95. Home: 5311 Belleville Ave Baltimore MD 21207-7046 Office: 5314 Belleville Ave Baltimore MD 21207-7046

BRADDOCK, NONNIE CLARKE, religious organization administrator; b. Rye, N.Y.; d. Peter Benedict and Nora Bridget (Devins) Clarke; m. Eugene Stephen Braddock, Sept. 7, 1962; children: Stephen E., Brian B., Glenn C. Adminstr. Beaver Farm Retreat and Conf. Ctr., Yorktown Heights, N.Y.; deputy city clk. City of Rye, N.Y.; founder, pres. Celebrations; dir. Security Enforcement Bur.; part-time therapist; with Marriage Encounter movement, co-founder, chmn. bd., team leader No. Westchester-Putnam (N.Y.) Interfaith Marriage Encounter, 1981-87. Vol. Boy Scouts Am., numerous polit. orgns. and cmty. groups, 1970—; chair Warmth for Christmas clothing drive, N.Y.C. shelters; facilitator mil. family support group; organizer food collections for needy, Heart to Heart, coord. Angel Fund; organizer, sponsor Weekly Cable TV program featuring peace, 1991; bd. dirs. Homeless Shelter; adv. com. Comty. Mem. Interfaith Clergy Coun., Rite Christian Initiation for Adults, Right to Life, North Am. Retreat Dirs. Assn., Pax Christi Metro, Westchester Assn. Vol. Adminstrs., Feminists for Life, Fedn. Christian Ministries. Office: Beaver Farm Retreat Ctr Underhill Ave Yorktown Heights NY 10598

BRADEN, BETTY JANE, legal association administrator; b. Sheboygan, Wis., Feb. 5, 1943; d. Otto Frank and Betty Donna (Beers) Huettner; children: Jennifer Tindall, Rebecca Leigh; m. Berwyn Bartow Braden, Nov. 5, 1983. BS, U. Wis., 1965. Cert. elem. tchr., Wis. Tchr. Madison (Wis.) Met. Sch. Dist., 1965-70, 71-72, sub. tchr., 1972-75; adminstrv. asst. ATS-CLE State Bar Wis., Madison, 1978, adminstrv. asst. Advanced Tng. Seminars-Continuing Legal Edn., 1979, coordinator, 1980, adminstr. coordinator, 1980-84, adminstrv. dir., 1984-87, dir. adminstrn., bar svcs., membership, 1987—; mem. rels. and pub. svcs. dir. Legal Edn., 1992—; speaker Bar Leadership Inst. of ABA. Mem. Meeting Planners Internat. (sec. Wis. chpt. 1981-82, pres. 1982-83); Adminstrv. Mgmt. Soc., Am. Mgmt. Assn., Am. Soc. for Personnel Adminstrn., Am. Soc. of Assn. Execs., Wis. Soc. of Assn. Execs., LWV, Nat. Assn. Bar Execs. (program chair 1995-96). Home: 52 Golf Course Rd Madison WI 53704-1423 Office: State Bar of Wis 402 W Wilson St Madison WI 53703-3614

BRADEN, BRENDA LOU, lawyer; b. Hutchinson, Kans., Dec. 6, 1940; d. Gene M. and Margaret (Smith) Rayl; m. Melvin M. Hoyt, Mar. 1, 1959 (div. Oct., 1977); children: Aron K., Lisa Hoyt Marlar, Brian G., Sean M.; m. John Buckley Braden, May 19, 1985. Student, Washburn U., 1971-73, JD, 1980; BA in Polit. Sci., U. Colo., 1976. Bar: N.Mex. 1980, Kans. 1981, Wash. 1988, Oreg. 1994. Assoc. Kirk & Williams P.A., Albuquerque, New Mex., 1980; asst. atty. gen. Office of Atty Gen., Topeka, Kans., 1981-84; dep. atty. gen. Office of Atty Gen., Topeka, 1984-88; asst. code reviser Statute Law Com., Olympia, Wash., 1988-91; city atty. City of Hoquiam, Wash., 1991-94, City of Tualatin, Oreg., 1994—; liason Kansas County and Dist. Attys. Assn., Topeka, 1984-88. Campaigner Robert Stephan for Atty. Gen., Topeka, 1986; bd. dirs. Am. Diabetes Assn., Topeka, 1987; mem. long range planning com. St. Mark's Episcopal Cathedral, Seattle, 1989-90; advisor Gray's Harbor Hist. Seaport, Aberdeen, Wash., 1991-94. Mem. Oreg. Bar Assn., Oreg. Mcpl. Attys., 120 Day Club. Office: City of Tualatin 18880 SW Martinazzi Tualatin OR 97062

BRADFORD, BARBARA REED, lawyer; b. Cleve., June 13, 1948; d. William Cochran and Martha Lucile (Horn) B.; m. Warren Neil Davis, Oct. 9, 1976 (div. 1989); m. S. Jack Odell, Dec. 12, 1991. BA, Pitzer Coll., 1970; JD, Georgetown U., 1975, MBA, 1985. Bar: N.Y. 1976, D.C. 1976. Staff asst. Sen. Edward M. Kennedy, Washington, 1970-71; assoc. Breed, Abbott & Morgan, N.Y.C., 1975-76, Verner, Liipfert Law Firm, Washington, 1976-78; atty. AID, Washington, 1978-83; regional dir. U.S. Trade & Devel. Agy., Washington, 1986—; pres. Georgetown Export Trading, Inc., Washington, 1984-86. Bd. dirs. Jr. League, Washington, 1977-78. Mem. Potomac Hunt Club. Democrat.

BRADFORD, BARBARA TAYLOR, writer, journalist, novelist; b. Leeds, Eng.; came to U.S., 1964; d. Winston and Freda (Walker) Taylor; m. Robert Bradford, Dec. 24, 1963. Student pvt. schs., Eng.; LittD (hon.), Leeds U., London, 1990. Women's editor Yorkshire (Eng.) Evening Post, 1951-53, reporter, 1949-51; editor Woman's Own, 1953-54; columnist London Evening News, 1955-57; exec. editor London Am., 1959-62; editor Nat. Design Center Mag., 1965-69; syndicated columnist Newsday Spls., L.I., 1968-70; nat. syndicated columnist Chgo. Tribune-N.Y. (News Syndicate), N.Y.C., 1970-75, Los Angeles Times Syndicate, 1975-81. Author: Complete Encyclopedia of Homemaking Ideas, 1968, A Garland of Children's Verse, 1968, How to Be the Perfect Wife, 1969, Easy Steps to Successful Decorating, 1971, Decorating Ideas for Casual Living, 1977, How to Solve Your Decorating Problems, 1976, Making Space Grow, 1979, Luxury Designs for Apartment Living, 1981; (novels) A Woman of Substance, 1979, Voice of the Heart, 1983, Hold the Dream, 1985, screen adaptation, 1986, Act of Will, 1986, To Be the Best, 1988, The Women in His Life, 1990, Remember, 1991, Angel, 1993, Everything to Gain, 1994, Dangerous to Know, 1995, Love in Another Town, 1995, Her Own Rules, 1996, A Secret Affair, 1996. Recipient Dorothy Dawe award Am. Furniture Mart, 1970, 71, Matrix award N.Y. Women in Communications, 1985. Mem. Authors Guild, Nat. Soc. Interior Designers (Distinguished Editorial award 1969, Nat. Press award 1971), Authors Guild Am. (coun. mem. 1989—), Am. Soc. Interior Designers. Office: 450 Park Ave New York NY 10022-2605

BRADFORD, CHRISTINA, newspaper editor; b. Dec. 23, 1942; d. J. Robert and Lesley (Jones) Merrill; m. Alan Bradford, Sept. 24, 1966 (div. 1973). AA, Stephens Coll., Columbia, Mo., 1962; BS in Journalism, U. Mo.-Columbia, 1964. Asst. city editor Detroit Free Press, 1975-80; asst. mng. editor Democrat and Chronicle, Rochester, N.Y., 1980-82, mng. editor, 1982-86; mng. editor/news Detroit News, 1986-89, mng. editor, 1989—. Mem. AP Mng. Editors, Am. Soc. Newspaper Editors, Detroit Athletic Club. Home: 208 Main Sail Ct Detroit MI 48207-5008 Office: Detroit News 615 W Lafayette Blvd Detroit MI 48226-3124*

BRADFORD, DEBRA BENSON, television executive; b. Huntsville, Ala., Oct. 14, 1953; d. Vernon and Betty Lou (Taylor) Benson. Student, Jacksonville State U., 1971-73; BS in Mktg., U. Ala., 1986. Blind aide Jacksonville (Ala.) State U., 1971-73; sec., Recreation Dept. City of Madison, Ala., 1974-77; sales fin. rep. First Nat. Bank, Huntsville, Ala., 1977-81; asst. program dir. Sta. WAAY-TV, Huntsville, Ala., 1981-84, promotion mgr., 1984-88, program dir., 1988-93, program dir. cable rels., 1993—; bd. dirs. TV Program Conf.; project dir. Sta. WAAY-TV Christmas Parade, Children First Task Force. Bd. dirs. Crime Stoppers, Huntsville, 1985-96. Recipient Addy Muscle Shoals Ad Club, Florence, Ala., 1985, Greater Huntsville Ad Club, 1986-87. Mem. Nat. Assn. TV Programming Execs., Viewers for Quality TV. Home: 109 Oakland Trace Madison AL 35758 Office: Sta WAAY-TV 1000 Monte Sano Blvd SE Huntsville AL 35801-6137

BRADFORD, DIANA JEANNE, marketing professional; b. Ridgewood, N.J., July 18, 1970; d. William Lloyd and Jeanne Alma (Eckel) B. BA, Sweet Briar Coll., 1992. Receptionist Kentshire Galleries, N.Y.C., 1993; adminstrv. asst. The Worth Collection, N.Y.C., 1993; asst. trader Advest Inc., N.Y.C., 1993-95; coord. Donna Karan, N.Y.C., 1995—. Vol., co-chair St. Bartholomew's Cmty. Club, 1994; vol., co-coord. The Children's Aid Soc., N.Y.C., 1995. Home: 272 First Ave Apt 2A New York NY 10009

BRADFORD, DIANE GOLDSMITH, multimedia marketing and product consultant; b. Provo, Utah, Apr. 20, 1951; d. Howard and Roxey Faye (Rosenbaum) B.; 1 child, Tamara. BS, U. Utah, 1973, MS, 1976, PhD, 1980. Instructional design intern InterWest Regional Med. Edn. Ctr., Salt Lake City, 1979; instr. Algebra divsn. continuing edn. U. Utah, Salt Lake City, 1980-81; project tng. coord. Automated Mfg. Resource Planning Project, O.C. Tanner Co., Utah, 1981-83; data processing dir. VA Med. Ctr., Salt Lake City, 1983-85; asst. dir. tng. and publs. IHC Affiliated Svcs. Inc., Salt Lake City, 1985-88; asst. dir. edn. and tng. GTE Health Systems Inc., Moss Rehab. Hosp., Phila., 1988-89; dir. edn. Wharton exec. edn. U. Pa., Phila., 1989-92; pres. Prime Resources Inc., Aspen, Colo., 1993—. Contbr. articles to profl. jours. Awards judge Coun. Internat. Nontheatrical Events. Mem. Am. Prodn. and Inventory Control Soc. (cert., edn. v.p. 1983-84). Home: 1145 Black Birch Dr Aspen CO 81611-3706 Office: 1412 Ouray Ave Grand Junction CO 81501-3341 also: 255 S 38th St Philadelphia PA 19104-3706

BRADFORD, GAIL IDONA, secondary school educator; b. Mobile, Ala., Sept. 12, 1947; d. Estes Paul and Doris (Roe) B.; m. Benjamin C. Lann, Jr., May 28, 1971 (div. May 1986). AA, Clarke Meml. Coll., Newton, Miss., 1967; BS, Miss. Coll., 1969; MA, La. Tech U., 1973; postgrad., Western Ky. U., 1979-82, 88-92; MDiv, So. Bapt. theol. Sem., 1996. Cert. tchr., sch. adminstr., counselor, home economist; ordained minister United Meth. Ch. Vocat. counselor Mobile Rehab., 1970-71; tchr. kindergarten Lincoln Parish Schs., Ruston, La., 1971-73; state staff coord. Head Start, U. South Ala., Mobile, 1973-74; dep. dir. Jefferson County Com. for Econ. Opportunity, Birmingham, Ala., 1975-76; instr. vocat. edn. Lawson State C.C., Birmingham, 1977; mental health technician Commonwealth of Ky., Louisville, 1978-79; exec. dir. Tchr. Corps, Western Ky. U., Bowling Green, 1979-82; tchr. spl. edn. Jefferson County Pub. Schs., Louisville, 1982-88, tchr. vocat. home econs., 1988-92; chaplain various hosps., 1994—; dir. children's ministry PRP United Meth. Ch., Louisville, 1995—; cons., condr. workshops various pub. programs, Ala., Ky., 1973—; tchr. workshops Ky. Tech., Jefferson State Campus, Louisville, 1989—; mem. com. practitioners Commonwealth of Ky. Workforce Cabinet, 1990-92. Bd. dirs. Ministries United South Ctrl., Louisville, 1989—; active various Rep. campaigns, La., Ky., 1971-86; mem. nat. adv. bd. Safe Places, 1991—; mem. campaign staff Rep. John Buchanan of Ala., 1975-77; dir. counselors Hugh O'Brian Youth Found., 1989-91, state chmn., 1991-93, state bd. sec., 1993-95. Recipient Tchr. award Louisville Commmunity Found., 1986, Leadership Edn. award Bellarmine Coll., Louisville, 1987; named Ky. col. Commonwealth of Ky., 1988. Mem. Ky. Vocat. Home Econs. Tchrs. (pres. region 6, 1990-91), Ky. Home Econs. Assn. (chmn. adult, secondary and elem. edn. 1988-92), Am. Vocat. Assn., Coun. for Exceptional Children, Am. Insts. Parliamentarians, Thomas Jefferson Parliamentarians (treas. 1986), Toastmasters (area gov. dist. 11, 1986-87, Able Toastmaster award 1984), Golden Key, Kappa Delta Pi. Methodist. Home: 3113 Osprey Rd Louisville KY 40213-1226

BRADFORD, JANET LYNN, financial company executive; b. Ames, Iowa, July 28, 1964; d. John Norman and Phyllis Ann (Cameron) Bradford; m. Christopher McDermot Hudson, Sept. 3, 1994. BA, Va. Poly. Inst. and State U., 1986. Internat. debt assoc. Bread for the World, Washington, 1987-88; from asst. underwriter to sr. underwriter Blue Cross Blue Shield of Nat. Capital Area, Washington, 1988—. Vol. Lutherplace Shelter, Washington, 1988-94; floor coord. AIDS Walk, 1995.

BRADFORD, LISA ANN, bank auditor; b. Coshocton, Ohio, Sept. 10, 1970; d. James F. and Sandra L. (Miller) B. BBA in acctg. cum laude, Kent State Univ., 1993. Bank auditor/sales audit Lane Bryant, Reynoldsburg, Ohio, 1993—. Recipient Leadership award Kent State Univ., 1992. Mem. Inst. of Mgmt. Accts., Ohio Bus. & Profl. Womens Club (v.p.), Alpha Xi Delta (asst. treas. 1991-93), Beta Alpha Psi (reporting sec. 1992-93), Omicron Delta Kappa. Office: Lane Bryant 5 Limited Parkway E Reynoldsburg OH 43068

BRADFORD, LOUISE MATHILDE, social services administrator; b. Alexandria, La., Aug. 3, 1925; d. Henry Aaron and Ruby (Pearson) B. BS, La. Poly. Inst., 1945; cert. in social work, La. State U., 1949; MS, Columbia U., 1953; postgrad., Tulane U., 1962, 64, La. State U., 1967; cert., U. Pa., 1966. Diplomate Am. Bd. Clin. Social Work; cert. social worker Acad. Cert. Social Workers. With La. Dept. Pub. Welfare, Alexandria, 1945-78; welfare caseworker La. Dept. Pub. Welfare, Alexandria, La., 1950-53; children's caseworker La. Dept. Pub. Welfare, Alexandria, 1957-59, child welfare cons., 1959-73, social svcs. cons., 1973-78, state cons. day care, 1963-66; dir. social svcs. St. Mary's Tng. Sch., Alexandria, 1978—; del. Nat. Day Care Conf., Washington, 1964; mem. early childhood edn. com. So. States Work Conf., Daytona Beach, Fla., 1968; mem. La. adv. com. 1970 White House Conf. on Children, also del.; mem. So. region planning com. Child Welfare League Am., 1970-73; mem. profl. adv. com. Cenla chpt. Parents Without Partners, 1970-95; adj. asst. prof. sociology La. Coll. Pineville, 1969-85; lectr. Kindergarten Workshop, 1970-72; mem. La. 4-C Steering Com.; social svcs. cons. La. Spl. Edn. Ctr., Alexandria, 1980-86; del. Internat. Conf. on Social Welfare, Nairobi, 1974, Jerusalem, 1978, Hong Kong, 1980, Brighton, 1982, Montreal, 1984. Bd. dirs. Cenla Cmty. Action Com., Alexandria, 1966-68; mem. kindergarten bd. Meth. Ch., 1967-87, ofcl. bd., 1974-75, 77-81, 83-85, 96—. Recipient Social Worker of Yr. award Alexandria br. NASW La. Conf. Social Welfare, 1984, Hilda C. Simon award, 1987, George Freeman award, 1987. Mem. NASW, DAR, Acad. Cert. Social Workers, La. Bd. Cert. Social Workers, So. La. Assn. Children Under Six, La. Conf. Social Welfare (George Freeman award 1987, Hilda C. Simon award 1987), Internat. Coun. on Social Welfare, Am. Pub. Welfare Assn. (S.W. region planning com. 1965), Am. Assn. on Mental Retardation (La. social work chair 1989-94), DAR, Ctrl. La. Pre-Sch. Assn. (dir. 1967-70), Rapides Golf and Country Club. Home: 5807 Joyce St Alexandria LA 71302-2510 Office: PO Box 7768 Alexandria LA 71306-0768

BRADFORD, MARJORIE TIDMORE, public relations executive; b. Cin., Oct. 9, 1947; d. Derry and Anna (Larkin) Tidmore; 1 child, Kimberley Tanya. BA, Oberlin, 1969; MA, U. Cin., 1974. Pub. svc. dir. Sta. WCPO-TV Scripps-Howard Broadcasting, Cin., 1969-72; pub. info. dir. Ctrl. Cmty. Health Bd., Cin., 1972-74; pub. rels. mgr. Procter & Gamble Co., Cin., 1974-86; corp. comm. dir. Adolph Coors Co., Golden, Colo., 1986-89; owner MTB Enterprises, Cin., 1989—; dir. comm. State Treasury, Columbus, Ohio, 1994-96; v.p. mktg. United Way of Franklin County, Columbus, 1996—; chmn. Silver Anvil Award com. Pub. Rels. Soc. Am., 1987. Trustee Children's Hosp., Inc., Columbus, 1995—; vis. prof. Nat. Urban League, N.Y.C., 1977—. Named One of 100 Most Influential Bus. Women Dollars & Sense Mag., 1987. Mem. Nat. Urban League (black exec. exch. program,, Gold Cup), Govt. Communicators. Republican. Methodist. Office: United Way of Franklin County 360 S 3d St Columbus OH 43215-5485

BRADLEY, ANN WALSH, justice. Former judge Wis. Cir. Ct., Madison; justice Wis. Supreme Ct., Madison. Office: PO Box 1688 Madison WI 53701-1688 also: 231 Northeast State Capital Madison WI 53702*

BRADLEY, KAREN SUE, liberal arts educator; b. Pontiac, Mich., Nov. 28, 1949; d. Lyle and Elaine (Cameron) Rose; m. Jack Alden Bradley, Dec. 12, 1970; children: Chad R., Guy R., Jay C., Alicia R. BA, Mich. State U., 1970, MA, 1973; EdD, Tex. A&M U., 1986. Cert. elem. edn., supr., mid-mgmt., reading, supt. Tchr. Lansing (Mich.) Pub. Schs., 1971-73; tchr., counselor Santa Rosa County Schs., Milton, Fla., 1973-82; tchr. Bryan (Tex.) Ind. Sch. Dist., 1982-83; lang. arts cons. Region VI Edn. Svc. Ctr., Huntsville, Tex., 1983-85; rsch. asst. Tex. A&M U., 1985-86; asst. supt. Marlin (Tex.) Ind. Sch. Dist., 1986-87; asst. prin. Hearne (Tex.) Ind. Sch. Dist., 1987-89; prin. Travis Magnet Elem. Sch. Ector County Ind. Sch. Dist., Odessa, Tex., 1989-93; asst. prof. U. Tex. Permian Basin, Odessa, 1993-94, Sul Ross State U., Del Rio, Tex., 1994—; in-svc. cons. pub. schs., Fla. and Tex., 1973—. Author: Kid's Lit, 1986; contbr. poetry to World of Poetry, 1992 (Golden Poet award 1992). Leader Girl Scouts Am., Odessa, 1992-94; com. mem. Cub Scouts, Odessa, 1992-94. Partnership grantee Jr. League, 1993. Mem. ASCD, Internat. Reading Assn. (exemplary reading program award 1993), Permian Basin Reading Assn. (Friends of Reading award 1994), Phi Delta Kappa. 1st United Methodist. Home: 211 Echo Valley Dr Del Rio TX 78840 Office: Sul Ross State U Rio Grande Coll 205 Wildcat Dr Del Rio TX 78840-8402

BRADLEY, KATHY ANNETTE, lawyer; b. Statesboro, Ga., Oct. 7, 1956; d. Johnny and Frances Elizabeth (Anderson) B. AB, Wesleyan Coll., 1978; JD, Mercer U., 1981. Bar: Ga. 1981, U.S. Dist. Ct. (no. and mid. dists.) Ga. 1981, U.S. Dist. Ct. (so. dist.) Ga. 1982. Assoc. Doremus & Jones, P.C., Metter, Ga., 1981-82, Franklin, Roach & Taulbee, Statesboro, 1982, Hal Roach Jr., Statesboro, 1983-86; ptnr. Roach & Bradley, Statesboro, 1986-94; sole practitioner Kathy A. Bradley, P.C., Statesboro, 1994—. Second v.p. exec. com. United Way S.E. Ga., Statesboro, 1987-89, 92-96. Recipient Deen Day Smith Svc. to Mankind award, 1990, Outstanding Young Careerist award Bus. and Profl. Women's Club S.E. Dist., 1990; named 1st Dist. Outstanding Clubwoman Ga. Fed. Women's Clubs, 1989, Outstanding Citizen, 1988, Cmty. Hero/Olympic Torch Bearer, 1996. Mem. Bulloch County Bar Assn. (pres. 1987-88), Ogeechee Cir Bar Assn., Rotary Club of Downtown Statesboro, Wesleyan Coll. Alumnae Assn. (pres. 1991-94), Leadership Bulloch (bd. dirs. 1992-95). Mem. Church of God. Office: 106B Oak St Statesboro GA 30458

BRADLEY, KIM ALEXANDRA, sales and marketing specialist; b. Glen Cove, N.Y., Aug. 27, 1955; d. Harold William and Helen Doris (Rosenthal) Shepard; m. Gary Morgan Bradley, Oct. 2, 1982; children: Hunter Morgan, Parker Davis, Preston Carter. BS, U. Ill., 1977. Media estimator Lee King & Ptnrs., Chgo., 1977-78; asst. buyer Grey North Advt., Chgo., 1978; broadcast negotiator J. Walter Thompson, Chgo., 1978-80; acct. exec. Katz Communications, Inc., Chgo., 1980-84, sales mgr., 1984-88, v.p. sales mgr., 1988-93; prin., pres. The Encore Group, Inc., Chgo., 1993; pres., owner Bradley Mktg. Group, Lake Forest, Ill., 1993—. Mem. mktg. com., bd. dirs. Child Abuse Prevention Svcs.; alliance mem. Art Inst. of Chgo.; vol. Infant Welfare Soc.; aux. bd. dirs. Juvenile Protection Assn. Mem. Am. Mgmt. Assn., Inst. Mgmt. Cons., Am. Mktg. Assn., Broadcast Advt. Club (bd. dirs., v.p., exec. v.p., pres., chair for Child Abuse Prevention Svcs. chairity com.). Home: 30 Barnswallow Ln Lake Forest IL 60045-2984

BRADLEY, L. ELLEN, academic administrator; b. Roanoke, Va., June 5, 1969; d. Don L. and Jenny (Hughes) B. BA, U. Richmond, 1991; MA, Va. Commonwealth U., 1992. Projects coord. The Innovation Groups, Richmond, Va., 1992-94; publs. asst. U. Richmond, 1994-95, housing coord., 1995-96, asst. dir. publs., 1996—. Mem. Internat. Assn. Bus. Communicators (dir. chmn. 1994-95), Omicron Delta Kappa. Office: U Richmond 28 Westhampton Way Richmond VA 23173

BRADLEY, LISA M., artist; b. Columbus, Ohio, Dec. 15, 1951; d. Phillip Raymond Bradley and Jean Lichtenstein. BA, Boston U., 1973. Assoc. dir. Pace Primitive, N.Y.C., 1977-84, dir., 1984—. One-woman shows include Boston City Hall, 1973, Harvard U., Cambridge, Mass., 1976, Boston Ctr. for the Arts, 1977, Ludlow Hyland Gallery, N.Y.C., 1978, 79, Bette Stoler Gallery, N.Y.C., 1979, Major-Saxbe Gallery, Urbana, Ohio, 1986, Phillip Dash Gallery, N.Y.C., 1987, Donahue Gallery, N.Y.C., 1989, Ratner Gallery, Chgo., 1991, Donahue Gallery, 1993, Galerie Kaj ForsBlom, Helsinki, Finland, 1995; exhibited in group shows Essex Inst., Salem, Mass., 1972, Cambridge Art Assn., 1972, 73, New Bertha Schaeffer Gallery, N.Y.C., 1975, Gallery 200, Columbus, 1975, Galeria Rosanna, Boston, 1976, Baak Gallery, Cambridge, 1977, 78, Betty Parsons Gallery, N.Y.C., 1978, 79, 80, 81, Bette Stoler Gallery, N.Y.C., 1979, 80, 81, 1st Women's Bank, N.Y.C., 1981, Fay Gold Gallery, Atlanta, 1982, Deicas Art, La Jolla, Calif., 1982, Elayne Marquis Gallery, San Francisco, 1982, Soker-Kaseman Gallery, San Francisco, 1983, Phillipe Guimiot Gallery, Brussels, 1983, Kouros Gallery, N.Y.C., Leonarda Di Mauro Gallery, N.Y.C., 1985, Chronocide Gallery, 1986, Mokotoff Gallery, 1986, Jan Baum Gallery, L.A., 1986, Phillip Dash Gallery, N.Y.C., 1986, Lavrov Gallery, Paris, 1987, Sensibilities Contemporaines, Cie Moderne & Contemporaine, Paris, 1991, Musee de Nationale de Dakar, Senegal, 1992, E.M. Donahue Gallery, N.Y.C., 1993, Solway Gallery, Cin., 1993; pub., The Art of Seeing, Fisher & Zelanski, "The Spiritual in Art", 1993. Jewish. Home: 356 W 20th St Apt 3B New York NY 10011-3385 Office: Pace Primitive 32 E 57th St New York NY 10022-2513

BRADLEY, MARILYNNE GAIL, advertising executive, advertising educator; b. Rockford, Ill., Apr. 12, 1938; d. Sherwin S. and Lillian (Leopold) Gersten; m. Charles S. Bradley, 1959 (div. Dec., 1994); children: Suzanne, Scott. BFA, Washington U., 1960; MAT, Webster U., St. Louis, 1975; MFA, Syracuse U., 1981; postgrad., St. Louis Tchrs. Acad., 1990. With Essayons Studio, St. Louis, 1968-69; tchr. Webster Groves (Mo.) H.S., 1970—; instr. Webster Coll., Webster Groves, 1973-82, U. Mo., 1980—, St. Louis U., 1978—, Washington U., St. Louis, 1984-87; sec. Mo. Art Edn., State of Mo., 1986-87; mem. Tchrs. Acad. 1990-92. Author, illustrator: Arpens and Acres, 1976, Packets on Parade, 1980; illustrator: St. Louis Silhouettes, 1977; editor: (videos) 12 Water Color Lessons, 1987, Techniques of American Watercolor, 1990, The Santa Fe Trail Series, 1993, Over Gauguin's Shoulder, 1994, Aboriginal Art Techniques, 1994, City of Century Homes, 1995, Australian Dreamings, 1996. Bd. govs. Webster Groves Hist. Soc., 1965-72, 94—; mem. St. Louis Philharm. Soc., 1956-72; commr. City of Webster Groves, 1995—. Named Tchr. of Yr., 1987. Mem. So. Watercolor Soc. (sec. 1978-80), St. Louis Woman Artists, St. Louis Artist Guild (sec. 1985-86, pres. 1989-92, Disting. Woman 1987, v.p. pres.'s coun. 1995—), Monday Club (chmn. 1979-83).

BRADLEY, SISTER MYRA JAMES, health science facility executive; b. Cin., Feb. 1, 1924; d. John Joseph and Mary (McMannus) B. BS in Edn., Atheneum Ohio, 1950; BS in Nursing, Mt. St. Joseph Hosp., 1954; MHA, St. Louis U., 1959; LHD (hon.), Coll. Mt. St. Joseph, Cin., 1993; HHD (hon.), Xavier U., 1993. RN, Ohio. Mem. faculty U. Dayton, Ohio, 1955-57, Good Samaritan Hosp., Dayton, 1955-57; asst. adminstr. St. Mary-Corwin Hosp., Pueblo, Colo., 1960; adminstr. St. Joseph Hosp., Mt. Clemens, Mich., 1960-65; pres., chief exec. officer Penrose Hosp., Colorado Springs, Colo., 1965-90, Penrose-St. Francis Cath. Healthcare, Colorado Springs, Colo., 1987-91; pres., CEO Good Samaritan Hosp., Cin., 1991—. Recipient Bus. Citizen of Yr. award Colo. Springs C. of C., 1990, Disting. Svc. award U. Colo., 1983, Civic Princeps award Regis Coll., Colorado Springs, 1984, Elizabeth Ann Seton nursing award for excellence dept. nursing Penrose Hosp. and Penrose Community Hosp., 1987, Sword of Hope Am. Cancer Soc., 1988; named woman of Distinction Soroptimist Internat., 1988. Mem. Cath. Hosp. Assn., Am. Hosp. Assn., Colo. Hosp. Assn. (trustee), Nat. Coun. Community Hosps. (trustee), Am. Coll. Hosp. Adminstrs., Healthcare Forum (trustee), Downtown Rotary Club. Office: Good Samaritan Hosp 375 Dixmyth Ave Cincinnati OH 45220-2475

BRADLEY, PATRICIA ELLEN, professional golfer; b. Arlington, Mass., Mar. 24, 1951; d. Richard Joseph and Kathleen Maureen (O'Brien) B. Assoc. in Phys. Edn, Miami-Dade North Jr. Coll., 1971; B.S., Fla. Internat. U., 1974. Mem. Sun-Star Japan-U.S. Team Matches, 1975-76, All-Am. Collegiate Team, 1971, U.S.A. Com., 1974, 76, Golf Mag.'s All Am. Team, 1976, 77-78, 79-81; qualified for Colgate Triple Crown Tournament, 1975, 76, 77, 78; staff mem. Dunlop Golf Co.; under contract with Nabisco. Winner N.H. Womens Amateur Championship, 1967, 69, Fla. Collegiate Championship, 1970, Mass. Womens Amateur Championship, 1972, New Eng. Amateur Championship, 1972, 73, Colgate Far East Tournament, 1975, Girl Talk Classic Tournament, 1976, Bankers Trust Classic Tournament, 1977, Lady Keystone Open, Hoosier Classic, Rail Charity Classic, 1978, 91, J.C. Penny Classic, 1978, 89, Balt. Classic, Peter Jackson Classic, 1980, U.S. Womens Open, 1981, Du Maurier Classic, 1985, LPGA Pro-Am, 1985, Rochester Invitational, 1985, Turquoise Classic, 1990, Centel Classic, 1991, Safeco Classic, 1991, MBS Classic, 1991, HEALTHSOUTH Inaugural, 1995; recipient Most Improved Player award Golf Digest, 1976; named Player of Yr., 1986, Mazda Series, 1986, Vare Trophy, 1986; named to Ladies Profl. Golf Hall of Fame, 1991. Mem. Ladies Profl. Golf Assn. Roman Catholic. *

BRADLEY, PAULA E., state legislator; b. New Haven, Conn., Oct. 11, 1924; m. William L. Bradley; children: James R., Dwight C., Paul W. BA, Hiram Coll., 1945; postgrad., Middlebury Coll., 1946, Hartford Seminary, 1963-64. Ret. rsch. assoc. univ. devel. Yale U.; mem. N.H. Ho. of Reps., mem. resources, recreation and devel. com. Coos County del.-at-large N.H. State Dem. Com., 1992—; treas. Randolph Dem. Party, 1992—; bd. dirs. Coos County Family Health Svcs., Berlin, N.H., 1993—, Weeks Meml. Hosp., Lancaster, N.H., 1993-95; mem. Gorham (N.H.) Congregational Ch. Mem. AAUW (Androscoggin br. 1990—), Randolph Mountain Club (bd. dirs. 1986-91, 92—, treas. 1989-91, pres. 1995—). Office: RR 1 Box 1060 Randolph NH 03570

BRADLEY, SANDRA LYNN, nursing administrator; b. Lubbock, Tex., Oct. 16, 1959; m. Clayton Allen Bradley, Feb. 11, 1994; children: Chelsea, Stephanie, Chance, Rachael. Cert. vocat. nursing, Frank Phillips Coll., 1980; BSN, Tex. Tech U., 1995. RN, Tex.; lic. vocat. nurse, Tex. Nurse aide Dumas (Tex.) Meml. Home, 1978-79, lic. vocat. nurse, 1980-81; lic. vocat. nurse K.W. Pieratt, M.D., Dumas, 1981-82; LPN Pawnee (Okla.) Mcpl. Hosp., 1982-84; LPN, child birth educator Dr. James P. Riemer, Pawnee, 1984-88; lic. vocat. nurse (med.-surg.) Meth. Hosp., Lubbock, 1988-91, lic. vocat. nurse (cardiac telemetry), 1991-94; RN supr. home health divsn. South Plains Cmty. Action Assn., 1995; program dir./coord. Alternative Home Health Svcs., Lubbock, Tex., 1995—. Mem. AACN (West Tex. chpt.), Nat. League Nursing, Nurse Ambs.

BRADLEY, WANDA LOUISE, librarian; b. Havre de Grace, Md., June 6, 1953; d. William Smith and Josephine Viola (Miller) B. BA, U. Md., 1975; MSLS, Atlanta U., 1976; postgrad., Cath. U.; MPA (scholar), U. Balt., 1986. Libr. Harford County Pub. Libr., Bel Air, Md., 1976, Harford County Bd. Edn., Bel Air, Md., 1977-81, Nat. Grad. U., Arlington, Va., 1982, Md. State Dept. Edn., Balt., 1982-83, U.S. Dept. Labor, Washington, 1984, Balt. Gas and Electric Co., 1984-85, Morgan State U., Balt., 1985, Coppin State Coll., Balt., 1985-86, Montgomery County Pub. Sch. System, Rockville, Md., 1985-86, Community Coll., Balt., 1987-88; grant adminstr. Howard County Pub. Libr., 1988; libr., media specialist Balt. City Pub. Sch. System, 1992—; acad. advisor George Mason U., Fairfax, Va., 1981-82. Dept. Edn. fellow, 1983-84; U. Balt. Merit scholar, 1984, Atlanta U. scholar, 1976, U. Md. scholar, 1971; Howard County Pub. Libr. grantee, 1988. Mem. ALA, ASIS, Md. Libr. Assn., Spl. Librs. Assn., Med. Libr. Assn. Methodist. Office: Balt City Pub Sch Sys Greenspring Mid Sch Greenspring Ave Baltimore MD 21231

BRADLEY-BENNETT, KATHARINE PHILLIPS, recycling services administrator; b. Boulder, Colo., Dec. 13, 1948; d. Stephen Joseph and Anne (Hurlburt) Bradley; m. Stuart Andrew Bennett; children: Cody James, Patrick Daniel. BA in Music, Colo. Coll., 1971. Supervising tech. Music Print, Boulder, Colo., 1974-76; customer svc. rep. Paragon, Inc., Westerly, R.I., 1978-80; caretaker, program dir. Kimball Wildlife Refuge, Charlestown, R.I., 1978-81; program mgr. Eco-Cycle, Inc., Longmont, Colo., 1984—; Mem. Longmont (Colo.) Solid Waste Task Force, 1992-94. Co-editor, contbr.: (newsletter) Eco-Cycle Times, 1984—; mem. Ever' Little Thing band, Longmont, Colo., 1986—. Mem. Boulder County (Colo.) Parks/Open Space Advisory Com., 1985-87, Drug Free Schs. adv. com., Longmont, Colo., 1990—, steering com. The Teacher's Pantry, Longmont, Colo., 1994—. Mem. Nat. Audubon Soc., NOW, Foothills Audubon Bird Club (bird count leader areas 10, 11). Democrat. Home: 1527 Emery St Longmont CO 80501

BRADLEY-RIVAS, ANDREA DENISE, elementary education educator; b. El Paso, Tex., June 26, 1960; d. Raymond Joseph and Erika (Paul) Bradley; m. Hector Richard Rivas, July 8, 1989. BE, U. El Paso, 1982; MEd, Lesley Coll., 1990. Tchr. Vista Hills Sch., El Paso, Tex., 1982-92, Presa Elem. Sch., El Paso, 1993—. Named Tex. Sci. Tchr. Tex. Sci. Tchrs. Assn., 1990. Roman Catholic. Office: Presa Elem Sch 128 Presa Pl El Paso TX 79907

BRADMAN, BARBARA, small business owner; b. N.Y.C.; d. Emil Otto and Winifred Lois (Canavor) B. LittB in Russian Lit. (hon.), U. of London, 1973; BA, Franklin Pierce Coll., 1974. Tour guide Conway Hunt Travel Agy., London, 1972-73; dancer Acad. of Music, Phila., 1975-85; film critic Certified Reports, Kind, N.Y., 1988-1991, Hollywood, Calif., 1988-1991; owner Animal Fare, Inc., Bklyn., 1991—; mgmt cons. Trenton (N.J.) State Coll., 1976-78. Office: Animal Fare, Inc. 153 Prospect Pk SW Brooklyn NY 11218

BRADSHAW, DOVE, artist; b. N.Y.C., Sept. 24, 1949; d. David Nelson and Jean Katherine (Cormack) B. BFA, Boston Mus. Sch. Fine Arts, 1973. Artistic advisor The Merce Cunningham Dance Co., N.Y.C., 1984—. Exhibited in pub. collections including Met. Mus. Art, N.Y.C., Mus. Modern Art, N.Y.C., Bklyn. Mus. Art, Whitney Mus. Am. Art, N.Y., Art Inst. Chgo., Phila. Mus. Art, Le Pompidou Ctr., Paris, The Getty Ctr., L.A., Mus. of Contemporary Art, L.A., Pier Ctr., Orkney, Scotland, Internat. Mus. Art, Balboa, Spain, Kunst Mus., Dusseldorf, Germany, Moderna Mus., Stockholm; artist marble sculptures and paintings; prodr., dir., artist: (film) Indeterminacy, 1995; prodr.: (postcard) Metropolitan Mus., 1992; artist, prodr. handmade books. Recipient Pollock/Krasner award, 1985; grant Nat. Endowment of Arts, 1975. Mem. Sandra Gering Gallery, Stalke Galerie (Copenhagen).

BRADSHAW, LILLIAN MOORE, retired library director; b. Hagerstown, Md., Jan. 10, 1915; d. Harry M. and Mabel E. (Kretzer) Moore; m. William Theodore Bradshaw, May 19, 1946. BA, Western Md. Coll., 1937, DLitt (hon.), 1987; BLS, Drexel U., 1938, LittD (hon.), 1978; LHD (hon.), So. Meth. U., 1990—. Asst. adult circulation dept. Utica (N.Y.) Pub. Libr., 1938-41, asst. head, 1941-43; adult libr. Enoch Pratt Free Libr., Balt., 1943-44; asst. coord. work with young adults Enoch Pratt Free Libr., 1944-46; br. libr. Dallas Pub. Libr., 1946-47, readers adviser, 1947-52, head dept. circulation, 1952- 55, coord. work with adults, 1955-58, asst. dir., 1958-62, dir., 1962-84; asst. mgr. City of Dallas, 1984-85; Med. bd. publs. So. Meth. U., 1970-78; mem. curriculm com. Leadership Dallas, 1978-79, mem. adv. com. 1978-82, mem. Tex. Gov.'s Commn. on Status of Women, 1970-72, Tex. Com. for Humanities, 1980-84, Nat. Reading Coun., Washington, 1970-73; pres. Tex. Humanities Allliance, 1986-88, bd. dirs., 1988-92; mem. Urban Design Adv. Coun., Dallas, 1987-92; conferee, asst. task force leader Goals for Dallas, 1966-69, vice chmn. achievement com. for. continuing edn., 1971, chmn., 1972, chmn. citizen info. and participation com., 1976-77, trustee, 1977-78, sec. 1977, treas., 1979-83, exec. com., 1977-84; hon. chair Literacy Vols. Am., Dallas, 1987-90; mem. Com. to Plan the Future Goals for Dallas, 1973-74; mem. Dallas County Hist. Found., 1987-93, treas. 1990-93; mem. adv. bd. Tex. Libr. Syss. Act., 1974-77; del. White House Conf. on Libr. and Info. Svcs.; mem. ad hoc com. for planning and monitoring White House Conf. follow-up activities, 1980; bd. dirs. Hoblitzelle Found., 1971—, U. Med. Ctr., 1987-87, Friends of Fair Pk., 1989—; trustee Lamplighter Sch., 1974-81, Friends of Dallas Pub. Libr., 1984—, pres., 1994-96, Dallas Ballet, 1986-88, Dallas Arbotetum and Bot. Garden, 1986-88, Employees' Retirement Fund, City of Dallas, 1989-91, mcpl. adv. bd. Dallas Pub. Libr., 1991-93. Mem. bd. publs. So. Meth. U., 1970-78; mem. curriculum com. Leadership Dallas, 1978-79, mem. adv. com., 1978-82; mem. Tex. Gov.'s Commn. on Status of Women, 1970-72, Tex. Com. for Humanities, 1980-84, Nat. Reading Coun., Washington, 1970-73; pres. Tex. Humanities Alliance, 1986-88, bd. dirs., 1988-92; mem. Urban Design Adv. Coun., Dallas, 1987-92; conferee, asst. task force leader Goals for Dallas, 1966-69, vice chmn. achievement com. for continuing edn., 1971, chmn., 1972, chmn. citizen info. and participation com., 1976-77, trustee, 1977-78, sec., 1977, treas., 1979-83, exec. com., 1977-84; hon. chair Literacy Vols. Am., Dallas, 1987-90; mem. Com. to Plan the Future Goals for Dallas, 1973-74; mem. Dallas County Hist. Found., 1987-93, treas., 1990-93; mem. adv. bd. Tex. Library Systems Act, 1974-77; del. White House Conf. on Library and Info. Services; mem. ad hoc com. for planning and monitoring White House Conf. follow-up activities, 1980; bd. dirs. Hoblitzelle Found., 1971—, Univ. Med. Ctr., 1984-87, Friends of Fair Pk., 1989—; trustee Lamplighter Sch., 1974-81, Friends of Dallas Pub. Library, 1984—, pres., 1994—, Dallas Ballet, 1986-88, Dallas Arboretum and Bot. Garden, 1986-88, Employees' Retirement Fund, City of Dallas, 1989-91, mcpl. adv. bd. Dallas Pub. Libr., 1991-93. Named Tex. Libr. of Year, 1961; recipient Disting. Alumnus award Drexel U. Libr. Sch., 1970; Titche's Arete award for epitome of excellence in chosen field, 1970; Public Adminstr. of Yr. award, 1981; Excellence in Community Svc. award Dallas Hist. Soc., 1981; citation of honor Dallas chpt. AIA, 1982; Lillian Moore Bradshaw chair in libr. and info. studies established in her honor Tex. Woman's U. Mem. ALA (v.p. adult svcs. div. 1966-67, pres. adult svcs. div. 1967, 68, coun. 1968-69, pres. 1970-71, endowment trustee 1984-88, Honor Roll, Freedom to Read Found. 1993), Tex. Libr. Assn. (pres. 1964-65, chmn. pub. librs. div. 1955-56, chmn. awards com. 1973-74, 79-80, Disting. Svc. award 1975), Tex. Soc. Architects (hon. 1992), Dallas Hist. Soc. (trustee 1984-87), Zonta (pres. Dallas I 1976-77, Svc. award 1981, Dallas Humanitarian award 1991). Home: 6318 E Lovers Ln Dallas TX 75214-2016

BRADSHAW, LINDA JEAN, English language educator; b. Beth Page, N.Y., Nov. 15, 1961; d. Howard Richard and Amy Elaine (Jennings) Corry and Jacque Dolores (Wheat) (stepmother) Corry; m. David Scott Waychoff, May 18, 1985 (div. Apr. 4, 1991); 1 child, Skyler Nicole Waychoff; m. Walter Claburn Bradshaw, Dec. 13, 1991; 1 child, Richard Claburn Bradshaw; 1 stepson, Benjamin Robert Bradshaw. BS in Elem. Edn., S.W. Tex. State U., 1984, MA in English, 1989. Cert. elem. tchr. and secondary tchr., Tex., Ohio. Learning lab. specialist S.W. Tex. State U., San Marcos, 1984-89; tchr. Judson Ind. Sch. Dist., San Antonio, 1990; project dir. The Psychol. Corp., San Antonio, 1990-91, lang. arts cons., writer, 1991-96; instr. English, lectr. II Sinclair C.C., Dayton, Ohio, 1991-96; dir. reading, lang. arts, soc. sci. product devel. Riverside Pub., Chgo., 1996; spkr. in field, 1983—. Acting mng. editor: (jour.) Family Relations: Journal of Applied Family and Child Studies, 1993-94. Instr. New Braunfels (Tex.) Ind. Sch. Dist. Cmty. Edn., 1986-88. Recipient Future Tchr. scholarship, 1980. Mem. ASTD (motivational spkr. 1993), Nat. Coun. Tchrs. English, Coun. of Coll. Tchrs. of English, Internat. Reading Assn.

BRADSHAW, OTABEL, secondary school educator; b. Magnolia, Ark., Oct. 27, 1922; d. Grover Cleveland and Mae (Staggs) Peterson; AA, Magnolia A&M Coll., 1950; BS in Edn., So. State Coll., 1953; MS in Edn., Henderson State U., 1975; postgrad. U. Ark.; PhD, Kensington U., 1983; m. Charles Howard Bradshaw, Aug. 14, 1948; children: Susan Charla, Michael Howard. Tchr., English and drama Walkers Creek Schs., Taylor Ark., 1945-46, primary grades Locust Baypere Schs., Camden, Ark., 1946-52, 2d grade Fairview Sch., Camden, 1962-73; tchr. 1st grade Harmony Grove Sch., Camden, 1973-83, coordinator Title IX, gifted children and handicapped; tchr. East Camden Accelerated Sch., 1983—; cons. econ. edn. workshop U. Ark., Fayetteville. Life mem., sec., historian chmn. bicentennial com. PTA; active vol. fund-raising drives Am. Cancer Soc., Birth Defects Soc.; leader Missionary Soc., Camden 1st United Methodist Ch.; mem. Camden and Ouachita County Library bd., 1974-77; active Boys Club Aux. Recipient Disting. Alumni Award So. Ark. U., 1981, Valley Forge Tchr. medal and George Washington Honor medal Freedom Found., 1973; Achievement citation Kazanian Found., 1969, citation for ednl. leadership Pres. of U.S., 1976, 77; profl. achievement citation Internat. Paper Co. Found., 1981. Mem. Assn. Supervision and Curriculum Devel. (speaker San Francisco conf.), NEA, Ark. Edn. Assn. (speaker 1969), Harmony Grove Edn. Assn. (pres. 1978-79), Nat. Council for Social Studies (mem. sexism com.), Am. Assn. Adminstrs., Alpha Delta Kappa (outstanding mem.). Club: Tate Park Garden (sec.). Home: 3188 Roseman Rd Camden AR 71701

BRADY, ADELAIDE BURKS, public relations agency executive, giftware catalog executive; b. N.Y.C., June 27, 1926; d. Earl Victor and Audrey (Calvert) Burks; B.S., Boston U., 1946; m. James Francis Brady, Jr., June 22, 1946 (div. 1953); 1 son, James Francis. Exec. v.p. Media Enterprises, 1952-55; dir. group relations Save the Children Fedn., N.Y.C., 1955-59; dir. pub. affairs div. Girl Scouts U.S.A., N.Y.C., 1959-69; pres. Communication Internat., Inc., Washington, 1969-73, Burks Brady Communications, N.Y.C., 1972—, Adelaide's Angel Shopper Catalog Inc., Wilton, Conn., 1976— ; exec. v.p. Arts in the Parks Inc., Washington, 1971—; bd. dirs. Lenox Hill Hosp., N.Y.C.; past bd. dirs. Achievement Rewards for Coll. Scientists Found.; pres. Animal Lovers Inc. Mem. Nat. Womens Rep. Club., N.Y.C. Recipient Silver Reel award for film The Children of Now, Save the Children Fedn.; decorated cmndr. Order St. John of Jerusalem (Eng.), 1974. Mem. Nat. Assn. Women Bus. Owners, Public Relations Soc. Am., AAUW, NEA, Am. Women in Radio and TV, Nat. Ednl. Broadcasters Assn., Am. Soc. Profl. and Exec. Women, Women Execs. in Public Relations, N.Y. Press Women, Nat. Fedn. Press Women (state pres.), Women's Econ. Roundtable, Nat. Assn. Profl. Women, Nat. Assn. Female Execs., DAR. Episcopalian. Club: Capitol Hill (Washington), Yacht and Country Club (Fla.), MDW Officers (Wash.). Home: 312 Harvest Commons Westport CT 06880-3954 also: Yacht Country Club 3664 SE Fairway E Stuart FL 34997-6116 Office: 785 Park Ave New York NY 10021-3552

BRADY, CHRISTINE ELLEN, language arts educator; b. Manchester, N.H., Feb. 23, 1943; d. George Lewis and Lucy Eleanor (Broderick) B. BA in English, Manhattanville Coll., 1964; MA in English, U. Pa., 1966; EdD in Curriculum and Instrn., No. Ariz. U., 1987. Cert. tchr., N.Y., Ariz., Mass.; cert. administr., N.Y., Ariz. English instr. Bryn Mawr (Pa.) Coll., 1966-67; lang. arts tchr. Tuba City (Ariz.) H.S., 1978-82; asst. dir. Reading/Learning Ctr., Flagstaff, Ariz., 1982-83; supervisory home living specialist Apache Agy. Dept. Indian Affairs, Whiteriver, Ariz., 1983-85; English and edn. lectr. Cortland (N.Y.) State Coll., 1988-89; asst. dir. Tchr. Ctr. Broome County, Binghamton, N.Y., 1990-91; English instr. Broome Cmty. Coll., Binghamton, N.Y., 1989-91; labor svc. rep. N.Y. State Dept. Labor, Ithaca, 1992-94; title I lang. arts tchr. N.Y. State Divsn. for Youth, Highland, N.Y., 1994—. Mem. ASCD, Nat. Coun. Tchrs. English, Internat. Reading. Assn., Phi Delta Kappa. Address: PO Box 543 Highland NY 12528-0543 Office: NY State Divsn for Youth Highland Residential Ctr N Chodikee Lake Rd Box 970 Highland NY 12528

BRADY, JEAN STEIN, retired librarian; b. Concord, Mass., Nov. 4, 1930; d. Walfred and Mary Selina (Jussila) Stein; m. Maurice Goodrich Klein, Feb. 22, 1957 (div. 1982); 1 child, Audrey Elaine; m. Lawrence Kevin Brady, Oct. 15, 1988. BS, Simmons Coll., 1952; cert. d'Etudes, U. Grenoble, France, 1954; MA, Northwestern U., 1957. Cert. pub. libr., N.Y. Sr. libr. N.Y. Pub. Libr., 1952-53, 57-60; cataloger Columbia U., N.Y.C., 1954-55; reference asst. Northwestern U., Evanston, Ill., 1955-57; cataloger U. W.Va., Morgantown, 1960-61; book reviewer ALA, Chgo., 1961-63; sr. cataloger Cleve. Pub. Libr., 1964-70; sr. catalog libr. Yale U. Libr., New Haven, Conn., 1970-92; cataloger Columbia U., N.Y.C., 1993-95; ret., 1995. Revision asst. Bibliographical Guide to Romance Langs. and Lits., 1956-57; reviewer: Booklist and Subscription Books Bulletin, 1961-63. Mem. ALA, New Eng. Libr. Assn. Democrat. Episcopalian.

BRADY, KIMBERLY ANN, editorial director; b. Omaha, Sept. 22, 1956; d. John Henry and Margaret Florence (Swatek) Robinson; 1 child, Jonathan Charles Brady. Student, Corcoran Sch. Art, Washington, 1974-75, George Mason U., 1974-76, Christopher Newport Coll., Newport News, Va., 1976-79. Editor-in-chief student newspaper Christopher Newport Coll., 1977-79; photojournalist Gloucester-Matthews Gazette-Jour., Gloucester, Va., 1979-80; mng. editor Journal of Analytical Toxicology Preston Publs., Niles, Ill., 1980-81; mng. editor Darkroom Techniques and Creative Camera Preston Publs., 1981-84; art dir., prodn. mgr. Profl. Photographers of Am., Des Plaines, Ill., 1984-86; sr. editor Professional Photographer Profl. Photographers of Am., 1990-91; editor-in-chief PHOTO Electronic Imaging Profl. Photographers of Am., Des Plaines, Atlanta, 1991-94; editorial dir. Atlanta, 1994—; editorial cons., photographer, graphic artist Chgo., 1986-90; instr. Winona Internat. Sch. Profl. Photography, Mt. Prospect, Ill., 1987; judge photography competitions, Chgo., 1981-84, electronic imaging competition, L.A., 1993-95. Exec. dir. Lake Shore Sr. Svc. Ctr., Chgo., 1988-93; vol. Adult Literacy Program, Chgo., 1988; coord. Mayor Harold Washington campaign, Chgo., 1983. Recipient Va. Press Assn. Journalism award, 1979, Christopher Newport Coll. Journalism award, 1977-78. Mem. Profl. Photographers of Am. Office: Profl Photographers of Am 57 Forsyth St NW Ste 1600 Atlanta GA 30303-2206

BRADY, M. JANE, state official; b. Wilmington, Del., Jan. 11, 1951; m. Michael Neal. BA, U. Del., 1973; JD, Villanova U., 1976. Dep. atty. gen. Wilmington and Kent County, 1977-87; chief prosecutor Sussex County, 1987-90; solo law practice, 1990-94; atty. gen. State of Del., Wilmington, 1995—. Office: Office of Atty Gen Carvel State Office Bldg 820 N French St Wilmington DE 19801

BRADY, MARY ISABELLE, special education educator; b. Hornell, N.Y., Oct. 17, 1963; d. Lee Francis and Donna Mae (Preston) Van Skiver; m. Steven Leonard Brady, Aug. 12, 1988; children: Christopher, Steven. ASN, SUNY, Alfred, 1987, BS in Health Sci. and Svcs., 1992; MEd in Spl. Edn., Mansfield (Pa.) U., 1994. Cert. tchr. spl. edn., elem. edn., biology, gen. scis.; RN, N.Y. Sch. nurse Steuben Allegany BOCES, Hornell, 1988-93, spl. edn. tchr., 1993—; prenatal healthcare tchr. Hornell H.S., 1990—, home sch. instr., 1992—; tutor SUNY at Empire State Coll., Alfred, 1994—; early intervention svc. provider N.Y. State Dept. of Health, 1995; 7th grade Life Science tchr. McCracken Middle Sch., Hilton Head. Designer Curriculum for Pregnant Teenagers, 1990. Bd. dirs. Hornell ARea Concern for Youth, 1991—. Mem. ASCD, Sigma Tau Epsilon. Home: 656 Queens Grant Hilton Head Island SC 29928 Office: HE McCracken Mid Sch Hilton Head Island SC 29928

BRADY, MARY SUE, nutrition and dietetics educator; b. Sedalia, Mo., Mar. 29, 1945; d. H. Wesley and K. Virginia (McGaw) Steele; m. Paul L. Brady, Sept. 2, 1967; 1 child, Chad W. BA, Marian Coll., Indpls., 1968; MS, Ind. U., Indpls., 1970, DMSc, 1987. Registered dietitian; cert. specialist in pediatric nutrition. Pediatric dietitian J.W. Riley Hosp. Children, Ind. U. Sch. Medicine, Indpls., 1970-75, acting dir. pediatric nutrition, 1975-78, 80-82, neonatal dietitian, 1978-80, dir. pediatric nutrition, 1982-96; asst. prof. Ind. U. Sch. Medicine, Indpls., 1975-88, assoc. prof., 1988-96, prof. 1996—. Contbr. articles to Jour. of Am. Dietetic Assn., Pediatric Pulmonology, Jour. of Pediatrics. Fellow Am. Dietetic Assn. (mem. jour. bd. 1988-94, Excellence in Practice of Clin. Nutrition award 1991, PNPG Outstanding Mem. of Yr. 1994); mem. Sigma Xi. Office: JW Riley Hosp for Children 702 Barnhill Dr Rm 3747 Indianapolis IN 46202-5200

BRADY, VICKI LEE, dental assistant; b. Ft. Worth, Jan. 9, 1958; d. James Riley and Vera Lorene (Perkins) B. Cert. in Dental Assisting, Tarrant County Jr. Coll., Hurst, Tex., 1977. Cert. dental asst. Nat. Bd. Chairside asst. James R. Moran, DDS, Hurst, 1977-90, Tom McDougal, DDS, Richardson, Tex., 1990-91; free-lance chairside asst. Dallas, 1991-94; chairside asst. William Wyatt Jr., Flower Mound, Tex., 1995-96, C. Fred Pietsch & Jay L. Nutt, DDS, Richardson, 1996—. Patent pending in field. Mem. Tex. Dental Assts. Assn. (bd. dirs. 1988-90), Ft. Worth Dental Assts. Soc. (sec. 1987-88, pres. 1989-90, Dental Asst. of Yr. award 1990)), Dental Assistanting Nat. Bd. Home: Rt 3 Box 169 C Whitesboro TX 76273 Office: C Fred Pietsch & Jay L Nutt DDS 1231 E Beltline # 103 Richardson TX 75081

BRADY, VIOLA CATT, lawyer, psychologist; b. Bremen, Ind., June 28, 1946; d. Clarence Earnald and Mary Jane (MacDonald) Rouch; m. Patrick Brady, Dec. 24, 1976; childrten: Bruce, Colleen, David. BA, Ind. U., 1968; MA, Denver U., 1972, PhD, 1973; JD, Ind. U., 1979. Asst. prof. Lycoming Coll., Williamsport, Pa., 1973-76; atty. Lincoln Nat. Life Ins., Fort Wayne, Ind., 1979-81, Helsell Fetterman Martin Todd Hokansen, Seattle, 1981-84; sr. atty. The Boeing Co., Seattle, 1984—. Contbr. article to profl. jour. cons. Adoption Advocates, Seattle, 1992-94. Rsch. grantee Nat. Inst. Mental Health, 1971-73. Mem. Wash. State Bar Assn., Ind. State Bar Assn.

BRADY-BORLAND, KAREN, reporter; b. Buffalo, Mar. 13, 1940; d. Charles A. and Mary Eileen (Larson) B.; m. Gregg Robinson Borland, Sept. 6, 1969 (div. July 1985); children: Caitlin Luise, Kristin Robinson, Leila Nell. BA in English, Daemen Coll., 1961; MS in Journalism, Columbia U., 1962. Summer reporter Buffalo News, 1961, reporter, 1965-68, columnist, 1968-81; editor Prentice-Hall, Inc., Englewood, N.J., 1962-65; press officer for Rep. Max McCarthy U.S. Ho. Reps., Washington, 1967. Recipient numerous awards Buffalo Newspaper Guild, 1960-79, N.Y. State award for Major Dailies Mag. Writing AP, 1982, numerous community awards. Office: Buffalo News 1 News Plz Buffalo NY 14203-2930

BRADY MCCREERY, KATHRYN MARY, ophthalmologist; b. Ballinasloe, Galway, Ireland, May 20, 1963; came to U.S., 1993; d. Joseph Gerard and Kathleen Elizabeth (Gill) Brady; m. Charles John McCreery, Dec. 28, 1989; children: Kate, Alexandra. MB Bch BAO, Royal Coll. Surgeons in Ireland, 1986. Intern in medicine and surgery Beaumont Hosp., Dublin, Ireland, 1986-87, resident in internal medicine, 1987-89; resident in ophthalmology Royal Victoria Eye & Ear Hosp., Dublin, 1989-93; fellow in pediat. ophthalmology Children's Hosp., Pitts., 1993-94, attending physician, 1994-95; clin. instr. Eye & Ear Inst., U. Pitts. Contbr. articles to profl. jours. Fellow Royal Coll. Surgeons in Ireland, Royal Coll. Ophthalmologists; mem. Am. Acad. Ophthalmology, Royal Coll. Physicians in Ireland, Irish Ophthalmology Soc. Roman Catholic.

BRAHAM, DELPHINE DORIS, government accountant; b. L'Anse, Mich., Mar. 16, 1946; d. Richard Andrew and Viola Mary (Niemi) Aho; m. John Emerson Braham, Sept. 23, 1967 (div. Dec. 1987); children: Tammy, Debra, John Jr. BS summa cum laude, Drury Coll., 1983; M in Mgmt., Webster U., St. Louis, 1986. Bookkeeper, Community Mental Health Ctr., Marquette, Mich., 1966-68; credit clk. Remington Rand, Marietta, Ohio, 1971-72; acctg. technician St. Joseph's Hosp., Parkersburg, W.Va., 1972-74; material mgr. U.S. Army, Ft. Leonard Wood, Mo., 1982-86, accountant, 1986-92; acct. Dept. Defense Indpls., 1992—; instr., adj. faculty Columbia Coll., 1987-92, Park Coll., 1988-92. Leader Girls Scouts U.S.A., Williamstown, W.Va., 1972-74, Hanau, Germany, 1977-79. Mem. AAUW (treas. Waynesville br. 1986-90), NAFE, Assn. Govt. Accts., Am. Soc. Mil. Comptrs., Waynesville Bus. and Profl. Women's Orgn. Home: PO Box 16234 Indianapolis IN 46216-0234

BRAICO, CARMELLA ELIZABETH LOFRANO, clergy member; b. Chgo., Oct. 15, 1947; d. Anthony Alexander and Margarita A. (Cracco) Lofrano; 1 child, Kamie Lynn Plys. Student, Thornton Cmty. Coll., 1979-79; BA, Elmhurst Coll., 1983; MDiv, Eden Theol. Sem., 1987. Ordained to ministry, United Ch. of Christ. Preacher Trinity United Ch. of Christ, Fayetteville, Ill., 1984; chaplain Good Samaritan Home for the Aged, St. Louis, 1983-84; youth minister Evangelical United Ch. of Christ, St. Louis, 1984-85; student minister Kirkwood (Mo.) United Ch. of Christ, 1985-87, Faith Presbyn. Ch., DesPeres, Mo., 1985-87; solo pastor First Congl. United Ch. of Christ, LaSalle, Ill., 1987-93, early ret., 1993; former pres. Clergy Coun. Ill. Valley. Contbr. poems to Dark Side of the Moon, 1994 (Editor's Choice award 1994), Best Poems of 1995 (Editor's Choice award 1995), Best Poems of 1996 (Editor's Choice award 1996). Former clergy coord. Hospice, St. Margaret's Hosp., Spring Valley, Ill.; past bd. dirs. Justice & Peace Network Ill.; former mem. missioner-in-residence com. No. Assn. United Ch. of Christ; mem. the church and higher edn. com. Elmhurst (Ill.) Coll.; founding mem., bd. dirs. SHARE Program, LaSalle County, Ill., The Excellence Found. LaSalle Sch. Dist.; bd. dirs. Cmty. Concert Series Ill. Valley; founder St. Paul Cmty. Players Theatrical Group, Homewood, Ill.; leader, preacher Heritage Manor Nursing Home, Peru, Ill.; leader Jr. Girl Scout Troop, Thornton, Ill.; founding bd. mem., sec. Thornridge Child Devel., Dolton, Ill. Lincoln scholar Elmhurst Coll., 1983. Mem. NAFE, Profl. Assn. Clergy, Internat. Soc. Poets (disting. mem. 1995), Acad. Am. Poets, Ill. Valley Newcomer's Club, LaSalle Federated Women's Club, Ill. Valley Christian Women's Club, The Women's Guild, Triple S Club, Evening Circle. Home: 314 N Water St Thornton IL 60476

BRAILSFORD, JUNE EVELYN, musician, educator; b. Wiergate, Tex., Apr. 11, 1939; d. Lonnie and Jessie (Coleman) Samuel; m. Marvin Delano Brailsford, Dec. 23, 1960; children: Marvin Delano, Keith, Cynthia. BA in Music, Prairie View A & M U., Tex., 1960; MA in Music, Trenton (N.J.) State Coll., 1981; postgrad., Jacksonville State U., summer 1971, Lamar U., Beaumont, Tex., summer 1963, Juilliard Sch., summer 1994. Jr. high music tchr. Lincoln Jr. High Sch., Beaumont, Tex., 1960-61; organist/choir dir. various chs., various locations, 1962-82; dir. adult edn. Morris County Human Resources, Dover, N.J., 1980-82; band and choral dir. Zweibruecken Am. High Sch., Ger., 1982-84; vocal soloist and pianist Am. Women's Activities, Ger., 1986-87; dir. female coir U.S. Army War Coll., 1978-79, U.S. Air Force Skylarks, Sembach, Ger., 1976-77. Hostess/fundraiser Quad City Symphony Guild 75th Ur., Rock Island, 1989, Links, Inc. Beautillion Scholarship, 1989, Installation Vol. Coord. Cons., Ft. Belvoir, Va., 1990-91; minister music First Bapt. Ch., Vienna, Va., 1995; active numerous charitable orgns. Recipient Molly Pitcher award U.S. Army F.A. Officers, 1986, Outstanding Civilian Svc. award Dept. Army, 1990, Disting. Civilian Svc. award Dept. Army, 1992. Mem. AAUW, NAACP (life mem. No. Va. Fairfax County chpt.), Music/Etude Club, Rock Island Arsenal Hist. Soc. (hon. mem.), Quad City Symphony Guild (USO com.). Baptist. Home: 9304 Hallston Ct Fairfax Station VA 22039-3148

BRAINARD, BARBARA, artist; b. Boston, Mar. 21, 1952; d. Snelling Robinson Brainard and Tatiana (Holmsen) Rhinelander; m. R.B. Fairchild, Feb. 14, 1981 (div. Oct. 1989); children: Alexandra, Berry; m. Victor J. Cook, Dec. 30, 1989. BFA, Newcom Coll., 1985; MFA, Tulane U., 1988; BA, U. Coll., 1991. Instr. Tulane U., New Orleans, 1986-89; asst. prof. Loyola U., New Orleans, 1989—; workshop Vanderbilt U., Nashville, 1995, Pensacola Jr. Coll., Fla., 1995. Solo shows include: recent monotypes, 1996, La. Monotypes, R.I., 1995, La., 1994, Paintings, Chgo., 1987, others. Auction donor ACLU, New Orleans, 1995, Art Against Aids, New Orleans, 1989-95, Children's Mus., New Orleans, 1991, La. SPCA, 1991. Recipient Juror's award Alexandria Mus. of Art, La., 1988, Purchase awards Austin Peay State, Clarksville, Tenn., 1991, Bloomsberg U., Pa., 1989, Rutgers U., Camden, N.J., 1988, Arts Coun. of New Orleans. Mem. Newport Hist. Soc., Arts Coun. New Orleans. Home: 35 Newcomb Blvd New Orleans LA 70118

BRAINARD, JAYNE DAWSON (MRS. ERNEST SCOTT BRAINARD), civic worker; b. Amarillo, Tex., Nov. 1; d. Bill Cross and Evelyn (McLane) Dawson; m. Ernest Scott Brainard, Nov. 26, 1950; children: Sydney Jane, Bill Dawson. AB, Oklahoma City U., 1950. Sec.-treas. E.S. Brainard Inc., from 1980, now v.p. pers. and mktg.; v.p. J. Thornton Cattle Co., 1981—. Guardian Camp Fire Assn., 1960-65; vol. N.W. Tex. Hosp. Aux., 1960-63; state chmn. Am. Heritage, DAR, 1963-67, regent chpt., 1966-67, parliamentarian chpt., 1975-79, state historian, state chmn. marshalls, 1967-70, 73-76, mem. state organizing com., 1967-70, nat. vice chmn. marshalls, 1969-79, state rec. sec., 1970-73, editor cookbook, 1972, nat. vice chmn. motion picture com., 1971-73, mem. nat. bd. mgmt., nat. chmn. state regent's dinner, 1980-81, mem. Nat. Officers Club, 1979—, Nat. Chmn.'s Assn., 1981—, mem. Tex. speakers staff, 1972-76, 76-79, Tex. vice-regent, 1976-79, pres. nat. vice-regents club 1977-78, vice chmn. state fin. com., 1976-79, Tex. DAR Gen. Conf. chmn., 1975, 78, state chmn. state regents project, 1973-76, area rep. nat. speakers staff, 1977-80, 82-83, editor Tex. Roster, 1976, mem. state by law com., 1973-76, pres. chpt. regents Club, 1973-74, pres. vice-regents club, 1977-78, Tex. state regent, 1979-82, pres. Tex. DAR State Officers Club, 1980-81, state parliamentarian, 1982-85; state bylaws chmn., 1991—; organizing pres. Children Am. Revolution, 1963-65, state chmn. mag. sustaining fund; organizing regent Daus. Am. Colonies, 1972, chmn., 1974-76; bd. dirs. Tamassee DAR Sch., Kate Duncan Smith Sch.; pub. relations Amarillo Little Theater, 1965-69, pres., 1968-69, dir., 1966-69; bd. mem., program com. chmn. Amarillo Camp Fire Council, 1965-67, 75—, vice chmn. council, 1976—, pres., 1977-78; chmn. Camp Fire Leaders Assn., 1964-65, bd. dirs., 1974-79, pres. Amarillo council, 1977-78; br. pres. AAUW, 1963-65, pub. relations, 1965-67, world affairs rep., 1965-67; sec.-treas. group League Dem. Women, 1964; pres. Panhandle Geol. Soc. Aux., 1959, Starlighters Dance Club, 1963-64; pres. Speaking of Living Study Club, 1962-63, sec., 1973-74, parliamentarian, 1976-77, pres., 1977-78; pres. Rep. Woman's Club, 1968, 73, v.p., 1972; steering com. Nat. Libr. Week, 1966, 67, 68, Amarillo Chischom Trail Centennial, 1967; vol. St. Anthony's Hosp. Aux., parliamentarian, 1991-92, bylaws chmn., 1991—, pres. 1993, 94, 2nd v.p., 1995; mem. Revitalize Amarillo Com., 1972, Amarillo Heart Bd., 1972-73, Historic Markers Task Force; mem. St. Anthony's Hosp. Found. Bd., 1995-96. Recipient Martha Washington award and medal of appreciation SAR. Mem. Internat. Platform Assn., U.D.C. (rep. to Amarillo Geneal. Adv. Bd. 1973-74, 75-76, 76-77, pres. Amarillo Geneal. Adv. Bd. 1982-84), Nat. Assn. Parliamentarians (profl., registered parliamentarian, chmn. dist. 6, conf. 1990, pres. Hazel Crowley unit 1980-81, unit v.p. 1986-87, Palo Duro unit, 1988—, Yearbook 1987-88, Parlimentarian of Yr. award 1987, 90, pres. 1990-91), Tex. State Assn. Parliamentarians (rec. sec. 1988-89, 2d v.p. 1989-90, 1st v.p. 1990-92, state chmn. edn. 1989-90, chmn. ext. 1990-92, chmn. long range planning com. 1990-91, state pres. 1991-92, nominating chmn. 1994-95, parliamentarian 1995-96), United Daus. 1812 (organizing regent, state chmn. 1984-86), Daus. Colonial Wars, Nat. Soc. So. Dames (nat. protocol chmn. 1984-85), Godparents Club (sec.-treas. 1991-92), Lone Star Ballet (bd. dirs. 1989—, parliamentarian 1989-91, sec. 1991-92, pres.-elect 1993, chmn. devel. commn. 1993—, pres. 1994—), Bravo! Amarillo Opera (bd. dirs. 1991—, parliamentarian, 1991-94, corr. sec. 1993-95, recording sec. 1995-96), Ladies Golf Assn. (partnership chmn. 1994-95), Amarillo Country Club (reporter 1988-89, 96, treas. 1990-91, v.p. 1992, pres. 1993, parliamentarian 1993, 94), Jr. Travel Study Club (pres. 1991-92, parliamentarian 1996—). Mem. Christian Ch. (bd. parliament 1965-66). Home: 2119 S Lipscomb St Amarillo TX 79109-2236 Office: PO Box 1101 Amarillo TX 79105-1101

BRAININ, CONSTANCE SPEARS, psychotherapist, educator, social worker, counselor; b. Princeton, N.J., Feb. 21, 1932; d. Alexander Joseph and Anna (Stuttman) Spears; m. Norman Herbert Brainin, May 29, 1955; children: Kenneth, Risa, Alissa. BA, Northeastern Ill. U., 1975, MA, 1979; PhD, Southeastern U., 1981. Lic. social worker, Ill.; cert. clin. mental health counselor; lic. clin. profl. counselor, Ill. Supr. counseling staff Park Med. Ctr., Chgo., 1980-83; pvt. practice psychotherapist Chgo., 1982—; mem. adj. faculty Oakton C.C., Des Plaines, Ill., 1982—, Northeastern Ill. U., 1984-88; mem. governing bd. Theatre 219, Skokie, Ill., 1984-88; v.p. Edgebrook/Sauganash chpt. Am. Cancer Soc., 1988-93; lectr. Edgebrook C. of C., Chgo., 1985, Am. Cancer Soc., Chgo., 1984. Workshop leader Hope Ctr., Long Grove, Ill., 1984. Mem. APA, ACA, Am. Orthopsychiat. Assn., Assn. for Humanistic Psychology, Nat. Acad. Cert. Clin. Mental Health Counselors, Ill. Psychol. Assn., Inst. for Logotherapy.

BRAISTED, MADELINE CHARLOTTE, financial planner; b. Jamaica, N.Y., Nov. 23, 1936; d. Melvin Vincent and Charlotte Marie (Klos) B. AAS, Nassau C.C., 1968; BA, Hofstra U., 1973, MA, 1975, grad. Command and General Staff Coll., 1985, Coll. for Fin. Planning, 1991. CFP. Enlisted, U.S. Marine Corps., Cherry Point, N.C., 1954-57; reservations agt. Airline Industry, N.Y.C., 1957-64; reservations controller Auto Lease Industry, N.Y.C., 1964-66; nuclear medicine technician Queens Gen. Hosp., Jamaica, N.Y., 1969-70; lab. mgr. CUNY, 1970-80; commd. capt. U.S. Army Res., 1977-80, advanced through grades to major, 1984; cons. Energy Etcetera, Flushing, N.Y., 1979-85; capt. U.S. Army Res., Fort Totten, N.Y., 1975-80; USA Health Profl. Support Agy., Office Surgeon Gen. Washington, 1980-92. Author, pub. Energy Etcetera catalog, 1981-85; artist On Shore painting (hon. mention 1974). Merit badge counselor Boy Scouts Am., Queens County, N.Y., 1980-83; active mem. PTA, Jamaica, 1980-84. Decorated Legion of Merit, Army Commendation medal with one oak leaf, Army Achievement medal with one oak leaf cluster; named Community Leader and Noteworthy Am., Hist. Preservation of Am., 1976. Mem. NAFE, APHA, Am. Acad. Med. Adminstrs., Internat. Assn. Fin. Planners, Assn. Mil. Surgeons of U.S., Res. Officers Assn., Soc. Nuclear Medicine. Roman Catholic. Avocations: painting; sculpture. Office: 1983 Marcus Ave Ste 260 New Hyde Park NY 11042-1016

BRAITERMAN, THEA GILDA, economics educator, state legislator; b. Balt., Sept. 11, 1927; d. Isaac E. and Clara (Fink) Bloom; m. Marvin Braiterman, Mar. 21, 1948; children: Kenneth, Marta, David. BS, Johns Hopkins U., 1949; MA, U. Md., 1966; PhD, Union Inst., 1977. Assoc. prof. econs. Balt. Coll. of Commerce, 1966-73; prof. econs. New England Coll., Henniker, N.H., 1973—; mem. N.H. Ho. of Reps., 1988-94; cons. on retirement, 1988—. Author: Workbook on Economic Theory, 1966; contbr. articles to profl. jours. Sec., bd. govs. United Way of Merrimack County, Concord, N.H., 1984-90; v.p., bd. govs. Cmty. Svcs. Coun., Concord, 1980-84. Jane Addams Peace Assn. grantee, 1976-77; Gilmore grantee New Eng. Coll., 1988-90. Mem. Am. Econ. Assn., Ea. Econ. Assn. Home: PO Box 686 Henniker NH 03242-0686 Office: New England Coll Henniker NH 03242

BRAKAS, NORA JACHYM, education educator; b. Schenectady, N.Y., Aug. 9, 1952; d. Thaddeus Michael and Theresa Mary (Patnode) J. BS in Elem. Edn., Plattsburg State U. Coll., 1974; MS in Reading, SUNY, Albany, 1977, Cert. Advanced Study in Reading, 1986, PhD in Reading, 1990. Cert. elem. sch. tchr., reading tchr. Elem. sch. and reading tchr. Lee (Mass.) Ctrl. Sch., 1976-82; rsch. asst., tchg. asst. SUNY, Albany, 1985-88; reading specialist Guilderland (N.Y.) Sch. Dist., 1988-89; instr. reading dept. SUNY, Albany, 1989-90; asst. prof. tchr. edn., reading specialist Southeastern La. U., Hammond, 1990-91, Marist Coll., Poughkeepsie, N.Y., 1991—; presenter, spkr. in field. Contbr. articles to profl. jours. Student Literacy Corp. grantee U.S. Dept. Edn., 1991, IBM/Marist Joint Study Project grantee, 1992. Mem. Internat. Reading Assn., Soc. Children's Book Writers and Illustrators. Home: PO Box 176 Rhinecliff NY 12574 Office: Marist Coll 341 Dyson Poughkeepsie NY 12601

BRALICH, SUSAN JEAN, underwriting manager; b. Muncy, Pa., Aug. 5, 1947; d. Robert Nathan and Olive Lucille (Eichenlaub) Campbell; m. James Anthony Bralich; children: Ryan, Rodney, Erin. BS in Edn., Lock Haven (Pa.) State Coll., 1969. CPCU, 1995. Tchr. Camp Hill (Pa.) Sch. Dist., 1969-72; leader family recreation Harford County Parks and Recreation Dept., Bel Air, Md., 1975-80; personal lines underwriter Harford Mut. Ins. Co., Bel Air, 1983-85, comml. lines underwriter, 1985-94, mgr. personal lines underwriting, 1994; presch. instr. YWCA, Bel Air, 1978-80; mem. personal lines panel Ins. Svcs. Offices, N.Y.C., 1996—. Mem. Churchville (Md.) Recreation Coun., 1983-92, v.p., 1987-90; treas. Churchville Gymnastics, 1987-90. Mem. Nat. Soc. CPCU's, Md. Soc. CPCU's, Pa. Assn. Mut. Ins. Cos. (underwriting com. 1995—). Lutheran. Home: 2002 Highland Ave Bel Air MD 21015 Office: Harford Mut Ins Co 200 N Main St Bel Air MD 21014

BRAM, ISABELLE MARY RICKEY MCDONOUGH (MRS. JOHN BRAM), civic worker; b. Oskaloosa, Ia., Apr. 4; d. Lindsey Vinton and Heddy (Lundee) Rickey; B.A. in Govt., George Washington U., 1947, postgrad., 1947-49; m. Dayle C. McDonough, Jan. 20, 1949; m. 2d, John G. Bram, Nov. 24, 1980. Dep. tax assessor and collector Aransas Pass Ind. Sch. Dist., 1939-41; sec. to city atty., Aransas Pass, Tex., 1939-41; info. specialist U.S. Dept. State, Washington, 1942-48. Treas. Mo. Fedn. Women's Clubs, Inc., 1964-66, 2d v.p., 1966-68, 1st v.p., 1968-70, pres., 1970-72; bd. dirs. Gen. Fedn. Women's Clubs. Mem. steering com. Citizens Com. for Conservation; mem. exec. com. Missourians for Clean Water. Pres., DeKalb County Women's Democratic Club, 1964. Bd. dirs. DeKalb County Pub. Library, pres., 1966; bd. dirs. Mo. Girls Town Found.; dir. DeKalb County Little Theater Inc. Mem. AAUW, Nat. League Am. Pen Women, DeKalb County Hist. Soc., Internat. Platform Assn., Law Soc. U. Mo., Jefferson Club of U. Mo., Zeta Tau Alpha, Phi Delta Delta, Phi Delta Gamma. Democrat. Episcopalian. Mem. Order Eastern Star. Clubs: Tri Arts, Shakespeare, Wimodausis, Gavel, Ledgers, Jefferson. Editor: Mo. Clubwoman mag. Home: Sloan and Cherry Sts PO Box 156 Maysville MO 64469

BRAMAN, HEATHER RUTH, technical writer, editor, consultant, antiques dealer; b. Wilmington, Ohio, Apr. 27, 1934; d. William Barnett and Violet Ruth (Davis) Hansford; m. Barr Oliver Braman, June 29, 1957 (div.); children: Sean Robert, Heather Paige. BA, Hiram Coll., 1956; postgrad., Sinclair Community Coll., Dayton, Ohio, 1977-85, Wright State U., Dayton, 1986. Pers. clk. USAF, Wright-Patterson AFB, Ohio, 1956, specifications editor, 1956-57, publs. editor, writer, 1957-63; vol. Children's Med. Ctr., 1963-67, Dayton Pubs. Schs., 1969-87; tchr. Gloria Dei Montessori Sch., Dayton, 1973-77; asst. mgr., acctg. mgr., mgr. tennis club USAF, Wright-Patterson AFB, Ohio, 1977-81; tech. writer Miclin, Inc., Alpha, Ohio, 1982, Indsl. Design Concepts, Dayton, 1982-83; tech. writer, cons. Belcan Corp., Cin., 1984—; owner Chimney Sweep Antiques Shoppe, Arcanum, Ohio, 1991—; real estate investor. Founder, bd. dirs. Trotwood (Ohio) Women's Open Tennis Tournament, 1976-81; mem. Harrison Twp. Parks Bd., 1980-82; ballpersons coord. Dayton Pro Tennis Classic, 1977-80; pres. Dayton Tennis Commn., 1978-80; mem. parents exec. com. Hiram (Ohio) Coll., 1985—; ct.-appointed Spl. Advocate/Guardian Ad Litem (CASA GAL), 1988—; tutor English as a second lang. citizenship classes, 1991—. Mem. NOW, NAACP, Dayton Pub. Schs. Orgns., Dayton Tennis Umpires Assn., Mothers Against Drunk Drivers., AARP, WWF, HALT, Sigil of Phi Sigma. Democrat. Mem. Soc. Friends. Home: 320 Elm Hill Dr Dayton OH 45415-2943 Office: Belcan Corp 10200 Anderson Way Cincinnati OH 45242-4700

BRAMBLE, PAMELA CHACE LEUBA, artist; b. Ft. Meade, Md., Nov. 29, 1955; d. Edward Russell and Millicent (Chace) Leuba; m. Francis Laurence John Bramble, June 27, 1981. BFA, U. Conn., 1979; MFA, Columbia U., 1986. Dir. Carlson Gallery U. Bridgeport, Conn., 1981-84; adj. faculty Sacred Heart U., Fairfield, Conn., 1987-89; assoc. prof. art U. Conn., Torrington, 1989—; juror various art orgns. throughout the state of Conn., 1990—. Recipient Emerging Artist-Pres.'s Gold medallion Grumbacker Co., N.Y.C., 1986, Rsch./travel grant U. Conn. Rsch. Found., Storrs, 1990. Office: U Conn 855 University Dr Torrington CT 06790

BRAMBLETT, BARBARA DOYLE, city official; b. Coral Gables, Fla., Nov. 27, 1951; d. D. E. and Joy (Baker) Doyle; m. William H. Frei. B.A., Auburn U., 1973. Asst. city mgr. City of Auburn, Ala., 1973-84; city mgr. City of Conyers, Ga., 1984-88; adminstr. City of Hastings, Neb., 1988—. Bd. dirs. Rockdale House, Conyers, 1984-88; bd. dirs. United Way, Auburn, 1979-84, chmn., 1984; bd. dirs. Hastings Symphony Orch.; active Mayor's adv. com. on community devel., Auburn., 1976-82; mem. adv. council pub. adminstr. U. Ga., 1985-88; mem Grad. Leadership Rockdale, 1987. NEH fellow, 1978. Mem. Internat. City Mgmt. Assn. (v.p. 1992-94), Govt. Fin. Officers Assn., Ala. City Mgmt. Assn. (pres. 1980-81), Neb. City Mgmt. Assn. (pres. 1991-92), AAWU (v.p. 1984), Hastings Bus. and Profl. Women (pres. 1991-92). Democrat. Methodist. Club: Pilot, Hastings Rotary. Home: 1411 Heritage Dr Hastings NE 68901-2852 Office: City of Hastings 220 N Hastings Ave Hastings NE 68901-5144

BRAME, GLORIA GLICKSTEIN, writer; b. N.Y.C., N.Y., Aug. 20, 1955; d. Norman and Lola (Sheinman) Glickstein; m. William D. Brame, 1989. Diplôme de langue, Alliance Francaise, Paris, 1976; BA in English with honors, CUNY, Jamaica, 1977; MA in English, Columbia U., 1978. Instl. sales coord. Drexel Burnham Lambert, N.Y.C., 1979-82; rsch. assoc. Oppenheimer & Co., N.Y.C., 1982-84; fin. analyst Morgan Stanley, N.Y.C., 1984-86; dir. rsch. Recruitment Rsch. Inst., N.Y.C., 1986-87; editl. dir., capital campaign Cooper Union for Sci. and Art, N.Y.C., 1988-89; assoc. prof. creative writing New Coll. at Hofstra, Hempstead, N.Y., 1988-91; adj. prof. NYU, 1989-91, CUNY, 1989-91; pvt. practice N.Y.C. and Atlanta, 1986—. Author: (poetry) Daedalus Anthology of Verse, 1996; author: (with others) Different Loving, 1993; adv. editor ELF: Eclectic Literary Forum lit. mag., 1991—, Boulevard lit. mag., 1988-91; contbr. articles to popular mags. Recipient Tennessee Williams Poetry scholarship, Univ. of the South Sewanee (Tenn.) Writers' Conf., 1991. Home and Office: PO Box 18552 Atlanta GA 31126

BRAME, MARILLYN A., hypnotherapist; b. Indpls., Sept. 17, 1928; d. David Schwalb and Hilda (Riley) Curtin; 1 child, Gary Mansour. Student, Meinzinger Art Sch., Detroit, 1946-47, U. N.Mex., 1963, Orlando (Fla.) Jr. Coll., 1964-65, El Camino Coll., Torrance, Calif., 1974-75; PhD in Hypnotherapy, Am. Inst. Hypnotherapy, 1989. Cert. and registered hypnotherapist. Color cons. Pitts. Plate Glass Co., Albuquerque, 1951-52; owner Signs by Marillyn, Albuquerque, 1952-53; design draftsman Sandia Corp., Albuquerque, 1953-56; designer The Martin Co., Orlando, 1957-65; pres. The Arts, Winter Park, Fla., 1964-66; supr. tech. publs. Gen. Instrument Corp., Hawthorne, Calif., 1967-76; pres. Camart Design, Westminster, Calif., 1977-86, Visual Arts, El Toro, Calif., 1978—; mgr. tech. publs. Archive Corp., Costa Mesa, Calif., 1986-90; adj. instr. Orange Coast Coll., Costa Mesa, 1985-90; hypnotherapist, Lake Forest, 1986—; bd. dirs. Orange County chpt. Am. Bd. Hypnotherapy. Author: Lemon and Lime Scented Herbs, 1994, (textbook) Folkdancing is for Everybody, 1974, Innovative Imagery, 1996; inventor, designer dance notation sys. MS Method. Mem. bd. govs. Lake Forest II Showboaters Theater Group, 1985-88, 90-95. Mem. Soc. Tech. Communication (v.p. programs, 1987, newsletter editor 1986-87, newsletter prodn. editor 1985-86).

BRAME, PATTI THOMAS, middle school educator; b. Winston-Salem, N.C., Aug. 18, 1946; d. Raymond Gray and Annie Ruth (Fulk) Thomas; m. John Milam Brame, Aug. 17, 1968; children: Michael Thomas, Jonathan Neal, David Scott. BA, Guilford Coll., Greensboro, N.C., 1968; MEd, U. N.C., Greensboro, 1970. Cert. mid. sch. tchr. comm. skills, math., social studies, N.C. Tchr. Operation Head Start, Walnut Cove, N.C., summer 1968, Prince William County, Dale City, Va., 1968-69, Onslow County, Sneads Ferry, N.C., spring 1969, Morongo Dist., Yucca Valley, Calif., 1970-71, Chesterfield County, Richmond, Va., 1971-73; tchr. Surry County, Dobson, N.C., 1982—, mem. sch. improvement team, 1994—, chmn. sch. improvement team, 1995—; faculty advisor Battle of Books, Dobson, 1991—; participant N.C. Tchg. Acad., 1994-95. Author: Teacher Ideas, 1986, 1990; contbr. Instr. mag., 1989, 90. Ch. trustee Dobson United Meth. Ch., 1990—, chmn. Coun. on Ministry, 1988, mem. ch. choir, 1974—. Named Tchr. of Yr., Dobson Elem. Sch., 1986-87. Mem. NEA, N.C. Edn. Assn. Home: 130 Ashley Dr Dobson NC 27017-8401 Office: Central Mid Sch PO Box 768 Dobson NC 27017

BRAMHALL, CATHERINE E., researcher; b. Morristown, N.J., Feb. 9, 1971; d. Jacques III and Toni Marie (Travaglia) B. BA magna cum laude, Princeton U., 1992. Mgr. N.Y. rsch. Russell Reynolds Assocs., N.Y.C., 1992—. Office: Russell Reynolds Assocs 200 Park Ave New York NY 10166

BRAMLETT, SHIRLEY MARIE WILHELM, interior decorator, artist; b. Scottsboro, Ala., June 14, 1945; d. Robert David and Alta (Reeves) Wilhelm; m. Paul Kent Bramlett, June 5, 1966; children: Paul Kent II (dec.), Robert Preston. BS, David Lipscomb U., 1966; postgrad., U. Miss., 1966-68; pvt. study art, 1976—. Decorator The Anchorage House, Oxford, Miss., 1966-67, Interiors by Shirley, Tupelo, Miss., 1971-80; tchr. Oxford City Schs., 1967-69; decorator, buyer Donald Furniture, Tupelo, 1969-71; owner, importer Bramblewood Interiors & Antiques, Belden, Miss., 1976-80; owner, decorator, artist The Cottage on Caldwell, Inc., Nashville, 1980—. Represented in art galleries Gallery Fine Art, Destin, Fla., Lyzon Gallery, Nashville, Magic Memories, Franklin, Tenn., elegant Creations Gallery, Brentwood, Tenn.; introduced and presented House of Parliament, Luxembourg; commd. for watercolor print fortnightly Musicale of Miss., 1991-92; European representation by Internet Internat. Bd. dirs. Found. for Christian Edn., 1988—, Ea. European Missions, Vienna, Austria, 1986— (commd. for watercolor print used in internat. fundraising); del. Miss. Dem. caucus, 1970; fundraiser Agape Artist, 1991. Named Woman of Decade, David Lipscomb Coll., 1986, one of Outstanding Young Women of Am., 1979; selected Centennial Artist, David Lipscomb U., Nashville, 1991, one of ten Master Tenn. Artists, Lyzon Gallery, Nashville, 1991. Mem. Nat. Mus. Women in Arts, Tenn. Watercolor Soc., Nat. Soc. Tole and Decorative Painters, Green Hills Garden Club (cover artist for nat. conv. garden clubs 1985), Assoc. Ladies Lipscomb (bd. dirs. 1991-92). Mem. Ch. of Christ. Home: 930 Caldwell Ln Nashville TN 37204-4016

BRAMMER, BARBARA ALLISON, secondary school educator, consultant; b. Pitts., Sept. 3, 1942; d. Harry Harlan Allison and Valedina J. (Kouloumbrides) Vorkapic; m. Wetsel Jerry Brammer, Jan. 14, 1968; 1 child, Jeffrey Scott. AA, Valencia Community Coll., 1975; BS in Limnology, Fla. Tech. U., 1977; Ms in Adminstrn. and Supervision, Nova U., 1982, postgrad., 1990—. Tchr. Maynard Evans High Sch., Orlando, Fla., 1977-87; facilitator Valencia Community Coll., Orlando, 1987; tchr. Miami Killian Sr. High Sch., 1987-88, Dade County Sci. Zoo Magnet, Miami, Fla., 1988-89; facilitator Miami Dade Community coll., 1989; tchr. Homestead (Fla.) Sr. High Sch., 1989—; cons. documentary Pub. TV, Orlando, 1982. Author: Marine Science, 1980. Bd. dirs. Butler Chain Conservation Assn., Windermere, Fla., 1983-84. Cpl. USMC, 1960-62. Mem. NSTA, Nat. Marine Educators Assn., United Tchrs. Dade, Fla. Assn. Sci. Tchrs., Fla. Marine Educators Assn. (treas. membership chmn. 1986-88, bd. dirs. 1988-91, Outstanding Marine Sci. Educator award 1995-96), NOAA Tchr. in the Sea Soc., Beta Sigma Phi. Republican. Home: 15022 SW 74th Pl Miami FL 33158-2139 Office: Homestead Sr High Sch 2351 SE 12th Ave Homestead FL 33034-3511

BRAMMER, BARBARA RHUDENE, retired secondary education educator; b. Dawson, Tex., Aug. 20, 1936; d. William Alpheus and Eunice (Priddy) Hargis; m. Jerry Lane Brammer, Apr. 15, 1960; children: Cathy DeLane Brammer Francis, David Wayne Brammer, Karen Ann Brammer Shelfer. BS in Secondary Edn., U. North Tex., 1958. Cert. math tchr., Tex. Tchr., coach N.W. Ind. Sch. Dist., Justin, Tex., 1957-62; tchr. math. N.W. High Sch., Justin, Tex., 1970-93, dept. head, 1984-93; tchr., coach Decatur (Tex.) Ind. Sch. Dist., 1966-68; substitute tchr. math. dept. N.W. High Sch., Justin, Tex., 1993—; coach Acad. Decathlon Team, World Book Ency., 1986-90; advisor Merrill Pub. Co., 1989-91. Recipient Tchr. award Tandy Computers & Tex. Christian U., 1989; named one of 36 Outstanding Alumnus, Sch. Edn. U. North Tex., 1990; coach of State Champion Acad. Decathlon team, 1988. Mem. NEA, Tex. State Tchrs. Assn. (life), Tex. Ret. Tchrs. Assn., Tex. Math. Tchrs., Rhome Womens Club (pres. 1981-82). Mem. Ch. of Christ. Home: RR 1 Box 130 Rhome TX 76078-9725

BRAMWELL, MARVEL LYNNETTE, nurse, social worker; b. Durango, Colo., Aug. 13, 1947; d. Floyd Lewis and Virginia Jenny (Amyx) B. Diploma in lic. practical nursing, Durango Sch. Practical Nursing, 1968; AD in Nursing, Mt. Hood Community Coll., 1972; BS in Nursing, BS in Gen. Studies cum laude, So. Oreg. State Coll., 1980; cert. edn. grad. sch. social work, U. Utah, 1987, cert. counselor alcohol, drug abuse, 1988, MSW, 1992; M in Social Work, 1992. RN, Utah, Oreg., Ind.; cert. social worker, Utah, Ind.; cert. clin. social worker, Ind. Staff nurse Monument Valley (Utah) Seventh Day Adventist Mission Hosp., 1973-74, La Plata Community Hosp., 1974-75; health coordinator Tri County Head Start Program, 1974-75; nurse therapist, team leader Portland Adventist Med. Ctr., 1975-78; staff nurse Indian Health Service Hosp., 1980-81; coordinator village health services North Slope Borough Health and Social Service Agy., 1981-83; nurse, supr. aides Bonneville Health Care Agy., 1984-85; staff nurse Latter Day Saints Adolescent Psychiat. Unit, 1985-86; coordinator adolescent nursing CPC Olympus View Hosp., 1986-87, 91; charge and staff nurse adult psychiatry U. Utah, 1987-88; nurse MSW Community Nursing Svc., Salt Lake City, 1989-90; with Community Nursing Svc. and Hosp., Clearfield, Utah, 1993-94; med. social worker Meth. Home Health, Indpls., 1994—; assisted with design and constrn. 6 high tech. health clinics in Ala. Arctic, 1982-83; psychiat. nurse specialist Community Nursing Svc. Contbr. articles to profl. jours. Active Mothers Against Drunk Driving, Program U. Alaska Rural Edn., 1981-83. Recipient Cert. Appreciation Barrow (Alaska) Lion's Club, 1983, U.S. Census Bur., Colo., 1970. Mem. NOW, Nat. Assn. Social Workers, Assn. Women Sci. Home: 925 N Alabama St Indianapolis IN 46202-3318

BRANCH, BRENDA SUE, library director; b. Buffalo, Apr. 27, 1947. BS in Edn., SUNY, Cortland, 1969; MLS, SUNY, Buffalo, 1972, postgrad., 1972; postgrad., S.W. Tex. State U., 1973-74, Stephen F. Austin State U., 1975-76; MPA, S.W. Tex. State U., 1985. Tchr. Kenmore Ind. Sch. Dist., 1969-70; asst. health scis. libr. SUNY, Buffalo, 1971-73; br. mgr. Austin Pub. Libr., 1973-75; acquisitions libr. Tex. Ea. U., 1975; humanities libr. Stephen F. Austin State U., 1975-76; dist. libr. coord. Longview Ind. Sch. Dist., 1976-77; program devel. coord. Austin Pub. Libr., 1977-80, supr. br. svcs., 1980-86, assoc. dir. pub. svcs., 1986-91, dir., 1991—; project mgr. reduction-in-force project City of Austin, 1988, co-chair customer svc. task force, coord. creativity program, 1990; mem. long range planning com. svcs. spl. populations Tex. State Libr., 1992. Active Travis County Continuing Edn. Adv. Bd., Austin, 1981—, Tex. Mcpl. League, Mayor's Coalition Workplace Literacy, 1990—, Literacy and Fundamental Edn. Speaker's Bur., 1991—, Leadership Austin, 1991—, chair kids program, 1993; tutor, trainer Travis County Adult Literacy Coun., 1986-89; chair City of Austin Workplace Literacy Task Force, 1989—; mem. speaker's bur. United Way, 1990—; mem. MPA adv. coun. S.W. Tex. State U., 1993—; bd. dirs. Big Bros./Big

Sisters, 1986-90, chair pub. rels. com., 1986-90, fundraiser, 1986-90, com. co-chair, 1986-90. Recipient Outstanding Achievement for Govt. Svc. award YWCA, 1991. Mem. ALA, Tex. Libr. Assn. (treas. dist. V 1976-77, mem. continuing edn. com. 1978-79, mem. membership com. 1986-89, mem. ann. conf. placement ctr. 1989—, mem. literacy com. 1990—, chair 1990-93, mem. resource sharing com. 1990—, mem. ad hoc property com. 1992, mem. minority recruitment com. 1992-93, co-chair legis. day 1992-93, chair-elect pub. libr. divsn. 1994-95, chair 1995—), Austin Soc. Pub. Adminstrn. (chair membership com. 1984-89, newsletter editor 1984-89), Toastmasters (v.p., pres., newsletter editor). Office: Austin Public Library PO Box 2287 800 Guadalupe St Austin TX 78768-2287

BRANCH, KIMBERLEY THOMAS, government official; b. Washington, Feb. 5, 1962; d. Irving Patrick and Sylvia Anne (Wilkinson) Thomas; m. Stephen Douglas Branch, May 26, 1986 (div. Oct. 1993); children: Johnathan Stephen, Kirsten Michelle. BSBA, Greensboro Coll., 1986; postgrad., Webster U., St. Louis, 1991—. Office asst. Shope, McNeil & Maddox, PA, Greensboro, N.C., 1984-85; clk.-typist Def. Investigative Agy., Alexandria, Va., 1986; adminstrv. asst. Nat. Coun. for U.S.-China Trade, Washington, 1986-87; contracts adminstr. Louis Berger Internat., Inc., Washington, 1987-91; contract specialist GSA, Washington, 1991-93; contracting officer FAA, Washington, 1993—; mem. women's exec. leadership program USDA Grad. Sch., Washington, 1995-96. Home: 7986 Copperfield Way Manassas VA 22110 Office: FAA 800 Independence Ave SW Washington DC 20591

BRAND, ALICE GLARDEN, English languge and literature educator; b. N.Y.C., Sept. 8, 1938; d. Alfred and Claire (Rindner) Glarden; m. Ira Brand, Apr. 10, 1960; children: Kerry, Janice Kaylor, Jonathan. Student, U. Rochester, 1956-58; BA cum laude, CCNY, 1960; EdM, Rutgers U., 1973, EdD, 1979. English and creative writing tchr. N.Y. and N.J. Pub. Schs., 1960-78; writing instr. Rutgers U., 1978-80, Somerset County Coll., Rider Coll., 1978-80; asst. prof. U. Mo., St. Louis, 1980-86; dir. comm. programs and program dir. Gateway Writing Project, 1980-87; assoc. prof. English, 1987; assoc. prof. English, dir. writing Clarion U. of Pa., 1987-89; assoc. prof. SUNY, Brockport, 1989-91, dir. of composition, 1989-92, prof. English, 1989-91, dir. composition, 1989-92, prof. English, 1992—; vis. scholar U. Calif., Berkeley, 1982-83. Author: Therapy in Writing: A Psycho-Educational Enterprise, 1980, (poetry) As it Happens, 1983, Studies on Zone, 1989, The Psychology of Writing: The Affective Experience, 1989; editor Assembly for Expanded Perspectives on Learning's jour., Presence of Mind: Writing and the Domain Beyond the Cognitive, 1994; reviewer for pubs. including Prentice Hall, Houghton Mifflin, Harper & Row, Simon & Schuster, and Macmillan; reader Jour. of Advanced Composition; many editl. and adv. bds. for textbooks, anthologies, and composition jours.; contbr. poems, articles and short stories to profl. publs. Dir. cmty. writing programs N.J. State Teen Arts Festival and Highland Park and East Brunswick Poet in the Schs., 1977-80. Home: 217 Brittany Ln Pittsford NY 15434 Office: SUNY Dept English Brockport NY 14420*

BRANDENBURG, LOIS SUE, educator; b. Bklyn., June 8, 1938; d. Bernard Robert and Audrey Esther (Cohen) Goldfinger; m. Harvey F. Brandenburg, Apr. 10, 1969; 1 child, Douglas Scott. EdB, U. Miami, 1960. Tchr. Dade County Elem. Sch., Miami, Fla., 1960-61, North Merrick (N.Y.) Elem. Schs., 1961-71; substitute tchr. Uniondale (N.Y.) Schs., 1977-83; substitute tchr. East Brunswick (N.J.) Schs., 1983-85, aide to retarded, 1985-88; tchr. Middlesex County Edn. Svcs. Com., Piscataway, N.J., 1988—; tchr. parent effectiveness tng. YMCA, Freeport, N.Y., 1975-78. Com. woman Dem. ORgn., Forest Hills, N.Y., 1965-69; pres. N.F. of Ileitis & Colitis, Nassau County, N.Y., 1975-82; v.p. North Merrick Tchrs. Assn., 1969-71; treas. Middlesex County Edn. Svcs. Com. Assn., 1996—. Mem. NOW, NEA, N.J. Edn. Assn., B'Nai B'rith, Hadassah, City of Hope (life)., Am. Med. Ctr. (life). Home: 10 Tall Oaks Dr East Brunswick NJ 08816

BRANDES, MARIE ELIZABETH HESS, medical disability specialist; b. Duluth, Minn., Jan. 29, 1954; d. Albert Guenther and Gisela (Oppens) Hess; m. Robert Lee Brandes, July 17, 1988. BS, Duquesne U., 1976; MS, Ohio U., 1983. Cert. trainer total quality mgmt., Fla. Music therapy intern Polk (Pa.) Gen. Hosp., 1977; activities coord. Highland Park Ctr., Pitts., 1977-78; recreation therapist State of N.Y., Thiells, 1978-79; vol. svc. coord. State of Fla., Orlando, 1982-84; human svcs. counselor State of Fla., Winter Park, 1984-86; specialist med. disability State of Fla., Orlando, 1986—; writer and photographer various publs., 1982—. Contbr. articles to profl. jours. Mem. Nat. Assn. for Music Therapy (registered music therapist 1978), Hadassah (corr. sec. 1995-96, program chairperson 1994-95). Jewish. Office: Disability Determinations 3438 Lawton Rd Ste 127 Orlando FL 32803

BRANDES-BOWEN, ILA ANN, entrepreneur; b. Charlotte, Apr. 3, 1954; d. Roddy Arthur and Marguerite (Johnson) Brandes; m. Timothy Ray Bowen, July 1, 1984; children: Timothy Brandes, Nathaniel Brandes. B.A., U. N.C., Greensboro, 1977. Asst. supr. quality control Ball Corp., Asheville, N.C., 1977-79, indsl. engr., Muncie, Ind., 1979-80, methods and standards engr., 1980-82, materials handling engr., 1982-85, customer service engr., 1983-85; cons. Porsche Market Group, Rockaway, N.J., 1985-86; owner, pres. IAM, Asheville, N.C., 1985-87; owner PIP, Statesville, N.C., 1986—, TAOF, Inc., Statesville, 1989—; addressed 1984 Internat. Exposition Food Processors (speech pub.). Counselor Young Life, Greensboro, 1972-77, Jr. Achievement, Muncie, 1979-81; bd. dirs. Muncie Symphony Membership Dr., 1981, Corp. Challenge, Muncie, 1981-83, United Way Fund Dr., Muncie, 1982-83, Downtown Statesville Devel Corp., 1988-91, officer, 1989-91, Fox Creek Farms, Inc., Troutdale, Va., 1989—. Republican. Presbyterian.

BRANDON, JUDITH MAUREEN, artist; b. Indpls., Mar. 3, 1963; d. John McCrary and Joan Mac (Rochefort) B. BFA, Cleve. Inst. Art, 1987. Artist, model, designer, painter Judith M. Brandon Self Help Found., Cleve., 1978—; cons. Sideline Design, Cleve., 1992—, Serpico Film Works, Cleve., 1994—. Author short stories. Bd. dirs., investigator Tremont Fairfield Ave. Planning Com., Tremont and Cleve., Ohio, 1995; vol. benefit set Spaces Art Gallery, Cleve., 1987—; mem. Nat. Dem. Com., 1990—, Nat. Rep. Com., 1990—. Recipient 3d pl. award Chagrin Valley Art Ctr., 1995, Could of Been a Primadonna award Specialty Painters of Cleve., 1995. Mem. Nat. Mus. Women in Arts, Nat. Humane Soc., So. Poverty Law Ctr., Cleve. Ctr. for Contemporary Art. Home: 2164 W 11th St Cleveland OH 44113-3604

BRANDON, KATHRYN ELIZABETH BECK, pediatrician; b. Salt Lake City, Sept. 10, 1916; d. Clarence M. and Hazel A. (Cutler) Beck; MD, U. Chgo., 1941; BA, U. Utah, 1937; MPH, U. Calif., Berkeley, 1957; children: John William, Kathleen Brandon McEnulty, Karen (dec.). Intern, Grace Hosp., Detroit, 1941-42; resident Children's Hosp. Med. Center No. Calif., Oakland, 1953-55, Children's Hosp., L.A., 1951-53; pvt. practice, La Crescentia, Calif., 1946-51, Salt Lake City, 1960-65, 86—; med. dir. Salt Lake City public schs., 1957-60; dir. Ogden City-Weber County (Utah) Health Dept., 1965-67; pediatrician Fitzsimmons Army Hosp., 1967-68; coll. health physician U. Colo., Boulder, 1968-71; student health physician U. Utah, Salt Lake City, 1971-81; occupational health physician Hill AFB, Utah, 1981-85; child health physician Salt Lake City-County Health Dept., 1971-82; cons. in field; clin. asst. U. Utah Coll. Medicine, Salt Lake City, 1958-64; clin. asst. pediatrics U. Colo. Coll. Medicine, Denver, 1958-72; active staff emeritus Primary Children's Hosp., LDS Hosp., and Cottonwood Hosp., 1960-67. Diplomate Am. Bd. Pediatrics. Fellow Am. Pediatric Acad., Am. Pub. Health Assn., Am. Sch. Health Assn.; mem. Utah Coll. Health Assn. (pres. 1978-80), Pacific Coast Coll. Health Assn., AMA, Utah Med. Assn., Salt Lake County Med. Soc., Utah Public Health Assn. (sec.-treas. 1960-66), Intermountain Pediatric Soc. Home and Office: PO Box 58482 Salt Lake City UT 84158-0482

BRANDT, BARBARA BERRYMAN, cultural organization administrator; b. Buffalo, Sept. 10, 1935; d. C. Edward and Helen Catherine (O'Connell) Berryman; m. Roger W. Se; children: Deborah Brandt Guckes, Roger William Jr., Edward Carl. AAS, Erie C.C., 1955; cert., SUNY, 1971. Asst. curator Theodore Roosevelt Inaugural Nat. Hist. Site, Buffalo, N.Y., 1972-74, curator, 1974-81, supt., 1981—, exec. dir., 1993—. mem. adv. bd. Buffalo Gen. Hosp. Coun., 1993—; bd. dirs. Eden Town Preservation bd., 1991—; exec. bd. mem. Jr. League Buffalo, 1968—; mem. Women for Downtown, Buffalo, 1992; com. mem. Arch. History Conv. Visitors Bur., Buffalo, 1993; mem. Ronal M. Donald House Centennial Com. Mem. Nat. Soc. Fund Raising Execs. (bd. dirs. 1990-96), Theodore Roosevelt Assn. (exec. com., trustee 1989—, v.p. 1995—), Landmark Soc., Assn. Vol. Adminstrn. (co-chmn. tours nat. conv. 1986), Women for Downtown, N.E. Mus. Conf., Assn. Interior Designers (hon.), Medaille Coll. Arts (adv. bd. 1986-88), Gyrettes Internat. (pres. Buffalo chpt. 1993), Red Jacket Ski Club (sec. 1969-84), Task Force Frank Lloyd Wright-Darwin Martin Restoration. Office: Theodore Roosevelt Inaugural Nat Hist Site 641 Delaware Ave Buffalo NY 14202-1001

BRANDT, GRACE BORGENICHT, art dealer; b. N.Y.C., Jan. 25, 1915; d. Samuel Lazarus and Jeanette (Salny) Lubell; m. J. Borgenicht, Jan. 20, 1938; children: Jan Schwartz, Berta Kerr, Lois Borgenicht; m. Warren Brandt, Dec. 27, 1960. MA, Columbia U., 1937. Dir., owner Grace Borgenicht Gallery, Inc., N.Y.C., 1951-95; adviser Tupperware Art Found. Scholarship, Bus. Meets the ArtYoung Pres.'s Orgn. One-woman shows include Laurel Gallery, N.Y.C., 1947, 48, 50, Philbrooks Mus., Tulsa, 1948, Everhart Mus., Scranton, Pa., 1948; exhibited in group shows at Nat. Assn. Women Artists, 1948, 49, L'Association Nationale des Femmes Artistes Americaines, 1949, Internat. Watercolor Exhbn., 1949, 53, 55, 59, Contemporary Am. Painting, 1951, N.Y. Soc. Women Artists, 1953, Whitney Mus. ann. exhbn., 1954, Aquarelles Contemporaines aux Etats-Unis, France, 1954, Martha Jackson Gallery, N.Y.C., 1955; represented in permanent collections Philbrook Mus., Everhart Mus. Mem. Nat. Assn. Women Artists (first prize watercolor 1949), Art Dealers Assn. Am., N.Y. Soc. Women Artists, N.Y.C. Artists Club.

BRANDT, IRENE HILDEGARD, secondary education educator; b. Meriden, Conn., June 6, 1942; d. Walter M. and Hildegard E. Brandt. BS, Ctrl. Conn. State U., 1964, cert. 6th yr. degree, 1989, MS, 1969, postgrad., 1989. Cert. 7-12 math. tchr., K-12 adminstrn. and supervision, intermediate supervision, Conn. Tchr. math. Jefferson Jr. H.S., Meriden, 1964-67, Platt H.S., Meriden, 1967—. Active Summit Club, Meriden, 1972—. Yearbook dedicated to her Platt H.S., 1971, named Oustanding Tchr. by Srs., 1990, 91, 92, 96. Mem. ASCD, Nat. Coun. Tchrs. Math., New Eng. Math. Tchrs. Assn., Assn. Tchrs. Math. in Conn. (conv. presider 1990-96), Am. Fedn. Tchrs., Conn. Fedn. Tchrs., Meriden Fedn. Tchrs. (sec. 1982-90). Home: 70 Genest St Meriden CT 06450-4538

BRANDT, KATHY A., public relations and events management executive, secondary school educator; b. Chgo., June 12, 1942; d. Leo J. and Helen J. (Briskin) Weisel; m. John M. Brandt, Nov. 28, 1967; children: Debra, Lee. BA, U. Iowa, 1963; MA, Fairfield U., 1975. Cert. secondary sch. tchr. Tchr. Golden Valley Jr. H.S., San Bernardino, Calif., 1963-64, Lake Forest (Ill.) H.S., 1964-68, Stamford (Conn.) H.S., 1968-72; pres. Brandt Assocs., Inc., Westport, Conn., 1984—. Vol. tchr., aide, mem. curriculum com. Westport Schs., 1976-83; editor newsletter Kings Hwy. Sch. PTA, Westport, 1984; mem. parent's com. Pine Manor Coll., Chestnut Hill, Mass., 1994—. Mem. LWV, N.Am. Ski Journalists Assn. Home and Office: Brandt Assocs Inc 29 Washington Ave Westport CT 06880-2549

BRANIGAN, HELEN MARIE, educational administrator; b. Albany, N.Y., Sept. 24, 1944; d. James J. and Helen (Weaver) B. BS in Bus. Edn., Coll. St. Rose, Albany, 1967, MA in English, 1972; postgrad., SUNY, Albany, 1973-81. Tchr., chair dept. bus. edn. S. Colonie Sch. Dist., Albany, 1968-81; assoc. Bur. Bus. Edn. N.Y. State Edn. Dept., Albany, 1981-87; assoc. Bur. Occupational Edn. Program Devel., Albany, 1987-91, Bur. Occupational Edn. Innovation and Quality, Albany, 1991-93, Cen./So. Regional Field Svcs., Albany, 1993-95, North Country/Regional Field Svcs., 1995—; mem. adv. coun. SUNY, Cobbleskill, 1985-94; bd. trustees St. Catherine's Found., 1993—; sr. cons. Internat. Cr. for Leadership in Edn., Schenectady, N.Y., 1991—. Editor McGraw-Hill Book Co., Glencoe Pub., 1986—; contbr. articles to profl. jours. Lay vol. Archdiocese of Anchorage, 1967-68; mem. N.Y. State Staff Devel. Coun. Mem. ASCD, Am. Vocat. Assn., Bus. Tchrs. Assn. N.Y. State, Delta Pi Epsilon. Roman Catholic. Home: 540 New Scotland Ave Albany NY 12208-2318 Office: NY State Edn EBA Rm 461 Albany NY 12234

BRANKER, LAURA MICHELE, lobbyist; b. N.Y.C., Nov. 26, 1966; d. Philip and Monica Orwin (Beckles) B. BS in Journalism, Fla. A&M U., 1993. Info. specialist Fla. Dept. Ins. Press Office, Tallahassee, 1991-92; editor Fla. Ho. of Reps. Clerk's Office, Tallahassee, 1992-93; pub. rels. asst. Fla. Commerce Fed. Credit Union, Tallahassee, 1993; legis. asst. Fla. Ho. of Reps., Ft. Lauderdale, 1993-96; legis. liaison Broward Co. Commn. Inter govt. Affairs. Mem. Women in Comm., 1993-96, Women in Comm., First Amendment chair, 1996—, United Lauderhill (Fla.) Homeowners Assn., 1996, Women's Polit. Caucus, Ft. Lauderdale, 1996; bd. mem. City of Lauderhill Arts and Cultural Com., 1996, Ashanti Cultural Arts, Ft. Lauderdale, 1996. Home: PO Box 525 Fort Lauderdale FL 33302 Office: Office of Inter Govtl Affairs Broward Co Commn 115 S Andrews Ave Rm 406 Fort Lauderdale FL 33301

BRANNACK-EPPOLITE, LISA ANN, clinical forensic nurse, intensive care nurse; b. Pontiac, Mich., Mar. 14, 1967; d. Kenneth Ralph and Carol Ann (Scott) Schwark. BSN magna cum laude, No. Mich. U., 1992; postgrad., Clayton Sch. Natural Healing, Birmingham, Ala. RN; critical care RN; cert. emergency nurse; cert. BLS; cert. Pediatric Advanced Life Support; cert. flight RN.; cert. ACLS. ACLS instr. George Washington U., 1993—; emergency and intensive care nurse Md. Profl. Staffing Svcs., Bethesda, 1995—. Vol. Montgomery County Coalition for the Homeless, Gaithersburg, Md., 1995—. Ensign, USNR. No. Mich. U. Academic Achievement scholar, 1988-92, Am. Business Women's scholar, 1989-92, USN Nursing scholar, 1990. Mem. Jr. Mil. Nurse's Orgn. (sec. 1992-93). Lutheran. Home: 20454 Summer Song Ln Germantown MD 20874

BRANNICK, ELLEN MARIE, management consultant; b. Rochester, Minn., Aug. 10, 1934; d. Daniel Ryther and Grace Ellen (Mills) Markham; m. Thomas L. Brannick,. BS in Health, Phys. Edn., MacMurray Coll., 1956, MS, 1959. Elem. phys. edn. Ritenour Consol. Sch. Dist., Overland, Mo., 1958-61; head tchr., summer dir. Civic League Day Nursery, Rochester, 1961-64; recreation therapist Rochester State Hosp., 1964-68; rehab. dir. Rochester State Hosp., 1968-70; rehab. therapist Napa State Hosp., Calif., 1971; indsl. therapy con. Napa State Hosp., 1971-73, community liaison rep., 1973—. Mem. Friends Napa County Library, 1977, Napa County Humane Soc., 1978. Mem. Napa Valley AIDS Project, Napa County Hist. Soc. Democrat. Office: Napa State Hosp 2100 Napa Vallejo Hwy Napa CA 94558-6234

BRANNOCK, REBECCA SUSAN, psychology educator; b. Boonville, Mo., Aug. 23, 1959; d. Glenn W. and Helen J. (Morris) Groves; m. James D. Brannock, Aug. 6, 1983; 1 child, Marlana D. BS, So. Mo. State U., 1980, MS, 1983; Edn. Specialist, Pittsburg (Kans.) State U., 1990; PhD, U. Ark., 1995. Lic. profl. counselor, Ark; cert. secondary sch. counselor, Mo. Home econs. tchr. Humansville (Mo.) H.S., 1980-82, Willow Springs (Mo.) H.S., 1981-83; sch. counselor Van-Far Schs., Vandalia, Mo., 1983-86, Neosho (Mo.) R.S. Schs., 1986-92; acad. counselor U. Ark., Fayetteville, 1992-95; asst. prof. psychology and counseling Pittsburg State U., 1995—. Mem. ACA, ACES, SMSCA (past pres., pres.-elect, pres., treas., career guidance chair, dist. pres. 1991-92), Chi Sigma Iota (chpt. pres. 1993-94). Episcopalian. Home: RR 1 Box 58A Webb City MO 64870 Office: Pittsburg State U Dept Psychology/Counseling Pittsburg KS 66762

BRANNON, TREVA LEE (WOOD), insurance company executive; b. Burleson, Tex., Oct. 6, 1932; d. William Albert and Virginia May (Garner) Wood; m. Lone J. Brannon, Aug. 3, 1951 (dec. Apr. 1989); 1 child, Ralph Eugene. Grad. high sch., Godley, Tex. Acctg. clk. Internat. Svcs. Life Ins. Co., Ft. Worth, 1950-63; sec. John Hancock Life Ins. Co., Ft. Worth, 1963-64; asst. v.p. Olympic Life Ins. Co., Ft. Worth, 1964-70; v.p. Transport Life Ins. Co., Ft. Worth, 1970—. Mem. Soc. Ins. Licensing Adminstrs. Home: 349 Heirloom Dr Fort Worth TX 76134-3950 Office: Transport Life Ins Co 714 Main St Fort Worth TX 76102-5217

BRANNON, WINONA EILEEN, electrical contractor; b. Austell, Ga., Jan. 3, 1948; d. John Milton and Vera Inez (Banks) McDaniel; m. Harold Wallace Smith, May 9, 1966 (div. June 1967); m. Jerry Edward Weddington, Feb. 24, 1968 (div. Feb. 1984); children: Michael Richard, Paula Daniell; m. David Lee Brannon, Dec. 9, 1985; 1 step-child, Kimberly Lorraine. Cert. in data processing, DeKalb Tech., Chamblee, Ga., 1968; cert. in keypunch, Ga. State, 1969; cert. in elec. codes, Cobb Voc. Tech., Marietta, Ga., 1983. Lic. hair stylist, Ga.; lic. elec. contractor, Ga. Hair stylist Casa Di Bella and Modella, Atlanta and Mableton, Ga., 1965-68; sec. and keypunch operator Ga. Sec. of State, Atlanta, 1968-70; data transcriber IRS, Chamblee, Ga., 1969-73, data processor, 1978-79, IDRS operation, 1980-82; sch. bus driver Cobb County Bd. Edn., Marietta, 1974-77; meat packer Cudahy (Bar-s Meats), Atlanta, 1979-80; electrician J&J Electric, Mableton, 1982-85; owner, elec. contractor Watts New Electric, Mableton, 1985—; cons. lighting design, home remodeling, 1995—. Trustee Trinity United Meth. Ch., Austell, 1992—; sponsor South Cobb Athletic Assn. T-Ball Team, 1994—; organizer, sponsor contractor's bowling league, Austell, Ga., 1994-95. Recipient First Pl. Hair Styling award, Mableton, 1965, 66. Mem. Adams Rainbow (worthy advisor 1965), Ea. Star (Assn. matron 1983). Republican. Home and Office: 5923 Ridge Dr Mableton GA 30059-3524

BRANNON-PEPPAS, LISA, chemical engineer, researcher; b. Houston, Sept. 19, 1962; d. James Graham and Patricia Ann (Hightower) Brannon; m. Nicholas A. Peppas, Aug. 10, 1988. BS, Rice U., 1984; MS, Purdue U., 1986, PhD, 1988. Sr. formulations chemist Eli Lilly & Co., Indpls., 1988-91; pres., founder Biogel Tech., Indpls., 1991—. Author, editor: Absorbent Polymer Technology, 1990; mem. editorial bd. Jour. Applied Polymer Sci., 1995—; contbg. editor Polymer News, 1989—; contbr. articles to profl. jours. Vol. Indpls. Mus. Art, 1990—, Humane Soc. Indpls., 1990—, Indpls. Zoo, 1994—. Recipient Harold B. Lamport award Biomed. Engring. Soc., 1989. Mem. AIChE (exec. bd. programming coun., dir. materials divsn., chmn. subcom. biomaterials divsn. 1990-93, dir.-at-large food, pharm. and bioengring. divsn. 1992-94, 2d vice chair materials divsn. 1994-95, 1st vice chair materials divsn. 1995-96), Am. Chem. Soc. (membership com. 1990—), Controlled Release Soc. (treas. 1995—, internat. planning com. 1991, bd. govs. 1992-95), Jr. League Indpls. (bd. dirs. 1992-94). Office: Biogel Tech PO Box 681513 Indianapolis IN 46268-7513

BRANSCOMB, ANNE WELLS, communications consultant; b. Statesboro, Ga., Nov. 22, 1928; d. Guy Herbert and Ruby Mae (Hammond) Wells; m. Lewis McAdory Branscomb, Oct. 13, 1951; children: Harvie Hammond, Katharine Capers. BA, Ga. Coll., 1949, U. N.C., 1949; postgrad., London Sch. Econs., 1950; MA, Harvard U., 1951; JD with honors, George Washington, 1962; LLD, U. Notre Dame, 1995. Bar: D.C. 1962, Colo. 1963, N.Y. 1973, U.S. Supreme Ct. 1972. Rsch. assoc. Pierson, Ball and Dowd, Washington, 1962; law clk. to presiding judge U.S. Dist. Ct., Denver, 1962-63; assoc. Williams & Zook, 1963-66; pvt. practice Boulder, 1966-69; assoc. Arnold and Porter, Washington, 1969-72; communications counsel Teleprompter Corp., N.Y.C., 1973; v.p. Kalba-Bowen Assocs. Inc., communication cons., Cambridge, Mass., 1974-77, chmn. bd., 1977-80, sr. assoc., dir., 1980-82; pres. The Raven Group, Concord, Mass., 1986—; trustee Pacific Telecomm. Coun., 1981-83, 86-93; mem. tech. adv. bd. Dept. Commerce, 1977-81; vis. scholar Yale U. Law, 1981-82; mem. program on info. resources policy Harvard U., 1986—; chmn. program com. Legal Symposium Telecom '87, Internat. Telecomm. Union, 1986-87; adj. prof. internat. law Tufts U., 1987-89; sr. scholar Annenberg Pub. Policy Ctr., Annenberg Sch. Comm., U. Pa., 1994-95. Author: Who Owns Information?, 1994; mem. editl. bd. Info. Soc.; editor: Toward a Law of Global Communications Network; contbg. editor Jour. Comm., 1980-90; contbr. articles to profl. jours. Bd. dirs. Nat. Pub. Radio, 1975-78; vice chmn. Colo. Dem. State Ctrl. Com., 1967-69; del. mem. permanent orgn. com. Dem. Nat. Conv., 1968; trustee, exec. com. Rensselaer Poly. Inst., 1980-89; trustee Telluride Inst., 1994—. Recipient Alumni Achievement award Ga. Coll., 1980, Belva Lockwood award George Washington U., 1995; Rotary Found. fellow, 1950-51; Inaugural fellow FreedomForum Media Studies Ctr., Columbia U., 1985. Mem. ABA (nat. conf. lawyers and scientists ABA/AAAS 1985-91, chmn. communications com. sci. and tech. sect. 1980-82, chmn. communications law div. 1982-84, mem. coun. and tech. sect. 1981-85), Am. Polit. Sci. Assn., Internat. Inst. Communication, Internat Intercommunications Union (legal symposium organizer 1983, chmn. program com. 1987), Soc. Preservation of First Wives and First Husbands (pres.), Order of Coif, Valkyries, Phi Beta Kappa, Alpha Psi Omega, Pi Gamma Mu. Office: Harvard U 200 Aiken 33 Oxford St Cambridge MA 02138-2901

BRANSCUM, CARLA JEANNE, special education educator; b. Sherman, Tex., Apr. 6, 1953; d. Carl Ellis and Bobbie Jeanne (Arnold) Little; m. Larry Marshall Branscum, July 19, 1975; children: Marshall Little, Larra Carljeanne. AA, Ea. Okla. State Jr. Coll., 1973; BS in Edn. in Spl. Edn., East Ctrl. State U., Ada, Okla., 1975, MEd in Learning Disabilities, 1977. Cert. tchr., Okla. Tchr. remedial reading Earlsboro (Okla.) Elem. Sch., 1975-77; tchr. spl. edn. Okemah (Okla.) Jr. H.S., 1977-79, Northwood Elem. Sch., Seminole, Okla., 1987-91; learning disabilities tchr. Bowlegs (Okla.) Elem. Sch., 1979-80; tchr. spl. edn. Bowlegs H.S., 1981-87; tchr. spl. edn., coach Odyssey of Mind, Seminole (Okla.) Mid. Sch., 1991-95; bd. dirs. Seminole County Spl. Edn. Found., 1989-93. Mem. Seminole Arts Coun. Named Tchr. of Yr., Bowlegs Assn. Classroom Tchrs., 1985, Seminole County Tchr. of Yr., Seminole Edn. Assn., 1985. Mem. NEA, AAUW (sec. 1990-92), Learning Disabilities Assn., Okla. Edn. Assn., Jasmine Moran Children's Mus., Beta Sigma Phi. Mem. Ch. of Christ. Home: 2804 William Blvd Seminole OK 74868

BRANSON-BERRY, KAREN MARIE, nurse; b. Phila., Aug. 22, 1956; d. Floyd Ralph and Regina (Marter) Banbury; m. John Joseph Branson III, Oct. 23, 1977 (div. 1991); children: John Joseph IV, Katherine Marie; m. Steven Wayne Berry, July 4, 1992. BSN, San Diego State U., 1991. RN, Calif.; EMT, Japan, BCLS EMT; cert. ACLS provider, BLS instr., Post Anesthesia Care Unit. Unit asst. Cooper Med. Ctr., Camden, N.J., 1975-76; pvt. duty nurse aide Nursing Staff, Annapolis, Md., 1977; ward clerk Community Hosp., Chula Vista, Calif., 1979-80; unit asst. Bay Gen. Hosp. ICA, Chulavista, 1985-86; med. asst. Dr. D. Burrows, ob.-gyn., San Diego, 1988-89; RN Scripps, Chula Vista, 1990; ensign nurse corp. Naval Hosp. Camp Pendleton, Oceanside, Calif., 1990-91, Naval Hosp. Camp. Pendleton, Oceanside, 1991-93; clin. cons. 21 Area Br. Med. Clinic, 1993—, lt. jr. grade, 1993, promoted to lt., 1994; mem. edn. and tng. com. Camp Pendleton, 1991—, mem. ward rm. social com., nurse corp. social com., 1991-92, chmn. social com., 1993-94, nurse corp. strategic task force, 1993-94; troop nurse Adult Girl Scout Troop #5053, 1991—; mem. command infection control com Naval Hosp. Camp Pendleton, 1994; interium clinic supr. 21 Area Br. Med. Clinic, 1994. Interviewer Navy Relief Soc., Pensacola, Fla. 1977-79; pres./sec. Helicopter Sq. 8/HS-10, San Diego, 1979-86; fundraiser Atsugi Wives Club, Japan, 1986-88; vol. ARC, Japan, 1986-88. Lt. USN, 1993-95. Decorated Meritorious Svc. medal USN, Achievement medal, 1995, 96; recipient Cert. Appreciation award Dept. Def. Schs., 1987, ARC, Japan, 1987, Alfred award Navy League U.S. Newport County Coun., 1991; named Jr. Navy Nurse of Yr. Naval Hosp. Camp Pendleton, 1991-92, 93-94. Mem. Am. Acad. Ambulatory Care Nurses (vice chmn. 1995-96), Calif. Nurses Assn., Navy Nurse Corps Social Com, Wardroom Com., Sigma Theta Tau Internat. Republican. Home: 523 Chantel Ct Chula Vista CA 91910-7438 Office: Naval Hosp Camp Pendleton Oceanside CA 92055

BRANT, DONNA MARIE, journalist; b. N.Y.C., Oct. 17, 1955; d. Earl Evans and Catherine Marie (Schatz) B. BA in Philosophy, George Washington U., 1977; MS in Broadcast Journalism, Boston U., 1979. Desk asst. nat. news desk NBC News, N.Y.C., 1979, news and feature asst. presdl. campaign, 1979-80; bur. coord. nat. news bur. NBC News, Pitts., 1980-82; futures editor nat. news desk NBC News, Washington, 1982-83, polit. assignment editor presdl. campaign, 1983-84, assignment editor nat. news desk, 1984-89; West Coast reporter, prodr. Am.'s Most Wanted, Fox Broadcasting Co., Washington, 1989-95, N.Y. reporter, prodr., 1995—. Sr. rschr.: Barter, 1978. Resident assoc. Smithsonian Instn., Washington, 1982. Recipient citation Internat. Assn. Asian Crime Investigators, citation Davis (Calif.) Police Dept., citation Multnomah County (Oreg.) Sheriff's Office, citation Riverside County (Calif.) Sheriff's Office, citation U.S. Marshals Svc. Mem. Washington Hist. Soc., Internat. Platform Assn., Sigma Delta Chi. Office: America's Most Wanted 5151 Wisconsin Ave NW Washington DC 20016-4124

BRANT, MARY JANE, psychotherapist; b. Camden, N.J., Feb. 27, 1947; d. Francis Vincent and Jane Elizabeth Hurley; m. Richard Thomas Brant, Sept. 13, 1969; children: Catherine Marie, Richard Thomas Jr. BA in Psychology,

Rutgers U., 1980; MS in Counseling and Human Rels., Villanova U., 1985. Counselor Help Counseling Ctr., Phoenixville, Pa., 1980-85; clin. coord., sr. psychotherapist Comprehensive Counseling Ctr., Chestnut Hill, Pa., 1985-91; adj. prof. grad sch. addictions program Chestnut Hill (Pa.) Coll., 1988; psychotherapist Pinebrook Ctr., Paoli, Pa., 1991-92, pvt. practice psychotherapist Ridgefield, Conn., 1992—. Paintings exhibited in one-women show at Sacco's Ristorante, Ridgefield, 1995. Mem. Nat. Women's Hall of Fame, 1993. Mem. AAUW (bd. dirs., chair women's issues 1993—), Am. Grop Psychotherapy Assn. (clin.), Carl Jung Found. Office: 148 Nursery Rd Ridgefield CT 06877-3400

BRANT, SANDRA J., magazine publisher. Publisher, Art in America, The Magazine Antiques, Interview. Office: Brant Publs 575 Broadway New York NY 10012

BRANT, SUSAN LANE, librarian; b. Flint, Mich., July 13, 1943; d. Sidney Raymond and Bettina Eleanor (Beebe) McCleary; m. Lawrence R. Heath, July 8, 1967 (div. Dec. 1984); children: Ellison M., Benjamin D.; m. John E. Brant, Aug. 2, 1986. BA in Am. Studies, U. Mich., 1965, MLS, 1966. Libr. circulation dept. Law Sch. Libr. U. Mich., Ann Arbor, 1966-67; libr. Madison (Wis.) Pub. Libr., 1967-69; dir. Law Sch. Criminal Justice Reference and Info. Ctr. U. Wis., Madison, 1969-71; reference libr. Nicolet Area Tech. Coll., Rhinelander, Wis., 1971—. Recipient Wis. Women Leaders in Edn. award AAUW Wis. chpt., 1987. Mem. ALA, NOW, Assn. Coll. and Rsch. Librs., Freedom to Read Found., Nat. Mus. of Women in Arts, Wis. Libr. Assn. (exec. bd. 1983-87, literary awards com. 1993-95, chair 1996-97), Wis. Intellectual Freedom Coalition (founder, pres. 1980-82). Episcopalian. Office: Nicolet Area Tech Coll PO Box 518 Rhinelander WI 54501

BRANTLEY, PENNIE ANN, artist; b. Caruthersville, Mo., Dec. 11, 1950; d. Fred Eugene and Leslie Qujette (Ready) B.; m. Eugene Simon Eventov, May 11, 1992. Attended, Ont. Coll. Art, Toronto, Ont., Can., Kansas City Art Inst., Mo. Women Artists, 1986. Exhbns. include Garret Gallery, 1985, Evansville (Ind.) Mus., 1985, 86, 88, Spiva Art Ctr., Joplin, Mo., 1986, Lotos Club, N.Y.C., 1986, St. Louis Art Mus., 1987, Art St. Louis, 1987, 88, 90, Nelson-Atkins Mus. Art, Kansas City, Mo., 1987, Fontbonne Gallery, St. Louis, 1987, Artemisia Gallery, Chgo., 1988, Wash. U. Gallery, 1989, MJF Gallery, St. Louis, 1990, Bromfield Gallery, Boston, 1995, Fed. Res. Bank Boston, 1995, Art Advisory, Boston, 1996. Bd. govs. St. Louis Artists' Guild, 1984-87; bd. dirs. Women's Caucus for Art, 1987-89. Mem. ARTcetera (mem. acquistions com. 1995-96), Bromfield Gallery.

BRANYON, DARLENE DIXON, radio broadcaster; b. Montgomery, Ala., Aug. 29, 1950; d. Joe Mac and Dorothy Marie (Gilbert) Dickinson; m. Robert Earl Branyon, Mar. 8, 1991. BS, Auburn U., 1974; postgrad., Ron Bailie Sch. Broadcasting, 1983-84. Acct. David Thames Builders, Montgomery, 1977-83; air personality KKBB Radio, Denver, 1983-84, WHHY Radio, Montgomery, 1984-86; air personality, music dir. WLWI Radio, Montgomery, 1986-93, ABC Real Country Network, Tempe, Ariz., 1993-95; air personality morning show Sta. WKSJ Radio, Mobile, Ala., 1995-96; program dir., morning show personality Sta. WJCC Radio, Montgomery, Ala., 1996—. Exec. v.p. Montgomery Jaycees, 1989; voter registration State of Ala., Montgomery, 1993-96; bd. dirs. Mobile Fine Arts, 1995-96; celebrity chmn. March of Dimes, Montgomery, 1991-92; celebrity fundraiser Pub. Broadcasting TV, Phoenix, 1993-95. Finalist Music Dir. of Yr. award Billboard Mag., 1990, finalist Personality of Yr. award Billboard Mag., 1991, Personality of Yr. award Montgomery Mag., 1992; master of ceremonies Ala. June Jam, 1993-95; recipient Morning Show Personality of Yr. award, 1996. Mem. Country Music Assn. (judging com. 1992, finalist Personality of Yr. 1991, 92), NOW (Montgomery pres. 1993-94), Kiwanis Club. Methodist. Home: 600 Lucy's Trl Wetumpka AL 36092 Office: Sta WJCC 3435 Norman Bridge Rd Montgomery AL 36105

BRASEL, JO ANNE, physician; b. Salem, Ill., Feb. 15, 1934; d. Gerald Nolan and Ruby Rachel (Rich) B. BA, U. Colo., 1956; MD, U. Colo., 1959. Diplomate Am. Bd. Pediatrics, Am. Bd. Pediatric-Endocrinology. Pediatric intern, resident Cornell U. Med. Coll.-N.Y. Hosp., N.Y.C., 1959-62; pediatric endocrine fellow Johns Hopkins U. Sch. Medicine, Balt., 1962-65, asst. prof. pediatrics, 1965-68; asst. prof. then assoc. prof. pediatrics Cornell U. Med. Coll., N.Y.C., 1969-72; assoc. prof. then prof. pediatrics Columbia U. Coll. Physicians and Surgeons, N.Y.C., 1972-79, asst. dir. Inst. Human Nutrition, 1972-79; prof. pediatrics Harbor-UCLA Med. Ctr., UCLA Sch. Medicine, 1979—, program dir. Gen. Clin. Research Ctr., 1979-93, prof. medicine, 1980—; mem. adv. com. FDA, Rockville, Md., 1971-75; mem. nutrition study sect. NIH, Bethesda, Md., 1974-78; mem. select panel for promotion of child health HEW, Washington, 1979-80; mem. life scis. D adv. screening com. Fulbright-Hays program, Washington, 1981-84, digestive disease and nutrition grant review group NIADDK, 1985-89, U.S. Govt. Task Force on Women, Minorities and the Handicapped in Sci. and Tech., 1987-89. Recipient Rsch. Career Devel. award NIH, 1973-77, Irma T. Hirschl Trust Career Sci. award, 1974-79, Sr. Fulbright Sabbatical Rsch. award, 1980. Mem. Soc. Pediatric Rsch. (sec.-treas. 1973-77, pres.-elect 1977-78, pres. 1978-79), Am. Fed. Clin. Rsch., Endocrine Soc., Am. Soc. Clin. Nutrition, Am. Inst. Nutrition, Western Assn. Physicians, Lawson Wilkins Pediatric Endocrine Soc. (bd. dirs., mem. bd. 1972-74, pres.-elect 1991-92, pres. 1992-93), Am. Pediatric Soc., Assn. Program Dirs. for Gen. Clin. Rsch. Ctrs. (pres. 1982-83), Western Soc. Pediatric Research, Phi Beta Kappa, Alpha Omega Alpha. Office: Harbor-UCLA Med Ctr Box 446 1000 W Carson St Torrance CA 90509-2910

BRASHEAR, DIANE LEE, marital and sex therapist; b. Parkersburg, W.Va., July 21, 1933; d. Ralph Elijah and Dorothea Esther (McDade) Blake; m. Richard Evers Brashear, Aug. 31, 1956; children: Allison, Meredith Kay. BS in Social Adminstrn., Ohio State U., 1955, MSW, 1957; PhD, Purdue U., 1971. Diplomate Am. Bd. Sexology. Chief social worker Ind. Sch. for Blind, Indpls., 1965-68; asst. prof. social work Ind. U., Indpls., 1970-72; dir. Brashear Ctr., Inc., Indpls., 1972-84; news reporter marriage & family coun. Sta. WTHR-TV, Indpls., 1980—; assoc. prof. ob-gyn and psychiatry Ind. U. Sch. Medicine, Indpls., 1984—; vis. prof. Purdue U., West Lafayette, Ind., 1971-72; bd. dirs. Alan Guttmacher Inst., National, 1985-93. Author: Social Worker as Sex Educator, 1977; editor Indpls. Mo., 1975-91; contbr. articles, book chpts. and video tapes. Pres. Planned Parenthood Greater Indpls., 1985-87; bd. dirs. Planned Parenthood Fedn. Am., 1983-88, 91-93; vice chmn. Greater Indpls. Progress Cmty., 1989-92, United Way, Indpls., 1989—; pres. Cmty. Svc. Coun., Indpls., 1989-91; chair adv. bd. Women's Fund Indpls. Found. Recipient Pauline Selby award, Big Sisters Greater Indpls., 1986, Leadership award YWCA, Ind., 1986, Disting. Svc. award Planned Parenthood Cen. Ind., 1991. Mem. Am. Assn. Marriage and Family, Am. Coll. Ob/Gyn., Soc. Sci. Study Sex, Soc. Sex Therapy & Rsch. Office: Ind U Blvd #2440 550 University Indianapolis IN 46202-5270

BRASSELL, ROSELYN STRAUSS, lawyer; b. Shreveport, La., Feb. 19, 1930; d. Herman Carl and Etelka (McMullan) Strauss. BA, La. State U., 1949; JD, UCLA, 1962. Bar: Calif. 1963. Atty. CBS, Los Angeles, 1962-68, sr. atty., 1968-76, asst. gen. atty., 1976-83, broadcast counsel, 1983-91; pvt. practice law L.A., 1991—; instr. TV Prodn. Bus. and Legal Aspects, UCLA Extension, 1992. Co-writer: Life After Death for the California Celebrity, 1985; bd. editors U. Calif. Law Rev., 1960-62. Named Angel of Distinction Los Angeles Cen. City Assn., 1975. Mem. Calif. Bar Assn., L.A. County Bar Assn. (exec. com. 1970—, sect. chmn. 1980-81), Inst. Corp. Counsel (adv. bd. 1980—, Beverly Hills Bar Assn., L.A. Copyright Soc. (treas. 1977-78, sec. 1978-79, pres. 1981-82), Am. Women in Radio and TV (nat. dir.-at-large 1971-73, nat. pub. affairs chmn. 1977-78, Merit award So. Calif. chpt. 1989), NATAS, Women in Film, Orange County World Affairs Coun. (trustee 1995—), U. Calif. Law Alumni Assn. (dir. 1971-74), Order of Coif, Alpha Xi Delta, Phi Alpha Delta. Republican. Home: 33331 Gelidum Cir Monarch Beach CA 92629-4451 Office: 645 Wilcox Ave Ste 1-D Los Angeles CA 90004-1131

BRASSFIELD, PATRICIA ANN, psychologist; b. Lebanon, Oreg., Apr. 22; d. John James and Mabel Dolores (Scott) Smith; children: Byron Scott, Robert Kent, Lisa Michelle Best. Student, U. Oreg.; BS, Oreg. State U.; MEd, U. Hawaii, 1974; PhD, U.S. Internat. U., 1980. Lic. psychologist, Hawaii, Ariz., Nev.; cert. substance abuse counselor, Hawaii, cert. hypnotherapist, marriage, family and child counselor, Calif., nat. cert. addiction counselor II. Family counselor Psychiat. Svcs., Honolulu, 1974-78, San Diego Ctr. for Psychotherapy, 1979-82; unit team mgr. Oahu Community Corrections, Honolulu, 1982-83; sch. counselor Kalaheo & Moanalua High Schs., Oahu, Hawaii, 1983-85; dir. Waipahu (Hawaii) Community Counseling Ctr., 1985-87; forensic psychologist criminal ct. Hawaii Dept. Health, Honolulu, 1987-91, State of Nev., 1996—; sch. psychologist San Diego City Schs., 1981-82; family counselor Fairlight, Inc., Honolulu, 1983-84; clin psychologist, pvt. practice, Oahu and Maui, Hawaii, 1982-95, Las Vegas, 1995—; cons. United Airlines, Honolulu, 1989-95, Sex Abuse Intervention, Wailuku, Maui, 1990—, Family Ct., Wailuku, 1990—. Contbr. articles to profl. jours. Mem. APA, Nat. Assn. Drug and Alcohol Counselors, Mensa. Office: Ste 225 1063 E Main Maui HI 96793 also: 6881 W Charleston Ste B Las Vegas NV 89117

BRASUNAS, ELLEN LYDIA, psychotherapist; b. Columbus, Ohio, Nov. 16, 1924; d. Arthur Theodore and Norma Caroline (Wagner) W.; m. Anton deSales Brasunas, Nov. 16, 1946; children: James Anton, Kay Ellen, Anne Elizabeth. BS in Nursing, Ohio State U., 1946; MA in Counseling, Webster U., 1978. RN. Pub. health nurse St. Louis County, 1971-75; pub. sch. nurse Normandy Sch. Dist., St. Louis, 1975-79; psychotherapist Christian Psychol. and Family Services, St. Louis, 1979-83, Creve Coeur Counseling, St. Louis, 1983—; pvt. practice, St. Louis, 1983—; vol. Nat. Council on Alcoholism, St. Louis, 1983—. Recipient Outstanding Vol. award Nat. Council on Alcoholism, St. Louis, 1984. Mem. Am. Assn. Marriage and Family Therapy (clin.), Ethical Soc. St. Louis (lic. profl. counselor). Democrat. Club: Dulcimer (St. Louis). Home: 8030 Daytona Dr Saint Louis MO 63105

BRASWELL, JACKIE TERRY, medical, surgical nurse; b. Raleigh, N.C., Oct. 15, 1961; d. Charles Thurman and Laura (Russell) Terry; 1 child, Matthew Russell Braswell. BSN, U. N.C., 1983. Cert. BCLS, med. surgical nursing ANA. Staff nurse orthopedics/neurology unit Wake County Med. Ctr., Raleigh, staff nurse cardiac telemetry step-down unit; asst. head nurse orthopedics unit Raleigh Community Hosp., staff nurse telemetry unit; charge nurse vent unit IHS, Raleigh, 1993-95. Mem. ANA, NCNA.

BRASWELL, PAULA ANN, artist; b. Decatur, Ala., May 6, 1955; d. Andrew Leon and Dorothy Faye (Fretwell) B.; m. Rober Armand Robichaud, June 22, 1996. BA, Jacksonville State U., 1978; postgrad., New Orleans Acad. Fine Arts, 1987, U. New Orleans, 1987-88; MFA, Fla. State U., 1990. Instr. art Butler Sch., Marrero, La., 1984, Fla. Keys Coll., Tavernier, 1985; grad. instr. Fla. State U., Tallahassee, 1989-90; adj. prof. Calhoun Coll., Decatur, Ala., 1990, Chattanooga State Coll., 1991, Cleveland (Tenn.) State Coll., 1991; studio artist Knoxville, Tenn., 1991—. Artist (video sculpture) New American Talent, 1996, Transforming Tradition, 1996, Combined Talents Fla. Nat., 1995, Art Current Contemporary Artists, 1994-95, Contemporary Arts Ctr., New Oreleans, 1992. Grantee Nat. Endowment Arts, 1991. Mem. AAUW, NOW, Women's Caucus for Arts (exhibitor), Knoxville Mus. Art (exhibitor), Knoxville Arts Coun. (exhibitor), Coll. Art Assn., Contemporary Arts Ctr. (exhibitor), People for Protection of Animals, Humane Soc. U.S. Democrat. Mem. Ch. of Christ. Home: 612 Loop Rd Knoxville TN 37922

BRATCHER, CARLA ELIZABETH, obstetrician and gynecologist; b. Wichita, Kans., Sept. 18, 1942; d. Carl E. and Armilda Elizabeth (Salmans) Dillon; m. Carl E. Bratcher III, Apr. 9, 1983. Student, U. Wash., 1960-62; BS, U. Fla., 1966; MD, U. Pa., 1979. Diplomate Am. Bd. Ob-Gyn. Rsch. technician Nat. Cancer Inst.-NIH, Bethesda, Md., 1967-73, Wistar Inst., Phila., 1973-75; ob-gyn intern Madigan Army Med. Ctr., Tacoma, 1979-80, resident in ob-gyn, 1980-83; chief ambulatory care svc. ob-gyn. 2d Gen. Hosp., Landstuhl, Fed. Republic Germany, 1984-87; pvt. practice, Grand Prairie, Tex., 1988-89; pvt. practice ob/gyn. Redmond, Oreg., 1990—; chief ob. dept. Ctrl. Oreg. Dist. Hosp., 1990—; vol. instr. dept. ob-gyn Dallas-Ft. Worth Med. Ctr., 1988-89. Maj. M.C., U.S. Army, 1979-87. Fellow Am. Coll. Obstetricians and Gynecologists; mem. AMA, AAUW, Oreg. Med. Assn., Am. Med. Women's Assn. Democrat. Office: Redmond Ob Gyn 215 NW Kingwood Ste 150 Redmond OR 97756

BRATHWAITE, HARRIET LOUISA, nursing educator; b. Rye, N.Y., Aug. 28, 1931; d. James Pierce and Mattie (Collins) Bowling; m. Leroy L. Brathwwaite, Feb. 18, 1950; 1 child, Helene Ann Brathwaite Ward. AAS in Nursing, Bklyn. Coll., 1959; BSN, L.I. U., 1965; postgrad., Tchrs. Coll. of Columbia U., 1965-68; MSN, Adelphia U., 1973. Staff nurse Kings County Hosp., Bklyn., 1959; head nurse City Hosp. at Elmhurst, Queens, N.Y., 1959-62; instr. Kings County Hosp. Sch. Nursing, 1963-65, Downstate Med. Ctr. Sch. Nursing, 1965-69; nurse community mental health South Beach Psychiat. Ctr., 1969-73; cons. psychiat. nursing service HEW and N.Y. State Health Dept., Albany, 1973-74; chief of service Creedmoor Psychiat. Ctr., Queens Village, N.Y., 1974-87; asst. prof. nursing L.I. U., 1987-92. Coleader Allied Dems., Jamaica, N.Y., 1959-62; bd. dirs. South Queens Dems., Howard Beach, N.Y.; mem. adv. bd. Transitional Services, Queens, 1983-85. Mem. AAUW, NAACP, ANA, Nat. Black Nurses Assn. (chmn. legis. com. Queens chpt. 1981—, Cert. of Appreciation 1989), N.Y. State Nurses Assn. (coun. on legislation 1990—, trustee Polit. Action Com. 1991—, 25-Yr. Membership award 1986, Legis. awrd 1988, Ruth W. Harper award for Disting. Svc. 1991), 100 Black Women of L.I., Bklyn. Coll. Alumni Assn. (bd. dirs. 1995), Knickerbocker Club (chmn. fin. and scholarship com.), Chi Eta Phi, Kappa Eta. Home: PO Box 1841 10 Cuffee Dr Sag Harbor NY 11963-0064

BRATTAIN, ARLENE JANE CLARK, interior designer; b. Phila., July 27, 1938; d. Franklin Corning Clark and Nora May Robertson; children: Kathy, Kurt, Karen, David. Cert. in interior design, N.Y. Sch. Interior Design, 1975; BS, U. Minn., 1986. Exec. United Way, Mpls., 1980; interior designer AB Interiors, Minnetonka, Minn., 1982—; pvt. practice color analyst, Minnetonka, 1984—; cons. showroom Rollin B. Child Tile, Plymouth, Minn., 1985; interior designer Room & Bd. Stores, Minnetonka, 1985-86. Designer Window Fashions mag., 1988—, Am. Soc. Interior Designers Showcase Home, 1987, Showcase Home for March of Dimes, 1988, Showcase Vignette, 1989. Trainer dist. Camp Fire Girls, Minnetonka, 1967-78; trainer, leader Boy Scouts Am., Mpls., 1967-80; pres. PTA, Minnetonka, 1970; pres. Music Boosters, Minnetonka, 1976-84. Recipient Silver Fawn award Boy Scouts Am., 1973. Mem. Am. Soc. Interior Designers (profl.), Internat. Furnishings and Design Assn. (exec. 1988—), Nat. Trust for Hist. Preservation, Mensa.

BRATTER, JANET ELLEN, musician, writer; b. Newark, Sept. 24, 1946; d. Morton M. and Dorothy Ruth (McGeary) B. Student, James Madison Coll., 1964-65, George Mason Coll., 1965-66; BA in English Lit., George Washington U., 1969. Musician New Orleans, 1976-78, San Francisco, Oakland, 1978-80, Washington, V.I., 1980-81, Washington, New Orleans, N.Y.C., Bermuda, 1981-83; writer River Cities Gazette, Miami (Fla.) News, Miami Herald, 1983-91; singer, songwriter, inventor, writer, investor Chapel Hill, N.C., 1992—; adjudicator Devel. of Excellence of Young People award Miami Dade C.C., 1989; news dir., prodr. Sta. KLPI, Ruston, La., 1981-83; singer/songwriter, Miami, 1983-91; prodr. Sta. WLRN-TV, Miami, 1987-89; music therapist Intergenerational Program of State of Fla., Miami Springs, 1987-90. Performer Carnegie Hall, 1981; prodr. (TV) Feminization of Power, 1988. Active ACLU, Nat. Abortion and Reproductive Rights Action League, Friends of Fla. Folk; officer NOW, 1983-91, del., 1984-93; founding mem. South Fla. Folk Soc., Miami, 1984—; officer Women's Polit. Caucus, Miami, 1988-90; activist South Fla. Peace Coalition, Miami, 1983-90, Fla. Coalition Peace & Justice, Miami, 1984-90; Nicaraguan peace del. Witness for Peace, 1987-88; bd. mem. Unity Ctr. of Peace, Chapel Hill, 1995—. Democrat. Jewish. Home: 3232 1/2 Grand Route Saint John New Orleans LA 70119

BRATTON, IDA FRANK, secondary school educator; b. Glasgow, Ky., Aug. 31, 1933; d. Edmund Bates and Robbie Davis (Hume) Button; m. Robert Franklin Bratton, June 20, 1954; 1 son, Timothy Andrew. B.A., Western Ky. U., 1959, M.A., 1962. Cert. secondary tchr., Ky. Tchr. math. and sci. Gottschalk Jr. High Sch., Louisville, 1959-65; tchr. math. Iroquois High Sch., Louisville, 1965-79; tchr. Waggener High Sch., Louisville, 1979—, chair math. dept. co-chair sch. based decision making coun. Waggener High Sch. Mem. NEA, Ky. Edn. Assn., Jefferson County Tchrs. Assn., AAUW. Democrat. Methodist. Avocations: travel, needle crafts. Home: 304 Paddington Ct Louisville KY 40222-5541 Office: Waggener High Sch 330 S Hubbards Ln Louisville KY 40207-4011

BRATZLER, MARY KATHRYN, publisher; b. Albuquerque, Sept. 16, 1960; d. William James and Nancy Jane (Hobbs) Colby; m. Zim Emig, May 30, 1987 (div. Nov. 1990); 1 child, Aeriel Kaylee Emig; m. Steven James Bratzler, Mar. 16, 1996. B of Univ. Studies, U. N.Mex., 1995. Comml. artist Modern Press, Albuquerque, 1978-80; asst. composition supr. Graphic Arts Pub., Albuquerque, 1980-84, composition supr., 1984-85, asst. plant mgr., 1985-86; typesetter Universal Printing and Graphics, Albuquerque, 1986-87; typeseter Bus. Graphics, Albuquerque, 1988-90; office asst. UNM Gen. Honors, Albuquerque, 1992-93; desktop pub., 1990—; cons. Mary Kay Cosmetics, 1991—. Participant N.Mex. Pub. Utilities Commn., Santa Fe, 1993; coord. clothing bank PTA, Zia Elem. Sch., 1995-96; parent rep. Unified Student Centered Classroom, 1996—. Mem. Golden Key, Phi Beta Kappa.

BRAUER, GWENDOLYN GAIL, real estate broker; b. Middletown, Ohio; d. Robert J. and Mary M. (Kurry) Flynn; 1 child, John. CFP. Sales assoc. Better Homes Realty, Fairfax County, Va., 1976-81, Town & Country Properties, Fairfax County, 1981-84, ReMax Xecutex Real Estate, Fairfax County, 1984—. Mem. Nat. Assn. Realtors (cert. residential specialist, Million Dollar Sales Club 1980—), Employee Relocation Coun. (cert. relocation profl.), Internat. Bd. CFPs, No. Va. Assn. Realtors (Top Producers Club 1985—), Va. Assn. Realtors, Remax 100 Club (Hall of Fame 1994—). Home: 2627 Five Oaks Rd Vienna VA 22181 Office: ReMax Xecutex Real Estate 2911 Hunter Mill Rd Ste 101 Oakton VA 22124-1719

BRAUER, RHONDA LYN, lawyer; b. Gary, Ind., Nov. 23, 1959; d. Hugh Donald and Charlotte Gloria (Danzig) B.; m. Gregory John Holch, Sept. 7, 1989; 1 child, Jillian Brauer Holch. BA magna cum laude, Cornell U., 1981; JD magna cum laude, Ind. U., 1984. Bar: N.Y. 1985, U.S. Dist. Ct. (so. and ea. dist.) N.Y. 1991, U.S. Supreme Ct. 1992. Assoc. Cleary, Gottlieb, Steen & Hamilton, N.Y.C., 1984-86, 89-92, Brussels, 1986-88; asst. sec. and sr. counsel The New York Times Co., N.Y.C., 1992—. Contbr. articles to profl. jours. Pro bono work Lawyers Com. for Human Rights, N.Y.C., 1984-86, ACLU, 1989-90, Vol. Lawyers for the Arts, N.Y.C., 1989-92, N.Y. Lawyers for the Pub. Interest, 1992—. Recipient Anne MacIntyre Litchfield prize of history Cornell U. Coll. Arts and Scis., 1981; Salzburg (Austria) Seminar fellow, 1988. Mem. Assn. of Bar of City of N.Y., N.Y. Women's Bar Assn.

BRAULT, G(AYLE) LORAIN, healthcare executive; b. Chgo., Jan. 3, 1944; d. Theodore Frank and Victoria Jean (Pribyl) Hahn; m. Donald R. Brault, Apr. 29, 1971; 1 child, Kevin David. AA, Long Beach City Coll., 1963; BS, Calif. State U.-Long Beach, 1973, MS, 1977. RN, Calif; cert. nurse practitioner. Dir. nursing Canyon Gen. Hosp., Anaheim, Calif., 1973-76; dir. faculty critical care masters degree program Calif. State U., Long Beach, 1976-79; regional dir.. nursing and support svcs. Western region Am. Med. Internat., Anaheim, Calif., 1979-83; v.p. Hosp. Home Care Corp. Am., Santa Ana, Calif., 1983-85; pres. Healthcare Assn. So. Calif., Torrance, 1986-92; v.p. Hosp. Coun. So. Calif., L.A., 1993—; invited lectr. China Nurses Assn., 1983; cons. AMI, Inc., Saudi Arabia, 1983; advisor dept. grad. nursing Calif. State U., L.A., 1988, advisor Nursing Inst., 1990-91; guest lectr. dept. pub. health UCLA, 1986-87; assoc. clin. prof. U. So. Calif., 1988—; lectr. Calif. State U., L.A., 1996-97; editl. advisor RN Times, Nurseweek, 1988—, chmn. editl. adv. bd. Contbr. articles to profl. jours., chpts. to books. Commr. HHS, Washington, 1988. HEW advanced nurse tng. grantee, 1978. Mem. Women in Health Adminstrn. (sec. 1989, v.p. 1990), Nat. Assn. Home Care, Am. Orgn. Nursing Execs., Calif. Assn. Health Svcs. at Home (task force chmn. 1988, bd. dirs. 1988-93, chmn. bd. dirs. 1990-93), Calif. League Nursing (bd. sec. 1983, program chmn. 1981-82), Am. Coll. Health Care Execs., ASAE, AONE, Phi Kappa Phi, Sigma Theta Tau. Republican. Methodist. Home: 1032 E Andrews Dr Long Beach CA 90807-2406

BRAULT, PATRICIA HELEN MARIE, parochial school educator; b. Appleton, Wis., Oct. 7, 1945; d. Clifford Leroy and Florence Ella Edna (Lau) Beahm; m. Leon John Vincent Brault, Oct. 30, 1965; children: Tina, Jody, Anthony, Christopher. BA, St. Norbert Coll., DePere, Wis., 1983; MS in Edn., U. Wis., Oshkosh, 1992. Tchr. St. Joseph Sch., DePere, 1984-89, Marquette Sch., DePere, 1989-93; adminstr., math. tchr. Holy Cross Sch., Mishicot, Wis., 1993—. Home: 728 Westwind Ct De Pere WI 54115-1024 Office: Holy Cross Sch 423 Church St Mishicot WI 54228-9688

BRAUN, ELAYNE, sculptor, educator; b. N.Y.C., Feb. 6, 1924; d. Benjamin Weinglass and Byrdie (Leff) Miller; m. Herbert Braun, Jan. 10, 1942; children: Richard F., Caryl B. Student, Greenwich House Potters and Sculptors, N.Y.; studied with Mr. Paul Frazier; student, L.I. Sch. Art & Design, Bellmore, N.Y.; studied with Mr. Lloyd Reiss; student, Queens (N.Y.) Coll. Cert. art instr. Educator Farmingdale (N.Y.) Nursing Home, 1961-62, Pvt. Art Studio, N.Y., 1963-74, 1977-81; educator Indian River Cmty. Coll., Fort Pierce, Fla., 1982-95, Palm Grove Country Club, Fort Pierce, 1995—; art cons. Allied Teenage Guidance Svc., N.Y.C., 1965-74; art exhbn. cons. Indian River Cmty. Coll., Fort Pierce, 1982-95. Prin. works include: The Nestlings, 1967 (Suffolk Mus. Craftsmanship award 1967), Repose & Sea Forms, 1968 (Greenwich House City Backyard 1968), Beginning, 1969 (Greenwich House 1st in Show award 1969), Four Figure Fountain, 1972 (Fellowship Gallery Group Show award 1972); group shows include Jersey City Mus., N.J., 1971, Tyringham Gallery, Mass., 1973-74, Guild Hall Mus., East Hampton, N.Y., 1975-76, Phoenicia Gallery, Atlanta, 1978-79, Bridge Store Art Gallery, Fort Pierce, Fla., 1986-87, The Colt Gallery, Jensen Beach, Fla., 1986-87, Lighthouse Gallery, Tequesta, Fla., 1982-96, Ctr. For the Arts, Stuart, Fla., 1985-86, Maple Ave. Art Gallery, Jensen Beach, 1985-86, Edward S. Frisch, Ltd., West Palm Beach, Fla., 1984-86, N.Y., 1978-82, Tequesta Gallery, 1984-86, Fort Pierce Art Gallery, 1982, Indian River C.C., 1982, Queens Mus., 1981, Lincoln Ctr., N.Y., 1981, Queens Coll., Jefferson Hall, 1980-81, Zoma Gallery, N.Y., 1980-81, Creative Gallery, Babylon, N.Y., 1981, numerous others; one woman shows include Lighthouse Gallery, Tequesta, 1983, Creative Gallery, Babylon, 1981-82, The In-Cellar Gallery, Forest Hills, N.Y., 1972-75, Scintilla Gallery, N.Y., 1973-75, Fellowship Gallery, Queens, 1973-74, Gallery Potpourri, St. James, N.Y., 1970-73, Fountainhead Gallery, Port Washington, N.Y., 1969-71, Hollis (N.Y.) Unitarian Ch., 1968; represented in numerous pvt. collections and pub. places such as Modern Art Foundry, N.Y., Temple Shaaray Tefila, N.Y., Monarch Country Club, Ea. Metalizing Co., others. Mem. St. Lucie Profl. Arts League, Artcore, Art Assocs. of Martin County, L.I. Craftsmen's Guild, Sculptor's Alliance, Queens Coun. on the Arts, Greenwich House Sculptors, Jamaica Art Mobilization, Alliance of Queens Artists, Alliance of Boca Artists.

BRAUN, EUNICE HOCKSPEIER, author, religious order executive, lecturer; b. Alta Vista, Iowa; d. George Phillip and Lydia (Reinhart) Hockspeier; student Gates Coll., 1932-34, Coe Coll., 1937-39, Northwestern U., 1944-47; m. Leonard James Braun, May 29, 1937. Freelance writer for mags., newspapers, 1947-52; bus. mgr. Baha'i Publishing Trust, Wilmette, Ill., 1952-55, mng. dir., 1955-71; internat. news editor Baha'i News, 1952-70; tchr. Baha'i schs., Alaska, Can., Europe and U.S., 1958—; lectr. Baha'i Faith in U.S., Central Am., Europe, Africa, Asia, 1953—; cons. Baha'i Pub. Trust, New Delhi, India, 1972; mem. aux. bd. Continental Bd. Counselors, Baha'i Faith in the Ams., 1972-86. Mem. Nat. League Am. Pen Women, Baha'i Faith, Iota Sigma Epsilon. Author: Know Your Baha'i Literature, 1959; The Dawn of World Peace, 1963; Baha'u'llah: His Call to the Nations, 1967; From Strength to Strength, Half Century of the Formative Age of the Baha'i Faith, 1978; A Crown of Beauty, 1982; The March of the Institutions, 1984; A Reader's Guide: The Development of Baha'i Literature in English, 1986; From Vision to Victory, 1993; contbr. essays to Baha'i World, Internat. Record. Home: 1025 Forestview Ln Glenview IL 60025-4433

BRAUN, HELENE AMY, artist; b. Bklyn., Feb. 22, 1956; d. Sheldon and Ida (Brotkin) Rosenspan; divorced; children: Penelope, Lorraine. AA in Textile Surface Design, Fashion Inst. Tech., 1988; BFA, Kean Coll. N.J., 1992, MA, 1995. Staff artist Bucilla, Secaucus, N.J., 1987-88, Annin, Roselle, N.J., 1988-89; claim examiner Chubb Ins., Parsippany, N.J., 1989-92. Exhbns. include Fine Arts Inst. San Bernadino CountyMus., Calif., 1995, Phila. Woodmere Mus., 1995, Visual Arts Ctr. Northwest Fla., 1995. Mem. Watchung Arts Ctr. (New Art Group 1995—), Salute to Women Arts Internat., Am. Penwomen, Phila. Watercolor Club. Jewish.

BRAUN, JANICE LARSON, language arts educator; b. Cook, Minn., Mar. 4, 1949; d. Roy Woodrow and Hazel Vivian (Huff) Larson; m. Joseph

Edmund Braun, July 17, 1975; 1 child, Elizabeth. BA in English and German, Concordia Coll., Moorhead, Minn., 1971. Lang. arts tchr. Dist. 742 Cmty. Schs., St. Cloud, Minn., 1971—, mem. K-12 lang. arts com., 1984—, mem. Tech. H.S. site com., 1988-92; mem. writer assessment grant com. State of Minn. and Dist. 742, 1993—; advisor Cultural Awareness and Racial Equity Com. Leader Wide Horizons 4-H Club, Benton County, Minn., 1990—; catechist Bethlehem Luth. Ch., St. Cloud, 1994—; mem. Archie Givens Origins project St. Cloud State U., 1993—. Mem. NEA, Minn. Edn. Assn., St. Cloud Edn. Assn., Nat. Coun. Tchrs. English, Amnesty Internat. (adult leader, advisor Tech. H.S. chpt. 1987—). Democrat. Office: Tech HS 233 12th Ave S Saint Cloud MN 56301-4286

BRAUN, MARY LUCILE DEKLE (LUCY BRAUN), therapist, consultant, counselor; b. Tampa, Fla.; d. Guthrie J. and Lucile (Culpepper) Dekle; children: John Ryan, Matthew Joseph, Jeffrey William, Douglas Edwin. AB, Brenau Coll.; MA, U. Cen. Fla.; EdD, U. Fla. Cert. ins. rehab. specialist; lic. mental health counselor; lic. marriage and family therapist; nationally cert. counselor. Coord. Orange County Child Abuse Prevention, Orlando, Fla., 1983-88; cons. Displaced Homemaker Program, Orlando, 1989—, DCS, Oviedo, Fla., 1990-92; adj. prof. U. Ctrl. Fla., Orlando, 1989—; clin. dir. Response Sexual Abuse Treatment Program, 1993-95; mem. adv. bd. Fla. Hosp. Women's Ctr., Orlando, 1989—; bd. dirs. Parent Resource Ctr., Orlando, Children With Attention Deficit Disorders, Orlando, 1989—. Author: Someone Heard, 1987, Humor Us Soup, 1989; contbg. author: Death from Child Abuse, 1986, Personality Types of Abusive Parents, 1993. Sustaining mem. Jr. League of Orlando and Winter Park, Fla., 1989—. Program recipient Community Svc. award Walt Disney World, 1987. Mem. ACA, Fla. Counseling Assn., Nat. Bd. Cir. Counselors, Phi Kappa Phi, Kappa Delta Pi, Chi Sigma Iota.

BRAUN, VIRGINIA VICKERS, publications professional; b. Little Falls, N.Y., Nov. 22, 1947; d. Harry Dan and Frances (Steele) Vickers; m. Eric R. Braun, Mar. 26, 1971; children: Eric Daniel, Alexander Crockett. BA in English, St. Lawrence U., 1969; MJ, U. Mont., 1984. Features editor The Lebanon (Tenn.) Democrat, 1974-78; editorial asst. U.S. Forest Svc., Missoula, Mont., 1978-80; news writer U. Mont., Missoula, 1981-83, publs. editor, 1983-89, publs. mgr., 1989-95, editor The Barrister, Sch. Law, also freelance editor, 1996—. Editor mags. including The Montanan, 1983-95, Vision, 1984-90. Recipient 1st place Lifestyles, Tenn. Press Assn., 1976, 77, 78, 2d place, 1975, 3d place U. Network Pub., 1984, 1st place Coun. for Advancement and Support of Edn., 1987. Mem. Missoula C. of C. (bd. dirs. conv. and visitors bur. 1989-92). Home and Office: 4425 Duncan Dr Missoula MT 59802-3287

BRAUNSTEIN, DIANE KAREN, government relations professional; b. Bklyn., Feb. 20, 1956; d. Elliott Bernard and Barbara (Stadin) B. Grad. in polit. sci., Kenyon Coll., 1977. Constituent aide Congressman Bill Green, N.Y.C., 1978; legis. aide Congressman Bill Green, Washington, 1979-80; social ins. planning specialist Social Security Adminstrn., Balt., 1981-84; staff asst. soc. security subcom. U.S. House Ways and Means Com., Washington, 1983; legis. analyst Office of Asst. Sec. for Legislation HHS, Washington, 1984-86, 88-89, acting dep. asst. sec. for human svc. legislation Office of Asst. Sec. Legislature, 1990; Congl. affairs advisor Social Security Adminstrn., Washington, 1987-88; dep. staff dir. U.S. Senate Com. on Aging, Washington, 1990-91; dir. rsch. and policy devel. White House Conf. on Aging, Washington, 1991-92; dir. Mich. Office of Svcs. to Aging, Lansing, 1993-95; sr. assoc. APCO Assocs., Inc., Washington, 1996—; mem. steering com. Inst. Gerantology, Wayne State U., Detroit, 1993—. Contbr. articles to profl. jours. Selected for goodwill exchange mission Konrad Adenhaver Found., B'nai Brith, Germany, 1994. Named 1995 honoree Mich. Assn. of Foster Grandparents/Sr. Companions Program. Mem. AARP (hon.), Nat. Acad. Social Ins. Office: APCO Assocs Inc 1615 L St NW Ste 900 Washington DC 20036

BRAVO, ROSE MARIE, retail executive; b. N.Y.C., Jan. 13, 1951; d. Biagio and Anna (Bazzano) LaPila; m. Charles Emil Bravo, June 13, 1971 (div. 1977); m. William Selkirk Jackey, Oct. 9, 1983. B.A. in English, Fordham U., 1971. Exec. trainee, dept. mgr. A&S, Bklyn., 1971-74; assoc. buyer Macy's, N.Y.C., 1974-75, buyer, 1975-79, councilor, 1979-80, adminstr., 1980-84, group v.p., 1984-85, sr. v.p. 1985-88; chmn., chief exec. officer, I. Magnin, San Francisco, 1988-92; pres., Saks Fifth Ave., Inc., N.Y.C., 1992—. Chmn. retail com. March of Dimes Birth Defects Found., 1980-81. Office: Saks & Co Inc 12 E 49th St Fl 19 New York NY 10017-1028*

BRAWER, CATHERINE COLEMAN, foundation executive, public affairs director, museum curator; b. N.Y.C., Feb. 19, 1943; d. Joseph A. and Beatrice R. Coleman; m. Robert A. Brawer, Sept. 7, 1962; children: Christopher Paul, Nicholas Andrew. BA, Sarah Lawrence Coll., 1964; MA in Art History, NYU, 1966. Publicity coord. Evehjem Mus. Art, Madison, Wis., 1970-75, curator Liebman Collection, 1974-75; mktg. mgr. Maidenform, Inc., N.Y.C., 1975-78; ind. curator N.Y.C., 1978; v.p. Ida and William Rosenthal Found., N.Y.C., 1981-90, pres., 1990—; dir. pub. affairs Maidenform Inc., N.Y.C., 1990—; curator Maidenform Mus.; dir. Maidenform, Inc., N.Y.C., 1970—; trustee Katonah (N.Y.) Mus. Art, 1982—, Ind. Curators, Inc., N.Y.C., 1989—, Inst. Fine Arts, NYU, 1993—, Musica Viva, 1995—. Author: (catalogues) The Auspicious Dragon in Chinese Decorative Arts, 1978, Many Trails: Indians of the Lower Hudson Valley, 1983, Trade Winds: The Lure of the China Trade, 1985; (book) Making Their Mark: Women Artist Move into the Mainstream 1970-85, 1989, Chinese Export Porcelain from the Liebman Porcelain Collection, 1992. Mem. Am. Ceramic Circle, N.Y. Regional Assn. Grantmakers (mem. com. 1990-91), Art Table N.Y.

BRAXTON, TONI, popular musician. Albums include Toni Braxton, 1993; contbr. Boomerang soundtrack, 1992. Recipient Grammy award Best Female R&B Vocal, 1994, 95. Office: Arista Records care of LaFace 6 W 57th St New York NY 10019-3913*

BRAY, CAROLYN SCOTT, educational administrator; b. Childress, Tex., May 19, 1938; d. Alonzo Lee and Frankie Lucile (Wood) Scott; m. John Graham Bray, Jr., Aug. 24, 1957 (div. May 1980); children: Caron Lynn, Kimberly Anne, David William. BS, Baylor U., 1960; MEd, Hardin-Simmons U., 1981; PhD, U. North Tex., 1985. Registered med. technologist. Adj. prof. bus. comm. Hardin-Simmons U., 1981-84; dir. career placement, 1979-82, assoc. dean students, 1982-85; assoc. dir. career planning and placement U. North Tex., Denton, 1985-95, adj. prof. higher edn. adminstrn., mem. Mentor program; dir. career svcs. U. Tex. at Dallas, Richardson, 1995—. Organizer, mem. Abilene Women's Network, 1982-85; mem. U. North Tex. League for Profl. Women, 1985-95; mem. pers. com. First Bapt. Ch., 1992-95; bd. dirs. Irving Christian Counseling, Inc., 1993-95. Mem. Assn. Sch., Coll. and Univ. Staffing (bd. dirs. 1989-94, treas. 1994-95), S.W. Assn. Colls. & Employers (vice chair ops. 1992, 93, chair ann. conf. registration, 1991, 92), Tex. MBA Consortium (treas. 1993-95, co-chmn. 1995-96, Tex. Am. Assn. for Employer of Edn., Staffing (v.p. 1986-87, pres. 1987-88), Nat. Assn. Colls. & Employers, North Cen. Tex. Assn. Sch. Pers. Adminstrs. and Univ. Placement Pers. (pres. 1987-88, sec. 1988-95), Denton C. of C. (pub. rels. com. 1988-95), Dallas Human Resources Mgmt. Assn., Leadership Denton (co-dir. curriculum 1988-89, chair membership selection com. 1990, 93, 94, steering com. 1990, 93, 94, Denton Cultural Arts Assn., Kappa Kappa Gamma (chpt. advisor, chmn. adv. bd. Zeta Sigma chpt. 1987-93). Republican. Avocations: skiing, tennis, golf, reading. Office: U Tex at Dallas Box 830688, LF 11 Richardson TX 75083-0688

BRAY, JOAN, state legislator; b. Sept. 16, 1945; m. Carl Hoagland; 2 children. BA, Southwestern U.; MEd, U. Mass. Former tchr., journalist, former dist. dir. for Congresswoman Joan Kelly Horn; mem. Mo. Ho. of Reps. Bd. dirs. Citizens for Modern Transit. Fleming fellow, 1995. Mem. PTO, Nat. Womens Polit. Caucus. Democrat. Home: 7120 Washington Ave Saint Louis MO 63130-4312 Office: Mo Ho of Reps State Capitol Bldg Rm 411 Jefferson City MO 65101-6806*

BRAY, NANCY A., oceanographic administrator. Dir., Scripps Inst. of Oceanography physical oceanography rsch. divsn. U. of Calif. San Diego, La Jolla, Calif. Office: U Calif San Diego Physical Oceanography Rsch Divsn Scripps Inst Oceanography La Jolla CA 92093*

BRAY, SHARON ANN, management company executive; b. Long Beach, Calif., June 12, 1944; d. George Knight and Oweta Izeda (Little) B.; m. Larry Dwane Collins, Jan. 29, 1967 (dec. July 1981); children: Elinor F., Claire J.; m. John C. Renner, May 20, 1989. BA in Sociology, San Jose (Calif.) State U., 1967; MEd, Mt. St. Vincent U., Halifax, Nova Scotia, 1981; EdD in Applied Psychology, U. Toronto, Can., 1986. Cert. tchr., Calif. Tchr. San Jose, Ottawa and Halifax Schs., 1967-80; psychologist Halifax County Sch. Bd., 1980-83; instr. St. Mary's U., Halifax, 1981-83; pvt. cons. Toronto, 1985-86; sr. cons. Stevenson, Kellogg, Ernst & Whinney, Toronto, 1985-86; dir. profl. svcs. Right Assocs., Toronto and Cupertino, Calif., 1988-90; v.p., dir. profl. svcs. Lee Hecht Harrison, San Jose, Calif., 1990-91, sr. v.p., gen. mgr., 1991-94, regional sr. v.p., 1994-95; sr. v.p. corporate dir. profl. svcs. and devel. Lee Hecht Harrison, N.Y.C., 1995—; disting. vis. lectr. Calif. Polytech. U., San Luis Obispo, 1987; keynote speaker Calif. Career Devel. Conf., Calif., 1992. Author: This Way to Canada, 1978; contbr. articles to profl. jours. Bd. dirs. Young Peoples' Theatre, Toronto, Ont., 1988-90, TheatreWorks, Palo Alto, Calif., 1990-92, Project Hired, Sunnyvale, Calif., 1992-95, Plays for Living, N.Y., 1996—. Mem. Internat. Assn. Career Mgmt. Profls., Am. Assn. Counseling and Devel., Am. Mgmt. Assn., Calif. Career Devel. Assn., Soc. for Human Resources Mgmt. Democrat. Methodist. Office: Lee Hecht Harrison 200 Park Ave Fl 26 New York NY 10166-0005

BRAZEAL, AURELIA ERSKINE, ambassador; b. Chgo., Nov. 24, 1943. BS, Spelman Coll., 1965; M of Internat. Affairs, Columbia U., 1967; postgrad., Harvard U., 1972. With Foreign Svc., 1968; consular and econ. officer U.S. Embassy, Buenos Aires, 1969-71; econ. reports officer Econ. Bureau U.S. State Dept., 1971-72, watch and line officer Office of Secretariat, 1973-74, desk officer Uraguay, Paraguay, 1974-77; dir. econs. Office Japan Affairs, 1984-86; review officer Office of Secretariat U.S. Dept. Treasury, 1977-79; econ. officer Tokyo, 1979-82; officer ECON Bur. U.S. Dept. State, 1982-84; dep. dir. Econ. Office Japan, 1984-86; mem. sr. seminar, 1986-87; min. counselor econ. affairs U.S. Embassy, Tokyo, 1987-90; U.S amb. to Micronesia, 1990-93, U.S. amb. to Kenya, 1993—. Office: Am Embassy Kenya, Moi/Haile Selassie Ave POB 30137, Nairobi Kenya

BRAZEAL, DONNA SMITH, psychologist; b. Greenville, S.C., Feb. 10, 1947; d. G.W. Hovey and Ollie Occena (Crane) Smith; m. Charles Lee Brazeal, June 27, 1970 (div. May 1980). BA, Clemson U., 1971, MEd, 1975; postgrad., Western Carolina U., 1974, Furman U., Greenville, 1977; PhD, Columbia Pacific U., 1994. Lic. sch. psychologist, S.C., N.C. Instr., head med. record dept. Greenville Tech. Coll., 1971-73; chief psychologist Greenville County Schs., 1975-80; coord. psychol. svcs. Union County Schs., Monroe, N.C., 1980—; pvt. practice psychology Monroe and Charlotte, N.C., 1986—; mem. learning disabilities com. Greenville County Schs., 1978-79; co-founder, bd. dirs. Ctr. for Spiritual Awareness of N.C., Monroe, 1982—. Co-author, co-editor: School Psychologist, 1980. Child find program coordinator Union County, 1980-85; mem. various coms. Assn. for Retarded Citizens, Monroe; mem. interagy. council Piedmont Mental Health, Monroe, 1983—. Catawba Bus. Women scholar, 1965; N.C. Dept. Pub. Instrn. Pre-Sch. Incentive grantee, 1984. Mem. Nat. Assn. Sch. Psychologists, N.C. Assn. Sch. Psychologist (mem. pub. relations com. 1984-85), Animal Protection Inst. Am., Greenpeace, Union County Humane Soc., River Hills Community Ch. (mem. adult edn. com. 1985-86), Delta. Libertarian. Unitarian. Home: PO Box 240173 Charlotte NC 28224-0173

BRAZEAU, FRANCES MINA, elementary school educator; b. Waterbury, Conn., Apr. 17, 1940; d. Lester Irving and Margaret Gertrude (Henry) Forst; m. Robert Ernest Brazeau, Feb. 18, 1967; children: Margaret, Elizabeth, Katherine. BS, So. Conn. State Coll., 1962; MS in Liberal Studies, Wesleyan U., 1967. Cert. secondary tchr. Tchr. Bd. Edn., Beacon Falls, Conn., 1962-64, Redding, Conn., 1964-65; tchr. State Hawaii Dept. Edn., Honolulu, 1965-66, Pittsfield (Mass.) Pub. Schs., 1967-69, Adult Learning Ctr., Pittsfield, 1975-81, North Canaan (Conn.) Elem., 1981—; recruiter Hartford (Conn.) Ins. Co., 1966-67. Class chair Parents Coun. Union Coll., Schenectady, N.Y., 1995-96. Office: North Canaan Elem Sch Pease St Canaan CT 06018

BRAZIER, MARY MARGARET, psychology educator, researcher; b. New Orleans, Feb. 4, 1956; d. Robert Whiting and Margaret Long (Mc Waters) B. BA, Loyola U., New Orleans, 1977; MS, Tulane U., 1985, PhD, 1986. Assoc. prof. Loyola U., 1986—. NSF grantee, 1987. Mem. APA, Am. Psychol. Soc., Southeastern Psychol. Assn., Midwestern Psychol. Assn., Ea. Psychol. Assn., Southwestern Psychol. Assn. (coun. 1988—), So. Soc. Philosophy and Psychology (exec. coun. 1989-92). Roman Catholic. Office: Loyola U Dept Psychology 6363 Saint Charles Ave New Orleans LA 70118-6143

BRDLIK, CAROLA EMILIE, accountant; b. Wuerzburg, Germany, Mar. 11, 1930; came to U.S., 1952; d. Ludwig Leonard and Hildegard Maria (Leipold) Baumeister; m. Joseph A. Brdlik; children: Margaret Louise, Charles Joseph. BA, Oberrealschule Bamberg, Fed. Republic Germany, 1948; MA, Bavarian Interpreter Coll., Fed. Republic Germany, 1949; Cert., Internat. Accts. Soc., Chgo., 1955. Interpreter, exec. sec. NCWC Amberg, Schweinfurt, Ludwigsburg and Munich, Fed. Republic Germany, 1949-52; exec. sec. Red Ball Van Lines, Jamaica, N.Y., 1952; interpreter Griffin Rutgers Inc., N.Y.C., 1952-53; office mgr., exec. sec. Rehab. Ctr. Summit Co., Inc., Akron, 1953-56; pvt. practice acctg. Cuyahoga Falls, Ohio, 1956-61, Uniontown, Ohio, 1961-81; sec., treas. Omaca, Inc., Uniontown and Deerfield Beach (Fla.), 1981-86; pres. Omaca, Inc., Uniontown and Jupiter, 1986—; sec.-treas. Shipe Landscaping, Inc., Greensburg, Ohio, 1968-92, Sattler Machine Products, Copley, Ohio, 1981-88; asst. treas. Mar-Lynn Lake Park, Inc., Streetsboro, Ohio, 1969—. Bd. dirs., trustee Czechoslovak Refugees, Cleve. and Cin., 1968. Mem. Nat. Soc. Tax Profls. (cert. accredited taxation and accountancy), Nat. Soc. Pub. Accts., Nat. Assn. Tax Preparer's, Nat. Assn. Enrolled Agts., Fla. Soc. Enrolled Agts., Fla. Soc. Acctg. and Tax Profls. Roman Catholic.

BREAKSTONE, KAY LOUISE, public relations executive; b. Allentown, Pa., Sept. 9, 1936; d. Morris H. and Mabel (Gruber) Senderowitz; B.S., N.Y. U., 1967; m. Jules L. Breakstone, Dec. 3, 1960; children—Enid, Jessica. With N.Y. Conf. Bd., 1967-69, Bache, Halsey Stuart, N.Y.C., 1969-70; securities analyst Dean Witter, N.Y.C., 1970-71; vice-pres. Burson Marsteller, Inc., N.Y.C., 1971-79; dir. investor relations Kennecott Corp., Stamford, Conn., 1979-81; sr. v.p. Burson-Marsteller, 1981-87, exec. v.p., 1987-92; pres., CEO Ludgate Comm., N.Y.C., 1993—. Mem. Nat. Investor Relations Inst. (pres. 1980-81). Office: Ludgate Comm 747 3rd Ave New York NY 10017-2803

BREARLEY, CANDICE, fashion designer; b. Trenton, N.J., Jan. 2, 1944; d. Joseph William and Lillian (Mieler) Szalay; m. Purvis Brearley, Sept. 2, 1965. BFA, Mus. Sch., Phila., 1965, MFA, 1968; BFA, Parsons Sch. Design, 1975, New Sch. Social Rsch., 1975. Freelance portrait artist Trenton, 1965-72; asst. designer Malcolm Starr, N.Y.C., 1974-75; designer Originala, N.Y.C., 1975-77, Vignette, N.Y.C., 1977-78; pres., designer Candice Brearley, Inc., Trenton, 1978—; pres. Wickford Corp. of N.J., Trenton, 1986—; bd. dirs. Beta Con Corp., Lawrenceville, N.J. One-woman shows Nat. State Bank, N.J., 1971; exhibited in group show at N.J. State Mus., Trenton, 1970. Mem. devel. com. Restoration of "The Brearley House," Lawrenceville, N.J. Recipient award Lane Bryant Design Competition, 1974. Fellow Phila. Mus. Art, Met. Mus. Art, Princeton U. Mus., N.J. State Mus. Roman Catholic. Office: Candice Brearley Inc 128 Buckingham Ave Trenton NJ 08618-3314

BRECHT, SALLY ANN, quality assurance executive; b. Trenton, N.J., Aug. 5, 1951; d. Charles L. and Helen (Orfeo) B. BBA, Coll. William & Mary in Va., 1973; MBA, Rider Coll., 1981. Cert. quality engr., quality auditor, quality mgr., software quality engr. Electronic data processing auditor McGraw Hill, Inc., Hightstown, N.J., 1976-79, State of N.J., Mercerville, 1979-80, NL Industries, Hightstown, 1980-84; systems tech. planning specialist Ednl. Testing Svc., Princeton, N.J., 1984-85, acting div. dir. application devel., 1985-87, mgr. computer standards and security, 1987-88, asst. dir. office corp. quality assurance, quality engr., 1988—. Contbr. articles to popular publs. Office: Ednl Testing Svc Rosedale Rd Princeton NJ 08540-6702

BRECKEL, ALVINA HEFELI, librarian; b. Chgo., Dec. 6, 1948; d. William Christ and Liselotte (Herrmann) Hefeli; m. Theodore A. Breckel, Feb. 10, 1973. BFA cum laude, Bradley U., 1970; MALS, Rosary Coll., River Forest, Ill., 1973. Cert. art tchr., media libr., Ill. Tchr. art Chgo. Pub. Schs., 1971-84; libr. Oakton Community Coll., Des Plaines, Ill., 1988—; bd. dirs. North Shore Bd. of Gads Hill Ctr., 1996—. Author: Looking for Glass on the Internet, 1996; editor News & Notes, 1988-89. Rep. election judge New Trier Twp., Ill., 1988; com. mem. Villagers for a Safe Winnetka, 1989; mem. women's bd. Howard Area Cmty. Ctr., 1990-95; chmn. Fuller Lane Ctr., Winnetka, 1991-92, 94-95; mem. Midwestern Antiques Club, 1993—; mem. women's bd. Winnetka Cmty. House, 1995—. Mem. AAUW (bd. dirs. New Trier chpt. 1989-90), Sandwich (Mass.) Hist. Soc., Winnetka Hist. Soc., Art Inst. Chgo. (life), Nat. Greentown Glass Assn., Internat. Platform Assn., Nat. Am. Glass Club (life, founding mem. James H. Rose chpt., chpt. sec. 1992—), Greater Chgo. Glass Collectors Club (v.p. 1995—), Pi Lambda Theta (life, art editor chpt. Notes 1977-84), Delta Zeta (v.p. Chgo. North Shore chpt. 1987-90). Home: 185 Fuller Ln Winnetka IL 60093-4212 Office: Oakton CC 1600 E Golf Rd Des Plaines IL 60016

BRECKENRIDGE, BETTY GAYLE, management development consultant; b. Austin, Tex., Dec. 8, 1945. BA, Baylor U., 1966; MA, So. Meth. U, 1984. Cons. leadership continuity program AT&T, 1993—; cons. Leadership Devel. Ctr. Bellsouth Corp., 1990—; cons. Devel. Dimensions Internat., Pitts., Pa., 1984—. Office: 302 E Marshall # 515 West Chester PA 19380

BREE, GERMAINE, French literature educator; b. France, Oct. 2, 1907; came to U.S., 1926, naturalized, 1952; d. Walter and Lois Marguerite (Andrault) B. Licence, U. Paris, 1930, Diplôme d'Etudes Supérieures, 1931, Agregation, 1932; postgrad., Bryn Mawr Coll., 1931-32; D.Litt., Smith Coll., 1960, Mt. Holyoke Coll., 1963, Allegheny Coll., 1963, Duke U., 1964, Colby Coll., 1964, Oberlin Coll., 1966, Dickinson U., 1968, Rutgers U., 1969, Wake Forest U., 1970, Brown U., 1971, U. Mass., 1976, Kalamazoo Coll., 1977, Washington U., 1978, U. of the South, 1979, Boston Coll., 1979, U. Wis.-Madison, 1981; L.H.D., Wilson Coll., 1960; LL.D., Middlebury Coll., 1965, U. Mich., 1971, Davis-Elkins Coll., 1972, U. Wis. at Milw., 1973, N.Y. U., 1975; LL.D. (all hon.). Tchr. Algeria, 1932-36; from lectr. to prof. Bryn Mawr Coll., 1936-53; faculty French summer sch. Middlebury Coll., 1937, 40, 41, 46; chmn. dept. French Washington Sq. Coll., 1953-60; head Romance lang. dept., grad. sch. arts and sci. N.Y. U., 1954-60, head dept. Romance langs. and Russian, 1958-60; Vilas prof. U. Wis. Inst. for Research in Humanities, Madison, 1960-73; Kenan prof. of Humanities Wake Forest U., Winston-Salem, N.C., 1973-84, Kenan prof. of Humanities emerita, 1984—; Disting. vis. prof. Ohio State U., 1981; Whitney Oates vis. prof. Princeton U., 1983; Bernhardt vis. prof. Williams Coll., fall 1983; mem. panel translation Nat. Endowment Humanities, 1978-79; cons. lang. depts. Conn. Coll., 1979; Mem. adv. bd. Am. Council Learned Socs. Author: Marcel Proust, 1952, André Gide, 1953, Camus, 1959, rev. edit., 1961, Twentieth Century French Literature: An Anthology of Prose and Poetry, 1961, (with Margaret Guiton) An Age of Fiction, (with Micheline Dufau) Voix d'aujourd'hui, 1964, The World of Marcel Proust, 1966, (with Alex Kroff) Twentieth Century French Drama, 1969, (with G. Bernauer) Defeat and Beyond, An Anthology of French Wartime Writing (1940-1945), 1970, Camus and Sartre: Crisis and Commitment, 1972, Women Writers in France, 1973, Littérature Française, Vol. 16, XX Siecle c.2, 1920-1970, 1978, others; editor series of French poets in transl. Wake Forest U. Press, 1989, L'univers fabuleux de Jean-Marie Le Clézio, 1990; contbr. (with G. Bernauer) articles to profl. publs.; book revs. to New Republic. Served with French Army, 1943-45. Decorated Bronze Star; chevalier Legion of Honor (France); commandeur dans l'Ordre des Palmes Académiques. Mem. MLA (pres. 1975), AAUP, PEN, Am. Assn. Tchrs. French, Société des Professeurs Français, Am. Philos. Soc., Alliance Française, Nat. Council Humanities, Am. Acad. Arts and Sci.

BREED, HELEN ILLICK, ichthyologist, educator; b. New Cumberland, Pa., Mar. 12, 1925; d. Joseph Simon and Della May (Brotzman) Illick; m. Henry Eltinge Breed, Jr., Nov. 23, 1957; children: Henry E., Joseph I., Brenda E. BS, Syracuse U., 1947, MS, 1949; PhD, Cornell U., 1953. Tchr. sci. Lyons (N.Y.) Cen. High Sch., 1949-50; instr. zoology and physiology Akron (Ohio) U., 1953-54; postdoctoral Ford Found. fellow, instr. physiology Vassar Coll., Poughkeepsie, N.Y., 1954-55; asst. prof. biology Russell Sage Coll., Troy, N.Y., 1955-57; asst. dir. systematic biology NSF, Washington, 1957; assoc. prof. conservation Cornell U., Ithaca, N.Y., 1957-61; rsch. assoc. biology Rensselaer Poly. Inst., Troy, 1964-68; environ. cons. Eltick Rsch. Corp., Troy, 1971-90; enivron. advisor, cons. Women's Environ. and Devel. Orgn., N.Y.C., 1991—; internat. environ. liaison and coord. N.Y. State Summit and Agenda's 21 Program, Albany, 1992—; ichthyology cons. Ichthyological Assocs., Lake George Project, Troy, 1969, Ithaca, 1971-80, Lima, Peru, 1973-73; internat. environ. liaison and coord. N.Y. State Summit and Agenda's 21 Program, Albany, 1992—. Contbr. articles to profl. jours. Capital dist. mem. Syracuse U. campaign for excellence, Troy, 1988-90. Nat. Wildlife Fedn. fellow, 1950, Sports Fishing Inst. fellow, 1951-53, Am. Scandinavian Found. fellow, Trondheim, Norway, 1959-60. Mem. AAAS, Am. Soc. Zoologists, Soc. Systematic Zoology, Am. Soc. Ichthyologists and Herpetologists, Am. Fisheries Soc., Brunswick Hist. Soc. Republican. Lutheran. Home and Office: RD 3 421 Tamarac Rd Troy NY 12180

BREEN, KATHERINE ANNE, speech and language pathologist; b. Chgo., Oct. 31, 1948; d. Robert Stephen and Gertrude Catherine (Bader) Breen; B.S., Northwestern U., 1970; M.A. (U.S. Rehab. Services trainee), U. Mo., Columbia, 1971. Speech/lang. pathologist Fulton (Mo.) pub. schs., 1971-73; co-dir. Easter Seal Speech Clinic, Jefferson City, Mo., summers 1972, 73; speech/lang. pathologist Shawnee Mission (Kans.) pub. schs., 1973-96; staff St. Joseph's Hosp., Kansas City, Mo., 1978-81, Midwest Rehab. Ctr., Kansas City, 1985; pvt. practice speech therapy; cons. East Central Mo. Mental Health Center; guest lectr. Fontbonne Coll., St. Louis. Clin. certification in speech pathology. Mem. Am., Kans. speech and hearing assns., NEA, Mo. State Tchrs. Assn., Kansas City Alumni Assn. of Northwestern U. (dir. alumni admissions council, Outstanding Leadership award for work on alumni admissions council 1981, Svc. award, 1991), Friends of Art Nelson/Atkins Art Gallery and Museum (vol.), Nat. Trust Hist. Preservation, Kansas City Hist. Found., Zeta Phi Eta. Methodist. Home: 6865 W 51st Ter Apt 1C Shawnee Mission KS 66202-1576

BREEN, MARILYN, mathematics educator; b. Anderson, S.C., Nov. 8, 1944; d. Marvin and Martha Louise (Lesser) B.; m. Walter Gill Kelley, May 24, 1975; 1 child, Joyce Elizabeth. BA, Agnes Scott Coll., 1966; MS, Clemson U., 1968, PhD, 1970. Mem. faculty dept. math. U. Okla., Norman, 1971—, instr., 1971-73, asst. prof., 1973-77, assoc. prof., 1977-82, prof., 1982—. Contbr. rsch. articles to math. jours. Mem. Am. Math. Soc., Math. Assn. Am., Phi Beta Kappa, Sigma Xi, Phi Kappa Phi. Presbyterian. Office: U Okla Dept Math 601 Elm Ave Norman OK 73019-3100

BREHM-GRUBER, THERESE FRANCES, minister, consulting psychologist; b. Milw., July 6, 1932; d. Stanley Leo and Frances Hedwig (Kulasiewicz) Maternowski; m. James Monroe Brehm, Aug. 17, 1968 (dec. Feb. 1983); children: Frank X. Brehm, Gretchen Brehm Duran, Eric Brehm; m. Harold John Gruber, July 2, 1994. BS, Marquette U., 1961, MEd, 1963; D of Ministry, Grad. Theol. Found., 1993. Cert. state sch. psychologist, Wis.; ministerial cert. Fedn. Christian Mins. Counselor, sch. psychologist Germantown (Wis.) St. Sch. Dist., 1963-68; sch. psychologist Neenah (Wis.) St. Sch. Dist., 1968-91; lay min. Green Bay Diocese/Parish, Neenah, 1973—; cons. Pvt. Counseling Agys., Appleton, Wis., 1990-94. Co-author: (with Irene Dill) The Sharing of Power in the Catholic Church, 1993. Vol. follow-up worker Best Friends, Neenah and Menasha, 1994—; dir. mem. bd. dirs. Big Bros./Big Sisters, screeners of vols., 1970-80. Named Dutch Uncle, Big Bros./Big Sisters, 1972, Vol. of Yr., 1975. Mem. Bd. Total Cath. Educators of Green Bay Diocese (bd. dirs., nominating com. 1993—), Altrusa Club Neenah Menasha (pres. 1990-92). Democrat. Roman Catholic. Home: 711 Congress St Neenah WI 54956

BREIDEGAM, MARY ELLEN, accountant; b. Reading, Pa., Apr. 23, 1951; d. John B. Jr. and Anna May (Diefenderfer) Stevens; m. William R. Breidegam, Mar. 17, 1979. BSBA, Kutztown U., 1991. Various positions Bank of Pa., Reading, Pa., 1969-75; adminstrv. clk. GPU Svc. Corp., Reading, 1975-79; sr. acct. GPN Svc. Corp., Reading, 1979—. Loaned-campaign specialist Berks County United Way, 1985, mem. comty. edn.

support, 1986—, small bus. unit chmn. ann. campaign, 1987; disaster svcs. chmn. Berks County ARC, 1988-95, bd. dirs., 1992—, vol. recruitment and strategic planning subcoms.; mass-care officer Berks County Emergency Mgmt. Planning Com., 1991-95, bd. pres. Reading Pub. Libr., 1994-95, bd. trustees, 1996—; co-chmn. Tulip Conf., 1996, chmn. planning com., 1996; mem. Friends of Reading-Berks Libr. Sys.; bd. dirs. Berks County Commn. for Women, 1996—, Mifflin Comty. Libr., 1996—. Recipient Rudy Berhalter Meml. award, 1994. Mem. NAFE, AAUW, Am. Bus. Womens Assn., Nat. Mus. Women in Arts, World Affairs Coun. Berks County, Hist. Soc. Berks County, Berks Women's Network, Pa. Libr. Assn., Toastmasters (past v.p. edn., past v.p. pub. rels., pres. GPU 1992-93, 94-95, area 13 gov. dist. 38 1994-95, v.p. edn. 1996, Able Toastmaster award 1995, Exemplary Svc. award 1995). Democrat. Home: 36 N Miller St Shillington PA 19607 Office: GPU Svc PO Box 15152 Rte 183 & Van Reed Rd Reading PA 19612-5152

BREMER, CELESTE F., judge; b. 1953. BA, St. Ambrose Coll., 1974; JD, Univ. of Iowa Coll. of Law, 1977. Asst. county atty. Scott County, 1977-79; asst. atty. gen. Area Prosecutors Div., Iowa, 1979; with Carlin, Liebbe, Pitton & Bremer, 1979-81, Rabin, Liebbe, Shinkle & Bremer, 1981-82; with legal dept. Deere and Co., 1982-84; corp. counsel Economy Forms Corp., 1985-89; magistrate judge U.S. Dist. Ct. (Iowa so. dist.), 8th cir., Des Moines, 1984—; instr. Drake Univ. Coll. of Law, 1985-96. Mem. ABA, Fed. Magistrate Judge Assn., Nat. Assn. Women Judges, Am. Judicature Soc., Iowa State Bar Assn. (bd. govs., 1987-90), Iowa Judges Assn., Iowa Supreme Ct. Coun. on Jud. Selection (chmn. 1986-90), Iowa Orgn Women Attys., Polk County Bar Assn., Polk County Women Attys. Office: US Courthouse 123 E Walnut St Ste 429 Des Moines IA 50309-2036

BREMER, JOANNA CHARLES, journalist; b. Roanoke, Va., Apr. 24, 1947; d. John Clyde Jr. and Ruth Vivian Forman; m. Robert M. Charles, June 3, 1967 (div. 1984); m. James Allen Bremer, Sept. 19, 1987. Student, Orange Coast Community Coll., Costa Mesa, Calif., 1964-65, U. Utah, 1966-69; BS in Journalism, Wayne State U., 1982. Staff writer Salt Lake Tribune, 1966-69, Mellus Newspapers, Lincoln Park, Mich., 1969; women's editor News-Herald Newspapers, Wyandotte, Mich., 1969-72; various editorial positions Detroit Free Press, 1972-89; pres. Joanna Charles Comms., Detroit, 1989-95, Wharton Enterprises, Galveston, Tex., 1995—; editor Pierpont Comms., Houston, 1996—; cons. pub. rels. Founders Soc. Detroit Inst. Arts/Art and Flowers Festival, 1992-93, Detroit Sci. Ctr., 1990-91; cons. newsletter Detroit Grand Prix Assn., 1989, cons., race dir., 1990; cons. Identity Com. St. John Health Sys., Detroit, 1994-95. Editor, cons. Health Alliance Plan, 1994-96. Vice chair Mems. Coun./Internat. Inst. Detroit, 1991-92, chair, 1993; mgr. media ctr. Detroit Grand Prix Assn., 1991-94; ad hoc com. Mich. Women's Studies Assn., Lansing, 1988-95; mem. Beginning Experience/Detroit team, 1985-87, Founders Soc./Detroit Inst. Arts, 1982-95; bd. dirs. Mich. Journalism Hall of Fame, 1991-93; mem. adv. com. St. John. Hosp., Detroit, 1993-95. Mem. Women in Comm., Inc. (pres. 1991-92), Mich. Freedom of Info. Com. (treas. 1991-92), Automotive Press Assn., Exec. Career Women (co-chair scholarship com. 1996—), Z Krewe for Galveston Mardi Gras, Galveston C. of C., Friends of Mich. Women's Hall of Fame. Office: Wharton Enterprises 4909 Wharton Galveston TX 77551

BRENDEL, TERRY ANNE, obstetrical and gynecological nurse; b. Elkhart, Ind., Nov. 7, 1952; d. Earl Jr. and Audrey Jane (Lichtenberger) Nichols; m. Gary Otto Brendel, June 8, 1974; children: Stephanie Lynn, Christina Renae. ASN, U. Indpls., 1974; postgrad., numerous seminars. RN, Ind. Relief charge med.-surg. nurse Marion (Ind.) Gen. Hosp., 1974-79; instructional asst. learning disabilities/kindergarten Perry Twp. Schs., Indpls., 1985-90; office nurse S.E. Ob-Gyn., Beech Grove, Ind., 1990-92, Southpointe Ob-Gyn., Indpls., 1992—. Fundraiser Crises Pregnancy Ctr., Indpls., 1992-94. Mem. ANA, Nat. Assn. of Physician Nurses, Assn. of Women's Health, Obstetric and Neonatal Nurses. Methodist. Home: 8120 Hi Vu Dr Indianapolis IN 46227-2617 Office: 8120 Southpointe Dr D-1 Indianapolis IN 46227

BRENDER, JEAN DIANE, epidemiologist, nurse; b. Bellingham, Wash., Nov. 23, 1951; d. Otto and Jennie Wilma Tolsma; m. Dennis Ray Brender, Aug. 30, 1975; 1 child, Valerie. BSN summa cum laude, Whitworth Coll., 1974; M of Nursing, U. Wash., 1979, PhD of Epidemiology, 1983. RN, Tex. Staff nurse, infection control Sacred Heart Med. Ctr., Spokane, Wash., 1974-80; instr. nursing Intercollegiate Ctr. for Nursing Edn., Spokane, 1979-80, asst. prof. nursing, 1982-84; teaching asst. epidemiology U. Wash., Seattle, 1981-82; rsch. health scientist Audie L. Murphy Vets. Hosp., San Antonio, 1984-85; staff epidemiologist bur. epidemiology Tex. Dept. Health, Austin, 1986-87, acting program dir. environ. epidemiology program, 1987, dir. environ. epidemiology program, 1987-93, dir. noncommunicable disease epidemiology and toxicology, 1993—, also state environ. epidemiologist; bd. dirs. Agriculture Resources Protection Authority; state environ. epidemiologist; adj. instr. allied health scis. and health adminstrn. S.W. Tex. State U., 1986-90; adj. asst. prof. epidemiology U. Tex. Health Sci. Ctr.-Houston Sch. Pub. Health, 1985-93, adj. assoc. prof., 1993—. Contbr. articles to profl. jours. Tchr., mem. adult choir St. Martin's Luth. Ch., Austin, 1991—. Recipient H.E.A.L.T.H. award, 1994; grantee in field. Mem. Soc. Epidemiologic Rsch., Coun. State and Territorial Epidemiologists, Exec. Women in Tex. Govt. Home: 6902 Alder Cv Austin TX 78750-8161 Office: Tex Dept Health 1100 W 49th St Austin TX 78756-3101

BRENKEN, HANNE MARIE, artist; b. Duisburg, Germany, July 6, 1923; arrived in U.S., 1977; d. Hermann and Luise (Werth) Tigler; m. Hans Brenken, Mar. 28, 1942 (div. 1985); children: Karin Brenken Schneider-Henn, Berndt; m. Ricardo Wiesenberg, May 20, 1986. Grad., Landschulheim, Holzminden, Germany, 1941; studied in pvt. art schs., Munich and Bonn, Germany. One-person shows include Contra Kreis Gallery, Bonn, Germany, 1958, Galerie Junge Kunst, Fulda, Germany, 1959, Universa-Galerie, Nurenberg, Germany, 1960, Galleria Monte Napoleone, Milan, Italy, 1961, Galerie Niedlich, Stuttgart, Germany, 1961, 63, Galerie am Jakobsbrunnen, Stuttgart, 1964, 67, Kunst und Kunstverein Mus., Pforzheim, Germany, 1969, Kunstverein Mus., Munich, 1972, Galerie Dorothea Leonhart, Munich, 1974, I.C.L. Gallery, East Hampton, N.Y., 1980, Anne Reid Gallery, Princeton, N.J., 1981, Adagio Gallery, Bridgehampton, N.Y., 1982, 84, Queens Mus., N.Y., 1983, Ericson Gallery, N.Y.C., 1984, 85, Benton Gallery, Southampton, N.Y., 1986, Vered Gallery, East Hampton, N.Y., 1988, Gallery Rodeo, Lake Arrowhead, Calif., Taos, N.Mex., Beverly Hills, Calif., 1990, Brian Logan Art Space, Washington, 1991, The Gallery, Leesburg, Va., 1992, Amerika Haus, Frankfurt, Germany, 1993, Ganser Haus, Wasserburg, Germany, 1993, Ann Norton Sculpture Gardens, West Palm Beach, Fla., 1993, Jean Chisholm Gallery, West Palm Beach, 1994, Okuda Internat. Gallery, Washington, 1995; group shows include Duisburg (Germany) Mus., 1959, Baden-Baden Mus., Germany, 1961, 62, Haus der Kunst, Munich, 1963, 64, 69, 70, 71, 72, 73, Kunstgebäude, Stuttgart, 1963, 71, Acad. Fine Arts, Berlin, 1964, 73, Forum Stadtpark, Graz, Austria, 1965, Folkwang Mus., Essen, Germany, 1965, Munich City Mus., 1967, Karlsruhe (Germany) Kunstverein, 1967, Galerie Heseler, Munich, 1968, Hannover (Germany) Mus., 1969, Modern Art Mus., Munich, 1969, Bonn Mus., 1970, Kunstkreis Gallery, Wasserburg, Germany, 1972, 73, Kunstverein Mus., Rosenheim, Germany, 1972, Mainz Mus., 1974, Kunstverein Mus., Frankfurt, Germany, 1977, Guild Hall Mus., East Hampton, N.Y., 1979, 80, 81, 82, 83, Parrish Art Mus., Southampton, N.Y., 1979, 80, 81, Elaine Benson Gallery, Bridgehampton, N.Y., 1980, 81, Kunstverein Mus., Munich, 1982, Ericson Gallery, 1984, Vered Gallery, East Hampton, 1985, 86, 87, 89, Franz Bader Gallery, Washington, 1989, Ganser Haus, Wasserburg, 1992; permanent collections include Solomon R. Guggenheim Mus., N.Y.C., The Queens (N.Y.) Mus., Phoenix Art Mus., Guild Hall Mus., various mus. in Europe; author: (book) Firlefranz, 1969. Studio: PO Box 3405 Warrenton VA 22186-8005

BRENNAN, ANN RICHARD, secondary education educator; b. Red Hill, Pa., June 12, 1947; d. Clarence Renninger and Helen Grace (Bucher) Richard; m. Peter Edward Brennan, Mar. 29, 1969; children: Amy Lynn, Wendy Ann. BS in Med. Tech., Lebanon Valley Coll., 1969; MS in Sci. Edn., Fla. State U., 1994. Sci. tchr. Etowah H.S., Woodstock, Ga., 1990—; dept. chair Etowah H.S., Woodstock, 1993—. Mem. Nat. Sci. Tchr. Assn. (presenter), Ga. Sci. Tchr. Assn. (presenter). Office: Etowah High Sch 1895 Eagle Dr Woodstock GA 30188-2307

BRENNAN, DONNA LESLEY, public relations company executive; b. Washington, Mar. 13, 1945; d. Don Arthur and Louise (Tucker) B.; m. Salil Gutt, Jan. 14, 1985. BA, Denison U., 1967. Tchr. Souderton Area High Sch., Pa., 1967-69; mgr. media rels. Ins. Co. N.Am., Phila., 1969-72; dir. press rels. Colonial Penn Group, Phila., 1972-75, 1975-81, dir. communications, 1981-83; v.p. corp. communications Norstar Bancorp, Albany, N.Y., 1983-85; v.p. communications Meritor Fin. Group, Phila., 1986-87; prin. Donna Brennan Assocs., 1988—. Mem. Pub. Rels. Soc. Am. (pres. Phila. chpt. 1988), Phila. Women's Network (founder, bd. dirs.), Women's Assn. for Women's Alternatives (vice chmn., bd. dirs.), Forum of Exec. Women (pres. 1992-93).

BRENNAN, EILEEN HUGHES, nurse; b. Atlanta, Sept. 26, 1951; m. David Lee Altizer, May 11, 1974 (div. Dec. 1978); m. Scott Curtis Brennan, Feb. 6, 1982; 1 child, Bonnie Joy. Student, North Ga. Coll., 1969-70; diploma, Ga. Bapt. Sch. Nursing, 1973; student, Tift Coll., 1970-73, Ga. State U., 1980-85, SUNY, Albany, 1986-91, Brenau Univ., 1994—. RN, Ga.; CNOR. Orthopedic charge nurse Grady Meml. Hosp., Atlanta, 1974; operating room nurse DePaul Hosp., Norfolk, Va., 1974-76; nurse orthopedics Cabell Huntington (W.Va.) Hosp., 1976; surg. charge nurse VA Hosp., Huntington, 1976-77; nurse VA Hosp., Decatur, Ga., 1978-82, team leader oper room, 1979—, mem. operating room open heart team, 1986-88, 89-91; orthopedic nurse specialist Peachtree Orthopedic Clinic, Atlanta, 1982; operating room charge nurse Drs. Meml. Hosp., Atlanta, 1982-85, chmn. operating room policy and procedures, 1982-84, 94—; vascular rsch. coord. # 141 Co-operative Study-a-Multi-Ctr. VA Study, Decatur, Ga., 1988-89, # 362, 1991-93; acting temporary chair Narcotic Inventory Com., 1994-95, team leader genitourological svc., 1995—. Developed multi-media slide presentation for the Perioperative Patient as well as a pamphlet for preop teaching purposes, 1979, rev., 1985; editor: urology pamphlet, 1986, Open Heart Instrumentation, 1987; wrote and presented slide teaching program for coop. study (a multi-ctr. Dept. VA study), 1993. Vol. ARC, Atlanta, 1970-95, Am. Heart Assn., Atlanta, 1987-88, Atlanta Lung Assn., 1985-88, Am. Lung Assn., Atlanta, 1988-91, Outreach Com., 1995—, North Fulton County Cmty. Charities, including Thanksgiving lunch, Brown Bag Cmty. Food Bank, Clothes Closet, Homestretch, Battered Women's Shelter, Adopt a Christmas Family, 1991—, horse show for charities, 1995—. Recipient Cert., United Fund Campaign, Atlanta, 1981, Spl. Incentive award VA Med. Ctr., Decatur, Ga., 1981, Performance award Nurse Profl. Standards Bd., Decatur, 1987, Achievement award, 1987. Mem. Assn. Operating Room Nurses (co-chmn. Project Alpha 1986-87, spl. com. ethics, HIV task force). Episcopalian. Home: 9250 Brumbelow Crossing Way Alpharetta GA 30202-6193

BRENNAN, MAUREEN, lawyer; b. Morristown, N.J., Aug. 7, 1949. BA magna cum laude, Bryn Mawr Coll., 1971; JD, Boston Coll., 1977. Bar: Pa. 1977, U.S. Dist. Ct. (ea. dist.) Pa. 1978, Ohio 1989. Atty. U.S. EPA, Washington, 1977-80; asst. dist. atty. Phila. Trial and Appellate Divs., 1980-84; in-house environ. counsel TRW, Inc., 1985-87; ptnr. Baker & Hostetler, Cleve., 1987—; adj. prof. Case Western Res. U., Cleve., 1990-92. Active Cleve. Tree Commn., 1991—, co-chair, 1993-95; trustee Clean-Land Ohio, 1990—. Recipient Bronze Medal for Achievement, U.S. EPA, 1980. Mem. ABA (natural resources and environ. sect.), Pa. Bar Assn. (environ. law com.), Ohio State Bar Assn. (environ. law com.), Cleve. Bar Assn. (environ. law sect., chair wetlands com. 1991-92), Cuyahoga County Bar Assn. (environ. law com.). Office: Baker & Hostetler 3200 Nat City Center 1900 E 9th St Cleveland OH 44114-3401*

BRENNAN, NANCY ANN, accountant; b. Bakersfield, Calif., Sept. 3, 1958; d. Kenneth James and Elaine A. (Westendorf) P.; m. Raymond Matthew Brennan, Oct. 24, 1992. BA in Bus. Accountancy Option magna cum laude, Calif. State U., Fresno, 1994. Asst. ops. officer Bank of Am., Bakersfield, 1974-81; ops. officer Am. Nat. Bank, Bakersfield, 1981-86; staff acct. Stoughton Davidson Accountancy Corp., Fresno, 1995—. acctg. cons., Fresno, 1996—. Mem. Inst. Mgmt. Accts. Republican. Office: Stoughton Davidson Accounting Corp 3433 W Shaw Ave Ste 100 Fresno CA 93710

BRENNAN, NORMA JEAN, professional society publications director; b. Helena, Mont., Apr. 16, 1939; d. Harland Sanford Herrin and Elizabeth (Wardlaw) Brumfield; m. Anthony E. Brennan, Dec. 4, 1964 (div. Mar. 1986); children: Christopher E., Kimberly A. BA, U. Pacific, 1960. Editorial asst. Am. Rocket Soc., N.Y.C., 1961-62, asst. mng. editor, 1962-65; mng. editor AIAA, N.Y.C., 1978-80; publs. divsn. dir. AIAA, N.Y.C., Washington,Reston, Va., 1980—. Mem. Young Republicans, Stockton, Calif., 1958-60; vol. Mt. Sinai Hosp., N.Y.C., 1962-64. Mem. AIAA (sr., Space Shuttle Flag award), Soc. for Scholarly Pub. (chair edn. com.), Coun. Biology Editors, Assn. Am. Pubs., European Assn. Sci. Editors, Coun. Engring. and Sci. Soc. Execs., N.Am. Serials Interest Group, Washington Women's Info. Network. Home: 11551 Links Dr Reston VA 20190-4820 Office: AIAA 1801 Alexander Bell Dr Reston VA 20191

BRENNER, ANNE MANON, pediatrician, allergist; b. Jacksonville, Fla., Oct. 21, 1944. BA, Tex. Tech. U., 1966; MD, U. Tex., 1971. Diplomate Am. Bd. Allergy and Immunology, Am. Bd. Pediatrics. Intern in family practice John Sealy Hosp. U. Tex., Galveston, 1971-72, resident in pediatrics, 1972-74; pediatric practice Galveston, 1974-77; fellow in immunology and respiratory medicine Nat. Asthma Ctr., Denver, 1977-80; sr. staff physician Nat. Jewish Ctr., Denver, 1981—; assoc. prof. pediatrics U. Colo. Health Scis. Ctr., Denver. Contbr. articles to profl. jours. Mem. Am. Acad. Pediatrics, Am. Acad. Allergy and Immunology. Roman Catholic. Office: Nat Jewish Ctr Immunology and Respiratory Medicine 1400 Jackson St Denver CO 80206-2761

BRENNER, ERMA, author; b. N.Y.C., Dec. 1, 1911; d. Robert and Amy (Schoenbrunn) Brandt; m. Charles Brenner, Sept. 8, 1935; children: Elsa Brenner Cohen, Lucy (Mrs. Barrie Biven). Student, Harvard, 1931-34; studied with, Eduard Steuermann, 1954-61. Dir., owner Camp Sherbo, Bridgeton, Maine, 1933-40; tchr. nursery sch. Children's Ctr., Roxbury, Mass., 1942-44, Colonial Heights Nursery Sch., Yonkers, N.Y., 1946-48; owner, developer Scenichrome, 1946-48; mem. staff White Plains (N.Y.) Day Care Ctr., 1976-77; coordinator play ctr. dept. child psychiatry, mem. staff therapeutic nursery Albert Einstein Med. Coll., 1977—; cons. to staff children's day hosp. N.Y. Hosp. Westchester Div., 1980-81; creator, dir. Small House Program for emotionally disturbed children N.Y. Hosp., Cornell Med. Ctr., Westchester divsn., Rockland State Children's Psychiat. Hosp., Queens Children's Psychiat. Hosp.; cons. Parent Child Ctr., N.Y. Psychoanalytic Inst., N.Y.C., 1993—, Therapeutic Nursery, 1994. Author: A New Baby! A New Life!, 1973, repub. as When Baby Comes Home, (with others) The Vulnerable Child, vol. 2, 1994. Recipient Christophers award, 1973. Home and Office: 35 East 85th St New York NY 10028-0954

BRENNER, ESTHER HANNAH, elementary school educator; b. N.Y.C., Apr. 12, 1940; d. Israel Eli and Elsie (Lipschitz) B. BEd, U. Miami, 1963. Cert. tchr., Fla. Elem. tchr. Dade County Bd. Pub. Instrn., Miami, Fla., 1963-96; ret. Dade County Bd. Pub. Instrn., Miami, 1996. Unit chmn. Jackson Meml. Hosp., Miami, 1963-73; instr. trainer first aid and CPR, Greater Miami chpt. ARC, 1987—, chmn. safety svcs. Homestead br., 1989-92, chmn. nursing and health programs S.W. br., youth chmn., 1988-90, vol. youth coord., 1996, disaster shelter mgr.; adult trainer South Fla. coun. Girl Scouts USA, 1987—, master trainer, 1995. Recipient Appreciation plaque Adv. for Victims, 1985, Clara Barton Honor award, 1985, Ayme Carroll Meml. award, 1988, Plaque of Appreciation, PTA, 1989, Health and Safety award ARC, 1989, Woman of Yr. award Am. Cancer Soc., 1990—, Sarah Cullipher award, 1992, Appreciation Pin, Girl Scouts of Am., 1992, Honor Pin, Girl Scouts of Am., 1995. Mem. NSTA, Fla. Assn. Sci. Tchrs., Dade County Sci. Tchrs. Assn. (Sci. Tchr. of Yr. award 1994), Advs. for Victims (plaque of appreciation 1987), Gamma Sigma Sigma (past historian, sec., v.p., pres. Greater Miami chpt., bd. dirs. so. region 1975-79, nat. pub. rels. dir. 1979-83, Woman of Yr. award 1973, Outstanding Alumnae award 1977, Disting. Svc. award 1987). Democrat. Jewish. Home: 12310 SW 111th S Canal Street Miami FL 33186-4826

BRENNER, JANE SEGREST, city council member; b. Tuskegee, Ala., Aug. 18, 1930; d. Benjamin Howell Segrest and Doris Spradley (Ray) Serrett; m. Edward John Brenner, June 1, 1951 (dec. June 1992); children: Beverly, Douglas, Carolyn, Mary. Student, La. State U., 1948-50. Mem. city council City of Punta Gorda, Fla., 1996—. Trustee, past pres. Charlotte County Mental Health Ctr., Punta Gorda, Fla., 1986-96; chair bd. dirs. Ctr. for Abuse and Rape Emergencies, Punta Gorda, 1984-89; co-chair United Way Campaign, Charlotte County, Fla., 1992-94; Rep. Exec. Com. Charlotte County, 1990—; v.p. Southwest Fla. League Cities, 1996—. Mem. DAR, Lawyers' Wives of D.C., Special Tng. and Rehab. Found., Kentucky Colonels, Burnt Shore Country Club, Isles Yacht Club. Republican. Office: City of Punta Gorda 326 W Marion Ave Punta Gorda FL 33950

BRENNER, JANET MAYBIN WALKER, lawyer; b. Arkansas City, Kans.; d. D. Arthur and Maybin (Gardner) Walker; children: Margaret Maybin Burns, Theodore Kimball Jonas, Amanda Nash Freeman; m. Edgar H. Brenner, Aug. 4, 1979. AB, U. So. Calif.; JD, George Washington U., 1978. Bar: D.C. 1978; U.S. Dist. Ct. (D.C.). Sole practice law, Washington, 1979—. Mem. women's com. Corcoran Gallery Art, Washington, 1969—, Pres.'s Cir., Planned Parenthood D.C., 1990—, Found. for Preservation of Historic Georgetown. Mem. D.C. Bar Assn., Women's Bar of D.C., Women's Legal Def. Fund, Sulgrave Club (Washington). Home: 3325 R St NW Washington DC 20007-2310 also: Shadow Ridge Farm Washington VA 22747

BRENNER, LYNNETTE MARY, reading specialist, educator; b. Woodbury, N.J., July 20, 1959; d. Bernhard A. and Anna Rose (Rickert) B. BS in Bible and Elem. Edn., Lancaster (Pa.) Bible Coll., 1981; MEd in Reading, Beaver Coll., 1991. Cert. Elem. and Reading Tchr., N.J., Pa. 2d grade tchr. Killian Hill Christian Sch., Lilburn, Ga., 1981-83, Bethel Bapt. Ch. Sch., Cherry Hill, N.J., 1984-92; reading specialist Cherry Hill Bd. Edn., 1992—; adj. faculty Ea. Coll., St. Davids, Pa., 1994—; mem. steering com. Cherry Hill Tchrs. applying Whole Lang., 1993-95. Sec. missions com. Columbus Bapt. Ch., 1992—, discipleship ministry, 1993—, Sun. sch. tchr., 1992-94. Recipient Recognition honor N.J. Senator for Geography Awareness, 1990, Gov.'s Tchr. Recognition Program award, 1995; named Tchr. of Yr., Kilmer Sch. Mem. NEA, N.J. Edn. Assn., West Jersey Reading Coun. (bd. dirs.), N.J. Reading Assn., Internat. Reading Assn. Republican. Baptist. Office: Joyce Kilmer Elem Sch Chapel Ave Cherry Hill NJ 08002

BRENNER, MARGIE LEIGH, mortgage company originator; b. Campbellsville, Ky., June 6, 1946; d. Bennie Lawrence and Evelyn Garnetta (Seay) DeWitt; m. Aaron Brenner, July 20, 1969; children: Susan Leigh, Tracy Lynne. Grad. in elem. edn., Western Ky. U., 1968; postgrad., U. Ky., Lexington, 1986, U. Ky., Elizabethtown, 1988. Real estate agt. Nat. Realtors Assn., Elizabethtown, Ky., 1986-92; mortgage originator Nat. Bankers Assn., McLean, Va., 1993—. Mem. adv. bd. Hardin County Sch., Elizabethtown, 1985-87. Recipient Apple award Elizabethtown Sch. Sys., 1985. Mem. Order Ea. Star, Ky. Cols. Republican. Baptist.

BRENNER, RENA CLAUDY, communications executive; b. Camden, N.J.; d. John Lawler and Louretta (Du Fresene) Morgan; m. Edgar W. Claudy (div. 1968); 1 child, Renee; m. Millard Brenner, Nov. 6, 1971 (dec. 1975); children: Sally, Malcolm, Hugh. Student, U. Pa., 1978, U. Mich., 1983. Reporter Tribune-Telegram, Salt Lake City, 1943-45, Times Chronicle, Jenkintown, Pa., 1950-55; free-lance writer Enfield, Pa., 1955-60; pub. relations dir., advt. mgr. Gen. Atronics/Magnavox, Phila., 1960-70; mgr. corp. pub. relations ITE-Imperial, Phila., 1970-73, dir. corp. comm., 1973-76; dir. corp. comm. Parker-Hannifin Corp., Cleve., 1976-83, v.p. corp. comm., 1983-85; pres. Brenner Assocs., Clearwater, Fla., 1986—. Recipient Creative Direction award Phila. Club Advt. Women, 1970, Clarion award Women in Communications, 1982, Gold Key award Pub. Relations News, 1984. Mem. Bus. Profl. Advt. Assn. (life), Pub. Relations Soc. Am. (life), Nat. Investors Relations Inst.. Office: Brenner Assocs 1501 Gulf Blvd Apt 607 Clearwater FL 34630-2903

BRENNER, RONA KATZEN, financial planner; b. Harrisburg, Pa., June 26, 1942; d. Henry Charles and Helen (Nassan) Katzen; m. Jerry Herbert Brenner; children: Lauri Brenner Rosenthal, Holly Brenner Udell. BA, George Washington U., 1966; cert. upper level math., U. Del., 1988; CFP, Coll. for Fin. Planning, 1992. CFP. V.p. fin. planning Fin. House, Wilmington, Del., 1989—; tchr. West Chester U., 1993, 94; speaker U. Del., 1992, 2d Ann. Entrepreneurial Women's Expo, Wilmington, Del., 1993. Columnist: Your Money Matters Kennett Square (Pa.) Newspaper, 1992—. Mem. AAUW, Deleware and So. Chester County Study Group for CFPS (chair 1993-94), Deleware Valley Soc. Inst. CFPs (bd. dirs. 1994-96, v.p. 1995—), Wilmington Women in Bus., Alliance for Women Entrepreneurs (bd. dirs. 1995—). Office: Fin House 5818 Kennett Pike Wilmington DE 19807-1116

BRENT, SUZANNE STOKES, sociology educator, consultant; b. Amarillo, Tex., Oct. 25, 1939; d. Clarence Norman and Sue Alice (Simpson) Stokes; m. Don Teel Curtis (div. Feb. 1983); children: Margaret Curtis McDermid, Stephen Teel Curtis II, Sara Curtis Robinson; m. Joseph Phillip Brent, Sr., Dec. 27, 1988. Ba, So. Meth. U., 1961; MHR, U. Okla., 1985; postgrad., U. North Tex., 1989—. Lic. marriage and family therapist, chem. dependency counselor. Tchr. Highland Park Jr. High, Dallas, 1961-62; coord. family programs Northwest Tex. Hosp., 1985-88; dir. life svcs. West Tex. A&M U., 1989-91; educator, family life specialist Amarillo (Tex.) Coll., 1994-95; mem. adj. faculty dept. sociology and behavioral scis. Amarillo Coll., 1994—; nat. planning com. U.S. Dept. Edn., 1990-91; bd. rep. Tex. Assn. Alcoholism and Drug Abuse Counselors, 1989-90. Bd. dirs. Amarillo Jr. League, 1967—, Amarillo Art Ctr., Amarillo Little Theatre. Consortium grantee U.S. Dept. Edn., 1990. Mem. Am. Sociol. Assn., Nat. Assn. Alcoholism & Drug Abuse Counselors (master addiction counselor), Internat. Coalition of Addition Studies Educators (bd. dirs. 1996—), Internat. Coun. on Alcohol and Addictions. Office: PO Box 15185 Amarillo TX 79105-5185

BRENTINE, ELLEN JOAN, elementary school educator; b. Tyler, Minn.; d. Henry and Clara A. (Lens) Bakker; m. Frank X. Brentine, Dec. 19, 1973. BA in History and Elem. Edn., Coll. St. Catherine, St. Paul, 1960; MEd, Washburn U. of Topeka, Kans., 1979. Cert. tchr. K-9. Tchr. Most Holy Trinity Sch., St. Louis Park, Minn., 1960-61, St. Bernard's Sch., St. Paul, 1961-66, Assumption Sch., Richfield, Minn., 1966-72, St. Bridget's Sch., Mpls., 1972-73, Unified Sch. Dist. #345, Topeka, 1973—; classroom tchr. adv. bd. for Super Science Red student mag. Scholastic, Inc., N.Y.C., 1992—. NDEA grant, summer 1965, NSF grant, summer 1966; named Dist. Tchr. of the Yr. Seaman Profl. Educators Assn. of Kans., 1989-90. Mem. NEA, Internat. Reading Assn. Democrat. Roman Catholic. Office: West Indianola Elem Sch 4201 NW Brickyard Rd Topeka KS 66618-3531

BRENTON, MARIANNE WEBBER, state legislator, technical librarian; b. Freeport, Maine, Feb. 25, 1933; d. Milton and Leah (Hamilton) W.; m. Richard P. Brenton, Mar. 4, 1955; children: Anne, Joan, Peter. BA in Biology, Bates Coll., 1955. Sci. tchr. Southboro (Mass.) High Sch., 1956-57; tech. libr. Trans-Sonics Inc., Burlington, Mass., 1957-59, MKS Instruments, Andover, Mass., 1978-90; state rep. Mass. Ho. of Reps., Boston, 1991—. Trustee Tewksbury (Mass.) State Hosp., 1967-83; mem. Burlington Sch. Com., 1972-81, also past chmn. Republican. Home: 16 Nelson Rd Burlington MA 01803-1726 Office: Rm 549B State House Boston MA 02133*

BRESLIN, ELVIRA MADDEN, lawyer, educator; b. Phila., Oct. 28, 1943; d. Daniel Joseph and Elvira Rose (Leichner) Madden; m. John Anthony Breslin, June 19, 1971; children: Kristen, John A.V. AB in English, Secondary Edn., Chestnut Hill Coll., Phila., 1961-65; MA in High Sch. Adminstrn., Villanova (Pa.) U., 1968; JD, Cath. U. Am., Washington, 1990; LLM in Taxation, Villanova U., 1996. Bar: Pa. 1991, U.S. Dist. Ct. Pa. 1994, U.S. Ct. Appeals (3d cir.) 1994, D.C. 1992, U.S. Dist. Ct. D.C. 1992. Tchr. Baldwin-Whitehall Pub. Schs./Cheltenham Pub. Schs., Pa., 1965-75; educator, prin. certification, tchr. Fairfax (Va.) Pub. Schs., 1979-94; computer/paralegal specialist Personnel Pool, Washington, 1987; rsch. assoc. Meade & Assocs., Fairfax, 1988, Akin, Gump, Strauss, Hauer & Feld, Washington, 1988; law clk. Fedn. of Tax Adminstrs., Washington, 1989, Beins, Axelrod, Osborne & Mooney, Washington, 1989-90; pvt. practice Washington and Pa., 1991—; rsch. assoc. Villanova U., 1994; legal/computer specialist Nat. Acad. Scis., Smithsonian Instn., Steptoe & Johnson, Akin, Gump, Strauss, Hauer & Feld, Office of Ind. Counsel; legal resource/rsch. specialist Dir. Testing and Evaluation, Walnut Hill Ctr. Mem. Oakton Glen (Va.) Homeowners Neighborhood Watch, 1987—, Oakton Glen Homeowners Assn., 1979—; mem., religious instr. Our Lady of Good Counsel

Roman Cath. Ch., Vienna; judge moot ct. competitions Cath. U. Columbus Sch. Law, Washington, 1993—; exec. treas. Thomas Jefferson H.S. for Sci. and Tech., also investment advisor. Mem. ABA (tax sect. and legal edn. sect.), Fed. Bar Assn. (tax sect.), D.C. Bar Assn. (tax sects.), Pa. Bar Assn. (tax sects., legal edn., edn. coms. and taxation coms.). Home and Office: 2655 Oakton Glen Dr Vienna VA 22181

BRESLIN, EVALYNNE L. W., retired psychiatric nurse; b. Richmond, Ohio, July 7, 1931; d. Evan P. and Ada Augusta (Huscroft) Wood-Robertson; m. Donald Joseph Breslin, Jan. 30, 1954; children: Lisa Karen, Mark Nathaniel (dec.), Paul Andrew Scott. Diploma, Cleve. Met. Gen. Hosp., 1952; student, Case Western Res. U., Akron U.; HHD (hon.), London Inst. of Applied Rsch., 1973. Lic. RN, Ohio, Mass; RN, Ohio, Mass. Head nurse Cleve. Met. Gen. Hosp., Cleve. State Receiving Hosp.; cons. mental illness and addictions Mass.; ret. Bd. dirs. Triple Trouble; ret. vol. monitor state hosp. facilities Alliance for Mentally Ill; vol. nursing/psychiat. work with abandonded adolescents, 1968-89. Mem. ANA, Nat. League Nursing, Mass. Nurses Assn. (coun. on mental health).

BRESLOW, MARILYN GANON, portfolio manager; b. Cleve., Apr. 23, 1944; d. Joseph M. and Edith (Rubin) Ganon; m. Jan L. Breslow, June 27, 1965; children: Noah J., Nicholas M. BA, Barnard Coll., 1965; MBA, Harvard U., 1970. Market rsch. analyst Polaroid Corp., Cambridge, Mass., 1965-68, project cons., 1973-78, bldg. W-4 mgr., 1978-80, dir. mktg. svcs., 1980-83; cons. Peat, Marwick, Mitchell & Co., Washington, 1970-71; assoc. ICF, Inc., Washington, 1971-73; cons. Brookline, Mass., 1983-84; v.p. Dillon, Read & Co., Inc., N.Y.C., 1984-90; gen. ptnr. Concord Ptnrs., 1984-90; portfolio mgr., analyst W.P. Stewart & Co., Inc., N.Y.C., 1990—; also bd. dirs. W. P. Stewart & Co., Inc., N.Y.C.; bd. dirs. Alteon, Inc., Ramsey, N.J. Mem. N.Y. Soc. Security Analysts, IEEE. Home: 10 Horseguard Ln Scarsdale NY 10583-2311

BRET, DONNA LEE, elementary education educator; b. Pottsville, Pa., Dec. 18, 1950; d. S. Allen and Georgene Katherine (Heiser) Zimmerman; m. Donald Louis Bret, Oct. 11, 1969; 1 child, Thomas Donald. AA, Glendale C.C., 1988; BEd, Ariz. State U., 1990, MEd, 1995. Cert. elem., ESL tchr., Ariz. Kindergarten tchr. Glendale (Ariz.) Elem. Dist., 1991-92, 1st grade ESL tchr., 1992-93, multi-age ESL tchr., 1993—. Mem. NEA, Ariz. State U. Alumni Assn., Bilingual Club. Office: Glendale Elem Sch Dist 7301 N 58th Ave Glendale AZ 85301-1893

BRETT, JAN CHURCHILL, illustrator, author; b. Hingham, Mass., Dec. 1, 1949; d. George and Jean (Thaxter) B.; m. Daniel Bowler, Feb. 27, 1970 (div. 1979); 1 child, Lia; m. Joseph Hearne, Aug. 18, 1980. Student, Colby Jr. Coll., 1968-69, Boston Mus. Fine Arts Sch., 1970. Author, illustrator: Fritz and the Beautiful Horses, 1981 (Parent's Choice award Parents' Choice Found., 1981), Good Luck Sneakers, 1981, Annie and the Wild Animals, 1985, The First Dog, 1988, Beauty and the Beast, 1989, The Wild Christmas Reindeer, 1990, The Twelve Days of Christmas, 1990, The Mitten, 1990, Goldilocks and the Three Bears, 1990, The Owl and the Pussycat, 1991, Berlioz the Bear, 1991, The Trouble with Trolls, 1992, Christmas Trolls, 1993, Town Mouse, Country Mouse, 1994, Armadillo Rodeo, 1995; Comet's Nine Lives, 1996; illustrator: Woodland Crossings, 1978, Inside A Sand Castle and Other Secrets, 1979, The Secret Clocks Time Senses of Living Things, 1979, St. Patrick's Day in the Morning, 1980 (Parent's Choice award Parents' Choice Found. 1981), Young Melvin and Bulger, 1981, In the Castle of the Cats, 1981, Some Birds Have Funny Names, 1981 (Amb. Honor award English Speaking Union U.S. 1983), I Can Fly, 1981, Prayer, 1983, The Valentine Bears, 1983, Some Plants Have Funny Names, 1983, Where Are All the Kittens, 1984, Old Devil Is Waiting, 1985, The Mother's Day Mice, 1985, Scary, Scary Halloween, 1986, Noelle of the Nutcracker, 1986, The Enchanted Book, 1987, Happy Birthday, Dear Duck, 1988. Overseer Boston Symphony Orchestra; trustee Thayer Acad., Braintree, Mass. Mem. Nat. Soc. Colonial Dames Am. Office: 132 Pleasant St Norwell MA 02061-2523

BRETTELL, CAROLINE B., anthropology educator; b. Montreal, Que., Can., June 11, 1950; came to U.S., 1967; d. Jacques Louis and Zoe (Browne-Clayton) Bieler; m. Richard Robson Brettell, June 9, 1973. BA, Yale U., 1971; MA, Brown U., 1972, PhD, 1978. Instr. U. Tex., Austin, 1976-78, postdoctoral rsch. assoc. Population Rsch. Ctr., 1978-80; lectr. Loyola U., Chgo., 1983-88; project dir. and rsch. assoc. Newberry Libr., Chgo., 1984-88; dir. women's studies So. Meth. U., Dallas, 1989-94; vis. assoc. prof. So. Meth. U., 1988-91, assoc. prof., 1991-93, prof., 1993—, chair dept. anthropology, 1994—. Author: Men Who Migrate, Women Who Wait, 1986, We Have Already Cried Many Tears, 1982, revised edit., 1995; co-author: Painters and Peasants, 1983, Gender in Cross-Cultural Perspective, 1992, Gender and Health: An International Perspective, 1995; editor: When They Read What We Write: The Politics of Ethnography, 1993; co-editor: International Migration: The Female Experience, and others. Recipient numerous grants including NIH, 1978, Wenner Gren Found., 1979, NEH, 1984, Social Sci. Rsch. Coun., 1988, 96, Am. Phil. Soc., 1990 and others. Mem. Soc. Sci. History Assn. (exec. com. 1988-92), Am. Anthropol. Assn., Coun. for European Studies (steering com. 1988-92, exec. com. 1994—), Literacy Instrs. for Tex. (pres. bd. dirs. 1994-95). Home: 5522 Montrose Dr Dallas TX 75209-5610 Office: Dept Anthropology So Meth U Dallas TX 75275

BRETTSCHNEIDER, CATHIE I., editor; b. Balt., Nov. 29, 1947; d. William Henry and Mary Irene (Kyle) B. BA in Religion and Philosophy, Catawba Coll., 1969; MA in Religion and Culture, Syracuse U., 1970, MPhil. in Religion and Culture, 1975. Promotion copywriter Princeton U. Press, N.J., 1977-80, manuscript editor, 1983-91, religion acquisitions editor, 1987-91; prodn. editor APA, Arlington, Va., 1981-83; humanities acquisitions editor Univ. Press Va., Charlottesville, 1991—; consulting editor (mag. book rev.) Belles Lettres, Gaithersburg, Md., 1985—. Mem. MLA, Am. Acad. Religion. Office: Univ Press Va Box 3608 University Sta Charlottesville VA 22903

BRETZ, KELLY JEAN RYDEL, actuary; b. Wadena, Minn., Oct. 30, 1962; d. Edmund Leroy and Glenyce Clara (Andrie) B.; m. Daniel Mark Bretz Rydel. BA in Math., Moorhead State U., 1984. Completed Assn. for Investment Mgmt. and Rsch. chartered fin. analyst level 1 and level 2. Asst. actuary Northwestern Nat. Life Ins. Co., Mpls., 1984-92; assoc. actuary TMG Life Ins. Co., Fargo, N.D., 1993-94, MSI Life Ins. Co., Arden Hills, Minn., 1994, MidAm. Mut. Life Ins. Co., Roseville, Minn., 1994-95; sr. staff actuary Fortis Fin. Group, Woodbury, Minn., 1996—; grader Soc. Actuaries' Exam 220, 1992, 93. Contbr. articles to co. jours. Organizer blood drive Mpls. Blood Bank, 1992; meal deliverer Meals on Wheels, Fargo, 1993; meal server Sharing and Caring Hands, Mpls., 1992. Fellow Soc. Actuaries (mem. fin. and investment mgmt. practice edn. com.); mem. Am. Acad. Actuaries, Twin Cities Actuarial Club, Life Ins. Mktg. and Rsch. Assn. (fin. mktg. and svcs. com. 1993). Office: Fortis Fin Group 500 Bielenberg Dr Woodbury MN 55125

BREWER, CAROL DEAN COAKER, secondary school English language educator; b. Mobile, Ala., Mar. 18, 1949; d. George M. and Cathy (Pennington) Coaker; widowed; 1 child, Jeremy Dean. BA in English, Earlham Coll., 1972; MA in Edn., Ball State U., 1976. Cert. secondary sch. English tchr., Tenn. Tchr. Wernle Children's Home, Richmond, Ind., 1972-73; English tchr. Centerville (Ind.) H.S., 1973-77, Montgomery Bell Acad., Nashville, 1987-91; English tchr. Father Ryan H.S., Nashville, 1991—, chair SACS evaluation com., 1993-94; English tchr., chair dept. Marianna (Fla.) H.S., 1977-86; rsch. tchr. Leonard Bernstein Ctr. for Arts, Nashville, 1994—. Design cons., 1993-94. Mem. Nat. Coun. Tchrs. English, Bellevue C. of C. (bicentennial mem.). Presbyterian. Home: 122 Morton Mill Cir Nashville TN 37221-6715

BREWER, CHERYL ANN, obstetrician and gynecologist, educator; b. New Rochelle, N.Y., Oct. 31, 1959; d. John Paul and Marie Elizabeth (Royance) B. BS, Miss. U. for Women, 1981; MD, Ind. U., Indpls., 1985. Resident in ob-gyn. SUNY Health Scis. Ctr., Syracuse, 1985-89, asst. prof. ob-gyn., 1989-91; asst. prof. dept. ob-gyn. Ind. U., Indpls., 1991-92; fellow in gynecologic oncology U. Calif., Irvine, 1992—. Fellow Am. Coll. Ob-Gyn. Home: 17632 Jordan Ave Apt 40B Irvine CA 92715-2976 Office: U Calif Med Ctr 101 The City Dr Irvine CA 92715

BREWER, CONSTANCE ANN, social studies educator; b. Erwin, Tenn., Sept. 25, 1948; d. James Hiram Jr. and Evelyn (Rice) Ford; m. Dwight Vernon Brewer, June 23, 1971; children: Kimberly, Scott. BS, East Tenn. State U., 1970; MAEd, Tusculum Coll., 1996. Cert. tchr. Tchr. Unicoi (Tenn.) Elem., 1970-71; guidance counselor Evans Elem., Erwin, Tenn., 1971-73; tchr. Rock Creek Elem., Erwin, Tenn., 1973-74, Evans Elem., Erwin, Tenn., 1977-88, Unicoi County H.S., Erwin, Tenn., 1988—; cons., vol. Unicoi County Heritage Mus., Erwin, 1993—; cons. Internat. Day, East Tenn. State U., Johnson City, 1991—; mem. adv. bd. Tenn. Tchr.'s Study Coun., Erwin, 1985-90. Mem. Friends of Libr., Erwin, 1992—; vol. Am. Cancer Soc., Erwin, 1992—, Jaycees, Erwin, 1991-93. Mem. NEA, Nat. Coun. for Social Studies Tchrs., Tenn. Edn. Assn., Unicoi County Edn. Assn. (sec. 1988-90, rep. 1993—, v.p. 1996-97). Home: 111 Hickory Springs Rd Erwin TN 37650-9117

BREWER, DEBORAH GREEN, secondary school educator; b. Friendship, N.Y., Mar. 21, 1950; d. Victor and Dilia (Savona) Green; m. Alden McKenzie Brewer, July 5, 1980. BS in Edn./Social Studies, SUNY, Geneseo, 1972; MS in Reading, St. Bonaventure U., 1976. Cert. K-12 reading, social studies tchr., N.Y. 7th grade social studies tchr. Allegheny (N.Y.) Ctrl. Sch.; 7-12 spl. areas tchr., 8th grade social studies tchr. Dundee (N.Y.) Cen. Sch.; mem. Com. on Spl. Edn., Dundee, chmn. mentor com. Mem. Lake Counties Reading Assn. (treas. 1993-94, Coun. Svc. award 1994, co-pres. 1994-95). Home: PO Box 386 Geneva NY 14456-0386

BREWER, JANICE KAY, state legislator, property and investment firm executive; b. Hollywood, Calif., Sept. 26, 1944; d. Perry Wilford and Edna Clarice (Bakken) Drinkwine; m. John Leon Brewer, Jan. 1, 1963; children: Ronald Richard, John Samuel, Michael Wilford. Med. asst. cert. Valley Coll., Burbank, Calif., 1963, practical radiol. technician cert., 1963; D in Humanities (hon.) L.A. Chiropractic Coll., 1970. Pres., Brewer Property & Investments, Glendale, Ariz., 1970—; mem. Ariz. Ho. of Reps., Phoenix, 1983-86, Ariz. Senate, 1987—, majority whip, 1993—. State committeeman, Rep. Party, Phoenix, 1970, 1983; legis. liaison Ponderosa Rep. Women, Phoenix, 1980; bd. dirs. Motion Picture & TV Commn. Active NOW. Recipient Freedom award Vets. of Ariz., 1994; named Woman of Yr., Chiropractic Assn. Ariz., 1983, Legislator of Yr., Behaviour Health Assn. Ariz., 1991, NRA, 1992. Mem. Nat. Fedn. Rep. Women, Am. Legis. Exch. Coun. Lutheran. Home: 6835 W Union Hills Dr Glendale AZ 85308-8058 Office: Ariz State Senate Capitol Phoenix AZ 85007

BREWER, KAREN, librarian; b. Janesville, Wis., Apr. 29, 1943; d. Gordon A. and Charlotte (Warren) Schultz; m. Eugene N. Brewer, June 22, 1963. BA, U. Wis., 1965, MA, 1966; PhD, Case Western Res. U., 1983. Libr. Middleton Med. Libr. U. Wis., Madison, 1966-67; libr. Med. Libr. U. Tenn., Memphis, 1968-69; libr. Cleve. Health Sci. Libr. Case Western Res. U., Cleve., 1970-76; dir. libr. Coll. Medicine Northeastern Ohio U., Rootstown, 1976-88; dir. libr. Med. Ctr. NYU, 1988—. Mem. editorial bd. Ann. Stats. Acad. Health Sci. Libr., 1986-91. Fellow N.Y. Acad. Medicine; mem. Assn. Acad. Health Sci. Librs. (sec.-treas. 1986-89, pres.-elect 1994, pres. 1995), Med. Libr. Assn. (bd. dirs. 1991-94), Acad. Health Info. Profls. (disting. mem.), Am. Med. Informatics Assn. Office: NYU Med Ctr Libr 550 1st Ave New York NY 10016-6481

BREWER, LINDA GUY, elementary education educator; b. Alexander City, Ala., June 20, 1951; d. Lowell Oliver and Janie (Allen) Guy; m. Kenneth Wayne Brewer, Dec. 22, 1969; children: Tracie Michelle B. Skinner, Stacie Janelle B. Honaker, Michael Wayne. Student, Alexander City State Jr. Coll., 1971, Gadsden State Jr. Coll., 1992; BS in Edn., Jacksonville State U., 1994. Cert. elem. and early childhood tchr., Ala. Substitute tchr. Talladega (Ala.) County Schs., 1974-81, 92-93, chpt. I instnl. asst., 1981-92. Sec.-treas. Munford (Ala.) PTA, 1983-85; tchr. Munford Ch. of Christ, 1985—; troop leader, cookie chmn. Girl Scouts U.S.A., Munford, 1980-84, svc. unit chmn., 1992-94. MIrriam Higgenbotham scholar, 1993; recipient Pres.'s award Cottaquilla Coun. Girl Scouts U.S.A., 1982, Leadership award, 1983. Home: PO Box 103 Munford AL 36268-0103

BREWER, MARGARET S., network management specialist, consultant; b. Elizabeth, N.J., June 24, 1948; d. William Carl and Margaret Jessie (Hipwell) Sussky. BS in Math., U. Ala., Tuscaloosa, 1970. Software programmer various cos., Houston, 1970-79; software specialist United Energy Resources, Houston, 1979-82; comm. specialist 1st City Nat. Bank, Houston, 1982-83; network sys. programmer Wis. Power & Light, Madison, 1983-84; lead network sys. programmer Blue Cross/Blue Shield N.C., Chapel Hiill, 1985-88, SAS Inst., Inc., Cary, N.C., 1988-90, VF Corp., Greensboro, N.C., 1993-94; supr. network mgmt. EPA, Research Triangle Park, N.C., 1990-93; co-founder, pres., tech. cons. Network Sys. Integrators, Inc., Franklinville, N.C., 1994-95, also bd. dirs.; founder Hawksview House Needleworks, Franklinville, 1995; systems programmer staff specialist Fed. Res. Bank Richmond, Va., 1996—; owner needlework design and sales show The Ebony Ewe, 1996—; data comms. cons. Ptnr. Spl. Olympics, N.C., 1995. Mem. IEEE (assoc.), Assn. for Computing Machinery, IEEE Computer Soc., NAFE, N.Y. Acad. Scis., Order of Internat. Fellowship. Home: 3305 Rufford Pl Chester VA 23831 Office: Fed Res Bank 701 E Byrd St Richmond VA 23219

BREWER, MARJORIE JOY, elementary school educator; b. Chgo., Dec. 4, 1940; d. LeRoy Kenneth and LaVonne Geraldine (Osborn) Moore; m. David Louis Brewer, July 1963 (div. Mar. 1979); children: David Brett, Holly Elaine, Brian Christian. BS in Spl. Edn., Speech and Hearing, Phillips U., 1963; MEd in Elem. Edn., Northeastern State U., 1990. Cert. tchr., Okla. Probation counselor Okla. County Children's Ct., Oklahoma City, 1963-66; elem. tchr. Walt Whitman Magnet Elem. Sch., Tulsa, 1990-92, Waite Phillips Elem. Sch., Tulsa, 1992—; mem. editl. com. citizenship edn. com. Okla. Bar Assn., 1992. Ordained deacon Presbyn. Ch. Kirk of the Hills, Tulsa, 1986-89; asst. scoutmaster Troop 16, Boy Scouts Am., New Haven Meth., Tulsa, 1985; pres. Baylor U. Parents League, Tulsa, 1987-88; chmn. 25th class reunion Phillips Univ., Enid, Okla., 1988. Recipient scholarship Okla. Bar Assn., 1991. Mem. Kappa Delta Pi, Delta Kappa Gamma (v.p. Alpha Lambda chpt. 1992-94, pres. 1994-96), Kappa Kappa Iota (sec. 1996—). Republican. Presbyterian. Home: 6006 S Jamestown Ave Tulsa OK 74135-7844 Office: Waite Phillips Elem Sch 3613 S Hudson Tulsa OK 74135

BREWER, PRISCILLA NAOMI, artist; b. Dallas, June 8, 1955; d. Jack James and Gladys Lubert (Wilson) B. Degree in comml. art, East Tex. State U., 1978. Designer various advt. agys., Dallas, 1978-89; pvt. practice Charlie, Ink, Gatlinburg, Tenn., 1990-95, Smokin Airbrush, Galveston, Tex., 1996—. Editor: The Airbrush Rag, 1994-96; contbr. articles to newspapers and mags. Mem. Am. Airbrush Assn. (charter, life). Office: Smokin Airbrush 6702 Seawall Blvd # 2 Galveston TX 77551

BREWSTER, ELIZABETH WINIFRED, English language educator, poet, novelist; b. Chipman, N.B., Can., Aug. 26, 1922; d. Frederick John and Ethel May (Day) Brewster. BA, U. N.B., 1946; MA, Radcliffe U., 1947; BLS, U. Toronto, 1953; DLitt, Ind. U., 1962; D.Litt., U. N.B., 1982. Cataloger Carleton U., Ottawa, Ont., 1953-57; cataloger Ind. U. Library, Bloomington, 1957-58, N.B. Legis. Library, 1965-68, U. Alta. Library, Edmonton, Can., 1968-70; mem. English dept. Victoria U., B.C., 1960-61; reference libr. Mt. Allison U. Libr., Sackville, N.B., 1961-65; vis. asst. prof. English U. Alta., 1970-71; mem. faculty U. Sask., Saskatoon, Can., 1972—, asst. prof. English, 1972-75, assoc. prof., 1975-80, prof., 1980-90, prof. emeritus, 1990—. Author: East Coast, 1951, Lilloot, 1954, Roads, 1957, Passage of Summer, 1969, Sunrise North, 1972, In Search of Eros, 1974, Sometimes I Think of Moving, 1977, The Way Home, 1982, The Sisters, 1974, It's Easy to Fall on the ice, 1977, Digging In, 1982, Junction, 1982, A House Full of Women, 1983, Selected Poems 1944-84, 2 vols., 1985, Visitations, 1987, Entertaining Angels, 1988, Spring Again, 1990, The Invention of Truth, 1991, Wheel of Change, 1993, Away from Home, 1995, Footnotes to the Book of Job, 1995. Recipient E.J. Pratt award for poetry U. Toronto, 1953, Pres. medal for poetry U. Western Ont., 1980, Lit. award Can. Broadcasting Corp., 1991, Lifetime award for excellence in the arts Sask. Arts Bd., 1995. Mem. League Can. Poets (life), Writers' Union Can., Assn. Can. Univ. Tchrs. English. Office: U Saskatchewan, Dept English, 9 Campus Dr, Saskatoon, SK Canada S7N 5A5

BREWSTER, MARGARET EMELIA, artist; b. Kaukauna, Wis., July 18, 1932. Attended, U. Wis., Fox Valley, 1951-53. Photographer, graphic artist Appleton Papers, Inc., Combined Locks, Wis., 1954-90. Exhbns. include Appleton Gallery Arts, 1965-94, Bank of Kaukauna, 1974-96, Frances Hardy Gallery, Ephraim, Wis., 1984, 86, 93, 95, Neville Pub. Mus. Brown County, Green Bay, 1986-87, 90, 92-95, Minn. State Capital, St. Paul, 1987, Brown County Libr., Green Bay, 1988, Ctr. Visual Arts, Wausau, Wis., 1991, Milw. Art Mus., 1991-92, Outagamie County Hist. Mus., 1991-95, Bank One Lobby Gallery, Neenah, Wis., 1993-94, 96, Wis. Arts Bd. Gallery, 1994, U. Wis., Platteville, 1996, William F. Boniface Arts Ctr., Escanaba, Mich., 1996. Bd. dirs. Friends of the 1000 Islands Environ. Ctr., Kaukauna, 1986—, chair art fair, 1986-94, sec., 1988-93. Mem. Kaukauna Creative Artists Group (sec. 1991-93, chair exhibit and publicity 1991—), Midwest Watercolor Soc., Wis. Women in Arts, Wis. Painters & Sculptors, Nat. Mus. Women in Arts. Studio: 400 W Division St Kaukauna WI 54130

BREWSTER, OLIVE NESBITT, retired librarian; b. San Antonio, July 19, 1924; d. Charles Henry and Olive Agatha (Nesbitt) B.; B.A., Our Lady of Lake Coll., 1945, B.S. in L.S., 1946. Asst. librarian aeromed. library U.S. Air Force Sch. Aviation Medicine, Randolph AFB, Tex., 1946-60, chief cataloger aeromed. library Sch. Aerospace Medicine, Brooks AFB, Tex., 1960-83, chief tech. processing, 1983-88; ret., 1988. Mem. ALA, Am. Soc. Indexers, Mensa. Anglican. Home: 1906 Schley Ave San Antonio TX 78210-4332

BREWSTER, PATRICIA D., health science association administrator; b. Englewood, N.J., July 28, 1943; d. Michael and Anne (Sebasian) Damian; m. Rodman Peabody Brewster, Nov. 24, 1965; children: Rodman P. Jr., Michael Grant. BA in English, Colo. Coll., 1965; MS in Mgmt., Regis U., 1992. Tchr. secondary sch. Arapahoc Sch. Dist. #6, Littleton, Colo., 1965-70, Jefferson County Sch. Dist. R-4, Golden, Colo., 1980-87; interior design/space planner pvt. practice, 1979-83; program coord. Homestead Mus., Evergreen, Colo., 1989-90; dir. cmty. devel. Mile High Transplant Bank, Denver, 1991-94; exec. dir. Transplant Found., Denver, 1994—; pres., CEO Mile High Transplant Bank, 1995—; mem. adv. bd. Cryolife, Inc., Atlanta, 1995-96; treas. Transplant Coun. Rockies, Denver, 1993—; pres. Dirs. of Vol. Agys., Denver, 1991—. Mem. Leadership Denver, 1995-96, Leadership Golden, 1995-96; mem. adv. coun. Hall of Life/Denver Mus. Natural History, 1995—; bd. dirs. NAt. Repertory Orch., Breckenridge, Colo., 1981-84. Mem. Am. Assn. Tissue Banks (com. mem. 1994—chair edn. com. 1994-96), Nat. Soc. Fundraising Execs., Nat. Assn. Transplant Coord., Alpha Phi Found. (chair 1988-92). Office: Mile High Transplant Bank 8085 E Harvard Ave Denver CO 80401

BREWSTER-WALKER, SANDRA JOANN, public relations executive, publishing executive, genealogist, historian, consultant; b. Copiaque, N.Y., June 16, 1942; d. Willis Hodges and F. Wilda (Scurlock) Brewster; m. Stuart M. Walker (div. 1984); children: Jeffrey, Carlton, Cassandra. Cert., Island Drafting Sch., 1965; BA, Dowling Coll., 1972; MA, SUNY, New Paltz, 1978. Acting asst. dir. Urban Ctr., Vassar Coll., Poughkeepsie, N.Y., 1972-74; tchr. Middletown Jr. High Sch., N.Y., 1974-78; elec. mfg. engr. Perkin-Elmer Corp., Norwalk, Conn., 1978-84; pub., editor Ram's Horn Pub. Co., Stamford, Conn., 1983-84; software mgr. Pergamon Press, Inc., Elmsford, N.Y., 1985-86; pres., owner The Brewster Group, Inc., Stamford, 1986-92; dep. dir. pub. affairs (apptd. by Pres. Clinton) USDA, Washington, 1993-95; pres., CEO L & P Internat., Inc., Washington, 1995—; sr. v.p. Lockhart & Pettus Advtsg., 1990-92. Pub., editor Conneticut Update, 1984; editor: Augustus M. Hodges Project, 1978-86, Fairfield County Black Biograph. Index Project, 1980—; contbr. to Westchester Women mag., 1985. Mem. Town of Walkill Bicentennial Com., 1976, Bicentennial Com., Middletown Pub. Schs., 1976; mem. Circleville Pub. Sch. PTA, 1975-77, v.p., 1977-78; instr. genealogy Greater Orange YMCA, Middletown, N.Y., 1975, 77, mem. planning bd., 1976; vice chmn. to corp. campaign advisor United Negro Coll. Fund, Lower Fairfield, Conn., 1980-81; mem. John Anderson for Pres. Com., 1980; exec. dir. Conn. Legis. Black Caucus, Hartford, 1981-82; aide to State Senator J.C. Daniels, 1981-82; founder, bd. dir. Bridgeport Black History Project, 1982-83; adv. com. Conn. Democrats, 1984; inaugural com. Mayor Serrani, Stamford, 1984-85; coord. Lower Fairfield County Mondale/Ferraro Campaign, 1984; state coord. Conn. Com. to Elect Jesse Jackson Pres., 1984; Stamford coord., 1988—; mem. Conn. chpt. Coalition of 100 Black Women, 1980-81, Nat. Project Vote, 1984, adv. com. black women's exhibit L.I. and Bklyn. Hist. Soc.; vol. Alberta Jagoes for Mayor campaign, Milford, Conn., 1982, Christine M. Niedermeier for Congress Com., 1984; mem. steering com. Margaret Morton for Congress, 1987; candidate state rep. 145th dist., 1988; advance team and convention operation Clinton for President '92, Clinton/Gore '92. Named Woman of Month, Conn. Women's Mag., 1983, Working Woman of Month, Essence mag., 1983. Mem. NAFE, NOW, Coalition of 100 Black Women (Lower Fairfield chpt. 1986, 89-90), Nat. Abortion Rights Actions League, Rainbow Coalition, Nat Advance Team Clinton/Gore. Home: 20927 Stanmoor Tr Sterling VA 20165

BRICCETTI, JOAN THERESE, symphony manager, arts management consultant; b. Mt. Kisco, N.Y., Sept. 29, 1948; d. Thomas Bernard and Joan (Filardi) B. AB in Am. History, Bryn Mawr Coll., 1970. Adminstrv. asst., program guide editor Sta. WIAN-FM, Indpls., 1970-72; adminstrv. asst. T. Briccetti, condr., Indpls., 1970-72; dir. pub. rels. The Richmond (Va.) Symphony, 1972-73, mgr., 1973-80; mgr. St. Louis Symphony Orch., 1980-84, gen. mgr., 1984-86, chief oper. officer, 1986-92; ind. cons. for arts & Edn., 1993 ; mng. dir. Metro Theater Co., St. Louis, 1996—; cons., panelist Arts Couns. Ohio, Va., Ky. Active orch. and planning sects., music programs Nat. Endowment fot the Arts, 1974-78, chmn. orch. panel, 1975-78, cons., evaluator, panelist, 1974—, mem. first challenge grant rev. panel, 1977, co-chmn. recording panel, 1983-84; mem. grant rev. panel Va. Commn. for the Arts, 1976-78; adv. bd. Eastern Music Festival, 1977-83, Richmond Friends Opera, 1979-80; adv. coun. Va. Alliance for Arts Edn., 1978, Federated Arts Coun. Richmond, 1979-80; steering com. BRAVO Arts, 1978-79 (gov.'s award); cons. Tenn. Arts Commn., 1979-80; bd. dirs. Theatre IV, Richmond, 1974-80, Am. Music Ctr, N.Y.C., 1980-84, St. Louis Forum, 1983—, New City Sch., St. Louis, 1987—, Metro Theatre Co., 1994—; mem. challenge grant evaluation panel Ky. Arts Commn., 1983; participant Leadership St. Louis, 1983-84, bd. dirs., 1987-89; commr. subdistrict Mo. History Mus., 1987—, sec., 1993; speaker, panelist, cons. numerous arts orgns. Mem. Am. Symphony Orch. League (chmn. orch. library info. svc. adv. com., recruiter, mem. final interview com., advisor mgmt. fellowship program), Regional Orch. Mgrs. Assn. (v.p. 1976, policy com. 1977-79), Women's Forum Mo. Office: Metro Theatre Co 524 Trinity Ave Saint Louis MO 63103

BRICKER, VICTORIA REIFLER, anthropology educator; b. Hong Kong, June 15, 1940; came to U.S., 1947, naturalized, 1953; d. Erwin and Henrietta (Brown) Reifler; m. Harvey Miller Bricker, Dec. 27, 1964. A.B., Stanford U., 1962; A.M., Harvard U., 1963, Ph.D., 1968. Vis. lectr. anthropology Tulane U., 1969-70, asst. prof., 1970-73, assoc. prof., 1973-78, prof., 1978—, chmn. dept. anthropology, 1988-91. Author: Ritual Humor in Highland Chiapas, 1973, The Indian Christ, The Indian King: The Historical Substrate of Maya Myth and Ritual, 1981 (Howard Francis Cline meml. prize Conf. Latin Am. History), A Grammar of Mayan Hieroglyphs, 1986; book rev. editor: Am. Anthropologist, 1971-73; editor: Am. Ethnologist, 1973-76; gen. editor: Supplement to Handbook of Middle American Indians, 1977—. Guggenheim fellow, 1982; Wenner-Gren Found. Anthropol. Rsch. grantee, 1971; Social Sci. Rsch. Coun.l grantee, 1972; NEH grantee, 1990. Fellow Am. Anthrop. Assn. (exec. bd. 1980-83); mem. NAS, Am. Soc. Ethnohistory (exec. bd. 1977-79), Linguistic Soc. Am., Seminario de Cultura Maya, Societe des Americanistes. Office: Tulane Univ Dept Anthropology New Orleans LA 70118

BRICKMAN, RAVELLE, public relations writer and consultant; b. N.Y.C., Aug. 26, 1936; d. Arthur M. and Eva S. (Kaplan) Silberman; m. Anthony Brickman, Mar. 4, 1962 (div. Sept. 1979); children: Joshua Mark, David Meyer; m. Michael J. Bonner, Nov. 25, 1993. BA, Smith Coll., 1958. Writer, editor various book and mag. pubs., N.Y.C. and London, 1958-71; editor Aphra, N.Y.C., 1971-73; various pub. relations positions YMCA Greater N.Y., N.Y.C., 1973-76, dir. mktg. services, 1976-79; account exec. Zachary & Front Pub. Relations, N.Y.C., 1979-81; account supr., v.p., sr. v.p., creative dir. Richard Weiner, Inc., N.Y.C., 1981-86; pres. The Brickman Group, Mktg. and Pub. Rels., N.Y.C., 1986-93; writer, cons. in pub. rels. pvt. practice, N.Y.C., 1993—; writer, cons. NYNEX, NSF, N.J. Inst. Tech.,

City of N.Y., YMCA Greater N.Y. Mem. Pub. Rels. Soc. Am. (bd. dirs. 1981-84, Silver Anvil award 1984, Big Apple awards 1988), Counselors Acad., Women Execs. in Pub. Rels. (bd. dirs. 1989-90), Publicity Club N.Y. (bd. dirs. 1986-87, v.p., treas. 1986-88, 1st v.p. 1992-93, pres. 1993-95), City Club N.Y., Smith Coll. Alumnae Assn. (chmn. 1998 reunion). Democrat. Jewish.

BRICKWEDDE, LANGHORNE VIRGINIA, computer programmer, analyst; b. Washington, Feb. 9, 1947; d. Ferdinand Graft and Marion Langhorne (Howard) B. BS, Pa. State U., 1969; MBA, U. Conn., 1979. Vol. Peace Corps, We. Samoa, 1969-70; researcher fgn. trade divsn. Bur. Census, Suitland, Md., 1980-82; computer programmer, analyst IRS, Washington, 1983-89. Vol. Sr. Day Care Ctr., State Coll., Pa., 1994, 96. Democrat. Mem. Unitarian Universalist Ch.

BRIDGEFORTH, PAMELA RENEÉ, arts center administrator; b. Newark, Nov. 8, 1967; d. Arthur and Rhodora (Newtown) Harris; m. Vincent E. Thompson, III, Jan. 11, 1992; children: Vincent E. Thompson, IV, William-Patrick Thompson. BA in English Lit., LaSalle U. Devel. assoc. Am. Music Theatre and Festival, Phila., assoc. dir. devel.; dir. devel. Walt Whitman Cultural Arts Ctr., Camden, N.J.; panel rep. N.J. State Coun. on Arts, Trenton, N.J., 1996—. Recipient Oscar Wolfberg scholarship, 1984, Bronze medal Nat. Honor Soc., 1984. Office: Walt Whitman Cultural Arts 2d and Cooper Sts Camden NJ 08102

BRIDGER, TERESA LYNNE, university program administrator; b. Oneonta, N.Y., Oct. 7, 1962; d. James Albert and Janice Elaine (Markham) B.; m. Edward John Maginnis Jr., May 19, 1990; 1 child, Conor Bridger Maginnis. BS in Spl. and Elem. Edn., Ind. (Pa.) U., 1983; MEd in Internat. Multicultural Studies, U. Pitts., 1988; postgrad., George Mason U., 1989—. Cert. spl. edn. and elem. tchr., supr., adminstr., Md. Spl. edn. tchr. Craig House-Technoma, Pitts., 1984-87; from spl. edn. tchr. to elem. tchr. Prince George's County Pub. Schs., Upper Marlboro, Md., 1987-91, multicultural edn. specialist, 1991-96; owner consulting business, 1990—; part-time kindergarten tchr., 1995-96; cons. in field. Named Tchr. of Yr. City of Bowie, Md., 1988-89. Mem. ASCD, Mid-Atlantic Assn. for Coop. in Edn., Internat. Assn. for the Study Coop. in Edn., Nat. Assn. for Multicultural Edn., Md. Multicultural Coalition.

BRIDGES, BERYL CLARKE, marketing executive; b. N.Y.C., Oct. 27, 1941; d. David and Edith (Foster) Clarke; m. R. Shaw Bridges, Sept. 2, 1962 (div. May 1985); children: Robert Shaw Jr., Margaret Clarke, John Morrison; m. Robert A. McMillan, July 25, 1992. BA in English, Philosophy, Wheaton Coll., 1963. Acct. exec. McMoran-Redington Pub. Rels., Greenwich, Conn., 1975-77; mgr. sales promotion Lindenmeyr Graphic Resource Ctr., Greenwich, 1977-79; corp. mgr. promotions Lindenmeyr Paper Corp., Greenwich, 1979-81; mgr. southeastern region Paper Sources Internat. subs. Lindenmeyr Paper Corp., 1981-83, v.p. mktg., 1983-84; pres. Zanders USA, Inc. (subs. Internat. Paper Co.), Wayne, N.J., 1984-95; account exec. Target Graphics, Boonton, N.J., 1996—; cons. and lectr. in field. V.p. Greenwich Hist. Soc., 1974-77; mem. Jr. League, Greenwich, 1971-78. Mem. Am. Inst. Graphic Arts. Republican. Unitarian. Home: 18 Lake Dr Boonton NJ 07005-1047 Office: 62 Parsippany Blvd Boonton NJ 07005

BRIDGES, DONNA MARIE, executive recruiter; b. Cedar Rapids, Iowa, Oct. 5, 1961; d. Ronald David and Dee Ann (Howard) B.; m. Michael Troas Newell, Dec. 14, 1985 (div. June 1988). BBA, S.W. Tex. State U., 1985. Staff acct. and auditor MBank/MCorp, San Antonio and Austin, Tex., 1985-88; fin. acct. Bekins Moving and Storage, Dallas, 1988-90; corp. acct. Gamma Internat., Dallas, 1990-91; exec. recruiter Accts. on Call, Atlanta, 1992—. Interim music dir. Our Redeemer Luth. Ch., Dallas, 1991; soloist and music leader Luth. Ch. of the Apostles, Atlanta, 1993—; cmty. and music leader Via de Christo, Atlanta, 1993—. Mem. Inst. Mgmt. Accts. (bd. mem. 1992-93, 95-96, spkr. 1995). Home: 6818-J Glenridge Dr Atlanta GA 30328 Office: Accts on Call Ste 630 3355 Lenox Rd Atlanta GA 30326

BRIDGES, JUDY CANTRELL, gifted and talented education educator; b. Dallas, Feb. 17, 1947; d. William and Jewel Alexandria (Autrey) C.; m. Gary L. Bridges, Aug. 17, 1969; children: John Drewry, Judith Alexandria. BA, Tex. Tech. U., 1969; gifted/talented endorsement, Sul Ross State U., Alpine, Tex., 1992, MEd, 1993; cert. in mid-mgmt., Sul Ross State U., 1994. Lic. secondary edn. math. and English. Tchr. New Deal (Tex.) Ind. Sch. Dist., 1969-70, Indpls. Pub. Schs., 1970, USDESEA, Zweibruecken, Germany, 1971-73, Lubbock (Tex.) Ind. Sch. Dist., 1973-76; tchr. Ector County Ind. Sch. Dist., Odessa, Tex., 1976-85, 87-90, tchr. gifted spl. edn., 1990-92, gifted/talented coord., 1992—; acct. Walter Smith CPA, Odessa, 1977-82; real estate appraiser Appraisal Assocs., Odessa, 1985-87; vis. lectr. Sul Ross State U., Odessa, 1994; mem. gifted/talented adv. com. Region 18 Edn. Svc. Ctr., Midland, Tex., 1993-94. Author: (poem) Paradigm Shifts in the West Texas Sand, 1991. Treas. Campaign to Elect County Judge, Odessa, 1991; mem. bd. Permian H.S. Football Booster Club, 1993; advisor, officer Jr. League of Odessa, Inc., 1980—, treas./treas. elect, 1986-88; assst. treas., bd. dirs. Odessa Symphony Guild, 1996. Recipient Dept. of Def. Commendation, U.S. Dependent Edn. System, Zweibruecken, 1973, Cert. of Appreciation-Stop of Felony Odessa Police Dept., 1992. Mem. ASCD, NEA, Tex. State Tchrs. Assn. (treas. Ector County unit 1991-92), Tex. Assn. Gifted and Talented, Am. Creativity Assn., Nat. Coun. Tchrs. Math. Baptist. Home: 4243 Lynbrook Ave Odessa TX 79762-7146 Office: Ector County Ind Sch Dist PO Box 3912 Odessa TX 79760-3912

BRIDGEWATER, NORA JANE, medical, surgical nurse; b. Rodgers, Tex., Feb. 27, 1924; d. Wiley Levi and Phoebajane (Owens) Shelgren; m. Joe Garland Bridgewater, Aug. 7, 1940; children: Garland, Janie William Clayton, Richard, Allen, Paula, Shewanna, Russell. AA in Psychology, Bakersfield Coll., 1970, BSN, 1978. Med. nurse Kern Med. Hosp., Bakersfield, Calif., 1964-68, Mercy Hosp., Bakersfield, 1969-78, Sherrif's Dept., Laredo, Calif., 1978-87; nurse Sheriff Facility, Bakersfield, 1986-87. Sgt. U.S. Army Nurses Corps, 1938-40. Mem. Calif. Nursing Assn. Democrat. Baptist.

BRIEND-WALKER, MONIQUE MARIE, French and Spanish language educator; b. Lamballe, France, Nov. 21, 1946; came to U.S., 1970; d. Francis Marie and Maria Françoise (Auffray) Briend; m. Robert A. Walker, Apr. 21, 1979; children: Charlotte Marie, Robert Anselle, Alexander Francis. Licence-es-lettres, U. Rennes, France, 1969; Maîtrise de lettres, U. Rennes, 1971. Asst. prof. U. Rochester, N.Y., 1970-71; prof. English and art Ecole Privée Louise de Bettignies, Paris, 1972-77; sr. lectr. U. Dartmouth, Hanover, N.Y., 1982-87; tchr. French St. Albans Sch., Washington, 1988-89; tchr. French and Spanish Landon Sch., Bethesda, Md., 1989—; asst. in mktg. CBS Records, Paris and N.Y., 1978-82; dir. summer cultural and linguistic program London-in-Europe, Bethesda, 1989—. Fulbright scholar U. Rochester, 1970-71. Roman Catholic. Home: 10818 Brewer House Rd North Bethesda MD 20852 Office: Landon Sch 6101 Wilson Ln Bethesda MD 20817

BRIER, PAMELA SARA, health facility administrator; b. L.A., Sept. 5, 1945; d. Harry M. and Patricia (Weisberger) E.; m. Stephen B. Brier, Sept. 11, 1966; 1 child, Jennifer. AB, U. Calif., Berkeley, 1967; MPH, UCLA, 1972. Dir. reimbursement N.Y.C. Health & Hosps. Corp., 1981-83, sr. asst. v.p. fin., 1983-84, v.p. pres. fin., 1984-88, sr. v.p. administrn., 1986-88, exec. v.p., 1988-89; exec. dir. Bronx (N.Y.) Mcpl. Hosp. Ctr., 1989—; exec. v.p. Maimonides Med Ctr., Brooklyn, NY. Mem. N.Y. State Hosp. Rev. and Planning Coun., 1991. Home: 214 E 11th St Apt 1C New York NY 10003-7338 Office: Maimonides Med Ctr 4802 10th Ave Brooklyn NY 11219*

BRIERRE, MICHELINE, artist; b. Jeremie, Haiti; d. Luc Brierre and Simone Lataillaide; m. Charles Lopez (div.); children: Liza Lopez Camus, Charles Lopez; m. Barry Kaplan. Studied with, Mr. Ramponeau, Haiti, 1951-53; student, Academie Nehemie Jean, Haiti, 1958-60, Miraflores Art Ctr., Peru. Author: I am Eve, 1980, Spanish translation, 1980; solo show Commonwheel, Manitou Springs, Colo., 1995; exhibited in group shows at Galerie Hotel Rancho, Haiti, 1961, Galerie Brochette, Haiti, 1962, Onze Femmes peintres, Haiti, 1963, Galerie Brochette, Haiti, 1964, Brierre/Castera, Haiti, 1965, Musee d'Art, Haiti, 1980, Galeria 70, Bogota, Colombia, S. Am., 1980, Galeria San Diego, Colombia, 1980, Woman's Way, Miami, Fla., 1982, Un Regard Soleil, Port-au-Prince, Haiti, 1983, Reflection On The Past, Aureus, Miami, 1983, Un Mundo Para Compartir, Lima, Peru, 1983, Festival Arts Gallery, Port-au-Prince, 1984, An Evening With The Artists, Naples, Fla., 1986, 87, Art in Jewelry, Island House, Bayside, Fla., 1987, Mixed Media Studio Show, Miami, 1989, 91, Collective Show, Commonwheel, Manitou Spings, Colo., 1994, Douglas County Art Ctr., Roby Mills Gallery and Bus. of Art Ctr., 1995. Mem. Fine Arts Ctr. Colo. Springs, Bus. of Art Ctr., Commonwheel Co-op. Home and Studio: All Things Beautiful 8050 Woody Creek Dr Colorado Springs CO 80911

BRIGEOIS, EVELYNE BRIGITTE, artist, publisher; b. Troyes, Aube, France, Feb. 18, 1946; came to U.S., 1984.; Student, B.E.P.C., Aix-en-Othe, France, 1951. Trilingual exec. sec., Eng., France, Germany, Spain, 1965-79; owner, mgr. Brigeois Pub., Vallejo, Calif., 1987—. One woman shows include Lawrence Gallery, Portland, Oreg., 1984, Scott Gallery, Orinda, Calif., 1985, Leslie Levy Gallery, Scottsdale, Ariz., 1986, 89, Charleston Heights Art Ctr., Las Vegas, Nev., 1987, Horvath Gallery, Sacramento, 1993; exhibited in group shows Transco Gallery, Houston, 1988, numerous others; represented by Vanier & Roberts Fine Art, Scottsdale, Ariz., Studio 42, Los Gatos, Calif. Recipient numerous awards, including Robert Wiegand Meml. award La. Watercolor Soc., 1985, award Detroit Inst. Arts Drawing and Print Club, 1985, award of honor Birmingham Mus. Art, 1986, 1st place award Assoc. Artists Southport, N.C., 1986. Mem. Nat. Watercolor Soc. (Helen Wurdeman award 1985), Ala. Watercolor Soc.

BRIGGS, CONNIE MICHELLE, education educator; b. Sherman, Tex., July 13, 1954; d. Alfred Clayton and Marvadeen Lee (Rind) Craft; m. Coy Wayne Briggs, Apr. 4, 1974; children: Justin Coy, Joshua Clayton. BS in Elem. Edn., Southeastern Okla. State U., 1976, MEd, 1981, MA in Reading, 1988; PhD in Reading, U. North Tex., 1994. Cert. tchr., Okla., Tex., Kans. Elem. tchr. Colbert (Okla.) Pub. Schs., 1976-89; 8th grade computer tchr. Denison (Tex.) Pub. Schs., 1989-90; teaching fellow U. North Tex., Denton, 1992; asst. prof. elem. edn. Southeastern Okla. State U., Durant, 1990-95; dir. profl. devel. sch., asst. prof. elem. edn. Emporia (Kans.) State U., 1995—. Contbr. articles and revs. to profl. jours. Mem. Kans. Higher Edn. Reading Profls. (pres. elect 1996-97), Bryan County Reading Assn. (pres. 1994-95), Assn. Tchr. Educators, Internat. Reading Assn., Nat. Coun. Tchrs. English, Coll. Reading Assn. (editl. bd. 1994-96), Alpha Upsilon Alpha, Delta Kappa Gamma. Roman Catholic. Office: Emporia State U 1200 Commercial St Box 47 Emporia KS 66081

BRIGGS, CYNTHIA ANNE, educational administrator, clinical psychologist; b. Berea, Ohio, Nov. 9, 1950; d. William Benajah and Lorraine (Hood) B.; m. Thomas Joseph O'Brien, Nov. 28, 1986; children: Julia Maureen, William Thomas. B Music Edn., U. Kans., 1973; MusM, U. Miami, 1976; D. Psychology, Hahnemann U., 1988. Lic. psychology, Mo.; bd. cert. music therapist. Music therapist Parsons (Kans.) State Hosp., 1973-74; grad. asst. U. Miami, Coral Gables, Fla., 1974-76; asst. prof., dir. Hahnemann U., Phila., 1976-85, assoc. prof., 1985-91; psychology resident Assocs. in Psychol. and Human Resources, Phila., 1988-91; clin. dir. Child Ctr. of Our Lady, St. Louis, 1991—. Author chpts. to books; contbr. articles to profl. jours. Mem. APA, Am. Assn. Music Therapy (pres. 1987-89), Nat. Coalition Arts Therapies Assns. (chair 1991-93). Democrat. Office: Child Ctr of Our Lady 7900 Natural Bridge Rd Saint Louis MO 63121-4628

BRIGGS, MARIAN, public relations executive. BA in Journalism, Marquette U. Editor Key This Week in Chgo. and Key Quad Cities, 1975-79; various pub. rels. and promotional positions Conwed Corp., 1979-85; sr. account exec. Brum & Anderson, 1985-87; account supr. Padilla, Speer, Burdick & Beardsley, Mpls., 1986; v.p. Padilla, Speer, Beardsley, Mpls., 1987-91, sr. v.p., 1991—. Office: Padilla Speer Beardsley 224 W Franklin Ave Minneapolis MN 55404-2331*

BRIGGS-ERICKSON, CAROL ANN, librarian; b. Muskegon, Mich., Aug. 20, 1952; d. Raymond John and Josephine (Dombrausky) Smith; m. Phillip George Briggs, Sept. 25, 1969 (div. Oct. 1977); 1 child, Christine Jeanette; m. Leif Stanley Erickson, Nov. 29, 1991. AA, Muskegon (Mich.) Cmty. Coll., 1978; BS, Grand Valley State U., 1984; M of Info. and Libr. Studies, U. Mich., 1994. With support staff Muskegon Cmty. Coll., 1985-94, libr., 1994—. Co-author: Environmental Guide to the Internet, 1996. Mem. Phi Kappa Phi, Beta Phi Mu (Excellence in Scholarship 1994). Office: Muskegon Cmty Coll Libr 221 S Quarterline Rd Muskegon MI 49444

BRIGGUM, SUE MARIE, corporate executive; b. Harrisburg, Pa., Apr. 8, 1950; d. John Gehring and Blanche Faye (Hess) B.; m. Martin Rose, Jan. 6, 1984; 1 child, Lauren. BA, U. Pitts., 1972; MA, U. Wis., 1973, PhD, 1979; JD, Harvard U., 1980. Bar: D.C. 1980. Lectr. U. Wis., Madison, 1973-77; assoc. Wald, Harkrader & Ross, Washington, 1980-86, Piper & Marbury, Washington, 1986-87; dir. govt. affairs WMX Techs., Inc., Washington, 1987—. Co-author: Concordance to Almayer's Folly, 1980, Hazardous Waste Regulation Handbook, 1983, rev. edit 1985; co-editor: Modernism in Literature, 1976. Office: WMX Technologies Inc 1155 Connecticut Ave NW Washington DC 20036-4306

BRIGHT, DEBORAH, artist, educator; b. Washington, Feb. 17, 1950; d. Albert Seymour and Lois Blanche (Jamison) B.; m. Hugh Reid Wilson, div. 1986. BA magna cum laude, Wheaton Coll., 1972; MFA, U. Chgo., 1975. Lectr. DePaul U., Chgo., 1979-86; asst. prof. U. Mass., Boston, 1986-88; asst. prof. RISD, Providence, 1989-93, assoc. prof., 1993—; cons. NEA, 1992, 93. Exhibited in solo shows at SUNY Binghamton, 1988, Rutgers U., 1992, U. Calif., Irvine, 1992, Colgate U., 1995, Bunting Inst./Radcliffe Coll., 1996, Atlanta Coll. Art, 1997; exhibited in group shows at Nat. Mus. Am. Art, Washington, 1992, Museet for Fotokunst, Denmark, 1992, Victoria and Albert Mus., 1995, Art in Gen., N.Y., 1995, Jan Kesner Gallery, L.A., 1995, Can. Mus. Contemporary Photography, 1996, others; works in permanent collections at Victoria and Albert Mus., Nat. Mus. Am. Art, Mus. Art/R.I. Sch. Design, Calif. Mus. Photography, Ill. State Mus., others; asst. editor The New Art Examiner, Chgo., 1985-86. Founding mem. Women's Cmty. Cancer Project, Cambridge, Mass., 1988; mem. Act-Up, Boston, 1989, Gay and Lesbian Caucus, CAA, N.Y.C., 1990—. Grantee New Eng. Found. for the Arts, 1992, Art Matters, Inc., 1994, Somerville Arts Coun., 1995 others; Mary Ingraham Bunting Inst. fellow, Cambridge, Mass., 1995—. Mem. Soc. Photographic Edn. (bd. mem. 1987-91), Coll. Art Assn. (program chmn. nat. conf. 1996). Democrat. Home: 72 Newton St Somerville MA 02143 Office: RISD 2 College St Providence RI 02903

BRIGHT, VENITA DARLENE, secondary educator; b. Lebanon, Ky., Sept. 25, 1947; d. Samuel A. and Edith (Phillips) B.; m. Michael A. Clark, June 7, 1986. BS, Ea. Ky. U., 1969, MEd, 1971. Tchr. Franklin County High Sch., Frankfort, Ky., 1970-80, Western Hills High Sch., Frankfort, 1980—; dept. chair Western Hills High Sch., Frankfort, 1992—, resource tchr. Ky. Tchr. Internship Program, 1984—. Pres. Frankfort Audubon Soc., 1990. Office: Western Hills High Sch 100 Doctors Dr Frankfort KY 40601

BRIGNONI, GLADYS, foreign language educator; b. Ponce, P.R., Apr. 9, 1965; d. Angel Manuel and Gladys Alejandrina (Roman) B. BA, Purdue U., 1987; MAT, Ind. U., 1992, PhD, 1996. Cert. in Spanish and ESL for secondary sch., Ind. Assoc. instr. Spanish dept. Ind. U., Bloomington, 1988—, Spanish instr. Continuing Studies, 1992—, instr. fgn. lang. methods, 1993-94, Spanish instr. Ctr. Internat. Bus. & Rsch., 1993-94, rsch. asst. Ctr. for Reading and Lang. Studies; prof. Spanish Old Dominion U., Norfolk, Va., 1996—; Spanish tchr. Internat. Ednl. Sys., Nashville, Ind., 1991-92; Spanish grammar instr. Ind. U. Honors Program in Mex., 1991-92; tchr. Spanish Bloomingh H.S. South, 1993-94; curriculum specialist, cons. Office of Workforce Devel., Gov.'s Commn. on Adult Literacy, Little Rock, 1994-95; Spanish translator Pan Am. Games, Indpls., summer 1987; presenter in field. Mem. Latinos Unidos, 1989-94; VITAL tutor for ESL Learners, Bloomington, 1994-95; Spanish instr. Older Am. Ctr., Bloomington, summer 1995. Ind. U. scholar, 1988-95. Mem. Ind. Fgn. Lang. Tchrs. Assn., Internat. Soc. for Intercultural Edn., Tng. and Rsch., Am. Coun. Tchg. Fgn. Langs., Sigma Delta Pi. Roman Catholic. Home: 349 Reflections Dr Apt 302 Virginia Beach VA 23452

BRILES, JUDITH, writer, speaker, consultant; b. Pasadena, Calif., Feb. 20, 1946; d. James and Mary Tuthill; MBA, Pepperdine U., 1980; PhD Nova U., 1990; children: Shelley, Sheryl, Frank (dec.), William (dec.). Brokers asst. Bateman, Eichler, Hill, Richards, Torrance, Calif., 1969-72; account exec. E. F. Hutton, Palo Alto, Calif., 1972-78; pres. Judith Briles & Co., Palo Alto, 1978-85, Briles & Assocs., Palo Alto, 1980-86; ptnr. The Briles Group, Inc., 1987—; instr. Menlo Coll., 1986-87, Skyline Coll., 1981-86; instr. U. Calif.-Berkeley Sch. Continuing Edn., U. Calif.-Santa Cruz Sch. Continuing Edn., U. Hawaii; mem. adv. coun. Miss Am. Pageant, 1989-95, No-nonsense Panty Hose, 1989-92, Colo. Women's News, 1993—. Pres., v.p., sec., bd. dirs. Foothill-DeAnza Coll. Found., Los Altos Hills, Calif., 1979-90, bd. dirs. Col. Nurses Task Force, Col. League Nursing; mem. adv. bd. Flint Ctr., Cupertino, Calif. Mem. NAFE (adv. bd. bus. woman's mag. 1981-86), Peninsula Profl. Women's Network, Nat. Speaker's Assn. (bd. dirs.). Republican. Club: Commonwealth. Author: The Woman's Guide to Financial Savvy, 1981; Money Phases, 1984, Woman to Woman: From Sabotage to Support, 1987, Dollars and Sense of Divorce, 1988, Faith and Savvy Too!, 1988, When God Says No, 1990, The Confidence Factor, 1990, Money Guide, 1991, The Workplace: Questions Women Ask, 1992, Financial Savvy for Women, 1992, The Briles Report on Women in Healthcare, 1994, Money Sense, 1995, Gender Traps, 1996, Raising Money Wise Kids, 1996.

BRILL, YVONNE CLAEYS, engineer, consultant; b. St. Norbert, Manitoba, Canada, Dec. 30, 1924; d. August and Julienne (Carette) Claeys; m. William Franklin Brill, Dec. 15, 1951; children: Naomi, Matthew, Joseph. BS, U. Manitoba, Canada, 1945; MS, U. So. Calif., 1951. Mathematician Douglas Aircraft, Santa Monica, Calif., 1945-46; research analyst Rand Corp., Santa Monica, 1946-49; group leader Marquardt Corp., Van Nuys, Calif., 1949-52; staff engr. UTC Research, East Hartford, Conn., 1952-55; project engr. Wright Aeronautical, Wood Ridge, N.J., 1955-58; mgr. propulsion systems RCA AstroElectronics, Princeton, N.J., 1966-81, staff engr., 1983-86; mgr. solid rocket motor NASA Hdqrs., Washington, 1981-83; with space engring segment Internat. Maritime Satellite Orgn., London, 1986-91; cons. Brill Assocs., Skillman, N.J., 1991—; mem. USAF Sci. Adv. Bd., Washington, 1982-83, Nat. Acad. Engring.; Com. on Internat. Orgns. and Programs, 1992-96; apptd. mem. aerospace safety adv. panel NASA, 1994—. Contbr. articles to sci. jours.; patentee in field. Bd. dirs. Princeton YWCA, 1981-82. Recipient Engr. of Yr. award Cen. Jersey Engring. Councils, 1979, Diamond Superwoman award Harpers Bazaar/DeBeers Corp., 1980, Marvin C. Demlar award AIAA, 1983. Fellow AIAA, Soc. Women Engrs. (dir. student affairs 1979-80, 83-84, treas. 1980-81, Engring. Achievement award 1986, Resnik Challenger medal 1993); mem. NAE, Internat. Astronautical Acad. (academician, edn. com. 1983-85), Sigma Xi, Tau Beta Pi. Republican. Home and Office: 914 Route 518 Skillman NJ 08558-2616

BRILLANTES, TERESITA BOBILA, physician; b. Oct. 3, 1944; came to U.S., 1967; d. Rosalio and Susana Bobila; m. Hermogenes Bilgera Brillantes, Dec. 28, 1968; children: Rosanna, Gerardo, Meliza. AA, U. St. Tomas, The Philippines, 1964, MD cum laude, 1967. Diplomate Am. Bd. Family Practice, Am. Bd. Internal Medicine, Am. Bd. Quality Assurance & Utilization Rev. Physicians. Attending dept. medicine St. James Hosp./St. Michaels, Newark, 1974—; dir. dept. medicine St. James Hosp., Newark, 1992—; attending dept. medicine Columbus Hosp., Newark, 1994—. Pres. U. St. Tomas '67 Found. USA, Short Hills, N.J., 1991-94. Mem. Filipino-Am. Med. Soc. N.J. (sec., v.p., pres.-elect), U. San Tomas Med. Alumni Assn. Found. Am. (charter), Assn. Filipino Physicians (life), Republican Club. Roman Catholic. Home: 114 Great Hills Rd Short Hills NJ 07078 Office: 159 Elm St Newark NJ 07105-0375

BRILLIANT, ELEANOR LURIA, social work educator; b. Bklyn., Nov. 25, 1930; d. Joseph and Leah (Cohen) Luria; m. Richard Brilliant, June 24, 1951; children: Stephanie, Livia, Franca, Myron. BA, Smith Coll., Northampton, Mass., 1952; MS, Bryn Mawr (Pa.) Coll., 1969; DSW, Columbia U., 1974. Asst. in prodn. course Harvard Bus. Sch., Cambridge, Mass., 1952-54; instr. Bryn Mawr Coll., 1969-71; adminstr., dir. Lower East Side Family Union, N.Y.C., 1974-75; dir. planning/evaluation United Way of Westchester, White Plains, N.Y., 1975-78, assoc. exec. dir., 1978-80; asst. prof. Columbia U., N.Y.C., 1980-84, assoc. prof., 1984-85; assoc. prof. social work Rutgers U., New Brunswick, N.J., 1986-95, prof., 1995—; faculty mem. women's studies program BSW program Rutgers U., New Brunswick, 1992—; dir. BSW program Rutgers U. Livingston Coll., New Brunswick, 1987-89; chair, adminstr. policy and planning area MSW program Rutgers U. Sch. Social Work, New Brunswick, 1992—; cons. United Way of Westchester, White Plains, 1980, Family Info. and Referral Svc. Teams, Inc., White Plains, 1980-83, 87, James Bell Assocs., 1994—; mem. scholar's adv. coun. Ind. U. Ctr. on Philanthropy. Author: The Urban Development Corporation: Private Interests and Public Authority, 1975, The United Way: Dilemmas of Organized Charity, 1990. Mem. Westchester County Homeless Crisis Action Group, 1985-86, chair long range planning com., 1986; mem. Westchester Commn. on the Homeless, 1986-87; bd. dirs. Hudson Valley Health Sys. Agy., 1978-86, Nat. Ctr. for Social Policy and Practice, 1986-88; mem. Commn. on Mental Health and Children, Senator Nicholas Spano chair, N.Y. State, 1989-92; mem. ho. of dels. Coun. Social Work Edn., 1987-89; mem. Scholars Adv. Coun. of the Ind. U. Ctr. on Philanthropy, 1993—. U.S. Fulbright grantee, 1972-73, NIMH grantee 1968-69; fellow Douglass Coll., Rutgers U., 1992—. Mem. NASW (rep. to del. assembly 1987, 90, nat. treas. 1989-91), Assn. for Rsch. on Non-Profit Orgns. and Vol. Action, Nat. Coun. for Rsch. on Women, Assn. for Cmty. Orgn. and Social Adminstrn. Home: 10 Wayside Ln Scarsdale NY 10583-2908 Office: Rutgers U Sch Social Work 536 George St New Brunswick NJ 08901-1167

BRILLIANT, MICHELLE KAREN, communications company executive; b. Boston, Jan. 28, 1969; d. Erwin and Barbara (Lecker) Brilliant. BA, McGill U., 1991; MBA, Columbia U., 1993. Investment banker The Jordan, Edmiston Group, N.Y.C., 1993-95; dir. spl. projects New World Comm. Group, L.A., 1995—. Mem. Beta Gamma Sigma Soc.

BRIN, PAMELA YALE, art dealer, mirror and glass designer; b. Mpls., Apr. 11, 1927; d. George Brooks and Florence Jacobs; m. Robert Brin, Dec. 5, 1948; children: Barbara Brin Beal, Nancy Brin Polski. BA, U. Minn., 1948. Owner Mirror Mirror, Mpls., 1972—, Poster for Gt. Walls, 1972—, Harmon Glass & Mirror, 1980-85. Mem. Humphry Inst. Mem. Nat. Home Fashion League, Poster Soc. Am., Nat. Women's League of Conservative Judaism, Nat. Coun. Jewish Women.

BRINDEL, JUNE RACHUY, author; b. Little Rock, June 5, 1919; d. Otto L. and Etta Mina (Balster) Rachuy; m. Bernard Brindel, Aug. 26, 1939; children: Sylvia Mina, Paul, Jill. BA, U. Chgo., 1945, MA, 1958. Prof. English Wright Coll., Chgo., 1958-81; tchr. drama Nat. Music Camp, Interlochen, Mich., 1957-67. Author: Ariadne, 1980 (nominated for Pulitzer prize), Phaedra, 1985, Nobody is Ever Missing, 1984, Luap, 1971; short stories in Sound of Writing, MSS, IA Rev., Carolina Quar., others. Recipient Lit. award Ill. Arts Coun., Chgo., 1985, fellow, 1984, 85, C.s. Lewis prize Ind. U., 1973. Mem. Soc. Midland Authors, Ind. Writers of Ill., The Writers (v.p. 1995), Phi Beta Kappa. Home: 2740 Lincoln Ln Wilmette IL 60091

BRINE, DOLORES RANDOLPH, chemist; b. Marion, N.C., Nov. 26, 1945; d. Carl Lee and Addie (Ritter) Randolph; m. George Atkins Brine, Aug. 31, 1968. BS, Duke U., 1968. Rsch. chemist Research Triangle Inst., Research Triangle Park, N.C., 1968—. Contbr. articles to profl. jours., chpts. to books. Mem. Am. Chem. Soc. Episcopalian. Home: 6505 Hunters Ln Durham NC 27713-9738

BRINK, MARILYN JEANNE, early childhood education educator, supervisor; b. Chgo., Jan. 24, 1950; d. Raymond Thomas and Jeanne Ethel (Reed) Tydd; m. Richard Anthony Brink, Aug. 12, 1972; children: Brian, Lindsay, Lauren. BS in Edn., So. Ill. U., 1972; MEd, Nat. Louis U., 1983. Adj. faculty mem. Coll. of DuPage, Glen Ellyn, Ill., 1990—, Waubonsee C.C., Sugar Grove, Ill., 1991—; dist. supr., trainer Two Rivers Head Start, Batavia, Ill., 1992—; mem. adv. bd. Child Care Resource and Referral, DuPage and Kane Counties, Ill., 1993-95. Mem. Nat. Assn. for Edn. of Young Children, Assn. for Childhood Edn. Internat., Fox Valley Assn. for Edn. of Young Children (bd. dirs. 1991—, pub. rels. com. 1992-94). Office: Two Rivers Head Start 6N656 Watseka Ave Saint Charles IL 60174-6685

BRINK, MARION ALICE, employee assistance professional; b. Boston, Feb. 15, 1928; d. Martin Bernhard and Astrid Marie (Bjaastad) Windedal; m. A. Rudie Shobaken, Feb. 5, 1947 (div. 1963); children: Richard Michael, Ron Eric; m. James A Brink, Jan. 29, 1977. Student, Cambridge Jr. Coll., 1945-47, Framingham State Coll., 1967, Boston U., 1967-69; BA, U. N.H., 1983; M in Theol. Studies, Harvard U., 1987. From lab tech. to chemist Liberty Mut. Rsch., Hopkinton, Mass., 1963-77; asst. to mgr. Rec. Sec. Office Harvard U., 1977-79; sec. Sloan Sch. MIT, 1980-82; owner tech. typing svc. New Castle, N.H., 1982-84; counseling intern Green Pastures Counseling Ctr., Dover, N.H., 1984-85; alcohol educator Freedom From Chem. Dependency Found., Inc., Needham, Mass., 1985-87; dir. devel., editor News Bulletin Freedom From Chem. Dependency Found., Inc., Needham, 1987-88; ptnr. Palmerbrink, Charlestown, Mass., 1989-90; founder MB Assocs., Charlestown, 1991—. Counselor Women's Resource Ctr., Portsmouth, 1980; treas., bd. dirs. Friends of Metro Boston, Inc.; mem. canteen com. Lindemann Mental Health Ctr. Mem. Employee Assistance Profls. Assn., Am. Acad. of Health Care Providers in the Addictive Disorders, Ctr. for Process Studies. Democrat. Unitarian. Home: 86 Wentworth Rd New Castle NH 03854

BRINKEMA, LEONIE MILHOMME, federal judge; b. Teaneck, N.J., June 26, 1944; d. Alexander Juste and Modeste Leonie (Macksoud) Milhomme; m. John Robert Brinkema, Dec. 22, 1966; children: Robert Aaron, Eugenie Alexandra. BA with honors, Douglass Coll., 1966; MLS, Rutgers U., 1970; JD with honors, Cornell U., 1976. Bar: D.C. 1976, Va. 1978. Trial atty. U.S. Dept. Justice, Washington, 1976-77, 1983-84; asst. U.S. atty. U.S. Atty's Office Ea. Va., Alexandria, 1977-83; prin. Leonie M. Brinkema Atty., Alexandria, 1984-85; U.S. magistrate judge U.S. Dist. Ct. (ea. dist.) Va., Alexandria, 1985-93, U.S. dist. judge, 1993—; legal lectr. Va. State Bar Professionalism Faculty, 1990-92, No. Va. Criminal Justice Acad., 1984-85; guest lectr. Alexandria Bar Assn., Alexandria Women Attys. Assn., Va. Women Attys. Assn., U.S. Dept. Justice Advocacy Inst., Va. Law Found. Active Fairfax Choral Soc., Alban Chorale. Woodrow Wilson grad. fellow, 1966, Danforth Found. grad. fellow, 1966. Mem. ABA, Va. State Bar, D.C. Bar, Nat. Assn. Women Judges, Va. Women Attys. Assn., George Mason Inn of Ct. (master), Phi Beta Kappa. Office: US Dist Ct 401 Courthouse Sq Alexandria VA 22314-5799

BRINKER, ANITA MARIE, phytochemist; b. Fort Wayne, Ind., Dec. 4, 1961; d. Robert Cyril and Mary Elizabeth (Lomont) B. BS, U. Mich., 1984; MS, Cornell U., 1985; PhD, U. Ill., 1990. Postdoctoral rsch. assoc. USDA Nat. Ctr. for Agrl. Utilization Rsch., Peoria, Ill., 1990-92; rsch. fellow Alexander von Humboldt Found. Westfälische Wilhelms U., Münster, Germany, 1992-94; prin. rsch. chemist Unilever Rsch. US, Edgewater, N.J., 1994—. Contbr. articles to profl jours. Recipient Ralph Alston award Botanical Soc. Am., 1989; Nat. Sci. Found. fellow, 1984. Mem. Phytochemical Soc. N.Am., Am. Soc. Plant Physiologists, U. Ill. Alumni Assn., Sigma Xi. Office: Unilever Rsch US 45 River Rd Edgewater NJ 07020

BRINKLEY, CHRISTIE, model; b. L.A., Feb. 2, 1953; d. Don and Marge B.; m. Jean François Allaux, 1974 (div. 1981); m. Billy Joel, 1985 (div.); 1 child, Alexa Ray; m. Ricky Taubman, 1994. Attended, U. Calif., Los Angeles, U. Calif., Northridge, La Grande Chaumiere. Model Elite Model Mgmt. modeled for over 200 mag. covers incl. Sports Illustrated's annual swimsuit issue, 1979, 80, 81, product promotions incl. Cover Girl makeup, Revlon cosmetics, Clairol hair care items, Chanel No. 19 perfume, Mastercard, Kinney Shoes, Anheuser-Busch beer; pub. Christie Brinkley's Outdoor Beauty and Fitness Book, 1983; cameo appearance (film) National Lampoon's Vacation, 1983, (video) Billy Joel's "Uptown Girl"; designed album cover Billy Joel's "River of Dreams"; introduced line of dolls (with Beverly Johnson) The Real Model Collection Matchbox Toys; past host Living in the 90's with Christie Brinkley CNN. Office: Ford Models Inc 344 E 59th St New York NY 10022-1570*

BRINTON, VICTORIA RUTH, secondary school educator; b. Provo, Utah, Aug. 8, 1951; d. J. Emerson and Eve (Bjorndal) B. BA, Brigham Young U., 1973; MEd, U. Utah, 1981. Cert. tchr., Utah, 1973. Tchr. Millard Sch. Dist., Fillmore, Utah, 1974-76, Granite Sch. Dist., Salt Lake City, 1977, Jordan Sch. Dist., Sandy, Utah, 1977—; adj. prof. S.L. C.C., Sandy, Utah, 1989; mem. Utah State Social Studies Curriculum Devel. Com., Salt Lake City, 1994—, Utah State Textbook Selection Com. for Social Studies, Salt Lake City, 1989-91. Recipient Outstanding Educator award Jordan Edn. Found. Kennecott Corp., 1992-93, Tchr. of Yr. award Jordan North Secondary Coun., 1993. Mem. NEA, Utah Edn. Assn., Jordan Edn. Assn., Libr. of Congress Assn., Mus. Art Brigham Young U.

BRIONES, ELLEN MARGARET, legal editor, researcher; b. Boston, June 17, 1962; d. Michael and Shirley Ann (Lasch) Menaker; m. Jon Eric Briones, June 22, 1985; children: Demetris Alexander, Nikkita Alisha. BA in English Lit., U. Oreg., 1985, JD, 1991. Loan processor Home Fed. Savs., Eugene, Oreg., 1985-86; rsch. asst. Grad. Sch. U. Oreg., Eugene, 1987 summer; vault and sr. teller West One BancCorp, Eugene, 1988; law clk., rsch. asst. various attys. Eugene, 1990-94; student rep. BARBRI, Eugene, 1991-92; vol. coord. L. Holland's Lane County Dist. Ct. Jud. campaign, 1992-93; legal asst. Sahlstrom & Dugdale, Eugene, 1994; legal asst./rschr. Buck, Hogshire & Tereskerz, Charlottesville, Va., 1994-95; lawyer, editor Michie Law Publs., Charlottesville, 1995—; part time telefund coord. U. Oreg. Found., Eugene, 1981-85; conf. planner sch. law U. Oreg., 1992-93. Mem. ABA, Oreg. Women Lawyers Assn., Lane County Women Lawyers Assn., Alpha Lambda Delta, Phi Eta Sigma. Home: 2675 Meriwether Dr Charlottesville VA 22901-9512

BRISCO, VALERIE, track and field athlete; b. Greenwood, Miss., July 6, 1960; d. Arguster and Guitherea Brisco; m. Alvin Hooks (div.); 1 child, Alvin. Student, Calif. State U., Northridge. Track competitions include Assn. for Intercollegiate Athletics for Women, 1979, Athletic Congress Nat. Championships, 1984, Olympic Games, Los Angeles, 1984, UCLA Invitational, 1985, Bruce Jenner Meet, San Jose, Calif., 1984, European Track Circuit, 1984, 85, Millrose Games, 1985, Times-Herald Invitational, 1985, Olympic Games, 1988. Co-chairperson Minnie Riperton Cancer Week, 1986-90. Recipient 3 Gold medals 1984 Olympics, Los Angeles, Silver medal 1988 Olympics, Seoul, Republic of Korea; Outstanding Mother's award Nat. Mother's Day Com., 1986; ranked #1 in U.S. in 400 meters, Track and Field News, 1986, #2 in U.S. in 200 meters, Track and Field News, 1986, #3 in U.S. in 100 meters, Track and Field News, 1986, #4 in U.S. in 200 meters, Track and Field News, 1988, #2 in U.S. in 400 meters, Track and Field News, 1988, #6 in world in 400 meters, Track and Field News, 1988. Office: World Class Athletes PO Box 18204 Long Beach CA 90807-8204

BRISCOE, AGATHA DONATTO, data processing executive, instructor; b. Liberty, Tex., Feb. 21, 1947; d. Alton Peter and Audrey Mary (Broussard) Donatto; m. Edward Gans Briscoe, Jan. 23, 1976; 1 child, Allison Marie. BS in Math. summa cum laude, Tex. So. U., 1969; student, UCLA, 1967-68, 69-70. Cert. secondary tchr., Tex. Scientific programmer The Aerospace Corp., El Segundo, Calif., 1971-73; tech. staff TRW Def. and Space Systems Group, El Segundo, 1973-76; instr. data processing Hawaii C.C., Hilo, 1979-86; analyst, programmer Cayman Islands Govt., Grand Cayman, 1986-87; dir. mgmt. info. svcs. V.I. Dept. Health, St. Thomas, 1987-89; systems analyst V.I. Telephone Co., St. Thomas, 1989-90; sr. applications specialist InfoTech (Kapioloni Health Care Systems), Honolulu, 1990-93, new projects coord., 1993-95; sr. programmer/analyst Sutter Health, Sacramento, 1995-96; advanced programmer-analyst Shared Med. Systems, Sacramento, 1996—; pres. Hawaii Vocat. Assn., Hilo, 1983-85; coord. data processing program Hawaii C.C., Hilo, 1979-86. Supr. com. mem. Big Island Ednl. Fedn. Credit Union, Hilo, 1979-86; troop leader Girl Scouts Am., Hilo, 1984-85; cmty. rep. African-Am. adv. com. U. Hawaii, Manoa, 1994; vol. tutor, Honolulu, 1991-94. Equipment grantee U. Hawaii Pres.'s Fund, Honolulu, 1985. Home: 2964 Bridlewood Dr Cameron Park CA 95682 Office: Sutter Health 2901 L St Sacramento CA 96816

BRISCOE, CONNIE, writer; b. Washington, Dec. 31, 1952; d. Leroy Fabian and Alyce Levinia (Redmond) B. BS, Hampton U., 1974; MPA, Am. U., 1978. Rsch. analyst Analytic Svcs. Inc., Arlington, Va., 1976-80; assoc. editor Joint Ctr. for Polit. and Econ. Studies, Washington, 1981-90; mng. editor Gallaudet U., Washington, 1990-94; writer, 1994—. Author: Sisters and Lovers, 1994, Big Girls Don't Cry, 1996.

BRISCOE, MARIAN DENISE, real estate agent, lyricist; b. Balt., Sept. 15, 1958; d. Donald and Bernice (Cofield) Cox; m. James McA. Briscoe, Nov. 2, 1979; children: Crystal Joy and Jennelle Denise. Student music, Morgan State U., 1977; cert. hotel mgmt., C.C.B., Balt., 1979. Therapeutic tech. Union Meml. Hosp., Balt., 1978-80; auditor Holiday Inn, Balt., 1979-81; lyricist J.J. Prodns., Balt., 1981—; realtor Homecoming Realty, Balt., 1995—; mgr. Brant Mgmt., Balt., 1991—. Mem. Nat. Assn. Realtors, Greater Balt. Bd. Realtors. Democrat. Home: 1214 N Calhoun St Baltimore MD 21217-2750 Office: Homecoming Realty 4134 Edmondson Ave Baltimore MD 21229-1807

BRISCOE, MARY BECK, federal judge; b. 1947. BA, U. Kans., 1969, JD, 1973; LLM, U. Va., 1990. Rsch. asst. Harold L. Haun, Esq., 1973; atty.-examiner fin. divsn. ICC, 1973-74; asst. U.S. atty. for Wichita and Topeka, Kans. Dept. Justice, 1974-84; judge Kans. Ct. Appeals, 1984-95, U.S. Ct. Appeals (10th cir.), Topeka, Kans., 1995—; mem. Coun. Chief Judges of State Intermediate Appellate Cts.; mem. civil code com. Kans. Jud. Coun., 1985-93. Fellow Am. Bar Found., Kans. Bar Found.; mem. ABA (mem. nominating com. appellate judges conf. 1994), Am. Judicature Soc., Nat. Assn. Women Judges, Topeka Bar Assn., Kans. Bar Assn. (mem. com. on professionalism, equality, and quality of life 1994—, Outstanding Svc. award 1992), Women Attys. Assn. Topeka, Kans. Hist. Soc., Topeka Lawyers Soc., Washburn Law Sch. Assn. (hon.), U. Kans. Law Soc. Office: US Ct Appeals 10th Cir 424 S Kansas Ave Topeka KS 66603

BRISKEY, LISA ANN, accountant; b. Detroit, Aug. 8, 1963; d. Robert Howard and Barbara Joan (Welsh) Parnell; m. John Francis Briskey, Sept. 10, 1994; 1 child, Jacob Paul. A in Acctg., Macomb C.C., 1985; B Acctg., Walsh Coll., 1988, M Fin., 1995. CPA, Ill.; cert. mgmt. acct. Inst. Mgmt. Accts. Asst. mgr. Burger Chef, Warren, Mich., 1979-85; acct. CMI Corp., West Bloomfield, Mich., 1985-88, Marathon Petroleum Co., Detroit, 1988-89, Blue Cross Blue Shield, Detroit, 1989—. Mem. Am. Soc. Women Accts. (bd. dirs., treas. 1989-93), Millpointe of Westland Assn. (bd. dirs., treas. 1992—), Nat. Mgmt. Assn. (bd. dirs., pub. rels. com. 1989-93). Home: 2021 Stockmeyer Westland MI 48186

BRISSETTE, MARTHA BLEVINS, lawyer; b. Salisbury, Md., Apr. 30, 1959; d. Reuben Wesley and Miriam Rebecca (Walters) Blevins; m. Henry Joseph Brissette III, May 24, 1980. BA, U. Richmond, 1981, JD, 1983. Bar: Va. 1983, U.S. Supreme Ct. 1987. Law clk. Supreme Ct. Va., Richmond, 1983-84; atty. Dept. Justice, Washington, 1984-88; staff atty. Office of the Exec. Sec., Supreme Ct. Va., Richmond, 1988; asst. atty. gen. Office of the Atty. Gen. of Va., Richmond, 1989-92; atty., v.p. govt. affairs counsel Lawyers Title Ins. Corp., Richmond, 1992—. Vol. Habitat for Humanity; bd. dirs. Highland Support Project Jr. Achievement Ctrl. Va. Mem. Phi Beta Kappa. Catholic. Home: 8221 Brookfield Rd Richmond VA 23227-1501 Office: Lawyers Title Ins Corp Nat Hdqs 6630 W Broad St Richmond VA 23230-1702

BRISSON, HARRIET ELDREDGE, art educator; b. South Kingstown, R.I., Aug. 11, 1932; d. Lucus Gilbert and Harriet Hapgood (House) Eldredge; m. David Winslow Brisson, June 8, 1953 (dec. May 1982); 1 child, Erik. BFA, R.I. Sch. Design, 1953; MFA, Ohio U., 1955; MA in Teaching, R.I. Sch. Design, 1966. Instr. Auburn (Ala.) U., 1958-63, Providence Pub. Schs., 1966-69; from asst. prof. to prof. art R.I. Coll., Providence, 1969—; Thorp prof. artistic work R.I. Coll., 1986-87; pres. bd. trustees Studio Potter Orgn., Goffstown, N.H., 1990—. Contbr. articles to profl. jours. Mem. Nat. Coun. Edn. Ceramic Arts (dir.-at-large 1983-84), Internat. Sculpture Ctr. Home: 155 Green Hill Ave Wakefield RI 02879 Office: RI Coll 600 Mt Pleasant Ave Providence RI

BRISTO, MARCA, healthcare executive; b. Albany, N.Y., June 23, 1953; d. Earl C. and Dorothy (Moore) B.; m. J. robert Kettlewell, Oct. 15, 1988; children: Samuel Clayton Kettlewell, Madeline Elizabeth Kettlewell. BA in Sociology, Beloit Coll., 1974; BSN, Rush Coll. Nursing, Chgo., 1976. Cert. nursing. RN Rush Presbyn. St. Luke's Med. Ctr., Chgo., 1976-77; RN Northwestern Meml. Hosp., Chgo., 1977, family planning nurse specialist, 1978-79; exec. dir. Access Living Met. Chgo., 1979-84; chmn. Nat. Coun. Disability, Washington. Mem. nat. adv. bd. Access Am., Austin, Tex.; bd. dirs. Donors Forum of Chgo.; bd. dirs., chairperson Ill. Pub. Action Coun.; co-founder, pres. Nat. Coun. on Ind. Living. Named Outstanding Young Citizen, Chgo. Jr. C. of C., 1984; recipient Commr.'s Disting. Svc. award U.S. Dept. Edn. Rehab. Svcs. Adminstrn., 1987, Cert. of Esteem & Recognition, Stte of Ill. Office of Sec. of State, 1987. Mem. Nat. Coun. on Ind. Living. Office: Access Living Met Chgo 310 S Peoria St Chicago IL 60607-3534 Office: Nat Coun Disability 1331 F St NW Ste 1050 Washington DC 20004-1107*

BRISTOL, LOUISE FITZGERALD, nurse; b. Moorestown, N.J., Mar. 24, 1935; d. Edward William and Katherine (D'Arcy) Fitzgerald; children: John Edward, Eric Charles. RN, W. Jersey Hosp., 1956; BSN, U. Pa., 1975; MS, U. Del., 1985; postmasters cert. in nursing adminstrn., Villanova U., 1987. RN, N.J. Nurse West Jersey Hosp., Camden, N.J., 1956-57, Mount Holly (N.J.) Hosp., 1957-59, Good Samaratin Hosp., Syracuse, N.Y., 1959-61, Syracuse VA Med. Ctr., 1961-64; med. staff nurse Phila. VA Med. Ctr., 1967-80, staff nurse ICU, 1969-70, surg. staff nurse ICU, 1970-73, night coord., 1973-80; nurse Wilmington (Del.) VA Med. Ctr., 1980-86; headnurse/supr. Coatesville (PA.) VA Med. Ctr., 1986-89; geriatric gerontol. clin. nurse specialist VA Med. Ctr., Coatesville, Pa., 1991—; bd. dirs. NOVA Nat. Com. Mem. Nurses of VA (bd. dirs., chair chpts. com.), ANA (gerontology coun.), Kansas City ANA (cert.), Brandywine Valley Assn. Roman Catholic. Office: Coatesville Vet Adminstn Med Ctr Coatesville PA 19320

BRISTOR, KATHERINE M., lawyer; b. Hampton, Va., 1953. BA magna cum laude, Carleton Coll., 1975; JD, Columbia U., 1980. Bar: N.Y. 1981. Ptnr. Skadden, Arps, Slate, Meagher & Flom, N.Y.C. Harlan Fiske Stone scholar. Office: Skadden Arps Slate Meagher & Flom 919 3rd Ave New York NY 10022*

BRISTOW, CAROLYN LUREE CUMMINGS, library media specialist; b. Jackson, Mich., Feb. 20, 1943; d. Leon Dewitt and Lulu Luree (Boyle) Cummings; m. Michael Barry Bristow, June 21, 1964; children: Michael Christopher, Jeffery Alan, Benjamin Aaron. AA, Jackson Jr. Coll., 1963; BA, Western Mich. U., 1965; postgrad., UCLA, 1969; MEd, Wright State U., Dayton, Ohio, 19960. Cert. tchr. 1-8, ed. tech. specialist K-12, Ohio. Libr. elem. sch. Portage (Mich.) Pub. Schs., 1965-67; substitute tchr. Redondo Beach (Calif.) City Schs., 1967, libr. elem. sch., 1968, libr. cons., 1968-69; dir. ednl. media svcs. Troy (Ohio) City Schs., 1975-78; libr. elem. sch. Bethel Local Schs., Tipp City, Ohio, 1974-75, K-8 media specialist, 1982-92, dir. info. svcs., 1992—. Youth music leader LDS Ch., Huber Heights, Ohio, 1976—; coun. tng. chmn. Boy Scouts Am., Springfield, Ohio, 1978-90; pres. Menlo Park PTO, Huber Heights, 1982-84. Recipient dist. award of merit Boy Scouts Am., 1986, Silver Beaver award, 1988, Tchr. of Yr. award Bethel Local Schs., 1987; 21st Century grantee Bethel Bd. Edn., 1992; Jennings scholar Martha E. Jennings Found., 1993. Mem. Ohio Ednl. Libr. Media Assn., Greater Miami Valley Ednl. Tech. Coun. Home: 6527 Rosebury Dr Huber Heights OH 45424-3540 Office: Bethel Local Schs 7490 State Route 201 Tipp City OH 45371-9300

BRITO, SILVIA, artistic director; b. Havana, Cuba, Dec. 2, 1933; d. Lillian and Osvaldo Brito. Student, Baldor Acad., 1951, Theatre Matrix, 1978. Sec., bookkeeper J. Mieres & Co., 1951-61; sec. typist Phoenix Assurance Co., 1961-62, Dodge & Seymour Ltd., 1962-64; data processor GM Corp., 1964-73; data processing asst. supr. Adsco Data Systems, 1973-75; data processor Lenox Hill Hosp., 1975-91. Actress Teatro Prometeo, 1959-61, Andres Castro Co., 1966-68, Dume Grupo Studio, 1968-70, 75-76; actress, dir. Repertorio Espanol, 1970-72; dir., producer Thalia Spanish Theatre, 1977—. Recipient El Tirmpo and Talia awards for best actress, 1970-71, Best Dir. ACE awards, 1981, 84, Best Prodn. ACE award, 1980-82, 84-86, 88-90, 95, Best Dir. Aplausos award, 1989, Artistic Merits award Arts and Bus. Coun., 1989, Citation of Honor Queens Borough pres., 1990, Best Prodn. award, 1992-93, Lifetime Achievement Latina Excellence award, 1995. Office: Thalia Spanish Theatre 41-17 Greenpoint Ave Sunnyside NY 11104-0368*

BRITT, DONNA MARIE, school nurse; b. Phila., Oct. 27, 1950; d. Joseph D. and Margaret M. (Cullen) Finn; divorced; children: Colleen Marie, Patricia Ann, Joseph James. BA in Biology, Holy Family Coll., 1972, BSN, 1974. cert. sch. nurse, N.J. Staff nurse Jeannes Hosp., Phila., 1975; tchr. Archdiocese of Phila., 1985-91; sch. nurse Camden City Bd. of Edn., N.J., 1991-93; sch. nurse, health tchr. Riverside (N.J.) Bd. edn., 1994-95; sch. nurse City of Burlington, N.J., 1995—; chairperson Mid. States Com. Our Lady Help of Christians, Phila., 1988-91, co-chairperson Mid. States Com. Camden City Sch., 1991-93. Cons.: (book) Tough Love for Teachers, 1989. Merit badge counselor Boy Scouts Am., Frontier Dist., Phila., 1990—. Mem. Nat. Sch. Nurses Assn., N.J. State Sch. Nurses Assn., Burlington County Sch. Nurses Assn., NEA, N.J. Edn. Assn., Burlington County Edn. Assn. Roman Catholic. Home: 9 Primrose Pl Delran NJ 08075-2817 Office: Capt James Lawrence Sch 315 Barclay St Burlington NJ 08016

BRITT, MAISHA DORRAH, protective services official; b. S.C.; d. Charles Joseph Britt and Versena (Kennedy) Dorrah; m. W. Benjamin Williams, Dec. 14, 1963 (div. June 1976); children: Terri Rochelle, Trina Michelle. AS, BS, Phila Coll. Textiles and Sci.; MA, Antioch U., Phila., 1986. Cert. in electronic surveillance. Police officer Phila. Police Dept., 1976-79; sgt. county detective Phila. Dist. Atty's Office, 1979-90; orgn. devel. cons., pres. M. Dorrah-Britt and Assocs., 1991—; cert. family devel. specialist Norristown Family Ctr., 1994—; founder, dir. Creative Awareness Workshop, Phila., 1978—. Poet: (included in anthology) Famous Poems of the Twentieth Century, 1996. Sec. bd. Horizon House, Phila., 1988—; vol. Women Against Abuse, Phila., 1983—, youth adv. New Gethsemane Bapt. Ch., Phila., 1978—; mem. bd. trustees Ctr. for Literacy, 1990—, vice chmn.; vol. security team program mem. Atlanta Com. Olympic Games, 1996. Recipient Woman of Yr. citation Pa. Fedn. Bus. and Profl. Women's Clubs Inc.; inducted into Murrell Dobbins H.S. Hall of Fame, 1988. Mem. Am. Soc. for Indsl. Security, County Detectives Assn. Pa. (exec. bd. 1990—), Fraternal Order of Police, Internat. Police Assn., Internat. Assn. Women Police, Nat. Women's Hall of Fame, Nat. Assn. Chiefs of Police, Bus. and Profl. Women's Club, Internat. Platform Assn. Republican. Address: PO Box 1381 Dover DE 19903-1381

BRITT, MARGARET MARY, accounting educator; b. Balt., Jan. 21, 1951; d. Joseph John and Lottie Elizabeth (Zielinski) B. BA in Elem. Edn., U. Mass., 1972; BSBA, Boston U., 1979, M. Human Resource Edn., 1990. Cert. tchr. elem. edn., music, Mass.; cert. vocat. tech. educator in bus. mktg., Mass. Internal auditor Digital Equip. Corp., Maynard, Mass., 1979-82, sr. fin. analyst FDP, 1982-83; sr. fin. analyst sales Digital Equip. Corp., Stow, Mass., 1983-85; cons. trainer Digital Equip. Corp., Maynard, 1985-87, fin. cons., trainer, 1987-90, mgr. corp. fin. edn., 1990-94; automated office instr. Mass. Job Tng., Worcester, 1995—; part-time instr. fin. continuing edn. dept. Syracuse U., 1990-91; adj. prof. bus. Ea. Nazarene Coll., Quincy, Mass., 1994—; bd. dirs. Am. Biog. Inst., 1990—. Sec. Parsons Hill Homeowners Assn., Worcester, 1985-90; presenter time mgmt. workshop MIT-Soc. Women Engrs. and Alumnae, Cambridge, 1988, 89. Named Outstanding Young Women of Am., 1984. Mem. ASTD, NAFE, Inst. Internal Auditors, Nat. Mus. for Women in the Arts. Home: 39 Parsons Hill Dr Worcester MA 01603-1245 Office: Mass Job Tng Inc 332 Main St Worcester MA 01603

BRITTAIN, NANCY HAMMOND, accountant; b. Athens, Pa., Oct. 29, 1954; d. Charles Avery Hammond and Leona May (Rolls) Mc Creary; m. Edward M. Brittain, Sept. 6, 1975. AS in Bus., Elmira Coll., 1989, BS in Acctg. summa cum laude, 1994. CPA, Pa. Legal sec. Friedlander, Friedlander, Reizes, Joch & Littman, P.C., Waverly, N.Y., 1973-84; bus. mgr. Foundry divsn. Ajax X-Ray, Inc., Sayre, Pa., 1984—. Mem. Athens Borough Zoning Bd., 1991—. Mem. Inst. Mgmt. Accts., Alpha Sigma Lambda (mem. exec. com. Beta Tau chpt., various offices 1988-95). Republican. Methodist. Home: 614 Church St Athens PA 18810-1806 Office: Ajax X-Ray Inc Foundry Divsn 150 Bradford St Sayre PA 18840-1802

BRITTELL-WHITEHEAD, DIANE PEEPLES, secondary education educator, addiction counselor; b. Binghamton, N.Y., Feb. 2, 1950, d. Berbie Winfred and Vera (Bufano) Peeples; m. Edward James Brittell, June 14, 1975 (div. 1991); children: Jesse, Aimeé, Jeneé; m. Paul Whitehead, July 20, 1996. BS in Mental Health, Hahnemann U., 1974; MEd, cert. reading specialist, Widener U., 1987, MEd. Cert. in spl. edn., allied addictions practitioner, Pa. Cashier Pantry Pride Markets, Norristown, Pa., 1964-74; tchr. Parkway Day Sch., Phila., 1973-77; diagnostic tchr. Sleighton Farms, Wawa, Pa., 1984-85; tchr., reading specialist Ridley Sch. Dist., Ridley Park, Pa., 1987—; mental health worker, tchr. Hahnemann Hosp., Phila., summers 1988-94; addictions counselor Crozer Chester (Pa.) Med. Ctr., 1991—, Keystone Rehab. Ctr., Chester, 1993—; tutor, Chester, 1985-87; lectr. state tchrs. convs., Pa., N.J., 1986-88, various rehab. workshops, 1986—. Contbr. articles to various publs. Vol. St. Mary's Orphanage, Ambler, Pa., 1967-69. Mem. NEA, ASCD, AAUW, Nat. Assn. Drug Abuse Counselors, Pa. Edn. Assn., Pa. Assn. Drug Abuse Counselors. Republican. Home: 400 E Hinckley Ave Ridley Park PA 19078 Office: Ridley Mid Sch Ridley Park PA 19078

BRITTIN, MARIE ELEANOR, communications, psychology, speech and hearing science educator; b. Wichita, Kans.; d. F. E. and A. M. Brittin. BS, Northwestern U.; MA, U. Iowa; PhD, Northwestern U. Lic. speech pathologist Ohio, Wash. Instr. U. Wis., Madison, 1950-53; coord. comm. disorders Tacoma Pub. Schs., 1956-64; dir. speech and hearing Coll. Edn. Ohio State U., Columbus, 1964-73, assoc. prof. speech and hearing sci., 1973-89; cons. Kent (Wash.) Pub. Schs., 1991; chair Chauncey D. Leake award for excellence in pharmacology, 1978-90; elected mem. compensation and benefits com. Ohio State U., 1985-89; adj. faculty comm. U. Wash., 1994—; pvt. cons. in field; presenter comm. seminars. Editor: Ohio Jour. Speech and Hearing, 1984-85. Pres., com. chair Zonta Internat., Tacoma, Columbus. Fellow Am. Speech-Lang.-Hearing Assn. (legis. coun. 1989, 90, 91, site visitor 1982-84, Ace award 1986); mem. APA, Internat. Assn. Logopedics and Phoniatrics (presenter), AAAS, Nat. Aphasia Assn., PEO, Christian Med. and Dental Soc., Ohio State U. Faculty Women's Club (pres. 1966-67), Pi Lambda Theta (pub. adv. bd. 1983-85), Delta Kappa Gamma (pres. Alpha Tau chpt. 1964). Home: 1220 7th Ave SW Puyallup WA 98371-6759 Office: Ohio State U Speech and Hearing Sci 1070 Carmack Rd Columbus OH 43210-1002

BRITTLE, LINDA VAUGHAN, reading and behavioral science educator; b. Suffolk, Va., Jan. 13, 1949; d. John Shelton Vaughan and Daphne (Williams) Dunn; m. M. Kenneth Brittle, Sr., July 24, 1971; children: Lorraine, Marshall. BS, Longwood Coll., 1971; MEd, U. Va., 1979; EdD, East Tenn. State U., 1994. 2d grade tchr. Spotsylvania County Pub. Schs., Fredericksburg, Va., 1971-74, 75-78; gifted instr. U. Va. Sch. for Gifted/Talented, Fredericksburg, Va., 1971-74, 75-78; 5th grade tchr. Henrico County Pub. Schs., Richmond, Va., 1979-80, 2d grade tchr., 1980-82; 1st grade tchr. St. Anne's Cath. Sch., Bristol, Va., 1983-90, 2d grade tchr., dir. enrichment, 1986-90; multi-age tchr. Bristol Va. City Schs., 1992-94, Chpt. I reading tchr., 1994-95, 1st grade tchr., 1995—; adj. asst. prof. dept. behavioral sci. King Coll., Bristol, 1996. Bd. dirs. Bristol Ballet, 1985-90, Highlands Cmty. Svcs., Bristol, 1993—; mem. Jr. League of Bristol, 1986—; mem. Patron's Cir., Mid-Atlantic Chamber Orch., Bristol, 1990-94; chair bd. dirs. Bristol Va. Youth Svcs., 1990-94. Recipient Doctoral fellowship East Tenn. State U., 1991, Tchr. of Yr. award Bristol Va./Tenn. Rotary, 1993, A. Margaret Boyd Internat., Delta Kappa Gamma, 1993. Mem. ASCD, Va. ASCD, Gifted Child Advocacy Assn., Va. Assn. for Edn. of Gifted, Assn. for Childhood Edn. Internat., Va. State Reading Assn., S.W. Reading Coun., Phi Delta Kappa, Kappa Delta Pi, Gamma Beta Phi. Presbyterian. Home: 16 Long Crescent Bristol VA 24201 Office: Bristol Va City Sch 16 Long Crescent Bristol VA 24201

BRITTON, DEE, arts school official, music educator; b. Danville, Ill., Dec. 19, 1956; d. Harry Edward and Elaine Joanne (Meyer) Peterson; m. Robert Kevin Britton, Sept. 3, 1977; children: Kirsten Dee, Lauren Marie, Erin Lynn. BSBA, Auburn U., 1978; MS in Fin., U. Ill., 1981. Mgr. Danville (Ill.) Symphony, 1984-86; pres. Trillium Performing Arts Ctr., Watertown, N.Y., 1986-91; exec. dir. Met. Sch. for Arts, Syracuse, N.Y., 1992—; tchr. music, Danville, Watertown, Syracuse, 1978—; cons., Danville, 1984-86, Syracyse, 1992—; mem. faculty various colls., 1980—; mem. faculty, program auditor Nat. Guild Cmty. Schs., Englewood, N.J., 1994-96, mem.

fin. com., 1996; mem. exec. com. Performing Arts Med. Assn., Syracuse, 1993—; presenter in field. Vol. Girl Scouts U.S.A., 1986—; mem; Syracuse Arts Coalition, 1992—; mem. Syracuse City Sch. Dist. Task Force, 1995, Cmty. Wide Dialogue, Syracuse, 1996; spkr. United Way Ctrl. N.Y., 1994-96, pres., 1992-96. Recipient ward for youth-at-risk programs President's Com. on Arts and Humanities, 1996. Mem. AAUW, NAFE. Presbyterian. Home: 126 Redfield Ave Fayetteville NY 13066 Office: Met Sch for Arts 320 Montgomery St Syracuse NY 13202

BRITTON, EVE MARCHANT, newspaper reporter; b. N.Y.C., June 25, 1965; d. Donald Robison and Susan Harriet (Marchant) B. Student, Allegheny Coll., 1983-85; BA in Journalism, San Francisco State U., 1990; postgrad., Monterey Coll. Law, 1995—. Reporter city coun. Carmel (Calif.) Pine Cone, 1990; reporter youth issues Monterey (Calif.) County Herald, 1990—; mem. newsroom task force Monterey County Herald, 1992-94. Mem. steering com. Beacon House 10K Run, Pacific Grove, Calif., 1986-94, 1st Night Monterey, 1993-96; tutor Seaside (Calif.) Homework Ctr., 1993-94; choir mem., lector All Sts. Episcopal Ch., Carmel, 1994—. Named Woman of Distinction, Soroptomists Internat., 1995; recipient 1st pl. honor Monterey County Literacy Assn., 1994. Mem. Student Bar Assn., Humane Soc. U.S., Women's Golf Connection, Richard Nixon Meml. Libr., Ctrl. Coast Press Club. Home: PO Box 125 Carmel Valley CA 93924 Office: Monterey County Herald PO Box 271 Monterey CA 93942

BRITTON, KATHERINE LELA QUAINTON, lawyer; b. Sydney, N.S.W., Australia, Mar. 21, 1960; d. Anthony Cecil Eden and Susan (Long) Quainton; m. Edward Charles Britton, Aug. 23, 1986; children: Peter Edward Quainton, Gillian Amanda Oates, Matthew Joseph McDonald. AB, Princeton U., 1982; JD, Harvard U., 1986. Bar: D.C. 1986. Assoc. Arnold & Porter, Washington, 1986—. Knox fellow Harvard U., 1985. Mem. ABA, D.C. Bar Assn. Home: 5000 Glenbrook Rd NW Washington DC 20016-3225 Office: Arnold & Porter 1200 New Hampshire Ave NW Washington DC 20036-6802

BRITZ, DIANE EDWARD, investment company executive; b. York, Pa., June 15, 1952; d. Everett Frank and Billie Jacqueline (Sherrill) B.; m. Marcello Lotti, Sept. 9, 1978 (dec. Apr. 1990); children: Ariane Elizabeth, Samantha Alexis. BA, Duke U., 1974; MBA, Columbia U., 1982. Asst. mgr. Columbia Artists, N.Y.C., 1974-76; gen. mgr. Ea. Music Festival, Greensboro, N.C., 1977-78; v.p. Britz Cobin, N.Y.C., 1979-82; pres. Pan Oceanic Mgmt., Inc., N.Y.C., 1983-90, Pan Oceanic Advisors, Ltd., N.Y.C., 1988-94; chmn. Pan Oceanic Mgmt. Ltd., N.Y.C., 1994—; also bd. dirs Pan Oceanic Advisors, Ltd., N.Y.C.; pres. Am. Capital Ptnrs., Ltd., 1996—; bd. dirs. Pan Oceanic Mgmt., Inc. Mem. bd. advisors Turtle Bay Music Sch.; bd. dirs. The 1148 Corp.; mem. bd. visitors Duke U. Mem. Fin. Women's Assn., Caramoor Ctr. for Music and Arts, Inc. (bd. dirs., steering com. capital campaign), Columbia Bus. Sch. Club of N.Y., Doubles Club. Quaker. Office: 1148 5th Ave # 14B New York NY 10128-0807

BRIUER, ELKE MOERSCH, editor; b. Darmstadt, Germany, Feb. 20, 1943; came to U.S., 1962; d. Karl Wilhelm and Ilse (Hohorst) Moersch; divorced; children: Patricia Mae Monroe, Kenneth Frank Gaston; m. Frederick L. Briuer, Oct. 9, 1986. BA in German cum laude, U. Md., 1977, postgrad., 1984; postgrad., U.T., 1980; MS in Comm., Miss. Coll., 1992. Accredited pub. rels. profl. Pub. affairs officer Med. Ctr. 97th Gen. Hosp., Frankfurt, Germany, 1982-84; supr. pub. affairs officer USMCA, Aschaffenburg, Germany, 1984-86; pub. affairs specialist 5th rctg. brigade U.S. Army, San Antonio, 1986-88; writer, editor (Technology Transfer Specialist) U.S. Army Engr. Waterways Expt. Sta., Vicksburg, 1988—. Author: (recruitment pamphlet) The Quick Answer Book of U.S. Army Recruiting Support Command Exhibits, 1989, (booklet) The Young Scientist's Introduction to Wetlands, 1993; dir. (video) The Black Swamp, 1995; editor: Caduceus, Ad Libs, Wetlands Rsch. Program Bull., 1991—; writer, editor: (multi-media CD-ROM) Wetlands Rsch. Program Summary, 1991-94; contbr. numerous articles to newspapers and mags. Sec. Vicksburg Art Assn., 1990-91, newsletter editor, 1990-93; mem. Soc. Wetland Sci., 1991—, Miss. Heritage Trust, 1991—, Heritage Herald editor, 1994—; 2d v.p. Vicksburg Cmty. Concert Assn., 1994-96. Mem. So. Pub. Rels. Fedn., Pub. Rels. Assn. Miss. Office: US Army Engr Waterways Expt Sta CEWES-IM-MV-E 3909 Halls Ferry Rd Vicksburg MS 39180-6133

BROADBENT, AMALIA SAYO CASTILLO, graphic arts designer; b. Manila, May 28, 1956; came to U.S., 1980, naturalized, 1985; d. Conrado Camilo and Eugenia de Guzman (Sayo) Castillo; m. Barrie Noel Broadbent, Mar. 14, 1981; children: Charles Noel Castillo, Chandra Noel Castillo. BFA, U. Santo Tomas, 1978; postgrad. Acad. Art Coll., San Francisco, Alliance Francaise, Manila, Karilagan Finishing Sch., Manila, Manila Computer Ctr.; BA, Maryknoll Coll., 1972. Designer market research Unicorp Export Inc., Makati, Manila, 1975-77; asst. advt. mgr. Dale Trading Corp., Makati, 1977-78; artist, designer, pub. relations Resort Hotels Corp., Makati, 1978-81; prodn. artist CYB/Young & Rubicam, San Francisco, 1981-82; freelance art dir. Ogilvy & Mather Direct, San Francisco, 1986; artist, designer, owner A.C. Broadbent Graphics, San Francisco, 1982—; faculty graphic design & advt. depts. Acad. Art Coll., San Francisco. Works include: Daing na Isda, 1975, (Christmas coloring) Pepsi-Cola, 1964 (Distinctive Merit cert.), (children's books) UNESCO, 1973 (cert.). Pres. Pax Romana, Coll. of Architecture and Fine Arts, U. Santo Tomas, 1976-78, chmn. cultural sect., 1975; v.p. Atelier Cultural Soc., U. Santo Tomas, 1975-76; mem. Makati Dance Troupe, 1973-74. Recipient Merit cert., Inst. Religion, 1977. Mem. NAFE, Alliance Francaise de San Francisco, Internat. Platform Assn., San Francisco Bus. & Profl. Women's Prayer Group. Roman Catholic.

BROADUS, LORRAINE HUTCHERSON, nursing educator; b. Ft. Worth, July 31, 1930; d. L.C. and Snodie Morine (Wright) Hutcherson; m. Clyde R. Broadus (div.); children: Clyde R. Jr., Reginald H., William G. BSN, MeHarr Med. Coll. Sch. Nursing, 1951; MS in Nursing, Tex. Woman's U., 1974. RN Tex. Staff nurse Air-EVAC MEd./Surg., Travis AFB, Fairfield, Calif., 1955, Ft. Worth Ind. Sch. Dist., 1955-70, 72-76; night supr. Elmood Psychiat. Hosp.-Tarrant County Hosp. Dist., Ft. Worth, 1970-72; asst. prof. nursing Tarrant County Jr. Coll., Ft. Worth, 1976-80, assoc. prof. nursing, 1980-90, assoc. prof. emeritus, 1990—; mem. adv. com. Tarrant County Hosp. Dist. Psychiat. Nursing Faciluty, Ft. Worth, 1988—; cons. psychiatric staff All Sts. Episcopal. Hosp., Ft. Worth, 1990. Author: (manual) Psychiatric Nurisng Staff Development Manual, 1990. Bd. dirs. YWCA/Tarrant Area Agy Aging, Ft. Worth, 1994. Recipient Pres. award-25 Ys. Svc. to Mankind, Meharry Med. Coll., 1976; named Health Educator of Yr. KNOK Radio Sta., 1967. Mem.ANA, Tex. Nurses Assn. (chair continuing edn. approval review com. 1975-78), Ft. Worth chpt. Links (pres. 1975-78), Progressive Lit. & Art Club (v.p. 1994). Democrat. Home: 2212 Fairway Dr Fort Worth TX 76119-4563

BROADUS-GARCIA, CASSANDRA ANN, art educator; b. New Orleans, Oct. 10, 1960; d. Lloyd Zedric and Earlene (Phillips) B. BFA in Art Edn., U. So. Miss., Hattiesburg, 1984; MA, U. North Tex., Denton, 1992; PhD, Ohio State U., 1994. Tchr. art Hattiesburg (Miss.) Pub. Schs., 1984-85, Irving (Tex.) Ind. Schs., 1985-86, Highland Park Ind. Schs., 1986-90; grad. teaching fellow U. North Tex., Denton, 1990-91; grad. teaching and rsch. asst. Ohio State U., Columbus, 1992-94; tchr. art Ctrl. Conn. State U., New Britain, 1994—; art cons. Capers for Kids, Dallas, 1985-90, Tex. Arts Coun., Austin, 1990-92. Contbg. author: (monograph) Art Education and Technology, 1994; Art-O-Gram columnist Ft. Worth Star-Telegram, 1991. Recipient Ameritech Doctoral prize for excellence in telecomms. rsch. Ohio State U., 1994. Mem. Nat. Art Edn. Assn., Am. Ednl. Rsch. Assn., Phi Kappa Phi, Delta Kappa Gamma. Office: Ctrl Conn State U 1615 Stanley St New Britain CT 06053-2439

BROADWAY, NANCY RUTH, landscape design and construction company executive, consultant, model and actress; b. Memphis, Dec. 20, 1946; d. Charlie Sidney and Patsy Ruth (Meadows) Adkins. BS in Biology and Sociology cum laude, Memphis State U., 1969; postgrad., Tulane U., 1969-70; MS in Horticulture, U. Calif.-Davis, 1976. Lic. landscape contractor, Calif. Claims adjuster Mass. Mut. Ins., San Francisco, 1972-73; community garden coord. City of Davis, Calif., 1976; seed propagation supr. Bordier's Wholesale Nursery, Santa Ana, Calif., 1976-78; owner, founder Calif. Landscape Co., 1978-88, Design & Mgmt. Consultare, 1988—. Actress: Visions of Murder, 1993, Eyes of Terror, 1994. NDEA fellow Tulane U., 1969-70. Fellow Am. Hort. Soc.; mem. Nat. Assn. Gen. Contractors, Calif. Native Plant Soc., Stockton C. of C. Democrat. Home and Office: 220 Atlantic Ave Unit 112 Santa Cruz CA 95062-3800

BROCHES, ALEXANDRA, artist; b. N.Y.C., Apr. 23, 1942; d. Aron and Caterina Johanna (Pothast) B.; m. Richard P. Calabro, Apr. 15, 1967 (div. Sept. 1981); 1 child, Rachel Calabro; m. Darrell Y. Matsumoto. BA, Bennington Coll., 1964; MA, Hunter Coll., 1968. Lectr. coll. continuing edn. U. R.I., Providence, 1969-81, 86-87, 89; lectr. C. C. of R.I., Warwick, 1979-82; acting co-dir. Bannister Gallery R.I. Coll., Providence, 1991, lectr., 1987—; freelance graphic designer, Wakefield, R.I., 1982—; trustee Photographic Insight Found., 1989-92; artist mem. Hera Gallery, Wakefield, 1974—, exec. dir., 1994-96. Exhibited in numerous painting and photography shows, including 17 one-woman and 60 group shows, 1965—, including Hera Gallery, Wakefield, R.I., 1992, 94, 96, Sarah Doyle Gallery, Providence, 1989. Chairwoman salute to R.I. women in arts and comm. Coalition R.I. Women's Year and State Adv. Commn. on Women, 1975; workshop presenter UN Fourth World Conf. on Women, Beijing, 1995. Mem. Women's Caucus for Art.

BROCK, AMY LONA, special education educator; b. Grand Rapids, Mich., Apr. 11, 1970; d. Charles Lewis and Debra Lynn (Alvarez) B.; d. Lona Sue (Schulz) B. BA, Western Mich. U., 1993; postgrad., Grand Valley State U., 1996—. Educator emotionally impaired Hawaii Dept. Edn., Honokaa, 1993-95, Grand Rapids (Mich.) Pub. Schs., 1995—. Mem. AAUW, NOW, Coun. Exceptional Children (spl. needs advocacy 1990-93), Kappa Delta Pi. Democrat.

BROCK, DEE SALA, television executive, educator, writer, consultant; b. Covington, Okla., June 7, 1930; d. Lester Edward and Vera Mae (Bowers) Sala; m. Robert Wesley Brock, June 8, 1952 (div. 1979); children: Baron Sala, Bishop Chapman, Bevin Bowers. BA, U. North Tex., 1950, MA, 1956, PhD, 1985. Tchr. high sch. Dallas Ind. Sch. Dist., 1952-66; mem. faculty, adminstr. Dallas County Community Coll. Dist., 1966-74, telecourse writer, producer, adminstr., 1974-75, dir. mktg. info., 1975-80; dir., v.p. PBS, Washington, 1980-89; sr. v.p. edn. PBS, Alexandria, Va., 1989-90; pres. Dee Brock & Assocs., Plano, Tex., 1991—; bd. dirs. Pub. Svc. Satellite Consortium, U.S. Basics; mem. adv. bd. Learning Link, 1987-90, Telcon Industry, 1990-91; chair exec. coun. U. of the World, 1989-91; mem. adv. coun. Triangle Coalition, 1989-91. Author: Writing for a Reason: Study Guide, 1974 (with Jeriel Howard) Writing for a Reason, 1978, (with Laura Derr) The World of F. Scott Fitzgerald, 1980; mem. editorial bd. Am. Jour. Distance Edn., 1987-90; producer (internat. teleconf.) Out of the Red, 1991; producer, writer (TV series and workbook) Communicating in English in the Healthcare Workplace, 1994; speaker in field; contbr. articles in field; co-patentee video indexing system. Trustee Coun. for Adult and Experiential Learning, 1989—; bd. dirs. Coalition for the Advancement of Citizenship, 1988-90, active Met. Police Chief's Boys and Girls Club, Washington, PTA, Dallas. Reynolds Econ. fellow U. N.C., 1966; Literacy award N. Tex. Reading Coun., 1980, Nat. Person of Yr. award Nat. Coun. on Community and Continuing Edn., 1985, Award for Excellence in TV Programming NEA, 1986; recipient Outstanding Career Achievement award ITC Am. Assn. Community and Jr. Colls., 1990. Mem. NEH (nat. bd. cons. 1980-85), U.S. Distance Learning Assn. (bd. dirs. 1989-91, mem. adv. bd. 1989), So. Assn. Colls. and Schs. (mem. Project 1990 task force 1984-86), Nat. Assn. Ednl. Broadcasters (steering com. 1979-81), Assn. Ednl. Communications Technology, Nat. Coun. Tchrs. English (pres. S.W. regional coun. 1972-74). Methodist. Home and Office: 3533 Piedmont Dr Plano TX 75075-6254

BROCK, HELEN RACHEL MCCOY, mental health and community health nurse; b. Cromwell, Okla., Dec. 10, 1924; d. Samuel Robert Lee and Ire Etta (Pounds) McCoy; m. Clois Lee Brock, Sept. 29, 1963; children: Dwayne, Joyce, Peggy, Ricki, Stacey. AS, Southwestern Union Coll., Keene, Tex., 1968; BS in Nursing, Union Coll., Lincoln, Nebr., 1970; postgrad., Vernon Regional Jr. Coll., Tex., 1972, 76; MPH, Loma Linda (Calif.) U., 1983. Cert. ARC nurse. Dir. nursing Chillicothe (Tex.) Clinic-Hosp., 1970-77, Pike County Hosp., Waverly, Ohio, 1977-79, Marion County Hosp., Jefferson, Tex., 1979-81; nurse III, nursing unit supr, patient health educator Vernon State Hosp., Maximum Security for Criminally Insane, 1981—; nurse, admissions and assessments Texhoma Community Health Svcs., 1987-94. Mem. Am. Nurses Assn., Tex. Nurses Assn. Home: PO Box 238 Chillicothe TX 79225-0238

BROCK, KERRY LYNN, broadcast executive; b. Ft. Lewis, Wash., Feb. 4, 1957; d. Frank Harvey and Carol Jean (Carpenter) B.; m. John Michael Seigenthaler, Jan. 4, 1992. BA in Speech, Communications, Washington State U., Pullman, 1979. Anchor, reporter KNDU TV, Kennewick, Wash., 1979-80, KIVI TV, Boise, Ind., 1980-81, WOWT TV, Omaha, 1981-83, KOMO TV, Seattle, 1983-93; broadcasting, programming dir. Freedom Forum First Amendment Ctr. Vanderbilt U., Nashville, 1993—. Exec. prodr., host (TV program) Freedom Speaks. Bd. dirs. Wash. State Leukemia Soc., Seattle, 1986-93, Sinking Creek Film Festival, Nashville, 1993—; trustee Wash. State U., Pullman, 1990—; adv. bd. dirs. Seattle Jr. League, 1992-93. Mem. NATAS (bd. dirs.), Soc. Profl. Journalists, Radio and TV News Dirs. Assn., Nat. Press Club. Office: The Freedom Forum First Amendment Ctr 1207 18th Ave S Nashville TN 37212-2807

BROCK, REBECCA JEAN, computer programmer analyst; b. Lawton, Okla., Nov. 30, 1954; d. Henry C. Hanks and Barbara Jean (Wilmoth) Barnett; m. Edward Allen Brock, June 21, 1974 (div. July 1994); children: Melody Lynn, Lindsay Allen. BS in Comoputer Sci., Ctrl. State U., Edmond, Okla., 1989. Help desk rep. Hertz Corp., Oklahoma City, 1989-91, assoc. computer programmer, 1992, computer programmer, 1992-94, computer programmer analyst, 1994—. Solo guitar and vocal concert; writer songs. Grantee Choctaw Nation Okla., 1987; schilar Data Processing Mgmt. Assn., 1988. Mem. Beta Sigma Phi. Democrat. Baptist. Home: 315 N Elm St Rt 1 Crescent OK 73028 Office: Hertz Corp 5601 Northwest Expy Oklahoma City OK 74100

BROCKA, M. SUZANNE, controller; b. Moline, Ill., May 25, 1960; d. Paul Edmund and Therese Clemence (Fleischman) St. Ledger; m. Bruce Brocka, Mar. 17, 1984; children: Melinda Athena, Bennett Paul. BA in Acctg., St. Ambrose U., Davenport, Iowa, 1981; postgrad., Teikyo-Marycrest U., Davenport, Iowa, 1984-86. CPA, Ill. Acct. Iowa-Ill. Gas and Elec. Co., Davenport, 1981-86; acctg. supr. Frank E. Basil/Gen. Dynamics, Rock Island, Ill., 1986-87, mgr. fin., 1988-90, mgr. fin./contracts, 1990-91; controller City of Davenport, 1991—; cons. Frank E. Basil Inc., Washington, 1990-91, Rocky Mountain Metals Inc., Raton, N.Mex., 1994—, Exec. Scis. Inst., Davenport, Iowa, 1987—. Author: Quality Management, 1992. Bd. dirs. Scott County Historic Preservation Soc., Davenport, 1985-88. Mem. Am. Mgmt. Assn., Fin. Mgmt. Assn., Am. Econ. Assn., Govt. Fin. Officers Assn., Alpha Chi. Home: 1005 Mississippi Ave Davenport IA 52803-3938 Office: City of Davenport 226 W 4th St Davenport IA 52801-1308

BROCKET, JUDITH ANN, elementary education mathematics educator; b. Muscatine, Iowa, Feb. 3, 1942; d. Kenneth McKay and Dorothy Pearl (Stewart) Uebe; m. Raymond Gene Brocket, July 28, 1963; 1 son, Jamie. AA, Muscatine Jr. Coll., 1962; BA, Parsons Coll., 1965; grad., Children's Inst. of Lit., 1987. Cert. tchr., Iowa. Swim instr. for handicapped ARC, Burlington, IA, 1965; 3d grade tchr. Burlington Community Sch. Dist., 1965-68, 5th grade tchr., 1970-80, chpt. I math. tchr., 1980—; 4th grade tchr. West Burlington (Iowa) Community Sch. Dist., 1968-70; presenter in field; mem. North Cen. Accreditation Com., 1984-87; mem. Lit. Mag. Com., 1988—. Contbr. articles to profl. publs.; author math. workbooks, curriculum guide. Pres. Burlington PTA, 1981-82, treas., 1988-89; mem., spokesperson Burlington Sch. Dist. Adv. Com., 1980—; mem. Burlington Parent Adv. Com., 1980—; nom. coun. Messiah Lutheran Ch. Recipient cert. of merit U.S. Dept. Edn., 1987; Fed. Govt. grantee, 1983, 84. Mem. NEA, Iowa State Edn. Assn., Burlington Edn. Assn., Burlington Art Guild. Democrat. Lutheran. Home: 13084 115th St Burlington IA 52601-8705

BROCKMAN, RUTH LATHEM, county official; b. Greenville, S.C., Oct. 7, 1965; d. James Lathem and Annie Catherine (Hester) B. BA in Bus., Furman U., 1987; MBA, Clemson U., 1993. Acctg. specialist County of Greenville, Greenville, 1987-91, adminstrv. coord., 1991-94, sr. mgmt. analyst, 1994—; adj. instr. Greenville Tech. Coll., 1992-93. Vol. March of Dimes, Greenville, 1991-95, Habitat for Humanity, Greenville, 1995; orgnl. coord. United Way, Greenville, 1994; area coord. Am. Cancer Soc., Greenville, 1995. Mem. Internat. City and County Mgmt. Assn., Govtl. Fin. Officers Assn., Phi Eta Sigma. Baptist. Office: County of Greenville Ste 100 301 University Ridge Greenville SC 29601

BROCKMEYER, ANN HARTMANN, financial planner; b. Detroit, Mar. 5, 1941; d. Robert Allan and Eunice Elizabeth (Seitz) Wilson; m. James Cline Hartmann, July 18, 1970 (dec.); m. Richard W. Brockmeyer, Oct. 1, 1994. BA, Montclair State Coll., 1962; MBA in Fin., Rutgers U., 1975. CLU; chartered fin. cons. Tchr. Bloomfield (N.J.) Bd. Edn., 1962-63; adminstr. Girl Scouts USA, Pa., Mich., 1963-72, YWCA of Am., N.J., Ohio, 1972-77; dir. fin. and field personnel Sycor, Inc., Ann Arbor, Mich., 1977-79; sr. cons. Health Systems Group, Ann Arbor, 1979-80; fin. planner Hartmann & Assocs., Toledo, 1980—; adj. faculty U. Toledo, 1983-87, Lourdes Coll., Sylvania, Ohio, 1987—; faculty Cigna Nat. Edn. Events, 1984—; speaker in field. Editor: (newletter) Money Talks, 1982—. Pres. Maumee Valley Girl Scout Coun., Toledo, 1990-96; 1st v.p. Girls Clubs of Am., N.Y.C., 1985-87; nat. aquatic sch. staff instr., trainer ARC, Mich., Pa., 1974-80. Named Hines award Honoree Nat. Bd. Child Welfare, 1986. Mem. Am. Arbitration Assn. (comml. panel), Am. Soc. CLU/ChFC (pres. Toledo chpt. 1988-90, nat. bd. dirs. 1993-96), Toledo Assn. Life Underwriters (v.p. 1991-94, pres. elect 1994, pres. 1995), Toledo Estate Planning Coun. (bd. dirs. 1992—), Zonta Club Toledo (bd. dirs. 1987-88). Republican. Methodist. Office: Hartmann & Assocs 6635 W Central Ave Toledo OH 43617-1029

BROCKWAY, LAURIE SUE, editor, journalist, author; b. N.Y.C., Dec. 18, 1956; d. Lee L. and Shirley Ruth Brockway; 1 child, Alexander Kent Garrett. AA, Laguardia Community Coll., 1978; student, Hunter Coll. CUNY, 1978-81. Features editor, crime reporter The Bklyn. Paper, 1978-81; editor-in-chief The Iniator, N.Y.C., 1982-83; pub., editor The Transformer, N.Y.C., 1983-84; co-producer, writer The Brockway Good News Report, N.Y.C., 1984-85; N.Y. bur. chief Women's News, N.Y.C., 1983-85, mng. editor, 1990, Manhattan corr., 1985—; account supr., Brockway Assocs., Inc., N.Y.C., 1985-88; free lance editor, writer, 1988—; editor/owner, syndicated writer Star Reporter News Svc. 1989-94; editor in chief Playgirl Mag., N.Y.C., 1994-95, editor at large, 1996—; tchr. erotica writing and sexuality. Co-producer, writer, host, news anchor/writer, moderator This Is the New Age, The One Show, Whole Life Expo., The Learning Annex Interview Series, N.Y.C., 1995—; author: Seductions, 1991, Women at Work, 1993, The Doctor is In, 1994, A Dangerous Day, 1995; co-author: Network Your Way to Endless Romance, 1997, The Couples Guide to Great Sex Over 40, 1997; med. correspondent Life in Medicine mag., 1992-94; editor: Playgirl's Favorite 50 Fantasies, 1996; contbr. articles to mags., newspapers. Recipient LaGuardia Meml. award, 1978, Laguardia Student Coun. scholar, 1978, Expository Writing award, LaGuardia English Dept., 1978.

BRODBECK, LEOLA CLARA, county official; b. Fredricksburg, Tex., Aug. 31, 1940; d. Anton and Augusta (Klein) Schmidtzinsky; m. Alfons F. Brodbeck, Oct. 27, 1963; children: Lloyd, Dale. Grad. h.s., Fredericksburg. Registered tax assessor, Bd. Tax Profl. Examiners. Sec. Orange County Title Co., Santa Ana, Calif., 1963-64; dep., tax assessor-collector Gillespie County, Fredericksburg, 1960-63, 65-84, tax assessor-collector, 1985—. Treas. Gillespie County Rep. Women, 1996. Mem. Tex. Assn. Assessing Officers, Tax Assessor-Collector Assn., Inst. Cert. Tax Adminstrs., Fredericksburg C. of C. Roman Catholic.

BRODBECK, MARY LOU, artist, furniture designer; b. Hastings, Mich., Nov. 25, 1958; d. Willard Nathan and Margaret Grace (Balduf) B.; m. John Joseph Schmitt, May 20, 1995; 1 child from previous marriage, Jack. BFA, Mich. State U., 1982. Assoc. indsl. designer Haworth, Holland, Mich., 1985-90; freelance designer, Kalamazoo, 1990—; cons. indsl. designer Steelcase, Inc., Grand Rapids, Mich., 1993-94. One-woman shows include Water Street Gallery, Saugatuck, Mich., 1992-93, UpJohn Corp., Kalamazoo, 1992, Deborah's Choice Gallery, Muskgeon, Mich., 1992; patentee for furniture designs. Vol. leader Campfire Girls, Douglas, Mich., 1988-89; mem. Douglas (Mich.) Planning Commn., 1995—. Recipient purchase award Holland Arts Coun., 1990, Krasl Art Ctr., St. Joseph, Mich., 1991, cash award Holland Friend of Arts, 1990. Home: 471 W South St Apt 507 Kalamazoo MI 49007

BRODER, GAIL STEINMETZ, lawyer; b. Bklyn., Oct. 18, 1944; d. Eric and Judith (Daskal) Steinmetz; m. Samuel Broder, Dec. 26, 1966; children: Karen R., Joanna S. BA, CUNY, 1966; MA, U. Mich., 1971; JD with honors, George Washington U., 1979. Bar: Md., 1980. Pvt. practice Rockville, Md., 1980-84; staff atty. Vet. Adminstrn., Washington, 1984-89; sr. atty. U.S. Dept. HHS, Washington, 1989-95; pres., exec. dir. Cancer Survivorship Alliance of South Fla., Ft. Lauderdale, 1995—. Bd. dirs. Nat. Coalition for Cancer Survivorship, Silver Spring, Md., 1995—; bd. dirs. Broward Homebound Program, Pompano Beach, Fla., 1996—; vol. Am. Cancer Soc., South Fla., 1995—; editl. bd. NCI Worldwide Web Editl. Bd., Bethesda, Md., 1996—; actor comm. theatre, Brighton Beach Memoirs, 1987, Medea, 1988. Office: Cancer Survivorship Alliance of South Fla 759 Heron Rd Fort Lauderdale FL 33326

BRODER, PATRICIA JANIS, art historian, writer; b. N.Y.C., Nov. 22, 1935; d. Milton W. and Rheba (Mantell) Janis; m. Stanley H. Broder, Jan. 22, 1959; children: Clifford James, Peter Howard, Helen Anna. Student, Smith Coll., 1953-54; B.A., Barnard Coll., Columbia U., 1957; postgrad., Rutgers U., 1962-64; DHL (hon.), St. Lawrence U., 1993. Stock brokerage trainee A.M. Kidder & Co., N.Y.C., 1958; registered rep. Thomson & McKinnon, N.Y.C., 1959-61; ind. registered investment advisor, 1962-64; art cons.; art investment advisor. Writer on art history; books include Bronzes of the American West (Best Art Book award Nat. Acad. Western Art, 1975), Great Paintings of the Old American West, American Indian Painting and Sculpture, Taos: A Painter's Dream (Western Heritage Wrangler award for best art book Nat. Cowboy Hall of Fame and Western Heritage Ctr., 1980, Art Book award Border Regional Libr. Assn., 1981), Hopi Painting: The World of the Hopis, Dean Cornwell: Dean of Illustrators, The American West: The Modern Vision (New award 1984, Trustees award Cowboy Hall of Fame 1984), Shadows on Glass: The Indian World of Ben Wittick, 1990. Recipient Herbert Adams Meml. medal for svc. to Am. sculpture Nat. Sculpture Soc., 1975, Western Heritage Wranglers award for best article on Am. west Nat. Cowboy Hall of Fame and Western Heritage Ctr., 1975, Trustees Gold medal for outstanding contbn. to the west Nat. Acad. Western Art, 1984. Mem. Western History Assn., AAUW. Home: 488 Long Hill Dr Short Hills NJ 07078-1227

BRODER, SHARI BRYANT, arbitrator, mediator; b. New Hyde Park, N.Y., June 10, 1955; d. Harold S. and Lorraine Natalie (Sidewitz) B.; m. Eric Joseph Bryant, Mar. 19, 1988; 1 child, Eliza Anna Bryant. BA, U. Md., 1977; JD, U. Maine, 1986. Bar: Maine 1986. Legis. aide Rep. Olympia Snowe, Washington, 1979-83; law clk. Pierce, Atwood, Portland, Maine, 1985-86, Justice Sidney W. Wernick, Portland, Maine, 1986-87, Maine Superior Ct., Portland, Maine, 1986-87; assoc. lawyer Brann & Isaacson, Lewiston, Maine, 1987-91; arbitrator, mediator, hearing officer pvt. practice, Freeport, Maine, 1991—; hearing officer Maine Dept. Labor, Freeport, 1993—. Bd. dirs., pres. Maine Arts, Inc., Portland, 1991-96; clk., bd. dirs. The Children's Rainforest, Lewiston, 1988—. Recipient Disting. Graduate award U. Maine, 1986. Mem. Soc. Profls. in Dispute Resolution, Am. Arbitration Assn. (arbitrator), Nat. Inst. Dispute Resolution, Maine State Bar Assn. (chair alternative dispute resolution com. 1996—), Maine Assn. Dispute Resolution Profls. (sec. 1992—). Office: PO Box 158 Freeport ME 04032

BRODIAN, LAURA, broadcasting and illustration studio executive, professional illustrator; b. Newark, Oct. 16, 1947; d. Sol and Jean Dolores (Posner) B.; m. Frank Kelly Freas, June 30, 1988. BA, Kean Coll., 1972; M in Music Edn., Ind. U., 1974, D in Mus. Edn., 1982. Lic. radio and TV operator. Tchr. various schs., N.J., 1967-72; assoc. instr. Ind. U., Bloomington, 1973-74; edn. dir. Ind. Arts Commn., Indpls., 1975-76; announcer, engr. Sta. WFIU-FM, Bloomington, 1979-80; announcer, producer Sta. KQED-FM, San Francisco, 1982-87; exec. producer, announcer Sta. KUSC-FM, L.A., 1987-88; exec. dir. fin., mktg., pub. rels. Kelly Freas Studios, 1988—. Host (syndicated classical music show) Music Through the Night, 1988, classical music in-flight program Delta Airlines, 1989—, illustrator, 1990—; announcer KKGO-FM, L.A., 1995—, KKHI-FM, San Francisco, 1995—. Toastmaster, Bay Con '94 SciFi conv., San Jose, Calif., 1994; artist guest of honor LepreCon 21, Sci Fiction conv., 1995, ConFurence, Irvine, Calif., 1996, MidSouth conv., Memphis, Tenn., 1996. Recipient Chesley award for best sci. fiction mag. cover Assn. Sci. Fiction and Fantasy Artists, 1990. Mem. Nat. Assn. broadcast Employees and Technicians, Assn. Sci. Fiction and Fantacy Artists (former we. regional dir.), Bay Area English Regency Soc. (founder), Southern Calif. Early Music Soc. (past pres.), Customer's Guild West (dir. at large).

BRODIE, NANCY S., insurance company executive; b. Cleve., 1951. Grad., Cleve. State U., 1975. Pres., also bd. dirs. Independence Square Properties; CFO Penn Ins. and Annuity Co.; sr. v.p., CFO Penn Mut. Life Ins. Co., Phila. Office: Penn Mutual Life Ins Co 530 Walnut St Philadelphia PA 19172*

BRODKIN, ADELE RUTH MEYER, psychologist; b. N.Y.C., July 8, 1934; d. Abraham J. and Helen (Honig) Meyer; m. Roger Harrison Brodkin, Jan. 26, 1957; children: Elizabeth Anne, Edward Stuart. BA, Sarah Lawrence Coll., 1956; MA, Columbia U., 1959; PhD, Rutgers U., 1977. Lic. psychologist, N.J. Sch. psychologist pub. schs., River Edge, Norwood, 1961-66, Morristown, Chatham, N.J., 1967-73; cons. psychologist United Hosp. Newark, 1973; assoc. dir. Infant Child Devel. Ctr. St. Barnabas Med. Ctr., Livingston, N.J., 1977-79; clin. asst. prof. dept. psychiatry U. Medicine and Dentistry N.J., Newark, 1979-90, clin. assoc. prof., 1990—; vis. scholar Hasting (N.Y.) Ctr. for Life Scis., 1979; mem. Essex County Mental Health Adv. Bd., Essex County, N.J., 1985-87; cons. Scholastic, Inc., 1988—; clin. assoc. prof. psychiatry UMDNJ-N.J. Med. Sch., 1990—. Author: Between Teacher and Parent, Supporting Young Children As They Grow, 1994, (with A.T. Jersild and E. Alina Lazar) The Meaning of Psychotherapy in the Teacher's Life and Work, 1962; author, prodr. (video documentary) Competing Commitments, 1984 (Best Ednl. Videotape award N.J. Cable); co-author, prodr. ednl. videotapes: Passage to Physicianhood, 1985, The Insidious Epidemic, 1986; columnist Between Tchr. and Parent, Pre-K Today mag., 1988-93, child devel. columnist, 1991-92; columnist You and Today's Child, Instr. mag., 1992-93, Kids in Crisis, Instr. mag., 1993-96; columnist Adolescent Devel., Mid. Yrs. mag., 1990-95; contbr. articles to profl. jours. Grantee Gannett Found., Cmty. Fund for N.J., Carter-Wallace, Inc., Schering Corp.; Adelaide M. Ayer fellow Columbia U., 1962-63, NIMH fellow, 1962, Louis Bevier fellow Rutgers U., 1976-77. Fellow Am. Orthopsychiat. Assn.; mem. APA, N.J. Psychol. Assn. (Psychol. Recognition award 1982, 86, 90), Am. Sociol. Assn. Home and Office: 2 Trevino Ct Florham Park NJ 07932-2724

BRODSKY, BEVERLY, artist. BA in Art, Bklyn. Coll., 1965; postgrad., Sch. Visual Arts, N.Y., 1969-70, The New Sch., 1969-70, The Bklyn. Mus., 1969-70. tchr. Parsons Sch. Design, 1979—, Adelphi U., 1980-85, Vt. Grad. Sch., Vt. CollO, others; lectr. in field. Author, illustrator: The Crystal Apple, 1974, Sedna, An Eskimo Myth, 1975, The Golem, 1976 (Caldencott honor medal 1977, notable book award 1977), Jonah, 1977, secret Places, 1979, The Purim Players, 1984, The Story of Job, 1986; illustrator Forest of the Night, 1975), Gooseberries to Oranges, 1982 (notable book award 1983); one woman shows include B.E.L. Gallery, Westport, Conn., 1979, Washington (Conn.) Art Assn., 1979, SUNY Plattsburgh, 1980, The Wilson Arts Ctr., Rochester, N.Y., 1982, The Open Gallery Parsons Sch. Design, N.Y.C., 1986, The Kimberly Gallery, N.Y.C., 1990, The Elizabeth Stone Gallery, Birmingham, Mich., 1991; group shows include 92nd St. YMCA, N.Y.C., 1982, The N.Y. Pub. Libr., N.Y.C., 1982, Ruth S. Harley U. Ctr. Gallery Adelphi U., 1983, Yeshiva U. Mus., N.Y.C., 1983, City Gallery, N.Y.C., 1984, The Houghton Gallery Cooper Union, N.Y.C., 1985, The Internat. Gallery, San Diego, 1987, The Triangle Artists' Workship, Pine Plains, N.Y., 1988, The Jewish Mus., N.Y.C., 1988, Parsons Sch. Design, N.Y.C., 1989, LÖrhl Gallery, MÖnchengladbach, Germany, 1990, M-13 Gallery, N.Y.C., 1992, Blondies' Contemporary Art, High, N.Y.C., 1992, Janice Scharry Epstein Mus., West Bloomfield, Mich., 1992, Art Ctr. Battle Creek, Mich., 1992, The Painting Ctr., Soho, N.Y.C., 1994, 1996 (juried show), ALJIRA Found., Newark, 1994, Elsa Mott Ives Gallery, N.Y.C., 1994; reviewed in Print Mag., Art Direction Mag., The N.Y. Art Review, 1988, N.Y. Times, The Villlage Voice, Publisher's Weekly, The Booklist, Juni Magazin Fur Kultur and Politik, 1991. Home: 55 Bethune St New York NY 10014

BRODY, ANITA BLUMSTEIN, judge; b. N.Y.C., May 25, 1935; d. David Theodore and Rita (Sondheim) Blumstein; m. Jerome I. Brody, Oct. 25, 1959; children—Lisa, Marion, Timothy. AB, Wellesley Coll., 1955; JD, Columbia U., 1958. Bar: N.Y. 1959, Fla. 1960, Pa. 1972. With Office Atty. Gen., State N.Y., 1958-59; dep. asst. atty. gen. State N.Y., 1959; sole practice, Ardmore, Pa., 1972-79; ptnr. Brody, Brown & Hepburn, Ardmore, 1979-81; judge Pa. Ct. Common Pleas 38th Jud. Dist., Norristown, 1981-92; judge U.S. Dist. Ct. (ea. dist.) Pa., Phila., 1992—; lectr. in law U. Pa., Phila., 1978-79. Mem. ABA, Am. Judicature Soc., Nat. Assn. Women Judges, Pa. Bar Assn., Montgomery Bar Assn. (bd. dirs. 1979-81), Temple Am. Inn of Ct. (pres. 1994-95). Republican. Jewish. Office: 3825 US Courthouse Philadelphia PA 19106

BRODY, JACQUELINE, editor; b. Utica, N.Y., Jan. 23, 1932; d. Jack and Mary (Childress) Galloway; m. Eugene D. Brody, Apr. 5, 1959; children: Jessica, Leslie. A.B., Vassar Coll., 1953; postgrad., London Sch. Econs., 1953-56. Assoc. editor Crowell Collier Macmillan, N.Y.C., 1963-67; writer Coun. Fgn. Rels., N.Y.C., 1968-69; mng. editor Print Collector's Newsletter, N.Y.C., 1971-72, editor, 1972-96, art writer, 1996—. Office: 119 E 79th St New York NY 10021-0339

BRODY, JANE ELLEN, journalist; b. Bklyn., May 19, 1941; d. Sidney and Lillian (Kellner) B.; m. Richard Engquist, Oct. 2, 1966; children: Lee Erik and Lorin Michael Engquist (twins). B.S., N.Y. State Coll. Agr., Cornell U., 1962; M.S. in Journalism, U. Wis., 1963; HHD (hon.), Princeton U., 1987; LHD (hon.), Hamline U., 1993. Reporter Mpls. Tribune, 1963-65; sci. writer, personal health columnist N.Y. Times, N.Y.C., 1965—; mem. adv. council N.Y. State Coll. Agr., Cornell U., 1971-77. Author: (with Richard Engquist) Secrets of Good Health, 1970, (with Arthur Holleb) You Can Fight Cancer and Win, 1977, Jane Brody's Nutrition Book, 1981, Jane Brody's The New York Times Guide to Personal Health, 1982, Jane Brody's Good Food Book, 1985, Jane Brody's Good Food Gourmet, 1990, (with Richard Flaste) Jane Brody's Good Seafood Book, 1994, Jane Brody's Cold and Flu Fighter, 1995. Recipient numerous writing awards, including; Howard Blakeslee award Am. Heart Assn., 1971; Sci. Writers' award ADA, 1978; J.C. Penney-U. Mo. Journalism award, 1978; Lifeline award Am. Health Found., 1978. Jewish. Office: NY Times 229 W 43rd St New York NY 10036-3913

BROENING, ELISE HEDWIG, writer; b. Bronx, N.Y., Feb. 10, 1941; d. Herman Berhardt and Lillian Marie (Kraft) B. BS in English, NYU, 1962, MA in Ednl. Psychology, 1969; postgrad., NYU Reading Inst., 1968-69, SUNY, Binghamton, 1986-87, Cornell U., Ithaca Coll., P.R., Cin. U. Tchr. English Jr. High Sch. # 104, N.Y.C., 1961-62, Union Endicott (N.Y.) Cen., 1962-63; tchr. English and Reading Johnson City (N.Y.) Schs., 1963-87; freelance writer San Diego, 1987—. Contbr. articles to profl. jours. Mem. Met. Opera Guild, San Diego Opera Guild, Tri-Cities Opera Guild, NYU Alumni Assn., Kappa Delta Pi. Home and Office: 606 3rd Ave Apt 201 San Diego CA 92101-6838

BROERING, NAOMI CORDERO, librarian; b. N.Y.C., Nov. 24, 1939; d. Julius and Emily (Perez) Cordero; B.A., Calif. State U., 1961, M.A. in history, 1963; postgrad. UCLA, 1964, M.L.S. in Library Sci., 1966, postgrad. (NIH fellow), 1967; postgrad. Sch. of Law, U. West Los Angeles, 1970; m. Arthur J. Broering, 1971 (dec. 1992). Acquisitions and reference librarian U. So. Calif., 1967-68; chief librarian Children's Hosp., Los Angeles, 1968-71; asst. librarian Walter Reed Gen. Hosp., Washington, 1972; chief reader services, grant officer VA, Washington, 1972-75; assoc. libr. Med. Ctr., Georgetown U., Washington, 1975-78, libr., 1978—; Med. Ctr. libr. Dahlgren Meml. Library, dir. Biomed. Info. Resources Ctr., 1983—, P.I. Georgetown, Integrated Acad. Info. Mgmt. System, 1986—; mem. adj. faculty Cath. U. Editor: Bull. Med. Libr. Assn. Fellow Am. Coll. Med. Informatics, Med. Libr. Assn. (dir. 1979-82); mem. ALA, Am. Med. Informatics Assn., Am. Soc. Info. Sci., AAAS, Assn. Acad. Health Sci. Library Dirs., Spl. Library Assn., Acad. Health Info. Profls. (disting. mem.). Author, editor: High Performance Medical Libraries, 1993; contbr. articles to profl. jours. Office: Georgetown U Med Ctr Libr 3900 Reservoir Rd NW Washington DC 20007-2187

BROERS, KIMBERLY ANN, editor, writer; b. Dayton, Ohio, Sept. 20, 1956; d. Deryl Dean and Valerie Carol (Devine) B. Cert., Univ. Bordeaux, France, 1977; BA in Writing and French summa cum laude, William Jewell Coll., 1978. Editor, proofer Johnson City Community Coll., Overland Park, Kans., 1978-79; sr. staff writer Women in Bus. mag., Kansas City, Mo., 1979-81; freelance writer, editor Kansas City, 1981-95; editor nat. mag. VFW Aux., Kansas City, 1984-96; copywriter Tappan Design, Shawnee Mission, Kans., 1989-96. Author, editor: Celebrate 75 Years, 1989; contbr. numerous articles to mags. Judge nat. publs. VFW, 1987-93. Mem. Women in Comm. Inc. (newsletter editor 1987-88, roster editor 1988-92), Nat. Soc. for Protection of Animals (newsletter editor 1989-96). Home: 2549 Charlotte St Kansas City MO 64108-2735 Office: VFW Aux 406 W 34th St Kansas City MO 64111-2721

BROGAN-WERNTZ, BONNIE BAILEY, police officer, municipal agency administrator; b. Pine Grove Mills, Pa., Mar. 28, 1941; d. Gilbert Chester and Rosalie Evelyn (Reed) Bailey; m. Donald M. Brogan, Aug. 12, 1960 (div. Oct. 1971); children: Donna Lynn Gregory, Rodney Marshall Brogan; m. Robert R. Werntz, Aug. 28, 1982 (dec. June 7, 1992). A in Criminal Justice, Ind. U., 1976, BS, 1981. Cert. instr. law enforcement tng., Ind. Stenographer South Bend (Ind.) Police Dept., 1970-73, police officer, 1973—, cpl. accident investigation, 1975-80, detective sgt., investigator sex crimes, 1980-85, lt., 1985—, field tng. officer adminstr., shift comdr., 1985-88, dir. tng., 1988-92, investigative supr., 1992-96, juvenile supr. sex crimes, chld abuse supr., 1996—; bd. dirs. Women's Com. on Sex Offenses, South Bend; vol., trainer rape crisis Sex Offense Svcs., South Bend, 1980-87; recorder, treas. Child Sexual Abuse Consortium, South Bend, 1982-85; mem. Giarretto Task Force/Family and Children Ctr., Mishawaka, Inc., 1985. Iniator ordinance St. Joseph County Funds for Examinations and Victims of Sex Crimes, 1983. Bd. dirs. Parents Anonymous, South Bend, 1982, Women's Shelter for Battered Women, South Bend, 1985, South Bend Credit Union Supervisory Commn., 1983; mem. Children and Adolescent Adv. Council, South Bend, 1984. Recipient Joseph J. Newman award Protective Bd./Council for Retarded St. Joseph County, 1982, Child Abuse Investigator award The Breakfast Exchange Club, 1982, award for Exceptional Quality in Investigative Child Abuse/Neglect, Child Protective Services of St. Joseph County Dept. Pub. Welfare, 1983, Outstanding Service award Women's Com. on Sex Offenses, 1983, Outstanding Officer of Yr. award, St. Joseph County Council of Clubs, 1985, Police Officer of Yr. award, Ind. Council Fraternal Vets. and Social Scis., 1985, Outstanding Achievement award YWCA Tribute to Women, 1986. Mem. Internat. Assn. of Women Police (Hon. Mention Officer of Yr. 1985), Fraternal Order of Police. Democrat. Home: 1709 Altgeld St South Bend IN 46614-1601 Office: South Bend Police Dept 701 W Sample St South Bend IN 46601-2821

BROGLIATTI, BARBARA SPENCER, television and motion picture executive; b. L.A., Jan. 8, 1946; d. Robert and Lottie (Goldstein) Spencer; m. Raymond Haley Brogliatti, Sept. 19, 1970. BA in Social Scis. and English, UCLA, 1968. Asst. press. info. dept. CBS TV, L.A., 1968-69, sr. publicist, 1969-74; dir. publicity Tandem Prodns. and T.A.T. Comm. (Embassy Comm.), L.A., 1974-77, corp. v.p., 1977-82, sr. v.p. worldwide publicity, promotion and advt. Embassy Comm., L.A., 1982-85; sr. v.p. worldwide corp. comm. Lorimar Telepictures Corp., Culver City, Calif., 1985-89; pres., chmn. Brogliatti Co., Burbank, Calif., 1989-90; sr. v.p. worldwide TV publicity, promotion and advt. Lorimar TV, 1991-92; sr. v.p. worldwide TV publicity, promotion and pub. rels. Warner Bros. Inc., Burbank, 1992—. Mem. bd. govs. TV Acad., L.A., 1984-86; bd. dirs. KIDSNET, Washington, 1987—, Nat. Acad. Cable Programming, 1992-94; vice chmn. awards com. TV Acad.; mem. Hollywood Women's Polit. Com., 1992-93. Recipient Gold medallion Broadcast Promotion and Mktg. Execs., 1984. Mem. Am. Diabetes Assn. (bd. dirs. L.A. chpt. 1992-93), Am. Cinema Found. (mem. bd. dirs. 1994—), Dirs. Guild Am., Publicists Guild, Acad. TV Arts and Scis. (vice chmn. awards com.). Office: Warner Bros Studios 4000 Warner Blvd Ste 1057 Burbank CA 91552

BROISMAN, EMMA RAY, economist, retired international official; b. Boston, July 11, 1922. BA in Sociology, U. Maine, 1944; MA in Econs., Columbia U., 1946. Rsch. asst., libr. Internat.Labor Orgn. Liason Office with UN, N.Y.C., 1947-57; program fellowship officer Internat. Labor Orgn. Asian Field Office, Bangalore, India, 1957-63; program officer Internat. Labor Orgn., Geneva, Switzerland, 1964-68; program officer Internat. Labor Orgn. Reg. Office for Asia and the Pacific, Bangkok, 1969, sr., pers. fin. and adminstrn. officer, 1970-72; chief rels. and info. sect. Internat. Labour Office, Bangkok, 1973-75; dep. dir. Internat. Labour Office, New Delhi, 1975-78; coord. women and youth programs Internat. Labour Orgn., Bangkok, 1978-83; UN rep. Internat. Coun. Women, 1985—; assoc. Ctr. for Study of Women and Soc., Grad. Ctr., CUNY, 1989—; internat. devel. cons., 1983—. Contbr. articles to profl. jours. Mem. LWV (dir. 1986-90), Nat. Coun. Women (sec., bd. dirs. 1991-94), Pan Pacific South-East Asia Women's Assn. (bd. dirs.), Am. Com. on Fgn. Policy, Acad. Coun. on UN Sys. Home: 301 E 48th St Apt 16B New York NY 10017-1736

BROKKE, CATHERINE JULIET, mission executive; b. Mpls., Dec. 25, 1926; d. Emil John and Alma (Brye) Eliason; m. Harold Joseph Brokke, Sept. 9, 1949; 1 child, Daniel. Diploma in nursing, Luth. Deaconess Hosp., Mpls., 1947; student, Concordia Coll., Moorhead, Minn., 1948-49, Bethany Coll. Missions, Mpls., 1949-51. RN, Minn. Sch. and occupational nurse Bethany Fellowship, Mpls., 1951-75; missions sec. Bethany Fellowship Missions, Mpls., 1963-86, dir., 1986—; bd. dirs. Bethany Corp., Ltd, STEM Ministries; instr. Bethany Coll. Missions, 1950-88. Mng. editor Message of Cross, 1990—; composer hymns. Organist Bethany Missionary Ch., Bloomington, Minn., 1956-89. Mem. Evang. Fellowship of Mission Agys. (trustee 1987-93), Evang. Missions Info. Svc. (bd. dirs. 1994—). Office: Bethany Fellowship Missions 6820 Auto Club Rd Bloomington MN 55438-2413

BRONKAR, EUNICE DUNALEE, artist, art educator; b. New Lebanon, Ohio, Aug. 8, 1934; d. William Dunham and Helen Kate (Hypes) Connor; m. Charles William Bronkar, Jan. 26, 1957; 1 child, Ramona. BFA, Wright State U., 1971, M in Art Edn., 1983, postgrad. art studies, 1989; postgrad. art studies, Dayton Art Inst., 1972. Cert. art tchr., Ohio. Part time tchr. Springfield (Ohio) Mus. of Art, 1967-77; adjunct instr. Clark State C.C., Springfield, 1974-84, lead tchr., 1984-94, asst. prof., 1989-94; ret., 1994; artist private practice, Urbana, Ohio, 1995—; edn. chmn. Springfield Mus. Art, 1973-74; image banks participant, Ohio Arts Coun., Columbus, Visual Arts Network, Dayton, Ohio, 1994; affiliated with Crescent BeachArt Gallery, St. Augustine, Fla. and Little Gallery, Springfield, Ohio. Artist: One woman shows include in Springfield, Ohio: Polo Club, Upper Valley Mall Cinema, Security Nat. Bank, Mr. C's Beauty Salon, Lakewood Beach, Springfield Mus. of Art, Clark State C.C.; Dayton, Ohio: Miami Valley Hosp., High St. Gallery, Stoeffer's Restaurant, Wegerzyn Garden Ctr., Meml. Hall, Wright State Univ., Urbana, Ohio: Champaign County Arts Coun., Urbana Cinema; South Charleston, Ohio: Cmty. Park Dedication, Philip Caldwell spl. guest speaker, Chmn. of the Bd. and CEO Ford Motor Co; accepted in over 86 area, state, regional, and nat. juried exhibitions including: Ohio Water Color Soc.'s Annual Traveling shows 1983-84, 86-87, Western Ohio Watercolor Soc., Hon. Mention 1983, Chase Patterson award, 1985, Spl. Merit award, 1990, 1st, 1996; Springfield Mus. of Art: awards 1965, 68; 2d pastel 1972, 2d pastel and 1st drawing 1976, Jurors award pastel 1979, 1st drawing 1986, 3d drawing 1987, 2d drawing 1989, 1st drawing 1990, 1st drawing and 2d painting 1991, 1st drawing 1992; Dayton Soc. Painters and Sculptors: Best of Show 1974, 1st painting, 2d painting 3d drawing 1978, Hon. Mention 1979, 3d Graphic 1980, Best of Show drawing and 1st pastel 1981, 1st drawing 1991, 3d painting 1993; Champaign County Fair: Best of show drawing and 1st pastel 1968; represented in six public and numerous private collections. Cleaned and restored art collections at Warder Pub. Libr., and the Masonic Temple, Penn House and Mus. of Art in Springfield, Ohio, 1970-90; mem. adv. com. comml. art, Clark County JVS Sch., Springfield, 1991-95; judge more than 10 pub. h.s.art shows, 1970's -90's. Recipient medal Bicentennial Com. and 4H Found. of Ohio, Springfield, 1976. Mem. Western Ohio Water Color Soc, Springfield (Ohio) Mus. of Art, Dayton Soc. Painters and Sculptors, Cin. Art Club, Ohio Water Color Soc., Nat. Mus. Women in Arts, Audubon Artists Soc., Pastel Soc. and others. Studio and Home: 5516 S US Hwy 68 Urbana OH 43078-9420

BRONNER, KATHERINE ELIZABETH, high school counselor; b. Waverly, Iowa, Dec. 20, 1943; d. Wesley Neil and Mary Catherine (Berge) Hagerty. BS, Mankato (Minn.) State U., 1966, MS, 1971; postgrad., St. Thomas U., St. Paul, U. Minn., 1971—. Phys. edn. and health instr. Zumbrota (Minn.) H.S., 1966-67; phys. edn. instr. St. Paul Park (Minn.) Jr. High and Oltman Jr. High, 1967-70; resident advisor Gage Ctr. Mankato State U., 1970-71; counselor Rosemont (Minn.) H.S., 1971-76, Apple Valley (Minn.) H.S., 1976—; counselor, instr. Women Sense of Identity program U. Minn., 1978-70. Contbr. to Teen Pregnance and Parenting Resource Handbook. Bd. dirs. Minn. Coalition of Orgns. for Sex Equality in Edn., St. Paul, 1980—; participant 2d Ann. Conf. for Drug Free Schs., Apple Valley, 1984; active Alanon, Mpls., 1980—. Mem. NEA, Minn. Edn. Assn. (bldg. rep.), Minn. Assn. Counseling and Devel. (govtl. chair), Minn. Sch. Counselor's Assn. (exec. bd. 1975-83, lt. chair 1975-80, govtl. rels. rep. 1975-80, treas. Dakota divsn. 1981-82, pres. 1982-83, facilities chair spring conf. 1992), Minn. Coalition of Sex Equality in Edn. (exec. bd. 1980-83, treas. 1982-83), Lake Area Counselors Assn. (facilities chair). Democrat. Methodist. Office: Apple Valley HS 14450 Hayes Rd Apple Valley MN 55124

BRONNERT-WALSH, LOIS M., speech-language pathologist; b. Terre Haute, Ind., Aug. 18, 1942; d. Lee E. and Marie W. (Strubbe) B.; m. Joseph E. Walsh, June 17, 1989. BS, Ind. State U., 1964, MS, 1966. Cert. clin. competence speech pathology; lic. speech pathologist, Mo. Speech and hearing therapist Lake County Schs., Crown Pt., Ind., 1964-65, Hammond (Ind.) pub. schs., 1966-68; instr., supr.depts. speech pathology, audiology, edn. Ea. Ill. U., Charleston, Ill., 1968-72; speech-lang. pathologist spl. sch. dist.St. Louis County (Mo.), 1972—. Contbr. articles to profl. jours. Fellow Nat. Speological Soc. (recording sec. exec. planning com. 1997 conv.); mem. Am. Speech Lang. Hearing Assn., Mo. Speech Lang. Hearing Assn. (chairperson awards com. 1975-76, contbr. poster session 1976), Coun. Exceptional Children, Mo. Speological Survey, Sierra Club. Home: 660 Green Hedge Dr Fenton MO 63026 Office: Spl Sch Dist 12110 Clayton Rd Saint Louis MO 63131

BRONSKI, BETTY JEAN, health care consultant; b. Chgo., Mar. 21, 1952; d. Joseph Jacob and Helen Margaret (Hruby) B. BS, Marquette U., Milw., 1974, MS, 1975; MS, Cardinal Stritch Coll., Milw., 1987. Speech pathologist Sch. Dist. BrownDeer, 1974-79; project analyst Eaton Corp., Milw., 1979-82; mktg. rsch. dir. SSM- Mgmt. Services, Milw., 1982-86; adminstr. asst. SSM-Ministry Corp., Milw., 1986-87; dir. planning & devel. St. Mary's Hill Hosp., Milw., 1987-89; pres. Carefinders, Inc., 1989—. Vol. Greater Milw. Area Spl. Olympics, 1979-82, Alzheimer's Assn. S.E. Wis., 1992-93; bd. dirs. St. Clare Mgmt., 1992-95. Roman Catholic. Home: 5150 N Berkeley Blvd Milwaukee WI 53217-5503 Office: Carefinders Inc PO Box 17900 # 146 Milwaukee WI 53217-0900

BRONSTER, MARGERY S, attorney general; b. N.Y., Dec. 12, 1957; married; 1 child. BA in Chinese Lang., Lit. and History, Brown U., 1979; JD, Columbia U., 1982. Assoc. Sherman & Sterling, N.Y., 1982-87; ptnr. Carlsmith, Ball, Wichman, Murray, Case & Ichiki, Honolulu, 1988-94; atty. gen. State of Hawaii, 1994—; bd. dirs. Hawaii Lawyers Care, past pres., 1992; co-chair planning com. Citizens Conf. Judicial Selection, 1993. Bd. dirs. Ballet Hawaii. Office: Office of the Attorney General 425 Queen Street Honolulu HI 96813*

BRONTSEMA, JENNIFER ANNE, graphic designer; b. Berkeley, Calif., Feb. 24, 1970; d. Donald Theodore and Joan (Richardson) B. BA in Philosophy, U. Calif., Santa Cruz, 1993. Coord. spl. projects Monterey (Calif.) County Legal Svcs., 1990-93; graphic designer Conari Press, Berkeley, Calif., 1993—. Contbg. author: More Random Acts of Kindness, 1994, Slowing Down in a Speeded Up World, 1994. Office: Conari Press 2550 9th St Ste 101 Berkeley CA 94710

BRONWELL, NANCY BROOKER, writer; b. Columbia, S.C., Oct. 11, 1921; d. Norton Wardlaw and Lucile Duty (Michaux) Brooker; m. Alvin Wayne Bronwell, June 21, 1943 (div. Mar. 1975); children: Betsy Randolph Bronwell Jones, Cynthia Alison. BS, Mary Washington Coll., 1942; postgrad., U. Ky., 1942-43, Tex. Tech. U., 1965, 87. Tchr. English, phys. edn. Louisville Pub. Schs., 1943-46; sec. edn. dept. Jos. S. Seagram & Sons Inc., Louisville, 1945-46; sec. to sales mgr. Marshall Field Corp., Chgo., 1946; sec. to dir. purchases Jos. E. Seagram & Sons., Inc., 1946-48; freelance writer Lubbock, Tex., 1978—. Author: Lubbock: A Pictorial History, 1980. Cofounder, bd. dirs. Young Women's Christian Assn., Lubbock, 1953; vol. Lubbock Jr. League, Lubbock Symphony Orch., Palsy Ctr., ARC, Tech. Mus., St. Paul's Ch. Mem. South Plains Writers Guild, Lubbock Heritage Assn. (Excellence award 1981), DAR, Friends of Libr. (life). Republican. Episcopalian. Home and Office: 4108 18th St # A Lubbock TX 79416-6009

BROOK, JUDITH SUZANNE, psychiatry and psychology researcher and educator; b. N.Y.C., Dec. 31, 1939; d. Robert and Helen E. (Zimmerman) Muser; m. David W. Brook, Dec. 15, 1962; children: Adam, Jonathan. BA, Hunter Coll., 1961; MA in Psychology, Columbia U., 1962, EdD in Devel. and Ednl. Psychology, 1967. Lic psychologist, N.Y. Asst. prof. psychology Queens Coll., CUNY, Flushing, 1967-69; rsch. assoc. Columbia U., N.Y.C., 1969-77, sr. rsch. assoc., 1977-80; assoc. prof. psychiatry Mt. Sinai Sch. Medicine, N.Y.C., 1980-90, adj. prof., 1990-94; prof. N.Y. Med. Coll., Valhalla, N.Y., 1990-94; prof. cmty. medicine Mt. Sinai Sch. Medicine, 1994—; rsch. scientist devel. Nat. Inst. on Drug Abuse, 1982-90, sr. rsch. scientist, 1992—, ad hoc reviewer, 1989—, chair study sect. epidemiology, prevention & rsch; ad hoc reviewer NIMH, NSF. Author: The Psychology of Adolescence, 1978, others; contbr. over 100 articles to profl. jours. Recipient 1st ann. Dean's Disting. Rsch. award N.Y. Med. Coll., 1992; grantee Nat. Inst. on Drug Abuse, 1979—. Fellow Am. Psychopathol. Assn.; mem. APA, Am. Psychol. Soc. (liaison officer 1989—), Assn. for Med. Edn. and Rsch. in Substance Abuse, N.Y. State Psychol. Assn. Office: Mt Sinai Sch Medicine Dept Cmty Medicine Box 1044 One Gustave Levy Pl New York NY 10029

BROOKE, JENNIFER, advertising executive. Exec. v.p. Earle Palmer Brown, Bethesda, Md. Office: Earle Palmer Brown 6935 Arlington St Bethesda MD 20814*

BROOKER, LENA EPPS, human services administrator; b. Lumberton, N.C., Oct. 13, 1941; d. Frank Howard and Grace Evelyn (Smith) Epps; m. James Dennis Brooker, July 30, 1966; children: Lora, Lindsey. AB, Meredith Coll., Raleigh, N.C., 1962. Cert. elem. sch. tchr., N.C. Elem. sch. tchr., Charlotte, Robeson County, N.C., Winchester, Va., Chevy Chase, Md., Raleigh, 1962-75; coord. human svcs. program N.C. Commn. Indian Affairs, Raleigh, 1975-78; planner, adminstr. human svcs. program N.C. Dept. Natural Resources and Community Devel., Raleigh, 1978-86; diversity mgt. dir. The Women's Ctr., Raleigh, 1990—; developer model program U.S. Dept. Labor, Raleigh, 1976; presenter Pres.'s Commn. on Status of Women, Raleigh, 1979; facilitator Internat. Yr. of Woman, Winston-Salem, N.C., 1977; speaker on status of Am. Indians to univs., schs., chs. and orgns., 1975—. Contbg. writer The Carolina Call. Chaplain, entertainment chmn. Dem. Women Wake County, Raleigh, 1989-91; mem. Task Force on Native Am. Ministry N.C. Conf. United Meth. Ch., chmn. ethnic minority local ch. concerns com., 1988-91, mem. bd. evangelism, 1986-91, audit com. coun. fin. and adminstrn., 1990-91, coun. ministries, 1992-94, mem. bishops task force on staff and structure, 1993-95; mem. Wake County Mammography Task Force, 1990-93; mem. cultural diversity com. Wake County Arts Coun., 1990; bd. dirs. Internat. Festival Raleigh, 1990-91, Triangle OIC, 1991-93, N.C. Civil Liberties Union, 1992-94, United Arts Coun. Wake County, 1996, sec. 1996; mem. steering com. for Yr. of native Am., N.C. Mus. Natural History, 1986; mem. city of Raleigh Human Resources & Human Rels. Commn., 1990-93; pres. bd. dirs. Women's Fund of N.C., 1993—; bd. advisors Heritage Arts Found., 1993, N.Am. Health Edn. Fund, 1994—, Women's Leadership Inst., Bennett Coll., 1995—. Grantee N.C. Arts Coun., Duke-Semans Fine Arts Found., 1986; recipient Personal Advocacy for Women in N.C. Carpathian award N.C. Equity, 1993. Mem. N.C. Natural Scis. Soc. (bd. dirs. 1987-90), Triangle Native Am. Soc. (past coord. spl. projects), Meredith Coll. Alumne Assn. (bd. dirs. 1994-95). Home: 2110

Fairview Rd Raleigh NC 27608-2235 Office: The Women's Ctr 128 E Hargett St Raleigh NC 27601-1460

BROOKER, SUSAN GAY, employment consulting firm executive; b. Washington, Sept. 4, 1949; d. Robert Morris and Mildred Ruby (Parler) B. BA, St. Mary's Coll., St. Mary's City, Md., 1971. News editor WPGC Radio, Lanham, Md., 1971; mgr. trainee Household Fin. Corp., Silver Spring, Md., 1972; career counselor Place-All, Bethesda, Md., 1972-73; exec. v.p. New Places, Inc./ Get-A-Job, Washington, 1973-89; employment cons., owner, pres. SGB Consultants, Reston, Va., 1989—; mem. Emploibank, Washington, 1978-79/. Outreach vestry chair Grace Episcopal Ch., 1992-94; conservation chairperson Silver Spring Woman's Club, 1993-94. Recipient Cert. Appreciation U.S. Fish and Wildlife Assn., 1985, Cert. of Recognition Chaplaincy Assocs., Howard Gen. Hosp, Letter of Appreciation Pres. Bill Clinton, 1996. Mem. Pell-Capital Pers. Svc. Asssn. (cert.), St. Mary's Coll. (Md.) Alumni Assn. (bd. dirs. 1987-91). Democrat. Home and Office: 2209 Coppersmith Sq Reston VA 20191-2305

BROOKES, RUTH HARDING, guidance counselor; b. prospect, ME, Mar. 14, 1915; d. Gerry Barker and Jennie Gertrude (Clifford) Harding; m. Kenneth Brookes, Dec. 27, 1938 (dec.); children: Gay, Gerry H., Kenneth C., Katherine H. BA, U. Maine, 1935; MEd, Boston U., 1936. Cert. Guidance Counselor, Maine. Tchr. Bristol (Conn.) H.S., 1936-38; guidance counselor C Westboro (Mass.) H.S., 1955-60, Buker Jr. H.S., Augusta, Maine, 1961-64, Cony H.S., Augusta, 1965-75. Co-chmn. Direct Svc. to Patients, Damariscotta, Maine, 1976-95; chmn. Adult Edn. Adv. Coun., U. Maine Sch. Dist. #74, 1980-95; vol. Miles Meml. Hosp., 1976-96. Democratic. Home: HC 61 Box 290 New Harbor ME 04554

BROOKINS, DOLORES, educational consulting organization executive; b. Memphis, Mar. 10, 1948; d. Adolphus Sr. and Katherine (Pierson) B. BA in Elem. Edn., Lane Coll., 1970; MS in Guidance and Counseling, Tenn. State U., 1973; PhD in Ednl. Adminstrn., Ohio State U., 1982. Cert. tchr., prin. grades Kindergarten through 9, Tenn; cert. counselor grades kindergarten through 12, D.C.; cert. HUD cons. Elem. tchr. Memphis City Schs., 1970-73; ednl. cons. Memphis Area Schs. and Tenn. State U., 1970-92; head resident counselor Tenn. State U., Nashville, 1973, test supr./counselor III, 1974-76; asst. dean students, dir. counseling ctr. Lane Coll., Jackson, Tenn., 1976-78; rsch. assoc., dir. evening fin. aid, night bldg. mgr. Ohio State U., Columbus, 1978-82; asst. dean students, dir. minority affairs U. Ark., Fayetteville, 1982-85; assoc. dir. instrnl. svcs., assoc. rschr. Ill. Cmty. Coll. Bd., Springfield, 1985-87; legis. aide/rschr. to chmn. appropriation II com. Ill. Gen. Assembly, Springfield, 1987-88; asst. to dir. budget, mgmt. acct. II City of Springfield, 1988, exec. dir. human rels. commn., fair housing bd., 1988-91; ednl. cons. B&A, Memphis, 1970-80, sr. ednl. cons., 1981-91; CEO, sr. ednl. cons. B&A, Washington, 1992-94; adj. prof. Sch. Social Work, U. Ill., 1988-91; assoc. grad faculty Coll. Grad. Studies, Ctrl. Mich. U. Author: (manual) Administrative Burnout: A Latent Dysfunction of Roles, Goals Disjunction and Organizational Routinization, 1982, Smile: A Peer Counseling Manual, 1985. Alt. del. from Memphis, Dem. Nat. Conv., 1966; Dem. election judge, pollwatcher, Washington, 1994. Named one of Outstanding Young Women of Am., 1983; named Outstanding Female Exec., NAFE, Washington. Mem. ASTD, Nat. Assn. Human Rights Workers (mem. com. 1989-91), Rotary, Phi Delta Kappa. Baptist. Home and office: 5294 Louise Dr Memphis TN 38109

BROOKS, ANDRÉE AELION, journalist, educator, author; b. London, Feb. 2, 1937; d. Leon Luis and Lillian (Abrahamson) Aelion; m. Ronald J. Brooks, Aug. 16, 1959 (div. Aug. 1986); children: Allyson, James. Journalism cert., N.W. London Poly., 1958. Reporter Hampstead News, London, 1954-58; story editor Photoplay mag., N.Y.C., 1958-60; N.Y. corr. Australian Broadcasting Co., N.Y.C., 1961-68; elected rep. Elstree, Eng., 1973-74; columnist N.Y. Times, N.Y.C., 1978-95; free-lance journalist, 1978—; adj. prof. journalism Fairfield U., Conn., 1983-87; assoc. fellow Yale U., 1989—; founder, pres. Women's Campaign Sch. Yale U., 1993—; v.p. Minuteman Media, 1995—. Author: Children of Fast Track Parents, 1989 (Best Non-fiction Book award 1990). Mem. exec. bd. Am. Jewish Com., 1987-91; trustee Temple Israel, Westport, Conn., 1991—. Recipient numerous awards including 1st place for news writing Conn. Press Women, 1980, 83, 85, 86, Outstanding Achievement award Nat. Fedn. Press Women, 1981, 1st place award Fairfield County chpt. Women in Comms., 1982, 83, 86, 87, 92, 2d place award in mag. writing Nat. Assn. Home Bldrs., 1983, Spl. Svc. award Conn. chpt. Am. Planning Assn., 1983, 1st place award for mag. writing Nat. Fedn. Press Women, 1983; named one of Am. Women of Achievement Am. Jewish Com., 1989. Mem. Conn. Press Women (chmn. nominating com. 1983-86), Women in Communications (contest co-chmn. 1983-84). Home: 15 Hitchcock Rd Westport CT 06880-2630

BROOKS, ANITA HELEN, public relations executive; b. N.Y.C.; d. Arthur and Bertha (Stewart) Sayle; m. Arnold Brooks, July 1, 1954 (div.). BA, Hunter Coll., 1950; MA, Columbia U., 1952, MLS, 1954. Tchr. Latin Hunter Coll. High Sch., N.Y.C., 1955; publicity rep. WOR Radio, N.Y.C., 1955; writer King Features Syndicate, N.Y.C., 1955-59; pub. relations writer NBC-TV, N.Y.C., 1956; dir. pub. relations N.Y. State Mental Health Fund Campaign, 1956, WMCA Radio, N.Y.C., 1957; account exec. various pub. rels. agys., N.Y.C., 1957-65; pres. Anita Helen Brooks assocs., Pub. Relations, N.Y.C., 1965—; lit. agt. Anita Brooks Lit. Agt., N.Y.C., 1956—. Writer radio-TV shows. Vice chmn. Sinatra for Meml. Sloan-Kettering Cancdr Hosp. Benefit; mem. patroness com. Harkness Ballet Found.; mem. benefit com. Mannes Coll. Music, N.Y.C.; mem. legis. adv. com. of Senator Roy M. Goodman, N.Y. State Senate. Decorated Dame Comdr. Knights of Malta; named hon. citizen Venezuela. Mem. Am. Women in Radio and TV, Pub. Rels. Soc. Am., Internat. Radio and TV Soc., Publs. Publicity Assn., Assn. Motion Picture Advertisers, Mystery Writers Am., Columbia U. Alumni Assn., Sisters in Crime Soc., Smithsonian Assocs., N.Y. Press Club, Eta Sigma Phi, Latin/Greek Honor Soc. Office: 155 E 55th St New York NY 10022-4038

BROOKS, DEBORAH ELMA, author, consultant; b. Queens, N.Y., Nov. 20, 1947; d. Elmer and Frances Earline (Thompson) B.; m. Jerry L. Lawrence, Jan. 8, 1977; 1 child, Samantha Brooke Lawrence. BA, Northland Coll., 1971; postgrad., New Sch. Social Rsch., 1971-72. Program investigator Human Resources, N.Y.C., 1970-71; rsch. assoc. Econ. Opportunity Commn., Nassau County, N.Y., 1972-73; mem. in-port staff World Campus Afloat, 1973; adj. instr. Antioch Coll.-Tchr.'s Inc., N.Y.C., 1973-74; asst. dir. Rock Valley Comm. Corrections, Beloit, Wis., 1974-76; lectr. N.Y.C. Bd. Edn., 1994-95; pres., founder JDI, N.Y.C., 1995—; cons. UN Assn U.S.A., N.Y.C., 1993-95; mem. exec. bd. Inwood (N.Y.) Buccaneers, 1991-92, advisor, 1988-92. Author: UNS-USA's Recommended List of Teaching Materials-UN's 50th, 1994; author, artist: This Tyme & Drip, 1977. Vol. Trinity Ch. Homeless Shelter, 1992-93, recreation dept. Penninsula Nursing Home, Far Rockaway, N.Y., 1992—. Recipient Hoberman award Rockville Ctr. Art Guild, 1984, Pastels/Drawings Merit award, 1984, Recognition award Internat. Platform Assn., 1978-79, numerous others.

BROOKS, DIANA D., auction house executive; b. Glen Cove, N.Y., 1950; m. Michael C. Brooks; 2 children. Student Miss Porter's Sch., Farmington, Conn., 1965-68, Smith Coll., 1968-69; AB in Am. Studies, Yale U., 1972. Lending officer nat. banking group Citibank, N.A., N.Y.C., 1973-79; with Sotheby's North & South Am., N.Y.C., 1979—, sr. v.p., chief fin. & adminstrv. officer, 1982-84, exec. v.p., 1984-85, chief oper. officer, 1985-87, pres., 1987-90, pres. & chief exec. officer, 1990—, also bd. dirs.; bd. dirs. Sotheby's Holdings, Inc., pres., CEO, 1994. Trustee Yale U., Allen-Stevenson Sch., Deerfield Acad. Office: Sotheby's Inc 1334 York Ave New York NY 10021-4806

BROOKS, GLADYS SINCLAIR, public affairs consultant; b. Mpls.; d. John Franklin and Gladys (Phillips) Sinclair; m. Wright W. Brooks, Apr. 17, 1941; children: Diane Brooks Montgomery, John, Pamela (Mrs. Jean Marc Perraud). Student U. Geneva, Switzerland, 1935; BA, U. Minn., 1936; LLD, Hamline U., 1966. Dir. Farmer's and Mechanics Bank, 1973-82; mem. Met. Council, 1975-83; lectr. world affairs, 1939—; mem. Mpls. City Council, 1967-73; mem. Met. Airports Commn., 1971-74; pres. World Affairs Ctr. U. Minn., 1976-83; instr. continuing edn. for women U. Minn.; lectr. on world tour as Am. specialist U.S. Dept. State, 1959-60; pres. Brooks/Ridder & Assocs., 1983-94. Mem. Mpls. Charter Commn., 1948-51; pres. YWCA, Mpls., 1953-57, 62-65, mem. nat. bd., 1959-71, del. world meeting, Denmark; pres. Minn. Internat. Ctr., 1953-63; chmn. Minn. Women's Com. for Civil Rights, 1961-64; mem. U.S. Com. for UNICEF, 1959-68; mem. Gov.'s Adv. Com. Children and Youth, 1953-58, Minn. Adv. Com. Employment and Security, 1948-50; Midwest adv. com. Inst. Internat. Edn.; mem. nat. com. White House Conf. Children and Youth, 1960; chmn. Gov.'s Human Rights Commn., 1961-65; dir. Citizens Com. Delinquency and Crime, 1969-93; chmn. Mpls. Adv. Com. on Tourism, 1976-82, Ctr. Women in Govt., 1987-92; chmn. adv. com. Office World Trade, 1988-92; vice chmn. Nat. Community Partnerships Seminars, 1977-82; mem. Midwest Selection Panel, White House Fellows, 1981. Del. Rep. Nat. Conv., 1952; state chmn. Citizens for Eisenhower, 1956; founder, pres. Rep. Workshop; co-chmn. Mpls. Bicentennial Commn., 1974-76; pres. Internat. Center for Fgn. Students; dir. Minn. Alumni Assn.; trustee United Theol. Sem., YWCA, Met. State U.; bd. dirs. Hamline U., Midwest China Ctr., Walker Health Services; mem. pres.'s adv. council St. Catherine's Coll.; trustee Hamline U., Met. State U. Recipient Centennial Women of Minn. award Hamline U., 1954, Woman of Distinction award AAUW, Mpls. 1956, Outstanding Achievement award U. Minn., 1962, Woman of Yr. award YWCA, 1973, Brotherhood award NCCJ, 1975, State Bar award for community leadership, 1976, Service to Freedom award Minn. State Bar Assn., 1976, Community Leadership award YWCA, 1981, Svc. Beyond Self award Rotary, 1990. Mem. World Affairs Council (pres. 1942-44), Minn. LWV (dir. 1940-45), Mpls. Council Ch. Women (pres. 1946-48), Nat. Council of Chs. (mem. gen. bd., v.p. 1961-69), Minn. Council of Chs. (1st woman pres. 1961-64, Christian service award 1967), Mpls. Council of Chs. (v.p. 1946-48), United Ch. Women (bd. mgrs.), Minn. UN Assn. (dir.), Nat. League Cities (human resources steering com. 1972-73), Am. Acad. Polit. Sci., Mpls. C. of C., Minn. Women's Polit. Caucus, Minn. Women's Econ. Roundtable, AAUW, Women's Symphony Assn., Delta Kappa Gamma (hon.). Presbyn. Clubs: Horizon 100, Women's. Home: 5056 Garfield Ave Minneapolis MN 55419-1253

BROOKS, GLENDA, elementary education educator; b. Mass., Dec. 24, 1950; d. William Lee and Dorothy (Wilder) B. BS in Elem. Edn., U. Mass., 1973, MA in Teaching with honors, 1983. Cert. elem. art tchr., Mass., N.Y. Intern Grant Sch., Williamstown, Mass., 1972-73; tchr. art North Adams Mid. Sch., 1974-77; resident tutor A Better Chance Program, Amherst, Mass., 1977-78; apprentice carpenter United Brotherhood of Carpenters, Greenfield, Mass., 1979-80; youth counselor, mktg. rep. Berkshire Tng. and Employment, Pittsfield, Mass., 1985-86; tchr. trainer U.S. Peace Corps., 1986-88; tchr. art. and ESL Hoosac (N.Y.) Sch., 1989-92; substitute tchr., tchr. asst. Berkshire Farm Sch., Canaan, N.Y., 1992-94; tchr. Hillcrest Ednl. Ctr., Lenox, Mass., 1995—; lectr. in field. Pottery exhibited at Berkshire Artisans, Pittsfield, 1994. Organizer Jesse Jackson Campaign, Western Mass., 1984. Mem. N.Y. State and Local Retirement System, U. Mass. Alumnus Assn., North Adams State Coll. Alumnus Assn.

BROOKS, GWENDOLYN, writer, poet; b. Topeka, June 7, 1917; d. David Anderson and Keziah Corinne (Wims) B.; m. Henry L. Blakely, Sept. 17, 1939; children: Henry L., Nora. Grad., Wilson Jr. Coll., Chgo., 1936; L.H.D., Columbia Coll., 1964. Instr. poetry Columbia Coll., Chgo., Northeastern Ill. State Coll., Chgo.; mem. Ill. Arts Council; cons. in poetry Library of Congress, 1985-86; Jefferson lectr., 1994. Author: (poetry) A Street in Bronzeville, 1945, Annie Allen, 1949 (Pulitzer prize 1950), Maud Martha: (novel) Bronzeville Boys and Girls, 1953; (for children) The Bean Eaters, 1956; poetry, 1960, Selected Poems, 1963, In the Mecca, 1968, Riot, 1969, Family Pictures, 1970, Aloneness, 1971, To Disembark, 1981; (autobiography) Report From Part One, 1972, The Tiger Who Wore White Gloves, 1974, Beckonings, 1975, Primer for Blacks, 1980, Young Poets' Primer, 1981, Very Young Poets, 1983, The Near-Johannesburg Boy, 1986, Blacks, 1987, Gottschalk and the Grande Tarantelle, 1988, Winnie, 1988, Children Coming Home, 1991, Report From Part Two, 1995. Named one of 10 Women of Yr. Mademoiselle mag., 1945; recipient Creative Writing award Am. Acad. Arts and Letters, 1946, Aninsfield-Wolf award, 1969, Essence award, 1988, Frost medal Poetry Soc. Am., 1989, Lifetime Achievement award Nat. Endowment for the Arts, 1989, Soc. for Lit. award U. Thessaloniki, Athens, Greece, 1990, Aiken-Taylor award, 1992, Jefferson lectr. award NEH, 1994, Nat. Book Found. medal for lifetime achievement, 1994, Am. Book award Gwendolyn Brooks Jr. H.S., 1995, Nat. medal of arts, 1995; Guggenheim fellow, 1946, 47; named poet laureate of Ill., 1968; inducted into Nat. Women's Hall of Fame, 1988; Gwendolyn Brooks chair in Black Lit. and Creative Writing established in her honor Chgo. State U., 1990; The Gwendolyn Brooks Ctr. established, 1992; Gwendolyn Brooks Elem. Sch. named in her honor, Aurora, Ill., 1995. Mem. Soc. Midland Authors. Home: 5530 S South Shore Dr Apt 2A Chicago IL 60637-1921

BROOKS, HELENE MARGARET, editor-in-chief; b. Jersey City, Apr. 1, 1942; d. Sinclair Duncan and Helen Margaret (McDermott) B.; m. Joseph F. Olivieri, Dec. 10, 1987 (dec. July 1991). BA, C.W. Post Coll., 1977; MBA, Dowling Coll., 1992. Asst. editor McCall's mag., N.Y.C., 1969-72, assoc. editor, 1972-75, editor features and travel, 1975-83; managing editor 50 Plus mag. Whitney Commn., N.Y.C., 1983; exec. editor 50 Plus mag. Whitney Comm., N.Y.C., 1983-87; editor in chief Network mag./Internat. Airlines Travel Agt. Network, N.Y.C., 1987—; editorial cons. Am. Hairdressing Industry , N.Y.C. 1983. Mem. Am. Soc. Mag. Editors, Delta Mu Delta, Phi Eta. Democrat. Presbyterian. Home: 84 Trellis Ln Wantagh NY 11793-1939 Office: Internat Airlines Travel 300 Garden City Plz Ste 342 Garden City NY 11530-3331

BROOKS, LAURA LEE, psychotherapist, mental health consultant; b. Columbus, Ohio, Oct. 16, 1962; d. Herbert Erwin and Linda Lee (Lilly) Urell. BA in Psychology with honors cum laude, U. N.C., Wilmington, 1991; MSW cum laude, East Carolina U., 1993. Cert. clin. social worker, N.C. Family therapist Family Svcs., Wilmington, N.C., 1993-94; dir., psychotherapist New Beginnings, Wilmington, 1993-95; pvt. practice psychotherapist Wilmington, 1995—; cons. Assn. for Retarded Citizens, Wilmington; therapist Vols. of Am., Wilmington; presenter N.C. Psychol. Assn., 1991; presenter, author rsch. posters. Vol. Spl. Olympics, Columbus, Ohio and Wilmington, 1986—. Pitt County Mental Health Social Work Student scholar, 1993, Milton H. Erickson Found. scholar, 1992, James Lee Love scholar U. N.C., 1990, U. N.C. rsch. scholar, 1990. Mem. NASW, Phi Alpha, Psi Chi (v.p. 1993). Democrat. Episcopalian. Office: Options in Counseling 1402 S 17th St Wilmington NC 28401

BROOKS, LORRAINE ELIZABETH, chaplain, educator; b. Port Chester, N.Y., Mar. 10, 1936; d. William Henry Sr. and Marion Elizabeth (Harrell) B. BS in Music Edn., SUNY, Potsdam, 1958; M of Performance, Manhattan Sch. Music, 1970. Dir. Camp Spruce-Mountain Lakes, North Salem, N.Y., 1964-73; youth adviser St. Peter's Episcopal Ch., Port Chester, N.Y., 1964-65, St. Andrew's-St. Peter's Ch., Yonkers, N.Y., 1970-73; v.p. South Yonkers Youth Council, 1970-76; assoc. Sisters Charity of N.Y., Scarsdale, 1978—; eucharistic minister, lector Our Lady of Victory Ch., Mt. Vernon, N.Y., 1981-93, eucharistic ministry lector, youth dir., 1988—; Roman Cath. chaplain White Plains (N.Y.) Med. Ctr., 1981—; cons. Quincy Tenants Assn., Mt. Vernon, 1986—. Soloist Greenhave Correctional Facility retreat, N.Y., 1994; recital St. Mary's Ch. Outreach Program, 1994. Vestrywoman St. Andrew's Episc. Ch., Yonkers, 1971-75; contralto soloist St. Peter's Episc. Ch., Port Chester, 1959-69, Cape Cod Roman Cath. Charismatic Conf., 1993; mem. Collegiate Chorale, N.Y.C., 1958-68; svc. team mem. Charismatic Cmty., Scarsdale, 1975-91; v.p. Willwood Tenant Assn., Mt. Vernon, 1981-82, pres., 1982-84; vol. speaker N.Y. Regional Transplant Program, 1992—; active Montefiore Med. Ctr. TRIO, 1991—, presenter kidney transplant program, 1995; active Teen/Twenty Encounter Christ, 1990—; lector, eucharistic min. St. Mary's Roman Cath. Ch., 1993—, facilitator RENEW program, 1994—, CORE team mem., 1996, coord. prayer group Day of Reflection; asst. coord. RENEW, St. Mary's Ch., Mt. Vernon, N.Y., 1995—. Mem. Westchester County Sch. Music Assn. (exec. bd.), Scarsdale Tchrs. Assn. (exec. bd.), Music Educators Nat. Conf. Democrat. Roman Catholic. Office: Scarsdale Pub Schs Mamaroneck Rd Scarsdale NY 10583-5008

BROOKS, MARY ELLEN, English educator; b. Mamaroneck, N.Y., Sept. 13, 1947; d. Cornelius J. and Mary Ellen (Higgins) Mahoney; m. Christopher C. Brooks, Aug. 29, 1970; children: Daniel, Shannon, Kevin. BA, SUNY, 1969; MA, San Francisco State U., 1973; MS, Calif. Lutheran U., 1982. English educator Eastchester (N.Y.) H.S., 1969-70; lang. arts educator Ben Franklin H.S., San Francisco, 1970-78; spl. edn. tchr. Lompoc H.S., 1978-85, English educator, 1985—; lang. arts 6-12 mentor, 1996—. Grantee NEH, 1994. Mem. AAUW (v.p. programs), Nat. Coun. Tchrs. English. Democrat. Roman Catholic. Office: Lompoc HS 515 W College Ave Lompoc CA 93436

BROOKS, NORMA NEWTON, legal assistant, secondary school educator; b. Granite, Okla., Oct. 30, 1936; d. Ralph David and Bessie M. (Elkins) Newton; m. Rex Dwain Brooks, May 16, 1964; children: Jonathan Douglas, Elizabeth Ann. Student, U. Okla., 1979, BS in Edn., 1970; MEd, Ctrl. State U., 1972. Cert. secondary sch. tchr., Okla. Legal asst. Rex D. Brooks Atty.-At-Law, Oklahoma City, 1974—. Mem. Am. Home Econs. Assn., Women in the Arts, Kappa Delta Pi. Baptist. Home: 2323 N Indiana Ave Oklahoma City OK 73106 Office: Rex D Brooks Atty-At-Law 1900 NW 23 Oklahoma City OK 73106

BROOKS, PATRICIA LAVERSE, systems analyst, network administrator; b. East St. Louis, Ill., Apr. 1, 1963; d. Leverse and Patricia Ann Brooks. BSBA, St. Louis U., 1985, MBA, 1991. Cert. network adminstr. Asst. mgr. Osco Drug Inc., Evanston, Ill., 1986-87; help desk coord. Osco Drug Inc., Oakbrook, Ill., 1987-88; in-store sys. coord. Osco Drug Inc., Oakbrook, 1988; mgr. computer resources St. Louis U., 1988-94; systems analyst CDSI, St. Louis, 1994-95; mgr. computer resources Glennon Co., Inc., St. Louis, 1995—. Mem. Nat. Black MBA Assn., Delta Sigma Theta. Home: 732A Greenway Manor Dr Florissant MO 63031-8905 Office: The Glennon Co Inc One City Ctr Ste 1600 Saint Louis MO 63101

BROOKS, PATRICIA SCOTT, principal; b. St. Louis, July 19, 1949; d. John Edward and Doris Louise (Webb) Scott; m. John Robert Brooks, May 22, 1986; 1 child, Ollie. BS, W.Va. State Coll., 1971; MA, Marshall U., 1974; adminstrv. cert., Ind. U., 1990. Cert. tchr., Ind. Tchr. spl. edn. Huntington (W.Va.) State Hosp., 1971; tchr. elem. edn. Kanawha County Sch., Charleston, W.Va., 1971-78; tchr. elem. edn. Washington Twp., Indpls., 1979-82, tchr. mid. sch., 1982-90, adminstrv. intern, 1989-90, asst. coord., 1990, 92, asst. prin., 1990-93; prin. Pike Twp., Indpls., 1993—; participant Ind. U. Tchr. as a Decision Maker Program, Bloomington, 1989; mem. Human Rels. Com., Indpls., 1996; presenter U.S. Dept. Edn. Panelist State PTA Conv. Recipient Tchr. Spotlight award Topics Newspaper, 1983; named one of 100 Outstanding Black Women in State of Ind., Nat. Coun. Negro Women, 1990; Danforth fellow Ind. U., 1989. Mem. Ind. Assn. for Elem. and Mid. Sch. Prins., Phi Delta Kappa, Delta Sigma Theta. Methodist. Home: 2711 Pomona Ct Indianapolis IN 46268-1248

BROOKS, SHELLEY, middle school educator; b. Boston, Aug. 20, 1955; d. Bernard and Carol Florence (Klass) B. BEd, U. Miami, Coral Gables, Fla., 1977; cert. in reading, U. Fla., Gainesville, 1978; postgrad., U. Tex., Dallas, 1990, U. Nev., Las Vegas, 1993. Cert. early childhood edn., elem., K-12 reading tchr., Nev. Elem. curriculum libr. U. Miami, 1977-78; classroom tchr. Citrus County Sch. Dist., Homosassa, Fla., 1978-80; reading tchr. Dallas Ind. Sch. Dist., 1982-90, Clark County Sch. Dist., Las Vegas, 1990—. Tchr. rep. Clark County Sch. Dist., 1991-93, Dallas Ind. Sch. Dist., 1982-90. Mem. NAFE, Internat. Reading Assn. Jewish. Office: James Cashman Mid Sch 4622 W Desert Inn Rd Las Vegas NV 89102-7115

BROOKS, SHIRLEY WALKER, health facility administrator; b. Gaston County, N.C., Dec. 25, 1929; d. Guy and Edna (Peters) W.; children: Nancy, Mary, William, Cort, Jennifer. RN, Riverside Hosp. Sch. Nursing, Newport News, Va., 1950; Diploma, Fla. State U., 1973; postgrad., U. So. Fla. Cert. gerontol. nurse. Instr. Pinellas County Schs., St. Petersburg, Fla.; dir. of nursing Beverly Enterprises, St. Petersburg; regional nurse cons. Nat. Health Corp., Murphysboro, Tenn.; dir. of nursing Welcare Mgmt., St. Petersburg. Bd. dirs. St. Petersburg Jr. Coll. Home: 705 W Warren St Shelby NC 28150

BROOKS, SUZANNE RAYETTA, small business owner; b. Phila., Jan. 20, 1941; d. John Christian Lemon and Rayetta (Ortiga) Anderson. BA in English and Edn., La Salle U., 1975; MA in English and Creative Writing, Wash. State U., 1979. Lic. pvt. investigator, Calif., tax preparer, Calif. Police woman juvenile aid divsn. Phila. Police Dept., 1965-72; dir. sci. supportive svcs. Wash. State U., Pullman, 1979-82; dir. affirmative action U. Nev., Reno, 1982-84, Pa. State U., University Park, 1984-89; dir. Multi-Cultural Ctr., Calif. State U., Sacramento, 1990-95; owner, cons. Creative Concepts/Systems, Sacramento, 1990—. Author: (poetry) Ins & Outs, 1983 (published in India); contbr. short story to mag. Bd. dirs. Nat. Inst. Women of Color, Washington, 1981-92, Nev. Women's Fund, Reno, 1982-84, Washoe County Pers. Com., Reno, 1982-84, Bakari Homes for Boys, Sacramento, 1992—; assoc. Smithsonian Inst., Washington, 1985-89; mem. mayor's action network State Coll. Pa., 1986-89; mem. planning com. August Women's Peace Event, Sacramento, 1992. Recipient Racial Justice award YWCA, Sacramento, 1992; Danforth fellow, 1975, Andrew Kozak fellow Pa. State chpt. Phi Delta Kappa, 1987. Mem. AAUW, NAACP, NAFE, Mensa. Democrat. Roman Catholic.

BROOKS, VICKI S., health educator; b. Salida, Colo., Dec. 25, 1946; d. C.S. Smith and Betty Jo (Evans) Shields; m. Monty Craig Johnson, June 26, 1994; children: Sabina Holesinger, Joseph Johnson. PhD, U. Wyo., 1992. Cert. counselor. Health educator Lewis Palmer H.S., Monument, Colo., 1979-89, Northeastern State U., Tahlequah, Okla., 1992-94; counselor Cherry Creek H.S., Englewood, Colo., 1994—. Help in crisis bd. dirs. Safe House, Tahlequah, 1992-94. Mem. AAHPERD, ACA, Mental Health Counseling Assn. Home: 4163 S Memphis St Aurora CO 80013 Office: Cherry Creek High Sch 9300 E Union Ave Englewood CO 80111

BROOKS-KORN, LYNNE VIVIAN, artist; b. Detroit, July 6, 1951; d. Loren Edward and Edith Zona (Gaub) Brooks; m. Howard Allen Korn, Apr. 17, 1977. BFA magna cum laude, U. Mich., 1973, MFA, 1976. Teaching fellow U. Mich. Sch. Art, Ann Arbor, 1976; vis. lectr. various history of art depts., over 150 solo and group shows since 1992. Numerous one-woman shows, including Grants Pass (Oreg.) Mus. Art, 1993, Red River Valley Mus., Vernon, Tex., 1993, Red River Valley Mus., Vernon, Tex., 1993, Coll. Ea. Utah, 1994, Aberdeen (Scotland) Arts Ctr., 1995, Napa County Librs., 1996, MacLaurin Art Gallery, Ayr, Great Britain, 1996, Carlsbad (N.Mex.) Mus., 1994; group shows include Foster City (Calif.) Mus. Gallery, 1993, San Bernadino County Mus., Redlands, Calif., 1993, Ohio State U., 1994, Bryn Mawr (Pa.) Coll., 1995, Haggin Mus., Stockton, Calif., 1996; represented in permanent collections San Bernadino County Mus., Longwell Mus., Downey Mus. Art, Red River Valley Mus., Yosemite Mus., Brit. Mus., Bryn Mawr Coll., others; work reviewed in numerous publs.; various commns. Recipient numerous awards for art, including Internat. Art Competition, 1987, 88, 89, Nepenthe Munki Soc., Wichita, Kans., 1989, Haggin Mus., Stockton, Calif., 1990, Menlo Park Civic Ctr., 1991, San Bernardino County Mus., 1992, Sweetwater County Art Guild, 1993, East Tex. State U., 1993, Breckenridge Fine Arts Ctr., 1993, Lake Worth Art League, Inc., 1993, 94, Amador County Arts Coun., 1993, Coastal Ctr. for Arts, St. Simons Island, Ga., 1993, Soc. We. Artists Signature Mem., 1994, Ea. Washington WC Soc., 1994, San Jacinto Coll., Pasadena, Tex., 1995, Peninsula Art Assn., Burlingame, Calif., 1996; Rackham grantee U. Mich., 1975. Mem. Coll. Art Assn. Democrat. Home and Studio: 700 Loma Vista Ter Pacifica CA 94044-2425

BROOME, CLAIRE VERONICA, epidemiologist, researcher; b. Tunbridge Wells, Kent, England, Aug. 24, 1949; came to U.S., 1951; d. Kenneth R. and Heather C. (Platt) B.; m. John F. Head, Apr. 2, 1988; children: Gabriel K., Steven G. BA, Harvard U., 1970, MD, 1975. Diplomate Am. Bd. Internal Medicine. Dep. chief spl. pathogens br. Ctrs. for Disease Control, Atlanta, 1979-80, chief meningitis, spl. pathogens br., 1981-90, assoc. dir. sci., 1991-94, acting dir., nat. ctr. injury prevention and control, 1992-93, dep. dir., 1994—; cons. vaccine devel. AID, 1988—, WHO, NIH, various univs.; mem. steering com. on encapsulated bacterial vaccines, WHO, Geneva, 1989-91, chmn., 1992—; mem. adv. com. on vaccines FDA, Washington, 1990-94. Contbr. numerous articles to profl. jours. Recipient M. C. Rockefeller fellowship, 1970-71, Meritorious Svc. medal USPHS, 1986, rsch. grants NIH, FDA, Dept. of State. Fellow Infectious Diseases Soc. Am. (Bristol-Myers Squibb award 1993); mem. ACP, Am. Epidemiologic Soc., Am. Soc. Microbiology, Common Cause, Phi Beta Kappa, Alpha Omega Alpha. Office: Ctrs for Disease Control # D14 Atlanta GA 30333

BROOME, LINDA BELFORD, bank fraud investigator; b. Columbia, S.C., Nov. 5, 1946; d. Warren Calvin and Inaweise (Wright) Belford; m. Robert Ezbon Wicker, Nov. 27, 1969 (div. June 1984); children: Jennifer Marie Wicker, Christopher Michael Wicker; m. Phillip Roy Broome, Oct. 13, 1984. A in Bus., Midlands Tech. Coll., Columbia, 1994. From adminstrv. asst. to v.p./security mgr. First Citizen's Bank, Columbia, 1972—; ambassador Midland Tech. Coll., 1992-94. Mentor Richland Sch. Dist., Columbia, 1994-95. Mem. Internat. Assn. Credit Card Investigators, S.C. Bank Security Group, Phi Theta Kappa. Baptist. Office: First Citizens Bank 1230 Main St Columbia SC 29201

BROONER, MARY E., lawyer; b. Bartlesville, Okla., Dec. 12, 1948; d. George Merle and Mildred E. (Ayers) B.; m. John P. Hannah, Oct. 15, 1982; 1 child, Jeffrey P. BA, Grinnell Coll., 1971; JD, U. Notre Dame, 1978. Bar: Pa. 1979, D.C. 1979. Program asst. African Am. Asst., N.Y.C., 1973-74; gen. atty. Hayes & White, PC, Washington, 1980-83; mgr. regulatory affairs Motorola, Washington, 1983-95, sr. mgr. wireless regulatory policy, 1993—; exec. dir. Thomas J. Watson Found., Providence, 1991-93. Chair Joseph Wall Sesquicentennial Svcs. awards Grinnell (Iowa) Coll., 1996; mem. bd. Christian edn. Westmoreland Congl. Ch., Bethesda, Md., 1993-96. Mem. Nat. Conf. Women Bar Assns. (bd. dirs. 1991-95), Fed. Comms. Bar Assn. Found. (bd. dirs. 1996—), Fed. Comms. Bar Assn., Women's Bar Assn. D.C. (chair comms. law forum 1982-85, chair working parents 1987-89). Democrat. Office: Motorola 1350 Eye St NE Washington DC 20005

BROSELOW, LINDA LATT, medical office technician, aviculturist; b. Harrisburg, Pa., July 9, 1940; d. Herman and Ricci (Buch) Latt; m. Robert Joel Broselow, Nov. 26, 1966; children: Andrew M., Katherine, Jordan. BS, Pa. State U., 1962; MA, Columbia U., 1965. Vol. Peace Corps, Ankara, Turkey, 1962-64; office mgr. Robert J. Broselow, M.D., Lubbock, Tex., 1984-88, med. office technician, 1990—. Vol. South Park Hosp., Lubbock, 1986-87, Ronald McDonald House, Lubbock, 1990-92. Mem. MADD, Am. Diabetes Assn., Am. Assn. Ret. Persons, Humane Soc. U.S., Audubon Soc., Arkadashlar, Assn. of Univ. Women. Home: 4609 9th St Lubbock TX 79416 Office: 3506 21st St Ste 506 Lubbock TX 79410

BROSH, RITA, performing company executive. Artistic dir. S.W. Jazz Ballet Co., Houston. Office: SW Jazz Ballet Co PO Box 38233 720 1/2 Pinemont Houston TX 77018*

BROSIOUS, LORRAINE K., counselor; b. Sunbury, Pa., Mar. 15, 1945; d. Lawrence W. and I. Aletha (Hollenback) Acker; m. Paul R. Brosious, Sept. 3, 1966 (dec. Oct. 1984); children: Lisa, Paul, Holly, Jonathan. BA, Susquehanna U., Selinsgrove, Pa., 1967; MA, Liberty U., Lynchburg, Va., 1991. Tchr. English Monroe Twp. Schs., Williamstown, N.J., 1967-68; nursery sch. tchr. and operator First Bapt. Ch., Peekskill, N.Y., 1978-82, 85-89; tutor for homebound students Strategic Learning, Granite Springs, N.Y., 1989-90; substitute tchr. Lakeland Sch. Dist., Shrub Oak, N.Y., 1977-78, 89-92; adult edn. counselor No. Westchester BOCES, Yorktown Heights, N.Y., 1994-95; individual and family counselor Christian Counseling Ctr., Peekskill, 1992—. H.S. tchr. 1st Bapt. Ch., Peekskill, 1993-95, active in various youth activities, 1975-95; coach Shrub Oak Athletic Club, 1980-84. Mem. ACA, Christian Assn. for Psychol. Studies, Am. Assn. for Christian Counselors. Conservative. Baptist. Home: 1345 Artis Rd Shrub Oak NY 10588 Office: Christian Counseling Ctr 690 Highland Ave Peekskill NY 10566

BROSKIN, KATHLEEN MARIE, elementary education educator; b. Indiana, Pa., Mar. 18, 1951; d. John David and Goldie Marie (Henry) Kinter; m. John James Broskin, Feb. 14, 1970; children: Chris Matthew, Mark Thomas, Rebecca Ann. BS in Edn., Indiana U. Pa., 1972, MEd, 1980. Tchr. remedial math. Marion Ctr. (Pa.) Schs., 1975-80, elem. tchr., 1980—; cons. South Ctrl. Pa. Writing Project, 1992—. Citizen Amb. People to People Internat., 1994. Mem. NEA, ASCD, Internat. Reading Assn., Assn. for Childhood Edn. Internat. (Hall of Excellence award 1994), Nat. Coun. Tchrs. English, Pa. Edn. Assn. (grantee 1993). Home: 436 Route 85 Home PA 15747-9420

BROSNAN, CAROL RAPHAEL SARAH, arts administrator, musician; b. Paterson, N.J., July 19, 1931; d. Basil Roger Warnock and Mary Ellen Carroll (McDonald) B. Student, George Washington U., Washington, 1956-61, U. Va., 1975, U. Oxford (Eng.), 1975; BA in History, George Washington U., 1981, postgrad., 1983-87; piano student of, Iris Brussels, 1940-53. Adminstrv. clk. Dept. of Army, Def., Pentagon, Office of asst. chief of staff intelligence, Washington, 1955-58; clk. fgn. sci. info. program NSF, Washington, 1958-60, adminstrv. clk., 1960-65, adminstrv. fellowship clk. grad. fellowship program, 1965-72; staff asst. to Jane Alexander, chmn. Nat. Endowment for the Arts, Washington, 1972—; music tchr. piano, Paterson, N.J., 1945-53; piano recitalist U.S., Heidelberg, W. Ger. Served with WAC, 1953-55. Recipient Young People's Concerts award, 1945. Hon. fellow Harry S. Truman Libr. Inst. Nat. and Internat. Affairs, 1975. Mem. Am. Assn. for Advancement Slavic Studies, Am. Hist. Assn., Am. Philol. Assn., Acad. Polit. Sci. (contbg. 1978-81), Am. Classical League, Friends of Bodleian Libr. (Oxford U.), Luther Rice Soc. of George Washington U. (life), Phi Alpha Theta. Home: 6030 Sunset Ridge Ct Centreville VA 22020-3051 Office: Nat Endowment for Arts 1100 Pennsylvania Ave NW Washington DC 20004-2501

BROTEMARKLE, MARY ANN, science educator; b. Montgomery County, Mo., Oct. 11, 1931; d. Thomas Jefferson and Rosa Viola (Winter) Powell; m. Jack Keith Brotemarkle, June 20, 1953; children: Jeff, Jill Lewis, Susan Forrester, Mark. BS in Edn., Truman State U., 1953; MEd in Secondary Sci., U. Mo., 1971, EdS in Curriculum and Instrn., 1978, M in Libr. and Info. Sci., 1990. Lifetime tchg. cert., Mo. Rural elem. sch. tchr. Cen. Pub. Sch., Fulton, Mo., 1950-51; tchr. sci. and English Kahoka (Mo.) Pub. Sch., 1963-64; rsch. libr., storyteller N. E. Regional Libr., Kahoka, 1964-66; tchr. secondary sci. Clark County R.I. Sch., Revere, Mo., 1966-67, Columbia (Mo.) Pub. Sch., 1967-85; thesis cataloger Farrell Libr. Kans. State U., Manhattan, 1986; tchr. English jr. h.s. Columbia Pub. Schs., 1986-90; children's libr. Dorothy Bramlage Pub. Libr., Junction City, Kans., 1990-92; ret. vol. VNA, CMAAA, LAC, LWV, Columbia, 1993—; sci. club sponsor Jefferson Jr. H.S., Columbia, 1971-85, tchr. supr., 1971-85, 87-90; sci. seminar leader U. Mo., Columbia, 1971-85; honors elem. sci. tchr. Columbia Pub. Schs., summers 1973, 79-84; mem. ALA, Kans. Libr. Assn., Kans. Reading Assn., Junction City, 1990-92. Sec., bookkeeper Girl Scouts Am., Kirksville, Mo., 1951-53, Girl Scout leader, 1968-71; pres. PTA, Kahoka, 1965; Webelos leader Boy Scouts Am., Kahoka, 1962; leader Clay County 4-H Club, Clay Center, Nebr., 1955-57; tutor Hospice Vis. Nurses Assn., 1996, Literacy Action Corp., Cen. Mo. Area Agy. on Aging, 1993—; mem. Friends of Librs., Manhattan, Kans., 1990-92; hon. mem. U.S. Army ROTC Cadet Command, Ft. Riley, Junction City, 1991; vol. in mission, Mexico, 1996, Vol. Overseas Cooperative Assn., 1993—. Mem. AAUW, LWV, Ret. Tchrs. Assn. Mo., Phi Delta Kappa. United Methodist. Home: 410 Parkade Blvd Columbia MO 65202-1454

BROTHERS, JOYCE DIANE, television personality, psychologist; b. N.Y.C.; d. Morris K. and Estelle (Rapoport) Bauer; m. Milton Brothers, July 4, 1949; 1 child, Lisa Robin. BS, Cornell U., 1947; MA, Columbia U., 1950, PhD, 1953; LHD (hon.), Franklin Pierce Coll., Gettysburg Coll., Lehigh U., 1994. Asst. in psychology Columbia U., N.Y.C., 1948-52; instr. psychology Hunter Coll., N.Y.C., 1948-52; ind. psychologist, writer, 1952—. Co-host: TV program Sports Showcase, 1956; appearances: TV program Dr. Joyce Brothers, 1958-63, Consult Dr. Brothers, 1960-66, Ask Dr. Brothers, 1965-75; hostess (TV syndication) Living Easy with Dr. Joyce Brothers, 1972-75; columnist TV syndication, N.Am. Newspaper Alliance, 1961-71, Bell-McClure Syndicate, 1963-71, King Features Syndicate, 1972—, Good Housekeeping mag., 1962—; appearances Sta. WNBC, 1966-70; radio program Emphasis, 1966-75, Monitor, 1967-75, Sta. WMCA, 1970-73, ABC Reports, 1966-67, NBC Radio Network Newsline, 1975—; news analyst radio program, Metro Media-TV, 1975-76, news corr., TVN, Inc., 1975-76, Sta. KABC-TV, 1977-82, Sta. WABC-TV, 1980-82, , 86-88, Sta. WLS-TV, 1980-82, NIWS Syndicated News Service, 1982-84, The Dr. Joyce Brothers Program, The Disney Channel, 1985, Sta. KCBS-TV News, 1987—; spl. feature writer Hearst papers, UPI; current affairs spl. corr. Fox TV Syndication, 1990—; author: Ten Days to a Successful Memory, 1959, Woman, 1961, The Brothers System for Liberated Love and Marriage, 1975, How to Get Whatever You Want Out of Life, 1978, What Every Woman Should Know About Men, 1982, What Every Woman Ought to Know About Love and Marriage, 1988, The Successful Woman, 1989, Widowed, 1990, Positive Plus: The Practical Plan to Liking Yourself Better, 1994. Co-chmn. sports com. Lighthouse for Blind; door-to-door chmn. Fedn. Jewish Philanthropies, N.Y.C.; mem. fund raising com. Olympic Fund; mem. People-to-People Program. Winner $64,000 Question TV Program, 1956, $64,000 Challenge, 1957; recipient Mennen Baby Found. award, 1959, Newhouse Newspaper award, 1959, Am. Acad. Achievement award, Am. Parkinson Disease Assn. award, 1971, Deadline award Sigma Delta Chi, 1971, Pres.'s Cabinet award U. Detroit, 1975, Woman of Achievement award Women's City Club Cleve., 1981, award Calif. Home Econs. Assn., 1981, award Distrubutive Edn. Clubs Am., 1981, Golden Gavel Excellence in Comm. award Toastmasters, 1982, Pub. Svc. award Ridgewood Women's Club, 1987, Women Who Make a Difference award Sen. Bill Bradley, 1990, Gt. Am. award Bards of Bohemia, 1993, Diamond award, 1994, George M. and Mary Jane Leader Healthcare Achievement award, 1995. Mem. Sigma Xi. Office: NBC Westwood One Radio Network 1700 Broadway New York NY 10019-5905

BROTMAN, BARBARA LOUISE, columnist, writer; b. N.Y.C., Feb. 23, 1956; d. Oscar J. and Ruth (Branchor) Brotman; m. Chuck Berman, Aug. 28, 1983; children: Robin, Nina. BA, Queens Coll., 1978. Writer, columnist Chgo. Tribune, 1978—. Recipient Ill. Newspapers Column Writing award UPI, 1984, Peter Lisagor award Sigma Delta Chi, 1984. Office: Chgo Tribune Co 435 N Michigan Ave Chicago IL 60611-4001

BROTMAN, PHYLLIS BLOCK, advertising and public relations executive; b. Balt., Mar. 23, 1934; d. Sol George Block and Delma (Herman) Brotman; student Balt. Jr. Coll., U. Va., Mary Washington Coll.; m. Don N. Brotman, Aug. 16, 1953; children: Solomon G., Barbara Brotman Kaylor. Assoc., Channel 13 TV, 1953-55; free-lance pub. relations, 1960-66; coordinator pub. relations Md. Council Ednl. TV, 1965-66; pres. Image Dynamics, Inc., Balt., 1966—; lectr., cons. Md. Gen. Assembly Legis. Info. Program, 1968-70. Panelist TV, radio; columnist Balt. Bus. Jour. Coord. spl. events Balt. Jr. Coll., 1965; state chmn. U.S. Olympics Com. Mid-Atlantic Region, 1989-92; chmn. mem. com. Greater Balt. Com., 1985-87, mem. econ. devel. coun., 1990-91; adv. bd. mem. Nat. Aquarium Balt., 1988—; bd. dirs. Nat. Adv. Review Bd., 1988-89; mem. Balt. Pub. Rels. Coun.; bd. dirs. Balt. Symphony Orch., 1989—, mem. mktg. com. 75th anniversary season, 1991; chmn. adv. bd. Children and Youth Trust Fund, 1989—; bd. dirs. Internat. Visitors Ctr., co-chair mktg. com., 1990—; founding mem. Chamber Symphony of San Francisco, 1984, bd. dirs. 1984-91; mem. pub. rels. com. U. Md. System, 1988—, mem. pres. adv. coun., 1988—; mem. 20th anniversary conf. com. Internat. Urban Fellows Program Johns Hopkins Inst. Policy Studies, 1989-90; mem. community resources bd. Jr. League Balt., 1982-87; bd. dirs. New Directions for Women, 1979, 1987-90, Stella Maris Hospice Oper. Corp., 1985-87, Jewish Family and Children's Soc., 1980-83; mem. communications United Way Ctrl. Md., 1981-83; mem. mktg., pub. rels. com. Balt. Mus. Art, 1982-84, hon. com. Joshua Johnson Coun. and Endowment Fund, 1988; mem. U. Md. Endowments Com., 1978-79; nat. commr. B'nai B'rith Youth Commn.; bd. electors Balt. Hebrew Congregation, pres. parents' assn., mem. religious sch. com., bd. congregation; bd. dir. Nat. Coun. Jewish Women, life mem. award; former bd. dirs. Assoc. Placement and Guidance Bur., Levindale Home and Infirmary Ladies Auxiliary, Sinai Hosp. Auxiliary, Nat. Jewish Welfare Fund; chmn. Balt. County Econ. Devel. Commn., 1987-91; appointed commn., 1980; appointed Mayor's Commn. Telecommunications, 1987-90; appointed State of Md. Legis. Compensation Commn., 1979-82, 83-86, 87-90, 91—; appointed Mayor's Com. Internat. Bus., 1988-90; appointed Balt. County Bd. Edn. Study Com.; appointed vice chmn. Nat. UN Day Com., 1978-81; appointed Mayor Balt. Bus. Delegation for Balt. Conv. Ctr., 1979; bd. trustees Loyola Coll. Balt., 198-86, 87-93, treas., 1981, 82-83; bd. adv. Towson State U., 1989—, bd. vis., mem. adv. coun. Sch. Bus. & Econs., 1983-85; Found. bd. dirs. Mary Washington Coll., 1985-87, 88-92, speaker jr. class ring ceremony, 1981; mem. exec. com. Inst. Politics and Govt. Coll. Continuing Edn. U. So. Calif.; commencement speaker U. Ky. Coll. Dentistry, 1982. Recipient Cert. of Achievement Young Women's Leadership Coun., Cert. Appreciation for Svc. to Md. Gen. Assembly by Md. Senate, Cert. Achievement in Profession Md. Ho. Dels., Cert. Achievement in Profession Legis. Info. Program Pub. Rels. Soc. Am. Maryland Chpt., Cert. Appreciation Pub. Svc. Md. Area Residences Youth, Pub. Rels. award Great Chesapeake Balloon Race Pub. Rels. Soc. Am. Md. Chpt., Leadership award nat. svc. to profession Internat. Orgn. Women Execs., 1980, Dedicated Svc. award Jewish Family and Children, 1983, Pres. Citation private sector initiatives, 1985, Guardian of Menorah Internat. award B'nai B'rith, 1986, Silver Anvil award Pub. Rels. Soc. Am., 1988; named One Balt. Most Powerful Women Balt. Mag., One Balt. Outstanding Women Mgrs. WMAR-TV, U. Balt., 1983, Woman of Yr. Arlene Rosenbloom Wyman Guild/Univ. Md. Cancer Ctr., 1984, Women of Yr. B'nai B'rith Internat., 1985, Media Advocate of Yr. for Md. U.S. Small Bus. Adminstrn., 1985, Most Admired Company Balt. Mag., 1987, 88, 89, Entrepreneur of Yr. Balt. County Econ. Devel., 1990, Woman of Yr. project Avon Products, Inc., 1990, Save-A-Heart Humanitarian of Yr., 1991, Woman of Yr. B'nai B'rith Women of Balt., 1994 Mem. Am. Assn. Adv. Agencies (chmn. mid-Atlantic region 1981-82, gov. eastern region 1982, 83, 84, chmn. eastern region 1986-87, bd. dirs. 1982-87, gov. rels. com. 1982-87), Ctr. Club Balt. (bd. dirs. 1983—, communications chmn. 1983—), Md. C. of C. (v.p. membership 1991—, v.p. leadership Md. bd. govs. 1992-93, v.p. ctrl. dist. 1985-91, legis. conf. chmn. 1990, exec. com. 1986—, bd. dirs. 1984—), Am. Assn. Political Cons. (pres. 1976-80, bd. dirs. 1974-76, 1980—), Pub. Rels. Soc. Am. Md. Chpt. (nat. chmns. rountable 1987-88, co-chmn. nat. conf., 1980, v.p. Md. chpt. 1968, lifetime achievement award 1993), Am. Adv. Fedn. (co-chair pub. rels. com. 1986-88, nat. govt. rels. coun. 1982—, chmn. legis. com. 1981), Meeting Planners Internat. (co-chmn. pub. rels. 1978-80, task force election by-laws 1979), Adv. Assn. Balt. (bd. dirs. 1974-76), Md.-DC-Del. Press Assn. (co-chmn. assocs. sect. 1982-83), Am. TraumaSoc. (nat. bd. dirs. 1981-87, Md. bd. dirs. 1982-89), Beta Gamma Sigma, Alpha Sigma Nu. Avocations: tennis, flying (cert. aviation solo flight single engine aircraft), wine competitions(tasting, selecting). Home: 8105 Mcdonogh Rd Baltimore MD 21208-1005 Office: Image Dynamics Inc 1101 N Calvert St Baltimore MD 21202-3840

BROUN, ELIZABETH, art historian, museum administrator; b. Kansas City, Mo., Dec. 15, 1946; d. Augustine Hughes and Roberta Catherine (Hayden) Gibson; m. Ronald Broun, June 5, 1968; 1 dau., Katherine. B.A., U. Kans., 1968, Ph.D., 1976; cert. advanced study, U. Bordeaux, France, 1967. Curator prints and drawings Spencer Mus. Art, Lawrence, Kans., 1976-83; asst. prof. U. Kans., Lawrence, 1978-83; asst. dir. chief curator Nat. Mus. Am. Art, Washington, 1983-88; acting dir., 1988-89; dir. Nat. Mus. Am. Art, Washington, 1989—. Author: exhbn. catalogues Prints of Zorn, 1979, Prints and Drawings of Pat Steir, 1983, Patrick Ireland; Drawings 1965-85, 1986, Albert Pinkham Ryder, 1989; co-author: Benton's Bentons, 1980, Engravings of Marcantonio Raimondi, 1981. Woodrow Wilson fellow, 1968-69; Ford. Found. fellow, 1970-72. Mem. Phi Beta Kappa. Office: Nat Mus Am Art 8th & G Sts NW Washington DC 20560

BROUSSARD, CAROL MADELINE, writer, literary consulting agent, photographer; b. Albany, Calif.; d. Roy E. Avila and Adele (Belfils) Cazet; children: Valerie Madeline, Sean Hunter Rutledge. Student, West Hill Coll., Coalinga, Calif., Coll. Sequoias, Visalia, Calif., Inst. Metaphysics, La Brea, Calif., Fresno City Coll., 1995—. Former pub. and investigative journalist; pub. TV Watch, Tyler, Tex., 1969-74; resource sec. John C. Fremont Sch., Corcoran, Calif., 1974-77; editor Coalinga (Calif.) Record, 1978-81; pub., prodn. mgr. Kern Valley Chronicle, Lake Isabella, Calif., 1981-84; freelance writer, 1990—; featured TV show Writing Procedures, 1992; instr. home pub. Calif. State U., Fresno, 1992, 95; instr. photography Clovis (Calif.) Adult Edn., 1993—, instr. ethnic watercolors, 1993-94, instr. investigative journalism. 1994, instr. freelance journalism, 1995; tchr. photog. lab. Clovis Teen Summer Sch., 1992. Author poetry; composer lyrics for Cajun Hoedown Man Century, summer 1990, theme song Karma for Cinnimin Skin, Lance Mungia film, 1994. Vol., Literacy Program for WIN/WIN, Fresno Unified Sch. Dist., 1992, Trained Domestic Violence Response Team, Marjoree Mason Ctr. YMCA, 1996—. Recipient Photo-Journalist award Calif. Newspaper Assn., 1983, Best Feature Photo award Calif. Justice System, 1984, World of Child Photo award Fresno City and County Offices, 1980, Poetic Achievement award Amherst Soc., 1990, award of merit World of Poetry, 1990, Golden Poet award, 1990, 91, Iliad Literary award, 1990, Poetry Editor's Choice award, 1992-93; spotlight interview Writers' Journal, 1992. Mem. Writers Internat. Network (speaker 1991, 92, coord. Vols. Conf. awards 1991). Republican.

BROUSSEAU, DIANE MARIE, nurse; b. Pawtucket, R.I., Mar. 8, 1963; d. Gerard Eugene and Sandra Elaine (Brown) B. BS, R.I. Coll., 1990. Asst. coord. Community Health & Home Svcs., Attleboro, Mass.; surg. oncology nurse Roger Williams Gen. Hosp., Providence, Nursing Placement, Inc., Providence, Oakland Grove Health Care Ctr., Woonsocket. Mem. ANA, NSNA, Oncology Nursing Soc., Nursing Club (pres. 1990), Kappa Delta Phi N.A.S., Sigma Theta Tau. Home: PO Box 3089 Attleboro MA 02703-0916

BROWAR, LISA M., librarian; b. N.Y.C., Jan. 22, 1951; d. Elliott Andrew and Shirley (Kahn) B. B in English Lit., Ind. U., 1973, MLS, 1977; M in English Lit., U. Kans., 1976. Asst. curator Beinecke Libr. Yale U., New Haven, Conn., 1979-81, archivist Sterling Meml. Libr., 1981-82; curator spl. collections Vassar Coll. Libr., Poughkeepsie, N.Y., 1982-87; asst. dir. rare books and manuscripts N.Y. Pub. Libr., N.Y.C., 1987—. Mem. ALA, Assn. Coll. and Rsch. Librs. (sec. rare books and manuscripts sect. 1987-89, chair, 1994-95), Am. Printing History Assn., Soc. Am. Archivists, Bibliog. Soc. Am. Democrat. Office: NY Public Lib Rare Book & Manuscript Divsn 5th Ave & 42nd St New York NY 10018

BROWDER, MARTHA CLINE HOLSINGER, retired librarian, association executive; b. Harrisonburg, Va., Dec. 31; d. Henry S. and Elizabeth (Cline) Holsinger; m. Edward Raney Browder, Jr., Oct. 2, 1950. BS, James Madison U., 1933; MEd, U. Va., 1963; postgrad., Coll. of William and Mary, summer 1947, U. Chgo., summer 1948. Cert. tchr., Va., libr., Va. Tchr. McGheysville (Va.) H.S., 1933-44, McIntire H.S., Charlottesville, Va., 1944-50; libr. Scottsville (Va.) H.S., 1950-51; tchr., asst. libr. Highland Springs (Va.) H.S., 1951-53; head libr. Waynesboro (Va.) H.S., 1953-70, Meadowbrook H.S., Chesterfield, Va., 1970-78; ret.; evaluator Nat. Audio Visual Assn., Atlantic City, 1965. Ch. libr. Waynesboro Ch. Brethren, 1993—; officer, com. mem. LWV, Waynesboro, 1979—. Mem. AAUW (mem., chmn. various coms.), ALA (chpt. del. 1968, 69), Va. Libr. Assn. (chmn. sch. libr. sect. 1968), Am. Assn. Ret. Persons (chmn. various coms.), Augusta Ret. Tchrs. (chmn. various coms.). Republican. Home: 1915 Park Rd Waynesboro VA 22980

BROWES, PAULINE, Canadian legislator; b. Harwood, Ont., Can., May 7, 1938; d. Robert Earle and Clara (Sandercock) Drope; m. George Harold Browes, Sept. 2, 1960; children: Tammy, Janet, Jeffrey. Student, Toronto Tchrs. Coll., York U., McLaughlin Coll. Mem. for cen. Scarborough Can. Ho. of Commons, 1984-93; min. of state (environment) Can. Ho. Commons, 1991-93, min. of state (employment and immigration), min. Indian affairs and Northern Devel., 1993. Chmn. Scarborough Bd. Health, 1979-84; vice-chair Ont. Environ. Assessment Bd., 1995-96. Mem. Progressive Conservative Party. Anglican. Club: Albany of Toronto, Scarborough Golf and Country Club. Address: 16 Cotteswood Pl, Scarborough, ON Canada M1G 3P7

BROWN, ALICE MARY, pharmacist; b. Kalamazoo, Mich., Jan. 2, 1947; d. Clarence Walter and Era Rice; m. Jack R. Brown, Apr. 14, 1971; children: Jennifer, Heather, Alice. BS in Pharmacy, Wayne State U., 1969; PharmD, U. Mich., 1971. Intern pharmacist Dearborn (Mich.) Pharmacy, 1966-69; staff pharmacist Lynn Hosp., Allen Park, Mich., 1968-71, Mt. Carmel Hosp., Detroit, 1969-71; staff/relief pharmacist Granger Nitz Pharmacy (later changed to Mey Pharmacy), Saginaw, Mich., 1972-74, 76-82, 1986-89; cons. pharmacist Caro (Mich.) Regional Ctr., 1974-76; relief pharmacist Meijer Pharmacy, Saginaw, 1982-83; clin. researcher, vascular technician Dr. Jack Brown, Saginaw, 1984—; relief pharmacist Arbor Drug (formerly Mey Pharmacy and Granger Nitz Pharmacy), Saginaw, 1990—; lectr. drug abuse prevention Wayne State U., Detroit, 1967-69; program producer WUCM-TV, Delta Coll., 1976-79, resident pharmacist, 1978; co-developer Poisoned Peter Puppet Show, 1979; cons. Citizens for Substance Abuse Svcs., Lansing, Mich., 1981-82; developer poison prevention tray liner. Contbr. articles to profl. jours. Homeroom mother Liskow Elem. and Shields Elem., Saginaw, 1980-86; co-troop leader Brownies, Saginaw, 1981; fellow Applied Pharmacy Practice Resolution Jount House & Senate State Mich. poison prevention. Grantee U./ Mich., 1983-84, KPR-L'eggs, 1989, ThorLo Hosiery Inc., 1991. Fellow Am. Farriers Assn., Mich. Pharmacists Assn. (com. mem., Pub. Svc. award 1980, Hall of Honor recognition 1992), Saginaw County Pharmacists Assn. (com. mem., past v.p., pres., and exec. bd. mem., Achievement award 1980, Pres. award 1985), Applied Pharmacy Practice. Office: 7974 Gratiot Rd Saginaw MI 48609-5026

BROWN, ANGELA ROSE, social services speaker, educator; b. Alexandria, Va., Sept. 15, 1946; d. Andre John and Dorothy Loyola (Hinken) Polichnowski; m. Everett Delanel Brown Jr., Sept. 15, 1979 (dec. Feb. 15, 1992); m. David Eugene Warnick, June 12, 1993. AD in Abnormal Behavioral Problems, U. Paris, 1970. Spokesperson Women's Health, Bowie, Md., 1989—; facilitator Jacobs Inst. Women's Health, Washington, 1993—; ct. advocate for battered women Prince George's Mental Health, Bowie, 1994—; spkr., trainer, educator Awakening Women, Bowie, 1995—. Author: When All the Doors Close Look to the Windows, 1996; creator therapeutic dolls for abused children; creator healing cards. Mem. Montgomery County Cmty. Partnership, Rockville, Md., 1994—. Mem. NOW (legal ct. watcher 1995-96). Republican. Roman Catholic. Home: 15903 Pointer Ridge Dr Bowie MD 20716

BROWN, ANITA ALTER ANDERSON, bank executive; b. L.A., Jan. 24, 1943; d. John Stark Alter and Fern Emily (Wood) Alter Hunter; m. Harold R. Anderson, Oct. 2, 1965 (div. Sept. 1987); children: Cynthia D. Anderson (dec.), Stacey Leigh Anderson; m. Walton Edward Brown, Sept. 29, 1990; stepchildren: Walton Edward Jr., Christopher M. BS, U. Ariz., 1964; MBA in Finance, U. So. Calif., 1982. CFA. Mgmt. trainee, equity security analyst First Interstate Bank, L.A., 1964-66; portfolio asst., fixed-income security analyst Security Pacific Investment Mgrs., L.A., 1973-76; portfolio mgr. trust dept. SPNB, L.A., 1976-80, sr. portfolio mgr., mgr. trust dept., 1980-84, sr. v.p., mgr. Pacific Century Advisors, 1984-86; sr. portfolio mgr., v.p. Citicorp Trust, L.A., 1987-95, Wells Fargo Bank, L.A., 1995—. Mem. St. Matthew's Episcopal Ch., 1995—. Recipient Woman of Yr. award YWCA, L.A., 1983. Mem. Assn. Investment Mgmt. and Rsch., L.A. Soc. Fin. Analysts (gov., treas. 1981-83, gov. 1993-96), L.A. Assn. Investment Women, Kappa Kappa Gamma. Office: Wells Fargo Bank IMG 8th Fl 9600 Santa Monica Blvd Beverly Hills CA 90210

BROWN, ANN, federal agency administrator; m. Donald Brown, 1959; children: Cathy, Laura. Student, Smith Coll., 1955-58; BA, George Washington U., 1959. Past v.p. Consumer Fedn. Am.; chmn. bd. Pub. Voice, 1983—; chmn. U.S. Consumer Product Safety Commn., 1994—; nat. and local chmn. consumer affairs com. Ams. for Dem. Action; past chmn. adv. bd. Washington Consumer Protection Office. Named Washingtonian of Yr., Washingtonian mag., 1989; recipient Merit award Washington City Coun., Mem. of Yr. award Ams. for Dem. Action. Mem. Inst. for Injury Reduction., Colaition for Consumer Health and Safety. Office: US Consumer Product Safety Commn 4330 East West Hwy Bethesda MD 20814

BROWN, ANN CATHERINE, investment company executive; b. St. Louis, Aug. 12, 1935; d. George Hay and Catherine Doratha (Smith) B. B.A., Northwestern U., 1956; M.B.A., U. Mich., 1958. Copywriter Fred Gardner Advt. Co., N.Y.C., 1959-61, Batten, Barton, Durstine & Osborn, N.Y.C., 1961-63, Ogilvy & Mather Co., N.Y.C., 1963-64; copy group head Benton & Bowles Co., N.Y.C., 1964-66; pvt. investor, 1966-69; with Baker, Weeks & Co., Inc., N.Y.C., 1969-76; v.p. Baker, Weeks & Co., Inc., 1973-76; exec. v.p., dir. Melhado, Flynn & Assocs., Inc., N.Y.C., 1976-83; chmn., investment exec. A.C. Brown & Assocs. Inc., 1983—. Columnist Forbes mag., 1976-90. Home: PO Box 30098 Sea Island GA 31561-0098

BROWN, ANNE ELIZABETH, accountant, controller; b. Albuquerque, Aug. 10, 1960; d. Robert Allen and Kathryn Louise (Plowman) Robertson; m. Lawrence Jay Brown, Sept. 21, 1985; children: Emily Kathleen, Christopher Allen. BS, Ind. State U., 1982. CPA, Ohio. Plant acct. S.W. Forest Industries, Dallas, 1982-83; acct. Weston Paper and Mfg. Co., Terre Haute, Ind., 1983-85; chief acct. Walker Knittle Products, Troy, Ohio, 1985-86; staff acct. I Reynolds and Reynolds Co., Dayton, Ohio, 1986-87; staff acct. II Reynolds and Reynolds Co., Dayton, 1987-88, acctg. supr., 1988-93, payroll supr., 1993-95; acctg. mgr. Dartmouth Hosp., Dayton, 1995-96; contr. RCOD Home Med. Oxygen, Dayton, 1996—. Treas. Sugar Creek Presbyn. Ch., Dayton, 1994—, liturgist, 1994—, vice-chair pastor nominating com.,

1996; leader Girl Scouts Am., Dayton, 1995—. Mem. AICPA, Ohio Soc. CPA's. Democrat.

BROWN, ANNE RHODA WIESEN, civic worker; b. Medford, N.J., Nov. 27, 1926; d. George William and Mary Rebecca (Hattman) W.; m. Richard C. Brown, Aug., 1995. BS, U. N.H., 1948; MRE, Andover Newton Theol. Sch., 1950. Cert. community coll. instr., Calif. Dir. Christian edn. Bapt. chs., Mass., R.I., 1950-54; tchr., recreator World Coun. Chs., France, 1955; dir. Christian edn. Bapt. chs., Norristown, Wayne, Pa., 1956-62; recreation worker U.S. mil. hosps. ARC, 1962-64, recreation supr. U.S. mil. hosps. and bases, 1964-1976; field dir. ARC, Wright Patterson AFB, Ohio, 1976-79; sta. dir. ARC, Osan AFB, Republic of Korea, 1979-80; asst. dist. dir. ARC, Camp Zama, Japan, 1981-83, March AFB, Calif., 1983-84; sta. mgr. ARC, Camp Pendleton, Calif., 1985-86; vol. resource assoc. ARC, Stuttgart, Germany, 1986-88; sec. European Recreation Soc., Heidelberg, Germany, 1973-74. Author: Children Around the World, 1960. Bd. dirs. Project Pup, 1993-95. Recipient medal for civilian svcs. in Vietnam, U.S. Govt., 1968. Mem. AAUW (v.p. 1991-93), Tiger Bay Club (bd. dirs.). Democrat. Baptist.

BROWN, ARLENE PATRICIA THERESA (RÉNI), artist; b. Elizabeth, N.J., Jan. 3, 1953; d. William J. and Adelaide Elizabeth (Von Krasa) B.; student Union Coll., 1971. BA, Kean Coll., 1980. Owner, pres. Reni Co., Roselle Park, N.J., 1979—; pvt. tchr. art, Glass and Mirror Abrasive Etching , air brush artist designer, metal and wood engraving, crystal, gunstock, gun metal engraving and carving, Roselle Park, 1979—; owner Twinks Trademark and Associated Characters. Exhibited in The Children's Mus., Ind.; patentee in field. Recipient 3d Place award Custom Car and Van Show, Meadowlands, N.J., 1981, 2d place award Custom Car and Van Show, Asbury Park, N.J., 1982. Mem. Graphic Artists Guild, Artists' Equity Assn., Summit Art Assn., Princeton Art Assn.,, Am. Women's Econ. Devel. Assn., Found. Christian Living, Positive Thinkers Club, N.J. Art Dirs. Club, Morris County C. of C., N.J. Jewelers Assn., Internat. Jet Sports Boating Assn., Assn. Jensen Owners, Westfield Art Assn., Alumni Assn. Kean Coll. Address: PO Box 186 Roselle Park NJ 07204-0186

BROWN, BETH MARIE, dietitian, hospital administrator; b. Pigeon, Mich., Oct. 2, 1952; d. Walton Durwood and Marion Anita (Schweitzer) B. BS, Cen. Mich. U., 1974; MS, S.W. Tex. State U., 1990. Registered dietitian; diplomate ACHE. Clin. dietitian Leonard Hosp., N.Y., 1975-76; edn. and staff devel. dietitian VA Med. Ctr., Iron Mtn., Mich., 1976-79, chief food prodn. & svc., 1979-81; chief adminstrv. dietetic svc. VA Med. Ctr., Phila., 1981-83; chief dietetic svc. VA Med. Ctr., Butler, Pa., 1983-86, Temple, Tex., 1986-94; adminstrv. officer managed care South Tex. Vets. Health Care System, San Antonio, 1995—; adj. lectr. Tex. A&M U., Temple, 1986-94. Mem. Big. T Toastmasters, Temple, 1989-93, assoc. dir. trainee, San Antonio,1994; bd. dirs. Altrusa Internat. of Temple, 1989-92, Butler Meals-on-Wheels, 1983-86. Recipient Pride & Pub. Svc. award Dept. Vets. Affairs, 1991, Leadership VA award, 1990; named Competent Toastmaster, 1990, Outstanding Young Woman of Am., 1988, Excellence in Improving Svc. to the Pub., 1979. Mem. Am. Coll. Healthcare Execs., Am. Dietetic Assn., Cen. Tex. Dietetic Assn. (officer 1987-89), Tex. Hosp. Assn., Tex. Dietetic Assn. Lutheran. Home: 3147 Morning Tr San Antonio TX 78247 Office: South Tex Vets Health Care System 7400 Merton Minter St San Antonio TX 78284-5700

BROWN, BETSY ETHERIDGE, dean; b. Statesville, N.C., Aug. 2, 1950; d. Guy Wetmore and Elizabeth (Hackney) Etheridge; m. Homer L. Brown, Aug. 13, 1972 (dec. Mar. 1987); 1 child, Elizabeth Leigh; m. Lawrence C. Timbs, Jr., July 30, 1995. BS in English, Appalachian State U., 1972; MA in English, Ohio State U., 1974, PhD in English, 1978. Cert. tchr., N.C. Asst. prof. English Pa. State U., University Park, 1978-85; asst. to v.p. Queens Coll., Charlotte, N.C., 1987-89, Winthrop U., Rock Hill, S.C., 1990-92; assoc. v.p. Winthrop U., Rock Hill, 1992-94, dean Coll. Arts and Scis., 1994—; bd. mem. Cmty. Bd. for Women's Svcs., Rock Hill, 1994—. Recipient Mgmt. Devel. Program award Harvard Grad. Sch. Edn., 1992, Forum award Am. Coun. on Edn.-Nat. Idenfification Program, 1995; Fulbright grantee, Bonn, Germany, 1994. Mem. AAUW, S.C. Women in Higher Edn. Adminstrn. (bd. sec. 1994—). Office: Winthrop Univ 107 Kinard Rock Hill SC 29733

BROWN, BETTY HARRISON, mental health counselor; b. Greenville, Miss., Apr. 10, 1939; d. John Grover and Margaret Elizabeth (Langford) Harrison; m. James Franklin Hopson, July 13, 1960 (div. Dec. 1983); children: James Kevin, Lisa Kay; m. Henry Earl Brown, June 27, 1987. BA, Miss. State U., 1961; MA, U. Miss., 1979. Lic. profl. counselor, Miss.; nat. cert. counselor Nat. Bd. Cert. Counselors. Substitute tchr. at various pub. schs. Wahiawa, Hawaii, 1968-71, Kaysville, Utah, 1971-72; exec. sec. MPI, Inc., Houston, Miss., 1974-76; outreach therapist Region 3 Mental Health, Tupelo, Miss., 1976-78, mental health counselor, 1984-89; dir. social svcs. Houston Cmty. Hosp., Miss., 1979-84; inpatient psychiat. counselor North Miss. Med. Ctr. Behavioral Health, Tupelo, Miss., 1989-94'; outpatient counselor NMMC Behavioral Health, Tupelo, Miss., 1995—, MidSouth Counseling Ctr., Tupelo, Miss., 1994; mem. Lee County Sexual Abuse Task Force, Tupelo, 1990—; co-chmn. Stop the Hurt! Child Sexual Abuse Conf. Com., Tupelo, 1991—; mem. adv. bd. Nat. Coun. on Alcoholism, Tupelo, 1994-95, Lee County Foster Care Rev. Bd., Tupelo, 1996. Mem. Am. Counseling Assn., Am. Clin. Mental Health Assn., Miss. Counseling Assn., Miss. Clin. Mental Health Assn. Methodist. Home: 340 CR114 Houlka MS 38850 Office: North Miss Med Ctr Behavioral Health Ctr 830 S Gloster St Tupelo MS 38801

BROWN, BETTY MARIE, government agency administrator; b. Siler City, N.C., June 11, 1952; d. Ardentries and Emma (Peoples) Mason; m. Tommy E. Brown, Aug. 8, 1968 (dec.); 1 child, Christopher T.; m. Roger L. Cook, June 10, 1973 (dec. Feb. 1981); 1 child, Felicia M. AAS, Phila. Community Coll., 1981; BS, Drexel U., 1986. Cert. early childhood edn. tchr., elem. edn. tchr., Pa. Mgr. Mr. Gourmet Deli, Phila., 1977-80; pres. Parents, Friends and Vols. Community Svc. Orgn., Phila., 1983—; tchr. Phila. Sch. Dist., 1988-89; remittance perfection clk. IRS, Phila., 1990-92; account analyst IRS-Automated Collection Sys., Phila., 1992—; tchr. Mid City YWCA, Phila., 1983-88. Sec. support community outreach project Dept. Human Svcs., Phila., 1990-91. Recipient Community Svc. award Dept. Human Svc., 1988. Baptist. Home: 1132 Easton Rd Apt B Philadelphia PA 19150-2708 Office: Parents of the 39th Dist 1132 Easton Rd Philadelphia PA 19150

BROWN, BEULAH LOUISE, retired elementary educator; b. Warren County, Ohio, Feb. 21, 1917; d. Fred Austin and Roba E. (Doughman) Birmingham; m. William Dale Brown, Aug. 14, 1942 (dec. Apr. 1984). Student, Ohio U., 1937-39, BS in Edn. cum laude, 1957. Cert. tchr., Ohio. Tchr. 2d grade Bainbridge (Ohio) Village Sch., 1939-43; rsch. lab. asst. Mead Paper Corp., Chillicothe, Ohio, 1944-45; tchr. 2d grade Chillicothe City Schs., 1945-46, Marysville (Ohio) Schs., 1946-49; tchr. 1st grade Riley Twp. Sandusky County Schs., Fremont, Ohio, 1951-52; tchr. 2d grade Fremont City Schs., 1952-59; tchr. 2d grade Lancaster (Ohio) City Schs., 1959-64, tchr. 1st grade, 1966-75; tchr. 2d grade Ashland (Ohio) City Schs., 1964-66; supervising tchr. Bowling Green (Ohio) State U., 1955-59, Ohio U., Athens, 1960-64, 66-75, Ashland Coll., 1964-66. Vol. Lancaster Hosp., Meals on Wheels, Pub. Libr. Mem. AAUW, Farifield County Ret. Tchrs., Ohio Ret. Tchrs., Clionian Literary Club, Kappa Delta Pi, Delta Kappa Gamma. Republican. Methodist.

BROWN, BONNIE JOAN, human resources director; b. N.Y.C.; 1 child, Andrew Martin. BA in Psychology and Sociology, U. Okla.; MBA, U. Mich., 1979. Rsch. assoc. Inst. for Social Rsch. U. Mich., Ann Arbor, 1971-74, dir. student svcs., 1974-77; human resources mgr. GE, Fairfield, Conn., 1979-90; dir. human resources Pub. Svc. Enterprise Group, Newark, 1990-94, Asea Brown Boveri Inc., Stamford, Conn., 1994-95; orgn. effectiveness cons. Cary, N.C., 1995—; cons. Dept. Human Svcs., Ann Arbor, 1978-79. Contbr. articles to profl. jours. Com. chair PTA, West Windsor, N.J., 1988; treas. Boy Scouts Am., Apalachin, N.Y., 1985; referee West Windsor Soccer Assn., 1989; peer arbitrator Mercer County Legal System, West Windsor, 1988; reader Recording for the Blind, Princeton, N.J., 1992-94, Libr. for Blind & Physically Handicapped, Raleigh, N.C., 1996—. Mem. ASTD, Human Resources Planning Soc., Orgn. Devel. Network, Assn. for Psychol. Type. Home and Office: 3131 Grande Valley Cir Cary NC 27513

BROWN, CALLIE CORRINNE WRATHER, medical, surgical nurse, derma-technologist; b. Rutherford County, Tenn., July 1, 1934; d. Horace Palmer and Gola Kate (Jones) Wrather; m. Trenton Larry Brown, Sept. 7, 1957; children: Bradley Trenton, Brenda Calantha, Gerald Truman. RN, East Tenn. Bapt. Hosp. Sch. Nursing, 1956; student, U. Tenn., 1953, 54, 62. RN, Tenn., N.C., S.C., Pa., Ohio, Ind. Supr. Maury County Hosp., Columbia, Tenn., 1957; office nurse Acuff Clinic, Knoxville, 1957-60; staff nurse oper. rm. East Tenn. Bapt. Hosp., Knoxville, 1961; plant nurse, stenographer wear-ever divsn. Aluminum Co. Am., Chillicothe, Ohio, 1964; pub. health nurse Blount County Health Dept., Maryville, Tenn., 1961-68; supr. Richmond (Ind.) State Hosp., 1970-71; staff nurse Med. Pers. Pool, Pitts., 1971-76, Aide Health Svc., Pitts., 1980-83; store mgr. Furniture Factory Outlet World of Waxhaw, N.C., Columbia, S.C. and Hickory, N.C., 1983-89; staff, charge nurse, designated facilitator St. Joseph's Hosp., Asheville, N.C., 1991—; pres., derma-technologist Derma-Graphics of Asheville, Inc., 1992—. Instr. mother and baby care, home nursing, swimming ARC, Columbia, Knoxville and Maryville, Tenn., 1957-60's; treas. Independence PTA, Aliquippa, Pa., 1978-80; pres. Hopewell Jr. High Parent, Tchr. and Student Assn., Aliquippa, 1980-83; mem. choir various chs., 1960-78. Mem. ANA, Nat. League Nursing (advocacy), Am. Coun. Dermagraphic Rsch. (diplomat), Soc. Permanent Cosmetic Profls., MCN Micropigmentation Assn. Baptist. Home: 73 Old Concord Rd Fletcher NC 28732-9421 Office: Derma-Graphics of Asheville Inc 206 E Chestnut St Asheville NC 28801-2444 also: St Joseph's Hosp Biltmore Ave Asheville NC 28801

BROWN, CANDICE LEIGH, novelist; b. Crawfordsville, Ind., June 4, 1963; d. James Earl and Mae Maxine (McAllister) B.; m. William Henry Epstein, Oct. 24, 1992. Student, Pima Cmty. Coll., 1990, U. Ariz., 1993. Ballet dancer U.S. and Europe, 1978-87; deli waitress L.A., 1982-84; ednl. advisor, sec. Pima Cmty. Coll., Tucson, 1987—; choreographer Tucson Met. Ballet, 1987—; ballet tchr. France Acad. of Dance, Tucson, 1987—. Author: The Body of Dancers, 1993. Creative Writing fellowship Ariz. Commn. on the Arts, 1996; recipient Martindale Literary award Martindale, 1978; scholarship San Francisco Ballet, Marint SS Ballet, 1979, 80, Harkness Ballet, N.Y., 1980. Democrat. Home and Office: 3748 E 4th St Tucson AZ 85716

BROWN, CAROL ELIZABETH, management educator; b. Boise, Idaho, Jan. 26, 1950; d. Mason Oliver Brown and Hazel (Metcalf) Henderson; m. Richard Bruce Wodtli, Aug. 16, 1989. BS in Art, U. Wis., 1972; MS in Acctg., U. Oreg., 1977; PhD in Computer Sci., Oreg. State U., 1989. CPA. Bookkeeper Stone Fence Inc., Madison, Wis., 1972-74; staff acct. Baillies, Denson, Erickson & Smith, Madison, 1974-75, Minihan, Kernutt, Stokes & Co., Eugene, 1977-78; instr. Oreg. State U., Corvallis, 1978-89, asst. prof., 1989-92, assoc. prof., 1992—. Assoc. editor Jour. Info. Sys., 1989-92; mem. editl. rev. bd. Internat. Jour. Intelligent Sys. in Acctg., Fin. and Mgmt., 1991—, Internat. Jour. Applied Expert Sys., 1994—; guest editor Expert Sys. With Applications, 1991, 95; contbr. articles to profl. jours. Bd. dirs. United Way of Benton County, Corvallis, 1989-96, sec.-treas., 1993-96; vol. acct., 1982-86. Recipient Outstanding Vol. Svc. award United Way of Benton County, 1986, 93; rsch. grant Oreg. State U., 1988, 90, Scholarship award, 1992, 93; rsch. grant TIAA-CREF, 1990, 91. Mem. IEEE Computer Soc., Am. Acctg. Assn. (program adv. com. 1990-91, artificial intelligence/expert sys. sect., vice chairperson 1991-92, chairperson-elect 1992-93, chairperson 1993-94, Pioneer Svc. award 1994), Am. Assn. Artificial Intelligence, Inst. Mgmt. Accts. (dir. manuscripts Salem, Oreg. area 1990—, bd. dirs. 1990—, Merit cert. 1990-91, Rsch. grantee 1993), Oreg. Soc. CPA (com. mem. 1989-94, vice chmn. computer svcs. com. 1990-91, Recognition cert. for Leadership Excellence 1989-90, Outstanding Svc. award 1990-91), Assn. Computer Machinery, others. Home: 1949 Ingalls Way Eugene OR 97405 Office: Oreg State U Coll Bus Bexell Hall # 200 Corvallis OR 97331-2603

BROWN, CAROLYN SMITH, communications educator, consultant; b. Salt Lake City, Aug. 12, 1946; d. Andrew Delbert and Olive (Crane) Smith; m. David Scott Brown, Sept. 10, 1982. BA magna cum laude, U. Utah, 1968, MA, 1972, PhD, 1974. Instr. Salt Lake Ctr., Brigham Young U., Salt Lake City, 1976-78; vis. asst. prof. Brigham Young U., Provo, 1978; asst. prof. Am. Inst. Banking, Salt Lake City, 1977—; prof., chmn. English, communication and gen. edn. depts. Latter Day Saints Bus. Coll., Salt Lake City, 1973—, dean acad. affairs, 1986-96, v.p. for acad. affairs, 1996—; founder, pres. Career Devel. Tng., Salt Lake City, 1979—; cons. in-house seminars 1st Security Realty Svcs., USDA Natural Resource Conservation Svc., Utah Power & Light, Utah Soc. Svcs., Adminstrv. Office of Cts., HUD, Intermountain Health Care, Fidelity Investments, Am. Inst. Banking; mem. NW Assn. Schs. & Colls. Liaison, 1980—, Utah Bus. Coll. Dean's com., 1990—. Author: Writing Letters & Reports That Communicate, 8th edit., 1994; contbr. articles to profl. jours. Demi-soloist Utah Civic Ballet (now Ballet West), Salt Lake City, 1964-68; active Mormon Ch.; C. of C. Bus. Edn. com., 1991-92. Named Tchr. of Month, Salt Lake City Kiwanis, 1981; NDEA fellow, U. Utah, 1972. Mem. Am. Bus. Communications Assn. (lectr. West/N.W. regional chpt. 1987), Delta Kappa Gamma (2d v.p. 1977-79), Lambda Delta Sigma (Outstanding Woman of Yr. 1983), Kappa Kappa Gamma (Outstanding Alumnus in Lit. 1974). Republican. Clubs: Alice Louise Reynolds Literary (Salt Lake City) (v.p. 1978-79, sec. 1985-86). Office: LDS Bus Coll 411 E South Temple Salt Lake City UT 84111-1302

BROWN, CATHERINE ALLETTO, elementary education educator; b. Chgo., Apr. 30, 1964; d. William Charles and Frances (Brown) Alletto; m. James Ronald Brown, April 24, 1993; 1 child, Emily Lauren. BA in edn., U. Ill., Chgo., 1987, MEd, 1990. Tchr. Archdiocese of Chgo. Bridgeport Cath. Acad., Chgo., 1987-91, Chgo. Bd. Edn.-Carson Sch., Chgo., 1991-95, Chgo. Bd. Edn.-Everett Sch., Chgo., 1995—; cheerleading coach Carson Sch., 1991-95, Everett Sch., 1995—. Nominated for Thanks to tchr. award, WBBM-TV, 1995. Mem. AAUW, Internat. Reading Assn., Ill. Coun. for Affective Reading Ednl. Roman Catholic. Office: Chgo Bd of Edn Everett Sch 3419 S Bell Chicago IL 60608

BROWN, CATHERINE HELEN MCKINNEY, publishing executive; b. Urbana, Ohio, Feb. 19, 1965; d. Clarence J. and Joyce Helen (Eldridge) B.; m. Clark Evan Brinnon, May 18, 1996. BS in Indsl. Engring., Northwestern U., 1987; MBA, Case Western Res. U., 1994. Engring. staff, engring. coord. Honda of Am., Mfg., Marysville, Ohio, 1987-92; rsch. analyst Brown Pub. Co., Cin., 1993, gen. exec., 1995—; human resource intern GE Lighting Co., Cleve., 1993; asst. dir. Ctr. for the Mgmt. of Sci. and Tech., Case Western Res. U., Cleve., 1994. Home: 3090 Stone Quarry Rd Urbana OH 43078

BROWN, CHARLINA PIERCE, education educator; b. Ironton, Ohio, Feb. 8, 1935; d. Charlton Louian and Ina (Hill) Pierce; m. July 29, 196l (div. Aug. 198l); children: Heather Pierce, Stacia Ketchersid. BS, Fla. State U., 1957, MS, 196l; PhD, Tex. Women's U., 1977. Elem. tchr. Leon County Bd. Pub. Instrn., Tallahassee, 1957-59, 6l-64; grad. asst. Inst. Human Devel., Fla. State U., Tallahassee, 1959-6l; asst. prof. div. edn. Tift Coll., Forsyth, Ga., 1960-6l, North Tex. State U., Denton, 1977-78; instr. Jacksonville (Fla.) U., 1965-66; cons. HEW, Livingston, Ala., 1967-68; grad. asst., adj. asst. prof. Tex. Woman's U., Denton, 1978-8l; asst. prof. edn. Bethune-Cookman Coll., Daytona Beach, Fla., 1988—; developer, dir. Coop. Presch., Livingston, Ala., 1967-68; owner, cons. Pupils, Parents, Preschs., Denton, 1980-8l; asst. head tchr. Rsch. Ctr. for Child Devel., Tallahassee, 1987; realtor assoc. Prudential Serpico Realty, Inc., Tallahassee; mem. Bd. of Realtors. Officer Denton Woman's Club, 1970-76; mem. Fla. State U. Seminole Booster. Tex. Woman's U. fellow, 1976-77. Mem. AAUW, Assn. for Childhooed Edn. Itnernat. (tchr. edn. com.), ASCD, Investment Club, Alpha Delta Kappa, Pi Lmabda Theta, Delta Gamma (alumni pres. 1957-59). Democrat. Baptist. Home: 2271 W Lake Hall Rd Tallahassee FL 32308-2992 Office: Bethune-Cookman Coll 640 2d Ave Daytona Beach FL 32017

BROWN, CORRINE, congresswoman; b. Jacksonville, Fla., Nov. 11, 1946; married; 1 child, Shantrel. BS, Fla. A & M U., 1969; EdS, U. Fla., 1974. Former mem. Fla. Ho. of Reps; del. Nat. Dem. Conv., 1988; mem. 103rd-104th Congress from 3rd Fla. dist., 1993—, mem. transp. and infrastructure com. aviation, surface transp., mem. VA com. hosp. and health care. Mem. Sigma Gamma Rho. Baptist. Home: 314 Palmetto St Jacksonville FL 32202-2619 Office: US Ho of Reps 1610 Longworth House Office Bldg Washington DC 20515-0903*

BROWN, D. ROBIN, elementary educator; b. Cleve., Oct. 31, 1949; d. William Michael and Darla G. (Carlson) Linsenmann; m. Ross H. Brown, Aug. 21, 1971. BA cum laude, W.Va. Wesleyan U., 1971; MA, Ashland U., 1988, postgrad., 1988-90; postgrad., Ohio State U., 1989-90. Cert. elem. tchr., Ohio, W.Va. Tchr. Lost Creek Elem. Sch., Clarksburg, W.Va., 1971-72, Leesburg (Va.) Middle Sch., 1972-75, Northmoor Elem. Sch., Dayton, Ohio, 1975-79, Jonathan Alder Local Schs., Plain City, Ohio, 1979—. Active TWIG # 158, Columbus, Ohio, 1990—, Salvation Army, Columbus, 1990—, Worthington Hills Women's Club, Columbus, 1985—. Recipient Sci. award Exxon, 1974. Mem. Internat. Reading Assn., Reading Recovery, Kappa Delta Pi, Sigma Eta Sigma, Pi Gamma Mu, Tri Beta. Home: 825 Highview Dr West Worthington OH 43235-1232 Office: Jonathan Alder Local Schs 4331 Kilbury Huber Rd Plain City OH 43064-9064

BROWN, DALE SUSAN, government administrator, educational program director, writer; b. N.Y.C., May 27, 1954; d. Bertram S. and Beatrice Joy (Gilman) B. BA, Antioch Coll., 1976. Rsch. asst. Am. Occupational Therapy Assn., Rockville, Md., 1976-79; writer Pres.' Com. on Employment of People with Disabilities, Washington D.C., 1979-82, program mgr., 1982—, program mgr. labor com., 1995; program mgr. work environment and tech. com. Ams. with Disabilities Act, 1986-94, program com. on libr. and info. svcs., 1984-86, youth devel. com., 1986-88, new products devel. team, 1987-90, agy. rep. 1991-93, with interagy. tech. assistance coordinating team, 1992-94; cons. in field; gen. assembly speaker nat. conv. Gen. Fedn. Women's Clubs, 1981; mem. Rehab. Svcs. Adminstrn. Task Force on Learning Disabilities, 1981-83. Author: Steps to Independence for People with Learning Disabilities, 1980, Pathways to Employment for People with Learning Disabilities, 1991, Working Effectively with People Who Have Learning Disabilities and Attention Deficit Hyperactivity Disorder, 1995, I Know I Can Climb the Mountain, 1995; writer film: They Could Have Saved Their Homes, 1982; dir. videotape Part of the Team People with Disabilities in the Workforce, 1990; editorial bd. Perceptions, 1981-83, Learning Disabilities Focus, 1988-90, In The Mainstream, 1994—; co-editor Learning Disabilities and Employment; cons. editor Learning Disabilities Rsch. and Practice, 1990—. Pres. Assn. Learning Disabled Adults, Washington, 1979-80; bd. dirs. Closer Look Nat. Info. Ctr., Washington, 1980-83, Am. Coalition of Citizens with Disabilities, 1985-86; chair 5th ann. conf. on Info. Tech. for User With Disabilities, 1989; spl. asst. for people with disabilites Federally Employed Women, 1991-92; mem. congrl. task force Rights and Empowerment of Ams. with Disabilities, 1988-90; mem. blue ribbon panel on Nat. Telecommunications Access for People with Disabilities, 1989-94. Found. for Children with Learning Disabilities grantee, 1982; recipient Margaret Byrd Rawson award, 1989, Personal Achievement award Womens Program USDOL, 1989, Individual Achievement award Nat. Coun. on Communication Disorders, 1991, Spl. Achievement award Pres.'s Com. on Employment of People with Disabilities, 1991, Gold Screen award Nat. Assn. Govt. Communicators, 1991, Arthur S. Fleming award, 1992, 94; named one of Ten Outstanding Young Ams., U.S. Jr. C. of C., 1994, Jaycees, 1994. Mem. Nat. Network of Learning Disabled Adults (founder, pres. 1980-81, rep. Inter-agy. com. on computer support handicapped employees 1988—), Nat. Assn. Govt. Communicators (Blue Pencil award 1986, rep. inter-agy. com. on handicapped employees 1989—, Learning Disabilities Assn. (bd. dirs. 1986-91), ALA. Democrat. Jewish. Office: Pres' Com Employment of People with Disabilities 1331 F St NW Washington DC 20004-1107

BROWN, DARMAE JUDD, librarian; b. Jefferson City, Mo., Sept. 14, 1952; d. William Robert and Dorothy Judd (Curtis) B. BA, W.Va. Wesleyan Coll., 1974; MA, U. Denver, 1975; M of Computer Info. Systems, U. Denver, 1992. Searching assoc. Bibliog. Ctr. for Rsch., Denver, 1975-76; libr. N.E. Colo. Regional Libr., Wray, 1976-81; head tech. svcs. Ector County Libr., Odessa, Tex., 1981-84, Waterloo (Iowa) Pub. Libr., 1984-89; systems coord. Aurora (Colo.) Pub. Libr., 1989—. Mem. ALA, Iowa OCLC Users Group (pres. 1986-87), Colo. Libr. Assn., Libr. & Info. Tech. Assn., Beta Phi Mu, Sigma Alpha Iota. Home: 12010 E Harvard Ave Aurora CO 80014-1808

BROWN, DEBORAH ELIZABETH, television producer, marketing professional; b. Aledo, Ill., Nov. 29, 1952; d. Kenneth M. and Mary Esther (Gilmore) B.; m. K. J. Lester, Nov. 28, 1975 (dec. Mar. 1982); children: Rebekah Jean, Aaron Mark, Jonathan Caleb. Student, Letourneau Coll., 1970; BA in Theater Arts, Sterling Coll., 1974; MA in Comm., Wheaton Coll., 1977. Producer, dir. Sta. WCFC-TV, Chgo., 1978-80; sales mgr. SNG Enterprises, St. Charles, Ill., 1980-82; pres., CEO Circle Family Video Stores, Niles, Mich., 1982-87; exec. producer Picture Radio Pictures, Lakeland, Fla., 1987-93; mgr. Computer Keyboard, Portland, Oreg., 1993—; vis. prof. comm. Wheaton (Ill.) Coll., 1980; video cons. Spring Arbor Distbrs., Belleville, Mich., 1985, Gospel Films, Muskegan, Mich., 1985. Producer, dir., writer (TV program and book) Crafts With Emilie, 1979 (Spl. Emmy nomination); video contbg. editor Christian Booksellers Assn. jour., 1984-85; set decorator Cindy Williams Comedy Spl., 1993. Corp. sponsor Pregnancy Care Ctr., Niles, 1985-87; producer Four Flags Area Apple Festival, Niles, 1987. Mem. Fellowship of Christians in Arts, Media and Entertainment, Christian Video Retailers Assn. (exec. dir. 1985-87), Fla. Motion Picture and TV Assn. Baptist. Office: Computer Keyboard 12000 SE 82nd Ave Ste 1121 Portland OR 97266-7736

BROWN, DEBORAH IONE, computer specialist; b. Washington, Nov. 29, 1952; d. Charles Curtis and Estella (Clark) Bradley; 1 child, Dwyte Aaron Jr. AAS, cert., Washington Tech. Inst., 1973; BBA, U. D.C., 1982. Records clk. Washington Tech. Inst., 1971-74; domputer aide U.S. Dept. of Treasury, Washington, 1974-75; computer programming trainee Exec. Office Budget and Mgmt., Washington, 1976-77; computer programmer Metro Police Dept., Washington, 1977-80; computer sys. analyst Nat. Guard Bur., Falls Church, Va., 1980-81; computer programmer analyst U.S. Computer Sys. Command, Falls Church, Va., 1981-85; computer specialist Exec. Office of the Pres., Washington, 1985-86; computer specialist, contracting officer rep. U.S. Dept. of Army, Alexandria, Va., 1987—. Fellow Internat. Biographical Inst. (bd. dirs. 1992—); mem. NAFE, Black Employee Program Mgmt. (Pesinscom rep. 1993). Democrat. Baptist. Home: 12604 Milburn Lane Bowie MD 20715 Office: HQ Persinscom ASQL-PLO-C 200 Stovall St Alexandria VA 22332

BROWN, DENISE SCOTT, architect, urban planner; b. Nkana, Zambia, Oct. 3, 1931; came to U.S., 1958; d. Simon and Phyllis (Hepker) Lakofski; m. Robert Scott Brown, July 21, 1955 (dec. 1959); m. Robert Charles Venturi, July 23, 1967; 1 child, James C. Student, U. Witwatersrand, South Africa, 1948-51; diploma, Archtl. Assn., London, 1955; M of City Planning, U. Pa., 1960, MArch, 1965, DFA (hon.), 1994; DFA (hon.), Oberlin Coll., 1977, Phila. Coll. Art, 1985, Parsons Sch. Design, 1985; LHD (hon.), N.J. Inst. Tech., 1984, Phila. Coll. Textiles and Sci., 1992; DEng (hon.), Tech. U. N.S., 1991; HHD (hon.), Pratt Inst., 1992; DFA (hon.), U. Pa., 1994. Registered architect, U.K. Asst. prof. U. Pa., Phila., 1960-65; assoc. prof., head urban design program UCLA, 1965-68; with Venturi, Rauch and Scott Brown, Phila., 1967—, ptnr., 1969-89; prin. Venturi, Scott Brown and Assocs. Inc., Phila., 1989—; vis. prof. arch. U. Calif., Berkeley, 1965, Yale U., 1967-70; asst. prof. U. Pa., 1960-65, vis. prof. Sch. Fine Arts, 1982, 83; Eliot Noyes design critic in arch. Harvard U., Cambridge, Mass., 1989-90; mem. visitors com. MIT, 1973-83; mem. adv. com. dept. arch. Temple U., 1980—; cons. to dean search com. Sch. Arch., Washington U., St. Louis, 1992; mem. adv. bd. dept. arch. Carnegie Mellon U., 1992—; mem. jury Prince of Wales Prize in Urban Design, Grad. Sch. Design Harvard U., Cambridge, 1993. Author: Urban Concepts, 1990; co-author: Learning from Las Vegas, 1972, rev. edit., 1977, A View from the Campidoglio: Selected Essays, 1953-84, 85, On Houses and Housing, 1992; contbr. numerous articles to profl. jours. Mem. curriculum com. Phila. Jewish Children's Folkshul, 1980-86; policy panelist design arts program NEA, 1981-83; mem. bd. advisors Architects, Designers and Planners for Social Responsibility, 1982—; mem. capitol preservation com. Commonwealth of Pa., Harrisburg, 1983-87; bd. dirs. Ctrl. Phila. Devel. Corp., 1985—, Urban Affairs Partnership, Phila., 1987-91; trustee Chestnut Hill Acad., Phila., 1985-89. Decorated commendatore Order of Merit (Italy); recipient numerous awards, citations, commendations for designs and urban planning, including Chgo. Architecture award, 1987, U.S. Presdl. award nat. medal of Arts, 1992, Hall of Fame award Interior Design mag., 1992, (with Robert Venturi) The Phila. award, 1993, The Benjamin Franklin medal Royal Soc. for Encouragement of Arts, Mfg. and Commerce, 1993, Am. Coll. Schs. of Architecture/AIA Topaz medallion, 1996. Mem.

Royal Inst. Brit. Archs., Am. Acad. Arts and Scis., Archs. Designers and Planners for Social Responsibility, Am. Planning Assn, Archtl. Assn. London, Internat. Women's Forum, Soc. Coll. and U. Planning, Soc. Archtl. Historians (bd. dirs. 1981-84), Carpenters Co. of City and County of Phila., Athenaeum of Phila., Royal Soc. Encouragement of Arts, Mfr. and Commerce. Democrat. Jewish. Office: Venturi Scott Brown & Assocs Inc 4236 Main St Philadelphia PA 19127-1603

BROWN, DIANE FONTENOT, religious organization administrator, lay worker, volunteer; b. Opelousas, La., Nov. 11, 1934; d. Jared Y. and Lucille (Dunbar) Fontenot; m. Herbert Graham Brown, Oct. 18, 1953; children: Debbie, Jared, Greg, Donna. Student, Coll. of the Sacred Heart, Grand Cateau, La., 1952-53; D of Christian Letters (hon.), Franciscan U., Steubenville, Ohio, 1996. Chmn. conf. Assn. Christian Therapists, Rochester, N.Y., 1978-89; dir., founder Our Lady of Divine Providence House of Prayer, Inc., Clearwater, Fla., 1980—, pres., 1981-96; founder, dir. Marian Servants of Divine Providence, St. Petersburg, Fla., 1987-90; founder Our Lady of Divine Providence Sch. Spirituality, Clearwater, Fla., 1991-96; bd. mem. Cath. charismatic commn. Diocese St. Petersburg, Fla.; spkr. in field. Pres., mem. bd. Cath. Edn. Found., St. Petersburg, Fla. Named 1 of 25 Most Influential Women of the Tampa Bay Area, 1993. Mem. Rotary Internat. (first lady 1995-96, vice chmn. women in future soc. com. 1996—). Democrat. Roman Catholic. Home: 1114 Mandalay Pt Clearwater FL 34630

BROWN, ELIZABETH ANN, foreign service officer; b. Portland, Oreg., Aug. 15, 1918; d. Edwin Keith and Grace Viola (Foss) B. A.B., Reed Coll., 1940; postgrad. (teaching fellow), Wash. State Coll., 1940-41; A.M., Columbia, 1943. Exec. asst. to chmn. 12th region WLB, Seattle, 1943-45; internat. affairs officer Dept. State, 1946-56; joined U.S. Fgn. Service, 1956; assigned Office UN Polit. Affairs, Dept. State, 1956-60; 1st sec. Am. embassy, Bonn, Germany, 1960-63; dep. dir. Office UN Polit. Affairs, 1963-65, dir., 1965-69; mem. State Dept. Sr. Seminar in Fgn. Policy, 1969-70; counselor for polit. affairs Am. embassy, Athens, Greece, 1970-75; dep. chief mission Am. embassy, The Hague, Netherlands, 1975-78; sr. insp. Dept. State, 1978-79, cons., 1980—; ret., 1979; adviser U.S. del. UN Gen. Assembly, 1946-50, 53, 55, 57-59, 64-65. Recipient 7th ann. Fed. Woman's award, 1967. Mem. Am. Fgn. Service Assn., Phi Beta Kappa. Home: 4848 Reservoir Rd NW Washington DC 20007-1561 Office: Dept State Washington DC 20007

BROWN, ELLEN HYNES, nursing administrator; b. Boston, Aug. 7, 1956; d. Patrick Joseph and Helen Elizabeth (Hoosen) Hynes; m. Donald E. Brown, May 30, 1992. BSN with honors, Northeastern U., 1981; MS in Primary Care Nursing, Simmons Coll., 1996. RN, Mass., cert. BLS, BLS instr., ACLS. Co-op gen. med. unit Carney Hosp., Dorchester, Mass., 1977; co-op cardiac stepdown unit Mt. Auburn Hosp., Cambridge, Mass., 1978-81; co-op health clinic John Hancock Ins. Co., Boston, 1981; staff nurse, gen. surg. unit Mass. Gen. Hosp., Boston, 1981-82; staff nurse, cardiac stepdown unit Mercy Hosp., New Orleans, 1982, Community Hosp. of S. Broward, Hallendale, Fla., 1983; staff nurse, SICU North Broward Med. Ctr., Pompano Beach, Fla., 1983-84; staff nurse, MICU/CCU Mass. Gen. Hosp., Boston, 1984-87, clin. supr. med. and emergency nursing, 1987—; occupational health nurse practitioner Children's Hosp. Med. Ctr., Boston, 1996—; instr. BLS, Mass. Gen. Hosp., Boston, 1991-93. Mem. Sigma Theta Tau. Roman Catholic. Home: 250 Court St Plymouth MA 02360-4038 Office: Mass Gen Hosp Fruit St Boston MA 02114

BROWN, ELLEN JOSEPHINE, public relations executive, fundraiser; b. San Angelo, Tex., Nov. 29, 1941; d. Loyd Miller and Sue Frances (Gilliam) Herring; m. Charles Stephen Brown, Nov. 21, 1962; 1 child, Charles Stephen Brown II. BS in Journalism, North Tex. State U., Denton, 1964. Asst. woman's editor Fort Worth (Tex.) Press, 1964-66; woman's editor, reporter Standard-Times, San Angelo, Tex., 1966-72; publs. dir., regional planner Concho Valley Coun. of Govts., San Angelo, Tex., 1972-81; from public relations coord. to dir. public relations West Tex. Rehab. Ctr., San Angelo, 1982—; mem. stewardship com. 1st Presbyn. Ch., San Angelo, Tex., 1995—. Mem. adv. coun. United Blood Svcs., San Angelo, Tex., 1990 , Mediation Ctr. of San Angelo, 1989—; chmn. adv. com. BBB, 1995-96. Recipient (5) Writing awards Tex. Associated Press Mng. Editors, Award Tex. Mental Health/Mental Retardation, 1967, Disting. Citizen award Mayor's Com. on Persons with Disabilities, 1983. Mem. Nat. Soc. Fund Raising Execs. Presbyterian. Home: 4705 Timber Ridge San Angelo TX 76904 Office: West Tex Rehab Ctr 3001 S Jackson San Angelo TX 76904

BROWN, GAY WEST, school psychologist; b. L.A., Nov. 20, 1953; d. James Dale and Ola Maye (Daniels) West; m. Lorenzo Hubbard, Nov. 26, 1977 (dec. Feb. 1990); 1 child, Loren Rochelle; m. Fred Lyndle Brown, Jr., Dec. 28, 1992. BA, Calif. State U., Dominguez Hills, 1975; MS, U. So. Calif., 1976; PhD, UCLA, 1991. Lic. ednl. psychologist; cert. sch. psychologist. Student counselor Dignity Ctr. for Drug Abuse, L.A., 1974-76; community health worker Am. Indian Free Clinic, Compton, Calif., 1974-76; student psychologist Martin Luther King Hosp., L.A., 1976-77; counselor aide Washington High Sch., L.A., 1974-77; vocat. counselor Skill Ctr., L.A., 1977-78; sch. psychologist L.A. Unified Sch. Dist., 1978—, tchr., advisor, 1988-90; psychol. asst. Verdugo Hills (Calif.) Mental Health, 1984-85; counselor, coord. Crenshaw High Sch., L.A., 1985-87; part-time instr. Calif. State U., Dominguez Hills, 1996—; asst. behavior sci. cons. Coalition Mental Profls., L.A., 1992-93; psychol. asst. Martin Luther King Hosp., L.A., 1992-93; part-time prof. Calif. State U., L.A., 1994-95. Mem. APA, Nat. Assn. Sch. Psychologists, Calif. Assn. Sch. Psychologists, L.A. Assn. Sch. Psychologists, Assn. Black Psychologists (sec. 1992-93, historian 1995-96), Pan African Scholars Assn., United Tchrs. L.A., Delta Sigma Theta. Democrat. United Methodist. Office: Sch Mental Health Clinic 439 W 97th St Los Angeles CA 90003-3968

BROWN, GERALDINE, nurse, freelance writer; b. Clemson, S.C.; d. Isaac and Gladys (Patterson) B. AS in Nursing, U. D.C., Washington, 1973; real estate cert., Long and Foster Inst., College Park, Md., 1984; cert. in TV broadcasting, Columbia Sch., Bailey's Crossroads, Va., 1987; BS in Nursing, Bowie State U., 1989, MA in Communications, 1991; PhD, Howard U., 1994. RN, D.C., FCC Third Class License. Supr. staff nurse Walter Reed Hosp., Washington, 1970-76; supr. clin. nurse Dept. Human Svcs., Washington, 1976-78, community health nurse, 1978-84; nursing instr. Phillips Bus. Sch., Alexandria, Va., 1984-85; pvt. nurse Washington, 1973—; faculty Howard U. Coll. Nursing, 1994—; dir. pub. affairs Bible Way Chs. Worldwide, Inc., Washington, 1978-91; soc. columnist As It Happens, Charlotte (N.C.) Post, 1964-66; soc. editor Washington Cafe Soc. mag, 1971; contbr. feature stories Capital Spotlight newspaper, 1978—; mem. faculty Coll. Nursing, Howard U., 1994—. Asst. organizer DC Mayor's United Nations Day, 1980; vol. Met. Boys and Girls Clubs, Washington, 1980—; vol. Nursing Instr., The Washington Saturday Coll., 1982-84; Co. ARC, 1973—, Big Sisters of the Washington Met. Area, 1988—. Recipient certs. of excellence Govt. of D.C., 1978-84; cert. of appreciation Mayor of D.C., 1980, meritorious pub. svc. award, 1980; svc. trophy Washington Saturday Coll., 1984. Mem. ANA, NAACP, Nat. Coun. Negro Women, Smithsonian Inst. (assoc.), Nat. Black Nurses Assn., Washington Urban League, Chi Eta Phi, Sigma Theta Tau. Democrat.

BROWN, GERRI ANN, physical therapist; b. N.Y.C., May 1, 1948; d. S. Stanley and Corinne (Carlin) Schkurman; m. Michael Edward Brown, Oct. 2, 1971. BS in Phys. Therapy, Ithaca Coll., 1969. Registered phys. therapist, Colo., N.Y. Lectr. U. Colo. Med. Sch., Denver, 1970-81; dir. phys. therapy and team facilitator Wheatridge (Colo.) Regional Ctr., 1969-81; phys. therapist Ptnrs. Home Health Care, Lakewood, Colo., 1982-83, Mt. Evans Home Health Care, Evergreen, Colo., 1983-88, Western Home Health, Arvada, Colo., 1988-93, Eccher Home Care, Lakewood, 1993—; Luth. Med. Ctr., Home Health Svcs., Wheatridge, Colo., 1995—; lectr. U. Colo., Denver, 1970-81, U. No. Colo., Greeley, 1977-81; tchr., cons. Eccher Home Care, Lakewood, 1993—, Western Home Health Care, Arvada, 1988-93, Mt. Evans Health Care, 1983-88; chairperson task force State of Colo., Denver, 1972-73. Mem. Citizens for Action, Idledale, Colo., 1975-76. Mem. Am. Phys. Therapy Assn. (sect. on geriatrics and home health care), Hiwan Golf Club. Home: PO Box 88 Idledale CO 80453

BROWN, GLENDA ANN WALTERS, ballet director; b. Buna, Tex., July 22, 1937; d. Jesse Olaf and Kathryn Jeanette (Rogers) Walters; m. David Dann Brown, Dec. 13, 1958 (div. Feb. 1994); children: Kathryn Jean, Vanessa Lea. Grad. high sch., Beaumont, Tex. Asst. tchr. Widman Sch., Beaumont, 1952-55; owner, tchr. Walters Sch. of Dance, Jasper, Tex., 1955-59; assoc. tchr. Emmamae Horn Sch., Houston, 1964-81; owner, tchr. Allegro Acad., Houston, 1981—; owner, dir. Allegro Ballet, Houston, 1974-81, artistic dir., 1981—; dir. Nat. Choreography Conf., 1987—. Mem. dance panel Cultural Arts Council, Houston, 1979, dance panel Tex. Commn. on the Arts, 1988-90; sec. Riedel Estates Civic Club, Houston, 1975-78; Rep. poll worker, Houston, 1970-81. Mem. Dance Masters Am. (exam. chmn. chpt. 3 1980-86), Southwestern Regional Ballet Assn. (exec. v.p. 1981—), Dance Am., Nat. Assn. Regional Ballet (bd. dirs. 1985-88), Regional Dance Am. (nat. bd. dirs., v.p. 1988-95, pres. 1995—). Methodist. Avocations: camping, singing, golf, travel. Office: Allegro Ballet and Dance Acad 1570 S Dairy Ashford St Ste 200 Houston TX 77077-3862

BROWN, GLORIA VASQUEZ, banker; b. Alice, Tex., Aug. 7, 1945; d. Mauro and Aurora (Canales) Vasquez; m. Larry R. Brown, July 5, 1986. BA in Math., Tex. Woman's U., 1967; postgrad., U. Tex., San Antonio, 1979. Tchr. math. Corpus Christi (Tex.) Ind. Sch. Dist., 1967-69, Columbus (Ohio) Ind. Sch. Dist., 1969-70; with Urban Mass Transp., Washington, 1971-77; owner/operator Derma Clinic, San Antonio, 1977-79; field svcs. officer Neighborhood Reinvestment Co., Dallas, 1979-89, spl. projects officer, 1989-91; cmty. affairs officer Fed. Res. Bank of Dallas, 1991—; lectr. in field; instr. So. Meth. U./Southwestern Grad. Sch. Banking. Creator: Breaking Ground, 1995 (Merit award 1995); creator/editor Banking and Cmty. Perspectives, 1992. Bd. dirs. Arts Dist. Friends, Dallas, 1991-94; mem. Region VI adv. coun. U.S. SBA, Dallas, 1992—; mem. program com. Dallas Nonprofit Capacity Bldg. Program, 1994-96; vice chair IMAGE de Dallas, 1993-94; mem. Hispanic 50, Dallas Friday Group. Recipient Women Making a Difference award Minority Bus. News, Dallas, 1995, Key to the City, City Coun. of Lafayette, La., 1980's; Leadership Tex. Found. for Women's Resources, Austin, 1996. Mem. Greater Dallas C. of C. (women's bus. issues adv. coun. 1994—), Tex. Woman's U. Alumnae Assn., Hispanic Bankers Assn. Roman Catholic. Home: 1012 Plantation Dr DeSoto TX 75115 Office: Federal Reserve Bank Dallas 2200 N Pearl Dallas TX 75201

BROWN, HELEN GURLEY, editor, writer; b. Green Forest, Ark., Feb. 18, 1922; d. Ira M. and Cleo (Sisco) Gurley; m. David Brown, Sept. 25, 1959. Student, Tex. State Coll. for Women, 1939-41, Woodbury Coll., 1942; LLD, Woodbury U., 1987; DLitt, L.I. U., 1993. Exec. sec. Music Corp. Am., 1942-45, William Morris Agy., 1945-47; copywriter Foote, Cone & Belding (advt. agy.), Los Angeles, 1948-58; advt. writer, account exec. Kenyon & Eckhardt (advt. agy.), Hollywood, Calif., 1958-62; editor-in-chief Cosmopolitan mag., 1965—; editorial dir. Cosmopolitan internat. edits., 1972—. Author: Sex and the Single Girl, 1962, Sex and the Office, 1965, Outrageous Opinions, 1967, Helen Gurley Brown's Single Girl's Cook Book, 1969, Sex and the New Single Girl, 1970, Having It All, 1982, The Late Show, 1993. Named 1 of 25 most influential women in U.S., World Almanac, 1976-81; recipient Francis Holmes Achievement award for outstanding work in advt., 1956-59, Disting. Achievement award U. So. Calif. Sch. Journalism, 1971, Spl. award for editl. leadership Am. Newspaper Woman's Club, Washington, 1972, Disting. Achievement award in journalism Stanford U., 1977, Matrix award in matg. category N.Y. Women in Comm., 1985, Henry Johnson Fisher award Mag. Pubs. of Am., 1995; Helen Gurley Brown Rsch. Professorship established in her name Northwestern U. Medill Sch. Journalism, 1986; inducted into Pubs.' Hall of Fame, 1988. Mem. Authors League Am., Am. Soc. Mag. Editors (Hall of Fame award 1996), AFTRA, Eta Upsilon Gamma. Office: Cosmopolitan The Hearst Corp 224 W 57th St New York NY 10019-3212

BROWN, HELEN SAUER, fund raising executive; b. Findlay, Ohio, Feb. 7, 1923; d. Joseph Thomas and Mary Magdalene (Sweeney) Sauer; m. Thomas Francis Brown, June 10, 1944; children: Mary Helen Anne, Thomas F., Joachim J., Mary Christine, Mary Kathleen, Mary Elizabeth, Timothy J., Martin J., John Fitzgerald Kennedy. BA magna cum laude, Mundelein Coll. for Women, 1944, MA summa cum laude, 1970. V.p. T.F. Brown Co., Chgo., 1962 84; tchr. Nazareth Acad., La Grange Park, Ill., 1968-72; pastoral min. Ill., 1970—; dir. religious edn. Divine Savior Parish, Downers Grove, Ill., 1972-76; pres. Herself's Doings Ltd., La Grange, Ill., 1972—; retail store owner/mgr. Nettle Creek Shop, La Grange, 1976-85; dir. resource devel. Cmty. Family Svc. & Mental Health Assn., Lyons and Riverside Townships, Ill., 1986—; cons., spkr. in field; pres. Religious Edn. Svcs., La Grange, 1972-86; adv. coun. U. Notre Dame Sch. of Theology, 1970-72. Author: Community and Social Justice, 1974. Trustee Mundelein Coll., Chgo., 1970-90; organizer ERA, Springfield, Ill., 1968—; peace activist, Washington, 1966—; commr. Lyons (Ill.) Mental Health Commn., 1978-80; commr. econ. devel. Village of La Grange, 1983-93; commr. program rev. Pvt. Industry Coun., Cook County, Ill., 1984-94; dir. Ill. Retirement Home Assn., Hinsdale, 1993—. Cardinal Meyer scholar Archdiocese of Chgo., 1970. Mem. NAACP, AAUW, LWV, Nat. Soc. Fund Raising Execs. (cert. 1991), La Grange West Suburban C. of C. (chair pres.'s coun. 1985-96, pres. 1986-87, Woman of Yr. 1983), Women for Peace, Amnesty Internat., Bus. and Profl. Women/USA (Outstanding Working Woman Ill. chpt. 1993), Phoenix Soc., Women's Bd., Clergy and Laity Concerned for Justice and Peace, Gannon Ctr. Women and Leadership, Mundelein Coll. Alumnae, La Grange Cath. Women's Club, Kappa Gamma Pi. Democrat. Roman Catholic. Home: 1571 W Ogden Ave # 2626 La Grange Park IL 60526

BROWN, HERMIONE KOPP, lawyer; b. Syracuse, N.Y., Sept. 29, 1915; d. Harold H. and Frances (Burger) Kopp; m. Louis M. Brown, May 30, 1937; children—Lawrence D., Marshall J., Harold A. BA, Wellesley Coll., 1934; LLB, U. So. Calif., 1947. Bar: Calif. 1947. Story analyst 20th Century-Fox Film Corp., 1935-42; assoc. Gang, Kopp & Tyre, Los Angeles, 1947-52; ptnr. to sr. ptnr. Gang, Tyre, Ramer & Brown, Inc., Los Angeles, 1952—; lectr. copyright and entertainment law U. So. Calif. Law Sch., 1974-77. Contbr. to profl. publs. Fellow Am. Coll. Trust and Estate Coun.; mem. Calif. Bar Assn. (chair probate law cons. group nd. legal specialization 1977-82, trust and probate law sect., exec. com. 1983-86, advisor 1986-89), L.A. Copyright Soc. (pres. 1979-80), Order of Coif, Phi Beta Kappa. Office: Gang Tyre Ramer & Brown Inc 132 S Rodeo Dr Beverly Hills CA 90212

BROWN, JAN WHITNEY, small business owner; b. Roundup, Mont., Mar. 16, 1942; d. John Estes and Janet Lillian (Snyder) Dahl; m. William A. Brown III; children: Erik Lane, Kimberly Elise. BA in Sociology, Social Work, Carroll Coll., 1976. Sec. 1st Nat. Bank, Bozeman, Mont., 1962, Office of Gov., Helena, Mont., 1963-69; pub. info. coord. Helena Model City Program, 1969-73; pub. relations and assn. mgmt. Mont. Bar Assn., Helena, 1973-76, Mont. Assn. Life Underwriters, Helena, 1973-76; legis. liaison Mont. Religious Legis. Coalition, Helena, 1975-81; exec. dir. Helena Food Share Inc., 1987; co-owner Jorud Photo and Gifts, Helena, 1971—; legislator Mont. St. Legislature, Helena, 1983-92; mem. legis. coun. Helena, 1989-92; bd. dirs. Helena Food Share, Inc., Bus. Improvement Dist.; chmn. state adminstrn. com. Mont. Ho. of Reps., 1989-92. Chmn. Mont. Medal of Valor Com., Helena, 1986-93; pres. United Way, Helena, 1982; bd. dirs. Mont. Area Health Edn. Ctr., Bozeman, 1988-93, Mont. Hunger Coalition, Helena, 1988-89, St. Peter's Comty. Hosp. Found. Bd., 1994—; Helena City Commr., 1993; vice chair Helena Citizens Coun., 1994—. Recipient Disting. Svc. award Mental Health Assn., 1976, Disting. Community Svc. award Jaycees, 1982, Ann. Appreciation award Child Support Enforcement, 1985, United Way award, 1988, Community Svc. award VFW, 1988. Mem. Helena Unlimited. Democrat. Episcopalian. Office: Jorud Photo and Gifts 327 N Last Chance Gulch St Helena MT 59601-5013

BROWN, JANE BOWDEN, artist, educator; b. Jersey City, N.J., Mar. 14, 1922; d. John Stanley and Caroline (White) Bowden; m. Wendell Stimpson Brown Jr., June 20, 1942 (dec. Aug. 1992); children: Wendell S., Caroline E. Calbos, Cynthia J., Barbara J. Valentine, Jeffrey L. BS in Phys. Edn., Doug Lass Coll., 1942; studies with Betty Abel, Douglass Coll., Little Silver, N.J., 1942; studies with John Terelak, Marblehead, Mass., 1968-70; studies with Amelia James, Atlanta, 1975-82, studies with Ouida Canaday, 1982-94, studies with Jospeh Perrin, 1984. Cert. tchr. phys. edn. and sci. K-12. Substitute tchr. Elem. Sch., Little Silver, N.J., 1965-68, Title I tchr., 1967-68; substitute tchr. Marblehead and Lynn, Mass., 1968-70, DeKalb County, Decatur, Ga., 1970—; publicity chmn., sec., v.p. DeKalb County Art Ctr., Atlanta, 1976—; sec., v.p. Artists Atelier of Atlanta, 1993—. exhibitor acrylics, watercolors, collages and drawings; contbr. articles to profl. jours. Mem., v.p., sec., bd. dirs. PTA, Little Silver, 1958-70; bd. AAUW, Little Silver, 1960-70. Mem. Callanwolde Guild (bd. dirs. 1976—), Atlanta Artists Club (Merit award 1995). Republican. Presbyterian. Home: 2110 Gunstock Dr Stone Mountain GA 30087 Art Studio: Artists Atelier Atlanta 857 Collier Rd NW Atlanta GA 30318

BROWN, JANET K., lawyer; b. Mpls., Sept. 15, 1950; d. Vernon K. and Alfie I. (Sletten) Whitaker; m. Richard E. Brown, July 4, 1973 (dec. Sept. 1992); m. Jonnie E. Hayes, Sept. 24, 1994. BA, Washington U., 1972; JD, St. Louis U. Bar: Mo. 1976. Pvt. practice, 1976; prosecuting atty. Wayne County, Greenville, Mo., 1977-78. Mem. Wayne County Bd. for the Sheltered Workshop, Greenville, 1975—, Sears Cmty. Liason Coun., Popular Bluff, Mo., 1985—. Home: PO Box 1164 Poplar Bluff MO 63902

BROWN, JANET MCNALLEY, retirement plan consultant; b. Denver, May 16, 1960; d. Michael Collins and Sharon Bess (Cook) McNalley. Student, Mt. Holyoke Coll., 1978-79; BA in Econs. with honors, Mills Coll., Oakland, Calif., 1982; MA in Social Scis., U. Calif., Irvine, 1987, elem. teaching credential, 1988. Teaching asst. U. Calif., Irvine, 1986-88; employee benefits adminstr. Western Co. N.Am., Ft. Worth, 1988-89; trust officer Ameritrust Tex. N.A., Ft. Worth, 1989-90; thrift and profit sharing analyst Burlington No. R.R., Ft. Worth, 1990-93; assoc. human resources group Coopers & Lybrand, Dallas, 1993-94; pension coord. Bell Helicopter Textron, Inc., Ft. Worth, 1994-95; adminstr., cons. Rogers & Assocs., Ft. Worth, 1995—. Dem. del., Ft. Worth, 1990; mem. Liberty Coalition, Bluebonnet Pl. Neighborhood Assn. (newsletter editor); neighborhood crime prevention coord. Citizens on Patrol. Mem. AAUW (membership v.p. 1990-92, charter Eleanor Roosevelt Found. 1990-92), Am. Soc. pension Actuaries (qualified pension adminstr., cert. pension cons.). Home: 3408 Cockrell Ave Fort Worth TX 76109-3003 Office: Rogers & Assocs 424 S Summit Ave Fort Worth TX 76104

BROWN, JANICE ANNE, sales director; b. Ponca City, Okla., Nov. 13, 1942; d. Rexford S. and Helen L. (Stickel) B.; m. Charles E. Carey, June 7, 1966 (div. 1978); 1 child, Kevin Scott Carey. Student, U. Sys. Casino employee Carson Nugget, Carson City, Nev., 1968-82; owner, operator Restaurant, Anchorage, 1974-76, Bookkeeping Tax Co., Carson City, 1982-88; sr. sales dir. Mary Kay Cosmetics, Las Vegas, 1988—. Mem. bd. dirs. Carson City Little League, 1978-84, treas., bd. dirs. Carson City Dem. Cen. Com., 1982-94, mem. Dem. State Cen. Com., 1986—, Common Cause, Carson City, 1988-94. Mem. Womens Polit. Cacus, Carson City Dem. Womens Club (pres. 1986-89), Dem. State Ctrl. Com. Roman Catholic. Home and Office: PO Box 70208 Las Vegas NV 89170-0208

BROWN, JANIECE ALFREIDA, pilot; b. Ellensburg, Wash., May 23, 1956; d. Don Elmer and LaRhee Deloris (Montgomery) Lewis; m. David E. Brown, Oct. 10, 1993. AA, Big Bend Community Coll., Moses Lake, Wash., 1980-82; BS, Cen. Wash. U., 1982-84. Pilot AAR Western Skyways, Troutdale, Oreg., 1984-87; airline capt. N.P.A., Inc., Pasco, Wash., 1987-89; flight engr. airline pilot Alaska Airlines, Seattle, 1989—, 1st officer Boeing 727 and MD-80; bus. mgr. David Brown & Assocs., 1994—. Lobbyist Save Our Watershed, Roslyn, Wash., 1978-80. Recipient Scholastic award CleElum (Wash.) High Sch., 1974. Mem. Airline Pilot Assn. (mem. dangerous goods com.), Alpha Eta Rho (pres. Ctrl. Wash. U. chpt. 1983-84). Home: 20912 NE Interlachen Ln Troutdale OR 97060-8731 Office: Alaska Airlines PO Box 61900 Seattle WA 98178

BROWN, JEANETTE GRASSELLI, university official; b. Cleve., Aug. 4, 1928; d. Nicholas W. and Veronica (Varga) Gecsy; m. Glenn R. Brown, Aug. 1, 1987. BS summa cum laude, Ohio U., 1950, DSc (hon.), 1978; MS, Western Res. U., 1958, DSc (hon.), 1995; DSc (hon.), Clarkson U., 1986; D Engring. (hon.), Mich. Tech. U., 1989; DSc (hon.), Wilson Coll., 1994, Notre Dame Coll., 1995, Kenyon Coll., 1995. Project leader, assoc. Infrared Spectroscopist, Cleve., 1950-78; mgr. analytical sci. lab. Standard Oil (name changed to BP Am., Inc. 1985), Cleve., 1978-83, dir. technol. support dept., 1983-85, dir. corp. rsch. and analytical scis., 1985-88; disting. vis. prof., dir. rsch. enhancement Ohio U., Athens, 1989-95; bd. dirs. B.F. Goodrich Co., AGA Gas, Inc., USX Corp., BDM Internat., Inc., McDonald & Co. Investments, Diatrac Holdings, Inc.; mem. bd. on chem. sci. and tech. NRC, 1986-91; chmn. U.S. Nat. Com. to Internat. Union of Pure and Applied Chemistry, 1992-94, mem. joint high level adv. panel U.S.-Japan Sci. and Tech., 1994—, Ohio Bd. Regents, 1995—. Author, editor 8 books; editor: Vibrational Spectroscopy; contbr. numerous articles on molecular spectroscopy to profl. jours.; patentee naphthalene extraction process. Bd. dirs. N.E. Ohio Sci. and Engring. Fair, Cleve., 1977—; trustee Holden Arboretum, Cleve., 1988—, Edison Biotech Ctr., Cleve., 1988-95, Cleve. Playhouse, 1990-96, Garden Ctr. Greater Cleve., 1990-93, Mus. Arts Assn., 1991—, Gt. Lakes Sci. Ctr., 1991—, Rainbow Babies and Children's Hosp., 1992-95, Nat. Inventors' Hall of Fame, 1993—; trustee Ohio U., 1985-94, chmn. 1991-92; chair Cleve. Scholarship Programs, 1995—. Recipient Disting. Svc. award Cleve. Tech. Soc. Coun., 1985; named Woman of Yr. YWCA, 1980; named to Ohio Women's Hall of Fame State of Ohio, 1989, Ohio Sci. & Tech. Hall of Fame, 1991. Mem. Am. Chem. Soc. (chair analytical divsn. 1990-91, Garvan medal 1986, Analytical Chem. award 1993), Soc. for Applied Spectroscopy (pres. 1970, Disting. Svc. award 1983), Coblentz Soc. (bd. govs. 1968-71, William Wright award 1980), Royal Soc. Chemistry (Theophilus Redwood lectr. 1994), Phi Beta Kappa, Iota Sigma Pi (pres. fluorine chpt. 1957-60, nat. hon. mem. 1987). Republican. Roman Catholic. Home: 150 Greentree Rd Chagrin Falls OH 44022-2424

BROWN, JOAN HALL, elementary school educator; b. Montgomery, Ala., Sept. 12; d. Leo Nathaniel and Bertha (Glaze) Hall; m. Tyrone Brown, Aug. 25, 1984. BS in Elem. Edn. cum laude, Ala. State U.; MEd cum laude, Auburn U., Montgomery, 1989. Cert. tchr., Ala. Tchr. Resurrection Sch., Montgomery, 1985-89, St. John the Bapt. Cath. Sch., Montgomery, 1989-91; tchr., former asst. prin. St. John Resurrection Cath. Sch., Montgomery, 1991-94; tchr. Highland Gardens Elem. Sch., Montgomery, 1994—; mem. sch. bd. Resurrection Sch., 1987-88, advisor, editor sch. newspaper; textbook com. Mobile Diocese, Montgomery, 1985-87, mem. English proficiency com., 1991-92; coord. State Spelling Bees, 1989, St. John the Bapt. Cath. Sch., 1990-91, St. John Resurrection Cath. Sch., 1991-94, textbook com. 1993-94; fin. com. Highland Gardens Sch., v.p. programs. Mem. Resurrection Cath. Ch.; mem. Montgomery County PTA. Grantee Arts Coun. Montgomery, 1991, 93, 94. Mem. NEA, Ala. Edn. Assn., Capitol Area Reading Educator, Nat. Honor Soc., Deka Philos. Svc. Orgn. (v.p. 1985—), Internat. Reading Assn., Kappa Delta Pi. Democrat. Roman Catholic. Home: 705 N Pass Rd Montgomery AL 36110-2906

BROWN, JOAN MYERS, performing company executive. Artistic dir. Phila. Dance Co. (Philadanco). Office: Philadanco Phila Dance Co 9 N Philadanco Way Philadelphia PA 19104-2210*

BROWN, JOANNE, financial analyst; b. Aiken, S.C., Dec. 17, 1954; d. Henry and Polly A. (Douse) B.; m. Jesse Hughes, Jr.; children: Ivana Hughes, Desmond Hughes. AA in Acctg., Durham Bus. Coll., 1973; BA in Acctg., Benedict Coll., 1978. Acct., mgr. Hughes Bus. Svcs., Augusta, Ga.; fin. analyst Westinghouse SRS, Aiken, S.C., 1989—.

BROWN, JOBETH GOODE, food products executive, lawyer; b. Oakdale, La., Sept. 15, 1950; d. Samuel C. Goode and Elizabeth E. (Twiner) Baker; m. H. William Brown, Aug. 4, 1973; 1 child, Kevin William. BA, Newcomb Coll. Tulane U., 1972; JD, Wash. U., 1979. Assoc. Coburn, Croft & Putzell, St. Louis, 1979-80; staff atty. Anheuser-Busch Cos. Inc., St. Louis, 1980-81, exec. asst. to v.p. sec., 1982-83, asst. sec., 1983-89, sec., v.p., 1989—. Trustee Anheuser-Busch Found., St. Louis, 1989—, Forsyth Sch., St. Louis, 1991; mem. adv. bd. Mo. Found. Women's Resources, St. Louis, 1990—; dir. Girl Scouts USA Coun., Greater St. Louis, 1991—. Mem. ABA, Mo. Bar Assn., Bar Assn. Met. St. Louis, Am. Soc. Corp. Secs. (pres. 1992), Algonquin Golf Club, Order of Coif. Republican. Presbyterian. Office: Anheuser-Busch Cos Inc 1 Busch Pl Saint Louis MO 63118-1849

BROWN, JOYCE LAYNA, substance abuse professional, consultant; b. Balt., Apr. 19, 1955; d. Cecil Everett and Bessie Melle (Ward) Keel. BS, U.

Md. Baltimore County, Balt., 1978. Cert. addictions counselor, Md. Clin. dir. First Step Inc. Youth Svc. Bur., Balt., 1979-88; cons., instr. State of Md. Drug Abuse Adminstrn., Balt., 1983-88, 96—; dir. project Raising Ambitions Instilling Self-Esteem Fund Ednl. Excellence, Balt., 1988-90; substance abuse coord. Howard County Govt., Ellicott City, Md., 1990—; exec. sec. Alcohol & Drug Abuse adv. bd., Howard County, 1990—; founder, chair Substance Abuse Partnership Forum, Howard County, 1992—; news commentator Cable 15, 1994—. Mem. Women's Leadership Cir., Howard County, 1996—, Criminal Justice/Treatment Coalition, Howard County, 1995; mem. Child Protection com., Howard County, 1994—, Interagy. Com. Sr. Citizens, Howard County, 1996; Md. state rep. Com. Anti Drug Coalitions Am., 1995—; bd. dirs. Md. State One Church/One Addict, 1996—; bd. dirs. Howard County Hwy. Safety ADv. Coun., 1991—. Mem. AAUW, MADD, Nat. Assn. Prevention Profls. & Advocates. Office: Howard County Govt 3430 Courthouse Dr Ellicott City MD 21043

BROWN, JULIE M., state legislator; b. Worcester, Mass., Feb. 20, 1935; divorced; 4 children. Student, Worcester State Tchrs. Coll. Mem. N.H. Ho. of Reps.; mem. children, youth and juvenile justice com. 1st woman chairperson Rochester (N.H.) Rep. City Com., 1974-76, vice chairwoman, 1976-78; ward 2 selectman Rochester, 1986-92; mem. Rochester Planning Bd., 1985-89; bd. dirs. Rochester Red Cross, 1985-90, Strafford County Cmty. Action Program, 1983-90, chmn. bd., 1991—; crusade chair Am. Cancer Soc., 1976, bus. chair, 1977, profl. chair, 1978; dir 1st Ch. Congl. Youth Group, 1971-75. Recipient N.H. Voice for Children award, 1996. Home and Office: 414 Lilac City E Rochester NH 03867-4552

BROWN, JUNE, journalist; b. Detroit, July 19, 1923; d. Simpson and Vela (Wilkerson) Malone; m. Warren C. Garner, June 28, 1961; 1 dau., Sylvia G. Mustonen. Student, Wayne State U., 1941. Columnist, classified advt. mgr. Mich. Chronicle, Detroit, 1945-74; columnist Detroit News, 1974-87, Mich. Chronicle, 1990-92; CFO Warner Garner Realty, Southfield, Mich., 1992—. Author: June Brown's Guide to Let's Read, 1981. Founder The Let's Read Summer Sch., 1980—. Recipient Best Column awards Detroit Press Club, 1971, 72, Nat. Newspaper Pubs. Assn., 1968, 69, Sch. Bell award Mich. Edn., Assn., 1989. Methodist. Home: PO Box 120 Holly MI 48442-0120

BROWN, JUNE GIBBS, government official; b. Cleve., Oct. 5, 1933; d. Thomas D. and Lorna M. Gibbs; children: Ellen Rosenthal, Linda Windsor, Victor Janezic, Carol Janezic. B.B.A. summa cum laude, Cleve. State U., 1971, M.B.A., 1972; postgrad., Cleve. Marshall Law Sch., 1973-74; J.D., U. Denver, 1978; postgrad. Advanced Mgmt. Program, Harvard U., 1983. Cert. govt. fin. mgr., 1995. Real estate broker, officer mgr. N.E. Realty, Cleve., 1963-68; staff acct. Frank T. Cicirelli, C.P.A., Cleve., 1970-71; asst. to comptroller S.M. Hexter Co., Cleve., 1971; grad. teaching fellow Cleve. State U., 1971-72; dir. internal audit Navy Fin. Ctr., Cleve., 1972-75; dir. fin. systems design Bureau of Land Mgmt., Denver, 1975-76; project mgr. Bureau of Reclamation, 1976-79; insp. gen. Dept. Interior, Washington, 1979-81, NASA, Washington, 1981-85; v.p. fin. and adminstrn. Systems Devel. Corp., a Burroughs Co., 1985-86; assoc. adminstr. for mgmt. NASA, 1986-87; insp. gen. U.S. Dept. Def., Arlington, Va., 1987-90; dep. insp. gen. USN-CINCPACFLT, 1990; insp. gen. USN Pacific Fleet, Pearl Harbor, Hawaii, 1991-93; inspector gen. HHS, Washington, 1993—, HHS, SSA, Washington, 1995-96; bd. dirs. Fed. Law Enforcement Tng. Ctr., 1984-85, Interagy. Auditor Tng. program Dept. Agr. Grad. Sch., 1983-85; chmn. interagy. com. on Info. Resource Mgmt., 1984-85; mem. bd. advisors Nat. Contract Mgmt. Assn., 1987-89; vice chair Pres.'s Coun. on Integrity and Efficiency, mem. audit com., rep. Nat. Intergovtl. Audit Forum; bd. dirs. Inspectors Gen. Auditor Tng. Inst. Mem. bd. advisors Howard U. Sch. Bus., 1987-89. Recipient award Am. Soc. Women Accts., 1969, 70, 71, Raulston award Cleve. State U., 1971, Pres.'s award Cleve. State U., 1971, Outstanding Achievement award U.S. Navy, 1973, Career Svc. award Chgo. region Fed. Exec. Bd., 1974, Outstanding Contbn. to Fin. Mgmt. award Denver region Fed. Exec. Bd., 1977, Donald L. Scantlebury award Joint Fin. Mgmt. Improvement Program, 1980, Outstanding Svc. award Nat. Assn. Minority CPA Firms, 1980, NASA Exceptional Svc. medal, 1985, Outstanding Achievement in Aerospace award, 1987, Woman of Yr. award, YWCA 1988, Bur. Land Mgmt., Dept. Interior, 1975, Disting. Pub. Svc. award Dept. Def., 1989, Meritorious Civilian Svc. award U.S. Navy, 1993, Nat. Capital Area chpt./Govt. Exec. Mag. award for leadership, 1994, George Washington U. Pi Alpha Alpha Pub. Svc. award, 1996; named Disting. Alumni Cleve. State U., 1990. Fellow Nat. Acad. Pub. Adminstrn. (standing panel exec. orgn. and mgmt.); mem. AICPAs, Assn. Govt. Accts. (nat. pres. 1985-86, nat. exec. com. 1977-87, vice chmn. nat. ethics com. 1978-80, 90, chmn. fin. mgmt. standards bd. 1981-82, service award 1973, 76, 93, outstanding achievement award 1979, Robert W. King Meml. award 1988, nat. ethics com. 1990, dir. Hawaii chpt. 1991-93), Hawaii Soc. CPAs (bd. dirs. 1991-93), Am. Accts. Assn., Nat. Contract Mgmt. Assn. (bd. advisors 1988-90), NASA Alumni Assn., Women in Aerospace, ASPA (at-large mem. nat. coun. 1994—, Profl. Responsibility Exemplary Practice award 1990, pres.-nat. capitol area chpt. 1989), Exec. Women in Govt., Beta Alpha Psi. Office: HHS Inspector Gen 330 Independence Ave SW Washington DC 20201-0001

BROWN, KAREN KENNEDY, judge; b. Houston, May 23, 1947. BA, U. Pa., 1970; JD, U. Houston, 1973. Bar: Tex. 1974, U.S. Dist. Ct. (so. and we. dists.) Tex. 1975, U.S. Ct. Appeals (5th cir.) 1974, U.S. Ct. Appeals (11th cir.) 1981, U.S. Supreme Ct., 1980. Law clk. Judge John R. Brown, Houston, 1973-75, Judge Woodrow Seals, Houston, 1975-76; asst. fed. pub. defender So. Dist. Tex., Houston, 1976-82; pvt. practice, Houston, 1982-83; U.S. magistrate U.S. Cts. So. Dist. Tex., Houston, 1984-90; U.S. Bankruptcy Judge, 1990—. Mem. LWV. Episcopalian. Office: US District Court PO Box 61252 515 Rusk Ave Houston TX 77208

BROWN, KAREN RIMA, orchestra manager, Spanish language educator; b. N.Y.C., Apr. 26, 1943; d. Alexander and Leona (Rosenfeld) Jaffe; m. Russell Vernon Brown, Aug. 13, 1966; children: Stephanie Leona and Gregory Russell. BA, Colby Coll., 1965; MA, U. Wis., 1966. Teaching asst. U. Wis., Madison, 1965-66; instr. Spanish U. Wis., Janesville, 1966-68, Baraboo, 1968-70, Eau Claire, 1970-71; instr. Spanish Ohio U., Zanesville, 1978—; mgr. Southeastern Ohio Symphony, New Concord, 1977—; lectr. Spanish Muskingum Coll., New Concord, 1984; mem., music panelist Ohio Arts Coun., Columbus, 1979-83, 90-93; pres. S.E. Ohio Regional Arts Coun., Zanesville, 1978-80. Bd. dirs. Muskingum County Visitors and Conv. Bur., Zanesville, 1987-90, bd. sec., 1989-90; bd. dirs. Assn. of Two Toledos, 1984-87, Ohio Citizens Com. for Arts, Canton, 1979-84; regional coord. Ohio Citizens for the Arts, 1995—. Mem. Am. Assn. Tchrs. Spanish and Portuguese, Ohio Valley Fgn. Lang. Assn., Bus. and Profl. Women, Phi Beta Kappa, Phi Sigma Iota, Sigma Delta Pi (hon.). Democrat. Office: Southeastern Ohio Sym Orch PO Box 42 New Concord OH 43762-0042

BROWN, KATE, state legislator; b. Torrejon de Ardoth, Spain, 1960. BA, U. Colo.; JD, Lewis and Clark Northwestern. Mem. Oreg. Ho. of Reps., 1991—; atty. Democrat. Address: PO Box 82699 Portland OR 97282-0699 Office: Oreg Ho of Reps State Capitol Salem OR 97310*

BROWN, KATHAN, publisher of artists' etchings and woodcuts; b. N.Y.C., Apr. 23, 1935; d. Elwood Stanley and Clarissa Brown; m. Jeryl Louis Parker, 1960 (div. 1965); 1 child, Kevin Powis Parker; m. Thomas Robert Marioni, June 14, 1983. BA, Antioch Coll., 1958; MFA, Calif. Coll. Arts and Crafts, Oakland, 1962, DFA (hon.), 1985; DFA (hon.), San Francisco Art Inst., 1990. Founder, dir. Crown Point Press, San Francisco, 1962—. Author: Ink, Paper, Metal, Wood--Painters and Sculptors at Crown Point Press, 1996. Democrat. Office: Crown Point Press 20 Hawthorne St San Francisco CA 94105

BROWN, KATHIE HAYS, health facility administrator; b. Wheeling, W.Va., June 16, 1953; d. Harold McElroy and Bernice Laura (Brown) Hays; m. Richard Samuel Brown Sr., June 5, 1976; children: Richard Samuel Jr., Kyle Hays. BSN, Alderson-Broaddus Coll., 1975; MS, Nova U., 1989. Lic. social worker, W.Va.; RN, Ohio, W.Va. Nurse Vis. Nurse Assn., Wheeling, 1975-79; nursing coord. Florence Crittenton Svcs., Wheeling, 1979-85, asst. exec. dir., 1985-91; chief exec. officer Wheeling Health Right, Inc., 1992—; mem. com. Gov.'s Task Force on Maternal and Child Health, Charleston, 1986. Author: Implementation of An Independent Living Program for Adolescent Mothers, 1989. Mem. Triadelphia PTA; pres. Park View PTA, 1989-91; chair ch. and soc., bd. dirs. Elm Grove United Meth. Ch., Wheeling, 1989-91, Wheeling Area Homeless Coalition, 1992-94; mem. gov.'s task force Children, Youth and Families, 1991—; adv. com. Wheeling Area Headstart, 1992-95, v.p. Leadership Wheeling Alumni, 1992-94; bd. dirs. St. John's Home for Children, 1994-96, Task Force on Adolescent Pregnancy and Parenting, Charleston, W.Va., 1985-94, Ohio Valley Interfaith Vol. Caregivers, 1995—. Mem. Soroptimists Internat. (rec. sec. Wheeling chpt. 1991-94, v.p. 1994-95, pres. 1995-96), Order of Ea. Star, Daus. of the Nile, Wheeling Kiwanis Morning Club (pres. 1994-95). Democrat. Home: 131 Grant Ave Wheeling WV 26003-5486 Office: Wheeling Health Right Inc 88 14th St Wheeling WV 26003-3406

BROWN, KATHLEEN, state treasurer, lawyer; d. Edmund G. and Bernice Brown; m. George Rice (div. 1979); children: Hilary, Alexandra, Zebediah; m. Van Gordon Sauter, 1980; 2 stepsons. BA in History, Stanford U., 1969; grad., Fordham U. Sch. Law. Mem. L.A. Bd. Edn., 1975-80; with O'Melveny & Myers, N.Y.C., then L.A.; commr. L.A. Bd. Pub. Works, 1987-89; elected Treas. of Calif., 1990-94; sr. v.p. investment mgmt. group Bank of Am., L.A., 1994—. Democrat. Office: Bank of Am 555 S Flower St 50th Fl Los Angeles CA 90071

BROWN, KAY, state legislator; b. Oct. 6, 1948; 3 children. BA in Edn., Dakota Wesleyan U. Ptnr. D.H. Gustafon, Kay Brown Assocs.; developer, cons.; mem. Minn. Ho. of Reps., 1992—. Home: 10714 Timberland Dr Northfield MN 55057 Office: 551 State Office Bldg Saint Paul MN 55155*

BROWN, KAY (MARY KATHRYN BROWN), state official; b. Ft. Worth, Tex., Dec. 19, 1950; d. H.C., Jr. and Dorothy Ruth (Ware) B.; m. William P. Dougherty, Dec. 15, 1978 (div. 1984); m. Mark A. Foster, Aug. 24, 1991; 1 adopted child, Kathryn Yucui. B.A., Baylor U., 1973. Reporter, UPI, Atlanta, 1973-76; reporter, feature writer Anchorage Daily Times (Alaska), 1976-77; reporter, co-owner Alaska Advocate, Anchorage, 1977; aide, researcher Alaska State Legislature, Juneau, 1979-80; dep. dir. div. of oil and gas (formerly div. minerals and energy mgmt.) Alaska Dept. Natural Resources, Anchorage, 1980-82, dir., 1982-86; elected Alaska Ho. of Reps., 1986; del. White House Conf. Libr. and Info. Svcs., 1991. Co-author: Geographic Information Systems: A Guide to the Technology, 1991. Office: House of Representatives State Capitol Juneau AK 99801-1182

BROWN, LILLIE MCFALL, elementary school principal; b. Feb. 29; d. Clayton and Septertee (Dewberry) McFall; m. Charles Brown, Oct. 4, 1958; 1 child, Eric McFall. BA in Home Econ., Sci., Langston Univ., 1956; MA in Spl. Edn., Chgo. Tchrs. Coll., 1964; MA in Adminstrn., Seattle Univ., 1976. Home econ. tchr. Altue (Okla.) Separate Pub. Schs., 1955-56, first grade tchr., 1956-57, fourth grade tchr., 1957-60; middle sch. tchr. Chgo. Pub. Sch.s, 1960-64; spl. edn. primary tchr. Seattle Pub. Schs., 1966-67, spl. edn. intermediate tchr., 1967-68, program coord., 1968-71, elem. asst. prin., 1971-76, elem. prin., 1976—; Mem. Project READ, Seattle, 1968. Contbr. articles to profl. jours. Treas. African Am. Alliance, 1980—; historian Wash. Alliance Black Sch. Educators, 1991—; vol. Olympic Games, Seattle, 1990; participant First African-African Am. Summit, Ibidijan, Cote d'Ivoire, 1991-92; mem. rsch. bd. advisors Am. Biog. Inst., 1995—. Recipient Sears Found. grant., 1967. Mem. NAACP, Nat. Assn. Elem. Sch. Prins., Assn. Wash. Sch. Prins., Elem. Prins. Assn. Seattle Pub. Schs., Prins. Assn. Wash. State, Prin. Assn. Seattle Pub. Schs., Ednl. Leadership, Phi Delta Kappa, Kappa Delta Pi, Delta Sigma Theta. Democrat. Baptist. Home: 2736 34th Ave S Seattle WA 98144-5561

BROWN, LINDA JEAN, nursing administrator; b. Pana, Ill., Mar. 13, 1947; d. William H. and Meribah J. (Wardall) Laughlin; m. Robert W. Brown, Aug. 25, 1968; children: William H., Jeffrey A. RN, Decatur (Ill.) Meml. Hosp. Sch. Nursing, 1969; BS, Millikin U., 1969. RN, Colo.; cert. Profl. Healthcare Quality, Colo. Dir. quality assurance, utilization rev. St. Vincent Meml. Hosp., Taylorville, Ill., 1975-81, Cedar Springs Hosp., Colorado Springs, Colo., 1982-89; dir. quality assurance Ft. Morgan (Colo.) Community Hosp., 1989-90; dir. nursing Bethesda Care Ctr., Paonia, Colo., 1990-91; asst. adminstr. Mountain Crest Hosp., Ft. Collins, Colo., 1991-95; adminstr. First Am. Home Care, Denver, 1995—; PRN cons., Brim & Associates., Portland, Oreg., 1989-90, conf. speaker, 1990; PRN cons. Horizon Mental Health Svcs., Denton, Tex., 1992; cons. Meritcare, Pitts., 1990. Author: (with others) Nurse Clinician Pocket Manual: Nursing Diagnosis, Care Planning and Documentation, 1989. Mem. Colo. Nurse Exec. Assn. Home: 12079 Forest St Denver CO 80241-3241

BROWN, LINDA JOAN, psychotherapist, psychoanalyst; b. Mineola, N.Y., Feb. 18, 1941; d. Charles Harold and Helen (Golbach) B. Student, Smith Coll., Northampton, Mass., 1958-60; BA, Barnard Coll., N.Y.C., 1962; MPS in Art Therapy, Pratt Inst., Bklyn., 1973; MSW, Hunter Coll., N.Y.C., 1976. Cert. social worker, psychoanalyst, N.Y.; lic. clin. social worker, Calif.; diplomate clin. social work Am. Bd. Examiners in Clin. Social Work. Singer, actress Broadway theatres, N.Y.C., 1962-65, pub. rels./community rels. specialist, real estate, publicist/editor, pub., edn. cons., 1965-71; art therapist Bronx (N.Y.) Psychiat. Ctr., 1972-74; clin. social worker North Richmond Community Mental Health Ctr., S.I., N.Y., 1977-79; staff therapist Lincoln Inst. Psychotherapy, N.Y.C., 1978-80; sr. staff therapist Ctr. for Study Anorexia and Bulimia, N.Y.C., 1983-85; staff therapist Inst. Contemporary Psychotherapy, N.Y.C., 1988—; pvt. practice psychotherapy N.Y.C., 1978—; mem. human svc. faculty Tristate Inst. Traditional Chinese Acupuncture, N.Y.C., 1986-89; mem. faculty N.Y. Open Ctr., N.Y.C., 1987—; adj. faculty Health Choices Ctr. for Healing Arts, Princeton, N.J., 1987-90; clin. cons. Personal Performance Cons., EAP, 1988; human resources cons. industry, N.Y.C., 1988—; workshop leader seminars on stress mgmt., assertiveness tng., comm. and counseling skills, intimate relationships skills, creative expression. Mem. NASW.

BROWN, LINDA LOCKETT, nutrition management executive, nutrition consultant; b. Jacksonville, Fla., Jan. 8, 1954; d. Willie James and Katie Lee (Taylor) Lockett; m. Thomas Lee Brown, Dec. 18, 1982; children: Ashanti, William, Timothy. BS in Agr., U. Fla., 1975, M of Agr., 1981. Lic. profl. nutritionist; cert. food svc. dir. III; registered dietitian. Chemist/microbiologist Green Giant Co., Alachua, Fla., 1975-77; lab. technologist II U. Fla., Gainesville, 1977-81, extension agt. I, Ft. Myers, 1981-85, extension agt. II, 1985-87, West Palm Beach, 1987-88; pres. CINET, Inc., 1985—; area supr. Palm Beach County Sch. Food Svc., 1988-90; adj. prof. Palm Beach Community coll., 1990, Fla. C.C., Jacksonville, 1993—; dir. sch. food svc. St. Johns County, 1990—; nutrition cons. Congregate Meals, Ft. Myers, 1984-87, Serenity House, Ft. Myers, 1985-87; cons. Performax, 1989—; vis. prof. U. Fla. Coop. Ext. Svc., Clay County, 1996—; treas. St. Augustine chpt. Internat. Food Svc. Execs. Assn., 1993—; apptd. by gov. Fla. Health and Human Svcs. Bd., elected vice chair, 1993-94, chair, 1994-96. Columnist Palm Beach Post, 1989—; contbr. articles to profl. jours.; host nutrition digest radio show Sta. WZNZ-AM, Jacksonville, Fla., 1996—. Mem. exec. bd. Community Coordinating Coun., Ft. Myers, 1985; Am. Heart Assn., Palm Beach, 1989-90; co-founder Friends of Hearing Impaired Youth, Gainesville, 1976; tutor-coord. Sampson, Gainesville, 1973; mem. Jr. League, Ft. Myers, 1987; mem. Jr. League, Palm Beach, Fla., 1987-90, mem. edn. tng. com., community rsch. com. 1989-90; mem. nutrition com. Am. Heart Assn., Palm Beach, 1989—. State U. System Bd. Regents grantee, 1980. Mem. NAFE, Soc. Nutrition Edn. (legis. network chmn.), Am. Diabetes Assn. (mem. profl. adv. com. Jacksonville affiliate 1996), Am. Dietetic Assn. (network of blacks in nutrition, chair legis. com. 1988-89, chair nominating 1989, sec. 1989-90, state profl. recruitment coord.), Fla. Dietetic Assn. (chair minority issues com., chair membership 1987-88, chair edn. and registration 1988-90, state profl. recruitment coord. rep. Fla. chpt., chair nominating com. 1994—), Palm Beach Dietetic Assn. (community nutrition chair 1988-89, chair legis. com. 1989-90), Caloosa Dietetic Assn. (sec.), Nat. Speakers Assn., Sch. Food Svcs. Assn. (1988—), Nat. Assn. Extension Home Econs. Agts., Internat. Platform Assn., Jacksonville Dietetic Assn., Nutrition Today Soc., Alpha Zeta, Epsilon Sigma Phi. Club: Greater Palm Beaches Bus. and Profl. Women (minority student mentor, role model mentor), Nat. Speakers Assn., N. Fla. Profl. Speakers Assn. Avocations: singing, violin. Office: 2234 George Wythe Rd Orange Park FL 32073-8507

BROWN, LOIS HEFFINGTON, health facility administrator; b. Little Rock, Mar. 28, 1940; d. Carl Otis and Opal (Shock) Heffington; M. Ivy Roy Brown, June 21, 1984; children: Carletta Jo Rice, Roby Lynn Rice, Pherby Allison Graham, Phelan Missy Graham. Student, Guilford Tech. Community Coll., Jamestown, N.C., 1974-75, 77, 80. Cert. hearing aid specialist. Sec. Berger Enterprises, West Memphis, Ark., 1962-65; office mgr. Beltone Hearing Aid Ctr., Greensboro, N.C., 1975-81; owner Hearing Care Ctr., Cullman, Ala., 1982-85, Miracle-Ear Ctr., Cullman, Decatur, Fultondale, Jasper and Birmingham, Ala., 1985-87; pres. L&I Corp., Cullman, Decatur, Fultondale, Jasper and Birmingham, 1987-90, L & I Corp. Miracle Ear Ctr., Cullman, Decatur, Jasper, Ala., 1991-93; owner Conway (Ark.) Hearing Aid Ctr., 1994—, Beltone Hearing Aid Ctr., Conway, 1995-96; distbr. Showcase Distbg. Co., Conway, North Little Rock, Ark. Gov.-appointed Ala. Bd. Hearing, chmn. of the bd., 1989-91. Mem. Nat. Hearing Aid Soc., Ark. Hearing Soc. (sec. 1996—), Ala. Hearing Aid Dealers Assn. (sec. 1984-86, v.p. 1986-88, bd. dirs. 1988-91), Ark. Hearing Aid Dealers Assn., Women of the Moose. Republican. Baptist. Home: 199 Highway 107 Enola AR 72047-8101

BROWN, LORENE B(YRON), library educator, educational administrator; b. Plant City, Fla., Nov. 9, 1933; d. Benjamin and Sallie (Barton) Byron; m. Paul L. Brown, Aug. 1, 1974. B.S., Fort Valley State Coll., 1955; M.S.L.S., Atlanta U., 1956; Ph.D., U. Wis., 1974. Cataloguer N.C. Central U., Durham, 1956-58, Gibbs Jr. Coll., St. Petersburg, Fla., 1958-60, Fort Valley State Coll., Ga., 1960-65, Norfolk State U., Va., 1965-70; assoc. prof., dean Atlanta U., 1970-89, prof., 1989—; dir. Info. Retrieval Workshops, Atlanta, 1976-78; evaluator Coop. Coll. Library Ctr., Atlanta, 1979-82; cons. United Bd. Coll. Devel., Atlanta, 1976-79. Author: Subject Access for African American Material, 1995. Mem. Friends of Library, Atlanta, 1982. Recipient Rachel Schenk award Library Sch. U. Wis., Madison, 1971; So. Fellowship Found. fellow Atlanta, 1972-74. Mem. ALA, Am. Soc. for Info. Sci., Assn. Library and Info. Sci. Edn., Ga. Library Assn., Met Atlanta Library Assn., Beta Phi Mu. Democrat. Baptist. Home: 855 Flamingo Dr SW Atlanta GA 30311-2402 Office: Atlanta U Sch Libr and Info Studies 223 James P Brawley Dr SW Atlanta GA 30314-4358

BROWN, LORRAINE ANN, office manager; b. Providence, Mar. 15, 1947; d. Leonard Francis and Elaine Frances (Pettis) Millen; m. Jeffrey Schofield Brown, May 22, 1976 (div. 1983); 1 child, Kaneeta Sage; m. Dieter Paul Wuennenberg, July 14, 1965; 1 child, Desiree Jacqueline Wuennenberg. Student, Manhattan Sch. Printing, 1972, L.A. Trade Tech. Coll., 1981-83. Communications rep. TransAmerica Occidental, Los Angeles, 1973-77; owner, jewelry designer The Lorraine Brown Co., El Segundo, Calif., 1979-83; mgr. Silk Lingerie Outlet, Sherman Oaks, Calif., 1982-83; office mgr. Am. Silk Label, L.A., 1984; asst. prodn. coordinator Pacific Coast Mills, L.A., 1984-85; asst. designer jr. wear Judy Knapp Inc., L.A., 1986-87; sales exec. Integrated Aquatic Systems, Marina Del Rey, Calif., 1987-88; adminstrv. svcs. coord. GTE Govt. Svcs., El Segundo, Calif., 1988-94; event coord. Jackson Nat. Life Dist., Westwood, 1995-96; office mgr. Ind. Jour. Newspapers, 1996—. Asst. leader Girl Scouts U.S., El Segundo, 1985-87; P.V.P. leader 4-H, 1991-94; vol. Tree Muskateers and Swift Project. Mem. Svcs. Employees Assn. (pres.), Young Exec. Singles, Advanced Degrees, Sierra Singles. Home: 756 Main St El Segundo CA 90245-3051

BROWN, LYNETTE RALYA, journalist, publicist; b. Beloit, Wis., Dec. 15, 1926; d. Lynn Louis and Ethel Clara (Meeker) Ralya; m. Donald Adair Brown, Jr., Dec. 20, 1947; children: Donald Adair III, Alison Laura, Julia Carol. BA in Journalism, Mich. State U., 1948; MA in Journalism, Michigan State U., 1985; MA in Mass Comm., Wayne State U., 1983. Actress, publicist Grand Traverse Playhouse, Traverse City, Mich., 1946 (summer), N.Y. Summer Playhouse, Mackinac Island, Mich., 1947 (summer); writer WILS Radio, Lansing, Mich., 1947-48; writer, performer WJBK Radio, TV, Detroit, 1948-49; editor Denby Ctr. News, Detroit, 1949-51; freelance writer Oakland County, Mich., 1952-78; editor Henry Ford Mus., Dearborn, Mich., 1979-81; writer, reporter Legal Advertiser Newspaper, Detroit, 1983-85; publicist Bloomfield (Mich.) and Birmingham (Mich.) Pub. Librs., 1986-89; freelance writer, publicist Lynette Brown Comm., Birmingham, Mich., 1989—. Columnist: (newspaper) At the Libraries, 1986-89. Probation sponsor Dist. Ct. Mich., 1960-70; publicist Oakland County Vol. Bur., 1979-82; leader sr. high/jr. high youth group Drayton Ave. Presbyn. Ch., Oakland County, 1952-54, 62-66, Pine Hill Congl. Ch., Oakland County, 1968-71, Northbrook Presbyn. Ch., Oakland County, 1976-77; polit. campaign worker Rep. candidates and non-partisan jud. candidates, 1952—; Cub Scout leader Royal Oak Emerson Sch., Oakland County, 1961-64; Girl Scout troop leader Bloomfield Twp. Meadow Lake Sch., Oakland County, 1966-71. Mem. AAUW (chair women's issues, pub. info. dir. 1995—), Oakland County C. of C. (Athena award 1995). Home and Office: 6120 Westmoor Rd Bloomfield Hills MI 48301

BROWN, MARCIA JOAN, author, artist, photographer; b. Rochester, N.Y., July 13, 1918; d. Clarence Edward and Adelaide Elizabeth (Zimber) B. Student, Woodstock Sch. Painting, summers 1938, 39; student painting, New Sch. Social Research, Art Students League; BA, N.Y. State Coll. Tchrs., 1940; student Chinese calligraphy, painting, Zhejiang Acad. Fine Arts, Hangzhou, Peoples Republic China, 1985, 87; studied painting with Judson Smith, Stuart Davis, Yasuo Kuniyoshi, Julian Levi; LHD (hon.), SUNY, Albany, 1996. Tchr. English, dramatics Cornwall (N.Y.) High Sch., 1940-43; library asst. N.Y. Pub. Library, 1943-49; tchr. puppetry extra-mural dept. U. Coll. West Indies, Jamaica, B.W.I., 1953; tchr. workshop on picture book U. Minn.-Split Rock Arts Program, Duluth, 1986, workshop on Chinese brush painting Brush Artists Guild, 1988; sponsor Chinese landscape painting workshops with Zhuo HeJun, 1988-89; sponsored workshops Chinese caligraphy with Wong Dong Ling, 1989, 90, 92; invited speaker exhbn. illustrations, Japan, 1990, 94. Illustrator: The Trail of Courage (Virginia Watson), 1948, The Steadfast Tin Soldier (Hans Christian Andersen), 1953 (Caldecott Honor Book award), Anansi (Philip Sherlock), 1954, The Three Billy Goats Gruff (Asbjornsen and Moe), 1957, Peter Piper's Alphabet, 1959, The Wild Swans (Hans Christian Andersen), 1963, Giselle (Théophile Gautier), 1970, The Snow Queen (Hans Christian Andersen), 1972, Shadow (Blaise Cendrars), 1982 (Caldecott award 1983), How the Ostrich Got His Long Neck (Aardema), 1995, (with others) Sing a Song of Popcorn, 1988, Of Swans, Sugar Plums and Satin Slippers (Violette Verdy); author, illustrator: The Little Carousel, 1946, Stone Soup, 1947 (Caldecott Honor Book award), Henry Fisherman, 1949 (Caldecott Honor Book award), Dick Whittington and His Cat (retold), 1950 (Caldecott Honor Book award), Skipper John's Cook, 1951 (Caldecott Honor Book award), The Flying Carpet (retold), 1956, Felice, 1958, Tamarindo, 1960, Once a Mouse (retold), 1961 (Caldecott award), Backbone of the King, 1966, The Neighbors, 1967, The Bun (retold), 1972, All Butterflies, 1974 (Boston Globe Honor Book, Horn Book), The Blue Jackal (retold), 1977, Walk Through Your Eyes, 1979, (with photographs) Touch Will Tell, 1979, (with photographs) Listen to a Shape, 1979, Lotus Seeds; Children, Pictures and Books, 1985, (with others) From Sea to Shining Sea, 1993; translator. illustrator: Puss in Boots, 1952 (Caldecott Honor Book award), Cinderella (Charles Perrault), 1954 (Caldecott award 1955), How, Hippo!, 1969 (honor book Book World Spring Book Festival); author, photographer: film strip The Crystal Cavern, 1974; woodcut prints exhibited, Bklyn. Mus., Peridot Gallery, Hacker Gallery, Library Congress, Carnegie Inst., Phila. Print Club; Chinese brush painting and calligraphy exhibited at Hammond Mus., North Salem, N.Y., 1988; prints in permanent collection, Library of Congress, N.Y. Pub. Library, pvt. collections; art work in Mazza Gallery Findlay (Ohio) Coll.; traveling exhibition, lectrs. illustration Japan, 1990, 94. Recipient Disting. Svc. to Children's Lit. award, U. So. Miss., 1972, Regina medal Cath. Libr. Assn., 1977, Disting. Alumnus medal SUNY, 1969, Laura Ingalls Wilder award, 1992; U.S. nominee Internat. Hans Andersen award illustration, 1966, 76; career rsch. material in spl. libr. collection, SUNY, Albany, de Grummond Collection, U. So. Miss., Hattiesburg, Kerlan Collection, U. Minn. Fellow Internat. Inst. Arts and Letters (life); mem. Author's Guild, Print Coun. Am., Art Students League, Oriental Brush Artists Guild, Sumi-e Soc. Am, Am. Artists of Chinese Brush Painting.

BROWN, MARGARET DEBEERS, lawyer; b. Washington, Sept. 24, 1943; d. John Sterling and Marianna Hurd (Hill) deBeers; m. Timothy Nils, Aug. 28, 1965; children—Emeline Susan, Eric Franklin. BA magna cum laude, Radcliffe Coll., 1965; postgrad. Harvard U. Law Sch., 1965-67; JD, U. Calif.-Berkeley, 1968. Bar: Calif. 1969, U.S. Ct. Appeals (9th cir.) 1971, U.S. Supreme Ct. 1972, U.S. Ct. Appeals (D.C. cir.) 1986, U.S. Ct. Appeals (2d cir.) 1987. Assoc. White, Hamilton, Wyche, Shell & Pollard, Petersburg, Va., 1968-70, Heller, Ehrman, White & McAuliffe, San Francisco, 1970-73; sole practice, San Francisco, 1973-77; atty. Pacific Telephone (name changed to Pacific Bell 1984), San Francisco, 1977-83, sr. atty., 1983-85; sr. counsel

Pacific Telesis Group, 1985—; speaker McGeorge Law Sch., Sacramento, 1983. Elder Calvary Presbyn. Ch., San Francisco. Mem. Calif. State Bar (mem. com. bar examiners), San Francisco Bar Assn. (chmn. corp. law dept. sect. 1993, judiciary com. 1993—, nominating com. 1993), Phi Beta Kappa. Office: Pacific Telesis Group 140 New Montgomery St Rm 1320 San Francisco CA 94105

BROWN, MARILYNNE JOYCE, emergency nurse; b. Algona, Iowa, Sept. 26, 1932; d. Michael Henry and Enid Hazel (Bonnette) Miller; m. Vaughn Hardgrove Brown; children: Jeffery Von, Steven Michael, Sindy Lynne, Timothy Ralph. Diploma in Nursing, St. Mary's Sch. Nursing, Rochester, Minn., 1953; AA, Grossmont C.C., El Cajon, Calif., 1981; BS in Health Sci. Edn., San Diego State U., 1983. Cert. emergency nurse. Dir. Algona Osteo. Clinic, 1953-55; staff nurse St. Ann's Hosp., Algona, 1955-60; emergency/relief charge nurse El Cajon Valley Hosp., 1960-65; emergency nurse Grossmont Hosp., La Mesa, Calif., 1965-90; ret.; coord. EMT program Grossmont C.C., El Cajon, 1970-83; cons. and lectr. in field. Mem. Emergency Nurses Assn. (life, past sec., v.p., pres.), Beta Sigma Phi. Home: 596 Dichter St El Cajon CA 92019-2572

BROWN, MARTHA S., dean; b. Great Falls, Mont., Aug. 6, 1946; d. Kenneth A. and Helen A. (Archibald) Small; m. James P. Henderson, Feb. 21, 1964 (div. Feb. 1969); children: James P., Christine M.; m. Theron J. Brown, Sept. 15, 1971. AS in Bus., Allan Hancock Coll., 1983, AA in Bus., 1983; BS in Bus. Mgmt., U. Md., Europe, 1988; M Adminstrn. Sci., U. Mont., 1992. Instr. Jr. Collegiate Sch., Santa Maria, Calif., 1983-84; with U.S. Govt. Procurement, Germany, 1987-88; sr. instr. curriculum devel. May Tech. Coll., Great Falls, 1990-92; instr. West Coast U., Vandenberg AFB, Calif., 1992-93; acad. dean Santa Barbara Bus. Coll., Santa Maria, 1993—; curriculum developer SBBC Corp., Santa Barbara, Calif., 1994—. Mem. NAFE. Office: Santa Barbara Bus Coll 303 E Plaza Santa Maria CA 93454

BROWN, MARY, library director. Dir. St. Petersburg (Fla.) Pub. Libr., 1991—. Office: Saint Petersburg Pub Libr 3745 9th Ave N Saint Petersburg FL 33713-6001*

BROWN, MARY BETTIE SMALL, real estate broker; b. Elizabeth City, N.C., Sept. 23, 1930; d. Clyde Vernon and Betty (Stanton) Small; m. Harry B. Brown, Sept. 7, 1985; children: Betty G. Dupuis, Charlie White, Jr., Clyde Small White. Grad., Va. Intermont Coll., 1948; postgrad., U. N.C., Greensboro, 1948-50; student, Harbardger Bus. Coll., 1953; Cert., Grad. Realtors Inst., 1974. Sec. U.S. Govt., Parris Island, S.C., 1953-55; bus. tchr. Charleston (S.C.) Bus. Inst., 1965-72; real estate broker Charleston, 1972-84, Leesburg, Fla., 1985-95; real estate broker Suntree Properties Waterside, Melbourne Beach, Fla., 1995—. Mem. LWV; pres. Ladies Aux. of Fleet Reserve, Melbourne Beach, 1996—. Mem. Nat. Assn. Realtors (cert. residential specialist), State S.C. Assn. Realtors, State Fla. Assn. Realtors, Melbourne Area Assn. Realtors, Order of Ea. Star, Toastmasters Internat. (past pres.). Democrat. Methodist. Home: 135 Heron Dr Melbourne Beach FL 32951 Office: Suntree Properties Waterside 503 Fifth Ave Indialantic FL 32903

BROWN, MARY CARNEY, former state representative; b. Midland, Mich., Aug. 18, 1935; d. Sheldon and Wilma Carney; m. Donald J. Brown; children: Linda, Jeff, Jim. Student, Albion Coll., 1953-55; AB in Recreation, Syracuse U., 1957, MS in Phys. Edn., 1961. Tchr. various cos., camps and colls.; asst. prof. dept. phys. edn. for women Western Mich. U., 1965-76; state rep. State of Mich., 1975-9; mem. legis. coms. Civil Rights and Women's Issues, Conservation, Environ. and the Great lakes, Human Svcs. and Children, Taxation; chmn. Ins. Com., Air Quality Subcom.; chair House Dem. Caucus, 1983-94. Mem. Friends of Kal-Haven Trail, Kalamazoo Womens Network; bd. dirs. Jobs for Mich. Grads., 1982-89; pres. Kalamazoo Area LWV, 1969-73, lobbyist, state bd. dirs., 1973-74; chairperson Kalamazoo County Dem. Party, 1975-76; founding mem. Kalamazoo Environ. Coun., 1991—; charter mem. Kalamazoo Nature Ctr.; mem. citizens adv. com. KRPH, 1987—; century club mem. Mich. Dem. Party, com. to assess need for constl. conv., 1977, co-chair policy com., 1986; spokesperson Mich. Dem. Women's Caucus, 1978-79,. Named Outstanding Freshman Legislator, State Capitol Bur. Booth newspapers, 1977, one of 10 Top Legislators, Detroit News poll, 1977, 79, Legislator of Yr., Mich. Assn. Children's Alliances, 1985, Woman of the Yr. NOW, 1982, Legislator of the Yr. Mich. Township Assn., 1989, Conservationist of the Yr. Sierra Club, 1990, recipient Cert. of Appreciation, Kalamazoo Alcohol and Drug Abuse Coun., Cert. of Svc. with distinction Assn. Student Govt. Western Mich. U., 1980; honored by Women Lawyers Assn. Mich., 1980, Community Svc. award Eagles Aerie 526 Kalamazoo, Cert. of Appreciation, County Rd. Assn. Mich., 1983, Woman of Achievement award Kalamazoo YWCA, 1993, The Brown Jacobs Equality in Edn. award Mich. NOW, 1994, Outstand Pub. Svc. award Planned Parenthood of Kalamazoo, 1994, Milliken award Planned Parenthood Affiliates of Mich., 1995, Lifetime Achievement award Sierra Club, 1994. Mem. AAUW (co-winner Outstanding Mich. Legislator 1982), ACLU, Am. Camping Assn. (bd. dirs. Mich. sect. 1972-76, 80-82), ACLU. Home: 1624 Grand Ave Kalamazoo MI 49006-4419 also: Mich State Ho of Reps State Capitol Lansing MI 48909

BROWN, MARY ELEANOR, physical therapist, educator; b. Williamsport, Pa., Jan. 1, 1906; d. Sumner Locher and Mary Kate (Eagles) Brown. Student U. Wis.-Madison, 1927-28; B.A., Barnard Coll., 1931; M.A., NYU, 1941, postgrad., 1942-45, Western Reserve U., 1960-61; postgrad. U. Miami, Miami-Dade Jr. Coll., 1971-72, Cuesta Community Coll., 1977-79. Supervising phys. therapist, rsch. asst. Inst. for Crippled and Disabled, N.Y.C., 1941-46; instr. edn. N.Y.U., 1942-46; phys. therapist Childrens Rehab. Inst., Cockeysville, Md., 1946; organizing dir. phys. edn. State Rehab. Hosp., West Haverstraw, N.Y., 1946-47; phys. therapy cons. Nat. Soc. for Crippled Children and Adults, Chgo., 1947-49; physical therapy cons., dir. prof. svcs., dir. cerebral palsy sch. N.Y. State Dept. Health, Albany, N.Y. and Eastern N.Y. Orthopedic Hosp. Sch., Schenectady, N.Y., 1949-53; chief phys. therapist Bird S. Coler Hosp. for Chronic Diseases, N.Y.C., 1953-54; chief phys. therapist, instr. edn. St. Vincents Hosp. and N.Y.U., 1954-58; chief rsch. assoc. hand rsch. Highland View Hosp., Cleve., 1958-64, cons. on kinesiology, hand rsch., 1964-65; supr. continuing edn. for phys. therapists, asst. prof. phys. therapy Case Western Res. U., Cleve., 1964-68; dir. phys. therapy Margaret Wagner House of Benjamin Rose Inst., Cleve., 1968-70; free lance writer, 1970—; 1st Mary Eleanor Brown lectr. clin. phys. therapy rsch. Inst. Rehab. and Rsch., Tex. Med. Center, Houston, 1979; Adv. bd. Community Svcs. Dept. Cuesta Community Coll., San Luis Obispo, Calif., 1977-92; vol. UN and Univ. for Peace, Costa Rica, 1982—. Author: Therapeutic Recreation and Exercise: Range-of-Motion Activities for Health and Well-Being, 1990; contbr. articles in field to profl jours. Recipient Award of Merit, Case-Western Res. U., 1970; award for clin. rsch. Inst. Rehab. and Rsch., Tex. Med. Ctr., Houston, 1979; Lucy Blair Svc. award Am. Phys. Therapy Assn., 1984, Disting. Alumna award Lancaster Country Day Sch., 1987. Mem. Inst. Gen. Semantics, Internat. Soc. Gen. Semantics, Am. Phys. Therapy Assn. (Catherine Worthingham fellow 1990), Women for Internat. Peace and Arbitration, Found. for Global Community. Home: 1235 3rd St Apt B Los Osos CA 93402-1115

BROWN, MARY JO, chemist, researcher; b. Portsmouth, Va., Dec. 27, 1946; d. Robert Luther and Jane Frances (Robinson) Allen; m. James William Brown Jr., Apr. 3, 1971. BA, Glenville State Coll., 1975; BA cum laude, Marietta Coll., 1978, MA, 1994. Lab. technician Borg Warner Chems., Washington, W.Va., 1966-72, rsch. asst., 1972-90; rsch. asst. GE Plastics, Parkersburg, W.Va., 1990-95, analytical technologist, 1995—; pres. Employee Activity Club, Washington, 1988-92, treas, 1992—; hazardous materials specialist GE Chem. Response, Washington, 1991-96. Editor, pub. Appalachian Roots, 1983—; contbr. articles to profl. jours. Mem. C. of C. Improvement Coun., Parkersburg, 1988-94. Mem. YWCA, W.Va. Mining Your History Found. (founder, bd. dirs. 1995-96), W.Va. Writers Inc., Mountain State Press (founder), Parkersburg Humane Soc. Home: PO Box 165 Davisville WV 26142 Office: GE Plastics State Rt 892 Washington WV 26181

BROWN, MARY THERESE, controller; b. L.A., Mar. 10, 1964; d. Robert David and Catherine Helen (Ferry) Hogue; m. Jonathan Robert Brock Brown, June 15, 1991. BS in Acctg., NYU, 1988. CPA, N.Y. Sr. assoc. Coopers & Lybrand, N.Y.C., 1988-93; sr. grants acct. Tchrs. Coll., Columbia U., N.Y.C., 1993-94; contr. Queens (N.Y.) Mus. Art, 1994—. Mem. fin. com. Cmty. Ch. N.Y., N.Y.C., 1995-96. Mem. AICPA, Inst. Mgmt. Accts., N.Y. State Soc. CPAs. Home: 112-20 72nd Dr Apt A26 Forest Hills NY 11375 Office: Queens Mus Art Flushing Meadows Corona Pk Queens NY 11368

BROWN, MELISSA CORRIE ANNE, writer; b. Sydney, Australia, Aug. 10, 1950; arrived in U.S., 1952; d. Douglas Edward and Cecelia Mary (O'Donnell) B.; m. Edward Joseph Baum, Aug. 12, 1991; 1 child, Iain Douglas Pedden. BA magna cum laude, Grand Valley State Univ., 1977; MS in journalism, Ohio Univ., 1990. Sr. acct. exec. Williams Mktg. Svcs., Grand Rapids, Mich., 1989-90; mgr. corp. editorial programs Herman Miller, Inc., Zeeland, Mich., 1979-84; writer/cons. Melissa Brown Communications, St. Joseph, Mich., 1985—; instr. writing course Lou Williams Seminars, 1992-94; adj. faculty Grand Valley State Univ., Allendale, Mich., 1990-93, Kendall Coll. Design, Grand Rapids, 1990-93; legal writing instr. Notre Dame Law Sch., 1996-97. Contbr. photographer The Design of Herman Miller, 1970, Pictures for Organizations, 1980, Product Design & Corporate Strategy, 1990; mng. editor Notre Dame Jour. of Law, Ethics and Pulic Policy, 1996-97. Co-chair Amerasian Resettlement com. Fountain St. Ch., Grand Rapids, 1988-89. White scholar Thomas J. White Ctr. on Law and Govt., Notre Dame Law Sch., 1995-97. Mem. Internat. Assn. Business Communicators (Award of Excellence, 1977, 80, 89, Awards of Merit, 1993, 88, West Mich. chpt. pres. 1993-94, sec. 1974-75), Kappa Tau Alpha. Home and Office: 614 Court St Saint Joseph MI 49085

BROWN, MELISSA ROSE, securities analyst; b. Manhasset, N.Y., Dec. 7, 1957; d. Frederick Robert and Cynthia (Barnett) B.; 2 children. BS in Econs., U. Pa., 1979; MBA, NYU, 1984. Tech. cons. Interactive Data Corp., N.Y.C., 1979-81; fin. analyst Nabisco Brands, N.Y.C., 1981-82; quantitative analyst Prudential Bache, N.Y.C., 1982-85; dir. quantitative rsch. Prudential Securities, N.Y.C., 1985—. Mem. Assn. for Investment Mgmt. Rsch. (chair subcom. Charlottesville Va. chpt. 1989-91), Chgo. Quantitative Alliance. Office: Prudential Securities 1 New York Plz 17th Fl New York NY 10292

BROWN, MICHELLE RENEE, interior designer; b. Lincoln, Nebr., Apr. 30, 1964; d. John Allen and Audrey Claudine (Baker) Rider; m. Edward Daniel Brown, Nov. 19, 1988; 1 child, William Andrew. Student, East Tenn. State U., 1982-84, 1985-87; BA in Home Econs., Tenn. Tech. U., 1986; MA in Interior Design, U. Ky., 1988; postgrad., W.Va. U., 1990-91 summers. Cert. Nat. Coun. for Interior Design Qualification, Home Economist, 1990. Teaching asst. U. Ky., Lexington, Ky., 1986-88; interior designer Interiors, Morgantown, W.Va., 1990—; asst. prof., interior design W.Va. U., Morgantown, 1988-95. Design Projects include: W.Va. U. Academic Affairs Office Design, U. Health Svcs. Records and Nurses Area, U. Svcs Ctr. Ctrl Adminstrn., Office Layout, Divsn. Family Resources Breakroon, Stalnaker Hall, Arnold Hall, Math Dept, Wise Library, Duncan Library; Hawkins County Courthouse Extension, Tenn.; Fairmont State Coll. Learning Resource Ctr.; Calvary Baptist Ch.; C&P Telephone Co., Morgantown, W.Va. Recipient Faculty Scholarship award Tenn. Tech. U., 1985-86, Outstanding Tchr. award W.Va. U., 1993. Mem. Am. Soc. Interior Designers, Am. Home Econs. Assn., W.Va. Home Econs. Assn., Phi Kappa Phi, Phi Upsilon Omicron. Home: 79 Gans St Westover WV 26505-4512 Office: Interiors 19 Ashebrooke Sq Morgantown WV 26505

BROWN, OPAL DIANN, medical technologist, nurse; b. Gassaway, W.Va., Aug. 9, 1958; d. Albert Lee and Elizabeth Lee (Kidd) Persinger; m. Thomas David Brown, July 31,1993. BS in Med. Tech., W.Va. U., 1981; BSN, U. S.C., 1993. Med. technologist Biomed. Reference Labs., Fairmont, W.Va., 1981-82, Fairmont (W.Va.) Gen. Hosp., 1982, B.G. Thimmappa, M.D., Inc., Bridgeport, W.Va., 1982-83, Pocahontas Meml. Hosp., Marlinton, W.Va., 1984-87, Alexandria (Va.) Hosp., 1987-88, Richland Meml. Hosp., Columbia, S.C., 1988—; part-time RN Midlands Regional Ctr., S.C. Dept. of Disabilities and Spl. Needs, Columbia, 1994—. Mem. Am. Soc. Clin. Pathologists, Sigma Theta Tau. Democrat. Presbyterian. Home: 232 Laurel Meadows Dr West Columbia SC 29169-2361

BROWN, PAMELA RAYE, safety and environmental engineer; b. Columbus, Ga., Apr. 5, 1955; d. A.W. and Rosalind Hazel (Lefferdink) B. AS, Polk C.C., Winter Haven, Fla., 1977, AA, 1978; BS in Crimonology/Law, Fla. State U., 1979; MS in Criminal Justice/Law, Calif. State U., Long Beach, 1984. Mfg. mgr. Frito-Lay, Rancho Cucamunga, Calif., 1989-90; safety dir. Sysco Corp., Walnut, Calif., 1990-94; safety environ. engr. Allied Signal Aerospace, Barstow, Calif., 1994—; drug/youth counselor County of Orange, Santa Ana, Calif., 1979-80; counselor Ex-Offenders, Garden Grove, Calif., 1980-81; youth job developer Saddlebuck C.C., 1981-82. Capt. U.S. Army, 1984-89. Decorated Army Commendation medal, Army Achievement medal, Airborne "Jump Wings", U.S. Army. Mem. Am. Soc. Safety Engrs., NOW. Office: Allied Signal Aerospace 850 East Main St Barstow CA 92392

BROWN, PAMELA SUE, accountant; b. Inglewood, Calif., Sept. 25, 1959; d. Bruce Kellner and Joyce (Wixom) B.; m. Victor Stanford Frake, Aug. 30, 1986; children: Emily Anne, Katie Nicole. AA, El Camino Coll., 1979; BS, Calif. State U., Long Beach, 1981. CPA, Calif. Staff acct. Richard H. O'Hara & Co., CPA, City of Industry, Calif., 1982-87; tax mgr. Fagan, Stiles & Co., CPA, Long Beach, Calif., 1987-88; pub. acct. Pamela Sue Brown, CPA, Long Beach, Calif., 1988—. Vol. Children's Miracle Network Telethon, Anaheim, Calif., 1988-89, Vol. Income Tax Assistance Program, Torrance, Calif., 1981. Mem. Am. Soc. Women Accts. (pres.-elect 1984-85, pres. 1985-87), Inst. Mgmt. Accts. (com. chairperson), Calif. Soc. CPAs, Long Beach Area C. of C. Office: 263 Belmont Ave Long Beach CA 90803-1523

BROWN, PATRICIA ANN, child health nurse; b. Kokomo, Ind., Apr. 4, 1938; d. John Conrad and Marie L. (Landseadel) B. BSN, Ind. U., 1959, MSN, 1969; Pediatric Nurse Assoc., U. Tenn., 1976. Staff nurse, asst. head nurse Ind. U. Children's Hosp., Indpls., 1960-66; chief nurse Child Devel. Ctr., Memphis, 1966-67; instr., asst. prof. child health nursing Ctr. for Health Scis., U. Tenn., Memphis, 1969-73; asst. prof. child health nursing U. Tenn., Knoxville, 1973-75, U. Tenn. Ctr. for Health Scis., Memphis, 1975-84; child health nursing faculty Holmes Jr. Coll., Grenada, Miss., 1985-89; dir. nursing East Ark. C.C., Forrest City, Ark., 1989—; chairperson Nursing Faculty Coun., Memphis. Hospice vol. Hospice of Memphis, 1981-84. Mem. Nat. League for Nursing, Tenn. Nurses Assn. (chairperson Maternal Child Health), Ark. State Bd. Nursing, Coun. Nursing Adminstrs. of Nursing Edn. Programs in Ark. (chairperson assoc. degree nursing coun. 1992-94), Ind. U. Alumni, Sigma Theta Tau, Pi Lambda Theta. Methodist. Home: 6984 Loddon Cv Memphis TN 38119-8517 Office: East Ark CC 1700 New Castle Rd Forrest City AR 72335-2204

BROWN, PATRICIA DONNELLY, software industry executive; b. Plainfield, N.J., Sept. 6, 1954; d. Vincent Joseph and Rita Joan (Carroll) Donnelly; m. Douglas P. Brown, Oct. 17, 1986; children: Douglas, Christopher. BA in Liberal Arts, Rosemont Coll., 1978. Sales rep. Control Data Corp., Phila., 1978-81; dir. mktg. Columbia Software, Bryn Mawr, Pa., 1981-82; dir. tech. support Cullinet Software, Westwood, Mass., 1982-89; dir. engring. AT&T GIS/Teradata, San Diego, L.A., 1989-95; v.p. AT&T GIS, San Diego, 1995-96; exec. dir. strategic relationships HNC Software, San Diego, 1996—. Vol. San Diego Urban League, 1994-95, Jackie Robinson YMCA, San Diego, 1994-95; exec. sponsor AT&T Alliance, 1994—. Republican. Unitarian Universalist.

BROWN, PATRICIA IRENE, lawyer, retired law librarian; b. Boston; d. Joseph Raymond and Harriet A. (Taylor) B. BA, Suffolk U., 1955, JD, 1965, MBA, 1970; MST, Gordon Conwell Theol. Sem., 1977. Bar: Mass. 1965. Libr. asst. Suffolk U., Boston, 1951-60, asst. libr., 1960-65, asst. law libr., 1965-85, assoc. law libr., 1985-92; human resources counselor Winthrop (Mass.) Sr. Ctr., 1993—. Dir. Referral/Resource Ctr., Union Congl. Ch., Winthrop, Mass.; vol. health benefits counselor Mass. Dept. Elder Affairs, 1994—. First Woman inducted into Nat. Baseball Hall of Fame, Cooperstown, N.Y., 1988, All- Am. Girls Profl. Baseball League, 1950-51. Mem. Assn. Am. Law Librs., Am. Congl. Assn. (bd. dirs. 1992—), Mass. Bar Assn.

BROWN, PAULA KINNEY, heating and air conditioning contractor; b. Portsmith, Va., June 19, 1953; d. Curtis Wade and Joan (Glascoe) Kinney; m. Wayne Howard Brown, Feb. 12, 1983; children: Rebecca Jo, Raina Jaye. AS, Lake Sumter Community Coll., 1973, 77; student Lake County Area Vocat. Ctr., 1979, 80. Cert. air conditioning and heating contrator. Pres. Kinney's Air Conditioning and Heating, Leesburg, Fla., 1981—, head computer system operator, 1986—, office mgr; sec.-treas. Wayne's Paint & Body, Inc., Leesburg, 1995—. Mem. adv. com. for Area Lake Air Conditioning and Heating Vo-Tech. Sch., Eustis, Fla., 1981-82, 1993—. Mem. Ch. of Christ. Home: 5 Lonesome Pine Trl Yalaha FL 34797-3058 Office: Kinney's Air Conditioning & Heating Inc 409 N 13th St Leesburg FL 34748-4968 also: Wayne's Paint & Body Inc 3831 W Main St Leesburg FL 34748

BROWN, RANDI ANN, artist, educator; b. Birmingham, Ala., Feb. 22, 1954; d. Earl Frederick Jr. and Edna Lorena (Gilland) B. BFA summa cum laude, U. Montevallo, 1990; M of Applied Tchg. in Art, U. Memphis, 1993. Cert. tchr. fine arts, Tenn. Graphic artist South Cen. Bell, 1973-78, John, Scott, Mitchell, N.Y.C., 1979-80; graphic artist Atlanta, 1980-83, Birmingham, 1983-85; art tchr., artist-in-residence Memphis City Schs., 1993—; judge art show Nat. Colored Pencil Assn., Memphis. Exhibited in group shows Tenn. All-State Exhbn., Parthenon, Nashville. Mem. Amnesty Internat., Memphis, 1993—. Recipient Koenig Studio award, 1988, 89, Virginia Barnes Overall Excellence in Art award, Excellence in Studio Art award, Serendipity Merit award, AAUW award for acad. excellence, 1989, 90, Fine Art Achievement award Binney and Smith Corp., 1990, Scholarship Achievement award, 1990-91. Mem. Tenn. Art League, Coalition for Visual Arts, Phi Theta Kappa (1st Pl. Art award 1987), Kappa Pi, Lambda Sigma Pi, Phi Kappa Phi, Omicron Delta Kappa, Kappa Delta Pi. Roman Catholic.

BROWN, (JERENE) ROXANNE, sales executive; b. L.A., July 5, 1947; d. John Phillip and Margaret Leona (Dalrymple) Ortiz; m. Terry Lee Wood, May 7, 1966 (div. Sept. 1969); 1 child, Tiffany Christine Wood Suraco; m. Christopher Corey Brown, July 17, 1984; children: Jason Michael and John Charles (twins); m. Richard L. Gibbs, Apr. 18, 1996. Student, Casper Coll., 1977. Info. operator Gen. Telephone, Baldwin Park, Calif., 1965-67; long distance operator Gen. Telephone, Santa Maria, Calif., 1967-69; office mgr. Monroe Calculator, Las Vegas, Nev., 1972-74; mgr. Exch. Club, Salt Lake City, 1977-81, Pouches Inc., Salt Lake City, 1981-82; asst. producer KSTU TV 20, Salt Lake City, 1982-84; sec. ADVO - Sys., Inc., Orange, Calif., 1984-85, terr. sales rep., 1985-88; major account exec. ADVO - Sys., Inc., Garden Grove, Calif., 1988-95; v.p. JRB & Assocs., Long Beach, Calif., 1995—; owner JRB & Assocs. Advt. Cons., 1995—, JRB Advt. Cons., 1995—; cons. Rice - Urmana Advt., Huntington Beach, Calif., 1989-91. Bd. dirs. ACLU, Salt Lake City, 1977; precinct worker Voter Registrar, Huntington Beach, 1988, Long Beach, Calif., 1990; bd. dirs., sec. Alamitos Bay Beach Peninsula Preservation Group, 1996—. Mem. ACLU, Platform Speakers Assn., Alamitos Bay Garden Club (v.p., ways and means com. 1996—). Home: 6119 E Seaside Walk Long Beach CA 90803-5654 Office: JRB & Assoc 6119 E Seaside Walk Long Beach CA 90803-5654

BROWN, RUBYE GOLSBY, secondary education educator, artist; b. Youngstown, Ohio; d. Clifford and Augusta Bell (Blalock) Golsby; m. Robert L. Brown; children: Harlean J. Preston, Charles, Louis, Carson, Gloria, Robin, Debbie. BA in Edn., Youngstown (Ohio) State Coll., 1956, BS, 1979, MS in Sociology, Edn. and Adminstrn., 1981; Cert. in History and Govtl. Econs., Youngstown State U., 1989. Credit mgr. Klivan's, Youngstown, 1953-56; sec. City Hall, Treasurer's Office, Youngstown, 1956; substitute tchr. Chaney High Sch., Youngstown, 1981-92; tchr. Round Rock High Sch., 1992—; instr. Austin (Tex.) Community Coll., 1993—; owner Custom Craft, Austin, 1993—; instr. in art, pub. speaker on crime and drug abuse. Mem. Ohio State Bd. Health, 1980—; pres. Mahoning County Courtwatch, 1987—; ednl. specialist Police Dept. Task Force, Youngstown, 1989—; vol. Olin E. Teaque Detention Ctr. Recipient Health Care award, Columbus State Bd. Health, 1988. Mem. Am. Soc. Curriculum and Devel., Am. Univ. and Coll. Women. Democrat. Baptist.

BROWN, RUTH ANN, pharmacist; b. Endicott, N.Y., Nov. 17, 1948; d. Herbert Matthew and Rose Marie (Murphy) B. BS in Pharmacy, Phila. Coll. Pharmacy & Sci., 1971; MBA in Health Adminstrn., Widener U., 1983. Lic. pharmacist, N.Y., Pa. Staff pharmacist Crozer Chester Med. Ctr., Chester, Pa., 1972-80, asst. dir. pharmacy, 1980-85, assoc. dir. pharmacy ops., 1985-91, acting dir., 1988-89; staff devel./QAI coord. pharmacy dept. Albert Einstein Med. Ctr., Phila., 1991-92; pharmacist, mgr. Willowcrest, Phila., 1992—; relief pharmacist Ctrl. Drug of Chester, Pa., 1980-91; site coord. dept. ext. svcs. Phila. Coll. Pharmacy and Sci., 1988-90, continuing edn. adv. bd. 1988-90, clin. instr. pharmacy, 1982-91; staff pharmacist Taylor Hosp., Ridley Park, Pa., 1989-90, Roxborough Meml. Hosp., Phila., 1992-93. Vol. LPGA Tournament to benefit Ronald McDonald Houses, 1987—. Fellow Am. Soc. Cons. Pharmacists; mem. Am. Soc. Hosp. Pharmacists (ho. of dels. 1983, 93, 94, 95, 96), Pa. Soc. Hosp. Pharmacists (mem. Pa. pharmacy liaison group, mem. profl. affairs coun., mem. orgnl. affairs coun., mem. ctrl. office task force, mem. fin. com., chmn. policy rev. com. 1995-96, chmn. constn. and bylaws com. 1991-92, 95-96, DVSHP chpt. rep. to bd. dirs. 1990-92, presdl. officer 1992-95, other coms.), Ctr. for Proper Medication Use (chmn. bd. dirs. 1994-95, chmn. subcom. on proper medication use in children 1995-96), Delaware Valley Soc. Hosp. Pharmacists (nominations com., mem. program com., sec. 1981-87, pres. 1988-89, chmn. bd. dirs. 1989-90, 96—, chpt. rep. to PSHP bd. dirs. 1990-92, Jonathan Roberts award 1991), Guild Phila. Hosp. Pharmacists, Delaware County Pharm. Assn., Alumni Assn. Phila. Coll. Pharmacy (various coms.), Am. Legion Aux., Lambda Kappa Sigma (grand v.p. for alumni 1986-88, grand pres. 1988-90). Roman Catholic. Office: Willowcrest-Albert Einstein Med Ctr 5501 Old York Rd Philadelphia PA 19141

BROWN, SANDRA, writer. Mgr. Merle Norman Cosmetics Studios, Tyler, Tex., 1971-73; weather reporter KLTV-TV, Tyler, 1972-75, WFAA-TV, Dallas, 1976-79; model Dallas Apparel Mart, 1976-87. Author: (romance novels) Breakfast in Bead, 1983, Heaven's Price, 1983, Relentless Desire, 1983, Tempest in Eden, 1983, Temptation's Kiss, 1983, Tomorrow's Promise, 1983, In a Class by Itself, 1984, Send No Flowers, 1984, Bittersweet Rain, 1984, Sunset Embrace, 1984, Words of Silk, 1984, Riley in the Morning, 1985, Thursday's Child, 1985, Another Dawn, 1985, 22 Indigo Place, 1986, The Rana Look, 1986, Demon Rumm, 1987, Fanta C, 1987, Sunny Chandler's Return, 1987, Adam's Fall, 1988, Hawk's O'Toole's Hostage, 1988, Slow Heat in Heaven, 1988, Tidings of Great Joy, 1988, Long Time Coming, 1989, Temperatures Rising, 1989, Best Kept Secrets, 1989, A Whole New Light, 1989, Another Dawn, 1991, Breath of Scandal, 1991, Mirror Image, 1991, French Silk, 1992, The Silken Web, 1992, Honor Bound, 1992, A Secret Splendor, 1992, Shadows of Yesterday (also published as Relentless Desire), 1992, Three Complete Novels, 1992, Charade, 1994, The Witness, 1995, "TEXAS!" series: Texas! Lucky, 1990, Texas! Sage, 1991, Texas! Chase, 1991, Texas! Trilogy, 1992, (as Laura Jordan) Hidden Fires, 1982, The Silken Web, 1982, (as Rachel Ryan) Love Beyond Reason, 1981, Love's Encore, 1981, Eloquent Silence, 1982, A Treasure Worth Seeking, 1982, Prime Time, 1983, (as Erin St. Claire) Not Even for Love, 1982, A Kiss Remembered, 1983, A Secret Splendor, 1983, Seduction By Design, 1983, Led Astray, 1985, A Sweet Anger, 1985, Tiger Prince, 1985, Above and Beyond, 1986, Honor Bound, 1986, The Devil's Own, 1987, Two Alone, 1987, Thrill of Victory, 1989. Home: 1000 N Bowen Arlington TX 76012*

BROWN, SANDRA JEAN, banker; b. Bridgeport, Conn., June 10, 1936; d. Victor James and Mildred Lillian (Norbeck) B. Various positions Peoples Bank, Bridgeport, 1953-72, corp. sec., 1972—; dir. Conn. Housing Fin. Authority, 1985—. Bd. dirs. Internat. Inst. Conn., 1981—, Barnum Mus. Found., 1986—; chmn. adv. com. Mut. Housing Assn. Southwestern Conn., 1993—; trustee YWCA of Ea. Fairfield County, 1994—; mem. Local Redevel. Auth. planning adv. com. Town of Stratford, Conn.; trustee Ctrl. Conn. Coast YMCA. Recipient Community Leadership award Sacred Heart U., Bridgeport, 1983, Ann. Achievement award Women's Network of Greater Bridgeport, 1990, Salute to Women award YWCA Greater Bridgeport, 1984. Mem. Fin. Women Internat. (state pres. 1981-82, Conn. State Woman of Yr. 1994), Assn. Bank Women Conn., Am. Soc. of Corp. Secs., Fairfield County Bankers Assn. (bd. dirs.).

BROWN, SANDRA LEE, educational consultant, watercolorist; b. Chgo., July 9, 1943; d. Arthur Willard and Erma Emily (Lange) Boettcher; m. Ronald Gregory Brown, June 21, 1983; 1 child, Jon Michael. BA in Art and Edn., N.E. Ill. U., 1966; postgrad., No. Ill. U. Cert. K-9 tchr., Ill. Travel agt. Weiss Travel Bur., Chgo., 1959-66; tchr. Chgo. Sch. System, 1966-68; tchr. Schaumburg (Ill.) Sch. Dist. 54, 1968-94, creator coord. peer mentoring program for 1st-yr. tchrs., 1992-96; cons./dir. Yardstick Ednl. Svcs., Monroe, Wis., 1994—; mem. adv. bd. Peer Coaching and Mentoring Network, Chgo. suburban region, 1992—; peer cons. Sch. Dist. 54, 1988-94. Exhibited in group shows Court House Gallery, Woodstock, Ill., Millburn (Ill.) Gallery, Gallerie Stefanie, Chgo. Campaign chmn. for mayoral candidate, Grayslake, Ill., 1989; campaign chmn. for trustee Citizens for Responsible Govt., Grayslake, 1991. Mem. Lakes Region Watercolor Guild, Delta Kappa Gamma (chmn. women in arts Gamma chpt. Ill. 1992-94, Alpha Mu chpt. 1995—). Home: PO Box 416 Monroe WI 53566 Office: Yardstick Ednl Svcs PO Box 416 Monroe WI 53566

BROWN, SANDRA LOUISE PALMER, small business owner, consultant; b. Royal Oak, Mich.; d. Michael Peter and Elizabeth Louis (Hampers) Palmer; m. Gregory Jacob Brown, June 9, 1990. BBA, Iowa State U., 1982; M in Human Resource Edn., Boston U., 1994. Transp. analyst Mass. Bay Transp. Authority, Boston, 1982-85; tech. support rep. Project Software & Devel., Cambridge, Mass., 1985-86; self-employed computer cons. Newton, Mass., 1986-87; account rep. IBM, Boston, 1987-92; pres. Am. Cons. and Tng., Concord, Mass., 1991-93; v.p. mktg. Drake Beam Morin, Inc., 1993-94; prin. Applied Interventions, Concord, 1994—; assoc. Human Resource Mgmt. Group. Mem. Mus. Fine Arts, Boston, 1987—, Jr. League Boston, 1985—; vol. Young Life, Westwood, Mass., 1984-86. Mem. ASTD, Human Resource Coun., New Eng. Human Resource Assn., Boston Human Resource Assn., Nat. Speakers Assn., New Eng. Speakers Assn. Republican.

BROWN, SARAH ANNE, director community resources; b. Troy, Mo., Oct. 19, 1964; d. John Edwin and Judith Ann (Yeast) Schofield; m. David Gene Brown, Feb. 20, 1989; 1 child, Abigail Frances. BA, Southeastern Mo. State U., 1986, MA, 1988. Dep. clk. Sangamon County Cir., Springfield, Ill., 1990-91; caseworker Kemmerer Village, Assumption, Ill., 1991-92; sr. counselor Chaddock, Quincy, Ill., 1992-93; vol. social worker The Salvation Army, Hannibal, Mo., 1993-94, Salvation Army flood relief family advocate, 1994-95; dir. cmty. resources Marion County Svcs., Hannibal, 1995—; mem. Pike County Unmet Needs Com., Bowling Green, Mo., 1994-95. Mem. Main St. design com., Hannibal, 1993-96; sec. Hope House Homeless Shelter, Hannibal, 1994—; chair fundraising com. Habitat for Humanity, Hannibal, 1995-96, bd. dirs., 1994—. Mem. Order of Ea. Star, Bus. and Profl. Women. Home: 233 N Griffith St Hannibal MO 63401 Office: Marion County Svcs for Devel Disabled 3175 Palmyra Rd Hannibal MO 63401

BROWN, SHARON ELIZABETH, software engineer; b. Lynn, Mass., Nov. 23, 1960; d. Leland James Brown and Vail (Wilkinson) Bartelson. B-SChemE, U. Mass., 1983. Software engr. K&L Automation div. Daniel Industry, Tucson, 1983-86, sr. software engr., 1986-87, asst. mgr. software systems, 1987; software mgr. Daniel Automation, Houston, 1987-91; sr. software engr. Praxis Instruments, Inc., Houston, 1991-93, Dresser Measurement, Houston, 1993—. Mem. NSPE, ISA. Republican. Home: 5735 Henniker Dr Houston TX 77041-6589 Office: Dresser Industries Inc PO Box 42176 Houston TX 77242-2176

BROWN, SHARON GAIL, company executive, consultant; b. Chgo., Dec. 25, 1941; d. Otto and Pauline (Lauer) Schumacher; B in Gen. Studies, Roosevelt U.; m. Robert B. Ringo, Aug. 2, 1984; 1 dau. by previous marriage, Susan Ann. Info. analyst Internat. Minerals & Chems., Northbrook, Ill., 1966-71, programmer analyst, 1971-74; programmer analyst Procon Internat. Inc. subs. UOP Inc., Des Plaines, Ill., 1974-76, systems analyst, 1976-77, project leader, 1977-78; mgr. adminstrv. services, 1978-82; spl. cons. to pres. IPS Internat., Ltd., 1982-83; spl. cons. to pres. CEI Supply Co. div. Sigma-Chapman, Inc., 1984-87, ptnr. and co-founder Brown, Ringo & Assocs., 1987—; data processing cons. Mem. Buffalo Grove (Ill.) Youth Commn., 1978-82; mem. adv. com. UOP Polit. Action Com., 1979-82; Mem. Rep. Senatorial Com. Inner Circle. Mem. Am. Mgmt. Assn., Chgo. Council on Fgn. Rels., Lake Forest-Lake Bluff Hist. Soc. Home: 90 Atteridge Rd Lake Forest IL 60045-1713

BROWN, SHELLY ANN, retail executive; b. Indianola, Miss., Sept. 8, 1951; d. Clarance L. House and Fannie M. (Berry) Benton; m. Howard H. Brown, Sept. 2, 1989; children: Frank D. Stephens, Deetra L. Tate, Howard H. Jr. AA, State Tech. Inst., Memphis, 1988; BA, U. Memphis, 1994, MS, 1996. Supr. Def. Depot Memphis, 1972-93, Williams-Sonoma, Memphis, 1994-95; asst. mgr. Nordstroms, Memphis, 1995-96; mgr. Creative Computer, 1996; educator Memphis City Schs., 1996. Mem. NOW. Home and Office: 1792 Keyes Dr Memphis TN 38116

BROWN, SHERI LYNN, accountant; b. Monroe, La., Apr. 13, 1959; d. Richard Larry and Virginia Ann (McIntosh) Mitchell; m. Peter Russell Brown, Oct. 22, 1982; children: Katy Elizabeth, Daniel Richard. BS in Acctg. cum laude, La. Tech. U., 1981. Comptr. All Star Cabinets & Millworks, Baton Rouge, 1990-94; dist. acctg. mgr. Browning-Ferris Industries, Monroe, 1994; dir. fin. & adminstrn. Monroe C. of C., 1994—. Mem. Mayor's Commn. Needs Women. Mem. Inst. Mgmt. Accts., Women Bus. Owners Assn., Profl. Bus. Women's Orgn., Beta Gamma Sigma, Beta Alpha Psi. Republican. Office: Monroe C of C 300 Washington St Ste 104 Monroe LA 71201

BROWN, SHIRLEY, state legislator; b. Oshkosh, Wis., Oct. 2, 1952; m. Jack W. Brown; children: Angela, Jack. Owner billing collection agy.; chair womens legis. caucus Fla. Ho. of Reps., 1992—; mem. Fla. State Coordinating Coun. Early Childhood, 1991, Fla. Entertainment Commn. bd. dirs. Sarasota Family counseling Ctr., Sarasota Friends Unity in Cmty., 1990—. Mem. Am. Bus. Women's Assn., Fla. Collectors Assn., Bus. and Profl. Women. Democrat. Presbyterian. Office: Fla House of Reps State Capitol Tallahassee FL 32301

BROWN, SHIRLEY ANN, speech and language pathologist; b. Bklyn., Oct. 9, 1935; d. Hyman and Lillian (Fuhrer) Rubak; m. Ronald Wallace Brown, Sept. 29, 1956; children: Abbie Howard, Daniel Mark. BA, Bklyn. Coll., 1956, MA, 1961. Lic. speech/lang. pathologist, N.Y., N.J. Speech pathologist Richmond County CP Treatment Ctr., S.I., N.Y., 1956-59, Coney Island Hosp., Bklyn., 1959-61, Mendham Boro Schs. and Chatham Twp. Schs., 1962-67; pvt. practice home care speech pathologist various hosps. and med. facilities, 1967-79; dir. speech pathology dept. Englewood (N.J.) Hosp., 1974-92; speech pathologist Holy Name Hosp., Teaneck, N.J., 1992-96, chief speech-lang. pathology dept., 1996—; speech pathologist Home Health Care Agys., Bergen County, 1992—; clin. supr. comm. disorders grad. program Hunter Coll., N.Y.C., 1993—, Kean Coll., N.J., 1993—, Montclair State U., 1996—. Chair svc. and rehab. Am. Cancer Soc., Hackensack, N.J. Recipient Nat. Honor citation for Profl. Edn., Am. Cancer Soc., 1985, Crimson Sword award Am. Cancer Soc., 1989. Mem. Am. Speech. Lang. and Hearing Assn. (cert., congl. action com., state chair career info., Continuing Edn. award 1983—, Outstanding Clin. Achievement award 1985), N.J. Speech, Lang. and Hearing Assn. Home: 6 Sisson Ter Tenafly NJ 07670-1810 Office: Holy Name Hosp Speech-Lang Pathology Dept 718 Teaneck Rd Teaneck NJ 07666-4245

BROWN, SHIRLEY JEAN, health care facility manager, nurse; b. Vallejo, Calif., Mar. 17, 1946; d. Celester Mackey and Lillie B. (Collins) Presley; m. Leo Brown, 1976; children: Vickie Hardin Williams, Altee Jr., Keith Hardin, La Tonya R. Brown. Diploma in nursing, Brackenridge Sch. Nursing, Austin, 1977; AA, Austin (Tex.) C.C., 1983. RN Tex. ORT/RN Holy Cross Hosp., Austin, 1966-78; RN Austin Women's Clinic, 1978-80; dist. health svc. mgr. Health & Human Svcs. Dept., Austin, 1980—; bd. mem. Child Inc. Health Care Adv. Bd. Co-chair Austin Interfaith, 1989—. Recipient Boss III award of distinction Austin Met. Bus. Resource Ctr., 1990, Civic & Human Endeavors, 1994. Mem. NAFE, Am. Coll. Health Care Execs., Brackenridge Hosp. Sch. Nursing Alumni Assn. Democrat. Baptist. Home: 7207 Hartnell Dr Austin TX 78723

BROWN, SHIRLEY MARK, retired science administrator; b. Phila., Apr. 25, 1924; d. Paul and Bertha Evelyn (Zucker) Mark; m. Bernard Beau, Sept. 1, 1947; children: Eric Joel, Aimee Susan. BA, Temple U., Phila., 1945, MA, 1947. Rsch. chemist U. Mich., Ann Arbor, 1947-50; instr. Upsala Coll., East Orange, 1960-74; acad. planner Rutgers U., New Brunswick, N.J., 1974-80, assoc. dir. Waksman Inst., 1980-88; exec. dir. Rutgers Rsch. and Ednl. Found., New Brunswick, 1980-94; assoc. dir. Office of Corp. Liaison and Technol. Transfer Rutgers U., 1988-91, adminstr. corp. contracts, 1991-94. sec. Joint Civic Com. Westfield 1962-66, Com. for Human Rights Westfield 1967-70; publicity chairperson. PTA Westfield 1963-67. Mem. LWV, Assn. Univ. Technol. Mgrs., Nat. Coun. Univ. Rsch. Adminstrs., Soc. Rsch. Adminstrs. Home: 146 Tudor Oval Westfield NJ 07090-2245

BROWN, SUSAN ELIZABETH S., secondary education educator; b. Niagara Falls, N.Y., Feb. 25, 1940; d. Harold Marvin and Thelma A. (Lowenberg) Sonnichsen; m. Edward J. Hehre, Jr., June 22, 1963 (div. Apr. 1977); children: Nancy Elizabeth, Edward James III; m. Robert Goodell Brown, July 30, 1988. BA, Cornell U., 1963; student, L.I. U., 1970-73; MALS, Dartmouth Coll., 1986; student, U. Geneva, Switzerland. Cert. profl. educator level II, Vt., libr./media specialist level I, Vt. Latin and French tchr. Pinkerton Acad., Derry, N.H., 1964-67; adminstrv. sec. New Eng. Bd. Higher Edn., New Eng. Coun. Higher Edn. Nurses, Durham, N.H., 1968; French tchr. Shelter Island (N.Y.) H.S., 1972; Latin, French, Journalism tchr. Woodsville (N.H.) H.S., 1974-88; Latin, French tchr. Thetford (Vt.) Acad., 1988—, telecomm. coord., 1993-94; alternative cert. bds., N.H., Vt. Contbr. articles to profl. jours. Trustee, chair Haverhill (N.H.) Libr. Assn., 1978-88; moderator Haverhill U.C.C., 1985; treas. Latham Libr., Thetford, 1992—. Mem. New Hampshire Classics Assn. (pres. 1966-68, hon. 1970, treas. 1977-87)), Classics Assn. New Eng. (exec. bd. 1981-87, 92-93), Sigma Tau Delta. Republican. Home: PO Box 239 Thetford Center VT 05075-0239 Office: Thetford Acad PO Box 190 Thetford VT 05074-0190

BROWN, SUSIE WARRINGTON, foundation executive; b. Lambert, Miss., Apr. 18, 1952; d. Richard Leon and Mary Josephine (White) Warrington; children: Melissa Jo, Ronny Leon. BBA, Delta State U., 1985; M of Health Sci., Wichita State U., 1987. Exec. dir. Harvey County United Way, Halstead, Kans., 1985-87, United Way Washington County, Greenville, Miss., 1987-90, United Way Kankakee (Ill.) County, 1991-94, United Way of Greater Utica, N.Y., 1994—; co-founder, dir. Christmas in Apr., Kankakee, 1991—; dir. Cmty. Resource Ctr., Kankakee, 1992—; chmn. mayor's adv. com. Cmty. Econ. Devel., Kankakee, 1994; founder Blueprint, 1994, Success by Six, 1995. Treas. Eastside Bus. Coun., Kankakee, 1991—. Recipient Point of Light award Pres. George Bush, 1990, Key to the City award Mayor Frank Self, 1992, Larry Power Comty. Excellence award Bourbonnais C. of C., 1994, Point of Light award Congressman Tom Ewing, 1992; Gus Shea Meml. scholar United Way Am., 1993. Mem. Manteno C. of C. (bd. dirs. 1992—), Kiwanis (com. chair 1991—). Baptist. Home: 97 Prospect St Utica NY 13501-6056 Office: United Way Greater Utica 270 Genesee St Utica NY 13502-4617

BROWN, SUZANNE WILEY, museum director; b. Cheyenne, Wyo., Aug. 28, 1938; d. Robert James and Catharine Helen (Schroeder) Wiley; BS with honors, U. Wyo., 1960, MS, 1964; postgrad. U. Cin. Med. Sch., 1965-66, U. Ill., 1969-72; m. Ralph E. Brown, July 19, 1968; 1 dau., Nina M. Rsch. asst. Harvard Med. Sch., 1962-63; rsch. asst. U. Cin. Med. Sch., 1964-65; sr. lab. asst. U. Chgo., 1966-67; rsch. assoc. U. Colo. Med. Sch., 1968; teaching asst. U. Ill., 1971-73; exec. asst. Chgo. Acad. Scis., 1974-82, asst. dir., 1982-84, assoc. dir., 1984-90, ret.; mem. adv. bd. Mitchell Indian Mus., Evanston, Ill., Fechin Inst., Taos, N.Mex.; mem. collectors com. Field Mus., Chgo. NDEA fellow, 1960-62. Mem. Achievement Rewards Coll. Scis. (corr. sec.), Brookfield Zool. Soc. (bd. govs.), Phi Beta Kappa, Sigma Xi, Phi Kappa Phi.

BROWN, TAMARA C., career counselor, nutritionist; b. Herrera, Panama, Apr. 29, 1965; came to U.S., 1979; d. Armando and Cecilia (Tello) Brown. BS in Human Ecology, Cook Coll., Rutgers U., 1988; student, Montclair State U. Dietetic asst. Morristown (N.J.) Meml. Hosp., 1988-92; employment svc. trainee N.J. State Dept. Labor, Jersey City, 1992-93, bilingual career counselor, 1993—. ESL tutor Literacy Vols. Am., Essex, N.J., 1995—.

BROWN, TANYA AYRES, accountant; b. Warren, Mich., Apr. 25, 1970; d. Ronald Earl and Ruth Ann (Stetson) Ayres; m. Mark Owen Brown, June 12, 1992. BA in Bus. Adminstrn., Ea. Nazarene Coll., Quincy, Mass., 1992, BS in Computer Info. Svcs., 1992. Acctg. mgmt. trainee Johnson & Johnson, New Brunswick, N.J., 1992-93, assoc. acct., 1993, acct., 1994—. Leader Immanuel Ch. of the Nazarene, Lansdale, Pa., 1992—. Mem. Inst. of Mgmt. Accts. Republican. Home: 36 B Darien New Hope PA 18938 Office: Johnson & Johnson One Johnson Plz New Brunswick NJ 08901

BROWN, TERESA ELAINE, state legislator; b. Oct. 6, 1953; d. Waid Stanley and Elaine Agusta (Swift) Fosburg; children: Christopher, Delaine. Student, Alliance Coll., Edinboro U. Legis. aide 6th Legis. Dist., Meadville, Pa., 1979-86, 5th Legis. Dist., Meadville, 1987; per diem employee Crawford County, Meadville, 1988-89, asst. dir. tax claim bur., 1989-90; mem. Pa. Ho. of Reps., Titusville, 1991—; mem. appropriations com., transp. com.; sec. Legis. Office for Rsch. Liaison; co-chmn. Emergency Svcs. Outreach Group; active Fire Fighters Caucus, Task Force on Jobs and Bus. Expansion, Task Force on Environ., Task Force on Welfare Reform, Anti-gambling Caucus. Former editor Crawford County GOP Newsletter. Former asst. coord. Cambridge Springs (Pa.) Little League and Little Griddlers; former mem. Miss Crawford County Pageant Scholarship Exec. Bd., Cambridge Springs Presbyn. Food Pantry; mem. adv. bd. U. Pitts., Titusville; past dist. leader GOP Cambridge Dist.; active Cambridge Springs Presbyn. Ch., also former mem. bd. deacons; active Meadville Med. Ctr. Aux., Pa. Ag Reps., Craford County GOP Exec. Bd., Northwest Coun. Rep. Women, Capitol Area Coun. Rep. Women in Govt. Mem. NRA, Bus. and Profl. Women, Meadville Sportsmen Club, Pa Ruffled Grouse Soc., Kiwanis Club of Cambridge Springs. Home: 629 State St Meadville PA 16335-2262 Office: Pa Ho of Reps State Capitol Harrisburg PA 17120*

BROWN, TINA, magazine editor; b. Maidenhead, Eng., Nov. 21, 1953; d. George Hambley and Bettina Iris Mary (Kohr) B.; m. Harold Evans, Aug. 20, 1981; children: George Frederick, Isabel Harriet. M.A., Oxford U. Columnist Punch Mag., London, 1978; editor in chief Tatler Mag., London, 1979-83, Vanity Fair Mag., N.Y.C., 1984-92; editor New Yorker mag., N.Y.C., 1992—. Author: (play) Under the Bamboo Tree, 1973 (Sunday Times Drama award), (play) Happy Yellow, 1977, (book) Loose Talk, 1979, (book) Life As A Party, 1983. Named Most Promising Female Journalist, recipient Kathrine Pakenham prize Sunday London Times, 1973; named Young Journalist of Yr., 1978, Mag. Editor of Yr. Advt. Age mag., 1988.recipient USC Distinguished Achievement in Journalism Award, USC Journalism Alumni Assoc., 1994. Office: The New Yorker 20 W 43rd St New York NY 10036-7400*

BROWN, TRISHA, dancer; b. Aberdeen, Wash., Nov. 25, 1936. B.A. in Dance, Mills Coll., Calif.; Ph.D. hon. in Fine Arts, Oberlin Coll. Founder, pres. Trisha Brown Dance Co., New York, NY, 1970—; founding mem. Judson Dance Theatre; choreographer Grand Union Improvisation Group, 1970-76; lectr. Mills Coll., Calif., Reed Coll., Oreg., NYU, Goucher Coll., Md., Carnegie Mellon U., Pa.; conductor workshops and seminars throughout world. Dancer worldwide; choreographer: Untitled, 1961, Trillium, 1962, Lightfall, 1963, Untitled Duet, 1963, Part of a Tango, 1963, Target, 1964, Rulegame Five, 1964, Motor, 1965, Homemade, 1965, Inside, 1966, Skunk Cabbage, 1967, Saltgrass and Waders, 1967, Medicine Dance, 1967, Snapshots, 1968, Ballet, 1968, Falling Duet, 1968, Sky Map, 1969, Dance with Duck's Head, 1968, Yellow Belly, 1969, Leaning Duets, 1970, The Stream, 1970, Man Walking Down the Side of a Building, 1970, Accumulation 4 1/2, 1971, Walking on the Wall, 1971, Leaning Duets II, 1971, Falling Duet II, 1971, Rummage Sale and the Floor of the Forest, 1971, Planes, 1968, Roof Piece, 1971, Primary Accumulation, 1972, Accumulating Pieces, 1973, Group Accumulation, 1973, Roof and Fire Piece, 1973, Spanish Dance, 1973, Structured Pieces, 1973, Figure 8, 1974, Drift, 1974, Spiral, 1974, Pamplona Stones, 1974, Locus, 1975, Line Up, 1976, Glacial Decoy, 1979, Opal Loop, 1980, Son of Gone Fishin', 1981, Set and Reset, 1983 (N.Y. Dance and Performance award 1984), Lateral Pass, 1985 (N.Y. Dance and Performance award 1986), Carmen, 1986, Newark, 1987, Astral Convertible, 1989, For M.G.: The Movie, 1991, Astral Converted, 1991, Another Story as in Falling, 1993, If you couldn't see me, 1994, Foray Forêt, 1990, You Can See Us, 1995, M.O., 1995, Twelve Ton Rose, 1996; featured TV show, M.O., Sta. WNET-TV, N.Y.C., Dance in America, Sta. WGBH-TV, Boston, Dancing on the Edge, Sta. WGBH-TV, Boston, Making Dances, Sta. WGBH-TV, Boston; drawings exhibited Venice Biennale, Toulon Museum; group exhibition: Numerals: Mathematical Concepts in Contemporary Art, Drawings: The Pluralist Decade, New Notes for New Dance, Art and Dance: Images From the Modern Dialogue; Avant-garde Theater and Dance Notes & Scores curated by Robert Rauschenberg; film Accumulation with Talking plus Watermotor, KCET, Los Angeles, and KTCA, Mpls. Fellow Guggenheim Found., 1975, 84, NEA Creative Artists Svc. Program, 1977, 81-84; MacArthur fellow, 1991; grantee NEA, N.Y. State Coun. on Arts, other founds. and corps.; recipient creative arts award Brandeis U., 1982, Dance Mag. award, 1987, Chevalier dans L'Ordre des Arts & des Lettres, Govt. France, 1988, Samuel H. Scripps Am. Dance Festival award, 1994. Home: 211 W 61st St 4th Fl New York NY 10023 Office: 211 W 61st St 4th Fl New York NY 10023*

BROWN, VALERIE ANNE, psychiatric social worker, educator; b. Elizabeth, N.J., Feb. 28, 1951; d. William John and Adelaide Elizabeth (Krasa) B.; BA summa cum laude (fellow), C.W. Post Coll., 1972; MSW (Silberman scholar), Hunter Coll., 1975; PhD, Am. Internat. U., 1996; Diplomate Am. Bd. Examiners, Am. Bd. Clin. Social Work, Nat. Assn. Soc. Work; cert. addictions specialist, cert. master hypnotherapist. Social work intern Greenwich House Counseling Center, N.Y.C., 1973-74, Metro Cons. Center, N.Y.C., 1974-75; sr. psychiat. social worker, co-adminstr. Saturday Clinic, Essex County Guidance Center, East Orange, N.J., 1975-80; pvt. practice psychiat. social work, psychotherapy, 1979—; sr. psychiat social worker John E. Runnells Hosp., Berkeley Heights, N.J., 1980-86; dir. social work Northfield Manor, West Orange, N.J., 1987; clin. coord. Project Portals East Orange Gen. Hosp., 1987-88; asst. dir. ARS/Century House Riverview Med. Ctr., Red Bank, N.J., 1988-93; sr. clin. case mgmt. specialist Prudential Ins. Co., Woodbridge, N.J., 1993-93; clin. dir. Greenhouse-KMC, Lakewood, N.J., 1994—, Shoreline-KBH, Toms River, N.J., 1996—; tech. advisor Nat. Comm. Network, 1988—; instr. Brookdale Coll., 1991—; co-founder Women's Growth Ctr., Cedar Grove, N.J., 1979; counselor Passaic Drug Clinic, 1978-80; field instr. Fairleigh Dickinson U., Madison, N.J., 1981-86, Brookdale Coll., 1989-92; field supr. Union Coll., Cranford, N.J., 1986; instr. Sch. Social Work, NYU, N.Y.C., 1980-83, asst. prof., 1983-85; evaluator Intoxicated Driver Resource Ctr., Essex County, N.J., 1987-88. Alt. Monmouth County profl. adv. bd. Mem. NASW, Psi Chi, Pi Gamma Mu, Sigma Tau Delta. Office: 20 Ellsworth Ct Red Bank NJ 07701-5403

BROWN, VALERIE SHARICE, marketing executive; b. Silver Spring, Md., Aug. 26, 1967; d. Leroy Jr. and Rose Ann (Lanier) B. BS in Econs., U. Pa. Wharton, 1988; postgrad. in econs., U. Zimbabwe, Harare, 1989; MBA, Harvard Bus. Sch., 1994. Assoc. intern mgmt. Citibank N.A., Libreville, Gabon, 1988; rsch. asst. The World Bank, Washington, 1990; bus. analyst McKinsey & Co., N.Y.C., 1990-92; bus. devel. intern Merck & Co., West Point, Pa., 1993; coord. N.Am. region Women's World Banking, N.Y.C., 1994-95; dir. internat. ops.; dir. internat. ops. Ben & Jerry's Homemade, South Burlington, Vt., 1995. Rotary Internat. fellow, 1989, Merck MBA fellow Merck & Co., 1992, AAUW fellow, 1992, George F. Baker scholar Harvard Bus. Sch., 1994. Mem. Harvard Bus. Sch. of Women Alumnae. Address: 12 Fayette Rd # 319 South Burlington VT 05403

BROWN, WENDY ELAINE, communications consultant; b. Los Alamos, N.Mex., Apr. 28, 1956; d. Leon J. and Dorothy (Stern) B.; m. Richard Swanson; children: Tasmin Amanda Swanson, Nathaniel Richard Swanson. BA, Northwestern U., 1978. Software engr. Prime Computer Inc., Natick, Mass., 1978-80; systems programmer Dialcom, Silver Spring, Md., 1980-85; systems programmer, analyst APA, Falls Church, Va., 1985-86; mem. tech. staff Corp. for Open Systems, McLean, Va., 1986-89; cons. PSC Internat. Inc., McLean, 1989-95; cons. J.G. Van Dyke and Assocs., Annapolis Junction, Md., 1995—. Author OSI Dictionary of Acronyms, 1992. Mem. IEEE Computer Soc., ACM, Assn. for Computing Machinery. Democrat. Jewish. Avocations: sewing, electronic networking. Home: 9417 Russell Rd Silver Spring MD 20910-1445 Office: JG Van Dyke & Assocs 141 National Business Pkwy Ste 210 Annapolis Junction MD 20701

BROWN, WENDY WEINSTOCK, nephrologist; b. N.Y.C., Dec. 9, 1944; d. Irving and Pearl (Levack) Weinstock; m. Barry David Brown, May 2, 1971 (div. Sept. 1995); children: Jennifer Faye, Joshua Reuben, Julie Aviva, Rachel Ann. BA, U. Mass., 1966; MD, Med. Coll. of Pa., 1970. Am. Bd. Internal Medicine, 1977. Intern U. Ill. Affiliated Hosps., Chgo., 1970-71; resident in internal medicine The Med. Coll. Wis. Affiliated Hosps., Milw., 1971-74; gen. practitioner Vogelweh (W. Germany) Health Clinics, 1975-76; fellow in nephrology Med. Coll. of Wis. Milw. County Med. Complex, Milw., 1976-78; staff physician St. Louis VA Med Ctr., 1978—, acting chief, hemodialysis sect., 1983-85, chief dialysis/renal sect., 1985-90; dir. clin. nephrology, 1990—; staff physician St. Louis U. Hosps., 1978—, St. Louis City Hosp., 1982-85, St Mary's Health Ctr., St. Louis, 1994—; assoc. prof. internal medicine St. Louis U. Health Sci. Ctr., 1985—. Reviewer Clin. Nephrology, Am. Jour. Kidney Disease, Jour Am. Geriatric Soc., Jour. Jour. Renal Replacement Theory, Jour. Am. Soc. Nephrology, Geriatric Nephrology and Urology, also mem. editl. bd.; contbr. articles to profl. jours. Mem. adv. coun. Mo. Kidney Program, 1985-91, chmn., 1988-89; numerous positions Nat. Kidney Found., 1984—, nat. chmn., 1995—; bd. dirs. Nat. Kidney Found. Ea. Mo. and Metro East, Inc., 1980—; bd. dirs. Combined Health Appeal Greater St. Louis, Inc., 1988, pres., 1989-92; bd. dirs. Combined Health Appeal Am., 1991—, sec., 1992-96, vice chmn., 1996—. Recipient Upjohn Achievement award Med. Coll. Wis. Affiliated Hosps. 1972, St. Louis YWCA Cert. of Leadership 1989, Chmn.'s award Nat. Kidney Found. of Ea. Mo. and Metro East 1990, Nat. Kidney Found., Washington 1990; named Casual Corner Career Woman of the Yr. 1986, Combined Health Appeal of Am. Vol. of Yr. 1991. Fellow ACP; mem. Am. Soc. Nephrology, Internat. Soc. Nephrology, Coun. on Kidney in Cardiovascular Disease, Am. Heart Assn., St. Louis Soc. Am. Med. Women's Assn., St. Louis Internists (v.p. 1983-84, pres. 1984-85), Women in Nephrology, Internat. Soc. for Peritoneal Dialysis, Am. Geriatrics Soc., Alpha Omega Alpha. Home: 100 Frontenac Frst Saint Louis MO 63131-3235 Office: Saint Louis VAMC 915 N Grand Blvd Saint Louis MO 63106-1621

BROWN-BLACK, LILLIAN (RUSTY), volunteer; b. Ft. Leavenworth, Kans., Oct. 10, 1920; d. Charles Robert and Lillie (Irvin) Brown; m. Robert Russell Black, Mar. 25, 1991. Club-recreation worker ARC, Philippines-Japan, 1945-47, Germany, 1947-48, Japan-Korea, 1950-52; sec.-civilian U.S. Army, Washington, 1952-53; sec. The White House, Washington, 1953-61; personal-pvt. sec. Office of Pres. D.D. and Mamie Eisenhower, Gettysburg, Pa., 1961-68; claims authorizer Social Security, Kansas City, Mo., 1968-73; caretaker The Brown Family, Kansas City, Kans., 1973-91; spkr. Eisenhower Years/Life on an Old Indian Fort/Philately, 1990—. Bd. mem. Eisenhower Soc., Gettysburg, 1991—; state contact Kans. ARC Overseas Assn., 1992—. Mem. Nat. Mus. Women in Arts. Republican. Baptist. Home: 2001 N Adams St # 1015 Arlington VA 22201-3751 also: 7614 Greeley Ave Kansas City KS 66112

BROWN-CHAPPELL, BETTY L., social worker, educator; b. San Francisco, Nov. 25, 1946; d. Benjamin Franklin and Clara Lucille (Williams) Brown; m. Michael James Chappell, Oct. 1, 1975; children: Michael Jahi, Aisha Ebony. BA, U. Mich., 1969, MSW, 1971; PhD, U. Chgo., 1991. Social caseworker Detroit Health Dept., 1971; cmty. svc. asst. Commn. on Cmty. Rels., Detroit, 1971-73; adminstrv. asst. Sr. Citizens Dept., Detroit, 1973-77; asst. dir. Walter Reuther Sr. Citizens Ctrs., Detroit, 1977-79; vis. instr., rsch. assoc. U. Ill. Chgo., 1979-80; coord. acad. adv., assoc. prof. Northeastern Ill. U., Chgo., 1980-84; asst. dean U. Chgo., 1984-89; field coord. Ill. State U., Normal, 1990-92; asst. prof. U. Mich., Ann Arbor, 1992-96; assoc. prof. Ea. Mich. U., Ypsilanti, 1996—; mgmt. cons. United Tenants Speak, Detroit, 1994; ednl. cons. C.O.T.S., Detroit, 1994. Contbr. articles to profl. jours. Fellow U. Mich., 1991-92, Ill. Consortium on Edn. Opportunity, 1989-90, Delta Sigma Theta, 1988, Ctr. Urban Rsch. and Policy Studies, 1987; recipient Citation Acad. All-Am., 1988, Detroit Bd. Edn.,

1975, Cert. Appreciation City Detroit Mayor's Office and Sr. Citizens Dept., 1976, Resolution of Merit Mich. State Rep., Jackie Vaughn, 1975. Mem. Nat. Assn. Black Social Workers (steering com. 1975-79, v.p. Detroit chpt. 1974-75). Office: Univ Mich 421A King Hall Ypsilanti MI 48197

BROWNE, ANN APRIL, purchasing manager; b. Washington, Apr. 9, 1945; d. Benjamin and Sarah (Barr) Mudrick. BA in Bus. Mgmt., Eckerd Coll., 1987. Cert. purchasing mgr.; accredited purchasing practitioner. Purchasing mgr. Gen. Kinetics, Rockville, Md., 1972-73; assoc. buyer Control Data Corp., Rockville, 1973-74; outside sales rep. Mid Atlantic Industries, Bladensburg, Md., 1974, U.S. C. of C., San Antonio, 1975; inside sales coord. Frabimore Equipment & Controls, Inc., Elk Grove Village, Ill., 1976-77; customer svc. rep. Viracon, Inc., Bensenville, Ill., 1977; purchasing mgr. Vectrol div. Westinghouse Elec. Corp., Oldsmar, Fla., 1978-83; purchasing agt. Helen Ellis Meml. Hosp., Tarpon Springs, Fla., 1987—. Mem. Material Mgmt. Assn. of Fla., Nat. Assn. Purchasing Mgmt. (cert.), Phi Theta Kappa.

BROWNE, JOY, psychologist; b. New Orleans, Oct. 24, 1950; d. Nelson and Ruth (Strauss) B.; Carter Thweatt, June 9, 1966 (div. 1979); 1 child, Patience. BA, Rice U.; PhD, Northeastern U.; postgrad., Tufts U. Registered psychologist, Mass. With research/optics dept. Sperry Rand, Boston, 1966-68; engr. space program Itek, Boston, 1968-70; head social services dept. Boston Redevel. Authority, 1970-71; staff psychologist South Shore Counselling Assocs., Boston, 1971-82; on-the-air psychologist Sta. WITS, Boston, 1978-82, Sta. KGO, San Francisco, 1982-84; host, news Sta. KCBS, San Francisco, 1984-85; on-air psychologist Sta. WABC, N.Y.C., 1985-87, ABC Talkradio, N.Y.C., 1987-92, WOR Radio Network, N.Y.C., 1992—, Sta. WABC-TV, 1995—; dir. Town of Hull Adolescent Outreach Program; cons. human sexuality PBS, 1994—. Author: The Used Car Game, 1971, The Research Experience, 1976, Nobody's Perfect, 1988, Why They Don't Call When They Say They Will and Other Mixed Signals, 1989. Named One of 25 Outstanding Broadcasters USA Today, 1995, 96, Legend La., 1996, Best Female Talk Show Host, Nartash, 1996. Mem. APA (bd. dirs. 1994-97), Phi Kappa Phi (Communicator of Yr. award 1992). Office: WOR Radio Network 1440 Broadway New York NY 10018

BROWNE, SHEILA, publishing executive, actress; b. High Point, N.C., Aug. 7, 1943; d. Peter Joseph and Mary Catherine (Walsh) B. BA, Marymount Manhattan Coll., N.Y.C., 1965; studied with Sanford Meisner, N.Y.C., 1969-70. Dir. cover copy Pocket Books, Inc., N.Y.C., 1982-96. Actor, writer Studio Arena Theater, 1968-69; actor Champlain Shakespeare Festival, 1971. Mem. Women in Comm. (N.Y. chpt.), Actor's Equity Assn.

BROWNE-MILLER, ANGELA CHRISTINE, author, educator, social research association executive, metaphysician, political analyst; b. Whittier, Calif., June 26, 1952; d. Lee Winston and Louisa Francesca (de Angelis) Browne; m. Richard Louis Miller, Feb. 22, 1986; 1 child, Evacheska. BA in Biology and Lit. with honors, U. Calif., Santa Cruz, 1976; postgrad. in spl. edn., Sonoma State U., 1976-77; MSW, U. Calif., Berkeley, 1981, MPH, 1983, Dr. Social Welfare, 1983, PhD in Edn., 1992. Lic. clin. social worker, Calif. Child and family counselor Clearwater Ranch Children's Home, Mendocino County, Calif., 1976-77; conselor, spl. edn. tchr. Bachman Hill Sch., Mendocino County, Calif., 1977-78; substitute tchr. Marin County (Calif.) Sch. Dist., 1978-79; founder Metatech/Metasome Corp. Services, 1982—; also bd. dirs. Whole Care Inst.; rsch. dir. Cokenders Alcohol and Drug Inst., Emeryville, Calif., 1983-89; exec. cons. Parkside Med. Svcs., Chgo., 1989-90; bd. dirs. Mataterra Prodns; policy and program analyst White House Conf. on Families, Washington, summer 1980 to spring 1981; research analyst Office for Families, Adminstrn. for Children Youth and Families HHS, 1981, grant reader, 1982, 84, 85, 86; day care program evaluator, budget cons. San Francisco Bay area, 1980-83; lectr. Sch. Social Welfare, Haas Sch. Bus. U. Calif., Berkeley, 1984—; program cons. Wilbur Hot Springs Health Sanctuary, 1984-93; pres. Cokenders Alcohol and Drug Inst., Emeryville, 1986-90; lectr. Sch. Pub. Policy U. Calif., Berkeley, 1986-88; guest White House Conf. for a Drug-Free Am., 1987-88; lectr. in field. Author: The Day Care Dilemma, 1990, Working Dazed, 1991, Transcending Addiction, 1992, Gestalting Addiction, 1993, Learning to Learn, 1994, Intelligence Policy, 1995, Omega Point, 1995, Shameful Admissions, 1996, Embracing Death, 1996, Flesh Trade, 1996; contbr. numerous articles to profl. jours.; panelist numerous nat. radio and TV appearances, Oprah Winfrey Show, Talk of the Nation. Pub. dir. Californians for Drug Free Youth Conf., 1986; mem. Nat. Task Force on Drug Abuse, 1984. Recipient Presdl. Mgmt. Internship award, 1982; grantee Adminstrn. for Children Youth and Family Welfare, 1980; NIMH postdoctoral fellow, 197-89. Mem. Am. Pub. Health Assn., Nat. Assn. Social Workers, Assn. Ednl. Rschrs. and Adminstrs., Am. Acad. Psychotherapists, Mensa. Office: 98 Main St # 315 Belvedere Tiburon CA 94920-2566

BROWNER, CAROL, federal agency administrator; d. Michael Browner and Isabella Harty Hugues; m. Michael Podhorzer; 1 child, Zachary. Grad., U. Fla., 1977, JD, 1979. Gen. counsel govt. ops. com. Fla. Ho. of Reps.; with Citizen Action, Washington; chief legis. aide environ. issues to Sen. Lawton Chiles, legis. dir. to Sen. Al Gore, Jr., 1988-91; sec. Dept. Environ. Regulation, Fla., 1991-93; adminstr. EPA, Washington, 1993—. Office: Environmental Protection Agency Office of the Administrator 401 M St SW Washington DC 20460 0001

BROWNING, CAROL ANNE, pediatrician, educator; b. Appleton, Wis., June 1, 1936; d. Bertie Lee and Margaret (Loscher) B. BA, Oberlin Coll., 1958; MD, U. Wis., 1962. Diplomate Am. Bd. Pediatrics, Am. Bd. Neonatal-Perinatal Medicine. Intern Highland-Alameda County Hosp., Oakland, Calif., 1962-63; resident Children's Hosp. East Bay, Oakland, 1963-65; pediatrician Kaiser-Permanente Med. Ctr., Walnut Creek, Calif., 1965-68; fellow in neonatology Stanford U., 1968-70; neonatologist Med. Coll. Wis., Milw., 1970-89; mem. staff Sinai Samaritan Med. Ctr., Milw., 1970—; assoc. prof. pediatrics U. Wis. Sch. Medicine, Milw., 1989—; bd. dirs. Perinatal Found., Madison, Wis., 1988—; med. dir. NICU, 1991—. Bd. dirs. Unitarian Ch. North, Mequon, Wis., 1987-89, St. Francis Children's Ctr., Milw., 1987-90. Fellow Am. Acad. Pediatrics; mem. Nat. Perinatal Assn., Wis. Assn. for Perinatal Care (pres. 1976-77, Callon-Leonard award 1989). Democrat. Office: Sinai Samaritan Med Ctr 2000 W Kilbourn Ave Milwaukee WI 53233-1625

BROWNING, NORMA LEE (MRS. RUSSELL JOYNER OGG), journalist; b. Spickard, Mo., Nov. 24, 1914; d. Howard R. and Grace (Kennedy) B.; m. Russell Joyner Ogg, June 12, 1938. A.B., B.J., U. Mo., 1937; M.A. in English, Radcliffe Coll., 1938. Reporter Los Angeles Herald-Express, 1942-43; with Chgo. Tribune, from 1944, Hollywood columnist, 1966-75; Vis. lectr. creative writing, editorial cons., mem. nat. adv. bd. Interlochen Arts Acad., Northwood Inst. Author: City Girl in the Country, 1955, Joe Maddy of Interlochen, 1963, (with W. Clement Stone) The Other Side of the Mind, 1965, The Psychic World of Peter Hurkos, 1970, (with Louella Dirksen) The Honorable Mr. Marigold, 1972, (with Ann Miller) Miller's High Life, 1972, Peter Hurkos: I Have Many Lives, 1976, Omarr: Astrology and the Man, 1977, (with George Masters) The Masters Way to Beauty, 1977, (with Russell Ogg) He Saw A Hummingbird, 1978, (with Florence Lowell) Be A Guest At Your Own Party, 1980, Face-Lifts: Everything You Always Wanted to Know, 1981, Joe Maddy Of Interlochen: Portrait of A Legend, 1991; Contbr. articles to nat. mags. Recipient E.S. Beck award Chgo Tribune. Mem. Theta Sigma Phi, Kappa Tau Alpha. Address: 226 E Morongo Rd Palm Springs CA 92264-8402

BROWNING, THERESA MICHELLE, public relations executive, marketing director; b. Indpls., Feb. 2, 1962; d. Grover and Helen Lucille (Kinser) B. BA, Ind. U., 1986. Adminstrv. asst. Clinic for Women, Indpls., 1985-86; dir. edn. Marion County Cancer Soc., Indpls., 1986-90; mktg. specialist Purdue U., West Lafayette, Ind., 1990-94, info. specialist, 1995—; pub. spkr. Ill. Grape Growers & Vintners, Navoo, 1994; presenter Ohio Grape & Wine Short Course, Cleve., 1995, Midwest Internat. Wine Exposition, Chgo., 1993. Contbr. articles to profl. jours. Mem. Gender Fairness Coalition Ind., 1994. Mem. NOW (bd. dirs. Ind. divsn. 1992—, pres. Indpls. chpt. 1989, bd. dirs. Indpls. chpt. 1987-89), Pub. Rels. Soc. Am. (Hoosier chpt.), Toastmasters. Home: 2830 W 38th St Indianapolis IN 46222 Office: Ind Wine Grape Coun 5610 Crawfordsville Rd #2004 Indianapolis IN 46224

BROWNLEE, PAULA PIMLOTT, professional society administrator; b. London, June 23, 1934; came to U.S., 1959; d. John Richard and Alice A. (Ajamian) Pimlott; m. Thomas H. Brownlee, Feb. 10, 1961; children: Kenneth Gainsford, Elizabeth Ann, Clare Louise. BA with honors, Somerville Coll., Oxford (Eng.) U., 1957; PhD in Organic Chemistry, Oxford (Eng.) U., 1959. Postdoctoral fellow U. Rochester, N.Y., 1959-61; rsch. chemist Am. Cyanamid Co., Stamford, Conn., 1961-62; lectr. U. Bridgeport, Conn., 1968-70; asst. prof., then assoc. prof. Rutgers U., N.J., 1970-76, assoc. dean, then acting dean Douglass Coll., 1972-76; dean faculty, prof. chemistry Union Coll., Schenectady, N.Y., 1976-81; pres., prof. chemistry Hollins (Va.) Coll., 1981-90; pres. Assn. Am. Colls. and Univs., Washington, 1990—; bd. dirs. Bell Atlantic of Va. Author lab. manual; contbr. articles to profl. publs. Bd. dirs. U. Rochester, Assn. Religion in Intellectual Life, Nat. Humanities Ctr. Hon. fellow Somerville Coll., Oxford, Eng., 1996—. Mem. Am. Chem. Soc., Royal Chm. Soc. London, Soc. Values in Higher Edn., Cosmos Club, Sigma Xi. Episcopalian. Office: Assn Am Colls and Univs 1818 R St NW Washington DC 20009-1604

BROWN-LEMACKS, LOIS BENAY, print and video designer; b. Houston, Mar. 11, 1970; d. Milton Shepard Brown-Knaebel and Nila Ann Willis Fleming. BFA in Video Prodn. cum laude, Savannah Coll. Art and Design, 1991. Prodn. asst. So. Cable Advt., Savannah, Ga., 1990-92; designer Eaton and Assocs., Savannah, 1992-94; v.p. creative designs Marcom, Cape Girardeau, Mo., 1994-96. Author: (poetry) Dreamcatcher, 1996. Vol., co-chmn. activities Peace Ctr., Wilkes-Barre, 1995-96. Recipient regional Addy award for best 30 second pub. svc. announcement, 1990. Mem. Internat. TV Assn. (treas. 1989-90, sec. 1990-91). Home and Office: Delphinus Inspirations 380A E Ridge St Nanticoke PA 18634

BROWN-PROVOST, LINDA, elementary school educator; b. Holyoke, Mass., Aug. 31, 1965; d. Allan Kingsbury and Irene Catherine (Pietrzyk) Brown; m. Christopher Jude Provost, Apr. 20, 1991. AS, Holyoke (Mass.) C.C., 1985; BS, U. Hartford, Conn., 1987, MEd, 1990, EdD in Ednl. Leadership, 1995. Tchr. Hartford Pub. Schs., 1988; ednl. therapist Forestville (Conn.) Rehab. Ctr., 1988-89; tchr. St. Brigid Sch., West Hartford, Conn., 1989-90, Simsbury (Conn.) Pub. Schs., 1990—; grad. asst. U. Hartford, West Hartford, 1992-94; condr. workshops in field; certification specialist Aerobics and Fitness Assn. Am. U. Hartford Dean's scholar, 1985, 86. Mem. Sigma Rho, Kappa Delta Phi. Republican. Roman Catholic. Home: 22 Sunrise Terr Weatogue CT 06089 Office: Squadron Line School 44 Squadron Line Rd Simsbury CT 06070-1636

BROWNRIGG, JUDITH HAMILTON, institutional sales executive; b. Roanoke, Va., June 14, 1950; d. Carl Cannaday and Mary Lee (Anderson) Hamilton; m. W. Grant Brownrigg, Apr. 28, 1984; children: Carter Grant, Taylor Hamilton, Kelsey Anderson. BS in Nursing, U. Va., 1972, MBA, 1982. RN, Va. Staff, charge nurse No. Va. Drs. Hosp., Falls Church, 1972; librarian John Hopkins Sch. Internat. Studies, Bologna, Italy, 1974-75; English instr. Politzer Sch. Langs., Bologna, 1975-76; staff, charge nurse Alexandria (Va.) Hosp., 1975, Roanoke (Va.) Meml. Hosp., 1972, 76-77; head nurse intensive care U. Va. Hosp., Charlottesville, 1972, 77-79, staff nurse clinic, 1979-80; mgmt. assoc. Equitable Life Assurance Soc., N.Y.C., 1982-84, product mgr., 1984-86; v.p. product devel. Equitable Real Estate Investment Mgmt., Inc., N.Y.C., 1986-87; v.p. instl. sales Equitable Real Estate, N.Y.C., 1987—. Baptist. Home: 305 N Mountain Ave Montclair NJ 07043-1021 Office: Equitable Real Estate Investment Mgmt Inc 787 7th Ave New York NY 10019-6018

BROWN-WAITE, VIRGINIA (GINNY BROWN-WAITE), state legislator; b. Albany, N.Y., Oct. 5, 1943; m. Harvey Waite; children: Jeannien Roxby Waite, Danene Mitchell, Sue Meaders, Lorie Sue. BS, SUNY, 1976; MS, Russell Sage Coll., 1984. Former commr. Hernando County; former legis. dir. N.Y. State Senate; mem. Fla. State Senate, 1992—. Active W Hernando GOP, United Way; bd. dirs. Hernando County Spouse Abuse Ctr. Mem. Bus. and Profl. Women's Club, Suncoast MG Club. Roman Catholic. Address: Fla State Senate State Capitol Tallahassee FL 32301

BROYLES, BONITA EILEEN, nursing educator; b. Ross County, Ohio, Sept. 29, 1948; d. Arthur Runnels and Mary Elizabeth (Page) Brookie; m. Roger F. Broyles, Dec. 29, 1984; children: Michael Richard Brown, Jeffrey Allen Brown. BSN, Ohio State U., 1970; MA with honors, N.C. Cen. U., Durham, 1988; EdD summa cum laude, LaSalle U., 1996. ADN instr., CPR instr. Piedmont C.C., Roxboro, N.C.; instr. nursing Watts Sch. Nursing, Durham; res. float staff nurse Durham County Gen. Hosp., Durham; dir. practical nursing edn., instr. Piedmont C.C., Roxboro, N.C.; maternity patient tchr. Mt. Carmel Med. Ctr., Columbus, Ohio; vice chmn. assoc. degree nursing faculty Piedmont Community Coll., 1990—. Contbr. articles to profl. jours. Named ADN Educator of Yr. N.C. Assoc. Degree Nursing Coun., 1993. Office: Piedmont CC Sch Nursing College St Roxboro NC 27573

BROZOWSKI, LAURA ADRIENNE, mechanical engineer; b. Yokohama, Japan, May 12, 1960; came to U.S., 1961; d. John and Muriel Sydney (Jackson) B. BSME, U. Calif., 1982; MS in Mech. Engring., Calif. State U., 1987; MBA, Pepperdine U., 1988. Registered profl. engr.; cert. profl. mgr. Mem. tech. staff Rocketdyne Divs. Rockwell Internat. Corp., Canoga Park, Calif., 1982—. Fellow Inst. Advancement Engring.; mem. ASME, Nat. Soc. Profl. Engrs., Nat. Mgmt. Assn. Home: 22036 Collins St # 230-n Woodland Hills CA 91367-4713

BRUBAKER, KAREN SUE, manufacturing executive; b. Ashland, Ohio, Feb. 5, 1953; d. Robert Eugene and Dora Louise (Camp) B. BSBA, Ashland Coll., 1975; MBA, Bowling Green State U., 1976. Supr. tire ctr. ops. BF Goodrich Co., Akron, Ohio, 1976-77, supr. tire ctr. acctg., 1977-79, asst. product mgr. radial passenger tires, 1979-80, product mgr. broadline passenger tires, 1980-81, group product mgr. broadline passenger and light truck tires, 1981-83, mktg. mgr. T/A high tech radials, 1983-86; product mktg. mgr. B.F. Goodrich T/A radials The Uniroyal Goodrich Tire Co., Akron, Ohio, 1986-91; product mktg. mgr. Michelin performance tires Michelin Americas Small Tires, Akron, Ohio, 1991-95. Sect. chmn. indsl. divsn. United Way, Akron, 1983-86; mem. adv. coun. to trustees Coll. Bus. and Econs, Ashland U., 1990-92; vol. Hospice Vis. Nurses Svcs.; fund raiser Nat. Heart Assist and Transplant Fund/Judi Reali Transplant Fund. Recipient Alumni Disting. Service award Ashland Coll., 1986; Alpha Phi Clara Bradley Burdette scholar, 1975. Mem. Am. Mktg. Assn. (pres. Akron/Canton chpt. 1982-83, Highest Honors award 1983, nat. bd. dirs., v.p. bus. mktg. 1984-86, v.p. profl. chpts. 1987-89), Sales and Mktg. Execs., Akron Women's Network, Zonta Internat., Beta Gamma Sigma, Omicron Delta Epsilon. Home: 822 Village Pky Fairlawn OH 44333-3297

BRUBAKER, LOU ANN, advertising executive, consultant; b. Mansfield, Ohio, Apr. 29, 1957; d. Louis Stanley and Doris Ellen (Schneider) B. BA in Polit. Sci. and Urban Planning, Kent State U., 1981. Zoning adminstr. City of Cuyahoga Falls (Ohio), 1980-81; v.p. mktg. Nat. Mgmt. and Mktg., Columbus, Ohio, 1981-86; dir. advt. Drustar Drug Control Systems, Grove City, Ohio, 1986-88; program dir. STN Internat. Chem. Abstract Svcs., Columbus, 1988-91; pres. Brubaker Advt. and Mktg., Laurel, Md., 1991—; bd. dirs. Woman Rising Inc., Balt. Home and Office: Brubaker Advt and Mktg 10422 Churchill Way Laurel MD 20723-5749

BRUCE, CHERYL MEYER, communications director; b. Enid, Okla., Oct. 11, 1952; d. DeWayne and Ramona (Kluver) Meyer; m. Wade Elkins, Dec. 29, 1972 (div. 1975); m. James E. Bruce, March 11, 1978; children: Maeghan, Jamie. BA, East Tex. State U., Commerce, 1975, MA, 1978. H.s. speech, drama tchr. Pine Tree H.S., Longview, Tex., 1975-76; grad. tchg. asst. East Tex. State U., Commerce, Tex., 1976-78; admin. asst., pers. East Tex. State U., 1977-78; admin. asst., provost Tex. Woman's U., Denton, Tex., 1978-79; asst. to pres. Tex. Woman's U., 1979-87; dir. comm. State Bar of N. Mex, Albuquerque, 1987—; judge partnership awards ABA, Chgo, 1996, judge N.Mex. mock trial, 1988—. Author: Bar Executive (newsletter), 1995; editor: Bar Bulletin (newsletter), 1987—, Bar Journal (mag.), 1995—. Mem. Nat. Assn. of Bar Execs. (exec. coun. 1987—, workshop chair, comm. & pub. rels., 1993, vice-chair 1994-95, chair 1995-96, scholarship com. 1994-97, publs. com. 1990). Republican. Methodist. Home: 5705 Carruthers NE Albuquerque NM 87111 Office: State Bar of New Mex PO Box 25883 Albuquerque NM 87125

BRUCE, RACHEL MARY CONDON, nurse practitioner; b. Bklyn., Dec. 18, 1940; d. Bernard Francis Sr. and Rachel Evelyn (Riggott) Condon; m. Donald Eugene Bruce, Sept. 27, 1966; children: Donald Eugene, Kevin Francis, Rachel Janine. BSN, Molloy Cath. Coll., 1962; MEd in Counselor Edn., U. Guam, Mangilao, 1975; cert. sch. nurse practitioner, U. Colo., 1984, cert. pediatric nurse practitioner, 1985. RN, N.Y., Guam; cert. nurse practitioner, Guam; cert. sch. nurse practitioner, pediatric nurse practitioner ANCC. Asst. head nurse med.-surg. unit Bklyn. Hosp., 1962-64; part-time nurse Guam Meml. Hosp., Tamuning, 1971-72; sch. health counselor IV, Dededo Jr. H.S., Tamuning Dept. Edn., Guam, 1973-76; asst. prof. nursing U. Guam, Mangilao, 1976-80; instr. first responder Police Acad. Guam C.C., Mangilao, 1981-84, prof., sch. health counselor, nurse practitioner Student Health Ctr., 1982-94; ednl. health cons., Mangilao, 1994-96; asst. prof. tng. project Peace Corps, Tumon, Guam, summer 1978; vis. nurse Indiana (Pa.) Vis. Nurses Assn., 1980-81; part-time pediatric nurse practitioner Family Med. Clinic, Tamuning, 1988-90; mem. adv. com. preparing Guam Nurse Practice Act, Nurse Practitioner Task Force, 1985-87, mem. revision com., 1993-96; mem. com. on family planning Guam Health Objectives for 1990, 1986-87; mem. grant writing com. Fipse (drug awareness) Guam C.C., 1989-91; Guam C.C. rep. to CEO's Task Force on Health Issues, 1989-90. Co-author: (booklet) Growing Together, 1987, (revised) Growing Together, 1995. CPR instr. ARC, Guam, 1978-81; BCLS instr. Guam Heart Assn., 1981-84; vol. rape counselor Counseling Advs. Reaching Out, Guam, 1982-84; founding bd. mem., co-vice chair Guam Arthritis Found., 1989; singer Guam Symphony Chorale, 1987-95. 1st lt. USAF Nurse Corps, 1964-66. Recipient proclomation for outstanding svc. in nursing Guam Legislature, 1988, for outstanding profl. and cmty. svc., 1989. Mem. ANA (nat. disting. svc. register 1988), AAUW (past pub. rels. officer), Guam Nurses Assn., Nat. Assn. Sch. Nurses, Guam Assn. Sch. Nurses, Am. Acad. Nurse Practitioners (state award for excellence of care and outstnding contbn. in practice 1991), Internat. Reading Assn. (grantee 1992), People to People Internat. (sch. health del. to Ea. Europe 1994). Roman Catholic. Home: 11 Timber Ln Conroe TX 77384

BRUCE, VERNA LEE SMITH HICKEY, media specialist, librarian; b. Corbin, Ky., Feb. 16, 1935; d. William Abaslom and Ruthie Marie (McKeehan) Smith; m. Ralph Milton Hickey, June 2, 1956 (dec. Sept. 1981); m. Edward Bruce, June 22, 1991; stepchildren: Judy, Gary, Alisa. BA in Bus., Cumberland Coll., 1955, BS in Edn., 1968; MA in Libr. Sci., Union Coll., 1970; cert. in supervision, Ea. Ky. U., 1977. Cert. media specialist, libr., tchr., Ky. Typist Whitley County Court Clerk Office, Williamsburg, Ky., 1955-62; head bookkeeper Harlan (Ky.) Daily Enterprise, 1963-65; elem. tchr. Harlan County Bd. Edn., 1966-70; reading tchr. Boone County Bd. Edn., Florence, Ky., 1970, media specialist, libr., 1970-95; coach girls basketball, Burlington (Ky.) Elem. Sch., 1974-79, coord. girls basketball, 1979-94. Active Florence Bapt. Ch., 1970-95, mem. single adult ministry, 1970-90, choir mem., 1970-91; active Corinth Bapt. Ch., 1935-62, Calvery Bapt. Ch., Loyall, Ky., 1963-68, Chevelot Bapt. Ch., 1968-70; pres. PTA, Loyall, 1967-69, active other chpts.; mem. salary/contract com. Boone County Edn. Assn., 1990-94. Recipient Lifetime Membership award PTA, 1994, No. Ky. Sch. Libr./Media Specialist award, 1995. Mem. NEA, Ky. Edn. Assn., No. Ky. Libr. Assn., Ky. Libr. Assn., Ky. Sch. Media Assn., Boone County Libr. Assn. (sec. 1980-91), Boone County Homemakers. Republican. Home: 209 Claxon Dr Florence KY 41042-1529

BRUCK, ARLENE LORRAINE, secondary education educator; b. Kingston, N.Y., June 26, 1945; d. Machileo and Lillian (Turco) Forte; m. Laurence J. Bruck; children: Jennifer Lynn, Jason Scott. BA in Latin, Coll. Mt. St. Vincent, Riverdale, N.Y., 1967; MS in Psychology, SUNY, New Paltz, 1971. Cert. in social studies, Latin, elem. edn. Tchr. 2d grade Kingston Schs. Consol., 1967-74, tchr. Latin, psychology and sociology, 1984—; mem. Mid-Hudson Social Studies Coun., 1992—. Placement chair Jr. League, Kingston, 1982-84; vol. Girl Scouts, Tillson, N.Y., 1981-86, Athletes Against Drugs, Kingston, 1984-87. Recipient Mary Dodge McCarthy award for gen. excellence, 1967, Mid-Hudson Social Studies Coun. Excellence in Tchg. award, 1994; named Outstanding Young Woman, 1974; N.Y. State Regents scholar, 1963-67, AAUW scholar, 1963-67; NEH fellow, 1992. Mem. APA, AAUW (v.p. 1970-74, sec. 1975-77, pres. program 1994, pres. 1995-96), N.Y. State Assn. Fgn. Lang. Tchrs. Roman Catholic. Home: 39 Beth Dr Kingston NY 12401-6148 Office: Kingston High Sch 403 Broadway Kingston NY 12401-4625

BRUCK, PHOEBE ANN MASON, landscape architect; b. Highland Park, Ill., Nov. 26, 1928; d. George Allen and Louise Townsend (Barnard) Mason; m. F. Frederick Bruck, June 30, 1956. Student Bard Coll., 1946-49; BS, Ill. Inst. Tech., 1954; MLA, Harvard U., 1963. Trainee, Nat. Gallery of Art, Washington, 1947, Mus. Modern Art, N.Y.C., 1948; head design dept. Design Research Inc., Cambridge, Mass., 1955-60; cons. The Architects Collaborative & Sert, Jackson Assocs., Inc., 1960-63; v.p. F. Frederick Bruck, Architect & Assoc., Inc., Cambridge, pres., 1993-96; vis. design critic dept. landscape architecture Harvard U. Grad. Sch. Design, 1971-79; v.p. The Buccaneers Co., 1989—, also bd. dirs; cons. The arts at Harvard and Radcliff, 1995—. Contbr. to New Landscapes for Living, 1980. Judge, New Eng. Flower Show, Mass. Hort. Soc., 1971-79, Thoreau Awards, Assn. Landscape Contractors, 1980; mem. Sci. Adv. Group for Edn., Cambridge Pub. Schs., 1981-82; chair Harvard Sq. Adv. Commn., 1987—; co-chair Quincy Sq. Design Com., 1991-95. Mem. Mass. Bd. Registration of Landscape Architects (chair 1992-95), Am. Arbitration Assn., Am. Soc. Landscape Architects, Boston Soc. Landscape Architects (pres. 1973-75, examining bd. 1978-81), Mass. Soc. Mayflower Descendants, Harvard Sq. Def. Fund (chmn. adv. ocm. 1987, bd. dirs. 1984-85, pres. 1985-86), Harvard U. Grad. Sch. Design Alumni Assn. (officer 1972-78), Soc. for Protection of New Eng. Antiquities (design adv. com). Episcopalian. Home & Office: 148 Coolidge Hl Cambridge MA 02138-5521

BRUCKERT, LUCINDA GETTY, artist; b. Niskayuna, N.Y., Oct. 28, 1952; d. George Clinton and Mary Wheeler (Walker) Getty; 1 child, Anita Genet Bruckert. Grad. h.s., 1970. Freelance artist Clay, N.Y., 1977-89; comml. driver Cicero-North Syracuse (N.Y.) Sch. Dist., 1989—; owner Handcrafted Glass, Clay, 1995—; Designer cross-stitch. Recipient 2d Place Masters award Old Forge Art Show, 1979, 3d Place, 1970, 79. Home: 209 Deerfield Rd # 6 East Syracuse NY 13057

BRUCK-LIEB, LILLY, retired consumer advisor, broadcaster, columnist; b. Vienna, Austria, May 13, 1918; came to U.S., 1941, naturalized, 1944; d. Max and Sophie M. Hahn; Ph.D. in Econs., U. Vienna; postgrad. Sorbonne, Paris, Sch. of Econs., London, Sch. of Bus., Columbia U., 1941-42, Sch. of Social Work, N.Y. U., 1964-66; m. Sandor Bruck, Mar. 7, 1943; 1 child, Sandra Lee (Mrs. John David Evans III); m. David L. Lieb, Dec. 7, 1985. Dir. consumer edn. Dept. Consumer Affairs, City of N.Y., 1969-78; project dir. Am. Coalition of Citizens with Disabilities, 1977-78; consumer advisor, broadcaster In Touch Networks, N.Y.C., 1978-90; consumer affairs commentator Nat. Public Radio, 1980-82; ret. Chmn. Westchester County, Bonds for Israel, 1960-64. V.p. Jewish Community Ctr., White Plains, N.Y. Recipient Eleanor Roosevelt award Bonds for Israel, 1963; Woman of Yr. award Anti Defamation League, 1972; Community Service award local council Girl Scouts U.S.A., 1974. Mem. Soc. of Consumer Affairs Profls. Democrat. Author: Access, The Guide to a Better Life for Disabled Americans, 1978; contbr. articles on disability and rehab. to books, ency., and mags. Home: 25 Murray Hill Rd Scarsdale NY 10583-2829

BRUDNAK, DORIS JEAN, counselor; b. Morrison, Ill., June 23, 1940; d. William Nathan and Hazel Blanche (Jacobs) Wade; m. Basil John Brudnak, June 18, 1966; children: Mark, Andrew, Matthew, Lucy. BS in Edn., No. Ill. U., 1962, MS in Edn., 1994. Tchr. phys. edn. High Sch. Dist. # 155, Crystal Lake, Ill., 1962-67; teaching asst. Cmty. Sch. Dist. # 300, Carpentersville, Ill., 1985-92; intensive day treatment therapist Janet Wattles Mental Health Ctr., Rockford, Ill., 1994—. Mem. Am. Counseling Assn., Ill. Counseling Assn. Democrat. Roman Catholic. Home: 504 Cheyenne Dr Lake In The Hills IL 60102 Office: Janet Wattles Ctr 526 W State St Rockford IL 61101

BRUECKNER, BONNIE LICHTENSTEIN, security administrator; b. Chgo., Mar. 5, 1936; d. Ralph Henry and Hazel May (Mullens) Lichtenstein; m. Keith Allen Brueckner, June 18, 1988; children: Deborah Norwood, J. Patrick Klavas. BA in Psychology, San Diego State U., 1981. Security mgr.

Phys. Dynamics, La Jolla, Calif., 1980-86, security cons., 1986—; sr. security coord. Lockheed, Burbank, Calif., 1986-87, United Tech., San Diego, 1987-89; div. adminstr. security Inst. for Def. Analyses Ctr. for Comm. Rsch. La Jolla, San Diego, 1989—. Mem. Nat. Classification Mgmt. Soc.

BRUEMMER, LORRAINE VENSKUNAS, funeral director, real estate broker, nurse; b. Waterbury, Conn., Jan. 25; d. Anthony George and Mary Agnes (Kritchman) Venskunas; m. Jay Porter Bruemmer, Oct. 28, 1973; 1 child by previous marriage: Linda L. Rocco Sovak. R.N., St. Francis Hosp. Sch. Nursing, 1950; B.S., Columbia U., 1958; M.Ed., U. Hartford, 1961. Head nurse pediatrics Cook Hosp., Hartford, Conn., 1953-56; instr. pediatrics Bellevue Hosp., N.Y.C., 1958-59; instr. med. surg. nursing New Britain Gen. Hosp., 1959-62; hosp. supr. New Britain Gen. Hosp., 1962-63; owner Venskunas Funeral Home, New Britain, 1962—; owner Bruemmer Venskunas Real Estate, New Britain, 1974—, Stanley Monumental Co., 1993—; commr. New Britain Health Dept., 1965-74; nurse blood bank ARC, N.Y.C., 1957-59, New Britain, 1960-69. Vol. Republican Party, New Britain. Mem. New Britain Funeral Dis. Assn. (pres. 1975-78), Conn. Funeral Dirs., Nat. Funeral Dirs., New Britain Bd. Realtors, Hartford Bd. Realtors, Nat. Bd. Realtors, Multiple Listing Service Greater Hartford. Roman Catholic. Clubs: Ladies Guild (pres. 1969), Shuttle Meadow Country. Avocations: antiques; golf; tennis; swimming; bicycling; gardening. Home: 36 Roslyn Dr New Britain CT 06052-1824 Office: Venskunas Funeral Home 665 Stanley St Ste 1612 New Britain CT 06051-2736

BRUESEWITZ-LOPINTO, GAIL C., marketing professional; b. N.Y.C., May 17, 1956; d. Arthur George and Blanche Juliana (Dobos) Bruesewitz; m. Joseph LoPinto, Sept. 1990; 1 child, Frank Joseph. BA in Eng. Lit., SUNY, Binghamton, 1978. Exec. sec. promotion and artist devel. Columbia Records/CBS Records, Inc., N.Y.C., 1979-82, dir. nat. dance music mktg., 1982-89; v.p., power station promotion Crossover Mktg. Inc., N.Y.C., 1989-90; pres. Brueser Prodns., 1990; nat. dir. promotion/artist devel. Ear Candy Records, 1990-91; prodn. coord. AIG Risk Mgmt., Inc. (divsn. Am. Internat. Group, Inc.), N.Y.C., 1991—; rep. record div. Women's Orgn. Coun. CBS, Inc., N.Y.C., 1980-82; adv. bd., dance/music, New Music Seminar, N.Y.C., 1989—. Editor newsletter Brueser's Boogie Backpage, 1983-90. Bd. dirs. Mt. Tremper (N.Y.) Lutheran Camp and Retreat Ctr., 1976-78, Camp Wilbur Herrlich, Pawling, N.Y., 1990; active Big Sisters, Binghamton (N.Y.) Social Svcs. dept., 1975-78. Named N.Y. rep. for Mademoiselle mag., 1975. Democrat. Lutheran. Office: Am Internat Group Inc 70 Pine St Lowr 3 New York NY 10270-0093

BRUETT, KAREN DIESL, sales and fundraising consultant; b. N.Y.C., May 15, 1945; d. Francis J. and Dorothy (Peterson) Diesl; m. William H. Bruett, Jr., Mar. 18, 1967; 1 child, Lindsey Diesl. BA in English, St. Lawrence U., 1966; MA, Hunter Coll., 1971. Tchr. English Freeport (N.Y.) pub. schs., 1966-70; exec. interviewer, researcher Louis Harris & Assocs., N.Y.C., 1970-72; dir. adult edn. West Side YMCA, 1972-76, mem. bd. mgrs., 1978-83; v.p. new bus. devel. Gaylord Adams & Assocs., Inc., N.Y.C., 1976-81; account exec. John Blair Mktg., N.Y.C., 1981-83, v.p. sales, 1983-84, sr. v.p., gen. sales mgr., 1984-86; ind. sales and fundraising cons.; bd. dirs. Resolution, Inc., S. Burlington, Vt., Kendall Mktg. Assocs., Inc., Cambridge, Mass. Trustee St. Lawrence U., 1978-95, vice chmn. trustees, 1995—, chmn. alumni fund, 1983-84, chmn. annual giving, 1984-88, chmn. planning com., 1987-88, mem. exec. com., 1987—, chmn. devel. com., 1988-95; trustee Vt. Coun. on Arts, 1986-91, vice chmn. bd. trustees, chmn. devel. com., 1988-91; del. Am.-Soviet Youth Forum, Baku, USSR, 1974. Mem. Internat. Women's Forum, 1991—. Home and Office: 110 Mosle Rd Far Hills NJ 07931-2229

BRUFF, BEVERLY OLIVE, public relations consultant; b. San Antonio, Dec. 15, 1926; d. Albert Griffith and Hazel Olive (Smith) B. BA, Tulane U., 1948; postgrad. Our Lady of Lake Coll., 1956, Okla. Center for Continuing Edn., 1960-70. Asst. dir. New Orleans Theatre Guild, 1948-50; dist. dir. San Antonio Area coun. Girl Scouts Am., 1958-70, public rels. dir., 1970-83; free-lance pub. rels., 1983—; mem. Coun. of Pres., v.p., 1981-82, 84—; mem. Coun. of Internat. Rels. Zoning commr. Hill Country Village, Tex., 1973-76, 83-85, 88—; councilwoman Hill Country Village, 1985-88; bd. dirs. Animal Def. League, Camp Fire, Inc. Mem. Pub. Rels. Soc. Am., Tex. Pub. Rels. Assn. (Silver Spur award), Women in Communications (historian 1969-70, v.p. 1970-71, treas. 1971-73), Tex. Press Women (recipient state writing contest awards 1971, 72, 73, 74, mem. exec. bd. dirs. 1970-71, 73-74, dist. treas. 1972-73, dist. v.p. 1973), Nat. Fedn. Press Women, Internat. Assn. Bus. Communicators, Speech Arts of San Antonio (pres. 1964-66, 70-72, 84—, dir. 1964-72, 88—, chmn. bd. dirs. 1966-69), Am. Women in Radio and TV (dir. chpt. 1974, sec. 1975, pres. 1979-80), San Antonio Soc. Fund Raising Execs., Assn. Girl Scout Exec. Staff. (exec. bd. 1963-72, nat. bd. 1972-74). Home: 508 Tomahawk Trl San Antonio TX 78232-3620

BRUM, BRENDA, state legislator, librarian; b. Parkersburg, W.Va., Jan. 3, 1954; d. Carl Henry Ogilvie and Helen Mae (Camp) B. BS, W.Va. U., 1975, MA, 1978. Libr., tchr. English, Hamilton Jr. H.S., Parkersburg, 1976-85; libr. Parkersburg South H.S., 1985—; mem. W.Va. Ho. of Dels., 1991-92, 93-94. Bd. dirs. Wood County chpt. Am. Cancer Soc.; foster parent Try Again Homes; mem. adv. bd. Wood County Vocat. Nursing. Mem. LWV, Wood County Edn. Assn. (past treas., exec. com.). Democrat. Home: 2600 17th Ave Parkersburg WV 26101-6419

BRUMBAUGH, KATHLEEN SEMO, journalist, historian, lay minister; b. Johnson City, N.Y., Apr. 5, 1951; d. George Thomas and Wanda Sophia (Surowka) Semo; m. Robert Alan Brumbaugh, July 31, 1980. BA in Cultural Journalism, SUNY, Binghamton, 1975, postgrad., 1994—. Cert. tchr. adult continuing edn., N.Y.; cert. sch. bus driver, N.Y. Owner, operator Wiggle Woggle Marionette Theater, Binghamton, 1976-89; news show host Weekend Newsbeat Spotlight WKOP Radio, Binghamton, 1979-80; freelance journalist Binghamton Press, 1979-81; editor Tioga County Gazette and Times Owego (N.Y.) Pennysaver Press, 1981-93; historian Tioga County, Owego, 1993-94; Arthro Pro patient ptnr. Searle Pharms., N.Y.C., 1993—; instr. adult continuing edn. Broome-Tioga Bd. Coop. Ednl. Svcs., Binghamton, 1994, bd. dirs., N.E. coord. Impact Med. Divsn./Internat. Svcs. of Hope, Maumee, Ohio. Co-author: Tioga County's Bicentennial Year-Celebration Information for Communities, 1992, Seasons of Change, the second hundred years of Tioga County, New York, 1990; coord. editor: Off Campus College Self-Help Survival Manual 1993-95, 1993; history columnist Tioga County Courier, 1993-94; exhibited in group photography shows, 1981—; contbr. articles to numerous mags. Fund rep. west ctrl. N.Y., The Fresh Air Fund, 1992-94; mem. adv. bd. Tioga County Pub. Transit, 1994, Tioga County D.A.R.E. program, 1991-93; v.p. Tioga County War Svc. Medal Commn., 1992-94; pres. Tioga County Bicentennial Commn., 1989-91; evaluator Tioga County 4-H Projects, 1982-94; vol. tchr. nursing homes and Boys and Girls Clubs; mem. Tioga County Rep. Com., 1992—; dir. Spreading Joy, Maumee, Ohio, 1994—. Recipient plaque Tioga County Bicentennial Commn., 1991, Tioga County Citizen of Yr. award Elks, 1991, 2d pl. photography award Nat. Assn. Advt. Newspaper Pubs., 1987, 3d pl., 1985, People Are Great award Sta. WBNG-TV, Binghamton, 1980. Mem. County Historians Assn. N.Y. State, Tioga County Writers Club (co-founder 1992—), Owego Camera Club, Rotary (pres. 1990-91, Paul Harris fellow 1993). Address: PO Box 35 Waterville OH 43566-0035

BRUMER, MIRIAM, artist, educator; b. N.Y.C., Oct. 7, 1939. BA, U. Miami, 1960; MFA, Boston U., 1964. Mem. faculty N.Y. Inst. Tech., 1969-75, Five Towns Music and Art Found., 1977—, Hunter Coll., 1976-81, Marymount Manhattan Coll., 1976-86, NYU, 1983—, Queens Mus. Art, 1987—; artist-in-residence N.Y. Found. for Arts, 1985. One-woman shows include Hankook Gallery, N.Y.C., 1982; exhibited in group shows Fordham U., 1980, Boston City Hall, 1983, Leonardo di Mauro Gallery, 1987, Schneyer & Shen, 1987, Barnard-Biderman Gallery, N.Y., 1994, Mus. Stony Brook, N.Y., 1996, also others; represented in permanent collection Chase Manhattan Bank, Bell Labs., N.Y. Bank for Savs., also pvt. collections. Ludwig Vogelstein Found. grantee, 1976-77; Com. Visual Arts grantee, 1979, 80. Home: 250 W 94th St New York NY 10025-6954

BRUMFIELD, SABRINA, information technology professional; b. Chgo., Apr. 30, 1966; d. Eddie and Rita Brumfield. BS Bus. Adminstrn., Ill. Inst. Tech., 1988. Programmer analyst Hewlett-Packard, Mountain View, Calif., 1988-91, software applications specialist, 1991-93, info. tech. engr., 1993—. Mem. NAFE. Office: Hewlett-Packard MS46UD 19091 Pruneridge Ave Cupertino CA 95014

BRUNDRETT, DOROTHY LOREEN, counselor, artist; b. Dilley, Tex., July 16, 1953; d. Horace A. Sr., and Laura Elizabeth (Johnson) B. BA in psychology, Corpus Christ State U., 1989, MS in counseling, 1990. Lic. profl. counselor, Tex. Student advisor counseling dept. Del Mar Coll., Corpus Christi, Tex., 1989; mental health assoc. Bayview Psychiat. Hosp., Corpus Christi, 1989-91; counselor La Raza Runaway Shelter, Corpus Christi, 1991; crisis Counselor Nueces County, Corpus Christi, 1991-92; assoc. clin. psychol. Tex. Dept. Criminal Justice, Dilley, Tex., 1995; counselor pvt. practice Brundrett Counseling, Pearsall, Tex., 1994—. Mem. C. of C., Dilley, 1994-95, vol. counselor Southwest Family Life Ctr., 1995—. Mem. Am. Counseling Assn., Tex. Counseling Assn. Office: Brundrett Counseling 313 E San Marcos Pearsall TX 78061

BRUNE, EVA, fundraiser; b. Bklyn., Apr. 20, 1952; d. Paul Mass and Edythe Siegel; m. David H. Brune, Oct. 30, 1988; children: Jared Alexander, Isaac Nicolai. BFA, Calif. Coll. Arts and Crafts, Oakland, 1978. Visual arts dir. Sonoma (Calif.) County Arts Commn., 1980-82; assoc. dir. Visual Arts Ctr. of Alaska, Anchorage, 1982-83; program dir. Internat. Sculpture Ctr., Washington, 1983; dir. Pro Arts, Oakland, 1983-85; devel. dir. A Traveling Jewish Theater, San Francisco, 1985-88; mng. dir. INTAR Hispanic Arts. Ctr., N.Y.C., 1988-94; dir. ann. fund The Big Apple Circus, N.Y.C., 1994-96; exec. dir. CityKids Found., N.Y.C., 1996—; instr. Calif. Coll. Arts and Crafts, Oakland, 1978-79. Past bd. dirs. Alliance Resident Theaters, N.Y.C., Citiarts, N.Y.C.; former panelist theater program Nat. Endowment for Arts, Washington; panelist OPERA Am., Fla. State Coun. on Arts, N.J. State Coun. on Arts, Westchester County Coun. on Arts, N.Y. Recipient fellowships Nat. Endowment for the Arts, Washington, 1980, 82. Jewish.

BRUNELLO-MCCAY, ROSANNE, sales executive; b. Cleve., Aug. 26, 1960; d. Carl Carmello and Vivan Lucille (Caranna) B.; divorced, 1991; m. Walter B. McCay, Feb. 26, 1994; 1 child, Angela Breanna. Student, U. Cin., 1978-81, Cleve. State U., 1981-82. Indsl. sales engr. Alta Machine Tool, Denver, 1982; mem. sales./purchases Ford Tool & Machine, Denver, 1982-84; sales/ptnr. Mountain Rep. Enterprises, Denver, 1984-86; pres., owner Mountain Rep. Ariz., Phoenix, 1986—; pres. Mountain Rep. Oreg., Portland, 1990—, Mountain Rep. Wash., 1991—; sec. Computer & Automated Systems Assoc., 1987, vice chmn., 1988, chmn., 1989. Active mem. Rep. Party, 1985—; mem. Phoenix Art Mus., Grand Canyon Minority Coun., 1994; vol. Make-A-Wish Found., 1995-96. Named Mrs. Chandler Internat. by Mrs. Ariz. Internat. orgn., 1996. Mem. NAFE, Soc. Mfg. Engrs. (pres. award 1988), Computer Automated Assn. (sec. 1987, vice chmn. 1988 chmn. 1989), Nat. Hist. Soc., Italian Cultural Soc., Tempe C. of C., Vocat. Ednl. Club Am. (mem. exec. bd., pres. 1987—). Roman Catholic. Office: Mountain Rep Ariz 410 S Jay St Chandler AZ 85224-7668

BRUNER, CATHERINE MURRAY, horticulturist; b. Madison, Wis., Nov. 25, 1948; d. Ervin Murray and Helen (Finkelstein) B.; m. Ronald Alan Richardson, Aug. 29, 1983. BA, U. Wis., 1972, MS, 1977. Cert. project mgmt. profl. From outdoor resource specialist to mgr. landscape svcs. CUNA Mutual Ins. Soc., Madison, 1984-96; lectr. U. Wis. Extension, 1975-80, U. Wis., Madison, 1994, 95; mem. City of Madison Ad Hoc Com. on Prairie Restoration and Natural Landscapes, 1978; interview com. City of Milw. Forestry Dept., 1988, 92. Vol. Unitarian Universalist Svc. Com., Tegucigalpa, Honduras, 1967, U. Wis. Arboretum Longenecker Gardens, Madison, 1985-95, Olbrich Botancial Gardens, Madison, 1995. Mem. Wis. Woody Plant Soc., Wis. Arborist Assn., Madison Perennial Soc., Am. Conifer Soc., Project Mgmt. Inst., Friends of Univ. Wis. Arboretum, Madison Area Profl. Horticultural Alliance. Home: 216 N Dickinson St Madison WI 53703

BRUNNER, AILEEN JOYCE, music educator; b. S.D., Jan. 6, 1951; d. Henry Edward and Mildred Eleanor (Baird) Salmo; m. Gary Lee Brunner, June 17, 1973; children: Michael, Ryan. BS in Edn., Black Hills State U., 1973. Cert. tchr. bus., music, econs., S.D. Tchr. bus. Belle Fourche (S.D.) H.S., 1974-81; fin. officer Town of Nisland, S.D., 1987-92; tchr. music Newell (S.D.) Sch., 1992—. Tchr., coord., organist 1st Bapt. Ch., Belle Fource, S.D., 1973—; mem. Child Evangelism Fellowship, 1984-90, sec. Black Hills Area , 1984-90, state com., Huron, 1985-88; officer (all roles) Sunshine Gang Extension Club, Nisland, S.D., 1985-92; troop leader Boy Scouts Am., Nisland, 1988-90. Mem. NEA, Nat. Bus. Edn. Assn., Black Hills Orff Assn., Music Educators Nat. Conf., Am. Choral Dirs. Assn. Home: HC 76 Box 11 Nisland SD 57762-9701 Office: Newell Sch PO Box 99 Newell SD 57760-0099

BRUNNER, ELIZABETH ANNE, anchor, reporter; b. Hartford, Conn., May 22, 1959; d. Galen Eames Jr. and Mary (Chacko) Russell. MusB, Lawrence U., 1981; postgrad., U. Ill., 1987. Dir. vocal music Rich South High Sch., Richton Pk., Ill., 1981-83; asst. mgr. U-S Splty. Retailing, Champaign, Ill., 1983-85; community svcs. rep. Sta. WCIA, Champaign, 1985-88, weather anchor, 1986-88; dir. community rels. Sta. WTVT, Tampa, Fla., 1988-93, news anchor, 1989-93; anchor Eye Opener Newscast Sta. WCVB-TV, Boston, 1993—, reporter, anchor Chronicle News mag., 1993—; host live auction Sta. WILL Champaign, 1985-88; membership drive Sta. WEDU, Tampa, 1989-90. Mem. com. United Way of Greater Tampa, 1988-90; bd. dirs. Am. Cancer Soc., 1986-88, United Way of Champaign, 1987, Friends of Tampa Recreation, 1989-90, Boys and Girls Club of Tampa, 1990, In the Best Interests of the Children, 1994—; mem. exec. com. Make a Wish Found. Greater Boston. Recipient Up and Comers award Tampa Bus. Jour., 1990; media award Am. Cancer Soc., 1990, Pub. Rels. award Am. Women in Radio and TV, 1990, Cert. of Appreciation, United Way of Greater Tampa, 1990, New Eng. Emmy award, 1995; named Best Newcomer to Boston Media Market, Boston mag., 1994. Office: Sta WCVB Channel 5 5 TV Place Needham MA 02194

BRUNNER, LILLIAN SHOLTIS, nurse, author; b. Freeland, Pa.; d. Andrew J. and Anna (Tomasko) Sholtis; m. Mathias J. Brunner, Sept. 8, 1951; children: Janet Brunner Cramer, Carol Ann Brunner Burns, Douglas Mathias. RN, diploma, U. Pa., 1940, BS, 1945, LittD (hon.), 1985; MS in Nursing, Case-Western Res. U., 1947; ScD (hon.), Cedar Crest Coll., 1978. RN, Pa. Head nurse U. Pa. Hosp., Phila., 1940-42, operating room supr., 1942-44; head, fundamentals of nursing dept. U. Pa. Hosp., 1944-46; asst. prof. surgical nursing Yale U. Sch. Nursing, New Haven, Conn., 1947-51; surgical supr. Yale-New Haven Hosp., 1947-51; rsch. project dir. Sch. Nursing Bryn Mawr (Pa.) Hosp., 1973-77; co-founder History of Nursing Mus., Pa. Hosp., Phila., 1974; mem. bd. overseers Sch. Nursing U. Pa., 1982-88; bd. overseers emeritus, 1988—; chmn. nursing adv. Presbyn.-U. Pa. Med. Ctr., Phila., 1970-88, 90-93, trustee, 1976-88, 90-95, vice chmn. bd. trustees, 1985-88; bd. mem. Presbyn. Found. for Phila., 1995—. Author: Manual of Operating Room Technology, 1966, (with others) Lippincott Manual of Nursing Practice, 1974, 4th edit., 1986, Textbook of Medical and Surgical Nursing, 1964, 6th edit., 1988; editl. bd. Nursing Photobook Series, 1978-90. Recipient Disting. Alumnus award Frances Payne Bolton Sch. Nursing, Case Western Res. U., 1980, Alumni award for merit Soc. Alumni Assns., U. Pa., and Am. Dream Achievement award Class of '45, U. Pa., 1995. Fellow Am. Acad. Nursing; mem. ANA, Nat. League for Nursing (judge nat. writing contest 1982-84, Disting. Svc. award 1979), Nat. League Am. Pen Women (sec. Phila. chpt. 1972-76, nat. sec. 1984-86), Assn. Oper. Rm. Nurses, Nurses Alumni Assn. U. Pa. Hosp., Ben Franklin Soc., Internat. Old Lacers Soc., Sigma Theta Tau, Pi Gamma Mu, Pi Lambda Theta. Home and Office: 645 Willow Vly Sq J-411 Lancaster PA 17602-4871

BRUNO, AUDREI ANN, nurse educator, administrator; b. Pitts., Oct. 31, 1946; d. Vincent Joseph and Julia Elizabeth (Karaffa) Mataya; m. Edward Orlando Bruno, Apr. 30, 1966; children: Brent Edward, Bradley Edward. AA, Community Coll. Alleghany County, 1976; BSN, Pa. State U., 1984; MSN, U. Pitts., 1988. Cert. nurse adminstr. Psychiat. nursing supr. Western Psychiat. Clinic and Inst., Pitts., 1976-81; staff charge nurse Magee Women's Hosp., Pitts., 1981-82; charge team leader Central Med. Pavillion, Pitts., 1982-84; clin. specialist Vis. Nurse Assn. of Alleghany County, Pitts., 1984-92; rschr. U. Pitts.; mem. speakers bur. Community Coll. Allegheny County; project developer WPIC Adolescent Module, 1980-81; CEO Psycho-Ednl. Cons., 1996; coord. grant Putting Cmty. Health into AD Curriculum, 1993-96. Chmn. North Huntington (Pa.) Suicide Awareness and Prevention Com., 1986-88; fieldworker Project Star, Pitts., 1986-88; mem. Pa. Task Force on Elder Abuse, Nurses Interest in Care of Elderly; mem. adv. com. Nat. Project DART. Mem. Nursing Quality Assurance (cons.), Sigma Theta Tau. Home: 14071 Ridge Rd North Huntingdon PA 15642

BRUNO, CATHY EILEEN, state official; b. Binghamton, N.Y. d. Martin Frank and Beverly Carolyn (Hamlin) Piza; m. Frank L. Delaney (div.); m. Paul R. Bruno, May 5, 1990. BA, SUNY, Binghamton; MSW, Syracuse U. Psychiat. social worker Willard (N.Y.) Psychiat. Ctr., 1968-73, Broome Devel. Ctr., Binghamton, 1973-74, 76; congl. legis. aide, 1975; asst. dir. Bur. Program and Fiscal audits N.Y. State Office Mental Retardation and Devel. Disabilities, Albany, 1976-80, statewide coord. Intermediate Care Facilities for Developmentally Disabled, 1980, cert. coord. Western County Svc. Group, 1980-83, Upstate unit dir. Bur. Cert. Control, 1983-85; dir. ICF/DD Survey and Rev., 1985-89; area dir. Bur. Program Cert., 1989-95; dir. Bur. Transitional Svcs., 1995—; adj. instr. SUNY Sch. Social Welfare, Albany, 1982-83. Grantee HEW, 1975-76. Mem. Am. Mgmt. Assn. Address: PO Box 3153 Albany NY 12203-0153 Office: 44 Holland Ave Albany NY 12229

BRUNO, GRACE ANGELIA, accountant, educator; b. St. Louis, Oct. 11, 1935; d. John E. and Rose (Goodwin) B. BA, Notre Dame Coll., 1966; MEd, So. Ill. U., 1972; MAS, Johns Hopkins U., 1983; PhD, Walden U., 1985. CPA, Mo., Md., N.J. Tchr. Sch. Sisters of Notre Dame (SSND) of St. Louis, 1962-80; pres. Bruno-Potter, Inc., Avon By The Sea, N.J., 1981—; asst. treas., instr. acctg. Coll. of Notre Dame of Md., Balt., 1978-79, treas., 1979-80; asst. prof. acctg. Georgian Ct. Coll., Lakewood, N.J., 1985-91; fin. advisor James Harry Potter gold medal award ASME, N.Y.C., 1980—. Elected to Internat. Platform Assn., 1987. Mem. AICPA, N.J. Soc. CPAs, St. Louis Bus. Educators (treas. 1972-73), Inst. Bus. Appraisers, Inc., Johns Hopkins Univ. Faculty Club. Democrat. Roman Catholic. Home and Office: 419 3rd Ave Avon By The Sea NJ 07717-1244

BRUNO, JUDYTH ANN, chiropractor; b. Eureka, Calif., Feb. 16, 1944; d. Harold Oscar and Shirley Alma (Farnsworth) Nelson; m. Thomas Glenn Bruno, June 1, 1968; 1 child, Christina Elizabeth. AS, Sierra Coll., 1982; D of Chiropractic, Palmer Coll. of Chiropractic West, Sunnyvale, Calif., 1986. Diplomate Nat. Bd. Chiropractic Examiners. Sec. Bank Am., San Jose, Calif., 1965-67; marketer Memorex, Santa Clara, Calif., 1967-74; order entry clk. John Deere, Milan, Ill., 1977; system analyst Four Phase, Cupertino, Calif., 1977-78; chiropractic asst. Dr. Thomas Bruno, Nevada City, Calif., 1978-81; chiropractor Chiropractic Health Care Ctr., Nevada City, 1987—; pvt. practice Cedar Ridge, Calif., 1991—. Area dir. Cultural Awareness Coun., Grass Valley, Calif., 1977—; vol. Nevada County Libr., Nevada City, 1987-88, Decide Team III, Nevada County, 1987-92, Active Parenting of Teen Facilitator Nev. Union H.S., 1989-93, judge sr. projects, 1992—; noetic scis. mem. women's forum, 1995—. Mem. Am. Chiropractic Assn., Women Health Practitioners of Nevada County (founder 1993—), Nevada County C. of C. (vol. task force health care 1993), Toastmasters (sec. 1988, pres. 1989, edn. v.p. 1990), Women's Forum, Noetic Scis. Republican. Office: Chiropractor Health Care PO Box 1718 Cedar Ridge CA 95924-1718

BRUNO, LINDA LEE, finance educator; b. East Orange, N.J., Feb. 6, 1947; d. Walter King and Virginia Grace (Stagg) Sherwood; m. Vincent William Bruno, Aug. 31, 1968; children:, Patrick, Peter, Vincent. BA in Bus. Edn., Montclair State Coll., 1969, MA in Bus. Edn., 1975. Cert. tchr. bus. edn., N.Y., N.J. Tchr. bus. edn. N. Warren Regional H.S., Blairstown, N.J., 1969-71, High Point Regional H.S., Sussex, N.J., 1971-75; tchr. bus. edn., dept. chair Dryden (N.Y.) Jr.-Sr. H.S., 1975—; bus. edn. tchr. Candor (N.Y.) Ctrl. Sch., 1975-76, Tompkins-Cortland C.C., Dryden, 1976-88; computer edn. adult tchr. TST BOCES, Ithaca, N.Y., 1980—; mem. Bus. Tech. Prep. Com., 1991—, Tompkins County Workforce Prep. Com., Ithaca, 1994—. Ednl. contact Rotary, Dryden, 1994—, Bus. Club, Dryden, 1994—. Mem. NEA, N.Y. Edn. Assn., Dryden Faculty Assn., Dryden Tchrs. Ctr. (trainer). Home: 364 Mcclintock Rd Dryden NY 13053-9736

BRUNO, MARILYN JOAN, foreign service officer, management consultant, trade specialist; b. Caracas, Venezuela, May 28, 1948; d. Philip Lee and Eugenia Alda (Micera) Bruno; m. Fernando Herrera (div. 1980); 1 child, Cynthia. BA, Mt. Holyoke Coll., 1969; MA, NYU, 1970, PhD, 1977; JD, N.Y. Law Sch., 1992. Lic. stockbroker, commodity broker, N.Y.; lic. real estate broker, Fla.; bar: N.Y. 1992, N.J. 1992, Fla. 1992, D.C. 1993. Adj. prof., asst. dir. NYU in Spain, Madrid, 1970-80; account exec. Dean Witter Reynolds/Shearson, N.Y.C. and Miami, 1980-82; v.p. Ace Am., Miami, Fla., 1982-84; v.p. precious metals dept. Capital Bancorp, Miami, Fla., 1983-84; pres. Bruno Cons. Co., Inc., Miami, Fla., 1984—; second sec., consular & econ. affairs Dept. of State, Athens, Greece, 1993-95; second sec., consular, econ. and polit. affairs Dept. of State, San Jose, Costa Rica, 1995—; lectr Tunderbird U., Mesa, Ariz., 1985—, Universidad de Los Andes, Bogota, 1984—. Author: Countertrade, 1984-86; columnist weekly col. in Jour. of Commerce, 1982-84; editorial asst.: Generally Accepted Accounting Principles, 1988; contbr. articles to profl. jours.; author travel guide. Named Woman Entrepreneur of the Yr., NOW, Palm Beach, 1986. Mem. Internat. Mgmt. Devel. Inst., Phi Alpha Delta. Office: Am Embassy-San Jose PSC 20 Box 407 APO AA 34020-0407

BRUNO, PAULA CELESTE, customer service representative; b. Erie, Pa., Jan. 13, 1966; d. Carmen Charles and Anna Lorene (Allgood) B. BA, Mercyhurst Coll., 1988. Adminstrv. asst. Tri-State Bus. Inst., Erie, 1990, Ecolab, Erie, 1992, Cmty. Caring, Erie, 1990-92; sales, customer svc. rep. Printing Techs., Erie, 1992-94; customer support rep. Hagan Bus. Machines, Erie, 1994—. Pres. Mercyhurst Prep. Alumni, Erie, 1994—; bd. dirs. Mercyhurst Prep., 1996; coach Mercyhurst Cheerleaders, 1984-94. Mem. NAFE, Erie Jaycees (pres. 1995-96), Pa. Jaycees (dist. dir. 1996). Democrat. Roman Catholic. Home: 3604 Allegheny Rd Erie PA 16508 Office: PO Box 1553 Erie PA 16507

BRUNS, CAROL ELIZABETH, artist; b. Des Moines, Iowa, Sept. 18, 1943; d. Leonard W. Ellen (Hansen) B.; 1 child, Zoe Bruns. BS, NYU, 1966. curator various shows. One-woman exhbns. San Miguel de Allende, Mex., 1991, Art Initiatives, N.Y.C., 1995; group exhbns. include OK Harris Gallery, N.Y.C., 1975, The Clocktower, N.Y.C., 1986, Hook Gallery, 1986, Thomson Gallery, Minn., 1989, Rempire Gallery, N.Y.C., 1990, The Gallery, Boca Raton, Fla., 1991, Archetype Gallery, 1994, Bklyn. Waterfront Artists Coalition, 1994, 95; commn. Figurative stairrail Tome residence, Irapuato, Mex., 1994; tching. 1979-93; numerous permanent collections. Home: 61 Pearl St Brooklyn NY 11201-1147

BRUSASCHETTI, MARILEE MARSHALL, media executive; b. Albuquerque, Sept. 16, 1962; d. John Lawrence and Carol Kay (Turner) Marshall; m. James Douglas Brusaschetti, July 22, 1995. BSBA, Ariz. State U., 1984. Asst. media planner DDB Needham, L.A., 1985-86; media planner Saatchi & Saatchi, DFS, Torrance, Calif., 1986-87; media planner, sr. Keye, Donna, Pearlstein, L.A., 1987-88; media dir. Owens & Assocs., Phoenix, 1988-90; assoc. media dir. Foote, Cone & Belding, Santa Ana, Calif., 1990-94; media supr. Goldberg, Moser, O'Neill, San Francisco, 1994—; lectr. mktg. dept. Ariz. State U., Tempe, 1988-89. Mem. Ariz. State U. Alumna Assn. (sec. 1993-94), Young Profls. Against Cancer, L.A. Ad Club, Delta Delta Delta. Republican. Methodist.

BRUSER, MADELINE, music educator; b. Oakland, Calif., Mar. 5, 1948; d. David and Freda (Belkin) Bruser; m. Parlan M. McGaw, Oct. 7, 1990. BMus, Juilliard Sch., N.Y.C., 1970; MMus, San Francisco Conservatory, 1978. Piano faculty East Bay Ctr. Performing Arts, Richmond, Calif., 1975-78, 92d St. Y Sch. Music, N.Y.C., 1978-84, Westchester Conservatory of Music, White Plains, N.Y., 1978-79, Manhattan Sch. Music Ext., N.Y.C., 1985-87; pvt. piano tchr. N.Y.C., 1971—; workshop presenter MedArt World Congress on Arts and Medicine, N.Y.C., 1992; condr. numerous other workshops. Author: The Art of Practicing: A Guide to Making Music from the Heart, 1997. Recipient First prize Denver Symphony N.Am. Young Artists Competition, 1973, Alfred Hertz Award for Music, U. Calif.-Berkeley, 1974-76. Buddhist. Home: 310 W 89th St New York NY 10024

BRUVOLD, KATHLEEN PARKER, lawyer. BS in Math., U. Denver, 1965; MS in Math., Purdue U., 1967; JD, U. Cin., 1978. Bar: Ohio 1978, U.S. Dist. Ct. (so. dist.) Ohio 1978, U.S. Dist. Ct. (ea. dist.) Ky. 1979. Mathematician bur. rsch. and engring. U.S. Post Office, 1967; instr. math. Purdue U., West Lafayette, Ind., 1967-68, asst. to dir., tng. coord., programmer Adminstrv. Data Processing Ctr., 1968-71; instr. math. Ind. U., Kokomo, 1969-70; atty. Union Light, Heat and Power/Cin. Gas & Electric, 1978-79; pvt. practice Cin., 1979-80; asst. dir. Legal Adv. Svcs. U. Cin., 1980-89, assoc. gen. counsel, 1989—; asst. atty. gen. State of Ohio, 1983—; chair Ohio pub. records com. Inter-univ. Coun. Legal Advisors, 1980-84; presenter various confs. and symposiums. Active com. group svcs. allocation United Way and Community Chest; v.p. Clifton Recreation Ctr. Adv. Coun., 1983-84; vice chair Cin. Bilingual Acad. PTA, 1989-90. U. Denver scholar, Jewel Tea Co. scholar. Mem. ABA (computer law div.), Nat. Assn. Coll. and Univ. Attys. (bd. dirs., co-chair taxation sect., com. ann. meeting arrangements, program com., publs. com., bd. ops. com., JCUL editl. bd. nominations com., honors and award com., intellectual property sect., com. continuing legal edn. 1992—), Cin. Bar Assn. (com. taxation, program chmn. 1985-86, sec. 1986-87, com. computer law). Home: 536 Evanswood Pl Cincinnati OH 45220-1527 Office: U Cin Office of Gen Counsel 300-A Adminstrn Bldg Cincinnati OH 45221-0623

BRYAN, BARBARA DAY, librarian; b. Livermore Falls, Maine, May 20, 1927; d. Lorey Clifford and Olga Elvira (Bergquist) Day; m. Robert S. Bryan, June 24, 1950. BA in Psychology, U. Maine, 1948; MS in Library Sci., So. Conn. State U., 1964. Catalog dept. asst. Yale U. Library, New Haven, 1948-49; departmental library cataloger Harvard U., Cambridge, Mass., 1949-51; descriptive cataloger Yale U. Library, New Haven, 1951-52; cataloger Fairfield (Conn.) Pub. Library, 1952-54, reference librarian, 1954-57, asst. librarian, order librarian, 1957-65; asst. dir. libraries Fairfield U., 1965-74, university librarian, 1974—; mem. Conn. State Libr. Bd., Hartford, 1978-82, chair, 1987-92; bd. dirs. Bibliomation, Inc., Stratford, Conn., 1987-91. Bd. dirs. Oak Lawn Cemetery Assn., 1994—. Recipient Disting. Alumnus award So. Conn. State U. Sch. of Libr. Sci., 1979; named Conn. Libr. Assn. Libr. of Yr., 1988. Mem. ALA (Conn. chpt. councilor 1977-80), Assn. Coll. and Rsch. Librs. (constrn. and by-laws com. 1986-90, mem. coll. libr. sect. stds. com. 1991-95), New Eng. Libr. Assn. (mem. com. 1981-85, coun. mem. 1975-77), Conn. Libr Assn., Fairfield Hist. Soc., Conn. Audubon Soc., Oak Lawn Cemetery Assn. (bd. dirs.), Phi Beta kappa, Phi Kappa Phi. Democrat. Home: 999 Merwins Ln Fairfield CT 06430-1919 Office: Fairfield Univ Univ Library Fairfield CT 06430

BRYAN, CAROLINE ELIZABETH, quality assurance professional; b. Washington, Dec. 4, 1951; d. Carter Royston and Anna Maria (Schneider) B. BA, Vassar Coll., 1973. Programmer Santa Barbara Rsch. Ctr., Goleta, Calif., 1975-77; tester, software developer and sr. test technician Johnson Controls, Inc., Milw., 1977-85; cons. Cap Gemini Am., Cranford, N.J., 1986-90; quality assurance engr. PRC, Inc., McLean, Va., 1990-91; software quality assurance engr. Unify Corp., Sacramento, 1991-94; software engr. Objective Systems Integrators, Folsom, Calif., 1994—; cons. AT&T, Lincroft and Middletown, N.J., 1986-90. Editor (newsletter) Captain America, 1989. Fellow Murphy Ctr. for Codification of Human and Organizational Law; mem. IEEE (assoc.), Assn. for Computing Machinery, Am. Philatelic Soc., QuiltNet. Democrat. Roman Catholic. Home: 112 Fargo Way Folsom CA 95630 Office: Objective Systems Integrators 100 Blue Ravine Rd Folsom CA 95630-4703

BRYAN, DOROTHY JEAN, artist; b. Bowling Green, Ohio, Aug. 27, 1924; d. Howard Thomas and Rae (Beauchamp) Uber; m. Ashel Gano Bryan; children: Rebecca Bryan Bergert, David A. Bryan, Katherine Bryan Hollingsworth. Grad. high sch., Bowling Green. pres. Medici Circle, Bowling Green State U.; com. mem. Arts Unltd., Friends of Music. Exhibited in group shows at Bowling Green State U., 1st Nat. Bank-Toledo, Mid-Am. Bank, Bowling Green, Art Expo, Toledo Mus. Area Artist Show, Toledo Mus. Collectors Corner, State House, Columbus. Com. mem. Heritage 1976, Bowling Green, 1975-75, Heritage 2000, Bowling Green, 1995—, Ohio Arts Coun. for Art Program, 1995-96, Aesthetic Devel. Ctr., 1995-96. Named Hon. Alumnus Bowling Green State U., 1987; recipient Outstanding Citizen City of Bowling Green, 1995, Govs. award for the Arts State of Ohio, 1994, Outstanding Philanthropist, 1994. Republican. Home: 42 Trafalgar Bend Bowling Green OH 43402

BRYAN, MARY ANN, interior designer; b. Dallas, Nov. 16, 1929; d. William C. and Harriet E. (Carter) Green; m. Frank Wingfield Bryan, Aug. 31, 1957; children: Frank Wingfield, Elizabeth F. BS in Interior Design U. Tex., 1950. Head of stock Foleys Dept. Store, Houston, 1952-53, asst. buyer, 1953-54, buyer, 1955-60, exec. tng. dir., 1960-61; owner, pres. The Bryan Design Assocs., Inc., Houston, 1961-96; mem. interior design Tex. Bd. Archtl. Examiners, 1993—. Trustee Houston Art Inst.; mem. interior design adv. bd. Stephen F. Austin Coll., Houston C.C.; U.S. del. Friendship Among Women; dir. profl. devel NCIDQ. Mem. Am. Soc. Interior Designers (nat. bd. dirs. 1984-86, 91-92, pres. Gulf Coast chpt. 1975), Chi Omega. Republican. Home: 5120 Woodway St 8009 Houston TX 77056

BRYAN, SHERRIE ANN, social worker, therapist; b. Mpls., Jan. 18, 1946; d. William Glen and Esther (Weng) Tramblie; m. John David Bryan (div. 1991); children: Tanya Michelle, Jennifer Colleen; m. Richard Earl La Tourette, May 29, 1994. BA, Columbia Union Coll., 1969; MSW, Md. U., Balt., 1982. Lic. clin. social worker, Md., Va., D.C., Nev. Social worker Psychiat. Inst., Washington, 1981-89; clin. dir., county advocate MacArthur Sch., Washington, 1989-91; ins. approval for residential treatment ctrs. Health Mgmt. Strategies, Alexandria, Va., 1991-92; clin. social work therapist No. Va. Psychiat. Assn., Fairfax, Va., 1992-93; pvt. practice as clin. social work therapist Alexandria, 1993-94, Incline Village, Nev., 1995—; emergency psychiat. evaluator West Hills Hosp., Reno, 1996; cons., group facilitator Tahoe Women's Svcs., Incline Village, 1996. Sec.-treas. Interagy. Com., North Lake Tahoe, Calif., 1995-96; mem. Child Abuse Prevention, North Lake Tahoe, 1995-96. Mem. NASW, AAUW, NOW, Assn. for Play Therapy, Assn. Childrens Residential Ctrs., Incline Village C. of C., Sierra Club. Democrat. Office: PO Box 1726 Crystal Bay NV 89402

BRYAN, SUKEY, artist; b. Summit, N.J., Apr. 4, 1961; d. Barry Richard and Margaret Susannah (Elliot) Bryan; m. James Duane Brooks, July 8, 1989; 1 child, Matthew Lyle Brooks. BA, Yale U., 1983; MFA, Md. Inst./Coll. of Art, Balt., 1990. Artist. Solo exhbns. include Essex (Md.) C.C., 1990, 91, Johns Hopkins U., Balt., 1992, H. Pelham Curtis Gallery, New Canaan, Conn., 1992, Peabody Rm., Balt., 1993, Galerie Francoise e.s.f., Balt., 1994, C. Grimaldis Gallery, Balt., 1995; exhibited in group shows The BauHouse, Balt., 1991, Ctr. for Creative Arts, Yorklyn, Del., 1992, Edinboro U. Pa., 1992, Dundalk (Md.) Art Gallery, 1993, Addison Gallery Arm Art, Andover, Mass., 1993, Kristal Gallery, Warren, Vt., 1994, Fifth Column, Washington, 1995, St. Mary's Coll. Md., 1995, Balt. Festival for the Arts, 1992, 93, 95, C. Grimaldis Gallery, 1995, Art Sites, Rockville (Md.) Art Place, 1996, others; represented in collections at Cathedral of the Incarnation, Balt., Piper & Marbury, Balt.; author, artist: Tidal Grass, 1993. Recipient Individual Artist award Md. State Arts Coun., 1991; Visual Artist fellow Nat. Endowment for Arts, 1993-94. Democrat. Episcopalian. Home and Studio: 2621 St Paul St Baltimore MD 21218

BRYANT, ANNAMARIE, purchasing agent; b. Santa Barbara, Calif., June 29, 1965; d. Benjamin Wiley Jordan and Jeannette Elizabeth Rutschke; m. Robert Allan Bryant, July 31, 1988 (div. 1996). File clk. San Luis Welding Supply, San Luis Obispo, Calif., 1983; customer svc. clk. The Living Picture, Alameda, Calif., 1984, 7-11, Alameda, 1985-86; clk. Def. Subs. Reg. Pacific, Alameda, 1987-88; pers. clk. Def. Depot Tracy, Alameda, 1988-90; adminstrv. clk. Gen. Svcs. Adminstrn., San Francisco, 1990, purchasing agt., 1990—. Co-coord. Fed. Recycling Coun., 1992, 93; operator Muscular Dystrophy Assn., Arroyo Grande, Calif., 1980. Democrat. Lutheran. Office: Gen Svcs Adminstrn 5th Fl W 450 Golden Gate Ave San Francisco CA 94102

BRYANT, ANNE LINCOLN, educational association executive; b. Jamaica Plain, Mass., Nov. 26, 1949; d. John Winslow and Anne (Phillips) B.; m. Peter Harned Ross, June 15, 1986; stepchildren: Charlotte Ross, George Ross. BA in English, Secondary Edn., Simmons Coll., 1971; EdD in Higher Edn., U. Mass., 1978. Intern U. Mass., Amherst, 1972; asst. to dean Springfield Tech. C.C., 1972-74; dir. Nat. Assn. Bank Women Ednl. Found., Chgo., 1974-86; v.p. P.M. Haeger, Chgo., 1978-86; exec. dir. AAUW, Washington, 1986-96, also exec. dir. Ednl. Found., Legal Advocacy Fund; exec. dir. Nat. Sch. Bds. Assn., Washington, 1996—. Contbr. articles to profl. jours. Mem. exec. com. Simmons Coll., Boston, 1971—; adv. commr. Edn. Commn. States, 1986—; mem. bd. govs. UNA of U.S.A., 1991—, Ind. Sector, 1988-94, Hosp. Corp. Am., 1993-94. Recipient William H. Cosby Jr. award U. Mass., 1983; named Woman of Yr. for Edn., YWCA, 1976. Fellow Am. Soc. Assn. Execs. (bd. dirs. 1985-88, Key award 1992); mem. Am. Assn. for Higher Edn. (bd. dirs. 1980-87). Episcopalian. Office: AAUW 1111 16th St NW Washington DC 20036-4873

BRYANT, BARBARA EVERITT, academic researcher, market research consultant, former federal agency administrator; b. Ann Arbor, Mich., Apr. 5, 1926; d. William Littell and Dorothy (Wallace) Everitt; m. John H. Bryant, Aug. 14, 1948; children: Linda Bryant Valentine, Randal E., Lois Bryant Chen. AB, Cornell U., 1947; MA, Mich. State U., 1967, PhD, 1970. Editor art Chem. Engring. mag. McGraw-Hill Pub. Co., N.Y.C., 1947-48; editorial rsch. asst. U. Ill., Urbana, 1948-49; free-lance editor, writer, 1950-61; with continuing edn. adminstrn. dept. Oakland Univ., Rochester, Mich., 1961-66; grad. rsch. asst. Mich. State Univ., East Lansing, 1966-70; sr. analyst to v.p. Market Opinion Rsch., Detroit, 1970-77, sr. vp., 1977-89; dir. Bur. of the Census, U.S. Dept. of Commerce, 1989-93; rsch. scientist Sch. Bus. Adminstrn. U. Mich., 1993—. Author: High School Students Look at Their World, 1970, American Women Today & Tomorrow, 1977, Moving Power and Money: The Politics of Census Taking, 1995; contbr. articles to profl. jours. Mem. U.S. Census Adv. Com., Washington, 1980-86, Mich. Job Devel. Authority, Lansing, Mich., 1980-85; state editor LWV of Mich., 1959-61. Mem. Am. Soc. for Quality Control, Women in Comms. (pres. Detroit 1974-75, Nat. Headliner award 1980), Am. Mktg. Assn. (pres. Detroit 1976-77, midwestern v.p. 1978-80, v.p. mktg. rsch. 1982-84), Am. Statis. Assn., Am. Assn. Pub. Opinion Rsch., Population Assn. Am., Cosmos Club (Washington), Cornell Club N.Y. Republican. Presbyterian. Avocation: swimming. Home: 1505 Sheridan Dr Ann Arbor MI 48104-4051 Office: U Mich Sch Bus Ann Arbor MI 48109-1234

BRYANT, BERTHA ESTELLE, retired nurse; b. Va., Jan. 11, 1927; d. E.F. and Julia B. Diploma, Sibley Meml. Hosp., Washington, 1947; B.S., Am. U., 1948; M.A., Tchrs. Coll., Columbia U., 1962. Staff nurse, head nurse NIH, Bethesda, Md., 1954-59; asst. dir. nursing USPHS Alaska Native Hosp., Mt. Edgecumbe, 1959-61; instr. Sch. Nursing, U. Mich., 1962-64; chief div. clin. nursing Bur. Nursing, D.C. Dept. Public Health, Washington, 1964-65; commd. Nurse Corps, USPHS, 1965, nurse dir., capt., 1974—; nurse cons., hosp. facilities services br., div. hosps. and med. facilities Bur. Health Services, HEW, Silver Spring; nurse cons., social analysis br., div. health services research and analysis Nat. Center Health Services Research, Health Resources Adminstrn., HEW, Rockville, Md.; nurse cons. div. extramural research Nat. Center Health Services Research, Office Asst. Sec. Health, HHS, Hyattsville, Md., 1977-81. Contbr. articles to profl. jours. Mem. AAUW, Assn. Mil. Surgeons U.S., Commd. Officers Assn. USPHS.

BRYANT, ESTHER, investment manager, retired correspondent; b. Chgo., Oct. 28, 1922; d. Joseph and Pauline (Smith) Gooder; m. Harold Bryant, Sept. 6, 1947; children: James, Janet. Typist Maremont Automotive, Chgo., 1942-44; salesperson Carson Pirie Scott & Co., 1945-47; coord. donations AMA, Chgo., 1979-81; corr. Rotary Internat., Evanston, Ill., 1982-88. Home: 2421 W Pratt Blvd Apt 251 Chicago IL 60645

BRYANT, EVELYN CHRISTINE, elementary education educator; b. Lakeview, S.C., Aug. 1, 1942; d. Jasper L. and Marcella (William) Page; m. James A. Bryant, Feb. 1, 1964; children: James Jr., Marc C., Linda E. AAS in Gen. Edn., Fayetteville Tech. C.C., Fayetteville, N.C., 1987; BS in Elem. Edn., Fayetteville State U., 1990, MA in Spl. Edn., 1994. Tchr.'s aide spl. edn. Ashley Sch., Fayetteville, 1976-81; substitute tchr. Cumberland County/Ft. Bragg, Fayetteville, 1989-90; data processor Census Bur., Fayetteville, 1990; tchr. chpt. I reading Midway Elem., Dunn, N.C., 1990-95, Cliffdale Elem. Sch., Fayetteville, N.C., 1995—. Active Parents Autism Children, 1970—, Mother's Mar. Dimes, 1990-91. Mem. NEA, Order Eastern Star (asst. sec. 1986-87), Heroine Jericho, Daus. of Zion, Kappa Delta Pi. Baptist. Home: 725 Glensford Dr Fayetteville NC 28314-0843

BRYANT, FRANCES JANE, retired newspaper editor; b. Cushing, Okla., Dec. 10, 1933; d. Edward Glahn and Dorothy Evelyn (McLean) B. AA, Christian Coll., Columbia, Mo., 1953; BJ, U. Mo., 1955. Reporter The Norman (Okla.) Transcript, 1955-57, wire editor, 1957-59, city editor, 1959-67, mng. editor, 1967-95; ret., 1995. Bd. dirs. Juvenile Svcs., Inc., Cleveland County, Okla., 1981-87, pres., 1984-85; bd. dirs. Cleveland County chpt. ARC, 1987-90. Named Oustanding Bus. Woman Bus. and Profl. Women, Norman, 1971, State Woman of Year Theta Sigma Phi, U. Okla., 1968; recipient Disting. Alumni award Columbia Coll. (formerly Christian Coll.), 1980; inducted Okla. Journalism Hall of Fame, 1994. Mem. AP Okla. News Execs. (pres. 1970-71, 91-92), Soc. Profl. Journalists, Altrusa Internat. (pres. Norman chpt. 1969-71). Democrat. Epsicopalian. Home: 606 Sherwood Dr Norman OK 73071-4905

BRYANT, JANET HOUGH, actress, voice teacher, performing artist; b. Rockford, Ill.; d. Roy Arthur and Ida Elissa Bertha (Bergman) Hough; m. Charles Herbert Bryant Jr., Dec. 28, 1938 (dec. 1942); 1 child, Janna Lee Wright. Student, U. Iowa, 1931; AM, Stephens Coll., 1934; BE, Drake U., 1937; student, Vassar Experimental Theatre, 1935, Am. Conservatory Music, Chgo., 1942; MS in Music Edn., U. So. Calif., 1961; cert., Ecole d'Art Am., Fontainebleau, France, 1965; student, Am. Inst. Musical Studies, Graz, Austria, 1979. Tchr. music Los Angeles Schs., 1955-76; pvt. voice tchr. Newport Beach, Calif., 1955—. Appeared in plays Born Yesterday, Rumpelstiltskin, Stage Door, The Heiress, Darling delinquent, You Can't Take It with You, So You Want to be a Mother; appeared in operas Dance of Death, La Boheme, Faust, Rape of Lucretia, La Traviata, Stabat Mater, Otello, 1996; performed as guest artist throughout Orange County, Calif.; exhibited in art shows at Lido Village, Bullock's Dept. Store, Jewel Court, City Hall of Newport, Orange County, Calif., Orange Coast Plaza; appeared in movies Sister Act II, Kangaroo Man, Strange Days; performer Hats, Hats, Hats, 1993-94. Pres. Musical Arts Orange County, 1980-82, chmn. program, 1978-80, rec. sec., 1977-78; chmn. program Orange County Philharm. Soc., 1984-86, 88-89, chmn. ways means, 1986-88, chmn. publicity, 1980-82; chmn. program Musical Theatre Guild Orange County, 1978-80; founder Opera Pacific; charter mem. Rep. Nat. Task Force, Nat. Mus. of Women in Arts, 1988—. Mem. Nat. Assn. Tchrs. Singing (exec. bd. dirs. 1984-89), Music Tchrs. Assn., Music Tchrs. Assn. Calif., Costa Mesa Art league, South Coast Repertory Theatre Guild, Internat. Congress Voice Tchrs., Camelot Chpt. Performing Arts Ctr., Soc. Mil. Widows of Orange County (pres. 1993-95, fundraiser), Delta Gamma. Home and Studio: 2022 Barranca Newport Beach CA 92660-4528

BRYANT, KAREN WORSTELL, financial consultant; b. Cadillac, Mich., Sept. 7, 1942; d. Harley Orville and Rose Edith (Bell) Worstell; children: Lynda Jean, Tracey Jo, Cynthia Jill, Troy Thomas; m. Robert Melvin Bryant, Nov. 29, 1968. Student, Cen. Mich. U., 1963-67, Mich. State U., 1966, Johns Hopkins U., 1982-83. Sales rep. Xerox Corp., Southfield, Mich., 1972-74; cons. and employment contracts IBM World Trade Asia, The Policy Study Grp., Johnson & Johnson Internat., Tokyo, 1974-79; area sales mgr. Universal Plastics, McLean, Va., 1979-81; exec. product mgr. The Western Union Telegraph Co., Upper Saddle River, N.J., 1981-86; dir. mktg. and sales support The Nat. Guardian Corp., Greenwich, Conn., 1986-88; fin. cons. Smith Barney, Paramus, N.J., 1988—; guest lectr. for orgns; guest on TV documentaries. Contbr. articles to profl. jours. Fundraiser chair Rep. Cand. Re-Election Com., Rockland County; bd. dirs., fundraising chair Ramapo Ctrl. Found., Hillburn, N.Y. Mem. World Wildlife Fedn., N.Y. State Horse Coun., Nature Conservancy, Suffern H.S. Parents Lacrosse Assn., Suffern H.S. Band Boosters Club. Republican. Home: 19 Sky Meadow Rd Suffern NY 10901-2520 Office: Smith Barney Inc South Tower 140 E Ridgewood Ave Paramus NJ 07652-3915

BRYANT, PAMELA ANNE, military career officer, retired, business owner; b. Detroit, July 15, 1950; d. Theodore Louis and Martha Marie (Nordstrom) Cogut; children: Tessa A. McGeaughay, Sean L. BS in Vocat. Indsl. Edn., U. Md., 1976; student, Mich. State U., East Lansing, 1969-71; MS, Troy (Ala.) State U., 1986. Commd. 2d lt. USAF, 1980, advanced through grades to maj., 1984; chief cargo ops., reports and systems div. 22d Air Force, Travis AFB, Calif., 1989-90; chief support div. directorate transp. Hdqrs USAF Res., Robins AFB, Ga., 1990-94; squadron commdr. 650th Transp. Squadron, Edwards AFB, Calif., 1994—; owner Bryant Enterprises, 1991—; lectr. Clifton-Morenci (Ariz.) Rotary Club, 1989. Soccer team coord. Am. Youth Assn., RAF Laken Heath, Eng., 1983; troop leader Girl Scouts U.S., RAF Laken Heath, 1982; membership chmn. Boy Scouts Am., RAF Laken Heath, 1983. U. Md. scholar, 1976. Mem. Nat. Def. Transp. Assn., NAFE, Air Force Assn. (life), Alpha Sigma Lambda.

BRYANT-FIELDS, REGINA L., lawyer; b. Cornwall, N.Y., Sept. 15, 1955. BA, Bowdoin Coll., 1977; JD, Columbia U., 1980. Bar: N.Y. 1981, Calif. 1982. Ptnr. Brown & Wood, N.Y.C. Office: Brown & Wood One World Trade Ctr New York NY 10048-0557*

BRYCE, TERESA A., lawyer; b. Norfolk, Va., July 31, 1959; d. Burie O'Neal and Dorothy Mae (Hicks) Bryce. BA, U. Va., 1981; JD, Columbia U., 1984. Bar: Md. 1985, D.C. 1985. Rsch. asst., Legis. Drafting Rsch. Fund Columbia U. Sch. Law, N.Y.C., 1983-84; law clk. to Chief Justice Robert N. Wilentz N.J. Supreme Ct., Perth Amboy, 1984-85; assoc. Piper & Marbury, Balt., 1985-90; v.p., assoc. gen. counsel The Prudential Ins. Co. of Am., Frederick, Md., 1990-94; v.p., gen. counsel PNC Mortgage Corp. of Am., Vernon Hills, Ill., 1994—. Bd. dirs. Parks and People Found., Balt., 1993-94, Chesapeake Bay Outward Bound Program adv. bd., Balt., 1988-93; bd. dirs. Total Health Care, Balt., 1988-90. Mem. ABA (forum on affordable housing and cmty. devel. law, fair housing practice divsn. 1989—, sect. of real property, probate and trust law 1986—, com. on secondary market financing of affordable housing 1995—, mortgages and financing of home ownership com. 1993—), Md. Bar Assn., D.C. Bar Assn., Am. Corp. Counsel Assn., Alliance of Black Women Attys. (treas. 1987-88), Mortgage Bankers Assn. (legis. com., chair state legis. and regulatory com., mem. legal issues com.), Delta Sigma Theta. Presbyterian. Office: PNC Mortgage Corp of Am 75 N Fairway Dr Vernon Hills IL 60061

BRYER, CAROL CLINE, medical technologist; b. Phila., Nov. 12, 1938; d. Howard Carr and Ethel Frances (Mathews) Cline; divorced; children: James Robert MacDonald, Juli Ann MacDonald. BS, Fla. So. Coll., Lakeland, 1960; Med. Technologist, Abington (Pa.) Meml. Hosp., 1961. Lic. med. technologist, supr., Fla.; reg. med. technologist ASCP. Med. technologist Holy Cross Hosp., Ft. Lauderdale, Fla., 1961-62, Lauderdale Med. Group, Ft. Lauderdale, 1962-73, Boca Med. Group, Boca Raton, Fla., 1973-93, South Fla. Health Care Assocs., Boca Raton, 1993-94, Physicians Specialty Group, Boca Raton, 1994—. Mem. Am. Soc. Clin. Pathologists (assoc.), Fla. Soc. Med. Technologists. Republican.

BRYFONSKI, DEDRIA ANNE, publishing company executive; b. Utica, N.Y., Aug. 21, 1947; d. Lewis Francis and Catherine Marie (Stevens) B.; m. Alexander Burgess Cruden, May 24, 1975. B.A., Nazareth Coll., Rochester, N.Y., 1969; M.A., Fordham U., 1970. Editorial asst. Dial Press, N.Y.C., 1970-71; editor Walker & Co., N.Y.C., 1971-73; editor Gale Research Co., Detroit, 1974-79, sr. editor, 1979, v.p., assoc. editorial dir., 1979-84, sr. v.p., editorial dir., 1984-86, exec. v.p., pub., 1986-94, pres., CEO, 1995—. Author: The New England Beach Book, 1974; editor: Contemporary Literary Criticism, Vols. 7-14, 1977-80, Twentieth Century Literary Criticism, vols. 1-2, 1977-78, Contemporary Issues Criticism, vol. 1, 1982, Contemporary Authors Autobiography Series, vol. 1, 1984. Bd. dirs. Friends of Detroit Pub. Libr., 1980-89, pres., 1984-86; bd. dirs. Friends of Librs. U.S.A., 1995—. Mem. ALA, Assn. Am. Pubs. (chmn. libraries com. 1983-85, exec. council gen. pub. div. 1985-87, co-chmn. joint com. resources and tech. services div. 1983-85). Home: 546 Lincoln Rd Grosse Pointe MI 48230-1218 Office: Gale Research Co 835 Penobscot Bldg Detroit MI 48226

BRYSON, DOROTHY PRINTUP, retired educator; b. Britton, S.D., Dec. 2, 1894; d. David Lawrence and Marion Harland (Gamsby) Printup; m. Archer Butler Hulbert, June 16, 1923 (dec. Dec. 1933); children: Joanne Woodward, Nancy Printup; m. Franklin Fearing Wing, Oct. 15, 1938 (dec. Mar. 1942); m. Arthur Earl Bryson, Feb. 15, 1964 (dec. Apr. 1979). AB, Oberlin Coll., 1915; AM, Radcliffe Coll., 1916; LHD (hon.), Colo. Coll., 1989. Instr. Latin, Tenn. Coll., Murfreesboro, 1916-18; tchr. Latin, prin. high sch., Britton, 1918-20; instr. classics Colo. Coll., Colorado Springs, 1921-22, 23-25, sec., instr., head resident, 1951-60; tchr. latin San Luis Prep. Sch., Colorado Springs, 1934-36, 41-42, Sandia Sch., Albuquerque, 1937-39, Westlake Sch., L.A., 1946-49; exec. dir. YWCA, Colorado Springs, 1942-46, 49-51; editor western history Stewart Commn., Colorado Springs, 1934-41; ret., 1960. Editor: Overland to the Pacific, 5 vols., 1934-41. Bd. dirs. Day Nursery, Colorado Springs 1933-37. Fellow Aelioian Lit. Soc., 1920-21; scholar U. Chgo., 1920-21. Mem. LWV (v.p., bd. dirs. Colorado Springs 1943-45), Women's Edn. Soc. Colo. Coll. (pres., bd. dirs. 1955—), Reviewers Club, Tuesday Discussion Club, Pikes Peak Posse Westerners, Women's Literary Club, Phi Beta Kappa, Gamma Phi Beta. Republican. Episcopalian. Home: 107 W Cheyenne Rd Apt 610 Colorado Springs CO 80906-2509

BRYSON-SHAHN, BERNARDA, artist; b. Athens, Ohio, Mar. 7, 1903; d. Charles Harvey and Lucy Wilkins (Weethee) B.; m. Victor Luster Parks (div. 1927); m. Benjamin Svie Shahn, 1935 (dec. 1969); children: Susannah, Jonathan, Abigail. Student, Ohio U., 1922-25, 29, DFA (hon.), 1992; DFA (hon.), Ohio U., 1994; student, Ohio State U., 1928, Cleve. Sch. Art, 1927, New Sch. for Social Rsch., 1940-41. Editor South Side Advocate, Columbus, Ohio, 1927-28; writer Ohio State Jour., Columbus, 1929-30; tchr. etching and lithography Columbus Gallery Fine Arts, 1930-31; sec., founder Artists Union, N.Y.C., 1933-34; lithographer spl. skills divsn. Resettlement Adminstrn., Washington, 1935-37; asst. to artist U.S. Resettlement Adminstrn., Washington, 1937; gov. Skowhegan Sch. Painting & Sculptore, 1965—; mem. Trenton Artists Workshop, 1995—, Roosevelt Art Project; spkr. in field. Author, illustrator: The Zoo of Zeus, Gilgamesh, Twenty Miracles, St N; author: Ben Shahn, 1972; illustrator Wuthering Hights & Pride & Prejudice; artist illustrator Fortune mag., Sci. Am., Harpers Mag.; permanent murals include Bronx (N.Y.) Post Office; represented by Midtown-Payson Gallery, 1987-96, John Payson & the Hobe Sound Fla. Gallery. Recipient Gold medal, Skowhegan (Maine) Sch. Painting & Sculptore, 1995, Soc. Illustrators award, 1995, Hon. award Columbus Sch. for Girls, 1982, Skowhegan Sch.Painting and Sculpture, 1996. Democrat.

BRZOSKA, DENISE JEANNE, paralegal, artist; b. Wilmington, Del., Mar. 21, 1945; d. Eugene Joseph and Marie Jeanette (Durr) B. Student, U. Del., 1971-84; grad., Citizen's Police Acad., New Castle, Del., 1995. Cert. graphic designer; cert. paralegal. Bookkeeping clk. Del. Div. of Revenue, Wilmington, 1963-66; tech. support personnel dept. physics and astronomy U. Del., Newark, 1966-91; paralegal Wilmington Trust Co./Trust Legal, 1992—; mem. geographic adv. coun. and by-laws com. New Castle County Police, 1996. Artist representing Del. at Colliseum Arts Internat., World Trade Ctr., 1981. Campaign worker Joe Biden for U.S. Senate, Del., 1978, S.B. Woo for Lt. Gov., Del., 1984, S.B. Woo for U.S. Senate, Del., 1988; mem. geographic adv. coun., by-laws com. New Castle County Police Dept., 1996. Mem. Del. Paralegal Assn., Wilmington Women in Bus., Pa. Horticultural Soc., Del. Art Mus., Wilmington Garden Day. Roman Catholic. Home: 422 Old Airport Rd New Castle DE 19720-1002

BRZUSTOWICZ, VICTORIA CECILE, artist; b. Rochester, N.Y., Sept. 28, 1954; d. Richard J. and Alice (Cinq-Mars) B. BA in Studio Art, Wells Coll., 1975. Art dir. Digitech Pub., Inc., Rochester, 1989-93, Corea & Eibl, Inc., Rochester, 1993—; trainer, cons. graphic design computer programs, Rochester, 1990—. Two woman show at Pyramid Gallery, Rochester, 1978; group exhibitions include Pyramid Arts Ctr., Inc., Rochester, 1978, 82, 83, 85, String Rm. Gallery Wells Coll., Aurora, N.Y., 1983, Zaner Gallery, Rochester, 1985, Albany (N.Y.) Inst. History and Art, 1986 (Village Frame Shop award 1986), Meml. Art Gallery, Rochester, 1982, 83, 84, 86, Germanow Gallery, Rochester, 1986, Cooperstown (N.Y.) Art Assn. Galleries, 1991, Art Dialogue Gallery, Buffalo, 1992; illustrator for books: Once-Upon-A-Time Saints, 1977, More Once-Upon-A-Time Saints, 1978. Home: 90 Forest Hills Rd Rochester NY 14625-1935

BUBLITZ, DEBORAH KEIRSTEAD, pediatrician; b. Boston, Feb. 28, 1933; d. George and Dorothy (Kingsbury) Keirstead; m. Clark Bublitz, Mar.

1, 1958; children: Nancy B. Dyer, Susan B. Schooleman, Philip K. Bublitz, Caroline D. Bublitz, Elizabeth E. Bublitz. BS, Bates Coll., 1953; MD, Johns Hopkins U., 1959. Resident St. Louis Children's Hosp., 1959-60, U. Colo. Health Sci. Ctr. and Dept. Health and Hosps., Denver, 1968-71; pvt. practice Littleton, Colo., 1974—; asst. clin. prof. pediatrics U. Colo. Health Sci. Ctr. and Children's Hosp., 1975-87, assoc. clin. prof. pediatrics, 1987—; creditials com. Swedish/Porter Hosp., Englewood, Colo., 1985-87, chief dept. pediatrics, 1985-87; med. assoc., advisor LaLeche League, 1975—. Author: (with others) Clinical Pediatric Otolaryngology, 1986. Fellow Am. Acad. Pediatrics; mem. AMA, Colo. Med. Soc. (women's governing coun. 1990-96, asst. chair women's governing coun. 1993-94, chair, 1994-95), Arapahoe Med. Soc., Am. Women's Med. Assn. Episcopalian. Home: 5621 Blue Sage Dr Littleton CO 80123 Office: Littleton Pediatric Med Ctr 206 W County Line #110 Highlands Ranch CO 80126

BUC, NANCY LILLIAN, lawyer; b. Orange, N.J., July 27, 1944; d. George L. and Ethel (Rosenbaum) B. AB, Brown U., 1965, LLD (hon.), 1994; LLB, U. Va., 1969. Bar: Va. 1969, N.Y. 1977, D.C. 1978. Atty. Fed. Trade Commn., Washington, 1969-72; assoc. Weil, Gotshal & Manges, N.Y., 1972-77, ptnr., 1977-78; ptnr. Weil, Gotshal & Manges, Washington, 1978-80, 81-94, Buc & Beardsley, Washington, 1994—; chief counsel FDA, Rockville, Md., 1980-81; mem. recombinant DNA adv. com. NIH, 1990-94. Mem. editl. bd. Food Drug and Cosmetic Law Jour., 1981-87, 94—, Jour. of Products Liability, 1981-92, Health Span: The Jour. of Health, Bus. & Law, 1984-95. Mem. adv. com. on new devels. in biotech. Office of Tech. Assessment, Washington, 1986-89, mem. adv. com. on govt. policies and pharm. R & D, 1989-93; mem. com. to study medications devel. and rsch. Nat. Inst. Drug Abuse, 1993-95; mem. com. on contraceptive R & D, Inst. Medicine, 1994-96. Fellow Brown U., 1980-92; recipient Disting. Svc. award Fed. Trade Commn., Washington, 1972, Award of Merit FDA, Rockville, 1981, Sec.'s Spl. citation HHS, Washington, 1981, Ind. award Associated. Alumni of Brown U., 1991. Mem. ABA (mem. spl. com. to study FTC 1988-89), Com. of 200 Va. Law Sch. Found. (bd. dirs.), Women's Legal Def. Fund (bd. dirs.). Office: Buc & Beardsley 919 18th St NW Ste 600 Washington DC 20006-5503

BUCCI, KATHLEEN ELIZABETH, lawyer, nurse; b. Malden, Mass., Nov. 1, 1952; d. Harold Edward and Elizabeth Marie (Keefe) B. ASN, Mass. Bay C.C., 1977; BA, U. Mass., 1985; JD, New Eng. Sch. Law, 1985. Bar: Mass. 1989, U.S. Dist. Ct. Mass. 1992, U.S. Ct. Appeals (1st cir.) 1992; cert. hemodialysis nurse. RN staff Nat. Med. Care Inc., Boston, 1977-78; RN ICU St. John's Hosp., Santa Monica, Calif., 1978-79; asst. head nurse UCLA Med. Ctr., Westwood, Calif., 1979-80; nurse coord. P.J. West & Assocs., Inc., Tarzana, Calif., 1980-81; RN mobile acute team Hemodialysis, Inc., Northridge, Calif., 1981-82, Hemostat, Inc., Burbank, Calif., 1982-84; med.-legal cons. Kathleen E. Bucci, RN, Malden, Mass., 1985-92; nurse atty. Ned. C. Lofton, P.C., Wakefield, Mass., 1992-94, Halström Law Offices, P.C., Boston, 1994—. Mem. Am. Assn. Nurse Attys. (New Eng. chpt. bd. dirs. 1991-93, pub. rels. chairperson 1989-93), Assn. Trial Lawyers Am., Mass. Bar Assn. Roman Catholic. Office: Halström Law Office PC 132 Boylston St Boston MA 02116-4616

BUCCI, MARY RUTH, primary education educator; b. New Castle, Pa., July 21, 1948; d. David Feyling and Mary Ann (Bintrim) Clausen; m. Richard Alan Bucci, May 24, 1975; children: Melissa Kay, Jeffrey Michael, Keren Ann. BS in Edn. cum laude, Slippery Rock U., 1971, MEd magna cum laude, 1974; MA in Edn. summa cum laude, Regents U., 1988. Cert. tchr., reading specialist, curriculum supr., Pa. Tchr. lang. arts Shenango Elem. Sch., New Castle, 1971-76; tchr. kindergarten Rhema Christian Sch., Coraopolis, Pa., 1984-95, curriculum specialist, 1988-91, tchr. computer sci., 1991-95; coord. gen. studies Hillel Acad. of Pitts., 1995—; pvt. tutor, home sch. evaluator; mem. sec. Rhema Christian Sch. Bd., Aliquippa, Pa., 1986-89. Mem. ASCD, Alpha Xi Delta (chpt. dir. 1976-77, province collegiate dir. 1974-76). Republican. Home: 206 Windy Hill Dr Coraopolis PA 15108-1146 Office: Hillel Acad Pitts 5685 Beacon St Pittsburgh PA 15217

BUCCIERI, M. ELAINE, lawyer; b. Ft. Worth, Dec. 8, 1960; d. D.S. and Patsy Lou (Howard) B. BBA in Land Mgmt. magna cum laude, Tex. Tech U., 1983, JD cum laude, 1986. Bar: Tex. 1986, Tenn. 1995, U.S. Dist. Ct. (no. dist.) Tex. 1988. Assoc. Clark, West, Dallas, 1986-87, Law, Snakard & Gambill, Ft. Worth, 1988-89; staff atty. Bishop, Payne, Ft. Worth, 1990; ptnr. Law Offices M. Elaine Buccieri, Ft. Worth, Tex. and Nashville, Tenn., 1990—. Assoc. editor Tex. Tech. U. Law Rev., 1985-86. Mem. Tex. Young Lawyer Assn. (local affiliates com., homeless com., elderly com.), Ft. Worth-Tarrant County Young Lawyers Assn. (bd. dirs. 1988, treas. 1989-90, sec. 1990, v.p. 1990-91, pres. 1991-92), Order of Coif, Beta Gamma Sigma. Office: Law Office of M Elaine Buccieri 608 Brentlawn Rd Nashville TN 37220-1947

BUCHANAN, CARLA WILLIAMS, data processing consultant; b. White County, Ill., Sept. 16, 1949; d. Clarence Arthur and Verna Pearl (Callicotte) W.; m. Robert Hall Gaston (div.); m. Danny LeRoy Buchanan, May 15, 1995. AS, Belleville (Ill.) Area Coll., 1969; BS in Edn., Ill. State U., 1971. Sec. Falstaff Brewing Corp., St. Louis, 1971-73; editor in-house Concordia Pub. Ho., St. Louis, 1974-75; programmer data processing St. Clair County Courthouse, Belleville, 1977; programmer to prin. cons. McDonnell Douglas Automation Co., St. Louis, 1978-89; reengring. and imaging cons. IBM, Kansas City, Mo., 1989-95; imaging cons. Electronic Data Systems, Mission, Kans., 1995-96; prin. Calicotte Buchanan Consulting, Mission, Kans., 1996—; cons., system architect Ill. Dept. of Revenue, Individual Income Tax System, Springfield, 1982-83, Bridge Mgmt. System, Pa. Dept. of Transp., Harrisburg, Pa., 1984-85; cons. imaging and reengring. J.B. Hunt Co., Inc., Fayetteville, 1992-93. Patentee in field. Vol., mem. Kansas City Ski Club, 1993-96; editor monthly newsletter Lenexa Optimist Club, 1993-96. Mem. Assn. for Info. and Image Mgmt. Home: 6334 Maple Dr Mission KS 66202-4314 Office: PO Box 9433 Mission KS 66201-2133

BUCHANAN, DIANE FRANCIS, secondary school counselor; b. Dallas, Mar. 1, 1945; d. Alwilder M. (Anderson) Thompson; m. James J. Buchanan. BS in Edn., U. North Tex., 1967; MEd, East Tex. U., 1978. Lic. profl. counselor, spl. edn. counselor, career counselor; elem. edn. Tchr. elem. edn. Arlington (Tex.) Ind. Schs., 1967-75; tchr. elem. edn. Richardson (Tex.) Sch. Dist., 1975-78, counselor elem. edn., 1978-79; counselor elem. edn. Northside Sch. Dist., San Antonio, 1979-80; counselor jr. h.s. Richardson Sch. Dist., 1980-93, counselor sr. h.s., 1993—. Mem. Tex. Assn. for Counseling and Devel., Richardson Edn. Assn., Phi Delta Kappa. Office: J J Pearce H S 1600 N Coit Richardson TX 75080

BUCHANAN, GLORIA JEAN, retail executive; b. Bowling Green, Ky., Nov. 3, 1950; d. Albert M. and Lenora (Hayes)Paschal; m. Michael C. Moonan (div.); 1 child, Shelly; m. Andrew George Buchnan. Mgr. Alexander Wallcovering, Falls Church, Va., 1976-81; decorator Duron Paints and Wallvocering, Beltsville, Md., 1982-84, sales rep., 1984-85, archtl. rep., 1985-86, dir., 1986-91; dir. archtl. sales dept. McCormick Paint Works Co., Rockville, Md., 1991—. Bd. govs. Washington Bldg. Congress, 1994—. Mem. NAFE, Constrn. Specification Inst. (industry dir. 1993-94, membership chmn. 1993-94, v.p. 1995—), Interior Design Soc., Washington Sales and Mktg. Council. Republican. Episcopalian. Home: 9823 Arrowood Dr Manassas VA 22111-2581 Office: McCormick Paint Works Co 7325 Lewis Ave Rockville MD 20705

BUCHANAN, LEE ANN, public relations executive; b. Albuquerque, July 6, 1955; d. William Henry Buchanan and Juanita Irene (Pilgrim) Wood; m. Charles Stanton Wood, Jan. 17, 1987. BA, U. Calif., Irvine, 1977. Exec. asst. to Congressman William Thomas, U.S. Ho. of Reps., Washington, 1979-83; dep. chief staff Gov. George Deukmejian, Sacramento, 1983-84; sr. v.p., ptnr. Nelson Comm., Costa Mesa, Calif., 1985-95. Bd. govs. Rep. Assocs. of Orange County, 1985—; founding sec. Orange County Young Reps., 1985. Mem. Internat. Assn. Bus. Communicators, Am. Assn. Polit. Cons., Pub. Relations Soc. Am., U. Calif.-Irvine Alumni Assn. Address: PO Box 1741 Mammoth Lakes CA 93546-1741

BUCHANAN, MICHELLE MARIE, secondary education language arts educator; b. Burbank, Calif., Aug. 5, 1968; d. James Murphy and Elaine Marie (Saccomanno) B. BA, Met. State Coll. of Denver, 1992. Cert. secondary level tchr., Colo., Tex. Tchr., substitute tchr. various Colo. pub. schs., elem. and h.s. levels, 1992—; English language tchr. Bonham Mid. Sch., Amarillo, Tex., Mullen H.S., Denver. Asst. editor prose (mag.) Metrosphere, 1990. Mem. AAUW, Colo. Lang. Arts Soc., Nat. Coun. Tchrs. of English, Clan Buchanan Socl, Phi Alpha Theta, Sigma Tau Delta. Democrat. Home: 4600 E Asbury Cir 306 Denver CO 80222

BUCHANAN, NANCY ELIZABETH, librarian; b. Vancouver, B.C., Can., Mar. 21, 1946; d. Frank Borden and Velma Lucille (Smyth) Clark; m. Robert Wayne Buchanan, Dec. 27, 1967 (div. 1977). BA, U. Ariz., 1967, MLS, 1973, MA, 1980. Cert. tchr. Ariz. C.C. Tchr. Spanish Dover (N.H.) High Sch., 1968-69; sec. Earl Fruit Co., San Francisco, 1970-71, U. N.H., Durham, 1971-72; circulation libr. Pima C.C., Tucson, 1973-80, reference libr., 1980-90, collection devel. libr., 1990—; instr. honors program Pima C.C., Tucson, 1984—; reviewer Booklist, 1982-83, Lector, 1984-86. Author: (with others) Vocational & Technical Resources for Community College Libraries, 1995. Mem. ALA, Phi Kappa Phi, Delta Sigma Pi. Office: Pima CC Libr 2202 W Anklam Rd Tucson AZ 85709

BUCHANAN, TERI BAILEY, communications executive; b. Long Beach, Calif., Feb. 24, 1946; d. Alton Hervey and Ruth Estelle (Thompson) Bailey; m. Robert Wayne Buchanan, Aug. 14, 1964 (div. May 1979). BA in English with highest honors, Ark. Poly. Coll., 1968. With employee communications AT&T, Kansas City, Mo., 1968-71; freelance writer Ottawa, Kans., 1971-73; publs. dir. Ottawa U., 1973-74; regional info. officer U.S. Dept. Labor, Kansas City, 1974; owner, operator PBT Communications, Kansas City, 1975-79; sr. pub. affairs rep., sr. editor, exhibit supr., communications specialist Standard Oil/Chevron, San Francisco, 1979-84; owner The Resource Group/Comms., Napa, Calif., 1984—; mem. faculty pub. rels. master's program Golden Gate U., San Francisco, 1987. Pub. rels. trainer Bus. Vols. for Arts, San Francisco, 1985-93; mem. Napa Conf. and Visitors Bur. Recipient Internat. Assn. Bus. Communicators Bay Area Gold and Silver awards, 1984. Mem. Yountville C. of C. (mktg. com.). Democrat. Episcopalian. Office: The Resource Group 134 Golden Gate Cir Napa CA 94558

BUCHBINDER-GREEN, BARBARA JOYCE, art and architectural historian; b. Bronx, N.Y., Dec. 23, 1944; d. Michael and Esther Buchbinder; m. Raymond Jerome Green, Dec. 18, 1970. BA cum laude, Vanderbilt U., 1965; PhD, Northwestern U., 1974. Teaching asst. Northwestern U., Evanston, Ill., 1967-68; lectr. Northwestern U., Chgo., 1975; freelance researcher and writer Evanston, 1977—; editor GreenAssoc. Architects, Inc., Evanston, 1979—; cons. nomination forms Nat. Register of Historic Places, 1983—; mem. architecture adv. com. Mus. Sci. and Industry, Chgo., 1980-86; trustee Evanston Hist. Soc., 1986-92, pres., 1988-90, mem. house walk com. 1981-83, 88-90, chmn., 1988-90, mem. restoration planning com., 1980-91, editor newsletter TimeLines, 1989-92. Author: Lucy Fitch Perkins, 1984, Evanston: A Pictorial History, 1989; editor, compiler Evanstoniana, 1984; guest curator "Lucy Fitch Perkins" exhibit, 1983-84, "Photographs from Evanstoniana" exhibit, 1984-87; pub. photographer: Evanstoniana, 1984, Evanston: A Pictorial History, 1989, Victorian Details, 1990; history editor Chgo. Yacht Club Blinker, 1993-95; editor Cruising Sail Fleet, 1993—; contbr. articles to profl. jours. Founding mem. Preservation League Evanston, 1982; commr. Evanston Preservation Commn., 1981-89, chmn. preservations awards com., 1983-84, mem. evaln. com., 1978-92, chmn., 1985-89; mem. Citizen's Adv. Com. on Pub. Pl. Names, 1989-92; bd. dirs. Dewey Cmty. Conf., 1981-84, mem. exec. com., 1981-82, rec. sec., 1982-83. Univ. fellow Northwestern U., 1968-69, Dissertation Year fellow, 1969-70; Vanderbilt U. scholar, 1962-65. Mem. Victorian Soc. in Am. (bd. dirs. Chgo. chpt. 1978-81), Chgo. Architecture Found. Aux. Bd. (sec. 1990-91, exec. com. 1990-92, v.p. for cmty. affairs 1991-92), Archtl. Soc. Art Inst. Chgo., Soc. Archtl. Historians, Women's Archtl. League (v.p. 1980-82), Chgo. Maritime Soc., Nat. Trust for Hist. Preservation, Lake Forest Found. for Hist. Preservation, Howard Van Doren Shaw Soc., Tibetan Terrier Club Am., Cliff Dwellers Club. Home and Office: 1026 Michigan Ave Evanston IL 60202-1436

BUCHERRE, VERONIQUE, environmental company executive; b. Casablanca, Morocco, Nov. 20, 1951; came to U.S., 1967; d. Maurice Daniel Bucherre and Lucette Jaqueline Piani; m. Douglas Lee Frazier; 1 child, Marc-Andrew. Diploma Para Profesores, Gregorio Maranon, Madrid, 1972; MA, San Francisco State U., 1974; PhD in Latin Am. Affairs, U. Paris-Sorbonne, 1980; diploma in conf. interpreting, London Sch. of Poly., 1983. Lic. real estate broker, Md. Instr. French Peace Corps, Baker, La., 1968; editorial asst. Newsweek mag., San Francisco, 1970-72; mem. faculty San Francisco State U., 1972-74, 77; conf. interpreter-translator France and U.S., 1974-85, rural developer, 1976-86; pres. Bucherre & Assocs., Washington, 1985-88; inventor The Rainbank System, 1985; bd. dirs. Rainbank System, 1986-88, CEO; pres. Rainbank Group Ltd., 1988—; vis. prof. Am. U., Washington, 1992, 93; student body rep. IHEAL, Sorbonne, Paris, 1974-75; mem. bd. mgmt. Inst. des Hautes Etudes de l'Amerique Latine, Paris, 1975-76; mem. Lab III, Centre Nat. de Recherche Scientifique, Paris, 1975-77; mem. civilian pers. rules editing com. Inter-Am. Def. Bd., 1991-94, pres. internat. civilian staff, 1987-92, bd. dirs., 1991-93. Author: Florence, 1979, Uruguay, 1980; co-author: Civilian Personnel Rules of the Inter-American Defense Board, Relief Ops. Manual. Named Hon. Citizen City of Mobile, Ala. Mem. Le Droit Humain (Paris), Droit Humain Club (Paris), GITE Club (Paris). Office: 6404 Western Ave Bethesda MD 20815-3307

BUCHWALD, MONITA, public relations executive. Account exec. Manning, Selvage & Lee Inc., N.Y.C., 1980-83, v.p., 1983-85, dep. group mgr., 1985-86; group mgr. Manning, Selvage & Lee, Inc., N.Y.C., 1986-87, sr. v.p., 1987-88, dir. health care divsn., worldwide acct. dir., 1988-92, sr. v.p., 1992-93, joint mng. dir. N.Y., 1993-94, sr. v.p., dep. dir. creative and strategic devel., 1994—. Office: Manning Selvage & Lee Inc 79 Madison Ave New York NY 10016-7802*

BUCHWALD, NAOMI REICE, judge; b. Kingston, N.Y., Feb. 14, 1944; BA cum laude, Brandeis U., 1965; LLB, cum laude, Columbia U., 1968. Bar: N.Y. 1968, U.S. Ct. Appeals (2d cir.) 1969, U.S. Dist. Ct. (so. and ea. dists.) N.Y. 1970, U.S. Supreme Ct. 1978. Litigation assoc. Marshall, Bratter, Greene, Allison & Tucker, N.Y.C., 1968-73; asst. U.S. atty. So. Dist. N.Y., 1973-80, dep. chief civil div., 1976-79, chief civil div., 1979-80; U.S. magistrate judge U.S. Dist. Ct. (so. dist.) N.Y., N.Y.C., 1980—, chief magistrate judge, 1994-96. Editor Columbia Jour. Law and Social Problems, 1967-68. Recipient spl. citation FDA Commrs., 1978, Robert B. Fiske Jr. Assn. William B. Tendy award, Outstanding Pub. Svc. award Seymour Assn. Mem. ABA, Fed. Bar Coun. (v.p. 1982-84), Assn. of Bar of City of N.Y. (trademarks and unfair competition com. 1988-89, mem. long range planning com. 1993-95, litigation com. 1994—), N.Y. State Bar Assn., Phi Beta Kappa, Omicron Delta Epsilon. Office: US Ct House Rm 2270 500 Pearl St New York NY 10007

BUCK, ALISON JENNIFER, technical writer; b. Bangor, Maine, Dec. 11, 1952; d. George Hill and Anna (Komisaruk) B. BS, U. Maine, Orono, 1974; MA, Brigham Young U., 1978. Cert. tchr., Maine, Mass. Vol. program coordinator Head Start/Hampshire Community Action Commn., Northampton, Mass., 1980; career edn. specialist, job developer Hampshire Ednl. Collaborative, Northampton, 1981; documentation specialist Amherst (Mass.) Assocs., 1981-84; sr. tech. writer Visual Intelligence Corp., Amherst, 1984-85; tech. documentation specialist Video Communications Inc., Feeding Hills, Mass., 1986-87; contract tech. writer Digital Equipment Corp., Westfield, Mass., 1987; mktg. coordinator, tech. publs. mgr. Millitech Corp., South Deerfield, Mass., 1988; contract tech. writer Carrier Corp., Farmington, Conn., 1988-89; author computer-based tng. materials AMS Courseware Developers, Manchester, Conn., 1989-92; learning tech. Aetna Ins. Corp., Hartford, Conn., 1992-94; application developer Health New Eng., Springfield, Mass., 1994—. Co-author: The Coffee Maker Cookbook, 1988. Mem. Soc. for Tech. Communication. Democrat. Office: Health New England One Monarch Pl Springfield MA 01144

BUCK, ANNE MARIE, library director, consultant; b. Birmingham, Ala., Apr. 12, 1939; d. Blaine Alexander and Marie Reynolds (McGeorge) Davis; m. Evan Buck, June 17, 1961 (div. Apr. 1977); children: Susan Elizabeth Buck Rentko, Stephen Edward. BA, Wellesley (Mass.) Coll., 1961; MLS, U. Ky., 1977. Bus. mgr. Charleston (W.Va.) Chamber Music Soc., 1972-74; dir. Dunbar (W.Va.) Pub. Libr., 1974-76; tech. reference libr. AT&T Bell Labs., Naperville, Ill., 1977-79; group supr. libr. AT&T Bell Labs., Reading, Pa., 1979-83; group supr. support svcs. AT&T Bell Labs., North Andover, Mass., 1983; dir. libr. network Bell Communications Rsch. (Bellcore), Morristown, N.J., 1983-89; dir. human resources planning Bell Communications Rsch. (Bellcore), Livingston, N.J., 1989-91; univ. libr. N.J. Inst. Tech., Newark, 1991-95, Calif. Inst. of Tech., Pasadena, 1995—; adj. prof. Rutgers U., New Brunswick, N.J., 1989-91; instr. U. Wis., Madison, 1988-90; v.p. Engring. Info. Found., N.Y.C., 1994—; mem. Engring. Info. Inc. (bd. dirs.), Castle-Point-on-the-Hudson, Hoboken, N.J., 1988—; spkr. profl. assn. confs., 1982—; libr. cons. North Port (Fla.) Area Libr., 1990-91. Mem. editorial adv. bd. Highsmith Press, 1991—; contbr. articles to profl. jours. Sect. mgr. United Way of Morris County, Cedar Knolls, N.J., 1984-95; advisor Family Svc. Transitions Coun., Morristown, 1987-90; libr. trustee Lisle (Ill.) Pub. Libr. Dist., 1978-80; bd. dirs. Kanawha County Bicentennial Commn., Charleston, W.Va., 1974-76. Recipient Vol.'s Gold award United Way, 1991. Mem. ALA (Grolier Nat. Libr. Week grantee 1975), Am. Soc. Info. Sci. (chpt. chmn. 1987-89, Chpt. of Yr. award 1988, treas. 1992-95), Conf. Bd. Inc. (chmn. info. svcs. adv. coun. 1987-89), Spl. Libr. Assn., Am. Soc. Engring. Edn., Archons of Colophon, Indsl. Tech. Info. Mgrs. Group, Wellesley Coll. Alumni Assn. (class rep. 1986-91), N.J. Wellesley Club (regional chmn. 1986-89, corr. sec. 1994-95), Beta Phi Mu. Unitarian. Home: 2254 Loma Vista Pasadena CA 91104 Office: Calif Inst of Tech Mail Stop 1-32 Pasadena CA 91125

BUCK, DOROTHY CECELIA, psychotherapist, writer; b. St. Louis, June 2, 1940; d. Martin and Cecelia (Bishop) B.; m. Achille Snyder, Mar. 10, 1967 (div. 1979); children: Raoul David, Ariane Marie. MA, Emmanuel Coll., 1987; PhD, Boston U., 1990. Ballet performer, tchr. internat. ballet cos., 1958-71; dir. Classical Ballet Acad., New Haven, 1971-85; pvt. practice psychotherapy, pastoral counseling Boston, 1990—; prof. Emmanuel Coll., Boston, 1992—. Author: The Dance of Life, 1987; contbr. articles to profl. jours. Mem. Am. Mental Health Assn. (bd. dirs.), Mass. Mental Health Counseling Assn., New Eng. Soc. Group Psychotherapy. Roman Catholic. Office: 520 Commonwealth Ave Boston MA 02215

BUCK, JANE LOUISE, psychology educator; b. Reading, Pa., Mar. 10, 1933; d. C. Robert and Viola Louise (Berger) B.; m. Leo Laskaris, Oct. 7, 1954 (div. Aug. 1978); 1 child, Julie. BA, U. Del., 1953, MA, 1959, MEd, 1966, PhD, 1971. Instr. U. Del., Newark, 1964-66; rsch. assoc. Rsch. for Better Schs., Phila., 1967-68; asst. prof. Del. State U., Dover, 1969-73, assoc. prof., 1973-77, prof. psychology, 1977—; cons. in stats. E.I. duPont de Nemours, Wilmington, Del., 1983-93; vis. prof. Ctr. for Sci. and Culture, U. Del., 1986. Author: Specifying the Risk, 1985; contbr. articles to profl. jours. Speaker, evaluator Del. Humanities Forum, 1980-88; pres. Del. Gerontol. Soc., Newark, 1987-88. Mem. AAUP (coun. 1987-90, 93—, pres. Del. State U. chpt. 1976-80, 95—, chief negotiator 1982—, mem. com. on historically Black colls. and univs. and status of minorities in the profession 1988-90, interim sec. Del. Conf 1991-92, pres. Del. conf. 1993—, mem. com. govtl. rels. 1994—, Sternberg award for collective bargaining 1994), APA (Div. Two), Am. Psychol. Soc., Am. Statis. Assn., Danforth Assocs., Kappa Delta Pi, Psi Chi, Alpha Chi Omega. Office: Del State Univ Psychol Dept DuPont Pkwy Dover DE 19901

BUCK, LINDA DEE, recruiting company executive; b. San Francisco, Nov. 8, 1946; d. Sol and Shirley D. (Setterberg) Press; student Coll. San Mateo (Calif.), 1969-70; divorced. Head hearing and appeals br. Dept. Navy Employee Rels. Svc., Philippines, 1974-75; dir. human resources Homestead Savs. & Loan Assn., Burlingame, Calif., 1976-77; mgr. VIP Agy., Inc., Palo Alto, Calif., 1977-78; exec. v.p., dir. Sequent Personnel Svcs., Inc., Mountain View, Calif., 1978-83; founder, pres. Buck & Co., San Mateo, 1983-91. Publicity mgr. for No. Calif., Osteogenesis Imperfecta Found. Inc., 1970-72; cons. Am. Brittle Bone Soc., 1979-88; active Florence (Oreg.) Area Humane Soc., 1994—, Friends of Libr., Florence, 1994—; bd. dirs. Florence Festival Arts, 1995; mem. Florence Area C. of C.; bd. dir., dir. women Rhododendron Scholarship Program, Florence, Oreg., 1995. Jewish.

BUCK, LORRAINE, sales representative; b. Columbus, Ohio, Sept. 15, 1968; d. Norman Whitney and Delphine Lorraine (Zelinski) B. BA in Journalism, Ind. U., 1990. Day care instr. Tabernacle Acad., Indpls., 1985-88; sales intern Sherwin-Williams, Indpls., 1989; sales rep. E.J. Brach, Inc., Cin., 1990-91; sales rep. J.M. Smucker Co., North Canton, Ohio, 1991-92, dist. sales mgr. (2 dists.), 1992-95, product brand mgr. traditional fruit spreads, 1995—. Mem. Women in Communications, Inc. (v.p. Ind. U. student affiliation 1988-90), Gamma Phi Beta. Republican. Methodist.

BUCK, MARY HELEN, physical therapist; b. Kiel, Wis., June 30, 1928; d. Henry Carl and Minnie Emma (Voelker) Meiselwitz; m. James J. Buck, Apr. 14, 1954; children: David William, Randall Henry, Laura Kay. BS in Phys. Medicine, U. Wis., 1950, cert. Physical Therapy, 1950. Registered phys. therapist, Wis., Ariz., Calif. Phys. therapist March of Dimes, Fond du Lac, Wis., 1950-51, St. Agnes Hosp., Fond du Lac, 1951-52, St. Joseph Hosp., Phoenix, 1952-54, Mercy Hosp., San Diego, 1954, Meml. Med. Ctr., Long Beach, Calif., 1960, 63, Bellflower (Calif.) Med. Group, 1969-72, Vis. Nurse Svc., Long Beach, 1972-87; bd. dirs. Stroke Assn. of Long Beach, 1985-95, mem. adv. bd. 1995-96. Active in Presbyn. Ch. on local level as well as on Presbytery level. Democrat.

BUCK, NANCY MARGARET TIMMA, accountant, banker; b. Seattle, June 16, 1945; d. Guy Church and Nancy L. (Fraser) B.; m. George L. Wittenburg (div. May 1972); 1 child, Guy Charles. Student, Stephens Coll., 1963-64. Legal adminstr. Mullen, McCaughey & Henzell, Santa Barbara, Calif., 1965-67; trust adminstr. First Interstate Bank of Calif., Santa Barbara, 1974-84; pres., owner, acct. N.T.B. Profl. Bus. Svc., Santa Barbara, 1984—; chief fin. officer Specialty Crane Corp., Santa Barbara, 1985—; pvt. tustee, conservator, 1984—; mem. Continuing Edn. Bar. Mem. Am. Inst. Banking, Nat. Assn. Female Execs, Nat. Notary Assn., Nat. Fedn. Ind. Bus. Republican. Episcopalian. Club: Santa Barbara Assocs., University (Santa Barbara).

BUCK, SARAH BETH, educational foundation development director; b. Thief River Falls, Minn., Mar. 16, 1948; d. Walter A. Ekeren and Lois M. (Schiager) Rand; m. Ray A. Boosinger, Sept. 20, 1969 (div. Nov. 1973); 1 child, David C. Boosinger; m. J. Ben Buck, June 7, 1975; stepchildren: Catherine, Kevin, Brian. BS in Indsl. Adminstrn., Iowa State U., 1981, MBA, 1995. Adminstrv. asst. Mary Greeley Med. Ctr., Ames, Iowa, 1972-80; dir. mktg. and info. svcs. Mary Greeley Med. Ctr., 1980-87; instr. health care mktg. Iowa State U., 1987, mgr. Internat. Trade Svc., 1987-89; dir. devel./edn. and adminstrn. Iowa State U. Found., Ames, 1989—; co-owner SafeGuard Films, Ames, 1983-91; spkr., guest lectr. U. No. Iowa, Cedar Falls, 1989, Iowa State U., 1989—; judge publ. competition Mo. Hosp. Assn., 1985. Mem. Golden Circle Internat. Visitors' Coalition, Des Moines, 1988-89, SAFE Coalition for Substance Free Cmty., Ames, 1995—; trustee Mary Greeley Med. Ctr., 1993—; bd. dirs. Am. Heart Assn., Story County, 1985-87; v.p. St. Andrew's Luth. Ch., Ames, 1996. Mem. Coun. for Advancement and Support of Edn. (Regional Bronze award 1996), Nat. Com. on Planned Giving, Am. Soc. Hosp. Mktg. and Pub. Rels. (cert., regional coun. coord. nat. publ. evaluation svc.), Nat. Assn. Hosp. Devel., Midwest Edn. Advancement Network, Iowa Soc. Hosp. Mktg. and Pub. Rels. (pres. various coms.), Mid-Iowa Planned Giving Coun., Ames C. of C. (various coms.), Iowa State U. Alumni Assn. (life, bd. dirs. 1993-94). Office: Iowa State U Found 2229 Lincoln Way Ames IA 50014

BUCKALEW, REBECCA POPEK, secondary school educator; b. Baton Rouge, June 29, 1943; d. Stanley Francis and Bertha Marie (Reeves) P.; m. Charles Donald Buckalew Sr.; children: Elizabeth Ann, Charles Donald Jr. BA, U. South Fla., 1975, MA in German Edn., 1978. Cert. tchr., Fla. Tchr. German and English Clearwater (Fla.) H.S., 1978—; coord. exch. program German Am. Partnership Program, N.Y.C., 1978—; test writer, cons. Dept. Edn., Fla., 1987-93; workshop leader Goethe Inst., 1991-93; program dir. for Program for Internat. Culture and Commerce, Clearwater H.S., 1992—. Mem. Fla. Fgn. Lang. Assn. (German Tchr. of Yr. 1987, 94), Pinellas County Fgn. Lang. Tchrs. Assn. (Tchr. of Yr. 1993), Am. Assn. Tchrs. of German (v.p. Fla. chpt. 1987-91, treas. 1991-93, sec. 1994—). Democrat. Methodist. Office: Clearwater HS 540 S Hercules Ave Clearwater FL 34624

BUCKERIDGE, MARGERY JANE, educator, journalist; b. Sheboygan, Wis., Sept. 24, 1931; d. Charles Rex and Helen Dora (Brunsell) B. BS, U. Wis., 1954. H.s. tchr. various locations, Wis., 1954-75; part-time journalist Evansville (Wis.) Rev. Pres. Rock County (Wis.) Women's Rep. Club, 1994—; del. Wis. State Rep. Conv., 1980—, Nat. Rep. Conv., 1996. Mem. Eastern Star (assoc. conductress). Republican. Congregational.

BUCKINGHAM, BARBARA RAE, educator; b. Union City, Ind., Jan. 27, 1932; d. Ray E. and Edith A. (Wagner) B. BA cum laude, Hanover Coll., 1954; MA, Ind. Univ., 1956. Tchr. City Sch. Dist., Marion, Ohio, 1956-64; social studies educator City Sch. Dist., Rochester, N.Y., 1966—. Editor: Revonah, 1954; art work Aldelphean, 1959. Vol. Peace Corps, Ethiopia, 1964-66; gov. bd. Rochester Returned Peace Corps Vols., 1968-76; election com. mem. Councilwoman Letvin, Gates, N.Y., 1980; steering com. Pub. Affairs Forum, Hanover, 1952. Mem. AAUW (pres. 1956-96), Nat. Peace Corps Assn., Friends of Ethiopia, Rochester Tchr. Assn., Pi Gamma Mu (Outstanding Grad. award 1954), Gamma Sigma Pi, Alpha Phi Gamma. Democrat. Presbyterian. Home: 64 Lyellwood Pkwy Rochester NY 14606

BUCKLER, MARILYN LEBOW, school psychologist, educational consultant; b. N.Y.C., Mar. 18, 1933; d. Herman and Gertrude (Abolitz) Lebow; m. Sheldon A. Buckler, June 1, 1952 (div. 1978); children: Julie, Eve, Sarah Buckler Welcome. BS cum laude, NYU, 1954; MEd in Counseling, Northeastern U., 1970. Cert. ednl. psychologist, Mass.; sch. guidance counselor, Mass., sch. psychologist, Mass. Kindergarten tchr. Washington Pub. Schs., 1955-56, Stamford (Conn.) Pub. Schs., 1956-58; guidance counselor Framingham (Mass.) Pub. Schs., 1969-70; sch. psychologist, guidance counselor Carlisle (Mass.) Pub. Schs., 1970—; parent workshop leader, mentor Wellesley Coll.-Stone Ctr., 1993—; tchr. parenting course Middlesex C.C., Bedford, Mass., 1990—, cons. LEAP program, 1992-93; workshop leader, creator parenting courses, various pvt. schs. and orgns., Mass., 1990—; parent educator "families first" Wheelock Coll., 1995—. Mem. ACA, Mass. Sch. Counselor Assn., Mass. Sch. Psychologists Assn., Pi Lambda Theta. Office: Carlisle Pub Schs 83 School St Carlisle MA 01741-1712

BUCKLEW, SUSAN CAWTHON, federal judge; b. 1942. BA, Fla. State U., 1964; MA, U. So. Fla., 1968; JD, Stetson U., 1977; LLD (hon.), Stetson Coll. Law, 1994. Tchr. Plant High Sch., 1964-65, 70-72, Seminole High Sch., 1965-67, Chamberlain High Sch., 1969; instr. Hillsborough C.C., 1974-75; corp. legal counsel Jim Walter Corp., 1978-82; county ct. judge Hillsborough County, 1982-86; circuit ct. judge 13th Jud. Circuit, 1986-93; judge U.S. Dist. Ct. (mid. dist.) Fla., 1993—; mem. Gender Bias Study Commn., 1988-90, Fla. Bar Bench Bar Commn., 1990-92; bd. overseers Stetson Coll. Law, 1994—. Recipient award Disting Svc., Fla. Coun. Crime and Delinquency, 1990, Disting. Alumnus award Stetson Lawyers Assn., 1994. Mem. ABA, Fla. Gar Assn., Fla. Assn. Women Lawyers, Hillsborough Assn. Women Lawyers (award Outstanding Pub. Svc. ADvancing Status Women 1991), Hillsborough County Bar Assn. (Robert W. Patton Outstanding Jursit award young lawyer's sect. 1990), Fla. State U. Alumni Assn., Am. Inns Ct. (LII, William Glenn Terrell chpt.), Athena Soc., Tampa Club, Delta, Delta, Delta Alumnae. Office: US Dist Ct 611 N Florida Ave Rm 109 Tampa FL 33602-4500

BUCKLEY, DEBORAH JEANNE MOREY, marketing manager; b. Bethesda, Feb. 26, 1952; d. Robert Earl and Carolyn Ann (Garrity) Morey; m. Robert Gill Buckley, Dec. 2, 1972; 1 child, Leigh Ann. AAS, Trident Tech. Coll., 1978; student, U. N.C., 1982-83. Nuclear chemistry specialist Duke Power Co., Charlotte, N.C., 1978-82; rsch. technician Graphic Arts Tech. Found., Pitts., 1984; sr. process technician U.S. Filter Corp., Warrendale, Pa., 1985-88, applications engr. in tech. svcs. group, 1988-92, market mgr. groundwater systems, sr. application engr., 1993-95, tech. mktg. specialist, 1995—. Sec. Seneca Valley Acad. Games Parents Assn., Harmony, Pa., 1992-93. With USN, 1970-74. Mem. NAFE, Am. Electroplaters Soc., Hazardous Materials Control Rsch. Inst. Republican. Office: US Filter Corp 181 Thorn Hill Rd Warrendale PA 15086-7527

BUCKLEY, ELIZABETH ANN, marketing executive; b. Duluth, Minn., Jan. 30, 1947; d. Robert Peers and Kate Wisdom (Holland) B.; m. Judson David Jones, Aug. 5, 1975 (div. Dec. 1981); 1 child, Felix David Buckley-Jones; m. Dennis Britton McGrath, Sept. 10, 1983; stepchildren: Daniel Scott McGrath, Amy Susan McGrath. BA, St. Norbert Coll., 1969; MA, Mankato State U., 1978. Dep. commr. Minn. Dept. of Corrections, St. Paul, 1972-79; v.p. sales and mktg. City Venture, Mpls., 1979-83; exec. cons. Comml. Credit, Mpls., Balt., 1983-85; investment officer Dain Bosworth, Mpls., 1985-90; sr. v.p., chief mktg. officer Mona Meyer McGrath & Gavin, Mpls., 1990-96; exec. v.p. Shandwick USA, Mpls., 1996—; speaker in field. Chair bd. trustees Cricket Theatre, Mpls., 1989-91; chair Women's Polit. Caucus Outstanding Women, 1990-91. Mem. Am. Mktg. Assn. (chair pub. rels. com. Minn. chpt. 1992—), Minn. Spkrs. Assn., Nat. Spkrs. Assn., Minn. Sales and Mktg. Execs. (editor newsletter 1991-92), Pub. Rels. Soc. Am. Counselors Acad. Home: 284 Pelham Blvd Saint Paul MN 55104-4935 Office: Shandwick USA Ste 500 8400 Normandale Lake Blvd Minneapolis MN 55437-1080

BUCKLEY, JANICE MARIE, school administrator; b. Chgo., Apr. 6; d. Charles Lawrence and Yolande Marie (Sarpy) B. BS, So. Ill. U., 1965; MA, Gov.'s State U., 1979, Roosevelt U., 1990; postgrad., Roosevelt U., 1991—, Beijing U., 1994. Cert. adminstr., supt., Ill. 3d-6th grade tchr. Hartigan Sch., Chgo., 1965-75, reading lab. coord., 1975-76, ESEA reading coord., 1976-77, chair English dept., 1977-80, 7th-8th grade tchr., 1980-84, tchr. facilitator, 1984-87, acting prin., 1988-89, acting asst. prin., 1989-93, asst. prin., 1992—; master tchr. Hartigan Sch.; lead tchr. summer sch. Chgo. Bd. Edn., 1984-89, coord. aftersch. reading program, 1985-89, worker coord., 1992. Mem. St. Clotilde Sch. Bd., Chgo., 1987-88; mem. Chatham Cmty. Coun., Chgo., 1990. Mem. ASCD, Am. Fedn. Tchrs., Chgo. Asst. Prins. Assn., Chgo. Tchrs.' Union, Phi Delta Kappa, Alpha Kappa Alpha (chpt. Basileus 1963-65). Democrat. Roman Catholic. Office: 8331 S King Dr Chicago IL 60619

BUCKLEY, LINDA TIBBETTS, public relations executive; b. Hartford, Conn., Dec. 2, 1954; d. Wesley Frederick and Noreen Philomena (Lowe) T.; m. Robert Bruce Buckley, Sr., Nov. 9, 1985; children: Brendan Patrick, Robert Bruce Jr. Student, U. South Fla., 1973-74. Office mgr. Inside Sports Mag. (divsn. Newsweek), L.A., 1979-80; sr. researcher, reporter Newsweek mag., L.A., 1980-92; dep. editor Newsweek on Campus, L.A., 1987-89; mgr. publicity and pub. rels. Universal Studios Fla., Orlando, 1992-94, dir. publicity and pub. rels., 1994—. Mem. L.A. Mayor's Christopher Columbus Bicentennial Com., 1990; bd. dirs. Reseda (Calif.) Homeowners Assn., 1987-91; asst. campaign mgr. L.A. City Coun. Candidate Peter Ireland, 1988; mem. adv. bd. Camp Good Days and Spl. Times. Recipient Spl. award Matsushita Pub. Rels. Competition, 1992, 2 Awards of Merit, Internat. Assn. Bus. Communicators, 1994. Mem. Pub. Rels. Soc. Am., Fla. Pub. Rels. Assn. Democrat. Roman Catholic. Home: 239 Lake Ellen Dr Casselberry FL 32707-2913 Office: Universal Studios Fla 1000 Universal Studios Plz Orlando FL 32819-7601

BUCKLEY, PRISCILLA LANGFORD, magazine editor; b. N.Y.C., Oct. 17, 1921; d. William Frank and Aloise (Steiner) B. BA, Smith Coll., 1943. Copy girl, sports writer UP, N.Y.C., 1944; radio rewrite staff mem. U.P., 1944-47; corr. U.P., Paris, France, 1953-56; news editor Sta. WACA, Camden, S.C., 1947-48; reports officer CIA, Washington, 1951-53; with Nat. Rev. Mag., N.Y.C., 1956—; mng. editor Nat. Rev. Mag., 1959-86, sr. editor, 1986—; mem. U.S. Adv. Commn. Pub. Diplomacy, 1984-91. Editor: The Joys of National Review, 1995; columnist One Woman's Voice Syndicate, 1976-80. Mem. Cosmopolitan Club, Sharon Country Club (Conn., sec. 1973-77, pres. 1978-80, 94-95). Home: Great Elm Sharon CT 06069 Office: Nat Review 150 E 35th St New York NY 10016-4178

BUCKLEY, REBECCA HATCHER, physician, educator; b. Hamlet, N.C., Apr. 1, 1933; d. Martin Armstead and Nora (Langston) Hatcher; m. Charles Edward Buckley III, July 9, 1955; children: Charles Edward IV, Elizabeth Ann, Rebecca Kathryn, Sarah Margaret. BA, Duke U., 1954; MD, U. N.C., 1958. Intern Duke U. Med. Ctr., Durham, N.C., 1958-59, resident, 1959-61, practice medicine, specializing in pediatric allergy and immunology, 1961—; dir. Am. Bd. Allergy and Immunology, Phila., 1971-73, chmn. exam. com., 1971-73, co-chmn. bd. dirs., 1982-84; chmn. Diagnostic Lab. Immunology, 1984-88; mem. staff Duke U. Med. Ctr.; asst. prof. pediatrics and immunology, 1968-72, assoc. prof. pediatrics, 1972-76, assoc. prof. immunology, 1972-79, prof. immunology, 1979—, J. Buren Sidbury prof. pediatrics, 1979—. Contbr. numerous articles to med. publs. Recipient Allergic Diseases Acad. award Nat. Inst. Allergy and Infectious Diseases, 1974-79, Merit Rsch. award NIH, 1990, Nat. Bd. award Med. Coll. Pa., 1991, Clemons von Pirquet award Georgetown, 1993, Disting. Tchr. award Duke U. Med. Alumni Assn., 1993, Outstanding Achievement award Immune Deficiency Found., 1994, Disting. Svc. award Am. Acad. Allergy and Immunlogy, 1996. Fellow Am. Acad. Allergy and Immunology (mem. exec. com. 1975-82, pres. 1979-80); mem. Am. Assn. Immunologists, Soc. Pediatric Rsch., Am. Acad. Pediatrics (Bret Ratner award 1992), Southeastern Allergy Assn. (pres. 1978-79), Am. Pediatric Soc. (coun. mem. 1991-97). Republican. Episcopalian. Home: 3621 Westover Rd Durham NC 27707-5032 Office: Duke U Med Ctr PO Box 2898 Durham NC 27715-2898

BUCKLEY, STEPHANIE DENISE, health care executive; b. Tulsa, Sept. 19, 1961; d. Richard Harvey and Judith Carol (Holtzinger) Welcher; m. Jeffery Lee Taylor, June 16, 1990 (div. July 1992); m. Dennis Ray Buckley, Oct. 30, 1995. BS, Okla. State U., 1983; MA, U. Okla., 1994. Reporter The Daily O'collegian, Stillwater, Okla., 1980-83; news anchor KOSU-FM, Stillwater, 1981, KRXO-FM, Stillwater, 1982; asst. producer KTVY-TV, Oklahoma City, 1983-84; anchor/reporter KTEN, Ada, Okla., 1985-86; producer America's Shopping Channel, Oklahoma City, 1987; pub. rels. coordinator S.W. Med. Ctr. Okla., Oklahoma City, 1988-89, pub. rels. assoc., 1990-91, mgr. pub. rels. and devel., 1991-93; exec. dir., CEO Neighborhood Alliance, Oklahoma City, 1994-95; cmty. devel. assoc. Integris Health, Oklahoma City, 1995—; cons. on brochure, Women to Woman, 1990. Mem. comms. com. United Way, Oklahoma City, 1989-90; bd. dirs. Nat. Clown and Laughter Hall of Fame, 1989—; bd. dirs. HUGS, 1992-94, Firesafe Found., 1994—, Internat. Ctr. for Humor and Health, 1995—, contact, 1996; bd. dirs. Youth Build Oklahoma City, 1996. Recipient Good Guy award, KTVY-TV, 1988, 89. Mem. Women in Comms. (v.p. 1981-82), Am. Hosp. Assn., Okla. Hosp. Assn., Am. Soc. Health Care Mktg. and Pub. Rels., Pub. Rels. Soc. Am., Oklahoma City C. of C., South Oklahoma City C. of C., Lions Internat., Am. Bus. Clubs (bd. dirs.), Rotary Internat. (group study exch. to Queensland, Australia 1995), West Oklahoma City Rotary Club. Methodist. Office: Integris Health C-30 3366 Northwest Expressway Oklahoma City OK 73112

BUCKLEY, SUSAN, lawyer; b. Rockville Center, N.Y., Dec. 24, 1951. BA, Mt. Holyoke Coll., 1973; JD, Fordham U., 1977. Bar: N.Y. 1978, D.C. 1980. Ptnr. Cahill Gordon & Reindel, N.Y.C. Mem. N.Y. State Bar Assn. (com. on law media 1992—). Office: Cahill Gordon & Reindel 80 Pine St New York NY 10005-1702*

BUCKLEY, VIKKI, state official. Sec. of state State of Colo., 1995—. Office: Office of the Sec of State 1560 Broadway Ste 200 Denver CO 80202-5135*

BUCKLEY, VIRGINIA LAURA, editor; b. N.Y.C., May 11, 1929; d. Alfred and Josephine Marie (Manetti) Iacuzzi; m. David Patrick Buckley, July 30, 1960; children: Laura Joyce, Brian Thomas. B.A., Wellesley Coll., 1950; M.A., Columbia U., 1952. Tchr. English Bennett Coll., Millbrook, N.Y., 1954-56, Berkeley Inst., Bklyn., 1956-58; copy editor World Pub. Co., N.Y.C., 1959-69; children's book editor Thomas Y. Crowell, N.Y.C., 1971-80; editorial dir. Lodestar Books, affiliate of Dutton Children's Books, div. Penguin Books USA, N.Y.C., 1980—. Author: State Birds; contbr. articles to profl. jours. Mem. ALA. Home: 33 Brook Ter Leonia NJ 07605-1504 Office: Lodestar Books 375 Hudson St New York NY 10014-3658

BUCKLEY-BRAWNER, KATHRYN YOLANDE, consulting executive; b. Waltham, Mass., July 31, 1953; d. William Anthony and Yolande (Bredillet) Buckley; m. William Harrison Brawner, June 19, 1976; 1 child, Kyrsten Virginia. BA in Polit.Sci., Monterey Inst. Internat. Study, 1978. Gen. mgr. Photonic Systems, Santa Clara, 1986-87; internat. sales Christopher Ranch, Gilroy, Calif., 1987-91; mgr. Skan-Dutch Trading Co., Morgan Hill, Calif., 1991-92; v.p. Snow Pearl Internat., Inc., San Jose, Calif., 1992—. Graphic designer corp. identity package, 1985—. Trustee Monterey (Calif.) Inst. Internat. Studies, 1980-83. Mem. AAUW (graphic designer newsletter 1981-88, T-shirt 1984—). Roman Catholic. Home: 250 Stebbins St Belchertown MA 01007 Office: Snow Pearl Internat Inc 6940 Claywood Way San Jose CA 95120-2209

BUCKLO, ELAINE EDWARDS, federal judge; b. Boston, Oct. 1, 1944; married. AB, St. Louis U., 1966; JD, Northwestern U., 1972. Bar: Calif. 1973, U.S. Dist. Ct. (no. dist.) Calif. 1973, Ill. 1974, U.S. Dist. ct. (no. dist.) Ill. 1974, U.S. Ct. Appeals (7th cir.) 1983. Law clk. U.S. Ct. Appeals (7th cir.), Chgo., 1972-73; lectr. law Northwestern U., Chgo., 1973; assoc. Morrison & Foerster, San Francisco, 1973-74; assoc., then ptnr. Miller, Shakman (previously Devoe, Shadur & Drupp), Chgo., 1974-79; ptnr. Coin, Crowley & Nord, Chgo., 1980-83; ptnr., counsel Johnson & Schwartz, Chgo., 1983-85; U.S. magistrate judge U.S. Dist. Ct. (no. dist.) Ill., Chgo., 1985-94, judge, 1994—; vis. prof. law, U. Calif., Davis, 1978-80. Editor, Litigation, 1979-85; contbr. articles to profl. jours. Bd. dirs. Midwest Women's Ctr., Chgo., 1980-82. Mem. Fed. Bar Assn. (bd. dirs. 1987-88, treas. 1988-89, sec. 1989-90, v.p. 1990-92, pres. Chgo. chpt. 1992-93), Chgo. Bar Assn. (chairperson devel. of law com. 1989-90), Chgo. Coun. Lawyers (pres. 1977-78), Order of Coif. Office: US Dist Ct No Dist Everett McKinley Dirksen Bldg 219 S Dearborn St Rm 1764 Chicago IL 60606*

BUCK-MOORE, JOANNE ROSE, nursing administrator, mental health educator; b. Cambridge, Mass., Jan. 3, 1939; d. Joseph J. and Louise L. (Buck) Verrochio; m. Donald P. Moore, June 15, 1985; children: Marie-Louise Buck, Victoria Buck, Katrina Buck, Edwin Buck. ASN, Middlesex Community Coll., Bedford, Mass., 1977; BSN magna cum laude, Worcester (Mass.) State Coll., 1980; MSN, U. R.I., 1983. RN, Mass. Dir. nursing Ctr. for Rehab. at Columbus, East Boston, Mass., Mt. Pleasant Hosp., Lynn, Mass.; nursr mgr. and program dir. Commonwealth of Mass. Dept. of Mental Health, Boston; mental health/addictions instr. Palm Beach C.C., Fla. Atlantic U.; lectr. at schs., clubs, seminars, confs.; legal cons. and expert witness. Author: Management by Objective: A Handbook for Nurses. Mem. ANA (cert. mental health psychiat. nurse), Mass. Nurses' Assn., Sigma Theta Tau. Home: 107 Amberjack Ln Jupiter FL 33477-7202

BUCKNAM, MARY OLIVIA CASWELL, artist; b. Modesto, Calif., Feb. 6, 1914; d. Charles Henry and Helen Anne (Cross) Caswell; m. William Nelson Bucknam, June 22, 1946 (dec. 1966); children: William Nelson Jr., Charles Henry. BA, Calif. State U., San Jose, 1936; postgrad., U. Calif., Berkeley, 1938, Calif. State U., Stanislaus, 1968-75, U. San Francisco, 1968-75. Tchr. Stanislaus County (Calif.), 1936-38, Modesto (Calif.) Schs., 1938-43, San Bernardino (Calif.) City, 1943-46; art tchr. Klamath Union Schs., Klamath River, Calif., 1960-61; co-owner Bigfoot Ranch and Resort, Klamath River, 1960-66, art tchr., tchr. Riverbank (Calif.) City Schs., 1966-79; art cons. Riverbank Elem., 1986; gallery artist Cen. Calif. Art League, Modesto, 1986—. Group shows include Siskiyow Artists Assn., 1961-66 (best of show award, first award, other awards), Stanislaus County Shows, 1975-90 (best of show award, first award, other awards); over 150 paintings held by pvt. individuals and pub. orgns., Three Sisters Show Gallery tour, 1991-93, Travels with my Paintbrush Show Tour, 1991-92. Donor with Caswell family of land for Caswell State Park, San Joaquin County, Calif., 1995; pres. Caswell Sch. PTA, Ceres, Calif., 1956-57, Ceres Study Club, 1952-53; v.p. Siskiyou Artists Assn., Yreka, Calif., 1963-65; pres. Modesto Tchrs. Assn., 1940-41; vol. tchr. adult watercolor classes; active Trinity Singers Choirm 1990—. Named Woman of Distinction Soroptimist Internat., Ceres, Calif., 1992, Outstanding Woman of Stanislaus County Stanislaus County Commn. for Women, 1994. Mem. AAUW (Modesto br., fellowships chair 1959-60, historian 1956), Ctrl. Calif. Art League (chmn. bank shows Modesto 1988-94, co-chair young artists show Modesto 1986, 88, 89, 90, head instr. 1994—), Calif. Ret. Tchrs. Assn., Stanislaus County Hist. Soc., Sierra Club, Tuolumne River Lodge, Delta Kappa Gamma (hist.-photography 1985-94, v.p. chpt. 1969-71), Kappa Delta Pi. Republican. Presbyterian. Home: 2704 La Palma Dr Modesto CA 95354-3229

BUCKNER, JENNIE, newspaper editor; m. Steven Landers; 1 child Katie. BS in Journalism with honors, Ohio State Univ. Mng. editor San Jose Mercury News, Calif.; v.p. news Knight-Ridder, Inc., 1989-93; v.p., editor The Charlotte Observer, N.C., 1993—; mem. adv. bd. New Directions for News. Bd. visitors Davidson Coll., 1994—. Mem. Am. Soc. Newspaper Editors. Office: Knight Ridder Newspapers News Department PO Box 30308 Charlotte NC 28230-0308*

BUCKNER, LINDA GALE, special agent, personnel director; b. Dalton, Ga., Sept. 10, 1957; d. Malcolm T. and B. Ruth (Hayes) B. BS, Ga. State U., 1981; MPA, Brenau U., 1987; grad., FBI Nat. Acad., 1992. Sgt. Chatsworth (Ga.) Police Dept., 1978-81; adj. prof. Ga. State U., Atlanta, 1991—, Mercer U., 1994—; asst. spl. agt. in charge Ga. Bur. Investigation, Decatur, 1981—; adj. prof. St. Francis Co., 1996—. Legis. liaison Ga. Bur. Investigation, Atlanta, 1994-96. Recipient Dirs. award Ga. Bur. Investigation, 1984. Mem. Internat. Assn. Women Police (pres. 1991-94), Ga. State U. Criminal Justice Alumni Orgn. (pres. 1992-93), Ga. Women in Law Enforcement (co-founder 1987, exec. dir. 1987-89), Nat. Alliance Non-Violent Programming (steering com. 1993-94), Coun. on Elder Abuse and Neglect (treas. 1992), Peace Officers Assn. Ga. (regional dir. 1992-93), Ga. League Families/POW-MIA, Ga. FBI Nat. Acad. Assocs. (conf. vice chair). Presbyterian. Office: Ga Bur Investigation 3121 Panthersville Rd Decatur GA 30034-3830

BUCKNER-REITMAN, JOYCE, psychologist, educator; b. Benton, Ark., Sept. 25, 1937; d. Waymond Floyd Pannell and Willie Evelyn (Wright) Whitley; m. John W. Buckner, Aug. 29, 1958 (div. 1970); children: Cheryl, John, Chris; m. Sanford Reitman, Aug. 13, 1994. BA, Ouachita Bapt. Coll., 1959; MS in Edn., Henderson State U., 1964; PhD, North Tex. State U., 1970. Lic. psychologist, Tex., marriage and family therapist; cert. Nat. Registry Health Svc. Providers in Psychology; master trainer in imago relationship therapy. Assoc. prof. U. Tex., Arlington, 1970-80, chmn. dept. edn., 1976-78; pvt. practice psychology, Arlington, 1974—; dir., chief profl. officer Southwest Inst. Relationship Devel., Weatherford, Tex.; author, profl. speaker; appeared on internat. TV shows, including Oprah Winfrey Show. Mem. APA, Nat. Assn. for Imago Relationship Therapy (pres.), Nat. Speakers Assn., Am. Assn. Marital and Family Therapy. Home: 2208 Farmer Rd Weatherford TX 76087

BUCKRIDEE, PATRICIA ILONA, international marketing/strategy consultant; b. N.Y.C., Oct. 19, 1960; d. Laszlo Carl and Evelyn Liane (Schauer) Varhegyi; m. Winston D. Buckridee, Dec. 29, 1991; children: Karolyn Liane, Elizabeth Rachel. BS, Seton Hall U., 1982; MBA, Rutgers U., Newark, 1987. Statis. analyst UN, Vienna, Austria, 1983-85; cons., tutor, N.J., 1985-87; assoc. mgr. strategy and devel. AT&T, Basking Ridge, N.J., 1987-88; market mgr. microelectronics AT&T, Berkeley Heights, N.J., 1988-89; sr. product mgr. data systems group AT&T, Morristown, N.J., 1989; sr. fin. analyst Am. Express Travel Related Svcs. Co., N.Y.C., 1989-91; ind. cons. Scotch Plains, N.J., 1991—; market rsch. mgr. AT&T, Parsippany, N.J., 1996—; internat. cons., N.J., 1985—; interpreter, translator, N.J., 1987—; pres. PIB Internat. Inc., 1991—. Mem. Am. Mktg. Assn. Office: PIB Internat 14 King James Ct Scotch Plains NJ 07076-1111

BUCOLO, GAIL ANN, biotechnologist; b. Port Chester, N.Y., July 27, 1954; d. Joseph Anthony and Jennie (Tomassetti) B. BS in French, Oneonta State Coll., 1976; MA in French, Middlebury Coll., 1977; postgrad., Columbia U., 1981-82; MS in Biotechnology, Manhattan Coll., 1995. Technician N.Y. Hosp., N.Y.C., 1983-86; rsch. technician NYU Hosp., N.Y.C., 1986; sr. rsch. technician Meml. Sloan Kettering, N.Y.C., 1986-88, Columbia U., N.Y.C., 1988—; corr. Scienceport, Rye, N.Y., 1994—. Mem. N.Y. Acad. Sci., Sigma Xi. Roman Catholic. Home: 3645 Corlear Ave Bronx NY 10463 Office: Columbia U 630 W 168th St Black Bldg New York NY 10032

BUCQUEROUX, BONNIE LEE, writer; b. Cleve., May 1, 1944; d. Henry and Helen L. (Young) McLanus; m. Jack Karlyle Pollard (div. 1986); children: Stephen, Kimberly Jean (dec.); m. Andrew Hunt Howard, Jul. 6, 1993. Mng. editor Mich. Farmer Mag., Lansing, 1970-83; freelance writer, 1984-86; assoc. dir. Nat. Ctr. for Cmty. Policing, 1986-95; exec. dir. Mich. Victim Alliance, Lansing, 1994—; asst. coord. sch. of journalism Mich. State U., 1995—; vice chair Critical Incident Analysis Group, 1994—, cons. Cmty. Policing Consortum, Washington, 1994—, Nat. Inst. of Correction, Washington, 1994—, Nat. Organ. of Black Law Enforcement, Washington, 1995. Co-author: Community Policing: A Step By Step Guide, 1994, Contbr. articles to profl. jours. Pres. Mich. Rural Safety Coun., Lansing, 1975-79. Named writer of the Year Am. Agrl. Editors Assn., 1976, Oscar in Argl., 1979, Young Writer of the Year, 1995. Mem. Internat. Soc. For Traumatic Stress Disorders. Democrat. Home: 1500 Sandhill Mason MI 48854

BUCUVALAS, TINA, folklorist; b. Berwyn, Ill., Feb. 18, 1951; d. Theodore and Lorraine Bucuvalas; m. Charles A. Curran, May, 1987; children: Alexandra, Chloe. BA, U. Calif., Santa Cruz, 1973; MA, UCLA, 1976; PhD, Ind. Univ., 1986. Curator Hist. Mus. So. Fla., Miami, 1986-91; freelance folkorist Maine, Fla., Washington, 1991—; bd. dirs. Cultural Resources Inc.; cons. Maine Indian Basketmakers, Portland Performing Arts. Author: Introduction to Arkansas Folklore: A Teacher-Student Guide, 1986, Native American Foodways and Recipes: Hopi, Navajo, Hualapai, Laguna, 1986. South Florida Folk Arts: A Teacher Guide, 1988, (with Peggy A. Bulgher and Stetson Kennedy) South Florida Folklife, 1994. Mem. Am. Folklore Soc., Fla. Folklore Soc. *

BUDD, ISABELLE AMELIA, research economist; b. Granite City, Ill., Feb. 8, 1923; d. Floyd Harry and Amelia Frederica (Bradvogel) Marx; BS, U. Mo., 1944; postgrad. U. Wis., 1946; m. Louis John Budd, Mar. 3, 1945; children: Catherine Lou, David Harry. Research economist Ralston Purina Co., St. Louis, 1945-46; govtl. legislator, Durham, N.C., 1975-79; fin. and govtl. cons., Durham, 1972-88. Troop leader Girl Scouts U.S.A., 1955-61; mem. environ. concerns com. Duke U., Durham, 1972-77, co-chmn., 1974-75; mem. Durham City Council, 1975-79; Durham del. Council Govts., 1976-78; mem. exec. com. regional govt. criminal justice com., 1976-78; chmn. personnel policy com. regional govt., 1977-78; bd. dirs. Durham County Sr. Citizens Coordinating Council, 1982-85, Raleigh-Durham Internat. Airport Authority, 1983-85; chmn. bd. trustees Raleigh-Durham Firemen's Relief Fund, 1983-89. Mem. AAUW (life), N.C. Center for Public Policy Research, Greater Durham C. of C., S.W. Durham Assn. (charter mem., treas. 1973-76), Mark Twain Circle of Am. (founding mem. 1986, govt. advisor), Nat. Trust for Historic Preservation, Historic Preservation Soc. Durham (charter mem.), N.C. Mus. Life and Sci., Friends of Duke U. Library (life), Ind. Scholars Assn. (life). Author articles on estates. Home: 2753 Mcdowell Rd Durham NC 27705-5715

BUDDINGTON, OLIVE JOYCE, shop owner, retired education educator; b. Norwich, Conn., June 11, 1925; d. William and Viola Jane (Turnbull) B. BS, Willimantic (Conn.) State Tchrs.' Coll., 1947; MA, Columbia U., 1951. Cert. tchr. nursery-6th grade, Conn. Tchr. Bd. Edn., Greenwich, Conn., 1947-49, 51-84; tchr. Agnes Russell Ctr. Tchr.'s Coll. Columbia U., N.Y.C., 1949-51; owner, mgr. 1840 House-Antiques, Norwich, Conn., 1965—. Photographer tourism and promotion, 1994. Chair Parking Commn. City Coun., Norwich, Conn., 1989-91, Tourism Commn., 1990—; chmn. environ. com., Norwich, 1989-91; justice of the peace. Recipient Caroline Bidwell Award Greenwich (Conn.) Assn. Pub. Schs., 1984, Svc. Above Help Norwich Rotary Club, 1995. Mem. Nat. Edn. Assn., Conn. Edn. Assn. Democrat. Home and Office: 47 8th St Norwich CT 06360

BUDGE, WENDY ANNE, medical technologist; b. Tacoma, Jan. 14, 1947; d. Robert Woodrow and Elsie Inez (Stein) B.; m. William Grayson Budge; children: William C., Amy M. BA in Secondary Art Edn., Boise State U., 1969; BS in Microbiology, U. Idaho, 1972. Art instr. Payette (Idaho) Pub. Schs., 1969-70; med. technologist Deaconess Med. Ctr., Spokane, Wash., 1974—, evening microbiology supr. Leader Inland Empire Camp Fire Boys and Girls, Spokane, 1982—, mem. dist. com., 1988—; vol. Am. Cancer Soc., Spokane, 1993—. Mem. Am. Valksport Assn. Methodist. Home: W 606 16th Ave Spokane WA 99203 Office: Deaconess Med Ctr W 800 5th St Spokane WA 99210

BUDNIAKIEWICZ, THERESE, author; b. Mons, Belgium, Sept. 28, 1948; came to U.S., 1961; d. Tadeusz Eugeniusz and Janina Antonina (Więckowska) B.; m. Bart S. Ng, July 6, 1972. BA in Math., U. Chgo., 1971; MA in Comparative Lit., U. Mich., 1972, PhD in Comparative Lit., 1986. Lectr. in English Ind. U.-Purdue U., Indpls., 1987-92. Author: Fundamentals of Story Logic, 1992. Mem. MLA, Semiotic Soc. Am., Can. Semiotic Assn., Internat. Assn. for Semiotics of Law, Internat. Assn. for Semiotic Studies. Home and Office: 5823 Dapple Trace Indianapolis IN 46228

BUDOFF, PENNY WISE, physician, author, researcher; b. Albany, N.Y., July 7, 1939; d. Louis and Goldene Wise. B.A., Syracuse U., 1959; M.D., SUNY-Upstate Med. Sch., 1963. Intern, St. Luke's Meml. Hosp., Utica, N.Y., 1963-64; practice medicine specializing in family practice and women's health, Woodbury, N.Y., 1964-85; clin. assoc. prof. family medicine SUNY at Stony Brook, 1980—; founder, dir. emeritus Penny Wise Budoff Women's Health Svcs., Bethpage, N.Y., ground-breaking women's health care facility, 1985—; affiliated with North Shore U. Hosp.; attending dept. ob/gyn North Shore U. Hosp., 1992—; asst. prof. ob/gyn family practice Cornell U. Medical Coll., 1993—; prin. investigator pilot study to determine heavy metals in breast cancer tissue from patients residing on Long Island 10 years or more North Shore Hosp. and Brookhaven Nat. Lab, 1994; lectr., TV guest on women's medicine and health issues; mem. panel menopause NIH, 1993; clin. rsch. on menstrual pain, premenstrual syndrome, menopause, breast cancer and osteoporosis. Author: No More Menstrual Cramps and Other Good News, 1980, No More Hot Flashes and Other Good News, 1983; author: World Book Health & Medical Annual, 1994; Contbr. articles to profl. jours. Bd. dirs. Coalition Against Domestic Violence. Named Women of Yr. C.W. Post Coll., 1981; recipient Nat. Consumers League award, 1983, Max Cheplove award Erie chpt. N.Y. State Acad. Family Physicians, 1983, Women of Distinction award Soroptomist Internat. of Nassau County, L.I., 1990, honoree Nassau County Coalition Against Domestic Violence, 1992, Fellow Nassau County Med. Soc., Am. Acad. Family Physicians (nat. com. on pub. rels.); mem. NOW (Equality Award in Health 1988, Unsung Heroine award), Am. Med. Women's Assn. (co-chmn. nat. women's health com., liaison), Nassau Acad. Family Physicians (past pres.). Home: 3 Sea Crest Dr Huntington NY 11743-9765 Office: Penny W Budoff MD Womens Health Service North Shore U Hosp 4300 Hempstead Tpke Bethpage NY 11714-5704

BUELL, DEBORAH M., lawyer; b. Kansas City, Mo., Apr. 19, 1955. BJ, U. Mo., 1977; JD magna cum laude, Georgetown U., 1981. Bar: N.Y. 1982. Law clk. U.S. Dist. Ct. (so. dist.) N.Y., 1981-83; ptnr. Cleary Gottlieb Steen & Hamilton, N.Y.C.; adj. prof. legal writing Bklyn. Law Sch., 1982-83. Mem. ABA (mem. litigation sect., bankruptcy and insolvency com.), Fed. Bar Coun., N.Y. State Women's Bar Assn. Office: Cleary Gottlieb Steen & Hamilton 1 Liberty Plz New York NY 10006-1404*

BUELL, EVANGELINE CANONIZADO, consumer cooperative official; b. San Pedro, Calif., Aug. 28, 1932; d. Estanislao C. and Felicia (Stokes) Canonizado; student San Jose State Coll., 1952-53; grad. U. San Francisco, 1978; m. Ralph D. Vilas, 1952 (dec.); m. Robert Alexander Elkins, July 1, 1961 (dec.); children: Nikki Vilas, Stacey Vilas, Danni Vilas Plump; m. William David Buell, Feb. 21, 1987. With Consumers Coop. of Berkeley (Calif.) Inc., 1958—, edn. asst. for community relations, 1964-73, supr. edn. dept., 1973-76, asst. to edn. dir., 1976-78, program coordinator edn. dept., 1980-81, personnel tng. coordinator, 1981-92; ret.; events coordinator Internat. House, U. Calif., Berkeley, 1984; also guitar tchr. Mem. Community Adv. Com., Bonita House, Berkeley, 1974; mem. steering com. for cultural and ethnic affairs Guild of Oakland Mus., 1973-74; dir. various activities YMCA, YWCA, Oakland City Recreation Dept., 1959-73; pres. Berkeley Community Chorus and Orch.; co-chair Berkeley Art Commn., 1992-94; bd. dirs. Philippine Ethnic Arts & Cultural Exch. Recipient Honor award U. Calif. Student Coop., 1965, Outstanding Staff award U. Calif. Berkeley Chancellor, 1992, Nat. Philanthropy Disting. Vol. award, 1993, Outstanding Instrn. Program Support award Cole Sch. Visual & Performing Arts, Outstanding Berkeley Woman award Berkeley Commn. on the Status of Women, 1996, other awards. Mem. Filipino Am. Nat. Hist. Soc. (pres. East Bay chpt. 1996, Silver Arts & Music award 1994), Coop. Educators Network Calif. Democrat. Unitarian. Columnist Coop. News, 1964—. Home: 516 Santa Barbara Rd Berkeley CA 94707-1746 Office: 2299 Piedmont Ave Berkeley CA 94720-2327

BUENDIA, IMELDA BERNARDO, clinical director, physician; b. Iloilo City, The Philippines, Nov. 12, 1944; d. Carlos P. and Coleta (De la Cruz) Bernardo; m. Arsenio G. Buendia, June 5, 1971; children: Mary Elaine, Joseph Carlo, Adrian Cesar. BS, U. The Philippines, 1964, MD, 1969. Resident in pediats. Philippine Gen. Hosp., Manila, 1969-71; resident in family practice St. Michael's Hosp., Milw., 1971-75; med. officer Talihina (Okla.) Hosp., 1975-78; med. officer Wewoka (Okla.) Indian Clinic, 1978-92, clin. dir., 1992—. Music dir. St. Joseph Cath. Ch., Wewoka, 1976—; active Phil-Am. Civic Orgn., Oklahoma City, 1978—. Recipient Dir. Excellence award USPHS, 1993. Fellow Am. Acad. Family Physicians; mem. Philippine Med. Assn. Okla. (treas. 1989, sec. 1990, pres.-elect 1994, pres. 1995). Home: 7 Oakhurst St Wewoka OK 74884-3714 Office: Wewoka Indian Clinic Hwy 270 Wewoka OK 74884

BUENO, ANA (MARIE), marketing executive, writer; b. N.Y.C., N.Y., Apr. 27, 1952; m. David M. Kreitzer, June, 1973 (div. Feb. 1979); 1 child, Anatol C. Kreitzer. Sr. writer healthcare Integral Sys., Inc., Walnut Creek, Calif., 1986-88; freelance writer L.A., 1989-92; cons. mktg. Health Net, L.A., 1992-96; ptnr., pres. Bueno and Wixen Mktg., L.A., 1996—. Author: Special Olympics: The First 25 Years, 1994. Sponsor, vol. Spl. Olympics, Calif., 1988-96. Recipient Disting. Vol. Svc. award Spl. Olympics, 1992. Mem. AAUW, Jewish Bus. and Profl. Women, The Jewish Fedn. Jewish.

BUESSING, MARJORIE B., state legislator; b. Kirkland, Wash., May 1, 1950; 4 children. Student, Bellevue (Wash.) C.C. Mem. N.H. Ho. of Reps., mem. edn. com. Sgt. CAP, Bellevue, 1966-68; vol. VISTA, Gary, Ind., 1970-71; treas., mem.-at-large Eastman PTO, 1989-92. Mem. Order of Women Legislators, Woman's Fedn. World Peace, PTO, East Concord Lamplighters, Concord Contemporary Woman's Club. Republican. Mem. Unification Ch. Office: NH Ho of Reps State Capitol Concord NH 03301-1805

BUFFALO, JO (JO WINSHIP), artist, art educator; b. Cleve., Dec. 2, 1948; d. Richard Trevor Gross and Dolores Rice. BFA in Ceramics, Syracuse U., 1973, MFA in Illustration, 1985. Surg. asst. Rocky Gorge Animal Hosp., Laurel, Md., 1970-72; instr. St. Lucys Raruowa, South Nyanza, Kenya, 1976-79; scientific illustrator, draftsman Centuries Rsch., Montrose, Colo., 1979-80; archeol. technician, illustrator Nickens & Assoc., Montrose, Colo., 1980-82; instr. ceramics Syracuse (N.Y.) U., 1983-86; prof., dir. visual comms. Cazenovia (N.Y.) Coll., 1986-96; bd. dirs. Cultural Resources Coun., Syracuse, N.Y., tchg. artist, 1985-91, v.p. bd., 1995-96; jurist N.Y. State Fair, Syracuse, 1993, tech. asst. installation A Century of Ceramics in U.S., 1878-1978 Everson Mus., 1979. Featured in (exhbn. catalogue) 13th Chunichi Internat. Exhbn. Ceramics, Nagoya, Japan, 1985, (Peter Dormer) The New Ceramics-Trends and Traditions, 1986, (book) American Ceramics The Collection of the Everson Museum, 1989; one-woman shows include Internat. House, N.Y.C., 1987-88, White Light Gallery, N.Y.C., CD/FS Gallery, Syracuse, 1984; group exhibitions include Artificie Gallery, Syracuse, 1995, Altered Space Gallery, Syracuse, 1994, Chapman Gallery, 1993, Ctrl. N.Y. Mensa, 1992, George Waters Gallery, Elmira, N.Y., Schweinfurth Meml. Art Gallery, Auburn, N.Y., 1990, Eureka Gallery, Syracuse, 1989, N.Y. State Sch. for the Arts, Fredonia, N.Y., 1987, CD/FS Gallery, Syracuse, 1985, 3th Chunichi Internat. Exhbn. of Ceramic Arts, Nagoya, Japan, 1985, Nin Freudenheim Gallery, Buffalo, 1983, Adelle M Fine Art, Dallas, 1982, Human Arts Gallery, Dallas, 1982, Western Slope Artists Invitational, Denver, 1982, Meyer, Brier, and Weiss Gallery, San Frnacisco, 1982, James Yaw Gallery, Birmingham, Mich., 1982, Everson Mus. of Art, Syracuse, 1982, The Clayworks Studio Workshop, Inc., N.Y.C., 1981. Recipient Mus. Purchase Everson Mus. Art, 1985. Mem. MENSA. Office: Cazenovia Coll Cazenovia NY 13035

BUFFUM, ELIZABETH V., federal agency administrator; b. Washington, July 27, 1941; d. Harry Leo and Mary Ellen (Carnell) Veihmeyer; children: Stephen Wilder Buffum, Kathleen Carnell Buffum. BS, Akron U., 1972, MA, 1975; postgrad., Harvard U., 1985, Brookings Inst., 1990, 94, Fed. Exec. Inst., 1991. Cert. tchr. Owner small business, Washington, 1975-78; policy advisor Energy Rsch. and Devel. Administrn., Washington, 1975-77; analyst Exec. Office of the Pres., Washington, 1977-78; policy asst. to asst. sec. U.S. Dept. Energy, Washington, 1978-81; assoc.mgr. U.S. DOE Office of Sci. Tech. Information, Washington, 1981-85; dep. mgr. U.S. DOE Office of Sci. Tech. Information, Oak Ridge, Tenn., 1986-89, dir. Office Sci.and Tech. Info., 1990—; chief operating officer Sci. Edn. & Tech. Info. Office, Washington, 1993—; U.S. rep. Internat. Energy Agy., Paris, 1990—, Internat. Atomic Energy Agy., Vienna, 1990—; bd. dirs., vice chair tech. com. Internat. Coun. Sci. and Tech. Info., 1994—. Pres. bd. dirs. Hope of Tenn., Oak Ridge, 1989-92; vol. FISH, Oak Ridge, 1988-94; fundraiser March of Dimes, 1989-94; fundraiser, tutor Norwood Elem. Sch., 1990-94. Recipient Administrv. and Mgmt. Excellence award Interagy. Com. on Info. Resources Mgmt., 1992, Orgnl. Excellence award Pub. Employees Round Table, 1992, Exceptional Svc. award Federally Employed Women, 1993, Presidential Rank award, 1994. Mem. AAAS, AAUW, NAFE, Am. Assn. Info. Sci. (policy chair 1985), Assn. Politics and Life Scis., Federally Employed Women, Acad. of Polit. Sci., Sr. Execs. Assn. Office: Dept Energy Sci & Tech Info Office 1000 Independence Ave SW Washington DC 20585-0001

BUFORD, EVELYN CLAUDENE SHILLING, jewelry specialist, merchandising professional; b. Fort Worth, Sept. 21, 1940; d. Claude and Winnie Evelyn (Mote) Hodges; student Hill Jr. Coll., 1975-76, Tarrant County (Tex.) Jr. Coll., 1992-93; m. William J. Buford, Mar. 1982; children by previous marriage: Vincent Shilling, Kathryn Lynn Shilling La Chappell. With Imperial Printing Co., Inc., Ft. Worth, 1964-70, 77-79, gen. sales mgr. comml. div., 1982-90, corp. sec., 1977-79; with Tarrant County Hosp. Dist., Fort Worth, 1973-77, asst. to asst. adminstr., 1981-84; merchandising asst. J.C. Penney Co., 1989—. Mem. Exec. Women Internat. (dir., publs. chmn., v.p. 1984, pres. 1985, chmn. adv. com. 1986, 87, scholarship dir. 1988-93, corp. publ. com. 1988-89, dir. S. ctrl. region 1993-94). Republican. Methodist. Home: 1025 Kenneth Ln Burleson TX 76028-8375 Office: JC Penney Co Hurst TX 76053

BUFORD, RONETTA MARIE, music educator; b. Kansas City, Mo., Sept. 17, 1946; d. Joseph Ronald and Violet Katheryne (Jennison) Coursey; 1 child, Frederrick Kenyatta. Bachelor of Music Edn., Lincoln U. of Mo., 1968. Cert. vocal and instrumental music tchr., Mo. Chmn. vocal music M.L. King Jr. High Sch., Kansas City, 1968-71; chmn. music dept. Southeast Jr. High Sch., Kansas City, 1971-75; chmn. fine arts Paseo High Sch., Kansas City, 1975-90; vocal music specialist Met. High Sch., Kansas City, 1990—, asst. girls basketball coach, asst. cross country coach, 1992—; summer music specialist Horace Mann Elem. Sch., Kansas City, 1972; mentor Students at Risk, Kansas City, 1988; vis. lectr. Lincoln U., Jefferson City, Mo., 1980, 85, 87, NE Mo. State U., Kirksville, 1986; panelist Sta. KPRS, Kansas City, 1987; min. music N.W. Mo. Conf. A.M.E. Ch., Kansas City, 1984—, choir dir., 1985—; dir. sr. choir Ward Chapel A.M.E. Ch., KAnsas City, 1985-87. Author: (curricula) Junior High Learning Task, 1972, Motivating the Unmotivated, 1986. Asst. troop scoutmaster Boy Scouts Am.; spl. cons. music United Meth. Ch. Women; active NAACP. Recipient Meritorious Service award Lincoln U. Vocal Ensemble, 1985, Outstanding Tchr. award Black Archives Mid-Am., 1987; named one of Outstanding Young Women of Am., 1983. Mem. AAUW, Am. Choral Dirs. Assn., Am. Fedn. Tchrs., Music Educators Nat. Conf., Nat. Assn. Negro Women, Order Eastern Star, Order Cyrenes, Heroines of Jericho, Tri-M Music Honor Soc., Order Golden Circle, Nat. Coaches Assn., Vocat. Indsl. Clubs Am., Alpha Kappa Alpha, Phi Delta Kappa, Sigma Alpha Iota. Home: PO Box 301054 Kansas City MO 64130-1054 Office: Kansas City Sch Dist 1211 Mcgee St Kansas City MO 64106-2416

BUFORD, TONJA YEVETTE, track and field Olympic athlete; b. Dayton, Ohio, Dec. 13, 1970; d. Georgianna B. Grad., U. Ill., 1993. Mem. U.S. Olympic Team, Barcelona, Spain, 1992, Atlanta, 1996. Recipient 16 individual Big Ten championships U. Ill., 9 relay Big Ten championships, conf. title indoor awards for 55 and 200 dashes, 55 hurdles, conf. title outdoor awards for 100, 200, 400 and both hurdles, bronze medal Pan Am. Games, Havana, Cuba, 1991, bronze medal 400 meter hurdles Olympic Games, Atlanta, 1996; ranked 7th in world for 400 meter hurdles, 1992, ranked 5th, 1993. Office: USA Track and Field PO Box 120 Indianapolis IN 46206*

BUGBEE, JOAN BARTHELME, retired corporate communications executive; b. Galveston, Tex., Dec. 31, 1932; d. Donald and Helen (Bechtold) Barthelme; m. George A. Bugbee, Apr. 2, 1966; children: Richard, John. BA in Journalism, U. Colo., 1955. Pub. rels. rep. Philco Corp., Phila., 1957-60; account exec. Jacobs Keeper Newell Assoc., Houston, 1960-63; pub. rels. rep. Tex. Ea. Corp., Houston, 1963-66; assoc. editor Oil and Gas Digest Mag., Houston, 1978-79; mgr. corp. communications Pennzoil Co., Houston, 1980-87, dir. corp. communications, 1987-90, v.p. corp. communication, 1990-96; ret., 1996. Mem. Pub. Rels. Soc. Am. (Outstanding Presentation award Phila. chpt. 1959), Forum Club of Houston (communications com.), Phi Beta Kappa.

BUGBEE-JACKSON, JOAN, sculptor; b. Oakland, Calif., Dec. 17, 1941; d. Henry Greenwood and Jeanie Lawler (Abbot) B.; m. John Michael Jackson, June 21, 1973; 1 child, Brook Bond. BA in Art, U. Calif., San Jose, 1964, MA in Art/Ceramics, 1966; student Nat. Acad. Sch. Fine Arts, N.Y.C., 1968-72, Art Students League, N.Y.C., 1968-70. Apprentice to Joseph Kiselewski, 1970-72; instr. art Foothill (Calif.) Jr. Coll., 1966-67; instr. design De Anza Jr. Coll., Cupertino, Calif., 1967-68; instr. pottery Greenwich House Pottery, N.Y.C., 1969-71, Craft Inst. Am., N.Y.C., 1970-72, Cordova (Alaska) Extension Center, U. Alaska, 1972-79, Prince William Sound Community Coll., 1979—; one-woman exhbns. in Maine, N.Y.C., Alaska and Calif.; group exhbns. include Allied Artists Am., 1970-72, Nat. Acad. Design, 1971, 74, Nat. Sculpture Soc. Ann., 1971, 72, 73, Alaska Woman Art Show, 1987, 88, Cordova Visual Artists, 1991-96, Alaska Artists Guild Show, 1994, Am. Medallic Sculpture Nat. Travelling Exhbn., 1994-95; pres. Cordova Arts and Pageants Ltd., 1975-76; commns. include Merle K. Smith Commemorative plaque, 1973, Eyak Native Monument, 1978, Anchorage Pioneer's Home Ceramic Mural, 1979, Alaska Wildlife Series Bronze Medal, 1980, sculpture murals and portraits Alaska State Capitol, 1981, Pierre De Ville Portrait commn., 1983, Robert B. & Evangeline Atwood, 1985, Armin F. Koernig Hatchery Plaque, 1985, Cordova Fishermen's Meml. Sculpture, 1985, Alaska's Five Govs., bronze relief, Anchorage, 1986, Reluctant Fisherman's Mermaid, bronze, 1987, Charles E. Bunnell, bronze portrait statue, Fairbanks, 1988, Alexander Baranof Monument, Sitka, Alaska, 1989, Wally Noerenberg Hatchery Plaque, Prince William Sound, Alaska, 1989, Russian-Alaskan Friendship Plaque (edit. of 4), Kayak Island, Cordova, Alaska and Vladivostok & Petropavlovsk-Kamchatskiy, Russia, 1991, Sophie-Last Among Eyak Native People, 1992, Alaska Airlines Medal Commn. 1993, Hosp. Aux. plaque, 1995; also other portraits. Bd. dirs. Alaska State Coun. on the Arts, 1991-95. Scholarship student Nat. Acad. Sch. Fine Arts, 1969-72; recipient J.A. Suydam Bronze medal, 1969; Dr. Ralph Weiler prize, 1971; Helen Foster Barnet award, 1971; Daniel Chester French award, 1972; Frishmuth award, 1971; Allied Artists Am. award, 1972; C. Percival Dietsch prize, 1973; citation Alaska Legislature, 1981, 82, Alaskan Artist of the Yr., 1991. Fellow Nat. Sculpture Soc. Address: PO Box 374 Cordova AK 99574-0374

BUGG, CAROL DONAYRE, interior designer; b. N.Y.C., June 8, 1937; d. Carlos G. and Frances M. (Burkhart) Donayre; m. James S. Bugg, Dec. 24, 1968; step-children: Karen, Ken, Darlene, Jim, Whitney. AA, Georgetown Visitation Coll., Washington D.C., 1957; student in Spanish, Georgetown U., Washington D.C., 1960; student interior design, Internat. Inst. of Interior Design, Washington, 1967; interior decorator, Parsons Sch. Design, Paris, 1984. Design asst. W&J Sloane, Washington D.C., 1967-68, The H. Chambers Co., Washington D.C., 1968-69; dir. design Internat. Cosmetic Co., Washington D.C., 1970-72; interior decorator Stix, Baer & Fuller, St. Louis, 1972-73, Burklew Design Assocs., Md., 1973-76; pres. Carol Donayre Bugg & Assocs., 1976-85; v.p., dir. design Decorating Den Systems, Inc., Bethesda, Md., 1984—. Author: (book) Dream Rooms For Real People, 1990, Divine Design, 1994; lectr. in field. Mem. decorating com. Congl. Women's Club, Washington D.C.; sponsor Leader Dogs For the Blind, Rochester, Mich.; active gourmet gala March of Dimes, Washington D.C. Mem. Am. Soc. Interior Design (Washington D.C. chpt. chmn. ways and means com. 1979), Color Mktg. Group. Home: 3717 Bradley Ln Chevy Chase MD 20815 Office: Decorating Den Systems Inc 7910 Woodmont Ave Bethesda MD 20814

BUHLER, JILL LORIE, editor, writer; b. Seattle, Dec. 7, 1945; d. Oscar John and Marcella Jane (Hearing) Younce; 1 child, Lori Jill Kelly; m. John Buhler, 1990; stepchildren: Christie, Cathie Vsetecka, Mike. AA in Gen. Edn., Am. River Coll., 1969; BA in Journalism with honors, Sacramento State U., 1973. Reporter Carmichael (Calif.) Courier, 1968-70; mng. editor Quarter Horse of the Pacific Coast, Sacramento, 1970-75, editor, 1975-84; editor Golden State Program Jour., 1978, Nat. Reined Cow Horse Assn. News, Sacramento, 1983-88, Pacific Coast Jour., Sacramento, 1984-88, Nat. Snaffle Bit Assn. News, Sacramento, 1988; pres., chief exec. officer Communications Plus, Port Townsend, Wash., 1988—; mag. cons., 1975—. Interviewer Pres. Ronald Regan, Washington, 1983; mng. editor Wash. Thoroughbred, 1989-90. Mem. 1st profl. communicators mission to USSR, 1988; bd. dirs. Carmichael Winding Way, Pasadena Homeowners Assn., 1985-87; mem. scholarship com. Thoroughbred Horse Racing's United Scholarship Trust; hosp. commr. Jefferson Gen. Hosp., 1995—. Recipient 1st pl. feature award, 1970, 1st pl. editorial award Jour. Assn. Jr. Colls., 1971, 1st pl. design award WCHB Yuba-Sutter Counties, Marysville, Calif., 1985, Photography awards, 1994, 95, 96. Mem. Am. River Jaycees (Speaking award 1982), Am. Horse Publs. (1st Pl. Editorial award 1983, 86), Port Townsend C. of C. (trustee, v.p. 1993, pres. 1994, officer 1996), Mensa (bd. dirs., asst. local sec., activities dir. 1987-88, membership chair 1988-90), Kiwanis Internat. (chair MEP com., treas. 1992—), 5th Wheel Touring Soc. (v.p. 1970). Republican. Roman Catholic. Home: 440 Adelma Beach Rd Port Townsend WA 98368-9605

BUHLER, LESLIE L., institute administrator. BA with honors in History and Art History, Syracuse U., 1969; postgrad., New Sch. for Social Rsch., 1971, Am. U., 1980. Asst. for cmty. programs Met. Mus. Art, N.Y.C., 1970-72; program coord. resident assoc. program Smithsonian Instn., Washington, 1972-75; instnl. devel. officer Nat. Archives and Records Svc., Washington, 1975-78; ind. cons., 1977-82; dir. membership and mktg. Alban Inst., Inc., Bethesda, Md., 1982-85, dir. devel., membership and mktg., 1985-88, dir. ops., 1988-89, exec. v.p., 1989—, acting pres., 1994-95; grante reviewer Office of Mus. Programs, NEH, Washington, 1973-74. Bd. dirs. Mus. of City of Washington, 1980-84; vol. advisor Nat. Mus. for Bldg. Arts, Washington, 1977-79. Recipient cert. of appreciation Am. Revolution Bicentennial Adminstrn., 1976. Home: 4701 32d St NW Washington DC 20008 Office: Alban Inst Ste 433N 4550 Montgomery Ave Bethesda MD 20814-3341

BUHR, FLORENCE D., county official; b. Strahan, Iowa, Apr. 7, 1933; d. Earnest G. and May (Brott) Wederquist; m. Glenn E. Buhr, 1955; children: Barbara, Lori Lynn, David. BA, U. No. Iowa, 1954. Precinct chair Polk County Dem. Ctrl. Com., Iowa, 1974-79; clerk, sec. Iowa Ho. Reps., 1974-79, 81-82; rep. dist. 85 State of Iowa, 1983-90, asst. majority leader Ho. Reps., 1985-90; state senator Iowa State Senate, 1991-95, asst. majority leader, 1992-95; Polk County supr. Des Moines, 1995—. Democrat. Presbyterian. Home and Office: 4127 30th St Des Moines IA 50310-5946

BUICHL, ANNA ELIZABETH, city official; b. Canonsburg, Pa., Aug. 9, 1940. AA, El Camino Jr. Coll., 1960; BA, Long Beach State Coll., 1963; MBA, Pepperdine U., 1985. Programmer analyst L.A. Dept. Airports, 1973-88, info. sys. mgr., 1988—; mem. adv. bd. Govt.-Bus. Tech. Expn., Sacramento, 1996; vice chmn. infotel com. Airports Coun. Internat. N.Am., Washington, 1996. Office: LA Dept Airports One World Way Los Angeles CA 90045

BUILER, DOROTHY MARION, business owner; b. Athens, Wis., Apr. 20, 1925; d. Edwin Herman and Katherine Dorothy (Dick) Mueller; m. Donald J. Builer, May 24, 1947; 1 child, Thomas Edwin. Grad. h.s., Athens. Owner, ptnr. Builer's Sport Shop, Wausau, Wis., 1959—, Campers Haven, Heafford Junction, Wis., 1967—. Mem. Internat. Platform Assn., Bus. and Profl. Women Club (pres. Marathon county 1968-69, pres. Northwood dist. 1973-74), Wausau Womans Club (pres.-elect 1988-90, pres. 1990-91), Am. Legion Aux. (pres. local unit 1958-59, pres. 8th dist. 1963-64, chmn. State of Wis. aux. conv. 1964), Valley Garden Club, Wausau Wheelers Bike Club (organizer). Home: 3919 Pine Cone Ln Wausau WI 54403

BUIS, PATRICIA FRANCES, geology educator, researcher; b. Jersey City, Dec. 29, 1953; d. George Herman Buis and Marie Agnes Fitzsimmons. BA in Geology, Rutgers U., 1976; MA in Geology, Queens Coll., 1983; PhD in Geology, U. Pitts., 1988; MS in Mining Engring., Mich. Tech. U., 1994, PhD in Mining Engring., 1995. Coal quality geochemist Pa. Geologic Survey, Harrisburg, 1989-91; asst. prof. U. Miss., Oxford, 1994-96, Japanese Sci. and Tech. Mgmt. Program scholar, 1996—; cons., reviewer of sci. textbooks prior to pub. Winston-Rinehart, Austin, Tex., 1994—. Dept. Edn. doctoral fellow in mining Mich. Tech. U., 1991-95, Provost Predoctoral fellow U. Pitts., 1988; Dept. Edn. grantee Mich. Tech. U., 1993; nat. merit scholar Schering-Plough, Rutgers U., 1971-75. Mem. Soc. Exploration Geochemistry, Nat. Water Wells Assn., Am. Mineralogist, Sigma Xi. Office: U Miss University MS 38677

BUIST, JEAN MACKERLEY, veterinarian; b. Newton, N.J., Dec. 24, 1919; d. Ackerson Jacob and Mary Morris (Morford) Mackerley; m. Richardson Buist, Oct. 2, 1948; children: Peter Richardson, Jean Morford Buist Earle, Mary Elizabeth Buist Lueth. DVM, Cornell U., 1942. Veterinarian Summit (N.J.) Dog and Cat Hosp., 1942-48; pvt. practice Sparta, N.J., 1948—. Mem. Sparta Twp. Bd. Health, 1962-82, chmn., 1972-82; mem., chmn., sec. N.J. State Bd. Vet. Med. Examiners. Recipient Gaines award Newton Kennel Club, 1970, Disting. Svc. award Assn. Women Veterinarians, 1989, Life Achievement award Baldwin Sch., 1992; Paul Harris fellow Newton N.J. Rotary Club, 1995. Mem. Nat. Assn. State Bds. (pres.-elect 1984, pres. 1985-86), Am. Vet. Med. Assn. (nat. bd. exam. com. 1987-91, chmn. 1990-91), N.J. Vet. Med. Assn. (treas. 1982-92), N.J. Acad. Vet. Medicine and Surgery (bd. dirs. 1972-92, sec. 1975-82), Sussex County 4-H Horse Club Leaders Assn. (pres. 1970-76), Sussex County Horse Show Assn. (v.p. 1980-82, pres. 1982-90), Sussex County Farm and Horse Show Assn. (v.p. 1980-94). Home: 68 Sand Pond Rd Hamburg NJ 07419 Office: 143 Stanhope Rd Sparta NJ 07871-2118

BUJOLD, LOIS MCMASTER, science fiction writer; b. Columbus, Ohio, Nov. 2, 1949; d. Robert Charles and Laura Elizabeth (Gerould) McMaster; m. John Fredric Bujold, Oct. 9, 1971 (div. Dec. 1992); children: Anne Elizabeth, Paul Andre. Author: (novels) Shards of Honor, 1986, The Warrior's Apprentice, 1986, Ethan of Athos, 1986, Falling Free, 1988 (Nebula award 1989), Brothers in Arms, 1989, Borders of Infinity, 1989, The Vor Game, 1990 (Hugo award 1991), Barrayar, 1991 (Hugo award 1992, Rickie award 1992, 1st place Locus poll 1992), Mirror Dance, 1994 (Hugo & Locus awards 1995), Cetaganda, 1996, Memory, 1996, (novellas) The Borders of Infinity, 1987, The Mountains of Mourning, 1989 (Nebula and Hugo awards 1990), Labyrinth, 1989 (Best Novella/Novelette Analytical Lab. 1990), Weatherman, 1990 (Best Novella Analytical Lab. 1991); contbr. short stories to sci. fiction mags., articles to profl. jours. Mem. Sci. Fiction and Fantasy Writers Am., Novelists, Inc. Office: Spectrum Literary Agency 111 8th Ave Ste 1501 New York NY 10011-5201

BUKAR, MARGARET WITTY, physician assistant, healthcare administrator, civic leader; b. Evanston, Ill., June 21, 1950; d. LeRoy and Catherine Ann (Conrad) Witty; m. Gregory Bryce Bukar, June 5, 1971 (dec. 1989); children: Michael Bryce, Caroline Nicole. BS, DePaul U., 1972, MBA, 1981; MS, Finch U. Health Scis., 1996. Staff med. technologist The Evanston (Ill.) Hosp., 1972-75, immunopathology lab. supr., 1975-77, lab. mgr., 1977-84, dir. lab. adminstrn., 1984-85; bookkeeper Ronald Knox Montessori Sch., Wilmette, Ill., 1986-87; beauty cons. Mary Kay Cosmetics, 1990-96; sec. Northwestern U., Evanston, 1991-94; physician asst. Women's Med. Group, P.C., Skokie-Evanston, Ill., 1996—. Den leader Cub Scouts, Boy Scouts Am., Wilmette, 1985-87, den leader coach, 1987-88; active PTA of St. Francis Xavier Sch., 1985—, chair rummage sale, 1987-88, scouting coord., 1991-92, mem. sch. bd., 1986-87, sec. 1988-89, vice chmn., 1989-90; eucharistic min. sick St. Francis Xavier Ch., 1990—, liturgical song leader, 1993—; troup co-leader, song leader Girl Scouts Am., 1992—. Recipient Emily Withrow Stebbins award Evanston Hosp., 1985. Mem. NAFE, Am. Soc. Clin. Pathologists, Am. Acad. Physician Assts., Ill. Acad. Physician Assts., Wilmette Hist. Soc., Elms Social Club (pres. 1992). Avocations: knitting, interior design, reading.

BUKER, LINDA SUE, elementary education educator; b. Allentown, Pa., May 22, 1956; d. Donald C. and Dorothy Ann (Brader) Hopkins; m. David T. Stevenson Jr., Aug. 12, 1978 (div. May 1993); children: Tracy, Patrick, Amanda; m. Dennis Ray Buker, June 25, 1993. BS in Edn., Kutztown (Pa.) State Coll., 1978; EdM, Millersville (Pa.) U., 1985; postgrad., Okla. State U., 1995—. Cert. elem. tchr., Okla., Pa. Substitute tchr. Phila. Sch. Dist., 1978-79, Upper Darby Sch. Dist., Phila., 1978-79, Penn Manor Sch. Dist., Millersville, Pa., 1982-89, Manheim Twp. Sch. System, Lancaster, 1982-89, Lancaster (Pa.) Sch. Dist., 1982-89, Union Pub. Schs., Tulsa, 1990-91; tchr., supt. adv. bd. Tulsa Pub. Schs., 1991—; elem. and middle sch. curriculum com. mem., elem. and middle sch. discipline com. mem., sch. newspaper sponsor, in-svc. instr. on integrated curriculum Tulsa Pub. Schs. Tri-county coord. Hands Across Am., Lancaster, 1983; coord. Millersville Food Bank, 1983-86. Grantee Tulsa Edn. Fund 1995; summer fellowship Inst. in Early Am. History, Williamsburg, Va.; recipient Cmty. award for vol. svc. Mem. NEA, ASCD, Nat. Coun. Tchrs. Reading, Nat. Jr. Honor Soc. (adv. bd.), Okla. Edn. Assn., Tulsa Classroom Tchrs. Assn. (rep. 1992-93), Tulsa Oratorio Chorus, Tulsa County Reading Coun., Okla. Reading Coun., Tulsa Meml. H. S. Band Parents Assn. (exec. bd.). Democrat. Lutheran. Home: 7361 S 74th E Ave Tulsa OK 74133

BUKOWSKI, ELAINE LOUISE, physical therapist; b. Phila., Feb. 18, 1949; d. Edward Eugene and Melanja Josephine (Przyborowski) B. BS in Phys. Therapy, St. Louis U., 1972; MS, U. Nebr., 1977. Lic. phys. therapist, N.J.; diplomate Am. Bd. Disabilities Analysts (sr. analyst, profl. adv. coun. 1995—). Clk. City of Phila., 1967; staff phys. therapist St. Louis Chronic Hosp., 1973, Cardinal Ritter Inst., St. Louis, 1973-74; dir. campus ministry musicals Creighton U., Omaha, 1974-75; tchg. asst. U. Nebr. Med. Ctr., Omaha, 1975-76; lectr. in anatomy U. Sci. and Tech., Kumasi, Ghana, 1977-78; chief phys. therapist Holy Family Hosp., Berekum, Ghana, 1978-79; coord. info. & guidance The Am. Cancer Soc., Phila., 1979-81; staff phys. therapist Holy Redeemer Vis. Nurse Assn., Phila., 1981-83; rehab. supr. Holy Redeemer Vis. Nurse Assn., Swainton, N.J., 1983-87; asst. prof. phys. therapy Richard Stockton Coll. N.J., Pomona, 1987-96, assoc. prof., 1996—; bd. dirs. The Bridge, Phila., 1979-80; vacation relief phys. therapist, N.J., summer 1988—; mem. profl. adv. coun. Holy Redeemer VNA, Swainton, N.J., 1982-93, chmn., 1985-91, mem. pers. com., cons. hospice program, 1985-87, rehab. cons., 1987-88; legis. adv. coun. subcom. on edn. and health care Cape May & Cumberland Counties, 1988-90; utilization rev. cons. rehab. svcs., 1990; mem. fitness screening team N.J. State Legislature, 1990; mem. geriatric rehab. del. Citizen Amb. Program, China, 1992. Co-author slide study program, 1976, (video) Going My Way? The Low Back Syndrome, 1976; contbr. articles to profl. jours. Vol. Am. Cancer Soc., Phila., 1979-82, Walk-a-Day-in-My Shoes prog. Girl Scouts Am., Cape May County, N.J., 1983-86; task force phys. therapy prog. Stockton State Coll., Pomona, N.J., 1985-88. U.S. Govt. trainee, 1971, 72; Physical Therapy Fund grantee, 1975, 76; recipient Vol. Achievement award Am. Cancer Soc., 1981. Mem. Am. Phys. Therapy Assn. (edn. sect., orthopedic sect., vice chair so. sect. 1993-96, chair so. sect. 1996—, ho. of dels. 1994-96), N.J. Arthritis Health Professions Assn. (reader adv. network Arthritis Today, key contact voting dist. 1, legis. network State of N.J. 1989—, vice chair so. dist. 1994-96, chair so. dist. 1996—, bd. dirs. 1996—, ho. of dels.), Smithsonian Assn., Phys. Therapy Club (sec. 1971-72), N.J. Phys. Therapy Assn. (rsch. com. 1995—). Office: Richard Stockton Coll NJ Phys Therapy Program Jim Leeds Rd Pomona NJ 08240

BULGER, PEGGY ANNE, cultural organization administrator; b. Albany, N.Y., Dec. 13, 1949; d. David J. and Hannah (Casey) B.; m. Douglas B. Leatherbury III, Apr. 21, 1979; children: (twins) Hannah Elizabeth and Meagan Chase. BA, SUNY, Albany, 1972; MA, Western Ky. U., 1975; PhD, U. Pa., 1992. Oral historian Bur. Cultural Affairs, Albany, 1975; rsch. and participants coord. Appalacian Mus., Berea, Ky., 1975-76; state folk arts coord. Fla. Dept. State, 1976-79; folklife programs adminstr. Bur. Fla. Folklife Programs, 1979-89; coord. Regional Folk Arts Program So. Arts Fedn., Atlanta, 1989-92, dir., 1992—; chairperson Folk Arts Steering Com. Atlanta Com. Olympic Games Cultural Olympiad, 1992-96; cons. Marine Resources Coun. Fla., Nat. Folk Festival, Nat. Black Arts Festival; bd. dirs. Nat. Coun. Traditional Arts, 1992—. Editor: Musical Roots of the South, 1992; author: (with Tina Bucuvalas and Stetson Kennedy) South Florida Folklife, 1994; contbr. books The Steamboat Era in Florida, 1984, The Conservation of Culture: Folklorists and the Public Sector, 1988; guest editor: Southern Folklore, 1992; producer documentary videotapes and films for educl. TV, radio networks ans sound recordings, videotapes for PBS including Four Corners of Earth: Folklife of Seminole Women, 1984, Fishing All My Days: Maritime Traditions of Florida's Shrimpers, 1985, Every Island Has Its Own Songs: The Tsinouris Family of Tarpon Springs, 1988, Music Masters and Rhythm Kings, 1993. Recipient Wayland D. Hand prize, 1991-92; Brit. Coun. fellow, Folklore Study Tour No. Ireland, 1992. Democrat. Episcopalian. Home: 4849 Pine Hill Ct W Stone Mountain GA 30088 Office: So Arts Found 181 14th St NE Ste 400 Atlanta GA 30309*

BULL, INEZ STEWART, special education and gifted music educator, coloratura soprano, pianist, editor, author; b. Newark, Apr. 13, 1920; d. Johan Randulf and Aurora (Stewart) B. Artist diploma in piano, Juilliard, 1946; diploma, U. Oslo, Norway, 1955; MusB, N.Y. Coll. Music, 1965; MA, NYU, 1972, EdD, 1979. Piano tchr. Juilliard Inst. Musical Art, N.Y., 1942-43; chmn. music dept. Casement's Coll., Ormond Beach, Fla., 1949-50; dir. music Essex County Girls Vocat. & Tech. H.S., Newark, 1953-57; dir. music, organist State of N.J. Institution for Retarded Girls North Jersey Tng. Sch., Totowa, N.J., 1953-68; spl. edn. gifted coord. Jefferson Magnet Sch. in Union City (N.J.) Pub. Sch. Sys., 1956—; dir. Upper Montclair Music Sch., Montclair, N.J., 1945—, Ole Bull Music Sch., Potter County, Pa., 1952-68; adjudicator Lycoming Coll., Williamsport, Pa., 1948—; conductor Whippany Symphony Orch., 1951-52; curator, builder Ole Bull Mus., Carter Camp, Pa., 1968—; dir. youth chorus, Union City, 1956—; dir. Hudson County Elem. Choral Festival, 1971—; artist-in-residence, Union City, N.J.; guest lectr. Columbia U., N.Y.C., Yale U. Grad. Sch. Music, Hartford, Conn., NYU, Lycoming Coll., Williamsport, Pa., Mansfield U., Pa., Princeton U., N.J., U. Scranton, Pa., Jersey City State Coll. Author 17 books; editor various newsletters and mags.; author (song): Evening Prayer, 1934, I Will Bow and Be Humble, 1954; recording artist Educo Records. Choir dir. Nutley Luth. Ch., 1940-41, First Congregational Ch., 1940-43; organist, choir dir. North Jersey Tng. Sch. Chapel, 1952-68; founder, dir. Ole Bull Music Festival, 1952—; dep. gov. and mem. rsch. bd. advisors Am. Biog. Inst., Raleigh; U.S. State Dept amb. of goodwill to Norway by order of Pres. Dwight D. Eisenhower, 1953, Norwegian Goodwill amb. of goodwill to U.S. by order of King Haakon VII, 1953. Recipient Freedom medal-Eisenhower medal, 1953, Sterling Silver plaque King Olav V of Norway, 1966, NJEA award, 1970, Performing Arts Prestige award in Edn., 1976, Olympic Gold medal Norwegian Govt., 1992, Medal of Honor in Silver, 1991, Gold medal of Honor, 1992, Pa. Senate Legis. citation, 1992, Outstanding Tchr. of the Handicapped in the U.S. Nat. Rsch. Coun., 1970, Woman of Distinction honorable mention award Girl Scout Coun. of Greater Essex County, 1996, Artisan award Oakeside Bloomfield Cultural Ctr., 1996, 50 Women You Should Know award Internat. YWCA; Fulbright scholar U. Oslo (Norway) Grad. Sch., 1955. Mem. Ole Bull Hist. Soc. (pres. 1972—), Phi Delta Kappa (pres. 1984-86, newsletter editor 1984-92), Kappa Delta Pi (pres. 1984—, newsletter editor 1984—), Pen & Brush Club, Internat. Percy Grainger Soc. (v.p.). Republican. Home: 172 Watchung Ave Montclair NJ 07043-1737 Office: Robert Waters Sch 2800 Summit Ave Union City NJ 07087-2323

BULL, MARY MALEY, radio executive; b. Munich, Mar. 26, 1956; came to U.S., 1956; d. John David and Mary (Kline) M.; m. Steven Tremaine, May 23, 1981; children: Ellen, Emily, Stephanie. BA in History & Music, Trinity U., San Antonio, Tex., 1978. Exec. trainee Joskes' of Tex., San Antonio, 1978-79; office mgr. Advance Mktg., Dallas, 1979-80; acct. exec., asst. advt. mgr., advt. dir. Fisher Publs., San Antonio, 1980-88; sr. account mgr. KSMG-FM, San Antonio, 1988—. Actress Harlequin Theatres, San Antonio, 1979—, San Antonio Little Theatre, 1985—, St. Andrew's Players, 1982—; model various Tex. TV commls., mags., newspapers. Mem. adminstrv. bd., family ministries chmn., St. Andrews Meth. Ch., San Antonio, mem. applause support group, choir pres., 1989, mem. bell choir, dir. children's choir, 1993—; active Girl Scouts USA, 1992—, leader, 1994—. Recipient Nat. Presby. scholarship Nat. Presby. Ch., 1974-78, Dow Jones Writing award Dow Jones, 1974, Addy award, 1989; named Top Salesman Recorder-Times, 1982-84, one of Outstanding Young Women Am., 1983, 85, 87. Mem. San Antonio Advt. Fedn. (bd. dirs. 1988-94, 2d v.p. 1989-90, 1st v.p. 1990-91, pres. 1991-92, 10th dist. dir. 1992-93), Women in Comm., San Antonio Radio and Broadcast Execs., Suburban Newspaper Am. Club. Republican. Methodist. Office: KSMG-FM Radio 8930 Fourwinds Dr Ste 500 San Antonio TX 78239-1973

BULL, VIVIAN ANN, college president; b. Ironwood, Mich., Dec. 11, 1934; d. Edwin Russell and Lydia (West) Johnson; m. Robert J. Bull, Jan. 31, 1959; children: R. Camper, W. Carlson. BA, Albion (Mich.) Coll., 1956; postgrad., London Sch. Econs., 1957; PhD, NYU, 1974. Economist Nat. Bank Detroit, 1955-59; with Bell Telephone Labs., Murray Hill, N.J., 1960-62; dept. econs. Drew U., Madison, N.J., 1960-92, assoc. dean, 1978-86; pres. Linfield Coll., McMinnville, Oreg., 1992—; bd. dirs. Chem. Bank N.J., Morristown; trustee Africa U., Zimbabwe; treas. Joint Expedition to Caesareu Maritima Archaeology, 1971—. Author: Economic Study The West Bank: Is It Viable?, 1975. Trustee, assoc. Am. Schs. Oriental Rsch., 1982-90; trustee Colonial Symphony Soc., 1984-92, The Albright Inst. of Archaeol. Record; commr. Downtown Devel. Commn., Madison, 1986-92; mem. Univ. Sen. United Meth. Ch., 1989-96, gen. bd. higher edn., 1988-92; mem. planning bd. Coll. Bus. Adminstrn., Africa U., Zimbabwe, 1990-91; exec. com. Nat. Assn. Commns. on Salaries, United Meth. Ch., 1986-92. Fulbright scholar, 1956, Paul Harris fellow Rotary Internat., 1988; named Disting. Alumna Albion Coll., 1979; recipient Salute to Policy Makers award Exec. Women in N.J., 1986, John Woolman Peacemaking award George Fox Coll., 1994, Equal Opportunity award Urban League of Portland, 1995. Mem. Nat. Assn. Bank Women, Phi Beta Kappa. Address: Linfield Coll Office of the Pres 900 S Baker St McMinnville OR 97128-6894

BULLARD, HELEN (MRS. JOSEPH MARSHALL KRECHNIAK), sculptor; b. Elgin, Ill., Aug. 15, 1902; d. Charles Wickliffe and Minnie (Cook) Bullard; student U. Chgo., 1921-29; m. Lloyd Ernst Rohrke, June 11, 1924 (div. Feb. 1931); children—Ann Louise (Mrs. Ross DeWitt Netherton), Barbara Jane (Mrs. Valtyr Emil Gudmundson); m. 2d, Joseph Marshall Krechniak, Jan. 30, 1932 (dec. Feb. 1964); 1 child, Mariana (Mrs. Wilfred Martin). With research dept. L.V. Estes, Inc., Chgo., 1920-22; operator Square D Co., Detroit, 1922-24; researcher Commerce and Adminstrn. library U. Chgo., Detroit, 1924-25, dir. Crossville (Tenn.) Play Ctr., 1949-50. Creator hand-carved dolls, 1949—, wood sculpture, 1959—; exhibited with Nat. Inst. Am. Doll Artists Exhbns., Los Angeles, 1963, Cin., 1964, Washington, 1965, Chgo., 1966, Boston, 1967, New Orleans, 1969, Detroit, 1970, Los Angeles, 1971, Omaha, 1972, Louisville, 1973, Miami, Fla., 1974, Milw., 1975, Watts Bar Dam, Tenn., 1976, Chgo., 1977, N.Y.C., 1979, others until 1987, also craftsmen's fairs, 1954-65, The Club, Birmingham, Ala., 1963, Oak Ridge Art Ctr., 1965, Children's Mus., Nashville, 1967, McClung Mus., Knoxville, 1969; one woman show Tenn. State Mus., 1972, Nashville, Knoxville, Asheville, N.C.; author: Dr. Woman of the Cumberlands, 1953, The American Doll Artist, 1965, Vol. II, 1974, A Bullard Family, 1966, Dorothy Heizer, the Artist and Her Dolls, 1972; Crafts and Craftsmen of the Tennesee Mountains, 1976, (monograph) My People in Wood, 1984, Faith Wick: Doll Artist Extraordinaire, 1986, Cumberland County, 1956-86, Vol. II, 1987, (with husband) Cumberland County's First Hundred Years, 1956. Campaign chmn. Cumberland County unit Am. Cancer Soc., 1947-52. Mem. So. Highland Handicraft Guild (dir. 1957-59), Highland Handicraft Guild, Nat. Inst. Am. Doll Artists (founder, pres. 1963-67, 69-71, chmn. bd. 1977-80, honoree Helen Bullard Scholarship Fund 1995), United Fedn. Doll Clubs (2d v.p. 1977-79), Am. Craftsmen's Coun., Tenn. Folklore Soc., Mensa. Democrat. Unitarian.

BULLARD, JUDITH EVE, psychologist, systems engineer; b. Oneonta, N.Y., Oct. 5, 1945; d. Kurt and Herta (Deutsch) Leeds; divorced; children: Nicholas A., Elizabeth A. BA in Polit. Sci., Spanish U., Oreg., 1966, MA in Psychology, 1973; MBA, George Washington U., 1994. Supr. residential program Skipworth Juvenile Home, Eugene, Oreg., 1966-68; research asst. Oreg. Research Inst., Eugene, 1968-69, 83-85; supr. residential program Ky. Correctional Facility, Lexington, 1969-70; research asst. U. Oreg., Eugene, 1970-73; asst. dir. Regional Mental Health Clinic, Frankfort, Ind., 1974-76; dir. mental health Lane County Mental Health, Eugene, 1977-80; cons. Managerial Communications, Eugene, 1980-83; sys. engr. AT&T Bell Labs., Holmdel, N.J., 1985 91, mgr. strategic/tech. planning, 1992-95, quality mgr., 1996—; mem. strategic task force Globa Bus. Comm. Sys., chairperson customer based panels edn. forum, 1991—, mgr. forward looking work/tech. mgmt. group, mgr. tech. ptnr. program, tech. and planning, info. platform sys., 1993—, innovation, 1994—, chairperson 2nd day software symposium, tech. strategy conf., rsch. and tech. planning, 1995, Breakthru Tech. project, 1996, svc. planned and executed Rsch. Tech. Exch. Symposium, mem. leadership team Cultural Change project; exec. prodr. 15TV Broadcast Solutions, 1996. Prodr. (video) The World is Our Work Place, 1991. Bd. dirs. Asbury Park 10K, Jersey Shore 1/2 Marathon, 1985—, Women's Resource and Survival Ctr., Keyport, N.J., 1986—; chairperson Area Affirmative Action Com., 1990—; pres. Affirmative Action Diversity Coun. Mem. Women's Profl. Network (trustee Holmdel br. 1987—), Partnership in Edn. & Bus., Corrections in Mental Health, Human Factors Soc. Office: AT&T BF409 200 Laurel Ave Middletown NJ 07748

BULLARD, MARY ELLEN, retired religious study center administrator; b. Elkin, N.C., Jan. 12, 1926; d. Roy Brannoch and Mattie Reid (Doughton) H.; m. John Carson Bullard Sr., Apr. 27, 1957; children: John Carson Jr., Roy Harrell. BS, U. N.C., Greensboro, 1947; postgrad., Union Theol. Sem., N.Y.C., 1956; MA, Troy State U., Montgomery, Ala., 1979. Dir. women's and girls' work Gilvin Roth YMCA, Elkin, 1947-49; dir. Christian edn. 1st United Meth. Ch., Salisbury, N.C., 1949-51, Charlotte, N.C., 1951-55; dir. youth ministry United Meth. Ch., Western N.C. Conf., 1956-57; dir. edn. ministries, div. continuing edn. Huntingdon Coll., 1979-88; dir. U.S. office Bibl. Resources Study Ctr., Inc., Jerusalem, 1988-92; bd. dirs. Ch. Women United Ala., 1970-71; del. World Meth. Coun., 13th World Meth. Conf., Dublin, 1976; mem. 15th World Meth. Conf., Nairobi, Kenya, 1986, 16th World Meth. Conf., Singapore, 1991, exec. com., 1991—, World Evangelism Inst., 1991—; del. Gen. Conf. United Meth. Ch., St. Louis, 1988, Louisville, 1992; del. Southeastern Jurisdictional Conf., United Meth. Ch., Lake Junaluska, N.C., 1988, 92, 96; mem. gen. coun. fin. and adminstrn. United Meth. Ch., 1992—. Bd. dirs. LWV, Montgomery, 1966-70, Am. Cancer Soc., Montgomery, 1975-81, Ala. Dept. Youth Svcs., Mt. Meigs Campus Chapel, 1984-86; mem. Montgomery Symphony League, 1984-96; mem. adv. bd. Resurrection Cath. Mission, 1993—; mem. Nat. Vision 2000 Long-Range Dream Team, United Meth. Ch., 1995—; del. Southeastern Jurisdictional Conf., The United Meth. Ch., 1988, 92, 96; bd. trustees Ala. West Fla. Con. The United Meth. Ch., 1995—. Recipient award of recognition Bd. Edn. We. N.C. Conf. The United Methodist Ch., 1956, Christian Higher Edn., Ala.-West Fla. Conf. United Meth. Ch., 1975, Conf. Coun. on Ministries, Ala. West Fla. Conf., 1987, Candler Sch. of Theology, Emory U., 1990, Alice Lee award Ala. West Fla. Conf. United Meth. Ch., 1994. Mem. Christian Educators Fellowship, Kappa Delta Pi. Home: 3359 Warrenton Rd Montgomery AL 36111-1736

BULLARD, SHARON WELCH, librarian; b. San Diego, Nov. 4, 1943; d. Dale L. and Myrtle (Sampson) Welch; m. Donald H. Bullard, Aug. 1, 1969. B.S.Ed., U. Central Ark., 1965; M.A., U. Denver, 1967. Media specialist Adams County Sch. Dist. 12, Denver, 1967-69; tchr., libr. Humphrey pub. schs., Ark., 1965-66, libr., 1969-70; catalog libr. Ark. State U., Jonesboro, 1970-75; head documents cataloging Wash. State U., Pullman, 1979-83; head serials cataloging U. Calif.-Santa Barbara Davidson Libr., 1984-88, head circulation dept., 1988—; cons. Ctr. for Robotic Systems Microelectronics Rsch. Libr., Santa Barbara, 1986, Calif. State Libr. retrospective conversion project, 1987, Ombudsman's Office U. Calif., Santa Barbara, 1988; distributor Amway, 1985-91. Canvasser, Citizens for Goleta Valley, 1985-86; adv. bd. Total Interlibr. Exch., 1994-96. Mem. ALA, Calif. Libr. Assn. (tech. svcs. chpt. southern Calif. sect.), Libr. Assn. U. Calif.-Santa Barbara (mem. subcom. on advancement and promotion 1987-91), NAFE, So. Calif. Tech. Processes Group (membership com. 1987), Assn. Coll. and Rsch. Librs. (intern membership com. 1993-94, extended campus libr. sect. guidelines com. 1995—), Libr. Adminstrn. and Mgmt. Assn. (mem. circulation/access svcs. systems and svcs. sect. 1993—, mem. equipment com. bldg. and equipment sect. 1993—), Notis Users Circulation Interest Group (presenter meeting 1992, mem. CIRC SIG steering com. 1993—, moderator meeting 1993—, chair elect 1994-95, chair 1995-96), Pi Lambda Theta (exec. bd., sec. Santa Barbara chpt. 1990-91, hospitality com. 1991-92). Avocations: t'ai chi, walking, camping, boogey boarding, swimming.

BULLITT-JONAS, MARGARET MORLEY, priest, educator; b. Cambridge, Mass., Oct. 24, 1951; d. John Marshall Bullitt and Sarah (Cowles) Doering; m. Robert Alan Jonas, Oct. 25, 1986; 1 child, Samuel; 1 stepchild, Christy. BA, Stanford U., 1974; MA, Harvard U., 1977, PhD, 1984; postgrad., Shalem Inst., 1988; MDiv, Episcopal Divinity Sch., 1988. Tchg. fellow Harvard U., Cambridge, Mass., 1977-82; curate Christ Ch., Andover, Mass., 1988-91; assoc. priest Emmanuel Ch., Boston, 1991-92; asst. rector Grace Ch., Newton, Mass., 1992-96; lectr. in pastoral theology Episc. Div. Sch., Cambridge, 1991-92, 94—; leader of spiritual retreats and workshops in various dioceses, 1986—. Contbr. articles to profl. jours. including Anglican Theol. Review, Human Devel., also others. Active Commn. on Ministry, 1994—, Examining Chaplain's Com., 1990—; bd. dirs. MECA, 1992-96. Mem. Soc. St. John the Evangelist Spiritual Colleagues Group, Spiritual Dirs. Internat., Episcopal Peace Fellowship. Home: 105 Garfield St Watertown MA 02172 Office: Episcopal Divinity Sch 99 Brattle St Cambridge MA 02138

BULLOCK, EDNA JEANETTE, photographer; b. Hollister, Calif., May 20, 1915; d. Fred A. and Gertrude A. (Chase) Earle; m. Wynn Bullock, 1943 (dec. 1975); children: Barbara Ann Bullock-Wilson, Lynne Harrington-Bullock; 1 stepchild, Mary Wynn Burnat Horner. AA, Modesto (Calif.) Jr. Coll., 1936; B of Edn., UCLA, 1938. Cert. tchr., Calif. Phys. edn., dance tchr. Fresno (Calif.) H.S., 1940-43; from phys. edn. to home econ. tchr. Monterey (Calif.) Peninsula Unified Sch. Dist., 1959-1974; pvt. practice as photographer Monterey, 1976—; lectr. in field. One-Women shows include Shado Gallery, Portland, Oreg., 1977, Pacific Grove (Calif.) Art Ctr., 1979, Photo-Synthesis Gallery, Clovis, Calif., 1979, Cafe Balthazar Gallery, Pacific Grove, 1980, Collectors Gallery, Pacific Grove, 1980, Focus Gallery, San Francisco, 1981, San Jose City Coll., 1981, Exposures Gallery, Libertyville, Ill., 1982, Jeb Gallery, Providence, 1982, Ledel Gallery, N.Y.C., 1983, Neikrug Gallery, N.Y.C., 1983, Spectrum Gallery, Fresno, 1985, Vision Gallery, San Francisco, 1985, Photography at Oreg. Gallery, Eugene, 1986, Betty Garland Gallery, San Francisco, 1987, Exposure Gallery, Orleans, Mass., 1987, Olive Hyde Art Gallery, Fremont, Calif., 1987, Foto Galerie, Chincoteague, Va., 1990, G. Ray Hawkins Gallery, Santa Monica, Calif., 1993, Halsted Gallery, Birmingham, Mich., 1993, 95, PhotoZone Gallery, Eugene, 1993, Marjorie Evans Gallery, Carmel, Calif., 1995, F Stops Here Gallery, Santa Barbara, Calif., 1995; exhibited in group shows including Stills Gallery, Edinburgh, Scotland, 1988, Dancing Man Gallery, Santa Cruz, 1989, Josephus Daniels Gallery, Carmel, Calif., 1989, Pacific Grove Art Ctr., 1987, 89, 91-92, Imagery Gallery, Lancaster, Ohio, 1992, Grant Gallery, Denver, 1992, Silver Image Gallery, Seattle, 1992, Photographic Image Gallery, Portland, 1993, Scott Nichols Gallery, San Francisco, 1994; photographer Combing the Coast I, 1981, Combing the Coast II, 1982, Combing the Coast I and II, 1985, Edna's Nudes, 1995. Bd. dirs. Friends the Arts U. Calif., Santa Cruz, 1983-87, Ctr. for Photographic Art, 1991-94. Recipient Lifetime Achievement award Gov. Pete Wilson State of Calif., 1995; named Local Hero, Coast Weekly, 1996. Democrat. Unitarian Universalist. Office: PO Box 222984 Carmel CA 93922-2984

BULLOCK, JUDY ROESKE, accountant, human resources executive; b. Monroe, Mich., Sept. 10, 1957; d. Ivan Kenneth and Nell Elizabeth (Giles) Roeske; m. Charles C. Bullock, Jr., Feb. 17, 1991; children: Charles Christopher Bullock, Catherine Christina Bullock. BA in Acctg., U. South Fla., 1982; ChFC, Am. Coll., 1987; postgrad., Keller, 1994—. ChFC, AICPA/PFS; CPA, Fla., Mo., SPHR (Sr. Profl. Human Res.). Sr. tax specialist KPMG Peat Marwick, Tampa, Fla., 1982-84; tax/tech. design dir. CIGNA Fin. Svcs., Tampa, 1984-87; sr. mgr. tax/exec. fin. svcs. Price Waterhouse, Tampa, St. Louis, 1987-93; mgr. compensation unit, exec. compensation practice leader, exec. benefits practice leader, sr. cons. Towers Perrin, St. Louis, 1994-95; dir. exec. compensation & benefits Deere & Co., Moline, Ill., 1995—; artist Innovative Solutions, Moline, 1991—. Loaned exec. United Way, Tampa, 1989. Mem. AICPA, Am. Compensation Assn., Am. Soc. CLU/ChFC, Mo. Soc. CPAs (mem. personal fin. svcs. com. 1993, mem. investment com. 1994, dir. programs exec. compensation mgmt. coun. conf. bd. 1996), Soc. Human Resource Mgmt. Republican. Roman Catholic. Home: 3850 35th Avenue Ct Moline IL 61265 Office: Deere & Co John Deere Rd Moline IL 61265

BULLOCK, MERRY, scientist; b. Springfield, Ohio, Feb. 5, 1950; d. Wilfred Marion and Nancy Louise (Bauer) B.; m. Toomas Hendrik Ilves, Dec. 31, 1980; children: Luukas, Juulia. BA, Brown U., 1971; MA, U. Pa., 1976, PhD, 1979. Prof. U. B.C., Vancouver, Can., 1979-84; vis. guest prof. Max Planck Inst., Munich, 1985-87; sr. rsch. assoc. Max Planck Inst., Munich, $D, 1987-93; programentist NSF, Arlington, Va., 1994-95; sr. scientist Am. Psychol. Assn., Washington, 1995—. Author, editor: The Development of Intentional Action: Cognitive, Motivational and Interactional Processes, 1991. Mem. Phi Beta Kappa.

BULLOCK, SANDRA, actress; b. Washington, July 26, 1966; d. John and Helga B. Grad., Washington-Lee H.S., Arlington, Va., 1982. Appearances include (TV movies) Bionic Showdown: The Six-Million Dollar Man and the Bionic Woman, 1989, (TV series) Working Girl, 1990, (feature films) Fire on the Amazon, 1991, Love Potion #9, 1992, The Vanishing, 1993, Demolition Man, 1993, The Thing Called Love, 1993, Wrestling Ernest Hemingway, 1993, Speed, 1994 (Best Female Performance, Most Desirable Female MTV Movie awards), While You Were Sleeping, 1995 (Favorite Actress in a Motion Picture award People Choice Awards 1996), The Net, 1995, Two if by Sea, 1996, A Time to Kill, 1996, In Love and War, 1996; actor, prodr. Kate and Leopold, 1996; actor, writer Making Sandwiches, 1996. Recipient Best Actress MTV's Big Picture, 1994-95, Best Actress US Mag., 1995, Favorite Actress in a Comedy/Drama Theatrical and Favorite Actress-Comedy Video awards BlockBuster Entertainment Awards, 1996. Office: UTA 9560 Wilshire Blvd Fl 5 Beverly Hills CA 90212*

BULLS, DEBBIE STOREY, nurse; b. Talladega, Ala., Jan. 16, 1959; d. Carthell and Virginia Pearl (Cunningham) Storey; m. George Blanchet Bulls, Oct. 22, 1989; 1 child, Taylor Anona Virginia. BS in Biology, Tuskegee U., 1988. Commd. 2d lt. U.S. Army, 1983, advanced through grades to capt., 1987; staff nurse Tuskegee (Ala.) VA Hosp., 1990-94, Bapt. Med. Ctr., Montgomery, Ala., 1992-93, Ctrl. Ala. Home Health, Tuskegee, 1992-93. Mem. Ala. Assn. Univ. Women. Episcopalian. Home: 806-H Phillips Dr Tuskegee AL 36088

BULMAHN, LYNN, journalist, freelance writer; b. Waco, Tex., Feb. 18, 1955; d. Franklin Harrold and Louise (Stolte) B. BA, SW Tex. State U., 1977. Med., health, feature writer and gen. assignment reporter Waco Tribune Herald, 1977—; vis. journalist fellowship Duke U., 1991. Bd. trustees Unity Ch. of Living Christ, Hewitt, Tex. Recipient Anson Jones Merit citation, Tex. Med. Assn., 1978, 91, Outstanding Contbn. award Nat. Found. March of Dimes, 1980, Pub. Health award for media excellence Tex. Pub. Health Assn., 1980, 85, 88, 89, 90, 91, 92, 93, 94, 95, First Place award Readers Digest Mag. Workshop Tex. Competition, 1981, Feature Writing award North and East Tex. Press Assn., 1983, Media Appreciation award McLennan County Med. Assn., 1985, Journalism Excellence award Am. Cancer Soc., 1989, 91, Silver Star of Tex. award Tex. Hosp. Assn., 1989, 92, Newspaper award, Mental Health Assn., 1989, 90, 91, 94, 95, Anson Jones award Tex. Med. Assn., 1992; co-recipient Tex. Katie award Press Club Dallas, 1993. Office: Waco Tribune-Herald 900 Franklin Ave Waco TX 76701-1906

BUMBRY, GRACE, soprano; b. St. Louis, Jan. 4, 1937; d. Benjamin and Melzia (Walker) B. Student, Boston U., 1954-55, Northwestern U., 1955-56, also fgn. countries, Music Acad. West, 1956-59; studied with, Lotte Lehmann, 1956-59; HHD (hon.), St. Louis U.; hon. doctorates in humanities, Rust Coll., Holly Spring, Miss., U. St. Louis, U. Mo.; MusD (hon.), Rockhurst Coll. Operatic debut, Paris Opera, 1960; debut Basel Opera, 1960, Bayreuth Festival, 1961, Vienna State Opera, 1963, Royal Opera House, Covent Garden, 1963, Salzburg Festival, 1964, Met. Opera, 1965, La Scala, 1966, Bess in Porgy and Bess, N.Y. Met. Opera, 1985; has appeared other opera houses in Europe, S.Am., Japan, U.S.; command performances The White House and London; recs. for Deutsche Grammophon, Angel, London and RCA. Recipient John Hay Whitney award, Richard Wagner medal, 1963, Grammy award, 1979, Royal Opera House medal, 1988. Mem. Zeta Phi Beta, Sigma Alpha Iota. Office: Herbert H Breslin Inc 119 W 57th St New York NY 10019-2303*

BUMGARNER, DORIS CAMPBELL, town manager, finance officer; b. Lincolnton, N.C., June 23, 1945; d. Tate William and Lora (Keener) C.; m. Ralph Lowell Bumgarner, Jr., June 23, 1963; children: Ralph Lowell III, Tania Lorraine. Town clk./asst. fin. officer Town of Maiden, N.C., 1990-92, acctg. clk., 1992—, town mgr./fin. office, 1992—. Bd. dirs. Catawba County Libr. Bd. Trustees, Newton, N.C., 1989—, mem. com. Maiden Recreation Adv. Com., 1993—; donor recruiter ARC Bloodmobile, Hickory, 1985-89; participant, team organizer March of Dimes Bowling for Babies, 1993; mem. Maiden Downtown Revitalization Com., 1994-96, Maiden Spring Festival Com., 1990-96. Recipient Sheriff's award for excellence in drug edn. and awareness Catawba County Sheriff's Dept., 1993, Centennial N.C. Found. award Gov.'s office, 1991. Fellow Internat. City Mgrs. Assn., Internat. Inst. of Mcpl. Clks.; mem. Am. Assn. Profl. Bookkeepers, Maiden Area coun. Catawba County C. of C. Republican. Lutheran. Office: Town of Maiden 113 W Main St Maiden NC 28650

BUNCH, LUANN VICTORY, marketing executive; b. Mpls., May 3, 1955; d. John F. and Theresa A. (Otten) Victory; m. Dennis Bunch, Dec. 24, 1986. AA, North Hennepin Community Coll., Brooklyn Park, Minn., 1975; BA magna cum laude, St. Cloud State U., 1976; MA with high honors, Southwestern Mo. State U., 1978. Dir. pub. rels. Park Cen. Hosp., Springfield, Mo., 1977-79; dir. community rels. and devel. Mt. Carmel Med. Ctr., Pittsburg, Kans., 1980-82; dir. physician mktg. and recruiting Coord. Svcs., Wichita, 1982-85; mgr. profl. rels. Rep. Health Corp., Dallas, 1985-86; dir. mktg. Timberlawn Psychiat. Hosp., Dallas, 1987-90; chief exec. officer, mktg. and pub. rels. cons. Victory Assocs., Plano, 1991-93; dir. physician recruitment Advocate Health Care, Oak Brook, Ill., 1994—. Editor: Insight (Telestar award 1988), 1987, Direct Mail Piece (Telestar award 1988, Bronze Quill award of Excellence for Brown Bag lectr. series Internat. Assn. Bus. Communicators 1989), 1987, Inner View, 1977-78, Spectrum, 1980; host radio and TV talk shows, Pittsburg. Bd. dirs. ARC, Pittsburg, 1981; dir. Pittsburg Community Theatre, 1981; instr. Pittsburg Children's Theatre Workshop, 1981; pub. relations cons. Am. Diabetes Assn., Springfield, 1979. Recipient Applause award Tex. Soc. Mktg. and Pub. Rels., 1988-89, 90-91, Telestar award and merit award Brown Bay Series, 1990, First Pl. award Nat. Assn. Pvt. Psychiat. Hosps., 1990. Mem. Am. Mktg. Assn., Am. Soc. Mktg. and Pub. Rels., Am. Soc. Planning and Mktg., Women in Communications, Tex. Soc. Hosp. Mktg. and Pub. Rels. Roman Catholic. Home: 1087 Camellia Pl Fox River Grove IL 60021-1348 Office: Advocate Health Care 2025 Windsor Dr Oak Brook IL 60521

BUNDESEN, FAYE STIMERS, investment and management company owner, educator; b. Cedarville, Calif., Sept. 16, 1932; d. Floyd Walker and Ermina Elizabeth (Roberts) Stimers; m. Allen Eugene Bundesen, Dec. 27, 1972 (dec. 1991); children: William, David, Edward Silvius; Ted, Eric Bundesen. BA, Calif. State U.-Sacramento, 1955; MA, Calif. State U.-San Jose, 1972. Licensed real estate broker, Calif. Elem. sch. tchr. San Francisco Pub. Schs., 1955-60; elem. and jr. h.s. tchr., lang. arts specialist Sunnyvale (Calif.) Schs., 1978-83; cons. Santa Clara County Office of Edn. and Sunnyvale Sch. Dist., 1983-86; v.p. Bundesen Enterprises, Elk Grove, Calif., 1975-81, pres., 1981—. Bd. dirs. Sunnyvale Sch. Employees' Credit Union, 1983-86, v.p., 1984-86; co-chmn. Elk Grove Taxpayers Assn. for Incorporation, 1994; pres. Elk Grove/Laguna Civic League, 1994—; pers. chmn. Bethany Presbyn. Ch., 1992-95; mem. City of San Jose Tenant/Landlord Hearing Com., 1983-86, v.p., 1984-85. Mem. Assn. Supervision and Curriculum Devel., Calif. Scholarship Fedn. (life), AAUW, Calif. Apartment Assn., Nat. Apartment Assn., Calif. Assn. Realtors, Nat. Assn. Realtors, Sacramento Assn. Realtors, Sacramento Valley Apt. Assn., Soroptimist Internat. Rio Cosumnes, Elk Grove C. of C. Presbyterian. Office: PO Box 2006 Elk Grove CA 95759-2006

BUNDI, RENEE, art director, graphic designer; b. Elmont, N.Y., Apr. 20, 1962; d. Anthony Joseph and Marion Rose (Graziano) B. Student, St. John's U., 1980-84. Creative dir. Coastal Communications, N.Y.C., 1985-86; art and prodn. coord. Cahner's Pub. Co./Datamation mag., N.Y.C., 1986-87; sr. prodn. editor CMP Publs./Var Bus. Computer Sys. News, Manhasset, N.Y., 1987-89, asst. art dir., 1989-91; assoc. art dir. Varbus. CMP Publs., 1991-94; art dir. Info. Week Mag., 1994—. Recipient Print Design award Print mag., 1988, 91, 92, 93, 94, 95, Ozzie Design award Mag. Design and Prodn., 1988, 89, 90, 91. Mem. Graphic Artist Guild, Soc. Publ. Designers (Excellence in Design award 1987, 88, 89, 92, 93, 94), Alex User's Group, MacIntosh User's Group. Roman Catholic.

BUNDY, HALLIE FLOWERS, biochemist, educator; b. Santa Monica, Calif., Apr. 2, 1925; d. Douglas and Phyllis (Flowers) B. BA in Chemistry, Mt. St. Mary's Coll., L.A., 1947; MS in Biochemistry, U. So. Calif., 1955, PhD in Biochemistry, 1958. Instr. sch. medicine U. So. Calif., L.A., 1959-60; asst. prof. Mt. St. Mary's Coll., 1960-63, assoc. prof., 1963-66, prof. biochemistry, 1966-90, emeritus prof., 1990—; asst. program dir. undergrad. rshc. participation NSF, Washington, 1965-66. Contbr. rsch. articles to profl. jours. USPHS predoctoral fellow, 1955-57; NSF Sci. Faculty fellow, 1969-70; grantee NIH, 1960-66, 86-89, NSF, 1961-78, 87-89, Grad. Women in Sci., 1974. Mem. Am. Chem. Soc., Pacific Slope Biochem. Conf., Sigma Xi. Office: Mt St Mary's Coll PO Box 4338 Sunriver OR 97707-1338

BUNDY, L. LANHAM, artist; b. Austin, Tex., Sept. 6, 1961; d. Jean D. Bundy and Ann H. (Becker) Crockett. BFA, RISD, 1984. Bookstore owner Providence, 1991-93; pub. Fish-Eye Lens Press, Providence, 1985-95; contbg. editor QuixArt Jour., 1993-96; vol., cons. Very Spl. Arts, R.I., 1993-96.

BUNDY, MARY LOTHROP, retired social worker; b. Boston, Apr. 9, 1925; d. Francis B. and Eleanor (Abbott) Lothrop; m. McGeorge Bundy, June 10, 1950; children: Stephen M., Andrew L., William L., James A. AB magna cum laude, Radcliffe Coll., 1946; MSW, Hunter Coll., 1980. Assoc. dir. admissions Radcliffe Coll., Cambridge, Mass., 1949-50; clin. social worker Jewish Bd. of Family and Children's Svcs., Bklyn., 1980-84; pvt. practice N.Y.C., 1984-95; ret., 1995; vice-chmn. and trustee Radcliffe Coll., Cambridge, 1962-80, acting v.p., 1978-79 ; overseer Harvard U., Cambridge, 1971-77; bd. dirs. Corning (N.Y.) Inc., 1973—; trustee and chair Edward W. Hazen Found., N.Y.C., 1985-95; bd. dirs. Found. for Child Devel., N.Y.C., 1985—. Trustee Metropolitan Museum of Art, N.Y.C., 1968-78. Mem. Nat. Assn. Social Workers, Assn. Cert. Social Workers, Forum for Women Dirs., Phi Beta Kappa.

BUNE, KAREN LOUISE, criminal justice official; b. Washington, Mar. 6, 1954; d. Harry and Eleanor Mary (White) B. BA in Am. Studies cum laude, Am. U., 1976, MS in Adminstrn. of Justice with distinction, 1978. Notary pub., Va. Case mgr. Arlington (Va.) Alcohol Safety Action Program, 1979-94; victim specialist Office of Commonwealth Atty., Arlington, Va., 1994—; case mgr. regional rep. of case mgmt. com. of Dirs. Assn. Commn. on Va. Alcohol Safety Action Program, Richmond, 1980-81, 84-85, 88-89, mem. subcom. studying treatment issues, 1988-94; chair career guidance subcom. alumni adv. com. Sch. Pub. Affairs Am. U., Washington, 1991-94. Sch. of Justice rep. alumni adv. com. Coll. Pub. Affairs, Am. U. Washington, 1982-86, chmn. student rels., 1982-86, mem. alumni steering com., 1991—. Recipient spl. achievement award Dept. Navy, 1973, merit award Arlington County, 1986, Woman of the Yr. Am. Biog. Inst., 1990, inducted into Hall of Fame for outstanding achievement in case management. Mem. ASPA (No. Va. chpt. coun.), NAFE, APHA, AAUW, Nat. Assn. Chiefs Police (award of merit 1986), Nat. Criminal Justice Assn., Nat. Orgn. Victim Assistance, Am. Police Hall of Fame (cert. of appreciation 1985), Acad. Criminal Justice Scis., So. Criminal Justice Assn., Am. Soc. Criminology, Va. Sheriffs Inst., No. Va. Crime Prevention Assn., No. Va. Fraternal Order Police, Va. Assn. Female Execs., Internat. Platform Assn., Am. U. Alumni Assn. (immediate past pres. sch. pub. affairs chpt. 1994-96), Women of Washington, Phi Kappa Phi, Phi Alpha Alpha, Phi Delta Gamma (1st v.p. 1981-82). Home: 926 16th St S Arlington VA 22202-2606 Office: Office of Commonwealth Atty 1425 N Court House Rd Arlington VA 22201-2605

BUNIM, MARY-ELLIS, television producer; b. Northampton, Mass., July 9, 1946; d. Frank Roberts and Roslyn Dena (LaMontagne) Paxton; m. Robert Eric Bunim, Jan. 31, 1971; 1 dau., Juliana. Pres. Bunim-Murray Prodns., L.A., 1988—. exec. prodr. daily CBS-TV series Search for Tomorrow, 1976-81, As the World Turns, 1981-84, NBC-TV series Santa Barbara, 1984-86, syndicated Crime Diaries, 198, ABC-TV series Loving, 1989-90, FBC series American Families, 1990; co-creator, exec. prodr. MTV series The Real World, 1992—, Road Rules, 1995—, NBC spl. Friends and Lovers, 1994, NBC Special High School Reunion: Class of '86, 1996.

BUNKER, BERYL H., retired insurance company executive, association executive; b. Chelsea, Mass., Aug. 18, 1919; d. Albert Crocker and Eva Agnes (Norris) Hardacker; m. John Wadsworth Bunker, Oct. 31, 1942. Student, Simmons Coll., 1936-38, Boston Coll. Law, 1948-49; grad., Bentley Sch. Acctg., Boston, 1958; BBA with highest honors, Northeastern U., 1962, MBA, 1967. CFA. Legal rsch. clerk Frank Shepard Co., N.Y.C., 1938-43; cost acct. Johns Manville Corp., Pittsburg, Calif., 1943-46; studio mgr. Wheelan Studios, Boston, 1946; clerical supr. Columbian Purchasing Group, Boston, 1946-48; office mgr. Wellesley (Mass.) Coll., 1948-51; statistician Eastman Kodak Co., Rochester, N.Y., 1951-53; investment officer John Hancock Mut. Life, Boston, 1953-74; sr. v.p. John Hancock Advisers, Boston, 1974-84. Nat. bd. dirs. YWCA of the U.S.A., 1988-94, mem. World Svc. Coun., 1992—; pres. bd. dirs. Boston YWCA, 1985-87, active 1977-96; bd. chair Visiting Nurses Assn. Cape Cod, South Dennis, Mass., 1995, Old South Meeting House Mus., Boston, 1989-92; trustee Simmons Coll., 1994—. Recipient Philanthropy award Women in Devel., 1990; named Woman of Achievement, Cambridge YWCA, 1991. Mem. AARP, LWV, NOW, AAUW, Assn. Investment Mgmt. Rsch., Mass. Women Polit. Caucus, Boston Security Analysts Soc. (treas. 1973-76), Mass. Women's State Wide Legis. Network (dir. 1987), Simmons Coll. Alumnae Assn. (pres. 1989-91, Alumnae Svc. award 1984, Planned Giving award 1993), Older Women's League, The Internat. Alliance, Harwich Hist. Soc., Project Vote Smart, Women's Ednl. & Indsl. Union, Friday Forum. Home: 790 Boylston St Apt 22F Boston MA 02199-7921 also: 22 Cross St Harwich Port MA 02646-1813

BUNKER, JANICE WATERS, publisher, editor; b. Kansas City, Mo., Nov. 28, 1940; d. Clark Cannon and Martha Lucile (Reid) Waters; m. Paul D. Bunker III, Oct. 27, 1956; 1 child, Robyn Lee Charest; m. David A. Fagan, Jan. 21, 1983. Mgr. U.S. sales program Digital Equipment Corp., Maynard, Mass., 1973-91; pub., editor, founder Digital Alumni, Amherst, N.H., 1992—. EMT Amherst Rescue Squad, 1993-96. Office: Digital Alumni PO Box 789 Amherst NH 03031 Home: 2 Cross St Amherst NH 03031

BUNKERS, SUZANNE LILLIAN, writer; b. Le Mars, Iowa, Apr. 20, 1950; d. Jerome Anton and Verna Mae (Klein) B.; 1 child, Rachel Susanna. BS, Iowa State U., 1972, MA, 1974; PhD, U. Wis., 1980. Tchg. asst. Iowa State U., Ames, 1972-74, Purdue U., W. Lafayette, Ind., 1974-75; tchg. asst. U. Wis., Madison, 1975-79, lectr., 1979-80; asst. prof. Mankato (Minn.) State U., 1980-85, assoc. prof., 1985-89, prof. English, 1989—; Mem. early childhood adv. com., Mankato, Minn., 1984-85. Author: All Will Yet Be Well, 1993, In Search of Susanna, 1996, Good Earth, Black Soil, 1981; editor: The Diary of Caroline Seabury, 1991, Inscribing the Daily, 1996. Leader Troop 396 Girl Scouts Am., Mankato, Minn. 1994—. Rsch. fellow Nat. Endowment Humanities, 1986-87, Fulbright fellow, 1988, Leadership fellow Bush Found., 1995-96. Mem. AAUW (co-chair equity com. 1994-95), YWCA, MLA (del. assembly). Home: 317 Carroll St Mankato MN 56001 Office: Mankato State U Dept English Box 53 Mankato MN 56002-8400

BUNKER-SCOTT, JENNIFER NICOLE, special education educator; b. Auburn, Wash., Oct. 31, 1966; d. Gordon Brock and Sandra Kay (Opie) Bunker; m. Robert Michael Scott, Oct. 31, 1993. AA, Walla Walla (Wash.) C.C., 1987; BA in Edn., Ctrl. Wash. U., 1989. Cert. in spl. edn./deaf edn. Deaf edn. tchr./interpreter Bow Lake Elem., Burien, Wash., 1989-90; behavioral specialist Ballard (Wash.) 1st Luth., 1990-91; deaf edn. tchr. Northwest Sch. for Hearing Impaired, Seattle, 1990-91; spl. edn. tchr. United Cerebral Palsy, Seattle, 1991—; traveling edn. specialist State of Wash., Seattle, 1993—. Authot, editor: (with Vivian Downing) Memories of My Life, 1994. Softball coach Pony League, Walla Walla, 1985-86; rsch. technician/lab asst. Friends of Washoe, Ellensburg, Wash., 1987-88; vol. Counterpoint Mental Health, Seattle, 1994-95; legal adv. Geriatric Legal Rights Group, Seattle, 1994-95. Office: United Cerebral Palsy 14910 1st Ave NE Seattle WA 98155

BUNN, ANN FALOR, artist, educator; b. Toledo, Ohio, Oct. 25, 1932; d. Falor E. and Anita R. (Reisig) Smyser; m. Dorrance Parks Bunn, Aug. 13, 1955; children: David, Anita, Steven. BFA, U. Colo., 1954; postgrad., U. Denver, 1955, U. St. Thomas, Houston, 1982-83; MA in Edn., Calif. State Poly. U., Pomona, 1990. Cert. art tchr., Tex. Art instr. Port Arthur (Tex.) Ind. Sch. Dist., 1955-57; art instr. Contemporary Arts Mus., Houston, 1964-69, curator of edn., 1970-81; pvt. practice cons. visual arts edn. Houston, 1981-83, Glendora, Calif., 1983-93, Evergreen, Colo., 1993—; edn. coord. Univ. Art Mus. Calif. State U., Long Beach, 1990-93; asst. prof., lectr. art edn. Calif. State U., L.A., 1991-93. Contbr. articles to profl. jours., chpt. to book; author mus. guide: Art on View: Handbook for Educators, 1990. Recipient Outstanding Mus. Educator award Calif. Art Edn. Assn., 1991, Cert. of Appreciation, Calif. Art Edn. Assn., 1993. Mem. Nat. Art Edn. Assn., Colo. Art Edn. Assn., Evergreen Artists Assn.

BUNN, DOROTHY IRONS, court reporter; b. Trinidad, Colo., Apr. 30, 1948; d. Russell and Pauline Anna (Langowski) Irons; m. Peter Lynn Bunn; children: Kristy Lynn, Wade Allen, Russell Ahearn. Student No. Va. Community Coll., 1970-71, U. Va., Fairfax, 1971-72. Registered profl. reporter; cert. shorthand reporter. Pres., chief exec. officer Ahearn Ltd., Springfield, Va., 1970-81, Bunn & Assocs., Glenrock, Wyo., 1981—; cons. Bixby Hereford Co., Glenrock, 1981-89, co-mgr., 1989—. Del., White House Conf. on Small Bus., Washington, 1986, 95, state chair, 1995; mem. Wyo. adv. coun. Small Bus. Adminstrn., 1994—. Mem. NAFE, Am. Indian Soc., Nat. Ct. Reporters Assn., Nat. Fedn. Ind. Bus., Xcel Internat. (1st v.p., 1994-95, dir. 1995-96, 1st v.p. 1994-95), Wyo. Shorthand Reporters Assn. (chmn. com. 1984-85), Nat. Cattlewomen, Wyo. Cattlewomen (Converse County), Nat. Fedn. Ind. Businesses (guardian 1991—), Nat. Fedn. Bus. and Profl. Women (1st v.p. Casper 1994-95, pres. 1995—, pub. rels. chair, Choices chair), Xscribe Users Assn.. Avocations: art, music. Home: PO Box 1618 Bixby Hereford Co Glenrock WY 82637 Office: Bunn & Assocs 81 Bixby Rd Glenrock WY 82637

BUNT, KATHLEEN ANN, foundation administrator; b. Caldwell, Idaho, Aug. 12, 1965; d. Joseph Laverne and Judith Ann Bunt. BBA, Austin Peay State U., Clarksville, TN, 1988. Student asst. Austin Peay State U., Clarksville, Tenn., 1983-88; asst. mgr. Walgreens Co., Nashville, 1988-89; job specialist, program mgr. PENCIL Found., Nashville, 1989—. Author (program curriculum) Resume Writing, 1992. Advisor Jobs for Tenn. Grads. Tenn. Career Assn., Nashville, 1989—. Mem. Nat. Assn. Female Execs.

BUNT, LYNNE JOY, insurance broker; b. Corning, N.Y., Sept. 25, 1948; d. William Henry and Cleo Ann (Williams) Prentice. AA, Foothill Coll., 1969; ins. studies, IIAAC, IEA, WAIB, 1969. Account exec., v.p. Jardine Ins. Brokers, Inc., San Francisco, 1979—. Congregationalist. Democrat. Office: 333 Bush St San Francisco CA 94104-2806

BUNTEN, BRENDA ARLENE, geriatrics nurse; b. Paris, Ill., May 7, 1947; d. Arthur Ray Sr. and Maxine L. (Bacon) B. A in Arts and Scis., Lakeland Coll., Mattoon, Ill., 1968; ADN, Kapiolani C.C., Honolulu, 1992. Charge nurse Meml. Med. Ctr., Springfield, Ill., 1968-76, Mattoon Health Care Ctr., 1977-79; agy. nurse Kahu Malama, Inc., Honolulu, 1983; charge nurse, staff devel. coord., infection control officer Hale Nani Health Ctr., Honolulu, 1979-93, also nursing staff scheduler, supr., 1979-93; unit mgr. Randal Mill Manor, Arlington, Tex., 1994—; supr. Heritage Oaks, Arlington, Tex., 1994—; fundraiser Challenger Run Hawaii, Honolulu, 1986—; co-owner, cons. retail sales Sunset Enterprises, Honolulu, 1982—. Mem. USS Lancelot, Citizens Police Acad. Alumni Assn., Citizens Fire Dept. Alumni Assn., Alpha Kappa Psi, Beta Sigma Phi (pres. 1985-86). Home: 2009 Newbury Dr Arlington TX 76014-3616

BUNTING, CAROLYN ELLEN, middle school administrator; b. Durham, N.C., Jan. 4, 1943; d. Glenn Woodburn and Emma Lucille (Garrard) B. BA, U. N.C., Greensboro, 1965; MEd, Duke U., 1971, PhD, 1977. Cert. social studies tchr., curriculum specialist, supr./adminstr., N.C. Tchr. Greensboro Pub. Schs., 1965-68; tchr. Durham (N.C.) Pub. Schs., 1969-71, mid. sch. adminstr., 1990—; supr. student tchrs. Appalachian State U., Boone, N.C., 1973-74; pvt. practice pub. sch. cons., 1974-75; tchr., supr. Sampson County Schs., Clinton, N.C., 1975-77; prof. edn. Campbell U., Buies Creek, N.C., 1977-87; exec. N.C. Assn. Sch. Adminstrs., Raleigh, N.C., 1987-89. Contbr. articles to numerous jours. Mem. ASCD, Nat. Mid. Sch. Assn., Kappa Delta Pi, Phi Kappa Phi. Home: 214 Morreene Rd Durham NC 27705-6105

BUNT SMITH, HELEN MARGUERITE, lawyer; b. L.A., Oct. 8, 1942; d. Alan Verbanks and Nettie Virginia (Crandall) Bunt; m. Charles Robert Smith, Jan. 12, 1974; children: John, Sharon. BS, U. Calif., L.A., 1964; JD, Southwestern U., 1972. Bar: Calif. 1972; cert. secondary tchr., Calif. Tchr. L.A. City Schs., 1965-72; pvt. practice Pasadena, Calif., 1973—. Sunday sch. tchr. Lake Ave. Congrl. Ch., Pasadena; sec. Pasadena Sister Cities Com., 1994-95. Office: 465 E Union St Ste 102 Pasadena CA 91101

BURBANK, JANE RICHARDSON, Russian and European studies educator; b. Hartford, Conn., June 11, 1946; d. John and Helen Lee (West) B.; m. Frederick Cooper, Sept. 3, 1985. BA, Reed Coll., 1967; MLS, Simmons Coll., 1969; MA, Harvard U., 1971, PhD, 1981. Tchg. fellow Harvard U., Cambridge, Mass., 1976-80, asst. prof., 1981-85; asst. prof. U. Calif., Santa Barbara, 1985-86, assoc. prof., 1986-87; assoc. prof. U. Mich., Ann Arbor, 1987—, dir. Ctr. for Russian and East European Studies, 1992—; reviewer Kritika, 1983, Russian Rev., 1984, Am. Hist. Rev., 1988, 91, Jour. Modern History, 1989, 92, 93, Slavic Rev., 1990, Harvard Ukrainian Studies, 1991; presenter Comparative Study of Social Transformation seminar, U. Mich., 1990, Conf. on the Relationships between the State and Civil Soc. in Ea. Europe and Africa, Comparative Perspectives, Villa Serbelloni, Bellagio, Italy, 1990, L'viv U., Ukraine, 1990, U. Minn., 1990, Stanford (Calif.) U., 1990, 91, U. Mich., 1991, 92, 93, U. Iowa, 1991, Northwestern U., 1992. Author: Intelligentsia and Revolution: Russian Views of Bolshevism, 1917-1922, 1986; editor: Perestroika and Soviet Culture, 1989; editor Kritika, 1978-80; mem. editl. bd. Ind.-Mich. Series in Russian and East European Studies; contbr. articles to profl. jours. Fulbright-Hayes Rsch. award, 1991, Sheldon Traveling fellow Harvard U., 1977-78, Krupp Found. fellow, Ctr. for European Studies, Harvard U., 1977-78, AAUW fellow, 1980-81, Whiting fellow, 1980-81, Am. Coun. Learned Socs. fellow, 1983-84, Hoover Inst. Postdoctoral fellow, 1990-91; grantee NEH, 1984, Harvard U., 1982-84, Internat. Rsch. and Exchs. Bd., Acad. Exch. with the USSR, 1987-88, 91, U. Mich., 1990. Mem. Am. Hist. Assn., Am. Assn. for the Advancement of Slavic Studies, Social Sci. Rsch. Coun. (joint com. on Soviet studies 1988-93), Phi Beta Kappa. Office: 31 Pearce Mitchell Pl Stanford CA 94305

BURBIDGE, E. MARGARET, astronomer, educator; b. Davenport, Eng.; d. Stanley John and Marjorie (Stott) Peachey; m. Geoffrey Burbidge, Apr. 2, 1948; 1 child, Sarah. B.S., Ph.D., U. London; Sc.D. hon., Smith Coll., 1963, U. Sussex, 1970, U. Bristol, 1972, U. Leicester, 1972, City U., 1973, U. Mich., 1978, U. Mass., 1978, Williams Coll., 1979, SUNY, Stony Brook, 1985, Rensselaer Poly. Inst., 1986, U. Notre Dame, 1986, U. Chgo., 1991. Mem. staff U. London Obs., 1948-51; rsch. fellow Yerkes Obs. U. Chgo., 1951-53, Shirley Farr fellow Yerkes obs., 1957-59, assoc. prof. Yerkes Obs., 1959-62; rsch. fellow Calif. Inst. Tech., Pasadena, 1955-57; mem. Enrico Fermi Inst. for Nuclear Studies, 1957-62; prof. astronomy dept. physics U. Calif. San Diego, 1964—, univ. prof., 1984—; dir. Royal Greenwich Obs. (Herstmonceux Castle), Hailsham, Sussex, Eng., 1984-90; rsch. prof. dept. physics U. Calif., San Diego, 1990—; Lindsay Meml. lectr. Goddard Space Flight Ctr., NASA, 1985; Abby Rockefeller Mauze prof. MIT, 1968; David Elder lectr. U. Strathclyde, 1972; V. Gildersleeve lectr. Barnard Coll., 1974; Jansky lectr. Nat. Radio Astronomy Observatory, 1977; Brode lectr. Whitman Coll., 1986. Author: (with G. Burbidge) Quasi-Stellar Objects, 1967; editor: Observatory mag., 1948-51; mem. editorial bd.: Astronomy and Astrophysics, 1969—. Recipient (with husband) Warner prize in Astronomy, 1959, Bruce Gold medal Astronomy Soc. Pacific, 1982; hon. fellow Univ. Coll., London, Girton Coll., Lucy Cavendish Coll., Cambridge; U.S. Nat. medal of sci., 1984; Sesquicentennial medal Mt. Holyoke Coll., 1987, Einstein medal World Cultural Coun., 1988. Fellow Royal Soc., Nat. Acad. Scis. (chmn. sect. 12 astronomy 1986), Am. Acad. Arts and Scis., Royal Astron. Soc.; mem. Am. Astron. Soc. (v.p. 1972-74, pres. 1976-78; Henry Norris Russell lectr. 1984), Internat. Astron. Union (pres. commn. 28 1970-73), Grad. Women Sci. (nat. hon. mem.). Office: U Calif-San Diego Ctr Astrophysics Space Scis Mail Code # 0111 La Jolla CA 92093

BURCH, JUDITH ANN, recreation therapist; b. Camp Chafee, Ark., June 3, 1955; d. Frankie Gene and Margaret Anne (Cathcart) B. BS in Pks., Recreation & Conservation, East Carolina U., 1977. Cert. therapeutic recreation specialist Nat. Coun. for Therapeutic Recreation. Chief expressive therapy Cumberland Psychiat. Hosp., Fayetteville, N.C., 1978-80; recreation therapist VA Hosp., Augusta, Ga., 1980-91, San Antonio, 1991—; adapted ski instr. Nat. Vets. Winter Sports Clinic, Crested Butte, Colo., 1986—; vol. Warm Springs Rehab. Hosp., San Antonio, 1991—. Contbr. chpt. to book. Mem. Delta Zeta Sorority Alumnae (v.p. 1995-96). Home: 11500 Huebner Rd Apt 1708 San Antonio TX 78230 Office: VA Hosp 7400 Milton Mintor Blvd San Antonio TX 78284

BURCH, JUDITH VARNEY, art dealer; b. Kewanee, Ill., Sept. 16, 1937; d. Harley Roosevelt and Elsie (Pendelton) Varney; m. Dana DeWitt Burch, Jr., Dec. 30, 1961; children: Dana DeWitt III, Jennifer Pendleton, Palmer Varney. BA, Duke U., 1958. Docent emeritus Va. Mus. Fine Art, Richmond, 1978-93; owner Arcic Inuit Art, Richmond, 1985—; curator, lectr. in field; judge arts festival Econ. Devel./Can., Rankin Inlet, 1995; leader Invit Studies Conf., St. John's, Newfoundland, 1996.

BURCHARD, ELLEN WILLIAMS, actress, producer, artist, writer; b. Newport, R.I., June 13, 1913; d. Clarence Raymond and Mary Christine (Stewart) Williams; m. John Church Burchard, Feb. 6, 1943; 1 child, John Church. studied acting U. Wis., 1944, Stella Adler Studio, 1954-56, Herbert Berghof Studio, 1957-65, Harold Clurman's Profl. Acting Classes, N.Y.C., 1960-62. Actress on Broadway, films and TV, also in Rome and London; founder Carriage House Theatre, Little Compton, R.I., 1958, producer, artistic dir., actress Pro Summer Repertory Co., 1958-76; off-Broadway producer, N.Y.C., 1958-76; producer, artistic dir. Actors Repertory Co., Little Compton, 1959-94; actress R.I. Playwrights Theatre Summer Festival, Providence, 1985; lyricist Morning Song, 1979; playwright Marguerite, 1978, Scenes from the Past, 1979; off-Broadway roles include Journey to Endor, 1987-88, Ashen Victors, 1993-94, Love Letters, 1994; editor (poetry) To Diana, 1985. Founder, pres. Young Women's Rep. Club, Newport, 1935-37, 46-54, Little Compton Rep. Club, 1946-57, Newport Players Guild, 1936-42, 46-52; founder, 1st v.p. New Eng. Council Young Reps., 1932-37; Young Rep. Nat. Committeewoman from R.I., 1932-43. Mem. Actors Equity Assn., Screen Actors Guild, AFTRA, R.I. Short Story Club (pres. 1982-85), R.I. Water Color Soc., Newport Art Mus., Westport Art Club, Bus. Womens Club (charter, Newport). Congregationalist. Club: Mosaic (charter mem.) (Newport).

BURCHARD, RACHAEL C., playwright; b. Hendersonville, N.C., Aug. 27, 1921; d. Henry Homer and Olive (Gowan) Ballenger; m. Waldo W. Burchard, May 24, 1945 (dec. Dec. 1985); children: Gina Michel, Petrea Celeste, Margot Theresa, Stuart Gregory. BA, Linfield Coll., 1945; MA in English, No. Ill. U., 1966. Cert. secondary tchr., Calif. Tchr. English and history San Diego H.S./Jr. Coll., 1945-46; tchr. English and social studies Vallejo (Calif.) Jr. H.S., 1947-48; demonstration tchr. U. Calif., Berkeley, 1948; English tchr. El Cerrito (Calif.) H.S., 1948-50; tchr. English, drama Acalanes H.S., Lafayette, Calif., 1951-53; demonstration tchr. No. Ill. Univ., Dekalb, 1958-70, supr. instr., 1970-72; ednl. cons. Ill. Office of Edn., Dekalb, 1978-80; adj. prof. Collin County C.C., Plano, Tex., 1989. Author: John Updike: Yea Sayings, 1971, Hallelujah Hopscotch, 1986, Green Figs and Tender Grapes, 1985, We the Real People I and II, 1991, 93, Troupers and Tramps, 1994; contbr. articles and poetry to numerous jours. Recipient Comm. Treasure award Portland Gen. Electric, Yamhill County, 1995; Oreg. Book awards finalist Literary Arts, Inc., Portland, 1994, Kay Snow awards finalist Willamette Writers, Portland, 1991, various poetry awards. Home: 1662 SW Bonnie Jean Pl McMinnville OR 97128

BURCHENAL, JOAN RILEY, science educator; b. N.Y.C., Dec. 11, 1925; d. Wells Littlefield and Bertha Barclay (Fahys) Riley; m. Joseph Holland Burchenal, Mar. 20, 1948; children: Elizabeth Payne, Joan Littlefield, Barbara Fahys, Caleb Wells, David Holland, Joseph Emory Barclay. BA, Vassar Coll., 1946; MAT, Yale U., 1971; MA, Fairfield U., 1981. Sci. tchr. New Canaan (Conn.) Country Sch., 1968-69, Low Heywood Sch., Stamford,

Conn., 1968-69, The Thomas Sch., Rowayton, Conn., 1972-73; sci. tchr. Darien Bd. Edn., Conn., 1973-91, ret.; mem. panel on grants for tchrs. enhancement program NSF, 1987, 92. Bd. dirs., chmn. standards com. A Better Chance, Darien, 1985—; bd. dirs. Darien Nature Ctr., 1975-91, Darien Audubon Soc., 1978-86, Darien LWV, 1951-62; hon. chmn. Darien Sci. Fair, 1986; mem. steering com. Holly Pond Saltmarsh Conservation Com., 1968-71; mem. acad. courses com. Darien Cmty. Assn., 1964-71, chmn., 1971; trustee Garrison Forest Sch., 1959-62; bd. dirs. Alumnae and Alumni Vassar Coll.; rep. Town Meeting of Darien, 1993—; cmty. rep. K-12 Sci. Curriculum Com., 1994—; elder First Presbyn. Ch. of New Canaan, 1994—, Stephen min., 1994—. Recipient Presdl. award for excellence in sci. teaching Nat. Sci. Tchrs. Assn., NSF, Washington, 1985. Mem. AAAS, N.Y. Acad. Sci., Nat. Assn. Biology Tchrs., Nat. Sci. Tchrs. Assn., Assn. Presdl. Awardees in Sci. Teaching (nominating com. 1987-90), Cosmopolitan Club, Ausable Club, Noroton Yacht Club, Phi Beta Kappa. Republican. Presbyterian. Home: 18 Juniper Rd Darien CT 06820-5707

BURCHER, HILDA BEASLEY, librarian; b. Va., June 5, 1938; d. Andrew and Virgie (Hall) Beasley; m. Eugene Stearns Burcher, June 18, 1960 (dec.); children: Eugene Andrew, Mark Eric. BA in English, U. Va., 1960; MSLS, U. Md., 1967. Tchr's. profl. cert., libr's. cert. Va. English tchr. Fairfax (Va.) County Pub. Schs., 1960-65, reference libr., 1969-75; head libr. St. Agnes Sch., Alexandria, Va., 1975-91; reference libr. part-time Fairfax Pub. Libr., 1987-96; libr. St. Stephens-St. Agnes Mid. Sch., Alexandria, 1991-95. Mem. Alexandria (Va.) Symphony League, 1987-96. Mem. ALA, Va. Ednl. Media Assn., Met. Washington Ind. Sch. Libr.'s Assn., Va. Libr. Assn. (sch. chairperson 1994), Beta Phi Mu.

BURDEN, JEAN (PRUSSING), poet, writer, editor; b. Waukegan, Ill., Sept. 1; d. Harry Frederick and Miriam (Biddlecom) Prussing; m. David Charles Burden, 1940 (div. 1949). BA, U. Chgo., 1936. Sec. John Hancock Mutual Life Ins. Co., Chgo., 1937-39, Young & Rubicam, Inc., Chgo., 1939-41; editor, copywriter Domestic Industries, Inc., Chgo., 1941-45; office mgr. O'Brion Russell & Co., Los Angeles, 1948-55; adminstr. pub. relations Meals for Millions Found., Los Angeles, 1955-65; editor Stanford Research Inst., South Pasadena, Calif., 1965-66; propr. Jean Burden & Assocs., Altadena, Calif., 1966-82; lectr. poetry to numerous colls. and univs., U.S., 1963—; supr. poetry workshop Pasadena City Coll., Calif., 1960-62, 66, U. Calif. at Irvine, 1975; also pvt. poetry workshops. Author: Naked as the Glass, 1963, Journey Toward Poetry, 1966, The Cat You Care For, 1968, The Dog You Care For, 1968, The Bird You Care For, 1970, The Fish You Care For, 1971, A Celebration of Cats, 1974, The Classic Cats, 1975, The Woman's Day Book of Hints for Cat Owners, 1980, 84, Taking Light from Each Other, 1992; poetry editor: Yankee Mag, 1955—; pet editor: Woman's Day Mag, 1973-82; contbr. numerous articles to various jours. and mags. MacDowell Colony fellow, 1973, 74, 76; Recipient Silver Anvil award Pub. Relations Soc. of Am., 1969, 1st prize Borestone Mountain Poetry award, 1963, Gold Crown award for lit. achievement, 1989. Mem. Poetry Soc. Am., Acad. Am. Poets, Authors Guild. Address: 1129 Beverly Way Altadena CA 91001-2517

BURDETT, BARBRA ELAINE, biology educator; b. Lincoln, Ill., Mar. 18, 1947; d. Robert Marlin and Klaaska Johanna Baker; m. Gary Albert Burdett, Sept. 27, 1968; children: Bryan Robert, Heather Lea, Amanda Rose. AA, Lincoln Coll., 1981; postgrad., Ill. State U. Edn. Core, 1982-83; BS, Millikin U., 1985; postgrad., Western U., 1994—. Cert. tchr., Ill. Tchr. advanced placement biology, botany and human physiology Brown County H.S., Mt. Sterling, Ill., 1985-95; tchr. biology and algebra Pleasant Plains (Ill.) H.S., 1995—; dir. Drama Club, Brown County H.S., 1988-90, dir. sci. fairs; ednl. advisor Nat. Young Leaders Conf. Author: Misty White, 1991, Possums Sing, 1994. Sponsor Children, Inc., Richmond, Va., 1985—, Internat. Wildlife Coalition, North Falmouth, Mass., 1991—; vol. Vets. Hosp., St. Louis, 1988—. Mem. ASCD, Nat. Assn. Biology Tchrs. (Biology Tchr. of Yr. in Ill. 1994), Ill. Sci. Tchrs. Assn., Phi Delta Kappa (newsletter editor 1990), Phi Theta Kappa. Episcopalian.

BURDETT, PHYLLIS W., secondary education educator; b. Swainsboro, Ga., Nov. 26, 1950; d. John David and Idell (Hudson) Walters; divorced; children: Amy Ladell, David Lewis. BA magna cum laude, Tift Coll., 1971; MEd, Ga. Coll., 1978; postgrad., Ga. State U., 1995—. Case worker child welfare Bibb County Dept. Family & Children Svcs., Macon, Ga., 1971-73; tchr. Houston County Bd. Edn., Warner Robins, Ga., 1975-82, 93—, Windsor Acad., Macon, 1982-93; literacy tutor Mid. Ga. Vocat. Tech., Warner Robins, 1994; vol reader GARR, Macon, 1990-91; adj. faculty Mercer U., Macon, 1993-95, Ga. Mil. Coll., Warner Robins, 1994-95, Macon Coll., 1987-94. Sponsor Interact-Jr. Rotary, Northside High Sch., 1993-95. Recipient Golden Pen award Macon Telegraph, 1984. Mem. NCTE, GCTE, Habitat for Humanity, Theta Chi Omega. Methodist. Office: Northside HS 126 Green St Warner Robins GA 31093-2604

BURDETTE, JANE ELIZABETH, nonprofit association executive, consultant; b. Huntington, W.Va., Aug. 17, 1955; d. C. Richard and Jewel Kathryn (Wagner) B. AAS, Parkersburg Community Coll., W.Va., 1976; BA, Glenville State Coll., W.Va., 1978; MA, W.Va. U., 1984. Fund raiser, recruiter Muscular Dystrophy Assn., Charleston, W.Va., 1973, 74, 75; sec., bookkeeper Nationwide Ins. Co., Parkersburg, 1975; v.p. Burdette Funeral Home, Parkersburg, 1976-85; intake and referral specialist Wood County Sheltered Workshop, Parkersburg, 1984-85; exec. dir. YWCA, Parkersburg, 1985-91; cons. in field, 1991—. Bd. dirs. Sheltered Workshop, Parkersburg, 1982-86, Western Dist. Guidance Ctr., Parkersburg, 1984-94; vol. St. Joseph's Hosp., 1991—; mem. W.Va. Coun. Ind. Living, 1992-94; mem. W.Va Muscular Distrophy Assn. task force on disability issues, 1992—; bd. advisors, vice chmn. Parkersburg Community Coll., 1980-89, Domestic Violence Interdisciplinary adv. com., 1987, Just Say No, 1987-91; chmn. Wood County Commn. on Crime, Delinquency and Corrections, Parkersburg, 1985—; chmn. Mid Ohio Valley United Fund Agy., 1986 Heads; v.p. Jr. League of Parkersburg, 1989—; mem. Sanctuary Soc., 1991—, All Saints Guild, 1991-95, St. Margaret Mary Parish Coun., 1992—; bd. dirs., v.p. Cmty. Svc. Coun., 1985-96; bd. dirs. Parkersburg Transit Authority, 1994—; liaison Gov. Commn. on Disabled Persons, Charleston, W.Va., 1981-85; mem. Career Adv. Network, 1987-91; treas. W.Va. Women's Conf., 1987; exec. com. W.Va. chpt. Muscular Dystrophy Assn., 1987—; mem. We've Been There Parent Support Group, 1987-90; v.p. A Spl. Wish Found., 1988—; mem. Parkersburg Consumer Adv. Group; mem. founding com. Banquet of Wealth, 1988-91; bd. dirs. Horizon's Ind. Living Ctr., v.p., 1990—; past transition plan team leader Wood County Bd. Edn.; past liason Internat. Yr. Disabled Persons; past treas. and program chmn. Gov.'s Conf.; former pres. Y Teen Club, YWCA; former adv. com. Mountwood Pk. White Oak Village, Organ Donor Com., 1989. Named Miss Wheelchair W.Va., 1981, Outstanding Young Woman of Yr. for W.Va., 1981, Outstanding Young Woman of the Yr, 1986; recipient Kenneth Hieges award Muscular Dystrophy Assn., 1982, Outstanding Citizen award Frat. Order of Police, 1984, Community Service award Moose Lodge, 1995, Cert. Appreciation State W.Va., Gov. Jay Rockefeller, Cert. Appreciation Am. Legion Aux., Trail of New Beginning award, Banquet of Wealth Trial Blazer award YWCA/Altrusa, 1989, Personal Achievement award for W.Va., MDA, 1993, 94, Mary Harriman Community Leadership award Jr. League Internat., 1994; named W.Va.'s Disabled Profl. Woman of Yr. Pilot Internats., 1989, Hometown Hero Sta. WSAZ-TV, 1993, One Who Makes a Difference, Sta. WTAP, 1994, Profl. and Bus. Woman's Internat. Hall of Fame, 1995;. Mem. NAFE, Toastmasters (Comm. and Leadership award 1989). Democrat. Roman Catholic. Avocation: designing. Home: 2500 Brooklyn Dr Parkersburg WV 26101-2913

BURDETTE, MARY KATHRYN, business owner; b. Wheeling, W.Va., Aug. 31, 1962; d. C. Richard and Jewel W. (Wagner) B. Student, W.Va. U., 1993-95, Marshall U., 1990. Mgr. Russell's Tuxedo, Columbus, Ohio; asst. mgr. 9th St. Bridal, Columbus; sales rep. Stone & Thomas, Vienna, W.Va., 1990-92; BRC clk. S.W. Resources, Parkersburg, W.Va., 1992-94; owner, manager Elite Bridal & Formals, Vienna, 1995—. Mem. Cmty. Svc. Coun., MS Assocs. Republican. Roman Catholic. Home: 2500 Brooklyn Dr Parkersburg WV 26101 Office: Elite Bridal & Formals 1007 Grand Central Ave Vienna WV 26105

BURGAR, RUBY RICH, college health service nurse; b. Boardman, N.C., Sept. 29, 1908; d. William Hardy and Lena (Carter) Rich; m. William Edward Burgar, June 29, 1935 (div. 1940). Diploma, Baker Sanatorium Sch. Nursing, 1929; BA in Sociology, Occidental Coll., 1955; postgrad., UCLA, 1957-64. RN, Calif. Indsl. nurse Manville-Jenkes Co., Gastonia, N.C., 1929-30; pub. health nurse Hampshire County Dept. Health, W.Va., 1931-32; staff nurse USPHS, San Francisco, 1932-35, Emergency Hosp., Washington, 1940-41, Queen's Hosp., Honolulu, 1941, St. Francis Hosp., San Francisco, 1941, Monterey (Calif.) Hosp., 1941-42; staff nurse, then head nurse Emmons Student Health Svc., Occidental Coll., L.A., 1942-66, nurse dir., 1966-74, relief nurse, 1976-77. Active L.A. chpt. ARC, 1952-91. Staff nurse USN, 1930-31; jr. nurse officer res. USPHS, 1954-74. Recipient Clara Barton medallion ARC, 1977, 40 Yr. pin, 1992; named Vol. of Yr. Am. Bapt. Home, 1992-93. Fellow Am. Coll. Health Assn. (emeritus; Ruth E. Boyington award 1968, Edward E. Hitchcock award 1971, Cert. of Appreciation 1993); mem. ANA, Pacific Coast Coll. Health Assn. (exec. dir. emeritus 1987, Ruby Rich Burgar Svc. award established 1977), Calif. Nurses Assn., Nat. League Nursing (charter), Calif. League for Nursing, L.A. Lung Assn., L.A. County Heart Assn., L.A. Art Mus., Alpha Tau Delta. Presbyterian.

BURGER, JILL PARSONS, librarian, researcher; b. Troy, N.Y., Sept. 30, 1969; d. Howard Kenwood and Angeline Marie (Laiacona) Parsons; m. James Jeffrey Burger. BA magna cum laude, SUNY, Buffalo, 1991; MLS, SUNY, Albany, 1995. Libr., weekly computer columnist The Record Newspaper, Troy, N.Y., 1993-95; info. specialist Norton Co., Watervliet, N.Y., 1995—. Mem. Spl. Libr. Assn. Office: Norton Co PO Box 808 Troy NY 12181-0808

BURGER, PAULA, artist; b. Novogrudek, Poland, July 27, 1934; came to U.S., 1949; d. Wolf and Sarah (Ginenski) Koladicki; m. David Zapiler, Nov. 25, 1951 (div. 1978); children: Susan, Freda A., Steven M.; m. Samuel Burger, Apr. 5, 1981. Student, U. Denver, 1977-78, U. Colo., 1979, Art Students League, Denver, 1989-91. Lic. health care adminstr., real estate agt., Colo. Artist Denver, 1978—; Holocaust survivor lectr. One-woman and group shows include U. Denver Law Libr., 1992, 94, Town Hall Arts Ctr., Colo., 1993-94, Jewish Women & Art, Colo., 1994, Cross Currents Gallery, Ill., 1991, Creative Design Gallery, Colo., 1990, Art Zone, Colo., 1990-93; represented in permanent collections at U. Denver Law Sch. Libr., BMH Congregation, Colo., Landmark Edn., Colo., Zapiler & Ferris Attys. at Law, Colo. State Capitol. Mem. Denver Art Mus., Mus. Modern Art N.Y. Studio: 160 S Monaco Pky Denver CO 80224-1125

BURGESON, JOYCE ANN, retired travel agency official; b. Jamestown, N.Y., Sept. 10, 1936; d. Walter Edward and Marion (Cree) Van Horn; m. David G. Burgeson, Sept. 10, 1955; children: Kathalene, Donna, Jeffrey, Karen, Christine. AS, Empire State Coll., SUNY, Saratoga Springs, 1990. Bookkeeper Burgeson Wholesale, Jamestown, 1962-88; realtor assoc. Kote Realty, Jamestown, 1982-89; real estate appraiser Goldome Bank, Jamestown, 1986-89; travel saleswoman, tour escort Cert. Travel Tours, Jamestown, 1983-90, 96—, Travelhost of Jamestown, 1990-95; payroll mgr. The Resource Ctr., Jamestown, 1988-95; prin. Burgeson Bus. Seminars, Jamestown, N.Y., 1990—. Mem. bd. Maple Grove H.S., Bemus Point, N.Y., 1979-82; mem. adminstrv. bd. 1st United Meth. Ch., Jamestown, 1985-95; cert. lay spkr. United meth. Ch., 1987—; mem. investment com. Jamestown Audubon Soc. Mem. Toastmasters Internat., Order of Vikings. Home: 88 Fluvanna Ave Jamestown NY 14701-9791 Office: Burgeson Bus Seminars 3280 W Oak Hill Rd Jamestown NY 14701-9791

BURGESS, ELEANOR CHANCE, engineering firm executive; b. Cambridge, Eng., Dec. 11, 1938; d. Britton Chance and Jane Lindenmayer; m. James Burgess; B.S., U. Pa., 1960; M.S., Columbia U., 1972; children—Jennifer, Bradford, Hannah. Founder, pres. Offshore Devices, Inc., Peabody, Mass., 1973-90; pres. Phosphoenergetics, Phila., 1986; owner Naval War Coll. Bookstore, 1987-92; bd. dirs. Non-Invasive Methods, Inc., chmn. 1990-93, Non Invasive Techs., Inc., 1993—, Fabric Workshop/Mus., 1994—. Home: 205 David Ln Marathon FL 33050-2917 Office: 12 Burch Dr Morris Plains NJ 07950

BURGESS, MARJORIE LAURA, protective services official; b. Whitakers, N.C., Nov. 24, 1928; d. Benjamin and Laura Lenora (Ford) Harrison; m. Bonus David Dixon, July 24, 1948 (div. Apr. 1970); children: David Kingsley (dec.), Terence David, Michael Jerome; m. William A. Burgess, June 6, 1970 (div. July 1976). AS in Correction Adminstrn., John Jay Coll. Criminal, Justice, N.Y.C., 1971; BA in Social Scis., John Jay Coll Criminal Justice, N.Y.C., 1972, postgrad. in pub. adminstrn., 1973-75. Correction officer N.Y. State Dept. Correction, Bedford Hills, N.Y., 1959-67, correction sgt., 1967-73, correction lt., 1973-82, 86-90, capt., 1982-86; ret., 1990. Vol. intergenerational program Martin Luther King Srs. Ctr. Mem. AAUW, Am. Correctional Assn., Alumni Assn. John Jay Coll., The Smithsonian Assocs., Retired Pub. Employees Assn., AARP. Democrat. Baptist.

BURGESS, MARY ALICE (MARY ALICE WICKIZER), publisher; b. San Bernardino, Calif., June 21, 1938; d. Russell Alger and Wilma Evelyn (Swisher) Wickizer; m. Michael Roy Burgess, Oct. 15, 1976; children from previous marriage: Richard Albert Rogers, Mary Louise Rogers Reynnells. AA, Valley Coll., San Bernardino, 1967; BA, Calif. State U., San Bernardino, 1975, postgrad., 1976-79; postgrad., U. Calif., Riverside, 1976-79. Lic. real estate salesman, Calif.; real estate broker, Calif. Sec.-treas. Lynwyck Realty & Investment, San Bernardino, 1963-75; libr. asst. Calif. State U., San Bernardino, 1974-76, purchasing agt., 1976-81; co-pub. The Borgo Press, San Bernardino, 1975—. Co-pub: (with Robert Reginald) Science Fiction and Fantasy Book Review, 1979-80; co-author (with M.R. Burgess) The Wickizer Annals: The Descendents of Conrad Wickizer of Luzerne County, Pennsylvania, 1983, (with Douglas Menville and Robert Reginald) Futurevisions: The New Golden Age of the Science Fiction Film, 1985, (with Jeffrey M. Elliot and Robert Reginald) The Arms Control, Disarmament and Military Science Dictionary, 1989, (with Michael Burgess) The House of the Burgesses, 2d edit., 1994; author: The Campbell Chronicles: A Genealogical History of the Descendants of Samuel Campbell of Chester County, Pennsylvania, 1989, (with Boden Clarke) The Work of Katherine Kurtz, 1992-93, (with Michael Burgess and Daryl F. Mallett) State and Province Vital Records Guide; editor: Cranberry Tea Room Cookbook, Still The Frame Holds, Defying the Holocaust, Risen from the Ashes: A Story of the Jewish Displaced Persons in the Aftermath of World War II, Being a Sequel to Survivors (Jacob Biber), 1989, Ray Bradbury: Dramatist (Ben P. Indick), 1989, Across the Wide Missouri: The Diary of a Journey from Virginia to Missouri in 1819 and Back Again in 1821, with a Description of the City of Cincinnati, (James Brown Campbell), Italian Theatre in San Francisco, Into the Flames: The Life Story of a Righteous Gentile, Jerzy Kosinski: The Literature of Violation, The Little Kitchen Cookbook, Victorian Criticism of American Writers, 1990, The Magic That Works: John W. Campbell and The American Response to Technology, 1993, Libido into Literature: The "Primera Época" of Benito Pérez Galdós, 1993, A Triumph of the Spirit: Stories of Holocaust Survivors, 1994, A Way Farer in a World in Upheaval, 1993, William Eastlake: High Desert Interlocutor, 1993, The Price of Paradise: The Magazine Career of F. Scott Fitgerald, 1993, The Little Kitchen Cookbook, rev. edit., 1994, An Irony of Fate: William March, 1994, Hard-Boiled Heretic: Ross Macdonald, 1994, We The People!, 1994, The Chinese Economy, 1995, Voices of the River Plate, 1995, Chaos Burning on My Brow, 1995; co-editor and pub. (with Robert Reginald) of all Borgo Press publs.; also reviewer, indexer, researcher and editor of scholarly manuscripts. Chmn. new citizens Rep. Women, San Bernardino, 1967; libr. San Bernardino Geneal. Soc., 1965-67; vol. Boy Scout Am., Girl Scouts U.S., Camp Fire Girls, 1960s. Recipient Real Estate Proficiency award Calif. Dept. Real Estate, San Bernardino, 1966. Mem. City of San Bernardino Hist. and Pioneer Soc., Calif. State U. Alumni Assn., Cecil County (Md.) Hist. Soc., Gallia County (Ohio) Hist. and Geneal. Soc., DAR (membership and geneal. records chmn. 1964-66, registrar and vice regent San Bernardino chpt. 1965-67). Office: The Borgo Press PO Box 2845 San Bernardino CA 92406-2845

BURGESS, MYRTLE MARIE, retired lawyer; b. Brainerd, Minn., May 3, 1921; d. Charles Dana and Mary Elzaida (Thayer) Burgess. BA, San Francisco State U., 1947; JD, Hastings Coll. Law, 1950. Bar: Calif. 1951. Pvt. practice law, San Francisco, 1951-52, Reedley, Calif., 1952—; judge pro tem Fresno County Superior Ct., 1974-77; now owner/operator Hotel Burgess. Bd. dirs. Reedley Indsl. Site Devel. Found., 1970-81; dir., 2d v.p. Kings Canyon unit Calif. Republican Assembly, 1973-75; pres., bd. dirs. Sierra Community Concert Assn., Reedley council Girl Scouts U.S.A., 1955-56, Fresno Cmty. Concert Assn., 1995—; commr. Fresno City-County Commn. Status of Women; bd. dirs., treas. Reedley Downtown Assn., 1983—; bd. dirs. Kinship Program, 1988; bd. dirs., sec. Kings View Found., bd. dirs. Calif. Hotel Motel Assn., 1993—. Recipient award for remodeling and preservation of old bldg. Fresno Hist. Soc., 1975, others. Mem. ABA, Calif. Bar Assn., Fresno County Bar Assn., World Jurist Assn., Am. Trial Lawyers, Reedley C. of C. (bd. dirs. 1958-63, 87-91, Woman of Yr. 1971, Athenian award 1988). Republican. Presbyterian. Clubs: Bus. and Profl. Women's (pres.). Lodge: Order Eastern Star. Office: 1107 G St Reedley CA 93654-3003

BURGESS, NANCY JO, elementary education educator; b. Alva, Okla., Jan. 11, 1953; d. Leonard Ray and Helena Bertha (Schick) Nelson; m. Dennis Wayne Burgess, May 20, 1975 (dec. Sept. 1992); children: Justin Dallas, Tia Denise. B in Music Edn., Southwestern Okla. State U., 1975. Music tchr. grades K-12 Aline/Cleo Springs, Okla., 1976-77; music tchr. grades 1-5 Hickok Sch. Unified Sch. Dist. 214, Ulysses, Kans., 1977-78; music tchr. grades 1-5 and trainable mentally handicapped Red Rock Sch. Unified Sch. Dist. 214, Ulysses, 1980—; music tchr. grades 6 and TMH Joyce/Kepley Sch., Ulysses, 1983—. Dir. ch. choir Grace Luth. Ch., Ulysses, 1987-90, Christian bd. edn., 1990-94, youth sponsor, 1992—; site coun. mem. H.S., Ulysses, 1993—. Named Outstanding Educator, Grant County C. of C., 1987. Mem. NEA, KNEA, Kans. Music Educators Assn., GCTA. Office: USD 214 111 S Baughman St Ulysses KS 67880-2402

BURGESS, RUTH LENORA VASSAR, speech and language educator; b. Pune, India, Aug. 6, 1939; d. Theodore R. and F. Estelle (Barnett) Vassar; m. Stanley Milton Burgess, Feb. 26, 1960; children: John Bradley, Stanley Matthew, Scott Vassar, Heidi Amanda Elizabeth, Justin David. BS in Edn., Tex. Tech. U., 1960; MA, U. Mo., 1968, PhD, 1979. Speech therapist Inkster (Mich.) Pub. Schs., 1961-62; mid. sch. tchr. Strafford (Mo.) Pub. Schs., 1962-63; speech therapist Fulton (Mo.) Pub. Schs., 1967-68; speech-lang. clinician Springfield (Mo.) Pub. Schs., 1963-66; asst. prof. Evangel Coll., Springfield, 1968-76; prof. curriculum and instruction S.W. Mo. State U., Springfield, 1976—, dir. Ctr. Rsch. and Svc., 1990—; mem. sci. adv. bd. Internat. Ctr. Enhancement of Jerusalem, Israel, 1993-96; field reviewer Dept. Edn., Washington, 1993-96, U.S. Vocat. Rehab., Washington, 1993, 94, 96; mem. evaluation team Title I Springfield Schs., 1994. Author: The Status of the Educational Resource Teacher, 1981; editor The Learner in the Process, 1978-80; contbr. articles to profl. jours. Ex-officio bd. dirs. Orphanage Assn., Pune, 1968—; mem. Kodaikanal-Woodstock Alumni Assn., Atlanta, 1956—; mem. exec. coun. Women Issues Network, Springfield, 1993—. Grantee Dept. Edn., 1978-83, 90-92, Dept. Elem. and Secondary Edn., 96, Mellon Found., 1988-90. Mem. AAUW, ASCD, Am. Speech, Lang. and Hearing Assn. (cert.), Internat. Assn. for Cognitive Edn. (field editor 1990-94). Office: SW Mo State U Dir Svc & Rsch 901 S National Ave Springfield MO 65804-0027

BURGESS, SANDRA JEAN, marketing consultant; b. Cleve., Sept. 26, 1953; d. Roy Thomas and Mary Lois (Quardits) B. BA in Polit. Sci., Oakland U., 1975; MBA, Mich. State U., 1990. Porject supr., publ. coord., asst. editor, writer William Beaumont Hosp., Royal Oak, Mich., 1977-86; editl. supr. St. Clair Health Corp., Detroit, 1986-88; owner Burgess Editl. Svcs., Troy, Mich., 1986—. Bd. dirs. Mich. State U. Advanced Mgmt. Program Alumni Club, East Lansing, 1993-95; chair Boys and Girls Club Troy, 1995—. Mem. Am. Advt. Fedn., Aircraft Club Detroit, Greater Detroit C. of C., Troy C. of C. (chmn. 1995—), Women in Communication. Lutheran.

BURGESS, VIRGINIA DIANE FORMANOWICZ, middle school English language educator; b. Dunkirk, N.Y., Mar. 21, 1959; d. Daniel Robert and Jacqueline Ann (Lancaster) Formanowicz; m. Laroy Carlton Burgess Jr., Oct. 9, 1982; 1 child, Elizabeth. BA in English cum laude, SUNY, Fredonia, 1980; MS in Edn., SUNY, Geneseo, 1986. 7th and 8th grade English tchr. Midlakes Mid. Sch., Phelps, N.Y., 1981-82, 84—; 7th-9th grade English tchr. Brockton (N.Y.) Ctrl. Sch., 1982-83; mem. gender equity com. Midlakes Mid. Sch., Phelps, 1992-94, mem. mentor tchr., 1994. Mem. Nat. Coun. Tchrs. English, N.Y. State English Coun., N.Y. State United Tchrs. Democrat. Roman Catholic. Office: Midlakes Mid Sch 1550 Rte 488 Clifton Springs NY 14432

BURGETT, BRENDA See CURKENDALL, BRENDA IRENE

BURK, SYLVIA JOAN, petroleum landman, freelance writer; b. Dallas, Oct. 16, 1928; d. Guy Thomas and Sylvia (Herrin) Ricketts; m. R. B. Murray, Jr., Sept. 7, 1951 (div. Jan. 1961); children: Jeffery Randolph, Brian BeVaughn; m. Bryan Burk, Apr. 26, 1973. BA, So. Meth. U., Dallas, 1950, MLA, 1974; postgrad. U. So. Calif., 1973-74. Cert. profl. landman. Landman, E. B. Germany & Sons, Dallas, 1970-73; asst. mgr. real estate Atlantic Richfield Co., L.A., 1973-74; landman GoldKing Prodn. Co., Houston, 1974-76; oil and gas cons./landman, co-owner Burk Properties, Burk Ednl. Properties, Houston, 1976—. Author: Petroleum Lands and Leasing, 1983; contbr. articles and photographs to profl. jours.; photographer; Author's Guild, 1984-93. Active Planning and Zoning Commn., Sugar Land, Tex., 1990-92; vol. media staff Economic Summit Industrialized Nations, Houston, 1990. Mem. Foremost Women 20th Century, Am. Assn. Petroleum Landmen (dir. 1980-82, 2d v.p. 1982-83, 71-94), Houston Assn. Petroleum Landmen (dir. 1976), Dallas Woman's Club, Sweetwater Country Club, Huisache Club, Sugar Creek Garden Club, HAPL Aux. (treas.). Republican. Presbyterian.

BURKE, ADRIENNE LEE, sculptor, painter; b. Landstuhl, West Germany, July 20, 1970; d. Hugh Gene and Lee Starr (Vanderhoef) B. BFA, Ind. U. Pa., 1993. Patineur Loveland (Colo.) Sculpture Works, 1993-96, Art Castings Colo., Loveland, 1996—; freelance sculptor, Ft. Collins, Colo., 1995—. Exhbns. include Alternative Arts Alliance, Denver, 1994-95. V.p. Amnesty Internat., Ind. U. Pa., 1990-91; disc jockey Sta. KTCL-FM, 1994—. Reynolds scholar, 1993. Home: 1816 Crestmore Pl Fort Collins CO 80521

BURKE, ARLENE L., osteopath, surgeon; b. Long Beach, Calif., Jan. 20, 1947; d. Luster B. and Margaret E. (Rives) Larch; children: David T. Burke, Christiene M. Burke, Sandra A. Hinsdale; m. Ronald H. Lloyd, Nov. 21, 1993. BA with honors, Loma Linda U., 1976; DO, U. Health Sci. Osteo. Medicine, Kansas City, Mo., 1981; MPH, The Johns Hopkins U., 1987. Commd. 2d lt. U.S. Army, 1977, advanced through grades to lt. col., 1993; resident in family practice Silas B. Hayes Army Cmty. Hosp., Fort Ord, Calif., 1981-83; family practice physician Weed Army Cmty. Hosp., Fort Irwin, Calif., 1983-85; med. dir. Med. Clinic, South Korea, 1985-86; resident in preventive medicine Madigan Army Med. Ctr., Tacoma, 1987-88; physician, occupl. health cons. Blanchfield Army Cmty. Hosp., Fort Campbell, Ky., 1988-91; preventive medicine physician Operation Desert Storm, 1990-91; occupl. health cons. Pueblo (Colo.) Health Clinic, 1991-93; physician, occupl. health cons. Evans Army Cmty. Hosp., Fort Carson, Colo., 1991-93; med. dir., staff physician several hosps., 1988-93; pvt. practice occupational medicine & adult primary care Colorado Springs, 1994-96; occpl. medicine clin. practice Peoria, Ill., 1996—. Contbr. articles to profl. jours. Mem. Am. Coll. Preventive Medicine, Colo. Soc. Osteo. Physicians, Colo. Pub. Health Assn., Colo. Med. Soc., El Paso County Med. Soc. Republican. Seventh Day Adventist. Office: 200 E Pennsylvania Ave Ste 101 Peoria IL 61603

BURKE, CHERYL C., lawyer; b. New Orleans, La., Nov. 17, 1947. BA, Oberlin Coll., 1969; JD, Northeastern U., 1973. Bar: Md. 1973, U.S. Dist. Ct. Md. 1974, D.C. 1975, U.S. Dist. Ct. D.C. 1975, U.S. Ct. Appeals (4th and D.C. cirs.) 1975, U.S. Supreme Ct. 1977, U.S. Ct. Appeals (10th cir.) 1979, U.S. Ct. Appeals (1st cir.) 1988. Mem. Akin, Gump, Strauss, Hauer & Feld, L.L.P., Washington; chair, hearing com., Bd. Profl. Responsibility. Mem. ABA, Maritime Law Assn. U.S., Federal Energy Bar Assn., Md. State Bar Assn., D.C. Bar. Office: Akin Gump Hauer Strauss & Feld # 400 1333 New Hampshire Ave NW Washington DC 20036

BURKE, DOROTHY DRECHSLER, acupuncturist, nurse; b. Balt., Nov. 9, 1949; d. William Edward and Helen Roberta (Kirkpatrick) Drechsler; m. Thomas R. Burke, Feb. 14, 1993. BA in Am. Studies, U. Md., 1971, BSN,

1974, MS in Nursing, 1983, M of Acupuncture, 1992. RN, Md.; cert. BLS instr.-trainer; nat. bd. cert. in acupuncture. Med. intensive care nurse U. Md. Hosp., Balt., 1974-77, Johns Hopkins Hosp., Balt., 1977-78; coronary care nurse clinician Frances Scott Key Med. Ctr., Balt., 1978-80; cardiac clin. specialist Greater Balt. Med. Ctr., 1980-82; instr., cardiac rehab. nurse Union Meml. Hosp., Balt., 1982-87; cardiac clin. specialist Harbor Hosp. Ctr., Balt., 1987-92; instr. Howard C.C., 1992—; pvt. practice acupuncture Frederick, Md., 1992—; staff in acupuncture and detox units Sheppard Pratt Hosp.; instr. RN Sch. Nursing-Harbor Hosp. Ctr., 1989. Author: (with others) Myocardial Infarction: A Guide to Patient Education, 1988. Mem. Am. Assn. Acupuncture and Oriental Medicine, Am. Holistic Nurses Assn., Sigma Theta Tau. Office: 176 Thomas Johnson Dr #203 Frederick MD 21702

BURKE, ELLEN KATHERINE, management consultant; b. Balt., Apr. 13, 1954; d. Bernard James and Joanne Patricia (McElveney) B. BS in Edn., SUNY, Cortland, 1977; MS in Applied Behavioral Sci., Johns Hopkins U., 1991. Activities therapist U. Rochester (N.Y.) Med. Ctr., 1977-79; therapeutic recreation specialist Md. Gen. Hosp., Balt., 1980-84; sales mgr. Monumental Life Ins. Co., Balt., 1984-87; mgmt. cons. Mega Mktg., Timonium, Md., 1987-90; mgmt. and orgn. devel. specialist Martin Marietta, Balt., 1990-93; human resources mgr. Ryland Group, Columbia, Md., 1993-95; v.p., gen. mgr. Career Ptnrs. Internat.-Chesapeake Group, Columbia, 1995—. Chair bd. dirs. Treatment Resources for Youth, Balt., 1993—; coach Cockeysville (Md.) Girls Youth Lacrosse, 1989—. Mem. Chesapeake Human Resources Assn., Exec. Women's Golf Network, NOW. Democrat. Home: 13 Rainflower Path Sparks MD 21152

BURKE, JACQUELINE YVONNE, telecommunications executive; b. Newark, Apr. 10, 1949; d. Trim and Viola (Smith) Russell; m. Harry Clifford Burke Jr., Aug. 20, 1968 (div. 1977); 1 child, Terence Christopher. Student, Howard U., Washington, 1966-67; HHD, London Inst. Applied Rsch., 1993; Cert. of License for Gospel Ministry, Annointed Tabernacle, Greensboro, N.C., 1994. Ordained to ministry Convent Ministries Internat., Faith Tabernacle Outreach Ministries, 1995. Teaching asst. Barringer High Sch., Newark, 1967; course developer Prudential Property and Casualty Ins., Newark, 1968-74; exec. Ad-A-System, Avenel, N.J., 1974-77; staff mgr. AT&T, Basking Ridge, N.J., 1977-83; quality assurance mgr. ops. and engring. Bell Communications Rsch., Morristown, N.J., 1984-86, dir. traffic routing adminstr., mem. tech. staff, 1986-91, tng./devel. specialist, 1991-93, performance technologist, 1993—; instr. Summer Tech. Edn. Program, Morristown, 1987; pres. Jacqueline Burke Enterprises, 1991—; pres., founder Liberation By Edn. Ministries, South Plainfield, N.J., 1995—; dean Divine Healing Temple Bible Tng. Outreach Ctr., Plainfield, 1994-95. Instr. Youth for Christ, Fanwood, N.J., 1984-86; cons., instr. Black Achievers/YMCA, Newark, 1985; pres. Archway Pregnancy Ctr., Elizabeth, N.J., 1985-89; mem. Faith Fellowship Ministries and World Outreach Ctr., 1987-95, Faith Tabernacle Ch., 1995—; exec. dir. edn. and tng. Faith Tabernacle Outreach Ministries, 1996—; tchr. neighborhood Bible study, 1989—; mem. bd. advisors Bros. and Sisters, Inc., 1989—; apptd. bd. advisors Am. Biog. Inst. Rsch., 1989; sec. Women Aglow, 1991-92, pres. Plainfield chpt. fellowship, 1992—; Am. del. to Africa African-Am. Summit, 1993; dean Divine Healing Temple Bible Tng. Outreach Ctr., 1994-95. Recipient Tribute to Woman in Industry award YWCA, 1985, Black Achiever award, 1985, Sojourner Truth award Nat. Assn. Negro Bus. and Profl. Women, 1989, Bellcore Synergy III cert., 1989, Recognition award YWCA, 1986, Cert. of Recognition Urban Women's Ctr., 1990, Bellcore Software Devel. and Software Com. Quality award, 1991, Recognition award Woman Aglow Fellowship, Plainfield chpt., 1993; named Outstanding Young Woman Am., 1985; Proclamation from City Mayor of Plainfield, 1990. Mem. NAFE, Nat. Assn. Negro Bus. and Profl. Women's Club, Inc., Career Options/YWCA, Am. Mgmt. Assn., Tribute to Women and Industry (speaker, mem. mgmt. forum 1985—), Internat. Platform Assn., Am. Biog. Inst. (rsch. bd. advisors 1989—). Democrat. Home: 229 West Ave South Plainfield NJ 07080-1924 Office: Bell Comm Rsch 6 Corporate Pl Rm 1M186 Piscataway NJ 08854-4120

BURKE, JANET LOIS, computer science educator; b. Chgo., Jan. 3, 1951; d. Joseph and Lorine Carol (Kalvin) Orenstein; m. Joseph D. Burke, Aug. 5, 1978; children: Kynan Neville, Alison Lyn, Owen Joseph. AAS in Liberal Arts, Westchester C.C., Valhalla, N.Y., 1976; BA in Psychology and Biology, SUNY, Purchase, 1978; cert. tchg., Lee Coll., 1993. Cert. tchr. grades 7-12 gen. sci., chemistry, biology, math., Tenn. Cert. trainer thematic/integrated curriculum, Nat. Sch. Conf. Inst.; cert. p.c. troubleshooting essential instr. Mainframe computer operator Pergamon Press, Inc., Elmsford, N.Y., 1977-78; programmer, documentation analyst Kane-Miller Inc., Tarrytown, N.Y., 1978-79; sys. analyst, on-line programmer Combe, Inc., White Plains, N.Y., 1979-81; sys. analyst, sr. programmer Technicon, Inc., Tarrytown, 1981-83; tchrs. aide Little Seaters Nursery, Belvidere, N.J., 1987-89; substitute tchr. various pub. elem. schs., Warren County, N.J., Chattanooga, Hamilton County, Tenn., 1987-94; personal computer applications support ComputerWorld, Dover, Del., 1983-85; vol. libr. Hamilton County Schs., Chattanooga, 1989-91; gifted tchr. Bradley County Sch., Cleveland, Tenn., 1993. Bd. dirs. Chattanooga City Coun. PTAs, 1993-94, unification analyst com. chair, 1993-94; pres. White Twp. PTO, 1987-89; organizer White Twp. Concerned Parents Group, 1988-89; chair Chattanooga Sch. Liberal Arts Enrichment, 1993-94. Recipient Pres.'s Vol. Action award WhiteHouse, 1994; mini-grantee Edna McConnell Clark Found., 1994, Pub. Edn. Found., Libr. Power, 1994, 95, 96. Mem. AAUW, ASCD. Home: 723 Hurricane Creek Rd Chattanooga TN 37421-4515

BURKE, JOHNNIE FOREMAN, guidance counselor; b. Tuscumbia, Ala., Dec. 24, 1938; d. John Henry Garner and Mary Earline (Poole) Neal; m. James Wallace Foreman, Jul. 29, 1956 (div. Jan. 1980); children: Christopher James, Sherri Foreman Quinones; m. Baxter Burke, Dec. 24, 1982. BS in health and physical edn., George Williams Coll., 1966; MS in counseling psychology, Chgo. State U., 1974; postgrad., Loyola U. Nat. cert. counselor. Internship Purdue U., West Lafayette, Ind., 1992; physical instr. Chgo. Park Dist., Chgo., 1958-65; physical edn. tchr., biology tchr. Chgo. Pub. Schs., 1966-69, guidance counselor, 1969—. Chmn. scholarship adv. com. Chgo. Urban League, 1993, mem. women's bd., 1995; mem. adv. bd. Harris YWCA, Chgo., 1994—; v.p. Chgo. Prairie Tennis Club, 1994—; election worker, Chgo., 1992. Recipient Disting. Svc. award Northeastern Ill. Univ., 1994, Award for Excellence South Side Help Ctr., Chgo., 1994, Beautiful People award Chgo. Urban League, 1996. Mem. Kappa Delti Pi. Home: 9842 S Van Vlissingen Rd Chicago IL 60617 Office: Chgo Vocat HS 2100 E 87th St Chicago IL 60617

BURKE, KAREN KEITH, graphic designer, administrator; b. Picayune, Miss., July 15, 1966; d. Charles Herbert Keith and Janice (Carroll) Goss; m. Barry Gene Burke, Mar. 28, 1992. BFA in Graphic Design, Miss. U. for Women, 1988. Acct. exec., graphic designer Huff Advt.and Promotions, Meridian, Miss., 1988-94; print coordinator Cobb County Govt. Comm. Office, Marietta, Ga., 1994—; v.p. TipMasters, Meridian, 1990-94, Women in Comm., 1995-96, bd. dirs., newsletter coord., 1995-96. Creative dir. Cobb County Ann. Report, 1995. Active Seatbelt Safety task force, Marietta, 1994—, Coalition for Child Abuse Prevention, Marietta, 1996—; bd. dirs. Jr. Miss program, Meridien, 1989-94, Safe Path Child Advocacy Ctr., Marietta, 1996—; mentor Visions Youth Leadership, Meridien, 1993-94; mem. mktg. com. United Way of Cobb County, Marietta, 1996—. Recipient award of Excellence Printing Industry Assn. of South, 1990, award of Merit Internat. Assn. Bus. Communicators, 1992, 94; named Outstanding Young Women of America, 1991. Mem. Kennesaw Fine Arts Soc., Jaycees (bd. dirs., Greater Meridian chpt., 1989-94, Miss. chpt., 1990-93). Republican. Presbyterian. Home: 2615 Dreux Ct Kennesaw GA 30152 Office: Cobb County Govt Comm Office 100 Cherokee St Marietta GA 30090

BURKE, KATE KANENGEISER, artist; b. St. Louis, July 21, 1952; d. Theodore Emery and Kathryn (Kanengeiser) B.; m. Charles Emmanuel Cavas, June 17, 1989. Student, Mus. Sch., Boston, 1971; BFA, Art. Inst. of Boston, 1974. Artist: 100 carved cast iron manhole covers/Hail Minn., Mpls., 1992, 10 carved bronze plaques/Breck Meml., Brighton, Mass., 1989, 5' diameter bronze medallion/Oak Sw. Medallion, Brighton, 1989, 100 carved bronze bricks/Boston Bricks, 1986. Recipient awards for Outstanding Contbrn. City of Mpls., 1992; monetary grantee Browne Fund, Brighton, 1989, 1986, Henderson Fund, Brighton, 1989. Mem. Internat. Sculpture Soc. Home: 767 Leesburg Sta Volant PA 16156

BURKE, KATHLEEN B., lawyer; b. Bklyn., Sept. 2, 1948. BA, St. John's U., 1969, JD, 1973. Bar: Ohio 1973. Ptnr. Jones, Day, Reavis & Pogue, Cleve. Mem. Ohio State Bar Assn. (pres. 1993-94). Office: Jones Day Reavis & Pogue North Point 901 Lakeside Ave E Cleveland OH 44114-1116

BURKE, KATHLEEN J., bank holding company executive. Exec. v.p., pers. rels. officer BankAmerica Corp., San Francisco, now vice chmn. Office: BankAmerica Corp 555 California St San Francisco CA 94104-1502*

BURKE, KATHLEEN MARY, lawyer; b. N.Y.C., Dec. 8, 1950; d. Hubert J. and Catherine (Painting) B. BA magna cum laude, Marymount Manhattan Coll., 1972; JD, U. Va., 1975. Bar: N.Y. 1976, Calif. 1979, U.S. Dist. Ct. (so. and ea. dists.) N.Y. 1977, U.S. Ct. Appeals (2d cir.) 1977, U.S. Ct. Appeals (9th cir.) 1980. Assoc. Donovan Leisure Newton & Irvine, N.Y.C., L.A., 1975-81, Kelley Drye & Warren, N.Y.C., 1981-84; assoc. counsel Soc. N.Y. Hosp., 1984-87, sec. and counsel, 1987—; sec. joint bd. N.Y. Hosp.-Cornell Med. Ctr.; sec. N.Y. Hosp-Cornell Med. Ctr. Fund, Inc., Soc. N.Y. Hosp. Fund, Inc., Royal Charter Properties, Inc., Royal Charter Properties-East, Inc., Royal Charter Properties-Westchester, Inc., Exec. Registry, Inc., N.Y. Hosp., Queens Med. Ctr., NYH Care Network, Inc., others; faculty Concern for Dying, N.Y.C., 1985-90, NYU Sch. Continuing Edn., 1994—; lectr. Cornell U. Med. Coll., 1994—. Contbr. articles to profl. jours. Trustee Marymount Manhattan Coll., N.Y.C., 1990—, N.Y. Meth. Hosp., 1995—. Mem. ABA, N.Y. State Bar Assn. (health law com. 1989-93), Am. Soc. Corp. Secs., Assn. of Bar of City of N.Y. (children and law com. 1986-89, law and medicine com. 1991-94), Am. Acad. Hosp. Attys. (speaker annual confs. 1987-92), Health Care Exec. Forum, Nat. Health Lawyers, Greater N.Y. Hosp. Assn. Legal Adv. Com. Roman Catholic. Office: Soc NY Hosp 525 E 68th St # 109 New York NY 10021-4873

BURKE, LILLIAN WALKER, retired judge; b. Thomaston, Ga., Aug. 2, 1917; d. George P. and Ozella (Daviston) Walker; m. Ralph Livingston Burke, July 8, 1948 (dec.); 1 son, R. Bruce. BS, Ohio State U., 1947; LLB, Cleve. State U., 1951, postgrad., 1963-64; grad., Nat. Coll. State Judiciary, U. Nev., 1974. Bar: Ohio 1951. Gen. practice law Cleve., 1952-62; asst. atty. gen. Ohio, 1962-66; mem., vice chmn. Ohio Indsl. Commn., 1966-69; judge Cleve. Mcpl. Ct., 1969-87, chief judge, 1981, 85, vis. judge, 1988—; guest lectr. Heidelburg Coll., Tiffin, Ohio, 1971; cons. Bur. Higher Edn., HEW, 1972. Pres. Cleve. chpt. Nat. Council Negro Women, 1955-57, recipient certificate of award, 1969; sec. East dist. Family Service Assn., 1959-60; mem. council human relations Cleve. Citizens League, 1959-79; mem. Gov.'s Com. on Status of Women, 1966-67; pres. Cleve. chpt. Jack and Jill of Am., Inc., 1960-61; v.p.-at-large Greater Cleve. Safety Council, 1969-79; mem. Cleve. Landmarks Commn., 1990—; woman ward leader 24th Ward Republican Club, 1957-67; mem. Cuyahoga County Central Com., 1958-68; sec. Cuyahoga County Exec. Com., 1962-63; alt. del. Rep. Nat. Conv., Chgo., 1960; bd. dirs., chmn. minority div. Nat. Fedn. Rep. Women, 1966-68; life mem., past bd. dirs. Cleve. chpt. NAACP; bd. dirs. Greater Cleve. Neighborhood Centers Assn., Catholic Youth Counselling Services; trustee Ohio Commn. on Status of Women, 1966-70, Consumers League Ohio, 1969-75, Cleve. Music Sch. Settlement; bd. mgmt. Glenville YWCA, 1960-70; mem. project com. Cleve. Orch. Recipient achievement award Parkwood Christian Meth. Episcopal Ch.., 1968, Martin Luther King Citizen's award, 1969, outstanding achievement award Ta-Wa-Si Scholarship Club, 1969, Outstanding Svc. award Morning Star Grand chpt., Cleve., 1970, award of honor Cleve. Bus. League, 1970, svc. award St. Paul AME Ch., Lima, Ohio, 1972, Woman of Achievement award Inner Club Coun., Cleve., 1973, cert. of award Nat. Coun. Negro Women, 1969; named Career Woman of Yr., Cleve. Women's Career Clubs, 1969. Mem. ABA, Nat. Assn. Investment Clubs (pres. Dynasty Investors Club 1992—, bd. dirs. N.E. Ohio Coun. 1993—), Nat. Bar Assn., Ohio Bar Assn., Cuyahoga County Bar Assn., Cleve. Bar Assn., Am. Judicature Soc., Am. Judges Assn. (bd. govs. 1982-86, chmn. conv. agenda com. 1981-83), Phillis Wheatley Assn., Women Lawyers Assn. (hon. adviser), Ohio State U. Alumni Assn. (life), Am. Bridge Assn. (life), Women's City Club (Cleve.), Altrusa, Alpha Kappa Alpha. Episcopalian. Home: 1357 East Blvd Cleveland OH 44106-4018

BURKE, LISA, communications executive; b. Gunnison, Colo., Aug. 31, 1963. BA in Econs., Stanford U., 1984, MS in Civil Engring. and Urban Planning, 1985. Land use and transp exec. asst. Orange County (Calif.) Supr. Gaddi Tazquez, 1985-91; mgr. planning Orange County Transp. Authority, 1991-93; v.p. Pacific/West Communications Group, Irvine, Calif., 1994—. Office: Pacific/West Comms Group 18301 Von Karman #340 Irvine CA 92715-2442*

BURKE, M. VIRGINIA, state legislator; b. Boston, Jan. 30, 1945; m. James G.; 2 children. Degree, Aquinas Coll., 1964. Roman Catholic. Home: 46 Meadowcrest Dr Bedford NH 03110-6316 Office: NH Ho of Reps State Capitol Concord NH 03301

BURKE, MARGARET ANN, computer and communications company specialist; b. N.Y.C., Feb. 25, 1961; d. David Joseph and Eileen Theresa (Falvey) B. BS in Computer Sci., St. John's U., Jamaica, N.Y., 1982; MBA, U. Md., 1994. Cert. data processor. Software specialist Bell Atlantic Corp., Washington, 1983—. Active Friends of Hillwood Mus., Washington. Mem. NAFE, Alliance Francaise, Nat. Fedn. Rep. Women, Am. Film Inst. Roman Catholic. Home: 6652 Hillandale Rd # A Bethesda MD 20815-6406 Office: Bell Atlantic 13100 Columbia Pike Silver Spring MD 20904-5247

BURKE, MARGARET LINDA, physician; b. Phila., Dec. 28, 1946; d. James Francis Sr. and Margaret Mary (Bolger) B. BFA, Moore Coll. Art, 1969; MD, Jefferson Med. Coll., 1991. Physician Cooper Family Medicine, Camden, N.J., 1995—. Mem. Am. Assn. Family Practitioners. Office: Cooper Family Medicine 725 Collings Ave West Collingswood NJ 08107

BURKE, MARGUERITE JODI LARCOMBE, writer, computer consultant; b. Pasadena, Calif.; d. Richard Albert and Marguerite (Colella) L.; m. M. Theodore Jockers, Dec. 5, 1954 (div. Nov. 1969); children: Richard Larcombe, Sir Blair; m. Roger Eugene Burke, Dec. 5, 1969. BA, Columbia U., 1949. Model Ford Agy., N.Y.C., 1949-54; freelance writer Savannah, Ga., 1969-80; pres. Jodi Larcombe Assocs., Murfreesboro, N.C., 1970—; freelance computer programmer Murfreesboro, 1981—; exec. asst. Resinall Corp., Severn, N.C., 1981—, computer programmer, 1981-89. Author: Sailing Cookbook, 1979; contbr. numerous articles to mags.; dir. Shotgun Theater Prodns., 1995. Dir. Shotgun Theater Prodns., N.Y., 1996—. Mem. Met. Opera Oncore Soc., Am. Film Soc., Met Opera Patron Assn. (2d century cir.), Met. Opera Nat. Coun., N.Y.C. Opera. Home: 306 Holly Hill Rd Murfreesboro NC 27855-2110 Office: Jodi Larcombe Assocs 306 Holly Hill Rd Murfreesboro NC 27855-2110

BURKE, MARIANNE KING, state agency administrator, financial executive; b. Douglasville, Ga., May 30, 1938; d. William Horace and Evora (Morris) King; divorced; 1 child, Kelly Page. Student, Ga. Inst. Tech., 1956-59, Anchorage C.C., 1964-66, Portland State U., 1968-69; BBA, U. Alaska, 1976. CPA, Alaska. Sr. audit mgr. Price Waterhouse, 1982-90; v.p. fin., asst. sec. NANA Regional Corp., Inc., Anchorage, 1990-95; v.p. fin. NANA Devel. Corp., Inc., Anchorage, 1990-95; sec.-treas. Vanguard Industries, J.V., Anchorage, 1990-95, Alaska United Drilling, Inc., Anchorage, 1990-95; treas. NANA/Marriott Joint Venture, Anchorage, 1990-95; v.p. fin. Arctic Utilities, Inc., Anchorage, 1990-95, Tour Arctic, Inc., Anchorage, 1990-95, Purcell Svcs., Ltd., Anchorage, 1990-95, Arctic Caribou Inn, Anchorage, 1990-95, NANA Oilfield Svcs., Inc., Anchorage, 1990-95, NANA Corp. Svcs., Inc., Anchorage, 1992-95; dir. divsn. ins. State of Alaska, 1995—; mem. State of Alaska Medicaid Rate Commn., 1985-88, State of Alaska Bd. Accountancy, 1984-87; bd. dirs. NAIC Edn. and Rsch. Found. Bd. dirs. Alaska Treatment Ctr., Anchorage, 1978, Alaska Hwy. Cruises; treas. Alaska Feminist Credit Union, Anchorage, 1979-80; mem. fund raising com. Anchorage Symphony, 1981. Mem. AICPA, Alaska Soc. CPAs, Govtl. Fin. Officers U.S. and Can., Fin. Execs. Inst. (bd. dirs.), Nat. Assn. of Ins. Commrs. Home: 7241 Foxridge Cir Anchorage AK 99518-2702 Office: State Office Bldg PO Box 110805 333 Willoughby Ave Juneau AK 99811-0805 also: 3601 C St Ste 1324 Anchorage AK 94503-5948

BURKE, MARJORIE HARDMAN, state legislator, farmer; b. Nov. 14, 1932; m. Billy B. Burke; children: Roberta Diane, Carolyn Sue. AB, Glenville State Coll., 1953. House mem. 9th Del. Dist. State of W.Va., Sand Fork, 1980—; majority whip 68th legislature; speaker pro tem 69th legislature; former chmn. state com. Agrl. Stabilization and Conservation Svc.; dir., sec., treas. W.Va. Livestock Round-up. Chair women's caucus Gilmer County Recreation Coun., 1985-86; mem. Dem. State Exec. Com. Mem. W.Va. Fedn. Dem. Women (pres.), Gilmer County Dem. Women's Club, Cen. W.Va. Livestock Mktg. Assn. (mgr.), W.Va. Simmental Assn., Gilmer County 4-H Leaders, Future Farmers of Am. Alumni, Order Eastern Star, Glenville Extension Homemakers Club. Baptist. Home: Titan Farm Sand Fork WV 26430 Office: PO Box 300 Sand Fork WV 26430-0300

BURKE, MARY GRIGGS (MRS. JACKSON BURKE), art collector; b. St. Paul. BA, Sarah Lawrence Coll.; MA in Clin. Psychology, Columbia U.; postgrad., New Sch. for Social Rsch. Pvt. collector Japanese art, St. Paul, 1966—; founder The Mary & Jackson Burke Found., N.Y.C., 1972—; mem. vis. com. Freer Gallery Art, Smithsonian Instn.; mem. Met. Mus. Art; pres. The Mary and Jackson Burke Found. Mem. nominating com., mem. membership com., mem. exec. com., mem. activities com. The Japan Soc., 1959-77, chmn. student and visitors com., 1957-63, chmn. art gallery adv. com., 1970-73, bd. dirs., 1968-77, also hon. life trustee; chmn. friend mem. Japan House Gallery, 1969-75, 87—; bd. dirs. The Cable (Wis.) Natural History Mus., 1968-92, also hon. life trustee, Sarah Lawrence Coll., Bronxville, N.Y., 1968-78, also hon. life trustee, The Internat. Crane Found., Baraboo, Wis., 1978-90, The Hobe Sound (Fla.) Nature Ctr., 1987—; mem. adv. coun. dept. art history and archeology Columbia U., N.Y.C., 1970—; mem. internat. coun. Mus. Modern Art, N.Y.C., 1970—; mem. vis. com. Freer Gallery of Art, Smithsonian Instn., Washington, 1971—, vice chmn., 1989-92; mem. vis. com. dept. Asiatic art Mus. Fine Arts, Boston, 1972-90, also friend, 1972-90; mem. vis. com. dept. Islamic art, mem. vis. com. dept. Asian art, mem. edn. com., mem. acquisitions com., bd. dirs. Met. Mus. Art, N.Y.C., 1976—, also friend Far Ea. dept., 1984—; mem. Smithsonian Assocs. nat. bd. Smithsonian Instn., Washington, 1977-83; mem. art gallery adv. com., mem. exec. com., mem. devel. com., bd. dirs. The Asia Soc., 1978-88, also hon. life trustee; friend Bklyn. Mus. Art, 1982—, Friends of Asian Art, Freer and Sackler Galleries, 1991—; William Beene fellows N.Y. Zool. Soc., 1986—. Decorated Order of The Sacred Treasure (Japan), Second Leve Gold and Silver Star (Japan). Home: 3 E 77th St New York NY 10021-1732*

BURKE, MARY THOMAS, university administrator, educator; b. Westport, County Mayo, Ireland, Nov. 28, 1928; d. Thomas J. and Anne (McGuire) B. BA, Belmont (N.C.) Abbey Coll., 1958; MA, Georgetown U., 1965; PhD, U. N.C., Chapel Hill, 1968. Elem. tchr. St Patrick's Sch., Charlotte, N.C., 1950-51, St Agnes Sch., Greenport, N.Y., 1951-54; tchr. Charlotte (N.C.) Cath. High Sch., 1954-64; academic dean Sacred Heart Coll., Belmont, N.C., 1967-70; assoc. prof. U. N.C., Charlotte, 1970-75; prof., chmn. human svcs. dept. U. N.C., 1975—; chmn. State Adv. Coun. on Pupil Pers. Svcs., 1972-76. Co-editor: (with Judith Miranti) Ethical and Value Issues in Counseling, 1992, Counseling: The Spiritual Dimension, 1995. Bd. dirs. McKlenburg chpt. and state divsn. Am. Cancer Soc., 1977-83, treas., 1983-86, crusade chmn., 1986; chairperson United Way, U. N.C., Charlotte, 1974; bd. dirs. St. Joseph Hosp. and St. Joseph's Health Svcs., Asheville, Selwyn Life Ctr., Charlotte, 1986-90; bd. dirs. Nat. Bus. Forms, Greeneville, Tenn., 1973—, asst. sec., treas. bd. dirs., 1975-92, sec., treas., 1992—; mem. bd. trustees Belmont Abbey Coll., 1994—. Recipient Anti-Defamation award B'nai B'rith Women, 1978, Ray Thompson Human Rels. award N.C. Assn. for Non-White Concerns, 1978, WBT Woman of Yr. award, 1979, Ella Stephen Barret Leadership award, 1983, AWO Good of Soc. award Am. Cancer Soc., 1981, Leadership award Am. Cancer Soc., 1988, Faculty Svc. award Gen. Alumni Assn. U. N.C., 1994, Silver Medalian Humanitarian award Nat. Conf. Christians and Jews, 1995, Meritorious award Assn. for Spiritual Ethical and Religious Values in Counseling, 1995; named Excellence in Teaching award finalist Nations Bank, 1995. Mem. AACD (human rights com. 1992-93), N.C. Pers. and Guidance Assn. (exec. com. 1973-90, editl. bd. jours. 1975-78, pres. Metrolina chpt. 1973-74, state pres.-elect 1980-81, pres. 1981-82, leadership award 1983), N.C. Guidance Assn. (program com. 1974-75), Nat. Cath. Guidance Assn. (state rep. 1974-79), N.C. Assn. Religious and Value Issues in Counseling (chairperson 1974—, pres. 1985-86, 93-94, bd. dirs. 1986-94), N.C. Assn. Counselors Educators and Suprs., Am. Pers. and Guidance Assn., Am. Counselor Educators and Suprs. Assn., Assn. Religious Values in Counseling, N.C. Assn. Group Work, N.C. Mental Health Assn., N.C. Sch. Counselors Assn. (Counselor Educator of Yr. award 1975), So. Assn. Counselor Educators and Suprs., Assn. for Religious Values in Counseling (bd. dirs. Metrolina AIDS Project 1989-90, pres. bd., 1990-92, pres.-elect 1989-90, pres. 1990-91, Pres.' award 1992), Coun. Accreditation of Counseling and Related Edn. Programs (bd. dirs. 1993—, vice chair 1994-96, chairperson 1996—, ACA liaison to Nat. Bd. Cert. Counselors 1994—), Phi Delta Kappa, Delta Kappa Gamma, Chi Sigma Iota, Mu Tau Beta (Devoted Svc. award 1994). Office: U NC Dept Counseling/Child Devel Charlotte NC 28223

BURKE, MONA, sales engineer; b. New Delhi, India, Jan. 28, 1969; came to U.S., 1978; d. Krishan Lal and Nirmal Kanta (Rawla) Adlakha; m. Damien Bahorich Burke, Oct. 11, 1992. BS in Chem. Engring., U. Va., 1990. Process engr. Monsanto, Sauget, Ill., 1990-93; sales engr. Monsanto Plastics, Auburn Hills, Mich., 1993-95; account mgr. Colorite Polymers, Burlington, N.J., 1996—. Advisor Jr. Achievement, East St. Louis, Ill., 1990-93; vol. Discover "E" Program, Ill., 1991-92; rep. United Way, Ill., 1991-92. Recipient YWCA Leadership award, St. Louis, 1992. Mem. AIChE (chair chem. show com. 1993, chair student rels. 1991-93), Soc. Plastic Engrs. Office: Monsanto 2401 Walton Blvd PO Box 215290 Auburn Hills MI 48326

BURKE, NANCY, psychologist, educator; b. Chgo., Feb. 13, 1957; d. Maurice Oscar and Elaine (Abelson) B. BA, Carleton Coll., 1979; MA, U. Chgo., 1984, PhD, 1990. Lic. clin. psychologist, Ill. Clin. psychologist in pvt. practice Chgo., 1992; staff psychologist Northwestern Meml. Hosp., Chgo., 1992; asst. prof. psychology Northwestern U. Sch. Medicine, Chgo., 1993—. Contbr. articles to profl. jours. Fellow De Karaman Found., 1989-90. Mem. APA, Chgo. Assn. for Psychoanalytic Psychology (coun. mem. 1994—), MLA. Office: Northwestern Meml Hosp 259 E Erie Chicago IL 60611

BURKE, NANCY JAYNE, gas and electric company executive; b. Balt., Dec. 16, 1944; d. James A. and M. Jane (Martin) B.; divorced. AA in Acctg., Johns Hopkins U., 1964; BS in Bus. Mgmt., Coll. of Notre Dame, Balt., 1980. CPA, Md.; cert. info. sys. auditor. Sec., programmer Balt. Gas and Electric Co., 1968-70, sr. programmer, 1970-71, programmer/analyst, 1971-73, analyst, 1973-74, electronic data processing auditor, 1975-92, sr. customer analyst, 1992—. Bd. dirs. Friends of Villa Maria, Balt., 1988—; co-founder Ctrl. Md. Electronic Data Processing Auditors Assn., 1977, sec., 1980; treas. Friends of Mercy, Balt., 1993, Villa Maria, Balt., 1991; chair Rodgers Forge S.A., Balt., 1987. Home: 7009 Heathfield Rd Baltimore MD 21212-1506 Office: Balt Gas & Electric PO Box 1475 Baltimore MD 21203-1475

BURKE, SANDRA SUE, nurse; b. Dubuque, Iowa, June 27, 1945; d. Merro Matthew and Marie Delia (Scherr) Koppes; m. William John Burke, June 24, 1967 (div. Sept. 1981); children: Daniel, David, Steven. Student, St. Anthony's Sch. Nursing, 1963-66; diploma, Des Moines Area C.C. Rn, Iowa. Staff nurse Xavier Hosp., Dubuque, 1966-67, 1972-3, U. Iowa, Iowa City, 1967-68, VA, Iowa City, 1968-70, Mercy Hosp., Iowa City, 1974-75; instr. lamaze Iowa Meth. Med. Ctr., Des Moines, 1980-81; office nurse internal medicine Iowa Physicians ClinicMed. Found., Des Moines, 1984—; supr. nursing Iowa Physicians Clinic, Des Moines, 1988-92. CCD instr. Sacred Heart Sch., West Des Moines, 1977-79. Roman Catholic. Office: Iowa Physicians Clinic Med Found 1221 Pleasant St Ste 200 Des Moines IA 50309

BURKE, SHEILA P., legislative staff member; b. San Francisco, Jan. 10, 1951; d. George Abbott and Mary Joan (Winfield) B.; m. David Chew, Jan.

1983; children: Daniel, Kathleen, Sarah. BSN, U. San Francisco, 1973; MA in Pub. Adminstrn., Harvard U., 1982. Staff nurse Alta Bates Hosp., Berkeley, Calif., 1973-74; dir. student affairs Nat. Student Nurses Assn., N.Y., 1974-75; dir. program and field svcs. Nat. Student Nurses Assn., 1975-77; legis. asst. Senator Bob Dole, 1977-78; profl. staff mem. for Senator Bob Dole Senate Com. Fin., U.S. Senate, 1979-82, dep. staff dir. for Senator Bob Dole, 1982-85; dep. chief of staff Senate Majority Leader Bob Dole, U.S. Senate, 1985-86; chief of staff Senator Bob Dole, 1986-96; sec. U.S. Senate, Washington, 1995; adj. nursing faculty Georgetown U.; rsch. asst. Ctr. Health Policy and Mgmt. John F. Kennedy Sch. Govt., Harvard U., 1980-81; sr. advisor Bob Dole for Pres. Campaign, 1996—; advisor to dean J.F. Kennedy Sch. Govt. Harvard U., 1996—. Address: 1323 Merrie Ridge Rd Mc Lean VA 22101

BURKE, SHIRLEY JEAN, health and physical education educator; b. St. Louis, Feb. 3, 1943; d. Leon and Lillie B. (Lampkin) B. BS, Tenn. State U., 1965; MS, Ea. Mich. U., 1975; ednl. specialist, Wayne State U., 1981. Tchr. Harry E. Davis Jr. H.S., Cleve., 1965-66, Glenville H.S., Cleve., 1966-69; tchr., coach Cass Tech. H.S., Detroit, 1969-89; dept. head phys. edn. Southeastern H.S., Detroit, 1989-92; head dept. health and phys. edn., athletic dir. Southwestern H.S., Detroit, 1992—; athletic dir. Southeastern H.S. Mem. AAHPERD, Mich. Interscholastic Athletic Adminstrs. Assn. (region 12 rep.), Nat. Interscholastic Athletic Adminstrs. Assn., Profl. Women's Network, Phi Delta Kappa, Delta Sigma Theta. Democrat. Home: 14336 Montrose Detroit MI 48227 Office: Southwestern HS 6921 W Fort Detroit MI 48209

BURKE, SUZANNE MAUREEN, art historian, dean; b. Commerce, Tex.; d. John Emmett and Evelyn (Perkins) B. BA, Miss. U. for Women, 1977; MA, NYU, 1980, PhD, 1994. Cert. in mus. studies Met. Mus. Art and NYU, 1982. Ind. scholar Rome, London, N.Y.C., 1983-92; prof. Savannah (Ga.) Coll. of Art and Design, 1992-93, art history dept. chairperson, 1993-95, dean spl. programs, 1995—. Regional coord. Ga. Save Outdoor Sculpture, Savannah. Fellow NEH, N.Y., 1978-81; Fulbright scholar Fulbright Commn., Rome, Florence, 1982-83. Mem. AAUW, Am. Assn. Mus., Coll. Art Assn., Phi Kappa Phi. Office: Savannah Coll Art-Design PO Box 3146 201 W Charlton Savannah GA 31410

BURKE, TAMARA LYNN, marketing professional; b. Appleton, Minn., July 4, 1960; d. Merlyn Eugene and Patricia Yvonne (Johnson) Munsterman; m. James Warren Burke, Jr., Mar. 26, 1983 (div. June 1993); 1 child, Madelyn Amanda. BA, U. Minn., 1982. Asst. acct. exec. Sheggeby Advt., Mpls., 1982-83, BBDO, Inc., L.A., 1983-84; program mgr. Cable Music Channel, Hollywood, Calif., 1984-85; acct. exec. Ogilvy & Mather, L.A., 1985-88; mktg. mgr. Teleflora, L.A., 1988-93; asst. mgr. mktg. & merchandising Jafra Cosmetics Internat. Inc. (A Gillette Co.), Westlake Village, Calif., 1993—. Recipient Silver Clio award, 1986, N.Y. Internat. Film and TV Festival bronze award, 1986, Ogilvy & Mather Creative Excellence award, 1986. Mem. Rho Lambda Hon. Soc. Office: Jafra Cosmetics Inter Inc 2451 Townsgate Rd Westlake Village CA 91361

BURKE, YVONNE WATSON BRATHWAITE (MRS. WILLIAM A. BURKE), lawyer; b. L.A., Oct. 5, 1932; d. James A. and Lola (Moore) Watson; m. William A. Burke, June 14, 1972; 1 dau., Autumn Roxanne. A.A., U. Calif., 1951; B.A., UCLA, 1953; J.D., U. So. Calif., 1956. Bar: Calif. 1956. Mem. Calif. Assembly, 1966-72, chmn. urban devel. and housing com., 1971, 72; mem. 93d Congress from 37th Dist. Calif., 94th-95th Congresses from 28th Dist. Calif., House Appropriations Com.; chmn. Congl. Black Caucus, 1976; county supervisor Jones, Day, Reavis & Pogue, L.A.; dep. corp. commr., hearing officer Police Commn., 1964-66; atty., staff McCone Commn. (investigation Watts riot), 1965; past chmn. L.A. Fed. Res. Bank; former U.S. adv. bd. Nestle. Vice chmn. 1984 U.S. Olympics Organizing Com.; bd. dirs. or bd. advisers numerous orgns.; former regent U. Calif., Bd. Ednl. Testing Svc.; Amateur Athletic Found.; former bd. dirs. Ford Found., Brookings Inst.; bd. supr's. 2d Dist., L.A. County Bd. of Supr's., 1992. Recipient Profl. Achievement award UCLA, 1974, 84; named one of 200 Future Leaders Time mag., 1974, Alumni of Yr., UCLA, 1996; recipient Achievement awards C.M.E. Chs.; numerous other awards, citations.; fellow Inst. Politics John F. Kennedy Sch. Govt. Harvard, 1971-72; Chubb fellow Yale, 1972. Office: Office Board of Supervisors 866 Kenneth Hahn Hall Admn 500 W Temple St Los Angeles CA 90012-2713

BURKEN, RUTH MARIE, retail company executive; b. Kenosha, Wis., Sept. 25, 1956; d. Richard Stanley and Anne Theresa (Steplyk) Wojtak; m. James H. Burken, Oct. 15, 1988. AAS, Gateway Tech. Inst., 1976; BA, U. Wis.-Parkside, 1980; AAS, Coll. of DuPage, 1995. Transp. aide Kenosha Achievement Ctr. (Wis.), 1977; lifeguard U. Wis.-Parkside, Kenosha, 1980, library clk., 1978-80; asst. mgr. K Mart Corp., Troy, Mich., 1980-88, regional office supr., 1988, internal auditor, 1989-92, sr. field auditor, 1992—. Mem. NAFE, Distributive Edn. Clubs Am. (parliamentarian 1976), U. Wis.-Parkside Alumni Assn. Roman Catholic. Office: K Mart Internat Hdqs 3100 W Big Beaver Rd Troy MI 48084-3004

BURKET, GAIL BROOK, author; b. Stronghurst, Ill., Nov. 1, 1905; d. John Cecil and Maud (Simonson) Brook; AB, U. Ill., 1926; MA in English Lit., Northwestern U., 1929; m. Walter Cleveland Burket, June 22, 1929; children: Elaine (Mrs. William L. Harwood), Anne, Margaret (Mrs. James Boyce). Pres. woman's aux. Internat. Coll. Surgeons, 1950-54, now bd. dirs. Mus.; nat. vice chmn. Am. Heritage of DAR, 1992-95; pres. Northwestern U. Guild, 1976-78; sec. Evanston women's bd. Northwestern U. Settlement, 1979-81, pres., 1984-86; mem. cen. com., 1986—. Mem. Nat. Trust Hist. Preservation, 1995—. Recipient Robert Ferguson Meml. award Friends of Lit., 1973. Mem. Nat. League Am. Pen Women (Ill. state pres. 1952-54, nat. v.p. 1958-60), Soc. Midland Authors, Poetry Soc. Am., Women in Communications Inc., AAUW (pres. N. Shore br. 1961-63), Ill. Opera Guild (bd. dirs. 1982—, 1st v.p. 1986-91, pres. 1991-93), Daus. Am. Colonists (state v.p. 1973-76), Colonial Dames Am. (chpt. regent 1974-80), Phi Beta Kappa, Delta Zeta. Author: Courage Beloved, 1949; Manners Please, 1949; Blueprint for Peace, 1951; Let's Be Popular, 1951; You Can Write a Poem, 1954; Far Meadows, 1955; This is My Country, 1960; From the Prairies, 1968. Contbr. articles, poems to lit. publs. Address: 1020 Lake Shore Blvd Evanston IL 60202-1433

BURKETT, EUGENIE INES, music educator; b. Van Nuys, Calif., Dec. 22, 1952; d. John Jacob Burkett and Isabelle Rubie (Roddy) Koons; m. Steven Wayne Trinkle, Nov. 7, 1982; 1 child, Isadora Lynn Trinkle. B of Music Edn., Baylor U., 1974; MusM, Manhattan Sch. Music, 1975; PhD, U. Wis., 1992. Cert. tchr., N.C., Tex. Instrumental and choral dir. Holy Name Sem., Madison, Wis., 1988-92; asst. prof. U. N.C., Pembroke, 1992—; lectr. Edgewood Coll., Madison, 1991-92; co-founder, prodr., musician, v.p. Trinkle Brass Works, Inc., Red Springs, N.C., 1977—; coord., prodr. choral, gen., instrumental clinicians U. N.C., Pembroke, 1992—. Timpanist, percussionist Augusta (Ga.) Symphony Orch., 1992—; piano accompanist Robeson Civic Chorale, Lumberton, N.C., 1993-95; dir. Orff Ensemble for Children, Pembroke, 1995—. Faculty Devel. and Rsch. grantee Pembroke State U., 1994-96, Florence Rogers Charitable Trust grantee, 1994-95, N.C. Arts Coun. grantee, 1994-95. Mem. AAUW, Am. Guild Organists (newsletter editor Cape Fear chpt. 1993, bd. dirs.), N.C. Music Edn. Nat. Conf., Coll. Music Soc., N.C. Percussive Arts Soc. (newsletter editor 1992, state exec. bd.), Phi Delta Kappa (v.p. membership 1993). Home: 414 S Main St Red Springs NC 28377 Office: U NC PO Box 1510 Pembroke NC 28372-1510

BURKETT, HELEN, artist; b. Washington, Feb. 15, 1942; d. Harding Theodore and Helen Louise (Torris) B.; m. J.D. Collins, Sept. 1, 1961 (Apr. 16, 1975); children: Mark W. Collins, Donna L. Collins; m. Charles Talbot Marshall, Dec. 24, 1975; 1 child, Gabrielle T. Marshall. Student, Strayer Sch. of Bus., 1960-61, Corcoran Sch. of Art, 1968-69, Md. U., 1970-73, Hilton Leech Studio-Gallery, 1976-80, Ringling Sch. Art, 1980-81. Asst. to dir. Hilton Leech Studio, Sarasota, Fla., 1975-80, workshop organizer, figure study coord., 1978-80; demonstrator, tchr., artist, owner/operator Helen Burkett Studios, Sarasota, Fla., 1975—. One person show at Manatee Jr. Coll., 1984, Ctrl. Fla. C.C., Ocala, 1987; exhibitor numerous art festivals, 1987—; subject of periodical The Artist Mag., 1992, The Am. Artist Mag., 1996. Tchr. Vis. Artist Program, Coconut Grove, Fla., 1990—; artist, tchr. Donne Bitner Studio, Cocoa Beach, Fla., 1996. Recipient 2d prize in watercolor U. Tampa, 1991, 93, 1st prize in watercolor Lowe Art Mus./U. Miami, 1992, Purchase award Festival of the Masters-Disney Corp., 1995, Purchase award Wayne State U.-Ford Motor Co., 1995. Mem. ACLU, NOW, Am. Watercolor Soc. (assoc.), Nat. Watercolor Soc. (assoc.), Nat. Assn. Ind. Artists, Sarasota Art Assn. (bd. dirs. 1980-82), Fla. Watercolor Soc. (life, Award of Distinction 1985, 92), So. Watercolor Soc., Mich. Guild Artists. Buddhist. Home and Studio: Helen Burkett Studio 2988 Oak St Sarasota FL 34237-7346

BURKETT, MARJORIE THERESA, nursing educator, gerontology nurse; b. Jamaica, West Indies, Mar. 21, 1931; d. David Cameron and Mabel Louise (McKenzie) Espeut; m. Leo A. Burkett, Apr. 4, 1962; 1 child, Catherine Ann. Diploma in Midwifery and Nursing, Kingston Sch. of Nursing, Kingston, Jamaica, 1953; diploma in Nursing Edn., U. Edinburgh (Scotland UK), 1963; diploma in Psychiat. Nursing, Royal Victoria Hosp., Montreal, Can., 1970; BA, U. West Indies, 1975; MSN Edn., U. Miami, 1977, PhD, 1990; adult health nurse practitioner, Fla. Internat. U., 1992. RN, Fla., Tenn., Eng. and Wales UK, Jamaica; cert. midwife, Jamaica. Assoc. prof. Fla. Internat. U., North Miami, 1988—, coord. adult med. and surg. nursing, 1990, coord. Childbearing Nursing, 1992—; faculty mem. numerous community colls. and profl. coms. Contbr. articles to profl. jours. Mem. ANA, Nat. League Nursing, Fla. League Nursing, Fla. Nurses Assn., Nat. Coun. on Aging, Golden Key Nat. Honor Soc., Sigma Theta Tau, Phi Lambda Pi, Phi Delta Kappa. Office: Fla Internat U Sch Nursing 3000 NE 145th St Miami FL 33181-3612

BURKETT, PATRICIA JEAN, office technology educator, distribution company executive; b. Lexington, Ky., Mar. 11, 1947; d. Samuel Clarence and Margaret Ellen (Miller) Cornett; m. Gordon Lee Burkett, July 29, 1967; 1 child, Kimberly Dawn. AS, Somerset C.C., 1967; BS, Campbellsville Coll., 1969; MA, Ea. Ky. U., 1973. Cert. tchr., Ky. Ins. clk. Somerset (Ky.) Hosp., 1965-67; sec. Taylor County Hosp., Campbellsville, Ky., 1967-69; owner, mgr. Kim's Hallmark Gallery, Cynthiana, Ky., 1974-84; owner, mgr. distbn. bus. Cynthiana, Ky., 1991—; office tech. tchr. Ky. Tech. Harrison Ctr., Cynthiana, 1969—; portfolio cons. Ky. Dept. Edn., 1994-95. Mem. Ky. Bus. Edn. (bd. dirs.), Ctrl. Ky. Bus. Assn. (v.p. 1976-78), Ctrl. Ky. Vocat. Assn., Future Bus. Leaders Am. (state exec. coun., advisor 1969—). Republican. Baptist. Home: Rt 6 Box 84 Cynthiana KY 41031 Office: Cynthiana Democrat Webster Ave Cynthiana KY 41031

BURKHARDT, ANN, occupational therapist, clinical educator; b. Providence, Dec. 21, 1954; d. Kenneth Ralph and Betty Jane (Neale) B. BA in Psychobiology, Wheaton Coll., 1976; MA in Occupational Therapy, NYU, 1979. Lic. occupational therapist, N.Y., R.I., Mass.; cert. neurorehab. therapist Am. Occupational Therapy Assn. Staff therapist Charlton Meml. Hosp., Fall River, Mass., 1979; staff therapist, sr. therapist Columbia U.-Harlem Hosp., N.Y.C., 1979-84; staff therapist, burn specialist Cornell Med. Ctr.-N.Y. Hosp., N.Y.C., 1984-86; dir. occupational therapy Greater Harlem Nursing Home, N.Y.C., 1986-87; chief occupational therapist Meml. Sloan-Kettering Cancer Ctr., N.Y.C., 1987-92; asst. dir. occupational therapy Columbia-Presbyn. Med. Ctr., N.Y.C., 1992—; clin. instr. Columbia U., N.Y.C., 1993—; pvt. practice N.Y.C., 1984—; del. Coll. of Occupl. Therapists, Edinburgh, Scotland, 1995, World Fedn. Occupl. Therapists, London, 1994; spkr. in field. Author: (chpt.) Occupational Therapy Intervention in Recreational Settings in Acute Care, 1993, (pamphlet) Lymphedema: Self-Care and Treatment, 1992; co-author: A Therapists Guide to Oncology, 1996; contbr. articles to profl. jours. Mem. Am. Occupl. Therapy Assn. (alt. rep. to rep. assembly 1992-94, polit. action com. 1994), N.Y. State Occupl. Therapy Assn. (Merit award 1990, alt. rep. 1992-94, pres.-elect. 1994-95, pres. 1995—), Metro N.Y. Dist. Occupl. Therapy Assn. (bd. dirs., sec. 1990-96), Am. Congress Rehab. Medicine, N. Am. Soc. Lymphology, Internat. Soc. Lymphology, Am. Phys. Medicine, Am. Soc. Assn. Execs., Am. Med. Writers Assn., Am. Burn Assn., Congress of Rehab. Medicine. Home: 160 E 91st St Apt 4B New York NY 10128-2458 Office: Milstein Hosp Bldg 8 Garden North 405 177 Fort Washington Ave New York NY 10032-3713

BURKHARDT, BARBARA JEAN, media specialist, librarian; b. Queens, N.Y., July 6, 1948; d. Alexander and Edythe Elizabeth (Taylor) McKinnon; children: Scott Alexander, Danielle Elizabeth, Ashley Taylor. BA in Edn., W.Va. Wesleyan Coll., 1970; MS, Queens Coll., 1975; MLS, Rutgers U., 1990. Cert. tchr., N.Y., N.J. Teaching asst. U. Del., 1977-79, Trenton State U., 1981; tchr. 1st grade Maurice Hawk Sch., Princeton Junction, N.J., 1985-87; libr. asst. Firestone Libr. Princeton (N.J.) U., 1988; libr., media specialist North Brunswick Twp. (N.J.) Pub. Schs., 1990-92, Hightstown (N.J.) High Sch., 1992-93, Fisher Sch., Ewing, N.J., 1993, Ewing H.S., 1994—. Author (poetry book) Wait for Me, 1975. Sect. leader Princeton Pro Musica chorus. Mem. ALA, Region V Libr. Coop., Mercer County Ednl. Media Assn., Edn. Media Assn. N.J. Home: 8 Hancock Ct Plainsboro NJ 08536-2306

BURKHARDT, DOLORES ANN, library consultant; b. Meriden, Conn., July 28, 1932; d. Frederick Christian and Emily (Detels) Burkhardt; B.A., U. Conn., 1955; M.S., So. Conn. State Coll., 1960; postgrad. Cen. Wash. State Coll., 1962, Columbia, 1964—; 6th yr. diploma U. Conn., 1972. Asst. librarian So. Conn. State Coll. Library, summers 1960, 62; sch. library tchr. Farmington High Sch., Unionville, Conn., 1955-65; library cons.; media specialist East Farms Sch., Farmington, Conn., 1967-70; sch. library coordinator K-12, Durham-Middlefield, Conn., 1970-72; media specialist regional dist. 10, Burlington-Harwinton, Conn., 1972-78; ednl. media cons., 1978—, librarymedia specialist Burr Elem. Sch., Hartford Pub. Schs., 1996—. Instr. Boston U. Media Inst. Spl. cons. Conn. Dept. Edn., 1965—. Mem. AAUW (sec. 1956-58), NEA, Conn. Edn. Assn., New Eng. (pres. 1969-70), Conn. (2d v.p. 1965—, chmn. sch. library devel.; chmn. standards com. 1970-72, chmn. instructional materials selection policy com. Region 10) sch. library assns., Am. Assn. Sch. Librarians, New Eng. Sch. Devel. Council, Phi Delta Kappa. Lutheran. Home and Office: 812 Savage St Southington CT 06489-4629

BURKHARDT, JAYNE LESLIE, lawyer; b. Muncie, Ind., Aug. 23, 1943; d. Robert Howell and Betty Lou (Pfeiffer) Leslie; m. Richard Wellington Burkhardt, Jr., Aug. 13, 1966; children: Richard, Frederick. BA, Tufts U., 1965; JD, U. Ill., Champaign, 1982. Bar: Ill. 1983. Rsch. analyst John Hancock Ins. Co., Boston, 1965-67; staff asst. Clifton-Gunderson Accts., Champaign, Ill., 1983-85; atty. Land of Lincoln Legal Assistance Found., Champaign, Ill., 1985-90. Pres. LWV, Champaign, 1993—, World Heritage Mus. Guild, Champaign, 1995—, sec. bd. dirs., 1995—; mem. allocations com. United Way, Champaign, 1993-95; bd. dirs. Champaign Conservation and Design Commn., 1995—. Home: 306 W Vermont St Urbana IL 61801

BURKHART, DOROTHY P., art critic; b. Newark, Oct. 16, 1924; d. James and Leena (Lemme) Pallante; m. William H. Burkhart; children: Douglas Kimball, Willow Rodriguez, Christopher William. Student, Boston U., 1946, 48; BA in Art, San Jose State U., 1976, MA, 1978; postgrad., Stanford U., 1977. Art critic San Jose (Calif.) Mercury News, 1980-92; ind. curator Triton Mus. Art, Santa Clara, Calif., 1992-94; juror artist residency program Villa Montalvo, Saratoga, Calif., 1993-94, mem. adv. com., 1995—; mem. com. for Soc. for Encouragement of Contemporary Art, San Francisco Mus. Modern Art, 1993-97; past tchr. art history San Francisco Art Inst.; spkr. in field. Author, editor: (catalogue) Robert Cottingham's Modernist On the Move, 1994; contbr. revs., features, column to San Jose Mercury News, ARTWEEK, ARTnews. Mem. Internat. Assn. Art Critics. Home: 225 Avalon Dr Los Altos CA 94022

BURKHART, SANDRA MARIE, art gallery director; b. Cleve., Dec. 29, 1942; d. John Joseph Norris and Audrey Eleanor Kegg McGuire Marshall; m. Thomas Henry Burkhart, Oct. 29, 1960 (div. Sept. 26, 1979); children: Bryan, Brad, Lisa, Michelle. Student, Evergreen Valley Coll., San Jose, 1978-80, San Jose City Coll., 1978-80, West Valley Coll., Saratoga, Calif., 1978-79. Med. technician Eye Med. Clinic, San Jose, 1980-83; ind. corp. art salesperson San Jose, 1983-92; corp. sales dir. Phoenix Gallery, San Jose, 1986-88; v.p. mktg. Whittlers Mother, San Francisco, 1989-90; dir. Martin Lawrence Galleries, Santa Clara, Calif., 1990—. Home: 1353 Greenwich Ct San Jose CA 95125

BURKHEAD, VIRGINIA RUTH, rehabilitation nurse; b. Marlow, Okla., Apr. 11, 1937; d. Norvin Woodrow Whitehead and Harriet Louise (Pittman) Mayes; m. Marvin Vern Foster, Oct. 16, 1956 (div. 1964); children: Deborah, Marcia, Marva, Laurie, Sheila; m. Robert Burdett Burkhead, Apr. 11, 1987. ADN, Casper Coll., 1971; BSN, Wash. State U., 1994. RN, Wash. Staff nurse, house supr., enterostomal therapy nurse Meml. Hosp. Natrona County, Casper, Wyo., 1971-79; enterostomal therapy nurse, coord. ostomy program Holy Family Hosp., Spokane, 1979—, coord. neurol. rehab. program, 1985—. Deaconess 1st Christian Ch., Spokane, 1986—. Mem. Assn. Rehab. Nurses, Wound, Ostomy and Contence Nurses Soc., Jacks and Jennys Square Dance Club (coun. del. 1992), Sigma Theta Tau. Mem. Christian Ch. (Disciples of Christ). Home: 2116 E Lincoln Rd Spokane WA 99207-7723 Office: Holy Family Hosp 5633 N Lidgerwood St Spokane WA 99207-1224

BURKHOLDER, HARRIETT ANN, elementary education educator; b. Richwood, W.Va., Nov. 26, 1936; d. Clemmie Harper and Louise Gibson; m. Edsel W. Burkholder; 1 child, Edsel. BS, Bowling Green (Ohio) Coll., 1965; M Elem. Edn., U. Pitts., 1975. Cert. tchr., W.Va., Ohio, Pa. Tchr. Nettie (W.Va.) Elem. Sch., 1959-62, Genoa (Ohio) Elem. Sch., 1962-70; tchr. chpt. 1 South Fayette (Pa.) Twp. Schs., 1970—. Home: RR 3 Box 38 Monongahela PA 15063-9703 Office: South Fayette Twp Elem Sch 2250 Old Oakdale Rd Mc Donald PA 15057

BURKLAND, PAMELA RODGERS, company executive; b. San Mateo, Calif., Apr. 22, 1943; d. Robert Charles and Mary Ellen (McNerney) Rodgers; m. Melvin Elwyn Ohlson, Jan. 20, 1969 (div. 1976); children: Ingrid Anna, Arik Mikkel; m. Arthur Steven Rolon, Oct. 9, 1991. BA in Internat. Rels., Marylhurst Coll., 1966. Internat. mktg. adminstr. Varian Assocs., Santa Clara, Calif., 1978-85; export licensing supr. Varian Assocs., Palo Alto, Calif., 1985-87, internat. order adminstr. supr., 1987-90, mgr. internat. svcs. and transp., 1990-95; ops. mgr. Peregrin Logistics Systems, Portland, Oreg., 1995—; corp. accounts mgr. Peregrin Logistics Systems, Portland, 1996. Author of poetry. Mem. NAFE, Coun. Logistics Mgmt., Profl. Assn. Exporters and Importers (corp. sec. 1988-94, corp. pres. 1995—, founder, dir. 1986—), Bus. Action Group, Portland Metro Bus. Women, Internat. Soc. Poets, Portland Art Mus. Republican. Office: Peregrin Logistics Systems 8933 NE Marx Ave Portland OR 97218

BURKS, KATHLEEN ANN, school counselor; b. Reno, Nev., Jan. 9, 1952; d. Elmer and Mary Catherine (Vanderwerff) B.; m. Glenn Francis McKnight, Aug. 23, 1975 (div. Feb. 1981). BS in Elem. Edn., U. Nev., Reno, 1973, MA in Counseling and Ednl. Psychology, 1995. Lic. ednl. pers., Nev. Elem. tchr. Mineral County Schs., Hawthorne, Nev., 1973-75, Rice Sch. Dist., San Carlos, Ariz., 1984-85, Galena Park Ins. Sch. Dist., Houston, 1985-86; substitute tchr. Humboldt County Schs., Winnemucca, Nev., 1975-77, elem. tchr., 1977-82, 86-95, sch. counselor, 1995—. V.p., Pres. Winnemucca Fine Arts Gallery, 1994, past-pres., 1995; mem. com. Shooting the West, Winnemucca, 1988-92. Mem. ACA, Am. Sch. Counselors Assn., Assn. for Specialists in Group Work, Phi Kappa Phi, Kappa Tau Alpha. Office: French Ford Mid Sch 5495 Palisade Winnemucca NV 89445

BURLAGE, DOROTHY DAWSON, clinical psychologist; b. San Antonio, Sept. 13, 1937; d. Joseph M. and Virginia (Hendrix) Dawson. BA, U. Tex., 1959; EdM, Harvard U., 1972, PhD, 1978. Lic. psychologist, Mass. Horace Lentz lectr. Harvard Coll., 1972-73; rsch. assoc. in psychiatry Harvard Med. Sch., Cambridge, Mass., 1976-78; rsch. assoc. Children's Hosp. Med. Ctr., Boston, 1978-79; clin. fellow psychology Harvard Med. Sch., 1978-80; staff psychologist Eliot Community Mental Health Ctr., Concord, Mass., 1980-85; instr. dept. psychiatry Harvard Med. Sch., 1984-88; mem. staff dept. psychiatry Newton Wellesley Hosp., 1986-92; now with Harvard U. Health Svcs.; pvt. practice clin. psychologist Cambridge; clin. supr. Children's Hosp., Boston, 1994—. Contbr. articles to profl. jours. Bd. dirs. Children's Mus., Boston, 1988-94, Profls. for Parents and Families, 1994; mem. scientist adv. bd. Mind Sci. Found., 1994. Grantee HEW, Bus. and Profl. Women's Found., 1976; fellow NIMH, 1972-73, 73-74, Zeta Tau Alpha, 1972-73; Woodrow Wilson fellow in Women's Studies, 1976-77. Mem. Am. Psychol. Assn., Mass. Psychol. Assn., AOA. Home: 10 Lancaster St Apt 5 Cambridge MA 02140-2816

BURLESON, DAPHNE, traffic assistant; b. Bklyn., July 3, 1962; d. Morris and Naomi B. BS, U. Colo., 1994. Teaching asst. Dept. Social Svcs., Denver, 1993-94; publ. asst. Morris Pub. Co., 1994-95; traffic asst. Multimedia, N.Y.C., 1995—. Author: Ebrona, 1994 (Author's award 1994). Mem. Am. Geophys. Union, Smithsonian Inst., Nat. Trust Historic Preservation. Republican. Methodist.

BURLINGAME, BARBARA C., state legislator; b. Woonsocket, R.I., June 6, 1947; divorced; children: Gregory, Jeffery. BSBA, Bryant Coll., 1989. Rep. dist. 62 State of R.I., dep. majority leader, mem. finance com.; rep. R.I. House; mem. task force on domestic violence R.I. Supreme Court; mem. R.I. Port Authority, R.I. Human Resource Investment Coun., House Dem. Caucus on Bus. Issues; v.p. adminstrn. and small bus. svc. No. R.I. C. of C.; mem. Adv. Coun. of Options for Working Parents. Mem. NAACP, R.I. Women's Pol. Caucus (pres.), Woonsocket Rotary Club, Greater Woonsocket YMCA, Lambda Class Leadership R.I. Democrat. Home: 565 Fairmount St Woonsocket RI 02895-4157 Office: RI House of Reps State Capitol Providence RI 02903*

BURMAN, DIANE BERGER, organization development consultant; b. Pitts., Dec. 7, 1936; d. Morris Milton and Dorothy June (Barkin) Berger; m. Sheldon Oscar Burman, Dec. 15, 1926; children: Allison Beth, Jocelyn Holly, Harrison Emory Guy. BA, Vassar Coll., 1958; MA, Middlebury Coll., 1961. Tchr. of French Allderdice High Sch., Pitts., 1960-61, Mamaroneck (N.Y.) High Sch., 1961-64; personnel specialist G.D. Searle & Co., Skokie, Ill., 1972-77, orgn. devel. tng. cons., 1977-78; personnel and orgn. devel. cons. Abbott Labs., North Chgo., 1978-82; orgn. devel. cons., v.p., mgr. career devel. Harris Bank, Chgo., 1982—. Mem. edit. bd. Orgn. Devel. Jour., 1987. Bd. advisors Grad. Sch. Bus. No. Ill. U. Mem. ASTD (bd. dirs. Chgo. career devel. profl. practice area 1987—), Orgn. Devel. Network (exec. dir. Chgo. chpt. 1986-89), Assn. Psychol. Type-Nat. Conf., Orgn. Devel. Inst. (adv. bd. 1987—, chmn. nat. conf. 1990), Nat. Assn. Bank Women, Internat. Assn. Career Mgmt. Profls., Vassar Club (bd. dirs. 1975-80, 95—). Jewish. Home: 247 Prospect Ave Highland Park IL 60035-3357 Office: Harris Bank 111 W Monroe St Chicago IL 60603-4003

BURMAN, MARSHA LINKWALD, lighting manufacturing executive, marketing development professional; b. Balt., Jan. 9, 1949; d. William and Lena (Ronin) Linkwald; m. Robert Schlosser, July 2, 1972 (div. 1980); children: Melanie, David. BS in Edn. cum laude, Kent State U., 1970, MA in Sociology summa cum laude, 1971. Cert. in secondary edn., Ohio. Spl. project dir. tng. and rsch. ctr. Planned Parenthood, Chgo., 1978; with mgmt. edn. ctr. Gould, Inc., Chgo., 1979, program adminstr., 1979-80; sys. trainer Lithonia Lighting, 1981; mgr. tng. and edn. Lithonia Lighting, Chgo., 1981-86; dir. mktg., tng. and devel., corp. tng., mgr. Lithonia Lighting Ctr., Atlanta, 1986—. Author: (booklet) Putting Your Best Foot Forward (award Am. Soc. Tng. and Devel.), 1982; author, editor: Dictionary of Lighting Industry Terminology, 1989, 3d edit., 1990. U.S. Office Edn. grantee, 1971. Mem. ASTD (bd. dirs. 1982, spl. projects dir. Atlanta chpt. 1982, Vol. of Yr., Cmty. Leader Am. 1987, 89, 92), Tng. Dirs. Roundtable (founding mem.), Lithonia Lighting Mgmt. Club (v.p. 1982-83), Toastmasters. Office: Lithonia Lighting Div Nat Svc Industries 1400 Lester Rd NW Conyers GA 30207-3908

BURNETT, CAROL, actress, comedienne, singer; b. San Antonio, Apr. 26, 1933; d. Jody and Louise (Creighton) B.; m. Joseph Hamilton, 1963 (div.); children: Carrie Louise, Jody Ann, Erin Kate. Student, UCLA, 1952-54. Introduced comedy song I Made a Fool of Myself Over John Foster Dulles, 1957; Broadway debut in Once Upon a Mattress, 1959; regular performer in Garry Moore TV show, 1959-62; appeared several CBS-TV spls., 1962-63; star Carol Burnett Show, CBS-TV, 1966-77, Carol & Co., 1990-91; appeared on Broadway, play Once Upon a Mattress, 1960, play Plaza Suite, 1970, musical play I Do, I Do, 1973, Same Time Next Year, 1977, television miniseries Fresno, 1986; films include Who's Been Sleeping in My Bed, 1963, Pete 'n' Tillie, 1972, Front Page, 1974, A Wedding, 1977, Health, 1979, Four Seasons, 1981, Chu Chu and the Phillyflash, 1981, Annie, 1982, Noises Off, 1992; TV movies Friendly Fire, 1978, The Grass is Always Greener Over the Septic Tank, 1979, The Tenth Month, 1979, Life of the Party, 1982, Between Friends, 1983, Hostage, 1988; club engagements, Harrah's Club, The Sands,

Caesar's Palace, MGM Grand. Recipient outstanding comedienne award Am. Guild Variety Artists, 5 times; Emmy award for outstanding variety performance Acad. TV Arts and Scis., 5 times; TV Guide award for outstanding female performer, 1961, 62, 63; Peabody award, 1963; Golden Globe award for outstanding comedienne of year Fgn. Press Assn., 8 times; Woman of Year award Acad. TV Arts and Scis.; 12 People's Choice awards; 1st ann. Nat. TV Critics Circle award for outstanding performance, 1977; San Sebastian Film Festival award for best actress for A Wedding, 1978; 1st Ace award Best Actress Between Friends, 1983, Horatio Alger award Horatio Alger Assn. Disting. Ams., 1988; named One of 20 Most Admired Women Gallup Poll, 1977. Address: Bill Robinson ICM 8942 Wilshire Blvd Fl 2 Beverly Hills CA 90211-1934*

BURNETT, CORRINE, healthcare administrator; b. Chgo, May 5, 1941; d. Napoleon Burnett and Henrietta (Forbush) Williams. BSN, Tuskegee U., 1964; MSN, Boston Coll., 1972; MBA, Marquette U., 1988. RN, Wis. Commd. 2d lt. U.S. Army, 1963, advanced through grades to lt. col.; supr., asst. prof., head nurse U.S. Army Nurse Corps, 1965-86; ret. U.S. Army, 1986; supr., acting divsn. chief Fort Logan Mental Health Hosp., Denver, 1977-78, nurse exec., 1980-84; asst. prof. U. Colo., Denver, 1978-80; v.p. patient svcs. St. Anthony Hosp., Milw., 1985; dep. health commr. City of Milw., 1988-92; pres., CEO Weiji, Inc., Milw., 1992—, Weiji Supportive Systems, Inc., Milw., 1993—, Front Door Health Systems, Inc., Milw., 1994—, ODI, Inc., Milw., 1995—; mem. quality assurance Humana, Milw., 1993—. Bd. dirs. Curative Rehab., Milw., 1991-93, DePaul Hosp., Milw., 1989-92, Milw. Access Telecomm., Milw., 1993-94, Isaac Coggs health Connection, Milw., 1991-93; fundraiser, founder WOMO Charities, Milw., 1995—. Decorated Bronze Star, 1970, Presdl. citation, 1967, 70. Office: Weiji Supportive Systems Inc 2214 N Terrace Ave Milwaukee WI 53202

BURNETT, ELIZABETH (BETSY BURNETT), counselor; b. Columbus, Ohio, July 17, 1953; m. Gilbert C. Burnett, Jan. 2, 1973; children: Jeffrey, Stephanie. BS in Med. Tech. with honors, Rutgers U., 1976; MA in Counseling with honors, Denver Sem., 1992. Med. technologist various hosps., Denver and Plainfield, N.J., 1976-92; missions dir. Bear Creek Ch. and Family of Faith Ch., Denver, 1985-89; counseling dir. Providence Homes, Denver, 1989—; dir. Providence Counseling Ministry, Denver, 1993—; program cons. various urban counseling svcs. and rehabs., Denver, Colorado Springs, Mich., Calif., Australia, 1992—; urban ministry cons. Denver Sem., 1991-95; contract counselor So. Gables Ch., Littleton, Colo., 1992-96, presenter divorce recovery workshops, 1992-96; spkr. in field. Author: Handbook of Urban Christian Counseling, 1992. Children's dir. mothers of preschoolers, vacation Bible sch., and missions edn. program Bear Creek Ch., Denver, 1982-85; deaconess, lay leader So. Gables Ch., Littleton, 1992-96. Recipient med. tech. award Muhlenberg Hosp., 1976. Mem. Am. Counseling Assn., Am. Assn. Christian Counselors, Internat. Assn. Addictions & Offender Counselors, Assn. Multicultural Counseling and Devel., Christians for Bibl. Equality, Am. Soc. Clin. Pathologists. Office: Providence Homes 801 Logan St Denver CO 80203-3114

BURNETT, IRIS JACOBSON, corporate communications specialist; b. Bklyn., Nov. 14, 1946; d. Milton and Rose (Dubroff) Groman; m. Allan Jacobson; 1 child, Seth Jacobson; m. David Burnett, Jan. 29, 1984; 1 child, Jordan Burnett. BS, Emerson Coll., 1968, MS in Comm. Theory, 1971. Instr. Boston U., 1971-73; dir. press and pub. rels. Dept. Parks and Recreation, Boston, 1975-77; dir. internat. visitors U.S. Dept. State, Washington, 1977-80; dir. security Dem. Nat. Conv., N.Y.C., 1980; sr. v.p. Arrive Unltd., Washington, 1980-84; pres. In Advance, Arlington, 1984-87; asst. prof. Am. U., Washington, 1987-90; pres. Sound Remarks, Arlington, 1990-92; exec. dir. Debates '92, Washington, 1992; chief staff USIA, Washington, 1993-96; sr. v.p. for corp. comm. USA Network, N.Y.C., 1996—. Author: Hart for President, 1984, National Surrogate Schedule, 1984, Inauguration, Transition: Clinton Gore Campaign, 1992. Active McGovern presdl. campaign, Boston, 1972; mem. nat. staff Udall for Pres., Washington, 1974-76, Carter-Mondale '76, 1976-77; bd. dirs. Tap Am. Project, 1994—; official del. 4th World Conf. on Women. Mem. Women's Fgn. Policy Group, Emily's List, Nat. Jewish Dem. Coalition.

BURNETT, JUDITH JANE, foundation administrator, consultant; b. Muncie, Ind., Aug. 21, 1947; d. Albert Ward and Jane M. (Collins) Burnett; student public schs. Saleswoman, Collins Mobile Home Sales, Muncie, 1970-73; sales mgr. HiWay, Inc., Anderson, Ind., 1973-75; service dir., then ops. mgr. Indiana Homemakers, Inc., Indpls., 1975-80, exec. v.p., 1980-83, also dir.; corp. sec. Mgmt. Alternatives, Inc., Indpls., 1984-85; exec. v.p., dir. Three—I Homemakers, Inc., Illini Homemakers, Inc., 1980-83; dir. Home Care Med. Products Co., 1980-82; adminstr. ECF Med. Billing, 1987-88; adminstrv. Extended Med. Svcs., 1988-92; owner Projects and Promotions, 1988—; exec. dir. Ryan White Found., 1994—; mem. council Central Ind. Health Systems Agy., 1980-83; mgr. Eynon for Congress Campaign, 1985-86; mem. Homemaker, Handyman, Home Health Aide Task Force, 1980-83, sec., 1980-81, Marion County Council Rep. Women, Marion County GOP Strategy Team; vol. access control mgr. Tenth Pan An. Games, 1987; mem. bd. Ind. AIDS Fund, 1994-96, Nat. Children's Film Festival, 1995—. Home: 9992 Estep Dr Indianapolis IN 46280

BURNETTE, CAROLYN LEE, rehabilitation nurse; b. Tulsa, July 27, 1967; d. Richard Lee and Mankie (Ray) Creech; m. Kenneth Junior Burnette, Dec. 2, 1989; children: Tyler Anthony, Shawn Allan. AAS, Tulsa Jr. Coll., 1988. Cert. Rehab. Nurs. Staff nurse orthopedics St. John Med. Ctr., Tulsa, 1988-89, charge nurse rehab., 1989-93; charge nurse rehab. N.E. Okla. Rehab. Hosp., Tulsa, 1993, dir. nursing rehab., 1993-94; staff nurse Quality Home Health, Cassville, Mo., 1994-96; rehab. nurse coord. Columbia Hosp. South, Springfield, Mo., 1996—; mem. cmty. adv. bd. N.E. Okla. Rehab. Hosp., Tulsa, 1993-94; mem. Tulsa Area Dirs. Nursing and Educators, Tulsa, 1993-94. Mem. Assn. Rehab. Nurses, Assn. Spinal Cord Injury Nurses, Nat. Stroke Assn., Okla. Head Injury Found. Republican. Home: PO Box 54 Cassville MO 65625 Office: Columbia Hosp South 3535 S National Springfield MO 65807

BURNEY, VICTORIA KALGAARD, business consultant, civic worker; b. Los Angeles, Apr. 12, 1943; d. Oscar Albert and Dorothy Elizabeth (Peterson) Kalgaard; children: Kim Elizabeth, J. Hewett. BA with honors, U. Mont., 1965; MA, U. No. Colo., 1980; postgrad. Webster U., St. Louis, 1983-84. Exec. dir. Hill County Community Action, Havre, Mont., 1966-67; community orgn. specialist ACCESS, Escondido, Calif., 1967-68; program devel. and community orgn. specialist Community Action Programs, Inc., Pensacola, Fla., 1968-69; cons. Escambia County Sch. Bd., Fla., 1969-71; pres. Kal Kreations, Kailua, Hawaii, 1974-77; instr., dir. office human resources devel. Palomar Coll., San Marcos, Calif., 1978-81; chief exec. officer IDET Corp., San Marcos, 1981-87; cons. County of Riverside, Calif., 1983. Mem. San Diego County Com. on Handicapped, San Diego, 1979; cons. tribal resource devel., Escondido, Calif., 1979; mem. exec. com. Social Services Coordinating Council, San Diego, 1982-83; mem. pvt. sector com. and planning and rev. com. Calif. Employment and Tng. Adv. Council, Sacramento, 1982-83; bd. mgrs. Santa Margarita Family YMCA, Vista, Calif., 1984-86; bd. dirs. North County Community Action Program, Escondido, 1978, Casa de Amparo, San Luis Rey, Calif., 1980-83; mem. San Diego County Pub. Welfare Adv. Bd., 1979-83, chairperson, 1981; mem. Calif. Rep. Cen. Com., Sacramento, 1989—; ofcl. San Diego County Rep. Cen. Com., 1985-93, exec. com., 1987-92, 2nd vice-chmn. 1991-92; chmn. 74th Assembly Dist. Rep. Caucus, 1989-90; chmn. Working Ptnrs., 1987-90; trustee Rancho Santa Fe Community Ctr., 1991-92; active Nat. Assistance League, 1993—; bd. dirs. Assistance League North Coast, 1994—, mem. 1993—. Mem. Nat. Assn. County Employment and Tng. Adminstrs. (chairperson econ. resources com. 1982-85), Calif. Assn. Local Econ. Devel., San Diego Econ. Devel. Corp., Oceanside Econ. devel. Council (bd. dirs. 1983-87), Oceanside C. of C., San Marcos C. of C. (bd. dirs. 1982-85), Carlsbad C. of C. (indsl. council 1982-85), Escondido C. of C. (comml. and indsl. devel. council 1982-87), Vista C. of C. (vice chairperson econ. devel. com. 1982-83), Vista Econ. Devel. Assn., Nat. Job Tng. Partnership, San Diego County Golden Eagle Club.

BURNHAM, JOY JONES, education educator; b. Alexander City, Ala., Oct. 6, 1962; d. William and Minnie Jones; m. Rick Burnham, Aug. 6, 1988. BS in Elem. Edn., Auburn U., 1986, PhD in Counselor Edn., 1995; MS in Counseling, Jacksonville State U., 1990. Lic. profl. counselor, Ala. Instr. Auburn (Ala.) U., 1992-93; adj. prof. Jacksonville (Ala.) State U., 1994-95, U. Ala., Gadsden, 1995—. Active Jr. League Anniston (Ala.)/ Calhoun County, 1991. Mem. Am. Counseling Assn., Am. Sch. Counseling Assn., Ala. Counseling Assn. (exec. coun. mem. 1992), Ala. Sch. Counseling Assn., Ala. Assn. Counselor Edn. and Supervison.

BURNHAM, PATRICIA WHITE, consultant on aging, business executive, author; b. Omaha, July 30, 1933; d. William Max and Berniece Irene (Shockey) Orr; m. William L. White, June 18, 1955 (div. Nov. 1979); children: Lucinda, Christopher, Duncan; m. Robert A. Burnham, Feb. 23, 1980. BA in English, DePauw U., Greencastle, Ind., 1955; MA in English, Ill. State U., 1966, PhD in Adminstrn., 1977. Tchr. Morton Grove (Ill.) and Evansville (Ind.) pub. schs., 1955-60; instr. Ill. State U., Normal, 1963-71, dir. Nat. Student Exchange, 1971-74, dir. continuing edn., 1974-76, asst. dean, 1976-79; assoc. dir. Ill. Bd. Higher Edn., Springfield, 1979-80; assoc. vice provost Ohio State U., Columbus, 1980-81; specialist bus. ins. Nationwide Ins. Co., Columbus, 1981-83; v.p. pvt. banking Chase Manhattan Bank, N.A., N.Y.C., 1983-88; pres. Transitions Group, Inc., East Burke, Vt., 1986—. Author: Life's Third Act, 1994; contbr. articles to publs. and seminars on adult policies and programs. Bd. dirs. Mennonite Hosp., Bloomington, Ill., Ind. Coll. Fund, N.Y.; pres. Coun. Vt. Elders, 1994—. Mem. Am. Assn. Higher Edn., Am. Edn. Rsch. Assn., League of Women Voters (v.p. 1991-92), Phi Beta Kappa, Phi Delta Kappa. Congregationalist. Office: Transitions Group Inc PO Box 239 East Burke VT 05832-0239

BURNHAM, SOPHY, writer; b. Balt., Dec. 12, 1936; d. George Cochran and Sophy Tayloe (Snyder) Doub; m. David B. Burnham, Mar. 12, 1960 (div. 1984); children: Sarah Tayloe, Molly Bright. BA cum laude, Smith Coll., 1958. Aquisitions editor David McKay, Inc., N.Y.C., 1971-73; contbg. editor Town and Country mag., N.Y.C., 1975-80, New Art Examiner mag., Washington, 1985-86, Mus. & Arts/Washington, 1987-89, New Woman mag., 1984-90; exec. dir. Fund for New American Plays, 1992—; author, playwright, Washington, 1970—. Author: (nonfiction) The Art Crowd (Book of Month Club alt. selection), 1973, The Landed Gentry, 1978, A Book of Angels, 1990, Angel Letters, 1991, For Writers Only, 1994, (novels) Buccaneer, 1977, The Dogwalker, 1979, Revelations, 1992, The President's Angel, 1993, (plays) The Study, The Nightingale, Beauty and the Beast, The Witch's Tale (Best Children's Radio Play 1980), Penelope (1st prize Women's Theatre, Seattle), Snowstorms (winner N.C. Festival of New Am. Plays 1993), (films) The Smithsonian Whale, The Leaf Thieves; contbr. articles, essays to mags. and jours. Mem. lit. panel D.C. Arts and Humanities Commn., 1986, 87; founding mem. The Studio Theatre, 1978-80, chmn. bd. dirs., 1979-80; founding mem. D.C. Community Humanities Coun., 1979-85, vice chair 1979-80. Recipient Daughter of Mark Twain award, 1974, Award of Excellence Communications Arts mag., 1980, Pub. Humanities award D.C. Cmty. Humanities Coun., 1988, Virginia Mann New Plays award N.C. Festival, 1993; D.C. Arts and Humanities Coun. grantee, 1980-81, Helene Wurlitzer Found. of Taos grantee, 1981, 83, 91, Office of Advanced Drama Rsch. grantee U. Minn., 1976. Mem. Women's Internat. Theatre Alliance (sec. 1979-81), Octagon Com. (bd. dirs. 1984-89), Cosmos Club.

BURNHAM, VIRGINIA SCHROEDER, medical writer; b. Savannah, Ga., Dec. 9, 1908; d. Henry Alfred and Natalie Morris (Munde) Schroeder; children: Douglass L., Peter B., Gilliat S. (dec.), William W., Virginia L., Daniel B. Student, Smith Coll., Barnard Coll. V.p., sales mgr., bd. dirs. Conn. Mfg. Co. Inc., Waterbury, 1952-61, pres., chief exec. officer, bd. dirs., 1961-73; pres. Burnham Industries, Watertown, Conn., 1956-59; pres., bd. dirs. NuTip Corp., Waterbury, 1962-64, Maretta Inc., N.Y.C., 1963-65; pres., treas., bd. dirs. Tech., Inc., Waterbury, 1969-73; sec. The Gaylord Hosp., Wallingford, Conn., 1970-81; pres. Tech. Internat. Corp., 1973-75, Tech. Interaction, Med. Cons., Greenwich, Conn., 1975—, The Paper Mill, Inc., 1989-92; dir. Community Mental Health Ctr., Inc., Stamford, Conn., 1974-78; mem. nat. adv. food and drug com. FDA, Dept. Health, Edn., and Welfare, Washington, 1973-76; mem. health rsch. facilities coun. NIH, Washington, 1959-61, nat. adv. heart coun., 1957-60; mem. ad-hoc com. cons. on med. rsch. Subcom. Labor, Health and Welfare, U.S. Senate Appropriations Com., Washington, 1959-60. Co-author: Knowing Yourself, 1992, The Two-Edged Sword, 1990, The Lake With Two Dams, 1993, Since Time Began, 1994; contbr. articles to Am. Health Found. Newsletter, Jour. Sci. Health, Conn. Med. Jour. Mem. adv. coun. steering com. The Episc. Ch. Found., 1970-76, Commn. to Reform the Ct. System, Gen. Assembly, State of Conn., 1974-78, nat. adv. coun. SBA, Washington 1976-77, chmn. dist. adv. coun., Hartford, Conn., 1976-77; pres. Conn. Citizens for Judicial Modernization, Inc., Hartford, 1976-78; mem. Presdl. Task Force on Rehab. of Prisoners, Washington, 1969-70; bd. dirs. Assn. to Unite the Democracies, Washington, 1982—; chmn. dist. adv. coun. Small Bus. Adminstrn., Hartford, 1976-77; pres. Conn. chpt. Am. Health Found., N.Y.C., 1971-73; dir. exec. com. Greater N.Y. Safety Coun., N.Y.C., 1971-79, dir., 1964-79; vice-chmn., dir. Conn. Coun. of Nat. Coun. Crime and Delinquency, Hartford, 1965-73; mem. adv. com. Conn. Regional Med. Program, 1973-76, FDA, Washington and many more civic and health orgns. Decorated Knighthood of Honour and Merit, Sovereign Hospitaler Order of St. John of Jerusalem, Knights of Malta, 1985; recipient Ira V. Hiscock award Conn. Pub. Health Assn., 1986; Silver Key award The Gaylord Hosp., 1970, Disting. Svc. award Conn. Heart Assn., 1960, Conn. Mother of Yr. award Am. Mothers Com., 1951, Cert. of Honor, Conn. Cancer Soc., 1950, Merit award Am. Heart Assn., 1960. Mem. AAAS, APHA, Am. Cancer Soc., Am. Heart Assn., Am. Holistic Med. Found., Am. Women in Sci., Conn. Bus. & Industry Assn., Conn. Pub. Health Assn., Nat. Assn. Mfrs., N.Y. Acad. Sci. Republican. Episcopalian. Home and Office: 41 Duncan Dr Greenwich CT 06831-3616

BURNS, BARBARA, lawyer; b. Jersey City, May 12, 1951; d. Thomas Jr. and Regina (Trzanowska) Gangemi; m. Damon Williams, Jan. 4, 1977 (div. 1986); 1 child, Jacob Williams; m. Matthew Burns, Feb. 7, 1987; 1 child, Olivia Burns. BA, Newton Coll., 1973; JD cum laude, New Eng. Sch. Law, 1976. Bar: Mass. 1977, N.J., 1984, U.S. Dist. Ct. Mass. 1977, U.S. Dist. Ct. N.J. 1984, U.S. Supreme Ct. 1988. Corporate counsel Acton (Mass.) Corp., 1977-79; asst. gen. counsel Greater Media, Inc., East Brunswick, N.J., 1984-88, assoc. gen. counsel, 1988-93, v.p., gen. counsel, 1993—. Mem. Am. Corporate Counsel Assn., Fed. Comm. Bar Assn., N.J. Bar Assn. Office: Greater Media Inc Two Kennedy Blvd East Brunswick NJ 08816

BURNS, BARBARA BELTON, investment company executive; b. Fredericktown, Mo., Dec. 10, 1944; d. Clyde Monroe and Mary Celestial (Anderson) Belton; m. Larry J. Bohannon; Mar. 27, 1963 (div.); 1 child, Timothy Joseph; m. Donald Edward Burns, Nov. 1, 1980; stepchildren: Brian Edward, David Keone (dec.). Student, Ohio State U., 1970-75. Dir. nat. sales Am. Way, Chgo., 1976-77; recruiter Bell & Howell Schs., Columbus, Ohio, 1978-80; pres., founder Bardon Investment Corp., Naples, Fla., 1980-90; founder Cambridge Mgmt. Co., Columbus, 1983-86; pres., CEO Charter's Total Wardrobe Care, Columbus, 1984-89; founder, exec. Phoenix Bus. Group, Inc., 1990—. Treas. Vicace-Columbus Symphony, 1981-82; fundraiser Grant Hosp., Columbus, 1986; chmn. Impresarios/Opera Columbus, 1986-87; founding mem. Columbus Women's Bd., 1986-87; mem. devel. com. Babe Zaharias/Am. Cancer Soc.; auction chmn. Opera Ball-Opera/ Columbus, 1989; tennis tournament chmn. NABOR Scholarship Fund, 1990, 91; mem. Philharmonic Chorale, Naples, Fla., 1992; spokesperson Diabetes Found. Collier Co., Fla., 1992—, pres., 1994; elder Vanderbilt Presbyn. Ch., 1994; prs. Diabetes Found., Inc., 1994—. Named Entrepreneur of Yr. Arthur Young/Venture mag., 1988, Outstanding Vol. Opera Columbus, 1986, Vol. of Yr. Diabetes Found., 1994; recipient Design award Reynoldsburg C. of C., 1988. Mem. Naples C. of C. (new bus. com. 1990—). Republican.

BURNS, BEBE LYN, journalist; b. Baytown, Tex., Nov. 2, 1952; d. L.L. and Edith Elizabeth (Smith) B.; m. George Frederick Rhodes Jr., Nov. 30, 1980; 1 child, Elizabeth Kathleen. BA, U. Houston, 1974; MS in Journalism, Northwestern U., 1975. Reporter, anchor Sta. WSPA-TV, Spartanburg, S.C., 1975-76, Sta. KHOU-TV, Houston, 1976-79; reporter Sta. KTVI-TV, St. Louis, 1979-82; bus. reporter Sta. KPRC-TV, Houston, 1982-95; prin. Burns Kopatic, Houston, 1996—. Bd. dirs. Presbyn. Sch., 1996—, Houston Area Parkinson's Soc., 1991-95, CanCare of Houston, Inc., 1995—; founding mem. Greater Houston Women's Found.; active Friends of Fleming Park, Boulevard Oaks Civic Assn. Recipient awards Headliners Club Tex. 1988, Tex. AP Broadcasters, 1988, Am. Women in Radio & TV, 1988, Press Club Houston, 1987, 88, Press Club Dallas, 1981, 93, Employee award for help to jobless Tex. Employment Commn., 1993, Bus. Advocacy award North Harris-Montgomery C.C. Dist. & Bus. & Industry Coun., 1993; named one of Women on the Move Houston Post and Tex. Exec. Women, 1988, Small Bus. Media Advocate of Yr. SBA, 1992. Mem. Soc. Profl. Journalists. Methodist. Office: Burns Kopatic 5599 San Felipe Ste 1210 Houston TX 77056

BURNS, B(ILLYE) JANE, museum director; b. Yeager, Okla., Nov. 1, 1940; d. William O. and Berniece (Floyd) French; m. Richard D. Burns, June 12, 1960 (div. 1990); children: Jennifer, Richard, Timothy, Daniel. AS, Okla. State U., 1960; BA in Bus., Goshen Coll., 1988. Treas. Woodlawn Nature Coun., Inc., Elkhart, Ind., 1975-82; cons. Am. art Midwest Mus. Am. Art, Elkhart, 1978-81, founding trustee, 1978—, dir., 1980-91; cons. Heritage Fine Arts, Elkhart; bd. dirs. Soc. Bank, Key Corp. Mem. Woodlaw Nature Coun., Inc., Elkhart, 4-Arts Club, Elkhart, Ind. Advs. for Art, Elkhart County Symphony. Mem. LWV (bd. dirs. 1985-91, v.p. 1990-91), Michiana Arts and Scis. Coun., Concert Club. Democrat. Methodist. Home: 2413 Greenleaf Blvd Elkhart IN 46514-4055 Office: MW Mus Am Art 429 S Main St Elkhart IN 46516-3210

BURNS, BRENDA, state legislator; b. LaGrange, Ga., Nov. 22, 1950; m. Bruce Burns; 3 children. Sen. dist. 17 State of Ariz.; chmn. profession and employment com.; ethics coms. judiciary com.; vice-chmn. com. and econ. devel. com. econ. devel., internat. trade & tourism, ways & means, appropriations, edn. coms.; mem. com. and fin. com., apptd. to western legis. conf. federalism task force; nat. dir. Am. Leg. Exch. Coun. Republican. Home: 8220 W Orange Dr Glendale AZ 85303-6006 Office: State Capitol 1700 W Washington St Phoenix AZ 85007-2812

BURNS, CANDICE, elementary and special education educator; b. Detroit, Oct. 1, 1950; d. Gerald Edgar and Irma Dee (Lyle) B.; m. Brian Maiville, Aug. 13, 1977; children: Marguerite Maiville, Joseph Maiville. BA, U. Mich., 1972; MA in Reading and Learning Disabilities, Oakland U., Rochester, Mich., 1980. Cert. tchr. elem. K-8, social studies, spl. edn./ learning disabilities, Mich. Elem. tchr. Willow Run Schs., Ypsilanti, Mich., 1972-78, Pinckney (Mich.) Schs., 1978-80; spl. edn. tchr. South Lyon (Mich.) Schs., 1980-87; elem. spl. edn. tchr. Dexter (Mich.) Cmty. Schs., 1987—; cons. Washtenaw Ind. Sch. Dist., Ann Arbor, Mich., 1992-94; co-chair Sch. Improvement Team, Dexter, 1992-93; presenter Nat. Coun. Exceptional Children, 1995, 96, State of Mich. Coun. Exceptional Children, 1995. Dir. jr. ch. Dexter United Meth. Ch., 1986-90. Mem. NEA, Mich. Edn. Assn., Learning Disabilities Assn., Mich. Reading Assn., Mich. Coun. Tchrs. Math. Office: Dexter Cmty Schs 2704 Baker Rd Dexter MI 48130-1535

BURNS, CAROLYN DIANE, music educator; b. Alton, Ill., Apr. 29, 1950; d. Robert Milton and Emma Rosalie (Weigand) Krase; m. Robert Joseph Burns, Aug. 14, 1982; children: Emily, Austin. Student, Cin. Coll. Music Conservatory, 1972-75; BS, Rocky Mountain Coll., 1980; M of Music Edn., U. Mont., 1987. Cert. music tchr. K-12, Mont. Sec., staff edn. Good Samaritan Hosp., Cin., 1973-76; sec. pub. rels. St. Vincent Hosp., Billings, Mont., 1976-78; sec. Luth. Social Svcs., Billings, Mont., 1978-80; tchr. music Sch. Dist. #14, Shelby, Mont., 1980—; adv. bd. Cadenza Mag., Mont., 1994—; cons. Fine Arts Curriculum, Shelby, 1995. Contbr. articles to Cadenza Mag., 1990-93. Choir dir. Sunshine Singers, Shelby, 1984—, Meth. Ch., Shelby, 1993—. Recipient scholarship Bus. & Profl. Women, 1987, Mont. Arts Coun. grant, 1993. Mem. Mont. Gen. Music Tchrs. (pres. 1990-92, spkr. 1993), Mont. Music Educators Assn. (exec. bd. mem. 1990-92), Soc. for Gen. Music (symposium participant 1993), Delta Kappa Gamma (rsch. chmn. 1993-95). Lutheran. Office: Meadow Sch 141 6th Ave N Shelby MT 59474-1802

BURNS, CASSANDRA STROUD, prosecutor; b. Lynchburg, Va., May 22, 1960; d. James Wesley and Jeanette Lou (Garner) Stroud; m. Stephen Burns; children: Leila Jeanette, India Veronica. BA, U. Va., 1982; JD, N.C. Cen. U., 1985. Bar: Va. 1986, N.J. 1986, U.S. Dist. Ct. (ea. dist.) Va. 1987, U.S. Ct. Appeals (4th cir.) 1987, U.S. Bankruptcy Ct. (ea. dist.) Va. 1987. Law clk. Office Atty. Gen. State of Va., Richmond, summer 1984; law intern Office Dist. Atty. State of N.C., Durham, 1985; staff atty. Tidewater Legal Aid Soc., Chesapeake, Va., 1987-89; asst. atty. Commonwealth of Va., Petersburg, 1989-90; assoc. atty. Bland and Stroud, Petersburg, 1990; asst. pub. defender City of Petersburg, 1990-91; Commonwealth's atty. City of Petersburg, Va., 1991—; founder BED Task Force on Babies Exposed to Drugs, 1991. Sec. Chesapeake Task Force Coun. on Youth Svcs., 1987-89; ch. directress and organist; mem. NAACP. Mem. Va. Bar Assn. (mem. coun. 1993—), Old Dominion Bar Assn., Va. Assn. Commonwealth Attys. (bd. dirs., mem. coun. 1993—), Legal Svcs. Corp. Va. (bd. dirs.), Southside Va. Legal Aid Soc. (bd. dirs.), Petersburg Bar Assn., Petersburg Jaycees, Order Eastern Star, Petersburg C. of C., Phi Alpha Delta, Alpha Kappa Alpha. Democrat. Baptist. Club: Buddies (Lynchburg). Home: 326 N Park Dr Petersburg VA 23805-2442 Office: Commonwealth's Atty 39 Bollingbrook St Petersburg VA 23803-4548

BURNS, DIANE, gifted education educator; b. N.Y.C., Feb. 20, 1946; d. John A. and Virginia Mae (Ridenour) De Gaetano; 1 child, Michele Young; m. Frank Anthony Burns, Apr. 6, 1980; 1 child, Michael John. BA, SUNY, New Paltz, 1968; MEd, U. Ctrl. Fla., 1984. Cert. tchr. elem., early childhood and gifted edn., Fla. Tchr. grade 3 Three Village Sch. Dist., Setauket, N.Y., 1968-69; reading tchr. Am. Heritage Sch., Hollywood, Fla., 1971-74; tchr. various grades Oak Park Elem., Leesburg, Fla., 1975-87; tchr. gifted 3d and 4th grades Dabney Elem., Leesburg, 1987-95; tchr. 3d grade Treadway Elem. Sch., Leesburg, Fla., 1995—; pvt. tutor, Leesburg. Author, editor: The Time Shifters, 1990 (Fla. Assn. of Gifted grant). Soloist, choir mem. Chancel Choir-Morrison United Meth. Ch., Leesburg, 1986—. Named Fla. Merit Master tchr. State of Fla., Tallahassee, 1983. Mem. Fla. Assn. Gifted, Lake County Edn. Assn., Lake County Reading Coun., Alpha Delta Kappa (chaplain 1986-88). Republican. Home: 819 Palm Ave Leesburg FL 34748-6857 Office: Treadway Elem Sch 10619 Treadway School Rd Leesburg FL 34788

BURNS, ELISA, music educator; b. Birmingham, Jan. 6, 1962. B of Mus. Edn., U. Montevallo, 1984; M of Music Edn., La. State U., 1986. Dir. band John Carroll, Birmingham, 1984-85, Warrior, Birmingham, 1986-88; from asst. to prof. La. State U., Baton Rouge, 1985-86; dir. orchestra The Altamont Sch., Baton Rouge, 1988—, chair fine arts dept., 1995—; guest conductor various orgns., Birmingham. Vol. Crisis Ctr., Birmingham, 1993—. Named Elite Music Educator, U. Montevallo, 1984. Mem. Music Educators Nat. Conf. Democrat. Office: The Altamont Sch 4801 Altamont Rd Birmingham AL 35222

BURNS, ELLEN BREE, federal judge; b. New Haven, Conn., Dec. 13, 1923; d. Vincent Thomas and Mildred Bridget (Bannon) Bree; m. Joseph Patrick Burns, Oct. 8, 1955 (dec.); children: Mary Ellen, Joseph Bree, Kevin James. BA, Albertus Magnus Coll., 1944, LLD (hon.), 1974; LLB, Yale U., 1947; LLD (hon.), U. New Haven, 1981, Sacred Heart U., 1986, Fairfield U., 1991. Bar: Conn. 1947. Dir. legis. legal svcs. State of Conn., 1949-73; judge Conn. Cir. Ct., 1973-74, Conn. Ct. of Common Pleas, 1974-76, Conn. Superior Ct., 1976-78; judge U.S. Dist. Ct. Conn., New Haven, 1978—, chief judge, 1988-92. Trustee Fairfield U., 1978-85, Albertus Magnus Coll., 1985—. Recipient John Carroll of Carrollton award John Barry Council K.C., 1973, Judiciary award Conn. Trial Lawyers Assn., 1978, Cross Pro Ecclesia et Pontifice, 1981, Law Rev. award U. Conn. Law Rev., 1987, Judiciary award Conn. Bar Assn., 1987, Raymond E. Baldwin Pub. Svc. award Bridgeport Law Sch., 1992. Mem. ABA, Am. Bar Found., New Haven County Bar Assn. Roman Catholic. Office: US Dist Ct 208 US Courthouse 141 Church St New Haven CT 06510-2030

BURNS, SISTER JACQUELINE, college president; b. Kearny, N.J., Sept. 1, 1927; d. John Francis and Elizabeth Louise (Calmar) B. BA in History, Coll. St. Elizabeth, 1957; MA in History, Cath. U. Am., 1963, PhD in History, 1967; LHD (hon.), Seton Hall U., 1987. Secondary sch. tchr. St. John Cathedral High Sch., Paterson, N.J, 1957-64; instr., asst. prof. history Coll. St. Elizabeth, Morristown, N.J., 1967-71, asst. dean of studies, 1971-76, dean of studies, 1976-81, pres., 1981—; bd. dirs. Chestnut Hill Coll., Phila., Assn. Cath. Colls. and Univs., 1993-96; del. Gen. Assemblies of

Sisters of Charity, 1971, 75, 79, 84, 87, 91, 95, Provincial Assembly, 1967-77, 81, 85, 89, 93, Coun. So. Province, 1970-74; mem. exec. bd. N.J. Pres.' Coun., 1994—. Trustee Good Samaritan Hosp., 1975-81, chairman planning com., 1978-81, exec. com., 1975-78; bd. dirs. Neylan Commn., 1986-92; trustee St. Joseph Hosp. and Med. Ctr., Paterson, N.J., 1984-90; bd. dirs. Morris County Consumer Credit Union, 1986-87; mem. Dept. Higher Edn. Preparation for Coll. Task Force, 1983-84; mem. acad. and student affairs com. of the bd. trustees Immaculate Conception Sem., 1981-83. Recipient Pres.'s award for ednl. leadership Northeast Coalition of Ednl. Leaders, 1987, Woman of Achievement award Bus. and Profl. Women's Clubs N.J., Morris County, 1984, honoree Kearny Friends of Erin, 1986; Fulbright scholar, France, 1964. Mem. Am. Hist. Asns., Am. Cath. Hist. Assn., Am. Assn. Higher Edn., Nat. Collegiate Honors Coun., N.J. Pres.'s Coun. (exec. bd. dirs. 1994—), Assn. Cath. Univs. and Coll. (bd. dirs. 1993-96), N.J. Bd. Higher Edn. (exec. com. 1990-94, chair acad. affairs com. 1990-94), Pub. Leadership Ednl. Network (bd. dirs. 1989—), Morris County C. of C. (bd. dirs. 1988—), Presdl. Adv. Coun. for Intercampus Telecom. Network, Pres.'s Planning Group for Intergroup Rels., Nat. Assn. Ind. Coll. and Univs. (bd. dirs. 1985-88), Assn. Ind. Coll. and Univs. N.J. (chairperson bd. dirs. 1985-87, bd. dirs. 1978—, exec. com. 1983—, chairperson acad. affairs com. 1978-81), N.J. Coun. Econ. Edn. (bd. dir.s 1984-88), N.J. Ind. Coll. Fund, N.J. Com. for the Humanities, Am. Coun. Edn. (nat. identification program for the advancement of women in higher edn. adminstrn. N.J. planning com.), N.J. Dept. Higher Edn. (lic. adv. cbd. 1979-82, health professions ednl. adv. coun. 1976-81), N.J. Coll. and Univ. Coalition on Women's Edn. (chairperson), Berkshire Conf. Women Historians. Office: Coll St Elizabeth Office of Pres 2 Convent Rd Morristown NJ 07960-6989

BURNS, KAREN FARTHING MACBETH, secondary education educator; b. Cleve., July 4, 1957; d. Thomas Dixon and Lucy Roxanna (Bingham) F.; m. John F. Burns; children: Peter F. MacBeth, Jeffrey D. MacBeth. MusB, Appalachian State U., 1979; MEd, U. Houston, 1981; MA, Appalachian State U., 1986. "G" cert. in lang. arts, social studies, reading, grades 4-9; music, grades K-12. Tchr. music Landrum Jr. H.S., Houston, 1979-81; tchr. 6-8 grades Cove Creek Elem. Sch., Sugar Grove, N.C., 1981-83; music dir. Bethesda Presbyn. Ch., Aberdeen, N.C., 1985-91; tchr. social studies, comms. skills 7th grade Aberdeen Mid. Sch., 1989-91, tchr. comms. skills 8th grade, 1991—; student govt. sponsor Aberdeen Mid. Sch., 1988—, com. mem., mentor tchr., 1992—; bd. dirs., pers. Bethesda After-Sch. Program, Aberdeen. Editor, compiler: (student poetry) A Gallery of Poetry, 1993, 94. Vol., mem. Moore County Arts Coun., Southern Pines, N.C., 1983-88; soloist, mem. Moore County Chamber Music Soc., Southern Pines, 1986-91; soloist Winston-Salem (N.C.) Symphony, Southern Pines, 1990; deacon, soloist Bethesda Presbyn. Ch., Aberdeen, 1993—. Named Outstanding Young Educator, Southern Pines Jaycees, 1992. Mem. NEA.

BURNS, KITTY, executive secretary; b. Chgo., Feb. 1, 1951; d. Joseph Lewis and Evelyn Marian (Smith) B. CNA, Bay City Coll., San Francisco, 1971. Adminstrv. asst. Syntex, Palo Alto, Calif., 1984-94; sec. to v.p. customer svcs. Visa Internat., Foster City, Calif., 1995—. Author: (plays) Terminal Terror, 1991 (Silver award San Mateo Playwriting Contest 1991), Psycho Night at the Paradise Lounge, 1994, If God Wanted Us to Fly He Would Have Given Us Wings!, 1996. Former fundraiser Arlen Gregorio for State Senate, Palo Alto; treas. Hillbarn Theatre, Foster City, 1986, social chmn., 1987-89, 96—. Mem. Dramatists Guild. Democrat. Office: Visa Internat PO Box 8999 San Francisco CA 94128-8999

BURNS, LESLIE KAYE, documentary video producer and director; b. Columbus, Miss., Sept. 21, 1953; d. Fayette Charles Jr. and Mary Theo (Wright) B. BFA in Printmaking/Advt. Art cum laude, Miss. U. for Women, 1975; MFA in Photography/Printmaking, U. Ala., 1978. Multi-image producer, photographer Pitluk Group Advt. Agy., San Antonio, 1981-87; dir. media prodn. Inst. Texan Cultures U. Tex., San Antonio, 1987—. Producer, dir., writer/co-writer numerous documentaries and ednl. videos including From the Ground Up: Theirs to Tell, Ours to Share, 1989, Panna Maria; The Heart of Polish Texans, 1990 (San Antonio Conservation Soc. citation), Circle of Life: The Alabama-Coushattas, 1991 (San Antonio Conservation Assn. citation, 41st Ann. Columbus Internat. Film and Video Festival honoree), Tex. Folklife Festival 1991-95 :30 Pub. Svc. Announcement (1st Pl. Internat. Festivals Assn. Media Competition 1991, Mktg. award Tex. Festivals Assn. 1991, 92), Train Your Brain: A Science, Engineering, and Mathematics Video, 1991, "I Remember...": The Impact of World War II on Children in Texas, 1991, The Day of the Dead, 1991 (San Antonio Conservation Soc. citation 1992, 41st Ann. Columbus Internat. Film and Video Festival honoree, Am. Assn. Mus. Muse award 3rd place cultural studies divsn. 1993), Big City Trail: The Urban Indians of Texas, 1992 (42d Annual Columbus Internat. Film and Video Festival honoree), Texas Children's Festival Promotional Video, 1992, People of the Sun: The Tiguas of Ysleta, 1992 (Soc. Visual Anthropology Film and Video Festival honoree 1993, 42d Annual Columbus Internat. Film and Video Festival honoree), Tejanos: Quiènes somos?, 1993, Noki Pematedieni (To Have a New Life), 1993, Scientists Are Everywhere!, 1994, Tex. Folklife Festival Promotional Video, 1995, Tex. Folklife Festival 1995 Pub. Svc. Announcement (1st place Pinnacle award Internat. Festivals and Events Assn. 1995), Workin' From Can't to Can't: African-American Cowboys in Texas, 1995 (Am. Assn. Mus. Muse award 2d place cultural studies divsn. 1996, Women in Comms., Inc. San Antonio profl. chpt. award of excellence TV documentary program, 1996, 44th Ann. Columbus Internat. Film and Video Festival Bronze plaque), American Indians in Texas Today, an Interactive Multimedia Exhibit, 1996 (Multimedia Profl. mag. Top 100 of 1996). Mem. Am. Assn. Museums. Office: U Tex Inst Texan Cultures 801 S Bowie St San Antonio TX 78205-3209

BURNS, LINDA LATTIN, secondary education English educator; b. McPherson, Kans., Nov. 6, 1942; d. Walter and Wilna (Borth) Lattin; m. Robert Allen Burns., Nov. 16, 1936. BS in Edn., Emporia (Kans.) State U., 1964, MA, 1965; PhD, U. Mo., Columbia, 1979. Tchr. English Wyandotte H.S., Kansas City, Kans., 1965-66; instr. English Mo. U., Columbia, 1966-68; asst. prof. English S.E. Mo. State U., Cape Girardeau, 1968-76, assoc. prof. English, 1976-80, prof. English, 1980-86, prof. English and secondary edn., 1986-92, 93—, acting chair dept. secondary edn., 1992-93. Editor: (newsletter) Professional Pursuits, 1985—; contbr. articles to Children's Lit. Quarterly. Mem. S.E. Mo. English Tchrs. Assn. (exec. sec. 1974—), Mo. Assn. Tchrs. of English (pres. 1981-82), Nat. Coun. Tchrs. of English (bd. dirs. 1980—). Home: 1546 Oak Lei Dr Cape Girardeau MO 63701-3018 Office: SE Mo State U One University Pla Cape Girardeau MO 63701-4017

BURNS, MARIAN LAW, legal administrator; b. Drexel Hill, Pa., Jan. 10, 1954; d. Vincent Charles and Agatha M. (Paoletti) Law; m. Lawrence Joseph Burns, Sept. 29, 1979; children: Peter Andrew, Rita Marie. Paralegal, legal sec. Tuso & Gruccio, Vineland, N.J., 1972-74; legal sec. Swartz, Campbell & Detweiler, Phila., 1974-80; adminstrv. mgr. Drinker Biddle & Reath (formerly Smith, Lambert, Hicks & Beidler, P.C.), Princeton, N.J., 1980-88; legal adminstr. Sherr, Joffe & Zuckerman, P.C., West Conshohocken, Pa., 1988-90, Groen, Laveson, Goldberg & Rubenstone, Bensalem, Pa., 1990—. Mem. ABA (assoc., sect. econs. of law practice), Assn. Legal Adminstrs. (sec. Independence chpt. 1991-93, pres.-elect 1993-95, pres. 1995—), Phila. Bar Assn. (assoc.). Office: Groen Laveson Goldberg & Rubenstone PO Box 8544 Ste 200 Bensalem PA 19020-8544

BURNS, MARIE T., secondary education educator; b. Nashua, N.H.; d. Charles Henry and Eleanor Agnes (Martin) O'Neil; m. Thomas M. Burns; children: Ann Burns Pelletier, Mary Burns Powlowsky, Catherine Burns Patten. BA, Regis Coll.; postgrad., Rivier Coll. Cert. tchr., N.H. Tchr. English Pelham (N.H.) Sch. Dept., City of Nashua. Trustee, chmn. of house com., Mary A. Sweeney Home. Mem. Nat. Assn. Tchrs. English, N.H. Assn. Tchrs. English, New Eng. Assn. Tchrs. English, Nashua Tchrs. Union (mem. secondary grouping practices com. Nashua Sch. Dist.).

BURNS, MARION G., management consultant, retired council executive; b. Tonawanda, N.Y., July 22, 1924; d. Herbert E. and Gertrude V. (Bristow) B. BA, Bethany Coll., W. Va., 1945; MS, Sch. Applied Social Sci. Western Res. U., 1948. Case worker family welfare dept. Salvation Army, Buffalo, 1945-46; dist. dir., functional dir. tng. and camping Akron (Ohio) Area Girl Scout Coun., 1948-53; exec. dir. Girl Scouts DuPage County Coun., Glen Ellyn, Ill., 1953-67, Seal of Ohio Girl Scout Coun., Columbus, 1967-71; mgmt. cons. Region V Girl Scouts U.S., Shawnee Mission, Kans., 1972-79; assoc. dir. ednl. svcs. Girl Scouts U.S., N.Y.C., 1979-82; interim exec. dir. Girl Scouts U.S., Tex. Wash., Ill., N.Y., 1983-87; exec. dir. Lake Erie Girl Scout Coun., Cleve., 1987-90; vol. mgmt. cons. Oklahoma City, 1991—. Mem. exec. com. coun. agy. execs. United Way Svcs., Cleve., 1989-90; mem. World Found. for Girl Guides and Girl Scouts, N.Y.C.; mem. Friends of Sangam Com., 1992—; life mem. Girl Scouts U.S.A; pres.'s assoc. Bethany Coll., 1995-96. Mem. NASW (cert. appreciation TEX 1984), Acad. Cert. Social Workers, Assn. Girl Scout Profl. Workers (pres. 1961-63, 64-66, v.p. 1957-60, Hall of Fame 1987), Zeta Tau Alpha (Theta chpt. Bethany Coll. Disting. Alumni Achievement award for youth svcs. Mem. Christian Ch. Home: 3021 Willow Brook Rd Oklahoma City OK 73120-5724

BURNS, MARY FERRIS, finance executive; b. Corpus Christi, Tex., Aug. 24, 1952; d. Wilbur Glenn and Lena (Faught) Ferris; m. Douglas Keith Burns, Dec. 26, 1975. BA, Baylor U., 1974; MLS, U. Tex., Austin, 1975; BS, U. Tex., Dallas, 1982; MA, U. Fla., 1978. CPA, Tex., Wash.; human resources profl. Reference libr., Latin Am. collection U. Fla., Gainesville, 1975-78; reference libr., Fondren Libr. So. Meth. U., Dallas, 1978-79; libr. Tex. A&M U., College Station, 1979-81; auditor, provider reimbursement divsn. Blue Cross & Blue Shield Tex., Dallas, 1983-84; internal auditor U. Tex. Health Sci. Ctr. at Dallas, 1984-85, adminstrv. svcs. officer Biomed. Comm. Resource Ctr., 1985-87; adminstrv. svcs. mgr. Div. of Lab. Animal Medicine Stanford U., 1988-89, adminstrv. svcs. mgr. Dept. of Microbiology and Immunology, 1989; dir. fin. and adminstrn. RIDES for Bay Area Commuters, Inc., San Francisco, 1989-93, Children's Home Soc. Wash., Seattle, 1993—; cons. Centro Intenacional de Desarrollo Humano en America Latina, Cuernavaca, Mex., 1975. Contbg. editor: Hispanic American Periodicals Index, 1975, 76. Bd. trustees, mem. Cmty. Svcs. for Blind. Mem. AICPA, Wash. Soc. of CPA's., Soc. for Human Resource Mgmt., King County Libr. Sys. Found.

BURNS, MARYANN MARGARET, elementary education educator; b. Portland, Maine, Mar. 4, 1944; d. William and Emma (Greco) B. Finishing sch. grad., Chandler Sch. for Women, Boston, 1963; BS in Edn. and English summa cum laude, U. Maine, 1974. Cert. elem. tchr., Maine. Pvt. sec. IBM, L.A., 1968-70; learning lab. tchr. Sch. Adminstrv. Dist. # 6, Bar Mills, Maine, 1974—, Frank Jewett Sch., W. Buxton, Maine. Mem. NEA, Maine Tchrs. Assn., U. Maine Alumni Assn., Polit. Action Com. Democrat. Roman Catholic. Home: 17 Wildrose Ave S Portland ME 04106-6619 Office: Sch Adminstrv Dist 6 PO Box 38 Bar Mills ME 04004-0038

BURNS, ROBIN, cosmetics company executive. Student, Syracuse U. Formerly with Bloomingdale's, N.Y.C., v.p.; pres. Calvin Klein Cosmetics; pres., CEO Estee Lauder USA, N.Y.C., 1990—. Office: Estee Lauder USA 767 5th Ave New York NY 10153*

BURNS, ROSALIE ANNETTE, neurologist, educator; b. Phila., July 29, 1932; married. BA, Smith Coll., 1953; MD, Yale U., 1956. Intern in medicine Cornell Med. divsn. Bellevue Hosp., N.Y.C., 1956-57; resident in neurology Neurol. Inst. N.Y.-Columbia-Presbyn. Med. Ctr., 1957-60; asst. in neurology, fellow Nat. Cerebral Palsy Study, 1959-60; fellow in cerebral vascular disease NIH-dept. neurology Tufts U.-New Eng. Ctr. Hosp., Boston, 1960-61; asst. dir. 2d neurology divsn. Bellevue Hosp., N.Y.C., 1962-64; instr. neurology dept. medicine Cornell U. Sch. Medicine, 1962-64; asst. neurologist to outpatients N.Y. Hosp., N.Y.C., 1962-64; electroencephalographer The Inst. of Pa. Hosp., 1964-65; instr. in neurology Med. Coll. Pa., 1964-65, dir. neurology clinics, 1965-74, assoc. in neurology, 1965-66, head sect. neurology, dept. psychiatry and neurology, 1965-71, asst. prof. neurology, 1966-70, assoc. prof. neurology, 1970-74, acting chmn. dept. neurology, 1971-74, prof. neurology, 1974-95, chmn. dept. neurology, 1975-95; univ. prof., exec. dir. Ctr. for Clin. Neurosci. Med. Coll. Pa./Hahnemann Univ., 1995—; program dir. NIH Devel. Grant Med. Coll. Pa., 1966-73; consulting physician in neurology Ea. Pa. Psychiat. Inst., 1965-76, Pathway Sch. for Learning Disorders, 1978-81, Phila. VA Med. Ctr., part-time staff, 1975-77, attending physician in neurology, 1967-68; cons. staff Inglis House, 1967 93, Phila. Geriatric Ctr., 1985; half time rsch. asst. neuropathology lab. Walter E. Fernald State Sch. Mental Retardation, Waverly, Mass., 1961-62; adj. attending neurologist dept. neurology Sloan-Kettering Cancer Ctr., 1986; presenter in field. Contbr. chpts. to books, articles to profl. jours. Nat. Found. fellow, 1955. Fellow Am. Acad. Neurology (edn. com. 1975-78, practice com. 1990-92, del. to Coun. of Acad. Socs. 1987-91, nominating com. 1993, 2d v.p. 1983-85, women's liaison officer 1991); mem. Am. Bd. Med. Specialties, Am. Bd. Psychiatry and Neurology (bd. dirs. 1993-97, nominating com. 1993, rev. appeals com. 1992, credential com. 1992 and many other coms.), Am. Neurol. Assn. (annals of neurology oversight com. 1993), Assn. Univ. Profs. Neurology (sec.-treas. 1983-88, pres.-elect 1988-90, pres. 1990-92), Phila. Neurol. Soc. (1st v.p. 1971, 2nd v.p. 1977, pres. 1979-80, chmn. nominating com. 1981, and other coms.), Smith Coll. Club Phila., Alumnae Assn. Woman's Med. Coll. (assoc., Delaware Valley chpt.), Phi Beta Kappa, Sigma Xi, Alpha Omega Alpha (Delta chpt., chmn. membership com. 1980-81). Office: Hahnemann Univ Broad & Vine Philadelphia PA 19102

BURNS, SALLY ANN, medical association administrator; b. Findlay, Ohio, Dec. 13, 1959; d. Van Larson and Marian (Delia) B. Student, Findlay Coll., 1980-82, Bowling Green State U., 1982-83; AAS, Houston C.C., 1985. Lic. physical therapist asst., Tex. Intern in clin. studies various Hosps., Houston, 1984-85; patient care Spring Br. Meml. Hosp., Houston, 1985-86; pres. Burns Phys. Therapy Clinic, Inc., Houston, 1986—; pres., bd. dirs. Phys. Therapy Plus, Inc., Houston, 1988—; pres. FYI Med. Suppliers, Inc., 1991—, Pain Stop Inc., 1994—; pres. FYI Med. Suppliers, Inc., 1991—, FYI Med., Inc., 1991, Pain Stop, Inc., 1994—; mem. adv. com. Houston C.C. Sys. Physical Therapist Asst. Program. Author: Physical Therapy for Multiple Sclerosis. Mem. adv. com. Houston C.C. Sys. Phys. Therapist Asst. Program. Mem. Inst. for Profl. Health Svc. Adminstrs. (charter mem.), Am. Judicature Soc., Am. Phys. Therapy Assn., Tex. Phys. Therapy Assn., Community Health Adminstrn. Home: 1914 Potomac Dr Houston TX 77057-2922 Office: Phys Therapy Plus Inc 3303 Audley St Houston TX 77098-1921

BURNSIDE, MADELEINE HILDING, museum director, educator; b. London, Oct. 18, 1948; came to U.S., 1970; d. George William Augustin Burnside and Signe Winifreda (Nyman) Smyth; m. William Joseph Lukan, May 18, 1973. BA, U. Warwick, Eng., 1970; PhD, U. Calif., Santa Cruz, 1976. Editorial assoc. Art News mag., N.Y.C., 1976-79, Arts mag., N.Y.C., 1979-80; performance critic Soho Weekly mag., N.Y.C., 1977-78; freelance curator Bronx Mus. Fine Arts, 1977-80; dir. Islip (N.Y.) Art Mus., 1980-91; assoc. prof. Dowling Coll., Oakdale, N.Y., 1985-91; exec. dir. Mel Fisher Maritime Heritage Soc., Key West, Fla., 1991—; assoc. prof. Union Inst., 1995—. Bd. dirs. People Take Action Against AIDS, Bellport, N.Y., 1988-90, Stopping AIDS Together, 1990—, Key West Bus. Guild, 1994—, Fla. Assn. Museums, 1995—. Harkness Found. fellow, 1970, Ford Found. fellow, 1973; NEA grantee, 1980. Mem. Media Alliance. Home: 536 White St Key West FL 33040 Office: Mel Fisher Maritime Heritage Soc 200 Greene St Key West FL 33040-6516

BURNSIDE, MARY, software company executive. BS, U. Calif., Berkeley. Formerly with System Industries Inc., Cygnet Systems; with Novell, Inc., San Jose, 1988—, material planning mgr., sr. v.p. ops., exec. v.p. corp. svcs., CEO. Recipient Tribute to Women in Industry award, 1992. Office: Novell Inc 2180 Fortune Dr San Jose CA 95131

BURNSIDE, MARY BETH, biology educator, researcher; b. San Antonio, Apr. 23, 1943; d. Neil Delmont and Luella Nixon (Kenley) B. BA, U. Tex., 1965, MA, 1967, PhD in Zoology, 1968. Instr. med. sch. Harvard U., Boston, 1970-73; asst. prof. U. Pa., Phila., 1973-76; asst. prof. U. Calif., Berkeley, 1976-77, assoc. prof., 1977-82, prof., 1982—, dean biol. scis., 1984-90; mem. nat. adv. eye coun. NIH, 1990-94; mem. sci. adv. bd. Lawrence Hall of Sci., Berkeley, 1983—, Whitney Labs., St. Augustine, Fla., 1993—; mem. bd. sci. councillors Nat. Eye Inst., 1994—. Mem. editl. bd. Invest. Ophthalmol. Vis. Sci., 1992-94; contbr. numerous articles to profl. jours. Mem. sci. adv. bd. Mills Coll., Oakland, Calif., 1986-90; trustee Bermuda Biol. Sta., St. George's, 1978-83; dir. Miller Inst., Berkeley, Calif., 1995—. Recipient Merit award NIH, 1989—, rsch. grantee, 1972—; rsch. grantee NSF. Fellow AAAS; mem. Am. Soc. Cell Biology (coun. 1980-84). Office: U Calif Dept Molecular & Cell Biology 335 Life Scis Addn Berkeley CA 94720-3200

BURR, JOAN ANN, artist, educator; b. N.Y.C.; d. John Joseph and Vivian (Monroe) Schneider; m. Raymond Aaron Burr, Feb. 14, 1956; children: Jesse, Jody, David, Donna, Terri. AA, Rose Coll., 1977; student, La. Tech., 1980, Scottsdale Artists Sch., 1982, 83, Norton Gallery of Art, West Palm Beach, Fla. Freelance artist, 1970—; art instr. pvt. classes, 1975-90. One person shows include Sakura, Stuart, Fla.; exhibited in group shows Okla. Festival of Arts Invitational, 1971-84, Arts Festival Cultural Ctr., Stuart, 1990, 92, 93, 1st Nat. Bank of Palm City Fla., 1993, Phippen Mus., Prescott, Ariz., 1995, Taos (N.Mex.) Watercolor Soc. Show, 1995, others; represented in pvt. collections including Gov.'s Mansion, Oklahoma City, Liberty Nat. Bank, Oklahoma city, Babbitt Trading Post, Ariz., Cordell (Okla.) Nat. Bank; featured in publs. Okla. Art Gallery Mag., Ency. of Living Artists in Am., Sunshine Artists Mag. Recipient David Gale award Western Fedn. Artists, 1st pl. award Lake Worth Nat. Art Exhbn., 1993, Grumbacher Gold medal award Ariz. Watercolor Show, 1st pl. award Sedona Ann., 1st pl. award Winslow Arts Assn., Best of Show award Crossroads Show, 1st pl. award Guthrie Ann. Mem. Am. Watercolor Assn. (assoc.), No. Ariz. Art Assn. Home: PO Box 286 Joseph City AZ 86032

BURR, JUDITH ELIZABETH, educational administrator; b. Riverside, N.J., Oct. 10, 1947; d. Norman and Mary Elizabeth (Knight) B. BA magna cum laude, Drew U., 1970; MAT, Trenton State Coll., 1974. Cert. tchr. biol. scis., prin., asst. supt., N.J. Tchr. sci. Glassboro (N.J.) Intermediate Sch., 1974-79; coord. state gifted programs Ednl. Info. and Resource Ctr., Sewell, N.J., 1979-83; assoc. dir. Nat. Talent Network Ednl. Info. and Resource Ctr., Sewell, 1983—; adv. coun. mem. Buehler Challenger and Sci. Ctr., Paramus, N.J., 1993—. Author: Symposium for Arts Scenarios, 1986-96; co-author: Marsville: The Cosmic Village, 1991, Planet X: A Fraternal Twin, 1992 (award 1995); editor, contbg. author: Cognetics Ann. Problems, 1984-96 (award 1989). Regional coord. Nat. Alumni in Admissions Drew U., Madison, N.J., 1992-96. Fellow Inst. for Ednl. Leadership, 1981-82; recipient Disting. Svc. Odyssey of the Mind Program, 1982-83. Mem. Soc. Mfg. Engrs. (hon. sr.), Challenger Ctr. for Space Sci. Edn. (internat. faculty), N.J. Assn. for Gifted Children. Episcopalian. Office: Ednl Info & Resource Ctr 606 Delsea Dr Sewell NJ 08080

BURR, LAURIE DIANE, information technology consultant; b. Bath, N.Y., Jan. 29, 1953; d. Jonathan Williams and Dorothy Evelyn (Daines) B.; m. Jeffrey Howard Halpern. AB, Vassar Coll., 1974; MBA, U. Va., 1983. Fin. planner Burlington, Vt., 1975-76; mktg. rep. IBM, Burlington, 1976-80; fin. planner IBM/Lab.-Mfg., Poughkeepsie, N.Y., 1983-84; marketer, analyst IBM/Regional & Br. Offices, Balt., 1984-86; proposal mgr. IBM/Pub. Sector Group, Balt., 1986-88; cons. pub. sector industry IBM, Bethesda, Md., 1988-93; pres. Renaissance Consulting Co., Inc., Annapolis, Md., 1993—. Mem. Eastport Yacht Club.

BURRI, BETTY JANE, research chemist; b. San Francisco, Jan. 23, 1955; d. Paul Gene and Carleen Georgette (Meyers) B.; m. Kurt Randall Annweiler, Dec. 1, 1984. BA, San Francisco State U., 1976; MS, Calif. State U., Long Beach, 1978; PhD, U. Calif. San Diego, La Jolla, 1982. Research asst. Scripps Clinic, La Jolla, 1982-83, research assoc., 1983-85; research chemist Western Human Nutrition Rsch. Ctr., USDA, San Francisco, 1985—; adj. prof. nutrition dept. U. Nev., 1993—; mem. steering com. Carotenoid Rsch. Interaction Group, 1994—. Co-editor Carotenoid News; contbr. articles to profl. jours. Grantee NIH, 1982, 85, USDA, 1986-95; affiliate fellow Am. Heart Assn., 1983, 84. Mem. Assn. Women in Sci. (founding dir. San Diego chpt.), N.Y. Acad. Sci., Carotenoid Rsch. Interaction Group, Am. Inst. Nutrition, Am. Soc. Clin. Nutrition. Office: Western Human Nutrition Rsch Ctr PO Box 29997 San Francisco CA 94129-0997

BURRIS, CHRISTINE TUVE, professional society administrator; b. Washington, Mar. 20, 1948; d. Richard Larsen and Maxine (Duvel) Tuve; m. James Frederick Burris, July 3, 1971; 1 child, Cameron William Tuve Burris. BA in Sociology, U. Md., 1971; MA in Rehab. Counseling, NYU, 1976. Social work intern Dept. Social Svcs., Montgomery County, Md., 1970; recreation leader Dept. Recreation, Montgomery County, Md., 1970-71; statis. asst. Nat. Soc. for Prevention of Blindness, N.Y.C., 1971-74; rehab. counseling intern Inst. for Crippled and Disabled, N.Y.C., 1975-76; rehab. counselor Fedn. Employment and Guidance Svc., Bronx, N.Y., 1976-77; rsch. asst. Indices, Inc., Falls Church, Va., 1977-79; sr. rsch. assoc. Rehab Group Inc., Falls Church, Va., 1979-82; staff assoc. Assn. Am. Med. Colls., Washington, 1984-87; exec. dir. D.C. Acad. Family Physicians, Washington, 1989—; cons. JWK Internat. Corp., Annandale, Va., 1984; Washington rep. Am. Fedn. for Clin. Rsch., Washington, 1984-87. Editor, pub. Newsletter of the D.C. Acad. of Family Physicians, 1989—, Newsletter of the Cove Point Beach Assn., Inc., 1994—, Newsletter of Cub Scout Pack 666, Nat. Capital Area Coun., 1995—. Vol. Fondation de la Recherche des Maladies Cardiovasculaires, Lausanne, Switzerland, 1983, Nature Conservancy, Md. Chpt., 1988, Beavoir Sch., Washington, 1992-96; bd. dirs. Cove Point Beach Assn., Inc., 1993-96; sec. pack com. Cub Scouts Am., 1995—. Recipient traineeship U.S. Rehab. Svcs. Adminstrn., 1975-76, Ann. Svc. award Nature Conservancy, 1988. Mem. Am. Soc. Assn. Execs., Assn. Am. Med. Soc. Execs., Greater Washington Soc. Assn. Execs., Nat. Rehab. Counseling Assn. (legis. com. mem. N.Y. chpt. 1975 77), Cove Point Beach Assn., Inc. (bd. dirs. 1993-96)., Assn. Am. Med. Soc. Execs. Democrat. Office: DC Acad Family Physicians 4803 Davenport St NW Washington DC 20016-4314

BURRIS, FRANCES WHITE, personnel director; b. Cuero, Tex., Oct. 18, 1933; d. Marian Cecil and Dorothy Christine (Pruetz) White; m. Berlie Burris Jr, Mar. 8, 1958 (div. 1982); children: William Alan, Joel Maurice. BA, Mary Hardin Baylor Coll., Belton, Tex., 1955; M in Eng., Trinity U., San Antonio, 1959. Cert. tchr., Tex. Elem. tchr. East and Mt. Houston Independent Sch. Dist., 1956, Edgewood Ind. Sch. Dist., San Antonio, 1956-57, 58-59; tchr. Edna (Tex.) Ind. Sch. Dist., 1957-58; elem. tchr. Northside Ind. Sch. Dist., San Antonio, 1960-62, Southside Schs., San Antonio, 1962-63; mgr. Michael's Dept. Store, Houston, 1980-81; eligibility worker Tex. Dept. Human Resources, Houston, 1981—. Mem. Meridith Manor Civic Club, Houston, 1966-78, Settlers Valley Civic Club, Katy, Tex., 1979-81. Mem. Tex. State Employees Union (exec. bd. 1984—, del. gen. assembly 1984-96, lobbyist 1985—). Democrat. Baptist. Club: Bridge (Houston).

BURRIS, KATHRYN ANN, professional association administrator; b. Fredricksburg, Tex., Dec. 1, 1957; d. Bryon Curthburn and Sara Lee (Matthews) Rinehart; m. Charles Anthony Burris, Nov. 4, 1989. BS, Howard Payne U., 1979; diploma, Ranger Jr. Coll., 1982. Cert. Okla. Bd. Nurse Registration and Nursing Edn. Educator Brownwood (Tex.) Home and Sch., 1979-80; critical care nurse Brownwood Regional Hosp., 1981-83; home healthcare nurse Healthcare, Inc., Tulsa, 1983-85; staff nurse Broken Arrow (Okla.) Med. Ctr., 1984-85; state dir. Am. Chronic Pain Assn., Tulsa, 1987-93; exec. dir. Pain Tamers Support Network, Inc., Tulsa, 1993—; mem. Rehabilitative Adv. Coun. State Okla., 1993—; mem. Assistive Tech. Coun. Okla., 1994—. Feature columnist (newspaper) The Tulsa Tribune, 1988-92; contbg. writer (newsletters) Nat. Chronic Pain Outreach Assn. Lifeline, 1988, Am. Chronic Pain Assn. Chronicle, 1989-93, Pain Tamers Support Network, Inc., 1993—. Make-up artist Brownwood Theater Co., 1980-81, wardrobe dir., 1980; mem. State of Okla. Rehab. Adv. Coun., 1993—, State of Okla. Assistive Tech. Adv. Coun., 1994-95. Mem. Reflex Sympathetic Dystrophy Syndrome Assn. (state dir. 1988—), Fibromyalgia Network. Democrat. Home: 5807 E 35th St Tulsa OK 74135-5303 Office: Pain Tamers Support Network Inc PO Box 55372 Tulsa OK 74155-1372 *Died Apr. 24, 1996.*

BURRIS, LAUREN BAYLERAN, business owner; b. Detroit, Mar. 30, 1952; d. Haig Aram and Dirouhi (Halajian) Bayleran; m. William James Burris, Feb. 14, 1981; children: Taron, Ian. BBA, U. Mich., 1973; MBA, Wayne State U., 1978. Sales rep. IBM Corp., Detroit, 1973-76; assoc. dir. U. Mich., Dearborn, 1976-78; owner Bayleran & Burris, Inc., Orchard Lake, Mich., 1978—, L.B. Burris & Co., Inc., Orchard Lake, 1982—, Servicelease, Inc., Orchard Lake, 1989—; cons. Rapidata, Southfield, Mich., 1980-82. Editor: A Practical Armenian & English Book, 1971. Head pub. rels. com. Oakland County C. of C., Pontiac, Mich., 1983; core leader Cmty. Bible Study, 1994—. Mem. Wayne State U. Alumnae Assn. (pres. Detroit chpt. 1981-83), Alpha Phi. Republican.

BURROWS, BARBARA ANN, veterinarian; b. Columbia, S.C., Dec. 15, 1947; d. Robert Beck and Betty Elizabeth (Rabon) Burrows; m. Richard M. Duemmler, Aug. 31, 1968 (div. Aug. 1975); 1 child, Sandra Lynn. BA, Hartwick Coll., 1969; VMD, U. Pa., 1983. Bacteriologist Johnson & Johnson, North Brunswick, N.J., 1969-70; microbiologist Ciba-Geigy, Summit, N.J., 1973-79; veterinarian Amboy Ave Vet. Hosp., Metuchen, N.J., 1983-84, Black Horse Pike Animal Hosp., Turnersville, N.J., 1984-93, San Juan Animal Hosp., San Juan Capistrano, Calif., 1993-94; relief vet., 1994—; relief veterinarian Alicia Pet Clinic, Laguna Hills, Calif., Crown Valley Animal Hosp., Laguna Niguel, Calif., Moulton Animal Hosp., Laguna Niguel. Capt. USAF. Mem. Am. Vet. Med. Assn., So. Calif. Vet. Med. Assn., Am. Assn. Feline Practitioners. Home: 25582 Breezewood St Dana Point CA 92629-2138

BURROWS, ELIZABETH MACDONALD, religious organization executive, educator; b. Portland, Oreg., Jan. 30, 1930; d. Leland R. and Ruth M. (Frew) MacDonald. Certificate, Chinmaya Trust Sandeepany, Bombay; PhD (hon.), Internat. U. Philosophy and Sci., 1975; ThD, Christian Coll. Universal Peace, 1992. Ordained to ministry First Christian Ch., 1976. Mgr. credit Home Utilities, Seattle, 1958, Montgomery Ward, Crescent City, Calif., 1963; supr. Oreg. Dist. Tng. West Coast Telephone, Beaverton, 1965; pres. Christian Ch. Universal Peace, Seattle, 1971—; prof. religion Christian Coll. Universal Peace, also bd. dirs.; pres. Archives Internat., Seattle, 1971—; v.p. James Tyler Kent Inst. Homeopathy, 1984-95. Author: Crystal Planet, 1979, Pathway of the Immortal, 1980, Odyssey of the Apocalypse, 1981, Maya Sangh, 1981, Harp of Destiny, 1984, Commentary for Gospel of Peace of Jesus Christ According to John, 1986, Seasons of the Soul, 1995, Voyagers of the Sand, 1996, Hold the Anchovies, 1996; author of poetry (Publisher's Choice award Poets of the New Era, Disting. Poets of Am.). Recipient Pres. award for literary excellence, 1994, 95. Mem. Internat. Speakers Platform, Internat. New Thought Alliance, Cousteau Soc., Internat. Order of Chivalry, The Planetary Soc. Home: 10529 Ashworth Ave N Seattle WA 98133-8937

BURSHELL, SANDRA, artist. Attended, Boston U., 1968-70; BA, Temple U., 1971; MEd, Tyler Sch. Art, Phila., 1975; postgrad., Art Inst. Chgo., New Orleans Acad. Fine Arts. Represented by Upper Edge Gallery, Aspen, Colo., Carol Robinson Gallery, New Orleans, Carol Schwartz Gallery, Phila. Solo shows include Gallery Shva, Beersheva, Israel, Carol Robinson Gallery, New Orleans, 1990, Terrebonne Mus., Houma, La., 1991; group shows include Downtown Gallery, New Orleans, 1988, 89, 90, St. Tammany Mus. Art Assn., Covington, La., 1987-92, 96, Arlington (Tex.) Mus. Art, 1989, Salmagundi Club, N.Y.C., 1990, 96, San Bernardino County Mus., 1990, 91, Degas Pastel Soc., New Orleans, 1988, 90, 94, Lincoln Ctr. for Performing Arts, Cork Gallery, N.Y.C., 1989, 91, Lauren (Miss.) Rogers Mus. Art, 1990, 92, Zigler Mus., Jennings, La., 1990-92, New Orleans Acad. Fine Arts, 1991-95, Arts Club of Washington, 1992-95, Pastel Soc. Am., N.Y.C., 1992, 94, 95, Galerie Melacon, Lake Charles, La., 1993, Carol Robinson Gallery, 1993, 95, Meadows Mus. Art, Shreveport, La., 1993, Patio Gallery, Covington, 1993, Longview Mus., 1994, Ft. Walton (Fla.) Mus. Art, 1994, 96, Helen Rose Gallery, Sacramento, 1995, Isabel Anderson Comer Mus., Ala., 1996, Hanson Gallery, New Orleans, 1996, Upper Edge Gallery (feature artist), Aspen, Colo., 1996; numerous pvt. and pub. collections; contbr. (CD-ROM) Showcase of American Pastel Artists, 1995; contbr. various publs.; subject of news articles and revs. Recipient First prize in graphics St. Tammany Art Assn., 1987, Watson-Guptil Pub. award Kans. Pastel Soc., 1988; finalist Artist's Mag. portrait painting competition, 1989. Mem. Pastel Soc. Am. (Strathmore Paper Co. award 1994, Sally Strand scholar 1995, Nat. Arts Club award 1995, World Trade Ctr. Purchase award 1995), Am. Artists Profl. League, Internat. Assn. Pastel Socs. (officer), Cassatt Pastel Soc., Degas Pastel Soc. (bd. dirs., Merit award 1989, Dixie Art award 1992-93, Excellence award 1993, La. Watercolor Soc. of Merit award 1995), Allied Artists Am. (assoc.), Artists' Fellowship, Inc. Studio: 4812 Haring Ct Metairie LA 70006

BURSLEY, KATHLEEN A., lawyer; b. Washington, Mar. 20, 1954; d. G.H. Patrick and Claire (Mulvany) B. BA, Pomona Coll., 1976; JD, Cornell U., 1979. Bar: N.Y. 1980, U.S. Dist. Ct. (ea. and so. dists.) N.Y. 1980, U.S. Ct. Appeals (5th and 11th cirs.) 1981, Fla. 1984, U.S. Dist. Ct. (mid. dist.) Fla. 1984, Tex. 1985, Mass. 1995. Assoc. Haight, Gardner, Poor & Havens, N.Y.C., 1979-81; counsel Harcourt Brace Jovanovich, Inc., N.Y.C. and Orlando, Fla., 1981-85; v.p. and counsel Harcourt Brace Jovanovich, Inc., San Antonio and Orlando, 1985-92, 92-94; assoc. gen. counsel pub. Harcourt Gen., Inc., Chestnut Hill, Mass., 1992—; gen. counsel Harcourt Brace & Co., Chestnut Hill, Mass., 1994—. Mem. Maritime Law Assn. (proctor). Office: Harcourt Gen Inc 27 Boylston St Chestnut Hill MA 02167-1719

BURSON, BETSY LEE, librarian; b. Olney, Tex., Dec. 16, 1942; d. James Hollis and Lora Elizabeth (Talbott) B.; m. Winston Rabb Henderson, June 26, 1976. BS in Edn., Kans. State Tchrs. Coll., 1964; MLS, Tex. Woman's U., 1967, PhD in Libr. Info. Studies, 1987. With Phoenix Pub. Libr., 1967-74; libr. dir. Glendale (Ariz.) Pub. Libr., 1974-75; project archivist Phoenix History Project, 1975-77; adj. faculty U. Ariz., Tucson, 1979, Tex. Woman's U., Denton, 1980; libr. cons. La. State Libr., Baton Rouge, 1982-85; libr. dir. El Paso (Tex.) Pub. Libr., 1987-90, Arlington (Tex.) Pub. Libr., 1990—. Named Librarian of the Yr. Tex. Library Assn., 1995. Office: Arlington Pub Libr 101 E Abram St Arlington TX 76010-1102

BURSTEIN, SHARON ANN PALMA, corporate communications specialist; b. Schenectady, N.Y., July 18, 1952; d. Harold Edward and Lois Ida (Hesner) Rieck; m. Joseph Carmen Palma, May 17, 1975 (div. Sept. 1982); m. Richard Lyle Burstein, Sept. 8, 1985; 1 child, Alexandra Blaire. BA, Nat. Lewis U., 1974; postgrad., Russell Sage Coll., 1974-78, Union Coll., 1980. Cert. tchr., N.Y. Elem. tchr. Saratoga Springs (N.Y.) Schs., 1974-80; ednl. cons. Whitcomb Assocs., Boston, 1980-81; ednl. mktg. specialist Monroe Systems for Bus., Newington, Conn., 1981-83; nat. mktg. mgr. Victor Techs., Hartford, Conn., 1983, Exclusives, Boston, 1984-85; dir. pub. rels. Lawrence Group, Albany, N.Y., 1985-87, dir. corp. comm., 1987-88; v.p. Lawrence Group, Albany, 1988-89; v.p investors rels. Lawrence Group, N.Y.C., 1987-89; pres. S.A. Burstein & Assocs., Albany, 1989-94, Neswick Ct., 1994—; adj. prof. Russell Sage Coll., Troy, N.Y., 1994—; cons. N.Y. Assn. Bus. Ofcls., 1982-83. Editor: Helpline newspaper, 1985, 87; co-prodr. Playing It Safe, 1986 (Nori award 1987), To Be As Independent As You Can be (Nori award 1989), Cookbook Capital Connoisseur (Nori award 1989), Camp Ever Young (Nori award 1993); acted in TV comml., 1981 (Addy award 1982). Bd. dirs. Multiple Sclerosis Soc., Albany, 1986—, Mohawk Pathways Girl Scouts U.S.; active N.Y. Spl. Olympics, 1987, Capital Womens Charity Found., Albany, 1987. Mem. NAFE, Nat. Investor Rels. Inst., Am. Mgmt. Assn., Assn. Profl. Communicators, Nat. Assn. Investment Clubs, Tennis Industry Assn., Albany C. of C. (womens bus. coun.), Steuben Club, Womens Press Club, Kappa Delta Pi. Democrat. Home: 4 Birch Hill Rd Loudonville NY 12211-2004

BURSTYN, ELLEN (EDNA RAE GILLOOLY), actress; b. Detroit, Dec. 7, 1932; m. Paul Roberts; m. Neil Burstyn; 1 child, Jefferson. LHD (hon.), Dowling Coll.; DFA (hon.), Sch. Visual Arts. Artistic dir. The Actor's Studio, N.Y.C., 1982-88. Appeared regularly on Jackie Gleason TV show, 1956-57; Broadway debut in Fair Game, 1957-58, (summer stock) John Loves Mary, 1960, (Broadway prodns.) Same Time, Next Year, 1975 (Tony award for Best Actress, Drama Desk award, Outer Circle Critics award), 84 Charing Cross Road, 1982, Shirley Valentine, 1989, Shimada, 1992, (off-Broadway) Park Your Car in Harvard Yard with Burgess Meredith, (Chgo.) Driving Miss Daisy, 1988, Shirley Valentine, 1990; film appearances include Goodbye Charlie (under name Ellen McRae), 1964, For Those Who Think Young, 1965, Tropic of Cancer, 1969, Alex in Wonderland, 1971 (named Best Supporting Actress N.Y. Film Critics, Nat. Soc. Film Critics, Acad. Award nominee for Best Supporting Actress), The Last Picture Show, 1971 (Acad. award nominee Best Actress), The King of Marvin Gardens, 1972, The Exorcist, 1973 (Acad. Award nominee for Best Actress), Harry and Tonto, 1974, Alice Doesn't Live Here Anymore, 1974 (Acad. Award as Best Actress, Golden Globe award, Brit. Acad. award), Providence, 1977, Same Time Next Year, 1978, Dream of Passion, 1978, Resurrection, 1980, Silence of the North, 1980, The Ambassador, 1984, Twice in a Lifetime, 1986, Hannah's War, 1987, The Color of Evening, 1990, Grand Isle, 1990, Dying Young, 1990, The Cemetery Club, 1993, When a Man Loves A Woman, 1994, Roommates, 1994, How to Make An American Quilt, 1995, The Baby-Sitters Club, 1995; TV movies include Thursday's Game, 1974, The People vs. Jean Harris, 1981 (Emmy award nominee), Into Thin Air, 1985, Surviving, 1985, Act of Vengeance, 1986, Something in Common, 1986, Pack of Lies, 1987 (Emmy nomination) When you Remember Me, 1990, Mrs. Lambert Remembers Love, 1991, Taking Back My Life: The Nancy Ziegrenmeyer Story, 1992, Grand Isle, 1992, Shattered Trust: The Shari Karney Story, 1993, Getting Gotti, 1994, Trick of the Eye, 1994, Getting Out, 1994; TV series include: The Doctors, The Ellen Burstyn Show, 1986-87; dir. off-Broadway play Judgement, 1981, Into Thin Air, 1985, When You Remember Me, 1990, Running Out, 1991; star TV series The Ellen Burstyn Show, 1986; narrator segment TV show Dear America: Letters Home from Vietnam, 1988; appearance documentary film Balls of Grace; original photography work featured in Darkroom Photography mag., June, 1989. Mem. individual artists grants and policy overview panels Nat. Endowment for the Arts, Theater Adv. Council City of New York. Mem. Actors Equity Assn. (pres. 1982-85). Office: CAA 9830 Wilshire Blvd Beverly Hills CA 90212-1804*

BURTON, BARBARA ABLE, psychotherapist; b. Columbia, S.C.; d. Eugene Walter Able and Mary Louise (Chadwick) Cantelou; 1 child, Stacia Louise. BA in Psychology, Ga. State U.; MSW, U. Ala., 1970. Diplomate Am. Bd. Examiners in Clin. Social Work, Internat. Acad. Behavioral Medicine, Counseling and Psychotherapy; cert. Am. Acad. Cert. Social Workers, NASW, diplomate clin. social work. Assoc. exec. dir. Positive Maturity, Inc., Birmingham, Ala., 1970-72; comm. org. planner Community Svc. Council, INc., Birmingham, Ala., 1972-75; adj. faculty U. Ala., Tuscaloosa, Ala., 1975-77; dir. Ensley Outpatient Drug Abuse Clinic, Birmingham, Ala., 1975-77, Sch. of Social Work, Miles Coll., Birmingham, Ala., 1977-78; prog. mgr. and clin. cons. Goodwill Industries of Ala., Birmingham, Ala., 1977-81; pvt. practice New Orleans, 1983--; cons. Omega Internat. Inst., New Orleans, 1988--. Author: Love Me, Love Me Not, and Other Matters That Matter, 1990. Past chmn. Policy and Program Com. Birmingham Urban League; Ala. Adv. Com. on Social Svcs.; Ala. Com. for the Dev. of Higher Ed.; Ala. Conf. of Social Work. NIMH fellow Inst. on Human Sexuality, U. Hawaii, 1976. Mem. Am. Assn. Sex Educators, Counselors and Therapists, Nat. Assn. Social Workers, Pvt. Practitioners Unit of New Orleans, Acad. Cert. Social Workers, Internat. Platform Com., Psi Chi. Office: 1631 Constantinople St New Orleans LA 70115-4707

BURTON, BARBARA ANNE, plumbing and heating company executive; b. Flushing, N.Y., Nov. 28, 1948; d. Victor Arthur and Anne (Inglima) Schettini; m. Maurice John Burton, Mar. 10, 1973; children: Anthony John, Christopher Maurice. Acad. diploma, Flushing High Sch., 1966. Loan payers. Household Fin. Corp., N.Y.C., 1966-67; sec. P.F. Collier Inc., London, 1968-69, exec. sec., 1969-70; sec. Bill Lutz Assocs., N.Y.C., 1970-72; exec. sec. merchandising Courtaulds N.Am., N.Y.C., 1972-75; sec.-treas. M. Burton Plumbing & Heating Corp., N.Y.C., 1975—. Republican. Roman Catholic. Home: 53-42 211th St Bayside NY 11364 Office: M Burton Plumbing & Heating 206-01 48th Ave Bayside NY 11364-1046

BURTON, KATHLEEN T., mental health professional; b. Lynn, Mass., Jan. 29, 1962; d. Charles W. and Mary L. (Mayer) B. BA in Psychology/Comms., Notre Dame Coll., South Euclid, Ohio, 1985; MEd in Counseling, Cleve. State U., 1990, EdS in Counseling Psychology, 1991; postgrad., Saybrook Inst., San Francisco, 1992—. Cert. cognitive-behavioral therapist. Human rels. & devel. coord. Kaiser Permanente, Cleveland Heights, Ohio, 1984-87; counselor Cleve. Treatment Ctr., 1989-90; tchg. asst., counselor intern Cleve. State U., 1989-91; community trainer Woodland (Calif.) Community Options, 1991-95; mental health profl., psychologist intern Davis, Calif., 1992-95; psychologist pvt. practice, 1995—; group facilitator for human sexuality course dept. psychiatry Davis Med. Sch., 1994—; group leader, facilitator anxiety, phobias and panic Woodland Sr. Ctr., 1993—; mental health cons., creator "Mental Health Matters" Pub. TV, 1995; founder Sr./Youth Fair, Woodland, 1995; mental health writer Davis Enterprise; lectr. anxiety, phobias, panic, drug addictions, Moscow, Kiev, 1994. Author of a poem; contbr. article to medical jour. 1st place winner Nat. Future Design competition, Washington, 1984. Mem. ACA, Internat. Assn. for Addictions & Offender Counselors, Ohi Counseling Assn. (past rep.), Am. Family Assn. Roman Catholic. Office: 14 Leisureville Cir Woodland CA 95776

BURTON, LYNDA M., lawyer; b. St. Helena, Calif., Feb. 7, 1953; d. Leonard D. and Helen Maxine (Ashton) B. BA with honors, U. of the Pacific, Stockton, Calif., 1975; JD, U. San Francisco, 1980. Bar: Calif. 1981. Law clk. ACLU, San Francisco, 1979; staff atty. Legal Aid Soc. of San Mateo County, Redwood City, Calif., 1981—; mem. exec. com. San Mateo County Task Force on Violence Against Women, 1991—. Contbg. author: Bargaining for Equality, 1981; editor: Domestic Violence Law Manual, 2d edit., 1988. VISTA vol. Tex. Rural Legal Aid, Alice, 1975-77; human rights/elections observer to El Salvador, 1989, 94, Nicaragua, 1992, Mexico, 1994; ofcl. observer to U.N. 4th World Conf. on Women, Beijing, 1995. Recipient Women Helping Women award Soroptimist Internat., 1994, Woman of Distinction Soroptimist Internat., 1994. Mem. Nat. Lawyers Guild (founding mem. pro-choice project 1988—, regional v.p. San Francisco 1990-92), Svc. League (bd. dirs. 1989—). Democrat. Office: Legal Aid Soc of San Mateo County 298 Fuller St Redwood City CA 94063

BURTON, SHEAROR FAY, school system administrator, educator, computer consultant; b. Eastpoint, Fla., Dec. 10, 1938; d. George Wilburn and Mary Virginia (Segree) Creamer; m. Thomas Eliot Gordon, Oct. 6, 1956 (div. Apr. 1969); children: Brenda Gale, Pamela Faith; m. Orlis Luell Burton, Dec. 25, 1969. AA, Gulf Coast Community Coll., Panama City, Fla., 1969; BA, Fla. State U., 1972; MA, U. West Fla., 1979. Cert. tchr., Fla. Tchr. aide Chapman Elem. Sch., Apalachicola, Fla., 1966-67, sec., 1967-71; libr. Brown Elem. Sch., Eastpoint, Fla., 1972-73; media specialist Apalachicola High Sch., 1972-90; dist. adminstr. Franklin County Sch. Dist., Apalachicola, 1990—; adj. instr. Gulf Coast Community Coll., Panama City, 1987-89, Apalachicola coord., 1990-91; dir. Drug Free Schs. Adv. Coun., Apalachicola, 1989—; mem. Franklin County Literacy Bd., Apalachicola, 1989—; trainer Disadvantaged Youth Program, Apalachicola, 1990-91. Author: (computer program) Winner's Edge, 1989; editor: (book) Classic Creamer Cookery, 1996, (newsletter) Good New's Report, 1991. Recipient Literacy Program Goal Achievement award Fla. Dept. Edn., Tallahassee, 1991. Mem. Fla. Assn. Sch. Adminstrs., Fla. Assn. Media in Edn., Fla. Literacy Coalition, Franklin County Literacy Bd., Philaco Woman's Club (parliamentarian 1988), Kappa Delta Pi, Delta Kappa Gamma (Alpha Lambda chpt. coor. sec. 1988). Baptist. Office: Franklin County Schs 155 Avenue E Apalachicola FL 32320-2069

BURTON, VALORIE RAQUEL, marketing director, writer; b. Panama City, Fla., Jan. 15, 1973; d. Johnny Agnew Burton and Leone Edwenia (Adger Burton) Murray. BA in Internat. Affairs, Fla. State U., 1993; MA in Journalism, Fla. A&M U., 1994. Freelance writer various publs., 1993—; mktg. dir. Lane Gorman Trubitt, L.L.P., Dallas, 1995—; mem. fundraising spl. events com., Women in Comm., Inc., Dallas, 1995—. Pub. rels. intern, Office of the Gov., Tallahassee, 1992. Cadet, USAF Acad., Colorado Springs, Colo., 1990-91. Miss Black Tex. USA, 1995, top 10 finalist Miss Black USA scholarship orgn., 1995; Delores Auzenne Grad. fellow, State of Fla., 1995-96. Mem. Assn. for Acctg. and Mktg., Pub. Rels. Soc. Am., Women in Comm., Inc. Baptist. Office: Lane Gorman Trubitt LLP 1909 Woodall Rodgers 4th fl Dallas TX 75201

BURTON LYLES, BLANCHE, pianist; b. Phila., Mar. 2, 1933; d. Anthony Huston and Ida Blanche (Taylor) Burton; m. Thurman W. Lyles, Dec. 7, 1957 (div. June 1967); 1 child, Thedric (dec.). B Music in Piano, Curtis Inst., 1954; B Music Edn., Temple U., 1970. Musical specialist Phila. Pub. Schs., 1966-92; bd. dirs. Settlement Music Sch., Phila. Leader Soc. Combo performed at Ross Perot Presidential Rally CNN-TV, 1992. Named Outstanding Virtuoso Musician Nat. Black Music Caucus, 1995. Mem. Nat. Assn. Negro Musicians, Curtis Alumni Soc., Delta Sigma Theta. Home: 1118 S 19th St Philadelphia PA 19146-2937

BURTT, ANNE DAMPMAN, special education educator; b. Phila., Nov. 22, 1950; d. Elmer and Anne (Scott) Dampman; m. James Burtt, Aug. 5, 1972. BS in Edn. cum laude, Duquesne U., 1972; MEd, U. Pitts., 1976, Temple U., 1985. Cert. spl. edn., elem. tchr., reading specialist. Tchr. Pitts. Pub. Schs., 1972-77, Montgomery County (Pa.) Intermediate Unit, 1977—. Mem. PTO, 1972—, Chpt. Attention Deficit Disorders, 1989—, CHADD Bux-Mont. Divsn., Behavioral Disorders/Learning Disorders. Recipient Pius X award Archdiocese Phila., Most Successful Grad. 25th Yr. Reunion West Phila. Cath. Girls' H.S. Mem. Pa. State Edn. Assn., Coun. for Exceptional Children, Behavior Disorders and Learning Disabilities. Home: 131 Maple Ave Willow Grove PA 19090-2902 Office: Montgomery County Intermediate Unit 1605-B W Main St Norristown PA 19403-3290

BURZYCKI, TRACY ANNE, business owner; b. Norwich, Conn., Oct. 19, 1970; d. Frank Daniel and Barbara June (Koziol) B. BS, U. Conn., 1992. Natural products chemist Pfizer, Groton, Conn., 1993—; owner Burzycki and Assocs., Mystic, Conn., 1995—. Vol. Spl. Olympics, Conn., 1994; mem. Lisbon (Conn.) Planning and Zoning Bd., 1995; mem., publicity chair Pfizer Players Theatrical Group, Groton. Mem. U. Conn. Alumni Group, Kappa Kappa Gamma (reference chair 1996—). Home: 32 Pearl St Mystic CT 06355

BURZYNSKI, SUSAN MARIE, newspaper editor; b. Jackson, Mich., Jan. 1, 1953; d. Leon Walter and Claudia (Kulpinski) B.; m. James W. Bush, May 22, 1976 (div. 1989); children: Lisa M., Kevin J.; m. George K. Bullard, Jr., Mar. 21, 1992. AA, Jackson C.C., 1972; BA, Mich. State, 1974. Reporter Saratogian, Saratoga Springs, N.Y., 1974, Gongwer News Svc., Lansing, Mich., 1975, The State Jour., Lansing, 1975-79; Metro editor Port Huron (Mich.) Times Herald, 1979-82, mng. editor, 1982-86; asst. city editor Detroit News, 1986-87, Sunday news editor, 1987, news editor, 1988-91, asst. mng. editor/news, 1991-96, asst. mng. editor, recruiting and tng., 1996—. Roman Catholic. Office: Detroit News 615 W Lafayette Blvd Detroit MI 48226-3124

BUSARD, ROBERTA ANN, artist, educator; b. Muskegon, Mich., Apr. 20, 1952; d. Thomas Richard and Dolores Mae (Fisher) B.; m. William VonWemp Suchmann, Dec. 19, 1992; 1 child Katherine Susan Busard Suchmann. BFA, Mass. Coll. Art, 1977; attended, San Francisco Art Inst., 1970, 73, Art Inst. Boston, 1971, Silvermine Coll. Art, 1972. Cert. art edn. K-12. Intern art tchr. Boston Pub. Schs., 1975, 77, The Internat. Sch. Genoa, Italy, 1976; art tchr., dir. The Kid's Art Studio, S. Burlington, Vt., 1990-91, The Women's Art Project, Ann Arbor, Mich., 1992-94; art tchr. Go Like The Wind Montesorri Sch., Ann Arbor, 1993-94; guest lectr. u. Mich., Ann Arbor, 1992; mem., advisor, curator The Vt. Artist's Collective, Burlington, Vt., 1989-90; freelance artist, curator, 1988—. Solo shows include Margolis Gallery, Vail, Colo., 1984, Hibberd-McGrath Galleries, Keystone, Colo., 1985, St. Mark's Gallery, N.Y.C., 1986, Lincoln Ctr., Ft. Collins, Colo., 1987, Reinike Gallery, New Orleans, 1988, Stowe (Vt.) Playhouse Gallery, 1988, Gallery One, Denver, 1988, Reinike Gallery, Atlanta, 1992, 95, Visual and Performing Arts Loft Gallery, Ann Arbor, Mich., 1995, Ford Amphitheater Gallery, U. Mich. Hosps., Ann Arbor, 1995, Chgo. Sch. Profl. Psychology, 1996; numerous group exhbns. include Woodstock (Vt.) Gallery, 1989, 90, Lone Pine Gallery, Newport Beach, Calif., 1989, 90, 91, Gallery One, Denver, 1989, 90, 91, Vt. Artists' Collective, Burlington, 1990, Burlington City Arts Coun., 1990, Reinike Gallery, Atlanta, 1990, 91, 92, 94, Art's Alive, Burlington, 1990, Impressions Gallery, Burlington, 1990, 91, 92, Stratton (Vt.) Arts Festival, 1991, U. Mich. Rackam Grad. Sch. Galleries, 1991, Art-Tech Gallery, Chgo., 1993, 94, Galleriea, Washtenaw Coun. for Arts, 1993, ARC Gallery, Chgo., 1994, Wells St. Art Festival, Chgo., 1994, Detroit Artists' Mkt., 1994, Chautauqua (N.Y.) Art Assn., 1994, Chgo.'s New EastSide Artworks, 1994, Anchorage Mus. History and Art, 1994-95, An Art Place Inc. Gallery, 1995, Art Inst. Boston, 1995, Elite Gallery and Russian-Am. Cultural Ctr., Moscow, 1995, Nat. Mus. of Women in the Arts, Washington, 1996, many others; permanent collections include Anchorage Mus. Art and History, Nat. Mus. Women in the Arts, Dieckmann & Assocs., Ltd., U.S. West Telecom. and many pvt. collections. Recipient Juror's Choice Mary Mellor Meml. Fund award for painting, mixed media and drawing San Francisco Women Artists Gallery, 1994, Juror's Choice award for painting Arts Alive, Burlington, 1990. Mem. Nat. Women's Caucus for Art, Mich. Women's Caucus for Art (founder Mich. chpt. 1994, pres. 1994-95, co-pres. 1996—), Detroit Focus Gallery (exbhn. com. mem. 1994-95), Chgo. Artist's Coalition, Coll. Art Assn., Mich. Bus. and Profl. Assn., Nat. Mus. for Women in the Arts, Artists' choice Mus., Alumni Assn. of San Francisco Art Inst., Alumni Assn. of Art Inst. Boston, Alumni Assn. of Mass. Coll. Art. Office: 118 S Main St Ste 346 Ann Arbor MI 48104

BUSBICE, DEBORAH LEE, public school educator; b. East Grand Rapids, Mich., Feb. 15, 1951; d. Richard and Bette Buchanan; m. Roger L. Busbice, Apr. 19, 1985; 1 child, Bonnye R. BS, Eastern Mich. U., 1973; MEd, Nicholls State U., Thibodaux, La., 1986, postgrad., 1991, 93. Cert. elem. tchr., supr. student teaching, elem. sch. prin., academically gifted. Tchr. Ypsilanti (Mich.) Sch. Dist., 1975-80; tchr. St. Mary Parish Sch. Bd., Patterson, La., 1981-90, Berwick, La., 1990—. Pres. Atchafalaya Women's Rep. Club, Morgan City, La., 1990-94. Recipient AT&T La. Awards for Excellence in Tchg. Econs., 1990-91, 91-92. Mem. Academically Gifted and Talented Assn., La. Sci. Tchrs. Assn., Nicholls Reading Coun. (parish dir. 1992-95), Internat. Reading Assn., Assoc. Profl. Edn. of La. (sec. 1987-95). Republican. Episcopalian. Home: PO Box 2315 Morgan City LA 70381-2315 Office: Berwick Elementary Sch 400 Texas St Berwick LA 70342-2526

BUSBY, ANN, film company executive. Sr. v.p., MCA Motion Picture Group Universal Pictures, Universal City, Calif. Office: Universal Pictures Motion Picture Group 100 Universal City Plz Universal City CA 91608*

BUSBY, MARJORIE JEAN (MARJEAN BUSBY), journalist; b. Kansas City, Mo., Jan. 31, 1931; d. Vivian Eric and Stella Mae (Lindley) Phillips; m. Robert Jackson Busby, Apr. 11, 1969 (dec. Feb. 1989). B.J., U. Mo., 1952. With Kansas City (Mo.) Star Co. (became div. Capital Cities Communications 1977, name changed to Capital Cities/ABC Inc.), 1952—, editor women's news, 1969-73, assoc. Sunday editor, People Sect. editor, 1973-77, fashion editor, 1978-81, feature and home writer, 1981—. Mem. Fashion Group (1st recipient Kansas City appreciation award 1978), Women in Communications, LSV, Mortar Board, Soc. Profl. Journalists, Kappa Alpha Theta (pres. Alpha Mu chpt. 1951-52). Presbyterian. Clubs: Leawood Country, Belle of Am. Royal Orgn. Home: 9804 Mercier St Kansas City MO 64114-3860 Office: 1729 Grand Blvd Kansas City MO 64108-1413

BÜSCH, ANNEMARIE, mental health nurse; d. Jurgen Julius and Anna (Stark) B. RN, Anschar Sch. Nursing, Kiel, Fed. Republic Germany, 1954; student, Traverse City State Hosp., Mich., 1959, Wayne State U., 1962, Colby-Sawyer Coll., New London, N.H., 1981. Lic. nurse, N.H., Vt., Fed. Republic Germany. Asst. head nurse Univ. Eye Inst., Kiel, 1954-56; nurse aide, grad. nurse Ontario Hosp., London, Can.; staff nurse, charge nurse Grace Hosp., Receiving Hosp., Detroit, 1962-67; coll. health nurse Wayne St. U., Detroit, 1967-70; staff nurse Mary Hitchcock Meml. Hosp., Hanover, 1970-71, nurse mental health dept., 1978-82; charge nurse Dartmouth Coll. Health Svc., Hanover, N.H., 1971-77; staff nurse, charge nurse Hanover Health Terrace; staff nurse Temporary Nurses, Inc., Hanover, Vis. Nurse Alliance of Vt. and N.H., White River Junction, Vt.; camp nurse Nat. Music Camp InterLochen, Mich.

BUSCH, ANNIE, library director; b. Joplin, Mo., Jan. 6, 1947; d. George Lee and Margaret Eleanor (Williams) Chancellor; 1 child, William Andrew Keller. BA, Mo. U., 1969, MA, 1976. Br. mgr. St. Charles (Mo.) City Coun. Libr., 1977-84; br. mgr. Springfield/Greene County (Mo.) Libr., 1985-89, exec. dir., 1989—; mem. exec. bd. Mo. Libr. Network Corp., St. Louis, 1991-96. Mem. adv. bd. Springfield Pub. Sch. Found., 1992-94; pres. Ozarks Regional Info. On-Line Network, Springfield, 1993—; mem. Gov.'s Commn. on Informational Tech.; mem. exec. bd. Mo. Rsch. and Edn. Network, pres., 1996-97; bd. dirs. Ozarks Pub. TV, 1994—; mem. task force Mo. Goals 2000, 1995. Mem. ALA, Mo. Libr. Assn. (pres. 1993-94, exec. bd. 1990-94), Forum, Pub. Libr. Assn., Rotary (treas. Springfield Club 1994). Office: Springfield-Greene Cty Libr 620 W Republic Rd Springfield MO 65807-5818

BUSCH, CAROLE ANN MCGOVERN, psychotherapist, art therapist, nurse, consultant; b. Manhattan, N.Y., June 6, 1945; d. James Lenahan and Claire Beatrice (Murphy) McGovern; m. Joseph Jacob Busch Jr.; children: James McGovern, Angela Maureen, Caroline Claire. Diploma in nursing, St. Mary's Sch. Nursing, 1966; BA in Art magna cum laude, U. Tenn., Chattanooga, 1985, MEd in Guidance, 1988. RN, Tenn.; cert. clin. nurse specialist in adult psychiat. and mental health nursing; registered art therapist; lic. art therapist; cert. art therapist; nat. bd. cert. med. psychotherapist; fellow and diplomate Am. Bd. Med. Psychotherapists. Med. and surg. staff nurse St. Marys Hosp. Med. Ctr., Knoxville, Tenn., 1966-67; med. and surg. charge nurse William F. Bowld Hosp., Memphis, 1967-69; coronary care nurse Bapt. Meml. Hosp., Memphis, 1969-71; pvt. practice med. psychotherapist, art therapy cons. Signal Mountain, Tenn., 1988—; art therapy cons. Valley Psychiat. Hosp., Chattanooga, 1989-90; coord. art expressions group adaopt a parent Alexian Bros. Health Care Ctr., Signal Mountain, 1989-91; nat. and internat. presenter on arts and medicine, 1991—; profl. artist and photographer, 1975—. Numerous one-woman and group art exhbns. regionally, nationally, and internationally; works in pub. and pvt. collections in U.S., Ireland and China. Ann. workshop leader Very Spl. Arts Festival, Orange Grove Ctr., Chattanooga, 1981—; career beginning mentor U. Tenn. Ctr. for Community Career Edn., Chattanooga, 1988-89; vol. mental health counselor Signal Crest Meth. Ch., Signal Mountain, 1988-90; amb. art therapy del. People to People, China, 1995. Recipient Disting. Leadership award in the mental health field, 1987. Mem. Tenn. Art Therapy Assn. (founder 1993, pres. 1995—), Golden Key Nat. Honor Soc., Kappa Delta Pi, Chi Sigma Iota, Alpha Soc., Girls Cotillion, Signal Mountain Tennis Club (bd. dirs. 1981). Roman Catholic. Office: Art Therapy Consults & Studio 715-B Mississippi Ave Signal Mountain TN 37377

BUSCH, JOYCE IDA, small business owner; b. Madera, Calif., Jan. 24, 1934; d. Bruno Harry and Ella Fae (Absher) Toschi; m. Fred O. Busch, Dec. 14, 1956; children: Karen, Kathryn, Kurt. BA in Indsl. Arts & Interior Design, Calif. State U., Fresno, 1991. Cert. interior designer Calif. Stewardess United Air Lines, San Francisco, 1955-57; prin. Art Coordinates, Fresno, 1982—, Busch Interior Design, Fresno, 1982—; art cons. Fresno Community Hosp., 1981-83; docent Fresno Met. Mus., 1981-84. Treas. Valley Children's Hosp. Guidance Clinic, 1975-79, Lone Star PTA, 1965-84,; mem. Mothers Guild Jan Joaquin Mem. Hosp., 1984-88. Mem. Am. Soc. Interior Designers, Illuminating Engring. Soc. N.Am. Republican. Roman Catholic. Club: Sunnyside Garden (pres. 1987-88).

BUSH, BARBARA PIERCE, volunteer, wife of former President of the United States; b. Rye, N.Y., June 8, 1925; d. Marvin and Pauline (Robinson) Pierce; m. George Herbert Walker Bush, Jan. 6, 1945; children: George Walker, John Ellis, Neil Mallon, Marvin Pierce, Dorothy Walker. Student, Smith Coll., 1943-44; hon. degrees, Stritch Coll., Milw., 1981, Mt. Vernon Coll., Washington, 1981, Hood Coll., Frederick, Md., 1983, Howard U., Washington, 1987, Judson Coll., Marion, Ala., 1988, Bennett Coll., Greensboro, N.C., 1989, Smith Coll., 1989, Morehouse Sch. Medicine, 1989. Author: C. Fred Story; Millie's Book; Barbara Bush: A Memoir, 1994. Hon. chair adv. bd. Reading is Fundamental; hon. mem. Bus. Coun. for Effective Literacy; mem. adv. coun. Soc. of Meml. Sloan-Kettering Cancer Ctr.; hon. mem. bd. dirs. Children's Oncology Svcs. of Met. Washington, The Washington Home, The Kingsbury Ctr.; hon. chmn. nat. adv. coun. Literacy Vols. of Am., Nat. Sch. Vols. Program; sponsor Laubach Literacy Internat.; nat. hon. chmn. Leukemia Soc. of Am.; hon. mem. bd. trustees Morehouse Sch. of Medicine; hon. nat. chmn. Nat. Organ Donor Awareness Week, 1982-86; pres. Ladies of the Senate, 1981-88; mem. women's com. Smithsonian Assocs., Tex. Fedn. of Rep. Women, life mem., hon. mem.; hon. chairperson for the Nat. Com. on Literacy and Edn. United Way, Barbara Bush Found. for Family Literacy, Washington Parent Group Fund, Girls Clubs of Am., 10th anniversay Harvest Nat. Food Bank Network; hon. chmn. Nat. Com. for the Prevention of Child Abuse and Childhelp U.S.A.; hon. pres. Girl Scouts U.S; hon. chair Nat. Com. for Adoption; mem. bd. trustees Mayo Clinic Found.; hon. chair Read Am., Boarder Baby Project; mem. bd. visitors M. D. Anderson Cancer Ctr.; hon. chair Leukemia Soc. Am., Children's Literacy Initiative; hon. mem. Reading is Fundamental; ambassador at large Americares; honorary mem. Barbara Bush Found. for Family Literacy. Recipient Nat. Outstanding Mother of Yr. award, 1984, Woman of Yr. award USO, 1986, Disting. Leadership award United Negro Coll. Fund 1986, Disting. Am. Woman award Coll. Mt. St. Joseph, 1987, Free Spirit award Freedom Forum, 1995. Mem. Tex. Fedn. Rep. Women (life), Internat. II Club (Washington), Magic Circle Rep. Women's Club (Houston), YWCA. Episcopalian. Office: 10000 Memorial Dr Houston TX 77024-3422*

BUSH, CRYSTAL REED, financial planner; b. Chgo., Dec. 14, 1957; d. Alonzo and Elmethra (Luster) Reed; m. Tony Bush, Aug. 12, 1989. BA in History, Roosevelt U., 1979; JD, DePaul U., 1995. Tchr. Chgo. Bd. Edn., 1979-90; pres. Buree Assocs., Chgo., 1990—. Fin. editor The Leguenet, 1991; contbr. articles to jours. Treas., chair program com. Women's Entrepreneur Network, Chgo., 1990-91; treas. League of Black Women, Chgo., 1991-92. Recipient Exceptional Contbn. award to Afro-Am. Cmty. AT&T, 1991, 92, 93. Mem. Nat. Assn. Women Bus. Owners (mem. Chgo. chpt.), Chgo. Bar Assn., Ill. Bar Assn. Home: 8644 S Kenwood Ave Chicago IL 60619-6416 Office: Buree Assocs 14 N Peoria St Ste 100 Chicago IL 60607

BUSH, JOANNE TADEO, financial consultant, corporate executive; b. Norristown, Pa., May 17, 1947; d. I.C. and Anne (DeJohn) Arena; 1 child, Ryan J. Tadeo; m. David F. Bush, Oct. 15, 1989. BS in Acctg. cum laude, Villanova U., 1979; MBA in Taxation, Drexel U., 1982. Lic. investment advisor, securities broker. Adminstrv. asst. Cen. Montgomery Mental Health and Mental Retardation Ctr., Norristown, 1970-80; grad. teaching asst. Drexel U., Phila., 1981-82; lectr. Pa. State U., Abington, 1982-83; asst. prof. Ursinus Coll., Collegeville, Pa., 1883-84; fin. cons. Merrill Lynch, Exton, Pa., 1984—. Mem. bd. dirs. Y.M.C.A. Central Chester County., bd. dirs. Chester County Estate Planning Coun., 1988—, Chester County Chamber for Bus. and Industry; West Chester charity ball com. Mem. Rotary, Alpha Sigma Lambda, Beta Gamma Sigma, Phi Kappa Phi. Office: Merrill LynchOakland Corp Ctr 101 Arrandike Blvd Exton PA 19341

BUSH, JUNE LEE, real estate executive; b. Philippi, W.Va., Sept. 20, 1942; d. Leland C. and Dolly Mary (Costello) Robinson; m. Jerry Lee Coffman, June 15, 1963 (div. 1970); 1 child, Jason Lance; m. Richard Alfred Bush, May 20, 1972. Grad., Fairmont State Coll., 1962, Dale Carnegie, Anaheim, Calif., 1988. Exec. sec. McDonnell Douglas, Huntington Beach, Calif., 1965-72; adminstrv. asst. Mgmt. Resources, Inc., Fullerton, Calif., 1978-80; bldg. mgr. Alfred Gobar Assocs., Brea, Calif., 1980-95; treas. Craig Park East, Fullerton, 1982, bd. dirs., 1982-84. Author instrn. manual Quality Assurance Secretarial Manual, 1971. Sec. PTA, La Palma, 1974. Mem. Gamma Chi Chi. Home: 563 Highland Ave Half Moon Bay CA 94019

BUSH, LINDA A., land use planner; b. Westfield, Mass., Dec. 4, 1951; d. Harold Arthur and Lucy (King) B. BS in Zoology, U. Mass., 1973; MS in Resource Mgmt., Antioch U., 1981. Planner Upper Valley-Lake Surapee Coun., Lebanon, N.H., 1980-81; local govt. advisor Tug Hill Commn., Watertown, N.Y., 1981-83; town planner Town of Wallingford, Conn., 1984—. Chmn. bd. YMCA, Wallingford, 1993-95; vice chmn. campaign United Way Meriden-Wallingford, 1995. Mem. AICP, Am. Planning Assn. Office: Town of Wallingford 45 S Main St Wallingford CT 06492

BUSH, MARJORIE EVELYNN TOWER-TOOKER, educator, media specialist, librarian; b. Atkinson, Nebr., Mar. 12, 1925; d. Albert Ralph and Vera Marie (Rickover) Tower-Tooker; m. Louis T. Genung, Feb. 2, 1944 (dec. Jan. 1982); 1 son, Louis Thompson; m. Laurence Scott Bush, Sept. 22, 1984; 1 stepson, Roger A. Bush. Student U. Nebr.,1951, Wayne State Coll., 1942-47; BA Colo. State Coll., 1966, U. No. Colo., 1970; postgrad. Doane Coll., 1967-68, U. Utah, 1973-74, PhD (hon.), 1973. Elem. tchr. Atkinson Public Schs., 1958-69; adminstr. libraries and audiovisual communications Clay County Dist. I-C, Fairfield, Nebr., 1972-81; media specialist Albion (Nebr.) City Schs., 1981—; mem. Neb. Gov.'s White House Conf. on Libraries. Chmn. edn. adminstrv. bd. Park Hill United Meth. Ch., Denver, also pres.; sec. Denver Symphony Guild. Mem. NEA (life), Nebr., Colo. edn. assns., Assn. Childhood Edn. Internat., ALA, Nebr., Mountain Plains library assns., Nat. Council Tchrs. English, AAUW, Nebr. Ednl. Media Assn., Assn. Supervision and Curriculum Devel., Assn. Ednl. Communications and Tech., Internat. Visual Literacy Assn., Nat. Council Exceptional Children, Alumni Assn. U. No. Colo. (life charter), Women Educators Nebr., United Meth. Women (pres.), Am. Legion Aux., Nebr. Lay Citizens Edn. Assn. (exec.), Am. Nat. Cowbelles, Nebr. Cowbelles, DAR (regent 1971, dist. treas. 1968-71), Internat. Platform Assn., LWV, Women's Soc. Christian Service, Ak-Sar-Ben. Club: Windsor Gardens (Denver). Lodges: Opti-Mrs. (pres.), Optimists Internat., Columbine Optimists (pres. 1987-88), Eastern Star. Home: 9655 E Center Ave Denver CO 80231-1276

BUSH, MARY ELIZABETH, English and writing educator, author; b. Canastota, N.Y., Sept. 13, 1949; d. Carmon Anthony and Pauline Theresa (Galavotti) B. BA, SUNY, Buffalo, 1972; MA, Syracuse U., 1980, ArtsD, 1984. Asst. prof. Hobart and William Smith Coll., Geneva, N.Y., 1985-89, Hamilton Coll., Clinton, N.Y., 1989-91, Memphis State U., 1991-93; assoc. prof. Calif. State U., L.A., 1993—; co-founder, co-dir. Cmty. Writers' Project, Syracuse, 1994-95. Author: (short stories) A Place of Light, 1990; contbg. author: (anthology) The Voices We Carry, 1994, (lit. jours.) Story, 1992, The Mo. Rev., 1996, also various others. Nat. Endowment for Arts writing fellow, 1995. Mem. PEN Internat. (Nelson Algren award 1985), Am. Italian Hist. Assn. Associated Writing Programs. Home: 1007 Palm Terr Pasadena CA 91104 Office: Calif State U LA English Dept 5151 State University Dr Los Angeles CA 90032

BUSH, SARAH LILLIAN, historian; b. Kansas City, Mo., Sept. 17, 1920; d. William Adam and Lettie Evelyn (Burrill) Lewis; m. Walter Nelson Bush, June 7, 1946 (dec.); children: William Read, Robert Nelson. AB, U. Kans., 1941; BS, U. Ill., 1943. Clk. circulation dept. Kansas City Pub. Library, 1941-42, asst. librarian Paseo br., 1943-44; librarian Kansas City Jr. Coll., 1944-46; substitute librarian San Mateo County Library, Woodside amd Portola Valley, Calif., 1975-77; various temporary positions, 1979-87; owner Metriguide, Palo Alto, Calif., 1975-78. Author: Atherton Lands, 1979, rev. edition 1987. Editor: Atherton Recollections, 1973. Pres., v.p. Jr. Librarians, Kansas City, 1944-46; courtesy, yearbook & historian AAUW, Menlo-Atherton branch (Calif.) Br.; asst. Sunday sch. tchr., vol. Holy Trinity Ch., Menlo Park, 1955-78; v.p., membership com., libr. chairperson, English reading program, parent edn. chairperson Menlo Atherton High Sch. PTA, 1964-73; founder, bd. dirs. Friends of Atherton Community Library, 1967—, oral historian, 1968—, chair Bicentennial event, 1976; bd. dirs. Menlo Park Hist. Assn., 1979-82, oral historian, 1973—; bd. dirs. Civic Interest League, Atherton, 1978-81; mem. hist. county commn. Town of Atherton, 1980-87; vol. Allied Arts Palo Alto Aux. to Children's Hosp. at Stanford, 1967—, oral historian, 1978—, historian, 1980—; vol. United Crusade, Garfield Sch., Redwood City, 1957-61, 74-88, Encinal Sch., 1961-73, program dir., chmn. summer recreation, historian, sec.; vol. Stanford Mothers Club, 1977-81, others; historian, awards chairperson Cub Scouts Boy Scouts Am.; founder Atherton Heritage Assn. 1989, bd. dirs., 1989—; mem. Guild Gourmet, 1971—. Recipient Good Neighbor award Civic Interest League, 1992. Mem. PTA (life). Episcopalian.

BUSHNELL, CAROLYN SUZANNE, bank executive; b. L.A., Sept. 1, 1940; d. William Commodore Bushnell and Mary (Kunellis) Oviatt. AA, Mt. San Antonio Jr. Coll., Walnut, Calif., 1961; BA, San Francisco State U., 1964; MEd, U. LaVerne, 1977. Cert. secondary tchr., Calif.; cert. elem. tchr., Calif.; lic. real estate agt., Calif. High sch. tchr. Santa Maria (Calif.) Union High Sch. Dist., 1965-67, Torrance (Calif.) Unified Sch. Dist., 1967-79; office leasing specialist Matlow-Kennedy Corp., Torrance, 1979-83; property mgr./leasing agt. Huntington Seacliff Corp., Torrance, 1983-85; v.p. comml. div. Lewis W. Ground & Assocs., San Diego, Calif., 1985-88; asset mgr. Travelers Ins. Cos., Santa Monica, Calif., 1988-90; v.p., corp. officer Home Savs. Am., Irwindale, Calif., 1990-92; asset mgr., dept. head Plus Investments, Inc., L.A., 1993-94; pres. Bushnell & Assocs. Comml. Real Estate, Glendora, Calif., 1994—; cons. and lectr., U.S., Can., 1978—; nat. alternate del. Nat. Network Women in Comml. Real Estate, L.A. chpt., 1992; selection com. Fulbright/Hays Internat. Ednl. and Cultural Exch. program, L.A., 1979—. Pres. bd. dirs. YWCA, Torrance, 1971-74; pres. So. Calif. Overseas Tchrs. Orgn., 1981-83, South Bay League of So. Calif. Forensic Assn., 1971-73. Scholarship Fulbright-Hays Internat. Ednl. and Cultural Exch. program, 1978-79; Coe fellowship Pepperdine U., 1973. Mem. AAUW (chpt. legis. com. chairperson 1989), Fulbright Alumni Assn., Nat. Soc. DAR (nat. resolutions com. 1990—, vice chmn. 1994—). Democrat. Greek Orthodox. Home and Office: PO Box 38 Glendora CA 91740-0038

BUSHNELL, CATHARINE, marketing consulting firm executive; b. Pullman, Wash, July 2, 1950; d. David and Catharine Howe (Goodfellow) B.; m. H. Michael Sisson, Oct. 31, 1975. BS in Speech, Northwestern U., 1972. Prodn. mgr. Mike White Advt., Chgo., 1972; stage actress, Chgo., 1972-73; ptnr., dir. photography Mome, Raths & Outgrabe, Chgo., 1973-75; exec. v.p. Sisson Assocs., N.Y.C., 1975—; pres. Illusion Gallery, Creative Resource Co., N.Y.C., 1981—, The Sisson Group Inc., 1986—; v.p. Ea. European Merchandising Corp., 1992—, also bd. dirs.; mem. bd. dirs. Digital Mktg. Assocs., 1993—; faculty New Sch.-Parsons Sch. of Design, 1985-86. Photographer motion picture stills for various films, N.Y.C., 1975—; author: Raggedy Ann and Andy in the Tunnel of Lost Toys, 1980; Raggedy Ann and Andy and the Pirates of Outgo Inlet, 1981; Linda's Magic Window, 1981; Frannie's Magic Kazoo, 1982. Judge ann. student photog. portfolio rev. High Sch. of Art and Design, N.Y.C., 1979-83. Mem. Licensing Industry Assn., Internat. Photographers Motion Picture Industry, Internat. Soc. Photography (charter), Actors Equity Assn., Northwestern U. Alumnae Assn., Delta Zeta. Office: The Sisson Group Inc 300 E 40th St New York NY 10016-2188

BUSHO, ELIZABETH MARY, nurse, consultant, educator; b. Ellendale, Minn., Feb. 26, 1927; d. Ruben Oscar and Lillian Katherine (Gahagan) B. RN, Kahler Hosps. Sch. of Nursing, 1948. RN, Minn. Oper. rm. staff nurse, Minn., Calif., Colo., 1948-53; oper. rm. head nurse, Mt. Sinai Hosp., Mpls., 1953-61; asst. supr. oper. rm. St. Barnabas Hosp., Mpls., 1961-71; asst. dir. surg. svcs. St. Mary's Hosp., Rochester, Minn., 1971-80, dir., 1980-90; sr. cons. oper. rms. Mayo Med. Ctr., Rochester, 1990-92; ind. cons. surg. svcs., 1992—; instr. Rochester Community Coll. Developer course in oper. rm. nursing. Mem. adv. bd. Rochester Area Vocat. Tech. Inst., Rochester Community Coll., Sigma Theta Tau. Republican. Methodist. Office: 2100 Valkyrie Dr NW Apt 415 Rochester MN 55901-2449

BUSHOR-GARDNER, SANDI J., biology educator; b. Chicago Heights, Ill., June 24, 1959; d. Robert S. and Lenore M. (D'Arcy) Bushor; m. Daniel E. Gardner, Apr. 16, 1988; 1 child, C(atherine) J. BS in Phys. Edn./Recreation, U. Ill., Chgo., 1981; MS in Environ. Biology, Govs. State U., University Park, Ill., 1989; postgrad., Ill. Inst. Tech., Chgo., 1993-95; PhD Candidate, Walden U., Mpls., 1995—. Profl. scout Wau Bon Girl Scout Coun., Fond Du Lac, Wis., 1981-82; pre-sch. tchr. Anita M. Stone Ctr., Flossmoor, Ill., 1982-84, Alsip (Ill.) Pre-Sch., 1984-85; teaching asst. Govs. State U., 1986-89; park ranger Ind. Dunes Nat. Lakeshore, Porter, 1986-92; prof. biology South Suburban Coll., South Holland, Ill., 1990-96; adj. prof. Ind. U.-N.W., Gary, 1990-92, Govs. State U., 1989-93; mem. spl. populations adv. bd. South Suburban Mental Health, South Holland, 1992-94; staff develop./curriculum specialist Purdue U., 1995-96, adj. faculty, 1996, Triton Coll., River Grove, Ill., 1996; workshop presenter, cons. in field. Co-author: Case Studies for Anatomy and Physiology, 1992, Lab Manual for General Biology, 1994. Leader, vol., trainer Calumet coun. Girl Scouts U.S., Highland, Ind., 1981-84, 93—. Recipient Spl. Achievement award Nat. Park Svc., 1988; Hand-On Sci. for Tchrs. award EPA, 1992. Mem. Nat. Sci. Tchrs. Assn., Nat. Assn. Biology Tchrs., Ill. Assn. C.C. Biology Tchrs. Home: 51 Terrace Dr Munster IN 46321-2112 Office: Triton Col 2000 5th Ave River Grove IL 60171

BUSKA, SHEILA MARY, controller; b. Brewer, Maine, May 9, 1941; d. George William Sanderlin and Margaret Owenita Harrah; m. Roland Michael Buska, Nov. 28, 1959; children: Bryan Michael, Craig William, Christine Mary, Paul Kevin. AA, U. San Diego, 1959; BS in Acct. magna cum laude with distinction, San Diego State U., 1984. Cert. mgmt. acct.; CPA, Calif. Sr. acct. Peak Health Plan, San Diego, 1984-86; legal entity acct. M/A-COM Govt. Sys., San Diego, 1986-87; sr. acct. Lois A. Brozey, CPA, San Diego, 1987-89; controller, treas. Soco-Lynch Corp. dba Crown Chem. Corp., Chula Vista, Calif., 1989—. Author: (poem) Young America Sings, 1957, Sermons in Poetry, 1957; contbr. articles to profl. jours. Mem. Inst. Mgmt. Accts. (dir. membership acquisition 1995-96, treas. 1993-94, dir. corp. devel. 1992-93, dir. cert. mgmt. accts., 1989-90, v.p. membership and mktg. 1985-86, Most Valuable Mem. 1990-91). Democrat. Roman Catholic. Home: 509 Burgasia Path El Cajon CA 92019 Office: Soco-Lynch Corp dba Crown Chem Corp 1888 Nirvana Ave Chula Vista CA 91911

BUSSE, EILEEN E., special education educator; b. Green Bay, Wis., Oct. 16, 1957; d. Ervin F. and Elaine I. (Behnke) Dohl; m. John F. Busse, July 5, 1980; children: Jessica Lynn, Jeremy John. BS in Elem. and Spl. Edn., U. Wis., Eau Claire, 1979; MS in Spl. Edn., U. Wis., Whitewater, 1985. Cert. tchr. elem. and spl. edn. Tchr. spl. edn./mentally retarded Ithaca (Wis.) Pub. Schs., 1979-80; spl. edn. tchr. Walworth County HCEB Walworth County HCEB, Whitewater, Wis., 1980—; spl. edn. tchr. Lakeview Elem. Sch., 1991—; coop. tchr. U. Wis., Whitewater, 1988—. Author: Student Owned Spelling, 1991, II, 1992, III, 1994. Mem. Gifted and Talented Parent Support Group, Whitewater, 1993—; sch. liaision, founder Caring Parents Support Group, Whitewater, Lakeview, 1988-94, student coun. advisor, Whitewater, 1995—; mem. First English Luth. Ch. edn. com., Whitewater, 1990-95, chmn. edn. com., 1993-95, mem. ch. coun., 1993-95; active Girl Scouts U.S.A., 1992—, Boy Scouts Am., 1995—. Recipient Excellence in Edn. award U.S. Dept. Edn., 1984-85. Mem. Coun. for Exceptional Children, Wis. Assn. Children with Behavioral Disorders. Home: 455 Ventura Ln Whitewater WI 53190-1548 Office: Lakeview Elem Sch PO Box 646 Whitewater WI 53190-0646

BUSTIN, BEVERLY MINER, state senator; b. Morrisville, Vt., Feb. 14, 1936; d. Donald Haze and Della Mae (Kenfield) Miner; children: Catherine Margaret, David Wayne. BS, Thomas Coll. Maine state senator, 1979—, chair joint select com. on alcoholism services, 1982-84, chair instl. services com., 1983-84, chair bus. and commerce commn., 1985-87. Mem. Kennebec County (Maine) Dem. Com., Hollowell (Maine) Dem. Com.; treas. Uplift, Inc., 1980-86; vice chair Kennebec County Regional Health Agy., 1984-88, chair audit program rev., 1987—, mem. banking and ins. com., 1987—, chair joint select com. on corrections, 1987—, chair Commn. on Overcrowding at AMHI-BMHI, 1987-89. Office: Maine State Senate 3 State House Station Augusta ME 04333*

BUSWELL, DEBRA SUE, small business owner, programmer, analyst; b. Salt Lake City, Apr. 8, 1957; d. John Edward Ross and Marilyn Sue (Patterson) Potter; m. Randy James Buswell, AUg. 17, 1985; 1 child, Trevor Ryan. BA, U. Colo., Denver, 1978. Programmer, analyst Trail Blazer Systems, Palo Alto, Calif., 1980-83; data processing mgr. Innovative Concepts, Inc., San Jose, Calif., 1983-86; owner Egret Software, Milpitas, Calif., 1986—. Mem. IEEE, No. Calif. Pick Users. Home and Office: 883 Del Vaile Ct Milpitas CA 95035-4518

BUTAUD, SUE ANN, social studies educator; b. Abbeville, La., Apr. 3, 1945; d. Floyd G. and Lucille (Reaux) B. BA, U. Southwestern La., 1967, MEd, 1976, postgrad., 1978-90; postgrad., U. Va., 1978. Tchr. social studies Vermilion Parish/Erath (La.) H.S., 1966—; participant Fed. Forum, Washington, 1978; coord. Parish Day Govt., Erath, 1980—, Boys and Girls State, Erath, 1980—; co-sponsor Beta and Jr. Beta Clubs, Erath, 1972-85; mem. insvc. planning com. Vermilion Parish, 1978-79, 93-94, mem. philosophy and objectives com., chair parental involvement in governance and advocacy com. and curriculum and instrn. com., 1989-90, mem. Vermilion pupil progression com., 1996-97, chmn. social studies dept., 1992—, mem. faculty adv. com., 1993-94. Recipient Good Citizenship award Am. Legion, 1985; named Outstanding Tchr. Am. History, La. Soc. DAR, 1995-96, Vermilion Parish tchr. of the Yr., 1986-87. Mem. NEA, Nat. Coun. Social Studies (chairperson S.E. Regional Conv. 1976), Vermilion Coun. Social Studies (sec.-treas. 1975-77, pres. 1977-79), La. Coun. Social Studies (sec. 1979-80, treas. 1978-79), La. Assn. Educators, Vermilion Assn. Educators, Alpha Epsilon chpt. Delta Kappa Gamma (corr. sec. Vermilion Parish 1994-96, pres. 1996-98). Roman Catholic. Home: 302 W Lastie PO Box 204 Erath LA 70533

BUTCH, MARY SUE, lawyer; b. Pitts., 1954. BA, Harvard U., 1976; JD, Boston U., 1981; LLM, NYU, 1985. Bar: N.Y. 1983. Ptnr. Skadden, Arps, Slate, Meagher & Flom, N.Y.C. Contbr. articles to law rev., 1980-81. Office: Skadden Arps Slate Meagher & Flom 919 3d Ave New York NY 10022*

BUTCHER, AMANDA KAY, retired university administrator; b. Lansing, Mich., Oct. 25, 1936; d. Foster Eli and Mayme Lenore (Taft) Stuart; m. Claude J. Butcher, Aug. 24, 1957; 1 child, Mary Beth. BS in Bus., Cen. Mich. U., 1981. Office asst. Dept. Dairy Sci., East Lansing, Mich., 1966-76; bus. mgr. dept. pathology Coll. Vet. Medicine Mich. State U., East Lansing, 1976-96. Mem. Adminstrv. Profl. Suprs. Assn. (v.p. 1982), Adminstrv. Profl. Assn. East Lansing (pres. 1976-80). Democrat. Home: 610 Emily Ave Lansing MI 48910-5404

BUTCHER, ANN PATRICE, elementary school educator; b. Aurora, Ill., May 14, 1965; d. Harry Neal and Patsy JoAnn (Smith) Patterson; m. Steven James Butcher, July 14, 1990; children: Todd Merrill, Seth Richard-James. BA, Aurora U., 1989; MA, No. Ill. U., 1994. Cert. in elem. edn., curriculum and supervision. Elem. sch. tchr. Sch. Dist. #129, Aurora, 1989—; gifted tchr. Aurora U., 1993—; tchr. Adv. Bd. for Sci. Edn., Sci.-Tech./Psychics of Aquatic Animals, Aurora; mem. Impact II adv. bd. Ill. Math. and Sci. Acad., Aurora, 1991, Leadership Inst. Integrating Internet, Instrn. and Curriculum participant, instr. Fermi Acceleration Lab., Batavia, Ill.; mem. consortium Aurora Cmty. Edn., 1996—. Impact II disseminator grantee Ill. Math. and Sci. Acad./State of Ill., 1991, 92, Aurora Found. grantee, 1993, Honor Roll of Tchrs. awardee Assn. Sci. and Tech. Ctrs., Washington, 1996. Mem. NEA, Ill. Edn. Assn., Ill. Sci. Tchrs. Assn., Ill. Reading Coun., Aurora Cmty. Edn. Consortium, Kappa Delta Pi. Lutheran. Home: 805 Acorn Dr North Aurora IL 60542-3030 Office: Nicholson Elem Sch 649 N Main St Montgomery IL 60538-1225

BUTCHER, SUSAN HOWLET, sled dog racer, dog kennel owner; b. Boston, Dec. 26, 1954; d. Charles and Agnes (Young) B.; m. David Lee Monson. Driver 1st dog team to summit Mt. KcKinley, Alaska, 1979; winner among top 10 finishers Long Distance Sled Dog Races, Alaska and Minn., 1978-87; 5th pl. Iditarod Race, Anchorage and Nome, Alaska, 1980, 81, 2d pl., 1988, 90, champion, winner 1st pl., 1986, 87, world record holder, 1986-87; champion, winner 1st pl. Coldfoot Classic Race, Brooks Range, Alaska, 1985; winner Iditarod, Alaska, 1988, Kusho 300, Bethel, Alaska, 1988, Portage 250, Alaska, 1988; bd. dirs. Iditarod Trail Com., Wasilla, Alaska, 1980-86, ambassador of good will Iditarod Sport of Sled Dog Racing, 1982—; mem. nutrition adv. panel Purina Pro Plan, St. Louis, 1986—; tech. advisor Allied Fibers, N.Y.C., 1985—. Contbr. articles to profl. jours. Hon. chmn. March of Dimes, Anchorage, 1986, Spl. Olympics, Anchorage, 1987. Named Musher of Yr. Team and Trail, N.H., 1987, one of Profl. Sports Women of Yr. Womens Sports Found., N.Y.C., 1987, Sports Woman of Yr., W.S.F, 1988, Sportswomen of Yr. U.S. Sports Acad.; recipient Victor award, Las Vegas, Nev., 1987, 88, legis. commendation States of Alaska and Mass., 1986-87, Moniqo Bedeaux prize French Sport Acad., 1989, Athletic Achievement award Tanguray, N.Y., 1989. Mem. Iditarod Trail Com., Iditarod Trail Blazers (life), Beargrease Race Com., Kuskokwim 300 Race Com. Club: Interior Dog Mushers (Manley, Alaska); Nome Kennel; Norton Sound Sled Dog. *

BUTCOFSKI, PAMELA JANE, sales executive; b. Washington, Jan. 20, 1967; d. John Alexander and Marilyn Larue (Wood) B. BS in Chemistry, Temple U., 1989. Application engr. Chemcut, State College, Pa., 1989-90; sales rep. Cole Med., Woodbine, Md., 1990-91; sr. sales mgr. Smith Kline Beecham, L.A., 1991-95; sales mgr. Mast Immunosystems, Mountain View, Calif., 1995—. Mem. Am. Bus. Women's Assn. Roman Catholic. Home: 12432 Browning Santa Ana CA 92705

BUTEAU, MICHELLE DIANE, energy company executive; b. Oakland, Calif., Mar. 6, 1952; d. Bernard Lamonthe and June (Dowler) B.; m. Barry Crawford Anderson, Nov. 1974 (div. 1982); 1 child, Damon Buteau-Anderson. BA in Liberal Arts, Cath. U. Am., 1974, MBA, Loyola/Notre Dame Coll., 1989. Dir. U.S. Summer Sch. Inst., U.S. Dept. State/USIA, Posnan, Poland, 1975-76; bookkeeper Internat. Energy Assocs. Ltd., Washington, 1980-83, rsch. assoc., 1983-85, project mgr., 1984-92, sr. cons., 1987-89, mgr. emergency planning, 1990-92, sr. project mgr., prin. cons. hydroelectric plant, New Martinsville, W. Va., 1992-94; sr. project mgr., mgr. market evaluation Ogden Energy, Inc., 1994—. Actress and dir. dinner theatres, 1974—. Intern to Senator Everett M. Dirksen, Washington, 1968; pres. Cath. Youth Orgn., Bethesda, Md., 1968-70; pres. Conduit Rd. Fire Bd., Glen Echo Fire Dept., 1995—. Mem. NAFE, Nat. Emergency Mgmt. Agy.,

Women's Coun. on Energy and the Environment, Elec. Generation Assn. (sec. 1996—). Buddhist. Avocations: acting, dancing, singing, firefighting. Office: Ogden Energy Inc 3211 Jermantown Rd Fairfax VA 22030-2844

BUTERA, ANN MICHELE, consulting company executive; b. Bayside, N.Y., Apr. 27, 1958; d. Gaetano Thomas and Josephine (Inserro) B. BA, L.I. U., 1979; MBA, Adelphi U., 1982. Dept. mgr. Abraham & Straus Stores, Huntington, N.Y., 1978-80; mgmt. cons. Chase Manhattan Bank N.A., Lake Success, N.Y., 1980-83, Nat. Bankcard Corp., Melville, N.Y., 1983-84; pres. Whole Person Project, Inc., Elmont, N.Y., 1984—. Bd. dirs. Nassau County coun. Girl Scouts U.S., 1985—. Recipient Bus. Achievement award Women on the Job, 1990. Mem. NAFE, ASTD, Fin. Women Internat., L.I. Networking Entrepreneurs (pres. 1984—), North Shore Bus. Forum, L.I. Ctr. for Bus. and Profl. Women. Republican. Roman Catholic. Home and Office: Whole Person Project Inc. 82 Cerenzia Blvd Elmont NY 11003-3631

BUTLER, BILLIE RAE, educational administrator; b. Waverly, Tenn., Aug. 2, 1941; d. Clifford Ronald and Pauline Elizabeth (Forsythe) Hunter; m. E.D. Longest (div.); children: Tamara Dianne, Teresa Denise, Tanya Darlene; m. William R. Butler, Dec. 16, 1979. AA, Hartnell Coll., Calif., 1973; BA, Chapman Coll., Calif., 1978. Cert. life permit Children's Ctr., Calif. Commn. for Tchr. Prep. and Licensing. Tchr. Monterey County Office of Edn., Salinas, Calif., 1973-78, coord., 1978-80, program dir., 1980—; mem. Monterey County Child Care Planning, 1992—; bd. dirs., officer Monterey Bay Parents as Tchrs., Monterey County, 1990-96. Mem., officer Salinas Valley Child Abuse Prevention Coun., Monterey County, 1980-84; mem. Family Self-Sufficiency Coord. Coun., Monterey Coun. Mem. AAUW, Calif. Head Start Assn. (bd. dirs. 1991-93), Cen. Coast Assn. for Edn. of Young Children (bd. dirs. 1984-90). Office: Monterey County Office Edn 901 Blanco Cir Salinas CA 93912

BUTLER, BRETT, comedian, actress; b. Montgomery, AL, 1958; d. Roland Decatur Anderson, Jr. and Carol; adoptive parent Bob Butler; m. Charles Wilson, 1978 (div. 1981); m. Ken Ziegler, 1987. Waitress Houston, TX, 1981-82; stand-up comedian, 1982—. TV appearances include: Grace Under Fire, 1992—. Office: ABC 2020 Avenue Of The Stars Los Angeles CA 90067-4704*

BUTLER, CAROL KING, advertising executive; b. Charlotte, N.C., May 29, 1952; d. Charles Snowden Watts and Marion (Thomas) King; m. James Rodney Butler, Aug. 12, 1972 (div. 1975). Student U. N.C., Greensboro, 1970-72. Sales rep. Sta.-WKIX, Raleigh, N.C., 1978-82, N.C. Box, Inc., Raleigh, 1982-84; radio sales account exec. WRAL-FM, Raleigh, 1984-88, team sales mgr., 1989; prin. Butler-Smith Assocs., Raleigh, 1988-89; ind. programming and video producer, Raleigh, 1989-90; prin., freelance presentation/video script writer, producer and sales person, Carol Butler Sales Writer/Photographer, 1991—; sales mgr. BW Territory of Lifetouch, 1996. Mem. NAFE. Democrat. Mem. Unity Ch. Avocations: water skiing, golf, tennis, boating, bicycling. Home: 6616 English Ivy Ln Raleigh NC 27615-6303

BUTLER, ELIZABETH VIRGINIA (BETSY BUTLER), government official, political consultant, fund raiser; b. Sacramento, June 14, 1963; d. Harold Samuel and Marguerite (Savage) B. BA in English, San Diego State U., 1987, BA in Polit. Sci., 1987. So. Calif. fin. dir. McCarthy for U.S. Senate, L.A., 1988-92; dep. Calif. fin. dir. Clinton for Pres., L.A., 1992; dir. outreach and devel. The Calif. Inst., Washington, 1993; spl. asst. to asst. sec. Internat. Trade Adminstrn., Dept. Commerce, Washington, 1993-96, spl. asst. to gen. counsel, 1996—. Active Clinton-Gore Adminstrn. Assn., Washington, 1993—, ARC Ball Com., Washington, 1994-96. Mem. Calif. State Soc. Democrat. Presbyterian. Office: Dept Commerce Office Gen Counsel Rm 5870 Washington DC 20230

BUTLER, GRACE CAROLINE, medical administrator; b. Lima, Peru, Dec. 19, 1937; (parents Am. citizens); d. Everett Lyle and Mary Isabella (Sloatman) Gage; m. William Langdon Butler, Dec. 28, 1961; children: Mary Dyer, William Langdon Jr. AA, Stephens Coll., 1957; BS in Nursing, Columbia U., 1960; postgrad., Union County Coll., 1984. Head nurse N.Y. State Psychiat. Inst., N.Y.C., 1960-61; clin. instr. Columbia U., N.Y.C., 1960-61; staff nurse, educator Vis. Nurse Service, Summit, N.J., 1962-63; health adminstr. Eagle Island Girl Scout Camp, Tupper Lake, N.Y., 1964; evening supr. Ashbrook Nursing Home, Scotch Plains, N.J., 1968-72; teaching asst. Scotch Plains-Fanwood (N.J.) Sch. System, 1975-78; staff nurse Westfield (N.J.) Med. Group, 1980-82, head nurse, 1982-83, supr., 1983-84; office adminstr. Harris S. Vernick, MD, PA, Westfield, 1984-86, corp. v.p., office adminstr., 1986-88; corp. v.p., office adminstr. Assocs. in Medicine, Westfield, 1988-90; pvt. researcher, 1990—; diabetes educator Boehringer Manneheim Diagnostics, 1984—, Eli Lilly and Co., Indpls., 1984—; microbiologist tester Med. Technol. Corp., Somerset, N.J., 1984—; computer advisor Cordis Corp., Miami, 1985—. Asst. leader Girl Scouts U.S., Fanwood, N.J., 1970-73; religious educator All Saints Episcopal Ch., Scotch Plains, 1967-82; bd. dirs. PTA, Scotch Plains and Fanwood, 1973-79; mem. altar guild All Saints Episcopal Ch., Scotch Plains, 1994—. Mem. League For Ednl. Advancement for Registered Nurses, Am. Soc. of Notaries, Columbia U./Presbyn. Hosp. Sch. of Nursing Alumni Assn. Republican. Episcopalian. Home: 125 Russell Rd Fanwood NJ 07023-1063

BUTLER, JAN MEREDITH, elementary education educator; b. Eunice, La., Jan. 21, 1971; d. Robert Milby and Anita Rae (Thibodeaux) B. BA in English Edn., McNeese State U., 1993. Tchr. Calcasien Parish Schs., Lake Charles, La., 1993—; mem. ACAP, Lake Charles, La., 1993—. Mem. NEA, La. Assn. Educators, Calcasien Assn. Educators, Nat. Coun. Tchrs. of English, Sigma Tau Delta. Home: 1518 Common St Lake Charles LA 70601

BUTLER, JODY TALLEY, gifted education educator; b. Columbus, Ga., Mar. 14, 1958; d. Bill Ray and Jacqueline (Hay) T.; m. Danny Butler. BS in Edn., West Ga. Coll., 1979, MEd, 1982; EdD, Auburn U., 1988. Cert. tchr., Ga. Tchr. Cen. Primary Sch., Carrollton, 1979-88; tchr. gifted student program QUEST Cen. Middle Sch., Carrollton, 1988—; co-owner Hay's Mill Antiques, Ga., 1994—. Mem. Internat. Reading Assn., Ga. Ptnrs. in Edn. Coun., Profl. Asshn. Ga. Educators, Carroll County Cmty. Chorus, Phi Delta Kappa (Dissertation of Yr. award 1989), Phi Kappa Phi, Alpha Gamma Delta. Presbyterian. Office: Ctrl Middle Sch 155 Whooping Creek Rd Carrollton GA 30116-8999

BUTLER, LINDA AXELSON, recreational facility manager; b. Statesboro, Ga., May 22, 1959; d. Joseph Allen and Malcolm Rae (Smith) Axelson; m. Aug. 29, 1981 (div. Feb. 1989). BA in Spanish, Baker U., 1981. Acct. Lois A. Brozey, CPA, San Diego, 1981-82; bus. mgr. San Diego Chicken, Inc., 1983; discount brokerage mgr. Union Bank and Trust, Bartlesville, Okla., 1984; bus. mgr. ARCO Arena, Sacramento, 1985-86, box office mgr., 1987-91; box office mgr. San Diego Sports Arena, 1991-92, Arrowhead Pond of Anaheim, Calif., 1993—; cons. Don Chargin Boxing Prodns., L.A., 1987—. Recipient scholarship Baker Univ., 1981. Mem. Box Office Mgrs. Internat., Alpha Chi Omega (sch. com. chmn. 1981), Sigma Delta Pi, Alpha Mu Gamma. Republican. Presbyterian. Home: 1105 Woodside Dr Placentia CA 92870-3719 Office: Arrowhead Pond of Anaheim 2695 E Katella Ave Anaheim CA 92806-5904

BUTLER, MARGARET KAMPSCHAEFER, retired computer scientist; b. Evansville, Ind., Mar. 7, 1924; d. Otto Louis and Lou Etta (Rehsteiner) Kampschaefer; m. James W. Butler, Sept. 30, 1951; 1 child, Jay. AB, Ind. U., 1944; postgrad., U.S. Dept. Agr. Grad. Sch., 1945, U. Chgo., 1949, U. Minn., 1950. Statistician U.S. Bur. Labor Statistics, Washington, 1945-46, U.S. Air Forces in Europe, Erlangen and Wiesbaden, Germany, 1946-48; statistician U.S. Bur. Labor Statistics, St. Paul, 1949-51; mathematician Argonne (Ill.) Nat. Lab., 1948-49, 51-80, sr. computer scientist, 1980-92; dir. Argonne Code Ctr. and Nat. Energy Software Ctr. Dept. Energy Computer Program Exch., 1960-91; spl. term appointee Indsl. Tech. Devel. Ctr. Argonne Nat. Lab., 1993—; cons. AMF Corp., 1956-57, OECD, 1964, Poole Bros., 1967. Author: Careers for Women in Nuclear Science and Technology, 1992; editor Computer Physics Communications, 1969-80; contbr. (chpt.) The Application of Digital Computers to Problems in Reactor Physics, 1968, Advances in Nuclear Sci. and Technology, 1976; contbr. articles to profl. publs. Treas. Timberlake Civic Assn., 1958; rep. mem. nomination com. Hinsdale (Ill.) Caucus, 1961-62; coord. 6th dist. ERA, 1973-80; del. Rep. Nat. Conv., 1980; bd. mgr. DuPage dist. YWCA Met. Chgo., 1987-90; mem. computer and info. sys. adv. bd. Coll. DuPage, 1987—; mem. industry adv. bd. computer sci. dept. Bradley U., 1988-91; vice-chair Ill. Women's Polit. Caucus, 1987-90; chair voter's svc. LWV, Burr-Ridge-Willowbrook, 1991-93. Recipient Cert. Leadership, Met. YWCA, Chgo., 1985, Merit award Chgo. Assn. Technol. Socs., 1988; named to Fed. 100, 1991; named Outstanding Woman Leader of DuPage County Sci., Tech. and Health Care, 1992; recipient spl. award Am. Nuclear Soc. Math and Comp. divsn., 1992. Fellow Am. Nuclear Soc. (mem. publs. com. 1965-71, bd. dirs. 1976-79, exec. com. 1977-78, chmn. bylaws and rules com., 1979-82, profl. women in ANS com. 1991-93, reviewer for publs.); mem. Assn. Computing Machinery (exec. com., sec. Chgo. chpt. 1963-65, publs. chmn. nat. conf. 1968, reviewer for publs.), Assn. Women in Sci. (pres. Chgo. area chpt. 1982, exec. bd. 1985-87), Nat. Computer Conf. (chmn. Pioneer Day com. 1985, tech. program chmn. 1987). Republican. Home: 17 W 139 Hillside Ln Hinsdale IL 60521-6062

BUTLER, MARY JANE, accountant; b. Orangeburg, S.C., Sept. 24, 1946; d. Woodrow and Mary (Smith) Dantzler; m. Young F. Butler, Mar. 16, 1968; children: Dwayne M., Darrell W. BS, S.C. State Coll., 1970, MEd, 1978. Cert. counselor, govt. fin. mgr., Notary Pub. Sec. Fayetteville (N.C.) State U., 1972-73; retail ops. Army/Air Force Exchange, Ft. Benning, Ga., 1974-75; vol. counselor Briarwood Elem. Sch., Charlotte, N.C., 1977; from acct. to sect. chief in acctg. Comptr. Dept. of Army, Ft. Monmouth, N.J., 1980-89, br. chief in acctg., 1989-93; acctg. br. chief Dept. of Def., Ft. Monmouth, N.J., 1993—; team leader fin. and acctg. div. Ft. Monmouth, 1990—; acting br. chief Dept. of Def., 1993—. Chmn. social action com. Delta Sigma Theta, Monmouth County, N.J., 1988-90. Recipient CECOM Command award, 1992, One Star Note, 1992, Quality Leadership award, 1995. Mem. NAFE, Assn. Govt. Accts. (sec. 1985-87, pres. 1988-90, 90—, Nat. award 1988-89), Am. Soc. Mil. Comptrs., Am. Soc. Notaries. Baptist. Home: PO Box 52 Middletown NJ 07748-0052 Office: HQDFAS-IN DFAS-IN/EM-BFBM Fort Monmouth NJ 07703

BUTLER, NANCY TAYLOR, gender equity specialist, program director; b. Newport, R.I., Oct. 31, 1942; d. Robert Lee and Roberta Claire (Brown) Taylor; m. Edward M. Butler, Aug. 22, 1964; children: Jeffrey, Gregory, Katherine. AB, Cornell U., 1964. Asst. dir. Career Equity Assistance Ctr. for Tng. Trenton (N.J.) State Coll., 1990—; owner Equity Resources, Tinton Falls, N.J., 1993—; mem. N.J. Gender Equity Adv. Comm., 1995—, sec., 1996—. Editor Equity Exch., 1991—. Mem. Monmouth County dist. ethics com. Supreme Ct. N.J., 1987-91; pres. Vol. Ctr. Monmouth County, Red Bank, 1985-89; mem. Cornell U. Coun., Ithaca, N.Y., 1987-91, 94—, adminstrv. bd., 1996—; dir. Cornell Assn. Class Officers, 1991—; chmn. Cornell Alumni Trustee Nominating Com., 1994. Recipient Woman of Achievement award Commn. on Status of Women, 1988, Women's History Tribute NOW-N.J., 1995, Woman Leader award N.J. Assn. Women Bus. Owners, 1996. Mem. AAUW (life; pres. N.J. chpt. 1988-90, Edn. Found. Named Gift 1982, 83, 84, 86, 87, 89, 91), Nat. Coalition for Sex Equity in Edn. Home: 20 Cedar Pl Tinton Falls NJ 07724-2807 Office: Trenton State Coll CEAC-Tng CN4700 Trenton NJ 08650-4700

BUTLER, NATALIE, legal assistant; b. Jersey City, Sept. 17, 1967; d. Michael A. Butler and Marie C. (Shackewyc) McDonnough. BA, Haverford Coll., 1989. Legal asst. Skadden, Arps, Slate, Meagher & Flom, Washington, 1989-92; legal asst. specialist environ. group Wilmer Cutler & Pickering, Washington, 1992—. Mem. Nat. Capitol Area Paralegal Assn. Roman Catholic. Office: Wilmer Cutler & Pickering 2445 M St NW Washington DC 20037

BUTLER, PAM, artist; b. N.Y.C., Jan. 12, 1955; d. Arthur D. and Kathleen (Lehman) Butler. Student, SUNY, Buffalo, 1976-78; BS in Fine Arts, Empire State Coll., 1982; MFA, Sch. Visual Arts, 1990. Guest lectr. Trinity Coll., Hartford, Conn., 1991; tchr. PS 87 After Sch. Art Program, N.Y.C., 1992-93; guest lectr. Internat. Ctr. for Photography, 1994, Empire State Coll., 1994, 95; adv. bd. PS 122 Gallery, N.Y.C., 1995—. Work exhibited at Adam L. Gimble Gallery, 1982, Visual Arts Gallery, 1990, Milkie Way Gallery, 1991, PS 122 Gallery, 1992, 95, Muranushi Lederman, Inc., 1992 Horodner Romley Gallery, 1992, Doley Le Cappellaine, 1992 (all N.Y.C.); Delta Axis Ctr. for Contemporary Art, Memphis, 1992, Art in General, N.Y.C., 1993, Artists Space, N.Y.C., 1993, Hallwalls, Buffalo, N.Y., 1993, 95, FDR Gallery, N.Y.C., 1994, Russet Lederman, N.Y.C., 1994, Contemporary Art Ctr. (catalogue), Moscow, 1994, White Columns, N.Y.C., 1994, 95, The Other Side Gallery, Memphis, 1994, Flamingo East, 1995, N.Y.C., Scotland Street Mus., Glasgow, 1995, 450 Broadway Gallery, N.Y.C., 1995, Collett Art Gallery, Ogden, Utah, 1996; pub. projects include (installed posters) Good Girl Project, N.Y.C., 1994-96, Memphis, 1994, Buffalo, 1995, (billboard) Art Belongs to the People, Moscow, 1994, (performance and posters) The Win Project, N.Y.C., 1994—. Office: Good Girl Project PO Box 1014 Village Sta New York NY 10014

BUTLER, PATRICIA, protective services official; b. Salem, Mass., Aug. 13, 1958; d. Frank Arthur and Ruth Elizabeth (Bartlett) B. Paramedic degree, Davenport Coll., 1984, AA in Mgmt. of Emergency Med. Svcs., 1987; Mich. Law Enforcement Officers Tng. Coun. cert., Grand Valley State U., 1988; BA in MHR, Spring Arbor Coll., 1994. CEO Whispering Winds, Inc., L'Anse, Mich., 1985—; firefighter Grand Rapids (Mich.) Fire Dept., 1985; security, data entry clerk Lacks Industries, Grand Rapids, 1985-88; loss prevention officer Woodland Mall Security, Kentwood, Mich., 1988-89, Butterworth Hosp., Grand Rapids, 1989; police officer Lakeview Police Dept., 1989, Edmore (Mich.)-Home Mcpl. Police Dept., 1989-90, Coopersville (Mich.) Police Dept., 1989-90; chief police Lakeview Village Police Dept., 1990-94, MSP L'anse Post, 1994—; mem. Mich. Paramedic, 1986—, Mich. Police Chaplains, 1992-94. Mem. NAFE, Nat. Assn. Chiefs, Mich. Chief's Assn. (v.p. 1991-94), Internat. Assn. Women Police, Mich. Assn. Chief of Police, Women Police Mich., Lions. Office: MSP-L'Anse PO Box 100 Lanse MI 49946

BUTLER, PATRICIA LACKY, mental health nurse, educator, consultant; b. Galesburg, Ill., Aug. 31, 1943; d. Allen Dale and Mary (Weaver) Lacky; m. Glen William Butler, Mar. 14, 1964 (div. Apr. 1974); children: Scott Lewis, Andrew William, Suzanne Elizabeth; m. Keith Warren Turner, Oct. 13, 1992. AA in Nursing/Journalism, Sacramento City Coll., 1965; BS in Sociology/Psychology, SUNY, Albany, 1992. Clin. nurse Mercy Gen. Hosp., Sacramento, Sacramento Med. Ctr.; Davis (Calif.) Cmty. Hosp.; clin. nurse Woodland (Calif.) Meml. Hosp., 1965-74; dir. nurses Woodland Skilled Nursing, 1978-79; head nurse/psychiatry St. Croix Mental Health, Christiansted, U.S. V.I., 1974-79; clin. program coord. Yolo County Mental Health, Woodland, 1980—; instr. Yuba C.C., Marysville, Calif., 1988—. Author curriculum; mem. editl. adv. bd. Daily Democrat. Bd. dirs. Concilio of Yolo County, Woodland, 1984-87; mem. Red Cross Nat. Disaster Mental Health, 1996—. Recipient Bell award Mental Health Assn. Yolo County, 1993; NIMH grantee, 1989-90. Mem. Forensic Mental Health Assn. Calif. (sec. 1991-93, conf. planning 1990-91, dir. edn. and tng. 1996—). Democrat. Roman Catholic. Home: North Lake Tahoe Homewood CA 96141 Office: Yolo County Mental Health 213 W Beamer St Woodland CA 95695-2510

BUTLER, PATRICIA O., management consultant; b. Liberty, N.Y., Feb. 3, 1953; d. Paul Stephen and Florence (Dunn) Obuhanich; m. William Reiley Butler, Aug. 4, 1984; 1 child, William Paul Langley. BA, Elmira (N.Y.) Coll., 1977. Mgr. product adminstrn. Savin Corp., Binghamton, N.Y., 1979-83; master scheduler Codman & Shurtleff, Randolph, Mass., 1983; mgr. ops. systems USCI div. C.R. Bard, Billerica, Mass., 1983-86; sr. cons./project mgr. Digital Corp., Maynard, Mass., 1986-87; cons. Coopers & Lybrand, Boston, 1987-89; pres., cons. MBC, Westboro, Mass., 1989—; cons. Coopers & Lybrand, 1987-89. Author tng. manuals: Cycle Counting, 1988, System Implementation, 1985. Vol. Food Bank, Westboro, Mass., 1989-91. Mem. Data Processing Mgmt. Assn., Am. Prodn. Inventory Control Soc. (bd. dirs. 1986-87), Profl. Women's Network, Newcomers Club (interest group coord. for golf and skiing 1987-91), Psi Chi.

BUTLER, SUSAN LOWELL, association executive, writer; b. Bklyn., Feb. 10, 1944; d. John William and Catherine (Mauro) Yost; m. Horace Hamilton Lowell (div. 1982); m. James Thomas Butler, Feb. 12, 1983; stepchildren: James, Kevin, Michael. BA, Lycoming Coll., 1965; postgrad., U. Pa., 1965-67. Tchr. English and Journalism Bristol Twp. Schs., Levittown, Pa., 1967-70; field rep. Nat. Edn. Assn., Washington, 1970-74, dir. communications, 1974-80; dir. western states region Nat. Edn. Assn., Austin (Tex.) and Denver, 1980-84; account supr. Dale Chrisman & Assocs., Austin, 1984-86; pvt. cons. Austin, 1986-88; exec. v.p. Women in Comm., Inc., Washington, 1988-91; nat. exec. dir. Nat. Women's Hall of Fame, Seneca Falls, N.Y., 1991-96; dir. Coalition For America's Children, Washington, 1996—; mem. bd. The Media Inst., Washington, 1989-91. Author: National Education Association: A Special Mission, 1987, Handbook of Association Communications, 1987, Pressing Onward: The Women's Historical Biography of the National Education Association, 1996. V.p. pub. affairs Mental Health Assn. of Tex., Austin, 1987-88; bd. dirs.Nat. Women's Hall of Fame; mem. adv. bd. Nat. Archives History Project, 1995—. Mem. Am. Soc. Assn. Execs., Pub. Rels. Soc. Am. (accredited), Nat. Press Club, Women, Men and Media (exec. com.), Women in Communications Inc. Episcopalian. Home: 406 Skyhill Rd Alexandria VA 22314-4920 Office: Coalition for Americas Children 1634 Eye St NW Washington DC 20006

BUTLER, TONI JEAN, transportation executive; b. Beaufort, S.C., July 14, 1963; d. Tony Lee and Betty Joe (Tramel) B. BS in Acctg., Akron U., 1986. CPA, Ohio. Gen. acct. Rail Van Consol., Inc., Twinsburg, Ohio, 1987-88, fin. analysts, 1988, asst. controller, 1988-90; 1993-95, 1993-95; systems cons. Data Systems Tech., Columbia, S.C., 1995—; project mgr. info. systems, 1993-95; cons. Data Sys. Tech., Columbia, S.C.; advisor Lamberts CPA Rev. Course, Columbus, Ohio, 1990. Chair subcom. Arthritis Found., Columbus, 1990-94; treas. Columbus chpt. Star Fleet, 1993, v.p., 1994; asst. to prodr. CareCon Found., Columbus, 1994.

BUTLER-THOMAS, JANNETTE SUE, human resources professional; b. Eugene, Oreg., Mar. 15, 1960; d. Robert Eugene and Dorothy Marilyn (Irvin) Butler; m. Robert Alan Thomas, Oct. 3, 1992. BS in Hotel Adminstrn., U. Nev., Las Vegas, 1982. Cert. health promotion dir., sr. profl. in human resources. Pers. mgmt. trainee The Sheraton Corp., San Diego, 1982-83; dir. pers. The Sheraton Corp., Palm Coast, Fla., 1983-85; dir. human resources The Sheraton Corp., Dallas, 1985-89; corp. dir. human resources Hilton Reservations Worldwide, Carrollton, Tex., 1989-95; human resource cons. Symantec Corp., Eugene, Oreg., 1995—. Mem., vol. Nat. Multiple Sclerosis Soc., Dallas, 1991—; mem. steering com. Lane County Career Ctrs. Recipient Volunteerism award Lodging Industry Tng. Ctr., 1988. Mem. Soc. for Human Resource Mgmt., Northwest Human Resource Mgmt. Assn. (bd. dirs.), Inst. for Internat. Human Resource Mgmt. Episcopalian. Office: Symantec Corp 175 W Broadway Eugene OR 97401

BUTTERFIELD, DIANE MARIE, financial executive, accountant, consultant; b. Albert Lea, Minn., Aug. 24, 1950; d. William Roland and Genevieve Elaine (Mahowald) B. BA in Acctg., S.W. State U., Minn., 1972. CPA, Minn. Various positions KMPG Peat Marwick, Mpls., 1972-80; sr. mgr. KMPG Peat Marwick, N.Y.C., 1980-83; cons. Edmond, Okla., 1983-84; dir. acctg. Policy and Rsch. dept. Household Internat., Prospect Heights, Ill., 1984-89; fin. dir. Chase Manhattan Bank, N.Y.C., 1989—; alt. mem. emerging issues task force Fin. Acctg. Standards Bd., 1984-88. Mem. AICPA (banking com. 1994—).

BUTTERWORTH, JANE ROGERS FITCH, physician; b. Louisville, Aug. 3, 1937; d. Howard Mercer and Jane Rogers (McCaw) Fitch; m. William Butterworth, Sept. 5, 1958 (div. Feb. 1968); children: Jane Rogers, William Stoddard, Robert Mercer, Benjamin Richard Mallory, Anne Lewis. BS, U. Louisville, 1971, MD, 1974. Rotating intern Humana Hosp. Audubon (formerly St. Joseph's Hosp.), Louisville, 1974-75, resident in radiology, 1975-76; resident in phys. medicine and rehab. Frasier Rehab. (formerly Inst. of Phys. Medicine and Rehab.), Louisville, 1976-80; staff physiatrist Rockford (Ill.) Meml. Hosp., 1980-83; clin. instr. Rockford Sch. Medicine, 1980-83; med. dir. phys. medicine and rehab. Western Res. Care System, Youngstown, Ohio, 1983-86, mem. teaching staff residency program, 1983-96; clin. instr. Northeastern Ohio U. Coll. of Medicine, Rootstown, 1983—, chairperson phys. medicine subcoun., mem. acad. rev. and promotions com., 1985-95; adj. faculty Youngstown State U., 1984—; regional med. advisor Rehab. div. Ohio Indsl. Commn., Youngstown, 1985—; mem. admissions com. Northeastern Ohio U. Coll. Medicine, 1988; cons. psychiatrist Vista Ctr., Lisbon, Ohio, 1994—. Mem. choir St. John's Episcopal Ch., Youngstown, vestrywoman, 1989-91; bd. dirs. Goodwill Industries, Youngstown, 1985-92, advisor rehab. divsn., 1986—, bd. advisors, 1993—; mem. med. rev. staff Hospice, Youngstown, 1984—; dir. med. svcs. Easter Seals Soc., Youngstown, 1987—; mem. med. bd. pub. TV, Youngstown, 1986—; violinist Youngstown State U. Cmty. Orch., 1985; mem. Youngstown Musica Sacra, 1989—; regional med. advisor Rehab. Divsn. Ohio Indsl. Commn., 1984-94, 95. Recipient Community Svc. award St. John's Episcopal Ch., 1988. Mem. AMA, Ohio Med. Assn., Mahoning County Med. Soc. (coun. 1989, alt. del to Ohio Med. Assn. 1990, pres. 1992), Ky. Med. Assn., Jefferson County Med. Soc., Am. Congress Rehab. Medicine, Colonial Dames Soc. Am., Phi Beta, Chi Delta Phi, Kappa Alpha Theta. Republican. Home: 186 Rockland Dr Boardman OH 44512-5921 Office: Western Res Care System Southside Hosp 345 Oak Ave Youngstown OH 44512-6124

BUTTNER, JEAN BERNHARD, publishing company executive; b. New Rochelle, N.Y., Nov. 3, 1934; d. Arnold and Janet (Kinghorn) Bernhard; m. Edgar Buttner, Sept. 13, 1958 (div.); children: Janet, Edgar Arnold, Marianne. BA, Vassar Coll., 1957; cert. bus. adminstrn., Harvard-Radcliffe program, 1958; Montessori diploma, Coll. Notre Dame, Belmont, Calif., 1967; D Bus. Adminstrn. (hon.), U. Bridgeport, 1994. Past v.p. Buttner Cos., Oakland, Calif.; pres., COO Value Line Inc. (subs. Arnold Bernhard & Co.), N.Y.C., 1985-87, chmn., pres., CEO, 1988—; chmn. Value Line Mutual Funds; chmn., CEO, pres. Arnold Bernhard & Co., Inc. (parent co. to Value Line, Inc.). Editor-in-chief The Value Line Investment Survey. Trustee Williams Coll., Radcliffe Coll.; past trustee Emma Willard Sch., Coll. Prep. Sch., Oakland, Calif., Com. Econ. Devel.; mem. N.Y.C. Partnership Com. of 200; past mem. adv. coun. Stanford Bus. Sch.; past mem. The Presdl. Roundtable; past vis. com. for bd. overseers Harvard Bus. Sch.; past bd. dirs. Harvard Bus. Sch. Club N.Y.; past pres. Piedmont (Calif.) Sch. Bd.; past dir. Berkeley Montessori Sch.; past west coast admissions rep. Vassar Coll., Harvard U., Harvard Bus. Sch. Named one of N.Y.'s Most Influential Women in Business, Crain's, 1996; recipient Alumni Achievement award, Harvard U. Grad. Sch. Bus. Adminstrn., 1995; recipienet Alumnae award Choate Rosemary Hall, Wallingford, Conn., 1995. Mem. Com. 200. Republican. Congregationalist. Office: Value Line Inc 220 E 42nd St New York NY 10017-5806

BUTTON, RENA PRITSKER, public affairs executive; b. Providence, Feb. 15, 1925; d. Isadore and Esther (Kay) Pritsker; m. Daniel E. Button, Aug. 16, 1969; children by previous marriage: Joshua, Bruce, David Posner. Student, Pembroke Coll., 1942-45; B.S., Simmons Coll., 1948; postgrad., Albany Law Sch., Union U., 1968-69. Spl. asst. to U.S. Rep., 1967-69; spl. projects coordinator United Jewish Appeal, 1971-74; exec. dir. Nat. Council Jewish Women, Inc., N.Y.C., 1974-76; pres. Button Assos., N.Y.C., 1976—; exec. v.p. Catalyst, N.Y.C., 1980-82; pres. Button & Button, Albany, N.Y., 1982—; mem. adv. coun. N.Y. State Senate Minority, 1980—; exec. dir. N.Y. State Coun. on Alcoholism and Other Drug Addictions, 1990-93. Co-producer, moderator: TV pub. affairs program Speak For Yourself, Albany, N.Y., 1963-66. Past mem. Mohawk-Hudson Coun. on Ednl. TV; chmn. pub. affairs com. Marymount Manhattan Coll.; past bd. dirs. Albany YWCA, Albany Coun. Chs. Devel. Corp., World Affairs Coun., Planned Parenthood Assn. Albany; trustee Jerusalem Women's Seminar, Citizens for Family Planning, N.Y. Com. Integrated Housing, Hist. Albany Found. Ctr. for Counseling; pres. Sr. Svc. Ctr. Albany Area; bd. dirs. Com. Modern Cts.; exec. dir. N.Y. Head Injury Assn., 1993-96; candidate N.Y. Stae Assembly 102d Dist., 1996. Clubs: Siasconset Casino (Siasconset, Mass.), Univ. (Albany). Home and Office: 16 Spruce Ct Delmar NY 12054-2614

BUTTRAM, DEBRA DORIS, fashion vendor and consultant, English educator, service dog trainer; b. Port St. Joe, Fla., Aug. 22, 1954; d. Wayne Morrison Sr. and Doris Mae (Amos) B.; m. David Cheuk Lun Kong, Dec. 29, 1979 (div. 1989); m. Marcello Galimberti, June 12, 1993. BS in Early Childhood Edn., Fla. State U., 1978. English tchr. Metta Found. for Refugees, Sydney, Australia, 1979; exec. asst. East West Freight Ltd., Hong Kong, 1981-82; boutique dir. Diane Fries Ltd., Hong Kong, 1985; buyer, boutique dir. Joyce Boutique Ltd., Hong Kong, 1985-87; mktg., sales exec. Icarus Ltd. (Chanel), Hong Kong, 1988-90; freelance wholesale fashion vendor Milan, Italy; trainer, sec. Italian Assn. for Use of Assistance Dogs, Bosisio Parini, Italy, 1991—. Home and Office: Via IV Novembre 26, 22040 Bosisio Parini Italy

BUTTS, CAROLYN ANNE, publishing executive; b. Bklyn., Oct. 18, 1966; d. Frank Curtis and Dorothy (Lloyd) B. BA, L.I. U., 1988. Reporter Amsterdam News, N.Y.C., 1988-92, N.Y. Post, N.Y.C., 1989-93; publisher, founder African Voices, N.Y.C., 1992—; press officer Manhattan Borough Pres., N.Y.C., 1994—; exec. officer Imani House, Inc., Bklyn., 1992—. Mem. N.Y. Assn. Black Journalists, Found. African-Am. Women, Black Women in Publishing. Roman Catholic. Office: African Voices Inc 270 W 96th St New York NY 10025

BUTTS, NINA, humanities educator; b. Dallas, Sept. 15, 1952; d. Edward Alexander Butts and Ruth Jane Laessle; m. Brian Dean East, Jan. 30, 1988; 1 child, Chloe Noelle. BA, U. North Tex., 1976, MA, 1979. Cert. secondary tchr., Tex. Tchr. Elgin (Tex.) H.S., 1977-78; tchg. fellow U. North Tex., Denton, 1978-79; instr. English Austin (Tex.) C.C., 1979—; mem. faculty U. Tex., San Antonio, 1982; alumni rep. Bennington (Vt.) Coll., 1981—; contbg. writer Tex. Observer, 1981-85. Founding mem. bd. dirs. Nuclear Weapons Freeze Campaign, Austin, 1982-86, Texans for Bilateral Nuclear Weapons Freeze, Austin, 1984-87; Dem. primary candidate for U.S. Ho. of Reps., Austin, 1986; vol. Children's Shelter Tex., Austin, 1995-96; pres. bd. dirs. Texans Against Gun Violence, Austin, 1996. Carey McWilliams fellow The Nation Inst., N.Y.C., 1983-84. Mem. Nat. Coun. Tchrs. English, Tex. Faculty Assn. Home: 4400 Shoalwood Ave Austin TX 78756-3217 Office: Austin CC 1212 Rio Grande Austin TX 78701

BUTTS, VIRGINIA, corporate public relations executive; b. Chgo.. BA, U. Chgo. Writer Dave Garroway radio show NBC, N.Y.C., 1953; writer, producer, talent Sta. WBBM-TV, Chgo.; midwest dir. pub. relations for mags. Time, Fortune, Life and Sports Illustrated, Time Inc., 1956-63; dir. pub. relations Chgo. Sun-Times and Chgo. Daily News, 1963-74; v.p. pub. relations Field Enterprises Inc., Chgo., 1974-84; v.p. pub. rels. The Field Corp., 1984-90; pub. rels. counsel Marshall Field V, Chgo., 1991—; mem. pub. affairs com. Art Inst. Chgo. Contbr. Lesly's Public Relations Handbook, 1978, 83, World Book Ency. Recipient Clarion award Women in Communications, Inc., 1975, 76, Businesswoman of the Yr. award Lewis U., 1976. Mem. Pub. Rels. Soc. Am. (nat. bd. ethics 1987-93), Publicity Club Chgo. (Golden Trumpet award 1968, 69, 75, 76, 80), Nat. Acad. TV Arts and Scis., The Chgo. Network.

BUTWELL, RUTH OAKES, college dean; b. Kalamazoo, Mich., June 19, 1929; d. Edwin Charles and Helen Louise (Thompson) Oakes; m. Richard Lee Butwell, July 3, 1954 (div. Dec., 1965, dec. Feb., 1987); children: John Dale, Ann Louise. BS, Eastern Mich. U., 1951; MS, Ind. U., 1953. Resident asst. Ind. U., Bloomington, 1951-53; dean of women Wilmington (Ohio) Coll., 1953-54; counselor in counseling office U. Ky., Lexington, 1954; instr. coll. of nursing Wayne State U., Detroit, 1955; asst. dean of women U. Md., College Park, 1955-57; dir. Christian edn. N.Y. Ave. Presbyn. Ch., Washington, 1957-58; asst. dean of men U. Ill., Urbana, 1960-61; asst. dean of women U. The Philippines, Quezon City, 1964-65; assoc. dean of students Mo. Valley Coll., Marshall, Mo., 1966-71; dean of student life Berea (Ky.) Coll., 1971-95; treas. Ky. Assn. Women Deans and Counselors, 1986-87, v.p. 1987-88, pres. 1988-89. Author: (with others) (book) Nicaragua: Five Central Kentuckians Observe the 1990 Nicaraguan Elections, 1990. Recipient Woman of Yr. award Mo. Valley Coll., Marshall, Mo., 1971. Mem. NOW, Nat. Assn. Student Pers. Adminstrs. (adminstrs. liason), Nat. Assn. Women Educators (mem. resolutions com.), Ky. Assn. Women Educators, Berea Coll. Women's Network (founder, chairperson 1978-80). Democrat. Mem. Ch. of Christ Union. Home: 300 Prospect Berea KY 40403

BUTZ, GLORIA K., elementary education educator; b. Salem, Oreg., Aug. 29, 1951; d. Mary Carolyn (Davis) Mann; m. Loren O. Butz, Aug. 18, 1973; children: Janiess Dielle, Karel Trevor. BA Music Edn., Seattle Pacific U., 1973, MEd, 1981. Cert. elem./secondary tchr., Wash.; profl. cert. Assn. Christian Schs. Internat. Music tchr., grades K-6 Auburn (Wash.) Sch. dist. #408, 1973-75, tchr. sixth grade, 1975-77; reading tutor Valley Christian Sch., Auburn, 1983-84, elem. tchr., fifth/sixth grades, 1984—; mem. sch. bd. Valley Christian Sch., 1982-84; young author's camp staff mem., Seattle Pacific U., Wash., 1981-83. Dir. Vacation Bible Sch., Auburn Free Meth. Ch., 1987, 89, 92, 94. Mem. Internat. Reading Assn., Washington Orgn. for Reading Devel., Auburn Coun. Internat. Reading Assn. Republican. Home: 1505 24th St SE Auburn WA 98002-7837

BUTZ, MARY, principal; b. Bklyn., Jan. 5, 1948; d. John and Eva (Cewe) B. BA, St. Joseph's Coll. Women, 1969; MA, Bklyn. Coll., 1972. Tchr. N.Y.C. Bd. Edn., 1969-82; asst. prin. E.R. Murrow H.S., N.Y.C., 1982-88; staff devel. specialist U.F.T., N.Y.C., 1988-90; staff devel. borough coord. Queens (N.Y.) High Sch., 1990-92; assoc. dir. ednl. issues Am. Fedn. Tchrs., Washington, 1992-93; dir., founder Manhattan Village Acad., N.Y.C., 1993-94, prin., 1994—; cons. in field. Kellog Found. fellow, 1988-91. Mem. Coalition Network. Office: Manhattan Village Acad 43 W 22nd St New York NY 10010

BUURMAN, ELOISE BERNHOFT, guidance counselor, retired; b. Tacoma, Wash., July 17, 1915; d. Georg Kristian and Ellen Victoria (Ekman) Bernhoft; m. Gerrit Buurman, Nov. 25, 1943 (dec. Oct. 1990); children: Gerrit B., Ellen J. Buurman Hulse. AA, Skagit Valley Jr. Coll., 1934; BA in Phys. Edn., U. Wash., 1936, cert. in teaching, 1937; cert. in counseling, Western Wash. U., Bellingham, 1970. Cert. tchr., Wash. Phys. edn. and sci. tchr. Monroe (Wash.) High Sch., 1937-43; phys. edn. tchr. Clover Park Sr. High Sch., Tacoma, 1943-44; phys. edn. and history tchr. Lynden (Wash.) High Sch., 1952-68; counselor Lynden High Sch., 1968-75; ret. Lynden (Wash.) High Sch., 1975; coach boy's basketball Monroe High Sch., 1943. Tournament chmn. Ladies Golf Club at Grandview, Custer, Wash., 1975-85. Mem. AAUW, Delta Kappa Gamma, Pi Lambda Theta. Lutheran. Home: 6911 Holeman Ave Blaine WA 98230-9005

BUVINGER, JAN, library director; b. Lampasas, Tex., Oct. 4, 1943; parents Orville Layne and Myriam (Hamer) Rogers. BS, Coll. Charleston, S.C., 1965; MLS, Emory U., 1970. Childrens asst. libr. Charleston (S.C.) County Libr., 1970-71, reference libr., 1972-75, head reference dept., 1976-77, dep. dir., 1977-79, dir., 1979—. Mem. Am. Libr. Assn., S.C. Libr. Assn., S.E. Libr. Assn. Office: Charleston County Libr 404 King St Charleston SC 29403-6422

BUXBAUM, DORIS LEAH, secondary school educator; b. N.Y.C., Oct. 12, 1941; d. Abe and Birdie Best; m. Lawrence David Buxbaum, Nov. 17, 1962; children: Lisa, Leslie. BA, Hunter Coll., 1962; MS in Edn., Queens Coll., 1966. Cert. secondary math. tchr., N.Y., N.J. Math. tchr. Martin Van Buren H.S., N.Y.C., 1962-64, Jr. H.S. 217Q, N.Y.C., 1964-65, P.S. 175Q, N.Y.C., 1972-75, Russell Sage Jr. H.S., N.Y.C., 1977-79, Norwood (N.J.) Pub. Sch., 1979—; staff developer, mentor No. Valley Regional Dists., Demarest, N.J., 1993—; del. NEA Rep. Assembly, 1993—. Grantee NSF, 1993-96. Mem. Norwood Edn. Assn. (treas. 1980-87, pres. 1987—). Office: Norwood Pub Sch 177 Summit St Norwood NJ 07648

BUYNY, MARIANNE JO, eating disorders therapist, addictions counselor; b. Connellsville, Pa., Mar. 19, 1949; d. Marion Alyowich and Stella Louise (Sowinski) Marchewka; m. Jerome Michael Buyny, Oct. 21, 1972; children: Janean Estell, Jared Michael, Allison Victoria. BA in Psychology and Sociology, Alliance Coll., Cambridge Springs, Pa., 1971; MA in Psychology, Marywood Coll., Scranton, Pa., 1976; postgrad., C.C. Allegheny County, Pitts., 1985. Cert. allied addictions practitioner, criminal justice specialist. Med. social worker Schneider Home Health Care Agy., Inc., Pitts., 1985-87; mental health specialist Intercare, Hillside Psychiat. Ctr., McKeesport, Pa., 1987-91, Intercare, Lakewood Psychiat. Hosp., Canonsburg, Pa., 1991-95; psychol. specialist counselor II Med. Ctr. U. Pitts., 1995—; sr. rsch. assoc. Western Psychiat. Inst. and Clinic, Pitts., 1990—; therapist Willough at Naples, Naples, Fla., 1994—; asst. dir. in tng. of Group Psychotherapy and Psychodrama, Pitts., 1991—; reconstrn. therapist, Pitts., 1991—. Mem. Dance Therapy Assn., Pi Gamma Mu, Lambda Alpha. Home: 1712 Hathaway Ln Pittsburgh PA 15241-2706

BUYSE, MARYLOU, pediatrician, clinical geneticist, medical administrator; b. N.Y.C., June 27, 1946; d. George J. and Barbara M. (Sauer) B.; AB, Hunter Coll., 1966; MD, Med. Coll. Pa., 1970; MS in Med. Adminstrn. U. Wis., 1993; m. Carl N. Edwards, Jan. 22, 1982. Intern, U. Mich., 1970-71; resident in pediatrics L.A. County-U. So. Calif. Med. Ctr., 1971-73, fellow, 1973-75; instr. Sch. Medicine U. So. Calif., 1973-75, Sch. Medicine Boston U., 1975-84; asst. prof. pediatrics U. So. Calif., 1973-75, Tufts U., 1976-84; coordinator Myelodysplasia Clinic, Tufts-New Eng. Med. Ctr., Boston, 1976-79, dir. Cystic Fibrosis Clinic and staff pediatrician Ctr. for Genetic Counseling and Birth Defects Evaluation, 1975-82, med. dir. Ctr. for Birth Defects Info. Service, 1978-82, dir. center, 1982-94; pres. Medx, Ltd., 1985—; pres. Ctr. for Birth Defects Info. Scis., Inc., 1985—; dir. clin. genetics Children's Hosp., Boston, 1985-86; mem. med. adv. bd. Mass. Cystic Fibrosis Found., 1977-79; med. dir. Ferald State Sch., 1988-94; assoc. med. dir. MassPRO, 1993-95; mem. Mass. Bd. Registration in Medicine, 1994-95; assoc. med. dir. Care Advantage Health Syss., Inc.; cons. in field. Recipient Physicians Recognition award AMA, 1975, Alumni Achievement award Med. Coll. Pa., 1987. Diplomate Am. Bd. Med. Genetics. Fellow Am. Acad. Pediatrics, Mass. Med. Soc. (asst. sec.-treas. 1991-94, trustee 1991—, sec.-treas. 1994-96, v.p. 1996—); mem. Am. Med. Woman's Assn. (pres. Mass. br. 39 1986-91), Am. Mgmt. Assn., Am. Soc. Human Genetics, AAAS, Am. Med. Writers Assn., Soc. Craniofacial Genetics (pres. 1986), Am. Coll. Physician Execs., Teratology Soc., Charles River Dist. Med. Soc. (pres. 1993-95), Alpha Omega Alpha. Asso. editor Birth Defects Compendium, 2d edit., 1979; assoc. editor Syndrome Identification Jour., 1977-82, editor, 1982; editor Jour. Clin. Dysmorphology, 1982-86, Dysmorphology and Clinical Genetics, 1986-94; editor-in-chief Birth Defects Encyclopedia, 1990. Office: Ctr Birth Defects Info Svcs Inc Dover Med Bldg Box 1776 Dover MA 02030

BUZALJKO, GRACE WILSON, editor, writer; b. Cambridge, Mass., Nov. 4, 1922; d. Charles and Elizabeth (Douglas) Wilson; m. Ahmed Buzaljko, Mar. 9, 1963 (div. Mar. 1980). BA cum laude, St. Mary Coll., Leavenworth, Kans., 1944; postgrad., U. Pitts., 1946-47, New Sch. for Social Rsch., 1949-50. Promotions asst. Pitts. Press, 1945-48; manuscript editor John Wiley & Sons, N.Y.C., 1948-52, Harcourt Brace Jovanovich, N.Y.C., 1952-60, U. Calif. Press, Berkeley, 1960-67; adminstrv. editor Harcourt Brace Jovanovich, San Francisco, 1967-72; editor dept. anthropology U. Calif., Berkeley, 1973-88, ret., 1988. Editor: Yurok Myths (A.L. Kroeber), 1976, Karok Myths (A.L. Kroeber and E.W. Gifford), 1980; contbr. articles to profl. jours. Co-clk. Berkeley Soc. of Friends Meeting, 1988-90. Mem. AAUW (v.p., program chmn. Berkeley br. 1981-83, legis. chmn. 1988-94), Miwok Archeol. Preserve of Marin, Am. Anthrop. Assn. Home: 612 Albemarle St El Cerrito CA 94530-3217

BUZAN, TAMMIE JO, nurse; b. Decatur, Ill., Jan. 22, 1965; d. Ronald Dale and Darlene C. (Crow) Spires; m. Jeffrey Stewart Buzan, Jan. 9, 1988; children: Hannah Marie, Kimberly Jo. BS in Nursing, Millikin U., 1987. RN, Ill. Staff nurse emergency rm. Decatur Meml. Hosp., 1987-89; asst. head nurse Cmty. Health Improvement Ctr., Decatur, 1989-91; office nurse Moweaqua (Ill.) Family Practice, 1991-94, Dr. Michael Wall, Forsyth, Ill., 1994—. Mem. Jr. Women's Club (v.p. 1994-95, pres. 1995—). Home: RR 1 Box 188 Moweaqua IL 62550-9503 Office: 113 Illini Dr PO Box 110 Forsyth IL 62535

BUZZELL, BARBARA FEDER, public relations executive; b. Bethesda, Md., Apr. 4, 1953; d. Harold William and Edith (Herman) Feder. BA, U. Md., 1975. Mem. staff U.S. Senator J. Glenn Beall, Jr., 1975-76; fashion coord. Bloomingdale's, Tysons Corner, Va., 1976-78; dir. pub. rels. I. Magnin, Rockville, Md., 1979-81; exec. v.p. Laurey Peat & Assocs., Dallas, 1982—. Bd. dirs. SPCA of Tex., Dallas, 1989-95, Diffa, Dallas, 1990-93, Friends of Fair Park, Dallas, 1986-88, North Tex. Food Bank, 1995—, AIDS Arms, Inc., 1995—. Recipient Matrix award Women in Comm., 1986, Achievement award Tex. Pub. Rels. Soc. Am. Mem. Pub. Rels. Soc. Am. Office: Laurey Peat & Assocs Inc 2001 Ross Ave # 3020 Dallas TX 75201-8001

BYARS, BETSY (CROMER), author; b. Charlotte, Aug. 7, 1928; d. George Guy and Nan (Rugheimer) Cromer; m. Edward Ford Byars, June 24, 1950; children: Laurie, Betsy Ann, Nan, Guy. Author: Clementine, 1962, The Dancing Camel, 1965, Rama, the Gypsy Cat, 1966, The Groober, 1967, The Midnight Fox, 1968 (Am. Book of Yr. selection Child Study Assn. 1968, Lewis Carroll Shelf award 1970), Trouble River, 1969 (Am. Book of Yr. selection Child Study Assn. 1969), The Summer of the Swans, 1970 (Am. Book of Yr. selection Child Study Assn. 1970, John Newbery medal 1971), Go and Hush the Baby, 1971, The House of Wings, 1972 (Am. Book of Yr. selection Child Study Assn. 1972, Nat. Book award nomination 1973), The 18th Emergency, 1973 (Am. Book of Yr. selection Child Study Assn. 1973, New York Times Outstanding Book of Yr. 1973, Dorothy Canfield Fisher Meml. Book award Vt. Conress of Parents and Teachers 1975), The Winged Colt of Casa Mia, 1973 (Am. Book of Yr. selection Child Study Assn. 1973, New York Times Outstanding Book of Yr. 1973), After the Goat Man, 1974 (Am. Book of Yr. selection Child Study Assn. 1974), The Lace Snail, 1975 (Am. Book of Yr. selection Child Study Assn. 1975), The TV Kid, 1976 (Am. Book of Yr. selection Child Study Assn. 1976), The Pinballs, 1977 (Woodward Park School Annual Book award 1977, Child Study Children's Book award Child Study Children's Book Com. at Bank Street Coll. of Edn. 1977, Ga. Children's Book award 1979, Charlie May Simon Book award Ark. Elem. School Coun. 1980, Surrey School Book of Yr. award Surrey School Librs. of Surrey 1980, Mark Twain award Mo. Assn. of School Librs. 1980, William Allen White Children's Book award Emporia State Univ. 1980, Young Reader medal Calif. Reading Assn. 1980, Golden Archer award Dept. Libr. Sci. Univ. of Wis.-Oskosh 1982), The Cartoonist, 1978, Goodbye Chicken Little, 1979 (New York Times Outstanding Book of Yr. 1979), The Night Swimmers, 1980 (Am. Book of Yr. selection Child Study Assn. 1980, Best Book of Yr. School Libr. Jour. 1980, Am. Book award for Children's Fiction 1981), The Cybil War, 1981 (Tenn. Children's Choice Book award Tenn. Libr. Assn. 1983, Sequoyah Children's Book award 1984), The Animal, the Vegetable, and John D. Jones, 1982 (Parents' Choice award for Lit. Parents' Choice Found. 1982, Best Children's Book Sch. Libr. Jour. 1982, CRABbery award Oxon Hill Br. of Prince George's County Libr. 1983, Mark Twain award Mo. Assn. of School Librs. 1985), The Two-Thousand-Pound Goldfish, 1982 (New York Times Outstanding Book of Yr. 1982), The Glory Girl, 1983, The Computer Nut, 1984 (Charlie May Simon award 1987), Cracker Jackson, 1985 (S.C. Children's Book award 1988, Md. Children's Book award 1988), The Not-Just-Anbody Family, 1986, The Golly Sisters Go West, 1986, The Blossoms Meet the Vulture Lady, 1986, The Blossoms and the Green Phantom, 1987, A Blossom Promise, 1987, Beans on the Roof, 1988, The Burning Questions of Bingo Brown, 1988, Bingo Brown and the Language of Love, 1989, Hooray for the Golly Sisters, 1990, Bingo Brown, Gypsy Lover, 1990, Seven Treasure Hunts, 1991, Wanted...Mud Blossom, 1991, The Moon & I, 1992, Bingo Brown's Guide to Romance, 1992, McMummy, 1993, The Golly Sisters Ride Again, 1994, The Dark Stairs: A Herculeah Jones Mystery, 1994, Coast to Coast, 1994, My Brother, Ant., 1996, Tornado, 1996, Dead Letter: A Herculeah Jones Mystery, 1996; editor: Growing Up Stories, 1995. Recipient Regina medal Catholic Libr. Assn., 1987. Home: 126 Riverpoint Dr Clemson SC 29631-1049*

BYARS, MERLENE HUTTO, accountant, visual artist, writer, publisher; b. West Columbia, S.C., Nov. 8, 1931; d. Gideon Thomas and Nettie (Fail) Hutto; m. Alvin Willard Byars, June 10, 1950 (dec.); children: Alvin Gregg, Robin Mark, Jay C., Blaine Derrick. Student, Palmer Coll., Midlands Tech., U. S.C., 1988—; diploma in Journalism, Internat. Corr. Sch., 1995, Longridge Writers Group, 1995. Acct. State of S.C., 1964-93; ret., 1993; pres. Merlene Hutto Byars Enterprises, Cayce, 1993—; designer Collegiate Licensing Co., U.S. Trademark, 1989—. Pub. Lintheads, 1986, Olympia-Pacific: The Way It Was 1895-1970, 1981; Did Jesus Drive a Pickup Truck, 1993, The Plantation Era in South Carolina; pub., produr. (play) Lintheads and Hard Times, 1986; creator quilt which hung in S.C. State Capital for bicentennial celebration, 1988; designer Saxe Gotha Twp. Flag, 1993; author: The State of South Carolina Scrap Book, Orangeburg District, 1990, A Scrap Book of South Carolina, Dutch Fork, Saxe Gotha, Lexington County, 1994. Life mem. Women's Missionary Soc., United Luth. Ch., 1954—; mem. edn. found. U. S.C., 1969-93; treas. Airport H.S. Booster Club, 1969-76; sec. Saxe Gotha Hist. Soc., Lexington County, 1994-96. Recipient numerous awards for quilting S.C. State Fair, 1976—, Cert. for rose rsch. test panel Jackson and Perkins, 1982, Formost Women in Comm. award, 1969-70, Cayce Amb. award, City of Cayce, 1994. Fellow Internat. Biog. Assn.; mem. Cayce Mus. History (contbr. books, award for contribution 1987), S.C. State Mus. Home: 1842 Evelyn St Cayce SC 29033-2008

BYAS, TERESA ANN URANGA, healthcare professional; b. Plainview, Tex., Mar. 20, 1955; d. Adam T. and Lucy (Sandoval) Uranga; m. Wesley W. Byas, Sept. 11, 1972 (div. 1992); children: Chad W., Christina Ann. Student, Tarrant County Jr. Coll., 1982-83, 87-88, 95—, Tex. Wesleyan U., 1983-88. Teller Allied Nat. Bank (now named 1st Interstate), Ft. Worth, 1985-87, Nowlin Savs. and Loans (now named Comerica), Ft. Worth, 1987-88; missionary United Meth. Ch. Global Bd. World Missions, Brazil, 1988-91; asst. mgr. Bag 'n Baggage, Ft. Worth, 1991-92, store mgr., 1992-93; med. record clerical coord. Total Home Health Svcs., Inc., Ft. Worth, 1993-94; nurses aide Total Home Svcs. In Med. Home Health, 1994-95, Nurture Care, Ft. Worth, Tex., 1995—; with svc. desk The Home Depot Store, Ft. Worth, 1996—. Mem. Women's Polit. Caucus, Ft. Worth, United Meth. Women's Group; hon. mem. Westcliff United Meth. Women's Group (chpt. named in her honor 1991). Mem. Am. Bus. Women's Assn. Democrat. Home: 3117 Sondra Dr # 207D Fort Worth TX 76107 Office: The Home Depot 4850 SW Loop 820 Fort Worth TX 76109

BYER, DIANA, performing arts company executive; b. Trenton, N.J., Aug. 31, 1946; d. Fred and Norma (Handis) B. Grad. high sch., Trenton. Soloist Manhattan Festival Ballet, N.Y.C., 1972, Les Grands Ballet Canadiens, Montreal, Can., 1975; dir. Ballet Sch. of N.Y., N.Y.C., 1978—, N.Y. Theatre Ballet, 1978—; dir., founder Project LIFT scholarship program for children living N.Y.C. homeless shelters, 1989—. Helen Weiselberg scholar Nat. Arts Club, 1988, 90, 93. Office: NY Theatre Ballet 30 E 31st St New York NY 10016-6825

BYINGTON, SALLY RUTH, association administrator, writer, consultant; b. Grand Rapids, Mich., Apr. 16, 1935; d. George and Evangeline (Boerma) Meyer; m. S. John Byington, Nov. 27, 1964 (div. Dec. 1988); children: Nancy Lee Rhodes, Barbra Ann. BA, Western Mich. U., 1957; MA, U. Md., 1962. Cert. tchr. k-8, Md. Grad. asst. U. Md., College Pk., 1959-60; tchr. U. Chgo. Lab. Sch., 1963-64, Grand Rapids, Mich., 1957-59. 64-65, Montgomery County Md. Pub. Schs., Rockville, Md., 1961-63; learning specialist Endeavor Learning Ctr., Rockville, 1987-88; asst. to pres. Women in Militry Svc., Arlington, Va., 1988-89; exec. asst. Korean War Vets. Meml. Adv. Bd., Washington, 1989-91; pub. safety cons., civic activist, 1991-93; cons. Children Early Edn. Program, Bur. Edn. for Handicapped, Dept. edn., Washington, 1975-80; diagnostician pvt. practice. Author: Marriage Through Divorce and Beyond. Pres. Greater Springfield (Va.) Rep. Women's Clubs, 1980s, v.p., 1980s; dist. dir. Fairfax County Rep. Com., 1988; vol. Fairfax County Pub. Schs. Enrollment Study, 1985; coord. Capitol Hill Cmty. Policing Coun.; mem. MPD's Chief of Police Citizens Adv. Coun.; project dir. Guns into Plowshares Sculpture Project; mem. Ward 6 Crime Task Force. Recipient vol. recognition award Fairfax Pub. Schs., 1985. Mem. LWV (study rep. 1980's), Capitol Hill Restoration Soc. (pub. safety issues chair). Home and Office: 1231 Maryland Ave NE Washington DC 20002-5335

BYMEL, SUZAN YVETTE, talent manager, film producer; b. Chgo.; d. Howard Behr and Jacqueline Shirley (Richards) B. Student, U. Ill., Chgo. Exec. asst. Kenny Rogers Prodns., 1981; prodn. exec. Pinehurst Prodns., 1982; music mgmt. assoc. Frontline Mgmt., 1983; pres. Suzan Bymel & Assocs., 1985-94; oper. ptnr. Bymel/O'Neill Mgmt., 1995—, Meg Ryan Prodns. (a.k.a. Fandango Films), 1988-93, Bymel/O'Neill Mgmt., 1995 ; freelance screenwriter, actress. Mem. Hollywood Woman's Polit. Com., L.A. Office: 1724 N Vista St Los Angeles CA 90046-2235

BYNUM, HENRI SUE, education and French educator; b. Columbia, Miss., Feb. 7, 1944; d. George Milton and Lois Marie (Newsom) Dearing; m. James Lamar Bynum Jr., Feb. 28, 1965; children: James Wesley, Charles Drew. BA, U. So. Miss., 1967, MEd, 1977, PhD, 1979. Cert. tchr., Fla. Tchr. French, Spanish, modern dance Natchez (Miss.) Adams Pub. Schs., 1972-76; tchr. ESL U. So. Miss., Hattiesburg, 1977-79, coord. academic programs English Lang. Inst., 1979-81, adj. prof., 1980-81; dir. internat. edn. So. Ctr. for Rsch. and Innovation, Hattiesburg, 1981-82; chmn., asst. prof. dept. ESL U. So. Ala., Mobile, 1982-85; tchr. French, Spanish Moss Point (Miss.) High Sch., 1985-86; tchr. French Vero Beach (Fla.) Jr. High, 1986-87; prof. edn., French, Indian River Community Coll., Ft. Pierce, Fla., 1987—; adj. prof. Mobile Coll., 1986; cons. for curriculum devel. Colegio LaCruz, Puerto LaCruz, Venezuela, Escuela Anaco (Venezuela); co-dir. ESL curriculum Workshop, Assn. Venezuelan Am. Schs., Anaco. Cons. Safe Space, Inc., Vero Beach, 1989—. Mem. Phi Delta Kappa, Kappa Delta Pi. Republican. Office: Indian River Community Coll 3209 Virginia Ave Fort Pierce FL 34981-5541

BYRD, BARBARA ANN, professional society administrator; b. Martinsburg, W.Va., Aug. 31, 1952; d. James Leonard and Elizabeth (Somerfield) Byrd; 1 child, Marjorie Lynn. BS, Old Dominion U., 1973, MS, 1975; postgrad., U. Maryland, 1976. Cert. assn. exec. Instr. Old Dominion U., Norfolk, Va., 1972-75; asst. prof. U. Maryland, Balt., 1975-76; assoc. dir. Am. Dental Hygienists Assn., Chgo., 1976-79; dir. edn. Am. Coll. Preventive Medicine, Washington, 1979-81; dir. profl. affairs Tex. Pharm. Assn., Austin, 1981-83; dir. edn. and research Tex. Med. Assn., Austin, 1983-86; exec. v.p. Internat. Assn. Hospitality Accts., Austin, 1986-90, Community Assns. Inst., Alexandria, Va., 1990—; chair Assns. Advance Am. Com., 1994—. Bd. dirs. Nat. Bd. Cardiopulmonary Credentialing, Gaitersburg, N.D., 1981-82, mem. exec. com. 1982; bd. dirs. South Tex. Arthritis Found., San Antonio, 1987-89, Capital Area Arthritis Found., Austin, 1986-89; founding chmn. Travis County Adult Literacy Coun., Austin, 1984-90, chmn. emeritus 1990—; bd. dirs. Am. Hotel and Motel Assn. Research Found., 1988-90. Recipient award Internat. Assn. Bus. Communicators, 1988; named one of Outstanding Young Women Am., 1981, Top 10 Bus. Women of Yr., Am. Bus. Women's Assn., 1986, Greater Washington Soc. of Assn. Execs. Monument award in edn., 1992. Fellow Am. Soc. Assn. Execs. (charter, vice chmn. 1991-92, planning com. 1985-88, 91-92, Assn. Advance Am. and planning com. 1991—, chair Assn. Advance Am. com. 1994, bd. dirs. 1985-86, 88—, chmn. ednl. sect. 1985-86, chmn. task force on social responsibility 1989—, chair fellows 1989-90, Excellence award 1985, 88, 94, CAE commr. 1991-93, Mgmt. Achievement award 1983, sec.-treas. 1993-94, gov. task force 1992-93, Key award 1996); mem. Town Lake Bus. Women's Assn. (Woman of Yr. 1986), Tex. Soc. Assn. Execs. (com. chair 1981—), Greater Washington Soc. Assn. Execs. (CAE cert. com., instr. and tutor 1991-92), Leadership Austin, Leadership Tex. (bd. dirs., tng. group 1987—), World Future Soc., Internat. Assn. Hosp. Accts. (hon. 1990). Home: 4203 Wilton Woods Ln Alexandria VA 22310-2942 Office: Community Assns Inst 1630 Duke St Alexandria VA 22314-3426

BYRD, CHRISTINE WATERMAN SWENT, lawyer; b. Oakland, Calif., Apr. 11, 1951; d. Langan Waterman and Eleanor (Herz) Swent; m. Gary Lee Byrd, June 20, 1981; children: Amy, George. BA, Stanford U., 1972; JD, U. Va., 1975. Bar: Calif. 1976, U.S. Dist. Ct. (ctrl., so. no., ea. dists.) Calif., U.S. Ct. appeals (9th cir.). Law clk. to Hon. William P. Gray, U.S. Dist. Ct., L.A., 1975-76; assoc. Jones, Day, Reavis & Pogue, L.A., 1976-82, ptnr., 1987-96; asst. U.S. atty. criminal divsn. U.S. Atty.'s Office-Cen. Dist. Calif., L.A., 1982-87; ptnr. Irell & Manella, L.A., 1996—. Author: The Future of the U.S. Multinational Corporation, 1975; contbr. articles to profl. jours. Mem. FBA, Calif. State Bar (com. fed. cts. 1985-88), Los Angeles County Bar Assn., Women Lawyers Assn. Los Angeles County, Am. Arbitration Assn. (large and complex case panel 1992—), Stanford Profl. Women Los Angeles County, Stanford U. Alumni Assn., 9th Jud. Cir. Hist. Soc. (bd. dirs. 1986—). Republican. Office: Irell & Manella LLP 1800 Ave of Stars Ste 900 Los Angeles CA 90067

BYRD, JUDY, civil rights activist; b. Canton, Ohio, Sept. 2, 1948; d. Louise Crowder Tadsen; children: Eric Byrd, Laura Henderson, Bryce Byrd. BA in Criminal Justice studies, Kent State U., 1994. Co-founder Domestic Violence project, Stark County, Ohio, 1977; congl. dist. coord Human Rights Campaign, Washington, 1994— (Dir.'s award, 1995). Mem. AAUW, NOW

(Akron area chpt., chair lesbian issues task force, 1995—, pres. 1996—; Woman of Yr., 1995), Women for Racial and Econ. Equality, People for Am. Way, Stonewall Akron, Inc., Ohio (charter mem. 1994, v.p. 1996—). Office: 900 Park Ave SW Canton OH 44706

BYRD, JULIE ANDERSON, nurse; b. San Diego, Feb. 18, 1949; d. Asa Lee and Connie (Alderete) Anderson; m. Richard Allan Byrd, June 8, 1970. Diploma, Mercy Coll. Nursing, San Diego, 1970. RN; registered diagnostic cardiac sonographer; registered vascular technologist. Staff nurse Howard Meml. Hosp., Biloxi, Miss., 1971, Santa Rosa Med. Ctr., San Antonio, 1972; office nurse Dr. Mario Cardenas, Princeton, W.Va., 1973-74; acting head nurse Radford (Va.) Community Hosp., 1975; staff nurse Nurses Ctrl. Registry, Phoenix, 1976, Greenbrier Valley Med. Ctr., Ronceverte, W.Va., 1981-82; chief noninvasive cardiovascular lab. The Greenbrier Clinic, While Sulphur Springs, W.Va., 1976-91; nurse for adolescent child care agy. Davis-Stuart Inc., Lewisburg, W.Va., 1992—. Recipient Am. Legion Sch. award, 1964. Mem. Soc. Vascular Tech., Greenbrier Health Club, Calif. Scholarship Fedn. (life). Democrat. Roman Catholic. Home: PO Box 647 Lewisburg WV 24901-0647 Office: Davis-Stuart Rte 2 Box 188-A Lewisburg WV 24901

BYRD, MARY JANE, education educator; b. Topeka, Apr. 21, 1946; d. Vernon Thomas and Mary Elizabeth (Caldwell) Wharton; m. Gerald David Byrd, June 24, 1965; children: Kari, Juli, Cori. BS, U. So. Ala., 1980, MBA, 1984; D of Bus. Adminstrn., Nova Southeastern U., 1991. Dental asst. Gerald E. Berger, DMD, Mobile, Ala., 1963-65; dental hygenist Robert P. Hall, DMD, Mobile, Ala., 1965-66; teller Am. Nat. Bank, Mobile, Ala., 1972-75; office mgr. Byrd Surveying, Inc., Mobile, Ala., 1975-80; div. acct. cafeteria Morrison, Inc., Mobile, Ala., 1980-82; mgmt. cons. pvt. practice Mobile, Ala., 1982-84; lectr. acctg. U. South Ala., Mobile, Ala., 1984; asst. prof. acctg. & mgmt. Univ. Mobile, Mobile, Ala., 1984-89; assoc. prof. acctg. and mgmt. Mobile Coll., 1989-95; prof. mgmt., 1995—; reviewer Internat. Jour. Pub. Adminstrn., 1991—; dir. Nat. Assn. Accts., Mobile, 1986-89. Author: Supervisory Management Study Guide/Southwestern, 1993, Small Business Management: An Entrepreneur's Guide to Success/Irwin, 1994, 2d edit. 1996, Human Resource Management, Dame, 1995; contbr. articles to profl. jours. Named Assoc. of the Month, Home Builders Assn., 1986, Charles S. Dismukes Outstanding Mem., Nat. Assn. Accts. Mem. AAUW, Acad. Mgmt., Am. Bus. Women Assn., Assn. for Bus. Grad. Dirs., Mortgage Lenders Assn., So. Acad. Mgmt. Office: Univ Mobile PO Box 13220 Mobile AL 36663-0220

BYRD, SANDRA JUDITH, information scientist; b. Detroit, July 14, 1960; d. Brian Kenneth and Ruth (Jocaitas) Paukstys; m. Michael Keith Byrd, Nov. 23, 1985; children: Kristin Michelle, Adam Keith. BA, So. Ill. U., 1994. Asst. mgr. Colony West Swim Club, 1979, mgr., summers, 1980-82; aquatic supr. So. Ill. U., Carbondale, 1982; asst. mgr. Body Shop, Vero Beach, Fla., 1984; office mgr. Insta-Med Clinics, Inc., Vero Beach, 1984; receptionist Redgate Communications Corp., Vero Beach, 1985, circulation asst., 1985-87, circulation mgr., 1987-88; circulation dir. TT Pubs., Inc., Longwood, Fla., 1988-89; supr. of nursing payroll Orlando (Fla.) Regional Med. Ctr., 1989—, computer specialist nursing adminstrn. computer support, 1990-91; info. specialist dept. ops. improvement Orlando Regional Healthcare System, 1993-96; bus. mgr. Treasure Coast Diagnostics, Inc., 1987-88. Ill. State scholar, 1979-82. Mem. NAFE. Home and Office: 180 SE Duxbury Ave Port Saint Lucie FL 34983

BYRNE, KATHARINE CRANE, lawyer; b. Chgo., Dec. 31, 1958; d. William Patrick and Jane M. (Burke) B.; m. William Vogt, June 24, 1995. BA, St. Mary's Coll., Notre Dame, Ind., 1980; JD, Loyola U., 1988. Bar: Ill. 1988, U.S. Dist. Ct. (no. dist.) Ill. 1988, U.S. Ct. Appeals (7th cir.) 1991, Fed. Trial Bar (no. dist.) Ill. 1992. Event planner Gaper's Caterers, Chgo., 1980-84; coord. Jane Byrne Campaign Com., Chgo., 1985-87; law clk. Cooney & Conway, Chgo., 1987-88, atty., 1988—; lectr. Andrews 8th Ann. Asbestos Litigation Conf., 1996. Author: Premises Liability, 1994. Lectr. Ill. Inst. for Continuing Legal Edn., Chgo., 1991; pres. Beautiful Chgo. (Ill.) Commn., 1994. Mem. ATLA, Ill. Trial Lawyers Assn. (lectr. seminar 1995), Celtic Lawyers. Democrat. Roman Catholic. Home: 1757 N Cleveland Ave Chicago IL 60614 Office: Cooney & Conway 120 N La Salle St Chicago IL 60602-2412

BYRNE, OLIVIA SHERRILL, lawyer; b. Trenton, N.J., Aug. 14, 1957; d. Stewart and Elizabeth (Sherrill) B. Student, Vanderbilt U., 1975-76; BA, Bowdoin Coll., 1979; JD, U. Toledo, 1982; LLM in Taxation, Georgetown U., 1987. Bar: Tex. 1982, Ohio 1984, Md. 1985. Assoc. Whiteford, Taylor & Preston, Balt., 1984-87, Linowes & Blocher, Silver Spring, Md., 1987-90, Weinberg & Jacobs, Rockville, Md., 1990-96; ptnr. Shulman Rogers Gandal Pordy & Ecker, Rockville, 1996—. Author: The At-Risk Rules Under the Tax Reform Act of 1986, The Door Closes on Tax Motivated Investments, IRS Issues New Guidelines for Management Contracts Used for Facilities Financed with Tax Exempt Bonds, 1993, RRA '93 Loosens Real Estate Rules for Exempt Organizations, 1993. Mem. Tax Coun. for State od Md., Leadership Montgomery, 1996. Mem. ABA (exempt orgn. com. taxation sect. 1991—), Md. Bar Assn. (coun. taxation sect.), Balt. City Bar Assn. (chmn. speakers bur. young lawyers sect.), Lawyers for Arts Washington, Comml. Real Estate Woman (bd. dirs., pres.), Profls. for Strathmore Hall (co-chmn.), D.C. Bowdoin Coll. Alumni Assn. (pres. 1992—), Howard County C. of C. (legis. com. 1989), Rotary. Home: 107 N Brook Ln Bethesda MD 20814-2610 Office: Shulman Rogers et al 11921 Rockville Pike Rockville MD 20852-2743

BYRNES, CHRISTINE ANN, internist; b. Darby, Pa., Dec. 18, 1951; d. John Edward and Olga (Rebechi) B. BA, U. Del., Newark, 1974; MD, Jefferson Med. Coll., Phila., 1978. Diplomate Am. Bd. Internal Medicine. Resident internal medicine Thomas Jefferson U. Hosp., Phila., 1978-81; coord. internal medicine residency program U. Med. & Dentistry of N.J./Cooper Med. Ctr., Camden, 1981-82; attending physician Thomas Jefferson U. Hosp., 1982-87, instr. medicine, 1982-85, clin. asst. prof. medicine, 1985-87; assoc. dir. Merck Human Health, West Point, Pa., 1987-89; sr. assoc. dir. Merck Human Health, 1989-91, dir., 1991-92, sr. dir., 1992—. Mem. ACP, Soc. Gen. Internal Medicine, Am. Soc. Internal Medicine, Am. Geriatrics Soc.

BYRON, BEVERLY BUTCHER, congresswoman; b. Balt., July 27, 1932; d. Harry C. and Ruth Butcher; m. Goodloe E. Byron, 1952 (dec.); children: Goodloe E. Jr., Barton Kimball, Mary McComas; m. B. Kirk Walsh, 1986. Student, Hood Coll., 1962-64. Mem. 96th-102nd Congresses from 6th Md. dist., 1979-93; Presdl. appt. to base closing and realignment commn., 1993; bd. dirs. McDonnell Douglas, Balt. Gas and Electric, Blue Cross/Blue Shield, UNC Corp., Farm and Mech. Nat. Bank, Def. Adv. Commn. on Women in the Mil.; exec. panel Chief of Naval Ops.; adv. bd. NASA. State treas. Md. Young Dems., 1962, 65; bd. assocs. Hood Coll.; bd. visitors USAF Acad., 1980-87; trustee Mt. St. Mary's Coll.; bd. dirs. Frederick County chpt. ARC; sec. Frederick Heart Assn., 1974-79; mem. Frederick Phys. Fitness Commn.; chmn. Md. Phys. Fitness Commn., 1979-89; mem. Frederick County Landmarks Found.; bd. dirs. Am. Hiking Soc.; bd. dirs. Adventure Sports Inst., 1992—; bd. advisors Internat. Studies Frostburg State U., 1990—, Am. Volkssport Assn., 1991—; mem. bd. vis., vice chair U.S. Naval Acad., 1995—. Episcopalian. Home: 306 Grove Blvd Frederick MD 21701-4813

BYRUM, DIANNE, state legislator; b. Mar. 18, 1954; d. Cecil Dershem and Mary D.; m. James E. Byrum; children: Barbara Anne, James Richard. AA, Lansing Cmty. Coll.; BS cum laude, Mich. State U. Rep. dist. 68 State of Mich., 1991-94; owner Blackhawk Hardware, Leslie, Mich., 1983—; senator 25th dist. State of Mich., 1995—; minority vice chair agr. and forestry, health policy and sr. citizens; mem. tech. and energy com., capitol com.; chair dem. caucus. Recipient Disting. Citizen award Ingham County Soil Conservation Dist., 1991, Disting. Alumnus award Lansing Cmty. Coll., 1993. Mem. Am. Cancer Soc. (Ingham-Delta br. mem. bd. dirs.), Mich. Retail Hardware Assn., Lansing Regional C. of C., Greater Lansing Safety Coun., S. Lansing Bus. Assn., S. Lansing-Everett Kiwanis, Women Bus. Owners. Democrat. Office: Mich State House 125 W Allegan PO Box 30036 Lansing MI 48909

BYRUM, JUDITH MIRIAM, accountant; b. Bismarck, N.D., Sept. 24, 1943; d. Adolph Mathew and Gertrude Cecelia (Lechner) H.; m. Richard W. Byrum, July 30, 1965 (div. Oct. 1984); children: Thomasin Jane, Toby Oliver; m. Danny D. Jansen, Oct. 21, 1989 (dec. Nov. 1989); m. Jack N. Sutton, June 26, 1993. BS in Acctg., Ariz. State U., 1967. CPA, Ariz., Kans. Underwriter Gt. SW Fire Ins. Co., Mesa, Ariz., 1963-65; staff auditor Touche Ross & Co., London, 1967-69, Arthur Andersen & Co., Kansas City, Mo., 1970-71; treas. John J. Peterson Real Estate, Overland Park, Kans., 1971-75; internal auditor Bus. Men's Assurance Co., Kansas City, 1975-78; chief exec. officer, owner Judith H. Byrum, CPA, Overland Park, 1978—. Contbr. articles to newsletter. Mem. adv. bd. Rockhurst Coll. Women's Ctr., Kansas City, 1977; mem. Congressman Larry Winn II Small Bus. Com., Washington, 1977-80; treas. Trinity Luth. Ch., Mission, Kans., 1990-94. Mem. AICPA (legis. liaison), Am. Woman's Soc. CPAs (treas., v.p. Chgo. 1977-83), Am. Soc. Women Accts. (pres. Kansas City 1980-81), Kans. Soc. CPAs (com. mem. 1977—, pres., v.p., treas. Metro chpt. 1989—, bd. dirs. 1994—), Kansas City Women's C. of C. (v.p. 1980), Beta Alpha Psi. Office: 10550 Marty St Ste 202 Shawnee Mission KS 66212-2557

BYSIEWICZ, SUSAN, state legislator; b. New Haven, Conn.. BA magna cum laude, Yale Coll., 1983; JD, Duke U., 1986. Pol. reporter N.Y. Times, Washington, 1985; campaign mgr., issues dir. White & Case, N.Y., 1986-88, Blumenthal, Hartford & Stamford, Conn., 1990, Robinson & Cole, Hartford, Conn., 1988-92; mem. staff law dept. Aetna Life and Casualty, 1992-94; mem. Middletown Dem. Com., 1989—; rep. dist., mem. judiciary com. State of Conn., 1993—, chair govt. adminstrn. and elections com., 1995—; atty. Author: Ella: A Biography of Governor Ella T. Grasso, 1984; contbr. chpt. to book. Conn. Bar Assn., N.Y. Bar Assn. Democrat. Address: Conn House of Reps State Capitol Hartford CT 06106

CAAMANO, KATHLEEN ANN FOLZ, gifted education professional; b. Rozellville, Wis., Dec. 20, 1944; d. Joseph and Isabel Ann (Brost) Folz; m. Gerald J. Caamano, Aug. 10, 1968; children: Michelle, David. BS, U. Wis., Stevens Point, 1968; MA, Cen. Mich. U., 1971. Cert. tchr., Ill. Tchr. Midland (Mich.) Pub. Schs., 1968-74, Newark (Ohio) City Schs., 1974-77; tchr. Minooka (Ill.) Sch. Dist., 1986—, coord. gifted edn., 1986—. Pres. Camelot Homeowners Assn., Joliet, Ill., 1985; tutor Big Bros./Big Sisters Assn. Will County, 1990; voter registrar Will County, Joliet, 1992—. Recipient Those Who Excel award Ill State Bd. Edn., 1992. Mem. Internat. Reading Assn., Ill. Edn. Assn. (tchr. rep. 1992—), Gifted Edn. Coun., Ill. Assn. Ednl. Rsch. and Evaluation, Will County Reading Coun., Delta Kappa Gamma (v.p.), Beta Sigma Phi (pres.). Roman Catholic. Home: 22257 S Galahad Dr Joliet IL 60431

CABANAS, ELIZABETH ANN, nutritionist; b. Port Arthur, Tex., Oct. 27, 1948; d. William Rosser and Frances Merle (Block) Thornton. BS, U. Tex., 1971; MPH, U. Hawaii, 1973; postgrad., Tex. Woman's U., 1991—. Registered dietitian. Clin. nutritionist Family Planning Inst. Kapiolani Hosp., Honolulu, 1972-74; dietitian Kauikeolani Children's Hosp.-Pacific Inst. Rehab. Medicine, Honolulu, 1974-75; dietitian San Antonio Ind. Schs., 1975-84, asst. food service adminstr., 1984-89; coord. equipment and facilities Dallas Ind. Sch., 1990-91; dietitian SureQuest Solutions in Software, Richardson, Tex., 1990-91; nutritionist div. endocrinology, metabolism and hypertension, clin. studies unit rsch. nutritionist, asst. prof. dept. health promotion & gerontology U. Tex. Med. Br., Galveston, 1991—; lectr. nutrition U. Hawaii, Honolulu, 1974-75, St. Mary's U., San Antonio Coll., 1984-90; adj. faculty Tex. Woman's U., 1994—; cons. nutritionist, 1980—; presenter in field. Contbr. articles to profl. jours. Recipient diabetes educator recognition Eli Lilly & Co., 1994. Mem. Am. Dietetic Assn., Am. Assn. Diabetes Educators, Assn. Sch. Bus. Ofcls. Internat., Nutrition and Food Svc. Mgmt. Com., Am. Diabetes Assn. (adv. com. U. Tex. Med. Br. children's diabetes mgmt. program 1993—, mem. Galveston County diabetes support group 1991—, Disting. Svc. award 1995), Coun. Nutritional Scis. and Metabolism (profl. sect., non-peer rev. com. 1993-94), Tex. Sch. Food Svc. Assn. (dist. bd. dirs. 1977-78), Tex. Nutrition Coun. (nominating com. 1996-99, sports and cardiovasc. nutritionists practice group, Tex. gerontol. nutritionists practice group), Houston Area Dietetic Assn. (legis. network com. 1995—), San Antonio Sch. Food Svc. Assn. (com. chmn. 1975-89), Tex. Assn. Sch. Bus. Ofcls., Tex. Restaurant Assn., San Antonio Area Food Svc. Adminstrs. Assn. (pres. 1989-90), Assn. Profls. in Positions of Leadership in Edn., Dallas Dietetic Assn. (cons. nutritionists practice group, chmn. 1990-91), San Antonio Mus. Assn., Randolph C. of C., Grand Opera House, Galveston (patron), Galveston Hist. Found., Space City Ski Club, Sierra Club, Hawaii Club (chmn. entertainment com. 1983). Republican. Methodist. Home: 711 Holiday Dr Apt 75 Galveston TX 77550-5579 Office: Univ Tex Med Br Rte 1060 301 University Blvd Galveston TX 77555-1060

CABRERA, CARMEN, secondary education educator; b. Havana, Cuba, Dec. 31, 1948; came to U.S., 1962; d. Armando and Carmen (Gomez) C. AA, East L.A. Coll., 1970; BA, Calif. State U., L.A., 1972; MA, Calif. State U., 1975. Cert. tchr., Calif. Tchr. Sacred Heart of Mary H.S., Montebello, Calif., 1973-91, acad. dean, 1989-91; tchr., curriculum dir. Cantwell Sacred Heart of Mary H.S., Montebello, 1991—; instr. East L.A. Coll., Monterey Park, Calif., 1974-77; chairperson dept. fgn. lang. Sacred Heart of Mary H.S., 1980-91, Cantwell Sacred Heart of Mary H.S., 1991-93, 95—. Assoc. Beverly Hosp. Found., Montebello, 1990-93. Mem. NASSP, ASCD, Am. Assn. Tchrs. Spanish and Portuguese (contest dir. 1987-89), Am. Coun. on Teaching Fgn. Langs., Nat. Cath. Ednl. Assn., Phi Kappa Phi. Office: Cantwell Sacred Heart Mary 329 N Garfield Ave Montebello CA 90640-3803

CACCAMISE, GENEVRA LOUISE BALL (MRS. ALFRED E. CACCAMISE), retired librarian; b. Mayville, N.Y., July 22, 1934; d. Herbert Oscar and Genevra (Green) Ball; m. Alfred E. Caccamise, July 7, 1974. BA, Stetson U., DeLand, Fla., 1956; MLS, Syracuse U., 1967. Tchr. grammar sch., Sanford, Fla., 1956-57, elem. sch., Longwood, Fla., 1957-58; tchr., libr. Enterprise (Fla.) Sch., 1958-63; libr., media specialist Boston Ave. Sch., DeLand, 1963-82; head media specialist Blue Lake Sch., DeLand, 1982-87, ret., 1987. Author Volusia County manual Instructing the Library Assistant, 1965, Echoes of Yesterday: A History of the DeLand Area Public Library, 1912-1995, 1995. Charter mem. West Volusia Meml. Hosp. aux., DeLand, 1962-81; leader Girl Scout U.S., 1955-56; area dir. Fla. Edn. Assn., Volusia county, 1963-65; bd. dirs. Alhambra Villas Home Owners Assn., 1972-75; bd. trustees DeLand Pub. Library, 1977-86, sec., 1978-80, v.p., 1980-82, pres. 1982-84; v.p. Friends of DeLand Pub. Library, 1987, pres., 1989, 90, 95, 96, bd. dirs., 1991—, newsletter editor 1992-95; charter mem. Guild of the DeLand Mus. Art, v.p., 1990, pres. 1991-92, mem. Guild of bd. dirs. 1991—, mus. bd. dirs., 1991-95; co-orgn. chmn. Friends DeLand Mus. Art, 1993. Mem. AAUW (2d v.p. chpt. 1965-67, rec. sec. 1961-65, 78-80, pres. 1980-82, parliamentarian 1982-84), Assn. Childhood Edn. (1st v.p. 1965-66, corr. sec. 1963-65), DAR (chpt. registrar 1969-80, asst. chief page Continental Congress, Washington 1962-65), Fla. Libr. Assn., Bus. & Profl. Women's Club (corr. sec. DeLand 1968-71, 2d v.p. 1969-70), Stetson U. Alumni Assn. (class chmn. for ann. fund drive 1968), Volusia County Assn. Media in Edn. (treas. 1977), Volusia County Retired Educators Assn. (pres. Unit II 1988-90, scholarship chmn. 1992-95), Soc. of Mayflower Descendants (lt. gov. Francis Cook Colony 1988-90), Pilgrim John Howland Soc., Colonial Dames XVII Century, Magna Charta Dames, Nat. Soc. New Eng. Women (v.p. Daytona Beach Colony 1990-91), Hibiscus Garden Circle (treas. 1988-89, v.p. 1990-93, 96—), Delta Kappa Gamma (pres. Beta Psi chpt. 1982-84), Nat. Soc. of U.S. Daus. of 1812. (rec. sec. Peacock chpt. 1989-90), DeLand Garden Club (corresponding sec. 1993-95, editor newsletter 1993-95), W. Volusia Hist. Soc. (sec. 1996, libr. 1995-96, bd. dirs.), Fla. Hist. Soc. Democrat. Episcopalian. Address: PO Box 241 Deland FL 32721

CACCIAMAN, CAROL, bank executive. Sr. v.p. State St. Boston Corp. Office: State St Boston Corp 225 Franklin St Boston MA 02110*

CACKENER, HELEN LEWIS, retired English educator, writer; b. Elmira, N.Y., July 4, 1926; d. Norman Pratt and Grace Genevieve (Oakes) Lewis; m. Daniel Glyndwr Lewis Jr., June 17, 1950 (div. Aug. 1959); children: Deborah Anne Poplasky, Elizabeth Laura Lewis-Michl, Margaret Grace Lewis-Price; m. Robert Millard Cackener, Apr. 17, 1960. BA in English Lit. magna cum laude, Oberlin Coll., 1948; MAT, Harvard U., 1950. Cert. secondary English tchr., N.Y. English tchr. Westbrook Coll., Portland, Maine, 1949-50, Schenectady (N.Y.) City Schs., 1950-51, 60, Hudson Falls (N.Y.) Sr. H.S., 1960-85. Contbr. articles to Glens Falls Today, Saratoga Style, and Schenectady Mag., 1985-88. Vol. PBS, Saratoga Performing Arts Ctr. John Hay fellow Ford Found., 1964. Mem. AAUW, P.E.O., Delta Kappa Gamma (Alpha Epsilon chpt., bd. mem. 1970-95, N.Y. state sec. 1983-87), Phi Beta Kappa. Republican. Presbyterian. Home: 895 W River Rd Gansevoort NY 12831

CACOSSA, PAULA, marketing executive; b. N.Y., Jan. 8, 1966; d. Francis and Caroline (Miranda) C. Student, Chinese U., Hong Kong, 1986-87; BS in Econs., Siena Coll., 1988; MBA, U. Pa., 1995. Customer svc. officer, China rep. Crown Pacific (China) Ltd., Beijing, 1988-91; mgr. Shandong Inc., N.Y.C., 1991-93; mgr. new bus. devel. Whirlpool Corp., Benton Harbor, Mich., 1995—. Home: PO Box 571 Saint Joseph MI 49085 Office: Whirlpool Corp 2000 M-63 North Benton Harbor MI 49022

CADDEO, MARIA ELIZABETH, critical care nurse; b. San Pedro, Calif., Oct. 26, 1967; d. Frank Paul Sr. and Lois Lee (Johnson) Caddeo. BSN, U. Md., 1989. Primary nurse I R.A. Cowley Shock Trauma Ctr., Balt., 1989—; staff nurse, coord. labor & delivery nursing edn. 67th CSH, Würzburg, Germany, 1992; staff nurse, unit orientation coord. North Arundel Hosp., 1995; dir. staff devel. Genesis Eldercare, Spa Creek, Annapolis, Md., 1996—; lectr. MIEMSS Snit program, trauma theory classes; instr. trauma prevention for high-risk adolescents. Nominee Flora Hoffman Tarun award, Award for Excellence in Care of Children, Edwin and L.M. Zimmerman award.

CADORA, KAREN MICHELE, literature educator; b. Castle Air Force Base, Calif., May 15, 1970; d. Donald Frank and Mavis Lancene (Hart) C. BS, Cornell U., 1991; MS, Stanford U., 1993, MA, 1996. Solar physics rschr. Stanford (Calif.) U., 1991-93, literature educator, 1993—. Home: PO Box 8403 Stanford CA 94309

CADORETTE, LISA ROBERTS, medical, surgical nurse; b. Johnson City, N.Y., June 12, 1966; d. John Lawrence and Dorothy Ellen (Ace) Roberts; m. Jeffrey Cadorette, May 31,1991; children: Jessica Renee, Jacqueline Elyse. BSN magna cum laude, Neumann Coll., 1989. RN, Pa.; cert. ACLS Am. Heart Assn. Commd. lt. USAF Nurse Corps., 1989; staff nurse USAF Nurse Corps., Andrews AFB, Md., 1989-90, Dover AFB, Del., 1990-91; asst. to chair divsn. nursing and health scis. Neumann Coll., Aston, Pa., 1992—; vol. emergency med. technician Lima (Pa.) Fire Co., 1988-91, Media (Pa.) Fire Co., 1988-91. Mem. Nightingale Soc., Sigma Theta Tau, Delta Epsilon Sigma. Office: Neumann Coll Divsn Nursing and Hlth Scis Aston PA 19014

CADWELL, CYNTHIA ANN, clinical applications manager; b. Norristown, Pa., Oct. 12, 1956; d. Richard Lee and Kathryn Mary (Skiffington) C.; 1 child, Cassandra Kathlee. LPN, Sacred Heart Hosp. Sch. Practical Nursing, Norristown, Pa., 1975; ADN, San Diego City Coll., 1978; BSN, USNY, Albany, 1996. RN, Calif. Nurse's aide Euclid Convalescent Ctr., San Diego, 1975-76; staff relief LVN Profl. Nurses Bur., San Diego, 1976-78; surgical ICU clin. nurse Sharp Meml. Hosp., San Diego, 1978-85, crit. care clin. educator, 1985-87; cardiac asst. clin. specialist Boston Sci. Corp., 1987-88, cardiac asst. applications specialist, 1988-92, clin. applications mgr., 1992—. Contbr. articles to profl. jours., chpt. to book. Mem. NOW, AAUW, AACN. Democrat. Roman Catholic.

CADWELL, FRANCHELLIE MARGARET, advertising agency executive, writer; b. Hamilton, Bermuda, Apr. 23, 1937; came to U.S., 1938; d. Margaret (Roulston) C.;. B.S., Cornell U., 1955. Pres. Cadwell Davis Ptnrs., N.Y.C., 1975—. Author: The Un-Supermarkets, 1969. Mem. Pres. Coun. Cornell Women; bd. dirs. N.Y. Humane Soc.; bd. govs. N.Y. Arthritis Found., N.Y.C.; bd. mem. Nat. Parks; mem. Pres.'s Com. Employment of People with Disabilities. Recipient Nat. Humanitarian award, YWCA award, Entrepreneurial award Women Bus. Owners of N.Y., 1983, Girl Scouts USA award. Mem. Advt. Women N.Y., Fashion Group, Cosmetic Toiletry and Fragrance Assn., Non-Prescription Drug Mfrs., Women in Comm. (Matrix award 1980). Home: 7 E 94th St New York NY 10128-1912 Office: Cadwell Davis Ptnrs (USA) Advt 375 Hudson St New York NY 10014-3658

CADY, MARY MARGARET, advertising executive; b. Deadwood, S.D., Feb. 3, 1947; d. Donald Phillip Hines and Lois Elaine (Morrill) Watson; m. Jean Poulin, July 3, 1993. Student, Augustana Coll., 1965-69. On-air talent, writer Sta. KSOO-TV, Sioux Falls, S.D., 1968-70; copywriter Campbell Mithun Advt., Mpls., 1970-71; copywriter, TV producer Smith, Kaplan, Allen & Renolds Advt., Omaha, Nebr., 1972-76; owner Creative Workshop, Omaha, 1976-80; v.p. creative svcs. Smith, Kaplan, Allen & Reynolds Advt., Omaha, 1980-85; sr. v.p., account svcs. Rollherser, Holland Kahler Advt., Omaha, 1985-89; pres. Blumenthal Cady Advt., Omaha, 1989—. Bd. dirs. Operators of Opera, Omaha, 1989-91, Ballet Omaha, 1989-91. Recipient numerous Addy awards Am. Fedn. of Advt., 1980—. Mem. Inst. for Career Advancement Needs (pres., bd. dirs. 1985—), Rotary. Episcopalian. Office: Blumentahl Cady Advt 10040 Regency Cir Omaha NE 68114-3732

CAFFEE, VIRGINIA MAUREEN, secretary; b. Kansas City, Mo., Feb. 25, 1948; d. Frederick Arthur Gladden and Ethel Elizabeth (Keithly) Courier; m. Jack B. Todd Jr., May 13, 1967 (div. Dec. 1973); m. Marcus Pat Caffee, May 31, 1975; 1 child, Katheryn Elizabeth. Student, Ctrl. Mo. State U., 1966-73, Okla. State U., 1977-78; BBA in Bus. Edn., Sam Houston State U., 1985. Cert. profl. sec., 1975. Land abstractor Johnson County Title Co., Warrensburg, Mo., 1967-68; dept. sec., bus. placement office Ctrl. Mo. State U., Warrensburg, 1968-69; exec. sec. European Exchange System, Giessen, Germany, 1969-70; confidential sec. Consolidated Freightways, Kansas City, 1972-73; exec. sec. Behring Internat., Houston, 1974-75; sr. sec. Tenneco Oil Co.-E&P, Houston, 1979-84; exec. sec. St. Petersburg (Fla.) Hilton & Towers, 1989-90; adminstrv. mgr. Tampa Bay Engring., Clearwater, Fla., 1990-92; office mgr., WP trainer Marcus Caffee, Consulting, Largo, Fla., 1992-95; sr. adminstrv. asst. BMH Inc., Dallas, 1995—; ad hoc instr. St. Petersburg (Fla.) Jr. Coll., 1993, Profl. Secs. Internat. chpt. liaison for CPS rev. course, 1993-94; presenter in field. Editor (performance programs) Suncoast Singers, 1991-94 (Cmty. Svc. award Arts Coun. Co-op 1993), Clearwater Cmty. Chorus, 1993-95, Ft. Worth Civic Chorus, Fall 1995, (newsletters) Clearwater Sparkler, 1992-93 (1st pl. award 1993), Fla. Divsn. The Secretariat, 1993-94. Sec. Montgomery County Choral Soc., Conroe, Tex., 1986-88, publicity co-chmn., 1987-89; pres. Anona Meth. Ch. Choir, Largo, 1990-91. Named Sec. of Yr., 1994; recipient Mo. State Tchrs. scholarship Mo. Congress Parents and Tchrs., 1966. Mem. NAFE, Nat. Assn. Exec. Secs., Profl. Secs. Internat. (chmn. secs. week, sec. Clearwater chpt. 1992-93, pres. 1994, chmn. seminar and v.p. Clearwater chpt. 1992-93, workshop spkr. Fla. divsn. 1993, program spkr. St. Petersburg chpt. 1993, alt. del. to internat. conv. 1993, alt. del. to divsn. meeting 1993, 94, del. dist. conv. 1994, Sec. of Yr. 1994-95, del. Fla. divsn. meeting 1995, program spkr. Trinity chpt. 1996, del. Tex.-La. meeting 1996, chmn. audit com. Denton chpt. 1996, divsn. treas. Tex.-La. divsn. 1996), CPS Soc. Tex. (poster chmn. 1983-85). Republican. Methodist. Office: BMH Inc 4004 Beltline Rd #125 Dallas TX 75244

CAFFERATA, J. FARRELL, massage therapist; b. Portland, Oreg., June 20, 1963; d. H. Treat and Patricia Dillon Cafferata. Grad. in Gen. Studies, U. Nev., 1989. Cert. EMT, Nev. Office mgr. H.T. Cafferata MD, Ltd., Reno, 1987-94, orgnl. cons., 1995—; moving crew U. Nev., Reno, 1994—; massage therapist J. Farrell Cafferata, Reno, 1994—; bd. dirs., CFO, Trellis Found., Reno, 1994—. Asst. treas. Cafferata for Congress, Patty Cafferata esq., Reno, 1995—. Home: 1929 Watt St Reno NV 89509

CAFFREY, LYNN REGINA, education educator; b. Queens, N.Y., May 31, 1961; d. Charles Daniel and Clare (Carney) Mailley; m. Robert Dennis Caffrey, Apr. 26, 1986; children: Katelyn Rose, Anna Leigh, Emily Joy. AA, Nassau C.C., 1982; BS in Edn., SUNY, Cortland, 1984; MS, St. John's Univ., 1989. Adminstrv. asst. Grumman Data Systems, N.Y.C., 1984-85; 1st grade tchr. Waverly Park Elem., Lynbrook, N.Y., 1985-88; reading specialist St. John's Univ., Jamaica, N.Y., 1988-90; instr. Tomlinson Coll., Cleveland, Tenn., 1990-92, Cleveland State Coll., 1990-92; instr., supr. student tchrs. Lee Coll., Cleveland, 1991-92; asst. prof., supr. of student tchr. York (Pa.) Coll., 1993—; mem. edn. policies bd. Christian Sch. of York (Pa.), 1993—. Recipient Excellence Edn. Tchg. award N.Y. State Edn.

Dept., 1986-87. Mem. ASCD, Tenn. Reading Assn. Office: York Coll Country Club Rd York PA 17403

CAFFREY, MARGARET MARY, humanities educator; b. Wilkes-Barre, Pa., July 5, 1947; d. James Anthony and Louise Elizabeth (Keil) C. BA, Coll. Misericordia, 1969; MA, U. Tex., 1979, PhD, 1986. Lectr. U. Tex., Austin, 1986-87; instr. Austin C.C., 1988; asst. prof. Memphis State U., 1988-93; assoc. prof. U. Memphis, 1993—. Author: Ruth Benedict: Stranger in This Land, 1989 (Critics Choice award). Faculty Rsch. grantee U. Memphis, 1993; named Oustanding Young Rschr., Memphis State U. Coll. Arts & Scis., 1989-90. Mem. Orgn. Am. Historians & Affiliate Coord. Coun. for Women in History, Am. Studies Assn., So. Hist. Assn., Assn. Southern Womens Historians. Office: U Memphis Dept History Memphis TN 38152

CAGGINS, RUTH PORTER, nurse, educator; b. Natchez, Miss., July 11, 1945; d. Henry Chapelle and Corinne Sadie (Baines) Porter; m. Don Randolph Caggins, July 1, 1978; children: Elva Rene, Don Randolph, Myles Thomas Chapelle. BS, Dillard U., New Orleans, 1967; MA, NYU, 1973; PhD Tex. Woman's U., 1992. Staff nurse Montefiore Hosp., Bronx, 1968-70, head nurse, 1970-72; nurse clinician Met. Hosp., N.Y.C., 1973-74, clin. supr., 1974-76; asst. prof. U. So. La., Lafayette, 1976-78; assoc. prof. Prairie View A&M U. Coll. Nursing, Houston, 1978—, apptd. project dir. LIFT Ctr. Active The Links Inc., Houston, 1982—, Cultural Arts Coun., Houston, Nat. Black Leadership Initiative on Cancer, Houston. Recipient Tchg. Excellence award Nat. Inst. Staff and Orgnl. Devel., 1992-93. Mem. ANA (clin. ethnic/racial minority fellow 1989-92, post doctoral proposal devel. program 1995), Nat. Black Nurses Assn., A.K. Rice Inst. (assoc. Ctrl. States Ctr., Tex. Ctr.), Assn. Black Nursing Faculty in Higher Edn. (Dissertation award 1990), Sigma Theta Tau, Delta Sigma Theta, Chi Eta Phi. Democrat. Baptist. Avocations: singing, sewing, traveling, aerobics, writing. Home: 5602 Goettee Cir Houston TX 77091-4523 Office: Prairie View A&M U Coll Nursing 6436 Fannin St Houston TX 77030-1519

CAGLE, BETTY WARE, school system administrator; b. Joplin, Mo., Aug. 31, 1942; d. Oliver Scherer and Mary Ponnie (Goodman) Ware; m. C. Warren Cagle, June 1, 1964; 1 child, C. Scott. BS, Drury Coll., 1963; MS, Pittsburg (Kans.) State U., 1969, EdS, 1977; EdD, U. Ark., 1985. Cert. elem. sch. tchr., adminstr., Mo. Tchr. Ferguson-Florrisant (Mo.) Sch. Dist., 1963-64, Strafford (Mo.) Pub. Sch. Dist., 1964-65; tchr. Neosho (Mo.) R-5 Sch. Dist., 1965-66, tchr. remedial reading, 1966-78, ednl. resource tchr., 1978-83, asst. supt., 1983-84, elem. prin., 1984-86; asst. prof. Mo. So. State Coll., Joplin, 1986-90; dir. elem. edn. Neosho R-5 Sch. Dist., 1990—; mem. policy coun. Head Start program, Neosho, 1992-95; mem. adv. bd. curriculum and assessment task force Mo. Dept. Elem. and Secondary Edn., Jefferson City, 1994-95. Contbr. chpt. to: Project Construct: A Curriculum Guide, 1992. Bd. dirs. Family Violence Coun., Joplin, 1993-96; com. mem. Gov.'s Goal 2000 Task Force, Jefferson City, 1994-95. Mem. Internat. Reading Assn. (pres. Mo. State chpt. 1975-76), Neosho C. of C. (mem. edn. com. 1990-96), Soroptomists (mem. various coms. 1991-96), Delta Kappa Gamma (scholarship chairperson 1991-93, Golden Anniversary scholar 1983, Delta State Achievement award 1996). Mem. Ch. of Christ. Office: Neosho R-5 Sch Dist 201 N Wood St Neosho MO 64850

CAGLE, JUDITH ANN, educator; b. Mechanicsburg, Pa., Mar. 3, 1946; d. John Walter and Juen Eletta (Hartman) Guy; m. Bernard LaDon Mince, May 15, 1964 (div. Jan. 1981); children: John Bernard, Stephanie Ann; m. Ronald Baldwin Cagle, Aug. 8, 1981; children: Ryan Bradly, Darren. AA in Bus. Adminstrn., Rollins Coll., 1983, BSBA, 1986; MS in Human Resources Mgmt., Fla. Inst. Tech., 1992. Television weather announcer Air Force Eastern Test Range, Cocoa Beach, Fla., 1966-70; cmty. vol. leader C of C., Melbourne, Fla., 1972-75; restaurant owner LaPlaza, Melbourne, Fla., 1975-77; mgr. human resources Harris Corp., Melbourne, Fla., 1977-91; cons. human resources pvt. practive, Palm Bay, Fla., 1991-95; instr. Christa McAuliffe Elem. Sch., Palm Bay, Fla., 1995—. Spokesperson GreaterMelbourne C. of C. Tourism Divsn., 1975. Mem. AAUW. Republican. Home: 390 Huntsville St NE Palm Bay FL 32907

CAGLE, PAULETTE BERNICE, mental health administrator and psychologist; b. Ft. Worth, July 14, 1944; d. James Frank and Cordelia Pauline (Bourke) C. BS, North Tex. State U., 1972; MA, So. Meth. U., 1976. Lic. chem. dependency counselor; cert. diagnostic and evaluation psychologist; qualified mental health profl. Part-time psychometrist Jack Waxler, Psychologist, Richardson, Tex., 1973-77; social worker Vernon (Tex.) State Hosp., 1977-78, psychologist, 1978-88; adminstr. tech. programs Wichita Falls (Tex.) State Hosp., 1988-91, assoc. dir. mgmt. and support, 1991—; cons. mem. quality improvement coun. Vernon State Hosp., 1992—. Co-founder and mem. Cmty. Svcs. Quality Assurance Dirs. of Tex., 1993—; designated contact Mental Health Disaster Assistance, Austin, 1994—; mem. Wichita County Mental Health Assn., 1992—. Named Sister of the Yr. Sisterhood of Freedom, 1991. Mem. Am. Counseling Assn., Am. Mental Health Counselors Assn., Tex. Assn. Alcoholism and Drug Abuse Counselors, Internat. Assn. of Marriage and Family Counselors. Office: Texas Dept Mental Health Wichita Falls State Hosp PO Box 300 Wichita Falls TX 76307-0300

CAHANA, ALICE LOK, artist; b. Budapest, Hungary, Feb. 7, 1929; d. Eugene Lok and Tereza (Schwartz) Lok; m. Moshe Cahana, Dec. 25, 1951; children: Ronnie michael, Rina. Student, Rice U., 1950, Houston U., 1970-78. Kindergarten tchr. Tel Aviv, 1950-52, Boras, Sweden; relgious schs. Sweden, 1952-56; speaker, 1971-81, artist, 1975-83; cons. Houston Ind. Sch., 1981. Art exhibits: From Ashes To The Rainbow, 1987-89, and various others, Sárvar-Auschwitz Yad-Vashem, Isreal, 1995, Remembering Not to Forget Opening Exhibit, Holocaust Mus., Houston, 1996. Recognized by Pres. Clinton at Am. Gathering of Holocaust Survivors as one who transcends the pain, is an internationally known artist, 1995. Mem. Holocaust Mus. Jewish. Home: 9002 Ferris Houston TX 77096

CAHELA, ROXANNE BOWDEN, home health nurse; b. Anniston, Ala., Nov. 24, 1963; d. Johnny Jeff and Naomi Wynelle (Craft) Bowden; m. Roy Wade Cahela, Dec. 8, 1984; children: Jessica Renee, Brandon Wade. BSN, U. Ala., Birmingham, 1986. Cardiovascular intensive care, open heart recovery nurse Med. Ctr. East, Birmingham, 1986-87; spl. care unit staff nurse Boaz-Albertville Med. Ctr., Boaz, Ala., 1987-89; home health nurse coord. Etowah County Health Dept., Gadsden, Ala., 1989-95; Area 5 home health mgr., Dept. Pub. Health State of Ala., Gadsden, 1995—. Bd. dirs. Caregivers in the Middle Inc. Support Group, Gadsden, 1993-94; coun. agy. execs. United Way, 1994-95. Mem. Home Health Care Nurses Assn. Republican. Baptist. Home: 1116 Broadwell Rd Boaz AL 35957 Office: Ala Dept Pub Health Area 5 PO Box 8425 Gadsden AL 35952

CAHILL, CATHERINE M., orchestra executive. Gen. mgr. N.Y. Philharmonic, N.Y.C. Office: New York Philharmonic Avery Fisher Hall 10 Lincoln Center Plz New York NY 10023-6912*

CAHILL, ELIZABETH MARY YOUNG, social service administrator; b. Las Vegas, Nev., Mar. 3, 1962; d. Ralph and Jessie (Tolan) Young; divorced. BA in English, U. Calif., Berkeley, 1984; postgrad., San Francisco State U., 1996—. Lic. real estate, Nev. Office mgr. C&F Sports, Las Vegas, 1984-86; bartender, mgr. Mirage Lounge, Las Vegas, 1987-88; advt. exec. Nat. Media, Inc., L.A., 1988-89; area coord. Women in Cmty. Svc., L.A., 1989-94; regional dir. Women in Cmty. Svc., San Francisco, 1994—. Recipient Regents scholarship U. Calif., Berkeley, 1980-84. Mem. NAFE, NOW. Democrat.

CAHN, MEREDITH, health consultant; b. Kew Gardens, N.Y., June 13, 1955; d. S. Lee Cahn and Eileen (Lurie) Finston; m. Samuel Isaac Doctors, Aug. 28, 1988; children: Rebecca, Olga Doctors-Cahn. BA, U. Pa., 1977; MPH, U. Calif. Berkeley, 1985. Program asst. James Bowman Assocs., San Francisco, 1984-86; program dir. family planning Somona County People for Econ. Opportunity, Santa Rosa, Calif., 1986-87; dir. Women's Needs Ctr. Haight Ashbury Free Clinics, San Francisco, 1987-91; cons. self-employed San Anselmo, Calif., 1991—; mem. Women's Health Com., San Francisco, 1987-91. Chair, bd. dirs. Vanguard Pub. Found., San Francisco, 1982-89; co-pres. Sisterhood Congregation Rodef Sholom, San Rafael, Calif., 1995—. Mem. APHA, NOW, Calif. Reproductive Health Assn. (bd. dirs. 1986-94, 96—), Am. Friends of the Royal Shakespeare Co., Overseas Mem. Royal Shakespeare Co., Women of Reform Judaism. Democrat. Jewish.

CAHN, RUTH PATRICIA, percussionist; b. McKeesport, Pa., Mar. 17, 1946; d. Thomas Allen and Vera Emilia (Schoeller) McLean; m. William L. Cahn, Sept. 9, 1968. BMus, Eastman Sch., 1968. Percussionist Rochester (N.Y.) Philharm., 1968—, devel. dir., 1993-94; tchr. Nazareth Coll., Rochester, 1972-76; sr. assoc. in percussion Eastman Sch. of Music, Rochester, 1977—; artist in residence City Sch. Dist., Rochester, 1977—; dir. music horizons Eastman Sch., Rochester, 1984-96. Bd. dirs. Operatheatre, Rochester, 1990-92, Rochester Philharm., 1988-92; pres. bd. dirs. Project UNIQUE, Rochester, 1995—. Grantee Arts for Greater Rochester, 1974. Mem. Percussive Arts Soc., Nat. Soc. of Fund Raising Execs., Mu Phi Epsilon (Musician of Yr. 1994). Office: Eastman Sch of Music 26 Gibbs St Rochester NY 14604

CAHOON, SUSAN ALICE, lawyer; b. Jacksonville, Fla., Oct. 14, 1948; d. Robert Harold and Alice (Dubberly) C. BA, Emory U., 1968; JD, Harvard U., 1971. Bar: Ga. 1971, U.S. Dist. Ct. (no. dist.) Ga. 1971, U.S. Dist. Ct. (no. & ea. dists.) Tex. 1977, U.S. Dist. Ct. (mid. dist.) Ga. 1978, U.S. Dist. Ct. (we. dist.) Wis. 1979, U.S. Supreme Ct. 1979, U.S. Ct. Appeals (4th cir.) 1980, U.S. Dist. Ct. (so. dist.) Ga. 1981, U.S. Ct. Appeals (5th, 11th & D.C. cirs.) 1981, U.S. Ct. Appeals (6th cir.) 1983. Assoc. Kilpatrick & Cody, Atlanta, 1971-76, ptnr., 1977—. Contbr. articles to law revs., chpts. to books. Chmn. Stone Mountain Park Authority, Atlanta, 1984-93; v.p. Fulton County Divsn. Am. Heart Assn., Atlanta, 1992-93, pres., 1993-95; v.p. USO Coun. Ga., Inc., Atlanta, 1992—; bd. dirs. Atlanta Conv. & Visitors Bur., 1992—, vice chmn. 1996, Metro Atlanta Crime Commn., 1990-92, Fed. Defender PRogram, 1987-92; pres. Atlanta Area Alumni Club, 1975; mem. Leadership Atlanta, 1982, LeadershipGa., 1989. Fellow Am. Coll. Trial Lawyers, Am. Bar Found., Ga. Bar Found.; mem. ABA (litigation sect. com. chair 1986-88, com. chair 1995—), Ga. Bar Assn. (com. chair 1980-81), Atlanta Bar Assn. (bd. dirs. 1981-87, Leadership award 1991), D.C. Bar Assn., Am. Law Inst., Phi Beta Kappa, Omicron Delta Kappa, Lumpkin Inns of Ct. (master bencher). Baptist. Home: 2040 Old Dominion Rd Atlanta GA 30350-4619 Office: Kilpatrick & Cody 1100 Peachtree St NE Ste 2800 Atlanta GA 30309-4528

CAIN, BECKY C., association executive; married; 1 child. BA in Polit. Sci., W.Va. U., 1969. Social studies tchr. Suttle Sch., Perry County, Ala., 1969-70; Am. govt., econs. tchr. Selma (Ala.) High Sch., 1970-72; nat. pres. League of Women Voters, Washington, 1992—; guest editorial columnist Charleston (W.Va.) Gazette Newspaper, 1984-88. Campaign coord. Citizens for Progress Through Edn., 1987-88, People for Better Govt., 1989; facilitator effectiveness program W.Va. Sch. Bd., 1989-91; active local League of Women Voters, W.Va., from 1975, mem. local bd. dirs., 1975-84, mem. state league bd. dirs., 1977-81, mem. legis. action com., 1977-81, local league pres., 1981-83, state league pres., 1983-87, chair League Women Voters W.Va. Endowment Trust, 1983-92, nominating com. chair, 1984-85, off-bd. dirs. League Women Voters U.S. Agrl. Study Com., 1986-88, mem. nominating com., 1986-87, bd. dirs. nat. league, 1988-92, trustee league edn. fund, 1988-92, chair nat. league program planning, 1989-90, chair nat. coun. planning, 1990-91, co-chair nat. 75th anniversary, 1991-92.; chair City of St. Albans Charter Rev. Com., 1979-80, W.Va. Citizens for Passage Constl. Amendment # 2, 1987; active City of St. Albans Parks and Recreation Com., 1982-86, Kanawha County Metro Govt. Com., 1985-86, W.Va. Legis. Higher Edn. Study Commn., 1986-87, Dept. Natural Resources Dir. Groundwater Policy and Tech. Adv. Com., 1986-87, State Bd. Edn. Blue Ribbon Commn. on Ednl. Reform, 1987, W.Va. Solid Waste Mgmt. Bd. Solid Waste Mgmt. Task Force, 1991-92, W.Va. C. of C. Health Care Task Force, 1990-92, W.Va. Election Commn., 1990—, W.Va. Divsn. Environ. Reorganization Adv. Bd., 1992-93, Nat. Recycling Adv. Coun., 1992—; mem. adv. bd. Ctr. Environ. Learning, Region III EPA, 1987-93; bd. dirs. Leadership W.Va., Inc., 1990-95, Citizens for Tax Justice, 1993—; mem. adv. commn. on election law ABA, 1992-95; mem. exec. com. Leadership Conf. on Civil Rights, 1992—, U.S. EPA Safe Drinking Water adv. com., 1993—, nat. adv. com. UNICEF, 1994—, bd. dirs. Health Alliance, 1994—. Recipient Common Cause Pub. Svc. award, 1988, W.Va. Celebrate Women Outstanding Achievement award, 1988, Corma A. Mowrey Meml. award W.Va. Edn. Assn., 1992, W.Va. U. Polit. Sci. Disting. Alumna award, 1994, Charleston Area W.Va. C. of C. Expect the Best award, 1996. Mem. League Women Voters U.S., Common Cause. Office: League of Women Voters 1730 M St NW Washington DC 20036-4505

CAIN, KAREN MIRINDA, musician, educator; b. Anna, Ill., Feb. 25, 1944; d. James Paul and Margaret Camilla (Sinks) C. MusB, So. Ill. U., 1966, MusM in Voice and Choral Conducting, 1967; postgrad., Trinity Coll., Washington, 1985. Cert. music tchr., Md. Choral music tchr. Prince George's County, Md., 1969-71; music tchr. class piano Montgomery County, Md., 1972-89; music tchr., founder of studio Rockville, Md., 1972—; co-founder, dir., arranger, mem. chorale staff, instr. music theory, profl. madrigal ensemble The Renaissance Revelers, 1985—; choral music dir. and soloist various chs. and synagogues, Rockville, Md., 1972-92; singer Paul Hill Chorale, Washington, 1982-90, mem. chorale staff, music theory instr., 1984-90; contbr. minstrel and history guilds, performer, mem., Md. Renaissance Festival, 1987—. Dir., editor: (CD) Renaissance Romance, 1994; arranger choral works featured on Renaissance Romance; dir.; performance at The Lutheran Reformation Svc. held at The Washington Nat. Cathedral, 1995, The White House, Kennedy Ctr.; co-author (with John Sinks): Sinks: A Family History, 1980. Mem. AAUW, Md. Music Tchrs. Assn., Montgomery County Class Piano Tchrs. Assn., Mu Phi Epsilon.

CAIN, MADELINE ANN, mayor; b. Cleve., Nov. 21, 1949; d. Edward Vincent and Mary Rita (Quinn) C. BA, Ursuline Coll., 1973; MPA, Cleve. State U., 1985. Tchr. St. Augustine Acad., Lakewood, Ohio, 1973-75; clk. coun. legis. aide Lakewood City Coun., 1981-85; legis. liaison Cuyahoga County Bd. Commrs., Cleve., 1985-88; mem. Ohio Ho. of Reps., Columbus, 1989-95; mayor City of Lakewood, Lakewood, Ohio, 1995—. Mem. Cudell Neighborhood Improvement Corp., West Blvd. Neighborhood Assn.; trustee Malachi House. Mem. Lakewood Bus. and Profl. Women, Lakewood C. of C., City Club. Democrat. Roman Catholic. Office: Ohio Ho of Reps Lakewood City Hall 12650 Detroit Ave Lakewood OH 44107

CAIN, PATRICIA JEAN, accountant; b. Decatur, Ill., Sept. 28, 1931; d. Paul George and Jean Margaret (Horne) Jacka; m. Dan Louis Cain, July 12, 1952; children: Mary Ann, Timothy George, Paul Louis. Student, U. Mich., 1949-52, Pasadena (Calif.) City Coll., 1975-76; BS in Acctg., Calif. State U., L.A., 1977, MBA, 1978; M in Taxation, Golden Gate U., Los Angeles, 1988; Diploma in Pastry, Hotel Ritz, France, 1991. CPA, Calif.; cert. personal fin. planner; cert. advanced fin. planner. Tax supr. Stonefield & Josephson, L.A., 1979-87; CFO Loubella Extendables, Inc., L.A., 1987-96; pvt. practice Pasadena, Calif., 1996—; participant program in bus. ethics U. So. Calif., L.A., 1986; trainer for A-Plus in house tax Arthur Andersen & Co., 1989-90; instr. Becker CPA Rev. Course, 1989-93. Bd. dirs. Sierra Madre coun. Girl Scouts U.S.A., 1968-73, treas., 1973-75, nat. del., 1975; mem. Town Hall, L.A., 1987—, L.A. Bus. Forum, 1991—. Listed as one of top six tax experts in L.A. by Money mag., 1987. Mem. AICPA (chair nat. tax teleconf. 1988, taxation com./forms subcom. 1994—), Am. Women's Soc. CPAs (bd. dirs. 1986-87, v.p. 1987-90), Calif. Soc. CPAs (chair free tax assistance program 1983-85, high road com. 1985-86, chair pub. rels. com. 1985-89, microcomputer users discussion group taxation com., fin. com./speaker computer show and conf. 1987-93, planning com. and speaker San Francisco Tax and Microcomputer show 1988, state com. on taxation 1991—, speaker Tax Update 1992, dir. L.A. chpt. 1993-95, v.p. 1995-96), Internat. Arabian Horse Assn., Wrightwood Country Club, Beta Alpha Psi. Democrat. Episcopalian.

CAIN, SANDRA KAY, secondary education educator; b. Beardstown, Ill., Mar. 30, 1949; d. Roy Martin and Helen Faye (Leatherman) Doll; m. Rodney Lee Cain, June 22, 1975; children: Matthew Martin, Philip John. BA, MacMurray Coll., 1971. Cert. edn., spl.-music grades K-12. Jr. and sr. high choir Virden (Ill.) Sch. Dist., 1971-74; sr. high vocal music Harlem H.S., Machesney Park, Ill., 1974-77; music and choir tchr. grades K-12 Faith Acad., Rockford, Ill., 1979-82, 84-85; jr. high vocal music tchr. Harlem Jr. High, Loves Park, Ill., 1985-88; sr. high vocal music and drama tchr. Harlem H.S., Machesney Park, 1988—; music dir. Faith Ctr., Rockford, 1978-89, Grace Family Ch., Belvidere, Ill., 1989—. Merit badge counselor Boy Scouts Am., Machesney Park, 1989-94. Recipient Those Who Excell Recognition, State Bd. Edn. Ill., 1990; named Most Inspirational Tchr., Western Ill. U., 1994. Mem. Am. Choral Dirs. Assn., Ill. Music Educators Assn., Music Educators Nat. Conf., Tri-Music Honor Soc. (state chair 1992—). Republican. Home: 4630 Illinois St Loves Park IL 61111-5851 Office: Harlem High Sch One Huskie Cir Machesney Park IL 61115

CAIN, SUSAN WATSON, mental health counselor; b. Fayetteville, N.C., Feb. 21, 1954; d. George David and Mary Leigh (Parnell) Watson; m. David Harold Cain, Jan. 23, 1993; 1 child, Angela Michelle; stepchildren: Sheila, David Jr., Devita, Debbie. BS in psychology, Pembroke State U., 1980, MA counseling, 1994, DHL, 1994. Nat. Acad. cert. family therapist; lic. profl. counselor, N.C. Dir. March of Dimes Found., Fayetteville, 1984-88; asst. dir., student affairs Pembroke (N.C.) State U., 1989-93; clin. intern Oaks Psychiat. Hosp., Wilmington, N.C., 1993-94; exec. dir. Cape Fear Regional Child Devel., Wilmington, N.C., 1994—; presenter Annual Conf. Child Abuse, N.C., 1993-94. Mem. Mid Carolina Coun. of Govt., 1992, legis. com. N.C. Dir. of Devel. Disabilities, 1994. Grantee Sara Lee Found., 1993, Cannon Found., 1994. Mem. ACA, APA, N.C. Lic. Profl. Counselors Assn., Psi Chi, Chi Sigma Iota, Internat Counseling Honor Soc. Office: Capr Fear Regional Child Devel. 6743 Amsterdam Way Wilmington NC 28405

CAIRNS, DIANE PATRICIA, motion picture executive; b. Fairbanks, Alaska, Mar. 2, 1957; d. Dion Melvin and Marsha Lala (Andrews) C. BBA, U. So. Calif., 1980. Literary agt. Sy Fischer Agy., L.A., 1980-85; sr. v.p. Internat. Creative Mgmt., L.A., 1985-96; sr. v.p. prodn. Universal Pictures, L.A., 1996—. Mem. Acad. Motion Picture Arts and Scis., Women in Film, NOW, Amnesty Internat., L.A. County Mus. of Art, Mus. of Contemporary Art (L.A.).

CAIRNS, PATRICIA WALTERS, artist, educator; b. Orange, Calif., Feb. 10, 1937; d. Milas Earl and Ruth Margaret (Albright) Walters; m. Edward Alan Cairns, July 15, 1956 (div. 1982); children: Peter Thompson, Kirby Edward, Robin Ruth; m. Gerald Walter Lant, Nov. 27, 1987. Student, Stanford U., 1954-56; BFA, U. Denver, 1965; secondary credential art edn., Calif. State U., San Luis Obispo, 1970. Artist, tchr. Denver Pub. Schs., 1966-69; art instr. Calif. State Poly. U., San Luis Obispo, 1970-72; artist, tchr. San Luis Coastal Schs., San Luis Obispo, 1972-94; painting instr. San Luis Obispo Art Ctr., 1994-95, Cuesta Coll. No. Co., Paso Robles, Calif., 1995—; chair art dept. San Luis Obispo H.S., 1983-94; presenter Calif. State Art Edn. Conf., San Diego, 1983. One-person shows include galleries in Morro Bay, Cambria, San Luis Obispo, Claremont, Santa Barbara, Paso Robles, 1987—; art work published in Best of Watercolor, People: in Watercolor, Artistic Touch II. Recipient Best of Show award Calif. Mid.-State Fair, 1991, awards for juried shows N.W. Watercolor Soc., Calif. Watercolor Assn., Women Artists of West. Mem. Nat. Mus. Women in Art, Nat. Watercolor Soc. (assoc.), Cen. Coast Watercolor Soc. (bd. dirs. 1980—, pres. 1996—), Gold Coast Watercolor Soc. (signature mem.), Watercolor West Soc. (juried assoc.), Paso Robles Art Assn., San Luis Obispo Art Assn. Office: Hill House Studio/Gallery 4895 El Verano Atascadero CA 93422

CAIRNS, SARA ALBERTSON, physical education educator; b. Bloomsburg, Pa., July 18, 1939; d. Robert Wilson and Sara (Porter) Albertson; m. Thomas Cairns, Apr. 13, 1968. BS in Edn., Pa. State U., 1961; MS in Edn., West Chester U., 1965. Cert. tchr., Pa., Del., prin., Del.; adaptive p.e. specialist. Phys. edn. tchr., coach Cen. Columbia County High Sch., Bloomsburg, Pa., 1961-64; phys. edn. tchr. Christina Sch. Dist., Newark, Del., 1964—; cons. U. Del., Newark, 1984—, coop. tchr., 1965—; area coord. New Castle (Del.) County Parks and Recreation, 1973—; presenter in field. Contbr. articles to profl. publs. Chair Leasure Elem. Sch. campaign United Fund, 1987-91. Recipient Outstanding Svc. award New CAstle County Parks and Recreation, 1985. Mem. NEA, AAUW, AAHPERD, Del. Assn. Health, Phys. Edn., Recreation and Dance (v.p. dance 1991-94, exec. bd.), Del. State Edn. Assn. Democrat. Presbyterian. Home: 40 Vansant Rd Newark DE 19711-4839 Office: Leasure Elem Sch 925 Bear Corbitt Rd Bear DE 19701-1323

CALABRESE, MARYLYN E. JONES, writing consultant; b. Scranton, Pa., Nov. 12, 1935; 1 child, David. AB, Bryn Mawr Coll.; MAT, Wesleyan U.; MA in English, U. Pa., PhD in Edn. Tchr., workshop leader, cons. Conestoga Sr. High Sch., Berwyn, Pa., 1967-76; chair English dept. Conestoga Sr. High Sch., 1982-91; writing cons. pvt. practice Malvern, Pa., 1991—. Contbr. articles to profl. jours. and papers to pubs. Recipient Decade of Equity award Mid-Atlantic Ctr. Sex Equity, Am. U., 1982. Home and office: 9 Madeline Dr Malvern PA 19355-2014

CALABRESE, ROSALIE SUE, arts management consultant, writer; b. N.Y.C., Feb. 17, 1938; d. Julius and Florence (Tuck) Hochman; m. Anthony J. Calabrese, June 15, 1960 (div.); 1 child, Christopher. BA in Journalism, CCNY, 1959. Asst. news editor Electronic News, N.Y.C., 1960; asst. to publicist Abner Klipstein, N.Y.C., 1963; asst. to producer Leonard Field, N.Y.C., 1964; mgr. Am. Composers Alliance, N.Y.C., 1969-85, exec. dir., gen. mgr., 1985-94; dir. Rosalie Calabrese Mgmt., N.Y.C., 1983—; music advisor Phyllis Rose Dance Co., N.Y.C., 1987—, also bd. dirs.; sec. bd. dirs. Am. Composers Orch., N.Y.C., 1987-93; bd. dirs. 1st Ave. Ensemble, Godlen Fleece Ltd., Friends Am. Composers, treas., 1991-94; mem. adv. bd. Downtown Music Prodns., 1991—, Joan Miller's Dance Players, N.Y.C., 1991-94; mem. adv. bd. Copland House, 1996—. Author, lyricist: (musicals) A Hell of An Angel, Simone, Not in Earnest, Murdering MacBeth, Pop Life, Does Anyone Here Speak Arabic?, Friends and Relations, Double-Play; assoc. producer, treas. box office: (play) Courtyard, 1959, The Mime and Me; co-producer: various plays at White Lake (N.Y.) Playhouse, also packaged tours for Prodn. Assocs.; dir. night club acts for Florence Hayle; lyricist with various composers; contbr. short stories and poetry to lit. and nat. mags. Mem. Dramatists Guild, Broadcast Music Inc., Am. Music Ctr., Poets and Writers, Poetry Soc. Am. Office: Rosalie Calabrese Mgmt Box 20580 Park West Sta New York NY 10025-1521

CALABRO, JOANNA JOAN SONDRA, artist; b. Waterbury, Conn., Dec. 2, 1938; d. Theodore Gruwien and Madeleine Elizabeth (Raynor) Reinhard; m. John Paul Calabro, Oct. 15, 1960; 1 child, Victor Theodore. Student, Paier Sch. Art, 1965-66, Mus. of Fine Arts Sch., 1976, Rice U., 1977; student of sculpture with, Bruno Lucchesi, Pietrasanta, Italy, 1982. Art instr. at gallery workshops Houston, 1975-78; co-owner Archway Gallery, Houston, 1975-78, Fine Arts of Rockport, Mass., 1989—. One woman shows include Five Star Gallery, Houston, 1974-75, Roberts Gallery, Houston, 1977, Dayton (Ohio) Soc. of Painters, 1983, Wilmington (Ohio) Coll., 1983, Rockport Art Assn., 1989, 92; represented in permanent collections at Am. Embassy, Bratislava, Slovak Republic. Sculpture instr. for merit badge Sam Houston Area coun. Boy Scouts Am., Houston, 1978; juror for scholastic art shows, Tex., 1975, Ohio, 1982, numerous other art shows, Conn., Tex., Ohio, Mass., 1970—; mem. art coun. Bd. Selectmen, Rockport, 1994. Recipient numerous awards including 1st Place award Champions Art, 1974, Am. Pen & Brush Women, 1975, Conn. Classic Art, 1978, Martha Moore Meml. award, 1989, Richard Ricchia Meml. award, 1990, R.V. T. Steeves award, 1990, William N. Ryan award, 1991. Mem. Am. Artist Profl. League, Rockport Art Assn. (bd. dirs. 1992-93), Guild Boston Artists, The Copley Soc. of Boston, Am. Medallic Sculpture Assn., Federation Internat. de la Me'daille. Studio: 32 Main St Rockport MA 01966-1441

CALAHAN, PATRICIA SUSAN, curriculum consultant; b. Cin., Mar. 31, 1961; d. Donald and Martha Calahan. BS, U. Mich., 1983; MEd, Ea. Mich. U., Ypsilanti, 1987. Tchr. presch. handicapped Houston Ind. Sch. Dist., 1983-85; tchr. 1st grade Banana Co., Panama, 1985-86; tchr. kindergarten to 4th grade Good News (Alaska) Ind. Sch. Dist., 1986; grad. asst. Ea. Mich. U., Ypsilanti, 1987-88; tchr. elem. emotionally impaired Fenton (Mich.) Ind. Sch. Dist., 1988; tchr. presch. emotionally impaired Redford Union (Mich.) Ind. Sch. Dist., 1989-90; tchr. juvenile delinquests State of Mich., Whitmore Lake, 1989-91; tchr. Maxey Boys Tng. Sch., Mich., 1990-94, U. Toledo, Ohio, 1994—; Instr. Columbia Coll., Mo. Fellow U. Toledo, 1993.

CALAMITA, KATHRYN ELIZABETH, nursing administrator; b. Portland, Maine, Oct. 12, 1943; d. Maurice Daniel and Eleanor Elizabeth (Sullivan) Casey; m. John Joseph Calamita, Jan. 9, 1965; children: Angela Marie, Carla Anne, Daniel John. RN, Mercy Hosp. Sch. Nursing, Springfield,

Mass., 1964; student, Midwestern State U., Wichita Falls, Tex., 1979-86, Vernon Regional Coll., 1987; BS in Bus., St. Joseph's Coll., Windham, Maine, 1992. Staff nurse Mercy Hosp., Springfield, 1964; med/surg. nurse Wichita Gen. Hosp., Wichita Falls, Tex., 1976-77, nurse ICU, 1977-79, supr. dept. nursing, 1979-86, assoc. adminstr. nursing dept., 1986-92; health facility adminstr. Wichita Falls Rehab. Hosp., 1992; rehab. nurse Bay Convalescent and Rehab. Ctr., Panama City, Fla., 1993-94; asst. DON L.A. Wagner Nursing and Rehab. Ctr., Panama City, Fla., 1994—. Mem. ANA (cert. in mgmt., 1995), FNA. Democrat. Roman Catholic.

CALBERT, CATHLEEN MARY, writing educator, poet; b. Jackson, Mich., June 2, 1955; d. Emile and Mary Helen (Weickart) Calbert; m. Christopher Lewis Mayo, Aug. 1, 1992. BA, U. Calif., Berkeley, 1977; MA, Syracuse U., 1984; PhD, U. Houston, 1989. Asst. prof. R.I. Coll., Providence, 1990-95, assoc. prof., 1995—. Author: Lessons in Space (poetry). Recipient Nation Discovery Prize in Poetry, 1990. Mem. MLA, Assoc. Writing Programs. Office: Rhode Island College 600 Mt Pleasant Providence RI 02908

CALCATERRA, REGINA MARIE, lobbyist; b. Central Islip, N.Y., Nov. 9, 1966; m. Louis G. Delli-Pizzi, Oct. 20, 1990 (div. Sept. 1994). BA, SUNY, New Paltz, 1988; JD, Seton Hall U., Newark, 1996. Assoc. advocate Ea. Paralyzed Vets. Assn., Jackson Heights, N.Y., 1988-91; asst. accessibility planner N.J. Transit, Newark, 1991-93; exec. asst. to dep. comptroller City of N.Y., 1994-95, dir. intergovtl. rels. to comptroller, 1995—; gymnastics coach All-Am. Gymnastics, Maspeth, N.Y., 1989-92. Chair bd. dirs. RFK Dem. Assn., Forest Hills, N.Y., 1992—; field ops. coord. Hevesi '93, Forest Hills, 1993; founder Westchester Advocacy Force on Disability Issues, 1990-91; bd. dirs. N.J. Transit Spl. Svcs. Adv. Com., Newark, 1988-91, Nassau County Transp. Citizen Adv. Com., Mineola, 1988-91, Suffolk County Handicapped Adv. Bd., Hauppauge, 1988-91, Chinese Asian Bi-Lingual Edn. Com./N.Y.C. Bd. Edn., Bklyn., 1996—. Mem. NOW, Govt. Affairs Profls. Assn. Home: 372 Fifth Ave #3L New York NY 10018 Office: New York City Comptroller One Centre St Rm 709 New York NY 10007

CALDWELL, ANGELA DAWN, dietetics educator, consultant; b. Pocahontas, Ark., June 21, 1966; d. Charles Floyd and Bonnie Faye (Hayes) Collins; m. Ricky Wayne Caldwell, June 30, 1984; children: Nicholas Wayne, Amanda Dawn. AA, Crowley's Ridge Coll., Paragould, Ark., 1986; BS, Harding U., Searcy, Ark., 1988; Cert. of internship, U. Ark. Med. Scis., Little Rock, 1989; MS, Ark. State U., Jonesboro, 1994. Reg. dietitian; lic. dietitian, Ark. Foodsvc. employee Randolph Co. Med. Ctr., Pocahontas, 1982-86; clin. dietitian St. Bernards Regional Med. Ctr., Jonesboro, 1989-91; cons. dietitian Black River Area Devel. Head Start, Pocahontas, Ark., 1994—; dietetics instr. Black River Technical Coll., Pocahontas, 1991—; mem. health adv. com. BRAD Head Start, Pocahontas, 1994—; program reviewer Dietary Mgrs. Assn., 1996—. Mem. bd. dirs. Am. Heart Assn., Randolph County, Ark., 1995—. Recipient Recognized Young Dietitian award Ark. Dietetic Assn., 1994. Mem. Am. Dietetic Assn., Ark. Consulting Dietitians (chair 1996—), Northeast Ark. Dietetic Assn. (pres. 1991-92). Mem. Ch. of Christ. Office: Black River Tech Coll Hwy 304 E PO Box 468 Pocahontas AR 72455

CALDWELL, ANITA M., journalism educator; b. Amityville, N.Y., Dec. 7, 1951; d. Irving and Ida (Horowitz) Schwartz. BS in Music Edn., Hartt Coll. Music, 1975; MS in Counseling, Ctrl. Conn. State Coll., 1980; MA in Journalism, U. Ariz., 1994. Pub. rels. assoc. Hartford (Conn.) Stage Co., 1984-85; freelance reporter Hartford, 1985-87; reporter Manchester (Conn.) Evening Herald, 1987-88, The Hartford Courant, 1989-92; freelance reporter Tucson (Ariz.) Citizen, 1992-95; asst. prof. journalism Okla. State U., Stillwater, 1995—; adj. instr. journalism Manchester (Conn.) C.C., 1987, 89, U. Hartford, 1989, 91, U. Ariz., Tucson, 1992-94; mem. media adv. bd. Manchester C.C., 1987-89. Spkrs. Newspapers for Edn., Conn., 1987-92; panelist S.W. Popular Culture Assn., Okla., 1996, LWV, Okla., 1996; rep. United Way Campaign, Okla., 1996. Dean's Incentive grantee Okla. State U., 1996. Mem. Assn. for Edn. in Journalism and Mass Comm., Soc. Profl. Journalists, Okla. State U. Student Svcs. Com. (sec. 1995—). Office: Okla State Univ 206 Paul Miller Bldg Stillwater OK 74078

CALDWELL, ANN W. CASE, academic administrator; b. Rochester, N.Y., Dec. 3, 1943; d. Ralph Everett and Constance Ann (McCoy) Wickins; m. Herbert Cline Caldwell, Sept. 17, 1966; children: Constance Haley, Robert James. BA in English Lit., U. Mich., 1965. Reporter Democrat & Chronicle, Rochester, 1961-64; asst. to dean Harvard Grad. Sch. of Edn., Cambridge, Mass., 1965-70; editor alumni quarerly Harvard Grad. Sch. of Edn., Cambridge, 1968-71; freelance editor, writer Harvard U. and Radcliffe, Cambridge, 1971-73; assoc. sec. Philips Acad., Andover, Mass., 1973-80; v.p. for planning and resources Wheaton Coll., Norton, Mass., 1980-90; assoc. dir. Mus. Fine Arts, Boston, 1990-91; v.p. for devel. Brown U., Providence, 1991—; trustee Women's Edn. and Indsl. Union, Boston, 1989-91. Contbr. chpt. to book. Chair Bicentennial Com., Newburyport, Mass., 1974-76, Citizens Adv. Com./Pub. Sch., Newburyport, 1979-80; mem. adv. com. Vols. in Action, Providence, 1995—. Mem. Coun. for Advancement and Support of Edn. (trustee, sec. dist. 1 1985-87, trustee, sec. nat. 1987-89), Women in Devel. Boston (founder, pres. 1984-86), Chilton Club, Univ. Club (Providence), Phi Delta Kappa. Office: Brown Univ Box 1893 Providence RI 02912

CALDWELL, ANNA MARIA LUISA, artist, sculptor; b. Charleston, W.Va., Dec. 23, 1961; d. Charles William and Stellina Giovanna (Hinter Wipflinger) C.; m. Robert Eric Hickman, July 24, 1993. BA, U. Iowa, 1986, MFA, 1988. mem. adv. com. Sculpture Ctr., N.Y.C., 1985. One-woman shows include U. Iowa, Iowa City, 1987, CSPS Gallery, Cedar Rapids, Iowa, 1992, U. Minn., Mpls., 1995, Art in General, N.Y.C., 1996; exhibited in group shows at U. Iowa, 1987, Johnson County Art Ctr., Iowa City, 1988, Epoché, Bklyn., 1990, Taller Latino Americano, N.Y.C., 1990, Minor Injury, Bklyn., 1990, 91, Davol Ctr. Art Gallery, Providence, 1991, The Right Bank Gallery, Bklyn., 1991, 92, Grand Street Fair, Bklyn., 1991, Keep Refrigerated, Bklyn., 1992, Galleria El Bohio, N.Y.C., 1992, Tribeca 148 Gallery, N.Y.C., 1992, Artist's Space, N.Y.C., 1992, Herron Test-Site, Bklyn., 1992, Mitchell White Gallery, N.Y.C., 1992, Lehman Coll. Art Gallery, Bronx, 1993, U. Ill., Urbana-Champagne, 1993, Tompkins Square Park, N.Y.C., 1993, Human Fest, Bklyn., 1993, Four Walls, Bklyn., 1993, 494 Gallery, N.Y.C., 1993, CSPS Gallery, 1993, White Columns, N.Y.C., 1993, 94, 95, U. West Fla., Pensicola, 1994, Roosevelt Island for Pub. Sculpture, N.Y.C., 1994, Crest Hardware Show, Bklyn., 1994, 95, 96, Sauce Gallery, Bklyn., 1994, Borbonico di Avellino, Italy, 1994, City Without Walls, Newark, 1994, Sculpture Ctr., N.Y.C., 1994, 96, Flamingo East, N.Y.C., 1995, McNeese State U., 1995, Arci-Gay Venezia, Venice, Italy, 1995, Art in Gen., N.Y.C., 1995, The Batroom, Bklyn., 1995, 450 Broadway Gallery, N.Y.C., 1995, L.I. Univ. Outdoor Sculpture, Bklyn., 1996. Dir. Williamsburg Art Festival, Bklyn., 1992-93; vol. counselor Creative Workshop for Homeless Children, N.Y.C., 1991. Recipient Artists Space grant, 1991, Best of Show award Roosevelt Island for Pub. Sculpture, 1994, Best of Show award City Without Walls, 1994. Mem. Womens Studio Group.

CALDWELL, CAREY TERESA, museum curator; b. McMinnville, Tenn., July 24, 1954; d. Harold Glenn Caldwell and Nancy Perkins (Bragg) Caldwell-Tedesco. BA in History, Queens Coll., Charlotte, N.C., 1974; postgrad., U. S.C., 1974-75, U. N.C., 1976; MA in Anthropology/Museology, U. Wash., 1987. Archaeology, field, lab. and rsch. asst. Ninety Six (S.C.) Hist. Site, 1974-75; tribal curator Suquamish (Wash.) Indian Tribe, 1977-78, dir. Suquamish Tribal Cultural Ctr. and Mus., 1979-85; cons. Bainbridge Island (Wash.) Japanese-Am. Heritage Project, 1986-87; cons. Fed. Cylinder Project Am. Folklife Ctr., Libr. of Congress, Washington, 1986-87; sr. curator of history The Oakland (Calif.) Mus., 1987—; cons., strategic planner, advisor to numerous mus., orgns., Indian tribes and cmty. groups including Nat. Mus. of Am. Indian, Smithsonian Instn., NEH, Wash. State Heritage Coun., 1978-85; panelist, reviewer NEH, 1986—; grants reviewer Inst. Mus. Svcs., 1986; cons. United Indians of All Tribes Found., Seattle, 1992-96; evaluator, cons. Osage Tribal Mus., 1993; cons. Native Am. Archives Project, 1981-82; cons. Minn. Hist. Soc., 1984-85, 94-95, Western Alliance of Art Adminstrs., 1993-95. Fellow Am. Anthropol. Assn.; mem. Am. Assn. Mus., Western Mus. Assn. (v.p. 1990-92), Coun. for Mus. Anthropology (bd. dirs. 1988-89), Internat. Coun. Mus., Am. Assn. for State and Local History (edn. com. 1981-82, publs. com. 1987-92, program com. 1989, ann. mtg., common agenda adv. bd. 1990-92, award of merit 1993), Wash. Mus. Assn. Democrat. Office: Oakland Mus Calif 1000 Oak St Oakland CA 94607-4820

CALDWELL, COURTNEY LYNN, real estate consultant, lawyer; b. Washington, Mar. 5, 1948; d. Joseph Morton and Moselle (Smith) C. Student, Duke U., 1966-68, U. Calif., Berkeley, 1967, 1968-69; BA, U. Calif., Santa Barbara, 1970, MA, 1975; JD with highest honors, George Washington U., 1982. Bar: D.C. 1984, Wash. 1986, Calif. 1989. Jud. clk. U.S. Ct. Appeals for 9th Cir., Seattle, 1982-83; assoc. Arnold & Porter, Washington, 1983-85, Perkins Coie, Seattle, 1985-88; dir. western ops. MPC Assocs., Inc., Irvine, Calif., 1988-91, sr. v.p., 1991—. Bd. dirs. Univ. Town Ctr. Assn., 1994; bd. dirs. Habitat for Humanity, Orange County, 1993-94, chair legal com., 1994. Named Nat. Law Ctr. Law Rev. Scholar, 1981-82. Mem. Calif. Bar Assn., Wash. State Bar Assn., D.C. Bar Assn., Urban Land Inst. Office: MPC Assocs Inc 1451 Quail St Ste 102 Newport Beach CA 92660-2741

CALDWELL, ETHEL LOUISE LYNCH, academic administrator; b. Chgo., July 16, 1938; d. Samuel Thomas and Louise (Brown) Lynch; m. Robert Caldwell Jr., Sept. 7, 1957 (div. 1968). BS in Bus. Edn., DePaul U., 1976; MS in Counseling Psychology, George Williams Coll., Downers Grove, Ill., 1979, MS in Adminstrn., 1979. Lic. tchr., Ill. Sec. Inland Steel Co., Chgo., 1957-68; adminstrv. asst. 1st Nat. City Bank, St. Thomas, V.I., 1968-71; pers./purchasing mgr. Peoples Bank of V.I., St. Thomas, 1971-73; bus. edn. tchr. Ctrl. YMCA Coll., Chgo., 1976, Chgo. Profl. Coll., 1976-78; rsch. asst. U. Ill., Chgo., 1978-79, rsch. assoc., 1980-81, asst. dir. early outreach, 1981-83, dir. early outreach, 1983—; pres. Lynch Enterprises, Summit, Ill., 1987—; mem. adv. bd. Ctr. for Ednl. R&D U. Ill., Chgo., 1989—, Project Canal, Chgo. Pub. Schs., 1990-92; mem. exec. bd. Chgo. Coun. Postsecondary Edn., 1989-91; lectr. African-Am. Studies Ctr., Smithsonian Inst., Washington, 1992; mem. counselor articulation bd. DePaul U., 1993—; field reader U.S. Dept. Edn., 1993—, U.S. Dept. Energy, 1995; mem. adv. coun. Greater Chgo. Youth Behavior Project, 1993—. Active Chgo. Urban League, Lulac Coun. 5201, 1988-91, Ill. Com. on Black Concerns in Higher Edn., 1989—. Recipient Health Careers Opportunity Program award U.S. Dept. Health and Human Svcs., 1987-80, 93—, Disting. Alumna award Argo Community High Sch., 1993. Mem. Am. Assn. for Higher Edn. (Achievement award 1991), Nat. Assn. for Coll. Admissions Counselors, Assn. Black Women in Higher Edn. (founding mem. Chgo. chpt.). Baptist. Office: U Ill 1919 W Taylor St M/C 969 Chicago IL 60612-7246

CALDWELL, EUGENIA DICKEY, information technology specialist; b. Texarkana, Tex., June 25, 1944; d. Kenneth Hall and Margaret Stuart (Wilson) Dickey; m. John Kershaw Ford, Aug. 17, 1967 (div. 1978); m. Peter Caldwell, Aug. 2, 1980. BA in Math. cum laude, Sweet Briar Coll., 1965; exchange student, St. Andrews (Scotland) Univ., 1993-94. Cert. info. tech. specialist. Database adminstr. U.S. Dept. Agr., New Orleans, 1970-85, Ochsner Med. Found., New Orleans, 1985-87; info. tech. specialist IBM/ISSC Consulting & Systems Integration, San Francisco, 1987—; mem. Info. Tech. Specialist Cert. Bd. Past mem. sustaining adv. previews com. Jr. League San Francisco; past chmn. profl. edn., past chmn. enrichment com., past placement advisor, past vol. preservation resource ctr. Jr. League New Orleans; past co-dir. Duncan Newburg Assn., past chmn. DNA garden com.; bd. dirs. Sweet Briar (Va.) Coll., 1995—. Mem. Nat. Audubon Soc., Golden Gate Audubon Soc., Audubon Canyon Ranch, Sierra Club, Nature Conservancy, World Wildlife Fund, Environ. Def. Fund, Save San Francisco Bay Assn., Nat. Park and Conservation Assn., Calif. Acad. Scis., San Francisco Beautiful, Friends of Urban Forest, Found. San Francisco's Archl. Heritage, Humane Soc., Soc. Calif. Pioneers (woman's aux.), Town & Country Club, Phi Beta Kappa. Office: IBM/ISSC 425 Market St San Francisco CA 94105

CALDWELL, JO ANN KENNEDY, elementary educator; b. Franklin, Va., Oct. 31, 1937; d. Benjamin and Bertha (Cicacco) Kennedy; m. Charles Gary Caldwell, Dec. 23, 1962; 1 child, Richard Blair. BA, Baylor U., 1959; MS, No. Mich. U., 1969, MA, 1970. Cert. tchr., Tex., Mich., Calif. Tchr. Univ. Jr. High Sch./Waco (Tex.) Sch. Dist., Gwinn (Mich.) Middle Sch., No. Mich. Lab. Sch., Marquette, Fairfield (Calif.)-Suisun Unified Sch. Dist.; mentor tchr.; presenter workshops; cons. creative oral langs. activities, choral reading, storytelling Readers Theatre. Recipient Solano County's Celebrate Literacy award, 1994. Mem. NEA, ASCD, Internat. Reading Assn., Calif. Reading Assn., Calif. Tchrs. Assn., Delta Kappa Gamma, Phi Delta Kappa.

CALDWELL, JOYCE A., religious association executive. Student, Luther Coll., Decorah, Iowa, 1968-70; BS in Secondary Edn.-English, U. Wis., Milw., 1973; MA in Edn., Marquette U., 1983. Commd. ch. staff assoc., Am. Luth. Ch.; rostered assoc. in ministry Evang. Luth. Ch. in Am. Sec. Automation Engring., Cedarburg, Wis., 1972-76; edn. and youth dir. Faith Luth. Ch., Cedarburg, 1975-86; tchr. English Cedarburg H.S., 1986-87; with Luth. Human Rels. Assn. Am., Milw., 1987-89; asst. dir. Luth. Human Rels. Assn. Am., 1989-90, exec. dir., 1990—; worship leader Congregation as Confirming Cmty., Am. Luth. Ch. So. Wis. dist., 1985; mem. Luth. Human Rels. Assn. Covenant Congregation Com., 1984-86; workshop leader numerous confs. and dist. events, Luth. Ch., 1977-86; developer tchr. tng. course, Christian Ednl. Media, Inc., A New Church/A New World anti-racism curriculum United Ch. of Christ. Cabinet rep. Greater Milw. Synod Interfaith Conf. Greater Milw., 1988—, mem. visioning com., 1988-90, mem. coun. and exec. com., 1987-89, com. Day of New Beginnings, 1987, mem. Beyond Racism Task Force, 1989—; mem. AIDS Task Force Wis. Conf. of Chs., 1987-90; chair Lakeshore Conf. Edn. Com., Am. Luth. Chs., 1977-82, mem. So. Wis. Dist. Edn. Network, 1978-86. Office: W70 N979 Washington Ave Cedarburg WI 53012

CALDWELL, JUDY CAROL, advertising executive, public relations executive; b. Nashville, Dec. 28, 1946; d. Thomas and Sarah Elizabeth Carter; 1 child, Jessica. BS, Wayne State U., 1969. Tchr. Bailey Mid. Sch., West Haven, Conn., 1969-72; editorial asst. Vanderbilt U., Nashville, 1973-74; editor, graphics designer, field researcher Urban Observatory of Met. Nashville, 1974-77; account exec. Holden and Co., Nashville, 1977-79; bus. tchr. Federated States of Micronesia, 1979-80; dir. advt. Am. Assn. for State and Local History, Nashville, 1980-81; dir. prodn. Mktg. Communications Co., Nashville, 1981-83; ptnr. Victory Images of Tenn., Inc., Nashville, 1990-92; owner, pres. Ridge Hill Corp., Nashville, 1983—.

CALDWELL, MARY ELLEN, English language educator; b. El Paso, Ark., Aug. 6, 1908; d. Clay and Mabel Grace (Coe) Fulks; m. Robert Atchison Caldwell, Feb. 22, 1936; 1 child, Elizabeth. PhB, U. Chgo., 1931, MA, 1933. Instr. English U. Ark., Fayetteville, 1940-42, U. Toledo, 1946-48; from instr. to asst. prof. to assoc. prof. U. N.D., Grand Forks, 1966-79, assoc. prof. emeritus, 1979—, prof. ext. divsn., 1979—. Author: North Dakota Division of the American Association of University Women, 1930-63, A History, 1964; co-author: The North Dakota Division of the American Association of University Women, 1964-84, 2d vol., 1984; contbr. revs. and articles to scholarly jours. Sec. citizen's com. Grand Forks Symphony Assn., 1960-66. Mem. AAUW (life, N.D. state pres. 1968-70), P.E.O., MLA (life), Soc. for Study of Midwestern Lit. (bibliography staff 1973—), Linguistic Cir. of Man. and N.D. (pres. 1981), Melville Soc. Democrat. Episcopalian. Home: 514 Oxford St Grand Forks ND 58203-2847

CALDWELL, NANCY ANN, social worker, nurse; b. Camden, N.J., Nov. 19, 1947; d. Thomas Frances and Nellie Daisy (Diehl) C.; m. Dennis Frank Molnar, Mar. 21, 1970 (div. 1977); 1 child, Rebecca Ann Molnar; m. John Conner Norcross, June 27, 1981; 1 child, Jonathon Andrew Caldwell Norcross. RN, Phila. Gen. Hosp., 1969; BA summa cum laude, R.I. Coll., Providence, 1984; MSW, Marywood Coll., Scranton, Pa., 1987. RN lic. social worker, Pa., profl. nurse, Pa.; cert. diplomate in social work. psychiatric and mental health nurse. Staff nurse med.-surg. and psychiatric units Princeton (N.J.) Hosp., 1970-71; pub. health nurse City of Trenton, N.J., 1972-76; sr. charge nurse mental health unit Cooper Med. Ctr., Camden, N.J., 1976-80; sr. staff nurse Butler Psychiatric Hosp., Brown U. Sch. Medicine, Providence, R.I., 1980-85; social work intern Women's Resource Ctr., Scranton, Pa., 1985-86; social work intern Family Svcs. of Wyoming County, Wilkes-Barre, Pa., 1986-87, family counselor, 1987-92; family therapist Family Svcs. of Lackawanna County, Scranton, 1992-94; supervising clinician Friendship House, Scranton, Pa., 1994-95; family counselor Family Svcs. of Wyoming Valley, Wilkes-Barre, 1995—. Recipient Polizzi Scholarship and Cmty. Svc. medal, 1987. Mem. NASW, ACA, Pa. Assn. Social Workers, Northeastern Pa. Counseling Assn., Internat. Assn. Marriage and Family Counseling, Acad. Cert. Social Workers, Soc. for the Exploration Psychotherapy Integration, Alpha Sigma Lambda. Home: Box 463-F RR3 Lake Ariel PA 18436

CALDWELL, PATRICIA FRANCES, financial consultant, lecturer; b. Columbus, Ohio, Aug. 21, 1942; d. Richard and Elizabeth Frances (McQuiniff) Smith; m. Terry Edward Caldwell, Dec. 19, 1970; children: Carrie Elizabeth, Christina Leigh. BS, Otterbein Coll., 1964; MEd, U. Okla., 1967; PhD, U. Calif., Riverside, 1981. Cert. secondary edn. tchr., Calif., Ohio. Secondary tchr. Copley (Ohio) Jr. High Sch., 1964-65, Apple Valley (Calif.) Jr. High Sch., 1967-68; tchr., counselor Victor Valley Coll., Victorville, Calif., 1968-74; dean of students San Bernardino (Calif.) Valley Coll., 1974-78; lectr. Calif. State U., San Bernardino, 1979-82, 85-86, La Verne U., Victorville, 1983-84, U. Redlands, Calif., 1988—; pvt. practice mgmt. cons. Victorville, 1987—; cons. Victor Valley Coll., Victorville, Palomar Coll., San Marcos, Calif., San Bernardino Valley Coll., 1992—, John Deere Corp., Moline, Ill., 1992—, Allan Hancock Coll., Santa Maria, Calif., 1994—, Victor Valley Union H.S. Dist., Victorville, 1993—, Pacific Oaks Coll., 1994, Barstow Coll., 1995—, Network Calif. C.C. Founds., 1995—, Western Fairs Assn., 1989—, Western Wash. Fair, 1992—, Pacific Nat. Exhbn., Vancouver, B.C., Can., 1990—, Calif. Assn. Racing Fairs, 1993-94, Calif. Constrn. Authority, 1994—, numerous county and state fairs. Leader Girl Scouts U.S., Victorville, 1980-93; pres. San Gorgonio Girl Scout coun., 1984-87; bd. dirs. Oro Grande Found., Victorville, 1984—; pres. Victor Valley Coll. Found., Victorville, 1994-96; pres. Victor Elem. Bd. Trustees, 1980-90. Recipient Lifetime Achievement award Desert Communities United Way, 1993; named Soroptomist Woman of Distinction, 1992. Mem. Nat. Sch. Bds. Assn., Am. Assn. Sch. Adminstrs., Calif. Sch. Bds. Assn., Victorville C. of C. (v.p., bd. dirs. 1994-96), Rotary. Republican. Presbyterian. Home: 13993 Burning Tree Dr Victorville CA 92392-4353 Office: 15476 W Sand St Victorville CA 92392-2314

CALDWELL, SARAH, opera producer, conductor, stage director and administrator; b. Maryville, Mo., Mar. 6, 1924. Student, U. Ark., Hendrix Coll., New Eng. Conservatory, Berkshire Music Ctr., Tanglewood, Mass.; D. Mus. (hon.), Harvard U., Simmons Coll., Bates Coll., Bowdoin Coll. Mem. faculty Berkshire Music Ctr.; dir. Boston U. Opera Workshop, 1953-57; created dept. music theater Boston U.; founded Boston Opera Group (later became Opera Co. of Boston), 1957, sinced served as artistic dir. and condr. Asst. to Boris Goldovsky in direction of New Eng. Opera Co.; operatic directorial debut with Rake's Progress, Opera Workshop, 1953; operatic debut as condr. with Opera Group of Boston, 1957, Carnegie Hall debut with Am. Symphony Orch., 1974; condr. and/or dir. maj. opera cos. in U.S., including N.Y. Met. Opera, Dallas Civic Opera, Houston Grand Opera, N.Y.C. Opera; condr. with maj. orchs. including: Indpls. Symphony, Milw. Symphony, Am. Symphony, N.Y. Philharmonic; condr. at Ravinia Festival, 1976. Recipient Rogers and Hammerstein award. *

CALDWELL, ZOE, actress, director; b. Hawthorn, Victoria, Australia, Sept. 14, 1933; m. Robert Whitehead, 1968; 2 sons: Sam, Charlie. Attended, Meth. Ladies Coll., Melbourne, Australia. Dorothy F. Schmidt Vis. Eminent Scholar in Theatre, Fla. Atlantic U., 1989-93. Theater debut as mem. of Union Theatre Repertory Co., Melbourne, 1953; other appearances in The Madwoman of Chaillot, Goodman Theatre, Chgo., 1964, The Way of the World, The Caucasian Chalk Circle, Mpls., Slapstick Tragedy, N.Y.C., 1966 (Best Supporting Actress Tony award 1966), Antony and Cleopatra, Richard III, The Merry Wives of Windsor, Stratford, Ont., Can., Shakespeare Festival, 1967, The Prime of Miss Jean Brodie, 1967 (Best Actress Tony award 1968), Colette, N.Y.C., 1970, A Bequest to the Nation, London, 1970, The Creation of the World and Other Business, N.Y.C., 1972, Love and Master Will, Washington, 1973, The Dance of Death, N.Y.C., 1974, Long Day's Journey Into Night, N.Y.C., Washington, 1976, Medea, N.Y.C., 1982 (Best Actress Tony award), Lillian, 1986, Come A-Waltzing With Me, A Perfect Ganesh, 1993, Master Class, 1995 (Best Actress Tony award 1996); dir. (plays): An Almost Perfect Person, N.Y.C., 1977, Richard II, Stratford, Ont., 1979, These Men, off-Broadway, 1980, The Taming of the Shrew, Hamlet, Am. Shakespeare Theatre, 1985, Vita and Virginia, N.Y.C., 1995. Decorated Order Brit. Empire; recipient Theatre World award, 1966. Address: Whitehead Stevens 1501 BroadwaySte 1614 New York NY 10036*

CALDWELL-PORTENIER, PATTY JEAN GROSSKOPF, advocate, educator; b. Davenport, Iowa, Sept. 28, 1937; d. Bernhard August and Leontine Virginia (Carver) Grosskopf; m. Donald Eugene Caldwell Mar. 29, 1956 (dec. Feb. 1985); children: John Alan, Jennifer Lynn Caldwell Lear; m. Walter J. Portenier, Oct. 3, 1992. BA, State U. Iowa, 1959. Hearing officer Ill. State Bd. Edn., Springfield, 1979-91, Appellate Court, 1986-91; pres., bd. dirs. Tri-County Assn. for Children With Learning Disabilities, Moline, Ill., 1972-79; adv. vol., Iowa and Ill., 1979-91; mem. adv. coun. Prairie State Legal Svcs., Inc., Rock Island, Ill., 1984-91; mem. profl. svcs. com. United Cerebral Palsy N.W. Ill., Rock Island, 1986-88; arbitrator Am. Arbitration Assn., Chgo., 1986-91, Better Bus. Bur., Davenport, 1986-91. Founder, pres. Quad Cities Diabetes Assn., Moline, 1969-72, bd. dirs., 1973—; mem. com. Moline Internat. Yr. Disabled, 1981; mem. Assn. for Retarded Citizens, Rock Island, 1987; mem. vol. Coun. on Children at Risk, Moline, 1988-91; reader for the blind Sta. WVIK, Rock Island, 1989-91. Mem. Ill. Assn. for Children with Learning Disabilities (bd. dirs., adv. 1980-83). Methodist. Home and Office: 2443 La Condessa Dr Los Angeles CA 90049-1221

CALDWELL-WOOD, NAOMI RACHEL, library media specialist; b. Providence, Mar. 31, 1958; d. Atwood Alexander II and Juanita (Johnson) Caldwell; m. Patrick William Wood, July 25, 1980; 1 child, William Earl Wood. BS, Clarion State Coll., 1980; MSLS, Clarion U. Pa., 1982; postgrad., Tex. A&M U., 1986-87, Providence Coll., 1990-92, U. Pitts., 1992—. Cert. teaching libr. Asst. dir., adult svcs. libr. Oil City (Pa.) Pub. Libr., 1984-85; microtest reference libr. Sterling C. Evans Libr., Tex. A&M U., College Station, 1985-87; libr. media specialist Nathan Bishop Mid. Sch., Providence, 1987-92; libr. sci. doctoral fellow dept. libr. sci. Sch. Libr. and Info. Sci. U. Pitts., 1992—; sch. library media specialist Feinstein H.S. for Pub. Svc., Providence, 1994—; mem. discovery award com. U.S. Bd. on Books for Young People, 1994; mem. com. R.I. Children's Book Award, 1990-92, R.I. Read-Aloud, 1990-92; participant Native Am. and Alaskan Native Pre-Conf. to White House Conf. on Librs. and Info. Scis., Washington, 1991, George Washington U. Nat. Indian Policy Ctr. Forum on Native Am. Librs. and Info. Svcs., Washington, 1991; hon. del. White House Conf. on Libr. and Info. Svcs., Washington, 1991; mem. U.S. nat. sect. Internat. Bd. on Books for Young People; bd. dirs. Ocean State Freenet; presenter in field. Mem. editorial adv. bd., reviewer Multicultural Rev., 1991—; mem. adv. bd. Native Ams. Info. Dir., 1992, OYATE, 1992—, Gale Ency. Multicultural Am.. Native N.Am. Ref. Libr.; reviewer Clarion Books, Greenwood Press, Random House, Harcourt Brace Trade Divsn., Browndeer Press, Oryx Press; contbr. articles to profl. jours. Mem. State of R.I. Libr. Bd., 1996, Spl. Presdl. Adv. Com. on Libr. of Congress, 1996—. Mem. Am. Indian Libr. Assn. (NMRT publicity com. 1986, NMRT minority recruitment com. 1986-88, OLOS libr. svcs. for Am. Indian people subcom. 1986-88, 90-91, chmn. 1992-94, sec. 1994—, ALCTS micropub. com. 1988-90, mem. coun. com. on minority concerns 1991-92, 94-96, chmn. ALA com. on Status of Women in Librarianship 1995, councilor-at-large 1992—), Am. Assn. Sch. Librs., Spl. Librs. Assn., Libr. Adminstrn. Mgmt. Assn. Home: 475 Sowams Rd Barrington RI 02806 Office: Feinstein HS for Pub Svc 544 Elmwood Ave Providence RI 02907-1820

CALEGARI, MARIA, ballerina; b. N.Y.C., Mar. 30, 1957; d. Richard A. and Marion (Gentile) C. Student, DuPons Dance Sch., Queens., 5 yrs., Ballet Acad., Queens, 6 yrs., Sch. Am. Ballet, 3 yrs. Mem. corps de ballet N.Y.C. Ballet, 1974-82, soloist, 1982-83, prin., 1983-94; assoc. dir. Carmel (N.Y.) Studio of Dance, 1996—. Dancer in N.Y.C. Ballet's Balanchine Celebration, 1993. Recipient Alumni award Profl. Children's Sch., 1986.

CALFEE, LAURA PICKETT, university administrator, photographer; b. Liberty, Tex., Oct. 30, 1952; d. Benjamin Ellis and Florence Ellen (Watson) Pickett; m. Gary Wayne Calfee, Dec. 21, 1981. B in Journalism, U. Tex.,

1979. Com. clk. Tex. Ho. of Reps., Austin, 1973-77; asst. to dir. Legis. Divsn. Ho. of Reps., Austin, 1977-83; com. coord. Tex. Ho. of Reps., Austin, 1983-87; spl. asst. for govtl. rels. Univ Houston System, Austin, 1987-92, asst. vice chancellor, 1992—; exec. producer Capitol Report, KUHT-TV, Houston, 1989—; moderator 1993. Co-author: (dance/theater) Chicken Tawk, performed at DIA Ctr. for Arts, N.Y.C., 1991; photographer: Gary's Best (hon. mention Best of Photography ann. 1992, Maria's Geese (hon. mention Best of Photography ann. 1994); permanent collections include Harry Ransom Humanities Rsch. Ctr. Photography Collection/U. Tex. at Austin, Tex. Midcontinent Oil and Gas Corp. Grantee: Tex. Hist. Commn., 1992-93; recipient Hon. Mention award Phoenix Gallery Ann. Juried Competition, 1994, State of the Art Nat. Juried Competition, 1994, State of the Art Nat. Juried Competition, Ithaca, N.Y., 1995, Grand award Govtl. Rels. Program, Coun. for Advancement and Support of Edn., Region IV, 1995, 1st pl./2d pl. Viewpoint 96 Bosque County Conservatory of Fine Art Competition, 1996. Mem. Tex. Fine Arts Assn., Tex. Photographic Soc., Laguna Gloria Art Mus. Home: 19001 FM 1826 Driftwood TX 78619 Office: U Houston System 1005 Congress Ave Ste 820 Austin TX 78701

CALHOUN, DEBORAH LYNN, emergency room nurse, consultant; b. Tulsa, Aug. 6, 1958; d. Charles Cooper Calhoun and Delores Susan (Deardorf) Metzger. BSN, Clemson U., 1982. RN, S.C.; cert. instr. ACLS, Am. Heart Assn., TNCC instr.; CEN; clin. coord. EMS and cmty. svcs., hyperbaric medicine. Staff nurse, clin. nurse III Roper Hosp., Charleston, S.C., 1982—; owner Charleston Med.-Lega. Consulting, 1994—; clin. coord. EMS/Cmty. Svcs. and Hyperbaric Medicine, Roper Hosp. Instr. ENCARE, 1993. Mem. ENA, TNCC, S.C. Emergency Nurses Assn. (pres. 1994), Low Country Emergency Nurses Assn. (pres. 1991. 92). Republican. Episcopalian. Home: 1212 Gilmore Rd Charleston SC 29407-5333 Office: Roper Hosp 316 Calhoun St Charleston SC 29401-1113

CALHOUN, JOAN MARIE, elementary education educator; b. Long Beach, Calif., June 10, 1969; d. Robert Warren and Barbara Ann C. BA summa cum laude in Diversified Edn., Mt. St. Mary's Coll., L.A., 1991; postgrad., Calif. State U., Long Beach, 1994—. Cert. elem. tchr., Calif. Child care worker Long Beach Unified Sch. Dist., 1987-91, recreation leader spl. edn., 1989-95; 4th grade tchr. Anaheim (Calif.) City Sch. Dist., 1991-92; 3rd grade tchr. St. Cyprian Sch., Long Beach, 1992—; pvt. tutor, Long Beach. Recipient Paul Douglas scholarship Aid of Student Commissioning, Sacramento, 1988-90. Mem. Delta Sigma Epsilon. Office: St Cyprian Elem Sch 5133 E Arbor Rd Long Beach CA 90808-1106

CALHOUN, NANCY, state legislator; b. Suffern, N.Y., July 10, 1944; d. Andrew Felix and Paula Mathilda (Kusmitsch) Coleman; children: Richard, Kathy Calhoun Wells, Glenn. Student, Empire State Coll., 1981-84. Tax collector Washingtonville (N.Y.) Sch. Dist., 1976-84; adminstrv. aide Office of the Assessor, Town of Blooming Grove, 1978-81; mem. Council, Town of Blooming Grove, 1982-85, supr., 1986-90; assemblywoman N.Y. State Assembly, Albany, 1991—. State committeewoman N.Y. State Rep. Com., 1985-91. Named Citizen of Yr., Monell Engine Co., 1988. Office: NY State Assembly State Capitol Albany NY 12248

CALHOUN, PATRICIA HANSON, secondary education educator; b. Detroit, Apr. 29, 1940; d. James William and Gordie Eugenia (Wiggins) H.; m. Hubert Calhoun, Jr., July 27, 1956; children: Phillip Wayne, Debra Jean, Donna Marie. BS in Comprehensive Bus. Edn., West Georgia Coll., 1981, MEd in Comprehensive Bus. Edn., 1982, EdS in Comprehensive Bus. Edn., 1984. Cert. tchr., performance based tchr., comprehensive bus. educator, Ga. Tchr. bus. edn. Bowdon (Ga.) H.S., 1982, Carroll County (Ga.) Vocat.-Tech. Sch., 1982-85, Chattahoochee Tech. Inst., Marietta, Ga., 1986-91, Paulding County H.S., Dallas, Ga., 1982-91; tchr. bus. edn. East Paulding H.S., Dallas, 1991—, also coord. coop. bus. edn., head dept. vocat. edn., 1991—; advisor Future Bus. Leaders Am., Dallas, 1984—. Mem. NEA, Ga. Assn. Educators, Ga. Bus. Edn. Assn., Nat. Bus. Edn. Assn., Nat. Vocat. Assn., Ga. Vocat. Assn., Phi Kappa Phi, Kappa Delta Pi. Republican. Home: 724 Burns Rd Carrollton GA 30117-2518 Office: East Paulding High Sch 6800 Dragstrip Rd Dallas GA 30132-4552

CALHOUN, PEGGY J., fundraising executive; b. La Salle, Ill., Sept. 14, 1957; d. Floyd Anthony and Sophia (Regula) Sarwinski; m. James R. Calhoun, Apr. 19, 1989. Student, Ill. Valley C.C., Oglesby, 1975, So. Ill. U., 1976, 77; MA, St. Mary's Coll., Minn., 1994. Cert. fund raising exec. Assoc. dir. United Way, Sarasota, Fla., 1979-85; devel. dir. Boy Scouts Am., Sarasota, 1985-86; assoc. campaign dir. United Way, Ft. Lauderdale, Fla., 1986-87; dir. devel. YMCA, Sarasota, 1987-88, Salvation Army, Ft. Lauderdale, 1988-91, Diabetes Rsch. Inst. Found., U. Miami Sch. Medicine, 1992-93; pres. Calhoun & Co., Inc., Ft. Lauderdale, 1993—; instr. Nova U., Ft. Lauderdale, 1991—. Com. mem. United Way, 1988-91. Mem. Nat. Soc. Fund Raising Execs. (pres., bd. dirs. 1990, Outstanding Profl. Fund Raiser 1991, bd. dirs. 1990—, pres. 1996), Women's Exec. Com. (mentor), Broward Planned Giving Coun. (bd. dirs. 1991), Pub. Rels. Soc. Am. (pres. 1993, bd. dirs. 1991—). Republican. Home and Office: 2741 NE 57th Ct Fort Lauderdale FL 33308-2723

CALINESCU, ADRIANA GABRIELA, museum curator, art historian; b. Bucharest, Romania, Dec. 30, 1941; came to U.S., 1973; d. Nicolae and Tamara Gane; m. Matei Alexe Calinescu, Apr. 29, 1963; children: Irena, Matthew. BA, Cen. Lyceé, Bucharest, 1959; MA in English, U. Bucharest, 1964; MLS, Ind. U., 1976, MA in Art History, 1983. Asst. prof. Inst. Theater and Cinema, Bucharest, 1967-73; rsch. asst. Ind. U. Art Mus., Bloomington, 1976-79, rsch. assoc., 1979-83, curator ancient art, 1983—; vis. assoc. mem. Am. Sch. Classical Studies, Athens, Greece, 1984. Author: The Art of Ancient Jewelry: An Introduction to the Burton Y. Berry Collection, 1994; author, co-editor: Ancient Art from the V. G. Simkhovitch Collection, 1988. NEA fellow, 1984; grantee Salzburg Seminar, 1970, NEA, 1987, 93, Kress Found., 1991, Internat. Rsch. and Exchanges Bd., 1991. Mem. Archaeol. Inst. Am., Classical Art Soc., Beta Phi Mu. Office: Ind U Art Mus E 7th St Bloomington IN 47405

CALISHER, HORTENSE (MRS. CURTIS HARNACK), writer; b. N.Y.C., Dec. 20, 1911; d. Joseph Henry and Hedvig (Lichtstern) C.; m. Curtis Harnack, Mar. 23, 1959; children by previous marriage: Bennet Hughes, Peter Heffelfinger. A.B., Barnard Coll., 1932; LittD (hon.), Skidmore Coll., 1980, Grinnell Coll., 1986; LittD, Adelphi U., 1988. Adj. prof. English Barnard Coll., N.Y.C., 1956-57; vis. lectr. State U. Iowa, 1957, 59-60, Stanford U., 1958, Sarah Lawrence Coll., Bronxville, N.Y., 1962, 67; adj. prof. Columbia U., N.Y.C., 1968-70, CCNY, 1969; vis. prof. lit. SUNY, Purchase, 1971-72, Brandeis U., 1963-64, U. Pa., 1965; Regent's prof. U. Calif., 1976; vis. prof. Bennington Coll., 1978, Washington U., St. Louis, 1979, Brown U., spring 1986; lectr., Fed. Republic of Germany, Yugoslavia, Rumania, Hungary, 1978; guest lectr. U.S./China Arts Exch., Republic of China, 1986. Author: (novels) False Entry, 1961, Textures of Life, 1962, The New Yorkers, 1969, Journal from Ellipsia, 1965, Queenie, 1971, Standard Dreaming, 1972, Eagle Eye, 1973, On Keeping Women, 1977, Mysteries of Motion, 1984, The Bobby-Soxer, 1986 (Kafka prize U. Rochester 1987), Age, 1987, (under pseudonym Jack Fenno) The Small Bang, 1992, In the Palace of the Movie-King, 1994; (novellas) The Railway Police, 1966, The Last Trolley Ride, 1966; short stories include In The Absence of Angels, 1951, Tale for the Mirror, 1962, Extreme Magic, 1963, Collected Stories, 1975, Saratoga Hot, 1985; autobiography: Herself, 1972; memoir: Kissing Cousins, 1988; contbr. short stories, articles, revs. to Am. Scholar, N.Y. Times, Harpers, Yale Rev., New Criterion, others. Guggenheim fellow, 1952, 55; Dept. of State Am. Specialist's grantee to S.E. Asia, 1958; recipient Acad. of Arts and Letters award, 1967, Nat. Council Arts award, 1967, Lifetime Achievement award Nat. Endowment for the Arts, 1989. Mem. Am. Acad. Arts and Letters (pres. 1987-90), PEN (pres. 1986-87). Office: care Donadio & Ashworth 231 W 22nd St New York NY 10011*

CALKINS, JOANN RUBY, nursing administrator; b. Mich., June 28, 1934; d. William Russell and Imajean (Dunkle) Armentrout; m. James W. Calkins, 1952; children: Russell, Jill, Cindy; m. W. Arthur Brindle, May 7, 1983. AS, Delta Coll., 1964, BS, Cen. Mich. U., 1972, MA, 1977. Staff nurse, L.P.N. clin. instr., asst. dir. Sch. Nursing, Midland (Mich.) Hosp., 1964-71; dir. nursing, dir. substance abuse unit Gladwin (Mich.) Hosp., 1972-76; prin. Calkins Profl. Counseling & Cons., Harrison, Mich., 1976-78, part-time, 1978-83; dir. nursing svc. Ctrl. Mich. Cmty. Hosp., Mt. Pleasant, 1978-83; dir. nursing Oaklawn Hosp., Marshall, Mich., 1983-87; asst. adminstr. profl. svcs. DON Betsy Johnson Meml. Hosp., Dunn, N.C., 1987-93, v.p. profl. svcs., 1993-95, pub. rels., 1995—; coord. Harnett County Alliance for Sch. Health Ctrs., 1995—; part-time prin. W. Arthur and Assocs. Cons.; conducted workshops Mich. Dept. Pub. Health, Mich. Hosp. Assn.; exec. dir. Holistic Health Agy., 1977-82. Trustee Mid-Mich. C.C.; vol. counselor student nurses Cen. Carolina Coll., 1988-93; friends of the libr., 1995; mem. health task force for Harnett County HelpNet; adv. bd. to schs. of nursing Johnston C.C., Sampson C.C., Cen. Carolina C.C.; mem. adv. bd. St. Joseph of the Pines Home Health Agy., 1988-93; cert. layity spkr. Meth. Ch., 1994; mem. adv. bd. Harnett County Coop. Ext., 1996—; bd. dirs. Harnett divsn. Am. Heart Assn., 1996—. Recipient Murial A. Grimmason Nursing Scholarship award, 1962; Cert. nursing adminstr. Mem. Mich. Soc. Hosp. Nursing Adminstrs. (mem. steering com. 1979-80, dir., 14 county rep. 1980-83, pres. 1983-84, chmn. devel. com.), Mich. Nurses Assn., Am. Orgn. Nurse Execs., N.C. Orgn. Nurse Execs. (exec. bd. dirs. 1990-93), Carolinas Healthcare Pub. Rels. and Mktg. Soc., Lioness Internat. (3d v.p. 1985). Office: 800 Tilghman Dr Dunn NC 28334-5510

CALLAGHAN, GEORGANN MARY, management consultant; b. Bklyn., June 25, 1944; d. George Louis and Jean (Russo) Carpenito; m. Matthew John Callaghan, June 7, 1969; children: Matthew, Michael, Christian. BS in Hist. Studies, SUNY Empire State Coll., 1994; postgrad. studies, Pace U. Law Sch., 1995—. Asst. to dir. pers. Kemper Ins., N.Y.C., 1962-65; asst. to assoc. gen. counsel Kemder Ins., N.Y.C., 1965; asst. to pres. Kalvin Miller, Meyer & Sacks, N.Y.C., 1969-70; asst. to ptnr. Dewey, Ballantine Bushby Palmer & Wood, N.Y.C., 1970-74; fashion cons. Bonwit Teller, Scarsdale, N.Y., 1979-91; self-employed office mgmt. cons. Scarsdale, 1980—. Den mother, exec. com. Boy Scouts Am. Mem. Maroon & White Athletic Assn. (bd. dirs.), Scarsdale PTA, Town and Village Club. Home and Office: 49 Carman Rd Scarsdale NY 10583-6328

CALLAGHAN, MARY ANNE, secondary school educator; b. Seattle, Mar. 14, 1947; d. John Joseph and Catherine Clara (Emard) C.; m. David Michael Buerge, Mar. 8, 1975; children: David John, Catherine Emily. BA in English Lit., U. Wash., 1970, Teaching Cert., 1973. Standard Wash. state teaching certification. Tchr. tng. intern Hazen H.S., Renton, Wash., 1968-70, tchr. English, 1970-71; tchr. English, theology Forest Ridge Sch. of the Sacred Heart, Bellevue, Wash., 1971-93, dean of students, 1988-92; tchr. English, theology Holy Cross H.S., Everett, Wash., 1993—; student life v.p., 1995—; chair English dept. Forest Rdige H.S. and Holy Cross H.S., 1980—; mem. accreditation team Holy Name Acad., Seattle, 1991, O'Dea H.S., Seattle, 1995; insvc. presenter for Archdiocese of Seattle, 1992, 93. Vol. Christian Movement for Peace, Montreal, Quebec, 1972; sch. bd. mem. St. Catherine Parish, Seattle, 1984-90. Recipient grants to initiate ethnic awareness programs Religious of the Sacred Heart, 1982, grant to study Asian lit. NEH, 1988. Mem. Nat. Cath. Edn. Assn., Nat. Coun. Tchrs. English. Roman Catholic. Office: Holy Cross Sch 2617 Cedar St Everett WA 98201-3137

CALLAHAM, BETTY ELGIN, librarian; b. Honea Path, S.C., Oct. 8, 1929; d. John Winfred and Alice (Dodson) C. B.A., Duke U., 1950; M.A., Emory U., 1954, Master Librarianship, 1961. Tchr. pub. schs. N.C., Ga. and S.C., 1951-60; field svcs. libr. S.C. State Libr., 1961-64, adult cons., 1964-65, dir. field svcs., 1965-74, dep. libr., 1974-79, dir., 1979-90, ret., 1990; Conf. coord. Gov.'s Conf. on Pub. Librs., 1965, S.C. White House Conf. Libr. and Info. Svcs., 1978-79; del. White House Conf. Libr. and Info. Svcs., 1979; mem. OCLC Users Coun., 1982-84, 86-87; chair del. SOLINET, 1983-84; bd. dirs. Southeastern Libr. Network, 1984-88, vice chmn., 1985-86, chmn. bd. 1986-87. Active S.C. Hist. Soc. Mem. ALA (coun. 1977-80), S.C. Libr. Assn. (fed. rels. coord. 1976-80, chmn. pub. libr. sect. 1985, mem. legis. com. 1984-90, v.p., pres.-elect 1987-88, pres. 1988-89, Intellectual Freedom award 1986, Educator of Yr. award 1987), Nat. Trust Hist. Preservation, Riverbanks Zool. Soc., Hist. Columbia Soc., Friends S.C. State Mus., Friends McKissick Mus., Friends Richland County Pub. Libr., S.C. Wildlife Fedn. Home: 733 Poinsettia St Columbia SC 29205-2067

CALLAHAN, CHRISTINE H., state legislator; b. N.Y.C., Oct. 19, 1944; divorced; children: Mary, James. AA, Centenary Coll., 1964; BS, U. R.I., 1989. Rep. dist. 99 R.I. Ho. of Reps., 1986—; mem. fin. com., joint com. on small bus. Acct. R.I. Philharmonic Orch. Home: 5 Cedar Ave Middletown RI 02842 Office: RI House of Reps State House Rm 106 Providence RI 02903*

CALLAHAN, KATE M., nurse; b. Buffalo, N.Y., Feb. 4, 1952; d. John Joseph and Carol Marie (Donnelly) C.; m. James Persse, June 23, 1972 (div. Nov. 1982); 1 child, Jason William; m. Peter M. Benjamin, Dec. 1, 1989. ADN, Trocaire Coll., 1972; BSN, U. Miami, 1994; MPA, Harvard U., 1996. RN, N.Y. Staff nurse, asst. head nurse Ill. Masonic Med. Ctr., Chgo., 1974-79; asst. DON Sandlewood Hosp., 1979-81; product mgr., sales rep. Am. Hosp. Supply Corp., Chgo., 1981-88; maternal child health specialist Hoag Meml. Hosp., Newport Beach, Calif., 1988-93; project dir. Camillus Health Concern, Miami, Fla., 1993-95. cons. Cmty. Partnership for the Homeless, Miami, 1994, 95, Providers Forum, Miami, 1994, 95. Recipient Alumnus award U. Miami, Coral Gables, Fla., 1994. Mem. ANA, Fla. Nurses Assn. (nurse rep. region I pub. health coun. 1993—), Assn. Women's Health Obstetric and Neonatal Nurses, Harvard Club Boson, Jr. League Miami, Woman's C. of C. Dade County (bd. dirs. 1995-96), Phi Kappa Phi, Sigma Theta Tau, Phi Delta Kappa. Democrat. Jewish. Home: 2111 Tiger Tail Ave Coconut Grove FL 33133

CALLAHAN, LEEANN LUCILLE, psychologist; b. San Diego, Calif., Dec. 7, 1950; d. Charlie A. Olsen and Delores A. (Libke) Turner; m. Chuck Callahan, Oct. 31, 1970; children: Clint, Devin, Chet. BS/MS in Psychology, San Diego State U., 1983; PhD in Psychology, USIU, San Diego, 1990. Lic. clin. psychologist. Clin. dir. Sharp Cabrillo Hosp., San Diego, 1989-91, Charter Hosp., San Diego, 1991-93; psychologist San Diego, 1989—; preferred provider Charter Hosp., San Diego, 1990—, speakers bur., 1990—; staff psychologist Sharp Cabrillo Hosp., San Diego, 1989-92. Editor Parentteen Mag.; contbr. articles to profl. jours. Pres. PTA, San Diego, 1985; citizen adv./city coun. City of San Diego, 1987; vol. Poway Unified Sch. Dist., San Diego, 1975—; speaker Rotary, San Diego, 1994. Mem. APA, Calif. State Psychol. Assn. Office: 9320 Carmel Mountain Rd Ste D San Diego CA 92129-2159

CALLAHAN, MARGUERITE ESTHER, nurse practitioner; b. Washington, Feb. 1, 1955; d. Daniel Francis and Mary Frances (Preston) C. BA, Converse Coll., 1977; BS, U. Tenn., 1980; postgrad., Weston Sch. Theology, 1981-82; MS, Pace U., 1991. Cert. adult nurse practitioner, Am. Nurse's Assn. Staff nurse Emory U. Hosp., Atlanta, 1980-81, Jackson Meml. Hosp., Miami, Fla., 1981-82; sch. nurse Carrollton Sch., Miami, 1981-82; staff nurse Pine St. Inn, Boston, 1982-83; sr. staff nurse The N.Y. Hosp., N.Y.C., 1984-88, 89-91; pub. health nurse Town of Greenwich (Conn.) Dept. Health, 1988-89; nurse practitioner Beth Israel Med. Ctr., N.Y.C., 1991-94, VA Med. Ctr., Nashville, 1994—; cons. Howard Area Community Ctr., Chgo., 1988, Town of Greenwich Dept. Health, 1991; adj. prof. grad. sch. nursing Pace U., Pleasantville, N.Y., 1993-94. Mem. Am. Acad. Nurse Practitioners, Middle Tenn. Advance Practice Nurses, Sigma Theta Tau. Roman Catholic. Home: 4487 Post Pl Apt 173 Nashville TN 37205-1621 Office: VA Med Ctr 1310 24th Ave S Nashville TN 37212-2637

CALLAHAN, MARSHA LYNN, property manager; b. Saginaw, Mich., Oct. 13, 1947; d. Leonard III and Phyllis Irene (Kristalyn) Mueller; m. James J. Callahan (div. 1983); children: Scott, Erich, Jason. Student, Temple U., 1975. Property mgr. Allstate Mgmt., 1983-86, JPC Property Mgmt., 1986-90; property mgr., leasing agt. Mertz Corp., 1990—. Author: (book of poetry) Garden of Life, 1995. Mem. Rotary (sec. 1983-85). Office: Mertz Corp 133-G Gaither Dr West Deptford NJ 08086

CALLANAN, KATHLEEN JOAN, retired electrical engineer; b. Detroit, Feb. 10, 1940; d. John Michael and Grace Marie (Kleehammer) C. BSE in Physics, U. Mich., 1963; postgrad. in physics Northeastern U., 1963-65; MSEE, U. Hawaii, 1971; diploma in Japanese lang. St. Joseph Inst. Japanese Studies, Tokyo, 1973; cert. in mgmt. Boeing Mil. Airplane Co. Employee Devel., 1985. Vis. scholar Sophia U., Tokyo, 1976-79; elec.-electronic components engr. Boeing Mil. Airplane Co. (named changed to Boeing Def. and Space Group-Product Support Div.), Wichita, Kans., 1979-83, instrumentation design engr., 1983-85, strategic planner for tech., 1985-86, research and engring. tech. supr., 1986-87, electromagnetic effects avionics mgr., 1987-89, elec. and electronics mgr., 1989, design tech. support mgr., 1990-92, engring. leader, 1992-95, ret. 1995. Contbr. articles to profl. jours. Mem. Rose Hill Planning Commn., Kans., 1982-85; coord. Boeing Employees Amateur Radio Soc., Wichita, 1982-83, sec., 1991. Fellow Soc. Women Engrs. (sr. mem., sect. rep. 1981-83, sec. treas. 1985-86, regional bd. dirs. 1983-85, sect. pres. 1987-88); mem. Bus. and Profl. Women, Quarter Century Wireless Assn. (communications com. 1985-86), Assn. of Old Crows (bd. dirs. 1988-91, chpt. pres. 1991). Lodge: Toastmasters (local pre pres. 1985-86, competent toastmaster 1985). Avocations: amateur radio, singing, bowling. Home: 456 Emden St Fort Myers FL 33903-2194

CALLANDER, KAY EILEEN PAISLEY, business owner, retired gifted talented education educator, writer; b. Coshocton, Ohio, Oct. 15, 1938; d. Dalton Olas and Dorothy Pauline (Davis) Paisley; m. Don Larry Callander, Nov. 18, 1977. BSE, Muskingum Coll., 1960; MA in Speech Edn., Ohio State U., 1964, postgrad., 1964-84. Cert. elem., gifted, drama, theater tchr., Ohio. Tchr. Columbus (Ohio) Pub. Schs., 1960-70, 80-88, drama specialist, 1970-80, classroom, gifted/talented tchr., 1986-90, ret., 1990; sole prop. The Ali Group, Kay Kards, 1992—; coord. Artists-in-the Schs., 1977-88; cons., presenter numerous ednl. confs. and sems., 1971—; mem., ednl. cons. Innovation Alliance Youth Adv. Coun., 1992—. producer-dir., Shady Lane Music Festival, 1980-88; dir. tchr. (nat. distbr. video) The Trial of Gold E. Locks, 1983-84; rep., media pub. relations liason Sch. News., 1983-88; author, creator Trivia Game About Black Americans (TGABA), exhibitor of TGABA game at L.A. County Office Edn. Conf., 1990; presenter for workshop by Human Svc. Group and Creative Edn. Coop., Columbus, Ohio, 1989. Benefactor, Columbus Jazz Arts Group; v.p., bd. dirs. Neoteric Dance and Theater Co., Columbus, 1985-87; tchr., participant Future Stars sculpture exhibit, Ft. Hayes Ctr., Columbus Pub. Schs., 1988; tchr. advisor Columbus Coun. PTAs, 1983-86, co-chmn. reflections com., 1984-87; mem. Columbus Mus. Art, Citizens for Humane Action, Inc.; mem. supt.'s adv. coun. Columbus Pub. Schs., 1967-68; presenter Young Author Seminar, Ohio Dept. Edn., 1988, Illustrating Methods for Young Authors' Books, 1986-87; cons. and workshop leader seminar/workshop Tchg. About the Constitution in Elem. Schs., Franklin County Ednl. Coun., 1988; sponsor Minority Youth Recognition Awards, 1994. Named Educator of Yr., Shady Lane PTA, 1982, Columbus Coun. PTAs, 1989, winner Colour Columbus Landscape Design Competition, 1990; Sch. Excellence grantee Columbus Pub. Schs.; Commendation Columbus Bd. Edn. and Ohio Ho. of Reps. for Child Assault Prevention project, 1986-87; first place winner statewide photo contest Ohio Vet. Assn., 1991; recipient Muskingum Coll. Alumni Disting. Svc. award, 1995. Mem. ASCD, AAUW, Assn. for Childhood Edn. Internat., Ohio Coun. for Social Studies, Franklin County Ret. Tchrs. Assn., Nat. Mus. Women in the Arts, Ohio State U. Alumni Assn., U.S. Army Officers Club, Navy League, Liturgical Art Guild Ohio, Columbus Jazz Arts Group, Columbus Mus. Art, Nat. Coun. for Social Studies, Columbus Art League, Columbus Maennerchor (Damen sect.). Republican. Home: 2323 Colts Neck Rd Blacklick OH 43004-9648 Office: The Ali Group Kay Kards PO Box 13093 Columbus OH 43213-0093

CALLARD, CAROLE CRAWFORD, librarian, educator; b. Charleston, W.Va., Aug. 8, 1941; d. William O. and Helen (Shay) Crawford; m. Donald Pope Callard, Apr. 20, 1966; children: Susan Lynne, Annie Laurie. BA in Am. History, U. Charleston, 1963; MLS, U. Pitts., 1966; MA in Social Founds., Ea. Mich. U., 1978. Tchr. Blessed Sacrament Sch., South Charleston, W.Va., 1962-64; grad. trainee W.Va. Libr. Commn., Charleston, 1964-65; reference libr. Tompkins County Pub. Libr., Ithaca, N.Y., 1966-69; head libr. U.S. Embassy, Addis Ababa, Ethiopia, 1969-70; head govt. documents Haile Sellassie U., Addis Ababa, 1970-71; br. libr. Ann Arbor (Mich.) Pub. Libr., 1973-83; documents libr. U. Mich., Ann Arbor, 1983-84; pub. svcs. supr. Libr. of Mich., Lansing, 1984-95; depository libr. inspector Govt. Printing Office, 1995—; chair around the world, around the campus U. Mich. Faculty Women's Club, Ann Arbor, 1974-76; tchr. genealogy Holt Pub. Schs., Okemos Pub. Schs., 1990-92, Washtenaw C.C., 1992-94; judge Mich. history Day, 1991, 93, 94. Author: Index to 150th Anniversary Issue Ithaca Jour., 1967, Guide to Local History, Sources in the Huron Valley, 1980; editor: Sourcebook of Michigan, 1986, Michigan Cemetery Atlas, 1991, Michigan 1870 Census Index, 1991-95, Michigan Cemetery Sourcebook, 1994; column editor Mich. History Mag. and Chronicle; contbr. articles to profl. jours. Membership chair LWV, Ann Arbor; v.p. Geneal. Soc. Washtenaw County, Mich., 1993, pres., 1993-94; v.p. Palatines to Am., 1987-90, Washtenaw Libr. Club, 1982-83; pres. Mich. Staff Assn., Lansing, 1985-86; pres. Govt. Documents Roundtable of Mich., pres., 1992-93; pres. Mich. Data Base Users Group, 1992-93; chmn. book sale Friends of Ann Arbor Pub. Libr. Recipient Notable Document award Govt. Documents Roundtable of Mich., 1991, Paul Thurston Documents award Govt. Documents Roundtable of Mich., 1993, Cert. of Merit Assn. State and Local History, 1995, Mich. Geneal. Coun., Libr. of Mich. Found. and Abrams Found. award, 1996; grantee U. Pitts., 1966, prof. staff grantee Ann Arbor Pub. Schs., 1980, edn. found. grantee Mich. Libr. Assn., 1982. Mem. ALA (state and local documents com.), AAUW (corr. sec., historian 1973-74, 82-83), DAR, Internat. Soc. Brit. Genealogy (trustee 1994-96), Mich. Libr. Assn. (chmn. govt. documents sect. 1982-84, leadership acad. 1991-93), Spl. Librs. Assn., D.C. Libr. Assn., Va. Libr. Assn., Fedn. Genealogy Socs. (del., corr. sec. 1986-87, v.p. regional affairs 1989-92), Nat. Genealogy Soc. (instr. devel. com. 1988-90, chmn. instns. com. 1992—, archives and libr. com. 1993-94), Mich. Geneal. Coun. (official good will ambassador 1995—).

CALLAWAY, KAREN A(LICE), journalist; b. Daytona Beach, Fla., Sept. 5, 1946; d. Robert Clayton III and Alice Johnston (Webb) C. BS in Journalism, Northwestern U., 1968. Copy editor Detroit Free Press, 1968-69; asst. woman's editor, features copy editor, news copy editor, asst. makeup editor Chgo. Am. and Chgo. Today, 1969-74; asst. makeup editor Chgo. Tribune, 1974-76, asst. news editor, 1976-81, assoc. news editor spl. sect., 1981—, assoc. news editor vertical publs., 1993—; adviser Jr. Achievement Tribune sponsored co., Chgo., 1976-77; editor Infant Mortality sect., 1989; vis. prof. student chpt. Soc. Profl. Journalists, Northwestern U., 1989. Chmn. class of 1968 20th reunion Northwestern U., 1989, mem. seminar day com., 1989-90, chmn., 1991, mem. alumni bd. dirs. Medill Sch. Journalism, 1991-95, ex-officio mem., 1995—; vol. Northwestern U. Settlement House. Mem. Soc. of Profl. Journalists, Sigma Delta Chi, Kappa Delta. Methodist. Office: Chicago Tribune 435 N Michigan Ave Ste 573 Chicago IL 60611-4001

CALLBECK, CATHERINE SOPHIA, Canadian government official; b. Central Bedeque, P.E.I., Can., July 25, 1939; d. Ralph and Ruth Callbeck. B Commerce, Mt. Allison U., Can., 1960; BEd, Dalhousie U., 1963; postgrad., Syracuse U. Mem. from 4th dist. of Prince P.E.I. Legislative Assembly, 1974-78, min. health and social svcs., min. responsible for disabled, 1974-78; with Callbeck's Ltd., Ctrl. Bedeque, 1978-88; M.P. from Malpeque dist. Ho. of Commons, Ottawa, Ont., Can., 1988-93; leader Liberal Party of P.E.I., Can., 1993—; 1st elected woman premier, pres. exec. coun. P.E.I., Can., 1993—; mem. legis. assembly 1st Dist. Queens, 1993—. Chair bd. dirs. Confedn. Ctr. of Arts; bd. regents Mt. Allison U.; bd. govs. U. P.E.I.; mem. Maritime Provinces Higher Edn. Commn.; bd. dirs. Inst. for Rsch. in Pub. Policy, P.E.I. United Fund, P.E.I. divsn. Can. Heart Found.; mem. provincial com. Internat. Yr. of the Disabled. Liberal. Mem. United Ch. of Can. Office: Office of the Premier, Shaw Bldg PO Box 2000, Charlottetown, PE Canada C1A 7N8

CALLEJON, DONNA M., federal agency administrator. BS in Managerial Econs., U. Calif., Davis, 1984. Various sales and trading positions Farmers Savs. Bank, Davis, 1984-86; sr. negotiator Western Regional Office Fed. Nat. Mortgage Assn., L.A., 1986; various risk mgmt. and negotiated transactions positions Fed. Nat. Mortgage Assn., Washington, 1986-90, v.p. product acquisition, 1990-91, sr. v.p. for single-family bus., 1991-96, sr. v.p. corp. devel, 1996—. Bd. dirs. Bus. for Social Responsibility, 1995—. Office: Fannie Mae 3900 Wisconsin Ave NW Washington DC 20016

CALLENDER, LORNA OPHELIA, nurse administrator; b. Potsdam, Jamaica, Dec. 15, 1944; d. Banaldino Aciento and Gladys Felicita (Juleye) Robinson; m. Robert Fitzgerald Callender, June 25, 1966; children: Gavin Shaun St. Elmo, Robert Fitzgerald II. AAS, N.Y.C. C.C., 1975; BA,

CUNY, 1978; MA, New Sch. for Social Rsch., N.Y.C., 1981. RN, Calif. Bank teller Mfrs. Hanover Trust, N.Y.C., 1968-70, proof clk., 1970-74; front office clk. Howard Johnson Hotel, Queens, N.Y., 1974-84; front office supr. Vista Internat. Hotel, N.Y.C., 1980-82, vocat. nurse Temporary Nursing Svc., East Orange, N.J., 1985-86, Calif. Psychiat. Placement Svc., Diamond Bar, 1986-90; team leader, nurse Casa Colina Hosp., Pomona, Calif., 1990-91; DON, United Care, Inc., Culver City, Calif., 1991-93; adminstr. Excelsior Home Health, Cucamonga, Calif., 1993-94, Calabar Home Health, Mira Loma, Calif., 1995—; dir. Inland AIDS Project, 1994—. Lobbyist Calif. Assn. Heath Svc. at Home, Sacramento, 1994, Home Care Assn. Am., Jacksonville, Fla., 1995. Mem. NAFE, AAUW. Democrat. Episcopalian. Home: 14213 Ranchero Dr Fontana CA 92337-0523

CALLENDER, NORMA ANNE, psychology educator, counselor; b. Huntsville, Tex., May 10, 1933; d. C. W. Carswell and Nell Ruth (Collard) Hughes Bost; m. B.G. Callender, 1951 (div. 1964); remarried 1967 (div. 1973); children: Teresa Elizabeth, Leslie Gemey, Shannah Hughes, Kelly Mari; m. E. Purfurst, June 1965 (div. Aug. 1965). BS, U. Houston, 1969; MA, U. Houston at Clear Lake, 1977; postgrad. U. Houston, 1970, Lamar U., 1972-73, Tex. So. U., 1971, St. Thomas U., 1985, 86, U. Houston-Clear Lake, 1979, 87, 89-93, San Jacinto Coll., 1988, 89, 94. Aerospace Inst., NASA, Johnson Space Ctr., 1986. Cert. profl. reading specialist, Tex.; lic. profl. counselor. Tchr., Houston Ind. Schs., 1969-70; co-counselor and instr. Ellington AFB, Houston, 1971; tchr. Clear Creek Schs., League City, Tex., 1970-86; cons., LPC intern Guidance Ctr., Pasadena (Tex.) Ind. Sch. Dist., 1993-95; part-time instr. San Jacinto Coll., Pasadena, Tex., 1980-81, 91-93; univ. adj., U. Houston, Clear Lake, 1986-91; owner, dir. Bay Area Tutoring and Reading Clinic, Clear Lake City, Tex., 1970—, Bay Area Tng. Assocs, 1982—, Bay Area Family Counseling, 1995—; cons. in field, 1994—. Contbr. poetry to profl. jours. State advisor U.S. Congl. Adv. Bd., 1985-87; vol., bd. dirs. Family Outreach Ctr., 1989-92; vol. Bay Area Coun. on Drugs and Alcohol, Nassau Bay, Tex., 1993-94; bd. dirs. Ballet San Jacinto, 1985-87; adv. bd. Cmty. Ednl. TV, 1990-92. Recipient Franklin award U. Houston, 1965-67; Delta Kappa Gamma/Beta Omicron scholar, 1967-68; PTA scholar, 1973; Berwin scholar, 1976; Mary Gibbs Jones scholar, 1976-77; Found. Econ. Edn. scholar, 1976; Insts. Achievement Human Potential scholar, Phila., 1987. Mem. APA (assoc.), ACA, Clear Creek Educators Assn. (past, honorarium 1976, 77, 85), Assn. Bus. and Profl. Women (mem. cmty. and ednl. affairs com.), Internat. Reading Assn., U. Houston Alumni Assn. (life), Leadership Clear Lake Alumni Assn. (charter, program and projects com mem. 1986-87, edn. com. 1985), Houston Mental Health Assn., Houston Psychol. Assn., Houston World Affairs Coun., Kappa Delta Pi, Phi Delta Kappa, Phi Kappa Phi (life), Psi Chi (life). Mem. Life Tabernacle Ch. Office: 1234 Bay Area Blvd Ste R Houston TX 77058-2538

CALLINAN, PATRICIA ANN, legal secretary; b. Harrisburg, Pa., Dec. 29, 1943; d. Albert Frances and Gilda Mary (Cifani) Pugliese; 1 child, Tricia Ann Corder. Comml. diploma, Bishop McDevitt, 1961. Chief enforcement sec. Commonwealth of Pa., Harrisburg, 1961-66; supt. sec. Cape May (N.J.) County Vocat. Tech. Ctr., 1966-67; asst. br. mgr. Continental Title Ins., Wildwood, N.J., 1967-91; legal sec. Corino & Dwyer, Esqs., Wildwood, 1991—. Past. pres., treas. Cape May County Legal Sec., 1968-70, St. Ann's PTA, Wildwood, 1980-84; past pres. Wildwood Cath. Parent Guild, 1986-88; bd. sec. Wildwood Crest Tourism Commn., 1990-93. Named Legal Sec. of Yr., Cape May County Legal Sec., 1970, 73. Mem. Victoria Village Homeowners (sec. 1994-96), Lower Township Rep. Club, Lower Township Rep. Orgn. (committeewoman 1994-96, 96—, mem. exec. com. rec. sec. 1994—). Roman Catholic. Home: 36 Canterbury Way Cape May NJ 08204 Office: Corino & Dwyer Esqs 9700 Pacific Ave Wildwood NJ 08260

CALLOWAY, DORIS HOWES, nutrition educator; b. Canton, Ohio, Feb. 14, 1923; d. Earl John and Lillian Ann (Roberts) Howes; m. Nathaniel O. Calloway, Feb. 14, 1946 (div. 1956); children: David Karl, Candace; m. Robert O. Nesheim, July 4, 1981. BS, Ohio State U., 1943; PhD, U. Chgo., 1947; DSc (Hon.), Tufts U., 1992. Head metabolism lab., nutritionist, chief div. QM Food and Container Inst., Chgo., 1951-61; chmn. dept. food sci. and nutrition Stanford Rsch. Inst., Menlo Park, Calif., 1961-63; prof. U. Calif., Berkeley, 1963-91, provost profl. schs. and colls., 1981-87; mem. expert adv. panel on nutrition WHO, Geneva, 1972-92, tech. adv. com. Consultative Group on Internat. Agrl. Rsch., 1989-93, Internat. Commn. on Health Rsch. for Devel., 1987-90, adv. coun. Nat. Inst. Arthritis, Metabolic and Digestive Diseases, Nat. Inst. Aging, NIH, Bethesda, Md., 1974-77, 78-82; trustee Internat. Maize and Wheat Improvement Ctr., 1983-88; trustee, bd. dirs. Winrock Internat. Inst.; cons. FAO, UN, Rome, 1971, 74-75, 81-83; lectr. Cooper Meml., 1983, Roberts Meml., 1985. Author: Nutrition and Health, 1981, Nutrition and Physical Fitness 11th edit., 1984; mem. editorial bd. Am. Dietetic Assn. Jour., 1974-77, Environmental Biology and Medicine, 1969-79. Recipient Meritorious Civilian Svc. Dept. Army, 1959, Disting. Achievement in Nutrition Rsch. award Bristol-Myers Squibb, 1994; named Disting. Alumna Ohio State U., 1974, Wellcome vis. prof. Fedn. Am. Soc. Exptl. Biol., U. Mo., 1980. Fellow Internat. Union of Nutritional Scis., Am. Inst. Nutrition (pres. 1982-83, sec. 1969-72, editorial bd. 1967-72, Conrad A. Elvehjem award 1986); mem. Inst. Medicine NAS, Sigma Xi. Office: U Calif Morgan Hall Berkeley CA 94720

CALMAS, ELLEN, public relations executive; b. Boston, May 10; d. Ted and June Calmas; two children. BS in Comm., Ithaca Coll. Comm., 1983. Mgr. Robert Wick Pub. Rels. Firm, N.Y.C., Rand Pub. Rels. Firm, N.Y.C.; dir. consumer divsn. Cone Comm., Boston, 1988-91, v.p., 1991-94, sr. v.p., 1994—. Bd. dirs. New Eng. chpt. Crohn's and Colitis Found. Named Nat. Cipreas Mercury Bell Ringer, New Eng. Bell Ringers. Office: 90 Canal St Boston MA 02114*

CALO, MARY ANN, art history educator; b. Chgo., Oct. 16, 1949; d. Peter L. and Mary R. (Baldwin) Vinciguerra; m. Michael J. Calo, Aug. 19, 1972; children: M. Ryan, Nina M. BS in Psychology, Denison U., 1971; MS in Info. Studies, Syracuse U., 1975, MA in History of Art, 1981, PhD in Humanities, 1991. Curator, registrar Syracuse (N.Y.) U. Art Coll., 1974-77; art libr. Everson Mus. Art, Syracuse, 1977-78; asst. prof. art history Colgate U., Hamilton, N.Y., 1991—. Author: Bernard Berenson and the 20th Century, 1994, (catalog) American Art: Works on Paper, 1994; contbr. articles to profl. jours. Mem. AUW, Am. Studies Assn., Coll. Art Assn. Home: 104 Westminster Ave Syracuse NY 13210 Office: Colgate U Art and Art History Dept Hamilton NY 13346

CALO, TINA CAROL, school counselor; b. Cleve., June 3, 1939; d. Vincent J. Calo and Marie A. (Caruso) Feudo. BSEd, Ohio U., 1961, MEd, 1969; postgrad., Calif. State U., Sacramento, 1979-80. Cert. tchr., counselor, spl. edn. tchr. Tchr. Maple Hts. (Ohio) Schs., 1961-67; counselor Dept. Def. Schs., Okinawa, Japan, 1967-70, Berlin, 1970-71; counselor Washington Schs., 1971-72; counselor Dept. Def. Schs., Hahn AB, Germany, 1972-79, Rhein Main AB, Germany, 1980-91; sch. counselor Myrtle Beach (S.C.) AFB, 1991-92. Mem. NEA, ACA (mem. European br., sec., bd. dirs.), Fed. Edn. Assn. Home: PO Box 15871 Surfside Beach SC 29587

CALVERT, LOIS PRINCE, geriatrics nurse; b. Lawrenceburg, Tenn., June 27, 1948; d. Virgil Miller and Beulah Mae (Fox) Prince; m. Albert Sidney Johnson, Sept. 26, 1970 (div. 1985); children: Kelley Nicole, Kristopher Scott; m. Malon Sherman Calvert, Oct. 19, 1990. Student, Bapt. Hosp. Sch. Nursing, 1966-67, Belmont Coll., 1966-67; ADN cum laude, Columbia State C.C., 1970; cert. in nursing home adminstrn., George Washington U., 1985. RN, Ala., Tenn. Psychiat. nurse, staff RN Bapt. Meml. Hosp., Memphis, 1970-71; staff RN, psychiat. staff nurse VA Hosp., Memphis, 1971-73; DON svc. Lawrenceburg (Tenn.) Health Care Ctr., 1975-80, nursing home adminstr., 1980-85; case mgr., aide supr., staff RN Lawrenceburg (Tenn.) Home Health Agy., 1985-86; staff RN, case mgr. home health patients, coord. home health Mid-South Home Health Agy., Florence, Ala., 1986-87; DON svcs. Lawrenceburg (Tenn.) Manor, Inc., 1987—; paramed. examiner ASB-Meditest, Nashville, 1989—; mem. NCLEX panel, item reviewer LPN State Bds., 1993. Sustaining membership chmn. Lawrence County coun. Girl Scouts U.S., 1977-78; pianist, dir. youth choir East Edn. Meth. Ch., 1985-94; vol. ARC, bd. dirs. Lawrence County chpt., 1995, also disaster health chmn. Fellow Am. Coll. Health Care Adminstrs. (profl. cert.); mem. Tenn. Employee Rels. Com., Nat. Assn. Dirs. Of Nursing Adminstrs. (founding mem. Tenn. chpt., corr. sec. 1995), Beta Sigma Phi (Girl of Yr. 1973, 76). Baptist. Home: 1613 Ann Rd Lawrenceburg TN 38464-3003 Office: Lawrenceburg Manor 3051 Buffalo Rd Lawrenceburg TN 38464-6189

CALVERT, LOIS WILSON, civic worker; b. Hartford, Conn., Sept. 12, 1924; d. Royal Wouldhave and Evelyn Charlotte (Danielson) Wilson; m. Wallace Erdix Calvert, Mar. 29, 1947; children: Pamela, Gary, Craig and David (twins). Grad., Bryant Coll., 1943. Registrar of voters Town of Simsbury, Conn., 1982—. Bd. dirs., mng. dir. Simsbury Hist. Soc., 1978—; mem. Simsbury Com. on Aging, 1980-89, Friends of Simsbury Libr.; trustee Simsbury Cemetery Assn., 1987—, Simsbury Land Trust, 1984-88; del. 6th dist. Dem. Conv., Bristol, Conn., 1984-86; justice of the peace Town of Simsbury, 1985—, mem. design rev. bd., 1989-93; mem. constl. conv. bicentennial comm. Hometown Hero, 1986, awards selection com., 1996; alt. Conn. Dem. Conv. for Gov., Hartford, 1986; del. State Dem. Conv., 1990, 92; mem. tourism com. Town of Simsbury, 1994-95, 96, ann. report com. 1994, 95, 325th ann. com., 1995; judge Regional History Day. 1993-96. Named a Simsbury Woman Hartford Woman mag., 1987. Mem. Registrar of Voters Assn. Conn., Soc. of Mary and John. Congregationalist. Home: 28 Riverside Rd Simsbury CT 06070-2517

CALVIN, DOROTHY VER STRATE, computer company executive; b. Grand Rapids, Mich., Dec. 22, 1929; d. Herman and Christina (Plakmyer) Ver Strate; m. Allen D. Calvin, Oct. 5, 1953; children: Jamie, Kris, Bufo, Scott. BS magna cum laude, Mich. State U., 1951; MA, U. San Francisco, 1988; EdD, U. San Francisco, 1991. Mgr. data processing. Behavioral Rsch. Labs., Menlo Park, Calif., 1972-75; dir. Mgmt. Info. Systems Inst. for Prof. Devel., San Jose, Calif. 1975-76; systems analyst, programmer Pacific Bell Info. Systems, San Francisco, 1976-81; staff mgr., 1981-84; mgr. applications devel. Data Architects Inc., San Francisco, 1984-86; pres. Ver Strate Press, San Francisco, 1986—. Instr., Downtown C.C., San Francisco, 1980-84, Cañada C.C., 1986-92, Skyline Coll., 1988-92, City Coll. of San Francisco, 1992—; mem. computer curriculum adv. coun. San Francisco City Coll., 1982-84. V.p. LWV, Roanoke, Va., 1956-58; pres. Bulliss Purissima Parents Group, Los Altos, Calif., 1962-64; bd. dirs. Vols. for Israel, 1986-87. Mem. NAFE, Assn. Computing Machinery, IEEE Computer Soc., Assn. Systems Mgmt., Assn. Women in Computing, Phi Delta Kappa. Democrat. Avocations: computing, gardening, jogging, reading. Office: Ver Strate Press 1645 15th Ave San Francisco CA 94122-3523

CALVIN, ROCHELLE ANN, development association adminstrator; b. St. Paul, Feb. 28, 1936; d. Peter Herbert and Leah (Noun) Schaffer; m. Arnold Orloff, 1957 (div. 1984); children: Robin, Nadine, Steven; m. Stafford R. Calvin, Nov. 25, 1988. BA, U. Minn., 1958. Dir. woman's divsn. United Jewish Fund, St. Paul, 1979-91, devel. dir., 1991—. Pres. Hadassah, St. Paul, 1977. Jewish. Office: United Jewish Fund 790 Cleveland Ave S Saint Paul MN 55116-1958

CAMACHO, DIANNE LYNNE, mathematics educator, administrator; b. Dundas, Ontario, Can., Mar. 21, 1948; d. Leslie Benjamin and Helen Isobel (Don) DeMille; m. Tate Stanley Casey, June 16, 1971 (div. June, 1975); 1 child, Marie Anne; m. Thomas John Camacho, Aug. 30, 1980; children: Patricia Suzanne, Tara Lynne. BA in Math., Whittier Coll., 1970, secondary tchg. cert., 1972; postgrad., Walden U. Math. tchr. Mater Dei H.S., Santa Ana, Calif., 1972-79, Santa Ana (Calif.) H.S., 1979; instr. math. Coast C.C., Costa Mesa, Calif., 1979-81; math. tchr. East Middle Sch., Downey, Calif., 1979-81, South Middle Sch., Downey, 1981-82, Warren H.S., Downey, 1982-93; specialist So. Calif. Regional Algebra Project Orange County Dept. Edn., Costa Mesa, 1993—; mem. math. adv bd. Downey Unified Sch. Dist., 1983—; cons., presenter confs., Orange County Dept. Edn., Costa Mesa, 1986—, Calif. State Dept. of Edn., Sacramento, 1989—; chief math devel. team Calif. Learning Assessment Sys.; chief reader, table leader Stds. Adv. Golden State Math. Exam.; mem. devel. team, chief reader Calif. State Regional Lead Assessment; reviewer Am. Coll. Testing. Author: (book) Batch Basic, 1973; author and project specialist (series of books and workbooks) So. Calif. Regional Algebra Project Focus on Algebra, Focus on Geometry, 1989—, (units in book) Math A, Investigating Mathematics, 1989. Recipient Wright Bros. Innovative Tchrs. award, Rockwell Co., L.A., 1991; grantee Rockwell Co., 1992. Mem. ASCD, Nat. Coun. Tchrs. of Math., Calif. Math. Coun. (Nominee Presidential award 1986). Home: 5243 Hersholt Ave Lakewood CA 90712-2732 Office: Orange County Dept Edn 200 Kalmus Dr Costa Mesa CA 92626-5922

CAMARA, BARBARA MCGUIRE, elementary education educator; b. DeFuniak Springs, Fla., July 22, 1942; d. Moses and Inez (Walton) McGuire; m. Aboubacar Camara; children: Renee, Leaurenza, Taryn. BS in Elem. Edn., U. Ala., 1975; MS in Math. Edn., U. Fla. A&M, 1985. Cert. tchr., Fla. Tchr. Franklin County Schs., Apalachicola, Fla., 1975-81, Leon County Schs., Tallahassee, Fla., 1981—. Recipient Educators award Bethel Missionary Baptist, 1987-88. Mem. Fla. State Math. Assn., Fla. State Sci. Assn., Fla. Tchrs. Assn., Leon County Tchrs. Union (sch. rep., bd. dirs. 1994-96), Phi Delta Kappa. Home: 3520 Cherokee Ridge Trl Tallahassee FL 32312 Office: Leon County Schs Tallahassee FL 32304

CAMBIO, BAMBILYN BREECE, state legislator; b. Johnston, R.I., Dec. 14, 1956; m. James V. Cambio. Cert. Am. Inst. Paralegal Studies. State rep. dist. 11 R.I. Ho. of Reps.; mem. HEW com., joint com. on environment and energy; commr. Exec. Dept. on Deaf and Hard of Hearing; sec. State Govt. Intern Commn.; freelance paralegal, title examiner. Chair North Providence Citizen's Environ. Com.; mem. North Providence Preservation Com., North Providence Women's Dem. Caucus, North Providence Dem. Town Com. Mem. Am. Polit. Item Collectors, R.I. Caucus Women Legislators, Nat. Order Women Legislators. Office: RI Ho of Reps State Capitol Providence RI 02903

CAMBIO, IRMA DARLENE, nursing consultant; b. Belleville, Kans., July 23, 1936; d. James and Agnes Marie (Morehead) Dooley; m. Anderson Cambio (div.); children: Jim, Connie Rae. AA, East L.A. Coll., 1960; student continuing ednl. courses, UCLA, 1966-69; student Coll. Nursing, U. Md., 1985. RN, Calif., Colo., Washington, N.Mex., Wyo. Nurse oper. rm. Beverly Cmty. Hosp., Montebello, Calif., 1960-63; DON Pico Rivera (Calif.) Cmty. Hosp., 1963-64, Burbank (Calif.) Convalescent Hosp., 1964-66; staff nurse oper. rm., then head nurse, insvc. instr. Huntington Meml. Hosp., Pasadena, Calif., 1966-68; staff nurse oper. rm. Sunrise Hosp., Las Vegas, Nev., 1969-71; supr. oper. rm. Valley Hosp., Las Vegas, 1971-72; head nurse med./surg. fl. Chino (Calif.) Gen. Hosp., 1972-73; staff nurse emergency rm. Dr.'s Hosp. Montclair, Calif., 1972-73; head nurse med. fl. Boulder (Nev.) Cmty. Hosp., 1973; staff nurse recovery rm. Holy Cross Hosp., Ft. Lauderdale, Fla., 1973; float nurse, then house shift supr. Imperial Point Hosp., Ft. Lauderdale, 1973-74; staff nurse oper. rm. Lauderdale Lakes (Fla.) Hosp., 1973-74; patient care coord. oper. rm., recovery rm. Imperial Point Hosp., Ft. Lauderdale, 1974-78; asst. head nurse level IV open heart surgery/transplant surgery dept. and transplant divsn. St. Anthony's Hosp., Denver, 1978-80; oper. rm. cons., equipment planner internat. divsn. Nat. Med. Enterprises, 1980-85; mem. oper. rm. staff, float nurse Rocky Mountain Hosp., Denver, 1985; mem. oper. rm. staff St. Joseph Hosp., Denver, 1985-86; head nurse level IV oper. rm. King Faisal Splty. Hosp., Riyadh, Saudi Arabia, 1986-93; cons. oper. rm., recovery rm. and ctrl. sterile supply mgmt. Denver, 1993—; cons. Gortex Graft Co., 1978-80; on-call staff nurse Nursefinders Nurses' Registry, L.A., 1984-85, Olsten Nurses' Registry, Denver, 1985—; travel nurse oper. rm. Georgetown U. Hosp., Washington, 1994, Penrose/St. Francis Hosp., Colorado Springs, Colo., 1994-95; past mem. commissioning team for start-up ops. of 5 new acute care hosps. Taif, Dhahran and Riyadh, Saudi Arabia, 1 acute care hosp. Kuala Lumpur, Malaysia; compiler book for new hosps. detailing equipment, instrumentation and supplies necessary for oper. suite and recovery rm., 1982; rschr./developer policy and procedure manuals for nursing svcs. several hosps., Saudi Arabia, 1983; cons. commd. hosps. and Royal Family Pvt. Med. Clinics, Saudi Arabia, 1986-87; cons. equipment purchase for expansion, cons. materials flow and mgmt. svs. various hosps., Saudi Arabia, 1986-91, NME New Hosp., Malaysia, 1991—, mem. commn. team. Contbr. articles to profl. publs. Participant Health Vols. Overseas, Washington. Mem. Assn. Oper. Rm. Nurses (pres. Las Vegas chpt. 1978-79, mem. mgmt. sys. assembly/divsn. 1994—, rschr. new products, developer plan for presentation and integration to hosps.). Republican. Methodist. Home and Office: 439 Wright St Apt 26 Lakewood CO 80228-1152

CAMERLENGO, HEIDI LYNNE, counselor, educator; b. Trenton, N.J., Mar. 17, 1965; d. Paul Albert and Shirley Ida (Conrad) Gunkel; m. Frank Richard Camerlengo, Aug. 8, 1987; 1 child, Frank Paul. BS magna cum laude, Trenton State Coll., 1987, MA, 1990. Nat. cert. counselor; master's addiction counselor. Residential counselor Anchor House, Trenton, N.J., 1988-90, outreach counselor, 1990-91, outreach dir., 1991—; co-adj. prof. Trenton State Coll., 1990-91; co-chmn. Mercer-Trenton (N.J.) Addiction Sci. Ctr. Adolescent Subcom., 1995—. Office: Anchor House 482 Centre St Trenton NJ 08611

CAMERON, JOANNA, actress, director; b. Greeley, Colo.; d. Harold and Erna (Borgens) C. Student, U. Calif., 1967-68, Pasadena Playhouse, 1968; Assoc. Degree in Bus., MPC, 1996. media cons. to Cath. Bishops on Papal Visit of Pope John Paul II, Calif., 1987. Starred in: weekly TV series The Shazam-ISIS hour, CBS, 1976-78; host, dir.: for TV equipped ships USN Closed Circuit Network Program, 1977, 78, 79, 80; guest star: numerous network TV shows, including Merv Griffin Show, The Survivors, Love American Style, Mission Impossible, The Tonight Show; appeared in numerous commls.; network prime time shows including Name of the Game, Medical Center, Bob Hope Special, The Bold Ones, Marcus Welby, Columbo, High Risk, Switch; motion picture debut in How to Commit Marriage, 1969; other film appearances include The Amazing Spiderman; dir. various commls., CBS Preview Spl.; producer, dir. documentaries include Razor Sharp, 1981, El Camino Real, 1987; discovered by Walt Disney while spl. tour guide at Disneyland; named in Guiness Book of Records for most nat. network programmed commls. Mem. Dirs. Guild Am., Acad. TV Arts and Scis., AFTRA, Screen Actors Guild, Delta Delta Delta. Club: Los Angeles Athletic. Address: Cameron Prodns PO Box 1011 Pebble Beach CA 93953-1011

CAMERON, JUDITH LYNNE, secondary education educator, hypnotherapist; b. Oakland, Calif., Apr. 29, 1945; d. Alfred Joseph and June Estelle (Faul) Moe; m. Richard Irwin Cameron, Dec. 17, 1967; 1 child, Kevin Dale. AA in Psychol., Sacramento City Coll., 1965; BA in Psychol., German, Calif. State U., 1967; MA in Reading Specialization, San Francisco State U., 1972; postgrad., Chapman Coll.; PhD, Am. Inst. Hypnotherapy, 1987. Cert. tchr., Calif. Tchr. St. Vincent's Catholic Sch., San Jose, Calif., 1969-70, Fremont (Calif.) Elem. Sch., 1970-72, LeRoy Boys Home, LaVerne, Calif., 1972-73; tchr. Grace Miller Elem. Sch., LaVerne, Calif., 1973-80, resource specialist, 1980-84; owner, mgr. Pioneer Take-out Franchises, Alhambra and San Gabriel, Calif., 1979-85; resource specialist, dept. chmn. Bonita High Sch., LaVerne, Calif., 1984—; mentor tchr. in space sci. Bonita Unified Sch. Dist., 1988—, rep. LVTV; owner, therapist So. Calif. Clin. Hypnotherapy, Claremont, Calif., 1988—; bd. dirs., recommending tchr., asst. dir. Project Turnabout, Claremont, Calif.; Teacher-in-Space cons. Bonita Unified Sch. Dist., LaVerne, 1987—; advisor Peer Counseling Program, Bonita High Sch., 1987—; advisor Air Explorers/Edwards Test Pilot Sch., LaVerne, 1987—; mem. Civil Air Patrol, Squadron 68, Aerospace Office, 1988—; selected amb. U.S. Space Acad.-U.S. Space Camp Acad., Huntsville, Ala., 1990; named to national (now internat.) teaching faculty challenger Ctr. for Space Edn., Alexandria, Va., 1990; regional coord. East San Gabiel Valley Future Scientists and Engrs. of Am.; amb. to U.S. Space Camp, 1990; mem. adj. faculty challenger learning ctr. Calif. State U., Dominguez Hills, 1994; rep. ceremony to honor astronauts Apollo 11, White House, 1994. Vol. advisor Children's Home Soc., Santa Ana, 1980-81; dist. rep. LVTV Channel 29, 1991; regional coord. East San Gabriel Valley chpt. Future Scientists and Engrs. of Am., 1992; mem. internat. invesigation Commn. UFOs, 1991. Recipient Tchr. of Yr., Bonita H.S., 1989, continuing svc. award, 1992; named Toyolaa Tchr. of Yr., 1994. Mem. NEA, AAUW, Internat. Investigations Com. on UFOs, Coun. Exceptional Children, Calif. Assn. Resource Specialists, Calif. Elem. Edn. Assn., Calif. Tchrs. Assn., Calif. Assn. Marriage and Family Therapists, Planetary Soc., Mutual UFO Network, Com. Sci. Investigation L5 Soc., Challenger Ctr. Space Edn., Calif. Challenger Ctr. Crew for Space Edn., Orange County Astronomers, Chinese Shar-Pei Am., Concord Club, Rare Breed Dog Club (L.A.). Republican. Home: 3257 N La Travesia Dr Fullerton CA 92635-1455 Office: Bonita High Sch 115 W Allen Ave San Dimas CA 91773-1437

CAMERON, KIMBERLY ANNETTE, construction manager; b. Milw., Nov. 15, 1967; d. James Lee Jr. and Georgia Mae (Parker) C. Degree in constrn. mgmt., U. Wis., 1990; MBA in Fin., Concordia U., 1996. Project mgr., estimator Hazardous Substance Abatement Contractors, Denver and Milw., 1991-92; dir. of real estate N.W. Side Comty. Devel. Corp., Milw., 1992-94; dir. home improvement svcs. Opportunities Industrialization Ctr. Greater Milw., 1994-96; pres. GQC Internat., Inc., Milw. and Chgo., 1996—; panelist women exploring apprenticeship Waukesha (Wis.) County Tech. Coll., 1994. Mem. Future Milw., 1995-96. Recipient Equity Initiative award AAUW, 1994-95, Mary Ellen Shadd Strong Pathfinder award OIC-GM, 1995. Mem. NOW (v.p. Milw. chpt. 1996), Nat. Assn. Women in Constn. (cert. constrn. industry technician, nat. chair competition Milw. chpt. # 105 1995-97, pres. 1996-97), Nat. Black MBA Assn. Home: Apt C 8125 N 107th St Milwaukee WI 53224 Office: Opp Indsl Ctr Greater Milw 3030 N Martin L King Dr Milwaukee WI 53212

CAMERON, LUCILLE WILSON, retired dean of libraries; b. Nashua, N.H., Dec. 21, 1932; d. Hugh Alexander and Louise Perham (Baldwin) C.; m. James Robert Doris, Aug. 19, 1976; children: Glenn A. Browning, Gail W. Browning, Valerie B. Cruickshank. BA, U. R.I., 1964, MLS, 1972. Social case worker R.I. Dept. Pub. Assistance, Providence, 1964-70; asst. circulation libr. U. R.I. Libr., Kingston, 1970-72, reserve libr., 1972-73, reference/bibliographer, 1973-88, head reference unit, 1983-86, chair pub. svcs., 1988-89, interim dean, 1989-90, dean, 1990-92, dean emerita. Coauthor: Labor and Industrial Relations Journals and Serials, 1989; contbr. articles to profl. jours. Recipient Computerized Intergrated Libr. System award Champlin Founds., Providence, 1989, 90, 91, Coll. Tech. Libr. Program award U.S. Dept. Edn., Washington, 1990, Disting. Alumna award Grad. Sch. Libr. and Info. Studies, U. R.I., Kingston, 1991. Mem. ALA, Assn. Coll. and Rsch. Librs., Consortium R.I. Acad. and Rsch. Librs., Higher Edn. Libr. Info. Network (chair), Univ. Press New England (gov.), Alpha Kappa Delta.

CAMERON, MINDY, newspaper editor; m. Bill Berg; 2 children; 1 stepchild. B in Journalism, Pacific U. Exec. prodr./anchor, writer pub. TV Rochester, N.Y. and Boise, Idaho; newspaper reporter Boise and Lewiston, Idaho; assoc. city editor Seattle Times, 1981-83, city editor, 1983-89, dep. editorial page editor, 1989-90, editorial page editor, 1990—; leader workshops Am. Press Inst.; writer, reporter PBS documentary, 1978. Bd. dirs. Pacific U., Northwest Pub. Affairs Network. Mem. Nat. Conf. Editl. Writers (bd. dirs. 1993-95), Am. Soc. Newspaper Editors, Soc. Profl. Journalists. Office: Seattle Times Fairview Ave N & John PO Box 70 Seattle WA 98111-0070

CAMERON, RITA GIOVANNETTI, writer, publisher; b. Washington; d. Joseph Angelo and Adeline Katherine (Fochett) C. BS with honors, U. Md., 1957; MEd, Am. U., Washington, 1962; DEd, Nova U., 1978. Tchr. D.C. pub. schs., Washington, 1959-64; prin. Prince George's County (Md.) Pub. Schs., 1964-73, 76-84; supr. instrn. K-12 Prince George's County pub. schs., 1973-76; free-lance writer ednl. materials Media, Materials Inc., Balt., 1965-75; Learning Well, Balt., 1995; free-lance writer travel articles AAA, Washington, 1978-83; owner, pub. Sch. House Global Enterprises, Fort Washington, Md., 1980—; presenter, cons. to sch. systems and ednl. orgns., 1985—. Author: Let's Learn About Maryland and Prince George's County, 1970, Let's Learn About Maryland, 1972, 95, Super Sub! Or How to Substitute Teach in Elementary School, 1974, AAA Traffic Safety Teacher Guide Grades 4-6, 1982, 83; author, pub.: The Master Teacher's Plan and Record Book, 1985, The School House Encyclopedia of Educational Programs and Activities, 1991; author numerous sci. and social studies kits and student programs, travel articles. Food preparer So Others Might Eat, Washington, 1985—, Missions of Charity Home for AIDS Victims, Washington, 1992—. Recipient Outstanding Citizenship award DAR, 1954, Nat. Tchr. award Expedition Nat. Tchr. Awards Program, 1960-61, Outstanding Tchr. Sci. award D.C. Coun. Engring. and Archtl. Soc. and Washington Acad. Scis., 1964, Outstanding Educator of Yr. award Prince George's County Bd. Edn., 1982-83, Am. Hist. award DAR, 1987, Outstanding Contbn. to Bicentennial Leadership Project award Couns. for Advancement of Citizenship, 1989. Mem. Md., Fla., N.C., N.Y., Pa. N.J., Va., Tex., Ga., Gt. Lakes, Mid.

States, S.E., and N.E. Regional Coun. for Studies, U. Md. Alumni Assn., Am. U. Alumni Assn., Nova U. Alumni Assn., Nat. Press Club, Phi Kappa Phi. Roman Catholic. Office: Sch House Global Enterprises PO Box 441028 Fort Washington MD 20749-1028

CAMERON, SUSAN KAY, public relations executive; b. Storm Lake, Iowa, Mar. 15, 1960; d. Charles William and Lois JoAnn (Reser) Hutchins; m. Michael J. Cameron, Aug. 12, 1989. BA, Buena Vista U., Storm Lake, 1982. Mgr. news and editl. svcs. Drake U., Des Moines, 1984-85; asst. dir. pub. rels. Buena Vista U., 1982-84, dir. pub. rels., 1985—; presenter Conf. for Women in Higher Edn., Cedar Rapids, 1988; chairperson com. for career advancement for minorities and women Mid.-Am. dist. Coun. for Advancement and Support of Edn., 1989, presenter leadership conf., sec., 1990, student scholarship chairperson 1992, chairperson conf. program track 1992-93, conf. program chairperson 1994-95; participant Nat. CASE Commn. on Philanthropy, 1995—. Alumni bd. dirs. St. Mary's Cath. Sch., Storm Lake, 1991-93. Recipient Young Alumnus award Buena Vista U., 1995. Mem. Storm Lake C. of C. (bd. dirs. 1992, chairperson pub. rels. com. 1986-87, amb. 1990—, Profl. Leadership award 1993). Roman Catholic. Office: Buena Vista Univ 610 W 4th St Storm Lake IA 50588-1713

CAMERON-GODSEY, MELINDA A. BRANTLEY, artist; b. El Dorado, Ark., Jan. 3, 1954; d. Austin Van and Jamie Lou (Middleton) Brantley; m. James Stephen Cameron, Jan. 5, 1973 (div. Nov. 1985); children: Kelly Van Cameron, Courtney Y. Cameron; m. William Paul Godsey, Jan. 1, 1995. BFA, La. Tech. U., 1979. Registered interior designer, Ark. Solo exhbns. include Riverside Art Gallery, Shreveport, 1990, Ark. River Valley Art Ctr., Russellville, 1989, Hot Springs (Ark.) Art Ctr., 1988, South Arkansas Art Ctr., El Dorado, 1991, 88, 95, Dishman Art Gallery, Beaumont, Tex., 1987, Ariel Gallery, N.Y.C., 1986, numerous others; art work published in American Artist's Annual Publication, Watercolor 90, Crazyhorse, Poet's Market, others. Mem. Knickerbocker Artists, Mid-Southern Watercolor Soc., Southwestern Watercolor Soc. Episcopal. Home and Office: 1217 Cypress El Dorado AR 71730

CAMINATI, LINDA MARY, mental health services administrator; b. Freeport, N.Y., Mar. 1, 1947; d. Oleg and Mary Theresa (Gabunas) Litt; m. Peter Louis Caminati, Apr. 20, 1974 (div. Oct. 1991); 1 child, Julie. BA in History, SUNY, Albany, 1969; MS in Tech. Mgmt., SUNY, Stony Brook, 1995. Resource and reimbursement agt. 1 Office Mental Health, West Brentwood, N.Y., 1969-76; sr. rsch. and reimbursement agt. 3 Office Mental Health, Kings Park, N.Y., 1976-80, ops. rev. supr., 1980-81; rsch. and reimbursement agt. 4 Office Mental Health, West Brentwood, 1982-89, sys. devel. mgr., 1990—. Mem. ASPA, Nat. Assn. Reimbursement Officers, Metro N.Y. Albany Alumni Assn. Roman Catholic. Home: 47 Imperial Dr Selden NY 11784 Office: NY State Office Mental Health Office Patient Resources West Brentwood NY 11717

CAMMARATA, JOAN FRANCES, Spanish language and literature educator; b. Bklyn., Dec. 22, 1950; d. John and Angelina Mary (Guarnera) Cammarata; m. Richard Montemarano, Aug. 9, 1975. BA summa cum laude, Fordham U., 1972; MA, Columbia U., 1974, MPhil., 1977, PhD, 1982. Preceptor, Columbia Coll., N.Y.C., 1974-82; adj. instr. Fordham U., N.Y.C., 1980-81; adj. asst. prof. Iona Coll., New Rochelle, N.Y., Manhattan Coll., 1982-84; asst. prof. Manhattan Coll., Riverdale, N.Y., 1982-90, assoc. prof., 1990-96, prof., 1996—. Author: Mythological Themes in the Works of Garcilaso de la Vega, 1983; editl. reviewer D.C. Heath; contbr. articles and revs. to profl. jours. Fellow arts and sci Columbia U., 1972-75; grantee Manhattan Coll., 1985, 91, NEH, 1987, 88, Rsch. Fellowship grantee N.Y.U. Faculty Seminars, 1992, 94; named univ. assoc. Faculty Resources Network Program NYU, 1985—, Andrew Mellon Found. vis. scholar, 1990; scholar-in-residence NYU, 1991-92; mem. adv. bd. Centro de Idiomas del Sureste, Mex. Mem. Cervantes Soc. Am., Am. Council Teaching of Fgn. Langs., N.E. MLA (Rsch. Fellowship grantee 1991), South Atlantic, South Ctrl. and Midwest MLA, Inst. Internat. de Lit. Iberoamericana, Renaissance Soc. of Am., Assn. Internat. de Hispanistas, MLA, Am. Assn. Tchrs. Spanish and Portugese, Hispanic Inst., N.Y. State Assn. Fgn. Lang. Tchrs. Roman Catholic. Avocations: piano, gardening, writing, needlework. Home: 135 Lawrence Pl New Rochelle NY 10801-1108 Office: Manhattan Coll Riverdale NY 10471

CAMMAROTA, MARIE ELIZABETH, health services administrator, nursing educator; b. Phila., Oct. 12, 1943; d. Angelo J. Cammarota and Angeline M. Cardile; m. Charles C. Cammarota, Aug. 14, 1965; 1 child, Sharon Marie. AS, Orange County Coll., Middletown, N.Y., 1963; BA, Glassboro State Coll., 1977, MA, 1981; EdD, Nova Southeastern U., 1995. Cert. sch. social worker, sch. nurse, pupil personal svcs., supr., FNP, sch. nurse practitioner, N.J.; RN, N.J., N.Y., Pa. Staff nurse to asst. head nurse Thomas Jefferson U. Hosp., Phila., 1963-65; instr. St. Joseph's Hosp., Sch. Nursing, 1965-66; sch. nurse Gloucester County Vocat. Tech. Sch., Sewell, N.J., 1974-88; asst. prof. Rowan Coll. N.J., Glassboro, 1988—; adj. prof. Gloucester County Coll., Sewell, 1985—, Glassboro (N.J.) State Coll., 1986-88; cons. com. on sch. health N.J. Acad. Pediatrics, Trenton, 1986—; cons. Edn., Info. and Resource Ctr., Sewell, 1989—; spkr. in field; state advisor N.J. Health Occupations Am. Recipient Golden Apple award Edn., Info. & Resource Ctr., Sewell, 1991. Mem. ANA, AAUW, Am. Acad. Pediatrics (affiliate sect. sch. health), Am. fedn. Tchrs., Gloucester County Sch. Nurse Assn. (pres. 1983-85), Phi Delta Kappa (Zeta Nu chpt. v.p. membership 1993-96, historian 1996—, Outstanding Leadership award 1984). Home: 44 Bryant Rd Turnersville NJ 08012-1447

CAMMERMEYER, MARGARETHE, nurse; b. Oslo, Mar. 24, 1942; came to U.S., 1951; d. Jan and Margrethe (Grimsgaard) C.; m. Harvey H. Hawken, Aug. 1965 (div. 1980); children: Matthew, David, Andrew, Thomas. BS, U. Md., 1963; MA, U. Wash., 1976, PhD, 1991. RN, Wash. Enlisted U.S. Army, 1961, advanced through grades to capt., 1965, resigned, 1968; staff nurse VA Hosp., Seattle, 1970-73, clin. nurse specialist in neurology, epilepsy, 1976-81; clin. nurse specialist in neuro-oncology VA Med. Ctr., San Francisco, 1981-86; clin. nurse specialist in neuroscis., nurse rschr. VA Med. Ctr., Tacoma, Wash., 1986-96; ret., 1996; capt. to col. USAR, 1972-88; asst. chief nurse, supr. Army Res. Hosp., Oakland, Calif., 1985-88; col. Wash. Army N.G. and N.G. Hosp., Tacoma, 1988-96. Co-author: Neurological Assessment for Nursing Practice, 1984 (named Book of Yr. ANA), Serving in Silence, 1994; co-editor, contbg. author: Core Curriculum for Neuroscience Nursing, 1990, 93; contbr. articles to profl. jours. Decorated Bronze Star medal; recipient presdl. cert. for outstanding community achievement of Vietnam era vets., 1979, "A" Proficiency designation Office of Surgeon Gen. Dept. of Army, 1986, Woman of Power award NOW, 1993; named Woman of Yr. Woman's Army Corps Vets. Assn., 1984, Nurse of Yr. VA, 1985. Mem. Feminist Majority Found., Am. Assn. Neurosci. Nursing (chair core task force), Am. Nurses Assn. (hon. human rights award 1994), U. Wash. Nursing Assn. (Disting. Alumna 1995), Assn. Mil. Surgeons. of U.S., Sigma Theta Tau. Home and Office: 4632 Tompkins Rd Langley WA 98260

CAMOES, NORMA ARCAMO, school nurse; b. Tagbilaran City, Bohol, The Philippines, Feb. 22, 1940; came to U.S., 1964; d. Florentino Cloma and Marcelina Basio Arcamo; m. Manuel F. Camoes, May 7, 1966; children: Manuel Norman, Marie-Noelle. BA, U. San Carlos, Cebu City, The Philippines, 1957; grad., So. Island Hosp. Sch. Nursing, Cebu City, The Philippines, 1962; postgrad. in pediatrics, Children's Meml. Hosp., Quezon City, The Philippines, 1963; sch. nurse practitioner cert., U. Colo., 1982. Staff nurse Children's Meml. Hosp., 1962-64; pvt. duty nurse San Juan De Dios Hosp. and Marian Hosp., Manila, 1963-64; staff nurse Newark City Hosp., 1964-68, head nurse prim. nursery, 1966-68; staff nurse Chas. Har. Meml. Hosp., St. Croix, V.I., 1968-78; pub. health nurse Dept. Pub. Health, St. Croix, V.I., 1970-78; sch. nurse Dept. Edn., St. Croix, V.I., 1978-95. Mem. Nat. Assn. Sch. Nurses, Am. Acad. Nurse Practitioners, Am. Fedn. Tchrs., St. Croix Fedn. Tchrs. Democrat. Roman Catholic.

CAMP, ALETHEA TAYLOR, executive organization development consultant; b. Wingo, Ky., Nov. 12, 1938; d. Wayne Thomas and Ethel Virginia (Austin) Taylor; children: Donna Paul, Sean Richard. BA, Murray State U., 1961; MA, So. Ill. U., 1975. Tchr. McLean and Hopkins (Ky.) County Schs., 1961-64; instr. homebound Harrisburg (Ill.) Community Sch. Dist., 1971-73; counselor evaluation Coleman Rehab. Ctr., Shawneetown, Ill., 1974-75; counselor corrections and parole Dept. Corrections, State Ill., Springfield, 1975-77, supr. casework, 1977, supr. parole, 1977-80; asst. warden programs Dept. Corrections, State Ill., Hillsboro, 1980-84, warden, 1984-91; correctional program specialist Nat. Inst. Corrections, Washington, 1991-95. Mem. NAFE, Assn. Exec. Women in Corrections, Am. Correctional Assn., Ill. Correctional Assn., N. Am. Wardens Assn.

CAMP, BARBARA ANN, municipal government official; b. Lancaster, Pa., Feb. 13, 1943; d. Linton Ferguson and Anna (Wills) Mennig; m. Nils Victor Anderson, Nov. 25, 1961 (div. 1972); children: Barbara Jean, Susan Michelle, Jennifer Eileen; m. Robert Tomlin Camp, Dec. 29, 1973. Cert. mcpl. clk., Sun Oil Corp., Phila., 1960-61; sales clk. Thomas Jewelers, Ocean City, N.J., 1969-71; composite typist Avalon Herald, N.J., 1971-72; exec. sec. Publs. Press., Pleasantville, N.J., 1972-74; clk.-typist Twp. of Upper Tuckahoe, N.J., 1977-78, mcpl. clk., 1978—. Editor twp. calendar, 1984-86. Mem. Mcpl. Clks. Assn. of N.J. (asst. treas. 1985-87, treas. 1987, asst. sec. 1988, sec. 1989, 2d v.p. 1990, 1st v.p. 1991, pres. 1992, N.J. Mcpl. Clk. of Yr., 1995), Internat. Inst. Mcpl. Clks. (bd. dirs. region II 1994, 95, 96), Cape May County Clks. Assn. (past sec., past v.p., past pres.), Assn. Twps. (sec.). Avocations: snow skiing, boating. Home: 223 Laurel Dr Marmora NJ 08223-1241

CAMP, HAZEL LEE BURT, artist; b. Gainesville, Ga., Nov. 28, 1922; d. William Ernest and Annie Mae (Ramsey) Burt; m. William Oliver Camp, Jan. 24, 1942; children: William Oliver, David Byron. Student, Md. Inst. Art, 1957-58, 62-63. One-woman shows at Ga. Mus. Art, Rockville Art Mus., Coll. Notre Dame (Balt.), U. Md., Balt. Vertical Gallery, Cleveland Meml. Gallery (Balt.), Unicorn Gallery, 1982, Hampton Ctr. for Arts and Humanities (Va.), 1985, Bendann Art Gallery, Balt., 1980, Cultural Art Center On The Hill Gallery, Yorktown, Va., 1995, others; exhibited in juried shows at Peale Mus., Balt., Wilmington (Del.) Fine Arts Ctr., Smithsonian Instn., City Hall Gallery, Balt., 1982, Balt. Watercolor Soc., 1983, 94, 95, Miniature Painters, Sculptors and Gravers Soc. at the Arts Club, Washington, 1987, 88, 89, 90, 91, 92, 93, 94, 95 (Honorable Mention award 1991), Hampton Bay Days Raddison Hotel Gallery, 1988, Twentieth Century Gallery, Williamsburg, Va., 1989, 90, 91, 92, 93, 94, 95, 96, D'Art Ctr., Norfolk, Va., 1989, Va. Watercolor Soc. at Va. Beach Ctr. for Arts, 1990, at Verona, Va., 1991, At William King Regional Arts Ctr., Abingdon, Va., 1992, Longwood Center Visual Arts, Farmville, Va., 1995, Lynchburg Fine Arts Center, Lynchburg, Va., 1996, Yorktown Cultural Arts Ctr. Va., 1991, 92, 93, 94, 95, 96, Goucher Coll. (1st prize in watercolor Nat. League Am. Pen Women Md. Juried Exhibit 1993, 94), Hermitage Found. Mus., Norfolk, 1994, Francis Land House, Va. Beach, 1994, Cork Gallery Lincoln Ctr., N.Y.C., 1994, Nat. Juried Exhibit of Nat. League Am. Pen Women, Turner Gallery, Balt., 1994, 95, Balt. Watercolor Soc., Pa. Watercolor Soc., 1994, Susquehanna U. Lore A. Degenstein Gallery, 1994, Suffolk Art League, 1994, Salmagundi Club, N.Y.C., 1995, others; represented in permanent collections Ga. Mus. Art, Athens, Peabody Inst., Balt., Rehoboth Art League, Del., numerous pvt. collections; work publ. in Artists of Mid-Atlantic, 1991; contbr. illustrations to mags., booklets. Recipient 1st prize Md. chpt. Artists' Equity, 1967, St. Marys County Art Assn., 1964, 67, 1st prize still life Cape May, N.J., 1969, Catonsville (Md.) Community Coll., 1969, Nat. League Am. Pen Women Exhibit at St. John's Coll., 1969, Best in Show York (Pa.) Art Assn. Gallery, 1972, 2d award Md. Inst. Alumni Founding Chpt., Balt., 1976, Best in Show Three Arts Club, Balt., 1978, Honorable Mention, Rehoboth Art League, Del., 1983, 93, Purchase award Old Point Nat. Bank, Hampton, Va., 1985, Merit award Hampton (Va.) City Hall, 1986, Juror's Choice award Twentieth Century Gallery, Williamsburg, Va., 1987, Award of Excellence Md. State Biennial Eliminations of Nat. League Am. Pen Women at Essex Community Coll., 1989, Montgomery Coll., Rockville, Md., 1987, Honorable Mention award Nat. Miniature Show, Jackson, Tenn., 1991, Honorable Mention award Suffolk Art League, 1992. Mem. Nat. League Am. Pen Women (pres. Carroll bd. 1968-70, editor The Quill 1975-76, editor Carroll br. 1982-83, rec. sec. nat. exec. bd. 1979-80, nat. nominating com. 1982, Md. art chmn. 1982, 3d prize oil Nat. Biennial exhibit Tulsa, Okla., 1966, miniature exhibit at Furman U., 1992 (1st prize Nat. Show, Excellence award and honorable mention 1993), Rehoboth Art League, Del. Hampton Arts League, Va. Watercolor Soc. (signature artist mem.), Balt. Watercolor Soc. (signature artist life mem., hon. mention 1982, sec. 1978-80), Peninsula Fine Arts Ctr., 20th Century Gallery, Yorktown Cultural Arts Ctr., Tidewater Art Assn., Miniature Painters, Sculptors and Gravers Soc. Washington, D.C. (assoc.), Pa. Watercolor Soc. Methodist. Home: 2 Bayberry Dr Newport News VA 23601-1006

CAMP, LINDA JOYCE, local government official; b. Plattsburgh, N.Y.; d. Maurice B. and Katherine E. (Trombley) C. BS, Cornell U., 1973, M of Pub. Sci., 1977. Media specialist N.Y. Sea Grant Program, Ithaca, 1973-76; mgr. comm., cable comm. officer City of St. Paul, 1980-87, purchasing systems mgr., 1988—; mem. met. coun. telecom. task force, St. Paul, 1982-85; mem. Minn. Telecom. Coun., St. Paul, 1984-85. Vol. Big Sister Program, St. Paul, 1980-83; bd. dirs. Minn. Ctr. for Women in Govt. Bush fellow, 1987. Mem. Nat. Assn. Telecom. Officers (pres. 1983, Pres.'s award 1985), Am. Mgmt. Assn., Am. Soc. for Pub. Adminstrn. (bd. dirs.), St. Paul Women in City Mgmt., Cornell U. Club (Minn.). Office: City of St Paul 280 City Hall Saint Paul MN 55102

CAMP, SHARON LEE, steel company technician, financial secretary; b. Denver, May 2, 1950; d. Edward Joseph and Wanda Marie (Young) C. Cert. millwright Parma (Ohio) Continuing Adult Edn. Millwright LTV Steel, Cleve., 1976—; fin. sec. United Steelworkers Am., Cleve., 1994—; coord. LTV Steel/United Steelworkers United Way, Cleve., 1994—; emergency responder LTV Steel, 1995—. Recipient Citizenship award Mary Rose Oakar, 1985. Mem. Scandanavia Health Club. Democrat. Roman Catholic. Office: United Steelworkers Local 185 1700 Denison Ave Rm 108 Cleveland OH 44109

CAMPAGNA, DEBRA, foundation administrator; b. Troy, Ala., July 18, 1949; d. Charles Edwin and Dorothy Carter (Sellers) Howard; m. Keith Alan Campagna, Oct. 30, 1976; children: Zoe, Asia, Kesa. BA, Vanderbilt U., Nashville, Tenn., 1971. CFRE. Public relations specialist Fireman's Fund Ins., San Francisco, 1974-77; freelance writer and public relations consultant San Francisco and Nashville, 1978-80; editl. dir. Dye, Van, Mol, Lawrence & Ericson, Nashville, 1980-81; freelance writer and public relations cons. Nashville, 1981-82; public relations cons. Holder Kennedy P.R., Nashville, 1982-83; mktg. dir. Nashville Symphony, 1983-86; dir. devel. Children's Hosp. Vanderbilt, Nashville, 1986-89, Conn. Children's Med. Ctr., Newington, Conn., 1989-92; v.p. Conn. Children's Med. Ctr., Hartford, 1992—; fellow Healthcare Forum, San Francisco, 1995-96; mem. bd. dirs. Inst. Cmty. Rsch., Hartford, 1992-95, CHILD Coun., Hartford Primary Care Consort. Mem. bd. dirs. Southside Instns., Neighboorhood Alliance, Hartford, YWCA Greater Hartford; founder Youth & Family Svcs., Haddam, Conn., 1992-95; grad. Leadership Greater Hartford, 1991. Mem. Nat. Soc. Fundraising Execs., Assn. Healthcare Philanthropy.

CAMPANELLI, PAULINE EBLE, artist; b. N.Y.C., Jan. 25, 1943; d. Joseph and Dorothy Eble; m. Dan Campanelli, May 24, 1969. Grad., Ridgewood Sch. of Art, 1964; student, Art Students League, 1965-67. fine arts pub. N.Y. Graphic Soc. Exhibited in group shows including Am. Art Gallery, Greenwich, Conn., Temple U., Lever House; represented in pub., corp. and pvt. collections throughout U.S.; author: Wheel of the Year, 1989, Ancient Ways, 1991, Circles, Groves and Sanctuaries, 1992, Rites of Passage, 1994, Halloween Collectibles, 1995, Art of Pauline and Dan Campanelli, 1995, Romantic Valentines, 1996; art work and home featured in Colonial Homes, Country Living, Country Almanac, Country Collectibles.

CAMPBELL, ALICE SHAW, retired accountant, poet; b. Crawfordsville, Ind., Aug. 29, 1918; d. Chester Monroe and Amy Susan (Peck) Shaw; m. George A. Campbell, Aug. 29, 1936. Student, Ind. U., 1958-74. With State and USDA Soil Conservation Svc., 1952-57, Dept. HEW-Social Security Adminstrn., Lafayette Motor Parts Co., Inc., West Lafayette, Ind., 1979-88. Author: (poetry) Kaleidoscope, 1989; contbr. poetry to publs. including Best Poems of 1995, Treasured Poems of Am., The Desert Sun, In the West of Ireland. Named Golden Poet, World of Poetry, 1989; recipient L.A. Poetry Acad. award presented by Milton Berle, 1993.

CAMPBELL, ANITA JOYCE, computer company executive; b. Jefferson City, Mo., Sept. 24, 1953; d. George Rigsby and Betty Jean (Heade) Sanders; m. Michael Joseph Campbell (div. 1986); children: Kim Erik Seaver, Daniel Joseph Campbell. AAS, Lincoln U., Jefferson City, 1985. Student lab. mgr. Lincoln U., 1985; integrated systems analyst Xerox Corp., St. Louis, 1988-89, ins. industry project mgr., western region ops. mgmt. staff, 1990-91, advanced product specialist, western regions ops. mgmt., 1991, advanced solutions tech. mgr., western region ops. mgmt., 1992-93, tech. market project mgr., rsch. & engring, integrated systems orgn., 1993-94, tech. mktg. mgr. integrated solutions, systems sales and support, 1994-95; tech. con., integrated document solutions Integrated Document Solutions, 1995—; project mgr. state and local govt. Xerox Profl. Doc. Svcs. Bridgeton, Mo., 1996—. Co-developer Delta Plan, 1988. Office staff campaign mgr. for Carter-Mondale Reelection Com., Washington, 1989-90; waterfront dir. Spl. Olympics, Lake of the Ozarks, Mo., 1987; bd. dirs. ARC, Jefferson City, 1986. Home: 912 Leawood Dr Saint Louis MO 63126-1114 Office: Xerox Corp 3221 McKelvey Rd Bridgeton MO 63044

CAMPBELL, ANN MARIE, artist; b. Burbank, Calif., June 14, 1956; d. Stephen and Ann Marie (Luis) C.; children: Richard Arthur, Robert Campbell, Victoria Ann. BA in Painting, Sculpture, Graphic Arts, UCLA, 1982. Artist: (murals) The Pickle Barrel, 1992, Old World Sky with Angels, 1996, Cottage Garden, 1995, Two Street Window, 1996, numerous others. Mem. Nat. Soc. Mural Painters, Am. Soc. Portrait Artists, Alpha Lambda Delta. Roman Catholic. Office: PO Box 581 Folsom CA 95630

CAMPBELL, BONNIE JEAN, former state attorney general; b. Norwich, N.Y., Apr. 9, 1948; d. Thomas Glenn and Helen Henrietta (Slater) Pierce; m. Edward Leo Campbell, Dec. 24, 1974. BA summa cum laude, Drake U., 1982, JD, 1984. Bar: Iowa 1985, U.S. Dist. (no. and so. dist.) Iowa 1985, U.S. Ct. Appeals (8th cir.) 1989, U.S. Supreme Ct. 1989. Clk. U.S. Dept. Housing and Urban Devel., Washington, 1965-67, U.S. Senate Subcom. on Inter Govtl. Relations, Washington, 1967-69; case worker Hon. Harold E. Hughes, Washington, 1969-74; field rep. U.S. Senator John C. Culver, Des Moines, 1974-80; assoc. Wimer, Hudson, Flynn & Neugent, P.C., Des Moines, 1984-89; of counsel Belin, Harris, Helmick, Des Moines, 1989-91; atty. gen. State of Iowa, 1991-94. Mem. awareness com. Powell III, Iowa Meth. Hosp., Des Moines, 1984; mem. adv. com. Des Moines Community Coll., Ankeny, Iowa, 1985; state chmn. Iowa Dems., Des Moines, 1987-89. Mem. Iowa Bar Assn. (lawyers helping lawyers 1985—), Phi Beta Kappa.•

CAMPBELL, CATHERINE B., marketing and corporate communications executive; b. Havre de Grace, Md., June 30, 1962; d. Jack and Carol Marie (Preston) Barham; m. Daniel Bostic Campbell II, Apr. 15, 1989; 1 child, Daniel Bostic Campbell III. BS in Journalism, U. Md., 1984, MA, 1991. Prodn. asst. Nat. Newspaper Assn., Washington, 1983-84; pub. rels. asst. The Ryland Group, Columbia, Md., 1984-86, pub. rels. coord., 1986-89, mgr. corp. comms., 1989-91; mgr. pub. rels. Blue Cross Blue Shield of Md., Owings Mills, 1991-92, dir. pub. rels., 1992-94; dir. mktg. and corp. comms. Green Spring Health Svcs., Owings Mills, 1995—. Bd. dirs. Developmental Svcs. Group, Inc., Columbia, 1991—. Mem. Women in Comms., Pub. Rels. Soc. of Am. (bd. dirs. Md. chpt. 1986—, com. mem. 1992—). Office: Green Spring Health Svcs 5565 Sterrett Pl Ste 500 Columbia MD 21044

CAMPBELL, CLAIRE PATRICIA, nurse practitioner, educator; b. Jan. 10, 1933; d. Hugh Paul and Clara Louise (Bell) Campbell. Student So. Meth. U., 1956-57; BS in Nursing, U. Tex. Sch. Nursing-Galveston, 1959, Family Nurse Practitioner, 1979, cert., 1984, 89; MS in Nursing, Tex. Woman's U. Sch. Nursing, 1971. Staff nurse Parkland Meml. Hosp., Dallas County Hosp. Dist., 1955-70, head nurse gen. surgery, chest surgery, neurosurgery, orthopedics, and internal medicine, until 1970; instr. nursing Tex. Woman's U. Sch. Nursing, Dallas, 1971-72; rschr. nursing diagnosis, Dallas, 1972-77; FNP Otis Engring. Health Svc., Dallas, 1979-86, nurse practitioner pain mgmt. program Dallas Rehab. Inst., 1986-95, HealthSouth SubAcute Unit, 1995—; adj. asst. prof. U. Tex. Sch. Nursing, Arlington, 1976—; cons. nursing diagnosis. Author: Nursing Diagnosis and Intervention in Nursing Practice, 1st edit., 1978, 2d edit., 1984. Mem. ANA, Tex. Nurses Assn. - Dist. 4, North Am. Nursing Diagnosis Assn., Sigma Theta Tau. Roman Catholic.

CAMPBELL, DEBRA LYNN, marketing and new venture consultant; b. Phoenix, Apr. 8, 1954; d. Joseph David and Elaine Lucinda (Krueger) C.; m. J. Frederick Stillman III, Oct. 26, 1985; 1 child, J. Frederick Stillman IV. BS, U. Ariz., 1975; MBA, Harvard U., 1980. Brand mgr. Procter & Gamble Co., Cin., 1975-78; project mgr. Dunham & Marcus, N.Y.C., 1980-81; v.p. Cox, Lloyd Assocs., N.Y.C., 1981-83; cons. Am. Cons. Corp., N.Y.C., 1983-85, dir., 1985-87, dir., CFO, 1987-88, pres., COO, 1988-90; pres. DCA, 1990—; pres. 173-175 Tenant's Corp.; bd. dirs. Amarillo Grill, Inc. Treasurer Phoenix Theatre Co., N.Y.C. Recipient Reggie award Promotion Mktg. Assn. Am. (Reggie award 1986, 87, 90). Mem. Am. Mktg. Assn. Office: DCA 175 Riverside Dr New York NY 10024-1616

CAMPBELL, DONNA MARIE, telecommunications executive; b. Somerville, N.J., Oct. 7, 1949; d. Howard E. and Joyce E. Bilbee; m. Charles Edward Campbell, Mar. 28, 1969; children: Carla Marie, Bradley James. Attended, Eckerd Coll. Bus. Mgmt., St. Petersburg, 1988. Personnel adminstr. The Bradenton Herald, 1979-82; dir. telecommunications HCA Blake Hosp., Bradenton, Fla., 1982-88; corp. mgr. telecomm. Snelling & Snelling Internat., Sarasota, Fla., 1988-90; mgr. telecomm. and ops. mgr. Health Resource Network Sarasota (Fla.) Meml. Hosp., 1990-94; dir. The Health Resource Network, 1994—; mem. SunHealth Alliance Task Force, 1991. Mem. Am. Bus. Women's Assn. (sec. 1983, pres. 1984, woman of yr. 1985), West Fla. Hosp. Comm. Assn. (sec. 1984-85, pres. 1986-87), Am. Hosp. Assn. (guest speaker nat. conf. 1991), IBX Users' Group (attendant console foucs com. 1993-94, nat. conf. hostess 1995, mem. exec. bd. 1995), Fla. Pub. Interest Rsch. Group, Am. Coalition for the Homeless. Republican. Baptist. Office: Sarasota Meml Hosp 1700 S Tamiami Trl Sarasota FL 34239-3509

CAMPBELL, DORIS KLEIN, retired psychology educator; b. Tazewell County, Ill.; d. Emil L. and Cora May (Osterdock) Klein. AB, Augustana Coll., 1930; MA, U. Ill., 1931; EdD, U. Fla., 1962. Instr. Arlington Hall, Washington, 1931-33, Cen. Coll., Mc Pherson, Kans., 1933-37; supr. student teaching Seattle (Wash.) Pacific Coll., 1937-39; tchr. The Harris Schs., Chgo., 1939-41; instr. to full prof. East Tenn. State Univ., Johnson City, 1960-77; Fulbright prof. psychology Silliman Univ., Dumaguete, Philippines, 1977-80; cons. Philippine-Am. Ednl. Found., Manila, 1968-69. Recipient Fulbright grant Coun. for Internat. Exchange of Scholars, Washington, 1968-69. Mem. APA, Am. Assn. Ret. Persons, Am. Coun. for the Blind, Fulbright Alumni Assn., Phi Kappa Phi, Delta Kappa Gamma, Tau Kappa Alpha, Kappa Delta Pi, Psi Chi. Methodist. Home: 16 Lake Hunter Dr Apt B213 Lakeland FL 33803

CAMPBELL, ELIZABETH ROSE, astrologer; b. Rocky Mount, N.C., Mar. 7, 1952; d. Walker Aylett Jr. and Sarah West (Davis) C. BA in Journalism, U. N.C., 1975, BA in Studio Art, 1975. Asst. editor The Sun: A Mag. of Ideas, Chapel Hill, N.C., 1977-82; dir. mktg., seminar prodr. Omega Inst. for Holistic Studies, Rhinebeck, N.Y., 1982-84; founder, counselor Wild Rose Cons., Carrboro, N.C., 1994—. Contbr. (anthology) The Best of the Sun, Vol. I, 1985, Vol. II, 1986, Dreams are Wiser than Men, 1988. Fellow Edna St. Vincent Millay Colony, 1986, Cummington Cmty. of Arts, 1988, Va. Ctr. for Creative Arts, 1996. Home: PO Box 175 Carrboro NC 27510

CAMPBELL, FELICIA FLORINE, English language educator, editor; b. Cuba City, Wis., Apr. 18, 1931; d. Frank Churchill and Irene (Bower) Florine; m. Ritsman Overmier Campbell, Dec. 1, 1962 (div. 1974); children: Adam, Jedediah, Catherine Burns, Tracy Campbell Tuttle. BS, U. Wis., 1955, MS, 1957; PhD, U.S. Internat. Univ., 1973. Tchg. asst. U. Wis., Madison, 1955-57, 59-61; instr. Wis. State Coll., Whitewater, 1957-59; prof. U. Nev., Las Vegas, 1962—; book critic Sta. KNPR Pub. Radio, Las Vegas, 1987—; film judge Las Vegas Ind. Film Festival, 1994. Editor: (jour.) Popular Culture Rev., 1989—; adv. editor: Jour. Popular Culture, 1992—; contbr. articles to profl. jours. Chair Nev. Gov.'s Commn. on Status of People, Las Vegas, 1975-77; pres. Nat. Soc. Profs., Las Vegas, 1974-75, 76;

pres. NOW, Las Vegas, 1973-75. Mem. Popular Culture Assn. (pres. 1993 95, del.-at-large 1990-92, bd. dirs.), Far West Popular Culture Assn. (CEO, dir. 1989—). Democrat. Home: Box 149 13 Montana Blue Diamond NV 89004-0149 Office: U Nev Dept English Box 455011 4505 Maryland Pkwy Las Vegas NV 89154-5011

CAMPBELL, FRANCES HARVELL, foundation administrator; b. Goldston, N.C.; d. George Henry and Evelyn (Meggs) Harvell; m. John T. Campbell, Jr., Apr. 27, 1968 (div. Aug. 1973). BS magna cum laude, U. Md., 1982. Asst. to Congressman Claude Pepper, U.S. Ho. of Reps., 1966-80, staff dir., 1980-89; dir. Claude Pepper Ctr., 1996—; chmn. bd., pres. Mildred and Claude Pepper Found., 1989—; exec. dir. Franklin D. Roosevelt Meml. Commn., 1988-92; Author: Young America Speaks, 1957. V.p. Dem. Women of Capitol Hill, 1982-83; bd. dirs. Fla. State U. Found., Nat. Com. to Preserve Social Security and Medicare, Econ. Club Fla.; del. White House Conf. on Aging, 1995, Fla. Coun. on Aging, Nat. Coun. on Aging. Mem. ACLU, AAUW, Gerontol. Soc. Am., So. Gerontol. Soc., Rotary Club Internat., Tiger Bay Club, Zonta, Phi Kappa Phi, Alpha Sigma Lambda. Avocations: orchid culture, reading, traveling. Home: 3943 Leane Dr Tallahassee FL 32308 Office: 210 S Woodward Ave Tallahassee FL 32304

CAMPBELL, GLENDA GAIL, medical and surgical nurse; b. Graham, Tex., July 28, 1953; d. Austin Bell and Margaret Louise (Ward) C. AA, Cisco (Tex.) Jr. Coll., 1974; BSN cum laude, Midwestern State U., 1992. Cert. NRP, PALS, TNCCP, ACLS. Asst. in lab. Graham Gen. Hosp., 1969-71; magnetic tape machine operator Graham Magnetics, 1972-73; sec./draftsman Dresser Atlas, 1974-84; sec. Campbell Rathole Drlg., Inc., 1984-91; clin. asst. Graham (Tex.) Gen. Hosp., 1991; grad. nurse, staff nurse RN Graham Gen. Hosp., 1992—. Recipient Nat. Collegiate Nursing award Midwestern State U., 1992. Mem. Nat. Student Nurses Assn., Midwestern State U. Nursing Honors Soc., Christian Broadcasting Network, Nat. Humane Edn. Soc., Nat. Bus. Assn., Sigma Theta Tau, Tex. Gamma Chpt. of Alpha Chi. Republican. Home: PO Box 52 Graham TX 76450-0052

CAMPBELL, JANE TURNER, former realtor; b. Macon, Mo., July 8, 1931; d. Thomas Freeman and Rena Ellen (Vandiver) Turner; m. Duard Ray McDonald, Aug. 25, 1952 (div. 1955); m. Ian MacCallum Campbell, Mar. 28, 1958; children: Colin Turner, Clay Ian. BS in Edn., U. Mo., 1953; postgrad., San Diego State Coll., 1955-57, UCLA, 1958. Cert. secondary sch. tchr., Calif., Ill., N.J.; lic. real estate salesperson, broker, N.J., lic. real estate salesperson, Pa. Tchr. Hallsville (Mo.) High Sch., 1953-54; co-owner McDonalds' Clothiers, Wewoka, Okla., 1954-55; tchr., class advisor Imperial (Calif.) High Sch., 1955-58, Temple City (Calif.) High Sch., 1958-59; prof. Coll. San Mateo, Calif., 1965-70, McHenry County Coll., Crystal Lake, Ill., 1972-76, Waubonsee Coll., Aurora, Ill., 1976-79; tchr., adminstr. Purnell Sch., Pottersville, N.J., 1980-86; realtor Sig Kuhne Realtors, Milford, N.J., 1986-89, Burgdorff Realtors, Inc., Pittstown, N.J., 1989-94; ret., 1994; co-founder Audio, Verbal, & Tutorial Ctr. McHenry County Coll., 1975-77. Author: Shorthand I, Shorthand II, Shorthand III, Office Procedures I, Bookkeeping I, Bookkeeping II, Bookkeeping III, Medical Sec., Legal Sec., Office Procedures II, Bus. Materials, Bus. Law, Office Machines I, Office Machines II. Chairperson Del. Valley Autumn Antique Show, Holland Twp., N.J., 1988-93, Holland Twp. Hist. Preservation Commn., 1989-95, Christmas Project, Hunterdon County, N.J., 1988—. Mem. Hunterdon County Bd. Realtors (Community Svc. award 1988), N.J. Assn. Realtors, Holland Twp. Women's Club (chairperson Clarence Carter Night 1988), Golden Talents (pres., v.p., trustee 1988-91), Pi Beta Phi. Republican. Episcopalian. Home: RR 2 Box 2672-6 Aitken Ln Edwards MO 65326-9588

CAMPBELL, JEAN, retired human services organization administrator; b. Fairhaven, Mass., Mar. 4, 1925; d. Elwyn Gilbert and Marion Hicks (Dexter) C. AA, Lasell Coll., Auburndale, Mass., 1944; BA, Brown U., 1946; MEd, U. Hartford, 1963. Field dir. Waterbury (Conn.) Area Coun. Girl Scouts, Inc., 1946-52; exec. dir. Manchester (Conn.) Girl Scouts, Inc., 1952-60; dist. dir. Conn. Valley Girl Scout Coun., Inc., Hartford, 1961-63; dir. field svcs. Plymouth Bay Girl Scout Coun., Taunton, Mass., 1963-64, exec. dir., 1964-68; exec. dir. New Bedford (Mass.) YWCA, 1968-87. Trustee Millicent Libr., Fairhaven, 1970—; corporator Compass Bank for Savs., 1976—, St. Luke's Health Found., 1986—; bd. dirs. Greater New Bedford Concert Series, 1978—; com. mem., past pres. Interchurch Coun. of Greater New Bedford, 1973—; bd. dirs., former treas. ICC Svcs. Corp., 1973—; bd. dirs. ICC Congregate Housing, Inc., 1991—, Fairhaven Improvement Assn., 1990-93; mem. 1st Congl. Ch. Fairhaven, chair history com., 1990-94; mem. Fairhaven/New Bedford--Tosashimizu (Japan) Sister City Com., 1991-94; asst. treas. Ladies Br. of the N.B. Port Soc., 1990-94, treas., 1994—. Recipient Thanks badge Girl Scouts U.S., 1956, Sidney Adams Cmty. Svc award Interch. Coun. of Greater New Bedford, 1984, AAUW Achievement award, 1987; named Woman of Yr., Internat. Women's Day Com., 1987; Annual Jean Campbell Svc. award established by YWCA of Southeastern Mass., 1995. Mem. AAUW (3d v.p. New Beford br. 1991-93), Fairhaven Hist. Soc. (investment com. 1992—), Lasell Coll. Alumnae Inc. (bd. mgmt. 1994—), Delta Kappa Gamma (pres. Eta chpt. 1986-88, chair family lit. project 1991—, state lit. coun. mem. 1991—, Alpha Upsilon State Achievement award 1992).

CAMPBELL, JILL FROST, academic administrator; b. Buffalo, July 29, 1948; d. Jack and Elaine Mary (Hamilton) Frost; m. Gregory H. Campbell, May 31, 1969; children: Geoffrey, Kimberly, Kristina. BS, SUNY, Brockport, 1970, MS in Edn., 1981; postgrad., SUNY, Buffalo, 1989—. Acct. clk. bursar's office SUNY, Brockport, 1974-75, sr. acct. clk., 1975-78, instl. rsch. asst., 1978-82, asst. dir. instl. rsch. office, 1982-86, acting assoc. pers. office, 1986-87, dir. contract and grant adminstrn. Rsch. Found., 1987—; adminstrv. svcs. coord. for profl. devel. SUNY, 1995—. Mem. exec. com. Nativity Home Sch. Assn., Nativity Blessed Virgin Sch., Brockport, 1985-87, mem. sch. pub. rels. and mktg. com., 1985-88; mem. Friends of Brockport Athletics, 1985—; coach Brockport Youth Summer Soccer, 1988-91; mem. com. Chancellor's Award for Excellence in Profl. Svc., Brockport, 1989-90. Grantee United Univ. Professions, 1985, 90, 93, 94. Mem. NAFE, Nat. Assn. Instl. Rsch. (mem. exec. com., co-originator and discussion leader books and current issues 1985-87, co-author profl. file, presenter papers, presenter panels 1979-87), SUNY Assn. Instl. Rsch. and Planning Officers (mem. exec. com., presenter papers, presenter panels 1984-87), Nat. Coun. Univ. Rsch. Adminstrs., North East Assn. Instl. Rsch. (mem. exec. com., sec. 1985-87, presenter papers, presenter panels 1978-87), Internat. Conf. for Women in Higher Edn. (presenter 1992), SUNY Brockport Alumni Assn., Brockport Profl. Women's Group, Rsch. Found. Cen. Office (users group 1987-90, sponsored program comm. com. 1990—, 4-yr. rsch. coun. 1988—, vice chair 1991, chair 1992), N.Y. State/United Univ. Professions (Excellence award 1990). Home: 5129 Redman Rd Brockport NY 14420-9601 Office: SUNY Rsch Found 350 New Campus Dr Brockport NY 14420-2932

CAMPBELL, JOANNA See SIMON, JO ANN

CAMPBELL, JUDITH MAY, physical education educator; b. Terre Haute, Ind., May 13, 1938; d. O.H. and D. Juanita C. B.S. in Phys. Edn., Ind. State U., 1960, M.S., 1963; D.Phys. Edn., Ind. U., 1978. Recreational dir. Terre Haute Park Dept., summers 1958-60; tchr. St. Louis pub. schs., 1960-61; instr. dept. phys. edn. Ind. State U., Terre Haute, 1961-66, asst. prof., 1968-75, assoc. prof., 1975-79, prof., 1979—, dir. undergrad. preparation; coach volleyball and basketball teams Univ. Sch., 1970-74, girl sports dir., 1974-78; founder Ind. Spl. Olympics, Inc., 1970; chmn. basketball Wabash Valley Bd. Women Ofcls., 1963-65, 68-74; nat. adv. bd. Spl. Olympics, Inc.; mem. nat. adv. bd. Joseph P. Kennedy, Jr. Found., 1972-74, chmn. Contbr. articles to profl. publs.; developer phys. edn. program in sch. curriculums. Bd. dirs. Ind. Spl. Olympics, 1968-74, state co-dir., 1970-74; bd. dirs. State Girls Sports Adv. Bd., 1975-77, Leadership Terre Haute, 1989—; mem. Air Pollution Bd. Vigo County, 1987-90; trustee Vigo County Sch. Bd., 1986-94. Recipient Lambert award Ind. State U., 1960; recipient Outstanding Phys. Fitness Leadership award Vigo County Jaycees, 1968, Service award Vigo County Assn. for Retarded Citizens, 1971, Community Service award Vigo County Jaycees, 1974, Eleanor St. John Disting. Alumni award, 1977, Katherine Hamilton Vol. award, 1989; Lilly Found. grantee, 1974; Chismar Found. grantee, 1972; Internat. Leadership Scholar; selected grand marshall Homecoming Parade Ind. State U., 1985. Mem. AAUP (pres. 1981—), Ind. Assn. Health, Phys. Edn. & Recreation (program devel. leadership award 1972, leadership award 1974), Mental Health Assn. Vigo County (bd. dirs. 1985 93), LWV (bd. dirs. Vigo County chpt. 1987 89), Delta Kappa Gamma (pres. 1980-82, grantee 1978), Phi Delta Kappa, Delta Psi Kappa. Home: 6745 E Manor Dr Terre Haute IN 47802-9019

CAMPBELL, KAREN ANN, marketing and promotion professional; b. Lynn, Mass., Nov. 8, 1951; d. Robert Franklin and Rita (Trebul) C. BS, U. N.H., 1973. Educator Danvers (Mass.) Pub. Schs., 1973-81; tournament dir. Boston 5 Classic, 1981-85, Golf Digest/Tennis Inc., Trumbull, Conn., 1985-91; ops. mgr. GD/T Sports Mktg., Trumbull, Conn., 1993—; dir. N.Y. Times Event/Sports Mktg., Trumbull, Conn., 1993—. Office: NY Times Mag Group 5520 Park Ave Trumbull CT 06611

CAMPBELL, KARLYN KOHRS, speech and communication educator; b. Blomkest, Minn., Apr. 16, 1937; d. Meinhard and Dorothy (Siegers) Kohrs; m. Paul Newell Campbell, Sept. 16, 1967. BA, Macalester Coll., 1958; MA, U. Minn., 1959, PhD, 1968. Asst. prof. SUNY, Brockport, 1959-63; with The Brit. Coll., Palermo, Italy, 1964; asst. prof. Calif. State U., L.A., 1966-71; assoc. prof. SUNY, Binghamton, 1971-72, CUNY, 1973-74; prof. communication studies U. Kans., Lawrence, 1974-86, dir. women's studies, 1983-86; prof. speech-communication U. Minn., Mpls., 1986—, dept. chair, 1993-96; inaugural Gladys Borchers lectr. U. Wis., Madison, 1974. Author: Critiques of Contemporary Rhetoric, 1972, rev. edit., 1997, Form and Genre, 1978, The Rhetorical Act, 1982, rev. edit. 1996, The Interplay of Influence, 1983, rev. edits., 1987, 92, 96, Man Cannot Speak for Her, 2 Vols., 1989, Deeds Done in Words, 1990, Women Public Speakers in the United States, 1800-1925: A Bio-Critical Sourcebook, 1993, Women Public Speakers in the United States, 1925—: A Bio-Critical Sourcebook, 1994; mem. editl. bd. Communication Monographs, 1977-80, Quar. Jour. Speech, 1981-86, 92-94, Critical Studies in Mass Commn., 1993—, Philosophy and Rhetoric, 1988-93; contbr. articles to profl. jours. Recipient Woolbert Rsch. award, 1987, Winans-Wichelns book award, 1990, Ehninger Rsch. award, 1991; Tozer scholar Macalester Coll., 1958, Tozer fellow, 1959; Fellow Shorenstein Barone Ctr., JFK Sch. of Govt., Harvard, 1992; Disting. Scholar award Human Communications, 1992. Mem. Speech Communication Assn. (disting. scholar award), Central States Speech Communication Assn., Ctr. Study of the Presidency, Phi Beta Kappa, Pi Phi Epsilon. Office: U Minn Dept Speech Commn 460 Folwell 9 Pleasant St SE Minneapolis MN 55455

CAMPBELL, KATHERINE MARIE LANGREHR, elementary and secondary education educator; b. N.Y.C., Dec. 4, 1947; d. Anton A. and Katherine (Batky) Langrehr; m. Frederick Augustus Campbell, Nov. 4, 1967; children: Julie Ann, Alicyn Katherine. BA in History, U. Bridgeport, 1970; MS in Lang. Arts Edn., Ctrl. Conn. State U., 1992. Tchr. grade 3 & 5 Holy Rosary Parochial Sch., Bridgeport, Conn., 1968-71; outreach worker Mignatory Children's Program Vernon (Conn.) Bd. Edn., 1980-81; sales rep. Proctor & Gamble, Wilton, Conn., 1982-86; reading/math tutor Bennet Jr. H.S., Manchester, Conn., 1986-87; tchr. lang. arts Elisabeth M. Bennet Mid. Sch., Manchester, Conn., 1987—, dept. head lang. arts, 1994-96; mem. content validation com. Nat. Bd. Profl. Teaching Stds., 1996; presenter in field. Mem. Gifted & Talented Bd. Vernon Bd. Edn., 1992-93; dir. Planning Bd. Emergency Shelter, Vernon, 1984-85; scout leader Girl Scouts Am., Vernon, 1979-80; treas., bd. dirs. PTO Vernon Elem. Sch., 1976-80. Recipient Celebration of Excellence award State of Conn., 1992; Conn. Writing Project fellow, 1989. Mem. AAUW, Nat. Coun. Tchrs. English, Internat. Reading Assn., New Eng. League Mid. Schs., Conn. Reading Assn. Office: Elisabeth M Bennet Mid Sch 1151 Main St Manchester CT 06040

CAMPBELL, KRISTINE KOETTING, pediatric nurse, administrator; b. Arcadia, Wis., Feb. 22, 1952; d. John Joseph and Dorothy Ann (Vogel) Koetting; m. Douglas William Campbell, Feb. 1, 1980; children: Colin William, Ryan Joseph. BSN, Viterbo Coll., La Crosse, Wis., 1974; MS in Nursing, Ohio State U., 1983; postgrad. studies in nursing, Oregon Health Scis. U., Portland, 1988—. RN Oreg., Wash.; TNCC (Emergency Nurses Assn.). Staff nurse Natal ICU Madigan Army Med. Ctr., Tacoma, Wash., 1974-76; head nurse nursery US Army Hosp., Augsburg, Germany, 1976-79; head nurse pediatrics US Army Hosp., Ft. Campbell, Ky., 1979-81; instr. pediatric and nursey nurses Columbus (Ohio) Tech. Inst., 1983-84; instr. pediatric nursing Ohio State U., Columbus, 1984-87; grad. rsch. asst. Oreg. Health Scis. Univ., Portland, 1988—; nursing supr. Landstuhl (Germany) Army Med. Ctr., 1990-91; chief nurse 396th Combat Support Hosp., Vancouver, Wash., 1995—; child educator tng. adults in positive parenting, Longview, Wash., 1992—. Co-author: (computer simulation) Lucy Web a four year old with Down's Syndrome undergoing a tonsillectomy. Mem. PTO, Longview, Wash., 1988—. Capt. U.S. Army, 1974-81; col. USAR. Recipient Instnl. Nat. Rsch. Svc. award, Oreg. Health Scis. U., 1990. Mem. ANa, Nat. Coun. on Family Rels., Res. Officers Assn., Assn. Mil. Surgeons U.S., Sigma Theta Tau. Democrat. Home: 3 Country Club Dr Longview WA 98632-5424 Office: Sch of Nursing Oreg Health Scis U 3181 SW Sam Jackson Park Rd Portland OR 97201-3098

CAMPBELL, LAURIE MARIE, artist; b. N.Y.C., Oct. 29, 1954; d. James Joseph and Beatrice Catherine (Anton) C. BA with honors, Brown U., 1976. One-woman show Vera Engelhorn Gallery, N.Y.C., 1995, 96; exhibited in group shows at Galerie Claudine Lustman, Paris, 1995, Galerie Jacob, Paris, 1994, Gallery K, Washington, 1994, Andrea Marquit Gallery, Boston, 1992, 93, others; represented in permanent collections Pfizer, Inc., N.Y.C., Champion Paper Corp, Conn., others. Home: 720 Ft Washington Ave #6E New York NY 10040

CAMPBELL, LINDA SUE, guidance counselor; b. Carbondale, Pa., Oct. 9, 1960; d. Charles Frederick and Grace Elizabeth (Mackle) Koehler; m. Terrance Lee Campbell, May 5, 1984. BS in Social Work, Mansfield U., 1982; postgrad., U. Scranton, 1988-93. Student caseworker Children's Svcs. Tioga County, 1981; live-in resident advisor Dauphin Residences, Inc., Harrisburg, Pa., 1982-83; live-in resident mgr. Human Resources Ctr., Inc., 1983-84, evaluator, placement officer, 1984-86, program specialist, 1986-93; guidance counselor Veritas Therapeutic Community Inc., Barryville, N.Y., 1993—. Mem. adminstrv. coun. Bethany United Meth. Ch., Honesdale, Pa., 1993-95, 95—. Mem. ACA, Am. Sch. Counselor Assn., Social Work/Anthropol./Sociol. Club (v.p. 1981). Republican. Home: RR 3 Box 760 Honesdale PA 18431-9521

CAMPBELL, MARGARET GEORGESON, retired librarian; b. Dayton, Ohio, Apr. 22, 1913; d. Andrew Gilbertson and Jessie (Taylor) C. BA, Ohio Wesleyan U., 1935; MLS, Western Res. U., 1952. Med. technologist Mt. Sinai Hosp., Cleve., 1936-39; med. technologist S.C. State Bd. Health, Columbia, 1939-45; club dir. ARC, Munich, Germany, 1945-46, Kunsan, Taegu, Korea, 1947-50; libr. U.S. Army Spl. Svcs., Germany, France, 1952-54; libr. dir. Shaker Heights (Ohio) Pub. Librs., Berlin, 1953-54; ret. Shaker Heights (Ohio) Pub. Librs., 1975; auditing student U. South Fla., Tampa, 1986—. Libr. vol. Sarasota (Fla.) Pub. Libr., 1976-78; interviewer Met. Ministries, Reading for the Blind, WUSF Radio, 1990—; vol. sr. care Univ. Cmty. Hosp., 1984—. Mem. Delta Zeta. Methodist. Home: 4000 E Fletcher Ave Apt G309 Tampa FL 33613-4818

CAMPBELL, MARGARET M., social work educator; b. New Orleans, Dec. 1, 1928; d. Walter and Caroline Louise (Seither) C. BA, St. Mary's Dominican Coll., 1950; MSW, Boston Coll., 1952; 3d yr. cert. clin. practice, N.Y. Sch. Social Work, 1959; DSW, Columbia U., 1970. Caseworker Charity Hosp., New Orleans, 1951-53, Cath. Social Services, San Francisco, 1953-55; supr. Spl. Service Club sect. U.S. Army Europe, 1956-58; caseworker Children's Bur., New Orleans, 1959-60, Associated Cath. Charities, New Orleans, 1960-63; lectr. Dominican Coll., New Orleans, 1961-66; spl. projects worker Associated Cath. Charities, New Orleans, 1964-65; dir. Fla. Family Ctr., New Orleans, 1965-67; asst. prof. Tulane U. Sch. Social Work, New Orleans, 1968, assoc. prof., 1971; dir. continuing edn. programs Tulane U., New Orleans, 1976-80; dir. Child Welfare Svcs. Tng. Ctr. Region VI, New Orleans, 1979-82; dean Tulane U. Sch. Social Work, New Orleans, 1982-94, prof., 1986—; dir. Ctr. on Aging, 1993-96, ret., 1996; chmn. various coms. sch. social work including Advanced Programs Continuing Edn., Ednl. Policy, NASW Student Liaison, Priorities Com. Author numerous publications and articles in profl. jours. in field. Mem. Kingsley House Bd., 1985, Area Agy. on Aging, 1988; bd. dirs. Tulane Ctr. Aging Rsch. and Svcs., 1993. Recipient Alumnae award Dominican Coll., 1970, Dominican Coll. Torchbearer award, 1985. Mem. NASW (chpt. pres. 1973-75, bd. dirs., treas., program dir., membership com., 1955-85; social worker of yr. Southeastern La. chpt. 1976; La. chpt. award 1978, La. chpt. Lifetime Achievement award 1992), Acad. Cert. Social Workers, Internat. Conf. on Social Welfare, New Orleans Children's Council, Child Welfare Info. Exchange Panel for La., Task Force on Adolescent Treatment Ctr., New Orleans Collaborative Tng. Program, Child Welfare League (chmn. southeastern conf. 1980-83), Council on Social Work Edn. (steering com. 1980-81, coordinator 1985), La. State Med. Soc. (geriatrics subcom. 1985-86), Nat. Council on Aging, Gerontological Soc. Am. (conf. com. 1985), Southern Gerontology Soc., Adult Protection Services Network, Coun. on Social Work Edn. (planning com. ann. meeting 1990-91), Am. Pub. Welfare Assn. (regional conf. com. 1989-90), Nat. Assn. Deans and Dirs. Schs. Social Work (chair 1991 meeting).

CAMPBELL, MARIA BOUCHELLE, lawyer, church executive; b. Mullins, S.C., Jan. 23, 1944; d. Colin Reid and Margaret Minor (Perry) C. Student, Agnes Scott Coll., 1961-63; AB, U. Ga., 1965, JD, 1967. Bar: Ga. 1967, Fla. 1968, Ala. 1969. Pvt. practice law Birmingham, Ala., 1968-94; law clk. U.S. Cir. Ct. Appeals, Miami, Fla., 1967-68; assoc. Cabaniss, Johnston and Gardner, 1968-73; sec., counsel Ala. Bancorp., Birmingham, 1973-79; sr. v.p., sec., gen. counsel AmSouth Bancorp., 1979-84, exec. v.p., gen. counsel, 1984-94; exec. v.p., gen. counsel AmSouth Bank, 1984-94; exec. asst. to rector Parish of Trinity Ch., N.Y.C., 1994—; lectr. continuing legal edn. programs; cons. to charitable orgns. Exec. editor Ga. Law Rev, 1966-67. Bd. dirs. St. Anne's Home, Birmingham, 1969-74, chancellor, 1969-74; bd. dirs. Children's Aid Soc., Birmingham, 1970-94, 1st v.p., 1988-90, pres., 1990-92; trustee Canterbury Cathedral Trust in Am., 1992—, Discovery 2000 Children's Mus., 1991-94, Soc. for Propagation of Christian Knowledge, 1991-93; bd. dirs. NCCJ, 1985-94, state chair, 1990-93; bd. dirs. Positive Maturity, 1976-78, Mental Health Assn., 1978-81, YWCA, 1979-80, Op. New Birmingham, 1985-87, pers. com., 1987-90, v.p., 1990-94; bd. dirs. Soc. for the Fine Arts U. Ala., 1986-89, Baptist Hospital Found. of Birmingham Inc., 1994-95, Alliance for Downtown N.Y., 1995—; commr. Housing Authority, Birmingham Dist., 1980-85, Birmingham Partnership, 1985-86, Leadership Birmingham, 1986—, program com., 1989-90, co-chair program com., 1990-91; mem. pres. adv. coun. Birmingham So. Coll, 1988-92, chair bd. overseers Masters Program, 1990-94; mem. pres.'s cabinet U. Ala., 1990-95; trustee Ala. Diocese Episcopal Ch., 1971-72, 74-75, mem. canonical revision com., 1973-75, 89-91, liturg. commn., 1976-78, treas., chmn. dept. fin., 1979-83, mem. coun., 1983-87, chancellor, 1987-91, cons. on stewardship edn., 1981-94, dep. to gen. conv., 1985, 88, 91; mem. Standing Commn. on Constn. and Canons, 1988-94; vestryman St. Luke's Episcopal Ch., 1991-94; bd. advisors So. region of Am. Soc. Corp. Secs., pres., 1992-94; community advisor Jr. League Birmingham, 1992-93; mem. adv. bd. Cahaba River Soc., 1991-94. Named One of Top 10 Women in Birmingham, 1989, One of Top 5 Women in Bus., 1993. Mem. ABA, State Bar Ga., Fla. Bar, Ala. Bar Assn., Birmingham Bar Assn., Am. Corp. Counsel Assn. (bd. dirs. Ala. 1984-89), Assn. Bank Holding Cos. (chmn. lawyers com. 1986-87), Greater Birmingham C. of C. (bd. dirs. 1988-94, exec. com. 1992-94, vice chmn., gen. counsel 1993-94), India House, Kiwanis, The Ch. Club N.Y., Order of St. John of Jerusalem. Home: 200 Rector Pl Apt 36E New York NY 10280-1174 Office: Parish of Trinity Ch 74 Trinity Pl New York NY 10006

CAMPBELL, MARILYN R., state legislator; b. Salem, N.H., July 31, 1932; married; 3 children. BS, U. N.H., 1954. Registered occupational therapy. Former dir. Salemhaven, Inc.; ret. farmer, pres. Turner Homestead, Inc., Salem; dir. Granite State Electric Co.; mem. N.H. Ho. of Reps., 1972-94; bd. dirs. Pelham Bank and Trust. V.p. N.H. Farm Bur., 1984-88; pres. N.H. Farm Bur. Assoc. Women, 1980-84; mem. women's com. Am. Farm Bur., 1984-90. Methodist. Home: 79 Brady Ave Salem NH 03079-4004

CAMPBELL, MARTHA MADISON, foundation program officer; b. Glen Ridge, N.J., May 9, 1941; d. Kenneth and Margaret Bruce (Macon) C.; m. Morton Park Iler, May 30, 1964 (div. July 1988); children: Douglas Gordon, Janet Madison, Bruce Campbell; m. David Malcolm Potts, March 25, 1995. BS, Wellesley Coll., 1963; MA, U. Colo., 1989, PhD, 1994. Statis. analyst A.C. Nielsen Co., N.Y.C., 1963; founder, dir. Population Speakout, Denver, 1988-93; mktg. cons. Specialized Comm., Denver, 1989-93; program officer population David and Lucile Packard Found., Los Altos, Calif., 1994—; vis. scholar U. Calif. Berkeley, 1994; cons. Planned Parent Fedn. Am., 1990-91. Contbr. articles to profl. jours. Office: David & Lucile Packard Fdn 300 Second St Los Altos CA 94022

CAMPBELL, MARY ANN, social psychologist; b. St. Louis, Oct. 28, 1950. BS in Edn. with honors, Drake U., 1972; MA in Sociology, Washington U., 1980, PhD in Sociology, 1988. Instr. Des Moines Area C.C., 1974-75; tchg. fellow Washington U., 1976-77, rsch. asst. dept. sociology and ctr. for the study of law in edn., 1979, instr., 1982, rsch. asst. dept. sociology, 1980-81; instr. Florissant Valley C.C., 1981; adj. instr. The Lindenwood Colls., 1982; instr. Kans. State U., 1983-84, co-dir. curriculum integration project dept. sociology, anthropology & social work, 1984; asst. prof. Rider Coll., 1985-86; asst. prof. U. Wis., Parkside, 1986-91, mem. women's studies faculty, 1986-91; rsch. asst. U. Ind.-Bloomington & Ctr. for Urban and Regional Studies U. N.C.-Chapel Hill, 1977, Dept. Sociology Drake U., 1974-75; rsch. cons. State Iowa Dept. Pub. Instrn., 1973-75; head rsch. asst. ACLU and Iowa Civil Liberties Union, 1973-74; legal advocate for abused women, St. Louis County, 1992-95. Contbr. chpts. to books, articles to profl. jours.; rev. (book) Doing Fieldwork: Warnings and Advice, 1980, (jour.) Jour. Contemporary Ethnography, 1988-90; assoc. editor: Jour. of Applied Sociology, 1991; presenter in field. Bd. dirs. Women & Recovery, Inc., St. Louis, 1978-79. Recipient Mary Will Dunkle scholarship for outstanding women in edn. Drake U., 1969-72. Mem. NOW, AAUW, Am. Sociolog. Assn., Nat. Women's Studies Assn.Soc. for the Study of Social Problems, Sociolog. Practice Assn. (mem. mental health interest group), Soc. for Applied Sociology, Midwest Sociolog. Soc., Clin. Sociology Soc., Wis. Sociolog. Assn., Alpha Kappa Delta.

CAMPBELL, MARY STINECIPHER, research chemist, educator; b. Chattanooga, Feb. 26, 1940; d. Jesse Franklin and Florence Gladys (Marshall) S.; m. John David Fowler Jr. (div. Mar. 1979); children: John Christopher, Jesse David; m. Billy M. Campbell, Jan. 1995. BA, Earlham Coll., 1962; PhD, U. N.C., 1967. Postdoctoral researcher Research Triangle Inst., Research Triangle Park, N.C., 1966-68, 74-76; mem. staff Los Alamos (N.Mex.) Nat. Lab., 1976—; adj. prof. organic, inorganic and phys. chemistry U. N.Mex. Grad. Ctr., Los Alamos, 1989—; instr. chemistry lab., 1989; vis. scientist AFOSR (AFATL), Eglin AFB, Fla., 1980-81. Contbr. articles to profl. jours.; inventor ammonium nitrate explosive systems and other explosive salts, fruit grower using organic methods. Mem. AAUW (sec. 1972-74), Am. Chem. Soc., N.Mex. Network Women in Sci. and Engring. (v.p. 1985-86, pres. 1986-87), Los Alamos Women in Sci. (pres. 1983-85), Toastmasters Internat. (pres. 1988, 696 Club), Los Alamos Folkdancers (treas. 1991-93), Bio-Integral Rsch. Ctr., N.Mex. Apple Coun. Democrat. Unitarian. Office: Los Alamos Nat Lab MS C920 Group DX-2 Los Alamos NM 87545

CAMPBELL, MILDRED CORUM, business owner, nurse; b. Warfield, Va., Feb. 24, 1934; d. Oliver Lee and Hazel King (Young) Corum; m. Hugh Stuart Campbell, Dec. 2, 1972. BSN, U. Va., 1956; operating rm. mgr. cert., U.S. Army Med. Svcs. Sch., San Antonio, 1967; gen. mgr. cert., Cedars of Lebanon Med. Ctr., L.A., 1968. Head nurse plastic surgery U. Va. Med. Ctr., Charlottesville, 1956-58, head nurse cardio-surg., 1958-61; staff nurs operating rm. NIH Heart Inst., Bethesda, Md., 1961-62; supr. operating and recovery rms. Med. Univ. of S.C., Charleston, 1962-64; head nurse cardio operating rms. Meth. Hosp., Tex. Med. Ctr., Houston, 1964-67; supr. operating and recovery rms. Cedars of Lebanon Med. Ctr., L.A., 1967-68; product-nurse cons. Ethicon, Inc., Somerville, N.J., 1968-69; nurse cons. Johnson & Johnson, New Brunswick, N.J., 1969-70; gen. mgr. Ariz. Heart Inst., Phoenix, 1970-72; owner, pres., bd. dirs. Highland Packaging Labs., Inc., Somerville, 1983—. Mem., moderator Nat. Assn. Operating Rm. Nurses, Denver, 1963-76; pres. Aux. Orgn., Muhlenberg Hosp., Plainfield, N.J., 1979-80; chmn. Assn. for Retarded Citizens Fund Raising Ball, Somerset County, N.J., 1982. Mem. Inst. Packaging Profls. Home: 58 Westcott Rd Princeton NJ 08540-3071 Office: Highland Packaging Labs Inc 1181 US Highway 202 Somerville NJ 08876-3909

CAMPBELL, NANCY EDINGER, nuclear engineer; b. Washington, May 9, 1957; d. Ralph Joseph and Eleanor (Brabble) Edinger; m. Larry Alan

Campbell, Feb. 25, 1984. BS in Nuclear Engring. with honors, Ga. Inst. of Tech., 1978; MBA, U. Pitts., 1985. Nuclear safety engr. Westinghouse Nuclear Tech. Div., Monroeville, Pa., 1978-81; nuclear fuel proposal engr. Westinghouse Nuclear Fuel Div., Monroeville, 1981-86; nuclear fuel project engr. Westinghouse Comml. Nuclear Fuel Div., Monroeville, 1986-90; reactor engr. U.S. Nuclear Regulatory Commn., Washington, 1990—; chmn. hospitality, rep. nuclear fuel div. Westinghouse Women's Career Devel. Com., Pitts., 1985-87. Mem. DAR, Am. Nuclear Soc., adv. com. U.S. N.R.C. Fed. Women's Program, Nat. Trust Hist. Preservation, Engring. Soc. Balt., Phi Kappa Phi, Tau Beta Pi, Phi Eta Sigma. Republican. Episcopalian. Office: US Nuclear Regulatory Commn Washington DC 20555

CAMPBELL, PATRICIA ELAINE, elementary education educator; b. Cin., Dec. 3, 1943; d. Jake T. and Margaret O. (Hunter) C.; 1 child, Andre. BA in Elem. Edn., Andrews U., 1968; MA in Edn., U. Cin., 1978. Cert. elem tchr., prin. and supr., Ohio. Tchr. elem. Cin. Pub. Schs., 1968—, consulting tchr. Math. Assessment Devel., 1988—; curriculum writer gifted and talented, career edn., programs in math. and sci.; mentor; youth program leader. Chmn. bd. Pvt. Parochial Sch., Cin., 1991-95. Mem. Ohio Maths. Group, Cin. Maths. Groupg, Nat. Coun. Tchrs. Maths. Adventist. Office: Cin Pub Schs 230 E 9th St Cincinnati OH 45202-2138

CAMPBELL, PATRICIA JEAN, critic, book editor; b. L.A., Nov. 20, 1930; d. Fred Duane and Frances (Griffith) Cowan; m. Billy Wilmon Campbell, Apr. 20, 1951 (div. Sept. 1971); children: Frederick, Bruce, Aisha, Cameron; m. David Lincoln Pildas Shore, Feb. 7, 1984. BA, UCLA, 1952; MLS, U. Calif., Berkeley, 1954. Freelance critic, editor, writer Fallbrook, Calif., 1979—; columnist (The Sand in the Oyster) Horn Book Mag., Boston, 1993—; lit. agt. Campbell Assocs. Lit. Agy., Fallbrook, 1995—; gen. editor Twayne's Young Adult Author series Simon & Schuster, N.Y.C., 1986—; cmty. orgn. cons. Fed. Office of Econ. Opportunity, L.A., 1969-70; instr. in adolescent lit. UCLA Extension, Westwood, Calif., 1976-81. Author: Sex Guides: Sex Education Books for Young Adults, 1979, Passing the Hat: Street Performers in America, 1981, Books and Films About Sexuality for Young Adults, 1986; co-author: (with David Shore) New Zealand by Motorhome, 1989, Europe by Van and Motorhome, 1991, 94; editor: The Fair Garden and the Swarm of Beasts, 1994; contbr. articles and revs. to newspapers and jours.; author and presenter (video) The Facts of Love in the Library, 1987; author and spkr. (audiotape) Sexuality in the Young Adult Novel, 1981; presenter and spkr. workshops for librarians in young adult lit., 1972—, other workshops in field; columnist Wilson Libr. Bull., Bronx, N.Y., 1978-88, 88-95; referee Jour. Youth Svcs. in Librs., 1990—; mem. editl. bd. Top of the News, 1980-81. Librarian, cataloger Libr. Hawaii, Honolulu, 1954-56; young adult libr., Westchester Br. L.A. City Pub. Libr., 1970-72; asst. coord. young adult svcs. L.A. Pub. Libr., 1972-77. Mem. ALA (Grolier Found. award 1989), Young Adult Libr. Svcs. Assn. (bd. dirs. 1979-82, Best Books for Young Adults com. 1978-80, TV com. 1980-84, publishers' liaison com., 1984-86, co-chair task force on adolescent pregnancy 1985-89, task force on adolescent health 1989-91, selection com. for Margaret Edwards award 1990, Grolier award com. 1994), Nat. Coun. of Tchrs. of English, Assembly on Lit. for Adolescents (bd. dirs. 1993-96, ALAN award com. 1994, chair 1996), Internat. Reading Assn., SIG, Network on Adolescent Lit., Soc. Children's Book Writers and Illustrators (San Diego chpt.), Phi Beta Kappa. Democrat. Episcopalian. Home and Office: 1842 Santa Margarita Dr Fallbrook CA 92028

CAMPBELL, PATRICIA LINDSEY, mechanical engineer; b. Little Rock, Oct. 16, 1952; d. Harvey Clay and Willie C. (Doyle) Pinkston; m. Dennis K. Campbell, July 3, 1971 (div. Oct. 1981); children: Casondra, Jeffrey; m. George O. Newsome, Mar. 14, 1991. AS in Engring., U. Ark., Little Rock, 1979; BS in Mech. Engring., Memphis State U., 1983; MS in Engring., U. Ark., 1989; JD, George Washington U., 1996. Registered profl. engr., Ark. Mech. engr. Entergy Ops./Ark. Power & Light, Russellville, Ark., 1983-91, U.S. Nuclear Regulatory Commn., Washington, 1991—. Leader Girl Scouts, Russellville, Ark., 1990. Scholar Inst. Nuclear Power Ops., Atlanta, 1982-83. Mem. ASME (sec. ops. and maintenance working group 1993—), Tau Beta Pi. Methodist. Home: 19213 Golden Meadow Dr Germantown MD 20876 Office: Mail Stop 07E23 Washington DC 20555

CAMPBELL, RENODA GISELE, recording industry executive; b. L.A., May 4, 1963; d. Rumby D. and Margarete (Alexander) C. BA, Loyola Marymount U., L.A., 1985. Mgmt. exec. Direct Mgmt. Group, L.A., 1989-90, media coord., 1990-91, assoc. pers. mgr., 1991—; label mgr. E Pluribus Unum Recordings, L.A., 1994—. Office: E Pluribus Unum Recordings 8424A Santa Monica Blvd #831 West Hollywood CA 90069-4700

CAMPBELL, RUTH ANN, budget analyst; b. La Plata, Md., Aug. 25, 1948; d. Lawrence Gilbert Pilkerton and Eleanor Garretter (Swann) Pilkerton-Grimm; m. Joseph Harvey Campbell, May 22, 1970 (dec. Oct. 1989); children: Joseph Lawrence, Timothy Craig. Clk.-stenographer Gen. Svcs. Adminstrn., Washington, 1966-68, sec., stenographer, 1968-70, program asst., 1970-71; adminstrv. asst. Gen. Svcs. Adminstrn., Mpls., 1971-72; adminstrv. asst. Gen. Svcs. Adminstrn., Washington, 1974-75, program analyst, 1975-78, corr. specialist, 1978-79, program analyst, 1979, budget analyst, 1979—. Sec. Fed. Women's Program/Gen. Svcs. Adminstrn., Washington, 1981-82, PTA, Waldorf, Md., 1981-83; treas. Cub Scout pack Boy Scouts Am., La Plata, Md., 1982-87; mem. vestry Christ Ch., Wayside, 1990-94, treas. Women's Guild, 1990-96; treas. Athletic Boosters Club, 1993-94; sec. Warrior Stadium Steering Com.; team capt. Thursday Nite Mixed Bowling League, 1976—. Mem. Am. Assn. Budget and Program Analysis. Episcopalian. Home: 7305 Saint Marys Ave La Plata MD 20646-3968 Office: Gen Svcs Adminstrn Rm 1105 Bldg 4 Washington DC 20406

CAMPBELL, SANDRA J., state legislator. State rep. dist. 53 R.I. Ho. of Reps.; dep. minority leader, mem. fin. com. Republican. Office: RI House of Reps State House Providence RI 02903*

CAMPBELL, SELAURA JOY, lawyer; b. Oklahoma City, Mar. 25, 1944; d. John Moore III and Gyda (Hallum) C. AA, Stephens Coll., 1963; BA, U. Okla., 1965; MEd, Chapel Hill U., 1974; JD, N.C. Cen. U., 1978; postgrad. atty. mediation courses, South Tex. Sch. of Law, Houston, 1991, Atty. Mediators Inst./Dallas, Dallas, 1992. Bar: Ariz 1983; lic. real estate broker, N.C.; cert. tchr. N.C. With flight svc. dept. Pan Am. World Airways, N.Y.C., 1966-91; lawyer Am. Women's Legal Clinic, Phoenix, 1987; charter mem. Sony Corp. Indsl. Mgmt. Seminar, 1981; guest del. Rep. Nat. Conv., Houston, 1992; judge all-law sch. mediation competition for Tex., South Tex. Sch. Law, Houston, 1994. Mem. N.C. Cen. U. Law Rev., 1977-78. People-to-People del. People's Republic of China, 1987; guest del. Rep. Nat. Conv., Houston, 1992. Mem. Ariz. Bar Assn., Humane Soc. U.S., Nat. Wildlife Fedn., People for the Ethical Treatment of Animals, Amnesty Internat., Phi Alpha Delta. Republican. Episcopalian. Home: 206 Taft Ave Cleveland TX 77327-4539

CAMPBELL, SHARON ELAINE, artist, researcher; b. Fort Myers, Fla., Sept. 20, 1943; d. Harrison Martin and Elaine Bressmer (Rawlins) Harp; m. Philip Waff Whitley, June 8, 1966 (div. 1980); children: Lise Johnson, Jason Whitley; m. James Davis Campbell, June 4, 1981; children: Kate, Jamie. BFA, Wesleyan Coll., Macon, Ga., 1965; MFA, U. N.C., 1968. Head exhbns. Greenville (S.C.) County Mus. Art, Mus. Sch. Art, 1971-90; art rschr. curatorial svcs. Greenville, 1990—; art cons. Fed. Reserve Bank, Charlotte, N.C., 1988—; art liaison Emrys Found., Greenville, 1993—; art adv. com. S.C. State Mus., Columbia, 1993—; mem. state art collection study com. S.C. Arts Commn., 1995-96. Curator Greenville County Mus. Art, 1983-90, Fine Arts Ctr., 1991—. Home and Office: 12 Whitsett St Greenville SC 29601

CAMPBELL, SUSAN CARRIGG, secondary education educator; b. Copaigue, N.Y., Dec. 8, 1946; d. Richard Carrigg and Mildred Josephine (Schneider) C. BS cum laude, SUNY, Oswego, 1968; MA, Adelphi U., 1992. Cert. secondary tchr., N.Y. Tchr. Brentwood (N.Y.) Pub. Schs., 1968—; co-developer learning skills program Brentwood (N.Y.) Pub. Schs., 1985-89, co-chairperson sch. improvement team, 1990-92, 93-94, 95, mem. summer curriculum writing project, 1993, adv. program com., 1993-94, conflict resolution trainee, 1994; adv. Student Leaders Club, Brentwood, N.Y., 1991; coord. Art Enrichment Show, 1986-91. Mem. L.I. Coun. Social Studies, Brentwood Tchrs. Assn., Kappa Delta Pi, Pi Gamma Mu. Democrat. Lutheran.

CAMPBELL, SUSAN PANNILL, banker; b. Richmond, Va., May 28, 1947; d. Raymond Brodie and Lucie Courtice (McDonald) C.; m. William F. Stutts Jr., May 16, 1992. A.B., Coll. William and Mary, 1969; M.Ed., U. Va., 1970, postgrad., 1974-75; postgrad. Summer Inst. of Coll. Admissions, Harvard U., 1972. Counselor, instr. Thomas Nelson Community Coll., Hampton, Va., 1970-71; asst. dean admissions U. Va., Charlottesville, 1971-78; banking officer, asst. v.p. Tex. Commerce Bank, Houston, 1978-82; asst. v.p. First City Tex., Houston, 1982-85, v.p., 1985-92; v.p. Franklin Fed. Bancorp, Austin, 1993-94; v.p. Nations Bank, 1994-96, sr. v.p. 1996—. Loaned exec. United Way, Houston, 1978; v.p. EnCorps, div. Houston Symphony League, 1981-82, pres., 1982-83, bd. dirs., 1983-85; bd. dirs. Houston Symphony League, 1982-83, Austin Lyric Opera, 1993—, Ct. Appointed Spl. Advocates, 1996—; bd. advisors Houston Symphony Soc., 1982-94. Honor award scholar Mary Baldwin Coll., Staunton, Va., 1965-66. Mem. Coll. William and Mary Alumni Assn., U. Va. Alumni Assn. (bd. dirs. Houston and Austin chpts.), Kappa Alpha Theta. Democrat. Methodist. Office: Nations Bank PO Box 908 Austin TX 78781

CAMPBELL, TISHA, actress; d. Mona C. Film appearances include Little Shop of Horror, House Party, Boomerang; TV program: Martin, 1992—. Office: care Michelle Mary Inc 8170 Beverly Blvd Ste 205 Los Angeles CA 90048-4524*

CAMPBELL, VIRGINIA KOLNICK, retired rehabilitation counselor; b. Smelterville, Idaho, Feb. 21, 1934; d. Dolph and Ruberta Rhoda (Hunt) Towles; m. Phillip Kolnick, Dec. 30, 1953 (div. Apr. 1963); children: Jo Ann, Phyllis Ann, Betty Sue; m. Robert Lloyd Campbell, Sept. 18, 1993. AA in Nursing, Phoenix Coll., 1961; BS in Sociology, Ariz. State U., 1966, MA in Edn., 1968, M of Counseling, 1971. RN Ariz.; cert. rehab. counselor. Coord. pvt. duty nursing Med. Personnel Pool, Phoenix, 1971-72; nurse health evaluation Ariz. Health Plan, Phoenix, 1973; instr. continuing edn. program Phoenix Coll., Maricopa County C.C. Dist., 1973-75; vocat. rehab. counselor III, cardio-pulmonary specialist State of Ariz., Phoenix, 1974-92, ret., 1992. Mem. Am. Assn. Cardiovascular Pulmonary Rehab. (fellow), Ariz. Cardiovascular Pulmonary Rehab. Assn. Home: 9224 E Bighorn Dr Prescott Valley AZ 86314-7302

CAMPER, GALE DIANA, critical care nurse, consultant; b. Detroit, Sept. 14, 1955; d. Isaac Melvin Jr. and Lilie Mamilonne; children: Corey, Canden. BSN, Mercy Coll. Detroit, 1978. RN, Mich.; CCRN; cert. ACLS. Charge nurse ICCU Sinai Hosp. Detroit, 1978-79; charge nurse, preceptor Providence Hosp., Southfield, Mich., 1980—; high tech case mgr. Renaissance Home Health Care, 1995—; arbitrator Mich. Med. Arbitration program, Detroit, 1985—. Mem. AACN (cert. critical care nurse), Am. Assn. Legal Nurse Cons., Mich. Nurses Assn.

CAMPER, MICHELLE GWEN, community health nurse, health administrator; b. Flushing, N.Y., Feb. 21, 1965; d. William Henry and Mamie Alexandria (O'Quinn) C. AAS, Queensboro C.C., N.Y., 1988. Staff nurse Dorchester Gen. Hosp., Cambridge, Md., 1990-93; HIV coord. Caroline County Health Dept., Denton, Md., 1993—; cmty. health edn. aids prevention Caroline County Health Dept., Denton, Md., 1993—. Voting mem. State of Md. Comty. Planning Group for Prevention of HIV Transmission, regional work group co-chair; active Comty. Planning Group State of Md. AIDS, 1994, 95, 96. Named Outstanding Minority student Queensboro C.C., Bayside, N.Y., 1988. Mem. Nat. Black Nurses Assn., Nat. Assn. Sickle Cell Disease, Assn. Nurses in AIDS Care. Democrat. Baptist. Home: 503 Penn St Hurlock MD 21643-3548 Office: Caroline County Health Dept PO Box 10 Denton MD 21629

CAMPION, JANE, director, screenwriter; b. Wellington, New Zealand; d. Richard and Edith Campion. BA in Anthropology, Victoria U., Wellington; Diploma of Fine Arts, Chelsea Sch Arts, London; Diploma in Direction, Australian Film and T.V. Sch., 1984. Dir., screenwriter Peel: An Exercise in Discipline, 1982 (also editor, Palme d'Or short film category Cannes Internat. Film Festival 1986, Diploma of Merit melbourne Film Festival, 1983, finalist Greater Union awards, Autralian Film Inst. awards), (video) Mishaps of Seduction and Conquest, 1983-84, A Girl's Own Story, 1983 (Rouben Mamoulian award 1984 Best overall short film Sydney Film Festival 1984, Unique Artist Merit Melbourne Film Festival 1984, Best Direction, Best-Screenplay, Best Cinematography Australian Film Inst. 1984, First Prize Cinestud Amsterdam Film Festival, 1985, Best Film Cinestud 1985, Fisert Prize Festival and Press prize), Passionless Moments, 1984 (also prodr., cinematographer, camera operator, Unique Artist Merit Melbourne Film Festival 1984, Best Exptl. Film Australian Film inst. 1984, Most Popular Short Film Sydney Film Festival 1985), After Hours, 1984 (XL Elders award Best Short Fiction, Best Short Fiction Melbourne Internat. Film Festival 1985), Sweetie, 1989, (Georges Sadoul prize Best Fgn. Film, Best Dir., Best Film Australian Critics awards 1990, New Generation award L.A. Film Critics, 1990, Best Fgn. Film Spirit of Independence awards 1990), The Piano, 1993 (Palme d'Or Cannes Internat. Film Festival 1993, Academy Award Best Original Screenplay 1994, Best Picture, Best Dir., Best Cinematography, 66th Acad. Awards, Australian Film Inst. awards, Australia Film Critics, Southeastern Film Critics Assn., others, Best Fgn. Film Chgo. Film Critics, Caesar awards); dir. An Angel at my Table, 1990 (Byron Kennedy award, Spl. Jury prize, Annual Elvira Notari award Best Woman Dir., Agia Scuola Italian Min. Culture, Best Film Si presci award Panel Internat. Critics, Best Film O.C.I.C. award Christian journalists, Best Film for Young Audiences Cinema e Ragazzi Italian film critcs prize, Critics award Toronto Film FEstival, Most popular film in the Forum, Otto Debelius prize Berlin Film Festival, Best Fgn. Film Spirit of Independence Awards), (TV) Two Friends, 1986 (Golden Plaque T.V. category Chgo. Internat. Film Festival 1987, Best Dir., Best Telemovie, Best Screenplay AFI awards 1987; composer: Feel the Cold (from A Girl's Own Story), 1983, (play) The Portrait of A Lady, 1995. Office: Creative Artists Agy 9830 Wilshire Blvd Beverly Hills CA 90212-1804

CAMPISE, ROSE ELLEN, art educator; b. Pitts., May 18, 1936; d. Joseph Anthony and Gertrude Frances (Kubiak) C. BEd, Duquesne U., 1963; ME, Pa. State U., 1978; cert. in art, Millersville U., 1985. Elem. educator Diocese of Pitts. Schs., 1955-69; art educator Eastern York (Pa.) Sch. Dist., 1969—. Mem. NEA, Nat. Art Educators Assn., Pa. State Edn. Assn., Ea. York Edn. Assn. Democrat. Roman Catholic. Home: 2585 Auburn Rd York PA 17402

CAMPOS, CHRISTINA RIVAS, finance officer, restaurant owner; b. Albuquerque, Nov. 1, 1964; d. Luz Ofelia (Gabaldon) Tuma; m. Jose A. Campos II, June 1, 1985; children: Analisa, Andrea, Jose III. BA in Latin Am. Econs., U. N.Mex., 1995. Owner Joseph's Restaurant, Santa Rosa, N.Mex., 1985—; chief fin. officer Guadalupe Health Svc., Santa Rosa, 1993-96; cmty. health liaison Guadlupe County, Santa Rosa, 1993-94; mem. geog. access task force State of N.Mex., 1993-94. Mem. Presdl. Rural Helath Care Panel, Bernalillo, N.Mex., 1993. Mem. Rotary Internat. (sec. 1993—), Santa Rosa C. of C. Democrat. Roman Catholic. Office: Joseph's Restaurant 865 Will Rogers Dr Santa Rosa NM 88435

CANAAN, ESTHER MAY, legal association administrator; b. Lewiston, Idaho, Oct. 25, 1951; d. Delby A. and Lillian M. Canaan. BS in Comm., Lewis-Clark State Coll., Lewiston, 1994. Sec. Ch. of the Nazarene, Lewiston, 1993-94; exec. dir. YWCA of Wenatchee Valley, Wash., 1994-95; adminstr. minimum continuing legal edn. Oreg. State Bar, Lake Oswego, 1996—; Bd. dirs. Northwest Non-Profit Resources, Spokane, Wash., 1995; coord., instr. LIFESTYLES employment readiness tng, Wenatchee, 1993-94. Women's advocate various ch. and civ. orgns., Idaho and Wash., 1975-95. Mem. Am. Assn. Christian Counselors, Nat. Assn. Female Execs., Women in Comm., Inc. (pres., membership chair 1992—), Orgn. Regulatory Adminstrs. for Continuing Legal Edn. Home: 14771 SW 109th Ave Apt 3 Tigard OR 97224-2330 Office: Oreg State Bar 5200 SW Meadows Rd Lake Oswego OR 97035

CANADA, MARY WHITFIELD, librarian; b. Richmond, Va., June 13, 1919; d. Waverly Thomas and Ruth Bradshaw (Smith) C. B.A. magna cum laude, Emory and Henry Coll., 1940; M.A. in English, Duke U., 1942; B.S. in L.S., U. N.C., 1956. Asst. circulation dept. Duke U. Library, 1942-45, undergrad. librarian, 1945-55, reference librarian, 1956-85, asst. head reference dept., 1967-79, head dept., 1979-85. Contbr. articles to profl. jours. Mem. exec. com. Friends of Duke U. Library. Duke U. grantee Can., 1979, 81. Mem. ALA (life; initiated performance evaluation discussion group), Southeastern Library Assn. (sec. coll. and univ. sect., chmn. nominating com. reference services div., also chmn. div.), N.C. Library Assn. (chmn. nominating com., chmn. newspaper com., chmn. coll. and univ. sect.), Alumni Assn. Sch. Library Sci. U. N.C. (pres.), Va. Hist. Soc. (life), Va. Geneal. Soc., DAR (chpt. regent), Friends of Va. State Archives, Campus club (Duke U.), Planning Adv. Com. N. Cen. Durham, Va. Mus. Beta Phi Mu. Methodist. Home: 1312 Lancaster St Durham NC 27701-1132

CANAHUATI, JUDY, lactation consultant; b. Phila., July 17, 1941; d. Max and Bessie S. (Creshkoff) Weiner; m. Pedro Felipe Canahuati, Sept. 6, 1969; children: Emilia, Pedro Cesar. BA, U. Pa., 1963; MPhil in Anthropology, Columbia U., 1974. Internat. bd. cert. lactation cons. Cmty. organizer Planned Parenthood, N.Y.C., 1966-67; instr. U. Nacional Honduras, San Pedro Sula, 1970-72; import-export mgr. Contessa Indsl., San Pedro Sula, Honduras, 1978-82; tech. adv. USAID, Tegucigalpa, 1982-85, Mgmt. Scis. for Health, Boston, 1986-88; bd. dirs. La Leche League Internat., Schaumburg, Ill., 1986, project dir., 1989-91; cmty. adv. Wellstart Internat., Washington, 1991-96; cons. Centro de Apoyo a la Lactancia Materna, San Salvador, 1981-83, Ednl. Devel. Ctr., Boston, 1985, UNICEF, N.Y.C., Tegucigalpa, 1989; researcher Inst. Reproductive Health Georgetown U., Washington, 1990-92. Co-author: Community-based Breastfeeding Support: A Planning Manual, 1996; contbr. articles to profl. jours.; co-prodr.: (video) Investing in the Future: Women, Work, and Breastfeeding, 1995. Bd. dirs. Escuela Internacional Sampedrana, San Pedro Sula, Honduras, 1980-85, Soc. Pro-Musica, San Pedro Sula, 1975-76. Fellow Nat. Inst. Mental Health, 1968-69. Mem. Internat. Lactation Cons. Assn., Consumer's Edn. and Protective Assn., Am. anthropol. Assn., Phi Beta Kappa. Home: 13702 Modrad Way #23 Silver Spring MD 20904 Office: Wellstart Internat 4062 First Ave San Diego CA 92103-2045

CANAVAN, CAROL ELAINE, college administrator; b. Marietta, Ohio, Sept. 22, 1947; d. Richard V. and Esther L. (Wilcox) Jacoby; m. Robert J. Canavan; children: Peter Andrew, Catherine Alaine. BA, Mich. State U., 1969; MA, U. S.D., 1972. Cert. Rsch. Adminstr. Tchr. Ky. Country Day Sch., Louisville, 1973-86, dept. chair, 1975-83, dir. student activities, 1983-86; asst. head Andrews Sch., Willoughby, Ohio, 1986-89; dir. grants acquisition Mt. Union Coll., Alliance, Ohio, 1990—. Active NOW. Recipient Brotherhood/Sisterhood Grand award NCCJ, 1984. Mem. Soc. Rsch. Adminstrs., Canton Coll. Women's Club. Office: Mt Union Coll 1972 Clark Ave Alliance OH 44601

CANAVAN, CHRISTINE ESTELLE, state legislator; b. Dorchestor, Mass., Jan. 25, 1950; m. Paul Canavan; 2 children. Grad., Massasoit C.C., 1983; BS summa cum laude, U. Mass. RN, Mass. Rep. dist. 10 Mass. Ho. of Reps., Boston, mem. personnel and adminstrn. com., ins. com., housing and urban devel. com.; mem. Brockton (Mass.) Sch. Com., 1990—, vice chair, 1992—. Mem. Amvets, Mass. Nurses Assn., Polish White Eagles Inc. Democrat. Roman Catholic. Home: 29 Mystic St Brockton MA 02402-2825 Office: Mass Ho of Reps Mass State House Boston MA 02133

CANCER, CATHY LYNN, elementary education educator; b. Vidalia, Ga., July 10, 1963; d. Jessie and Hattie Lee Hunt; m. Anthony Gerald Cancer, June 8, 1990; 1 child, Hunter Tyrez. BBA, Savannah State Coll., 1987; Tchg. Cert., Ga. So. U., 1989, MEd in Sch. Nursing, 1996. Elem. tchr. Toombs County Bd. Edn., Lyons, Ga., 1989—; bus. cons. H&K Package Store, Lyons, 1989—. Fellow ASCD, GSCA. Home: 117 Cascade Dr Lyons GA 30436-1634

CANDRIS, LAURA A., lawyer; b. Frankfort, Ky., Apr. 5, 1955; d. Charles M. and Dorothy (King) Sutton; m. Aris S. Candris, Dec. 22, 1974. AB with distinction in polit. sci., Transylvania Coll., 1975; postgrad., U. Pitts., 1975-77, U. Fla., 1977-78; JD, U. Pitts., 1978. Bar: Fla. 1978, U.S. Dist. Ct. (mid. dist.) Fla. 1978, U.S. Ct. Appeals (4th cir.) 1980, Pa. 1981, U.S. Dist. Ct. (we. dist.) Pa. 1982, U.S. Ct. Appeals (3d cir.) 1983. Assoc. Coffman, Coleman, Andrews & Grogan, Jacksonville, Fla., 1978-80, Manion, Alder & Cohen, Pitts., 1981-85; assoc. Eckert, Seamans, Cherin & Mellott, Pitts., 1985-86, ptnr., 1987-96, vice chmn. labor and employment law dept, mem. practice mgmt. com., mem. strategic planning com.; ptnr., mem. employment law sect. Meyer Unkovic & Scott, LLP, Pitts., 1996—; counsel Nat. Assn. Women in Constrn. (chpt. 161), Pitts., 1985-86. Contbr. over 30 articles to profl. jours. including Forum Reporter, Pers. Law Update, Hot Topics in Employment Law, and Reference Manual for the 30th Annual Mid-West Labor Law Conf. Coun. mem. O'Hara Twp., 1986-90; mem. O'Hara Twp. Planning Commn., 1990; bd. dirs. Tri-State Employers Assn., 1991-93, Parent and Child Guidance Ctr., 1991—; treas., mem. exec. com. SMC Bus. Couns., 1993-94, bd. dirs., 1993—. Nat. Merit Found. scholar 1972-75; named Ky. Col., 1974. Mem. ABA (EEO com. labor sect., labor and employment law com. litigation sect.), Fla. Bar Assn., Pa. Bar Assn. (employment sect.), Allegheny County Bar Assn. (CLE com., coun. on professionalism, employment and fed. cts. sect., hdqrs. com. and pers. subcom.), Soc. Hosp. Attys. Western Pa., Pitts. Pers. Assn. Republican. Office: Meyer Unkovic & Scott 1300 Oliver Bldg Pittsburgh PA 15222

CANETTO, SILVIA SARA, psychology researcher, educator; b. Ferrara, Italy, July 18, 1955; came to U.S., 1981; d. Amalio and Edda (Sucsi Leonelli) C. D. in Exptl. Psychology, U. Padua (Italy), 1977; MA, Hebrew U. of Jerusalem, 1983; PhD in Clin. Psychology, Northwestern U., 1987. Lic. psychologist. Family psychologist Martha Washington Hosp., Chgo., 1986-88; vis. asst. prof. dept. psychology U. Mont., Missoula, 1988-89, U. Vt., Burlington, 1989—; assoc. prof. dept. psychology Colo. State U., Ft. Collins, 1996—. Co-editor: (with David Lester) Women and Suicidal Behavior, 1995; contbr. chpts. in books and articles to profl. jours. Active The Italian Program, Mont. Pub. Radio, 1988-89. Internat. scholar Min. Fgn. Affairs, Italy, Israel, 1977-80; grantee Israeli Ctr. for Psychobiology, Rotary Internat., APA, European Chemoreception Rsch. Orgn. Mem. APA, Am. Assn. Suicidology, Gerontol. Soc. Am., Assn. for Women in Psychology, Internat. Coun. Psychologists. Office: Colo State U Dept Psychology Fort Collins CO 80523-1876

CANFIELD, JUDY OHLBAUM, psychologist; b. N.Y.C., May 15, 1947; d. Arthur and Ada (Werner) Ohlbaum; m. John T. Canfield (div.); children: Oran David, Kyle Danya. BA, Grinnell Coll., 1963; MA, New Sch. Social Rsch., 1967; PhD, U.S. Internat. U., 1970. Psychologist Mendocino State Hosp., Talmage, Calif., 1968-69, Douglas Coll., New Westminster, BC, Can., 1971-72, Family & Childrens Clinic, Burnaby, BC, Can., 1971-72; psychologist, trainer, cons. VA Hosp., Northampton, Mass., 1972-75; dir. New England Ctr., Amherst, Mass., 1972-76; dir., psychologist Gateways, Lansdale, Pa., 1977-78; asst. prof., psychologist Hahnemann Med. Ctr., Phila., 1978-84; pres., dir. Inst. Holistic Health, Phila., 1978-85; psychologist, cons. Berkeley, Calif., 1986—. Mem. task force, tng. com. Berkeley Dispute Resolution Svc., 1986-89; mem. measure H com. Berkeley United Sch. Dist., 1987-88. Mem. APA, Nat. Register Health Svc. Providers in Psychology, Nat. Assn. Advancement Gestalt Therapy (steering com. 1990), Calif. Psychol. Assn., Alameda County Psychol. Assn. (info.-referral svc. 1989—), Assn. Humanistic Psychology. Office: 2031 Delaware St Berkeley CA 94709-2121

CANFIELD, STELLA STOJANKA, artist; b. Varna, Bulgaria, Jan. 17, 1950; came to U.S., 1985; d. Stamat and Pepa-Despenna (Blisnacova) Bogdanov; m. Peter Petrov, Feb. 28, 1971 (div. Mar. 1988); children: Nicoletta, Peter; m. Michael Canfield, Mar. 27, 1988; adopted children: Jennifer, Paul. M, U. Phys. Edn. and Sports, Sofia, 1973. Lic. sport phys. therapy, Bulgaria. Phys. edn. and sports pedagogue H.S., Tolbuhin, Bulgaria, 1974-75, Med. U., Sofia, Bulgaria, 1975-76, middle and H.S., Sofia, 1976-80; restaurant owner Stella, Dusseldorf, Germany, 1982-83; with Oberheid Ceramic Studio, Dusseldorf, 1983-85; retail sales rep. The Ltd., Walnut Creek, Calif., 1989-90; savs. rep. Calif. Savs. & Loans, Montclair, 1990-92. Bd. dirs. Coupeville (Wash.) Arts Ctr., 1993—; treas., exhibitor Penn Cove Gallery, Coupeville, 1995—. Recipient 3 awards Tulip Festival,

La Conner, Wash., 1994, 2 awards, 1995, 96, 3 awards. Mem. Youth Coalition, Northwest Watercolor Soc.

CANGUREL, SUSAN STONE, human resources executive; b. Madison, Wis., Sept. 11, 1946; d. John Mather and Lois Marie (Wiessinger) Murray; m. Mel Cangurel; children: Lora Rae, Julie Lynn. Student U. Wis., 1964-66; BS, U. Wis., Milw., 1978; MBA, Century U., Albuquerque, 1990; PhD, Century U., 1994. Adminstrv. asst. Madison C. of C., 1967-72; v.p. loan adminstrn. Kensington Mortgage, Milw., 1972-79; v.p. adminstrn. Mortgage Investment Co., El Paso, 1979-85; mgr. personnel svcs. Summa Corp., Las Vegas, 1985-88, v.p. human resources MGM Desert Inn, 1988-91; human resources dir. The Miles Group, El Paso, 1991-95, The Orleans, Las Vegas, 1995—. Mem. Soc. Human Resource Mgrs., Am. Soc. for Tng. & Devel. (cert. profl. human resources 1992, cert. sr. profl. human resources 1993). Author poems and short stories. Home: 1409 Termas Dr Las Vegas NV 89117

CANN, NANCY TIMANUS, retail yacht sales executive; b. Balt.; d. E. Frank Timanus and Ruth F. (Herman) Schell; 1 child, Justin Ronald. Grad., Balt. Bus. Coll., 1967. Pres. Crusader Yacht Sales, Inc., Annapolis, Md., 1982—; bd. dirs. Bayfarers. Mem. Yacht Architects and Brokers Assn. (v.p. 1989-91, 92—, chmn. membership com. 1989-92, bd. dirs. 1992—, pres. 1994—). Home and Office: 7078 Bembe Beach Rd Annapolis MD 21403-3616

CANN, SHARON LEE, health science librarian; b. Ft. Riley, Kans., Aug. 14, 1935; d. Roman S. and Cora Elon (George) Foote; m. Donald Clair Cann, May 16, 1964. Student Sophia U., Tokyo, 1955-57; BA, Calif. State U., Sacramento, 1959; MSLS, Atlanta U., 1977; EdD, U. Ga., 1995. Cert. health scis. libr. Recreation worker ARC, Korea, Morocco, France, 1960-64; shelflister Libr. Congress Washington, 1967-69; tchr. Lang. Ctr., Taipei, Taiwan, 1971-73; libr. tech. asst. Emory U., Atlanta, 1974-76; health sci. libr. Northside Hosp., Atlanta, 1977-85; libr. cons., 1985-86; libr. area health edn. ctr., learning resource ctr. Morehouse Sch. Medicine, 1985-86; edn. libr. Ga. State U., 1986-93; head libr. Ga. Bapt. Coll. Nursing, 1993—. Editor Update, publ. Ga. Health Scis. Libr. Assn., 1981; contbr. articles to publs. Chmn. Calif. Christian Youth in Govt Seminar, 1958. Named Alumni Top Twenty Calif. State U.Sacramento, 1959. Mem. ALA, AAUW, Med. Libr. Assn., Spl. Libr. Assn. (dir. South Atlantic chpt. 1985-87), Ga. Libr. Assn. (spl. libr. divsn. chmn. 1983-85), Ga. Health Scis. Libr. Assn. (chmn. 1981-82), Atlanta Health Sci. Libr. (chmn. 1979, 95), Am. Numis. Assn., ARC Overseas Assn. Home: 5520 Morning Creek Cir Atlanta GA 30349-3538

CANNAROZZI, SUSAN FLORENCE SANGILLO, biologist, educator; b. Jersey City, July 2, 1949; d. John and Alice (Bustin) Sangillo; m. Matthew Michael Cannarozzi, Aug. 4, 1972 (div. Mar. 1992); 1 child, Matthew Emil. BA in Edn. magna cum laude, Montclair State U., 1970, MA in Biology summa cum laude, 1975. Cert. secondary tchr., N.J. Tchr. biology Hackensack (N.J.) H.S., 1970-73, New Milford (N.J.) H.S., 1975-77; tchr. chemistry Meml. H.S., West New York, N.J., 1993-94; tutor Master Tchr. Inc., Hoboken, N.J., 1992—. Hoboken Tchrs. Assn. grantee, 1966, State of N.J. scholar, 1966-70. Mem. NOW, Am. Chemistry Tchrs. Assn., Cousteau Soc. Roman Catholic. Home and Office: 910 Hudson St Hoboken NJ 07030

CANNING, MARJORIE ELIZABETH, health care administrator; b. Blue Earth, Minn., Mar. 18, 1931; d. Edgar A. and Esther M. (Frandle) VonFeldt; m. Leonard J. Canning, Mar. 14, 1953; children: Michael, Mark, Helen, Patricia, Colleen, Susan, Margaret, Kathleen, Maureen. RN, St. Mary's Coll., 1952; BS, Coll. St. Francis, 1982; MA, U. St. Mary's, 1985. Regional adminstr. Park Nicollet Med. Ctr., Mpls., 1980-89; exec. dir. PruHeart Ctr., Mpls., 1989-95; v.p. Health Sys. Minn., Mpls., 1995—; pres. Minn.Med. Group Mgmt., 1990, Women's Health Leadership Trust. Minn. Recipient Women of Achievement award West C. of C., Mpls., 1990, YWCA Cmty. Leaders Recognition award, 1984. Fellow Am. Coll. Med. Practice Execs.; mem. CSCA (pres. 1995-96), MGMA. Roman Catholic. Home: 6505 Gleason Ct Edina MN 55436 Office: Health Sys Minn 6500 Excelsior Blvd Minneapolis MN 55426

CANNING, TRACI A., designer; b. Norristown, Pa., Apr. 6, 1963; d. William and Joyce (Kobus) C. BA in English, Ursinus Coll., 1985; postgrad., West Chester U., 1995—. Devel. dir. Developmental Enterprises Found., Norristown, Pa., 1985-86; dir. interactive video Flight Safety Internat., Malvern, Pa., 1986-88; graphic artist, cons. Custom Designs Ink, Phila., 1988-89; videographer Custom Videography, Conshohocken, Pa., 1988-89; reporter Times Herald, Norristown, 1989-92; page designer Reading (Pa.) Eagle/Times newspaper, 1992—. Contbr. book and music revs. to Reading Eagle/Times newspaper, 1993—. Mem. com., corr. sec. Area 1 Dem. Com., Pottstown, 1994—; mem. Y.E.S. Mentor Program, 1996—. Recipient 2d Pl. Front Page Design award Pa. Newspaper Pubs. Assn., 1994, 2d Pl. Group award Nat. Assn. Real Estate Editors, 1995. Mem. NOW (newspaper co-editor 1994—), Women's Press Assn., Grad. Student Assn., Grizzly Network. Office: Reading Eagle/Times PO Box 582 Reading PA 19603

CANNISTRACI, DIANE FRANCES, sales account executive; b. Bronx, N.Y., Jan. 9, 1950; d. John and Dorothy (Romano) C. Student, Orlando (Fla.) Jr. Coll., 1968-70, Teiko Post Coll., 1991-92. Ea. regional sales mgr. Kierulff Airline/Internation Supply, 1979-86; western regional sales mgr. C & K Unimax, Wallingford, Conn., 1989-90; sales and mktg. rep. U.S. C. of C., 1990-91; store mgr. Petite Sophisticate, Manchester, Conn., 1991-92; internat. and airline mktg. Richey Cypress Electronics, Wallingford, 1992-96; sales account exec. Midway Indsl. Electronics, Plainview, N.Y., 1996—. Committeewoman Rep. Party, Huntington, N.Y.; fund raiser Am. Heart Assn., Rocky Hill, Conn., Am. Diabetes Assn., Rocky Hill; vol. Hartford (Conn.) Hist. Soc., With USNG, 1981-86. Recipient All Around Womanhood award PTA, Huntington Station, N.Y., 1968. Mem. Air Carrier Purchasing. Republican. Roman Catholic. Home: 345 Depot Rd Huntington Station NY 11746 Office: Midway Indsl Electronics 137 Express St Plainview NY 11803

CANNIZZARO, LINDA ANN, geneticist, researcher; b. S.I., N.Y., Aug. 4, 1953. BS, St. Peter's Coll., 1975; MS, Fordham U., 1977, PhD, 1981. Postdoctoral fellow Dartmouth U. Med. Sch., Hanover, N.H., 1981-83; fellow in human genetics Children's Hosp. Phila., 1983-84; co-dir. cytogenetics Milton S. Hershey (Pa.) Med. Ctr., 1984-86; dir. gene mapping S.W. Biomed. Rsch. Inst., Scottsdale, Ariz., 1986-89; asst. prof. Fels Inst. Temple U. Med. Sch., Phila., 1989-91; asst. prof. Jefferson Cancer Inst., Phila., 1991-93; assoc. prof. Albert Einstein Coll. Medicine, Bronx, N.Y., 1993—; dir. cancer and molecular cytogenetics Albert Einstein Coll. Medicine and Montefiore Hosp., Bronx, N.Y., 1993—. Editor-in-chief Cytogenetics Cell Genetics, 1995—; contbr. articles to profl. jours. Grantee Am. Cancer Soc., 1989-90, 94—. Mem. AAAS, AAUW, Am. Soc. Human Genetics. Office: Albert Einstein Coll Med Dept Pathology 1300 Morris Park Ave Bronx NY 10461-1926

CANNON, CHRISTINE ANNE, veterinarian; b. Chgo., Nov. 13, 1952; d. Joseph Phillip and Mildred Eileen (Toll) C.; m. Robert L. Van Grinsven, Mar. 25, 1989. BS in Animal Sci., Purdue U., 1974; BS in Vet. Medicine, U. Ill., 1975, DVM, 1977. Vet. Bellemore Animal Hosp., Granite City, Ill., 1977-79, Humane Soc. of Mo., St. Louis, 1979-81, Wheaton Way Vet. Hosp., Bremerton, Wash., 1981-82, Rose Hill Animal and Bird Hosp., Kirkland, Wash., 1982-83; relief vet. Wash., 1983-87; vet., owner Bird and Exotic Pet Care Clinic, Lynnwood, Wash., 1987-92; vet. owner A Pet Care Clinic, Mountlake Terrace, Wash., 1992—. Asst. editor Avian Emergency Care A Manual for Emergency Clinics, 1990. Group leader Canine Coll., Kirkland, 1986-87; mentor Project Discovery, Edmonds, Wash., 1989, 95-96; leader Explorer scout troop Boy Scouts Am., St. Louis, 1981; chair King County Animal Control Citizens Adv. Com., 1991—; bus. cons. Jr. Achievement, 1994-95, 95-96. Mem. AVMA, Assn. Avian Veterinarians (pub. rels. com. 1989-95, chmn. client edn. com. 1994-96), Wash. State Vet. Med. Assn. (editors and pub. com. newsletter), Seattle-King Couny Vet. Med. Assn. (rep. South Snohomish chpt. 1990—, chmn. ethics com. 1991-94, pres. 1995-97), Finch Lovers Pugeg Sound (co-founder, sec.-treas. 1987-91), Avicultural Soc. Puget Sound, N.W. Exotic Bird Soc., Pacific N.W. Herpetological Soc., Rotary (charter Mountlake Terrace, sgt.-at-arms 1994-96). Office: A Pet Care Clinic 23502 56th Ave W Mountlake Terrace WA 98043-5204

CANNON, GRACE BERT, immunologist; b. Chambersburg, Pa., Jan. 29, 1937; d. Charles Wesley and Gladys (Raff) Bert; m. W. Dilworth Cannon, June 3, 1961 (div. 1972); children: Michael Quayle, Susan Radcliffe, Peter Bert Cannon. AB, Goucher Coll., 1958; PhD, Washington U., St. Louis, 1962. Fellow Columbia U., N.Y.C., 1962-64, Columbia U. Coll. Physicians and Surgeons, N.Y.C., 1964-65; staff fellow NIH Nat. Cancer Inst., Bethesda, Md., 1966-67; cell biologist Litton Bionetics, Inc., Kensington, Md., 1972-80, head immunology sect., 1980-85; dir. sci. ImmuQuest Labs., Inc., Rockville, Md., 1985-88; pres. Biomedical Analytics, Inc., Silver Spring, Md., 1988-94; mgr. ATLIS Fed. Svcs., Inc., Silver Spring, Md., 1991-95; dir. ATLIS Fed. Svcs., Inc., Rockville, Md., 1995—; Mem. contract rev. coms. Nat. Cancer Inst., 1983-87. Contbr. articles to profl. jours. Mem. Pub. Svc. Health Club, Bethesda, Md., 1984—, sec., 1990—; mem. bd. Cmty. Ministries Rockville. Grantee USPHS, 1959-65, NSF, 1959. Mem. AAAS, Am. Assn. for Cancer Rsch., N.Y. Acad. Sci., Sigma Xi. Home and Office: 4905 Ertter Dr Rockville MD 20852-2203

CANNON, ISABELLA WALTON, mayor; b. Dunfermline, Scotland, May 12, 1904; came to U.S., 1916; d. James and Helen Bett (Seaman) Walton; m. Claude M. Cannon. BA, Elon Coll., 1924, LLD (hon.), 1978. Tchr. pub. schs.; head dept. stats. French Purchase Commn., Washington; fin. officer UN, Washington; with N.C. State U. Library; mayor of Raleigh, N.C., 1977-79. V.p. Women in Bus. Adv. Council, N.C. Conservation Council, Women's Polit. Caucus; charter mem. Wake County Dem. Women; organizer, pres. Univ. Park Assn., Raleigh; civic sponsor, mem. bldg. com. Raleigh Little Theatre; mem. Univ. Neighborhood Planning Council, N.C. Child Advocacy, N.C. Commn. Bicentennial of U.S.; bd. dirs. Mordecai Sq. Hist. Soc.; chmn. Wade CAC; mem. devel. bd. YWCA Acad. of Women; chairperson Keep Am. Clean Sweep; bd. dirs. Raleigh Symphony Orch.; mem. Women's Forum of N.C.; mem. Coll. Presdl. Electors, Centennial Com.; bd. dirs., historian St. Luke's Home, Raleigh liaison RSVP bd., Raleigh Bicentennial Task Force 1988-92, Martin Luther King Jr. Celebration Com., 1989-92; precinct chair numerous polit. orgns. Recipient. Disting. Alumnus award Elon Coll., 1983, Medallion award, 1991, Isabella Cannon Rm. named in her honor Elon Coll., 1987, Isabella Cannon Leadership Fellows Program established in 1991, Lifetime Achievement award Theatre in the Park, Govt. award YWCA Acad. Women, 1988, Role Model Leader award N.C. State U., 1991, Mentor of Distinction award Women Bus. Adv. Coun., 1994; Isabella Cannon Arboretum Intership established in her honor N.C. State U., 1991. Mem. N.C. Sr. Citizens Assn. (pres.), Elon Coll. Alumni Assn., Delta Kappa Gamma. Mem. United Ch. of Christ.

CANNON, NANCY GLADSTEIN, insurance agent; b. San Francisco; d. Richard and Caroline Gladstein; m. Robert L. Cannon; 1 child, Richard Michael. BA, San Francisco State U.; JD, U. West Los Angeles, 1980. Agt. State Farm Ins. Co., Pacific Palisades, Calif., 1984—. Mem. bd. govs. Pacific Palisades Civic League, 1987-91, Community Coun., 1988-89; bd. dirs. YMCA, Pacific Palisades, 1989-93, Sunset Mesa Property Owners Assn., 1991-93. Mem. Pacific Palisades C. of C., Santa Monica C. of C., Malibu C. of C., L.A. Athletic Club. Republican. Office: 15415 W Sunset Blvd Pacific Palisades CA 90272-3525

CANNON, NORA CAMILLE, art educator; b. Chgo., Aug. 11, 1955; d. Robert R. and Anna J. (Schmitt) Miller; m. Douglas L. Cannon, Sept. 1, 1973. BFA, Mass. Coll. Arts, Boston, 1990; MA, Tufts U., 1992. Cert. tchr. art K-12, Mass. Art tchr. Waltham (Mass.) Pub. Schs., Brookline, Mass., 1983-86; substitute tchr. Boston Area Schs., 1987-90; art instr. Mass. Coll. Art, Boston, 1989, gallery tour guide, 1989-90; art edn. specialist Tobin After Sch. Program, Boston, 1990; art instr. Jamaica Plain Arts, 1989-90; art activity dir. Dedham (Mass.) Country Day Camp, 1988-92; Gardner Monk fellow Mus. of Sci., Boston, 1991-92; expressive art therapist A.B.C.D. Headstart, Boston, 1991-93; spl. needs art educator Beverly (Mass.) Sch. for Deaf, 1992-93; guest spkr. in field. Contbg. author: The Hundred Languages of Children: Education for all the Children of Reggio Emilia, 1992. Tufts U. Edn. scholar, 1990, Christa McAuliffe Tchr. Incentive grantee, 1989, 90, Art Sch. Assocs. Trust Fund awardee, 1987. Mem. Nat. Art Edn. Assn., Mass. Art Edn. Assn., Early Childhood Ednl. Exch. Home: 7 Vale Ct Gloucester MA 01930-1238

CANNON, SAMANTHA KARRIE, management consultant, entrepreneur; b. Dayton, Ohio, Aug. 27, 1948; d. Emerson Lee and Elizabeth Ann (Riecken) Poppler; m. Peter Marcellus Cannon, Oct. 30, 1988. BA in Psychology, Calif. State U., Sacramento, 1977, MPA, MSW, 1982. Editor, pub. Equitable Life, Sacramento, 1972-76; mgmt. cons. State of Calif., Sacramento, 1976—; pvt. practice mgmt. cons. Sacramento, 1990—; founder, owner Your Best Friend, Sacramento, 1991—; mgmt. cons. United Way, Sacramento, 1985-88. Editor, pub.: (jour.) The Westerner, 1972-76. Past bd. dirs. Aquarian Effort; vol. comty. rape, suicide, family crisis, substance abuse and ex-offender programs; bd. dirs. Diogenes Youth Svcs., 1992-94. Recipient numerous local, state and nat. poetry awards. Lutheran. Office: Calif Dept Alcohol & Drug Programs 1700 K St Sacramento CA 95814-4022

CANO, KRISTIN MARIA, lawyer; b. McKeesport, Pa., Oct. 27, 1951; d. John S. and Sally (Kavic) C. BS in Biochemistry, Pa. State U., 1973; MS in Forensic Sci., George Washington U., 1975; JD, Southwestern U., 1978; LLM in Securities Regulation, Georgetown U., 1984. Bar: Calif. 1978, U.S. Dist. Ct. (cen., no. and so. dists.) Calif. 1984, U.S. Supreme Ct. 1988, U.S. Ct. Appeals (9th cir.) 1992. Assoc. Yusim, Cassidy, Stein & Hanger, Beverly Hills, Calif., 1979-81, Walker and Hartley, Newport Beach, Calif., 1981-82, Milberg, Weiss, Bershad, Spethrie & Lerach, San Diego, 1984; pvt. practice Newport Beach, 1984—. Bd. dirs., v.p. Sandcastle Community Assn., Corona del Mar, Calif., 1987-95. Mem. Orange County Bar Assn., Orange Coast Venture Group, Balboa Bay Club. Democrat. Roman Catholic. Office: 1 Corporate Plaza Dr Ste 110 Newport Beach CA 92660-7924

CANO, MARTA MENDENDEZ, securities company executive, financial consultant; b. Havana, Cuba, July 29, 1941; came to U.S., 1961; d. Jose F. and Maria C. (Llanio) Menendez; m. Peter J. Cano, Nov. 30, 1960 (div. Jan. 1982); children: Marta, Eileen, Marianne, Peter, Andres. BA in English cum laude, U. Havana, 1961; MEd, U. P.R., 1970. Lic. securities profl., mgmt., life and health ins., notary pub. Dir. ESOL program Colegio Rosa-Bel, Bayamon, P.R., 1966-75; v.p. import/export Distribuidora Delmar, Inc., Bayamon, 1975-79; advanced sales specialist Sun Life of Can., Morristown, N.J., 1980-87; sr. fin. cons. Smith Barney, West Palm Beach, Fla., 1987-94; v.p. investments Prudential Securities, Inc., North Palm Beach, Fla., 1995—; speaker in field. Founder Hispanic Coalition, Palm Beach County; nominated bd. dirs. Pal, Beach County, 1994; participant Directions 94, 1994; bd. commrs. Palm Beach County Health Care Spl. Taxing Dist., 1993—, Housing Authorities, City of West Palm Beach, 1994—; bd. dirs. Citizens Adv. for Health and Human Svcs., Palm Beach County, 1993—, Palm Beach County Budget Task Force, 1991—; mem. St. Ignatius Cathedral Parish coun., 1989-91; mem. Healthy Start Coalition, 1991—, others. Mem. Internat. Businessmean's Assn. (v.p. 1989-93), Internat. Assn. Fin. Planners. Roman Catholic. Office: Prudential Securities Inc 200 PGA Blvd Ste 2104 West Palm Beach FL 33408

CANO, SUSAN BAHR, educational administrator; b. Montpelier, Vt., Aug. 8, 1955; d. Roger Albert and Alice Joyce (Strong) Seamans; m. Paul Victor Cano, June 7, 1975; 1 child, Audrey Marie. MS in Spl. Edn., Plattsburgh (N.Y.) State U., 1987, MS in Spl. Edn. and Sch. Adminstrn., 1991. Spl. edn. tchr. Clinton-Essex-Warren-Washingron Bd. Coop. Ednl. Svcs., Plattsburgh, 1987-91; coord. Clinton-Essex-Warren-Washington Spl. Edn. Tng. Resource Ctr., Plattsburgh, 1991-95; internal mgr. of state and fed. monies for spl. edn. Dept. Edn., State of Vt., Montpelier, 1995—; spl. edn. network leader North Country Tchr. Resource Ctr., Plattsburgh, 1991-95; mem. budget task force Saranac (N.Y.) Ctrl. Sch., 1992. Mem. ASCD, Adirondack Assn. Spl. Educators (program com. 1992-95). Home: PO Box 53 Lake Elmore VT 05657 Office: State of Vt Dept Edn Family and Ednl Support Tm 120 State St Montpelier VT 05620-2501

CANTLIFFE, JERI MILLER, artist, art educator; b. Alliance, N.C., Nov. 25, 1927; d. Rufus Faye Miller and Viola Elizabeth (Ireland) Miller Smith; m. Lawrence R. Cantliffe Jr., Sept.1, 1949; children: Eileen M., David L., Geri Lyn, Lisa Ann, Jonathan M. BA, Meredith Coll., 1949; M in Art Teaching, Wesleyan U., 1967; postgrad., Paier Sch. Art, New Haven, 1974-76. Designer Stephenson Appliance Co., Raleigh, N.C., 1949-50; lab. asst. N.C. State Coll., Raleigh, 1950, Hoffman-LaRoche Pharms., Clifton, N.J., 1951-52; art tchr. Horace Wilcox Tech. Sch., Meriden, Conn., 1962-66; workshop tchr. Park & Recreation Dept., Haddam and Wallingford, Conn., 1970-84, YWCA, Meriden, 1970-85, Middletown (Conn.) Art Guild, 1970-90, instr. in arts and crafts, 1989; workshop tchr. Community Art Ctr., Kensington, Conn., 1977-79; freelance artist specializing in home portraits, 1980—. One-woman shows include Cen. Bank, Meriden, 1977, 79, 82, Meriden Pub. Libr., 1981, 84 (commd. artists, Woman of Yr. in Arts award 1979), Cheshire (Conn.) Pub. Libr., 1982, Phoenix Mut. Life Inst. Co., Hartford, Conn., 1982, New Haven Pub. Libr., 1983, 86, Greene Art Gallery, Guilford, Conn., 1984, Meredith Coll., Raleigh, 1984, Lord Proprietor's Inn, Edenton, N.C.; juried mem. shows include Salamagundi, N.Y.C., New Haven Paint & Clay, Friends of New Britain (Conn.) Mus., Meriden Arts & Crafts (Frederick Flatow award 1979, Butler Paint award 1980, Alan Reid Meml. prize watercolor 1986), Middletown (Conn.) Art Guild (1st prize watercolor 1977, 78, 92, 93), Guilford Art League, 1994, Brush & Palette, New Haven, Milford (Conn.) Fine Arts, Mt. Carmel Art Assn., Hamden, Conn., Wis. Watercolor Show, Glastonbury (Conn.) Art Guild, The New Group, New Haven, Conn. Classic Arts, Conn. Acad. Fine Arts, Am. Penwomen, Fairfield, Conn.; invitational shows include Jewish Home for the Aged, New Haven, Art-on-the-Mountain, Wilmington, Vt., Wesleyan Showcase, Middletown Showcase (Most Popular award 1979), Glastonbury C. of C., AAUW Art Show, Soundview Ann. Art Show, Greeley Nat. Art Show, 1990, Brownstone Group, Meriden, 1990-94, Art Cache Gallery, Vt., 1990-94, Ariz. Arts & Crafts Market Gallery, 1990-92; illustrator Meriden Calendar, Meriden City Hall Christmas Card, Meriden Centennial Quilt. Co-chmn. Commn. on the Arts, Meriden, 1975-76. Recipient Redstone Mfg. award Mum Art Festival, Bristol, Conn., 1978, Best in Show award Middletown Annual Winter Show, 1978, Judges Tri-color award Community Art League, Kensington, 1978, Most Popular Vote award Middletown Showcase, 1979, Middletown Art Guild, 1992, Rick Ciburi 1st prize award Cheshire Art League, 1981, Best in Show (watercolor) Bridgeport Art League, 1982, Women in Leadership award Middlesex County C. of C., 1992, Women in Leadership award YMCA, 1993; named Woman Yr. in Arts Meriden-Record Jour., 1981, Meriden Girls Club, 1982, Meredith Coll., 1984, Meriden YWCA, 1992, 100 Exceptional Women 1893-1993, 1993. Mem. Nat. League Am. PEN Women (nat. membership chair for the arts 1990-94, bd. dirs., sec. 1990-92, 92-94, nat. art show com. 1990-94, br. membership chair 1993-94, judge nat. art show Fayetteville, Ark. br. 1995, pres. Fairfield County br. 1988-92, corr. sec. 1992, v.p. 1986-88, 1st prize watercolor 1993, nat. art bd. 1990-94), PEN Women (state art co-chair 1988-89), Colo. Artists Assn., Rotary (youth exch. com., internat. com. chair youth exch. officer Meriden club, club svc. chair 1993, mem. scholarship com. 1993-94, dist. internat. com. 1993-94, Paul Harris fellow Meriden Rotary 1992). Congregationalist.

CANTO, MINERVA, reporter; b. Mexico City, July 28, 1970; came to U.S., 1976; d. Ignacio and Irene C. BA in Print Journalism, U. So. Calif., 1993. Adminstrv. asst., newsletter editor Calif. Chicano News Media Assn., L.A., 1989-91; editl. advisor Youth News Svc., L.A., 1991-92; newspaper reporter Albuquerque Jour., Santa Fe, 1993—. Mem. Nat. Assn. Hispanic Journalists, Calif. Chicano News Media Assn. Office: Albuquerque Jour 328 Galisteo Santa Fe NM 87501

CANTONE, CARMELA F., elementary education educator; b. Abington, Pa., Dec. 15, 1967; d. Salvatore V. and Florence (Searle) C.; m. Richard A. Calore, Aug. 29, 1992. BS, Cabrini Coll., 1989; MEd, Widener U., 1990, certificate, 1994; student, U. Pa., 1995—. Cert. elem. tchr. Pa., N.J. Tchr. Ctrl. Nursery Sch., Wayne, Pa., 1989-90; kindergarten tchr. Sonshine Presch., Bensalem, Pa., 1990-91; tchr. Huntington Learning Ctr., Abington, Pa., 1991-92, Camden (N.J.) C.C., 1991; elem. tchr. Phila. Sch. Dist., 1989—; edn. adv. bd., Radnor, Pa., 1989—, Cabrini Adv. Bd., Radnor, 1988-89; adj. faculty, Camden; presenter confs. in classroom rsch. Widener U., educating children for parenting Huey Elem., 1995—; participant Penn-Merk Collaborative, 1996. Asst. Spl. Olympics, St. Joseph's U., 1981-89, Hand-in-Hand Festival, Villanova U., 1981-89. Recipient Sesame Place award, 1993. Mem. Del. Reading Assn., Internat. Reading Assn. Home: 9 Station Rd Ardmore PA 19003-2317

CANTOR, ELEANOR WESCHLER, medical association executive; b. N.Y.C., Dec. 30, 1913; d. Samuel Peter and Anna (Rauchwerger) W.; m. Alfred Joseph Cantor, June 9, 1938; children—Pamela Corliss, Alfred Jay. B.A., Hunter Coll., N.Y.C., 1938. Producer radio quiz show CBS, N.Y.C., 1936-41; exec. officer Internat. Acad. Proctology, N.Y.C., 1948—, Internat. Bd. Proctology, 1950—; co-founder Acad. Psychosomatic Medicine, 1954.

CANTOR, LINDA C., history educator; b. N.Y.C., Nov. 25, 1947; d. Henry and Sylvia (Pepper) C. BA in History, Bklyn. Coll., 1968; MA in History, U. Ill., Urbana, 1969; MLS, Queens Coll., 1973. Tchr. history Sarah J. Hale H.S., Bklyn., 1969—; program chair S.J. Hale H.S., Bklyn., 1976—. Editor: (newsletter) LINEAGE (Jewish Genealogy Soc. L.I.). Mem. Jewish Genealogy Soc. L.I. (bd. dirs. 1988-90, sec. 1990-91, pres. 1992-94, past pres. 1995—), Assn. Jewish Genealogical Socs. (dir. 1995—). Home: 1129 Linden St Valley Stream NY 11580

CANTOR, MIRA, artist, educator; b. N.Y.C., May 16, 1944; d. Milton and Sara (Hochhauser) C.; m. Otto Piene, July 18, 1976 (div. 1983); 1 child, Chloe. BFA, U. Ill., 1966; MFA, U. Ill., 1969. Instr. U. Hawaii, Honolulu, 1970-71; with Northeastern U., Boston, 1983—, lectr. art, 1987-88, asst. prof., 1988-90, assoc. prof., 1991—. Ctr. for Advanced Visual Studies MIT fellow, 1978-80, Fulbright fellow, Eqypt, 1994. Office: Northeastern U 360 Huntington Ave Boston MA 02115-5005

CANTOR, PAMELA CORLISS, psychologist; b. N.Y.C., Apr. 23, 1944; d. Alfred Joseph and Eleanor (Weschler) C.; m. Howard Feldman, Sept. 11, 1969; children: Lauren Jaye, Jeffrey Lee. BS cum laude, Syracuse U., 1965; postgrad. in medicine, Johns Hopkins U., 1969-70; MA, Columbia U., 1967, PhD, 1972; postgrad., Harvard U. Children's Hosp. Med. Ctr., 1973-74, Instr. Radcliffe Inst., Harvard U., 1977-78; assoc. prof. psychology Boston U., 1970-80; pvt. practice clin. psychology, Needham, Mass., 1980—; faculty Med. Sch., Harvard U.; lectr. in field, also TV and radio appearances. Author: Understanding A Child's World- Reading in Infancy through Adolescence, 1977; cons. editor: Suicide and Life-Threatening Behavior; columnist: For Parents Only; contbr. chpts. to handbooks and numerous articles to profl. jours. Apptd. mem. Mass. Gov.'s Office for Children Statewide Adv. Bd., 1980—; adv. bd. Samaritans of Boston; pres. Nat. Com. Youth Suicide Prevention; mem. HHS Presdl. Task Force on Youth Suicide. Mem. Am. Psychol. Assn., Am. Assn. Suicidology (pres. 1985-86), Am. Orthopsychiat. Assn., Mass. Psychol. Assn., Am. Assn. Suicidology (bd. dirs.). Home: 11 Parkman Way Needham MA 02192-2863

CANTRELL, LANA, actress, singer; b. Sydney, Australia, Aug. 7, 1943; d. Hubert Clarence and Dorothy Jean (Thistlethwaite) C. JD, Fordham Law Sch., 1993. Of counsel Ballon Stoll Bader & Adler, N.Y.C., Sendroff & Assocs. PC, N.Y.C., 1996. Singer supper clubs, TV programs, Australia, 1958-62; U.S. debut: TV show The Tonight Show, NBC, 1962; rec. artist RCA and Polydor Records, 1967—(Grammy award as Most Promising New Female Artist, Nat. Assn. Rec. Arts and Scis. 1967); recs. include Lana!, Act III, And Then There Was Lana, The Now of Then!. Pres. Thrush, Inc.; U.S. rep. Internat. Song Festival, Poland, 1966, UN Internat. Women's Year Concert, Paris, France, 1975. Recipient 1st prize Internat. Song Festival Poland, 1966; 1st Internat. Woman of Yr. award Feminist Party, 1973. Office: Sendroff & Assocs PC 1500 Broadway New York NY 10036*

CANTRELL, LINDA MAXINE, counselor; b. Ann Arbor, Mich., June 20, 1938; d. Donald LaVerne and Lila Maxine (Crull) Katz; m. Douglas D. Cantrell, Dec. 28, 1963; children: Douglas David Jr., Warren Vincent, Bryan LaVerne. BA, U. Mich., 1960, MA, 1963, postgrad., 1963-65. Cert. secondary tchr., Mich. Caseworker Cook County Dept. Pub. Aid, Chgo., 1960; psychometrist Evanston (Ill.) Schs., 1960-61; rsch. assoc. U. Mich., Ann Arbor, 1961-64; guidance counselor Radcliff Mid. Sch., Garden City, Mich., 1964-66; dir. guidance and counseling St. Mary Acad., Monroe, Mich., 1985-87; counselor, head counselor, instr. Ypsilanti (Mich.) Adult Edn., 1987—; tchr. young adult program Ypsilanti Pub. Schs., 1995—. Rep. precinct leader Ann Arbor, 1971; clk., marker, rec. sec. Thrift Shop of Ann Arbor, 1981—; bd. dirs. Ypsilanti Adult/Cmty. Edn. Adv. Com., 1990—; treas. Burns Park Sch., Ann Arbor, 1978-79; rec. sec. Chapel of Love Ch., 1989—;

co-chmn. benefits Ann Arbor Chamber Orch., 1981-82; chmn. ann. benefit Rudolf Steiner Sch. Ann Arbor, 1984-85; treas. Burns Park PTO, 1978-79; vol. Greenhills Schs., 1978-81, St. Paul's Luth. Sch., 1972-73, among others. Recipient Gil Bursley award Rep. Party, 1972, scholarship Chi Omega, 1957. Mem. AAUW (fellowship chmn. 1971-73), Mich. Assn. for Counseling and Devel. (membership chmn. Monroe County chpt. 1986-87), Ypsilanti Fedn. Tchrs. (rec. sec. 1989-91), Mich. Assn. for Acad. Advisors Community Edn., Washtenaw Counselors Assn., Monroe County Counselors Assn. (membership chmn. 1985-87), Ann Arbor Women's City Club (membership com. 1985-87), Ea. Mich. U. Coll. Bus. Wives (program chmn. 1974, pres. 1975), Phi Kappa Phi, Pi Lambda Theta. Office: Ypsilanti Adult Edn Ypsilanti Pub Schs Perry Sch Ypsilanti MI 48197

CANTRELL, SHARRON CAULK, secondary school educator; b. Columbia, Tenn., Oct. 2, 1947; d. Tom English and Beulah (Goodin) Caulk; m. William Terry Cantrell, Mar. 18, 1989; 1 child, Jordan; children from previous marriage: Christopher, George English, Steffenee Copley. BA George Peabody Coll. Tchrs., 1970; MS Vanderbilt U., 1980; EdS Mid. Tenn. State U., 1986. Tchr., Ft. Campbell Jr. High Sch., Ky., 1970-71, Whitthorne Jr. High Sch., Columbia, Tenn., 1977-86, Spring Hill (Tenn.) High Sch., 1986—; chmn. edn. Homecoming '86 Maury County Schs., Columbia, 1984-86. Mem. NEA, AAUW (pres. Tenn. div. 1983-85), Maury County Edn. Assn. (pres. 1983-84), Tenn. Edn. Assn., Assn. for Preservation Tenn. Antiquities, Maury County C. of C., Friends of Children's Hosp., Phi Delta Kappa. Mem. Ch. of Christ. Home: 5299 Main St Spring Hill TN 37174-2449 Office: Spring Hill High Sch 1 Raider Ln Columbia TN 38401-7346

CANTU, KATHLEEN MARIE, academic administrator; b. Gary, Ind., May 23, 1956; d. John and Nellie Rose (Lopez) C. BS in Retail Mgmt., U. Wis., 1982. Page Wis. State Senate, Madison, 1980; store mgr. Fanny Farmer Candy Shops, Inc., Madison, 1980-85; recruiter, advisor Office of Admissions U. Wis., Madison, 1985-90, program mgr. Sch. Nursing, 1990—. Commr. City of Madison Cmty. Svcs. Commn., 1990—; bd. dirs. Dane County Human Svcs. Bd., Madison, 1993—; cmty. mem. Cmty. Assessment for Health and Human Svcs. Planning in Dane County, Madison, 1993, Latino Adv. Com. to U.S. Senator Russ Feingold, Madison, 1994—. Continuing adult edn. grantee U. Wis., 1991; recipient George Washington Carver award in chemistry, U. Wis.-Madison, 1992. Mem. Nat. Coalition of Hispanic Health and Human Svcs. Orgn., Wis. Indian Edn. Assn., Nat. Assn. Hispanic Nurses. Democrat. Roman Catholic. Home: 928 Erin St Madison WI 53715-1842 Office: U Wis Sch Nursing K6 262 Clin Sci Ctr 600 Highland Ave Madison WI 53792-2455

CANTÚ, NORMA V., federal official; b. Brownsville, Tex., Nov. 2, 1954. BS summa cum laude, Pan Am. U., 1973; JD, Harvard U., 1977. Bar: Tex. 1978, U.S. Dist. Ct. (so. dist.) Tex. 1979, U.S. Dist. Ct. (we. dist.) Tex. 1981, U.S. Ct. Appeals (5th and 11th cirs.) 1982, Calif. 1985, U.S. Ct. Appeals (10th cir.) 1986, U.S. Dist. Ct. (no. dist.) Tex. 1992. Tchr. English Brownsville, 1974, San Antonio, 1979; intern nursing home task force Office of Atty. Gen. Tex., 1977-78; staff atty. Chicana rights project Mex. Am. Legal Def. and Ednl. Fund, 1979-83, nat. dir., 1983-92, regional counsel, 1985-93; asst. sec. for civil rights Office for Civil Rights U.S. Dept. of Edn., Washington, 1993—; cons. NEA, Nat. Assn. Sch. Lawyers, Dept. of Edn., CRESST ctr. testing UCLA. Mem. exec. com. Avance Parent Child Tng. Program, 1990, 92, bd. dirs., 1990—; pro bono legal counsel YWCA San Antonio; mem. City San Antonio Health Facilities Commn., City of San Antonio Com. Drafting Regulations, Tex. Human Rights Commn., 1992, Ctr. Hispanic Health Policy Devel., 1992. Recipient Appreciation award Tex. Senate, 1993, Leadership award Hispanic Mag., 1993, Reynaldo G. Garza award Hispanic issues sect. State Bar Tex., 1993. Office: Dept of Education Office for Civil Rights 330 C St SW Ste 5000 Washington DC 20201-0001

CANTU, SANDRA LOU, special education educator; b. Searcy, Ark., June 19, 1962; d. Stewart Kenneth Smith and Bettye Lou (Hulsey) Ramsey; m. Dino Antonio Cantu, May 12, 1984; children: Derek Anthony, Dylan Alex. BS in Edn., Ark. State U., 1984; MA in Tchg., Webster U., 1992. Cert. tchr., Mo. Spl. edn. tchr. Maynard (Ark.) Pub. Schs., 1988-89, North St. Francois County Schs., Bonne Terre, Mo., 1989-90; spl. edn. tchr. Ste. Genevieve (Mo.) R-II Sch., 1990—, profl. devel. rep., 1994—. Author: Alarm: A Behavior Strategy, 1994. Mem. Found. for Restoration of St. Genevieve, 1993—; mem. S.E. Mo. Regional Profl. Devel. Mem. Coun. for Exceptional Children, Mo. Subdivsn. Learning Disabilities (pres. 1994, chairperson dist. profl. devel. com.). Democrat. Home: 748 Claymont Dr Sainte Genevieve MO 63670-1815 Office: Ste Genevieve Mid Sch 211 N 5th St Sainte Genevieve MO 63670-1203

CANTUS, JANE SCOTT, management consultant; b. Phila., Aug. 31, 1965; d. H. Hollister and Barbara Jane (Park) C. BA in History, Duke U., 1987; MBA, U. Va., 1990. Lyndon B. Johnson intern U.S. Congress, Washington, summer 1986; Dwight D. Eisenhower intern Rep. Nat. Com., Washington, summer 1986; legal asst. Crowell & Moring, Washington, 1987-88; fin. mgmt. asst. Martin Marietta Corp., Bethesda, Md., summer 1989; bus. devel. rep. def. and space divsn. Bechtel Nat., Inc., San Francisco, 1990-91; project control engr. Bechtel Savannah River Site, S.C., 1991; market analyst; bus. devel. rep. def. and space divsn. Bechtel Power Corp., Gaithersburg, Md., 1992-93; sr. assoc. Bechtel Financing Svcs., Inc., Gaithersburg, 1993-94, Korn/Ferry Internat., Washington, 1994—. Active Jr. League, 1987—. Recipient Sr. Leadership award, Duke U., 1987; named to Outstanding Young Women of Am., 1988. Mem. DAR (insignia com. chmn. McLean, Va. chpt., 1983—). Republican. Episcopalian.

CANTWELL, MARY, journalist; b. Providence; d. I. Leo and Mary G. (Lonergan) C.; m. Robert Lescher, Dec. 19, 1953 (div.); children: Katherine, Margaret. B.A., Conn. Coll., 1953. Copywriter Mademoiselle, N.Y.C., 1953-58; chief copywriter Mademoiselle, 1962-67, mng. and features editor, 1968-77, sr. editor features, 1978-80; mem. editiorial bd. N.Y. Times, 1980—, columnist, 1988-90. Author: American Girl, 1992, Manhattan, When I Was Young, 1995; contbr. articles and fiction to mags. Recipient Conn. Coll. medal, 1983, Walker Stone Editorial Writing award Scripps Howard, 1987. Office: NY Times 229 W 43rd St New York NY 10036-3913

CANTWELL, SANDRA LEE, legal assistant; b. Kansas City, Mo., June 12, 1938; d. Julius Erven and Olive Mae (Ragan) Henderson; m. Donald Howard Simmons, June 17, 1956 (div. Jan. 1970); children: Gary Howard Simmons, Juli Diane Simmons Mace, Stacey Jolene Simmons Coffman; m. Bert D. Cantwell. AA, Washburn U., 1987. Unclaimed property adminstr. Kansas State Treas., Topeka, 1979-80, exec. sec. to Kans. state treas., 1981-82; adminstrv. asst. to the CEO Kansas Sheriffs' Assn., Topeka, 1983-87; chief dep. county treas. Wyandotte County Courthouse, Kansas City, Kans., 1988-94, legal asst. to county counselor, 1994—. Author: Linthicum, Ragan Family History, 1985. Bd. dirs. Cancer Action, Inc., Kansas City, 1993—. Mem. Kansas Legal Assts. Soc., Nat. Fedn. of Paralegal Assn., Kansas City Women's C. of C. (bd. dirs. 1995—), Wyandotte County Hist. Soc. Democrat. Presbyterian. Home: 1219 South 105th St Edwardsville KS 66111 Office: Wyandotte County Counselors Office 710 North 7th St Kansas City KS 66101

CANUP, SHERRIE MARGARET, foreign languages educator; b. Thomaston, Ga., Dec. 18, 1946; d. J.B. and Lucille Evelyn (Parham) C. BA, Ga. Coll., 1969, MEd, 1976; EdS, West Ga. Coll., 1990. Tchr. Griffin (Ga.)-Spalding County Sch. System, 1969-91; head. dept. fgn. lang. Griffin H.S., 1992—. Mem. NEA, Ga. Assn. Educators, Fgn. Lang. Assn. Ga., Profl. Assn. Ga. Educators, Griffin Spalding Assn. Educators. Republican. Home: 1110 W Poplar St Apt K4 Griffin GA 30223-2666 Office: Griffin HS 1617 W Poplar St Griffin GA 30223-2038

CANUTE, LINDA MARIE, sales representative; b. Balt., Mar. 5, 1949; d. Emory Mayo Lamb-Murphy and Shirley Isabelle (Mulcare) Canier; m. William Eugene Hammer (dec. Aug. 1984); children: Tina Marie Dorman, Carey Dyan, Amanda Laura, Matthew James; m. Jack Russell Canute; 1 child, Derek Russell. Student, Des Moines Area C.C., 1991—. Machine operator Blue Bell Inc., Elkton, Va., 1966-72; cert. nurse's aide Eastern Star Nursing Home, Boone, Iowa, 1974-80; prodn. worker Sonoco Products Co., Boone, Iowa, 1980-82, manual trimmer, 1982-90, T.Q.M. coord., 1990-91, quality technician, 1990-91, head shipping clk., 1991-94, sales svc. rep., 1994—; mem. T.Q.M. steering com. Sonoco Products Co., 1990—, 3M/Sonoco core adv. team, Boone, 1994—, Sonoco base wage adv. team, 1984—; chair Safety/Housekeeping awareness team, 1982-86. Office: Sonoco Products Co 2105 Industrial Park Rd Boone IA 50036

CAPALDI, ELIZABETH ANN DEUTSCH, psychological sciences educator; b. N.Y.C., May 13, 1945; d. Frederick and Nettie (Tarasuck) Deutsch; m. Egidio J. Capaldi, Jan. 20, 1968 (div. May 1985). A.B., U. Rochester, 1965; Ph.D., U. Tex., 1969. Asst. prof. dept. psychol. scis. Purdue U., West Lafayette, Ind., 1969-74, assoc. prof., 1974-78, prof., 1979-86, asst. dean Grad. Sch., 1982-86, head dept. psychol. scis., 1983-88, sec.-treas. council of grad. dept. psychology, 1986-88; prof. U. Fla., Gainesville, 1988—; mem. basic behavioral neuroscis. fellowship rev. panel NIH, reviewer's res. NIMH, 1991; spl. asst. to pres., U. Fla. Author: Psychology, 1984, 3d edit., 1991; cons. editor Jour. Exptl. Psychology, 1991; assoc. editor Psychonomic Bull. Rev., 1993; contbr. articles to profl. jours. NIMH grantee, 1984-94, NSF grantee, 1995—. Fellow AAAS, APA, Am. Psychol. Soc. (mem. governing bd. 1991—); mem. Psychonomic Soc. (mem. governing bd. 1992—), Midwestern Psychol. Assn. (sec.-treas. 1988-90, pres. 1991), Sigma Xi. Home: 4140 NW 44th Ave Gainesville FL 32606-4518 Office: U Fla Dept Psychology Gainesville FL 32611

CAPECE, MARIA LYNN, financial analyst; b. Providence, Jan. 22, 1968; d. Raymond Anthony and Diane Edith (Puleo) C. BA, Brown U., 1990. Internat. buyer Victoria Creations, Warwick, R.I., 1990-92; fixed income analyst Eaton Vance Mgmt., Boston, MA, 1992—; interviewer Nat. Alumni Schs. Program. Mem. Boston Security Analysts Soc. Home: 50 Park Row W #426 Providence RI 02903

CAPEHART, HARRIET JANE HOLMES, economics educator; b. Springfield, Ill., Sept. 29, 1917; d. Walter Creager and Mary Gladys (Copeland) Holmes; m. Homer Earl Capehart Jr., June 17, 1950; children: Craig Earl, Caroline Mary, John. AB, Vassar Coll., 1938; MA, Harvard U., 1945, PhD, 1948; LLD (hon.), U. Indpls., 1986. Instr. Wheaton Coll., Norton, Mass., 1945-46, Wellesley (Mass.) Coll., 1947-48; assoc. prof. Western Coll. for Women, Oxford, Ohio, 1948-50; assoc. prof. econs. Butler U., Indpls., 1950-53; staff adult edn. div. U. Indpls. (formerly Indiana Cen. U.), 1973-75, adj. faculty, 1983—; lectr. summer sch. Butler U., 1948-50; bd. dirs. Indpls. Power and Light Co., IPALCO Enterprises Inc. Bd. trustees U. Indpls., 1969—; exec. bd. Women's Com. Indpls. Symphony Orch., 1964—; bd. dirs. Utility Women's Conf., 1986—; mem. Children's Mus. Guild, aux. Indpls. Day Nursery, others. Mem. Am. Econ. Assn., Econometric Soc., AAUP, Indpls. Mus. Art, Nat. Soc. Colonial Dames Am. (bd. mgrs. Ind.), Kappa Alpha Theta, Phi Beta Kappa. Republican. Clubs: Ind. Vassar (past pres.) Radcliffe of Ind. (past pres.). Home: 445 Pine Dr Indianapolis IN 46260-1450 Office: IPL 25 Monument Circle PO Box 15958 Indianapolis IN 46206

CAPELL, CYDNEY LYNN, editor; b. Jacksonville, Fla., Dec. 20, 1956; d. Ernest Clary and Alice Rae (McGinnis) Capell; m. Garrick Philip Martin, July 16, 1983 (div. Jan. 1988). BA, Furman U., 1977. Mktg. rep. E.C. Capell & Assocs., Greenville, S.C., 1977-80; sales rep. Prentice-Hall Publs., Cin., 1980-81; sales, mktg. rep. Benjamin/Cummings, Houston, 1981-83; sales rep. McGraw-Hill Book Co., Houston, 1983-85, engring. editor, N.Y.C., 1985-87; acctg. and infosystems editor Bus. Pubs., Inc., Plano, Tex., 1988-89; sr. editor Gorsuch Scarisbrick Pubs., Scottsdale, Ariz., 1989-90; editor-in-chief rsch. dept. Rauscher, Pierce, Refsnes Stock Brokers, 1990-94; editor-in-chief, dir. mktg. Marshall & Swift, L.A., 1994—; editor lit. mag. Talon, 1972; news editor Paladin newspaper, 1977. Named Rookie of Yr., McGraw-Hill Book Co., 1985. Mem. NOW, NAFE, Women in Pub., Women in Communications, Mensa. Republican. Avocations: tennis, ballet.

CAPELLE, MADELENE CAROLE, opera singer, educator, music therapist; b. Las Vegas, Nev., July 29, 1950; d. Curtis and Madelene Glenna (Healy) C. BA, Mills Coll., 1971; MusM, U. Tex., 1976; postgrad., Ind. U., 1976-77; diploma cert., U. Vienna, Austria, 1978; postgrad. in creative arts, Union Coll. Cert. K-12 music specialist, Nev. Prof. voice U. Nev. Clark County C.C., Las Vegas, 1986 ; music therapist Charter Hosp., Las Vegas, 1987—; pvt. practice music therapy, Las Vegas, 1989—; music specialist Clark County Sch. Dist., Las Vegas, 1989—; contract music therapist Nev. Assn. for Handicapped, Las Vegas, 1990; guest voice coach U. Basel, Switzerland, 1992; presenter concerts in Kenya, self-esteem workshops for children and adult women; artist-in-residence, Nev., Wyo., S.D., Oreg., Idaho, N.D., Utah, 1988—; mem. cons. roster Wyo. Arts Cou., 1988—; cons. U.S. rep. Princess Margaret of Romania Found.; workshops in music therapy and humor therapy Germany, Austria, Switzerland; workshop day treatment program dir. Harmony Health Care; judge Leontyne Price Nat. Voice Competition. Opera singer, Europe, Asia, S.Am., U.S., Can., Australia, 1978—; roles include Cio Cio San in Madama Butterly, Tosca, Turandot and Fidelio, Salome Electra; community concerts artist; featured PBS artist Guess Who's Playing the Classics; featured guest All Things Considered PBS radio, 1985; co-writer (one-woman show) The Fat Lady Sings, 1991 (Women's Awareness award); concerts Africa, Kenya, Somalia; concerts for Jugaslavian Relief throughout Europe; guest soloist national anthem San Francisco 49ers. Pres., founder, cons. Children's Opera Outreach, Las Vegas, 1985—; artist Musicians Emergency Found., N.Y.C., 1978-82; vol. Zoo Assn., Allied Arts, Ziegfeld Club (first Junior Ziegfeld Young Woman of Yr.), Las Vegas, 1979—; clown Very Spl. Arts, Nev., Oreg., S.D., 1989-90; goodwill and cultural amb. City of Las Vegas, 1983; panelist Kennedy Ctr., Washington, 1982; artist Benefit Concerts for Children with AIDS; mem. Nev. Arts Alliance, Make a Wish Found., Lyric Opera of Las Vegas. Named Musician of Yr. Swiss Music Alliance, 1993. Mem. Internat. Platform Assn., Nat. Assn. Tchrs. Singing (featured guest spkr.), Performing Arts Soc. Nev., Cultural Arts Soc. (co-founder 1995), Brown Bag Concert Assn. (bd. dirs.), Make a Wish Found., Las Vegas Lyric Opera (bd. dirs.). Democrat. Home: 3266 Brentwood St Las Vegas NV 89121-3316

CAPELLO, LINDA, artist; b. Bklyn., July 12, 1949; m. John Capello; 1 child, Joanna. AAS, Fashion Inst. Tech., N.Y.C., 1968. art tchr. figure drawing; art tchr. Guild Hall's Young At Art Program; art tutor Empire State Coll.; art tchr., dept. head Bialik Sch., Bklyn., 1985-87; illustrator for children's newspaper The Waldo Tribune; artist Karl Mann studios, 1978-80; freelance fashion illustrator. Exhibited in group shows at ann. Guild Hall shows, East Hampton, ann. Goat Alley Gallery 725 shows, Sag Harbor, ann. Southampton Artists group shows, Adelphia U. Gallery, L.I., 1973, Belanthi Gallery, Bklyn., 1979-81, BACA Small Works show, Bklyn., 1986, AFA at Lever House, N.Y.C., 1989, Mark Humphries Gallery, Southampton, 1993, Goodman Deisgn Gallery, Southampton, 1993, Clayton-Libratore Gallery, Bridgehampton, N.Y., 1993, 51st Ann. Audubon Exhibit, N.Y.C., 1993, Ashwagh Hall, East Hampton, 1994, Catherine Lorillard Wolf Art Club ann. show, N.Y.C., 1994, Am. Pen Women show, Farmingville, N.Y., 1995, Sundance Gallery, Bridgehampton, 1995, EEAC Juried Show, Riverhead, N.Y., 1995; oil paintings, drawings in pvt. collections; murals on pub. and pvt. walls. Mem. Southampton Artists.

CAPITOL-JEFFERSON, VIOLA WHITESIDE, secondary education art educator; b. Greenville, Pa., Feb. 23, 1947; d. Claude Henry Sr. and Geraldine (Carter) Whiteside; m. William H. Capitol Jr., Aug. 29, 1970 (div. 1982); m. Porter James Jefferson, Sept. 17, 1983. BS in Art Edn., Youngstown State U., 1971; MA in Art Edn., Trinity Coll., 1977. Cert. tchr. art, Md. Gen. office staff Greenville Hosp., 1965-70; pvt. sec. Gibbs Paving and Demolition, West Middlesex, Pa., 1970-71; tchr. art Lackey High Sch., Indian Head, Md., 1971-76; tchr. art, chair dept. McDonough High Sch., Pomfret, Md., 1976-88; tchr. art Surrattsville High Sch., Clinton, Md., 1988-90, 91-92, Largo High Sch., 1990-91; art tchr., chair dept. Friendly High Sch., Ft. Washington, Md., 1992—; multi-cultural curriculum writer Prince George's County, Upper Marlboro, Md., 1988—; multicultural liaison, Friendly H.S., Ft. Washington, Md., 1993—; sr. class sponsor, 1992-93; resource person Black Male Achievement Program, Prince George's County, 1990—, Cultural Experiences Program, 1988—; spkr., presenter ann. Md. Art Edn. Vol. Photo Archive, Nat. Mus. African Art, Washington, 1987, docent, 1985—; vol. Cross-Cultural Ctr., Washington, 1989—; sponsor youth ministries in assn. with Terry and Assocs., Inc., Wyo., Mich., 1992. scipient Disting. Svc. award Charles County Tchr. of Yr., Jaycees, 1982, Cert. of Outstanding Svc. Mid. States Assn. Colls. and Secondary Schs., 1974-89, Educator of Yr. award Prince George's Art Coun., 1995. Mem. NEA, Nat. Art Edn. Assn. (J. Eugene Grigsby award 1995), Md. Tchrs. Assn., Md. Art Edn. Assn. (COMC rep. exec. com. 1992—, Outstanding New Art Tchr. in Prince George's County 1989), Smithsonian Assocs., Black Women United for Action, Delta Sigma Theta. Home: 9200 Genoa Ave Fort Washington MD 20744-3777

CAPLAN, PAULA JOAN, actress, playwright, psychologist, educator; b. Springfield, Mo., July 7, 1947; d. Jerome Arnold and Theda Ann (Karchmer) C.; children: Jeremy Benjamin, Emily Julia. AB in English cum laude, Harvard U., 1969; MA in Psychology, Duke U., 1971, PhD in Psychology, 1973. Clin. psychology intern John Umstead Hosp., Butner, N.C., 1972-73, N.C. Meml. Hosp., Chapel Hill, 1972-73; fellow neuropsychology divsn. Rsch. Inst. Hosp. for Sick Children, Toronto, Can., 1974-76; psychologist Toronto Family Ct. Clinic Clarke Inst. Psychiatry, Can., 1977-80; lectr. dept. psychiatry U. Toronto, Can., 1978-79; asst. prof. dept. applied psychology Ontario Inst. for Studies in Edn., 1980-81; prin. investigator Toronto Multi-Agy. Child Abuse Rsch. Project, Can., 1979-84; lectr. women's studies U. Toronto, Can., 1979-95, asst. prof. psychiatry, 1979-95; assoc. dir. Ontario Inst. for Studies in Edn.'s Ctr. for Women's Studies in Edn., Can., 1984-85; head Ctr. for Women's Studies in Edn. Ontario Inst. for Studies in Edn., Can., 1985-87, assoc. prof. applied psychology, 1982-87, full prof. dept. applied psychology, 1987-95; vis. scholar Brown U. Pembroke Ctr., Providence, R.I., 1993-94, affiliated scholar, 1944-95; spkr. in field. Author: The Myth of Women's Masochism, 1985, 93, German edit., 1986, Swedish edit., 1987, Between Women: Lowering the Barriers, 1981, Don't Blame Mother: Mending the Mother-Daughter Relationship, 1989, 90, Brazilian edit., 1990, German edit., 1990, Dutch edit., 1991, Lifting a Ton of Feathers: A Woman's Guide to Surviving in the Academic World, 1993, You're Smarter than They Make You Feel: How the Experts Intimidate Us and What We Can Do About It, 1994, German edit., 1995, They Say You're Crazy: How the World's Most Powerful Psychiatrists Decide Who's Normal, 1995, (with Jeremy B. Caplan) Thinking Critically About Research on Sex and Gender, 1994, (with Marcel Kinsbourne) Children's Learning and Attention Problems, 1979, Spanish edit., 1984; mem. editl. bd. Can. Jour. Cmty. Mental Health, 1990-93, Women and Therapy, 1992-95; mem. internat. adv. bd. Feminism and Psychology, 1993-95; cons. Can. Jour. Behavioural Sci., 1984; editor Resources for Feminist Rsch./Documentation sur la Recherche Feministe, 1982-84, 85-86, adv. bd. mem. 1986-87; reviewer of grant proposals Hosp. for Sick Children Found., Social Scis. and Humanities Rsch. Coun. Can.; contbr. articles to profl. jours. and chpts. to books, and numerous others. Mem. Brown U. Parents Coun., 1992-94. Recipient fellowship Nat. Inst. Mental Health, 1969-71, fellowship Nat. Inst. Child Devel., 1971-73. Fellow APA (cons. to adv. group on self defeating personality disorder 1989-90, advisor to adv. group on late luteal phase dysphoric disorder 1989-90, Gninent Woman Psychologist 1996), Am. Orthopsychiatric Assn. (program com. mem., reviewer conv. 1983-84, program com. mem., reviewer Women's Inst. 1984-85), Can. Psychol. Assn. (newsletter editor interest group on women and psychology 1979-80, inst. organizer sect. on women and psychology 1980-81, coord.-elect sect. on women and psychology 1981-82, mem. com. on status women 1982-84, coord. sect. on women and psychology 1982-83, past coord. sect. on women and psychology 1983-84, mem. com. on nominations 1990-91); mem. Harvard-Radcliffe Club Toronto (mem. schs. com. 1981-82). Home: 95 Slater Ave Providence RI 02906

CAPLINGER, ALICE ANN, conductor, educator; b. San Bernardino, Calif., Dec. 5, 1958; d. Phillip Carlton and Eleanor Jeanette (Reiss) Hunt; m. Raymond Harold Caplinger, June 3, 1978; children: Christina, Robert, Michael, Patrick. MusB, Hardin-Simmons U., 1989, MusM, 1991. Cert. tchr. music, Tex., Colo. Specialist orchestral music Abilene (Tex.) Ind. Sch. Dist., 1991-92, Sch. Dist. # 11, Colorado Springs, Colo., 1992—; condr. Colo. Springs Youth Symphony, 1992—, dir. Little Mozart String Program, 1994-95. Recipient Ongoing Support of the Arts awardColorado Springs C. of C., 1996. Mem. Am. String Tchrs. Assn., Suzuki Assn. of Ams., Tex. Music Educators Assn., Kappa Delta Pi. Home: 6010 Canyon Springs Pl Colorado Springs CO 80918 Office: Palmer HS 301 N Nevada Ave Colorado Springs CO 80903

CAPLINGER, PATRICIA E., family nurse practitioner; b. St. Louis, Oct. 6, 1956; d. Julius G. and Wanda L. (Guthrie) Kissel; child from previous marriage, Jeremy Michael Frederiksen; m. Ray E. Caplinger, Dec. 26, 1995. ADN, St. Louis C.C., 1977; BSN, U. State N.Y., 1982; FNP, U. Colo., Denver, 1985. RN, Colo.; CNOR, CNRN; cert. family nurse practitioner. Med. case mgmt. supr. Intracorp., Denver; clin. mgr. Rehab. Svcs. Corp., Eureka, Calif.; family nurse practitioner Burre Clinic, Eureka; pvt. practice Eureka; dir. PM&R Marian Health Ctr., Sioux City, Iowa; family nurse practitioner Lebanon (Mo.) Med. Ctr. Mem. ANA (nursing scholar), ARN, AANP. Home: 23241 Red Oak Dr Lebanon MO 65536

CAPO, HELENA FRANCES, comedienne; b. N.Y.C., July 29, 1959; d. Frank Remo Capo and Rose Nellie (Aguilar) Richards; m. William Patterson, Oct. 18, 1986; 1 child, W. Spencer Patterson. BA, Queens Coll., 1981. Engr., disc jockey Sta WQMC-AM, N.Y.C., 1980; writer Sta. WBLS-FM, N.Y.C., 1984-86; assoc. editor Laugh Factory Mag., Los Angeles, 1985-87; pres. Precision Production Inc., N.Y.C., 1985—; producer N.Y.C. 1st Official Comedy Day, 1984; tchr. Learning Annex, N.Y.C., 1984; creator Availiabilities Hotline, N.Y.C., 1985. Author: Training Your Pet Flea, 1984, Dogslapping, 1987, Fast Talking for Fun and Profit, 1990, How to Get Publicity without a Publicist, 1995, Humor in Business Speaking, 1995; (audio tape) Fran's Fast Fractured Fairy Tales, 1991; (record album) Rappin' Mae, 1985; producer: Stand-Up for Animals, 1988. Named Worlds Fastest Talker Guinness Book World Records, N.Y.C. and London, 1989, 91. Roman Catholic. Office: Precision Prodns Inc PO Box 314 Flushing NY 11358-0314

CAPOBIANCO, LOIS JANE, school system administrator; b. Paterson, N.J.; d. John Joseph and Louise (D'Amelio) C. BA in Early Childhood and Elem. Edn., William Paterson Coll., 1974, MA in Edn. and Reading, 1978. Cert. sch. adminstr., supervisor, reading specialist, elem. sch. tchr., nursery sch. tchr. Tchr. Bishop Navagh Regional Sch., Paterson, 1974-75, Rockaway Borough (N.J.) Bd. of Edn., 1975-81; tchr., reading specialist Chester (N.J.) Twp. Bd. of Edn., 1981-88; edn. program specialist State of N.J. Dept. Edn., Trenton, 1988-91; supr. elem. edn., adminstrv. asst. to supt. Bloomfield (N.J.) Bd. of Edn., 1991-92; coord. edn. svcs. New Providence (N.J.) Bd. of Edn., 1992-94, dir. edn. svcs., 1994—; presenter State of N.J. Dept. of Edn., Edison, 1988-91, N.J. Edn. Assn. Conv., Atlantic City, 1991. Chairperson registration October Walk, Am. Diabetes Assn., Morristown, N.J., 1992, 93, 94. Mem. ASCD, Nat. Staff Devel. Coun. (presenter conf. 1991), N.J. Staff Devel. Coun., N.J. Assn. Supervision and Curriculum Devel. (presenter conf. 1991), N.J. Assn. Sch. Adminstrs., Phi Delta Kappa. Office: New Providence Bd of Edn 340 Central Ave New Providence NJ 07974-2322

CAPODILUPO, JEANNE HALTON, public relations executive; b. McRae, Ga., May 3, 1940; d. Lewis Irby and Essee Elizabeth (Parker) Hatton; m. Raphael S. Capodilupo, Jan. 21, 1967. Grad., Dale Carnegie Inst., 1976. Sec. A.R. Clark Acct., Fernandina Beach, Fla., 1958-59; receptionist, girl Friday Sta. WNDT-TV, N.Y.C., 1960-62, Coy Hunt and Co., N.Y.C., 1962-69; clk. Woodlawn Cemetery, Bronx, N.Y., 1969-71, historian, community affairs coord., 1971—, editor newsletter, 1979—, asst. to pres., 1984, dir. pub. rels., 1984; grad. asst. Dale Carnegie Inst., 1977-78. Researcher Woodlawn Cemetery's Hall of Fame; contbr. articles to profl. jours. Chmn. ann. Adm. Farragut Honor Ceremony, Bronx, 1976—; founder, chmn. Toys for Needy Children, 1983-91; bd. dirs. Bronx Mus. Arts, v.p., 1983-84; pres. Bronx Coun. Arts, 1987-90; mem. adv. bd. Salvation Army, 1985, Bronx Arts Ensemble, 1985; bd. mgrs. Bronx YMCA, 1985, life mem., vice chmn., 1989—; bd. dirs. Bronx Urban League, 1985; bd. dirs. Bronx Coun. on Arts, 1985, pres., 1987-90; mem. Bronx Landmarks Task Force, 1994—. Recipient award citation VFW, 1976, Voice of Democracy Program judge's citation, 1980, Disting. Community Svc. award N.Y.C. Council, II Leone di Sanmarco award Italian Heritage & Culture Com. Bronx, 1989; named Woman of Yr., YMCA, Bronx, 1986, Woman of Yr., Network Orgn. of Bronx Women, 1986, Jeanne and Ray Capodilupo named as Mr. & Mrs. Bronx 1989-90 proclaimed by Borough Pres., named Pioneer of the Bronx, 1992; cert. appreciation Dale Carnegie Inst., 1977; Outstanding Citizenship award Bronx N.E. Kiwanis Club, 1981; Service to Youth award YMCA of Bronx, 1983; recipient proclamation City Council of N.Y., Italian Heritage and Culture Com. of the Bronx, 1989; Outstanding Cemeterian award Am. Cemetery Assn., 1987-88; Citation of Merit Bronx Borough Pres.'s Office, 1988; Spl. Hons. for Outstanding Vol. Work Ladies Aux. Our Lady of Mercy Med. Ctr.; named Hon. Grand Marshall Bronx Columbus Day Parade, 1987-89, Bronx Meml. Day Parade, 1989; apptd. to commn. celebrating 350 yrs. of the Bronx by Borough Pres., recipient Pioneer award for Women's History Month for Outstanding Humanitarian Svcs., 1991. Mem. Bronx County Hist. Soc., Network Orgn. Bronx Women, Women in Communication, Bronx C. of C. (sec. 1988), YMCA (life mem.), N.Y. Press Club, Italian Big Sisters Club, Women's City Club, Order Eastern Star. Methodist. Office: Woodlawn Cemetery PO Box 75 Bronx NY 10470-0075

CAPOLUPO, GABRIELLE MARY, marketing professional; b. Winchester, Mass., Aug. 14, 1964; d. Michael Joseph and Virginia Ruth (Murray) C. BA, U. Mass. Amherst; MBA, San Jose State U., 1994. Asst. mgr. K Mart Apparel, Boston, 1986-87; store mgr. Fields Hosiery, Boston, 1987-88; from customer cost svc. rep. to product mktg. mgr. Novell, Inc., San Jose, Calif., 1988-95; program mgr. Cisco Sys., San Jose, 1995—. Judge Internat. Collegiate Bus. Policy Competition, San Jose, 1995. Mem. Alpha Lambda Delta. Roman Catholic. Home: 310 Elan Village Ln #212 San Jose CA 95134

CAPONE, MARGARET LYNCH, civic worker, parliamentarian; b. Wilkinsburg, Pa., May 21, 1907; d. John Edward and Anna Freda (Dunstrup) Lynch; m. Carmen R. Capone, July 21, 1936 (dec. May 1983); children: David Michael, Mary Ann Capone Sperling, Donald William. Student U. Pitts., 1925-33, 1949-53, Carnegie Inst. Tech., 1955-56. Parliamentarian Pa. Nurses Assn., 1960-68, Allegheny County Law Wives, Pa., 1975-89; treas. Allegheny County LWV, 1965-69, v.p., 1969-73, pres., 1973-79, parliamentarian, 1979—, historian, 1980; parliamentarian St. Lucy Guild to Blind, Pitts., Allegheny County Lawyers Aux., Diocese Coun. Cath. Women, Marian Manor Guild; cons. parliamentarian. Author: So You've Joined A Club, 1954; Parliamentary Pointers, 1972; editor Clea News, 1954-72. Named Woman of Yr., Clea News, 1973; Personality of Yr., Pitts. chpt. K.C., 1979. Mem. Nat. Assn. Parliamentarians (profl. registered parliamentarian, local pres. 1959-61, state pres. 1963-64, nat. v.p. 1977-79), Am. Inst. Parliamentarians (cert. profl. parliamentarian), Duquesne U. Women's Guild. Republican. Roman Catholic. Lodges: K.C. Women's Guild, Toastmistresses (pres. local club 1950-51, nat. bd. dirs. 1953-63, nat. sec. 1954-56, nat. v.p. 1956-57, editor Toastmistress Mag. 1958-62). Home: 6530 Zupancic Dr Pittsburgh PA 15236-3652

CAPONE, MARY THERESE, foreign language educator, editor; b. Uniondale, N.Y., Feb. 16, 1954; d. Everett Carl and Anna Marie (Connelly) Arndt; m. Robert Albert Capone, Sept. 5, 1975; children: Lara Therese, Kristy, Jessica, Ryan. Bachelors, Iona Coll., 1975; Masters, C.W. Post, 1991. Editor South Bay Newspaper, Lindenhurst, N.Y., 1985-88, This Week, Farmingdale, N.Y., 1988-91, Massapegua (N.Y.) Post, 1991-96; tchr. Lindenhurst (N.Y.) Pub. Sch., 1993—; pres. MRC Multi Media, Lindenhurst, 1996—. Contbr. articles to newspapers. Mem. Am. Assn. Tchrs. of German, Soc. Profl. Journalists, N.Y. State Assn. Fgn. Lang. Tchrs., Orton Gillingham Soc.

CAPORINO, GRACE CONNOLLY, secondary education educator, consultant; b. Red Bank, N.J.; d. Daniel Joseph and Mary Agnes (Martinez) Connolly; m. Gabriel Anthony Caporino, July 19, 1960 (dec. Mar. 1974); children: Melanie Brezovsky, Pamela. BA in Lit., Purchase Coll., 1974; MA in Secondary English, Manhattanville Coll., 1978. Cert. H.S. English tchr., N.Y. H.S. English tchr. Carmel (N.Y.) H.S., 1974—; lit. cons. Advanced Placement English Lit. Exam Reader, The Coll. Bd., Princeton, N.J., 1988—; cons. Tchr. Task Force, U.S. Holocaust Meml. Mus., Washington, 1990—; project dir. NEH masterwork grant CUNY Grad. Ctr., N.Y.C., 1989-91; project dir. NEH Humanities Focus Grant Holocaust Perspectives: The Word and the Image, Manhattanville Coll., Purchase, N.Y., 1995-96, adj. prof. edn. Contbg. editor: (pamphlets) Guidelines for Teaching the Holocaust, 1993, Teacher's Guide for Artifact Poster Series, 1993. Summer fellow Haifa U. and Yad Vashem, Jerusalem, Israel, 1987, summer NEH fellow Hollins Coll., Roanoke, Va., 1988; recipient Louis Yavner Teaching award Regents of SUNY, 1991. Mem. Nat. Coun. Tchrs. English (mem. Tchg. about Genocide and Intolerance com. 1994—), Internat. Consortium Nat. Coun. Tchrs. English (host European profs. English U.S. visit 1994), N.Y. State United Tchrs., Westchester Coun. English Tchrs. Home: 213 California Rd Yorktown Heights NY 10598-4907 Office: Carmel HS Fair St Carmel NY 10512

CAPPARELL, LORRAINE SUSAN, artist, sculptor, painter; b. Rochester, N.Y., July 26, 1947; d. Edmond Seth and Ruth Myrtle (Goettel) Spencer; m. James Capparell, Aug. 23, 1969 (div. 1995). BS, Cornell U., 1969. Exec. trainee McCurdy's, Rochester, 1969-70; prodn. artist Coakley-Heagerty, San Jose, Calif., 1971-73; freelance graphic designer Palo Alto, Calif., 1974—; photographer Palo Alto, 1978—, sculptor, painter, 1980—. Artist, creator Hands, 1982, The Three Ages of Women, 1986, Dream Shower: Tree of Life, 1994, Erato, 1994, Observer, 1995, Yin and Yang, 1996. Bd. dirs. Cult. Odyssey San Francisco, 1985—, Women's Caucus for the Arts, Palo Alto, 1986—. Mem. Kappa Kappa Gamma. Buddhist. Home: 698 Kendall Ave Palo Alto CA 94306

CAPPEL, MARY LOU, recreation therapy educator; b. St. Louis, May 12, 1949; d. Lawrence Hughes and Verna Adeline (Scheltens) Schuler; m. Timothy Raymond Cappel, Jan. 23, 1971; children: Ashley Lauren, Kirsten Michelle. BS, U. Mo., 1971; MS, U. N.C., 1980; PhD, U. So. Calif., 1988. Cert. therapeutic recreation specialist. Recreation therapist N.C. Meml. Hosp., Chapel Hill, 1973-75; tchg. asst. U. So. Calif., L.A., 1981-85; pvt. fitness cons., 1982-89; prof. Calif. State U. Dominguez Hills, Carson, 1988—. Author: More Than Aerobics, 1994, Principles of Leisure; editor Jour. Recreation and Leisure, 1991-93; guest editor Jour. Phys. Edn., Recreation and Dance, 1996. Vol. Watts (Calif.) Cmty., 1989—; mem. exec. bd. Watts Friendship Sports League, L.A., 1990—; bd. dirs. People for Parks, L.A., 1994—. Recipient Svc. Proclamation, City of L.A., 1991, 95, Vol. Svc. award L.A. Parks and Recreation, 1995. Mem. AAHPERD (bd. dirs. 1993-95, Honor S.W. area 1996), Calif. Assn. Health, Phys. Edn., Recreation and Dance (v.p. 1990-95, Svc. award 1996), Calif. Park and Recreation Soc. (edn. program chair 1995-96), Women in Leisure Svcs. (profl. devel. chair 1996), World Recreation and Leisure Assn., Am. Assn. Recreation and Leisure (editl. bd. 1994—). Roman Catholic. Office: Calif State U Dominguez Hills 1000 E Victoria St Carson CA 90747

CAPPELLO, EVE, international business consultant; b. Sydney, Australia; d. Nem and Ethel Shapira; children: Frances Soskins, Alan Kazdin. BA, Calif. State U.-Dominguez Hills, 1974; MA, Pacific Western U., 1977, PhD, 1978. Singer, pianist, L.A., 1956-76; profl. devel., mgmt./staff tng., 1976—; instr. Calif. State U., Dominguez Hills, 1977-95; counselor Associated Tech. Coll., L.A. instr. Mt. St. Mary's Coll., U. of Judaism, U. So. Calif., Loyola Marymount U.; founder, pres. A-C-T Internat.; invited speaker World Congress Behavior Therapy, Israel, Melbourne U., Australia. Mem. Internat. Platform Assn., Book Publicists So. Calif., Pasadena C. of C., Alpha Gamma. Author: Let's Get Growing, 1979, The New Professional Touch, 1988, 2d edit., Dr. Eve's Garden, 1984, Act, Don't React, 3d edit., 1988, The Game of the Name, 1985, The Perfectionist Syndrome, 1990, Why Aren't More Women Running The Show?, 1994; newspaper columnist, 1976-79; contbr. articles to profl. jours. Home: 518 S El Molino Ave # 303 Pasadena CA 91101

CAPPETTA, ANNA MARIA, art educator; b. New Haven, Feb. 14, 1949; d. Alfonso M. and Elvira (Bove) Cavaliere; m. Vincent John Cappetta, July 17, 1971. BS in Art Edn., So. Conn. State U., 1971, MS in Spl. Edn., 1973, MS in Supervision/Adminstrn., 1980, MS in Art Edn., 1981. Sub. tchr. West Haven (Conn.) Sch. System, 1971; art educator/coord. North Haven (Conn.) Sch. System, 1971—; adj. prof. art So. Conn. State U., New Haven, 1984-92; cons. Area Coop. Ednl. Svcs., Conn., 1987—. Co-author: (mag.) Art Education, 1990, School Arts, 1986—, Impace II Experienced Teachers Handbook, 1992; contbg. editor School Arts mag., 1991—. Recipient North Haven Tchr. of Yr. award, 1986, Conn. Celebration of Excellence award, 1987, 90, 92, Nat. Art Educator award, 1988, 89, Conn. Art Educator award, 1989, 95, North Haven Tchr. of Yr. award, 1989. Fellow Nat. Coun. Basic Edn.; mem. Nat. Art Edn. Assn. (nat. elem. dir. 1991-95, Nat. Art Educator award 1988, 89, advisory 1994, Briefing Paper Series 1993), Conn. Art Edn. Assn. (Conn. Art Educator award 1989, 95), Nat. Women's Art Caucus, Phi Delta Kappa (co-editor newsletter 1987-89), Delta Kappa Gamma. Home: PO Box 1399 19 Johnson Ln Madison CT 06443

CAPPETTA, PAMELA GUYLER, counselor; b. Huntington, Pa., May 16, 1949; d. Thomas Winslow and Lois Olene (Lukens) G.; m. Christopher John Boll, Aug. 16, 1969 (div. Aug. 1985); 1 child, Kirstin Boll Kochanek; m. Robert Christopher Cappetta, May 4, 1991. BS, Shippensburg U., 1971; MEd, Coll. William & Mary, 1980, EdD, 1990. Lic. profl. counselor, Va. Social worker York-Poquoson Social Svcs., Grafton, Va., 1981-84; coord. PACES family counseling ctr. Coll. William & Mary, Williamsburg, Va., 1984-87; family therapist TMJ rsch. ctr. Med. Coll. Va., Sch. Dentistry, 1984-88; clin. assoc., counselor Family Living Inst., Williamsburg, Va., 1985-88; clin. asst. prof. Med. Coll. Va., Sch. Dentistry, Richmond, Va., 1990-94; med. family therapist Norge Family Practice, Williamsburg, 1992-94; co-owner, counselor Family Living Inst., 1988-94; allied health profl. Williamsburg Place, 1993—; counselor pvt. practice, Williamsburg, 1995—; dir. coord. Transitions, Williamsburg, 1992-94. Contbr. articles to profl. jours. Vol. Va. Breast Cancer Found., Williamsburg, 1995; bd. dirs. Va. Cancer Pain Initiative, Richmond, 1996. Mem. Am. Acad. Pain Mgmt., Am. Counseling Assn., Am. Pain Soc., Nat. Bd. of Cert. Counselors, Va. Counseling Assn., Assn. Transpersonal Psychology, Assn. for Holotropic Breathwork Internat. Democrat. Office: 161-B John Jefferson Rd Williamsburg VA 23185

CAPPIELLO, ANGELA, church grants administrator; b. New Hyde Park, N.Y., July 6, 1954; d. Augustine and Angela (Tamburello) C. Cert. meeting and conv. mgmt., NYU, 1988, cert. assn. mgmt., 1989, cert. food and beverage mgmt., 1989, cert. travel mgmt., 1990, cert. hotel and motel mgmt.; 1991; cert. in fin. controls, NYU, 1992. Cert. meeting profl. Mgr. meetings and convs. N.Y. Libr. Assn., N.Y.C., 1987-89; conf. coord. ASCE, N.Y.C., 1989; mgr. meetings and confs. Coun. Cons. Orgns., N.Y.C., 1990-91; asst. to pres. Goodstein Devel. Corp., N.Y.C., 1991-93; asst. meetings mgr. Nat. Episcopal Ch., N.Y.C., 1993-96, dir. grants program, 1996—. Mem. NAFE, Am. Soc. Assn. Execs., Meeting Planners Internat. (bd. dirs. N.Y. chpt. 1991-93), N.Y. Soc. Assn. Execs., Profl. Conf. Mgrs. Assn., Internat. Soc. Meeting Planners, Religious Conf. Mgrs. Assn., Nat. Assn. for Advancement Fat Acceptance (bd. dirs. 1983-86). Home: 36 New Hyde Park Rd New Hyde Park NY 11040-4935 Office: Nat Episcopal Church 815 2nd Ave New York NY 10017-4503

CAPRIATI, JENNIFER MARIA, professional tennis player; b. N.Y.C., Mar. 29, 1976; d. Stefano and Denise (Deamicis) Capriati. Profl. tennis player, 1990—. Winner: (jr. singles) French Open, 1989, U.S. Open, 1989, (jr. doubles, with McGrath) Italian Open, 1989, Wimbledon, 1989, (singles) P.R. tournament, 1990, San Diego, 1991, Can. Open, 1991, (doubles, with M. Seles) Italian Open, 1991; finalist (singles) Phila., 1990; semifinalist (jr. singles) French Open, 1988, (singles) Wimbledon, 1991, U.S. Open, 1991, Boca Raton, 1991, German Open, 1991; recipient Gold medal 1992 Olympics. Office: Internat Mgmt Group care Barbara Perry 22 E 71st St New York NY 10021-4911*

CAPSOURAS, BARBARA ELLEN, college official; b. Niagara Falls, N.Y., Nov. 10, 1951; d. Joseph John and Wanda M. (Sczepanska) Horvath; m. John David Capsouras, Nov. 20, 1981; children: Cristina, Alexi. Student, Trenton State Coll., 1969-70; AA in Bus. Adminstrn. with high honors, County Coll. of Morris, 1982; postgrad., Fairleigh Dickinson U., 1983-84. Cert. family day care provider, N.J. Adminstrv. asst. tech. ops. Warner-Lambert Co., Morris Plains, N.J., 1970-79, adminstrv. asst. internat. mfg., 1979-80, adminstrv. asst. internat. mktg., 1980-83, pub. affairs coord., 1983-89; dir. alumni rels. County Coll. Morris, Randolph, N.J., 1990—, bd. dirs., mem. adv. bd. Child Care Ctr., 1990-93. Mem. AAUW, N.J. Consortium Alumni Profls., County Coll. of Morris Alumni Assn. (adv. bd. 1990—, mgr. campaign steering com. 1990-93, mgr. alumni annual fund 1990—), NOW, Nat. Parks and Conservation Assn., High Life Ski Club (officer 1972—, mem. race team, recipient various tennis and skiing awards). Office: County Coll Morris 214 Center Grove Rd Randolph NJ 07869-2007

CAPURRO, CLAUDIA CLELIA, internist; b. Chgo., 1960; d. Pietro Ubaldo and Dorothy Pauline (Spagnuolo) C.; m. Daniel Stuart Cohen, 1989. BS in Environ. Toxicology, U. Calif., Davis, 1983; MD, Chgo. Med. Sch., North Chicago, Ill., 1991. Diplomate Am. Bd. Internal Medicine, Nat. Bd. Med. Examiners. Intern in internal medicine Med. Coll. Wis., Milw., 1991-92, resident, 1992-94; fellow in geriatrics U. Ariz., Tucson, 1995—. Mem. ACP, AMA, AAAS, Am. Geriatrics Soc., Ariz. Med. Assn. Office: U Ariz Health Scis Ctr 1501 N Campbell Ave Tucson AZ 85724

CAPUTI, MARY ANDREA, humanities educator; b. Ithaca, N.Y., Mar. 1, 1957; d. Anthony Francis Caputi and Marjein Cecilia O'Neill. BA, Cornell U., 1979, PhD, 1988; MA, U. Chgo., 1981. Asst. prof. St. Mary's Coll., South Bend, Ind., 1991-95, Calif. State U., Long Beach, 1995—; vis. asst. prof. Colby Coll., Waterville, Maine, 1988-90. Author: Voluptuous Yearnings: A Feminist Theory of the Obscene, 1994; contbr. numerous articles to profl. jours. Mem. APSA. Democrat. Catholic. Office: CSULB - Political Sci 1250 Bellflower Blvd Long Beach CA 90840

CAPUTO, ANNE SPENCER, academic and library program director; b. Eugene, Oreg., Jan. 14, 1947; d. Richard J. and Adelaide Bernice (Marsh) Spencer; m. Richard Philip Caputo, July 15, 1977; 1 child, Christopher Spencer Caputo. BA in History, Lewis and Clark Coll., Portland, Oreg., 1969; MA, U. Oreg., 1971; MALS, San Jose State U., 1976. Librarian San Jose State U., Calif., 1972-76; online instr. DIALOG Info. Services, Palo Alto, Calif., 1976-77, chief info. scientist, Washington, 1977-85, mgr. classroom instrn. program, 1986-89, dir. acad. programs, 1990—; asst. prof. info. sci. Catholic U. Am., Washington, 1978—; online cons. Nat. Com. Library-Info. Sci., Washington, 1980-82; bd. dirs. ASK!, Washington, 1981—. Author: Brief Guide to DIALOG Searching, 1979. Contbr. articles to profl. jours. Named Info. Sci. Tchr. of Yr., Catholic U. Am., 1983. Mem. Am. Soc. for Info. Sci. (officer, chair Potomac Valley chpt. 1985-86), ALA, Spl. Library Assn., D.C. Library Assn., Am. Assn. Sch. Librarians. Episcopalian. Avocation: photographing architectural details on National Trust buildings. Home: 4113 Orleans Pl Alexandria VA 22304-1618 Office: Knight-Ridder Info Inc 1525 Wilson Blvd Ste 650 Arlington VA 22209-2411

CAPUTO, KATHRYN MARY, paralegal; b. Bklyn., June 29, 1948; d. Fortunato and Agnes (Iovino) Villacci; m. Joseph John Caputo, Apr. 4, 1976. AS in Bus. Adminstrn., Nassau C.C., Garden City, N.Y., 1989. Legal asst. Jacob Jacobson, Oceanside, N.Y., 1973-77; legal asst., office mgr. Joseph Kaldor, P.C., Franklin Square, N.Y., 1978-82, William H. George, Valley Stream, N.Y., 1983-89; exec. legal asst., office adminstr. Katz & Bernstein, Westbury, N.Y., 1990-93; sr. paralegal and office adminstr. Blaustein & Weinick, Garden City, N.Y., 1993—; instr. adult continuing edn. legal sec. procedures Lawrence (N.Y.) H.S., 1992—. Spl. events coord. Bklyn.-Queens Marriage Encounter, 1981, 82, 83, 85, 86; mem. Lynbrook Civic Assn. Mem. L.I. Paralegal Assn. Office: Blaustein & Weinick 1205 Franklin Ave Garden City NY 11530-1629

CARACO, VIRGINIA, artist; b. Gloversville, N.Y., Aug. 31, 1951; d. Fred Ernest and Evelyn Eve (Franko) Marshall; m. Joseph Charles Caraco, Oct. 16, 1970; 1 child, Donald Joseph. Cert. indsl. drafting, Trident Tech. Coll., 1970, cert. archtl. drafting, 1970. Exhbns. include Fine Art Ctr. of Kershaw County, 1985-95, Canty Bldg. S.C. State Fair, 1994-95, Sumter Galley of Art, 1981-85, Nations Bank, Aug., 1985. Chmn. NBSC Oil Painter's Invitational, Sumter Gallery Art, 1983-86; exhbn. com. chmn. Fine Art Ctr., Camden, S.C., 1986-89; pres. Sumter Art Guild, 1983-84, v.p., 1984-85; chmn. Congl. Art Comp., 1983; chmn. Iris Festival, Fine Arts Swan Lake Gardens, Sumter, 1984. Named Artist of Month, Sumter Art Gallery, 1985. Mem. Camden Art Assn. (v.p. 1986-87, pres. 1994-95), Colored Pencil Soc. Am., S.C. Watercolor Soc., Trenholm Art Guild. Home: Cedar Cottage 200 Poplar Ln Camden SC 29020

CARAVAS, PAMELA WIMER, elementary school educator; b. Dover, Del., May 27, 1966; d. Jerald Wain and Constance Faye (Rowe) Wimer. BS, James Madison U., Harrisonburg, Va., 1989; MEd, Old Dominion U., Norfolk, Va., 1993. Tchr. 3d grade Georgetown Elem. Sch., Chesapeake, Va., 1989-91, tchr. 4th grade, 1991-92; tchr. 4th grade Sparrow Road Intermediate Sch., Chesapeake, 1992—; Coach Odyssey of Mind Team. Contbr. (book): What America's Teachers Wish Parents Knew, 1993. Mem. NEA, Va. Edn. Assn., Chesapeake Edn. Assn., Chesapeake Reading Coun., PTA (life, faculty rep.), Internat. Reading Coun. Democrat. Greek Orthodox. Home: 1021 Angler Ln Virginia Beach VA 23451-6512

CARAWAY, MARGARET TAPPAN, special education administrator; b. Jefferson City, Tenn., Sept. 26, 1937; d. Edward Ivan and Isabella Dobson (Thomas) C.; m. Douglas Delano Dasinger, Apr. 5, 1958 (div. 1970); children: Ann Isabella Dasinger, Harry Mark Dasinger. MA in Edn., U. Mont., Billings, 1974. Cert. sch. psychologist. Coord., preschool day treatment S. Ctrl. Mont. Regional Mental Health Ctr., Billings, 1973-77; sch. psychologist Sch. Dist. # 56, Billings, Mont., 1980-85; tchr. emotionally disturbed Yuma (Ariz.) Dist. One, 1986-89, spl. edn. dir., 1989—; pres., bd. dirs. Achievement Place Home, Billings, Mont., 1982-84; mem., bd. dirs. Alpha House, Billings, Mont., 1984-86. Mem. Rotary Internat., Yuma, Ariz., 1994. Mem. Phi Delta Kappa. Episcopalian. Home: 1266 S Sunset Dr Yuma AZ 85364-4485

CARAY, LINDA, minister, author, poet; b. Oakland, Calif., Dec. 27, 1947; d. Philip Courtney and Melba Caray (Eble) Rude; m. Melford Duane Barker, Oct. 26, 1968 (div. 1981); children: Jeffrey Duane Barker, Scott Duane Barker (dec.). Student, U. Calif., Westwood, 1965; cert. interior design, Internat. Corr. Sch., 1987; postgrad., U. Metaphysics, Studio City, Calif., 1994-96. Ordained minister, metaphysical practitioner. Nurse various dr.'s offices, Azusa, Calif., 1969-82; owner beauty salon Upland, Calif., 1972-81; owner Italian restaurant Montclair, Calif., 1983-86; mgr., interior designer Standard Brands Paint Co., Calif., 1986-89; interior designer Upland, Calif., 1987-90; author, artist Flagstaff, Ariz., 1992—; pastoral counselor, 1995. Author: Crisis to Creativity, 1993; contbr. poetry to anthologies including The Coming of Dawn Anthology, Poetic Voices of American, Memories Anthology, Helicon, Inspirations in Ink. Bd. dirs., coach Upland Am. Little League, Calif., 1981-82. With U.S. Army, 1967-68. Recipient Editor's Choice award Nat. Libr. Poetry, 1993, Accomplishment of Merit award Creative Arts and Sci. Enterprises, 1993. Mem. Internat. Soc. Poets (charter lifetime mem., adv. panel 1993—), Alumni Assn. U. Metaphysics, Internat. Order Job's Daus. (honored queen 1962-66), Beta Sigma Phi (pres. 1965).

CARBO, TONI (TONI CARBO BEARMAN), information scientist, college dean; b. Middletown, Conn., Nov. 14, 1942; d. Anthony Joseph and Theresa (Bauer) Carbo; m. David A. Bearman, Nov. 14, 1970 (div. Nov. 1995); 1 child, Amanda Carole. AB, Brown U., 1969; MS, Drexel U., 1973, PhD, 1977. Bibliog. asst. Am. Math. Soc., Math. Revs., 1962-63; supr. Brown U. Phys. Scis. Library, Providence, R.I., 1963-66, 67-71; subject specialist U. Wash. Engring. Library, Seattle, 1966-67; teaching and research asst. Drexel U., 1971-74; exec. dir. Nat. Fedn. Abstracting and Indexing Services, Phila., 1974-79; cons. for strategic planning and new product devel. Instn. Elec. Engrs., London, 1979-80; exec. dir. U.S. Nat. Commn. on Libraries and Info. Sci., Washington, 1980-86; dean Sch. Library and Info. Sci. U. Pitts., 1986—; mem. adv. com. U.S. Dept. Commerce, Patent and Trademark Office, 1987-90; trustee Engring. Info., Inc., 1985-87; Lazerow lectr. U. Ind., 1984; Schwing lectr. La. State U., 1988; lectr. No. Ohio Am. Soc. Info. Sci./Spl. Librs. Assn., 1990, Beta Phi Mu, Phila., 1992; mem. U.S. Adv. Coun. Nat. Info. Infrastructure, 1994; mem. U.S. del. G-7 Info. Soc. Conf.; bd. mem. Pa. Info. Hwy. Consortium, 1994—. Co-editor Internat. Info. and Libr. Rev., 1989-92, editor, 1993—; contbr. articles to profl. jours., mem. editorial bds. profl. jours. Bd. dirs. Greater Pitts. Literacy Coun.; mem. presdl. adv. com. Carnegie Libr. of Pitts. Recipient Disting. Alumni award Drexel U. Coll. Info. Studies, 1984, 100 Most Disting. Alumni award, 1992, 100th Anniversary medal Drexel U., 1992. Fellow AAAS (chmn. sect. T 1992-93), Inst. Info. Scientists, Spl. Librs. Assn.; mem. ALA (coun. 1988-92), Am. Soc. for Info. Sci. (chmn. planning and nominations com. 1990-91, chmn. networking com., chmn. 50th ann. conf., pres. 1989-90, Watson Davis award 1983), Pa. Libr. Assn. (adv. bd. Pa. Gov.'s Conf. on libr. and info. svcs.), Nat. Info. Standards Orgn. (bd. dirs. 1987-90), Spl. Librs. Assn. (rsch. com. 1987-92, internat. rels. com., 1991—), Internat. Fedn. for Info. and Documentation (vice chair U.S. nat. com. 1990—, chair info. policy com. 1991—, chair global info. infrastructure and superhwys. taskforce 1993—), Assn. for Libr. and Info. Sci. Edn. (bd. dirs. 1996—), Laurel Initiative (bd. dirs.). Home: 1309 N Sheridan Ave Pittsburgh PA 15206-1759 Office: U Pitts Sch Info Sci 135 N Bellefield Ave Pittsburgh PA 15260

CARBOY, BEVERLY J., humanities educator; b. Pompton Plains, N.J., Aug. 7, 1943; d. James Francis and Glenna M. (Cullen) C. BA, William Paterson Coll., Wayne, N.J., 1965; MA, Seton Hall U., South Orange, N.J., 1969, William Paterson Coll., 1977. Cert. tchr. grades 7-12, N.J. Tchr. English Morris Hills H.S., Rockaway, N.J., 1965—, adv. lit. mag., 1968-84; adv. Helping Hands, 1985-90. Recipient Geraldine R. Dodge grantee Dodge Found., 1986. Mem. NEA, NJEA, Morris Hills Edn. Assn., Morris County Edn. Assn. (rep.). Office: Morris Hills HS 520 W Main St Rockaway NJ 07866

CARDANINI, TINA ANN, controller; b. Redwood City, Calif., Sept. 17, 1965; d. Pasquale Antone and Norma Edith (Canvin) Balzarini; m. Michael Robert Cardanini, April 9, 1988; children: Nicholas, Tiffany. BS, San Francisco State U., San Francisco, 1988, MS, 1994. CMA, Calif. Staff acct. Pvt. Svcs. Inc., San Mateo, Calif., 1987-88; sr. acct. Ross Stores, Inc., Newark, Calif., 1988-92; reg. acctg. mgr. Rollins Environ. Svcs., Inc., Wilmington, Del., 1992-94; corp. acctg. mgr. Mayne Nickless Courier Svcs., Inc., Foster City, Calif., 1994-96; contr. ctrl. svcs. Philips Semicondrs., Sunnyvale, Calif., 1996—. Sch. bd. mem. 1994—, coun. person 1995—, St. Charles Parish, San Carlos, Calif. Mem. Inst. of Mgmt. Accts. Home: 75 Bayport Ct San Carlos CA 94070

CARDEN, CONNIE TURNER, sales support manager, marketing executive, consultant; b. Eden, N.C., Sept. 28, 1961; d. James Robert and Sarah Wilma (Pruitt) Turner; m. Clinton Mark Carden. BSBA, Appalachian State U., 1983. Sr. account mgr. D & B Software, Atlanta, 1983-87; sr. mgr. Price Waterhouse, Atlanta, 1987-90; profl. svcs. mgr. Amdahl, Atlanta, 1990-94; dir. sales BSG Alliance IT, Atlanta, 1994-95; sales mgr. Data Gen., Maitland, Fla., 1995-96; v.p. sales and mktg. Simms Industries, Inc., Winter Park, Fla., 1996—; real estate agent, Fla., 1995—. Office: Simms Industries 110 University Park Dr Ste 180 Winter Park FL 32792

CARDEN, JOY CABBAGE, educational consultant; b. Livermore, Ky., Dec. 15, 1932; d. Henry L. and Lillie (Richardson) Cabbage; m. Donald G. Carden, Dec. 19, 1954; children: Lynn Kehlenbeck, Tom Carden, Bob Carden, Jan Blount, Jim Carden. BA, Ky. Wesleyan, 1955; MA, U. Ky., 1975. Instr. music Owensboro (Ky.) City Schs., 1955-57; founder, dir. Musical Arts Ctr., Lexington, Ky., 1980-88; edn. specialist Roland Corp., L.A., 1989, dir. edn., 1990-94, edn. cons., 1994—. Author: Music in Lexington Before 1840, 1980, Guide to Electronic Keyboards, 1988; editor, author: Carden Keyboard Ensemble Series; editor: Ensemble the Resource of Keyboard Instructors; composer ensembles for electronic keyboards. Mem. Music Tchrs. Nat. Assn. (commd. composer 1987), Nat. Guild Piano Tchrs. (state chmn. 1980-88), Nat. Conf. Piano Pedagogy (com. chmn. 1990-94), Ky. Music Tchrs. Assn. (state chmn. 1980-88). Home and Office: 112 La Fontenay Ct Louisville KY 40223-3020

CARDENAS, DIANA DELIA, physician, educator; b. San Antonio, Tex., Apr. 10, 1947; d. Ralph Roman and Rosa (Garza) C.; m. Thomas McKenzie Hooton, Aug. 20, 1971; children: Angela, Jessica. BA with highest honors, U. Tex., 1969; MD, U. Tex., Dallas, 1973; MS, U. Wash., 1976. Diplomate Nat. Bd. Med. Examiners, Am. Bd. Phys. Medicine & Rehab., Am. Bd. Electrodiagnostic Medicine. Asst. prof. dept. rehab. medicine Emory U., Atlanta, 1976-81; instr. dept. rehab. medicine U. Wash., Seattle, 1981-82, asst. prof. dept. rehab. medicine, 1982-86, assoc. prof. dept. rehab. medicine, 1986-92, prof. rehab. medicine, 1992—; med. dir. rehab. medicine clinic U. Wash. Med. Ctr., Seattle, 1982; project dir. N.W. Regional Spinal Cord Injury System, Seattle, 1990—. Editor: Rehabilitation & The Chronic Renal Disease Patient, 1985, Maximizing Rehabilitation in Chronic Renal Disease, 1989; contbr. articles to profl. jours. Co-chairperson Lakeside Sch. Auction Student Vols., Seattle, 1991; bd. dirs. CONSEJO Counseling & Referral Svc., 1994. Mem. Am. Spinal Injury Assn. (chairperson rsch. com. 1991), Am.

Acad. Phys. Medicine and Rehab., Am. Congress of Rehab. Medicine (chairperson rehab. practice com. 1980-84, Ann. Essay Contest winner 1976), Am. Assn. Electrodiagnostic Medicine. Office: Univ Wash Dept Rehab Med Box 356490 1959 NE Pacific St Seattle WA 98195-0004

CARDENAS, LYNDA LEIGH, pediatrics nurse; b. Van Nuys, Calif., Apr. 17, 1959; d. Jack Thomas and June Lee (Smith) Strayer; m. Ramon A. Cardenas, Jan. 21, 1988 (div. 1991). Diploma in med. assisting, Western Tech. Coll., 1983; lic. vocat. nurse, Simi Valley Adult Edn., 1991. LVN, Calif. Med. asst. La Serena Retirement Village, Thousand Oaks, Calif., 1982-84, Registry/Pvt. Geriatrics, Simi Valley, Calif., 1984-88; nurse, staff coord. Valley Children's Home, Inc., Simi Valley, 1988—. Office: Valley Children's Home Inc 3224 Wilmot St Simi Valley CA 93063-2656

CARDENAS, MARY PATRICIA, engineering educator; b. Lake City, Iowa, Dec. 15, 1964; d. Cesar Augustus and Patricia Anne (Rexroad) C. BS in Aerospace Engring., Iowa State U., 1987; MSME, U. Calif., Santa Barbara, 1993, PhD in Mech. and Environ. Engring., 1994. Engr. in tng., Iowa. Mem. tech. staff Rocketdyne, Rockwell Internat., Canoga Park, Calif., 1987-90; rsch. assoc. U. Calif., Santa Barbara, 1991-94, teaching asst., 1993, rsch. scientist, 1994-95; Parsons asst. prof. engring. Harvey Mudd Coll., Claremont, Calif., 1995—. Co-author: Modern Design of Liquid-Propellant Rocket Engines, 1992. Pres.'s scholar U. Calif., 1990-94. Mem. Soc. Women Engrs. (counselor 1995—). Office: Harvey Mudd Coll 301 E 12th St Claremont CA 91711

CARDER, PAMELA KAY, family therapist; b. Iowa City, Iowa, Sept. 6, 1965; d. Paul George and Frances Effie (Guthrie) C. BA in Psychology/Human Svcs., Buena Vista Coll., Storm Lake, Iowa, 1988. Home visitor S.I.E.D.A. Head Start, Ottumwa, Iowa, 1988-89; domestic violence/sexual assault counselor Crisis Ctr. & Women's Shelter, Ottumwa, 1989-93; family preservation therapist Children and Families of Iowa, Ottumwa, 1993—; domestic violence, sexual assault trainer Crisis Ctr. & Women's Shelter/Indian Hills C.C., Ottumwa, 1989-93; pub. spkr. Crisis Ctr., Ottumwa, 1989-93; mem. Iowa Coalition Against Domestic Violence and Sexual Assault, Crisis Ctr. and Women's Shelter, Ottumwa and Des Moines, 1989-93; dir. Battered Women's Support Group, Crisis Ctr. and Women's Shelter, Ottumwa, 1990-93; mem. HIV Task Force/S.E. Iowa, 1992; chairperson Gay, Lesbian and Bisexual Soc., 1991-93. Writer statewide HIV inserts for sexual assault evidence collection kits Iowa Coalition Against Sexual Assault, Des Moines, 1993. Democrat. Home: 1011 E Second Ottumwa IA 52501

CARDILLO, CLAIRE SANDRA, arts administrator; b. N.Y.C., Nov. 20, 1944; d. Antonio and Mabel Theresa (Beretta) Di Bernardi; m. Joseph Louis Boscia, Oct. 16, 1965 (div. Mar. 1980); children: Joseph Alan, Gregory; m. Carmelo Cardillo, Apr. 25, 1982. Grad., Theodore Roosevelt H.S., 1962. Sec. MacManus, John & Adams Advt., N.Y.C., 1962-63; exec. sec. Sperry & Hutchinson, N.Y.C., 1964-67; office mgr. Future Contracting Corp., Bronx, N.Y., 1976-78; adminstrv. asst. Bronx Coun. on Arts, 1978-83, adminstrv. dir., 1983-87, asst. dir., 1987—. Bd. dirs. Bronx Spl. Olympics, 1990-94, Bronx Tourism Coun., 1989-96; vice chair Visions-Bronx Adv. Bd., 1991-96; mem. N.E. Bronx Cmty. Coalition, 1993-96; celebrity waitress Leukemia Soc. Am., N.Y.C., 1989. Recipient Cmty. Leadership award Bronx House, 1988, citation of merit Bronx Borough Pres., 1988, Exemplary Support award Visions Svcs. for Blind, Bronx, 1993. Mem. Network Orgn. of Bronx Women (membership dir. 1992-94, pres. 1994-96), Notary Assn. Am. Roman Catholic. Office: Bronx Coun on Arts 1738 Hone Ave Bronx NY 10461

CARDINAL, SHIRLEY MAE, education educator; b. Morann, Pa., May 6, 1944; d. Thomas Joseph and Mary Louise (Nemish) Giza; m. Charles Edward Cardinal, June 11, 1966; children: Julie Ann, Karen Lee. BS, Lock Haven U., 1966; MEd, Pa. State U., 1970. Tchr. Bald Eagle Nittany Corp., Mill Hall, Pa., 1966-68; tchr., supr. Pa. State U., University Park, 1968-76; tchr., chairperson State Coll. (Pa.) Area Schs., 1968-76; primetime educator Oregon-Davis Corp., Hamlet, Ind., 1984—; instr., cons. Dept. Edn., Indpls., 1979—, cons. energy edn., 1980-85, educator linker, 1981—, rep. prime time, 1987—; instr. Ancilla Coll., Donaldson, Ind., 1976—; chair for evaluation North Ctrl. Accreditation Assn., 1988-89, leadership team, 1996; mem. leadership team North Ctrl. Regional Lab., 1991-92, 93-94, 94—, Fermi Nat. Accelerator Lab., 1994—, North Ctrl. Regional Ednl. Lab. Author: Energy Activities with Learning Skills, 1980. Chmn. publicity com. Rep. Orgn. Plymouth, Ind., 1983—; mem. Teacher Talk, Ind. Gov's. Com., 1988-89. Recipient Mankind and Edn. award U.S. Jaycees and Ind. Jaycees, 1981. Mem. Ind. State Tchr. Assn., Marshall County Reading Assn., Pa. State U. Club, Proficiency Bd. Accreditation (chairperson 1996), Phi Delta Kappa (v.p. programs South Bend chpt. 1992-93, v.p. membership 1994-95), Pi Lambda Theta, Sigma Kappa (chmn. Parent Club), Tri Kappa. Roman Catholic. Home: 10101 Turf Ct Plymouth IN 46563-9494

CARDINEAU, DONNA EVELYN, elementary school educator; b. Huntington, N.Y., Nov. 14, 1953; d. Albert and Lorraine E. (Terrell) Curson; m. Thomas J. Cardineau, Mar. 18, 1978; children: Sean, Denis. BA in Phys. Edn., Gettysburg Coll., 1975; MALS, SUNY, Stony Brook, 1980; postgrad., CUNY, 1993—. Cert. elem. tchr., N.Y. Health and phys. edn. tchr. Port Jefferson (N.Y.) Schs., 1976—, swimming tchr., student coun. adviser, sch. store adviser, intramural supr., bldg. union rep., 1989—, bldg. level team, 1991-92, coord. various fundraisers for student coun., 1989—. Alumni vol. Gettysburg (Pa.) Coll., 1990—; PTA liaison Port Jefferson Elem. Sch., 1993—, pres., 1990; coord. Jump Rope for Heart program Am. Heart Assn., Bohemia, N.Y., 1989—; coord. Math-a-Thon St. Jude's Hosp., Tenn., 1992—; coord. Daffodil Days program Am. Cancer Soc., Huntington, N.Y., 1991—; den leader, exec. com. Cub Scout Pack 41, Boy Scouts Am., 1990—; Sunday sch. tchr. First United Meth. Ch., 1991—, supt. schs., 1990-91. Office: Port Jefferson Pub Schs Scraggy Hill Rd Port Jefferson NY 11789

CARDWELL, NANCY LEE, editor, writer; b. Norfolk, Va., Apr. 2, 1947; d. Joseph Thomas Cardwell and Martha (Bailey) Underwood. B.A. in Econs., Duke U., 1969; M.S. in Journalism, Columbia U., 1971. Copy editor Wall Street Jour., N.Y.C., 1971-73, reporter, 1973-76, editor fgn. dept. and Washington bur., 1977-80, night news editor, 1981-83, nat. news editor, 1983-87, asst. mng. editor, 1987-89; sr. editor Bus. Week mag., N.Y.C., 1989-91; editor Habitat World, Habitat for Humanity Internat., Americus, Ga., 1991-94; dir. comms. Craver, Matthews, Smith & Co., Falls Church, Va., 1994-95; freelance editor/writer, 1994—. Episcopalian. Home: 1529 N Kenilworth St Arlington VA 22205-2820

CARDWELL, SANDRA GAYLE BAVIDO, real estate broker; b. Vinita, Okla., July 14, 1943; d. Amos Calvin Wilkins and Gretta Odell (Pool) Wilkins Kudlemyer; m. Phillip Patrick Bavido, Nov. 26, 1964 (div. Dec. 1973); 1 child, Phillip Patrick Bavido Jr.; m. Max Loyd Cardwell, Jan. 18, 1979 (div. Apr. 1992). AA, Tulsa Jr. Coll., 1973; BS cum laude, U. Tulsa, 1975. Sec. with various cos., 1966-69; sec. U.S. Dept. Fgn. Langs., West Point, N.Y., 1969-70; dep. ct. clk. civil div. Tulsa County Dist. Ct., Tulsa, 1975-76, dep. ct. clk. U.S. Passport Office, 1976-77; broker-assoc. Gordona Duca, Inc., Realtors, Tulsa, 1977—. Mem. Polit. Action Com., Tulsa, 1980—; vol. in children's rights and child abuse legis. and statutes. Mem. AAUW, Tulsa Met. Bd. Realtors, Okla. Bd. Realtors, Tulsa Christian Women's Club (contact advisor 1988-89), Stonecroft Ministries (life publs. 1987-88), United Meth. Women (bd. dirs. 1986-87), Phi Theta Kappa (pres.), Pi Sigma Alpha (treas. 1974). Republican. Methodist. Home: RR 4 Box 253-1 Vinita OK 74301-9585 Office: Gordona Duca Inc Realtors 7103 S Yale Ave Tulsa OK 74136-6308

CAREY, ALIDA LIVINGSTON, political scientist, writer, reporter; b. Phila., June 29, 1928; d. Henry Reginald and Margaret Howell (Bacon) C.; m. Isaac Kleinerman, Febr. 29, 1964 (div. Aug. 1967). Attended, Chatham (Va.) Hall Sch., 1947, Grad. Inst. of Internat. Studies, Geneva, Switzerland, 1949-50; BA, Smith Coll., Northampton, Mass., 1951. Promotion mgr. The Reporter Mag., N.Y.C., 1951-52; rschr., writer Newsweek Mag., N.Y.C., 1952-54; rschr. Edward R. Murrow series "See It Now" CBS-TV, Paris, 1954; reporter, writer Agence France-Presse, Paris, 1955; nat. U.S. correspondent The Reporter Mag., N.Y.C., 1968; reporter, writer Forbes Mag., N.Y.C., 1969-70; freelance writer various publs., 1955—. Contbr. numerous articles to profl. jours. including N.Y. Times Sunday Mag., Christian Sci. Monitor. Mem. Coun. to Oppose Sale of Saint Bartholomew's Ch., Inc., N.Y., 1986-91; vol. Saint James Ch. Soup Kitchen, N.Y., 1986—. Mem. ACLU, French Inst./Alliance Francaise, Mcpl. Art Soc., Editl. Freelancer's Assn.

CAREY, DAWN J., cultural organization administrator; b. Penn Yan, N.Y., Dec. 20, 1950; d. Chester E. and Claire L. (Lamb) C. Student, Cedar Crest Coll., 1968-70; BA in History & Psychology, Syracuse U., 1975; postgrad., U. South Fla. Cert. spl. edn. tchr., N.Y. Title I reading tchr. Lake Placid (N.Y.) Ctrl. Sch., 1973-75; tchr. Sarasota (Fla.) County Sch. Bd., 1975-83; ops. officer Barnett Bank, Sarasota, 1983-88; spl. edn. tchr. Franklin, Hamilton, Essex BOCES, Lake Placid, 1988-90; residential counselor YMCA Youth Shelter, Sarasota, 1991-94; residential program dir. YMCA Youth & Family Svcs., Sarasota, 1994—; mem. steering com. Alliance for Learning About Sexual Orientation, Sarasota, 1994—; voting mem. case rev. com. Family Svcs. Planning Team, Sarasota, 1994—; mem. human resource devel. com. Fla. Network for Youth & Family Svcs., Tallahassee, 1995—. Mem. Southeastern Network Youth & Family Svcs. (trainer, resource exch. facilitator). Episcopalian. Office: YMCA Youth & Family Svcs 41 N School Ave Sarasota FL 34237

CAREY, ELIZABETH BORGMANN, organization executive; b. Pitts., Jan. 13, 1938; d. Carl Williams and Mable Dorothy (Gaiser) Borgmann; children: Marc, Jeff, Ann, Julie. BA, U. Colo., 1959; postgrad., U. Denver, 1986-87. Dir. Cmty. Resources Inc., Denver, 1979-81; cmty. cons. Denver Pub. Schs., 1982-83; bookseller Tattered Cover Bookstore, 1983-84; pub. Woman Source, A Guide to Women's Resources, 1982-85; owner, pub. Metro Source Publs., 1985-88; devel. dir. Am. Heart Assn., 1988-90; exec. dir. Colo. Tennis Assn., 1990-94; dir. capital campaign Colo.'s Ocean Journey, 1994-95; devel. dir. Denver Victims Svc. Ctr., 1995—. Pub. Solo in the City, 1986, Having a Baby in Denver, 1986, Learning in the Mile High City, 1987. Bd. dirs., publicity chmn. Denver Women's Career Ctr., 1979-83; bd. dirs., mem. exec. com. Colo. Outward Bound, 1985-92; bd. dirs. Friends of Big Sisers, 1987-88, Citizens Appreciate Police, 1995-96, Parenting After Divorce, Denver, 1995-96; bd. dirs., chmn. award sect. Women's Found., 1988-90; mem. Martin Luther King Jr. Commn., Cmty. Edn. Coun.; founder, 1st chmn. Montclair Cmty. Assn., Denver. Home: 520 Glencoe St Denver CO 80220

CAREY, ERNESTINE GILBRETH (MRS. CHARLES E. CAREY), writer, lecturer; b. N.Y.C., Apr. 5, 1908; d. Frank Bunker and Lillian (Moller) Gilbreth; m. Charles Everett Carey, Sept. 13, 1930; children: Lillian Carey Barley, Charles Everett. B.A., Smith Coll., 1929. Buyer R. H. Macy & Co., N.Y.C., 1930-44, James McCreery, N.Y.C., 1947-49; Carey writer and lectr. Book reviewer, 1949—, syndicated newspaper articles, 1951, (with Lillian Moller Gilbreth) (McElligott medallion Assn. Marquette U. Women 1966); author: Jumping Jupiter, 1952, Rings Around Us, 1956, Giddy Moment, 1958, (with Frank B. Gilbreth, Jr.) Cheaper by the Dozen, 1949 (Prix Scarron French Internat. Humor award 1951, over 50 translations), Belles on Their Toes, 1951; contbg. author: Smith Voices—Selected Works by Smith College Women, 1990; lifetime papers represented in collections at Smith Coll.; also mag. articles and book revs. Bd. dirs. Right to Read, Inc., 1968—, co-chmn., 1967; lay adv. com. Manhasset (N.Y.) Bd. Edn.; trustee Manhasset Pub. Libr., 1953-59, v.p., 1956-59; trustee Smith Coll., 1967-72; active in care-preservation and current student use of Frank B. and Lillian M. Gilbreth lifetime papers at various worldwide librs. and univs. Montgomery award Friends if Phoenix Pub. Libr., 1981, honored guest Ariz. Lib. Friends, 1994; recipient Internat. Mgmt. award: the Gilbreth Medal, Soc. for advancement of Mgmt., 1996. Mem. Authors Guild Am. (life mem., mem. guild council 1955-60), P.E.N. Republican. Conglist. Clubs: North Shore, Smith College (L.I.) (asst. chmn. scholarship com. 1950-59); Smith Coll. (N.Y.); Smith College Phoenix (Phoenix) (vice chmn. scholarship com. 1967), 7 College Conf. Council (Phoenix). Home: 6148 E Lincoln Dr Paradise Valley AZ 85253-4258

CAREY, JANET L., physical education educator; b. Johnson City, N.Y., Jan. 8, 1949; d. Charles B. and Mary Jane (Pritchard) W.; m. Howard J. Barner, July 10, 1971 (div.); children: Stacy Patrice, Christie Suzanne; m. Clifford W. Carey, July 28, 1984; 1 child, Colleen Alice. BA in Math. and Secondary Edn., SUNY, Oswego, 1970; postgrad., SUNY, New Paltz, 1976—. Cert. tchr. math. grades 7-12, phys. edn. grades K-12, N.Y. Tchr. math. Marcellus (N.Y.) Ctrl. Sch., 1970-71, Liberty (N.Y.) Cen. Sch., 1971-81; tchr. GED Sullivan County Boces, Liberty, 1976-85; tchr. phys. edn. Jeffersonville (N.Y.)-Youngsville Cen. Sch., 1981-87, dir. tennis Browns Resort Hotel, Loch Sheldrake, N.Y., 1979-89; tennis profl. Stevensville Resort Hotel, Loch Sheldrake, 1990; tchr. phys. edn. Fallsburg (N.Y.) Cen. Sch., 1987—; assoc. adj. instr. phys. edn. Sullivan County C.C., Loch Sheldrake, N.Y., 1976—; mem. ad hoc adv. com. N.Y. Dept. Edn., Albany, 1990—; instr. cross country and alpine skiing Pines Resort Hotel, 1976-94, tech. dir., 1980-94, ski sch. dir., 1993-94; tech. dir. ski sch. Granit Hotel Winter Fun Park, 1994—, dir. ski sch., 1995—, dir. cross country, 1994—. Mem. Sullivan County Youth Bur., Monticello, 1987—, Tri-Valley Youth Commn., Grahamsville, N.Y., 1982—, tennis instr., 1992—, swimming dir., 1990—; co-chair Sullivan County Aquatic Com., Monticello; coach varsity girls tennis Hudson Valley Girls Tennis Empire State Games, 1992-94; coach varsity boys skiing, 1989-90, varsity girls tennis, 1991—, varsity boys tennis, 1994—; state tennis chair Empire State Games, 1994—; vol. ARC, instr. water safety, 1969—, instr. trainer, 1976—, lifeguard instr., first aid safety instr.; CPR instr. Am. Heart Assn.; co-chair health, wellness com. Fallsburg High Sch., 1992—, super team advisor, 1994—. Mem. AAUW, AAHPERD (coord., nat. del. 1995, 96, aquatic coun.), N.Y. State Assn. for Health, Phys. Edn., Recreation and Dance (program planner 1992—, secondary pres.-elect 1994-95, exec. coun. 1995—, secondary pres. 1995—, bd. dirs. 1996—), Ea. Profl. Ski Instrs. Assn., Nat. Ski Patrol, ARC (safety trainer 1968—), Nat. Water Fitness Assn. (instr. 1990—, coord. 1991—), Aquatic Exercise Assn. (instr.), N.Y. State Pub. High Sch. Athletic Assn. (sect. 9 safety chmn. 1983—, chairperson boys tennis, 1994—), Nat. Profl. Bus. Womens Assn., U.S. Ski Instrs. Am., U.S. Ski Coaches Assn., N.Y. State Coaches Assn., Assn. Univ. Women. Office: Fallsburg Ctrl Sch Brickman Rd Fallsburg NY 12733

CAREY, JEAN LEBEIS, management consulting executive; b. Charleston, W.Va., June 2, 1943; d. Edward H. and Marian (Lendved) Lebeis; m. Robert W. Carey, Nov. 1971 (dec. Mar. 1990); 1 child, Megan Rose. BA, Pa. State U., 1965. Programmer Penn Mut. Life Ins., Phila., 1967-68; sr. analyst/programmer U. Pa., Phila., 1969-72; sr. systems analyst Acme Markets, Phila., 1972-74; programming mgr. Bryn Mawr Coll., Pa., 1976-77; project adminstr. Smith Kline Beckman, Phila., 1977-83; project mgmt. cons. Arco Chem. Co., Phila., 1983-87; chief exec. officer Carey Project Orgn., Ardmore, Pa., 1987—; chmn. Sys. Methodology Users Mid-Atlantic, 1984-86, PMI Sys. Tech. Papers, 1983; co-dir. Cobol project U. Pa., Phila., 1969-72; lectr. in field. Author: Quality Management and Performance Measurement in Information Services, 1991, Making Quality Happen in Information Services, 1992, Project Manager's Handbook, 1993; contbr. articles to profl. jours. Bd. dirs. Danceteller/Dance Theater, Phila., 1985-88, Self Help Crafts of the World/Phila., Inc., 1994—, chmn. bd. dirs., 1995—; Scan/Child Abuse Treatment Ctr., Phila., 1983-94; mem. exec. com. SCAN Devel. Fund, Inc., 1989—; mem. Leadership, Phia. vol. svcs. group, 1985-91. Recipient Excel award, Arco, 1986. Mem. Project Mgmt. Inst. Soc. of Friends. Home and Office: Carey Project Orgn 663 Cricket Ave Ardmore PA 19003-1806

CAREY, KATHRYN ANN, advertising and public relations executive, editor, consultant; b. Los Angeles, Oct. 18, 1949; d. Frank Randall and Evelyn Mae (Walmsley) C.; m. Richard Kenneth Sundt, Dec. 28, 1980. BA in Am. Studies with honors, Calif. State U., L.A., 1971; postgrad. Georgetown U., Boston Coll. Cert. commercial pilot instrument rated. Tutor Calif. Dept. Vocat. Rehab., L.A., 1970; teaching asst. U. So. Calif., 1974-75, UCLA, 1974-75; claims adjuster Auto Club So. Calif., San Gabriel, 1971-73; corp. pub. rels. cons. Carnation Co., L.A., 1973-78; cons., adminstr. Carnation Community Svc. Award Program, 1973-78; pub. rels. cons. Vivitar Corp., 1978; sr. advt. asst. Am. Honda Motor Co., Torrance, Calif., 1978-84; exec. dir. Am. Honda Found., 1984—; adminstr. Honda Matching Gift and Vol. Program, Honda Involvement Program; mgr. Honda Dealer Advt. Assns., 1978-84; cons. advt., pub. rels., promotions. Editor: Vivitar Voice, Santa Monica, Calif., 1978, Rod Machado's Instrument Pilots' Survival Manual, c. 1991; editor Honda Views, 1978-84, Found. Focus, 1984—; asst. editor Friskies Research Digest, 1973-78; contbg. editor Newsbriefs and Momentum, 1978—, Am. Honda Motor Co., Inc. employees publs. Calif. Life Scholarship Found. scholar, 1967. Mem. Advt. Club L.A., Pub. Rels. Soc. Am., So. Calif. Assn. Philanthropy, Coun. on Founds., Affinity Group on Japanese Philanthropy (pres.), Ninety-Nines, Am. Quarter Horse Assn., Aircraft Owners and Pilots Assn., Los Angeles Soc. for Prevention Cruelty to Animals, Greenpeace, Ocicats Internat., Am. Humane Assn., Humane Soc. U.S., Elsa Wild Animal Appeal. Office: Am Honda Found 1919 Torrance Blvd Torrance CA 90501-2722

CAREY, SHIRLEY ANNE, nursing consultant; b. Syracuse, N.Y., Sept. 27, 1939; d. John Crotty and Eva Mae (Pratt) Walsh; m. John Paul Carey, July 23, 1966; children: Jason Leo, Jonathan Paul, Jennifer Anne. BSN, Nazareth Coll., 1961. RN, Calif. Charge nurse surg. svcs. L.A. County Hosp., 1962-64; instr. nursing L.A. County-U. So. Calif. Med. Ctr. Sch. Nursing, 1964-70; rschr./developer nursing edn. films Concept Media, Irvine, Calif., 1971-78; cmty. health educator Huntington Beach (Calif.) Hosp. and Med. Ctr., 1983—; nursing cons., health educator, writer Huntington Beach, 1988—; dir. staff devel. Huntington Beach (Calif.) Hosp. and Med. Ctr., 1995—, Samaritan Med Ctr., San Clemente, Calif., 1995—; instr. basics of babysitting Huntington Beach Med. Ctr., 1986—; instr. basic life support Am. Heart Assn., Huntington Beach, 1986—; HIV/AIDS educator ARC, Tustin, Calif., 1991—; bd. dirs. West Orange County Consortium Spl. Edn., Huntington Beach, 1991-92, clk., 1992, alt., 1993; bd. trustees Huntington Beach City Sch. Dist., 1990-94, 94—, clk., 1992, pres., 1993. Author, rschr.: (film series) Impaired Mobility, 1993, Basic Patient Care, 1994, Infection Control, 1995; film coord.: (film series) Human Development: Conception to Neonate, 1992, Human Development: First 2 1/2 Years, 1992, Human Development 2 1/2 to 6 Years, 1993. Pres., bd. dirs. Harry W. Montague Basketball Meml. Scholarship Com., Huntington Beach, 1989—, sec., bd. dirs. Huntington Beach Sister City Assn., 1993-95; mem., past officer Orange County (Calif.) Adoptive Parents, 1975—; active Girl Scouts Am., Costa Mesa, 1984-96, PTA, Huntington Beach, 1976—; commr. Huntington Beach Comty. Svcs. Commn., 1994—; mem. Huntington Beach Children's Needs Task Force, 1995—, com. Orange County Sch. Orgn., 1994—; exec. bd. dirs. Huntington Beach PRIDE/DARE Found., 1995—. Recipient Hon. Svc. award PTA, 1989, 2nd Place award Am. Jour. Nursing Film Festival, 1996. Mem. AAUW (exec. bd. dirs. 1995—), Nat. Sch. Bd. Assn. (mem. fed. rels. network 1993—), Women in Leadership, Calif. Sch. Bd. Assn. (mem. legis. network 1990—, del. assembly 1993—). Home and Office: 21142 Brookhurst St Huntington Beach CA 92646-7407

CARFAGNO-BUCK, CHRISTINA MARIE, social worker; b. Syracuse, N.Y., Mar. 19, 1970; d. Michael Jr. and Marian Edith (Harvard) Carfagno; m. Richard Francis Buck, Apr. 22, 1995. BS in Psychology, St. Lawrence U., 1992; MSW, SUNY, Albany, 1994. Cert. social worker, N.Y. Geriatric social worker Loretto Geriatric Ctr., Syracuse, 1994—. Mem. NASW, NOW, Phi Beta Kappa. Home: 106 Academy Green Syracuse NY 13207

CARIELLI, CAROL LEGGIO, guidance counselor; b. Bklyn., Oct. 27, 1956; m. Dominick Carielli, July 17, 1988. BA, Bklyn. Coll., 1977, MS, 1980; MS, Long Island U., 1983; profl. diploma, Fordham U., 1993, postgrad., 1994—. Cert. in sch. psychology, N.Y., supervision and adminstrn., N.Y. Tchr. comm. arts Bishop Ford Ctrl. Cath. High Sch., Bklyn., 1979-83, guidance counselor, 1984—; adj. lectr. Kingsborough Cmty. Coll./CUNY, Bklyn. Teach grantee Prins. Cath. High Sch./Diocese of Bklyn. Mem. Cath. Secondary Sch. Counselors N.Y.C. (Leadership award, past pres. 1990 92). Office: Bishop Ford Ctrl Cath High Sch 500 19th St Brooklyn NY 11215

CARING, LILLIAN COTT, psychologist; b. Poughkeepsie, N.Y.; d. Samuel and Mary Cott; widowed; children: Mary Louise, Joanne. BA, Hunter Coll., 1940; MA, Hofstra U., 1958; PhD, NYU, 1970. Psychologist Amityville (N.Y.) Schs., 1963-67, East Meadow (N.Y.) Schs., 1970-81; psychologist pvt. practice, 1981-87, Rockville Centre, N.Y., Northport, N.Y. Mem. APA, N.Y. Acad. Scis., N.Y. State Psychol. Assn., Nassau County Psychol. Assn., Suffolk County Psychol. Assn., Pi Lambda Theta, Psi Chi. Home: 250 E 87 St #27A New York NY 10128

CARINO, AURORA LAO, psychiatrist, hospital administrator; b. Angeles, The Philippines, Jan. 11, 1940; came to U.S., 1967; d. Pedro Samson and Hilaria Sanchez (Paras) Lao; m. Rosalito Aldecoa Carino, Dec. 2, 1967; children: Robert, Edwin, Antoinette. AA, U. of the East, Manila, 1961; degree in medicine, U. of the East, Quezon City, The Philippines, 1966. Lic. psychiatrist N.Y., Conn., Fla.; cert. Am. Bd. Psychiatry and Neurology. Resident in pediatrics U. of the East-R.M. Meml. Hosp., Quezon City, 1966-67; rotating intern Stamford (Conn.) Hosp., 1967-68; resident in psychiatry Norwich (Conn.) Hosp., 1968-71, staff psychiatrist, 1971-75; staff psychiatrist, unit chief, acting clin. dir. Harlem Valley Psychiat. Ctr., Wingdale, N.Y., 1975-80; svc. chief Fla. State Hosp., Chattahoochee, 1982-83; unit chief Hudson River Psychiat. Ctr., Poughkeepsie, N.Y., 1983-89, dep. med. dir., acting clin. dir., 1989-90, asst. to clin. dir., 1990-93, dep. med. dir.-admissions, 1993—; cons. Dept. Mental Hygiene, Dutchess County, Poughkeepsie, 1976—. Active N.Y. State Psychiat. Polit. Action Com., 1990—. Mem. Am. Psychiat. Assn., Am. Acad. Psychiatry and Law. Republican. Roman Catholic. Home: 10 Millbank Rd Poughkeepsie NY 12603-5112

CARINO, LINDA SUSAN, financial software and telecommunications company executive; b. San Diego, Nov. 4, 1954; d. DeVona (Clarke) Dungan. Student, San Diego Mesa Coll., 1972-74, 89-90. Various positions Calif. Can. Bank, San Diego, 1974-77, ops. supr., 1977-80, ops. mgr., 1980-82; asst. v.p. ops. mgr. First Comml. Bank (formerly Calif. Can. Bank), San Diego, 1982-84; v.p. data processing mgr. First Nat. Bank, San Diego, 1984-91; v.p. conversion adminstr. Item Processing Ctr. Svc. Corp., Denver, 1991-92; mgr. computer ops. FIserv, Inc., Van Nuys, Calif., 1992-93; v.p., data processing mgr. So. Calif. Bank, La Mirada, Calif., 1993-94, v.p. tech. support mgr., 1994—. Democrat. Home: 8400 Edinger Ave # X104 Huntington Beach CA 92647 Office: So Calif Bank PO Box 588 La Mirada CA 90637-0588

CARLCANO, CARLOTTA MIGUELINA (CARLOTTA BOTOE), educator, reading specialist; b. N.Y.C.; d. Carl and Marietta (Guilyard) C. BA, St. John's U., 1969; MS, L.I. U., 1973; postgrad., St. John's U. Cert. tchr., guidance counselor, N.Y. Mktg. rep. IBM Corp., N.Y.C., 1963-71; tchr. Bklyn., 1971-75; reading specialist Title I, Chpt. 1, Bklyn., 1975-77; coord. Open Enrollment, Bklyn., 1977; tchr., reading specialist N.Y.C. Pub. Schs., Bklyn., 1977—; mem. adj. prof. Essex County Coll., 1995-96. Chairperson Community Sch. Improvement Project, 1984-85. Mem. ASCD, NAFE, Nat. Inst. Bus. Mgmt. Democrat. Roman Catholic.

CARLEN, SISTER CLAUDIA, librarian; b. Detroit, July 24, 1906; d. Albert B. and Theresa Mary (Ternes) C. AB in Library Sci., U. Mich., 1928, MA in Library Sci., 1938; LHD (hon.), Marygrove Coll., 1981, Loyola U., Chgo., 1983, Sacred Heart Major Sem., 1989; LittD (hon.), Cath. U. of Am., 1983. Asst. librarian St. Mary Acad., Monroe, Mich., 1928-29; asst. librarian Marygrove Coll., Detroit, 1929-44, librarian, 1944-69, library cons., 1970-71; on leave as index editor New Cath. Ency., 1963-67, Cath. Theol. Ency., 1968-70; library cons. grad. div. Casa Santa Maria, N.Am. Coll., Rome, 1971-72; libr. St. John's Provincial Sem., Plymouth, Mich., 1972-80, libr. emeritus, 1980-82, scholar-in-residence, 1982-85, archivist, 1985-88; rsch. affiliate Bentley Hist. Libr., U. Mich., Ann Arbor, 1989—; supr. orgn. and servicing Community Ctr. Libraries staffed by vols.; bd. dirs. Corpus Instrumentorum, Inc., v.p., 1969-70; mem. instructional materials com. Mich. Curriculum Study; cons. McGraw Hill Ency. World Biography, 1968-72, World Book Ency., 1969-70; mem. working group on uniform headings for liturgical works Internat. Fedn. of Libr. Assns., 1972-75. Author: Guide to Encyclicals of the Roman Pontiffs, 1939, Guide to the Documents of Pius XII, 1951, Dictionary of Papal Pronouncements, 1958; editor: Papal Encyclicals, 1740-1981, 1981, Papal Pronouncements, 1991; editor: column At Your Service, Cath. Library World, 1950-52; Reference Book Rev. Sect., 1952-64, 66-72; Books for the Home column; monthly news release, Nat. Cath. Rural Life Conf., 1952-61; adv. bd.: The Pope Speaks, 1953-88, Pierian Press; contbr.: Catholic Bookman's Guide, 1961, Dictionary Western Chs, 1969, Ency. Dictionary of Religion, 1979, Translatio Studii, 1973. Trustee Marygrove Coll., Detroit, 1976-79, vice chmn. bd., 1977-79. Recipient Disting. Alumna award U. Mich. Sch. Libr. Sci., 1974, Domitilla award Marygrove Coll., 1991. Mem. ALA (coun. 1958-61, 68-71), Cath. Libr. Assn. (chmn. com. membership 1946-49, chmn. Mich. unit 1952-54, chmn. coll. and univ. sect. 1954-56, chmn. publs. com. 1961-62, pres. 1965-67,

Jerome award 1993), Mich. Libr. Assn. (chmn. coll. sect. 1956-57, chmn. recruiting com. 1959-60), Accademia Olubrense (charter), Am. Friends of Vatican Libr. (co-founder, v.p.), Phi Beta Kappa, Phi Kappa Phi, Beta Phi Mu. Home: 2301 Sandalwood Cir Apt 215A Ann Arbor MI 48105-1379

CARLETON, MARY RUTH, dean, consultant; b. Sacramento, Feb. 2, 1948; d. Warren Alfred and Mary Gertrude (Clark) Case; m. Bruce A. Hunt, Jan. 21, 1989. BA in Polit. Sci., U. Calif.-Berkeley, 1970, MJ, 1974; postgrad., San Diego State U. TV news anchorwoman, reporter Sta. KXAS-TV, Ft. Worth, 1974-78, Sta. KING-TV, Seattle, 1978-80, Sta. KOCO-TV, Oklahoma City, 1980-84; news anchor, reporter Sta. KTTV-TV, L.A., 1984-87; news anchor Sta. KLAS-TV, Las Vegas, Nev., 1987-91, KTNV-TV, 1991-93, Sta. UNLV-TV, 1993-94; broadcast instr. Okla. Christian Coll., 1981-84, UCLA, 1985-87, U. Nev.-Las Vegas, 1991-94; pub. speaking cons.; dir. UNLV Women's Ctr., 1991-94; news dir. univ. news Sta. UNLV-TV, 1992-94; asst. dean devel. San Diego State U., 1994—. Bd. dirs. World Neighbors, Oklahoma City, 1984-89, Allied Arts Coun. So. Nev.-Las Vegas, 1988-94, Nev. Inst. for Contemporary Art, 1988-94; bd. dirs. United Way, Las Vegas, 1991-94, secret witness bd., 1991-94, Las Vegas Women's Coun., 1993-94, Friends of Channel 10, 1991-94. Named Best Environ. Reporter, Okla. Wildlife Fedn., 1983, Disting. Woman of So. Nev., Woman of Achievement Las Vegas Women's Coun., 1990; recipient Broadcasting award UPI, 1981, Nat. award for best documentary, 1990, Tri-State award for best newscast, 1990, Emmy award, L.A., 1986, L.A. Press Club award 1986, 90, Nat. award for documentaries UPI, 1990, Woman of Achievement Media award Las Vegas C. of C., 1990. Mem. AARP (mem. nat. econ. issues team 1992-94, state legis. com.)Women in Comm. (Clarion award 1981, Best Newscaster 1990), Soc. Prol. Journalists, Press Women, Investigative Reporters, Sigma Delta Chi. Democrat. Roman Catholic. Avocations: tennis, gourmet cooking. Office: San Diego State U Coll Health & Human Svcs 5500 Canpanile San Diego CA 92182-4124

CARLICK, JEAN MEYERS, writer; b. Paducah, Ky., Sept. 29, 1937; d. Horace Daniel and Rebecca Carline (Bartlett) Meyers; m. Samuel Carlick, Apr. 11, 1965; 1 child, Bethany Anne. BA, U. Tex., 1958; MA, Murray State U., 1989. Tchr. fgn. lang. various schs., 1958-68; writer, author Paducah, Ky., 1989—; adj. composition tchr. Paducah C.C., 1990-91. Mem. ACLU, Am. Jewish Hist. Soc. Democrat. Jewish. Home: 292 New Mark Esplanade Rockville MD 20850

CARLILE, JANET LOUISE, artist, educator; b. Denver, Apr. 26, 1942; d. Jessie Crawford and Alice Essie (Locker) C.; m. David Hildebrand, Sept. 1, 1963 (div. 1968). BFA, Cooper Union, 1966; MFA, Pratt Inst., 1971. Prof. Bklyn. Coll., CUNY, 1971—; founder Incline Village (Nev.) Fine Arts Ctr., 1966-68; instr. Sch. Visual Arts, N.Y.C., 1968-70, Printmaking Workshop, N.Y.C., 1971, Scarsdale (N.Y.) Studio Workshop, 1971-73, SUNY-Stony Brook, L.I., 1976, Bard Winter Coll., Rhinebeck, N.Y., 1980; head printmaking, asst. dir. Bklyn. Mus. Art Sch., 1971-77; dir. Bklyn. Coll. Press, 1977—; cons. Woodstock (N.Y.) Sch. Art, 1980-84; judge Alpine Artists Show, Ouray, Colo., 1989, Landscape Ptg. Show, Woodstock Art Assn., 1995. One-woman shows include Blue Mt. Gallery, N.Y.C., 1980, Stetson U., DeLand, Fla., 1995, Fairleigh Dickinson Coll., Teaneck, N.J., 1995; exhibited in group shows at Associated Am. Artists Gallery, N.Y., 1971-81, Bklyn. Mus., 1976, Ulster County Artists Show, N.Y. State Coun. Show, 1984, Alpine Artists Show Ouray County, 1987; design for IRT Bklyn. Mus. Sta. Sec. San Juan Vista Landowners Assn., Ridgway, Colo., 1980-86. Recipient full scholarship Cooper Union, N.Y.C., 1962-66, Hirshorn Purchase prize, Soc. Am. Graphic Artists, 1969, Grad. fellowship Pratt Inst., Bklyn., 1971, Best of Show award, Alpine Artists Show Ouray County, 1987, NEA Workshop grant Colo. Coun. Arts, 1991, Creative Incentive award CUNY, 1992. Mem. Ouray (Colo.) County Arts Assn. (pres. 1991-93). Home: PO Box 1805 Ouray CO 81427-1805 also: 12 Bellows Ln Woodstock NY 12498-1204 Office: Brooklyn Coll Art Dept Bedford at Ave H Brooklyn NY 11210

CARLILE, SUSAN, secondary education educator; b. Peoria, Ill., May 14, 1967; d. James E. and Mary Lynn (Obery) C. BA, Taylor U., 1989; MA, Ariz. State U., 1995. EFL tchr. Fundacion Ponce de Leon, Madrid, 1989-92; English tchr. Maryvale High Sch., Phoenix, 1992-95, co-chair English dept., 1994-95; English tchr. Metro Tech. High Sch., Phoenix, 1995—. Active Camelback Bible Ch., Phoenix, 1994, Anytown USA, Phoenix, 1992. Home: 1214 S Roosevelt Tempe AZ 85281 Office: Metro Tech High Sch 1900 W Thomas Rd Phoenix AZ 85015

CARLIN, BETTY, educator; b. N.Y.C.; d. Samuel and Rose Sara (Bernstein) Grossberg; m. Arthur S. Carlin, July 18, 1953 (dec.); children: Lisa Anne Skinner, James Howard. BA, UCLA, 1952; MA, U. Calif., Berkeley, 1955. Educator L.A. Sch. Dist., 1952-55; owner Carlin's Shoes, L.A., 1952-68; educator Berkeley (Calif.) Sch. Dist., 1957-58; master tchr. spl. programs Calif. State Coll., Hayward, 1967-84; educator U. Calif., Berkeley, 1984-86; co-owner Art-Car Corp., 1978-88. Mem. Nat. Tchrs. Assn., Calif. Tchrs. Assn., Commonwealth Club, San Francisco Opera Guild.

CARLIN, CAROL RUTH, secondary education educator; b. Milw., Nov. 12, 1946; d. Robert and Ruth A. (Walsh) C. BS in Social Studies/English, U. Wis., 1969; MA in Communication, U. Wis., Milw., 1975. Tchr. Waterford (Wis.) High Sch., 1969-72, Badger High Sch., Lake Geneva, Wis., 1972—. Organizer Leadership Dynamics Program, Lake Geneva, 1992—; vol. assessor level III Alverno Coll., Milw., 1990—; Women in Edn. del. U.S.-China Joint Conf. on Women's Issues, 1995. Recipient Robert J. Webster Mentor award Screen Printing Assn. Internat., 1992, Wis. Women Leaders in Edn., AAUW, 1996; Christa McAuliffe fellow, 1995-96. Mem. NEA (bd. dirs. 1981-87), Nat. Assn. Experimental Edn., Wis. Edn. Assn. Coun. (bd. dirs. 1981-87, vol. grass roots organizer 1976—). Democrat. Home: 6914 W Coldspring Rd Greenfield WI 53220-2911 Office: Badger H S 220 E South St Lake Geneva WI 53147-2436

CARLISLE, JUDY ANN, federal agency administrator; b. Milw., July 23, 1948; d. Robert Frank and Emily Mathilda (Wolfgram) Steinkrauss; div.; children: Michael, Julie, Linda, Alan, Mark, Scott, Amanda. Student, Marquette U., 1965-67, U. Alaska, 1973-74; AA, Western Nev. Cmty. Coll., Fallon, 1980-82; student, U. Nev., 1983. Tchg. cert., Nev. Music tchr. The Studio, Fallon, 1978-84; libr. asst. Washoe County Libr., Reno, 1984-86; asst. dir. VETS/U.S. Dept. of Labor, Carson City, 1988—; writer, proofreader Fallon Eagle Standard, 1982; pub. rels. coord. Churchill County Recreation, Fallon, 1982-85; substitute tchr. Nev. Dept. Edn., Carson City, 1983-88; poetry tchr., 1983—. Author: Voices in Am. Poetry, 1991, Desert Wood, 1991; contbr. articles to popular publs. Vol. Carson City Libr., 1990—; mentor UNR Pregnant Teen Program, Carson City, 1992-94; surrogate advocate Carson City Sch. Dist., 1995—. With USN, 1967-68. Recipient Outstanding Literary Achievement award Western Nev. Cmty. Coll., Carson City, 1982, 1st prize in poetry Calliope Magazine, 1990, Editor's Choice award Voices of Am., 1994. Mem. AAUW, Vietnam Vets. Am. Lutheran. Home: 718 Hot Springs Rd # 3 Carson City NV 89706 Office: VETS US Dept Labor 1923 N Carson # 205 Carson City NV 89701

CARLISLE, LILIAN MATAROSE BAKER (MRS. E. GRAFTON CARLISLE, JR.), author, lecturer; b. Meridian, Miss., Jan. 1, 1912; d. Joseph and Lilian (Flournoy) Baker; student Dickinson Coll., 1929-30, Peirce Coll. Bus. Adminstrn., 1930-31; B.A., U. Vt., 1981, M.A., 1986; m. E. Grafton Carlisle, Jr., Jan. 9, 1933; children: Diana, Penelope. Adminstrv. sec. RAF Ferry Command, Montreal, Can., 1942; exec. staff mem. in charge collections, research Shelburne (Vt.) Mus., 1951-61; exec. sec. Burlington Area Community Health Study, 1963, coordinator, 1964; asst. coordinator Vt. Mental Retardation Planning Project, 1965; project dir. 4-county Champlain Valley Medicare Alert, 1966; dir. public relations Champlain Valley Agrl. Fair, 1968-77; lectr. U. Vt. Elder Hostel program, 1976-77, mem. faculty Vacation Coll., 1980-83. Pres., Burlington Community Council for Social Welfare, 59-61, 71-73; chmn. bd. Champlain Sr. Citizens, 1977-79; justice of peace, 1979-81; pres. Chittenden County Extension Adv. Com., 1977-78; chmn. publs. com. Vt. Bicentennial Commn., 1974-77; mem. Vt. Ho. of Reps., 1968-70. Recipient Community Council Disting. Citizen award, 1978. Mem. Vt. (trustee, chmn. mus. com. 1967), N.Y. (faculty seminar) Chittenden (pres. 1969-72, editor Heritage Series of 10 books about Chittenden County towns 1972-76) hist. socs., Vt. Old Cemetery Assn., Vt. Folklore Soc., League Vt. Writers (dir. 1962; v.p., pres. 1967-69). Am. Pen Women (pres. Green Mountain br. 1980-82), Order Women Legislators (pres. Vt. br. 1972-74), Meml. Soc. Vt. (pres. 1989-94), Chi Omega. Conglist. Club: Zonta (pres. 1964-65). Co-author: The Story of the Shelburne Museum, 1955; Profile of the Community, 1964; Environmental and Personal Health of the Community, 1964; Vermont Clock and Watchmakers, Silversmiths and Jewelers, 1970; also numerous catalogs on collections at Shelburne Mus.; editorial cons. Burlington Social Survey, 1967; editor: Historic Guide to Burlington Neighborhoods, 1991; contbr. articles to profl. jours. Home: 117 Lakeview Ter Burlington VT 05401-2901

CARLISLE, MARGO DUER BLACK, chief senatorial staff; b. Providence; d. Thomas F. Jr. and Margaret MacCormick Black; m. Miles Carlisle; children: Mary Hamilton, Tristram Coffin. BA, Manhattanville Coll. Legis. asst. Senator James A. McClure, Washington, 1973; staff mem. budget comm. task force U.S. Senate, Washington, 1974-75, exec. dir. steering com., 1975-80; staff dir. Senate Rep. Conf., Washington, 1981-84; exec. dir. Coun. for Nat. Policy, Washington, 1985-86; asst. sec. for legis. affairs Dept. Def., Washington, 1986-89; v.p. for govt. rels. The Heritage Found., Washington, 1989-90; chief staff Senator Thad Cochran, Washington, 1991—; staff dir. nat. security and fgn. policy subcoms. for Rep. platform, 1984, Washington. Contbr. articles on govt. policy to profl. jours. Trustee Phila. Soc., Washington, 1987-88, 93—, pres., 1995-96; bd. advisors, Marine Corps U., 1995—. Catholic. Home: 3221 Garfield St NW Washington DC 20008-3514 Office: Office of Sen Thad Cochran 326 Russell Bldg Washington DC 20510-0008

CARLISLE, PATRICIA KINLEY, mortgage company executive, paralegal; b. Royston, Ga., Sept. 21, 1949; d. Luther Clark Kinley and Ann Busby Carey; children: Angela Renee, William Clark, Matthew Vincent. Grad., Suburban Inst. Real Estate, Tucker, Ga., 1978; grad. with honors, Lanier Tech. Sch., Oakwood, Ga., 1983; postgrad., Gainesville Coll., 1986, Maryville Coll., 1986. Lic. real estate salesperson, Ga. Fin. analyst, then pers. mgr. Citicorp Acceptance Co., Inc., St. Louis, 1983-89; exec. v.p., v.p. purchasing, regional sales mgr. George-Ingraham Corp., Stone Mountain, Ga., 1989-90; sr. loan officer Terrace Mortgage Co., Atlanta, 1990-92; dir. client svcs. Feagin & Assocs., P.C., 1992-96, Cumming, Ga., 1996—; dir. client svcs. Feagin & Assocs., PL, 1996—; rsch. bd. advisors Am. Biog. Inst., Inc. Mem. NAFE, Forsyth County Bd. Realtors, Aircraft Owners and Pilots Assn., Female Execs. North Atlanta, AAPMW, Ga. Mortgage Brokers Assn., MBAG. Home: PO Box 467364 Atlanta GA 31146-7364

CARLOZZI, CATHERINE LAUREL, public relations, communications consultant; b. Berea, Ohio, July 25, 1953; d. Charles Henry and Carol Louise (Jones) Bader; m. Nicholas Carlozzi, Jan. 4, 1975. BA in English summa cum laude, Denison U., 1975; MA in English with distinction, U. Wis., 1976. Teaching asst. U. Wis., Madison, 1976-77; editor Visual Edn. Cons., Madison, 1977-78; copywriter advt. Walnut Equipment Leasing, Ardmore, Pa., 1978-79; assoc. nat. dir. publications Laventhol & Horwith, Phila., 1979-84; sr. assoc., mgr. spl. projects, v.p. Brown Boxenbaum, N.Y.C., 1984-91; prin. Carlozzi Comm. Cons., Cedar Grove, N.J., 1991—. Trustee Montclair, N.J. Art Mus., 1993—, chmn. audience devel. com., mem. nominating com. Recipient Dir.'s award Montclair Art Mus., 1994. Mem. N.Y. Women in Comm. (comm. com. 1992—), Phi Beta Kappa. Home and Office: Carlozzi Comms Cons 334 Crestmont Rd Cedar Grove NJ 07009-1908

CARLSEN, JANET HAWS, insurance company owner, mayor; b. Bellingham, Wash., June 16, 1927; d. Lyle F. and Mary Elizabeth (Preble) Haws; m. Kenneth M. Carlsen, July 26, 1952; children: Stephanie L. Chambers, Scott Lyle, Sean Preble, Stacy K., Spencer J. Cert., Armstrong Bus. Sch., 1945; student, Golden Gate Coll., 1945-46. Office mgr. Cornwall Warehouse Co., Salt Lake City, 1950-55, Hansen's Ins., Newman, Calif., 1969-77; owner Carlsen Ins., Gustine, Calif., 1978—. Mem. city coun. City of Newman, 1980-82, mayor, 1982-94; bd. dirs. ARC, Stanislaus, Calif., 1982-83, Tosca, 1993—; bd. dirs. Stanislaus County Area Agy. on Aging, 1995—, chairperson, 1996-97; bd. dirs. Calif. state com. TACC Commn. on Aging, 1996—; grand marshal Newman Fall Festival, 1989; v.p. ctrl. divsn. League of Calif. Cities, 1989-90, pres. 1990, 91; bd. dirs. Sr. Opportunity Svc. Ctr., 1993-96, Sr. Opportunity Svc. Program of Stanislaus County, 1995-96. Named Soroptimist Woman of Achievement, 1987, Soroptimist Woman of Distinction, 1988, Outstanding Woman, Stanislaus County Commn. for Women, 1989, Newman Rotary Club Citizen of Yr., 1993-94, Woman of Yr. Calif. State Assembly Dist. 26, 1994. Morman. Club: Booster (Newman). Lodge: Soroptimist. Home: 1215 Amy Dr Newman CA 95360-1003 Office: 377 5th St Gustine CA 95322-1126

CARLSEN, MARY R(OHENTA), social welfare administrator; b. Miami, Okla., Apr. 3, 1921; d. Edwan and Leila M. (Burkman) Trebilcox; m. Roger S. Carlsen, Sept. 13, 1947; 1 child, Nancy. Attended, N.E. Okla. Jr. Coll. Sec. Prodn. Mgmt., Washington, 1941-43, War Prodn. Bd., Washington, 1943-45; exec. officer HUD, Washington, 1945-70; co-owner, office mgr. Riverdale (Md.) Dry Cleaner, 1970-80. Bd. dirs. several agys. dealing with poor and homeless; chair Outreach Ch., Washington, vol., 1980—; mem. Balt. Washington Ann. Conf. United Meth. Ch.; B-W conf. pres. Asbury Guild, Asbury Meth. Village, 1996—. Mem. Rotary Inner Wheel. Democrat. Home: 415 Russell Ave Apt 611 Gaithersburg MD 20877

CARLSON, CLARE, state legislator; b. Grand Forks, N.D., Apr. 27, 1956. BS, N.D. State U. Rep. dist. 18 N.D. Ho. of Reps.; farmer. Republican. Lutheran. Home: 201 Chestnut St Grand Forks ND 58201-4661 Office: ND Ho of Reps State Capitol Bismarck ND 58505*

CARLSON, DALE BICK, writer; b. N.Y.C., May 24, 1935; d. Edgar M. and Estelle (Cohen) Bick; children: Daniel, Hannah. BA, Wellesley Coll., 1957. Lic. wildlife rehabilitator, 1991. Pres. Bick Pub. House, 1993—; founder, pres. Bick Pub. House, 1993—. Author children's books, adult books 1961—, including: Perkins the Brain, 1964, The House of Perkins, 1965, Miss Maloo, 1966, The Brainstormers, 1966, Frankenstein, 1968, Counting Is Easy, 1969, Your Country, 1969, Arithmetic 1, 2, 3, 1969, The Electronic Teabowl, 1969, Warlord of the Genji, 1970, The Beggar King of China, 1971, The Mountain of Truth (Spring Festival Honor book, named Am. Library Assn. Notable Book), 1972, Good Morning Danny, 1972, Good Morning, Hannah, 1972, The Human Apes, 1973 (named Am. Library Assn. Notable Book), Girls Are Equal Too, 1973 (named Am. Library Assn. Notable Book), Baby Needs Shoes, 1974, Triple Boy, 1976, Where's Your Head?, 1977, The Plant People, 1977, The Wild Heart, 1977, The Shining Pool, 1979, Lovingsex for Both Sexes, 1979, Boys Have Feelings Too, 1980, Call Me Amanda, 1981, Manners That Matter, 1982, The Frog People, 1982, Charlie the Hero, 1983, 1984-85: The Jenny Dean Science Fiction Mysteries, The Mystery of the Shining Children, The Mystery of the Hidden Trap, The Secret of the Third Eye, The James Budd Mysteries, The Mystery of Galaxy Games, The Mystery of Operation Brain, 1985, Miss Mary's Husbands, 1988, Basic Manuals in Wildlife Rehabilitation Series (6 vols.), 1993-94, Basic Manuals for Friends of the Disabled Series, 1995-96, others. Mem. Authors League Am., Authors Guild, Wind Over Wings. Address: 307 Neck Rd Madison CT 06443-2755

CARLSON, DESIREE ANICE, pathologist; b. Clinton, Iowa, June 10, 1950; d. Donald Richard and Bernice Elfriede (Jacobs) C.; m. Helmut Gunther Rennke; stepchildren: Stephanie Rennke, Christianne Rennke. MD, Duke U., 1975. Resident in pathology U. Wash., Seattle, 1975-76, N.E. Deaconess Hosp., Boston, 1976-77, Peter Bent Brigham Hosp., Boston, 1977-79; pathologist W. Roxbury VA Med. Ctr., Boston, 1979-82; med. dir. blood bank Univ. Hosp., Boston, 1982-90; assoc. chief pathology N.E. Meml. Hosp., Stoneham, Mass., 1990-93; chief pathology Brockton (Mass.) Hosp., 1993—; asst. prof. pathology Boston U. Sch. Med., 1982—; cons. pathology Brigham and Women's Hosp., Boston, 1984—; mem. adv. bd. ARC, Dedham, 1982—. Contbr. articles to profl. jours., book chpts. Recipient Outstanding Contbd. Article award Med. Lab. Observer, 1988. Mem. Coll. Am. Pathologists (N.E. regional commr. 1991—), Am. Med. Women's Assn., Am. Assn. Blood Banks, Mass. Med. Soc. (coms.), Mass. Pathology Soc., N.E. Pathology Soc. Republican. Presbyterian. Office: Brockton Hosp 680 Centre St Brockton MA 02402-3308

CARLSON, HANNAH BICK, developmental disabilities director; b. N.Y.C., July 13, 1963; d. Albert William David and Dale Elissa (Bick) C. BA in Psychology, U. Rochester, 1985; MA, Columbia U., 1986, MEd in Counseling Psychology, 1988; postgrad., Ctr. for Gestalt Psychotherapy, N.Y.C., 1986-88. Cert. rehab. counselor. Alcoholism counselor N.Y. Hosp., Payne Whitney Psychiat. Clinic, N.Y.C., 1986-87; sr. rehab. counselor NYU Med. Ctr. Rusk Inst., N.Y.C., 1988-91; vocat. rehab. counselor New Medico Rehab. Svcs., Great Neck, N.Y., 1991, program case mgr., 1991-93; devel. disabilities dir. West Haven (Conn.) Comty. House, West Haven, Conn., 1993—; lectr. NYU Med. Ctr., Rusk Inst., 1989-91, Manhasset Pub. Schs., 1991—. Co-author: (handbooks) I Have a Friend Who Has Mental Retardation, I Have a Friend Who is Deaf, I Have a Friend Who is Blind, I Have a Friend in a Wheel Chair, I Have a Friend with a Learning Disability, I Have a Friend with Mental Illness, 1996; contbr. articles to profl. jours. Mem. APA, Am. Assn. Mental Retardation, Nat. Rehab. Assn., Conn. Counseling Assn. Home: 101 Sport Hill Rd Easton CT 06612-2204 Office: West Haven Community House 227 Elm St West Haven CT 06516-4635

CARLSON, JANET FRANCES, psychologist, educator; b. Newport, R.I., Oct. 3, 1957; d. Robert Carl and Alice Marion (Orina) C.; m. Kurt Francis Geisinger, Sept. 22, 1984. BS summa cum laude, Union Coll., Schenectady, 1979; MA in Clin. Psychology, Fordham U., 1982, PhD in Clin. Psychology, 1987. Lic. psychologist, N.Y.; cert. sch. psychologist, N.Y., Conn. Clin. psychology intern Conn. Valley Hosp., Middletown, Conn., 1983-84; research fellow Schering-Plough Found., Bronx, N.Y., 1984-85; psychologist I Creedmoor Psychiat. Ctr., Queens Village, N.Y., 1985-86; psychologist Hallen Sch., Mamaroneck, N.Y., 1986-88; asst. prof. psychology Fordham U., Bronx, N.Y., 1988-89; asst. prof. sch. and applied psychology Fairfield (Conn.) U., 1989-93, dir. sch. and applied psychology programs, 1989-90; asst. prof. counseling and psychol. svcs. SUNY, Oswego, 1993-95, assoc. prof. counseling and psychol. svcs., 1995—; cons. N.Y.C. Bd. Edn. Office Rsch., Evaluation and Assessment, 1988-92; vis. asst. prof. psychology LeMoyne Coll., Syracuse, N.Y., 1992-93. Recipient Sugarfree scholarship, 1984-85, Sigma Xi Grant-in-Aid of Research, 1984-85. Mem. APA, Am. Ednl. Rsch. Assn., Nat. Assn. Sch. Psychologists, Ea. Psychol. Assn., N.Y. State Psychol. Assn., Northeastern Ednl. Rsch. Assn. (editor newsletter 1988-91, bd. dirs. 1990-93, pres. 1995-96), N.Y. Assn. Sch. Psychologists, Sigma Xi, Psi Chi (charter), Phi Kappa Phi (charter, pres. 1995-96).

CARLSON, JEANNIE ANN, writer; b. Bklyn., Jan. 13, 1955; d. Lloyd Arthur and Ruth Frances (Riley) C.; m. Kenneth D. Williams, May 15, 1976 (div. 1981); 1 child, Carl Philip; m. H. Daniel Hopkins, Dec. 16, 1987 (div. 1994). BA, Randolph-Macon Woman's Coll., 1977. Mktg./editing rep. Harris Pub., White Plains, N.Y., 1982; adminstrv. asst. Ray Fried Assocs., Inc., Eastchester, N.Y., 1980-84; proofreader Nat. Pennysaver, Elmsford, N.Y., 1983-84; chief writer Profl. Resume and Writing Service, St. Petersburg, Fla., 1984-87; exec. writer, pres. Viking Comm., Inc., 1987—; feature writer Asbury News, Crestwood, N.Y., 1983-84; editorial asst. Children's Rights Am., Largo, Fla., 1984; pub. rels. coord. The Renaissance Cultural Ctr., Clearwater, Fla., 1985; com. mem. work area on comm. Pasadena Community Ch., St. Petersburg, Fla., 1986-88, Christian edn. bd. Our Savior Luth. Ch., St. Petersburg, 1991-93; editorial advisor Grief Recovery Ctrs. Fla., 1992. Recipient Golden Poet award World of Poetry, 1985, 88, 89, 91, 92, Silver Poet award, 1986, 90, Recognition award Nat. Soc. Poets, 1979, poetry awards Internat. Publs., 1976-77, Achievement Certs. Profl. Resume and Writing Service, 1985, 86, 87, World of Poetry awards of merit, 1983 (2), 85, 87, 88 (2), 91, 92, Editor's Choice award Nat. Libr. Poetry, 1994, Woman of Yr. award ABI, 1995, 96. Mem. City News Service (affiliate writer), Profl. Assn. Resume Writers, Phi Beta Gamma. Methodist. Avocations: theatre, culinary arts, music. Office: Viking Communications Inc 300 31st St N Ste 212 Saint Petersburg FL 33713-7624

CARLSON, JENNIE PEASLACK, lawyer; b. Ft. Thomas, Ky., June 11, 1960; d. Roland A. and Shirley (Willen) Peaslack; m. Charles I. Michaels, Aug. 13, 1983 (div. May 1989); m. Richard A. Carlson, May 2, 1992. BA in English, Centre Coll., 1982; JD, Vanderbilt U., 1985. Bar: Ohio 1985. Atty. Taft, Stettinius & Hollister, Cin., 1985-91; sr. v.p., dep. gen. counsel Star Banc Corp., Cin., 1991—. Home: 8 Elmhurst Ave Cincinnati OH 45208-3211 Office: Star Banc Corp 425 Walnut St Fl 9 Cincinnati OH 45202-3904

CARLSON, KELLY J., insurance company executive; b. Providence, R.I., 1943. Grad., Providence Coll., 1967, Am. Coll., 1973. Sr. v.p. Phoenix Mut. Life Ins. Co., Hartford, Conn. Office: Phoenix Home Life Mut Ins Co One American Row Hartford CT 06115*

CARLSON, LINDA MARIE, language arts educator, consultant; b. St. Paul, Dec. 24, 1951; d. Kenneth Leroy Carlson and Margaret (Herbison) Berget. BS in English and Polit. Sci., U. Minn., Duluth, 1973, MEd in Rhetorical Theory, 1979; MBA, U. St. Thomas, 1987; postgrad., Rensselaer Poly. Inst., 1992—. Cert. Myers-Briggs Type Indicator adminstrn., cert. tchr., Minn. Tchr. English, curriculum leader Ind. Sch. Dist. 13, Columbia Heights, Minn., 1973-76, publs. advisor, coach, 1974-76; exec. asst. to provost Univ. Minn., Duluth, 1977-80; tech. editor EG and G (U.S. Dept. Energy), Idaho Falls, Idaho, 1980; tchr. English, gifted and talented Ind. Sch. Dist. 11, Coon Rapids, Minn., 1980—, lang. arts curriculum developer, 1981—, publs. advisor, 1982-84, learning styles cons., 1986—, assessment cons., 1989—; performance assessment cons. Minn. State Dept. Edn., St. Paul, 1990—; writing assessment cons. Minn. State Graduation Rulie Pilot Site, St. Paul, 1994—; lang. arts cons. pvt. and pub. schs. Minn. Mem. Minn. Arthritis Found., St. Paul, 1981-90, Commn. on Health and Healing, Mpls., 1984-86, Anoka (Minn.) Handicapped Assn., 1992—. Recipient Golden Apple Teaching award Ashland Oil Co., 1994; All-Univ. scholar Rensselaer Poly. Inst., 1992. Mem. NEA, ASCD, Nat. Coun. for Tchrs. of English, Anoka-Hennepin Edn. Assn. (pub. rels. com. 1980—), Coll. Compositional Comm. Home: 11117 Cottonwood St NW Coon Rapids MN 55448

CARLSON, NATALIE TRAYLOR, publisher; b. St. Paul, Feb. 15, 1938; d. Howard Ripley and Maxine (Johnson) Smith; m. James S. Carlson, Oct. 6, 1990; children: Drew Michael, Dacia Lyn, Dana Ann. BA, Jacksonville (Ala.) State U., 1975. Dir. Madison County Assn. of Mental Health, Huntsville, Ala., 1966-67; campaign mgr. U.S. Senatorial Race, No. Ala., 1968; pub. rels. Anniston Acad., 1970-76; journalist The Anniston Star, 1970-74, The Birmingham News, 1972-76; dir. Ala. affiliate, Am. Heart Assn., Birmingham, 1976-77; mgr. San Vicente New Home div., San Diego County Estates Realty, 1978-79; dir. sales Blake Pub. Co., San Diego, 1980-86; pres. Century Publ., San Diego, 1986—. Alternate del. at large Rep. Nat. Conv., San Francisco, 1964; fin. chmn. Madison County Rep. Exec. Com., Huntsville, Ala., 1966-69; pres. Madison County Rep. Women, Huntsville, 1967, 68; Diocesan Conv. del. Grace Episcopal Ch., Ala., 1975; active Nat. Rep. Party, 1962—; mem. St. James Episcopal Ch., Newport Beach, 1990—. Recipient 1st Pl. Newswriting award AP, 1971, 72, 73; nominee Outstanding Woman of Yr., Huntsville Area Jaycees, 1967. Mem. Long Beach Area C. of C., Palm Springs C. of C., Greater Del Mar C. of C., Huntington Beach C. of C., Kappa Kappa Gamma.

CARLSON, P(ATRICIA) M(CELROY), writer; b. Guatemala City, Guatemala, Feb. 3, 1940; (parents Am. citizens); d. James Benjamin and Alene (Jones) McElroy; m. M.A. Carlson, Aug. 20, 1960; children: Geoffrey, Richard. BA, Cornell U., 1961; MA, Cornell, 1966, PhD, 1974. Instr., lectr. psychology and human development Cornell U., Ithaca, N.Y., 1973-78; mem. bd. dirs. Bloomington Restorations, Inc., 1982-84. Author: (with M. Potts, R. Cocking and C. Copple), Structure and Development in Child Language, 1979, Audition for Murder, 1985, Murder is Academic, 1985, Murder is Pathological, 1986, (with Richard Darlington) Behavioral Statistics, 1987, Murder Unrenovated, 1988, Rehearsal for Murder, 1988, Murder in the Dog Days, 1991, Murder Misread, 1991, Bad Blood, 1991, Gravestone, 1993, Bloodstream, 1995, nine short stories. Chair Ithaca Environ. Commn., 1975-78; bd. dirs. Historic Ithaca, 1976-77. Mem. Mystery Writers Am. (bd. dirs. 1990-92), Sisters in Crime (internat. sec. 1990-91, v.p. 1991-92, pres. 1992-93). Address: Vicky Bijur Literary Agy 333 W End Ave New York NY 10023-8128

CARLSON, REVEANN JODI, radon technologist; b. Fargo, N.D., May 29, 1959; d. Robert Edward and Jorjann Reve (Vaala) C.; m. Frederick John Elliott, Oct. 1994. Student, Pierce Coll., Reseda, Calif., 1979-80, Am. U., Washington, 1981. Svc. mgr. F&F Heating & Air Conditioning, Camarillo, Calif., 1982-91; owner Radon Testing Svcs., Thousand Oaks, Calif., 1991—. Mem. Am. Assn. Radon Scientists and Technologists (bd. dirs. 1994-96).

Republican. Roman Catholic. Office: Radon Testing Services Ste 282 2219 E Thousand Oaks Blvd Thousand Oaks CA 91362

CARLSON, STACY, legislative staff director; b. Burbank, Calif., Sept. 6, 1960. BA in Econ., Calif. State U., 1982; MBA, Stanford U., 1988. Legis. asst. to Rep. Bill Thomas, 1982-84; chief of staff Kern County Bd. Suprs., 1984-86; various positions including sr. v.p. strategic planning and spl. projects Silicon Valley Bank, Santa Clara, Calif., 1989-93; minority staff dir. Com. House Adminstrn., 1993-94; staff dir. Com. House Oversight, 1995—. Office: Com on House Oversight 1309 Longworth House Washington DC 20515

CARLSON, SUZANNE OLIVE, architect; b. Worcester, Mass., Aug. 20, 1939; d. Sigfrid and Helga (Larson) C. BS, R.I. Sch. Design, 1963. Jr. ptnr. Dingnam-Fauteux & Partners, Worcester, 1969-70; ptnr. Richard Lamoureux Asso., Worcester, 1970-75, Herron & Carlson (AIA), Worcester, 1975—; Guest lectr. Holy Cross Coll., 1969-70. Chmn. Worcester Hist. Commn., 1976-88; trustee Worcester Heritage Soc., 1982-88, Park Spirit of Worcester Inc., 1987—; trustee Worcester Girls Inc. of Worcester, pres. 1989-92, sec. 1994—; trustee Performing Arts Sch. Worcester, 1977-86, v.p. 1980-85; trustee Cultural Assembly Greater Worcester, 1981-86, v.p., 1982-83. Recipient European Honors Program grant Rome, Italy, 1961-62; recipient AIA School medal for excellence, 1963. Mem. AIA (exec. bd. Ctrl. Mass. chpt. 1969-71, sec.-treas. 1970-71, v.p. 1971-72, pres. 1972-73), Mass. Soc. Architects (exec. bd. 1972-74, v.p. 1975, pres. 1976), New Eng. Regional Coun. Architects (pres. 1977), New Eng. Antiquities Rsch. Assn. (membership chair 1982-84, 90-94, resource devel. chair 1994—, graphics dir. jours. 1982—, trustee 1990—). Home and Office: Herron & Carlson 2 Oxford Pl Worcester MA 01609-2008

CARLSON ARONSON, MARILYN A., English language educator; b. Gothenburg, Nebr., July 24, 1938; d. Harold N. and Verma Elnora (Granlund) C.; m. Paul E. Carlson, July 31, 1959 (dec. Sept. 1988); 1 child, Andrea Joy; m. David L. Aronson, July 8, 1995. BS in Edn., English and Psychology, Sioux Falls Coll., 1960; MA in History, U. S.D., 1973, MA in English, 1992; postgrad., U. S.D. English and social scis. instr., curriculum coord. Beresford (S.D.) Pub. Sch., 1960-78; English and social scis. instr. Sioux Empire Coll., Hawarden, Iowa, 1979-85; instr. of English and ESL Midwest Inst. for Internat. Studies, Sioux Falls, 1985-89; asst. prof. English Augustana Coll., Sioux Falls, 1989—; part time instr. psychology Northwestern Coll., 1985; part time instr. English and lit. Nat. Coll., 1985-88; part time instr. English and history Augustana Coll., 1986-89; presenter in field. Author: Visions of Light: Flannery O'Connor's Themes and Narrative Method, also rev.; published Heroines in Willa Cather's Prairie Novels-Heritage of the Great Plains, 1995 author critiques. Named Tchr. of Yr., 1976; S.D. Humanities scholar, 1993; Bush mini-grantee, 1993; Internat. Studies grantee, 1994. Mem. AAUP, Nat. Coun. Tchrs. English, Nat. Fedn. Music Clubs, Am. Assn. Univ. Profs. Home: 29615 469th Ave Beresford SD 57004-9205 Office: Augustana Coll Dept English 29th St and Summit Ave Sioux Falls SD 57197

CARLUCCI, LYNETTE M., foundation administrator; b. Lynwood, Calif., Oct. 3, 1956; d. Elaine Ownby. AA in Mktg., Fullerton (Calif.) Coll., 1978; BA in Human Resources, Calif. State U., Long Beach, 1981; Advanced Exec. Tng., Exec. Inst. Boy Scouts Am.; Nat. Mgmt. Cert., Nat. Fin. Practitioners Forum. Assoc. coun. exec. Boy Scouts Am., Costa Mesa, Calif., 1981-82; coun. exec. Boy Scouts Am., Costa Mesa, 1982-83, 85-86, program dir., 1984, devel. dir, 1987-89, dir. devel., 1990; exec. dir. Orange County March of Dimes Birth Defects Found., 1993—. Mem. Nat. Soc. Fund Raising Execs. (bd. dirs.), Am. Soc. Tng. and Devel., Nat. Philantrophy Day Com. (co-chair 1995). Office: Orange Cty March of Dimes Birth Defects Found 2031 Orchard Dr Ste 250 Newport Beach CA 92660

CARLUCCI, MARIE ANN, nursing administrator, nurse; b. N.Y.C., Apr. 22, 1953; d. Clarence Hugh and Anna Rebecca (Mills) McNamee; m. Paul Pasquale Carlucci, Aug. 18, 1973; children: Christine, Patricia. Diploma in nursing, Mt. Vernon Hosp. Sch. Nursing, N.Y., 1974; BS in Behavioral Sci. summa cum laude, Mercy Coll., 1991; postgrad., N.Y. Med. Coll., 1991—. Cert. emergency nurse; cert. nurse adminstr. Staff nurse Mt. Vernon (N.Y.) Hosp., 1974-82, Lawrence Hosp., Bronxville, N.Y., 1982-84; staff nurse No. Westchester Hosp., Mt. Kisco, N.Y., 1984-91, asst. dir. nursing, mem. nurse mgmt. and ethics coms., 1991-94; asst. DON svcs. Ferncliff Manor, Yonkers, N.Y., 1994-95, dir. nursing svcs., 1995—. Religious edn. tchr. St. John and St. Mary's Ch., Chappagua, N.Y., 1984-94; campaign mgr. Com. to Elect Paul P. Carlucci, Chappagua, 1990; mem. Surrogate Decision Making Com., N.Y. Commn. Quality Care for Mentally Disabled; mem. bd. trustees Field Home-Holy Comforter, 1995—; mem. Hastings Ctr. Mem. N.Y. Orgn. Nurse Execs., N.Y. State MR/DD Nurses Assn., St. John and St. Mary's Women's Assn., Psi Chi, Phi Gamma Mu. Roman Catholic. Home: 23 Pine View Rd #5 Mount Kisco NY 10549-3935 Office: Ferncliff Manor 1154 Saw Mill River Rd Yonkers NY 10710-3210

CARLUCCIO, SHEILA COOK, psychologist; b. Carbondale, Pa., Nov. 10, 1954; d. Harry Thomas and Elizabeth Mary Cook; m. Robert Carluccio, Feb. 28, 1987; 1 stepchild, Robert Jr. BA, Marywood Coll., 1982, MA, 1987. Lic. psychologist. Sign lang. interpreter for hearing-impaired Scranton (Pa.) State Sch. for Deaf, 1984-86, psychology intern, 1986; staff clin. psychologist Devereux Found., Chester, N.J., 1987-88; staff psychologist Hope House, Dover, N.J., 1989-94, U. Scranton, Pa., 1994-95; pvt. practice Carbondale, 1993—. One woman art shows include Sterling Hotel, Wilkes-Barre, Pa., Sol Hemma, Uniondale, Pa., 1980; exhibited at Suraci Gallery, Scranton, Pa., 1979; contbr. poems to lit. jours. Human svc. team mem. Morris County Human Svc. Orgn./Assn., Dover, 1992. Mem. Am. Psychol. Assn. (assoc.), Am. Deafness and Rehab. Assn. (assoc.), Pa. Psychol. Assn. Psi Chi. Roman Catholic. Office: 123 Huntington Dr Dickson City PA 18519

CARMAN, SUSAN HUFERT, nurse coordinator; b. Detroit, Oct. 2, 1940; d. Theodore Louis and Margaret L. (O'Connor) Hufert; children: Amy E., Holly C., John T. BSN, Johns Hopkins U., 1964; MEd, Northeastern U., 1975; MS in Health Care Adminstrn., Simmons Coll., 1988. Instr. psychiat. nursing Salem (Mass.) Hosp. Sch. Nursing, 1975-78, Curry Coll., Milton, Mass., 1978-80; editor Beacon Comm. Corp., Acton, Mass., 1980-84; writer health promotion Honeywell Inc., Waltham, Mass., 1984-85; mgr. mental health unit Heritage Hosp., Somerville, Mass., 1986-87; specialist adult psychiatry Mass. Dept. Mental Health, Boston, 1987-93; clinician intensive clin. svcs. MHMA, Boston, 1994-96; with SHC Assocs., Boston, 1993—; bd. dirs. Com. to End. Elder Homelessness, Boston, Mass. Dept. Social Svcs., Lowell, sec., 1982-92. Chair health com. Jamaica Plain (Mass.) Tree of Life/Arbol da Vida, 1994-96; docent Arnold Arboretum, Boston, 1989—. Mem. ANA, Mass. Nurses Assn.

CARMEL, KATE MARY, museum curator; b. N.Y.C., Feb. 15, 1940; d. Philip David and Barbara (Wagner) C.; m. Norbert S. Weissberg, June 11, 1960 (div. 1979); children: John Wagner, Jed Wagner Weissberg. BA, Skidmore Coll., 1960; MA, NYU, Inst. Fine Arts, 1963; BFA, Parsons Sch. Design, N.Y.C., 1972; MA, grad. studies F.I.T., N.Y.C., 1986. Archtl. lighting designer Design Decisions, Inc., N.Y.C., 1972-75; prin. video prodn. co. Googleplex, Inc., N.Y.C., 1976-85; curator David A. Hanks & Assoc., N.Y.C., 1986-93; sr. curator Am. Craft Mus., N.Y.C., 1993-95, dir., 1995—; bd. mem., Am. Craft Mus., 1995—. Co-author: What Modern Was: Design 1935-1940, 1990, Craft in the Machine Age 1920-1945, 1995; designer: (theater) The Club (Tommy Tune, dir.), 1978 (Obie award 1978), NightClub Cantata (Elizabeth Swados, dir.), 1978 (Obie award 1978). Mem. Am. Assn. Art Museums, Art Table, Decorative Arts Soc. Office: Am Craft Mus 40 W 53rd St New York NY 10019

CARMEN, ELAINE (ELAINE HILBERMAN), psychiatrist, educator; b. N.Y.C., Mar. 26, 1939. BS, CCNY, 1959; MD, NYU, 1964. Diplomate Am. Bd. Psychiatry and Neurology. Instr. psychiatry U. N.C. Sch. Medicine, Chapel Hill, 1972-74, asst. prof., 1974-79, assoc. prof., 1979-84, prof., 1984-86; prof. psychiatry Boston U. Sch. Medicine, 1987—; asst. med. dir. S.C. Fuller Mental Health Ctr., Boston, 1987-90, med. dir., 1990-94; med. dir. Brockton (Mass.) Multi-Svc. Ctr., 1995—; mem. tech. expert group Women Violence and Mental Health, Nat. Women's Resource Ctr. Author: The Rape Victim, 1976; co-editor: The Gender Gap in Psychotherapy, 1984; contbr. articles to profl. jours. Chair Restraint, Seclusion and Abuse Task Force Mass. Dept. Mental Health, 1995—; co-chair mental health com. Boston AIDS Consortium, 1992-93. Recipient McNeil award for excellence in community psychiatry Am. Assn. Community Psychiatrists, 1993. Fellow Am. Psychiat. Assn. (chair com. on women 1978-80); mem. Mass. Psychiat. Soc., Mass. Med. Soc. Office: Brockton Multi-Svc Ctr 165 Quincy St Brockton MA 02402

CARMEN MARIA, LOPEZ, general manager; b. Havana, Cuba, Apr. 30, 1959; came to U.S., 1960; d. Roberto Diego and Milagros Antonia (Gonzalez) L. BS in Psychology, Georgetown U., 1981; MBA in Internat. Bus., George Washington U., 1986. Group mgr. C&P Telephone Co., Washington, 1981-84; asst. staff mgr. AT&T, Fairfax, Va., 1984-87; product mgr. AT&T, Fairfax, Va. and Basking Ridge, N.J., 1987-89; quality mgr. AT&T, Silver Spring, Md., 1989-92; dist. mgr. AT&T, Pleasanton, Calif., 1992-93; gen. mgr. tech. svc. orgn. AT&T, Denver, 1993-95; gen. sales mgr., no. New England Lucent Technologies (formerly AT&T), Waltham, Mass., 1995—. First co-chmn. Republican Nat. Hispanic Assembly, Washington, 1990-92; founding mem. N.Y. Relay Svc. Adv. Bd., 1988-89; chmn. HISPA Leadership Forum, 1993-95. Mem. Hispanic Assn. AT&T Employees (pres. nation's capital chpt. 1991-92). Home: 11 Donovan Ln Natick MA 01760 Office: Lucent Technologies 51 Sawyer Waltham MA 02154

CARMICHAEL, NANCY LOUISE, secondary school educator; b. Melrose Park, Ill., July 25, 1945; d. Leslie James and Viola Beth (Terrel) David; m. Robert Nelson Carmichael, Oct. 3, 1964; children: Rhonda Carmichael Scurek, Robert Leslie, Robyn Carmichael Keller. A degree, Ancilla Coll., 1980; B in Edn., Ind. U., South Bend, 1982, M in Edn., 1990. Tchr. English, sociology and psychology Oregon Davis H.S., Hamlet, Ind., 1983—. Office: Oregon Davis HS 5990 N 750 E Hamlet IN 46532-9524

CARNAHAN, BONNIE, systems analyst; b. Evansville, Ind., May 14, 1954; d. Ernest Everett and Betty Louise (Yelch) Carnahan; m. Gary Ray Smith, May 8, 1982 (div. Oct. 1986). Student, U. So. Ind., 1972-75, 84; BS in Biology, U. Evansville, 1979; AS in Computer Sci., Lockyear Coll., 1986. Nurses aide Welbourn Hosp., Evansville, 1976-79; vault teller Citizens Nat. Bank, Evansville, 1979-87; sr. telecom. devel. analyst LDDS/Worldcom, Inc., Tulsa, Okla., 1987—. Mem. Assn. Systems Mgmt., Project Mgmt. Inst. Republican. Methodist. Home: 6213 S Yorktown Ave Tulsa OK 74136 Office: LDDS/Worldcom Mail Drop 3.2.414 PO Box 21348 Tulsa OK 74121

CARNELLIE, DIANE MARIE, addiction counselor; b. Astoria, N.Y., Sept. 24, 1968; d. Joseph and Eugenia L. (Libowicz) Tymczyszyn; m. Paul Francis Carnellie, Sept. 10, 1994. BA in Psychology, Rutgers U., 1990; MA in Counseling, Kean Coll., 1993. Addiction counselor III Raritan Bay Med. Ctr., Perth Amboy, N.J., 1993-94, adolescent specialist, 1994-95. Mem. Am. Counseling Assn., Internat. Assn. Eating Disorders Profls. Home: 508 Holly Blvd Bayville NJ 08721

CARNES, DEBORAH POSEY, environmental scientist; b. Clarksville, Tenn, Nov. 18, 1952; d. John Everett and Lessie Inez (Dean) Posey; m. Wilson Clarence Carnes, Jr., Oct. 25, 1974; children: Clare Kay, Aliya Ann, Sarah Lyn. BS in Environ. Sci., Austin Peay State U., 1974; postgrad. in mgmt., Bristol U., 1989. Cert. tchr., Tenn.; lic. real estate salesperson, Tenn. Civil engring. technician U.S. Army C.E., Ft. Campbell, Ky., 1974-75; tchr. Internat. Sch., Riyadh, Saudi Arabia, 1977; health physicist/supr. Oak Ridge (Tenn.) Nat. Lab., 1980-82; environ. engr. Bechtel Nat. Inc., Oak Ridge, 1982-84; project mgr./sr. environ. analyst IT Corp., Knoxville, 1984-88; program mgr. hazardous waste remedial action program Ebasco, Oak Ridge, 1988-89; dir. regulatory compliance dept. Advanced Scis. Inc., Oak Ridge, 1989-91; ea. Dept. of Energy program mgr. Harding Lawson Assocs., Oak Ridge, 1991-92; mgr. fed. programs Rust Remedial Svcs., Inc., Oak Ridge, 1992-94; program mgr. tech. assurance Enterprise Adv. Svcs., Inc., Oak Ridge, 1994—. Co-author: (tech. manuals) Oak Ridge Nat. Lab. Tech. Manual, 1982. Exec. advisor to bd. Am. Mus. of Sci. and Energy Ambassador's Bd., Oak Ridge, 1995-96. Harding Lawson Corp. Oliver E. Merwin scholar, 1992. Mem. Oak Ridge Waste Mgmt. Assn., Nat. Contract Mgmt. Assn., Am. Nuclear Soc., Am. Soc. Quality Control, Beta Beta Beta, Kappa Delta Pi. Republican. Baptist. Office: Enterprise Advisory Svsc Inc 663 Emory Valley Rd Oak Ridge TN 37830

CARNES, JULIE E., federal judge; b. Atlanta, Oct. 31, 1950; m. Stephen S. Cowen. AB, U. Ga., 1972, JD, 1975. Bar: Ga. 1975. Law clk. to Hon. Lewis R. Morgan U.S. Ct. Appeals (5th cir.), 1975-77; asst. U.S. Atty. U.S. Dist. Ct. (no. dist.), Ga., 1978-90; spl. counsel U.S. Sentencing Commn., 1989, commr., 1990—; judge U.S. Dist. Ct. (no. dist.), 1992—. Office: US Courthouse 75 Spring St Ste 2167 Atlanta GA 30303

CARNEY, ANN VINCENT, secondary education educator; b. Slippery Rock, Pa., Feb. 17, 1933; d. Arthur Porter and Leila Felicia (Watson) Vincent; m. Charles Lucien Carney Jr., Dec. 15, 1954 (div. 1974); children: Adrienne Ann, Stephen Vincent. BS, Drexel Inst. Tech., 1955; MEd, U. Pitts., 1972. Cert. tchr., reading specialist, Pa. Tchr. English Allegheny Valley Sch. Dist., Springdale, Pa., 1957-62; reading specialist Gateway Sch. Dist., Monroeville, Pa., 1972—. Mem. AAUW, Internat. Reading Assn., Keystone State Reading Assn., Three Rivers Reading Coun., Phi Kappa Phi, Omicron Nu. Republican. Home: 4013 Impala Dr Pittsburgh PA 15239-2705 Office: Gateway Sch Dist 2609 Mosside Blvd Monroeville PA 15146-3307

CARNEY, JEAN KATHRYN, psychologist; b. Ft. Dodge, Iowa, Nov. 10, 1948; d. Eugene James and Lucy (Devlin) C.; m. Mark Krupnick, Jan. 1, 1977; 1 child, Joseph Carney Krupnick. BA, Marquette U., Milw., 1970; MA, U. Chgo., Chgo., 1984; PhD, U. Chgo., 1986. Registered Clin. Psychologist, Ill. Reporter Milw. Jour., 1971-76, editorial writer, 1976-79; asst. prof. psychology St. Xavier Coll., Chgo., 1985-86; dir. Lincoln Park Clinic, Chgo., 1986-87; pvt. practice psychotherapist Chgo., 1987—; mem. sci. staff Michael Reese Hosp. Med. Ctr., Chgo., 1987—; instr. Northwestern U. Med. Sch., 1991—; lectr. U. Ill. Coll. Medicine, 1993—. Recipient Best Series Articles, 1975, Best Editorial, 1978, Milw. Press Club, William Allen White Nat. Award for Editorial Writing, 1978, Robert Kahn Meml. Award for Research on Aging, Univ. Chgo., 1985. Mem. APA, Ill. Psychol. Assn., Chgo. Assn. Psychoanalytic Psychology. Home: 915 Burns Ave Flossmoor IL 60422-1107 Office: 55 E Washington St Ste 1219 Chicago IL 60602-2108

CARNEY, KATE, actress, director, educator; b. Rice Lake, Wis., Aug. 2, 1933; d. Rexford Hugh and Margot Caroline (Haanstad) C. BS, U. Wis., 1955; MA, Mt. Holyoke Coll., 1958; postgrad., Centre du Théâtre Nationale, 1970, Columbia U. and Case-Western Res. U., 1957-63; Creative Arts fellow U. Colo., 1963. Actress performing in London, Paris, Istanbul, Ankara, Tel Aviv and Nicosia, 1970-72, Off Off-Broadway! An Anthology with Kay Carney, N.Y.C., Boston, Chgo., San Francisco, Vancouver, Balt., Phila., Boston and various U.S. colls., 1973—; performed Tonques, 1985, Camptown Ladies, 1986, Age of Enlightenment, 1986, Vacancy, 1987, Taste of Honey, 1988, N.Y.C., And A Nightingale Sang, 1992, My Fair Lady, 1992, Boston, Washed Up Middle Aged Women, 1993, Dr. Owens-Adair, 1994, Two Boston Immigrants, 1995; dir. Mourning Pictures, Broadway and Lenox Arts Ctr., 1974, A Pretty Passion, Interart Theatre, N.Y.C., 1982, Quilt Pieces, Theatre of Open Eye, N.Y.C., 1983, Superwoman Bites the Dust, Playwright's Platform, Boston, 1984, The Mothers, Ubu Repetory Theatre, 1987, Airport, Theater at St. Peter's, 1988, A Good Time, Playwright's Horizons, 1988, Sleep Disturbances, Am. Renaissance Theatre, 1989, Man with the Killer Pen, New Dramatists, 1991, numerous others; tchr. acting, directing and psychophys. work Hunter Coll., Henry St. Playhouse, SUNY, Purchase, U. Calif.-Santa Cruz, 1977-80; assoc. prof. dept. theatre Smith Coll., Northampton, Mass., 1980-82, Bklyn. Coll., 1983-87; tchr. Ensemble Studio Theatre Inst., 1987, Brandeis U., 1989-92, Pine Manor Coll., 1993—; condr. workshops for profls. in U.S. and abroad, Coll. of Charleston, 1989, Marymount Manhattan Coll., 1988; organizer, trainer La Mama theatre groups, Paris and Tel Aviv; bd. dirs. Bear Rep. Theatre, 1977-79; performed with Open Theater, 1965-67; seminarian with Jerzy Grotowski, 1970. Moratorium organizer, performer Angry Artists Against the War, 1966-70; mem. Performing Artists for Nuclear Disarmament, 1981—, St. Clements Arts in Religious Action Com., 1972-75; organizer Bay Area Women in Theatre Orgn., 1978-80; contbr. articles to profl. jours. Kosciuszko Found. grantee, 1979, SUNY Rsch. Found. grantee, 1976. Mem. Soc. Stage Dirs. and Choreographers, Actors Equity, AFTRA, New England Theatre Conf., Women and Theatre Program, Assn. for Theatre in Higher Edn. (presenter nat. convs.), League Profl. Theatre Women/N.Y. Democrat. Unitarian. Office: Pine Manor Coll Theatre Dept 400 Heath St Chestnut Hill MA 02167-2332

CARNEY, KATHLEEN L., interior designer; b. Cleve., Dec. 19, 1947; d. Joseph Smythe and Irene (Smith) Walsh; m. James A. Carney, July 18, 1970: 1 child, James Kenneth. BA, Barat Coll. Sacred Heart, Lake Forest, Ill., 1969. Cert. interior designer, Ohio, Ill. Tchr. Cleve. Bd. Edn., 1969-71; owner The Mart - Antiques & Interiors, Rocky River, Ohio, 1985—. Jr. League Cleve., 1978—; fundraiser, liaison Malachi House Cleve., 1987—; patron mem. women's com. Cleve. Orch.; active Pioneer Womens bd. Western Res. Acad., Hudson, Ohio, 1987-88; bd. dirs. Cleve. Montessori Assn. Cleve., 1977—; active ARC; mem. Leukemia Soc. Women's Bd., 1994—. Mem. Am. women's Econ. Devel. Corp., Allied Bd. Trade, Nat. Fedn. Ind. Bus., Am. Soc. Interior Designers (allied practitioner), Interior Design Soc. (assoc. mem.), Westwood Country Club. Democrat. Roman Catholic. Home: 65 Kensington Oval Cleveland OH 44116-1504 Office: The Mart 28691 Center Ridge Rd Cleveland OH 44145-3810

CARNEY, MARGARET E., administrative assistant, small business owner; b. Herkimer, N.Y., Apr. 2, 1938; d. Donald Francis and Helen Mary (McLaughlin) Kane; m. John J. Carney Jr., July 18, 1959; children: John III, Caralee, Julie, Christy. BS, Geneseo Coll., 1960. Co-owner, book dealer Carney Books, Oneonta, N.Y., 1978—; sec. United U. Professions, Albany, N.Y., 1983—. election inspector City of Oneonta, 1980—; vol. Planned Parenthood. Mem. NOW, Comm. Workers Am. Democrat. Home: 44 Elm St Oneonta NY 13820 Office: United Univ Professions State Univ Coll Oneonta NY 13820

CARNEY, PHILLITA TOYIA, marketing communications management company executive, business and ministry consultant; b. Chgo., Apr. 18, 1952; d. Phillip Leon Carney and Margaret Clarice (Ewing) Brown. Student, U. Utah, 1971-74; BS in Bus., Westminster Coll., 1976. Ordained to ministry Full Gospel Ch., 1989; state cert. sexual assault advocate counselor and tgn., Chgo., Ill. Corp. tng. dir. U&I Sugar Corp., Salt Lake City, also Moses Lake, Wash., 1976-77, cert. Crisis Intervention, state cert. christian coun. therapist, Indep. Mo.; program coord. Div. on Aging, Seattle, 1977-78; bus. devel. officer Del Green Assoc., Foster City, Calif., 1978-79; regional v.p. Equitec Fin. Group, San Francisco, Irvine and Oakland, Calif., 1979-84, United Resources, Oakland, San Francisco, Nev., 1984-86; owner, mgr. Carney & Assocs., Oakland, 1986; regional v.p. Eastcoast Ops. Benefits Comms. Corp. divsn. Great West Life Ins. Co., Washington, 1986-87; nat. dir. enrollment svcs., nat. plan adminstr. U.S. Conf. Mayors Fringe Benefits Program, MCW Internat., Ltd., 1988—; dir. pub. rels. nat./internat. Liberty Temple Full Gospel Ch. and World Out Reach Ministries, Chgo., 1989—; dep. dir. Ams., Internat. Biog. Centre, 1992; dir. Total One, San Francisco; corp. cons., advisor Am. Intermediation Svcs., San Francisco, 1986; cons. Washington Literacy Council; sr. bus. cons., ptnr. Performance Strategies Inc., San Diego, 1986; ministry cons. Crusaders Ch., Chgo., 1991—; assoc. pastor Higher Love Ministries, Chgo., 1993—, Rsrch Master of Christian Counseling Psychology from Christian Bible Coll. and Seminary, Mo., 1996 ; bus. and ministry cons., 1989—; ch. elder, cons. New Covenant Life Ch., Chgo., 1994—; bd. dirs. Pastors Englewood, 1993—; exec. prodr., host "Focus" Radio Broadcast, Chgo., 1994—, "Viewpoint" Radio Broadcast, Ind., 1995, exec. prodr., host "Life Empowerment ", additional Radio Broadcast, Chgo., 1996; moderator, creator pub. affairs radio program, 1975-76 (Best Pub. Affairs Program award Nat. Pub. Radio 1976); del. White House Conf. on Small Bus., Washington, 1986; mem., lobbyist Concerned Women for Am., 1987—; founder Englewood Cares, Inc., Chgo., 1994—; appointed chairperson media rels. Chgo. Legis. for Chgo. Alternative Policing Strategies, 1995—; columnist CAPS Newsletter Chgo. Defender Citizens Newspaper, 1995—; exec. com. Say Yes Chicago Campaign, 1995—. Recipient award Am. Legion, 1970, DAR, 1970; named Most Admired Woman of Decade, Am. Biog. Inst. Fellow Am. Biog. Inst. Rsch. Assn. (assoc., nat. advisor); mem. Internat. Assn. Fin. Planning, Women Entrepreneurs, Internat. Biog. Ctr. (del. 1992), Bus. and Profl. Women, Sales Mktg. Exec. Assn., Zonta Internat. (pres. 1985—). Avocations: jogging, swimming, reading, writing. Home: 10925 S Wood St Chicago IL 60643-3419

CAROL, JOY HAUPT, cultural organization administrator; b. Lincoln, Nebr., Apr. 28, 1938; d. Wilson J. and Alma J. (Weilage) Haupt. BA in Edn., Nebr. Wesleyan U., 1959; postgrad., Scarritt U., 1960-61; MA in Counseling Psychology, U. Md., 1968; postgrad., NYU, 1974-75, Gen. Theol. Sem., 1996—; LHD (hon.), Nebr. Wesleyan U., 1994. Tchr., dir. Project Head Start various pub. schs., 1959-60, 64-68; project dir. Meth. Ch. Edn. Sys., Karachi, Pakistan, 1961-63; psychol. counselor pub. and pvt. schs., 1969-73; founder, dir. Union Ctr. for Women, Bklyn., 1973-76; assoc. exec. dir. YWCA Bklyn., 1978; mem. staff UN Devel. Program, Suva, Fiji, 1979-80; program officer Ford Found., N.Y.C., 1980-82; program devel. officer Cultural Info. Svcs., N.Y.C., 1983-84; dir. Asia/Pacific region Save the Children, Westport, Conn., 1984-93; dir. internat. programs Christian Children's Fund, Richmond, Va., 1993-95; dir. devel. Internat. Women's Tribune Ctr., N.Y.C., 1996—; cons. UN/World Coun. Chs., N.Y. and Asia, 1976-77, 84, women's orgns., Oslo, 1974. Author: You Don't Have to be Rich to Own a Brownstone, 1971, (Women in Devel. publ.) But We're Not Afraid to Speak Anymore, 1976, (booklet) Already I Feel the Change, 1989; author ofcl. report on end of Internat. Women's Decade, UN Devel. Program, 1985; contbr. numerous articles to mags. Bd. dirs. Vietnamese Meml. Assn., Ctrl. Europe Inst., 1990—; mem. nat. adv. coun., bd. dirs. Nebr. Wesleyan U., 1992—; co-founder self-help cmty. ctr. CHIPS, Bklyn., 1972-75; nat. convernor U.S. Forum on Vietnam, Cambodia, Laos, N.Y., 1990-95; co-founder, vol. Project Reach Youth, N.Y.C., 1965-68; vol. support groups for brain tumor patients at area hosps., Richmond, 1992-94. Named one of Outstanding Women of Am., 1966; named Outstanding Educator in U.S., U.S. Jaycees, Colo., 1966, Outstanding Woman, Bklyn. City Coun., 1970. Mem. AAUW, NOW, Women's Internat. League for Peace and Freedom, Soc. for Internat. Devel. Home: 549 W 123rd St Apt 13-H New York NY 10027 Office: Internat Womens Tribune Ctr 777 UN Plz New York NY 10017

CAROLAN, MADELEINE SOLOWAY, art educator, artist; b. Rochester, N.Y., Oct. 6, 1954; d. Albert Herman and Barbara (Berkowicz) Soloway; m. Christopher Lee Carolan, Oct. 10, 1982; children: Micaela Rose, Naomi Ruth. BFA, Mass. Coll. Art, 1978; MFA, Wash. U., 1981; cert., U. Ga. Cert. tchr., Ga. Art instr. Newton (Mass.) Cmty. Schs., 1974-76, San Francisco Children's Art Ctr., 1989; artist San Francisco, 1983—; art instr. Quinlan Art Ctr., Gainesville, Ga., 1991-93; art tchr. Pace Acad., Atlanta, 1993—; vis. artist Middlesex Sch., Concord, Mass., 1977, Laumeier Sculpture Park, St. Louis, 1980, U. Ark., Little Rock, 1980, Mass. Coll. Art, Boston, 1984. One-woman shows include Jeremy Stone Gallery, San Francisco, 1985, 87, 89 ; exhibited in group shows at R.I. Sch. Design, Woods Gerry Gallery, Providence, 1977, Boston City Hall, 1978, Prudential Life, Boston, 1978, U. Mass., Boston, 1979, Maryville Coll., St. Louis, 1980, Wash. U., 1981, 42nd Cedar City (Utah) Nat., 1983, Meyer Breier Weiss Gallery, San Francisco, 1983, Messing Gallery, St. Louis, 1985, Triton Mus., Santa Clara, Calif., 1985-86, Palo Alto (Calif.) Cultural Ctr., 1986, Jeremy Stone Gallery, 1987, 89, Anushka Gallerie, La Jolla, Calif., 1989, Quinlan Art Ctr., Gainesville, Ga., 1991, Artspace Gallery, Atlanta, 1991, Virginia Breier Gallery, San Francisco, 1992; permanent collections include Norton Agy., Gainesville, Montgomery Securities, San Francisco, Morrison and Foerster Attys., San Francisco, and pvt. collections. Mem. Nat. Art Edn. Assn., Ga. Art Educators Assn. Home: 338 Declaire Way Marietta GA 30067 Office: Pace Acad 966 W Paces Ferry Rd NW Atlanta GA 30327-2648

CARONE, PATRICIA, state legislator; b. Greenville, Pa., Mar. 21, 1943. BA, George Washington U.; MA, Georgetown U. Rep. dist. 12 Pa. Ho. of Reps., 1990—; tchr. Office: 2525 Rochester Rd Ste 201 Cranberry Township PA 16066 also: Pa Ho of Reps State Capitol Rm 18 East Wing Harrisburg PA 17120*

CAROON, LYNNE STANLEY, secondary and elementary educator, coach; b. Tulsa, Jan. 13, 1950; d. Robert James and Mary Helen (Holloway) Stanley; m. Larry Spencer Caroon, July 14, 1984 (dec. June 1990); stepchildren: Joseph Roland, Kathleen Michelle. BS in Edn., Okla. State U., 1972. Comml. loan processer First Nat. Bank (Liberty), Tulsa, 1972-73, intra-bank account processer, 1973-74; tchr., coach, athletic and phys. edn. coord. Holland Hall Sch., Tulsa, 1975—; presenter in field. Mem. BAMC Chancel Choir, Tulsa, 1980—. Holland Hall Sch. summer travel/study grantee, Singapore, 1993. Mem. Quota Internat. (pres. Tulsa 1990-92, gov. 1993-94, sec.-treas. 1995-96, presenter), English Speaking Union. Republican. Methodist. Office: Holland Hall Sch 5666 E 81st St Tulsa OK 74137

CAROSA, ROSINA M., nun, artist; b. Bklyn., July 1, 1940; d. Giocondo Jack and Carmela Lily Carosa. Student, Marymount Coll., 1958-60, Caldwell (N.J.) Coll., 1971-72. Joined Order of St. Clare, 1960. Head art dept. Monastery of St. Clare, Bordentown, N.J., 1973-74, mem. liturgy com., 1981—; retreat dir., novice mistress Monastery of St. Clare, Bolivia, 1975-80; mem. Holy Name Fedn. of Poor Clares, vocation dir., 1988—; instr. Monastery of St. Clare, 1988—; guest spkr., cons. One-woman show The Upstairs Gallery, Bordentown, N.J., 1994; group shows include St. Joseph's Coll., Phila., 1992, Assn. Uniting Religion and Art, Phila., 1992, Engrs. Armory, Phila., 1992, Midwestern Franciscan Fedn., Viterbo Coll., La Crosse, Wis., 1993, Trenton (N.J.) City Mus., 1993, 94, Peter Madero Gallery, N.Y.C., 1994, Smithville Mansion Festival '94, Easthampton, N.J., 1994 (Merit award 1994), N.J. Network, Trenton, 1995, numerous others; contbr. poetry to pubs. Recipient numerous grants; recipient painting awards Gardenstate Water Color Soc. Mems. Show, 1991, 16th Ann. Juried Art Show, Burlington County (N.J.) Cultural and Heritage Dept., 1992, 17th Ann. Juried Art Show, 1993. Mem. Gardenstate Watercolor Soc., Assn. Uniting Religion and Art, Trenton Artist Workshop Assn., New Arts Program. Roman Catholic. Home: 253 Weber Ave Ewing NJ 08638

CARPANZANO, CHRISTINA STEITZ, college administrator; b. Chgo., Dec. 3, 1952; d. Ronald Arthur and Anne Elizabeth (Wolk) Steitz; m. Jay Boundy, May 19, 1979 (div. Jan. 1986); m. Sergio Carpanzano, Dec. 31, 1992; children: Alexander, Anastasia. BA, Lake Forest Coll., 1974; MPA, DePaul U., 1983. Cert. travel cons. Reservation mgr. Internat. Travel Svc., Chgo., 1975-79; sales mgr. Transamerica Air, Chgo., 1979-83; sales profl. United Airlines, Elk Grove Village, Ill., 1983-90; sales mgr. Paging Network, Westchester, Ill., 1990-93; assoc. dean Robert Morris Coll., Chgo., 1992-95; adminstr. Joliet (Ill.) Jr. Coll., 1995—; cons. and advisor Bus. Network, Chgo. Presenter Chgo. Area Bus. Educators, mem. 1993—; mem. Community Svcs., Will County, 1994—. Recipient Outstanding Student award Am. Soc. Pub. Adminstrs., 1983. Mem. AAUW. Democrat. Roman Catholic. Office: Inst Econ Technology Joliet Jr Coll 214 N Ottawa Joliet IL 60432

CARPENTER, CAROL SETTLE, communications executive; b. Schenectady, Oct. 22, 1953; d. Carl Oscar and Ursula Elsen (McEldowney) Settle; m. R. Jay Carpenter, May 4, 1985; children: Reilly, Evie. BBA, Rochester Inst. Tech., 1975, postgrad. Inst. Children's Lit., 1988-91. Mgmt. trainee Lincoln First Bank, Rochester, N.Y., 1976-77; investment sec. Blyth Eastman Dillon, Scottsdale, Ariz., 1977-79; stockbroker E.F. Hutton, Scottsdale, 1979; stockbroker Rauscher Pierce Refsnes, Scottsdale, 1979-81; exec. v.p. RL Kotrozo Inc., Scottsdale, Ariz., 1981-85; asst. v.p. United Bank Ariz., Phoenix, 1985-88; asst. v.p. investments Citibank, Phoenix, 1988-91; freelance greeting card designer, Phoenix, 1991; CFO Warning Comm., Inc. Phoenix, 1992—. Staff vol. Crisis Nursery, Phoenix, 1987; co-pres. Khalsa Sch. Parent Coun., 1994-95; bd. dirs. Khalsa Montessori Elem. Schs., 1995—; mem. Contemporary Art Forum. Named Khalsa Sch. Parent of Yr., 1994-95. Mem. Phi Gamma Nu. Republican. Presbyterian. Club: Phoenix Country. Avocations: music, art, writing for children. Home: 374 E Verde Ln Phoenix AZ 85012-3012

CARPENTER, DAWN MICHELLE, investment banker, political scientist; b. Akron, Ohio, Jan. 9, 1971; d. William Louis and Cheryl Louise (Cameron) Carpenter; m. Edmund John Trepacz, II, July 3, 1993. BA, Am. U., 1992, MA, 1993; M of Pub. Mgmt. in Fin., U. Md., 1996. Mem. congressman's staff U.S. Congress, Washington, 1990, staff mem. House Subcom. on Census, 1991; legal asst. Latham & Watkins, Washington, 1992-94; pub. fin. investment banker Alex. Brown & Sons, 1995—; adj. prof. Am. govt. George Mason U., 1994—; grad. fellow Sch. Pub. Affairs, U. Md., 1995-96; vice-chmn. Arlington County Indsl. Devel. Authority, Arlington, 1993-99. Mem. Golden Key. Democrat. Home: 135 E Baltimore St Baltimore MD 21202

CARPENTER, DOROTHY FULTON, former state legislator; b. Ismay, Mont., Mar. 13, 1933; d. Daniel A. and Mary Ann (George) Fulton; m. Thomas W. Carpenter, June 12, 1955; children: Mary Ione, James Thomas. BA, Grinnell Coll., 1955. Tchr. elem. schs., Houston, and Iowa City, 1955-58; mem. Iowa Ho. Reps., 1980-94, asst. minority floor leader, 1982-88, chair ethics and state govt. coms., 1992-94; ret., 1994. Pres. Planned Parenthood of Iowa, 1970; bd. dirs. Planned Parenthood Fedn. Am., 1977-80; fin. chmn. Episcopal Diocese of Iowa, 1979-80. Recipient Grinnell Coll. Alumni award, 1980. Republican.

CARPENTER, DOROTHY SCHENCK, special education educator; b. Tewksbury, Mass., Feb. 17, 1942; d. William Edmond and Grace (Scott) Schenck; m. Booker Stephen Carpenter, Sept. 12, 1964; children: B. Stephen II, Sean D., Dreux S., Seth B. BA, George Washington U., 1987; MS, Johns Hopkins U., 1996. Cert. tchr., sch. counselor, Md. Sec. U.S. Dept. State AID, Washington, 1960-67; spl. edn. instr. asst. Montgomery County, Md. Pub. Schs., Gaithersburg, 1980-87; spl. edn. tchr. Montgomery County, Md. Pub. Schs., Rockville, 1987—. ballot box judge Mont. Co. Md. Bd. Elections, Clarksburg, 1980-87. Bd. Trustees grantee George Washington U., 1986, Columbia Women's scholar, 1986; Montgomery Coll. grantee, 1979, 80. Mem. NEA, Nat. Art Edn. Assn., Coun. for Exceptional Children, Mont. Co. Edn. Assn., Pi Lambda Theta (sec. 1989-90). Home: 12200 Greenridge Dr Boyds MD 20841-9032

CARPENTER, ELIZABETH JANE, digital equipment company communications executive, operations manager; b. Cleve., Mar. 29, 1949; d. Robert E. and Joan Jaffe. BA, Western Coll., Oxford, Ohio, 1970. Pub. rels. asst. Lennen & Newell/Pacific, Honolulu, 1970-73; account exec. Marschalk Advt., Cleve., 1973-76; cons. Carpenter Advt. & Pub. Rels., Cleve., 1976-80; internat. pub. rels. mgr. Wang Labs., Inc., Boston, 1980-82, advt. mgr., 1982-87; mgr. worldwide comm. CSS Digital Equipment Corp., Merrimack, N.H., 1987-92, advt. mgr. U.S. Svcs. group, 1992—; assoc. producer Am. Treasure, TV spl., 1986, The Entrepreneurs, TV spl., 1986-87; owner Carpenter Antiques, Dennis, Mass. Mem. Cape Cod Antiques Dealers Assn., Boston Advt. Club, Boston Club. Office: Digital Equipment Corp 3 Results Way Marlborough MA 01752-3047

CARPENTER, ELIZABETH MEGGS, secondary school educator; b. Lincolnton, N.C., May 10, 1945; d. Ernest Lee and Chloe Shelton (Barlow) Meggs; m. S. Richardson Carpenter, Sept. 4, 1965; children: Shelley, Susan. BA in French, Radford U., 1966; MA in English, Va. Tech., 1971; student, U. N.C., Greensboro. Cert. adminstr., N.C. Tchr. remedial reading Ironto (Va.) Elem. Sch., 1966-67; English and drama tchr. Floyd (Va.) County H.S., 1967-69; English, French and drama instr. Project Upward Bound., Va. Tech., Blacksburg, 1969-72; English instr. Va. Tech., Blacksburg, 1969-71; English and French tchr. Blacksburg H.S., 1971-76, Wallace O'Neal Day Sch., Southern Pines, N.C., 1979-80, Glenn H.S., Kernersville, N.C., 1985—; lang. arts cons. Sandhills C.C., Southern Pines, 1978; English tchr., chair dept. Bishop McGuinness H.S., Winston-Salem, N.C., 1980-85. Editor ednl. materials. Mem. NEA, ASCD (assoc.), Nat. Coun. Tchrs. English, N.C. Assn. Educators, Forsyth Assn. Classroom Tchrs., Forsyth Assn. Tchrs. English (treas. 1986-88, pres. 1988-92, Outstanding Svc. award 1992), Delta Kappa Gamma (rec. sec. Zeta chpt. 1994—). Office: Glenn HS 1600 Union Cross Rd Kernersville NC 27284

CARPENTER, JOANNE LAVENTIS, art educator, painter; b. Salem, Mass., June 24, 1939; d. Constantine George and Katherine (Stratigakis) Laventis; m. William Morton Carpenter III, Aug. 19, 1962 (div. 1988); 1 child, Matthew. BA, U. Mass., 1961; MA, U. Minn., 1969; MFA, U. Pa., 1993. Tchr. asst. U. Minn., Mpls., 1963-67; instr. Roosevelt U., Chgo., 1968-70; asst. editor Ency. Brittanica, Chgo., 1970-71; faculty Coll. of the Atlantic, Bar Harbor, Maine, 1972—. Mem. Rep. Dem. State Convention, 1982, 92. Mem. Coll. Art Assn., Visual Artists Union. Home: 86 Seawall Rd Southwest Harbor ME 04679 Office: Coll of the Atlantic Eden St Bar Harbor ME 04609

CARPENTER, KATHLEEN ALICE, developer; b. Elmhurst, Ill., May 31, 1949; d. Stephen Joseph and Virginia Alice (Tyler) C. Student, U. Ky., 1968-71. Adminstr. U. Chgo. Hosp. and Clinics, 1973-79; dir. development Andrew Glover Youth Program, N.Y.C., 1980-81, U. Chgo. Grad. Sch. Bus., 1981-91; v.p. Mus. Sci. and Industry, Chgo., 1991-94; pub. Chgo. Philanthropy, 1995—. Mem. Coun. for Advancement and Support of Edn., Alpha Xi Delta. Office: Chgo Philanthropy 60 E Chestnut #409 Chicago IL 60611

CARPENTER, KATHY HARRISON, civil engineer; b. Russellville, Ala., July 15, 1965; d. James Porter and Peggy Evelyn (Jones) Harrison; m. Harvey Clayton Carpenter, Jr., June 10, 1989. BSE, U. Ala., Huntsville, 1990, MSE, 1995. Engr. (coop. student) U.S. Army Space and Strategic Defense Command, Huntsville, 1987-90; engr. U.S. Army Space and Strategic Defense Command, Huntsville, 1990—. Mem. NAFE, ASCE, Jr. League of Morgan County, Decatur (Ala.) Jr. Women's Club, Phi Kappa Phi, Alpha Pi Mu. Methodist. Home: 529 Main St Moulton AL 35650

CARPENTER, MARY CHAPIN, singer, songwriter; b. Princeton, N.J., 1958; d. Chapin and Mary Bowie. BA, Brown U., 1981. Owner GETAREALJOB Music and Why Walk Music. Albums: Hometown Girl, 1987, State of the Heart, 1989, Shooting Straight in the Dark, 1990, Come On Come On, 1992, Stones in the Road, 1994; recs. on CBS, 1987—. Grammy recipient for Best Female Country Vocal Performance for four consecutive years, 1992, 93, 94, 95, Country Album of the Yr., "Stones in the Road", 1995; named Top Female Vocalist by Country Music Assn., 1992, 93, Acad. of Country Music Awards Top New Female Vocalist, 1990, Top Female Vocalist, 1993. Mem. ASCAP. Office: care Clarysage PO Box 42240 Washington DC 20015 also: care Borman Entertainment 1250 6th St Ste 401 Santa Monica CA 90401

CARPENTER, PAMELA PRISCO, bank executive, foreign language educator; b. Norwood, Mass., July 12, 1958; d. Francis Joseph and Helene Louise (Swartz) Prisco; m. Charles Gilbert Carpenter, Oct. 18, 1981; children: Charles, Craig, Cameron. BA summa cum laude, Harvard U., 1980; grad. cert., U. Salamanca, Spain, 1980; postgrad., Boston State Coll., 1980-81. Cert. Spanish tchr., Mass.; lic. real estate sales assoc., Mass. Asst. v.p., account mgr., internat. corr., banking cons. First Nat. Bank of Boston, 1980—; bilingual edn. substitute tchr. Boston English H.S., 1979-80; grades K-2 Spanish tchr. IES Lang. Sch., Westwood, Mass., 1991-92; pvt. Spanish and French tutor, 1980—. Pres. parent adv. bd. Mulberry Childcare and Pre-sch. Ctr., Norwood, 1991-94; mentor Bank of Boston/Hyde Park H.S. Partnership, 1990; sec. C.J. Prescott Elem. Sch. PTO, 1995—. Radcliffe Club of Boston scholar, 1976. Mem. Phi Beta Kappa. Home: 549 Neponset St Norwood MA 02062-5201

CARPENTER, ROXANNE SUE, realtor; b. Lebanon, Pa., Mar. 16, 1952; d. John Harold and Viola Helen (Miller) Ristenbatt; m. Richard Lee Carpenter, Jan. 30, 1971 (div. May 1989); children: Keith Scott, Jeffrey Alan. Lic. real estate salesperson, Pa. Computer operator Good Samaritan Hosp., Lebanon, 1969-82; legal sec. Allen H. Krause, Esquire, Lebanon, 1982; personal sec. Judge John Walter, Lebanon County Courthouse, Lebanon, 1983-87; realtor Suburban Realty, Annville, Pa., 1986-95, Re/Max of Lebanon County, Cleona, Pa., 1995—. Deaconess, mem. consistory St. Mark's United Ch. of Christ, Lebanon, 1990-93; solicitor United Way Lebanon County, 1985-92; pres. Lebanon Women of Today, 1986-87, chmn. Today's Woman, 1985, 86; mem. Lebanon County Dem. Com., 1988—; mem. adv. bd. Big Bros. and Big Sisters, sec.-treas., 1984-86; project chmn. Muscular Dystrophy Lebanon County, 1982-86. Recipient various awards, including Outstanding Officer of Yr. award Lebanon Women of Today, 1987, Pa. Assn. Realtors Excellence Club award, 1988, 89, 90, Pa. Assn. Realtors Excellence Club "Gold" award, 1990. Mem. Nat. Assn. Realtors, Pa. Assn. Realtors (excellence club life mem. 1990), Lebanon County Bd. Realtors, Lebanon Jaycee Women (chmn. Serena Lodge auction 1985), Lebanon Jaycettes (v.p. 1982, pres. 1984, project chmn. 1985, 86, Jaycette of Yr. 1983, Pres. of Yr. 1984). Democrat. Home: 670 Prescott Dr Lebanon PA 17046-8710 Office: Re Max Lebanon County 209 W Penn Ave Cleona PA 17042

CARPENTER, SHIRLEY ANN, grain merchandiser, nurse; b. Logansport, Ind., June 25, 1949; d. Raymond Eugene and Margery Ann (Ruff) Penn; m. James R. Carpenter, Mar. 30, 1968; children: Bret, Brian. ADN, Ind. U., Indpls., 1991. RN, Ind. Mgr. grain origination Ind. Farm Bur. Co-op, Logansport, 1975-87; office mgr., contr. Cole Harwood, Inc., Logansport, 1987-89; obstet. nurse Logansport Meml. Hosp., 1992; staff nurse Ind. U. Hosp., Indpls., 1992; patient care mgr., dir. human resources Chase Ctr., Logansport, 1992-93; grain merchandiser Countrymark Co-op, Indpls., 1993—; CPR instr. AHA, Logansport, 1991—. Mem. allocation com. Cass County United Way, Logansport, 1989; mem. Leadership 2000, N.W. Ind., 1995. Recipient Clin. and Acad. Excellence award Meth. Hosp., Indpls., 1991; Florence Nightengale scholar, 1990. Mem. Nat. Futures Assn., Ind. Hist. Soc., Sierra Club, Alpha Sigma Lambda. Democrat. Home: RR 2 Box 61 Kewanna IN 46939 Office: Pulaski Co Coop and Countrymark Coop Winamac IN 46996

CARPENTER, SUSAN KAREN, lawyer; b. New Orleans, May 6, 1951; d. Donald Jack and Elise Ann (Diehl) C. BA magna cum laude with honors in English, Smith Coll., 1973; JD, Ind. U., 1976. Bar: Ind. 1976. Dep. pub. defender of Ind. State of Ind., Indpls., 1976-81, pub. defender of Ind., 1981—; chief pub. defender Wayne County, Richmond, Ind., 1981; bd. dirs. Ind. Pub. Defender Coun., Indpls., 1981—; Ind. Lawyers Comm., Indpls., 1984-89; trustee Ind. Criminal Justice Inst., INdpls., 1983—. Mem. Criminal Code Study Commn., Indpls., 1981—, Supreme Ct. Records Mgmt. Com., Indpls., 1983—. Mem. Ind. State Bar Assn. (criminal justice sect.), Nat. Legal Aid and Defender Assn., Nat. Assn. Defense Lawyers, Phi Beta Kappa. Office: State Pub Defender 1 N Capitol Ave # 800 Indianapolis IN 46204-2026

CARPENTER-BOGGS, LYNNE ALANE, soil microbiologist; b. Weiser, Idaho, Sept. 24, 1970; d. Wade Ira David and Jacklyn Mae (Westphal) Carpenter; m. Charles Thomas Boggs, Aug. 9, 1992. BS in Biophys. Environ. Studies, Northland Coll., 1991; MS in Soil Sci., Iowa State U., 1994; pre-doctoral student in Soil Sci., Wash. State U., 1994—. Core tutor Northland Coll., Ashland, Wis., 1989-91; tchg. asst. Iowa State U., Ames, 1991-94; fellow Nat. Sci. Found., Iowa State U.,, Ames, Iowa, 1992-94, Nat. Sci. Found. Wash. State U., Pullman, Wash., 1994—. Contbr. articles to profl. jours. Office: Wash State U Dept Crop & Soil Scis 201 Johnson Hall Pullman WA 99164

CARPENTER-MASON, BEVERLY NADINE, health care/quality assurance nurse consultant; b. Pitts., May 23, 1933; d. Frank Carpenter and Thelma Deresa (Williams) Carpenter Smith; m. Sherman Robert Robinson Jr., Dec. 26, 1953 (div. Jan. 1959); 1 child, Keith Michael; m. David Solomon Mason Jr., Sept. 10, 1960; 1 child, Tamara Nadina. Grad. in nursing, Shadyside Hosp. Sch. Nursing, Pitts.; BS, St. Joseph's Coll., North Windham, Maine, 1979; MS, So. Ill. U., 1981; PhD, Columbia Pacific U., 1995. RN, Pa., D.C., Fla. Staff nurse med. surgery, ob-gyn neonatology and pediatrics Pa., N.Y., Wyo., Colo. and Washington, 1954-68; mgr. clinician dermatol. svcs. Malcolm Grow Med. Ctr., Camp Spring, Md., 1968-71; pediatric nurse practitioner Dept. Human Resources, Washington, 1971-73; asst. dir. nursing Glenn Dale Hosp., Md., 1973-81; nursing coord. medicaid div. Forest Haven Ctr., Laurel, Md., 1981-83, spl. asst. to supr. for med. svcs., 1983-84; spl. asst. to supt. for quality assurance Burr. Habilitation Svcs., Laurel, 1984-89; exec. asst. quality assurance coord. Mental Retardation Devel. Disabilities Adminstrn., Washington, 1989-91; also bd. dirs., 1989—; asst. treas. Am. Bd. Quality Assurance Utilization Rev. Physicians, 1988-94, chair exam. com., 1990-93; ret. Mental Retardation Devel. Disabilities Adminstrn., Washington, 1991; bd. dirs. Quality Mgmt. Audits, Inc., 1991-94; coord. quality assurance health svcs. div. UPARC, Clearwater, Fla., 1993-94; owner, prin. BCM Assocs., 1992—; cons., lectr. in field; case study editor, mem. jour. editorial bd. Am. Coll. Med. Quality, 1985—, chmn. publs. com., 1987—, asst. treas., 1988-93; mem. Am. Bd. Quality Assurance and Utilization Rev. Physicians, 1984—; chief proctor ABQAURP exam. com., 1995—; mem. exec. com. Am. Found. for Edn. in Healthcare Quality, 1995—. Contbr. articles to profl. jours. Mem., star donor ARC Blood Drive, Washington, Md., 1975-91; chair nominations com. Prince Georges Nat. Coun. Negro Women, Md., 1984-85. Recipient awards Dept. Air Force and D.C. Govt., 1966-92, Della Robbia Gold medallion Am. Acad. Pediatrics, 1972, John P. Lamb Jr. Meml. Lectureship award East Tenn. State Y., 1988, Woman of Yr., 1990, 91, 92, 93, 94, 95, 96. Mem. NAFE, Am. Assn. Mental Retardation (conf. lectr. 1988), Am. Coll. Utilization Rev. Physicians, Assn. Retarded Citizens, Healthcare Quality Inst., Top Ladies of Distinction (1st v.p. 1986-91), Internat. Platform Assn., Order Ea. Star (Achievement award Deborah chpt. 1991), Am. Bd. Quality Assurance Utilization Rev. Physicians (Chmn. of Yr. award 1992, presdl. citation, Calvin R. Openshaw Svc. award 1993). Democrat.

CARPER, GERTRUDE ESTHER, artist, marina owner; b. Jamestown, N.Y., Apr. 13, 1921; d. Zenas Mills and Virgie (Lytton) Hanks; m. J. Dennis Carper, Apr. 5, 1942; children: David Hanks, John Michael Dennis. Student violinist, Nat. Acad. Mus., 1931-41; diploma fine arts, Md. Inst. of Art, 1950; voice student, Frazier Gange, Peabody Inst. Music, 1952-55. Interior decorator O'Neill's (Importers), Balt., 1942-44; auditor Citizens Nat. Bank, Covington, Va., 1945-46; owner, developer Essex Yacht Harbour Marina, Balt., 1955—, owner, developer St. Michael's Sanctuary wildlife preserve, 1965—. Jewelry designer, 1987—; portrait artist, 1947—; exhibited one-woman shows Ferdinand Roten Gallery, Balt., 1963, Highfield Salon, Balt., 1967, Le Salon des Nations a Paris, 1985, Ducks and Geese of North Am., 1986, Series of Lighthouses, 1991; exhibited group shows Md. Inst. Alumni Show, 1964, Essex Libr., 1981, Hist. Preservation of Am., Hall of Fame, 1989, others; works included in collections including Prestige de la Peinture d'Aujourd'hos dans le Monde, 1990, Artists and Masters of the Twentieth Century, 1991; author: Expressions for Children, 1985, Fidere, 1993, Mentation, 1993; contbr. articles and poetry to ch. publs. and newspapers. Vol. tchr. of retarded persons, 1942—; leader Women's Circle at local Presbyn. chs., 1952-87, mem. 40 yrs. of choir svc. Mem. Md. Inst. Art Alumni Assn. (life), Grand Coun. World Parliament of Chivalry (Nobless of Humanity citation). Office: Essex Yacht Harbour Marina 500 Sandalwood Rd Baltimore MD 21221-5830

CARPIO, CECILIA, counselor; b. El Paso, Tex., June 4, 1949; d. Pedro and Maria de la Luz (Mendoza) C. BS, U. Tex. El Paso, 1977. Cert. tchr., Tex. Tchr. El Paso Ind. Sch. Dist., 1978-93, coord. at-risk, 1993—. Mem. NEA, PTA, Tex. State Tchrs. Assn., El Paso Tchrs. Assn. (v.p., bd. dirs.), El Paso Consultation Assn. (chairperson), Transmountain Optimist, Nat. Dem. Club (pres. 1991-93), Alpha Delta Kappa (historian, v.p., pres.). Democrat. Roman Catholic. Home: 11231 Peacepipe El Paso TX 79936 Office: Magoffin Mid Sch 4931 Hercules El Paso TX 79904

CARR, BESSIE, retired middle school educator; b. Nathalie, Va., Oct. 10, 1920; d. Henry C. and Sirlena (Ewell) C. BS, Elizabeth City Coll., N.C., 1942; MA, Columbia U. Tchrs. Coll., 1948, PhD, 1950, EdD, 1952. Cert. adminstr., supr., tchr. Prin. pub. sch., Halifax, Va., 1942-47, Nathalie-Halifax County, Va., 1947-51; prof. edn. So. U., Baton Rouge, 1952-53; supr. schs. Lackland Schs., Cin., 1953-54; prof. edn. Wilberforce U., Ohio, 1954-55; tchr. Leland Sch., Pittsfield, Mass., 1956-60; chair math. dept., tchr. Lakeland Mid. Sch., N.Y., 1961-83. Founder, organizer, sponsor 1st Math Bowl and Math Forum in area, 1970-76; founder Dr. Bessie Carr award Halifax County Sr. High Sch., 1962. Mem. Nat. Women's Hall of Fame. Mem. AAUW (auditor 1970-85), Delta Kappa Gamma (auditor internat. 1970-76), Assn. Suprs. of Math. (chair coordinating council 1976-80), Ret. Tchrs. Assn., Black Women Bus. and Profl. Assn. (charter mem. Senegal, Africa chpt.). Democrat. Avocations: travel, photography, souvenirs.

CARR, BONNIE JEAN, professional ice skater; b. Chgo., Sept. 29, 1947; d. Nicholas and Agnes Marie (Moran) Musashe; m. James Bradley Carr, Dec. 8, 1984; children: Brittany Jean, James Bradley II, Brooke Anderson. BS, Northwestern U., 1969; JD (hon.), Loyola U., Chgo., 1978. Skater Adventures on Ice, Mpls., 1961; prin. skater Jamboree on Ice, Chgo., 1961-68; society editor The Free Press, Colorado Springs, Colo., 1969; prin. skater, publicist on tour, asst. lighting dir., tour ednl. tutor Holiday on Ice Internat., 1970-74; skating dir. William McFetridge Sports Ctr., Chgo., 1975-86; choreographer, prin. skater Ice Time, USA, Mundelein, Ill., 1975—; skating coach St. Bronislava Athletic Club, Chgo., 1967-69; publicity dir. Amateur Skating Assn. Ill., Chgo., 1968; founder, dir. skating programs for blind, hearing impaired and mentally handicapped, Chgo., 1975-85; physical fitness advisor Exec. Health Seminars, Chgo., 1979; founder, dir. skating programs Fred Hutchinson Cancer Rsch. Ctr., Seattle, 1985-86; guest speaker Am. Cancer Soc., Columbia, S.C., 1973; conditioning coach Riverside Wellness and Fitness Ctr., Richmond, Va., 1989-91, Southampton Rec. Assn., Richmond, 1991-94; figure & speed skating coach Va. Spl. Olympics, 1991—. Recipient Key to City, Mobile, Ala., 1973, Service Recognition award Special Olympics, Chgo., 1984. Mem. Am. Guild Variety Artists, Am. Coun. on Exercise (cert. 1990-96). Roman Catholic. Home: 1931 Albion Rd Midlothian VA 23113-4148 Office: Ice Time USA 28800 N Gilmer Rd Mundelein IL 60060-9558

CARR, CAMILLE RUSS, elementary education educator; b. Montgomery, Ala., Mar. 20, 1942; d. Kirvin Clarence Hobbie and Dorothy Mildred (Russ) Armstrong; m. Thomas Edward Bumpass, Aug. 27, 1960 (div. May 1979); children: Dorothy Elizabeth, Thomas Edward Jr.; m. Charles Howard Carr, Aug. 15, 1979. AS, Kilgore (Tex.) Coll., 1973; BS, U. Tex., Tyler, 1975. Cert. elem. edn. Elem. tchr. Mozelle Johnston Elem. Sch., Longview, Tex., 1975-79, Spring Shadow Elem. Sch., Houston, 1979-82; elem. gifted tchr. Francone Elem., Houston, 1982-85, Gilmer (Tex.) Elem., 1985—; cons. Region VII Svc. Ctr., Kilgore, 1992-94; trainer N.J. Writing Project in Tex., Spring, 1992—. Co-author: The Spring Branch-Texas Express, 1982. Dir. Boys and Girls Missionary Crusade Assembly of God Ch., Gilmer, 1985—. Mem. Internat. Reading Assn., Assn. Tex. Profl. Educators (campus rep. 1985—).

CARR, GLADYS JUSTIN, publishing company executive; b. N.Y.C.; d. Jack and Mollie (Marmor) C. B.A., Smith Coll., M.A.; postgrad., Cornell U. Sr. editor Prentice-Hall, Inc., Englewood Cliffs, N.J., 1969; exec. editor Cowles Communications, Inc., N.Y.C., 1969-71; editorial dir. Am. Heritage Press, N.Y.C., 1971-75; sr. editor McGraw-Hill, Inc., N.Y.C., 1975-81, editor in chief, editorial dir., chmn. editorial bd., 1981-89, v.p., pub., 1988-89; v.p., pub. HarperCollins Pubs., Inc., N.Y.C., 1989—. Pub. and editor books by James Baldwin, Anthony Burgess, Erica Jong, Erma Bombeck, Philip Caputo, Brenda Maddox, Stuart Woods, Leon Uris, others; contbr. articles, revs. and poetry to profl. jours. Marjorie Hope Nicholson trustee fellow Smith Coll.; vis. Ford Found. fellow, Walter Francis Wilcox fellow. Mem. PEN Am. Ctr., Women's Media Group, Phi Beta Kappa. Club: Smith Coll. (N.Y.C.). Home: 920 Park Ave New York NY 10028-0208 also: 1 Boulder Ln East Hampton NY 11937-1047 Office: HarperCollins Pubs Inc 10 E 53rd St New York NY 10022-5244

CARR, IRIS CONSTANTINE, artist, writer; b. Smyrna, Turkey, Aug. 4, 1922; d. John and Julia Kyrides Constantine; m. Herman Edgar Carr Jr., 1947; 3 children. Diploma in dental nursing, Boston Sch. Dental Nursing, 1942; BA, Simmons Coll., 1970, postgrad., 1990-91; postgrad., DeCordova Mus. Sch., 1986—. Anesthetist for oral surgeon, Boston, 1942-43; exec. med. sec. Boston Evening Clinic, 1943-44; lab. sec., dir. Boston Dispensary, 1944-45, Children's Hosp., Boston, 1944-47; editl. asst. Internat. Rsch. and Publs., 1947—; developed improved interlibr. loan svc. Wellesley Coll. Libr., 1964. One woman show at Needham Village Gallery, 1991; contbr. articles to profl. pubsl. Mem. Mass. Med. Soc. Alliance (pub. rels. com. 1985-94, contbg. editor 1995—), Dedham Art Assn. (featured artist), Wellesley Soc. Artists (bd. dirs., registration com. 1994—), Needham Art Assn. (bd. dirs., publicity com., pres. 1989-90, co-inaugurated 1st art gallery 1990). Democrat. Home: 14 Ingleside Rd Needham MA 02192

CARR, JACQUELYN B., psychologist, educator; b. Oakland, Calif., Feb. 22, 1923; d. Frank G. and Betty (Kreiss) Corker; children: Terry, John, Richard, Linda, Michael, David. BA, U. Calif., Berkeley, 1958; MA, Stanford U., 1961; PhD, U. So. Calif., 1973. Lic. psychologist, Calif; lic. secondary tchr., Calif. Tchr. Hillsdale High Sch., San Mateo, Calif., 1958-69, Foothill Coll., Los Altos Hills, Calif., 1969—; cons. Silicon Valley Companies, U.S. Air Force, Interpersonal Support Network, Santa Clara County Child Abuse Council, San Mateo County Suicide Prevention Inc.,Parental Stress Hotline, Hotel/Motel Owners Assn.; co-dir. Individual Study Ctr.;

supr. Tchr. Edn.; adminstr. Peer Counseling Ctr.; led numerous workshops and confs. in field. Author: Learning is Living, 1970, Equal Partners: The Art of Creative Marriage, 1986, The Crisis in Intimacy, 1988, Communicating and Relating, 1984, 3d edit., 1991, Communicating with Myself: A Journal, 1984, 3d edit., 1991; contbr. articles to profl. jours. Mem. Mensa. Club: Commonwealth. Home: 4788 Raspberry Pl San Jose CA 95129 Office: Foothill College 12345 El Monte Ave Los Altos CA 94022-4504

CARR, LINDA JULIA, human resources specialist; b. Lansing, Mich., June 7, 1950; d. Joseph Garner and Ann Lucille (Shipley) Brooks; m. Alan Barry Carr, Jan. 17, 1937; children: Trevor Andres Douglass, Tara Lynn Zimmerman. AA, Howard Cmty. Coll., Columbia, Md., 1985; BS in behavioral sci., Univ. Md. Univ. Coll., 1981; AA in bus. adminstrn., Howard Cmty. Coll., 1994; postgrad., Tex. A&M Internat. Univ., 1996—. Sec. to divsn. head Libr. of Congress HR Divsn., Washington, 1984-87, head employment office, 1987-89, human resources specialist, 1989-91; adminstrv. officer Libr. of Congress Manuscript Divsn., Washington, 1991-94; human resources specialist Tex A&M Internat. Univ., Lardeo, Tex., 1994—. Mem. Hickory Ridge Architecutral Com., Columbia, Md., 1986-89, chair., 1988-93; mem. Hickory Ridge Architecutral Appeals Com., 1988-93, vice chair., 1988-90. Recipient Pres.'s scholarship Univ. Md., 1989, 90, 91. Mem. AAUW, Laredo Assn. Human Resources, Phi Kappa Phi, Alpha Sigma Lamda, Phi Theta Kappa. Home: 704 Dellwood Laredo TX 78045 Office: Tex A&M Internat Univ 5201 University Blvd Laredo TX 78041-1999

CARR, LISA COLETTE, college administrator; b. East Orange, N.J., Dec. 9, 1961; d. Carson Jr. and Josephine Earlene (Washington) Carr; m. Donald Allen Tutt, May 12, 1990; 1 child, Paige Temperance Angelique Tutt. AAS, SUNY, Delhi, 1981; BA, SUNY, Albany, 1988; MS, SUNY, Troy, 1995. Asst. mgr. Wendy's, Albany, N.Y., 1982-83, Pizza Hut, Saratoga, N.Y., 1983-85; shift supr. Pizza Hut, Menands, N.Y., 1985-88; asst. dir. admissions Siena Coll., Loudonville, N.Y., 1988-90; asst. dir. HEOP Russell Sage Coll., Troy, N.Y., 1990-92, dir. higher edn. opportunity program, 1992-95, assoc. dir. admissions, 1995-96, dir. admissions, 1996—. Facilitator support groups Boy's and Girl's Club, Albany, N.Y., 1988-93, Liberty Partnership, Troy, 1993-95, Troy H.S.-Transisions, 1994-95; lobbyist Higher Edn. Opportunity, Albany, N.Y., 1990-93. Mem. AAUW, Nat. Acad. Advising Assn., Nat. Alliance Black Sch. Educators, Capital Dist. Assn. Counseling and Devel., N.Y. State Assn. Woman in Higher Edn., Troy Area United Ministries (bd. dirs.), Alpha Kappa Alpha (asst. sec. 1994-95). Democrat. Office: Russell Sage Coll 51 First St Troy NY 12180

CARR, MARIE PINAK, book distribution company executive; b. Buffalo, June 17, 1954; d. Henry and Hildegard (Poech) Pinak; m. Richard Wallace Carr, Oct. 18, 1980; children: Katharine Marie, Ann Louise, Elizabeth Ashby. BS, Syracuse U., 1976. Cancer microbiologist Nat. Cancer Inst., Rockville, Md., 1976-78; mktg. specialist Precision Sci., Washington, 1978-80; art importer Dicmar Trading Co., Inc., Washington, 1981-83; book dist. Dicmar Trading Co., Inc., Silver Spring, Md., 1983—. Co-author: The Willard Hotel, 1986. Bd. dirs. Salvation Army Women's Aux., Washington, 1982-94, pres., 1990-91; bd. dirs. Am. Cancer Soc., Washington, 1988-90; co-chmn. Nat. Cancer Ball, 1989, 90; active Jr. League Washington, 1987-90. Mem. Washington Club. Republican. Roman Catholic. Office: Dicmar Trading Co Inc 8850 Brookville Rd Silver Spring MD 20910-1803

CARR, MARSHA HAMBLEN, special education educator; b. Dunlap, Tenn., Nov. 28, 1961; d. Jackie Robert and Molly Ann (Johnson) Hamblen; m. Lonnie Gerron Carr, Feb. 26, 1980; 1 child, Gerra Sheree. BS in Spl. Edn. magna cum laude, Tenn. Tech. U., 1989, MA in Supervision of Instrn., 1992. Resource tchr. Sequatchie County Bd. Edn., Dunlap, 1989-90; early childhood spl. edn. tchr. Project CHILD Sequatchie County Bd. Edn., Dunlap, 1990-91, coord., 1991—; presenter Tenn. Young Children Assn., Chattanooga, 1992—; mem. adv. bd. Tenn. Early Intervention System, Chattanooga, 1990—; behavior mgmt. cons., Dunlap, 1990—. Active First Bapt. Ch. of Dunlap. Mem. NEA, Tenn. Edn. Assn., Sequatchie County Edn. Assn., Phi Kappa Phi, Delta Kappa Gamma, Pi Lambda Theta, Kappa Delta Pi. Democrat. Baptist. Home: 1043 Tram Trl Dunlap TN 37327-4446 Office: Project CHILD PO Box 819 Dunlap TN 37327-0819

CARR, PATRICIA WARREN, adult education educator; b. Mobile, Ala., Mar. 24, 1947; d. Bedford Forrest and Mary Catherine (Warren) Slaughter; m. John Lyle Carr, Sept. 26, 1970; children: Caroline Elise, Joshua Bedford. BS in Edn., Auburn U., 1968, MEd, 1971. Tchr. DeKalb County Schs., Atlanta, 1969-70; counselor Dept. Defense Schs., Okinawa, Japan, 1972-75; tchr. Jefferson County Schs., Jefferson, Ga., 1975-76; counselor Clarke County Schs., Athens, Ga., 1976-78; tchr. Fairfax County Schs., Adult and Community Edn., Fairfax, Va., 1980—; instrnl. supr. Vol. Learning Program; coord. Enrichment for Srs. Program Fairfax Area Agy. on Aging and Adult and Cmty. Edn., 1985-89; cons. State Va. Dept. Edn., 1984—, Va. Assn. Adult and Cmty. Edn., 1987, Commn. on Adult Basic Edn., 1988; instr. George Mason U., Fairfax, 1985. Tchr. Met. Meml. United Meth. Ch., Washington, 1981—; co-leader McClean, Va. troop Girl Scouts U.S., 1985-88. Mem. Am. Assn. Adult and Community Edn., Smithsonian Nat. Assocs., No. Va. Assn. Vol. Adminstrs., Va. Assn. Adult and Community Edn., Greater Washington Reading Coun. Methodist. Office: Fairfax County Adult & Community Edn Woodson Adult Ctr 9525 Main St Fairfax VA 22031

CARRAHER, MARY LOU CARTER, art educator; b. Cin., Mar. 9, 1927; d. John Paul and Martha Leona (Williams) Carter; m. Emmett Pearl Carraher, Nov. 6, 1943 (div. July 1970); children: Candace Lou Holsenbeck-Smith, Michael Emmett, Cathleen Kruska. Student, U. Cin., 1946-48, Calif. State U., 1973-74. Lifetime credential in adult edn.: art, ceramics, crafts. Office clk. Foy Paint Co., Norwood, Ohio, 1945-47; substitute tchr. Cobb County Schs., Smyrna, Ga., 1961-63; art tchr. pvt. lessons Canyon Country, Calif., 1968-72; adult edn. art tchr. Wm. S. Hart H.S. Dist., Santa Clarita, Calif., 1973-96; children's art and calligraphy cmty. svcs. Coll. of the Canyons, Santa Clarita, Calif., 1976-96; founder, bd. dirs. Santa Clarita Art Guild, 1972-80; art dir. European tours Continental Club, Canyon Country, 1977-81; art tour guide and travel cons. Northridge (Calif.) Travel, 1981-91; vol. art tchr. stroke patients Henry Newhall Meml. Hosp., Valencia, Calif., 1993-96; art tchr. for respite care program, Newhall, Calif., 1995-96, Respite Care Ctr., Santa Clarita Valley Sr. Ctr., 1995-96. Artist, author: History of Moreland School District, San Jose, California, 1965; artist: Paintings for each season of Church Year, 1970's, Baptismal painting, 1988, Sr. Center Watercolor; Center Scenes, 1993, Watercolors of Christmas Charity Home Tour, 1993. Tchr., mem. Santa Clarita United Meth. Ch., 1966-96; judge for art contests and exhibits, Santa Clarita, 1973-96; mem. Santa Clarita Valley Hist. Soc., 1989-96; mem. Alumni Assn., Norwood (Ohio) City Schs., 1993-96. Recipient Bravo award nomination for Outstanding Achievement in Art, 1995, Sr. of the Yr. Santa Clarita Valley Sr. Ctr., 1995, Christian Svc. award Santa Clarita United Meth. Ch., 1988. Mem. Santa Clarita Valley Arts Coun., Hosp. Home Tour League, Nat. Women in the Arts. Republican. Methodist.

CARREL, GAEL SMITH, community volunteer; b. Detroit, Mar. 30, 1938; d. Gale Clifton and Dorothy Elizabeth (Butler) Smith; m. Jack James Carrel, Apr. 11, 1959; children: Jack James, Catherine Gale Carrel-Montano. pres. bd. dirs. Sunshine Town, Bogalusa, La., 1987-91, Bogalusa Mental Health Adv. Bd., 1991-94; sec. Region IX mental health adv. bd., Five Parish Region, La., 1993—; pres. bd. dirs. Northlake AIDS Network, 1994-96; chair Christmas in the Park Commn., Bogalusa, 1995—. Home: 1415 Colorado St Bogalusa LA 70427

CARRERE, TIA (ALTHEA JANAIRO), actress; b. Honolulu, 1967; d. Alexander and Audrey Janairo. Profl. model. Film appearances include: Zombie Nightmare, 1987, Aloha Summer, 1988, Showdown in Little Tokyo, 1991, Harley Davidson and the Marlboro Man, 1991, Wayne's World, 1992, Rising Sun, Fatal Mission, 1990, Instant Karma, 1990, True Lies, My Generation, The Immortals; TV guest appearances include The A-Team, 1986, MacGyver, 1986, 88, Tour of Duty, 1987, Tales for the Crypt, 1992, The New Hollywood Squares, Murphy's Law, General Hospital, 1983-85, The Road Raiders, 1989, Fine Gold, 1990; presenter The MTV Movie Awards, 1992, (spl.) Circus of the Stars. Recipient Female Star 1994 award NATO/Sho West. Office: United Talent Agy 9560 Wilshire Blvd 5th Fl Beverly Hills CA 90212*

CARRICK, KATHLEEN MICHELE, law librarian; b. Cleve., June 11, 1950; d. Michael James and Genevieve (Wenger) C. BA, Duquesne U., Pitts., 1972; MLS, U. Pitts., 1973; JD, Cleve.-Marshall U., 1977. Bar: Ohio 1977, U.S. Ct. Internat. Trade 1983. Rsch. asst. The Plain Dealer, Cleve., 1973-75; head reference SUNY, Buffalo, 1977-78, assoc. dir., 1978-80, dir., asst. prof., 1980-83; dir., assoc. prof. law Case Western Res. U., Cleve., 1983—; cons. Mead Data Central, Dayton, Ohio, 1987-91. Author: Lexis: A Research Manual, 1989; contbr. articles to profl. jours. Fellow Am. Bar Found.; mem. ABA, Am. Law Inst., Am. Assn. Law Librs., Assn. Am. Law Schs., Scribes. Home: 1317 Burlington Rd Cleveland OH 44118-1212 Office: Case Western Res U 11075 East Blvd Cleveland OH 44106-5409

CARRICO, DEBORAH JEAN, special education teacher; b. East St. Louis, Ill., Dec. 6, 1948; d. Leo Anthony and Edna Linda (Willett) C. BS, Murray State U., 1972; MA, Calif. State U., L.A., 1978. Cert. tchr., Calif. Tchr. Bonita Unified Sch. Dist., San Dimas, Calif., 1973-74, L.A. County Office Edn., Downey, 1974—; mentor L.A. County Office of Edn., 1989—. Bd. dirs. Hope House, Anaheim, Calif., 1988—. Mem. Coun. for Exceptional Children, Phi Kappa Phi. Democrat. Roman Catholic. Office: LA County Office Edn 9300 Imperial Hwy Downey CA 90242-2813

CARRINGTON, BETTY WATTS, nurse midwife, educator; b. W.Va., Mar. 14, 1936; d. James Henry and Odessa E. Watts; m. Homer S.I. Carrington, Aug. 17, 1958; children: Michael S., Lynn Ellen. BSN, U. Mich., 1958; MS, Columbia U., 1971, EdD, 1986. Cert. nurse-midwife. Dir. nurse-midwifery svc. Maternity-Infant Care Project/Brookdale Hosp. Affiliation, Bklyn., 1972-79; assoc. prof. nurse-midwifery SUNY Health Sci. Ctr., Bklyn., 1979-86; dir. grad. program in nurse-midwifery Columbia U. Sch. Nursing, N.Y.C., 1986-91; nurse-midwife rsch. assoc. dept. obstetrics and gynecology Harlem Hosp. Ctr., N.Y.C., 1989—; cons. minority recruitment and retention, 1981—. Contbr. articles to profl. jours. WHO fellow, Tanzania, 1983. Fellow Am. Coll. Nurse Midwives (nat. v.p. 1973-74); mem. NAUW (L.I. br. pres. 1986-90, chairperson nat. program standards com. 1994—), Sigma Theta Tau. Home: 11931 220th St Jamaica NY 11411-2010

CARRINGTON, MARIAN DENISE, university administrator, counselor, motivational speaker; b. Smithfield, N.C., Aug. 12, 1960; d. Thomas Martin and Marian Louise (Revels) Whitley; m. William Earl Carrington III; children: Wynnona Alexis, Crystal Elizabeth. BS, Old Dominion U., 1982; MA, Hampton U., 1991. Coord. cooperative edn. and internships Hampton (Va.) U., 1982-90; corporate recruitment coord. Christopher Newport U., Newport News, Va., 1990-91, dir. multicultural student affairs, 1991—; founder MARVEL M. Presentations, Hampton, 1990—, The Coun. for Humanity, Urban Renewal and Cmty. Wholeness, 1994—; founder, dir. New Beginnings for God's Women, Hampton, 1994—; cons. U. Ala., Tuscaloosa, 1985. Mem. exec. bd. YWCA Phyllis Wheatley Br., Newport News, 1992—, Hampton Coalition for Youth, Hampton, 1993—, Machen Elem. Sch. PTA, Hampton, 1994-95, Colonial Coast Girl Scout Coun., Norfolk, Va., 1994. Grantee U.S. Dept. Edn., 1983-90, State Coun. Higher Edn., 1990-94, 93-96. Mem. Va. Assn. Black Faculty and Adminstrs., Va. Counselor's Assn., Vocat. Edn. Adv. Coun. Home: 56 Banister Dr Hampton VA 23666 Office: Christopher Newport U Office Multicultural Student Affairs Newport News VA 23606

CARROLL, ADORNA OCCHIALINI, real estate executive; b. New Britain, Conn., Aug. 24, 1952; d. Antonio and Mary Ida (Reney) Occhialini; m. Christoper P. Buchas, Sept. 7, 1974 (div. Nov. 1982); 1 child, Jenna Rebecca; m. John Francis Carroll, Oct. 15, 1983; children: Jordan Ashley, Sean William. BA in Philosophy, Cen. Conn. State U., 1975; grad., Realtors Inst., 1989. Lic. real estate broker, real estate agt. Dir. therapeutic recreation program Ridgeview Rest Home, Cromwell, Conn., 1974, Meadows Convalescent Home, Manchester, Conn., 1975, Andrew House Health Care, New Britain, 1976; owner, mgr. Liquor Locker, Newington, Conn., 1977-87; owner, broker A.O. Carroll & Co., Newington, 1985-93, A. O. Carroll & Agostini Co., Kensington, Conn., 1994—; ptnr. Marco Realty & Devel. Co., Newington, 1978—. Mem. Nat. Assn. Realtors (dir. 1995, 96, multiple listing policy forum 1993, legis./polit. forum 1993, mem. svcs. com. 1994, 96, mem. recruitment and retention forum 1994, mem. state fiscal affairs com. 1995, personal asst. working group 1995, vice chair membership devel. and promotion forum 1996, edn. forum 1995), Conn. Assn. Realtors (v.p.-at-large 1992-94, vice-chair legislation 1991, mem. legis. policy & RPAC comss. 1991, conv. com. 1990, pres.-elect 1996, polit. affairs com. 1988, 89, chair state MLS task force 1994, chair agy. task force 1994, 95, chair personal assts. 1995, chair comms./tech. com. 1995), Greater New Britain Assn. Realtors (local dir. 1991, 92, chair legislation & nominating coms. 1991-92, pres. 1990, 93, 96, chair bylaws com. & state conv. 1990, pres.-elect 1989, chair programs & polit. affairs & AM HM WK 1988, spkr. 1989—, Realtor of Yr. 1991, state dir. 1995), Nat. Package Store Assn., Conn. Package Store Assn. (legis. lobbyist 1984-88, pres. 1986-88, Disting. Svc. award 1985), Greater Hartford Package Store Assn. (pres. 1981-82), Marchegian Soc. New Britain (pres. 1992, corr. sec. & chair budget 1991), Newington C. of C. (bd. dirs. 1987-88, chmn. legis. 1988). Home: 23 Occhialini Ct Newington CT 06111-4754 Office: AO Carroll & Agostini Co 742 Worthington Rdg Berlin CT 06037-3233

CARROLL, AILEEN, retired librarian; b. Mason, Wis., Aug. 7, 1914; d. John P. and Mary (Noonan) C. BA, De Paul U., 1938; MA, Northwestern U., 1940; MLS, Rosary Coll., 1965. Tchr. Chgo. Pub. Schs., 1940-52; systems media dir., libr. organizer Cook County Pub. Schs., 1952—. Author and pub. of children's poetry. Vol. St. Vincent's Orphanage, Chgo., Sacred Heart Home for the Aged, Chgo. Recipient scholarship AAUW, 1991. Mem. AAUW (Western Springs, Ill.), LWV, Rep. Club of Oak Park, Art Group of Western Springs. Home: 712 Courtland Cir Western Springs IL 60558-1945

CARROLL, BARBARA, musician, composer, singer; b. Worcester, Mass., Jan. 25, 1925; d. David Louis and Lillian Rose (Lavine) Coppersmith; m. Joseph Shulman, Sept. 20, 1954 (dec. Aug. 2, 1957); m. Bertram Joseph Block, Oct. 7, 1960 (dec. July 9, 1986); 1 child, Suzanne Elizabeth. Student, New Eng. Conservatory of Music, 1943-44; D in Music (hon.), Pine Manor Coll., 1980. Leader Barbara Carroll Trio, 1951-60. Appearances for 3 months Bemelmans Bar, The Carlyle, N.Y.C., spring and fall; Broadway appearances in Me and Juliet; TV appearances include All My Children, 1983, Today Show, Tonight Show, CBS Sunday Morning, 1995; (albums) Have You Met Miss Carroll, It's a Wonderful World, (CDs) Live At the Carlyle, This Heart of Mine, Everything I Love, Old Friends. Bd. mem. Duke Ellington Meml. Fund. Mem. ASCAP, Songwriter's Guild, Friars Club.

CARROLL, BONNIE, publisher, editor; b. Salt Lake City, Nov. 20, 1941. Grad. high sch., Ogden, Utah. Owner The Peer Group, San Francisco, 1976-78; pub., editor The Reel Directory, Cotati, Calif., 1978—. Pub., editor The Reel Thing newsletter, San Francisco, 1977-78. Mem. Assn. Visual Communicators (bd. dirs. 1987-90), No. Calif. Women in Film, San Francisco Film Tape Council (exec. dir. 1979-81). Office: The Reel Directory PO Box 866 Cotati CA 94931-0866

CARROLL, FOREST ANN, travel company executive; b. St. Augustine, Fla., June 20, 1981; d. John Franklin and Betty Sue (Murrell) Loyd; m. Daniel Otis Carroll, June 20, 1981; children: Laura Raine, Timothy Marshall. AD, Midway Coll., 1981. Paralegal Hastie, Murray and Carter, Lexington, Ky., 1981-83; paralegal litigation Stites & Harbison, Louisville, 1985-87; bookkeeper, receptionist Daniel O. Carroll, Louisville, 1987-95; travel cons. Woodside Carlson-Wagonlit, Louisville, 1995—.

CARROLL, GLORIA CRAUGH, school system administrator; b. Dallas, Nov. 14, 1937; d. John McAdams and Sara (Thompson) Craugh; m. Roger Wescott Carroll, July 14, 1956; children: Debra Patton (dec. 1991), Christopher John. BA in Secondary Edn., Kevka Coll., 1974; MEd, Elmira Coll., 1976; SDA, SUNY, Brockport, 1985; EdD, Columbia U., 1996. Tchr. 7-12 social studies Penn Yan (N.Y.) Ctrl. Sch., 1974-85, dir. 6-8 gifted programming, 1985-86, adminstr., curriculum instr., 1986-91, asst. supr., 1991, supr., 1991—; owner Am. Coll. Rsch. Assn., Penn Yan, 1982—. Mem. Yates County Tomorrow, Penn Yan, 1990—. Named Extraordinary Person Chronical Express Newspaper, 1993. Mem. ASCD, NYSCOSS. Roman Catholic. Office: Penn Yan Ctrl Schs 1 School Dr Penn Yan NY 14527-1099

CARROLL, JANE HAMMOND, artist, author, poet; b. Greenville, S.C., May 15, 1946; d. Charles Kirby and Margaret (Cooper) Hammond; m. Robert Lindsay Carroll Jr., Feb. 3, 1968; children: Jane-Gower, Robert Lindsay III. BA, U. S.C., 1968. Tchr. A.C. Flora High Sch., Columbia, S.C., 1968-70; exec. field dir. N.E. Ga. Girl Scout Coun., Athens, 1970-71; asst. dir. AID-Vol. Greenville, 1971-73; author, artist Winston Derek Pubs., Nashville, 1985—. Author, artist: Grace, 1987 (Gov.'s Collection 1988), Intimate Moments, 1987 (Gov.'s Collection), (art book) Dayspring, 1989; one-person shows include Williams Salon, Atlanta, 1989, 92, 93, 94, 95, Galerie Timothy Tew, Jenny Pruitt Realty, 1989, Ariel Gallery, Atlanta, 1996; group shows include Fine Art Mus. of the South, Mobile, Beyond the Wall, 1990, Mus. Archives, Washington, 1992, Internat. Pastel Show, Ga., 1991, 95, Internat. Southeastern Pastel Soc. Exhbn., 1993, Savannah Nat. (1st pl. award in mixed media), Telfare Mus. Savannah, 1995, Telfare Art Fair, 1995; permanent collections represented Greenville Meml. Hosp., S.C., Embassy Suites, Ill., Macan Motor Cars, Ga., Jenny Pruitt Reality, Ga., and others; commns. include Landscape, Portraits; pub. and pvt. collections. Bd. mgr. Greenville Jr. League, 1971-73; artist for fundraiser Rehab. Edn. for Handicapped Adults and Children, Atlanta, 1992-95; vol. artist Arts in the Atlanta Project, 1993. Mem. Nat. League Am. Pen Women (chair art's program 1984—, Achievement award 1987, 89, 93, 94, 95, 96), Atlanta Artist Club (v.p. 1984-85, Merit mem.). Presbyterian. Home and Office: 2979 Majestic Cir Avondale Estates GA 30002

CARROLL, JEANNE, public relations executive; b. Oak Park, Ill., May 20, 1929; d. John P. and Mary (Noonan) Carroll; BA, U. London, 1950; MA, Northwestern U., 1951; m. Harold M. Kass, Apr. 1966. Bus. girls editor Charm Mag., N.Y.C., 1951-53; pub. relations dir. Rosary Coll., River Forest, Ill., 1953-66; chmn. publicity Am. Cancer Soc., bd. dirs. W. and S.W. Suburban Unit, 1967—; med. adminstr., asst. to Dr. Harold Kass, Oak Park, Ill., 1969—; pub. rels. cons., 1993—. Pub. relations counselor in Midwest for Brown U., 1962; dir. pub. relations Mundelein Coll., 1968; producer radio show for teen-agers, Chgo., 1954; lectr. sci. devels. Bell Labs. for AT&T, 1954; participant annual Sun-Times seminars for coll. journalists MacMurray Coll., Jacksonville Ill. Chmn. March of Dimes campaign for Chgo., ednl. TV Channel 11, River Forest, 1963; trustee DePaul U., Chgo., chmn. Soc. Fellows dinner; chmn. Oak Park Hosp. Ben Din Dan, 1971-80; mem. com. library Internat. Relations, 1975-82; mem. bd. Arden Shores, sch. for boys, 1984—; bd. dirs. Globe Theatre Ctr.; mem. adv. bd. USO, mem. com. USO Celebration D-Day Activities, Chgo., 1994. Recipient Excellence award for coll. brochures Am. Coll. Pubs. Com., 1957; medal of recognition for work in pub. relations Bishop Fulton Sheen, 1960; Humanitarian award Performing Arts Ctr. and Citizens Com., Chgo., 1976; award DuSable Mus., 1978. Mem. Ill. Assn. Coll. Admissions Counsellors (pres.), Assn. Coll. Pub. Relations Assn., Family Service Assn. Am. (past bd. dirs.), Acad. Hosp., Pub. Relations, Ill. (pres.), Chgo. (pub. relations dir., med. soc. auxs.), Oak Park Hosp. (pres. women's aux. 1986-89), West Suburban Hosp. Med. Ctr. Aux. (life). Home: 712 Courtland Cir Western Springs IL 60558-1945

CARROLL, KAREN COLLEEN, physician, infectious disease educator, medical microbiologist; b. Balt., Nov. 7, 1953; d. Charles Edward and Ida May (Simms) C.; m. Bruce Cameron Marshall, Feb. 13, 1982; children: Kevin Charles Marshall, Brian Thomas Marshall. BA, Coll. Notre Dame of Md., 1975; MD, U. Md., 1979. Diplomate Am. Bd. Internal Medicine, Am. Bd. Infectious Diseases, Am. Bd. Pathology. Intern internal medicine U. Md., 1979-80; intern primary care internal medicine U. Rochester, AHP, 1980-82, chief med. resident internal medicine, 1982-83; fellow infectious diseases U. Mass., 1984-86; fellow med. microbiology Health Scis. Ctr. U. Utah, 1989-90; asst. prof. pathology U. Utah Med. Ctr., Salt Lake City, 1990—, adj. asst. prof. infectious diseases, 1990—; dir. microbiology lab. Associated Regional and Univ. Pathologists, Inc., Salt Lake City. 1990—. Contbr. articles to profl. jours. Fellow Coll. Am. Pathologists; mem. Am. Soc. for Microbiology, Infectious Diseases Soc. Am. Office: U Utah Med Ctr Dept Pathology 50 N Medical Dr Salt Lake City UT 84132-0001

CARROLL, KAREN JEORGIANNA, pension fund adminstrator; b. Morristown, N.J., d. Leonard Joseph and Gladys Louise (Lemanski) Kalechitz; m. James Douglas Carroll, Oct. 21, 1973 (div. Dec. 1984). Grad., Gibson Career/Finishing Sch., Phila., 1967. Asst. to pres. H. Lane Enterprises, West Caldwell, N.J., 1967-68; adminstrv. asst. Titanium Metals Corp., Caldwell, N.J., 1968-69; libr. USAF Base, Udornthai, Thailand, 1969-70; asst. to libr. U. of Calif., Rohnert Park, 1970-71; pres.'s asst. Gordon Labs., Mass., 1971-72; corp. sec. Titanium Industries, Fairfield, N.J., 1972-86; asst. to chmn. CBA Industries, Paramus, N.J., 1986-89; fund adminstr., asst. to chmn. Firemark Group, Parsippany, N.J., 1989—.

CARROLL, KIM MARIE, nurse; b. Ottawa, Ill., Feb. 13, 1958; d. John J. and Charin E. (Reilley) Marmion; m. Thomas Christopher Carroll, Aug. 25, 1979; children: Christopher John, Meaghan Elizabeth. BSN, U. Denver, 1983; diploma Copley Meml. Hosp. Sch. Nursing, Aurora, Ill., 1979. RN, Ill., Ind., Colo.; critical care practitioner. Staff nurse Penrose Hosp., Colorado Springs, Colo., 1979-83, asst. head nurse cardiac floor, 1983-84; asst. dir. nurses Big Meadows Nursing Home, Savanna, Ill., 1985-86, dir. nurses, 1986-88; clin. dir. Ind. Heart Physicians, Inc., Beech Grove, Ind., 1989-95; ambulatory care adminstr. The Gates Clinic, Denver, 1995—. Mem. Am. Orgn. Nurse Execs., Soc. Ambulatory Care Profls., Profls. In Workers' Compensation, Beta Sigma Phi (chpt. pres. 1988-89, rec. sec. 1991-92), Sigma Theta Tau. Roman Catholic. Avocation: skiing. Home: 5293 S Cathay Way Aurora CO 80015-4859 Office: The Gates Clinic 1000 S Broadway Denver CO 80209

CARROLL, LUCY ELLEN, choral director, music coordinator, educator; b. N.Y.C., Oct. 11; d. Edward Joseph and Lucy Sophie (Czapszys) C. B in Music Edn., Temple U., 1968; MA, Trenton State Coll., 1973; D in Musical Arts, Combs Coll. Music, Phila., 1982. Cert. tchr. music, N.J., Pa., Nat. Cert., 1991. Tchr. music Log Coll. Jr. High Sch., Pa., 1968-72, Ind. (Pa.) High Sch., 1972-73; tchr. music William Tennent High Sch., Warminster, Pa., 1973—, dir. mus. theater, 1973—; music coord. Centennial Schs., 1991; founder, dir. Madrigal Singers, Warminster, Pa., 1971—; choral dir. Cabrini Coll., Radnor, Pa., 1974-77, First Day Singers, Phila., 1979-83, Combs Coll. of Music, Phila., 1981-84, 87-88; choral adjudicator various Music festivals, 1973—; guest lectr. mus. seminars, convs., and writers' confs.; del. Internat. Arts Conf., Cambridge, Eng., 1992. Singer (operas Ambler Festival) Street Scene, 1970, Death of Bishop of Brindisi (premiere); (Robin Hood Dell) La Boheme; dir. (jazz theater piece N.Y.C.) Murder of Agamemnon, 1980, (musi. drama) Power of Love (1705), 1986, (outdoor music theater) Vorspiel (Pa. Historic Commn. 1989); contbr. articles to profl. jours., also sci. fiction to sci. fiction mags. and anthologies. Recipient awards Writers of Future, 1985, 87, Andrew Ferraro award Combs Coll. Music, 1989, plaque for svc. to music Bucks County Commr., 1991, Disting. Citizen prize Southampton Twp., 1994, Harmony award Country Gentlemen Nat. Soc. for Preservation and Encouragement Barbershop Quartet Singing in Am., 1994. Mem. Am. Choral Dirs. Assn., Sci. Fiction Fantasy Writers of Am., Theatre Assn. Pa., Del. Valley Composers (choral cons. 1988-90), Pa. Edn. Assn. Centennial Edn. Assn., Bucks County Music Educators Assn., Hist. Soc. Pa., Smithsonian Assocs., Music Fund Soc. of Phila., The Sonneck Soc. for Am. Music, Pa. Music Educators Assn. (adv. bd. 1986-87), Ephrata Cloister Assocs., Sigma Alpha Iota. Republican. Roman Catholic. Home: 712 High Ave Hatboro PA 19040-2418 Office: William Tennent High Sch Music Dept 333 Centennial Rd Warminster PA 18974-5408

CARROLL, MARIE-JEAN GREVE, educator, artist; b. Paterson, N.J., Dec. 19, 1930; d. William John and Charlotte Marie (Kranich) McGill; m. Theodore R. Greve, Nov. 4, 1950 (div. Oct. 1979); children: Richard W. Greve, Helen E. Greve Beard, Theodore A. Greve; m. William P. Carroll, 1981 (div. 1989). BA in Art Edn., William Paterson Coll., Wayne, N.J., 1971; MA in Visual Art, 1976. Cert. art tchr., N.J. Art tchr. Pequannock (N.J.) Elem. Sch., 1971-72, Passaic Valley High Sch., Little Falls, N.J., 1972-77, 85-86, Ramapo High Sch., Franklin Lakes, N.J., 1986—. Works exhibited at shows in Fla. galleries, 1983, Longboat Key Art Gallery, 1983, 84, Manatee Art Gallery, 1984, Pike County Art Show, Milford, Pa., 1994, 95, 96, others. Recipient art awards. Mem. NEA, Bergen County Edn. Assn., N.J. Edn. Assn., Nat. Art Edn. Assn.

CARROLL, MAUREEN PATRICIA, lawyer, editor; b. North Tarrytown, N.Y., Dec. 10, 1947; d. John F. and Grace M. C.; m. William L. Stull, Dec.

26, 1987. BA, Ohio Dominican Coll., 1970; MA, Cath. U. Am., 1978, PhD, 1985; JD, Columbia U., 1988. Bar: N.Y. 1989, D.C. 1990, Conn. 1990. Asst. prof. Coll. Holy Cross, Worcester, Mass., 1983-85; assoc. LeBeouf, Lamb, Leiby & MacRae, N.Y.C., 1987-89; counsel Aetna Law and Regulatory Affairs, Hartford, 1989—. Editor: Remembering Ray: A Composite Biography of Raymond Carver, 1993; editor, compiler article in profl. jour. Mem. AAUW, NY State Bar Assn., DC Bar Assn., Conn. Bar Assn., Nat. Health Lawyers Assn. Republican. Home: #32234 465 Buckland Hills Dr Manchester CT 06040 Office: Aetna Law and Regulatory Affairs RE4C 151 Farmington Ave Hartford CT 06156-3124

CARROLL, MAUREEN STEPHANIE, secondary education educator; b. Superior, Ariz., Jan. 16, 1948; d. Kenneth and Lydia (Partington) Nobs; children: Sydney Minckler, Tobia Minckler. BA in English, San Francisco State U., 1977, secondary edn. credential, 1978; MA in Ethics and Policy Studies, U. Nev., Las Vegas, 1993. Tchr. Clark County Sch. Dist., Las Vegas, 1978—. Vol. Nev. Desert Experience, Las Vegas, 1983—, Las Vegas Cath. Worker, 1985—, Pace e Bene, Las Vegas, 1992—. Grantee NEH, Duke U., 1990, Nev. Humanities Com., Las Vegas, 1992. Mem. NEA, Nat. Coun. for the Social Studies, Nat. Coun. Tchrs. English, Clark County Classroom Tchrs. Assn., Phi Kappa Phi. Office: Clark County Sch Dist 2832 E Flamingo Rd Las Vegas NV 89121

CARROLL, SALLY REGE, state agency administrator; b. Kharagpur, India, Jan. 1, 1960; d. Madhukar Anant and Gladys Constance (Sharp) Rege; m. Kevin Charles Carroll, Nov. 26, 1988. BA in Journalism and English, U. Mass., 1992; MA in Urban Affairs/Environ. Mgmt., Boston U., 1993. Sec. corp. comm. EG&G, Inc., Wellesley, Mass., 1983-84; editor Officer of the State Auditor, Boston, 1984-87; proofreader Interface Group, Inc., Needham, Mass., 1987-89; adminstrv./fin. asst. Boston U. Sch. of Law, 1989-92; newsletter editor Mass. Natural Heritage & Endangered Species Program, Boston, 1992-94; contractor Mercury Workgroup Mass. Water Resources Authority, Boston, 1994, adminstrv. mgr., editor dept. environ. quality, 1995—. Freelance writer: Mass. Audubon Soc., 1994—. Active First Parish Unitarian Ch., Saugus, Mass., 1995-96. Office: Mass Water Resources Authority Charleston Navy Yard Boston MA 02129

CARROLL, SHIRLEY DEVAUX STRONG, realtor; b. La Jolla, Calif., June 30, 1930; d. Fred Buhl and Leoda Carolyn (Hissong) Strong; m. Dorrence Coney Talbut, June 19, 1954 (div. Sept. 1969); children: Gregory Harrison Mack, Jeffrey Mitchell Strong, March Foster Chad; m. John Lawrence Carroll, Aug. 16, 1973. Student, Stephens Coll., 1948-49; BEd, U. Toledo, 1951; cert. in land use planning and devel., Am. Planning Assn., 1979. Lic. real estate sales broker, Tex. Tchr. Monroe (Mich.) Pub. Schs., 1951-52, Columbus (Ohio) City Schs., 1952-55, Greenwich (Conn.) Pub. Schs., 1955-56; producer Young People's Concert Series, Toledo, 1968-70; realtor Danberry Real Estate and Ins., Toledo, 1970-73; v.p., mgr. Rilco Mfg. Inc., Clute, Tex., 1974-76; coord. Sandusky County Econ. Devel., Fremont, Ohio, 1984-85; realtor Bolte Real Estate and Ins., Fremont, 1987—; exec. dir. Arts Coun. Sandusky County, Fremont, 1988-91; Treas. Internat. Energy Conservation Soc., Houston, 1977-82; commr. Planning and Zoning Commn., Missouri City, 1979-84, Ballville Zoning Commn., Fremont, 1984-89; dir. devel. Tex. Solar Energy Soc., Austin, 1982-84; mem. steering com. Elder Coll. Terra C.C., 1995—. Dir., writer, producer: (tv shows) Music for Young People, 1968-70. Campaign mgr. Bette (Graham White) for Mayor, Houston, 1976; mem. Tax Equalization Bd., Missouri City, Tex., 1980. Recipient appreciation award Am. Solar Energy Soc., Boulder, Colo., 1982. Mem. NAFE, Women in Networking, Fremont Area Artists and Fireland Artists, Fremont Country Club Women's Assn. (pres. 1989-90), Friends of Birchard Libr. (pres. 1988-90), Firelands Assn. of Realtors, Spectrum Gallery (Toledo). Home: 1829 Buckland Ave Fremont OH 43420-3503 Office: Bolte Real Estate 2378 W State St Fremont OH 43420-1441

CARROLL-DOVENMUEHLE, BETTYE TURPIN, counselor; b. Baton Rouge, La., Sept. 17, 1943; d. Baynard T. Jr. and Mary Elizabeth (Barnett) Turpin; m. Robert H. Dovenmuehle, July 31, 1988. BA, La. State U., 1964; MEd, U. N.C., Greensboro, 1989. Instr. Rockingham C.C., Wentworth, N.C., 1969-73; exec. dir. Eden (N.C.) Child Devel. Ctr., 1973-76; cons. Office for Children, Greensboro, 1976-77; trainer N.C. State Tng. Office for Head Start, Greensboro, 1977-80; counselor Fellowship Hall, Greensboro, 1980-86; rehab. counselor, behavior modification therapist The Hatcher Ctr., Danville, Va., 1989—; vol. therapist Mental Health Assocs., 1990—. Mem. ACA, Nat. Bd. Cert. Counselors, Va. Psychol. Assn., Assn. Nondirective Counselors, Nat. Assn. Drug Abuse Counselors, Va. Counselors Assn. Home: 147 Acorn Ln Danville VA 24541-6201

CARRUTHERS, CLAUDELLE ANN, occupational and physical therapist; b. Chgo., Nov. 23; d. Veronica Josephine Walker. AA, Golden Valley Luth. Coll., Minn., 1981; BS in Occupational Therapy, U. Minn., 1984; M in Phys. Therapy, U. Iowa, 1991; PhD, U. Minn., 1995. Lic. occupational therapist, Iowa, phys. therapist, Iowa, Minn.; cert. occupational therapist, Minn. Dir., supr., occupational therapist Rehab. Specialists, Inc., Minnetonka, Minn., 1984-86; supr., occupational therapist St. Therese Home, Inc., Mpls., 1986-88; dir., supr., occupational therapist Allied Health Alternatives, Inc., Mpls., 1988-89; occupational therapist St. Luke's Hosp., Cedar Rapids, Iowa, 1989-91; occupational therapist, phys. therapist Fairview Riverside Med. Ctr., Mpls., 1991—; instr., rschr. U. Minn., 1992-95; prof. occupational and phys. therapy Coll. of St. Catherine, 1995—; research in field of virtual reality, neurology/kinesiology; mem. adv. bd. occupational therapy program Anoka Tech. Coll., 1992—; mentor for occupational and phys. therapy students Coll. of St. Catherine's, St. Paul, 1992; mentor for occupational and phys. therapy and women athlete's of color U. Minn. Author publs. in field. Human rights commr. City of Plymouth, 1994—; mem. allocation panel United Way Mpls., 1992; mem. Minn. Zoo, 1986—. Recipeint Vol. Basketball award Courage Ctr., Golden Valley, Minn., 1981, 89. Mem. Am. Phys. Therapy Assn. (student rep. 1981-83), Iowa Occupational Therapy Assn., Minn. Occupational Therapy Assn., Am. Occupational Therapy Assn., Occupational Therapy Minn.-Dak Assn. (panel presentor 1992), Glende Ski Club (2d v.p. 1987), Martin Luther King Tennis Club, Alpha Kappa Alpha. Office: College Of St Catherine Dept of Physical Therapy Saint Paul MN 55105

CARSEY, MARCIA LEE PETERSON, television producer; b. South Weymouth, Mass., Nov. 21, 1944; d. John Edwin and Rebecca White (Simonds) Peterson; m. John Jay Carsey, Apr. 12, 1969; children: Rebecca Peterson, John Peterson. B.A. in English Lit., U. N.H., 1966. Exec. story editor Tomorrow Entertainment, L.A., 1971-74; sr. v.p. prime time series ABC-TV, L.A., 1978-81; founder Carsey Prodns., L.A., 1981; co-owner Carsey-Werner Co., 1982—; co-exec. producer TV series Oh Madeline, 1983; exec. producer The Cosby Show, 1984-92, A Different World, 1987-93, Roseanne, 1988—, Chicken Soup, 1989-90, Grand, 1990, Davis Rules, 1991, You Bet Your Life, 1992-93, Frannie's Turn, 1992, Grace Under Fire, 1993—, Cybill, 1995—, 3rd Rock From The Sun, 1996—, Cosby, 1996—, Men Behaving Badly, 1996—, Townies, 1996—. Office: care CBS Studio Ctr 4024 Radford Ave Bldg 3 Studio City CA 91604-2101

CARSON, AMELIA JANE, nurse, consultant; b. Greenville, S.C., Apr. 10, 1941; d. Lloyd Darwin Carson and Beulah Amelia (Long) Schaadt. RN, Greenville Gen. Hosp. Sch. Nursing, 1962; BSN, U. Wash., 1969; MS, U. Colo., Denver, 1971; student, Greenville Tech. Coll., 1996. Registered profl. nurse; cert. nursing administr. Med. staff nurse Letterman Gen. Hosp., San Francisco, 1962-63; med.-surg. nurse 121st Evacuation Hosp., Korea, 1963-64; emergency rm. nurse Brooke Army Med. Ctr., Fort Sam Houston, Tex., 1964-65; army nurse corps counselor First Recruiting Dist., Newark, 1966-67; head nurse & relief supr. 312th & 91st Evacuation Hosps., Chu Lai, Vietnam, 1969-70; pers. mgmt. officer Office Surgeon Gen., Washington, 1971-74; asst. inspector gen. Health Svcs. Command, Fort Sam Houston, 1975-77; chief nurse Kimbrough Army Hosp., Fort Meade, Md., 1977-80; asst. chief nurse Tripler Army Med. Ctr., Hawaii, 1980-83; chief nurse U.S. Army N.G., Washington, 1983-86; chief nurse, nursing cons. 18th Med. Command, 121st Evacuation Hosp., Korea, 1986-87; br. chief, nursing edn. cons. Office Surgeon Gen. Edn. & Tng. Divsn., Washington, 1987-89; vice chair, chair Vol. Sister Search Coms. Vietnam Women's Meml. Project, Inc., Washington, 1990—; rschr. Kimbrough Army Hosp., 1978-80. Mem. fin. com. First Bapt. Ch., Crofton, Md., 1989-90; cmty. svc. worker Altrusa Internat., Greenville, 1995. Decorated Bronze Star, 1970, Vietnam Campaign medal with 3 stars, 1969, Legion of Merit with Oak Leaf Cluster, 1986, N.G. Bur. Eagle award, 1986, UN Unit Citation, 1969. Mem. ANA, Holistic Nurses Assn., Sigma Theta Tau. Home and Office: PO Box 1621 Greer SC 29652-1621

CARSON, CYNTHIA LEE, physician's assistant; b. Pitts., Oct. 10, 1956; d. Charles Raymond and Mary Arlene (Parry) C. B.Med. Sci. summa cum laude, Alderson Broaddus Coll., 1978. Cert. physician's asst., Conn. Physician's asst. surg. resident Norwalk Hosp./Yale U., 1978-79, clin. coord./instr., 1995—; staff physician's asst. in surgery Norwalk (Conn.) Hosp., 1978—; staff physician asst. rep. operating rm. com. Hahnemann U. Physician Asst. Program, 1984—, clin. asst. instr., 1981—; adj. asst. prof. health care scis. George Washington U., 1991—. Contbr. articles to profl. jours. Recipient Yoichi Katsube Meml. award Pa. Surg. Residency, 1979, Frank J. Scallon Med. Writing award, 1984, 86. Mem. Am. Acad. Physician's Assts., Conn. Acad. Physician's Assts. Home: 30 Nearwater Rd Rowayton CT 06853 Office: Norwalk Hospital Norwalk CT 06850

CARSON, GAIL MARIA, fashion designer, marketing consultant; b. Detroit, Nov. 27, 1954; d. Samuel Salvador and Dorothy Marie (Mallard) Dasher; m. Calvin Jerome Carson, Feb. 15, 1975; 1 child, Meredith Jojuan. Student, U. Detroit, 1972-74, Siena Heights Coll., 1982-83; cert. in merchandising, Fashion Inst. Am., 1986. Hostess coffee shop J.C. Penney Co., Southfield, Mich., 1975-78; exec. dir. office ethnic minority higher edn. Wayne State U., Detroit, 1982-86; fashion show coord. Prodns. Plus, Inc., Birmingham, Mich., 1986-91; internat. mktg. cons. Internat. Mktg. Assn., Southfield, 1976—; designer knitwear Needle Classics, Detroit, 1986—, Rio Boutique, Detroit, 1993—. Mem. Winship Cmty. Coun., Detroit, 1976-80; fundraiser, campaigner Judge Bruce Morrow, Detroit, 1992; co-chairperson Mumford High Sch. Alumni, Detroit, 1992—; co-chairperson coun. Scott Meml. United Methodist Ch., Detroit, 1989-91. Recipient Outstanding Leadership award E.B.O.N. Assocs., 1980, Outstanding Achievement award Amway Corp., 1981, Outstanding Young Woman of Am. award, 1983. Mem. Knitter's Guild Am., Mumford H.S. Alumni Assn. and Endowment (co-chairperson 1992—, Outstanding Leadership award 1992), Mom and Dad Club Gesu Sch.

CARSON, LINDA FRANCES, gynecologic oncologist; b. Manchester, Conn., Feb. 8, 1952; d. Culley Clyde and Dorothy (Scarbourough) C.; m. Bruce Allen MacFarlane, June 2, 1974 (div. 1988); children: Megan Carson, Ian Scarbourough; m. Roderick Allen Barke, Jan. 13, 1989. BA, Conn. Coll., 1974; MD, George Washington U., 1978. Intern and resident Sinai Hosp. Balt., 1978-82; fellow in gynecologic oncology Barnes Hosp., St. Louis, 1982-83, U. Minn., 1983-86; dir. gynecologic oncology Hennepin County Med. Ctr., Mpls., 1986-89; dir. VA Gynecologic Svc., Mpls., 1989-90, dir. gynecol., 1990—, v.p. ob/gyn., 1994—; dir. div. gynecologic oncology U. Minn., Mpls., 1990—, assoc. prof. div. gynecologic oncology, 1991—; co-prin. investigator Gynecologic Oncology Group, 1990—; co-dir. Upper Midwest Trophoblastic Diseases Ctr. U. Minn., 1986—; dir. Women's Cancer Ctr., 1988—. Reviewer: Am. Jour. Obstetrics and Gynecology, 1989—, Gynecologic Oncology, Cancer, 1989—; contbr. articles to profl. jours. Fellow Am. Cancer Soc.; mem. AMA, Hennepin County Med. Soc., Internat. Soc. for Study Vulvar Disease, Mpls. Coun. Obstetrics and Gynecology, Minn. State Med. Soc., Minn. Women's Med. Soc., Soc. of Gynecologic Oncologists, Western Assn. Gynecologic Oncologists. Office: U Minn Dept Ob-Gyn Box 395 Mayo 420 Delaware St SE Minneapolis MN 55455-0374

CARSON, MARGARET MARIE, gas industry executive, marketing professional; b. Windber, Pa., Dec. 30, 1944; d. Peter and Margaret (Olenik) Buben; m. Claude Carson, Dec. 30, 1967 (div. 1974); m. Brian Charles Scruby, June 6, 1975; stepchildren: Debbie, Victor, Chris, Kenneth. BA, U. Pitts., 1971; MS in Mgmt., Houston Bapt. U., 1985. Petroleum analyst Gulf Oil Co., Pitts., 1973-75, crude oil analyst, 1971-74, environ. coordinator, 1974-79, mgr. oil acquistition, Houston, 1980-84, mktg. dir., 1985; sales dir. Cabot Cons. Group, Houston, 1985-86; dir. competitor analysis and corporate strategy dept., Enron Corp., Houston, 1987—; adj. prof. bus tech. Houston Community Coll., 1985-91. Columnist: The Collegian, 1984-85. Bd. dirs. Indiana U., Pa., 1980-81. Mem. Am. Competitiveness Soc. (bd. dirs.), Internat. Energy Economists, Gas Processors Assn. (speaker tech. sessions 1985-94), Gas Rsch. Inst., Univ. Club.

CARSON, MARY SILVANO, career counselor, educator,; b. Mass.; d. Joseph and Alice V. (Sherwood) Silvano; m. Paul E. Carson (dec.); children: Jan Ellen, Jeffrey Paul, Amy Jayne. BS, Simmons Coll., Boston; MA, U. Chgo., 1970; postgrad., Ctr. Urban Studies, 1970, U. Chgo., 1971, 72, DePaul U., Chgo., 1980. Cert. acad. counselor, Ill.; nat. cert. counselor. Mgr. S.W. Youth Opportunity Ctr., Dept. Labor, Chgo., 1965-67; careers' counselor Gordon Tech. High Sch., Chgo., 1971-74; dir. Career and Assessment Ctr., YMCA Coll., Chgo., 1974-81; project coord. Career Ctr., Loop Coll., Chgo., 1981-82; mem. adv. bd. City-Wide Coll. Career Ctr. Bd. dirs. Loop YWCA, Chgo., coord. employment project, 1985-87; ESL tchr., Greece, 1990. Mem. ACA, TESOL, Internat. Counseling Assn., Internat. Lyceum (London), Am. Ednl. Rsch. Assn., Nat. Vocat. Guidance Assn., Chgo. Bus. and Profl. Women's Club, Met. Club (San Francisco), Commonwealth Club, Browning Soc., World Coun., English Speaking Union, Pi Lambda Theta (chpt. pres. 1975).

CARSON, MARY SMITH, marketing and communications consultant; b. Evansville, Ind., Oct. 15, 1939; d. Richard and Edith (Miller) Smith; m. Roger Warren Carson, Feb. 1, 1958; children: John Brett, Richard Charles, Cheryl Lee. BA, Mary Washington Coll., 1971; MBA, Marymount U., 1990. Dir. United Way, Fredericksburg, Va., 1971-75; dir. alumni Mary Washington Coll., Fredericksburg, Va., 1976-81; assoc. dir. Am. Gas Assn., Arlington, Va., 1981-94; v.p. WE & Assocs., Ltd., Arlington, Va., 1995—. Small bus. coord. Bob Dole for Pres., Washington, 1988; ethnic campaign coord. Reagan for Pres., Washington, 1979, head Washington office, 1980. Inducted into Hall of Honor Am. Gas Assn., 1993. Mem. Nat. Coun. Housing Industry (co-chair 1994), Marymount U. Alumni Assn. (bd. dirs. 1993—). Republican. Roman Catholic. Home: 8225 Madrillon Estates Dr Vienna VA 22182 Office: WE & Assocs Ltd 1555 Wilson Blvd Ste 300 Arlington VA 22209

CARSON, REGINA EDWARDS, healthcare administrator, pharmacist, educator; b. Washington; d. Reginald Billy and Arcola (Gold) Edwards; m. Marcus T. Carson; children: Marcus Reginald, Ellis K., Imani R. BS in Pharmacy, Howard U., 1973; MBA in Mktg., Loyola Coll., Balt., 1987, MBA in Health Care Adminstrn., 1987. Asst. prof., asst. dir. pharmacy U. Md., Balt., 1986-88; asst. prof., coord. profl. practice Howard U., Washington, 1988-95; prin. Marrell Consulting., Randallstown, Md., 1993—; mng. ptnr. Marrell Cons., Randallstown, Md., 1995—; exec. v.p. Marrell, Inc., Randallstown, Md., 1985-93; drug utilization rev. cons. Md. Pharmacy Assn., Balt., 1986—; cons. pharmacist Balt. County Adv. Coun. Drug Abuse, Towson, 1984-86; adv. com. long-term care com. Nat. Assn. Retail Druggists. Bd. dirs. Northwest Hosp. Ctr. Aux., Randallstown, Joshua Johnson Coun. Balt. Mus. Art. Fellow Am. Soc. Cons. Pharmacists; mem. Nat. Assn. Retail Druggists, Am. Assn. Colls. Pharmacy, Nat. Pharm. Assn. (life, Outstanding Women in Pharmacy 1984), Nat. Assn. Healthservice Execs.

CARSON, VIRGINIA HILL, oil and gas executive; b. L.A., Dec. 4, 1928; d. Percy Albert McCord and Flora May (Newking) Schultz; m. John Carson, Dec. 30, 1950 (dec.). BA in Internat. Relations, U. Calif., Berkeley, 1949; postgrad. Stanford U., 1948, UCLA, 1951. Gen. office worker UN, San Francisco, 1949; ind. oil and gas profl., U.S., Can., Cuba, 1953-73; supr., specialist Sun Exploration & Prodn. Co. (name changed to Oryx Energy Co.), Dallas, 1978-83, profl. analyst, 1983-92; freelance editor, 1992—. Mem. Dallas Coun. World Affairs, 1984—, Dallas Mus. Fine Arts, 1984—; vol. North Tex. Taping and Radio for the Blind, 1992—, Thanks Giving Sq., 1996—. Nominated to pres.'s coun. Am. Inst. Mgmt., N.Y.C., 1974. Address: PO Box 12530 Dallas TX 75225-0530

CARSTARPHEN, KATHLEEN CECILE, social worker; b. Portsmouth, Va., Oct. 7, 1953; d. William Cecil and June Matura (Brown) Farnsworth; m. Rodger Dale Welton, Dec. 18, 1971 (div. 1977); 1 child, Brandy Lee Carstarphen Bergeron; m. Robert Bruce Carstarphen Jr., Oct. 2, 1982; 1 child, Scott Robert. AA in Human Svcs., N.H. Coll. Human Svcs., 1982, BS, 1984. Cert. guardian for superior ct. Chid protective social worker divsn. children, youth, family State of N.H., Manchester, 1988—; case mgr. devel. disabled adults Wm. J. Moore Ctr., Manchester, supr. work program, staff day habilitation for devel. disabled adults; mem. Commn. on Domestic Violence, Manchester, 1995; mem. negotiation team State Employees Assn., Concord, N.H., 1995. Den leader, com. mem. Boy Scouts Am., Manchester, 1990—; Sunday sch. tchr. Unitarian-Universalist Ch., Manchester, 1988. Mem. Nat. Abortion Rights Assn. Lobby, Children and Adults with Attention Deficit Disorder, Planned Parenthood. Democrat.

CARSTEN, ARLENE DESMET, financial executive; b. Paterson, N.J., Dec. 5, 1937; d. Albert F. and Ann (Greutert) Desmet; m. Alfred John Carsten, Feb. 11, 1956; children: Christopher Dale, Jonathan Glenn. Student Alfred U., 1955-56; Exec. dir. Inst. for Burn Medicine, San Diego, 1972-81, adv. bd. mem., 1981-92; founding trustee, bd. dirs. Nat. Burn Fedn., 1975-83; chief fin. officer A.J. Carsten Co. Inc., San Diego, 1981-91; chief fin. officer A.J. Carsten Co., Ltd., Powell River, B.C., Can., 1992—. Contbr. articles to profl. jours. Organizer, mem. numerous community groups; chmn. San Diego County Mental Health Adv. Bd., 1972-74, mem., 1971-75; chmn. community relations subcom., mem. exec. com. Emergency Med. Care Com., San Diego, Riverside and Imperial Counties, 1973-75; pub. mem. psychology exam. com. Calif. State Bd. Med. Quality Assurance, 1976-80, chmn., 1977; mem. rep. to Health Services Agy. San Diego County Govt., 1980; mem. Calif. Dem. Cen. Com., 1968-74, exec. com., 1971-72, 73-74; treas. San Diego Dem. County Cen. Com., 1972-74; chmn. edn. for legislation com. women's div. So. Calif. Dem. Com., 1972; dir. Muskie for Pres. Campaign, San Diego, 1972; organizer, dir. numerous local campaigns; councilwoman City of Del Mar, Calif., 1982-86, mayor, 1985-86; bd. dirs. Gentry-Watts Planned Indsl. Devel. Assn., 1986-90, pres., 1987-90; commencement speaker Alfred U., 1984. Recipient Key Woman award Dem. Party, 1968, 72, 1st Ann. Community award Belles for Mental Health, Mental Health Assn. San Diego, 1974, citation Alfred U. Alumni Assn., 1979. Office: RR# 2 Malaspina Rd C-13, Powell River, BC Canada V8A 4Z3

CARSTENS, JANE ELLEN, retired library science educator; b. New Iberia, La., Apr. 19, 1922; d. Charles John and Marie Claudia (Blanchet) C. BA in Elem. Edn., U. Southwestern La., 1942; BS in LS, La. State U., 1945; MS in LS, Columbia U., 1955, DLS, 1975. Asst. libr. Hamilton Lab. sch. and instr. libr. sci. U. Southwestern La., Lafayette, 1942-54, asst. prof., 1954-65, assoc. prof., 1965-75; children's librarian/storyteller N.Y. Pub. Libr., N.Y.C., 1947, 48-49; vis. lectr. U. Minn., Mpls., 1955-56, summer 59, La. State U., Baton Rouge, summer 1958, State Coll. Iowa, Cedar Falls, summer 1963; prof. libr. sci. U. Southwestern La., Lafayette, 1975-94; vis. lectr. Syracuse U., summers 1962, 64, U. Tex., Austin, summers 1976-86, 89. Named Tchr. of Yr., Amoco, 1982, Outstanding Alumna, U. Southwestern La., 1986; recipient Essae Culver Disting. Svc. award La. Libr. Assn., 1987, Alumni Faculty Excellence award Blue Key, 1990, Faculty Advisor of Yr. award U. Southwestern La. Student Govt. Assn., 1992, Point of Excellence award Kappa Delta Pi, 1992, Outstanding Tchr. award USL Found., 1994; Blue Key Faculty/Student Staff Directory dedicated to her, 1994-95. Mem. ALA, Assn. Libr. and Info. Sci. Edn., Assn. Libr. Svc. to Children (mem. Newbery award com. 1989-90), Am. Assn. Sch. Librs., La. Libr. Assn. (pres. 1959-60), Young Adult Libr. Svc. Assn., Phi Kappa Phi (pres. USL chpt. 1984-85), Delta Kappa Gamma (pres. Alpha chpt. 1988-90). Roman Catholic. Home: 214 St Joseph St Lafayette LA 70506-4535 Office: U Southwestern La PO Box 40298 Lafayette LA 70506-4535

CARSWELL, LOIS MALAKOFF, botanical gardens executive, consultant; b. N.Y.C., Mar. 2, 1932; d. Arthur and Dora (Krechevsky) Malakoff; m. Donald Carswell, Oct. 12, 1957; children: Anne Carswell Tang, Alexander, Robert Ian. AB magna cum laude, Radcliffe Coll., 1953; cert. in bus. adminstrn., Harvard U. and Radcliffe Coll., 1954. Editor Dell Pub. Co., N.Y.C., 1954-56; publicist Ruth E. Pepper Co., N.Y.C., 1957-58; vol. Bklyn. Botanic Garden, 1964—, co-chmn. plant sales, 1967—, co-chmn. capital campaign, 1984-88, chmn. bd. dirs., 1989—; chmn. Coalition Living Mus. N.Y. State, N.Y.C., 1980—; cons. N.Y. State Natural Heritage Trust, 1982—. Office: Bklyn Botanic Garden 1000 Washington Ave Brooklyn NY 11225-1008

CARTAINO, CAROL ANN, editor; b. N.Y.C., Dec. 7, 1944; d. Pietro Michael and Ann Wanda (Scotch) C.; 1 child, Clayton Collier-Cartaino. BA, Rutgers U., 1966; postgrad., NYU, 1967-68. Cert. English tchr., N.J. Prodn. editor trade book Prentice-Hall, Inc., Englewood Cliffs, N.J., 1966-68, from asst. to assoc. editor trade book, 1968-72, editor trade book, 1972-77; editor-in-chief Writer's Digest Books, Cin., 1978-86, freelance editor and collaborator, 1986-87; editl. dir. Don Aslett, Inc., Pocatello, Idaho, 1987-93, Marsh Creek Press, Pocatello, Idaho, 1993—; assoc. Collier Assoc. Literary Agy., Seaman, Ohio, 1987-94; proprietor White Oak Edits., 1987—, Carol Cartaino, Lit. Agt., 1994—; speaker in field; instr. in writing So. State C.C., Hillsboro and Wilmington, Ohio, 1989—. Vol. nurses aide Hackensack (N.J.) Hosp. State of N.J. scholar, 1962-66, Emerson (N.J.) PTA scholar, 1962. Roman Catholic. Home and Office: 2000 Flat Run Rd Seaman OH 45679-9551

CARTER, ANNETTE WHEELER, state legislator; b. May 24, 1941; divorced. Grad., Ala. State Coll. Mem. Conn. Ho. of Reps., 1988—; mem. pub. safety, cmty. and exportation coms., vice chmn. appropriations com., asst. majority leader; housing advisor Capitol Region Conf. Chs.; mem. nat. black Caucus, State Legis. Recipient Outstanding Accomplishments award Hope SDA Ch., 1990, Crispus A. Tucks award, 1991, Conn. State Black Dem. award, 1992. Mem. NAACP (award 1993), Greater Hartford Black Dem. Club. Episcopalian. Home: 207 Branford St Hartford CT 06112-1406 Office: House Democrats Legislative Office Bldg Hartford CT 06106*

CARTER, ARLENE FRANCES, nursing practitioner; b. Middletown, N.Y., May 16, 1940; d. James Albert Arnott and Florence Ethel (Nielsen) Wilcox; m. Timothy E. Stover, May 10, 1974 (div. July 1975); m. Arthur Philip Carter, Sept. 30, 1975; children: Alfred J. Stover, Diahanna L. Stover, Kenneth C., Shannon E., David I. Stover, Karri-Mae Carter. AAS, Orange County C.C., 1979; cert. women's health nurse practitioner, UCLA Med. Ctr., 1994. Cert. nursing adminstr., psychiat. nursing ANA. Staff nurse Montrose (N.Y.) VA Hosp., 1979-80, Mid Hudson Pyschiat. Ctr., New Hampton, N.Y., 1980-81, Middletown (N.Y.) Psychiat. Hosp., 1981-83; head nurse psychiat. Dept. Univ. Med. Ctr., Las Vegas, Nev., 1983-87; clinic supr., advanced practitioner of nursing Clark County Health Dist., Las Vegas, 1987—; mem. task force practice issues Nev. State Bd. Nursing, Carson City, 1994, 95; mem. task force on reducing teen pregnancy in Nev., Nev. State Dept. Health, Carson City, 1995—. Mem. Nat. Family Planning and Reproductive Health Assn., Nev. Nurses Assn., Nev. Assn. Female Execs., Nev. Maternal Child Coalition (treas. 1989—), Nev. Pub. Health Assn. Democrat. Baptist. Home: 337 Revere Dr Las Vegas NV 89107

CARTER, CARLA CIFELLI, management consultant; b. Chicago Heights, Ill., June 2, 1949; d. John Louis and Irene Frances (Romandine) Cifelli. BA, Western Mich. U., 1971; MBA, Ariz. State U., 1985. Tchr. Limestone (Maine) High Sch., 1971-75; mgr. employment and tng. Chubb Life Ins., Concord, N.H., 1975-78; employee relations supr. TRW, Inc., Plainville, Conn., 1978-79; asst. dir. corp. tng. Cigna, Bloomfield, Conn., 1979-82; cons. to human resources dept. Sentry Ins. Co., Scottsdale, Ariz., 1983-84; asst. v.p. Bank of Am., Phoenix, 1984-87; employee devel. adminstr. City of Phoenix, 1987-90; dir. Am. Productivity and Quality Ctr., Houston, 1990-95; v.p. Murro Consulting, Inc., 1996—; sr. examiner Ariz. Quality Alliance, 1994-95, regional presenter, 1994-96. Author: Human Resources and the Total Quality Imperative, 1994, Understanding the Organization, 1982, The Responsive City, Am. Productivity and Quality Ctr., 1990, Seven Basic Tools, HR mag., 1992, Measuring and Improving the HR Function Continous Journey, 1993, Using TQM Principles to Develop Executives, Employment Relations Today, 1994. Advisor Literary Vols., Phoenix, 1989; mem. Gov.'s Conf. on Quality, Ariz., 1993-94. Mem. ASTD (govtl. affairs dir. 1988-89), Am. Quality and Participation Soc. (nat. presenter 1992), Orgn. Devel. Network (nat. presenter 1989), Soc. Human Resource Mgmt. (regional presenter 1992, nat. presenter 1994), The Conf. Bd. (nat. presenter 1995), LOMA Human Resources Forum. Home: 6040 N Camelback Manor

Dr Paradise Vly AZ 85253-5148 Office: Murro Consulting Inc Ste 145 2111 E Highland Ste 145 Phoenix AZ 85016

CARTER, CAROLYN HOUCHIN, advertising agency executive; b. Louisville, Nov. 2, 1952; d. Paul Clayton and Georgia Houchin C.; m. Jeffrey Starr, Dec. 8, 1988. BSJ, Northwestern U., 1974, MSJ, 1975. Asst. account exec. SSC&B Advt., Inc., N.Y.C., 1975-76, account exec., 1976-77; account exec. Grey Advt., Inc., N.Y.C., 1977-79, account supr., 1979-81, v.p., account supr., 1981-82, v.p., mgmt. supr., 1982-85, v.p., group mgmt. supr., 1985-87, sr. v.p., 1987-92, exec. v.p., 1992—; mem. Nat. Advt. Rev. Bd., 1983-87; mem. adv. bd. advt. history Smithsonian Nat. Mus. Am. History, 1988-94. Chair March of Dimes Media Adv. Council, 1981-86; mem. U.S. Coun. World Comm. Yr., 1983; active YMCA Acad. Women Achievers, 1992. Recipient Clairol Mentor award Clairol, Inc., 1991. Mem. Women in Communications (pres. N.Y. chpt. 1982-83, N.Y. Matrix award in Advt. 1988, Nat. Headliner award 1991), Advt. Women of N.Y. (bd. dirs. 1987-88), Internat. Womens Forum (bd. dirs. N.Y. chpt. 1994). Office: Grey Advt Inc 777 3rd Ave New York NY 10017

CARTER, CATHERINE LOUISE, elementary school educator; b. Oakland, Calif., Mar. 31, 1947; d. Robert Collidge and Mae (Reidy) C. BA, Ohio Wesleyan U. Tchr. Barclay Elem. Sch., Cherry Hill, N.J., 1969-72, Malberg Elem. Sch., Cherry Hill, N.J., 1972-80, Beck Mid. Sch., Cherry Hill, N.J., 1980-89, 94-95, Carusi Jr. H.S., Cherry Hill, N.J., 1989-94, 95-96; coord. Nat. Women's History Month Cherry Hill Jr. Schs., 1993-94. Mem. dist. Recycling Program Cherry Hill Pub. Schs., 1990-94. Mem. NEA, NOW, N.J. Edn. Assn., Camden County Edn. Assn., Cherry Hill Edn. Assn., World Wildlife Fedn., Global Fund for Women, Planned Parenthood, Alice Paul Centenial Found., Seeking Edn. Equity and Diversity (study group 1994), Freedom from Hunger, Population Comms. Internat. Home: 1015 Oaklyn Ct Voorhees NJ 08043-1817 Office: Carusi Jr Sch Jackson and Roosevelt Rds Cherry Hill NJ 08002

CARTER, CHERYL A., medical/surgical nurse; b. Morgantown, W.Va., Apr. 11, 1960; d. Kenneth W. and Dorothy Eloise (Phillips) Smyth; m. James L. Carter, Oct. 15, 1988. BSN, W.Va. U., 1982. Staff nurse Ohio Valley Med. Ctr., Wheeling, W.Va., Riverside Meth. Hosp., Columbus, Ohio. Mem. ANA, Sigma Theta Tau. Home: 1974 Brittany Rd Columbus OH 43229-5706

CARTER, CHRISTINE SUE, cardiac recovery nurse; b. Dover, Ohio, Feb. 22, 1958; d. Theodore Louis and Mary Louise (Rossi) Rondinella; m. Robert Keith Carter, Aug. 16, 1986; children: Amanda Marie, Timothy Robert. BSN, U. Akron, 1980. CCRN. Staff nurse gen. med. unit Riverside Meth. Hosp., Columbus, Ohio, 1980-82, staff nurse, charge nurse intermediate care unit, 1982-84, staff nurse, occassional charge nurse coronary care unit, 1984-87, asst. nurse mgr. invasive recovery unit, 1987—, mem. critical care edn. com., 1992—; speaker, lectr. in field; CPR instr. Mem., conf. speaker Am. Heart Assn., Columbus, 1985. Mem. AACN (cert.), Ohio Nurses' Assn., Sigma Theta Tau. Democrat. Roman Catholic. Home: 4039 Kilbannan Way Dublin OH 43016-4160 Office: Riverside Meth Hosp 3535 Olentangy River Rd Columbus OH 43214-3925

CARTER, CYNTHIA HICKS, secondary education educator; b. Houston, Aug. 30, 1954; d. Weldon Betts and Nona Gay (Hunt) Hicks; m. William Frazier Carter, Jan. 5, 1974; children: Emily Gay, Weldon Bryan, William Benjamin. BS, Tex. Ea. U., Tyler, 1975; MS, U. Tex. at Tyler, 1978. Cert. in secondary math., phys. sci., elem. math., edn., Tex. Secondary math. and sci. tchr. Tyler Ind. Sch. Dist., 1983-84, Winona (Tex.) Ind. Sch. Dist., 1976-83, 84—; mem. textbook selection com. Winona Ind. Sch. Dist., 1984—. Author: (curriculum guides) Honors Physics, 1988, Honors Geometry, 1993. Tchr. Friendship Sunday sch. class Pleasant Retreat United Meth. Ch., 1982—, mem. adminstrv. bd., 1982-85. Mem. Nat. Coun. Tchrs. Math., Tex. State Tchrs. Assn. Home: 6134 County Road 1150 Tyler TX 75704-9307 Office: Winona Ind Sch Dist PO Box 218 Winona TX 75792-0218

CARTER, DEBRA DEEN, investment sales professional; b. Stoughton, Wis., Aug. 21, 1950; d. John Edward and Doreen Jane (Sveum) Karlslyst; m. Henry Edward Bjoin, Sept. 20, 1975 (div. Mar. 1981); m. Richard Wiley Carter, Apr. 26, 1986. BA in English, U. Wis., 1973. CFP. Account exec. Merrill Lynch, Hollywood, Calif., 1978-80; dir. mktg. Minoco Oil, L.A., 1980-83; v.p. mktg. May Petroleum, Dallas, 1983-86, Am. Residential Mgmt., Dallas, 1986; mktg. specialist Prudential-Bache, Dallas, 1987; v.p. Mass. Fin. Svcs., Boston, 1988-93, Franklin/Templeton, San Mateo, Calif., 1993—. Democrat.

CARTER, EDITH HOUSTON, statistician, educator; b. Charlotte, N.C., Oct. 12, 1936; d. Z. and Ellie (Hartsell) Houston; BS, Appalachian State U., 1959, MA, 1960; PhD, Va. Poly. Inst. and State U., 1976; m. Fletcher F. Carter, Apr. 2, 1961. Transcript analyst Fla. Dept. Edn., Tallahassee, 1961-65; instr. Radford U., 1969-70, 91-94, asst. prof., 1994—; prof. New River C.C., Dublin, Va., 1970-83, dir. instl. research, 1974-78, asst. dean Coll. Arts and Scis., 1978-79, statistician, 1979-83. Violist New River Valley Symphony, Va. Poly. Inst. and State U. Orch., Radford U. Orch., S.W. Va. Opera Soc. Orch.; sec./treas. Radford New River Valley chpt. Am. Sewing Guild, 1991-94, pres., 1994-96. Mem. Am. Ednl. Rsch. Assn., State and Regional Ednl. Rsch. Assn. (sec./treas. 1989-93, pres. 1993-95), Assn. Instl. Research (exec. bd. 1976-78), Southeastern Assn. C.C. Rsch. (exec. bd. 1976-78, Outstanding Service award, Disting. Service award 1981), Nat. Coun. Rsch. and Planning (Outstanding Svc. award 1992), Coll. Music Soc., Am. String Tchrs. Assn., Va. Ednl. Rsch. Assn. (pres.-elect 1996—), Va. Fedn. Women's Clubs (dir. 1968-70), Va. Tech. U. Alumni (pres. New River Valley chpt. 1982-83), Radford Jr. Woman's Club (pres. 1967-68). Methodist. Clubs: Radford Garden. Editor Community Coll. Jour. Research and Planning, 1981-93, Am. Assn. Community Colls. Jour. (rsch. review editor 1991—), Newsletter Southeastern Assn. C.C. Research, 1972—; mem. editorial bd. C.C. Rev., 1990-93. Home: 6924 Radford Univ Radford VA 24142 Office: Radford U Russell Hall Radford VA 24142

CARTER, ELEANOR ELIZABETH, business manager; b. Durham, N.C., July 16, 1954; d. Joseph William Jr. and Sheila Dale (Swartz) C. BS in Social Work, N.C. State U., 1977. Field worker family planning Wake County Health Dept., Raleigh, N.C., 1975-76; sales rep. Bristol-Myers Products, N.C., 1977-80; regional adminstn. asst. Bristol-Myers Products, Dallas, Tex., 1980; regional trainer Bristol-Myers Products, Washington, N.C., Va., 1980; sales adminstrn. mgr. corp. hdqrs. Bristol-Myers Products, N.Y.C., 1980-81; dist. supr. Bristol-Myers Products, Cin., 1981-82; account rep. Fuji Photo Film U.S.A., Inc., Cin., 1982-83; spl. account mgr. Fuji Photo Film U.S.A., Inc., Chgo., 1983-90; nat. account mgr. Fuji Photo Film U.S.A., Itasca, Ill., 1991—. Mem. Nat. Assn. Female Execs., Alpha Kappa Delta. Presbyterian. Office: Fuji Photo Film USA Inc 1285 Hamilton Pky Itasca IL 60143-1150

CARTER, IVY VERONICA, artist, educator; b. Dayton, Ohio, Oct. 19, 1944; d. Horace Wesley and Mildred (Collins) C. BSc in Fine Arts Edn., Ohio State U., 1965; MSLS, Wayne State U., 1971; postgrad., Sch. Art Inst. Chgo., 1988-89. Cert. substitute tchr. libr. media and visual art, Ohio. Grad. studies libr. Bowie (Md.) State Coll., 1970-80; supervisory libr. U.S. Army Libr., Uijongbu, Korea, 1980-81; libr./instr. So. Ohio Coll., Columbus, 1981; reference coord. Bowie State Coll., 1981-84; slide curator U. Akron /Sch. Art, 1986-88; libr. adminstr. Nat. Afro-Am. Mus., Wilberforce, Ohio, 1990-92; catalog/archives libr. Ohio Hist. Soc., Columbus, 1994; artist, info. broker, tchr. Columbus, 1994—; coord. arts festival Unitarian Universalist Congregation, East Columbus, Ohio, 1994; participant/alumni Americorps. One person shows include Columbus Driving Park Libr. Gallery, 1994, Vet. Hosp. Gallery, Ohio State U., Columbus, 1996; two-person shows include CCNY, 1994; contbg. author: New Museum's Artists Writings, 1986, The Ency. of African-Am. Culture and History, 1995, others. Active Walkathon, United Negro Coll. Fund, Columbus, 1995. Recipient awards for art; Puffin Found. grantee, 1995. Mem. Columbus Art League, Art for Comty. Expression, Artists Equity Assn. Home and Studio: 1286 Geers Ave Columbus OH 43206

CARTER, J. DENISE, lawyer; b. Kansas City, Mo., Mar. 21, 1963; d. Ronald Ira and Sharon Kay (Williams) C. AA, Longview C.C., 1986; BA, U. Mo., Kansas City, 1989, JD, 1992. Bar: Mo. 1992. Pvt. practice Powers & Carter, Kansas City, 1993—. Republican. Office: Powers & Carter 324 E 11th St Ste 1609 Kansas City MO 64106

CARTER, JEAN GORDON, lawyer; b. Fort Belvoir, Va., July 30, 1955; d. Thomas Laney and Cleone (Hunter) Gordon; m. Michael L. Carter, Sept. 17, 1977; children: Christina Jean, William Gordon. BS magna cum laude with honors in Accountancy, Wake Forest U., 1977; JD with high honors, Duke U., 1983. Bar: N.C. 1983; CPA; bd. cert. specialist in estates. Acct. Arthur Andersen & Co., Charlotte, N.C., 1977-80; atty. Moore & Van Allen, Raleigh, N.C., 1983-90; ptnr. Hunton & Williams, Raleigh, N.C., 1990—; councilor tax sect. N.C. Bar Assn., 1993—; coun. Estates sect. N.C. Bar Assn., 1990-92; pres. Wake County Estates Coun., Raleigh, 1991-92. Mem. Am. Coll. Trusts and Estates Attys., Order of the Coif, Phi Beta Kappa. Democrat. Methodist. Home: 3913 Stratford Ct Raleigh NC 27609 Office: Hunton & Williams 1 Hannover Sq Raleigh NC 27601

CARTER, JEANNE WILMOT, lawyer, publisher; b. Iowa City, Iowa, Oct. 25, 1949; d. John Robert and Adelaide Wilmot (Briggs) Carter; m. Daniel Halpern, Dec. 31, 1982; 1 child, Lily Wilmot. BA cum laude, Barnard Coll., N.Y.C., 1973; MFA, Columbia U., 1977; JD, Yeshiva U., N.Y.C., 1986. Bar: N.Y. 1987. Assoc. Raoul Lionel Felder, P.C., N.Y.C., 1986—; pres., co-owner, dir. Ecco Press, Hopewell, N.J., 1992—; dir. Nat. Poetry Series, Hopewell, 1981—. Author: Reading the Fights, 1987; editor: On Music, 1994; contbr. articles to profl. jours. including N.Am. Rev., Antaeus, Antioch Rev., Arts and Entertainment Law Jour., Ontario Rev., Denver Quar. Bd. dirs. AIDS Helping Hand, N.Y.C., 1987-95; vol. litigator Womanspace, Princeton, N.J., 1994; mem. Jr. League of N.Y.C., 1980—. N.Y. Found. of the Arts fellow, 1989. Mem. ABA, N.Y. State Bar Assn. Home: 60 Pheasant Hill Rd Princeton NJ 08540-7502

CARTER, JOY EATON, electrical engineer, consultant; b. Comanche, Tex., Feb. 8, 1923; d. Robert Lee and Carrie (Knudson) Eaton; m. Clarence J. Carter, Aug. 22, 1959; 1 child, Kathy Jean. Student, John Tarleton Agrl. Coll., 1939-40; B Music cum laude, N. Tex. State Tchrs. Coll., 1943, postgrad., 1944-45; postgrad., U. Tex., 1945; MSEE, Ohio State U., 1949, PhDEE and Radio Astronomy, 1957. Engr. aide Civil Service Wright Field, Dayton, Ohio, 1945-46; instr. math. Ohio State U., Columbus, 1946-48, asst., then assoc. Rsch. Found., 1947-49, from instr. to asst. prof. elec. engring., 1949-58; rsch. engr. N.Am. Aviation, Columbus, 1955-56; mem. tech. staff Space Tech. Labs. (later TRW Inc.), Redondo Beach, Calif., 1958-68; sect. head, staff engr. electronics rsch. labs. The Aerospace Corp., El Segundo, 1968-72, staff engr. and mgr. system and terminals, USAF Satellite Communications System Program Office, 1972-77, mgr. communications subsystem Def. Satellite Communications System III Program Office, 1978-79; cons. Mayhill, N.Mex., 1979—. Active Mayhill Vol. Fire Dept., 1986—; bd. dirs. Mayhill Cmty. Assn., 1988—, sec. bd. dirs., 1988—; co-chair music com. Mayhill Bapt. Ch., 1988—, trustee, 1989-92, 94—; bd. dirs. Otero County Farm Bur., 1987—. Named Cow Belle of Yr. Otero Cow Belles, 1988. Mem. IEEE (sr., life), Am. Astron. Soc., Am. Nat. Cattle Women (sec. otero CowBelles chpt. 1986-87, 1st v.p. 1988, historian 1989), Calif. Rare Fruit Growers, Native Plant Soc. N.Mex., Sacramento Mountains Hist. Soc. (bd. dirs. 1986—), High Country Horseman's Assn., Sigma Xi (life), Eta Kappa Nu (life), Sigma Alpha Iota (life), Alpha Chi, Kappa Delta Pi, Pi Mu Epsilon, Sigma Delta Epsilon. Home and Office: PO Box 23 Mayhill NM 88339-0023

CARTER, JULIA MARIE, secondary education educator; b. Topeka, May 2, 1958; d. Jack Earnest and Bonita Aileen (Hatfield) Estes; m. Dan W. Carter; children: John-Thomas, Jessica Raye. Student, Ouachita Bapt. U., 1982. Cert. tchr. K-12, Ark., Fla., Md., Va. Tchr. French Dunbar Jr. High, Little Rock, 1989-91; tchr. Mt. Vernon (Ark.) Schs., 1991; tchr. French Cathedral Sch., Little Rock, 1991-92; tchr. St. Mark's Episcopal Sch., Oakland Park, Fla., 1992-93; tchr. French Miramar (Fla.) High Sch., 1993-96, Benjamin Franklin Sch., 1996—; author, presenter in field. Vol. Chicot Elem., Little Rock, 1989-90, Silver Lake Mid. Sch., North Lauderdale, Fla., 1992-93, Miramar High Sch., 1993-95; mem. Ednl. Materials Equality Com., Little Rock, 1990-91. Fullbright scholar, 1989. Mem. Am. Assn. Tchrs. French (Prof. du Laureat 1989, 92), Am. Fedn. Tchrs. Democrat. Methodist. Home: 135 Chestnut Park Dr Rocky Mount VA 24151

CARTER, KATHRYN ANN, home health nurse, mental health counselor; b. Milw., June 10, 1953; d. Adrian H. and Eleanor R. (Kurth); m. G.R. Lewellyn, Oct. 14, 1972 (div.); children: Anna, Cynthia; m. David Lee Carter, June 15, 1985; children: Ryan, Rebekah; stepchildren: Dana, Derek, Angel. Med. asst., Sch. Nursing, San Diego, 1973; AS, Madison Area Tech. Coll., 1979; BS, Coll. St. Francis, 1989; MS, U. Wis., Whitewater, 1994. RN, Wis., N.Mex.; lic. profl. counselor, N.Mex. RN Mendota Mental Health, Madison, 1983-89, U. Wis. Hosps., Madison, 1989-94, Presbyn. Healthcare, Springer, N.Mex., 1995—; pvt. practice counselor Raton, N.Mex., 1995—; cons. Citizens for the Developmentally Disabled, Raton, 1995—. Leader Girl Scouts, Columbus, Wis., 1992-94. Mem. AAUW (membership v.p. 1994-95), ACA, NRA, Internat. Inst. Wis., Internat. Tae Kwon Do Assn. Home: 420 S 4th St Raton NM 87740 Office: Mental Health Counseling PO Box 854 Raton NM 87740

CARTER, LINDA SUSAN, journalist, educator; b. Columbus, Ohio, Nov. 18, 1950; d. Edward Herman and Jane Lewis (Joseph) C.; m. Jerome Ronald Piasecki, June 5, 1976 (div. Feb. 1983); 1 dau., Amanda. B.A., Mich. State U., 1984; JD Wayne State U., 1988, MA in History, 1991. News dir. WAVZ-AM, New Haven, Conn., 1977-78, WABX-FM, Detroit, 1978—; news anchor WWJ-AM, Detroit, 1978-81, 83-85; talk show host WXYZ-AM, Detroit, 1981-82; press sec. Office of the Gov., Lansing, Mich., 1982-83; dir. pub. affairs Sta. WDIV-TV, Detroit, 1985-86, dir. editorials, 1986-88; news anchor Sta. WWJ-AM, Detroit, 1988-90; lectr. journalism Wayne State U., 1990-91; asst. prof. journalism Mich. State U., 1991—. Mem. AFTRA (exec. bd. 1982-84), Nat. Acad. TV Arts and Scis., State Bar Mich., Sigma Delta Chi. Home: 28646 Rollcrest Rd Farmington Hills MI 48334 Office: Mich State U Sch Journalism 305 Comm Arts Bldg East Lansing MI 48824

CARTER, MAE RIEDY, retired academic official, consultant; b. Berkeley, Calif., May 20, 1921; d. Carl Joseph and Avis Blanche (Rodehaver) Riedy; BS, U. Calif., Berkeley, 1943; m. Robert C. Carter, Aug. 19, 1944; children: Catherine, Christin Ann. Ednl. adv., then program specialist div. continuing edn. U. Del., Newark, 1968-78, asst. provost for women's affairs, exec. dir. commn. status women Office Women's Affairs, 1978-86; adv. bd. Rockefeller Family grant project, 1979-83. Regional v.p. Del. PTA, 1960-62; pres. Friends Newark Free Library, 1968-69; mem. fiscal planning com. Newark Spl. Sch. Dist., 1972. Recipient Outstanding Service award Women's Coordinating Council, 1977, 79; Spl. Recognition award, Nat. U. Extension Assn., 1977, award for credit programs, 1971, Creative Programming award, 1971; AAUW grantee, 1968; Fulbright grantee, 1976; named to Delaware Women Hall of Fame, 1995. Mem. AAUW (past br. pres.), LWV, NOW, Nat. Assn. for Women Edn., Women's Legal Def. Fund, Nat. Women's Polit. Caucus. Republican. Author: Research on Seeing and Evaluating People, 1982, (with Geis and Butler) Seeing and Evaluating People, 1982, revised, 1986, (with Haslett and Geis) The Organizational Woman: Power and Paradox, 1992; also papers, reports in field. Home: 604 Dallam Rd Newark DE 19711-3110

CARTER, MARTHA ELOISE, retired curriculum specialist, reading consultant; b. Fulton, Miss., Aug. 9, 1935; d. Charles Tilmon and Vola Mae (Warren) Cooper; m. Hubert W. Carter, Aug. 3, 1957 (div.); 1 child, Bryan W. BS, U. Wis., 1957, MA, 1971. Classroom tchr. Milw. Pub. Schs., 1957-73, reading supr., 1973-76, generalist, supr., 1976-83, curriculum specialist/reading, 1983—; cons. New Reading Program, N.Y.C., 1993-94; adv. bd. Cardinal Stritch Coll., Milw., 1992-94; mem. tchrs. as readers com. Internat. Reading Assn., Newark, Del., 1994-97. Sunday sch. tchr., choir mem. Bapt. ch. Recipient Celebrate Literacy award Internat. Reading Assn. and Milw. Area Reading Coun., 1992; named Woman of Yr., Bd. Christian Edn., 1990. Mem. ASCD, Wis. State Reading Assn., Milw. Area Reading Coun., Phi Delta Kappa, Delta Kappa Gamma (corr. sec. 1994-95). Home: 3867 N 68th St Milwaukee WI 53216-2009 Office: Mt Zion Child Devel Ctr 2207 N 2nd St Milwaukee WI 53212

CARTER, MELODY BAKER, school system administrator; b. Ft. Hood, Mar. 12, 1956; d. Billy Joe Baker and Betty (Holder) Short; m. Benjamin P. Carter; m. Courtney, Casey. BEd, Miss. State U., 1977, MEd, 1979. Cert. ednl. administr.; cert. secondary tchr. math. Jr. high math. instr. Shivers Jr. H.S., Aberdeen, Miss., 1977-85; math. instr. Aberdeen H.S., 1985-90, Greenwood (Miss.) H.S., 1990-93; headmaster Carroll Acad., Carrollton, Miss., 1993—; supt. adv. coun. Aberdeen Schs., 1987-90. Youth dir. First Meth. Ch., Aberdeen, 1978-87; pres. Jr. Aux., Aberdeen, 1987, v.p., 1986, sec.-treas. 1984-85; pres. Jr. Women's League, Aberdeen, 1986, sec.-treas. 1988-90; sec.-treas. Cherokee Rose Garden Club, Carrollton, 1992—; sponsor Beta Club, student coun. Aberdeen and Greenwood Schs.; pres. N.E. Miss. Coun. Tchrs. of Math., 1985-86. Named Outstanding Woman of Yr. Jr. Aux., 1989. Mem. Delta Kappa Gamma (v.p. 1986-90), Phi Delta Kappa. United Meth. Office: Carroll Acad PO Box 226 Carrollton MS 38917-0226

CARTER, PAMELA LYNN, state attorney general; b. South Haven, Mich., Aug. 20, 1949; d. Roscoe Hollis and Dorothy Elizabeth (Hadley) Fanning; m. Michael Anthony Carter, Aug. 26, 1971; children: Michael Anthony Jr., Marcya Alicia. BA cum laude, U. Detroit, 1971; MSW, U. Mich., 1973; JD, Ind. U., 1984. Bar: Ind. 1984, U.S. Dist. Ct. (no. dist.) Ind. 1984, U.S. Dist. Ct. (so. dist.) Ind. 1984. Rsch. analyst, treatment dir. U. Mich. Sch. Pub. Health and UAW, Detroit, 1973-75; exec. dir. Mental Health Ctr. for Women and Children, Detroit, 1975-77; consumer litigation atty. UAW-Gen. Motors Legal Svcs., Indpls., 1983-87; securities atty. Sec. of State, Indpls., 1987-89; Gov.'s exec. asst. for health and human svcs. Gov.'s Office, Indpls., 1989-91, dep. chief of staff to Gov., 1991-92; with firm Baker & Daniels, 1992-93; atty. gen. State of Ind., Indpls., 1993—. Author poems. mem. Cath. Social Svcs., Indpls., Jr. League, Indpls., Dem. Precinct, Indpls. Recipient Outstanding Svc. award Indiana Perinatal Assn., 1991, Community Svc. Coun. Ctrl. Ind., 1991, non-profl. healthcare award Family Health Conf. Bd. Dirs., 1991, award for excellence Women of the Rainbow, 1991; named Outstanding Young Woman of America, 1977, Breakthrough Woman of the Year, 1989. Mem. Nat. Bar Assn., Ind. Bar Assn., Coalition of 100 Black Women. Democrat. Office: 402 W Washington St Rm C553 Indianapolis IN 46204-2739

CARTER, ROBERTA ECCLESTON, therapist, counselor; b. Pitts.; d. Robert E. and Emily B. (Bucar) Carter; divorced; children: David Michael Kiewlich, Daniel Michael Kiewlich. Student Edinboro State U., 1962-63; BS, California State U. of Pa., 1966; MEd, U. Pitts., 1969; MA, Rosebridge Grad. Sch., Walnut Creek, Calif., 1987. Tchr., Bethel Park Sch. Dist., Pa., 1966-69; writer, media asst. Field Ednl. Pub., San Francisco, 1969-70; educator, counselor, specialist Alameda Unified Sch. Dist., Calif., 1970—; master trainer Calif. State Dept. Edn., Sacramento, 1984—; personal growth cons., Alameda, 1983—. Author: People, Places and Products, 1970, Teaching/Learning Units, 1969; co-author: Teacher's Manual Let's Read, 1968. Mem. AAUW, NEA, Calif. Fedn. Bus. and Profl. Women (legis. chair Alameda br. 1984-85, membership chair 1985), Calif. Edn. Assn., Alameda Edn. Assn., Charter Planetary Soc., Oakland Mus., Exploratorium, Big Bros. of East Bay, Alameda C. of C. (svc. award 1985). Avocations: aerobics, gardening, travel. Home: 1516 Eastshore Dr Alameda CA 94501-3118

CARTER, ROSALYNN SMITH, wife of former President of United States; b. Plains, Ga., Aug. 18, 1927; d. Edgar and Allie (Murray) Smith; m. James Earl Carter, Jr., July 7, 1946; children: John William, James Earl III, Donnel Jeffrey, Amy Lynn. Grad., Ga. Southwestern Coll.; DHL (hon.), Morehouse Coll., 1980; LLD (hon.), U. Notre Dame, 1987. Disting. fellow Inst. Women's Studies Emory U., Atlanta, 1990—; vice chair, bd. dirs. The Carter Ctr., chair Mental Health Task Force Carter Ctr.; hon. chair, bd. dirs. Rosalynn Carter Inst. of Ga. Southwestern Coll.; co-founder Every Child by Two Campaign for Early Immunization. Author: First Lady from Plains, 1984, (with Jimmy Carter) Everything to Gain: Making the Most of the Rest of Your Life, 1987, Helping Yourself Help Others: A Book for Caregivers, 1994. Bd. dirs. friendship Force, Gannett Co.; bd. advisors Habitat for Humanity; trustee Menninger Found.; hon. trustee Scottish Rite Children's Med. Ctr.; m. Ga. Gov.'s Commn. to Improve Svcs. for Mentally and Emotionally Handicapped, 1971; hon. chmn. Pres.'s Commn. on Mental Health, 1977-78. Recipient Vol. of Decade award Nat. Mental Health Assn., 1980, Presdl. Citation APA, 1982, Nathan S. Kline medal of merit Internat. Com. Against Mental Illness, 1984, Disting. Alumnus award Am. Assn. State Colls. and Univs., 1987, Dorothea Dix award Mental Illness Found., 1988, Dean's award Columbia U. Coll. Physicians and Surgeons, 1991, Notre Dame award for internat. humanitarian svc., 1992, Eleanor Roosevelt Living World award Peace Links, 1992, Nat. Caring award, The Caring Inst., 1995, Kiwanis World Svc. medal, Kiwanis Internat. Found., 1995. Hon. fellow Am. Psychiat. Assn.

CARTER, RUTH B. (MRS. JOSEPH C. CARTER), foundation administrator; b. Charlotte, Vt.; d. Ira E. and Sadie M. (Congdon) Burroughs; m. Joseph C. Carter, June 28, 1935. PhB, U. Vt., 1931. Prin. Newton Acad., Shoreham, Vt., 1931-35; substitute tchr. Spaulding High Sch., Barre, Vt., 1931-35, Woodbury (Vt.) High Sch., 1935-36; tchr. Craftsbury Acad., Craftsbury Common, Vt., 1936-38; sales mgr., buyer Vt. Music Co., Barre, 1939-44; statistician Syracuse U., 1944-46; instr. English Temple U., Phila., 1946-47; records clk. sec. Phila., 1947-56; tchr. English Cen. High Sch., Phila., 1957, Springfield Twp. Sr. High Sch., Montgomery County, Pa., 1964-65; exec. dir. White-Williams Found., 1966-82, trustee, 1982-95. Author: (with Joseph C. Carter) Anchors Aweigh Around the World with Ernest Vail Burroughs, 1960, Pilgrimage to the Lovely Lands of our Ancestors, 1984. Recipient Humanitarian award Chapel of Four Chaplains, 1981, city coun. citation City of Phila., 1982, citation White-Williams Found., 1994. Mem. AAUW (admissions chmn. Phila. chpt. 1959-61, sec. 1961-64, treas. 1965-67), DAR (treas., historian, com. chmn., budget dir., treas., historian, com. chmn., regent Germantown chpt. 1983-86, 89-92, treas. 1992-95, registrar 1995-98, pub. rels. chmn. 1986—), Women for Greater Phila., New Eng. Hist. Geneal. Soc., Geneal. Soc. Vt., Soc. Mayflower Descs. (bd. dirs. 1983-84, sec. 1985-91), Temple U. Faculty Wives Club (rec. sec. 1983-86, pres. Old York group), Temple U. Women's Club, The English Speaking Union, Regent's Club (Phila. chaplain 1986-88). Republican. Methodist. Home: 40 Mount Carmel Ave Apt D2 Glenside PA 19038-3429

CARTER, SARALEE LESSMAN, immunologist, microbiologist; b. Chgo., Feb. 19, 1951; d. Julius A. and Ida (Oiring) Lessman; B.A., National Coll., 1971; m. John B. Carter, Oct. 7, 1979; children: Robert Oiring, Mollie. Supr. lab. immunology Weiss Meml. Hosp., Chgo., 1973-80; lab. immunology supr. Henrotin Hosp., Chgo., 1980-84; tech. dir. Lexington Med. Labs., West Columbia, S.C., 1984—; mem. nat. workshop faculty Am. Soc. Clin. Pathologists; clin. instr. faculty Med. U. S.C. Mem. Am. Soc. Clin. Pathologists (subspecialty cert. in microbiology and immunology, cert. med. technologist). Researcher Legionnaires Disease and mycoplasma pneumonia World Soc. Pathologists, Jerusalem, Israel, 1980. Contbr. articles to profl. jours.; Mem. Rep. Senoritorial Inner Circle, co-chmn. S.C. Young Profls. for George Bush. Office: 110 Medical Ln E Ste 100 West Columbia SC 29169-4817

CARTER, SHIRLEY RAEDELLE, retired elementary education educator; b. Pueblo, Colo., Oct. 28, 1937; d. John Clay and Velda Edythe (Bussard) Apple; m. Carrol Joseph Carter, Apr. 26, 1958; children: Margaret Carol, Norma Katherine, Michael Clay. AA in Edn., Pueblo Jr. Coll., 1957; BA in Elem. Edn., Adams State Coll., 1960, MA in Elem. Edn., 1971. Cert. tchr., Colo. 2d and 3d grade tchr. Beulah (Colo.) Elem. Sch., 1957-58; 3d grade tchr. Westcliffe (Colo.) Elem. Sch., 1961-62; substitute tchr. Dist. RE 11J, Alamosa, Colo., 1974-77; 6th grade English tchr. Evans Intermediate Sch., Alamosa, 1977-78, 5th grade English tchr., 1978-80; 5th grade tchr. Evans Elem. Sch., Alamosa, 1980-90, 4th grade tchr., 1990-95; retired, 1995; owner Shirley's Selectables Joe's Junk, Creede, Colo., 1993—.k. Editor, pub. newspaper Evans Eagle, 1984, newspaper anns. Tasanti, 1957, El Conquestor, 1959. Leader San Luis Valley Girl Scout Columbine Coun., 1972-77, adult trainer, 1974-87; dir. San Luis Valley Girl Scout Camp, 1974-75, program dir., 1976-87; parish Coun. Sacred Heart Ch., Alamosa, Colo., 1982-84. Mem. Creede C. of C. (bd. dirs. 1994—), Internat. Reading Assn. (bd. dirs. San Luis Valley chpt. 1980-90, pres., 1983-84, presenter Colo. Coun. 1982-88, Sweetheart 1985-86, 90-91). Democrat. Roman Catholic. Home: P O Box 53 Creede CO 81130

CARTER, STACEY MONICA, master printmaker; b. Cape May Court House, N.J., Aug. 20, 1969; d. Russell Harry and Ann Christine (Kinnamon) C. BFA, Temple U., 1991. Master printmaker Soma Fine Art Press, San Francisco, 1991-95, Billy Mudd Prodns., Oakland, Calif., 1995, Fine Art Press, San Francisco, 1991—; asst. curator Reflection Exhbn., U. Calif. Mus. of Art, Sci. and Culture, Danville, Calif., 1995. Printmaker (collaboration) Retrospective of Sculptor Yu Yu Yang's Life Work in Prints, 1994, Experimental Explosion Prints, 1994.

CARTER, SYLVIA, journalist; b. Keokuk, Iowa; d. Charles Sylvester and Frances Elizabeth (Smith) C. B of Journalism, U. Mo., 1968. Intern Quincy (Ill.) Herald-Whig, 1966, Detroit Free Press, 1967; reporter The N.Y. Daily News, 1968-70; successively gen. assignment reporter, edn. reporter, food writer, restaurant critic Newsday, Melville, N.Y., 1985-95, N.Y. Newsday, N.Y.C., 1985—; founder, editor Kidsday Newsday, Melville. Author: Eats: The Best Little Restaurants in New York, 1988, Eats N.Y.C.: A Guide to the Best, Cheapest, Most Interesting Restaurants in Brooklyn, Queens and Manhattan, 1995; contbr. to Family Circle and other publs. Trustee Anne O'Hare McCormick Scholarship Fund, N.Y.C., 1988—. Mem. Newswomen's Club N.Y. (pres. 1990-92, bd. dirs., Front Page award 1982). Democrat. Presbyterian. Home: 111 Waverly Pl New York NY 10011-9142 also: 46 Crescent Bow Ridge NY 11961-2915 Office: Newsday 235 Pinelawn Rd Melville NY 11747

CARTIER, CELINE PAULE, librarian, administrator, consultant; b. Lacolle, Que., Can., May 10, 1930; d. Henri Rodolphe and Irene (Boudreau) Robitaille; m. Georges Cartier, Nov. 29, 1952; children: Nathalie, Guillaume. Diplome superieur en pedagogie, U. Montreal, 1948, certificats en litterature et linguistique, 1952; diplome de bibliothecaire-documentaliste, Inst. Catholique, Paris, 1962; maîtrise en adminstrn. publique, Ecole Nationale d'Adminstrn. Publique, 1976; maîtrise en bibliothéconomie, U. Montreal, 1982. Dir. Bibliotheque Centrale, Commn. des ecoles catholiques, Montreal, 1964-73; dir. spl. collections U. Quebec, 1973-76, dir. sector librs., 1976-77; chief gen. libr. U. Laval, Que., 1977-78; gen. dir. libraries U. Laval, 1978-89; cons. Conseil CRC Cons., 1989—. Contbr. articles to profl. jours. Mem. Corp. des Bibliothecaires Profs. de Quebec.

CARTLIDGE, SHRILEY ANN BELL, school administrator; b. Indianola, Miss., July 26, 1940; d. Albert and Betty (Newsome) Bell; 1 child, Carol W. Rowe; m. Arthur J. Cartlidge, Mar. 16, 1991. BS, Miss. Valley State U., Itta Bena, 1964; MEd, Delta State U., Cleveland, Miss., 1975. Tchr. English Greenville (Miss.) Pub. Schs., 1964-93, chmn. dept. English, 1971-87, dist. chmn. dept. English, 1987-93; instr. supr. Yazoo City (Miss.) Schs., 1993-94, chpt. 1 coord., 1994-96; dir. fed. programs, 1996—; tchr./cons. Writing Across the Curriculum, MAS (state testing sys.). Bd. dirs. Miss. PTA, 1987—, v.p. edn., 1993-95, editor bull., 1993-95, state treas., 1995—. Mem. NEA, Nat. Coun. Tchrs. English, Internat. Reading Assn., Miss. Assn. Sch. Adminstrs., Eta Phi Beta (past pres., sec.). Baptist. Office: Yazoo City Mcpl School 1133 Calhoun Ave Yazoo City MS 39194-2939

CARTWRIGHT, MARY LOU, laboratory scientist; b. Payette, Idaho, Apr. 5, 1923; d. Ray J. and Nellie Mae (Sherer) Decker; BS, U. Houston, 1958; MA, Ctrl. Mich. U., 1976; m. Chadwick Louis Cartwright, Sept. 13, 1947. Med. technologist Methodist Hosp., Houston, 1957-59, VA Hosp., Livermore, Calif., 1960-67, Kaiser Permanente Med. Ctr., Hayward, Calif., 1967-71, United Med. Lab., San Mateo, Calif., 1972-73; sr. med. technologist Oakland (Calif.) Hosp., 1974-86; cons. med. lab. tech. Oakland Public Schs. Chmn., Congressional Dist. 11 steering com. Common Cause, 1974-77; consumer mem. Alameda County (Calif.) Health Systems Agy., 1977-78. Served with USNR, 1945-53. Mem. Calif. Soc. Med. Tech., Calif. Assn. Med. Lab. Tech. (Technologist of Yr. award 1968, 78, Pres.'s award 1977, Svc. award chpt. 1978, 79), Am. Soc. Med. Tech. (by-laws chmn. 1981-83), Disabled Am. Vets. (adjutant treas. of chpt. 122, 1993-96), Am. Bus. Women's Assn., Nat. Assn. Female Execs. Democrat. Home and Office: 350 Bennett St Apt 9 Grass Valley CA 95945-6870

CARTWRIGHT, TALULA ELIZABETH, writing and career development educator, communication and leadership consultant; b. Asheville, N.C., Oct. 25, 1947; d. Ralph and Sarah Helen (Medford) C.; m. Edwin Byram Crabtree, May 23, 1976 (div. Sept. 1984); children: Charity, Baxter; m. Richard Thomas England, Apr. 27, 1986; 1 child, Isaac. BA, U. N.C., 1971, MEd, 1974, EdD, 1988. Instr. McDowell Tech. Inst., Marion, N.C., 1972-73, Guilford Tech. C.C., Jamestown, N.C., 1973-89, Guilford Coll., Greensboro, N.C., 1982-87, U. N.C.-Greensboro, 1982-87, N.C. A&T State U., Greensboro, 1984-85; cons. Communication Assocs., Lenoir, Shelby, Asheboro, 1981—; dean continuing edn. Caldwell C.C., Lenoir, N.C., 1989-92; v.p. acad. programs Cleve. C.C., 1992-95; program assoc. Ctr. for Creative Leadership, Greensboro, N.C., 1996—; mem. bd. dirs. N.C. Quality Coun., Carolinas Quality Consortium, Parents-As-Tchrs.; mem. funding bd. United Way; chmn. bd. dirs. Cleve. Abuse Prevetion Coun. Precinct chmn. Dem. Party, Greensboro, 1973-74. Winfield scholar U. N.C. at Greensboro, 1970; recipient Escheats award U. N.C.-Greensboro, 1971; Tchr. of Yr. award Greensboro Tech. C.C. Edn. Assn., 1982, Edn. Honor Roll award, 1988, Educator of the Yr. award, 1989; Civitan Citizenship award, 1966; winner Human Rights Writing Contest, 1988, 89. Mem. NAFE, ASCD, NCAE (pres. local unit 1988-89, chair higher edn. commn. 1989-90, 92-95), Am. Coun. Edn., N.C. Assn. C.C. Adult Edn. Assn., Am. Assn. Women in C.C., Women's Adminstrs. in N.C. (exec. bd. 1995), Higher Edn., N.C. Assn. Colls. & Univs., Am. Mgmt.

CARTY, MARY ELLEN, psychologist; b. N.Y.C., Aug. 7, 1958; d. Walter Vincent and Sally Rita (Clarke) C. BA, Coll. of New Rochelle, 1980, MS, 1991; postgrad., Yeshiva U., 1994—. Cert. sch. psychologist, N.Y. Grad. asst. Coll. of New Rochelle, N.Y., 1989-90, rsch. asst., 1990-91; sch. psychologist intern Pawling (N.Y.) Ctrl. Sch. Dist., 1990-91; sch. psychologist Pawling Jr./Sr. H.S., 1991-93, Clarkstown H.S. South, West Nyack, N.Y., 1993-94, Link Elem. Sch., New City, N.Y., 1996—; behavior specialist, psychologist Esperanza Ctr., N.Y.C., 1993-96; cons. acad. counselor Iona Coll., New Rochelle, N.Y., 1990-94, 96—. Vol. English tchr. Immaculate Conception H.S., Jamaica, W.I., 1983-85; trustee, mem. ch. coun. St. Pius X Ch., Jamaica, 1983-85. Empire Challenger fellow N.Y. State Edn. Dept., 1988-89. Mem. N.Y. Assn. Sch. Psychologists (Ted Bernstein award 1996), Psi Chi. Democrat. Roman Catholic. Home: 434 N High St Mount Vernon NY 10552 Office: Ctr for Preventive Psychiatry 19 Greenridge Ave White Plains NY 10605

CARUANA, JOAN, educator, psychotherapist, nurse; b. Bklyn., Dec. 11, 1941; d. Gaetano and Fanny Caruana. RN, St. Vincent Hosp. Sch. Nursing, 1961; BS, Boston Coll., 1964; MA, NYU, 1975; grad., Psychoanalytic Psychotherapy Study Ctr., 1992. Cert. clin. specialist in adult psychiat. mental health nursing. Instr. St. Vincent's Hosp. Sch. Nursing, N.Y.C., 1965—; psychotherapist N.Y.C., 1987—; Editor St. Vincent's Hosp. Alumnae Assn. Newsletter, 1978—. Office: St Vincents Hosp Sch Nursing 27 Christopher St New York NY 10014-3518

CARUSO, AILEEN SMITH, managed care consultant; b. Albany, N.Y., July 25, 1949; d. Robert Vincent and Mary (Prince) Smith; m. George Michael Caruso, Apr. 24, 1971; 1 child, Patrick Michael. AAS in nursing, Russell Sage Jr. Coll., Albany, 1970; BSBA cum laude, Coll. St. Rose, 1994. RN, N.Y.; cert. case mgr. Staff nurse neuro and thoracic surgery units VA Hosp., 1970-71; staff nurse family practice Milton F. Gipstein, MD, Schenctady, N.Y., 1971-74; psychiat. nurse Peter F. Andrus, MD, Albany, 1977-81; coll. health nurse State U. N.Y., Albany, 1979-82; orthopedic staff nurse Rosa Road Orthopedics, Schenectady, 1980-82; coll. health nurse Union Coll., Schenectady, 1982-87; customer svc. rep. Empire Blue Cross, Albany, 1987-88; fin. planner N.Y. Life Ins., Albany, 1988-89; sr. mgr. Corp. Health Demensions, Troy, N.Y., 1989-94, dir. implementation and tng., 1994-96, dir. implementation and corp. case mgmt., 1996—; adv. Gen. Elec. Corp. Rsch. & Devel. Safety Com., Schenectady, 1992-94; chmn. profl. devel. Northeast N.Y. Health Promotion, Albany, 1994—; com. chair Schenectady Health Coalition, 1993-95; edn. and by laws com., chair govt. affairs Am. Occupational Health Nurses, Albany, 1994—. Co-author: Occupational Health Services Administrative/Patient Management Manual. PRes. Ch. Women, St. George's Episcopal Ch., 1994—, mem. exec. bd. dirs., 1989—, sr. vestryman; chmn. worksite program N.E. N.Y. Tobacco-Free Coalition, 1993-94; co-mgr. The Bookshop at St. Georges, 1993-95. Recipient Rector's Recognition award St. George's Ch., 1991. Mem. Am. Assn. Occupational Health Nurses, Schenectady County Health Promotion Consortium, Health Promotion Coun. of N.E. N.Y., Schenectady County Bus. and Profl. Women, Capital Dist. Case Mgmt. Assn., Sacandaga Boat Club, Alpha Sigma Lambda. Home: 392 Lucille Ln Schenectady NY 12306 Office: Corp Health Dimensions 500 Federal St Troy NY 12180-2832

CARUSO, CAROL ELAINE, elementary education educator; b. Jersey City, Dec. 11, 1958; d. Adrian T. and Catherine J. (Dobstetter) Mets; m. Frank J. Caruso, 1 child, Monica C. AA in Social Scis., Brookdale C.C., 1989; BA in Psychology, Rutgers U., 1994; postgrad., Monmouth U., 1994—. Assoc. mgr. tng. Bellcore, Piscataway, N.J., 1983-92; tech. specialist Monmouth County Vocat. Sch., Freehold, N.J., 1992-93; tchr., tech. coord. Fair Haven (N.J.) Elem. Sch., 1993—. Mem. Internat. Soc. Tech. in Edn., N.J. Assn. for Ednl. Tech., Assn. Supervision and Curriculum Devel., Monmouth Tech. in Edn. Coun. (v.p. 1993-95). Roman Catholic. Office: Fair Haven Pub Schs 242 Hance Rd Fair Haven NJ 07704-3147

CARUSO, KAY ANN PETE, elementary education educator; b. New Orleans, Sept. 23, 1944; d. John R. and Dorothy E. (LeBlanc) Pete; m. Frank J. Caruso III, Nov. 11, 1967; 1 child, Brian Joseph. BA, Southeastern La. U., 1966; MEd, U. New Orleans, 1981. Tchg. cert. La. Elementary tchr., libr., fifth grade reading tchr. Jefferson Parish Pub. Sch. Sys., Metairie, La., 1966—. Sec. Brother Martin H.S. Parent Club, New Orleans, 1992-94; tchr. rep. Alice Birney Sch. Parent Club, Metairie, 1979-83; vol. Rep. Nat. Conv., New Orleans, 1990. Named tchr. of yr. Jefferson Parish C. of C. 1988, 95-96; recipient Barbara McNamara award for reading promotion Reading Is Fundamental program, 1989, Disting. Tchg. award Gifted and Talented Program Northwestern State U., 1995. Mem. Jefferson Librs. Assn. (v.p., pres. 1984-88), Jefferson Fedn. Tchrs. (librs. chpt. rep. 1985-87), So. Assn. Colls. & Schs. (evaluator, com. chair 1980-96), AAUW (chpt. sec. 1996—), Delta Kappa Gamma (chpt. sec. 1984-86, v.p. 1988-90, pres. 1994-96). Office: Alice Birney Elem Sch 4829 Hastings St Metairie LA 70006

CARVALHO, MARIE JUSTINE, English language educator, poet; b. Omaha, Sept. 11, 1969; d. Eugene Wade and Ann Clare (McManus) C. Student, Trinity Coll., Rome, 1989; BA in Art, Pomona Coll., 1990. Program coord. Undergrad. Sch. Bus. U. Wash., Seattle, 1990-91; pub. rels. officer Western Wyo. C.C., Rock Springs, 1993-96, English instr., 1995-96; English instr. Duke U., Durham, N.C., 1996—; participant Wyo. Writers Cir., 1995; presenter Am. Sociology Assn. Conv., 1989. Big Sister Big Bros./Big Sisters Sweetwater County, Wyo., 1994-95. Ford Found. Sociology fellow, 1989, Wyo. Arts Coun. Lit. for Poetry fellow, 1994-95. Mem. Phi Beta Kappa. Democrat.

CARVER, DOROTHY LEE ESKEW (MRS. JOHN JAMES CARVER), retired secondary education educator; b. Brady, Tex., July 10, 1926; d. Clyde Albert and A. Maurine (Meadows) Eskew; student So. Ore. Coll., 1942-43, Coll. Eastern Utah, 1965-67; BA, U. Utah, 1968; MA, Cal. State Coll. at Hayward, 1970; postgrad. Mills Coll., 1971; m. John James Carver, Feb. 26, 1944; children: John James, Sheila Carver Bentley, Chuck, David. Instr., Rutherford Bus. Coll., Dallas, 1944-45; sec. Adolph Coors Co., Golden, Colo., 1945-47; instr. English, Coll. Eastern Utah, Price, 1968-69; instr. speech Modesto (Calif.) Jr. Coll., 1970-71; instr. personal devel. men and women Heald Bus. Colls., Oakland, Calif., 1972-74, dean curricula, Walnut Creek, Calif., 1974-86; instr. Diablo Valley Coll., Pleasant Hill, Calif., 1986-87, Contra Costa Christian H.S.; ret., 1992; communications cons. Oakland Army Base, Crocker Bank, U.S. Steel, I. Magnin, Artec Internat.; presenter in field. Author: Developing Listening Skills. Mem. Gov.'s Conf. on Higher Edn. in Utah, 1968; mem. finance com. Coll. Eastern Utah, 1967-69; active various cmty. drives. Bd. dirs. Opportunity Ctr., Symphony of the Mountain. Mem. AAUW, Bus. and Profl. Womens Club, Nat. Assn. Deans and Women Adminstrs., Delta Kappa Gamma. Episcopalian (supt. Sunday Sch. 1967-69). Clubs: Soroptimist Internat. (pres. Walnut Creek 1979-80 sec., founder region 1978-80); Order Eastern Star. Home: 20 Coronado Ct Walnut Creek CA 94596-5801

CARVER, ELIZABETH C., lawyer; b. Mo., 1959; Bar: Mo. 1985. BA with honors, U. Notre Dame, 1981; JD, Coll. of William and Mary, 1984. Jud. clk. hon. Floyd R. Gibson 8th Cir. Ct. of Appeals, 1984-86; ptnr. Bryan Cave LLP, St. Louis. Recipient Am. Jurisprudence Book award. Mem. Order of Coif. Office: Bryan Cave LLP One Met Square 211 N Broadway Saint Louis MO 63102-2750*

CARVER, JUANITA ASH, plastic company executive; b. Indpls., Apr. 8, 1929; d. Willard H. and Golda M. Ashe; children: Daniel Charles, Robin Lewis, Scott Alan. Student Ariz. State U., 1948, 72, Mira Mar Coll., 1994. Cons. MOBIUS, 1983—; pres. Carver Corp., Phoenix, 1977—. Bd. dirs. Scottsdale Meml. Hosp. Aux., 1964-65, now assoc. Republican. Methodist. Patentee latch hook rug yarner, Pressure Lift. Home: 9866 Reagan Rd Apt 126 San Diego CA 92126-3143

CARVER, LISA ANNE, professional society administrator; b. Newport, RI, Aug. 27, 1965; d. George Andrew and Judith Anne (Murphy) B.; m. George Allen Carver III, Oct. 2, 1993. BS in Mktg. Mgmt., Va. Tech., 1987, BA in Comms. Studies, 1987. Licensing coord. DeRand/Pennington/Bass, Inc., Arlington, Va., 1988-91, asst. compliance dir., 1991-92; securities fraud examiner Nat. Assn. Securities Dealers, Rockville, Md., 1992—. Roman Catholic. Home: 4663 Newington Rd Jefferson MD 21755

CARVER, MELISSA TOWNSEND, management consultant; b. Providence, Feb. 1, 1971; d. Paul Townsend and Phyllis Joan (Albrecht) C. BA in Econs., Cornell U., 1993. Systems analyst JP Morgan, Inc., N.Y.C., 1992; cons. Price Waterhouse, N.Y.C., 1993—. Mem. Inst. Mgmt. Cons. Office: Price Waterhouse 1177 Ave of Americas New York NY 10036

CARVER, PATRICIA ANN PULLEN, accountant; b. Louisville, Oct. 13, 1954; d. Carsue Sr. and Agnes I. (Elery) Pullen; m. Richard L. Carver, Aug. 5, 1972; children: Toni R., Michael A. BS in Commerce, U. Louisville, 1982. CPA, Ky. Revenue field auditor Ky. Revenue Cabinet, Louisville, 1983-87; acct. Met. Sewer Dist., Louisville, 1987-88, accts. payable supr., 1988-89, revenue adminstr., 1989-90, fin. analyst, 1990-91, chief internal auditor, 1991—. V.p safe place oversight com. YMCA Safe Place Svcs., Louisville, 1994—; bd. dirs. African Am. Cath. Ministries, Louisville, 1994—; acct. Ky. Edn. Reform All at Risk Childrens Caucus, Louisville, 1994—. Recipient Black Achiever award YMCA, Louisville, 1990. Mem. AICPAs, Ky. Soc. CPAs, Bellarmine Coll. African-Am. Leadership Inst., River City Bus. and Profl. Women, Delta Sigma Theta (alumni chpt.). Democrat. Office: Louisville & Jefferson Co Met Sewer Dist 400 S 6th St Louisville KY 40202-2319

CARY, LORENE EMILY, writer; b. Phila., Nov. 29, 1956; d. John William and Carole Joan (Hamilton) C.; m. Robert C. Smith, Aug. 27, 1983; children: Laura Hagans, Zoe Drayton; 1 stepchild, Geoffrey. BA, MA in English, U. Pa., 1978; MA in Victorian Lit., U. Sussex, 1980; LittD (hon.), Colby Coll., 1992. Apprentice writer Time, 1980; assoc. editor TV Guide, 1980-82; tchr., dormitory master, coach St. Paul's Sch., Concord, N.H., 1982-83; contbg. editor Newsweek, 1993-94; lectr. U. Pa. Dept. English, Phila., 1995—; adj. prof. U. Arts, Phila., 1984-88, Antioch U., Phila., 1984-88; guest lectr. in field. Author: Black Ice, 1991, The Price of a Child, 1995; contbr. essays to mags. Trustee St. Paul's Sch., Concord, N.H., 1987-91. Pew Found. fellow for Arts fellow, 1995-96. Mem. PEN, Authors Guild. Office: U Pa Dept English 34th and Walnut Sts Philadelphia PA 19104

CASADONTE, SUSANA TIGELEIRO, financial analyst; b. Newark, Mar. 2, 1967; d. Armando and Helena (Ferreira) Tigeleiro; m. Edward F. Casadonte, June 1995. BS, Seton Hall U., 1989, postgrad., 1996—. CPA, cert. mgmt. acct., N.J. Sr. acct. Arthur Andersen, Roseland, N.J., 1989-91; sr. auditor Johnson & Johnson, New Brunswick, N.J., 1991-94; sr. analyst Ethicon, Inc., Somerville, N.J., 1994-95, Ortho-McNeil Pharm., Raritan, N.J., 1995—. Telethon vol. Children's Miracle Network, Somerville, N.J., 1992-94. Mem. AICPA, Inst. Mgmt. Accts. Roman Catholic. Office: Ortho-McNeil Pharm 202 South Raritan NJ 08869

CASCIO, DONNA LEE, secondary education educator; b. Elizabeth, N.J., Mar. 11, 1948; d. Gerald and Doris Ethel Cascio. BS in Biology and Chemistry, Fairleigh Dickinson U., 1970; MA in Environ. Studies, Montclair State Coll., 1976. Cert. elem. tchr., supr., N.J. Secondary tchr. Woodbridge (N.J.) High Sch., 1972—; ednl. programming cons. Metlar House Mus., Piscataway, N.J., 1990—. Marine Sci. Consortium tchr. exch. grantee, Russia, 1992. Democrat. Roman Catholic. Home: 29 Keith Jeffries Ave Cranford NJ 07016-2708 Office: Woodbridge High Sch St George and Kelly St Woodbridge NJ 07095

CASE, ELIZABETH, artist, writer; b. Long Beach, Calif., July 24, 1930; d. Nelson and Sarah Lee (Odend'hal) C.; children: Walter J. Zwicker Jr., Keith Allen Zwicker, Pat James Cioffi, Susan Cioffi Onopa. Student, French Inst., 1946, Art Students League, 1948-49, Elmira Coll., 1949-51, Syracuse U., 1951, Chaffey Coll., Ontario, Calif., 1954. With animation dept. Walt Disney Prodns., Burbank, Calif., 1956-58; mem. faculty Lighthouse Art and Music Camp, 1961, New Hope Art Sch., Pa., 1961; asst. mgr. promotion, copywriter Reinhold Pub. Co., N.Y.C., 1962-63; copywriter Columbia U. Press, 1963; advt. coord. Orbit Imperial Design Corp., 1964; prin., dir. Gadfly Prodns., 1969-89, ECHO, 1989—; mem. faculty Ft. Lee Adult Sch., 1975-82; sr. copywriter/designer spl. projects coll. textbook advt. Prentice-Hall, Inc., Englewood Cliffs, N.J., 1975-77; mem. promotion and design staff Rutherford Mus., 1979; mgr. sales promotion M. Grumbacher, Inc., 1979-81; typographer Graphic Tech. Inc., N.Y.C., 1983-90, The Graphic Word, 1990-91; Ace Typographers, N.Y.C., 1991-92; copy editor Times-Beacon Newspapers, Manahawkin, N.J., 1993-94. USN combat artist, 1974—; one-man show rsch. libr. exhbns. facility Walt Disney Prodns., 1957, 58, Swain's Gallery, New Hope, Pa., 1963, D'Alessio Gallery, N.Y.C., 1963, Gallery 8, N.Y.C., 1969, Ft. Lee Pub. Libr., 1975, Ridgefield Pub. Libr., 1977, Old Bridge Pub. Libr., 1978, Edgewater (N.J.) Nat. Bank, 1983, Edgewater Pub. Libr., 1984, Ea. Va. Med. Ctr., Norfolk, 1984, Ocean County Artists' Guild, Island Hgts., N.J., 1994, Ocean County Libr. Manchester Br., 1996; exhibited in group shows at Friends Cen., Phila., 1960, Hist. Soc. Ann. Exhbn., Philips Mill, Pa., 1962-63, Englewood Armory Show, 1967-68, Hadassah, Paramus, N.J., 1969, Bergen C.C., 1970, traveling exhbn. Bicentennial Am. Freedoms, 1975-76, So. Vt. Art Ctr., 1980, Edgewater Arts Coun. 1982 (1st prize), 93-94, Bergen County Mus., 1984-85, Notes Mus., 1993, Jane Law Long Beach Island Watercolor Ann., 1993-94, Batsto Outdoor Art Show, 1993 (prize), 95 (prize), Jane Law Long Beach Island Ann. Miniature Art Show, 1993-94, Ocean County Art Guild, 1993 (prize), 94, 95 (prize), Ocean County Coll. Srs. Exhibit, 1993-94, 95 (2d prize), 96, N.J. State Show, 1993, 94, Nat. Soc. Mural Painters Centennial Exhbn. and Symposium, Art Students League Gallery, 1995, St. Francis Ann. Spring Art Show, Brant Beach, N.J., 1996, Women Oil Painters of N.J. Jane Law's Long Beach Island Gallery, 1996; represented in permanent collections at Washington Navy Yard Combat Art Collection, Ch. of Christ, Jersey City, Edgewater Pub. Libr., Intrepid Sea-Air-Space Mus. Am. Freedoms Collection; executed murals at INSCON, San Dimas, Calif., L.A. County Hosp., with Walt Disney team Delaware Canal, New Hope; mural design Allegheny Airlines, Lumberville, Pa., 1960; mural corner Main and 202, New Hope, 1960, Lumberville Meth. Ch., 1961, swimming pool, Jerico Valley, Pa., 1961, Orbit Imperial Design Corp., N.Y.C., 1965, Fabric Shop, Ft. Lee, 1969, 72, Ch. of Good Shepherd, 1971, Old Bridge Pub. Libr., 1977, reinstalled new libr. bldg., 1995, History of Women Voting (tryptych design) for traveling exhbn. Momentous Events in American History, Nat. Soc. Mural Painters, 1980-82, History of Typography, GTI, N.Y.C., 1985 (reinstalled at Bergen County Tech. Schs. Acad. for Advancement of Sci. and Tech. 1991); illustrator cover Bucks County Life, Doylestown, Pa., 1961, Vanity Fair Books, 1962, Am. Scandinavian Rev., 1962, Molecular Kinetic Theory, 1963, Theory of Lanthinides and Chemical Energy, 1963, Harle Publs., 1969-70, Programmed Algebra vols. 1 and 2, 1977, vol. 3, 1979, Use and Misuse of Statistics, 1978; illustrator, designer What Do I Do with a Major in ... (Malnig), 2d edit., 1984; pub. VeggieTree, ECHO Posters and Cards, 1988—. Recipient Spring Concours award Art Students League, 1949, Outstanding Achievement award Elmira Coll., 1976, Merit award Edgewater Coun., 1976; subject of 35-minute films The Wrong Elf, 1978, Stroke of Color, 1984 (included in N.Y. Art Rev. 1988), WLVW Leisure Village West The Joy of Painting, 1996. Mem. Nat. Soc. Mural Painters (publicity chmn. 1973—, sec. 1975, bd. dir. pub. rels. 1981-83, 92, editor newsletter 1980-81, 95—, author brochure and guide, curator bicentennial collection Intrepid Sea, Air, Space Mus. 1993, sec. 1995—). Home and Studio: 9-D Dartmouth St Whiting NJ 08759-3130

CASE, SARA ANN, critical care nurse, emergency nurse; b. Lake Charles, La., Nov. 24, 1963; d. Floyd Jerome and Dorothy Carol (Patrick) C. BSN, McNeese State U., 1989. RN, N.Y.; CCRN; cert. ACLS. Staff RN ICU Lake Charles (La.) Meml. Hosp., 1989-90; traveling nurse neurotrauma ICU, Md. Inst. for Emergency Med. Svcs. Sys. Shock Trauma Hosp., Balt., 1990; traveling nurse CCU and med. ICU, NYU Med. Ctr., N.Y.C., 1990-91; traveling nurse neurosurg. ICU, Zale Liphy U. Hosp., Dallas, 1991; traveling nurse burn ICU N.Y. Hosp.-Cornell Med. Ctr., N.Y.C., 1992; staff nurse cardiothoracic ICU, St. Vincent's Hosp. and Med. Ctr., N.Y.C., 1992—; per diem nurse emergency and critical care dept. N.Y. Hosp.-Cornell Med. Ctr., N.Y.C., 1992—. Mem. AACN. Democrat. Roman Catholic. Home: 104 Sullivan St Apt 4 New York NY 10012-3631

CASEBEER, DEANNA FERN GENTRY, elementary education educator; b. Albert Lea, Minn., July 18, 1945; d. Floyd Chester and Evelyn Vera (Bressel) Gentry; m. Roger Ned Casebeer, Oct. 2, 1965; children: Nita Ankrom, John Casebeer. Bs in Edn., SMS, 1969; MS in Edn., SMSU, 1985. Elem. tchr. Nicholes Junction Sch., Willard, Mo., 1969-70, West Ctrl. Sch., Joplin, Mo., 1970-72, Raymondville (Mo.) Pub. Schs., 1972-78, Houston (Mo.) Pub. Sch., 1978-81, Marion C. Early Sch., Morrisville, Mo., 1981-84, Bolivar (Mo.) Pub. Schs., 1986—. Mem. Internat. Reading Assn. (sec. 1994). Republican. Home: 1228 E 473d Rd Bolivar MO 65613-9672

CASELLA, JEAN, editor, writer; b. N.Y.C., Oct. 10, 1961; d. Stephen and Dolores Josephine (Hess) C. BA in English, Cornell U., 1983; postgrad., NYU, N.Y.C., 1988-90. Arts program specialist N.Y.C. Dept. Cultural Affairs, 1985-86; mng. editor Fiction Collective, N.Y.C., 1986-88, Thunder's Mouth Press, N.Y.C., 1988-91, Heresies mag., N.Y.C., 1993-95; freelance editor/writer Bklyn., 1991-95; sr. editor The Feminist Press, N.Y.C., 1995-96; guest lectr. NYU Ctr. for Pub., N.Y.C., summer 1990, Columbia U. Writing Program, N.Y.C., 1992; benefit organizer Free 2 Read - Writers & Pubs. Against Censorship, N.Y.C., 1993, 94. Co-editor: (with James Ridgeway) Cast A Cold Eye: American Opinion Writing, 1991; author spl. book revs. Mpls. City Pages, 1993-95; assoc. prodr. documentary film H-2 worker, 1990 (Best Documentary Sundance Film Festival, 1990). Mem. Nat. Writers Union. Office: The Feminist Press 311 E 94th St New York NY 10128

CASELLA, MARGARET MARY, artist, photographer; b. Bklyn., May 12, 1940; d. John August and Ann Elizabeth (Krajci) Butkovsky; m. Anthony Joseph Casella, Nov. 23, 1961; children: Paul Joseph, David John, Gregory Anthony. Cert. in Merchandising, Tobe-Coburn Sch., N.Y.C., 1961; BFA, L.I. U., 1982, MFA, 1984. lectr. in field. Photographer: (book) Garbage or Art?, 1990 (Gold award Photo Design Mag. 1990); exhibited in solo exhbns. Media Port Gallery, Port Washington Libr., 1989, Midtown Y Photography Gallery, N.Y.C., 1991, Grand Ctrl. Terminal, N.Y.C., 1991, others; group shows include U. Tex. at Arlington, Deutser Art Gallery, Houston, Heckscher Mus., Huntington, N.Y., Konica Plz., Tokyo, Elaine Benson Gallery, Bridgehampton, N.Y., Firehouse Gallery, Garden City, N.Y., The Visual Club, N.Y.C.; works in permanent collections of Mus. for Photographs, Branschweig, Germany, Yergeau Musee Internat. d'Art, Montreal, Fine Art Mus. of L.I., N.Y., Hempstead Houston fotofest Permanent Archives, Houston, Glyndor Gallery, Wave Hill, N.Y. Founder, dir. Art Upstairs Gallery, East Williston, 1983-91; co-chmn. Diet of the Arts, C.W. Post campus of L.I. U., 1992—. Mem. Advt. Photographers of N.Y., Profl. Women Photographers. Office: Casella Photography 889 Broadway New York NY 10003

CASEY, BARBARA ANN, lawyer; b. Amarillo, Tex., Feb. 4, 1958; d. Ewell E. Parker and Barbara (Massoud) Foster; m. Michael F. Casey, Oct. 29, 1994; 1 child, Claire Sophia. BA in econ., U. Cin., Cin., 1981; JD, Rutgers U. Sch. of Law, Camden, 1985. Bar: Pa., 1985, N.J., 1985. Staff supr. econ. analysis Cin. Bell, Inc., Cin., 1981-82; atty., assoc. Duane, Morris & Heckscher, Phila., 1985-88, Drinker, Biddle & Reath, Voorhees, N.J., 1988-90;

atty., assoc. Levin & Hluchan, P.C., Voorhees, 1990-92, atty., shareholder, 1992—; bd. dirs. Voorhees Bus. Assn., Voorhees. Mem. Burlington County Bar Assn., Camden County Bar Assn., Phila. Bar Assn., Penn. State Bar Assn., N.J. State Bar Assn. Republican. Roman Catholic. Office: Levin & Hluchan PC 1200 Laurel Oak Rd Ste 100 Voorhees NJ 08043

CASEY, BEVERLY ANN, postmaster; b. Decaturville, Tenn., Aug. 6, 1949; d. Willie Hugh and Lillian Blanche (Ivy) Tillman; m. John Robert Casey, Jan. 19, 1969 (div. 1982); children—John Gary, Kimberly Jean. Student Jackson State Community Coll., 1982-84. Sec. State of Tenn., Western Institute, 1969-76; post office clk. U.S. Postal Service, Western Institute, 1977-82, postmaster, 1982-84; postmaster U.S. Postal Service, Pickwick Dam, Tenn., 1984—; officer-in-charge U.S. Postal Service, Michie, Tenn., 1984. Bd. dirs. Pickwick Med. Clinic, 1986; vol. Hardeman chpt. Saint Jude, Bolivar, Tenn., 1983, Hospice, 1996; mem. parents advancement com. Wesleyan Coll., 1991-94; town chmn. Reelfoot council Girl Scouts U.S., 1980-84, activities chmn., 1980-84, recipient Appreciation award, 1983. Named Outstanding 3d Class Postmaster 380 area U.S. Postal Service, 1984; recipient Vol. Service award Cystic Fibrosis Found., Tenn. Chpt., 1982, Vol. Appreciation Cert. Western Mental Health, 1984. Mem. Nat. League of Postmasters (v.p. Tenn. br. 1984-86), 380 Postmasters Assn. (pres. 1983-84), U.S. Postal Service (dir.-at-large women's adv. coun. 1983-88). Baptist. Avocations: walking; tennis. Home: PO Box 363 Pickwick Dam TN 38365-0363 Office: US Postal Service Pickwick Dam TN 38365

CASEY, DARLA DIANN, elementary education educator; b. West Linn, Oreg., Mar. 21, 1940; d. Karl F. and Lucille Iona (Wilson) Lettenmaier; m. Charles Emerson Casey, July 30, 1965; children: John, Michael, Kim. BSEd, U. Wis., Milw., 1965; MEd, Oreg. State U., postgrad.; postgrad., U. Oreg., West State, Port State. Cert. tchr. grades K-9, basic art grades 1-12. Tchr., grade 3, swimming instr., grades 4-6 Lakeside (Oreg.) Elem.; tchr., readiness rm. K-1 Siuslaw Elem., Florence, Oreg.; tchr., grades K-1, spl. reading, art Washington Elem., Canon City, Colo.; tchr., grade 1 Sam Case Elem. Sch., Lincoln County Sch. Dist., Newport, Oreg.; mentor tchr. N.W. Sci. Survey Com.; speaker in field. Contbr. articles to profl. jours. Named Oreg. Elem. Sci. Tchr. of Yr. Am. Electronics Assn. and Dept. Edn., 1989; NASA scholar, 1992, 95, Oreg. Cadre for All tchrs. of sci. scholar, 1993, NASA Flight Opportunities for Sci. Tchr. Enrichment Project scholar, 1995, Am. Astron. Soc. Tchr. Resource Agt. scholar, 1996. Mem. NEA, Oreg. Edn. Assn., Oreg. Sci. Tchrs. Assn., Oreg. Reading Assn., Oreg. Seacoast Reading Coun. (past pres.), Oreg. Math. Tchrs. Assn., Phi Delta Kappa. Home: PO Box 514 Siletz OR 97380-0514

CASEY, KAREN ANNE, banker; b. Bklyn., Oct. 5, 1955; d. Stanley Joseph and Helen Katherine (Kosowski) Mozeleski; m. Dennis Joseph Casey, May 14, 1977; children: Christopher Sean, Erin Michelle. BBA, Baruch Coll., CUNY, 1977. CPA, N.Y., CFP. Jr. acct. Coopers & Lybrand, N.Y.C., 1977-78, sr. acct., 1978-79, supr., 1979-81; asst. fin. contr. Gulf Internat. Bank, N.Y.C., 1981-82, fin. contr., 1982; v.p., fin. contr. Allied Irish Banks plc, N.Y.C., 1982-87, sr. v.p., fin. contr., 1988-89, sr. v.p. mgmt. support svcs., 1989-92, sr. v.p., CFO, Allied Irish Bank, 1992-94, sr. v.p., head pvt. fin. svcs., 1994—; bank rep. to Inst. Fgn. Bankers, 1984—, Inst. Cert. Fin. Planners, 1991—. Mem. Am. Inst. CPAs. Roman Catholic. Avocations: gardening, golf, tennis, reading. Office: Allied Irish Banks Plc 405 Park Ave New York NY 10022-4405

CASEY, LYNN M., public relations executive; b. Bismark, N.D., June 18, 1955. BA, U. N.C., 1976; MA, U. Minn., 1979; postgrad., Coll. St. Thomas. Comms. specialist Burlington Northern, 1979-80, asst. editor employee comms., 1980-81, asst. mgr. mktg. comms., 1981-82, mgr. mktg./comms., 1982-83; with Brum & Anderson, 1983-87; v.p. Padilla Speer, 1987-91; sr. v.p. Padilla Speer Beardsley, 1991—. Mem. Pub. ReEls. Soc. Am., Phi Beta Kappa. Office: Padilla Speer Beardsley 224 W Franklin Ave Minneapolis MN 55404-2331*

CASEY, MARGARET ELLEN, elementary school educator, real estate agent; b. New Brunswick, N.J., Sept. 23, 1951; d. Patrick T. and Eleanor G. (Crosson) C. BA, Georgian Ct. Coll., 1973; MS in Edn., Monmouth U., 1977. Elem. tchr. Toms River (N.J.) Regional Schs., 1973-78, elem. guidance counselor, 1978-89, supr. instrn., 1989—; cons. in field. Mem. ASCD, Nat. Coun. Tchrs. Math., Nat. Alliance Mentally Ill (N.J. chpt.), N.J. Bd. Realtors, Prins. & Suprs. Assn. Roman Catholic. Home: 891 Royal Ln Toms River NJ 08753 Office: Toms River Regional Schs 1144 Hooper Ave Toms River NJ 08753

CASEY, PATRICIA A., lawyer; b. Detroit, Nov. 10, 1949. BA, U. Mich., 1970; MA, U. Rochester, 1974; JD, Duke U., 1982. Bar: D.C. 1982, U.S. Dist. Ct. (fed. dist.) 1983. Ptnr. Aiken, Gump, Strauss, Hauer & Feld, L.L.P., Washington. Mem. ABA, D.C. Bar. Office: Akin Gump Strauss Hauer & Feld Ste 400 1333 New Hampshire Ave NW Washington DC 20036-1511*

CASEY, PATRICIA LEE, film producer; b. N.Y.C.; d. Joseph and Johanna Lina (Tanner) C.; m. Judd Bernard, Feb. 18, 1972; 1 child, Alicia; stepchildren: Adrianna, Michael. Student, L.A. City Coll. Ballet dancer Radio City Music Hall, N.Y.C.; ballerina L.A. Ballet Co., 1959-64; producer Kettledrums Films, Valley Village, Calif. Dancer, choreographer (film) Double Trouble, 1965; assoc. prodr. Blue, 1967, Man Who Had Power Over Women, 1969, Glad All Over, 1970, Inside Out, 1973, Marseilles Contract, 1975, The Class of Miss MacMichaels, 1979; asst. prodr. Point Blank, 1966; co-star Fade In, 1967; prodr. Monty Python's And Now For Something Completely Different, 1971, The Playboy Guide to Amsterdam, 1980, Blood Red, 1989. Office: Kettledrum Films 4961 Agnes Ave Valley Village CA 91607

CASEY, RITA JO ANN, nursing administrator; b. Paulsboro, N.J., Nov. 19, 1942; d. George John and Louise Elizabeth (De Santis) Centofanti; m. Robert Joseph Casey, June 5, 1965; children: Joseph, Thomas. Diploma, Woman's Med. Coll. Hosp., 1963; BSN, Holy Family Coll., 1985. RN Pa. Staff nurse Woman's Med. Coll. Hosp., Phila., 1963-68; sch. nurse Bensalem (Pa.) Sch. Dist., 1979-83; coord. health svcs. Holy Family Coll., Phila., 1983—; sec. HFC Student Svcs. Mid. States Evaluation Com., Phila., 1991-92; mem. HFC Cmty. Svc. Adv. Bd., 1991—; mem. HFC Strategic Planning Com., Phila., 1993; ARC CPR instr., 1991—. Chartered orgn. rep. Boy Scouts Am., 1976—; pres. Bensalem H.S. Football Booster Club, 1988-89; sec. Bensalem Meml. Day Parade Com., 1989-94, Phila. Archdiocesan Cath. Com. Scouting, 1992—; co-founder Bensalem Tricentennial Commemorative Hist. Trail, 1993. Mem. Am. Coll. Health Assocs., Nat. Assn. Sch. Nurses, Nat. Athletic Trainers Assn., Southeast Coll. Health Nurses Assn., Med. Coll. Pa. Sch. Nursing Alumni Assn. (banquet chair 1963-94). Roman Catholic. Home: 2370 Ogden Ave Bensalem PA 19020-5211 Office: Holy Family Coll Grant & Frankford Aves Philadelphia PA 19114

CASEY, SHANNON GLORIA, visual effects producer; b. Edmonton, Alberta, Canada, Apr. 2, 1957; Came to the U.S., 1988; d. Dennis and Gloria June (Brooks) C.; m. John Harold Copeland, Nov. 20, 1987. Attended, Sch. Phys. Edn., U. Alberta, 1975-77; Diploma in Dance, Grant McEwan Coll., Alberta, 1980. Rschr., story editor mag. show Pizzazz, Toronto, Ontario, Canada, 1984-85; freelance script coord. Toronto, Canada and L.A., 1985-88; mgr. devel. Rattlesnake Prodns., L.A., 1988; mktg. coord. Hemdale Film Corp., L.A., 1988-89; feature devel. asst. Hollywood Pictures, L.A., 1989; film finance assoc. Internat. Creative Mgmt., L.A., 1991-92; visual effects prodr., prin. Air Age Images, Inc./Found. Imaging, Valencia, Calif., 1992—; story analyst various, L.A., 1986-92; word processing tnr. various, Toronto, 1985-88. Mem. ACLU, Acad. Television Arts & Scis. (Emmy award 1993).

CASH, AUDREY SUTTON, secondary school educator; b. Ellenton, Ga., Mar. 16, 1926; d. James Young and Martha Anne (Baker) Sutton; m. Thomas Bell, Dec. 24, 1948; children: Thomas M., Martha C. Reubert, Melanie C. Hill, Richard J. Diploma, Baldwin Jr. Coll., 1944; BS, U. Ga., 1947, MS, 1950; postgrad., Va. Commonwealth U., 1967-68, Fla. State U., 1969. Tchr. Moultrie (Ga.) High Sch., 1947-49, Cook High Sch., Adel, Ga., 1950-52, Juliette Lowe Sch., Savannah, Ga., 1955-57, Terry Parker High Sch., Jacksonville, Fla., 1968-88; ret., 1988; pres. Hope Enterprises of Jacksonville, Fla. Inc., 1977-87; lectr. Elderhostel, 1994. Author: (cookbook) Southern Literary, 1978. Active Jacksonville Rep. Com., 1968-88; tchr. adult Sunday sch. class Bapt. Ch., 1987—; active Salvation Army Aux., poverty relief, community recreation for sr. citizens, 1989—. Mem. AAUW (v.p. Jacksonville chpt. 1986-87, pres. 1988-89), Phi Kappa Phi, Phi Upsilon Omicron. Baptist. Home: 7210 White Birch Dr Jacksonville FL 32277-2820

CASH, CAROL VIVIAN, sociologist; b. Port Arthur, Tex., Jan. 22, 1929; d. Mano Nathan and Floris Duval (Akin) C.; m. Robert Morrow Welch, Dec. 21, 1951 (div. 1966); children: Catherine Carol, Robert M. III, Candice Claire. AA, Lamar Jr. Coll., 1951; BS in Sociology, U. Houston, 1971. Sec. Port Arthur SS Co., 1948-50; with Gov's Office State of Tex., Austin, 1951-52; legal sec. Wesley W. West, Houston, 1953-55. Author numerous children's books. Active Houston area Boy Scouts Am., Girl Scouts U.S., 1960-76, Port Arthur Hist. Soc.; mem. Tex. Sesquicentennial Com., 1986; active in restoration of Tex. historic homes. Mem. AAUW (chmn. Port Arthur fund raiser 1982), Tex. Artist Mus. Soc., Planetary Soc., Fed. Women's Clubs, Writer's Club (v.p. 1983-84, pres. 1984-85, treas. 1985-90), U. Houston Alumni Assn.

CASH, DEANNA GAIL, nursing educator; b. Coatesville, Pa., Nov. 28, 1940. Diploma, Jackson Meml. Hosp., 1961; BS, Fla. State U., 1964; MN, UCLA, 1968; EdD, Nova U., Ft. Lauderdale, Fla., 1983. Staff and relief charge nurse Naples (Fla.) Community Hosp., 1961-62; staff nurse Glendale (Calif.) Community Hosp., 1964-65; instr. Knapp Coll. Nursing, Santa Barbara, Calif., 1965-66; staff nurse, team leader Kaiser Found. Hosp., Bellflower, Calif., 1968-69; prof. nursing El Camino Coll., Torrance, Calif., 1969—; coord., instr. Internat. RN Rev. course, L.A., 1974-76; mentor statewide nursing program, Long Beach, Calif., 1981-88; clin. performance in nursing exam. evaluator Western Performance Assessment Ctr., Long Beach, 1981—. Mem. ANA.

CASH, JUNE CARTER, singer; b. Maces Springs, Va., June 23, 1929; d. Ezra and Maybelle (Addington) Carter; m. John R. Cash; children: Rebecca Carlene, Rozanna Lea, John Carter. Student, Neighborhood Playhouse Sch. Dramatics, 1955-56; HHD (hon.), Nat. U., San Diego, 1977. Propr. June Carter Cash Antiques and Gift Shop, Hendersonville, Tenn. Singer with, Carter Family, 1939-43, with Carter Sisters (and mother), after 1943; performed on, Sta. XERF, Del Rio Tex., Sta. KWTO, Springfield, Mo.; mem. Grand Ole Opry, Sta. WSM, Nashville; TV appearances include John Davidson Show, Tennessee Ernie Show, Johnny Cash Show, others; films include: Thaddeus, Rose and Eddie, Country Music Holiday; TV movies: Stage Coach, Murder Coweta Country, The Baron, The Last Days of Frank and Jessie James, Keep on The Sunny Side, Appalachian Pride, Gospel Road, Country Music Caravan, Road to Nashville, Tennessee Jamboree, Gospel Road; TV spl. The Best of The Carter Family; songs recorded include: Baby It's Cold Outside, Music Music Music, Love Oh Crazy Love, Let Me Go Lover, Leftover Loving; contbr. to album Johnny Cash is Coming to Town, 1987; author: Among My Klediments, 1979, From the Heart, 1986, Mother Maybelle's Cookbook, 1989; co-author: Ring of Fire. Address: House of Cash Inc 700 Johnny Cash Pkwy Hendersonville TN 37075

CASH, (CYNTHIA) LAVERNE, physicist; b. Statesville, N.C., Oct. 7, 1956; d. William J. and Martha Lee (Stroud) C. BS, Appalachian State U., 1979; MS, Clemson U., 1982; AA, Mitchell Community Coll., 1976; postgrad., Johns Hopkins U. Physicist U.S. Army Material Systems Analysis Activity, Aberdeen Proving Ground, Md., 1984-88; rsch. physicist U.S. Army Edgewood Rsch., Devel. and Enging. Ctr., Aberdeen Proving Ground, 1988—. Contbr. articles to profl. publs. Mem. Oak Grove Bapt. Ch, Bel Air, Md., singer in choir, sound engr., numerous others. Mem. Am. Phys. Soc., Sigma Phi Sigma, Pi Mu Epsilon, Phi Theta Kappa, Gamma Beta Phi. Baptist. Home: 100 Drexel Dr Bel Air MD 21014-2002

CASH, ROSANNE, country singer, songwriter; b. Memphis, May 24, 1955; b. May 1955; d. John R. Cash and Vivian (Liberto) Distin; m. Rodney J. Crowell, Apr. 7, 1979 (div. 1992); children: Caitlin Rivers, Chelsea Jane, Carrie Kathleen. Student, Vol. State C.C., 1974, Vanderbilt U., 1976, Lee Strasberg Theatre Inst., 1977. Rec. artist Ariola Records, Europe, 1978-84, CBS Records, worldwide, 1979—. Songwriter Blue Moon with Heartache, 1979, Seven Year Ache, 1980 (Gold Record award Rec. Industry Assn. Am. 1981), I Don't Know Why You Don't Want Me, 1984, (Grammy award 1985), Hold On (Robert J. Burton award 1987), others; Albums: Right Or Wrong, The Wheel, Seven Year Ache, 1980, Somewhere in the Stars, Rythym & Romance, 1985, King's Record Shop, 1987, Hits 1979-89, 1989, Interiors, 1990. Bd. advisors Nashvillians for Nuclear Arms Freeze, 1987-90. Mem. AFTRA, Nat. Acad. Rec. Arts and Scis. (Grammy award 1985), Am. Fedn. Musicians, Screen Actors Guild, Broadcast Music, Inc. (Spl. Achievement awards), Nashville Songwriters Assn. Internat. Democrat. *

CASHMORE, PATSY JOY, speechwriter, editor, author, consultant, educator; b. Milw., July 20, 1943; d. Anthony J. and Eva Irene (Arseneau) Peters; m. Gary Roy Cashmore, July 5, 1963 (div. Feb. 1983); children: Jay Allen, Jeffery Scott. Student U. Ill.-Chgo., 1961-62, Inst. Broadcast Arts, Milw., 1966-67, U. Wis.-Milw., 1970, U. Wis.-Madison, 1971-76,labor studies N.Y.C. Grad. Ctr., 1978. Copy writer H. Vincent Allen & Assocs., Chgo., 1961-63; asst. program coord. Sta.-WRIT, Milw., 1967-69; asst. news assignment editor WITI-TV, Milw., 1969-72; pub. rels. asst. Deaconess Hosp., Milw., 1972-73; asst. editor Milw. Labor Press, 1973-81, editor, 1981-90, coord. spl. comm. United Assocs., Washington, 1990—; voice talent on radio and TV commls.; instr., mem. faculty adv. com. U. Wis. Extension-Sch. for Workers, Madison; panelist NEH; guest Israeli govt., 1976, Govt. Fed. Republic Germany, 1980, pre-NATO talks Friedrich Ebert Found., 1981, 87, Peoples Republic of China, 1983, All Union Cen. Coun. of Trade Unions of Soviet Union, 1985; studied in East Africa, 1987. Contbr. articles to nat. publs. Chmn. comm. com., treas. Milw. Coun. on Drug Abuse, 1981-83, bd. dirs., 1984-87, Milw. Coun. on Alcoholism, 1985-88; mem. community affairs com. United Way, 1983-86; active Variety Club, 1983-87; chmn. community adv. bd. Sta.-WVTV pub. TV, 1982-85; bd. dirs. Goals 2000 Comm.tions Com., 1983; participant U.S. Del. to observe elections in El Salvador, 1989; ednl. specialist U.S. State Dept., Lesotho, 1990; vol. Earthwatch, Borneo, 1988. Mem. Internat. Labor Comm. Assn. (v.p. 1985, 87, 89, Best Signed Column award 1973, Best Feature Story award 1975, award of Merit for best use of art 1982, Best Headline award 1982, First award for gen. excellence newspaper 1982, 83, 87, 88, 1st award Labor History best instl. profile 1986, 87, 88, Best Graphics award 1987, Best Original Cartoon 1987, 88), U.S. Treasury Dept. (Liberty Bell award, 1986), Midwest Labor Press Assn. (pres.), Wis. Labor Press Assn. (treas.), Indsl. Rels. Rsch. Assn. (bd. dirs.), Milw. Jr. Acad. Club (past sec.-treas.). NAFE, Sigma Delta Chi, Wapatule Ski Club (newsletter editor 1984-85), Nat. Press Club, Milw. Press Club, Milw. Pen and Mike Club (Milw.). Avocations: travel, skiing, golf, swimming. Office: United Assn Journeymen & Apprentices 901 Massachusetts Ave NW Washington DC 20001-4307

CASKEY, PRISCILLA C., lawyer; b. Balt., June 3, 1946. Student, Johns Hopkins U., JD with honors, 1977; grad., U. Md. Bar: Md. 1977. With Whiteford, Taylor & Preston, Balt. Mem. ABA, Nat. Assn. Bond Lawyers, Md. State Bar Assn. Address: Whiteford Taylor & Preston Ste 1400 7 Saint Paul St Ste 1400 Baltimore MD 21202-1626

CASOLA, PAULA SUSANN, accountant; b. Gary, Ind., Feb. 29, 1968; d. Paul and Susan Ann (Bassala) C. BSBA in Acctg., Cen. Mich. U., 1990; MSF in Fin., Walsh Coll., 1995. Gen. accounts analyst Blue Cross Blue Shield Mich., Detroit, 1990-92, cost acctg. analyst, 1992-94, sr. cost acct., 1994-95; sr. acct. Blue Cross Blue Shield Mich., Southfield, Mich., 1995—. Mem. Inst. Mgmt. Accts. (cert.). Home: 34454 Koch Ave Sterling Heights MI 48310

CASON, MARILYNN JEAN, technological institute official, lawyer; b. Denver, May 18, 1943; d. Eugene Martin and Evelyn Lucille (Clark) C.; married. BA in Polit. Sci., Stanford U., 1965; JD, U. Mich., 1969; MBA, Roosevelt U., 1977. Bar: Colo. 1969, Ill. 1973. Assoc. Dawson, Nagel, Sherman & Howard, Denver, 1969-73; atty. Kraft, Inc., Glenview, Ill., 1973-75; corp. counsel Johnson Products Co., Inc., Chgo., 1975-86, v.p., 1977-86; mng. dir. Johnson Products Co., Inc., Lagos, Nigeria, 1980-83; v.p. internat. Johnson Products Co., Inc., Chgo., 1986-88; v.p., gen. counsel DeVry, Inc., Chgo., 1989—. Bd. dirs. Ill. chpt. Arthritis Found., Chgo., 1979—, chmn., 1991-93, trustee, Atlanta, 1993—; bd. dirs. Internat. House, Chgo., 1986-92; bd. dirs. Ill. Humanities Coun., Chgo., 1987-96, chmn., 1993-96. Mem. ABA, Nat. Bar Assn., Cook County Bar Assn. (pres. community law project 1986-88). Club: Stanford (Chgo.) (pres. 1985-87). Home: 3108 Colfax St Evanston IL 60201-1842 Office: DeVry Inc 1 Tower Ln Ste 1000 Oakbrook Terrace IL 60181-4624

CASON, NICA VIRGINIA, nursing educator; b. Edna, Tex.; 1 child, Cynthia Diane. Diploma, Lillie Jolly Sch. Nursing, 1965; BSN, U. Tex. Med. Br., Galveston, 1967; MSN, U. So. Miss., 1981. RN, Miss. Pub. health nurse Miss. State Dept. Health, Pascagoula; nursing instr. Miss. Gulf Coast Community Coll.-Jackson County Campus, Gautier, chair ADN program; comdr. 403d Aeromed. Staging Squadron, Keesler AFB, Miss. Col. USAFR, 1968—. Mem. NOADN, Nat. League Nursing, Sigma Theta Tau, Phi Kappa Phi.

CASPER, MARIE LENORE, middle school educator; b. Honesdale, Pa., Mar. 26, 1954; d. Frank J. and Ellenore L. (Austin) Shedlock; m. Gerald Joseph Casper, Oct. 9, 1976; children: Julia Anne, Jennifer Marie. BA, Marywood Coll., 1976; masters equivalency cert., State of Pa., 1982. Cert. elem. and secondary social studies tchr., Pa. Substitute tchr. Western Wayne Sch. Dist., South Canaan, Pa., 1976-81, secondary and elem. tchr., 1981-86, chpt. 1 math. specialist, 1986-90, middle sch. social studies tchr., 1990—; social studies tchr. Wallenpaupack Area Sch. Dist., Hawley, Pa., 1980-81; corp. sec. Simply Elegant Homes & Constrn., Inc., Kresgeville and South Canaan, Pa.; coord. Western Wayne Middle Sch. (WW II commemorative com.). Contbr. articles to profl. publs. Mem. PTA R.D. Wilson Sch., Western Wayne Mid. Sch. Mem. NEA, AAUW (treas. Hawley-Honesdale br. 1981-83), Pa. State Edn. Assn., Western Wayne Edn. Assn., Wayne County Hist. Soc., Smithsonian Instn., Audubon Soc., Nat. Geog. Soc., Platform Assn., Am. Legion Aux. (life). Republican. Roman Catholic. Home: PO Box 31 Salem Mt Rd South Canaan PA 18459-0031 Office: Western Wayne Mid Sch PO Box 376B Lake Ariel PA 18436-0376 also: Simply Elegant Homes & Cnst PO Box 937 Kresgeville PA 18333-0937

CASPERS, ANITA ELIZABETH, marketing communications executive; b. Fullerton, Calif., Mar. 16, 1964; d. Edward Mathias and Maria Elena (Vicencio) C. Student, Fullerton (Calif.) Coll., 1982-84, Long Beach City Coll., 1995—. From sales clk. to buying asst. Nordstrom Dept. Store, Brea/Santa Ana/Costa Mesa, Calif., 1984-90; sales/mktg. asst. Yalevideo, Anaheim, Calif., 1990; acct. coord. DeSalvo Comm., Costa Mesa, Calif., 1991-93; account exec. Killingsworth Presentations, Long Beach, Calif., 1993—; anchor woman, voice over, broadcaster, City of Costa Mesa, Calif., 1994—. Republican. Roman Catholic. Office: Killingsworth Presentations 3834 Long Beach Blvd Long Beach CA 90807

CASSELL, KAY ANN, librarian; b. Van Wert, Ohio, Sept. 24, 1941; d. Kenneth Miller and Pauline (Zimmerman) C. B.A., Carnegie-Mellon U., 1963; M.L.S., Rutgers U., 1965; M.A., Bklyn. Coll., 1969. Reference librarian Bklyn. Coll. Library, 1965-68; adult svcs. cons. N.J. State Libr., Trenton, 1968-71; libr. cons.-vol. Peace Corps, Rabat, Morocco, 1971-73; adult svcs. cons. Westchester Libr. System, White Plains, N.Y., 1973-75; dir. Bethlehem Pub. Libr., Delmar, N.Y., 1975-81, Huntington (N.Y.) Pub. Libr., 1982-85; exec. dir. Coordinating Coun. Lit. Mags., N.Y.C., 1985-87; univ. libr. New Sch. for Social Rsch., 1987-88; assoc. dir. programs and svcs. br. librs. N.Y. Pub. Libr., 1989—; adj. faculty Grad. Sch. Libr. Sci., SUNY, Albany, 1976-78, Palmer Sch. Libr. and Info. Scis., L.I. U., 1986-90, Grad. Sch. Info. and Libr. Sci., Pratt Inst., 1994—; chmn. cmty. adv. com. Capital Dist. Humanities Program, Albany, 1980-81; bd. dirs. Literacy Vols. of Suffolk, Bellport, N.Y., 1981-85; chmn. N.Y.C. Sch. Libr. Sys. Coun., 1991-94; treas. Libr. Pub. Rels. Coun., 1993—. Mem. ALA (pres. reference and adult svcs. divsn. 1983-84, chair membership com. 1991-95, coun. 1992—), N.Y. Libr. Assn. (pres. reference and adult svcs. sect. 1975-76), Feminist Press (bd. dirs.), Beta Phi Mu. Office: NY Pub Libr Office Programs & Svcs 455 5th Ave New York NY 10016-0109

CASSELL, LUCILLE RICHARDSON, small business owner; b. Sikeston, Mo., Feb. 23, 1958; d. Glen and Cenia (McCaster) Richardson; m. Arthur Earl Cassell, Apr. 12, 1986; children: Christopher Glen, Bryan Mitchell, David Arthur, Aaron Lamar. A in Bus. and Computer Sci., S.E. Mo. State U., 1980; deaconess lic., Green Meml. Bible Inst.-Coll., Sikeston, 1982. Shoe packer Wohl Shoe Co., Sikeston, 1980-84; sales clk. J.C. Penney, Sikeston, 1984-85; bookeeper, teller Bank of Sikeston, 1985-86; computer operator Sta. KBSI-TV, Cape Girardeau, Mo., 1986-89; data clk. Falcon Cable TV, Sikeston, 1989-90; owner, mgr. Wee=Care Daycare Ctr., Charleston, 1990-95; pres. CBD Enterprises, Inc., Charleston, 1995—. Author: The Best That I Can Be, 1995; inventor disposable diapers, adult diapers. Vol. Mo. Delta Med. Ctr., Sikeston, 1990; participant walk-a-thons Cystic Fibrosis Found., Charleston, 1992; Sunday sch. tchr. Green Meml. Ch., Sikeston, 1985-86. Mem. Ch. of God in Christ. Home and Office: PO Box 284 1210 Warren Charleston MO 63834

CASSELL, SHARON KOTELES, water testing business owner; b. Wheeling, W.Va., Dec. 11, 1948; d. Julius Michael and Mary Lee (Howe) Koteles; m. Richard Hudgins Cassell, Mar. 29, 1975; 1 child, Daniel H. BS, West Liberty State Coll., 1972. Registered med. technologist. Microbiologist Johns Hopkins Hosp., Balt., 1973-76; med. technologist Md. Med. Lab., Balt., 1976-79; chemist EA Engring., Sci. & Tech., Sparks, Md., 1981-85; pres. Cassell Testing Inc., Hunt Valley, Md., 1985—. Office: Cassell Testing Inc 10940 Beaver Dam Rd Hunt Valley MD 21030

CASSELMAN, SHARON MAE, recreational specialist; b. Cin., June 27, 1954; d. Alvin Maurice and Rosella Ann (Ruhe) C. Grad high sch., Cin. Instr. aquatics Powell Crosley YMCA, Cin., 1970-79; instr. phys. edn. St. John the Bapt. Elem. Sch., Cin., 1976-84; asst. aquatic dir., coach Jewish Cmty. Ctr., Cin., 1979-81; aquatic dir. City of Springdale, Cin., 1979-86; coach Roger Bacon High Sch., Cin., 1984-86; product cons. sales mktg. World Wide Aquatics, Inc., Cin., 1984-86; asst. dir. sports info. for women Vanderbilt U., Nashville, 1986-91, head coach men's and women's diving, 1986-91; program supr. recreation City of Springdale (Ohio), 1991—; mem. spl. events com. City of Springdale, 1992-95; pres. Nashville Diving League, 1989-91; cons. in field. Vol. Big Bros., Nashville, 1990, Fund Raisers for Youth Sports, Springdale, 1994, 95; sponsor Muscular Dystrophy Assn. Lock-Up, Cin., 1995. Recipient Bronze medal Sports Challenge Cystic Fibrosis Found., Nashville, 1989; named Regional Champion U.S. Volleyball Assn., 1976, All Tournament Team U.S. Slow-Pitch Softball Assn., Cin., 1986. Mem. Ohio Parks and Recreation Assn. (aquatic sect.), Greater Cin. Pool Operators Assn. (advisor). Republican. Lutheran. Office: City of Springdale Parks & Recreation 11999 Lawnview Ave Springdale OH 45246

CASSENS, SUSAN FORGET, artist; b. Ft. Pierce, Fla., May 11, 1956; d. Louis Conrad and Joan Hancock Forget; m. Steven Dale Cassens, Mar. 4, 1979; children: Christopher, Michael, Scott. AA, U. Fla., 1976; BA in Edn. with honors, Fla. Atlantic U., 1978. Tchr. Garden City Elem., Ft. Pierce, 1978-79; owner Brush Strokes Art Gallery, Ft. Pierce, 1993-95; co-owner Indian River Crafters Guild, Ft. Pierce, 1995—; bd. mem. St. Lucie County Cultural Affairs Coun., Ft. Pierce, 1993, chair, 1996—. Cover artist: Cracker Cuisine, 1993; exhbns. include A.E. Backus Gallery, Ft. Pierce, Treasure Coast Art Gallery, Ft. Pierce. Chpt. sec. Philanthropic Ednl. Orgn., Ft. Pierce, 1987, chpt. pres., 1989; mem. Vero Beach Ctr. for the Arts, A.E. Backus Art Gallery, Mainstreet (Ft. Pierce) Inc., St. Lucie Hist. Soc.; chair St. Lucie Mural Soc., Ft. Pierce, 1994. Mem. Nat. Mus. of Women in the Arts (charter mem.), Vero Beach Art Club, Heathcote Botanical Gardens (charter mem.). Presbyterian. Home: PO Box 593 Fort Pierce FL 34954-0593 Office: Indian River Crafters Guild 201 N 2nd St Fort Pierce FL 34954

CASSERLY, CONSTANCE DIANE, secondary school educator; b. Indiana, Pa., May 4, 1948; d. Wilbert Thomas and Mary (Ginalick) Neal; m. Timothy James Casserly, Aug. 29, 1969; children: Kimberly Alison, Matthew Timothy. BS in Edn., Indiana U. of Pa., 1970. Cert. secondary sch., English tchr. Tchr. Boys Village of Md., Cheltenham, Md., 1970-72, Homer Ctr. High Sch., Homer City, Pa., 1980-81; substitute tchr. Fairport (N.Y.) Schs., 1982-84; tchr. Graydon Manor, Leesburg, Va., 1984-85, The Enterprise Sch., Vienna, Va., 1985-88, Herndon (Va.) Middle Sch., 1988-92, Herndon H.S., 1992—. Author: A Fine Line, 1993. Mem. Nat. Coun. Tchrs. English (contbr. to Ideas Plus 1991, Notes Plus 1994). Democrat. Presbyterian. Home: 1105 Landerset Dr Herndon VA 20170-2083

CASSFORD, BETH ANN, middle school educator; b. Niagara Falls, Sept. 20, 1952; d. George E. and Mira M. (Herl) C. BA, Calif. State U., Fullerton, 1974. Tchr. Lakeside Mid. Sch., Norwalk, Calif., 1975—, Little Lake City Sch. Dist., Santa Fe Springs, Calif., 1975—; mentor tchr. Little Lake City Sch. Dist., 1985-89. Named Tchr. of Yr., Calif. State Dept. Edn., 1994, L.A. County Office Edn., 1994; honoree Disney Channel Salutes the Am. Tchr., 1994. Home: 662 Quincy Ave Long Beach CA 90814 Office: Lakeside Mid Sch 11000 E Kenney Norwalk CA 90650

CASSIDY, ESTHER CHRISTMAS, government official; b. Upper Marlboro, Md., Aug. 5, 1933; d. Donelson and Esther (Brooke) Christmas; divorced; children: William Keeling, Carroll Cassidy Drewyer, Daniel Clark. BA, Manhattanville Coll., 1955. Phys. scientist, R&D Nat. Bur. Standards, Gaithersburg, Md., 1955-73; sci. advisor U.S. Congressman Teno Roncalio, Washington, 1973-74; asst. dir. congl. affairs Energy R&D Adminstrn. Dept. Energy, Washington, 1974-78; dir. congl. and legis. affairs Nat. Inst. Stds. and Tech., Gaithersburg, 1978—. Contbr. articles to profl. jours. Mem. IEEE (sr.). Office: Nat Inst Standards and Tech Adminstrv Bldg Rm A-1111 Gaithersburg MD 20899

CASSIDY, MARY E., lawyer; b. Mineola, N.Y., Oct. 18, 1955. BA, SUNY, Binghamton, 1977, MS, 1980; JD, George Washington U., 1986. Bar: N.Y. 1987, D.C. 1988; CPA, N.Y. Spl. counsel Arnold & Porter, Washington. Mem. Order of the Coif. Office: Arnold & Porter 555 12th St NW Washington DC 20004*

CASSTEVENS, KAY L., federal official; b. Ft. Worth, July 4, 1949; d. Floyd C. and Shirley D. (Jackson) C. BJ cum laude, U. Tex., 1971; JD, George Washington U., 1979. Bar: D.C. 1980. Legis. aide Senator George McGovern, S.D., 1973-77; legis. dir. Rep. John F. Seiberling, Ohio, 1977-85; legis. dir. Sen. Tom Harkin, Iowa, 1986-91, chief of staff, 1991-92; asst. sec. legis. and congrl. affairs Dept. of Edn., Washington, 1993—; dep. issues dir. to Geraldine Ferraro, Mondale-Ferraro Campaign, fall 1984; mem. rsch. staff Dukakis for Pres. Campaign, fall 1988; dep. campaign mgr. Ams. for Harkin Presdl. Campaign, 1991-92. Office: Dept of Education Legislative & Congressional Affairs 600 Independence Ave SW Washington DC 20202-0004

CAST, ANITA HURSH, small business owner; b. Columbus, Ohio, July 11, 1939; d. Charles Walter and Hulda Marie (Ramsey) Hursh; m. William R. Cast, Apr. 1, 1961; children: Jennifer, Carter, Meghan. BA, DePauw U., 1961. Ptnr. Cast Hursh and Assocs., Ft. Wayne, Ind., 1982—; pianist Words and Music, Ft. Wayne, 1983—; owner Anita Cast's Wearable Art, Ft. Wayne, 1986—; cons. for bd. tng. Bd. dirs., pres. Am. Symphony Orch. League, vol., v.p., 1985-86; bd. dirs. WBNI Nat. Pub. Radio, Ft. Wayne; commr. Ind. Gov.'s Mansion Commn., 1987, Ind. Arts Commn., 1979-87; chmn., bd. dirs. Fine Arts Found., Ft. Wayne, 1988; pres. Ft. Wayne Philharmonic, 1977-79; pres., bd. dirs. Friends of Music, Ind. U.; v.p. Leadership Ft. Wayne Adv. Bd., Ind. Endowment of the Arts; chmn. bd. Arts United of Greater Ft. Wayne, 1988-90; pres. Met. YMCA, Ft. Wayne, 1986—; mem. Mayor's Bicentennial Exec. Bd., 1989-94; mem. Ind. Cultural Congress Hon. Com. Lily Endowment Leadership fellow. Republican. Episcopalian. Home and Office: Anita Cast Wearable Art 4401 Taylor Rd Fort Wayne IN 46804-1913

CASTALINE, BEATRIX ANNA, accountant, artist; b. Oldenburg, Germany, June 17, 1963; came to U.S., 1969; d. Brigitta Maria (Rahms) Terry; m. Eric Scott Castaline, Aug. 15, 1992; 1 child, Britta Anne. BA in Mktg., U. South Fla., 1986, BA in Acctg., 1993. Credit mgr. Hyatt Regency Tampa, Fla., 1982-87; computer operator, promotional advisor Carl T. Watkins, CPA, Tampa, 1984-87; rservation sales agt., counselor WORLDSPAN Travel Agy. Info. Svcs./N.W. Airlines, Inc., Kansas City, Mo., 1987-90; sr. staff acct. Associated Marine Inst., Inc., Tampa, 1992-94, Carl T. Watkins, CPA, Tampa, 1990—. Republican. Roman Catholic.

CASTANEDA, SHEILA ELIZABETH, educator; b. Dubuque, Iowa, Aug. 26, 1952; d. Merlin John and Florence T. Jaeger; m. J.M. Castaneda, Aug. 12, 1972; children: Kristina, Ben, JoAnna. BA, Clarke Coll., 1973; MS, U. Wis., 1979. Programmer, analyst AID Ins. Co., Des Moines, 1974-76, Telectro, Guatemala City, Guatemala, 1977-78; teaching asst. U. Wis., Madison, 1978-79; assoc. prof., chair dept. computer scis. Clarke Coll., Dubuque, Iowa, 1980—; pres. steering com. Small Coll. Computing Symposium, 1990-96; cons. trainer William C. Brown Comms., Dubuque, 1994, John Deere Dubuque Works, 1994-96, Honeywell Inc., 1996. Mem. Assn. Computing Machinery, Upsilon Pi Epsilon. Roman Catholic. Office: Clarke Coll 1550 Clarke Dr Dubuque IA 52001-3117

CASTANO, ELVIRA PALMERIO, art gallery director, art historian; b. Cin., July 23, 1929; d. John and Josephine C.; m. Carlo Palmerio, June 1, 1958 (dec.); 1 child, Marina. B Lit. Interpretation, Emerson Coll., 1950; postgrad., Pius XII Inst., Florence, Italy, 1954-55; student opera with Cesare Sturani. Curator Castano Art Gallery, Boston, 1965-78; dir. Castano Art Gallery, Needham, Mass., 1978—; rschr.mem Smithsonian Instn., Boston, 1988-89; Vatican translator; interpreter Italian art specializing in Macchiaioli art; Italian interpreter Ritz Carlton Internat. Festival, (Italian) Mayor's Office Sister Cities Internat. Conv.; appointed sec. World Affairs Coun., Boston. Mem. Rep. Presdl. Task Force, Nat. Rep. Senatorial Com., Presdl. Inner Circle; bd. dirs. Needham Hist. Soc.; vol. Sail Boston, 1992; del. Presdl. Trust, 1992; aapptd. Gov.'s Com. on Women's Issues; vol. Italian Interpreter for Mayor's Office Sister Cities Internat. Conv. Cardinal Spellman scholar. Mem. Boston U. Women's Coun., Boston Mus. Fine Arts, Boston Browning Soc., Fogg Art Mus. of Harvard U., Friends of Needham Libr., Archives Am. Art Boston, Alliance Francaise Boston, World Affairs Coun. Boston (sec.), Nat. Mus. Women in Arts, Needham Hist. Soc. (bd. dirs.). Address: 245 Hunnewell St Needham MA 02194-1425

CASTELLAN, DEBORAH MARY, nurse anesthetist; b. Wallace, Idaho, Dec. 4, 1949; d. Mike Robert and Patricia Eileen (Batchelor) C. BSN, U. Portland, 1972; MSN, U. Ariz., 1977, U. of N.Y., Buffalo, 1983. Cert. registered nurse anesthetist. Commdr. 2d lt. U.S. Army, 1975, advanced through grades to lt. col., 1989, ret., 1995; instr. nursing ADN program Portland C.C., 1974-89; staff nurse anesthetist U.S. Army, Ft. Dix, N.J., 1983-85; chief anesthesia 121st Evac Hosp., Seoul, Korea, 1985-86, 2nd Gen. Hosp., Landostul, West Germany, 1986; chief trauma svc. U.S. Army 86th Evac. Hosp., Saudi Arabia, 1991; head nurse Fitzsimmons Army Med. Ctr., Denver, 1989-91, chief ambulatory nursing svc., 1991-94, asst. chief nurse, 1994-95; anesthesia asst. head Providence Hosp., Toppenish, Wash., 1995—; cons. AACN, 1974-79; adv. bd. liaison Wash. Nurse Anesthetist, 1995. Contbr. articles to profl. jours. Vol. Spl. Olympics, Mt. Holly, N.J., 1983-85, Landstul, West Germany, 1986-89. Recipient Kuwait Liberation medal Kuwait Govt., 1991. Mem. ANA, Am. Assn. Nurse Anesthetist, Colo. Assn. Nurse Anesthetist, Washington Assn. Nurse Anesthetist (chairperson liasion), Ret. Army Nurse Corps Assn., Sigma Theta Tau. Roman Catholic. Home: 1019 Schoentrup Zillah WA 98953

CASTELLANO, MARIE TANNER, elementary school educator; b. Santa Barbara, Calif., Oct. 29, 1939; d. Thornton Addison and Gladys Rosamund (McKeown) Tanner; m. Pasquale Allen Castellano, June 29, 1962; children: Derek Michael, Mark Addison, Kurt Pasquale. AA, Fullerton Coll., 1959; BA, San Diego State U., 1961. Cert. elem. tchr., Calif. 4th grade tchr. La Mesa (Calif.) Dals Elem. Sch., 1961-62, Bradford Ave. Elem. Sch., Placentia, Calif., 1962-63; substitute tchr. Rio Linda Sch. Dist., North Highlands, Calif., 1972-74; ESL/learning lab. tchr. Oneonta and Arroyo Vista Schs., South Pasadena, Calif., 1980-84; 5th grade tchr. Arroyo Vista Elem. Sch., South Pasadena, 1984-86, 4th/5th grade tchr. gifted and talented class, 1986-92, 5th grade tchr. gifted and talented class, 1992—; adj. faculty mem. Calif. State U., L.A., 1991-94, Mt. St. Mary's Coll., L.A., 1991-94; state cons. L'Starss Consortium of Schs., San Gabriel Valley, Calif., 1991-94; presenter at confs. in field. Author: Comprehensive Resource Personnel Directory, 1984, History/Social Science Guides, K-5, 1990; contbr. articles to profl. publs. Elder Calvary Presbyn. Ch., South Pasadena, 1991-94. Named County Tchr. of Yr., L.A. County Office of Edn., 1995, Tchr. of Yr. Oneonta Men's Club, 1994, South Pasadena Tchr. of Yr., 1995. Mem. NEA, ASCD, Calif. Assn. for Gifted, Nat. Assn. for Gifted, World Coun. for Gifted, Calif. Tchrs. Assn. Presbyterian. Home: 1000 Stratford Ave South Pasadena CA 91030-3412

CASTELLINI, PATRICIA BENNETT, business management educator; b. Park River, N.D., Mar. 25, 1935; d. Benjamin Beekman Bennett and Alice Catherine (Peerboom) Bennett Breckinridge; m. William McGregor Castellini; children: Bruce Bennett Subiani, Barbara Lea Ragland. AA, Allan Hancok Coll., Santa Maria, Calif., 1964; BS magna cum laude, Coll. Great Falls, 1966; MS, U N D., 1967, PhD, 1971. Fiscal acct. USIA, Washington, 1954-56; pub. acct., Bremerton, Wash., 1956; statistician USN, Bremerton, 1957-59; med. svcs. accounts officer U.S. Air Force, Vandenberg AFB, Calif., 1962-64; instr. bus. adminstrn. Western New Eng. Coll., 1967-69; vis. prof. econs. Chapman Coll., 1970; vis. prof. U. So. Calif. systems Griffith AFB, N.Y., 1971-72; assoc. prof., dir. adminstrv. mgmt. program Va. State U., 1973-74; assoc. prof. bus. adminstrn. Oreg. State U., Corvallis, 1974-81, prof. mgmt., 1982-90, emeritus prof. mgmt., 1990—, univ. curriculum coord., 1984-86, dir. adminstrv. mgmt. program, 1974-81, pres. Faculty Senate, 1981, Interinstl. Faculty Senate, 1986-90, pres., 1989-90; exec. dir. Bus. Enterprise Ctr., 1990-92, Enterprise Ctr. L.A., Inc., 1992-95, Castellini Co., 1995—; commr. Lafayette Econ. Devel. Authority, 1994—, treas., 1995-96; cons. process tech. devel. Digital Equipment Corp., 1982. Pres., chmn. bd. dirs. Adminstrv. Orgnl. Svcs., Inc., Corvallis, 1976-83, Dynamic Achievement, Inc., 1983-92; bd. dirs. Oreg. State U. Bookstores, Inc., 1987-90, Internat. Trade Devel. Group, 1992—, BBB of Acadiana, 1994—, sec., 1994-95, vice chmn. 1995—; dir., cons. Oregonians in Action, 1990-91. Cert. adminstrv. mgr. Pres. TYEE Mobil Home Park, Inc., 1987-92. Fellow Assn. Bus. Communication (mem. internat. bd. 1980-83, v.p. Northwest 1981, 2d v.p. 1982-83, 1st v.p. 1983-84, pres. 1984-85); mem. Am. Bus. Women's Assn. (chpt. v.p. 1979, pres. 1980, named Top Businesswoman in Nation 1980, Bus. Assoc. Yr. 1986), Assn. Info. Systems Profls., Adminstrv. Mgmt. Soc., AAUP (chpt. sec. 1973, chpt. bd. dirs. 1982, 84-89, pres. Oreg. conf. 1983-85), profls. chpt. 1985-86, administrv., Am. Vocat. Assn. (nominating com. 1976), Associated Oreg. Faculties, Nat. Bus. Edn. Assn., Nat. Assn. Tchr. Edn. for Bus. Office Edn. (pres. 1976-77, chmn. public relations com. 1978-81), La. Bus. Incubation Assn. (sec.-treas. 1993-95), Corvallis Area C. of C. (v.p. chamber devel. 1987-88, pres. 1988-89, chmn. bd. 1989-90, vice chmn., 1996-96, v.chm., 1996—, Pres.' award 1986), Boys and Girls Club of Corvallis (pres. 1991-92), Sigma Kappa, Rotary Corvallis (bd. dirs. 1990-92, dir. voc. svcs. 1991-92, pres.-elect 1992), Rotary Lafayette (bd. dirs. 1993—, cmty. svc. dir. 1993-94, treas. 1995-96, sec. 1996—). Roman Catholic. Contbr. numerous articles to profl. jours. Office: Castellini Co 1007 W St Mary Blvd Lafayette LA 70506-3420

CASTELLON, CHRISTINE NEW, information systems specialist, real estate agent; b. Pittsfield, Mass., June 22, 1957; d. Edward Francis Jr. and Helen Patricia (Cordes) New; m. John Arthur Castellon, Oct. 1, 1988. BS in Elec. and Computer Engring., U. Mass., 1979; MBA, Northeastern U., 1986. Engr. microwave radio system design New Eng. Telephone Co., Framingham, Mass., 1979-82; mgr. minicomputer support group New Eng. Telephone Co., Dorchester, Mass., 1982-85; mgr. current systems planning/network svcs. NYNEX Svc. Co., Boston, 1985-87; mem. tech. staff computing environments Bellcore, Piscataway, N.J., 1987-90; assoc. dir. info. systems provisioning NYNEX Telesector Resources Group, N.Y.C., 1990-93; sales assoc. Weidel Realtors, Flemington, N.J., 1994—; speaker New Eng. Telephone Careers-In-Engring. Program, 1980-82. Leader 2d violin sect. Cen. Jersey Symphony Orch., Raritan Valley Community Coll., N.J., 1988—; prin. 1st violinist New Eng. Conservatory Extension Div., Boston, 1979-87; violinist Civic Symphony Orch., Boston, 1982-87; active UMASS Coll./Industry Adv. Com. Named Monument Mountain High Sch. valedictorian, 1975; recipient Arion Music award, 1975, cert. Applied Music and Theory Pittsfield Community Music Sch., 1975, Exceptional Merit award NYNEX, 1987. Mem. IEEE, U. Mass. Alumni Assn. (coll./industry adv. com. for women), Northeastern U. MBA Alumni Assn. Roman Catholic. Home: 622 Old York Rd Neshanic Station NJ 08853-3600

CASTIGLIONE, JOANNE FRANCES, accountant; b. Methuen, Mass., May 17, 1960; d. Rocco Joseph and Frances Gladys C. BS in Bus. Adminstrn., U. Lowell, 1982, MBA in Fin., 1987. Cert. Am. Prodn. Inventory Ctrl., Prodn. and Inventory Mgmt. Gross margin analyst programmer Compo Industries, Lowell, Mass., 1982-85; sr. fin. analyst Textron Def. Sys., Wilmington, Mass., 1985-94; sr. cost analyst Heidelberg Harris, Dover, N.H., 1994-96; cost acct. Astex, Woburn, Mass., 1996—; cert. tax preparer H&R Block Exec. Tax Svc., Andover, Mass., 1988—. mem., clerk Sunpoint Condo Assoc., Hampton, N.H., 1988—, fin. comm. mem. St. Augustine Parish, Lawrence, Mass., 1995—; bd. dirs. St. Mary Immaculate Cemetery, 1985—. Office: Applied Sci and Tech ASTEX 35 Cabot Rd Woburn MA 01801-1053

CASTIGLIONE-DEGAN, ANNETTE, reading specialist, county freeholder; b. Bklyn., Feb. 20, 1953; d. Vito and Victoria (Maggiore) C.; m. John Robert Degan Jr., July 10, 1976; children: Genna, Alexis, Patrick John. BA, Canisius Coll., Buffalo, N.Y., 1975; MA, Temple U., Phila., 1981. 2d grade tchr. Scotchtown Ave. Sch., Goshen, N.Y., 1975-76, Epiphany Elem., Phila., 1977-78; lang. arts coord. E.S. Miller H.S., Phila., 1978-82; adj. instr. Burlington County Coll., Pemberton, N.J., 1984-86; reading coord. Mill Creek Sch., Phila., 1992; high sch. reading tchr. Camden Bd Edn., N.J., 1992—; freeholder Camden County, 1993—. Pres., v.p. Haddon Heights (N.J.) Jr. Women's Club, 1983-92; chair Women For Andrews, Cherry Hill, N.J., 1994—. Recipient Maria Vizcarranto deSota award N.J. Statewide Women's Summit, 1995, Outstanding Woman of Achievement award Camden County Coun. of Girl Scouts, 1996, Women's Recognition award in politics City of Camden & Cmty. Affairs, 1996. Mem. AAUW, South Jersey Fedn. Democrat Women, Third Dist. Past Presidents. Democrat. Roman Catholic. Office: Office Board Freeholders 12th Flr 520 Market St Camden NJ 08102

CASTILLO, DIANA MAY, religious organization administrator; b. Pontiac, Mich., July 22, 1945; d. John Robert and Ellen May (Steele) Burkhart. AA in Humanities magna cum laude, U. Cin., 1992, BA in English magna cum laude, 1994; postgrad. studies Journalism, No. Ariz. U., 1996—. Lic. real estate sales agt., W. Va. Delayed birth cert. clk. State of W. Va. Dept. Health, Charleston, 1979-86; proofreader Anderson Publ. Co., Cin., 1987-88, Press Cmty. Papers, Cin., 1987-88; word processing specialist U. Cin., 1990-94; supr. Hope Cottages Women's Gospel Mission, Flagstaff, Ariz., 1996—; writer, editor St. John Social Svc. Ctr., Cin., 1989; proofreader, desktop publisher Dept. English, U. Cin., 1994, Florence (Ky.) Bapt. Temple, 1994-95, editor, desktop publ., Beechgrove (Ky.) Boosters, 1995; editor Inst. for Creation Rsch., Cajun, Calif., 1996. Voter registration notary State of W. Va., 1981-91; CPR instr. Am. Heart Assn., Charleston, W. Va., 1983, vol. respite care provider, United Home Care, Cin., 1987; vol. worship leader Women's Gospel Mission, Flagstaff, 1995-96. Recipient Presidential scholarship W. Va. State Coll., Institute, W. Va., 1985. Mem. Women in Comm., Inc., Freelance Edtl. Assn., Golden Key, Alpha Sigma Kappa, Phi Kappa Epsilon. Republican. Baptist. Home: 4 S San Francisco St # 330 Flagstaff AZ 86001

CASTLE-HASAN, ELIZABETH E., religious organization administrator; b. Balt., Nov. 1, 1950; d. John Thomas and Elizabeth Eliza (Wilson) Castle; m. Osborne Samuel James, Jr., Dec. 20, 1980 (div. Nov. 1993); children: Claudia C. Boulware, Richsharia D. Boulware, Kurtson E. Boulware, Curtis R. Boulware II; m. Edward N. Hasan, Dec. 12, 1994. AA in Criminal Justice, Valencia C.C., 1982; D of Systematic Theology (hon.), Interdenominational Theol. Sem. and Coll. of Theism, 1990; student, Love of God Theol. Sem. Account exec. Sta. WEBB, Balt., 1975-77; liaison coord. Balt. City Jail, 1977-79; case mgr. Health and Rehabilitative Svcs., Cocoa, Fla., 1980-88; CEO Yissakar Ministries, Gainesville, Fla., 1989-94, Jabbok Ministries, Gainesville, 1991-94, Resurrected Life Ministries, Inc., Sarasota, Fla., 1994—; pres. The House of Bavaka (formerly, The House of La E'Shika), Sarasota, 1992—; CEO Resurrected Life Ministries Inc., 1994—, HEAT Ministries, 1996; bd. dirs. Jay Ministries, West Palm Beach, Fla., 1993. Author: The Prophet's Fast, 1996; co-author: Reflections in Lace, 1992; author: (poetry) Power, 1990 (honorary mention 1990); columnist, religious editor Mahogany Revue, Ocala, Fla., 1992-93; author short story, 1987 (honorary mention 1987); contbr. articles to newspaper. Chairperson com. for Aged and Disabled Persons, Gainesville, 1993, Sarasota Employment and Econ. Devel., 1996; chmn. grant com. Student Adv. Com. of Howard Bishop Mid. Sch., Gainesville, 1993; candidate City Commr. Dist. I, Gainesville, 1993, 95; mem. leadership bd. Sarasota County Coalition for the Homeless, 1994—, mem. exec. bd., 1995; mem. exec. com. Democratic Club, Sarasota, 1994; pres., bd. dirs. Family Self-Sufficiency Project, Sarasota, 1994—; cmty. liasion for Newtown Task Force; bd. dirs. Common Ground Cmty. Assn.; mem. Nat. Coalition Neighborhood Women. Recipient 1st Willie Bruton award U. Ctrl. Fla., 1982, Dr. Martin L. King scholarship, 1982. Mem. NAFF, Nat. Coalition of Neighborhood Women, God's Women of Power (pres. 1993), Gainesville Women's Network, Royal Venice Assn., Phi Beta Kappa, Chi Epislon. Democrat. Office: Venice Housing Authority PO Box 49796 Sarasota FL 34230-6796

CASTLEN, PEGGY LOU, insurance company executive; b. Parkersburg, W.Va., Sept. 7, 1939; d. Ted and Nina Leone (Wehler) Swartz; m. Tom Mefford Castlen, June 16, 1962 (div. Oct. 30, 1987); children: Michael Alan, Thomas Matthew, Cynthia Anne. BS in Edn., Miami U., 1961; M of Human Resource Devel., Univ. Assocs., San Diego, 1983. Lic. personal lines ins. agt.; CPCU. Elem. tchr. various sch. systems, Dearborn, Mich., 1961-62, Chgo., 1962-64, Oxford, Bluffton, Ohio, 1964-65, 65-66; dir. Bluffton (Ohio) Community Nursery Sch., 1969-71; coord. Assn. for Effectiveness Trainers, Columbus, Ohio, 1974-77; ind. tng. cons. Columbus and Portland, Oreg., 1971-80; office svcs. supr. NERCO, Inc., Portland, Oreg., 1980-85; personnel div. mgr. Nationwide Mut. Ins. Co., Portland, Oreg., 1985-89, field sales mgr., 1989-90; life co. human resources officer Nationwide Ins., Columbus, 1990-95, EEO/human resources officer, 1995—; cons., com. bd. mem. Jr. Achievement, Portland, 1981-85; assessor-cons., bd. dirs. Employment Connection, Beaverton, Oreg., 1980-85. Chairperson United Way Campaign Nationwide Regional Office, Portland, 1989; chairperson adv. com. Lake Oswego (Oreg.) Sch. Dist., 1985-88; elder, trustee United Presbyn. Ch., Beaverton, 1978-91, Columbus, 1975-77; mem. adv. bd. Downtown Cmty. Based Program, 1993—; com. mem., bd. dirs., YWCA, 1995—; com. mem. ARC, 1987-90. Recipient Vol. of Yr. award Nationwide Civic Action Program, 1989; named to Drummer's Soc., 1990. Mem. Soc. for Human Resource Mgmt., Am. Mgmt. Assn., Profl. Ins. Pers. Adminstrs., CPCU Soc. (bd. dirs., editor newsletter), Nationwide Ins. Enterprise Human Resources Coun., Nat. Fed. Credit Union (mem. com.). Presbyterian. Office: Nationwide Ins Co 1-01-13 One Nationwide Plz Columbus OH 43216

CASTNER, LINDA JANE, instructional technologist, nurse educator; b. Abilene, Tex., Feb. 16, 1943; d. Joseph Arthur and Jane Theora (Stickdorn) Kidwell; m. Harvey Robert Castner, June 12, 1965; children: Raymond Scott, David Alan, Susan Marie. BSN summa cum laude, Ohio State U., 1965, PhD in Edn., 1992; MSN, Marquette U., Milw., 1984. RN, Ohio. Pub. health nurse I Columbus Pub. Health Nurses, 1965-66; med./surg. instr. St. Joseph Hosp. Sch. Nursing, Joliet, Ill., 1967-68; part-time instr. Waukesha County Tech. Inst., Pewaukee, Wis., 1974-83; staff nurse med./surg. West Allis (Wis.) Meml. Hosp., 1981-82; asst. dir. TLC/instr. U. Rochester, N.Y., 1984-86; instructional designer Fuld Inst., Athens, Ohio, 1992—, ednl. cons. in nursing, 1992—. Author/designer interactive videos: Physical Examination, 7 programs, 1994-95, Pediatric Assessment, 1994. Mem. ANA, Nat. League Nursing, Assn. Ednl. Comm. and Tech., Health Scis. Comm. Assn., N.Am. Nursing Diagnosis Assn., Sigma Theta Tau. Home: 433 Olenwood Ave Worthington OH 43085 Office: Castner Cons Instrnl Tech 433 Olenwood Ave Worthington OH 43085

CASTOR, BETTY, academic administrator. Pres. Univ. South Fla., Tampa. *

CASTORINO, SUE, communications executive; b. Columbus, Ohio, May 5, 1953; m. Randy Minkoff, Oct. 29, 1983. BS in Speech, Northwestern U., Evanston, Ill., 1975. Grad. fellow Ohio Gov.'s Sch., Columbus, 1975; producer, community affairs WBBM-TV (CBS all-news)), Chgo., 1975; news anchor, reporter Sta. WBBM, Chgo., 1981-86; news reporter WHTH-AM/FM, Newark, Ohio, 1975; news anchor, reporter WERE-AM (NBC all-news), Cleve., 1975-78, WWWE-AM (ABC), Cleve., 1978-81; founder, pres. Sue Castorino: The Speaking Specialist, Chgo., 1986—; guest lectr. various groups in bus., medicine, govt., law, sports, fin., worldwide, 1986—; leader media and presentation skills seminars; pvt. voice coach, 1986—; internat. exec. comm. tng. in media, crisis and issue mgmt. Author: North Shore Mag., 1987—; voice-over and on-camera talent, 1986—. Recipient Golden Gavel award Chgo. Soc. Assn. Execs., 1991, various news reporting awards AP, UPI, Chgo., 1981-86. Mem. Sigma Delta Chi. Office: The Speaking Specialist 435 N Michigan Ave Ste 2700 Chicago IL 60611-4001

CASTRATARO, BARBARA ANN, lawyer; b. Bethpage, N.Y., Apr. 25, 1958; d. Vincent James and Theresa (Chiarini) C. BA in Music, C.W. Post Coll. Sch. Music, 1984; JD, N.Y. Law Sch., 1989. Bar. N.Y. 1990, U.S. Dist. Ct. (so. dist.) N.Y. 1990. Music dir. CBS Network, N.Y.C., 1979-83, exec. officer ops., 1984-88; music dir. NBC Network/Score Prodns., L.A., 1979-83, Score Prodns./ABC Network, N.Y.C., 1982-83; atty. Donald Frank Esq., N.Y.C., 1989-93, Bender & Bodnar, White Plains, N.Y., 1993—; lectr. on divorce and separation; adj. faculty mem. Berkley Coll., White Plains, N.Y. Emmy Nomination N.Y. Acad. TV Arts & Sci., 1979, 82-83. Mem. ABA, Womens Bar Assn., N.Y. State Bar Assn., N.Y. County Lawyers Assn. Home: 31 Birchwood Rd Stamford CT 06907-1902 Office: 11 Martine Ave White Plains NY 10606-1934

CASTRO, AMUERFINA TANTIONGCO, geriatrics nurse; b. Morong, Rizal, Philippines, July 30, 1942; d. Eusebio and Juana (Victorio) Tantiongco; m. El B. Castro, Apr. 6, 1966; children: Cesar, El Jr., Christopher. BSN, U. East, Quezon City, Philippines, 1963; MA in Nursing, NYU, 1975. Cert. in oncology and gerontology nursing. Mem. staff U. East Ramon Magsaysay Meml. Med. Ctr., Quezon City, 1963-64; mem. faculty St. Catherine Sch. Nursing, Quezon City, 1964-65; operating room nurse Fordham Hosp. and Union Hosp., Bronx, N.Y., 1966-69; staff nurse in chemotherapy rsch. Meml. Hosp.-Sloan Kettering, N.Y.C., 1969-74; charge nurse Greenbrook (N.J.) Manor Nursing Home, 1989—. Vice-chmn., trustee Found. Philippine-Am. Med. Soc. N.J., 1990—. Mem. ANA, N.J. Nurses Assn., Philippine Nurses Assn. Am. (bd. dirs., Nat. Svc. award 1988-90), Philippine Nurses Assn. N.J. (pres., adv. bd., Outstanding Mem. award 1986—), U. East Ramon Magsaysay Meml. Med. Ctr. Nursing Alumni Assn. U.S.A. (pres. 1988-92, mem. adv. bd., Outstanding Alumni in Cmty. Svc. award 1993), Philippine Am. Med. Soc. N.J. Aux. (pres.-elect), Sigma Theta Tau.

CASTRO, JAN GARDEN, author, arts consultant, educator; b. St. Louis, June 8, 1945; d. Harold and Estelle (Fischer) Garden; 1 child, Jomo Jemal. Student, Cornell U., 1963-65; B.A. in English, U. Wis., 1967; publishing cert., Radcliffe Coll., 1967; M.A.T., Washington U., St. Louis, 1974, MA, 1994. Life cert. tchr. secondary English, speech, drama and social studies, Mo. Tchr., writer St. Louis, 1970—; dir. Big River Assn., St. Louis, 1975-85; lectr. Lindenwood Coll., 1980—; co-founder, dir. Duff's Poetry Series, St. Louis, 1975-81; founder, dir. River Styx P.M. Series, St. Louis, 1981-83; arts cons. Harris-Stowe State Coll., 1986-87. Contbg. author: San Francisco Rev. Books, 1982-85, Am. Book Rev., 1990—, Mo. Rev., 1991, News Letters, 1993, Tampa Rev., 1994—, The Nation, Am. Poetry Rev.; author books including Mandala of the Five Senses, 1975, The Art and Life of Georgia O'Keeffe, 1985, paperback edit., 1995; editor: River Styx mag., 1975-86; co-editor: Margaret Atwood: Vision and Forms, 1988; TV host and co-prodr. The Writers Cir., Double Helix, St. Louis, 1987-89. Mem. University City Arts and Letters Commn., Mo., 1983-84. NEH fellow UCLA, 1988, Johns Hopkins U., 1990, Camargo fellow, Cassis, France, Assis. Fin., 1996; recipient Arts and Letters award St. Louis Mag., 1985, Editor's award and editor during G.E. Younger Writers award to River Styx Mag., Coordinating Coun. for Lit. Mags., 1986, Arts award Mandrake Soc. Charity Ball, 1988, Leadership award YWCA St. Louis, 1988. Mem. MLA, Margaret Atwood Soc. (founder). Home: 7420 Cornell Ave Saint Louis MO 63130-2914 Office: Lindenwood College Saint Charles MO 63301

CASWELL, FRANCES PRATT, retired English language educator; b. Brunswick, Maine, June 25, 1929; d. Harold Edward and Marian Elizabeth (Nicoll) Pratt; m. Forrest Wilbur Caswell, June 30, 1956; children: Lucy Caswell Hilburn, Helen Caswell Watts, Harold F. BA, U. Maine, 1951; MA, U. Mich., 1955. Tchr. English, Bridgton (Maine) High Sch., 1951-54, Grosse Point (Mich.) High Sch., 1955-56; instr. South Maine Tech. Coll., South Portland, 1968-84, chmn. dept., 1984-93; bd. dirs. Maine Vocat. Region 10. Athor: Growing Through Faith, A History of the Brunswick United Methodist Church, 1821-1996, 1996; contbg. author: Brunswick, Maine, 250 Years A Town, 1989. Pres. United Pejepscot Housing Inc.,

Brunswick, 1987-93. Mem. AAUW, Nat. Coun. Tchrs. English, Casco Bay Art League. Republican. Methodist.

CASWELL, LINDA KAY, insurance agency executive; b. Canton, Ohio, Sept. 29, 1952; d. Lloyd Norman and Eva Mae (Clark) C. Grad. high sch., Canton, Ohio. Office mgr., sec. Harold Dickinson Architect, Canton, 1970-73; dist. mgr., sec., clk. Met. Life Ins., Canton, 1973-80, office mgr., 1980-86; brokerage assoc. Met. Brokerage, Canton, 1986-89; owner, pres. Golden Horizons Ins. Agy., Canton, 1987—. Office: Golden Horizons Ins Agy 5874 Fulton Dr NW Canton OH 44718-1735

CATALANO, JANE DONNA, lawyer; b. Schenectady, N.Y., Feb. 21, 1957; d. Alfred and Joan (Futscher) Martini; m. Peter Catalano, June 18, 1988. BA, SUNY, Plattsburgh, 1979; JD, Albany Law Sch., 1982. Bar: N.Y. 1983, U.S. Dist. Ct. 1983. Atty. Pentak, Brown & Tobin, Albany, N.Y., 1982-87, Niagara Mohawk Power Corp., Albany, 1987—. Mem. N.Y. State Bar Assn., Albany County Bar Assn. Home: 7 Blackburn Way Latham NY 12110-1943 Office: Niagara Mohawk Power Corp Ste 304 111 Washington Ave Albany NY 12210

CATALDI, SUZANNE LABA, philosophy educator; b. Somerville, N.J., Nov. 9, 1951; d. Michael and Ann (Bialy) Laba. BA, George Mason U., Fairfax, Va., 1981; PhD in Philosophy, Rutgers U., New Brunswick, N.J., 1991. Asst. prof. Moorhead (Minn.) State U., 1991-95, So. Ill. U., Edwardsville, 1995—. Author: Emotion, Depth and Flesh: A Study of Sensitive Space, 1993. Office: So Ill U Edwardsville IL 62026

CATALFO, BETTY MARIE, health service executive, nutritionist; b. N.Y.C., Nov. 2, 1942; d. Lawrence Santo and Gemma (Patrone) Lorefice; children—Anthony, Lawrence, Donna Marie. Grad. Newtown High Sch., Elmhurst, N.Y., 1958. Sec., clk. ABC-TV, N.Y.C., 1957-60; founder, lectr., nutritionist Weight Watchers, Manhasset, N.Y., 1964-75; founder, pres. Every-Bodys Diet, Inc. dba Stay Slim, Queens, N.Y., 1976—; dir. in-home program N.Y. State Dept. Health, N.Y.C., 1985—; founder, pres. Delitegul Diet Foods, Inc., 1988—; lectr. in field. Author: 101 Stay-Slim Recipes, 1983, Get Slim and Stay Slim Diet Cook Book, rev. ed., 1987, Diet Revolution, 1991, Holiday Cookbook, 1992, Fat Counts in Fast Food Spots, 1992, Choose to Loose!, 1993, You Are Not Alone, 1993, Eating Out, 1994, Change or Select, 1994, Calories Do Count!, 1994, Fat Free Receipes, 1994; author, dir., producer: (video) Dancersize for Overweight, 1986, Get Slim and Stay Slim Diet Cook Book, Eating Right for Your Life, Hello It's Me and I'm Slim, (videos) Stay Slim Line Dancing, 1989, Stay Slim Food Facts, 1989, Help Me Before I Give In, 1990, A New Year A New You!, 1991, Relax and Meditate, 1991, Come Shop with Me, 1991, Change or Accept, 1993, The Bag Lady, 1993, Sneak Eater, 1993, Sins That Every Dieter Makes, 1994, Stay Slim from Start to Finish, 1994, Here's Some Helpful Diet Tips, 1994, What Every Smart Dieter Knows, 1994, Mirror Mirror on the Wall, 1994, Weight Management Techniques, 1995; author, editor: (video) Eating Right For Life, 1985, Isometric Techniques for Weight Reduction, Dance Your Calories A-Weigh; author, producer: (video) Eating Habits, 1986—; (video) Isometric Techniques for Weight Reduction, 1986, Patience Is a Virtue When Weight Loss is the Goal, 1986, Slow Down you Eat to Fast, 1994, Always Giving Never Receiving, 1994, Relax and Don't You Worry, 1994; producer, dir.: (video) Positive and Negative Diet Forces, 1987, (video) Hello It's Me and I'm Thin, 1987, (video) Dance Your Calories A-Weigh, 1987, (video) Positive and Negative Diet Forces, 1987. Sponsor, lectr. St. Pauls Ctr., Bklyn., 1981—, Throgs Neck Assn. Retarded Children, Bronx, 1985—; active ARC, LWV, Am. Italian Assn., United Way Greenwich, Council Chs. and Synagogues, Heart Assn., N.Y. Meals on Wheels, 1985—, Health Assn. Fairfield County, Food Svcs. for Homeless People, 1993, 94, 95; chairperson, sponsor Battered Women, 1994—. Named Woman of Yr., Bayside Womens Club, N.Y., 1983, O, PK Woman of Yr., 1986—, Woman of Yr. Richmond Boys Club, 1987, Woman of Yr. Bronx Press Club Assn., 1987; recipient Merit award for Svc. Cath. Archdiocese of Bklyn., 1985, Merit award Svcs. Cath. Archdioces of Bklyn. and Queens, 1992, 93, 94, Community Service award Sr. Citizens Sacred Heart League Bklyn./Queens Archdiocese. N.Y. State Nutritional Guidance for Children Nat. Assn. Scis. Mem. Nat. C. of C. for Women (Woman of Yr. 1987, 90), Pres.'s Coun. on Nutrition, Roundtable for Women in Food Service, Bus. and Profl. Women's Club, Pres. Council for Phys. Fitness, Nat. Assn. Female Execs., Assn. for Fitness in Bus. Inc., Nat. Assn. Female Bus. Owners. Democrat. Roman Catholic. Club: Mothers Sacred Heart Sch. (chairperson 1979-82). Avocations: reading, travel, golf, family. Home: 21422 27th Ave Flushing NY 11360-2608 also: 58 Riverview Ct Greenwich CT 06831-4127 Office: 10005 101st Ave Ozone Park NY 11416-2610

CATALINA, LYNN JOHNSTON, public relations and marketing professional; b. Jackson, Miss., Apr. 25, 1948; d. Erle Ennis Jr. and Fay (Martin) Johnston; m. Ben H. Catalina Jr., Jan. 31, 1970; children: Charles Jeffrey, Jamie Lynn. BS in Journalism Edn., Miss. U. for Women, 1970. Journalism and speech tchr. Orange County Schs., Orlando, Fla., 1970-71; reporter, theater critic Herald Pub. Co., San Antonio, 1978-80; freelance writer and advt. cons. various mags., newspapers and agys., Hartford, Conn., 1981-83; dir. comms. First Presbyn. Ch., Albuquerque, 1985-87; contract writer Psychol. Corp., San Antonio, 1989; info. writer III Inst. Texan Cultures, San Antonio, 1990-92, dir. comms. and mktg., 1992—; mem. adv. com. Things Remembered TV program KLRN/PBS, San Antonio, 1995; surveyor mus. assessment program Am. Assn. Mus., Washington, 1996—. Author: How To Speak Air Force, 1984. Elder John Calvin Presbyn. Ch., San Antonio, 1989-91, moderator, pastor nominating com., 1995-96, advt./pub. rels. coord., 1989—; mem. promotions com. walk for women's athletics U. Tex., San Antonio, 1995. Mem. Women in Comms., Inc. (Proliner award of merit 1995), Tex. Pub. Rels. Assn. (mem. winter conf. com. 1995-96, bd. dirs. 1996—). Home: 8510 Aesop Ln Universal City TX 78148 Office: Inst Texan Cultures 801 Bowie St San Antonio TX 78205

CATER, E. JANICE, adult education educator; b. Hot Springs, Ark., Nov. 28, 1945; d. Cecil Lowery and Euna Corine (Lowe) Suitt; m. Brent Alan Cater, July 2, 1967; 1 child, Kenneth Jefferson. BSE, Henderson State U., 1966; MA, Ea. Mich. U., 1979; EdD, U. Ark., 1992. Adult edn. staff Flint (Mich.) Community Schs., 1971-87, field worker, 1981-87; coord./producer Home Learning Ctr., Flint, 1981-82; faculty, prof. of radio, TV and film U. of the Ozarks, Clarksville, Ark., 1982—; chmn. student media bd., U. Clarksville, 1983—, dir. Video Svcs., 1987—. Producer news and pub. affairs program, U. Clarksville, 1989—. Mem. Ark. Instrnl. Media Assn., Alpha Chi, Phi Delta Kappa (historian 1986-89). Office: Univ of Ozarks 415 College Ave Clarksville AR 72830

CATER, JUDY JERSTAD, librarian; b. San Francisco, Jan. 20, 1951; d. Theodore S. and Estelle E. (Christian) Jerstad; m. Jack E. Cater, Nov. 24, 1973; children: Joanne Jerstad, Jennifer Jerstad. AB, Mount Holyoke Coll., 1973; MS, Simmons Coll., 1974; MA, U. San Diego, 1984. Cert. libr., libr. tech., supr. chief adminstrv. officer. Cataloging libr. Palomar Coll., San Marcos, Calif., 1975-76, fine arts, evening reference libr., 1976-77, acquisitions libr., 1977-86, media svcs., acquisitions libr., 1988-90, chair, v.p. instrn. svcs., 1987-88, dir. libr. media ctr., 1986-88, 90-92, media svcs. libr., 1993—; cons., manuscript asst. Presidio Army Mus., Calif. Hist. Soc., San Francisco, 1974-75; rschr. Charles H. Brown Archaeol. Site, San Diego, 1977; adj. faculty mem. history dept., 1990—. Pres. Mount Holyoke Club of San Diego, 1982-86. Recipient stipend Simmons Coll. Sch. Libr. Sci., 1979, Girl Scouts of San Diego and Imperial Counties Disting. Leader award, 1990, Faculty Svc. award Palomar Coll., 1990, NISOD Excellence award, 1991. Mem. ALA, Calif. Libr. Assn. (sec. treas. 1986, membership chair 1987, minority scholarship com. 1991-93, awards and scholarships com. 1993—), Calif. Tchrs. Assn. (pres. Palomar Coll. chpt. 1979-80), Faculty Assn. Calif. Cmty. Colls., Am. Assn. Women in Cmty. and Jr. Colls. Episcopalian. Office: Palomar Coll Libr 1140 W Mission Rd San Marcos CA 92069-1415

CATES, JO ANN, librarian, management consultant; b. Ft. Worth, June 25, 1958; d. Charles Kimbrough and Lydia Joe (Sachse) C.; m. Joseph Daniel Frank, Oct. 28, 1989; 1 child, Jacob Abraham Frank, Dec. 9, 1993. BS in Journalism, Boston U., 1980; MLS, Simmons Coll., 1984. Advt. asst. Boston Phoenix, 1978-79; med. serials asst. Mass. Gen. Hosp., Boston, 1979-80; editorial asst. Exceptional Parent Mag., Boston, 1980-81; libr. reference asst. Lesley Coll., Cambridge, Mass., 1981-84; head reference libr. Lamont Libr., Harvard U., Cambridge, Mass., 1984-85; chief libr. Poynter Inst. for Media Studies, St. Petersburg, Fla., 1985-91; head transp. libr. Northwestern U., Evanston, Ill., 1991-94; tchr. News Libr. and Newsroom Seminars Poynter Inst., 1990-91; mem. Harvard Com. on Instrn. Libr. Use, 1984, mem. adv. com. on book and serial budgets, 1991-94; cons. journalism orgns. Calif., Fla., Mass., 1984—; book reviewer Libr. Jour., Choice, 1985—, Am. Reference Book Annual, 1993—. Author: Journalism: A Guide to the Reference Literature, 1990; editor Transp. Divsn. Bull., 1992-94; mem. editorial bd. Footnotes, 1991-94; contbr. articles to profl. jours. Mem. Transp. Rsch. Bd. Info. Svcs. Com., 1991-94; media intern Dem. Nat. Com., Boston, 1979-80. Scholar Women in Comm., 1976-78; Trustee scholar Boston U., 1978-80; Simmons Coll. grantee, 1982-84. Mem. Spl. Librs. Assn., Assn. for Edn. in Journalism and Mass Comm., Suncoast Info. Specialists (pres. 1990-91). Home: 500 Sheridan Rd Apt 1E Evanston IL 60202-3181

CATES, MICHELLE RENEE, air force reserve officer, consultant; b. Peoria, Ill., June 30, 1956; d. Roy Frederick and Dorothy Eleanor (Powell) C. BS in Phys. Edn., Taylor U., Upland, Ind., 1978; MA in Curriculum and Instrn., Chapman U., Orange, Calif., 1991. Par profl. West Chicago (Ill.) High Sch., 1978-79; tchr. lang. arts 1st Bapt. Christian Sch., Downers Grove, Ill., 1979-80; grad. asst. Whitworth Coll., Spokane, Wash., 1980; teaching fellow N.W. Nazarene Coll., Nampa, Idaho, 1981-83; commd. officer USAF, 1983-92, advanced through grades to capt., 1989; intelligence officer Operation Desert Shield and Storm, King Fahd Air Base, Saudi Arabia, 1991; ret. USAF, 1992; asst. prof. aerospace studies U. Ariz., Tucson, 1992; tactical officer Comdt.'s Office, Tex. A&M U., College Station, 1992; resigned from active duty; sr. cons. with Booz Allen & Hamilton, 1995—. Maj. USAR. Democrat. Baptist. Home: 5903 Mt Eagle Dr # 711 Alexandria VA 22303

CATEURA, LINDA BRANDI, writer, painter; b. New Haven; d. Albert and Alice (Capobianco) Brandi; m. Henry Joseph Cateura; 1 child, Patricia. BA, Albertus Magnus Coll., New Haven, 1944. Assoc. lit. editor Harper's Bazaar Mag., N.Y.C., 1949-57; assoc. editor Woman's Day Mag., N.Y.C., 1957-60, Family Circle Mag., N.Y.C., 1961-63; free lance book reviewer N.Y. Times, Sat. Rev., N.Y.C., 1957-61; adminstrv. aide State Sen. William Giordano, N.Y.C., 1969-73; press aide N.Y. Sec. of State, N.Y.C., 1977-79; pub. info. officer Dept. State, State of N.Y., N.Y.C., 1979-82; lectr. on ethnic, religious and family issues; guest numerous TV and radio shows. Author: Oil Painting Secrets from a Master, 1984, Growing Up Italian, 1987, Catholics U.S.A., 1989; painter portraits and still lifes, 1980—; exhibited in art shows, N.Y.C.; portraits on commn. Recipient Bklyn. Woman Writer of Yr. award Dist. Atty.s' Office of Kings County, N.Y.C., 1993. Mem. Am. Soc. Portrait Painters, Artists Talk on art, Oral History Assn., The Nature conservancy. Democrat. Roman Catholic. Home and Studio: 136 Willow St Brooklyn NY 11201-2202

CATHOU, RENATA EGONE, chemist, consultant; b. Milan, Italy, June 21, 1935; d. Egon and Stella Mary Egone; m. Pierre-Yves Cathou, June 21, 1959. BS, MIT, 1957, PhD, 1963. Postdoctoral fellow, research assoc. in chemistry MIT, Cambridge, 1962-65; research assoc. Harvard U. Med. Sch., Cambridge, 1965-69, instr., 1969-70; research assoc. Mass. Gen. Hosp., 1965-69, instr., 1969-70; asst. prof. dept. biochemistry Sch. Medicine, Tufts U., 1970-73, assoc. prof., 1973-78, prof., 1978-81; pres. Tech. Evaluations, Lexington, Mass., 1983—; sr. cons. SRC Assocs., Park Ridge, N.J., 1984-93; sr. investigator Arthritis Found., 1970-75; vis. prof. dept. chemistry UCLA, 1976-77; mem. adv. panel NSF, 1974-75; mem. bd. sci. counselors Nat. Cancer Inst., 1979-83; ind. cons. and writer. Mem. editorial bd. Immunochemistry, 1972-75; contbr. chpts. to books and articles to profl. jours. MIT Company Founders citation, 1989; NIH predoctoral fellow, 1958-62; grantee Am. Heart Assn., 1969-81, USPHS, 1970-81. Mem. AAAS, Am. Soc. for Biochemistry and Molecular Biology, Am. Assn. Immunologists, U.S. Power Squadron (past dist. lt. comdr.), Charles River Squadron (past comdr.). Office: Tech Evaluations PO Box 23 Lexington MA 02173-0001

CATINA, VICKIE GAYLE, accountant; b. Dallas, Aug. 21, 1969; d. Luke Wayne and Patsy Earline (Creighton) C. BS, MS, U. North Tex., 1993. CPA, Tex. Staff acct. Westinghouse Security Sys., Irving, Tex., 1993-95, sr. acct., 1995, sr. acct., a/r supr., 1996—. Recipient Acctg. Excellence award Tex. Soc. CPAs, 1993. Mem. Inst. Mgmt. Accts. (cert.), Inst. Internal Auditors (cert.). Home: # 2088 2922 W Royal Irving TX 75063 Office: Westinghouse Security Sys Inc 4221 W John Carpenter Frwy Irving TX 75063

CATLEY-CARLSON, MARGARET, professional organization administrator; b. Nelson, B.C., Oct. 6, 1942; d. George Lorne and Helen Margaret (Hughes) Catley; m. Stanley F. Carlson, Oct. 30, 1970. BA with honors, U. B.C., 1966; postgrad., Inst. Internat. Relations, U. W.I., St. Augustine, Trinidad and Tobago, 1970; LLD (hon.), U. Regina, 1985; LittD (hon.), St. Mary's U., 1985; Fellow, Ryerson Poly. Inst. Concordia U., 1986, Mt. St. Vincent U., 1990. Joined Dept. External Affairs., Can., 1966; second sec. Can. High Commn., Colombo, Sri Lanka, 1968; with aid and devel. div. Dept. External Affairs, 1970-74; econ. counsellor Can. High Commn., London, 1975-77; v.p. Can. Internat. Devel. Agy., 1978, sr. v.p., acting pres., 1979-80; asst. under-sec. Dept. External Affairs, 1981-82; asst. sec. gen. UN; dep. exec. dir. ops. UNICEF; pres. Can. Internat. Devel. Agy., 1983-89; dep. minister Health and Welfare Country of Canada, 1989-92; pres. The Population Coun., N.Y.C., 1993—. Office: The Population Coun 1 Dag Hammarskjold Plz New York NY 10017-2201

CATLIN, SUSAN LYNN, alcohol and drug abuse psychotherapist; b. Chgo., Dec. 15, 1954; d. Charles Sexton and Dorothy Mary (Good) C. BA, U. Ill., 1977; postgrad., George Williams Coll., 1983; MA, Roosevelt U., 1995. Cert. alcohol and drug counselor. Psychiat. tech. Forest Hosp., Des Plaines, Ill., 1979-85; alcohol counselor Ptnrs. in Psychiatry, Des Plaines, 1985-90; dir., pres. S.L. Catlin and Assocs., Des Plaines, Schaumburg, Ill., 1990—; cons. Advanced Psychiat. Svcs., 1990-94. Fellow Div. of Ill. Addictions, Nat. Assn. Alcoholism and Drug Abuse Counselors. Republican. Methodist. Home: 258 Sierra Pass Dr Schaumburg IL 60194

CATO, LEANNA SAMPSON, special education eductor; b. Bellamy, Ala., Sept. 16, 1941; d. Otto Carlo and Magnolia Eloise Sampson; (legally separated); children: Willeah Eloise, Cedric Sampson C. BEd, Arkansas A.M.& N. U., Pine Bluff, 1964; MEd, Bowie (Md.) State U., 1974; postgrad. studies in Edn., Johns Hopkins U. CASE, 1976-77. Cert. advanced tchr., Md. Secondary sch. tchr. Md., 1966—; spl. edn. tchr. Bladensberg (Md.) H.S., 1981—; spl. edn. self-contained tchr. Prince George's County Pub. Schs., Bladensburg, 1996—; landlord Ocean Pines, Md., Burgess, Va.; chmn. faculty recognition com. Bladensburg H.S., 1991-94, initiator job awareness program, 1994—. Ch. sch. tchr. St. John Bapt. Ch., Columbia, Md., 1993-95. flower guild mem., 1985—; campaign vol. Dem. Com. Howard County. Mem. NEA, Md. Educators Assn.. Democrat. Baptist. Home: 5018 Hayload Ct Columbia MD 21044 Office: Bladensburg HS 5610 Tilden Rd Bladensburg MD 20780

CATOLINE, PAULINE DESSIE, small business owner; b. Ft. Worth, Dec. 17, 1937; d. Byron Hillis and Dessie Elizabeth (Plumlee) Doggett; children: Sherry Lou, Brenda Lynn; m. Donald Ralph Ackerman, Feb. 19, 1993. BA in Bus. Mgmt. (labor rels. specialty), Hiram Coll., 1989. Notary public, Ohio. Sec. Gen. Am. Life Ins. Co., Ft. Worth, 1956-57, Kelly Girl Svcs., Youngstown, Ohio, 1965-69; legal sec. Burgstaller, Schwartz & Moore, Youngstown, 1962-65, Green, Schiavoni, Murphy & Haines, Youngstown, 1969-71, Flask & Policy, Youngstown, 1971-83; sec. Western Res. Care System, Youngstown, 1983-87, exec. sec., 1987-90; owner, mgr. Pauline's Place, Youngstown, 1993—; legal sec. Henderson, Covington, Stein, Donchess & Messenger Law Firm, 1993-94; exec. adminstrv. asst. to pres. CEO, sr. v.p. Internat. Renaissance Developers, Youngstown, 1994-96; owner Pauline's Place, 1996—. Pres. PTA, Cottage Hills, Ill., 1968-69, brownie and scout leader, 1968-69. Mem. Mahoning County Legal Secs. Assn. (v.p. 1973-74, editor monthly booklet 1974-75), Exec. Link, Missionary Group Club. Democrat. Methodist. Home: 3961 Cannon Rd Youngstown OH 44515-4604 also: Internat Renaissance Developers 237 E Front St Youngstown OH 44503

CATTANEO, JACQUELYN ANNETTE KAMMERER, artist, educator; b. Gallup, N.Mex., June 1, 1944; d. Ralph John and Gladys Agnes (O'Sullivan) Kammer; m. John Leo Cattaneo, Apr. 25, 1964; children: John Auro, Paul Anthony. Student Tex. Woman's U., 1962-64. Portrait artist, tchr. Gallup, N. Mex., 1972; coord. Works Progress Adminstrn. art project renovation McKinley County, Gallup, Octavia Fellin Performing Arts wing dedication, Gallup Pub. Library; formation com. mem. Multi-modal/Multi-Cultural Ctr. for Gallup, N.Mex.; exch. with Soviet Women's Com., USSR Women Artists del., Moscow, Kiev, Leningrad, 1990; Women Artists del. and exch. Jerusalem, Tel Aviv, Cairo, Israel; mem. Artists Del. to Prague, Vienna and Budapest.; mem. Women Artists Del. to Egypt, Israel and Italy, 1992, Artist Del. Brazil, 1994, Greece, Crete and Turkey, 1996, Spain, 1996. One-woman shows include Gallup Pub. Libr., 1963, 66, 77, 78, 81, 87, Gallup Lovelace Med. Clinic, Santa Fe Station Open House, 1981, Gallery 20, Farmington, N.Mex., 1985—, Red Mesa Art Gallery, 1989, Soviet Restrospect Carol's Art & Antiques Gallery, Liverpool, N.Y., 1992, N.Mex. State Capitol Bldg., Santa Fe, 1992, Lt. Govt. Casey Luna-Office Complex, Women Artists N.Mex. Mus. Fine Arts, Carlsbad, 1992, Rio Rancho Country Club, N.Mex., 1995; group shows include: Navajo Nation Library Invitational, 1978, Santa Fe Festival of the Arts Invitational, 1979, N.Mex. State Fair, 1978, 79, 80, Catharine Lorillard Wolfe, N.Y.C., 1980, 81, 84, 85, 86, 87, 88, 89, 91, 92, 4th ann. exhbn. Salmagundi Club, 1984, 90, 3d ann. Palm Beach Internat., New Orleans, 1984, Fine Arts Ctr. Taos, 1984, The Best and the Brightest O'Brien's Art Emporium, Scottsdale, Ariz., 1986, Gov.'s Gallery, 1989, N.Mex. State Capitol, Santa Fe, 1987, Pastel Soc. West Coast Ann. Exhbn. Sacramento Ctr. for Arts, Calif., 1986-90, gov.'s invitational Magnifico Fest. of the Arts, Albuquerque, 1991, Assn. Pour La Promotion Du Patrimone Artistique Français, Paris, Nat. Mus. of the Arts for Women, Washington, 1991, Artists of N.Mex., Internat. Nexus '92 Fine Art Exhbn., Trammell Corw Pavilion, Dallas, Carlsbad (N.Mex.) Mus. Fine Art; represented in permanent collections: Zuni Arts and Crafts Ednl. Bldg., U. N.Mex., C.J. Wiemar Collection, McKinley Manor, Gov.'s Office, State Capitol Bldg., Santa Fe, Historic El Rancho Hotel, Gallup, N.Mex., Sunwest Bank. Fine Arts Ctr., En Taos, N.Mex., Armand Hammer Pvt. Collection, Wilcox Canyon Collections, Sadona, Ariz., Galaria Impi, Netherlands, Woods Art and Antiques, Liverpool, N.Y., Stewarts Fine Art, Taos, N.Mex. Mem. Dora Cox del. to Soviet Union-U.S. Exchange, 1990. Recipient Cert. of Recognition for Contbn. and Participation Assn. Pour La Patrinome Du Artistique Français, 1991, N.Mex. State Senate 14th Legislature Session Meml. # 101 for Artistic Achievements award, 1992, Award of Merit, Pastel Soc. West Coast Ann. Membership Exhbn., 1993. Mem. Internat. Fine Arts Guild, Am. Portrait Soc. (cert.), Oil Painters of Am., Pastel Soc. of W. Coast (cert.), Mus. N.Mex. Found., N.Mex. Archtl. Found., Mus. Women in the Arts, Fechin Inst., Artists' Co-op. (co-chair), Gallup C. of C., Gallup Area Arts and Crafts Council, Am. Portrait Soc. Am., Pastel Soc. N.Mex., Catharine Lorillard Wolfe Art Club of N.Y.C. (oil and pastel juried membership), Chautaugua Art Club, Knickerbocker Artists and Oil Painters of Am., Soroptimists (Internat. Woman of Distinction 1990). Address: 210 E Green St Gallup NM 87301-6130

CATTANI, MARYELLEN B., lawyer; b. Bakersfield, Calif., Dec. 1, 1943; d. Arnold Theodore and Corinne Marilyn (Kovacevich) C.; m. Frank C. Herringer; children: Sarah, Julia. AB, Vassar Coll., Poughkeepsie, N.Y., 1965; JD, U. Calif. (Boalt Hall), 1968. Assoc. Davis Polk & Wardwell, N.Y.C., 1968-69; assoc. Orrick, Herrington & Sutcliffe, San Francisco, 1970-74, ptnr., 1975-81; v.p., gen. counsel Transamerica Corp., San Francisco, 1981-83, sr. v.p., gen. counsel, 1983-89; ptnr. Morrison & Foerster, San Francisco, 1989-91; sr. v.p. gen. counsel Am. Pres. Cos., Ltd., 1991-95, exec. v.p., gen. counsel, 1995—; bd. dirs. Golden West Fin. Corp., World Savs. & Loan Assn., ABM Industries Inc. Author: Calif. Corp. Practice Guide, 1977, Corp. Counselors, 1982. Regent St. Mary's Coll., Morega, Calif., 1986—, pres., 1990-92, trustee, 1990—, chmn., 1993-95; trustee Vassar Coll., 1985-93, The Head-Royce Sch., 1993—; bd. dirs. The Exploratorium, 1988-93; active Ctr. Pub. Resources San Francisco. Mem. ABA, State Bar Calif. (chmn. bus. law sect. 1980-81), Bar Assn. San Francisco (co-chair com. on women 1989-91), Calif. Women Lawyers, San Francisco C. of C. (bd. dirs. 1987-91, gen. counsel 1990-91), Am. Corp. Counsel Assn. (bd. dirs. 1982-87), Women's Forum West (bd. dirs. 1984-87). Democrat. Roman Catholic. Club: Women's Forum West.

CATTELL, HEATHER BIRKETT, psychologist; b. Carlisle, eng., Dec. 16, 1936; came to U.S., 1955; d. Wilfred B. and Anne Birkett; m. Russel B. Shields, June 10, 1953 (div. 1963); children: Vaughn, Gary, Heather Luanne; m. Raymond B. Cattell, May 9, 1981. BA, U. Hawaii, 1974, MA, 1977, PhD, 1979. Lic. clin. psychologist, Hawaii. Dir. rsch. Salvation Army, Honolulu, 1979-81; pvt. practice Honolulu, 1981—; lectr., workshop leader, U.S., Australia, Can., and United Kingdom, 1989—. Author: The 16PF: Personality in Depth, 1989. Mem. Phi Beta Kappa. Office: 1188 Bishop St Ste 1702 Honolulu HI 96813-3307

CATTERALL, MARLENE, Canadian legislator; b. Ottawa, Ont., Can., Mar. 1, 1939; d. Paul and Isobel Petzold; m. Ron Catterall, July 14, 1962; children: Karen, Chris, Cheryl. Ed., Carleton U. Alderman City of Ottawa, 1976-85; coun. mem. Regional Municipality Ottawa-Carleton, 1976-85; mem. from Ottawa West Ho. of Commons, 1988—, apptd. parliamentary sec. to pres. of treasury bd.; apptd. dep. govt. whip, 1994; vice chair Procedure and House Affairs Com. Mem. Ottawa Women's Network, Bus. and Profl. Women's Club. Liberal. Roman Catholic. Office: House of Commons, Rm 451-S Centre Block, Ottawa, ON Canada K1A 0A6

CATTERTON, MARIANNE ROSE, occupational therapist; b. St. Paul, Feb. 3, 1922; d. Melvin Joseph and Katherine Marion (Bole) Maas; m. Elmer John Wood, Jan. 16, 1943 (dec.); m. Robert Lee Catterton, Nov. 20, 1951 (div. 1981); children: Jenifer Ann Dawson, Cynthia Lea Uthus. Student, Carleton Coll., 1939-41, U. Md., 1941-42; BA in English, U. Wis., 1944; MA in Counseling Psychology, Bowie State Coll., 1980; postgrad., No. Ariz. U., 1987-91. Registered occupational therapist, Occupational Therapy Cert. Bd. Occupational therapist VA, N.Y.C., 1946-50; cons. occupational therapist Fondo del Seguro del Estado, Puerto Rico, 1950-51; dir. rehab. therapies Spring Grove State Hosp., Catonsville, Md., 1953-56; occupational therapist Anne Arundel County Health Dept., Annapolis, Md., 1967-78; dir. occupational therapy Eastern Shore Hosp. Ctr., Cambridge, Md., 1979-85; cons. occupational therapist Kachina Point Health Ctr., Sedona, Ariz., 1986; regional chmn. Conf. on revising Psychiat. Occupational Therapy Edn., 1958-59; instr. report writing Anne Arundel Community Coll., Annapolis, 1974-78. Editor Am. Jour. Occupational Therapy, 1962-67. Active Md. Heart Assn., 1959-60; mem. task force on occupational therapy Md. Dept. of Health, 1971-72; chmn. Anne Arundel Gov. Com. on Employment of Handicapped, 1959-63; mem. gov.'s com. to study vocat. rehab., Md., 1960; com. mem. Annapolis Youth Ctr., 1976-78; mem. ministerial search com. Unitarian Ch. Anne Arundel County, 1962; curator Dorchester County Heritage Mus., Cambridge, 1982-83; v.p., officer Unitarian-Universalist Fellowship Flagstaff, 1988-93; co-moderator, founder Unitarian-Universalist Fellowship of Sedona, 1994—, respite care vol., 1994—; citizen interviewer Sedona Acad. Forum, 1993, 94. Mem. P.R. Occupl. Therapy Assn. (co-founder 1950), Am. Occupl. Therapy Assn. (chmn. history com. 1958-61), Md. Occupl. Therapy Assn. (del. 1953-59), Ariz. Occupl. Therapy Assn., Pathfinder Internat., Dorchester County Mental Health Assn. (pres. 1981-84), Internat. Platform Assn., Ret. Officers Assn., Air Force Assn. (Barry Goldwater chpt., sec. 1991-92, 94-96), Severn Town Club (treas. 1965, sec. 1971-72, 94-95), Internat. Club (Annapolis, publicity chmn. 1966), Toastmasters, Newcomers (Sedona, pres. 1986), Pathfinder, Zero Population Growth, Delta Delta Delta. Republican. Home: 415 Windsong Dr Sedona AZ 86336-3745

CATTO, PATRICIA JANE, literature educator; b. Auburn, N.Y., Mar. 17, 1952; d. William Tripoli and Pauline Jane (Ferri) C. MA, SUNY, Oswego, 1978. Creative writer Hallmark Cards, Inc., Kansas City, Mo., 1984-87; assoc. prof. Kansas City (Mo.) Art Inst., 1987—; panelist, spkr. Sch. of Visual Arts Nat. Conf., N.Y.C., 1992, 93, 95; Fulbright advisor Kansas City (Mo.) Art Inst., 1994—; cons. Hallmark Cards, Inc., Kansas City, 1995. Author: Wife of Geronimo's Virile Old Age, 1991; author of poetry. Poetry reader Nat. Clothesline Project, Kansas City, 1995. Mem. NOW, AAUW, Founds. and Theory in Art Edn. (convener/spkr. 1995). Home: 23 E 69 Terr Kansas City MO 64113 Office: Kansas City Art Inst Kansas City MO 64111

CATTS, LOIS MAY, critical care nurse specialist; b. Portland, Oreg., May 3, 1952. BSN, Seattle Pacific U., 1974; MSN, U. Calif., 1989. CCRN. Staff nurse, charge nurse Good Samaritan, Portland, 1974-87; staff nurse U. Calif., San Francisco, 1987-90; critical care educator Sequoia Hosp., Redwood City, Calif., 1990; critical care CNS Providence Yakima (Wash.) Med. Ctr., 1990—. Mem. AACN, Am. Heart Assn. (chmn. ACLS task force 1992—). Office: Providence Yakima Med Ctr 110 S 9th Ave Yakima WA 98902-3315

CAULFIELD, ELLEN RESCIGNO, retired public information officer; b. Yonkers, N.Y., Jan. 16, 1936; d. Rocco E. and Mildred F. (Foley) Rescigno; m. George F. Caulfield, July 14, 1959 (div. 1983); 1 child, Kevin; m. Douglas J. Maloney, May 14, 1988. BA, Syracuse U., 1957. Editor ITT, N.Y.C., 1957-59; pub. rels. staff Catalina, L.A., 1959-60; devel. officer Childrens Home Soc., L.A., 1970-73; planner, coord. Marin Sr. Coord. Coun., San Rafael, Calif., 1975-77; dir. County of Marin Divsn. of Aging, San Rafael, 1977-95; ret., 1995. Bd. mem. Ecumenical Assn. for Housing, San Rafael, 1980-85, United Way, San Rafael, 1989-95; mem. Wed. Morning Dialogue, Marin County, 1980—, Marin (Calif.) Forum, 1994—. Home: 204 Forbes Ave San Rafael CA 94901

CAULFIELD, JOAN, academic relations coordinator, educator; b. St. Joseph, Mo., July 17, 1943; d. Joseph A. and Jane (Lisenby) Caulfield; BS in Edn. cum laude, U. Mo., 1963, MA in Spanish, 1965, PhD, 1978; postgrad. (Mexican Govt. scholar) Nat. U. Mexico, 1962-63. TV tchr. Spanish, Kansas City (Mo.) pub. schs., 1963-68; tchr. Spanish, French Bingham Jr. High Schs., Kansas City, 1968-78; asst. prin. S.E. High Sch., Kansas City, 1984; prin. Nowlin Jr. High Sch., Independence, Mo., 1984-86, Lincoln Coll. Preparatory Acad., Kansas City, Mo., 1986-88, asst. supt., Kansas City, 1988-89; part-time instr. U. Mo.-Kansas City; dir. English Inst., Rockhurst Coll., summers, 1972-75, coord. sch. coll. rels., 1989—; mem. nat. steering com. Brain-Based Learning Network; assessor dept. elem. and secondary edn. State Mo. Mem. Sister City Commn., Kansas City, 1980—, Kans.' Quality Performance Assessment Team; ofcl. translator to mayor on trip to Seville, Spain, 1969; bd. dirs. Kansas City chpt. NCCJ, Expo '92 World's Fair, Seville, Spain (translator 1992), St. Theresa's Acad., 1991-94, Kansas City Acad. of Learning; selected leadership training Greater Mo.; trainer Harmony in a World of Difference, 1989-93; mem. task force C. of C.bd. dirs. Girls to Women. Named Outstanding Secondary Educator, 1973. Mem. ASCD, Romance Lang. Assn., Nat. Assn. Secondary Sch. Prins., MLA (contbr. jour.), Am. Assn. Tchrs. Spanish & Portuguese, Friends of Seville, Friends of Art, Magnet Schs. Am. (contbr. jour.), Mo. Mid. Sch. Assn. (contbr. jour.), Phi Sigma Iota, Phi Delta Kappa, Delta Kappa Gamma (state scholar 1977-78, contbr. jour. Bulletin), Phi Kappa Phi, Sigma Delta Pi. Presbyterian. Home: 431 W 70th St Kansas City MO 64113-2022 Office: 1100 Rockhurst Rd Kansas City MO 64110-2545

CAUTHEN, CARMEN WIMBERLEY, legislative staff member, jewelry designer; b. Raleigh, N.C., Aug. 4, 1959; d. William Peele and Cliffornia (Grady) Wimberley; m. Ricky Leon Cauthen, May 26, 1990; 1 child, Kena Elizabeth. Student, Ga. Inst. Tech., 1977-78; BA in Polit. Sci., N.C. State U., Raleigh, 1986. Asst. sgt.-at-arms N.C. Ho. of Reps., Raleigh, 1981, 82, computer calendar clk., various yrs.; owner, jewelry designer Accessories and Things, Raleigh, 1984—; sec. Coll. Humanities/Social Sci. N.C. State U., Raleigh, 1989-91; owner bookkeeping/typing svc. CTYPE, Raleigh, 1990—; jour. clk. N.C. Ho. of Reps., Raleigh, 1992-94, adminstrv. clk., 1992—. Mem. Am. Soc. Legis. Clks. and Secs. Democrat. Christian. Home: 703 Latta St Raleigh NC 27607-7203 Office: NC Gen Assembly House Prin Clks Office Legis Bldg Jones St Raleigh NC 27603-5924

CAUTHORN, DOROTHY NICKELSON, communications executive, public relations educator; b. Phila., Oct. 6, 1950; d. Vernon Clinton and Dorothy (Smyth) Nickelson; divorced; 1 child, Francis Scott. BS, LaSalle Coll., 1975; MEd, Beaver Coll., 1978; postgrad., U. Pa., Phila. Cert. English tchr., Pa. Tchr. Sch. Dist. Phila., 1975-82; comm. specialist Penn Mutual Life Ins., Phila., 1982-84; prin. Applied Comm., Phila., 1984-93; mgr. internal comm. Core States Fin. Corp., Phila., 1993-95; comms. mgr. Vanguard Group Investment Cos., Valley Forge, Pa., 1995—; cons. CIGNA, 1991-92. Editor City Mag., 1975; contbg. editor Merck World mag., 1989-90. Bd. dirs., pub. rels. chair Children's Hosp. Phila. Oncology Divsn., 1993—; bd. dirs., treas. Women in Comm., 1991—; bd. dirs., program chair I.A.B.C., 1990-92; com. mem. Rep. Party, 1993—; mem. edn. program com. Chestnut Hill Friends Meeting, 1988-90. Recipient Svc. award Mayor's Commn. Literacy, 1989, Women in Comm., 1996. Mem. Soc. of Friends. Home: 8217 Ardleigh St Philadelphia PA 19118 Office: Vanguard Group Investment Cos PO Box 2900 Valley Forge PA 19482

CAUTHORNE-BURNETTE, TAMERA DIANNE, family nurse practitioner, healthcare consultant; b. Richmond, Va., Apr. 13, 1961; d. Robert Francis Cauthorne and Lois Avery (Lloyd) Cumashot; m. William Nichols Burnette, Dec. 3, 1983. BSN, U. Va., 1983; postgrad., Med. U. S.C., 1988; MSN, Old Dominion U., 1993, grad. cert. in women's studies, 1994; postgrad., Med. Coll. Va., 1994—. RN, Va.; family nurse practitioner. Staff nurse, charge nurse gynecology-oncology unit U. Va. Med. Ctr., Charlottesville, 1983, staff nurse, charge nurse high-risk labor and delivery, ICU, 1984-85; staff nurse, charge nurse, preceptor med. ICU Med. U. S.C., 1985-87, staff nurse ICU, 1988; staff nurse, charge nurse med.-surg. ICU, progressive care Stuart Cir. Hosp., Richmond, Va., 1988-90; staff nurse pediatric and neonatal ICU Childrens' Hosp. of the King's Dau., Norfolk, Va., 1990, staff nurse, team leader neonatal ICU, 1990-91; pvt. health care cons., 1993—; with Delmar Pub., 1994—; pres. The Foxmont Co., LLC, 1995—; with Sussex Ctrl. Health Ctr., 1995; men's responsibility clinic coord. Planned Parenthood, 1996; cons. Old Dominion U. Coll. Health Sci., Sch. Nursing, 1993—, undergrad. clin. facility, 1994—; condr. analysis of Russian and Ukrainian health care system; breast self-exam instr. Am. Cancer Soc., 1982—; presenter at profl. confs.; mng. mem. The Foxmont Co., L.L.C.; mem. adj. faculty Sch. Nursing U. Va., 1996. Contbg. author for med. texts Delmar Pub.; contbr. articles to profl. jours. Vol. Ronald McDonald House, 1980-83; docent Spoleto Festival USA, 1984-92, MacArthur Meml. Mus., 1991; vol. receptionist info. ctr. Gibbes Art Gallery, 1987-89; vol. ARC Blood Donation Ctr., 1986-92; mem. U. Va. Coll. of Health Scis. Coun. Fellow Internat. Pedagogical Acad./Moswoc. Order of Omega Nat. Honor Soc.; mem. AACN, DAR, AAUW, Va. Coalition for Nurse Practitioners, U. Va. Sch. Nursing Alumnae Assn. (pres., CEO 1994—), Jr. League Va. (chair state pub. affairs com.), Virginians Patient Choice Coalition, Jr. League Norfolk and Virginia Beach (state pub. affairs vice chmn./lobbyist 1995), Daus. of Confederacy, Carolina Art Assn., S.C. Hist. Soc., Confederate Meml. Lit. Soc., U. Va. Coll. Health Scis. Coun., Alpha Delta Pi (chmn. nat. panhellenic rels. com., nat. by-laws and resolutions com.), Sigma Theta Tau.

CAUTHRON, ROBIN J., federal judge; b. Edmond, Okla., July 14, 1950; d. Austin W. and Mary Louise (Adamson) Johnson. BA, U. Okla., 1970, JD, 1977; MEd, Cen. State U., Edmond, Okla., 1974. Bar: Okla. 1977. Law clk to Hon. Ralph G. Thompson U.S. Dist. Ct. (we. dist.) Okla., 1977-81; staff atty. Legal Svcs. Ea. Okla., 1981-82; pvt. practice law, 1982-83; spl. judge 17th Jud. Dist. State Okla., 1983-86; magistrate U.S. Dist. Ct. (we. dist.) Okla., Oklahoma City, 1986-91, judge, 1991—. Editor Okla. Law Rev. Bd. dirs. Juvenile Diabetes Found. Internat., 1989—; mem. nominating com. Frontier Coun. Boy Scouts Am., 1987, Edmond Ednl. Endowment; trustee, sec. First United Meth. Ch., 1988-90. Mem. ABA, Okla. Bar Assn. (vice chmn. 1990), Okla. County Bar Assn. (bd. dirs. 1990— bench and bar com.), McCurtain County Bar Assn. (pres. 1986), Am. Judicature Soc., Nat. Assn. Women Judges, Fed. Bar Assn., Okla Assn. Women Lawyers, Nat. Coun. Women Magistrates (bd. dirs. 1990-91), Okla. Jud. Conf. (v.p. 1985), Am. Inns of Ct. (pres. elect 1990-91), Order of Coif, Phi Delta Phi. Office: US Courthouse 200 NW 4th St Ste 3122 Oklahoma City OK 73102-3029*

CAVALLARO, MARY CAROLINE, retired physics educator; b. Everett, Mass., Feb. 2, 1932; d. Joseph and Domenica Cavallaro. BS, Simmons Coll., 1954, MS, 1956; EdD, Ind. U., 1972; postgrad., Tufts U., 1980-81. Inst. math. and physics Sweet Briar (Va.) Coll., 1955-56; instr. physics Simmons Coll., Boston, 1956-58, Randolph-Macon Woman's Coll., Lynchburg, Va., 1958-59; lectr. Boston U., 1960-61; asst. prof. physics Framingham (Mass.) State Coll., 1961-63; prof. physics Salem (Mass.) State Coll., 1963-94; ret., 1994; cons. Introductory Phys. Scis. group Edn. Devel. Ctr., Newton, 1966; asst. to dean grad. studies Salem State Coll., 1971-78, coord. pre-engring. program, 1980-89, coord. secondary edn. program, 1988-91; vis. scholar Harvard U. Grad. Sch. Edn., Cambridge, Mass., 1989-90. Grantee NSF, 1962. Mem. AAUW, Am. Phys. Soc., Am. Assn. Physics Tchrs., Nat. Sci. Tchrs. Assn., Am. Inst. Physics, Soc. Coll. Sci. Tchrs., Simmons Coll. Alumnae Assn., Ind. U. Alumnae Assn., Pi Lambda Theta.

CAVALLON, BETTY GABLER, interior designer; b. Waverly, N.Y., July 17, 1918; d. Wallace Frederick and Harriet (Heaton) Gabler; grad. Parisien Sch. Design, Detroit, 1939; m. Michel Francis Cavallon, Dec. 26, 1946 (dec. 1981); children: Claire, Carol (dec.); stepchildren: Michael, Mary; m. John W. Crist, Nov. 20, 1982. Lic. interior designer, Conn. Fabric coordinator Montgomery Ward, 1940-46; interior designer Betty Cavallon Interiors Ltd., Stamford, Conn., 1946—. Mem. Am. Soc. Interior Designers (corp.). Republican. Episcopalian. Home and Office: 69 Riverside Ave Stamford CT 06905-4413

CAVANAUGH, ELLEN, religious organization administrator. Exec. dir. Cath. Network of Vol. Svc. Office: 4121 Harewood Rd NE Washington DC 20017*

CAVANAUGH, JEAN, medical secretary; b. Lake City, Iowa, June 27, 1924; d. Orrin Ellsworth and Golda Mae (Howard) VanHorn; m. Clair Joseph Cavanaugh, 1947; children: Thomas Paul, Kathleen Ann Bowman, Michael John, Terrence Joseph, James Clair. BS in Bus. Edn., Ft. Hays State U., Hays, Kans., 1970, MS in Guidance and Counseling, 1971, Edn. Specialist, 1975. Cert. tchr. Clk., fingerprint classifier FBI, Washington, 1942-44; pollster Gallup Polls, Great Bend, Kans., 1974-82; substitute tchr. Great Bend Sch. Dist., 1971-84; med. sec. Cen. Kans. Med. Ctr., Great Bend, 1974—; bd. dirs. First Bank & Trust Co., Glidden, Iowa. Bd. mem. Unified Sch. Dist. 428, Great Bend, 1979—; exec. sec. Golden Belt Cmty. Concerts, 1979—; sec. Barton County Health Fair Bd., 1983-90, Ret. Sr. Vol. Program, 1985—; bd. dirs. Smoky Hills Pub. TV, 1991—, vp. bd.; active Sr. Ctr. Adv. Bd.; cmty. mem. Wellness Com., 1995-96. Named Woman of Yr., Bus. and Profl. Women, Great Bend, 1976. Mem. AAUW, Am. Med. Assn. Aux. (regional v. p. Midwestern regional 1985-87), So. Med. Assn. Aux. (councilor 1986-89, 92-96, by-laws com. 1992), Northwest Family Cmty. Edn. Unit (sec.), C. of C. (edn. com. 1989—), Pilot Internat. of Great Bend (dir., pres.-elect 1989-90, pres. 1991-92, gov.-elect Kans.-Mo. dist. 1993, pilot gov. Kans.-Mo. dist. 1994-95), Kans. Assn. Middle Level Edn., Nat. Middle Sch. Assn., Kans. Assn. Sch. Bd. Region 8 Legis. (chmn. 1996-97), Athenian and Cosmopolitan Study Clubs, Phi Delta Kappa. Roman Catholic. Home: 5103 Telstar Great Bend KS 67530

CAVANAUGH, LINDA MARIE, secondary school educator; b. Bridgeport, Conn., May 13, 1951; d. James Gordon and Dorothy Marian (Quinn) C. BA, Trinity Coll., 1973; MA, West Conn. State U., 1982; postgrad., Wesleyan U., 1991. Cert. secondary tchr., Conn. Tchr., coach Immaculate H.S., Danbury, Conn., 1979-84; tchr. Mt. Anthony Union H.S., Bennington, Vt., 1984-85; tchr., coach St. Joseph's Ctrl. H.S., Pittsfield, Mass., 1985-86; tng. instr. Subway World Hdqrs., Milford, Conn., 1986-88; tchr., coach St. Paul Cath. H.S., Bristol, Conn., 1988-94, Canton (Conn.) Jr./Sr. H.S., 1994—; coach boys/girls track Avon H.S., spring 1996. Mem. Conn. Assn. Reading Rsch., Delta Kappa Gamma. Home: 15 Scherone Ct Plainville CT 06062

CAVANAUGH MITCHELL, JODI ANNELIESE, lawyer; b. Frankfurt, Germany, Oct. 27, 1969; came to U.S., 1970; d. Charles Irving and Evelyn Beatrice (Welch) Cavanaugh; m. Michael Bowen Mitchell Jr., May 21, 1994; 1 child, Evan Anneliese. B, Coll. Notre Dame Md., Balt., 1990; JD, U. Md., Balt., 1993. Bar: Md. 1993. Jud. law clk. Cir. Ct. Balt. County, 1993-95; claims rep. State Farm Ins.Co., Frederick, Md., 1995—. Mem. Alpha Alpha Alpha. Home: 2210 Angelica Ter Baltimore MD 21209

CAVASINA, MARY MAGDALENE, surgeon; b. Canonsburg, Pa., Dec. 26, 1927; d. Joseph Edward and Rose (Staffen) C. BS, U. Pitts., 1948; MD, Women's Med. Coll. of Pa., 1952. Diplomate Am. Bd. Surgery. Intern Mercy Hosp., Pitts., 1952-53, resident in gen. surgery, 1953-57; teaching fellow U. Pitts., 1953-57; sr. surg. staff mem. Canonsburg Gen. Hosp., 1957-92, chief surgery, 1962-75. Asst. chief and fire surgeon Canonsburg Vol. Fire Dept. Mem. Cath. Daus. of Am., Bus. and Profl. Women's Club, Pitts. Surg. Soc., Am. Coll. Surgeons. Republican. Roman Catholic. Office: 160 W Pike St Canonsburg PA 15317-1328

CAVERS-HUFF, DASIEA YVONNE, philosopher; b. Cleve., Oct. 24, 1961; d. Lawrence Benjamin and Yvonne (Warner) Cavers; m. Brian Jay Huff, July 26, 1986. BA, Cleve. State U., 1984, MA, 1990; postgrad., U. Md., 1986-90; PhD, U. Calif., Riverside, 1996. Teaching asst. Cleve. State U., 1983-86; instr. Upward Bound program Case Western Res. U., Cleve., 1986; instr. U. Md., Coll. Park, Md., 1987-89; mem. faculty Charles County Community Coll., 1989-90; asst. prof. Riverside Community Col., 1990—. U. Md. grad. fellow, 1986-87; Ford Found. predoctoral fellow, 1987-89. Mem. Am. Philos. Assn., Minority Grad. Student Assn. (co-chmn. U. Md. 1987-88). Democrat. Home: 25969 Andre Ct Moreno Valley CA 92553-6824 Office: Riverside City Coll Humanities and Social Scis Div Riverside CA 92506

CAVNAR, MARGARET MARY (PEGGY CAVNAR), business executive, former state legislator, nurse, consultant; b. Buffalo, July 29, 1945; d. James John and Margaret Mary Murtha Nightengale; BS in Nursing, D'Youville Coll., 1967; MBA, Nat. U., 1989; m. Samuel M. Cavnar, 1977; children: Heather Anne Hicks, Heide Lynn Gibson, Dona Cavnar Hambly, Judy Cavnar Bentrim. Utilization rev. coord. South Nev. Meml. Hosp., Las Vegas, 1975-77; v.p. Ranvac Publs., Las Vegas, 1976—; ptnr. Cavnar & Assocs., Reseda, Calif., 1976—, C & A Mgmt., Las Vegas, 1977—; pres. PS Computer Svc., Las Vegas, 1978-86; bd. mem. Nev. Eye Bank, 1987-89, exec. dir., 1990-91; dir. of health fairs Centel & CH13TV, 1991-94; bd. dirs. Bridge Counseling Assocs., 1992—, pres., 1994-95. Mem. Clark County Republican Cen. Com., 1977-87, Nev. Rep. Cen. Com., 1978-80; mem. Nev. Assembly, 1979-81; Rep. nominee for Nev. Senate, 1980; Rep. nominee for Congress from Nev. 1st dist., 1982, 84; bd. dirs., treas. Nev. Med. Fed. Credit Union; v.p. Cmty. Youth Activities Found., Inc., Civic Assn. Am.; mem. utilization rev. bd. Easter Seals; trustee Nev. Sch. Arts, 1980-87; nat. adviser Project Prayer, 1978—; co-chmn. P.R.I.D.E. Com., 1983—; co-chmn. Tax Limitation Com., 1983, Personal Property Tax Elimination Com., 1979-82, Self-Help Against Food Tax Elimination Denial Com., 1980; mem. nat. bd. dirs., co-chmn. Nev. Pres. Reagan's Citizens for Tax Reform Com., 1985-88; mem. Nev. Profl. Stds. Rev. Orgn., 1984; co-chmn. People Against Tax Hikes, 1983-84; bd. dirs. Nev. Eye Bank, 1988-90. Mem. Nev. Order Women Legislators (charter, parliamentarian 1980—), Cosmopolitantly Hers Info. (pres.), Sigma Theta Tau.

CAYCE, KAY C., accountant; b. Hopkinsville, Ky., Sept. 13, 1950; d. Ralph and Dot Cochran; m. Ken O. Cayce, Aug. 15, 1969 (div. Feb. 1994); children: Ken IV, Chris. Student, U. Ky., 1968-71; BBA in Acctg., Austin Peay State U., 1982. CPA, Ky., Tenn. CPA Thurman, Campbell and Co. PSC, Hopkinsville, 1982-94, Strothman and Co., PSC, Louisville, 1994-95, Carpenter & Mountjoy, PSC, 1995—. Mem. AICPA, Ky. Soc. CPAs. Home: 912 Burning Springs Circle Louisville KY 40223 Office: Carpenter & Mountjoy PSC 2300 Waterfront Plz Louisville KY 40202-4256

CAYLEFF, SUSAN EVELYN, women's studies educator; b. Boston, Mar. 4, 1954; d. Nathan and Frieda (Kates) C. BA, U. Mass., 1976; MA, Sarah Lawrence Coll., 1978, Brown U., 1979; PhD, Brown U., 1983. Teaching fellow Brown U., Providence, 1981-83; asst. prof. Inst. for the Med. Humanities, U. Tex. Med. Br., Galveston, 1983-87; assoc. prof. dept. women's studies San Diego State U., 1987—; faculty advisor varsity women's crew team, 1988—; mem. adj. faculty Inst. for the Med. Humanities, U. Tex. Med. Br., 1987—; humanities rep. com. for the protection of human subjects San Diego State U., 1988—;. Author: Wash and Healed..., 1987, Wings of Gauze: Women of Color and the Experience of Health and Illness, 1993, Babe: The Life and Legend of Babe Didrikson Zaharias, 1995 (Pulitzer Prize nominee 1995-96); editl. cons. Tex. Medicine, 1985-87; mem. editl. bd. Med. Humanities Rev., 1986-87. Nat. Endowment for Humanities grantee, 1984, Babe Didrikson Zaharias Meml. Found. grantee, 1986, San Diego State U. Found. grantee, 1988, Kennedy Inst. for Bioethics scholar Georgetown U., 1984, Calif. State U. scholar, 1989—; named Outstanding Prof. San Diego State U. Assoc. Students, 1993, prof. nominee San Diego State U. Trustees, 1994. Nat. Endowment for Humanities grantee, 1984, Babe Didrikson Zaharias Meml. Found. grantee, 1986, San Diego State U. Found. grantee, 1988, Kennedy Inst. for Bioethics scholar Georgetown U., 1984, Calif. State U. scholar, 1989—; named Outstanding Prof. San Diego State U. Assoc. Students, 1993, San Diego State U. Trustees, 1994. Mem. Am. Assn. for the History of Medicine, Nat. Women's Studies Assn., Coordinating Group for Women in the Hist. Profession, Western Assn. for Women's Historians, Soc. for Menstrual Cycle Rsch., Brown U. Alumni Assn., Phi Kappa Phi. Democrat. Jewish. Office: San Diego State U Dept Womens Studies San Diego CA 92182

CAYLOR, DEE JERLYN, accountant; b. Calhoun, Ga., Dec. 22, 1942; d. George Herbert and Annie Mae (Shirley) Darnell; widowed; children: Mark Gerald, George Alexander, Gregory Wayne. Student, Am. Inst. Banking, 1961, Dalton Jr. Coll., 1979, Continual Learning Inst., Nashville, 1985. Asst. mgr. Holidy Inn, Calhoun, Ga., 1969-72; asst. gen. mgr. Gentry Inn, Nashville, 1973-74; resident mgr. Am. Homes, Nashville, 1975-77; office mgr. Liberty Carpets, Dalton, Ga., 1978-79; owner, operator Age Olde Traditions, Antiques, Calhoun, 1980-83; resident mgr. Allied Mgmt. Co., Nashville, 1984-85; acct. Vawter, Gammon, Norris & Collins, Nashville, 1986, Robert Half & Accountemps, Nashville, 1987-88; resident mgr. Carter Co., Nashville, 1989—; office mgr. Bridal Path Wedding Chapel, Nashville, 1991—; acct. Gaddy, Gaydou & Assoc., 1993; pvt. practice acct. Nashville, 1994—. Exec. dir. spl. TV musical Tribute to Women in Country Music, 1990. Mem. Women of Music and Entertainment Network (founder, pres. 1988-94), Nashville Apt. Assn. (community svc. com. 1990). Republican. Baptist.

CAZDEN, COURTNEY B(ORDEN), education educator; b. Chgo., Nov. 30, 1925; d. John and Courtney (Letts) Borden; m. Norman Cazden (div. 1971); children: Elizabeth, Joanna. BA, Radcliffe Coll., 1946; MEd, U. Ill., 1953; EdD, Harvard U., 1965. Elem. tchr. pub. schs., N.Y., Conn., Calif., 1947-49, 54-61, 74-75; asst. prof. edn. Harvard U., Cambridge, Mass., 1965-68, assoc. prof., 1968-71, prof., 1971-95, Charles William Eliot prof. emerita, 1996—; vis. prof. U. N.Mex. summer 1980, U. Alaska, Fairbanks, summer 1982, U. Auckland, N.Z., spring 1983, Bread Loaf Sch. of English, Vt., 1986—; chairperson bd. trustees Ctr. Applied Linguistics, Washington, 1981-85. Author: Child Language and Education, 1972, Classroom Discourse: The Language of Teaching and Learning, 1988, Whole Language plus Essays on Literacy in the US and New Zealand, 1992; co-editor: Functions of Language in the Classroom, 1972, English Plus: Issues in Bilingual Education, 1990; editor: Language in Early Childhood Education, rev. edit., 1981. Trustee Highland Ednl. and Rsch. Ctr., New Market, Tenn., 1982-84; bd. dirs. Feminist Press, Old Westbury, N.Y., 1982-84; clk. New Eng. regional office Am. Friends Svc. Com., Cambridge, 1989-92. Recipient Alumna Recognition award Radcliffe Coll., 1988; fellow Ctr. Advanced Study in Behavioral Scis., Stanford, Calif., 1978-79; Fulbright research fellow, New Zealand, 1987. Mem. Nat. Acad. Edn., Coun. on Anthropology and Edn. (pres. 1981, George & Louise Spindler award 1994), Am. Assn. Applied Linguistics (pres. 1985), Nat. Conf. on Rsch. in English (pres. 1993-94), Am. Ednl. Rsch. Assn. (exec. com. 1981-84, award for disting. contbns. to ednl. rsch. 1986). Quaker. Office: Harvard U Grad Sch Edn Appian Way Cambridge MA 02138

CAZENAVE, ANITA WASHINGTON, secondary school educator; b. Austin, Tex., Nov. 9, 1948; d. Willis Hunt and Henry Etta Washington Littleton; m. Noël Anthony Cazenave, July 20, 1971; 1 child, Anika Tené. BA in Early Childhood/Elem. Edn., Dillard U., New Orleans, 1971; MEd in Reading Edn., Loyola U. of New Orleans, 1976; PhD in Psychology of Reading Edn., Temple U., 1993. Cert. tchr., La., Pa., reading tchr., Conn. Dir. Second Bapt. Day Nursery, Ann Arbor, Mich., 1971-72; reading cons. New Orleans Pub. Schs., 1972-78; reading instr. Temple U., Phila., 1979-80; reading specialist Operation Re-Entry Career Svcs., Inc., Phila., 1980-81; coord. ednl. svcs. Phila. O.I.C. Project new Pride, 1981; reading and math. tchr. Reading Edn. and Diagnostic Svcs. Inc., Phila., 1981-84; lang. arts/reading tchr. FitzSimons Middle Sch., Phila., 1985-91; reading tchr. Putnam (Conn.) Middle Sch., 1991-92; reading cons. Bloomfield (Conn.) H.S., 1992—; presenter workshops Bloomfield Bd. Edn., 1993-94, others; reader SAT II writing tests Ednl. Testing Svcs. Leader Girl Scouts U.S., New Orleans, 1977-78, Brownie troop leader, 1983-90; Sunday sch. supt. Mt. Airy United Meth. Ch., Phila., 1980-82; campaign worker Wilson Goode for Mayor, Phila., 1982. Named Outstanding Leader, Troop Parents Girl Scouts, Phila., 1985. Mem. ASCD, Internat. Reading Assn., Phila. Coun. of Internat. Reading Assn. (com. chair 1983-85), Greater Hartford Coun. Internat. Reading Assn. (recording sec. 1994—), Delta Sigma Theta (Hartford Alumnae chpt. chaplain and collegiate advisor 1994—, parliamentarian 1996—, chair state coun. chpts. heritage & archives 1994—, chair SAT tng. com. 1995—). Democrat. Home: 37 Storrs Heights Rd Storrs Mansfield CT 06268-2305 Office: Bloomfield High Sch 5 Huckleberry Ln Bloomfield CT 06002-3131

CECERE, JENNIFER, artist, art educator; b. Richmond, Ind., Oct. 31, 1950; d. Andrew Carl and Bettina Jane (Mastropier) C.; m. David Walker Prendergast, Aug. 25, 1981 (div. 1985). BFA, Cornell U., 1973. Artist in the schools N.Y.C., 1987; instr. art The New School, N.Y.C., 1995—; ind. contractor Hunt Mfg. Co., Phila., 1976-83. One-woman shows include Snug Harbor Cultural Ctr., S.I., N.Y., Rathbone Gallery, Albany, N.Y., Robert Freidus Gallery, N.Y.C., Pub. Sch. 1 Mus., Long Island City, others; exhibited in group shows at Archer M. Huntington Art Gallery, Austin, Hudson River Mus., Yonkers, N.Y., traveling exhibit, 1993-96, The Cooper-Hewitt Mus., N.Y.C., The Herbert F. Johnson Mus., Ithaca, N.Y., The Addison Gallery of Am. Art, also others; represented in pub. collections, N.Y.; inventor photo screen printing process. Recipient Ind. Exhbn. Program award, 1980, award Com. for Visual Arts, 1988, Artists New Work award N.Y. Found. for the Arts, 1994; Creative Artists Public Svc. fellow N.Y. State, 1982. Mem. Cornell U. Fedn. Bd.

CECIL, DORCAS ANN, property management executive; b. Greensboro, N.C., Mar. 31, 1945; d. George Joseph and Marianne Elizabeth (Zimmerman) Ernst; m. Richard Lee Cecil, June 8, 1968; children: Sarah, Matthew. BA, U. Ark., 1967. Pres. B & C Enterprises Property Mgmt., Ltd., O'Fallon, Ill., 1977-93, Cecil Mgmt. Group, Inc., O'Fallon and St. Louis, 1993—. Bd. dirs. O'Fallon Pub. Libr., 1983—, v.p., 1986-87, pres., 1987—; sec. St. Vincent de Paul Soc., 1987—; bd. dirs. Leadership Coun. Southwestern Ill., 1994—. Named Realtor of Yr., Belleville Area Assn. Realtors, 1994. Mem. Inst. Real Estate Mgmt. (cert., v.p. 1987, pres. St. Louis chpt. 1990, vice chmn. Nat. IREM std. coms. 1991—, regional v.p. 1992-93, governing councillor 1994—, nat. ethics and discipline hearing bd. 1994—), St. Louis Multi-Housing Coun., Profl. Housing Mgmt. Assn., Cmty. Assns. Inst., Nat. Assn. Realtors, Ill. Assn. Realtors (housing com. 1994—), Belleville Assn. Realtors (bd. dirs. 1991-94, Realtor of Yr. 1994), Mo. Assn. Realtors, Belleville Bd. Realtors C. of C. (bd. dirs. 1987-96, v.p. 1988—, pres. 1992-93), O'Fallon C. of C. Office: Cecil Mgmt Group Inc PO Box 459 O'Fallon IL 62269

CECOLA, MARY ANN, nurse anesthetist; b. Shreveport, La., Oct. 19, 1965; d. Russell A. and Mary Rose M. (Moran) C. BSN, Our Lady of Holy Cross Coll., New Orleans, 1990; postgrad., Xavier U. RN, La.; CCRN, 1995, ACLS, 1993. RN Ochsner Med. Foun., New Orleans, 1990—. Mem. Our Lady of Holy Cross Coll. Honor Soc. (chmn. eligibility com. 1992, v.p. 1993-95), Sigma Theta Tau. Home: 1401 Lake Ave #E-11 Metairie LA 70005

CEDARBAUM, MIRIAM GOLDMAN, judge; b. N.Y.C., Sept. 16, 1929; d. Louis Albert and Sarah (Shapiro) Goldman; m. Bernard Cedarbaum, Aug. 25, 1957; children: Daniel Goldman C., Jonathan Goldman C. BA, Barnard Coll., 1950; LLB, Columbia U., 1953. Bar: N.Y. 1954, U.S. Dist. Ct. (so. dist.) N.Y. 1956 U.S. Ct. Appeals (2d cir.) 1956, U.S. Ct. Claims 1958, U.S. Supreme Ct. 1958, U.S. Dist. Ct. (ea. dist.) N.Y. 1980, U.S. Ct. Appeals (5th and 11th cirs.) 1981. Law clk. to judge Edward Jordan Dimock U.S. Dist. Ct. (so. dist.) N.Y., 1953-54, asst. U.S. atty., 1954-57; atty. Dept. Justice, Washington, 1958-59; part-time cons. to law firms in litigation matters, 1959-62; 1st asst. counsel N.Y. State Moreland Act Commn., 1963-64; assoc. counsel Mus. Modern Art, N.Y.C., 1965-79; assoc. litigation dept. Davis, Polk & Wardwell, N.Y.C., 1979-83, sr. atty., 1983-86; acting justice Village of Scarsdale, N.Y., 1978-82, justice, 1982-86; judge U.S. Dist. Ct. (so. dist.) N.Y., 1986—; mem. com. defender svcs. Jud. Conf. U.S., 1993—; bd. vis. Columbia Law Sch.; trustee Barnard Coll.; co-counsel Scarsdale Open Soc. Assn., 1968-86. Mem. adv. com. on labor rels. Scarsdale Bd. Edn., 1976-77; mem. Scarsdale Bd. Archtl. Rev., 1977-78. Recipient Medal of Distinction Barnard Coll., 1991. Mem. Am. Law Inst., ABA (chmn. com. on pictorial graphic sculptural and choreographic works 1979-81), N.Y. State Bar Assn. (chmn. com. on fed. legislation 1978-80), Assn. of Bar of City of N.Y. (com. on copyright and literary property, 1982-84, com. on the Bicentennial 1988-92), Fed. Bar Coun., Copyright Soc. U.S.A. (trustee, mem. exec. com. 1979-82), Supreme Ct. Hist. Soc. Jewish. Office: US Dist Ct US Courthouse 500 Pearl St Rm 1330 New York NY 10007-1312

CEGLOWSKI, DEBORAH ANN, educational consultant; b. Lowell, Mass., Aug. 23, 1953; d. Leonard Ernest and Emily Rose (Thibodeau) C.; m. John Ernest Seem, May 19, 1979; children: James Donald, Emily Junice. BA in Elem. Edn., Johnson State Coll., 1974; MEd, Harvard U., 1977; PhD in Curriculum and Instruction, U. Ill., 1995. Vol. early childhood edn. U.S. Peace Corps, Jamaica, West Indies, 1974-76; instr. early childhood edn. Doane Coll., Crete, Nebr., 1977-80; dir. early childhood family edn. Lewiston (Minn.) Pub. Schs., 1980-83; dir. Deb's DayCare, Winona, Minn., 1983-86; parent educator Winona Pub. Schs., 1984-88; dir. early childhood family edn. Rushford (Minn.) Pub. Schs., 1988-91; instr. early childhood edn. Winona State U., 1984-91; lead cons. Emprise Designs, Milw., 1993—; mem. health adv. com. Head Start, 1990-92; chair Fillmore County Interagy. Com., Minn., 1990-91. Contbr. articles to profl. jours. Founder Winona Christmas Store, 1986; vol. Hokah (Minn.) Head Start Program, 1993—. Bagley fellow U. Ill., 1993, Bush Found. Leadership fellow, St. Paul, 1992; Blanchard Found. Meml. scholar, Boxborough, Mass., 1971. Mem. AAUW (pres. local chpt. 1977-81), Am. Edn. Rsch. Assn., Nat. Assn. Edn. Young Children, Nat. Head Start Assn., Nebr. Assn. Edn. of Young Children (legis. liaison 1977-80), Winona DayCare Providers (edn. chair 1983-86). Home and Office: 410 S Elm St La Crescent MN 55947-1264

CEKAUSKAS, CYNTHIA DANUTE, social worker; b. Detroit, Mar. 24, 1954; d. Vladas Algimantas and Isabel Gana (Stasiulis) C. BA in Sociology, Madonna Coll., Livonia, Mich., 1976; MSW, U. Mich., 1979. Bd. cert. social worker, La.; lic. clin. social worker, Fla. Psychiat. social worker Charity Hosp. New Orleans, 1982-84; social worker child and adolescent svc. DePaul Hosp., New Orleans, 1986-87; social worker, family advocacy programmgr. Army Cmty. Svcs., Friedberg, Fed. Republic Germany, 1988-89; social worker, mgr. family adv. program, chmn. family adv. case mgmt. team Cmty. Counseling Ctr., Camp Zama, Japan, 1989-90; social worker, exceptional family mem. program mgr. Army Cmty. Svcs., Bamberg, Germany, 1990-91; alt. family adv., on-call crisis counselor Desert Storm Army Cmty. Svcs., Bamberg, Fed. Republic Germany, 1990-91; social worker, family advocacy rep., head dept. family adv. Naval Med. Clinic, New Orleans, 1991-96; presenter child abuse prevention Bad Nauheim Elem. Sch., 1988-89. Contbr. articles to newspapers. Hosp. corspman USN, 1979-82. Recipient Customer Svc. award Giessen Mil. Cmty., 1988-89, Friend Bad Nauheim Elem. Sch. award, 1989, commendation for exceptional svc. Cam Zama, 1990, Scroll of Appreciation for Desert Storm/Desert Shield, Bamberg, Germany, 1990-91, Outstanding Performance award, 1993, 94, Presdl. Sports Award for racewalking, 1996, for aerobic dance, 1996. Mem. NAFE, NASW, NOW, Acad. Cert. Social Workers, Federally Employed Women, New Orleans Track Club, Greater New Orleans Runners' Assn., Am. Racewalk Assn., Nat. Audubon Soc. Democrat. Roman Catholic. Home: 102 Amy Ln Sunny Hills FL 32428

CELMER, VIRGINIA, psychologist; b. Detroit, June 26, 1945; d. Charles and Stella (Kopicko) C. BA in English, Marygrove Coll., 1968; MA in Theological Studies, St. Louis U., 1977; PhD in Counseling Psychology, Tex. Tech. U., 1986. Lic. psychologist; lic. chem. dependency counselor; cert. diplomate in managed care; cert. alcoholism and drug abuse counselor; internat. cert. alcoholism and drug abuse counselor; cert. group psychotherapist. Chaplain Mercy Ctr. for Health Care Svcs., Aurora, Ill., 1977-81; grad. asst. counselor U. Counseling Ctr., Tex. Tech. U., Lubbock, 1982-86, pre-doctoral intern in counseling psychology, 1985-86; post-doctoral intern Consultation Ctr., San Antonio, 1986-89, staff psychologist, 1989-90; pvt. practice psychologist San Antonio, 1989—; instr. dept. psychology Tex. Tech. U., Lubbock, 1981-85, Oblate Sch. Theology, San Antonio, 1989-90. Contbr. articles to profl. jours. Mem. APA, Tex. Psychol. Assn., Bexar County Psychol. Assn., Am. Group Psychotherapy Assn., San Antonio Group Psychotherapy Assn., Nat. Assn. Alcoholism and Drug Abuse Counselors, Tex. Assn. Alcoholism and Drug Abuse Counselors, Leadership Conf. Women Religious (region XII), Intercongregational Leadership Group San Antonio. Office: 1603 Babcock Rd Ste 270 San Antonio TX 78229-4750

CENTERBAR, ALBERTA ELAINE, education educator; b. Ilion, N.Y., Dec. 8, 1949; d. Raymond A. and Gladys J. (Orcutt) Pettengill; m. Richard E. Centerbar, Nov. 2, 1985. BFA, Fla. Atlantic U., 1971, MEd, 1975, EdS, 1993, EdD, 1995. Tchr. 3d grade St. Anastasia Sch., Ft. Pierce, Fla., 1971-74; spl. edn. tchr. St. Lucie County Schs., Ft. Pierce, 1975-80, music specialist, 1980—; adminstr./dir. First United Meth. Ch., Ft. Pierce, 1971-81; adj. prof. (undergrad.) Fla. Atlantic U., Boca Raton, 1990—, adj. prof. (grad.), rsch. specialist, 1993—; tchr. evaluator Fla. performance mgmt. cert. St. Lucie County Schs., 1990—; evaluator, rsch. specialist S.E. Assn. Colls. and Schs., Fla., 1993; revised state cert. tchr. exam. Guest organist chs. from Fla. to Ga., 1981—; accompanist local theater and state band groups, 1975—; adminstrv. bd. First United Meth. Ch., Ft. Pierce, 1971—; chair and vice chair edn. leadership adv. coun. Fla. Atlantic U., 1991-94, co-chair Prof. of Yr. selection com., 1993. Phi Kappa Phi Nat. Grad. scholar, 1992—. Mem. AAUW, ASCD, Fla. Music Educators Assn. Home: 1923 S Ocean Dr Fort Pierce FL 34949-3362 Office: Village Green Elem School 1700 SE Lennard Rd Port Saint Lucie FL 34952-6535 Also: Fla Atlantic Univ 500 NW University Blvd Port Saint Lucie FL 34986

CENTERS, BONNIE JEAN, nursing administrator; b. Mt. Sterling, Ky., June 23, 1947; d. Harrison Williams and Viola (Alfrey) Conway; m. Arlie Edward Centers, Feb. 5, 1962; 1 child, Arlie Edward Jr. AAS, Morehead State U., 1980. RN, Ky.; cert. rehab. nurse; cert. case mgr.; cert. ACLS instr., BCLS instr. Staff nurse CCU/ICU Mary Chiles Hosp., Mt. Sterling, 1980-83, staff nurse surgery/preceptor, 1983-90; asst. dir. nursing svc. Winchester (Ky.) Health Care Ctr., 1990-92, case mgr. subacute, 1992-95; nurse, ref. liaison Cardinal Hill Rehab. Hosp., Lexington, Ky., 1995—; method of instrn. instr. nurses aides Montgomery Area Vocat. Sch., Mt. Sterling, 1989-91, cert. medication aide instr., 1991-92; speaker in field; mem. faculty conf. on rehab. continuum U. Ky., Lexington, 1994; cons. Christopher East Health Care Facility, 1994; field reviewer Joint Accreditation on Hosps., Cert. and Accreditation for Rehab. Facilities. Co-author tng. manual: Nurse Management, 1991; author orientation programs Guardian Angel, 1991, Nurse Aide Orientation, 1991. Vol. Big Bros./Big Sisters, Winchester, 1991-94, Winchester Health Care, 1991-94. Mem. Assn. Rehab. Nursing, Internat. Case Mgmt. Assn. Home: 865 Bedford Rd PO Box 101 Jeffersonville KY 40337

CEPAITIS, ELIZABETH A., state legislator; b. Lowell, Mass., Apr. 22, 1943; 3 children. BS in Edn., Salem State Coll., 1964; MBA, Rivier Coll., 1978. Mem. N.H. Ho. of Reps., 1993—; mem. mcpl. com. and county govt. com.; fin. controller. Former treas., bd. dirs. Nashua Children's Assn.; former vol. Humane Soc. New England. Office: NH Ho of Reps State Capitol Concord NH 03301*

CERADSKY, SHIRLEY ANN, psychiatric nursing; b. Gravette, Ark., Feb. 8, 1944; d. Albert Raymond and Pansy Blanch (McGhee) Kelley; m. Kenneth Meade Ceradsky, June 15, 1968; children: Shane Thomas, Cameron Lee, Eric Tanner. Diploma, Wesley Sch. Nursing, 1966; student, Wichita State U., 1967-78, Carl Menninger Sch. Psychiatry, 1992-96. Cert. psychiat. nursing ANCC. Staff nurse Wesley Med. Ctr., Wichita, Kans., 1966, Siloam Meml. Hosp, Siloam Springs, Ark., 1966-67, Swedish Convenant Hosp., Chgo., 1967-68, U. Iowa Hosp., Iowa City, 1968-71, Charter Hosp., Wichita, 1988-89; charge nurse, staff nurse St. Joseph Med. Ctr., Wichita, 1971—, mem. quality assurance program, 1992-93, staff nurse adv. coun., 1994—; presenter nursing at night clin. ann. sessions Menninger Clinic, 1994. Contbr. article to profl. jours. Mem. Am. Psychiatric Nurses Assn. Democrat. Home: 7121 E 40th Street Cir N Wichita KS 67226-2414 Office: St Joseph Medical Ctr 3600 E Harry St Wichita KS 67218-3713

CEREZO, CARMEN CONSUELO, federal judge; b. 1940. BA, U. P.R., 1963, LLB, 1966. Pvt. practice, 1966-67; law clk. U.S. Dist. Ct., San Juan, 1967-72; judge Superior Ct., P.R., 1972-76, Ct. Intermediate Appeals, 1976-80; judge U.S. Dist. Ct., P.R., 1980-93, chief judge, 1993—. Office: Federico Degetau Fed Bldg Rm CH-131 150 Carlos Chardon Ave Hato Rey San Juan PR 00918-1761*

CERNY, CHARLENE ANN, museum director; b. Jamaica, N.Y., Jan. 12, 1947; d. Albert Joseph and Charlotte Ann (Novy) Cerny; children: Elizabeth Brett Cerny-Chipman, Kathryn Rose Cerny-Chipman. BA, SUNY, Binghamton, 1969. Curator Latin-Am. folk art Mus. Internat. Folk Art, Santa Fe, 1972-84, mus. dir., 1984—; adv. bd. C.G. Jung Inst., Santa Fe, 1990—. Mem. Mayor's Commn. on Children and Youth, Santa Fe, 1990-93, adv. bd. Recipient Exemplary Performance award State of N.Mex., 1982, Internat. Ptnr. Among Mus. award; Smithsonian Instn. travel grantee, 1976; Florence Dibell Bartlett Meml. scholar, 1979, 91; Kellogg fellow, 1983. Mem. Am. Assn. Mus. Internat. Coun. Mus. (bd. dirs. 1991—, exec. bd. 1991-95), Am. Folklore Soc., Mountain-Plains Mus. Assn., N.Mex. Assn. Mus. (chair membership com. 1975-77). Office: Mus Internat Folk Art PO Box 2087 Santa Fe NM 87504-2087

CERNY, MARY ANN, administrator; b. Kendalia, Tex., Nov. 8, 1948; d. Frank Joseph and Stella (Piper) Lombardino; m. Owen Edward Cerny, Oct. 20, 1968; children: Kelly Marie, Allen Shane. Student, U. Houston, 1966-67, Del Mar Coll., 1980—. Gen. mgr. Corpus Christi (tex.) Creditors Assn., Check Stop, Inc., 1979-95; exec. v.p. Check Stop, Inc., San Antonio, 1992—; pres. San Antonio Creditors Assn., 1992—; mem. Credit Women Internat./Credit Profls., Corpus Christi, 1987-88. Pres. bd. trustees Calallen Independent Sch. Dist., Corpus Christi, 1992, sec. bd. dirs., 1990-91. Mem. Am. Collectors Assn. Roman CAtholic. Office: Check Stop Inc 400 S Padre Island Dr #202 Corpus Christi TX 78405

CERULLI, PATRICIA ANN, secondary education educator; b. Phila.; d. Raymond Gaeton and Nancy Marie (Juliano) Christinzino; m. Robert Luciano Cerulli, June 17, 1967; children: Nicholas Raymond, Nancy Marie. BA in Edn., Rowan Coll., 1984, MA in Edn., 1992, MA in Sch. Adminstrn., 1995. Cert. tchr. music K-12, elem. edn., supr., prin., N.J. Tchr. parochial schs., Pa., N.J., 1961-80; substitute tchr. pub. and parochial schs., N.J., 1980-84; tchr. Mt. Holly Mid. Sch., N.J., 1984-85, Pennsauken Schs., N.J., 1985-86; tchr./dir. Medford Schs., N.J., 1986-87, Lenape Regional High Sch. Dist., Medford, N.J., 1987—; mem. strategic planning com. Lenape Regional High Sch. Dist., 1996; mem. adv. coun. Phila. Orchestra Edn. Coun., 1991-94; master tchr. bd. N.J. Symphony Orchestra, 1991-94; edn. resource team N.J. Performing Arts Ctr., 1993-94. Author various music compositions, poetry. Chmn. Music Core Course Proficiencies Panel, Trenton, N.J., 1992; mem. Curriculum Content Standards Panel, Trenton, 1993, Music Resource Guide for Proficiencies, Trenton, 1993, Performance Assessment Panel, Trenton, 1993, Tech. Tng. for Proficiencies, Trenton, 1994, Core Course Proficiencies for World Langs., Trenton, 1991, all N.J. Dept. Edn.; mem. adv. bd. Rowan Coll. N.J. Beginning Tchrs. Induction Ctr., 1996. Recipient Sch. Leader award N.J. Sch. Bd. Assn., 1991, five ednl. grants, Lenape Bd. Edn., 1988-90, self-awareness for students grant, Mt. Holly Bd., 1984, music for spl. edn. grant, Pennsauken, 1985. Mem. ASCD, Music Educators Nat. Conf., N.J. Assn. Sch. Adminstrs. (sem. presenter and clinician), N.J. Music Educators Assn. (sem. presenter and clinician), N.J. Alliance for Arts Edn. (rep.), Am. String Tchrs. Assn. (pres.-elect 1993-94, nat. grant 1987), Phi Delta Kappa (v.p. Zeta Nu chpt., internat. seminar scholar, sem. presenter and clinician). Home: 7 Little John Dr Medford NJ 08055-8529

CERVENKA, ANN MARIE, early childhood development specialist; b. Warren, Ohio, Feb. 7, 1964; d. George Andrew and Marilyn Ann (Krauss) C. BS in Human Devel. Spl. Edn., Vanderbilt U., 1986; MEd in Early Childhood Edn., Kent State U., 1988, postgrad. Cert. multiple handicapped K-12, developmentally handicapped K-12, pre-kindergarten, early edn. of handicapped birth-5 yrs. Tchr. infant/toddler spl. needs Lucas County Bd. MR/DD, Toledo, 1986-87; tchr./therapist infant toddler spl. needs Kent (Ohio) State U., 1987-88; tchr. spl. needs 3-5 yr.-olds Cleveland Heights (Ohio)-U. Hts. Bd. Edn., 1988-90; early childhood spl. needs specialist Lake County Ednl. Svc. Ctr., Painesville, Ohio, 1990—. Dir., instr. Diabetes Assn. Greater Cleve., 1979-80; dir. Cleve. Sight Ctr., 1989-92; counselor, instr. Camp Sue Osborn-East Shore Ctr., Kirtland, Ohio, 1992-95, dir., 1996; coord. spl. programs YMCA, Geauga County, 1991—. Mem. Nat. Assn. for Edn. of Young Children, Coun. for Exceptional Children, Divsn. of Early Childhood. Home: 38375 Tamarac Blvd 204-2 Willoughby OH 44094 Office: Lake County Ednl Svc Ctr 150 Main St Painesville OH 44077-3403

CERVILLA, CONSTANCE MARLENE, marketing consultant; b. Lafayette, Ind., Dec. 28, 1951; d. Norman Cimmino and Marilyn Jane (Stonebraker) C. AB, Harvard U., 1974, postgrad., 1974-75. Mktg. asst. Gen. Mills, Inc., Mpls., 1975-76; product dir. Pillsbury Co., Mpls., 1976-78; asst. v.p. Citicorp, N.A., Rochester, N.Y., 1978-80; cons. Bain & Co., Boston, 1980-81; owner, pres. Core Group Mktg., Inc., Mpls., 1981—; co-founder, v.p. Mil. Communications Ctr., Inc., Mpls., 1983-89; co-founder Gift Certificate Ctrs., Inc., 1990—; speaker to bank mktg. orgns. Patentee in field. Mem. Bank Mktg. Assn., Harvard/Radcliffe Club Minn., Mpls. Inst. Arts, Woman's Club Mpls., Wilderness Soc., Nat. Rowing Assn., Harvard Club (N.Y.C.). Office: Core Group Mktg Inc 6436 City West Pky Eden Prairie MN 55344-7712

CESINGER, JOAN, author; b. Oswego, N.Y., July 2, 1936; d. Guy Wesley and Gladys Matilda (Redlinger) Wagner; m. John Robert Cesinger, July 7, 1956; children: Michael, Richard, Steven. BA in Edn., Northwestern U., 1957. Asst. editor, feature writer Frontier Enterprise, Vernon Town Crier, Mundelein News, Lake Zurich, Ill., 1966-69; editor Lamp of Learning, Lake Zurich, 1967-68; mag. columnist Allen Raymond Inc., Darien, Conn., 1972-77; treas., office mgr., editor Dynamic Resources, La Verne, Calif., 1980-92. Author: Games and Activites for Early Childhood Education, 1967, If I Were . . ., 1975, Kindling Patriotism with Challenging Activties, 1976, Fostering Spelling Achievement with Challenging Games, 1980, American Government: Puzzles, Games, and Individual Activities, 1982, World Cultures: Puzzles, Games, and Individual Activities, 1985, The Plant Kingdom, 1985, Earth and Its Surface, 1985, Air and Weather, 1985, Civics and Citizenship, 1986, World Geography: Puzzles, Games, and Individual Activities, 1985, World History: From the Fall of Rome to Modern Times, 1986, Let's Learn About Dinosaurs, 1987, Holiday Sparklers, 1988, Book 2, 1989. Mem. Brookfield West Garden (v.p. 1978-79), P.E.O., Kappa Kappa Gamma, San Vicente Valley Club, Book Marks Club, Conversations Club. Home and Office: 23347 Barona Mesa Rd Ramona CA 92065-4345

CÉSPEDES, MELINDA BROWN, elementary school educator, dancer; b. San Jose, Calif., Sept. 9, 1942; d. Oren Able and Mildred Virginia (Bayless) Tolliver; m. Luis Pascual Céspedes, Dec. 3, 1981 (div. Sept. 1991); 1 child, Cara Thäis Brown. BS, Calif. State Poly., San Luis Obispo, 1964; std. elem. credential, U. Calif., Berkeley, 1967, adminstrv. svcs. credential, 1986; studies in belly dancing with, Bert Balladine, Sonya Ivanovna, Sabah, Najia, Amina; studied acting with John Parkinson. Cert. tchr. English Lang. Devel., Calif. Tchr. kindergarten Orinda (Calif.) Union Sch. Dist., 1968-76; tchr. 3rd grade Oakland (Calif.) Unified Sch. Dist., 1983-85, tchr. kindergarten, 1985-89; tchr. 1st grade Hayward (Calif.) Unified Sch. Dist., 1989-90, program coord., 1990-92, tchr. Charquin program, tchr. 2nd and 3rd grade, 1992-93, tchr. 1st grade English lang. devel., 1993-94, tchr. 1st and 2nd grades English lang. devel., 1994—; chairperson faculty adv. coun. Webster Sch., Oakland Unified Sch. Dist., 1984-86, chairperson sch. site coun., 1984-87, circuit chairperson, 1985-86, 87-88, certification trainer, 1986-87, acting asst. prin., 1986, coord. Gifted and Talented Edn. program, 1988-89, coord. collaborative self-study, 1987-89, asst. prin. adminstrv. intern-fine arts summer sch., 1988, implementer cognitive coaching model, 1995; coord. Gifted and Talented Edn. program Burbank Sch., Hayward Unified Sch. Dist., 1990-92, dir. Markham Variety Show, 1993, mem. bilingual advisor-leadership team Markham Elem. Sch., 1994-95, conflict mgmt. trainer, 1992-95, curriculum coun. rep., 1995-96; performer, instr. Middle Ea. dance Ibiza, Spain, Berkeley, Sausalito, Larkspur and Corte Madera. Author: Common Ground, 1996; dir. Troupe Latifa, Ibiza, Veiled Threats, Sausalito, Dancers of DeNile, 1991-96, Larkspur and Sausalito; past mem. Sabah Ensemble, Berkeley; performed at Club Vasilas, Athens, Greece, BAzouki Club, Kos, Greece; regular featured performer at El Morocco, concord, Grapeleaf, San Francisco, El Mansour, San Francisco, Cleopatra, San Francisco, Cairo Cafe, Mill Valley, Mykonos, Berkeley, Powell Station, San FranciscoGreek Taverna, San Francisco, Bagdad, San Francisco, various clubs in Ibiza, Tenerife, Marbella, and Madrid, various dance festivals. Marcus Foster grantee for kindergarten marine biology program, Oakland, 1987. Mem. Calif. Tchrs. Assn., Common Cause, Amnesty Internat., Global Exchg., Phi Delta Kappa (v.p. programs 1988-90, editor newsletter 1987-88).

CETTEL, JUDITH HAPNER, artist, secondary school educator; b. Langley, Va., Aug. 28, 1945; d. Francis S. and Mary Louise (Ellers) Hapner. BFA, Miami U., Oxford, Ohio, 1967, MEd, 1972; student, La Varenne Cooking Sch., Paris, 1976, Alliance Francais, Paris, 1976. Cert. tchr. art K-12, Ohio. Artist WMUB TV, Miami U., Oxford, 1966-67; grad. tchg. asst. Miami U., 1971-72; graphic designer, asst. to editor Miami U. Dept. Alumni Affairs, Oxford, 1967-69; grad. tchg. asst. Miami U., 1970-71; tchr. art Mason (Ohio) H.S., 1969—; chair dept. fine arts K-12 Mason City Schs., Mason, Ohio, 1980—; ptnr. Life Style Designs, Cin., 1978—; graphic designer/advt. dir. Hurrah! Gourmet Kitchenware and Cooking Sch., Cin., 1973-80; freelance fine artist, Cin., 1967—; mem. crisis intervention team Mason City Schs., 1993—, mem. faculty adv. bd., 1994—. Artist murals in various comml. and residential settings, 1982—; represented in pvt. collections, Ohio, N.H., N.J., N.C.; featured in article in Arts and Activities Mag., 1994. Mem., vol. Mt. Adams Civic Assn., Cin., 1976—; adv. coun. mem. Assn. for Advancement of Arts in Edn., 1995—, mem. long range planning team, 1996—. Recipient Golden Apple award Mason City Schs., 1988, Shining Star award, 1995, 96, Contemporary Design award Homerama-Cin. Home Builders Assn., 1980; Arts in Edn. grantee Ohio Arts Coun., 1987. Mem. NEA, Ohio Edn. Assn., Mason Edn. Assn., Nat. Art Edn. Assn., Ohio Art Edn. Assn., S.W. Ohio Art Edn. Assn. Office: Mason HS 770 S Mason Montgomery Rd Mason OH 45040-1728

CETTO, LORRAINE MARY, music educator; b. Athol, Mass., Jan. 12, 1956; d. Edward Francis and Eleanor (Ryder) C. B in Music Edn., Anna Maria Coll., 1978; cert., U. Hartford, 1982; M in Performance, U. Conn., 1983. Cert. pub. educator. Vocal music tchr. Quaboag H.S., Warren, Mass., 1978-80, West Brookfield (Mass.) Elem. Sch., 1979-80; grad. asst. U. Conn., Storrs, 1980-83, part time prof., 1982-84; music dir. Our Lady Rosary Parish, Spencer, Mass., 1980-86, West Avon (Conn.) Congregation, 1987—; dir. choral activities Hall H.S., West Hartford, Conn., 1983—; guest conductor various Conn. high schs., 1985—; bd. mem. Woodland Concert Series, Hartford, 1991-94. Mem. Am. Choral Dirs. Assn. (exec. bd. 1988—, pres.-elect Conn. chpt. 1995—), Conn. Music Educators Assn., Music Educators Nat. Conf., Kodaly Educators. Democrat.

CEVERA, EILEEN LEVY, special education educator; b. Balt., June 29, 1952; d. Julius and Jean Feinstein Levy; children: Jason Adam, Jonathan Lucas. BS in Spl. Edn. and Elem. Edn., U. Md., 1974; MS in Comm. Disorders, Johns Hopkins U., 1982. Tchr. moderate lang. disorders Baltimore County Pub. Sch., Towson, Md., 1974-75; tchr. comm. disorders Anne Arundel County Pub. Schs., Annapolis, Md., 1975-81; tchr. handicapped Mercer County Spl. Svcs. Sch. Dist., Trenton, N.J., 1982-92; tchr. resource room Carroll County Pub. Schs., Westminster, Md., 1989-89; tchr. handicapped West Windsor-Plainsboro Sch. Dist., Princeton Junction, N.J., 1992—; coord. prodn. Through The Broken Looking Galss interdisciplinary inclusion project. Producer Through the Broken Looking Glass, an Inclusion prodn., 1995. Vol., supporter Spl. Olympics, N.J., 1991—. Recipient N.J. gov.'s tchr. recognition award, 1987, 94. Home: 422 Clarksville Rd Princeton Junction NJ 08550-1515 Office: West Windsor-Plainsboro Mid Sch 55 Grovers Mill Rd Plainsboro NJ 08536-3105

CEYER, SYLVIA T., chemistry educator. Grad. summa cum laude, Hope Coll., Holland, Mich.; PhD, U. Calif., Berkeley. Postdoctoral fellow Nat. Bur. Standards; faculty mem. dept. chemistry MIT, Cambridge, Mass., 1981—, asst. prof., now prof. and Keck Found. prof. of energy. Recipient Recognition award for young scholars AAUW Ednl. Found., 1988, Nobel Laureate Signature awd. for Graduate Education in Chemistry, Am. Chemical Soc., 1993. Fellow Am. Phys. Soc., Am. Acad. Arts and Scis. Office: MIT Dept Chemistry 77 Massachusetts Ave Cambridge MA 02139-4301

CHABROW, SHEILA SUE, English language educator; b. Chgo., Mar. 24, 1940; d. Fred and Florence (Arenson) Steinberg; m. Penn Benjamin Chabrow, June 18, 1961; children: Michael Penn, Carolyn Debra, Frederick Penn; BA, U. Miami (Fla.), 1961; student Harvard U., 1960-61, George Washington U., 1961-62, Va. Poly. Inst., 1972-74; MS, Barry U., 1976. Writer, No. Va. Newspapers, Fairfax, 1969-73; dir. Olam Tikvah Sch., Fairfax, 1973-74; tchr. Palmetto Sr. H.S., Miami, 1979-80; instr. psychology Barry U., Miami, 1980-81; instr. intensive English, U. Miami, Coral Gables, Fla., 1981—; instr. English Fla. Internat. U., 1986-89; v.p. Cutler Bay Estates, Miami, 1975-76, Parent Co-Op. Preschools Internat., 1972-73; pres. No. Va. Co-Op. Schs., 1969-70. Mem. Women in Communications, AAUW (sec. Annandale, Va. 1972), Theta Sigma Phi. Office: U Miami Dept Intensive English Coral Gables FL 33146

CHACE, MARGARET YVONNE, reading teacher, consultant; b. Acushnet, Mass., Feb. 24, 1943; d. Leo Joseph and Yvonne Theresa (St. Amand) Blais; m. Charles Robert chace, Aug. 6, 1971; children: William, David. BA, Salve Regina Coll., 1965; MEd, Bridgewater (Mass.) State Coll. Elem. tchr. Diocese of Providence, Cranston, R.I., 1965-67, Pawtucket, R.I., 1967-68; elem. tchr. Diocese of Fall River, New Bedford, Mass., 1968-70, New Bedford (Mass.) Pub. Schs., 1970-71, Prince Frederick (Md.) Pub. Schs., 1971-77; chpt. 1 reading tchr. Middleboro (Mass.) Pub. Schs., 1978—. Dog club leader 4-H, Middleboro, 1984—, town. com. scholarship sec., 1985—; v.p., organizer Middleboro Music Guild, 1979—; ch. chair Choral Group, Lakeville, Mass., 1979—. Recipient Beyond the Call of Duty award 4-H County Extension, Plymouth County, 1989, Honor award Tchrs. Assn., Plymouth County, 1990. Mem. NEA, Internat. Reading Assn., Plymouth County Edn. Assn., Middleboro Edn. Assn., Mass. Edn. Assn. Roman Catholic. Home: 104 Wall St Middleboro MA 02346-3022 Office: Burkland Sch Mayflower Ave Middleboro MA 02346

CHACHAS, CATHERINE VLAHOS, environmental manager; b. Kaloskopi, Phokidos, Greece, Aug. 18, 1946; arrived in U.S., 1965; d. Peter and Maria (Priovolos) Vlahos; m. Gregory A. Chachas, Aug. 22, 1970; children: Angelo, Maria. BSChemE, U. Utah, 1970. Eviron. engr. Utah Dept. Transp., Salt Lake City, 1970-78, EPA Region 8, Salt Lake City, 1978-80, N.W. Energy, Salt Lake City, 1980-81; environ. dir. Ute Energy, Salt Lake City, 1981-82, Geokinetics, Salt Lake City, 1982-85; environ. program mgr. Hercules Aerospace, Magna, Utah, 1985-88, quality assurance mgr., 1988-92; self-employed Environ. Mgmt., Salt Lake City, 1992—; Utah br. mgr. Environ. Resource Mgmt., Salt Lake City, 1994—. Greek Orthodox. Home: 1416 E Farm Meadow Ln Salt Lake City UT 84117 Office: Environ Resource Mgmt 102 W 500 S Salt Lake City UT 84101-2334

CHACKO, ANNA S., lawyer; b. Penang, Malaysia, Oct. 21, 1959. BSc with honors, U. Aston, Birmingham, Eng., 1981; barrister at law, Inns of Ct. Sch. Law, London, 1982; LLM, Duke U., 1985. Bar: Eng. and Wales 1982, High Ct. of Malaya 1983, Ohio 1986, N.Y. 1988. Ptnr. Anderson, Kill, Olick & Oshinsky, P.C., N.Y.C. Mem. ABA, N.Y. State Bar Assn., Bar Coun. Malaya, Hon. Soc. Lincoln's Inn. Office: Anderson Kill Olick & Oshinsky PC 1251 Avenue of the Americas New York NY 10020-1182*

CHAFFIN, VIRGINIA LOUISE, licensed practical nurse; b. Miami, Ariz., Dec. 29, 1936; d. Angelita Cutbirth; m. Patrick R. Chaffin, July 21, 1956; children: Denise M., Mary Therese, Diana M., Gina Lee, Cecilia R. Real estate broker, Western Coll., 1984; LPN, Gateway C.C., 1992. Real estate broker Ariz. Dept. Real Estate, Phoenix, 1983—; LPN Ariz. State Bd. Nursing, Phoenix, 1992—. Contbr. articles to newspapers and mags. Dep. registrar Voter Registration, Phoenix, 1985—; vol. Get Out the Vote Activities, Phoenix, 1980—, Girl Scouts U.S.A.m, Phoenix, 1965-70; active Cath. Women's Groups, Phoenix, 1965-73, Hear My Voice, Ann Arbor, Mich., 1995—. Mem. Sierra Club.

CHAGNON, LUCILLE TESSIER, literacy and developmental learning specialist; b. Gardner, Mass., June 1, 1936; d. Fred G. Tessier and Alfreda C. (Ross) Noel; m. Richard J. Chagnon, Sept. 16, 1978; children: Daniel, David. BMus, Rivier Coll., Nashua, N.H.; adv. cert. in Human Resource Mgmt. and Cmty. Devel., Inst. Cultural Affairs, Chicago, 1969; MEd, Boston Coll., 1972. Edn. specialist, N.H., 1960-73; internat. cons. Inst. Cultural Affairs, Chgo., 1973-79; staff tng. dir. CO-MHAR, Inc., Phila., 1979-81; pres., owner Chagnon Assocs., Collingswood, N.J., 1981-86; prin. Sacred Heart Sch., Camden, N.J., 1986-87; founder, dir. Lifeline Literacy Project, Phila., 1988-94; literacy and learning specialist Rutgers U., Camden, 1989—; adj. grad. faculty dept. counseling psychology Temple U. Sch. Edn., Phila., 1985-90; sr. project staff Right Assocs., Phila., 1983-93. Author: Easy Reader, Writer, Learner, 1994; (with Richard J. Chagnon) The Best is Yet to Be: A Pre-Retirememt Program, 1985. Bd. dirs. Camden County Literacy Vols. of Am., 1987-91, Handicapped Advocates for Ind. Living, 1988—; mem. Collingswood Bd. Edn., 1985-89. Mem. Nat. Coun. Tchrs. English, Nat. Learning Found., Brain-Based Edn. Network, Inst. Noetic Scis., Inst. Cultural Affairs, New Horizons for Learning, Internat. Alliance for Learning. Home and Office: 1 Courtland Ln Willingboro NJ 08046-3405

CHAIKEN, MARCIA R., social scientist, researcher; b. Bronx, N.Y.; d. Harold and Mollie Kuratin Rosenblum; m. Jan M. Chaiken, June 16, 1963; children: David, Shama Beth. BA in Zoology with honors, Douglass Coll., Rutgers U., 1960; MA in Biology, U. Calif., L.A., 1962; PhD, UCLA, L.A., 1979. Resident social scientist RAND, L.A., 1979-83; sr. social scientist Abt Assocs., Cambridge, Mass., 1984-89; dir. rsch. LINC, Alexandria, Va., 1989—; presenter in field. Contbr. numerous articles to profl. jours, chpts. to books. Troop leader Girl Scouts U.S.A., L.A., 1973-81; Havurah coord. Stephen Wise Temple, L.A., 1982-84, Temple Emunah, Lexington, Mass., 1990-92. Mem. Am. Soc. Criminology (exec. coun. 1995—, co-chair task force on prevention rsch., policy and practice 1994-95, com. on criminological policy 1993-94, program chair 1993, chair panel on early intervention for high-risk youth 1990, com. for the Gene Carte student paper competition 1988-89, chair com. on ethical consideration in criminological rsch. 1983-84), Am. Sociological Assn. (chair mem. com. sect. on crime, law and deviance 1989-90), Soc. for the Study of Social Problems. Democrat. Jewish. Office: LINC PO Box 924 Alexandria VA 22313

CHAIT, ANDREA MELINDA, special education educator; b. Buffalo, May 7, 1970; d. Marvin and Rochelle (Benatovich) C. BS in Health Edn., Ithaca (N.Y.) Coll., 1992; MEd in Spl. Edn., U. Fla., 1995. Cert. tchr. health edn., N.Y.; cert. N.Y. State Mandatory Child Abuse and Neglect Tng. Program K-12; cert. tchr. spl. edn., Ga. Substitute tchr. Cortland (N.Y.) H.S., 1992; tchrs. aid/substitute Stanley G. Falk, Cheektowaga, N.Y., 1993; pvt. spl. edn. tutor Buffalo and Gainesville, 1992—; behavioral disorders tchr. Paul P. West Middle Sch., East Point, Ga., 1995-96, chairperson discipline com. spl. edn. dept., 1995—. Vol. Task Force for Battered Women, Ithaca, 1991, nursing homes, Ithaca, 1991-92, Human Rights Orgn., Gainesville, 1993-94. Mem. ASCD, Coun. for Exceptional Children, Coun. for Children with Behavioral Disorders, Pi Lambda Theta, Kappa Delta Pi, Phi Kappa Phi. Jewish. Home: 823 SW 56th Ter Gainesville FL 32607

CHAKOS, ARRIETTA, assistant to the city manager; b. Chgo., Oct. 4, 1951; d. George Chakos and Linda (Sarafis) Bayou; m. Adlai Stevenson Leiby, Oct. 16, 1981; 1 child, Sophia. BA in English, Calif. State U., Arcata, 1976, postgrad., 1976-78. Lectr. Calif. State U., Arcata, 1976-78; freelance editor Berkeley, Calif., 1978-79; editor, book buyer Bookpeople, Berkeley, Calif., 1979-83; project mgr. Live Oak Co., Berkeley, Calif., 1984-89; editor, writer MacMillan/McGraw Hill, Berkeley, Calif., 1989-90; legis. liaison Berkeley Unified Schs., Calif., 1990-94; asst. to city mgr. City of Berkeley, Calif., 1994—. Chair emergency prep task force Berkeley Pub. Schs., 1990; mem. citizens disaster prep task force City of Berkeley, 1990-94, founder town & gown preparedness group, 1991-95; policy adv. bd. alternate Bay Area Earthquake Prep Project, Oakland, Calif., 1991; mem. blue ribbon task force, emergency prep Cities of Berkeley and Oakland, 1991-92; mem. loss study project oversight com. Nat. Inst. Bldg. Scis./FEMA, Washington, 1993—. Mem. AAUW, LWV, Nat. Women's Polit. Caucus, Earthquake Engring. Rsch. Inst., Ctr. for Ethics and Social Policy. Office: City of Berkeley 2180 Milvia St Berkeley CA 94704

CHALFANT, LINDA KAY, Spanish educator, retired, legal secretary; b. New Kensington, Pa., Oct. 9, 1943; d. Fred and Evelyn V. (Peters) C.; m. Charles V. Utley, Sr., Jan. 26, 1963 (div.); children: Charles V. Utley, Yvette Melissa Utley. BA in Child Study, Vassar Coll., 1965; MS in Spanish and Linguistics, Georgetown U., 1971. Cert. tchr., N.Y., D.C. Bilingual rsch. asst. Georgetown U., Washington, 1966-71; curriculum writer D.C. Pub. Schs., 1969-70, 91; asst. prof., rsch. assoc. U. D.C., 1982-85; asst. to dir. Latin for Modern Sch., McLean, Va., 1968-94; tchr. D.C. Pub. Schs., 1965-95, ret., 1995; freelance cons., editor, 1961—; bilingual legal sec. Wilkinson, Barker, Knauer & Quinn, Washington, 1996—; proposal review panelist Nat. Endowment for Humanities, Washington, 1984, 87, 89, U.S. Dept. Edn., Washington, 1986. Founder, 1st pres. Fgn. Lang. Action Group, Washington, 1978-79; Sunday sch. tchr., Washington, 1972-93; mem. book sale com. Washington Vassar Club, 1984—. Recipient Grad. Study fellowship King Juan Carlos Found., Spain, 1994, Travel grant Spain '92 Found., 1994. Roman Catholic. Office: Wilkinson Barker et al 1735 New York Ave NW Washington DC 20006-5209

CHALIDZE, LISA LEAH, lawyer; b. Salem, Oreg., Nov. 14, 1958; d. David Harding and Carmen Elaine (Stafford) Barnhardt; m. Valery Nikolaevich Chalidze, May 1, 1981. Student, U. Leningrad, USSR, 1979; BA cum laude, U. Oreg., 1980; JD cum laude, N.Y. Law Sch., 1983. Bar: Vt. 1984, U.S. Dist. Ct. Vt. 1984, U.S. Ct. Appeals (2d cir.) 1986. Ptnr. Hull, Webber & Reis and predecessor firm Dick, Hackel & Hull, Rutland, Vt., 1984—; treas. Chekhov Pub. Corp., N.Y.C., 1987—, Inst. for Dem. Devel., Benson, Vt., 1988—. Co-editor: The Federalist Papers (Russian edit.), 1991; contbr. articles to profl. pubs. Nat. dir. Law for Kids Project, 1995—. Alfred Gross scholar N.Y. Law Sch., 1980-83. Mem. ABA, Vt. Bar Assn. Office: Hull Webber & Reis 60 N Main St Rutland VT 05701-3249

CHALLELA, MARY SCAHILL, maternal, child health nurse; b. Hopedale, Mass., Nov. 30, 1927; d. James and Sarah Mary (Norton) Scahill; m. Charles V. Challela, May 29, 1976. BS, Boston U., 1954, MS, 1967, D in Nursing Sci., 1979. Staff nurse Mass. Gen. Hosp., Boston, 1949-51, U.S. Indian Svc., Ariz., 1951-52; sr. instr. Cleve. Met. Gen. Hosp. Sch. Nursing, 1954-66; asst. prof. Northeastern U., Boston, 1967-70; cons. Shriver Ctr., Waltham, Mass., 1970-72, dir. nursing univ. affiliated program, 1972-93; ret., 1993; mem. staff continuing edn. New Eng. Regional Genetics Group, 1990-92. Contbr. articles to profl. jours. Pres. Sacred heart Guild, Hopedale, 1972-74; chair Commn. on Disabilities, Hopedale, 1987-95; bd. dirs. Coun. on Aging, Hopedale, 1993—. Recipient Citizen Achievement award Mass. Assn. for Retarded Citizens, 1987, Excellence in Nursing award Sigma Theta Tau, 1987; Am. Assn. Mental Retardation fellow, 1988. Mem. ANA, Mass. Nurses Assn., Internat. Assn. Nurses in Genetics.

CHALMERS, DIANA JEAN, accountant; b. Harvey, Ill., Aug. 25, 1955; d. Melvin Earl and Rita Caroline (Zulfer) Besse; Michael Jon Chalmers, Mar. 18, 1972; children: Mikki Lynn, Robert Michael. Mgr. Pizza Hut, Richton Park, Ill., 1975-77; owner, operator D-Dusters, Hazel Crest, Ill., 1985-91; trustee Village of Hazel Crest, 1987-94; adminstrv. dir. Hazel Crest Area C. of C., 1990—; accounts asst. AAA Galvanizing, Joliet, Ill., 1995—. Author of poems. Founder Neighbors United Party, Hazel Crest, 1989; chmn. Hazel Crest Hazelnut Festival, 1986-90; coord. Hazel Crest Blood Donor Program, 1990-93; pres. Hazel Crest Girl's Softball. Mem. Chgo. Southland Chamber. Home: 22853 Judith Dr Plainfield IL 60544-9637 Office: AAA Galvanizing 625 Mills Rd Joliet IL 60434

CHALONE, RHONDA CHRISTINE, music educator; b. Ithaca, N.Y., Nov. 8, 1968; d. Frederick Erle Chalone and Joy Frances (Lanphear) Toscano. MusB, U. Ill., 1990, MusM, 1991. Grad. tchg. asst. U. Ill., Champaign, 1990-91; gen. music tchr., choir dir. St. Matthew's Sch., Champaign, 1991-92; keyboard instr., music history and midi tech. Wayland Acad., Beaver Dam, Wis., 1992-95; program assoc. Wis. Sch. Music Assn., 1995; pvt. piano tchr., Madison; freelance arranger Hal Leonard Corp., Milw., 1995. Playground coord. City Beaver Dam, Wis., 1994; ch. organist Grace Presbyn. Ch., Beaver Dam, 1994. Mem. NAFE, MENC, Nat. Piano Guild, Music Theory Midwest, Phi Kappa Phi, Pi Kappa Lambda, Golden Key. Home: 237 N Thompson Dr #4 Madison WI 53714 Office: Wis Sch Music Assn 4797 Hayes Rd Madison WI 53704

CHAMBERLAIN, BARBARA KAYE, small business owner; b. Lewiston, Idaho, Nov. 6, 1962; d. William Arthur and Gladys Marie (Humphrey) Greene; m. Dean Andrew Chamberlain, Sept. 13, 1986 (div.); children: Kathleen Marie, Laura Kaye. BA in English cum laude, BA in Linguistics cum laude, Wash. State U., 1984. Temp. sec. various svcs., Spokane, Wash., 1984-86; office mgr. Futurepast, Spokane, 1986-87; dir. mktg. and prodn. Futurepast: The History Co., Melior Publs., Spokane, 1987-88, v.p., 1988-89; founder, owner PageWorks Publ. Svcs., Coeur d'Alene, Idaho, 1989—; mem. dist. 2 Idaho State Ho. of Reps., 1990-92; mem. Idaho State Senate, 1992-94; adj. faculty North Idaho Coll., 1995. Author North Idaho's Centennial, 1990; editor Washington Songs and Lore, 1988. Bd. dirs. Mus. North Idaho, Coeur d'Alene, 1990-91; bd. dirs. Ct. Apptd. Spl. Advocates, 1993—, pres., 1995-96. Named Child Advocate Legislator of Yr., Idaho Alliance for Children, Youth and Families, 1993. Mem. AAUW, NOW, LWV, Nat. Women's Polit. Caucus, Idaho Women's Network, No. Idaho Pro-Choice Network, Idaho Conservation League, Mensa, Post Falls C. of C., Kiwanis. Democrat. Office: PageWorks Publ Svcs PO Box 2730 Coeur D Alene ID 83816

CHAMBERLAIN, ELIZABETH SIMMONS, retired English language educator; b. St. Louis, June 15, 1929; d. George Edwin and Myrtle Coline (Smith) Simmons; m. Barnwell Rhett Chamberlain Jr., Aug. 11, 1956; 1 child, Edwin Rhett. AB, Wellesley Coll., Mass., 1951; AM, U. Mich., 1955; PhD, U. N.C., Chapel Hill, 1979. Tchr. English and Bible history, adminstr. Kingswood Sch. Cranbrook, Bloomfield Hills, Mich., 1951-55, Ashley Hall, Charleston, S.C., 1955-56; tchr. English and social studies Charlotte (N.C.) Country Day Sch., 1956-58; instr. English Meredith Coll., Raleigh, N.C., 1962-68; asst. prof. English N.C. Cen. U., Durham, 1981-95. Mem. Human Rels. Com., Durham, 1983-88, 91-94, chair, 1986-88, 93-94; mem. Civic Ctr. Authority, Durham, 1988-91; mem. merger com. City and County Planning Commn., Durham, 1983-84; mem. Nursing Home Adv. Com., Durham, 1982-85. Democrat. United Methodist. Home: 340 Blackberry Inn Rd Weaverville NC 28787

CHAMBERLAIN, ISABEL CARMEN (ISA CHAMBERLAIN), environmental chemist; b. Buenos Aires; came to U.S., 1974; Degree in biochemistry, Tucuman (Argentina) U., 1974; MS in Analytical Chemistry, U. Wash., 1987. Biochemist Olympic Med. Labs., Bremerton, Wash., 1974-81; microbiologist Saudi Med. Svcs., Saudi Arabia, 1982-84; analytical chemist Puget Sound Naval Shipyard, Bremerton, 1987-88, EPA, Manchester, Wash., 1988—; instr. Pierce Coll., Tacoma, 1988; spkr. USA-Mex. Environ. Symposium, 1995; drinking water labs. cert. officer. Vol. speaker career day to schs. and colls., 1987—. Recipient regional exch. award EPA, Washington, 1995. Mem. Assn. Analytic Chemists Internat. (chmn. 1994, past chmn. 1995, edtl. bd. 1995). Office: EPA Region 10 7411 Beach Dr E Port Orchard WA 98366-8204

CHAMBERLAIN, JEAN NASH, county government department director; b. Chgo., Oct. 14, 1934; d. William Edmund and Virginia Jean (La Fon) Nash; m. James Staffeld Chamberlain, Dec. 29, 1953; children: James W., William S., Caren T., Martha J. Student, U. S.C., 1951-53. Polit. dir. Tribune/United Cablevision, Huntington Woods, Mich., 1982; orgn. dir. polit. campaign, Oakland, Mich., 1983-84; dir. fin. Dan Murphy for Gov., Mich., 1985-86; exec. mgr. Greater Royal Oak (Mich.)/Oak Park C. of C., 1986-93. Vice chair Rep. com., Oakland County, Mich., 1971-73; chair Rep. 18th congl. dist., 1973-77; del. Rep. Nat. Conv., Kansas City, Mo., 1976; bd. dirs. Oakland County Mental Health Bd., 1976-93, chair 1984-86. Mem. U.S. C. of C., Mich. State C. of C., South Oakland Boys and Girls Club (bd. dirs.), South Oakland Salvation Army (bd. dirs.), Harnack Firefighters Scholarship Fund (bd. dirs.), Woodward Dream Cruise (bd. chair). Roman Catholic. Office: Oakland County Exec Office Bldg 1200 N Telegraph Rd Pontiac MI 48341

CHAMBERLAIN, JILL FRANCES, financial services executive; b. Chgo., Mar. 25, 1954; d. Chester Emery and Mary Edythe (Hurd) C. B.A. in Math. with honors, Ill. State U., 1975; M.B.A., U. Chgo., 1981. Programmer Arthur Andersen, Chgo., 1975-76; cons. Laventhol & Horwath, Chgo., 1976-77; fin. systems analyst U. Chgo. Hosp., 1978-80; v.p. CHI/COR Info. Mgmt., Inc., Chgo., 1980-87; systems designer GECC, Stamford, 1987-88; mgr. Customer Resolution Ctr., GE Capital Corp., 1988—; cons. RMS Bus. Systems, Chgo., 1976-77. Mem. NAFE. Libertarian. Methodist. Avocations: reading, traveling, needlework. Office: GE Capital 1600 Summer St Stamford CT 06905-5125

CHAMBERLAIN, KATHRYN BURNS BROWNING, retired naval officer; b. Rapid City, S.D., Jan. 17, 1951; d. George Alfred III and Mildred Doty Browning; m. Thomas Richard Masker, Apr. 19, 1975 (widowed Sept. 1978); m. Guy Caldwell Chamberlain III, Mar. 25, 1980 (div. Oct. 1988); children: Burns Doty, Anne Caldwell. BA, La. Tech. U., 1973; postgrad., Naval Postgrad. Sch., Monteray, Calif., 1978-79; MA, Auburn U., 1984; postgrad., U. Ill., 1994-96, Govs. State U., 1995-96. Ensign USN, 1974, ltjg., 1976, lt., 1978, advanced through grades to lt. comdr., 1983, surface warfare designation, 1980, joint staff officer, 1986; comdg. officer Mil. Sealift Command Office USN, Alaska, 1986-88; comdr., exec. officer USNAVFAC USNAVFAC, Newfoundland, Nfld., Can., 1991-94. Mem. AAUW, ASPA, Am. Planning Assn., Am. Mgmt. Assn., Internat. City/County Mgmt. Assn. Home and Office: PO Box 6586 Champaign IL 61826-6586

CHAMBERLAIN, LINDA ANN, nursing administrator, consultant; b. Newark, N.J., Dec. 9, 1947; d. Alfred Dante and Terri Kathryn (Argyros) Spatola; children: Marc E. Chamberlain, Christopher W. Chamberlain. BSN, Seton Hall U., South Orange, N.J., 1969; MS in Human Orgnl. Science, Villanova (Pa.) U., 1989. Cert. nursing adminstr. Critical care nurse Clara Maass Hosp., Belleville, N.J., 1972-79; adult critical care nurse Hershey (Pa.) Med. Ctr., 1979; rehab. nurse Heatherbank, Columbia, Pa., 1979, head nurse, 1979, nursing svcs. coord., 1979-81, dir. nursing svcs., 1981-87; mgr. nursing svcs. Wilmac Corp., York, Pa., 1987-90; asst. adminstr. Lancashire Hall Wilmac Corp., Nettsville, Pa., 1990-92; adminstr. Heatherbank Nursing & Rehab. Ctr. Wilmac Corp., Columbia, Pa., 1992-94; dir. spl. projects Wilmac Corp., York, 1994—; mem. bd. dirs. Lancaster Co. Office of Aging, 1996—; v.p. Pa. Assn. Dirs. of Nursing Adminstrn.; pres. Am. Soc. Long Term Care Nurses. Mem. Pa. Dept. of Health Long Term Care Licensure/Cert. Panel, 1988—, Long Term Care Network, Harrisburg, Pa., 1994—. Mem. Pa. Adult Day Svcs. Assn., Coalition of Pa. Nurses, York Coll. of Pa. Nursing Honor Soc., Sigma Theta Tau. Democrat. Roman Catholic. Office: Wilmac Corp 209 N Beaver St York PA 17403

CHAMBERLIN, MARJORIE RUTH, educator; b. Easton, Pa., Mar. 1, 1949; d. William Hermon and Ruth Elizabeth (King) Werner; m. Kermit Jay Chamberlin, Nov. 27, 1974; 1 child, Jay William. BA, Glassboro (N.J.) State U., 1971; MEd, Pa. State U., 1979. Cert. tchr., N.J., Pa. Tchr. Warren County Vo-Tech., Washington, N.J., 1971-83; supr. Monroe County Vo-Tech., Bartonsville, Pa., 1987-88; substitute tchr. East Stroudsburg (Pa.) Sch. Dist., 1995—; adj. Northampton County C.C., Bethlehem, Pa., 1986-87; cons. N.J. Dept. Edn., Trenton, 1979. Bd. dirs. Fine Arts Discovery Series, Reeders, Pa., 1993-96. Mem. LWV (Monroe county treas. 1991-93, pres. 1993-95), United Meth. Women (treas. 1990-91). Home: PO Box 88 Delaware Water Gap PA 18327

CHAMBERS, ANNE COX, newspaper executive, former diplomat; b. Dayton, Ohio. Student Finch Coll., N.Y.C.; hon. degrees: D Pub. Service, Wesleyan Coll., 1982; DHL, Spelman Coll., 1983; LLD, Oglethorpe U., 1983, DHL, Brenau Coll., 1989, LLD, Clark Atlanta U., 1989. Chmn. bd. Atlanta Jour.-Constn.; Am. ambassador to Belgium, 1977-81; bd. dirs. Cox Enterprises, Inc. Bd. dirs. Atlanta Arts Alliance, High Mus. Art, Cities in Schs., Am. Ditchley Found., MacDowell Colony, Forward Arts Found., Emory Mus. Art and Archaeology, N.Y. Bot. Garden, Coun. Am. Ambs., Chairman's Coun., Met. Mus. Art; trustee Mus. Modern Art; mem. internat. council Mus. Modern Art, nat. com. Whitney Mus. Am. Art. Decorated Legion of Honor (France). Mem. Council Fgn. Relations. Office: Atlanta Newspapers 1400 Lake Hearn Dr NE Atlanta GA 30319-1464

CHAMBERS, CAROLYN SILVA, communications company executive; b. Portland, Oreg., Sept. 15, 1931; d. Julio and Elizabeth (McDonnell) Silva; widowed; children: William, Scott, Elizabeth, Silva, Clark. BBA, U. Oreg. V.p., treas. Liberty Comm., Inc., Eugene, Oreg., 1960-83; pres. Chambers Comm. Corp., Eugene, 1983-95, chmn., 1996—; chmn., bd. dirs. Chambers Constrn. Co., 1986—; bd. dirs., dep. chair bd. Fed. Res. Bank, San Francisco, 1982-92; bd. dirs. Portland Gen. Corp.; bd. dirs. U.S. Bancorp. Mem. Sacred Heart Med. Found., 1980—, Sacred Heart Gov. Bd., 1987-92, Sacred Heart Health Svcs. Bd., 1993-95, PeaceHealth Bd., 1995—; mem. Oreg. Found., 1980—, pres., 1992-93; chair U. Oreg. Found., The Campaign for Oreg., 1988-89; pres., bd. dirs. Eugene Arts Found.; bd. dirs., treas., dir. search com. Eugene Symphony; mem. adv. bd. Eugene Hearing and Speech Ctr., Alton Baker Park Commn., Pleasant Hill Sch. Bd.; chmn., pres., treas. Civic Theatre, Very Little Theatre; negotiator, treas., bd. dirs., mem. thrift shop Jr. League of Oreg. Recipient Webfoot award U. Oreg., 1986, U. Oreg. Pres.'s medal, 1991, Disting. Svc. award, 1992, Pioneer award, 1983, Woman Who Made a Difference award Internat. Women's Forum, 1989, U. Oreg. Found. Disting. Alumni award, 1995, Tom McCall awrd Oreg. Assn. Broadcasters, 1995, Disting. Alumni award U. Oreg., 1995, Outstanding Philanthropist award Oreg. chpt. Nat. Soc. Fund Raising Execs., 1994. Mem. Nat. Cable TV Assn. (mem. fin. com., chmn. election and by-laws com., chmn. awards com., bd. dirs. 1987—, Vanguard award for Leadership 1982), Pacific Northwest Cable Comm. Assn. (conv. chmn., pres.), Oreg. Cable TV Assn. (v.p., pres., chmn. edn. com., conv. chmn., Pres.'s award 1986), Calif. Cable TV Assn. (bd. dirs., conv. chmn., conv. panelist), Women in Cable (charter mem., treas., v.p., pres., recipient star of cable recognition), Wash. State Cable Comm. Assn., Idaho Cable TV Assn., Community Antenna TV Assn., Cable TV Pioneers, Eugene C. of C. (first citizen award, 1985). Home: PO Box 640 Pleasant Hill OR 97455-0640 Office: Chambers Comm Corp PO Box 7009 Eugene OR 97401-0009

CHAMBERS, CLARICE LORRAINE, clergy, educational consultant; b. Ossining, N.Y., Oct. 7, 1938; d. Willie and Louise (McDonald) Cross; m. Albert W. Chambers, June 9, 1962; children: Albert W., Cheryl L. Fultz. Diploma, Manna Bible Inst., Phila.; BS in Bibl. Studies, Trinity Coll. of Bible, Newburgh, Ind., 1983; MA in Bibl. Theology, Internat. Bible Inst. and Sem., Orlando, Fla., 1986. Ordained to ministry Pentecostal Ch., 1975. Master data specialist Naval Supply Dept., Phila., 1957-65; dir. tng., tchr. Opportunities Indsl. Ctr., Harrisburg, Pa., 1969-72; pub. info. asst. Pa. Dept. Revenue, Harrisburg, 1972-79; pastor Antioch Tabernacle United Holy Ch. of Am., Harrisburg, 1979—; Fin. sec. United Holy Ch. of Am., Greensboro, N.C., 1978-92, treas. no. dist., Linden, N.J., 1992-96; mem. screening team La. Dept. Edn., Baton Rouge, 1995. Mem. Harrisburg Sch. Bd., 1975—; pres. Pa. Sch. Bds. Assn., New Cumberland, 1992; bd. dirs. Nat. Sch. Bds. Assn., Alexandria, Va., 1993—; trustee Shippensburg (Pa.) U., 1989-96. Recipient Cmty. Sv. award Ctrl. Pa. chpt. Nat. Assn. Black Accts., 1984, Harrisburg chpt. Black United Fund. Pa., 1989, Outstanding Leadership award Greater Harrisburg NAACP, 1987, award of svc. Coun. of Pub. Edn., 1995. Democrat. Home: 147 Sylvan Terr Harrisburg PA 17104 Office: Antioch Tabernacle UHC of Am 1920 North St Harrisburg PA 17103

CHAMBERS, IMOGENE KLUTTS, school system administrator, financial consultant; b. Paden, Okla., Aug. 6, 1928; d. Odes and Lillie (Southard) Klutts; BA, East Central State U., 1948; MS, Okla. State U., 1974, EdD, 1980; m. Richard Lee Chambers, May 27, 1949. High sch. math. tchr. Marlow (Okla.) Sch. Dist., 1948-49; with Bartlesville (Okla.) Sch. Dist., 1950-94, asst. supt. bus. affairs, treas. Ind. Sch. Dist. 30, 1977-87, treas., 1985-94; fin. acctg. cons. Okla. State Dept. Edn., 1987-92; dir. Plaza Nat. Bank, 1984-94; adv. dir. Bank Okla., 1994-96. Bd. dirs. Mutual Girls Club, 1981—; treas. Okla. Schs. Ins. Assn., 1982—, adminstr., 1993—. Mem. Okla. Assn. Sch. Bus. Ofcls., Assn. Sch. Bus. Ofcls. Internat., Okla. Assn. Retired Sch. Adminstrs., Okla. State U. Alumni Assn., E. Ctrl. Univ. Alumni Assn. (bd. dirs. 1994—), Rotary. Democrat. Methodist. Office: 911 SE Greystone Pl Bartlesville OK 74006-5141

CHAMBERS, INGRID CLAUDIA, nurse administrator; b. Jamaica, West Indies, Dec. 1, 1947; d. Cleland and Lurline Earle; m. Calvin Chambers, Dec. 23, 1970; children: Earle, Mark. Student, So. Gen. Hosp., Glasow, Scotland, 1968; BS, Columbia Union Coll., 1990. Med. rep. Mead Johnson Pharma., 1969; critical care nurse So. Gen. Hosp., Glasgow, Scotland, 1970; tech. dir. cardiology Wash. Adventist Hosp., Takoma Pk., Md., 1978; adminstrv. dir. Wash. Adventist Hosp., Takoma Pk., 1987; dir. Adventist Healthcare Mid-Atlantic; faculty mem. Johns Hopkins U., 1977-81, Inst. for Med. Studies, Calif., 1987-88. Contbr. articles to profl. jours. Mem. Am. Assn. Cardiovascular Adminstrsn., Am. Soc. Echocardiography. Home: 14708 Prince John Ct Burtonsville MD 20866-1831

CHAMBERS, JILL LOUGH, graphic artist; b. New Castle, Ind., Nov. 15, 1947; d. Sheldon Lawrence and Margaret Clara (McDowell) Lough; m. Barry Alden Chambers, July 1, 1967; children: Barry A. Jr., Alice Paul. BS, Ball State U., 1970. Tchr. art K-12 Switz City (Ind.) Schs., 1971-72; substitute tchr. Indpls. Pub. Schs., 1972; restaurant auditor Indpls. Hilton Hotel, 1973; caseworker Hendricks County Dept. Pub. Welfare, Danville, Ind., 1973-74; receptionist Doctor's Office, Columbus, Ohio, 1974; caseworker Big Sisters Gr. Indpls., 1977-79; campaign staffer Va. Dill McCarty for Gov., Indpls., 1983-84; lobbyinst Gender Fairness Coalition Ind. and Ind. Nat. Orgn. Women, Indpls., 1979, 89; office mgr. Ind. Nat. Orgn. Women, Indpls., 1984-86; owner Creatrix Graphic Design, Indpls., 1986-95. Bd. dirs., newsletter editor B-T neighborhood Assn., Indpls., 1979-81; Dem. precinct com. woman St. Joseph County, South Bend, Ind., 1994-95; candidate state senate, Indpls., 1996. Recipient Jeanine Rae Meml. award Justice, Inc., Indpls., 1986. Mem. AAUW (South Bend chpt.), LWV (South Bend chpt. adv. bd.), Ind. Hist. Soc. Women's History Archives, Ind. Nat. Orgn. Women (pres. 1972, editor newsletter, 1986—, Sagawitch of the Wabash, 1986), Art Dirs. Club Ind., Gender Fairness Coalition Ind. (chmn. bd. 1989—). Unitarian. Home: 4619 Blvd Pl Indianapolis IN 46208

CHAMBERS, JOAN LOUISE, dean of libraries; b. Denver, Mar. 22, 1937; d. Joseph Harvey and Clara Elizabeth (Carleton) Baker; m. Donald Ray Chambers, Aug. 17, 1958. B.A. in English Lit., U. No. Colo., Greeley, 1958; M.S. in Library Sci., U. Calif.-Berkeley, 1970; M.S. in Systems Mgmt., U. So. Calif., 1985. Librarian U. Nev., Reno, 1970-79; asst. univ. librarian U. Calif., San Diego, 1979-81; univ. librarian U. Calif., Riverside, 1981-85; dean of librs. Colo. State U., 1985—; mgmt. intern. Duke U. Libr., Durham, N.C., 1978-79; sr. fellow UCLA Summer, 1982; cons. tng. program Assn. of Rsch. Libraries, Washington, 1981; libr. cons. Calif. State U., Sacramento, 1982-83, U. Wyo., 1985-86, 94, 95, U. Nebr., 1991-92, Calif. State U. System, 1993-94, Univ. No. Ariz., 1994, 95. Contbr. articles to profl. jours., chpts. to books. U. Calif. instl. improvement grantee, 1980-81; State of Nev. grantee, 1976, ARL grantee, 1983-84. Mem. ALA, Assn. Coll. and Rsch. Librs. IFLA (com. mem.) CNI, Libr. Adminstrn. and Mgmt. Assn., Colo. Libr. Assn., United Way, Sierra Club, Beta Phi Mu, Educom, Phi Lambda Theta, Kappa Delta Phi, Phi Kappa Phi. Home: PO Box 1477 Edwards CO 81632-1477 Office: Colo State U William E Morgan Libr Fort Collins CO 80523

CHAMBERS, JOHNNIE LOIS, elementary education educator, rancher; b. Crocket County, Tex., Sept. 28, 1929; d. Robert Leo and Lois K. (Slaughter) Tucker; m. R. Boyd Chambers; children: Theresa A., Glyn Robert, Boyd James, John Trox. BEd, Sul Ross State U., Alpine, Tex., 1971. Tchr. 1st and 2d grades Candelaria (Tex.) Elem. Sch., 1971-73; head tchr. K-8 Ruidosa (Tex.) Elem. Sch., 1973-77; head tchr. K-8 Presidio Ind. Sch. Dist. at Candelaria Elem. Sch., 1977-91, tchr. 2d and 3d grades, 1991-93, tchr. pre-kindergarten, kindergarten and 1st grade, 1993—; acting prin. Candelaria Elem. & Jr. High, 1995—; mem. sight-base decision making, Presidio, 1991-94; mem. Chihuahuan Desert Rsch. Inst., Alpine, 1982-94. Leader Boy Scouts Am., Ruidosa and Candelaria, 1973-91, Cub Scout leader, 1973-91;chpt. mem. Sheriffs Assn. Tex., Austin, 1980. Recipient awards Boy Scouts Am., 1969, 83, winner Litter Gitter award, 1994-95. Mem. Tex. State Tchrs. Assn., Phi Alpha Theta. Home and Office: Number 1 Education Ave Candelaria TX 79843

CHAMBERS, LINDA DIANNE THOMPSON, social worker; b. Mexia, Tex., Apr. 21, 1953; d. Lee and Essie Mae (Hopes) Thompson; m. George Edward Chambers, Nov. 30, 1978; 1 child, Brandon. AS cum laude, Navarro Coll., Tex., 1974; B in Social Work magna cum laude, Tex. Woman's U.,

1976; cert. gerontology and Human Svcs. Mgmt., Sam Houston U., 1982; M in Social Work, U. Tex.-Arlington, 1990. Lic. marriage and family therapist, social worker-advanced practitioner; cert. family life ducator; registered sex offender treatment provider. Mem. social work staff Dept. Human Resources, Ft. Worth, Tex., 1975, Children's Med. Ctr., Dallas, 1976, Mexia State Sch., Tex., 1976-93, Methodist Home, Waco, Tex., 1993-96, Tes. Dept. Health, Waco, 1996—. Pres., Raven Exquisites, Mexia, 1983-84, sec.-treas., 1984-85; bd. dirs. Limestone County Child Welfare Bd., Hospice, Inc.; pres. bd. dirs. Limestone County unit Am. Cancer Soc.; bd. dirs. Gibbs Meml. Libr., Teen Pregnancy Prevention Coun., Childcare Mgmt. Svcs.; mem. Tex. Dem. Women; vol. McLennan County Pub. Health Dist. AIDS Clinic; coord., founder Limestone County Teen Parent Program; co-founder Limestone County Parenting Coalition; mem. Limestone County Youth Adv. Com.; PTO sec. Ctrl. Tex. Literacy Coalition, 1992—; vol. Ctr. for Action Against Sexual Assault, Family Abuse Ctr.; mem. Tex. Hist. Found., Nat. Mus. Women in Arts, 1985—; Recipient numerous awards for scholarship and profl. excellence. Fellow Internat. Biog. Assn. (dep. bd. gov., life); mem. Am. Sociol. Soc. (sec. 1975-76), Univ. Woman's Assn., Am. Childhood Edn. Internat., Nat. Assn. Social Workers, NAFE, Am. Assn. Mental Retardation, Nat. Assn. Future Women, Am. Soc. Profl. and Exec. Women, Nat. Assn. Negro Bus. and Profl. Women's Clubs, AAUW, Tex. Woman's U. Nat. Alumnae Assn., Mortar Bd. Honor Soc. (sec.-treas. 1975-76), Tex. Soc. Clin. Social Workers, Internat. Platform Assn., Internat. Assn. Bus. and Profl. Women, Am. Biog. Assn. (dep. bd. govs.), Nat. Mus. Women Arts, Los Amigos, Limestone County Parenting Coalition (co-founder), Phi Theta Kappa, Alpha Kappa Delta, Alpha Delta Mu, Young Dems. Club. Avocations: reading, gardening, gourmet cooking. Home: 102 Harding Mexia TX 76667

CHAMBERS, LOIS IRENE, insurance automation consultant; b. Omaha, Nov. 24, 1935; d. Edward J. and Evelyn B. (Davidson) Morrison; m. Peter A. Mscichowski, Aug. 16, 1952 (div. 1980); 1 child, Peter Edward; m. Frederick G. Chambers, Apr. 17, 1981. Clk. Gross-Wilson Ins. Agy., Portland, Oreg., 1955-57; sec., bookkeeper Reed-Paulsen Ins. Agy., Portland, 1957-58; office mgr., asst. sec., agt. Don Biggs & Assocs., Vancouver, Wash., 1958-88, v.p. ops., 1988-89, automation mgr., 1989-91, mktg. mgr., 1991-94; automation cons. Chambers & Assocs., Tualatin, Oreg., 1985—; chmn. adv. com. Clark Community Coll., Vancouver, 1985-93, adv. com., 1993-94. Mem. citizens com. task force City of Vancouver, 1976-78, mem. Block Grant rev. task force, 1978—. Mem. Ins. Women of S.W. Wash. (pres. 1978, Ins. Woman of Yr. 1979), Nat. Assn. Ins. Women, Nat. Users Agena Systems (charter; pres. 1987-89), Soroptimist Internat. (Vancouver)(pres. 1978-79, Soroptimist of the Year 1979-80). Democrat. Roman Catholic. Office: Chambers & Assocs 8770 SW Umatilla St Tualatin OR 97062-9338

CHAMBERS, MARJORIE BELL, historian; b. N.Y.C., Mar. 11, 1923; d. Kenneth Carter and Katherine (Totman) Bell; m. William Hyland Chambers, Aug. 8, 1945; children: Lee Chambers-Schiller, William Bell, Leslie Chambers Trujillo, Kenneth Carter. AB cum laude, Mt. Holyoke Coll., South Hadley, Mass., 1943; MA, Cornell U., 1948; PhD, U. N.Mex., 1974; LLD honoris causa, Ctrl. Mich. U., 1977; LHD (hon.), Wilson Coll., 1980, Northern Michigan U., 1982. Staff asst. Am. Assn. UN, League of Nations Assn., N.Y.C., 1944-45; program specialist dept. rural sociology Cornell U., Ithaca, N.Y., 1945-46, rsch. asst. dept. speech and drama, 1946-48; substitute tchr. Los Alamos (N.Mex.) Pub. Schs., 1962-65; project historian U.S. AEC, Los Alamos, 1965-69; adj. prof. U. N.Mex., Los Alamos, 1970-76, 84-85; pres. Colo. Women's Coll., Denver, 1976-78; dean Grad. Sch. Union Inst., Cin., 1979-82, mem. core faculty Grad. Sch., 1979—; interim pres. Colby-Sawyer Coll., New London, N.H., 1985-86; vis. prof. Cameron U., Lawton, Okla., 1974; commr., vice-chair N.Mex. Commn. on Higher Edn., Santa Fe, 1987-91; chair citizen adv. bd. U.S. Army Command and Gen. Staff Coll., Ft. Leavenworth, Kans., 1990—; mem. bd. dirs. Coun. Ind. Colls. and Univs., Santa Fe, 1991—; rep. Los Alamos County Labor Mgmt. Bd. Contbr. articles to profl. jours. Chair Los Alamos County Coun., 1976, councilor, 1975-76, 79; candidate N.Mex. 3d Congl. Dist., 1982, lt. gov. N.Mex., 1986; chair Sec. of Navy's Advisor Bd. on Edn. and Tng., Washington and Pensacola, Fla., 1987-89; chair Citizen Bd. of U.S. Army Command and Gen. Staff Coll., Fort Leavenworth, Kans.; acting chair, vice-chair adminstrn. Pres. Carter's Com. for Women, Washington, 1977-80; chair Pres. Ford's Nat. Adv. Bd. on Women's Ednl. Programs, Washington, Los Alamos County Pers. Bd., 1983-90; mem. nat. adv. coun . U.S. SBA, 1990—; mem., editor Los Alamos and N.Mex. Rep. Ctrl. com., 1982—; trustee Colby-Sawyer Coll., New London, N.H., 1980-89; pub. mem. U.S. Dept. State Fgn. Svc. selection bd., 1978; mem. U.S. del. UN Conf. Women, Copenhagen, 1980. Recipient Teresa d'Avila award Coll. St. Teresa, Winona, Minn., 1978, Disting. Woman award U. N.Mex. Alumni Assn., Albuquerque, 1990, N.Mex. Disting. Pub. Svc. award Gov. and Awards Coun., Albuquerque, 1991; named Outstanding N.Mex. Woman Gov. and Com. on Status of Women, Albuquerque, 1988, 89. Mem. AAUW (life), U.S. rep. coun. 1973-75, nat. pres. 1975-79, pres. Edn. Found.), DAR, Bus. and Profl. Women (Los Alamos parliamentarian and dist. parliamentarian 1991-93), Women's Polit. Caucus (gov. bd. conv., keynoter, vice-chair Rep. caucus 1971—), Internat. Women's Forum, N.Mex. Hist. Soc., Los Alamos Hist. Soc. (pres., Sangre de Cristo Girl Scouts "Woman of Distinction" 1996). Presbyterian.

CHAMBERS-PHILLIPS, SHERRIE MARIE, professional athlete, sports executive; b. New Guinea, Australia, July 15, 1963; U.S. citizen.; d. Paul Eugene Chambers and Frances Rose Fielden; m. Dean Phillips, June 22, 1991. BA in Psychology, U. Colo., Colorado Springs, 1991; postgrad., U. Okla., Norman. Mem. facility mgmt. divsn. U.S. Olympic Com., 1994—; mem. world ranking 5th) World Univ. Judo Championships, Tiblisi, Russia, 1988, Brussels, 1990; mem. (world ranking 9th) USA World Championship Judo Team, Belgrade, Yugoslavia, 1989, Hamilton, Can., team capt. U.S. Olympic Tng. Squad, Colorado Springs, 1992-96; mem. operation gold program U.S. Olympic Com., Colorado Springs, 1995; alt. Olympic Judo Team, Atlanta, 1996; asst. coach U.S. Olympic Tng. Squad, 1996. Spokesperson Woman's Sports Found., Denver; resident athletes coun. mem. U.S. Olympic Tng. Ctr., Colorado Springs, 1992-96. Recipient Silver medal Pan Am. Games, Mar Del Plata, Argentina, 1995, 48 kg. category U.S. Nat. Judo Championships, 1989, 90, 92, 95; grantee Woman's Sports Found., N.Y., 1992. Mem. Am. Univ. Women, U.S. Judo Fedn., U.S. Judo Assn. Roman Catholic. Office: US Olympic Tng Ctr-Judo Team 1 Olympic Plaza Colorado Springs CO 80909

CHAMBLESS, VALERIE HEPBURN, state official; b. Iowa City, Oct. 5, 1961; d. Lawrence Ronald and Mary Elizabeth (Zoghby) Hepburn; m. Thomas Sidney Chambless, Sept. 21, 1991. BA in Polit. Sci., Agnes Scott Coll., 1983; MPA, Ga. State U., 1987; postgrad., U. Ga., 1989—. Legis. aide, rsch. asst. Ga. Gen. Assemby, Atlanta, 1980-82; dir. govt. rels. Office Ga. Sec. of State, Atlanta, 1983-84, dir. adminstrn., 1984-90; asst. commr. Ga. Dept. Human Resources, Atlanta, 1990-92; dist. health planner S.W. Ga. Health Dist., Albany, 1992-93; exec. dir. S.W. Ga. Regional Bd., Albany, 1993—; health care cons. to pvt. agys. and State of Ga., 1992-94; vice chmn. Albany Area Primary Health Care, Inc., 1992—; bd. dirs. SOWEGA Health Edn., Inc., Albany, 1992—; mem. resource coun. Ga. Future Cmtys. Commn., 1995—. Campaign cons. state and local candidates, 1980—; mem. steering com. Albany/Dougherty 2000, 1992—; bd. dirs. Ga. Rural Health Assn., 1992-95; founding mem., officer S.W. Ga. Cmty. Health, Albany, 1993-95. Recipient outstanding svc. award Gov. State of Ga., 1987, Disting. Svc. award Easter Seal Soc. S.W. Ga., 1994, Cmty. Leadership award Ctr. Dirs. Ga., 1994, leadership award Dougherty Leadership Inst., 1995. Mem. ASAP, Southeastern Conf. on Pub. Adminstrn., Pi Alpha Alpha. Democrat. Roman Catholic. Office: SW Ga Regional Bd 507 3d Ave Ste 5 Albany GA 31701

CHAMLIN, SUZANNE, artist, educator; b. Long Branch, N.J., Feb. 18, 1963; d. George Maynard and Gloria Yvonne (Rosenwasser) C. BA, Barnard Coll., 1985; MFA, Yale U., 1989. vis. lectr. Yale U., New Haven, 1991, 92, 93, 95; adj. lectr. NYU-Sch. Continuing Edn., N.Y.C., 1993-96, The New Sch., N.Y.C., 1994-96, Cooper Union Extended Studies, N.Y.C., 1994-96; adj. faculty Purchase (N.Y.) Coll.-SUNY, 1994-96. One-woman shows include The Fine Arts Mus. of L.I., 1987-88, Paul/Sanger Gallery, N.J., 1990; group shows include The Painting Ctr., N.Y.C., 1993, Gallery A, Chgo., 1994. Recipient Presdl. Purchase award Temple U., Phila., 1985, residency The Va. Ctr. for the Creative Arts, Va., 1986, 90, 95, The Millay Colony, Austerlitz, N.Y., 1987, The Ragdale Found., 1996, 1st prize 4th annual juried show Fine Arts Mus. of L.I., Hempstead, 1987-88; finalist NEA MidAtlantic Regional fellow, 1996. Home: 146 Mulberry St New York NY 10013

CHAMPAGNE, VIRGINIA GREELEY, speech/language pathologist; b. Boston, Jan. 8, 1955; d. Thomas Horace and Marie Celine (Dwyer) Greeley; m. Alan James Champagne, July 14, 1984; 1 child, Colin Greeley. BA, Boston Coll., 1976; MS, U. Southwestern La., 1978. Cert. speech-lang.-hearing pathologist, Mass., R.I., La. Speech/lang. pathologist, early childhood specialist Lincoln (R.I.) Pub. Schs., 1978-80, Andover (Mass.) Pub. Schs., 1980—. Mem. Am. Speech-Lang.-Hearing Assn. Home: 6 Dartmouth Rd Andover MA 01810-2515

CHAMPION, NORMA JEAN, communications educator, state legislator; b. Oklahoma City, Jan. 21, 1933; d. Aubra Dell and Beuleah Beatrice (Flanagan) Black; m. Richard Gordon Champion, Oct. 3, 1953 (dec.); children: Jeffrey Bruce, Ashley Brooke. BA in Religious Edn., Cen. Bible Coll., Springfield, Mo., 1971; MA in Comm., S.W. Mo. State U., 1978; PhD in Tech., U. Okla., 1986. Producer, hostess The Children's Hour, Sta. KYTV-TV, NBC, Springfield, 1957-86; asst. prof. Cen. Bible Coll., 1968-84; prof. broadcasting Evangel Coll., Springfield, 1978—; mem. Springfield City Coun., 1987-92, Mo. Ho. of Reps., Jefferson City, 1992—; adj. faculty Assemblies of God Theol. Sem. Springfield, 1987—, pres. coun.; chmn. bd. Berean U.; frequent lectr. to svc. clubs, ednl. seminars; seminar speaker Internat. Pentecostal Press. Assn. World Conf., Singapore, 1989; announcer various TV commls. Contbr. numerous articles to religious publs. Mem. bd Mo. Access to Higher Edn. Trust, 1990—; regional rep. Muscular Dystrophy Assn.; mem. adv. bd. Chameleon Puppet Theater, 1987; mem. exec. bd. Univ. Child Care Ctr., 1987; hon. chmn. fund raising Salvation Army, 1986; also numerous other bds., hon. chairmanships.; judge Springfield City Schs. Recipient commendation resolution Mo. Ho. of Reps., 1988; numerous award for The Children's Hour; Aunt Norma Day named in her honor City of Springfield, 1976. Mem. Nat. Broadcast Edn. Assn., Mo. Broadcast Edn. Assn., Nat. League Cities, Mo. Mcpl. League (human resource com. 1989, intergovtl. rels. com. 1990), Nat. Assn. Telecom. Officers and Advisors, Internat. Pentesostal Press Assn., Josephson Inst. for Advancement Ethics, Springfield C. of C., Mo. PTA (life). Republican. Mem. Assemblies of God Ch. Home: 3609 S Broadway Ave Springfield MO 65807-4505 Office: Evangel Coll 1111 N Glenstone Ave Springfield MO 65802-2125

CHAMPLIN, MARY ANN, human resources executive; m. William Champlin; 3 children. B of Fgn. Svc., Georgetown U. Acct. exec. computer systems divsn. RCA; asst. dir. Conn. Gen. Corp., 1975-80; with Aetna Life and Casualty, 1971—, with office of chmn., 1988, sr. v.p. human resources, 1991—. Mem. adv. bd. The Catalyst, U. Conn. Bd. Overseers, Child Care Collaborative; trustee Com. on Econ. Devel.; bd. dirs. Urban League; past co-chair fundraising HArtford Easter Seals. Mem. Ins. Conf. Group, Greater Hartford Forum Bus. Ethics and Econ. Justice, Bus. Roundtable (employee rels. com.). Office: Aetna Life & Casualty Co 151 Farmington Ave Hartford CT 06156-0001

CHAMPNEY, LINDA LUCAS, reading educator; b. El Paso, Tex., Dec. 18, 1946; d. William Franklin and Caroline (Clements) Lucas; m. Rod Wayne Champney, Aug. 4, 1967; children: Kimberley Anne, Krisa Marie, Kari Lyn. BA, U. Tex., 1968; MEd, U. Colo., 1989. Cert. lang. arts and elem. edn. educator; nat. bd. cert. tchr. early adolescent lang. Tchr. MacArthur Jr. H.S., El Paso, 1968-69, 78-79; dir., tchr. St. Paul's United Meth. Ch., El Paso, 1976-78; subs. tchr. Irvine (Calif.) Unified Sch. Dist., 1981; reading tutor Mark Twain Elem. Sch., Littleton, Colo., 1982-83; lang. arts, reading tchr. Powell Mid. Sch., Littleton, 1983-93; reading specialist, cons. EdSource, Inc., Littleton, 1996—; instr. C.C. Aurora, Colo., 1990-91, C.C. Denver, Colo., 1995—. Mem. ASCD, Internat. Reading Assn. (study & rsch. com., program com.), Littleton Edn. Assn. (faculty rep.). Home and Office: 1657 W Canal Ct Littleton CO 80120

CHANATRY-HOWELL, LORRAINE MARIE, artist, designer, educator; b. Utica, N.Y., Aug. 6, 1934; d. Elias and Catherine (Esso) Chanatry; m. James Burt Howell, Feb. 18, 1995. BFA, Syracuse U., 1955; MA, Cath. U. Am., 1958; postgrad., Temple U., 1963, U. San Francisco-Guadalajara, Mex., 1965; EdD, U. South Fla., 1966; postgrad., U. Valencia, Spain, 1966, Am. U. Beirut, 1968. Cert. art tchr. Art supr./tchr. New Hartford (N.Y.) Ctrl. Sch., 1955-56; guidance counselor Washington-Lee H.S., Arlington, Va., 1959-60; interior designer B. Altman & Co., N.Y.C., 1960-61; chmn. art depts. Maitland (Fla.) Jr. H.S., 1962-64; chmn. art dept. Mid-Fla. Tech. Inst., Orlando, 1964-70, Liverpool (N.Y.) H.S., 1970-72; owner, dir. Lorraine Marie Art Ctr., Liverpool, 1972-73, Utica, N.Y., 1973-94; freelance artist and designer, cons., 1994—; cultural amb., Egypt, Syria, Lebanon, Jordan, 1961; adj. prof. fine arts Mohawk Valley C.C., Utica, 1988-94, Utica Coll., 1976-77. Bd. govs. Cath. U. Am., Washington, 1995—. Mem. Syracuse U. Alumni Assn. (pres. 1964-70, sec. 1980-88), Alpha Omicron Pi (charter 2d Century Soc., corp. bd. Chi chpt., v.p. alumni chpt. Orlando 1966-69, pres. Syracuse 1970-72). Greek Melchite Catholic. Home: 23 Shadow Brooke Dr Bridgeton NJ 08302 also: 429 San Jose Winter Haven FL 33884

CHANCE, M. SUE, psychiatrist, author, publisher; b. Paris, Tex., Apr. 27, 1942; d. John Bruce and Sally (McDaniel) Scott; m. Thomas E. Chance, Jr., Jan. 1, 1976 (div. Apr. 1989); m. Arthur J. Overgaag, July 18, 1992; 1 child, Jim Scott (dec.). BA, Angelo State U., San Angelo, Tex., 1971; MD, U. Tex., Galveston, 1978. Diplomate Am. Bd. Psychiatry and Neurology. Intern U. Okla. Health Sci. Ctr., Oklahoma City, 1978-79; resident in psychiatry Menninger's Clinic, Topeka, 1980-81, 82-83; pvt. practice, Houston, 1983-86, Tyler, Tex., 1986-87, Dallas, 1987-92; med. dir. adult psychiatry Mainland Ctr. Hosp., Texas City, Tex., 1984-86; unit chief adult chem. dependency unit Willowbrook Hosp., Waxahachie, Tex., 1987-90; med. dir. adult svcs. The Cedars Hosp., De Soto, Tex., 1990-91; dir. geriatric cons. svc. Chestnut Hill Hosp., Travelers Rest, S.C., 1995-96. Author: Stronger Than Death: When Suicide Touches Your Life, 1992 (Menninger Popular Press award 1993), A Voice of My Own: A Verbal Box of Chocolates, 1993, (novel) Stoneflowers, 1994; columnist Bonne Chance, Psychiat. Times, 1986—. Recipient Esther Haar award Am. Acad. Psychoanalysis, 9195, award for cover design Nat. Assn. Ind. Pubs., 1994. Fellow Am. Psychiat. Assn.

CHANDLER, ALICE, university president, educator; b. Bklyn., May 29, 1931; d. Samuel and Jenny (Meller) Kogan; m. Horace Chandler, June 10, 1954; children: Seth, Donald. A.B., Barnard Coll., 1951; M.A., Columbia U., 1953, Ph.D., 1960. Instr. Skidmore Coll., 1953-54; lectr. Barnard Coll., 1954-55, Hunter Coll., 1956-57; from instr. to prof. CCNY, 1961-76, v.p. instl. advancement, 1974-76, v.p. acad. affairs, 1974-76, provost, 1976-79, acting pres., 1979-80; pres. SUNY Coll., New Paltz, 1980—; bd. dirs. Coun. on Internat. Ednl. Exch. Author: The Prose Spectrum: A Rhetoric and Reader, 1968, The Theme of War, 1969, A Dream of Order, 1970, The Rationale of Rhetoric, 1970, The Rationale of the Essay, 1971, From Smollett to James, 1980, Foreign Student Policy: England, France, and West Germany, 1985, Obligation or Opportunity: Foreign Student Policy in Six Major Receiving Countries, 1989. Lizette Fisher fellow. Mem. Regional Plan Assn. (bd. dirs. 1987), Lotos, Phi Beta Kappa. Office: SUNY Coll at New Paltz Office of Pres 75 S Manheim Blvd New Paltz NY 12561-2449

CHANDLER, ANNE LOUISE, counselor, educator; b. Memphis, Nov. 23, 1947; d. Roland Bagwell and Louise (Ballard) C.; m. John William Moore, Dec. 17, 1977; children: J. Chandler Moore, Scott C. Moore, Elisabeth C. Moore. BA, Vanderbilt U., 1969; MA, Mich. State U., 1974, PhD, 1978. Lic. profl. counselor, Va.; cert. rehab. counselor. Disability examiner State of Mich., Lansing, 1972-75; instr. Mich. State U., East Lansing, 1976-77; asst. prof. Va. Commonwealth U., Fishersville, 1979-81, U. S.C., Columbia, 1982-84; asst. prof. Va. Commonwealth U., Richmond, 1985-88, assoc. prof., 1988—; counselor, cons., Richmond, 1985—. Mem. editl. bd. Rehab. Counseling Bull., 1991—, Vocat. Evaluation and Work Adjustment Bull., 1986—; contbr. articles to profl. jours. Mem. ACA, Am. Rehab. Counseling Assn. (exec. bd. 1986-89), Nat. Rehab. Assn. Office: Va Commonwealth Univ PO Box 980330 Richmond VA 23298-0330

CHANDLER, ELISABETH GORDON (MRS. LACI DE GERENDAY), sculptor, harpist; b. St. Louis, June 10, 1913; d. Henry Brace and Sara Ellen (Sallee) Gordon; m. Robert Kirkland Chandler, May 27, 1946 (dec.); m. Laci de Gerenday, May 12, 1979. Grad., Lenox Sch., 1931; pvt. study sculpture and harp. Mem. Mildred Dilling Harp Ensemble, 1934-45; instr. portrait sculpture Lyme Acad. Fine Arts, 1976—; dir. Abbott Coin Counter Co., Inc., 1941-55. Exhibited sculpture NAD, Nat. Sculpture Soc., Allied Artists Am., Nat. Arts Club, Pen and Brush, Lyme Art Assn., Mattatuck Mus., Catherine Lorillard Wolfe Art Club, Am. Artists Profl. League, Hudson Valley Art Assn., USIA, 1976-78, Lyme Art Ctr., 1979, retrospective exhbn. Lyme Acad. Fine Arts, 1987, Madison Gallery, 1987, Old State House, Hartford, Conn., 1989, Mellon Art Ctr., Wallingford, Conn., 1989, Fairfield U. Walsh Gallery, 1991, Brit. Mus., London, Am. Medallic Sculptors Assn. Traveling Exhbn., 1994, Slater Mus. Cropsey Found., 1995, Nat. Sculpture Exhbn. Lyme Acad. Fine Arts, 1995-96; represented in permanent collections Aircraft Carrier USS Forrestal, Gov. Dummer Acad., James Forrestal Research Ctr. of Princeton U., Lenox Sch., James L. Collins Parochial Sch., Tex., Storm King Art Ctr., Columbia U., Pace U., White Plains, N.Y., St. Patrick's Cathedral, N.Y.C., McAuley Ctr., St. Joseph's Coll., West Hartford, Conn.; designed relief mural Our Lady of Mercy Hosp, N.Y.C., 1996, Forrestal Meml. Medal, Timoschenko Medal for Applied Mechanics, Benjamin Franklin Medal, Albert A. Michelson Medal, Jonathan Edwards Medal, Shafto Broadcasting Award Medal, Woodrow Wilson Sch. of Princeton U., Ga. Pacific Bldg., Atlanta, Messiah Coll., Grantham, Pa., Adlai E. Stevenson High Sch., Ill., Queen Anne's County Courthouse Square, Md., pvt. collections. With mus. therapy div. Am. Theatre Wing, 1942-45; trustee The Lenox Sch., 1953-55; chmn. Associated Taxpayers Old Lyme, 1969-72; mem., trustee Brookgreen Gardens, S.C., 1989—. Recipient 1st prize Bklyn. War Meml. competition, 1945, 1st prize sculpture Catherine Lorillard Wolfe Art Club, 1951, 58, 63, Gold medal, 1969, Founders prize Pen & Brush, 1954, 76, 78, Gold medal, 1957, 61, 63, 69, 74, 76, Am. Heritage award, 1968, Solo Show award, 1961, 69, 75, Thomas R. Proctor prize NAD, 1956, Dessie Greer prize, 1960, 79, 85, Sculpture prize Nat. Arts Club, 1959, 60, 62, Gold medal, 1971, Gold medal Am. Artists Profl. LEague, 1960, 69, 73, 75, prize, 1981, Anna Hyatt Huntington prize, 1970, 76, Harriet Mayer Meml. prize, 1961, Gold medal Hudson Valley Art Assn., 1956, 69, 74, Mrs. John Newington award, 1976, 78, Lindsey Morris Meml. prize Allied Artists Am., 1973, Gold medal, 1982, Sculpture prize Acad. Artists, 1974, Sydney Taylor Meml. prize Knickerbocker Artists, 1975, New Netherlands DAR Bicentennial medal, 1976, Pietro Montana Meml. prize Hudson Valley Art Assn., 1995; named Citizen of Yr., Town of Old Lyme, Conn., 1985. Fellow NAD (academician), Nat. Sculpture Soc. (council 1976-85, Tallix Foundry award 1979, John Spring Founder's award 1986, John Cavanaugh Meml. prize 1991, Silver medal, citation 1992), Am. Artists Profl. League, Internat. Inst. Arts and Letters; mem. Federation International de la Medaille, Nat. Arts Club, Allied Artists Am., Am. Medallic Art Soc., Pen and Brush, Catherine Lorillard Wolf Art Club, Lyme Art Assn. (pres. 1973-75), Council Am. Artists Socs. (dir. 1970-73), Am. Artists Profl. League (dir. 1970-73), Lyme Acad. Fine Arts (trustee 1976—, chair sculpture dept.). Home and Studio: 2 Mill Pond Ln Old Lyme CT 06371-1118

CHANDLER, ESTELLE T., artist; b. Redlands, Calif., Feb. 22, 1961. Exhibited in one-woman shows and group exhbns. in U.S., Japan, German, Hong Kong and Mexico, Ctr. Contemporary Arts, Seattle, 1986-88, Tacoma Art Mus., 1987, Julliard Sch., N.Y.C., 1990, Neiman-Marcus, Dallas, 1991, Barney's, N.Y.C., 1992, Catalina Island Jazz Festival, Calif., 1992, The Guggenheim Mus., 1993, The Kennedy Ctr. for the Performing Arts, Washington, 1993, Carnegie Hall, N.Y.C., 1994, Asia Soc., N.Y.C., 1994, Met. Opera House, N.Y.C., 1994, Arranz Gallery, Buenos Aires, 1995, The Jayson Gallery, Chgo., 1995, Woodburn Gallery, Ohio, 1995, Bloomingdale's, N.Y., 1995, Gallery Cosmos, Tokyo, 1995, Paramount Hotel, N.Y.C., 1995. Republican. Sephardic/Creole. Office: ETC Inc PO Box 2771 Seattle WA 98111

CHANDLER, KAREN REGINA, career guidance specialist; b. Billings, Mont., Nov. 10, 1937; d. James Daniel Romine and Regina (Graham) Middleton; m. Dave Chandler, June 28, 1959; children: Dan, Lance, Trina. BS in Social Sci., Mont. State U., 1959; cert. summa cum laude, Seattle U., 1982. Employment specialist Magna & Assocs. Vocat. Rehab., Federal Way, Wash., 1983-84; instr., employment specialist Pvt. Industry Coun., Auburn, Wash., 1985; career guidance specialist Kent (Wash.) Pub. Schs., 1986—. Chmn. LWV, Kent, 1978. Mem. Wash. Career specialist Assn. (legis. chmn. 1986—, founder), Wash. Vocat. Assn. (sec. 1993-94, Occupational Info. Specialist award 1993), Wash. State Guidance Task Force, Wash. Vocat. Assn. Guidance (sec. 1993-94, pres.-elect 1994-95, pres. 1995—), Wash. Guidance & Counseling Plan (mem. writing team), W.Va. Guidance Assn. (pres. 1995-96). Democrat. Presbyterian. Home: 13306 12th Ave E Tacoma WA 98445-3559 Office: Kent Pub Schs 12430 SE 208th St Kent WA 98031-2231

CHANDLER, MARCIA SHAW BARNARD, farmer; b. Arlington, Mass., Aug. 22, 1934; d. John Alden and Grace Winifred (Copeland) Barnard; m. Samuel Butler Chandler, Aug. 31, 1952 (dec. 1986); children: Shawn Chandler Seddinger, Mark Thurmond, Matthew Butler. BA, Francis Marion Coll., Florence, S.C., 1976; MEd, U. S.C., 1985. Resource person United Cerebral Palsy of S.C., Dillon, 1976-79; instr. English Horry-Georgetown Tech. Coll., Conway, S.C., 1980-81; farm owner, mgr. Dillon. Author: (with others) Best of Old Farmer's Almanac, First 200 Years, 1991; cover artist So. Bell Telephone Directory, 1988, 90. Bd. dirs., publicist, artist Dillon County Theatre, Inc., 1985—; publicist, bd. dirs., artist MacArthur Ave. Players, Dillon, 1990—; bd. dirs. Friends of Francis Marion U., 1985—; pres. Dillon Area Arts Coun., 1980-85, Jr. Charity League of Dillon, 1960-75; nat. poetry judge DAR, 1982. Recipient Honorable Commendation for civic involvement S.C. Ho. Reps., Mar. 22, 1990. Mem. Cousteau Soc., Ctr. Environ. Edn., Internat. Fund Animal Welfare, World Wildlife Fund, Nature Conservancy, Sea Shepherd Conservation Soc. Home: 309 E Reaves Ave Dillon SC 29536-1919

CHANDLER, MARGUERITE NELLA, real estate corporation executive; b. New Brunswick, N.J., May 16, 1943; d. Edward A. and Marguerite (Moore) C.; m. Ronald Wilson, May 30, 1964 (div. Nov. 1973); children: Mark, Adam; m. Richmond Shreve, Nov. 22, 1979; 1 child, Laura. BS in Acctg., Syracuse U., 1964, MS in Polit. Mgmt., 1988. Tax acct. Peat Marwick Mitchell, Providence, 1964; grant adminstr., psychology dept. Brown U., Providence, 1965; intern in devel. cons. Washington, 1973-75; prin., tng. cons. M. Chandler Assocs., 1975-76; mgmt. cons. Edmar Corp., Bound Brook, N.J., 1976-78, pres., chief exec. officer, 1978-90, pres., 1991—. Peace Corps vol., 1966-68; established Food Bank Network of Somerset County, 1982, pres., 1982-85; established Worldworks Found., Inc., 1983; founder PeopleCare Ctr., 1984, pres., 1984-86; bd. dirs. N.J. Coun. for Arts, 1986-87; pres. bd. trustees N.J. Coun. of Chs., 1985-90; bd. dirs. United Way Somerset Valley, 1984-91, gen. campaign chmn., 1985-86; recorder Blue Ribbon Com. on Ending Hunger in N.J., 1984-86; vol. Somerset Community Action Program, 1969-71, Missionaries of Charity, Calcutta, India, 1981; treas. Somerset County Day Care Assn., 1969-71; mem. N.J. Gov.'s Task Force on Pub./Pvt. Sector Initiatives, 1986-91; Dem. candidate for U.S. Congress Dist. 12, 1990; mem. adv. bd. US-USSR Youth Exch., Ptnrs. in Peacemaking, The Giraffe Project; mem. Gov.'s Adv. Coun. on Solid Waste Mgmt., 1991-92; chairperson numerous fund-raising events to combat world hunger; established Heritage Trail Assn. of Somerset County, pres. 1994—. Named Woman of Yr., Women's Resource Ctr. Somerset County, 1983, Citizen of Yr., Somerset County C. of C., 1985, N.J. Chpt. Nat. Assn. Soc. Workers, 1986, Bus. and Profl. Women's Club, 1987, Person of Decade, Courier-News, 1989, Bus. Person of Yr., Bus. for Ctrl. N.J. mag., 1993; recipient People's Champion award Somerset Family Planning Svc., 1985, Disting. Svc. award N.J. Speech-Lang.-Hearing Assn., 1986, N.J. Women of Achievement award Douglass Coll. and N.J. Fedn. Women's Clubs, 1986, Brotherhood award Cen. Jersey chpt. Nat. Conf. Christians and Jews, 1986, Presdl. End Hunger award, 1987, Somerset Alliance for the Future Quality of Life award, 1996. Mem. Assn. N.J. Recyclers (pres. 1991-93), Somerset C. of C. (chmn. bd. 1989-90, chmn. strategic planning cultural and heritage com., tourism coun.), World Bus. Acad. (bd. dirs. 1988-89), Rotary (pres. Bound Brook-Middlesex club 1993-94), Regional Plan Assn. (bd. dirs. 1994—), Heritage Trail Assn. Somerset County (founder, pres. 1994—). Mem. Soc. of Friends. Home: 6 Lisa Ter Somerville NJ 08876-2515 Office: PO Box 149 Bound Brook NJ 08805-0149

CHANDLER, MARLENE MERRITT, construction executive; b. Greenville, S.C., Dec. 13, 1949; d. Harvey Allen and Gladys Iona (Stewart) Merritt; m. Charles Mack Owens, June 8, 1968 (div. Oct. 1984); 1 child, Heather

Michelle; m. Ray Lewis Chandler, Apr. 25, 1985. Grad. high sch., Piedmont, S.C. Asst. billing and computer operator Dillard Paper Co., Greenville, 1968-70; exec. asst. Daniel Constrn. Co., Greenville, 1970-74; co. sec., pres. asst. M.L. Garrett Constrn. Co., Greenville, 1974-78; asst. to purchasing mgr. P.Y.A. Monarch Co., Inc., Greenville, 1978-83; mgr., owner, pres. RAM Builders, Easley, S.C., 1985—; owner, pres. RAM Builders of Greenville, Inc., Greenville, 1986—. Author poem: Poetry Contest, 1989. Tutor Greenville Lit. Assocs., Inc., 1988-90; dir. S.C.'s Living Doll Pageant, S.C.'s Most Beautiful Girl Pageant, S.C.'s Baby of the Yr., S.C.'s Baby Bumpkin Contest. Named Mrs. I Love You Greenville, Greenville Bus. Assn., 1981, Mrs. S.C., S.C. Little Miss/Beauty Pageant, Greenville, 1982. Republican. Baptist. Home and Office: RAM Builders Greenville Inc 10129 Anderson Rd Easley SC 29642-8237

CHANEY, ETHEL SCOTLAND, English language educator; b. Cleve., Mar. 16, 1914; d. Bayard Scott and Beatrice Louise (Homan) Scotland; m. William Stanton Chaney, Oct. 8, 1939 (div. Mar. 1988); children: Scott Clay, Karen Marie Kauffman, Norma Chaney Shear, Ruth Margot Walker. BS, U. Ill., 1935; MA, Roosevelt U., 1966. Tchr. 4th grade Raynor Park Sch., Joliet, Ill., 1936-39; tchr. 8th grade Culbertson Sch., Joliet, 1936-39; tchr. English Joliet Twp. H.S. and Jr. Coll., 1959-80, Gulf H.S., New Port Richey, Fla., 1980, Pasco C.C., New Port Richey, Fla., 1981, Rutledge Jr. Coll., Raleigh, N.C., 1987, Huntington Learning Ctr., Raleigh, 1988; substitute tchr. Wake City Schs., Raleigh, 1987-96. Docent N.C. Mus. Art, Dickens Soc., Jane Austen Soc., Crime Writers Soc. Mem. Univ. Women (life), U. Ill. Alumni (life), Roosevelt U. Alumni (life), Pi Beta Phi (life). Democrat. Unitarian-Universalist. Home: 2406 F Wesvill Ct Raleigh NC 27607

CHANG, BARBARA KAREN, medical educator; b. Milltown, Ind., Jan. 6, 1946; m. M.F. Joseph Chang-Wai-Ling, Oct. 6, 1967; children: Carla Marie Yvonnette, Nolanne Arlette. BA, Ind. U., 1968; MA, Brandeis U., 1970; MD, Albert Einstein Coll. Medicine, 1973. Diplomate Am. Bd. Internal Medicine, Am. Bd. Med. Oncology, Am. Bd. Hematology. Resident in internal medicine Montefiore Med. Ctr., Bronx, N.Y., 1973-75; fellow in hematology/oncology med. ctr. Duke U., Durham, N.C., 1975-78; staff physician VA Med. Ctr., Augusta, Ga., 1978—, chief hematology/oncology, 1980-89, assoc. chief of staff edn., 1990-95; prof. medicine Med. Coll. Ga., Augusta, 1978—; chief of staff VA Med. Ctr., Albuquerque, 1995—; prof., assoc. dean U. N.Mex. Sch. Medicine, Albuquerque, 1995—; mem. Sci. Adv. Bd., Washington, 1983-88; mem. expert panels computer applications Dept. Vets. Affairs, Washington, 1988—. Contbr. numerous articles on cancer rsch. to profl. jours. Youth coord. Am. Hemerocallis Soc., Augusta, 1993-95. Grantee Nat. Cancer Inst., Am. Cancer Soc., 1978-93. Fellow ACP, Am. Soc. Hematology, Am. Assn. Cancer Rsch., Am. Soc. Clin. Oncology, Bioelectromagnetic Soc. (bd. dirs. 1983-86). Office: Dept Vets Affairs Med Ctr 2100 Ridgecrest Dr SE Albuquerque NM 87108

CHANG, JANICE MAY, lawyer, law educator, psychologist; b. Loma Linda, Calif., May 24, 1970; d. Belden Shiu-Wah and Sylvia (Tan) C. BA, Calif. State U, San Bernardino, 1990, cert. paralegal studies, 1990, cert. creative writing, 1991; JD, LaSalle U., 1993, D in Common Law, 1993, D in Homeopathic Medicine, 1993, D in Psychology, 1993; D Naturopathy, Clayton Sch. Natural Healing, 1993; PhD Psychology, Internat. U., 1994; D of Preventive Medicine, Bernadean U., 1994; DO, Anglo-Am. Inst. Drugless Ther., 1994; M of Herbology, Emerson Coll. Herbology, 1996; postgrad., Calif. Coast U., 1995—. Diplomate Brit. Guild Drugless Practitioners. Victim/witness contact clk.-paralegal Dist. Atty.'s Office Victim/Witness Assistance Program, San Bernardino, Calif., 1990; gen. counsel JMC Enterprises, Inc., 1993—; law prof. LaSalle U., 1994—. Contbr. poetry to anthologies, including Am. Poetry Anthology, 1987-90, The Pacific Rev., 1991, The Piquant, 1991, River of Dreams, 1994, Reflections of Light, 1994, Musings, 1994 (Honorable Mention award 1994), Best Poems of 1995 (Celebrating Excellence award 1995, Inspirations award 1995), Am. Poetry Annual, 1996, Best New Poems of 1996, Interludes, 1996, Meditations, 1996, Perspectives, 1996 (Honorable Mention award 1996). Recipient Poet of Merit award Am. Poetry Assn., San Francisco, 1989, Golden Poet award World of Poetry, Washington, 1989, Publisher's Choice award Watermark Press, 1990, Editor's Choice award The Nat. Libr. of Poetry, 1990-96, Pres.'s award for lit. excellence Iliad Press, 1996; Rsch. Coun. on Botanic Medicine fellow. Fellow Emerson Coll. Rsch. Coun. on Botanic Medicine; mem. APA, ATLA, Am. Psychology-Law Soc., Am. Coll. Legal Medicine, Am. Naturopathic Med. Assn., Am. Soc. Law, Medicine and Ethics, Calif. Trial Lawyers Assn. (med. law sect.), Delta Theta Phi. Republican. Seventh-Day Adventist. Home: 11466 Richmont Rd Loma Linda CA 92354-3523

CHANG, JEANNETTE, publishing executive. BS, CCNY. Advt. sales rep. Cosmopolitan mag. Hearst Mags., N.Y.C., 1973-77, fashion advt. mgr., 1977-79; dir. fashion mktg. Bazaar mag. Hearst Mags., N.Y.C., 1979-84; assoc. pub. Harper's Bazaar mag. Hearst Mags., N.Y.C., 1984-94, v.p., 1992-94, v.p., pub., 1994—; spkr. in field. Active City Meals on Wheels, Meml. Sloan Kettering Found., Susan G. Komen Breast Cancer Found. Named to YWCA Acad. of Women Achievers, 1992. Mem. Fashion Group Internat. (bd. dirs., chair cosmetic exec. women's com.). Office: Harper's Bazaar 1700 Broadway 37th Fl New York NY 10019*

CHANG, LINDA GALE, marketing, sales promotion manager; b. San Francisco, Aug. 12, 1952; d. Ralph M. and Mable H. (Mark) Joe; m. Jerold M. Chang; 1 child, Kevin. AA in Art, Hartnell Coll., 1972; BA in Graphic Design, San Jose State U., 1975. Mktg. Becker CPA Review, 1996—; sales planning & promotions mgr. Neutrogena; sales promotion supr. Avery Internat. Creative designer, Art Dir.: Avery Internat., Composition Arts, William Blumhoff Design, Typothetae. Address: 138 Paseo Perdido Walnut CA 91789-2234

CHANG, LING WEI, sales executive; b. Taiwan, China, July 27, 1960; came to U.S., 1976; d. Thomas T.P. and Hou Hsin (Wang) C. BE, Cooper Union, 1982; MS, Syracuse U., 1989. Engr. Data Systems div. IBM Corp., Poughkeepsie, N.Y., 1982-85; sys. engr. U.S. mktg. and svcs. IBM Corp., N.Y.C., 1985-90; adv. mktg. rep. N.Y. gov. br. IBM U.S., N.Y.C., 1991-92, acct. mgr. N.Y. Pub. Svcs., 1993-94; br. mgr. LEXIS-NEXIS, N.Y.C., 1994-95; nat. account mgr. Computer Assocs. Internat. Inc., N.Y.C., 1996—. Vol. City Hosp. Ctr. at Elmhurst, N.Y., 1978; jr. judge Nat. Energy Found., 1979-82; bd. mgrs. Queens Ctr. Pla. Condominium, 1990-92. Mem. Women, Inc., Tau Beta Pi, Eta Kappa Nu. Home: 87-08 Justice Ave Apt 10D Elmhurst NY 11373-4580 Office: Computer Assocs Internat Inc North Plz 2 Penn Plz 2nd Fl New York NY 10121

CHANG, LYDIA LIANG-HWA, school social worker, educator; b. Wuhan, Hubei, China, Sept. 25, 1929; came to U.S., 1960; d. Shu-Tze Yu-Rou and Yuen (Young) C.; m. David P. Ausubel, Nov. 27, 1979 (div. Sept. 1984); children: Elizabeth L. Ip, George Lee. Diploma in Spanish and Lit., U. Sorbonne, Paris, 1959; MSW, NYU, 1963; cert. in advanced social work, Columbia U., N.Y.C., 1977, PhD in Social Work, 1980. Cert. social worker, cert. sch. social worker, N.Y. Supr. Cath. Charities, N.Y.C., 1969-71; dir. mental health cons. ctr. Univ. Settlement, N.Y.C., 1971-73; psychotherapist Luth. Med. Ctr., Bklyn., 1974-78; assoc. prof. U. Cin., 1978-80; asst. prof. Borough of Manhattan C.C., N.Y.C., 1983-86; bilingual sch. social worker N.Y.C. Bd. Edn., 1987—, instr. for staff devel. program, 1991—; cons. Cath. Social Svc. Bur., Cin., 1978-80; faculty advisor Borough of Manhattan C.C., 1983-86. Contbr. articles and poetry to various publs. Mem. adv. bd. Pub. Sys. of Schs., Cin., 1978-80, Orange County Asian Am. orgn., Goshen, N.Y., 1980-82; treas. U.S.-China Ednl. Fund, Hastins-on-Hudson, N.Y., 1994—; mem. Asian-Am. Dem. Assn., Queens, 1993—, Am. Voters Assn., Queens, 1986—. Mem. NASW, Nat. Assn. Sch. Social Workers, Columbia Alumni Assn., Nankai Alumni Assn. (v.p. 1991-94). Episcopalian. Home: 77-11 35th Ave Apt 2P Jackson Heights NY 11372 Office: NYC Bd Edn CSE D24 72-52 Metropolitan Ave Middle Village NY 11379

CHANG, MARIAN S., filmmaker, composer; b. Atlanta, Aug. 19, 1958; d. C.H. Joseph and C.S. (Chun) C. BA in Music, Harvard U., 1981; MFA in Filmmaking, Columbia U., 1994. Composer, choreographer Exptl. Theatre, Dance, Boston, 1981-88; composer for modern dance co. Performing Arts Ensemble, Boston, 1986-88; co-dir., choreographer, performer Theatre S., Boston, 1987-88; prodr., dir., screenwriter N.Y.C., 1991—; founder, prodr. Shy Artists Prodns., Boston, N.Y.C., 1988-94. Mass. Artists Fellowship Program fellow in choreography, 1987, in music composition, 1988; recipient First Prize Kans. City Music Scholarship Competition, 1976. Home: 220 E 27th St #7 New York NY 10016

CHANG, SYLVIA TAN, health facility administrator, educator; b. Bandung, Indonesia, Dec. 18, 1940; came to U.S., 1963; d. Philip Harry and Lydia Shui-Yu (Ou) Tan; m. Belden Shiu-Wah Chang, Aug. 30, 1964; children: Donald Steven, Janice May. Diploma in nursing, Rumah Sakit Advent, Indonesia, 1960; BS, Philippine Union Coll., 1962; MS, Loma Linda (Calif.) U., 1967; PhD, Columbia Pacific U., 1987. Cert. RN, PHN, ACLS, BLS instr., cmty. first aid instr., IV, TPN, blood withdrawal/. Head nurse Rumah Sakit Advent, Bandung, Indonesia, 1960-61; critical care, spl. duty and medicine nurse, team leader White Meml. Med. Ctr., L.A., 1963-64; nursing coord. Loma Linda U. Med. Ctr., 1964-66; team leader, critical care nurse, relief head nurse Pomona (Calif.) Valley Hosp. Med. Ctr., 1966-67; evening supr. Loma Linda U. Med. Ctr., 1967-69, night supr., 1969-79, adminstrv. supr., 1979-94; sr. faculty Columbia Pacific U., San Rafael, Calif., 1986-94; dir. health svc. La Sierra U., Riverside, Calif., 1988—; site coord. Health Fair Expo La Sierra U., 1988-89; adv. coun. Family Planning Clinic, Riverside, 1988-94; blood drive coord. La Sierra U., 1988—. Counselor Pathfinder Club Campus Hill Ch., Loma Linda, 1979-85, crafts instr., 1979-85, music dir., 1979-85; asst. organist U. Ch., 1982-88. Named one of Women of Achievement YWCA, Greater Riverside C. of C., The Press Enterprise, 1991, Safety Coord. of Yr. La Sierra U., 1995. Mem. Am. Coll. Health Assn., Assn. Seventh-day Adventist Nurses, Pacific Coast Coll. Health Assn., Adventist Student Pers. Assn., Loma Linda U. Sch. Nursing Alumni Assn. (bd. dirs.), Sigma Theta Tau. Republican. Seventh-day Adventist. Home: 11466 Richmont Rd Loma Linda CA 92354-3523 Office: La Sierra U Health Svc 4700 Pierce St Riverside CA 92505-3331

CHANG, VICTORIA KIM, biochemistry educator, researcher; b. N.Y.C., Oct. 7, 1961; d. Victor C.L. and Theresa Eun Sook (Kim) C. BS, Wellesley Coll., 1983; PhD in Biochemistry, Molecular and Cell Biology, Cornell U., 1993. Undergrad. rsch. scientist MIT, Cambridge, 1982-83; rsch. technician Children's Hosp., John Enders Rsch. Inst., Boston, 1983-84; grad. and postdoctoral rsch. scientist, teaching asst. introductory biochemistry, sect. leader advanced biochem. methods lab. dept. biochemistry Cornell U., Ithaca, N.Y., 1984-94, outdoor edn. sr. instr. outdoor edn. program, 1989-92, postdoctoral rsch. scientist, 1993-94; prin. rsch. investigator Colo. Coll., Colorado Springs, 1994-96, asst. prof. biochemistry, 1994-96; asst. prof. biochemistry/chemistry dept. Drew U., Madison, N.J., 1996—. Zimmerman Found. Undergrad. Rsch. fellow Wellesley Coll., 1982, Grad. Rsch. Asst. fellow Cornell U., 1984-92; Faculty R&D grantee Barnes Found., 1994, Howard Hughes Faculty Rsch. grantee Colo. Coll., 1995, Natural Sci. Divsn. Rsch. grantee, 1995, Minority Scholar Faculty Rsch. grantee, 1995. Democrat. Presbyterian. Office: Drew U Chemistry Dept Madison NJ 07940

CHANIN, LEAH FARB, law library administrator, lawyer, consultant, law educator; b. Galveston, Tex., Nov. 29, 1929; d. A. C. and Celia (Rubenstein) Farb; m. Louis Chanin, Feb. 4, 1951 (dec. Jan. 1991); children: Scott, Leonard, Johanna, Rebecca. BA, So. Meth. U., 1950; LLB, Mercer U., 1954. Bar: Ga. 1954, U.S. Dist. Ct. (mid. dist.) Ga. 1954. Practice, Macon, Ga., 1959-63; mem. Kenmore & Culpepper, 1959-63; mem. faculty Walter F George Sch Law, Mercer U., 1964-92, asst. prof. law, 1969-72, assoc. prof., 1972-77, prof., 1977-92, dir. Law Libr., 1964-92, dean pro tem, 1986-87; disting. prof., dir. libr. U. D.C. Sch. Law, 1992—. mem. Fed. Merit Rev. Com., 1979-81; bd. visitors Mercer Law Sch., 1992—. Author: Specialized Legal Research, 1987, Georgia Legal Research, 1990, Legal Research in D.C., Maryland and Virginia, 1995; contbr. articles to profl. jours. Mem. State Bar Ga. (adv. ethics opinions bd., pres. author's ct. 1985-86), Am. Assn. Law Librs. (pres. 1982-83), Internat. Assn. Jewish Lawyers. Democrat. Jewish. Home: 3001 Veazey Ter NW Apt 1027 Washington DC 20008-5405 Office: UDC Sch Law Bldg 39B 4200 Connecticut Ave NW Washington DC 20008

CHANNING, CAROL, actress; b. Seattle, Jan. 31, 1923; d. George and Adelaide (Glaser) C.; m. Charles F. Lowe, Sept. 5, 1956; 1 son, Channing George. Student, Bennington Coll. Actress: (Broadway prodns.) No for an Answer, 1941, Let's Face It, 1941, Proof Through the Night, 1942, So Proudly We Hail, Lend an Ear, 1948 (Theatre World award, Critic's Circle award), Gentlemen Prefer Blondes, 1949, 51-53, Wonderful Town, 1953, Pygmalian, 1953, The Vamp, 1955, Show Business, 1959, Show Girl, 1961, George Burns-Carol Channing Musical Revue, 1962, The Millionairess, 1963, Hello Dolly, 1964-67, also revivial (Tony award for Best Actress, N.Y. Drama Critics Cir. award for Best Actress), Carol Channing with Her Stout-Hearted Men, 1970 (London Critics award), Four on a Garden, 1971, Cabaret, 1972, Festival at Ford's, 1972, Carol Channing and Her Gentlemen Who Prefer Blondes Revue, 1972, Jerry's Girls, 1984-85, Legends, 1986, (theatre tours) Lorelei, 1973-75, Carol's Broadway Revue; (films) First Travelling Saleslady, 1956, Thoroughly Modern Millie, 1967 (Golden Globe award as Best Supporting Actress 1967), Skidoo, 1968, Shinbone Alley (voice), 1971, Sgt. Peppers Lonely Hearts Club Band, 1978, Happily Ever After (voice), 1990, Hans Christian Andersen's Thumbelina (voice), 1994, others; (TV prodns.) Svengali and the Blonde, Three Men on a Horse, Crescendo; (TV appearences) The Love Boat, 1977, Alice in Wonderland, 1985, Where's Waldo? (voice), 1991, Addams Family (voice), 1992, The Magic School Bus (voice), 1994. Recipient Best Night Club Act award, 1957, 64, Spl. Tony award, 1968, Theatre World award for Bronze medallion City of N.Y., 1978, Lifetime Achievement Tony award, 1995. Christian Scientist. Office: William Morris Agy 151 S El Camino Dr Beverly Hills CA 90212-2704*

CHANTRY, ELIZABETH ANN, operational staff officer; b. Houston, May 18, 1956; d. William Amdor and Patricia Claire (Von Lorenz) C. BA, U. N.C., 1979. Student Dept. Def., Washington, 1979-80, lang. analyst, 1981-92, sr. staff officer, 1992—. Mem. Friends to Washington Ednl. Telecommunications Assn., Balt. Internat. Affairs Internat., World Affair Coun. Washington; donor to Col. Williamsburg Found., Am. Soc. for Prevention Cruelty to Animals, Carter Ctr., Am. Cancer Soc., Am. Heart and Lung, Am. Diabetes Assn., Multiple Sclerosis Soc., Habitat, St. Judes Hosp. Mem. Nat. Pks. Assn., Nat. Trust for Hist. Preservation, Smithsonian Resident Assn., Chesapeake Bay Assn. Democrat.

CHANTRY, RHONDA S., accountant; b. May 26, 1953; d. Robert D. and Lottie J. (Stifle) C.; children: Melissa M. Nihsen, Jenae L. Nihsen. BSBA cum laude with honors, U. Nebr., 1994. Spl. accounts rec. bookkeeper Met. Utilities Dist., Omaha, 1983-89, mktg. analyst, 1989—. Mem. Sarpy County Econ. Devel. Corp., Papillion, Nebr. Mem. Inst. Mgmt. Accts. (CMA), Omaha C. of C., Lavista (Nebr.) C. of C.

CHAPDELAINE, LORRAINE ELDER, gerontology nurse; b. Yonkers, N.Y., Sept. 29, 1939; d. Alexander Lindsay Elder and Evelyn Emma Flower Bellini; m. Bernard Grant Dostal, May 15, 1960 (div. Nov. 1972); children: Dana Arthur Dostal, Jeffrey Alexander Dostal. Diploma, Mass. Genl. Hosp. Sch. Nursing, Boston, 1961; BS cum laude, Elms Coll., Chicopee, Mass., 1990; MS, U. Mass., 1992. RN, Mass.; cert. gerontol. clin. specialist. Staff nurse Cooley Dickinson Hosp., Northampton, Mass., 1961-67, Holyoke (Mass.) Hosp., 1967-74; health svc. supr. Mountain View Nursing Home, Montgomery, Mass., 1979-85; staff nurse, supr. Port Charlotte (Fla.) Care Ctr., 1985-87; staff nurse Holyoke Geriatric Authority, 1987-89; temporary staff O'Connell Profl. Svc., Holyoke, 1987-90; asst. prof. clin. nursing U. Mass. Sch. Nursing, Amherst, 1992-93; clin. specialist/wound cons. Hampshire County Vis. Nurse Assn., Northampton, 1992—; clin. specialist, vis. staff Vis. Nurse Svcs Western Mass., Holyoke, Mass., 1989—; grant writer, adminstr. Nurse Managed Well Elderly Foot Clinics, 1993—; lectr. in field; initiator, adminstr. grant-funded nurse-managed foot clinics for elderly poor. Mem. Nat. Gerontol. Nurses Assn., Advanced Practice Gerontol. Nurses Interest Group, Order Eastern Star (Worthy Matron 1981, 84), Sigma Theta Tau. Episcopalian. Home: 3 Vassar Cir Holyoke MA 01040-2627 Office: Vis Nurse Svcs Western Mass 330 Whitney Ave Holyoke MA 01040-2751

CHAPIN, DIANA DERBY, city official; b. St. Joseph, Mich., Nov. 15, 1942; d. David Norman and Gladys Ruth (Henke) Derby; B.A. cum laude (Woodrow Wilson fellow), U. Mich., 1964; M.A., Cornell U., 1966, Ph.D. (Woodrow Wilson dissertation fellow), 1971; m. James Burke Chapin, Mar. 16, 1968; children—James Derby, David Sheffield. Asst. prof. Queens Coll., N.Y.C., 1969-74; dist. adminstr. 8th Congl. Dist., N.Y.C., 1974-76; asst. commr. N.Y.C. Dept. Parks and Recreation, 1978-81, Queens Borough commr., 1981-86 ; dep. commr. planning Dept. Parks and Recreation, N.Y.C., 1986-90, dep. commr. planning and capital projects, 1990-94; dep. commr. policy and adminstrn. N.Y.C., Dept. Bldgs., 1994-96; 1st dep. commr. N.Y.C. Dept. Environ. Protection, 1996—. Del. Democratic Nat. Conv., Miami, Fla., 1972; dist. leader 35th Assembly Dem. Dist., N.Y.C., 1972-78; mgr. various campaigns, 1977-78. Recipient ann. employee award N.Y.C. Dept. Parks and Recreation, 1982. Congregationalist. Contbr. articles to profl. publs. Home: 35-46 79th St Jackson Heights NY 11372-4849 Office: 60 Hudson St New York NY 10013

CHAPIN, JUNE ROEDIGER, education educator; b. Chgo., May 19, 1931; d. Henry and Stephanie L. (Palke) Roediger; m. Ned Chapin, June 12, 1954; children: Suzanne, Elaine. BA in Liberal Arts, U. Chgo., 1952, MA in Social Sci., 1954; EdD in Edn., Stanford U., 1963. Tchr. credentials, Calif., Ill. Tchr. Chgo. (Ill.) Pub. Schs., 1954-56, Redwood City (Calif.) Schs., 1956-60, San Francisco (Calif.) State U., 1963-65, U. Santa Clara, Calif., 1965-67; prof. edn. Coll. Notre Dame, Belmont, Calif., 1967—. Author, co-author twelve books including Elementary Social Studies, 1996. Recipient Hilda Taba award Calif. State Social Studies Coun., 1976. Mem. Am. Sociol. Assn., Am. Ednl. Rsch. Assn., Nat. Coun. for the Social Studies, Social Sci. Edn. Consortium, Phi Delta Kappa. Home: 1190 Bellair Way Menlo Park CA 94025-6611

CHAPIN, SUZANNE PHILLIPS, retired psychologist; b. Syracuse, N.Y., Aug. 9, 1930; d. Harold Bridge and Charlotte Virginia (Warner) Phillips; m. Richard Hilton Chapin, June 13, 1953 (div. 1964); children: Bruce Phillips Chapin, Linda Chapin Fry. BA, Syracuse U., 1952; MA, Columbia U., 1965. Statis. asst. Syracuse Bd. of Edn., 1952-53; psychol. examiner Stamford (Conn.) Pub. Schs., 1965-68, psychologist Head Start program, 1967-68; psychologist Southbury (Conn.) Tng. Sch., 1968-74, Onondaga Assn. for the Retarded, Syracuse, 1974, Harlem Valley Psychiatric Ctr., Wingdale, N.Y., 1974-93, Mid-Hudson Psychiat. Ctr., New Hampton, 1993; ret., 1993. Mem. LWV, Audubon Soc., Sierra Club. Democrat. Home: 10 S Bearwood Dr Palmyra VA 22963

CHAPKIS, WENDY LYNN, women's studies educator; b. Pasadena, Calif., Sept. 2, 1954; d. Robert Lynn and Marjorie Jean (King) C.; m. Gabriel Demaine, Oct. 1989. BA, U. Calif., 1977, MA, 1989, PhD, 1995. Project dir. Transnat. Inst., Amsterdam, The Netherlands, 1979-86; lectr. U. Calif., Santa Cruz, 1989-95; asst. prof. U. Southern Maine, Portland, 1995—; resource development Santa Cruz AIDS project, 1986-90, WomenCare Cancer Advocacy, Santa Cruz, 1994. Author: Beauty Secrets: The Politics of Appearance, 1986, Live Sex Acts: Women Performing Erotic Labor, 1996; editor: Loaded Questions, 1981, Of Common Cloth, 1983. Fulbright Found. fellow, 1993-94. Mem. Am. Sociol. Assn., Soc. for Study of Social Problems, Nat. Lesbian & Gay Task Force. Office: U Southern Maine 94 Bedford St Portland ME 04103

CHAPLIN, GERALDINE, actress; b. Santa Monica, Calif., July 3, 1944; d. Charles and Oona (O'Neill) C.; 1 child, Shane. Ed. pvt. schs., Royal Ballet Sch., London. Motion pictures include Doctor Zhivago, 1965, Stranger in the House, 1967, I Killed Rasputin, 1968, The Hawaiians, 1970, La casa sin fronteras, 1971, Sur un arbre perche, 1971, Innocent Bystanders, 1972, Z.P.G., 1972, Le Marriage a la Mode, 1973, Ana y los lobos, 1973, The Three Musketeers, 1974, Verflucht dies Amerika!, 1974, La Banda de Jaider, 1974, The Four Musketeers, 1975, Nashville, 1975, Noroit, 1976, Buffalo Bill and the Indians, 1976, Welcome to L.A, 1977, Cria Cuervos, 1977, Elisa, Vida Mia, 1977, Roseland, 1977, In Memorium, 1977, Une Page d'Amour, 1977, Remember My Name, 1978, A Wedding, 1978, Los Ojos Vendados, 1978, L'Adoption, 1978, Mais ou et donc ornicar, 1979, Mama Cumple 100 Anos, 1979, La Viuda de Montiel, 1979, The Mirror Crack'd, 1980, Voyage en Douce, 1981, Les Uns et les Autres, 1981, Bolero, 1982, La Vie est un roman, 1983, Buried Alive, 1984, L'Amour par terre, 1984, Gentile Alouette, 1985, White Mischief, 1988, The Moderns, 1988, I Want to Go Back Home, 1989, The Return of the Musketeers, 1989, The Children, 1990, Buster's Bedroom, 1991, Chaplin, 1992, Hors Saison, 1992, The Age of Innocence, 1993; TV appearances include: (miniseries) The Word, 1978, (specials) My Cousin Rachel, 1985, (movies) The Corsican Brothers, 1985, Duel of Hearts, 1992, A Foreign Field, 1994. Office: William Morris Agy 151 S El Camino Dr Beverly Hills CA 90212-2704*

CHAPMAN, BETTY TRAPP, historian, writer; b. Tupelo, Miss., Oct. 18, 1936; d. Charles Wilson and Mamie Elizabeth (Bates) Trapp; m. Billy Klingman Chapman, Dec. 29, 1960; children: Laura Chapman Foster, Elizabeth Chapman. BA, Millsaps Coll., Jackson, 1958. Tchr. Spring Branch Ind. Sch. Dist., Houston, 1959-61; substitute tchr. St. John's Sch., Houston, 1973-77; continuing studies tchr. Houston, 1984-95, ind. historian, freelance writer, 1989—; columnist Houston Bus. Jour., 1993—; mem. bd. trustees Harris County Heritage Soc., Houston, 1983-85, 87-91; mem. bd. dirs. Greater Houston Preservation Alliance, Houston, 1992-94; rsch. cons. Houston Women Project, 1987-91; archivist St. Luke's United Methodist Ch., Houston, 1989—. Author: Houston Then and Now, 1993; co-author: Upon This Rock, 1995, Two-minute Histories of Houston, 1996. Mem. bd. dirs. Houston Jr. Forum, 1969-72, 82-85, chair Lifelong Learning Classes, 1991-95; com. mem. League of Women Voters, Houston, 1996; speaker on local history various cmty. orgns., Houston, 1986—. Recipient Outstanding Mem. for 1978 award Houston Jr. Forum, 1978, Friend of the Soc. award Harris County Heritage Soc., 1991. Mem. AAUW, Nat. Women's History Network, Tex. State Historical Assn., So. Assn. Women Historians. Democrat. Methodist. Home: 6166 Olympia Dr Houston TX 77057

CHAPMAN, DELINDA (ANN), state official; b. Decatur, Ill., Apr. 25, 1947; d. Roy Wesley and Margere Jane (Daunt) C.; m. Lewis Steven Shelton, June 21, 1969 (div. May 1974); m. John Edward Erickson, Aug. 31, 1979; stepchildren: Linda Dumich, Debra Schoonover, Pamela Sitch, Scott, Paula Martin. BA, Ill. Coll., 1969; MA, Sangamon State U., Springfield, Ill., ž974; EdD, U. Ill., 1979. Cert K-9 tchr., supt.'s endorsement, gen. adminstrv., Ill. Tchr., asst. prin., acting prin. Sch. Dist. 186, Springfield, 1969-76; rsch. asst. U. Ill. Coll. Edn., Champaign, 1976-78; supr. elem. edn. Charles County Bd. Edn., La Plata, Md., 1978-80; vis. prof. U. Guam, Mangilao, 1980-81; regional coord., adminstr. field svc., assoc. dept. Ill. Dept. Children and Family Svcs., Springfield, 1982-86, mgr., 1991-92; dir. data processing Office Sec. State, State of Ill., Springfield, 1986-91; assoc. dir. Ill. Liquor Control Commn., Springfield, 1992-93; spl. asst. to dir. Ill. Dept. Pub. Aid, Springfield, 1993—; mem. textbook selection com. State of Ill., Springfield, 1973-74; coord. Charles County Afro Am. Heritage Exhibit, Pomonkey, 1979-80; mem., sec. sch. attendance adv. com. Chgo. Pub. Schs., 1985-86; presenter in field. Chmn. Ill. Commn. for Celebration 75th Anniversary of 19th Amendment, Springfield, 1994-95; mem. coun. Inter-Civic Club, 1994-96; organizer Springfield Edn. Advocacy Coalition, 1995-96; vice chmn., sec. So. div. March of Dimes, 1989—. Recipient cert. of appreciation Afro Am. Heritage Soc., Charles County, 1980, gov.'s cert. of appreciation State of Ill., 1995; named Vol. of Yr., Greater Ill. chpt. March of Dimes, 1993. Mem. AAUW (pres. Springfield br. 1994-96, Ill. dir. planning and devel. 1995-98), Ill. Coll. Alumni Assn. Home: 77 Cottage Grove Springfield IL 62707 Office: Ill Dept Pub Aid 100 S Grand Ave E Springfield IL 62762

CHAPMAN, DIANE P., lawyer; b. Lowell, Mass., Dec. 31, 1952. BA, Duquesne U., 1974; JD, Cleve. State U., 1978. Bar: Ohio 1978. Ptnr. Baker & Hostetler, Cleve. Office: Baker & Hostetler 3200 Nat City Ctr 1900 E 9th St Cleveland OH 44114-3401*

CHAPMAN, HOPE HORAN, psychologist; b. Chgo., Feb. 13, 1954; d. Theodore George and Idelle (Poll) H.; m. Stuart G. Chapman, Dec. 4, 1983. BS, U. Ill., Champaign-Urbana, 1976; MA, No. Ill. U., 1979; student lawyer's asst. program Roosevelt U., Chgo. 1996. Lic. counselor, Ill. Psychologist Glenwood (Iowa) State Hosp. Sch., 1979-83, Gov. Samuel H. Shapiro Devel. Ctr., Kankakee, Ill., 1985-86; dir. staff tng. and devel. Glenkirk, 1988-90; clin. assoc. Bennett & Assoc., 1990-91; psychologist Singer Mental Health & Devel. Ctr., Rockford, Ill., 1992-93; forensic psychologist Elgin (Ill.) Mental Health Ctr., 1993-94; Scholar State of Ill. Active Omaha Symphonic Chorus, 1981-83; mem. Omaha Public Schs. Citizens Adv. Com., 1980-81; mem. edn. com. Anti-Defamation League, 1980-85, chmn. com. anti-Semitism and Jewish youth, 1981-84; commr. youth commn. Village of Hoffman Estates, Ill., 1988-94; vice-chmn. oversight com. Vogelei Teen. Ctr., 1988-94; commr. Environ. Commn., Village of Hoffman Estates, 1994—, chmn. Schaumburg Twp. Mental Health Bd., 1993-94. Mem. APA, Midwest Psychol. Assn., Am. Assn. on Mental Retardation, Am. Psychology-Law Soc., Am Coll. Forensic Examiners, Phi Kappa Phi, Psi Chi. Jewish. Contbr. papers to profl. confs., articles to jours.

CHAPMAN, JOYCE EILEEN, community college educator, administrator; b. Red Bluff, Calif., June 11, 1940; d. Joseph L. and Elaine C. (Potter) Cole; m. William H. Chapman, July 15, 1961; 1 child, Gregory W. AA in Bus. Edn., Shasta Coll., Redding, Calif., 1960; BA in Bus. Edn., Chico (Calif.) State Coll., 1962; MA in Edn. with distinction, Calif. State U., Chico, 1991. Cert. C.C. instr., office svcs. and related techs., banking, fin., ct. reporting, office adminstr. Calif. Tchr. bus. edn. Red Bluff (Calif.) Union H.S., 1962-63; traffic mgr. WOHP Radio, Bellefontaine, Ohio, 1963; tchr. bus. edn. Indian Lake H.S., Lewistown, Ohio, 1963-64; adminstrv. and transp. supr. Tumpane Co., Inc., Adana, Turkey, 1964-66; telephone claims rep. Allstate Ins. Co., San Antonio, Tex., 1966-70; tchr. vocat. office edn. Somerset (Tex.) H.S., 1975-80; instr. bus. edn. Shasta Coll., Redding, Calif., 1980-94; instr. office info. systems Butte Coll., Oroville, Calif., 1987-90; instr. ct. reporting Butte Coll., Oroville, 1990—; mem. Butte Coll. Curriculum Com. Oroville, 1990-91; facilitator ct. reporting Adv. Com., Oroville, 1990—, Butte Coll. Ct. Reporting, Oroville, 1990—; mem. Butte FLEX Com. (staff devel.), Oroville, 1993—. Author: (book) Introduction to Computer-Aided Transcription, 1991; (degree program) Court Reporting: A Macro Curriculum for Butte C.C. Dist., 1990. Mem. ASCD, NEA, Nat. Ct. Reporters Assn., Calif. Ct. Reporters Assn., Calif. Tchrs. Assn., North State Ct. Reporters Assn., Reporting Assn. Pub. Schs. Calif. (sec.-treas.). Republican. Office: Butte Coll 3536 Butte Campus Dr Oroville CA 95965-8303

CHAPMAN, KAREN LOUISE, lawyer; b. Denver, Apr. 1, 1954; d. Arthur Alec and Kathleen Joan (Weiss) C.; m. Stuart Donovan Jenkins, June 30, 1984. BS, U. Colo., 1976; JD, Stanford U., 1979. Bar: Colo. 1979, D.C. 1980. Atty. bur. competition FTC, Washington, 1972-82; assoc. Morrison & Foerster, Denver, 1982-84; assoc. Kirkland & Ellis, Denver, 1984-85, ptnr., 1875-94; ptnr. Bartlit Beck Herman Palenchar & Scott, Denver, 1994—. Pres. Stanford Pub. Interest Law Found., Calif., 1978-79. Regents scholar, 1972-73, Boettcher scholar, 1972-76; recipient Wall Street Journal award, 1976. Mem. ABA, D.C. Bar Assn., Colo. Bar Assn. Office: Bartlit Beck Herman 511 16th St Ste 700 Denver CO 80202-4232

CHAPMAN, KATHLEEN HALLORAN, state legislator, lawyer; b. Estherville, Iowa, Jan. 19, 1937; d. Edward E. and Meryl (McConoughey) Halloran; m. Allen Ray Chapman, Apr. 29, 1961; children: Christopher, Stuart. BA, U. Iowa, 1959, JD, 1974. Bar: Iowa 1974, U.S. Ct. Appeals (8th cir.) 1974. Prin. Booth & Chapman, Cedar Rapids, Iowa, 1974—; mem. Iowa Ho. of Reps., Des Moines, 1983-92, vice chmn. judiciary com., 1983-86, vice chmn. ethics com., 1985-88, vice chmn. ways and means com., 1987-88, chmn. rules and adminstrn. com., 1987-88, asst. majority leader, 1989-90, chmn. edn. appropriations, 1991-92; Legis. Coun. Iowa Gen. Assembly, 1987-92; participant Atlantic Exch., 1989. Trustee East Cen. Regional Libr., Cedar Rapids, 1974-80, Tanager Place, Cedar Rapids, 1978—. Toll fellow Coun. State Govts., 1988; named Woman of Yr. Linn County, 1995. Mem. Iowa Bar Assn. (chair adminstrv. law sect. 1995-96). Democrat. Roman Catholic. Office: 425 2d St SE 1010 The Ctr 425 2nd St SE Cedar Rapids IA 52401

CHAPMAN, KRISTIN HEILIG, public relations consultant; b. New Orleans, Nov. 4, 1966; d. Brady Alexander and Margaret Faye (Fisher) Heilig; m. Mark Richard Chapman, Sept. 16, 1989. BA in Journalism and Pub. Rels., Auburn U., 1988. Acct. exec. Ketchum Pub. Rels., Atlanta, 1988-90; mktg. coord. IBM, El Paso, Tex., 1991; v.p. The Randolph Partnership, Atlanta, 1992—. Vol. The Atlanta Project, 1992-94, Jr. League Gwinnett and North Fulton Counties, Duluth, Ga., 1992—. Recipient Gold Touchstone award Am. Hosp. Assn., 1993-94, Gold Flame award Internat. Assn. Bus. Communicators, 1990, 93, 95, Clarion award Women in Comm., 1994. Mem. Pub. Rels. Soc. Am. (com. 1989—, Phoenix award 1990, 91, 92, 93, 94, 95, Silver Anvil award 1994). Republican.

CHAPMAN, LUCY IRENE, secretary, office manager; b. Va., Feb. 7, 1937; d. Isaac Dewey and Margie Almeada (Bobbitt) Spencer; m. Harold Paul Chapman, June 22, 1957; children: Paul, Phillip, Jonathon, Cheerilyn. Student, Columbia Coll., 1953-57. Nurse El Paso, Tex., 1958; artist Danbury, Conn., 1961; nurse Alta Craig Hosp., Ridgefield, Conn., 1962-64; artist West Palm Beach, Fla., 1972-81; real estate agt. Merrill Lynch, Century 21, Brandon, Tampa, Fla., 1984-87, Prudential, Charlotte, N.C., 1987-90; sec. Capitol Asset Mgmt. Corp., Charlotte, N.C., 1990-92, Front Royal, Va., 1992—. Organizer, Christian Womens Clubs, Roanoke, Va., 1970, Bible coord.; den mother Boy Scouts Am. Runner up for Poet Laureate of Fla., 1980. Mem. Garden lub, Shenandoah Writers Club, Kiwanis Club, Calvary Ch. Home: 409 Rogers Mill Rd Strasburg VA 27657 Office: Ste 204 824 John Marshall Hwy Front Royal VA 27630

CHAPMAN, MARY KATHRYN, elementary education educator; b. Birmingham, Ala., May 31, 1958; d. Vincent and Mary Helen (Treadwell) York; m. Jere Clark Chapman, Dec. 18, 1982; children: Lacy Dawn, John Luke. BS in Edn., Auburn U., Montgomery, Ala., 1980, MS, 1982. Cert. tchr., Ala., Tex. Elem. tchr. Fews Elem Sch., Montgomery, 1980-83; elem. tchr., computer rep. Morningview Elem. Sch., Montgomery, 1988-91; tchr. phys. edn. Jackson Elem. Sch., Abilene, Tex., 1983-85, Austin Elem. Sch., Abilene, 1986-87; tchr. W.L. Radney Elem. Sch., Alexander City, Ala., 1991—, tchr. drama, 1991-94, mem. bldg. leadership team, 1994-95; workshop presenter Montgomery Schs., 1990. Sunday sch. and Bible sch. tchr. Alexander City Ch. of Christ, 1991—; adult leader Girl Scouts U.S.A., Alexander City, 1992—; sponsor Alexander City Cheerleaders, 1992. Named Tchr. of Yr., Alexander City Sch., 1993, Alexander City C. of C., 1993; recipient Class Act award Sta. WSFA-TV, Montgomery, 1994. Mem. NEA, Ala. Edn. Assn. Home: 1953 Morningside Dr Alexander City AL 35010 Office: Radney Elem Sch 140 Alison Dr Alexander City AL 35010

CHAPMAN, PAULA ANNE, cultural organization administrator; b. Tiffin, Ohio, Sept. 15, 1960; d. Paul Everett and Mary Virginia (Brosious) Young; m. James Nelson Cook, Sept. 16, 1977 (div. Dec. 1981); children: Nichole Adele, Jessica Theresa, Samantha Rebekah; m. Harry N. Chapman, Dec. 10, 1988. BS in Psychology, Heidelberg Coll., 1982; MA in Polit. Sci., Bowling Green (Ohio) State U., 1987; postgrad., Ball State U., 1994—. Child therapist Sandusky (Ohio) Youth Referral Svc., 1982-83; parole officer State of Ohio, Columbus, 1983-86; dep. dir. Seneca, Sandusky and Wyandot Commn. Mental Health Bd., Tiffin, 1986-87; program dir. WSOS Cmty. Action Commn., Fremont, Ohio, 1987-88; dir. community devel. Seneca Indsl. and Econ. Devel. Corp., Tiffin, 1988-90; exec. dir. Tiffin Area C. of C./Seneca Indsl. & Econ. Devel. Corp., Tiffin, 1988-90; pres. Chapman Cmty. Devel. Cons., Tiffin, 1990-93; dir. devel. St. Francis Health Care Ctr., Green Springs, Ohio, 1993-94, St. Francis Coll., Ft. Wayne, Ind., 1994—; adj. prof. econs. Tiffin U., 1987-94; mem. ednl. adv. bd. Vanguard/Sentinel Vocat. Sch., Fremont, 1989-90; chmn. Tiffin Fair Housing Bd., 1985-90; bd. dirs. Ohio Indsl. Tng. Program, Sandusky, 1988-90, Pvt. Industry Coun., Fremont, Seneca County Revolving Loan Fund, Tiffin; chairperson adv. bd. WSOS. Candidate Seneca County Commr., 1992; docent Ft. Wayne Children's Zoo; active Ft. Wayne Women's Bur.; vol. Legal Svcs. Maumee Valley, Ft. Wayne; mem. fin./devel. com. Ft. Wayne YWCA; mem. mktg. com. Sci. Ctrl., Ft. Wayne; mem. Grad. Ft. Wayne Leadership Works, 1994; vol. house mgr. Ft. Wayne Civic Theatre. Mem. NAFE, Nat. Soc. Fundraising Execs. (mem. N.W. Ind. cluster steering com.), Bus. and Profl. Women's Assn. (Young Career Woman of Yr. 1987, 89), Ft. Wayne C. of C. (mem. VIP com. Ambs. Club), Kiwanis Internat. (mem. Ind. dist. steering com., Iodine Deficiency Disease project, bd. dirs. Ft. Wayne Downtown chpt.). Home: 1721 Woodland Crossing Fort Wayne IN 46825-7228

CHAPMAN, VERA F., realtor, interior designer; b. Vienna, Austria, Feb. 16, 1940; d. Moses and Schifra (Kossowsky) Friedmann; m. Philip Lawrence Chapman, June 14, 1960; 1 child, Avery Spencer. BA, Hunter Coll., 1960; grad., Sch. Interior Design, N.Y.C., 1976. Lic. realtor, N.J. Rsch. asst. WGBH-TV, Boston, 1960, Yeshua Wurzweiler Sch. Social Work, N.Y.C., 1961-65; interior designer, 1974-89; realtor Weichert Realtors, Short Hills, N.J., 1994—. Pres. nat. women's divsn. Albert Einstein Coll. Medicine, N.J., 1989-91, mem. nat. bd., 1990—; co-founder Friends of Cardozo Law Sch., N.Y.C., 1992. Mem. Bd. Realtors Oranges and Maplewood, Met. Women's Golf Assn., Preakness Hills Golf Club. Office: Weichert Realtors 505 Millburn Ave Short Hills NJ 07078

CHAPPELL, BARBARA KELLY, child welfare consultant; b. Columbia, S.C., Oct. 17, 1940; d. Arthur Lee and Katherine (Martin) Kelly; 1 child, Kelly Katherine. BA in English and Edn., U. S.C., 1962, MSW, 1974. Tchr. English, Dept. Edn., Honolulu, 1962-65, Alamo Heights High Sch., San Antonio, 1965-67; caseworker Dept. Social Services, Columbia, S.C., 1969-70; supr. Juvenile Placement and Aftercare, Columbia, 1970-72; child welfare cons. Edna McConnell Clark Found., N.Y.C., 1974-75; dir. Children's Foster Care Rev. Bd. System, Columbia, 1975-85; child welfare cons., 1985-89; adminstr. Dept. Human Resources and Juvenile Svcs., Balt., 1989-92; exec. dir. New Pathways, Inc., Balt., 1992—; lectr. in field. Contbr. articles to profl. jours. Coordinator Child's Rights to Parents, Columbia, 1970-75. Episcopalian. Home and Office: 3215 Girardeau Ave Columbia SC 29204-3314

CHAPPELLE, GLORIA ANN, medical/surgical nurse; b. Newark, Aug. 14, 1948; d. Oceola Clayton and Alberta (Horne) C. Diploma, Orange Meml. Sch. Nursing, 1969; BS, Rutgers U., 1990. Cert. med.-surg. nurse, ANCC. Staff nurse Orange (N.J.) Meml. Hosp., 1969-71; staff nurse, clin. nurse I to clin. nurse II Morristown (N.J.) Meml. Hosp., 1971-89, unit educator, 1989—, tng. coord. patient focused care, 1995; chairperson practice coun. nursing divsn. Shared Governance at Morristown (N.J.) Meml. Hosp., 1990-92. Bd. mem., sec. Mary Queen of All Nations Missionary Alliance, Dover, N.J.; Eucharistic min. St. Margaret's of Scotland, Morristown. Recipient Gov.'s Nursing Merit award N.J. Dept. Health's Nursing Adv. Com., 1992. Mem. ANA, N.J. State Nurses Assn. Office: Morristown Meml Hosp 100 Madison Ave Morristown NJ 07960-6013

CHAPPLE, KAREN VIRGINIA, non-profit administrator; b. Dayton, Ohio, Feb. 16, 1949; d. Milton Summers and Virginia Lee (Chafin) C.; m. Steven Timothy Bower, May 27, 1994; children: Neil, Brook, Avril. BS, U. Tampa, 1971; MA, U. South Fla., 1974. Exec. dir. Epilepsy Found., Tampa, 1977-88; dir. affiliate svcs. Epilepsy Found. Am., Landover, Md., 1988-91; statewide CEO Summit House, Greensboro, N.C., 1991—; bd. dirs., treas. N.C. Cmty. Sentencing Assn., 1992-95; bd. dirs. Take It Upstream, Greensboro, 1996—. Pres. Zonta Club of Tampa, 1985-87; v.p. Dem. Women of Guilford, Greensboro, 1994. Recipient Pres.'s Svc. award Points of Light Found., Washington, 1996, Boss of the Yr. award Greensboro (N.C.) Jaycees, 1996. Mem. Am. Correctional Assn., Am. Probation and Parole Assn., Internat. Cmty. Corrections (state contact 1994). Office: Summit House 612-B West Friendly Greensboro NC 27401

CHAPPUIS, ERICA JEAN, artist; b. Arlington, Va., Feb. 18, 1959; d. Eric John and Jean Catherine (Dingwall) Hall; m. Laurent Bernard Chappuis; 1 child, Merlin. BFA, Carnegie-Mellon U., 1981. Artist, 1981—. One-woman shows include Impact Art Gallery, Grosse Pointe, Mich., 1993, 1995; contbg. artist: Erotic Art by Living Artists, 2d edit., Ency. Living Artists, 6th edit.; represented on-line by Art Comm. Internat., Phila., 1996; represented in numerous pvt. collections; contbr. Paramour mag., Jam Rag mag. Recipient Paxton Travel award, 1980, 1st award of honor Birmingham-Bloomfield Art Assn. Studio: 5545 Radnor Detroit MI 48224

CHAR, CARLENE, writer, publisher, editor; b. Honolulu, Oct. 21, 1954; d. Richard Y. and Betty S.M. (Fo) C. BA in Econs., U. Hawaii, 1977; MA in Bus. Adminstrn., Columbia Pacific U., 1984, PhD in Journalism, 1985, B in Gen. Studies in Computer Sci., Roosevelt U., 1986. Freelance writer, Honolulu, 1982—; editor Computer Book Rev., Honolulu, 1983—; instr. Chaminade U., Honolulu, 1996—.

CHARBONNET, GABRIELLE, writer; b. New Orleans, July 24, 1961; d. J. Arthur and Grace (Raffalovich) C.; m. Barry John Varela, May 5, 1991. BA, Loyola U., 1985. Prodn. asst. Random House, N.Y.C., 1987-88; assoc. editor Daniel Weiss Assocs., Inc., N.Y.C., 1988-89, mng. editor, 1989-93, writer, 1993—. Author: Snakes Are Nothing to Sneeze At, 1990, (adapter) Else-Marie and Her Seven Little Daddies, 1991, Boodil, My Dog, 1992, Tutu Much Ballet, 1994. Mem. DES Action Network. Office: Henry Holt & Co 115 W 18th St 6th Fl New York NY 10011*

CHAREST, GABRIELLE MARYA, educational administrator; b. Westfield, Mass., Jan. 3, 1943; m. Leonard Kenneth Charest, Aug. 21, 1965 (div.); children: Leonard Kenneth Jr., Douglas John. BA, St. Joseph Coll., West Hartford, Conn., 1964; MEd, Westfield State Coll., 1978; EdD, U. Mass., 1996. Cert. tchr., adminstr., Mass., Vt., N.H., Conn. Tchr. French, West Springfield (Mass.) Jr. High Sch., 1964-65, Agawam (Mass.) Jr. High Sch., 1967-69; tchr. French, Latin, Spanish, and English, Agawam High Sch., 1973-81, chmn. dept. fgn. langs., 1981, asst. prin., 1981-95; prin. Springfield (Vt.) H.S., 1996—; mem. adj. faculty Westfield State Coll., 1986—; rsch. asst. U. Mass., Amherst, 1991-92; workshop presenter on mentoring, 1990; chmn. steering com. for re-evaluation by New Eng. Assn. Schs. and Colls., 1986-88; presenter profl. devel. workshops Agawam Pub. Schs., 1992-93, restructuring sys. analysis, 1994, at Huntington , Mass. for Gateway Regional Schs., 1995, Belchertown (Mass.) Schs., 1996. Sec. West Springfield Conservation Commn., 1971-73; mem. Friends West Springfield, Libr., 19990—, Springfield Libr. and Mus., 1994—. Grantee New Eng. Assn. Schs. and Colls., 1991-92. Mem. ASCD, NEA, Nat. Assn. Secondary Sch. Prins., Am. Ednl. Rsch. Assn., Vt. Prins. Assn., Vt. Prins. Acad., New Eng. Native Am. Inst., Phi Delta Kappa. Home: PO Box 594 Springfield VT 05156

CHARKES, SUSAN DIANE, publishing executive; b. Washington, Mar. 14, 1958; d. N. David and Nancy Ellen (Amsterdam) C.; m. Terence Alan Stevick, Apr. 3, 1957; 1 child, Nicholas. BA, U. Chgo., 1979; JD, Columbia U., 1983; MLS, Rutgers U., 1993. Bar: N.Y. 1984, U.S. Dist. Ct. N.J. 1984, U.S. Ct. Appeals (3d cir.) 1984. Law clk. U.S. Ct. Appeals, Newark, 1983-84; assoc. Debevoise & Plimpton, N.Y.C., 1984-88, Christy & Viener, N.Y.C., 1988-92; electronic database analyst AT&T Bell Labs., Murray Hill, N.J., 1993; sr. literature scientist Warner-Lambert Co., Morris Plains, N.J., 1993-96; internet product developer Reed Reference Pub., New Providence, N.J., 1996—. Contbr. articles to profl. publs. Vol. Electronic Info. and Edn. Svc. of N.J., South Orange, N.J., 1993—. Mem. Spl. Librs. Assn. (pres.-elect N.J. chpt. 1996—). Office: Reed Reference Pub 121 Chanlon Rd New Providence NJ 07974

CHARLES, BLANCHE, retired elementary education educator; b. Spartanburg, S.C., Aug. 7, 1912; d. Franklin Grady and Alice Florida (Hatchette) C. BA, Humboldt State U., 1934; adminstrv. cert., U. So. Calif., 1940. Tchr. Jefferson Elem. Sch., Calexico (Calif) Unified Sch. Dist., 1958-94; libr. Calexico Pub. Libr., El Centro Pub. Libr. Elem. sch. named in her honor, 1987. Mem. NEA, ACT, Calif. Tchrs. Assn., Nat. Soc. DAR, Nat. Soc. Daus. of Confederacy, Delta Kappa Gamma. Home: 37133 Hwy 94 Campo CA 91906-2809

CHARLES, ISABEL, university administrator; b. Bklyn., Mar. 10, 1926; d. James Patrick and Isabel (Roney) C. B.A., Manhattan Coll., 1954; M.A., U. Notre Dame, 1960, Ph.D., 1965; postgrad., U. Mich., 1968-69. Chmn. dept. English Bishop Watterson High Sch., Columbus, Ohio, 1954-59, St. Mary of the Springs Acad., Columbus, 1959-62; asst. prof. English Ohio Dominican Coll., Columbus, 1965-68; acad. dean, exec. v.p. Ohio Dominican Coll., 1969-73; asst. dean Coll. Arts and Letters, U. Notre Dame, 1973-75, acting dean, 1975, dean, 1976-82, asst. provost, 1982-87, assoc. provost, 1987-95; assoc. provost emerita U. Notre Dame, 1995—. Contbr. articles to profl. jours. Mem. MLA, Assn. Am. Colls. Home: 1802 Stonehedge Ln South Bend IN 46614-6341

CHARLES, MARY LOUISE, newspaper columnist, photographer, editor; b. L.A., Jan. 24, 1922; d. Louis Edward and Mabel Inez (Lyon) Kusel; m. Henry Loewy Charles, June 19, 1946; children: Susan, Henry, Robert, Carol. AA, L.A. City Coll., 1941; BA, San Jose (Calif.) State U., 1964. Salesperson Bullock's, L.A., 1940-42, Roos Bros., Berkeley, Calif., 1945-46; ptnr. Charles-Martin Motors, Marysville, Calif., 1950-54; farm editor Indep. Herald, Yuba City, Calif., 1954-55; social worker Sutter County, Yuba City, 1955-57; social worker Santa Clara County, San Jose, 1957-61, manual coordinator, 1961-73, community planning specialist, 1973-81; columnist Sr. Grapevine various weekly newspapers, Santa Clara County, 1981-86; editor Bay area Sr. Spectrum Newspapers, Santa Clara, 1986-90; columnist, 1990-94; columnist Santa Clara Valley edit. Senior Mag., 1994-95; columnist San Jose Mercury News, 1994—, Prime Times Monthly Mag. (now Prime Monthly), 1994—; founder, pres. Triple-A Coun. Calif., 1978-80. Vice chmn. Santa Clara County Sr. Care Commn., 1987-89, chmn., 1989-91, mem. social svcs. com., 1993—; mem. adv. coun. Coun. on Aging of Santa Clara County, 1995—; mem. aging and disabled adv. com. Met. Transp. Agy., 1995—. With WAVES, USNR, 1942-45. Recipient Social Welfare award Daniel E. Koshland Found., 1973, Friends of Santa Clara County Human Rels. Commn. award, 1992, first ann. Angelina Aguilar Yates Humanitarian award, 1995; named 24th State Assembly Dist. Woman of Yr., 1990. Mem. NASW, LWV (San Jose/Santa Clara Bd. 1993-96, Bay Area bd. transp. chmn. 1996), Nat. Coun. Sr. Citizens (bd. dirs. 1988—), Svc. Employees Internat. Union (mem. local 535, state exec. bd. dirs. 1973—, pres. sr. mems. and retiree chpt. 1982—), Congress of Calif. Srs. (bd. dirs. 1987—, region IV pres. 1992—, trustee 1993—), Older Women's League (bd. dirs. 1980-84), Older Women's League of Calif. (edn./resource coord. 1987-89, pres. 1990-91, Golden Owl award 1995), Am. Soc. on Aging (co-chair women's concerns com. 1985-86, awards com. 1990-93), Nat. Coun. on the Aging, Calif. Specialists on Aging (treas. 1985-93), Calif. Srs. Coalition (chmn. 1986, treas. 1993—), Calif. Writers Club (cen. bd. dels. 1995—). Home and Office: 2527 Forbes Ave Santa Clara CA 95050-5547

CHARLES, SALLY ALLEN, real estate company executive; b. Atlanta, Jan. 9, 1950; d. Thomas Roach Jr. and Lucille (Blake) Allen; m. Darrell Charles, Dec. 28, 1974; children: Carey Robert, Jane Allen. BA in Speech Comm., Auburn U., 1972; MBA, Kennesaw State U., 1989. Sect. editor, writer Campus Crusade for Christ, San Bernardino, Calif., 1972-74; staff writer, photographer The Cherokee Tribune, Canton, Ga., 1984-86; dir. mktg. Citizens Bank, Ball Ground, Ga., 1986-89; cons. Small Bus. Devel. Ctr. Kennesaw (Ga.) State U., 1990-96, dir. Small Bus. Inst., 1992-96; v.p. Purchasers Rep., Atlanta, 1996—; adj. faculty dept. mgmt. and entrepreneurship Kennesaw State U., 1991-94; chmn. Cobb County Seminar on Employer Sponsored Child Care, Kennesaw, 1992; preliminary judge Small Bus./Family Bus. of the Yr., Kennesaw State U. Family Bus. Forum, 1993; mem. small bus. adv. coun. Apple Computers, Napa Valley, Calif., 1994. Editor: (assn. newsletter) The Momentum, 1995—; reviewer Jour. of Strategy Small Bus., 1996—. Press credentials chair Woodstock (Ga.) Welcome for Pres. and Mrs. George Bush, 1992; spkr., instr. annual tng. Ga. Soc. CPA's, Atlanta, 1993; spkr. Interfedn. Chinese Students and Scholars, Chapel Hill, N.C., 1994; advisor facilities Kappa Alpha Theta, Emory U., Atlanta, 1994—. Recipient Best Writing award for Weekly Paper, Ga. Cancer Soc., Atlanta, 1985; named Outstanding Young Citizen, Woodstock (Ga.) Jaycees, 1985, Small Bus. Inst. Cases of the Yr., Ga.-U.S. Small Bus. Adminstrn., Atlanta, 1992, 93, 95; Small Bus. Inst. grantee U.S. Small Bus. Adminstrn., Washington and Atlanta, 1991-95. Mem. Small Bus. Inst. Dirs. Assn. (adv. com. 1994-96, newsletter editor 1995—, coord. new dir. tng. 1995, v.p. 1996, Showcase award 1994), Inst. Mgmt. Cons., Sales and Mktg. Execs., Kappa Alpha Theta (asst. treas. 1993). Republican. Baptist. Home: 530 Dogwood Hills Ln Alpharetta GA 30201 Office: Purchasers Rep Ste 3B 350 Northridge Rd Atlanta GA 30350

CHARLESWORTH, MARION HOYEN, secondary education educator; b. Lowell, Mass.; d. Francis Emmanuel and Elizabeth (Donabed) Hoyen; A.A. in Acctg. summa cum laude, Worcester Jr. Coll., 1950; B.A. in English cum laude, Worcester State Coll., 1976; m. Donald W. Charlesworth, Sept. 7, 1952 (dec. May 24, 1974); 1 son, Donald W. Jr. Office mgr. Worcester Shoe Co. (Mass.), 1945-46; asst. fin. sec. YMCA Worcester, 1946-56; substitute tchr. Haverhill High Sch. (Mass.), 1965—, tchr. acctg., evening div. Haverhill High Sch., 1979-85, tchr. English evening divsn., 1985-89. Vol. clk. Haverhill Pub. Library Fund Raising, 1966-69, vol. pub. libr. gift shop, 1989-91; mem. Haverhill Skating Rink Com., 1969-70; vol. Merrimack Wastewater Mgmt. Study, U.S.C.E., Commonwealth of Mass. and Merrimack Valley Planning Commn. in cooperating with EPA, 1973-75; vol. Haverhill Recycling, 1971-75, Haverhill Cmty. meals, 1983—; vol. hostess USO, 1941-52; fin. sec. 1st Presbyterian Ch., Worcester, 1942-46; sec. Planetary Minds, Worcester YWCA, 1951, treas. Bus. and Profl. Girls, 1951; deacon First Congregational Ch., Haverhill, 1967-70, 74-75, 81-83, mem. outreach com., 1978-81, auditor women's guild, 1987—; bd. dirs. Steven-Bennett Home, Inc., Haverhill, 1977 , Winnekenni Found., Inc., 1977—, sec. 1991-93; vol. USD Ctr., Worcester, Mass., WWII; bd. dirs. Children's Aid and Family Soc. of Haverhill, 1987—, clk. of bd., 1992-93; mem. Hale Hosp. Aux., Haverhill, 1971—, Haverhill Growth Alliance, 1979-82, Haverhill Neighborhood Coalition, 1979-82, Friends of Haverhill Pub. Libr., 1979—, vol., 1989-91, Merrimack River Watershed Council, 1980—, Northeast Cultural Arts Ctr., 1982-93; charter mem. Statue of Liberty Ellis Island Found., 1984—; mem. Widowed Life Line Program Affiliate Children's Aid and Family Soc., 1974-88, vol., 1983-88. Mem. NAM, Mature Students Orgn. (chmn. parliamentary procedure 1974), Haverhill Parent Tchr. Assns. (exec. bd. 1964-71); pres. Caleb Dustin Hunking PTA, 1968-71; Mass. Congress PTA, Tau Lambda Omega (sec. 1950-52). Clubs: Haverhill Garden (pres. 1973-75, chmn. pub. relations 1972-84, dir. 1975-82), Women's City of Haverhill (2d v.p. 1971-73, life mem. 1985); Assyrian-Am. Ind. (treas. 1948-72) (Worcester). Mass. reporter The Assyrian Star, 1963-64. Recipient Cert. appreciation Haverhill Kiwanis Club, 1986, Citation Commonwealth of Mass. State Senate, 1988. Instrumental while club pres. in numerous awards being bestowed on Haverhill Garden Club, including regional, state and nat. awards, 1979, also nat. publicity award from Nat. Council of State Garden Clubs and Sperry and Hutchinson Co., 1979, 80. Home: 35 Columbia Park Haverhill MA 01830-3303

CHARLETON, MARGARET ANN, child care administrator, consultant; b. Orange, Calif., Aug. 3, 1947; d. Arthur Mitchell and Isabelle Margaret (Esser) C.; (div. Sept. 1985). AA in Liberal Arts, Orange Coast Coll., 1968; BA in Psychology, Chapman Coll., 1984. Head tchr. Presbyn. Ch. of the Master, Mission Viejo, Calif., 1977-81; child care program adminstr. Crystal Stairs, Inc., L.A., 1981—; mem. adv. bd. Children's Home Soc., Santa Ana, Calif., 1982-83; cons. Calif. Sch. Age Consortium, Coast Mesa, 1987, Calif. State Dept. of Edn., 1988; trainer preschool edn. program Sesame Street PBS, 1994-96; lectr. in field. Contbr. articles to profl. jours. Mem. South Orange County Community Svc., Mission Viejo, 1983—; liaison Family Svcs.-Marine Base, El Toro, Calif., 1989—. Recipient Plaque of Recognition, Vietnamese Community of Orange County, 1984. Mem. NAFE. Roman Catholic. Office: Crystal Stairs Inc 5105 W Goldleaf Cir Ste 200 Los Angeles CA 90056-1272

CHARLEY, NANCY JEAN, communications professional; b. LaCrosse, Wis., Jan. 6, 1956. A in Bus. Adminstrn., Midway Coll., 1992, A in Computer Info. Systems, 1993, BBA, 1994, postgrad. Office mgr. for neurologist, Lexington, Ky., 1985-88; health unit coord. acute care hosp., Lexington, 1979-91, health unit coord. trainer, 1992-93, coord. order comms., order mgmt. trainer mgmt. info. system, 1988-95; system support analyst Mgmt. Info. Systems, 1994-96, sys. support analyst, patient auditor trainer, 1996—; freelance cons. Mem. Nat. Assn. Health Unit Coords. (support cons. 1990, edn. bd. 1990-95, chmn. continuing edn. com. 1991-93, mem. several ad hoc coms.), Midway Coll. Alumnae Assn. Office: Baptist Healthcare Systems 4007 Kresge Way Louisville KY 40207-4604

CHARLTON, BETTY JO, retired state legislator; b. Reno County, Kans., June 15, 1923; d. Joseph and Elma (Johnson) Canning; BA, U. Kans., 1970, MA, 1976; m. Robert Sansom Charlton, Feb. 24, 1946 (dec. 1984); children: John Robert, Richard Bruce. Asst. instr. polit. sci. and western civilization U. Kans., Lawrence, 1970-73; legis. adminstrv. svcs. employee State of Kans., Topeka, 1977-78, legis. aide gov's. office, 1979; mem. Kans. Ho. of Reps., 1980-95, ret., 1995.

CHARMOLI, MARGARET CHARITY, psychologist; b. Virginia, Minn., Dec. 8, 1951; d. Arnold Amadeo and Orvokki Katri (Harju) C. BA, Macalester Coll., 1974; MA, U. Minn., 1979, PhD, 1986. Lic. psychologist, Minn.; lic. marriage and family therapist, Minn. Adminstrv. intern Ramsey County Adminstrs. Office, St. Paul, 1974-76; adminstrv. asst. Ramsey County Comty. Human Svcs. Dept., St. Paul, 1976-82; grad. asst. Pers. Decisions, Inc., Mpls., 1980-85; counselor Office Students with Disabilities,

U. Minn., Mpls., 1982-85, Vocat. Assessment Clinic, Mpls., 1984-86; psychologist employee asst. program Met. Clin. Counseling, Mpls., 1985-86, psychologist, 1986-88; psychologist Maplewood (Minn.) Psychol. Assocs., 1988— Bd. dirs. Neighborhood Health Clincs, St. Paul, 1974-78, Ramsey Action Programs, St. Paul, 1975-76; mem. adv. com. Exodus, Inc., St. Paul, 1977-78; pres. Family Tree Health Clinic, St. Paul, 1977-78; appointments chair Ramsey County Women's Polit. Caucus, St. Paul, 1978-80, co-chair, 1980-81; vice chair Equal Opportunities Coalition, St. Paul, 1981-83; mem. blue ribbon task force on affirmative action St. Paul Mayor's Office, 1981; founder, chair Rainbow Forum, St. Paul, 1994-95; active St. Paul Human Rights Commn., 1980-89. Recipient Recognition of Svc. award Ramsey Action Programs, 1975, City of St. Paul, 1983, 85, Senator Nicholas Coleman Meml. Svc. award St. Paul Gay and Lesbian Communities, 1985, Vol. Recognition cert. State of Minn., 1986, Svc. award St. Paul Human Rights Commn., 1989. Mem. APA, Minn. Womens Psychologists (mem. steering com. 1986-88, 93-96, 1st Ann. Rsch. award 1984), Minn. Psychol. Assn. (mem. ann. meeting com. 1983-84, 93-96, chair ann. meeting 1994, mem. APA rep. to task force on psychology and the handicapped 1983-86, mem. exec. coun. 1994—, pres.-elect 1995, pres. 1996), Minn. Soc. Clin. Hypnosis, Minn. Coun. Sexual Addiction/Compulsivity (bd. dirs. 1995-96), Phi Kappa Phi. Home: 1870 Roblyn Ave Saint Paul MN 55104-3504

CHARNIN, JADE HOBSON, magazine executive; b. N.Y.C., Mar. 12, 1945; d. John Louis Campo and Elizabeth (Anne) Stanton; m. David Alan Hobson, Dec. 30 (div. 1972); m. Martin Charnin, Dec. 18, 1984. BA, NYU, 1967. Asst. editor Glamour mag., N.Y.C., 1970; accessory editor Vogue mag., N.Y.C., 1970-78, fashion editor, 1978-81, fashion dir., 1981-86, creative dir. fashion, 1987-88; v.p., dir. creative svcs. for fashion and design group Revlon, Inc., 1988; exec. creative dir. Mirabella Mag., 1988-94; fashion dir., N.Y. Mag., 1994—; cons. editor Self mag., N.Y.C., 1979-81. Costumer coord. for off broadway shows Laughing Matters, 1989, Martin Charnin, the Hits and the M.S.'s, 1990. Mem. NAFE, ASPCA, Am. Horticultural Soc., Nat. Mus. Women in the Arts, Horticultural Soc. N.Y. (bd. dirs.), Internat. Platform Assn., Humane Soc. (mem. pres.'s adv. bd. of N.Y.), Animal Protection Inst. Democrat. Avocations: gardening, opera, ballet, theater, skiing. Office: NY Mag 755 2nd Ave New York NY 10017-5906

CHARPENTIER, GAIL WIGUTOW, private school executive director; b. N.Y.C., Mar. 10, 1946; d. Jacob M. and Ethel (Israel) Wigutow; m. Peter Jon Charpentier; children: Elisabeth Marie, Matthew Kyle. BA, CUNY, 1967; MA, New Sch. Social Research, N.Y.C., 1976. Lic. social worker; cert. adminstr. of spl. edn. Tchr. Spl. Service Pub. Sch., Bronx, N.Y., 1967-73; adminstr. Boston City Hosp., 1973-76; dir. Monson Devel. Ctr., Palmer, Mass., 1976; residential dir. Kolburne Sch., New Marlboro, Mass., 1976-79; exec. dir. Berkshire Meadows, Housatonic, Mass., 1979—; researcher Nat. Opinion Research Ctr., N.Y.C. and Boston, 1973-76; trainer residential child care, Mass., 1978—; mem. human rights bd. Oakdale Found., Great Barrington, Mass., 1980—. Recipient Community Criminal Justice award Justice Resource Inst., 1984. Mem. NAFE, Am. Assn. Mental Retardation, Mass. Assn. Approved Pvt. Schs. (bd. dirs. 1982-84, ins. trustee 1984-87, svc. award 1982), New Eng. Assn. for Child Care, Internat. Assn. for Retts Syndrome, Berkshire Profl. Women, Hop Brook Club (pres.). Home: Orchard House PO Box 406 Tyringham MA 01264-0406 Office: Berkshire Meadows 249 N Plain Rd Housatonic MA 01236-9736

CHARTERS, KAREN ANN ELLIOTT, critical care nurse, health facility administrator; b. Chelsea, Mass., Apr. 3, 1946; d. Albert Charles and Hazelle Marie (Kraus) Elliott; m. Byron James Charters, Feb. 4, 1972. Diploma, Grace New Haven Sch. Nursing, New Haven, Conn., 1967; student, So. Conn. State Coll., 1968, U. New Haven, 1974, St. Leo Coll., 1988—. Cert. CCRN. Asst. head nurse Yale New Haven (Conn.) Hosp., 1972-76; staff nurse critical care unit Hosp. Corp. Am., 1982—; relief clin. coord. Columbia New Port Richey (Fla.) Hosp., 1987—. Mem. AACN (bd. dirs. Gulf Coast chpt. 1990-91, treas. 1991-93), Am. Heart Assn. (past bd. dirs.). Home: 13318 Hillwood Cir Hudson FL 34667-1421 Office: Col New Port Richey Hosp 5637 Marine Pkwy New Port Richey FL 34653

CHARTIER, JANELLEN OLSEN, airline service coordinator; b. Chgo., Sept. 12, 1951; d. Roger Carl and Genevieve Ann (McCormick) Olsen; m. Lionel Pierre-Paul Chartier, Nov. 6, 1982; 1 child, Régine Anne. B.A. in French and Home Econs., U. Ill., 1973, M.A. in Teaching French, 1974; student U. Rouen (France), 1971-72. Cert. tchr., Ill. Flight attendant Delta Airlines, Atlanta, 1974—, French qualified, 1974—, Spanish qualified, 1977-82, German qualified, 1980—, in-flight svc. coord., 1980—, European in flight svc. coord., 1983—; French examiner In-Flight Svc., 1984-95; interpreter Formax, Inc., Mokena, Ill., 1976-82; staff interpreter Acad. Legal and Tech. Translation, Ltd., 1991—, part time instr. French Northea. Ill. U., 1995—. Bd. dirs. One Plus One Dance Co., Champaign, Ill., 1977-78. Mem. Am. Assn. of tchrs. of French, NAFE, Alliance Maison Francaise de Chgo., Phi Delta Kappa, Alpha Lambda Delta. Roman Catholic. Home: 155 N Harbor Dr Apt 3506 Chicago IL 60601-7323

CHASANOW, DEBORAH K., federal judge; b. 1948. BA, RUtgers U., 1970; JD, Stanford U., 1973. Pvt. practice atty. COle & Groner, Washington, 1975; asst. atty. gen. State of Md., 1975-79; chief criminal appeals divsn. Md. Atty. Gen.'s Office, 1979-87; U.S. magistrate judge U.S. Dist. Ct. Md., 1987-93, dist. judge, 1993—; instr. law schs. U. Balt., U. Md., 1978-84. Mem. Fed. Magistrate Judges Assn., Md. Bar Assn., Prince George's County Bar Assn., Montgomery County Bar Assn., Women's Bar Assn., Marlborough Am. Inn. Ct. (pres. 1988=90), Wrangler's Law Club, Phi Beta Kappa. Office: US Courthouse 6500 Cherrywood Ln Rm 465A Greenbelt MD 20770-1249*

CHASE, ALYSSA A., editor; b. New Orleans, Dec. 23, 1965; d. John Churchill and Alexandra Andra (de Monsabert) C.; m. Robert Brian Rebein, July 1, 1995. BA in Lit. in English, U. Kans., 1988; BA in Studio Art magna cum laude, SUNY, Buffalo, 1994. Asst. editor Dial Books for Young Readers, N.Y.C., 1989-90; assoc. editor Holiday House, Inc., N.Y.C., 1990-92, Buffalo Spree Mag., Buffalo, N.Y., 1992-95; copy editor, writer The Riverfront Times, St. Louis, Mo., 1995—; freelance copy writer, proofreader, copy editor and/or rschr. Harper Collins Children's Books, N.Y.C., 1990-92, Morrow Jr. Books, N.Y.C., 1990-92, Tambourine Books, N.Y.C., 1990-92, Lothrop, Lee & Shepherd Books, N.Y.C., 1990-92, Dorling Kindersley, Inc., N.Y.C., 1990-92, The Humanist: Prometheus Books, 1993, Printing Prep, Buffalo, 1994, Georgette Hasiotis, Buffalo, 1994, August Tavern Creek Developers, St. Louis, 1996; tchg. artist, docent coord., tour guide The Arts in Edn. Inst. of Western N.Y., Cheektowaga, N.Y., 1995. Mem. Phi Beta Kappa. Home: 7130 Dartmouth Ave University City MO 63130

CHASE, BETH ELAINE, mental health counselor, artist; b. Camp Hill, Pa., Dec. 3, 1969; d. Robert O'Neil Anderson and Clarice Elaine (Hughes) Cooper; m. Joey Ray Chase, June 4, 1993. BA, Messiah Coll., 1992; MS, Shippensburg U., 1995. Cert. Nat. Counselor. Youth counselor United Meth. Home For Children, Mechanicsburg, Pa., 1992-93; mental health counselor Capital Area Pregnancy Ctr., Camp Hill, 1992—, Mazzitti & Sullivan EAP and Counseling Svcs., Hummelstown, Pa., 1994—. Mem. Am. Counseling Assoc., Pa. Counseling Assoc. Republican. Home: 5120 Simpson Ferry Rd Mechanicsburg PA 17055 Office: Mazzitti & Sullivan Couns Ste 3 1305 Middletown Rd Hummelstown PA 17036

CHASE, DORIS TOTTEN, sculptor, video artist, filmmaker; b. Seattle, 1923; d. William Phelps and Helen (Feeney) Totten; m. Elmo Chase, Oct. 20, 1943 (div. 1972); children: Gregory Totten, Randall Jarvis Totten. Student, U. Wash., 1941-43. lectr. tours for USIA in S.Am., 1975, Europe, 1978, India, 1972, Australia, 1986, Eastern Europe, 1987; vis. lectr., presenter U. Colo., Boulder, Mary Mount Coll., N.Y., the Kitchen Ctr. for Film & Video, Nat. Film Bd. of Can., Toronto, N.Y. Grad. Sch. One-woman shows include Seligmann Gallery, Seattle, 1959, 61, Gallery Numero, Florence, Italy, 1961, Internat. Gallery, Italy, 1962, Hall Coleman Gallery, Seattle, 1962, Gallery Numero, Rome, 1962, 66, Formes Gallery, Tokyo, 1963, 70, Bangkok Ctr. Mus., Thailand, 1963, Bolles Gallery, San Francisco, 1964, Collectors Gallery, Seattle, 1964, 66, 69, Suffolk (N.Y.) Mus., 1965, Smolin Gallery, N.Y.C., 1965, Tacoma Art Mus., 1967, Ruth White Gallery, N.Y.C., 1967, 69, 70, Fountain Gallery, Portland, Oreg., 1970, U. Wash. Henry Gallery, 1971, 77, Wadsworth Athenum, Hartford, Conn., 1973, Hirshhorn Mus., Washington, 1974, 77, Anthology Film Archives, N.Y.C., 1975, 80, 83, Donnell Libr., N.Y.C., 1976, 79, 83, 92, Performing Arts Mus. at Lincoln Ctr., 1976, Mus. Modern Art, N.Y.C., 1978, 80, 87, 93, High Mus., Atlanta, 1978, Herbert Johnson Mus., 1982, A.I.R. Gallery, N.Y.C., 1983-85, Art in Embassies, USIS, 1984-88, Inst. Contemporary Art, London, 1989, Woodside/Braseth Gallery, 1990, 92, John F. Kennedy Ctr., 1990, Seattle Arts Mus., 1990, 92, 95, Mus. N.W. Art La Conner Wash., 1995; circulating exhibit Western Mus. Assn., 1970-71, Am. Inst. Archs., Seattle, 1994; represented in permanent collections Finch Coll. Mus., N.Y.C., Mus. Modern Art, N.Y.C., Seattle Art Mus., Ashai Shimbum, Tokyo, Georges Pompidou Ctr., Paris, Battelle Inst., Mus. Fine Arts Boston, Milw. Art Inst., Art Inst. Chgo., Mus. Fine Arts Houston, Frye Art Mus., Seattle, Nat. Collection Fine Arts, Smithsonian Instn., Washington, Wadsworth Athenum, N.C. Mus. Art, Raleigh, Mus. Modern Art, Kobe, Japan, Pa. Acad. Art, Phila., Portland Art Mus., Vancouver (B.C.) Art Gallery, Montgomery (Ala.) Mus. Fine Art, Hudson River Mus., N.Y.C., Tacoma Art Mus.; works represented in archival collections Ctr. for Film and Theatre Rsch., U. Wis., Madison, U. Wash., Seattle; works reproduced in various art mags. & books; executed monumental kinetic sculpture Kerry Park, Seattle, Anderson, Ind., Expo '70, Osaka, Japan, Sculpture Park, Atlanta, Lake Park, Ind., Met. Mus. Art, N.Y.C., Montgomery Mus. Fine Arts, Seattle Ctr. Theater; multi-media sculpture for 4 ballets, Opera Assn. Seattle; included in Sculpture in Park program N.Y.C., Playground of Tomorrow ABC-TV, L.A.; work in video TV Exptl. Lab., Sta. WNET-TV; TV prodn. Lies, 1980, Window, 1980; Doris Chase Dance Series produced at Bklyn. Coll., U. Mich., Ann Arbor, Sta. RTSI-TV, Switzerland, Sta. WCET-Cin., Sta. WGBH-TV, Boston, Sta. WNYC, N.Y.C., NET; prodr. Doris Chase Dance Series, 1971-81, Concept Series, 1980-84; prodr. By Herself Series: Table for One (with Geraldine Page), 1985, (with Anne Jackson) Dear Papa, 1986, (with Luise Rainer) A Dancer, 1987, (with Priscilla Pointer) Still Frame, 1988, (with Joan Plowright) Sophie, 1989, The Chelsea, 1994. Recipient honors and awards at numerous festivals in U.S. and fgn. countries; grantee Nat. Endowment for Arts, Seattle Arts Commn., Am. Film Inst., 1988, N.Y. State Coun. for Arts, Mich. Arts Coun., Seattle Art Commn., 1992, Jerusalem Film Festival, 1987, Berlin Film Festival, 1985, 87, Athens Film Festival, 1995, London Film Festival, 1986, Am. Film Inst. Festival, 1987, 94, Retirement Rsch. Found., 1994; subject of documentary Doris Chase: Portrait of the Artist, PBS, 1985, book & video Doris Chase: Artist in Motion (by Patricia Failing), 1992; recipient Wash. Gov.'s Art award, 1992. Mem. Actors Studio (writer, dirs. wing 1986). Address: Chelsea Hotel 222 W 23rd St New York NY 10011-2301

CHASE, GAIL, retired fine art photographer; b. Seattle, Apr. 10, 1929; d. Charles Eugene and Geraldine (Smithson) Matheus; m. Keith Chase, May 11, 1950; children: Su, Cathy, Charles, Cammi. Student, The Annie Wright Sch., 1943-47, Mills Coll., 1947-48, U. Wash., 1948-50. Owner Gail Chase Gallery, Bellevue, Wash., 1969-83; freelance photgrapher Bellevue, 1989-95. Author: The Eye and The Eyebrow, 1989; one-person shows Benham Gallery, 1992, 94, Cunningham Gallery, 1993, Safeco, 1994, numerous others; group shows include Am. Craft Gallery, 1991, Erector Square Gallery, 1991, Art 54 Gallery, 1992, Kansas City Miss., 1992, Bellevue Art Mus., 1994, 95; represented in collections at Palmer Mus. Pa. State U., Am. Embassy, Istanbul, Marlboro Corp. Home: 9901 NE 4th St #4 Bellevue WA 98004

CHASE, JEAN COX, retired English educator; b. Charlottesville, Va., July 2, 1925; d. Joseph Lee and Wirt (Davidson) Cox; m. John Bryant Chase Jr., June 16, 1951 (dec. June 1978); children: Nancy Davidson Chase, Jean Cox Chase. BA magna cum laude, U. N.C. Woman's Coll., 1946; MA in Eng. Lang. and Lit., U. Mich., 1947; postgrad., U. Va., 1950, 53, various univs. Cert. tchr., Va., N.C. Instr. English Carroll Coll., Waukesha, Wis., 1947-49, housemother, 1948-49; teaching asst. English U. Wis., Madison, 1949; editorial proof reader Michie Legal Publs., Charlottesville, Va., 1951; tchr. of English and Latin Lane High Sch., Charlottesville, Va., 1950-53; critic tchr. for sch. edn. in English U. Va., Charlottesville, Va., 1951; tutor Chapel Hill, N.C., 1958-66; teaching English, gifted, remedial Jordan High Sch., Durham, N.C., 1966; tchr. English Orange County High Sch., Hillsborough, N.C., 1966-67; instr. Cen. Piedmont Community Coll., Charlotte, N.C., 1970-87; co-chmn. fall faculty conf., Cen. Piedmont Community Coll., 1974, vice-chmn. faculty senate, 1976-77, chmn., 1977-78, chmn. writing across the curriculum, 1980-84 and others; judge Charlotte Writers Club Contest, 1984. Co-editor, author: The Communication Course, 1974; contbg. author, The Jane Doe Papers, 1977, Women of Mecklenburg: Making a Difference, 1980. Active N.C. state legis. coun., N.C. Coun. Women's Orgns., World Affairs Conf. Planning Com., Univ. League, Jr. Svc. League, Creative Retirement Hilton Head, Dem. Party of Hilton Head, others; vol. English, Latin tutor. Recipient scholarship U. Mich., Ann Arbor, 1946-47, fellowship Nat. Endowment for Humanities, Carnegie Mellon Univ., Pitts., 1981. Mem. MLA, AAUW (various offices, coms. Hilton Head br.), Nat. Coun. Tchrs. English, Great Books Study Group, Opera Guild Study Group, Daus. of the King (life), Phi Beta Kappa, Kappa Delta Pi, Chi Omega (advisor local chpt. 1959-69), others. Episcopalian. Home: 300 Wood Haven Dr Apt 3405 Hilton Head Island SC 29928-7516

CHASE, JOAN B., psychologist; b. N.Y.C., June 11, 1936; d. Noah and Anne (Witkin) C. BS, CCNY, 1959; EdD, Rutgers U., 1968. Lic. psychologist N.J., Fla.; registered psychologist Ont., Can. Edn. counselor NJ Commn. for the Blind, Newark, 1959-66; rsch. assoc. SUNY Downstate Med. Ctr., Bklyn., 1966-70; assoc. prof. UMDNJ - Robert Wood Johnson Med. Sch., Piscataway, 1971-93; cons. Ctr. for Mental Health, Tampa, 1993—; instr. Jersey City State Coll., 1966-70; assoc. prof. U. Tex., Austin, 1969-70; asst. prof. Hunter Coll. CUNY, 1967-71; course writer, instr. Hadley Sch. for the Blind, Winnetka, Ill., 1993—; clin. coord. Youth Support Project U. South Fla., Tampa, 1996—; adj. assoc. prof. Rutgers U., New Brunswick, N.J., 1972-92, adj. faculty Nova Southeastern U.; cons. psychologist N.J. Commn. for the Blind, Newark, 1967-95, W. Ross MacDonald Sch., Brantford, Ont., Can., 1986-90, Cerebral Palsy of Middlesex, Edison, N.J., 1968-86. Author: Retrolental Fibroplasia, 1972. Profl. adv. bd. ARC Somerset, Manville, N.J., 1974-92. Grantee U.S. Dept. Health & Human Svcs., 1984-91. Mem. APA, AAUP (v.p., chair com. 1985-92), Assn. for Edn. & Rehab. of the Blind and Visually Impaired, Nat. Assn. Sch. Psychologists, Coun. for Exceptional Children. Home: 2598 Gary Circle #504 Dunedin FL 34698 Office: Youth Support Project Univ South Florida 8620 N Dixon Ave Tampa FL 33604

CHASE, KAREN HUMPHREY, educator; b. New Bedford, Mass., Nov. 17, 1948; d. Clifton Humphrey and Alice (Duffy) C. BA in Sociology, Stonehill Coll., 1970. Cert. tchr. K-8, Mass. Tchr., grade 3 Minot (Maine) Consold. Sch., 1970-72; tchr. grade 6 social studies George R. Austin Mid. Sch., Lakeville, Mass., 1972—; dept. leader social studies, Austin Mid. Sch., Lakeville, 1976-80; supt. search team Freetown-Lakeville Sch. Dist., 1995. Actor/dir.: Your Theatre, Inc. New Bedford, Mass., 1985—; mem. Sippican Lands Trust, Marion, Mass., Marion Arts Ctr., 1973—; 2nd v.p. Educators Assn. Freetown-Lakeville, 1991—. Named Young Careerist of Yr., Bus. and Profl. Women, Wareham, Mass., 1979. Mem. Plymouth County Educators Assn. (Significant Svc. Honor award 1995), Mass. Tchrs. Assn., NEA, Nat. Coun. for Social Studies. Home: 62 Converse Rd Marion MA 02738 Office: George R Austin Mid Sch 112 Howland Rd Lakeville MA 02347

CHASE, KAREN SUSAN, English literature educator; b. St. Louis, Oct. 16, 1952; d. Stanley Martin and Judith C.; m. Michael H. Levenson, Dec. 30, 1984; children: Alexander Nathan, Sarah Sophie. BA, UCLA, 1974; MA, Stanford U., 1977, PhD, 1980. Asst. prof. U. Va., Charlottesville, 1979-85, assoc. prof., 1985-91, prof., 1992—. Author: Eros and Psyche, 1984, George Eliot's Middlemarch, 1990; co-editor: Victorian Culture and Literature Series. Office: Univ of Va English Department 219 Bryan Hall Charlottesville VA 22903

CHASE, MARIA ELAINE GAROUFALIS, publishing company executive; b. Chgo., Jan. 9, 1957; d. Byron L. and Irene (Mathews) Garoufalis. BS, Manchester Coll., 1979. CPA, Ill. Sr. mgr. Ernst & Young, Chgo., 1979-92; contr., v.p. fin. Fox Valley Press, Inc., Plainfield, Ill., 1994—. Bd. trustees rep., Alumni Assn. bd. dirs. Manchester Coll.; bd. dirs. St. Nectarios Greek Orthodox Ch. Ladies' Soc., Palatine, Ill., 1985-92, pres., 1989-90. Mem. AICPA, AMA, NAFE, Internat. Newspaper Fin. Execs., Ill. CPA Soc., Manchester Coll. Acctg. Alumni Assn., Greek Women's Univ. Club. Office: Fox Valley Press Inc 3101 N Us Highway 30 Plainfield IL 60544-9604

CHASE, MARY ANN, physician; b. Boston, Aug. 15, 1945; d. Roscoe Moses and Dorothy Elinor (Carney) C.; m. John R. Vinton, July 18, 1964; children: Nathaniel, Andrew. BA, NYU, 1970; MD, Med. Coll. Pa., 1974. Diplomate Am. Bd. Internal Medicine. Intern Montefiore Hosp. and Med. Ctr., N.Y.C., 1974-75, resident, 1975-77; staff physician Augusta (Maine) Mental Health Inst., 1977-78; pvt. practice Miles Meml. Hosp., 1978-85; physician FHP, Salt Lake City, 1985—. Mem. ACEP, Utah Med. Assn. Democrat. Episcopalian. Office: 7495 S State St Midvale UT 84047

CHASE, NICOLE MARIE, mental health association worker, counselor; b. Amsterdam, N.Y., Jan. 2, 1954; d. Roger Stephen and Frances Marie (Rotonde) C. BS in Psychology, Sociology, Elem. Edn., Russell Sage Coll., 1975, MS in Health Edn., 1979; postgrad., SUNY, Albany, 1982-83; MEd in Profl. Counseling, Coll. William & Mary, 1992, EdD in Profl. Counseling, 1995, postgrad., 1996—. Cert. sch. adminstr., N.Y., elem. & health edn. tchr., N.Y., prin. Tchr. Broadalbin (N.Y.) Elem. Sch., 1975-85; policy analyst, devel. specialist N.Y. Commn. Quality of Care Mentally Disabled, Albany, 1985-88; mental health counselor HCA Peninsula Psychiat. Hosp., Hampton, Va., 1992-94; mental health counselor New Horizons Family Counseling Ctr. Coll. William & Mary, Williamsburg, Va.; policy analyst Va. Bd. People with Disabilities, Richmond, Va., 1995—; asst. chair com. students with spl. needs, advisor primary student coun., chair policy review & update com., dir. reading & textbook com., sch. rep. planning & devel. com. regional staff Broadalbin Elem. Sch. Group counselor Adults Molested as Children, 1995-96. Kellas scholar Russell Sage Coll., 1975. Mem. ACA, Am. Mental Health Counseling Assn., Kappa Delta Pi.

CHASE, NORAH CAROL, English language educator; b. Bklyn., Dec. 18, 1942; d. Homer Bates Chase and Dorothy (Teitelbaum) Weiner; m. M. Alan Ettlinger, Dec. 26, 1970 (div. Nov. 1985); 1 child, Gabrielle Ettlinger. Attended, Rutgers U., New Brunswick, N.J., 1966-75; MA in Comparative Lit., U. Minn., Mpls., 1969; PhD in Women's Studies, The Union Inst., Cin., 1995. Assoc. prof. Kingsborough Cmty. Coll., Bklyn., 1968—; assoc. prof. Extension Program Queen's Coll., N.Y.C., 1992-96; mem. exec. com. and grievance counselor Profl. Staff Congress, N.Y.C., 1994—; co-facilitator Women Writing Women's Lives Seminar. Recipient Rsch. grantee CUNY, 1984, 86, 96, The Ford Found., 1985-87. Mem. NOW. Office: English Dept Kingsborough CC Oriental Blvd Brooklyn NY 11235

CHASE, SYLVIA B., journalist; b. St. Paul, Feb. 23, 1938; d. Kelsey David and Sylvia (Bennett) C. B.A., UCLA, 1961. Aide to Calif. State Assembly Com. on Fin. and to Senator Thomas Rees, 1961-65; active polit. campaigns Calif., 1961-68; coordinator Kennedy for Pres., 1968; advance person Atty. Gen. Tom Lynch of Calif., 1966; action reporter Sta. KNX Los Angeles, 1969-71; corr. and anchorwoman CBS News, N.Y.C., 1971-77; corr. 20/20 ABC News, N.Y.C., 1977-86; anchorwoman Sta. KRON-TV News, San Francisco, 1986-90; corr. Primetime Live ABC News, N.Y.C., 1990—. Recipient Emmy award 1978, 80, 86, 87; Headliners award, 1979, 83, 94; Front Page award, 1979; Gainsbrugh award, 1979; consumer award Nat. Press Club, 1982; Pinnacle award, 1983; Russell L. Cecil award, 1983; Communications award Better Health and Living Mag., 1986, Award of Courage, NOW, 1987; Peabody award, 1989, Robert F. Kennedy award, 1989, Matrix award Women in Communications, 1992, AWRT award, 1994. Mem. Am. Women in Radio & Television. Office: PrimeTime Live 147 Columbus Ave Fl 3 New York NY 10023-5900

CHASE-JENKINS, LINDA MARIE, management consultant; b. Damariscotta, Maine, Sept. 6, 1967; d. Leverett Paul and Audrey Jane (Hall) Chase; m. Arthur Lester Jenkins III, June 5, 1993. BS, Cornell U., 1989; MBA, Columbia U., 1993. Underwriter marine ins. Cigna Co., Phila., 1989-91; mgmt. cons. Coopers & Lybrand, L.L.P., N.Y.C., 1993—. Mem. Cornell U. Alumni Club, Columbia U. Alumni Club, Kappa Alpha Theta. Republican. Office: Coopers & Lybrand 1301 Sixth Ave New York NY 10019

CHASEK, ARLENE SHATSKY, academic director; b. Newark, N.J., June 1, 1934; d. Herman and Rose (Sporn) Shatsky; m. Marvin B. Chasek, Apr. 10, 1960; children: Pamela S., Laura N., Daniel J. BA, Cornell U., 1956; MA, Columbia U., 1957; postgrad., U. N.D., 1972-74, Rutgers U., 1981-91. Tchr. English and journalism Elizabeth (N.J.) Pub. Schs., 1978-80, Summit (N.J.) Pub. Schs., 1978-80; coord. MA program Fairleigh Dickinson U., Teaneck, N.J., 1979-81; editor AT&T, Murray Hill, N.J., 1980-81; project coord. Consrotium for Ednl. Equity, Rutgers U., New Brunswick, N.J., 1981-85, project dir., 1985-88, dir. spl. projects, 1988-93; dir. family involvement programs in math., sci. and tech. Rutgers Consortium for Ednl. Equity, 1993-95; dir. Ctr. for Family Involvement in Schs., 1995—. Author, editor: Rutgers Family Tools and Technology, 1994, Rutgers Family Science, 1993, Mathematics in Art/Art in Mathematics, 1986 (U.S. Dept. Edn. award 1987), From Jumping Genes to Red Giants: A Guide to High School Science Research; author: The Recruitment and Retention Challenge, 1982, Futures Unlimited, 1985 (Curriculum award am. Ednl. Rsch. Assn. 1986). Recipient Golden Apple award for Family Involvement Programs, Working Mother mag., U.S. Dept. Edn., and Tchrs. Coll. Columbia U., 1996. Mem. AAUW, LWV, NSTA, Nat. Assn. Equity Educators, Coop. Learning Assn., Internat. Tech. Edn. Assn., Assn. Math. Tchrs. N.J. Home: 9 Schindler Pl New Providence NJ 07974-1738 Office: Rutgers Univ Consortium for Ednl Equity 4090 Livingston Campus New Brunswick NJ 08903

CHASE-RIBOUD, BARBARA DEWAYNE, sculptor, writer; b. Phila., June 26, 1939; d. Charles Edward and Vivian May (West) C.; m. Marc Eugene Riboud, Dec. 25, 1961 (dec. 1981); children: David, Alexis; m. S.G. Tosi, July 4, 1981. MFA, Yale U., 1960; PhD (hon.), Temple U., 1981, Muhlenberg Coll., 1993, U. Conn., 1996. Exhibited in one-woman shows Berkeley (Calif.) Mus., 1973, Mass. Inst. Tech., 1973, Detroit Art Inst., 1973, Indpls. Art Mus., 1973, Mus. Modern Art, Paris, 1974, Kunstmuseum Dusseldorf, 1974, Bronx Mus., 1979, Pasadena Coll., Calif., 1990, Kiron Arts and Comm., Paris, 1994; exhibited in group shows Whitney Mus., N.Y.C., Smithsonian Mus., Washington, Mus. Modern Art, N.Y.C., Carnegie Inst., Pitts., Centre Pompidou, Paris, Wellesley U. Mus., Nat. Mus. Art, Smithsonian Mus., L.A. Mus. Contemporary Art, Detroit Art Inst., New Orleans Mus. Art, Milw. Art Mus., Ft. Wayne Mus. Chgo. Cultural Ctr.; represented in permanent collections Met. Mus., Mus. Modern Art, Lannan Found., Los Angeles, Centre Pompidou, Nat. Collections, France, others; author: From Memphis and Peking, Poems, 1974, Sally Hemings, 1979, new edit., 1994, Study of a Nude Woman as Cleopatra, Verse, 1987, Valide, 1986, Echo of Lions, 1989 (citation State Legislature, Gov. Conn., 1989), The President's Daughter, 1994, Egypt's Nights, 1994. Decorated Knight Order of Arts and Letters (France), 1996; John Hay Whitney Found. fellow, 1958, Nat. Endowment for Arts fellow, 1973; recipient Kafka prize for best fiction written by Am. women, 1979, Academic of Italy with Gold medal, 1979, The Carl Sandburg Poetry prize, 1988, Van Der Zee Sculpture prize, 1995. Mem. PEN, The Century Assn., Yale Alumni Assn., Am. Ctr. N.Y.

CHASEY, JACQUELINE, lawyer. Formerly counsel Bertelsmann, Inc.; sr. counsel Bertelsmann, Inc., 1990-93; v.p., legal affairs, 1994—. Office: Bertelsmann Inc 1540 Broadway New York NY 10036-4039

CHASSE, FRANCES REILLY, elementary education educator; b. Glendale, W.Va., June 30, 1947; d. Leo F. Reilly and Evelyn L. Miller Beckley; m. Clifford G. Chasse, June 19, 1970. BS, Ctrl. Conn. State U., New Britain, 1971; MEd in Reading, U. Maine, Orono, 1982, CAS in Lang. Arts, 1991, postgrad., 1991—. Cert. literacy specialist, curriculum specialist, classrm. tchr., prin., Maine. Tchr. 5th grade Madawaska (Maine) Sch. Dept., 1971-83, tchr. 3d grade, 1983-85, reading specialist, 1985-88, tchr. 2d grade, 1988-96, Chpt. I summer dir., 1992; mem. com. St. John Valley Profl. Devel. Com., Ft. Kent, Maine, 1991-93; dir. Aroostook Right to Read, Aroostook County, Maine, 1987-88; Reading Is Fundamental coord. Madawaska Sch. Dept., 1985—; chair, com. mem. Madawaska Support System, 1985-88, 92-95. Grantee New England Reading Assn., 1985; Alpha Psi State scholar Delta Kappa Gamma Soc., 1991. Mem. ASCD, Maine Assn. for Supervision and Curriculum Devel., Delta Kappa Gamma Soc. (parliamentarian, sec., v.p., pres.). Roman Catholic. Home: 15 Fox St Madawaska ME 04756-1326 Office: Madawaska Sch Dept 96 Saint Thomas St Madawaska ME 04756-1242

CHATER, SHIRLEY SEARS, former vice chancellor, federal commissioner; b. Shamokin, Pa., July 30, 1932; d. Raymond and Edna Sears; m. Norman

Chater, Dec. 5, 1959 (dec. Dec. 1993); children: Cris, Geoffrey. BS, U. Pa., 1956; MS, U. Calif., San Francisco, 1960; PhD, U. Calif., Berkeley, 1964. Asst., assoc., prof. dept. social and behavioral scis. Sch. Nursing U. Calif.-San Francisco, Sch. Edn.-Berkeley, 1964-86; asst. vice chancellor acad. affairs U. Calif., San Francisco, 1974-77, vice chancellor acad. affairs, 1977-82; council assoc. Am. Council Edn., Washington, 1982-84; sr. assoc. Presdl. Search Consultation Svc. Assn. Governing Bds., Washington, 1984-86; pres. Tex. Woman's U., Denton, 1986-93; chair Gov's health policy task force State of Texas, 1992; commr. Social Security Adminstrn., Washington, 1993—. Bd. dirs. Carnegie Found. for Advancement of Teaching, United Educators Ins. Risk Retention Group, Denton United Way, 1986-93; mem. commn. on women Am. Coun. on Edn. Mem. Inst. Medicine, NAS, Dallas Forum, Charter 100 of Dallas, Internat. Alliance, Nat. Acad. Pub. Adminstrn., Nat. Acad. Social Ins. Home: 5175 Macomb St NW Washington DC 20016-2611 Office: Social Security Adminstrn Altmeyer Bldg 6401 Security Blvd Baltimore MD 21235-0001

CHATFIELD, MARY VAN ABSHOVEN, librarian; b. Bay Shore, N.Y.; d. Cornelius and Elma Elizabeth (Sumner) van Abshoven; m. Robert W. Chatfield, June 22, 1963 (div. 1981); 1 child, Robert Warner Jr.; m. Alexander Watts, Jan. 6, 1996. A.B., Radcliffe Coll., 1958; S.M., Columbia U., 1961; M.B.A., Harvard U., 1972. With library system Harvard U., Cambridge, Mass., 1961-92, librarian Bus. Sch., 1963-78, head libr., 1978-92; acting libr. Countway Libr. Harvard Med. Sch., 1988-89; head libr. Angelo State U., San Angelo, Tex., 1992-95. Mem. Daughters of Brit. Empire, Rotary. Episcopalian. Home: 95 Ironia Rd Mendham NJ 07945

CHATFIELD, RUTH CHRISTINA, nurse, researcher; b. Atlanta, July 9, 1956; d. Gene Hall and Norma Jean (Bryant) C. Diploma in nursing, Ga. Bapt. Med. Ctr., Atlanta, 1979; BS in Nursing, Emory U., 1983. RN, Ga. Staff nurse Windy Hill Hosp., Marietta, Ga., 1979-80; charge nurse Ga. Bapt. Med. Ctr., 1980-83, oncology clinician, 1983-85; clin. educator Humana Women's Hosp., Tampa, Fla., 1985-86; team nurse, coord. nutrition support and pain teams H. Lee Moffit Cancer Ctr. and Rsch. Inst., Tampa, 1986-88; mktg. rep. Am. Home Patient Ctrs., Inc., Franklin, Tenn., 1988-89; mgr. Sims Deltec, Inc., St. Paul, 1989—; presenter in field. Contbr. articles to profl. jours. Vol. Am. Cancer Soc., 1982-84; instr. basic cardiac life support Am. Heart Assn., 1985-86. Mem. Internat. Assn. for Study Pain, Am. Soc. for Parenteral and Enteral Nurtition (Fla. bd. dirs. 1988-90), Oncology Nurses Soc., Fla. Assn. Nutrition Support (nurse counselor 1988, 89, newsletter editor 1989, 90, bd. dirs. 1988-90). Republican. Home: 2913 Coral Shores Dr Fort Lauderdale FL 33306 Office: Sims Deltec Inc 1265 Grey Fox Rd Saint Paul MN 55112-6967

CHATFIELD-TAYLOR, ADELE, arts administrator, historic preservationist; b. Washington, Jan. 29, 1945; d. Hobart Chatfield-Taylor and Mary Owen (Lyon) C.-T.; m. John Guare, May 20, 1981. BA, Manhattanville Coll., 1966; MS in Historic Preservation, Columbia U., 1974; postgrad. (Loeb fellow), Harvard U., 1978-79; ArtsD (hon.), Lake Forest Coll., 1995. Archtl. historian Historic Am. Bldg. Survey, Washington, 1967; co-founder, dir. Urban Deadline Architects, Inc., 1968-73; landmarks preservation specialist N.Y.C. Landmarks Preservation Commn., 1973-74, asst. to chmn., 1974-79, dir. policy and programs, 1979-80; adj. prof. historic preservation program Grad. Sch. Architecture and Planning, Columbia U., 1976-84; founder and exec. dir. N.Y. Landmarks Preservation Found., 1980-84; dir. design arts program Nat. Endowment for Arts, 1984-88; pres. Am. Acad. in Rome, N.Y.C., 1988—; bd. dirs. Preservation ACTION, 1976-84, regional v.p., 1978-83, sec., 1983-84; trustee Ctr. for Bldg. Conservation, 1978-84; mem. U.S. del. to China, Women in Architecture, 1977, 80, U.S. del. to China, Historic Preservationists, 1982; mem. exec. com. U.S./Internat. Coun. on Monuments and Sites, 1979-84; mem. China adv. com. Nat. Endowment Arts, 1980-84, vice chmn. design arts policy panel, 1978-82; bd. dirs. Nat. Alliance of Preservation Commns., 1983-84; trustee Tiber Island History Mus., 1983—; guest lectr. Harvard U., MIT, Columbia U., NYU, U. Va. Contbr. articles to profl. jours. Mem. restoration com. South Street Seaport Mus., 1975-84; mem. Nat. Com. on U.S.-China Relations, 1982—; mem. lawn adv. bd. U. Va., 1982-86; mem. adv. bd. Jeffersonian Restoration, 1989—, Law and the Arts, 1989—; bd. dirs. Greenwich Village Trust for Historic Preservation, 1983-84, Internat. Design Conf. Aspen, 1986-90, Nat. Bldg. Mus., 1989—; mem. adv. bd. Jeffersonian Restoration, 1989—; mem. Commn. Fine Arts, 1990-94. Archtl. fellow Ednl. Facilities Lab Acad. Ednl. Devel., 1982-83; Rome prize Am. Acad. in Rome, 1983-84; fellow N.Y. Inst. Humanities, 1983-89. Fellow Am. Acad. Arts & Scis.; mem. Nat. Trust Historic Preservation, Friends of Cast Iron Architecture, Preservation League N.Y. State, Met. Mus. Art, Century Assn. Club: Pug Dog of Greater N.Y. Office: Am Acad in Rome 7 E 60th St New York NY 10022-1001

CHATHAM, CAROL LEE, accountant; b. Newnan, Ga., Sept. 29, 1962; d. Fredrick William and Lucy Ann (Yarbrough) Lange. BBA in Acctg., West Ga. Coll., 1988, M of Profl. Accountancy, 1995. Advanced staff auditor Ga. Dept. of Audits, Atlanta, 1988-93; fiscal officer Cmty. Action for Improvement, LaGrange, 1993-94; grant acct. Columbus (Ga.) Consol. Govt., 1994—. Mem. Inst. Mgmt. Accts., Ga. Govt. Fin. Officers Assn. Republican. Baptist.

CHATTERTON, JANINE K., elementary education educator; b. N.Y.C., Aug. 19, 1968; d. Francis Peter and Jean Julia (Napoli) C. BA in Elem. Edn. and Psychology, Hunter Coll., 1991; MS in Elem. Edn. and Reading, St. John's U., 1995. Cert. tchr., N.Y., reading tchr., N.Y. Tchr. grades 7-8 St. Teresa Sch., Woodside, N.Y.; tchr. grade 2 St. Raphael Sch., L.I. City, N.Y.; reading tutor St. John's U., Jamaica, N.Y.; tchr. grade 3 reading Pub. Sch. 143 Q; coord. after-sch. program. Mission moderator, lector eucharistic ministries St. Raphael Ch., L.I. City, 1991—. Mem. Internat. Reading Assn., Tng. Tomorrow's Tchrs., Home Sch. Assn. (tchr. rep. 1993—), Kappa Delta Phi. Democrat. Roman Catholic. Home: 39-35 51st St Woodside NY 11377-3152

CHATTON, BARBARA ANN, education educator; b. San Francisco, Aug. 4, 1948; d. Milton John and Mildred (Vick) C.; m. Andrew M. Bryson, May 1, 1993. BA, U. Calif., Santa Cruz, 1970; MLS, UCLA, 1971; PhD, Ohio State U., 1982. Libr. John Steinbeck Pub. Libr., Salinas, Calif., 1971-79; prof. U. Wyo., Laramie, 1982—. Author: Using Poetry Across the Curriculum, 1993; co-author: Creating Connections, 1986. Mem., past chair Friends of Libr.,, Albany County, Wyo., 1989—. Recipient Ellbogen award U. Wyo., 1990. Mem. ALA, Nat. Coun. Tchrs. English, Internat. Reading Assn., Phi Delta Kappa. Office: U Wyo Coll Edn PO Box 3374 Laramie WY 82071-3374

CHAUDRY, BUSHRA, artist; b. Lahore, Pakistan, Feb. 4, 1967; d. Chaudry Mohammad Ali and Tahira (Jafri) Mohammed Ali. BA, Lahore Coll. Women, 1987; BFA, Nat. Coll. Arts, Lahore, 1991; MFA, Pratt Inst., Bklyn., 1996. Tchr. Lahore Grammar Sch., 1984-88; workshop instr. South Asian Planning, Lahore, 1991; designer World Wildlife Fund, Lahore, 1992; tchr. Rainbow Ctr., Binghampton, N.Y., 1993; printmaking asst. Tapir Editions, N.Y.C., 1994—; freelance contbr. The Republic Mag., Lahore, 1991. Exhbns. include Shakir Ali Mus., Lahore, 1989, Nat. Art Gallery, Islamabad, Pakistan, 1990, Nat. Coll. Arts, Pakistan, 1992, Nairang Gallery, Lahore, 1992, Am. Ctr., Lahore, 1993, Manhattan Graphics Ctr., N.Y.C., 1994, Nagoya Univ. Arts, Japan, 1994, 450 Broadway Gallery, N.Y.C., 1995, Kentler Internat. Drawing Space, Bklyn., 1995, Northeastern U., Boston, 1995, Nat. Inst. Arts., Taipei, Taiwan, 1995, Gallery Hogbergsgatan, Stockholm, 1995. Mem. Guggenheim Mus., Pratt Artists League. Home: 318 Birch Dr Roselle NJ 07203

CHAUNCEY, PAULA E., bank executive. Sr. v.p. loan rev. Bay Banks, Inc., Boston. Office: Bay Banks Inc 175 Federal St Boston MA 02110*

CHAVARRIA, DOLORES ESPARZA, financial service executive; b. Levelland, Tex., Nov. 13, 1952; d. Thomas Medina and Hermenejilda (Estrada) Esparza; m. Margarito R. Grimaldo (div. Feb. 1975); children: Maurice Patrick, Margarito; m. Frank Sedillo Chavarria; 1 child, Mecca Esparza. AS, South Plains C.C., 1977; student, Tex. Tech U., 1977-78. Notary public, Tex. Supr. cen. supply South Park Med. Ctr., Lubbock, Tex., 1980-84, dir. materials mgmt. dept., 1984-90; buyer City of Lubbock, 1990-94, recruiter, 1994—; prin. D.E.E. Enterprises, Lubbock, 1992—. Chmn. S.W. Voter's Registration, Lubbock, 1988. Mem. Nat. Assn. Purchasing Mgmt. (2d v.p. South Plains chpt.), Am. Bus. Women's Assn., Tex. Purchasing Mgmt. Assn., Hispanic Assn. of Women. Democrat. Roman Catholic. Office: 1625 13th St Lubbock TX 79401-3830

CHAVE, CAROLYN MARGARET, lawyer, arbitrator; b. Chgo., Jan. 30, 1948; d. Grant Carruthers and Priscilla Morrison (Shaw) C.; m. Robert Edmund Hand; children: Joshua, Chloe, Robert, Grant. BA, U. Chgo., 1970; MAT, Oakland U., 1971; JD, Loyola U., Chgo., 1976. Bar: Ill. 1976, N.Y. 1979. Tchr. corps intern Pontiac (Mich.) Pub. Schs., 1970-71; sec., receptionist Grad. Sch. Bus., U. Chgo., 1971; counselor Sonia Shankman Orthogenic Sch., Chgo., 1972; pvt. practice Chgo., 1976-78; asst. v.p., assoc. counsel Bank of Tokyo, N.Y.C., 1978-85; substitute tchr. N.Y.C. Pub. Schs., 1986-88; with Breckenridge Law Offices, 1986-88; sr. v.p., counsel, mgr. human resources Tokai Bank, N.Y.C., 1988—; arbitrator Am. Arbitration Assn., N.Y.C., 1986—. Vol. lawyer Chgo. Vol. Legal Svcs., 1977-78; designer playground PS 41 Parent Assn., Greenwich Village, N.Y., 1987. Mem. N.Y. County Lawyers Assn. Office: Tokai Bank Ltd 55 E 52nd St New York NY 10055-0002

CHAVERS, BLANCHE MARIE, pediatrician, educator, researcher; b. Clarksdale, Miss., Aug. 2, 1949; d. Andrew and Mildred Louise (Cox) C.; m. Gubare Robert Mpambara, May 21, 1982; 1 child, Kaita. B.S. in Zoology, U. Wash., 1971, M.D., 1975. Diplomate Am. Bd. Pediatrics. Intern, U. Wash., Seattle, 1975-76, resident in pediatrics, 1976-78; fellow in pediatric nephrology U. Minn., Mpls., 1978-81, instr., 1981-82, asst. prof. pediatrics, 1983—, assoc. prof. pediatrics, 1990—; attending physician dept. pediatrics, U. Minn. Sch. Medicine, Mpls., 1981—. Contbr. articles to profl. jours. Recipient Clin. Investigator award NIH, 1982. Mem. Am. Acad. Pediatrics, Am. Soc. Nephrology, Am. Soc. Pediatric Nephrology, Internat. Soc. Nephrology, Internat. Soc. Pediatric Nephrology. Democrat. Mem. African Methodist Episcopal Zion Ch. Avocations: tennis, reading, collecting African artifacts, art. Home: 9218 Fawnridge Cir S Bloomington MN 55437-1825 Office: Univ Minn Box 491 Mayo 515 Delaware St SE Minneapolis MN 55455-0348

CHAVEZ, ANTIONETTE LOUISE, marketing manager; b. Milw., Nov. 17, 1962; d. Louis Paul C. and Patricia Michelle (Johnson) Dolenshek. AD, Milw. Area Tech. Coll. Interviewer Consumer Pulse, Inc., Milw., 1987-89; tchrs. aide Milw. Area Tech. Coll., 1989-90; saleswoman Hardwear Design, Milw., 1990-92; restaurant mgr. Café Phyllis, Milw., 1993-95; mktg. mgr. AMRE, Milw., 1996—. Sec., treas. Art Club, Shorewood, Wis., 1979; driver Women's Transit Authority, Madison, 1981; v.p. Distributive Edn. Club Am., Milw., 1987; vol. Milw. AIDS Project, 1995—. Mem. Cream City Bus. Assn. Democrat. Roman Catholic. Home: 830A W. Pierce St Milwaukee WI 53204

CHAVEZ, DOROTHY VAUGHAN, elementary school educator, environmental educator; b. Columbus, Miss., Jan. 13, 1942; d. Robert Clayton and Sara (Harris) Vaughan; m. Samuel Patrick Chavez, Nov. 18, 1961; children: Sarah Rose Chavez Brundage, Samuel Clayton. BS, Miss. U. for Women, 1962; MEd, U. North Tex., 1968; PhD, Tex. A&M U., 1995. Cert. tchr., supr., Tex. Tchr. Littleton (Colo.) Ind. Sch. Dist., 1962-64, Albuquerque Ind. Sch. Dist., 1964-65, Richardson (Tex.) Ind. Sch. Dist., 1965-69, Austin (Tex.) Ind. Sch. Dist., 1973-89, 92, Round Rock (Tex.) Ind. Sch. Dist., 1992—. Author: Nature's Classroom: Locations and Programs in Texas, 1991; editor: Directory of Environmental Education and Interpretive Centers, 1992, Take Children to the Wilds... to Discover Wildflowers and Native Plants, 1993; contbr. articles to environ. publs. Dir. vol. ushers staff Austin Symphony Orch. Soc., 1991-95. Mem. Tex. Assn. Environ. Edn. (editor 1991-93, bd. dirs., Outstanding Contbns. award 1992), Tex. Edn. Agy (environ. edn. adv. com.), Tex. Outdoor Edn. Assn., Nat. Sci. Tchrs. Assn., Tex. Sci. Tchrs. Assn., N.Am. Environ. Edn. Assn., Am. Nature Study Soc., Roger Tory Peterson Inst., Tex. PTA (hon. life), Alpha Delta Kappa, Delta Kappa Gamma, Gamma Sigma Delta. Home: 4107 Mark Rae St Austin TX 78727-1802 Office: Gattis Elem Sch 2920 Round Rock Ranch Blvd Round Rock TX 78664-7820

CHAVEZ, NELBA, federal agency administrator. BA in Sociology and Psychology, U. Ariz.; MSW, UCLA; PhD in Social Work, U. Denver; student sr. exec. program in state and local govt., Harvard U. From clin. dir. to exec. dir., COO La Frontera Ctr., Tuscon, 1972-89; prin. Chavez and Assocs., 1989-90; dir. juvenile probation svcs. City and County of San Francisco, 1990-92; adminstr. Substance Abuse and Mental Health Svcs. Adminstrn., U.S. Dept. Health and Human Svcs., Washington, 1994—; bd. dirs. Nat. Coalition of Hispanic Mental Health and Human Svc. Orgns.; active U.S. Senate Hispanic Adv. Com., Pres. Nat. Coun. on Handicapped, White House Prevention Com. on Drug-Free Am. Active Tuscon Mayor's Task Force on Children. Recipient Outstanding Leadership award Ariz. State U., 1985, Dedication and Commitment award Tenth Ann. Chicano Conf., 1989, Disting. Svc. award Nat. Assn. Profl. Asian Am. Women, 1995, Mujer 95 award League United L.Am. Citizens, 1995, Rafael Tavares, MD, Meml. award Assn. Hispanic Mental Health Profls., 1995. Office: Dept Health and Human Svcs Substance Abuse Svcs Adminstrn 5600 Fishers Ln Rm 12-105 Rockville MD 20857

CHAVIS, GERALDINE ELLEN, government employee; b. Balt., July 6, 1960; d. Frederick Anthony and Catherine Eva (Weigmann) Hall; m. Alonzo Duront Chavis, Sept. 28, 1983; children: Anthony Daniel, Amber Dionna. Grad. high sch., Balt. Payroll asst. Youth Entitlement Program, Balt., 1979-80; receptionist Cashier Tng., Balt., 1980-81; office clk. Katzenberg Bros., Inc., Balt., 1981-85; distbn. clk. U.S. Postal Svc., Balt., 1985—; rep. Avon Products, Inc., Newark, Del., 1990—. Block capt. City Govt. Recycling, Balt., 1992—. Mem. Am. Postal Workers Union (local rep. 1990—). Democrat. Roman Catholic. Home: 3209 Independence St Baltimore MD 21218

CHAVIS, KATHERINE (KITTY CHAVIS), disability consultant, artist; b. Bklyn., Dec. 4, 1938; d. Allen Joseph Holmes and Doris Viola (Hobson) Holmes Osborne; m. Herbert Chavis, Dec. 16, 1956 (dec. Feb. 1972); m. Johnnie Jones Jr., Apr. 24, 1977 (dec. Oct. 1988). IBM coder Met. Life Ins. Co., N.Y.C., 1955-62; receptionist Assemblyman Mills Calif. State Legis., San Diego, 1963-65; traffic coord. Air Products & Chems., Inc., N.Y.C., 1965-67; exec. sec. Dept. Water, Gas and Electricity, N.Y.C., 1967-68; statis. typist Haryou Act Inc., N.Y.C., 1968-70; typist Worker's Compensation Bd., N.Y.C., 1970-82; police adminstrv. aide N.Y.C. Police Dept., 1982-91; assoc. dir. Inst. disability Advocacy, Bklyn., 1992—; pres. Kandi Creations, Bklyn., 1995—. Participant: (book) American Negro Art, 1959; solo exhbns. include Fournier's Studio, Greenwish Village, N.Y., 1966, Madau Gallery, Bklyn., 1967-70; group shows include Soul Gallery, N.Y.C., 1961, Manor Gallery, Bklyn., 1962, Atelier d'Arts Gallery, N.Y.C., 1967, Bklyn. Mus., 1968, Design Masters Gallery, N.Y.C., 1988, Creative Concerns Gallery, Bklyn., 1989, ACCAA Gallery, Bklyn., 1990-91, Ctr. of Arts Gallery, Bklyn., 1992, 94; work represented in several permanent collections, including Met. Opera House, N.Y.C., UNESCO, Brussels, Bklyn. chs. Sec. S.E. San Diego Cmty. Guild, 1963-65, Classon/Franklin/Greene Aves. Block Assn., Inc., Bklyn., 1988; 2d v.p. young adult coun. NAACP, 1967; trustee N.Y.C. Guardian Assn., Inc., 1986; acting chmn. BedStuy chpt. Citizens Action Taskforce, Pub. Advocates Office, N.Y., 1995; co-editor Bed-Stuy Interagy. Coun. of Aging, 1995—. Recipient Tillman award Pub. Sch. 167 Bd. of Edn., Bklyn., 1952, 1st prize Wall St. Art Assn. U.S. Trust Co., 1962, 2d prize Hunter Coll. Irish Feis, 1961, 62. Mem. N.E. Assn. Women Police (life), African Peoples Christian Orgn., Nat. Conf. Artists (asst. newsletter 1989—), Ancient Order of Foresters (chief ranger 1981-82). Office: Kandi Creations PO Box 022517 Brooklyn NY 11202

CHAVOOSHIAN, MARGE, artist, educator; b. N.Y.C., Jan. 8, 1925; d. Harry Mesrob and Anna (Tashjian) Kurkjian; m. Barkev Budd Chavooshian, Aug. 11, 1946; children: J. Dean, Nora Ann. Student Art Students League, 1943, Reginald Marsh, N.Y.C., 1943, Mario Cooper, N.Y.C., 1977. Designer Needlework Arts Co., N.Y.C., 1943-44; illustrator John David Men's Store, N.Y.C., 1944-45; illustrator, layout artist Fawcett Publs., N.Y.C., 1945-47; designer, illustrator Pa. State U., University Park, 1947-49; art tchr. Trenton pub. schs., N.J., 1958-68, art cons. Title One Program, 1968-74; painting instr. Princeton Art Assn., N.J., 1974-77, 96, Jewish Cmty. Ctr., Ewing, N.J., 1974-85, Contemporary Club, Trenton, 1974-85, YMCA, YWCA, Trent Ctr., Trenton, 1974—, various watercolor workshops, N.J., 1990—; artist-at-large Alliance For Arts Edn., N.J., 1979-80; adj. asst. prof. art instr. Mercer County Coll., West Windsor, N.J., 1985-93; tchr. watercolor workshops Chalfonte, Cape May, N.J. One woman shows include Rider Coll., 1974, Jersey City Mus., 1980, N.J. State Mus., 1981, Trenton City Mus., 1984, 87, Arts Club, Washington, D.C., 1991, Coryell Gallery, Lambertville, N.J., 1993, Chalfonte Cape May, 1993, 94, 95, Chalfonte, 1996; exhibited in group shows at Douglas Coll., N.J., 1977, Bergen Mus., Paramus, N.J., 1980, 81, 82, Hunterdon Art Ctr., Clinton, N.J., 1982, 95, Morris Mus., Morristown, N.J., 1984, Allied Artists of Am., 1984, 86, 89, 91-95, Salmagundi Club, N.Y.C., 1988, 91, 92, 94, 95, Berman Mus., 1995, Balt. Watercolor Soc., 1995, Barron Art Ctr., Woodbridge, N.J. (Ida Wells and Clara Stroud award 1993), Ridgewood (N.J.) Art Inst. (Ruth Ratay Meml. Fund award 1994), Art Works of Princeton and Trenton, 1995, Hunterdon County Cultural and Heritage Commn. Show, Clinton, N.J., 1995; represented in permanent collections Mercer County Cultural and Heritage Commn., Arts Club of Washington, N.J. State Mus., Jersey City Mus., Trenton City Mus., Morris Mus., Rider Coll., Art Mus. San Lazarre, Italy, Bristol Myers Squibb, Johnson and Johnson, Schering Plough Corp, Pub. Svc. Electric and Gas, Co., U.S. Trust. Recipient numerous awards Union Coll., Mercer County Cultural and Heritage Commn., Phillips Mill (Walter E. Martin Meml. award 1992, Patrons award for watercolor 1994), Am. Watercolor Soc., Phila. Watercolor Club, Ligorno and Solansky award Hunterdon County Cultural and Heritage Commn., 1991, Cynthia Goodgal Meml. award Ridgewood Art Inst., 1992, Ruth Ratay award Cmty. Arts Assn. Mid Atlantic Show, 1994, Elliot Liskin Meml. award Salmagundi Open Show, 1995; named Woman of Month Women's Newspaper of Princeton, 1984. N.J. State Council Arts fellow, 1979. Fellow Am. Artists Profl. League (Am. Arts Clon. award 1973, Winsor Newton award 1980, Gold medal, Barron Art Ctr. award 1991, 93, Merit award 1992, Am. Artists Profl. League award 1994, Best in Show award, Best in Watercolor 1995, others); mem. Nat. Assn. Women Artists (two yr. nat. travel award 1985, S. Winston Meml. award 1988, two yr. travel award 1996—), Catherine Lorillard Wolfe Art Club (Bee Paper Co. award 1977, Anna Hyatt Huntington Bronze medal 1979, Cynthia Goodgall Meml. award 1995), Allied Artists Am. (elected mem., Henry Gasser Meml. award 1992), N.J. Watercolor Soc. (Newton Art Ctr. award 1972, Helen K. Bermel award 1984, Howard Savs. Bank award 1986-87), Lambertville Historical Soc. award Coryell Gallery, Lambertville, 1995, Painters and Sculptors Soc. (Medal of Honor, Digby Chandler medal, others), Garden State Watercolor Soc. (Triangle Art Ctr. award 1976, 89, 94, Grumbacher Silver medal 1981, Merit award 1982, Trust Co. award 1987, Triangle award 1994, Art Express award, 1995, Rider U. Gallery award 1995), Midwest Watercolor Soc., Nat. Arts Club (John Elliott award 1988), Phila. Watercolor Club (Village Art award 1991). Filmed Watercolr Workshop aired on State of the Arts N.J. Workshop. Democrat. Mem. Apostolic Ch. Armenia. Home: 222 Morningside Dr Trenton NJ 08618-4914

CHEASEBRO, MARGARET ANN, elementary school counselor; b. Spokane, Wash., July 22, 1945; d. William Harbison Jr. and Margaret Eloise Philips; m. Clarence Wallace Cheasebro, June 12, 1971; 1 child, Philip Wallace. BA in Humanities, Sterling (Kans.) Coll., 1967; MA in Psychology, Counseling, Guidance, U. No. Colo., 1971. Cert. elem. sch. counselor, N.Mex. Tchr., counselor Bur. Indian Affairs, Toyei, Ariz., 1967-68; elem. sch. tchr. Chinle (Ariz.) Pub. Schs., Mary Farms, Ariz., 1968-70, 71-73; elem. sch. counselor Farmington (N.Mex.) Mcpl. Schs., 1973-77, 92—; weekly newspaper reporter Aztec (N.Mex.) Ind. Rev., 1977-79; Aztec bur. chief Farmington Daily Times, 1980-84; weekly newspaper mng. editor Ind. Rev., Aztec, 1984-86; newspaper corr. Albuquerque Jour., 1989-92; freelance writer-photographer Aztec, 1986—. Author: Puppet Scripts by the Month, 1985, Puppet Scripts by the Situation, 1989, 25 Puppet Plays About Bible People, 1991, Prodigal Son and Other Parables As Plays, 1992; writer, photographer drama Broadman Press, Ch. Recreation Mag., Contemporary Drama Svc., Hosanna, Lillenas, Std. Pub., Book Prodn. Sys. Inc.; contbr. articles and photos to profl. jours.; photographer Augsburg Pub. Ho., Camp Quality, Family Day Caring, Warner Press; writer short stories; creator puzzles. Bd. dirs. Aztec Mus. Assn., 1991—. Recipient Guy Rader award N.Mex. Med. Soc., Farmington, 1978, 1st pl. award feature writing, daily paper N.Mex. Press Women, 1984, 1st pl. award feature, personality profile, editing, 1986, 1st pl. award feature article N.Mex. Press Assn., 1988, 1st pl. award monolog Colo. Christian Communicators, Colorado Springs, 1994. Mem. S.W. Christian Writers Assn. (pres. 1987-89), Farmington Writers Assn. (past pres.). Republican. Home: 246 Road 2900 Aztec NM 87410-9711 Office: Bluffview Elem Sch 1204 Camina Real Farmington NM 87401-8145

CHECCHIA, BENITA V. See VALENTE, BENITA

CHEDIAK, CRISTINA GODÍNEZ, media and communications executive; b. Havana, Cuba, Feb. 18, 1953; came to U.S., 1961; d. Mario Alberto and Consuelo (Mayol) G.; m. Natalio R. Chediak, Mar. 18, 1975 (div. 1987); 1 child, Natalie Cristina. BA, MDCC, 1979. Promotions mgr. WNJV-TV, N.Y.C., 1989-95, programming and promotions dir., 1991-95; programming mgr. Gems Internat. TV, Miami, Fla., 1995—. Roman Catholic. Office: Gems Internat TV 10360 USA Today Way Miramar FL 33026

CHEE, CAROLYN JEAN, aerospace engineer; b. Sacramento; d. Donald Ning and Joan Tai (Gin) Lee; m. Lyndon Y. Chee, Oct. 15, 1989. BS, U. Calif., Berkeley, 1986, MS, 1987, postgrad., 1991—. Engring. tutor, advisor U. Calif., Berkeley, 1982-86, rsch. asst., 1986-88, 91—; project engr. Golden Grain Macaroni Co., San Leandro, Calif., 1984; engring. aide Aerojet Strategic Propulsion Co., Sacramento, 1985; engr., scientist Jet Propulstion Lab., Pasadena, Calif., 1986, 88-90, McDonnell Douglas Space Systems Co., Huntington Beach, Calif., 1990-91; mem. Tiger Team McDonnell Douglas Space Systems Co., 1990. Recipient Jet Propulsion Lab./NASA Recognition award, 1989, Honor award NASA, 1991; GTE fellow, 1992. Mem. AAUW, ASME, AIAA, Soc. Women Engrs. Office: U Calif Dept Mech Engring 6124C Etcheverry Hall Berkeley CA 94720

CHEE, SHIRLEY, real estate broker; b. Ridley Park, Pa., Dec. 29, 1941; d. Richard E. and Lillian G. (Laudeman) Foehl; married, Nov. 26, 1967 (div. Nov. 1986). BS, Susquehanna U., 1963; grad., Real Estate Inst., 1975, postgrad., 1976-77. Music tchr. Nether Providence (Pa.) Sch. System, 1963-65, Anne Arundel Sch. System, Annapolis, Md., 1965-67; 1st cellist Annapolis Symphony Orch., 1967; bank teller Guaranty Bank & Trust Co., Morgan City, La., 1967-68; real estate agt. Joe J. Relle, Inc., Gretna, La., 1969-71; real estate broker Clyde Casey Real Estate, Inc., Gretna, 1972-75; pres. Chee, Inc. Realtors, 1976—, Harvey, La., 1976—; pres. West Bank Profl. Real Estate Sch., Inc., Gretna, 1976-87; mem. merger task force New Orleans and Jefferson Bds. Realtors, 1992. Chmn. small bus. Am. Cancer Soc., New Orleans, 1978, 79; pres. West Bank Rep. Women's Club, Gretna, 1976; mem. Harvey Canal Indsl. Assn., 1988. Mem. Jefferson Bd. Realtors (chmn. edn. 1979, dir. 1989-90, chmn. profl. standards 1989, 91), La. Realtors Assn., Nat. Assn. Realtors, ERA-S.E. La. Brokers Coun. (pres. 1990, sec. 1989-90, treas. 1990, Multi-Million Dollar award 1989), New Orleans Met. Assn. Realtors (bd. dirs. 1993-94). Home: 728 Hickory St Terrytown LA 70056-5113 Office: Chee Inc Realtors 1600 4th St Harvey LA 70058-4410

CHEEK, BARBARA LEE, college reading program director, educator; b. Springfield, Mo., Oct. 25, 1935; d. Curtis Earl and Gertrude Helen (Ahonen) Nelson; m. Lee Roy Clyde, June 16, 1961; children: Michael, Paul, Daniel. BA in Edn. cum laude, Pacific Luth. U., 1957; postgrad., U. Wash., Seattle, 1961-62; MA in Elem. Reading Edn., Boise (Idaho) State U., 1982; postgrad., Ea. Oreg. U., 1983, Seattle U., 1989. Cert. elem. and secondary edn. tchr., Wash. Sec. engring. dept. Boeing Aircraft Co., Seattle, 1957; instr. Edmonds (Wash.) Sch. Dist., 1957-61, Clover Pk. Sch. Dist., Tacoma, Wash., 1961-62, Payette (Idaho) Sch. Dist., 1970-74; bookkeeper Cheek Dairy Supply, Payette, 1970-71; instr. Ontario (Oreg.) Sch. Dist., 1975-79; prof. Treasure Valley Community Coll., Ontario, 1979-89; prof. Pierce Coll., Tacoma, 1989—, dir. reading dept., 1989—; dir. Alternative Learning Ctr. Pierce Coll., 1996—; instr. Profl. Excellence Program Tacoma (Wash.) Sch. Dist., 1994; sec. Malheur Reading Coun., Ont., 1986-87; faculty exec. bd. Treasure Valley C.C. Faculty, Ont., 1986-88; mem. Peer Evaluation Oreg. Devel. Edn., Ont., 1986; cons. Tacoma Sch. Dist. Profl. Excellence Program, 1993—; exec. Interior Design Nutritionals/Nu-Skin, 1994—. Moderator Ont. candidate's fair AAUW, 1985, state sec., Payette, 1972-74, sec. N.W.

region, 1974, br. pres., 1970-72, 75-77; bd. dirs. Boy Scouts Am., Oregon, Idaho, 1971-84; deacon, v.p. Luth. Ch., 1986; mem. basic literacy steering com. Tacoma, 1992; mem. Pierce County Literacy Coalition, bd. dirs., Tacoma; mem. Scandinavian Cultural Ctr., Pacific Union U. Recipient Faculty Devel. award Higher Edn. State of Wash., 1990-91. Mem. AAUW (chpt. pres. 1970-72), ASCD, Western Coll. Reading Assn., Wash. State C.C., Faculty Devel. (state com.), Wash. Devel. Edn. Assn., Am. Assn. Women in Comty. and Jr. Colls., Wash. Fedn. of Tchrs., Coll. Reading and Learning Assn., Tchr. English to Spkrs. of Other Langs., Sweet Adelines, Internat., Alpha Delta Kappa (v.p. 1986). Republican. Office: Pierce Coll 9401 Farwest Dr SW Tacoma WA 98498-1919

CHEEK, NORMA JEAN, retired educator; b. Ada, Okla., Feb. 7, 1928; d. John Herbert and Jewell Esther (Hobbs) Winters; m. George A. Cheek, Dec. 5, 1947; children: George Allen III, Michael Kirby. AA, Conners Jr. Coll., 1948; BS, Ctrl. State Coll., Edmond, Okla., 1961, MEd, 1964. Tchr. Mid-Del Schs., Midwest City, Okla., 1961-89, coach, 1978-87. Salesman vol. YMCA, 1970—; bldg. rep. Midwest City Assn. Classroom Tchrs., 1980. Mem. AAUW, Alpha Delta Kappa (various positions including v.p. 1980). Democrat. Baptist. Home: 604 Traub Pl Midwest City OK 73110-2738

CHEELY, LYNNETTE MARIE, counselor, basketball coach; b. Petersburg, Va., June 29, 1968; d. James Conway and Karen Lynette (Spencer) C. BA, U. S.C., 1990, MEd, EdS, 1992. Registered guidance counselor, S.C. Counselor S.C. Vocat. Rehab., Aiken, 1992-93; guidance counselor Jasper County Sch. Dist., Ridgeland, S.C., 1993-94, Kershaw County Sch. Dist., Camden, S.C., 1995—; instr. U.S. C., Beaufort/Hilton Head, S.C., 1995; basketball coach North Ctrl. H.S., Kershaw, 1995-96, Ridgeland Mid. Sch., 1993-94; riding instr. and trainer. Mem. ACA, S.C. Sch. Counseling Assn. Home: 3009 Earlewood Dr Columbia SC 29201

CHEESEMAN, RUTH ANN, special education educator, drug-free counselor; b. Stryker, Ohio, Dec. 10, 1943; d. Verne Ernest and Esther Pauline (Garner) Leininger; m. Robert Warwick Cheeseman Jr., July 22, 1972; children: Robert Warwick III, Kevin Alexander, Brian Mitchell. BS in Edn., Manchester Coll., 1965; MS in Edn., Purdue U., 1968. Cert. 1-8 gen. edn. tchr., mental retardation and learning disabilities endorsements, Ind. Master tchr., program developer for fed. grant in spl. edn. Ft. Wayne (Ind.) State Hosp. & Tng. Ctr., 1965-71; mildly mentally handicapped primary tchr. Ft. Wayne (Ind.) Cmty. Schs., 1971-77; tchr. learning disabilities edn. N.W. Ind. Spl. Edn. Coop., Crown Point, 1978-96, mem. learning disabilities adv. bd., 1991-93; tchr. math., spl. edn. Northwest Ind. Spl. Edn. Coop., 1996—; mem. curriculum com. Lake Ridge Sch. Corp., Gary, Ind., 1989-91, mem. drug-free bd., 1991—, Snowflake dir., 1993—. Tchr. Sunday sch., youth dir. Beacon Heights Ch. of Brethren, Ft. Wayne, 1966-72; tchr. Sunday sch., youth dir. Ross Ref. Ch., Gary, 1980-90, dir. vacation Bible sch., 1988; Ind. rep. Marigold Soc. Am., 1982-89; leader Cub Scouts Am., Boy Scouts Am., Gary, 1980-88. Mem. ASCD, Instnl. Tchrs. Assn. (sec. 1968-70), N.W. Coop. Tchrs. Union. Home: 5835 W 45th Ave Gary IN 46408-3424

CHEHEBAR-VALDES, JACQUELINE, neuropsychologist, consultant, researcher; b. Bklyn., Sept. 17, 1962; d. Gabriel and Rosy (Mosseri) Chehebar; m. Manuel Valdes, June 3, 1990. BA, U. Conn., 1983; cert. in substance abuse studies, Nova U., 1987, MS, 1988; PhD, Nova U., Ft. Lauderdale, 1992. Therapist asst. Cedars Med. Ctr., Miami, Fla., 1983-84; children's outpatient coord. Jewish Family Svc., Miami Beach, Fla., 1988-89; neuropsychology apprentice Robert A. Levitt, Ph.D., PA, Miami Beach, Fla., 1989-90; intern Columbia Presbyn. Med. Ctr., N.Y.C., 1990-91; fellow and resident Robert A. Levitt, PhD, PA, Ft. Lauderdale, 1991-93; pvt. practice, 1993—; dir. neuropsychology svcs. Hollywood (Fla.) Meml. Med. Ctr., Rehab. Unit, 1995—; psychology supr., educator Sunrise (Fla.) Rehab. Hosp., 1992—; rschr., asst. dir. internship North Broward Med. Ctr., Memory Disorders Ctr. Neurolog. Inst., Pompona, Fla., 1993—, dir., 1994—; neuropsychologist Neurologic Cons., Fort Lauderdale, Fla., 1992—, Hollywood, Fla., 1992—, Memory Disorder Ctr., 1992—; neuropsychology cons. Sunrise (Fla.) Rehab. Hosp., 1992-94. Contbr. articles to profl. jours. Sec. Spanish Speaking Neuropsychology Interest Group, L.A., 1993-94; apptd. Child Sexual Abuse Svc. Provider Task Force, 1989. Mem. APA, Internat. Neuropsychol. Soc., Nat. Acad. Neuropsychologists, Nat. Head Injury Found., Fla. Psychol. Assn. Democrat. Jewish. Home: 520 E Mt Vernon Dr Plantation FL 33325 Office: No Broward Med Ctr Neurol Inst and Memory Disorder Ctr 201 E Sample Rd Pompano Beach FL 33064

CHEILEK, HAZEL K., secondary school educator, musician; b. Cleve., Jan. 20, 1933; d. W. Worley and Edna (Fischer) Kerlin; m. Harold A. Cheilek, Dec. 26, 1964; children: Alan Joseph, Anne Tila. BS, Case Western Reserve U., 1954; MM, U. Tex., Austin, 1956. Tchr. stringed instruments Cleve. Pub. Schs., 1956-58; violist Philharmonia Hungarica, Vienna, Austria, 1958-59, San Pietro Chamber Orch., Naples, Italy, 1959-63; tchr. Buffalo Schs., 1963-65; freelance violist Buffalo, 1964-70, Washington, 1970—; viola instr. DC Youth Orch., Washington, 1970-81; orch. dir. Fairfax County Schs., Fairfax, Va., 1980-84, Thomas Jefferson H.S. for Sci. & Tech., Alexandria, Va., 1984—. Mem. Music Tchrs. Nat. Assn., Music Educators Nat. Conf., Am. String Tchrs. Assn., Chamber Music Am. (Heidi Castleman award 1993). Office: Thos Jefferson HS for Sci and Tech 6560 Braddock Rd Alexandria VA 22312

CHELL, BEVERLY C., lawyer; b. Phila., Aug. 12, 1942; d. Max M. and Cecelia (Portney) C.; m. Robert M. Chell, June 21, 1964. BA, U. Pa., 1964; JD, N.Y. Law Sch., 1967; LLM, NYU, 1973. Bar: N.Y. 1967. Assoc. Polur & Polur, N.Y.C., 1967-68, Thomas V. Kingham Esq., N.Y.C., 1968-69; v.p., sec., asst. gen. counsel, dir. Athlone Industries Inc., Parsippany, N.J., 1969-81; asst. v.p., asst. sec., assoc. gen. counsel Macmillan Inc., N.Y.C., 1981-85, v.p., sec., gen. counsel, 1985-90; vice chmn., gen. counsel K-III Holdings, N.Y.C., 1990-92, K-III Comm. Corp., N.Y.C., 1992—. Mem. Assn. of Bar of City of N.Y., Am. Soc. Corp. Secs. Home: 1050 5th Ave New York NY 10028-0110 Office: K-III Comm Corp 745 5th Ave Fl 23 New York NY 10151-0002*

CHELSTROM, MARILYN ANN, political education consultant; b. Mpls., Dec. 5; d. Arthur Rudolph and Signe (Johnson) C. BA, U. Minn., 1950; LHD, Oklahoma City U., 1981. Staff asst. Mpls. Citizens Com. Public Edn., 1950-57; coord. policies and procedures Lithium Corp. Am., Inc., Mpls., N.Y.C., 1957-62; exec. dir. The Robert A. Taft Inst. Govt., N.Y.C., 1962-77, exec. v.p., 1977-78, pres., 1978-89, pres. emeritus, 1990—; polit. edn. cons., 1990—; pres. Chelstrom Connection, 1992—. Editor: Teaching the Excitement of Politics in America, 1984, Political Parties, Two Party Goverment and Democracy in United States, 1988. Active LWV, Mpls., 1950-60, N.Y.C., 1972—; charter mem. Citizens League Greater Mpls., 1952-60; del. White House Conf. on Edn., 1955; vice chmn. Minn. Women for Humphrey, 1954; treas. councilman Luth. Ch. Recipient Cert. of Recognition for Svc. to Mpls. Pub. Schs., Mpls. Citizens Com., 1957; named Town Topper, Mpls. Star, 1958. Mem. Am. Polit. Sci. Assn., Minn. Alumni Assn. (gov. N.Y. 1963—, pres. 1971-73, nat. dir. 1971-75), Minn. Alumni Club (Mpls.). Lutheran. Home: 9600 Portland Ave Minneapolis MN 55420-4564 Office: 155 E 38th St New York NY 10016-2660

CHELTON, ELAINE, pianist; b. Bklyn., June 23, 1955; d. Jack and Sylvia C.; m. Bob Mastrogiacomo, Aug. 21, 1983. MusB, Queens Coll., 1978, MA, 1986. Piano instr. Aaron Copeland Sch. Music, N.Y., 1982-88; pianist Am. Dance Machine, Eglevsky Ballet, L.I., N.Y., 1982-90; solo pianist N.Y.C. Ballet, 1990; keyboard nat. tour Evita, 1988. Recordings as pianist include (film) Nutcracker, 1992, (CD) Ballet Music for Barre and Center Floor, 1996. Mem. ASCAP, Dramatists Guild. Office: NYC Ballet 20 Lincoln Plz New York NY 10023

CHEN, BARBARA MARIE, anesthesiologist; b. Youngstown, Ohio, May 17, 1960; d. Ching Chi and Kim Lian Chen. BS summa cum laude, Youngstown State U., 1981; MD, St. Louis U., 1985. Diplomate Am. Soc. Anesthesiologists. Resident in surgery Bklyn.-Caledonian Hosp., Bklyn., 1985-88; resident in anesthesia Georgetown U. Hosp., Washington, 1989-92; staff anesthesiologist NIH, Bethesda, Md., 1992-93; staff anesthesiologist, researcher Georgetown U. Hosp., Washington, 1992-95; staff anesthesiologist Providence Hosp., Anchorage, Alaska, 1996—. Vol. Spl. Olympics, Arlington, Va., 1992, Cmty. for a Creative Nonviolence, Washington, 1989-95, Holiday Project, 1989-95, Martha's Table, 1994-95. Recipient Robert Dripps Meml. award Janssen Pharm., 1991. Mem. AMA, Am. Soc. Anesthesiologists, Am. Regional Soc. Anesthesiologists, Am. Heart Assn., Am. Med. Women's Assn., Soc. Cardiovascular Anesthesiologists. Office: Providence Hosp 3300 Providence Dr Ste 107 Anchorage AK 99508-4619

CHEN, CHING-CHIH, information science educator, consultant; b. Foochow, Fukien, China, Sept. 3, 1937; came to U.S, 1959; d. Han-chia and May-ying (Liu) Liu; m. Sow-Hsin Chen, Aug. 19, 1961; children: Anne, Catherine, John. BA, Nat. Taiwan U., Taipei, 1959; MLS, U. Mich., 1961; PhD, Case Western Res. U., 1974. Asst. Sch. Libr. Sci. U. Mich., Ann Arbor, 1960-61, svc. libr., 1961-62; sci. reference libr. McMaster U., Hamilton, Ont., Can., 1962-63, head sci. libr., 1963-64; sr. sci. libr. U. Waterloo, Ont., Can., 1964-65; head engring., math. and sci. libr. U. Waterloo, Can., 1965-68; assoc. sci. libr. MIT, Cambridge, Mass., 1968-71; asst. prof. Sch. Libr. and Info. Sci. Simmons Coll., Boston, 1971-76, asst. dean for acad. affaris Sch. Libr. and Info. Sci., 1977-79, assoc. dean, prof. Sch. Libr. and Info. Sci., 1979—; cons. Am. Soc. Info. Sci./Cath. U. Am., 1976-77, Chung-Shan Inst. Sci. Rsch., Taiwan, 1977-87, Abt Assocs., Inc., 1980-82, Sci. and Tech. Info. Ctr. Nat. Sci. Coun., Taiwan, 1973-77, S.E. Asia Region WHO, 1980, 81, Engring. Info. Inc., 1982, UNESCO, Paris, 1984, Nat. Geographic Soc., 1985, Norman Bethuen U. Med. Scis. Libr., 1986, Getty Trust, 1988, USIA, 1988, Ont. Coun. Gradual Studies, 1989, FID, 1989, World Bank, 1990, UNESCO, 1991, DataConsult, Mex., 1991, Soros Found., 1992-93, USIA, 1993-95. Author, editor 26 books including Biomedical, Scientific and Technical Book Reviewing, 1976, Sourcebook on Health Sciences Librarianship, 1977, Quantitative Measurement and Dynamic Library Service, 1978, Scientific & Technical Information Sources, 2d edit., 1987, (with others) Numeric Databases, 1984, HyperSource on Hypermedia/Multimedia Technologies, 1989, HyperSource on Optical Technologies, 1989, Optical Technologies in Libraries: Use & Trends, 1991, Planning Global Information Infrastructure, 1995; editor-in-chief: Microcomputers for Information Management, 1983—; also editor numerous conf. proceedings; contbr. over 100 articles to profl. jours. Barbour scholar U. Mich., 1959-61, Case Western Res. U. fellow, 1973-74, NATO fellow, 1975, AAAS fellow, 1985; Emily Hollowell Rsch. grantee, 1972—, Simmons Coll. Fund Rsch. grantee, 1972-81; recipient Disting. Svc. award Chinese-Am. Librs. Assn., 1982, Cert. of Appreciation, Asian-Pacific-Am. Librs. Assn., 1983, Disting. Alumni award U. Mich., 1983, Outstanding Svc. award Nat. Cen. Libr., 1986, Disting. Svc. award Asian-Am. Libr. Assn, 1992, Cindy award Assn. Visual Comm., 1992. Fellow AAAS; mem. ALA (disting. svc. award 1989, Humphrey award 1996), AAUP, Am. Soc. Info. Sci. (best Info. Sci. Tchr. award 1983), Assn. Am. Libr. Schs., Assn. Coll. and Rsch. Librs., Libr. Info. Tech. Assn. (Gaylord Libr. and Info. Tech. Achievement award 1990, Outstanding Achievement Libr. Hi Tech. award 1994), New Eng. Libr. Assn. (Emerson Greenaway award 1994). Home: 1400 Commonwealth Ave Newton MA 02165-2830 Office: Simmons Coll 300 Fenway Boston MA 02115-5820

CHEN, CONCORDIA CHAO, mathematician; b. Peiping, China; came to U.S., 1955, naturalized, 1969; d. Chun-fu and Kwie Hwa (Wong) Chao; BA in Bus. Adminstrn., Nat. Taiwan U., 1954; MS in Math., Marquette U., 1958; postgrad. Purdue U., 1958-60, M.I.T., 1961-62; m. Chin Chen, July 2, 1960; children: Marie Hui-mei, Albert Chao. Teaching asst. Purdue U., Lafayette, Ind., 1958-60; system analysis engr. electronic data processing div. Mpls.-Honeywell, Newton Highlands, Mass., 1960-63; mgmt. planning asst. Lederle Labs., Am. Cyanamid Co., Pearl River, N.Y., 1964, computer applications specialist, 1967, ops. analyst, 1967; staff programmer IBM, Sterling Forest, N.Y., 1968-73, adv. programmer Data Processing Mktg. Group, Poughkeepsie, 1973-80, mgr. systems programming and systems architecture, Princeton, N.J., 1980-82, sr. systems analyst, 1982-83, data processing mktg. cons., Beijing, 1983-88; sr. planner IBM DSD, Poughkeepsie, 1988-92; program mgr. Chiang Indsl. Charity Found Ltd., 1993-94; mgr. software engring. China Weal Bus. Machinery Co., Ltd., Hong Kong, 1995—. Chmn. ednl. council Hudson region MIT. Mem. Am. Math. Soc., Soc. Indsl. and Applied Maths., MIT Club Hudson Valley (pres.). Home: 85 Moulton St Newton Lower Falls MA 02162-1407 Office: 9 Queens Rd 8th Fl Ctrl, Hong Kong Hong Kong

CHEN, EDNA LAU, art educator, artist; b. Lanai City, Hawaii, Apr. 20, 1932; d. George S.H. and Amy (Choy) Lau; m. Francis F. Chen, Mar. 31, 1956; children: Sheryl Frances, Patricia Ann, Robert Francis. BA, U. No. Colo., 1954; MA, Columbia U., 1955. Cert. tchr., Calif. Tchr. Somerville (N.J.) H.S., 1955-56, Littlebrook Sch., Princeton, N.J., 1956-57, L.A. County Mus., 1978-81, Beverly Hills (Calif.) Adult Sch., 1976—; vol., founder, dir. Garret 21, Warner Sch., L.A., 1971-77; artist-in-residence Volcano (Hawaii) Art Ctr., 1978, 80. Solo shows include Gallery 100, Princeton, N.J., 1964, 68, 72, 73, Jacqueline Anhalt Gallery, L.A., 1975, Elaine Starkman Gallery, N.Y.C., 1983, Art Loft, Honolulu, 1983, 85, 87. Named Tchr. of Yr., Beverly Hills Kiwanis Club, 1979. Democrat. Unitarian. Home: 638 Westholme Ave Los Angeles CA 90024

CHEN, FANNY YING, accountant; b. Shanghai, China, Feb. 26, 1969; came to the U.S., 1988; d. De Fang Chen and Pei Qin Lin; m. Ricky Z. Ma, Sept. 16, 1995. BS in Commerce, DePaul U., 1992, postgrad., 1996—. Assoc. acct. Ecker Enterprise Corp., Chgo., 1990-92; sr. tax acct. Blackman, Kallica, Bartelstein, LLP, Chgo., 1993-95; fin. analyst McDonald's Corp., Oak Brook, Ill., 1996—; officer Silver-Shield Internat. Corp., Chgo., 1994—, China Capital Devel. Investment Corp., St. Louis, 1995. Recipient Tchr.'s Union award Tchr.'s Union City Colls., Chgo., 1990, The Nat. Dean's List award, Nat. Gold Key Honor Soc. Mem. Asian Am. Profl. Assn., Acctg. Club, Beta Alpha Psi. Office: McDonalds Corp Oak Brook Acctg Ctr #943-A McDonalds Plz CS 9030 Oak Brook IL 60522

CHEN, JOAN (CHEN CHONG), actress; b. Shanghai, China, 1961; came to U.S., 1981; Appeared in films including Little Flower, 1978, Awakening, 1980, Dim Sum: A Little Bit of Heart, 1985, Tai-Pan, 1986, The Last Emperor, 1987, Night Stalker, 1987, Blood of Heroes, 1990, Turtle Beach, 1993, Where Sleeping Dogs Lie, 1993, On Deadly Ground, 1994, Golden Gate, 1994, Heaven and Earth, 1994, The Hunted, 1995, Judge Dredd, 1995, Wild Side, Precious Find; TV appearances include Twin Peaks, Miami Vice, (TV movie) Shadow of a Stranger. Office: 2601 Filbert St San Francisco CA 94123-3215*

CHEN, LYNN CHIA-LING, librarian; b. Peking, China, Dec. 3, 1932; came to U.S., 1955; d. Shu-Peng Wang; m. Di Chen, June 14, 1958; children: Andrew A., Daniel T. BA, Nat. Taiwan U., 1955; MLS, U. Minn., 1957. Cataloger Hennepin County Libr., Edina, Minn., 1972-80; libr./programmer Prorodeo Hall of Champions, Colorado Springs, Colo., 1981-83; ref. libr. Meml. Hosp., Colorado Springs, 1983-85; asst. libr. Am. Numismatic Assn., Colorado Springs, 1985-90, head libr., 1991—. Mem. Colo. Libr. Assn., Spl. Libr. Assn. Home: 302 Sunbird Cliffs Ln W Colorado Springs CO 80919-8017 Office: American Numismatic Assn 818 N Cascade Ave Colorado Springs CO 80903-3208

CHENAULT, MARILYN MATHIS, legal administrator; b. Mt. Vernon, Ill., Oct. 21, 1949; d. Nathan Bullock and Marguerite (Woodberry) Chenault; m. Tom Dee McFall, Aug. 29, 1969; children: Shannon, Nathan; m. Troy David Phillips, Aug. 14, 1981; stepchildren: Todd, Brittany. BS with honors, Okla. State U., 1970. Retail analyst Opticks, Inc. div. G. D. Searle, Dallas, 1977-78; dir. of adminstr. Glast, Phillips and Murray, Dallas, 1978-81; exec. dir. Haynes and Boone L.L.P., Dallas, 1981-94; prin. Chenault and Co., 1994-95; exec. dir. Wolf, Greenfield & Sachs, P.C., 1995—; adj. prof. So. Meth. U. Sch. Law, Dallas, 1981-94; instr. paralegal program So. Meth. U., 1981-85; legal adv. coun. Wang Labs., 1985-91, Pitney Bowes, 1991—; mem. Tech. Task Force, 1989-93; chair Practicing Law Profitability Conf., 1984, Large Law Firm Tech. Conf., 1990; co-chair Law Net Inc. Conf., 1988. Contbr. articles to Nat. Law Jour. Lou Wentz scholar Coll. Bus., Okla. State U., Stillwater, 1969-70, also C.V. Richardson scholar, 1969-70; named Outstanding Coll. Bus. Grad., 1970. Mem. NAFE, State Bar Tex. (law office mgmt. com. 1991-94), Dallas Bar Assn. (strategic planning com. 1990-94, chair mktg. subcom.) Tex. Lawyer Law Tech. Planning Com. 1992, Nat. Assn. Legal Adminstrs. (dir. of adminstrn. sect. 1979-85, large firm adminstrn. sect. 1985-91, com. mem. 1986-88, vice-chmn. 1989-90, chmn., 1990-91, chair in-house tng. task force, 1990-91, communication/governance/structure issues task force 1988-89, instr. law office adminstrn. course 1984, 87, pres. Dallas chpt. 1985-86, prin. adminstrs. team 1992—, nat. nominating co. 1992-93, nat. certification task force 1996—). Home: 36 Mount Vernon St # 2 Charlestown MA 02129 Office: Federal Reserve Plz 600 Atlantic Boston MA 02210

CHENEY, CAROL, endocrinologist; b. St. Louis, June 29, 1948; d. Robert Simpson and Nancy Ann (Bisel) C.; m. Joshua Aaron Bardin, June 9, 1979; children: Joseph, Jonathan. BA summa cum laude, Oberlin Coll., 1970; MD, U. Calif., San Diego, 1976. Diplomate Am. Bd. Internal Medicine, Am. Bd. Endocrinology. Intern, resident in internal medicine U. Calif., San Diego, 1976-82, asst. clin. prof. medicine, 1982-83; pvt. practice endocrinology Encinitas, Calif., 1984-86; endocrinologist Scripps Clinic and Rsch. Found., La Jolla, Calif., 1986—; assoc. clin. prof. U. Calif., San Diego, 1986—. NSF fellow, 1970-71, Woodrow Wilson Found. fellow, 1970-71. Fellow ACP; mem. Am. Diabetes Assn. (chair patient edn. 1987-91, bd. dirs. 1987-93), Juvenile Diabetes Assn. (bd. dirs. 1994—), Endocrine Soc., N.Am. Menopause Soc., Jacobs Inst. for Women's Health. Democrat. Office: Scripps Clinic 10666 N Torrey Pines Rd La Jolla CA 92037-1027

CHENEY, ELEANORA LOUISE, retired secondary education educator; b. Seneca Falls, N.Y., June 3, 1923; d. Guy Darrell and Alice Augusta (McCoy) Stevenson; m. John C. Dinsmore, Jan. 13, 1941 (div. 1953); children: Patricia Walter, Nancy Shannon, Jon Dinsmore (dec.); m. Daniel Laverne Cheney, Aug. 8, 1959. BA, Rutgers U., 1966; MA, U. Glassboro, 1971. Account clk. GE, Auburn, N.Y., 1953-58; supr. accounts payable Sylvania Electric, Camillus, N.Y., 1958-60; cost acctg. clk. RCA, Cherry Hill, N.J., 1960-64; honors English tchr. Lenape Regional High Sch., Medford, N.J., 1966-74; guidance counselor Shawnee High Sch., 1974-81; owner Another World of Travel, Marlton, N.J., 1981-86; co-founder, trustee, sec. Danellie Found., 1991—; part-time travel agt., 1986—; notary pub., 1983—. Counselor Contact Ministries, Moorestown, N.J., 1976—; mem. fin. com., nominating com. Haddonfield (N.J.) United Meth. Ch., 1987-92, supr. ch. sch., 1980-82; bd. dirs. Fellowship House, Camden, N.J., 1994—; mem. adminstrv. coun. Haddonfield (N.J.) United Meth. Ch., 1996—. Named to Nat. Woman's Hall of Fame, 1994. Mem. AAUW. Republican. Methodist. Home: 445 Westminster Ave Haddonfield NJ 08033-4024

CHENEY, LOIS SWEET, infection control nurse; b. Clifton Springs, N.Y., Oct. 26, 1933; d. Merton E. Sr. (dec.) and Jennie M. (Smith) S. (dec.); divorced; children: Linda Cheney Thorpe, Susan Cheney Post, Douglas A. Cheney. Diploma in nursing, Rochester (N.Y.) Gen. Hosp., 1954; BS in Edn. with high honors, Mansfield (Pa.) State Coll., 1973; MS, Columbia Pacific U., Mill Valley, Calif., 1982. RN, N.Y. With Meml. Hosp., Towanda, Pa., 1974-82; coord. infection control and employee health Clifton Springs Hosp. and Clinic, 1982-87; now infection control officer Monroe Cmty. Hosp., Rochester, 1987—; spkr. on mgmt. AIDS in long term care, 1987, 88, 89, 92; spkr. and cons. in infection control. Contbr. articles to profl. jours. Mem. Assn. Profls. in Infection Control and Epidemiology (cert., Rochester-Finger Lakes chpt.), Bus. and Profls. Women's Club, Toastmasters Internat. Intravenous Nurses Soc., N.Y. State Pub. Health Assn.

CHENHALLS, ANNE MARIE, nurse, educator; b. Detroit, May 26, 1929; d. Peter and Beatrice Mary (Elliston) McLeod; m. Horacio Chenhalls, 1953 (dec.); children: Mark, Anne Marie Chenhalls Delamater. Student Detroit Conservatory Music, 1946-47; grad. Grace Hosp. Sch. Nursing, 1951; B. Vocat. Edn., Calif. State U.-Los Angeles, 1967, B.S. in Nursing, 1968; M.A., Calif. State U.-Long Beach, 1985. R.N., Calif. Nurse, Grace Hosp., Detroit, 1951-52; pvt. duty nurse, Mexico City, 1953-54; nurse St. Francis Hosp., Lynwood, Calif., 1957-63; assoc. prof. nursing Compton Coll. (Calif.), 1964-72; health educator, sch. nurse Santa Ana Unified Sch. Dist. (Calif.), 1972-76, 79—; med. coord., internat. health cons. Agape Movement, San Bernardino, Calif., 1976-79; instr. community health, Uganda, 1982; med. evaluator Athletes in Action, 1979; pub. health nurse Orange County Health Dept., Calif., 1990-95 . Assoc. staff mem. Campus Crusade for Christ. Solo vocalist, Santa Ana, Orange, Seal Beach, Dinner Theater, Calif., Civic Light Opera, Buena Park, Calif.; acting Master's Repertory Theater, 1990—, Santa Ana. U.S. govt. grantee, 1968. Mem. Calif. Sch. Nurses Assn., Nat. Educators Assn., Calif. Tchrs. Assn. Democrat. Home: 30802 S Coast Hwy Trlr A2 Laguna Beach CA 92651-4207 Office: Santa Ana Unified Sch Dist 1405 French St Santa Ana CA 92701-2414

CHENOWETH, ELIZABETH REARICK WINELAND, retired retail administrator; b. Des Moines, Sept. 9, 1933; d. Harold Haggard and Luella Jane (Burt) Rearick; m. William Harrison Wineland, May 30, 1956 (dec. Oct. 1969); children: Nora Elizabeth, Jonathan David: m. Maynard B. Chenoweth, Mar. 2, 1985 (dec. Apr. 1988). BS, Beloit Coll., 1955. Analytical chemist Dow Chem. Co., Midland, Mich., 1956-58; bookstore mgr. Saginaw Valley State Coll., University Ctr., Mich., 1967-88, bookstore dir., 1988-92. Mem. Midland Bd. Edn., 1974-86, pres., 1980-82; class agt. 1955 Beloit Coll., 1984—. Mem. AAUW (parliamentarian 1974-76, 85-87, chmn. legis. program 1987-89, sec. 1989-91, treas. 1992-94, co-pres. 1995—), Nat. Assn. Coll. Stores (cert. store profl.).

CHENOWETH, HELEN, congresswoman; b. Topeka, Kans., Jan. 27, 1938; 2 children. Attended, Whitworth Coll., 1975-79; cert. in law office mgmt., U. Minn., 1974; student, Rep. Nat. Com. Mgmt. Coll., 1977. Bus. mgr. Northside Med. Ctr., 1964-75; state exec. dir. Idaho Rep. Party, 1975-77; chief of staff Congressman Steve Symms, 1977-78; campaign mgr. Symms for Congress Campaign, 1978, Leroy for Gov., 1985-86; v.p. Consulting Assocs., Inc., 1978—; bd. dirs. Ctr. Study of Market Alternatives. Deacon Capitol Christian Ctr., Boise. Office: US Ho of Reps 1719 Longworth Washington DC 20515

CHEOROS, EDITH MARIE, elementary school educator; b. Delmont, S.D., Jan. 14, 1940; d. John Louis and Eleanor Sophia (Mosel) Fuchs; m. Peter Joseph Cheoros, Dec. 14, 1941; 1 child, Lisa Maria Cheoros Yamamoto. BS, Concordia Tchrs. Coll., 1962. Tchr. St. John's Luth. Sch., Long Beach, Calif., 1962-69, Wilson Elem. Sch., Lynwood (Calif.) Unified Sch. Dist., 1969—; participant Oropus (Greece) Project; vis. educator European Inst., Berlin. Writer curriculum Apple, 1975-78. Organist St. John's Ch., Long Beach, 1962-66; life mem. Lynwood PTA. Named Tchr. of Yr., Lynwood C. of C., 1972. Mem. NEA, Nat. Coun. Social Studies, Calif. Tchrs. Assn., Lynwood Tchrs. Assn. (tchr. adv. 1970-76), Cousteau Soc., Friends of Calypso. Lutheran.

CHEPIGA, PAMELA ROGERS, lawyer; b. N.Y.C., July 15, 1949; d. Edward and Stella (Renner) Rogers; m. Michael J. Chepiga, Nov. 21, 1970; children: Geoffrey, Emily. BA cum laude, Fordham U., 1970, JD cum laude, 1973. Bar: N.Y. 1974, U.S. Dist. Ct. (so. and ea. dists.) N.Y. 1974, U.S. Ct. Appeals (2d cir.) 1974. Law clk. to judge U.S. Dist. Ct. N.Y. (so. dist.), N.Y.C., 1973-75; assoc. Hughes, Hubbard & Reed, N.Y.C., 1975-77; asst. U.S. atty. So. Dist. N.Y. U.S. Atty.'s Office, N.Y.C., 1977-84, chief securities and commodities fraud unit, 1982-84; counsel Cadwalader, Wickersham & Taft, N.Y.C., 1984-85, 91-94, ptnr., 1985-91; lectr. in securities and white-collar criminal field. Mem. Assn. Bar City of N.Y. (young lawyers com. 1975-78, com. fed. legis. 1980-84, com. minorities in prof. 1985-89, criminal law com. 1988-90), N.Y. State Bar Assn. (com. fed. constn. 1980-83).

CHERE, ANN MARGARET, sculptor, educator; b. Bklyn., June 11, 1958; d. Jerome Vito and Jean (Guido) Colonna; m. Russell William Chere, Feb. 27, 1991. BA, SUNY, Stony Brook, 1980. Mgr. B. Dalton Bookseller, Queens, N.Y., 1981-82, N.Y.C., 1983-84; mgr. Walden Books, L.I., N.Y., 1982-83; freelance studio mgr./exhbn. coord. N.Y.C., 1983-87; asst. showroom mgr. Nat. Craft Show Room, N.Y.C., 1987; gallery dir. Pindar Gallery, N.Y.C., 1988-90; sculpting apprentice Vera Lightstone, Sculptor, N.Y.C., 1983-89; ceramics tchr. Kinnelon (N.J.) Sch. Enrichment Program, 1994-96; sculptor, pvt. instr. Warwick, N.Y., 1990—; tchr. enrichment program Warwick (N.Y.) Sch., 1996. Solo shows include Unitarian Soc. of Orange County exhbn., 1993; group exhibits include Unitarian Soc. exhbns., 1991, Trotting Horse Mus., Goshen, N.Y., 1992, 93, 94, 95, Studio 18 Visual Arts Ctr., Middletown, N.Y., 1992, Orange Classic Festival Art Show, 1993, Lake George (N.Y.) Arts Project, 1993, Middletown (N.Y.) Arts Ctr., 1993, 94, 95, Times Herald-Record, Middletown, 1994, 95, Sullivan County Art and Cultural Ctr., Hurleyville, N.Y., 1994, 96, Lill St. Gallery, Chgo., 1994, Applewood Winery, Warwick, 1995, Herter Gallery, U. Mass./Amherst,

1995, Chilton Pub. Co., Wayne, Pa., 1996, Gallery JJENTH, Peekskill, N.Y., 1996, Cooperstown Art Assn. Nat. Exhbn., N.Y., 1996. Vol. coord. Cmty. 2000: Arts and Culture Task Force, Warwick, 1995-96; sec., newsletter editor Warwick Art League, 1995-96, treas., 1992-94; vol. tchr. Warwick Valley Sch. Dist., 1991-96; vol. NOW, N.Y.C., 1984-87, treas., 1987-89; mem. N.Y. Found. for the Arts. United Fedn. tchrs. scholar, 1976, N.Y. State Bd. Regents scholar, 1976. Mem. Empire State Crafts Alliance. Democrat.

CHEREM, BARBARA BROWN, education educator; b. Detroit, May 4, 1949; d. Max Frederick and Dorothy Catherine (Bender) Brown; m. Gabriel Jerome Cherem, May 1973; children: Mariah, Max. BA in English and Secondary Tchg., U. Mich., 1971; MA Ed. in Spl. Edn., Mich. State U., 1975, PhD in Edn., 1991. Tchr. Romulus (Mich.) H.S., Hawthorn Children's Psychiat. Sch., Northville, Mich., Wittenberg (Wis.)-Birnamwood H.S.; pres., owner Leaning Shop, Columbus, Ohio; tchr. cons. Jackson (Mich.) Pub. Schs., 1977-79; rsch. and curriculum devel. grantee Ea. Mich. U., Ypsilanti, 1979-83; prof., dir. assessment Spring Arbor (Mich.) Coll., 1983—; v.p. Interp Ctrl., Chelsea, Mich., 1979-89; cons. in field. Trustee Chelsea Pub. Schs., 1986-90; mem. adminstrv. bd. First United Meth. Ch., Chelsea, 1983-85. Mem. AAUW, Am. Assn. Adult Continuing Edn. (trustee 1993—), Phi Delta Kappa, Alpha Delta Pi (philanthropy chair 1967). Office: Spring Arbor Coll 102 N Main Spring Arbor MI 49283

CHERIS, ELAINE GAYLE INGRAM, business owner; b. Ashford, Ala., Jan. 8, 1946; m. Samuel David Cheris, June 8, 1980; 1 child, Zachariah Adam Abraham. BS, Troy State U., 1971. Aquatics dir. Yale U., New Haven, 1976-79; owner, mgr. Cheyenne Fencing Soc., Denver, 1980—; chmn. organizing com. World Fencing Championships, 1989, World Jr./Cadet Fencing Championships, 1993. Author: Handbook for Parents - Fencing, 1988, 2d edit., 1992; editor Yofen Mag., 1988-90, 1992—. Mem. Gov.'s Coun. on Sports and Fitness, Colo., 1990—; commr. Colo. State Games-Fencing, 1989—. Mem. U.S. Olympic Team, 1980, 88 (6th place fencing), 96 (mem. women's epee team), mem. U.S. Pan-Am. Games Team, 1987 (Gold medal women's foil team), 1991 (Gold medal women's epee team); named Sportswoman of Yr. Fencing, YWCA, 1980, 81, 82, to Sportswoman Hall of Fame, 1982; mem. U.S. World Championship Fencing Team, 1982, 85, 87, 90, 91, 92, 93, U.S. Maccabiah Fencing Team, 1981 (1 gold, 1 silver medal); recipient Gold Medal of Honor from Fedn. Internat. d'Escrime, 1993. Mem. AAPHERD, U.S. Fencing Assn. (youth chmn. 1988-90, editor Youth mag., 1988-90, 92—, chmn. Colo. divsn., 1992-94), Fedn. Internat. d'Escrime (chmn. Atlanta fencing project '96, chmn. World Fencing Day 1994). Jewish. Office: Cheyenne Fencing Soc 5818 E Colfax Ave Denver CO 80220-1507

CHERKEZIAN-KILLIGAN, BEATRICE MICHELLE, artist; b. Buenos Aires, Jan. 31, 1966; came to U.S., 1966; d. Sebuh and Catherine (Balderian) Cherkezian; m. Albert Richard Killigan, Dec. 19, 1963. AA and Art Edn., Miami-Dade C.C., 1993; BFA, Fla. Internat. U., 1995; postgrad., U. Miami, 1995—. Designer ready-to-wear sportswear, Buenos Aires, Avignon, France, Chgo., 1965-83; dir. sch. ballet Dance Experience of Coral Gables, Fla., 1975-82; dir. Gables Art Gallery, Coral Gables, 1978-82; tchg. asst. U. Miami, Fla., 1995—; pvt. art tutor, art cons. and evaluator, Coral Gables, 1980—. Exhibited in group shows Salon des Independents, Paris, 1988—, Gallery Ariel and Nesle, Paris, 1980—; contbr. articles to various publs. Vice chmn. cultural bd. City of Coral Gables, 1995-97, mem. adv. bd. cultural affairs. Fellow U. Miami, 1995-97.

CHERMAYEFF, ALEXANDRA SASHA, artist; b. N.Y.C., Feb. 17, 1960; d. Ivan and Sara Anne (Duffy) C.; m. Philip W. Howie, May 10, 1992; children: Phineas Alexander, Olivia Isabel. BA, U. Vt., 1982; postgrad., N.Y. Studio Sch., 1983-86. Cert. appraiser N.Y. Univ. Sch. Appraisal Studies. Cons. Alexandra Chermayeff Artist Svcs., N.Y.C., 1987—; asst. to chmn., bd. dirs. Andy Warhol Found., N.Y.C., 1991-93; collection mgr., curator Frederick Hughes, N.Y.C., 1991—; curatorial asst. Heiner Bastian Fine Art, Berlin, 1991—. Exhibited in group shows Bowery Gallery, N.Y., 1992, Addison Gallery, Andover, Mass., 1993, Parrish Art Mus., N.Y., 1994 (award 1994), N.Y. Studio Sch. Gallery, 1995. Recipient Allied Artist award Nat. Arts Club, 1985; Ellen Battell Stoeckel fellow Yale U., 1985. Mem. Greene County Coun. on the Arts. Office: Fred Hughes Ste 905 286 Fifth Ave New York NY 10001

CHERNAY, GLORIA JEAN, association executive; b. Cleve., Oct. 14, 1938; d. Joseph and Angela M. (Fiorelli) Iuliano; m. Terry A. Chernay, July 11, 1959 (div. 1973); children: Debbie Jean, Vickie Ann. BS, Ind. State U., 1959; MS, Ind. U., South Bend, 1971; PhD, Mich. State U., 1977. Tchr. Mishawaka (Ind.) Pub. Schs., 1960-74; instr. Mich. State U., E. Lansing, 1974-76; asst. prof. George Mason U., Fairfax, Va., 1976-82; dep. dir. Nat. Coun. for Accreditation of Tchr. Edn., Washington, 1982-86; dir. constituent svcs. Coun. on Postsec. Accreditation, Washington, 1986-90; exec. dir. Assn. of Tchr. Educators, Reston, Va., 1990—; ednl. cons. fed., state, local edn. agencies and higher edn. instns. Contbr. articles to profl. jours. Bd. dirs. Lake Audubon Terrace Cmty. Assn., 1995—; pres. Hawthorne Village, Fairfax, 1987-88, bd. dirs. 1988-92. Mem. Phi Delta Kappa (area coord. 1988-90). Office: Assn Tchr Educators 1900 Association Dr Ste ATE Reston VA 20191-1502

CHERNENKO, ANN MARIE, artist, entertainer, writer; b. L.A.. BFA, UCLA; MFA, U. Calif., Irvine. coord. Laguna Art Mus. Juried Show, Laguna Beach, 1983, Orange County Arts Commn. Arts Festival, Calif., 1984. One-woman shows include Ivy Gallery, L.A., 1987, 88, San Francisco State U., 1988, Convergence Gallery, San Francisco, 1988, 89, Diane Nelson Gallery, Laguna Beach, Calif., 1989, Williams-Lamb Gallery, Long Beach, Calif., 1989, 90; two-person shows include Newport Harbor Art Mus., Newport Beach, Calif., 1983; group shows include Laguna Art Mus., Laguna Beach, 1983; performed leading and feature roles in Santa Fe local and cmty. theatres; performer Good Morning N.Mex. comml. KOAT-TV Sta., Albuquerque, 1995. Recipient Purchase award Wash. State Arts Commn., 1983; named Artist of the Month KOCE-TV Sta., Orange, Calif., 1984. Office: 289 S Robertson Blvd # 155 Beverly Hills CA 90211

CHERNOFF-PATE, DIANA, interior designer, small business owner; b. San Mateo, Calif., Apr. 7, 1942; d. Fred Eugene and Nadine (Chernoff) Pate; 1 child, Kim Renee. BA in Design, U. Calif., Berkeley. Lic. cosmetologist, Calif. Owner, mgr. Diana Interiors/Design, Napa, Calif.; co-owner, v.p., mgr. ops. Stickney Enterprises, Redwood, Calif., Stickney Restaurants and Bakeries, Redwood; pub. rels. specialist, coord. passenger svc. tng. TWA, San Francisco; adminstr. Internat. Fed. Employees Benefits, 1973, Pension Funds, 1982. Author: Cooking for Profit. Co-sponsor Stanford Athletic Fund, Stanford U.; mem. Frank Lloyd Wright Found. Mem. LWV (Carmel br.), NAFE, Internat. Platform Assn., Am. Soc. Phys. Rsch., Embroiderers Guild Am. (founder San Mateo and Santa Clara chpts.), Internat. Parliament Safety and Peace, Maison Internat. Intellectuels Acad. Midi, Germany Inst. Applied Rsch., World Affairs Coun., Designers Lighting Forum, Inst. Noetic Scis., San Francisco De Young Mus., San Francisco Asian Mus., San Francisco Ballet, Commonwealth Club of Calif. Home: 1220 Cayetano Dr Napa CA 94559-4263

CHERNUSHIN, HEIDEMARIE ELISABETH, public affairs assistant; b. Cleve., Sept. 2, 1957; d. Walter Stephan and Ilse Margarethe (Stamminger) Kostendt; m. Mark Chernushin, Nov. 29, 1980 (dir. Sept. 1990); children: Nikolas Sylvester, Alexander John. BA, Kent State U., 1979, postgrad., 1990—. Auto travel counselor AAA-Ohio Motorists Assn., Parma, 1988-89; pub. affairs asst. AAA-Ohio Motorists Assn., Cleve., 1989—. Pres. BBG Adult Svc. Club, Parma, 1993—; rec. sec. bd. Christian edn. St. Paul United Ch. of Christ, Parma, 1992—. Mem. Women in Comm., Inc. Home: 8252 Ridge Rd North Royalton OH 44133 Office: AAA Ohio Motorists Assn 6000 S Marginal Rd Cleveland OH 44133

CHERRY, BARBARA WATERMAN, speech and language pathologist, physical therapist; b. Norfolk, Va., June 25, 1949; d. Robert Bullock and Dorothy Estelle (Walsh) Waterman; m. Albert Glen Cherry, Sept. 17, 1977; 1 child, Dorothy Louise. BS in Phys. Therapy, U. Fla., 1972, MA in Speech-Lang. Pathology, 1982. Lic. phys. therapist, speech and lang. pathologist, Fla.; cert. tchr., Fla. Staff phys. therapist Retreat for the Sick Hosp., Richmond, Va., 1973-75; clin. instr. in phys. therapy Sch. of Rehab. Scis., Tehran, Iran, 1975-76; staff phys. therapist Sulmaniya Hosp., Manama, Bahrain, 1976-77, Cathedral Rehab. Ctr., Jacksonville, Fla., 1978-80; staff speech-lang. pathologist S. Allen Smith Clinic, Jacksonville, 1982-87, Mt. Herman Exceptional Child Ctr., Jacksonville, 1987-91, Duval County Sch. System, Jacksonville, 1991—. Mem. Am. Speech, Lang., and Hearing Assn., Am. Phys. Therapy Assn., Phi Kappa Phi. Episcopalian. Home: 8821 Ivey Rd Jacksonville FL 32216-3369 Office: Moncrief Elem Sch 5443 Moncrief Rd Jacksonville FL 32209-3160

CHERRY, CAROL LYNN, principal; b. Camden, N.J., Aug. 21, 1948; d. Daniel Joseph and Louise Agnes (Smith) Brown; m. Norman Reddick Cherry, Apr. 19, 1969; children: Talenthea Melaine Cherry Hollis, Aletha Renee Cherry. BS summa cum laude, N.C. AT&T State U., 1974; MEd, Savannah-Armstrong State U., 1979; EdS, U. Ga., 1989; postgrad., Ga. State U., 1992—. Cert. adminstrn. and supervision, early childhood edn., data collector. Tchr. Dept. Def., Babenhausen, West Germany, 1975-77, Chatham County Schs., Savannah, Ga., 1979-80, Clayton County Schs., Jonesboro, Ga., 1980-83, Dept. Def., Fort Buchanan, P.R., 1983-84, Beachwood and University Heights (Ohio) Schs., 1984-86, Houston County Schs., Perry, Ga., 1986-88; instrnl. coord. Houston County Schs., Perry, 1988-94, prin., 1994—; strategic planning mem. Houston County Schs., Perry, 1990-92; adv. coun. mem. Coop. Ext. Svc., Athens, Ga., 1991-94; leadership acad. Ga. Dept. Edn., Atlanta, 1992-94. Recipient J. Everette DeVaughn Outstanding Doctoral Student award Ga. State U., 1995; named to New Leaders Inst. Ga. Dept. Edn., 1995-96. Mem. NEA, Ga. ASCD, Ga. Assn. Educators, Internat. Reading Assn. (pres. Houston-Peach reading coun. 1990-91), Am. Ednl. Rsch. Assn., Ga. Assn. Elem. Sch. Prins. (sec. 3d dist. 1994-96, pres.-elect 3d dist. 1996—), Nat. Assn. Elem. Sch. Prins. Methodist. Home: 102 Cliff Ct Bonaire GA 31005-9719

CHERRY, KAREN ANN, bank officer; b. Salina, Kans., Oct. 13, 1957; d. Lawrence Francis and Pearl Anna (Fortin) Wallerius; m. Ronald Gail Cherry, June 2, 1979; children: Lauren Renee Cherry, Sarah Marguerite Cherry. BS in Acctg., Kans. State U., 1979. Bookkeeper/staff acct. Kennedy & Coe, Salina, 1979; pharmacy technician Morris Prescription Shop, Salina, 1980-83; supplies mgr. Mowery Clinic, Salina, 1983-85; bookkeeper Bennington (Kans.) State Bank, 1985-95, asst. v.p./data processing supervisor, 1995—. Home: 604 N Lincoln Bennington KS 67422 Office: Bennington State Bank 2130 S Ohio Salina KS 67401

CHERRY, LINDA LEA, federal agency administrator; b. Davenport, Iowa, Apr. 6, 1956; d. Francis Eugene and Joan Grace (Rottman) Johnson; m. Bradley Scott Cherry, Mar. 1, 1980; children: Jacob Carl, Lucas Andrew. AA, Des Moines Area Community Coll, 1981; BS, Upper Iowa U., 1992. Cert. peace officer; cert. sex crimes investigator. Cashier Frontier Grocery Store, Polk City, Iowa, 1976; clk. typist Deere Employees Credit Union, Ankeny, Iowa, 1974-76; gas sta. attendant Go-Tane, Ankeny, 1977; radio operator Ankeny Police Dept., 1976-78, detective, 1980-85, 89-90, patrol officer, 1978-80, 85-89; guard U.S. Marshals Svc., Des Moines, 1983-90, dep. U.S. marshal, 1990—, recruiter, pub. info. officer, spl. emphasis program mgr., 1990-95, student intern coord., 1992-95, seized asset specialist, 1994-96; motor vehicle officer Des Moines, 1995—; witness security contact U.S. Marshals Svc., Des Moines, 1995—, sexual harassment point of contact, 1996—; instr. Ankeny Police Dept., 1980-90; apptd. mem. coun. Iowa Law Enforcement Acad., 1988-90; apptd. mem. E-911 Commn., 1986-88. Named Officer of Yr., Optimist Club, Ankeny, 1981. Mem. NRA (life), Iowa Assn. Police Women (life, pres. 1982-88, Officer of Yr. 1989, fundraising/publicity officer 1992-95), Iowa State Policemen's Assn. (del. 1989), Iowa Assn. Chiefs and Police Officers (legis. com. 1989-90), Internat. Assn. Women Police (life, regional coord. 1986-88, chmn. membership com. 1991-94, rec. sec. 1992-94, pres. 1994-96, immediate past pres. 1996—, life trustee 1996—). Republican. Lutheran. Home: RR 2 Box 30 Elkhart IA 50073-9802 Office: US Marshals Svc 208 US Courthouse Des Moines IA 50309

CHERRY, REGINA SIBYLLE, painter, photographer; b. Ranis, Germany, Aug. 30, 1946; came to U.S., 1976; d. Hans Herrman Melchior Schneider and Ursula Schneider-Bruni; m. Herman Cherry, Nov. 21, 1976 (dec. Apr. 1992). Meister schuler, Hochschule der Bildenden Kunste, Berlin, 1976. Editl. asst. rsch. jours. Pergamon Press, N.Y.C., 1978-80; asst. to dir. Carys Gallery, N.Y.C., 1981-87, Sadenberg Gallery, N.Y.C., 1989—. Home: 121 Mercer St New York NY 10012-3818

CHERRY, RONA BEATRICE, magazine editor, writer; b. N.Y.C., Apr. 26, 1948; d. Manuel M. and Sylvia Zelda C. B.A., Am. U., 1968; M.S., Columbia U., 1971. Reporter No. Va. Sun, Arlington, 1968; reporter Akron Beacon Jour., Ohio, 1969-70, Wall St. Jour., N.Y.C., 1971-72; assoc. editor Newsweek mag., N.Y.C., 1972-74; reporter N.Y. Times, N.Y.C., 1976-77; exec. editor Glamour mag., N.Y.C., 1977-88; editor-in-chief Longevity mag., v.p., dir. new mag. devel. Gen. Media Internat., N.Y.C., 1988-92; editor-in-chief Fitness Mag., N.Y.C., 1992-96; lectr. New Sch. Social Rsch., 1978, Sch. Continuing Edn., NYU, 1980; faculty Summer Pub. Inst., 1980, 83, Reader's Digest Writer's Workshops; mem. screening com. Nat. Mag. awards, 1980-82, 90-92, judge, 1991-92, 94-96; judge Nat. Media awards Am. Speech-Lang.-Hearing Assn., 1988. Co-author: The World of American Business, 1977; contbg. author: Woman in the Year 2000; contbr. articles to publs. including N.Y. Times Sunday mag., Parade, Ms. mag., Christian Sci. Monitor; contbr. book revs. to Sunday N.Y. Times. Mem. nat. comms. coun. March of Dimes, 1981-92; v.p. Newswomen's Club N.Y., 1985-87. Recipient Media award Nat. Assn. Recycling Industries, 1973, Bus. Journalism award U. Mo., 1977, Am. Coll. Radiology, 1986, Writer's award Am. Soc. Anesthesiologists, 1983, Maggie award Planned Parenthood Fedn. Am., 1985, Media award Am. Coll. Radiology, 1986. Mem. Am. Soc. Mag. Editors (bd. dirs. 1990-92). Home: 140 Riverside Dr # 8J New York NY 10024-2605

CHERRY, VIVIAN, photographer, jeweler; b. N.Y.C., July 27, 1920; d. Samuel and Ida (Agranovitch) C.; m. Herb Tank; m. 2d Eric Schmidt; 1 child, Steven Schmidt; m. 3d Louis Finger; m. 4th Alex Redein. Prodr., photographer: (children's film) Hello Halloween, 1970s; one-person shows include 44th St. Gallery, N.Y.C., 1940s, The Gallery, St. Mary's Coll. of Md., St. Mary's City, Md., 1990, Z Gallery, N.Y.C., 1992, 93, 94, Donnell Libr., N.Y.C., 1996; represented in permanent collections Nat. Portrait Gallery, Smithsonian Instn., Washington, Internat. Mus. Fine Arts, Pretoria, Bergen County Mus. Fine Arts, Paramus, N.J., The N.Y. Pub. Libr., Bklyn. Mus., Mus. Modern Art; photographer: Parents Guide to Child Problems, The Long Loneliness (Dorothy Day); works featured in Popular Photography, Salon Photography, Colliers, Jubilee, Amerika Pageant, Coronet, numerous others. Home: 343 E 30th St New York NY 10016

CHERRYH, C. J., writer; b. St. Louis, Sept. 1, 1942; d. Basil L. and Lois Ruth (Van Deventer) C. BA in Latin, U. Okla., 1964; MA in Classics, Johns Hopkins U., 1965. Cert. tchr., Okla. Tchr. Oklahoma City Pub. Schs., 1965-77; lectr. in field. Author: (novels) Gate of Ivrel, 1976, Well of Shiuan, 1978, Brothers of Earth, 1976, Hunter of Worlds, 1976, The Faded Sun: Kresrith, 1977, The Faded Sun: Shon'Jir, 1978, Fires of Azeroth, 1979, The Faded Sun: Kutath, 1979, Hestia, 1979, Sunfall, 1981, Downbelow Station, 1981 (Hugo award for best novel 1982), Wave Without a Shore, 1981, The Pride of Chanur, 1982, Merchanter's Luck, 1982, Port Eternity, 1982, Forty Thousand in Gehenna, 1983, The Dreamstone, 1983, The Tree of Swords and Jewels, 1983, Chanur's Venture, 1984, Cuckoo's Egg, 1985, Visible Light, 1985, The Kif Strike Back, 1985, Angel with the Sword, 1985, Chanur's Homecoming, 1986, Exile's Gate, 1988, Cyteen, 1988 (Hugo award 1988, 89), Smuggler's Gold, 1988, Rimrunners, 1989, Rusalka, 1989, Chernevog, 1990, Yvgenie, 1991, Heavy Time, 1991, Rumrunners, 1991, Hellburner, 1992, Chanur's Legacy, 1992, Goblin Mirror, 1993, Faery in Shadow, 1993, Tripoint, 1994, Foreigner, 1994, Rider at the Gate, 1995, Invader, 1995, Fortress in the Eye of Time, 1995, Inheritor, 1996, Cloud's Rider, 1996, Lois & Clark, 1996; editor: Flood Tide, 1990; translator: Stellar Crusade by Pierre Barbet, 1980, The Green Gods by Nathalie & Charles Henneberg, 1980, The Book of Shai by Daniel Walther, 1982; contbr. short stories to numerous mags. Woodrow Wilson fellow, 1965; recipient John W. Campbell award for best new writer, 1977, Hugo award for short story, 1979, for novel, 1982, 89, Locus award for best sci. fiction novel, 1988. Mem. Sci. Fiction Writers Assn., Alpha Lambda Delta, Phi beta Kappa.

CHERTOK, BARBARA LISS, special education educator; b. Boston, Nov. 7, 1935; d. Wolf and Pauline (Garber) Liss; m. Benson T. Chertok, June 4, 1961 (dec. 1981); children: Victoria Chertok May, Maxwell Benjamin. Student, Boston U., Am. U. Cert. oral interpreter: visible to spoken. Speechreading (lipreading) instr. Montgomery Coll., Rockville, Md., 1986—; pvt. practice Bethesda, Md., 1986—; coord. oral interpreting workshops Bethesda; bd. dirs. Am. Hearing Rsch. Found., Sta. WRC-TV Deaf and Hard of Hearing Cmty. Adv. Bd., SHHH Montgomery County Chpt. Bd.; spkr., presenter in field; cons. in field. Contbr. articles to profl. jours. Vol. Clinton Campaign, Washington, 1992. Featured in numerous newspaper and jour. articles and on TV. Mem. Alexander Graham Bell Assn. for Deaf (mem. Oral Hearing Impaired Sect., Internat. Orgn. Edn. Hearing Impaired), Self Help for Hard of Hearing People, Auditory-Verbal Internat., Assn. Late Deafened Adults, Washington Area Group Hard of Hearing, Telecommunications for Deaf, Inc., League for Hard of Hearing. Home and Office: 4940 Sentinel Dr Apt 205 Bethesda MD 20816-3552

CHESHIRE, CYNTHIA LYNNE, medical technologist, applications specialist; b. Jacksonville, Fla., Feb. 8, 1960; d. Barton William and Carolyn Lucille (Copeland) C. BS in Microbiology, Brigham Young U., 1981, MBA, 1988. Med. technologist Mountain View Hosp., Payson, Utah, 1983-88, Utah Valley Regional Med. Ctr., Provo, Utah, 1987-88; evening shift supr. St. Vincent's Med. Ctr., Jacksonville, Fla., 1988-90; hematology supr. Meml. Med. Ctr., Jacksonville, 1990-92; hematology support specialist Baxter, Waukegan, Ill., 1992-94; hematology applications specialist Sysmex Corp., Long Grove, Ill., 1994-95, area applications coord., 1995—; mem. adv. bd. MLT program Fla. Jr. Coll., Jacksonville, 1991-92. Mem. Am. Soc. Clin. Pathologists, Clin. Lab. Mgmt. Assn. Mem. LDS Ch. Office: Sysmex Corp Am 6699 RFD Gilmer Rd Long Grove IL 60047

CHESKY, EVELYN G., state legislator. Chmn. bd. Hoyoke Pub. Works, 1978; alderman-at-large, 1985; state rep. dist. 5 Mass. Ho. of Reps., Boston, mem. counties com., pub. safety and fed. fin. assistance com. Mem., bd. dirs. Holyoke Boys and Girls Club. Recipient Polish Heritage Citizens award Holyoke Hosp. Aux. Democrat. Office: Mass Ho of Reps State Capitol Rm 33 Boston MA 02133*

CHESKY, PAMELA BOSZE, school system administrator, curriculum specialist; b. Perth Amboy, N.J., June 17, 1942; d. Jospeh John and Irene (Konazeski) Bosze; m. Frederick Alan Chesky, Aug. 20, 1966; children: Rick, Scott. BA, Coll. Notre Dame, Balt., 1964; MLS, Rutgers U., 1992. Cert. ednl. media specialist. Tchr. social studies Woodbridge (N.J.) Bd. Edn., 1964-69, ednl. media specialist, 1969-93, supr. librs. guidance and nursing svcs., 1993-95; curriculum specialist for strategic planning Media Ctrs and Student Assistance Counselors, 1995—; mem. membership com. Infolink, Piscataway, N.J., 1995—, vice chair, 1996; mem. adv. com. Sch. Comm., Info. Libr. Svc. Rutgers U., 1994—. Contbr. articles to profl. jours. Commr. Woodbridge Cultural Arts Commn., 1992—; vice-chair Middlesex County Dem. Orgn., New Brunswick, N.J., 1992-95; parliamentarian Woodbridge Dem. Orgn., 1993—; program co-chair Friends Librs. Woodbridge Twp.; mem. Colonia chpt. Hadassah. Mem. ALA (affiliate assembly), Am. Assn. Sch. Librs. (membership com. 1993-95, chair task force on libr. advocacy 1995), Edn. Media Assn. N.J. (pres. 1993-94, scholarship 1992), Hadassah, Gamma Phi Beta. Democrat. Roman Catholic. Home: 135 Midwood Way Colonia NJ 07067-3116 Office: Woodbridge Bd Edn PO Box 428 School St Woodbridge NJ 07095

CHESLER, PHYLLIS, psychology educator; b. Oct. 1, 1940; d. Leon Chesler and Lillian Hammer; 1 child, Ariel. BA in Comparative Lit. and Lang., Bard Coll., 1963; MA in Psychology, New Sch. for Social Rsch., 1967, PhD in Psychology, 1969. Instr. in psychology Inst. for Devel. Studies, 1965-66; fellow in neurophysiology N.Y. Med. Coll., 1967-68; tchg. fellow in psychology New Sch. for Social Rsch., 1968-69; prof. psychology, sociology, anthropology & women's studies Coll. of S.I./Richmond Coll., CUNY, 1969—; intern dept. psychotherapy Washington Sq. Inst. for Psychotherapy and Mental Health, 1968-69; rsch. asst. New Sch. for Social Rsch., 1966-67; rsch. assoc. grad. dept. physiology Yeshiva U., 1965, Brain Rsch. Lab., N.Y. Med. Coll., 1966-69, Inst. for Devel. Studies, 1965-66; intern, clin. rsch. assoc. N.Y. Med. Coll./Met. Hosp., 1968-69; lectr., presenter in field. Author: Women and Madness, 1972, 2d edit., 1989, paperback edit., 1972, Eng., 1974, Germany, 1974, The Netherlands, 1974, France, 1975, Italy, 1977, Japan, 1983, Israel, 1987, Women, Money and Power, 1976, paperback edit., 1977, About Men, 1978, 2d edit., 1990, Eng., 1978, Germany, 1979, The Netherlands, 1979, Denmark, 1980, paperback edit., 1980, France, 1982, Sweden, 1983, With Child: A Diary of Motherhood, 1979, paperback edit., 1981, Germany, 1980, The Netherlands, 1981, Sweden, 1982, France, 1983, Mothers on Trial: The Battle for Children and Custody, 1986, 2d edit., 1991, paperback edit., 1987, Sacred Bond: The Legacy of Baby M., 1988, 2d edit., 1989, Eng., 1990, Patriarchy: Notes of an Expert Witness, 1994; co-editor, contbr.: Feminist Foremothers in Women's Studies, Psychology and Mental Health, 1996; editor-at-large On the Issues mag.; contbr. articles to profl. jours.; mem. adv. bd. Jour. Women and Therapy, Feminism and Psychology, An Internat. Jour. Mem. APA, AAUP, PEN (judge Am. Ctr. 1993 Martha Albrand award), Am. Assn. for Abolition of Involuntary Mental Hospitalization, Assn. for Children of Enforcement of Support (bd. dirs.), Assn. for Women in Psychology (co-founder), Ctr. for Study of Psychiatry (bd. dirs.), Nat. Women's Health Network (co-founder), Vet. Feminists of Am., N.Y. State Psychol. Assn., N.Y. Women's Action Alliance (charter), Women's History Rsch. Ctr. (adv.), N.Y. Women's Forum/Internat. Women's Forum (charter). Home: 732 A Carroll St Brooklyn NY 11215

CHESNA-SERINO, EDNA MAE, nurse; b. Chelsea, Mass.; d. John 1st and Edna Winifred (Daly) Chesna; m. Robert E. Serino Sr., May 1, 1960; children: Robert Jr., Marie Elena, Susan Olivia. Assoc. Nursing, North Shore C.C., 1977; BSN, Salem State Coll., 1995. RN. Med./surg. nurse Mass. Soldiers Home, Chelsea, 1973-82; allergy nurse cons. Respiratory Care Physicians, Lynn, Mass., 1983-88, Allergy Assocs., Lynn, 1983-88; sch. nurse Abraham Lincoln Elem. Sch., Revere, Mass., 1988-89; adult day health nurse Cmty. Family Adult Care, Everett, Mass., 1990-91; assessment/evaluation nurse Chelsea, Revere, Winthrop Home Care, 1992-93; founder, CEO The Vital View Corp., Revere, 1983-88; clin. instr. Essex Agrl. & Tech. Inst., Danvers, Mass., 1996—; substitute sch. nurse, Winthrop and Revere, Mass. Mem. Rep. Presdl. Task Force, Washington, 1985—; treas. Friends of Revere Pub. Libr., 1993-94. Mem. Mass. Nurses Assn. (bd. dirs. 1985-86), Rotarian, Rotary (disting. svc. award 1991-94, nurse and women rep., London and Paris 1989). Roman Catholic. Office: PO Box 92 Revere MA 02151-0001

CHESNEY, SUSAN TALMADGE, human resources specialist, technical writer; b. N.Y.C., Aug. 12, 1943; d. Morton and Tillie (Talmadge) Chesney; m. Donald Lewis Freitas, Sept. 17, 1967 (div. May 1976); m. Robert Martin Rosenblatt, Apr. 9, 1980. AB, U. Calif., Berkeley, 1967. Placement interviewer U. Calif., Berkeley, 1972-74, program coord., 1974-79; pers. adminstr. Hewlett-Packard Co., Santa Rosa, Calif., 1982-84; pres. Mgmt. Resources, Santa Rosa, 1984—; human resources mgr. BioBottoms Inc., Petaluna, Calif., 1990-91; human resources adminstr. Parker Compumotor, Rohnert Park, Calif., 1991-93; cons. Kensington Electronics Group, Healdsburg, Calif., 1984-85, Behavioral Medicine Assocs., Santa Rosa, 1985-86, M.C.A.I., Santa Rosa, 1986-87, Bowdon Designs, Santa Rosa, 1987-88, Bass & Ingram, Santa Rosa, 1988—, Eason Tech., Inc., Healdsburg, 1995—, Interim Svcs., Inc., Santa Rosa, 1995—, Flex Products, Inc., Santa Rosa, 1996—, Optical Coating Lab., Inc., Santa Rosa, 1996—. Mem. Nat. Soc. Performance Instrn., No. Calif. Human Resources Coun., Pers. Assn. Sonoma County. Avocations: cooking, gardening, music.

CHESNUT, CAROL FITTING, lawyer; b. Pecos, Tex., June 17, 1937; d. Ralph Ulf and Carol (Lowe) Fitting; m. Dwayne A. Chesnut, Dec. 27, 1955; children: Carol Marie, Stephanie Michelle, Mark Steven. BA magna cum laude, U. Colo., 1971; JD, U. Calif., San Francisco, 1994. Rsch. asst. U. Colo., 1972; head quality controller Mathematica, Inc., Denver, 1973-74; cons. Mincome Man., Winnipeg, Can., 1974; cons. economist Energy Cons. Assocs. Inc., Denver, 1974-79; exec. v.p. tng. ECA Intercomp, 1980-81; gen. ptnr. Chestnut Consortium, S.F., 1981—; sec., bd. dirs. Critical Resources, Inc., 1981-83. Rep. Lakehurst Civic Assn., 1968; staff aide Senator Gary Hart, 1978; Dem. precinct capt., 1982-88. Mem. ABA, ACLU, AAUW (1st v.p. 1989-90), Am. Mgmt. Assn., Soc. Petroleum Engrs., Am. Nuclear Soc. (chmn. conv. space activities for 1989, chair of spouse activities 1989), Am.

Geophys. Union, Assn. Women Geoscientists (treas. Denver 1983-85), Associated Students of Hastings (rep. 1994), Calif. State Bar, Canyon Ranch Homeowners Assn. (sec. bd. dirs. 1994—), Phi Beta Kappa, Phi Chi Theta, Phi Delta Phi. Unitarian. Office: 7537 Dry Pines Cir Las Vegas NV 59329

CHESNUT, NONDIS LORINE, writer, consultant, former English language educator; b. South Daytona, Fla., June 29, 1941; d. Anthony Valentine and Myrtle Marie (Allen) Campbell; m. Raymond Otho Chesnut, Aug. 25, 1962; 1 child, Starlina Mintina Chesnut Kladler. BS in English and Speech, Concord Coll., 1962; postgrad., Frostburg U., 1967; MEd, Shippensburg U., 1972; postgrad., W.Va. U., 1973; Advanced Grad. Specialist Degree, U. Md., 1974. Cert. administr., secondary prin., elem. prin., reading specialist, tchr. English and speech. Tchr. English and speech Harpers Ferry (W.Va.) H.S., 1962-64; libr. Great Mills (Md.) H.S., 1968-69; tchr. English and reading North Hagerstown H.S., Hagerstown, Md., 1964-73; tchr. South Hagerstown H.S., Hagerstown, 1974-77; reading resource tchr. Woodland Way Elem. Sch., Hagerstown, 1977-83; adj. instr. grad. sch. Hood Coll., Frederick, Md., 1982-83; reading specialist Fountain Rock Elem. Sch., Hagerstown, 1983-85; tchr. Williamsport (Md.) H.S., 1985-95; reading and lang. arts cons., Md., 1973-95, Fla., 1996—; spkr., presenter local, nat. and internat. workshops, 1973-95; lectr. main campus and south campus Daytona Beach C.C., 1996—; speech and debate coach. Writer for radio programs and advertisements for reading, 1986—, TV programs, 1974-78, 90-91; appeared on TV programs, 1974-78; co-editor column Beckley Post Herald, 1957-59; contbr. articles to newspapers and mags., 1964—; appeared in film Guarding Tess, 1993. Mem. debating team Concord Coll., 1961-62, mem. newspaper staff, 1959-61; mem. Washington County Network of Orgns., 1984-88; co-dir. Billy Bud, 1962; v.p. Women's Ind. Club, 1962, treas., 1961; sec.-treas. Fgn. lang. Club, 1961, Debate Club, 1961-62; treas. Meth. Youth Fellowship, 1961; pres. Tri-Hi-Y, 1959; legis. chairperson State of Md. Reading Coun., 1977-78; active Life in Spirit Group, St. Ann's Roman Cath. Ch., 1994-95, Grace United Meth. Ch., 1995, Lady of Hope Cath. Ch., 1996—. Recipient Pres.'s award State of Md. Reading Coun., 1981, Washington County Reading Coun., 1981, Voice of Democracy award VFW/Ladies Aux., 1992, Am. Heritage Writing award Williamsburg Lions Club, 1995, numerous others; W.Va. Legislature scholar, 1959-62. Mem. AAUW (ednl. chairperson 1983-85, legis. v.p. 1986-87, cmty. chairperson 1987-89), NEA (mem. publicity and scholarship coms., Washington County Tchrs. Assn., bldg. rep. 1989-95, del.), ASCD, VFW (chairperson Voice of Democracy 1989-95, VFW award 1989-95), Md. Dist. Am. Heritage Lions (Region II Lions award, Williamsport Am. Heritage Lions award 1995), State of Md. Tchrs. Assn., Md. State Tchrs. Assn., State of Md. Internat. Reading Assn. Coun. (sec. 1975-79, v.p. elect 1979-80, v.p. 1980-81, pres. 1981-82, nominating chairperson 1982-83), Washington County Tchrs. Assn., Internat. Reading Assn. (sec.-treas. sex differences in reading group 1976-77, 83-85, mem. gender differences in reading group 1985-86, mem. readability interest group, mem. mastery learning interest group, del. convs., mem. internat. rsch. com. 1976-77, 84-85, mem. disabled learners interest group 1975-82), Assn. Rsch. and Enlightenment (Guidance Helping award 1989), Coll. Reading Assn., Md. Assn. English Tchrs., United Dem. Assn., Internat. Platform Assn., Am. Legion (chairperson oratorial contest 1989-95, speech coach). Democrat. Home: 107 Old Sunbeam Dr Daytona Beach FL 32119 Office: Daytona Beach Community College Dept Reading Bldg 14 109A 1200 W International Blvd Daytona Beach FL 32120-2811

CHESNUTT, JANE, publishing executive; b. Kenedy, Tex., Oct. 10, 1950; m. W. Mallory Rintoul. BJ, U. Tex., 1973. Editorial asst. Am. Jour. Nursing, N.Y.C., 1975-78; asst. editor Woman's Day mag., N.Y.C., 1978-82, health editor, 1982-89, beauty, health, fashion editor, 1989-91, editor-in-chief, 1991—. Mem. bus. adv. coun. Washington Irving H.S., N.Y.C. Mem. Am. Soc. Mag. Editors, Women in Comms., Inc. (chair mentoring com. N.Y. chpt., bd. dirs. N.Y. Women in Comms., Inc., Clarion award 1985), Fashion Group Internat., YWCA Acad. of Achievers. Office: Woman's Day Mag Hachette Filipacchi Mags Inc 1633 Broadway New York NY 10019-6708

CHESTER, LYNNE, foundation executive, artist; b. Fargo, N.D., May 29, 1942; d. Harry Batten and Margaret Emily (White) Welliver; m. R. Craig Chester, Feb. 25, 1984; 1 child, Benjamin. BA in Music, Hillsdale Coll., 1964; MA in Guidance Counseling, Mich. State U., 1965; PhD in Psychology, U. Mich., 1971. Tchr. Warren (Mich.) Consol. Schs., 1965-70; curriculum advisor Royal Oak (Mich.) Pub. Schs., 1974-75; co-founder, exec. dir. Peace Rsch. Found., Carmel, Calif., 1993—; assoc. Hillsdale Coll., 1989—; guest lectr. ceramics James Milliken U., Decatur, Ill., 1991; guest lectr. creative convergence Carl Cherry Ctr. for Art, Carmel, 1991; co-founder, bd. mem. Monterey (Calif.) Peninsula Coll. Art Gallery, 1991—; fundraiser Monterey (Calif.) Peninsula Coll. Student Art Gallery, 1992-94. Artist of three commd. sculptures for pvt. collections; also ceramics, sculpture and photographs in pvt. and corp. collections; represented in permanent collection at Krammert Art Mus., Champaign, Ill., Fresno (Calif.) Mus. Art; juried show Ctr. for Photographic Art, Carmel, Calif., 1996; author of poetry. Pres., bd. dirs. Carl Cherry Ctr. for Arts, Carmel, 1988-94, 95—; bd. dirs. Carmel Pub. Libr. Found., 1992-93, Monterey Inst. for Rsch. in Astronomy, 1985-95, Monterey County Cultural Commn., 1994—; bd. dirs. Monterey Peninsula Mus. Art, 1991-93; co-founder, bd. dirs. Monterey Bay Artists Day, KAZU-FM Radio Sta., 1987-89; co-founder Southfield (Mich.) Symphony, 1972. Recipient Citizens Adv. Coun. award City of Royal Oak, 1978-83, Best of Show award for monoprint Monterey Peninsula Coll., 1990, Poetry prizes Carl Cherry Ctr. for Arts, 1990-94, Benefactor of Arts award Monterey County Cultural Coun., 1992, 93, 94, Soccer Mgr./Coach of Yr. 1976-81; others. Mem. Internat. Sculpture Ctr., Nat. Mus. Women in Art (charter mem.), Sigma Alpha Iota (Ruby Sword of Honor). Home: 3037 Forest Way Pebble Beach CA 93953-2904 Office: Peace Rsch Found 225 Crossroads #145 Carmel CA 93923

CHESTER, NIA LANE, psychology educator; b. L.A., Dec. 8, 1945; d. Thomas Henry and Virginia (Chalmers) Lane; m. C. Ronald Chester, Aug. 9, 1969 (div. July 1988); children: Caben Paul, Ian Thomas. BA magna cum laude, Smith Coll., 1967; MA, Columbia U., 1968; PhD, Boston U., 1981. Tchr. Elmont (N.Y.) Meml. High Sch., 1967-70; master tchr. Ednl. Collaborative Greater Boston, Cambridge, Mass., 1971-75; teaching fellow Harvard U., Cambridge, 1976-78; rsch. assoc. Boston U., 1981-83, 88—; rsch. scholar Radcliffe Coll., Cambridge, 1983-84; assoc. prof. psychology Pine Manor Coll., Chestnut Hill, Mass., 1983—, Lindsey prof., 1990, chair divsn. Natural and Behavioral Scis., 1993-94, dir. internship program, 1994—, dean learning & assessment, 1996—; reviewer Jour. Personality and Social Psychology, 1985—; vis. prof. Boston U., 1986-88. Editor: Experience and Meaning of Work in Women's Lives, 1990; contbr. articles to profl. jours., chpts. to books. Bd. dirs. Peabody Aftersch. Program, Cambridge, 1983-85, Tobin Aftersch. Program, Cambridge, 1989—. NIMH fellow, 1979; recipient Ruth Allinger Gibson '26 Teaching award, 1992; Women's Coll. Coalition grantee, 1992. Mem. APA, Ea. Psychol. Assn. (program com. 1989-93). Office: Pine Manor Coll Dept Psych 400 Heath St Chestnut Hill MA 02167-2332

CHESTON, SHEILA CAROL, lawyer; b. Washington, Nov. 5, 1958; d. Theodore C. and Gabrielle Joan (Hellings) C. BA, Dartmouth Coll., 1980; JD, Columbia U., 1984. Bar: N.Y. 1986, D.C. 1986, U.S. Dist. Ct. D.C. 1987, U.S. Ct. Appeals (D.C. cir.) 1987, U.S. Dist. Ct. (so. and ea. dists.) N.Y. 1989, U.S. Ct. Appeals (2d cir.), U.S. Supreme Ct. 1989. Law clk. to judge U.S. Ct. Appeals for 9th Cir., L.A., 1984-85; assoc. Wilmer, Cutler & Pickering, Washington, 1985-92, ptnr., 1992-93; gen. counsel Def. Base Closure and Realignment Commn., 1993; spl. assoc. counsel to Pres. of U.S., 1994; dep. gen. counsel Dept. Air Force, 1993-95, gen. counsel, 1995—; adj. prof. in internat. litigation Georgetown Law Sch., 1991—. Mem. ABA, D.C. Bar Assn., Women's Bar Assn., Am. Soc. Internat. Law. Democrat. Episcopalian. Office: Gen Counsel Dept Air Force 1740 Air Force Pentagon Washington DC 20330-1740

CHETTA, HOLLY ANN, transportation executive; b. New Orleans, Aug. 18, 1945; d. Henry John and Ernestine Rose (Blaise) C. BS, Tulane U., 1967, MS, 1970, MPH, 1977. Assoc. realtor Latter & Blum, New Orleans, 1978-83; administr. loan svc. First Fin. Bank, New Orleans, 1981-83; administr. USDA, New Orleans, 1982-84, U.S. Dept. Transp., New Orleans, 1984-91; pers. evaluator U.S. Coast Guard, New Orleans, 1991—. Author: (poems) Toward the Twenty-First Century, 1985, New Year's Eve, 1984. Republican. Roman Catholic. Home: 120 N Livingston Pl Metairie LA 70005 Office: US Dept Transp US Coast Guard Exam Ctr 1615 Poydras St New Orleans LA 70112

CHEUNG, JUDY HARDIN, special education educator; b. Santa Rosa, Calif., Feb. 3, 1945; d. Robert Stephens and Edna Rozella Hardin. BA, Calif. State U. at Sonoma, Rohnert Park, Calif., 1966; MA, U. San Francisco, 1981. Tchr. St. Thomas (V.I.) Dept. Edn., 1967-71; spl. edn. tchr. Sonoma Devel. Ctr., Eldridge, Calif., 1971—; administr. Redwood Empire Chinese Assn. Sch., 1996—; co-chairperson Ednl. Svcs. Profl. Practice Group, Eldridge, Calif., 1989-90, 93-94. Author, pub.: Acorn to Embers, 1987, Welcome to the Inside, 1984; author, photographer, pub. Captions, 1986. Recipient awards Silver Pegasus, 1983, Poets of the Vineyard, 1986, 87, Ark. Writers Conf., 1988. Mem. Calif. Fedn. Chaparral Poets (pres. 1989-91, 93-95), Ina Coolbrith Cir. (pres. 1988-90), Calif. Writers Club (treas. Redwood writers br. 1985-86), Bay Area Poets Coalition, Artists Embassy Internat. (Amb. of Arts award 1992), World Congress of Cultures and Poetry (internat. bd. dirs. 1993—, Grand Cultures medal 1993). Home and Office: 704 Brigham Ave Santa Rosa CA 95404-5245

CHEVALIER, DEBORAH MARIE, critical care nurse; b. Ansonia, Conn., Apr. 27, 1965; d. Richard Wilson and Mary Grace (Pettinella) R. RN, Bridgeport Hosp. Sch. Nursing, 1990; student, So. Conn. State U., 1993—. RN, BLS, ACLS, CCRN. Nurse gen. surg. fl. Hosp. St. Raphael, Hew Haven, 1989-93, nurse Surg. ICU, 1993—; nurse AAA Nursing Care Agy., Stratford, Conn., 1993—; preceptor Hosp. of St. Raphael, New Haven, 1992-94. Mem. AACN, Assn. Diploma Nursing Schs. Roman Catholic. Home: 29 Condon Dr Ansonia CT 06401-2636 Office: Hosp of St Raphael 1450 Chapel St New Haven CT 06511-4405

CHEVERS, WILDA ANITA YARDE, probation officer; b. N.Y.C.,; d. Wilsey Ivan and HerbertLee (Perry) Yarde; m. Kenneth Chevers, May 14, 1950; 1 child, Pamela Anita. BA, CUNY, 1947; MSW, Columbia, 1959; PhD, NYU, 1981. Probation officer, 1947-55; supr. probation officer, 1955-65; br. chief Office Probation for Cts. N.Y.C., 1965-72, asst. dir. probation, 1972-77, dep. commr. dept. probation, 1978-86; prof. pub. administrn. John Jay Coll. Criminal Justice CUNY, 1986-91; conf. faculty mem. Nat. Council Juvenile and Family Ct. Judges; mem. faculty N.Y.C. Tech. Coll., Nat. Coll. Juvenile Justice; mem. adv. com. Family Ct., First Dept. Sec. Susan E. Wagner Adv. Bd., 1966-70. Sec., bd. dirs. Allen Community Day Care Ctr., 1971-75; bd. dirs. Allen Sr. Citizens Housing, Queensboro Soc. for Prevention Cruelty to Children; chairperson, bd. dir. Allen Christian Sch., 1987-91. Named to Hunter Coll. Hall of Fame, 1983. Mem. ABA (assoc.), N.Y. Acad. Pub. Edn., Nat. Council on Crime and Delinquency, Nat. Assn. Social Workers, Acad. Cert. Social Workers. Middle Atlantic States Conf. Correction, Alumni Assn. Columbia Sch. Social Work, N.Y.U. Alumni Assn., NAACP, Am. Soc. Pub. Administrn. (mem. council), Counseliers, Hansel and Gretel Club (pres. 1967-69, Queens, N.Y.). Delta Sigma Theta. Home: 9012 Covered Wagon Ave Las Vegas NV 89117-7010

CHEW, MARGARET SARAH, geography educator, retired; b. Evanston, Ill., Aug. 20, 1909; d. Nathaniel Durbin and Nettie Jane (Trumbauer) C. BS, Northwestern U., 1930, MS, 1936; PhD with distinction, Clark U., 1960. Maths. and social studies tchr. Iron Belt (Wis.) High Sch., 1930-36; geography tchr. SUNY, Buffalo, 1937-38; social studies tchr. Haven Sch., Evanston, 1938-45; prof. geography U. Wis., La Crosse, 1945-79, chmn. geography dept., 1952-65; emeritus prof. geography U. Wis., 1979—; geography tchr. St. Teresa Coll., Winona, Minn., summer 1939; leader geography credit earning tours U. Wis., La Crosse, summers 1963-80; lectr. in field. Contbr. articles to profl. jours. Recipient fellowships in geog. Clark U., Worcester, 1936-37, 50-51; named fellowship grant presented to outstanding women La Crosse Br. AAUW, 1976. Mem. AAUW, Am. Assn. Geographers, Nat. Coun. Geography (chmn. map com. 1952-54), Wis. Geog. Soc. (founder, several offices), Delta Kappa Gamma (state scholarship chair, summer scholarship award 1951), Philanthropic Ednl. Orgn. (sec., many coms.).

CHIANELLO-SANTOS, MARINA, sales executive; b. Milan, Italy, June 9, 1964; came to U.S., 1965; d. Ettore and Elena (Falletti) Chianello; m. William Roland Santos, Apr. 22, 1995. AA, Monroe C.C., Rochester, N.Y., 1984; B in Polit. Sci., St. John Fisher, 1986; M in Comm., SUNY, Brockport, 1994. Cmty. dir. March of Dimes, Pittsford, N.Y., 1986-89; cmty. rels. rep. Tops Friendly Markets, Rochester, N.Y., 1989-92; coord. cmty. svcs. Rochester Inst. Tech., 1993-94; dir. sales Vet. Outreach Ctrs. Stars and Stripes The Flag Store, Rochester, 1994—; project coord. St. John Fisher, Rochester, 1995—; chairperson issues Women in Comm., Rochester, 1995—; coord. Ad Coun. Rochester, 1990-94. Mem. Arts Reach, Inc. (bd. dirs., vice chair 1993-94), Monroe County Spl. Olympics (pub. rels. 1990-95). Democrat. Roman Catholic. Home: 3181 E River Rd Rochester NY 14623 Office: Veterans Outreach Ctr 459 Sath Ave Rochester NY 74620

CHIAPELLA, ANNE PAGE, epidemiologist; b. Oakland, Calif., Oct. 12, 1942; d. Karl Josef and Anne Elizabeth (Gorrill) C. BA in Polit. Sci., Stanford U., 1964, PhD in Neurosci., 1982, MS in Stats., 1985; MPH in Epidemiology, Johns Hopkins U., 1986. Med. rschr. Stanford (Calif.) U., 1966-75, postdoctoral fellow, 1983-85; postdoctoral fellow Johns Hopkins U., Balt., 1986-88; program officer Inst. Medicine NAS, Washington, 1989-91; sr. analyst Nat. Inst. on Alcohol and Alcohol Abuse, Rockville, Md., 1991—; statis. and intellectual property cons. various orgns., Washington, 1983—. Writer humorous, tech. and travel speeches, 1985—; reviewer grants and sci. jours., 1992—; contbr. articles to sci. jours. Pres. Nebr. Ave. Neighborhood Assn., Washington, 1987-91; assoc. Smithsonian Instn., Washington, 1987—; active in Friends of Kennedy Ctr., Washington, 1987—, Friends of Nat. Zoo, Washington, 1987—, Textile Mus., Washington, 1986—. Grantee and fellow NIH, 1975, 77, 83, 86; grantee Environ. Health Sci. Ctr., 1986. AAAS, APHA, Soc. Epidemiologic Rsch., Toastmasters Internat. (officer 1987-89). Home: 5126 Nebraska Ave NW Washington DC 20008-2047

CHIAPPERINI, PATRICIA BIGNOLI, real estate appraiser, consultant; b. N.Y.C., Jan. 16, 1946; d. Gennaro and Giovanna (Resburgo) Bignoli; m. Joseph M. Chiapperini, Dec. 14, 1968. BS in Acctg. and Econs., St. John's U., 1968; postgrad., U. Ala., 1969, Rutgers U., 1980, Am. Inst. Real Estate Appraisers, 1983. Cert. gen. real property appraiser, N.J., instr. real property appraising, N.J., gen. real property appraiser, N.J. Staff acct. Cleary, During & Co., N.Y.C., 1967-69; chief acct. Montgomery Bapt. Hosp. (Ala.), 1969-70; internal auditor Scottex Corp., N.Y.C., 1970-73; office mgr. Mid-Jersey Realty, East Brunswick, N.J., 1973-79; self-employed real estate appraiser, North Brunswick, N.J., 1979—; guest lect. Middlesex County Coll., 1979—; adj. prof. Jersey City State Coll. Chmn. Arts and Cultural Com., Milltown, N.J., 1979-83; active Am. Legion Aux., Milltown, 1973—. Recipient John Marshall award St. John's U., 1968. Mem. Nat. Assn. Ind. Fee Appraisers, Cen. Jersey Ind. Fee Appraisers (treas., 1982-83, v.p., 1984), Milltown C. of C. (v.p. 1987), Lions. Roman Catholic. Office: 735 Georges Rd New Brunswick NJ 08902

CHIAPPETA, JESSICA ANNE, secondary education educator; b. Warren, Mich., Sept. 11, 1970; d. Jeffrey James and Elaine Martha (Michelini) C. BS in Math. with honors, U. Notre Dame, Ind., 1992. Provisional cert. in secondary edn., Ind., Mich. Asst. mgr. Pier 1 Imports, Sterling Heights, Mich., 1988-91; summer intern Chrysler Motors, Highland Park, Mich., 1989; camp counselor Detroit Country Day, 1991; tchr. Univ. Liggett Sch., Grosse Pointe, Mich., 1992-95, Grosse Pointe North H.S., 1995—. Home: 14492 Bournemuth Shelby Township MI 48315-4603 Office: Grosse Pointe North HS 707 Vernier Rd Grosse Pointe MI 48236-2509

CHIAVARIO, NANCY ANNE, business and community relations executive; b. Centralia, Ill., Aug. 17, 1947; d. Victor Jr. and Alma Maria (Arsenault) C. Asst. mgr. rent supplement B.C. Housing Mgmt. Commn., Vancouver, 1975-81, administrv. asst., 1981-84, mgr. tenants and ops. svc., 1985-86, administrv. asst., 1986-87; commr., vice chmn. Vancouver Park Bd., 1986-90, chair, 1991-93; city councillor Vancouver, 1993—. Pres. B.C. Recreation and Parks Assn., 1989-90; exec. dir. B.C. Sport and Fitness Coun. for the Disabled, 1989-90; dir. B.C. Wheelchair Sports Assn., 1991-92, Tree Can. Found., 1995—; mem. Non-Partisan Assn. Mem. Inst. Housing Mgmt. (cert. administr. 1983, cert. finance 1985), West End Commn. Ctr. Assn. (pres. 1985-86), Mt. Pleasant Commn. Ctr. Assn. (pres. 1981-83). Democrat. Home: 206-90 E 11th Ave, Vancouver, BC Canada V5T 2B8 Office: Vancouver City Coun, 453 W 12th Ave, Vancouver, BC Canada V5Y 1V4

CHIECHI, CAROLYN PHYLLIS, federal judge; b. Newark, Dec. 6, 1943; d. Michele A. and Dominica (DeFilippis) C. BS magna cum laude, Georgetown U., 1965, JD, 1969, LLM in Taxation, 1971. Bar: D.C. 1969, U.S. Dist. Ct. D.C., U.S. Ct. Fed. Claims, U.S. Tax Ct., U.S. Ct. Appeals (D.C. cir., Fed. cir., 5th cir., 6th cir., and 9th cirs.), U.S. Supreme Ct. Atty., advisor to Judge Leo H. Irwin U.S. Tax Ct., Washington, 1969-71; assoc. Sutherland, Asbill & Brennan, Washington, 1971-76, ptnr., 1976-92; judge U.S. Tax Ct., 1992—; mem. bd. regents Georgetown U., Washington, 1988-94, 95—, mem. nat. law alumni bd., 1986-93; bd. dirs. Stuart Stiller Meml. Found., Washignton, 1986—; prin. Coun. for Excellence in Govt., Washington, 1990-92. Dept. editor Jour. of Taxation, 1986-92; contbr. articles to profl. jours. Fellow Am. Bar Found., Am. Coll. Tax Counsel; mem. ABA, D.C. Bar Assn., Fed. Bar Assn., Women's Bar Assn., Nat. Assn. Women Judges, Am. Judicature Soc., Georgetown U. Alumni Assn. (bd. govs. 1994—). Office: US Tax Ct 400 2nd St NW Washington DC 20217-0001

CHIERIGHINO, BRIANNE SIDDALL, voice-over, actress, assistant location manager; b. Encino, Calif., Aug. 25, 1963; d. Earl Richard and Loretta Jeanette Siddall; m. D. Deven Chierighino, Apr. 4, 1987. AA in Art cum laude, L.A. Valley Coll., Van Nuys, Calif., 1985; student, Glendale (Calif.) C.C., 1990-94; BA in Art magna cum laude, Calif. State U., Northridge, 1995; postgrad., Loyola Marymount U., L.A., 1995—. Freelance asst. sound editor L.A., 1985-89, illustrator, 1985—; voice over artist, actor Tisherman Agy., L.A., 1990—; location asst., 1996—. Art exhibited at San Bernardino (Calif.) County Mus., 1995. Civic vol. fundraiser AIDS Meml. Quilt, Northridge, 1995. Recipient Outstanding Citizen award Coun. City L.A., 1987, L.A. Police Dept., 1987. Mem. SAG, AFTRA, Golden Kay Nat. Honor Soc., Phi Kappa Phi, Psi Chi. Office: 2219 W Olive Ave Ste 110 Burbank CA 91506

CHILD, JULIA MCWILLIAMS (MRS. PAUL CHILD), cooking expert, television personality, author; b. Pasadena, Calif., Aug. 15, 1912; d. John and Julia Carolyn (Weston) McWilliams; m. Paul Child, Sept. 1, 1945. BA, Smith Coll., 1934. With advt. dept. W.&J. Sloane, N.Y.C., 1939-40; with OSS, Washington, Ceylon, China, 1941-45; co-founder Am. Inst. Wine & Food, 1982. Hostess TV program The French Chef, WGBH-TV, Boston, from 1962, Julia Child & Co., 1978-79, Julia Child & More Co., 1980, Dinner at Julia's, PBS, 1983; occasional cooking segment Good Morning America, ABC-TV, 1980—; video cassettes The Way to Cook, 1982; author: (with Simone Beck and Louisette Bertholle) Mastering the Art of French Cooking, 1961, The French Chef Cookbook, 1968, Mastering the Art of French Cooking, Vol. II, 1970, (with Simone Beck) From Julia Child's Kitchen, 1975, Julia Child & Company, 1978, Julia Child & More Company, 1979, Mastering the Art of French Cooking I & II, 1983, The Way to Cook, 1989; columnist McCall's mag., 1975-82, Parade mag., 1982-86. Recipient Peabody award, 1964, Emmy award, 1966, French Ordre de Merite Agricole, 1967, Ordre National de Merite, 1974. Office: Good Morning Am 147 Columbus Ave New York NY 10023-5900 also: care Knopf Inc 201 E 50th St New York NY 10022-7703*

CHILDEARS, LINDA, banker; b. Council Bluffs, Iowa, Jan. 25, 1950; d. Nolan Glen and Mary Lucile (Dunken) Jackson. Grad., U. Wis., Am. Inst. Banking; student, U. Colo., U. Denver. Various positions First Nat. Bank Bear Valley (name changed to United Bank Bea, Colo., 1969-79; v.p. administrn. First Nat. Bancorp., 1979-83; pres., CEO, Equitable Bank of Littleton, 1983—; founder The Fin. Consortium; pres., CEO, Young Ams. Bank, Denver, 1987—, also vice-chmn. bd. dirs.; chmn. bd., pres. Young Ams. Edn. Found. Contbr. articles to Time and Newsweek. Bd. dirs. Cherry Creek Art Festival, Denver, 1989—; chmn. Grad. Sch. Banking; chmn. Nat. Assembly; past chair Jr. Achievement, Panorama Products and Svcs., Mile High United Way; mem. adv. bd., nat. past pres. Camp Fire Coun. Colo. Named hon. life mem. Nat. CampFire, past chmn., numerous other awards Camp Fire Inc. Mem. Am. Bankers Assn. (past chmn. Edn. Found., edn. coun.), Found. Tchg. Econs. (trustee), Colo. Bankers Assn. Republican. Office: Young Ams Bank 311 Steele St Denver CO 80206-4414

CHILDERS, SUSAN LYNN BOHN, special education educator, administrator, human resources and transition specialist, consultant; b. Zanesville, Ohio, Mar. 1, 1948; m. Lawrence J. Childers; 1 child, Jeffrey Scott. AA, Ohio U., 1978, BS in Edn. cum laude, 1982; MEd in Supervision, Ashland U., 1991. Profl. cert. 1-8 elem. tchr., K-12 edn. handicapped and supervision; spl. edn. tchr., Ohio. Educator learning disabilities, developmentally handicapped Maysville Local Sch. Dist., South Zanesville, Ohio, 1982-89; work-study coord. Holmes County Office Edn., Millersburg, Ohio, 1990, editor spl. edn. newsletter, 1990-93, cons., supervisor work-study programming, 1991-93; spl. edn. supr. Wayne County Bd. Edn., Wooster, Ohio, 1993-94; administr. severe behavior handicapped program, supr. special edn. Ashland-Wayne County Bd. Edn., Wooster, 1994-95; cons. Tri-County Ednl. Svc. Ctr., Wooster, 1996—; mem. Holmes County Spl. Edn. Adv. Coun., 1990-93, E. Holmes Local Sch. Dist. Strategic Planning Action Team Job/Life Skills, 1993; spkr. in field; rep. Ohio Devel. Handicapped Issues Forum; mem. steering com. Ohio Speaks, 1991-94; mem. strategic planning com. Ashland-Wayne County Bd. Edn., 1994-95; mem. Chippewa Local Sch. Dist. Child Care Bd., 1995-96; chmn. Direct Student Svcs. Strategic Planning Com., 1995-96; mem. safety com. Ashland-Wayne Ednl. Svc. Ctr., 1994-96; mem. svc. coordination com. Wayne County Children and Family First Initiative, 1995, 96. Editor Spl. Edn. Newsletter Holmes County Office Edn., 1990-93. Mem. adv. bd. Holmes County Job Placement, Holmes County Litter Prevention Cmty. Action Plan com., 1993; vol. Ohio Buckeye Book Fair, 1991-93, Holmes County Spl. Olympics, 1990-93, chairperson vols., 1993; mem. jr. assembly Bethesda Hosp., 1970-78; mem. Beaux Arts Zanesville Art Ctr., 1972-78; mem. spl. needs adv. bd. Ashland-West Holmes Career Ctr., 1990-93; mem. Transition and Comm. Consortium on Learning Disabilities, Ohio U. Alumni Career Resource Network, Holmes County Abuse Prevention Cmty. Action Plan com., 1993, Ohio Staff Devel. Coun., Wayne County Family and Children First Coun. (Clin. Cluster), 1994-96; co-chairperson fundraising com. Creating Connections Symposium, Akron, Ohio, 1994; mem. Ashland-Wayne-Holmes Counties Adv. Com. for Tech. and Tng. subcom., Ohio, 1996—; adv. com. for tech. 3-county rep., Ashland, Wynd, Holmes, Ohio, 1996—, mem. A-site tech. tng. com., 1996—, regional rep. for School/Net Communities of Practice, 1996—. Recipient award Muskingum County Office Litter Prevention, 1988, Kids Care Project, 1989, Maysville Bd. Edn. commendation, 1989, Merit award Keep Ohio Beautiful program, 1991, Ohio Future Forum's Exemplary Transition from Sch.-to-Work Model award, 1993, Model Program designation Ohio's Employability Skills Project, 1987, Franklin B. Walter Outstanding Educator award, 1996. Mem. ASCD, Career Edn. Assn., Coun. Exceptional Children, Ohio Rural Edn. Assn., Ohio Sch. Suprs. Assn., Ohio Assn. Vocat. Edn. Spl. Needs Pers., Ohio Assn. Suprs. and Work-Study coords. (award of Excellence 1992, reg. pres. 1993-94), Am. Assn. Univ. Women, Wayne-Holmes Elem. Administrs. Assn., Phi Delta Kappa. Home: PO Box 192 Millersburg OH 44654-0192 Office: Kinney Meml Bldg 2534 Burbank Rd Wooster OH 44691-1675

CHILDRESS, BEVERLEY BURNS, assistant headmaster, counselor, educator; b. Mobile, Ala., July 30, 1951; d. Willard Timothy and Avril Beverley (Chenoweth) Burns; m. George Boyd Childress, Aug. 10, 1974. BS, U. Ala., 1973, MA in Counseling, 1975. Tchr., counselor Holy Spirit Sch., Tuscaloosa, Ala., 1975-76, tchr., 1980-81; tchr., counselor St. Joseph Sch., Bowling Green, Ky., 1976-80; tchr., counselor Chambers Acad., Lafayette, Ala., 1980-88, acad. administr., 1989-95, asst. headmaster, 1995-96; acad. advisors Coll. Scis. and Math. Auburn (Ala.) U., 1996—; computer cons. C&L Enterprises Inc., Lafayette, Ala., 1989-90. Editor: The Smith Group, Auburn, Ala., 1995—, designer first issue newsletter, 1996. V.p. Auburn (Ala.) League of Women Voters, 1985-87; vol. Tuscaloosa (Ala.) V.A. Hosp., 1974-76, driver for elderly St. Michael's Ch., Auburn, 1990—; pres. St. Vincent de Paul Soc. St. Michael's Ch., Auburn, 1993-94. Recipient 100 Hours Vol. Cert. VA, Tuscaloosa, Ala., 1975. Mem. Nat. Acad. Advising Assn. Roman Catholic.

CHILDRESS, ELIZABETH LUSH, community volunteer, investor; b. Eugene, Oreg., Sept. 10, 1939; d. William A. and Norma L. (Dane) Lush; m.

Martin L. Pernoll, June 25, 1961 (div. Feb. 1987); children: Kristin Ann Pernoll Manzano, Martin W.; m. William A. Childress, Apr. 14, 1990; stepchildren: Anita C. Norman, Roger W. Childress. BA, U. Oreg., 1961; postgrad., Reed Coll., 1965, Tulane U., 1985-86. Lic. real estate sales agt., La. H.S. tchr. Texas City, Tex., 1961-63; real estate sales agt. New Orleans, 1980—, tax preparer, 1987-90. Bd. dirs. Tulane Med. Ctr., 1984-85, New Orleans East Rotary Club, 1987-90, Mid. Tenn. Symphony, Murfreesboro, 1992-95; bd. dirs., pres. Mid. Tenn. Med. Ctr. Ambassadors, 1995—, Jr. League Murfreesboro, 1992; vice chmn. bd. dirs. ARC, Murfreesboro, 1994—, mem. Tenn. State Coun.; pres. bd. dirs. 1st United Meth. Ch. United Meth. Women, 1995—; active Habitat for Humanity, Murfreesboro, 1993-95. Recipient Rotarian of Yr. award New Orleans East Rotary, 1990, Presdl. award Jr. League of Murfreesboro, 1992. Mem. Phi Beta Kappa. Republican. Home: 1510 Shagbark Tr Murfreesboro TN 37130

CHILDRESS, KERRI J., federal agency administrator; b. Sydney, Nebr.; d. Jack L. and Florence (Paris) Lindley; children: Kelly Nicole, Patrick Tyler. BA in History and Polit. Sci. summa cum laude, U. Md., 1983. Assoc. editor Navy Times newspaper, Springfield, Va., 1977-80; tchr. history and journalism Dept. Def. High Sch., Wuerzburg, Germany, 1982-84; historian Mt. Vernon Ladies' Assn., Va., 1984-85, Arlington Nat. Cemetery, 1985-89; media rels. officer Mil. Dist. of Washington, Ft. McNair, 1989-91; pub. affairs officer Office Gov. U.S. Soldiers' and Airmen's Home, Washington, 1991—; mem. pub. affairs staff Presdl. Inaugural Com., 1977. Contbr. articles to profl. jours. With USN, 1973-77, lt. Res. Recipient Hon. Tomb Guard ID Badge from sentinels, Tomb of the Unknowns, Arlington Cemetery, Achievement medal, Dept. Army, 1990; named Sailor of Yr., Naval Res. Unit, 1978. Mem. Phi Kappa Phi, Phi Alpha Theta. Office: Office of the Gov US Soldiers & Airmen's Home Washington DC 20317

CHILDS, DEBORAH WILDMAN, special education educator; b. Warham, Mass., Sept. 2, 1956; d. Roland E. Jr. and JoAnn (Ward) Wildman; m. Austin S. Childs, July 28, 1979; children: Brett E., Lindsey A., Erica A. BA in Health and Phys. Edn. K-12, Ohio No. U., 1978; Learning and Behavior Disorders 7-12 (Rank II), U. Ky., 1984; MEd, Wright State U., 1990, cert. prin. and asst. supr., 1992. Cert. prin. K-12, asst. supt., spl. edn. K-12, phys. edn. and health K-12. Tchr. elem. phys. edn. Union County Schs., Richwood, Ohio, 1978-79; tchr. spl. edn. Jessie Clark Jr. H.S./Lafayette Sr. H.S., Lexington, Ky., 1981-82, Fayette Sch., Lexington, 1982-85, Day Treatment Ctr., Lexington, 1986-89, Piqua (Ohio) City Schs., 1992—. Vacation Bible Sch. dir. Greene St. Ch., Piqua, 1992-94. Mem. ASCD. Methodist. Home: 727 W Greene St Piqua OH 45356-1849 Office: Bennett Jr H S 615 S Main St Piqua OH 45356-3849

CHILDS, RHONDA LOUISE, motivational speaker, consultant; b. Albany, N.Y., Sept. 29, 1946; d. David Cornelius and Rhoda Louise (Rodeniser) Curley; m. Lindsay N. Childs, July 22, 1972; children: Ashley Louise, Nathan Shreeve David Curley, Justin David Curley. BA in Sociology and Anthropology, Cath. Convent Coll., Buffalo, 1966; cert. proficiency exam, McGill U., Montreal, Que., Can., 1968; student, Siena Coll., Loudonville, N.Y., Russell Sage Coll. Adminstrv. asst. Hypersonic Lab., McGill U., 1966-68; adminstrv. asst. dept. comparative religions Sir George Williams U., Montreal, 1966-68; with various cmty. svc. orgns., Europe, Can., Africa, 1968-71; rechr. N.Y. State Mental Hygiene Dept., Albany, 1971-72; non-teaching profl. SUNY, Albany, 1973-75; cmty. liaison Collins Bay Penitentiary, Kingston, Ont., Can., 1976-77; ct. monitor Family Ct., 1975-78; pres. Concerned Citizens Against Crossgates, Guilderland, N.Y., 1978-80; adminstrv. asst. St. Catherine's Ctr. for Children, Albany, 1980-85; dir. govt. and cmty. affairs Empire Blue Cross and Blue Shield, Albany, 1985-94; devel. counsel St. Peter's Hosp., Albany, 1994-96; prin. New Visions, A Childs Co., Slingerlands, N.Y.; cons. to numerous nonprofit orgns.; founder, coord. Family Agys. Committed to Svc., 1983-86; founder, pres. Corp. Vol. Coun.; lectr. numerous ednl. and exec. seminars; motivational spkr. in field. Author: My Own Telephone Book, 1988. Bd. dirs. Salvation Army, Sr. Svc. Ctrs. Found., Albany Symphony Orch., Northeastern N.Y. chpt. Arthritis Found., March of Dimes; mem. br. coun. Am. Heart Assn.; bd. dirs., mktg. cons. Annie Schaffer Sr. Ctr.; grad. Capital Leadership, 1988-94; pres. Child Abuse and Neglect Coun., 1987-90; trustee Capital Dist. chpt., mem. pub. rels. com. Nat. Multiple Sclerosis Soc.; mem. devel. com. N.Y. State Mus. Inst.; mem. adv. bd. Ret. Sr. Vol. Programs; trustee, pres. St. Anne Inst.; pres. N.Y. State Legis. Forum, 1993-96, numerous others. Recipient Outstanding Svc. award Family Agys. Committed to Svc., 1985, Community Svc. award Cystic Fibrosis Found., 1988, Tribute to Women award, YWCA, 1991, Franklin D. Roosevelt Vol. award March of Dimes, 1991, June A. Bonneau award Sr. Svc. Ctrs. Albany, Citizen of Yr. award Samaritans, 1994, Golden Rule award, 1994, Lifetime Achievement award Women of Excellence, 1994, Outstanding Svc. award St. Anne Inst., 1994. Mem. APHA, Nat. Soc. Fund Raising Execs., Albany-Colonie Regional C. of C. (numerous coms., guest lect.), Corp. Vol. Couns. Am., NAFE, SUNY Women's Club, Women's Press Club, Enterprising Women's Leadership Inst., Rotary (pres. elect Albany chpt., coms. Dist. 7190 Citizen of Yr. award 1990, Airport Citizen of Yr. award 1990, Paul Harris fellow 1990). Democrat. Roman Catholic. Office: New Visions A Childs Co 308 Quidor Ct Slingerlands NY 12159-9554

CHILDS, SHIRLE MOONE, educational administrator; b. N.Y.C., Aug. 2, 1936; d. Harold McDaniel and Bessie Mary (Batts) Moone; m. William Childs, Sept. 5, 1971; children by previous marriage: Duane Kelby Milner, David Kent Milner. BS, U. Hartford, 1968, MS, 1970; PhD, U. Conn., 1978. Tchr., Hartford (Conn.) Public Schs., 1968-71, vice prin., acting prin. Mark Twain Elem. Sch., 1973-77, early childhood edn. specialist, 1978-84; asst. supt. instrnl. svcs. East Orange (N.J.) Pub. Schs., 1984-87; adminstrv. asst. for instruction Teaneck (N.J.) Pub. Schs., 1987-89; dir. curriculum, instrn. evaluation Windham (Conn.) Pub. Schs., 1990-94; cons. early childhood edn. Conn. State Dept. Edn., 1994—; dir. curriculum, instrn. lectr., adj. prof., instr. Conn. Coll. for Women, Eastern Conn. State Coll., U. Hartford. Past pres. bd. dirs. Women's League Day Care; trustee Hartford Conservatory Teaneck Libr. Coun., 1987-89; trustee Windham History and Textile Mus., 1990-95; bd. dir. Windham Heights Day Care Ctr., Windham United Way, bd. dir. Windham Region United Way, Women's League Day Care; Hartford Dist. dir. Christian Edn., A.M.E. Zion Church; Validator Nat. Assn. for the Edn., of Young Children; assessor State of Conn.; mem. Windsor Dem. Club; mem. Commr.'s Task Force on High Sch. Graduation Requirements N.J. Dept. Edn., 1987; assessor Md. and N.J. Assessment Ctrs., 1987; bd. dirs. Assault on Illiteracy, 1980—. Rockefeller Found. fellow, 1977-78; Kettering Found. fellow, 1976-85. Mem. Nat. Assn. Edn. Young Children, Am. Assn. Sch. Adminstrs., ASCD (facilitator early childhood edn. network 1988—), Hartford Assn. Edn. Young Children, Conn. Assn. Suprs./Instrs. in Spl. Edn., Urban League, NAACP, Nat. Council Negro Women, Delta Sigma Theta (nat. sec. 1979-83), Phi Delta Kappa, Pi Lambda Theta. Methodist. Lodge: Order Eastern Star. Avocations: Chinese cooking, needlepoint, quilting. Home: 26 Regency Dr Windsor CT 06095-3844 Office: 25 Industrial Park Rd Middletown CT 06457

CHILOW, BARBARA GAIL, social worker; b. Grand Forks, N.D., June 7, 1936; d. Alfred Thomas and Florence (Micken) Seeley; m. Steven Chilow, Aug. 15, 1987; children: John Mark Doss, Timothy Stephen Doss, Elizabeth De La Cruz, David Chilow. BS, UCLA, 1957; MSW, U. So. Calif., 1970; MPA, Calif. State U., Long Beach, 1985. Lic. social worker, Calif., Utah, marriage, family and child counselor, Calif. Social worker Dept. Pub. Welfare, San Diego, 1957, Dep. Pub. Assistance, Whitman, Mass., 1966-68; psychiat. social worker State of Calif., Pomona, 1971-73; clin. social worker Orange County Dept. Mental Health, Santa Ana, Calif., 1973-74, sr. clin. social worker, 1974-79; dep. dir. mental health Orange County Human Svcs. Agy., Santa Ana, 1979-80, dep. regional mgr., 1980-82, adminstrv. mgr. II, 1982-93; clin. coord. Brightway at St. George, Utah, 1993—; pvt. practice clin. social worker Newport Beach, Calif., 1977-93; chair So. Calif. Case Mgmt. Coun., 1987-89, Orange County Bd. and Care Quality Com., Santa Ana, 1984-89. Pres. Winchester Hills Homeowners Assn., St. George, 1995. Mem. NASW, AAUW, DAR, Alliance for Mentally Ill (pres. Orange County chpt. 1994-95), Phi Alpha Alpha. Democrat. Presbyterian. Home: 1110 W 5830 N Saint George UT 84770 Office: Brightway at St George 115 W 1470 S Saint George UT 84770

CHIN, CECILIA HUI-HSIN, librarian; b. Tientsin, China; came to U.S., 1961; d. Yu-lin and Ti-yu (Fan) C. B.A., Nat. Taiwan U., Taipei, 1961; M.S.L.S., U. Ill., 1963. Cataloger, reference librarian Roosevelt U., Chgo., 1963; reference librarian, indexer Ryerson & Burnham Libraries, Art Inst. Chgo., 1963-70, head reference dept. indexer,, 1970-75; acting dir. libraries Art Inst. Chgo., 1976-77, assoc. librarian, head reference dept., 1975-82; chief librarian Nat. Mus. Am. Art and Nat. Portrait Gallery, Smithsonian Inst., Washington, 1982—. Compiler: The Art Institute of Chicago Index to Art Periodicals, 1975. Reciipient awards Nat. Portrait Gallery, Smithsonian Instn., 1984, 89. Mem. Art Librs. Soc., D.C. Libr. Assn., Washington Rare Book Group. Office: Nat Mus Am Art & Nat Portrait Gallery Smithsonian Instn Washington DC 20560

CHIN, CINDY LAI, accountant; b. Kowloon, Hong Kong, Dec. 2, 1957; came to U.S., 1964; d. Sau Kuen and Koon On C. BS in Acctg., CUNY, 1980; grad., Real Estate Inst., 1990, NYU, 1995. Real estate acct. Milford Mgmt., Inc., N.Y.C., 1980-82; staff acct. Occidental Petroleum Corp., N.Y.C., 1983-85; portfolio acct. Yarmouth Group Inc., N.Y.C., 1985-91; sr. portfolio acct. CPC, N.Y.C., 1993—; cons. C&M Real Estate Joint Venture, N.Y.C., 1985-89. Mem. China Inst., N.Y.C., 1986. Mem. NAFE, Hunter Coll. Acctg. Alumni Assn. Home: 32 Gary Ct Staten Island NY 10314-1616 Office: CPC 5 W 37th St New York NY 10018-6222

CHIN, JANET SAU-YING, data processing executive, consultant; b. Hong Kong, July 27, 1949; came to U.S., 1959; d. Arthur Quock-Ming and Jenny (Loo) C. BS in Math, U. Ill., Chgo., 1970; MS in Computer Sci., U. Ill., Urbana, 1973. System programmer Lawrence Livermore (Calif.) Lab., 1972-79; sect. mgr. Tymshare Inc., Cupertino, Calif., 1979-83, Fortune Systems, Redwood City, Calif., 1983-85; div. mgr. Impell Corp, Berkeley, Calif., 1985; pres. Chin Assocs., Oakland, Calif., 1985-88; bus. devel. mgr. Sun Microsystems, Mountain View, Calif., 1988-92; engrng. dir. Cadence Design Systems, San Jose, Calif., 1992-94, quality dir., 1994-95; sr. dir. adminstrv. svcs. Avant! Corp., Sunnyvale, Calif., 1995—; Vice-chmn. Am. Nat. Standards Inst. X3H3, N.Y.C., 1979-82, internat. rep. X3H3, 1982-88. Co-author: The Computer Graphics Interface, 1991; contbr. tech. papers to profl. publs. Mem. Assn. Computing Machinery, Sigma Xi.

CHIN, JENNIFER YOUNG, public health educator; b. Honolulu, June 22, 1946; d. Michael W.T. and Sylvia (Ching) Young; BA, San Francisco State Coll., 1969; M.P.H., U. Calif., Berkeley, 1971; m. Benny Chin, Nov. 16, 1975; children: Kenneth Michael, Lauren Marie, Catherine Rose. Edn. asst. Am. Cancer Soc., San Francisco, 1969-70; intern Lutheran Med. Ctr., Bklyn., 1971; community health educator Md. Dept. Health and Mental Hygiene, Balt., 1971-74; community health educator Northeast Med. Svcs., San Francisco, 1975; pub. health educator Child Health and Disability Prevention, San Francisco Public Health Dept., 1975-83; health educator maternal and child health, 1991—. USPHS grantee, 1970-71. Mem. Soc. No. Calif. Pub. Health Edn. (treas. 1976, 77), Am. Public Health Assn. Office: 680 8th St Ste 200 San Francisco CA 94103-4942

CHIN, KATHY HIRATA, lawyer; b. Frankfurt-am-Main, Germany, July 3, 1953. BA magna cum laude, Princeton U., 1975; JD, Columbia U., 1980. Bar: N.Y. 1981, U.S. Dist. Ct. (so. and east. dists.) N.Y. 1981, U.S. Dist. Ct. (no. dist.) N.Y. 1984. Ptnr. Cadwalader, Wickersham & Taft, N.Y.C.; mem. Gov. Mario M. Cuomo's judicial screening com. for 1st Judicial Dept., 1992-94, mem. Magistrate Judge Merit Selection Panel for E.D. N.Y., 1992—, mem. N.Y.C. Planning Commn., 1995—. Editor-in-chief Columbia Jour. Transnational Law, 1980. Harlan Fiske Stone scholar, Columbia U., 1980. Mem. Asian Am. Bar Assn. of N.Y., N.Y. State Bar Assn., N.Y. County Lawyers Assn. Office: Cadwalader Wickersham & Taft 100 Maiden Ln New York NY 10006*

CHIN, SUE SOONE MARIAN (SUCHIN CHIN), conceptual artist, portraitist, photographer, community affairs activist; b. San Francisco; d. William W. and Soo-Up (Swebe) C. Grad. Calif. Coll. Art, Mpls. Art Inst., (scholar) Schaeffer Design Ctr.; student, Yasuo Kuniyoshi, Louis Hamon, Rico LeBrun. Photojournalist, All Together Now show, 1973, East-West News, Third World Newscasting, 1975-78, Sta. KNBC Sunday Show, L.A., 1975, 76, Live on 4, 1981, Bay Area Scene, 1981; graphics printer, exhbns. include Kaiser Ctr., Zellerbach Pla., Chinese Culture Ctr. Galleries, Capricorn Asunder Art Commn. Gallery (all San Francisco), Newspace Galleries, New Coll. of Calif., L.A. County Mus. Art, Peace Pla. Japan Ctr., Congress Arts Communication, Washington, 1989; SFWA Galleries, Inner Focus Show, 1989—, Calif. Mus. Sci. and Industry, Lucien Labaudt Gallery, Salon de Medici, Madrid, Salon Renacimento, Madrid, 1995, Life Is a Circus, SFWA Gallery, 1991, 94, UN/50 Exhibit, Bayfront Galleries, 1995, Sacramento State Fair, AFL-CIO Labor Studies Ctr., Washington, Asian Women Artists (1st prize for conceptual painting, 1st prize photography), 1978, Yerba Buena Arts Ctr. for the Arts Festival, 1994; represented in permanent collections L.A. County Fedn. Labor, Calif. Mus. Sci. and Industry, AFL-CIO Labor Studies Ctr., Australian Trades Coun., Hazeland and Co., also pvt. collections; author (poetry) Yuri and Malcolm, The Desert Sun. 1994 (Editors Choice award 1993-94). Del. nat., state convs. Nat. Women's Polit. Caucus, 1977-83, San Francisco chpt. affirmative action chairperson, 1978-82, nat. conv. del., 1978-81, Calif. del., 1976-81. Recipient Honorarium AFL-CIO Labor Studies Ctr., Washington, 1975-76; award Centro Studi Ricerche delle Nazioni, Italy, 1985; bd. advisors Psycho Neurology Found. Bicentennial award L.A. County Mus. Art, 1976, 77, 78. Mem. Asian Women Artists (founding v.p., award 1978-79, 1st award in photography of Orient 1978-79), Calif. Chinese Artists (sec.-treas. 1978-81), Japanese Am. Art Coun. (chairperson 1978-84, dir.), San Francisco Women Artists, San Francisco Graphics Guild, Pacific/Asian Women Coalition Bay Area, Chinatown Coun. Performing and Visual Arts. Chmn., Full Moon Products; pres., bd. dir. Aumni Oracle Inc. Address: PO Box 421415 San Francisco CA 94142-1415

CHIN, SUSAN HO, linguist, educator; b. N.Y.C.. BA, U. Mich.; MA, Ga. State U. Instr. Dept. ESL and applied linguistics Ga. State U., Atlanta, 1982-89; sr. prof. English, speech and tech. comm., assoc. dean gen. studies DeVry Inst. of Tech., Decatur, Ga., 1989—; presenter in field; workshop facilitator in field and in issues of cultural diversity. Contbr. articles to English Leadership Quar., Hawaiian English Jour. and other profl. jours. Mem. Nat. Coun. Tchrs. English, Ga. Coun. Tchrs. of English, Conf. on English Leadership, Tchrs. of English to Spkrs. of Other Langs., Ga. Tchrs. English to Spkrs. of Other Langs. (v.p. 1985-87, bd. dirs. 1991-93). Office: DeVry Inst Tech 250 N Arcadia Ave Decatur GA 30030-2115

CHIN, SYLVIA FUNG, lawyer; b. N.Y.C., June 27, 1949; d. Thomas and Constance (Yao) Fung; m. Edward G.H. Chin, July 10, 1971; children: Arthur F., Benjamin F. BA, NYU, 1971; JD, Fordham U., 1977. Bar: N.Y. 1978, U.S. Dist. Ct. (so. and ea. dists.) N.Y. 1979, U.S. Supreme Ct. 1990. Law clk. to dist. judge U.S. Dist. Ct. (so. dist.), N.Y.C., 1977-79; assoc. White & Case, N.Y.C., 1979-86, ptnr., 1986—; adj. assoc. prof. law Fordham U., N.Y.C., 1979-81. Co-author (article in book) Negotiating Business Transactions, 1988; mem. editorial bd. Bus. Law Today, 1996—. Mem. ABA, N.Y. County Lawyers Assn., Fordham Law Alumni Assn. (bd. dirs.), Asian Am. Bar Assn. N.Y. (pres. 1994-96, bd. dirs.). Office: White & Case 1155 Ave of the Americas New York NY 10036-2711

CHING, CALLEEN JANN, lawyer; b. Honolulu, July 19, 1951; d. Calvin K.H. and Katherine K. (Kam) C. BA in Urban Studies, U. So. Calif., 1973; JD, William S. Richardson Sch. Law, 1976. Bar: Hawaii 1976. Supervising atty. Legal Aid of Hawaii, Honolulu, 1976-86, Handicapped Rights Project, Honolulu, 1986-90; family ct. per diem judge 1st Cir. Ct. Hawaii, Honolulu, 1991-92; enforcement atty. Hawaii Civil Rights Comm., Honolulu, 1990-95; program dir. AmeriCorps Domestic Violence Clinic, Honolulu, 1995—; mem. Judiciary Gender and Other Fairness, Honolulu, 1993—; facilitator Kids 1st, Honolulu, 1995—. Co-author: Effective Legal Writing for Paralegals, 1996; contbg. author: Our Rights, Our Lives, 1991. Mem. Associated Chinese Univ. Women (chair 1989—). Office: Americorps Domestic Violence Clinic 1040 Richards St Ste 306 Honolulu HI 96813

CHINITZ, JODY ANNE KOLB, data processing manager; b. Bay City, Mich., July 8, 1953; d. Adam H. and Evelyn I. (Sylvester) Kolb; m. William A. Chinitz, Feb. 11, 1979. Student Saginaw Valley State Coll., 1972, Bklyn. Coll., 1973-76; BA in Russian Lang. and Lit. summa cum laude, CUNY, 1980. With personnel dept. N.Y. Life Ins. Co., N.Y.C., 1972-77, computer programmer, 1977-80; computer systems cons. Soroban Data Systems, Inc., N.Y.C., 1980-82; project leader Midlantic Nat. Bank, West Orange, N.J., 1982-89, asst. v.p., 1989-96; project leader M&I Tri-State Resource Ctr., Cedar Knolls, N.J., 1996—. Home: 31 Norwood Ave Montclair NJ 07043-1921 Office: M&I Tri-State Resource Ctr 2 Ridgedale Ave Cedar Knolls NJ 07927

CHINN, PEGGY LOIS, nursing educator, editor; b. Columbia, S.C., Feb. 25, 1941; d. Hubert R. and Margaret (Gasteiger) Tatum; m. Philip C. Chinn, June 15, 1964 (div. 1974); children: Kelleth Roger, Jonathan Mark (dec.). AA, Mars Hill Coll., 1960; BS, U. Hawaii, 1964; MS, U. Utah, 1970, PhD, 1971. From instr. to asst. prof. U. Utah, Salt Lake City, 1971-74; assoc. dir., prof. Tex. Woman's U., Denton, 1974-78; prof. Wright State U., Dayton, Ohio, 1978-81, SUNY, Buffalo, 1981-90, U. Colo., Denver, 1990-96; founder, editor Advances in Nursing Sci., Rockville, Md., 1978—; cons., lectr. in field. Author: Child Health Maintenance, 1974, 2d edit., 1978, Theory in Nursing, 1983, 4th edit., 1995, Peace and Power, 3d edit., 1991; contbr. articles to profl. jours. Co-founder Cassandra: Radical Feminist Nurses Network, nationwide 1982, Margaret Daughters Inc., Buffalo, 1984. Fellow Am. Acad. Nursing (governing coun. 1987-90); mem. Am. Nurses Assn., Nat. League for Nursing, Sigma Theta Tau. Office: U Conn Nursing Health Sci Ctr 231 Glenbrook Rd Storrs Mansfield CT 06269

CHINN, PHYLLIS ZWEIG, mathematics educator; b. Rochester, N.Y., Sept. 26, 1941; d. Julian and Gladys Elizabeth (Weinstein) Z.; m. Daryl Ngee Chinn, Dec. 31, 1968; children: Allison Hai-Ting, Wesley Chee. BA, Brandeis U., 1962; MAT, Harvard U., 1963; MS, U. Calif., San Diego, 1966, PhD, Santa Barbara, 1969. Asst. prof. Towson State Coll. Balt., 1969-75; assoc. prof. Humboldt State U., Arcata, Calif., 1975-83, prof., 1984—; exch. prof. U. Cen. Fla., Orlando, 1983-84. Dir. Redwood Area Math Project, 1988—. Author: (bibliography) Women in Science and Math, 1979, 3rd edit., 1988; also monograph. Contbr. articles to profl. jours. Conf. coord. Nat. Women's Studies Assn., Arcata, 1982, Expanding Your Horizons in Sci. and Math, Arcata and Orlando, 1980-89. Calif. State U. grantee, 1977. Mem. Assn. for Women in Math., Women and Math., Assn. for Women in Sci., Nat. Council of Tchrs. of Math., Math. Assn. Am., Profs. Rethinking Options in Math. for Prospective Tchrs. (dir. project 1992—), Assn. Math. Tchr. Educators, Phi Beta Kappa, Phi Kappa Phi. Office: Humboldt State U Math Dept Arcata CA 95521

CHINN-HECHTER, MAMIE MAY, nonprofit organization executive; b. Oakland, Calif., Aug. 20, 1951; d. Bing T. and Georgia S. (Ong) C.; m. Marc S. Hechter. BS in Bus., U. Nev., 1974. Loan processor First Fed. Savs. and Loan, Reno, 1974-75, loan processor supr., 1975-76, sr. loan counselor, affirmative action officer, 1977-78; jr. loan officer First Fed. Savs. and Loan, Carson City, Nev., 1976-77; loan officer State of Nev. Housing Divsn., Carson City, 1978-79, loan adminstr., 1979-83, dep. adminstr., 1983-93; pres., CEO Nev. Comty. Reinvestment Corp., Las Vegas, 1993—; mem. exec. com. Housing and Devel. Fin., Ethics Com., Media and Comms. Com., Carson City, 1987-93. Bd. mem. Nev. Cmty. Reinvestment Corp., 1991—; bd. com. Nev. Housing and Neighborhood Devel., Inc., 1994—, state low income housing trust fund, 1994—; mem. United Way Planning Coun., 1995—; mem. cmty. adv. bd. Nev. State Bank; participant C. of C. Leadership Las Vegas, 1996. Mem. Capitol City (Carson City sec. 1984-88), Women's Bowling Assn. (bd. dirs. 1983-84), Nat. 600, Asian C. of C. Office: Nev Comty Reinvestment Corp 5920 W Flamingo Rd Ste 8 Las Vegas NV 89103-0109

CHINNIS, PAMELA P., religion organization administrator; b. Springfield, Mo.; children: Ann, Cabell. BA, Coll. William and Mary, 1946; DHL (hon.), Va. Theol. Sem., 1983, Yale U., 1990, Ch. Divinity Sch. of Pacific, 1992, St. Paul's Coll.; DD, Gen. Theol. Sem., 1992. Sr. warden Ch. Epiphany, Washington, 1972-78, 90-95, v.p. Province III, 1985-91; now pres., House of Deputies Episcopal Church, N.Y.C.; mem. exec. coun., 1979-85; chair stewardship and devel. com., venture in mission process com.; alternate lay del. to Anglican Consultative Coun., 1979-85, lay del., 1985-93; mem. search com. for new Sec. Gen. Anglican Communion, 1992-93; presiding officer 1976 triennial meeting of women of ch., Mpls.; chair Venture in Mission; chair legis. com. on ecumen. rels. Ho. of Deputies 1985 Conv.; chair com. for full participation of women in ch., 1985-88; mem. gen. bd. and exec. coordinating com. Nat. Coun. Chs., 1988—; del. to Anglican Coun. N.Am. and Carribean, 1982-85, sec. exec. com.; del. to World Coun. Chs., Faith and Order Commn., India, 1978, Ptnrs. in Mission Consultation of Nippon Sei Ko Kai, 1980, Internat. Consultation of Community of Women and Men in Ch., Sheffield, Eng., 1980, Anglican Coun. N.Am. and Carribean com. on Refugees, Belize, Ctrl. Am., 1983. Bd. dirs. Coll. William and Mary Alumni Soc., Am. Friends of Diocese Jerusalem, Washington Theol. Consortium; gov. Va. Bd. Visitors Coll. William and Mary; bd. trustees Gen. Theol. Sem., 1987-90, Bekeley Divinity Sch., Yale U., 1991-93, Greater S.E. Community Hosp., Washington; mem. adv. bd. St. Barnabus Ctr., Wis., Conf. of Deaf, Episc. Radio-TV Found. Recipient Disting. Christian Svc. award Seabury-Western Theol. Sem. Mem. Am. Soc. Order of St. John, Cathedral chpt. Washington Nat. Cathedral. Office: Episcopal Ch 815 2nd Ave New York NY 10017-4503

CHINSAMY, ANUSUYA, paleobiologist, researcher; b. Pretoria, Transvaal, South Africa, Aug. 27, 1962; came to U.S., 1992; d. Krishna and Sushilla (Pillay) C.; m. Yunus Nadi Turan, July 2, 1992. Higher diploma in Edn., Westville U., Durban, South Africa, 1985; BSc with honors, U. Witwatersrand, Johannesburg, South Africa, 1984, MSc, 1988, PhD, 1991. Jr. lectr. U. Witwatersrand, 1988-90, lectr., 1991-92; postdoctoral fellow U. Pa., Phila., 1992. Editor: Palaeontological Newsletter of PSSA, 1991-92, co-editor, 1990; contbr. articles to profl. jours. Rsch. grantee NSF, 1992-94, Coun. for Sci. and Indsl. Rsch., 1984, 86, 87. Mem. Palaeontological Soc. of S.A. (recipient Lystrosaurus shield 1986), Soc. Vertebrate Palaeontology. Office: Univ of Pennsylvania 3800 Spruce St Philadelphia PA 19104*

CHIOCCO, BERNADETTE M., tax accountant; b. Darby, Pa., Aug. 11, 1961; d. William Joseph and Marie Antoinette (Prodoehl) Medrow; m. Timothy Michael Chiocco, Oct. 21, 1989; 1 child, Elizabeth Anne. BS, St. Joseph's U., 1983; M in Taxation, Villanova U., 1992. CPA. Sr. tax mgr. Asher & Co., Ltd., Phila., 1983—. Bd. dirs. Darby Libr. Co., 1992—. Mem. AICPAs, Pa. Inst. CPAs, Rotary. Office: Asher & Co 1845 Walnut St Philadelphia PA 19103

CHIORAZZI, MARY LORRAINE, psychiatrist; b. New York. BS, Marymount Manhattan Coll., 1966; MD, Georgetown U., 1970. Diplomate Am. Bd. Psychiatry. Pvt. practice child, adolescent, adult psychiatry Englewood, N.J., 1975—. Office: 163 Engle St Englewood NJ 07631-2530

CHIPMAN, DEBRA DECKER, paralegal; b. Oneonta, N.Y., Sept. 21, 1959; d. Leon Hannibal and Patricia Elizabeth (Ainsworth) Decker; m. Michael A. Chipman, May 24, 1980 (div. Sept. 1990); 1 child, Amanda Michelle. Student, Robert Morris Coll., 1988-94. Sec., receptionist Power Engrng. Corp., Binghamton, N.Y., 1977-78; accounts payable clk. Old Dominion U. Rsch. Found., Norfolk, Va., 1978-80; adminstrv. asst. U. Pitts., 1980-81; paralegal Papernick & Gefsky, Attys. at Law, Pitts., 1981-93; mgr. Preferred Settlement Svcs., Inc., Pitts., 1993—. Recipient award Otsego County Bankers Assn., 1977. Mem. Nat. Assn. Legal Assts, Pitts. Paralegal Assn. (co-chair fundraising com. 1990), Pa. Assn. Notaries, Pa. Land Title Assn., Pa. Land Title Inst. (western Pa. chpt. edn. com.). Methodist. Home: 2593 Hunters Point Ct S Wexford PA 15090 Office: 9401 Mcknight Rd Ste 302 Pittsburgh PA 15237-6000

CHISHOLM, MARGARET ELIZABETH, retired library education administrator; b. Grey Eagle, Minn., July 25, 1921; d. Henry D. and Alice (Thomas) Bergman; children: Nancy Diane, Janice Marie Lane. BA, U. Washington, 1957, MLS, 1958, PhD, 1966. Libr. Everett (Wash.) C.C., 1961-63; asst. and assoc. prof. edn. U. Oreg., Eugene, 1963-67; assoc. prof. edn. U. N.Mex., Albuquerque, 1967-69; prof., dean Coll. Libr. and Info. Svcs. U. Md., College Park, 1969-75; v.p. univ. relations and devel. U. Washington, Seattle, 1975-81; dir. and prof. Grad. Sch. Libr. and Info. Sci., U. Wash., Seattle, 1981-92; ret., 1992; adv. com. White House Conf. on Libr. and Info. Sci., 1989-91, Pub. Broadcasting Svc. Archive; commr. Western Interstate Commn. Higher Edn., Colo., 1981-85. Author: Information Technology: Design and Applications (with Nancy Lane), 1990. Mem. USIA del. to Mexican-Am. Commn. on Cultural Coop., 1990. Civilian aide

U.S. Army, 1978-88. Recipient Ruth Worden award U. Wash., Seattle, 1957, Disting. Alumni award St. Cloud (Minn.) U., 1977, Disting. Alumni award U. Wash., 1979, John Brubaker award Cath. Libr. Assn., 1987, Pres.'s award Wash. Libr. Assn., 1991. Mem. ALA (exec. bd. 1989-90, pres. 1988-89, v.p. 1986-87), Assn. Pub. TV Stas. (trustee 1975-84, 87-93), White House Conf. on Libr. and Info. Svcs. (adv. com. 1989-91), U. Wash. Retirement Assn. (v.p. 1995-96, pres. 1996—). Home: 5892 NE Park Point Pl Seattle WA 98115-7845

CHISHOLM, SHIRLEY ANITA ST. HILL, former congresswoman, educator, lecturer; b. Bklyn., Nov. 30, 1924; d. Charles Christopher and Ruby (Seale) St. Hill; m. Conrad Chisholm, Oct. 8, 1949 (div. Feb. 1977); m. Arthur Hardwick, Jr., Nov. 26, 1977. B.A. cum laude, Bklyn. Coll.; M.A., Columbia U.; LL.D. (hon.), Talladega (Ala.) Coll., Hampton (Va.) Inst., LaSalle Coll., Phila., U. Maine, Portland, Capital U., William Patterson Coll., Pratt Inst., Coppin State Coll., N.C. Coll., Kenyon Coll., Wilmington (Ohio) Coll., Acquinas Coll., Grand Rapids, Mich., Reed Coll., Portland, Oreg., U. Cin., Smith Coll., Northampton, Mass. Former nursery sch. tchr., dir. nursery sch.; ednl. cons. Div. Day Care, Bur. Child Welfare, N.Y.C.; mem. N.Y. State Assembly, 1964-68, 91st-98th Congresses from 12th Dist. N.Y., 1969-83; Purington chair Mount Holyoke Coll., South Hadley, Mass., 1983-87; Lectr. Spellman Coll., Atlanta. Author: Unbought and Unbossed, 1970, The Good Fight, 1973. Hon. mem. bd. dirs. Cosmopolitan Young People's Symphony Orch., N.Y.C.; adv. bd. Fund. for Research and Edn. in Sickle Cell Disease; bd dirs. Bklyn. Home for Aged; mem. Central Bklyn. Coordinating Council; mem. nat. adv. council Inst. for Studies in Edn., Notre Dame; mem. adv. com. Washington Workshops; nat. bd. dirs. Ams. for Democratic Action; mem. adv. council NOW; hon. com. mem. United Negro Coll. Fund.; Presdl. candidate Dem. Party, 1972. Named Alumna of Year Bklyn. Coll. Alumni Bull., 1957; recipient award for outstanding work in field of child welfare Women's Council of Bklyn., 1957, Key Woman of Year award, 1963, Woman of Achievement award Key Women, Inc., 1965. Mem. Nat. Assn. Coll. Women, Bklyn. Coll. Alumni, LWV, Key Women, NAACP, Delta Sigma Theta. Methodist. *

CHISHOLM, STEPHANIE MCKAY, elementary school educator; b. Waukegan, Ill., Aug. 3, 1963; d. Thomas McKay and Ruth M. (Meade) C. BS, U. Ill., Chgo., 1988; postgrad., Nat. Louis U. Tchr. 1st grade St. Mary of the Lake Sch., Chgo., 1989; tchr. 6th grade Sch. Dist. #60, Waukegan, 1990-91, tchr. 4th grade, 1991-95, tchr. 2d/3d grade, 1995-96; tutor Ednl. Cons. Svc., Vernon Hills, Ill., 1990—. Editor: Project Care, 1991—. Waukegan Found. grantee, 1994.

CHISOLM, BARBARA WILLE, world affairs organization executive; b. Albany, N.Y., Dec. 8, 1936; d. Edmund James and Marian Virginia (Titter) Bowen; m. Roland Frank Wille, July 2, 1969 (dec. July 1988); children: Serena Bowen, Alison Brevard; m. Oliver Beirne Chisolm, Aug. 10, 1991. BA, Smith Coll., 1958; MA, U. London, 1960. Acting dir. catalogue rsch. dept. Met. Mus., N.Y.C., 1966-69; dir. Art Gallery of the China Inst., N.Y.C., 1969-71; N.Y.-New Eng. dir., lectr. Nat. Fine Arts Assocs., Washington, 1974-88; exec. sec., dir., pres. Forum for World Affairs, Stamford, Conn., 1989—; invited guest NATO, Brussels, 1996. Mem. Nat. Coun. World Affairs Orgns. (bd. dirs. 1996—), English Speaking Union Greenwich-Stamford (bd. dirs. v.p. ednl. com. 1986-96). Republican. Episcopalian. Home: 21 Stepping Stone Ln Greenwich CT 06830-2401 Office: Forum for World Affairs 3 Landmark Sq Ste 330 Stamford CT 06901-2707

CHISWICK, NANCY ROSE, psychologist; b. East Orange, N.J., May 8, 1945; d. Haim Hershel and Beatrice May (Levinson) C.; m. Arthur Howard Patterson, Aug. 5, 1973; children: Michael Chiswick-Patterson, Emily Chiswick-Patterson. AB, Smith Coll., 1966; MA, U. Ill., Chgo., 1970; PhD, U. Ill., 1973. Lic. psychologist, Pa. Intern Northwestern U. Med. Sch., Chgo., 1973; mental retardation specialist The Counseling Svc., Bellefonte, Pa., 1973-75; clin. staff psychologist Pa. State U., 1975-80; dir. clin. psychologist Child, Adult and Family Psychol. Ctr., State College, Pa., 1980—; adj. prof. psychology and human devel. Pa. State U., 1974—; mem. allied staff Ctr. Cmty. Hosp., State College, 1985—; staff Meadows Psychiat. Hosp., Centre Hall, Pa., 1985—. Creator, co-host pub. TV Series About Women, 1979-80. Del. White House Conf. Families, 1980, bd. dirs. Meadows Psychiat. Hosp., 1983-85, Jewish Cmty. Ctr., 1989-96. Named Guest in Residence W. Marlin Butts Com. Oberlin (Ohio) Coll., 1978. Fellow Ctrl. Pa. Psychol. Assn. (sec. 1987-89); mem. APA, Pa. Psychol. Assn. Home: 2443 Hickory Hill Dr State College PA 16803-3361 Office: Child Adult & Family Psychol Ctr 315 S Allen St Ste 218 State College PA 16801-4850

CHITTICK, ELIZABETH LANCASTER, association executive, women's rights activist; b. Bangor, Pa., Nov. 11, 1918; d. George and Flora Mae (Mann) Lancaster. Student, Columbia U., 1944-45, N.Y. Inst. Fin., 1950-51, Hunter Coll., 1952-56, Upper Iowa U., Fayette, 1976. Adminstrv. asst., chief clk U.S. Naval Air Stas., Seattle and Banana River, Fla., 1941-45; v.p. treas. W.A. Chittick & Co., MAnila, 1945-52; 31062Smith; real estate salesperson La Jolla, Calif., 1949; registered rep. Bache & Co., N.Y. Stock Exch., N.Y.C., 1950-62, Shearson & Hamil, 1962-63; investment adviser, 1962-65; revenue officer IRS, N.Y.C., 1965-72; pres. Nat. Woman's Party, Washington, 1971-89, Woman's Party Corp., 1978-91; commr. Washington Commn. on Status of Women, 1982-86; pres., adminstr. Sewall-Belmont House; bd. dirs. Wexita Corp., N.Y.C., Pan Am. Liason Com. of Women's Orgns. Inc.; 1st v.p., bd. dirs. Nat. Coun. Women U.S. Lectr., TV and radio commentator on Equal Rights Amendment; author: Answers to Questions About the Equal Rights Amendment, 1973, 76. Mem. Coalition for Women in Internat. Devel., Internat. Women's Yr. Continuing Com., 1978-81, Women's Campaign Fund, Washington, 1975-80, Women's Nat. Rep. Club, N.Y.C., Women Govt. Rels., Washington; mem. U.S. com. of cooperation to Inter-Am. Commn. of Women, OAS, 1974-80; del. U.S. World Conf. of Internat. Women's Yr., Mexico City, 1975; mem. women's history ctr. task force Am. Revolution Bicentennial Adminstrn., 1973-76; mem. adv. com. U.S. Ctr. for Internat. Women's Yr., 1973-76; vice convenor com. on law and status of women Internat. Coun. of Women; chmn. UN Drive for war orphans and widows, Manila, 1949;. Mem. Greater Washington Soc. Assn. Execs., Internat. Coun. Women (Paris), Nat. Fedn. Bus. and Profl. Women's Clubs, Gen. Fedn. Women's Clubs, Women's Press Club (N.Y.C.), Am. Newswomen's Club, Nat. Press Club, Order Eastern Star. Home and Office: 3590 S Ocean Blvd Apt 107 Palm Beach FL 33480-5743

CHITTY, (MARY) ELIZABETH NICKINSON, university historian; b. Balt., Apr. 27, 1920; d. Edward Phillips and Em Turner (Merritt) Nickinson; m. Arthur Benjamin Chitty, June 16, 1946; children: Arthur Benjamin, John Abercrombie, Em Turner, Nathan Harsh Brown. BA cum laude, Fla. State U., 1941, MA, 1942; DCL, U. of South, 1988. Tchr. Fla. Indsl. Sch. for Girls, Ocala, 1942-43; psychometrist neuropsychiat. dept. Sch. Aviation Medicine, Pensacola (Fla.) Naval Air Sta., 1943-46; assoc. editor Sewanee (Tenn.) Alumni News, U. of South, 1946-62; bus. mgr., mng. editor Sewanee Rev., 1962-65, dir. fin. aid and career svcs., 1970-80, assoc. univ. historiographer, 1980—; freelance editor. Editor: (with H.A. Petry) Sewanee Centennial Alumni Directory, 1954-62; Centennial Report of the Registrar of the University of the South, 1959; (with Arthur Ben Chitty) Too Black, Too White (Ely Green), 1970; author: (with Moultrie Guerry and Arthur Ben Chitty) Men Who Made Sewanee, 1981, (with A.B. Chitty and W. Givens) Ninety-Nine Iron, 1992; columnist Sewanee Mountain Messenger, 1985—. Bd. dirs. Sewanee Civic Assn., 1979-80, 86-88; CONTACT-Lifeline of Coffee and Franklin Counties, 1981-84; mem. adv. coun. St. Andrew's Sewanee Sch., 1988—. Recipient Cmty. Svc. award Sewanee Civic Assn., 1996. Mem. Assn. Preservation Tenn. Antiquities (trustee 1985-88), AAUW (pres. Sewanee br. 1975-77), Fla. State U. Alumni Assn. (dir. 1941—, permanent pres. Class of 1941), Mortar Bd., Phi Beta Kappa, Phi Kappa Phi, Phi Alpha Theta, Kappa Delta. Democrat. Episcopalian. Home: 100 South Carolina Ave Sewanee TN 37375-2045 Office: Univ of South Sewanee TN 37385-1000

CHITWOOD, LERA CATHERINE, marketing information professional; b. Columbiana, Ala., Sept. 14, 1942; d. Roy P. and Lizzie Hearn (Erwin) C.; m. John N. Mathys, Mar. 17, 1984 (div. 1992); 1 child, Jonathan Roy Chitwood Mathys. BA in English, Carson-Newman Coll., 1964; MLS, Emory U., 1967; MBA, DePaul U., 1985. Asst. head dept. bus. and sci. Atlanta Pub. Libr., 1964, 66-69; tchr. English, Sequoyah High Sch., Doraville, Ga., 1965; libr. Ill. Inst. Tech. Stuart Sch. Mgmt. and Fin., Chgo., 1970-79; sr. reference libr., asst. prof. bibliography U. Ala., Huntsville, 1979-82; mgr. bus. rsch. Motorola Inc., Schaumburg, Ill., 1985-95; mgr. mktg. John Crane Internat., Morton Grove, Ill., 1995—. Libr. sch. scholar Atlanta Pub. Libr., 1966. Mem. Soc. Competitive Intelligence (CI Rev. columnist, 1991-95), Assn. Global Strategic Info. Home: 208 E Crescent Ave Elmhurst IL 60126-4054

CHIU, DOROTHY, pediatrician; b. Hong Kong, Aug. 8, 1917; came to U.S., 1946; d. Yan Tse Chiu and Connie Kwai-Ching Wan; m. Kitman Au; children: Katherine, Margo, Doris, James, Richard. BS, Lingnan U., 1939; MD, Nat. Shanghai Med. Coll., 1945. Diplomate Am. Bd. Pediats. Sch. physician L.A. Sch. Dist., 1954-55; pvt. practice Burbank, Calif., 1954-55, San Fernando, Calif., 1955—; staff pediatrician Holy Cross Med. Ctr., Mission Hills, Calif., 1961—. Bd. dirs. Burbank Cmty. Concert, 1970-80. Fellow Am. Acad. Pediats.; mem. Calif. Med. Assn., L.A. County Med. Assn. Republican. Office: 11273 Laurel Canyon Blvd San Fernando CA 91340-4300

CHIU, TERRI-ANN ANTHONY, critical care nurse; b. Trenton, N.J., Dec. 24, 1963; d. Walter Leon and Margaret Louise (Kohler) Anthony; m. William Chien-Chen Chiu, May 25, 1991. BSN, Trenton State Coll., 1990. RN, Pa., N.Y., N.J., Md. Nurse extern Thomas Jefferson U. Hosp., Phila., 1989-90, staff nurse, 1990-93; staff nurse N.Y. Hosp.-Cornell Med. Ctr., N.Y.C., 1991-92, Robert W. Johnson U. Hosp., New Brunswick, N.J., 1992-94, Johns Hopkins Hosp., Balt., 1994—. Mem. AACN, Nat. League Nursing, Sigma Theta Tau. Democrat. Roman Catholic. Home: 2410 Old Frederick Rd Catonsville MD 21228-5420 Office: Johns Hopkins Hosp SICU 600 N Wolfe St Baltimore MD 21205

CHIZAUSKAS, CATHLEEN JO, manufacturing company executive; b. Little Rock, Dec. 26, 1954; m. Alan Michael Chizauskas, Nov. 11, 1978; children: Marc Alan, Danielle Kelley. Diploma in Mgmt., Simmons Coll., Boston, 1981. Clk. typist to direct materials buyer Gillette Safety Razor Co., Boston, 1972-79, buyer capital equipment, 1979, mgr. MRO and purchasing svcs., 1979-85, adminstrv. asst. to v.p. mktg., 1985-87, exec. asst. to pres., 1987-88, assoc. brand mgr. shave creams, 1988-89, bus. mgr., 1989-91, product mgr., 1991-94, nat. trade mktg. mgr. grooming products, 1994-95; dir. ethnic mktg. Gillette Co., Boston, 1995—. Mem. Am. Mgmt. Assn., Simmons Coll. Grad. Sch. Alumnae Assn. Roman Catholic. Office: Gillette Co Gillette Park Boston MA 02106

CHO, MARGARET, comedian, actress; b. San Francisco, 1970; d. Sueng-Hoon Cho and Young-Hie. Comedian, 1991—. TV appearances include All-American Girl, 1994—. Named Best Female Comedian Am. Comedy Awards, 1993. *

CHOICE, PRISCILLA KATHRYN MEANS (PENNY CHOICE), gifted education educator, international consultant; b. Rockford, Ill., Nov. 8, 1939; d. John Z. and Margaret A. (Haines) Means; m. Jack R. Choice, Nov. 14, 1964; children: William Kenneth, Margaret Meta. BA, U. Wis., 1963; MEd, Nat.-Louis U., 1990; MA, N.E. Ill. U., 1995. Field rsch. dir. Tatham-Laird and Kudner Advt., Chgo., 1964-69; drama specialist Children's Theatre Western Springs (Ill.), 1969-81; gifted teaching asst. Sch. Dist. 181, Hinsdale, Ill., 1980-84; tchr. Sch. Dist. 99, Cicero, Ill., 1984-85; gifted edn. program coord. Community Consolidated Sch. Dist. 93, Carol Stream, Ill., 1985—; drama specialist, cons. Choice Dramatics, Hinsdale and Clarendon Hills, Ill., 1976—; producing dir. Mirror Image Youth Theatre, Hinsdale, 1986-88; adj. prof. Coll. DuPage, Glen Ellyn, Ill., 1990-92, Nat.-Louis U., Evanston, Ill., 1991—, Aurora (Ill.)úU., 1995—, Govs. State U., University Park, Ill., 1992-93; internat. cons. in gifted edn. and drama-in-edn., 1989—. Contbg. author Gifted/Arts Resource Guide, 1990; contbg. editor Ill. Theatre Assn., Followspot News, 1992-95. Bd. dirs. Ill. Theatre Assn., Chgo., 1983-87; mem. gifted adv. com. Ednl. Svc. Ctr., Wheaton, Ill., 1987-90, 92-95, Regional Office of Edn., Wheaton, 1995—, Northeastern Ill. U., Chgo., 1993-95. Recipient Ill. State Bd. Edn. gifted edn. fellowship, 1988, AAUW continuing edn. scholarship, 1986, 90, Excellence award Ill. Theatre Assn., 1991, Excellence award Ill. Math. and Sci. Acad., 1990, Recognition of Excellence, No. Ill. Planning Commn. Gifted Edn., 1990. Mem. ASCD, World Coun. on Gifted Edn., Nat. Assn. Gifted Children, Ill. Assn. Gifted Children (membership chmn. 1992-94, advocacy com. 1995—), Ill. Coun. Gifted, AAm. Assn. Theatre in Edn., Ill. Theatre Assn. (bd. dirs. 1983-87, Outstanding Achievement award 1991), Inst. for Global Ethics, Ill. Alliance Arts Edn., Theatre Western Springs, Phi Delta Kappa. Home: 113 S Prospect Ave Clarendon Hills IL 60514-1422 Office: Cmty Consol Sch Dist 93 Jay Stream Sch 283 El Paso Ln Carol Stream IL 60188-1736

CHOITZ, LESLIE JANE, development assistant; b. South Bend, Ind., Mar. 16, 1954; d. Alfred H. and Martha J. (Carr) C. BA in English, Berry Coll., Rome, Ga., 1976; MS in Adminstrn., U. Notre Dame, 1987. Accounts payable bookkeeper A.H. Choitz & Co. Inc., South Bend, 1977-81; asst. to exec. dir. Southhold Restorations, Inc., South Bend, 1976-77, exec. dir., 1981-89; dir. arts program Michiana Arts and Scis. Coun., South Bend, 1989-95; devel. asst. Sisters of the Holy Cross, Notre Dame, Ind., 1995—; grant application rev. panelist Ind. Arts Commn., Indpls., 1995. Co-author: Our Bend in the River, 1986. Bd. dirs. Ind. Assembly of Local Arts Agys., Indpls., 1991-95; bd. dirs. South Bend Civic Theatre, Inc., 1986-89, 96—, treas., 1996; chronicler St. Joseph County Healthy Cmtys., 1993-95. Mem. AAUW (bd. dirs. 1981-86, 88-89). Republican. Lutheran. Home: 208 Napoleon Blvd South Bend IN 46617

CHOLDIN, MARIANNA TAX, librarian, educator; b. Chgo., Feb. 26, 1942; d. Sol and Gertrude (Katz) Tax; m. Harvey Myron Choldin, Aug. 28, 1962; children: Kate and Mary (twins). BA, U. Chgo., 1962, MA, 1967, PhD, 1979. Slavic bibliographer Mich. State U., East Lansing, 1967-69; Slavic bibliographer, instr. U. Ill., Urbana, 1969-73, Slavic bibliographer, asst. prof., 1973-76, Slavic bibliographer, assoc. prof., 1976-84, head Slavic and East European Libr., 1982-89, head, prof., 1984—, dir. Russian and East European Ctr., 1987-89, C. Walter and Gerda B. Mortenson Disting. prof., 1989—, dir. Mortenson Ctr. for Internat. Libr. Programs, 1991—. Author: Fence Around the Empire: Russian Censorship, 1985; editor: Red Pencil: Artists, Scholars and Censors in the USSR, 1989, Books, Libraries and Information in Slavic and East European Studies, 1986. Mem. ALA, Am. Assn. for Advancement of Slavic Studies (pres. 1995), Internat. Fedn. Libr. Assns. and Instns., Phi Beta Kappa. Jewish. Home: 1111 S Pine St Champaign IL 61820-6334 Office: U Ill Libr 1408 W Gregory Dr Urbana IL 61801-3607

CHONMAITREE, TASNEE, pediatrician, educator, infectious disease specialist; b. Bangkok, Thailand, Dec. 9, 1949; came to U.S., 1975; d. Surajit and Arporn (Maitong) C.; m. Somkiat Laungthaleong Pong, June 27, 1981; children: Ann L. Pong, Dan L. Pong. BS, Mahidol U., Bangkok, 1971; MD, Siriraj Med. Sch., Bangkok, 1973. Diplomate Am. Bd. Pediatrics, Am. Bd. Pediatric Infectious Diseases. Rotating intern Siriraj Hosp., Bangkok, 1973-74, resident in pediatrics, 1974-75; resident in pediatrics Lloyd Noland Hosp., U. Ala., Birmingham, 1975-78; fellow infectious disease U. Rochester (N.Y.), 1978-81; asst. prof. pediatrics U. Tex. Med. Br., Galveston, 1981-87, asst. prof. pathology, 1985-87, assoc. prof. pediatrics and pathology, 1987-94; prof. pediatrics and pathology, 1994—; assoc. dir. clin. virology lab. U. Tex. Med. Br., Galveston, 1985-92, dir. divsn. pediatric infectious disease, 1985-92. Contbr. 50 articles to profl. jours. Grantee NIH, 1994-99. Fellow Am. Acad. Pediatrics, Pediatric Infectious Diseases Soc., Infectious Diseases Soc. Am.; mem. Soc. Pediatric Rsch., European Soc. for Pediatric Rsch., Tex. Infectious Disease Soc. Buddhist. Home: 1906 Cherrytree Park Cir Houston TX 77062-2327 Office: U Tex Dept Pediatrics Med Br Ninth Street & Market Galveston TX 77555-0371

CHONSKI, DENISE THERESA, primary school educator, artist; b. Albany, N.Y., Jan. 26, 1962; d. Stanley V. and Rosemary K. (Dyda) C. BSBA, BS in Art Edn., Coll. of St. Rose, Albany, N.Y., 1984, MS in Elem. Edn., 1994. Cert. elem., K-12 art tchr.; permanent cert. in elem. edn. N-6 with early childhood annotation, N.Y. K-8 art tchr. St. Luke's Sch., Schenectady, N.Y., 1984-92, Holy Spirit, East Greenbush, N.Y., 1984-85, Vincentian Inst. Grammar Sch., Albany, 1985-86, St. Paul the Apostle, Schenectady, 1986-90, St. Helen's, Niskayuna, N.Y., 1987-89; 5-8 art educator Cohoes (N.Y.) Cath. Schs., 1985-86; 7-12 art educator Notre Dame Bishop Gibbons H.S., Schenectady, 1989-90; pre-K and nursery sch. and K-8 art educator St. Teresa of Avila Sch., Albany, 1990—; workshop presenter/guest speaker Cath. Sch. Office, Diocese of Albany, 1992—; del. Lakeside Health Inst., Delhi, N.Y., 1993. Mem. Albany Inst. History and Art, 1995—; bd. dirs. Cmty. Maternity Svcs., Albany, 1989-95. Recipient Bldg. Amb. award Edn. Ctr. Inc., 1993-94. Mem. N.Y. State Art Tchrs. Assn., Nat. Cath. Educators Assn., Kappa Delta Pi. Roman Catholic. Home: 64 Hurst Ave Albany NY 12208-1537

CHOPARD, CHERYL LYNNE, counselor; b. Manchester, Iowa, June 22, 1964; d. Roger W. and Lois L. (Gissible) C. BA, U. No. Iowa, 1986; MS, Iowa State U., 1995. Therapeutic recreation specialist Richard Young Hosp., Omaha, Nebr., 1987; youth counselor Linn County Juvenile Detention Ctr., Marion, Iowa, 1988-90; activity therapist Chicago Read Mental Health Ctr., 1990; counselor intern Hawkeye C.C., Waterloo, Iowa, 1993, C.A.S.S., Waterloo, 1993-94; adminstr. No. Iowa Transition Ctr., Mason City, 1994-95; crisis counselor Integrated Crisis Svc., Waterloo, 1985-86; pet therapist Cedar Sch., Cedar Falls, Iowa, 1986; grief group counselor Covenant Med. Ctr., Waterloo, 1993. Vol. Cedar Valley Hospice, Waterloo, 1993-94. Recipient J. Nivens scholarship Iowa Parks and Recreation Assn., 1986, Acad. scholarship Am. Bus. Women's Assn., 1993. Mem. Am. Counseling Assn.

CHOUDHURY, SHARMIN AHMAD, elementary education educator; b. Dhaka, Bangladesh, Feb. 29, 1960; came to U.S., 1984; d. Tajuddin Ahmad and Zohra (Khatun) Ahmad; m. Munirul Islam Choudhury, Oct. 24, 1977; children: Taj C., Aumrita. B in Liberal Arts, Navran Coll., 1980; MA, George Washington U., 1990. Tchr. Maple Leaf Internat. Sch., Dhaka, 1980-84; head counsellor Green Acre Sch. Summer Camp, Rockville, Md., 1986; elem. tchr. Muslim Community Sch., Potomac, Md., 1990-92; advisor Primary Sch., Dhaka, 1987-91; sponsor, co-dir. Dardaria Primary Sch., Dhaka, 1987—. Contbr. poetry to lit. jours., books; writer, spkr. on spirituality and women's rights. Mem. SahHati Women's Orgn., Bethesda, Md., 1987—; bd. dirs. Minaret of Freedom Inst., 1995—. Fellow George Washington U., 1987, fellow, 1988; recipient Women of Distinction award Soroptimist Internat. of Am., 1996. Mem. Muslim Women's Georgetown Study Project, Women of Vision, Lifeline Network: World Alliance for Humanitarian Assistance for Bosnia. Office: Muslim Cmty Sch 7917 Montrose Rd Potomac MD 20854-3360

CHOUGH, HEESUNG, secondary school educator; b. Seoul, Dec. 22, 1937; m. Euiwon Chough; children: Grace, Regina, Michael. BA, Ewha Womans U., 1959; BS, Limestone Coll., 1961; MS, Columbia U., 1965. Registered dietician; cert. tchr. N.Y. Dietitian Lemuel Shattuck Hosp., Jamaica Plain, Mass., 1961-62; therapeutic dietitian Luth. Med. Ctr., Bklyn., 1963-66; rsch. dietician Downstate Med. Ctr., N.Y.C., 1966-67; pub. health nutiritionist Downstate Med. Ctr., Bklyn., 1967-68; tchr. h.s. Beacon (N.Y.) City Sch. Dist., 1968-72; dietetic cons. various hosps., Orange County, Calif., 1973-75; jr. h.s. tchr. Santa Ana (Calif.) Unified Sch. Dist., 1976—; bd. dirs. Internat. Found. for Ewha Womans U., 1992—; social com. mem. Carr Intermediate Sch., Santa Ana, 1989. Bd. dirs. Korean Am. Mus. Aux. Bd., 1994—; mem. Orange Rep. Fedn. for Woman, Orange, Calif., 1993—, Canyon Hills Cmty. Coun., Anaheim Hills, Calif., 1995—; mem. Olive Crest Fundraising Com., Olive Crest Treatment Ctr., Inc., Santa Ana, 1993-94; bd. dirs. Korean Family Counseling at Legal Advice Ctr., Garden Grove, 1992-95, Korean Am. Youth Found., L.A., 1989—; guest spkr. Cmty. Edn. Events, Orange County, 1990—. Mem. AAUW, Ewha Womans U. Alumnae Assn. of So. Calif. (advisor 1996—, chairperson, bd. dirs. 1991-95, pres. 1989-90), Ewha Girls H.S. Alumnae Assn. of So. Calif., chairperson, bd. dirs. 1993-95, pres. 1982-83), Phi Kappa Theta, Delta Kappa Gamma. Home: 315 S Avenida Margarita Anaheim CA 92807-3708

CHOVAN, CONNIE DEE, account executive; b. Dallas, Feb. 2, 1963; d. LaVerne Melvin and Sara Lou (Wheeler) C. BSBA in Mktg., San Diego State U., 1989. Sales asst. San Diego Marriott Hotel & Marina, 1989-93; asst. mgr. Transam. Fin. Svcs., National City, Calif., 1993-95; account exec. Culver Pers. Svcs., San Diego, 1995—. Mem. NOW, Nat. Notary Assn. Office: Culver Pers Svcs 4540 Kearny Villa Rd Ste 207 San Diego CA 92123

CHOW, AMY, gymnast, Olympic athlete; b. San Jose, Calif., May 15, 1978. Mem. USA Team, Hamamatsu, Japan, 1993, World Championships Team, Dortmund, Germany, 1994, Pan Am. Games Team, Mar del Plata, Argentina, 1995, U.S. Olympic Team, Atlanta, 1996. Placed 1st vault U.S. Gymnastics Championships, Ohio, 1992, 1st all around, vault, uneven bars, balance beam, 2d floor exercise, Mex. Olympic Festival, 1992, 3rd all around, vault, 1st floor exercise, USA/Japan Competition, Hamamatsu, Japan, 1993, 3rd vault Coca-Cola Nat. Championships, Nashville, Tenn., 1994, 1st vault, 2d uneven bars, 3rd all around Pan Am. Games, Mar del Plata, Argentina, 1995; recipient Gold medal Women's Gymnastics Team competition and Silver medal uneven bars, Olympic Games, Atlanta, 1996. Office: care USA Gymnastics Pan American Plaza 201 S Capitol Ave Ste 300 Indianapolis IN 46225*

CHOW, RITA KATHLEEN, nurse consultant; b. San Francisco, Aug. 19, 1926; d. Peter and May (Chan) C. BS, Stanford U., 1950, nursing diploma, 1950; MS, Case Western Res. U., 1955; profl. diploma in nursing edn. adminstrn, Columbia U., 1961, EdD, 1968; B of Individualized Studies, George Mason U., 1983. Asst. in teaching Stanford U., Calif., 1951-52; instr., dir. student health Fresno (Calif.) Gen. Hosp. Sch. Nursing, 1952-54; instr. Wayne State U. Coll. Nursing, Detroit, 1957-58; rsch. assoc., project dir. cardiovascular nursing rsch. Ohio State U., Columbus, 1965-68; commd. officer USPHS, 1968, advanced through grades to nurse dir., capt., 1974; spl. asst. to dep. dir. Nat. Ctr. Health Svcs. Rsch., Health Svcs. and Mental Health Adminstrn., HEW, Rockville, Md., 1969-73; dep. dir. manpower utilization br., 1970-73; dep. dir. Office Long Term Care; dep. chief nurse officer USPHS, Rockville, 1973-77; chief quality assurance br. div. long-term care Office of Standards and Certification, Health Standards and Quality Bur., Health Care Fin. Adminstrn., HHS, 1977-82; supervisory clin. nurse and spl. asst. to health systems adminstr. USPHS Indian Hosp., HRSA, HHS, Rosebud, S.D., 1982-83; dir. patient edn., asst. dir. nursing G.W. Long Hansen's Disease Ctr., USPHS, Carville, La., 1984-89; dir. nursing Fed. Med. Ctr., Ft. Worth, 1989-95; now pvt. cons. Author: Identifying Nursing Action with the Care of Cardiovascular Patients, 1967, Cardiosurgical Nursing Care: Understandings, Concepts, and Principles for Practice, 1975; mem. editorial bd. Nursing and Health Care, 1983-95; contbr. to publs. in field. Served with Nurse Corps U.S. Army, 1954-57. Recipient Nursing Svc. award Assn. Mil. Surgeons U.S., 1969, Commendation medal USPHS, 1972, citation for outstanding contbn. to cardiovasc. nursing Am. Heart Assn., 1972-79, Nursing Edn. Alumni Assn. award for disting. achievement in nursing rsch. Columbia U. Tchrs. Coll., 1973, Meritorious Svc. medal USPHS, 1977, Disting. Alumnus award Case Western Res. U. Sch. Nursing, 1979, Disting. Svc. medal USPHS, 1987, Artist of Life award Internat. Women's Writing Guild, 1987, Women's Honors in Pub. Svcs. award ANA, 1988, Commendable Svc. medal U.S. Dept. Justice, Bur. Prisons, 1995; AAUW scholar, Nat. League Nursing fellow, 1959-61; rsch. grantee Sigma Theta Tau, 1966.

CHOWNING, DONNA SINGLETON, accountant; b. Vallejo, Nov. 13, 1942; d. Donald Holt and Anna Berneice (Groves) Singleton; m. Joseph H. Chowning, Feb. 29, 1980; (div. June, 1992). Student acctg., Golden Gate U., San Francisco; BS, U. San Francisco, 1984. CPA, Calif. Acct. Frederikson & Co. CPA, San Francisco, 1976-82; ptnr. Chowning & Rianda, San Francisco, 1982—; mem. adv. bd. Calif. Soc. CPAs Non-Profit Com., San Francisco, 1988-94. Office: Chowning & Rianda 1717 17th St San Francisco CA 94103

CHOWNING, ORR-LYDA BROWN, dietitian; b. Cottage Grove, Oreg., Nov. 30, 1920; d. Fred Harrison and Mary Ann (Bartels) Brown; m. Kenneth Bassett Williams, Oct. 23, 1944 (dec. Mar. 1945); m. Eldon Wayne Chowning, Dec. 31, 1959. BS, Oreg. State Coll., 1943; MA, Columbia U., 1950. Dietetic intern Scripps Metabolic Clinic, LaJolla, Calif., 1944; sr. asst. dietitian Providence Hosp., Portland, Oreg., 1945-49; contact dietitian St. Lukes Hosp., N.Y.C., summer 1949; cafeteria food svc. supr. Met. Life Ins. Co., N.Y.C., 1950-52; set up food svc. and head dietitian McKenzie-Willamette Meml. Hosp., Springfield, Oreg., 1955-59; foods dir. Erb Meml. Student Union, Eugene, Oreg., 1960-63; set up food svc. and head dietitian Cascade Manor Retirement Home, Eugene, 1967-68; owner, operator Veranda Kafe, Inc., Albany, Oreg., 1971-80; owner, operator, sec.-treas. Chownings Adult Foster Home, Albany, 1984—. Contbr. articles to profl. jours.

Lin County Women's chmn. Hatfield for Senator Spaghetti Rally, Albany H.S., 1966; food preparation chmn. Yi for You, Mae Yih for State Senate, Albany Lebanon, Sweet Home, 1982; Silver Clover Club sponsor Oreg. 4-H Found., Oreg. State U., Corvallis, 1994, 95. Recipient coll. scholarship Nat. 4-H Food Preparation Contest, Chgo., 1939. Mem. Am. Dietetic Assn. (registered dietitian, gerontol. nutritionist dietetic practice group 1988—), Oreg. Dietetic Assn. (diet therapy chairperson, newsletter editor 1963-64), Willamette Dietetic Assn., Kappa Delta Pi (Kappa chpt.), Mu Beta Beta. Republican. Mem. Disciples of Christ. Home and Office: Chownings Adult Foster Home 4440 Woods Rd NE Albany OR 97321-7353

CHOYKE, PHYLLIS MAY FORD (MRS. ARTHUR DAVIS CHOYKE, JR.), management executive, editor, poet; b. Buffalo, Oct. 25, 1921; d. Thomas Cecil and Vera (Buchanan) Ford; m. Arthur Davis Choyke Jr., Aug. 18, 1945; children: Christopher Ford, Tyler Van. BS summa cum laude, Northwestern U., 1942. Reporter City News Bur., Chgo., 1942-43, Met. sect. Chgo. Tribune, Chgo., 1943-44; feature writer OWI, N.Y.C., 1944-45; sec. corp. Artcrest Products Co., Inc., Chgo., 1958-88, v.p., 1964-88; pres. The Partford Corp., Chgo., 1988-90; founder, dir. Harper Sq. Press div., 1966—. Author: (under name Phyllis Ford) (with others) (poetry) Apertures to Anywhere, 1979; editor: Gallery Series One, Poets, 1967, Gallery Series Two, Poets—Poems of the Inner World, 1968, Gallery Series Three Poets: Levitations and Observations, 1970, Gallery Series Four, Poets, I am Talking About Revolution, 1973, Gallery Series Five/Poets—To An Aging Nation (with occult overtones), 1977; (manuscripts and papers in Brown U. Library). Bonbright scholar, 1942. Mem. DAR (corr. sec. Gen. Henry Dearborn chpt. 1991-92, treas. 1992-96), Soc. Midland Authors (bd. dirs. 1987-96, treas. 1988-93, pres. 1993-95), Mystery Writers Am. (assoc.), Chgo. Press Vets. Assn., Arts Club Chgo., John Evans Club (Northwestern U.), Poetry Soc. Am. (N.Y.C.), Friends of Lit., Acad. Am. Poets (N.Y.C.). Home: 29 E Division St Chicago IL 60610-2316

CHRABASZCZ, MONICA, accountant; b. Poland, Nov. 9, 1975; Came to the U.S., 1991; d. Michal and Barbara (Radlowska) C. BS in Acctg., Pa. State U., University Park, 1996; MEd, Bloomsburg (Pa.) U., 1996. Sec. Paskowsky Med. Ctr., Bklyn., 1992; staff acct. mentor program Robin Yevak, CPA, Hazleton, Pa., 1994—; student adv. Pa. State U., University Park, 1995—, mem. major event com. 1995—. Mem. Inst. Mgmt. Accts., Golden Key Nat. Honor Soc. Home: 512 N Broad St West Hazleton PA 18201

CHRISCOE, CHRISTINE FAUST, industrial trainer; b. Atlanta, Oct. 29, 1950; d. Henry Charles and Shirley Faye (Birdwell) Faust; BA, Spring Hill Coll., 1973; postgrad. Ga. State U., 1974—; m. Ralph D. Chriscoe, June 25, 1983. Trainer, Fed. Res. Bank, Atlanta, 1973-77; project mgr., tng. dept. Coca Cola U.S.A., Atlanta, 1977-79, sr. project mgr., 1979-81, mgr. tech. tng., 1981-84, mgr. sales, mgmt. and mktg. tng., 1984-85, mgr. bottler tng., 1984-85; mgr. human resources devel., 1986-88; mgr. tng. and devel., 1988-90; pres. Christine Chriscoe and Assocs., 1990—, Ga. Pacific Corp., 1990—, dir. human resources devel., 1990-92, dir. human resources devel. and planning, 1992—, dir. strategic human resources, 1995—; speaker Best of Am. Human Resource Conf., Ga. State U., Nat. Soc. Performance Improvement. Trustee Ga. Shakespeare Festival. Mem. ASTD (speaker), Internat. TV and Video Assn., Soc. for Applied Learning Techs., Tng. Dirs.' Forum (bd. dirs.), Atlanta Human Resources Planning Soc. (bd. dirs.), The Bridge (bd. dirs.). Roman Catholic.

CHRISMAN, DIANE J., librarian; b. Lackawanna, N.Y., June 20, 1937; d. Floyd R. and Elizabeth R. (Nowakowski) Schutta. B.A., U. Vt., 1959; M.S.L.S., Simmons Coll., 1960. Asst. head Crane br. Buffalo & Erie County Pub. Library, 1961-64, asst. head young adult dept., 1964-65, asst. head order dept., 1965-68, coordinator children div., 1968-79, dep. dir., 1979—; lectr. SUNY-Buffalo, 1966-68, 80, 90-94. Contbr. articles to profl. jours. Mem. ALA, N.Y. Libr. Assn., Rotary, Zonta (past pres.). Home: 78 Rainbow Ter Orchard Park NY 14127-2517 Office: Buffalo & Erie County Pub Libr Lafayette Sq Buffalo NY 14203-1821

CHRISMAN, NANCY CAROL, medical administrator; b. Walnut Ridge, Ark., Mar. 22, 1943; d. Williford Ray and Syble Oleeta (Atkinson) Cooksey; m. Herbert Dale Chrisman, June 4, 1961; children: Stanley Ray, Eric Dale. Student, Ark. State U., 1963. Payroll clk. GE, Jonesboro, Ark., 1965-66, 68; sec., bookkeeper 1st Christian Chr., Jonesboro, 1969-76; payroll clk. GE, Jonesboro, 1976-77; office mgr. Barrett, Wheatley, Smith and Deacon, Jonesboro, 1977-88; adminstrv. asst. Richard Stevenson, M.D., P.A., Jonesboro, 1988-89; adminstr. N.E. Ark. Women's Clinic, P.A., Jonesboro, 1989—; dir. Mid South Bank, Jonesboro, 1995—; mem. Widowed Persons Adv. Bd., Jonesboro, 1990—. Charter bd. dirs., past sec., past chmn. Crime Stoppers, Jonesboro, 1991-95; pres. Showtime divsn. Found. Arts, Jonesboro, 1992. Recipient Good Neighbor Spotlight award Sta. KAIT-TV, 1993. Mem. Med. Group Mgmt. Assn., Univ. Rotary Club (Paul Harris fellow 1995), Jonesboro C. of C. (dir., treas. 1994—, mem. Leadership Jonesboro 1993), Pi Omega Pi. Democrat. Baptist. Office: N E Ark Womens Clinic PA 3104 Apache Dr Jonesboro AR 72401

CHRISTEN, LYNNE ROBBINS, banking officer, public relations specialist; b. Opp, Ala., Jan. 9, 1946; d. Farrell Gaston and MaryNell (Woodham) R.; m. Johnny David Hughes, July 15, 1971 (div. Feb. 1974); m. Henry Tiffany Christen Jr., Jan. 26, 1975; children: Eric Robbins, Ryan Gallagher. Student, Auburn U., 1964-65; AA, Clayton State U., 1975; interior design cons. designation, ICS Inst., Scranton, Pa., 1981. Accredited pub. rels. profl. Flight attendant, supr. Eastern Air Lines, Atlanta, 1965-86; career devel. cons. Careers Plus, Mary Esther, Fla., 1987—; pvt. banking asst. v.p. for Okaloosa-Walton County AmSouth Bank of Fla., Ft. Walton Beach; prof. pub. speaker N.W. Fla., 1988—. Author: (manual) Be Your Own Decorator, 1984; columnist local periodical, 1988; contbr. bus. related articles to various jours. Mem. adv. bd. Ft. Walton Beach H.S., Okaloosa Econ. Devel. Program Com.; bd. dirs. ARC, Emerald Coast chpt. Recipient award of distinction N.W. Fla. Pub. Rels. Assn., 1990. Mem. NAFE, Ft. Walton Beach C. of C. (editor Coast Lines mag. 1990-93, Outstanding Mem. of Yr. 1989), Greater Ft. Walton Beach C. of C. (pres. 1993), Leadership C. of C. (grad. 1989). Republican. Methodist. Home: 390 Angela Ln Mary Esther FL 32569-1612 Office: AmSouth Bank 25 NE Beal Pkwy PO Box 4069 Fort Walton Beach FL 32548

CHRISTENSEN, DONNA RADOVICH, crafts consultant, educator; b. Midvale, Utah, Sept. 16, 1925; d. Daniel and Clara Ellen (Turley) Radovich; B.A., U. Utah, 1947; M.A. Columbia U., 1951; m. John Whittaker Christensen, Feb. 2, 1952; children: Carlyn M. Christensen Szalanski, John Chipman, Craig Whittaker. Tchr. and guidance counselor Jordan High Sch., Sandy, Utah, 1947-50; sec. Placement Bur. of Columbia U. Tchr.'s Coll., N.Y.C., 1950-51; free-lance designer of needlecrafts, 1970—; tchr. of needlecraft, 1965—; tchr. 18th Century painted finishes Isabel O'Neil Found. for Art of Painted Finish, N.Y.C., 1975-77; cons. in crafts, 1965—. V.p. Silvermine Guild of Artists, 1965-68, hospitality chmn., 1958-65. Recipient Service award Silvermine Guild, 1963, Journeyman's medallion O'Neil Studio, 1974. Mem. Embroider's Guild of Am., Needle and Bobbin Club (v.p. 1977-82, pres. 1982-89, bd. dirs. 1989-91), New Canaan Sewing Group (exec. bd. 1977-81), Phi Kappa Phi, Pi Lambda Theta, Kappa Delta Pi. Mormon. Club: New Canaan Garden (exec. bd. 1972-77, v.p. 1987-89, pres. 1989-91), Federated Garden of Conn. Inc. (asst. civic devel. chmn. 1991-93). Home: 788 Ponus Ridge New Canaan CT 06840-3412

CHRISTENSEN, DONNA RAY, educator; b. Chgo., Oct. 26, 1940; d. Raymond and Eleanor Grace (Kuempel) C. BA, Rosary Coll., 1986; MA, Concordia U., 1993. Instr. adult edn. Ctrl. YMCA Coll., Chgo., 1965-68; adminstr. St. James-Christie Acad., Oak Park, Ill., 1969-86; educator Sch. Dist. #89, Maywood, Ill., 1986-91; reading specialist Sch. Dist. #92, Broadview, Ill., 1991—; adj. faculty Concordia U., River Forest, Ill., 1995, Aurora (Ill.) U., 1996. Bd. dirs. Oak Park-River Forest Symphony, 1992-94; mem. festival chorus Concordia U., 1988—. Mem. West Suburban Reading Coun. (bd. dirs. 1994-96), Internat. Reading Assn.

CHRISTENSEN, JANICE DAYON, foreign language educator; b. Ozamis City, Mindanao, Philippines, Jan. 2, 1970; d. Wilfredo Librero and Linda (Vente) Dayon; m. Jason Thomas Christensen, July 28, 1995. BA in Spanish Edn., U. Ill., 1992; MEd in Curriculum and Instruction, Nat. Louis U., Evanston, Ill., 1995. Fgn. lang. educator Dist. 99, Downers Grove, IL, 1992-96; presenter conf. session A Clear and Present Stranger, 1995. Mem. Am. Assn. Tchrs. of Spanish and Portuguese, Ill. Coun. of Tchrs. of Fgn. Lans. Methodist. Office: Community HS Dist 99 South 1436 Norfolk Downers Grove IL 60516

CHRISTENSEN, JENNIFER ELIZABETH, producer; b. La Grange, Ill., June 29, 1972; d. Alan Wayne Christensen and Susan Elizabeth (Kudlacz) Lindsay; life ptnr. Nancy C. Demers. BS in Polit. Sci. Radio and TV, Butler U., 1994. Cert. fgn. policy London Sch. Econs., 1993. Assoc. prodr., assignment editor, field prodr., prodr. WXIN-TV, Fox News, Indpls., 1993—; rschr. Chgo. Bd. Elections, 1991-92, R.E.S. Co. Fellow Scholars, Indpls., 1992-93; policy analyst The Atlantic Coun., London, 1993. Co-author: Women Public Speakers in the United States, 1925-93, 1994; segment prodr. (TV news series) Youth Matters, 1995-96. Pres., founding mem. Demia Feminist Alliance, Indpls., 1990-94; treas. Indy Pride, Inc., Indpls., 1995-96; vol. literacy tutor Vets. Upward Bound, Indpls., 1995-96; bd. dirs., co-pres. local chpt. NOW, Indpls., 1995-96. Summer fellow Butler U., 1993, 94; recipient Emmy nomination, 1995, City of Indpls. Mayor's award for Volunteering, 1995. Democrat. Home: 137 W 47th St Indianapolis IN 46208 Office: WXIN 1440 N Meridian Indianapolis IN 46208

CHRISTENSEN, JOAN K., state legislator; children: Cara, David, Laura, Michael. Grad., Met. Bus. Coll., Chgo.; student, Syracuse U. Mem. Syracuse Common Coun., Syracuse Bd. Assessment Rev.; mem. 119th dist. N.Y. State Assembly, 1990—, chair legis. women's caucus, chair task force on women's issues, chair adminstrv. regulations rev. commn., mem. aging, housing, higher edn., labor, real property taxation, and small bus. coms., hon. mem. Puerto Rican/Hispanic task force, mem. task force worker's compensation reform; mem. local govt., cities, small bus., labor and aging coms.; hon. mem. N.Y. State Assembly P.R./Hispanic Task Force. Liaison to Mayor's Syracuse Commn. for Women; mem. City of Syracuse (N.Y.) Bd. of Assessment Rev., 1984, Syracuse Common Coun., chair fin., taxation and assessment com., Vets. Airport, Pub. Safety, Pub. Works and Transp. Coms.; bd. dirs. Am. Heart Assn., Meals on Wheels, Paul Robeson Performing Arts Co., Eric Trust Meml. Found.; bd. dirs., vice chair Neighborhood Watch Groups of Syracuse; hon. co-chair Pregnancy Hotline Task Force; active Thursday Morning Roundtable. Recipient Svc. award Greater Eastwood C. of C., 1990, Valley Dem. of Yr. award, 1991, Onondaga County Dem. of Yr. award, 1992, Jeannette Rankin award Onondaga County Women's Polit. Caucus, 1992. Mem. VFW Post 1955 Ladies Aux., South Side Bus. Assn., Urban League of Onondaga County, Inc. Democrat. Office: NY State Assembly Legislative Office Bldg Albany NY 12248*

CHRISTENSEN, KAREN KAY, lawyer; b. Ann Arbor, Mich., Mar. 9, 1947; d. Jack Edward and Evangeline (Pitsch) C.; m. Kenneth Robert Kay, Sept. 2, 1977; children: Jeffrey Smithson, Braden, Bergen. BS, U. Mich., 1969; JD, U. Denver, 1975. Bar: Colo. 1975, D.C. 1976, U.S. Supreme Ct. 1979. Atty., advisor office of dep. atty. gen. U.S. Dept. of Justice, Washington, 1975-76, trial atty. civil rights div., 1976-79; legis. counsel ACLU, Washington, 1979-80; staff atty. D.C. Pub. Defender Service, Washington, 1980-85; asst. gen. counsel Nat. Pub. Radio, Washington, 1985-93; gen. counsel Nat. Endowment Arts, Washington, 1993—; mem. D.C. Bd. Profl. Responsibility, 1990—. Mem. D.C. Bar Assn., NCA/ACLU (exec. bd. 1986-93, chair 1993), Phi Beta Kappa. Office: 1100 Pennsylvania Ave NW Washington DC 20004-2501

CHRISTENSEN, LORRAINE ROGERS, singer, voice instructor; b. Portland, Oreg., Dec. 11, 1936; d. Merrill Fay and Helen L. (Rounds) Rogers; m. James Christensen, Feb. 14, 1965 (div. 1978); children: Vera Jean, Linda Ruth. Student, Oreg. State U., 1955-57; MusB, Coll. Conservatory of Music, Cin., 1960; postgrad., Portland State U., 1963, U. Oreg., 1966-67. Contralto soloist several major chs., Portland and Cin., 1954-65; voice instr. Siuslaw Schs., Florence, Oreg., 1966-72; singer of recitals Portland, 1970-75; voice instr. Technique Classes, Portland, 1975-82; opera devel., role preparations San Francisco, 1977-81; singer, voice instr. Montrose Studio, Guilford, Conn., 1983—; founder Western Lane Music League, Florence, Oreg., 1966-70, founder, dir. Siuslaw Singers, Florence, 1967-69, founder, Voice Technique Classes, Portland, 1975-81. Operatic role: Azucena in Il Trovatore, 1977, Ulrica in Un Ballo in Maschera, 1978, Leonora in La Favorita, 1978-79, Amneris in Aida, 1985-87. Recipient Dr. Anne Baecker German Lied award, CCM, Cin., 1960, First Place Dist. Met. Opera Auditions, 1968, First Place Hermann Reutter award U. Oreg., 1970. Mem. AAUW (cultural chairperson 1991-94), Women in the Arts, Nat. Assn. Tchrs. Einging, Mu Phi Epsilon. Democrat. Methodist. Home: 121 Whitethorn Dr Guilford CT 06437-1705

CHRISTENSEN, MARTHA, mycologist, educator; b. Ames, Iowa, Jan. 4, 1932; d. Leo Martin and Eva (Patterson) C. BS, U. Nebr., 1953; MS, U. Wis., 1956, PhD, 1960. High sch. sci. tchr. Ralston (Nebr.) Pub. Schs., 1953-54; research assoc. U. Wis. Dept. Botany, Madison, 1960-62; asst. prof. U. Wyo. Dept. Botany, 1963-68, assoc. prof., 1968-76, prof., 1976-89, prof. emerita, 1989—. Mem. Ecol. Soc. Am., Brit. Mycol. Soc., Mycol. Soc. Am. (pres. 1987-88). Office: U Wyoming Dept Botany Laramie WY 82071

CHRISTENSEN, SALLY HAYDEN, government executive; b. Washington, Apr. 25, 1935; d. Sharp Adolphus and Grayce Elizabeth (Long) Hayden; m. John William Christensen, Mar. 24, 1969; children—John Stephen, Donna Isabelle. Student Dunbarton Coll. of Holy Cross, 1953-54, Am. U., U. Va. Chief higher edn. br. U.S. Office Edn., 1966-68, dep. dir. budget office, 1968-72, chief budget rev. br., 1974-80, dep. asst. sec., 1980-81, acting asst. sec., 1981, 93, dep. asst. sec., dir. budget service, 1981—, acting dept. under sec., 1991, cons. to rules and regulations task force, 1972-74. Author Congl. reports. Recipient Spl. citations Sec. Edn. and U.S. Commr. Edn., 1972, 1980, 81, 84; Pres.'s Disting. Exec. award, 1982, 88; HEW Superior Service award, 1965. Club: Arlington County Com. of 100. Home: 5415 18th St N Arlington VA 22205-3032 Office: US Dept Edn 600 Independence Ave SW Washington DC 20202-0004

CHRISTENSEN, TINA S., secondary education educator; b. Wheatridge, Colo., Apr. 10, 1970; d. Deborah L. Hunter; m. Terry L. Christensen, Aug. 8, 1992. BA in Secondary English Edn., U. No. Colo., 1992. Lang. arts tchr. 8th grade Evergreen (Colo.) Middle Sch., 1993-94, Oberon Middle Sch., Arvada, Colo., 1994—. Office: Oberon Middle Sch 7300 Quail Arvada CO 80005

CHRISTENSON, CAROL ANN, information systems professional; b. Cleve., June 20, 1970; d. Bernard Lee and Nella Jean (Burgess) Toppings; m. John Michael Christenson, May 20, 1995. BA, Cumberland Coll., 1992. Info. systems cons. I dept. of adminstrn. State of W.Va., Charleston, 1992-93, info. systems cons. II, 1993—; svc. adminstr. Digitz, Raleigh, N.C., 1996—; chairperson Gov.'s EEO/AA coun., Charleston, 1994—; EEO counselor, trainer State of W.Va., 1993—. Dir. children's ch. North Charleston Bapt. Ch., 1995. Mem. Internat. Pers. Mgmt. Assn., Assn. Info. and Imaging Mgmt. Republican. Baptist. Home: 1128 Waterford Forest Cir Cary NC 27513 Office: Digitz 3016 Hillsborough St Cary NC 27513

CHRISTIAN, BETTY JO, lawyer; b. Temple, Tex., July 27, 1936; d. Joe and Mattie Manor (Brown) Wiest; m. Ernest S. Christian, Jr., Dec. 24, 1960. B.A. summa cum laude, U. Tex., 1957, LL.B. summa cum laude, 1960. Bar: Tex. 1961, U.S. Supreme Ct. 1964, D.C. 1980. Law clk. Supreme Ct. Tex., 1960-61; atty. ICC, 1961-68; asst. gen. counsel ICC, Washington, 1970-72; assoc. gen. counsel ICC, 1972-76, commr., 1976-79; partner firm Steptoe & Johnson, Washington, 1980—; atty. Labor Dept., Dallas, 1968-70. Mem. ABA, Fed. Bar Assn. (Younger Fed. Lawyer award 1964), Tex. Bar Assn., Am. Law Inst., Am. Acad Apellate Lawyers, Adminstrv. Conf. U.S., City Tavern Assn. Office: 1330 Connecticut Ave NW Washington DC 20036-1704

CHRISTIAN, MARY JO DINAN, educator, real estate professional; b. Denver, May 7, 1941; d. Joseph Timothy and Margaret Rose (Ryan) Dinan; m. Ralph Poinsett Christian, Aug. 27, 1966. BA, Loretto Heights Coll., Denver, 1964; MA, George Washington U., 1983. Cert. English educator, adminstrn. and supervision secondary edn. English tchr. Denver Pub. Schs., 1964-67, Prince George's County Pub. Sch., Md., 1967-81; vice-prin. Prince George's County High Sch., Md., 1981—; presenter gender/ethnic expectations and student achievement Nat. Conf. Columnist: WomenSpeak, 1981-91. Rep. Prince George's County Commn. Women UN Fourth World Conf. Women Forum, Beijing, 1995. Md. Ho. of Dels. recognition. Mem. NAFE, ASCD, NEA (chair adminstrs. caucus 1991-92, adminstr.-at-large resolutions com. 1986-92, polit. action com. 1984-86, coord.-at-large women's caucus 1981-91, chair adminstr.'s caucus 1991-93, Creative Leadership award 1989), Md. State Tchrs. Assn. (state coord. Sen. Sarbane campaign 1982, state voter registration coord. 1984, issue coord. Tom McMillen campaign 1986, Women's Rights award 1988), Vail Racquet Club, Capitol Hill Garden Club, Phi Delta Kappa, Alpha Delta Kappa. Home: 504 Independence Ave SE Washington DC 20003-1143 Office: Prince Georges County 5211 Boydell Ave Oxon Hill MD 20745-3700

CHRISTIAN, SUZANNE HALL, financial planner; b. Hollywood, Calif., Apr. 28, 1935; d. Peirson M. and Gertrude (Engel) Hall; children: Colleen, Carolyn, Claudia, Cynthia. BA, UCLA, 1956; MA, Redlands U., 1979; cert. in fin. planning, U. So. Calif., 1986. CFP. Instr. L.A. City Schs., 1958-59; instr. Claremont (Calif.) Unified Schs., 1972-84, dept. chair, 1981-84; fin. planner Waddell & Reed, Upland, Calif., 1982-96, sr. account exec., 1986; br. mgr. Hornor, Townsend & Kent, Claremont, 1996—; corp. mem. Pilgrim Place Found., Claremont; lectr. on fin., estate and tax planning for civic and profl. groups. Author: Strands in Composition, 1979; host Money Talks with Suzanne Christian on local TV cable, 1993—. Mem. legal and estate planning com. Am. Cancer Soc., 1988—; profl. adv. com. YWCA-Inland Empire, 1987; treas. Fine Arts Scripps Coll., 1993-94. Mem. Inst. CFP's, Internat. Assn. Fin. Planners, Planned Giving Roundtable, Estate Planning Coun. Pomona Valley, Claremont C. of C. (pres., bd. dirs. 1994-95), Curtain Raisers Club Garrison (pres. 1972-75), Circle of Champions (president's coun. 1994-95, Silver Crest award 1985-87, 94, 95), Rotary, Kappa Kappa Gamma (pres. 1970-74). Home: PO Box 1237 Claremont CA 91711-1237 Office: Hornor Townsend & Kent 419 Yale Claremont CA 91711

CHRISTIANO, MARY HELEN, systems analyst; b. Geneva, N.Y., Sept. 14, 1956; d. Anthony Joseph Christiano and Lucy Ann (Benge) Christiano Farris; 1 child, Andrew Joseph. Cert., Syracuse Sch. Automation, 1975; student, Augsburg Coll., 1990—. Cert. computer programmer, sys. analyst. Asst. head cashier Neisner's Dept. Store, Waterloo, N.Y., 1973-74; lead computer operator Geneva Gen. Hosp., 1976-78; sys. analyst 3M Co., St. Paul, 1979—; v.p. Westbridge Inc., St. Paul, 1992-94. Author, editor: (newsletter) Qualifier, 1985-87. Tutorial adviser St. Paul schs., 1987-92; chpt. leader Riverview Crime Watch, St. Paul, 1989-90; vol. United Negro Coll. Fund, St. Paul, 1993—, Spl. Olympics, Bloomington, Minn., 1992, Toys for Tots, St. Paul, 1991—; mem. Sci. Mus. of Minn., 1991. Mem. Women in Tech. Home: 1572 McAfee St Saint Paul MN 55106 Office: 3M Info Tech 3 Med Ctr Bldg 224-4S-19 Saint Paul MN 55133-3224

CHRISTIANSEN, LARA IRENE, journalist; b. Ridgewood, N.J., Aug. 9, 1969; d. Larry E. and Lois I. (Combs) C. BA in English and Journalism, Oral Roberts U., 1991. Pub. rels. rep. Oral Roberts U., Tulsa, 1987-91; staff writer, religion editor Broken Arrow (Okla.) Daily Ledger, 1991; staff writer, bridal editor Tulsa World, 1991—. Asst. news editor (newsletter) The Oracle, 1988-89, news editor, 1989-90, asst. features editor, 1990-91. Mem. Women in Comms., Inc., Oral Roberts U. Alumni (adv. coun.), Tulsa Press Club. Mem. Assemblies of God Ch.

CHRISTIE, CYNTHIA A., sales and marketing executive; b. Olean, N.Y., Dec. 13, 1957; d. James A. and A. Phyllis (Walker) Christie; m. John B. Warwick, Aug. 16, 1986. BS in English, Murray State U., 1979; MBA in Bus. Mgmt., LaSalle U., 1995. Sales specialist AT&T, St. Louis, 1980-83; tng. design specialist AT&T, Cin., 1983-87; nat. acct. exec. AT&T, Orlando, Fla., 1987-91; v.p. IMA, Melbourne, Fla., 1992—. Author: (sales mgmt. tng. program) Relationship Analysis and Creative Problem Solving '94, Advanced Voice Telecommunications '95. Membership chair Melbourne (Fla.) Civic Theatre, 1991; co-chair small bus. coun. tng. program Melbourne C. of C., 1992-93. Office: IMA Inc 2525 Aurora Rd Ste 102 Melbourne FL 32935

CHRISTINE, VIRGINIA FELD, actress; b. Stanton, Iowa, Mar. 5, 1920; d. George Allen Ricketts and Helga (Ossian) Kraft; m. Fritz Feld, Nov. 10, 1940; children: Steven, Danny. Student, UCLA, 1939-40. Actress appearing in Edge of Darkness, Mission to Moscow, The Killers, Cover Up, High Noon, The Mummy's Curse, Not as a Stranger, Cyrano, The Men, Three Brave Men, Cobweb, Body Snatchers, The Spirit of St. Louis, Johnny Tremaine, Judgement at Nuremberg, Guess Who's Coming to Dinner?, The Prize, Rage to Live, Four for Texas, 300 TV shows; spokeswoman, role of Mrs. Olson TV comml. Proctor & Gamble (Folgers), Cin., 1964-85. Hon. mayor, Brentwood, Calif.; bd. dirs. Family Planning Ctrs. Greater Los Angeles; judge Am. Coll. Theatre Festival. Recipient 1st place award Forensic League, 1937, Hall of Fame award Long Beach City Coll., 1977, citation-cultural award City of Los Angeles, 1979. Democrat.

CHRISTOFF, BETH GRAVES, artist; b. Galveston, Tex., Jan. 29, 1936; d. James Warren Patterson and Wilna Margaret (Heatherly) Day; m. Lawrence D. Graves, Jr., June 22, 1954 (div. 1975); children: Jacqueline, Keith Alan, Stephen Lee; m. Nicholas Christoff, Nov. 22, 1980; 1 stepchild, Steven Gregory. Student, U. Calif., Tokyo, 1952-54, Blair Bus. Coll., Colorado Springs, Colo., 1969-70; student art, Temple Coll., 1980-84. Owner, mgr. Christoff Fashion Hideway, Belton, Tex., 1985-91; Exhibited in group shows in ctrl. Tex., 1980-96. Works exhibited in various exhbns. Ctrl. Tex., 1980-96; gallery representation The Howling Cow Gallery, Temple, Christoff Arts Studio/Gallery, Bell Fine Arts Abbey Gallery. Active Tex. Orch. Soc., Temple Civic Theatre, Friends of the Mus., Bell County Local and State Med. Auxs. Mem. Allied Artists Am. (assoc.), Pastel Soc. S.W., Am. Soc. Portrait Artists, Salado Village Artists, Bell Fine Arts, Women in the Arts, Knickerbocker Artists N.Y. (assoc.), Internat. Soc. Poets, PEO, Order Ea. Star, Rotary (Paul Harris fellow). Democrat. Methodist. Home and Studio: 312 E 22nd St Belton TX 76513-2034

CHRISTOFFEL, KATHERINE KAUFER, pediatrician, epidemiologist, educator; b. N.Y.C., June 28, 1948; d. George and Sonya (Firstenberg) Kaufer; m. Tom Christoffel, Oct. 11, 1970 (div. Dec. 1992); children: Kevin, Kimberly. BA, Radcliffe Coll., 1969; MD, Tufts U., 1973; MPH, Northwestern U., 1981. Diplomate Am. Bd. Med. Examiners; bd. cert. pediatrics. Intern Columbus (Ohio) Children' Hosp., 1972-73; resident then fellow Children's Meml. Hosp., Chgo., 1973-76; asst. prof. Sch. Medicine U. Chgo., 1976-79; asst. prof., then assoc. prof. Northwestern U. Med. Sch., Chgo., 1979-91, prof., 1991—; dir. Nutrition Evaluation Clinic Children's Meml. Hosp., Chgo., 1982—; med. dir. violent injury prevention ctr. Children's Meml. Med. Ctr., Chgo., 1993—; chmn. steering com. Handgun Epidemic Lowering Plan, Chgo., 1993—; dir. Pediatric Practice Rsch. Group, Chgo., 1984—; dir. statis. scis. and epidemiology program Children's Meml. Inst. for Edn. and Rsch., 1994—. Contbr. numerous articles to med. jours. Rsch. grantee Nat. Insts. Child Health and Human Devel., 1989-94. Fellow Am. Acad. Pediatrics (spokesperson on firearms 1985—, injury com. 1985-93, chair adolescent violence task force 1994, 1st Injury Control award 1992); mem. APHA (Disting. Career award 1991), Am. Coll. Epidemiology, Soc. for Pediatric Rsch., Ambulatory Pediatric Assn. Office: Childrens Meml Hosp 2300 N Childrens Plz # 46 Chicago IL 60614-3318

CHRISTOFFERSEN, SUSAN GRAY, small business owner; b. Oakland, Calif., Aug. 11, 1942; d. Edward Kiley Gray and Mabel Genevieve (Griffiths) Lee; m. Timothy Robert Christoffersen, July 24, 1965; children: Jenny, Shannon. BA, Stanford U., 1964, MA, 1965. U.S. history tchr. Leonia High Sch., N.J., 1965-67; frontier intern Nat. and World Coun. Chs., Brazil, India, Switzerland, 1967-68; U.S. history tchr. Pacifica High Sch., West Pittsburg, Calif., 1969-70; advt. chairwoman Kennedy-King Found.; bus. officer Pacific Sch. Religion, Berkeley, Calif., 1977-78; tax preparer Expatriate Tax Dept. Chevron Corp., San Francisco, 1983; from engring. dept. to quality cons. AT&T, San Francisco, Pleasanton, Calif., 1983-88; pres. Quality Efficiency, Alamo, Calif., 1988—; substitute tchr., counselor Juvenile Hall, Martinez, Calif., 1969-75; mgr. rental properties, 1977—. Chairwoman land use subcom. East Bay Regional Parks Adv. Com., 1978-80; co-founder Las Trampas Ridgelands Assn., 1980-82; singer Gospel Choir, Community Presbyn. Ch., Danville, 1989-92. Mem. AAUW (bd. dirs. Danville, Calif. br. 1992-93), Stanford Women of East Bay. Democrat. Episcopal. Home: 234 Via Bonita Alamo CA 94507-1840

CHRISTOPHER, IRENE, librarian, consultant; b. Greece, Nov. 17, 1922; came to U.S., 1923; d. George and Helen (Stephens) C. AB, Boston U., 1944; BLS, Simmons Coll., 1945. Gen. asst. Robbins Pub. Libr., Arlington, Mass., 1945-46; gen. asst. Boston U. Chenery Libr., 1946-47, head circulation dept., 1947-48, head reference dept., 1948-62; dir. libr. Emerson Coll., Boston, 1962-68; Gordon McKay libr. Harvard U., Cambridge, Mass., 1968-70; chief libr. Boston U. Med. Ctr., 1970-92. Mem. AAUW, ALA (various coms. 1962-82, coun. 1970-74), Spl. Librs. Assn. (various coms. Boston chpt. 1952-75), Am. Soc. Info. Sci., North Atlantic Health Scis. Librs., Med. Libr. Assn., New Eng. Online Users Group, Inc., Mass. Libr. Assn., Boston U. Women's Coun. Home: 790 Boylston St Apt 11C Boston MA 02199-7911

CHRISTOPHER, MARY JULIA, elementary school educator; b. Columbus, Ga., Feb. 21, 1948; d. Madison Henry and Mary Julia (Fields) Hortman; m. Cecil Thomas Christopher Jr., July 24, 1971 (div.); children: Clayton, Travis, Meghan. BS in Elem. Edn., Ga. So. Coll., 1970; M in Early Childhood Edn., Ga. Coll., 1981; specialist in edn. cert., Ga. Southwestern Coll., 1994. Cert. elem. sch. tchr., Ga. Tchr. grade 4 Gould Elem. Sch., Savannah, Ga., 1969-72; tchr. grade 3 Hartley Elem. Sch., Macon, Ga., 1972, Windsor Acad., Macon, 1973; tchr. grade 2 Barden Elem. Sch., Macon, 1985-87; tchr. grade 4 Bonaire (Ga.) Elem. Sch., 1987-93, Perdue Elem. Sch., Warner Robins, Ga., 1993—. Mem. Ga. Reading Assn. (v.p. Hope chpt. 1991-94), Internat. Reading Assn. Home: 201 Mount Zion Rd Bonaire GA 31005

CHRISTOPHER, SHARON A. BROWN, bishop; b. Corpus Christi, Tex., July 24, 1944; d. Fred L. and Mavis Lorraine (Krueger) Brown; m. Charles Edmond Logsdon Christopher, June 17, 1973. BA, Southwestern U., Georgetown, Tex., 1966; MDiv, Perkins Sch. Theology, 1969; DD, Southwestern U., 1990. Ordained to ministry United Meth. Ch., 1970; elected bishop 1988. Dir. Christian Edn. First United Meth. Ch., Appleton, Wis., 1969-70, assoc. pastor, 1970-72; pastor Butler United Meth. Ch., Butler, Wis., 1972-76, Calvary United Meth. Ch., Germantown, Wis., 1972-76, Aldersgate United Meth. Ch., Milw., 1976-80; dist. supt. Ea. Dist. Wis. Conf. United Meth. Ch., 1980-85; asst. to bishop Wis. Conf. Wis. Confs. United Meth. Ch., Sun Prairie, Wis., 1986-88; bishop North Cen. jurisdiction United Meth. Ch., Minn., 1988—. Contbr. articles and papers to religious publs. Bd. dirs. Nat. Coun. Chs. of Christ, 1988—, United Meth. Ch. Bd. of Ch. & Soc., 1988-92, bd. discipleship, 1992—; bd. dirs. Walker Meth. Health Ctr., Mpls., 1988—, Meth. Hosp., Mpls., 1988—, Nat. United Meth. Clergywomen, 1992—; trustee Hamline U., St. Paul, 1988—; gen. and jurisdictional conf. del., 1976, 80, 84, 88; mem. N. Cen. Jurisdiction Com. on Episcopacy, 1984-88, Com. on Investigation, 1980-88, Gen. Bd. Global Ministries, 1980-88, chmn. Mission Pers. Resources Program Dept., 1984-88. Named one of Eighty for the Eighties, Milw. Jour., 1980.

CHRISTY, AUDREY MEYER, public relations consultant; b. N.Y.C., Mar. 11, 1933; d. Mathias J. and Harriet Meyer; m. James R. Christy, Apr. 19, 1952; children: James R., III, Kathryn M. Smith, John T., Alysia A. Coleman, William J. BA, U. Buffalo, 1967. Pub. rels. officer Turgeon Bros., Buffalo, 1968-69; mem. pub. rels. staff Sch. Fine Arts, U. Nebr., Omaha, 1972; pub. rels. exec. Mathews & Clark Advt., Sarasota, Fla., 1974-75; profiles editor Tampa Bay mag., Tampa, Fla., 1972; pub. rels. cons. Bildex Corp., 1973-79; owner, operator Christy & Assocs., Venice, Fla., 1976—; dir. mktg. comm. Northern Trust Bank, Naples, 1994—. Trustee Big Bros./Big Sisters of Sarasota; vice chmn. Erie County March of Dimes, 1970; bd. dirs. Sarasota chpt. Am. Cancer Soc., Manasota (Pvt.) Industry Coun., 1987-89; mem. S.W. Fla. Ambulance Adv. Com., 1981; pres. Community Health Edn. Coun. Recipient various advt. awards. Mem. Pub. Rels. Soc. Am. (Outstanding Pub. Svc. award 1984), Fla. Hosp. Assn., Nat. Assn. Women Bus. Owners (charter mem. Sarasota chpt.), Sarasota County C. of C. (v.p., bd. dirs. 1990-91, vice chmn. mktg. 1984-85, 85-86, 86-87, 88-90, 90, vice chmn. 1989-90), Sarasota Manatee Press Club, LWV (editor Sarasota publ. 1978-79). Home: 216 Bayshore Cir Venice FL 34285-1407 Office: Christy & Assoc 100 W Venice Ave Ste L Venice FL 34285-1928

CHRONISTER, ROCHELLE BEACH, state legislator; b. Neodesha, Kans., Aug. 27, 1939; m. Bert Chronister, 1961; children: Pam, Phillip. AB, U. Kans. State rep. dist. 13 Kans. Ho. of Reps.; former asst. majority leader; sec. for social and rehab. svcs. Kans. Cabinet, 1995—; chmn. Kans. Rep. Party, 1989—. Named Woman of Yr., Neodesha C. of C. Mem. AMA (aux.), Bus. and Profl. Women. Methodist. Home: RR 2 Box 321 A Neodesha KS 66757-9562

CHRONISTER, VIRGINIA ANN, school nurse, educator; b. York, Pa., Sept. 25, 1940; d. Ernest B. and Mary L. (Anderson) Stokes; m. Burton F. Chronister, June 13, 1964; children: Scott E., Karen A. Student, York Jr. Coll., Millersville (Pa.) Coll.; diploma, Harrisburg (Pa.) Hosp., 1961; BS in Profl. Arts, St. Joseph's Coll., North Windham, Maine, 1985; M. (equivalency), Pa. State U., 1989; postgrad., St. Joseph's Coll., North windham, Maine. RN, Pa.; cert. sch. nurse (edn. specialist II), Pa. Charge nurse Harrisburg Hosp., 1961-64; instr., practical nurses York City Sch. Dist., 1964-68; instr., med. secs. Yorktowne Bus. Inst., York, 1985; sch. nurse West York Sch. Dist., York, 1985—; substitute sch. nurse, 1972-85. Recipient Cardiac Nursing award. Mem. NEA, AAUW, Pa. State Edn. Assn. (sch. nurse sect.), Pa. Sch. Health Assn., Nat. Assn. Sch. Nurses, Harrisburg Hosp. Alumnae Assn., York County Sch. Nurse Assn. (pres. 1991-92), United Ostomy Assn. (charter mem.), West York Area Edn. Assn. (pres. 1991—), York County Coord. Coun., Beta Sigma Phi. Home: 2090 Loman Ave York PA 17404-4214

CHRZANOWSKA-JESKE, MALGORZATA EWA, electrical engineering educator, consultant; b. Warsaw, Poland, Nov. 26, 1948; came to U.S., 1985; d. Waclaw and Halina (Siedlanowska) Chrzanowska; m. Witold Norbert Jeske, July 21, 1978; children: Marcin, Olaf. MS in Electronics, Warsaw Tech. U., 1972; MS in Elec. Engring., Tuskegee (Ala.) Inst., 1976; PhD in Elec. Engring., Auburn (Ala.) U., 1988. Rsch. and tchg. instr. Warsaw Tech. U., 1972-75; rsch. and tchg. asst. Tuskegee Inst., 1975-76; rsch. and tchg. asst. Auburn U., 1976-77, rsch. asst., postdoctoral fellow, 1985-89; sr. rschr. Inst. Electron Tech., Warsaw, 1977-82, CAD project leader, 1983-85; asst. prof. Portland (Oreg.) State U., 1989-95, assoc. prof. elec. engring., 1995—; cons. Inst. Electron Tech., Warsaw, 1985—; lectr. Tuskegee Inst., 1977; profl/lectr. Oreg. Ctr. for Advance tech., Beaverton, 1991-94. Contbr. articles to profl. jours. Troop leader Polish Scout Assn., Warsaw, 1958-66; sci. and activity com. chmn. Polish Student Assn., Warsaw, 1966-75; mem. Solidarity, Poland, 1980-85. Recipient First Level award Polish Dept. Sci., Higher Edn. and Tech., 1983; named to Women of Distinction in Engring. Columbia coun. Girl Scouts U.S., 1993. Mem. ACM, IEEE (Oreg. sect. exec. com. 1994—), IEEE Electron Device Soc. (chair edn. com. Oreg. sect. 1989—), IEEE Circuits and Sys. Soc. Office: Portland State Univ Dept Elec Engring 1800 SW 6th Ave Portland OR 97207

CHRZANOWSKI, JOANNA BLANDYNA, English language educator; b. Lodz, Poland, Apr. 4, 1953; came to U.S., 1975; d. Romuald and Blandyna Franciszka (Jaracz) Wasniewski; m. Mark Andrew Chrzanowski, Apr. 12, 1975; 1 child, Karoline Joanna. Student, U. Lodz, 1972-75; BA, SUNY, 1976, MA, 1977; PhD, Syracuse U., 1995. Cert. tchr. English, Polish, Russian, N.Y. English tchr. Frankfurt (N.Y.)-Schyuler H.S., 1977-78; adj. prof. English Onondaga C. C., Syracuse, N.Y., 1978-80; prof. English Jefferson C.C., Watertown, N.Y., 1980—. Author: JCC Guide TO Documentation, 1989, Freshman English Workbook, 1993. Sec. of Hope Appeal St. Ann's Cath. Ch., Parish, N.Y., 1991, organizer of food drive, 1990-94; pres. JBC Industries of Parish, Mexico, N.Y., 1994—; religious edn. instr. St. Mary's Cath. Ch., Mexico, 1993-95. Recipient Outstanding Fac. award Phi Theta Kappa, 1991, Constance Dorothea Weinman For Grad. Study in Ednl. Tech. award, 1993, 94, 95, Outstanding Tchr. of the Year The N.Y. State Assn. of Two Year Coll., 1993, Nat. Inst. Staff Organ. and Devel. award For Ecellence in Teaching U. Tex., 1993, Gov. Cuomo's Cert. of merit, 1994; Burton Blatt scholar, Syracuse U., 1993, 95, Emil and Maud Beck Merit scholar, 1994, Grad. Sch. scholar, 1994. Mem. Assn. for Ednl. Comm. and Tech., Soc. For Tech. Comm., Nat. Coun. of Tchrs. of English, World Assn. for Case Study Method Rsch. and Application, Phi Lambda Theta. Office: Jefferson CC Coffeen St Watertown NY 13601

CHU, ESTHER BRINEY, retired history educator; b. Bluff City, Ill., Jan. 27, 1911; d. John and Charlotte (Shaw) Briney; m. H.T. Chu, Apr. 19, 1935 (dec. May 1983); children: David S.C., Edna S.C., George S.T. BA, U. Ill., 1935, MA, 1936; PhD, Northwestern U., 1942. Prof. history Hunter Coll., N.Y.C., 1943-45, 55-58; prof. history Jersey City (N.J.) State Coll., 1959-75, prof. emeritus, 1976; pres., faculty assoc. day coun., exec. com. Jersey City State Coll., 1960-75; founder Can. studies program, New Jersey Colls. Author: Briney Families, 1976, Briney Patriots Pioneers and Families, 1979, Briney Families Coast to Coast, 1989. Past pres. YWCA, Mt. Vernon, N.Y.; bd. dirs. Pilgrim Place, Claremont, Calif., 1984-92; chmn. Young People's Dem. Club, Schuyler County, Ill., 1932-33, UN Women's Guild, Westchester County, N.Y., 1951-60. Named Outstanding Educator of Am., 1971, Ill. Coll. scholar, 1931; Northwestern U. fellow, 1938. Mem. Am. Hist. Assn. (life), AAUP (pres. coll. chpt. 1970-72, nat. com. W 1972-75), AAUW, Assn. Can. Studies in U.S., LWV (pres. 1982-83), Phi Alpha Theta. Democrat. Episcopalian. Home: 2734 Mountain View Dr La Verne CA 91750-4312

CHUDY, ROBIN VICTORIA, harpist, artist; b. Chgo., Apr. 21, 1955; d. Victor Frank Chudy and Leah Fuehrer. BA, U. Calif., Santa Cruz, 1977; MMus, Eastman Sch Music, U. Rochester (N.Y.), 1979. Harpist Saunders at Rye Harbor, N.H., 1980-84, Apley's at the Sheraton, Boston, 1984-86, Sonesta Hotel, Cambridge, Mass., 1986-88, Ritz-Carlton Hotel, Boston, 1988—. Mem. Am. Harp Soc. Home: 10 Hall St # 1 Somerville MA 02144-3221

CHUMAS, LINDA GRACE, elementary school educator; b. Floral Park, NY, May 3, 1944; d. Vincent Armond and Alisandra (Simonelli) DeAngelis; m. Spero Nicholas Chumas; children: Spero Chris, Kara Alisandra. BS, Ea. Ky. U., 1967; MA, SUNY, New Paltz, 1983. Cert. health and phys. edn. Tchr. phys. edn. Valley Ctrl. H.S., Montgomery, N.Y., 1968-70, varsity girls tennis coach, 1968-70, jr. varsity girls sports coach, 1968-70, tchr. adult edn. and phys. edn., 1968-75; phys. edn. tchr. Leptondale Elem. Sch., Wallkill, N.Y., 1983—; aerobics, line dance tchr. Wallkill H.S. PTO, 1993-96, tchr. ballroom dancing, 1995-96; tennis tchr. Town of Shawangunk Recreation, Wallkill, 1993-96; tennis tchr. children and adults Wallkill Arts Cmty., 1996—; Jump Rope for Heart coord. Am. Heart Assn., 1983—; mem. Wallkill Ctrl. Sch. Dist. Strategic Planning Com., 1991—; tchr. tennis Walkill Arts Cmty., summer, 1996—. Treas. Am. Field Svc., Wallkill, 1989-93; chairperson flower sales Am. Heart Assn., Leptondale Elem. Sch., 1990—; co-dir. road race Shamrock Scramble, Wallkill, 1988-96; solicitor Multiple Sclerosis Soc., Capital region, 1990-92. Recipient Outstanding Devel. award Am. Heart Assn., Kingston, N.Y., 1990, Straight from Heart flowers award, 1992-95. Mem. AAHPERD (mem. coun. svcs. for eastern dist. assn. 1995—), N.Y. State Assn. Health, Phys. Edn., Recreation and Dance (sec. 1993-95, Jump Rope for Heart Task Force 1992—, Jump Rope for Heart Catskill zone coord. 1992—), N.Y. State United Tchrs. (health ins. rep. Ulster County 1991—), Nat. Dance Assn. Democrat. Greek Orthodox. Home: PO Box 163 11 Berry St Wallkill NY 12589 Office: Leptondale Elem Sch RD #2 Mill St Wallkill NY 12589

CHUN, SUGHOK KOH, internist; b. Seoul, Republic of Korea, Jan. 20, 1929; d. Bak-Han and Shin-ai C. Koh; m. Byungkyu Chun, Oct. 20, 1957; children: David J., James J. BS, Seoul Nat. U., 1951; MD, Korea U., Seoul, 1952. Diplomate Am. Bd. Internal Medicine. Internship Seoul Nat. Univ. Hosp., Seoul, Korea, 1952-53, Alexandria Hosp., Alexandria, Va., 1957-58; residency Seoul Nat. Univ., 1953-56, Alexandria Hosp., 1958-59, D.C. Gen. Hosp., Washington, 1959-62; staff physician CCU Howard U. Hosp., Washington, 1968-74; med. officer FDA, Rockville, Md., 1974—. Methodist. Office: FDA 5600 Fishers Ln Rockville MD 20904

CHUNG, AMY TERESA, lawyer, property manager; b. San Francisco, Sept. 1, 1953; d. Burk Him and Mary Angeline (Lin) C.; m. Andrew Nathan Chang, May 5, 1979; children: Adrian Thomas, Alison Nicole. AB in Psychology, U. Calif., Berkeley, 1975; JD, U. Calif., San Francisco, 1978. Bar: Calif. Legal counsel M & B Assocs., San Francisco, 1978—; v.p. Anza Parking Corp., Burlingame, Calif., 1993—. Mem. adv. com. U. Calif., San Francisco, 1992—; v.p. York Peak Homeowners Assn., West Hills, Calif., 1987-89; v.p. Chinatown Stockton St. Mchts. Assn., San Francisco, 1981—; vice chair Chinese CMty. Housing Corp., San Francisco, 1991—; bd. dirs. Park Day Sch., Oakland, Calif., 1993—; mem. mayor's citizens adv. com. Mid-Market, San Francisco, 1996—. Mem. Calif. Bar Assn. Office: M & B Assocs 835 Washington St San Francisco CA 94108

CHUNG, CONNIE (CONSTANCE YU-HWA CHUNG), broadcast journalist; b. Washington, Aug. 20, 1946; d. William Ling and Margaret Chung; m. Maurice Richard Povich. B.S., U. Md., 1969; D.J. (hon.), Norwich U., 1974, Providence Coll., 1988; LHD, Brown U., 1987; LLD (hon.), Wheaton Coll., 1989. TV news copyperson, writer, reporter Sta. WTTG-TV, Metromedia Channel 5, Washington, 1969-71; corr. CBS News, Washington, 1971-76; TV news anchor Sta. KNXT-TV, CBS, L.A., 1976-83; anchor NBC News, NBC News at Sunrise, NBC Nightly News (Saturday), NBC News Digests, NBC News Mag. 1986, NBC News Spls., N.Y.C., 1983-89, Saturday Night with Connie Chung (CBS-TV), 1989-90, CBS Evening News (Sunday edit.), 1989-93, Face to Face, 1990-91, Eye to Eye, 1993-95; co-anchor CBS Evening News, 1993-95. Recipient Achievement cert. for series of broadcasts U.S. Humane Soc., 1969, Metro Area Mass Media award AAUW, 1971, Outstanding Young Woman of Am. award, 1971, Atlanta chpt. Nat. Assn. Media Women award, 1973, Outstanding Excellence in News Reporting and Pub. Svc. award Chinese-Am. Citizens Alliance, 1973, Hon. award for news reporting Chinese YMCA Boston, 1974, Woman of Distinction award Golden Slipper Club-Phila., 1975, Best TV Reporting award Sta. KNXT-TV and L.A. Press Club, 1977, Outstanding TV Broadcasting award Valley Press Club, 1977, Golden Mike award for best documentary, 1978, Emmy award for individual achievement L.A. chpt. NATAS, 1978, 80, Mark Twain trophy Calif. Associated Press. TV and Radio Assn., 1979, Best News Broadcast 4:30 p.m., 1980, Women in Comm. award Calif. State U. at L.A., 1979, George Foster Peabody award for programs on environ. Md. Ctr. Pub. Broadcasting, 1980, Portraits of Excellence award Pacific S.W. Region B'nai B'rith, 1980, Newscaster of Yr. award Temple Emanuel Brotherhood, 1981, First Amendment award Anti-Defamation League of B'nai B'rith, 1981, Best Newscast 6:00 p.m. award AP, 1981, Calif. Associated Press TV and Radio Assn., 1981, Golden Mike award for best news broadcast, 1981, Disting. Contbns. in area of Comm. Media award L.A. Basin Equal Opportunity League, 1983, Women in Bus. award, 1983, L.A. Press Club award for 4:30 p.m. broadcast, 1983, L.A. Press Club award for 6:00 p.m. broadcast, 1983, Emmy award, 1986, Emmy award for outstanding interview, 1989, 90, Silver Gavel award ABA, 1991, Ohio State of Achievement of Merit award, 1991, Nat. Headliner award NCCJ, 1991, Clarion award Women in Comm., 1991, Commendation award for AIDS and rape Am. Women in Radio and TV, Commendation award for breast implants, 1991. Office: Geller Media Mgmt 250 W 57th St New York NY 10019*

CHUNG, CYNTHIA NORTON, communications specialist; b. Milton, Mass., Apr. 14, 1955; d. Ralph Arnold and Mary Elizabeth (McDonald) N.; m. Chinsoo Chung; children: Sara Jane, Steven Joonmok. BFA in Archtl. and Graphic Design, U. Mass., 1977. Graphic designer Garber Travel, Inc., Brookline, Mass., 1977-78; graphic and exhibit designer Rust Craft, Inc., Dedham, Mass., 1978-80; corp. advt. artist Morse, Inc., Canton, Mass., 1980-83; pvt. practice designer Boston, 1983-84; asst. art dir. Cahners Pub. Co., Newton, Mass., 1984-86, art dir., 1986-87; art dir. Knapp, Inc., Brockton, Mass., 1987-89; customer svc. rep. TWA, Boston, 1990; communications specialist Boston Fin. Data Svcs., Quincy, Mass., 1992—. Designer graphs and charts for Vols. I and II State Budget Commonwealth of Mass., 1982; art dir. Mini Micro Systems, 1984-87. Mem. Kappa Kappa Gamma (pres. 1975-76). Roman Catholic. Home: 134 Samoset Ave Quincy MA 02169-2452 Office: Boston Fin Data Svcs Inc Two Heritage Dr Quincy MA 02170

CHUNG, GRACE H., psychotherapist, occupational therapist; b. Pusan, Korea, Oct. 22, 1964; came to US, 1971; d. Chun and Myung (Bae) C. BS, Loma Linda U., 1987; MA, U. No. Colo., 1995. Staff occupl. therapist, registered U. Calif., Irvine, 1987; staff O.T.R. Northbrook Hand Therapy, Thornton, Colo., 1988-90, Mapleton Hand Ctr., Boulder, Colo., 1990-93; contractual cons. Denver and Boulder, Colo., 1993-95; pvt. practice psychotherapist Boulder, Colo., 1995—; lectr. in field, Boulder, 1996—, contract occupl. therapist, 1993—. Recipient Women's Resource Funds Boulder (Colo.) County Health Dept., 1995. Mem. Am. Counseling Assn., Am. Occupl. Therapist Assn. Office: 703 Walnut Boulder CO 80302

CHUN OAKLAND, SUZANNE NYUK JUN, state legislator; b. Honolulu, June 27, 1961; d. Philip Sing and Mei-Chih (Chung) Chun; m. Michael Sands Chun Oakland, June 11, 1994; children: Mailene Nohea Pua Oakland, Christopher Michael Sing Kamakaku Oakland. BA in Psychology and Comm., U. Hawaii, 1983. Adminstrv. asst. Au's Plumbing and Metal Works, Hawaii, 1979-90; community svc. specialist Senator Anthony Chang, Hawaii, 1984; adminstrv. asst. Smolenski and Woodell, Hawaii, 1984-86; rsch. asst., office mgr. City Coun. Mem. Gary Gill, Hawaii, 1987-90; mem. Hawaii Ho. of Reps., 1990—. Named Legis. of Yr. Hawaii Long Term Care Assn., 1993, Healthcare Assn. Hawaii, 1993, 95, Hawaii Psychiat. Med. Assn., 1994, Autism Soc. Hawaii, 1994; recipient Friend of Social Workers award NASW, 1995. Democrat. Episcopalian. Office: State House Reps State Capitol Honolulu HI 96813-2437

CHURCH, BARBARA RYAN, organizational psychologist; b. Vallejo, Calif.; d. William Russell and Geraldine Hall (Hatcher) Ryan; divorced; children: Gabrielle Church Russell, Elizabeth Broward McGhie. BA, U. Fla., 1974; MA in Psychology, West Ga. Coll., 1981; EdD, U. Ga., 1985. Pub. svc. dir., news editor WJKS-TV, Jacksonville, Fla., 1969-71; dir. cmty. rels. Atlanta Assn. Ret. Citizens, 1977-78; coord. pub. info. Mental Health Assn., Atlanta, 1978-80; edn./testing specialist Federal Law Enforcement Tng. Ctr., Glynco, Ga., 1984-86; dir. evening coll., asst. prof. psychology Brewton-Parker Coll., Mt. Vernon, Ga., 1986-88; tng. rsch. analyst Federal Law Enforcement Tng. Ctr., 1988-90; researcher, edn. specialist U.S. Dept. Justice, Immigration & Naturalization Svc., Glynco, 1990—; tchr., cons. adult edn. courses Ga. State U., Atlanta, 1978—, Brunswick (Ga.) Coll., 1978—. Convenor, cons. Kettering Found., 1987-88; mem. adv. bd. HRD degree, dept. adult edn. U. Ga. Recipient award for best campaign of non-profit orgn. Am. Mktg. Assn., 1978, ann. award for innovative programming Ga. Adult Edn. Assn., 1983; named communicator of yr. United Way, 1980. Mem. U. Ga. Lifelong Learning Assn., Ga. Adult Edn. Assn. (bd. dirs. 1989-91), Soc. Police & Criminal Psychology, Commn. Profs. of Adult Edn. Episcopal. Office: US Dept Justice Immigration & Naturalization Svc Federal Law Enforcement Bldg T-706 Tng Ctr Glynco GA 31524

CHURCH, IRENE ZABOLY, personnel services company executive; b. Cleve., Feb. 18, 1947; d. Bela Paul and Irene Elizabeth (Chandas) Zaboly; children: Irene Elizabeth, Elizabeth Anne, Lauren Alexandria Gadd, John Dale Gadd II. Grad. high sch. Pers. cons., recruiter, Cleve., 1965-70; chief exec. officer, pres. Oxford Pers., Pepper Pike, Ohio, 1973-89, Oxford Temporaries, Pepper Pike, 1979—, Oxford Group Ltd., Inc., 1989—; guest lectr. in field, 1974—; expert witness for ct. testimony, 1982—. Troop leader Lake Erie coun. Girl Scouts U.S., 1980-81; mem. Christian action com. Federated Ch., United Ch. Christ, 1981-85, sub-com. to study violence in rels. to women, 1983, creator, presenter programs How Work Affects Family Life and Re-entering the Job Market, 1981, mem. Women's Fellowship Martha-Mary Circle, 1980—, program dir., 1982-84, 87—; chpt. leader Nat. Coalition on TV Violence, 1983—; mem. The Federated Ch., United Ch. of Christ, Chagrin Falls, Ohio, program dir Mary-Martha Circle, 1982—, christian action com. 1981-85, mem. Mary-Martha Circle, Women's fellowship, 1980—; mem Better Bus. Bur., 1973-82. Mem. Nat. Assn. Pers. Cons. (cert., mem. ethics com. 1976-77, co-chairperson ethics com. 1977-78, mem. bus. practices and ethics com. 1980-82, mem. cert. pers. cons. soc. 1980-82, regional leader for membership 1987—, Pres.'s award 1988), Ohio Assn. Pers. Cons. (trustee 1975-80, 85—, sec. 1976-77, 85-87, chairperson bus. practices and ethics com. 1976-77, 81-82, 1st v.p., chairperson resolutions com. 1981-82, chairperson membership com. 1985-89, 2d v.p. 1987—, Outstanding Svc. award 1987, pres. 1988-89), Greater Cleve. Assn. Pers. Cons. (2nd then 1st v.p., 1974-76, state trustee 1975-80, pres. 1976-77, bd. advisor 1977-78, chairperson bus. practices and ethics com. 1974-76, chmn. nominating com., 1983-88, membership com. 1987-87, arbitration com., 1980, 85-87, fundraising, 1980-89, bd. dirs. 1980-89, trustee 1985-89, program chair 1987-89, Vi Pender Outstanding Svc. award 1977), Euclid C. of C. (small bus. com. 1981, chairperson task force com. evaluating funding in social security and vet.'s benefits 1981), Internat. Platform Assn., Am. Bus. Women's Assn., Nat. Assn. Temp. Svcs., Chagrin Valley C. of C. (leader Chagrin Blvd./East chpt. 1987—, Pres.'s award for Outstanding Contbns. 1988, pres. bd. dirs 1990—), Greater Cleve. Growth Assn. Coun. Small Enterprises, Rotary (vocat. svc. chairperson, program com. 1987—, membership chairperson 1988-89). Home: 8 Ridgecrest Dr Chagrin Falls OH 44022-4218

CHURCH, MARTHA ELEANOR, retired academic administrator, scholar; b. Pitts., Nov. 17, 1930; d. Walter Seward and Eleanor (Boyer) C. BA, Wellesley Coll., 1952; MA, U. Pitts., 1954; PhD, U. Chgo., 1960; DSc (hon.), Lake Erie Coll., 1975; LittD (hon.), Houghton Coll., 1980; LHD (hon.), Queens Coll., 1981, Ursinus Coll., 1981, St. Joseph Coll., 1982, Towson State U., 1983, Dickinson Coll., 1987, Coll. Notre Dame Md., 1995; LLD (hon.), Hood Coll., 1995. Instr. geography Mt. Holyoke Coll., South Hadley, Mass., 1953-57; lectr. geography Ind. U. Gary Ctr., 1958; instr., then asst. prof. geography Wellesley Coll., 1958-59; dean coll., prof. geography Wilson Coll., 1965-71; assoc. exec. sec. Commn. Higher Edn., Middle States Assn. Coll. and Secondary Sch., 1971-75; pres. Hood Coll., Frederick, Md., 1975-95, pres. emerita, 1995—; sr. scholar Carnegie Found. for Advancement of Tchg., Princeton, 1995—; bd. dirs. Farmers and Mechanics Nat. Bank, 1982—, Montgomery Mut. Ins. Co., 1989-90; cons. for Choice: Books for Coll. Librs.; co-chmn. nat. adv. panel nat. Ctr. for Rsch. to Improve Postsecondary Teaching and Learning, U. Mich., 1985-90; mem. bd. vis. Def. Intelligence Coll., 1988-91; mem. adv. bd. dirs. Automobile Club Md., 1991—. Author: The Spatial Organization of Electric Power Territories in Massachusetts, 1960; Co-editor: A Basic Geographical Library: A Selected and Annotated Book List for Am. Colls, 1966; cons. editor, Change mag., 1980 . Bd. dirs. Coun. for Internat. Exch. of Scholars, 1979-80, Japan Internat. Christian U. Found., 1977-91, Nat. Ctr. for Higher Edn. Mgmt. Sys., 1980-83; bd. dirs. Am. Coun. on Edn., 1976-79, vice chmn., 1978-79, mem. nat. identification panel, 1977—, Nat. Rsch. Com., 1993-96; bd. advisors Fund for Improvement of Postsecondary Edn., HEW, 1976-79; mem. Sec. of Navy's Adv. Bd. on Edn. and Tng., 1976-80; chmn. Md. Commn. on Civil Rights, 1981-82; trustee Bradford Coll., Mass., 1982-87, Peddie Sch., N.J., 1982—, Carnegie Found. for the Advancement of Tchg., 1986-96, vice chairperson, 1990-92, chairperson, 1992-94, immediate past chairperson, 1994-96; trustee Nat. Geog. Soc., 1989—, chair audit rev. com., 1993—; trustee Nat. Geog. Soc. Edn. Found., 1989-96; chmn. bd. dirs. Medici Found., Princeton, N.J., 1985—; trustee United Bd. for Christian Higher Edn. in Asia, 1995—, chmn. East and Intra-Asia program subcom., 1996—; mem. Md. Humanities Coun., 1985-86, Md. Jud. Disabilities Commn., 1985-94; commr. Edn. Commn. States, Md., 1981—; exec. com. Campus Compact: Project for Pub. and Cmty. Svc., 1986-89. Mem. AAUW, Am. Assn. Advancement of Humanities (bd. dirs. 1979-81), Am. Assn. Higher Edn. (chmn. 1980-81, bd. dirs. 1979-83), Assn. Am. Geographers, Nat. Assn. Ind. Colls. and Univs. (bd. dirs. 1983-86), Md. Ind. Colls. and Univs. Assn. (pres. 1979-81, mem. exec. com. 1988-92), Assn. Am. Colls. and Univs. (mem. adv. com. project on status and edn. of women 1980-85), Women's Coll. Coalition (mem. exec. com. 1976-80, 87-89), Am. Conf. Acad. Deans (sec., editor 1969-71), Coun. Protestant Colls. and Univs. (bd. dirs. 1969-71), Soc. Coll. and Univ. Planning (mem. editl. bd. 1979-95), Cosmos Club (mem. jour. editl. bd. 1990-94), Inst. Ednl. Leadership (bd. dirs. 1982-87), Sigma Delta Epsilon, Delta Kappa Gamma (hon.). Home: 104 Mercer Ct Apt 15-6 Frederick MD 21701-4003 Office: Carnegie Found for the Advancement of Tchg 5 Ivy Ln Princeton NJ 08540

CHURCHILL, CAROL ANN, lawyer, volunteer; b. Louisville, Ky., Apr. 11, 1953; d. Charles James and Anna Catherine (Riefling) C. BS, Colo. State U., 1975; JD, U. West L.A., 1983. Bar: Calif. 1983; cert. specialist in probate, estate planning and trust law. Assoc. Ball, Hunt, Hart, Brown & Baerwitz, Long Beach, Calif., 1983-90, Cameron, Madden, Pearlson, Noblin & Sellars, Long Beach, 1990-94; ptnr. Churchill & Boskovich, Long Beach, 1994—. Planning commr. City of Signal Hill, Calif., 1987-90, coun. mem., 1990-94, mayor, 1993-94; bd. dirs. Found Theatre, 1985-87, Family Svcs. of Long Beach, 1988-90, VNA Found., Long Beach, 1990—, United Cambodian Comty., Inc., 1990-91; advisor to bd. United Cambodian Comty., Inc., 1995—. Named Outstanding Bus. Woman, Impact Coun. Am. Bus. Woman Assn., 1994. Mem. Long Beach Bar Assn. (bd. govs. 1995—), Women Lawyers of Long Beach (Pro Bono award 1994, Lawyer of Yr.

1995), Soroptimist Internat. (coms.). Home: 1979 Raymond Ave Signal Hill CA 90806 Office: Churchill & Boskovich 100 Oceangate Ste 1000 Long Beach CA 90802

CHURCHILL, KAREN LYNN, curator, educator; b. Ft. Worth, July 18, 1956; d. Richard Lionel and Yonova (Muncy) C. Student, Mills Coll., 1973-75; AB in British Lit., Colgate U., 1977; MA in Art History, Ariz. State U., 1986; MA in Arts Adminstrn., So. Meth. U., 1987, MBA, 1987; postgrad. in art history, Case Western Res. U., 1992—. Coord. cultural programs So. Meth. U., Dallas, 1987-89; dir. Gray Gallery, Univ. Mus. East Carolina U., Greenville, N.C., 1989-90; faculty assoc. Ariz. State U., Tempe, 1991; asst. prof. Kent (Ohio) State U., 1993-94; photography rsch. asst. Cleve. Mus. Art, Cleve., 1995—; mem. adv. bd. Scottsdale (Ariz.) Cultural Coun., 1991-93, Internat. Friends of Transformative Art, Paradise Valley, Ariz., 1991—; gallery cons. Ind. State U., Terre Haute, 1994; exhibn. cons. J. Paul Getty Mus., Malibu, Calif., 1994—. Curator (art exhibns.) So. Meth. U., 1987-89, Gray Gallery, 1989-91, Eco-Logic: Ariz. Artists as Environmental Activists, 1992, The Cleve. Mus. of Art, 1996—. Commn. appointee Christopher Columbus Quincentary Commn., Dallas, 1987-89. N.C. Arts Commn. rsch. grantee, 1990; Case Western Res. U. scholar, 1992—; Andrew Mellon fellowship, 1996. Mem. Am. Assn. Mus., Coll. Art Assn. Home: 1551 Maple Rd Cleveland Heights OH 44121 Office: The Cleve Mus of Art 11150 East Blvd Cleveland OH 44106

CHURCHILL, SALLY JO, lawyer; b. Saginaw, Mich., Oct. 29, 1955; d. James P. and Annabel I. (Muir) C.; m. Edward L. Kulka, Jan. 14, 1989. B of Gen. Studies, U. Mich., 1977; MA, Tufts U., 1980; JD, U. Mich., 1987. Bar: Mich. 1987. Resource specialist Ecological Rsch. Svcs. Inc., Iron River, Mich., 1980-82; resume specialist Mich. United Conservation Clubs, Lansing, Mich., 1986; asst. atty. gen. Office of Atty. Gen., Lansing, Mich., 1987-91; atty. Rosi, Olson & Levine, Traverse City, Mich., 1991-92; land protection specialist Little Traverse Conservance, Harbor Springs, Mich., 1992-93; ptnr. Honigman Miller Schwartz & Cohn, Detroit, 1993-96; univ. atty. U. Mich., Ann Arbor, 1996—; spkr. in field. Mem. State Bar of Mich. (mem. environ. law sect. program com. 1992-93, chair-elect environ. law sect. 1995-96, chair 1996-97). Office: U Mich Office of Gen Counsel 4010 Fleming Adminstrn Bldg Ann Arbor MI 48191-3400

CHURCHVILLE, LIDA HOLLAND, librarian; b. Dallas, May 5, 1933; d. Norbert R. and Agnes J. (Buckley) Holland; m. Joseph J. Churchville, Oct. 6, 1952 (dec. 1974); children: Lisa, Zoe, Anthony (dec.), Stephen. BA in History, Russell Sage Coll., Troy, N.Y., 1965; MLS, SUNY, Albany, 1967. Libr. Office Legis. Rsch., N.Y. Senate, Albany, 1967-75; chief law libr. U.S. Army Libr., Washington, 1975-78; coord. fed. women's program Dept. Def., The Pentagon, 1976-78; chief libr. Nat. Archives and Records Svcs., 1978-81; reference and spl. project libr. Nat. Archives Libr., 1981-83; spl. project libr. publs. unit Nat. Archives Trust Fund, 1983—, info. specialist Patent & Trademark Office, 1989; with Archives Libr. Info. Ctr., Nat. Archives, 1989-93; chief librarian, 1993-95. Mem. Women's Issues Task Force, 1981-83, Women's Nat. Dem. Club, 1981-92, Eleanor Roosevelt Dem. Club, Greenbelt, Md.; mem. Paint Branch Unitarian Ch., Adelphi, Md., sec. to Bd. of Trustees, 1991-93; docent Greenbelt Mus., 1988—; active Bd. of Elections, Greenbelt, 1993—; vol. Arena Stage. Recipient Outstanding Performance award The Pentagon, 1977; active mem. FEDLINK adv. coun. Lib. of Congress, 1994—; sec. Fed. Lib. Info. coun. com., 1994—; Mem. D.C. Libr. Assn. (program com. 1993), Soc. Am. Archivists, Nat. Archives Assembly, DC Online Users Group. Home: 19Q Ridge Rd Greenbelt MD 20770-0710 Office: Nat Archives Library NNUL Rm 2380 8601 Adelphi Rd College Park MD 20740-6001

CHWATSKY, ANN, photographer, educator; b. Phila., Jan. 11, 1942; BS in Art Edn., Hofstra U., 1965, MS, 1971; postgrad. L.I. U., 1973-74. Cert. tchr. Photography editor L.I. mag., 1976-80; instr. Internat. Ctr. Photography, N.Y.C., 1979-80, Parrish Art Mus., Southampton, N.Y., 1984—; ; dir. master art workshop Southampton Coll., 1985—; mem. art faculty NYU, 1991—. Author, photgrapher The Man In The Street, 1989; photographer The Four Seasons of Shaker Life; photographs featured in Time, Newsweek, Newsday, Manchete, N.Y. Times, MD Medical Times; one person shows include Photographers Gallery, London, 1985, Shakers, Nassau County Mus. Fine Arts, 1987, Greater Lafayette (Ind.) Mus. Art, 1988, Brooklyn Coll., 1990, Kiev, USSR Exhibition Hall, 1991, Brooklyn Coll., Lincoln Ctr., Buenos Aires, 1993; group shows include The Other, Houston Ctr. Photography, 1988, L.I. Fine Arts Mus., 1984, Women's Internat Ctr., N.Y.C., 1976, 80, Parrish Art Mus., Southampton, 1979, Internat. Ctr. Photography, N.Y.C., 1980, 82, Nassau County Mus. Fine Arts, 1983, Soho 20 Gallery, N.Y.C., 1984, New Orleans World's Fair, 1984, Southampton Gallery, 1988, 89, Lizan Tops Gallery, L.I., 1994, Apex Art, N.Y.C., 1995; represented in permanent collections: Forbes N.Y.C. Midtown YWCA, Nassau County Mus. Fine Arts, Susan Rothenberg, others. Bd. dirs. Rosa Lee Young Day Care Ctr., Rockville Centre, 1982—. Recipient Estabrook Disting. Alumni award Hofstra U., 1984; Kodak Profl. Photographers award, 1984; Eastman Found. grantee, 1981-82; Polaroid grantee, 1980. Mem. Assn. Am. Mag. Profls., Picture Profls. Am., Profl. Women Photographers N.Y.C. Democrat. Jewish. Avocations: tennis, gardening. Home & Studio: 29 E 22nd St Apt 3N New York NY 10010-5305

CHYPRE, ELIZABETH, designer, silversmith, business owner; b. N.Y.C., July 30, 1938; d. Henry and Irma Mendez; m. John R. Petrak, June 1, 1957 (div. 1972); children: John H. Petrak, James E. Petrak; m. Louis J. Chypre, Mar. 13, 1977. AA, Dutchess Community Coll., Poughkeepsie, N.Y., 1973; BS in Human & Community Svc., Empire State Coll., 1976; MS in Criminal Justice, L.I. U., 1979. Ceramist Chypre & Chypre Assocs., Rhinebeck, N.Y., 1981-87; designer, silversmith, graphic designer The Wordsmiths, Rhinebeck, 1988—. Editor newsletter Hudson Valley Artisan's Guild, 1991—; contbr. Against the Night, 1969, Hudson Valley Arts Rev., 1993; author: Business Sense for Craftsmen, 1992; publisher: Choices for Craftsmen and Artists, 1996—. Intern vol. Dutchess County Dept. Probation, Poughkeepsie, 1976; vol. judo instr. YMCA, 1969-71; mem. Hope Lodge Cancer Support Group, 1988—. Scholar Fashion Inst. Tech., 1955; recipient Disting. Svc. award YMCA, 1971, Freddie award Hudson Valley Ceramic Assn., 1981, 17 Blue Ribbons, 1982-86. Mem. Hudson Valley Artisan's Guild (v.p. 1991-93). Office: Chypre & Chypre PO Box 484 Rhinebeck NY 12572-0484

CIAGLIA, JOANNA, social worker; b. Chgo., Nov. 19, 1947; d. Ernest Albert and Joanna Marie (Vervieri) C. AB, St. Louis U., 1969, MSW, 1971; MPH, U. Calif., 1979. Occpl. therapy Ridgeway Hosp., Chgo., 1968; resident asst. St. Louis U., 1969-71; satelite program coord. Buckilew House, 1972-76. Co-author: Social Functioning of Lobotomized Individuals, 1970, Low Cost Housing For the Mentally Disabled, 1980. Mem. NASW.

CIAIO, LAURA ASHMORE, accountant; b. Laramie, Wyo.; d. Glenn L. Ashmore and Angela L. (Edwards) Bennett; m. Andrew Charles Ciaio, aug. 5, 1989; 1 child, Nathan Andrew. BSBA, Rochester Inst. Tech., 1989. CPA, N.Y. Staff acct. Coopers & Lybrand, Rochester, N.Y., 1989-92; gen. acctg. mgr. Lewis Tree Svc., Inc., Rochester, 1992-95; mgr. fin. reporting MDT Biologic Co., Rochester, 1995—. Tutor, bd. dirs., treas., chmn. fin. com. Literacy Vols. Am.-Rochester, N.Y., Inc., 1989—. Mem. ICP, Inst. Mgmt. Accts., N.Y. State Soc. CPA's. Office: MDT Biologic Co 1777 E Henrietta Rd Rochester NY 14623

CIAK, BRENDA SUSAN, nurse; b. Springfield, Mass., Jan. 29, 1955; d. Stanley Peter and Jessica Evelyn (Jorkowski) Ciak; divorced, 1989. BS in Pub. Health, U. Mass., 1976, BSN, 1979, RN, 1979; MSN, Boston U., 1986. RN, Mass.; cert. in infection control; cert. gerontological nurse. Staff nurse Miriam Hosp., Providence, 1979-80; head nurse Western Mass. Kidney Ctr., Springfield, 1980-85; nurse epidemiologist Providence Hosp., Holyoke, Mass., 1985-86; infection control program mgr. VA Med. Ctr., Northampton, Mass., 1986-94; clin. nurse supr. infection control, quality & case mgmt. Mercy Hosp., Springfield, Mass., 1995—; presenter at profl. confs. Contbr. to profl. publs. Co-founder, co-chair AIDS/HIV Positive Support Group VA Med. Ctr., Northampton, 1989-92. Featured in article in Women Unltd. mag., 1991; contbr. articles to profl. jours. Mem. NAFE, Assn. Practitioners in Infection Control (elected mem. New England chpt. nominating com. 1993-94), Advanced Nursing Practice Group of Western Mass. (chairperson 1989-94), Zonta Club Internat. (bd. dirs. 1992-94), Springfield Mus. and Libr. Assn., Sigma Theta Tau (chpt. archivist 1990-92). Home: 102 Wolcott St Springfield MA 01104-2418 Office: Mercy Hosp Dept Quality & Case Mgmt 271 Carew St Springfield MA 01104

CIALELLA, ROSEANN MARGARET, educational administrator; b. Bklyn., Oct. 9, 1947; d. Vincent James and Mary Rose (Cuoco) Internicola; m. Edward Charles Cialella, Feb. 27, 1971. BS, SUNY, Brockport, 1969; MEd, Rutgers U., 1977; EdD, Nova Southeastern U., Ft. Lauderdale, Fla., 1994. Cert. tchr., prin, supt. schs., N.J. Tchr. Penns Grove (N.J.) Bd. Edn., 1973-76, Gloucester County Vo-Tech, Sewell, N.J., 1976-78; prin. Mullica Twp. Bd. Edn., Elwood, N.J., 1978-79, Washington Twp. Bd. Edn., Sewell, 1979-84; supt. Berkeley Twp. Bd. Edn., Bayville, N.J., 1984-87, Merchantville (N.J.) Bd. Edn., 1987-89; supr. U. Pa., Phila., 1989-90; supt. schs. Estell Manor (N.J.) Bd. Edn., 1990—; mem. prof. devel. com. N.J. State Dept. Edn., Trenton, 1992—. Charter mem. Estell Manor Cmty. Drug Alliance, 1990-93. Mem. AAUW, Am. Assn. Sch. Adminstrs., N.J. Assn. Sch. Adminstrs. (various coms.), Phi Delta Kappa. Home: 14 Caraway Ct Thorofare NJ 08086-2403 Office: Estell Manor Bd Edn 128 Cape May Ave Estell Manor NJ 08319

CIAVARELLI, RITA MURPHY, maternal/infant health nurse; b. Titusville, Pa., Sept. 26, 1954; d. Francis Cassidy and M. Irene (Lavery) Murphy; m. Louis Paul Ciavarelli, Feb. 14, 1987. BSN, Villa Maria Coll., 1976; MS, Va. Commonwealth U., 1988. RN, Pa., Va.; RNC, Nat. Cert. Corp.; lic. clin. nurse specialist, Va. Staff nurse urology St. Vincent Health Ctr., Erie, Pa., 1976-77, postpartum/gynecol. nurse, 1977-82; newborn nursery/neonatal ICU nurse Richmond (Va.) Meml. Hosp., 1983-92, clin. nurse specialist, clin. educator, 1992—; asst. clin. instr. Med. Coll. Va. Sch. Nursing, Richmond, 1986, preceptor BS/MS students, 1992—; hosp. instr. in neonatal resuscitation Am. Heart Assn., 1994—; instr. in perinatal continuing edn., Richmond, 1992—; mem. Regional Perinatal Coord. Coun., 1992—, Richmond Infant Mortality Rev. Com., 1992—. Christian marriage formation team instr. Cath. Diocese of Richmond, 1989—. Mem. Assn. Women's Health, Obstetric and Neonatal Nurses, Va. Soc. for Healthcare Edn. and Training, Sigma Theta Tau. Home: 912 Walton Creek Dr Midlothian VA 23113-7129 Office: Richmond Meml Hosp 1300 Westwood Ave Richmond VA 23227-4612

CIAVOLA, LOUISE ARLENE, foundation executive; b. Summit Station, Ohio, July 16, 1933; d. Orus Allen and Marie Elizabeth (White) Helser; m. Rex George Ciavola, May 20, 1961; children: Rex George Jr., Todd Colby, Christina Adelina. BS in Edn. with honors, Ohio U., 1954; postgrad., U. Mich., 1959-60, 84, Western Mich U., 1960, Wayne State U., 1984. Cert. elem. and secondary tcr., Ill., Ohio, Mich. Tchr. pub. schs., Northlake, Ill., 1954-55, Cuyahoga Falls, Ohio, 1955-57, Newark, Ohio, 1957-59, Kalamazoo, 1959-60, Grosse Pointe, Mich., 1960-85; asst. dir. vols. Children's Hosp. Mich., Detroit, 1978-82; assoc. exec. dir. Cystic Fibrosis Found., Grand Rapids, Mich., 1988-89, assoc. exec. dir., Greater Mich. Chpt., 1989-92; cmty. site dir. Am. Heart Assn., San Jose, Calif., 1995—. Bd. dirs., officer Jr. Women's Assn. for Detroit Symphony Orch., 1964-70, Tennis and Crumpets, Inc., Detroit, 1975-82; bd. dirs. Midland (Mich.) Hosp. Ctr., 1985-87, Mother's Club Grosse Pointe South High Sch., 1983-84; co-founder, bd. dirs. Grosse Pointe Found. for Acad. Enrichment, 1970-85; chmn. United Found., Grosse Pointe Park, Mich., 1968; deacon Grosse Pointe Meml. Ch., Grosse Pointe Farms, Mich., 1970. Recipient award for devoted svc. Children's Hosp. Mich., 1982. Mem. NAFE, Ctrl. U.S. Ski Assn. (bd. dirs. 1977-81), Silver Creek Valley Country Club, 20th Century Club (Midland), Contemporary Rev. (Midland), Otsego Ski Club (Gaylord, Mich.), Chimes, Kappa Delta Pi, Phi Alpha Theta, Tau Beta. Republican. Presbyterian. Office: Am Heart Assn Calif Affiliate One Almaden Blvd Ste 500 San Jose CA 95113

CICCHELLA, DENISE, mortgage service representative, poet; b. Paterson, N.J., Apr. 30, 1969; d. Louis Nicholas and Bernice Marie (Silagyi) C. BBA in Acctg., Loyola Coll., 1991; MBA in Internat. Bus., Farleigh Dickinson U., 1996; postgrad., Am. Banking Assn., 1992—. Loan adminstr. UJB Fin., Hackensack, N.J., 1991-96; rsch. specialist Summit Mktg. Co., Cranford, N.J., 1996—; ind. mktg. cons. Author: (anthology) Between a Laugh and a Tear, World of Poetry, 1988 (Silver award); contbr. articles to profl. jours. Blood drive coord. Am. Red Cross, Balt., 1988-91; active Spl. Olympics, U. Md., 1990, Project Appalachia, Cumberland, Md., 1991, Romero Peace March, Washington, 1990. Recipient Cura Personalis award, 1988, Leadhership honors, 1990; scholar Warren Point Sq. Club, 1987-91. Mem. Assn. Accts., Women Banker's Assn., Mensa. Roman Catholic. Home: 1-32 Hartley Pl Fair Lawn NJ 07410

CICCIARELLI, MARIA ELENA, cultural arts administrator; b. Detroit, Mar. 27, 1952; d. Edwin Nicholas and Grace Catherine C. BS in Leisure Svcs. and Studies, Fla. State U., 1981. Cert. leisure profl. Site mgr. N.W. Recreational Ctr. City of Austin Parks and Recreation Dept., 1981-83, unit mgr., recreation ctrs., 1984-89, program mgr. cultural arts, 1989—; HIV in the workplace trainer City of Austin Parks and Recreation Dept., 1992—. Recipient Arts Basic Schs. award Tex. Commn. on the Arts, 1995, Cert. of Appreciation U. YWCA, 1994. Mem. Tex. Alliance for Edn. and the Arts (regional 13 chair 1995—), Nat. Recreation and Park Assn. (bd. dirs. arts and humanities divsn., newsletter chair 1993—, S.W. Regional Artist Humanities award 1993, Nat. Mullen Arts and Humanities award 1995). Office: City of Austin Parks andRecr Dept PO Box 1088 Austin TX 78767

CICCONE, MADONNA LOUISE VERONICA See MADONNA

CIELINSKI-KESSLER, AUDREY ANN, technical writer, publisher, small business owner; b. Cleve., Sept. 10, 1957; d. Joseph and Dorothy Antoinette (Hanna) Cielinski. BJ with high honors, U. Tex., 1979. Reporter, writer Med. World News mag., N.Y.C., 1979; asst. copy chief Med. World News mag., Houston, 1983-84; free-lance writer, editor, 1984—; editorial asst. Jour Health and Social Behavior, Houston, 1980-81; sec. dept. psychiatry Baylor Coll. Medicine, Houston, 1980-81; procedures analyst, tech. writer, tech. librarian Harris County Data Processing Dept., Houston, 1981-83; communications specialist III, Wang systems adminstr. office of planning and rsch. Houston Police Dept.; tchr. tech. writing class, 1985-89; tech. writer Chevron Exploration and Prodn. Svcs. Co., Houston, 1990-92; freelance tech. writer, 1992—; owner The Write Hand, Kent, Ohio, 1992—. Contbr. stories and articles newspapers and mags.; editor newsletters Signals, CEPS Synergy, PCLIBtm Letter, Insights, Steps & Specs. Vol. writer, graphic designer, office religious edn. St. Ambrose Roman Cath. Ch., Houston, 1983-92; vol. editor newsletters Greater Houston area Am. Cancer Soc. and VGS, Inc. Recipient Commendation award Chief of Police, Houston, Chief's Command Employee of Month award June, 1989. Mem. NAFE, Women in Comms., Nat. Assn. Desktop Pubs., Am. Med. Writers Assn., Soc. for Tech. Comm., Soc. Children's Book Writers (assoc.), Sigma Delta Chi, Phi Kappa Phi, Alpha Lambda Delta. Home and Office: 1638 S Lincoln St Kent OH 44240-4449

CIESZEWSKI, SANDRA JOSEPHINE, manufacturing company manager; b. Cleve., June 7, 1941; d. Chester L. and Cecilia (Laska) C. BA in Chemistry, Ursuline Coll., 1962; BA in Art History, Cleve. State U., 1981; Exec. MBA, Baldwin Wallace Coll., 1989. Chemist Harshaw Chem. Co., Cleve., 1962-65, Union Carbide Corp., Parma, Ohio, 1965-79; project mgr. Gould, Inc., Eastlake, Ohio, 1979-91; product engrng. mgr.- lithium Duracell U.S.A., Lexington, N.C., 1992—. Mem. Soc. of Women Engrs. (N.E. Ohio sect.) Cleve. Garden Ctr., Cleve. Mus. Art. Mem. Am. Chem. Soc., Soc. Applied Spectroscopy, Electrochem. Soc. (treas 1980), Women's Club (sec. Walton Hills chpt. 1985, treas. 1991), Assoc. Artists of Winston-Salem.

CIESZYNSKI, IZABELA, library director. Dir. Newport News Pub. Libr. System, Norfolk, Va. Office: Newport News Public Library Sys 2400 Washington Ave Newport News VA 23607-4305*

CIGANA, KATHLEEN L., international business educator; b. Canonsburg, Pa., Jan. 22, 1946; m. Angelo Cigana. BBA, Washington and Jefferson Coll., 1988; M Pub. Mgmt., Carnegie Mellon U., 1989; PhD in Internat. Devel., U. Pitts., 1992. Adminstr. ALCOA, Pitts., 1973-89; rschr. Duquesne U., Pitts., 1990—, assoc. adj. prof., 1994—; pvt. practice bus. cons. Washington and Canonsburg, Pa., 1990—; career cons., mem. admissions coun. Carnegie Mellon U., Pitts., 1990—; mem. legis. network U. Pitts., 1990—; bd. dirs., sec. Canonsburg Diversified Svcs., Inc.; adj. faculty mem. Washington & Jefferson Coll., Washington, Pa., 1990—. Bd. dirs. Canonsburg Gen. Hosp., 1995—. U. Pitts. rsch. grantee, 1992. Mem. AAUW, Am. Ednl. Rsch. Assn., U. Pitts. Doctoral Assn., Washington and Jefferson Coll. Gen. Alumni Assn. (mem. exec. com. 1990—), Comparative Internat. Edn. Assn. Home and Office: 6 Morgan St Canonsburg PA 15317

CILIBERTI, PATRICIA, social researcher, clinical social worker; b. Wilmington, N.C., Sept. 12, 1959. BA in English and Psychology, U. Mont., 1988; MSW, Portland State U., 1990, postgrad., 1993—. Residential care worker Rosemont Sch., Portland, 1989-90; family therapist Tualatin Valley Mental Health, Tigard, Oreg., 1990—; contract therapist Tualatin Valley Mental Health, Beaverton, Oreg., 1991—; project mgr. Child Welfare Partnership, Portland, 1994-95; rechr. Regional Rsch. Inst., Portland, 1995—; rsch. and statistics cons. Portland State U., 1996—; vol. grant writer Cath. Charities, Portland, 1996; adj. faculty U. Portland and Portland State U., 1996—. Crisis counselor YWCA Battered Women's Shelter, Missoula, Mont., 1987-88. Recipient Oreg. honors scholarship Portland State U., 1988-89, 89-90. Mem. NOW, NASW, CSWE. Office: Regional Rsch Inst Portland State U PO Box 751 Portland OR 97207-0751

CIMA, BROOKS DEMENT, art educator; b. Pt. Arthur, Tex., Feb. 3, 1957; d. Marvin Raye and Shirley M. (Haydel) Dement; m. Dennis Louis Cima, July 11, 1987; 1 child, Caitlin Raye. BS in Dance, Lamar U., 1979, tchr. cert., 1987. Cert. tchr. art K-12, Fla., cert. tchr. art K-12, secondary dance, Tex. Instr. dance dept. Lamar U., Beaumont, Tex., 1979; tchr., owner Brooks Dement's Dance Factory, Pt. Arthur, 1979-87; dance tchr. Magnet Sch. Woodrow Wilson Mid. Sch., Pt. Arthur, 1984-87; artistic dir., founder Applause Jazz Dance Theatre, Panama City, Fla., 1987-89; art tchr. Hiland Park Elem. Bay County Ind. Sch. Dist., Panama City, 1987-89; art tchr., chair fine arts dept., drill team instr. Waller (Tex.) H.S., Waller Ind. Sch. Dist., 1989-91; art tchr. Cimarron Elem. Sch. Katy (Tex.) Ind. Sch. Dist., 1991-94, art tchr. West Meml. Elem. Sch., 1994—; dance tchr. Step in Time Studio, Katy, 1991—; bd. dirs. Bus. Growth Network, Katy; cons. Renaissance Finishes/Katy, 1991—; presenter, instr. Kindergarten Tchrs. of Tex. State Conf., Houston, 1993, Dance Troupe, Inc., 1981-85. Choreographer: (ballet) The Legend of the Lake, 1986; dir., choreographer: (opera) H.M.S. Pinafore, 1994; dir. Into the Woods, 1994; choreographer 12 shows for comty. theatre groups, 1979—. Supt. of edn. Living Word Luth. Ch., 1993-96; bd. dirs. Cimarron PTA, Katy, 1992-94; reflections chmn. Katy coun. PTA, 1994-95. Named Houston West Tchr. of Yr., Houston West C. of C., 1993-94, Outstanding Spl. Area Tchr., Assn. of Bay County Educators, 1989. Mem. Nat. Art Edn. Assn., Dance Masters Am., Tex. State Tchrs. Assn., Tex. Art Educators Assn., Houston Art Educators Assn. Lutheran.

CINGARI, SUSAN G., television producer, writer, actress; b. Stamford, Conn., Dec. 22, 1959; d. Rocco and Christine Helen (Battaglia) C. BA in Am. Govt. and Philosophy, Wheaton Coll., Norton, Mass., 1981. Video journalist CNN/Atlanta, 1981-83; creative svcs. dir. WTWS-TV, New London, Conn., 1983-85; producer KRDO-TV, Colorado Springs, 1985-87, WPEC-TV, West Palm Beach, Fla., 1987, WPBF-TV, West Palm Beach, 1987-90; pres. Starquest Prodns., West Palm Beach, 1990—, Starquest Prime Time Prodns., West Palm Beach, 1993—. Recipient Best Newscast award AP, Colorado Springs, 1987, Silver and Bronze award Natl. Mature Media, TV divsn., 1996. Mem. Am. Women in Radio and TV, Women in Comms. Home: 5003 Wheatley Ct Lantana FL 33462

CINO, MARIA, legislative staff member; b. Buffalo, Apr. 19, 1957; d. Richard J. and Lucy M. (Tripi) C. BA in Polit. Sci., St. John Fisher Coll. Project supr. Rep. Nat. Com., 1981-82, dir. local programs, 1983-84, exec. asst. field dir., 1985-86; rsch. analyst Am. Viewpoint, Inc., 1986-88; adminstrv. asst. Rep. L. William Paxon, 1989-93; exec. dir. Nat. Rep. Congl. Com., 1993—. Mem. Ho. Adminstrv. Assts. Assn., Pi Gamma Mu. Office: Nat Rep Congl Com 320 1st St SE Rm 203 Washington DC 20003-1838

CINOTTI, AMINTHA K., urban planner; b. New Haven, Nov. 8, 1957; d. Daniel A. and Jeanne M. (Boisclair) C. BA, U. R.I., 1979, M in Cmty. Planning, 1983. Cmty. devel. dir. Town of Weymouth, Mass., 1984—. Fair housing commr., Weymouth, 1990—; vol. tour guide Fall River (Mass.) Hist. Soc., 1988—. Mem. Nat. Cmty. Devel. Assn. (bd. dirs. 1990—), Sigma Kappa (collegiate province officer 1986—, collegiate dist. dir. 1993-96), , Newport Yacht Club. Home: 864 Robeson St Fall River MA 02720

CINTAVEY, KATHLEEN OTTERSON, secondary education educator. BA, Colby Coll.; MEd, Bowling Green State U., 1989; PhD in Urban Edn., Cleve. State U., 1995. Cert. K-12 tchr., Ohio. Tchr. Lorain (Ohio) City Schs., 1984—, Admiral King H.S., Lorain, 1984; policy writer Lorain City Schs., 1986, creator discipline ladder, 1991—, presenter, 1994, lang. arts curriculum guide co-creator, 1992; rschr. Cuyahoga County Juvenile Ct., Cleve., 1993; adj. prof. ednl. psychology Oberlin (Ohio) Coll., instrnl. devel. and reading methods Cleve. State U., 1995—. Soccer coach North Olmsted (Ohio) Soccer Assn., 1990; open forum mem. Midwest Conf. Comparative and Internat. Edn. Soc., 1992. Grantee Endowment Fund, 1993, Cleve. Mus. Health, 1993, Nord Found., 1993, Lorain City Schs. Endowment Fund, 1989. Mem. ASCD, NEA, Am. Ednl. Rsch. Assn., Ohio Ednl. Assn., Cleve. State U., Alpha Omega (founding mem. 1994), Phi Delta Kappa. Home: 30041 Wellington North Olmsted OH 44070-5082 Office: Admiral King HS 2600 Ashland Ave Lorain OH 44052-4450

CIOCIOLA, CECILIA MARY, science education specialist; b. Chester, Pa., Feb. 9, 1946; d. Donato Francis Pasqual and Mary Theresa (Dugan) C. BA, Immaculata Coll., 1975; MA, West Chester U., 1984. Tchr. Archdiocese of Phila., 1964-72, Harrisburg (Pa.) Diocese, 1972-74, Camden (N.J.) Diocese, 1974-76; tchr., elem. sci. chairperson Archdiocese of Phila., 1976-86; ednl. cons. Macmillan Pub. Co., Delran, N.J., 1986-88; program officer PATHS/PRISM, Phila., 1988-90; asst. exec. dir. minority engring., math., sci. program Prime, Inc., Phila., 1988—; instr. edn. dept. Chestnut Hill Coll., Phila; mem. tchr. cert. adv. com. Phila. Coll. Pharmacy and Sci.; cons. Delaware County Intermediate Unit, Media, Pa.; chairperson elem. (grades 1-8), sci. com. Phila. Archdiocese, 1985-86, mem., 1984-86; coord. Chester County Cath. Schs.: Computer Edn., Pa., 1982-84, Fed. Nutrition Program, St. Agnes Sch., West Chester, Pa., 1982-84, Justice Edn. Teaching Strategies, St. Agnes Sch., West Chester, 1983-84. Author, editor: (curriculum) Elementary Life and Earth Science, 1984. NSF grantee Operation Primary Phys. Sci., La. State U., 1997—. Mem. AAUW, ASCD, Nat. Sci. Tchrs. Assn., Pa. Biotech. Assn. (edn. coun.), Phila. Coll. Pharmacy and Sci. (sci. edn. adv. com.), Pa. Sci. Tchrs. Assn. Office: Prime Inc The Wellington 135 S 19th St Ste 250 Philadelphia PA 19103-4907

CIOLLI, ANTOINETTE, librarian, retired educator; b. N.Y.C., Aug. 20, 1915; d. Pietro and Mary (Palumbo) C.; A.B., Bklyn. Coll., 1937, M.A., 1940; B.S. in L.S., Columbia U., 1943. Tchr. history and civics Bklyn. high schs., 1943-44; circulation librarian Bklyn. Coll. Library, 1944-46; instr. history Sch. Gen. Studies, Bklyn. Coll., 1944-50, asst. prof. library dept., 1965-73, assoc. prof., 1973-81, prof. emerita, 1981—; reference librarian Bklyn. Coll. Library, 1947-59, chief sci. librarian, 1959-70, chief spl. collections div., 1970-81, hon. archivist, 1981—. Mem. ALA, Am. Hist. Assn., Spl. Libraries Assn. (museum group chpt. sec. 1950-51, 52-54), N.Y. Library Club, Beta Phi Mu. Author: (with Alexander S. Preminger and Lillian Lester) Urban Educator: Harry D. Gideonse, Brooklyn College and the City University of New York, 1970; contbr. articles to profl. jours. Home: 1129 Bay Ridge Pky Brooklyn NY 11228-2337

CIPARICK, CARMEN BEAUCHAMP, judge; b. N.Y.C., 1942. Grad., Hunter Coll., 1963; JD, St. John's U., 1967; LLD honoris causa, CUNY, Queens Coll., 1994. Staff atty. Legal Aid Soc., N.Y.C.; asst. counsel Office of the Judicial Conf., 1969-72; chief law asst. N.Y.C. Criminal Ct., 1972-74; counsel Office of N.Y.C. Adminstrv. Judge, 1974-78; judge N.Y.C. Criminal Ct., 1978-82, N.Y. Supreme Ct, 1982-94; assoc. judge N.Y. Ct. Appeals, N.Y.C., 1994—; former mem. N.Y. State Commn. Judicial Conduct; adj. prof. paralegal studies dept. N.Y.C. Tech. Coll., Bklyn. Trustee Boricua Coll.; bd. dirs. St. John's U. Sch. of Law Alumni Assn. Named to Hunter Coll. Hall of Fame, 1991. Mem. N.Y. Assn. Women Judges (bd. dirs.). Office: 60 Centre St New York NY 10007

CIPLIJAUSKAITE, BIRUTE, humanities educator; b. Kaunas, Lithuania, Apr. 11, 1929; came to U.S., 1957; d. Juozas and Elena (Stelmokaite) C. B.A., Lycee Lithuanien Tubingen, 1947, M.A., U. Montreal, 1956; Ph.D., Bryn Mawr Coll., 1960. Permanent mem. Inst. Rsch. in Humanities U. Wis., Madison, 1974, asst. prof., 1961-65, assoc. prof., 1965-68, prof., 1968-73, John Bascom prof., 1973—. Author: La Soledad y la poesia española contemporánea, 1962, El poeta y la poesia, 1966, Baroja, un estilo, 1972, Deber de plenitud: La poesia de Jorge Guillén, 1973, Los noventayochistas y la historia, 1981, La mujer insatisfecha, 1984, La novela femenina contemporánea (1970-85), 1988, Literaturos eskizai, 1992; editor: Luis de Gongora, Sonetos completos, 1969, critical edit., 1981, Jorge Guillén, 1975, (with C. Maurer) La voluntad de humanismo: Homenaje a Juan Marichal, 1990, Novisimos, postnovisimos, clásicos: la poesia de los 80 en España, 1991; translator: Juan Ramón Jiménez, Sidabrinukas ir as, 1982, María Victoria Atencia, Svenciausios Karalienes Ekstazes, 1989, Voces en el silencio: Poesia lituana contemporánea, 1991, Birute Pukeleviciute, Planto, 1994. Guggenheim fellow, 1968. Mem. Assn. For Advancement Baltic Studies (v.p. 1981), Asociación Internacional de Hispanistas. Office: U Wis Inst Rsch in Humanities 1401 Observatory Dr Madison WI 53706-1525

CIRCLE, LILIAS WAGNER, honor society administrator; b. Ann Arbor, Mich., Apr. 26, 1928; d. Herbert Phillip and Lilias Julia (Kendall) Wagner; m. Robert L. Jones, Dec. 29, 1951 (div. Jan. 1967); children: Lilias, Robert G., Eric D.; m. T. Robert Circle, Dec. 14, 1968; 1 child, Phillip T.; stepchildren: Jane Circle Asmuth, Thomas Rhys. BA in Speech, U. Mich., 1950. Student Interlochen (Mich.) Music Camp, 1944-47, staff, 1950; tchr. English, history Ann Arbor Pub. Schs., 1950-51; tchr. speech Eastern Mont. Coll., Billings, 1957; writer pub. rels. Chgo. Symphony Orch., 1967-68; adminstrv. asst. Leadership Greater Chgo., 1984; nat. sec. and treas. Pi Kappa Lambda, Evanston, Ill., 1984—; essayist, spkr. Lyric Opera Chgo., other orgns., 1986—; violist Evanston Symphony, 1960—; prodr. Savoy-aires, Evanston, 1964-89, soloist choral groups, 1974—. Author program notes Evanston Symphony, 1963—, Symphony II, 1992—, Allied Arts, Chgo. Symphony Chorus, Stagebill, Mostly Music Chamber Music Series, 1993—. Active St. Augustine's Ch., Wilmette, 1973—; class officer U. Mich., 1949—; mem. alumni bd. Interlochen Music Camp, 1979-81. Republican. Episcopalian. Club: Mich. Shores. Office: Pi Kappa Lambda Northwestern U Sch Music Evanston IL 60208-1200

CIRILO, AMELIA MEDINA, educational consultant, supervisor; b. Parks, Tex., May 23, 1925; d. Constancio and Guadalupe (Guerra) C.; m. Arturo Medina, May 31, 1953 (div. June 1979); children: Dennis Glenn, Keith Allen, Sheryl Amelia, Jacqueline Kim. B.S. in Chemistry, U. North Tex., 1950; M.Ed., U. Houston, 1954; Ph.D. in Edn. and Nuclear Engring., Tex. A&M U., 1975; cert. in radioisotope tech. Tex. Woman's U., Denton, 1962; cert. in Pub. Speaking Dale Carnegie, 1993. Cert. in supervision, bilingual Spanish, Tex.; cert. permament profl. tchr., Tex. Tchr. sci., dept. Starr County Schs., Rio Grande City, Tex., 1950-53; elem. tchr. San Benito-Brownsville, Tex., 1953-54, Kingsville (Tex.) Schs., 1954-56; tchr. sci. dept. head chem. physics LaJoya (Tex.) Pub. Schs., 1956-70; teaching asst. Tex. A&M U., College Station, 1970-74; instr. fire chemistry Del Mar Jr. Coll., Corpus Christi, Tex., 1974-75; exec. dir Hispanic Ednl. Research Mgmt. Analysis Nat. Assn., Inc., Corpus Christi, 1975-79; head dept. chem. physics San Isidro (Tex.) High Sch., 1979-82; tchr. chemistry W.H. Adamson High Sch., Dallas, 1982-84, Skyline High Sch. 1984-92; ednl. cons., 1992—; chmn. faculty adv. com., 1983-84; tchr. high intensity lang. sci. Skyline High Sch., Dallas, 1984-86, chem. tchr. 1986-92; mem. core faculty Union Grad. Coll., Cin., P.R., Ft. Lauderdale, and San Diego, 1975-79; mathematician Well Instrument Devel. Co., Houston, summers 1950-54; panelist, program evaluator Dept. of Edn., Washington, 1977-79; program evaluator, Robstown, Tex., 1975-79; tchr. trainer Edn. 20 and 2 Region Ctrs., Corpus Christi and San Antonio, 1975-79; researcher, writer Coll. Edn. and Urban Studies, Harvard U., Cambridge, Mass., 1978-80; vis. prof. bilingual dept. East Tex. State Coll., Commerce, 1978; ednl. cons. and supv. Adult Basic Edn. Lincoln Ctr., Dallas Pub. Schs., 1994—; conf. presenter program evaluation, 1977-79; rschr. Harvard U., 1983. Author: Comparative Evaluation of Bilingual Programs (named one of best U.S. books), 1978; Reflections (poetry), 1983; contbr. chpt. to book. NSF grantee The Women's U., 1963-65. bd. dirs. Meth. Home for Elderly, Weslaco, Tex., 1968, Am. Cancer Soc. fund drive, College Station, 1971-74; Brazos County advisor Tex. Constl. Revision Commn., 1973-74; sec. Goals for Corpus Christi Com. of 100; Corpus Christi rep. Southwestern Ednl. Authority, Edinburg, Tex., 1977-79; co-founder, bd. dirs. Women's Shelter, Corpus Christi, 1977-78; exec. bd. Nat. Com. Domestic Violence, 1978-80; pres. Elem. PTA, 1972-75; mem. Women's Polit. Caucus, Mex. Am. Democrats; Mem. Tex. Tchrs. Assn., NEA, Tex. Assn. Bilingual Educators, AAUW, Chem. Soc., Pan Am. Round Table, So. Sociol. Assn., Rocky Mountain Sociol. Assn., Metroplex Educators Sci. Assn., League United Latin Am. Citizens (pres. College Station 1973-74, past dist. dir. Corpus Christi), Fiesta Bilingual Toastmasters; bd. trustees Sci Cluster Skyline H.S., 1994—; Srs. Active in Life Adv. Com. Dallas City Parks & Recreation. Avocations: ballroom dancing, comedy. Home and Office: 4959 Lomax Dr Dallas TX 75227-2711

CIRONA, JANE CALLAHAN, investment vice president; b. Detroit, Feb. 23, 1949; d. Earl J. and Madeline Katherine (Freihaut) Callahan; children from previous marriage: Christopher Randall, Elisabeth Anne; m. James M. Cirona, Aug. 29, 1992. BA, Albion Coll., 1970; postgrad., Aquinas Coll., 1989—. Asst. mgr. Nat. Bank of Detroit, 1971-75; program coord. Muskegon (Mich.) Community Coll., 1978-79; services coord. Muskegon (Mich.) County Community Mental Health, 1979-81; supr. engring. services Teledyne Continental Motors, Muskegon; v.p. investment PaineWebber Inc., Muskegon, Mich., 1982—. Dir. Muskegon Econ. Growth Alliance, 1987—, Every Woman's Place, Muskegon, 1979-86; mem. Albion Coll. Planned Giving Adv. Bd., 1989—; mem. Commn. on Growth and Devel. Episcopal Diocese of Western Mich., 1985-88, Consumers Power Citizen Adv. Panel, Muskegon, 1983-84; bd. dirs. Mercy Hosp., Muskegon. Mem. Zonta Internat. Office: PaineWebber Inc PO Box 959 Muskegon WI 49443-0959

CISLER, THERESA ANN, osteopath, former nurse; b. Tucson, Dec. 20, 1951; d. William George and Lucille (Seeber) C.; 1 child, Daniel Luttrell. BSN, U. Ariz., 1974; DO, Kirksville Coll. Osteopathy, 1983. Operating room technician St. Joseph's Hosp., Tucson, 1973-74, operating room nurse, 1974-78, operating room inservice coordinator, 1978-79; intern Tucson Gen. Hosp., 1983-84; family practice and manipulation Assoc. Jane J. Beregi, D.O., Tucson, 1984-87; practice medicine specializing in osteo. manipulation Tucson, 1987—; active med. staff Tucson Gen. Hosp., 1984-91, med. records chmn., 1986-87; part-time med. staff Westcenter Drug & Rehab., Tucson, 1984-88; vol. med. staff St. Elizabeth Hugary Clinic, 1984-87; mem. substance abuse com. Westcenter-Tucson Gen. Hosp., 1986-88, osteo. concepts com., 1986-91, osteo. manipulative cons., 1986-91. Eucharistic min. St. Pius X Ch., Tucson, 1984-86, eucharistic min. coord., 1987-90. Mem. Am. Osteo. Assn., Am. Acad. Osteopathy, Ariz. Osteo. Med. Assn. (at-large ho. of dels. 1985-93, med. econs. com. 1993—), Kirksville Coll. Osteopathy-Century Club, Cranial Acad. Roman Catholic. Home and Office: 4002 E Grant Rd Ste D Tucson AZ 85712-2549

CISMARU, PAT KLEIN, municipal official; b. N.Y.C., Sept. 27, 1933; children: Jay, David. BBA, CCNY, 1958; MEd, CUNY, 1960; MS, Tex. Tech U., 1985, PhD, 1991. Lic. social worker, Tex.; OAMT mgmt. cert.; notary public, Tex. Owner Masonry Constrn. Co., Lubbock, Tex., 1980—; dir. respite unit LRMHMR Ctr., Lubbock, 1980-89; acad. dir. Park Coll., Lubbock, 1985-90; programs adminstr. RRIP Lubbock Housing Authority, 1989-93; owner rental property, N.J., Vt., Tex., Colo., 1972—; owner residential and comml. laundromats, Colo., 1991; convenience store, Colo., 1993—; tanning salons, Tex., 1993—; galaxy grocer. Mem. NAFE, AARP, LWV, NASW, Goodwill Industries. Home: 5108 79th Dr Lubbock TX 79424-3022 Office: PO Box 620693 Littleton CO 80162

CISNA, SUSAN JO, language arts educator; b. Mattoon, Ill., Jan. 24, 1950; d. William F. and Wanda L. (Bartimus) Grimes; m. Dennis E. Cisna, June 6, 1970; children: Michelle, Douglas. BS in Edn., Ea. Ill. U., 1971, MEd, 1992. 4th grade, 5th grade, 8th grade lang. arts tchr. Tuscola (Ill.) Dist. 301, 1970—; writing cons. Power Writing, Palo Alto, Calif., 1992-94. Citizens cons. com. Villa Grove (Ill.) City Coun., 1993-94. Mem. Nat. Coun. Tchrs. English, Ill. Reading Assn., Tuscola Edn. Assn., Phi. Delta Kappa. Home: 408 McCoy Cir Villa Grove IL 61956-9701 Office: East Prairie Sch 409 S Prairie St Tuscola IL 61953-1770

CISNEROS, EVELYN, dancer; b. Long Beach, Calif., 1955. Mem. San Francisco Ballet Co., 1977—. Performances include Scherzo, Mozart's C Minor Mass, Romeo and Juliet, Medea, The Tempest, 1980, Stars and Stripes, In the Night, A Midsummer Nights Dream, Cinderella, A Song for Dead Warriors, 1984, Confidences, 1986, Sleeping Beauty, 1992, Swan Lake, 1993. Office: San Francisco Ballet 455 Franklin St San Francisco CA 94102-4438 also: Peter S Diggins Assocs 133 W 71st St New York NY 10023-3834

CISZEK, SISTER BARBARA JEAN, educational administrator; b. Berwyn, Ill., June 8, 1946; d. Walter Arthur and Bernice Therese (Demski) C. AB, Loyola U., Chgo., 1971; MA, Concordia U., River Forest, Ill., 1987, CAS, 1994. Cert. tchr., adminstr., supr., Ill. 2d and 4th grade tchr. Our Lady of Mt. Carmel, Melrose Park, Ill., 1968; 1st grade tchr. St. Francis Xavier Sch., LaGrange, Ill., 1968-69; primary tchr. Alexine Montessori Sch., LaGrange Park, Ill., 1971-73, adminstr., tchr., 1973-79; dir. MECA Montessori Sch., Hinsdale, Ill., 1979-86; ednl. cons. CEDA, Chgo., 1988-91; exec. dir. Chgo. Metro Assn. for Edn. of Young Children, 1991—; adj. faculty mem. Concordia U., 1991—, mem. early childhood adv. bd., 1986—; mem. early childhood adv. bd. DePaul U., Chgo., 1994—; mem. adv. bd. Ill. Family-to-Family, 1993—; mem. McCormick Fellows bd. Nat. Louis U., Chgo., 1994. Co-author: Facilitating Montessori All Day, 1989. Mem. ASCD, Nat. Assn. for Edn. of Young Children (validator), Am. Montessori Soc. (cons., cert.), Ill. Montessori Soc. (bd. dirs. 1988-93), Chgo. Assn. for Edn. of Young Children (exec. dir.), Nat. Assn. Early Childhood Tchr. Educators. Office: Chgo Metro Assn Edn Young Children 410 S Michigan Ave Ste 525 Chicago IL 60605-1401

CITRIN, BETH EMILY, reading specialist; b. Schenectady, N.Y., Feb. 7, 1964; d. Lester Irving and Miriam (Friedenthal) C. AB, Duke U., 1985; EdM, Harvard U., 1989. Cert. tchr., reading specialist, adminstr., supr., Md., elem. tchr., reading tchr., Mass. Tchr. grades 2, 4, and 5 Bannockburn Elem. Sch., Bethesda, Md., 1985-88; reading specialist Highland Elem. Sch., Wheaton, Md., 1989-93, Kemp Mill Elem. Sch., Silver Spring, Md., 1993—; tchr. trainer Montgomery County Pub. Schs., Rockville, Md., 1993—; pvt. tutor, Bethesda, 1992—. Recipient Winfred Quinton Holton award Duke U., 1985, People Who Read Achieve award Southland Corp., Fairfax, Va., 1991, 92, 96; Edn. Found. grantee, 1995, Md. Coun. Maths. grantee, 1995. Mem. Phi Delta Kappa.

CITRON, BEATRICE SALLY, law librarian, lawyer, educator; b. Phila., May 19, 1929; d. Morris Meyer and Frances (Teplitsky) Levinson; m. Joel P. Citron, Aug. 7, 1955 (dec. Sept. 1977); children: Deborah Ann, Victor Ephraim. BA in Econs. with honors, U. Pa., 1950; MLS, Our Lady of the Lake U., 1978; JD, U. Tex., 1984. Bar: Tex. 1985; cert. all-level sch. libr., secondary level tchr., Tex. Claims examiner Social Security Adminstrn., Pa., Fla. and N.C., 1951-59; head libr. St. Mary's Hall, San Antonio, 1979-80; media, reference and rare book libr., asst. and assoc. prof. St. Mary's U. Law Libr., San Antonio, 1984-89; asst. dir. St. Thomas U. Law Libr., Miami, Fla., 1989-96, assoc. dir., 1996—, head pub. svc. Mem. ABA, Am. Assn. Law Librs. (publs. com. 1987-88, com. on rels. with info. vendors 1991-93, bylaws com. 1994-96), S.W. Assn. Law Librs. (continuing edn. com. 1986-88, chmn. local arrangements 1987-88), S.E. Assn. Law Librs. (newsletter, program and edn. coms. 1991-94), South Fla. Assn. Law Librs. (treas. 1992-94, v.p. 1994-95, pres. 1995-96). Office: St Thomas U Law Libr 16400 NE 32nd Ave Miami FL 33160

CITRON, DIANE, lawyer; b. Cin., Oct. 9, 1953; d. Carl and Georgia (Reid) C. B.A., Franklin and Marshall Coll., 1975; J.D., Case Western Res. U., 1978. Bar: D.C. 1978, Calif 1985. Assoc. Wasserman, Orlow, Ginsberg & Rubin, Washington, 1978-80; staff atty. U.S. SEC, Washington, 1980-83; sr. counsel Freddie Mac, Washington, 1983-84; assoc. Orrick, Herrington & Sutcliffe, San Francisco, 1984-85; assoc. Brown & Wood, San Francisco, 1985-87; spl. counsel Skadden, Arps, Slate, Meagher & Flom, San Francisco, 1987-92; ptnr. Mayer, Brown & Platt, Chgo., 1992—. Mem. ABA (bus. law sect., real property sect., subcom. securitization), Fed. Bar Assn., Women's Bar Assn. D.C., Bar Assn. D.C., Pi Gamma Mu. Democrat. Jewish. Office: Mayer Brown & Platt 190 S La Salle St Chicago IL 60603-3410

CIULLO, ROSEMARY, psychologist; b. Chgo.. BA, U. Ill., Chgo., 1974; MA, Gov.'s State U., University Park, Ill., 1977; PsyD with high distinction, Forest Inst. Profl. Psychology, 1986. Pvt. practice clin. psychologist North Shore Counseling & Consulting, Lake Zurich, Ill., 1995—. Mem. APA, Ill. Psychol. Assn., Orthopsychiatry. Office: 830 Main St Lake Zurich IL 60047

CIURCZAK, ALEXIS, librarian; b. Long Island, N.Y., Feb. 13, 1950; d. Alexander Daniel and Catherine Ann (Frangipane) C. BA Art History magna cum laude, U. Calif., L.A., 1971; MA Libr. Sci., San Jose State U., 1975; cert. tchr. ESL, U. Calif., Irvine, 1985. Intern IBM Rsch. Libr., San Jose, Calif., 1974-75; tech. asst. San Bernardino Valley Coll. Libr., Calif., 1975; tech. svcs. librarian Palomar Coll., San Marcos, Calif., 1975-78, pub. svcs. librarian, 1978-81, libr. dir., 1981-86, pub. svcs. librarian, 1987—, instr. Libr. Technology Cert. Program, 1975—; exchange librarian Fulham Pub. Libr., London, 1986-87; coord. San Diego C.C. Consortium Semester-in-London Am. Inst. Fgn. Study, 1988-89. Mem. ALA, San Diego Libr. Svcs. com., Calif. Libr. Media Educators Assn., Patronato por Niños, Kosciuszko Found., So. Calif. Tech. Processes Group, Pacific Coast Coun. Latin Am. Studies, Libros, Reforma, Libr. Assn. (British), Calif. Libr. Assn., Calif. Tchrs. Assn., Phi Beta Kappa, Beta Phi Mu. Office: Palomar CC 1140 W Mission Rd San Marcos CA 92069-1415

CIVISH, GAYLE ANN, psychologist; b. Lynnwood, Calif., Sept. 29, 1948; d. Leland and Arline (Frazer) Civish; children: Nathan Morrow, Shane Morrow. BA, U. Nev., Reno, 1970; MA, U. Colo., 1973, PhD, 1983. Lic. psychologist, Colo.; cert. sch. psychologist, Colo. Sch. psychologist Jefferson County (Colo.) Schs., 1983-89; psychologist in pvt. practice Lakewood, Colo., 1983—. Contbr. articles to profl. jours. Mem. APA, Colo. Psychol. Assn. (bd. dirs. 1990-93), Colo. Women Psychologists (past external liaison), Am. Soc. Clin. Hypnosis, Feminist Therapy Inst. (steering com. 1994—), Assn. for Women in Psychology, Phi Kappa Phi, Phi Delta Kappa. Democrat. Office: PO Box 713 Easton PA 18044

CLAASSEN, SHERIDA DILL, newspaper executive; b. Columbia, Mo., Nov. 27, 1948; d. Wilben Hubert and Dorothy Louise (Richardson) Dill; m. Arthur Norman Claassen, June 22, 1985; children: April Dill, Christopher Wilben. BJ, U. Mo., 1970; MBA, Pepperdine U., 1981. Editor Graphic Herald, Downers Grove, Ill., 1970-73; area editor Suburban Trib/Chgo. Tribune, 1973-78; copy editor San Jose (Calif.) Mercury, 1978-79, asst. metro. editor, 1979-81; city editor Wichita (Kans.) Eagle, 1981-82, asst. mng. editor, news, 1982-85, dir., R & D, 1985-91, exec. editor, 1991-94, v.p., assoc. pub., 1995—. Bd. dirs. Boys and Girls Club of Wichita, 1995—, Kids Voting Kans., 1995—, Roots & Wings, Wichita, 1989-91, Leaderhip Kans. Class 1989, Leadership 2000 Class 1991, Wichita; bd. advisors Salvation Army of Wichita, 1995—; v.p., bd. dirs. Wichita Festivals, Inc., 1988-91. Recipient Excellence in Entrepreneurship award Knight-Ridder, Inc., 1990. Office: Wichita Eagle PO Box 820 Wichita KS 67201-0820

CLAES, GAYLA CHRISTINE, writer, editorial consultant; b. L.A., Oct. 17, 1946; d. Henry George and Glorya Desiree (Curran) Blasdel; m. Daniel John Claes, Jan. 19, 1974. AB magna cum laude, Harvard U., 1968; postgrad., Oxford (Eng.) U., 1971; MA, McGill U., Montreal, 1975. Adminstrv. asst. U. So. Calif., L.A., 1968-70; teaching asst. English lit. McGill U., Montreal, 1970-71; editorial dir. Internat. Cons. Group, L.A., 1972-78; v.p. Gaylee Corp., L.A., 1978-81, CEO, 1981-88; writer, cons. L.A. and Paris, 1988—; dir. pub. rels. Centre Internat. for the Performing Arts, Paris and L.A., 1991—. Author: (play) Berta of Hungary, 1972, (novel) Christopher Derring, 1990; contbr. articles to lit. and sci. jours. Mem. Harvard-Radcliffe Club of So. Calif., Commonwealth Trust (London).

CLAIBORNE, LIZ (ELISABETH CLAIBORNE ORTENBERG), fashion designer; b. Brussels, Mar. 31, 1929; came to U.S., 1939; d. Omer Villere and Louise Carol (Fenner) C.; m. Arthur Ortenberg, July 5, 1954; 1 son by previous marriage, Alexander G. Schultz. Student, Art Sch., Brussels, 1948-49, Academie, Nice, France, 1950; DFA, R.I. Sch. Design, 1991. Asst. Tina Lesser, N.Y.C., 1951-52, Omar Khayam, Ben Reig, Inc., N.Y.C., 1953; designer Juniorite, N.Y.C., 1954-60, Dan Keller, N.Y.C., 1960-76, Youth Guild Inc., N.Y.C., 1976-89; designer, pres., chmn. Liz Claiborne Inc., N.Y.C., 1985-89, pres., 1976-89, chmn., chief oper. officer, until 1989; chmn. Liz Claiborne Cosmetics, 1985-89; guest lectr. Fashion Inst. Tech., Parsons Sch. Design; bd. dirs. Coun. of Am. Fashion Designers, Fire Island Lighthouse Restoration Com. Recipient Designer of Yr. award Palciode Hierro, Mexico City, 1976, Designer of Yr. award Dayton Co., Mpls., 1978, Ann. Disting. in Design award Marshall Field's, 1985, One Co. Makes a Difference award Fashion Inst. Tech., 1985, award Coun. Fashion Designers, 1986, Gordon Grand Fellowship award Yale U., 1989, Jr. Achievement award Nat. Bus. Hall of Fame, 1990, Frederick A.P. Barnard award Barnard Coll., 1991, Hon. Doctorate, R.I. Sch. of Design, 1991; named to Nat. Sales Hall of Fame, 1991. Mem. Fashion Group. Roman Catholic. *

CLAMAR, APHRODITE J., psychologist; b. Hartford, Conn.; d. James John and Georgia (Panas) Clamar; m. Richard Cohen, June 24, 1973. BA, CCNY, 1953; MA, Columbia U., 1955; PhD, NYU, 1978; student, Stella Adler Conservatory of Acting and Playwrights Horizon Thetare Sch., 1987-91. Mgmt. cons., psychologist Milla Alihan Assocs., N.Y.C., 1957-62; rsch. psychologist coord. Inst. Devel. Studies N.Y. Med. Coll., N.Y.C., 1964; intern psychologist Bellevue Psychiat. Hosp., N.Y.C., 1964-66; assoc. prof. Fashion Inst. Tech., N.Y.C., 1966-69; supervising psychologist Lifeline Ctr. Child Devel., N.Y.C., 1966-67; chief psychologist I Spy Health Program Beth Israel Med. Ctr., N.Y.C., 1967-70; dir. community-sch. mental health programs Soundview Community Svcs., Albert Einstein Coll. Medicine Yeshiva U., N.Y.C., 1970-73; dir. treatment program court-related children, dept. child psychiatry Harlem Hosp.; mem. faculty dept. psychiatry Coll. Physicians and Surgeons Columbia U., N.Y.C., 1973-76; pvt. practice psychotherapy N.Y.C., 1976-95; pres. Richard Cohen Assocs. Pub. Rels., N.Y.C., 1995—; cons. to pub. health and mental health agys., N.Y.C., 1976-91; mem. faculty Lenox Hill Hosp. Psychoanalytic and Psychotherapy Tng. Program, 1982-88; theater producer, artistic dir. Tom Cat Cohen Prodns., Inc., 1990—. Author: (with Budd Hopkins) Missing Time, 1981; contbr. articles to profl. jours. Fellow AAAS; mem. APA, Dramatists Guild, Authors Guild. Democrat. Greek Orthodox. Home: 162 E 80th St New York NY 10021-0439 Office: 40 W 55th St New York NY 10019

CLAMON, HARLEYNE DIANNE, retired social service supervisor; b. Camden, Tex., Feb. 12, 1940; d. Harley and Ada Virginia (Handley) C. BA, Sam Houston U., 1961. Lic. master social worker, Tex. Tchr. Big Sandy Ind. Sch., Dallardsville, Tex., 1961-62; social worker Tex. Dept. Human Svcs., Tex. City, 1962-75; social service supr. Tex. Dept. Human Svcs., Galveston, 1975-79, Tex. City, 1979-80, Livingston, 1980-92. Mem. adv. com. Mental Health, Mental Retardation, Livingston, Tex., 1980-87, chmn., 1982-87; vol. Polk County Meml. Hosp., 1982—; adult ladies Sunday sch. tchr. Leggett Bapt. Ch., 1984-95, song leader, 1994-95. Mem. AAUW (pres. Livingston 1984-86), DAR (Indian chmn. 1984-86, chaplain Livingston chpt. 1992-94), Bus. and Profl. Women (pres. Livingston 1983-85, Woman of Yr. 1982-83), Am. Pub. Welfare Assn., Tex. Pub. Employees Assn. (bd. dirs. 1970-75), Polk County Hist. Commn. (vice chmn. 1994-95, chmn. 1996—), Sam Houston State U. Alumni. Democrat. Baptist. Home: 616 W Calhoun St Livingston TX 77351-2751

CLANCY, HEATHER ANNE, editor; b. Mpls., July 21, 1965; d. Gerald Patrick Clancy and Beth Ann (Hazzard) Richardson. BA in English Lit., McGill U., 1987. Bus. writer United Press Internat., N.Y.C., 1987-89; assoc. editor Computer Reseller News, Manhasset, N.Y., 1989-91; sr. editor Computer Reseller News, San Jose, Calif., 1991-93; emerging technologies editor Computer Reseller News, San Mateo, Calif., 1993-95; editor spl. reports Computer Reseller News, Jericho, N.Y., 1995—. Democrat. Roman Catholic.

CLANCY, MARY CATHERINE, Canadian Parliament member; b. Halifax, N.S., Can., Jan. 13, 1948; d. Douglas and Catherine (Casey) C. BA with honors, Mt. St. Vincent U., Halifax, 1970; LLB, Dalhousie U., Halifax, 1974; LLM, U. London. Lawyer, broadcaster, univ. lectr., columnist; mem. Parliament, Ottawa, Ont., Can., 1988—; apptd. parliamentary sec. Min. of Citizenship & Immigration, Ottawa, 1993—; apptd. chair standing com. Nat. Defence & Veteran's Affairs, 1996—. Bd. govs. Dalhousie U.; bd. govs. Mt. St. Vincent U., pres. nat. bd. alumni; v.p. Atlantic region Nat. Women's Liberal Commn.; pres. St. Joseph's Children's Ctr.; bd. dirs. YWCA, Atlantic Ballet Co., Home of Guardian Angel, Seaweed Theatre. Mem. N.S. Barristers Soc. Liberal. Roman Catholic. Home: 6066 Coburg Rd, Halifax, NS Canada B3H 1Z2 Office: House of Commons, 461 Confederation Bldg, Ottawa, ON Canada K1A 0A6 also: 2131 Gottingen St Ste 210, Halifax, NS Canada B3K 5Z7

CLAPPER, MARIE ANNE, magazine publisher; b. Chgo., Nov. 21, 1942; d. Chester William and Hazel Alice (Gilso) Reinke; m. William Neil Petersen, Aug. 17, 1963 (div. 1975); children: Elaine Myrtice, Edward William; m. Lyle N. Clapper, Jan. 1, 1980; children: Jeffrey Leland, Anne Reinke; stepchildren: John Scott, Susan Louise. Student, Augustana Coll., Rock Island, Ill., 1960-63; EdB, Northeastern U., 1964. Writer Pack-o-Fun mag., Park Ridge, Ill., 1976-77; editor Pack-o-Fun mag., Des Plaines, Ill., 1977-78, pub., 1990—; asst. to pub., circulation dir. Crafts 'n Things mag., Des Plaines, Ill., 1978-82, pub., 1982—; pub. Decorative Arts Painting mag., Des Plaines, 1990—, The Cross Stitcher mag., Des Plaines, 1991—, Bridal Crafts mag., Des Plaines, 1991—; pub., pres. Clapper pub. Host TV show The Crafts 'n Things Show, 1984-86, Crafting for the 90s, 1990-94. Mem. Mag. Pubs. Am. (bd. dirs.), Hobby Industry Am. (bd. dirs.), Soc. Craft Designers. Office: Crafts 'n Things Ste 375 2400 Devon Des Plaines IL 60018-4618

CLAPS, JUDITH BARNES, educational consultant; b. N.Y.C., Sept. 8, 1938; d. Milton and Marguerite (Goodkind) Tarlau; m. Wayne C. Barnes, July 17, 1957 (div. 1968); children: David, Dan; m. Francis S. Claps, June 25, 1978. BA, Antioch Coll., 1961; MEd, Lehigh U., 1964; AA, Inst. Reality Therapy, Calif., 1984. Tchr. Cedarville (Ohio) Schs., 1960-61, Quakertown (Pa.) Schs., 1961-62; tchr. Bethlehem (Pa.) Schs., 1962-91, social worker, 1991-95; in-svc. cons. JB Claps & Assocs., Hellertown, Pa., 1982—; adj. prof. East Stroudsburg U., Pa., 1982-90; pre. Lehigh Valley Coun. for Social Studies, 1990-92; judge Nat. History Day, U. Md., 1989—. Author: Becoming a Better Parent: Take Control One Decision at a Time, 1996; creator: (video) Rap It Up, 1993, (pamphlet) Rap It Up, 1984, Bethlehem, 1986, Freemansburg-A Canal Town, 1984. Ednl. creator, bd. dirs. Burnside Plantation, Bethlehem, 1982; mem. adv. coun. Ret. and Sr. Vol. Program. Named History Tchr. of Yr., DAR, Bethlehem, 1984, Pa. Soc. Studies Tchr. of Yr., Pa. Coun. for Social Studies, 1989, nominated for Pa. Tchr. of Yr., 1990. Mem. Inst. Realty Therapy and Control Theory, NEA, Pa. State Edn. Assn., Bethlehem Edn. Assn., Phi Delta Kappa. Home: 3430 Drifting Dr Hellertown PA 18055-9601

CLARDY, MARY JOANNE, gifted education educator; b. Kansas City, Mo., Sept. 11, 1955; d. Norris Alger and Mary Jane (Brewster) Smith. AA, Miss. County Coll., 1985; BA, Gov.'s State U., University Park, Ill., 1988, MA in English, 1992. Cert. tchr, Ill., Mo.; cert. gifted students tchr., Ill. Tchr. Sch. Dist. #160, Country Club Hills, 1989-94; tchr., coord. gifted program Sch. Dist. #159, Mokena, Ill., 1994—; instr. Mississippi County C.C., summers 1993—; instr. Joliet Jr. Coll. Active NOW. Mem. NEA, Internat. Platform Assn. Home: 206 N East St Wilmington IL 60481

CLARE, CONSTANCE VIOLET, writer, dancer; b. N.Y.C., Mar. 28, 1962; d. Don Creighton and Frances Lorraine (Skerrett) Marsh. BA in Women's Lit. with honors, Mills Coll., 1996. Horse trainer, riding instr. various riding schools, Calif. and Europe, 1981-89; dancer Anne Bluethenthal & Dancers, San Francisco, 1991-94, Purple Moon Dance Project, San Francisco, 1992-95; bookseller, event coord. Old wives Tales Bookstore, San Francisco, 1992-95; painter, co-owner Mico Painting, San Francisco, 1993—. Contbr. chpt. The Femme Mystique, 1995. Vol. Green Party, Santa Barbara, Calif., 1990. Recipient Women's Studies Essay prize Mills Coll., 1995. Home: 91 Coleridge St San Francisco CA 94110

CLARE, JAN ROSE, secondary school educator; b. Sulphur Springs, Tex., Jan. 2, 1947; d. Ernest Alton and Rachel Frances (Spinks) Purdy; m.

Richard William Clare, July 26, 1969; children: Seth, Rhett, Shane. BS in Home Econs. Edn., North Tex. State U., 1969; MS in Edn., Stephen F. Austin State U., 1977. Cert. presch. dir. H.S. tchr. Garland (Tex.) Ind. Sch. Dist., 1969-74; presch. tchr. St. Peter's Sch., McKinney, Tex., 1986-88, presch. dir., 1988-91; tchr., presch. dir. McKinney H.S., 1991—; mem. tech. prep. steering com., mem. tech. prep. adv. bd. Collin County C.C., McKinney, 1993—; mem. Early Childhood Adv. Coun., 1990—, Teenage Parent Adv. Com., 1990—; Global Edge Steering Com., 1993—. Bd. dirs. St. Peter's Sch., 1979-89; sponsor Future Homemakers Am., McKinney, 1990—. Office: McKinney Ind Sch Dist McKinney HS 1400 Wilson Creek Pky Mc Kinney TX 75069-5320

CLARIZIO, JOSEPHINE DELORES, corporate services executive, former manufacturing and engineering company executive, foundation executive; b. Montclair, N.J., Dec. 15, 1922; d. Thomas and Raffaela (Caruso) D'Andrea; m. N. Robert Clarizio, June 3, 1951. Cert., Katharine Gibbs Sch., 1942; B.S., Seton Hall U., 1947; postgrad., Fordham U. Sch. Law, 1947-48, N.Y. Inst. Fin., 1964. Registered rep. Drexel, Burnham & Co., N.Y.C., 1965-70; asst. to pres. Wheelabrator-Frye Inc., Hampton, N.H., 1970-78, corp. sec., 1981-83; pres. Wheelabrator Found. Inc., Hampton, 1978-84; cons. Signal Cos. Inc., N.Y.C., N.H., 1984-86. Mem. Seton Hall U. Alumni Assn. Republican. Roman Catholic.

CLARIZIO, LYNDA M., lawyer; b. Newark, Aug. 19, 1960. AB summa cum laude, Princeton U., 1982; JD, Harvard U., 1985. Bar: D.C. 1985. Ptnr. Arnold & Porter, Washington. Articles editor Harvard Internat. Law Jour., 1984-85. Mem. Phi Beta Kappa. Office: Arnold & Porter 555 12th St NW Washington DC 20004-1202*

CLARK, BARBARA JUNE, elementary education educator; b. Leoti, Kans., May 29, 1934; d. Robert Carter and Adlee Belle (Wilson) C. BS in Edn., Ft. Hays State U., 1958, MS in Edn., 1967. Fourth grade tchr. McKinley Elem., Liberal, Kans., 1954-56; fourth grade tchr. Lincoln Elem., Liberal, 1958-61, 62—, fifth grade tchr., 1961-62; mathfest chmn. Unified Sch. Dist. 480, Liberal, 1987-88, grade level chmn., 1988-89, social studies textbook selection com., 1990-92, Lincoln Sch. site coun., 1993-94, Lincoln preassessment team, 1992—, Lincoln strategic action com., 1994—, reading textbook selection com., 1995-96, others. Editor: Wilson History, 1970—. Singer Meth. Chancel Choir; rec. sec. United Meth. Ch. Circle 9, 1986-88, v.p., 1996—. Recipient Representative Young Tchr. award Jr. C. of C., Liberal, 1962, PTA Life Membership, Lincoln Elem., Liberal, 1962. Mem. NEA, Kans. Edn. Assn., Liberal Edn. Assn. (Master Tchr. award 1989), Bus. and Profl. Women's Club (pres. 1979-80, treas. 1989-90, 94—, v.p. 1991-94, fin. chair 1992—, Woman of Yr. award 1974), Beta Sigma Phi (treas. 1981-91, pres. 1991—, Silver Circle award 1992, Order of Rose award 1974), Delta Kappa Gamma (rec. sec. 1986-88, music chmn. 1992-94, Phi state conv. registration chmn. 1994-95). Office: Lincoln Elem Sch Eleventh and Calhoun Liberal KS 67901

CLARK, BARBARA MARLENE, state legislator; b. Beckley, W.Va., June 12, 1939; m. Thomas Clark; children: Jan, Crystal, Thomas II, Brian. Mem. N.Y. State Assembly, 1986—; past mem. assembly standing com. on aging, housing, small bus., and social svcs.; mem. standing com. on children and families, corps., authorities and commns. edn. and labor. V.p. Parents Assn.; mem. exec. bd., prin. consultative coun. Andrew Jackson H.S., Sprinfield Garden Jr. H.S., P.S. 176, Cambria Heights, N.Y.; mem. adv. coun. Teen Pregnancy Prevention Program; active NAACP, Nat. Coun. Negro Women. Democrat. Home: 12056 224th St Cambria Heights NY 11411-2141 Office: NY State Assembly State Capitol Albany NY 12248*

CLARK, BEVERLY ANN, lawyer; b. Davenport, Iowa, Dec. 9, 1944; d. F. Henry and Arlene F. (Meyer) C.; m. Richard Floss; children: Amy and Barry (twins). Student, Mich. State U., 1963-65; BA, Calif. State U.-Fullerton, 1967; MSW, U. Iowa, 1975, JD, 1980. Bar: Iowa 1980; lic. social worker, Iowa. Probation officer County of San Bernardino, San Bernardino, Calif., 1968, County of Riverside, Riverside, Calif., 1968-69; social worker Skiff Hosp., Newton, Iowa, 1971-73; social worker State of Iowa, Mitchellville, 1973-74, planner, Des Moines, 1976-77, law clk., Des Moines, 1980-81; instr. Des Moines Area C.C., Ankeny, Iowa, 1974-75; corp. counsel Pioneer Hi-Bred Internat., Inc., Des Moines, 1981—; adj. prof. Drake Law Sch.; pub. Sweet Annie Press; owner Annie's Place, The B&B Connection Gift Catalog. Editor: Proceedings: Bicentennial Symposium on New Directions in Juvenile Justice, 1975; contbr. articles to profl. jours. Founder Mothers of Twins Club, Newton, Iowa, 1971; co-chmn. Juvenile Justice Symposium, Des Moines, 1974-75; mem. Juvenile Justice Com., Des Moines, 1974-75; mem. Nat. Offender Based State Corrections Info. System Com., Ia. rep., 1976-78; incorporator, dir. Iowa Dance Theatre, Des Moines, 1981; mem. Pesticide User's Adv. Com., Fort Collins, Colo., 1981-88; co-developer Iowa Migrant Ombudsmen Project, Pioneer, Inc. and Proteus, Inc. Recipient Disting. Alumni award U. Iowa, 1990, Nat. award Ctr. for Pub. Resources. Mem. ABA (subcom. on devel. individual rights in work place, termination-at-will subcom. 1982—), Iowa Bar Assn., Polk County Bar Assn., Polk County Women Atty.'s Assn., Am. Trial Lawyers Assn., Am. Assn. Agrl. Lawyers, Am. Seed Trade Assn., Am. Corp. Counsel Assn., Ctr. for Pub. Resource. Home: 7750 Highway F24 W Baxter IA 50028-8558 Office: Pioneer Hi-Bred Internat Inc 700 Capital Sq 400 Locust St Ste 700 Des Moines IA 50309-2331

CLARK, BEVERLY JEAN, lawyer, mediator; b. Detroit, May 21, 1939; d. Harry and Evelyn Blanche (Mabin) C. BA, U. Mich., 1961, MA, 1963; JD, Wayne State U., 1972. Bar: Mich. 1973, U.S. Dist. Ct. (ea. dist.) Mich. 1973, U.S. Dist. Ct. (we. dist.) Mich. 1990, U.S. Ct. Appeals (6th dist.) 1973. Pvt. practice Detroit, 1973—; bd. dirs. Mich. Indian Legal Services, Traverse City. Co-founder Mich. Women's Campaign Fund, Detroit; mem. Mich. Civil Rights Commn., 1981-91, chmn., 1991. Named Ford Scholar, Ford Motor Co., 1957-61. Fellow Am. Acad. Matrimonial Lawyers; mem. Acad. Family Mediators, Mich. Trial Lawyers Assn. (pres. 1983-84), Women Lawyers Assn. (pres. 1978-79, First in Leadership 1987), Mich. Coun. for Family and Divorce Mediation (pres. 1996—), Mediation Works (dir.). Democrat. Office: 440 E Congress St Ste 4R Detroit MI 48226-2917

CLARK, CANDY, actress; b. Norman, Okla.; d. Thomas Prest and Ella Lee (Padberg) C. Student public schs., Ft. Worth. Appeared in movies Fat City, 1971, American Graffiti, 1973 (nominated for best supporting actress), The Man Who Fell to Earth, 1975, Citizens Band, 1976, The Big Sleep, 1977, When Ya' Coming Back Red Ryder, 1978, More American Graffiti, 1978, National Lampoon Goes to the Movies, 1981, Blue Thunder, 1981, Amityville 3-D, 1983, Stephen King's Cat's Eye, 1984, At Close Range, 1986, The Blob, 1988, Cool-As-Ice, 1991, Buffy the Vampire Slayer, 1992, Radioland Murders, 1994; appeared in TV movies Amateur Night at the Dixie Bar and Grill, 1978, Where The Ladies Go, 1980, Rodeo Girl, 1980, Popeye Doyle, 1986, Plan of attack, 1992; appeared in off-Broadway show A Coupla White Chicks Sitting Around Talking, 1981, (play) It's Raining on Hope Street, 1988, Loose Lips, 1995.

CLARK, CAROL GRACE, marketing engineer; b. Honolulu, Hawaii; m. Michael James Clark, Feb. 29, 1996. BS in Geol. Scis., U. Wash., 1984; MSE in Materials Sci. and Engring., U. Mich., 1987; MS in Engring. Mgmt., Nat. Tech. U., 1994. Intern Lunar and Planetary Inst. NASA Johnson Space Ctr., Houston, 1984, vis. grad. fellow Lunar and Planetary Inst., 1985; sr. process engr. Intel Corp., Aloha, Oreg., 1988-94; Pentium Pro processor product mgr. Intel Corp., Hillsboro, Oreg., 1994—. Democrat. Roman Catholic.

CLARK, CAROLYN CHAMBERS, nurse, author, educator; b. Superior, Wis., Mar. 25, 1941; d. John and Phyllis (Olsen) Stark. BS, U. Wis., 1964; MS, Rutgers U., Newark, 1966; EdD, Columbia U., 1976. RN, Fla.; cert. advanced registered nurse practitioner, Fla. Instr. Bergen Community Coll., Paramus, N.J., 1972-74; pvt. practice wellness nursing, 1972—; found, dir. The Wellness Inst., Sloatsburg, 1979-84; assoc. prof. Pace U., Pleasantville, N.Y., 1983-84; prof., wellness coord. U. Tampa, Fla., 1984-85; cons. VA Med. Ctr., Bay Pines, Fla., 1988-89, provider continuing programs for nurses, 1990—; nurse practitioner/cons. Bay Area Psychol. Svcs., 1994—; dir. Women's Wellness Ctr. of the Resource Ctr. for Women, 1994—. Author: Nursing Concepts and Processes, 1977, The Nurse as Group Leader, 1977, 3rd edit., 1994 (also pub. in Swedish, German), Mental Health Aspects of Community Health Nursing, 1978, Classroom Skills for Nurse Educators, 1978, Assertive Skills for Nurses, 1978, Management in Nursing, 1979, The Nurse as Continuing Educator, 1979, Enhancing Wellness: A Guide for Self-Care, 1981, Wellness Nursing: Concepts, Theory, Research and Practice, 1986, Deadlier than Death, 1993, Dangerous Alibis, Cast Into The Fire, 1994, Wellness Practitioner, 1996; editor, pub. The Wellness Newsletter, 1980-94; editor Alternative Health Practitioner: The Jour. of Complimentary and Natural Care, 1995—; pres. Wellness Resources, 1992—; contbr. articles to profl. jours.; mem. editorial bd. Am. Jour. Holistic Nursing, 1985-88, Women's Health Care Internat., 1985—. Grantee, N.J. Blue Cross, 1982, Robert Wood Johnson Found., 1983; recipient award Fla. Free Lance Writers Assn., 1988, 92. Fellow Am. Acad. Nursing; mem. Mystery Writers Am., Sisters in Crime. Office: 3451 Central Ave Saint Petersburg FL 33713-8522

CLARK, CAROLYN COCHRAN, lawyer; b. Kansas City, Mo., Oct. 30, 1941; d. John Rogers and Betty Charleton (Holmes) Cochran; m. L. David Clark, Jr., Dec. 29, 1967; children: Gregory David, Timothy Rogers. BA, U. Mo., 1963; LLB, Harvard U., 1968. Bar: N.Y. 1968, Fla. 1979. Assoc. Milbank, Tweed, Hadley & McCloy, N.Y.C., 1968-76, ptnr., 1977—. Mem. deferred giving com., former regional chmn. major gifts com. Harvard Law Sch. Fund; mem. vis. com. Harvard Law Sch., 1982-88; mem. com. on trust and estate gift plans Rockefeller U.; trustee Madison Ave. Presbyn. Ch., 1984-86, N.Y. Botanical Garden, 1993—, Vis. Nurse Assn. N.Y. and Vis. Nurse Health Care, 1991—, Riverdale Country Sch., 1994—, Milbane Meml. Fund, 1996—; del. John D. Rockefeller Conf. Philanthropy in the 21st Century, N.Y., 1989; bd. advisors NYU program Philanthropy and the Law; chmn. NYU Tax Inst. program Taxation of Exempt Organizations. Recipient Disting. Alumna award U. Mo., 1989. Fellow Am. Coll. Trust and Estate Counsel (chmn. com. on charitable giving and exempt orgns.), N.Y. Bar Found., Am. Bar Found.; mem. ABA (chmn. subcom. income taxation of charitable trusts 1976-78, chmn. com. charitable instns. 1989-94), Assn. Bar City of N.Y. (chmn. com. on non-profit orgns. 1986-89, sec. com. philanthropic orgns. 1976-82, mem. com. trusts, estates and surrogates cts. 1977-80, 85-86), N.Y. State Bar Assn. (com. estate planning, trusts and estates sect. 1978-89), Am. Law Inst., Practising Law Inst. (lectr.), Harvard U. Law Sch., Assn. Greater N.Y. (trustee 1978-80, v.p. 1980-81, pres. 1981-82), NYU Tax Inst. (chmn. conf. tax planning charitable orgns. 1993-95), Nat. Harvard Law Sch. Alumni Assn. (exec. com. 1978-80, v.p. 1986-90, pres. 1990-92), Soc. Colonial Dames Am. in Mo., Maidstone Club. Home: 161 E 79th St New York NY 10021-0421 Office: Milbank Tweed Hadley & McCloy 1 Chase Manhattan Plz 54th Fl New York NY 10005

CLARK, CHARLENE ELIZABETH, nursing educator; b. Spokane, Wash., Jan. 8, 1941; d. Carl G. and Anna E. (Miller) Miller; m. Robert S. Clark, Apr. 14, 1962; children: Robert S. Jr., Jeffrey C. Diploma in nursing, Sacred Heart Sch. Nursing, Spokane, 1962; BS, Whitworth Coll., 1965, MEd, 1974. RN, Wash. Instr Sacred Heart Sch. Nursing, Spokane, 1962-66; instr. RN refresher course Spokane Community Coll., 1968; from instr. to prof. Intercollegiate Ctr. for Nursing Edn. Wash. State U., Spokane, 1969-94, dir. learning resource Intercollegiate Ctr. for Nursing Edn., 1981-95, asst. dean for instrnl. resources, 1995—; cons. in field. Contbr. articles to profl. jours. Recipient nurse excellence award: edn. Mem. ANA, Assn. Ednl. Comm./Tech. (continuing edn. com.), Am. Acad. Nursing, Sigma Theta Tau. Office: Wash State U W 2917 Fort George Wright Spokane WA 99204

CLARK, CHRISTINE MAY, editor, author; b. Peoria, Ill., Apr. 25, 1957; d. Darrell Ronald and Alice Venita (Burkitt) French; m. Terry Randolph Clark, Aug. 28, 1982. BA, Judson Coll., 1978. Assoc. editor David C. Cook Pub., Elgin, Ill., 1978-80; editor Humpty Dumpty, 1980-94; editor Children's Digest, 1980-83, Jack and Jill , 1983-86, Turtle mag., 1990—; editorial dir. Children's Better Health Inst., Indpls.; assoc. editor Highlights for Children, Honesdale, Pa., 1994-96; mng. editor Highlights for Children, 1996—; speaker Pacific Northwest Writers' Conf., 1986, Soc. Children's Book Writers Confs., Tex., 1987, 88, Reader's Digest Writers' Confs., S.C., 1989, W.Va., 1990, Seattle Pacific U., 1991, Highlights Found. Writers Workshop at Chautauqua, 1993. Author: (religious curriculum) Come, Follow Me, 1983, Living in Covenant, 1985. Contbr. articles and stories to children's and adult religious mags., also to Indpls. Monthly, Indpls. Woman, This Is Indianapolis, Key Horizons. Asst. scout leader Fox Valley Council Girl Scouts U.S., 1972; vol. Elgin Mental Health Ctr., 1975-76; big sister Big Sister-Little Sister Program, Elgin, 1980. Recipient journalism award EDPRESS, 1986, 87, 88, 89, 90, 92, Outstanding Reporting award Soc. Profl. Journalists, 1990; Aurora Found. scholar, 1975. Mem. Am. Soc. Mag. Editors, Soc. Children's Book Writers and Illustrators, Ednl. Press Assn., Judson Coll. Alumni Assn. Reorganized Ch. of Jesus Christ of Latter-day Saints. Avocations: Piano; travel. Office: Highlights for Children 803 Church St Honesdale PA 18431-1824

CLARK, DEBRA FEIOCK, marketing professional; b. Frankfurt, Fed. Republic Germany, June 19, 1958; came to U.S., 1960; d. Ray Donald Feiock and Joanne (Hackler) MacNiven; m. Steven D. Clark, Sept. 5, 1981 (div. 1986). BA in Communications, Calif. State U., Fullerton, 1981; cert. in mktg., U. Calif., Berkeley. Mgr. Foto Hall, Inc., Tustin, Calif., 1979-82; copy products sales rep. Kodak Copy Products, Los Angeles, 1982-85; electronic pub. sales Kodak Copy Products, Whittier, Calif., 1985-88; comml. mktg. Kodak Electronic Photography, Fremont, Calif., 1988—; regional account mgr. Thermal Printing Systems Eastman Kodak Co., 1990-92, bus. devel. mgr. Printer Producers Divsn., 1992-96, nat. sales mgr. digital and applied imaging, 1996—; guest speaker Fullerton (Calif.) Community Coll., 1988. Vol. Internat. Spl. Olympics, Reno, 1989, Girl Scouts U.S., 1989-90; mem. leadership team Young Adults Fellowship, Menlo Park Presbyn. ch., 1995. Mem. Sigma Kappa Sorority Alumni Assn. (pres. 1987-88). Presbyterian. Office: Eastman Kodak 37741 Madera Ct Fremont CA 94536-6637

CLARK, DESMOND LAVERNE, immigration legal secretary, editor, minister; b. Omaha, May 4, 1951; d. Thomas Edward and Louise Gwendolyn (Jackson) C. BS, Tenn. State U., 1973. Sec. Atlanta (Ga.) Housing Authority, 1973, modernization asst., 1974, contract coord., 1977; word processor, proof reader Touche Ross & Co., Miami, 1981, word processing supr., 1989; asst. editor Innerself Publs., Hollywood, Fla., 1991-93; legal sec. immigration law, 1996—; editor Innerself Publs., Hollywood, Fla., 1993-96; interfaith minister Interfaith Seminary, N.Y.C., 1993—; profl. entertainer Curtain Call Prodns., Ft. Lauderdale, Fla., 1990-96. Mem. exec. com. Dem. Party, Miami, 1980-88. Mem. Asn. Interfaith Ministry. Home: 3150 NW 135th St # 1 Opa Locka FL 33054-4884 Office: TK Mahon PA 2929 E Commercial Blvd #PHE Fort Lauderdale FL 33308

CLARK, DIANNA LEA, broadcast executive; b. Lincoln, Ill., June 27, 1956; d. Raymond Burnell and Patricia JoAnn (Bartlc) Kirby; m. Robert Allen Clark, Nov. 25, 1978. AA, Springfield (Ill.) Coll., 1976; BA, Sangamon State U., Springfield, 1979. With broadcast svcs. Sangamon State U., 1977-80; traffic dir. Sta. WIL-FM, St. Louis, 1980-85; ops. dir. Sta. KCLC Lindenwood Coll., St. Charles, Mo., 1985-86; radio sta. mgr. St. Louis C.C. at Flo Valley, St. Louis, 1986—. Mem. Am. Legion Aux. Mem. Am. Bus. Women's Assn. (sec. regional conf. 1990-92, Woman of Yr. 1986, 92), St. Charles Women's Bowling Assn. (bd. dirs. 1993—), When In Need of Service Bowling Club (sec.- treas., bd. dirs. 1983—), Nat. Broadcasting Soc./Alpha Epsilon Rho (nat. v.p. 1995—, coord. nat. conv. 1987, 93, chmn. nat. project on Tourette syndrome 1984-92, dir. regional conv. 1989-91, 94, Nat. Outstanding Mem. 1986, Nat. Honor Lifetime Mem. 1990). Office: St Louis CC Sta KCFV 3400 Pershall Rd Saint Louis MO 63135-1408

CLARK, ELIZABETH ANNETTE, insurance company administrator; b. Mpls., Oct. 6, 1934; d. Walter Burdette and Daveda Marguerite (Hansen) Garver; m. Forrest Halter, May 17, 1958 (div. Feb. 1973); children: Gregory, Linda Halter Balsiger; m. Leslie Matthew Clark, Sept. 28, 1976. AA, Montgomery Coll., 1954; AAS, Greenville (S.C.) Tech. Coll., 1973; B in Gen. Studies, Furman U., 1979; MBA, Clemson (S.C.) U., 1987. CLU. Data processor Liberty Life Ins. Co., Greenville, 1973-84, mgr. quality improvement dept., 1984-88, dir. project mgmt., 1989, asst. v.p. policy forms, 1989—; instr. computer programming part-time Greenville Tech. Coll., 1980-81. Sec. S.C./Piedmont chpt. Nat. Multiple Sclerosis Soc., Greenville, 1974-76; bd. dirs. Greenville Little Theatre, 1974-76; chmn. invitation com. Bicentennial Ball, Greenville, 1976; mem. Speakers' Bur., Family Counseling Ctr., 1991—. Fellow Life Mgmt. Inst.; mem. Life Office Mgmt. Assn. (rep. so. systems devel. commn. 1985-90, program chmn. 1987-88, sec. 1988-89, chmn. 1989-90), EFS Users (v.p. 1992-95), Life and Health Compliance Assn. (mem. exec. com.), Am. Coun. Life Ins. (task force on policy forms filing 1994-95), Mensa, Beta Sigma Phi (pres. Greenville chpt. 1975-76, 93-94, v.p. coun. 1975-76, Woman of Yr. 1975, 89, 90, 93, Alpha-Omega award 1977). Unitarian. Home: 121 Rockwood Dr Greenville SC 29605-1942

CLARK, ETHEL T., realtor; b. Marion, S.C., Jan. 18, 1946; d. Ellie C. and Helen B. (Davis) Fore; m. James Thomas, Aug. 14, 1964 (div.) children: Jonathan V., James D.; m. David L. Clark, Sept. 5, 1981. Cert. resdl. specialist Realtors Inst. Office mgr., realtor, fin. svcs. dir. Hall Real Estate, Spring Lake, NC, 1972—. Alderman Spring Lake, 1981—; fin., adminstrn. & intergovtl. rels. com. N.C. League Municipalities, 1985-91, horizons and strategies com., 1987; sec. Spring Lake Cmty. Ctr. Found., 1984—; trustee Williams Chapel Free Will Baptist Ch., Spring Lake. Mem. N.C. Assn. Realtors (external affairs com. 1985, 86, state conv. com. 1985, 94, state and local legis. com. 1987-93, state dir. 1989-95, co-chair equal opportunity com. 1995, chmn. 1996, issues and mobilization com. 1996), Women's Coun. Realtors (treas. N.C. chpt. 1985-87, v.p. 1988, pres. 1989, gov. 1990, v.p. Fayetteville chpt. 1983, 91, pres. 1984, 92, treas. 1986-96), Fayetteville Assn. Realtors (nominating com. 1984, 86, edn. com. 1976-84, 87, profl. standards com. 1982-96, v.p. membership 1985, dir. 1986-89, long range planning 1989-90, equal opportunity com. 1988, chmn. by-laws com. 1995-96, legis. and polit. affairs com. 1995-96). Democrat. Baptist. Office: Hall Real Estate 300 N Main St Spring Lake NC 28390

CLARK, EUGENIE, zoologist, educator; b. N.Y.C., May 4, 1922; m. Hideo Umaki, 1942; m. Ilias Konstantinou, 1949; 4 children; m. Chandler Brossard, 1966; m. Igor Klatzo, 1969. BA, Hunter Coll., 1942; MA, NYU, 1946, PhD (Pacific Sci. Bd. fellow 1949), 1950; DSc (hon.), U. Mass., Dartmouth, 1990, U. Guelph, 1995, U. South Hampton, 1995. Rsch. asst. in ichthyology Scripps Instn. Oceanography, 1946-47; with N.Y. Zool. Soc., 1947-48; research asst. in animal behavior Am. Museum Nat. History, N.Y.C., 1948-49; research assoc. Am. Museum Nat. History, 1950-80; instr. Hunter Coll., 1954; exec. dir. Cape Haze Marine Lab., Sarasota, Fla., 1955-67; asso. prof. biology City U. N.Y., 1966-67; asso. prof. zoology U. Md., 1968-73, prof. zoology, 1973-92, prof. emerita, sr. rsch. scientist, 1992—; vis. prof. Hebrew U., 1972. Author: Lady with a Spear, 1953, The Lady and the Sharks, 1969, Desert Beneath the Sea, 1991; subject of biography, Shark Lady (Ann McGovern), 1978. Recipient Myrtle Wreath award in sci. Hadassah, 1964, Nogi award in art Underwater Soc. Am., 1965, Dugan award in aquatic sci. Am. Littoral Soc., 1969, Diver of Yr. award Boston Sea Rovers, 1978, David Stone medal, 1984, Stoneman Conservation award, 1982, Gov. of S. Sinai medal, 1985, Lowell Thomas award Explorers Club, 1986, Wildscreen Internat. Film Festival award, 1986, medal Gov. Red Sea, Egypt, 1988, Nogi award in Sci., 1988, Women's Hall of Fame award State of Md., 1989, Women Educators award, 1990, Alumnae award, Franklin Burr award Nat. Geographic Soc., 1993; named to Hunter Coll. Hall of Fame Nat. Assn. Underwater Instrs., 1990, DEMA Hall of Fame, 1993; Fellow AEC, 1950; Saxton Fellow, 1952; Breadloaf Writer's fellow; Fulbright scholar Egypt, 1951 . Fellow AAAS; mem. Am. Soc. Ichthyology and Herpetology (life), Soc. Woman Geographers (Gold medal 1975, U. Md. Pres.'s medal 1993), Internat. Soc. Profl. Diving Scientists, Nat. Pks. and Conservation Assn. (vice chmn. 1976), Am. Littoral Soc. (v.p. 1970-89), Am. Elasmobranch Soc. Home: 7817 Hampden Ln Bethesda MD 20814-1108 Office: Univ Md Dept Zoology College Park MD 20742

CLARK, EVE VIVIENNE, linguistics educator; b. Camberley, U.K., July 26, 1942; came to U.S., 1967; d. Desmond Charles and Nancy (Aitken) Curme; m. Herbert H. Clark, July 21, 1967; 1 child, Damon Alistair. MA with honors, U. Edinburgh, Scotland, 1965, PhD, 1969. Rsch. assoc. Stanford (Calif.) U., 1969-71, from asst. prof. to assoc. prof., 1971-83, prof., 1983—. Author: Ontogenesis of Meaning, 1979, Acquisition of Romance, 1985, The Lexicon in Acquisition, 1993; co-author: Psychology and Language, 1977. Fellow Ctr. for Advanced Study in the Behavioral Scis., 1979-80, Guggenheim Found., 1983-84. Mem. Dutch Acad. Scis. (fgn.). Office: Stanford U Dept Linguistics Stanford CA 94305-2150

CLARK, FAYE LOUISE, drama and speech educator; b. La., Oct. 9, 1936; student Centenary Coll., 1954-55; BA with honor, U. Southwestern La., 1962; MA, U. Ga., 1966; PhD, Ga. State U., 1992; m. Warren James Clark, Aug. 8, 1969; children: Roy, Kay Natalie. Tchr., Nova Exptl. Schs., Fort Lauderdale, Fla., 1963-65; faculty dept. drama and speech DeKalb C.C., Atlanta, 1967—, chmn. dept., 1977-81. Pres. Hawthorne Sch. PTA, 1983-84. Mem. Ga. Theatre Conf. (sec. 1968-69, rep. to Southeastern Theatre Conf. 1969), Ga. Psychol. Assn., Ga. Speech Assn., Atlanta Ballet Guild, Friends of the Atlanta Opera, Southeastern Theatre Conf., Atlanta Hist. Soc., Atlanta Artists Club (sec. 1981-83, dir. 1983-89), Young Women of Arts, Speech Communication Assn., Phi Kappa Phi, Pi Kappa Delta, Sigma Delta Pi, Kappa Delta Pi, Thalian-Blackfriars. Presbyterian. Club: Lake Lanier Sailing. Home: 2521 Melinda Dr NE Atlanta GA 30345-1918 Office: DeKalb Coll Humanities Divsn North Campus Dunwoody GA 30338

CLARK, GLORIA JEAN FROLEK, school occupational therapist; b. Breckenridge, Minn., Nov. 25, 1954; d. Frank Charles Jr. and Florence Elizabeth (Bohnenstingl) Frolek; m. Steven R. Clark, Nov. 17, 1979; children: Nadia, Nathan, Natalie. BS, U. N.D., 1977; MS, Iowa State U., 1995. Registered occupl. therapist; cert. in infant massage, sensory integration and neuro-devel. treatment. Staff occupational therapist Easter Seals, Fargo, N.D., 1977-78; chair, occupational therapy dept. Easter Seals, Sioux City, Iowa, 1978-82; sch. occupational therapist Area Edn. Agy. 3, Spirit Lake, Iowa, 1982-83, Area Edn. Agy. 4, Sioux Center, Iowa, 1982-85; pvt. practice Ankeny, Iowa, 1983—; sch. occupational therapist Area Edn. Agy. 5, Storm Lake, Iowa, 1985-91; cons. Bur. Spl. Edn. Dept. of Edn., Des Moines, Iowa, 1989-91; sch. occupational therapist Heartland Area Edn. Agy., Johnston, Iowa, 1991—; cons. Blank Children's Hosp., Des Moines, 1992—; cons. rural environ. grant U. Kans., Kansas City, 1988; cons. fed. office of spl. edn. training grant St. Ambrose U., Davenport, Iowa, 1990-93; co-instr. Iowa State U., Ames, 1993-94. Author: (with others) Classroom Applications for School-Based Practice, 1993; co-author: (newsletter) Developmental Disability SIS Newsletter, 1993; co-editor: (manual) Resource Manual for Physical and Occupational Therapists Working in the Schools, 1990, (book) Occupational Therapy Services for Children and Youth Under IDEA, 1995. Vol. Westwood Sch., Ankeny, 1991—; sec. Westwood PTA, Ankeny, 1994-95; mem. Our Lady's Immaculate Ch., Ankeny, 1991-95, St. John's Cath. Ch., Adel, 1995—, tchr. catechism, 1995-96. Recipient Outstanding Leadership award Heartland Area Edn. Agy., 1992. Mem. Internat. Assn. Infant Massage Instrs., Am. Occupational Therapy Assn. (chair sch. system spl. interest sect., Outstanding Occupational Therapist of Yr. 1989, Roster of Fellows 1993), Iowa Occupational Therapy Assn. (v.p., sch. liaison, dist. chair), Neuro-Devel. Treament Assn., Sensory Integration Internat. Roman Catholic. Home: 2385 Scenic View Dr Adel IA 50003

CLARK, HARRIETT ANNE STOVALL, social worker; b. Columbus, Apr. 18, 1928; d. Mack Roger and Josephine Althea (Maugans) Stovall; m. Harry Lee Moore, Feb. 4, 1950 (div. 1963); children: Rebecca, Kristen, Nathan, Todd; m. Maurice Coates Clark, Oct. 17, 1965; 1 child, Sarah Lydia. BSN, Ohio State U., 1949, MSW, 1966. RN, Ohio; lic. social worker, Ohio; diplomate in clin. social work. Clin. social worker Children's Psychiat. Hosp., Columbus, 1966-67, Upham Hall, Ohio State U. Hosps., Columbus, 1967-68, Jess Parrish Hosp., Brevard County Mental Health, Titusville, Fla., 1972-77; pvt. practice social worker Columbus and Cocoa, Fla., 1971—; clin. social worker, sr. social worker child/adolescent div. Harding Hosp., Columbus, 1980-91; clin. social worker cardiovascular unit Toronto (Ont., Can.) Gen. Hosp., 1978-79; presenter workshops, 1980—. Contbr. articles to profl. jours. Trustee East Dublin (Ohio) Civic Assn., 1975—. Mem. NASW, Acad. Cert. Social Workers, Am. Group Therapy Assn., Tri-State Group Psychotherapy Assn. Democrat. Unitarian. Home: 7200 Riverside Dr Dublin OH 43016-9043

CLARK, HOPE ELIZABETH, dancer; b. Beirut, Lebanon, Aug. 1, 1964; came to U.S., 1968; d. Warren Clark and Alice Louise (Saulnier) Ritchie. BA, Bennington Coll., 1987. Performing arts tchr. Patuxent (Md.) Instn., 1988-90; gymnastics tchr. Discovery Programs, N.Y.C., 1990-94; gymnastics edn. tchr. Hunter Coll., N.Y.C., 1994-95; dancer Elizabeth Streb/

Ringside, N.Y.C., 1991—; gymnastics coach The Trinity Sch., N.Y.C., 1993-94; kid action coord. Streb/Ringside, N.Y.C., 1993-96, asst. choreographer, 1996; asst. dir. Ann Carlson, N.Y.C., 1994; choreographer Laurie Feirston's Prodns., N.Y.C., 1995. Home: 58 E 3d St New York NY 10003 Office: Streb/Ringside 584 Broadway Ste 1008 New York NY 10012

CLARK, JANE ANGELA, medical group administrator, educator; b. Linton, Ind., Sept. 18, 1955; d. Frank William and Doris Louise (French) Barlich; m. William H. Clark, June 4, 1977; children: William Daniel, Stephanie Lynne. BA, Purdue U., 1976; postgrad., U. Wis., 1978-79, U. Pa., 1985-90. Cert. employee benefits specialist. Rsch. asst. Purdue U., West Lafayette, Ind., 1977; pers. specialist Sentry Ins., Stevens Point, Wis., 1977-81; adminstr. Indianhead Med. Group, Rice Lake, Wis., 1981-88, Emergency Room Physicians Group, Rice Lake, 1985—; instr. mgmt. Wis. Indianhead Tech. Coll., Rice Lake, 1985—; cert. instr. Zenger-Miller courses; mem. suprs. mgmt. adv. com. Wis. Indianhead Tech. Coll., 1985-87. Chairperson Am. Heart Assn., Shell Lake, Wis., 1989; bd. dirs. United Way, Rice Lake, 1987-88. Mem. After Five Club (bd. dirs.), Alpha Lambda Delta, Phi Alpha Theta, Kappa Delta Pi. Republican. Baptist. Home: RR 1 Box 267A Shell Lake WI 54871-9780

CLARK, JANET, retired health services executive; b. Detroit, Oct. 3, 1941; d. John Francis Bullock and Martha Barbara (Bauer) Clark; m. Donald Bruce Tyson, Feb. 29, 1964; children: William John, Barbara June; m. Herman John Husmann, Nov. 11, 1988. AAS in Dental Hygiene, Broome C.C., 1961; BS in Health Edn., SUNY, Cortland, 1963; MPA in Mgmt., SUNY, Albany, 1993. Dental hygiene tchr. West Genessee Ctrl. Schs., Camillus, N.Y., 1964-65; health educator N.Y. State Dept. of Health, Syracuse, 1965-70; sr. sanitarian N.Y. State Dept. of Health, Monticello, 1977-80; prin. sanitarian N.Y. State Dept. of Health, N.Y.C., 1980-86; field ops. rep. N.Y. State Dept. of Health, Albany, 1986-89, mgr. Indian health, 1990-95, ret., 1995; sanitarian, health educator Onondaga County Health Dept., Syracuse, 1970-77; chmn., CEO Hažawi Found. for Econ. Deve. in Indigenous Nations, 1994—. Mem. Nat. Environ. Health Assn., N.Y. Soc. Profl. Sanitarians (sec. 1970-84), N.Y. State Registry of Sanitarians (treas. 1987-90, pres. 1990-95, Meritorious Svc. award 1986). Home: 355 Manning Blvd Albany NY 12206-1815 Office: PO Box 2033 Albany NY 12220

CLARK, JANET EILEEN, political scientist, educator; b. Kansas City, Kans., June 5, 1940; d. Edward Francis and Mildred Lois (Mack) Morrissey; AA, Kansas City Jr. Coll., 1960; AB, George Washington U., Washington, 1962, MA, 1964; PhD, U. Ill., 1973; m. Caleb M. Clark, Sept. 28, 1968; children: Emily Claire, Grace Ellen, Evelyn Adair. Staff, U.S. Dept. Labor, Washington, 1962-64; instr. social sci. Kansas City (Kans.) Jr. Coll., 1964-67; instr. polit. sci. Parkland Coll., 1970-71; asst. prof. govt., N.Mex. State U., Las Cruces, 1971-77, assoc. prof., 1977-80; assoc. prof. polit. sci. U. Wyo., 1981-84, prof., 1984-94; prof. polit. sci., head dept. State U. West Ga., Carrollton, 1994—. Co-author: Women, Elections and Representation, 1987, The Equality State, 1988, Women in Taiwan Politics: Overcoming Barriers to Women's Participation in a Modernizing Society, 1990; editor Women & Politics, 1991—. Wolcott fellow, 1963-64, NDEA Title IV fellow, 1967-69. Mem. Internat. Soc. Polit. Psychology Gov. Coun., 1987-89. Mem. NEA (pres. chpt. 1978-79), Am. Polit. Sci. Assn., Western Polit. Sci. Assn. (exec. coun. 1984-87), Western Social Sci. Assn. (exec. coun. 1978-81, v.p. 1982, pres. 1985), Women's Caucus for Polit. Sci. (treas. 1982, pres. 1987), LWV (exec. bd. 1980-83, treas. 1986-90, pres. 1991-93), Women's Polit. Caucus, Beta Sigma Phi (v.p. chpt. 1978-79, sec. 1987-88, treas. 1988-89, v.p. 1989-90, pres. 1990-91), Phi Beta Kappa, Chi Omega (prize 1962), Phi Kappa Phi. Democrat. Lutheran. Book rev. editor Social Sci. Jour., 1982-87. Contbr. articles to profl. jours. Home: 333 Foster St # D-23 Carrollton GA 30117-2861 Offiice: West Ga Coll Dept Polit Sci Carrollton GA 30118

CLARK, JANET KAYE, music educator; b. Oklahoma City, May 8, 1950; d. Delno Lane and Velma Fae (Lierle) Wells; m. Stephen Lee Clark, Aug. 8, 1968; children: Julie Ann, James Scott. B of Music Edn. with honors, U. Cen. Okla., 1977; postgrad., Tenn. Tech. U., 1984-85; MA in Edn. with honors, Austin Peay State U., 1990. Cert. gen. music 1-8, instrumental music K-12, elem. edn. Band tchr. grades 7-8 Highland West Mid. Sch., Moore, Okla., 1977-81; woodwind specialist grades 7-12 Moore Pub. Schs., 1981-83; music tchr. grades 1-12 The Clarksville (Tenn.) Acad., 1987-88; tchr. 2d grade Minglewood Elem. Sch., Clarksville, 1988-92; music tchr. grades K-5 Barksdale Elem. Sch., Clarksville, 1992-96, team leader for specialists, 1994-95; chmn. music profl. devel. Clarksville, Montgomery County Schs., 1995; reporter Adopt-A-Sch. Newspaper, 1993—. Author: The Star Program, 1993. Asst. den leader Boy Scouts Am., 1993-95; musician Mus. Meth. Handbell Choir, Clarksville, 1993-95; clarinetist Austin Peay State U., Cmty. Orch., 1985—, Austin Peay State U. Clarinet Choir, 1985-95; soloist Sch. Bd. Dinner at Minglewood, 1992. Mem. NEA, Tenn. Edn. Assn., Tenn. Music Edn. Assn., Mid. Tenn. Music Edn. Assn., Middle Tenn. Vocal Assn., Clarksville-Montgomery County Edn. Assn. (Disting. Classroom Tchr. 1993-94), Music Educators Nat. Conf. Home: 1226 Southern Pky Clarksville TN 37040-4339 Office: Barksdale Elem Sch 1920 Madison St Clarksville TN 37043-5065

CLARK, JANICE LAUREE, elementary school educator; b. Lindsborg, Kans., Oct. 21, 1949; d. Amos E. and Ada S. (Danielson) Dahlsten; m. Randy A. Clark, May 29, 1969; children: Peter A., Brian L. BA, Bethany Coll., 1971; MS, Ft. Hays State U., 1984. Tchr. reading, sci. Unified Sch. Dist. 209, Moscow, Kans., 1973-74; sub. tchr. Kans., 1972-79; 1st grade tchr. Unified Sch. Dist. 354, Claflin, Kans., 1979-86; elem. libr. Unified Sch. Dist. 290, Ottawa, Kans., 1986-87, 1st grade tchr., 1987-89, 96—, devel. 1st grade tchr., 1989-95, 2d grade tchr., 1995—; adj. instr. Ottawa U., Kansas City, Kans., 1995-96; 2nd grade tchr. Unified Sch. Dist. 305, Salina, Kans., 1995-96, 1st grade tchr., 1996—; summer sch. reading, math. tchr. Unified Sch. Dist. 290, 1993-95. Active Salina Chorale, 1996—, Friends Pub. Libr., 1991—; bd. dirs., com. chair Luth. Ch., women's group pres., choir. Recipient Earth Awareness grant WalMart, 1994, Outstanding Young Educator award Jaycees, 1989, Tackling Home Involvement grant Southwestern Bell Telephone, 1990, grant Ottawa Pub. Edn. Trust, 1988, 91, 92, Word processors grant, 1996. Mem. NEA, Internat. Reading Assn., Kans. Edn. Assn., Kans. Reading Assn. (zone coord. 1990-94, rec. sec. 1994—). Office: Franklin Elem 830 S 9th Salina KS 67401

CLARK, JEANENNE FRANCES, community health nurse specialist; b. St. Louis, Oct. 1, 1954; d. Pete Jr. and Marie (Risch) Stoplos; m. Richard Edward Clark, June 9, 1974; childen: Richard Paul, Jason Nicholas. Diploma, Jewish Hosp. Sch. Nursing, St. Louis, 1975; BSN cum laude, U. Mo., St. Louis, 1992; MPH, MSN, St. Louis U., 1996. Cert. critical care nurse. Staff nurse, acute medicine Jewish Hosp., St. Louis, 1975-77; critical care nurse, med.-coronary ICU St. Anthony's Med. Ctr., St. Louis, 1977-88; staff nurse level III burn/trauma, respiratory ICU Barnes Hosp., St. Louis, 1988-91; staff nurse trauma ICU St. Louis U. Hosp., 1991-94; pub. health nurse Family Care Health Ctrs., 1994, community health supr., 1994—, acting health svcs. dir., 1995; amb., mem. Critical Care Nursing Delegation, Russia, Hungary, 1992; program coord. Immunization Info. Sys., St. Louis U., 1996. Contbr. articles to profl. jours. Recipient St. Anthony's Star of Excellence award, 1986, Recognition award Barnes Hosp. Nursing Svc., 1990, Dean's Disting. Nurse award U. Mo., St. Louis, 1992; AACN scholar. Mem. ANA (inst. constituent mems. on nursing practice 1991-94), APHA, AACN (clin. practice spl. interest cons. region 14 1990-92, pres. St. Louis chpt. 1991-92, chmn. pub. rels. 1988-90, health care policy and legis. editor St. Louis chpt. 1989-95; cert. corp., exam. writer 1990-92), Mo. Nurses Assn. (2 v.p. 3d dist. 1994-96, coun. nursing practice 1987-91, med.-surg. chmn. 1989-91), Mo. Pub. Health Assn. (2d v.p. St. Louis chpt. 1995-96), LWV, Sigma Theta Tau. Home: 9939 Affton Pl Saint Louis MO 63123-4305

CLARK, JEANNE (BARBARA), police deputy chief; b. Chgo., Nov. 15, 1948; d. James John and Margaret Jessilyn (Sullivan) McGough; m. Patrick M. Clark, May 15, 1992. BA, St. Xavier U., Chgo., 1971; MA, U. Ill., 1975; cert. police mgmt., Northwestern U., 1982. Officer Chgo. Police Dept., 1975-78, youth officer, 1978-80, sgt., 1980-88, lt., 1988-89, comdr., 1989-95; asst. dep. supt. Bur. of Operational Svcs., Chgo. Police Dept., 1995-96, dep. chief patrol divsn., 1996—; sec.-treas. Comdg. Officers and Sgts. Chgo. Police Dept. Credit Union, 1986-88; chmn. Ill. Anti Car Theft Com., Chgo., 1989-91; bd. dirs. St. Jude Police League, 1990—. Office: Chgo Police Dept Patrol Divsn 1121 S State St Chicago IL 60605

CLARK, JOYCE NAOMI JOHNSON, nurse; b. Corpus Christi, Tex., Oct. 4, 1936; d. Chester Fletcher and Ermal Olita (Bailey) Johnson; m. William Boyd Clark, Jan. 4, 1958; (div. 1967); 1 child, Sherene Joyce. Student, Corpus Christi State U., 1975-77. RN, CNOR, ACLS; cert. instrument flight instr. Staff nurse Van Nuys (Calif.) Community Hosp., 1963-64, U.S. Naval Hosp., Corpus Christi, 1964-68; patient care coord. Meml. Med. Ctr., Corpus Christi, 1968—. Leader Paisano Coun. Girl Scouts U.S.A., Corpus Christi, 1968-74; past comdr. 3rd group USAF Aux., CAP Air Search and Rescue, wing chief pilot, ret. lt. col. 1993. Recipient Charles A. Mella award Meml. Med. ctr., 1981, Paul E. Garbert award CAP, 1986, cert. of appreciation in recognition of Support Child Guard Missing Children Edn. Program Nat. Assn. Chiefs of Police, Washington, 1987, Charles E. Yeager Aerospace Edn. Achievement award, 1985, Grover Loenig Aerospace award, 1986, Cert. of World Leadership Internat. Biographical Ctr., Cambridge, Eng., 1987, Gill Robb Wilson award #1021, 1988, Merit award Drug Free Am. Through Enforcement, Edn., Intelligence Nat. Assn. Chiefs of Police, Sr. Mem. of Yr. USAF Aux., CAP Air Search and Rescue, 1986. Mem. USAF Aux., CAP Air Search and Rescue (past comdr. 3rd group, wing chief pilot, Sr. Mem. of Yr. 1986), Am. Assn. Oper. Rm. Nurses (v.p. 1969), Am. Fed. Police, Aircraft Owners and Pilots Assn. Home: 1001 Carmel Pky Apt 33 Corpus Christi TX 78411-2152 Office: Meml Med Ctr 4606 Hospital Blvd Corpus Christi TX 78405-1818

CLARK, KAREN HEATH, lawyer; b. Pasadena, Calif., Dec. 17, 1944; d. Wesley Pelton and Lois (Ellenberger) Heath; m. Bruce Robert Clark,Dec. 30, 1967; children: Adam Heath, Andrea Pelton. Student, Pomona Coll., Claremont, Calif., 1962-64; BA, Stanford U., 1964-66; MA in History, U. Wash., 1968; JD, U. Mich., 1977. Bar: Calif. 1978. Instr. Henry Ford Community Coll., Dearborn, Mich., 1968-72; assoc. Gibson, Dunn & Crutcher, Irvine, Calif., 1977-86, ptnr., 1986—. Bd. dirs. Dem. Found. Orange County, 1989-91, 94—, Planned Parenthood Orange County, Santa Ana, Calif., 1979-82, New Directions for Women, Newport Beach, 1986-91, Women in Leadership, chair, 1995—. Mem. Women in Leadership (founder 1993), Women in Comml. Real Estate, Bldg. Industries Assn. So. Calif., Internat. Coun. Shopping Ctrs., Calif. Mortgage Bankers Assn. Office: Gibson Dunn & Crutcher 4 Park Plz Irvine CA 92714-8560

CLARK, KATHLEEN MULHERN, foreign language and literature educator; b. Phila., Oct. 10, 1948; d. John Joseph Jr. and Rosalie (Callahan) Mulhern; m. Robert Lee Clark, Oct. 7, 1972; children: Matthew, Kelly. AB, Immaculata Coll., 1970; MA, Villanova U., 1981; postgrad., U. Laval, Que., Can., 1969, Ecole Francaise des Attachés de Presse, Paris, 1991. Cert. French tchr. French tchr. Great Valley H.S., Devault, Pa., 1971-72, Conestoga Sr. H.S., Berwyn, Pa., 1970-71, 72-78; lectr. fgn. lang. Immaculata (Pa.) Coll., 1973-89, prof. fgn. lang., lit., 1989—; translator Burroughs Corp., Paoli, Pa., 1976-78; translator, cons. Smith, Kline Animal Health Products, West Chester, Pa., 1985; co-developer, designer Leadership Core Curriculum, Immaculata, 1990—. Class rep. Immaculata Coll. Alumnae Assn., 1970—, mem. bd. govs. 1996—. Recipient grant U. Laval, 1969, Pew Meml. Trust, 1990. Mem. AAUP, MLA, AAUW, Am. Assn. Tchrs. French, Am. Coun. on Teaching of Fgn. Langs., Alliance Française, Pi Delta Phi, Lambda Iota Tau. Roman Catholic. Home: 65 Rossiter Ave Phoenixville PA 19460-2509 Office: Immaculata Coll Faculty Ctr # 17 Immaculata PA 19345

CLARK, LETITIA Z., federal judge; b. 1945. BA, Rice U., 1967; MA, Rutgers U., 1970; JD, Syracuse U., 1973. Atty. EPA, Dallas, 1974-76; asst. U.S. atty. Southern District of Texas, 1982-85; bankruptcy judge Southern District of Texas, Houston, 1985—. Office: US Bankruptcy Ct PO Box 61010 515 Rusk St Houston TX 77002

CLARK, LOYAL FRANCES, public affairs specialist; b. Salt Lake City, July 16, 1958; d. Lloyd Grant and Zina (Okelberry) C. Student, Utah State U., 1976-78. Human resource coord. U.S. Forest Svc., Provo, Utah, 1984—, fire info. officer, 1987—, pub. affairs officer, interpretive svcs. coord., edn. coord., 1988—; mem. Take Pride in Utah Task Force, Salt Lake City, 1989—; chairperson Utah Wildlife Ethics Com., Provo, 1989—. Instr. Emergency Svcs., Orem, Utah, 1990—. Recipient Presdl. award for outstanding leadership in youth conservation programs Pres. Ronald Reagan, 1985, Superior Svc. award USDA, 1987, Exemplary Svc. award U.S. Forest Svc., 1992, Nat. Eyes on Wildlife Achievement award USDA Forest Svc., 1993. Mem. Nat. Wildlife Fedn., Nat. Assn. Interpretation, Utah Soc. Environ. Educators, Utah Wildlife Fedn. (bd. dirs. 1981-85, v.p. 1985-87, Achievement award 1983, 85, 87), Utah Wilderness Assn., Am. Forestry Assn., Nature Conservancy, Women in Mgmt. Coun. Office: Uinta Nat Forest 88 W 100 N Provo UT 84601-4452

CLARK, MARCIA RACHEL, prosecutor; b. Berkeley, Calif., 1954; d. Abraham I. Kleks; m. Gabriel Horowitz, 1976 (div. 1980); m. Gordon Clark (div. 1994); 2 children. BA in Polit. Sci., UCLA, 1974; JD, Southwestern U., 1979. Atty. Brodey and Price, L.A., 1979-81; atty. L.A. County Dist. Attys. Office, 1981—, now dep. dist. atty. Office: Criminal Cts Bldg 210 W Temple St Los Angeles CA 90012-3210

CLARK, MARTHA FULLER, state legislator, architectural historian, preservation consultant; b. York, Maine, Mar. 14, 1942; m. Geoffrey Clark; 3 children. BA, Mills Coll., 1964; MA, Boston U., 1977. Mem. N.H. Ho. of Reps., asst. Dem. leader, 1995—. Bd. dirs. Strawbery Banke, 1976-92; founder, pres. Inherit N.H., 1989-96; trustee Friends of Music Hall, 1989-96; bd. dirs. Preservation Action, 1988—, Wiss Inst., 1995—; mem. Hist. Dist. Commn., 1977-80, Portsmouth Mus. Commn., 1985-89, Gov.'s Commn. on 21st Century Living Landscape Task Force, 1989-90; mem. state exec. com. N.H. Dem. Party, 1995—. Mem. N.H. Hist. soc. (trustee 1992—), Leadership Seacoast. Demcrat. Office: NH House of Reps State Capitol Concord NH 03301

CLARK, MARY HIGGINS, author, business executive; b. N.Y.C., Dec. 24, 1931; d. Luke J. and Nora C. (Durkin) Higgins; m. Warren Clark, Dec. 26, 1949 (dec. Sept. 1964); children: Marilyn, Warren, David, Carol, Patricia. BA, Fordham U., 1979; hon. doctorate, Villanova U., 1983, Rider Coll., 1986, Stonehill Coll., 1992, Marymount Manhattan Coll., 1992, Chestnut Hill, 1993, Manhattan Coll., 1993, St. Peter's Coll., 1993. Advt. asst. Remington Rand, 1946; stewardess Pan Am., 1949-50; radio scriptwriter, prodr. Robert G. Jennings, 1965-70; v.p., ptnr., creative dir., prodr. radio programming Aerial Communications, N.Y.C., 1970-80; chmn. bd., creative dir. D. J. Clark Enterprises, N.Y.C., 1980—. Author: Silent Night, Aspire to the Heavens, A Biography of George Washington, 1969 (N.J. Author award 1969), Where Are the Children?, 1976 (N.J. Author award 1977), A Stranger Is Watching, 1978 (N.J. Author award 1978), The Cradle Will Fall, 1980, A Cry in the Night, 1982, Stillwatch, 1984, Weep No More, My Lady, 1987, While My Pretty One Sleeps, 1989, The Anastasia Syndrome and Other Stories, 1989, Loves Music, Loves to Dance, 1991, All Around the Town, 1992, I'll Be Seeing You, 1993, Remember Me, 1994, The Lottery Winner, 1994, Bad Behavior, 1995, Let Me Call You Sweetheart, 1995, Moonlight Becomes You, 1996; (with Thomas Chastain and others) Murder in Manhattan, 1986; editor: Murder on the Aisle: The 1987 Mystery Writers Anthology, 1987. Recipient Grand Prix de Litterature Policiere, France, 1980. Mem. Mystery Writers Am. (pres. 1987, dir.), Authors League, Am. Soc. Journalists and Authors, Acad. Arts and Scis. Republican. Roman Catholic. *

CLARK, MARY MORRIS, humanities educator; b. Tuscaloosa, Ala., Dec. 28, 1941; d. John William and Lilian Lucile (Burnett) Morris; m. Raymond Walter Clark (div. May 1979); children: Susannah, Jonathan, Kathryn; m. Bernard Franklin Wideman, Oct. 13, 1984. BA, U. N.H., 1962; PhD, U. Mass., 1978. Tchr. Kennett H.S., Conway, N.H., 1962-63, U.S. Peace Corps, Owerri, Nigeria, 1964-65; instr. Sch. Internat. Tng., Brattleboro, Vt., 1966-72; asst. prof. English U. N.H., Durham, 1978-84, assoc. prof., 1984-91, prof., 1991—. Author: A Dynamic Theory of Tone, 1978, The Tonal System of IGBO, 1990. Mem. Linguistic Soc. Am. Home: RR2 Box 35 North Berwick ME 03906 Office: U NH English Dept Durham NH 03824

CLARK, MAXINE, retail executive; b. Miami, Fla., Mar. 6, 1949; d. Kenneth and Anne (Lerch) Kasselman; m. Robert Fox, Sept. 1984. B.A. in Journalism, U. Ga., 1971. Exec. trainee Hecht Co., Washington, 1971, hosiery buyer, 1971-72, misses sportswear buyer, 1972-76; mgr. mdse. planning and research May Dept. Stores Co., St. Louis, 1976-78, dir. mdse. devel., 1978-80, v.p. mktg. and sales promotion Venture Stores div., 1980-81, sr. v.p. mktg. and sales promotion Venture Stores div., 1981-83, exec. v.p. mktg. and softlines, 1983-85; exec. v.p. apparel Famous-Barr, St. Louis, 1985-86; v.p. mdsing. Lerner Shops div. Limited Inc., N.Y.C., 1986-88; exec. v.p. Venture Stores, St. Louis, 1988-92; pres. Payless ShoeSource, Topeka, Kans., 1992-96; founder, CEO Ideas2 retail cons. firm. Sec., Lafayette Sq. Restoration Com., 1978-79; mem. Com. 200 Nat. Coun. Coll. Arts and Scis. Washington U.; bd. trustees U. Ga. Found., 1995—, mem. Nat. Advisory Coun. Girl Scouts of Am., 1995—; bd. dirs. The Earthgrains Co., 1996—, The Tandy Brands Accessories Co., 1996—, Creve Coeur Camera, Inc., 1996—.

CLARK, MAYREE CARROLL, investment banking executive; b. Norman, Okla., Mar. 9, 1957; d. Benton C. Clark and Joan M. (Harris) Richards; m. Jeffrey P. Williams, Apr. 28, 1984. BS, U. So. Calif., 1975; MBA, Stanford U., 1981. Econ. analyst Nat. Econ. Rsch., L.A., 1976-79; assoc. Kidder Peabody & Co., N.Y.C., 1980; assoc. Morgan Stanley, N.Y.C., 1981-84, v.p., 1985-87, prin., 1987-89, mng. dir., 1990—; adj. prof. Columbia U., N.Y.C., 1988-89. Chmn. Student Sponsor Partnership, N.Y.C., 1996—; trustee The Common Fund, 1992—; vol. I Have a Dream Program, N.Y.C., 1986-88. Republican. Office: Morgan Stanley and Co 1585 Broadway Fl 14 New York NY 10020-1104

CLARK, NANCY ELISABETH, dean; b. Bronx, N.Y., Sept. 8, 1965; d. Sheldon Erwin and Josephine Ena (Francis) C. BA in Urban Affairs, Barnard Coll., 1987; MS in Elem. Edn., Hunter Coll., 1993. Account coord. Cass Comms., N.Y.C., 1988; music and reading tchr. P.S. 31, Bronx, 1988-94; asst. dean music Moravian Coll., Bethlehem, Pa., 1994—; asst. prodr. Clark Enterprises, N.Y.C., 1989-93. Photographer jour. 1994 Debutantes Cotillion Jour. of United Moravian Ch., 1994, Lincoln Ctr. Family Art Show, 1995-96. Mem. ASCD, Nat. Assn. Sch. Music Tchrs., United Fedn. Tchrs., Barnard Alumni Assn. Mem. Moravian Ch. Office: Moravian Coll Music Dept 1200 Main St Bethlehem PA 18018-6614

CLARK, NANCY K., librarian; b. St. Louis, Aug. 27, 1952; d. Harry W. and Iona K. (Knobeloch) C. BA, So. Ill. U., 1973; MSLS, U. Ill., 1974. Cert. tchr. and media specialist, Ill. Libr. Mascoutah (Ill.) Unit Dist. #19, 1974—. Sec., bd. dirs. Mascoutah Meml. Scholarship Fund, 1977-88; sec. bd. trustees O'Fallon (Ill.) Pub. Libr., 1992—. Mem. ALA, AASL, Ill. Libr. Assn., NEA, Mo. Hist. Soc., Nat. Trust for Hist. Preservation, Am. Guild of Organists, Beta Phi Mu. Home: 1006 E Third St O'Fallon IL 62269

CLARK, PRISCILLA ALDEN, elementary school educator; b. Ray, Ariz., June 4, 1940; d. Edmund A. and Rena F. (Travis) White; m. Larry C. Clark, Sept. 5, 1959; children: Russell, Kenneth, Clifford, Thomas. BS, Tex. Woman's U., 1987. Cert. elem. tchr., ESL tchr. Tchr. kindergarten and prekindergarten, grade level chair Irving (Tex.) Ind. Sch. Dist.; kindergarten tchr. Shady Grove Day Care, Irving; tchr. Irving (Tex.) Sch. Dist. Active in ch. and boy scouts. Recipient Silver Beaver award. Mem. Internat. Reading Assn., Sci. Tchrs. Assn. Tex., Kindergarten Tchrs. Tex., North Tex. Reading Assn., Assn. Tex. Profl. Educators (state del.), Mortar Bd., Irving Theatre Guild, Pi Lambda Theta (chair nat. com., chair region VII, nat. spkr., pres. Alpha Sigma chpt., pres. Region 7), Alpha Chi, Delta Delta Delta, Omega Rho Alpha, Delta Kappa Gamma (pres. Mu Omicron chpt., Internat. Woman of Yr. 1992-93). Home: 2717 Peach Tree Ln Irving TX 75062-3230

CLARK, REBECCA LEIGH, sociology educator; b. Danville, Va., Nov. 22, 1949; d. Clyde Odell and Lillian Evelyn (Turner) C.; 1 child, Jon Clark Sells. BA magna cum laude, Stratford Coll., 1972; MA, Ariz. State U., 1975, PhD, 1987. Cert. C.C. tchr., Ariz. Vis. staff mem. Maricopa County (Ariz.) C.C. Dist., 1974-89; Phoenix area field rschr. HRS, Inc., L.A., 1982; faculty assoc. dept. sociology Ariz. State U., Tempe, 1976, 79, 86-89, faculty rsch. assoc. adolescent and family devel. project, 1988-89; assoc. prof. sociology Averett Coll., Danville, Va., 1989—; presenter in field; manuscript reviewer Harper Collins Pubs., 1989—. Interviewed on local TV program; contbr. articles, book revs. to profl. jours. Mem. nurturing com. Habitat for Humanity, Danville, 1994—; chair cheerleading com. Dixie Intercollegiate Athletic Conf., 1993-95; project dir. survey on quality of life Danville C. of C. 1991. Recipient Leadership award Danville C. of C., 1992. Mem. Alpha Kappa Delta. Home: 215 Montague St Danville VA 24541 Office: Averett Coll 420 W Main St Danville VA 24541

CLARK, SANDRA JEAN, humanities educator; b. Niagara Falls, N.Y., Mar. 28, 1942; d. Stanley LaVerne and Jean Elizabeth (Kelman) Stephens; m. Ronald Keith Clark, June 27, 1964; 1 child, Christopher Keith. BS in English, Anderson Coll., 1964; MA in English, Ball State U., 1967, PhD in Composition and Rhetoric, 1995. Cert. lang. arts tchr., Ind. English tchr. Highland H.S., Anderson, Ind., 1964-72; prof. English Anderson (Ind.) U., 1975—, writing program dir., 1985—. Founder, bd. dirs. Women's Alternatives, Anderson, 1977-85. Mem. Ind. Tchrs. of Writing (sec. 1986-88. v.p. 1995-96, pres. 1996—). Mem. Ch. of God. Office: Anderson U English Dept Anderson IN 46012

CLARK, SANDRA MARIE, school administrator; b. Hanover, Pa., Feb. 17, 1942; d. Charles Raymond Clark and Mary Josephine (Snyder) Clark Wierman. BS in Elem. Edn., Chestnut Hill Coll., 1980; MS in Child Care Adminstrn., Nova U., 1985; MS in Ednl. Adminstrn., Western Md. Coll., 1992. Cert. elem. tchr., elem. prin., Pa. Tchr. various elem. schs., Pa., 1962-75; asst. vocation directress Mt. St. Joseph Motherhouse, Chestnut Hill, Pa., 1975-76; tchr. St. Catharine's Sch., Spring Lake, N.J., 1976-77; asst. mgr. Jim's Truck Stop, New Oxford, Pa., 1977-81; adminstr. Little People Day Care Sch., Hanover, 1981-88, sec., treas. bd. dirs., 1985-86; coord. regional resource Magic Yrs. Child Care & Learning Ctrs., Inc., Hanover, 1987-88; prin. St. Vincent de Paul Sch., Hanover, Pa., 1988—; presenter Hanover Area Seminar for Day Care Employees, 1983-86. coord. sch. safety patrols St. Vincent's Sch., Hanover, 1969-75, vice-chmn. bd., 1982-84; multi-media instr. first aid ARC, Hanover, 1983-86, bd. dirs., 1984-88; exec. sec. of bd. of dirs. ARC, Hanover, 1988; 1st v.p. Hanover Area Coun. of Chs., 1988, pres., 1989; validator accredidation program Nat. Acad. Early Childhood Programs, Washington, 1987—; bd. dirs. Life Skills Unltd. Handicapped Adults, 1988—; facilitator Harrisburg Diocesan Synod, Hanover, 1985-88, parish del., 1988. Pa. Dept. Pub. Welfare tng. grantee, 1986. Mem. NAFE, Nat. Cath. Ednl. Assn. Democrat. Roman Catholic. Club: Internat. Assn. Turtles (London). Home: 348 Barberry Dr Hanover PA 17331-1302 Office: St Vincent De Paul Sch Hanover PA 17331

CLARK, SARA MOTT, retired home economics educator; b. Mahaffey, Pa., Sept. 19, 1915; d. William Benjamin and Anna Pearl (Murray) M.; m. Maximilian Steineger, Dec. 13, 1941; children: Max III, Benjamin Alan, Betsy Ann, Kathryn Louise. BS, Juniata Coll., Huntingdon, Pa., 1933-37, Ind. U. Pa., 1940-41. Dietician, Home Econ. Tchr., Internat. Porcelain Art Tchr. Dietician Adrian Hosp., Punxsutawney, Pa., 1937-40; home econs. tchr. Scio High Sch., Ohio., 1941-42, Punxsutawney (Pa.) Area Dist. Sch., 1960-77; artist, tchr. Internat. Porcelain Artist, Bradenton, Fla.; pres. N.W. Pa. Hosp. Dietetics Orgn., Punxsutawney, 1938-40; chmn. Am. Home Econs. Ctr. We. Dist., Punxsutawney, 1967-68; chmn. art com. The Shores, Bradenton, Fla. Vol. Art Display Internat. Porcelain Artist Atlanta Ga. 1986, Art in Action Festival Arts State Coll. 1981-82; Author: Various Porcelain Paintings China and Fla. 1986. Den mother Boy Scouts Am., Punxsutawney, 1951-56; Brownie leader Girl Scouts U.S., Punxsutawney, 1959; tchr. Sunday Sch. 1st Bapt. Ch., Punxsutawney, 1957-60; chmn. art com. The Shores at Bradenton Retirement Facility, 1996. Recipient Tribute to Porcelain Artist award Punxsutawney Spirit, 1987. Mem. AAUW (historian Bradenton 1991-93, chair bridge group 1993-94), Progressive Study Club (pres. 1953-54, 75-76, farewell luncheon award), Treasures of Porcelain Artists, Gulf Coast Porcelain Artists, New Floridians Club (1st v.p. 1994), The Shores (art chmn.). Republican. Home: Apt 1017 1700 3rd Ave W Bradenton FL 34205-5944

CLARK, SHELIA ROXANNE, sports association executive, legislative analyst; b. June 28, 1959; d. Milton Cornell and Mable Juanita (Grubb) C. BS in Polit. Sci., Radford U., 1983; MPA, James Madison U., Harrisonburg, Va., 1987. Dir. Black Teenage World Scholarship Program, Va., 1977-88; intern Field Found., New River Valley, Va., 1984-85, Rep. Rick Boucher, Washington, 1987; adminstrv. asst. OMB Watch, Washington, 1988; legis. asst. Nat. Community Action Found., Washington, 1988-93;

exec. dir. Gary Clark's Sports Camp, 1990—; project coord. Student Coalition Against Tobacco, 1994-95; cons., asst. Nat. Children's Day Found., Washington, 1991-93. program dir. Project Unity, Va., 1984; bd. mem. VA Action, 1985, Grassroots Leadership Project, N.C., 1987; campaign worker Clinton Presdl. Campaign/Transition, Washington, 1992. Internship The Field Found., 1984-85, Congressman Rick Boucher, Washington, 1987. Mem. Nat. Council Negro Women. Home: PO Box 1865 Dublin VA 24084 Office: Gary Clarks Sports Camp 212 Broad St # C Dublin VA 24084-3203

CLARK, SUSAN (NORA GOULDING), actress; b. Sarnia, Ont., Can., Mar. 8, 1943; d. George Raymond and Eleanor Almond (McNaughton) C. Student, Toronto (Ont.) Children's Players, 1956-59; student (Acad. scholar), Royal Acad. Dramatic Art, London. partner Georgian Bay Prodns. Producer: Jimmy B. and Andre, 1979, Word of Honor, 1980, Maid in America, 1982; star Webster, ABC-TV, 1983-89; appeared in Brit. TV prodns., repertory theatre; appeared in Brit. premiere of play Poor Bitos; appeared in Can. TV prodns., including Heloise and Abelard, Hedda Gabler; starred in Taming of the Shrew; appeared in Sherlock Holmes, Williamstown Theatre Festival, (taped for HBO), 1981, Meetin's on the Porch, Canon Theater, Beverly Hills, 1990, Lion in Winter, Walnut St. Theater, Phila., 1992; Getting Out, Mark Taper Forum, Los Angeles, 1978, The Vortex, Walnut Street Theatre, 1994; films include The Apple Dumpling Gang, Night Moves, The North Avenue Irregulars, Airport '75, Midnight Man, Porky's, Murder by Decree, Tell Them Willie Boy is Here, Skin Game, City on Fire, Madigan, Coogan's Bluff, Skullduggery, Promises in the Dark, Valdez is Coming, Showdown, Double Negative, Nobody's Perfekt, The Canadian Conspiracy; appeared in segments of TV series Columbo, Marcus Welby, Barnaby Jones, Webster; appeared in Double Solitaire, Pub. Broadcasting System; TV films include: Something for a Lonely Man, 1968, The Astronaut, 1972, Trapped, 1973, Babe, 1975 (Emmy award), McNaughton's Daughter, 1976, Amelia Earhart, 1976 (Emmy nom.), Jimmy B. & Andre, 1980 (also co-prodr.), The Choice, 1981, Maid in America, 1982 (also co-prodr.), Snowbound, The Jim and Jennifer Stolpa Story, 1993, Tonya and Nancy, The Inside Story, 1994, The Butterbox Babies, 1994 (Gemini nomination). Mem. ACLU, Am. Film Inst. Office: care Georgian Bay Prodns 3814 W Olive St Ste 202 Burbank CA 91505-4648*

CLARK, SUSAN MATTHEWS, psychologist; b. Newton, Kans., Aug. 5, 1950; d. Glenn Wesley Matthews and Jane Buckles; m. S. Bruce Clark, Aug. 14, 1971; children: Casandra Jane, Ryan Matthews. BME, Wichita State U., 1971, MME, 1975, MA, 1982; PhD, North Tex. State U., 1985. Elem. tchr. Derby (Kans.) Pub. Schs., 1972-74; profl. musician Amarillo (Tex.) Symphony, 1974-77; psychol. cons. Achenbach Ctr., Hardtner, Kans., 1983-85; psychologist VA Med. Ctr., Wichita, Kans., 1984-85, St. Francis Acad., Inc., Salina, Kans., 1986-89, Psychiat. Clinic Wichita, 1989-93; gen. mgr. Affiliated Psychiat. Svcs., Wichita, 1993-95; psychologist Charter Clinic, Wichita, Kans., 1995—; bd. dirs. Salina Coalition for the Prevention of Child Abuse, 1986-87. Author: Grant, 1987. Bd. deacons Plymouth Congl. Ch., Wichita, 1989-92, mem. bd. Christian Edn., 1993. Recipient: Phi Kappa Phi, Mu Phi Epsilon, Psi Chi. Mem. APA, Nat. Acad. Neuropsychology, Southwestern Psychol. Assn., Kans. Psychol. Assn., Wichita Area Psychol. Assn., Kans. Assn. Profl. Psychologists. Republican. Congregationalist. Office: Charter Clinic 8911 E Orme Ste C Wichita KS 67207

CLARK, SUSANNE L., bank executive. Sr. v.p. investor rels. State St. Boston Corp. Office: State St Boston Corp 225 Franklin St Boston MA 02110*

CLARK, SUZANNE, accountant; b. San Bernadino, Calif., Sept. 10, 1948; d. Richard Grant and Dorothy Jean (Gast) C.; children: Chelsea A. Clark-James, Graeme W. Clark-James. BS in Mktg. and Acctg., U. Colo., 1970, M in Urban Affairs, 1978. CPA, Colo., CFP, Colo.; personal fin. specialist. Dir. adminstrv. svcs. Suburban Cmty. Tng. & Svc. Ctr., Englewood, 1973-78; staff adminstr Solar Energy Rsch. Inst., Golden, Colo., 1979-80; rschr. Cmty. Coll. Denver, 1980-81; staff acct. R.E. Weise & Co., CPAs, Denver, 1982-83; owner Clark & Assoc., CPA, P.C., Denver, 1983—. Author: Providing Personal Financial Planning Services in Your CPA Practice, 1987, Providing Fiduciary Accounting and Tax Services, 1990, The Personal Financial Planning Process An Introduction, 1993, Personal Financial Planning in Crisis Situations, 1993, Estates and Trusts: A Guide to Fiduciary Advisors, 1996. Bd. dirs. Children's Ctr., Denver, 1982-84, Hospice of Peace, Denver, 1987-88. Mem. AICPA (personal fin. specialist edn. subcom. 1988-93), Colo. Soc. CPAs (specialization oversight bd. 1984-87, pers. fin. planning com. 1987-88, comms. com. 1994—). Office: Clark & Assoc CPA PC 50 S Steele St Ste 430 Denver CO 80209-2808

CLARK, TERESA WATKINS, psychotherapist, clinical counselor; b. Hobart, Okla., Dec. 18, 1953; d. Aaron Jack Watkins and Patricia Ann (Flurry) Greer and Ralph Gordon Greer; m. Philip Winston Clark, Dec. 29, 1979; children: Philip Aaron, Alisa Lauren. BA in Psychology, U. N.Mex., 1979, MA in Counseling and Family Studies, 1989. Lic. profl. clin. counselor, N.Mex. Child care worker social svcs. divsn. Family Resource Ctr., Albuquerque, 1978-79; head tchr., asst. dir. Kinder Care Learning Ctr., Albuquerque, 1979-80; psychiat. asst. Vista Sandia Psychiat. Hosp., Albuquerque, 1980-87; psychotherapist outpatient clinic Bernalillo County Mental Health Ctr.-Heights, 1989-91; therapist adolescent program Charter/Heights Behavioral Health Sys., Albuquerque, 1991—. Mem. ACA, Am. Assn. Multicultural Counseling and Devel., N.Mex. Health Counselors Assn. (former cen. regional rep. bd. dirs., ethics chairperson, bd. dirs.), Mental Health Coundelor's Assn., Phi Kappa Phi, "Billy The Kid Outlaw Gang" Hist. Soc. Democrat. Office: Charter/Hlth Behav Hlth Sys 103 Hospital Loop Albuquerque NM 87109

CLARK, THREESE ANNE, occupational therapist, disability analyst; b. Bath, N.Y., Jan. 16, 1946; d. Frank George and Beulah Irene (Harris) Brown; m. Jacob Clark, Mar. 11, 1966 (div. Mar. 1977); 1 child, Jayson Todd. BS in Occupational Therapy, U. N.D., 1967, MS in Counseling and Guidance, 1977. Lic. occupational therapist, Pa., Md.; diplomate Am. Bd. Disability Analysts (charter adv. bd. mem. 1995—). Occupational therapist U. N.D. Med. Ctr., 1968; chief occupational therapist, program developer Corning (N.Y.) Hosp., 1968-69, Arnot-Ogden Hosp., Elmira, N.Y., 1969-71; staff occupational therapist VA Ctr., Bath, N.Y., 1971-74; instr. occupational therapy U. N.D., Grand Forks, 1974-77; prin. investigator occupational therapy Ohio State U., 1977-79; occupational therapist Regional Ednl. Assessment and Cons. Team, Hillsboro, Ohio, 1979-81; occupational therapist, phys. medicine and rehab. Saint Mary's Hosp., West Palm Beach, Fla., 1981-82; chief occupational therapist Mercy Med. Ctr., Oshkosh, Wis., 1982-87; dir. occupational/recreational therapy HealthSouth Rehab. Hosp., Altoona, 1987-95, clin. dir. spinal injury program, 1987-95; pres. and owner Life Care Planning and Mgmt. Inc., Altoona, 1993—; assoc. prof., program chair profl. occupl. therapy program Mt. Aloysius Coll., Cresson, Pa., 1995—; cons. Founders Pavillion, Corning, 1969, Grafton (N.D.) State Sch. for the Retarded, 1975-76, Heart of Am. Rehab. Ctr., Rugby, N.D., 1976-77, Andrea Clifford program, 1978; guest lectr. support groups, community groups, ednl. programs, 1987—; presented numerous papers on occupational therapy. Contbr. articles to profl. jours. Charter mem. profl. adv. coun. Am. Bd. Disability Analysts; pres. adv. bd. Occupational Therapy Asst. Program, Mt. Aloysius Jr. Coll., 1988-92, 94-96; mem. adv. profl. com. Home Nursing Agy., Altoona, 1988-93; mem. Com. Health Care Adv. Com., 1994—; bd. dirs. Ctr. for Internat. Living of South Cen. Pa., 1992—; mem. med. svc. com. Evergreen Manor, Oshkosh, 1985-87; chair home/family life and human rels. Northtowne Elem. Sch. PTA, Columbus, Ohio, 1978, others. Mem. Am. Occupational Therapy Assn. (coun. edn. 1974-76, coun. affiliate pres. 1976), Nat. Rehab. Assn., Ohio Occupational Therapy Assn., Columbus Dist. Occupational Therapy Assn., Pa. Occupational Therapy Assn., Am. Assn. Hand Therapists. Baptist. Home: 5300 5th Ave Altoona PA 16602-1312 also: Life Care Planning Mgmt Inc 5300 5th Ave Altoona PA 16602-1312 Office: Mt Aloysius Coll 7373 Adm Peary Hwy Cresson PA 16630

CLARK, VIOLET CATHRINE, retired school administrator, volunteer; b. Mpls., Oct. 16, 1915; d. John Albert and Ellen Charlotte (Carlson) Lundgren; m. Robert Edward Clark, May 6, 1944 (div. June, 1954); children: Linda Cathrine Kovach, Sharon Roberta Drake. BS in Horticulture, U. Minn., 1942; MS, U. Minn., St. Paul, 1948. Cert. tchr., adminstr., Calif. Rsch. asst. horticulture U. Minn., Mpls., Duluth, 1942-44; elementary sch. tchr. Riverside (Calif.) Pub. Schs., 1953-58, prin., 1958-81; rschr. raspberries, MMMs Sponsor U. Minn., Duluth, 1942-44. Contbr. articles to newspapers and Hortculture jours., 1942-46. Vol. Ecumenical Ctr. Homeless Shelter and Meals, Oceanside, 1982—, Country Friends, Rancho Santa Fe, 1982—. Reading, Carlsbad, 1991-94, vote solicitor, Carlsbad, 1985-86. Recipient plaque Ecumenical Ctr., 1989, cert., 1995. Mem. Altrusa (com. chair 1943-83), Eastern Star, Alpha Delta Kappa (pres. 1947). Lutheran. Home: 4740 Birchwood Cir Carlsbad CA 92008

CLARK, WILMA JEAN MARSHALL, English language educator; b. Akron, Ohio, Apr. 18, 1928; d. Paul Marshall and Laura Mae Haught; m. Gerald F. Clark, Apr. 11, 1947; children: Thomas M., G. Michael, Kathleen S., Deborah J. BA, Akron U., 1961; MA, Morgan State U., 1970; PhD, U. Md., 1980. Tchr. English, Journalism, French Overlea Sr. H.S., 1961-67; tchr. English and Journalism Perry Hall Sr. H.S., 1967-68; chair English dept. Towsontown Jr. H.S., 1968-70; asst. prof. English Dundalk (Md.) C.C., 1970-72; assoc. prof. English Morgan State U., Balt., 1970-94; prof. English Ea. Christian Coll., Belair, Md., 1989—; adj. prof. English Lincoln (Ill.) Christian Coll. and Seminary-East Coast, 1995—; mem. Mountain Christian Sch. Bd., Hartford County, Md., 1992—; founding mem. Mountain Christian High Sch., Hartford County, 1996—. Contbr. articles to profl. jours. Mem. AAUP, Balt. Alliance of H.S./Coll. Educators, Coll. English Assn. (panel mem. nat. conf., treas./exec. bd. mid-Atlantic group). Home: 11518 Chapman Rd Kingsville MD 21087-1526

CLARKE, CORDELIA KAY KNIGHT MAZUY, managment executive; b. Springfield, Mo., Nov. 22, 1938; d. William Horace and Charline (Bentley) Knight; m. Logan Clarke, Jr., July 22, 1978; children by previous marriage—Katharine Michelle Mazuy, Christopher Knight Mazuy. A.B. with honors in English, U. N.C., 1960; M.S. in Statistics, N.C. State U., 1962. Statistician Research Triangle Inst., Durham, N.C., 1960-63; statis. cons. Arthur D. Little, Inc., Cambridge, Mass., 1963-67; dir. mktg. planning and analysis Polaroid Corp., Cambridge, 1967-70; dir. mktg. and bus. planning Transaction Tech. Inc., Cambridge, 1970-72; pres. Mazuy Assos., Boston, 1972-73; v.p. Nat. Shawmut Bank, Boston, 1973-74; sr. v.p., dir. mktg. Shawmut Corp., 1974-78; sr. v.p., dir. retail banking Shawmut Bank, 1976-78; v.p. corp. devel. Arthur D. Little, Inc., 1978-79; v.p. Conn. Gen. Life Ins. Co., 1979-85; pres. CIGNA Securities, 1983-85; chmn. Templeton, Inc., 1985-92, 95—; exec. v.p. McGraw-Hill Inc., 1988-90; pres. micromarketing divsn. ADVO, 1990-95; faculty Williams Sch. Banking; adv. com. Bur. of Census, 1978-84; bd. dirs. Guardian Life Ins. Co., Providence Jour. Co., Age Wave, Inc., Cybex, Inc.; tchr. Amos Tuck Grad. Sch. Bus., Dartmouth Coll., 1964-65, exec.-in-residence, 1978, 80; bd. overseers, 1979-85; exec.-in-residence Wheaton Coll., 1978; vis. prof. Simmons Grad. Sch. Mgmt., 1978; mem. schs. adv. coun. Bank Mktg. Assn., 1976-78; mem. corp. adv. bd. Hartford Nat. Bank & Trust Co., 1980-87. Columnist Am. Banker, 1976-78. Mem. Mass. Gov.'s Commn. on Status of Women, 1977-79; bd. corporators Babson Coll., 1977-80; adv. bd. Boston Mayor's Office Cultural Affairs, 1977-79; bd. dirs. Blue Shield of Mass., 1976-79, Greater Hartford Arts Coun., 1979-93; trustee Children's Mus. Hartford, 1980-82; corporator Inst. of Living, 1981-92; regent U. Hartford, 1982—; bd. dirs. Hartford Art Sch., 1982-94, Hartford Stage Co., 1985—, Manhattan Theatre Club, 1988-91, Inst. for Future, 198-92, N.Y. Internat. Festival of Arts, 1988-91, Goodspeed Opera, 1988—, Inst. Design, 1990—. Mem. Phi Beta Kappa, Phi Kappa Phi, Kappa Alpha Theta. Home and Office: 89 River Rd East Haddam CT 06423-1402

CLARKE, INGRID GADWAY, academic ombudsman, consultant; b. Bad Homburg, Hesse, Fed. Republic Germany, Sept. 21, 1942; came to U.S., 1964, naturalized, 1982; d. Johann Kajetan and Irmgard (Schneider) Rebholz; m. David Scott Clarke, Dec. 24, 1984. B.A. equivalent, Johann Wolfgang Goethe Universität, Frankfurt, Fed. Republic Germany, 1964; M.A., Memphis State U., 1965; postgrad. Tulane U., 1965-69; Ph.D., So. Ill. U., 1984. Instr. So. Ill. U., Carbondale, 1969-74, univ. ombudsman, 1974—, also chairperson bd. dirs. students' legal assistance program, 1980-86 . Mem. Carbondale Human Relations Com., 1974-76; chairperson Carbondale Fair Housing Bd., 1978-82. Fulbright scholar, 1964-67. Mem. Fulbright Alumni Assn., Univ. and Coll. Ombudsman Assn. (founder and first pres. 1985-86), Soc. Profls. in Dispute Resolution Delta Phi Alpha. Avocations: opera; tennis; skiing. Office: So Ill U Office Univ Ombudsman Carbondale IL 62901

CLARKE, JANE CAROL, educational administrator, principal; b. Shelby, Ohio, Mar. 20, 1940; d. Clyde Eugene and Hazel Ruth (Johnson) Smith; m. Edward Dean Clarke, July 15, 1971; children: Suzanne, Karla, Jeff, Ethan, Jeremy. Assoc. degree, Lansing C.C., 1977; BS, Ea. Mich. U., 1980, MA, 1982. Cert. dir. spl. edn., elem. adminstr., K-12 spl. edn. tchr. Dir. spl. edn., prin., dir. alt. edn. Stockbridge (Mich.) Schs., 1988—; dir. Mich. Alt. Edn. Orgn., 1995-96; recommended to Dissertation Nat. Rsch. Conf.-Ednl. Rsch. Assn., 1995. Mem. AAUW, Mich. Adminstrs. of Spl. Edn., Mich. Elem. and Mid. Sch. Prins. Home: 4678 Pine Eagles Dr Brighton MI 48116 Office: Stockbridge Comty Schs 303 W Elizabeth Stockbridge MI 49285

CLARKE, JANICE CESSNA, principal; b. Inglewood, Calif., Sept. 8, 1936; d. Eldon W. and Helen V. Cessna; m. Jack F. Clarke, Mar. 30, 1958; children: Scott Alan, Kristin Ann, Kerry Suzanne. BA, U. of Redlands, 1958; MA in Teaching, Reed Coll., 1963; EdD, U. Nev., Reno, 1993. Cert. tchr., adminstr., Nev. Elem. tchr. Portland (Oreg.) Pub. Schs., 1959-62, Eugene (Oreg.) Pub. Schs., 1964-66; music tchr. Tempe (Ariz.) Pub. Schs., 1969-70; music tchr. Washoe County Sch. Dist., Reno, 1971-80, tchr. gifted and talented program, 1980-89, coord. gifted and talented program, 1989-93; prin. Brown Elem. Sch., Reno, 1993—; bd. dirs. Far West Lab. for Ednl. Rsch., San Francisco, 1983-90. Mem. Nev. State Bd. Edn., 1982-90, pres., 1984-86. Recipient Disting. Svc. award Washoe County Tchr. Assn., 1974, Tchr. of Month award Reno/Sparks C. of C., 1984; named to El Segundo High Sch. Hall of Fame, 1989. Mem. NEA, Nev. State Edn. Assn., Nev. Assn. Sch. Adminstrs., Nev. Sch. Bds. Assn. (bd. dirs. 1982-90), Nat. Assn. Elem. Sch. Prins., Phi Delta Kappa, Delta Kappa Gamma. Office: Brown Sch 13815 Spelling Ct Reno NV 89511-7232

CLARKE, JOYCE ANNE, biochemist; b. Sheffield, Eng., Sept. 17, 1947; came to U.S., 1968; d. Fred A. and Annie (Johnson) C.; m. Frank Ogawa, 1982. BA with honors, Girton Coll., Cambridge U., Eng., 1968, MA, 1972; PhD (fellow) in Biochemistry, U. Calif., Riverside, 1974. Research asst. dept. biochemistry U. Calif.-Riverside, 1968-73; lectr. dept. life scis. Middle East Tech. U., Ankara, Turkey, 1974-76; Dept. Energy research asso. Plant Research Lab., Mich. State U., East Lansing, 1976-78; assoc. biochemist dept. plant scis. U. Calif., Riverside, 1979-82, comm. coord. Internat. Club, 1979-82; biochemist Sci. Applications Internat. Corp., 1985-86, 91—; lectr. dept. biochemistry Va. Polytech. Inst. and State U., Blacksburg, 1986-89. Exec.-on-loan to Rebuild L.A., 1992-93. NSF fellow, 1976-78; Phi Beta Kappa scholar, 1972-73. Mem. Anglo-Am. Friendship Club, Oxford and Cambridge Club of L.A. (treas. 1992-95, v.p. 1996—). Episcopalian. Contbr. articles on plant psysiology and jojoba biochemistry to profl. jours. Home: 14901 Newport Ave Apt 101 Tustin CA 92680-6189

CLARKE, KIT HANSEN, radiologist; b. Louisville, May 24, 1944; d. Hans Peter and Katie (Bird) Hansen; AB, Randolph-Macon Woman's Coll., 1966; MD, U. Louisville, 1969; m. John M. Clarke, Feb. 14, 1976; children: Brett Bonnett, Blair Hansen, Brandon Chamberlain; stepchildren: Gray Campbell, Jeffrey William John M. Intern, Louisville Gen. Hosp., 1969-70; resident in internal medicine and radiology U. Tenn., Knoxville, 1970-73; resident in radiology U.S. Fla., Tampa, 1973-74; staff radiologist, chief spl. procedures Palms of Pasadena, St. Petersburg, Fla., 1974—, chmn. radiology dept., 1992—. Active Fla. Competitive Swim Assn. of AAU. Diplomate Am. Bd. Radiology. Fellow Am. Coll. Radiology; mem. AMA, Fla. West Coast Radiology Soc., Radiol. Soc. N.Am., Fla. Med. Assn., Pinellas County Med. Soc., Fla. Radiology Soc., Am. Horse Show Assn. (hunter, jumper divsn). Episcopalian. Home: 7171 9th St S Saint Petersburg FL 33705-6218 Office: 1609 Pasadena Ave S Saint Petersburg FL 33707-4565

CLARKE, MARJORIE JANE, environmental consultant, author, researcher; b. Miami, Fla., July 14, 1953; d. Garnet Winston Clarke and Janice Marie (Platt) Johnson. BA in Geology, Smith Coll., 1975; MA in Environ. Sci., Johns Hopkins U., 1978; MS in Energy Tech., NYU, 1982; MPhil, CUNY, 1996. Cert. qualified environ. profl. Intern EPA, Washington, 1974-75, 76; phys. scientist U.S. EPA, N.Y.C., 1978; sr. economist Tri-State Regional Planning Commn., N.Y.C., 1979-81; policy coord. N.Y. Power Authority, N.Y.C., 1981-83; environ. scientist N.Y.C. Dept. Sanitation, 1984-88; dir. solid waste rsch. INFORM, Inc., N.Y.C., 1988-90; tech. rsch. cons. WNET-Channel 13, N.Y.C., 1990; environ. cons. Natural Resources Def. Coun., N.Y.C., 1990—; sr. solid waste cons. INFORM, 1990-94; cons. Air and Waste Mgmt. Assn., 1993-94; rsch. fellow Ctr. for Applied Studies of the Environment, CUNY, 1992—; cons. Hampshire County (Eng.) Coun., 1994-95; cons. to Commonweal, 1996; mem. steering com. Citywide Recycling Adv. Bd., N.Y.C., 1991—; mem. Camden County Environ. Tech. Adv. Com., 1993-95; mem. N.J. Sept. Environ. Protection and Energy Mercury Emission Standard-Setting Task Force, 1992-95; mem. N.Y. State Adv. Bd. on Operating Requirements, Albany, 1988-92; examiner Qualified Environ. Profls. Program, 1995—; peer reviewer Environ. Def. Fund, N.Y.C., 1988—, Nat. Resources Def. Coun., N.Y.C., 1988-90; chair Manhattan Citizens' Solid Waste Adv. Bd., 1992-94, vice chair, 1994-96, chair waste prevention com., 1991—. Contbr. articles to profl. confs. and jours., 1983—. Mem. USEPA/Nat. Recycling Coaliton's Nat. Task Force to develop and promote a source reduction procurement strategy, 1996—. Recipient citation Dartmouth Coll., 1974; featured on cover Money Mag., 1981; U.S. EPA grantee, 1991—; Gilleece fellow CUNY, 1991-95. Mem. ASME (indsl. and mcpl. waste rsch. com. 1986—, operator cert. com. 1988—), Nat. Acad. Scis. (nat. rsch. coun. com. health effects waste incineration 1995—), Air and Waste Mgmt. Assn. (sec. 1988-89, session chair annual meeting 1988—, vice chair 1989-90, chmn. solid waste and thermal treatment com. 1990-92, vice chair solid waste intercom. task force 1992-94, chair integrated waste mgmt. com. 1994—, tech. dir. video 1993-94), N.Y. State Solid Waste Combustion Inst. (tech. adv. com. 1988-92), Riverside-Inwood Neighborhood Gardens (founder, pres. 1984—), N.Y. Cycle Club (ride leader 1982—). Democrat. Home and Office: 1795 Riverside Dr Apt 5F New York NY 10034-5334

CLARKE, MARY ELIZABETH, retired army officer; b. Rochester, N.Y., Dec. 3, 1924; d. James M. and Lillian E. (Young) Kennedy. Student U. Md., 1962; D.Mil.Sci., Norwich U., Northfield, Vt., 1978. Joined U.S. Army as pvt., 1945, advanced through grades to maj. gen., 1978; exec. asst. to Chief of Plans and Policies, Office of Econ. Opportunity, 1966-67; comdr. WAC Tng. Bn., 1967-68; office dep. chief of staff for pers., 1968-71; WAC staff adviser 6th Army, 1971-72; comdr., comdt. U.S. Women's Army Corps Ctr. and Sch., 1972-74; chief WAC Adv. Office, U.S. Army Mil. Pers. Ctr., Washington, 1974-75, dir. Women's Army Corps, Washington, 1975-78; comdr. U.S. Army Mil. Police and Chem. Sch. Tng. Ctr., Ft. McClellan, Ala., 1978-80; dir. human resources devel. Office of Dep. Chief of Staff for Personnel, Washington, 1980-81, ret., 1981; hon. prof. mil. sci. Jacksonville (Ala.) State U. Mem. Def. Adv. Com. on Women in the Svcs., 1984—, vice chmn., 1986—; mem. adv. com. Women Veterans, 1989—, chmn., 1991; mem. The Presidential Commn. on the Assignment of Women in the Armed Forces. Decorated D.S.M.; recipient Toastmasters Internat. award, 1984, Nat. Veteran's award, 1994. Mem. Assn. of U.S. Army (coun. trustees), United States Automobile Assn. (bd. dirs. 1978-88), WAC Assn., WAC Mus. Found., Bus. and Profl. Women's Club. Address: 514 Fairway Dr SW Jacksonville AL 36265-3301

CLARKE, MARY PATRICIA, sports league communications executive; b. N.Y.C., May 31, 1966; d. Peter Francis and Ellen Marie (Murphy) C. BA, Fordham U., 1988; MS, Syracuse U., 1991. Asst. prodr. Good Morning Am. ABC/Capital Cities, N.Y.C., 1986-89; acct. supr. Edelman Pub. Rels., N.Y.C., 1991-92; Cohn & Wolfe Pub. Rels., N.Y.C., 1992-93; dir. corporate comm. NHL, N.Y.C., 1993—. Recipient Outstanding Tchg. Asst. award Syracuse U., 1991. Roman Catholic. Office: NHL Enterprises 1251 6th Ave New York NY 10019

CLARKE, URANA, writer, musician, educator; b. Wickliffe-on-the-Lake, Ohio, Sept. 8, 1902; d. Graham Warren and Grace Urana (Olsaver) C.; artists and tchrs. diploma Mannes Music Sch., N.Y.C., 1925; cert. Dalcroze Sch. Music, N.Y.C., 1950; student Pembroke Coll., Brown U.; BS, Mont. State U., 1967, M of Applied Sci., 1970. Mem. faculty Mannes Music Sch., 1922-49, Dalcroze Sch. Music, 1949-54; adv. editor in music The Book of Knowledge, 1949-65; v.p., dir. Saugatuck Circle Housing Devel.; guest lectr. Hayden Planetarium, 1945; guest lectr., bd. dirs. Roger Williams Park Planetarium, Providence; radio show New Eng. Skies, Providence, 1961-64, Skies Over the Big Sky Country, Livingston, Mont., 1964-79, Birds of the Big Sky Country, 1972-79, Great Music of Religion, 1974-79; mem. adv. com. Nat. Rivers and Harbors Congress, 1947-58; instr. continuing edn. Mont. State U. Chmn. Park County chpt. ARC, 1967-92, chmn. emeritus 1992—, co-chmn. county blood program, first aid instr. trainer, 1941-93; instr. ARC cardio-pulmonary resuscitation, 1976-84; mem. Mont. Commn. Nursing and Nursing Edn., 1974-76; mem. Park County Local Govt. Study Com., 1974-76, chmn., 1984-86, vice-chair, 94-96; chmn. Park County Red Cross, 1995—. Mem. Am. Acad. Polit. Sci., Am. Musicol. Soc., Royal Astron. Soc. Can., Inst. Nav., Maria Mitchell Soc. Nantucket, N.Am. Yacht Racing Union, AAAS, Meteoritical Soc., Internat. Soc. Mus. Research, Skyscrapers (sec.-treas. 1960-63), Am. Guild Organists, Park County Wilderness Assn. (treas.), Trout Unlimited, Nature Conservancy, Big Sky Astron. Soc. (dir. 1965—), Sierra Club. Lutheran. Club: Cedar Point Yacht. Author: The Heavens are Telling (astronomy), 1951; Skies Over the Big Sky Country, 1965; also astron. news-letter, View It Yourself, weekly column Big Skies, 1981—, contbr. to mags. on music, nav. and astronomy. Pub. Five Chorale Preludes for Organ, 1975; also elem. two-piano pieces. Inventor, builder of Clarke Adjustable Piano Stool. Address: Log-A-Rhythm 9th St Island Livingston MT 59047

CLARK-JACKSON, SUSAN, publishing executive. Pres., pub. Reno Gazette-Jour., 1985—; sr. group pres. Pacific Newspaper Group, Gannett; bd. dirs. Harrah's Entertainment, Inc.; bd. visitors John S. Knight Fellowships for Profl. Journalists, Stanford U. Office: Gannett Co Inc Box 22000 955 Kuenzli Reno NV 89520

CLARKSON, CAROLE LAWRENCE, insurance company professional; b. Fredericksburg, Va., Dec. 18, 1942; d. Jerry Allen and Gladys Mae (Eubank) Lawrence; m. David Wendell Morris, Aug. 14, 1965 (div. 1977); 1 child, Peyton Lawrence; m. Lawrence Herbert Clarkson, Aug. 14, 1982. BA, Purdue U., 1965; postgrad., Ind. U., Indpls., 1970, U. Ill., 1971-73, U. Louisville Sch. of Bus., 1980-82. Pub. sch. tchr. various, Ind., Okla., Ill., N.C., Italy, 1965-75; librarian documentation U. Louisville Computing Ctr., 1980-82, IBM Corp., Austin, Tex., 1983-85; ins. mgr. Ohio State Life Ins. Co., Columbus, 1985-88, Community Life Ins. Co., Columbus, 1988-90; hosp. audit/stop loss coord. Health Adminstrn. Svcs., Houston, 1991—; supervisory mgr. Ins. Inst. of Am., 1987—. Mem. Internat. Claims Assn. (assoc. life and health claims 1987), Nat. Assn. Female Execs., Purdue U. Alumni Assn. Home: 2006 Kelona Dr Spring TX 77386-2541

CLARKSON, EDITH WEST, nursing administrator; b. Refugio, Tex., Feb. 8, 1942; d. Edward Allison and Jeannette Frances (Marsden) C. BSN, U. Tex., 1965, MSN, 1975. RN, Tex. Head nurse, staff nurse U. Tex. Med. Br., Galveston, 1965-68, 70-74; staff nurse Dr. Michael DeBakey's first heart transplant team in U.S. Meth. Hosp., Houston, 1968-70; staff nurse-surg. ICU Audie Murphy VA Hosp., San Antonio, 1976-79; quality assurance coord. VA Med Ctr., Albuquerque, 1980-81; staff nurse-surg. ICU De Tax Hosp., Victoria, Tex, 1983-84; quality assurance coord. Spohn Hosp., Corpus Christi, Tex., 1984; staff nurse med.- surg. Santa Rosa Hosp., San Antonio, 1984-86; nursing supr. Meth. Hosp., San Antonio, 1986-92; dir. patient care svcs. Refugio (Tex.) County Meml. Hosp., 1992-93; patient care coord.-hospice AIM Hospice/Home Health, Beeville, Tex., 1993-96; dir. adult psychology and chem. dependency Columbia Bayview Hosp., Corpus Christi, Tex., 1996—; clin. preceptor RN refresher program, Meth. Hosp., San Antonio, 1989-92, mem. instl. rev. bd., 1991-92; mem. bus. & industry adv. coun. San Antonio Coll., 1990-92. Bd. dirs. USDA Natural Resources Conservation Svc., Refugio, 1992-96. Mem. ANA (congl. dist. coord. 1992-96), Tex. Nurse Assn. (dist. 17 chmn. govtl. affairs com. 1992—, Tex. so. region rep. state govtl. affairs com. 1993—, dist. 17 pres.-elect 1994-95, pres. 1995-96), Sigma Theta Tau. Home: PO Box 883 Refugio TX 78377-0883 Office: Columbia Bayview Hosp 6226 Saratoga Corpus Christi TX 78414

CLARKSON, ELISABETH ANN HUDNUT, civic worker; b. Youngstown, Ohio, Apr. 20, 1925; d. Herbert Beecher and Edith (Schaaf) Hudnut; AB, Wilson Coll., 1947; MA, State U. N.Y., 1973, also postgrad.; LHD (hon.),

Wilson Coll., 1985; m. William M.E. Clarkson, Sept. 23, 1950; children: Alison H., David B., Andrew E. With J.L. Hudson Co., Detroit, 1947-50; writer The Minute Parade, daily Sta. WGR, Detroit, 1948-50; trustee Wilson Coll., Chambersburg, Pa., 1970-83, chmn. bd. trustees, 1979-82; bd. dirs. Buffalo Mus. Sci., 1972-87, 90—; mem. Trinity Episcopal Ch., 1950—, Trinity Vestry, 1996—, Racism Commn. Episcopal Diocese of W. N.Y., 1989-92, Cultural Leadership Group, 1994—; bd. dirs., companion-in-charge Soc. Companion of the Holy Cross, 1986-90, N.Y. State Mus., 1985-90; past chmn. jr. group Alright Knox Art Gallery; collector, curator Graphic Controls Corp. collection art, 1976-83; bd. dirs. Bischoff Clarkson Hudnut Corp., North Creek, N.Y., 1973-83; bd. trustees Clarkson Ctr. for Human Svcs., 1995—. Author: You Can Always Tell a Freshman, 1949, An Adirondack Archive: The Trail to Windover, 1993; also articles, dramatic presentations, archival materials Adirondack Mus., 1950-77. Recipient Trustee award for disting. svc. Wilson Coll., 1983, trustee emeritus. Mem. Buffalo Art Commn., 1983—, chmn. 1990-96; mem. cmty. adv. panel Niagara Frontier Transp. Authority, 1991-94; mem. exec. bd. arts adv. coun. SUNY at Buffalo, 1985-95; bd. dirs. N.Y. State Mus. Assn., Albany, 1985-90; mem. Garret Club, Buffalo Tennis and Squash Club; sustainer Jr. League, 1983—. Episcopalian. Home: 156 Bryant St Buffalo NY 14222-2003

CLARKSON, JOCELYN ADRENE, medical technologist; b. Bennettsville, S.C., July 9, 1952; d. Henry Louis and Frankie Allene (Carter) C. BA in Biology, Columbia (S.C.) Coll., 1973; cert. med. tech., Presbyn. Hosp., Charlotte, N.C., 1975. Coll. tutor of Germanic language Columbia Coll., 1970-73, switchboard operator, 1972-73; lab aide Richland Meml. Hosp., Columbia, 1974, now, med. technologist; profl. model. Appeared (TV commls.) Back Porch Restaurant and Meat Market, 1992, (film) The Chasers; author: poems, compilation, short stories, Messages from Hijac, 1989. Mem. Am. Soc. Clin. Pathologists (assoc.), Assn. for Studies of Classical African Civilization, African Am. Resource Inst. Roman Catholic. Home: 201 H L Clarkson Rd Hopkins SC 29061-9723

CLARNO, BEVERLY ANN, state legislator, farmer; b. Langlois, Oreg., Mar. 29, 1936; d. Howard William and Evelyn June (Young) Boice; m. Ray Clarno, July 15, 1983; children: Dan, Don, Randy, Cindi. Student, Marylhurst Coll., 1985, Lewis & Clark Law Sch., 1985-87. Real estate broker Lake Realty and Hatfield & Skopil, Lake Oswego, Oreg., 1984-85; pres. T & H Hog Farms, Wasco, Oreg., 1973-76; securities examiner State of Oreg., Salem, 1981-83; circuit ct. clerk Deschutes County, Bend, Oreg., 1987-88; state legislator State of Oreg., 1988—; spkr. Oreg. House, 1995—. Recipient Cost Cutting award, Citizens for Cost Effective Govt., Portland, 1991. Mem. Boys & Girls Aid Soc., Kiwanis Club, Lions Club, High Desert Mus., Eastern Star. Republican. Methodist. Home: 25325 Dodds Rd Bend OR 97701-9370 Office: Oregon House Reps State Capitol Salem OR 97310

CLARY, ALEXIA BARBARA, management company executive; b. Waterbury, Conn., Sept. 17, 1954; d. John Joseph and Veza (Mandzik) Zurlis; 1 child, Jason Farrell. BBA, U. Miami, Coral Gables, Fla., 1976; postgrad., U. New Haven, 1978-80, Mercer U., 1988-89. Buyer Hewlett Packard, Cupeztino, Calif., 1981-83; sr. buyer Mannesman Tally, Seattle, 1983; purchase mgr. ICI, Redmond, Wash., 1983-84; commodity mgr. No. Telecom, St. Mountain, Ga., 1985-88; mfg. rep. Montgomery Mktg., Norcross, Ga., 1988-90; internat. purchasing agt. Sci. Atlanta, Norcross, Ga., 1990-91; pres. Farrell Mgmt. Group, Lawrenceville, Ga., 1991-92; sr. buyer Amphenol, Danbury, Conn., 1992-94; purchasing mgr. Danaher-Gulton Graphic, East Greenwhich, R.I., 1994-96, King's Electronics, Tuckahoe, N.Y., 1996—. U. Miami scholar, 1974-75. Mem. Women in Electronics (v.p. sponsors 1989-90, guest speaker 1989), Nat. Assn. Female Execs., Nat. Assn. Purchasing Mgrs. Republican. Roman Catholic. Home: 18 Cynthia St Waterbury CT 06708

CLARY, ROSALIE BRANDON STANTON, timber farm executive, civic worker; b. Evanston, Ill., Aug. 3, 1928; d. Frederick Charles Hite-Smith and Rose Cecile (Liebich) Stanton; BS, Northwestern U., 1950, MA, 1954; m. Virgil Vincent Clary, Oct. 17, 1959; children: Rosalie Marian Hawley, Frederick Stanton, Virgil Vincent, Kathleen Elizabeth. Tchr., Chgo. Public Schs., 1951-55, adjustment tchr., 1956-61; faculty Loyola U., Chgo., 1963; v.p. Stanton Enterprises, Inc., Adams County, Miss., 1971-89; author Family History Record, genealogy record book, Kenilworth, Ill., 1977—. also lectr. Leader Girl Scouts U.S., Winnetka, Ill., 1969-71, 78-86, Cub Scouts, 1972-77; badge counselor Boy Scouts Am., 1978-87; election judge Rep. Com., 1977—; vol. Winnetka Libr. Genealogy Projects Com., 1995—. Mem. Nat. Soc. DAR (Ill. rec. sec. 1979-81, nat. vice chmn. program com. 1980-83, state vice regent 1986-88, state regent 1989-91, rec. sec. gen., 1992-95), Am. Forestry Assn., Forest Farmers Assn., North Suburban Geneal. Soc. (governing bd. 1979-86), Winnetka Hist. Soc. (governing bd. 1978-90, 95—), Internat. Platform Assn., Delta Gamma (mem. nat. cabinet 1985-89). Roman Catholic. Home: 509 Elder Ln Winnetka IL 60093-4122 Office: PO Box 401 Kenilworth IL 60043-0401

CLAUS, CAROL JEAN, small business owner; b. Uniondale, N.Y., Dec. 17, 1959; d. Charles Joseph and Frances Meta (Fichter) C.; m. Armand Joseph Gasperetti, Jr., July 7, 1985. Student pub. schs., Uniondale. Asst. mgr. Record World, L.I., N.Y., 1977-82, mgr. Info. Builders Inc., N.Y.C., 1982-92; pres. Carol's Creations, Belen, N.Mex. Mem. NAFE, Nat. Organization for Women. Democrat. Roman Catholic.

CLAUSEN, BETTY JANE HANSEN, retired social worker, travel consultant; b. Brooklyn, Wis., Oct. 25, 1925; d. Arthur John and Kathryn (Hefty) Hansen; m. Henry Albert Clausen, Jan. 31, 1948 (div. 1976); 1 child, Scott Alyn. BA, Beloit Coll., 1947. Psychometric sec. Vocat. Counseling Bur., Rockford (Ill.) Coll., 1947-48; classified ad-taker Beloit (Wis.) Daily News, 1948-49; copy-writer WROK, Rockford, 1955-60; tchr. elementary schs., Rockford, Elmhurst, Ill., 1960-61; exec. mgr. Melrose Park (Ill.) C. of C., 1961-67; mng. dir. S.W. Sr. Center, Parma Heights, Ohio, 1967-77; exec. dir. Sr. Citizens, Inc., Hamilton, Ohio, 1977-90, ret. 1990. Founder, pres. Easter Seal Parents Group Rockford, 1957-60, project chmn. Villa Park, Ill., 1963-65; treas. Easter Seal Aux., 1965-66; treas. United Cerebral Palsy, Rockford, 1959-60, bd. dirs. Ill. Soc., 1959-60; co-chmn. 53-Minute March, Elmhurst, 1963; pres. Freeman Sch. PTA., Rockford, 1959-60; chmn. exceptional child PTA, Elmhurst, 1962-66; hon. life mem. Ill. PTA.; mem. S.W. Community Resource Coun., 1968-77, Butler County Coun. on Aging, 1977-83; bd. dirs. Coun. Exceptional Children, New Neighbors League, S.W. Cleveland chpt., 1967; mem. coun. on aging Cin. Area Adv. Coun., 1979-83, coun. task force on aging Butler County Human Svcs. Named Citizen of Week, Elmhurst Press, 1966, Outstanding Sr. Citizen of Butler County by Cin. Area Coun. on Aging, 1991. Mem. Ill. C. of C., Ill. Assn. C. of C. Execs., West Suburban Coun. Chambers, Ohio Assn. Sr. Citizens Ctrs., Altrusa, Delta Delta Delta. Methodist. Home: 1224 Beissinger Rd Hamilton OH 45013-1106

CLAUSSEN, LISA RENEE, engineering executive; b. Cedar Grove, Wis., Mar. 28, 1964; d. Erwin John and Shirley Ann (Winkelhorst) C. BS in Indsl. Engring., U. Wis., Platteville, 1987; MS in Ops. Mgmt., U. Ark., Fayeteville, 1990. Registered profl. engr., Wis. Quality engring. process coord. Speed Queen Co., Ripon, Wis., 1987-88; plant quality control engr. Speed Queen Co., Searcy, Ark., 1988-90; quality engring. rep. Snap-on Inc., Kenosha, Wis., 1990-92, quality engr. med. products divsn., 1992-94; quality assurance supr. Snap-on Inc., Elizabethton, Tenn., 1994—. Active Nat. Kidney Found. Wis., Milw., 1994—. Mem. NAFE, Am. Soc. Quality Control (cert. quality engr., cert. quality auditor, membership chair N.E. Tenn. 1995-96, chair-elect 1996—), Inst. Indsl. Engrs. (dir. support Tri-Cities Tenn. 1995—). Office: Snap On Inc 2195 State Line Rd Elizabethton TN 37643

CLAWSON, ROXANN ELOISE, college administrator, computer company executive; b. Dallas, Oct. 15, 1945; d. Robert Wellington Clawson and Jeannette Irene (Rodenhauser) Clawson Clayton. BFA, Mich. State U., 1968. Library asst. Cooper Union, N.Y.C., 1970-75, asst. librarian, 1976-82, asst. to dean, 1985—; computer cons., 1986—. Acting appearance in The Dragon's Nest, La MaMa Theatre, 1989. Mem. NAFE, N.Y. Personal Computer Group. Democrat. Lutheran. Avocation: administration.

CLAX, FREDA MARIE, graphic designer, small business owner; b. Red Bank, N.J., Nov. 19, 1959; d. Joseph and Anita (Desbordes) C. Assoc. Specialized Tech., Art Inst. Pitts., 1981; BFA, Sch. Visual Arts, N.Y.C., 1987. Freelance graphic designer and illustrator various cos. various cos., N.Y.C., 1981-85; freelance designer Self Mag., Conde Nast Publs., N.Y.C., 1987; freelance designer communications design dept. Citicorp, N.Y.C., 1987, Weight Watchers Mag., N.Y.C., 1987; freelance designer Boating Mag., 1987; jr. designer Prima Mag., Gruner and Jahr Publs., N.Y.C., 1987-88; freelance designer In Fashion and Internat. Sportswear Mag., Murdoch Publs., N.Y.C., 1988, Mademoiselle mag., 1989, Episodes mag., 1990; asst. art dir. Footwear News mag. and newspaper Fairchild Publs., N.Y.C., 1988-89; sr. designer Essence Mag., N.Y.C., 1989-90; freelance cons. Mademoiselle mag., 1990—; freelance designer various clients, Hackensack, N.J., 1991—; freelance creative dir. Liquid mag., 1995; owner, creative dir. Sandbox Designs, Tinton Falls, N.J., 1995—; freelance creative dir. Liquid mag., 1995. Mem. NAFE, Inst. Graphic Arts, Eastern Monmouth Area C. of C. Office: Sandbox Designs 79 William St Tinton Falls NJ 07724

CLAXTON, HARRIETT MAROY JONES, retired English language educator; b. Dublin, Ga., Aug. 27, 1930; d. Paul Jackson and Maroy Athalia (Chappell) Jones; m. Edward B. Claxton, Jr., May 27, 1953; children—E. B. III, Paula Jones. AA, Bethel Woman's Coll., 1949; AB magna cum laude, Mercer U., 1951; MEd, Ga. Coll., 1965. Social worker Laurens County Welfare Bd., Dublin, 1951-56; high sch. tchr., Dublin, 1961-66; instr. Middle Ga. Coll., Cochran, 1966-71, asst. prof. English, lit. and speech, 1971-85, assoc. prof. 1985-86; research tchr. Trinity Christian Sch., 1986, 92, sr. English tchr., 1986-87; part-time tchr., Ga. Coll., 1987, Emanuel County Jr. Coll., 1988-96, Middle Ga. Coll., 1985-96. Weekly columnist Dublin Courier Herald, 1993—; contbr. articles to profl. jours. and newspapers; editor Laurens County History, II, 1987. Pres. bd. Dublin Assn. Fine Arts, 1974-76, 82-84, Dublin Hist. Soc., 1976-78; mem. Laurens County Library Bd., 1960-68; chmn. Dublin Hist. Rev. Bd., 1980—; sec. Am. Assn. Ret. Persons, 1987-90; v.p. Dublin Cmty. Concert, 1991—. Named Woman of Yr., St. Patrick's Festival, Dublin, 1979, Most Popular tchr., Dublin Ctr., 1985, Olympic Torch Bearer 1996; recipient Outstanding Service award Cancer Soc., Dublin, 1985, 93, Ga. Coll. Outstanding Alumni award for cmty. svc., 1996. Mem. DAR (historian, regent, state, dist. and nat. awards), Sigma Mu, Alpha Delta Pi, Phi Theta Kappa, Chi Delta Phi, Delta Kappa Gamma. Democrat. Baptist. Clubs: Woman's Study (pres.), Erin Garden (pres.) (Dublin). Home: 101 Rosewood Dr Dublin GA 31021-4129

CLAY, JOAN SANDERS, social studies educator; b. Princeton, Ark., Feb. 21, 1944; d. John Edward and Loreader (Fuller) Sanders; m. James H. Clay, Sept. 29, 1967 (div. Feb. 1992); children: Alwana Katrina Elizabeth, Jayme Anjanette. BA in History, U. Ark., Pine Bluff, 1965; MEd, N.E. La. U., 1975; postgrad., So. U., 1980, Grambling State U., 1981-83. Cert. secondary sch. tchr., Ariz. Classroom tchr. Hot Springs (Ark.) Sch. Dist., 1965-69, Morehouse Parish Schs., Bastrop, La., 1969-92; master tchr., evaluator La. Dept. Edn., Baton Rouge, 1990-92; substitute tchr., homebound tchr. Tolleston (Ariz.) Union Sch. Dist., 1992—; mem. faculty MEd program U. Phoenix, 1993—; coord. extended day program Roosevelt Sch. Dist., Phoenix, 1992; adj. faculty Ottawa U., Tempe, Ariz., 1993—; developer, presenter workshops in field. Author social studies curriculum State of La., 1980-86. Bd. dirs. Morehouse Edn. Assn., Bastrop, 1976-92, La. Coun. for Social Studies, 1980-92, program coord., 1976-78; cons. Delta Sigma Theta, Monroe, La., 1987-92; parental involvement worker St. Mary Ch., Bastrop, 1976. Recipient Svc. award La. Coun. for Social Studies, 1983, Voice of Democracy award VFW, 1988, Svc. award La. Dept. Edn., 1991; grantee U.S. Bicentennial Commn., 1988. Mem. Nat. Coun. for Social Studies (mem. profl. ethics com. 1990—, chair subcom. 1994), Alpha Kappa Alpha. Democrat. Methodist. Home: 4296 N 103rd Ave # 67 Phoenix AZ 85037-5510 Office: U Phoenix 4615 E Elwood St Phoenix AZ 85040-1958

CLAY, SUSAN JOSE, legislator; b. Lowell, Mass., Oct. 13, 1946; d. John Laughton and Maria Dolores (Abreu) C.; children: Jeffrey Alan, Dana Anthony Demers. BS, U. N.H., 1968. Pub. rels. cons. Clay-Wells Assocs., Durham, N.H., 1968-71; career/life counselor Women for Higher Edn., Hooksett, N.H., 1975-76; assoc. dir. St. Joseph Cmty. Svcs., Merrimack, N.H., 1976-78; cmty. rels. dir. Social Welfare Coun., Concord, N.H., 1978-80; lobbyist, exec. dir. Common Cause/N.H., Concord, 1981-95; legislator N.H. Gen. Ct., Concord, 1996—; owner, cons. Granite Profiles, Concord, 1992—; apptd. to legis. wetlands coun., legis. adv. commn., N.H. Comparative Risk Project. Editor: (rules handbook) Learning the Legislative Ropes, 1984, (commn. report) Committee on Legislative Reform, 1986; contbr. poetry to N.H. Profile mag., 1963-64. Mem. LWV, Concord, 1982-84, N.H. Bipartisan Comm. on Voter Participation, Concord, 1988, Commn. on Legis. Reform, Concord, 1986. Named Young Poet of Yr., N.H. Poetry Soc., 1964, Outstanding Young Woman in Am., 1984. Mem. Nat. Abortion and Reproductive Rights Action League, ACLU, N.H. Women's Lobby, Orgn. Women Legislators, Assn. of Women Lobbyists (organizer, pres.). Republican. Roman Catholic. Home: 150 Bunker Hill Rd New Boston NH 03070-4118 Office: NH House of Reps State House Mail St Concord NH 03301

CLAYBURGH, JILL, actress; b. N.Y.C., Apr. 30, 1944; d. Albert Henry and Julia (Door) C.; m. David Rabe, Mar., 1979. B.A., Sarah Lawrence Coll., 1966. Former mem., Charles Playhouse, Boston; Off-Broadway plays include The Nest; Broadway debut in The Rothschilds, 1970; stage appearances include In the Boom Boom Room (David Rabe), Design for Living (Noel Coward); film appearances include The Wedding Party, 1969, The Telephone Book, 1971, Portnoy's Complaint, 1972, The Thief Who Came to Dinner, 1973, The Terminal Man, 1974, Gable and Lombard, 1976, Silver Streak, 1976, Gable and Lombard, 1976, Semi-Tough, 1977, An Unmarried Woman, 1978, Luna, 1979, Starting Over, 1979, It's My Turn, 1980, First Monday in October, 1981, I'm Dancing as Fast as I Can, 1982, Hannah K, 1983, In Our Hands, 1984, Where Are The Children, 1986, Shy People, 1987, Beyond the Ocean, 1990, Whispers in the Dark, 1992, Le Grand Pardon II, 1992, Rich in Love, 1993, Naked in New York, 1994; appeared in TV films Snoop Sisters, 1972, The Art of Crime, 1975, Hustling, 1975, Griffin and Phoenix, 1976, Miles to Go..., 1986, Who Gets the Friends?, 1988, Fear Stalk, 1989, Unspeakable Acts, 1990, Reason for Living: the Jill Ireland Story, 1991, Trial: The Price of Passion, 1993, Firestorm: A Catastrophe in Oakland, 1993, For the Love of Nancy, 1994, Honor Thy Father and Mother: The True Story of the Menendez Brothers, 1994; TV documentary: Ask Me Anything: How to Talk to Kids About Sex, 1989. Recipient Best Actress award for An Unmarried Woman, Cannes Film Festival; Golden Apple award for best film actress in An Unmarried Woman. Office: care William Morris Agy 151 S El Camino Dr Beverly Hills CA 90212-2704*

CLAYPOOL, NANCY, social worker; b. Monterey, Calif., Aug. 6, 1957; d. Harold Herbert and Nancy Jeanne (Klohe) C.; 1 child, James Paul. BA in Social Welfare cum laude, San Francisco State U., 1980; M Social Work, U. Calif., Berkeley, 1985. Program developer Women's Found., San Francisco, 1984-85; foster care coord., house supr. Charila Svcs. for Girls, San Francisco, 1985-87; therapist Sierra Clinic, San Francisco, 1987-88; clin. social worker Youth Homes, Inc., Walnut Creek, Calif., 1988-90; homebased early childhood devel. tchr. Thurgood Marshall Family Resource Ctr., Oakland, Calif., 1990-92; psychiat. social worker Eden Med. Ctr., Castro Valley, Calif., 1992-94; chief clinician, primary therapist Transitions Geropsychiatry Alameda (Calif.) Hosp., 1994-96; program dir. Transitions Geopsychiatry Alameda (Calif) Hosp., 1996—. Contbr. articles to profl. publs. Mem. Alameda County Mental Health Bd., 1992—, chair, 1993-94, vice chair, 1994-95. Named Regional Clinician of Yr., Horizon Mental Health Svcs., 1994; Health-Social Networking grantee, 1984. Mem. Nat. Assn. Social Workers, Internat. Platform Assn. (appointee 1995). Home: 3946 35th Ave Oakland CA 94619-1435

CLAYTON, CANDACE SUE LINE, elementary school educator; b. Lima, Ohio, Aug. 27, 1948; d. Billy Jr. and Juanita Jean (Metcalfe) Line; m. Dennis Eldon Clayton, Aug. 12, 1972; children: Christopher Dennis, Adam Michael. BS in Edn., Miami U., Oxford, Ohio, 1970; MA in Edn., U. Dayton, 1993. Cert. elem. tchr. grades kindergarten through 8, Ohio; cert. media specialist grades kindergarten through 8, Ohio. Tchr. kindergarten Jackson Center (Ohio) Schs., 1970-79; tchr. 4th grade Hardin-Houston Schs., Houston, Ohio, 1987—; mem. Hardin Faculty Adv. Com., Sidney, Ohio, 1993-95. Recipient Hardin Houston Tchr. of Yr., 1996; Martha Holden Jennings grantee for Up to Our Elbors in Sci. program Jennings Found., 1994; Martha Holden Jennings scholar, 1995-96. Mem. Nat. Coun. Tchrs. English, Internat. Reading Assn. (Ohio coun., v.p. Shelby County chpt. 1989-91, pres. 1991-93), Delta Kappa Gamma. Home: 14450 Kirkwood Rd Sidney OH 45365-8930 Office: Hardin-Houston Elem Sch 10207 State Rt Sidney OH 45365

CLAYTON, EVA M., congresswoman, former county commissioner; b. Savannah, Ga., Sept. 16, 1934; m. Theaoseus T. Clayton; children: Theaoseus Jr., Martin, Reuben, Joanne. BS, Johnson C. Smith U.; MS, North Carolina Central U. Former commr. Warren County, N.C.; mem. 103rd Congress from 1st N.C. dist., Washington, D.C., 1993—; mem. agriculture com. resource conservation, rsch. and forestry, risk mgmt. and specialty crops 103rd Congress from 1st N.C. dist., mem. house democratic policy com.; ranking minority mem. Small Bus. subcom. on Procurement, Exports & Bus. Opportunities. Democrat. Office: US Ho of Reps 222 Cannon Washington DC 20515*

CLAYTON, JUDITH KAMM, arts administrator; b. Camden, N.J., Dec. 31, 1959; d. John Edward Jr. and Virginia (Kamm) C. Student, Montclair State Coll., 1978-80; AA, Ocean County Coll., 1991; BA, Rutgers U., 1994. Pharmacy technician Island Pharmacy, Ship Bottom, N.J., 1983-86, Chemist Shoppe, Medford, N.J., 1986-88, Comty. Med. Ctr., Toms River, N.J., 1988-95; curatorial asst. Painted Bride Art Ctr., Phila., 1994; curatorial asst., registrar Stedman Art Gallery, Camden, N.J., 1992-95; adminstrv. coord. Walt Whitman Ctr., Camden, 1995-96; exec. dir. South Jersey Cultural Alliance, 1996—; mem. benefit com. Mus. Edn. & Enrichment Program, Camden, 1992-95. Co-author: Johnson Park Restoration Project, 1994. Methodist.

CLAYTON, KATY, elementary education educator; b. Bellefonte, Pa., Feb. 21, 1956; d. Everette Lee and Donna June (Trowbridge) Swinney; m. Charles Edward Clayton Jr., July 15, 1977; children: Quinton, Meredith, Zachary. BS in Edn., Southwest Tex. State U., 1978, MEd in Reading, 1983. Tchr. kindergarten Lockhart (Tex.) Pub. Schs., 1978-80; owner pvt. day care San Marcos, Tex., 1980-84; tchr. 1st grade Crockett Elem. Sch., San Marcos, Tex., 1984-89, tchr. 2d grade, 1989-93, reading specialist, 1993—; dept. leader Crockett Elem. Sch., 1995—; cons. S.W. Tex. Tchr. Ctr., San Marcos, 1991-92; trainer Helping One Student to Succeed, 1995, tchr., 1996—. Bd. dirs. Little League, San Marcos, 1987-89; deacon 1st Christian Ch., San Marcos, 1988-92; presenter 23d Annual Tex. State Reading Assn. Conf., The Young Child and Literacy. Mem. Tex. Classroom Tchrs. Assn. (pres. 1990-91), Internat. Reading Assn., Reading Recovery Tchrs., Key Communicators. Democrat. Mem. Disciples of Christ. Home: 109 E Hillcrest San Marcos TX 78666-3239 Office: Crockett Elem Sch 1300 Girard St San Marcos TX 78666-2813

CLAYTON, LISA KATHLEEN, statistician, computer programmer; b. Apple Valley, Calif., June 19, 1962; d. Robert Alexander and Donna Ruth (Rudd) C.; m. Celia (Sally) Elvira Canjura, Apr. 20, 1993. Student, UCLA, 1982-85; BA, San Francisco State U., 1996. Data mgr. UCLA AIDS Ctr., L.A., 1985-91; rsch. statistician U. Calif., San Francisco, 1991—; computer cons. Deepthought Computing, L.A., 1987-91. Prodr. performance Dance Along Nutcracker, 1994, 95; lead clarinet Dixieland Dykes + 3, 1995. Pres., bd. dirs. Jon Sims Ctr. Performing Arts, San Francisco, 1995-96; pres. San Francisco Lesbian/Gay Freedom Band, 1994, bass clarinet player, 1992—. Mem. Assn. Computing Machinery.

CLAYTON, NORMA TOWNE, academic administrator, retired secondary education educator; b. Naples, Maine, Aug. 16, 1941; d. Norman Pingree and Elsie Adeline (Treadwell) Towne; m. John Middleton Clayton Jr., Aug. 17, 1968; 1 child, Signe Louisa. BA in Math., U. Maine, 1963; MEd in Natural Scis., U. Del., 1969, MBA, 1982. Cert. profl. secondary math. tchr., Del. Tchr. math. Alexis I. duPont High Sch., Red Clay Consol. Sch. Dist., Wilmington, Del., 1963-91; ret., 1991; program director Rape Crisis CONTACT Del., Wilmington; dir. planned giving Smith House, West Chester (Pa.) U. Deacon First and Cen. Presbyn. Ch., 1970-74, ruling elder, 1977-81, chairperson mission study and pastor search, 1989-90; mem. ministry unit New Castle Presbytery, 1990—, mem. new ch. devel. com., 1991— (chair 1993-94); mem. adminstrv. commn., 1992—, vice-moderator, 1992-93, moderator 1993-94. Mem. NEA (del. to assembly 1963—), Del. State Edn. Assn. (legis. liaison 1990), Nat. Coun. Tchrs. of Math., Del. Coun. Tchrs. of Math., Red Clay Edn. Assn. Home: 217 Walker Way Newark DE 19711-6121 Office: Devel Office Smith House West Chester U West Chester PA 19383

CLAYTON, VERNA LEWIS, state legislator; b. Hamden, Ohio, Feb. 28, 1937; d. Matthews L. and Yail (Miller) Lewis; m. Frank R. Clayton, Feb. 4, 1956; children: Valerie Clayton Euneman, Barry L. Office mgr., Village of Buffalo Grove, Ill., 1972-78, village clk., 1971-79, village pres., 1979-91; mem. Ill. Ho. of Reps., Springfield, 1993—. Mem. Lake County Solid Waste Planning Agy. (chmn. tech. com., chmn. agy.), Nat. League of Cities (chmn. transp. and communications steering com.). Recipient Disting. Service award Amvets, 1981. Mem. Northwest Mcpl. Conf. (pres. 1983-84), Chgo. Area Transp. Study Council Mayors (vice chmn. 1981-83, chmn. 1985-91), Mcpl. Clks. Ill. (treas. 1978-79), Mcpl. Clks. Lake County (pres. 1977-78), Ill. Mcpl. League (bd. dirs., v.p. 1985-90, pres. 1989-90), Buffalo Grove Rotary Club (hon. mem.), Buffalo Grove C. of C. (bd. dirs.). Republican. Methodist. Home: 2831 Acacia Ter Buffalo Grove IL 60089-6634 Office: 314 McHenry Rd Ste D-1 Buffalo Grove IL 60089-6749 also: 2119 N Stratton Bldg Springfield IL 62706

CLEARY, AUDREY, state legislator, nurse volunteer; b. Menominee, Mich., June 1, 1930; d. Edmund James and Laura Elizabeth (Mushynski) Boucher; m. Joseph Wolter Cleary, June 19, 1954; children: Patrick, Susan, Barbara, Paul, William, Philip, Richard, David, Mary, Peter, Steve. BSN, Marquette U., 1952. Staff nurse obstetrics St. Joseph's Hosp., Milw., 1952-55; state legislator State of N.D., Bismarck, 1991—. Coord. Birthright Bismarck, 1972—; city chairperson Cancer Crusade, Bismarck, 1982; vice chmn. dist. 49 Dem. Non-partisan League, Bismarck, 1988—; bd. dirs. Friends of N.D. Gov.'s Residence, Bismarck, 1988—, St. Vincent's Nursing Home, Bismarck, 1991—; pres. gov.'s counsel Commn. on Status of Women, Bicmarck, 1989-92, Bishop's Commn. on Cath. Schs., Bismarck, 1989—; mem. Bismarck-Mandan Symphony League. Mem. Cath. Daughters of the Ams., N.D. Mental Health Assn., 6th Dist. Med. Aux., Toastmasters (pres. # 581 1992—), Kiwanis (Golden "K"). Home: 104 Seminole Ave Bismarck ND 58501-3544*

CLEARY, BEVERLY ATLEE (MRS. CLARENCE T. CLEARY), author; b. McMinnville, Oreg., 1916; d. Chester Lloyd and Mable (Atlee) Bunn; m. Clarence T. Cleary, Oct. 6, 1940; children: Marianne Elisabeth, Malcolm James. BA, U. Calif., 1938; BA in Librarianship, U. Wash., 1939. Children's librarian Pub. Libr., Yakima, Wash., 1939-40; post librarian U.S. Army Regional Hosp., Oakland, Calif., 1942-45. Author: Henry Huggins, 1950 (Honor Book award New Eng. Round Table Children's Librs. 1972), Ellen Tebbits, 1951, Henry and Beezus, 1952, Otis Spofford, 1953, Henry and Ribsy, 1954 (Young Readers' Choice award Pacific Northwest Libr. Assn. 1957), Beezus and Ramona, 1955, Fifteen, 1956 (Dorothy Canfield Fisher Meml. Children's Book award 1958), Henry and the Paper Route, 1957 (Young Readers' Choice award Pacific Northwest Libr. Assn. 1960), The Luckiest Girl, 1958, Jean and Johnny, 1959 (ALA Notable Book citation 1961), The Real Hole, 1960, Hullabaloo ABC, 1960, Two Dog Biscuits, 1961, Emily's Runaway Imagination, 1961, Henry and the Clubhouse, 1962, Sister of the Bride, 1963, Ribsy, 1964 (Dorothy Canfield Fisher Meml. Children's Book award 1961, Nene award Hawaii Assn. Sch. Librs. and Hawaii Libr. Assn. 1968), The Mouse and the Motorcycle, 1965 (ALA Notable Book citation 1966, Young Readers' Choice award Pacific Northwest Libr. Assn. 1968, Youth award So. Ctrl. Iowa Assn. of Classroom Tchrs. 1968, William Allen White award Kans. Assn. Sch. Librs. and Kans. Tchrs. Assn. 1968, Nene award Hawaii Assn. Sch. Librs. and Hawaii Libr. Assn. 1969, Sue Hefley award La. Assn. Sch. Librs. 1972, Honor Book award New Eng. Round Table Children's Librs. 1973, Surrey Sch. Book award Surrey Sch. Dist. 1974), Mitch and Amy, 1967, Ramona the Pest, 1968 (Ga. Children's Book award Coll. Edn. U. Ga. 1970, Sequoyah Children's Book award Okla. Libr. Assn. 1971, Young Readers' Choice award Pacific Northwest Libr. Assn. 1971, Nene award Hawaii Assn. Sch. Librs. and Hawaii Libr. Assn. 1971, Mass. Children's Book award nomination 1977), Runaway Ralph, 1970 (Nene award Hawaii Assn. Sch. Librs. and Hawaii Libr. Assn. 1972, Charlie Mae Simon award Ark. Elem. Sch. Coun.

1973), Socks, 1973 (William Allen White award Kans. Assn. Sch. Librs. and Kans. Tchrs. Assn. 1968, Golden Archer award U. Wis. 1977), (play) The Sausage at the End of the Nose, 1974, Ramona the Brave, 1975 (Golden Archer award U. Wis. 1977, Mark Twain award Mo. Libr. Assn. and Mo. Assn. Sch. Librs. 1978), Ramona and Her Father, 1977 (ALA Notable Book citation 1978, Newbery Honor Book award ALA 1978, Boston Globe/Horn Book Honor award 1978, Young Readers' Choice award Pacific Northwest Libr. Assn. 1980, Nene award Hawaii Assn. Sch. Librs. and Hawaii Libr. Assn. 1980, Honor Book award Internat. Bd. on Book for Young People 1980, Tenn. Children's Book award Tenn. Libr. Assn. 1980, Utah Children's Book award Children's Libr. Assn. Utah 1980, Garden State award N.J. Libr. Assn. 1980, N. Mex. Land of Enchantment Children's award 1981, Tex. Bluebonnet award 1981), Ramona and Her Mother, 1979 (Am. Book award 1981, Garden State Children's Choice award N.J. Libr. Assn. 1982, Buckeye Children's Book award 1985), Ramona Quimby, Age 8, 1981 (Newbery Honor Book award ALA 1982, Am. Book award nomination 1982, Charlie Mae Simon award Ark. Elem. Sch. Coun. 1984, Garden State Children's Choice award N.J. Libr. Assn. 1984, Mich. Young Readers award 1984, Buckeye Children's Book award 1984), Ralph S. Mouse, 1982 (Calif. Assn. Tchrs. English award 1983, Golden Kite award Soc. Children's Book Writers 1983, Iowa Children's Choice award Iowa Ednl. Media Assn., 1984, Garden State Children's Choice award N.J. Libr. Assn. 1985), Dear Mr. Henshaw, 1983 (Dorothy Canfield Fisher Meml. Children's Book award 1985, ALA Notable Book citation 1984, N.Y. Times Notable Book 1983, Horn Book's Honor list 1984, Best Books list Sch. Libr. Jour. 1983, Christopher award 1983, John Newbery medal 1984, Commonwealth Silver medal Commonwealth Club Calif. 1984), Cutting Up with Ramona!, 1983, Ramona Forever, 1984, Lucky Chuck, 1984, The Ramona Quimby Diary, 1984, Beezus and Ramona Diary, 1986, Janet's Thingamajigs, 1987, The Growing Up Feet, 1987, A Girl from Yamhill: A Memoir, 1988, Muggie Maggie, 1990, Strider, 1991, Petey's Bedtime Story, 1993. Recipient Disting. Alumna award U. Wash., 1975, Laura Ingalls Wilder award ALA, 1975, Children's Choice Election 2nd Place award, 1978, Regina medal Cath. Libr. Assn., 1980, De Grummond award U. Miss., 1982, U. So. Miss. medallion, 1982, George C. Stone award Claremont Colls., 1983, Hans Christian Andersen medal nominee, 1984, Everychild Honor citation Children's Book Coun., 1985, Ludington award Ednl. Paperback Assn., 1987. Mem. Authors Guild of Authors League Am. Office: William Morrow & Co 1350 Avenue Of The Americas New York NY 10019-4702

CLEARY, LYNDA WOODS, financial advisor, consultant; b. Birmingham, Ala., June 18, 1950; d. Eugene and Elizabeth (Wright) Woods; m. George Cassius Riley, Nov. 29, 1975 (div. 1979); m. Richard Charles Cleary, Dec. 12, 1987. Student, Dartmouth Coll., 1970-71; BA, Tougaloo (Miss.) Coll., 1972; postgrad., Rutgers U., 1981-83; MBA, N.Y. Inst. Tech., 1992. Comml. underwriter Continental Ins. Co., N.Y.C., 1973-74; lectr. John Ericson Sch., Ostersund, Sweden, 1974; asst. underwriting cons. Prudential Property and Casualty, Holmdel, N.J., 1975-80; market rsch. analyst Continental Ins. Co., Piscataway, N.J., 1981-86; bus. systems analyst Am. Internat. Group, N.Y.C., 1986-87; ins. agt. Equitable Fin. Cos., N.Y.C., 1988; spl. agt. Northwestern Mut. Life, Princeton, N.J., 1988-89; cons. Cleary Woods Cons., Princeton, 1989—; account exec. Dean Witter, N.Y.C., 1992-93; fin. cons. Fahnestock & Co., Inc., Red Bank, N.J., 1993-95, Securities Am., Inc., Princeton, N.J., 1995—; cons. Nat. Torque Tech. Labs., Piscataway, 1989—. Mem. fin. com. Princeton Walk Homeowners Assn., 1988-95; fundraiser Crossroads Theatre, New Brunswick, N.J., 1988—; asst. troop leader Girl Scouts U.S., West Windsor. Recipient Cert. of Appreciation Concerned Community Women of Jersey City, Inc., 1990. Mem. Women Life Underwriters Confedn., Am. Mgmt. Assn., NAFE, Nat. Assn. Life Underwriters. Democrat. Baptist. Office: 22 Springwood Ct Princeton NJ 08540-9403

CLEARY, MANON CATHERINE, artist, educator; b. St. Louis, Nov. 14, 1942; d. Frank and Crystal (Maret) C. BFA, Washington U., St. Louis, 1964; MFA, Tyler Sch. Art, Temple U., 1968. Instr. fine arts SUNY, Oswego, 1968-70; from instr. to assoc. prof. D.C. Tchrs. Coll., Washington, 1970-78; from assoc. prof. to prof. art U. D.C., Washington, 1978—, acting chmn. dept., 1985-86, 90-91; assoc. dean Coll. Liberal and Fine Arts U. D.C., 1992-94, acting coord. art program, 1994—. One woman shows include Mus. Modern Art Gulbenkian Found., Lisbon, Portugal, 1985, Iolas/Jackson Gallery, N.Y.C., 1982, Osuna Gallery, Washington, 1974, 77, 80, 84, 89, Univ. D.C., 1987, Tyler Gallery SUNY at Oswego, 1987, J. Rosenthal Fine Arts, Washington, 1991, Addison/Ripley Gallery, Washington, 1994, others; group exhibits include Twentieth Century Am. Drawings: The Figure in Context, Traveled Nat. Acad. Design, 1984-85, others. Artist-in-residence Herning Hojskole, Denmark, 1980, Ucross Found., Wyo., 1984. Recipient Faculty Rsch. award, U. D.C., 1983, 89. Mem. Coll. Art Assn., Pi Beta Phi. Democrat. Presbyterian. Home: 1736 Columbia Rd NW Washington DC 20009-2846 Office: UDC Art Dept Rm 7812 4200 Connecticut Ave NW Bldg 48 Washington DC 20008-1174

CLEARY, MARGARET ELLEN, marketing professional; b. Mpls., Sept. 2, 1967; d. Michael John and Suzanne Clare (Williams) C. BA, Miami U., Oxford, Ohio, 1989; MBA, John Carroll U., 1995. Copywriter, editor Crystall Communications, Inc., Lakewood, Ohio, 1989-90; mktg. editor URS Cons., Inc., Shaker Heights, Ohio, 1990-92; mktg. comm. specialist Picker Internat., 1992-95; mktg. comm. mgr. Adalet-PLM Divsn. Scott Fetzer Co., 1995—. Mem. Women in Communications, Inc. (bd. dirs. newsletter 1990-91, chair scholarship 1991-92, bd. dirs. scholarship 1992-93, chair regional conf. 1993-94, program com. 1994-95, chair Communicators awards 1995-96), Cleve. Advt. Club, Pi Sigma Alpha. Roman Catholic. Home: 2842 Pease Dr Unit 107 Rocky River OH 44116

CLEARY, SUSAN, lawyer, consultant; b. Kearny, N.J., Mar. 30, 1966; d. Hugh Patrick and Jessica (Banaski) C. BA in Polit. Sci., Rutgers U., Newark, 1988, MA in Am. Studies, 1990; JD, Southwestern U., 1993. Bar: Calif. 1994. Clearance coord., asst. bus. & legal affairs Saban Entertainment, Inc., Westwood, Calif., 1993-94; dir. bus. & legal affairs World of Wonder Prodns., L.A., 1995; assoc. counsel Motion Picture Assn., Encino, Calif., 1995—; legal cons., 1994—. Mentor Southwestern U. Sch. Law, 1996. Mem. ABA, L.A. County Bar Assn., Beverly Hills Bar Assn. Democrat.

CLEGHORN, CHEREE BRIGGS, healthcare executive; b. Phoenix, June 25, 1945; d. Dale Sheaffer and Jeannetta Jeanne (Sebaugh) Briggs; m. George Reese Cleghorn, Mar. 15, 1975; stepchildren: Nona Elizabeth, John Michael. BA, Newcomb Coll., 1966; BJ, U. Mo., 1969. Reporter The Charlotte (N.C.) Observer, 1969-72; dir. pub. affairs Sch. Medicine U. N.C., Chapel Hill, 1972-75; spl. asst. to pres. Queens Coll., Charlotte, 1975-76; dir. pub. affairs WSU Health Care Inst., Detroit, 1976-79; cons. pub. affairs Detroit Med. Ctr. Corp., 1979-81, Johns Hopkins Med. Instns. Office of Pub. Affairs, Balt., 1982-83; v.p. pub. affairs Washington Healthcare Corp., 1983-86; pres. Cleghorn Health Communications, Bethesda, Md., 1986-88; pres. pub. rels. div. Rosenthal, Greene & Campbell, Bethesda, 1988-90; pres. Cleghorn & Assocs., Bethesda, 1990-94; sr. v.p. corporate affairs Loudoun Healthcare, Inc., Leesburg, Va., 1994—. Mem. communications com. Greater Washington Bd. Trade, 1988-90. Healthcare Forum fellow, 1996. Mem. Soc. Profl. Journalists, Am. News Women's Club, Pub. Rels. Soc. Am., Assn. Am. Med. Coll.'s Group on Pub. Affairs. Democrat. Presbyterian. Office: Loudoun Healthcare Inc 224 Cornwall St NW Leesburg VA 22075-2701

CLEHANE, DIANE CATHERINE, communications executive, journalist, writer; b. N.Y.C., Sept. 2, 1960; d. Charles and Rita (Morley) C. BA in Journalism and Sociology, U. Mass., 1982. Asst. buyer Macy's N.Y., N.Y.C., 1982-84; dir. pub. rels. Anne Klein II, N.Y.C., 1984-85; dir. publicity, pub. rels. Liz Claiborne, Inc., N.Y.C., 1985-87; dir. pub. rels. Esmark, N.Y.C., 1987-88; sr. promotion writer Vogue, N.Y.C., 1988; mktg. promotion mgr. Elle Mag., N.Y.C., 1989; pres., creative dir. Madeline Comms., N.Y.C., 1989—; style reporter, columnist Movieline Mag., 1996—. Editor: (spl. sect.) Fashion Inst. Tech. 50th Ann. N.Y. Times, 1995. Fundraiser, mktg. cons. Adopt-A-Dog, Greenwich, Conn., 1994-96; fundraiser, pub. rels. Montefiore Hosp., N.Y.C., 1994-96. Mem. Fashion Group Internat. (editor newsletter 1990-91, events com. 1994—), Women in Comm. (co-chair program com.) Cosmetic Exec. Women, Alpha Chi Omega. Office: Madeline Comms 700 Scarsdale Ave #3H Scarsdale NY 10583

CLELAND, NORA TEMPLE, writer, editor; b. Longton, Kans., Feb. 1, 1929; d. Oakes Richard and Lela Alice (Millikan) Temple; m. William Miles Cleland, Mar. 10, 1951; children: Sara A., Linda A., Anita L., William Ross. BS in Journalism, U. Kans., 1949. News and feature writer Lawrence Jour.-World, Kans., 1949-53, agrl. news writer, 1954; pub. rels. writer U. Kans. Sch. Arch. & Engring., Lawrence, 1953-58; home town news editor Divsn. of U. Rels./U. Kans., Lawrence, 1974-80; newsletter editor U. Kans., Lawrence, 1984-93, acting news divsn. coord., 1992-93; freelance news and feature writer Baldwin, Kans., 1993-96; agrl. news corr. Farm Talk, Parsons, Kans., 1996—; columnist Grass and Grain, Manhattan, Kans., 1996; Youth Projects Dir. Nat. Fedn. of Press Women, Overland Park, Kans., 1992—; pres. Kans. Press Women, Inc., Topeka, 1988-90, profl. devel. dir. 1994—; pub. rels. writer U. Kans., 1974-85, editor Oread newsletter, 1985-93. Writer, editor: Vinland Telephone Company History, Kan. Com., 1982 (Nat. Fedn. Press Women Comms. Contest award 1983); editor: Hometowning Pub. Rels. Sys., 1977, others. Co-pres. Vinland Fair Assn., Baldwin, 1985—. Mem. AAUW (ednl. fund dir. 1995-96), Kans. Press Women. Republican.

CLEM, ELIZABETH ANN STUMPF, music educator; b. San Antonio, July 9, 1945; d. David Joseph and Elizabeth Burch (Wathen) Stumpf; m. D. Bruce Clem, June 17, 1972; children: Sean David, Jeremy Andrew. BA in Music Edn., St. Mary-of-the-Woods (Ind.) Coll., 1970; MEd, Drury Coll., Springfield, Mo., 1979. Elem. tchr. St. Christopher Sch., Speedway, Ind., 1970-71; elem. and jr. high sch. tchr. Indpls. Sch. System, 1971-72; elem. tchr. Augusta (Ga.) Sch. System, 1972-73, Wabash (Ind.) Sch. System, 1976-77; pvt. practice piano tchr. Wabash, Ind., 1975-77, Honolulu, 1983-86, Burke, Va., 1986-90, Manhattan, Kans., 1990-93, Fayetteville, N.C., 1993-96; pvt. practice piano tchr. Meth. Coll. Performing Arts, 1993-96; co-chmn. Manhattan Musicianship Auditions, 1991, chmn., 1992. Dist. fundraiser rep. Wabash chpt. Am. Cancer Soc., 1975; leadership coord. Wabash coun. Girl Scouts U.S.A., 1976; music coord. Ft. Shafter Sacred Heart Chapel, Honolulu, 1985-86; mem. exec. bd. Little Apple Invitational Soccer Tournament, 1992; vol. N.C. Symphony. Mem. Nat. Guild Piano Tchrs., Music Tchrs. Nat. Assn. (cert.), N.C. Music Tchrs. Assn. (rep. to nat. assn.), Okla. Music Tchrs. Assn., Raleigh Piano Tchrs. Assn., Fayetteville Piano Tchrs. Assn. (v.p. 1994, pres. 1995), Lawton Music Tchrs., Schubert Music Club. Republican. Roman Catholic.

CLEM, GLORIA DARLENE, volunteer; b. Ft. Bragg, Calif., Apr. 11, 1938; d. Ernest and Ethel Irene (Remstedt) Bartolomie; m. Neil G. Clem, Mar. 9, 1958; children: Krista Darlene, Daneen Rene, Alison Paige. Occupational Therapist, San Jose (Calif.) State U., 1957. At large bd. dirs. U.S. Diving, 1982-83, 95—, Jr. Olympic internat. chair, 1984-90, law and legis. chair, 1990-91, v.p. Jr. Olympics, 1992-95; team mgr. U.S. Olympic Diving Team U.S. Diving, Barcelona, 1992; grant com. U.S. Diving, 1990—, bd. dirs., 1982—; mem. adv. bd. Diablo Valley Panhellenic, Contra Costa, Calif., 1993—. Author: U.S. Diving Rules & Codes, 1990. Guardian Jobs Daus., Lafayette, Calif., 1990-93. Mem. No. Calif. Diving Assn. (scholarship dhmn. 1994-95, bd. dirs., Svc. award 1990-95). Democrat. Presbyterian. Home: 122 Del Centro Ct Lafayette CA 94549

CLEM, HARRIET FRANCES, library director; b. Akron, Ohio, Nov. 8, 1940; d. Paul Milton and Mary Eva (Koppes) Miller; m. Ross Lynn Clem, June 23, 1979. BA cum laude, Kent State U., 1963, MLS, 1965. Teletype operator Babcock & Wilcox Co., Barberton, Ohio, 1958-59; bookmobile libr. Wadsworth (Ohio) Pub. Libr., 1963-64; head ext. dept. Rodman Pub. Libr., Alliance, Ohio, 1965-68, libr. dir., 1969—; instr. children's lit. Mt. Union Coll., Alliance, 1970-71; instr. libr. sci. Kent (Ohio) State U., 1975-7. Trustee YMCA, Alliance, 1974-84; pres. ARC, Alliance, 1975-77; chmn. program day Leadership Stark County, Canton, Ohio, 1995. Named Boss of Yr., Assn. Secs., Alliance, 1982. Mem. Ohio Libr. Coun. (founder acctg. divsn.), Alliance C. of C. (pres. 1983, 93, Athena award 1990), Beatrix Potter Soc., C.S. Lewis Soc., Alliance Women's Club (pres. 1977), Alliance Country Club, Beta Phi Mu (nat. coun. 1978-80). Episcopalian. Home: 13484 Louisville St Paris OH 44669 Office: Rodman Pub Libr 215 E Broadway Alliance OH 44601

CLEMENS, SYDNEY GUREWITZ, early childhood educator, consultant; b. Washington, Oct. 21, 1939; d. Clarence Darrow Gurewitz and Helen (Levitov) Sobell; children: Alexander Jeremy, Jennifer Martine. BA, U. Chgo., 1959; MA, Columbia U., 1969. Tchr. Bd. of Edn., N.Y.C., 1962-71; co-founder, dir. Discovery Room for Children, N.Y.C., 1969-71; tchr. San Francisco Unified Sch. Dist., 1972-83; mem. faculty Pacific Oaks Coll., Pasadena, Calif., 1988-92; founder, prin. educator, 1st grade tchr. San Francisco Charter Early Childhood Sch., 1993-95; cons., 1995—; Instr. child devel. dept. Merritt Coll., Oakland, 1981; extnsion faculty assocl. prof. Fresno State U., Sonoma State U., Sant Francisco State U., 1985-90; presenter, spkr. in field. Author: Pay Attention to the Children: Lessons for Parents & Teachers from Sylvia Ashton-Warner, 1996, The Sun's Not Broken, A Cloud's Just in the Way; On Child-Centered Teaching, 1983, Centering on the Children, 1985; consulting editor Young Children; contrbr. articles to profl. jours. Mem. Pasadena City Commn. on Children, Youth and Families, 1991-92. Home and Office: 73 Arbor St San Francisco CA 94131

CLEMENT, BETTY WAIDLICH, literacy educator, consultant; b. Honolulu, Aug. 1, 1937; d. William G. Waidlich and Audrey Antoinette (Roberson) Malone; m. Tom Morris, Jan. 16, 1982; 1 child, Karen A. Bratesani. BA in Elem. Edn., Sacramento State U., 1960; MA in Elem. Reading, U. No. Colo., 1973, MA in Adminstrn., EdD in Edn. & Reading, 1980. Elem. sch. tchr. pub schs., Colo., Calif., 1960-66; reading specialist, title I European area U.S. Dependent Schs., various locations, 1966-75; grad. practicum supr. U. No. Colo. Reading Clinic, Greeley, 1976-77; grant cons. Colo. Dept. Edn., Denver, 1978-81; adult edn. tutor, cons. various orgns., Boulder, Colo., 1983-87; student tchr. supr. U. San Diego, 1989-90; adult literacy trainer for vols. San Diego Coun. on Literacy, 1988—; adj. prof. U. Colo., Denver, 1981-82, U. San Diego, 1994—; adj. prof. comm. arts Southwestern Coll., Chula Vista, Calif., 1990—; presenter various confs. Coauthor, editor: Adult Literacy Tutor Training Handbook, 1990. Grantee Fed. Right-to-Read Office Colo. Dept. Edn., 1979, curriculum writing Southwestern Coll., 1992. Fellow San Diego Coun. on Literacy (chair coop. tutor tng. com. 1991-93); mem. Whole Lang. Coun. San Diego, Calif. Reading Assn. Office: U San Diego Alcala Park San Diego CA 92110

CLEMENT, CATHLEEN MCMULLIN, fundraiser; b. Inglewood, Calif., Dec. 14, 1946; d. Everett Keith and Patricia (Gibson) McM.; m. Kenneth Alfred Ross III, Apr. 21, 1968 (div. 1989); children: Patrick Ian, Rachel Marie; m. Paul Wayne Clement, July 28, 1990; stepchildren: Paul Wayne Jr., Blake Jordan, Erika Dawn. BA, Pepperdine Coll., 1968; MA, Fuller Theol. Sem., 1977. Cmty. resources dir. Fuller Psychol. Ctr., Pasadena, Calif., 1984-87; assoc. dir. devel. Fuller Theol. Sem., Pasadena, Calif., 1987-88; dir. devel. Five Acres, Altadena, Calif., 1988—; consulting mentor L.A. Unified Sch. Dist., 1993—. Pres. Pepperdine U. Alumni Bd., Malibu, Calif., 1981-82; vestry mem. All Saints Episcopal Ch., Pasadena, 1988-92. Recipient Svc. award Pepperdine U., 1983. Mem. Nat. Assn. Fund Raising Execs., San Gabriel Valley Estate Planning Coun., Planned Giving Roundtable. Home: 750 Galaxy Heights Dr La Canada CA 91011

CLEMENT, EDITH BROWN, federal judge; b. Birmingham, Ala., Apr. 29, 1948; d. Erskine John and Edith (Burrus) Brown; m. Rutledge Carter Clement Jr., Sept. 3, 1972; children: Rutledge Carter III, Catherine Lanier. BA, U. Ala., 1969; JD, Tulane U., 1972. Bar: La. 1973, U.S. Dist. Ct. (ea., mid. and we. dists.) 1973, U.S. Ct. Appeals (5th cir.) 1975, U.S. Supreme Ct. 1978, U.S. Ct. Appeals (11th cir.) 1981. Law clk. to Hon. H.W. Christenberry U.S. Dist. Ct., New Orleans, 1973-75; ptnr. Jones, Walker, Waechter, Poitevent, Carrere & Denegre, New Orleans, 1975-91; judge U.S. Dist. Ct. (ea. dist.) La., New Orleans, 1991—; speaker at seminars and profl. meetings. Mem. dean's coun. Tulane U. Law Sch., 1991-95. Life fellow La. Bar Found.; mem. ABA, La. State Bar Assn., Maritime Law Assn. U.S., Fed. Bar Assn. (pres. New Orleans chpt. 1990-91), New Orleans Bar Assn. (v.p. 1980-81). Roman Catholic. Office: US Dist Ct 500 Camp St Rm C-455 New Orleans LA 70130-3313

CLEMENT, HOPE ELIZABETH ANNA, librarian; b. North Sydney, N.S., Can., Dec. 29, 1930; d. Harry Wells and Lana (Perkins) C. BA, U. of King's Coll., 1951; MA, Dalhousie U., 1953; BLS, U. Toronto, 1955; D of Civil Law (hon.), U. King's Coll., 1992. With Nat. Library of Can., Ottawa, Ont., 1955-92; chief nat. bibliography div. Nat. Library of Can., 1966-70, asst. dir. research and planning br., 1970-73, dir. research and planning br., 1973-77, assoc. nat. librarian, 1977-92. Editor: Canadiana, 1966-69. Mem. Can. Libr. Assn. (Outstanding Svc. to Librarianship award 1992), Internat. Fedn. Libr. Assns. (medal 1991).

CLEMENT, KATHERINE ROBINSON, social worker; b. Balt., Dec. 19, 1918; d. Alphonso Pitts and Sue Seymour (Ashby) Robinson; m. Harry George Clement, 1941 (dec. 1992). BA, Coll. of Wooster, Wooster, Ohio, 1940; MS in Social Work, Smith Coll., 1953; post grad., Washington Sch. of Psychiatry, 1951. Lic. clin. social worker, Calif. Social worker Family Svc., Cin., 1953-55, Hamilton, Ohio, 1955-57; social worker Orange County, Calif., 1957-60; counselor pvt. practice, Fullerton, Calif., 1959-63; social worker Family Svc., Long Beach, Calif., 1961-1963; child welfare worker San Mateo (Calif.) County Welfare Dept., 1963-1967; supr. child protection Yolo County Dept. Social Svcs., Woodland, Calif., 1967-79; pvt. practice Woodland, Calif., 1980—; cons. psychiatric social svc. State Dept. Social Svcs., Sacramento, 1984—. Active Yolo County Dem. Ctrl. Com.; treas. Feminist Legal Svcs.; founding bd. dirs. Yolo County Ct. Apptd. Spl. Advocates; bd. dirs. Yolo County ARC; mem. Yolo County Health Coun. Mem. NASW, NOW, LWV, Mensa, Toastmasters, Soroptimist Internat. Democrat. Unitarian. Home: 205 Modoc Pl Woodland CA 95695-6662

CLEMENT, SHIRLEY GEORGE, educational services executive; b. El Paso, Tex., Feb. 14, 1926; d. Claude Samuel and Elizabeth Estelle (Mattice) Gillett; m. Paul Vincent Clement, Mar. 23, 1946; children: Brian Frank, Robert Vincent, Carol Elizabeth, Rosemary Adele. BA in English, Tex. Western Coll., 1963; postgrad. U. Tex., El Paso, N.Mex. State U.; MEd in Reading, Sul Ross State U., 1987. Tchr. lang. arts Ysleta Ind. Schs., El Paso, 1960-62; tchr. adult edn., 1962-64, tchr. reading/lang. arts, 1964-77; owner, dir. Crestline Learning Systems, Inc., El Paso, 1980-90; dir. Crestline Internat. Schs. (formerly Crestline Learning Systems, Inc., now Internat. Acad. Tex. at El Paso), 1987-90; instr. Park Coll., Ft. Bliss, Tex., 1992—, U. Phoenix, 1995; dir. tutorial for sports teams U. Tex., El Paso, 1984; bd. dirs. Southwest Inst., pres., 1993; dir. continuing edn. program El Paso Community Coll., 1985; mem. curriculum com. Ysleta Ind. Schs., El Paso, 1974; mem. Right to Read Task Force, 1975-77; mem. Bi-Centennial Steering Com., El Paso, 1975-76; presenter Poetry in the Arts, Austin, Tex., 1992; judge student poetry contest, Austin, Tex., 1995; Poetry Soc. Tex. program presenter Mesilla Valley Writers, 1993-96, El Paso Writers, 1994-95, Poetry Soc. Tex., 1993; instr. writing Paris Am. Acad., summer 1994, 95; cons. Ysleta Schs. 1995; lectr. on reading in 4 states. Author: Beginning the Search, 1979; contbr. articles to profl. jours.; contbr. poems to Behold Texas, 1983. Treas. El Paso Rep. Women, 1956; facilitator Goals for El Paso, 1975; mem. hospitality com. Sun Carnival, 1974, Cotton Festival, 1975. Mem. Internat. Reading Assn. (pres. El Paso County council 1973-74, presentor 1977-87), Assn. Children with Learning Disabilities (tchr. 1980), Poetry Soc. Tex. (Panhandle Penwomen's first place award 1981, David Atamian Meml. award 1991), Nat. Fedn. State Poetry Soc. (1st place award ann. contest 1988, 1st prize El Paso Historical Essay contest 1991, judge, 1997), Chi Omega Alumnae (pres. 1952-53). Home: PO Box 1645 114 Casas Bellas Ln Santa Teresa NM 88008-1645

CLEMENT, TRACY SHARP, laser physics researcher; b. Tampa, Fla., Jan. 11, 1966; d. Donald De and Betsy (Poe) Sharp; m. Justin Chiwaki Clement, July 24, 1993. BS, Rice U., 1988, MS, 1990, PhD, 1993. Dir. postdoctorial fellow Los Alamos (N.Mex.) Nat. Lab., 1993-95; physicist quantum physics divsn. Nat. Inst. Stds. and Tech., 1995—; asst. prof. adj. physics dept. Joint Inst. for Lab. Astrophysics U. Colo., Boulder, 1995—. Contbg. author: Dye Laser: 25 Years, 1992; contbr. articles to profl. jours. V.p. Houston Women's Soccer Assn., 1991-92, vol. Houston Women's Ctr., 1992-93. IBM TJ Watson Grad. fellow, 1992-93, Texas Engr. Found. Grad. Scholarship, 1989. Mem. IEEE, Lasers and Electro-Optics Soc., Optical Soc. of Am., Assn. for Women in Sci., Soc. of Women Engrs., Tau Beta Pi. Office: JILA U Colo Campus Box 440 Boulder CO 80309-0440

CLEMENTS, JENNIFER LYNNE, accountant; b. Rochester, N.Y., Apr. 24, 1969; d. Truman F. and Neva L. (Zarpentine) C. BSBA, U. of Buffalo, 1991, MBA, 1992. Accounts mgr. Kavinoky & Cook, Buffalo, 1992-94; acct. Damon & Morey, Buffalo, 1994—. Home: 570 Ontario St Buffalo NY 14207 Office: Damon & Morey 1300 Cathedral Pl Buffalo NY 14202

CLEMENTS, LYNNE FLEMING, family therapist, programmer; b. Bklyn., Aug. 8, 1945; d. Daniel Gillies and Dorothy Frances (Zitzmann) Fleming; m. Louis Myrick Clements, Feb. 19, 1972; children: Ryan Louis, Glenn Fleming. BA in Sociology, Bradley U., 1967; MSW, Fordham U., 1973; postgrad. studies, Columbia U., 1970-71; cert. family therapy, Inst. for Mental Health Edn., 1990. Lic. clin. social worker, N.J., 1994—. Computer programmer Employer's Comml. Union Group Ins. Cos., Boston, 1967-69, Harvard Bus. Sch., Cambridge, Mass., 1969-70, Volkswagon of Am., Englewood Cliffs, N.J., 1971; psychiatric social worker Associated Cath. Charities Family and Children's Svcs., Paramus, N.J., 1973-74, Christian Health Ctr., Wyckoff, N.J., 1976; owner, mgr. Wicker Wagon, Bergenfield, N.J., 1977-85; psychotherapist The Psychotherapy Counseling Ctr., Bergenfield, N.J., 1982-89; programmer analyst Atlas Computing Svcs., Secaucus, N.J., 1984 86; program coord., family therapist Div. of Family Guidance, Hackensack, N.J., 1986-91; pres. Corp. Family Resources, Ridgewood, N.J., 1989—; family therapist cons. Family Recovery of Valley View, White Plains, N.Y., 1992-94, Furman Clinic, Fair Lawn, N.J., 1995-96, Van Ost Inst. for Family Living, Englewood, N.J., 1996—; part-time family therapist N.J. Ctr. for Psychotherapy Inc., Ridgefield Park, 1990; family therapist cons. Family Recovery of Valley View, White Plains, N.Y., 1992-94; family therapist, cons. Furman Clinic, Fair Lawn, N.J., 1995—. Sunday sch. tchr. All Saints Ch., 1982-89, 94—, chmn. bd. community play ctr., 1977-78; mem. Twin-Boro Youth Ministry Coun., 1989—, Bergen County Family Day Care Coalition, 1989—; apptd. sec. Mayor's Beautify Bergenfield Com., 1991-95; chmn. entertainment Bergen County Children's Festival, 1993; apptd. chmn., designer Bergenfield's Coun. for Arts, 1993—; chmn. curriculum enhancement com. Bergen County Acad. for Advancement of Sci. and Tech., 1992—. Recipient 1st and 2nd pl. awards Bergenfield 1980 Art Contest; NIMH grantee, 1973. Mem. AAUW, Gifted Child Soc. (parent workshop coord. 1989—, bd. dirs. 1991—), Nat. Assn. Social Workers, Acad. Cert. Social Workers, Am. Orthopsychiat. Assn., Fordham U. Alumni Assn., N.J. Commerce and Industry Assn. (child care com. 1990—, human resources com. 1990—), N.J. Soc. Clin. Social Workers, Zonta (Amelia Earhart chmn. 1987-88, literacy com. 1995—, status of women in China com. chmn. 1993-94), Women of Accomplishment (founder, pres. 1990—, chmn. women's coalition conf. 1993—). Episcopalian. Home: 148 Harcourt Ave Bergenfield NJ 07621-1917 Office: Corp Family Resources 15 Godwin Ave Ste 1 Ridgewood NJ 07450-3817

CLEMENTS, MARY MARGARET, retired educator; b. Glasgow, Scotland, Dec. 23, 1925; came to U.S., 1928; d. Peter MacIntyre and Margaret Service (Mackay) Somerville; m. Carl Emery Clements, Aug. 28, 1954; children: Robert Peter, Margaret Ann Clements Fleming. BA in Edn., U. Akron, 1946; MA in History, U. Mich., 1950. Permanent cert. tchr., Ohio. Tchr. English, history and Spanish, Brunswick (Ohio) H.S., 1946-47, Covington (Ohio) H.S., 1947-51, Xenia (Ohio) Ctrl. H.S., 1951-58, Notre Dame Acad., Chardon, Ohio, 1970-74; tchr. Spanish, Villa Angela Acad., Cleve., 1968-70; tutor for pupil pers. Euclid (Ohio) Sch. System, 1963-67, 91-94, chmn. English dept. summer sch., 1980-91; ret., 1994; tchr. Spanish, English, and History Euclid (Ohio) Sch. System, 1995-96. Sec., coord. united thank offering Diocesan Episcopal Ch. Women, 1981-94; editor Episcopal Ch. Women's News Notes, 1984-94; mem., host family Am. Field Svc., Euclid, 1961-94; pres. PTA Coun., Euclid, 1974-76; provost Deanery Episcopal Ch., Cleve., 1993-95; trustee Ctr. for Human Svcs., Cleve., 1976-86; mem., past pres. Meridia Euclid Hosp., 1976-94; mem. Women's Caucus, Euclid, 1978-82; circulation mgr. Church Life Episcopal newspaper Diocese of Ohio, 1995; chmn. mission and ministry mem. Com. Against Racism. Recipient award for civic leadership Du Pont, 1980. Mem. AAUW (pres. 1978-80, Faculty Wives Assn. (pres. 1963-65). Home: 55 E 213th St Euclid OH 44123-1064

CLEMON-KARP, SHEILA RHEA, literature educator; b. Boston, Apr. 17, 1938; d. Simon R. and Celia (Wise) Clemon; m. Lawrence E. Karp, Dec. 22, 1957; children: Robert Bruce, Linda Clemon-Karp. AB, Radcliffe Coll.,

1959; MA, Northeastern U., 1971; PhD, Brandeis U., 1980. Adj. prof. U. Mass., Lowell, 1973-78; dir. congl. offices Office of Congressman James M. Shannon, Lowell, 1978-83; asst. sec. of elder affairs Commonwealth of Mass., Boston, 1983-87; dir. govt. rels., exec. asst. to univ. pres. Clark U., Worcester, Mass., 1987-90; cons. and lectr. in field, 1990-94; adj. prof. Fla. Atlantic U., Boca Raton, 1994—; pres. Cons. for Equal Edn., Mass., 1970-75; dir. Elder Svcs. of Merrimac Valley, Lawrence, Mass., 1979-83. Vice chair, legis. chair Govs. Commn. on the Status of Women, Mass., 1977-80; Dem. Town Com. Woman, Lexington, Mass., 1980-87, Dem. State Com. Women, 1987-89; elected rep. to Town Meeting, Lexington, 1977-86. Mem. Brandeis U. Nat. Womens Com. (v.p. 1992-94, dir. 1996—). Democrat. Jewish.

CLEMONS, JANE ANDREA, state legislator; b. Poughkeepsie, N.Y., Apr. 2, 1946; d. Mary (Longendyke) Martin; m. Michael R. Clemons, Oct. 15, 1966; children: Bret, Nick, Benjamin. Student, Moore Gen. Hosp., Grasmere, N.H., 1966. Nurse various orgns., Nashua, N.H., 1967-89; accounts mgr. D & M Cleaning Co., Nashua, 1989-92; mem. N.H. Ho. of Reps., Nashua, 1990—. Sponsor Sr. Citizen Computer Health Care Program, Nashua, 1983-84; ward chair Dem. City Com., Nashua, 1988; del. Dem. State Conv., Nashua, 1988; vol. Merrimack (N.H.) Friars Club, 1990-92; del. State Dem. Pary, 1993. Greek Orthodox. Home: 177 Kinsley St Nashua NH 03060-3649 Office: NH House Reps State House Concord NH 03301*

CLEMONS, JULIE PAYNE, telephone company manager; b. Attleboro, Mass., June 13, 1948; d. John Gordon and Claire (Paquin) P.; m. W. Richard Johnson, Oct. 10, 1970 (div. Oct. 1980); m. E.L. Clemons, Apr. 23, 1988. BBA, U. R.I., 1970. Svc. rep. New England Telephone, East Greenwich, R.I., 1970-71; svc. rep. So. Bell, Jacksonville, Fla., 1971-73, bus. office supr., 1973-77, bus. office mgr., 1978-84, staff mgr. assessment, 1984-86, mgr. assessment ctr., 1987-89; dir. human resource assessment State of Fla., Jacksonville, Fla., 1987-89; dir. human resource assessment Customer Svcs. Revenue Recovery Ctr., 1989-93, mgr. small bus. sales and svc., 1994-95, br. mgr. small bus. No. Fla., 1995—. Vol. Learn to Read; bd. dirs. Duval Assn. of Retarded Citizens, Jacksonville, 1981-86, treas. 1983-84; mem. Leadership Jacksonville, 1996—. Mem. NAFE, Am. Mgmt. Assn., Pioneers of Am., Jacksonville C. of C. Roman Catholic. Office: So Bell Tower 301 W Bay St # B1 Jacksonville FL 32202-5184

CLEVELAND, CEIL MARGARET, author, journalist, education administrator, English language educator; b. Tex., Jan. 10, 1942; d. Joe Donaldson Cleveland and Margaret Ellen (Gowdy) Slack; m. Donald R. Waldrip; children: Wendy Gentile, James Hardy, Timothy Owen; m. Jerrold K. Footlick, Nov. 24, 1984; stepchildren: Robbyn Footlick, Jill Footlick. BA, Whitworth Coll., 1968; MA magna cum laude, Midwestern U., 1971; postgrad., NYU, Columbia U., 1978-82. Assoc. editor Univ. Press, U. Cin., 1975-77; sr. devel. officer, founding editor-in-chief Columbia mag. Columbia U., N.Y.C., 1976-85; founder, pres. Cleveland Comms., Centerport, N.Y., 1987-91; v.p. instnl. rels. Queens Coll., CUNY, Flushing, N.Y., 1991-95; prof. English, v.p. univ. affairs SUNY, Stony Brook, 1995—; dir. curriculum Cin. Arts and Humanities Consortium, 1972-74; adj. prof. English Xavier U., 1972-77, U. Cin., 1972-77, Queens Coll., 1990—; co-founder Syzygy, Women's Press; founder, pub. fiction and poetry The Mill Pond Press. Author: In the World of Literature, 1991, Whatever Happened to Jacy: A Memoir, 1995; editor: English Musical Culture 1776-1976, 1976, Managing With Power, 1979; editl. bd. Liberal Edn., 1987-92. Trustee CNET, Cin., 1973-76, Cin. Symphony, 1973-76, Sch. for Creative and Performing Arts, Cin., 1973-76; founder Inner City Sch. Enrichment Project; mem. Coun. of Racial Equality, 1973-76; active Playhouse in the Park, 1973-76, Internat. Children's Village, Cin., 1973-76. Recipient Writer of Decade and Mag. editor of Decade, Coun. for Advancement and Support of Edn., 1976-86; recipient Edn. Comms. award Ed Press, 1993, Internat. Bus. Comms. award, 1994. Fellow Woodrow Wilson; mem. MLA, Coun. for Advancement and Support of Edn. (trustee 1981-83), Nat. Edn. Roundtable, N.Y.C. Women Leader's Roundtable, Am. Coun. Edn. (cons. 1994), Phi Beta Kappa. Home: 11 Prospect Rd Centerport NY 11721-1129 Office: SUNY 330 Adminstrv Bldg Stony Brook NY 11794

CLEVELAND, CHARLENE S., community health nurse; b. Haverhill, N.H., Aug. 20, 1945; d. Thomas D. and Willie E. (Smith) Sargent; children: Laura, Mary Ann. Diploma, Sylacauga Hosp. Sch. Nursing, 1967; student, Gadsden State Jr. C.C., 1979-82; BSN magna cum laude, Jacksonville State U., 1995. Staff nurse Sylacauga (Ala.) Hosp.; pub. health nurse Ala. Dept. Pub. Health, Sylacauga; staff nurse TCRC Child Devel. Ctr., Talladega, Ala.; homebound nurse Ala. Dept. Rehab., Anniston. Mem. Ala. State Nurses Assn., ARA, ASEA.

CLEVELAND, PEGGY ROSE RICHEY, cytotechnologist; b. Cannelton, Ind., Dec. 9, 1929; d. "Pat" Clarence Francis and Alice Marie (Hall) Richey; cert. U. Louisville, 1956; B. Health Sci., U. Louisville, 1984; m. Peter Leslie Cleveland, Nov. 25, 1948 (dec. 1973); children: Pamela Cleveland Litch, Paula Cleveland Bertloff, Peter L. Cytotechnologist cancer survey project NIH, Louisville, 1956-59; chief cytotechnologist Parker Cytology Lab., Inc., Louisville, 1959-75; mgr. cytology dept. Am. Biomed. Corp., 1976-78, Nat. Health Labs., Inc., Louisville, 1978-89; clin. instr. cytology Sch. Allied Health U. Louisville, 1989—; leader cytotechnologist del. to People's Republic of China, 1986; with various hosps. and labs., 1990—; ptnr. Sham Star Stable thoroughbred horse breeding and racing. Mem. Am. Soc. Clin. Pathologist (cert. cytotechnologist), Internat. Acad. Cytology (cert. cytotechnologist), Am. Soc. Cytology (del.-person to person cytology delegation, amb. USSR, 1990), Kentuckiana Cytology Soc., Cytology Soc. Ind., Horseman's Benevolent and Protective Assn. Democrat. Roman Catholic. Home: 8774 Lieber Hausz Rd NE Lanesville IN 47136-8522

CLEVELAND, SUSAN ELIZABETH, library administrator, researcher; b. Plainfield, N.J., Mar. 14, 1946; d. Robert Astbury and Grace Ann (Long) Williamson; m. Stuart Craig Cleveland, Aug. 21, 1971; children: Heather Elizabeth, Catherine Elisa. BA, Douglass Coll., Rutgers U., 1968; MLS, Rutgers U., 1969. Acquisitions libr. Jefferson U., Phila., 1970-71; biomed. libr. VA Hosp., Hines, Ill., 1972; med. cataloger U. Ariz., Tucson, 1973-74; dir. U. Pa. Hosp. Libr., Phila., 1974-87; exec. dir. Cleveland, Lamb, Urban Assocs., 1987-89; libr. dir. Mt. Sinai Hosp., Phila., 1989, West Jersey Health System, Voorhees, N.J., 1990—; cons. in field, Phila. USPHS fellow, Detroit, 1969-70; recipient Chapel of 4 Chaplains Legion of Honor. Mem. Med. Libr. Assn. (Phila. chpt.), Spl. Libr. Assn., Basic Health Sci. Libr. Consortium, S.W. N.J. Consortium for Health Info. Svcs., Health Scis. Libr. Assn. N.J., Acad. Health Info. Profls., Caravan Club. Home: 9 Sylvan Ct Laurel Springs NJ 08021

CLEVEN, CAROL CHAPMAN, state legislator; b. Hanover, Ill., Nov. 2, 1928; d. Edward William and Vivian (Strasser) Chapman; m. Walter Arnold Cleven; children: Kern W., Jeffrey P. BS, U. Ill., 1950, postgrad., 1950-56. Elem. sch. tchr. Derinda Ctr., Ill., 1946-47; with rsch. staff U. Ill., Urbana, 1950-56; exec. dir. Crittenton Hasting House, Brighton, Mass., 1975-86; mem. Mass. Ho. of Reps., Boston, 1987—; mem. edn. com., com. pub. svcs. edn. com., HUD com., mem. rules com.; mem. Commn. on Indoor Air Pollution, Rep. Task Force on AIDS, Mass. Caucus of Women Legislators, Spl. Commn. on Worker Availability in Human Svcs. Professions, Commn. on Mobile Home Parks, Adolscent Health Adv. Coun., Spl. Commn. on Pub. Assiatance, Spl. Com. on Women and the Criminal Justice System, Legis. Caucus on Older Citizens' Concerns, Dept. Social Svcs. Working Group, steering com. Mass. Legis. Children's Caucus. Mem. Chelmsford (Mass.) Sch. Com., 1969-87, mem. elem. needs com., 1969-71, mem. sch. bldg. com., 1971-76; bd. dirs. Camp Paul for Exceptional Children, 1987—; past pres. Lowell (Mass.) YWCA, Lowell Coll. Club; mem. Merrimack River Watershed Coun., Mass. Coalition for Pregnant and Parenting Teens, Alliance for Young Families; treas. Boston Ctr. Blind Children; bd. dirs. Chelmsford Ednl. Found.; bd. mem. Greater Lowell Alzheimer Assn.; mem. spl. adv. bd. Cmty. Teamwork, Inc. Mem. Mass. Assn. Sch. Coms. (life), Friends of the Library, Chelmsford Hist. Soc., Chelmsford LWV, Florence Crittenton League of Lowell, Phi Sigma, Sigma Delta Epsilon. Congregationalist. Home: 4 Arbutus Ave Chelmsford MA 01824-1113 Office: State House Rm 167 State Capitol Boston MA 02133

CLEVENGER, PENELOPE, international business consultant; b. Denver, Dec. 6, 1940; d. Harold Friedland and Charlotte (Glatt) Friedland Beskin; m. Willie K. Clevenger, Oct. 15, 1961 (div.). AA, Stephens Coll., 1960. Office mgr. Malcolm S. Gerald, Chgo., 1977-79; pers. mgr. Rolm/Midwest, Chgo., 1979-82; office adminstr. Nutech Engrs., Chgo., 1982-83; office mgr. Am. Acad. Orthopaedic Surgeons, Chgo., 1983-85, dir. adminstrn. Telecommunications Industry Assn. (formerly U.S. Telecommunications Suppliers Assn.), Chgo., 1985-88; pres. InterWorld Svcs., Ltd., 1988—. Bd. dirs. Ctr. Tng. and Rehab. of Disabled, Chgo., 1981-84; vol. Northwestern Meml. Hosp., 1985-87, Christian Industrial League, 1992—. Mem. Meeting Profls. Internat. (Chgo. chpt.), Meeting Profls. Internat. (nat. orgn.), Chgo. Coun. on Fgn. Rels. Democrat. Jewish. Home and Office: 233 E Wacker Dr Apt 3913 Chicago IL 60601-5116

CLEVENGER, SARAH, botanist, computer consultant; b. Indpls., Dec. 19, 1926; d. Cyrus Raymond and Mary Beth (Stevens) C. A.B., Miami U., 1947; Ph.D., Ind. U., 1957. Tchr sci. Radford Sch., El Paso, Tex., 1949-51, Hillsdale Sch., Cin., 1951-52; asst. prof. Berea (Ky.) Coll., 1957-59, 61-63, Wittenberg U., Springfield, Ohio, 1959-60, Eastern Ill. U., 1960-61, Ind. State U., Terre Haute, 1963-66; assoc. prof. Ind. State U., 1966-78, prof., 1978-85, prof. emerita, 1985—. Mem. Am. Inst. Biol. Sci., Am. Soc. Plant Taxonomists, Bot. Soc. Am., Internat. Assn. Plant Taxonomy, Phytochem. Soc. N.Am. (past sec.). Home: 717 S Henderson St Bloomington IN 47401-4838

CLEVER, LINDA HAWES, physician; b. Seattle; d. Nathan Harrison and Evelyn Lorraine (Johnson) Hawes; m. James Alexander Clever, Aug. 20, 1960; 1 child, Sarah Lou. AB with distinction, Stanford U., 1962, MD, 1965. Diplomate Am. Bd. Internal Medicine, Am. Bd. Preventive Medicine in Occupational Medicine. Intern Stanford U. Hosp., Palo Alto, Calif., 1965-66; resident Stanford U. Hosp., Palo Alto, 1966-67, fellow in infectious disease, 1967-68; fellow in community medicine U. Calif., San Francisco, 1968-69, resident, 1969-70; med. dir. Sister Mary Philippa Diagonostic and Treatment Ctr. St. Mary's Hosp., San Francisco, 1970-77; chmn. dept. occupational health Calif. Pacific Med. Ctr., San Francisco, 1977—; clin. prof. medicine Med. Sch., U. Calif., San Francisco; NIH rsch. fellow Sch. Medicine, Stanford U., 1967-68; mem. San Francisco Comprehensive Health Planning Coun., 1971-76, bd. dirs.; mem. Calif.-OSHA Adv. Com. on Hazard Evaluation System and Info. Svc., 1979-85, Calif. Statewide Profl. Stds. Rev. Coun., 1977-81, San Francisco Regional Commn. on White House Fellows, 1979-81, 83-89, 92, 95, chmn., 1979-81, bd. scientific counselors Nat, Inst. of Occupl. Safety and Health, 1995—. Editor Western Jour. Medicine, 1990—; contbr. articles to profl. jours. Trustee Stanford U., 1972-76, 81-91, v.p. 1985-91; trustee Marin Country Day Sch., 1978-85; bd. dirs. Sta. KQED, 1976-83, chmn., 1979-81; bd. dirs. Ind. Sector, 1980-86, vice chmn. 1985-86; bd. dirs. San Francisco U. H.S., 1983-90, chmn. 1987-88; active Womens Forum West, 1980—, bd. dirs. 1992, 93; mem. Lucile Packard Children's Hosp. Bd., 1993—; mem., co-chair U. Calif. Berkeley Sch. of Pub. Health Dean's Policy Adv. Coun.; mem. Nat. Inst. Occupl. Safety and Health Bd. of Scientific Counselors, 1995—. Fellow ACP (gov. No. Calif. region 1984-89, chmn. bd. govs. 1989-90, regent 1990-96, vice chair bd. regents 1994-95), Am. Coll. Occupl. and Environ. Medicine; mem. Inst. Medicine NAS, Calif. Med. Assn., Calif. Acad. Medicine, Am. Pub. Health Assn., Western Occupl. Medicine Assn., Western Assn. Physicians, Stanford U. Women's Club (bd. dirs. 1971-80), Chi Omega. Office: 2351 Clay St San Francisco CA 94115-1931

CLEWIS, CHARLOTTE WRIGHT STAUB, mathematics educator; b. Pitts., Aug. 20, 1935; d. Schirmer Chalfant and Charlotte Wright (Rodgers) Staub; student Memphis State Coll., 1953-54, U. Wis., 1957-59; BA, Newark State Coll., 1963; MAT, Loyola Marymount U., 1974; m. John Edward Clewis, Aug. 11, 1954; 1 dau., Charlotte Wright. Asst. to dir., housemother Leota Sch. and Camp, Evansville, Wis., 1957-59; tchr. math. Rahway Jr. H.S. (N.J.), 1963-70; tchr. math. Torrance (Calif.) Unified Sch. Dist., 1970-95, coord. math. dept., 1977-95, mem. math. steering com., 1978-83, 86-89, mem. proficiency exam writing com., 1977-91; mem. instructional materials rev. panel State of Calif., 1986; instr. Weekend Coll. Marymount-Palos Verdes, 1992-94; coach math. teams. Sec., pres. Larga Vista Property Owners Assn., 1975-84; mem. Rolling Hills Estates City Celebration Com., 1975-81; treas. adult leaders YMCA, Metuchen, N.J., 1967-69; bd. dirs. Peninsula Symphony Assn., 1978-84, sec., 1993—; commr. Rolling Hills Estates Parks and Activities, 1981—, chmn., 1985, 90, 96. Named Tchr. of Yr., Rahway Jr. H.S., 1966; recipient Appreciation award PTA, 1984, Hon. Service award PTA, 1986. Mem. Nat. Coun. Tchrs. Math., Calif. Math. Coun. Avocations: bicycling, camping, reading, horseback riding, computers. Home: 1 Gaucho Dr Rolling Hills Estates CA 90274-5113

CLICK, MARIANNE JANE, credit manager; b. Marion, Ohio, Aug. 2, 1949; d. Raymond E. and Martha C. (Robinson) C. BS in Edn., Ohio State U., 1971. Various positions Western Auto Supply, Delaware, Ohio, 1973-87; dept. mgr. Western Auto Supply, Kansas City, Mo., 1988-89, dir. revolving ops., 1989—. Bd. dirs. Consumer Credit Counseling Svcs., Kansas City, 1992—, sec., 1995-96. Mem. Internat. Credit Assn. (cert. consumer credit exec.), Credit Assn. Greater Kansas City (bd. dirs. 1991—, 2nd v.p. 1995-96, 1st v.p. 1996-97), Internat. Assn. Credit Card Investigators, Mchts. Rsch. Coun., Alpha Lambda Delta. Office: Western Auto Supply Co 5777 Deramus Ave Kansas City MO 64120-1261

CLIFF, JOHNNIE MARIE, mathematics and chemistry educator; b. Lamkin, Miss., May 10, 1935; d. John and Modest Alma (Lewis) Walton; m. William Henry Cliff, Apr. 1, 1961 (dec. 1983); 1 child, Karen Marie. BA in Chemistry, Math., U. Indpls., 1956; postgrad., NSF Inst., Butler U., 1960; MA in Chemistry, Ind. U., 1964; MS in Math., U. Notre Dame, 1980. Cert. tchr., Ind. Rsch. chemist Ind. U. Med. Ctr., Indpls., 1956-59; tchr. sci. and math. Indpls. Pub. Schs., 1960-88; tchr. chemistry, math. Martin U., Indpls., 1989—, chmn. math. dept., 1990—, divsn. chmn. depts. sci. and math., 1993—; adj. instr. math. U. Indpls., 1991. Contbr. rsch. papers to sci. jours. Grantee NSF, 1961-64, 73-76, 78-79, Woodrow Wilson Found., 1987-88; scholarship U. Indpls., 1952-56, NSF Inst. Reed Coll., 1961, C. of C., 1963. Mem. AAUW, NAACP, NEA, Assn. Women in Sci., Urban League, N.Y. Acad. Scis., Am. Chem. Soc., Nat. Coun. Math. Tchrs., Am. Assn. Physics Tchrs., Nat. Sci. Tchrs. Assn., Am. Statis. Assn., Am. Assn. Ret. Persons, Neal-Marshall-Ind. U. Alumni Assn., U. Indpls. Alumni Assn., U. Notre Dame Alumni Assn., Ind. U. Chemist Assn., Notre Dame Club Indpls., Kappa Delta Pi, Delta Sigma Theta. Democrat. Baptist. Home: 405 Golf Ln Indianapolis IN 46260-4108 Office: Martin U 2171 Avondale Pl Indianapolis IN 46218-3867

CLIFFORD, CHERYL KUCHTA, Christian education administrator; b. Winsted, Conn., July 30, 1947; d. George Henry and Gertrude Marie (Weaving) Kuchta; m. Steven Dale Clifford, July 22, 1989; children: Ruth Marie, Paul Arthur, Heidi Lynn, Robert Steven (quadruplets). BS in Elem. Edn., U. Hartford, 1970; MS in Remedial Reading, Ctrl. Conn. State U., 1978; MDiv, Gordon-Conwell Theol. Sem., 1986. Ordained to ministry United Ch. of Christ, 1988; cert. tchr., Conn. Tchr. East Hartland (Conn.) Elem. Sch., 1970-81; assoc. pastor St. John's United Ch. of Christ, Massillon, Ohio, 1988-91; interim pastor Emmanual United Ch. of Christ, Akron, Ohio, 1992; dir. Christian edn. First United Ch. of Christ, Canton, Ohio, 1994—; co-owner tax acctg. firm Clifford & Assocs., Canton, 1991—. Editor newsletter The Witness of Ohio, 1990-93. Recipient Cory Meml. Scholarship award for excellence in Christian edn. Scripture Press Ministries, 1986. Mem. Nat. Assn. Evangelicals. Republican. Office: First United Ch of Christ 901 E Tuscarawas St Canton OH 44707

CLIFFORD, GARRY CARROLL, publishing executive; b. Washington, May 25, 1934; d. Thomas Patrick and Agnes (McGarry) Carroll; m. George Clifford, Jr. (dec. Aug. 1985); children: George III, Thomas Carroll, Eamon M. Reporter Ottawa Jour., 1956-59; press officer Kennedy Campaign, Washington, 1960; freelance writer Chevy Chase, Md., 1961-74; corr. Time, Inc., People Mag., Washington, 1974-94, bur. chief, 1979-88, 91—. Trustee Lab. Sch. Washington, 1984-93. Roman Catholic. Home: 146 Grafton St Chevy Chase MD 20815-3424 Office: People Mag 1050 Connecticut Ave NW Washington DC 20036-5303

CLIFT, ELEANOR, magazine correspondent. Former White House corr. now contbg. editor Newsweek; commentator The McLaughlin Group. Office: Newsweek Washington Bur 1750 Pennsylvania Ave NW Washington DC 20006-4502

CLIFTON, ANNE RUTENBER, psychotherapist; b. New Haven, Dec. 11, 1938; d. Ralph Dudley and Cleminette (Downing) Rutenber; 1 dau., Dawn Anne. BA, Smith Coll., 1960, MSW, 1962. Diplomate in Clin. Social Work. Psychiat. case worker adult psychiatry unit Tufts-New Eng. Med. Ctr., Boston, 1962-68, supr. students, 1967-68; pvt. practice psychotherapy, Cambridge, Mass., 1966—; supr. med. students, staff social workers outpatient psychiatry Tufts New Eng. Med. Ctr., 1973—, also mem. exec. bd. Women's Resource Ctr., interim co-dir., 1986-88. Lic. clin. social worker, Mass. asst. clin. prof. psychiatry Tufts U. Med. Sch., 1974—, research dept. psychiatry, 1966-68, 73, 77—. Mem. Acad. Cert. Social Workers, Nat. Assn. Social Workers, Phi Beta Kappa, Sigma Xi. Clubs: Cambridge Tennis, Mt. Auburn Tennis. Contbr. articles to profl. jours. Home: 126 Homer St Newton MA 02159-1518 Office: 59 Church St Ste 4 Cambridge MA 02138-3724

CLIFTON, JUDY RAELENE, association administrator; b. Safford, Ariz., Nov. 8, 1946; d. Ralph Newton and Fayrene (Goodner) Johnson; student Biola Coll., 1964-65; BA in Christian Edn., Southwestern Coll., 1970; married. Editl. asst. Accent Publications, Denver, 1970-73; expediter Phelps Dodge Corp., Douglas, Ariz., 1974-78; exec. asst. So. Ariz. Internat. Livestock Assn., Inc., Tucson, 1978-81; adminstrv. asst. Phelps Dodge Corp., 1981—; sec. exec. bd. PAC, Phelps Dodge, 1985-90. Mem. adv. bd. Ariz. Lung Assn.; mem. Silver City Arts Coun., 1986-90; mem. Am. Security Council, 1979-85; leader 4-H, Douglas; mem. Rep. Nat. Com., 1978—, Conservative Caucus, 1979-85; del. Quadrennial N.Mex. State Rep. Con., 1988, 92. Recipient Am. Legion Good Citizen award, 1964, DAR award, 1964. Mem. NAFE, DAR, Nat. Assn. Evangelicals, U.S. Tennis Assn., Nat. Right to Life, So. Ariz. Internat. Livestock Assn., AAUW, Eagle Forum, Freedom Found., N.Mex. Eagle Forum, Mus. N.Mex. Found., Lordsburg/Hidalgo County C. of C. (1st v.p bd. dirs. 1990-93), Concerned Women of Am., Sigma Lambda Delta. Baptist. Clubs: Trunk & Tusk, Pima County Republican, Centre Ct., Westerners Internat., So. Ariz. Depression Glass, Tucson Tennis, Rep. Senatorial. Home: Drawer M Playas NM 88009

CLINE, CAROL ANN, music educator; b. Evansville, Ind., July 30, 1960; d. Orval Louis and Mary Jane (Adcock) Meier; m. Douglas Lynn Cline, May 18, 1985. B in Music Edn., Murray State U., 1982; M in Elem. Edn. summa cum laude, William Carey Coll., 1988. Cert. tchr. elem. edn., music edn. grades K-12, gifted/talented edn., Miss., Alaska, Ill. Music tchr. Shawneetown (Ill.) Grade Sch., 1983-85; tchr. grade 2 Nativity Blessed Virgin Mary Elem. Sch., Biloxi, Miss., 1986-87; music tchr. Biloxi (Miss.) Separate Schs., 1987-90; tchr. grade 2 and 5, music tchr. Hastings Sch., Madrid, Spain, 1990-92; reading band inst. Fort Greely Sch., Delta Junction, Alaska, 1992-93; choral dir. grades 7-12 Bay Jr. High/H.S., Bay St. Louis, 1993—; tchr. Sylvan Learning Ctrs., Slidell, La., 1994—. Choral dir. Torrejon Airbase (Spain) Chapel, 1991-92, Fort Greely (Alaska) Chapel, 1992. Music scholar Murray (Ky.) State U., 1978. Mem. NEA, Music Educators Nat. Conf., Assn. Curriculum and Devel., Am. Choral Dirs. Assn., Miss. Assn. Educators, Sigma Alpha Iota (life mem.). Home: 305 Drury Ln Slidell LA 70460-8463 Office: Bay Jr and Sr HS 750 Blue Meadow Rd Bay Saint Louis MS 39520-1606

CLINE, CAROLYN JOAN, plastic and reconstructive surgeon; b. Boston; d. Paul S. and Elizabeth (Flom) Cline. BA, Wellesley Coll., 1962; MA, U. Cin., 1966; PhD, Washington U., 1970; diploma Washington Sch. Psychiatry, 1972; MD, U. Miami (Fla.) 1975. Diplomate Am. Bd. Plastic and Reconstructive Surgery. Rsch. asst. Harvard Dental Sch., Boston, 1962-64; rsch. asst. physiology Laser Lab., Children's Hosp. Research Found., Cin., 1964, psychology dept. U. Cin., 1964-65; intern in clin. psychology St. Elizabeth's Hosp., Washington, 1966-67; psychologist Alexandria (Va.) Community Mental Health Ctr., 1967-68; research fellow NIH, Washington, 1968-69; chief psychologist Kingsbury Ctr. for Children, Washington, 1969-73; sole practice clin. psychology, Washington, 1970-73; intern internal medicine U. Wis. Hosps., Ctr. for Health Sci., Madison, 1975-76; resident in surgery Stanford U. Med. Ctr., 1976-78; fellow microvascular surgery dept. surgery U. Calif.-San Francisco, 1978-79; resident in plastic surgery St. Francis Hosp., San Francisco, 1979-82; practice medicine, specializing in plastic and reconstructive surgery, San Francisco, 1982—. Contbr. chpt. to plastic surgery textbook, articles to profl. jours. Mem. Am. Soc. Plastic and Reconstructive Surgeons, Royal Soc. Medicine, Calif. Medicine Assn., Calif. Soc. Plastic and Reconstructive Surgeons, San Francisco Med. Soc. Address: 490 Post St Ste 735 San Francisco CA 94102-1408

CLINE, CATHIE B., hospital administrator; b. Detroit, Jan. 2, 1943; d. Harold Norman Brodie and Fannie Bokatuik; m. Ted Allen Bingham, June 11, 1983; children: John, Peter, Fannie. BSN, Ohio State U., 1964, MHA, 1981. Staff nurse Tb facility Means Hall Ohio State U. Hosps., Columbus, 1964-65, head nurse Columbus Cancer Clinic, 1965-66, staff nurse coronary care step-down unit, 1972-75, asst. head nurse, constant care nursing, 1975-76, asst. dir., surg. nursing, 1978-79, interim assoc. hosp. adminstr./nursing, 1979, dir. critical care nursing, 1979-81; assoc. v.p. Cuyahoga County Hosp. System, 1981-82; v.p. patient svcs. MetroHealth Med. Ctr., Cleve., 1982-89, v.p. inpatient/hosp. based svc., 1989-92, sr. v.p. ops., 1992—; interim pres. MHS, 1993-94, sr.v.p., cOO, 1993; clin. instr. nursing Frances Payne Bolton Sch. Nursing Case Western Reserve U., Cleve., 1982, mem. exec. com. BSN consortium, 1989, asst. dean, 1990; vice chmn. nursing com. Ctr. Health Affairs, Greater Cleve. Hosp. Assn., 1983, chair nursing com., 1989-91; mem. nursing adv. com. Nursing Edn. Program Cuyahoga C.C., Cleve., 1983; lectr. continuing edn. Cleve. State U., 1984; clin. instr. dept. nursing Cleve. State U., 1990; bd. dirs. Vis. Nurses Assn. Hospice, Cleve., 1990; apptd. Opportunity for Change com. State of Ohio Health Care Access Com., Columbus, 1991; chair Cleve. State U./Metrohealth Acad. Com., 1991; membership com. Midwest Alliance Nursing, Indpls., 1992; chair steering com. Robert Wood Johnson Grant, 1993. Bd. dirs. Cleve. Area Citizen's League of Nursing, 1985-87; mem. task force clinical reimbursement, Cuyahoga C.C., Cleve., 1985; chair Greater Cleve. Nursing Roundtable, 1986-88; mem. steering com. United Way, 1990, rep. to campaign for health affairs, 1991-93; mem. adv. com. MSNMBA program Case Western Reserve U., 1990; apptd. by mayor City Tree Commn., City of Westlake, 1993. Johnson & Johnson Wharton fellow, 1986; recipient spl. recognition contbns. and support nursing edn. MetroHealth Sch. Nursing, 1989. Mem. Lake Erie Orgn. Nurse Execs. (charter, pres.-elect), Ohio State U. Alumni Assn. (life), Alpha Delta Pi, Sigma Theta Tau. *

CLINE, DOROTHY MAY STAMMERJOHN (MRS. EDWARD WILBURN CLINE), educator; b. Boonville, Mo., Oct. 19, 1915; d. Benjamin Franklin and Lottie (Walther) Stammerjohn; grad. nurse U. Mo., 1937; BS in Edn., 1939, postgrad., 1966-67; MS, Ark. State U., 1964; m. Edward Wilburn Cline, Aug. 16, 1938 (dec. May 1962); children: Margaret Ann (Mrs. Rodger Orville Bell), Susan Elizabeth (Mrs. Gary Lee Burns), Dorothy Jean. Dir. Christian Coll. Infirmary, Columbia, Mo., 1936-37; asst. chief nursing svc. VA Hosp., Poplar Bluff, Mo., 1950-58; tchr.-in-charge staff State Tng. Ctr. No. 4, Poplar Bluff, 1959-66, Dorothy S. Cline State Sch. #53, Boonville, 1967-85; instr. U. Mo., Columbia, 1973-74; cons. for workshops for new tchrs., curriculum revision Mo. Dept. Edn. Mem. Butler County Council Retarded Children, 1959-66; v.p. Boonslick Assn. Retarded Children, 1969-72; sec.-treas. Mo. chpt. Am. Assn. on Mental Deficiency, 1973-75. Mem. NEA, Mo. Tchrs. Assn., Am. Assn. on Mental Deficiency, Council for Exceptional Children, AAUW (v.p. Boonville br. 1968-70, 75-77), Mo. Writers Guild, Creative Writer's Group (pres. 1974—), Columbia Creative Writers Group, Eastern Center Poetry Soc., Laura Speed Elliott High Sch. Alumni Assn., Bus. and Profl. Women's Club, Smithsonian Assn., U. Mo. Alumni Assn., Ark. State U. Alumni Assn., Internat. Platform Assn., Mo. Hist. Soc., Boonslick Hist. Soc., Friends Historic Boonville, Delta Kappa Gamma, PEO. Mem. Christian Ch. Home: 603 High St Boonville MO 65233-1212

CLINE, JANE LYNN, state official; b. Kingwood, W.Va., June 25, 1956; d. Robert Denzil and Helen Jane (Phillips) C. BSBA, W.Va. U., 1978, MBA, 1986. Acct. W.Va. Dept. Hwys., Charleston, 1978-79, comptr., 1979-89; dep. commr. W.Va. Divsn. Motor Vehicles, Charleston, 1989, commr., 1989—. Field rep. Caperton for Gov., 1987-88, 92-93; active W.Va. Young Dems., 1980-87, Caperton Inaugural Com., Charleston, 1988, 93. Named Outstanding Young Dem., W.Va. Young Dems., 1983. Mem. Am. Assn. Motor Vehicle Adminstrn. (Region III v.p. 1993-94, pres. 1994—), Internat.

Pers. Mgmt. Assn., Bus. and Profl. Women. Methodist. Office: WVa Divsn Motor Vehicles State Capitol Complex Rm 113 Charleston WV 25317-9514*

CLINE, JANICE CLAIRE, education educator; b. Wausau, Wis., Aug. 22, 1945; d. George Leroy Cline and Irma Olga (Brummond) Doering; m. Brent Buell, Jan. 28, 1979. BS, U. Wis., 1967; MA, NYU, 1972; student of Eli Siegel, 1978; student of Ellen Reiss, Aesthetic Realism Found., N.Y.C., 1977—; student of Aesthetic Realism Teaching Method, 1977—. Tchr. Hyde Park High Sch., Chgo., 1967-69; instr. Chase Manhattan Bank JOB Tng. Program, N.Y.C., 1969-71; evaluator York Coll. Title I Evaluation Team, Jamaica, N.Y., 1972; adj. lectr. N.Y.C. Community Coll., CUNY, Bklyn., 1971-72; lectr. York Coll., CUNY, Jamaica, 1972—; Aesthetic Realism cons.-in-tng., N.Y.C., 1977—; guest speaker WVON, Chgo., 1980. Contbr. articles to profl. jours. Coord. Conf. in Support of the Liberation of S. Africa and Namibia, York Coll., Jamaica, N.Y., 1985, Student/Faculty Consortium on Central Am., York Coll., 1986. Recipient Outstanding Contribution award Afro-Am. Club, York Coll., 1985, Outstanding Contribution award Conf. of African People, Jamaica, N.Y., 1986. Mem. AAUP, Profl. Staff Congress, Internat. Reading Assn. (Manhattan coun.), CUNY Women's Coalition. Office: CUNY York Coll Dept English 94-20 Guy R Brewer Blvd Jamaica NY 11451-0001

CLINE, PAULINE M., educational administrator; b. Seattle, Aug. 25, 1947; d. Paul A. and Margaret V. (Reinhart) C. BA in Edn., Seattle U., 1969, MEd, 1975, EdD, 1983. Cert. tchr., prin., supt., Wash. Tchr., Marysville High Sch., Wash., 1969-70; tchr./adminstr. Blanchet High Sch., Seattle, 1970-78; asst. prin. Edmonds High Sch., Wash., 1978-84; prin. College Place Middle Sch., Edmonds, 1984-85, Mountlake Terrace High Sch., Wash., 1985-93; asst. supr., Mount Vernon Sch. Dist., 1993—. Recipient Washington award for excellence in edn. Gov. and Supt. Pub. Instruction, 1992. IDEA Kettering fellow, 1984, 86, 87, 90, 92, 93, 94, 95. Mem. Am. Assn. Sch. Adminstr., Assn. Supervision and Curriculum Devel., Phi Delta Kappa. Roman Catholic. Club: Women's University (Seattle). Lodge: Rotary (charter mem., past pres. Alderwood club). Avocations: skiing; kayaking; backpacking. Office: Mt Vernon Sch Dist 124 East Lawrence Mount Vernon WA 98273

CLINE, SANDRA WILLIAMSON, elementary education educator; b. San Francisco, Dec. 10, 1944; d. Wilburn Woodrow and Hazel Stewart (Cochrane) Williamson; m. Charles William Cline, June 11, 1966; 1 child, Jeffrey Charles. BA, Western Mich. U., 1970, MA, 1973; MA, Western Mich. U., 1986. Cert. tchr., Mich. 1st-3rd grade tchr. Portage Mich. Pub. Schs., 1971—, mem. sch. effectiveness team and report card rev. com., 1988-92, mem. sci. writing team, 1989—; mentor coach Western Mich. U.; mus. co-dir. Lake Ctr. Elem. Sch., Portage, 1982-83, student tchr., mentor, safety patrol advisor, 1st grade chairperson, state com. for social studies, writing chairperson, 1988-94. Vol. Portage Police, 1992—; assoc. coord. city emergency sys., 1995—. Recipient Congress medallion for disting. participation, 1992-93. Mem. NEA, ASCD, NSTA, Am. Fedn. Police (Nat. Patriotism award 1994), Nat. Coun. Tchrs. English, Assn. for Study of Coop. in Edn., Mich. Edn. Assn., Portage Edn. Assn. (exec. bd., membership chairperson, elem. grievance chair, negotiating team), Mich. ASCD (conf. com.), Phi Delta Kappa. Home: 2170 Sanibel Is # A-3 Kalamazoo MI 49024-8616 Office: Lake Ctr Elem Sch 10011 Portage Rd Kalamazoo MI 49002-7249

CLINE, VIVIAN MELINDA, lawyer; b. Seneca, S.C., Oct. 6, 1953; d. Kenneth H. and Wanda F. (Simmons) Fuller; m. Terry S. Cline, June 15, 1974 (div. Oct. 1986); 1 child, Alicia C. BSBA, Calif. State U., Northridge, 1974; JD, Southwestern U., L.A., 1983. Bar: Calif. 1983, Tex., 1990. Paralegal Internat. House Pancakes, North Hollywood, Calif., 1976-78; assoc. Tuohey & Prasse, Santa Ana, Calif., 1983-85; paralegal Smith Internat., inc., Newport Beach, Calif., 1978-83; corp. counsel Smith Internat., inc., Houston, 1985—. Bus. cons. Jr. Achievement, Houston, 1992-94. Mem. Exec. Women's Network (sec. 1993, pres. 1994, dir. programs 1995, sec. 1996), Am. Soc. Corp. Secs. Inc. (sec. Houston chpt. 1995-96, treas. 1996—). Republican. Presbyterian. Office: Smith Internat Inc 16740 Hardy Rd Houston TX 77032-1125

CLINEFELTER, RUTH ELIZABETH WRIGHT, historian, educator; b. Akron, Ohio, Nov. 2, 1930; d. Cyril and Ruth Elizabeth (Dresher) Wright. BA, U. Akron, 1952, MA, 1953; MLS, Kent State U., 1956. Serials libr. U. Akron, 1953-61, social scis. rsch. libr., 1961-76, humanities rsch. libr., 1977-83, social scis. humanities bibliographer, 1983—; lectr. in gen. studies U. Akron, 1960, instr. bibliography, 1956-59, asst. prof. bibliography, 1959-77, assoc. prof. bibliography, 1977-84, prof. bibliography 1984—; resource person NEH, Ohio; mem. joint study com. Am. History Rsch. in Ohio Ohio Hist. Soc., 1969-70; mem. acad. affairs com. Ohio Faculty Senate, 1971-72; mem. hist. abstracts bibliographic svc. ABC Clio Users Bd., 1978-79. Contbr. articles to profl. jours. Trustee Akron Area Women's History Project; active Citizens AGainst Sys. Abuse, Humane Soc. Greater Akron, Nat. Trust for Hist. Preservation, Progress Through Preservation, Summit County Hist. Soc., Cascade Locks Park Assn., Pet Guards Shelter. Mem. Acad. Libr. Assn. Ohio, AAUP, Am. Hist. Assn., Assn. for Bibliography of History, North Am. Conf. British Studies, North Cen. Women's Studies Assn., Ohio Acad. History, Ohio Classical Assn. Democrat. Episcopalian. Home: 1377 Hadden Cir Akron OH 44313-6505 Office: U Akron Bierce Libr Akron OH 44325

CLINES, CINDY COLLINS, elementary school administrator, educator; b. Lawrenceville, Ga., May 8, 1961; d. David Roger Collins and Mary Wood Verenna; 1 child, Ashleigh Merci Collinwood Clines. BS in Edn. in Early Childhood, U. Ga., 1982, MEd in Reading and Early Childhood, 1988, MEd in Supervision, 1990. Cert. instrnl. supr., early childhood edn. tchr., reading specialist, data collection specialist. Tchr. Auburn (Ga.) Elem. Sch., 1982-92; adminstr., instrnl. lead tchr. Bramlett Elem. Sch., Auburn, 1992—; after sch. program dir. Bramlett Elem. Sch., 1995—, tchr. support specialist supr., 1992—, Barrow County mentor supr., 1994—; mem. Ga. Edn. Leadership Acad., Atlanta, 1992-93. Leader/dir. Girl Scouts, Auburn, 1990-93; Sunday sch. tchr. Harmony Grove United Meth. Ch., Auburn, 1993—, co-chairperson adminstrv. bd., 1993-94, dir. children's ministry, 1995—. Recipient Cert. of Appreciation, Barrow County Assn. Educators, 1992. Mem. Profl. Assn. Ga. Educators, Alpha Delta Kappa, Golden Key Nat. Honor Soc. Democrat. Home: 1427 Harmony Grove Ch Rd Auburn GA 30203 Office: WB Bramlett Elem 622 Freeman Brock Rd Auburn GA 30203

CLINKENBEARD, BETH ANN, management analyst; b. Cleve., Apr. 3, 1957; d. John Alex and Ellen Martha (Stacy) C. BA, Hope Coll., 1979; MA in Libr. Scis., U. Mich., 1980. Program analyst/mgmt. analyst U.S. Army Tank-Automotive Command, Warren, Mich., 1981-86; mgmt. analyst Hdqrs., 21st Support Command, Kaiserslautern, Germany, 1986-88, Hdqrs., VII Corps, Stuttgart, Germany, 1988-92, U.S. Army Tank-Automotive and Armaments Command, Warren, 1992—. Recipient achievement medal for Desert Shield/Storm Support, U.S. Army, 1991. Mem. Am. Soc. Mil. Comptrs., Phi Alpha Theta.

CLINTON, HILLARY RODHAM, First Lady of United States, lawyer; b. Chgo., Oct. 26, 1947; d. Hugh Ellsworth and Dorothy (Howell) Rodham; m. William J. Clinton, Oct. 11, 1975; 1 child, Chelsea Victoria. BA with high honors, Wellesley Coll., 1969; JD, Yale U., 1973; LLD (hon.), U. Ark., Little Rock, 1985, U. Pa., 1993, U. Mich., 1993, San Francisco State U., 1995, U. Minn., 1995, U. Ill., 1994; D Pub. Svc. (hon.), George Washington U., 1994; San Francisco State U., 1995, U. Minn., 1995. Bar: Ark. 1973, U.S. Dist. Ct. (ea. and we. dists.) Ark. 1973, U.S. Ct. Appeals (8th cir.) 1973, U.S. Supreme Ct. 1975. Atty. Children's Def. Fund, Cambridge, Mass. and Washington, 1973-74; legal cons. Carnegie Coun. on Children, New Haven, 1973-74; counsel, impeachment inquiry staff Judiciary Com. U.S. Ho. of Reps., Washington, 1974; asst. prof. law, dir. Legal Aid Clinic U. Ark., Fayetteville, 1974-77; asst. prof. law U. Ark. Sch. of Law, Little Rock, 1979-80; ptnr. Rose Law Firm, Little Rock, 1977-92; headed Com. on Health Care, Washington, D.C., 1993-94; bd. dirs. Wal-Mart Stores, Inc., 1986-92, TCBY Enterprises Inc., 1989-92; chair ABA Commn. on Women in the Profession, 1987-91; chair Legal Svcs. Corp., Washington, 1978-80, bd. dirs., 1977-81. Author: Handbook on Legal Rights for Arkansas Women, It Takes a Village: And Other Lessons Children Teach Us, 1996; contbr. articles to profl. jours. Bd. dirs. Childrens Def. Fund, Washington, 1976-92, Child Care Action Campaign, 1986-92, Nat. Ctr. on Edn. and the Economy, 1987-92, Children's TV Workshop, 1989-92, Pub./Pvt. Ventures, 1990-92, Ark. Children's Hosp., 1988-92, Franklin and Eleanor Roosevelt Inst., 1988-92; mem. commn. on quality edn. So. Regional Edn. Bd., 1984-92; chmn. Ark. Edn. Stds. Com., 1983-84. Named Outstanding Layman of Yr. Phi Delta Kappa, 1984, One of 100 Most Influential Lawyers in Am., Nat. Law Jour., 1988, 91; recipient Lewis Hine award Nat. Child Labor Law Com., 1993, Albert Schweitzer Leadership award Hugh O'Brian Youth Found., 1993, Iris Cantor Humanitarian award UCLA Med. Ctr., 1993, Friend of Family award Am. Home Econs. Assn., 1993, Charles Wilson Lee Citizen Svc. award Com. for Edn. Funding, 1993, Claude D. Pepper award Nat. Assn. for Home Care, 1993, Commitment to Life award AIDS Project L.A., 1994, Disting. Svc., Health Edn. and Prevention award Nat. Ctr. for Health Edn., 1994, First Ann. Eleanor Roosevelt Freedom Fighter award, 1994, Brandeis award U. Louisville Sch. of Law, 1994, Social Justice award United Auto Workers, 1994, Ernie Banks Positivism trophy Emil Verban Meml. Soc., 1994, Humanitarian award Alzheimer's Assn., 1994, Elie Wiesel Found., 1994, Internat. Broadcasting award Hollywood Radio and TV Soc., 1994, Ellen Browning Scripps medal Scripps Coll., 1994, Disting. Pro Bono Svc. award San Diego Vol. Lawyer Program, 1994, Hippy U.S.A. award, 1994, C. Everett Koop medal, 1994, Women's Legal Def. Fund award, 1994, Martin Luther King, Jr. award Progressive Nat. Bapt. Conv., 1994, 30th Anniversary Women at Work award in Pub. Policy, 1994, Greater Washington Urban League award, 1995, Servant of Justice award N.Y. Legal Aid Soc., 1995, Presdl. award Bklyn. Coll., 1995, Outstanding Mother award Nat. Mother's Day Com., 1995. Fellow Am. Bar Found.; mem. Ark. Bar Assn., Ark. Trial Lawyers Assn., Ark. Women Lawyers Assn., Am. Trial Lawyers Assn., Pulaski County Bar Assn. Home and Office: The White House 1600 Pennsylvania Ave NW Washington DC 20500-0002*

CLINTON, MARIANN HANCOCK, educational association administrator; b. Dyersburg, Tenn., Dec. 7, 1933; d. John Bowen and Nell Maurine (Johnson) Hancock; m. Harry Everett Clinton, Aug. 25, 1956; children—Carol, John Everett. B.Mus., Cin. Conservatory Music, 1956; B.S., U. Cin., 1956; M.Mus., Miami U., Oxford, Ohio, 1971. Tchr. music public schs. Hamilton County, Ohio, 1956-57; tchr. voice and piano Butler County, Ohio, 1964—; instr. music Miami U., 1972-75; exec. dir. Music Tchrs. Nat. Assn., Cin., 1977-86; mng. dir. Am. Music Tchr., 1977-86. Mem. adminstrv. bd. Middletown (Ohio) 1st United Methodist Ch., 1968-72; bd. dirs. Friends of the Sorg Opera House. Mem. Music Educators Nat. Conf., Am. Ednl. Research Assn., Am. Soc. Assn. Execs., Nat. Fedn. Music Clubs, Pi Kappa Lambda, Kappa Delta Pi, Mu Phi Epsilon, Phi Mu. Republican. Home: 6543 Niderdale Way Middletown OH 45042-9400

CLINTON, MARY ELLEN, neurologist; b. Evanston, Ill., Feb. 15, 1950; d. Merle P. and Corinne E. (Wolf) C.; m. William J. Wade Jr. BS, Loyola/Marymount U., 1972; MD, U. So. Calif., 1976. Intern internal medicine Vanderbilt U. Hosp., Nashville, 1976-77, resident in neurology, 1979-81, chief resident, 1981-82, fellow in neuromuscular disease and electrodiagnostics, 1982-83, asst. prof. neurology, 1983-91; staff physician emergency medicine Donelson Hosp., St. Thomas Hosp., Nashville, 1977-79; asst. clin. prof. Vanderbilt U., Nashville, 1991—; dir. electrodiagnostic testing Neurosurg. Assocs., Nashville, 1991—; reviewing physician Mid South Found. for Med. Care, Inc., Memphis, 1991-95; med. expert Social Security and Disability Determination State of Tenn., 1987-95; dir. Vanderbilt Muscle Biopsy Lab., 1984-89; dir. neurodiagnostic labs. Nashville VA Hosp., 1989-91; mem. staff Parkview/West Side HCA Hosps., Nashville, So. Hills Med. Ctr.; cons. staff Bapt. Hosp., Nashville; consultant Williamson Med. Ctr., Franklin, Tenn. Contbr. articles and abstracts to profl. jours. Co-dir. Nashville br. Muscular Dystrophy Assn., 1983-91. Recipient Physician's Recognition award AMA, 1984, 88. Mem. Am. Soc. for Internal Medicine, Soc. for Neurosci., Am. Med. Women's Assn., Nashville Acad. Medicine, Tenn. Med. Assn., AMA, So. Clin. Neurol. Soc., Am. Acad. Clin. Neurophysiology, Am. Assn. for Electrodiagnostic Medicine, Am. Acad. Neurology, Kappa Gamma Pi. Office: Neurosurg Assocs 4230 Harding Rd Nashville TN 37205-2013

CLONTS, SUSAN ZAENGLEIN, physical education educator; b. Dayton, Ohio, Dec. 7, 1955; d. William Charles and Mary Elizabeth (Wood) Zaenglein; m. Thomas Richard Clonts, Dec. 20, 1975; children: David, Kasey. BS in Edn., U. Ga., 1977; MEd in Phys. Edn., West Ga. Coll., 1995. Cert. health and phys. edn. P-12, Ga. Tchr. phys. edn. Wheeler H.S. Cobb County Schs., Marietta, Ga., 1978-81; tchr. phys. edn. Powder Springs (Ga.) Elem. Sch. Cobb County Schs., 1982—; coach softball, gymnastics and basketball Wheeler H.S., Marietta, 1978-81; coach basketball McEachern H.S., Powder Springs, 1982-84, asst. coach fast-pitch softball, 1995, head-coach, 1996—. Mem. PTA, Powder Springs, 1982—; leader, svc. unit dir. Girl Scouts Am., Powder Springs, 1990-94; mem., coach Powder Springs Youth Orgn., 1989—; coach West Cobb Girls Softball Assn., 1995. Mem. AAHPERD, Ga. Assn. for Health, Phys. Edn., Recreation and Dance, Alpha Delta Kappa (chaplain, sgt.-at-arms 1987-94). Home: 2261 New Macland Rd Powder Springs GA 30073-1420 Office: Powder Springs Elem 4570 Grady Grier Dr Powder Springs GA 30073-2555

CLOPINE, MARJORIE SHOWERS, librarian; b. N.Y.C., June 25, 1914; d. Ralph Walter and Angelina (Jackson) Showers; m. John Junior Clopine, June 19, 1948 (div.); m. Frank Mason Storck, Sept. 14, 1985. BA, Pa. State U., 1935; MS, Drexel U., 1936; MS, Columbia U., 1949. Gen. asst. Libr., Drexel U., Phila., 1937-42; asst. libr. Gen. Chem. Div., Allied Chem. Corp., Morristown, N.J., 1943-46; bibliographer U.S. Office Tech. Svcs., Washington, 1946; med. libr. VA Hosp., Washington, 1946-49; asst. libr. U.S. Naval Obs., Washington, 1949-52, libr., 1952-63; cons. in astronomy Dewey Decimal Classification Editorial Office, Library of Congress, Washington, 1956, assoc. libr. Bethany (W.Va.) Coll., 1967-69. Alice B. Kroeger Meml. scholar Drexel U., 1935-36. Mem. AAUW, LWV, Inst. Retired Execs. and Profls., Women's Resource Ctr. of Sarasota, Friends of the Arts and Scis., Spl. Libraries Assn., Beta Phi Mu. Contbr. articles to profl. jours. Home and Office: 8400 Vamo Rd Apt 540 Sarasota FL 34231-7816

CLOPINE, SANDRA LOU, religious organization administrator; b. Ft. Wayne, Ind., May 12, 1936; d. Clarence Melvin and Gwendola Louise (Copp) Burry; m. Sidney Ray Goodwin, July 12, 1957 (dec. 1963); 1 child, Gwenda Lynn Goodwin Stewart; m. Myron Stanley Clopine, Aug 7, 1982; stepchildren: Charles, Dan, Linda Clopine Palser, Lynnette Clopine Blackstone. BA, Southwestern Assemblies of God, Waxahachie, Tex., 1958; BS, West Tex. State U., 1968; MA, Assemblies of God Theol. Sem., Springfield, Mo., 1979. Ordained to ministry West Tex. Assemblies of God, 1971. Fgn. missionary Assemblies of God Ch., Ghana, West Africa, 1961-65; social worker Tex. Ctr. Human Devel., Amarillo, 1968-69, dir. vol. svcs., 1969-70; instr. Arusha Bible Sch., Tanzania, East Africa, 1970-80; instr. sociology Evang. Coll. Assemblies of God, Springfield, 1979-80; office of info. coord. Internat. Corr. Inst., Brussels, 1980-82; state dir. Women's Ministries, Nebr., 1984-85; nat. sec., dept. head for denomination Assemblies of God Women's Ministries, Springfield, Mo., 1986-94, coord. Nat. Prayer Ctr., 1994—; speaker women's convs., leadership seminars, other orgns. Recipient Outstanding Contbn. award Internat. Corr. Inst., 1983, Leadership Friend of Yr. award Highland Child Placement Ctr., Kansas City, Mo., 1989; named Disting. Alumnus Southwestern Assemblies of God Coll., 1989. Mem. Nat. Assn. Evangs. Women's Commn. (chair 1992-95, bd. adminstrs. 1992—), Evang. Press Assn., Nat. Women's Leadership Task Force (steering com. 1990-92), Internat. Pentecostal Press Assn., Delta Epsilon Chi. Republican. Office: Assemblies of God 1445 N Boonville Ave Springfield MO 65802-1894

CLORE, GAINES REYNOLDS, artist, educator, museum consultant; b. Lamesa, Tex., Jan. 13, 1946; d. Hugh Elbert and Ruth Lee (Hodges) Gaines; 1 child, Meredith Gaines Clore. BA in Fine Arts, Tex. Tech U., 1968; MFA, Ariz. State U., 1971, postgrad., 1972. Cert. in secondary edn., Md., D.C. Created art dept. for Urban League Sch. Washington Urban League, 1973-75; chair dept. art Calvert H.S., Prince Frederick, Md., 1975-80; owner, gallery dir. Ocean Hand Art Gallery, Ocean City, Md., 1980-82; freelance graphic designer Laurel, Md., 1982-85; h.s. programs coord. Nat. Mus. Women in the Arts, Washington, 1986-90, mus. programs cons., 1990—; chair dept. fine arts Forestville (Md.) H.S., 1990—; curator Expanding Visions Exhbn. WCA honorees at Nat. Mus. Women in the Arts, 1991, Corinne Mitchel: A Glimpse of Joy Exhbn., at Nat. Mus. Women in the Arts, 1992, Pulse Point exhbn. Harvard Coll., 1996, writer exhbn. catalogue, 1996. Author: Gumba Ya Ya-- Anthology of African American Women Artists, 1994 (exhbn. catalog), Corinne Mitchel : A Glimpse of Joy, 1992: exhibited paintings in shows at West Beth Gallery, N.Y.C., 1990, 92, Rahr-West Art Mus., Manitowoc, Wis., 1990, Appleton (Wis.) Gallery of Art, 1991, Charles Allis Art Mus., Milw., 1991, Susan Conway Gallery, Washington, 1992, Bowie (Md.) State U., 1993; creator, producer Role Model Series Nat. Mus. Women in the Arts, 1988. Founder Art Honor Soc., 1975 now Nat. Art Honor Soc., 1978. Mem. DAR, Nat. Art Edn. Assn. (Presdl. award 1995), Women's Caucus for Art (membership chair 1990—, nat. bd. dirs.). Democrat. Episcopalian.

CLOSE, BEVERLY JEAN, secondary education educator; b. Portland, Oreg., July 1, 1958; d. Bertrand J. and Charlotte J. (Mollett) C. BA in Psychology, U. Oreg., 1980. Cert. English, social studies and journalism tchr., Oreg. Tchr. Glencoe High Sch., Hillsboro, Oreg., 1991, J.B. Thomas Jr. High Sch., Hillsboro, Oreg., 1991-92, Yamhill (Oreg.)-Carlton High Sch., 1992—; adv. mem. for Reflections (literary mag.), Yamhill-Carlton H.S., 1993—; adviser The Expression (newspaper) Yamhill-Carlton H.S., 1992—. Writer (newspaper) Hollywood Star, 1987-89. Mem. Jr. League of Portland, 1986—; bd. dirs. Friends of Extension, Hillsboro, 1994-95, 4-H (Washington County), Hillsboro, 1994-95. Mem. Nat. Coun. Tchrs. English. Office: Yamhill-Carlton High Sch 275 N Maple St Yamhill OR 97148-7601

CLOSE, GLENN, actress; b. Greenwich, Conn., Mar. 19, 1947; d. William and Bettine Close; m. Cabot Wade (div.); m. James Marlas, 1984 (div.); 1 child, Annie Maude Starke. B.A., Coll. William and Mary, 1974. Profl. actress, also accomplished mus. performer (lyric soprano); co-owner The Leaf and Bean Coffee House, Bozeman, Montana, 1991—. Joined New Phoenix Repertory Co., 1974; made Broadway debut in Love for Love; other Broadway appearences include The Rules of the Game, The Member of the Wedding, 1974-75, Rex, Barnum, 1980-81 (Tony award nominee), The Real Thing, 1984-85 (Tony award for Best Actress in Drama), Benefactors, 1986, Wine Untouched, Death and the Maiden, 1992 (Drama League N.Y. Distinguished Performance award, 1992, Tony award for Best Actress in Drama, 1992), Sunset Boulevard, 1994-95 (Tony award Lead Actress in a Musical, 1995); other theatre appearences include Uncommon Women and Others, The Singular Life of Albert Nobbs, 1982 (Obie award), Childhood, 1985, one performance oratorio Joan of Arc at the Stake, 1985, Sunset Boulevard (L.A.), 1993-94, and other repertory and regional theatres; films include The World According to Garp, 1982 (Acad. award nominee), The Big Chill, 1983 (Acad. award nominee), The Natural, 1984 (Acad. award nominee), Greystoke: The Legend of Tarzan, Lord of the Apes (voice), 1984, The Stone Boy, 1984, Maxie, 1985, Jagged Edge, 1985, Fatal Attraction, 1987, Light Years (voice), 1988, Dangerous Liaisons, 1988, Immediate Family, 1989, Reversal of Fortune, 1990, Hamlet, 1990, Hook (cameo), 1991, Meeting Venus, 1991, The House of the Spirits, 1994, The Paper, 1994; TV films include Too Far To Go, 1979, Orphan Train, 1979, The Elephant Man, 1982, Something about Amelia, 1984 (Emmy award nominee), The Elephant's Child (host), 1987, The Emperor's New Clothes (host), 1987, The Legend of Sleepy Hollow (narrator), 1988, Stones for Ibarra, 1988, (also exec. prodr.) Sarah, Plain and Tall, 1991, Skylark, 1993 (Emmy award nomine for Lead Actress in a Miniseries, 1993), Serving in Silence: The Margarethe Cammermeyer Story, 1995 (Emmy award). Recipient Woman of Yr. award Hasty Pudding Theatricals, 1990, Dartmouth Film Soc. award, 1990. Mem. Phi Beta Kappa. Office: CAA 9830 Wilshire Blvd Beverly Hills CA 90212-1804*

CLOSSER, GLORIA JEAN, media specialist; b. Wheeling, W.Va., Sept. 15, 1947; d. John Straface and Mary (Felici) John; m. Craig Alan Closser, Jul. 11, 1970; children: Carla Jo, Christine Marie. B, Ohio U., 1969; M, W.Va. U., 1971; adminstr./supervision, U. Dayton, 1983. Tchr. Indian Creek Sch. Dist., Mingo Junction, Ohio, 1968-69; media specialist/dist. media dir./tech. coord. Buckeye Local Sch. Dist., Rayland, Ohio, 1969—; libr. supr. Buckeye Local Sch. Dist., Rayland, 1983. Contbr. article to profl. jours. Mem. East Ohio Reg. Hosp. Auxilary, Martins Ferry, Ohio, 1989; registration chmn. Southern Jefferson Co. Political Club, Yorkville, 1982—; audit chmn. Yorkville United Meth. Ch., 1987; mem. Dem. Ctrl. Com., 1996—. Recipient grant, Jefferson Co. Bd. Edn., 1984,86; Martha Holden Jennings Found., Kent State U., 1990. Mem. Ohio Edn. Libr. Assn. (nominating com. 1985), Ohio Edn. Assn., Nat. Edn. Assn., Buckeye Local Classroom Tchrs. Assn., Gamma Delta (phone com. 1993—). Democrat. Home: 324 Market Yorkville OH 43971

CLOSSON, HELGA C., councilwoman; b. Oneida, N.Y., July 13, 1945; d. Kurt Adolf and Viola May (Merthiew) Rissman; m. Arthur E. Closson, Jr., Aug. 20, 1963; children: Christine, Tammy, Arthur III, Kurt. Cert. tchrs. aide. Councilwoman City of Oneida, 1991—; mem. ways and means com. City of Oneida, 1991-96, cable com., 1991-96, fin. com. 1991-96; mem. Woman Polit. Caucus, Nelson, N.Y., 1992-96. Author poems. Co-founder, chairwoman United Neighbors Orgn., Oneida, 1989-96; mem. Dem. Com., Oneida and Madison County, 1991—; vol. Kaffet Civic Ctr., Oneida, 1993—; liaison city water bd. coll. courses planning and land mgmt., U. S.C., Morrisville. Mem. Atlantic States Orgn. Lutheran. Home: 512 Fitch St Oneida NY 13421

CLOUD, LINDA BEAL, retired secondary school educator; b. Jay, Fla., Dec. 4, 1937; d. Charles Rockwood and Agnes (Diamond) Beal; m. Robert Vincent Cloud (Aug. 15, 1959 (dec. 1985). BA, Miss. Coll., 1959; MEd, U. So. Fla., 1976; EdS, Nova U., 1982; postgrad., Walden U., 1983. Cert. tchr., Fla. Tchr. Ft. Meade (Fla.) Jr.-Sr. H.S., 1959-67, 80-89, Lake Wales (Fla.) H.S., 1967-80; pres. Cloud Aero Svcs., Inc., Babson Park, Fla., 1992—; part-time tchr. Spanish, English, Polk County Adult Schs., 1960-76; instr. Spanish Warner So. Coll., Lake Wales, 1974; instr. vocal music, drama, composition Webber Coll., Babson Park, Fla.; cons., pvt. tutor in field. Contbr. articles to profl. and equine publs.; author, dir. numerous pageants for schs. Charter mem., bd. dirs. Lake Wales Little Theatre, Inc., 1976; dir. Four Sq. swing choir; entertainer for various local orgns.; ring announcer Fla. State Fair, 1987-88; judge poetry and essay contests; bd. dirs. Defenders of Crooked Lake; mem., soloist Babson Pk. Cmty. Ch. Recipient Best Actress award Lake Wales Little Theatre, Inc., 1978-79. Mem. AAUW, Nat. Coun. Tchrs. English, Fla. Coun. Tchrs. English, Polk Coun. Tchrs. English, Polk Fgn. Lang. Assn., Babson Park Womans Club, Sassy Singers, Southeastern Peruvian Horse Club (life). Republican. Home: 1654 Seminole Rd Babson Park FL 33827-9793

CLOUGH, SARALYN LOUISE, speech-language pathologist; b. Fontana, Calif., Nov. 8, 1971; d. Robert Lee Clough and Pamela Melindagale (Warren) Salazar. BA, Chico State U., 1993; MA, San Jose State U., 1995. Lic. speech-lang. pathologist. Speech-lang. pathologist aide West Valley Jr. Coll., Saratoga, Calif., 1993-95; speech-lang. pathologist Ortho-Neurol. Rehab., Los Gatos, Calif., 1996—. Educator Chico Women's Ctr., Napa (Calif.) State Hosp., 1990-93; bd. dirs. Gay Lesbian Bisexual Alliance, Chico, 1992-93, Chico Hate Crimes Com., 1992-93; emotional supporter AIDS Resources and Info. Svcs., Santa Clara, Calif., 1994-95. Mem. Am. Speech and Hearing Assn., Lesbian and Gay Audiologists and Speech Pathologists, NOW (v.p., Outstanding Feminist Activity award 1992). Democrat. Buddhist. Office: Sierra Sunrise Health Ctr 2850 Sierra Sunrise Ter Chico CA 95928

CLOUSE, VICKIE RAE, biology and paleontology educator; b. Havre, Mont., Mar. 28, 1956; d. Olaf Raymond and Betty Lou (Reed) Nelson; m. Gregory Scott Clouse, Mar. 22, 1980; 1 child, Kristopher Nelson. BS in Secondary Sci. Edn., Mont. State U. No., Havre, 1989; postgrad., Mont. State U., Bozeman, 1991-94. Teaching asst. biology and paleontology Mont. State U.-No., Havre, 1986-90; rsch. asst. dinosaur eggs and embryos Mus. of the Rockies, Bozeman, 1992-95; instr. biology and paleontology Mont. State U.-No., Havre, 1990—. Bd. trustees H.E. Clack Mus., Havre, 1991-97, H.E. Clack Mus. Found., Havre, 1991-97, Mont. Bd. Regents of Higher Edn., Helena, 1989-90, Mont. Higher Edn. Student Fin. Assistance Corp., Helena, 1989-90; mem. Ea. Mont. Hist. Soc., 1993—. Named Young Career Woman of Yr., Bus. and Profl. Woman's Club, 1986. Mem. Soc. Vertebrate Paleontologists, Mont. Geol. Soc. Office: Mont State U-No Hagener Sci Ctr Havre MT 59501

CLOWERS, EVEALYN, civic worker; b. Athens, Tenn., Oct. 20, 1935; d. Fred M. and Mabel (Hickman) Plank; m. Joe Little, Dec. 22, 1955 (div. Apr. 1973); children: Joseph Plank, Anna Laurie Little Watkins; m. H. Freddie Clowers, May 1, 1973. Cert. interior design, NYU. Mem. faculty staff U.

Md., Munich, Germany, 1959-60; office mgr. Dr. S. Harris Pierce, Cleve., Tenn., 1960-65; co-owner, operator Hickory Hollow Restaurant and Antiques, Cleve., Tenn., 1966-73, Clowers Interiors, Cleve., Tenn., 1973-83, Cherokee Inn Motel, Cleve., Tenn., 1983-86. East Tenn. vice chair Tenn. Dem. Party, committeewoman; mem. and chmn. Cleve. Pub. Libr.; past chmn. Ft. Loudon Regional Bd.; del. White House Conf. on Librs., 1991; Tenn. del. Dem. Nat. Conv., 1996; mem. Tenn. Adv. Coun. on Librs.; active Friends of Tenn. Librs., Tenn. Dem. Women; speaker on censorship; chair Tenn. Pub. Awareness com. on librs., 1996. Recipient Freedom of Info. award Tenn. Libr. Assn., 1994, Bill of Rights award ACLU, 1995. Mem. Disabled Am. Vets. Aux., Tenn. Libr. Assn. (pres. 1996), Fairfield Glade Golf & Country Club, McDonald Ruritan Club, Order Eastern Star. Episcopalian. Home: 2205 Brentwood Dr Cleveland TN 37311

CLOYD, HELEN MARY, accountant, educator; b. Austria-Hungary, 1918; d. Valentine and Elizabeth (Kretschmar von Kienbusch) Yuhasz; came to U.S. 1922, naturalized, 1928; BS, Eastern Mich. U., 1953; MA, Wayne State U., 1956; PhD, Mich. State U., 1963; m. George S. Smith, Mar. 4, 1939 (dec.); children: George, Nora; m. Chester L. Cloyd, Apr. 16, 1960 (dec.). Pub. accounting Haskins & Sells, Detroit, 1945-53; tchr. Marine City (Mich.) High Sch., 1954-59; instr. acctg. Central Mich. U., Mt. Pleasant, 1959-60; asst. prof. Wayne State U., Detroit, 1960-61; tchr. Grosse Pointe (Mich.) High Sch., 1961-64; assoc. prof. acctg. Ball State U., Muncie, Ind., 1964-71; prof. Shepherd Coll., Shepherdstown, W.Va., 1971-76; assoc. prof. George Mason U., Fairfax, Va. Recipient McClintock Writing award CPA, Mich., Ind., W.Va. Mem. AICPA, Am. Acctg. Assn., Am. Econs. Assn., AAAS, Assn. Sch. Bus. Ofcls., Delta Pi Epsilon, Pi Omega Pi, Pi Gamma Mu. Clubs: Order Eastern Star, White Shrine. Contbr. numerous articles to publs. Home: PO Box 186 Inwood WV 25428-0186

CLURFELD, ANDREA, editor, food critic; b. N.Y.C., Mar. 13, 1954; d. Jerome and Geraldine R. Clurfeld. BA in Art History, Wells Coll., 1976. Reporter, arts editor Hunterdon County Democrat, Flemington, N.J., 1977-82; night and Sunday editor New Jersey Herald, Newton, N.J., 1982-86; restaurant critic/food editor Asbury Park Press, Neptune, N.J, 1986—; editor Wine Taster mag., 1995—, The Guide to The Jersey Shore; Mem. Internat. Assn. Culinary Profls., Assn. Food Journalists, James Beard Found., Monmouth County Cooks Coop. (founding), Field Spaniel Soc. Am. Recipient award N.J. Press Assn., 1978-94, Nat. Newspaper Assn., 1981, Soc. Profl. Journalists, 1991, 94. Mem. Internat. Assn. Culinary Profls., Assn. Food Journalists, James Beard Found., Monmouth County Cooks Coop. (founding). Avocations: fine American crafts, travel, gardening. Home: Jolly Cackle Farm 103 Bowne Rd Locust NJ 07760 Office: Asbury Park Press Inc PO Box 1550 3601 Hwy 66 Neptune NJ 07754-1550

CLYMER, JUDITH ELAINE, elementary school educator; b. Defiance, Ohio, June 3, 1957; d. Lester Earl and Ruth Annabelle (Desgrange) Brinkman; m. Jack David Rishel, Aug. 14, 1982 (div. Jan. 1986); m. Burley Benjamin Clymer, Apr. 30, 1994; children: Mark, Robin, Ben, Terri. BA, Ohio No. U., 1978; MA, Bowling Green State U., 1988. Tchr. grade 2 Cory-Rawson Local Sch., Rawson, Ohio, 1978-82, 84—; substitute tchr. Calhoun County Pub. Schs., Battle Creek, Mich., 1982-84; young author liaison U. Findlay, Ohio, 1992, Mazza enthusiast, 1992—. Mem. Am. Fedn. Tchrs., Ohio Fed. Tchrs., Cory-Rawson Edn. Assn. (bargaining team 1986—). Republican. Mennonite. Home: 12038 Township Rd 130 Findlay OH 45840-9009

CLYNE, DIANNA MARIE, psychiatrist; b. Lincoln, Nebr., Mar. 16, 1959; d. John Clayton Clyne and Marilynn Paula (Matt) Hoenig; m. Jerry Lee Govier, Oct., 1981 (div. Sept. 1984); 1 child, Chanda Marie; m. Jerry Lee Smith, Sept. 9, 1991; children: Cassandra Lee, Crystal Renee, Catrina Diane, Corrin Pauline. Student, U. Nebr., 1977, 80, Southeast C.C., Lincoln, Nebr., 1978, 79-80; BS in Comprehensive Biology summa cum laude, Kearney State Coll., 1983; MD, U. Nebr. Med. Ctr., 1989. Diplomate Am. Bd. Forensic Examiners. Intern, then resident in psychiatry Maricopa Med. Ctr., Phoenix, Ariz., 1989-93; adult sr. med. investigator Cmty. Care Network/Maricopa Clin. Mgmt./ComCare, Phoenix, 1991-95, Urgent Care Ctr. Southwest Behavioral Health, Phoenix, 1995; adult sr. med. investigator rehab. Chemical Dependency Unit Hastings (Nebr.) Regional Ctr., 1996—; lectr., rschr. in field. With USNG, 1977-85, capt. Res. Mem. AMA, NAFE, Am. Psychiat. Assn., Am. Neuropsychiat. Assn., Am. Soc. Clin. Psychopharmacology, Am. Profl. Practice Assn., Am. Med. Women's Assn., Am. Assocs. Suicidology, Am. Field Svc., Assn. Am. Physicians and Surgeons, Nat. Assn. Residents and Interns, Nat. Assn. of Drs., Nat. Found. Depressive Illness, Inc., Nat. Family Assn., Ariz. Med. Assn., Ariz. Psychiat. Assn., Ariz. Med. Polit. Action Com., Phoenix Psychiat. Coun., Physicians Planning Svc. Corp., Women in the Arts, U. Nebr. Alumni, Kearney State Alumni, Southeast C.C. Alumni Assn. Roman Catholic. Home: 309 N 6th Ave Hastings NE 68901 Office: Hastings Regional Ctr PO Box 579 Hastings NE 68902-0579

CMAR, JANICE BUTKO, home economics educator; b. Pitts., Nov. 10, 1954; d. Edward Michael and Ruth Lillian (Pickard) Butko; m. Dennis Paul Cmar, children: Michael, Nicole. BS, Mansfield U., 1976; MS, Duquesne U., 1990. Cert. home economist. Home econ. tchr. Duquesne (Pa.) Sch. Dist., 1978-83; special edn. tchr. Allegheny Intermediate Unit, Pitts., 1985-95; home econs. tchr. Peters Twp. Sch. Dist., McMurray, Pa., 1995—; sponsor Duquesne High Sch., Y-Teens and Future Homemakers Am., 1979-83, Pathfinder Student Coun., Bethel Park, Pa., Mon-Valley Secondary Sch. Yearbook and Prom, Jefferson, Pa. Vol. Allegheny County Dept. Cmty. Svcs., Pitts., 1986—; mem. com. Allegheny County Dem. Orgn. Mem. Am. Fedn. Tchrs., Am. Assn. Family and Consumer Scis., State Assn. Family and Consumer Scis., Allegheny County Assn. Family and Consumer Scis. (pres. 1991-92), Phi Delta Kappa, Alpha Sigma Tau. Democrat. Home: Jefferson Borough 918 Old Hickory Ln Clairton PA 15025-3437 Office: 625 E McMurray Rd McMurray PA 15317

COATES, DONNA ALEXANDRIA, owner mechanical and construction equipment company; b. Joppa, Md., Oct. 27, 1946; d. Jesse Lee and Marian Colleen (Matthews) Reid; divorced; 1 child, Tracey Geneen. Grad., Western H.S., Balt., 1964. Master heating, ventilation and air conditioning mechanic; notary pub.; journeyman gasfitter. File clk. Social Security Adminstrn., Balt., 1965-66, 69-73; resident apt. mgr. Furguson & Assoc. and Grady Mgmt., Silver Spring, Md., 1977-85; adminstrv. dir. DD A/C & Heating, Inc., Balt., 1985-88; pres., owner, CEO Dime, Inc., Balt., 1987—. Mem., asst. sec. missionary bd. Greater Harvest Bapt. Ch., 1995; chair Mayor's Empowerment Zone Com., Balt., 1994. Recipient Thank You for Caring award City of Balt., 1980, Christmas in Apr., 1995; included in Great Blacks in Wax Mus., 1995. Mem. NAFE, Nat. Assn. Women Constrn. (bd. dirs. 1994—, v.p. 1995—), Bldg. Congress & Exch. Balt. Democrat. Office: Dime Inc 14 N Carey St Ste 103 Baltimore MD 21223-1818

COATES, GARDENIA EVANS, customer technical support manager; b. Lynchburg, S.C., Oct. 9, 1954; d. Thomas James Evans and Delphine (Evans) Rouse; m. Gerald Coates, May 23, 1981; children: Stephanie, Jarreau. BS in AMS and Econs., Carnegie-Mellon U., 1977. Computer operator Colonial Penn Ins., Phila., 1977-78, mktg. support analyst, 1978-79; sys. analyst Ins. Co. of N.A., Phila., 1979-82; quality assurance analyst AGS Mgmt. Sys., King of Prussia, Pa., 1982-83, project leader, 1983-86, sr. client support rep., 1986-89; project mgmr. cons. Coates Enterprise, Raleigh, N.C., 1989-90; mktg. support rep. Post Software Internat., Youngsville, N.C., 1990-91, devel. mgr., 1991-94, account leader, 1994—. Mem. membership com. PTA, N.C., 1991; mem. Women Missionary Soc., Raleigh, 1990-94; group leader Young People Dept., 1991. Recipient Jr. Fellowship award, 1972-77. Mem. Network of Minority Women in Sci. and Technol. (treas. 1976-77), Jr. Achievement (leader, advisor 1978-79). Methodist.

COATES, VERONA ANGES, educator; b. Boyd, Oreg., June 21, 1916; d. Willard Eli and Agnes Viola (Hastings) Adkisson; m. William Stanley Coates, June 29, 1941; children: William, Anne Olson, Jane Ormiston, David. AA, Sacramento Jr. Coll., Sacramento, Calif., 1936; BS, Oreg. State Univ., 1940, MS, 1942. Cert. tchr. Oreg., Calif. Extension asst. Oregon State Univ., Corvallis, 1944-45; adult edn. tchr. Hayward (Calif.) Sch. Dist., 1950-59; jr. high tchr. Mt. Eden Sch. Dist., Hayward, 1960-63, Union Sch. Dist., San Jose, Calif., 1963-69, Petaluma (Calif.) Sch. Dist., 1969—; vocational edn. tchr. Sonoma County, Santa Rosa, Calif., 1977-82; fashion merchandising tchr. Santa Rosa Jr. Coll., 1978-80; sub. tchr. Sonoma County, Santa Rosa, Calif. Active Self Help for Heard of Hearing, Napa, Calif., 1990—. Recipient Dist. Woman of Yr., Calif. State Leg., 1991. Mem. Am. Assn. Univ. Women, Am. Home Econs. Assn., Calif. Tchrs. Assn., Nat. Edn. Assn. Democrat. Protestant. Home: 203 Nicole Way Napa CA 94558

COBB, CECELIA ANNETTE, counselor; b. Dayton, Ohio, June 22, 1944; d. Fred E. and Margaret Laverne (Ogle) C.; m. Robert A. Fackler, June 25, 1966 (div. Mar. 1981); m. James A. McCluskey, June 18, 1983; 1 child, James Christian. BS, Ohio U., 1967; MA in Teaching, Saginaw Valley State Coll., 1978; MA in Counseling, Oakland U., 1993. Lic. profl. counselor, Mich.; cert. tchr., Mich. Tchr. L'Anse Creuse Pub. Schs., Mt. Clemens, Mich., 1966-91, counselor, 1993—; cons. Establishment Crisis Ctr., Mt. Clemens, 1968-70; supr. tchr. Mich. State U., Lansing, 1970-72; leader pilot project Quest Inc., Findlay, Ohio, 1982-83. Provider shelter for homeless, Mt. Clements, 1983—. Mem. NEA, Am. Sch. Counseling Assn., Mich. Edn. Assn., Mich. Sch. Counseling Assn., Macomb County Assn. Counseling and Devel., Chi Sigma Iota. Democrat. Home: 38098 Lakeshore Dr Harrison Township MI 48045-2855 Office: L'Anse Creuse Pub Schs 36727 Jefferson Ave Harrison Township MI 48045-2917

COBB, JANE OVERTON, legislative staff member; b. Charleston, S.C., July 23, 1962; d. Dolphin Dunnaha and Sue (Hagood) Overton; m. Robert Watson Cobb, July 15, 1989; children: Robert Watson, Jr., Johnson Hagood. BA, Vanderbilt U., 1984, MEd, 1985. Cert. secondary tchr., Ga. Tchr. English Columbia High Sch., Atlanta, 1985-86; tchr. ESL Hangzhou, China, 1986-87; govt. affairs asst. Hewlett Packard Co., Washington, 1987-89; mem. congrl. staff U.S. Ho. Reps., Washington, 1989—. Office: US Ho Reps Govt Reform & Oversight Com 2157 Rayburn Ho Office Bldg Washington DC 20515

COBB, KARINA NÖEL, photographer, journalist; b. Edina, Minn., Dec. 11, 1968; d. Nathan Allen and Saundra Lea (Olson) C.; m. Paul Frederick Peterson. BS in Journalism and Sociology, U. Wis., River Falls, 1995. Freelance reporter, prodr. Cable Access/Stillwater (Minn.), 1987-96; editor, inventor Sin Mag., River Falls, 1992; photographer Friends of the Saddle Horse, Cannon Falls, Minn., 1992, Saddle and Bridle Mag., 1992, Courage St. Croix, Stillwater, 1993—, Twin Cities Reader, Mpls., 1994; prodr. Campus TV News, River Falls, 1995, Cable Access Ctr., Stillwater, 1996; promotions person Soc. Profl. Journalist, River Falls, 1993-94; pres. New Music Alliance, River Falls, 1992-93; prodr., dir. Kaptain's Korner show, Stillwater, 1995; photographer Quarter Abroad, Europe, 1990; pres., inventor Crisis Ctr., 1992. Contbr photographs to essays and exhibits (hon. mention award 1990, 1st pl. award 1991, 3d pl. award 1989). Vol., mem. Courage St. Croix, Stillwater, 1993—; mission work our Savior's Luth. Ch., Cuernavaca, Mex., 1986. Recipient Am. Saddle Horse Assn., 1989. Mem. Women in Comms., Internat. TV Assn., River Valley Art Coun., Tri-State Horseman's Assn. (award of excellence 1990), Children's Home Soc.

COBB, KAY B., former state senator, lawyer; m. Larry Cobb; children: Barbara Cobb Murphy, Elizabeth Cobb DeBusk. BS, Miss. U. Women; JD, U. Miss. Former spl. asst. atty. gen. North Miss.; atty. Oxford, Miss. Mem. Nat. Alliance/Model State Drug Laws, Vets. Aux., C. of C. Republican. Baptist. Address: PO Box 1173 Oxford MS 38655-1173 Office: 914 Van Buren Ave Oxford MS 38655

COBB, MADELYN ADAMS, marketing director; b. Seattle, Oct. 14, 1964; d. John Hurst and Dolly Jacqueline (Desselle) Adams; m. Timothy F.S. Cobb, Oct. 3, 1992; 1 child, Harrison Avery Adams. AB in Polit. Sci., Duke U., 1986; MBA in Mktg., U. Pa., 1989. Mktg. mgr. 20th Century Fox Film Corp., L.A., 1989-91; account dir. Atlanta Com. Olympic Games, 1991-94, dir. media & mktg., 1995—. Mem. Links, Inc., Atlanta, 1994—. Mem. Nat. Black MBA Assn. African Methodist Episcopal.

COBB, ROWENA NOELANI BLAKE, real estate broker; b. Kauai, Hawaii, May 1, 1939; d. Bernard K. Blake and Hattie Kanui Yuen; m. James Jackson Cobb, Dec. 22, 1962; children: Shelly Ranelle Noelani, Bret Kimo Jackson. BS in Edn., Bob Jones U., 1961; broker's lic., Vitousek Sch. Real Estate, Honolulu, 1981. Lic. real estate broker, Honolulu; cert. residential broker. Bus. mgr. Micronesian Occupl. Ctr., Koror Palau, 1968-70; prin. broker Cobb Realty, Lihue, Hawaii, 1983—; sec. Neighbor Island MLS Svc., Honolulu, 1985-87, vice chmn., 1987-88; chmn. MLS Hawaii, Inc., Honolulu, 1988-90. Assoc. editor Jour Entymology, 1965-66. Sec. Koloa Cmty. Assn., 1981-89, pres., 1989; mem. Kauai Humane Soc., YWCA, Kauai Mus., Kauai Visitors Bur.; bd. dirs. Wong Care Home; vice chairperson Kauain Schs. Adv. Coun., 1995-98. Mem. Nat. Assn. Realtors (grad. Realtors Inst., cert. residential specialist), Hawaii Assn. Realtors (cert. tchr., state bd. dirs. 1984, v.p. 1985, dir. 1995-96), Kauai Bd. Realtors (v.p. 1984, pres. 1985, bd. dirs. 1995-97, Realtor Assoc. of Yr. award 1983, Realtor of Yr. award 1986), Kauai C. of C., Soroptomists (bd. dirs. Lihue chpt. 1986-89, treas. 1989). Office: PO Box 157 Koloa HI 96756-0150

COBB, SHARON YVONNE, screenwriter; b. DeLand, Fla., Apr. 19, 1958; d. Charles William and Bonnie (Elizabeth (Lyons) C. Grad. high sch., Pierson, Fla. Owner, mgr. Sharon Cobb Advt., Jacksonville, Fla., 1978-81; fiber sculptor Key West, Fla., 1981-86; dir. Keys Advt. & Mktg., Key West, 1986-87; pub. Fla. Travel Directory, Jacksonville, 1987-89; screenwriter Neptune Beach, Fla., 1989-93; film writer Jacksonville Today mag., Beverly Hills, Calif., 1993—; editor Jacksonville Today mag., 1991-92; lectr. screenwriting UCLA. Co-author: Secrets of Selling Your Script to Hollywood. Founder, bd. dirs. Earth Ctr. Inc., Jacksonville, 1978-81. Recipient Addy award Jacksonville Advt. Fedn., 1976, 77, Golden Image award Fla. Pub. Rels. Assn., 1978, 1st place pub. rels. program award So. Pub. Rels. Fedn., 1978. Mem. Fla. Freelance Writers Assn. (award for mag. feature writing 1992), Fla. Motion Picture and TV Assn. (Crystal Reel award for best screenplay 1993).

COBB, SHIRLEY ANN, public relations specialist, journalist; b. Oklahoma City, Jan. 1, 1936; d. William Ray and Irene (Fewell) Dodson; m. Roy Lampkin Cobb, Jr., June 21, 1958; children: Kendra Leigh, Cary William, Paul Alan. BA in Journalism with distinction, U. Okla., 1958, postgrad., 1972; postgrad., Jacksonville U., 1962. Info. specialist Pacific Missle Test Ctr., Point Mugu, Calif., 1975-76; corr. Religious News Svc., N.Y.C., 1979-81; splty. editor fashion and religion Thousand Oaks (Calif.) News Chronicle, 1977-81; pub. rels. cons., Camarillo, Calif., 1977—; media mgr. pub. info City of Thousand Oaks, 1983—. Contbr. articles to profl. jours. Trustee Ocean View Sch. Bd., 1976-79; pres. Point Mugu Officers' Wives Club, 1975-76, 90— ; bd. dirs. Camarillo Hospice, 1983-85; sec. Conejo Valley Hist. Soc., 1993-96, Ednl. TV for Conejo, 1996—. Recipient Spot News award San Fernando Valley Press Club, 1979. Mem. Pub. Rels. Soc. Am. (L.A. chpt. liaison 1991), Calif. Assn. Pub. Info. Ofcls. (pres. 1989-90, Paul Clark Lifetime Achievement award 1993), Sigma Delta Chi, Phi Beta Kappa, Chi Omega. Republican. Clubs: Las Posas Country, Spanish Hills Country, Town Hall of Calif. Home: 2481 Brookhill Dr Camarillo CA 93010-2112 Office: 2100 E Thousand Oaks Blvd Thousand Oaks CA 91362-2903

COBURN, JENNIFER, public affairs administrator; b. N.Y.C., June 28, 1966; d. Shelley and Carol (Krickett) C.; m. William O'Neil, Mar. 14, 1993. BA, U. Mich., 1988. Sales rep. Harmon Homes Mag., San Diego, 1988-92; freelance writer San Diego, 1992-93; coord. pub. affairs Planned Parenthood, $, 1993—. Author: Take Back Your Power: A Working Woman's Response to Sexual Harrassment, 1995, The History of San Diego NOW, 1995; contbr. articles to San Diego Union-Tribune, San Diego Rev., North County Times, Gay & Lesbian Times, 1993-96. Pres. San Diego chpt. NOW, 1994, 95, bd. dirs., 1993-96; 2d v.p. Coalition for Reproductive Choice, San Diego, 1995, 96; founder, dir. Feed the Homeless/Ch. of Today, San Diego, 1992, 93. Recipient Leadership award ABC-Channel 10, San Diego, 1993, Write Women Back in to History award Nat. Women's History Project, Windsor, Calif., 1995, Susan B. Anthony award NOW, San Diego, 1996. Democrat.

COBURN, MARJORIE FOSTER, psychologist, educator; b. Salt Lake City, Feb. 28, 1939; d. Harlan A. and Alma (Ballinger) Polk; m. Robert Byron Coburn, July 2, 1977; children: Polly Klea Foster, Matthew Ryan Foster, Robert Scott Coburn, Kelly Anne Coburn. B.A. in Sociology, UCLA, 1960; Montessori Internat. Diploma honor grad. Washington Montessori Inst., 1968, M.A. in Psychology, U. No. Colo., 1979; Ph.D. in Counseling Psychology, U. Denver, 1983. Licensed clin. psychologist. Probation officer Alameda County (Calif.), Oakland, 1960-62, Contra Costa County (Calif.), El Cerrito, 1966, Fairfax County (Va.), Fairfax, 1967; dir. Friendship Club, Orlando, Fla., 1963-65; tchr. Va. Montessori Sch., Fairfax, 1968-70; spl. edn. tchr. Leary Sch., Falls Church, Va., 1970-72, sch. administr., 1973-76; tchr. Aseltine Sch., San Diego, 1976-77, Coburn Montessori Sch., Colorado Springs, Colo., 1977-79; pvt. practice psychotherapy, Colorado Springs, 1979-82, San Diego, 1982—; cons. spl. edn., agoraphobia, women in transition. Mem. Am. Psychol. Assn., Am. Orthopsychiat. Assn., Phobia Soc., Council Exceptional Children, Calif. Psychol. Assn., San Diego Psychological Assn., The Charter 100, Mensa. Episcopalian. Lodge: Rotary. Contbr. articles to profl. jours.; author: (with R.C. Orem) Montessori: Prescription for Children with Learning Disabilities, 1977. Office: 826 Prospect St Ste 101 La Jolla CA 92037-4206

COCAIN HASTLER, CYNTHIA LUCILLE, artist, graphic designer; b. Akron, Ohio, Aug. 18, 1956; d. Harry William Vincent and Sally Lucille (Houghland) Cocain; m. Ronald Ernest Hastler, Oct. 9, 1979. BFA in Drawing, U. Akron, 1983. Coord. display design Lighthouse Pools, Cuyahoga Falls, Ohio, 1975-77; 3-D casting drafter Indsl. Artcraft, Akron, Ohio, 1977-80; freelance graphicist R.C.H. Studios, Akron, 1980—; art dir. Shrine Circus, Tadmor Temple, Akron, 1993—; cons., advisor home restoration Ohio Hist. Soc., Columbus, 1980, Summit County Hist. Soc., Akron, 1980; cons. Harvey Whitehill Painting, Sonoma, Calif., 1991—. Contbr. articles to popular mags.; artist logos for small bus. Assoc. fellow Bee Sharp Prodns., 1995. Mem. Akron Men's Garden Club, Highland Sq. Garden Club. Office: R C H Studios 294 Grove St Akron OH 44302

COCCO, CLAUDIA LIVIA, manufacturing executive; b. Newark, Jan. 3, 1957; d. Livio and Irma Angela Cocco. BS, Montclair State U., 1978; MBA, Claremont Coll., 1996. Lic. single engine pilot. Asst. br. mgr. Household Fin. Corp., Clifton, N.J., 1978-80; with legal adminstrn. dept. Hertz Leasing, Parsippany, N.J., 1980-84; with cost analysis dept. Rockwell Internat., El Segundo, Calif., 1984-86; with indsl. engring. dept. Northrop Corp., Pico Rivera, Calif., 1986-89; with contract mgmt. dept. McDonnell Douglas Corp., Long Beach, Calif., 1989—. Adult vol. Campfire Boys and Girls, Long Beach, 1990-91. Mem. Nat. Contracts Mgmt. Assn., McDonnell Douglas Mgmt. Club, McDonnell Douglas Women in Network Group. Republican. Roman Catholic.

COCCO, JACQUELINE M., state legislator; b. Bridgeport, Conn.. Grad., St. Vincent's Sch. Nursing. State rep. dist. 127 Conn. Ho. of Reps., 1987—; chmn. family and workplace com., mem. labor and pub. employees com., pub. health com., asst. majority leader; mem. Dem. Town Com., 1984—; mem. Bd. Humane Affairs, 1986-90; mem. Charter Rev. Com., 1988-89; vis. nurse. Home: 93 Heppenstall Dr Bridgeport CT 06604-1007 Office: Conn Ho of Reps Legislative Office Bldg Hartford CT 06106*

COCCO, MARIE ELIZABETH, journalist; b. Malden, Mass., Jan. 15, 1956; d. Morris Alfred and Dorothy Anne (Colameta) C.; m. Thomas Neal Burrows, Sept. 4, 1982; children: Matthew C. Burrows., Michael C. Burrows. BA, Tufts U., 1978; MS, Columbia U., 1979. Journalist Daily Register, Shrewsbury, N.J., 1979-80, Newsday, L.I., N.Y., 1980—. Recipient Excellence in Editorial Writing award N.Y. State Pubs. Assn., 1992, Nat. Reporting award Sigma Delta Chi, 1991. Mem. White House Corrs. Assn. (Barnet Nover award 1991), Nat. Press Club (Washington Corr. award 1991). Office: Newsday Washington Bur 1730 Pennsylvania Ave NW Washington DC 20006

COCHÉ, JUDITH, psychologist, educator; b. Phila., Sept. 2, 1942; d. Louis and Miriam (Nerenberg) Milner; m. Erich Coché, Oct. 16, 1966 (dec.); 1 child, Juliette Laura; m. John Anderson, Jan. 1, 1994. BA, Colby Coll., 1964; MA, Temple U., 1966; PhD, Bryn Mawr Coll., 1975. Diplomate Am. Bd. Profl. Psychology. Rsch. asst. Jefferson Med. Coll., 1965-66; diagnostician Law Ct., Aachen, Germany, 1967-68; staff psychologist N.E. Community Mental Health Ctr., Phila., 1969-74; family clinician Inst. Pa. Hosp., 1974-76; instr. psychology Drexel U., 1976-77; lectr. Med. Coll. Pa., 1977-78; asst. clin. prof. Hahnemann Med. Coll., Phila., 1979—; pvt. practice Phila., 1974—, N.J., 1985—; assoc. prof. psychiatry U. Pa., 1985—; mem. faculty Family Inst. of Phila., 1990—; sr. cons. Phila. Child Guidance Clinic, 1992—; clin. cons. Hilltop Prep Sch., 1977-86; clin. supr. Am. Assn. Marriage and Family Therapy. Co-author: Couples Group Psychotherapy, A Clinical Practice Model, 1990, Co. author Powerful Wisdom: Voices of Distinguished Women Psychotherapists, (1993); contbr. chpts. to books, articles to profl. jours. Bd. dirs. Whitemarsh Art Ctr., 1977-78, Please Touch Museum, 1982-89; mem. prof. adv. bd. Parents Without Ptnrs., 1977-86; mem. adv. com. Pa. Ballet/Shirley Rock. Grantee Del. Children's Bur. Bryn Mawr Coll., 1974-75, Pa. Hosp., 1975-77. Fellow Am. Group Psychotherapy Assn.; mem. APA, Am. Assn. Marriage and Family Therapy (approved supr.), Am. Family Therapy Assn., Phila. Soc. Clin. Psychologists (pres. 1980-81), Family Inst. Phila., Pa. Psychol. Assn. (chmn. legis. com. 1982), Soc. Rsch. in Psychotherapy. Address: 210 W Rittenhouse Sq Ste 404 Philadelphia PA 19103

COCHRAN, ANNE WESTFALL, public relations executive; b. Cairo, Ill., Sept. 16, 1954; d. Howard Thurston and Flora Isabelle (Stone) Westfall; m. Charles Eugene Cochran, June 14, 1975; 2 children. BA in Advt., So. Ill. U., 1974; MA in Communications, U. Wis., Milw., 1975. Dir. advt. Sight and Sound Systems Inc., Milw., 1975-76; nat. publicity/promotions mgr. 20th Century Fox Classics, L.A., 1981-85; nat. publicity dir. Cannon Films Inc., L.A., 1985-86; publicist, staff writer Warner Bros. Inc., Burbank, Calif., 1986-87; v.p. mktg. Cinetel Films, Inc., L.A., 1987; v.p. publicity and promotion U.S. U.S. Cineplex Odeon Films, Inc., L.A., 1987-89; ptnr. Jones Cochran Assocs., Beverly Hills, Calif., 1989-92; sr. v.p. corp. and motion picture divsns. Bender, Goldman & Helper, L.A., 1992-95; ptnr. Mission Appraisal Group, L.A., 1995—; mktg. cons., L.A., 1976-81. Bd. dirs. Casa de Rosas Sunshine Mission, L.A., 1990. Mem. Publicists Guild. Democrat. Mem. Ch. Religious Sci. Home: 13935 Hatteras St Van Nuys CA 91401

COCHRAN, CAROLYN, library director; b. Tyler, Tex., July 13, 1934; d. Sidney Allen and Eudelle (Frazier) C.; m. Guy Milford Eley, June 1, 1963 (div.). BA, Beaver Coll., 1956; MA, U. Tex., 1960; MLS, Tex. Woman's U., 1970. Libr., Canadian (Tex.) High Sch., 1970-71; rep. United Food Co., Amarillo, Tex., 1971-72; libr. Bishop Coll., Dallas, 1972-74; interviewer Tex. Employment Commn., Dallas, 1975-76; libr. St. Mary's Dominican, New Orleans, 1976-77, DeVry Inst. Tech., Irving, Tex., 1978—; with Database Searching Handicapped Individuals, Irving, 1983—; vol. bibliographer Assn. Individuals with Disabilities, Dallas, 1982-85. Mem. Am. Coalition of Citizens with Disabilities, 1982-85, Assn. Individuals with Disabilities, 1982-86, Vols. in Tech. Assistance, 1985—, Radio Amateur Satellite Corp., 1985-86; sponsor 500, Inc., 1988—. HEW fellow, 1967; honored Black History Collection, Dallas Morning News, Bishop Coll., Dallas, 1973. Mem. ALA, Spl. Libr. Assn., Am. Coun. of Blind and Coun. Citizens with Low Vision. Club: Toastmistress (pres. 1982-83) (Irving). Reviewer Library Jour., 1974, Dallas Morning News, 1972-74, Amarillo Globe-News, 1970-71. Office: DeVry Inst Tech 4801 Regent Blvd Irving TX 75063-2440

COCHRAN, JACQUELINE LOUISE, management executive; b. Franklin, Ind., Mar. 12, 1953; d. Charles Morris and Marjorie Elizabeth (Rohrbaugh) C. BA, DePauw U., 1975; MBA, U. Chgo., 1977. Fin. analyst Pan Am World Airways, N.Y.C., 1977-79, Gen. Bus. Group W. R. Grace & Co., N.Y.C., 1979-80; sr. fin. analyst Gen. Bus. Group div. W. R. Grace & Co., N.Y.C., 1980-81, mgr. fin. analysis, 1981-82; dir. fin. planning and analysis Gen. Bus. Group div. W. R. Grace & Co., N.Y.C., 1982-85; v.p. fin. Am. Breeders Svc. div. W. R. Grace & Co., DeForest, Wis., 1985-87, v.p. feed ops. Grace Animal Svc. div., 1987-89; gen. mgr., chief ops. officer SoftKat div. W. R. Grace & Co., Chatsworth, Calif., 1990; pres. SoftKat div. W.R. Grace & Co., Chatsworth, Calif., 1990-92; vice-chmn., chief adminstrv. officer Baker & Taylor, Inc., Thousand Oaks, Calif., 1992, pres. SoftKat div., 1992; exec. cons. Jacqueline Cochran Cons., Westlake Village, Calif., 1993—; gen. mgr. Attica Cybernetics, Inc., Chatsworth, Calif., 1995. Bd. visitors DePauw U., 1993-96. Recipient Women of Distinction award Madison (Wis.) YWCA, 1987; named to Acad. Women Achievers YWCA N.Y., 1984. Mem. Nat. Assn. Corp. Dirs., ABCD, The Microcomputer Industry Assn.

(adv. coun. 1992), AAUW, Phi Beta Kappa, Alpha Lambda Delta, Delta Delta Delta (advisor scholarship com. Madison chpt. 1985-89, treas. 1986-89, ho. corp. bd. dirs. 1986-89, fin. advisor 1986-89). Republican. Methodist. Office: 9234 Deering Ave Chatsworth CA 91311

COCHRAN, JILL TEAGUE, legislative staff member; b. Waco, Tex., May 3, 1946; d. Olin E. and Freddie (Dunman) Teague. BA, U. Tex., 1968. Med. illustrator's asst. U. Tex., San Antonio, 1972-74; staff asst. Ho. Vets.' Affairs Com., 1974-81, Dem. staff dir. Subcom. Edn., Tng., Employment and Housing, 1981—. Office: Subcom Edn Tng Employment & Housing Rm 333 Cannon House Office Bldg Washington DC 20515

COCHRAN, MARTHA L., lawyer; b. Knoxville, Tenn., Aug. 24, 1948. BS, U. Fla., 1970, JD, 1973. Bar: Fla. 1973, D.C. 1976, Md. 1987. Spl. counsel divsn. enforcement SEC, Washington, 1975-81; sr. fin. counsel subcom. telecomms. and fin., com. on energy and commerce U.S. Ho. Reps.; legis. dir. U.S. Senator Christopher Dodd, 1987-88; chief counsel, staff dir. subcom. on securities, com. on banking, housing and urban affairs U.S. Senate, 1989-94; ptnr. Arnold & Porter, Washington. Mem. editl. bd. and rsch. editor U. Fla. Law Rev., 1972-73; contbr. articles to profl. jours. and publs. Mem. ABA (chmn. SEC adminstrn., budget and legislation, fed. securities com.), Fed. Bar Assn. Office: Arnold & Porter 555 12th St NW Washington DC 20004-1202*

COCHRAN, MARY ANN, nurse educator; b. Chgo., Dec. 12, 1951; d. Lawrence Donovan and Mary Gracz (Capizzi) Lee; m. Thomas Lee Cochran, Mar. 12, 1971; 1 child, Nathan Edgar. Diploma in nursing, St. Joseph's Hosp., Joliet, Ill., 1973. RN, Ill.; cert. post anesthesia nurse; cert. ambulatory perianesthesia. Staff nurse Silver Cross Hosp., Joliet, 1973—, stafff nurse ICU, 1979—, in-svc. educator post anesthesia care unit, 1987-92, BLS instr., 1987—, postanesthesia care unit charge nurse, 1994—. Mem. AACN, Am. Soc. Post Anesthesia Nurses, Ill. Soc. Post Anesthesia Nurses (membership chair 1990-92, ways & means chair 1992-95, Ill. dist. 1 dir. 1995—). Office: Silver Cross Hosp 1200 Maple Rd Joliet IL 60432-1439

COCHRAN, MELISSA RICK, set designer, educator; b. San Diego, Oct. 12, 1956; d. William Bruce and Susan (Ulrich) Rick; m. John Henry Cochran, June 23, 1979; children: David William, Deborah Suzanne, Rachel Michelle. BA, Stanford U., 1978; MFA, Yale U., 1981. Resident designer, adj. lectr. Biola U., La Mirada, Calif., 1984-89; resident designer, adj. lectr. Westmont Coll., Santa Barbara, Calif., 1991—; advisor Cmty. Adv. Com., Santa Barbara, 1993-95, U. Calif. Santa Barbara Spl. Edn. Task Force, 1996; reviewer USITT portfolio revs., Wichita, Kans., Nashville, 1993-94. Scenic and lighting designer Broken Arrow Prodns. True West, 1992, Open Fist Theatre Co. True West, 1990. Comprehensive Sys. of Pers. Devel. Adv. Com. grantee, 1994. Mem. Actors Equity Assn., U.S. Inst. Theatre Tech. Republican. Episcopalian. Office: Westmont College 955 La Paz Rd Santa Barbara CA 93108

COCHRAN, SHIRLEY JEAN, accountant; b. Franklin, Tenn., Sept. 28, 1943; d. Leslie O. and N. Pearl (Henson) Layne; m. John F. Cochran, Aug. 30, 1963; children: Karla Jean, John Gregory. Cert. in Acctg., Columbia State U., 1982, Athens State U., 1990. CPA, Tenn. Sr. clk. Prudential Ins. Co., Nashville, 1961-65; comm. and quality control E.I. DuPont DeNemours Co., Columbia, Tenn., 1965-66; legal sec./paralegal Courtney and Fleming, Columbia, Tenn., 1974-83; CPA, mgr. Kraft CPA's, Columbia, Tenn., 1983—. Mem. Exch. Club, Columbia, 1993; mem. exec. com. Frank Cochran for Gov. Campaign, Maury County, 1994; grad. Leadership Maury Class, 1992-93. Recipient Outstanding Mem. award Nat. Assn. Accts., 1989. Mem. Inst. Mgmt. Accts. (pres., v.p. edn., bd. dirs. 1991—, Past Pres. award 1990), Tenn. Soc. CPA, Maury-Lawrence Legal Secs. Assn. (charter), Columbia State Alumni Assn. (bd. dirs., scholarship com. 1990—, Am. Preservation Tenn. Antiquities (tour hostess 1991—), Maury County C. of C. (small bus. com. 1994, home tour com. 1994), Gamma Beta Phi. Mem. Ch. of Christ. Office: Kraft Bros Esstman Patton & Harrell PO Box 1559 Columbia TN 38401-3222

COCHRANE, ALISON LEE, gas pipeline company marketing manager; b. Superior, Wis., Feb. 4, 1961; d. Wesley Charles and Mary (Hoch) C. BS in Petroleum Engring., U. Okla., 1984; MBA, U. Tex. Permian Basin, Odessa, 1988. Registered profl. engr., Okla. Prodn. engr. BP Exploration, Inc., Midland, Tex., 1984-87, prodn. engr. BP Exploration, Inc., Houston, 1987-89, gas coord., 1989-90; sr. rep. for mktg. Panhandle Eastern Pipe Line Co., Houston, 1990-91, coord. mktg., 1991-93; mgr. mktg., 1993—. Mem. Soc. Petroleum Engrs., Natural Gas Transp. Assn., Natural Gas Assn. Houston. Roman Catholic. Office: Panhandle Eastern Pipe Line 5400 Westheimer Ct Houston TX 77056-5310

COCHRANE, BETSY LANE, state senator; b. Asheboro, N.C.; d. William Jennings and Bobbie (Campbell) Lane; m. Joe Kenneth Cochrane, 1958; children: Lisa, Craig. BA cum laude, Meredith Coll., 1958. Mem. N.C. Ho. of Reps., Raleigh, 1980-88; house minority leader N.C. Ho. of Reps., Raleigh, N.C., 1985-88; mem. N.C. Senate, Raleigh, 1988—, chmn. Commn. on Aging, 1989—, vice chmn. higher edn. com., 1991-92; senate minority whip, 1993-94, senate minority leader, 1995-96; tchr. Winston-Salem Sch. System, Highland Presbyn. Ch. Sch.; mem. Nat. Rep. Platform Com.; chmn. Joint Legis. Ethics Com., 1991. Trustee Davie County Hosp. Recipient Woman in Govt. award N.C. Jaycees, 1985; named One of 10 Outstanding Legislators in Nation, 1987, Disting. Citizen of Yr. N.C. Libr. Dirs., 1991, Legislator of Yr. N.C. Divsn. Aging, 1991, N.C. Assn. for Home Care, 1992, Citizen of Yr. N.C. Health Facilities Assn., 1993, Legislator of Yr. award N.C. Wildlife Fedn., 1995, Legislator of Yr. award Austism Found., 1995. Baptist. Home and Office: 122 Azalea Cir Advance NC 27006-9582 Office: NC Senate 1127 Legislative Bldg Raleigh NC 27601

COCKBURN, EVE GILLIAN, newsletter editor; b. Astley, Eng., Mar. 3, 1924; came to U.S., 1948; d. Thomas and Alice (Speakman) Fairhurst; m. Aidan Cockburn, June 26, 1945 (dec. 1981); children: Gillian Margaret, Erika June, Vivien Jo, Alistair Aidan, Alison Francesca. BA with honours, Oxford U., 1945, MA, 1958. Sci. and health columnist Berkshire Evening Eagle, 1954-55; syndicated sci. and health columnist Pakistani newspapers, including Civil and Mil. Gazette, 1958-60; founder, editor Dance Newsletter, Detroit, 1969-74; co-founder, editor newsletter Paleopathology Assn., Detroit, 1973—, dir., 1981-; Mem. Antiquaries Bd., Detroit Inst. of Arts, 1971—. Editor Woman and Health, 1959-60, Mummies, Disease, and Ancient Cultures, 1980 (Med. Writers Am. award 1981); mem. editl. bd. Jour. Paleopathology, 1988—, contbg. editor, 1991; mem. sci. com. Cronos, 1990-92. Mem. World Coun. on Mummy Studies, 1992—, hon. com. The Origin of Syphilis in Europe, Toulon, France, 1993; mem. sci. com. The Evolution and Paleoepidemiology of Tb, Szeged, Hungary, 1996—. Fellow Zool. Soc. London; mem. Am. Assn. Phys. Anthropologists. Office: Paleopathology Assn 18655 Parkside Detroit MI 48221-2208

COCKER, BARBARA JOAN, marine artist, interior designer; b. Uxbridge, Mass.; A.A., Becker Jr. Coll., 1943; student Mt. St. Mary Coll., 1944-45, Clark U., 1945, N.Y. Sch. Interior Design, 1965-67. Owner, operator Barbara J. Cocker, Interior Design, Rumson, N.J., 1966—; owner Barbara J. Cocker Paintings of the Sea Gallery, Nantucket, Mass., 1975-96, 91, 95; tchr. adult edn. courses in interior design, 1965-68; artist, pvt. instr. marine art; pres. Maximus Praetorius Corp., Nantucket, Mass., 1979—; one-man shows marine paintings: Little Gallery, Barbizon, N.Y., 1971, Old Mill Assn., 1971, Pacem en Terris Gallery, N.Y.C., 1972, Central Jersey Bank & Trust Co., Rumson, 1971, 72, 74, 77, 79, Little Gallery, Nantucket Art Assn., 1975, 77, 79, 81, 84, 87, 89, 91, 92, 95, Caravan House Galleries, N.Y.C., 1975, 79, Guild of Creative Art, Shrewsbury, N.J., 1976, 81, 85, 88, 93, 95, IBM Corp., N.J., 1977, South St. Seaport Mus., N.Y., 1977, 80, Provident Nat. Bank, Phila., 1978, Gallery 100, Princeton, 1978, Bell Telephone Research Labs., 1982, 86, AT&T, 87, Midlantic Bank, N.J., 1988, 93, 94, 95, Art Alliance N.J., 1983, 91, Gilpin House Gallery (Va.), Swain Art Gallery, N.J., 1984, Oceanic Libr., N.J., 1989, 91, 93, Red Bank Libr., N.J, 1989, 91, Captiva (Fla.) Civic Assn., 1994, Captiva Community Ctr., 1994, Pen and Brush Club, 1996; group shows include: Guild Creative Art N.J., Composers, Authors and Artists Am. NAD, Salmagundi Club N.Y.C., Monmouth Coll. Festival of Arts, Caravan House Galleries, N.Y.C., Pen and Brush Club, N.Y.C., Lever House Galleries, N.Y.C., Nat. Arts Club, N.Y.C., Ocean County Artists Guild, N.J., Chelsea Gardens Gallery, Fla., Frank Lewis, Killarney, Ireland; painting selection for publication Clean Ocean Action, N.J., 1994. Named Woman of Yr. Zonta Internat., 1986. Mem. Catharine Lorillard Wolfe Arts Club, Am. Artists Profl. League, Nantucket Art Assn., Composers, Authors and Artists Am., Allied Artists Am., Monmouth Arts Found. (N.J.), So. Vt. Artists Inc., Pen and Brush Club (N.Y.C.), Big Arts Ctr. (Sanibel, Fla.), Sanibel-Captiva Art League. Address: PO Box 574 Nantucket MA 02554-0574 also: Paintings Of Sea Studio 10 Old South Wharf # 574 Nantucket MA 02554-3834

COCKRELL, DIANE ELYSE, librarian; b. Easton, Pa., Aug. 6, 1953; d. Russell Schafer and Janet Marjorie (Bittner) Dech; m. Joel Mark Cockrell, Oct. 16, 1983; 1 child, Bryan Russell. BS in Edn./Libr. Sci. and Spanish, Shippensburg (Pa.) U., 1975; MLS, U. Ala., 1982. Permanent cert. teaching libr. sci./Spanish, Pa. Elem. sch. libr. Easton Area Sch. Dist., 1976-79, tchr. Spanish, 1979-82; libr. Herner & Co., Arlington, Va., 1982-84; tech. info. specialist Nat. Inst. Standards and Tech., Gaithersburg, Md., 1984-86; tennis adj. prof. Montgomery Coll., Germantown, Md., 1982-89, reference libr., 1989—; mem. steering com. Alliance for Ednl. Excellence, Montgomery County, 1995—; advisor Montgomery Coll. Students in Free Enterprise, Germantown. Author: Testimonies Before Board of Education and County Council, 1994-95. Cluster coord., pres. PTA, Damascus, Md., 1993—; campaign chair, mem. Bd. Edn., Montgomery County, 1994; mem. Mongomery County Cmty. Partnership, 1994-95; precinct chair Montgomery County Dem. Party, Kensington, Md., 1992—; cluster coord. Montgomery County Ctrl. PTA, Silver Spring, Md., 1995—; rep. Upcounty Citizens Adv. Bd., Germantown, 1995—, 2d vice chair 1996; chair legis. coun. Montgomery County Council of PTAs. Mem. ALA, PTA (hon. life). Home: 10820 Longmeadow Dr Damascus MD 20872

CODERRE, ELAINE ANN, state representative; b. Providence, Oct. 11, 1947; d. Henry N. and Mary A. (McDonald) Daigneault; m. Raymond Russen Coderre, Feb. 3, 1967; children: Robert, Thomas, Karen. Student, U. R.I., 1965-68. Bank teller Pawtucket (R.I.) Inst. for Savs., 1970-82; pres. Dano USA, Pawtucket, 1982—; rep. R.I. Ho. Reps., 1985—; bd. dirs. Sr. Inn., Pawtucket, 1985—. Mem. Heart Fund Drive, Pawtucket, 1985, Pawtucket Tenants Affairs Bd., 1985—; sec. Child Support Enforcement Commn., 1985—. Named one of Outstanding Young Women in America, 1981. Mem. Vis. Nurses Assn. (bd. dirs. 1986—), VFW Aux. (sr. v.p. 1984-87, legisl. chair 1986-87), Jaycee Women. Democrat. Roman Catholic. Home: 18 Angle St Pawtucket RI 02860-3006 also: State House 323 State House Providence RI 02903*

CODY, HARRIETT M., judge; b. Norfolk, Va., Aug. 23, 1945; d. Hiram S., Jr. and Mary V. (Jacoby) C.; m. Harvey J. Sadis, Nov. 24, 1972; 1 child, Halley Jean Cody. BA, Stanford U., 1967; JD cum laude, Seattle U., 1975; grad., Nat. Jud. Coll., 1993. Bar: U.S. Supreme Ct., 1978; cert. tchr. Wash., 1968. Tchr. Seattle Pub. Schs., 1968-72; city atty. City of Seattle, 1976-77; lawyer Evergreen Legal Svcs., Seattle, 1977-79; pvt. practice Seattle, 1979-92; judge King County Superior Ct., Wash., 1993—. Contbr. article to MS. mag. Vol. Seattle AIDS Support Group, 1990-96. Mem. Am. Bar Assn., Superior Ct. Judges Assn., Wash. State Bar Assn., Wash. Women Lawyers (pres. 1979-80), Rotary (internat. dist. of Seattle). Office: King County Superior Ct 516 Third Ave Seattle WA 98104-2381

COE, ELIZABETH ANN, elementary education educator; b. El Paso, Tex., Feb. 25, 1944; d. Charles William Murray and Jeanne (Roman) Moore; children: Christopher E. Sanchez, Christine Angela Sanchez. BS in Edn., N.Mex. State U., 1968; postgrad., U. N.Mex., 1987-88; MA in Edn., N.Mex. State U., 1992; postgrad., East N.Mex. U., 1970-95, U. Phoenix, 1995, Ctr. for Bilingual Multicultural Studies, Cuernavaca, Mex., 1995. Cert. elem. educator, lang. arts. educator Kindergarten thru grade 12, social studies educator Kindergarten thru grade 12, N.Mex. Tchr. Hatch (N.Mex.) Schs., 1968-70, Ruidoso (N.Mex.) Mcpl. Schs., 1970-84; real estate agt., 1978-88; tchr. Tularosa (N.Mex.) Schs., 1988—; workshop leader Region IX, Ruidoso, 1989, 90; rep. Project L.E.A.D., U. N.Mex., Albuquerque, 1991, N.Mex. State BA Restructuring Conf., Albuquerque, 1990, Mesilla Valley Regional Coun. on Bilingual Edn., 1968-70; co-chair Internat. Reading Assn. Young Authors Conf., Tularosa, 1990-91; cons. N.Mex. State Writing Project, 1993; mem. task force on writing and portfolio assessment N.Mex. State Dept. Edn., 1993—; mem. com. for ednl. plan for student success Tularosa Mcpl. Schs. Author: (short story) Los Desesperados, 1989 (1st prize Tri-State award), Tortillitas Quemaditas, 1991 (Honorable Mention). Mem. N.Mex. State Dept. Edn. Task Force on Writing. Mem. NEA, LWV, Phi Kappa Phi. Home: PO Box 929 Ruidoso NM 88345-0929

COE, MARGARET LOUISE SHAW, community service volunteer; b. Cody, Wyo., Dec. 25, 1917; d. Ernest Francis and Effie Victoria (Abrahamson) Shaw; m. Henry Huttleston Rogers Coe, Oct. 8, 1943 (dec. Aug. 1966); children: Anne Rogers Hayes, Henry H.R., Jr., Robert Douglas II. AA, Stephens Coll., 1937; BA, U. Wyo., 1939. Asst. to editor The Cody Enterprise, 1939-42, editor, 1968-71. Chmn. bd. trustees Buffalo Bill Hist. Ctr., Cody, 1966—, Cody Med. Found., 1964—; commr. Wyo. Centenniel Commn., Cheyenne, 1986-91. Recipient The Westerner award Old West Trails Found., 1980, Gold Medallion award Nat. Assn. Sec. of State, 1982, disting alumni award U. Wyo., 1984, exemplary alumni award, 1994, Gov.'s award for arts, 1988; inducted Nat. Cowgirl Hall of Fame, 1983. Mem. P.E.O., Delta Delta Delta. Republican. Episcopalian. Home: 1400 11th St Cody WY 82414-4206

COE, SYLVIA BETTIS, management consultant; b. Hardwick, Vt., Jan. 17, 1949; d. Erwin Elwin and Alice Helen (Allen) Bettis; m. Steven L. Clough, Apr. 24, 1976 (div. Aug. 1989); children: Sarah Lee, Kimberlee Allison. BSBA, Johnson (Vt.) State Coll., 1984; MS in Adminstrn., St. Michael's Coll., Winooski, Vt., 1986; cert. in exec. mgmt., Duke U, 1988. Clk. of ct. Vt. Dist. Ct., Rutland, 1980-84; exec. v.p., treas. Valley Bank, White River Junction, Vt., 1986-91; owner, mgr. Smart Bus. Cons., Lexington, Ky., 1991—. Mem. Am. Mgmt. Assn., Robert Morris Assocs. Office: Smart Bus Cons 1818 Parkers Mill Rd Lexington KY 40504-2042

COEYMAN, EMILY NOLLIE ROGERS, civic worker; b. Waynesboro, Miss., Jan. 10, 1921; d. Olin Deauward and Ethel Louise (Finkbohner) Rogers; m. William Henry Coeyman, Apr. 5, 1941 (div. June 1952); children: Louis Brooke Roger, Louise Edna Coeyman Thomas. Student, Tomlinson Vocat. Inst., St. Petersburg, Fla., 1951, LaSalle Ext. Law U., 1957-59, St. Petersburg Jr. Coll., 1970-75, 85. Sec. Shorthand Reporter-Ct. Reporter, Washington, 1939-40, Colonial Decorating Co., Washington, 1940-41; clk-typist fin. and transp. dept. War Dept., Washington, 1941-43; clk. carrier U.S. P.O., Washington, 1943-44, ry. and postal clk. ry. mail svc., 1944; mdse. control clk. Hecht Co. Dept. Store, Washington, 1945-46; transcribing machine oprtor, clk.-typist REA, Washington, 1946; clk.-stenographer Glenn Dale (Md.) Tb Sanitorium, 1946-48; clk.-cashier, admitting clk. Mound Park Hosp., St. Petersburg, 1948-51; clk.-typist VA, Pass-A-Grille, Fla., 1951-52; med. sec. to chief physiatrist Gallinger Hosp. (name now D.C. Gen. Hosp., Washington, 1955-60; ret., 1960. Bd. dirs. Met. Planning Orgn., Clearwater, Fla., 1981-90, bd. dirs.-at-large, mem. citizens adv. com., 1984—; St. Petersburg rep. Tampa Bay Regional Planning Coun. Area Agy. on Aging, Pinellas County, 1981-90; bd. dirs.-at-large, mem. citizens adv. com. Pinellas Suncoast Transit Authority, Clearwater, 1988-94, Fast Speed and High Speed Monorail, Clearwater, 1993—; active participant numerous city and county govt. meetings, including Environ. Devel. Commn., Bd. Adjustment, Pinellas County Sch. Bd., Pinellas Suncoast Transit authority, Juvenile Welfare Bd., Com. Neighborhood Assn. Named to Hon. Hall of Fame, City of St. Petersburg, 1987, Hall of Faame, 1988; recipient hon. proclamation as a vol. Pinellas County Commrs., 1991, hon. proclamation Pinellas Sports Authority, 1992. Mem. Nat. Assn. Ret. Fed. Employees, Am. Assn. Ret. Persons, Pinellas Geneal. Soc., Sr. Citizens Sunshine Ctr. Club, St. Petersburg Stamp Club, Suncoast Tiger Bay Club, Women of Moose, St. Petersburg Rock, Gem & Mineral Soc. Republican. Baptist. Home: 6936 40th Ave N Saint Petersburg FL 33709-4610

COFFEE, VIRGINIA CLAIRE, civic worker, former mayor; b. Alliance, Nebr., Dec. 8, 1920; d. James Maddigan and Adelaide Mary (Forde) Kennedy; BS, Chadron State Coll., 1942; m. Bill Brown Coffee, June 21, 1942; children: Claire, Sara, Virginia Anne, Sue. High sch. prin., Whitman, Nebr., 1942; bookkeeper Coffee & Son, Inc., Harrison, Nebr., 1965—, officer, 1967—, pres., 1987—; dir. Friends of Agate Fossil BEOS, Inc., 1988, v.p. 1988—; mayor City of Harrison, 1978-80. Leader, Girl Scouts U.S.A., 1953-63; mem. Harrison Elem. Sch. bd., 1958-64; mem. liaison com. Chadron State Coll., 1975; pub. rels. chmn. Nebr. Cowbelles, 1968; sec. NW Stock Growers, 1971-73; corp. officer Ft. Robinson Centennial, 1973-88; officer Gov.'s Ft. Robinson Centennial Commn., 1973-75; hon. gov. Nebr. Centennial, 1967; chmn. Sioux County Bicentennial, 1973-77; trustee Nebr. State Hist. Soc. Found., 1975—, Village of Harrison, 1973-80, Chadron State Coll. Found., 1995—; bd. dirs. Harrison Cmty. Club, Inc., 1983-86, officer, 1984-86; apptd. Sioux County Vis. com. 1989—; apptd. adm. Nebr. Navy, 1992. Recipient Disting. Svc. award Chadron State Coll., 1994. Mem. Nebr. State Hist. Soc. (life, dir. 1979-85, 2d v.p. 1982-84, 1st v.p. 1984-85, com. for marker to honor Harrison centennial 1985-86), Wyo. State Hist. Soc., Cardinal Key Honor Frat., Sioux County Hist. Soc. (bd. dirs. 1975-81, 83-84, 87-90, pres. 1988-90, co-pres., sec., v.p.) Sioux county history book com. 1985-86, contbr. articles. Roman Catholic. Clubs: Nebr. Cattle Women, Ladies Community, Westerners Corral Internat., Harrison Cmty. Inc. Chmn. compilation com. book Sioux County Memoirs of Its Pioneers, 1967; coordinator Harrison sect. book Nebraska Our Towns, 1988. Address: PO Box 336 Harrison NE 69346-0336

COFFEL, PATRICIA K., retired clinical social worker; b. Bismarck, N.D., Sept. 14, 1934; m. Raymond A. Kobe, 1956; children: Anne, Elizabeth, Colleen, Denise, Tim, Heidi; m. Mitchel D. Coffel, 1983. Student, U. N.D., 1954-55; BA in Sociology, Coll. St. Benedict, 1956; MSW, Wayne State U., 1981. Diplomate Clin. Social Work; cert. social worker, Mich. Dir. social svcs. dept. Pontiac Nursing Ctr., 1978-84; dir. of med. social work dept. Advanced Profl. Home Health Care, Troy, Mich., 1985-86; med. social worker Visiting Nurses of Met. Detroit, 1987; family worker, therapist Camp Oakland Youth Svcs., Oxford, Mich., 1987-89; client svcs. case mgr. Macomb-Oakland Regional Ctr., Mt. Clemens, Mich., 1989-90; clin. social worker, case mgr. Oakdale Regional Ctr., Lapeer, Mich., 1990-91; clin. social worker Clinton Valley Ctr., Pontiac, Mich., 1991-96; retired, 1996; counselor Suicide Prevention, Inc., St. Louis, 1971-72, Macomb County Crisis Ctr., Warren, Mich., 1973-74; geriatric counselor Beverly Enterprises, Pontiac and Novi, Mich., 1981-83; grief and loss counselor Hospice SE Mich., Southfield, 1982-83. Grad. profl. scholar Wayne State U. Sch. Social Work, 1980. Mem. NASW (qualified clin. social worker), Acad. Cert. Social Workers. Home: 645 Oakwood Rd Ortonville MI 48462-8589

COFFEY, JEAN SHEERIN, pediatric nurse, educator; b. Bklyn., May 27, 1957; d. William Raymond and Theodora Julia (Woitazek) Sheerin; m. Jay W. Coffey, Aug. 6, 1977; 3 children. AS, U. Vt., Burlington, 1977; BS, Norwich U., 1992; MSN, U. Vt., 1996. RN, Vt.; cert. pediatric nurse, ANA. Staff nurse Med. Ctr. Hosp. Vt., Burlington, 1977-82, Courville at Nashua, N.H., 1982-86, Med. Ctr. Hosp. Vt., Burlington, 1986-91, Pediatric Medicine, South Burlington, Vt., 1989-95; care coord., program dir. pediatric high tech. home care Profl. Nurses Svc., Burlington, 1988-89; clin. instr. U. Vt., Burlington, 1992-95; nurse adminstr. pediatrics Fletcher Allen Health Care, Burlington, 1995—; adj. prof. U. Vt., 1995—. Co-creator asthma edn. for asthma camp and workshops, 1986—. Pres. Am. Lung Assn. of Vt., bd. dirs., vol., chair Christmas Seal, 1988; BCLS instr. Am. Heart Assn. of Vt., Williston, 1986—; youth coach Essex Recreation/Nashua Recreation, 1985—; religious educator St. Pius X Parish, Essex, 1988—. Presdl. fellow Norwich U., 1991-92; Comolli scholar, 1988-92; recipient Women in Sports award Essex Sch. Dist., 1993; named Outstanding Young Vermonter Jaycees, 1988. Mem. AACN, Sigma Theta Tau. Roman CAtholic. Home: 260 Browns River Rd Essex Junction VT 05452

COFFEY, JOANNE CHRISTINE, dietitian; b. Cambridge, Mass., Aug. 18, 1942; d. Timothy Patrick and Helen (Stevens) C. BS in Nutrition, Simmons Coll., 1964, M in Libr. and Info. Sci., 1994; MPH, U. Calif., Berkeley, 1966. Registered dietitian. Dietitian, clin. sect. chief VA Med. Ctr., Manchester, N.H., 1976-80; chief dietetic svc. VA Med. Ctr., Altoona, Pa., 1980-82, Providence, 1982-89; asst. chief dietetic svc. VA Med. Ctr., Boston, 1989—. Mem. Nature Conservancy, Nat. Trust for Hist. Preservation, Smithsonian. Mem. ALA, Am. Dietetic Assn. Democrat. Roman Catholic. Office: VA Med Ctr 150 S Huntington Ave Boston MA 02130-4817

COFFEY, NANCY ANN, commercial real estate broker, model; b. Palm Springs, Calif.; d. Arthur Johnson and Joan (Hunter) C. BA, Stanford U., MS in Engring. Indsl. real estate broker Coldwell Banker, Houston, 1977-79; comml. broker Coldwell Banker, San Francisco, 1980-87, Cushman & Wakefield, N.Y.C., 1987-90; model Gilla Roos, N.Y.C., 1991—; self-employed real estate broker, 1990—. Active Jr. League, San Francisco, 1981-87, N.Y.C., 1987-92; mem. spl. projects bd. Meml. Sloan Kettering Cancer Ctr., N.Y.C.

COFFEY-JOHNSON, CAROL LYNN, school counselor; b. Wooster, Ohio, Dec. 17, 1951; m. John Kenyon and Marjorie May (Reese) Coffey; m. Robert B. Johnson, May 3, 1986; children: Katie Nicoll, Russell Alexander. BS in Edn., U. Akron, 1973; MA in Edn., Colo. State U., 1983, PhD in Edn., 1995. Cert. tchr. Tchr. North Ctrl. Sch. Dist., Creston, Ohio, 1973-78; tchr., counselor, adminstrv. asst. Park Sch. Dist., Estes Park, Colo., 1978-94, tchr., transition coord., 1993—, counselor, 1995—. Dodge grantee Geraldine R. Dodge Found., N.J., 1993, 94, Pub. Svc. grantee Channel 7/ Pub. Svc. Co., Denver, 1993, 94. Mem. AAUW (sec. 1995, Educator of Yr. 1995), Colo. Assn. Sch. Execs., Colo. Edn. Assn., Colo. Sch. Counselors Assn., Delta Kappa Gamma (edn. com.), Phi Delta Kappa. Home: 169 1/2 Stanley Cir Estes Park CO 80517

COFFIELD, MARY ELEANOR, speech clinician, educator; b. Ft. Smith, Ark., July 28, 1921; d. Willard M. and Edith Isabel (Stemmons) C. Student, No. Ariz. State U., 1941-42; BE, Cen. Mo. State U., 1948; MA in Speech Pathology, U. Denver, 1960. Lic. speech pathologist, Mo. Tchr. music pvt. kindergarten Carthage, Mo., 1940-41; tchr. Columbian Elem. Sch., Carthage, 1943-47; fellowship tchr. Lab. Sch. Cen. Mo., Warrensburg, 1947-48; elem. tchr. Roswell (N.Mex.) Schs., 1948-49, Kansas City (Mo.) Sch., 1949-50; speech clinician Carthage Schs., 156-59, 60-86. Editor Jasper County Jour., 1983—. Pres. Rep. Women, Carthage, Carthage Social Agys.; hon. mem. United Presbyn. Ch., mem. choir, commr. synod; treas. McCune-Brooks Hosp. Aux.; mem. Presbytery Com., Profl. Devel. and Support Com.; moderator, enabler Gathering of Presbyn. Women in Carthage; mem. com. planning World Day of Prayer, Jasper County Sheltered Facilities Bd.; past pres., v.p., sec. Jasper County Crisis Intervention Bd.; past sec.-treas. Hard of Hearing Parents and Friends Group; instr. home nursing, chmn. water safety, staff aide ARC; pres. Friends of Libr., 1994-96. Named Citizen of Yr. Carthage Lions, 1985; recipient citation Future Farmers Am., 1985, Recognition Outstanding Svc. award Region V Coun. Devel. Disabilities, 1989. Mem. AAUW (pres., Woman of Distinction 1990), Internat. Platform Assn., Coun. Exceptional Children (state treas. 1969, 89, Merit award 1982, Mo. Tchr. of Yr. 1986, Nat. Tchr. of Yr. 1987, participant ann. meeting 1992, 93, 94), Am. Speech and Hearing Assn. (life), Mo. Assn. Social Welfare (life, chmn. state membership), Four State Stroke Club (sec. 1975—), Joplin Area Assn. Retarded Citizens (pres. 1978-81, 87-89, bd. dirs.), Carthage Tchrs. (Outstanding Ret. Mem.), Jasper County Hist. Soc., Ret. Tchrs. Assn. (pres. 1992-96). Home: 1718 S Garrison Ave Carthage MO 64836-3045

COFFIELD, SHIRLEY A., lawyer; b. Portland, Oreg., Mar. 31, 1945. BA, Willamette U., 1967; MA, U. Wisc.-Madison, 1969; JD, George Washington U., 1974. Bar: D.C. 1975. Law clk. Stitt, Hemmendinger and Kennedy, Washington, 1973-74; asst. gen. counsel Office of U.S. Trade Rep., 1975-79; ptnr. Reaves & Coffield, Washington, 1979-82; sr. counsel to dep. asst. sect. textiles and apparel U.S. Dept. Commerce, Washington, 1982-85; spl. counsel Skadden, Arps, Slate, Meagher and Flom, 1985-87; ptnr. Piper & Marbury, Washington and Balt., 1987-90, Baker & Hostetler, 1990-94, Keller and Heckman, L.L.P., Washington, 1994—; adj. prof. internat. econ. law Georgetown U. Law Sch., 1982—. Mem. ABA, Fed. Bar Assn., Am. Soc. Internat. Law, D.C. Bar, Pi Gamma Mu, Phi Delta Phi. Office: Keller & Heckman 1001 G St NW Ste 500 West Washington DC 20001-4545

COFFIN, BERTHA LOUISE, telephone company executive; b. Atlanta, Aug. 19, 1919; d. William Wesley and Bertha Louise (Marsh) Mendenhall; m. J. Donald Coffin, Feb. 14, 1943 (dec. Sept. 1978). BA, U. Kans., 1940. Med. technologist Midwest Research Lab., Emporia, Kans., 1940-43; ins. agt. Coffin Ins. Agy., Council Grove, Kans., 1943—, sole owner, mgr., 1978-

82; treas. Council Grove Telephone Co., 1947-50, sec.-treas., 1950-78, pres., gen. mgr., chmn. bd., 1978—; del. legis. confs. Nat. Tel. Coop. Assn., 1986, 88, 91-92, 94, comem. comml. co. com., 1987-91, mem. govt. affairs com., 1991—, exec. com., 1996—; founder, pres., chmn. bd. Kans. Personal Comm. Svcs. Ltd., 1995—. Copy preparation for book The Story of the Santa Fe Trail, 1982; author: History of Council Grove Telephone Company, 1991; ann. civic sects. tel. directory. Pres. various lit. clubs, Council Grove, 1945-72; speaker various civic, polit. and religious groups, 1962—; mem. adv. coun. Manhattan Christian Coll., 1983-86, trustee, 1986-92, 93—, chmn., 1991-92. Mem. Kans. Telecomm. Assn. (bd. dirs. 1992-95), Ind. Tel. Pioneers (dir. 1984-92). Democrat. Office: PO Box 272 Council Grove KS 66846-0272

COFFIN, JUDY SUE, lawyer; b. Beaumont, Tex., Aug. 17, 1953; d. Richard Wilson and Genie (Mouton) C.; m. Gary P. Scholick, Nov. 10, 1983; children: Jennie Sue, Kate Frances. BA, U. Tex., 1974; JD, So. Meth. U., 1976. Bar: Tex. 1977, Calif. 1982. Atty. NLRB, Tex., 1977-80; shareholder Littler, Mendelson, Fastiff, Tichy & Mathiason, San Francisco, 1980—, also bd. dirs. Office: Littler Mendelson Fastiff Tichy 20th Fl 650 California St San Francisco CA 94108-2693

COFFIN, LORI ANN, police officer; b. Gardner, Mass., Apr. 26, 1959; d. Leslie Gordon Jr. and Lucille (Allain) C. Dispatcher Rindge (N.H.) Police Dept., 1976-82, Peterborough (N.H.) Police Dept., 1982-89; patrol officer Greenfield (N.H.) Police Dept., 1990-92; desk officer Jaffrey (N.H.) Police Dept., 1992—. Firefighter Rindge Fire Dept., 1986-93; assoc. advisor Pub. Safety Explorer Post #308, Rindge, 1983-86; com. mem. Jaffrey Police Explorers, 1996—. Mem. N.H. Police Assn., Jaffrey Police Assn. Home: 633 Route 119 Rindge NH 03461-4100 Office: Jaffrey Police Dept 26 Main St Jaffrey NH 03452

COFFINGER, MARALIN KATHARYNE, retired air force officer, consultant; b. Ogden, Iowa, July 5, 1935; d. Cleo Russell and Katharyne Frances (McGovern) Morse. BA, Ariz. State U., 1957, MA, 1961; diploma, Armed Forces Staff Coll., 1972, Nat. War Coll., 1977; postgrad., Inst. for Higher Def. Studies, 1985. Commd. 2nd lt. USAF, 1963, advanced through grades to brig. gen., 1985; base comdr., dep. base comdr. Elmendorf AFB, Anchorage, Alaska, 1977-79; base comdr. Norton AFB, San Bernardino, Calif., 1979-82; chmn. spl. and incentive pays Office of Sec. Def., Pentagon, Washington, 1982-83; dep. dir. pers. programs USAF Hdqrs., Pentagon, Washington, 1983-85; command dir. NORAD, Combat Ops., Cheyenne Mountain Complex, Colo., 1985-86; dir. pers. plans USAF Hdqrs., Pentagon, Washington, 1986-89; ret. USAF, 1989. Keynote speaker, mem. dedication ceremonies Vietnam Meml. Com., Phoenix, 1990. Decorated Air Force D.S.M., Def. Superior Svc. medal, Legion of Merit, Bronze Star.; recipient Nat. Medal of Merit. Mem. NAFE, Air Force Assn. (vet./retiree coun., pres. Sky Harbor chpt. 1990), Nat. Officers Assn., Ret. Officers Assn., Maricopa County Sheriff's Exec. Posse, Ariz. State U. Alumni Assn. (Profl. Excellence award 1981). Roman Catholic. Home: 8059 E Maria Dr Scottsdale AZ 85255

COFFMAN, JENNIFER B., federal judge; b. 1948. BA, U. Ky., 1969, MA, 1971, JD, 1978. Ref. libr. Newport News (Va.) Pub. Libr., 1972-74, U. Ky., 1974-76; atty. Law Offices Arthur L. Brooks., Lexington, Ky., 1978-82; ptnr. Brooks, Coffman and Fitzpatrick, Lexington, 1982-92, Newberry, Hargrove & Rambicure, Lexington, 1992-93; judge U.S. Dist. Ct. (ea. dist. and we. dist.) Ky., London, 1993—; adj. prof. Coll. Law, U. Ky., 1979-81. Bd. dirs. YWCA Lexington, 1986-92; elder Second Presbyn. Ch., 1993. Mem. ABA, Ky. Bar Assn., Fayette County Bar Assn., U. Ky. Alumni Assn. Office: 207 US Courthouse 300 S Main St London KY 40741-1924

COFFMAN, (ANNA) LOUISE M., retired elementary education educator; b. Turlock, Calif., Aug. 11, 1924; d. Christopher Ezekial and Annie Laurie (Curtice) Mann; m. Dean Wilton Coffman, Feb. 10, 1945; children: Dane Wilbur, Nancy J. Coffman Hildreth, Janet L. Coffman Dempsey. AA, Modesto Jr. Coll., 1944; BS, Millersville State U., 1961; MEd, Western Md. Coll., 1966. Elem. tchr. Laird Sch. Stanislaus County, Modesto, Calif., 1944-45; tchr. 4th grade Cen. Sch. Dist., York, Pa., 1957-66; tchr. 3d grade Spring Grove (Pa.) Sch. Dist., 1966-84, ret., 1984; part-time tchr. Grace Acad. Christian Discipleship, York, 1985—; free-lance writer, 1979—; columnist "Notes From the Country," York Sunday News, 1977-88. Vol. Bell Shelter, York, 1985—, Access-Shelter for Abused Women, York, 1985—; tchr. rep. ARC, York, 1966-84; v.p. women's fellowship St. Paul's-Wolf's United Ch. of Christ, York, 1990-92, editor newsletter, mem. consistory; del. Pa. Ctrl. Conf., 1995; mem. United Ch. of Christ Mission and Outreach Com., 1986—, St. Paul's Wolf's United Ch. of Christ, York, 1980. Mem. AAUW (sec. Invest-Hers group 1994—), Women in Comm., Inc., Delta Kappa Gamma (Eta chpt., parliamentarian 1987-89, 2d v.p. 1990-92). Republican. Home: 3897 Barachel Dr York PA 17402-4403

COFFMAN, ORENE BURTON, hotel executive; b. Fluvanna, Va., Mar. 13, 1938; d. John C. and Adele (Melton) Burton; m. John H. Emerson, Aug. 5, 1955 (div. 1972); 1 child, Norman Jay; m. Mack H. Coffman, Oct. 26, 1986. Degree in hotel and motel mgmt., Michigan State U., 1966-70. Cert. hotel mgr., Mich. State U., 1970. Telephone operator Colonial Williamsburg (Va.) Hotel, 1962-64; room clk. Colonial Williamsburg (Va.) Hotel, 1964-68; mgr. front office Colonial Williamsburg (Va.) Hotel, 1968-83; asst. mgr. Williamsburg Inn, 1983—; pres. Colonial Williamsburg Employees Fed. Credit Union, 1980-85. Mem. Am. Hotel Motel Assn. (nat. acctg. award 1970). Democrat. Baptist. Office: Williamsburg Inn PO Box 1776 Williamsburg VA 23187-3704

COFFMAN, VESTA MAE, bank officer; b. Sutton, W.Va., Sept. 1, 1935; d. Lawrence and Nora Berry (Keener) Barnette; m. Francis Johnson, Oct. 2, 1954 (div. May 1979); children: Dennis, Donna, Dianne; m. Jack Eugene Coffman, Dec. 7, 1985. Grad. high sch., Sutton, W.Va. Credit mgr. Stutz Jewelry Stores, Cleve., 1954-64, Credit Union Cons., Cleve., 1965-78; collection mgr. One Valley Bank, Summersville, W.Va., 1978—. Mem. Ladies Aux. VFW (pres. local club 1978, treas. local club, dist. sec.). Democrat. Baptist. Home: Box 319 Birch River WV 26610

COFFRIN, ALOHA B., shop owner; b. Scotland County, Mo., Aug. 23, 1928; d. James Calvin Brown and Lena Belle Jeffrey; m. Rex R. Coffrin, Feb. 21, 1948 (dec. Aug. 1987); children: Thomas E., Terry R. Grad. high sch., Memphis, 1946. With Bank of Memphis, 1946-48, Smoot Atty. at Law, Memphis, 1957-63; bookkeeper Pepsi Cola, Memphis, 1964-65, Gerth & Baskett, Memphis, 1966-74; owner Coffrin Shoe Store, Memphis, 1974—. V.p. Bus. and Profl. Women, Memphis, 1976; mem. Ch. of Ea. Star, Memphis, 1975—; mem. choir Ch. and Cmty. Players, 1970-75. Home: R 3 Memphis MO 63555

COGGIN, CHARLOTTE JOAN, cardiologist, educator; b. Takoma Park, Md., Aug. 6, 1928; d. Charles Benjamin and Nanette (McDonald) Coggin; BA, Columbia Union Coll., 1948; MD, Loma Linda U., 1952, MPH, 1987; DSc (hon.), Andrews U., 1994. Intern, L.A. County Gen. Hosp., L.A., 1952-53, resident in medicine, 1953-55; fellow in cardiology Children's Hosp., L.A., 1955-56, White Meml. Hosp., L.A., 1955-56; rsch. assoc. in cardiology, house physician Hammersmith Hosp., London, 1956-57; resident in pediatrics and pediatric cardiology Hosp. for Sick Children, Toronto, Ont., Can., 1965-67; cardiologist, co-dir. heart surgery team Loma Linda (Calif.) U., asst. prof. medicine, 1961-73, assoc. prof., 1973-91, prof. medicine, 1991—, asst. dean Sch. Medicine Internat. Programs, 1973-75, assoc. dean, 1975—, spl. asst. to univ. pres. for internat. affairs, 1991, co-dir., cardiologist heart surgery team missions to Pakistan and Asia, 1963, Greece, 67, 69, Saigon, Vietnam, 1974, 75, to Saudi Arabia, 1976-87, People's Republic China, 1984, 89-91, Hong Kong, 1985, Zimbabwe, 1988, Kenya, 1988, Nepal, 1992, 93, China, 1992, Zimbabwe, 1993; mem. Pres.'s Advisory Panel on Heart Disease, 1972—; hon. prof. U. Manchuria, Harbin, People's Republic China, 1989, hon. dir. 1st People's Hosp. of Mundanjiang, Heilongjiang Province, 1989. Apptd. mem. Med. Quality Rev. Com.-Dist. 12, 1976-80. Recipient award for service to people of Pakistan City of Karachi, 1963, Medallion award Evangelismos Hosp., Athens, Greece, 1967, Gold medal of health South Vietnam Ministry of Health, 1974, Charles Elliott Weinger award for excellence, 1976, Wall Street Jour. Achievement award, 1987, Disting. Univ. Svc. award Loma Linda U., 1990; named Honored Alumnus Loma Linda U. Sch. Medicine, 1973, Outstanding Women in Gen. Conf. Seventh-day Adventists, 1975, Alumnus of Yr., Columbia Union Coll., 1984. Diplomate Am. Bd. Pediatrics. Mem. Am. Coll. Cardiology, AMA (physicians adv. com. 1969—) Calif. Med. Assn. (com. on med. schs., com. on member services), San Bernardino County Med. Soc. (chmn. communications com. 1975-77, mem. communications com. 1987-88, editor bull. 1975-76, William L. Cover, M.D. Outstanding Contbn. to Medicine award 1995), Am. Heart Assn., AAUP, Med. Research Assn. Calif., Calif. Heart Assn., AAUW, Am. Acad. Pediatrics, World Affairs Council, Internat. Platform Assn., Calif. Museum Sci. and Industry MUSES (Outstanding Woman of Year in Sci. 1969), Am. Med. Women's Assn., Loma Linda Sch. Medicine Alumni Assn. (pres. 1978), Alpha Omega Alpha, Delta Omega. Author: Atrial Septal Defects, motion picture (Golden Eagle Cine award and 1st prize Venice Film Festival 1964); contbr. articles to med. jours. Democrat. Home: 11495 Benton St Loma Linda CA 92354-3682 Office: Loma Linda U Magan Hall Rm 105 11060 Anderson St Loma Linda CA 92350

COGSWELL, ANN, music educator; b. Cardston, Alta., Can., May 31, 1934; came to U.S., 1934; d. Andrew John and Marian Elizabeth (Wagner) Kovatch; m. Edward Borden Cogswell, Jr., Aug. 12, 1955; children: Edward Borden, III, Paul Gilliam, Amy Barker Law. B in Music Edn., U. Mont., 1959, MA in Music History, 1988. Pvt. practice Gt. Falls, Mont., 1968—; founder The Mont. Chorale, 1976; pres. bd. dirs. Mont. Chorale, Inc., Gt. Falls, 1990—. Author, photographer Savor Sweet Christmas, 1996. Gov.'s appointee Mont. Com. for the Humanities, Missoula, Mont., 1991, 92. Recipient 1st place award in photography Mont. State Fair, 1990, 93, Outstanding Woman in the Arts award Gt. Falls Mont. YWCA, 1993, 1st place award in photography The Gt. Falls Tribune, 1995. Mem. Music Tchrs. Nat. Assn. (nat. cert. tchr. music), Nat. Assn. Tchrs. of Singing, Chorus Am., Mont. State Music Tchrs. Assn. (chmn. advocacy com. 1994-95), Mont. Arts Coun. (gov.'s appointee 1993, chmn. advocacy com. 1994—), Gt. Falls Music Tchrs. Assn. (pres., v.p. 1979, 86, 90, 96), Gt. Books Found. (area coord. 1990—), Gt. Falls Camera Club. Episcopalian. Home and Office: 1108 Adobe Dr Great Falls MT 59404

COHANY, SHARON RUTH, economist; b. N.Y.C., Dec. 12, 1952; d. Harry Pye and Reeva (List) C.; m. Glen Mark Richardson, Aug. 17, 1986. BA, U. Pa., 1974. Economist U.S. Bur. Labor Stats., Dallas, 1976-85, Washington, 1985—. Contbr. articles to profl. jours. Pres. Nat. Capital area sect. Nat. Coun. Jewish Women, Washington, 1990-92; co-chmn. Home Instrn. Program for Presch. Youngsters, Washington, 1994—. Recipient Lawrence Klein award Monthly Labor Rev., 1988. Mem. Washington Statis. Soc., Clearinghouse on Women's Issues, U. Pa. Alumni Club, B'nai B'rith Women. Office: US Bur Labor Stats 2 Massachusetts Ave NE Washington DC 20212

COHEN, BARBARA ANN, artist; b. Milw., Feb. 18, 1953; d. Joseph and Irene Marion (Brown) C. BS in Art, U. Wis., 1975. One-woman shows include 1st Wis. Nat. Bank, 1981; exhibited in group shows at San Francisco State, 1975-76, Comprehensive Employment Tng. Act, Milw., 1979, San Dieguito Art Guild, 1981, Imperial Valley Art Show, 1982, La Jolla Light Photo Contest, 1986, Clairemont Art Guild, 1993. Recipient 1st Pl. award for oil painting Imperial Valley Art Show. Democrat. Jewish. Home: 8627D Via Mallorca La Jolla CA 92037

COHEN, BONNIE R., government official; b. Brockton, Mass., Dec. 11, 1942; d. Harold I. and Irma (Sims) Rubenstein; m. Louis R. Cohen, Sept. 29, 1965; children: Amanda, Eli. BA, Smith Coll., 1964; EdM, Harvard U., 1965; MBA, Harvard Bus. Sch., 1967. Analyst RMC, Inc., Washington, 1967-71; asst. to vice supt. Washington Pub. Schs., 1971-72; sr. cons. Levin & Assocs., Washington, 1972-76; treas. UMWA Funds, Washington, 1976-81; advisor Stanford U. Treas., Palo Alto, Calif., 1981; sr. v.p. Nat. Trust for Historic Preservation, Washington, 1981-93; asst. sec. of interior Dept. of the Interior, Washington, 1993—; trustee ARC Retirement System, Washington, 1986-89; investment chair DC Retirement System, 1984-87. Bd. dirs. Beauvoir Sch., Washington, 1985-88, Nat. Cathedral Sch., Washington, 1985-88, Environ. Defense Fund, Washington, 1982-86, Ctr. for Marine Conservation, Washington, 1987-93. Mem. City Club. Democrat. Home: 3060 Garrison St NW Washington DC 20008-1050 Office: Dept of the Interior 1849 C St NW Washington DC 20240-0001*

COHEN, CARLA LYNN, publisher; b. N.Y.C., Feb. 27, 1937; d. Barnet and Florence (Skolnick) Ellowis; children—Beth Diane, Jeffrey. Student Clark U., Adelphi U. Editor, Oceanside (N.Y.) Beacon, 1975-77; adminstrv. asst. pub. relations Bd. Suprs. Nassau County, 1977-78; pres. Carla Cohen Communications, Oceanside, N.Y., pres. Cotar Publs., Nassau Borders Papers, Floral Park, N.Y., 1981—; editor Voters Guide, Lawrence, N.Y., 1979-80. Grand Marshall Meml. Day parade, 1986; panelist weekly Town Meeting radio talk show Sta. WGBB; founding mem. Resident Referral Network, 1995. Recipient Patriotic Service award VFW, 1976; Outstanding Achievement award Am. Cancer Soc., 1976-77; Pub. Service award USAF, 1983; named Woman of Yr., B'nai B'rith, 1985, Sons of Italy, 1985, Businessperson of the Yr. Nassau County Coun. C. of C., 1989-90. Mem. C. of C. (v.p. 1982—), LWV (v.p. 1979), Woodbury Republican Club (pres. syosset), Internat. Platform Assn. Republican. Jewish. Office: PO Box 155 Franklin Square NY 11010-0155

COHEN, CAROLYN ALTA, health educator; b. Boston, Aug. 25, 1943; d. Haskell Mark and Sarah (Siegal) Cohen. BS, Boston U., 1965; postgrad., Boston State Coll., U. Mass., 1978, Boston Leadership Acad., 1989. Health and phys. edn. tchr., coach, girls athletic coord. Roslindale H.S., Boston, 1965-76; health and phys. edn. tchr., coach, athletic coord. West Roxbury H.S., Boston, 1976-87; asst. dir. health phys. edn. athletics Madison Park Campus, Boston, 1979-87; health educator dept. phys. edn./athletics West Roxbury H.S., Boston, 1989-90, 90—; commr. girls' basketball Boston Pub. Schs., 1979—; cheerleading judge various orgns., 1963, 64, 65, 70, 74, 80, 69-74; coach recreational programs N.E. Deaconess Hosp. Sch. Nursing, 1962-64, Beth Israel Hosp. Sch. Nursing, 1961-64; basketball ofcl. Bay State League, Pvt. Sch. League, Cath. H.S., 1961-80; coach phys. edn. dept. Boston U., 1962-65, 65-68; ofcl. Boston Park and Recreation Dept., 1962-75, summer playgrounds instr., 1961-65; instr. garening, athletic specialist agr. dept. Boston Schs., 1965-76. Instr. ARC, 1965—; trustee Adaptic Environ. Ctr., Boston, 1986—, treas., mem. exec. bd., 1990—; rep. Office Children-Area IV, Roslindale, Boston, 1974-76; liaison West Roxbury H.S. and Cmty. Sch. New Move Unltd. Theatre, Boston, 1981-84; liaison spl. arts project West Roxbury H.S., Boston, 1993-94; trustee Friends of Boston Harbor Islands Inc. Recipient Spl. Citation Boston U. Sargent Coll. Alumni Assn., Boston, 1980, Cert. of Appreciation ARC Mass Bay, 1986, Disting. Svc. to Alma Mater award Boston U., 1994, New Agenda award Boston Salute to Women in Sport, 1993. Mem. AAHPERD (bus. mgr. nat. conv. 1988-89, Presdl. medallion Ea. Dist. 1976), Mass. Assn. Health, Phys. Edn. Recreation and Dance (state and exec. com. 1969-94, treas. 1981-94, coord. registration ann. state conv. 1975-94, Honor award recognition 1978, Presdl Citation 1988), Boston U. Alumni Assn. (v.p. 1980-82, 87-89, v.p. cmty. 1995—), Boston U. Nat. Alumni Coun (v.p. scholarships 1981-83, 88—), Sargent Coll. Alumni Assn. (class sec., editor class newsletter 1965—, Spl. Citation 1980, Black Gold award, 1995), Boston U. Women's Grad. Club. Home: 100 Corey St West Roxbury MA 02132-2330

COHEN, CHRISTINE LOUISE, controller; b. Caracas, Venezuela, Jan. 10, 1957; came to U.S., 1976; d. Stein Leonard and Louise (Dybing) Halvorssen; m. James Boyer Cohen, June 3, 1978; children: Jonathan Trent, Jessica Grace. BA, Mt. Vernon Coll., 1978; MBA, George Washington U., 1979. Cert. govt. fin. mgr. Libr. asst. law library George Washington U., Washington, 1978-79; acct. I auditor-contr.'s office County of Ventura (Calif.), 1979-80, acct. II, 1980-81, fin. analyst, 1981-83, supr. acctg., 1983-89; chief dep. auditor contr. auditor's office County of Ventura, Ventura, 1989-94; asst. auditor-contr. auditor-contr.'s office County of Ventura, 1994—. Bd. dirs. Palmer Drug & Alcohol Abuse Program, 1994-96, T.E.A.C.H. scholarship orgn. for foster children, 1994-96. Mem. AAUW, Assn. Govt. Accts., Calif. Soc. Muni Fin. Officers, Govt. Fin. Officers Assn. Office: County of Ventura L #1540 800 S Victoria Ave Ventura CA 93009

COHEN, CYNTHIA MARYLYN, lawyer; b. Bklyn., Sept. 5, 1945. AB, Cornell U., 1967; JD cum laude, NYU, 1970. Bar: N.Y. 1971, U.S. Ct. Appeals (2d cir.) 1972, U.S. Supreme Ct. 1975, U.S. Dist. Ct. (so. and ea. dists.) N.Y. 1972, (cen. and no. dists.) Calif. 1980, U.S. Ct. Appeals (9th cir.) 1980, U.S. Dist. Ct. (so. dist.) Calif. 1981, U.S. Dist. Ct. (ea. dist.) Calif. 1986. Assoc. Simpson Thacher & Bartlett, N.Y.C., 1970-76, Kaye, Scholer, Fierman, Hayes & Handler, N.Y.C., 1976-80; assoc. Stutman, Treister & Glatt, P.C., L.A., 1980-81, ptnr., 1981-87; ptnr. Hughes Hubbard & Reed, N.Y.C. and L.A., 1987-93, Morgan, Lewis & Bockius, LLP, L.A., Phila., N.Y.C., 1993—. Bd. dirs. N.Y. chpt. Am. Cancer Soc., 1977-80. Recipient Am. Jurisprudence award for evidence, torts and legal instns., 1968-69; John Norton Pomeroy scholar NYU, 1968-70, Founders Day Cert., 1969. Mem. ABA (antitrust and litigation sects.), Assn. of Bar of City of N.Y. (trade regulations com. 1976-79), L.A. County Bar Assn. (antitrust, comml. law and bankruptcy sects.), Assn. Bus. Trial Lawyers, Fin. Lawyers Conf., N.Y. State Bar Assn. (chmn. class-action com. 1979), State Bar Calif. (antitrust and bus. law sects.), Delta Gamma, Order of Coif. Home: 4818 Bonvue Ave Los Angeles CA 90027-1105 Office: Morgan Lewis & Bockius LLP 801 S Grand Ave Fl 22 Los Angeles CA 90017-4613

COHEN, D. ASHLEY, clinical neuropsychologist; b. Omaha, Oct. 2, 1952; d. Cenek and Dorothy A. (Bilek) Hrabik; m. Donald I. Cohen, 1968 (div. 1976); m. Lyn J. Mangiameli, June 12, 1985. BA in Psychology, U. Nebr., Omaha, 1975, MA in Psychology, 1979; PhD in Clin. Psychology, Calif. Coast U., 1988. Lic. psychologist, Calif.; lic. marriage and family therapist, Nev. Family specialist Ea. Nebr. Human Svcs. Agy. Consultation & Edn., 1979-80; psychotherapist Washoe Tribe, Gardnerville, Nev., 1980; therapist Family Counseling Svc., Carson City, Nev., 1980-93; psychotherapist Alpine County Mental Health, Markleeville, Calif., 1981-89, dir., 1990-93; psychologist Golden Gate Med. Examiners, San Francisco, San Jose, Calif., 1993—; conf. presenter and spkr. in field; presenter rsch. findings 7th European Conf. Personality, Madrid, 1994, Oxford (Eng.) U. ISSID Conf., 1991; site coord. nat. standardization Kaufmann brief intelligence test A.G.S., 1988-90. Vol. EMT, Alpine County, 1983-93. Recipient Svc. to Youth award Office Edn., 1991. Mem. APA, Internat. Neuropsychol. Soc., Internat. Soc. Study Individual Differences, Am. Psychol. Soc., Nat. Acad. Neuropsychology. Office: 127 Carson Ct Sunnyvale CA 94086

COHEN, DIANA LOUISE, mental health administrator, psychology, educator, psychotherapist; b. Phila., Apr. 8, 1942; d. Nathan and Dorothy (Rubin) Blasberg; m. Jules L. Frankel, July 3, 1987; 1 child, Jennifer. BA, Temple U., 1964, MEd, 1969; PhD, Temple Univ., 1996. Lic. psychologist, Pa., N.J.; nat. cert. mental health counselor. Caseworker Phila. Gen. Hosp., 1964-69, staff psychologist, 1969-70; staff psychologist Atlantic Mental Health Ctr., McKee City, N.J., 1970-80, unit dir., 1980-87, v.p. profl. svcs., 1987-91; pvt. practice Pa., N.J., 1991—; mem. adj. faculty Glassboro (N.J.) State Coll., 1988—; cmty. & family mediator Cmty. Justice Inst., Atlantic County, N.J., 1990—. Com. chmn. Atlantic County Commn. for Missing and Abused Children, 1984-89. Grantee N.J. Dept. Edn., 1988-89, N.J. Job Tng. Partnership Act, 1990. Mem. APA (assoc.), NJCA, N.J. Mental Health Counselors Assn. (pres.-elect 1996), South Shore Region Mental Health Counselors Assn. (sec. 1994—). Home: 569 Gravelly Run Rd Mays Landing NJ 08330-1654 Office: 2106 New Rd Linwood NJ 08221-1046 also: 1718 Welsh Rd Philadelphia PA 19115-4213

COHEN, ELAINE HELENA, pediatrician, pediatric cardiologist; b. Boston, Oct. 14, 1941; d. Samuel Clive and Lillian (Stocklan) C.; m. Marvin Leon Gale, May 7, 1972; 1 child, Pamela Beth Gale. AB, Conn. Coll., 1963; postgrad., Tufts U., 1963-64; MD, Women's Med. Coll. Pa., 1969. Diplomate Am. Bd. Pediats. Intern in pediats. Children's Hosp. of L.A., 1969-70, resident in pediats., 1970-71; fellow in pediat. cardiology UCLA Ctr. Health Scis., 1971-72, L.A. County/U. So. Calif. Med. Ctr., L.A., 1972-74; pediatrician Children's Med. Group of South Bay, Chula Vista, Calif., 1974—; clin. instr. dept. pediats. UCLA Sch. Medicine, 1971-72, U. So. Calif., L.A., 1972-74; clin. asst. prof. dept. pediats. U. Calif., San Diego, 1974—, preceptor dept. pediats., 1992—. Fellow Am. Acad. Pediats.; mem. Calif. Med. Assn., San Diego County Med. Soc. Office: Children's Med Group South Bay 280 E St Chula Vista CA 91910-2945

COHEN, ESTHER SIMA, art educator emeritus; b. N.Y.C., Dec. 29, 1913; d. Solomon Avigdor and Mary (Beshunsky) C. BA, NYU, 1940, MS in Supervision, 1949, postgrad., 1949-52; postgrad., Alfred U. Instr. NYU, N.Y.C., 1947-49, Fieldston Sch., N.Y.C., 1946-47; prof. Ea. Conn. State U., Willimantic, 1949-78; prof. emeritus, 1978—. Exhibited ceramics in group shows; contbr. articles to mags. Vol. Wadsworth Atheneum Art Libr., 1978—. Recipient Silver Apple award Conn. Edn. Assn., 1957. Mem. AAUP (retirees coun., organizer, bd. dirs.), AAUW, NEA (retirees coun. Washington chpt.), Nat. Art Edn. Assn. (com. mem.). Jewish. Home: 2363 Albany Ave West Hartford CT 06117-2714

COHEN, HELEN HERZ, camp owner, director; b. N.Y.C., Oct. 29, 1912; d. Fred W. and Florence (Hirsch) H.; m. Albert F. Schliefer, Sept. 22, 1933 (dec. Nov. 1941); m. Edwin S. Cohen, Aug. 31, 1944: children: Edwin C., Roger, Wendy. PhB, Brown U., 1933; MA, Columbia U., 1934; postgrad., NYU, Columbia. Counselor Camp Walden, Denmark, Maine, 1930-38, owner, 1939—; tchr. social studies Alcuin Prep. Sch., 1935; office mgr. Lewis P. Weil Importer, 1935-40; pres. The Main Idea, 1968—; founder, pres. Main Idea, Inc., 1969—. Author of several books; co-author: camp cookbook; contbr. articles to instrnl. booklets, mags. Active alumni coun. Pembroke Coll., 1960; chmn. camp divns. Bridgton (Maine) Hosp. Fund, 1962—; trustee Fund for Advancement Camping, 1980-90. Recipient Gold Key award Columbia Scholastic Press, 1972, award Fund for Advancement of Camping Patron, 1982. Mem. Am. Camping Assn. (regional bd. dirs. 1947-50, 52-55, 56-59, 60-63, standards visitor 1957-93, chmn. pvt. camps 1961, bd. dirs. 1963—, v.p. N.Y. 1963-75, Va. sect. 1975), Pioneers of Camping, Maine Camp Dirs. Assn. (legis. com. 1960-63, bd. dirs. 1963—, Halsey Gulick award 1991), Pembroke Coll. Club (co-founder), Cosmopolitan (Westchester, N.Y.) Club, Cornell Club, Farmington Country Club, Boar's Head Sports Club. Home: Ednam Forest 104 Stuart Pl Charlottesville VA 22903-4740 Office: Camp Walden Bos 3427 Charlottesville VA 22903 also: Rt 1 Box 129 Denmark ME 04022

COHEN, HELENE Z., lawyer; b. Jacksonville, Fla., Aug. 13, 1935. BSBA, U. Fla., 1956; JD, Emory U., 1976. Bar: Ga. 1976, U.S. Ct. Appeals Ga., U.S. Dist. Ct. (no. dist.) Ga. 1976, U.S. Ct. Appeals (11th cir.) 1983, U.S. Supreme Ct. 1984. Ptnr. Alston & Bird, Atlanta. Mem. State Bar of Ga., Atlanta Bar Assn. Office: Alston & Bird 1 Atlantic Ct 1201 W Peachtree St NW Atlanta GA 30309-3424*

COHEN, HOLLACE T., lawyer; b. Bklyn., May 10, 1948; d. Benjamin Carl and Esther (Abramowitz) Topol; m. Steven L. Cohen, June 22, 1969; children: Harlan Grant, Lauren Cecily. BA, CCNY, 1969; JD, NYU, 1972. Bar: N.Y. 1973. Assoc. Whitman & Ransom, N.Y.C., 1972-81, ptnr., 1981—. Mem. ABA, Am. Bankruptcy Inst., N.Y. State Bar Assn., Assn. Bar City N.Y. (com. women in profession), Sky Club. Office: Whitman Breed Abbott Morgan 200 Park Ave New York NY 10166-0005

COHEN, IDA BOGIN (MRS. SAVIN COHEN), import and export executive; b. Bklyn.; d. Joseph and Yetta (Harris) Bogin; student St. Johns U.; B.S., N.Y.U.; m. Barnet Gaster, June 26, 1941 (div. May 1955); m. 2d, Savin Cohen, Aug. 30, 1964. Sec.-treas. J. Gerber & Co., Inc., N.Y.C., 1942-54, v.p., dir., 1954-73; pres., dir. Austracan U.S.A., Inc., N.Y.C., 1960-73; v.p. Parts Warehouse, Inc., Woodside, N.Y., 1970-72, sec.-treas., 1972-83; also engaged in pvt. investments. Contbr. articles to South African Outspan, newspapers. Home: 12 Shorewood Dr Sands Point NY 11050-1909

COHEN, JOYCE E., former state senator, investment executive; b. McIntosh, S.D., Mar. 27, 1937; d. Joseph and Evelyn Petik; children: Julia Jo, Aaron J. Grad., Coll. Med. Tech., Minn., 1955; student, UCLA, 1957-58, Santa Ana Coll., 1957-62. Med. rsch. technician dept. surgery U. Minn., 1955-58; dept. immunology UCLA, 1958-59; dept. bacteriology U. Calif., 1959-61; med. rsch. scientist Allergan Pharms., Santa Ana, Calif., 1961-70; ptnr. Co-Fo Investments, Lake Oswego, Oreg., 1978-84; mem. Oreg. Ho. of Reps., 1979-81, Oreg. State Senate, 1983-94, Northwest Power Planning Coun., 1994—. Chmn. trade amd econ. devel., govt. reorgn. and reinvention com., senate judiciary com.; mem. senate revenue and sch. fin. com.; vice-chair agr. & natural resources com., health care & bio-ethics com.; mem. bus., housing & fin. com., rules com.; co-chair joint task force on lottery oversight; mem. joint com. on asset forfeiture oversight adv.; mem. Senate Exec. Appointments; mem. joint com. on land use, alt. joint com. legis.

audit; mem. Energy Policy Rev. Bd.; appointed to Oreg. Coun. Econ. Edn., Oreg. Criminal Justice Coun., adv. com. Ctr. for Rsch. on Occupational and Environ. Toxicology; mem. Jud. Br. State Energy Policy Rev. Com., 1979, Gov's. Commn. on Child Support. Woodrow Wilson Lecture series fellow, 1988. Mem. LWV, Assn. Family Conciliation Cts. (founding mem.), Oreg. Environ. Coun., Oreg. Women's Polit. Caucus. Democrat. Office: 620 SW 5th Ave Ste 1025 Portland OR 97204-1424

COHEN, JUDITH BETH, educator, writer; b. Detroit, Aug. 22, 1943; d. Harry S. and Gertrude (Milstein) Cohen; m. Jeff Weiss (div.); m. Mark Schneider. BA, U. Mich., 1965, MA, 1966; PhD, Union Inst., Cin., 1993. Asst. prof. SUNY, New Paltz, 1967-69; mem. faculty Goddard Coll., Plainfield, Vt., 1970-79; sr. preceptor Harvard U., Cambridge, Mass., 1979-89; assoc. prof. Lesley Coll., Cambridge, Mass., 1989—; assoc. Bard Coll. Inst. on Writing and Thinking, Annandale, N.Y., 1988—. Author: Seasons, 1984; contbr. articles, short story to lit. pubs.; reviewer Women's Rev. of Books. Fulbright fellow, Israel, 1987, fellow Hawthornden Castle Writer's Retreat, Scotland, 1995; recipient PEN Fiction prize, 1987. Mem. Nat. Coun. Tchrs. of English, New Eng. PEN. Jewish. Office: Lesley Coll 29 Everett St Cambridge MA 02138

COHEN, JUDITH W., academic administrator; b. N.Y.C., May 14, 1937; d. Meyer F. and Edith Beatrice (Elman) Wiles; BA, Bklyn. Coll., 1957, MA, 1960; cert. advanced studies Hofstra U., 1978; MA Columbia U., 1986, postgrad. 1986—. m. Joseph Cohen, Oct. 19, 1957; children: Amy Beth (dec.), Lisa Carrie, Adam Scott Frank, Elyssa Lily. Tchr. N.Y.C. Pub. Schs., Bklyn., 1957-60; tchr. Mid. Country Sch. Dist., Centereach, N.Y., 1970-93, retired 1993; prof. psychology 5 Towns Coll., Dix Hills, N.Y., 1994—. Title IX compliance officer, 1980-86, team leader 1987-91; dir. Long Island U. Summer Adventure Program, 1994—. Bus. adv. Women's Equal Rights Congress, Suffolk County Human Rights; chmn. bd. edn., Temple Beth David, trustee, 1975-79; pres. CHUMS, 1979-82; Tchr. of Gifted Post-L.I. U. Saturday Program, 1985—; L.I. Writing Project fellow, Dowling Coll., 1979—; cert. sch. dist. adminstr., supr., adminstr., N.Y. State; adj. prof. Five Towns Coll., 1994—. Mem. Nassau Suffolk Coun. Adminstrv. Women in Edn. (pres. 1979-81), Assn. for Supervision and Curriculum Devel., Assn. Gifted/Talented Edn., Women's Equal Rights Congress Com. (exec. bd.), Suffolk County Coordinating Council Gifted and Talented, Phi Delta Kappa, Delta Kappa Pi. Author: Arts in Education Curriculum in Social Studies and Language Arts, 1981. Home: 35 Gaymor Ln Commack NY 11725-1305

COHEN, JUNE LAURA, medicaid coordinator; b. D.C., Aug. 20, 1946; d. Bernard and Anne (Wald) Silkes; m. David Jack Cohen, Sept. 1, 1968; children: Cheryl Lynn, Amy Beth. BS, Pa. State U., 1968, MEd, 1973. Tchr. Juniata Mifflin VoTech., Lewistown, Pa., 1969-71; instr. Fairfax (Va.) County Adult Edn., 1974-75; tchr. Anne Arundel County, Annapolis, Md., 1976-84; jr. acct. Annapolis Fed. Savs. Bank, 1985-86, sr. acct., 1986-87; fin. adminstr. Juvenile Justice Adv. Coun., Balt., 1987-91; fin. analyst Gov.'s Office for Children, Youth and Families, Balt., 1991-95; medicaid coord. Md. State Dept. of Edn., Balt., 1995—. Author: (instrnl. material) UNIPAC, 1971, (handbook) Financial Management Handbook, 1991, instrnl. guide for video, 1989. PTA corr. sec. Broadneck El. Sch., Arnold, Md., 1978-80; rec. sec. Colonial Nursery Sch., Annapolis, 1981-83; fin. sec. Hadassah, Annapolis, 1985-88; chair edn. com. Temple Solel, Bowie, Md., 1992-93. Democrat. Office: Md State Dept of Edn 200 W Baltimore St Baltimore MD 21201

COHEN, LAUREL, case manager; b. Chgo., Dec. 1, 1943; d. Carl Eugene and Joan Adele (Arenz) Patterson; m. Sidney Henry Cohen, June 29, 1968 (div. Nov. 1981); children: Elizabeth Ann Cohen Jonsson, David Arthur Patterson, Douglas Edward, Deborah Sue; m. Frederick Joseph Foti, Jan. 19, 1985 (div. June 1994). Diploma in nursing, Swedish Covenant, 1967; BS, Moody Bible Inst., 1976. RN, N.J. Staff nurse Overlook Hosp., Summit, N.J., 1980-82; pub. health nurse Patient Care Svc., West Orange, N.J., 1982-83; hospice nurse The Hospice, Inc., Montclair, N.J., 1984-92; fin. svc. rep. Primerica Fin. Svcs., Duluth, Ga., 1985-89; coord. home care Vis. Nurse Assn. Essex Valley, East Orange, N.J., 1993-96; Medicare case mgr. U.S. Healthcare, Fairfield, N.J., 1996—. State coord. La Leche League, N.J., 1976-78; hospice vol. The Hospice, Inc., 1992—; mem. MADD, Rep. Presdl. Task Force, 1989. Lt. (j.g.) USNR, 1967-69. Mem. Adoptees Liberty Movement Assn. (spokesman 1977-83), DAR. Republican. Lutheran. Home: 79 Broad St Summit NJ 07901-4044 Office: US Healthcare 55 Lane Rd Fairfield NJ 07004

COHEN, LILA BELDOCK, writer; b. Bklyn., Apr. 1, 1927; m. Marshall J. Cohen, Oct. 28, 1956; children: Tamar, Howard. BA magna cum laude, U. Conn., 1972. owner, operator Paperback Alley, South Windsor, Conn., 1981-95. Author: The King Who Loved His Lollipops, 1971; contbr. stories to popular mags. including Nat. Jewish Monthly, Balt. Jewish Times, Hartford Courant, Hartford Mag. Pres. LWV, Manchester, 1968; chairperson A Conn. Party, Manchester, 1992-94. Home: 19 Cushman Dr Manchester CT 06040

COHEN, LISA BETH, English language educator; b. N.Y.C., Feb. 6, 1948; d. Paul and Sylvia Sarah (Singer) Sonenthal; m. Edmund Stephen Cohen, June 30, 1968; children: Ellen Paige, Paul Lawrence. BA in English cum laude, Smith Coll., 1968; MA in English, Boston U., 1969, cert. in advanced studies, Hofstra U., 1982, profl. diploma, 1991. Cert. English 9-12 tchr., Mass., N.Y. English tchr. Marshfield (Mass.) H.S., 1970-71; English tchr. Hewlett (N.Y.) H.S., 1971-84, English chair, 1984—. Author: Bible as Literature, 1975, (cable TV program) Extra Help in English, spring 1995—. Bd. edn. chair Hewlett East Rockaway (N.Y.) Jewish Ctr., 1985-92, bd. dirs., 1988-92. NEH fellow, 1995; named Educator of Excellence in English N.Y.S. English Coun., 1994. Mem. Nat. Coun. Tchrs. English, Long Island Lang. Arts Coun. Office: Hewlett HS 60 Everit Ave Hewlett NY 11557-2100

COHEN, LISA JANET, psychologist, educator; b. Chgo., Dec. 27, 1961; d. Morrel Herman and Sylvia Pauline (Zwein) C. AB, U. Mich., 1985, BFA, 1985; MA, CUNY, 1992, MPhil, 1992, PhD, 1992. Lic. psychologist, N.Y. Supervising psychologist Beth Israel Med. Ctr., N.Y.C., 1996—; asst. prof. psychiatry Albert Einstein Coll. of Medicine, 1996—; pvt. practice psychology, N.Y.C., 1994—; adj. asst. prof. psychology in psychiatry Mount Sinai Sch. of Medicine, 1996. Contbr. articles to profl. jours., chpts. to book. Mem. APA. Office: Dept Psychiatry Beth Israel Med Ctr 1st Ave and 16th St New York NY 10003

COHEN, LITA INDZEL, state legislator; m. Stanley S. Cohen; children: Reuven, Shoshana. AB in Polit. Sci. cum laude, U. Pa., 1962, postgrad., JD, 1965. Bar: Pa. 1965. Clk. Henderson, Wetherill & O'Hey, Norristown, 1964, Levi, Mandel & Miller, Phila., 1965; asst. regional counsel HUD, 1966-67; asst. counsel Sch. Dist. Phila., 1967-71; pvt. practice Merion, Pa., 1971-76; exec. v.p., gen. counsel, COO Ind. Broadcasting Co., Inc. and Banks Broadcasting Co., 1976-82; pres. Orange Prodns., Inc.-Nat. Radio Syndication Co., 1983-87, Lita Cohen Radio Svcs., Merion, Pa., 1987-93; mem. Ho. of Reps., Conshohocken, Pa., 1992—. Bd. dirs. Merion Civic Assn.; mem. citizens fire prevention com. Phila. Fire Dept.; active Lower Merion/Narberth Watershed Assn., Lower Merion Twp. Police Pension Assn., Har Zion Temple; v.p. bd. dirs. Phila. Child Guidance Ctr.; Lower Merion Twp. commr., 1986-93; capt. Heart Fund Block; mem. women's adv. com. Montemery County C.C.; hon. pres. Golda Meir Profl. Women's Hadassah; past bd. dirs. Kaiserman JYC, Atwater Kent Mus. Mem. Pa. Bar Assn., Phila. Bar Assn., Montgomery County Bar Assn. Office: Pa Ho of Reps House Box 202020 Harrisburg PA 17120 also: 1010 Fayette St Conshohocken PA 19428*

COHEN, LIZABETH ANN, history educator. AB, Princeton U., 1973; MA, U. Calif., Berkeley, 1981, PhD, 1986. Asst. curator Fine Arts Mus. San Francisco, 1975-77; dir. Camron-Stanford House Mus., Oakland, Calif., 1976-78; mus., pub. history cons.; mem. faculty dept. history Carnegie-Mellon U., from 1986; now prof. dept. history NYU, N.Y.C. Author: Making A New Deal: Industrial Workers in Chicago 1991-1939, 1990; contbr. numerous articles to profl. jours. Recipient Philip Taft Labor History award Cornell U., 1990, Bancroft prize in Am. history Columbia U., 1991; fellow NEH, 1993, Am. Coun. Learned Socs., 1994, Guggenheim Found., 1995. Office: NYU Dept History 19 University Pl New York NY 10003-4501

COHEN, MADELINE ROSE, arts educator; b. N.Y.C., Aug. 21, 1950; d. Ira Saul and Louise Olga (Giventer) C.; m. Ross Thomas French, May 21, 1989. BA in Comparative Lit., Brandeis U., 1972; MFA in Costume Design, U. Wis., 1976. Tchg. artist Lincoln Ctr. Inst., N.Y.C., 1978—, Nashville Inst. for the Arts, 1983—; arts edn. cons. Scarsdale (N.Y.) Union Free Sch. Dist., 1985-87, Tchrs. Coll./Columbia U., N.Y.C., 1989—, Chamber Music Am., N.Y.C., 1994; adv. bd. mem. Leonard Bernstein Ctr. for Learning, Nashville, 1992-94; edn. dir. Symphony Space, N.Y.C., 1989—. Costume designer theatrical prodns., 1977—. Organizer and 1st pres. chpt. of United Fedn. of Tchrs., Lincoln Ctr. Inst., N.Y.C., 1984; steering com. mem. N.Y.C. Arts in Edn. Roundtable, 1992—. Office: Symphony Space 2537 Broadway New York NY 10025

COHEN, MARCY SHARON, lawyer, bank executive; b. N.Y.C., Apr. 29, 1954; d. Morton Gilbert and Sue (Krumstock) C. AB, Lehman Coll., 1975; JD, N.Y. Law Sch., 1978. Bar: N.Y. 1979, U.S. Dist. Ct. (ea. and so. dists.) N.Y. 1979, U.S. Supreme Ct. 1982. Assoc. Marcus & Marcus, N.Y.C., 1978-80; v.p., assoc. gen. counsel Bank Leumi Trust Co. N.Y., N.Y.C., 1980-84; sr. v.p., gen. counsel Atlantic Bank N.Y., N.Y.C., 1984—; v.p., dep. gen. counsel Republic Nat. Bank N.Y., N.Y.C.; mem. faculty Am. Inst. Banking, N.Y.C., 1984-88. Mem. ABA (corp. bankig and bus. law com.), Assn. Bar of City of N.Y. (banking law com.), N.Y. State Bar Assn. (chair internat. and fgn. bus. law), Assn. Comml. Fin. Attys. Office: Republic Nat Bank NY 452 Fifth Ave New York NY 10018

COHEN, MARIE CAROL, elementary education educator; b. Passaic, N.J., Dec. 24, 1935; d. Salvatore Peter and Marie Camille (DiPietro) Tuzzeo; m. Victor David Cohen; children: Lawrence, Lori, Wendy. BA, William Paterson Coll., 1960; MS, L.I. U., 1971. Cert. student personnel svcs., 1991. Tchr. elem. Dept. Edn. N.J., Trenton, 1964—; purchaser antiques ABC Antiques, Garfield, N.J., 1960—. Exhibited in group shows at William Paterson Coll., Wayne, N.J., 1959-60, L.I. Univ., N.Y., 1970-71, Las Vegas Pub. Libr., 1976-77, L.D.S. Ch., Caldwell, N.J., 1985, L.D.S. Ch., Franklin Lakes, N.J., 1986, Louis Rey Libr., Hawthorne, N.J., 1996; one-person exhibit at Half Hollow Hills Libr., Dix Hills, N.Y., 1972-73. Mem. LWV, AAUW (facilitator arts and crafts shows 1992-94), Alumni Assn. William Paterson Coll., Alumni Assn. L.I. U. Democrat. Home: 70 Boonstra Dr Wayne NJ 07470

COHEN, MARLENE SHERI, retail executive; b. Hartford, Conn., Oct. 21, 1956; d. Alexander and Myra C.; married, 1989 (div. 1993). BA in Liberal Arts, U. Conn., 1978. Exec. trainee/asst. buyer G. Fox & Co., May Co., Hartford, Conn., 1978-81, buyer womens wear, 1981-82; buyer mens wear Reads Allied Stores Corp., Trumbull, Conn., 1982-87, Mitchells of Westport (Conn.), 1987-91; buyer product devel. mens wear Brooks Bros., N.Y.C., 1991-93, sr. buyer product devel. mens wear, 1993-95; dir. product devel. mens wear pvt. label Saks 5th Avenue, N.Y.C., 1995—. Active in influencing legislation in areas of domestic violence: restraining orders, stalking, harrassment. Republican. Home: 285 Rowayton Ave Rowayton CT 06853

COHEN, MARY ANN, judge; b. Albuquerque, July 16, 1943; d. Gus R. and Mary Carolyn (Avriette) C. BS, UCLA, 1964; JD, U. So. Calif., 1967. Bar: Calif. 1967. Ptnr. Abbott & Cohen, P.C. and predecessors, Los Angeles, 1967-82; judge U.S. Tax Ct., Washington 1982—, chief judge 1996—. Mem. ABA (sect. taxation), Legion Lex. Republican. Office: US Tax Ct 400 2nd St NW Washington DC 20217-0001

COHEN, NANCY JANE, filmmaker; b. Phila., May 17, 1951; d. Harold David C. and Rochea Neiman. BA, Pa. State U., 1972; postgrad., U. Manchester, Eng., 1972. Prin. MDWA Prodns., N.Y.C., 1986-93; mem.-poet N.Y.C. Unbearables, 1995; owner, pres. Lambstar Prodns., N.Y.C., 1994—. Dir. (films) Deep in the Deal, 1994, My Dinner with Abbie, 1990. Home: 435 E 9th St New York NY 10017

COHEN, RACHEL RUTSTEIN, financial consultant; b. Phila., June 10, 1968; d. Charles Lawrence and Ronna Newman Rutstein (stepmother) and Susan Ellen (Yokel) Sansweet; m. Kipp B. Cohen, Oct. 22, 1995. BS in Bus. Adminstrn., Pa. State U., 1990; student, U. Tel Aviv, 1989; postgrad., Temple U., 1994—. Registered rep., registered investment advisor; cert. fin. mgr. Sr. fin. cons. Merrill Lynch, Bala Cynwyd, Pa., 1990—. V.p. bd. dirs. Phila. chpt. Shaare Zedek Hosp.Charity, 1992—, co-chair Phone-A-Thon, 1993. Mem. Phila. C. of C. (diplomat 1991-95), Associated Builders and Contractors, Phila. Fin. Asn. (co-chair dinner com.), Green Valley Country Club, Pa. State U. Alumni Assn. Republican. Office: Merrill Lynch 2 Bala Plaza Bala Cynwyd PA 19610

COHEN, RACHELLE SHARON, journalist; b. Phila., Oct. 21, 1946; d. Hyman and Diane Doris (Schultz) Goldberg; m. Stanley Martin Cohen, June 22, 1968; 1 dau., Avril Heather. BS, Temple U., 1968. Editor, Somerville Jour. (Mass.), 1968-70; reporter Lowell Sun (Mass.), 1970-72, AP, Boston, 1972-79; state house bur. chief Boston Herald Am., 1979-80, editorial page editor, 1980-82; editorial page editor, columnist Boston Herald, 1982—. Mem. Mass. Bar Assn. (bench, bar, press com.), Mass. Assn. Mental Health (bd. dirs. 1993—). Office: Boston Herald 1 Herald St Boston MA 02118-2200

COHEN, ROBIN L., lawyer; b. Phila., Oct. 27, 1961. BA magna cum laude, U. Pa., 1983, JD, 1986. Bar: Pa. 1986, N.J. 1989, N.Y. 1989. Ptnr. Anderson, Kill, Olick & Oshinsky, P.C., N.Y.C. Office: Anderson Kill Olick & Oshinsky PC 1251 Avenue of the Americas New York NY 10020-1182*

COHEN, RONNI K., gifted education educator; b. Cambridge, Mass., June 3, 1947; d. Harry and Judith (Krulfeld) C. BS in Elem. Edn., U. Del., 1969; MEd in Gifted Studies and Creativity, Widener U., 1988. Tchr. Brandywine Sch. Dist., Claymont, Del., 1969—; adj. faculty coll. edn. U. Del., Newark, 1990-93, Wilmington Coll., New Castle, Del., 1993; cons. Zeisler Assocs., Wilmington, 1993—, E.E. Cats, Claymont, 1993—; econs. Am. cons. Del. Ctr. for Econ. Edn., Newark, 1984—; mem. tchr. adv. bd. Fed. Res. Bank Phila., 1992-94. Author: (workbooks) Econo M & Mics, 1992), Inventor's Portfolio, 1996; contbg. writer: Econs. for Kids, 1992-94. Named Entrepreneurship Educator of Yr. Inc. Mag., Ernst & Young, Merrill Lynch, Kauffman Found., 1993-94, Elem. Winner Nat. Fedn. Ind. Bus., 1992; recipient Innovative Teaching award Bus. Week, 1990, Excellence in Teaching award Del. Coun. Social Studies, 1994. Mem. Del. Elem. Econ. Educators (founding), Am. Creativity Assn. Home: 141/2 Forrest Ave Claymont DE 19703

COHEN, SELMA, reference librarian, researcher; b. N.Y.C., Mar. 14, 1930; d. George and Rose (Cohen) Unger; m. Irwin H. Cohen, Nov. 19, 1950; children: Barbara Katzeff, Joel. Grad. high sch., William Howard Taft High Sch., 1948. Asst. bookkeeper acctg. dept. Severud, Perrone et al, N.Y.C., 1970-75; asst. bookkeeper acctg. dept. Russell Reynolds Assocs., Inc., N.Y.C., 1976-77, rsch. asst., 1977—, reference libr., 1985—. Chairwoman Scott Tower Charity Com., Bronx, 1976-84, Scott Tower Property Improvement Com., Bronx, 1983-84. Home: 3400J Paul Ave Bronx NY 10468-1002 Office: Russell Reynolds Assocs 200 Park Ave New York NY 10166-0005

COHEN, SELMA JEANNE, dance historian; b. Chgo., Sept. 18, 1920; d. Frank A. and Minna (Skud) C. A.B., U. Chgo., 1941, M.A., 1942, Ph.D., 1946. Free lance writer, 1949—; editor Dance Perspectives, N.Y.C., 1959-76; founder, dir. Dance Critics Conf., Am. Dance Festival, 1970-72, U. Chgo. Seminars in Dance History, 1974-76; disting. vis. prof. Five Colls., Inc., 1976-77; editor Internat. Ency. Dance, N.Y.C., 1981—; dance editor World Ency. Contemporary Theatre, 1985—; adj. prof. U. Calif., Riverside, 1983-89, disting. scholar, 1990—. Author: The Modern Dance: Seven Statements of Belief, 1966, Doris Humphrey, An Artist First, 1972, Dance as a Theatre Art, 1974, Next Week, Swan Lake: Reflections on Dance and Dances, 1982. Rockefeller Found. grantee, 1969; Am. Dance Guild award, 1976; Guggenheim fellow, 1980; recipient Profl. Achievement award U. Chgo., 1974; award Dance mag., 1981. Mem. Am. Soc. Aesthetics, Am. Soc. Theatre Rsch., Dance History Scholars, Am. Coun. Learned Socs., Internat. Fedn. for Theatre Rsch., World Dance Alliance. Home and Office: 29 E 9th St New York NY 10003-6350

COHEN, SHARLEEN COOPER, interior designer, writer; b. L.A., June 11, 1940; d. Sam and Claretta (Ellis) White; m. R. Gary Cooper, Dec. 18, 1960 (dec. Feb., 1971); m. Martin L. Cohen, Aug. 27, 1972; children: Cami Gordon, Dalisa Cooper Cohen. Student, U. Calif., Berkeley, 1957-58, UCLA, 1958-60, L.A. Valley Film Sch., 1976-78. Owner, mgr. Designs on You, L.A., 1965-77; writer L.A., 1977—; prodr. Jewish Repertory Theatre, N.Y.C., 1996. Author: (books) The Day After Tomorrow, 1979, Regina's Song, 1980, The Ladies of Beverly Hills, 1983, Marital Affairs, 1985, Love, Sex and Money, 1988, Lives of Value, 1991, Innocent Gestures, 1994; (play) Solomon and Sheba, 1990; (musical) Sheba. Mem. exec. com. Women of Distinction United Jewish Appeal, 1990—; chair L.A. chpt. Nat. Gaucher Found., 1991-95; bd. dirs., mem. com. chair Calif. Coun. for the Humanities, San Francisco, 1992—. Recipient Hon. Mention, Santa Barbara Writers Conf., 1978. Mem. PEN, Writers Guild of Am.

COHEN, SHIRLEY, musician, educator; b. N.Y.C., Jan. 29, 1918; d. Abraham and Rose (Feldstein) Aronoff; m. Oscar J. Cohen; 1 child, Deborah Natalie Cohen Marcus. Student, NYU; studied piano, composition, harmony, with eminent musician-coaches, 1936-96. Authorized affiliate artist tchr. for SUNY (Purchase) candidates for Master's Degree in piano performance. Music dir. Raquette Lake Girls Club, 1936-38; music tchr. Woodward Sch., Bklyn., 1954-56; tchr. master classes, piano techniques, and interpretation IRPE Bklyn. Coll., Bklyn, 1985-96. Piano debut Steinway Hall, 1935. Recipient Silver medal for piano performance, theory and ear tng., 1934, dramatic arts radio performance WSGH, Bklyn., WLTH, Bklyn., WNYC, Manhattan, 1932-34. Mem. Music Tchrs. Nat. Assn., Bklyn. Music Tchrs. Guild. Home and Office: 1274 E Ninth St Brooklyn NY 11230

COHEN, SHIRLEY MASON, retired educator, civic worker; b. Jersey City, June 24, 1924; d. Herman and Esther (Vinik) Mason; m. Herbert Leonard Cohen, June 24, 1951; children: Bruce Mason, Annette Pauline, Carol Elyse, Debra Tamara. BA, Rutgers U., 1945; MA, Columbia U., 1946; postgrad., U. Calif., Berkeley, 1946-51. Instr. U. Calif., Berkeley, 1946-51, American River Coll., Sacramento, 1962; tchr. various high schs., Sacramento, 1975-92; ret., 1992; mentor tchr. Sacramento City Unified Sch. Dist., 1987, 88. Bd. dirs. Sacramento Cmty. Concerts, 1965—. Mem. Phi Beta Kappa.

COHEN, SUSAN LOIS, author; b. Chgo., Mar. 27, 1938; d. Martin and Ida Handler; m. Daniel E. Cohen, Feb. 2, 1958; 1 child, Theodora (dec.). BA, New Sch. for Social Rsch., 1960; MA in Social Work, Adelphi U., 1962. Social worker N.Y.C., 1962-67; various social work positions in N.Y.C., 1962-68. Author: The Liberated Couple, 1969, reassued under title Liberated Marriage, 1973; (under name Elizabeth St. Clair) Stonehaven, 1974, The Singing Harp, 1975, Secret of the Locket, 1975, Provenance House, 1976, Mansion in Miniature, 1977, Dewitt Manor, 1977, The Jeweled Secret, 1978, Murder in the Act, 1978, Sandcastle Murder, 1979, Trek or Treat, 1980, Sealed with a Kiss, 1981; (with Daniel Cohen) The Kids' Guide to Home Computers, 1983, The Kids' Guide to Home Video, 1984, Teenage Stress, 1984, Screen Goddesses, 1984, Rock Video Superstars, 1985, Wrestling Superstars, Vol. 1, 1985, Vol. 2, 1986, Hollywood Hunks and Heroes, 1985, Heroes of the Challenger, 1986, A Six-Pack and a Fake ID, 1986, The Encyclopedia of Movie Stars, 1986, A History of the Oscars, 1986, Teenage Competition: A Survival Guide, 1987, Young and Famous: Hollywood's Newest Superstars, 1987, Going for the Gold, 1987, What You Can Believe about Drugs, 1988, What Kind of Dog is That, 1989, When Someone You Know Is Gay, 1989, Zoo Superstars, 1989, Zoos, 1992, Where to Find Dinosaurs Today, 1992, Going for the Gold: Medal Hopefuls for Winter '92, 1992. Mem. Wodehouse Soc., Watson's Erroneous Deductions, Chapter One, The Capers of Sherlock Holmes, Clumber Spaniel Club of Am. Address: 877 W Hand Ave Cape May Court House NJ 08210-1865

COHEN, SUZETTE FRANCINE, reading specialist; b. Cleve., June 23, 1943; m. Irwin J. Cohen, July 7, 1963; children: Kathryn E. Fenton, Gregory M. BA, Cleve. State U., 1975; MEd, John Carroll U., 1979; PhD, Kent State U., 1986. Tchr. English Mayfield Bd. Edn., Mayfield Village, Ohio, 1975-78; tchr. reading South Euclid/Lyndhurst Bd. Edn., Lyndhurst, Ohio, 1978-79; reading specialist Cleve. State U., 1979—; adj. faculty Ursuline Coll., Pepper Pike, Ohio, 1990, Notre Dame Coll., South Euclid, Ohio, 1994; lectr. John Carroll U., University Heights, Ohio, 1987; field reader dept. edn., Washington, 1992—; textbook reviewer Houghton Mifflin Co., Wadsworth Pub. Co., 1982—; seminar leader Adult Gt. Books Found., Chgo., 1990-91; ednl. cons. Ivy Tech. State Coll., Muncie, Ind. Editor GARDN Newsletter. Sec. N.E. Ohio coun. NAIC, Cleve., 1993—; pres. Earn and Learn Investment Club, Highland Heights, 1993—; rschr. Rags to Riches Investment Club, Highland Heights, 1993—; mem. Greater Cleve. PC Users Group, 1994—; leader Beginners Telecomms. Spl. Interest Group. Mem. ASCD, Internat. Reading Assn. (pres. Ohio coll. coun. 1987), Coll. Reading Assn., Pi Lambda Theta (pres. Cleve. area chpt. 1988-90, nat. rsch. awards chair 1990-91, Exemplary Projects grantee 1989), Phi Delta Kappa (historian Cuyahoga Valley chpt. 1992-93, rsch. grantee, 1992). Home: 6339 Ashdale Rd Mayfield Hts OH 44124-4101 Office: Cleve State U E 24th and Euclid Ave Cleveland OH 44115

COHEN, SYLVIA ANN, artist; b. Bronx, N.Y., Aug. 22, 1936; d. Saul and Catherine (Palokas) Shanfield; m. Marvin Miles Cohen, June 2, 1957; children: Jay Gordon, Alan Seth, Eric Louis. BA, St. Thomas Aquinas Coll., 1976; MA, William Paterson Coll., 1982. Cert. tchr. k-12, N.Y. Solo shows include The Gallery Valley Cottage (N.Y.) Libr., Finklestein Meml. Libr., Spring Valley, N.Y., Piermont Fine Arts Gallery, Piermont, N.Y.; group shows include Mcpl. Gallery, Athens, Greece, Saddle River Valley Cultural Ctr., N.J., Rockland C.C., Broome Street Gallery. Mem. Nat. Assn. Women Artists (Gladys B. Blum Meml. award 1994), Nat. Mus. women in the Arts, Assn. Craftsmen and Artists (1st place for painting 1990), Piermont Fine Arts Gallery, Ringwood Manor Arts Assn.

COHN, CHERI WILSEY, crime analyst; b. Chgo.; d. Allen Gerald and Emily J. (Schwab) Wilsey; m. Jeffrey S. Cohn, Oct. 28, 1979; children: Meryl, Seth. BS, So. Ill. U.; MPA, U. Colo., Denver, 1991. Crime analyst Jefferson County Sheriff's Dept., Golden, Colo., 1992—. Bd. dirs. Jefferson Ctr. for Mental Health, Arvada, Colo., 1986—. Mem. ASPA, Internat. Crime Analysts Assn., Colo. Crime Analysts Assn. Jewish. Office: Jefferson County Sheriffs Dept 200 Jefferson County Pkwy Golden CO 80401

COHN, JANE SHAPIRO, public relations executive; b. N.Y.C., May 19, 1935; d. Harry I. and Ann (Safanie) Shapiro; m. Albert M. Cohn, June 30, 1957 (div. 1972); children: Theodore David, William Alan. BA, Brandeis U., 1956; postgrad., Coll. of New Rochelle, 1974-76. Dir. pub. rels. Hudson River Mus., Yonkers, N.Y., 1976-79; account exec. Dudley-Anderson Yutzy Pub. Rels. Agy. subs. Ogilvy Mather, N.Y.C., 1979-81; dir. communications Haines Lundberg Wachler, N.Y.C., 1981-91; prin. Jane Cohn Pub. Rels., Sherman, Conn., 1991—; cons. Inst. Contemporary Art, Phila., 1983; speaker, mktg. promotion strategies conf., 1989. Contbr. articles to profl. jours., chpts. to books. Fellow Soc. Mktg. Profl. Svcs. (bd. dirs. N.Y. chpt. 1988-89, 92-95, spkr. 1994 annual convention, Gold Medal award 1994); mem. AIA (assoc. 1988, speaker annual conv.), Am. Mktg. Assn. (panelist ann. conv. 1987, moderator profl. services sect. ann. conv. 1988, exec. mem.), Practice Mgmt. Assn. (spkr. promotion strategies conf. 1989). Democrat. Jewish. Office: Jane Cohn Pub Rels 31 Spring Lake Rd Sherman CT 06784-1201

COHN, JOAN KIRSCHENBAUM, mental health services professional; b. New Rochelle, N.Y., Sept. 28, 1943; d. David and Beatrice (Edelmann) Kirschenbaum; m. Peter Frank Cohn, Mar. 28, 1968; children: Alan Douglas, Clifford David. BA, Tufts U., 1965; MA, Columbia U., 1969; MSW, Boston U., 1975; D Social Work, Adelphi U., 1986; postgrad., Framingham Youth Guidance Ctr., Framingham, Mass., 1973-74, Judge Baker Guidance Ctr., Harvard Med. Sch., 1974-75, Pederson-Krag Clinic, Huntington, N.Y., 1983-84. Lic. psychotherapist, N.Y., Mass. Rsch. asst. Governor's Com. Law Enforcement Adminstrn. Justice, Boston, 1969; guidance counselor U. Mass., Boston, 1970-71; staff supervising social worker Judge Baker Guidance Ctr., Harvard Med. Sch., Boston, 1975-78; pvt. practice Huntington, N.Y., 1977—; staff supervising social worker

Boston Hosp for Women, Harvard Med. Sch., Boston, 1978-79; clinical instr. medicine, pediatrics SUNY, Stony Brook, 1982-95; supr., instr. L.I. Inst. Psychoanalysis, East Meadow, N.Y., 1992-95; asst. prof., medicine, cmty. medicine Mt. Sinai Sch. Med., N.Y.C., 1995—; cons., lectr. Children's Garden/Upper Story, Cambridge Sch. Weston, Mass., 1974-78; cons. Fisher Jr. Coll., Family Svc. Assn. Boston, 1980-81; lectr. various orgns. Author: (with Peter Frank Cohn) Heart Talk: Preventing and Coping With Silent and Painful Heart Disease, 1988, Fighting the Silent Killer, 1993; contbr. articles to profl. jours.; appeared on numerous TV shows including Dr. Ruth. Mem. Alumni Coun. Suffolk County, Tufts U., 1983-93. Mem. NASW, Am. Bd. Examiners Clin. Social Work, Soc. Clin. Social Work Psychotherapists. Office: 23 Green St Ste 103 Huntington NY 11743

COHN, MARIANNE WINTER MILLER, civic activist; b. Denver, Jan. 15, 1928; d. Henry Abraham II and Esther (Sheflan) Winter; m. Benjamin K. Miller, Dec. 29, 1948 (dec. Dec. 1972); children: Judy Ellen, Philip Henry; m. Isidore Cohn Jr., Jan. 3, 1976; children: Ian Jeffrey, Lauren Kerry. Student, Colo. U., 1946-47. Mem. exec. bd. Greater New Orleans Tourist and Conv. Commn., 1985; chmn. spouse program arrangements Am. Coll. Surgeons, La., 1985; mem. exec. bd. NCCJ, New Orleans, 1987—, sec., 1991-92, treas., 1993-94, nat. bd. dirs., 1993; bd. dirs. Jewish Endowment Found., New Orleans, 1987-88; mem. Arts Coun. of New Orleans, 1988—, v.p. devel. 1991-92, v.p. grants, exec. bd., 1995; pres. La. Mus. Found. of La. State Mus., 1989-90, bd. dirs., 1994—; mem. Sisterhood of Temple Emanuel Denver (pres. 1957-60); women's bd. dirs. Nat. Jewish Hosp. at Denver, 1951-80, pres. women's div., 1960-61, mem., sec. gov. bd., 1972-76; bd. dirs. New Orleans Symphony Aux., 1980; mem. nat. bd. Nat. Jewish Ctr., 1976—; chmn. Odyssey Ball of New Orleans Mus. Art, 1992; bd. dirs. La. Coun. for Music and Performing Arts, 1991-92; mem. exec. bd. New Orleans Arts Coun., 1991-92, 95—; mem. governing bd. La. State Mus., 1992—; exec. bd. Arts Coun. 95' V.P. Grants, 1995. Recipient Woman of Fashion award Men of Fashion, 1989. Republican.

COHN, MARJORIE BENEDICT, curator, art historian, educator; b. N.Y.C., Jan. 10, 1939; d. Manson and Marjorie (Allen) Benedict; m. Martin Cohn, Dec. 19, 1960. BA, Mt. Holyoke Coll., 1960; AM, Radcliffe Coll., 1961; DFA, Mt. Holyoke Coll., 1996. Conservator works of art on paper Art Mus. Harvard U., Cambridge, Mass., 1963-89, lectr. fine arts, 1974-77, sr. lectr., 1977—, print curator, 1989—, acting dir., 1990-91; vis. lectr. Boston U., 1972, 73, Wellesley (Mass.) Coll., 1973; vis. asst. prof. Brown U., Providence, 1975. Author: Wash & Gouache, 1977, A Noble Collection: The Spencer Albums of Old Master Prints, 1992, (with S.L. Siegfried) Works by J.A.D. Ingres in Collection of the Fogg Art Museum, 1980, Francis Calley Gray and Art Collecting for America, 1986. Sec. Arlington (Mass.) Hist. Commn., 1972-85. Mem. Am. Acad. Arts and Scis., Print Coun. Am. Democrat. Office: Harvard U Fogg Art Mus 32 Quincy St Cambridge MA 02138-3845

COHN, MILDRED, biochemist, educator; b. N.Y.C., July 12, 1913; d. Isidore M. and Bertha (Klein) Cohn; m. Henry Primakoff, May 31, 1938; children: Nina, Paul, Laura. BA, Hunter Coll., 1931, ScD (hon.), 1984; MA, Columbia U., 1932, PhD, 1938; ScD (hon.), Women's Med. Coll., 1966, Radcliffe Coll., 1978, Washington U., St. Louis, 1981, Brandeis U., 1984; Hunter Coll., 1984; ScD (hon.), U. Pa., Phila., 1984, U. N.C., 1985; PhD (hon.), Weizmann Inst. Sci., Israel, 1988; ScD (hon.), U. Miami, 1990. Rsch. asst. biochemistry George Washington U. Sch. Medicine, 1937-38; rsch. assoc. Cornell U., 1938-46; rsch. assoc. Washington U., 1946-58, assoc. prof. biol. chemistry, 1958-60; assoc. prof. biophysics and phys. biochemistry U. Pa. Med. Sch., 1960-61, prof., 1961-68, prof. biochemistry and biophysics, 1971-82; emerita, 1982—; Benjamin Rush prof. physiol. chemistry U. Pa. Med. Sch., 1978-82; sr. mem. Inst. Cancer Research, Phila., 1982-85; vis. prof. biol. chemistry Johns Hopkins U. Med. Sch., 1985-91; research assoc. Harvard U. Med. Sch., 1950-51; established investigator Am. Heart Assn., 1953-59, career investigator, 1964-78. Editorial bd. jour. Biol. Chemistry, 1958-63, 67-72. Recipient Hall of Fame award Hunter Coll., 1973, Disting. Alumni award, 1975, Cresson medal Franklin Inst., 1975, award Internat. Assn. Women Biochemists, 1979, Nat. Medal Sci., 1982, Chandler medal Columbia U., 1986, Disting. Svc. award Coll. Physicians, 1987, Women in Sci. award N.Y. Acad. Sci., 1992, Gov.'s award for excellence in sci., Pa., 1993, Founders medal Magnetic Resonance in Biology, 1994. Mem. NAS, Am. Philos. Soc. (v.p. 1994—), Am. Chem. Soc. (Garvan medal 1963, Remsen award Md. sect. 1988, chmn. divsn. of biological chem. 1975-76), Harvey Soc., Am. Soc. Biol. Chemists (pres. 1978-79), Am. Biophys. Soc., Am. Acad. Arts and Scis., Phi Beta Kappa, Sigma Xi, Iota Sigma Pi (hon. nat. mem. 1988). Office: U Pa Med Sch Dept Biochemistry & Biophys Philadelphia PA 19104-6089

COHN, ROBIN ALYSE, elementary education educator; b. Bklyn., July 23, 1971; d. Melvin Paul and Ellen (Cohen) C. BS, Long Island U., 1993. Tchr. grades 5 and 6 Wm. F. Halloran Sch. # 22, Elizabeth, N.J., 1993-94; tchr. grade 1 Abraham Lincoln Sch. #14, Elizabeth, 1994—. Mem. ASCD, Nat. Coun. Tchrs. of English, Internat. Reading Assn., Elizabeth Edn. Assn.

COIN, SHEILA REGAN, management consultant; b. Columbus, Ohio, Feb. 17, 1942; d. James Daniel and Jean (Hodgson) Cook; m. Tasso H. Coin, Sept. 17, 1967 (div.); children: Tasso, Alison Regan. BS, U. Iowa, 1964. RN Staff nurse VA Hosp., Boston, 1964-66; field rep. ARC, Chgo., 1966-67, adminstr., 1967; asst. div. dir. Am. Hosp. Assn., sec. Am. Soc. Hosp. Dirs. Nursing, Chgo., 1967-69; owner Coin & Assocs., Chgo., 1975-77; ptnr. Coin, Newell & Assocs., Chgo., 1977—; instr. dept. continuing edn. Loyola U., Chgo., 1975-77, Rock Valley Coll. Mgmt. Inst., Rockford, Ill., 1978-80, Ill. Central Coll. Inst. Personal and Profl. Devel., Peoria, 1979-85, Triton Coll. Continuing Edn., River Grove, Ill., 1983-86, No. Ill. U. Continuing Edn., DeKalb, 1983-86; mem. editorial bd. Tng. Today mag., 1992-94, assoc. editor, 1994—. Vol. Art Inst., Chgo., 1968-69; mem. Chgo. Beautiful Com., 1968-73; chmn. Mayor Daley's Chgo. Beautiful Awards Project, 1972; mem. jr. bd. Girl Scouts Assn., Chgo., 1975-76; mem. jr. governing bd. Chgo. Symphony Orch., 1971-81, pres., 1977-78; governing mem. Orchestral Assn., Chgo., 1977-81; bd. dirs. Mid-Am. chpt. ARC, Chgo., 1979-81, 91-94, vice chmn. 1986-89, mem. planning & evaluation subcom., 1991—, chmn. quality mgmt. steering com., 1992-94, bd. dirs. Chgo. dist., 1981-89, chmn. fin. devel. com., 1982-85, vice chmn. dist. bd., 1986-89; bd. dirs. Ill. chpt. Lupus Found. Am., 1991-93; bd. dirs., mem. Survive Alive House Found., 1989—; dir. Com. for Thalossemia Chgo. Bd., 1981-82; mem. Women's bd. Nat. Com. Prevention Child Abuse, Chgo., 1981-82; mem. State of Ill. Disabled Persons Adv. Coun. , 1988—; academic specialist in mgmt. devel. U.S. Info. Agy., 1994. Mem. ASTD (exec. com. of mgmt. devel. profl. practice area 1992-95), Ill. Tng. and Devel. Assn., Organizational Devel. Network Chgo. Democrat. Roman Catholic. Office: Coin Newell & Assocs 919 N Michigan Ave Chicago IL 60611-1601

COKER, GURNELLE SHEELY, retired secondary education educator; b. Ballentine, S.C., Nov. 17, 1915; d. George Johnston and Vennie Blanche (Amick) S.; m. Theron Hemingway Coker, Sr., Apr. 10, 1938; 1 child, Theron Hemingway Jr. BA, Winthrop Coll., 1936; M Edn., U. S.C., 1953. Cert. tchr., S.C. Tchr. 5th grade Hebron Consolidated Sch., Cades, S.C., 1936-38; elem. prin. Lexington County, Gilbert, S.C., 1938-41; jr. stock tracer 21st Sub Depot, Columbia (S.C.) Army Air Base, 1942-43; med. technician Station Hosp. Lab., Ft. Jackson, S.C., 1944-46; English tchr. Chapin (S.C.) High Sch., 1948-55; English tchr. Brookland-Cayce High Sch., West Columbia, S.C., 1955-69, English tchr., counselor, 1958-69, dir. guidance, 1969-81, ret., 1981. Sec. Earlwood Little Boys Baseball League, Columbia, 1954-55; mem. Lexington (S.C.) County Mental Health, 1970-75; active fund dr. Am. Heart Assn., Columbia, 1975—. Recipient Life Svc. award Ascension Luth. Ch. Women, 1955, Our Saviour Luth. Ch. Women of Evang. Luth. Ch. Am., 1990; appreciation So. Interscholastic Press Assn., 1964, Meritorious Svc. award Brookland-Cayce Sch. Bd. Trustees, 1981; Spl. Study scholar Lexington Sch. Dist. II, 1959; named Tchr. Yr. Lexington County Dist. II, 1968. Mem. Lexington County Ret. Educators Assn. (pres. 1985-87), S.C. Ret. Educators Assn. (coun. dels. 1981-96, sec. 1989-90), Gen. Fedn. Womens Clubs Sc.C. (v.p. West Columbia 1992-94, pres. 1994-96, Best Creative Writing award 1995-96, 1st pl. essay, 1995-96, cert. award for Outstanding Accomplishment in Legacy Writing Contest), U. S.C. Alumni Assn., S.C. ClassroomTchr. Assn. (pres. 1964-66), Alpha Delta Kappa (chpt. pres. 1984-86), Delta Kappa Gamma (contbr. articles and editorials to Alpha Eta state digest 1966-71, pres. chpt. 1994-96, Svc. award 1971, 2d v.p. Alpha Eta state S.C. 1987-89, Internat. Svc. award 1989), Order Eastern Star (worthy matron Earlwood chpt. 1959-60). Republican. Lutheran. Home: 1440 Cardinal Dr West Columbia SC 29169-6016

COKER, LYNDA, state legislator; b. Oct. 2, 1946; m. Gene V. Coker; 2 children. BS, Fla. State U., 1969; MEd, Ga. State U., 1982. Exec. asst. Cobb County Sheriff; mem. Ga. Ho. Reps., 1990-92, 1993—, mem. agrl. and consumer affairs com., mem. game, fish and parks com., mem. pub. safety com., mem. indsl. rels. com. Mem. Ga. Sheridd's Assn., Legal Sec. Assn., Civitan. Republican. Home: 4560 Ponte Vedra Dr Marietta GA 30067-4636 Office: Ga House of Reps 18 Capitol Sq Ste 611 LOB Atlanta GA 30334*

COKER, MELINDA LOUISE, counselor; b. Springfield, Mo., Apr. 28, 1946; d. Joe H. and Margaret L. (Owens) Bull; m. Richard H. Coker, Aug. 12, 1967; children: Shay, Candace, Logan. BA, Baylor U., 1968; MS, East Tex. State U., 1994. Nat. cert. counselor Nat. Bd. Counselor Cert.; lic. profl. counselor, Tex. Tchr. Houston Ind. Sch. Dist., 1968-71; owner, mgr. Greenleaves, Tyler, Tex., 1978-84; realtor Coldwell Banker, Tyler, 1989-91; counselor intern Hunt County Mental Health Mental Retardation, Greenville, Tex., 1993, Andrews Ctr., Tyler, 1994; career counselor intern Tyler (Tex.) Jr. Coll., 1994-95, spl. populations counselor, 1995—. Mem. ACA, Nat. Career Devel. Assn., Chi Sigma Iota. Home: 6701 La Costa Dr Tyler TX 75703

COLACECCHI, MARY BETH, editor; b. Corning, N.Y., Aug. 15, 1961; d. Joseph John and Mary Louise (Alotto) C.; m. James Stuart Hamilton, Oct. 8, 1988. AB, Cornell U., 1983. Freelance writer-editor daily newspapers and mags., newsletters and wire svc. East Coast area, 1984-96; writer World Wide Website, 1996; copy desk paginator News-Jour., Daytona Beach, Fla., 1984; reporter Press and Sun-Bull., Binghamton, N.Y., 1984-86; copy editor So. Conn. Newspapers, Greenwich, Stamford, 1986-89; asst. metro editor for layout Gannett Westchester Newspapers, White Plains, N.Y., 1989; assoc. editor Catalog Age Mag. div. Cowles Bus. Media, Stamford, 1990-94; freelance website writer, 1996. Freelance writer St. Petersburg (Fla.) Times, 1984, Daytona Beach (Fla.) News-Jour., 1984, Greenwich (Conn.) Time, 1986-89; freelance editor Stamford (Conn.) Advocate, 1990. Mem. Emmaus Comty., Stamford, 1986—; soup kitchen coord. New Covenant House, Stamford, 1993-96. Fellow Poynter Inst. for Media Studies, 1984, ethics fellow, 1988. Mem. Investigative Reporters and Editors, Nat. Fedn. Press Women, Editl. Freelancers Assn., Women in Comms. (bd. dirs. 1996—, v.p. job bank 1996—), Conn. Press Club (bd. dirs. 1993—, newsletter editor 1993-96, hospitality chair 1996—, Comm. Excellence award 1991-96).

COLAMARINO, KATRIN BELENKY, lawyer; b. N.Y.C., Apr. 29, 1951; d. Allen Abram and Selma (Burwasser) Belenky Lang; m. Leonard J. Colamarino, Mar. 20, 1982; m. Barry E. Brenner, June 1, 1974 (div. June 1979); 1 child, Rachel Erin. BA, Vassar Coll., 1972; JD, U. Richmond, 1976. Bar: Ohio 1976, U.S. Ct. Apls. (Fed. cir.), 1982. Staff atty. AM Internat. Inc., Cleve., 1976-78; atty. Lipkowitz & Plaut, N.Y.C., 1980-81; atty. Docutel Olivetti Corp., Tarrytown, N.Y., 1981-84; atty. NYNEX Bus. Info. Systems, White Plains, N.Y., 1984-85; corp. counsel, sec. Logica Data Architects, Inc., N.Y.C., 1986-90; corp. counsel SEER Technologies, Inc., N.Y.C., 1990-91; v.p. chief tech. counsel global relationship bank Citibank N.A., N.Y.C., 1991—. Class agt. Fieldston Sch., N.Y.C., 1980—, exec. bd. Ethical Fieldston Alumni Assn., 1980-90, 92-95, v.p. 1987-90; alumnae coun. rep. Vassar Coll., 1982-86, class corr. Vassar Quar., 1992—. Mem. ABA, Computer Law Assn. Office: Citibank NA 909 3rd Ave # 29/2 New York NY 10022-4731

COLANDUONI, BERNADETTE LOUISE, school nurse; b. Somerville, N.J., Dec. 3, 1942; d. Woodrow Wilson and Anna Elizabeth (Poltorak) Connelly; m. Donald John Colanduoni, May 15, 1965; children: Bernadette Marie Colanduoni-Danner, Donald John. RN, St. Francis Sch. Nursing, Trenton, N.J., 1963; BA, Jersey City State, 1976; MEd, Trenton State U., 1984. Cert. sch. nurse and tchr., N.J. Staff nurse Muhlenberg Hosp., Plainfield, N.J., 1963-65; occupl. nurse Art Color Printing Co., Dunellen, N.J., 1965-69; sch. nurse Middlesex (N.J.) Bd. Edn., 1971—; liaison Middlesex Borough Bd. Health, 1995—. Life mem. Bound Brook chpt. Deborah Heart and Lung Hosp.; mem. Middlesex Borough Bd. of Health Commn., 1995—. Recipient Meritorious award Deborah Heart and Lung Hosp., 1969, Gov. Tchr. Recognition award State of N.J., 1991. Mem. NEA, N.J. Edn. Assn., Middlesex Edn. Assn. (mem. negotiating team 1989—, liaison to Middlesex Borough Drug Alliance 1991—), Nat. Assn. Sch. Nurses, N.J. State Sch. Nurses, Middlesex County Sch. Nurses (rec. sec. 1980-84),. Home: 223 Woodland Ave Middlesex NJ 08846-1911 Office: Von E Mauger Mid Sch Fisher Ave Middlesex NJ 08846

COLANGELO, JAYNE ANNE PARKER, accountant, auditor; b. Glens Falls, N.Y., July 27, 1953; d. Harley Cyrus and Cecilia Loretta (Del Signore) Parker; m. Nicholas J. Colangelo, Aug. 23, 1980. AA in Liberal Arts, Adirondack C.C., 1973; BBA in Acctg., Siena Coll., 1984; postgrad., N.Y. State U., Albany, 1995—. Cert. fraud examiner; cert. govt. fin. mgr. Exec. sec. to dean Rensselaer Poly. Inst., Troy, N.Y., 1975-77; jr. programmer County of Warren, Lake George, N.Y., 1978-79; computer programmer/sys. analyst Glens Falls (N.Y.) Hosp., 1979-82; owner Letter Perfect, Saratoga Springs, N.Y., 1983-84; acct. Urbach, Kahn & Werlin, CPAs, Albany, N.Y., 1984-87; contr. The Carl Co. Dept. Stores, Schenectady, N.Y., 1987-89; assoc. auditor N.Y. State Dept. Environ. Conservation, Albany, 1990—; task force advisor on internal controls N.Y. State Dept. Environ. Conservation, Albany, 1996, mem. task force on sporting lic. Bd. dirs. Friends of Saratoga Springs (N.Y.) Pub. Libr., 1991—. Mem. Assn. Cert. Fraud Examiners, Assn. Govt. Accts., Inst. Mgmt. Accts., Albany Area chpt. Cert. Fraud Examiners (sec. to bd. 1996). Home: 156 Ballston Ave Saratoga Springs NY 12866

COLBENSON, MARY ELIZABETH DREISBACH, manufacturing engineer; b. New Haven, Nov. 27, 1966; d. Raymond Allen and Dorothy Louise (Seal) Dreisbach; m. Paul Carroll Colbenson, Sept. 7, 1991. BS in Mech. Engring./Materials Sci., U. Conn., 1989; MS in Materials Engring., Rensselaer Poly. Inst., 1995. Registered engr.-in-tng., Conn. Mfg. engr. United Technologies Corp., Pratt & Whitney, East Hartford, Conn., 1988-93; sr. mfg. engr. Haydon Switch and Instrument Inc., Waterbury, Conn., 1993—. Mem. Am. Soc. Materials, Materials Rsch. Soc., Soc. Mfg. Engrs. (cert. mfg. engr.). Home: 492 Prospect St Willimantic CT 06226 Office: Haydon Switch & Instrument 1500 Meriden Rd Waterbury CT 06705

COLBURN, JULIA KATHERINE LEE, volunteer, educator; b. Columbus, Ohio, Feb. 8, 1927; d. Fred Merritt and Lillian May (Getrost) Lee; m. Joseph Linn Colburn, Sept. 5, 1947; children: Joseph Linn, Jr., David Laird, Andrew Lee, Julia LeeAnne. BS in Edn., Ohio State U., 1948. Substitute tchr. Columbus Pub. Schs., 1965-69, 79-81, vol. resource person, 1979—. Author: The Six Who Signed, Christmas at Valley Forge; editor, compiler (state pub.) Ohio Daughters of 1812, Star and Anchor, 1983-85 (nat. first award, 1984, 85). Presiding judge Franklin County Bd. Elections, Columbus, 1959—; pres. Linden Jr. Civic Club, Columbus, 1953, Rhapsody Unit, Columbus Symphony, 1975-77, Arlington Park PTA, Columbus, 1963-64, Linden-McKinley Jr.-Sr. High PTA, Columbus, 1964-66, Northland High PTA, Columbus, 1972-73; organizing pres. Lazarus Cancer Ray, Columbus, 1953; leader Northland coun. Girl Scouts U.S., 1968-70; vol. Vision Ctr., Columbus, 1969-72 (Named Vol. of Yr. 1971); v.p. Linden United Meth. Women, Columbus, 1965-66, pres. 1966-68, 96—, various coms. 1963—; pres. Meth. Youth Fellowship, Columbus, 1944-45; adminstrv. bd. Linden United Meth. Ch., Columbus, 1944-45, 52—, spl. membership awards 1971, 77; dist. chmn. Christian Global Concerns Columbus North Dist. United Meth. Women, 1973-77. Recipient Silver Good Citizenship medal Ohio Soc. SAR, 1978, Medal of Appreciation, Benjamin Franklin chpt. SAR, 1978, Martha Washington meda. Ohio SAR, 1989. Mem. Ohio Geneal. Soc. (spkrs. staff 1978—), First Families of Ohio, DAR (Good Citizenship cert. 1945, state rec. sec. 1983-86, state vice regent 1986-89, state regent 1989-92, v.p. gen. 1992-95, nat. vice chmn. Valley Forge belltower restoration 1995—, various offices and coms. 1976—), NSDAR (spkrs. staff 1983—, chaplain v.p. club 1993-94, parliamentarian nat. vice chmn. club 1994—, v.p. gen. club), Children of Am. Revolution (sr. pres. state 1976-78, sr. nat. rec. sec. 1982-84, various coms. 1974—, Ohio Svc. award 1979, maj. benefactor 1986, nat. vice chmn. 1980-83), U.S. Daus. of 1812 (parliamentarian, chmn. nat. membership 1985-88, state pres. 1983-85, treas. Nat. Hdqrs. Endowment Trust Fund 1988-91, pres. Assn. of State Pres. 1991-93), Colonial Dames of Am., Dames of the Ct. of Honor, Colonial Dames XVII Century (state first v.p. 1985-87, 95—), Daus. Colonial Wars (state historian 1984-86, nat. vice chmn. 1989-92, state custodian 1992—, state 2d v.p. 1995—), Women Desc. Ancient and Honorable Arty. Co. (state rec. sec. 1983-86, state pres. 1986-89, nat. parliamentarian 1989-92, chaplain nat. 1992-95, nat. organizing sec. 1995—), Daus. Am. Colonists (Old Trails chpt. treas. 1981-85, vice regent 1985-87, regent 1987-89), New Eng. Women (pres. Columbus colony 1984-87, nat. chmn. 1987-95), Colonial Daus. Seventeenth Century, Daus. Union Vets., Zeta Phi Eta. Republican. Club: Ohio Fedn. Women's (trustee, chmn. 1974-83), Noreast Women's (v.p. 1994-96). Lodges: Order of Eastern Star (star point 1961-62), Linden Lawanis (Kiwanis Aux. pres. 1964). Avocations: genealogy; music; writing. Home: 1887 Northcliff Dr Columbus OH 43229-5332

COLBURN, KATHLEEN ANN, hospice consultant, administrator, psychologist; b. Clinton, Mass., Sept. 23, 1950; d. Clinton Franklin and Kathryn (Melanson) C. BA in English Lit., U. Mass., 1973; MA in Psychology, Drake U., 1976. Supr. of psychol. svcs. Polk County Juvenile Home, Des Moines, 1977-79; clin. dir. Survival, Inc., Quincy, Mass., 1979-80; dir. resident svcs. Broadlawns Med. Ctr., Des Moines, 1980-81; legis. analyst Legis. Fiscal Bur., Des Moines, 1981-84; chief of adminstrn. Iowa Dept. of Substance Abuse, Des Moines, 1984-86; exec. dir. Hospice of Ctrl. Iowa, Des Moines, 1986-95; dir. hospice programs Arthur Clark Home Care Svcs., North Kansas City, Mo., 1995—; bd. dirs. AIDS of Greater Des Moines, 1991-94, sec. bd., 1993-94; keynote spkr. 1st East/West Internat. Hospice Conf., Tianjin, China, 1992. Contbr. articles to profl. jours. Vol. Bernie Lorenz Recovery House, Des Moines, 1986-87, Sherman Hill Neighborhood Assn., Des Moines, 1989—; vol. mental health adv. coun. Broadlawns Med. Ctr., Des Moines, 1991-92; vol. spkr. United Way of Ctrl. Iowa, Des Moines, 1987-95. Grantee Iowa Pharmacy Assn., 1989, Aetna Ins. Co., 1991, Kresge Found., 1992, Mid-Iowa Health Found., 1993. Mem. Nat. Assn. Home Care (bd. dirs. Washington chpt. 1991-95, Spl. Contbn. to Hospice Field award 1993), Hospice Assn. Am. (bd. dirs. Washington chpt. 1990-95, chmn. bd. dirs. 1991-95), Greater Des Moines Rotary. Office: Arthur Clark Home Care Svcs 2700 Rock Creek Pkwy Kansas City MO 64117

COLBY, BARBARA DIANE, interior designer, consultant; b. Chgo., Dec. 6, 1932; d. Raymond R. and Mertyl Shirley (Jackson) C.; 1 son, Lawrence James. Student Wright Jr. Coll., 1950, Art Inst. Chgo., UCLA. Owner, F.L.S., Los Angeles, 1971-77; ptnr. Ambiance Inc., Los Angeles, 1976-77; owner Barbara Colby, Ltd., Los Angeles, 1977-81; bus. adminstr. Internat. Soc. Interior Designers, Los Angeles, 1982—; owner Chromanetics, Glendale, Calif., 1981—; instr. Otis/Parsons Sch. Design, Los Angeles Fashion Inst. Design and Merchandising; dir. color Calif. Coll. Interior Design, Costa Mesa, Calif., 1987; also lectr. in field. Author: Color and Light Influences and Impact, 1990; contbg. editor Giftware News. Instr. L.A. County Regional Occupation Program, 1990-94; tng. cons. United Edn. Inst., 1994—. Recipient award for Best Children's Room, Chgo. Furniture Show, 1969, award Calif. Design Show '76, 1976. Mem. Am. Soc. Interior Designers (cert.), Color Mktg. Group of U.S. Author: Color and Light: Influences and Impact, 1990; contbr. articles to profl. jours. Office: Colby Handcrafted Miniatures 245 W Loraine St Apt 309 Glendale CA 91202-1849

COLBY, JOY HAKANSON, art critic; b. Detroit; d. Alva Hilliard and Eleanor (Radtke) Hakanson; m. Raymond L. Colby, Apr. 11, 1953; children: Sarah, Katherine, Lisa. Student, Detroit Soc. Arts and Crafts, 1945; B.F.A., Wayne State U., 1946. Art critic Detroit News, 1947—; originator exhibit Arts and Crafts in Detroit, 1906-1976; at Detroit Inst. Arts, 1976; Mem. visual arts adv. panel Mich. Council for Arts, 1974-79; mayor's appointment Detroit Council for Arts, 1974; mem. Bloomfield Hills Arts Council, 1974. Author: Art and A City, 1956, lead essay in Arts and Crafts in Detroit catalog, 1976; Contbr. articles to art periodicals. Recipient Alumni award Wayne State U., 1967, Art Achievement award, 1983, Headliner award, 1984, award for arts reporting Detroit Press Club, 1984, Art Leadership award Ctr. for Creative Studies, 1989. Office: 615 W Lafayette Blvd Detroit MI 48226-3124

COLBY, KAREN LYNN See WEINER, KAREN COLBY

COLBY, LESTINA LARSEN, secondary education educator; b. Mt. Sterling, Ky., Apr. 19, 1937; d. Harold L. and Opal Kearney (Caudel) Larsen; m. Bruce Redfearn Colby, Dec. 28, 1962; children: Charles, Harold, Pamela. BS, U. Chgo., 1958, postgrad., 1958-62. Sci. tchr., debate coach Community High Sch., Midlothian, Ill., 1958-61; biology tchr., debate coach U. Chgo. Lab. Sch., 1961-66; sci. tchr. Springer Jr. High Sch., Wilmington, Del., 1977; biology and math. tchr. McKean High Sch., Wilmington, 1978; biology tchr., debate coach, student coun. advisor U. Liggett Sch., Grosse Pointe, Mich., 1979-93, Edsel B. Ford endowed sci. chair, 1990; biology tchr., chmn. sci. dept. Episcopal High Sch., Jacksonville, Fla., 1993—. Author: Teacher's Manual for Encyclopaedia Britannica's Evolution Unit, 1966, Plants and Animals, 1968. Mem. Nat. Assn. Biology Tchrs. (Mich. Outstanding Biology Tchr. 1990), Nat. Sci. Tchrs. Assn., Fla. Assn. Sci. Tchrs. Baptist. Office: Episcopal HS Jacksonville 4455 Atlantic Blvd Jacksonville FL 32207-2121

COLBY, MARVELLE SEITMAN, business management educator, administrator; b. N.Y.C., Oct. 31, 1932; d. Charles Edward and Lily (Zimmerman) Seitman; m. Robert S. Colby, Apr. 11, 1954 (div. Apr. 1979); children: Lisa, Eric; m. Selig J. Alkon, Dec. 6, 1986. BA, Hunter Coll., 1954; MA, U. N.Colo., 1973; PhD in Pub. Adminstrn., Nova U., 1977; cert., Harvard Grad. Sch. Bus., 1979. V.p. SE Region URC Mgmt. Services Corp., Washington, 1972-77; dir. devel. Hunter Coll. Woman's Ctr. Community Leadership, N.Y.C., 1977-78; dir. tng. and career devel. Girl Scouts U.S., N.Y.C., 1978-79; dir. Overseas Tour Ops. Am. Jewish Congress, N.Y.C., 1979-81; chief exec. officer Girl Scout Council Greater N.Y.C., 1981-82; prof. bus. mgmt. Marymount Manhattan Coll., N.Y.C., 1982—, chmn. bus. mgmt. and acctg. div., 1982-89, 93—; adj. prof. NYU, 1986-92; mem. exec. com. Assn. Recreation Mgmt., N.Y.C., 1982; cons. Rockport Mgmt., Washington, 1974-78. Author: Test Your Management IQ, 1984; co-author: Lovejoy's Four Year College Guide for the Learning Disabled, 1985, Introduction to Business, 1991; contbr. articles to profl. jours. Chmn. Met. Dade County Commn. Status Women, Miami, 1975-77; chief planner Met. Dade County U.S. SBA 1st annual conf. Future Women Bus., 1977. Named to Hunter Coll. Hall of Fame, 1986. Mem. Acad. Mgmt., Hunter Coll. Alumni Assn. (bd. dirs. 1978-79), Phi Delta Kappa. Club: Lotos (mem. literary com. 1983-89). Home: 242 E 72nd St New York NY 10021-4574 Office: Marymount Manhattan Coll 221 E 71st St New York NY 10021-4501

COLBY-HALL, ALICE MARY, Romance studies educator; b. Portland, Maine, Feb. 25, 1932; d. Frederick Eugene and Angie Fraser (Drown) C.; m. Robert A. Hall, Jr., May 8, 1976; stepchildren: Philip, Diana Hall Goodall, Carol Hall Erickson. B.A., Colby Coll., 1953; M.A., Middlebury Coll., 1954; Ph.D., Columbia U., 1962. Tchr. French, Latin Orono (Maine) High Sch., 1954-55; tchr. French Gould Acad., Bethel, Maine, 1955-57; lectr. French Columbia U., 1959-60; instr. Romance lit. Cornell U., Ithaca, N.Y., 1962-63, asst. prof., 1963-66, assoc. prof., 1966-75, prof. Romance studies, 1975—, chmn. Romance studies, 1990-96. Author: The Portrait in Twelfth Century French Literature: An Example of the Stylistic Originality of Chrétien de Troyes, 1965; mem. editorial bd.: Speculum, 1976-79, Olifant, 1974—. Fulbright grantee, 1953-54; NEH fellow, 1984-85; recipient Médaille des Amis d'Orange, 1985. Mem. Modern Lang. Assn., Medieval Acad. Am. (councillor 1983-86), Internat. Arthurian Soc., Société Rencesvals, Académie de Vaucluse, Phi Beta Kappa. Republican. Congregationalist. Home: 308 Cayuga Heights Rd Ithaca NY 14850-2107 Office: Cornell U Dept Romance Studies Ithaca NY 14853

COLE, BARBARA ANN, lawyer, educator; b. New Orleans, Sept. 16, 1954; d. Keith Martin Cole and Peggy St. Amant Ducote. BA, Southeastern U., 1976; JD, Loyola U., New Orleans, 1983. Bar: La. 1984. Social studies tchr. Slidell (La.) High Sch., 1976-81; instr. Southeastern U., Hammond, La., 1984-85; sole practice Hammond, La., 1983-96. Pres. Mayor's Commn. on Needs of Women, Hammond, 1985-86; mem. edn. com. Hammond C. of C.,

1985-86; chmn. Domestic Violence Task Force, 1985-86; pres. The Citizens Law Ctr. Mem. La. State Bar Assn. (Young Lawyers sect.), Fed. Bar Assn., La. Assn. Women Attys., La. Trial Lawyers Assn. Roman Catholic. Lodge: Krewe Iris, Krewe of Omega (captain).

COLE, BARBARA TODD, bookseller; b. Evanston, Ill., Dec. 26, 1912; d. Charles Cameron and Mary Barkley (Miller) Todd; m. John Allen Cole, Oct. 9, 1943 (dec.); children: Charles Allen, Susan Hale Cole Oliver. Grad. h.s., Evanston. Decorator Carson Pirie Scott, Chgo., 1930-32; bookseller E.P. Judd Bookseller, New Haven, 1933-39; with acquisition dept. Yale U. Libr., New Haven, 1939-42; dir. Chgo. office Army Mad Svc., Washington, 1942-45; bookseller, owner John Cole's Book Shop, La Jolla, Calif., 1946—. Bd. dirs. La Jolla Mus. Art, La Jolla Hist. Soc., Friends of the Libr., U. Calif. San Diego, Athenaeum, La Jolla. Mem. Am. Booksellers Assn., San Diego Booksellers Assn., So. Calif. Booksellers Assn., Athenaeum Art and Music Libr., San Diego Mus. Contemporary Art, San Diego Mus., numerous others. Congregational. Office: John Coles Book Shop 780 Prospect La Jolla CA 92037

COLE, BETTY LOU MCDONEL SHELTON (MRS. DEWEY G. COLE, JR.), judge; b. Elwood, Ind., June 5, 1926; d. Bernard Miller and Vee Marie (Robertson) McDonel; m. Elbert Shelton, Dec. 13, 1944; children: Steven Elbert, Jeanette Louise; m. 2d, Dewey G. Cole, Jr., Dec. 24, 1975. Student, Ind. U., 1947-50, LLB, 1969; student, Ball State U., 1964-65. Bar: Ind. 1969, Fed. Cts., 1969; cert. sr. judge. Pvt. practice, Muncie, Ind., 1969—, Betty L. Shelton Law Office, 1970-78; sr. ptnr. firm Dunnuck, Cole, Rankin and Wyrick, Muncie, 1978-80; judge Delaware County Superior Ct., 1980-95, ret., 1995. Mem. ABA, Ind. Bar Assn., Muncie Bar Assn., Ind. Judges Assn., Am. Trial Lawyers, Ind. U. Law Alumni Assn., Nat. Assn. Women Judges, LWV (league pres. 1963-64), Bus. and Profl. Women., Riley-Jones Club, Columbia Club.

COLE, CAROL WOOD, health services administrator; b. Cin., July 30, 1941; d. John Wood and Lillian Eliza (Flummer) Reynolds; m. Wayne Everett Cole, June 14, 1968; children: Spencer, Elizabeth. BSN, U. Cin., 1963; MPH, Loma Linda U., 1992. RN, Ohio, Wash., Oreg. From cmty. health nurse to health svcs. adminstr. Multnomah County Health Dept., Portland, Oreg., 1981—. co-chair East County Sr. Coalition, Gresham, Oreg., 1995—; steering com. East County Caring Cmty., Gresham, 1992—; chair Mid County Caring Com., Portland, 1996; adv. bd. YWCA East County Dist. Ctr., Portland, 1989—; bd. dirs. Mt. Hood Pops Cmty. Orch., Gresham, 1983-90, 94—, East Metro Arts & Culture Coun., Gresham, 1995—; mem. Cmty. Devel. & Housing Com., Gresham, 1992—; cmty. adv. com. Gresham H.S., 1988—. Mem. Am. Pub. Health Assn., N.Am. Nursing Diagnoses Assn., Oreg. Pub. Health Assn., Assn. Oreg. Pub. Health Nurse Supervisors (chair 1992-92, outstanding svc. award 1993). Home: 1819 SW 20th Ct Gresham OR 97080 Office: Multnomah County Health Dept 620 NE 2d Gresham OR 97030

COLE, CAROLYN JO, brokerage house executive; b. Carmel, Calif.; d. Joseph Michael, Jr., and Dorothea Newport (James) C.; A.B., Vassar Coll., 1965. Mgr. tech. services Aims Group, N.Y.C., 1965-67; editor Standard & Poor's Corp., N.Y.C., 1968-74; sr. v.p. PaineWebber, Inc., N.Y.C., 1975-95; exec. v.p. Tucker Anthony Inc., Boston, 1995—; guest lectr. Harvard U. Bus. Sch.; former chmn. bd. dirs. N.Y. Women's Bldg; adv. bd. Named to YWCA Acad. Women Achievers. Mem. NOW, DAR, N.Y. Soc. Security Analysts (past bd. dirs.), Assn. for Investment Mgmt. and Rsch., Soc. Fgn. Analysts, Aspen Inst. Humanistic Studies, Fin. Women's Assn., Women's Econ. Roundtable, Econ. Club N.Y., Women in Need (past bd. dirs.). Democrat. Episcopalian. Club: Vassar (N.Y.C.). Office: Tucker Anthony Inc One Beacon St Boston MA 02108

COLE, DIANA L., lawyer; b. Tacoma, Jan. 13, 1946; d. James Donald and Lillian Julia (Runyan) C. AA, Tacoma C.C., 1966; BA, U. Puget Sound, 1968; MA, Calif. State U., Long Beach, 1971; postgrad., Southwestern Sch. Law, 1976. Bar: Calif. 1977. Spl. edn. tchr. Tacoma Sch. Dist., 1968-69; home econs. and consumer edn. tchr. L.A. Unified Sch. Dist., 1969-76; pvt. practice law L.A., 1976—; br. mgr. Commodity Trading Advisor, L.A., 1996—. Sec. Homeowners Bd., Park Oakhurst. Mem. Consumer Attys. Assn. L.A., Phi Alpha Delta. Office: 3960 Wilshire Blvd # 507 Los Angeles CA 90010

COLE, DIANE JOYCE, writer; b. Balt., July 11, 1952; d. Alfred J. and Roselda (Katz) C.; m. Peter Baida, Aug. 7, 1977; 1 child, Edward Aaron. AB, Radcliffe Coll., 1974; MA, Johns Hopkins U., 1975. Author: After Great Pain, 1992, Hunting the Headhunters, 1988. Home: 305 E 86th St New York NY 10028

COLE, DONNA, librarian, library director; b. Amsterdam, N.Y., July 21, 1952; d. Frank Harry and Betty (Haig) C.; m. William Fite, Mar. 24, 1991. BA summa cum laude, Fitchburg State Coll., 1980; M in Libr. Svc., Rutgers U., 1983. Libr. Sch. Nursing, St. Francis Hosp. and Med. Ctr., Hartford, Conn., 1983-85; asst. br. libr. Upper Cape br. Cape May County Libr., Petersburg, N.J., 1986-87; head circulation, reference libr. Joint Free Pub. Libr. Morristown (N.J.) and Morris Twp., 1987-90, acting dir., 1990-91; asst. libr. dept. bus. and econs. Birmingham (Ala.) Pub. Libr., 1991-92; dir. Leeds (Ala.) Pub. Libr., 1992—. Contbr. articles and book revs. to various publs. Charter mem. Leeds Pub. Libr. Found., Inc., sec., 1996—; mem. Lupus Found., Birmingham, 1992—. Mem. AAUW, ALA, NOW, Pub. Libr. Assn., Southea. Libr. Assn., Ala. Libr. Assn. (2nd v.p. 1995-96), Jefferson County Pub. Libr. Assn. (sec. 1994), Greater Leeds Area C. of C., Leeds Area Bus. and Profl. Women (charter). Democrat. Mem. United Ch. of Christ. Home: 921 Bienville Ct Birmingham AL 35213-2009 Office: Leeds Pub Libr 802 Parkway Dr SE Leeds AL 35094

COLE, ELMA PHILLIPSON (MRS. JOHN STRICKLER COLE), social welfare executive; b. Piqua, Ohio, Aug. 9, 1909; d. Brice Leroy and Mabel (Gale) Phillipson; m. John Strickler Cole, Oct. 3, 1959. AB, Berea Coll., 1930; MA, U. Chgo., 1938. Various positions in social work, 1930-42; dir. dept. social svc. Children's Hosp. D.C., Washington, 1942-49; cons. pub. coop. Midcentury White House Conf. on Children and Youth, Washington, 1949-51; exec. sec. Nat. Midcentury Com. on Children and Youth, N.Y.C., 1951-53; cons. recruitment Am. Assn. Med. Social Workers, 1953; assoc. dir. Nat. Legal Aid and Defender Assn., 1953-56; exec. sec. Marshall Field Awards, Inc., 1956-57; dir. assoc. orgns. Nat. Assembly Social Policy and Devel., 1957-73; assoc. exec. dir. Nat. Assembly Nat. Vol. Health and Social Welfare Orgns., 1974; dir. edn. parenthood project Salvation Army, 1974-76, asst. sec. dept. women's and children's social svcs., 1976-78, dir. rsch. project devel. bur., 1978-92, ind. cons., 1993—; mem. Manhattan adv. bd., 1975—, sec., 1984—, mem. hist. commn., 1976—, exec. com., 1988-94; cons. nat. orgns. Golden Anniversary White House Conf. on Children and Youth, 1959-60; mem. adv. coun. pub. svc. Nat. Assn. Life Underwriters and Inst. Life Ins.; judges com. Louis I. Dublin Pub. Svc. awards, 1961-74; v.p. Blue Ridge Inst. So. Cmty. Svc. Execs., 1977-79, exec. com., 1979-81; mem. awards jury Girls Clubs Am., 1981-93; adv. bd. Nat. Family Life Edn. Network, 1982—. Mem. com. pub. rels. and fundraising Am. Found. for Blind Commn. on Accreditation, 1964-67; mem. task force on vol. accreditation Coun. Nat. Orgns. for Adult Edn., 1974-78; adv. bd. sexuality edn. project Ctr. for Population Options, 1977-86; bd. dirs., sec. James Lenox House, 1985-89, pres., 1989-94, treas., 1994—; bd. dirs., sec. James Lenox House Assn., 1985-89, pres., 1989-94, sec., 1994—; bd. dirs. Values and Human Sexuality Inst., 1980-85, Sexuality Info. and Edn. Coun. of U.S., 1993—, mem. exec. com. Mem. Pub. Rels. Soc. Am. (cert.), Nat. Assn. Social Workers (cert.), Nat. Conf. Social Welfare (mem. pub. rels. com. 1961-66, 69-82, chair adminstrn. sect. 1966-67), Jr. League N.Y., Women's Club of N.Y., Pi Gamma Mu, Phi Kappa Phi. Home: 19 Washington Sq N New York NY 10011-9170

COLE, ELSA KIRCHER, lawyer; b. Dec. 5, 1949; d. Paul and Hester Marie (Pellegrom) Kircher; m. Roland J. Cole, Aug. 16, 1975; children: Isabel Ashley, Madeline Aldis. AB in History with distinction, Stanford U., 1971; JD, Boston U., 1974. Bar: Wash. 1974, U.S. Supreme Ct. 1980, Mich. 1989. Asst. atty gen., rep. dept. motor vehicles State of Wash., Seattle, 1974-75, asst. atty. gen., rep. dept. social and health svcs., 1975-76, asst. atty. gen., rep. U. Wash., 1976-89; gen. counsel U. Mich., Ann Arbor, 1989—; presenter ednl. issues various confs. and workshops. Contbr. articles to profl. jours. Mem. Nat. Assn. Coll. and Univ. Attys. (chair profl. devel. com. 1990-91, mem. nominations and site selection coms. 1987-88, 95-96, program 1988-89, 89-90, 91-92, 92-93, 95-96, board ops. 92-93, fin., articles and by-laws coms. 1988-89, CLE com. 1995-96, 96-97, co-chair student affairs sect. 1987-88, 88-89, honors and awards ethics com. 1991-92, continuing legal edn. com. 1995-96, 96—, pub. com. 1996—, bd. dirs. 1988-91), Wash. State Bar Assn. (chair law sch. liaison com. 1988-89), Wash. Women Lawyers (pres. Seattle-King County chpt. 1986, v.p. membership, state bd. 1987, 88, state chair candidate endorsement com. 1987, 88), Seattle-King County Bar Assn. Congregationalist. Office: U Mich Office of the Gen Counsel 4020 Fleming Bldg Ann Arbor MI 48109

COLE, GRETCHEN BORNOR, distribution and service executive; b. Detroit, Nov. 12, 1927; d. Maurice Frank and Dora Levina (Richardson) Bornor; m. Ernest James Cole, Mar. 31, 1951; (div. May, 1981); children: Cynthia, Sara Ann. BA, DePauw U., 1949; MSW, Wayne State U., 1980. Cert. social worker, Mich. Regional sec. Kenyon and Eckhardt, Detroit, 1951-52; office mgr. W.O. Earl Assocs., Detroit, 1952-54; social worker St. Joseph Mercy Hosp., Pontiac, Mich., 1981-82; with Detroit Air Compressor and Pump Co., Ferndale, Mich., 1963-80, sec., 1981, v.p., 1982, chmn., pres., 1990—, also chmn. bd. dirs.; regional dir., v.p. Atlas Copco Distbr. Assn., 1987-90; mem. Atlas Copco Compressors Coun. Bd., 1990-92. Named one of Top 50 Woman Bus. Owners State of Mich., 1986, 94, one of Top 25, 1996. Mem. Women's Econ. Club, Nat. Assn. Women Bus. Owners, Econ. Club Detroit, Founder's Soc., Detroit Inst. Arts, Oakland County C. of C. (exec. bd. 1994—, chair mktg. com., bd. dirs. 1994—), Alpha Chi Omega. Republican. Episcopalian. Office: Detroit Air Compressor & Pump Co 3205 Bermuda St Ferndale MI 48220-1060

COLE, HEATHER ELLEN, librarian; b. Rochester, N.Y., Nov. 7, 1942; d. Donald M. and Muriel Agnes (Kimball) C.; m. Stratis Haviaras; 1 child, Elektra Maria Muriel. BA, Cornell U., 1964; MS, Simmons Coll., 1973. Mgr. Brentano's, Boston, 1968-70; intern Harvard Coll. Libr., Cambridge, Mass., 1970-73, reference libr., 1973-77, libr., 1977—; libr. Hilles and Lamont Librs., 1977—. Mem. AAUW, ALA, Am. Soc. Info. Sci. (New England chpt.), Assn. Coll. Rsch. Librs. Democrat. Episcopalian. Home: 19 Clinton St Cambridge MA 02139-2303 Office: Harvard Coll Lamont Library Cambridge MA 02138

COLE, HELEN, state legislator; b. Tishomingo, Okla., July 13, 1922; m. John Cole; 2 children. Former mayor, Moore, Okla., mem. Okla. Ho. of Reps., 37-39th sessions; mem. Okla. Senate, 1984—. Active Cleveland County Republican Women's Club. Mem. Yukon C. of C., Am. Legion Aux. Office: Okla Senate State Capitol Oklahoma City OK 73105 also: 3026 SW 89th St Apt A Oklahoma City OK 73159-6351*

COLE, JANET See HUNTER, KIM

COLE, JEAN ANNE, artist; b. Greeley, Colo., Jan. 30, 1947; d. Philip Owen and Rose Margaret (Maser) Dahl; m. Nelson Bruce Cole, June 22, 1968; children: Ashley Paige, Travis Allyn. BA in Interior Design, U. Calif., Berkeley, 1968. Interior designer K.S. Wilshire Design, L.A., 1969-70; interior designer Milton Swimmer Planning & Design, Beverly Hills, Calif., 1970-73, Denver, 1973-75; tchr. watercolor workshops, 1991—. Exhibited in numerous shows at Foothills Art Ctr., Golden, Colo., 1989, 91, 93, 94, 96, Brea (Calif.) Civic and Cultural Ctr., 1989, 90, Nevile Pub. Mus., Green Bay, Wis., 1990, 93, Nat. Watercolor Soc., 1991, Denver Mus. Natural History, 1991, Pikes Peak Ctr. Performing Arts, Colorado Springs, Colo., 1992, Colo. History Mus., 1992, 93, 94, 95, 96, Kneeland Gallery, Las Vegas, Nev., 1993, 94, 95, Salmagundi Club, N.Y.C., 1994, Met. State Coll. Ctr. for Visual Arts, Denver, 1994; contbr. articles to mags.; artist greetings cards Lcanin'Trec. Recipient 2d pl. watercolor award Art Zone Regional Show, 1988, 1st pl. watercolor award Colo. ARtists Convention, 1989, 1st pl., hon. mention People's Choice awards Denver Allied Artists, 1989, Best of Show award Pikes Peak Watercolor Invitational, 1992, Quaintance award Rocky Mountain Nat. Watermedia Exhibit, 1993, Paul Schwartz Meml. award Am. Watercolor Soc., 1994, Founder's award Watercolor West XXVI Ann. Nat. Transparent Watercolor Exhbn., Calif., 1994. Mem. Nat. Watercolor Soc., Colo. Watercolor Soc. (pres., treas., award of merit 1993). Republican. Home: 78 Ash St Denver CO 80220

COLE, JENNIFER JANE, elementary education educator; b. La Junta, Colo., Dec. 10, 1948; d. Ervin W. and Marjorie K. (Elliott) Bevlin; m. David L. Cole, Aug. 17, 1968; children: Amy Kathleen, Colin Christopher, Laura Elizabeth. BA in Elem. Edn., Colo. State Coll., 1969; MA, U. No. Colo., 1985. Cert. elem. tchr., Okla., Colo.; nat. bd. tchg. standards cert. early adolescence/English lang. arts, 1995. 1st grade tchr. Indiahoma (Okla.) Pub. Sch., 1969-70; K-6 substitute tchr. Heidelberg (Germany) Am. Sch., 1970-71, reading tutor, 1971-72; 1st grade tchr. Mirich Elem. Sch., La Salle, Colo., 1983-91; 3d grade tchr. Platteville (Colo.) Elem. Sch., 1991-92, 5th grade tchr., 1992—; mem. lang. arts curriculum, Gilcrest, Colo., 1987-88, 94, co-chmn. budget com., 1993; supr. student tchrs., La Salle, 1987-88, Platteville, 1994-95; presenter at profl. convs. Leader Girl Scouts, La Salle, 1982-83, 86-87; active No. Colo. Concert Band, Windsor, 1993—; elder 1st Presbyn. Ch., La Salle, 1994—. Mem. NEA, Internat. Reading Assn., Colo. Coun. Internat. Reading Assn., Colo. Edn. Assn., Valley Edn. Assn. (treas. 1991-94), Nat. Coun. Tchrs. English, Tchrs. Applying Whole Lang., Mothers of Twins Club (pres. 1981-82). Republican. Home: 19829 Scotch Pine Dr La Salle CO 80645-3130 Office: Platteville Elem Sch 1202 Main St Platteville CO 80651

COLE, JOAN (ELLEN) BLYLER, financial executive; b. Phila., Sept. 27, 1946; d. Charles Frederick and Ellen Elizabeth (Leavitt) Blyler; m. Charles Chatfield Cole Jr., Jan. 27, 1968; children: Charles Chatfield III, Christopher Andrew. BA, Rosemont (Pa.) Coll., 1968; BS, Kutztown (Pa.) U., 1984; MBA, Lehigh U., 1996. Cert. mgmt. acct. With Lehigh Portland Cement Co., Allentown, Pa., 1984—, various fin. positions, mgr. treasury. Mem. Inst. of Mgmt. Accts. (pres. Lehigh Valley chpt. 1992-93), Treasury Mgmt. Assn. Home: 4300 Rosewood Ln Allentown PA 18103 Office: Lehigh Portland Cement Co 7660 Imperial Way Allentown PA 18195

COLE, JOHNNETTA BETSCH, academic administrator; b. Jacksonville, Fla., Oct. 19, 1936; d. John Thomas and Mary Frances (Lewis) Betsch; m. Robert Eugene Cole (div. 1982); children: David, Aaron, Ethan; m. Arthur J. Robinson, Jr., 1988. Student, Fisk U., 1953; BA in Sociology, Oberlin Coll., 1957; MA in Anthropology, Northwestern U., Evanston, Ill., 1959, PhD, 1967. Instr. U. Calif., Los Angeles, 1964; dir. black studies Wash. State U., Pullman, 1969-70; prof. anthropology U. Mass., Amherst, 1970-83, assoc. provost undergrad. edn., 1981-83; vis. prof. Hunter Coll., N.Y.C., 1983-84, prof. anthropology, 1983-87, dir. Inter-Am. Affairs Program, 1984-87; pres. Spelman Coll., Atlanta, 1987—; corp. bd. dirs. Coca Cola Enterprises, NationsBank South, Mgmt. Tng. Corp., Merck & Co., Inc., Home Depot; trustee Rockefeller Found. Author, editor: Anthropology for the Eighties, 1982, All American Women, 1986, Anthropology for the Nineties, 1988, Conversations: Straight Talk with America's Sister President, 1993; mem. editorial bd. The Black Scholar. Recipient numerous hon. degrees. Fellow Am. Anthrop. Assn.; mem. Assn. Black Anthropologists (past pres.). Baptist. Office: Spelman Coll Office of the President 350 Spelman Ln SW Atlanta GA 30314-4399

COLE, JUNE ROBERTSON, psychotherapist; b. Dothan, Ala., Sept. 29, 1931; d. C. Pete and Mary (Danzey) Robertson; m. Robert Walker Cole, Jr., Feb. 11, 1956; children: Robert Pete, Mary Cathlyn. AA, Del Mar Coll., 1974; BA, Tex. A&I U., 1976; MA, Corpus Christi State U., 1978; postgrad Fielding Inst., Santa Barbara, 1985—. Lic. marriage and family therapist, profl. counselor. Actress, singer, radio, films, TV, stage, 1933-55; rec. artist Gold Label Records, 1951-55; pres. Coastal Bend Security Co., Corpus Christi, 1969-71; dir. Reality Therapy Ctr., Corpus Christi, 1975—; co-dir. Counseling and Psychology Resource Ctr., Corpus Christi, 1984—; pvt. practice psychotherapy, 1976—; mem. mental health staff Bayview Psychiatric Hosp., Corpus Christi, 1986—, Southside Community Hosp., Corpus Christi, 1989—, Charter Psychiatr. Hosp., Corpus Christi, 1990—; faculty Park Coll., Naval Air Sta., Corpus Christi, 1987-92. Bd. dirs. Coastal Bend Jazz Soc., 1978-79; presenter papers on Post Traumatic Stress Disorder, Compatibility Psychotherapy & 12 Step Programs in alcohol, drug addictions. Mem. AACD, APA, NOW, Am. Assn. for Mental Health Counselors, Am. Assn. Behavior Therapists, Tex. Psychol. Assn., Internat. Assn. for Group Psychotherapists, Corpus Christi Council Women, Nueces County Psychol. Assn., Tex. Assn. Counseling and Devel., Gulf Coast Assn. Counseling and Devel., Tex. Mental Health Counselors Assn., Coastal Bend Marriage and Family Therapists Assn., Internat. Inst. Reality Therapists. Office: 5934 S Staples St Ste 216 Corpus Christi TX 78413-3842

COLE, KATHERINE MARTHA (KIT COLE), communications professional; b. Newport Beach, Calif., May 1, 1970; d. John M. Cole and Madeline L. Cole Maxfield. BA, U. Calif., Davis, 1992; MPA, U. So. Calif., 1995. Dir. Nat. Lobby Office Associated Student U. Calif., Davis, 1990-91; dir. ednl. programming City of Davis, 1991-92; policy analyst Assembly Com. on Local Govt. Calif. State Legislature, Sacramento, 1992-94; assoc. Nelson Comm. Group, San Diego, 1994-96; coalition devel. specialist Calif. Coalition for Childhood Immunization, San Diego, 1996—. Co-author: (with others) New Towns in California: Planning, Governance and Infrastructure, Approaches and Concerns, 1994. Bd. dirs. NOW, San Diego, 1995—, Access Ctr. San Diego, 1996. Recipient Bernays award Pub. Rels. Soc. Am., San Diego chpt., 1995; Jesse Marvin Unruh Assembly fellow, 1993-94. Mem. Air and Waste Mgmt. Assn., Asian Bus. Assn. Democrat.

COLE, KATHLEEN ANN, advertising agency executive; retired social worker b. Cin., Nov. 22, 1946; d. James Scott and Kathryn Gertrude (Borisch) Cole; BA, Miami U., 1968; MSW, U. Mich., 1972; MM, Northwestern U., 1978; m. Brian Brandt, Mar. 21, 1970. Social worker Hamilton County Welfare Dept., Cin., 1969-70, Lucas County Children Svcs. Bd., Toledo, 1970-74, East Maine Sch. Dist., Niles, Ill., 1974-77; account supr. Leo Burnett Advt. Agy., Chgo., 1978-93; primary therapist, Lifeline, Chgo., 1994-95; acct. supr. GreenHouse Comm., 1995—; field instr. Loyola U., Chgo., 1976-77. Mem. Acad. Cert. Social Workers (chair pub. rels. task force), Nat. Assn. Social Workers, Miami U. Alumni Assn. (dir. 1976—), Northwestern U. Prof. Women's Assn., Kellogg Alumni Assn., North Shore United Meth. Congregation. Home: 414 Kelling Ln Glencoe IL 60022-1113

COLE, LORETTA P., health services administrator, researcher; b. N.Y.C.. BS, Brooklyn Coll., 1966; MA, U. Calif., 1968; MHA, U. Pitts., 1988. Health policy fellow Inst. Pitts., 1986-87; dir. health policy devel. N.Y. County Med. Soc., N.Y.C., 1988-90; human services program coordinator Clallan County, Wash., 1992-93; prepaid health plan coord. Oreg. Dept. Human Resources, Salem, 1993-94, mgr. analysis and evaluation, 1994—. Office: Oreg Office Med Assistance 500 Summer St NE Salem OR 97310

COLE, LYDIA N., cable television executive. V.p. programming Black Entertainment TV, Washington. Office: Black Entertainment TV 1899 9th St NE Washington DC 20018*

COLE, MARILYN BUSH, occupational therapy educator; b. N.Y.C., Jan. 29, 1945; d. George Lyman and Theis Odette (Maurer) Bush; m. Carl E. Cole, Aug. 31, 1968 (div. June 1981); children: Charlot E. Cole, Bradley Eric Cole; m. Martin M. Schiraldi Sr., July 3, 1982. BA, U. Conn., 1966; grad. cert., U. Pa., 1969; MS, U. Bridgeport, 1982. Registered occupational therapist, Conn. Staff occupational therapy Ea. Pa. Psychiat. Inst., Phila., 1968-69; dir. occupational therapy Middlesex Meml. Hosp., Middletown, Conn., 1973-76; supervising occupational therapist Lawrence & Meml. Hosps. Day Treatment Ctr., New London, Conn., 1976-79; staff occupational therapist Newington Children's Hosp., Newington, Conn., 1980-82; asst. prof. occupational therapy Quinnipiac Coll., Hamden, Conn., 1982-95, assoc. prof., tenured, 1995—; cons. psychiat. svcs. VA Med. Ctr., West Haven, Conn., 1983-91; cons. Fairfield Hills Hosp., Newtown, Conn., 1989-91. Author: (textbook) Group Dynamics in Occupational Theray, 1993; co-author Structured Group Experiences, 1982, chpt. in Group Process and Structure, 1988; contbr. articles to profl. jours. Grantee Quinnipiac Coll, 1986. Mem. Am. Occupational Therapy Assn. (Communications award 1976, cert.), Conn. Occupational Therapy Assn. (sec. 1978, nominations chair 1982-89), World Fedn. Occupational Therapists, AAUW (cultural chair 1972, publicity chair 1973-76, edn. chair 1989-91, nominations 1993-96), Ctr. for Study Sensory Integrative Dysfunction (cert. 1979). Republican. Episcopalian. Office: Quinnipiac Coll Dept Occupl Therapy Mount Carmel Ave Hamden CT 06518

COLE, MAX, artist; b. Hodgeman County, Kans., Feb. 14, 1937; d. Jack Delmont C. and Bertha (Law) Fakes; m. Richard Cole, Sept. 4, 1955 (dec. April 1958); children: Douglas, Janet, Cindy. B.A., Fort Hays State U., 1961; M.F.A., U. Ariz., 1964. Asst. prof. Pasadena (Calif.) City Coll., 1967-78; guest lectr. Claremont (Calif.) Grad. Sch., 1978, Coll. Creative Studies, U. Calif., Santa Barbara, 1977, 79, Contemporary Arts Council, Los Angeles County Mus. Art, 1979, Miami Dade Coll., 1982. One-man shows include Louver Gallery, L.A., 1978, 80, Sidney Janis Gallery, N.Y.C., 1977, 80, Oscarsson Siegeltuch Gallery, N.Y.C., 1986, Zabriskie Gallery, N.Y., 1987, Haines Gallery, San Francisco, 1988, 93, 96, Galerie Schlegl, Zurich, 1990, 96, Mus. Folkwang, Essen, Germany, 1993, Kunstraum Kassel (Germany), 1992, Kyo Higashi Gallery, L.A., 1991, 93, 94, Roswell (N.Mex.) Mus. and Art Ctr., Galerie Conrads, Düsseldorf, Germany, 1996, Stark Gallery, N.Y.; exhibited in group shows including L.A. County Mus. Art, 1976, Corcoran Gallery Art, Washington, 1977, La Jolla Mus., 1980, Santa Barbara Mus., 1980, Mus. Fine Arts of N.Mex., 1984, Neuberger Mus., Purchase, N.Y., 1984, Marilyn Pearl Gallery, N.Y.C., 1985, Pratt Manhattan Ctr. Gallery, 1985, UCLA, 1988, Nat. Gallery Modern Art, New Delhi, 1988, Panza Found., Verese, Italy, 1995, Aagauer Kunsthaus, Aarau, Switzerland, 1995, Trento (Italy) Mus., 1996, Galerie Conrads, Düsseldorf, 1996, Stark Gallery, N.Y., 1996, Galerie Schlegl, Zurich, 1996; represented in permanent collections L.A. County Mus. Art, Newport Harbor Mus. Art, La Jolla Mus. Contemporary Art, Mus. N.Mex., Dallas Mus. Art, Santa Barbara Mus., Everson Mus., Tel Aviv Mus., La. Mus., Denmark, Panza Collection, Italy. Address: 195 E 3d St New York NY 10009

COLE, NATALIE MARIA, singer; b. L.A., Feb. 6, 1950; d. Nathaniel Adam and Maria (Hawkins) C.; m. Marvin J. Yancy, July 30, 1976 (div.); m. Andre Fisher (div.). B.A. in Psychology, U. Mass., 1972. Rec. singles and albums, 1975—; albums include Dangerous, 1985, Everlasting, 1987, Inseparable, Thankful, Good To Be Back, 1989, Unforgettable, 1991 (4 grammys, 3 grammys 1992), Too Much Weekend, 1992, I'm Ready, 1992, Take A Look, 1993 (Grammy award nominee best jazz vocal 1994), Holly and Ivy, 1994; television appearances include Lily in Winter, USA, 1994, Stardust, 1996. Recipient Grammy award for best new artist, best Rhythm and Blues female vocalist 1975, 76; recipient 1 gold single, 3 gold albums; recipient 2 Image awards NAACP 1976, 77; Am. Music award 1978, other awards. Mem. AFTRA, Nat. Assn. Rec. Arts and Scis., Delta Sigma Delta. Democrat. Baptist. Office: care PMK care Jennifer Allen 955 S Carrillo Dr Ste 200 Los Angeles CA 90048*

COLE, PATRICIA ANN, elementary school educator; b. Huntington, W.Va., Dec. 26, 1957; d. Albert James and Nancy Suzanne (Linsenmeyer) Aluise; m. Dennis Franklin Cole, Aug. 1, 1981; 1 child, Dennis Franklin Jr. BA in Elem. Edn./Math. magna cum laude, Marshall U., 1980, MA in Elem. Edn. summa cum laude, 1986. Cert. elem. tchr., math. tchr., W.Va. Bank teller First Huntington Nat. Bank, 1980; elem. and jr. H.S. tchr. Our Lady of Fatima Sch., Huntington, 1980—, tutor, math. olympiad coach and moderator, 1988—; presenter W.Va. Sci. Tchrs. Convention, Huntington, 1994. Vol. Marshall Artist Series, Huntington, 1982, W.Va. Spl. Olympics, 1988, 89, Huntington Mus. of Art, 1984, 86; sec. Ladies Guild Sacred Heart Ch., Huntington, 1988; area chmn. Heart Fund, Huntington, 1980. Grantee Diocese of Wheeling, 1991, 95. Mem. Cabell County Reading Coun., Women's Club of Huntington (com. chmn. 1984-86, treas. 1985, social chmn. 1986, 3d vice chmn. 1987, 2d vice chmn. 1988, 1st vice chmn. 1989, chmn. 1990, Outstanding Chmn. award 1984, 86, Bd. Mem. of Yr. 1987, Dist. Mem. of Yr. 1991), Gamma Beta Phi. Home: 5112 Nickel Plate Dr Huntington WV 25705-3134

COLE, SALLY ANN, critical care nurse; b. Phila., Jan. 9, 1940; d. William Joseph and Sara Erma (Jones) C.; m. Daniel Cesarini, Feb. 18, 1955 (div. Dec. 1966); children: Daniel Lee, Robert Harold, Richard Dale. Grad., North Montgomery County Area Vocational Tech. Sch., Lansdale, Pa., 1969; ASN, Univ. State N.Y., Albany, 1989. RN, Fla. Nurse North Penn Hosp., Lansdale, 1969-73; LPN St. Petersburg (Fla.) Gen. Hosp., 1974-89,

ICU nurse, 1974-95, RN, 1989-95; RN, Fla.; cert. ACLS, Am. Heart Assn. Recipient Best Bedside Nursing Care award North Montgomery County Nursing Assn., 1969. Fellow AACN. Republican. Home: 4231 44th Ave N Saint Petersburg FL 33714-3548

COLE, SHARON GRACE CAYTON, secondary education educator; b. Sutton, W.Va., Jan. 3, 1945; d. Benjamin I. and Grace (Marple) Cayton; m. David P. Cole; children: Valerie Cole Poindexter, Leslea Cole Ashton, Jamin W. AB, Glenville (W.Va.) State Coll., 1966; MS, Marshall U., 1975. Fin. sec. Gilmer County Bd. Edn., Glenville, W.Va., 1966-68; tchr. bus. edn. Mason County schs., Pt. Plesant, W.Va., 1968—; coord., tchr. Gov.'s Summer Enhancement Program, 1990, 91, 92, 93, 94. Benedum Found. scholar, 1962. Mem. NEA, AAUW (1st v.p. 1993-95), W.Va. Edn. Assn. (past officer), Masons. Democrat. Baptist. Home: Rt 1 3 Belle Rd Point Pleasant WV 25550 Office: Mason County Vocat Tech Ctr Ohio River Rd Point Pleasant WV 25550

COLE, SUSAN A., university president, English language educator. BA in English and Am. Lit., Columbia U., 1962; MA in English and Am. Lit., Brandeis U., 1964, PhD in English and Am. Lit., 1972. Tchg. asst. Clark U., 1964-65; assoc. prof. CCUNY-N.Y.C. Tech. Coll., 1968-77; assoc. dean for acad. affairs Antioch U., 1977-80; v.p. for univ. adminstrn. and pers. Rutgers U., New Brunswick, N.J., 1980-92; pres., prof. English Met. State U., Mpls. and St. Paul, 1993—; guest adj. assoc. prof. Pace U., fall 1977; vis. sr. fellow in acad. adminstrn. Office Acad. Affairs, CUNY, 1991-93; bd. dirs. Western State Bank; presenter in field. Contbr. articles to profl. jours. Chmn. edn. resolutions sessions, coord. edn. panels N.Y. State meeting Internat. Women's Year, Albany, 1977; agy. mem. N.J. Gov.'s Mgmt. Improvement Program, 1982; v.p., bd. dirs. Bklyn. Ecumenical Coops., 1988-90; mem. cmty. health care policy task force Robert Wood Johnson Univ. Hosp., New Brunswick, 1991; mem. blue ribon task force Mpls. Pub. Libr., 1994-95; mem. steering com. Greater St. Paul Tomorrow, 1994—; trustee Twin Cities Pub. TV, 1994—, Sci. Mus. Minn., 1994; bd. dirs., mem. exec. com. St. Paul Riverfront Corp., 1994—; v.p., founding bd. dirs. St. Paul Pub. Schs. Found., 1995—; bd. dirs. St. Paul Found., 1995—. Mem. Am. Assn. State Colls. and Univs. (urban and met. steering com. 1993—), Am. Coun. on Edn. (Commn. on Women in Higher Edn. 1993—), Greater Mpls. C. of C. (enterprise devel. task force 1994—). Office: Met State U 700 E 7th St Saint Paul MN 55106-5000

COLE, SUSIE CLEORA, retired government employee relations official; b. Bloomsburg, Pa.; d. Harry E. and Chloe Ann (McKinstry) Cole; m. Richard Edward Miller, July 31, 1959 (div. Aug. 1977); 1 child, Terri Lee Miller; m. Gerald Edward Nelson, Feb. 18, 1978 (div. June 1982). Student in history No. Va. Community Coll., 1982; also govt. courses. With Dept. Navy, Washington, 1957-74, clk., technician U.S. Dept. Navy, Washington, 1957-67, Navy mil. pay regulations specialist, 1962-71; mgr. error detection and reduction program for mil. pay, allowances and travel, 1967-71, fiscal acct. 1971-74, fiscal clk. Dept. State, Washington, 1975-77, sr. retirement claims examiner, 1977-83, employee rels. officer, 1983-94, also mgr. fed. health benefits program and mgr. fed. life ins. program, 1983-94, ret., 1994. Active Citizen's Band Radio Club, Fairfax, Va., 1974-82, Retarded Children's Ctr., Fairfax, 1981-82. Recipient various govt. awards, including Sustained Exceptional Achievement award Dept. State, 1983-93. Democrat. Avocations: reading, travel, history, music, art. Home: 4910 N Arnold Dr #3 Prescott Valley AZ 86314 Office: US Dept State Bur Pers Office Employee Rels 2201 C St NW Washington DC 20520-0001

COLE, TERRI LYNN, organization administrator; b. Tucson, Dec. 28, 1951; m. James R. Cole II. Student, U. N.Mex., 1975-80; cert., Inst. Orgn. Mgmt., 1985. Cert. chamber exec. With SunWest Bank, Albuquerque, 1971-74, employment adminstr., 1974-76, communications dir., 1976-78; pub. info. dir. Albuquerque C. of C., 1978-81, gen. mgr., 1981-83, pres., 1983—; pres. N.Mex. C. of C. Execs. Assn., 1986-87, bd. dirs., 1980—; bd. regents Inst. for Orgn. Mgmt., Stanford U., 1988—, vice chmn., 1990-91, chmn., 1991; bd. dirs. Hosp. Home Health, Inc. Recipient Bus. Devel. award Expn. Mgmt. Inc., 1985, Women on Move award YWCA, 1986; named one of Outstanding Women of Am., 1984. Mem. Am. C. of C. Execs. Assn. (chmn. elect bd. 1992—). Republican. Office: Greater Albuquerque C of C PO Box 25100 Albuquerque NM 87125-0100

COLEMAN, ARLENE FLORENCE, nurse practitioner; b. Braham, Minn., Apr. 8, 1926; d. William and Christine (Judin) C.; m. John Dunkerken, May 30, 1987. Diploma in nursing, U. Minn., 1947, BS, 1953; MPH, Loma Linda U., 1974. RN, Calif. Operating room scrub nurse Calif. Luth. Hosp., L.A., 1947-48; indsl. staff nurse Good Samaritan Hosp., L.A., 1948-49; staff nurse Passavant Hosp., Chgo., 1950-51; student health nurse Moody Bible Inst., Chgo., 1950-51; staff nurse St. Andrews Hosp., Mpls., 1951-53; pub. health nurse Bapt. Gen. Conf. Bd. of World Missions, Ethiopia, Africa, 1954-66; staff pub. health nurse County of San Bernadino, Calif., 1966-68, sr. pub. health nurse, 1968-73, pediatric nurse practitioner, 1973—. Contbr. articles to profl. jours. Mem. bd. dist. missions Bapt. Gen. Conf., Calif., 1978-84; mem. adv. coun. Kaiser Hosp., Fontana, Calif., 1969-85, Bethel Sem. West, San Diego, 1987—; bd. dirs. Casa Verdugo Retirement Home, Hemet, Calif., 1985—; active Calvary Bapt. Ch., Redlands, Calif., 1974—; mem. S.W. Bapt. Conf. Social Ministries, 1993—. With USPHS, 1944-47. Calif. State Dept. Health grantee, 1973. Fellow Nat. Assn. Pediatric Nurse Assocs. and Practitioners; mem. Calif. Nurses Assn. (state nursing coun. 1974-76). Democrat.

COLEMAN, BARBARA MCREYNOLDS, artist; b. Omaha, May 5, 1956; d. Zachariah Aycock and Mary Barbara (McCulloh) McR.; m. Stephen Dale Dent, Mar. 12, 1983 (div. Dec. 20, 1992); children: Madeleine Barbara, Matthew Stephen; m. Ross Coleman, Oct. 16, 1993; 1 child, Marie Jeanne Coleman. Student, U. N.Mex., 1979, MA in Community and Regional Planning, 1984. Artist, 1986-92; lectr. U. N.Mex. Sch. of Architecture, Albuquerque, 1979-82, 91—; assoc. planner, urban designer City of Albuquerque Planning Div., 1982-84; city planner, urban designer City of Albuquerque, N.Mex. Redevel. Div., 1984-88; cons. City of Albuquerque Redevel. Dept., 1987-88; urban design cons. Southwest Land Rsch., Albuquerque, 1991. Columnist for "Kids and Art", 1990-92; author: Coors Corridor Plan (The Albuquerque Conservation Assn. urban design award 1984), Electric Facilities Plan, Downtown Core Revitalization Strategy and Sector Development Plan; contbg. author: Anasazi Architecture and American Design, 1994; contbr. articles to profl. publs.; exhibited in shows at Dartmouth St. Gallery, Brandywine Galleries, Albuquerque, Laurel Seth Gallery, Santa Fe, Chimayo (N.Mex.) Trade and Mercantile, JoAnne Chappel Gallery, San Francisco, Southwest Arts Festival, Albuquerque. Vol. art tchr. Chaparral Elem. Sch., Albuquerque, 1989-92. Recipient First Pl. for Pastels, 20th Ann. Nat. Small Painting Exhibition, N.Mex. Art League, 1991, Best of Show awards Pastel Soc. of N.Mex., 1990, Award of Merit, Pastel Soc. of S.W., 1989, TACA award for Urban Design, 1984. Mem. Pastel Soc. of Am., Pastel Soc. N.Mex. (pres. 1991-92). Democrat. Episcopalian. Office: U NMex Sch Architecture Albuquerque NM 87131

COLEMAN, BERNICE E., psychiatrist; b. Jersey City, June 15, 1925. BA, Cleve. State U., 1955; MD, Howard U., 1968; MPH, Yale U., 1973. Diplomate Am. Bd. Psychiatry and Neurology. Lectr., instr. Yale U., New Haven, 1972-73; med. dir. Salvation Army Addiction Treatment Facility, Honolulu, 1973-95; pvt. practice psychiatry Honolulu, 1973—; asst. prof. psychiatry U. Hawaii Sch. Medicine, 1974-82; chief of psychiatry Queens Med. Ctr., Honolulu, 1982-89, asst. chief psychiatry, 1989-91; chief of psychiatry, 1991-95; assoc. clin. prof. psychiatry, U. Hawaii, 1982—; disability determination cons. Div. Vocat. Rehab., State of Hawaii, 1978—. Fellow Am. Psychiat. Assn.; mem. Hawaii Psychiat. Soc. (pres. 1979-82), Hawaii Med. Assn., Am. Med. Soc. on Alcoholism and Other Drug Dependencies, ACLU (Hawaii bd. dirs. 1980—), Honolulu County Med. Soc. (bd. govs.). Home: 4182-1 Keanu St Honolulu HI 96816 Office: 1314 S King St Ste 759 Honolulu HI 96814

COLEMAN, BETH ANN, graphic artist; b. Clifton, N.J., June 27, 1970; d. John Joseph and Jane (Nicolas) C. BA in Fine Arts and Mktg., Albright Coll., 1992; cert. computer graphics, Moore Coll. Art, 1995. Typesetter U.S. Election Corp., West Chester, Pa., 1993-94; graphic artist Genex Svcs., Inc., Wayne, Pa., 1994—. Vol. Spl. Olympics, Main Line Chpt., 1995-96, Habitat for Humanity, Phila., 1995. Mem. Oracle Investment Club, Chester County Art Soc. Office: Genex Svcs Inc 735 Chesterbrook Blvd Wayne PA 19087

COLEMAN, BRENDA FORBIS, gifted and talented educator; b. Dallas, May 17, 1951; d. Thomas Carlyle and Dorothy Jean (Tillerson) Forbis; m. Rufus Andrew Coleman, July 2, 1971; 1 child, Christopher Andrew. BS, Dallas Bapt. U., 1972; MEd, East Tex. State U., 1979; cert. gifted and talented, Tex. Woman's U., 1990. Elem. tchr. Plano (Tex.) Ind. Sch. Dist., 1972-79; elem. tchr. Lewisville (Tex.) Ind. Sch. Dist., 1983-86, gifted and talented facilitator, 1986-89; elem. tchr. Lake Dallas (Tex.) Ind. Sch. Dist., 1989-91, gifted and talented EXCEL program coord., 1991—; presenter in field, Univ. Interscolastic League acad. coach, 1995-96. Organizer canned food dr. Lake Dallas Families, 1989. Mem. Tex. Assn. for Gifted and Talented, Assn. of Tex. Profl. Educators, Phi Delta Kappa. Republican. Methodist. Home: 109 Woody Trl Lake Dallas TX 75065-3123 Office: Lake Dallas Ind Sch Dist 190 Falcon Dr Lake Dallas TX 75065

COLEMAN, CAROLYN, state legislator; b. Oklahoma City, Oct. 15, 1952; d. Irwin Arthur and Beulah Wyatt; m. Richard E. Coleman; children: Mary Rachel, Sarah Elizabeth. Student, Rose State Coll., Southwestern Bible Coll. Mem. Okla. Ho. of Reps., Oklahoma City, 1990—. Mem. Metro South Crisis Ctr., Okla. Fedn. Rep. Women. Home: 1617 SE 5th St Moore OK 73160-8337 Office: Okla Ho of Reps State Capitol Oklahoma City OK 73105*

COLEMAN, CLAIRE KOHN, public relations executive; b. New Castle, Pa., Nov. 19, 1924; d. Louis and Florence (Frank) K.; BA, Pa. State U., 1945; m. Frederick H. Coleman, Mar. 10, 1957; children: Franklin, Elliot. Market editor Fairchild Publs., N.Y.C., 1945-48; asst. home editor N.Y. Times, 1949-50; public relations dir. United Wallpaper, Chgo., 1950-53; pub. rels. dir. Assoc.. Am. Artists, N.Y.C., 1953-54; dir. Wallpaper Info. Bur., N.Y.C., 1954; dept. head Roy Bernard, Inc., N.Y.C., 1955-58; pub. rels. dir. The Siesel Co., N.Y.C., 1972—, sr. v.p., 1981-88; pres. Tisch Trask Comm. Resources Pub. Rels. Group, 1988-89; sr. v.p. Anthony M. Franco, N.Y.C., 1989-90; pres. Coleman Comm., N.Y., 1990—. Mem. ctrl. steering com., Sch. Dist. Critical Assessments, New Rochelle, N.Y., 1969-71; bd. dirs., v.p. Beechmont Assn., 1960-74; mem. Mayor's Adv. Coun. on Aging, 1966; mem. Mayor's Adv. Com. on Bd. Edn. Appointments, 1969; v.p. Coun. of PTAs, 1969-70; chmn. women's divsn. United Jewish Appeal, New Rochelle, 1971. Fellow Internat. Furnishings and Design Assn. (formerly Nat. Home Fashions League: founder 1947, nat. treas. 1977-78, nat. pres. 1980-81, N.Y. chpt. v.p. 1994, Cir. of Execellence award 1994); mem. Women Execs. Pub. Rels. (bd. dirs. 1983-84, sec. 86-87, pres.-elect 1994-95, pres. 1996-97), Woman Execs. Pub. Rels. Found. (v.p. 1992-93, pres. 1993-94).

COLEMAN, DONNA LESLIE, artist, art educator; b. Phila., Nov. 16, 1954; d. Ernest Albert Coleman and Sonia Donna (Dimon) Prauser; m. Jeffrey Carlton Mumford, Nov. 23, 1985; 1 child, Josephine Blythe Coleman-Mumford. Student, U. Zurich, 1972-73, Mercy Coll., 1987-89; BFA, RISD, 1977; MFA, Bklyn. Coll., 1982. Cert. art tchr. N.Y. Art tchr. Germantown Acad., Ft. Washington, Pa., 1983-86, Rye (N.Y.) Country Day Sch., 1986-89, Fillmore Arts Ctr., Washington, 1991—, Browne Acad., Alexandria, Va., 1989—. Art Matters Inc. fellow, N.Y.C., 1992, 95; D.C. Commn. on the Arts grantee, 1992-93, 95-96, tech. assistance grantee, 1994.

COLEMAN, ELISABETH CHARLOTTE, corporate communications executive; b. Woking, Surrey, Eng., May 26, 1945; came to U.S., 1949; d. David and Anne Lise (Bojesen) C.; m. Rock Brynner, Dec. 24, 1978 (div. Jan. 1984). BA, Vassar Coll., 1966. Researcher Newsweek Mag., N.Y.C., 1967-70; corr. Newsweek Mag., San Francisco, 1970-73; reporter Sta. KQED-TV, San Francisco, 1973; radio-TV reporter ABC News, N.Y.C., 1973-74; reporter Sta. KABC-TV News, L.A., 1974-76; press sec. to Gov. Edmund G. Brown, Jr. Sacramento, 1976-78; producer Inside Story, PBS series, N.Y.C., 1980-82, Jack Hilton Prodns., N.Y.C., 1982-85; pres. Coleman Prodns., N.Y.C., 1985-88; dir. pub. rels. Ernst & Whinney, N.Y.C., 1988-90; v.p. internat. pub. affairs Am. Express, N.Y.C., 1990—. Contbr. articles to N.Y. Sunday Times Mag., Columbia Journalism Review, Family Weekly, N.Y. Daily News. Mem. PRSA, AFTRA. Office: Am Express Travel Related Svcs American Express Tower New York NY 10285*

COLEMAN, ELIZABETH ANN, museum curator; b. Takoma Park, Md., Sept. 13, 1941; d. Andrew Joel and Dorothy (Smith) C. BA, Elmira Coll., 1963; postgrad., U. Del., 1966. Asst. curator decorative arts Newark Mus., 1965-69, assoc. curator decorative arts, 1969; asst. curator decorative arts Bklyn. Mus., 1969-71, assoc. curator decorative arts/costumes and textiles, 1971-73, curator costumes and textiles, 1973-90; curator textiles and costumes Mus. Fine Arts, Houston, 1991—; cons. collections for various mus., hist. socs., 1975—; adj. prof. Fashion Inst. Tech., Rice U., Houston, 1990—; grants reviewer Nat. Endowment Arts, Washington, 1978—; cons. Getty Art Mus., Williamstown, Mass., 1992—. Co-author: The Collector's Encyclopedia of Dolls, 1969; author: The Genius of Charles James, 1982, The Opulent Era, 1989. Named Greens Honor Prof., Tex. Christian U., 1995. Fellow Costume Soc. Am. (founder, bd. dirs. various offices); mem. Costume Soc., Textile Soc. Am. (bd. dirs. 1989—), Internat. Coun. Mus. (costume com. 1978—). Office: Mus Fine Arts Houston 1001 Bissonnet Houston TX 77005

COLEMAN, FRANCES MCLEAN, secondary school educator; b. Jackson, Miss., Feb. 17, 1940; d. Robert Beatty and Dorothy Trotter (Witty) McLean.; m. Thomas Allen Coleman, Aug. 29, 1964; children: James Plemon, Robert McLean, Dorothy Witty McLean, Josiah Dennis, Leonidas McLean. BA, U. Miss., Oxford, 1962; MS, U. Miss., Jackson, 1964, PhD, 1970. Cert. tchr., Miss. Coord. Title I ESEA Choctaw County, Ackerman, Miss., 1970-73; instr. anatomy and physiology Wood Jr. Coll., Mathiston, Miss., 1977-78, instr. math. Miss. State U., Starkville, 1978-81; tchr. Choctaw City Sch. Dist., Ackerman, 1982—. Author: (jour.) Surgery, 1966. Active Miss. State Bd. of Health, Jackson, 1980-94. Recipient Presdl. award for excellence in sci. teaching NSF, 1990, Sci. Tchr. awards Disney, 1993; Coun. for Basic Edn. Sci.-Math. fellow, 1994; named Educator of Yr. Milken Family Founds., 1991; Tandy scholar, 1991; Tapestry grantee, 1995; Access Excellence fellow Genentech, 1995; Am. Physiol. Soc. fellow, 1995. Mem. Nat. Sci. Tchrs. Assn., Am. Assn. German Tchrs., Am. Assn. French Tchrs., Am. Assn. Physics Tchrs., Nat. Assn. Biology Tchrs., Miss. Edn. Computer Assn. (Miss. Computer Educator of Yr. 1990, pres.-elect 1995, pres. 1996), Miss. Fgn. Lang. Assn. (pres. secondary sect. 1992-94). Episcopalian. Home: PO Box 268 Ackerman MS 39735-0268 Office: Choctaw County Sch Dist PO Box 398 Ackerman MS 39735-0398

COLEMAN, JEAN BLACK, nurse, physician assistant; b. Sharon, Pa., Jan. 11, 1925; d. Charles B. and Sue E. (Dougherty) Black; m. Donald A. Coleman, July 3, 1946; children: Sue Ann Lopez, Donald Ashley. RN, Spencer Hosp. Sch. Nursing, Meadville, Pa., 1945; student Vanderbilt U., 1952-54. Nurse, dir. nursing Bulloch Meml. Hosp., Statesboro, Ga., 1948-51, nurse supr. surgery, 1954-67, dir. nursing, 1967-71; physicians asst., nurse anesthetist to Robert H. Swint, Statesboro, 1971—; mem. Pa. adv. com. Ga. Med. Bd., 1989—. Recipient Dean Day Smith Svc. to Mankind award, 1995; named Woman of Yr. in Med. Field, Bus. and Profl. Women, 1980. Mem. ANA, Ga. Nurses Assn., Am. Acad. Physicians Assts., Ga. Assn. Physicians Assts. (bd. dirs. 1975-79, v.p. 1979-80, pres. 1980-81), Ga. Bd. Med. Examiners (mem. physician assts. adv. com. 1987—, ex-officio mem. 1994). Democrat. Roman Catholic.

COLEMAN, K(ATHERINE) ANN, educator; b. Plattsburg, N.Y.; d. John and Anna C. BS, Elms Coll., 1963; MS, Springfield Coll., 1964; PhD, Boston Coll., 1971; MPH, Harvard U., 1978. Psychologist Exec. Office of the Pres., Washington, 1964-66; research assoc. Harvard U., Cambridge, Mass., 1970-71; asst. prof. SUNY, Stony Brook, 1971-75, assoc. prof., 1975-78; assoc. prof. Boston U., 1978—; owner, pres. La Di Da Properties, Cambridge, 1986—. Co-author: (with others) Behavioral Statistics: The Core, 1994, Fundamentals of Behavioral Statistics, 8th edit., 1996; contbr. articles to profl. jours. Mem. New Eng. Ednl. Rsch. Orgn. (bd. dirs. 1974-86, v.p. 1985-86, pres. 1986-87), Ea. Ednl. Rsch. Orgn. (div. chmn. 1979-91, bd. dirs. 1985-91). Home: 32 Shepard St Cambridge MA 02138-1518 Office: Boston U Dept Psychology 64 Cummington St Boston MA 02215-2407

COLEMAN, LILLIAN SIMONS, editor, writer; b. Atlanta, Jan. 26, 1955; d. Henry Mazyck and Martha Jane (Mack) Simons; m. John Dozier Coleman III, Nov. 29, 1975; children: Keating Simons, Lillian Marshall, John Dozier IV. BA in English, Columbia (S.C.) Coll., 1977; M in Mass Communications, U. S.C., 1980. Instr. journalism U. S.C., Sumter, 1979-82; communications mgr. Assn. for Edn. in Journalism and Mass Communication, Columbia, 1982-84, asst. editor, 1984-87, editor AEJMC News and Journalism and Mass Communication Directory, 1987-93; prodn. mgr. Journalism and Mass Comm. Quar., Columbia, 1994—; freelance writer, photographer Sandlapper mag., Columbia, 1980-82, Carolina Lifestyle mag., Columbia, 1983. Office: Assn Edn in Journalism and Mass Comm LeConte Coll U SC Columbia SC 29208-0251

COLEMAN, LINDA, state legislator. BA, U. Miss.; JD, Miss. Coll. State rep., mem. penitentiary com., vice chairwoman county affairs, judiciary, pub. bldgs., grounds & lands coms. Miss. Ho. of Reps., Jackson. Mem. Nat. Bar Assn., Magnolia Bar Assn. Democrat. Baptist. Office: Miss Ho of Reps State Capitol PO Box 382 Jackson MS 38762*

COLEMAN, NANCY CATHERINE, actress; b. Everett, Wash., Dec. 30, 1912; d. Charles Sumner Coleman and Grace Sharpless; m. Whitney French Bolton, Sept. 16, 1943 (dec. Nov. 1969); children: Charla Elizabeth, Grania Theresa. BA, U. Wash., 1934. Actress; films include KIng's Row, 1941, Dangerously They Live, 1941, The Gay Sisters, 1942, Desperate Jouney, 1942, The Edge of Darkness, 1943, In Our Time, 1944, Devotion, 1946, Her Sister's Secret, 1947, That Man from Tangier, 1953, Slaves, 1968; various TV shows including Valiant Lady, 1954-55; plays include Susan and God with Gertrude Lawrence, 1938, Liberty Jones, 1941, Desperate Hours, 1955. Mem. AFTRA, SAG, N.Y. TV Acad., Actors' Equity, Motion Picture Arts and Scis.

COLEMAN, WINIFRED ELLEN, administrator; b. Syracuse, N.Y., Oct. 3, 1932; d. Peter Andrew and Josephine (Fahey) C. BA, Lemoyne Coll., Syracuse, N.Y., 1954; MA, Marquette U., 1956. Dean of students Cazenovia (N.Y.) Coll., 1957-71; dean of students Trinity Coll., Washington, 1971-81; exec. dir. Nat. Coun. Catholic Women, Washington, 1981-85; pres. St. Joseph Coll., West Hartford, Conn., 1991—; bd. trustees, Lemoyne Coll., Syracuse, 1980-86; mem. Nat. Assn. Women Deans, Washington, 1957-81; mem. bd. dirs. Nat. Conf. ITT Hartford Mutual Funds Bd. Vice chmn. Syracuse Commn. for Women, 1986—; commr. Metro Commn. for Aging, Syracuse, 1987—; bd. dirs. Cen City Girl Scout Coun. Hon. Trinity Coll. Alumnae, Washington, 1978, Cazenovia (N.Y.) Coll. Alumnae, 1968, Naming of Winifred E. Coleman Student Union, Cazenovia Coll., 1961; recipient Chantal Award, Catholic Daughters of the Am. 1963. Mem. Alpha Sigma Nu (nat. bd. dirs. 1980-82). Roman Catholic. Home: 27 Buckingham Ln West Hartford CT 06117-2758 Office: St Joseph Coll 1678 Asylum Ave West Hartford CT 06117-2764

COLEMAN-HILL, ANDREA ELEAN, special education educator; b. Detroit, Mar. 7, 1954; d. Ronald and Hazel (Hallums) Coleman; m. Rodney I. Hill, July 21, 1990; children: Rodney Alexander, Chelsea Andrea. BS in Edn., Kutztown U., 1988; MEd and prin. cert., Cheyney U., 1995; internat. studies, Cambridge U., England. Long-term substitute tchr. Colonial Northampton Sch. Dist. 20, Easton, Pa., 1988-89; tchr. Overbrook Sch. for Blind, Phila., 1989-91, Cora Svcs., Phila., 1991-93, Reading (Pa.) Sch. Dist., 1993—. Mem. NEA, Pa. Edn. Assn., Reading Edn. Assn., Pa. Speech, Lang., Hearing Assn. Office: Thomas Ford Elem Sch Reading Sch Dist 911 Margaret St Reading PA 19611-1500

COLEMAN-JOHNSON, DEBRA LYNN, electrical engineer; b. Mobile, Ala., Apr. 7, 1966; d. Fred and Mattie Lois (Carter) C.; married, June 2, 1990. BSEE, Boston U., 1988. Test engr. Raytheon Corp., Andover, Mass., 1987-88; liaison design engr. Boeing Co., Everett, Wash., 1988-89; software engr. Boeing Co., Seattle, 1989-90; sr. sys. engr. Boeing Co., Renton, Wash., 1990-95; specialist engr. Boeing Co., Everett, Wash., 1995—; pres., owner Beacon Pub. and Media House, Seattle, 1994—; lectr. Math., Engring. and Sci. Achievement Orgn., 1989—; v.p. Seattle City Tours, 1990-93. Vol. MATHCOUNTS, Seattle, YMCA Black Achievers Program, 1994—. Mem. Nat. Soc. Black Engrs. Home: 3020 21st Ave S Seattle WA 98144-5906 Office: Boeing Co PO Box 3707 #MS 07-30 Seattle WA 98124-2207

COLEMAN-STEWART, ELIZABETH DIXON, civic worker; b. Washington, Aug. 9, 1963; d. John Sheridan and Jacquelyn (Hastings) C.; m. Keith Robert Stewart, Mar. 26, 1996. Student, Coll. of Wooster, 1981-83, Temple U., 1983-86. Store mgr. J.G. Hook, Phila., 1984-86; buyer Joshua Slocum, Phila., 1986-89; collectibles buyer QVC, West Chester, Pa., 1989-94; dir. programming Buckeye Comm. Inc., Media, Pa., 1994-95. Vol. ARC, West Chester, Pa. Home: 503 Polo Run West Chester PA 19380

COLEMAN WOOD, KRISTA ANN, physical therapy educator; b. Decatur, Ill., July 28, 1956; d. Wayne Dudley and Shirley Margaret (Doner) Coleman; m. Earl Andrew Wood, Mar. 21, 1987; 1 child, Karolyn Christine. BS, Eastern Ill. U., Charleston, 1978; BS in Phys. Therapy, U. Ill., Peoria, 1980; MSc in Bioengring., U. Strathclyde, Glasgow, Scotland, 1986; MS in Phys. Therapy, U. Minn., Mpls., 1988, PhD in Biomechanics, 1994. Lic. phys. therapist, Minn., Wis. Staff phys. therapist Bellin Meml. Hosp., Green Bay, Wis., 1980-82, Rehab. Specialists, Anoka, Minn., 1982-83, Fairview Hosp., Mpls., 1983-85; grad. rsch. and teaching asst. U. Minn., Mpls., 1984-85, 86-89, instr. phys. therapy curriculum, dept. phys. medicine, 1989-92, clin. specialist faculty phys. therapy curriculum, 1992—; cons. Recreational Opportunities for Physically Disabled, Green Bay, Wis., 1980-82; mem. survey team Green Bay Area Accessibility Guide, 1982. Rotary Found. grad. fellow, 1985-86, Charles and Constance Murcott Found. scholar Found. Phys. Therapy, 1988-89; recipient Acad. Mentoring award U. Minn. Inst. Tech., 1995. mem. Women in Sci. and Engring., Am. Phys. Therapy Assn., Am. Coll. Sports Medicine, Rehab. Engring. Soc. N.Am., Internat. Soc. Biomechanics, Soc. Orthopedic Medicine, Minn. Orthopedic Phys. Therapy Study Group (pres. 1994—), Phi Sigma. Methodist. Office: Univ Minn Minneapolis MN 55455

COLES, ANNA LOUISE BAILEY, university official, nurse; b. Kansas City, Kans., Jan. 16, 1925; d. Gordon Alonzo and Lillie Mai (Buchanan) Bailey; children: Margot, Michelle, Gina. Diploma, Freedmen's Hosp. Sch. Nursing, 1948; B.S. in Nursing, Avila Coll., Kansas City, Mo., 1958; M.S. in Nursing, Cath. U. Am., 1960, Ph.D. in Higher Edn., 1967. Instr. VA Hosp., Topeka, 1950-52; supr. VA Hosp., Kansas City, Mo., 1952-58; asst. dir. inservice edn. Freedmen's Hosp., Washington, 1960-61; adminstrv. asst. to dir. nursing Freedmen's Hosp., 1961-66, assoc. dir. nursing services, 1966-67, dir. nursing, 1967-69; dean Howard U. Coll. Nursing, Washington, 1968-86, dean emeritus, 1986—; cons. pvt. practice, Kansas City, Kans.; dir. minority devel. U. Kans., 1991-95; cons. Gen. Research Support Program, NIH, 1972-76, VA health care com. NRC-Nat. Acad. Scis., 1975-76, VA Central Office continuing edn. com., 1976—; pres. Nurses Examining Bd., 1967-68; mem. Inst. Medicine, Nat. Acad. Scis., 1974—; Mem. D.C. Health Planning Adv. Com., 1968-71, Tri-State Regional Planning Com. for Nursing Edn., 1969, Health Adv. Council, Nat. Urban Coalition, 1971-73. Contbr. articles to profl. jours. Bd. dirs. Iona Whipper Home for Unwed Mothers, 1970-72; bd. dirs. Nursing Edn. Opportunities, 1970-72; trustee Community Group Health Found., 1976-77, cons., 1977—; bd. regents State Univ. System Fla., 1977; adv. bd. Am. Assn. Med. Vols., 1970-72. Recipient sustained superior performance award HEW, 1962, Meritorious Pub. Svc. award Govt. of D.C., 1968, medal of honor Avila Coll., 1969, Disting. Alumni award Howard U. Nat. Assn. for Equal Opportunity in Higher Edn., 1990, cmty. svc. award Black Profl. Nurses Kansas City, 1991, lifetime achievement award Assn. Black Nursing Faculty in Higher Edn., 1993, svc. award Midwest Regional Conf. on Black Families and Children, 1994. Mem. Nat. League Nursing (dir.), Am. Nurses Assn., Freedmen's Hosp. Nursing Alumni Assn., Am. Congress Rehab. Medicine, Am. Assn. Colls. of Nursing (sec. 1975-76), Societas Docta, Inc. (charter, pres. 1996—), Sigma Theta Tau, Alpha Kappa Alpha. Home: 15107 Interlachen Dr #205 Silver Spring MD 20906

COLES, BERTHA SHARON GILES, visual information specialist; b. Paris, Tenn., Aug. 13, 1949; d. Charles Ray and Etter Bell (Lightfoot) Giles; divorced. Student, Profl. Edn. Divsn. Dallas, 1979, Dynamic Graphics Ednl. Found., 1980, No. Va. C.C., 1981. Typesetter, illustrator Def. Printing, Washington, 1979-83; editl. asst. Exec. Office of Pres., Washington,

1983; visual info. specialist Naval Media Support Ctr., Washington, 1983—. Design, layout, paste-up specialist for various publs., including U.S. Navy Medicine, 1981, 83, Bull., 1983, Playbook, 1995. Bd. dirs. London Woods Cmty. Assn., Capitol Heights, Md., 1995. Democrat. Home: 5634 Onslow Way Capitol Heights MD 20743 Office: Naval Media Support Ctr Pentagon Rm 2E-325 Washington DC 20350

COLEY, LINDA MARIE, secondary school educator; b. Albany, Ga., Apr. 19, 1945; d. Leonard Earl and Hazel (Brady) C. BS in Math., Piedmont Coll., 1966; MS in Math., U. Ga., 1972, postgrad. Cert. tchr., Ga. Tchr. Toccoa (Ga.) Pub. Schs., 1966-67, Hall County Sch. Dist., Gainesville, Ga., 1967-68, Clarke County Sch. Dist., Athens, Ga., 1968—. Sec., 1st v.p. Clarke County Dem. Com., Athens, 1981—. Mem. NEA, Ga. Edn. Assn., Clarke County Assn. Educators (treas., sec.), Alpha Delta Kappa (treas., sec., pres.). Democrat. Baptist. Home: 135 Ravenwood Pl Athens GA 30605-3344

COLEY, MAURITA K., broadcast executive. Exec. v.p. Black Entertainment TV Networks Black Entertainment TV, Inc., Washington. Office: Black Entertainment TV Networks Black Entertainment TV Holdings Inc One BET Plz 1900 W Pl NE Washington DC 20018-1211*

COLFACK, ANDREA HECKELMAN, elementary education educator; b. Yreka, Calif., July 17, 1945; d. Robert A. Davis and June (Reynolds) Butler; m. David Lee Heckelman, Sept. 5, 1965 (div. Nov. 1982); children: Barbara, Julie; m. Neal Cleve, Jan. 1, 1984; 1 stepchild, Karl. AB, Calif. State U., L.A., 1966; MA, Calif. State U., Fresno, 1969. Life standard elem. credential, Calif. cert. competencs: Spanish, Calif.; ordained to ministry Faith Christian Fellowship Internat., 1987. Tchr. Tulare (Calif.) City Schs., 1966-67, Palo Verde Union Sch. Dist., 1967-70, Cutler-Orosi (Calif.) Union Sch. Dist., 1979-82, Hornbrook (Calif.) Union Sch. Dist., 1982-84; sales mgr. Tupperware, Fresno, Calif., 1973-79; bilingual tchr. West Contra Costa (Calif.) Unified Sch. Dist., 1984—; prin. Bayview Elem. Sch., San Pablo, Calif., 1995—; site mentor Bayview Elem. Sch., Richmond, 1990-92, prin. Bayview Elem. Sch., San Pablo, Calif.; ELD mentor, Richmond, 1992-94, mentor selection com., 1994-95; summer sch. prin. Grant Elem. Sch., Richmond, 1995. Co-author: Project Mind Expansion, 1974. East Bay C.U.E. Tech. grantee, 1995. Mem. United Tchrs. Richmond, Calif. Assn. Bilingual Educators (sec. Richmond 1990-91), AAUW (pres. Tulare br. 1967-68). Democrat. Pentecostal. Home: 5461 Hackney Ln Richmond CA 94803 Office: Bayview Elem Sch 3001 16th St San Pablo CA 94806

COLGATE, DORIS ELEANOR, retailer, sailing school administrator; b. Washington, May 12, 1941; d. Bernard Leonard and Frances Lillian (Goldstein) Horecker; m. Richard G. Buchanan, Sept. 6, 1959 (div. Aug. 1967); m. Stephen Colgate, Dec. 17, 1969. Student Antioch Coll., 1958-60, NYU, 1960-62. Rsch. supr. Geyer Mover Ballard, N.Y.C., 1962-64; adminstrv. asst. Yachting Mag., N.Y.C., 1964-68; v.p. Offshore Sailing Sch. Ltd., Inc., N.Y.C., 1968-78, pres., Ft. Myers, Fla., 1978—; pres., CEO On and Offshore, Inc., Ft. Myers, 1984—; v.p. Offshore Travel, Inc., City Island, 1978-88. Author: The Bareboat Gourmet, 1983; contbr. articles to profl. jours. Mem. Royal Ocean Racing Club (London chpt.), Nat. Women's Sailing Assn. (chair nat. women's adv. bd. 1990-94, chair, 1991-94, pres. 1994—), Am. Women's Econ. Devel. Corp. (adv. bd. 1980-86, Betty Cook Meml. Lifetime Achievement award 1994, Boat/U.S. Nat. adv. coun. 1995—), Internat. Women Boating (bd. dirs., Sail Industry Leadership award 1996). Avocations: sailing, photography, writing, cooking. Home: 1555 San Carlos Bay Dr Sanibel FL 33957-3423 Office: Offshore Inc 16731 Mcgregor Blvd Fort Myers FL 33908-3843

COLGATE, JESSIE M., insurance company executive, lawyer; b. Buffalo, N.Y., May 13, 1950; d. Richard M. Colgate and Rosemary (Hall) Evans. AB, Harvard U., 1972; JD, Georgetown U., 1977. Bar: D.C. 1977. Assoc. Shea Gould, Washington, 1977-79, Steptoe & Johnson, Washington, 1979-86, Miller & Chevalier, Washington, 1986; sr. v.p. N.Y. Life Ins. Co., Washington, 1987—. Bd. dirs. Columbia Hosp. for Women, Washington, 1986-96. Mem. ABA, D.C. Bar Assn. Episcopalian. Office: NY Life Ins Co 1001 Pennsylvania Ave NW Washington DC 20004-2505

COLISH, MARCIA LILLIAN, history educator; b. Bklyn., July 27, 1937; d. Samuel and Daisy (Kartch) C. BA magna cum laude, Smith Coll., 1958; MA, Yale U., 1959, PhD, 1965. Instr. history Skidmore Coll., Saratoga Springs, N.Y., 1962-63; instr. Oberlin Coll., Ohio, 1963-65, asst. prof., 1965-69; assoc. prof. Oberlin Coll, Ohio, 1969-75; prof. history Oberlin Coll., Ohio, 1975—; Frederick B. Artz prof. history Oberlin Coll., 1985—, chmn. dept. history, 1973-74, 78-81, 85-86; vis. scholar Am. Acad. Rome, 1968-69; lectr. history Case Western Res. U., Cleve., 1966-67; editorial cons. W.W. Norton & Co., 1973, John Wiley & Sons, Inc., 1981, SUNY Press, 1983, 85, U. Chgo. Press, 1988, U. Calif. Press, 1988, Princeton U. Press, 1988, U. Notre Dame Press, 1991, 92, 94, U. Ill. Press, 1995, U. Pa. Press, 1995; cons. dept. history Grinnell Coll., 1974, Knox Coll., 1981, St. John's U., 1981, Whitman Coll., 1982, Hope Coll., 1995, Kenyon Coll., 1996; mem. exec. bd. Ohio Program Humanities, 1976-81, exec. bd., 1978-81, vice chmn., 1979-81; writing residency, Villa Serbellonia, Bellagio, 1995. Author: The Mirror of Language: A Study in the Medieval Theory of Knowledge, 2d rev. edit., 1983, The Stoic Tradition from Antiquity to the Early Middle Ages, 1985, enlarged paperback edit., 1990, Peter Lombard, 1994. Mem. exec. bd. Oberlin ACLU, 1970-74, chmn., 1972-74, rec. sec., 1976-77, vice chmn., 1979-80; mem. exec. bd. Oberlin YWCA, 1966-70. Recipient Wilbur Cross medal Yale Grad. Sch. Alumni Assn., 1993; Samuel S. Fels fellow Yale U., 1961-62, Younger Scholar fellow Inst. for Rsch. in Humanities, U. Wis., 1974-75, Nat. Humanitiess Ctr. fellow, 1981-82, Guggenheim fellow, 1989-90, Woodrow Wilson Ctr. fellow, 1994-95; NEH summer grantee U. Calif., 1993. Fellow Medieval Acad. Am. (coun. 1987-89, 2d v.p. 1989-90, 1st v.p. 1990-91, pres. 1991-92); mem. Am. Hist. Assn., Medieval Assn. Midwest (coun. 1978-81), Midwest Medieval Conf. (pres. 1978-79), Renaissance Soc. Am., Cen. Renaissance Conf., Soc. Internat. pour Etude Philosophie Medievale, Internat. Soc. for Classical Tradition, Phi Beta Kappa. Home: 143 E College St Apt 310 Oberlin OH 44074-1759 Office: Oberlin Coll Dept History Oberlin OH 44074

COLLAMER, SONJA MAE SOREIDE, veterinary facility administrator; b. Rapid City, S.D., Sept. 3, 1937; d. Louis Severin and Mae Marie (Barber) Soreide; m. John Harry Collamer, Dec. 30, 1959; children: Debra, Michael, Kenneth, Kerry. BS in Bacteriology, Colo. State U., 1959. Practice mgr. Saratoga (Wyo.) Vet. Clinic, 1966-94, ret., 1994; mem. Wyo. Bd. Medicine, 1995—. Pres., mem. Wyo. Jaycettes, 1962-70; elder, clk. session First Presbyn. Ch., Saratoga, 1966—; neighborhood chmn., leader Girl Scouts Am., Saratoga, 1967-77; sec., mem. Snowy Range Cattlewomen, Carbon County, Wyo., 1967—; active bd. of edn. Sch. Dist. #9, Saratoga, 1968-72; chmn., treas. bd. edn. Sch. Dist. #2, Carbon County, 1972-81; mem. Carbon County Rep. Ctrl. Com., 1980—; vice chair, mem. Saratoga Sr. Ctr. Bd., 1982-86; pres., mem. Snowy Range Ambs., Saratoga, 1984—; chair Region VIII Child Devel. Program, Carbon County, 1985-90; mem., fundraiser Saratoga Cmty. Choir, 1988—; mediator Wyo. Agrl. Mediation Bd., 1988—; co-chair Thomas for Congress Com., Carbon County, 1990; chair Saratoga Hist. and Cultural Assn. Bd., 1990—; active Planning & Devel. Commn., Carbon County, 1994. Mem. Am. Vet. Med. Assn. Auxiliary, Wyo. Vet. Med. Assn. Auxiliary (pres.), Kappa Delta. Republican. Presbyterian. Home: PO Box 485-806 Rangeview Saratoga WY 82331

COLLAS-DEAN, ANGELA G., state commissioner, small business owner; b. Manila, The Philippines, Oct. 20, 1933; came to the U.S., 1960; d. Juan Damocles and Soledad Garduño (Martinez) Collas; m. Bruce Goring Dean, Aug. 8, 1961; children: Heather Frances, Jennifer Ashton. BA in English Lit. and Humanities, U. of the Philippines, Diliman, Quezon City, 1955; MA in Drama, Baylor U., 1962. Owner Philippine Party Foods, Eugene, Oreg., 1984—; instr. U. of the Philippines, Diliman, Quezon City, 1963-65, Baylor U., Waco, Tex., 1965-68. Com. mem. Affirmative Action Adv. Com., Lane County, Oreg., 1972-76; bd. mem. Sign Code Bd. Appeals, Eugene, 1985-87; city commr. Human Rights Commn., Eugene, 1985-87, Cultural Arts Commn., Eugene, 1989-93; com. mem. Joint Soc. Svc. Fund, Lane County, Eugene and Springfield, 1986-88. Fulbright/Smith-Mundt grantee U.S. Dept. Edn., Manila, 1959, Fulbright grantee U.S. Dept. Edn., Manila, 1960. Mem. Philippine Am. Assn. (founding mem., officer Eugene 1983—), Asian Coun. (founding mem., officer Eugene and Springfield 1985—), Asian Am. Found. (founding mem., officer Eugene 1993—). Office: Philippine Party Foods 2092 Roland Way Eugene OR 97401-2061

COLLAZO, VERONICA O., federal agency administrator; b. San Antonio. BA, Am. U., MS in Adminstrn. of Justice; PhD, U. Denver. Dep. dir. internat. mcpl. devel. Internat. City Mgmt. Assn., Washington; dep. dir. Office Human Resource Devel., Washington; dep. chief, pers. liaison and tng., civil divsn. Dept. Justice; dir. Office of Tng. Sys. U.S. Postal Svc., Washington, 1991-92, v.p. diversity devel., 1992—.

COLLETTE, FRANCES MADELYN, retired tax consultant, lawyer; b. Yonkers, N.Y., Aug. 5, 1947; d. Morris Aaron and Esther (Gang) Volbert; m. Roger Warren Collette, Dec. 25, 1971; children: Darren Roger, Bonnie Frances. BEd summa cum laude, SUNY-Buffalo, 1969; JD, cum laude, U. Miami, 1980. Bar: Fla. 1980. Employment counselor Fla. Bur. Employment Security, Miami, 1969-73; unemployment claims adjudicator Fla. Bur. Unemployment Claims, Miami, 1973-77; Fla. unemployment tax and personnel cons.; owner Unemployment Svcs. Fla., Inc., Miami, 1977-93; lectr. in field. Mem. BBB S. Fla. (1st v.p. 1980-81, bd. govs., 2d vice chmn. 1990-91). Jewish.

COLLIER, BEVERLY JOANNE, elementary education educator; b. Grand Haven, Mich., Oct. 28, 1936; d. Joseph Frank and Anne (Mary) Snyder; divorced; children: Ann, Cindy. Student, U. Mich., 1955-57; BA, Western Mich. U., 1965. Cert. elem. tchr., Mich. 1st grade tchr. Fruitport (Mich.) Community Schs., 1965-93; retired, 1993. Contbr. articles to local newspapers. Active Grand Haven (Mich.) Presbyn. Ch., 1955—. Mem. ASCD, NEA, Muskegon Edn. Assn., Mich. Edn. Assn. (past regional rep.), Mich. Assn. Ret. Sch. Personnel (Muskegon County chpt.). Home: 1235 Washington Ave Grand Haven MI 49417-1627 Office: Fruitport Cmty Sch 305 Pontaluna Rd Fruitport MI 49415-9652

COLLIER, DIANA GORDON, publishing executive; b. Ottawa, Ont., Can., June 15, 1945; came to U.S., 1984; d. Edward Cecil and Vera (Lowrie) C.; m. Y. Naim, Apr. 17, 1982; 1 child, Sundiata. BA, U. B.C., 1963; MA, U. Montreal, 1975. Writer, 1972-83; editor Black Rose Books, Montreal, Que., Can., 1973-75; bus. mgr. Studies Polit. Economy, Ottawa, Ont., Can., 1980-82; pub. Clarity Press, Inc., Atlanta, 1984—; dir. communications, editor newsletter Internat. Human Rights Assn. of Am. Minorities, Chgo., 1988—. Author: Invisible Women of Washington, 1989 (Best of U.S. Small Press 1989), Minnesota Review, 1988; editor: Restructuring of America, 1991, Shelter in the Light, 1991, Israeli Peace-Palestinean Justice, 1994, A Popular Guide to Minority Rights, 1995, American Indians: Stereotypes and Realities, 1996. Bell Can. fellow, Montreal, 1973, 74; Can. Coun. grantee, Ottawa, 1975, 77. Mem. NAACP, Soc. Scholarly Pub., Pub. Mktg. Assn. Multicultural Pubs. Exch., COSMEP. Office: Clarity Press Inc 3277 Roswell Rd NE Ste 469 Atlanta GA 30305-1840

COLLIER, EVELYN MYRTLE, elementary school educator; b. Newton, Ala., Dec. 11, 1942; d. Palmer Lee and Jessie Beryl (Williams) C. BA, Samford U., 1965; M Religious Edn., Southwestern Sem., 1967; MS, Troy State U., 1977. Youth dir. Calvary Bapt. Temple, Savannah, Ga., 1967-69; tchr. Newton Elem. Sch., 1969-77, prin., 1977-94; asst. prof. elem. edn. Fla. Bapt. Theol. Coll., Graceville, Fla., 1994—. Mem. ASCD, Ala. Assn. Elem. Sch. Prins. (exec. bd. 1984-94, sec. 1985, dist. IX prin. 1983, dist. IX Disting. Prin. award 1986, 89, 92), Ala. Coun. Sch. Adminstrs. and Suprs. (bd. dirs. 1991-94), Nat. Assn. Elem. Sch. Prins., Delta Kappa Gamma (Alpha Kappa chpt., Beta state exec. bd. 1987—, pres. Ala. chpt. 1987-93, 1st v.p. 1989-91, 2d v.p. 1987-89, Golden Gift Fund award 1983, Internat. scholar 1996), Phi Delta Kappa. Baptist. Office: Fla Bapt Theol Coll 5400 College Dr Graceville FL 32440-1831

COLLIER, MARCIA KIM, genealogist; b. Washington, Apr. 26, 1956; d. James Clyde and Lois Earlene (Chambers) Smith; m. Joseph L. Collier. Profl. genealogist Montgomery, Ala., 1985—; owner So. Genealogy Svcs., Montgomery, 1991—; Event planner various orgns., Montgomery, 1990—. Author: Our Chambers Family Remembered, 1991; editor, pub.: The Known Descendants of Garrison & Isabella Piggott Deens/Deen/Dean, 1990; compiler, editor: Alabama County Data and Resources, 1996; compiler: Alabama Genealogy Society, Inc. Membership and Surname Directory, 1992, 4th edit., 1995; contbr. to various trade publs. Inst. Genealogy and Hist. Rsch. scholar, 1995, 96. Mem. NAFE, Nat. Geneal. Soc., Fedn. Geneal. Socs., Assn. Profl. Genealogists, Ala. Geneal. Soc. (2d v.p. 1992-94, 1st v.p. 1994-96, pres. 1996—). Office: So Genealogy Svcs PO Box 3122 Montgomery AL 36109-0122

COLLIER, RUTH BERINS, political science educator; b. Hartford, Conn., June 20, 1942; d. Maurice and Esther (Meyers) Berins; m. David Collier; children: Stephen, Jennifer. AB, Smith Coll., 1964; MA, U. Chgo., 1966, PhD, 1974. Asst. prof. rsch. Ind. U., Bloomington, 1975-78; asst. to assoc. rsch. polit. scientist U. Calif., Berkeley, 1979-83, lectr., 1983-90, assoc. prof., prof., 1990—. Author: Regimes in Tropical Africa, 1982, The Contradictory Alliance: Labor Politics and the Regime Change in Mexico, 1992 (Hubert Herring award, 1993); co-author: Shaping the Political Arena: The Labor Movement, Critical Junctures, and Regime Dynamics in Latin America, 1991 (Comparative Politics Sect. award Am. Polit. Sci. Assn., 1993). Named fellow Ctr. for Advanced Study in the Behavioral Scis., Stanford, 1994-95.

COLLIER, ZENA, author; b. London, Jan. 21, 1926; came to U.S., 1946; d. Benjamin and Rebecca Feldman; m. Louis Shumsky, May 3, 1945 (div. 1967); children—Jeffrey A. (dec.), Paul E.; m. Thomas M. Hampson, Dec. 30, 1969. Tchr. Writers Workshop, Adult Edn., Rochester, N.Y., 1968-78, Writers Workshop, Nazareth Coll., Rochester, N.Y., 1984-94; guest lectr. Chautauqua Inst., 1991. Author: (novels) A Cooler Climate, 1990, Ghost Note, 1992; (children's books) The Year of the Dream (as Jane Collier), 1962; (as Zena Shumsky with Lou Shumsky) First Flight, 1962, Shutterbug, 1963; A Tangled Web (as Jane Collier), 1967; Next Time I'll Know, 1981; Seven for the People, 1979; contbr. short stories in Prairie Schooner, Southwest Rev., Lit. Rev., So. Humanities Rev., McCalls, others; contbr. articles in Pubs. Weekly, Money, Family Circle, L.A. Times Book Rev., others. Bd. dirs. Friends of Rochester Pub. Library, 1967-70, 79-85; mem. community adv. bd. WXXI Pub. TV-AM-FM, 1983-95. Resident fellow MacDowell, Yaddo, Va. Ctr. Creative Arts; writer-in-residence Just Buffalo lit. ctr., 1984, Niagara-Erie Writers, 1986, N.Y. State, So. Tier Libr. System, 1985. Recipient Hoepfner prize, Citation on Honour Roll of Best Am. Short Stories; nomination for Pushcart prize. Mem. Authors Guild, Writers & Books, Poets and Writers Inc. Democrat. Jewish. Address: c/o Harvey Klinger 301 W 53rd St New York NY 10019-5766

COLLIER-EVANS, DEMETRA FRANCES, veterans benefits counselor; b. Nashville, Dec. 18, 1937; d. Oscar Collier and Earllee Elizabeth (Williams) Collier-Sheffield; m. George Perry Evans, Dec. 21, 1966; 1 child, Richard Edward. AA in Social Sci., Solano Community Coll., Suisun City, Calif., 1974; BA in Social Sci., Chapman Coll., Orange, Calif., 1981. Cert. tchr., Calif. Specialist placement, case responsible person employment devel. dept. City of San Diego, 1975-82; vocat. tchr. San Diego Community Coll., 1982-83; specialist placement N.J. Job Service, Camden, 1984-86, mgr. job bank, 1985; specialist placement Abilities Ctr., Westville, N.J., 1987-88; veteran's benifits counselor VA, Phila. 1988—; mem. bd. dirs. Welfare Rights; cons. Bumble Bee Canning Co., San Diego, 1982. Developer women's seminar Women's Opportunity Week, City of San Diego, 1982, network seminar Fed. Women's Week, City of Phila., 1986. Bd. dirs. Welfare Rights Orgn., San Diego, 1982; mem. Internat. YWCA. Served with USAF, 1956-59. Recipient Excellence cert. San Diego Employer Adv. Bd., 1981, Leadership cert. Nat. U., San Diego, 1981. Mem. Black Advs. State Service (charter, corr. sec. San Diego chpt. 1981-82), Nat. Assn. Female Execs., AAUW, NAACP (life, rec. sec. San Diego 1982), Chapman Coll. Alumni Assn., Alpha Gamma Sigma. Democrat. Avocation: calligraphy. Office: VA 5000 Wissahickon Ave Philadelphia PA 19144-4867

COLLINE, MARGUERITE RICHNAVSKY, maternal, women's health and pediatrics nurse; b. Bayonne, N.J., Nov. 30, 1953; d. John P. and Margaret M. (Conaghan) Richnavsky; m. Richard L. Colline, Oct. 8, 1977; children: Jennifer, Nicole, Danielle, James Michael. Diploma in practical nurse, Union County Tech. Inst., Scotch Plains, N.J., 1973; BSN, Seton Hall U., 1978. RN, N.J., Md. Practical nurse oncology unit John E. Runnell's Hosp., Berkley Heights, N.J.; staff nurse infant unit Johns Hopkins Hosp., Balt.; staff nurse neonatal unit Overlook Hosp., Summit, N.J. Mem. Nat. Assn. Neonatal Nurses, Sigma Theta Tau. Home: 8 Overlook Dr Bridgewater NJ 08807-2105

COLLING, CATHARINE MARY, nurse, hospital administrator; b. Broomfield, Colo., Jan. 15, 1909; d. Patrick and Margaret Mary (Ryan) Kirby; m. Anthony Joseph Colling; 1 child, Mary Helen Colling Nightingale. BA, Ursuline Coll., 1934. RN, Calif. Supr. Mary's Help Hosp., 1945-50; adminstrv. indsl. nurse Standard Oil Co. of Calif., San Francisco, 1951-62; ward conservator Bank of Am. Trust Dept., 1964-67; instr. indsl. nursing Univ. San Francisco, 1954-69; adminstr. White Sands Convalescent Hosp., Pleasant Hill, Calif., 1967-70, Hillhaven Lawton Convalescent Hosp., San Francisco, 1970-91; dir. Hillhaven, San Francisco, 1991-95; ret., 1994. Founder, chmn. Vols. Aux. for Hillhaven, San Francisco, 1994—. Recipient numerous nursing awards. Mem. Am. Coll. Nursing Home Adminstr., No. Calif. Assn. Indsl. Nurses, Western Indsl. Nurses, Calif. Nurses Assn., Mary's Help Hosp. Alumni Assn., Calif. Assn. Hosp. Facilities. Republican. Roman Catholic. Office: 1359 Pine St San Francisco CA 94109-4807

COLLINS, AUDREY B., judge; b. 1945. BA, Howard U., 1967; MA, Am. U., 1969; JD, UCLA, 1977. Asst. atty. Legal Aid Found. L.A., 1977-78; with Office L.A. County Dist. Atty., 1978-94, dept. dist. atty., 1978-94, head dep. Torrance br. office, 1987-88, asst. dir. burs. ctrl. ops. and spl. ops., 1988-92, asst. dir. atty., 1992-94; judge. U.S. Dist. Ct. (Ctrl. Dist.) Calif., 1994—; dep. gen. counsel Office Spl. Advisor, L.A. Police Dept. Bd. Commrs., 1992. Advisor Spl. Assistance to Victims in Emergency, 1992-93; pres. L.A. Dist. Atty.'s Crimie Prevention Found., 1993. Acad. scholar Howard U.; named Lawyer of Yr., Langston Bar Assn., 1988; honoree Howard U. Alumni Club So. Calif., 1989. Mem. Nat. Bar Assn., Calif. Women Lawyers, State Bar Com. Bar Examiners (chair subcom. on moral character 1992-93, co-chair 1993-94), L.A. County Bar Assn., L.A. County Bar Judiciary Com., Assn. L.A. County Dist. Attys. (pres. 1983), Black Women Lawyers L.A. County, L.A. County Dist. Atty.'s Conf. (sec. 1993), Women Lawyers L.A., Order of Coif, Phi Beta Kappa. Office: US Dist Ct Edward R Roybal Fed Bldg 255 E Temple St Rm 690 Los Angeles CA 90012-3334

COLLINS, BARBARA-ROSE, congresswoman; b. Detroit, Apr. 13, 1939; d. Lamar N. Sr. and Versa (Jones) R.; widowed; children: Cynthia Lynn, Christopher Loren. Student, Wayne State U. Commr. Human Rights Commn., Detroit, 1974-75; Mich. state rep., 1975-81; councilwoman City of Detroit, from 1982; mem. 102nd-103rd Congresses from 13th (now 15th) Mich. dist., 1991—, ranking minority mem. govt. reform & oversight subcom. on postal svc., mem. transp. & infrastructure com.; regional coord. Nat. Black Caucus of Local Elected Officials, 1984. Chmn. Detroit City Coun. Task Force on Teenage Violence, 1985. Recipient Disting. Cmty. Svc. award Shrines of Black Madonna Pan African Orthodox Christian Ch., 1981, Devoted Svc. award Metro Boy Scouts Am., 1984, Invaluable Svc. award Pershing H.S., Detroit, 1985. Office: 401 Cannon Washington DC 20515-2215 also: Dist Office One Kennedy Sq 719 Griswold Ste 2006 Detroit MI 48226*

COLLINS, CARDISS, former congresswoman; b. St. Louis, Sept. 24, 1931; m. George W. Collins (dec.); 1 child, Kevin. Ed., Northwestern U.; hon. degree, Winston-Salem State U., Spelman Coll. Barber Scotia Coll.; sec. Ill. Dept. Revenue, then acct., revenue auditor; mem. 93d-103d Congresses from 7th Ill. Dist., 1973-96; ret., 1996; ranking minority mem. govt. reform & oversight com.; former chair. govt. activity and transp. subcom.; former majority whip-at-large; former chair Congl. Black Caucus, sec.; former chair Mems. Congress for Peace through Law. Mem. NAACP, The Chgo. Network, The Links. Mem. Nat. Coun. Negro Women, Chgo. Urban League, Black Women's Agenda, Alpha Gamma Pi, Alpha Kappa Alpha. Democrat. Baptist. Office: US Ho of Reps 2308 Rayburn Bldg Washington DC 20515-0005*

COLLINS, CAROLYN HERMAN, school media specialist, legislative aide; b. Lenoir, N.C., May 25, 1944; d. William Richard and Madeline Edith (Harris) Herman; m. Walter William Collins, Dec. 30, 1989. BA in English, Old Dominion U., Norfolk, Va., 1968; MS in Library Science, Fla. State U., Tallahassee, 1977; CAS Ednl. Adminstrn., Old Dominion U., 1992. Cert. sec. prin. and librarian, tchr. English, French, profl. librarian. Librarian Southampton County (Va.) Schs., 1973-79, TRADOC Army Library, Fort Monroe, Va., 1980-81; media specialist Portsmouth (Va.) Pub. Schs., 1981—; legis. aide Va. House of Dels., Richmond, 1984—; moderator White House Conf. on Libraries, Washington, 1991; state del. Gov's. Conf. on Libraries, Richmond, Va., 1990; York regional dir. Va. Ednl. Media Assn. (VEMA), 1992-94. Del. Virginia Beach City Rep. Conv., 1985-87; mem. Red, White and Blue Club, Virginia Beach, 1987-88; elected rep. Rep. City Com., Virginia Beach, 1987-89. Mem. Va. Ednl. Media Assn. (regional dir. 1992-94), Va. Reading Assn., Va. Assn. Tchrs. of English, Va. Square Dancing Assn., Libr. of Congress Assocs., Old Dominion Alumni Assn. (v.p. English chpt. 1987-89, House Dels. 1993—), Alpha Delta Kappa (chpt. pres. 1978-80, dist. sec. 1980-82), Beta Phi Mu Honor Soc. Republican. United Methodist. Home: 4026-B Tanglewood Trl Chesapeake VA 23325

COLLINS, CARRIE LINDA CLARK, administrative assistant; b. El Paso, Tex., Dec. 16, 1958; d. Robert Lewis and Joyce Elizabeth (Carter) Clark; m. Mitchél Anthony Collins, Oct. 11, 1985; 1 child, Cheyenne Lynn. Student, U. Tex., El Paso, 1977-79, Del. State Coll., 1979-80, Rutgers U., Camden, N.J., 1980-85; BS in Applied Sci. and Environ. Tech., Thomas Edison State Coll., 1996. Daycare worker, supr. Mainz (Germany) Am. Nursery, 1972-74; writer Pegasus Lit. and Arts mag., El Paso, 1975-77; recreation aide El Paso Dept. Parks and Recreation, 1978-79; credit analyst, managerial asst. Sears Credit Ctrl., Moorestown, N.J., 1980-88; cons., legal sec. green acres program, poet laureate State of N.J., Trenton, 1987-94; adminstrv. asst. Regional Indsl. Devel. Corp., Turtle Creek, Pa., 1996—; freelance writer, 1973—. Contbr. poetry to various anthologies. Mem. choir, soloist Tabernacle Missionary Bapt. Ch., Alton, Ill., 1965-68, 1st United Bapt. Ch., El Paso, 1976-79, 2d Bapt. Ch., Mt. Holly, N.J., 1985—. Mem. NAACP, Lit. Vols. Am., Delta Sigma Theta. Democrat. Office: Regional Indsl Devel Corp 600 Braddock Ave Turtle Creek PA 15000

COLLINS, CONNIE WOODS, educational administrator; b. Brewton, Ala., May 24, 1957; d. Wilford S. Woods and Evelyn Marshall Woods Watson; m. Edward L. Collins, Jr., Dec. 23, 1977; children: Candace, Michael. BA in Sociology, U. West Fla., 1977; MEd in Ednl. Leadership, U. Ctrl. Fla., 1993. Tchr. Orange County Pub. Schs., Orlando, Fla., 1984-94; asst. prin. Seminole County Pub. Schs., Altamonte Springs, Fla., 1994—. Delores Auzanne fellow State of Fla., 1992-93. Mem. ASCD, Nat. Assn. Secondary Sch. Prins., Seminole Adminstrs. and Suprs., Phi Delta Kappa, Alpha Kappa Alpha. Democrat. Mem. Ch. of Christ. Home: 7037 Hiawassee Oak Dr Orlando FL 32818-8355 Office: Teague Mid Sch 1199 Sand Lake Rd Altamonte Springs FL 32714-7025

COLLINS, EARLEAN, state legislator; b. Rolling Fork, Miss.; m. John Grant, July 31, 1978; 1 child, Dwarrye. BA in Sociology, U. Ill., Chgo. Social service adminstr. State of Ill., Chgo., 1972-76, elected state senator, 1977—, asst. majority leader; bd. dirs. Nat. Caucus of Black Legislators, Westside Bus. Assn. of Chgo., Nat. Conf. State Legislators. Sponsor Unwed Mothers United, Chgo., 1977—, Collins Queenettes, Chgo., 1977—, Westside Progressive Women's Orgn., Chgo., 1980—. Numerous best legislator & recognition awards from profl. & civic groups. Mem. Intergovtl. Coop. Council, Operation PUSH, Ill. Job Tng. Council, NAACP, Conf. Women Legislators. Democrat. Baptist. Office: Ill State Senate State Capitol Springfield IL 62706*

COLLINS, EILEEN MARIE, astronaut; b. Elmira, N.Y., Nov. 19, 1956; d. James Edward and Rose Marie (O'Hara) C.; m. James Patrick Youngs, Aug. 1, 1987. AS in Math., Sci., Corning C.C., 1976; BA in Math., Econs., Syracuse U., 1978; grad., USAF Undergrad. Pilot Tng., Vance AFB, Okla., 1979, USAF Test Pilot Sch., Edwards AFB, Calif., 1990; MS in Ops. Rsch., Stanford U., 1986; student, USAF Inst. Tech., 1986; MA in Space Systems Mgmt., Webster U., 1989. Commd. 2d lt. USAF, 1978, advanced through grades to lt. col., 1993; instr. pilot 71st flight tng. wing USAF, Vance AFB, 1979-82; aircraft comdr. 86th mil. airlift squadron USAF, Travis AFB,

Calif., 1983-85; asst. prof. math. USAF Acad., Colorado Springs, Colo., 1986-89; astronaut Johnson Space Ctr. NASA, Houston, 1990—; second in command, space shuttle Discovery, 1995. Decorated Air Force Commendation medal with one oak leaf cluster, Meritorious svc. medal with one oak leaf cluster, Air Force Expeditionary medal. Mem. U.S. Space Found., Am. Inst. Aeronautics and Astronautics, Air Force Assn., Women Mil. Aviators, Order Daedalians.

COLLINS, GRACE ELIZABETH, English educator, writer; b. Newark, July 2, 1935; d. James Albert and Jessie Elizabeth (Summey) C. BA, Morgan State U., 1969; MA in English, U. Mich., 1970, PhD in English, 1974. Asst. prof. English SUNY, Stony Brook, 1973-76, Clark Coll., Atlanta, 1976-77, Coppin State Coll., Balt., 1983-92; assoc. prof. English Howard Cmty. Coll., Columbia, Md., 1992-95; coord. writing program Coppin State Coll, 1984-90; rschr. book articles Notable Black Am. Women, 1991, 95; reader Ednl. Testing Svc., Princeton, N.J., 1987—. Vol. Big Brothers/Big Sisters Md., 1986-91; vol. cons. Garrison Forest Sch., Owings Mills, Md., 1991—; vol. tutor, Columbia, Md., 1994—. Fellow Danforth Found., 1969-74; Harvard-Yale-Columbia Summer Studies grantee, 1968. Mem. Nat. Coun. Tchrs. English, Md. Writing Project, Mensa, Alpha Kappa Mu. Home: Apt 821 11379 Little Patuxent Pky Columbia MD 21044-3758

COLLINS, GWENDOLYN BETH, health administrator; b. Akron, Ohio; d. Emmert Samuel and Lillice Elizabeth (Matthews) Shaffer; divorced; 1 child, Holly Marie. BA, Case Western Res. U. Exec. dir. Canton Area Regional Health Edn. Network, 1981-88; project dir. Region VII Cancer Registry, Canton, Ohio, 1984-88; program dir. Diabetes Mgmt. Ctr., St. Petersburg, Fla., 1988-89, 92-94, Pasadena Sr. Health Ctr., St. Petersburg, 1995-96; pvt. practice health program mgmt. cons. Largo, Fla., 1995—; health mgmt. cons., 1986-88, 95—; mem. continuing med. edn. com. Aultman Hosp., 1983-88; planner and evaluator Directions for Mental Health, Inc., Clearwater, Fla., 1990-92. Mem. adv. com. Camp Y-Noah, 1985-86. HHS grantee, Canton, 1986-88. Mem. Cancer Control Consortium Ohio (mem. cancer incidence mgmt. com. 1986-87). Republican. Home: 13013 89th Ave N Largo FL 34646-2706

COLLINS, JOAN HENRIETTA, actress; b. London, May 23, 1933; came to U.S., 1938; d. Joseph William and Elsa (Bessant) C.; m. Anthony Newley (div.); children: Tara, Sacha; m. Ronald S. Kass, Mar., 1972 (div.); 1 child, Katy; m. Peter Holm (div.); m. Maxwell Reed. Ed., Francis Holland Sch., London; student, Royal Acad. of Dramatic Art. Films include: Cosh Boy, Our Girl Friday, I Believe in You, Girl in the Red Velvet Swing, Sea Wife, Rally Round the Flag Boys, Island in the Sun, Seven Thieves, Road to Hong Kong, Sunburn, The Stud, Game for Vultures, The Bitch, The Big Sleep, The Good Die Young, Land of the Pharoahs, The Bravados, Esther and the King, Warning Shot, The Executioner, Subterfuge, Revenge, Quest for Love, Tales From the Crypt, The Bawdy Adventures of Tom Jones, The Opposite Sex, The Virgin Queen, Quest for Love, Decadence, 1994, In the Bleak Mid-Winter, 1995; theater appearances include: Jassey, Claudia, The Skin of Our Teeth, The Praying Mantis, The Last of Mrs. Cheyney, The 7th Veil, A Doll's House, Private Lives (London, Broadway, also tour); TV films include: Drive Hard, Drive Fast, 1973, The Man Who Came to Dinner, Paper Dolls, 1982, The Wild Women of Chastity Gulch, 1982, The Cartier Affair, The Making of a Male Model, 1983, Her Life as a Man, 1984; miniseries: The Moneychangers, 1976, Sins, 1986, Monte Carlo, 1986, Tonight at 8:30, 1991, Dynasty: The Reunion, 1992; appeared in Faerie Tale Theater (Showtime TV), 1982; star TV series: Dynasty, 1981-89; other TV appearances: Roseanne (ABC), 1993, Mama's Back spl., 1993, Annie: A Royal Adventure (TV movie), 1995, Hart to Hart spl. (TV movie), 1995; video spl. Secrets of Fitness and Beauty, 1994; author: Past Imperfect (autobiography), 1978, Katy, A Fight for Life, Joan Collins Beauty Book, (novels) Prime Time, 1988, Love and Desire and Hate, 1991, My Secrets, 1994, Too Damn Famous, 1995, Second Act (autobiography), 1996. Recipient Emmy nomination, Golden Globe award, Ace award, People's Choice award.

COLLINS, JUDY MARJORIE, singer, songwriter; b. Seattle, May 1, 1939; d. Charles T. and Marjorie (Byrd) C.; m. Peter A. Taylor, Apr., 1958 (div.); 1 son, Clark Taylor. Pvt. study piano, 1953-56. Debut as profl. folk singer, Boulder, Colo., 1959; has since appeared in numerous clubs, U.S. and around world; performer concerts including Newport Folk Festival, maj. concert halls and summer theatres, throughout U.S. and Europe; also appeared radio and TV, including HBO TV spl. Judy Collins: From the Heart, 1989; recording artist, Elektra; profl. acting debut as Solveig in N.Y. Shakespeare Festival prodn. of Peer Gynt, 1969; producer, dir. documentary movie Antonia: A Portrait of the Woman, 1974; composer songs including Albatross, 1967, Since You've Asked, 1967, My Father, 1968, Secret Gardens, 1972, Born to the Breed, 1975; albums include Bread & Roses, Colors of the Day, So Early in the Spring/The First Fifteen Years, 1977, Hard Times for Lovers, 1979, Running for My Life, 1980, Trust Your Heart, 1987, Sanity and Grace, 1989, Recollections, Fires of Eden, 1990, Judy Sings Dylan: Just Like a Woman, 1993; author autobiography Trust Your Heart, 1987. Recipient Grammy award, 1968, 6 Gold Lps., Silver medal Atlanta Film Festival, Blue Ribbon award Am. Film Festival, N.Y.C., Christopher award. Office: care Charles Rothschild Prodns 330 E 48th St New York NY 10017-1729*

COLLINS, KATHLEEN ANNE, artistic director; b. Elmira, N.Y., Dec. 20, 1951; d. James G. and Joyce (Balmer) C.; m. Andrew Stephon Elston, May 28, 1977; children: Megan, Kate. BA, SUNY, Albany, 1974; MA in Theatre, U. Wash., 1976, MFA in Theatre, 1979. Dir. edn. Seattle Children's Theatre, 1975-78; instr. drama Lakeside Sch., Seattle, 1978-79; artistic dir. Honolulu Theatre for Youth, 1979-83, Fulton Opera House, Lancaster, Pa., 1983—; guest lectr. U. Wash., Seattle, 1979, U. Hawaii, Honolulu, 1981. Contbg. author: Drama With Children, 1979. Bd. dirs. PTO, Lancaster, 1990—. Mem. Am. Assn. Theatre Educators, Assn. and Soc. for Theatre and Children. Democrat. Roman Catholic. Office: Fulton Theatre Co PO Box 1865 Lancaster PA 17608-1865

COLLINS, LINDA LOU POWELL, contract manager; b. Michigan City, Ind., May 6, 1957; d. Ronald Edward Powell and Betty Louise (Gruenberg) Will; m. Aug. 15, 1981 (div. May 18, 1983); m. Edward T. Collins, oct. 14, 1989; 1 child, Elizabeth Louise. BA in English, Purdue U., 1980; MBA, St. Francis Coll., Fort Wayne, Ind., 1988. Cert. purchasing mgr.; cert. profl. contracts mgr. Head expeditor Graham Electronics, Ft. Wayne, Ind., 1981-82; expeditor solid state Hughes Def. Comms. (formerly Magnavox Electronic Sys. Co.), Ft. Wayne, 1982-83, assoc. buyer, 1983-85, buyer, 1985-87, subcontract adminstr., 1987-88, sr. contract adminstr., 1988-93, contract mgr., 1993—; bus. writing instr. Ind.-Purdue U., Ft. Wayne, 1990-91; seminar instr. Nat. Contract Mgmt. Assn., 1991-92. Mem. Civic Theater Dirs.' Cir., Ft. Wayne, 1989—; property trustee St. Joseph United Meth. Ch., Ft. Wayne, 1992, choir mem., 1993-95. Recipient Woman of Achievement award YWCA, 1996. Fellow Nat. Contract Mgmt. Assn. (program chair 1990-91, v.p. 1991-92, mem. chair 1992-93, v.p. programs/facilities 1993-94, v.p./sec. 1994-95, regional mem. chair 1994-96, nat. functional dir. mem. retention 1994-95, v.p. membership 1995-96, nat. dir. 1996—, regional fellows chair 1996—, James E. Cravens Mem. award 1993, Blanch Witte Hon. Mention award 1996); mem. Purdue U. Alumni Assn., Magna Health Club (v.p. 1990-91, mem. chair 1991-95, sec. 1995-96), Magnavox Mgmt. Club Ind. (facilities chair 1990-91, bd. dirs. 1993-96), Alpha Gamma Delta (altruism chair 1977-78). Republican. Office: Hughes Def Comms 1010 Production Rd Fort Wayne IN 46808-1164

COLLINS, LISA DIANE, art educator; b. Long Beach, Calif., Sept. 20, 1967; d. Jimmy Royce and Cloa Mae (Westbrook) C. BS Art Edn., BA Comml. Art, Kennesaw State Coll., Marietta, Ga., 1991; student, U. Ga. Studies Abroad, Cortona, Italy, 1988, Kennesaw State Coll. Studies, San Miguel, Mex., 1989; postgrad., State U. West Ga., Carrollton. Instr. studio art for children Kennesaw State Coll., 1988—; art educator Josh Powell Camp, Kennesaw, 1990-92; art tchr. Floyd Middle Sch., Mableton, Ga., 1991—; freelance artist; prodn. asst. Share Mag., Kennesaw State Coll., 1990-91, coop. tchr. to upcoming art tchrs., 1993—; dir. Floyd Celebrates Arts at Mable House Gallery, 1991—; judge Paulding County Fine Arts Assn. Exhibit, 1993. Bd. dirs. South Cobb Arts Alliance, 1996—. Named Tchr. of Yr., Floyd Mid. Sch., 1996. Mem. ASCD, Profl.. Assn. Ga. Educators., Nat. Art Edn. Assn. Home: 3800 Parks Dr Powder Springs GA 30073-2720

COLLINS, MARIBETH WILSON, foundation president; b. Portland, Oreg., Oct. 27, 1918; d. Clarence True and Maude (Akin) Wilson; m. Truman Wesley Collins, Mar. 12, 1943; children: Timothy Wilson and Terry Stanton (twins), Cherida Lynne, Truman Wesley Jr. BA, U. Oreg., 1940. Pres. Collins Found., Portland, Oreg., 1964—; dir. Collins Pine Co., Collins Holding Co., Ostrander Resource Co. Mem. exec. com., sec. bd. trustees Willamette U., Salem, Oreg., also mem. coms. on orgn. and campus religious life. Mem. Univ. Club, Gamma Phi Beta. Republican. Methodist. Home: 2275 SW Mayfield Ave Portland OR 97225-4400 Office: Collins Found Ste 305 1618 SW 1st Ave Portland OR 97201-5708

COLLINS, MARILYN, youth development administrator; b. Versailles, Ky.; d. Dan Douglas Sr. and Christine Creth Collins. BS in Biology, Western Ky. U., 1975; AA in Computers, BA in Bus. Adminstrn., Midway Coll., 1995. Diagnostic technician U. Ky., Lexington, 1976-93; bank teller Woodford Bank and Trust Co., Versailles, Ky., 1993-94; stock replenisher K-Mart, Versailles, Ky., 1995; 4-H youth devel. agt. Coop. Ext. Svc., Lebanon, Ky., 1995—. Advisor Glasscock Family Resource Ctr., Lebanon, 1995. Recipient Midway Coll. Acad. Excellence award Midway Women's Club, 1994. Mem. Ky. Assn. Ext. 4-H Agts., Gamma Beta Phi. Democrat. Methodist. Home: 116 S Harrison St Apt 2 Lebanon KY 40033 Office: Coop Ext Svc 135 E Water St Lebanon KY 40033

COLLINS, MARTHA, English language educator, writer; b. Omaha, Nov. 25, 1940; d. William E. and Katheryn (Essick) C.; m. Theodore M. Space, Apr. 1991. AB, Stanford U., 1962; MA, U. Iowa, 1965, PhD, 1971. Asst. prof. N.E. Mo. U., Kirksville, Kirksville, 1965-66; instr. U. Mass., Boston, 1966-71, asst. prof. English, 1971-75, assoc. prof., 1975-85, prof. English, 1985—, co-dir. creative writing, 1979—, 1994-96; dir. Martha's Vineyard Writers' Workshop, Vineyard Haven, Mass., summer 1984. Author (poetry): The Catastrophe of Rainbows, 1985, The Arrangement of Space, 1991, A History of Small Life on a Windy Planet, 1993. Fellow Bunting Inst., 1982-83, Ingram Merrill Found., 1988, NEA, 1990; recipient Pushcart prize, 1985, 96, Di Castagnola award, 1990, others. Mem. Poetry Soc. Am., Assoc. Writing Programs. Democrat. Office: U Mass-Boston Dept English Boston MA 02125

COLLINS, MARTHA ANN, features editor; b. Canton, Ga.; d. John William and Nellie Esther Mae (Fields) Disharoon; m. David Lee Collins; children: Richard Joseph (dec.), Gregory Keith, Leigh Ann. AA, Reinhardt Coll.; BA, U. Ga. Staff writer Marietta (Ga.) Daily Jour.; free-lance writer; substitute tchr. Cobb County Schs., Marietta; features writer Marietta Daily Jour., features editor. Mem. Hospice Steering Com. Promina Northwest, Marietta; mem., officer PTA, Austell, Ga.; den leader Cub Scouts, Austell; vol. performing arts program Cobb County Schs., Marietta; ch. youth dir., Austell. Mem. Phi Beta Kappa, Phi Kappa Phi, Kappa Tau Alpha. Baptist. Office: Marietta Daily Jour 580 Fairground St Marietta GA 30060

COLLINS, MARTHA TRAUDT, lawyer; b. Colorado Springs, Colo., July 23, 1952; d. Verne O.M. and Helen Louise (Post) Traudt; m. Alexander F. Rolle; children: Joseph T. Collins, Alexander S. Rolle. BS in Math., U. Nebr., 1974; JD, U. Colo., 1977. Bar: Colo. 1977. Assoc. Holme Roberts & Owen LLC, Denver, 1977-82, mem., 1983—. Contbg. author: Rocky Mountain Mineral Law Foundation's Law of Federal Oil and Gas Leases, 1988; author: Hedging Transactions for Oil and Gas Producers: Rocky Mountain Mineral Law Foundation Special Institute, 1995; contbr. articles to profl. jours. Bd. dirs. Human Svcs., Inc., Denver, 1988-92, pres. bd., 1993; mem. law alumni bbd. U. Colo. Sch. Law, 1987-91; mem. Leadership Denver, 1993-94; bd. dirs. Family and Cmty. Edn. and Support, Denver, 1996—. Mem. Colo. Bar Assn., Denver Bar Assn., Women's Bar Assn., Order of Coif, Phi Beta Kappa. Office: Holme Roberts & Owen LLP 1700 Lincoln St Ste 4100 Denver CO 80203-4541

COLLINS, MARY, health association executive, former Canadian legislator; b. Vancouver, B.C., Can., Sept. 26, 1940; d. Fredrick Claude and Isabel Margaret (Copp) Wilkins; children: David, Robert, Sarah. Student, U. B.C., Queen's U., Kingston, Ont., Can.; LLD (hon.), Royal Rds. Mil. Coll., 1994. Mem. Can. Ho. of Commons, 1984-93; pres., CEO B.C. Health Assn., 1994—; mem. fed. cabinet Can., assoc. min. nat. def., 1989-92, min. Western econ. diversification, 1993, min. state environ., 1993, min. responsible for status of women, 1990-93, min. of health, 1993; dir. Vancouver Bd. Trade. Trustee Queen's U.; bd. dirs. Vancouver Libr. Mem. Progressive Conservative Party. Home: 201-1315 W 7th Ave, Vancouver, BC Canada V6H 1B8 Office: BC Health Assn, 600-1333 W Broadway, Vancouver, BC Canada V6H 4C7

COLLINS, MARY ELLEN, human resources executive; b. Indpls., Jan. 24, 1949; d. Carl William and Hester (Dawson) McConn; m. Thomas N. Winger, June 19, 1971 (div. 1981); m. Larry Wayne Collins, Dec. 15, 1983; 1 child, Ann Marie. Diploma in nursing, Holy Cross Coll., 1969; BS, Coll. of St. Francis, 1981; MS, Ind. U., 1984; PhD in Orgnl. Behavior, Union Inst., Cin., 1993. Edn. coord. Cmty. Hosp., Indpls., 1969-84; dir. tng. Middletown (Ohio) Regional Hosp., 1984-87; pres. People Power Cons. Svc., Cin., 1987—; adj. prof. Coll. Mt. St. Joseph, Ohio, 1988-93; faculty MBA program Xavier U., Cin., 1996—. Editl. bd. Strategic Governance for Non Profit Orgns., (newsletters) Teamwork, Quality One. Adminstrv. chair Deerfield Ch., Maineville, 1987-89. Mem. ASTD (bd. dirs. Cin. chpt. 1988-89), Assn. for Psychol. Type (pres., founder Greater Cin. chpt. 1992—, bd. dirs. Gt. Lakes region, Internat. New Leader award 1993, internat. conf. chair 1997), Assn. Quality Participation (healthcare adv. bd., Disting. Faculty mem.), Internat. Visitors Ctr., Women Entrepreneurs, Inc. Methodist.

COLLINS, MARY ELLEN KENNEDY, librarian, educator; b. Pitts., Feb. 28, 1939; d. Joseph Michael and Stella Marie (Kane) Kennedy; m. Orpha Collins. BA, Villa Maria Coll., 1961; MLS, U. Pitts., 1970, PhD, 1980. Tchr., Pitts. Catholic Schs., 1962-65; tchr., Anne Arundel County Schs., Annapolis, 1965-67; legal sec., firm Joseph M. Kennedy, Pitts., 1967-70; cataloger Newport News (Va.) Libr. System, 1970-71; reference librarian Glenville (W.Va.) State Coll., 1971-80; asst. prof. libr. sci. Ball State U., Muncie, Ind., 1980-83; reference librarian, asst. prof. Purdue U., West Lafayette, Ind., 1983-88, assoc. prof., 1988—. Author: Education Journals and Serials: An Analytical Guide, 1988; contbr. articles to profl. jours. Sec. Presbyn. Ch., 1973-74, pres., 1974-76, bd. deacons, 1979-80; chmn. library com., Muncie, 1981-83; mem. belle com. W.Va. Folk Festival, 1973-80. Recipient Title III advanced study grant, 1977-78, Disting. Edn. and Behavioral Scis. Libr. award Assn. Coll. and Rsch. Librs., ALA, 1994. Mem. ALA (reference books rev. com. 1979-82, profl. devel. com. 1983-87, mem. Ednl. Behavioral Scis. (sect.-problems of access and control of ednl. materials 1984-88, curriculum materials com. 1988—, adult libr. materials com. 1988—), Ind. Library Assn., Spl. Libraries Assn., Assn. Coll. and Rsch. Libraries, Am. Assn. U. Profs., Assn. Ind. Media Educators, Assn. Am. Libr. Schs., AAUW (corr. sec. 1981-82), Delta Kappa Gamma, Sigma Sigma Sigma, Beta Phi Mu. Republican. Office: Purdue U HSSE Libr West Lafayette IN 47907

COLLINS, MONICA ANN, journalist; b. Rockville Center, N.Y., June 21, 1951; d. Louis Andrew and Eileen Ann (Hellawell) C. B.A., Vassar Coll., 1973. Writer, editor The Real Paper, Cambridge, Mass., 1975-79; TV critic Boston Herald Am., 1979-83, USA Today, Arlington, Va., 1983-89; columnist Boston Mag., 1983-85, TV Guide, 1989-93; TV critic, editl. page columnist Boston Herald, 1989—. Roman Catholic. Office: The Boston Herald 1 Herald St Boston MA 02118-2200

COLLINS, NANCY LEE, mathematician; b. St. Louis, May 17, 1925; d. Charles Alonzo and Leno Rosie (Squires) Roberts; m. Major Charles Brown Sr., Dec. 23, 1946 (dec. Feb. 1984); children: Major Charles Brown Jr., Victor Ivy Brown; m. James Pickett Collins, Nov. 29, 1986. BA, Harris Stowe State Coll., 1947; MEd, St. Louis U., 1955; MA in Counseling, Washington U., St. Louis, 1968. Cert. elem. and secondary counselor, Mo. Elem. tchr. St. Louis Bd. Edn., 1947-87, adult basic edn. tchr., 1967-72, secondary counselor, 1967-87; supr. computer math. lab. Meramec C.C., St. Louis, 1989—; counselor seven up program Villa Duschesne, Ladue, Mo., summer, 1970; tutor continuing edn. program. Univ. City, Mo., 1972-74. Co-editor: Profiles and Silhouettes: The Contribution of Black Women in Missouri, 1979. Spl. advocate vol. Juvenile Ct., St. Louis, 1989-95. Parsons Blewett scholar St. Louis Bd. Edn., 1977; NSF fellow, 1963; recipient Top Teens Thrust award Top Ladies of Distinction, Inc., St. Louis, 1993, Black History in Mo. Appreciation award AAUW, 1994, Cert. Appreciation Ct. Appointed Spl. Advocates, 1994. Mem. Mo. Conf. Womens Missionary Soc. (membership, recruitment chair 1995), Mo. Conf. Lay Orgn. (local pres. 1993-95), Delta Sigma Theta (choir mem. 1986-95, 50 Yr. Mem. award 1995, Cert. Appreciation award 1993). Democrat. African Methodist Episcopalian. Home: 955 Jeanerette Dr University City MO 63130 Office: Meramec CC 11333 Big Bend Blvd Kirkwood MO 63122

COLLINS, NAOMI F., higher education administrator; b. N.Y.C., Jan. 16, 1942; d. Maurice Milton and Ruth (Kalish) Feldman; m. James Franklin Collins, May 31, 1963; children: Robert Seaton, Jonathan Charles. BA magna cum laude, Queens Coll., 1962; MA, Ind. U., 1963, PhD in History, 1970. Lectr. U. Md., College Park, 1969-70; legis. rsch. analyst Md. Constitution Conv., Annapolis, 1967-68; info. program coord. USIA, Moscow/Am. Embassy, Moscow, 1974-75; legis. program analyst Md. State Legis., Annapolis, 1977; legis. liaison Congrl. Rsch. Svc./Libr. Congress, Washington, 1977-79; dep. dir. Am. Inst. for Islamic Affairs/Am. Univ., Washington, 1979-84; exec. dir. Md. Humanities Coun., Balt., 1984-92; exec. dir., CEO NAFSA: Assn. Internat. Educators, Washington, 1992—; commr. CETS NAS, Nat. Rsch. Coun., Washington, 1994—; adv. com. NSF, 1992—; commr. Commn. Internat. Edn./Am. Coun. Edn., 1994; chmn. trilateral working group N.Am. Student and Scholar Mobility, Washington, 1994—; v.p. Alliance for Internat. Ednl. and Cultural Exch.; adv. com. Md. State Dept. Edn., numerous other coms. in field; panelist NEH, 1987, 89, 95, Am. Assn. Mus., 1989, others. Author profl. publs.; contbr. articles, papers to profl. jours. Mus. adv. com. Md. Trust for Hist. Preservation. Recipient fellowships AAUW, Ind. U., Woodburn Meml./Ind. U., scholarship N.Y. State. Mem. Phi Beta Kappa, Phi Alpha Theta. Office: NAFSA: Assn Internat Educators Ste 1000 1875 Connecticut Ave Washington DC 20009

COLLINS, PATRICIA A., lawyer, judge; b. Camp Lejeune, N.C., Mar. 12, 1954; d. Thomas and Margaret (Parrish) C. BA, U. Va., 1976; JD, Gonzaga U., 1982. Bar: Alaska 1982, U.S. Dist. Ct. Alaska, U.S. Ct. Appeals (9th cir.) 1982. Assoc. Guess & Rudd, Anchorage and Juneau, 1982-84, 85-87; asst. pub. defender Alaska Pub. Defender's Office, Ketchikan, 1984-85; prin. Collins Law Office, Juneau, 1987-95; judge Alaska Dist. Ct., Ketchikan, 1995—; part time fed. magistrate judge U.S. Cts., Juneau, 1988-95, Ketchikan, 1996—; adj. prof. U. Alaska, Juneau, 1991-95. Mem. Alaska Bar Assn., Ketchikan Sailing Club. Office: State Ct 415 Main St #400 Ketchikan AK 99901

COLLINS, PATRICIA LOUISE, home health nurse; b. Dennison, Iowa, Dec. 14, 1954; d. Donald Nelson and Joan (McDonald) Wingrove; m. Kim Brian Collins, May 16, 1975; children: Kim Brian Jr., Chad Allan. ADN, Marshalltown (Iowa) C.C., 1992. RN, Iowa; LPN, Iowa; cert. BCLS instr, HIV/AIDS instr., Iowa. Nurse Eldora (Iowa) Regional Med. Ctr., 1990-91; ICU nurse, charge nurse Mercy Med. Ctr., Des Moines, 1991-93; cmty. health nurse Sac & Fox Tribe of the Miss. in Iowa, Tama, 1993-95; home health nurse Interim Healthcare of Iowa, Marshalltown, 1995—. Choir dir. Calvary Bapt. Ch., 1994; educator adult related devel. disabilities Indian Health Svcs., Aberdeen, S.D., 1993-95. Mem. Am. Diabetis Assn., Am. Heart Assn., ARC. Baptist. Home: 1858 105 St Union IA 50258 Office: Interim Healthcare of Iowa 16 E Main Ste 100 Marshalltown IA 50158

COLLINS, PATTI ANN, health nurse; b. Waltham, Mass., Sept. 8, 1958; d. Richard Leo and Maureen Gertrude (McCarthy) C.; m. Stephen Paul Baccari, Apr. 12, 1980 (div. Feb. 1993); children: Stephen Paul Baccari Jr., Thomas Joseph Baccari; m. Brian Robert Norris, Aug. 19, 1995; children: Jessica Lynn Norris, Michelle Lee Norris. BSN, Salem State Coll., 1994. RN, Mass. Staff nurse W.E. Fernald State Sch., Waltham, Mass., 1989—; program dir. sub acute svcs. Sun Corp., Lexington, Mass. Dir. family and youth activities Parents Without Partners, Framingham, Mass., 1991. Mem. Sigma Theta Tau Internat. Honor Soc. of Nursing. Home: 473 North Rd Bedford MA 01730-1031

COLLINS, PAULA JEANNE, executive assistant; b. Rock Island, Ill., Nov. 18, 1951; d. Paul Kenneth and Dorothy Jean (Hinton) Heinze; m. Larry Dean Collins, May 5, 1974 (div. May 1990); 1 child, Paul Ashley. BA, Augustana Coll., 1973. Supr. WFG Securities Corp., Middleton, Wis., 1987-94, v.p., 1994—; exec. asst. Wis. Fin. Group, Inc., 1996—; entertainer, 1972—. Dir. Yahara River Chorus, 1994—. Home: 131 Jenna Dr #210 Verona WI 53593

COLLINS, QUEENIE PETTWAY, financial analyst; b. Catherine, Ala., Jan. 11, 1960; d. Madeline Decree (Pettway) Davis; m. Julius Collins Jr., June 7, 1986; children: Michael Julius, Melissa Joy. BBA, Pace U., 1984; MBA, Cornell U., 1986. Cost analyst Procter-Gamble, Cin., 1986-87; sr. fin. analyst Pratt & Whitney, East Hartford, Conn., 1987-90, spl. projects analyst, 1990-95, bus. unit fin. analyst, 1995—. Pres. PTO, East Hartford/Glastonbury Elem. Magnet Sch., 1994-96, chmn. adv. com., 1994. Mem. Inst. Mgmt. Accts. Democrat. Baptist. Home: 35 Chapel St East Hartford CT 06108 Office: Pratt & Whitney MS 184-31 400 Main St East Hartford CT 06108

COLLINS, ROSE ANN, minister; b. Pitts., July 5, 1935; d. Joseph and Rochelle (McCrary) Covington; m. Frank Collins, June 30, 1960 (div. 1978); children: Gar Andre, Guy Tracy. BA, Ctrl. Bible Coll., Springfield, Mo., 1987; MDiv, Assemblies of God Theol. Sem., Springfield, Mo., 1989. Ordained to ministry, 1990. Assoc. minister Deliverance Temple World Outreach Ministries, Springfield, 1988-90; evangelist Deliverance Temple World Outreach Ministries, Springfield and Pitts., 1991-93; chaplain Western Ctr., Canonsburg, Pa., 1993-96; trustee Northside Ch. of God in Christ, Pitts., 1982-84, bd. dirs., 1983-84. Vol. Ctr. Victims Violent Crime. Mem. Soc. Chaplains (Western chpt.), Pa. Coun. Chs., Ret. Enlished Assn. (hon., Steel City chpt. 72 chaplain 1994). Home: 1105 Greentree Rd Pittsburgh PA 15220

COLLINS, SANDRA ANN, librarian; b. Bethelehm, Pa., July 10, 1951; d. Robert J. and Doris (Hottle) C. BS, Kutztown State Coll., 1973; MLS, U. Pitts., 1975; MPA, U. Utah, 1993. Children's libr. Bethlehem Pub. Libr., 1976-82, br. libr., 1982-87; children's libr. Weber County Libr., Ogden, Utah, 1982-87, tech. svcs., 1987-96, assoc. dir., 1989-96, asst. dir., 1996—; chair intellectual freedom com. Assn. of Libr. Svc. to Children, 1989; catloging needs of pub. librs. Pub. Libr. Assn., 1990—. Mem. ALA, LWV (bd. dirs. 1982), Utah Libr. Assn. (conf. co-chair ann. conf. 1994), Mountain Plains Libr. Assn., Pa. Libr. Assn., Soroptomist Internat. (sec., v.p. 1992—). Democrat. Home: 984 28th St Ogden UT 84403-0270 Office: Weber County Libr 2464 Jefferson Ave Ogden UT 84401-2488

COLLINS, SARAH B., bank executive. Sr. v.p. mktg. Mellon Bank Corp., Pitts. Office: Mellon Bank Corp One Mellon Bank Ctr Pittsburgh PA 15258*

COLLINS, SARAH RUTH, education educator; b. Northumberland, Pa., May 13, 1939; d. Walter Brown and Alice Marie (Neighbour) Knight; m. Frank Gibson Collins, June 13, 1960; children: James, Pamela Collins Williams. BA, Wheaton Coll., 1960; MA, U. Tex., Austin, 1974; PhD, Vanderbilt U., 1980. Tchr. various levels Evanston, Ill., 1960-61, Berkeley, Calif., 1961-71; tchr. pre-sch. and kindergarten Austin, Tex., 1969-73; tchr. in early childhood U. Tex., Austin, 1972-74; tchr. reading Motlow State C.C., Tullahoma, Tenn., 1977-91, prof. edn., 1982-93, coord. social scis., 1986-93; mem. state-wide adv. coun. for tchr. edn. and cert., 1987-90, state-wide adv. coun. for minorities in tchr. edn., 1990-91; adj. prof. edn. Mid. Tenn. State U., 1979—; presenter at profl. confs. Columnist feature articles for local newspapers. Actress Cmty. Playhouse, Tullahoma, 1973-87; storyteller various librs. and pub. schs., 1974—; violinist Mid. Tenn. Symphony Orch., Murfreesboro, 1987-89; presenter programs on grief and loss at various profl. confs. and cmty. orgns.; bd. mem., yearly speaker Compassionate Friends, 1985—; v.p. in charge of programs Unitarian

Universalist Ch. of Tullahoma, 1994. Recipient Gov. Ned McWherter's cert. of recognition Tenn. Collaborative Leadership Acad., 1991. Mem. AAUP (v.p. 1986-87, sec. 1990-91), Assn. Tchr. Educators, Bus. and Profl. Women's Club, Phi Delta Kappa, Kappa Delta Pi. Home and Office: 1703 Country Club Dr Tullahoma TN 37388-4831

COLLINS, SHARON MCCOY, producer, correspondent; b. Charlottesville, Va., Apr. 27, 1952. Dir. news Sta. WDVA Radio, Danville, Va., 1978-81; dir. news, reporter Sta. WAKG-FM Radio, Danville, 1981-83; reporter Sta. WVTM-AM Radio, Danville, 1981-83; reporter Sta. WSET-TV, Lynchburg, Va., 1979-91, bur. chief, 1983-89, mng. editor, 1989-91; prodr. weekly environ. mag. programs, correspondent Sta. CNN/TBS, Atlanta, 1991—. Prodr., correspondent Flood Spl. (Emmy award 1994), Earth Summit Spl. (ACE award 1992), Save the Earth Spl. (EMA award 1992). Pres. Danville Devel. Coun., 1990; bd. dirs. Crimestoppers, Danville. Recipient AP awards including Radio Best News Operation award, 1981, Radio Continuing Story award, 1981, Radio Outstanding Effort by Reporter award, 1981, 82, Feature award, 1987, Best In-Depth Report award, 1986, Best Documentary award, 1990, Douglas Freeman award, 1990; recipient Best In-Depth Report award UPI, 1985, Continuing Story award, UPI, 1987, Crimestoppers Prodn. of Yr. award SE Conv., 1985; named BPW Woman of Yr., 1982, Jaycees Woman of Yr., 1990. Mem. Danville C. of C. (bd. dirs.). Home: 1331 Briers Dr Stone Mountain GA 30083-1840 Office: CNN Earth Matters 1 Cnn Ctr NW Atlanta GA 30303-2705

COLLINS, SUSAN MARGARET, archaeologist; b. Trenton, N.J., June 26, 1948; d. Thomas Raymond and Marjorie Ann (Lakness) C. BA cum laude, U. Colo., 1969, MA, 1971, PhD, 1975. Spl. researcher Sch. Am. Rsch., Santa Fe, N.Mex., 1972-73; teaching assoc. U. Colo., Denver, 1973-75, instr., 1975; instr. U. Colo., Boulder, 1974; vis. asst. prof. U. Colo., Denver, 1978-79; asst. prof. Western Carolina U., Cullowhee, N.C., 1975-78; acting dir. lab. pub. archaeology Colo. State U., Ft. Collins, 1980-82; dir. archaeology program Pueblo of Zuni, N.Mex., 1982-84; state archaeologist Colo. Hist. Soc., Denver, 1988—; dep. state historic preservation officer Colo. Hist. Soc., Denver, 1989—; adj. assoc. prof. U. Colo., Denver, 1990—. Contbr. articles to profl. jours. Mem. Lt. Gov.'s Task Force Ute Mountain Pk., Ute Indian Reservation, 1990—. Mem. Nat. Assn. State Archaeologists (sec.-treas. 1990-92), Soc. Am. Archaeology, Colo. Coun. Profl. Archaeologists (pres. 1985-86), Col. Archaeol. Soc., Soc. for Hist. Archaeology. Democrat. Office: Colo Hist Soc 1300 Broadway Denver CO 80203-2104

COLLINS, WINIFRED QUICK (MRS. HOWARD LYMAN COLLINS), organizational executive, retired navy officer; b. Great Falls, Mont.; m. Howard Lyman Collins (dec.). BS, U. So. Calif., 1935; grad. Harvard-Radcliffe Program in Bus. Adminstrn., 1938; MA, Stanford U., 1952. Commd. ensign U.S. Navy, 1942, advanced through grades to capt. 1957; personnel dir. Midshipman's Sch., Smith Coll., 1942-43; chief Naval Personnel for Women, 1957-62; ret.; nat. v.p. U.S. Navy League, 1964-70, nat. dir. and chmn. nat. awards com., 1964-95; chmn. newsletter com. Nat. Navy League, 1995—; nat. dir. Ret. Officers Assn.; former cons. HEW; former trustee Helping Hand Found.; former mem. Sec. Navy's Bd. Advs. and Tng. of Naval Personnel; dir. CPC Internat., Inc., 1977-84, chmn. employee investment com., mem. audit, exec. compensation and exec. coms.; bd. dirs. Leadership Found.; trustee U.S. Naval Acad. Found., 1977—. 1st v.p. Republican Women of D.C. Decorated Legion of Merit, Bronze Star, Sec. Navy Commendation medal; recipient Navy's Disting. Civilian Pub. Service award, 1971, Disting. Service award Navy League of U.S., 1973, Hall of Fame award Nat. Navy League, 1990; named to Hall of Fame Internat. Bus. and Profl. Women's Assn., 1994. Mem. Harvard Grad. Bus. Sch. Washington Club (past dir.), Army Navy Town Club, Army Navy Country Club, Capital Spkrs. Club, Chevy Chase Club. Home: Harbour Sq 540 N St SW Washington DC 20024-4557

COLLINSON, VIVIENNE RUTH, education educator, researcher; b. Kitchener, Ont., Can., July 30, 1949; d. Earl Stanley and Mary Magdalena (Sauder) Feick; m. Charles L. Collinson, May 21, 1983. BA, Wilfrid Laurier U., Waterloo, Ont., 1974; MEd, U. Windsor, Ont., 1989; PhD, Ohio State U., 1993. Cert. adminstr., Md. Tchr. Waterloo County Bd. Edn., 1969-84, Windsor Bd. Edn., 1984-89; vis. asst. prof. U.Windsor, 1989-90; vis. asst. prof. U. Md., College Park, 1993-94, asst. prof. edn., 1994—. Author: Teachers As Learners, 1994, Reaching Students, 1996. Charter mem. Eleanor Roosevelt Found., 1989—; benefactor Stratford (Ont.) Shakespearean Festival Found. Recipient Ont. Silver medal for piano U. We. Ont. Conservatory of Music, 1965, McGraw-Hill awrd, 1969; Ont. scholar, 1968; Wilfrid Laurier U. grad. scholar. Mem. AAUW, Am. Ednl. Rsch. Assn., Fedn. Women Tchrs. Assn. Ont. (provincial resource leader 1988-94), Nat. Soc. for Study of Edn., Delta Kappa Gamma (Doctoral Dissertation award 1994), Phi Kappa Phi. Office: U Md Coll of Edn College Park MD 20742

COLLOTON, PATRICIA NELSON, lawyer, writer, chemist; b. Chgo., Sept. 18, 1944; d. Edwin F. and Helen (O'Brien) Nelson; m. Patrick G. Colloton, Aug. 12, 1972; children: John, Katy. BS in Psychology and Chemistry, U. Wis., 1961, JD, 1970. Bar: Wis. 1970, N.Y. 1971, Ill. 1981, Kans. 1985. Organic chemist Eli Lilly & Co., Indpls., 1966-67. Mem. Northbrook (Ill.) Sch. Bd., 1983-85, Longmeadow (Mass.) Sch. Bd., 1989-91; vice chmn. Pioneer Valley Spl. Edn. Collaborative, Longmeadow, 1990-91; mem. Johnson County Transition Coun., Overland Park, Kans., 1991-95; pres. PTO, Leawood, Kans., 1996-97. Home: 2513 W 118th St Leawood KS 66211-3033

COLON, ELSIE FLORES, American and English literature educator; b. N.Y.C., Oct. 26; d. Juan and Rosa Catalina (Caban) Flores; m. Daniel Colon, July 16, 1977. BA magna cum laude, Hunter Coll., 1992; postgrad., Grad. Sch. and Univ. Ctr., N.Y.C., 1992—. Cons. Clairol, Inc. Bristol-Myers Co., N.Y.C., 1983-91; tchr.-counselor Manhattan North Ctr. Assn. for Children with Retarded Mental Devel. Inc., N.Y.C., 1992; adj. prof. Touro Coll., N.Y.C., 1993—. Scholar Estate of J. Raymond Gerberick, 1992-93, Jewish Found. for Women, 1992-94; rsch. fellow Columbia U., 1991; Mellon assoc. Mellon Found., 1990-92. Mem. MLA, AAUW, Nat. Coun. Tchrs. of English, Am. Mus. Natural History (assoc.). Office: Touro Coll 240 E 123rd St New York NY 10035-2038

COLÓN, PHYLLIS JANET, city official; b. Taylor, Tex., Sept. 1, 1938; d. Jack and Lydia Windmeyer; m. Henry J. Coló, Feb. 12, 1977; children: Walter N. Barnes III, Bradley H. Barnes, Mark A. Barnes. AA in Pub. Adminstrn., Del Mar Coll.; postgrad. in Acctg., Durham Jr. Coll.; BAAS in Pub. Adminstrn., Tex. A&I U., 1987; postgrad., Art Inst. Dayton. Registered profl. appraiser, Tex., assessor, Tex.; cert. tax adminstr., Tex.; lic. real estate borker, Tex. Mgr. info. Med. Arts Lab., Dayton, Ohio, 1970-73; appraiser Nueces County Appraisal Dist., Corpus Christi, 1973-82; tax assessor, collector Flour Bluff Ind. Sch. Dist., Corpus Christi, 1982, dir. spl. svcs., 1992-93; tax assessor, collector City of Laredo, Tex., 1993—; mem. profl. stds. com. Bd. Tax Profl. Examiners, 1991, vice chmn., 1992, chmn. 1994—. Mem. advance planning bd. Corpus Christi Libr.; chmn. ad hoc planning com. Del Mar Coll., 1989—. Recipient achievement award State of Tex., Hero award City of Corpus Christi. Mem. NAFE, AAUW (bd dirs. Corpus Christi br.), Tex. Assn. Assessing Officers, Tex. Sch. Assessors Assn., Inst. Cert. Tax Adminstrs., Am. Soc. Notaries, Corpus Christi C. of C., Art Mus. South Tex., Kiwanis (treas. Corpus Christi 1989-90, pres. 1990—; 2d v.p. Laredo United Way, 1995—). Republican. Lutheran. Home: 8728 Martinique Dr Laredo TX 78045-8008 Office: City of Laredo PO Box 329 1110 Houston St Laredo TX 78040-8019

COLONEL, SHERI LYNN, advertising agency executive; b. Bklyn., Sept. 3, 1955; d. Irwin Murray Glaser and Rosalind (Mendelson) Krasik; m. Peter T. Colonel, Sept. 20, 1981 (dec.). B.A. in Psychology, SUNY-Cortland, 1977. Account exec. Ted Bates Co., N.Y.C., 1978-80; account exec. SSC&B Advt. (name now Ammirati & Puris/LINTAS), Inc., N.Y.C., 1980-82, v.p. account supr., 1982-83, v.p. mgmt. supr., 1983-84, sr. v.p. mgmt. supr., 1984-88, exec. v.p., 1988—, bd. dirs. 1990-94; pres. Gotham Inc., 1994—. Named to AAF's Hall of Achievement, 1993, 40 Under 40 List, Crain's N.Y. Bus., 1994. Mem. NAFE, Advt. Women N.Y. Home: 280 Park Ave S New York NY 10010-6121 Office: Gotham Inc 260 Madison Ave New York NY 10016

COLONY-COKELY, PAMELA CAMERON, medical researcher; b. Boston, Apr. 18, 1947; d. Donald Gifford Colony and Priscilla (Adams) Pratley; m. E. Paul Cokely Jr., Apr. 26, 1986; children: Daniel Patrick, John Travis. BA, Wellesley (Mass.) Coll., 1969; PhD, Boston U., 1976. Rsch. asst. sch. medicine Boston U., 1969-71, U. Hosp., 1971-73, Peter Bent Brigham Hosp., Boston, 1973-75; instr. dept. anatomy Harvard Med. Sch., 1975-77; assoc. staff in medicine Peter Bent Brigham Hosp., Boston, 1976-79; sr. fellow, instr. Harvard Med. Sch., Boston, 1979-81; asst. prof. anatomy and medicine Pa. State Coll. Medicine, Hershey, Pa., 1981-88; assoc. prof. rsch., pre-health advisor Franklin and Marshall Coll., Lancaster, 1988-91; adj. assoc. prof. of surgery Pa. State Coll. Medicine, Hershey, 1988-91, sr. rsch. assoc. dept. surgery, 1991-95; program dir. histotechnology SUNY, Cobleskill, 1995—; ind. assessor Nat. Health and Med. Rsch. Coun., Australia, 1985—; ad-hoc reviewer NIH, Nat. Cancer Inst., Bethesda, Md., 1986; lectr., adj. instr. Harrisburg Area Cmty. Coll., 1991—. Contbr. articles to profl. jours. Fellow Nat. Found. Ileitis and Colitis, 1979-81; grantee Fed. Republic Germany, 1978, Cancer Rsch. Ctr., 1982-83, NIH, 1982-91. Mem. AAAS, Am. Soc. Cell Biology, N.Y. Acad. Sci., Am. Gastroent. Assn., Nat. Assn. Advisors Health Profls. Office: SUNY Cobleskill Dept Liberal Arts and Sci Cobleskill NY 12043

COLOSIMO, LISA MARIE, software engineer; b. Buffalo, N.Y., Apr. 15, 1969; d. Donald Domenico and Donna Louise (Glinski) C. BS in Applied Math./Computer Sci., Carnegie Mellon U., 1991; MSE in Computer and Info. Sci., U. Pa., 1993. Systems engr. GE Aerospace, Valley Forge, Pa., 1991-93; software engr. Mars Electronics Internat., West Chester, Pa., 1993-94; cons. Integrated Sys. Consulting Group, Wayne, Pa., 1994—. Mem. IEEE, Soc. Women Engrs. (career guidance chairperson 1993-96, sec. Phila. sect. 1996—), Chi Omega. Roman Catholic. Office: Integrated Sys Cons Group Ste 200 575 E Swedesford Rd Wayne PA 19087

COLOSKI, MARY-ELLEN, elementary educator; b. New Haven, Conn., May 7, 1959; d. Vincent and Sue Meriano; m. John Paul Coloski, July 12, 1985. BS, So. Conn. State U., 1981, MS, 1988, postgrad., 1991. 7th grade tchr. St. Rose Sch., New Haven, 1982-85; 5th grade tchr. St. Stanislaus Sch., New Haven, 1985-87; health tchr. grades 6-8 West Shore Middle Sch., Milford, Conn., 1987-94, sci. and lang. arts tchr., 1994—, team leader, 1995—; PIMMS fellow Wesleyan U., Middletown, Conn., 1986—. Mem. NEA, Conn. Edn. Assn., Milford Edn. Assn. Office: West Shore Mid Sch Kay Ave Milford CT 06460

COLPITTS, GAIL ELIZABETH, artist, educator; b. Chgo., Nov. 26, 1954; d. Robert Moore and Mary Lee (Means) C. BA, Greenville Coll., 1976; MA, No. Ill. U., 1984, MFA, 1990. Grad. tchg. asst. No. Ill. U., DeKalb, Ill., 1982-83, asst. to publs. editor, 1988-90, tchg. intern, 1990, instr. Office Campus Recreation, 1989-90; artist-tchr. MFA program Vt. Coll., Montpelier, 1993; instr. Harold Washington Coll., Chgo., 1993, Columbia Coll., Chgo., 1995; artist, lectr. Judson Coll., Elgin, Ill., 1995, asst. prof. art, 1996—. One-person shows include Bethel Coll., Arden Hills, Minn., 1995, Greenville (Ill.) Coll., 1993, No. Ill. U., DeKalb, 1990; assoc. editor: Shoal Dance, 1995—, c ontbr. revs. and news; contbr. poetry to mags. Grad. sch. fellow No. Ill. U., 1987-88. Mem. Coll. Art Assn., Christians in Visual Arts, Chgo. Artists Coalition. Wesleyan. Office: Art Dept Judson Coll 1151 N State St Elgin IL 60123

COLSON, ELIZABETH FLORENCE, anthropologist; b. Hewitt, Minn., June 15, 1917; d. Louis H. and Metta (Damon) C. BA, U. Minn., 1938, MA, 1940; MA, Radcliffe Coll., 1941, PhD, 1945; PhD (hon.), Brown U., 1978, D of Sociology, 1979; D.Sc., U. Rochester, 1985, U. Zambia, 1992. Asst. social sci. analyst War Relocation Authority, 1942-43; research asst. Harvard, 1944-45; research officer Rhodes-Livingstone Inst., 1946-47, dir., 1948-51; sr. lectr. Manchester U., 1951-53; assoc. prof. Goucher Coll., 1954-55; research assoc., assoc. prof. African Research Program, Boston U., 1955-59, part-time, 1959-63; prof. anthropology Brandeis U., 1959-63; prof. anthropology U. Calif.-Berkeley, 1964-84, prof. emeritus, 1984—; vis. prof. U. Zambia, 1987; Lewis Henry Morgan lectr. U. Rochester, 1973; vis. rsch. assoc. Refugee Studies Program Queen Elizabeth House, Oxford, 1988-89. Author: The Makah, 1953, Marriage and the Family Among The Plateau Tonga, 1958, Social Organization of the Gwembe Tonga, 1960, The Plateau Tonga, 1962, The Social Consequences of Resettlement, 1971, Tradition and Contract, 1974, A History of Nampeyo, 1992; jr. author Secondary Education and the Formation of an Elite, 1980, Voluntary Efforts in Decentralized Management, 1983, sr. author For Prayer and Profit, 1988; sr. editor: Seven Tribes of British Central Africa, 1951; jr. editor People in Upheaval, 1987. AAUW travelling fellow, 1941-42, fellow Ctr. Advanced Study Behavioral Scis., 1967-68, Fairchild fellow Calif. Inst. Tech., 1975-76. Fellow Am. Anthrop. Assn., Brit. Assn. Social Anthropologists, Royal Anthrop. Inst. (hon.); mem. Nat. Acad. Sci., Am. Acad. Arts and Scis., Am. Assn. African Studies (Disting. Africanist award 1988), Soc. Applied Anthropology, Soc. Woman Geographers, Phi Beta Kappa. Office: U Calif Dept Anthropology Berkeley CA 94720

COLTON, BONNIE MYERS, writer, folklorist; b. Oswegatchie, N.Y., Dec. 7, 1931; d. Charles Mason Myers and Marjorie Virginia (Seaman) Stevens; m. Donald M. Colton, Jan. 4, 1952; children: Cherie Binns, Tricia Kennison, Jean Balch, Roger, Ben, Lin Sawyer, Neil. Student, Newspaper Inst. of Am., N.Y.C., 1961, Dale Carnegie Inst., Watertown, N.Y., 1978, Jefferson C.C., Lowville, N.Y., 1985. Record keeper, tax acct. Homewood Farm, Boonville, N.Y., 1952-89; cons./oral history interviewer Tug Hill Commn., Watertown, 1988-91; freelance writer/columnist, photographer Lowville, 1981—, newsletter editor, program coord. THRIFT newsletter, Lowville, 1991-94; ind. oral history interviewer, folklorist Lowville, 1991—; writer weekly col. Jour. and Republican, Lowville, 1990—. Contbr. numerous articles to profl. jours.; author/editor/pub.: Christmas Treasures, 1995. Vol. newsletter editor First Presbyn. Ch., Lowville, 1990-93; vol. critic Nat. Writers Club, Aurora, Colo., 1988—; mem. legis. adv. com. Chloe Ann O'Neil, N.Y. State Assemblywoman, 1995-96; pub. poetry readings at Lewis County Hist. Soc., Ogdensburg Libr., Lowville Libr., 1993-95; article writer/cons. THRIFT, N.Y. Forest Owners Assn., 1983—. Mem. Lewis County Hist. Assn. (life, videotape and hist. programs), N.Y. Forest Owners Assn. (Heiburg Award for svc. to forestry 1992), Acad. Am. Poets, Adirondack Mus., Nat. Trust for Hist. Preservation, Nat. Writers Club. Home and Office: 5595 Trinity Ave Lowville NY 13367-1416

COLTRANE, TAMARA CARLEANE, intravenous therapy nurse; b. Greensboro, N.C., Oct. 18, 1963; d. Charles Floyd and Nancy Jane (Lemons) C. BS in Nursing, U. N.C., Greensboro, 1986. RN, N.C.; cert. in intravenous therapy. Nursing asst. (summer) Mary Field Nursing Home, High Point, N.C., 1984; med.-surgical nurse Wesley Long Cmty. Hosp., Greensboro, 1986-88, IV team nurse, 1988—; mem. nursing policy com. Wesley Long Cmty. Hosp., Greensboro, 1987-88, nursing adv. com., 1987-89, 91-93, mem. nursing edn. coun., 1996—. Mem. coun. on ministries, pianist, coord. comm. Sandy Ridge United Meth. Ch., High Point, N.C., 1990—, mem. adminstrv. bd., 1986-88, 90—; vol. worker Starmount Villa Nursing Home, Greensboro, 1984. Mem. Nat. Intravenous Nurses Soc., N.C. Intravenous Nurses Soc., Sigma Theta Tau. Office: Wesley Long Cmty Hosp 501 N Elam Ave Greensboro NC 27403-1118

COLUCCIO, JOSEPHINE CATHERINE, primary and elementary education educator; b. Bklyn., Oct. 21, 1952; d. Dominic Anthony and Catherine (Pomponio) Ferone; m. Frank Anthony Coluccio, June 26, 1976; 1 child, Nancy Marie. BA in Edn. cum laude, Bklyn. Coll., 1974. Cert. nursery, kindergarten, and elem. tchr., N.Y., nursery and elem. tchr., N.J. Elem. math. and sci. tchr.-coord. Our Lady of Perpetual Help Sch., Bklyn., 1974-77; pub. rels. coord. McDonald's Corp., S.I., N.Y., 1977-78; day care group tchr. Congress of Italian Am. Orgns., Bklyn., 1979-80; elem. math. and sci. tchr.-coord. Resurrection Elem. Sch., Bklyn., 1980-83; owner, dir. Little Yellow House, Toms River, N.J., 1984-90, Little Explorers-An Ed U Care Program, Toms River, 1990—. Active Rep. Nat. Com., Washington, 1991—. Mem. ASCD, Nat. Assn. for Edn. Young Children, Nat. Safety Coun., Soc. Children's Book Writers and Illustrators (assoc.). Republican. Roman Catholic.

COLVIN, GRETA WILMOTH, entrepreneur; b. Odessa, Tex., Mar. 24, 1962; d. Charles Hayden and Sherry Beth (Browning) Wilmoth; m. Michael Anthony Colvin, Aug. 16, 1986; 1 child, Michael Anthony Jr. AA in Radio-TV-Film, San Antonio Coll.; BS, U. Tex.; grad., Dale Carnegie, 1993. Lic. broadcaster, paralegal, pvt. investigator. Various media positions W.M. Entertainment, San Antonio, 1978-86; co-owner Image Nightclubs, San Antonio, 1986-88; owner W.C. Advt., San Antonio, 1980-88; retail mgr. Hastings, San Antonio, 1989-94; pres. Paradigm Enterprises, Flagstaff, Ariz., 1994—. Democrat. Address: 2800 Cerrillos Rd Santa Fe NM 87505-2313 also: 11623 Whisper Valley St San Antonio TX 78230-3737

COLWELL, JUDY RAE, accounting educator; b. Truth or Consequences, N. Mex., Mar. 4, 1953; d. William E. and Velda Rae (Luallen) Barber; m. Jerry A. Colwell, Aug. 7, 1971; 1 child, Jill Dyana. AS, No. Okla. Coll., 1973; BS in Edn., U. Ctrl. Okla., 1974; MBA, Phillips U., 1984. CPA, Okla. Bus. instr. Unified Sch. Dist. 509, South Haven, Kans., 1978-88; acctg. instr. Cowley County C.C., Ark. City, Kans., 1988-90; acctg. instr. No. Okla. Coll., Tonkawa, 1990—, chair bus. divsn., 1996—; chair Acctg. Assoc. Program, No. Okla. Coll., Tonkawa, 1990—, mem. Faculty Affairs Com., sec. 1992-93, chair 1993-94, mem. Curriculum Coun., 1992—; mem. Faculty Assn. No. Okla. Coll., v.p. 1993-94. Mem. AICPA, Okla. Soc. Cert. Pub. Accts., Higher Edn. Alumni Coun. of Okla. Republican. Mem. Ch. of Christ. Home: 16698 W Ferguson Blackwell OK 74631-5439 Office: No Okla Coll 1220 E Grand Ave Tonkawa OK 74653-0310

COLWELL, RITA ROSSI, microbiologist, molecular biologist, educator; b. Nov. 23, 1934; m. Jack H. Colwell, May 31, 1956; children: Alison E.L., Stacie A. BS in Bacteriology with distinction, Purdue U., 1956, MS in Genetics, 1958; PhD, U. Wash., 1961; DSc, Heriot-Watt U., Edinburgh, Scotland, 1987; DSc (hon.), Hood Coll., 1991; DSc, Purdue U., 1993; LLD, Notre Dame Coll., 1994; DSc (hon.), U. Surrey, Eng., 1995. Rsch. asst. genetics lab. Purdue U., West Lafayette, Ind., 1956-57; rsch. asst. U. Wash., Seattle, 1957-58, predoctoral assoc., 1959-60, asst. rsch. prof., 1961-64; asst. prof. biology Georgetown U., Washington, 1964-66, assoc. prof. biology, 1966-72; prof. microbiology U. Md., 1972—, v.p. for acad. affairs, 1983-87; dir. Ctr. Marine Biotech., 1987-91; pres. Md. Biotech. Inst. U. Md., 1991—; hon. prof. U. Queensland, Brisbane, Australia, 1988; cons., advisor Washington area comms. media, congressman, legislators, 1978—; external examiner various univs. abroad, 1964—; mem. coastal resources adv. com. dept. natural resources State of Md., 1979; NAS ocean scis. bd., 1977-80, vice-chair polar rsch. bd., 1990-94; mem. Nat. Sci. Bd., 1984-90, sci. adv. bd. Oak Ridge Nat. Labs., 1988-90, 93-96, adv. com. FDA, 1991-92, food adv. com., 1993-96. Author 16 books including (manual numerical taxonomy) Collecting the Data, 1970, (with M. Zambruski) Rodina-Methods in Aquatic Microbiology, 1972, (with L. H. Stevenson) Estuarine Microbial Ecology, 1973, (with R. Y. Morita) Effect of the Ocean Environment on Microbial Activities, 1974, (with A. Sinsky and N. Pariser) Marine Biotechnology, 1983, Vibrios in the Environment, 1985, Nucleic Acid Sequence Data, 1988, (with others) Marine Biotechnology, 1995; mem. editorial bd. Microbial Ecology, 1972-91, Applied and Environ. Microbiology, 1969-81, Oil and Petrochemical Pollution, 1980-91, Jour. Washington Acad. Scis., 1981-87, Johns Hopkins U. Oceanographic Series, 1981-84, Revue de la Fondation Oceanographique Ricard, 1981-92, Estuaries, 1983-89, Zentralblatt fur Bacteriologie, 1985—, Jour. Aquatic Living Resources, 1987—, System. Applied Microbiology, 1985—, World Jour. Microbiology and Biotechnology, 1988—; contbr. articles and revs. to profl. jours. including Can. Jour. Fisheries and Aquatic Scis., Soc. Gen. Microbiology, Jour. Bacteriology, others. Recipient Gold medal Internat. Biotech. Inst., 1990, Purkinje Gold medal Achievement in Scis. Czechoslavakian Acad. Scis., 1991, Civic award Gov. Md., 1990, Cert. Recognition, NASA, 1984, Alice Evans award Am. Soc. Microbiol. Com. on Status of Women, 1988, Andrew White medal Loyola Coll., 1994, medal of distinction Barnard Coll./Columbia U., 1996; named Phi Kappa Phi Scholar of Yr., 1992, Outstanding Women on Campus U. Md., 1979. Fellow AAAS (chmn. sect. biol. scis. 1993-94, pres. 1995, chmn. bd. 1996), Grad. Women Sci., Can. Coll. Microbiologists, Am. Acad. Microbiology (chmn. bd. govs. 1989-94), Washington Acad. Scis. (bd. mgrs. 1976-79), Marine Tech. Soc., (exec. com. 1982-88), Sigma Delta Epsilon; mem. Am. Soc. Microbiology (various sci. coms. 1961—, pres. 1985, chmn. program com. REGEM-1 1988, Fisher award 1985), World Fedn. Culture Collections, Internat. Union Microbiol. Soc. (v.p. 1986-90, pres. 1990-94), Am. Inst. Biol. Scis. (bd. govs. 1976-82), Am. Soc. Limnology and Oceanography, Internat. Coun. Sci. Unions (gen com., exec. bd. 1993—), U.S. Fedn. Culture Collections (governing bd. 1978-88), Soc. Indsl. Microbiology (bd. govs. 1976-79), Classification Rsch. Group Eng. (charter), Soc. Gen. Microbiology, Phi Beta Kappa, Sigma Xi (Ann. Achievement award 1981, Rsch. award 1984, nat. pres. 1991), Omicron Delta Kappa, Delta Gamma. Office: U Md Biotech inst Ste 550 4321 Hartwick Rd College Park MD 20740-3210

COLY, LISETTE, foundation executive; b. N.Y.C., Apr. 6, 1950; d. Robert Raymond and Eileen (Lyttle-Garrett) C.; children: George Robert Damalas, Anastasia Eileen Damalas. BA cum laude, Hunter Coll., 1973. Sec. Parapsychology Found., Inc., N.Y.C., 1972-75, assoc. editor, 1975—, v.p., 1978—. Assoc. editor Parapsychology Rev. and Procs. Ann. Internat. Parapsychology Found. Confs., 1978—; editor, conf. coord. Proceedings Ann. Internat. Confs., 1989—. Office: Parapsychology Found Inc 228 E 71st St New York NY 10021-5136

COMBS, JEANNE MARIA, nurse; b. Hamilton, Ohio, Oct. 31, 1955; d. Eugene and Shirley Jean (Lattuga) Hacker Lewis; 1 child, Melinda Renee Wood, from previous marriage. AS in Nursing, Miami U., Oxford, Ohio, 1976. Cert. gerontol. nurse. Staff nurse Bethesda North Hosp., Cin., 1976-78; dir. staff devel. Mt. Pleasant Retirement Village, Monroe, Ohio, 1980-83; shift supr. Adventist Convalescent Hosp., Glendora, Calif., 1983-86; dir. nursing svcs. Colonial Manor, West Covina, Calif., 1986-88, Brethren Hillcrest Homes, La Verne, Calif., 1988-90; dir. nursing svcs., dir. human resources Cumberland Valley Dist. Health Dept., 1990-93; supr. Jackson County Home Health Program, McKee, Ky., 1990-93; dir. edn. Health Directions, Corbin, Ky., 1993—; Contbr. articles to mags. Named Woman of Yr. Trenton Ch. of God, 1983, Outstanding Dir. Nursing So. Calif. Coun. Activity Coords., 1988. Mem. Calif. Coun. Long Term Care Nurses (sec. 1986-90), Calif. Nurses Assn., Am. Soc. Aging, Calif. Assn. Health Facilities, Ky. Home Health Assn., Ky. Pub. Health Assn., Ky. Home Health Assn., West Covina C. of C. (membership com.), Covina Women's Club. Republican. Home: 895 George Mcqueen Rd Annville KY 40402-8711 Office: Health Directions PO Box 187 East Bernstadt KY 40729-0187

COMBS, LINDA JONES, management company executive, researcher; b. Jonesboro, Ark., Apr. 12, 1948; d. Dale Jones and Neva Craig; 1 child, Nathan Isaac. BSBA, U. Ark., 1971, MBA, 1972, PhD in Bus. Adminstrn., 1983. Assoc. economist Bur. Bus. and Econ. Rsch., Fayetteville, Ark., 1973-76; pres. Combs Mgmt. Co., Springdale, Ark., 1976-83; asst. prof. fin. U. Ark., Fayetteville, 1983-87; asst. prof. fin. and mktg. Western Ill. U., Macomb, 1987-88; asst. prof. bus. adminstrn. Cen. Mo. State U., Warrensburg, 1988-89; assoc. prof. bus. adminstrn. N.E. State U., Tahlequah, Okla., 1989—; cons. in credit and polit. rsch. Fayetteville Adv. Coun., 1975-76; cons. in fin. and banking, Fayetteville, 1973-76. Contbr. articles to profl. jours. Mem. Ark. Gov.'s Inaugural Com., Little Rock, 1985; county co-chmn. Clinton for Gov., Washington County, Ark., 1984, 86, 90; bd. dirs. Shiloh Mus., Am. Cancer Soc., South Washington County, North Ark. Symphony Soc.; bd. dirs. Ark. State Hosp. Sys., sec., chmn., 1991-95; active numerous polit. campaigns for candidates and issues. Mem. Am. Mktg. Assn. (health care mktg.), Transp. Rsch. Forum. Office: Combs Mgmt Co PO Box 1452 Fayetteville AR 72702-1452

COMBS, SANDRA LYNN, state parole board official; b. Lancaster, Pa., Aug. 31, 1946; d. Clyde Robert and Violet (Sensenig) Boose; m. Allen Evans Combs, Aug. 30, 1969; children: Evan McKenzie, Leslie Ann. AAS in Nursing, Thomas Nelson C.C., Hampton, Va., 1980; BS in Psychology, Juniata Coll., 1968. RN, Va. Dir. vols. in probation Yorktown (Va.) Juvenile Ct., 1973-74; emergency nurse assoc. to pvt. practice physician Hampton, Va., 1980-82; chmn. bd. dirs., CEO Hampton Roads Gulls Profl. Hockey Team, Hampton, 1981-82; mem. sch. bd. York County Pub. Schs., Yorktown, 1985-94; vice chmn. Va. Parole Bd., Richmond, 1994—; mem. supt.'s adv. coun. York County Pub. Schs., 1984-94, mem. long range strategic planning com., 1989-94; trustee New Horizons Tech. Ctr., Gov.'s Sch., Hampton, 1991-94; mem. Va. edn. tech. adv. com. Va. Dept. Edn., 1992-95; mem. Va. Bd. Correctional Edn., 1994—, Va. Adult Basic Edn. and Literacy Adv. Coun., 1994—. Pres. Hampton Med. Soc. Aux, 1977-78, Dare Elem. PTA, York County, 1979-81, York County Coun. PTA, 1983-84; chmn. York County Rep. Com., 1984-90, 1st Dist. Rep. Congl. Com., Va.,

1990-94; adviser edn. policy George Allen for Gov., Richmond, 1992-93. Capt. USAF, 1968-73, Vietnam. Decorated Bronze Star medal, Cross of Gallantry (Vietnam), Air Force Commendation medal. Mem. ASCD, VFW, Va. Sch. Bds. Assn. (bd. dirs. 1990-94, award of Excellence 1990, 91, 92), Mil. Order World Wars. Methodist. Home: 9925 Groundhog Dr Richmond VA 23235-3972 Office: Va Parole Bd 6900 Atmore Dr Richmond VA 23225-5644

COMDEN, BETTY, writer, dramatist, lyricist, performer; b. Bklyn., May 3, 1917; d. Leo and Rebecca (Sadvoransky) C.; m. Steven Kyle, Jan. 4, 1942; children: Susanna, Alan. Student, Bklyn. Ethical Culture Sch., Erasmus Hall High Sch.; B.S., N.Y. U. Writer, performer nightclub act, Revuers; writer: (with Adolph Green) book and lyrics Broadway shows On The Town, 1944-45, Billion Dollar Baby, Two on the Aisle, Bells are Ringing, Fade-Out-Fade-In, Subways are for Sleeping, On the Twentieth Century, A Doll's Life, 1982 (Tony award nomination), lyrics for Peter Pan, lyrics for Hallelujah, Baby!, lyrics for The Will Rogers Follies, 1991 (Tony award); screenplays Auntie Mame, Good News, The Barkleys of Broadway, Singin' in the Rain, The Band Wagon, others; screenplay and lyrics for On the Town, Bells are Ringing, Fade-Out-Fade-In, Subways are for Sleeping, It's Always Fair Weather, What a Way to Go; co-author: book for Applause, 1970; co-author (with Adolph Green) book for Lorelei, 1973, book and lyrics On the 20th Century, 1978; appeared in: On the Town, 1944; performed with Adolph Green, 1959, 77; also appeared in play Isn't it Romantic, 1983, in movie Garbo Talks, 1985, The Band Wagon; author: Off Stage, 1995. Recipient Donaldson award and Tony award for Wonderful Town, as co-lyricist Best Score 1983; Tony award for Hallelujah, Baby, as co-writer Best Score 1968, Tony award Applause 1970, Tony award Lyrics and Book On the 20th Century, A Doll's Life, Tony award for Best Original lyrics The Will Rogers Follies, 1991; Woman of Achievement award NYU Alumnae Assn. 1978; N.Y.C. Mayor's award Art and Culture 1978, Lifetime Achievement award Kennedy Ctr., 1991, Grammy award for Will Roger Follies, 1992; named to Songwriters Hall of Fame 1980, Theatre Hall of Fame. Mem. Dramatists Guild (council, v.p. Dramatists Guild Fund).

COMEAU, KATHY DARR, publishing executive; b. Miami, Fla., Dec. 26, 1956; d. William Holmes and Susan Marie (Standish) Darr; m. Mark Lesin Comeau, Dec. 30, 1978 (div. July 1985); children: Ryan William, Chase Lesin. Student, George Mason U., No. Va. C.C. Asst. mgr., trainer Times Cmty. Newspapers, Leesburg, Va.; asst. mgr. Connection Newspapers, McLean, Va.; regional mgr. PT Bull., Alexandria, Va. Office: PT Bulletin Ste 400 333 N Fairfax St Alexandria VA 22314

COMEAU, LORENE ANITA EMERSON, real estate developer; b. Haverhill, Mass., Sept. 6, 1952; d. Russell Paul and Jeannette (La Course) Emerson; m. Peter Robert Comeau, May 6, 1950; children: Stephen David, Michelle Patricia. BA with honors, Northeastern U., 1975. Lic. real estate broker. Housing rep., pub. liaison U.S. Dept. HUD, Boston, 1975-78; devel. mgr. John M. Corcoran & Co., Milton, Mass., 1978-84, v.p., 1984-94; ptnr. Corcoran Realty Assocs., Milton, 1994—; co-owner, treas. Refrigeration Engring. & Contracting Co., Inc., 1995—; bd. dirs. Stoneham Coop. Bank, 1992—, mem. bd. affairs com., 1992-93, mem. security com., 1993—; v.p. Merrimack Valley Housing Partnership, Lowell, Mass., 1986-89. Treas. Andover (Mass.) br. Merrimack Valley YMCA, 1986-88, vice chair, 1988-90, chair, 1990-92; assoc. mem. Andover Fair Housing Com., 1982-87, Andover Housing Partnership Com., 1990—, Andover Planning Bd., 1993-96; mem. Andover Master Plan Com., 1982-84, chmn. com. housing component and master plan, 1989-90; mem. Andover Zoning Bd. Appeals, 1984-87; mem. fin. com., cor. bd. Merrimack Valley YMCA, Lawrence, Mass., 1984-86, 91-94, treas. corp. fin. com., 1992-94; mem. low income housing subcom. corp. bd. 1992—; mem. adv. bd. Caritas Cmtys., 1994—, The Fessenden Sch. Parent's Orgn., 1995—. Mem. LWV (fin. chmn. Andover chpt. 1981-83, budget chmn. 1983-84, 86-87), New England Women in Real Estate (seminars com. 1992, cmty. rels. com., program com. 1992-96), Nat. Assn. Indsl. and Office Properties (pub. affairs com. 1992—), Svc. Club of Andover, Sanborn Sch. PTO (curriculum enrichment com. 1988-95), West Mid. Sch. PAC (curriculum enrichment com., women's history month 1993-95). Republican. Episcopalian. Home: PO Box 4108 Andover MA 01810 Office: John M Corcoran & Co 500 Granite Ave Milton MA 02186-5610

COMEAU, SUSAN, bank executive. Exec. v.p. State St. Boston Corp., Boston. Office: State St Boston Corp 225 Franklin St Boston MA 02110-2804

COMEAU-LUIS, ODETTE YVONNE, critical care nurse; b. Repentigny, Que., Can., Feb. 8, 1964; came to U.S., 1982; d. Lester Joseph and Yvonne Marie (Saulnier) Comeau; m. Robert John Luis, Aug. 27, 1994. ADN, Midland Coll., 1984; BSN, U. Tex., Galveston, 1987; MS, Loma Linda U., 1995. CCRN. Staff nurse, charge nurse Midland (Tex.) Meml. Hosp., 1984-85; staff nurse, charge nurse, tng. specialist U. Tex., Galveston, 1987-92; staff and charge nurse, coord. Emergency Cardiac Care Ctr., Loma Linda (Calif.) U., 1992—; BCLS instr. Am. Heart Assn., 1988-94; facilitator, founder ICU family support group Med. ICU U. Tex., Galveston, 1991-92, sec. interdisciplinary com., 1990-92. Mem. AACN (chair local edn. com. 1991-92), Sigma Theta Tau. Roman Catholic.

COMEAUX, KATHARINE JEANNE, realtor; b. Richland, Wash., Jan. 18, 1949; d. Warren William and Ruth Irma (Remington) Gonder; m. Jack Goldwasser, May 25, 1992; 1 child, Thelma Morrow. AA, West Valley Coll., 1970; student, San Jose State U., 1970-71. Cert. realtor. Realtor Value Realty, Cupertino, Calif., 1975-79, Valley of Calif., Cupertino, 1979-81, Coldwell Banker, Cupertino, 1981-82, Fox & Carskadon, Saratoga, Calif., 1984-90. With Los Gatos-Saratoga Bd. Realtors Polit. Action, 1984-89; v.p. Hospice of Valley Svc. League, Saratoga, 1984-89; Big Sister Big Bros./Big Sisters, San Jose, Calif., 1976-90; bd. dirs. Mountain Energy Inc., United Way of Josephine County, Energia Natural, Honduras, Boys and Girls Club. Home: 4330 Fish Hatchery Rd Grants Pass OR 97527-9547

COMER, DEBRA RUTH, management educator; b. Phila., Apr. 11, 1960; d. Nathan Lawrence and Rita (Ellis) C.; m. James Michael Maloney. BA, Swarthmore Coll., 1982; MA, Yale U., 1984, MPhil, 1985, PhD, 1986. Instr. Yale U., New Haven, 1983-84; orgnl. devel. cons. Port Authority of N.Y. & N.J., N.Y.C., 1984-87; asst. prof. mgmt. Hofstra U., Hempstead, N.Y., 1987-93; assoc. prof. mgmt. Hofstra U., Hempstead, 1993—, chairperson dept. mgmt. and GB, 1995—. Contbr. articles to profl. jours. Yale U. fellow, 1982-86, Joshua B. Lippincott fellow Swarthmore Coll., 1982; Hofstra U. grantee, 1988-96. Mem. APA, Acad. Mgmt., Ea. Acad. Mgmt., Organizational Behavior Teaching Soc. Jewish. Office: Hofstra U Dept Mgmt and GB 228 Weller Hall Hempstead NY 11550

COMET, CATHERINE, conductor; m. Michael Aiken; 1 child, Caroline. MusM in Orch. Conducting, Juilliard Sch. Music; studied with Pierre Boulez, Nadia Boulanger, Igor Markevich. Former music dir., condr. U. Wis. Symphony & Chamber Orch.; EXXON-Arts Endowment condr. St. Louis Symphony Orch., 1981-84; music dir. St. Louis Youth Orch.; assoc. condr. Balt. Symphony Orch., 1984-86; music dir. Grand Rapids (Mich.) Symphony Orch., 1986-90, 91—, Am. Symphony Orch., N.Y.C., 1990-91; guest condr. Pasadena Symphony, Buffalo Philharm., Ala. Symphony, Nat. Symphony, others. Recipient 1st prize Internat. Young Condrs.' Competition, France, 1966, Dmitri Mitroupolos Internat. Contest prize, 1968. Office: Grand Rapids Symphony Orch 220 S Lyon NW Ste 415 Grand Rapids MI 49503*

COMFORT, JANE, artistic director. BFA in Painting, U. N.C. Artistic dir. Jane Comfort & Co., N.Y.C.; presenter materials at Lincoln Ctr.'s Serious Fun! Festival, Off-Broadway at Classic Stage Co., The Joyce Theater, Performance Space 122 and Dance Theater Workshop in N.Y., The Am. Ctr./Paris, Antwerp's Dance/USA Festival, Jacob's Pillow Dance Festival, The Walker Art Ctr., The Balt. Art Mus. and Dancers Collective in Atlanta. Choreographer (Broadway musical): Passion (recipient four Tony awards, including Best Musical), (theater dance musicals) Faith Healing, 1993, S/he, 1994-95. Grantee Nat. Endowment for the Arts, N.Y. Found. for Arts, N.Y. State Coun. on the Arts, Phillip Morris Cos., Inc., Joyce Mertz-Gilmore Found., Dance Mag. Found., Harkness Founds. for Dance, Found. for Contemporary Performance Art, Consolidated Edison of N.Y. and Beards Fund. Office: Jane Comfort and Co 55 N Moore St New York NY 10013

COMFORT, PRISCILLA MARIA, college official, human resources professional; b. Ft. Dix, N.J., Feb. 20, 1947; d. Jennie Rita (Manes) McGuire; children: James, Aimee. BS, Montclair State Coll., 1969; MEd, Trenton State Coll., 1980. Cert. tchr., guidance counselor, pub. mgr., N.J. Tchr. Burlington (N.J.) Twp. and City Schs., 1969-72; employment svc. interviewer N.J. Dept. Labor and Industry, Trenton, 1972-74; prin. career devel. specialist N.J. Dept. Civil Svc., Trenton, 1974-76, prin. pers. technician, 1976-79; dir. pers. svcs. Stockton State Coll., Pomona, N.J., 1979-89; asst. v.p. human resources Stockton Coll., Pomona, 1990-95, assoc. v.p. human resources, 1995; with N.J. Gov.'s task force on sexual harassment, 1993. Mem. Betty Bacharach Rehab. Hosp. Found. Bd., 1993; tchr. CCD Assumption Ch., Pomona, 1981-84, mem. CCD adv. bd., 1983-84; active Little League, PTO, 1977-84; mem. pers. com. Big Bros./Big Sisters Adv. Com., 1988; mem. community adv. bd. Jewish Family Svcs., 1991—; mem. adv. bd. pers. com. Atlantic City C. of C., 1985; mem. Nat. Found. Bd., 1996. Recipient Tribute to Women in Industry award YWCA (twin), 1987, Mgmt. Merit award, 1986, 88, SUN Mag. award, 1988, Community Recognition award Chapel of the Four Chaplains, 1988. Mem. ASPA, Cert. Pub. Mgrs. Assn., N.J. Atlantic County Pers. Assn., Assn. Affirmative Action in Higher Edn. (panelist), N.J. Pers. Adv. Bd., N.J. Coll. and Univ. Pers. Assn. (chmn., sec.-treas., chmn. mem. sect.), Coll. and Univ. Pers. Assn. (nat. bd. dirs. 1993, nat. legis. com. 1989-93, bd. dirs. ea. region 1990-96, sec. 1990-93, active other coms.), CUPA Ea. Acad. for Human Resource Excellence (chair 1994-95). Roman Catholic. Office: Richard Stockton Coll NJ Jim Leeds Rd Pomona NJ 08240

COMINI, ALESSANDRA, art historian, educator; b. Winona, Minn., Nov. 24, 1934; d. Raiberto and Megan (Laird) C. BA, Barnard Coll., 1956; MA, U. Calif., Berkeley, 1964; PhD with distinction, Columbia U., 1969. Teaching asst. U. Calif., Berkeley, 1964; vis. instr. U. Calif., 1967; preceptor Columbia U., 1965-66, 67-68, instr., 1968-69, asst. prof., 1969-74; vis. asst. prof. So. Methodist U., summers 1970, 72, assoc. prof. art history, 1974-75, prof., 1975—, Univ. disting. prof., 1983—; Alfred Hodder resident humanist Princeton U., 1972-73; disting. vis. lectr. Oxford U., 1996; vis. asst. prof. Yale U., 1973; vis. humanist various univs.; lectr. in English, German and Italian; keynote spkr. Gewandhaus Symposia, Leipzig, Germany, 1983, 85, 87, 89, Mahler Internat Congress, Amsterdam, 1988, 95, Hamburg, 1989, Oxford, 1996, Montpellier, 1996; feature spkr. Purchase, N.Y., 1989, Leningrad, 1990, Stockholm, 1991, Berlin, 1993, Bethoven Extravaganza, Milw., 1994, Schiele Symposium, Indpls., 1994, Helsinki, 1996; panelist NEH Mus. and Pub. Programs, 1978—. Author: Schiele in Prison, 1973, Egon Schiele's Portraits, 1974 (Nat. Book award nominee 1975, reissued 1990, Charles Rufus Morey Book award 1975), Gustav Klimt, 1975, reissued 1986, 90, 93, also German, French and Dutch edit., Egon Schiele, 1976, reissued 1986, 94, also German, French and Dutch edits., The Fantastic Art of Vienna, 1978, The Changing Image of Beethoven, 1987; contbg. author: World Impressionism, 1990, Käthe Kollwitz, 1992, Egon Schiele, 1994, Violetta and her Sisters, 1994, Egon Schiele: Nudes, 1995, Salome, 1996; contbr. numerous articles to Stagebill, Arts Mag., English Nat. Opera; also author various catalogue and book introductions, also book revs. for N.Y. Times, Women's Art Jour. Awarded Grand Decoration of Honor for svcs. to Republic of Austria, 1990; recipient Charles Rufus Morey Book award Coll. Art Assn. Am., 1976, Laural award AAUW, 1979; named Outstanding Prof., 1977, 79, 83, 85, 86, 87, 88, 90; AAUW travel fellow, 1966-87; NEH grantee, 1975; named Meadows Disting. Teaching Prof., 1986-87, Tchr./Scholar of Yr., United Meth. Ch., 1996. Mem. ASCAP, Coll. Art Assn. Am. (bd. dirs. 1980-84), Women's Caucus for Art (bd. dirs. 1974-78, Life Achievement award 1995), Tex. Inst. Letters. Democrat. Home: 2900 McFarlin Blvd Dallas TX 75205-1920 Office: So Meth U Dept Art History Dallas TX 75275

COMISKY, HOPE A., lawyer; b. Phila., Apr. 23, 1953; married; three children. BA with distinction, Cornell U., 1974; JD, U. Pa., 1977. Bar: Pa. 1977, U.S. Dist. Ct. (ea. dist.) Pa. 1978, D.C. 1979, U.S. Ct. Appeals (3d cir.) 1979, U.S. Supreme Ct. 1987, U.S. Dist. Ct. (mid. dist.) Pa. 1991, N.Y. 1993. Law clerk ea dist. U.S. Dist. Ct., Pa., 1977-78; assoc. Dilworth, Paxson, Kalish & Kauffman, Phila., 1978-84, ptnr., 1985-91; ptnr. Anderson Kill & Olick, P.C. (formerly, Anderson Kill Olick & Oshinsky P.C.), Phila., 1992—, also bd. dirs., 1994—; mng. ptnr. Phila. office Anderson Kill & Olick, P.C. (formerly, Anderson Kill Olick & Oshinsky P.C.), 1995—; spkr. in field. Contbr. articles to profl. jours. Bd. dirs. Phila. Sch.; hon. bd. dirs. Fedn. Day Care Svcs., mem. exec. com., chmn. pers. practices com., 1985-91; bd. dirs. Ctr. for Literacy, 1996—; mem. Phila. Regional Employment Adv. Com., Am. Arbitration Assn., 1996—. Mem. Phi Beta Kappa, Mortar Bd. Office: Anderson Kill & Olick PC 1600 Market St Fl 32 Philadelphia PA 19103-7240

COMMARE, MARY ELLEN, social service administrator; b. Chgo., May 10, 1952; d. S. Harry and Eleanor (Zywiciel) Powell; m. Arthur Commare Jr., May 25, 1974; children: Ben, Coryn, Lauren. BS in Edn., Ea. Ill. U., 1973; MS in Mental Health, No. Ill. U., 1982. Cert. alcohol and drug counselor, Ill. Tchr. Marquardt Middle Sch., Bloomingdale, Ill., 1974-77, Yorkville (Ill.) High Sch., 1979-81; counselor, assoc. dir. Kendall County Human Svcs., Yorkville, 1982-95; exec. dir. Youth Svcs. Network, Rockford, Ill., 1995—. Active Belvidere Sports Boosters, 1995—, Belvidere Music Boosters, 1995—. Mem. Rockford Network, Womanspace. Office: Youth Svcs Network Inc 4302 N Main Rockford IL 61103

COMMIRE, ANNE, playwright; b. Wyandotte, Mich.; d. Robert and Shirley (Moore) C. BS, Eastern Mich. U., 1961; postgrad., Wayne State U., NYU. Author: (plays) Shay, 1973, Put Them All Together, 1978, Transatlantic Bridge, 1977, Sunday's Red, 1982, Melody Sisters, 1983, Starting Monday, 1988; (book) (with Mariette Hartley) Breaking the Silence, 1990, (teleplays) Rebel for God, 1980, Hayward's, 1980, editor. Something About the Author, 1970-90, Yesterday's Authors of Books for Children, 1977-78, Historic World Leaders, 1994, Women in World History, 1997. Recipient Eugene O'Neill Theatre award, 1973, 78, 83, 88; Creative Artists Program grantee, 1975; Rockefeller grantee for playwriting, 1979. Mem. PEN, Authors Guild, Dramatists Guild, Writers Guild Am. Home: 11 Stanton St Waterford CT 06385-1400 Also: 274 W 95th St New York NY 10025-6305

COMOLA, JACQUELINE PETERMANN, management consultant; b. Yazoo City, Miss., Aug. 8, 1937; d. John Winfred and Flo (Pearce) Petermann; divorced; children: James Paul Comola II, Jon Ronald Comola. BA in Polit. Sci., U. Tex., 1969, MA in Urban Inst., 1975, postgrad. in Orgn. Behaviour. Dir. tng. U.S. Dept. Energy, Dallas, Tex., 1973-74; project dir. U.S. Office Pers. Mgmt., Dallas, 1974-79; project dir. Am. Productivity and Quality Ctr., Houston, 1979-82, 85-86, v.p. White Collar Improvement, 1986-90, sr. v.p. Adv. Svc. and Rsch., 1990-91, dir. Internat. Svcs. Practice, 1991-93; exec. v.p. Psychol. Cons., Inc., Houston, 1982-83; pres. Collaborative Resources, Inc., Houston, 1993—; rev. panel mem. U.S. Dept. Edn., Washington, 1990-93; task force mem. Gov.'s Task Force on Productivity Improvement, Austin, Tex., 1989. Co-author: (books) Improving Productivity in Healthcare, 1988, Educating for Excellence, 1991; contbg. author: Handbook of Management Audits, 1993; contbr. articles to profl. jours. Bd. dirs. City Planning and Zoning Bd., Euless, Tex., City Libr., Bedford, Tex.; pres. PTA, Bedford. Mem. ASQC, Am. Mgmt. Assn., Founders Bus. Club, Mus. of Art. Episcopalian.

COMOSS, PATRICIA B., cardiac rehabilitation nurse, consultant; b. Shamokin, Pa., Apr. 20, 1947; d. William J. and Lucille M. (Shipulski) McCall; m. Eugene J. Comoss, Nov. 25, 1970. Diploma, St. Joseph's Hosp., Reading, Pa., 1968; BS in Health Care Mgmt., Pa. State U., Harrisburg, 1982. CCU staff nurse Polyclinic Med. Ctr., Harrisburg; head nurse, cardiac rehab. Rehab. Hosp., Mechanicsburg, Pa.; dir. edn. AMSCO/Rehab., Mechanicsburg; founder, pres. Nursing Enrichment Consultants, Harrisburg. Co-author: Cardiac Rehabilitation: A Comprehensive Nursing Approach, 1979; contbr. articles to profl. jours. Fellow Am. Assn. Cardiovascular and Pulmonary Rehab. (bd. dirs. 1986-88, v.p. 1988-90, pres.-elect 1990-91, pres. 1992, chair fed. project on clin. practice guidelines on cardiac rehab. 1992-95); mem. ANA, AACCN, Am. Coll. Sports Medicine, Am. Heart Assn. Home: 4100 Elmerton Ave Harrisburg PA 17109-1327

COMPTON, ANN WOODRUFF, news correspondent; b. Chgo., Jan. 19, 1947; d. Charles Edward and Barbara (Ortlund) C.; m. William Stevenson Hughes, Nov. 25, 1978; children: William Compton, Edward Opie, Ann Woodruff, Michael Stevenson. BA, Hollins (Va.) Coll., 1969. Reporter, anchorwoman WDBJ-TV (CBS), Roanoke, Va., 1969-70; polit. reporter, state capitol bur. chief WDBJ-TV (CBS), Richmond, Va., 1971-73; fellow Washington Journalism Center, 1970, trustee, 1978-93; corr. ABC News, N.Y.C., 1973-74; White House corr. ABC News, Washington, 1974-79, 81-84, 89—, congl. corr., 1979-81, 84-86, chief Ho. of Reps. corr., 1987-88. Trustee Hollins Coll., 1987-93; bd. dirs. Freedom Forum Ctr. for Media Studies, Columbia U., 1984—. Named Mother of Yr., Nat. Mother's Day Com., 1987. Mem. White House Corrs. Assn. (dir. 1977-79), Radio-TV Corrs. Bd. (chmn. 1987). Office: ABC News Washington Bur 1717 Desales St NW Washington DC 20036-4401

COMPTON, CHARLOTTE PATTON, special education educator; b. Bluefield, Va., June 17, 1953; d. Charles Everett and Lillian Rebecca (Mathena) Patton; children: Kris Compton, Monica Compton. BS, Concord Coll., Athens, W.Va., 1975; MS, Morehead State U., 1995. Cert. tchr. secondary edn.; rank I spl. edn. Home econs. tchr. Big Creek H.S., War, W.Va., 1975-76, Richlands (Va.) Mid. Sch., 1976-80; spl. edn. tchr. Montgomery County H.S., Mt. Sterling, Ky., 1987—; rsch. dietitian U. Ky., Lexington, 1987-89. Mem. Coun. for Exceptional Children, Ky. Edn. Assn. Episcopalian.

COMPTON, LORRAINE RHODAS, musician, educator; b. Bklyn., Apr. 22, 1957; d. John Frank and Joan Mildred (Casey) Rhodas; m. Asoka Compton, July 19, 1981. Student, Queens Coll., 1975-77. exec. dir. Yuko Daiko, Inc., St. Petersburg, Fla., 1993—. Democrat. Office: Yuko Daiko Inc 10460 Roosevelt Bvd # 222 Saint Petersburg FL 33716

COMPTON, MARY BEATRICE BROWN (MRS. RALPH THEODORE COMPTON), public relations executive, writer; b. Washington, May 25, 1923; d. Robert James and Abia Eliza (Stone) Brown; m. Ralph Theodore Compton, Mar. 18, 1961. Grad. Thayer Acad., Chandler Sch., Leland Powers Sch. Radio, TV and Theatre, Boston, 1942. Radio program dir. Converse Co., Malden, Mass., 1942-45; head radio continuity dept. Sta. WAAB, Yankee Network, Worcester, Mass., 1945-46; asst. dir. radio Leland Powers Sch. Radio, TV and Theatre, Boston, 1946-49, dir., 1949-51; program asst. Sta. KNBH, Hollywood, Calif., 1951-52; v.p. Acorn Film Co., Boston, 1953-54; dir. women's communications, editor Program Notes, radio interviewer NAM, N.Y.C., 1954-61. Celebrities pub. rels. Nat. Citizens for Nixon, 1968, Kennedy Ctr. Pub. Info., 1985-89, Washington Nat. Cathedral Visitor's Svcs., 1989—. Mem. Soc. Old Plymouth Colony Descs., Magna Carta Dames, Congl. Country Club (Bethesda, Md.). Home: 15300 Wallbrook Ct Apt 3F Silver Spring MD 20906-1455

COMPTON, NORMA HAYNES, retired university dean; b. Washington, Nov. 16, 1924; d. Thomas N. and Lillian (Laffin) Haynes; m. William Randall Compton, Mar. 27, 1946; children: William Randall, Anne Elizabeth. AB, George Washington U., 1950; MS, U. Md., 1957, PhD, 1962. Rschr. Julius Garfinckel & Co., Washington, 1955; tchr. Montgomery Blair High Sch., Silver Spring, Md., 1955-57; instr. U. Md., 1957-60, teaching and rsch. fellow Inst. Child Study, 1960-61, assoc. prof., 1962-63; psychology extern St. Elizabeths Hosp., Washington, 1962-63; assoc. prof. Utah State U., 1963-64, prof., 1964-68, head dept. clothing and textiles, 1963-68, dir. Inst. for Rsch. on Man and His Personal Environment, 1967-68; dean Sch. Home Econs. Auburn (Ala.) U., 1968-73; dean Sch. Consumer and Family Scis. Purdue U., 1973-87, prof. family studies, 1987-90; faculty The Edn. Ctr., Longboat Key, Fla., 1991—, mem. ednl. adv. bd., 1995—; cons. Burgess Pub. Co., Mpls., 1975-81, Nat. Advt. Rev. Bd., N.Y.C., 1978-82; bd. dirs. Armour & Co., Phoenix, 1976-82, Home Hosp., Lafayette, Ind., 1983-89; pres. adv. com. Women's Resource Ctr. of Sarasota, Fla., 1992—; chair Adv. Commn. Status Women, Sarasota, 1993—; mem. advocates coun. Family Law Network Sarasota, 1994—. Author: (with Olive Hall) Foundations of Home Economics Research, 1972, (with John Touliatos) Approaches to Child Study, 1983, Research Methods in Human Ecology/Home Economics, 1988; contbr. articles to profl. jours. Mem. APA, AAUW, PEO, Am. Assn. Family and Consumer Sci., Phi Beta Kappa, Sigma Xi, Phi Kappa Phi, Omicron Nu, Psi Chi. Episcopalian.

COMSTOCK, REBECCA ANN, lawyer; b. Mpls., Mar. 13, 1950; d. Clark Franklin and Ruth Carolyn (Sundt) C.; m. John A. Aronld, Mar. 2, 1991. Student, Conn. Coll., 1968-70; BA summa cum laude, U. Minn., 1973; JD Order of St. Ives, U. Denver, 1977. Bar: Minn. 1978, U.S. Dist. Ct. Minn. 1978. Ptnr.; atty. Dorsey & Whitney, Mpls., 1982—. Mem. ABA, Minn. Bar Assn. (chmn. adminstrv. law sect. 1989-90, exec. coun. environ. and natural resources law sect. 1992-94), Hennepin County Bar Assn., Legal Aid Soc. of Mpls. (bd. dirs. 1988-93), Minn. Women Lawyers Assn. (bd. dirs. 1979-81). Office: Dorsey & Whitney 220 S 6th St Minneapolis MN 55402-4502

CONANT, TARA PATRICIA, photographer; b. Boston, July 13, 1964; d. Ronald and Patricia C. (Madsen) Conant. BA, Westfield State, 1987; MFA, Bard Coll., 1996. Owner TC Photography, Springfield, Mass., 1994—. Author, photographer "Murder Sites of Twenty Women", 1995; one-woman shows include Marcuse Gallery, N.Y., Westfield State Coll., Mass.; exhbns. include Sites of Violence Against Women, 1995. Bard fellow, 1993-95. Mem. Kodak Profl. Photographers Assn., Ilforo Photographers Assn. Home: 60 Wrenwood St Springfield MA 01119

CONARD, KATHLEEN ANN, secondary education educator; b. Phoenix, Aug. 16, 1949; d. William Franklin and Helen Ruth (Highberger) C. BA, Ariz. State U., 1971; MA, U. Phoenix, 1990. Cert. secondary tchr., Ariz. Mid. sch. lang. arts and social studies tchr. Scottsdale (Ariz.) Pub. Schs., 1972-77, secondary tchr. lang. arts, social studies and Am. studies, 1977-94, mem. planning team Desert Mountain H.S., 1994—, lang. arts coord. Desert Mountain H.S., 1995-96; mentor Scottsdale Schs., 1995—. Bd. dirs. NOW, Phoenix, 1974-76, Women's Ctr., Phoenix, 1976-78; founding mother Women Take Back the Night, Phoenix, 1984-86, Woman Rising Newspaper, Ariz., 1975-78. Mem. NEA, Nat. Coun. Tchrs. English. Democrat.

CONAWAY, JANE ELLEN, elementary education educator; b. Fostoria, Ohio, July 9, 1941; d. Robert and Virginia Conaway; B.A. in Elem. Edn., Mary Manse Coll., Toledo, 1966; M.Ed. in Elem. Edn., U. Ariz., 1969; postgrad. in reading, U. Toledo, 1975-77; postgrad. U. Wis., 1987—. Tchr. Sandusky pub. schs., Ohio, 1966-67, Bellevue City Schs., Ohio, 1969-70; coord. 1st grade small group instrn. program St. Mary's Grade Sch., Sandusky, 1970-71; tchr. Chpt. I remedial reading Eastwood Local schs., Pemberville, Ohio, 1971-87, also dist. dir. Right to Read program; reading specialist Middleton-Cross Plains (Wis.) Area Sch. Dist., 1987—. Mem. NEA, Wis. Edn. Assn., Middleton Edn. Assn., Madison Area Reading Coun., Delta Kappa Gamma. Cert. as reading specialist in diagnostic and remedial reading, Wis. Home: 1302 Wexford Dr Waunakee WI 53597-1842 Office: Middleton Cross Plains Sch Dist 6701 Woodgate Rd Middleton WI 53562-3818

CONBOY, JUNE MAC MILLAN, counselor, therapist, community relations specialist; b. Jamaica, Queens County, N.Y., Apr. 25, 1933; d. Howard Samuel and Barbara Louise (Eifler) Mac M.; m. James Vincent Conboy, June 19, 1954 (dec. Aug. 1984); children: June K., Karen, Diana, Maureen, Christopher, George. BA in Fine Art, Georgian Court Coll., Lakewood, N.J., 1954; MPS in Counseling, N.Y. Inst. Technology, Old Westbury, N.Y., 1981; student, Nat. Inst. Expressive Therapy, Honolulu, 1995—. Diplomate Nat. Inst. Expressive Therapy; cert. expressive therapist. Fine art instr. Columbus (Ga.) Sch. Art, 1954-55; illustrator Mack Friedman Dept. Stores, Niagara Falls, N.Y., 1955-56; art instr. Home Studio and Town of Oyster Bay, L.I., N.Y., 1956-81; alcoholism counselor Alcoholism Counseling Svcs., Glen Cove, N.Y., 1980-81, Ctrl. L.I. Counseling Svc., Floral Park, N.Y., 1981-85; cmty. rels. specialist Dept. Cmty. and Youth Svcs., Town of Oyster Bay, Massapequa, N.Y., 1981—; art therapist Kings Park (N.Y.) Psychiat. Ctr., 1983; counselor and expressive therapist Muttontown, N.Y., 1981—; facilitator, trainer, mem. bd. dirs. Beginning Experience of L.I., 1980-92; presenter, lectr. N.Y.S. Assn. Counseling, 1990—. Mem. parent's coun. Locust Valley Sch. Dist., 1974-81; instr. Greenville Bakers Boys Club, Locust Valley, 1976-77. Mem. Nat. Expressive Therapy Assn. (presenter,

1991, 95), N.Y. Soc. Clin. Hypnosis (trainer, presenter 1990-96), L.I. Component Study Group (sec. 1989—), L.I. Mental Health Counselors Assn., Internat. Soc. for Study of Dissociation (presenter 1995). Roman Catholic. Home: RR1 Orchard Ln Oyster Bay NY 11771

CONDIE, VICKI COOK, nurse, educator; m. Michael J. Condie; children: Jennifer, Jamie, Stephen. Diploma, Deaconess Hosp. Sch. Nursing, 1969; BSN summa cum laude, SUNY, 1983; MS, Syracuse U., 1986; CAS in Nursing Edn., Widener U., 1991. RN, N.Y. Dir. nursing edn. Cayuga Community Coll., N.Y., 1987—, prof. nursing; SIDS educator Western N.Y. Sids Ctr., 1987—; mem. utilization rev. com. Cayuga County Dept. Health, 1985—, profl. adv. com. for Cert. Home Health Agy., 1987—; adj. prof. SUNY Health Sci. Ctr., Syracuse.; active N.Y. State Coun. ADN Programs. Active Florence Nightengale Mus. Assn., London. Mem. ANA, N.Y. State Nurses Assn. (mem. coun. nursing edn.), SUNY Health Sci. Ctr. Honor Soc., Sigma Theta Tau.

CONDIT, DORIS ELIZABETH, historian; b. Balt.; d. Harlan Whitney and Dorothy Elizabeth (Witte) Morgan; m. Kenneth W. Condit, Aug. 22, 1953; children: Caroline Walbridge, Victoria Whitney. Student, Johns Hopkins U., 1945-46; AB, George Washington U., 1949, MA, 1952. Historian U.S. Corps of Engrs., Hist. Div., Balt., 1949-51; ops. analyst Johns Hopkins U. Ops. Research Office, Chevy Chase, Md., 1952-56; research scientist, sr. research scientist Am. Univ. Center for Research in Social Systems, Washington, 1956-69; sr. research scientist Am. Inst. for Research, Kensington, Md., 1969-74; cons. Office of Sec. of Def., Washington, 1974-77, 85-87; contract historian Office of Sec. of Def., Washington, 1977-85; cons. Braddock, Dunn & McDonald, 1973-74, Am. Insts. for Research, 1974, Ops. Research Office, 1956-57; assoc. prof. research Am. U., 1960-69; research area chmn. Center for Research in Social Systems, 1966-70; mem. ad hoc group for Sci. and Tech. Info., 1962. Recipient Gardiner G. Hubbard Meml. prize in Am. history, George Washington U., 1949. Mem. Soc. for History in Fed. Govt., Soc. for Historians of Am. Fgn. Relations, Phi Beta Kappa. Episcopalian. Author: Allied Supplies for Italian Partisans During World War II, 1954; A System for Handling Data on Unconventional Warfare, 1956; Case Study in Guerrilla War: Greece During World War II, 1961; Modern Revolutionary Warfare: An Analytical Overview, 1973; The Test of War, 1950-53, History of the Office of the Secretary of Defense, Vol. II, 1988, (with Bert H. Cooper, Jr. and others) Challenge and Response in Internal Conflict, 3 Vols., 1967-68, U.S. Military Response to Overseas Insurgencies, 1970, Strategy and Success in Internal Conflict, 1971, Population Protection and Resources Management in Internal Defense Operations, 1971.

CONDITT, MARGARET KAREN, scientist, policy analyst; b. Mobile, Ala., Aug. 7, 1953; d. Abraham King and Catherine Patricia (Sullivan) C.; m. Richard Wayne Shoults, May 18, 1976 (div. Feb. 15, 1979); m. David Joseph Bruno, Feb. 13, 1988; 1 stepchild, Josh. BS in Chemistry, U. Ala., Tuscaloosa, 1975; PhD in Chemistry, U. Colo., 1984. Receptionist Mobile Infirmary, summer 1973; field hydrologist U.S. Geol. Survey, Tuscaloosa, 1975; sci. aide II Geol. Survey Ala., Tuscaloosa, 1975-77; tchg. asst. U. Ala., Tuscaloosa, 1977-79; rsch. asst. U. Colo., Boulder, 1979-84; sr. scientist Procter & Gamble, Cin., 1984—; reviewer sci. edn. grant proposals NSF, Washington, 1988; mem. water sci. and tech. bd. com. Nat. Acad. Scis., Washington, 1989-91. Author: (chpt.) Advanced Techniques in Synthetic Fuels Analysis, 1983; contbr. articles to profl. jours. Intern Colo. Gov.'s Sci. and Tech. Adv. Coun., 1981-83; appointee Liberty Twp. Bd. Zoning Appeal, 1994—; trustee, sec. Woodmoor Ter. Homeowner's Assn. Bd., 1993-96, pres. 1996—. Recipient fellowship Mining and Mineral Resources and Rsch. Inst., 1980, Rsch. fellowship U. Colo. Grad. Sch., 1981, Browns-Rickett grant AAUW, 1982. Mem. Am. Chem. Soc. Roman Catholic. Home: 6959 Rock Springs Dr Hamilton OH 45011

CONDON, MARIA DEL CARMEN, retired elementary school educator; b. Laredo, Tex., Aug. 31, 1929; d. Florencio and Carmen (Diaz) Briseno; m. James Robert Condon, July 24, 1967 (dec. Apr. 1978). BA, Tex. Woman's U., 1962. Tchr. Laredo Ind. Sch. Dist., 1963-9; supervising tchr. Laredo State U., 1984—. Mem. Tex. ASCD, Tex. Ret. Tchrs. Assn., Tex. Classroom Tchrs. Assn., Nat. Alumnae Assn. of Tex. Woman's U. Democrat. Roman Catholic. Home: 1514 Hibiscus Ln Laredo TX 78041-3325

CONDOS, BARBARA SEALE, real estate investment consultant, broker; b. Kenedy, Tex., Feb. 24, 1925; d. John Edgar and Bess Rochelle (Ainsworth) Seale; m. George James Condos, Dec. 24, 1955 (dec.); 1 child, James Alexander. MusB magna cum laude, U. Incarnate Word, San Antonio, 1946. Lic. real estate broker, Tex. Ptnr., CEO Mountain Top-V.I. Devel. Properties, V.I., 1977-85; pres. Investment Realty Co., San Antonio, 1978—; pres. Hallmark Realty, Inc., San Antonio, 1978—. Choreographer, dancer San Antonio Symphony's Youth Concerts and Opera Festival; actress San Antonio Little Theatre-Patio-Players 1948—. Trustee San Antonio Little Theatre, 1953-76; trustee Incarnate Word Coll., 1977-89, vice chair, 1980-82, trustee emerita, 1989—; mem. coun. McNay Mus., 1986—, chair coun., 1987—; chair coun. McNay Art Inst., 1988—; trustee McNay Art Mus., 1989—; bd. dirs. San Antonio Performing Arts Assn., 1978—. Mem. Internat. Real Estate Fedn., Internat. Inst. of Valuers, Real Estate Securities and Syndication Inst., Nat. Assn. Realtors, Tex. Assn. Realtors, San Antonio Bd. Realtors, The Argyle Club. Avocation: painting. Home: 217 Geneseo Rd San Antonio TX 78209-5913 Office: Investment Realty Co 1635 NE Loop 410 San Antonio TX 78209-1625

CONDRAN, CYNTHIA MARIE, gospel musician; b. Avon Park, Fla., Apr. 29, 1953; d. Kenneth Dale and Ruth Mae (Garber) Grubb; m. Lee Light Condran, July 3, 1971. Student, Lebanon Valley Coll., 1970-72. Piano tchr. Sebring, Fla., 1968-70, Annville, Pa., 1971—; gospel musician, writer, arranger Condran Music Co., Annville, Pa., 1972—, also recording engr.; writer comml. jingles. Sang by spl. invitation at Elipse of The White House, 1982; composer The Only Thing Holding You Back, 1977, Just A Few More Rivers, 1975, The Patchwork Quilt, 1978, Freedom, 1976, The Little Things, 1980, We're America, Heavens Fiesta, He's the Lord of Everyday, 1989, I've Never Known Such Love, 1990, I Just Want To Talk To You, 1990, Sweep Our Sins, 1990, Eternal Friends, 1991, The Precious Jewels At Christmas Time, 1992, Lost On My Way Back Home, 1993, I Believe in the Power of Love, 1993, To Speak Your Name, 1994, Forever, 1994, We Praise You Lord, 1994. Recipient Contemporary Country Artists of Yr. award Internat. Country Gospel Music Assn. Mem. Gospel Music Assn., Broadcast Music Inc., Christian Bus. and Prof. Women (music chmn.), So. Gospel Music Guild. Republican. Home: RR 3 Box 602 Annville PA 17003-9590

CONDREA, LYDIA, linguist, educator, researcher; b. Chisinau, Moldova, May 26, 1949; came to U.S., 1988; d. Vladislav and Ecaterina (Rusu-Ciobanu) Chiricenco; m. Arcady Condrea, June 8, 1980; children: Gabriela, Daniel. MA in French Philology, Chisnau State U., 1977, BA in Edn., 1977; MA in Romance Linguistics, U. Wash., 1990, PhC, 1993. Cert. tchr., Wash. Tchr. English, Italian, French, Spanish, Russian, Romanian various schs., Moldova, Moldova, Ukraine, 1977-78; lectr. French, English Art Inst., Chisinau, 1978-80; tchr. French U. Wash., Seattle, 1988-93; interpreter French, Romanian, Russian Seattle Mcpl. Ct. & Bereitz, 1989—; adj. faculty mem. Wash. Acad. Langs. and Seattle Pacific U., 1993—; dir. French studies Canoe French Camp, San Juan Islands, Wash., 1995. Home: 12563 B Densmore Ave N Seattle WA 98133

CONDRILL, JO ELLARESA, logistics executive, speaker; b. Hull, Tex., Oct. 25, 1935; d. Freddie (dec.) and Ida (Donatto) Founteno; m. Edwin Leon Ellis, Jan. 9, 1955 (div. 1979); children: Michael Edwin, James Alcia, Resa Ann, Thomas Matthew; m. Donald Richard Condrill, Sept. 21, 1980 (div. 1985). BSBA, Our Lady of the Lake U., 1982; grad. Logistics Exec. Devel. Course, Army Logistics Mgmt. Ctr., 1985; MS in Pub. Adminstrn., Ctrl. Mich. U., 1987; grad. program mgmt. course, Def. Sys. Mgmt. Coll., 1989; grad., U.S. Army War Coll., 1993. Cert. seminar coord. Sec. USAF, Wiesbaden, Fed. Republic Germany, 1968-73; sec. mil. tng. ctr. USAF, San Antonio, 1973-77; editorial asst. Airman Mag., San Antonio, 1978; mgmt. analyst San Antonio Air Logistics Ctr., San Antonio, 1979-82; inventory mgr. ground fuels Detachment 29, Alexandria, Va., 1982-83; logistics plans officer Mil. Dist. Washington, 1983-85, chief logistics plans ops. and mgmt., 1985-88, hdqrs. dept. of the army staff Office of the Dep. Chief of Staff for Logistics, 1988—; chief integration br. Office of the Dep. Chief of Staff for Logistics, 1990-95; owner Seminars by Jo, Alexandria, Va., 1984-86, Jo Condrill Presents, Alexandria, Va., 1996—; field instr. Golden State U., L.A., 1985-86; instr. Fairfax County Adult Edn., Springfield, Va., 1984; vol. aide ARC Wilford Hall Hosp., San Antonio, 1978; constn. drafter KC Women's Aux., San Antonio, 1977; den mother Boy Scouts Am., San Antonio, 1967; docent Nat. Mus. Am. History, 1988. Author: Civilians in Support of Military Field Operations, 1993, Leadership: From Vision to Victory in Six Simple Steps, 1995; numerous speeches. Civilian v.p. student coun. Army War Coll., Carlisle, Pa. Recipient Achievement medal for civilian svc. Dept. Army, 1984; Best Speaker award Def. Logistics Agy. Mem. Nat. Capital Spkrs. Assn., Internat. Platform Assn., Toastmasters (area gov. 1984-85, adminstrv. lt. gov. 1989-90, dist. 27 ednl. gov. 1990-91, dist. 27 gov. 1991-92, internat. dir. 1994-96, top ranking dist. gov. in internat. orgn. 1991-92, Internat. Pres. Disting. Dist. award 1991-92). Roman Catholic. Home: 6138 Talavera Ct Alexandria VA 22310-1887

CONDRON, BARBARA O'GUINN, metaphysics educator, school administrator, publisher; b. New Orleans, May 1, 1953; d. Bill Gene O'Guinn and Marie Gladys (Newbill) Jackson; m. Daniel Ralph Condron, Feb. 29, 1992; 1 child, Hezekiah Daniel. BJ, U. Mo., 1973; MA, Coll. Metaphysics, Springfield, Mo., 1977, DD, D Metaphysics, 1979. Cert. counselor; ordained min. Interfaith Ch. Metaphysics. Field rep. Sch. Metaphysics, New Orleans, 1978-80; dir. Interfaith Ch. Metaphysics, 1884-89; pres. Nat. Hdqs., Sch. Metaphysics, Windyville, Mo., 1980-84, chmn. bd., prof., 1989—; CEO SOM Pub., Windyville, 1989—; guest lectr., instr. Wichita State U., 1977, U. New Orleans, 1979, La. State U., 1981, Am. Bus. Womens Assn., 1982, U. Mo., Kansas City, 1984, Unity Village, 1985, Kans. Dept. Social Svcs. Conf., Topeka, 1986, U. Mo., Columbia and St. Louis, 1986, Mo. Tchrs. Conf., St. Louis, 1991, U. Okla., Norman, 1988-89, Parliament of World's Religions, Chgo., 1993, many others; creator Sch. Metaphysics Assocs., 1992; initiator Universal Hour Peace, 1995; initiator, advisor Nat. Dream Hotline, 1988—; radio and TV guest, 1977—. Author: What will I do Tmorrow?, Probing Depression, 1977, Search for a Satisfying Relationship, 1980, Strangers in My Dreams, 1987, Total Recall: An Introduction to Past Life & Health Readings, 1991, Kundalini Rising, 1992, Dreamers Dictionary, 1994, The Work of the Soul: Past Life Recall & Spiritual Enlightenment, 1996, Uncommon Knowledge, 1996, First Opinion, 1996; series editor When All Else Fails; editor-in-chief Thresholds Jour., 1990—; editor Wholistic Health and Healing Guide, 1992—; also numerous poems. Mem. Internat. Platform Assn., Am. Bus. Women's Assn., Interfaith Ministries, Kundalini Rsch. Network, Planetary Soc., Heritage Found., Sigma Delta Chi. Office: Sch Metaphysics Nat Hdqs Windyville MO 65783

CONE, CAROL LYNN, public relations executive; b. N.Y.C., June 7, 1950; d. William Addison Cone and Harriet (Gurney) Brown. BA, Brandeis U., 1972; MS, Boston U., 1978. Account exec. Newsome and Co., Boston, 1977-80; pres., CEO Cone Communications, Boston, 1980—. Mem. Gov.'s Entrepreneurial Adv. Council, Boston, 1982, Dukakis for Pres. campaign nat. fin. com., Boston, 1987. Named Outstanding Female Entrepreneur La Salle Jr. Coll., Newton, Mass., 1986, YWCA Achievement Entrepreneur, Boston, 1986, Entrepreneur of Yr. Arthur Young/Venture Mag., 1988; recipient Golden Quill award Internat. Assn. Bus. Communicators, 1987. Mem. Counselor's Acad. of Pub. Relations Soc. Am., Pub. Relations Soc. Am. (Silver anvil 1987), Am. Mktg. Assn. Office: Cone Comm Inc 90 Canal St Boston MA 02114-2022*

CONE, FRANCES MCFADDEN, data processing consultant; b. Columbia, S.C., Oct. 20, 1938; d. Joseph Means and Francis (Graham) McFadden; m. Charles Cone Jr., May 1962 (div. Sept. 1964); 1 child, Deborah Ann Cone Craytor. BS, U. S.C., 1960, MEd, 1973, M Math., 1977. Systems svc. rep. IBM, 1960-62; programmer/analyst Ga. Power Co., Atlanta, 1964-68, S.C. Fin. and Data Processing, Columbia, 1968-69; instr., head dept. Midlands Tech. Coll., Columbia, 1969-75; tng. coord. S.C. Nat. Bank, Columbia, 1975-79; systems analyst S.C. Dept. Health and Environ. Control, Columbia, 1979-80; project analyst So. Co. Svcs., Atlanta, 1980-89; cons. George Martin Assocs., Atlanta, 1989-93; sr. programmer, analyst Emory U., Atlanta, Ga., 1993—; adj. prof. Golden Gate U., Sumter, S.C., 1976-80. Vol. Ga. Wildlife Found. Mem. Nat. Mgmt. Assn. (sec., treas., awards comn. 1981-89). Republican. Episcopalian. Office: Emory U Computing Ctr Atlanta GA 30322

CONE, HEATHER JANE, educator of academically gifted; b. Sylvania, GA, Dec. 14, 1969; d. George Edward and Mary Christine (Hutchinson) C. BA, Clemson U., 1992. Cert. tchr. elem., academically gifted, S.C. Adminstrv. asst. Ogletree Johnson & Co., Hilton Head, S.C., 1992; tchr. Sandhills Farm Life Sch., Carthage, N.C., 1993—; sponsor Beta Club Carthage, N.C., 1993, 94, Cheerleading 1993-94, 94-95. Mem. N.C. Educators Assn. Home: 11 Cameron Ln Pinehurst NC 28374

CONE, VIRGIE HORNE HYMAN, former educator, civic worker; b. Brooksville, Fla.; d. George G. and Virgie (Horne) Hyman; m. Edward Elbert Cone, Dec. 20, 1930 (dec. Feb. 1962); children: Molly Gentile (dec. Jan. 1989), Edward Elbert. BS, Fla. State Coll. Women; MEd, U. Fla., 1956. Tchr., Meml. Jr. H.S., Hillsborough County, 1929-31; tchr. Duval County Robert E. Lee Sr. H.S., Jacksonville, Fla., 1943-55, dean, 1955-70; prin. Lee High Sch. (1st woman secondary sch. prin. in county), 1971-74; owner Cone's Antiques. Chmn., ARC night vols. St. Vincent's Hosp., 1969-71; mem. task force Mayor's Community Planning Coun., 1969; pres. Hamilton County unit Am. Cancer Soc., 1974-76; v.p. Hamilton County Meml. Hosp. Aux., 1975-76; mem. adv. coun. Health and Rehab. Svcs., Dist. 3, Fla.; dir. Area Agy. on Aging, 1977-82, bd. dirs., 1982—; del. White House Conf. on Aging, 1981, 95; mem. adv. coun. Social Security; mem. state legis. com. Am. Assn. Retired Persons, 1983-87, chmn., 1986-87; mem. State Longterm Care Ombudsman Coun., 1983-87, chmn. 1985-87 mem. adv. coun. State Civil Rights Commn.; pres. North Fla. Mental Health Bd., 1978-80; mem. Hamilton County Planning Coun., Gov.'s Commn. on Status Women, 1978-80; mem. exec. bd. North Central Fla. Health Planning Coun., 1979-80; bd. dirs. Mid. Fla. Area Agy. on Aging, State Comprehensive Health Assn., State Nursing Home Adv. Com.; mem. pub. issues com. Am. Cancer Soc.; mem. Banking Sunset Task Force, Fla., 1990-91; mem. aging commn. Fla. Med. Assn., 1988-93; mem. state com. to rewrite rating scale for nursing homes; bd. dirs. United Way Suwannee Valley; adv. com. health Hamilton County Sch. Sys. Health ctr. named in her honor, Jasper, Fla., 1993. Mem. Fla. Coun. Tchrs. Math. (curriculum chmn. 1952, sec. 1949), AAUW (Jacksonville v.p. 1953), Duval Tchrs. Assn. (chmn. profl. rights and responsibilities com. 1965-66), Jacksonville Panhellenic Assn. (pres. 1959-60, mem. scholarship com. 1963-68), Duval Personnel and Guidance Assn. (organizing chmn. 1966-69), Nat. Assn. Secondary Prins., Fla. Assn. Secondary Prins., Hamilton Ret. Tchrs., Fla. Assn. Area Agy. Dirs. (pres.), Fla. Ret. Educators Assn. (state legis. chair 1990-92), Am. Assn. Ret. Persons (capitol city task force, state legis. com.), Pilot Club of Jacksonville, Suwanee Valley Country Club (dir. 1978-80), Delta Kappa Gamma (chpt. pres. 1959-61), Sigma Kappa (nat. scholarship chmn. 1963-77). Home: 3D NW St Jasper FL 32052

CONERLY-PERKS, ERLENE BRINSON, retired chemist; b. Jackson, Miss., Nov. 16, 1938; d. Alvin Bryan and Erlene (Brinson) Conerly; m. Paul Allen Perks, May 4, 1991. BS, Millsaps Coll., 1959; MS in Tech. Mgmt., Am. U., 1978. Chemist NIH, Bethesda, Md., 1962-78; research biologist Dynamac, Rockville, Md., 1979-80; chemist EPA, Washington, 1980-94; ret., 1994. Democrat. Episcopalian.

CONETTA, TAMI FOLEY, lawyer; b. Akron, Ohio, Aug. 29, 1965; d. Charles David and Roxanne (Onyett) Foley; m. Anthony Joseph Conetta, July 29, 1989; 1 child, Emory Elizabeth Conetta. BA in Polit. Sci., Furman U., 1987; JD with honors, U. Fla., 1990. Bar: Fla. 1991. Lawyer Gassman & Conetta, P.A. (previously Alan S. Gassman, P.A.), Clearwater, Fla., 1990—. Contbr. articles to profl. jours. Profl. ptnr. Moffitt Cancer Ctr., Tampa, Fla., 1995—. Mem. Clearwater Bar Assn. (ch'r law week 1990—, Pres.'s award 1994), Clearwater Bar Probate Com. (chair 1994, 96-97), Pinellas County Estate Planning Coun., Clearwater Bar Young Lawyers (pres.-elect 1995). Office: Gassman & Conetta PA Ste 102 1245 Court St Clearwater FL 34616

CONEY, CAROLE ANNE, accountant; b. Berkeley, Calif., Aug. 11, 1944; d. Martin James and Ida Constance (Ditora) Skuce; m. David Michael Coney, June 20, 1964; children: Kristine Marie, Kenneth Michael. BS cum laude, Calif. State Poly. U., 1985, MBA, 1988. Tax cons., instr. H&R Block, Portland, Oreg., 1969-71; acct., asst. sec.-treas. Surety Ins. Co., La Habra, Calif., 1973-76; bookkeeper Homemakers Furniture, Downers Grove, Ill., 1976-79; office mgr., acct. Helen's Pl. Printing, Upland, 1979-80; bookkeeper Vanguard Cos., Upland, 1980-82; dir. acctg. Coll. Osteopathic Medicine of Pacific, Pomona, Calif., 1982-89; acctg. mgr. City of Ontario, Calif., 1989—. Pres. Brea/La Habra Newcomers, 1975; treas. Alta Loma (Calif.) Com. to Elect Robert Neufeld, 1981. Mem. NAFE, Nat. Assn. Coll. and Univ. Bus. Officers, Calif. Soc. Mcpl. Fin. Officers, Govt. Fin. Officers Assn., Assn. Coll. and Univ. Auditors, Coun. Fiscal Officers, Soroptomists, Ontario Kiwanis, Delta Mu Delta, Alpha Iota. Democrat. Roman Catholic. Home: PO Box 4910 24581 San Moritz Dr Crestline CA 92325-4910 Office: City of Ontario 303 E B St Ontario CA 91764-4105

CONEY, STEPHNÉ RENIÁ, education educator; b. Camden, N.J., Oct. 29, 1963; d. Douglas Tyrone and Bette Louise Coney; 1 child, Sescily Reneé. BA, Johnson C. Smith U., Charlotte, N.C., 1986; MA, Tex. So. U., Houston, 1988. Prof. edn. Hargest Coll., Houston, 1988-90; tax examiner IRS, Phila., 1990-96; founder, exec. dir. Nat. Stop the Violence Alliance, Inc., Camden, 1991—; founder, exec. dir. Camden County Internat. Nat. Festival, 1994—, Actors, Artists and Athletes Against Violence, 1995—, Facing Attitudes Concerning Ednl. Spirits, 1996. Recipient Stop the Violence award Assembly of N.J./Camden City Coun., 1995. Mem. Delta Sigma Theta. Democrat. African Methodist Episcopal. Office: Nat Stop the Violence PO Box 1293 Camden NJ 08105

CONFORTI, JOANNE, advertising executive; b. N.Y.C., Apr. 17, 1944; d. Ralph and Josephine (Amico) C. Student, Bklyn. Coll., 1961-63. Trainee, Gen. Motors, N.Y.C., 1960-62, adminstrv. asst., 1962-66, personnel asst., 1966-70; staff asst. Bozell & Jacobs, Inc., N.Y.C., 1973-75, personnel and office mgr., 1975-77, personnel and office v.p., 1977-79, human resources dir., v.p., 1979-81, corp. human resources dir., sr. v.p., from 1981, now exec. v.p. corp. human resources, also bd. dirs. Mem. Advt. Women of N.Y. Home: 440 E 62d St New York NY 10021-8558 Office: Bozell Jacobs Kenyon & Eckhardt 40 W 23rd St New York NY 10010-5200

CONGER, CYNTHIA LYNNE, financial planner; b. Omaha, Dec. 8, 1948; d. Bob Bruce Ashton and Cleo (Artz) Ashton Taplin; m. Terry H. Conger, Dec. 21, 1969 (div. June 1989); children: Cynthia T., Scott A. BA in Acctg., U. Ark., Little Rock, 1980, MBA in Fin. and Econ., 1983. CPA, Ark.; cert. fin. planner. Staff acct. Leaseway Ark., Inc., Little Rock, 1981-83; rsch. asst. Indls. Rsch. and Econ. Com., Little Rock, 1983; agt. Conn. Mutual Life, Little Rock, 1983-84; v.p., fin. planner Ark. Fin. Group, Inc., Little Rock, 1984—; pres. Cynthia L. Conger, CPA, PA, Little Rock, 1989—. Mem. Civitan, Little Rock, 1985-89. Mem. Internat. Assn. Fin. Planning (Ark. chpt., v.p. 1986-87, pres. 1987-89, nat. bd. dirs. 1994—, Delphi rsch. task force 1991), Registry Fin. Planning Practitioners. Methodist. Office: Ark Fin Group Inc 225 E Markham St Ste 375 Little Rock AR 72201-1635

CONGER, NANCY ANN, legal secretary; b. Washington, Sept. 18, 1964; d. Hubert Wilburn Jr. and Janice Elaine (Rudolph) Hendricks; m. David Victor Conger, May 19, 1990. AAS, Blue Ridge Cmty. Coll., 1992. Data entry supr. PSA/Smartnames, Capitol Heights, Md., 1982-87; computer operator Ebasco, Inc., Arlington, Va., 1987-88; legal sec. Stables & Assocs., Harrisonburg, Va., 1989-90, Obergh & Berlin, Washington, 1991, Melrod, Redman & Gartlan, Washington, 1991-93, Crowell & Moring, Washington, 1993—. Active Fairfax County Dem. Com., Va., 1993. Democrat. Home: 7614 Lee Landing Dr Falls Church VA 22043 Office: Crowell & Moring 10th Fl 1001 Pennsylvania Ave NW Washington DC 20004

CONGLETON, LAURA HELEN, freelance writer, film editor; b. Stamford, Conn., Jan. 14, 1962; d. Edward Blackburn and Lois Helen (Foster) C. BA, Mt. Holyoke Coll., S. Hadley, Mass., 1984; cert. in film prodn., NYU, 1992. Mgr. svc. stds. Chase Manhattan Bank, N.Y.C., 1984-87; mng. editor Sci. DataLink, N.Y.C., 1987-89; multimedia cons. N.Y.C., 1989-93. Film editor The Original Cast Album, 1992; 1st asst. editor The West Film Project, 1993-96; avid advisor To Wong Foo Thanks for Everything Julie Newmar, 1995; asst. editor Path to Paradise, 1996; film evaluator THX Lucasfilms Theatre Alignment Program, 1994—. vol. The Pearl Theatre Co., N.Y.C., 1988-94, InTouch Networks, N.Y.C., 1990-92; audio describer for visually-impaired theatre goers, 1992—. Mem. IATSE (Local 771).

CONIGILARO, PHYLLIS ANN, retired elementary education educator; b. Ilion, N.Y., Nov. 27, 1932; d. Gus Carl and Jennie Margaret (Marine) Denapole; m. Paul Anthony Conigilaro, July 16, 1983. BS cum laude, SUNY, Cortland, 1955; MA in Edn., Psychology, Cornell U., 1961. Cert. tchr., N.Y. Elem. classroom tchr. Mohawk (N.Y.) Central Sch., 1955-88. Contbr. articles to profl. jours. Bd. dirs. United Fund of Ilion, Herkimer, Mohawk and Frankfort, 1984-86, pres., 1986; pres. bd. edn. St. Mary's Parochial Sch., 1978; mem. Herkimer County Hist. Soc., 1988—, bd. trustees, 1994—; bd. dirs. local Federal Emergency Mgmt. Agy., 1987—. Mem. N.Y. State United Tchrs., Mohawk Tchrs. Assn. (past pres.), AAUW (pres. Herkimer chpt. 1981-82), N.Y. State Ret. Tchrs. Assn. (past legis. chmn. Herkimer County chpt.), Rep. Women's Club, Kappa Delta Pi. Republican. Roman Catholic. Home: RR 1 Box 285 Frankfort NY 13340-9557

CONKLIN, MARA LORAINE, public relations executive; b. Vallejo, Calif., July 28, 1962; d. Kenneth J. and Laura T. (Siegrist) Cichosz; m. Rex D. Conklin, Sept. 6, 1986; children: Elisabeth, Emily, Margaret. BA, Marquette U., 1984. Nat. news editl. staff Nat. Safety Coun., Chgo., 1984-85; corp. comm. specialist Household Internat., Prospect Hgts., Ill., 1985-86; acct. supr. Posner McGrath Ltd., Lincolnshire, Ill., 1986-90, v.p., 1990-92, sr. v.p., 1992-94, exec. v.p., 1994—. Recipient Spectra award Internat. Assn. Bus. Communicators, 1992, 94, Silver Trumpet award Publicity Club Chgo., 1993. Mem. Marquette Club Chgo. (chair alumni com. 1986-94, pres. 1994—). Office: Posner McGrath Ltd 300 Tri-State Internat Lincolnshire IL 60069

CONKLIN, SUSAN JOAN, psychotherapist, corporate staff development; b. Bklyn., Feb. 7, 1950; d. Joseph Thomas Hallek and Stella Joan (Kubis) Kuceluk; m. John Lariviere Conklin, July 25, 1981; children: Genevieve Therese, Michelle Therese. BA, CCNY, 1972; MSW, CUNY, 1975. Lic. ind. clin. social worker; cert. diplomat. Shop counselor Assn. for Help of Retarded Citizens, N.y.C., 1971-75; dir. social svcs., acting exec. dir. North Berkshire Assn. for Retarded Citizens, North Adams, Mass., 1975-77; project dir. Title XX tng. grant State of Mass., North Adams, 1978-79; pvt. practice psychotherapy Williamstown, Mass., 1979—; human resources cons., 1996—; asst. prof. North Adams State Coll., 1977-85, Berkshire C.C., Pittsfield, Mass., 1985-86, 95; therapeutic touch practitioner, 1978—; human resources cons., 1996—. Pres. Williamstown PTO, 1989-91; bd. dirs., edn. com., spl. events coord. Hospice No. Berkshire, Inc., 1989—. Mem. NASW (bd. dirs. 1981-83, regional coun. mem. 1980-83, 93—), LWV, Nurse Healers-Profl. Assn., Inc. (trustee 1981-83, rec. sec., editor-in-chief Coop. Connection newsletter 1983-88). Democrat. Episcopalian. Home and Office: 85 Hawthorne Rd Williamstown MA 01267-2700

CONKLING, SARA ANN, management educator; b. Orlando, Fla., Mar. 23, 1960; d. Homer Caples Jr. and Martha Elizabeth (Fort) C. BS in Econs., U. Pa., BA in Internat. Rels.; postgrad., U. Vt. Econ. cons. pvt. practice, Phila., 1979-85; sr. cons. Future Planning Assocs., Inc., Williston, Vt., 1985-90; v.p. Hackett and Co., Inc., South Burlington, Vt., 1990-91; employee benefit cons. pvt. practice, Burlington, Vt., 1991-94; instr. Vt. Ins. Inst., 1993-94, Champlain Coll., Burlington, Vt., 1993-94; exec. dir. Brevard Ecumenical AIDS Ministry, Inc., Cocoa, Fla., 1995—; adj. instr. pub. adminstrn. U. Ctrl. Fla., Orlando, 1995—. Contbr. articles to profl. jours. Direct svc. vol. Vt. Com. AIDS Resources, Edn. and Svcs., 1990-94; counselor Camp Ta-Kum-Ta, Vt., 1992—; chair svc. to hungry and homeless com. Episcopal Diocese Pa., 1983-85; lay leader Asbury Meth. Ch., Phila., 1981-82; vestry St. Stephen's Ch., Phila., 1984-85. Grad. Teaching fellow of yr. Dept. Pub. Adminstrn., U. Vt., Burlington, 1991-92; Benjamin Franklin scholar U. Pa., 1978-82; recipient Community Svc. award United Way, 1992. Mem. Am. Soc. Pub. Adminstrn. (Vt. chpt. v.p. 1992-94, Marshall E. Dimock award 1992), Pi Alpha Alpha. Unitarian.

CONLEY, GLORIA JEAN, special education educator; b. Memphis, Sept. 12, 1949; d. Henry and Leeanna (Ramsey) Edwards; m. Jesse Newson, Sept. 2, 1972 (div. Aug. 1974); m. Joe Conley, Feb. 18, 1981 (dec. Nov. 1991); m. Larry, Michael, Sharon, Lontina, Angela, Marcus, Joe. BS in Elem. Edn., Rust Coll., Holly Springs, Miss., 1976; BS in Spl. Edn., U. Miss., Oxford, 1989. Cert. elem. edn., spl. edn. Tchr. Mt. Olive Elem. Sch., Chgo., 1976-78, Tate County Schs., Senatobia, Miss., 1978—; chairperson spl. edn. dept. Coldwater (Miss.) Elem. Sch., 1984—, v.p. PTA, 1993-94, chmn. programs com., 1993-94. Mem. Coun. Exceptional Children, Alpha Kappa Mu. Democrat. Mem. Ch. of Christ. Home: PO Box 124 Coldwater MS 38618-0124

CONLEY, MARTHA RICHARDS, lawyer; b. Pitts., Jan. 12, 1947; d. Writt Adam Richards and Mary Jane (Brunges) Jennings; m. Charles Donald Conley, Jan. 20, 1978; children: David, Daniel. BA, Waynesburg Coll., 1968; JD, U. Pittsburgh, 1971. Bar: Pa. 1972, U.S. Dist. Ct. (we. dist.) Pa. 1972, U.S. Supreme Ct. 1977. Asst. solicitor Sch. Dist. of Pitts., 1972-73; ptnr. Brown & Cotton, Pitts., 1973-74; staff asst. U.S. Steel Corp., Pitts., 1974-76, asst. mgr. arbitration, 1976-84, asst. mgr. compliance, 1984-85, mgr. compliance, 1985-87, atty., 1987-94; gen. atty., 1994—; hazard commn. com. mem. Am. Iron and Steel Inst., Washington, 1984-87; bd. dirs. Shooting Star Prodns., Inc. Mem. resource devel. com. YWCA, Pitts., 1984-86. Mem. Nat. Bar Assn. (life), Allegheny County Bar Assn., Aurora Reading Club (pres. 1983-84). Democrat. Presbyterian. Home: 6439 Navarro St Pittsburgh PA 15206-1813 Office: 600 Grant St Ste 1580 Pittsburgh PA 15219-2703

CONLEY, PATSY GAIL, elementary education educator; b. Oceana, W.Va., Mar. 10, 1943; d. Ruble and Ruth (Hatfield) C.; m. Jose L. Abelleira (div. Feb. 1978); 1 child, Joseph L. Abelleira. BA, Glenville State Coll., 1965; MS, Nova Southeastern U., 1983, EdD, 1987. Tchr. kindergarten Head Start, Miami, Fla., 1965-67, facilitator, 1967-68; tchr. kindergarten Dade County, Miami, 1969-75, tchr. 1st grade, 1975-84, tchr. kindergarten, 1984—; mem. faculty con. Schoolsite, Miami, sch. adv. com., writing com., dept. chair; mem. clin. tchr. program U. Miami Dade County Pub. Schs., U. Miami; adj. prof. Nova Southeastern. Author: (rsch.) ERIC Listening A Program for First Grade, 1987.

CONLIN, ROXANNE BARTON, lawyer; b. Huron, S.D., June 30, 1944; d. Marion William and Alyce Muraine (Madden) Barton; m. James Clyde Conlin, Mar. 21, 1964; children: Jacalyn Rae, James Barton, Deborah Ann, Douglas Benton. BA, Drake U., 1964, JD, 1966, MPA, 1979; LLD (hon.), U. Dubuque, 1975. Bar: Iowa 1966. Assoc. firm Davis, Huebner, Johnson & Burt, Des Moines, 1966-67; dep. indsl. commr. State of Iowa, 1967-68, asst. atty. gen., 1969-76; U.S. atty. So. Dist. Iowa, 1977-81; ptnr. Conlin, P.C., Des Moines, 1983—; adj. prof. law U. Iowa, 1977-79; guest lectr. numerous univs. Chmn. Iowa Women's Polit. Caucus, 1973-75, del. nat. steering com., 1973-77; cons. U.S. Commn. on Internat. Women's Year, 1976-77; gen. counsel NOW Legal Def. and Edn. Fund, 1985-88, pres., 1986-88. Contbr. articles to profl. publs. Nat. committeewoman Iowa Young Dems.; also pres. Polk County Young Dems., 1965-66; del. Iowa Presdl. Conv., 1972; Dem. candidate for gov. of Iowa, 1982; bd. dirs. Riverhills Day Care Ctr., YWCA; chmn. Drake U. Law Sch. Endowment Trust, 1985-86; bd. counselors Drake U., 1982-86; pres. Civil Justice Found., 1986-88, Roscoe Pound Found., 1994—. Recipient award Iowa ACLU, 1974, Iowa Citizen's Action Network, 1987, Alumnus of Yr. award Drake U. Law Sch., 1989, ann. award Young Women's Resource Ctr., 1989, Verne Lawyer award as Outstanding Mem. Iowa Trial Lawyers Assn., 1994; named one of Top Ten Litigators Nat. Law Jour., 1989, 100 Most Influential Attys., 1991; scholar Reader's Digest, 1963-64, Fishcher Found., 1965-66. Mem. NOW (bd. dirs. 1986-88), ABA, ATLA (chmn. consumer and victims coalition com. 1985-87, chmn. edn. dept. 1987-88, parliamentarian 1988-89, sec. 1989-90, v.p. 1990-91, pres.-elect 1991-92, pres. 1992-93), Iowa Bar Assn., Assn. Trial Lawyers Iowa (bd. dirs.), Internat. Acad. Trial Lawyers, Iowa Acad. Trial Lawyers, Higher Edn. Commn. Iowa (co-chmn. 1988-90), Inner Circle of Advocates, Phi Beta Kappa, Alpha Lambda Delta, Chi Omega (Social Svc. award). Office: 300 Walnut St Ste 5 Des Moines IA 50309-2239

CONLON, KATHRYN ANN, county official; b. Mankato, Minn., July 30, 1958; d. Ralph Raymond and Joan Margaret (Meyer) Walter; m. James Alan Conlon, Oct. 1, 1977; children: Jessica Marie, Brian Michael. Student, Mankato Vocat. Sch., 1976-77. Teller Minn. Valley Fed. Credit Union, 1977; clk. Nicollet County Credit Bur., 1977-78; abstracter Lorna Holmquist, St. Peter, Minn., 1978-82; dep. recorder, abstracter Nicollet County, 1982-84, county recorder, abstracter, 1984—, sec. to dept. heads, 1985, chmn. dept. heads, 1986. Mem. Spina Bifida Assn. Minn., 1981—, Spina Bifida Assn. S.W. Minn., 1983—; bd. dirs. Children's Cen. Child Care, 1985-87, United Way, 1990-91. Mem. Minn. Assn. County Recorders (2nd v.p. 1994, pres. 1995), VFW Aux., Am. Legion Aux., St. Peter Lions. Avocations: handcrafting, camping, volleyball. Home: RR 3 Box 116 Saint Peter MN 56082-9542 Office: Nicollet County Recorder PO Box 493 Saint Peter MN 56082-0493

CONLON, SUZANNE B., federal judge; b. 1939. AB, Mundelein Coll., 1963; JD, Loyola U., Chgo., 1968; postgrad., U. London, 1971. Law clk. to judge U.S. Dist. Ct. (no. dist.) Ill., 1968-71; assoc. Pattishall, McAuliffe & Hostetter, 1972-73, Schiff Hardin & Waite, 1973-75; asst. U.S. atty. U.S. Dist. Ct. (no. dist.) Ill., 1976-77, 82-86, U.S. Dist. Ct. (cen. dist.) Calif., 1978-82; exec. dir. U.S. Sentencing Commn., 1986-88; spl. counsel to assoc. atty. gen., 1988; judge U.S. Dist. Ct. (no. dist.) Ill., 1988—; asst. prof. law De Paul U., Chgo., 1972-73, lectr., 1973-75; adj. prof. Northwestern U. Sch. Law, 1991—; vice chmn. Chgo. Bar Assn. Internat. Inst., 1993—. Mem. ABA, FBA, Fed. Judges Assn., Nat. Assn. Women Judges, Am. Judicature Soc., Internat. Bar Assn. Judges Forum, Chgo. Bar Assn., Law Club Chgo., Legal Club Chgo. (pres 1996-97). Office: US Dist Ct No Dist Everett McKinley Dirksen Bldg 219 S Dearborn St Ste 2356 Chicago IL 60604-1802

CONNALLY, SANDRA JANE OPPY, art educator; b. Crawfordsville, Ind., Feb. 10, 1941; d. Thomas Jay and Helen Louise (Lane) Oppy; m. Thomas Maurice Connally, Nov. 9, 1962; children: Leslie Erin Connally Hosier, Tyler Maurice. BS, Ball State U., 1963, MA, 1981. Freelance writer Muncie, Ind., 1971-76, art/freelance, 1964-81; substitute tchr. Muncie (Ind.) Community Schs., 1980-81, art tchr., 1981—. Two women shows include Emens Auditorium, Ball State U., 1983; juried shows include Ball State U. Small Drawing and Sculpture, 1964, Alford House/Anderson (Ind.) Fine Arts Ctr., Winter Show, 1979, 80, 81, Summer Show, 1981, Historic 8th St. Exhbn., 1981, Patrons Watercolor Gala, Oklahoma City, 1983, Whitewater Valley Annual Drawing, Painting and Printmaking Competition, Richmond, Ind., 1983; represented in numerous pvt. collections; contbr. short stories to profl. publs. Grantee Container Corp. Am., 1981, Ball State U. Mus. Art/Margaret Ball Meml. Fund, 1992, Robert B. Bell, 1993, 94, 95; recipient achievement award Ind. Dept. Edn., 1992-93, 94, Nat. Gallery Videodisc Competition, 1993; named disting. UniverCitizen Ball State U., 1992. Mem. NEA, Ind. State Tchr. Assn., Muncie Tchrs. Assn., Internat. Platform Assn., Nat. Art Edn. Assn., Art Edn. Assn. Ind. Republican. Methodist. Home: 2351 W Warwick Rd Muncie IN 47304-3346

CONNEALY, MARGARET JANE, educator, school administrator; b. Columbus, Ohio, Jan. 17, 1952; d. James Albert and Margaret Jane (Rohrbacher) Rutledge; m. Brien Ura Connealy, June 22, 1974; children: Molly Frances, Sean Patrick. BS, Nebr. Wesleyan, 1974; MEd in Elem. Edn., U. Nebr., 1982, MEd in Adminstrn., 1991. Tchr. Plattsmouth (Nebr.) Schs., 1974-76, York (Nebr.) Schs., 1976-83; tchr., adminstr. Internat. Sch., Düsseldorf, Germany, 1983-89; tchr. Lincoln (Nebr.) Schs., 1989-93, asst. prin., 1993—. Mem. ASCD, Phi Delta Kappa. Democrat. Home: 2435 Winding Way Lincoln NE 68506

CONNELL, KAREN W., medical services professional; d. Forrest and Mary M. Whaley; m. Roger Connell; three children. Student, Mo. U., Lincoln U. Mgr. Oak Tree Villas Retirement Ctr., Jefferson City, 1983-85; social work svcs. Villa Marie SNF/SSM Health Care Sys., Jefferson City, 1985-91; casualty tort analyst State Mo. Divsn. Med. Svcs., Jefferson City, 1991-93, physician program rep., 1993—. Office: State Mo Div Med Svcs 615 Howatan Ct Jefferson City MO 65109

CONNELL, MARY ELLEN, diplomat; b. Laconia, N.H., Jan. 20, 1943; d. Howard Benjamin and Jessie Louise Smith Naylor; m. O. J. Connell III, Nov. 4, 1969 (div. Aug. 1988); 1 child, Piers Andrew. BA, Smith Coll., Northampton, Mass., 1964; MPhil, U. Kans., 1969; MS, Nat. War Coll., 1992. Info. ctr. dir. U.S. Fgn. Svc., Nairobi, Kenya, 1978-80; pub. affairs officer U.S. Fgn. Svc., Bujumbura, Burundi, 1980-82; officer African affairs USIA, Washington, 1982-85, exec. asst. to assoc. dir. for policy, 1985-86; counselor pub. affairs U.S. Fgn. Svc., Copenhagen, 1986-90; vis. scholar St. Deiniol's Wales, 1991; exec. sec. USIA, Washington, 1992-95; pub. affairs advisor U.S. Mission to NATO, Brussels, 1995—. Mem. Am. Fgn. Svc. Assn., Atlantic Coun., Army and Navy Club. Episcopalian. Office: US Mission to NATO APO AE 09724

CONNELL, SHIRLEY HUDGINS, public relations professional; b. Washington, Oct. 5, 1946; d. Orville Thomas and Mary (Beran) H.; m. David Day Connell, Dec. 13, 1980 (div. 1985). BA, U. R.I., 1968, MA, 1970. Clk., editor MGM Studios, Culver City, Calif., 1970-72; scriptor, talent Monarch Records, Studio City, 1972-73; communications specialist U. So. Calif., L.A., 1973-81; dir. pub. rels. Six Flags Movieland, Buena Park, Calif., 1981-82; dir. pub. rels. Donald J. Fager & Assocs., N.Y.C., 1982-93, dir. policy holder/pub. rels., 1993—; cons. Children's TV Workshop, N.Y.C., 1978; ind. beauty cons. Mary Kay Cosmetics, 1991—; instr. Princeton Rev., 1990-91. Editor: Coastal Ocean Space Utilization III, 1995; contbr. articles to profl. jours.; contbg. editor Greater N.Y. Doctor's Shopper mag., 1987—. Pres. bd. trustees Oaks at North Brunswick Condominium Assn., 1987—; founding mem. Mcpl. Svcs. Com., North Brunswick; mgr. Animal Rescue Force, 1988—; chair environ. com. Twp. of North Brunswick, 1990—; snuggler pediat. and neonatal units St. Peter's Hosp. Mem. NAFE, Marine Tech. Soc. (vice chmn. 1980-81), Mensa (pub. rels. adv. com. 1989—, pub. rels. coord. Ctrl. N.J. chpt. 1992—, bd. dirs. 1992—), Oceanic Soc. (bd. dirs. 1979-81), Stony Brook Millstone Watershed Assn. (water qualification monitor 1994—).

CONNELLY, BARBARA CATHERINE, organization administrator; b. Somerville, Mass., Sept. 15, 1940; d. Sebastiano and Mary (Igo) DeFilippo; m. James Patrick Connelly, Oct. 19, 1961 (dec. Feb. 1987); children: Kathleen, James (murdered), Patricia, Barbara, Terence. Student, Empire State Coll. Cert. bereavement therapist. Sec. Brookhaven Hosp. Home Care, Patch, N.Y., 1987-89; sec. dept. rehab. St. Charles Hosp., Point Jefferson, N.Y., 1990-92; exec. dir. Outreach program for the secondary victim Parents of Murdered Children, 1996—. Exec. dir. Children Have Feelings Too, 1990—; sec. L.I. chpt. Parents of Murdered Children, 1981-86, treas., 1987-96, pres., 1991-96, state coord., 1996—. Recipient Newsday Leadership award L.I. Newsday, 1992; named Point of Light for volunteerism George Busch, 1992. Mem. NAFE. Democrat. Roman Catholic.

CONNELLY, CATHY ANN, public relations executive; b. Glendale, Calif., Dec. 10, 1956. BA in Comm. Studies, UCLA, 1979. Dir. client svcs. Jack McGrath & Assocs., 1979-80; pres. Connelly Comm., L.A., 1980-92; v.p. Wessell Co., L.A., 1992-93; v.p. pub. affairs Stoorza, Ziegause, Metzger & Boyer, L.A., 1993-94, sr. v.p. pub. affairs, 1994-95, sr. exec. v.p., gen. mgr., 1995—. Office: Stoorza Ziegaus Metzger & Boyer 333 So Grand Ste 2920 Los Angeles CA 90071*

CONNELLY, ELIZABETH ANN, state legislator; b. N.Y.C.; d. John Walter and Alice Marie (Mallon) Keresey; m. Robert Vincent Connelly; children: Alice, Robert, Margaret, Therese. Grad. high sch., Bronx. Telephone sales Pan Am. World Airways, N.Y.C., 1946-54; mem. N.Y. State Assembly, Albany, 1973—, chair com. on mental health, retardation/devel. disabilities, 1977-92, chair com. on standing coms., 1993-95, speaker pro tem, 1995—, chair intern com., 1995—; chair Legis. Women's Caucus, N.Y. State, 1993-95. Recipient over 200 awards and honors including S.I. Hosp. Vol. of Yr. award, 1972-73, Cert. Appreciation Willowbrook chpt. Benevolent Soc. Retarded Children, 1978, Legilator of Yr. award N.Y. State Coun. on Alcoholism, 1983, Woman of Yr. award Epilepsy Ctr., 1984, Disting. Humanitarian of Yr. award S.I. Ctr. Ind. Living, 1987, Alliance for Mentally Ill of N.Y. State award, 1988, Thomas G. Gilbert Meml. award N.Y. State Mental Health Soc., 1989, Nat. Barrier Awareness Found., 1990, Irish Am. Heritage Mus., 1991, N.Y. State Head Injury Assn. Pub. Policy award, 1994, N.Y. State Cath. Conf. Pub. Policy award 1996. Democrat. Office: NY State Assembly 1150 Forest Hill Rd Staten Island NY 10314

CONNELLY, KATHLEEN FITZGERALD, public relations executive; b. Springfield, Mass., Dec. 26, 1948. BA, Newton Coll.; MA in Polit. Sci., Rutgers U.; postgrad., U. Chgo. Legis. aide Mass. State Legis.; officer, corp. comm. and bond dept. Continental Bank & Trust Co. of Chgo., 1972-78; acct. exec. Hill & Knowlton, 1978, v.p., 1979-81, sr. v.p. group dir., 1981-86; mng. dir., sr. v.p. Hill & Knowlton, Inc., 1987-89, dep. gen. mgr., sr. v.p., 1990, exec. v.p., dir. worldwide bus. devel., bd. dir., 1990-92; pres. Dilenschneider Group, 1991—. Office: Dilenschneider Group 3 First Nat Plz 70 W Madison St Chicago IL 60602-4205

CONNELLY, PATRICIA LORRAINE, travel executive; b. Phila., Mar. 29, 1948; d. Robert H. and Helen (Kinsley) Nickerson; m. Joseph J. Connelly, Jan. 10, 1986. BA, Western State U., 1987; postgrad., Holy Family Coll., 1988. Mgr. Transeair Travel Inc., Phila.; assn. tax acct. Gen. Refractories Co., Phila.; travel mgr. Morgan, Lewis & Bockius, LLP, Phila.; adv. bd. Four Seasons Hotel. Mem. Nat. Passenger Traffic Assn., Delaware Valley Corp. Travel Mgrs. Assn. (asst. v.p.), Am. Soc. Travel Agts. (cert.), Meeting Planners Internat., Internat. Soc. Meeting Planners (cert. meeting planner).

CONNER, JANET HIGGINBOTHAM, secondary school educator; b. Jacksonville, Fla., Oct. 4, 1954; d. Louis Farres and Helen Marie (Keen) Higginbotham; m. Geald Dale Conner, May 3, 1991; 1 child, Miraj Kirsten. AA, U. Fla., 1974, BS, 1977. Cert. tchr., Fla. Tchr. Waycross (Fla.) City Schs., 1977-78, Callahan (Fla.) Jr. H.S., 1978-79, Fernandine Beach (Fla.) H.S., 1979-84; tchr., sci. chair person Hilliard (Fla.) Middle Sr. H.S., 1984—. Chairperson of com. N.E. Fla. Fair Assn., Callahn, 1988—; mem. West Nassau Hist. Soc., Callahan, 1995—. Mem. Fla. Assn of Sci. Tchrs., Nat. Sci. Tchrs. Assn. Democrat. Baptist. Home: Rte 2 Box 311 Hilliard FL 32046 Office: Hilliard Middle Sr HS 106 W Illinois Hilliard FL 32046

CONNER, KATHRYN ANN (NELSON), auditor; b. Knoxville, Tenn., Apr. 9, 1953; d. Fred McKinley and Rose Marie (Anderson) Nelson; m. Thomas Richard Conner, Jan. 7, 1977. Student, Hiwassee Coll., 1971-73, U. Tenn., 1973-74, Akron U., 1986; BS in Applied Orgn. Mgmt., Tusculum Coll., 1991. Tax preparer, acct. Richard Goldstein CPA, Knoxville, Tenn., 1982-83, Jim Cover, CPA, Gatlinburg, Tenn., 1982—; office mgr., sales rep. R & R Distributing, Inc., Knoxville, 1983-85; spl. projects coord. Schlegel Tenn., Inc., Maryville, 1985; markets coord. Schlegal Tenn., Inc., Maryville, 1985, tech. coord., 1990; systems coord. BTR Sealing Systems Tenn., Maryville, 1991, cost estimator, 1994, lead auditor, 1996—. Mem. AAUW. Methodist. Home: 3705 Forestdale Ave Knoxville TN 37917 Office: BTR Sealing Systems Tenn 1713 Henry G Lane St Maryville TN 37801

CONNER, KELLEY S., elementary education educator; b. Tyler, Tex., Sept. 3, 1971; d. Coye and Sue (Cook) C. BS in Applied Learning and Devel., U. Tex., 1992. Reading specialist San Marcos (Tex.) City Ind. Sch. Dist., 1993-94, 5th grade tchr., 1994-95. Mem. Dyslexia Adv. Com., San Marcos Civic Found., 1993—; provisional mem. Jr. Svc. League, San Marcos, 1993—. Mem. Kappa Delta Pi. Office: Maria Hernandez Intermed Sch 333 Stagecoach Tr San Marcos TX 78666

CONNERLY, DIANNA JEAN, business official; b. Urbana, Ill., June 7, 1947; d. Ellsworth Wayne and Imogene (Sundermeyer) Connerly. Student Ill. Comml. Coll., 1967. Bookkeeper, Jerry Earl Pontiac, 1968-72; officer mgr. Jack Nicklaus Pontiac, 1972-76; office mgr. Simon Motors Inc., Palm Springs, Calif., 1977-83; bus. mgr., 1983—. Vol. counselor How Found., 1992. Mem. Am. Bus. Women's Assn. (pub. rels. dir. Trendsetter chpt. 1983—). Office: 78611 Us Highway 111 La Quinta CA 92253-2068

CONNERTON, ANNE CRAGAN, secondary education educator; b. N.Y.C., Jan. 17, 1940; d. Henry James and Vera (Vargas) Cragan; m. James Edward Connerton, Sept. 5, 1959; children: Jane Connelly, Christine Smith, Mary Scott. BA, Univ. R.I., 1973; ME, Bowie State Univ., 1976. Social studies, govt. tchr. Va. Beach City Schs., Va., 1976-86, Fairfax (Va.) County Schs., 1986—; grant reviewer U.S. Bicentennial Commn. for the Constitution, Washington, 1990-91; TV panelist on "Democracy's Students" Libr. Congress, Mind Extension Univ., Washington, 1991; co-presenter Nat. Ednl. Assn. Tech. Conf., San Francisco, Calif., 1991. Exhibited: Woodlawn Needlework Exhibition (1st place, 1994). Mem. Stonington Conn. Hist. Soc., Hastings Hist. Soc., Friends of Woodlawn Plantation. Mem. Am. Needlework Guild, Va. Coun. for Social Studies. Roman Catholic. Home: 6016 Balsam Dr Mc Lean VA 22101 Office: Fairfax High Sch 3500 Old Lee Hwy Fairfax VA 22030

CONNERY, CAROL JEAN, foundation director; b. Amarillo, Tex., Oct. 22, 1948; d. William Wayne and Joyce Jean (Forney) Connery. AA, Christian Coll., 1969; BJ, U. Tex., Austin, 1971. Asst. dir. admissions Columbia (Mo.) Coll., 1971-80; exec. dir. nat. office Teenworld Scholarship Program, Overland Park, Kan., 1980-82; account exec. Mktg. Comm., Inc., Lenexa, Kans., 1983-86; account supr. Krupp/Taylor USA, Dallas, 1986-90; mktg. cons., 1990-93; dir. devel. St. Anthony's Found., Amarillo, Tex., 1994-95; dir. devel. Am. Quarter Horse Found., Amarillo, 1995—. Trustee Columbia Coll.; mem. coun. on ministries Polk St. United Meth. Ch. Mem. Assn. Healthcare Philanthropy (mem. regional bd.), Nat. Soc. Fund Raising Execs. (mem. regional bd.), United Way, Ctr. City Bus. and Profl. Women, Zeta Tau Alpha, Phi Theta Kappa (past nat. v.p.). Home: 3507 Brennan Gardens Amarillo TX 79121

CONNOLLY, JODY, education advisor; b. Erie, Pa., Sept. 26, 1961; d. Michael Joseph and Mary Ann (Sharaff) C. BS, Indiana U. Pa., 1983, postgrad., 1990—. Home base visitor Allegheny Intermediate unit Head Start, Pitts., 1984-87; tchr. AIU Head Start, Pitts., 1987-89, home base advisor, 1989—; mem. family living adv. bd. Pa. State U. Coop. Ext., Pitts., 1989-94. Vol. registration Vintage Sports Car Club Am., Pitts., 1993. Mem. Pa. Assn. for Edn. Young Children (coun. 1989-91, chmn. registration, Irish activities). Home: # 8 214 McCully St Pittsburgh PA 15216 Office: AIU Head Start 4 Station Sq 2d Fl Pittsburgh PA 15219

CONNOLLY, RUTH CAROL, critical care nurse; b. Pitts., Oct. 2, 1944; d. Chester John and Mary Elizabeth (Sansbury) Williams; separated; children: Patrick L., Sean M. Diploma in nursing, Allegheny Gen. Hosp., Pitts., 1965; cert. nurse practitioner, Allegheny Gen. Hosp., 1983, La Roche Coll., Pitts., 1983. RN, Pa. Staff nurse critical care Divine Providence Hosp., Pitts.; asst. clin. supr. Allegheny Gen. Hosp., clin. supr. neuroscis. unit; nurse practitioner Triangle Urol. Group, Pitts. Contbr. articles to nursing jours. Mem. AACCN, Am. Assn. Urology Allied Nurses, Am. Urol. Assn. Allied (founding mem. and pres.-elect Pitts. chpt.), Am. Assn. Office Nurses. Home: 5549 Pocusset St Pittsburgh PA 15217-1912

CONNOLLY-O'NEILL, BARRIE JANE, interior designer; b. San Francisco, Dec. 22, 1943; d. Harry Jr. and Jane Isabelle (Barr) Wallach; m. Peter Smith O'Neill, Nov. 27, 1983. Cert. of design, N.Y. Sch. Interior Design, 1975; BAF in Environ. Design, Calif. Coll. Arts and Crafts, 1978. Profl. model Brebner Agy., San Francisco, 1963-72; TV personality KGO TV, San Francisco, 1969-72; interior designer Barrie Connolly & Assocs., Boise, Idaho, 1978—; bd. dirs. Zoo Boise. Recipient Best Interior Design award Mktg. and Merchandising Excellence, 1981, 84, 91, Best Interior Design award Sales and Mktg. Coun., 1985, 86, Best Residential Design award Boise Design Revue Com., 1983, Grand award Best in Am. Living, Nat. Assn. Home Builders, 1986, 89, 2 Gold Nuggett Merit awards, 1990, Street of Dreams, People's Choice award, 1991, Award for Best Interior Merchandising MAME, Portland, 1991, Nat. Merit award, 1992. Mem. Nat. Assn. Home Builders (Nat. Silver award for best interior design 1991), Am. Soc. Interior Designers (affiliate), Inst. Residential Mktg. (Silver awrd 1991).

CONNOR, CAROL J., library director. BA in History, Molloy Coll., 1964; MA in History, Georgetown U., 1970; MS in Libr. Sci., Drexel U., 1972. Various adminstrv. positions in ednl. fields various U.S. Cities, 1964-72; spl. asst. tech. processes divsn. Lincoln (Nebr.) City Librs., 1972-73, coord. tech. processes divsn., 1973-76, asst. dir., 1976-78, dir., 1978—. Mem. Mayor's Com. for Internat. Friendship, Lincoln, 1973—; adv. com. U. Nebr., search for dean of librs., 1984-85; del. to cmty. retreat, Star Venture, 1986, edn. task force, 1987-88, vocat. edn. task force, 1988-89, downtown child care task force, 1988-89; mem. cmty. adv. com. Lincoln Pub. Schs. Search for English Cons., 1991, Search for Media Dir., 1992; mem. Nebr. Ctr. for Book Bd., 1990-95, Nebr. Libr. Commn. state adv. coun. 1985-86, Nebr. Lit. Festival Com., 1990-92; bd. dirs. Postsecondary Ednl. Librs. and Resource Ctrs. of Nebr. 1981-84, chair 1982; mem. edn. com. Am. Cancer Soc., Lancaster County, Nebr., 1989-91, Family Svcs. Bd., 1991—, vice chair chair elect 1992, chair, 1994; leadership Lincoln VI 1990-91; mem. Lincoln Cancer Ctr. adv. bd., 1988-94, vice chair 1991-94. Mem. ALA, (bylaws com., membership com., LITA/LAMA conf. com. 1996-97), Mountain Plains Libr. Assn. (chair continuing edn. com. 1984-85; membership devel. com. 1986-87, vice chair and chair of pub. libr. sect. 1975-77, v.p./ pres. elect 1996-97, pres. 1997-98), Nebr. Libr. Assn. (chair intellectual freedom com. 1975-76, state rep. to Mountain Plains Libr. Assn., 1984-86, vice chair and chair of pub. libr. sect. 1987-89), Urban Librs. Coun. (leadership programs 1994-95), Capitol Bus. and Profl. Women (v.p. 1983), Downtown Lincoln Assn. (mktg. com. 1988-89). Office: Lincoln City Librs 136 S 14th St Lincoln NE 68508-1899

CONNOR, CATHERINE BROOKS, educational media specialist; b. Dothan, Ala., Oct. 29, 1955; d. James Bolling and Margaret Elizabeth (Jones) Brooks; m. Joseph Yauger Whealdon, Jr., June 12, 1983 (div. Aug. 1990); 1 child, Joseph Yauger III; m. William Christopher Connor, Dec. 28, 1991. BS, Fla. State U., 1980, MS in Libr. Sci., 1990. Cert. profl. media specialist, Fla. Asst. br. mgr. City Fed. Savs. and Loan, Birmingham, Ala., 1976-77; elem. tchr. Louise S. McGehee Sch., New Orleans, 1981-85; kindergarten tchr. Lafayette Elem. Sch., New Orleans, 1986; grad. asst. Sch. Libr. Sci. Fla. State U., Tallahassee, 1990; media specialist Lely H.S., Naples, Fla., 1990-91; media specialist Frank M. Golson Elem. Sch., Marianna, Fla., 1991—, chmn. sch. adv. coun., 1995—, mem. leadership team, 1994—. Bd. dirs. Jackson County Pub. Libr./Friends of the Libr., Marianna, 1992-94; sustaining mem. Planned Parenthood Fedn. of Am., Washington, 1992—; charter mem. Libr. of Congress, Washington, 1994—. Mem. Daus. of Am. Revolution, Colonial Dames, Descendants of the Knights of the Garter. Democrat. Episcopalian. Home: PO Box 507 Marianna FL 32447 Office: Frank M Golson Elem Sch 4258 2d Ave Marianna FL 32446

CONNOR, LOUISE, small business owner; b. Kingstree, S.C., Dec. 26, 1951; d. Wallace Darlington and Polly (McGill) C. BA, Coll. of Charleston, 1975; MA, Columbia U., 1979. Pres. Jane Adams Ctr. for Battered Women, N.Y.C., 1977-80, The Showroom for Kids Clothes, Inc., N.Y.C., 1980—. Vol. God's Love We Deliver, N.Y.C., 1988-89; fund raiser Empire State Pride Agenda, N.Y.C., 1995. Mem. Bur. Wholesale Sales Reps. Democrat. Office: The Showroom 131 W 33d St Ste 310 New York NY 10001

CONNOR, MARIANNE, filmmaker, scriptwriter, educator; b. Schenectady, N.Y., Feb. 17, 1960; d. Thomas Elwood Connor Jr. and Marilyn Helen (Cadieux) Connor Long. BS in Fgn. Svc., BA in Honors English, Georgetown U., 1982; MFA in Film and Media Arts, Temple U., 1990. Ind. prodr. film/video Andromeda Prodns., Phila., 1986—; instr. Temple U., Phila., 1989; devel. assoc. Dave Bell Assocs., Hollywood, Calif., 1990; mem. faculty Drexel U., Phila., 1995—; dir., fundraiser Friday Afternoon Theatre, Washington, 1981; scriptwriter U.S. Info. Agy., Washington, 1985, 87, InVision Comms., Bala Cynwyd, Pa., 1995; mem. faculty ESF Concepts for Children, Phila., 1993-94. Writer, dir., cinematographer: (video documentary) Impressions of Jordan, 1989 (Nat. Coll. Emmy Acad. TV Arts & Scis.); writer, dir., editor: (short film) Time 'til Light, 1991; dir., cinematographer: (film documentary) La Salsa de Marabella, 1987; assoc. editor AMIDEAST, Inc., Washington, 1983-84. Campaign field mgr. Karen Selvaggi for State Rep., Langhorne, Pa., 1992. John Mitchell intern in TV devel. NATAS, 1990; Mid-Atlantic Region Media Arts fellow NEA/Am. Film Inst., 1988, Pa. Scriptwriters fellow Pa. Coun. on Arts, 1991, 94; Pa.'s Prodn. grantee Pa. Coun. on Arts, 1995. Home: 241 Periwinkle Ave Langhorne PA 19067 Office: Andromeda Prodns 241 Periwinkle Ave Langhorne PA 19067

CONNOR, MARY RODDIS, foundation administrator; b. Marshfield, Wis., May 14, 1909; d. Hamilton and Catherine S. (Prindle) Roddis; m. Gordon R. Connor, July 20, 1929 (dec. 1986); children: Mary I. Pierce, Gordon P., Catherine Dellin, David (dec.), Sara W. Connor. Student, Wellesley Coll., 1927-28; student, U. Wis., 1929. Corp. sec. Connor Lumber and Land Co., Connor Forest Industries, Wausau, Wis., 1954-78; co-founder, exec. dir. Camp Five Mus. Found., Inc., Laona, 1968—; bd. dirs., v.p. Hamilton Roddis Found.; pres. Connor Found., Forest History Assn. Wis., 1975-87; v.p. Gordon R. Connor Charitable Found.; mem. Nat. Women's Adv. Coun., Am. Forest Products Inst., 1960-78; active Mary Roddis Connor U. Wis. Endowment Fund, 1992. Author: A Century with Connor Timber, 1972, Forestry Futures and Conservation Misconcepts, 1946, 2d rev. edition, 1947; contbr. articles to various publs. Legis. chmn. 7th Dist. Wis. Fedn. Rep. Women, 1963-65, bd. dirs., 1955-65, vice chmn. 1955-59; del. Rep. county, state, nat. conventions, 1962; vice chmn. Marathon County; Rep. vice chmn. Recipient Gov.'s Wis. Heritage Tourism award, 1993, State Hist. Soc. Wis. award of merit, 1970, 90, U.S. EPA, 1987, Forest History Assn. Wis. Mus. award, 1978, Nat. Award in Edn. Arbor Day Found., 1975. Mem. Wis. Mayflower Soc., Colonial Dames (Wis. Soc.), The Hugenot Soc. of Wis., Bascom Hill Soc. (U. Wis.), Lake States Resource Alliance, Inc., Lake States Women in Timber, Inc., Forest History Assn. of Wis., State Hist. Soc. of Wis., Nat. Trust for Hist. Preservation, Wausau chpt. DAR (nat. vice chmn. resolutions 1965-68, Wis. state chmn. nat. def., 1962-65, nat. conservation chmn. 1974-77, recipient many awards). Home: 1220 Easthill Dr Wausau WI 54403-4956

CONNOR, SARA EDWARDS, college administrator; b. Tucson, Aug. 10, 1951; d. Charles and Mary Eugenia (Shirley) Edwards; m. William Christian Timberlake, Sept. 18, 1970 (div. 1984); 1 child, Brian Christian Timberlake; m. John Michael Connor, June 8, 1986; stepchildren: John Michael, Brian Shore. ASN, Floyd Coll., Rome, Ga., 1974; BSN, Med. Coll. Ga., Augusta, 1978, MSN, 1979; EdD, U. Ga., 1988. RN, Ga.; cert. med.-surg. clin. specialist. Asst. v.p. Armstrong Atlantic State U., Savannah, Ga.; mem. edn. com. Ga. Bd. Nursing, Atlanta, 1989-95. Contbr. articles to profl. jours. Bd. dirs. Savannah chpt. Am. Diabetes Assn., 1992—, pres., exec. bd., 1995-96. Mem. Am. Bus. Women's Assn. (pres. Bus. Woman of Yr. 1995), Sigma Theta Tau (scholarly activities chair 1992—), Alpha Eta. Home: 3005 River Dr # 309 Savannah GA 31404 Office: Armstrong Atlantic State U 11935 Abercorn St Savannah GA 31404

CONNOR, WILDA, government health agency administrator; b. Pleasantville, N.J., Apr. 9, 1947; d. Herman Smith and Rubina (Miraglilo) Cooney; m. James J. Connor Jr., Nov. 5, 1966; 1 child, James J. III. BSBA cum laude, Glassboro (N.J.) State Coll., 1985; postgrad., U. Pa., 1988-93. Employee services coord. Turning Point Drug Outpatient Program, Collingswood, N.J., 1976-78; mgmt. specialist Camden County Ctr. Addictive Diseases, Lakeland, N.J., 1978-87; adminstr. Family Practice Ctrs. Camden (N.J.) County Health Dept., 1988—. Com. fund raiser Camden County Dem. Congl. Campaign, Stratford, N.J., 1986; mem. Solid Waste Adv. Coun., Camden County; mem. Coastal Resources Adv. Commn. Dept. Environ. Protection. Mem. N.J. Assn. Alcoholism Counselors, N.J. Substance Abuse Cert. Bd. (cert. 1987, 89 MSA), LWV, Solid Waste Adv. Council. Roman Catholic. Home: 228 E Vasey Ave Clementon NJ 08021 Office: Camden County Dept Policy Planning & Devel Bldg 6981 N Park Dr Fl 3 Pennsauken NJ 08109

CONNORS, DORSEY, television and radio commentator, newspaper columnist; b. Chgo.; d. William J. and Sarah (MacLain) C.; m. John E. Forbes; 1 dau., Stephanie. BA cum laude, U. Ill. Fl. reporter WGN-TV Rep. Nat. Conv., Chgo., Dem. Nat. Conv., L.A., 1960. Conducted: Personality Profiles, WGN-TV, Chgo., 1948-49, Dorsey Connors Show, WMAQ-TV, Chgo., 1949-58, 61-63, Armchair Travels, WMAQ-TV, 1952-55, Homeshow, NBC, 1954-57, NBC Today Show, Dorsey Connors program, WGN, 1958-61, Tempo Nine, WGN-TV, 1961, Society in Chgo, WMAQ-TV, 1964; writer: column Hi! I'm Dorsey Connors, Chgo. Sun Times, 1965—; Author: Gadgets Galore, 1953, Save Time, Save Money, Save Yourself, 1972, Helpful Hints for Hurried Homemakers, 1988. Founder Ill. Epilepsy League; mem. woman's bd. Children's Home and Aid Soc., mem. women's bd. USO. Named one of Am.'s Outstanding Irish Am. Women, World of Hibernia mag., 1995. Mem. AFTRA, NATAS (Silver Cir. award 1995), SAG, Mus. Broadcast Comm. (founding mem.), Soc. Midland Authors, Chgo. Hist. Soc. (guild com., costume com.), Chi Omega. Roman Catholic. Office: Chgo Sun Times 401 N Wabash Ave Chicago IL 60611-3532

CONOMIKES, MELANIE REMINGTON, marketing consultant; b. Chgo., Sept. 3, 1966; arrived in Australia, 1995; d. George Spero Conomikes and Cynthia Stoll Chandler. BFA, NYU, 1988; postgrad., UCLA, 1993-94. Publs. dir. Conomikes Assn., Inc., L.A., 1987-92; comm. mgr. Frank O. Gehry & Assoc., Santa Monica, Calif., 1992-95; pres. Melanie Conomikes Consulting, L.A., Melbourne, Australia, Australia, 1995—; mktg. dir. DTC Multimedia, Melbourne, 1996—. Active L.A. planning com. Share Our Strength's "Taste of The Nation", 1995. Office: Melanie Conomikes Cons 11687 Bellagio Ste 13 Los Angeles CA 90049

CONOVER, JUDITH A., association executive. BA in Sociology, U. Cin. Statis. analyst; media monitor Mondale-Ferraro Campaign, 1984; adminstr. Environ. & Energy Study Inst., Washington, 1984-86; dir. adminstrn. Women's Ctr., 1986-94; dept. exec. dir. LWV U.S., LWV Voters Edn. Fund, Washington, 1994, exec. dir., 1994—. Chair Mount Vernon Dem. Party; bd. pres. Rte. One Corridor Housing, Inc.; mem. Commn. Women, Commn. Child Abuse. Office: 1730 M St NW St 1000 Washington DC 20036*

CONOVER, MONA LEE, retired adult education educator; b. Lincoln, Nebr., Nov. 9, 1929; d. William Cyril and Susan Ferne (Floyd) C.; m. Elmer Kenneth Johnson, June 14, 1953 (div. 1975); children: Michael David, Susan Amy, Sharon Ann, Jennifer Lynne. AB, Nebr. Wesleyan U., 1952; student, Ariz. State U., 1973-75; MA in Edn., No. Ariz. U., 1985. Cert. tchr., Colo., Ariz. Tchr. Jefferson County R-1 Sch., Wheat Ridge, Colo., 1952-56, Glendale (Ariz.) Elem. Sch. # 40, 1972-92; dir. Glendale Adult Edn., 1987-92; ret., 1992. Author: ABC's of Naturalization, 1989. Mem. AAUW, Phoenix Bot. Gardens, Heard Mus., Phoenix Zoo, Order of Ea. Star. Republican. Methodist.

CONOVER, NANCY ANDERSON, secondary school counselor; b. Manhattan, Kans., July 8, 1943; d. Howard Julius and Wilma June (Katz) Anderson; m. Gary Hites Conover, Aug. 10, 1968; children: Chad Anderson, Cary Hites. BS in Edn., Kans. State U., 1965; MEd, Wichita State U., 1991. Cert. sch. counselor, tchr., Kans. Tchr. Flint (Mich.) Sch. Dist., 1965-66, Unified Sch. Dist. 259, Wichita, Kans., 1967-68, Overland Park (Kans.) Sch. Dist., 1968-70; bus. mgr., sec.-treas. Gary Conover, D.D.S., Wichita, 1985-94; sch. counselor Unified Sch. Dist. 259, Wichita, 1991-94; secondary sch. counselor Unified Sch. Dist. 385, Andover, Kans., 1994—. Mem. Am. Counselors Assn., Kans. Assn. Counselors, Kans. Dental Aux. (sec. 1970-74), Wichita Dist. Dental Aux. (pres. 1970-75), Jr. League Wichita (adminstrv. v.p. 1978-82), Gamma Phi Beta, Phi Kappa Phi Honor Soc. Republican. Lutheran.

CONOVER, NELLIE COBURN, retail furniture company executive; b. Lebanon, Ohio, Dec. 21, 1921; d. Frank C. and Isabel (Murphy) Coburn; student public schs.; m. Lawrence E. Conover, Jan. 11, 1941; children—Lawrence R., Carol, David C., Constance, Christina. Co-founder, 1949, since exec. sec.-treas. Larry Conover Furniture & Appliance, Inc., and predecessor, Milford, Ohio, also trustee co. pension fund. Mem. Milford C. of C., Cin. Hist. Soc., Milford Hist. Soc., DAR. Democrat. Roman Catholic. Address: 438 Main St Milford OH 45150-1128

CONRAD, CHERYL DIANE, neuroscientist; b. West L.A., Mar. 18, 1963; d. Dale DeVere and Anita Clarice (Hudgin) C.; m. Curtis James Condon, Sept. 14, 1985 (div. July 1993); m. Stuart Greenstein, Aug. 23, 1996. BS in Chemistry, U. Calif., Irvine, 1986, BS in Biology, 1986; PhD in Neuroscience, U. Ill., 1994. Technician U. Calif., Irvine, 1986-87; postdoctoral fellow Rockefeller U., N.Y.C., 1994—. Contbr. articles to profl. jours. Recipient Doolen Scholarship for the Study of Aging, U. Ill., 1991-92. Mem. Am. Psychol. Soc., Soc. for Neurosci., Phi Kappa Phi. Democrat. Protestant. Office: Rockefeller U Neuroendocrinology Lab 1230 York Ave New York NY 10021

CONRAD, ELLEN ROSE, health educator; b. Buffalo, Feb. 23, 1944; d. Erwin William and Elizabeth May (Zilker) C.; m. Richard Joseph Anderson, Nov. 23, 1967 (div. Mar. 1993); children: William Anderson, Richard Anderson, Kie Anderson. BS in Health and Phys. Edn., SUNY, Brockport, 1966; MS in Edn., SUNY, Buffalo, 1986. Cert. tchr., N.Y. Health and phys. edn. instr. Lake Shore Ctrl. Schs., Angola, N.Y., 1966—; advisor numerous sch. orgsn. Recipient 5 Yr. Faithful Svc. award Somerset Labs., 1995. Mem. AAUW, Adirondack Mountain Club. Home: 596 Seymour Ter Angola NY 14006

CONRAD, JANE KATHRYN, writer; b. Phila., Mar. 12, 1916; d. Charles and Alice Leah (Hachenburg) Goodman; m. R. Conrad, 1942 (dec. Jan. 1952); children: Ruthie, Kathy. BA in Polit. Sci., Met. State U., 1974. Mem. staff Office of Commandant, USMC and Secret Svc., Washington, 1939-43; liaison to state agys. State of Del., Dover; columnist Mobile Home Life, Denver, 1971-79. Author: Pillars of Religion, 1978, Skeptics, Scoffers and Deists, 1983, Mad Madalyn, 1982, rev. edit., 1996, Child Abuse Hysteria, 1989, rev. edit., 1990; contbr. articles to profl. publs.; editor newsletter Quest for Truth, 1976—. Leader Girl Scouts U.S., 1936-52; lobbyist Mobile Home Owners, Denver, 1974; mayor Town of Lochbuie, Colo., 1985; mem. Colo. Mobile Home Licensing Bd., Denver, 1975-78; consumer rep. Nat. Fire Protection Assn., Boston, 1973-75; mem. HUD Mobile Home Commn., 1977. Mem. ACLU, Ams. United for Separation of Ch. and State, Rocky Mountain Skeptics, Anti-Defamation League.

CONRAD, LISA ANN, nurse, case manager; b. Elyria, Ohio, Dec. 19, 1959; d. Leo Amato and Margaret Mary (Gallagher) Baptiste; m. Donald W. Conrad Jr., Oct. 8, 1988. Diploma, MB Johnson Sch. Nursing, 1981. RN, Ohio. RN staff nurse Elyria (Ohio) Meml. Hosp., 1981-86, RN staff nurse surgery, 1986-90; RN staff nurse surgery Lutheran Medical Ctr., Cleve., 1990-95; case mgr. Healthsource-Provident Ins. Co., Cleve., 1995—. Recipient Chauncey Smythe Meml. scholarship Elyria Meml. Hosp., 1980-81. Mem. Assn. Oper. Rm. Nurses, N.E. Ohio Case Mgmt. Network. Lutheran. Home: 449 Xavier St Elyria OH 44035-8829

CONRAD, MARY, advertising executive. Sr. v.p., group acct. dir. Bayer Bess Vanderwarker, Inc., Chgo. Office: Bayer Bess Vanderwarker Inc 225 N Michigan Ave Ste 1900 Chicago IL 60601-7601*

CONRAD, SUSAN BARBARA, union adminstrator; b. Brighton, Mass., Nov. 11, 1954; d. Harold Birdges and Catherine Eileen (Coyne) C.; m. Dennis Francis Devine, Nov. 13, 1976 (div. July 1982); 1 child, Matthew David. Accts. payable clk. Inmont Corp., Cambridge, Mass., 1974-76; from claims devel. clk. to social ins. rep. HHS/Social Security Adminstrn., Boston, Cambridge, 1976-91; exec. v.p. Am. Fedn. Govt. Employees Local 1164, Boston, 1991—; regional equal opportunity coord. Am. Fedn. Govt. Employees, 1994—, women's coord., 1994—, exec. bd. dirs. 1991—. Mem. NOW. Democrat. Roman Catholic. Home: 43 Seven Pines Ave Cambridge MA 02140

CONRAD-ENGLAND, ROBERTA LEE, pathologist; b. Meriden, Conn., Aug. 25, 1950; d. Hans and Emma Ann (Bort) Conrad; m. Gary Thomas England, June 6, 1976; children: Eric Bryan, Christopher Ryan. BS in Microbiology, U. Ky., 1972, MD, 1976. Diplomate Nat. Bd. Med. Examiners, Bd. Am. Pathologists. Resident anatomic and clin. pathology Emory U. Affiliated Hosps., Atlanta, 1976-80; pathologist Western Bapt. Hosp., Paducah, Ky., 1980—; cons. Marshall County Hosp., Benton, Ky., 1985—. Mem., com. chairperson PTA, Poducah, Ky., 1993-94; mother's asst. Boy Scouts Am., Poducah, 1991-94. Fellow Coll. Am. Pathologists, Am. Soc. Clin. Pathologists; mem. Ky. Med. Assn., Ky. Soc. Pathologists, Ky. Mentors Women in Sci., Alpha Omega Alpha, Phi Beta Kappa.

CONRON, SHANA RIMEL, lawyer; b. St. Louis; m. Michael Conron, Jan. 22, 1964; 1 child, Rachel. AB, Washington U., 1960; MA, U. Ill., 1961; JD, Columbia U., 1978. Assoc. editor Polit. Sci. quar., N.Y.C., 1969-72; editor Parker Sch., Columbia U. Law Sch., N.Y.C., 1972-74; assoc. Chadbourne & Parke, N.Y.C., 1978-83; v.p., divsn. counsel Citibank, N.A., N.Y.C., 1983—. Mem. ABA, Assn. Bar City of N.Y. Office: Citibank NA 153 E 53rd St New York NY 10022-1148*

CONROY, CATHERINE MARTIN, public relations executive; b. Bklyn., Dec. 29, 1948; m. Robert Ellsworth Conroy, 1972; 1 child, Amy Elizabeth. BA, Bklyn. Coll., 1970. Adminstrv. dir. Met. Golf Assn., N.Y.C., 1970-74; v.p. Blyth, Eastman Dillon & Co., Inc., N.Y.C., 1975-78; asst. v.p. Merrill Lynch, N.Y.C., 1978-83; sr. v.p. Donaldson, Lufkin & Jenrette, Inc., N.Y.C., 1983—. Mem. Pub. Rels. Soc. Am., Fin. Comm. Soc. Office: Donaldson Lufkin & Jenrette Inc 277 Park Ave New York NY 10172

CONROY, MARY A., state legislator. Mem. ways & means com., joint com. health care cost containment Md. House of Dels., Annapolis, 1987—. Democrat. Office: Md Ho of Reps Lowe House Office Bldg Ste 208 Annapolis MD 21401*

CONROY, SARAH BOOTH, columnist, novelist, speaker; b. Valdosta, Ga., Feb. 16, 1927; d. Weston Anthony and Ruth (Proctor) Booth; m. Richard Timothy Conroy, Dec. 31, 1949; children: Camille Booth, Sarah Claire. B.S., U. Tenn., 1950. Continuity writer Sta. WNOX, 1945-48; commentator, writer Sta. WATO, 1948-49; reporter, architecture columnist Knoxville News Sentinel, 1949-56; assoc. editor The Diplomat mag., 1956-58; columnist Washington Post, 1957-58, design editor, columnist, 1970-82, feature writer, columnist, 1982—; reporter, art critic Washington Daily News, 1968-70; regular contbr. N.Y. Times, 1968-70; mem. adv. bd. Horizon mag., 1978-85. Author: Refinements of Love A Novel about Clover and Henry Adams, 1993. Recipient Raven award Mystery Writers Am., 1990, U. Tenn. Disting. Alumni award, 1995. Mem. AIA (hon.). Home: 5016 16th St NW Washington DC 20011-3842 Office: The Washington Post 1150 15th St NW Washington DC 20071-0001

CONROY, TAMARA BOKS, artist, special education educator, former nurse; b. Most, Bohemia, Czechoslovakia; came to U.S., 1947; d. Alois and Tatiana (Shapilova) Boks; m. John P. Conroy, Aug. 19, 1950 (dec. Oct. 1973); 1 child, Michael Thomas (dec.). Student, U. Graz, Austria, 1945-47; RN, New Rochelle (N.Y.) Med. Ctr., 1950; student, Coll. of William & Mary, 1958, 59, Cath. U. Am., 1960; BS in Nursing Edn., Columbia U., 1963, MA in Spl. Edn., 1965. RN, N.Y.; cert. spl. edn. tchr., N.Y. Nurse accident rm. New Rochelle Hosp./Med. Ctr., 1950-51; pub. health nurse Va. Dept. of Health, Richmond, 1958-59; tchr. spl. edn. Southern Westchester Bd. Coop. Edn. Svcs., Portchester, N.Y., 1965-83; freelance artist and painter N.Y.C. and Pelham, N.Y., 1969—; asst. to chmn. math. dept. Columbia U., N.Y.C., 1975-76. Author math. program Learning Numbers-Step by Step, 1977. Pres., founder Classical Music Lovers' Exch., Pelham, 1980—. Mem. Am. Fedn. Tchrs., N.Y. State United Tchrs., BOCES Tchrs. Assn. (profl.), Women's Mus. Group, Mamaroneck Artists Guild, Silvermine Artists Guild, Westchester Musicians Guild (assoc.), Kappa Delta Pi. Office: Classical Music Lovers' Exch PO Box 31 Pelham NY 10803-0031

CONSAGRA, SOPHIE CHANDLER, academy administrator; b. Radnor, Pa., Apr. 28, 1927; d. Alfred D. and Carol (Ramsay) Chandler; children: Maria, Pierluigi, Francesca, George. B.A., Smith Coll., 1949; M.A., Cambridge (Eng.) U., 1952. Exec. dir. Del. Arts Council, 1972-78; dir. visual arts and architecture N.Y. State Council Arts, 1978-80; dir. Am. Acad. in Rome, 1980-84, pres., 1984-88, pres. emerita, vice chmn./spl. projects, 1988-90; cons. Nat. Endowment Arts. Recipient Smith Coll. award, 1986, Centennial medal Am. Acad. in Rome, 1995. Address: 955 Lexington Ave New York NY 10021-5107

CONSIDINE, SUSAN MARY, entrepreneur; b. Queens, N.Y., Jan. 21, 1958; d. Richard Thomas and Mary Michael (Zappulo) C.; 1 child, Shane Anthony. Diploma in Nursing, Samaritan Hosp., Troy, N.Y., 1979; BS, SUNY, Utica, 1981; MBA, Rensselaer Poly. Inst., 1989. RN. Nurse St. Elizabeth Hosp., Utica, 1980-81, Marcy Psychiat. Ctr., Utica, 1981-84; sales mgr. Lincoln Logs Ltd., Chestertown, N.Y., 1984-86, v.p. dealer devel., 1986-87, v.p. customer svc., 1987-90, exec. v.p., 1990-92, also bd. dirs.; owner Tokens of Friendship, Bolton Landing, N.Y., 1992—. Home: RR # 1 Box 60 Horicon Ave Bolton Landing NY 12814 Office: Tokens of Friendship Main St Bolton Landing NY 12814

CONSILIO, BARBARA ANN, legal administrator, management consultant; b. Cleve., June 22, 1938; d. Joseph B. and Anna E. (Ford) C. BS, Kent State U., 1962; MA, U. Detroit, 1973. Cert. social worker, Mich. Tchr. Chagrin Falls (Ohio) High Sch., 1962-64; probation officer Macomb County Juvenile Ct., Mt. Clemens, Mich., 1965-68, casework supr., 1968-74; dir. children's svcs. Macomb County Juvenile Ct., Mt. Clemens, 1974-79; mgr. foster care and instns. Oakland County Juvenile Ct., Pontiac, Mich., 1979-83; ct. adminstr. Oakland County Probate Ct., Pontiac, 1983-93, ret., 1993. Bd. dirs. Children's Charter Cts. of Mich., Lansing, Statewide Adv. Bd. on Sexual Abuse, Lansing, Havenwyck Hosp., Auburn Hills, Orchards Children's Svcs., Southfield, Oakland County Coun. Children at Risk, Pontiac; mem. Nat. Women's Polit. Caucus, N.Y.C.; bd. dirs. Care House, Pontiac. Mem. Nat. Coun. Juvenile and Family Ct. Adminstrs. Group, Mich. Probate and Juvenile Register's Assn., Mich. Juvenile Ct. Adminstrs. Assn., Nat. Assn. Ct. Mgrs., Supreme Ct. Task Force on Racial and Ethnic Bias, Office of Children and Youth Svcs. (state foster care system rev. com.), Nat. Coun. Juvenile and Family Ct. Judges (Outstanding Ct. Adminstr. award, 1993). Home: 4045 Chestnut Hill Dr Troy MI 48098-4205

CONSTABLE, ELINOR GREER, federal official, diplomat; b. San Diego, Feb. 8, 1934; d. Marshall Raymond and Katherine (French) Greer; m. Peter Dalton Constable, Mar. 8, 1958; children: Robert, Philip, Julia. B.A., Wellesley Coll., 1955. Mem. staff Dept. Interior, 1955-57, Dept. State, 1957-58, OEO, 1964-68; sr. assoc. Transcentury Corp., Washington, 1971-72; with Dept. State, Washington, 1973—, dir. investment affairs, 1978-80; dep. asst. sec. Internat. Fin. and Devel., 1980-83; dep. asst. sec. for econ. and bus. affairs Dept. State, from 1983-93, asst. secr. for Oceans, International Environmental and Scientific Affairs Bureau, 1993—; ambassador to Kenya, 1986-89; rsch. prof. diplomacy Georgetown U., Washington, 1989-91; capital devel. officer US AID, Pakistan, 1977-78; sr. inspector Office Inspector Gen., 1992; asst. sec. Oceans, Environ., Sci. and Tech., 1993—. Office: Oceans Internat Environ Sci Affairs Office of Asst Secr 2201 C St NW Washington DC 20520-0001*

CONSTABLE, MARIANNE, rhetoric educator; b. Manchester, England, Nov. 10, 1957; came to U.S., 1963; d. William Charles and Antoinette (Rist) C. AB in Philosophy and Polit. Sci., U. Calif., Berkeley, 1978, JD, 1987, PhD in Jurisprudence and Social Policy, 1989. Lectr. sociology bd. U. Calif., Santa Cruz, 1986; asst. prof. dept. rhetoric U. Calif., Berkeley, 1988-94, assoc. prof., 1994—. Author: The Law of the Other: The Mixed Jury and Changing Conceptions of Citizenship, Law, and Knowledge, 1994; contbr. articles to profl. jours. Grantee ACLS, 1994, NEH, 1996—; vis. fellow Davis Ctr. for Hist. Studies Princeton U., 1993. Mem. Am. Polit. Sci. Assn., Law and Soc. Assn. (trustee 1995—), others. Office: U Calif at Berkeley Dept Rhetoric 2125 Dwinelle Hall Berkeley CA 94720-2650

CONSTANCE, BARBARA ANN, financial planner, small business owner, consultant; b. Springfield, Mass., Dec. 24, 1945; d. Edward F. and Margaret E. (Price) Corcoran; m. Thomas F. Tiedgen, Apr. 27, 1968 (div. 1975); m. G. Lawrence Gadsby Jr., May 5, 1978 (div. 1991); m. F. David Constance, Dec. 6, 1991. AA, Vt. Coll., Montpelier, 1965. CLU; chartered fin. cons. Adminstrv. asst. Mass. Mut. Life Co., Springfield and Hartford, Conn., 1965-75; office mgr. Am. Nat. Life Ins. Co., Springfield, 1976; traveling trainee Conn. Gen. Life Ins. Co., Bloomfield, 1976; sales rep. Conn. Gen. Life Ins. Co., Springfield, 1976-77; dir. mktg. NN Life Ins. Services, Johnston, R.I., 1978-80; sales rep. New Eng. Mut. Life Co., Providence, 1980-82; pvt. practice fin. planner Tiverton, R.I., 1982—; pres., founder Heritage Prodns., Ltd., Tiverton, R.I., 1988-91; cons. Northwestern Mutual Life Ins. Co., Providence, 1986-87; co-founder, bd. dirs. Career Connections, Inc. Bd. dirs. YWCA of Greater R.I., Big Sister Assn. of R.I. Mem. Am. Soc. CLUs and ChFC (past pres. R.I. chpt.), Nat. Assn. Life Underwriters, R.I. Life Underwriters, Assn. Health Ins. Agts., Newport County Women's Network (co-founder), R.I. Woman's Career Network, R.I. Bus. Exch., R.I. Estate Planning Coun. Republican. Episcopalian. Home: 177 Highland Rd Tiverton RI 02878-4413 Office: Kings Grant Office Park 21 Kings Charles Dr Portsmouth RI 02871

CONSTANTINE, JAN FRIEDMAN, lawyer; b. N.Y.C., Jan. 22, 1948; d. Howard J. and Elayne (Sercus) Friedman; m. Lawrence Levien, Oct. 11, 1970 (div. Sept. 1974); m. Lloyd E. Constantine, June 22, 1975; children: Isaac, Sarah, Elizabeth. BA, Smith Coll., Northampton, Mass., 1970; JD, George Washington U., 1973. Bar: N.Y. 1974, U.S. Dist. Ct. (so. and ea. dists.) N.Y. 1975, U.S. Ct. Appeals (2d cir.) 1975. Staff atty. div. spl. projects FTC, Washington, 1973-75; staff atty. N.Y. office FTC, N.Y.C., 1975-77; asst. atty. U.S. Dist. Ct. (ea. dist.) N.Y., Bklyn., 1977-82; litigation counsel Macmillan, Inc., N.Y.C., 1982-84, assoc. gen. counsel, 1985-90, dep. gen. counsel, 1990-91; dep. gen. counsel The News Corp. Ltd., N.Y.C., 1991-92; sr. v.p. and gen. counsel News Am. Pub. Inc., N.Y.C., 1992-96; sr. v.p. The News Corp. Ltd., N.Y.C., 1996—; vis. asst. prof. George Washington U. Law Sch., Washington, 1974. Mem. Assn. of Bar of City of N.Y. (mem. consumer protection com. 1981-84, corp. law com. 1987-90, media law com. 1991—). Home: 10 W 66th St New York NY 10023-6206 Office: The News Corp Ltd 1211 Ave Of The Americas New York NY 10036-8701

CONSTANTINE, LYNNE MARY, writer, consultant; b. Queens, N.Y., July 29, 1953; d. Arthur Anthony and Anne Jasmine (D'Angelo) C.; partner Suzanne Scott, Nov. 15, 1980; stepchildren: Elizabeth, William, Stephanie, David. BA summa cum laude, Canisius Coll., 1973; MA, Yale U., 1975, MPhil, 1976. Asst. prof. English James Madison U., Harrisonburg, Va., 1977-80; mng. dir. Health Edn. Found., Washington, 1981-83; exec. dir. Energy Conservation Coalition, Washington, 1983-85; ptnr., creative dir. Cmty. Scribes, Arlington, Va., 1985—; cons. APA Pres.'s Commn. on Violence in the Family, Washington, 1994-95, Commn. on Violence and Youth, 1992-93, Carnegie Coun. on Adolescence, Washington, 1994-95, D.C. Area Rape Crisis Ctr., 1985-95. Co-author: Migraine: The Complete Guide, 1994; mng. editor: Woman's Monthly, 1992—, Passages award, 1995. Mem. Nat. Lesbian and Gay Journalists Assn., Nat. Soc. for Hosp. Mktg. Comm. and Pub. Rels., Washington Ind. Writers, Washington Metro Soc. for Hosp. Mktg. Comm. and Pub. Rels. Home: 4600 S Four Mile Run Dr 636 Arlington VA 22204 Office: Community Scribes 1001 N Highland St Ste PH Arlington VA 22201

CONSTANTINI, JOANN M., information management consultant, speaker; b. Danbury, Conn., July 30, 1948; d. William J. and Mathilda J. (Ressler) C. BA, Coll. White Plains, N.Y., 1970; postgrad. Central Conn. State Coll., 1977-78, U. Hartford, 1985-88, U. Jacksonville, 1991; MS, Nova Southeastern U. Sch. Psychology, 1996; doctoral candidate Union Inst., 1996—. Cert. records mgr., 1987; lic realtor, N.C. Psychiat. social worker N.Y. State Dept. Mental Hygiene, Wassaic, 1970-73; with Northeast Utilities, Hartford, Conn., 1973-88, methods analyst, 1979-82, records and procedures mgmt. adminstr., 1982-88; document contr., mgr. Ralph M. Parsons Co., Fairfield, Ohio, 1990-91, St. Johns River Power Park, Jacksonville, 1991—; bd. dirs. Micrographics, Inc., Gainesville, Fla.; dir. Meriden (Conn.) YWCA, 1976-77, My Sisters Place, 1984-87; mem. faculty Cen. Piedmont C.C., 1989-90, Fla. C.C., Jacksonville, 1993-95. Bd. dirs. Meriden YWCA, Conn., 1978-79; vol., 1984—, Queen City Friends, Charlotte, 1988-89; mem. Greater Charlotte Bd. Realtors; mem. adv. coun. Clermont Coll., Cin., 1990-91, Jacksonville C.C. 1991—, Greater Hartford C.C., 1986. Mem. AAUW, Assn. Record Mgmt. and Adminstrs. (sec. 1984-85, bd. dirs., 1984-86, internat. chair industry action program 1989-93, chair industry action com. for pub. utilities, 1986-89), Assn. Image and Info. Mgmt. (dir. 1984-86), Women Bus. Owners, Assn. Configurement Data Mgmt., Electric Coun. New Eng. (chair records mgmt. com. 1985-87), Coll. White Plains Alumnae Assn., Nat. Trust for Hist. Preservation, Inst. Cert. Records Mgrs., Am. Platform Assn., Beta Sigma Phi. Democrat. Roman Catholic. Club: Northeast Utilities Women's Forum. (treas. 1983-88). Avocations: antiques, fund raising, traveling, investing. Home: 11538 Jonathan Rd Jacksonville FL 32225-1314

CONSTANTINO-BANA, ROSE EVA, nursing educator, researcher; b. Labangan Zamboanga del Sur, Philippines, Dec. 25, 1940; came to U.S.,

1964; naturalized, 1982; d. Norberto C. and Rosalia (Torres) Bana; m. Abraham Antonio Constantino, Jr., Dec. 13, 1964; children: Charles Edward, Kenneth Richard, Abraham Anthony III. BS in Nursing, Philippine Union Coll., Manila, 1962; MNursing, U. Pitts., 1971, PhD, 1979; J.D., Duquesne U., Pitts., 1984. Lic. clin. specialist in psychiatric-mental health nursing; registered nurse. Instr. Philippine Union Co., 1963-65, Spring Grove State Hosp., Balt., 1965-67, Montefiore Sch. Nursing, Pitts., 1967-70; instr. U. Pitts., 1971-74, asst. prof., 1974-83, assoc. prof., 1983—, chmn. Senate Athletic Com., 1985-86, 89-90, univ. senate sec., 1991-92, univ. senate v.p., 1993-95; project dir. grant divsn. of nursing HHS, Washington, 1983-85; prin. investigator NIH NINR, 1991-94; bd. dirs. Internat. Coun. on Women's Health Issues, 1986—. Author: (with others) Principles and Practice of Psychiatric Nursing, 1982; contbr. chpts. to books and articles to profl. jours. Mem. Republican Presdl. Task Force, Washington, 1980, Rep. Senatorial Com., Washington, 1980. Fellow Am. Acad. Nursing; mem. ABA, ATLA, Allegheny County Bar Assn. (bd. cert. forensic examiner), Pa. Bar Assn., Women's Bar Assn., Am. Assn. Nurse Attys., Am. Nurses Assn., Pa. Nurses Assn., Nat. League Nursing, Pa. League Nursing (chairperson area 6), Allegheny County Bar Assn., U. Pitts. Sch. Nursing Alumni Assn., U. Duquesne Law Alumni Assn., Sigma Theta Tau, Phi Alpha Delta. Seventh-Day Adventist. Avocations: cooking, playing the piano. Home: 6 Carmel Ct Pittsburgh PA 15221-3618 Office: U Pitts Sch Nursing 415 Victoria St Pittsburgh PA 15261

CONTE, ALLISON, artist, educator, art therapist; b. Bklyn., Mar. 2, 1960; d. Salvatore R. and Sarah (Intersimone) C. BA in Studio Art, U. St. Thomas; MS in Art Therapy, Coll. of New Rochelle, 1996. Lic. N.Y. in art grades K-12; N.Y.C. lic. Asst. art dir., editl. asst. The Cath. News Pub. Co., New Rochelle, N.Y., 1984-85; personal sec. The Broadhurst Theatre, N.Y.C., 1985-86. Prin. works include Set and Tech. Designer for Showcase, 1991, 92; costume designer for Ann. Dance Shows, 1990, 91, 92; set and tech. design for Peter Rouget Middle Sch. prodn., 1993, 94; costume designer, 1993, 94. Asst. to univ. curator Link-Lee Gallery, U. St. Thomas Campus, Houston, 1981-83;directed students in painting Neighborhood Murals to combat graffiti--"Irises" Windsor Place and Prospect Park West, Bklyn., "Landscape" 15th St. and Prospect Park West, Bklyn., "Trees of Life" established Peter Rouget Middle School as a Peace Zone in conjunction with Crown Heights Peace Zone Project. Recipient Golden Apple Tchr.'s award Peter Rouget Middle Sch., 1994, citation Howard Golden, Pres. of Borough of Bklyn., 1995, Neighborhood Revitalization award. Office: Peter Rouget Middle Sch 544 7th Ave Brooklyn NY 11215

CONTE, ANDREA, retail executive, health care consultant; b. Great Barrington, Mass., Feb. 13, 1941; d. Louis William and Rosalie (Salvini) C.; m. Philip Norman Bredesen, Nov. 22, 1974; 1 child, Benjamin Conte. BS in Nursing, U. Wash., 1968; MBA, Tenn. State U., 1983. RN. Nurse various hosps. and med. ctrs., Mass. and Calif., 1961-68, Vis. Nurse Service, Boston, 1968-70; clin. coordinator RMP Boston City Hosp., 1970-72; trainer computer systems Searle Medidata, Lexington, Mass., 1973-75; dir. nursing mgmt. services Hosp. Corp. Am., Nashville, 1975-78; cons. various health care cos., Nashville, 1978-81; mgr. Ernst and Whinney, Nashville, 1981-83; pres. Conte Philips, Nashville, 1983—; founder, pres. You Have The Power, Inc. Bd. dirs. Family and Children's Svc., 1988-91, Cumberland Sci. Mus., 1988-93, Shepherd's Ctr. of West Edn., 1989-91, Cable, 1989—, Tenn. Performing Arts Ctr., NCCJ, St. Thomas Hosp.; active Commn. on Future of Tenn. Jud. Sys.; chair You Have The Power com. Roman Catholic.

CONTI, ISABELLA, psychologist, consultant; b. Torino, Italy, Jan. 1, 1942; came to U.S., 1964; d. Giuseppe and Zaira (Melis) Ferro; m. Ugo Conti, Sept. 5, 1964; 1 child, Maurice. J.D., U. Rome, 1966; Ph.D. in Psychology, U. Calif.-Berkeley, 1975. Lic. psychologist. Sr. analyst Rsch. Inst. for Study of Man, Berkeley, Calif., 1967-68; postgrad. rsch. psychologist Personality Assessment and Rsch. Inst., U. Calif.-Berkeley, 1968-71; intern U. Calif.-Berkeley and VA Hosp., San Francisco, 1969-75; asst. prof. St. Mary's Coll., Moraga, Calif., 1978-84; cons. psychologist Conti Resources, Berkeley, Calif., 1977-85; v.p. Barnes & Conti Assocs., Inc., Berkeley, 1985-90; pres. Lisardco, El Cerrito, Calif., 1989—; bd. dirs. ElectroMagnetic Instruments, Inc., El Cerrito, Calif., 1985—. Trustee Monterey Inst. Internat. Studies, 1996—. Author: (with Alfonso Montuori) From Power to Partnership, 1993; contbr. articles on creativity and mgmt. cons. to profl. jours. Regents fellow U. Calif.-Berkeley, 1972; NIMH predoctoral rsch. fellow, 1972-73. Mem. APA. Office: Lisardco 1318 Brewster Dr El Cerrito CA 94530-2526

CONWAY, ANNE CALLAGHAN, federal judge; b. Cleve., July 30, 1950. AB, John Carroll U., 1972; JD, U. Fla., 1975. Bar: Fla. 1975, U.S. Supreme Ct. 1981, U.S. Ct. Appeals (5th and 11th cirs.), U.S. Dist. Ct. (mid., no. and so. dists.) Fla. Law clk. to justice U.S. Dist. Ct., Orlando, Fla., 1975-77; from assoc. to ptnr. Wells, Gattis & Hallowes, Orlando, 1978-81; assoc. Carlton, Fields, Ward, Emmanuel, Smith & Cutler, P.A., Orlando, 1982-85, ptnr., 1985-91; judge U.S. Dist. (Mid. Dist.) Fla., Jacksonville, 1991—; mem. adv. com. on local rules U.S. Dist. Ct., Orlando, 1990-91, grievance com. Orlando div., mid. dist., 1986-91. Bd. dirs. So. Ballet Theatre, Winter Park, Fla., 1985-89, adv. bd., 1985-89; bd. dirs. Greater Orlando Area Legal Svcs., 1978-85. Mem. ABA, Orange County Bar Assn. (chairperson state and fed. trial practice com. 1989-90). Office: US Courthouse 80 N Hughey Ave Rm 646 Orlando FL 32801-2231*

CONWAY, LENORA WEBB, executive recruiter; b. Memphis, Tex., May 28, 1933; d. Omri Kenneth and Lenora (Jourdan) Webb; m. Julian Attaway Cave, Sept. 5, 1958 (div. 1992); m. Patrick Joseph Conway, July 7, 1993. BA in Music, Furman U., 1954; MRE, So. Bapt. Theol. Sem., 1957. Divsn. mgr. CDI, Columbus, Ohio, 1975-82; v.p. Search Pro, Charlotte, N.C., 1992—; pres. Nat. Med. Search, Annapolis, Md., 1995—, Nat. Exec. Svcs., Annapolis, Md., 1992—. Author: (plays) The Sixth Day, 1970, The Search, 1975; (musical play) Orphan Queen, 1996; hostess TV talk show Panorama, 1970-75; columnist, 1970-80. Mem. Nat. Press Club (travel com.), Capital Spkrs. Club (bd. dirs.), Dramatists Guild. Democrat. Episcopalian. Home: 7034 Harbour Vl Ct #202 Annapolis MD 21403

CONWAY, LOIS LORRAINE, piano teacher; b. Caldwell, Idaho, Oct. 20, 1913; d. William Henry and Auttie Arrola (Bierd) Crawford; m. Edward Owen Conway, June 23, 1994; children: Michael David, Judith Ann, Steven Edward, Kathleen Jean. Degree, Albertson Coll. of Idaho, 1960's; student, Shorwood Music Sch., Chgo., Coll. of Notre Dame, San Francisco. Pvt. piano tchr. Ontario, Oreg., 1940-74, Pendleton, Oreg., 19774-92; ret., 1992; Nat. Guild Piano Tchrs. adjudicator spring auditions Am. Coll. Musicians, Austin, Tex., 1972-96. Author: (poetry) Pacifica-The Voice Within (Semifinalist 1995). Chmn. Nat. Guild Auditions, Ontario, Oreg., 1959-72, Pendleton, Oreg., 1972-80; v.p., publicity Community Concerts Assn., Ontario, 1960-72, membership work, 1972-75. Democrat. Home: 32600 Highway #74 Hemet CA 92545-9605

CONWAY, MARY PATRICIA, speech educator; b. Springfield, Mass., May 11, 1953; d. George Martin and Mary Josephine (Sweeney) C. BA, Boston Coll., 1975; MS, Worcester State Coll., 1984. Cert. elem. edn. and speech, Mass., speech pathologist, Mass. Speech-lang. pathologist Springfield (Mass.) Sch. Dept., 1975—. Corporator Springfield Libr. and Mus., 1980—; divsn. leader Quadrangle Quest, Springfield, 1988—; active Dem. Com., 1980—. Grantee Mass. State Dept., 1986; named Outstanding Young Woman Am., 1984. Mem. Am. Speech-Lang.-Hearing Assn. (cert.), Coun. Exceptional Children, Assn. for Children with Learning Disabilities, Delta Kappa Gamma (Alpha chpt. officer 1989-93). Roman Catholic. Home: 82 Pilgrim Rd Springfield MA 01118-1414

CONWAY, NANCY ANN, editor; b. Foxboro, Mass., Oct. 15, 1941; d. Leo T. and Alma (Goodwin) C.; children: Ana Lucia DaSilva, Kara Ann Martin. Cert. in med. tech., Carnegie Inst., 1962; BA in English, U. Mass., 1976, cert. in secondary edn., 1978. Tchr. Brazil-Am. Inst., Rio de Janeiro, 1963-68; freelance writer, editor Amherst, Mass., 1972-76; staff writer Daily Hampshire Gazette, North Hampton, Mass., 1976-77; editor Amherst Bull., 1977-80, Amherst Record, 1980-83; features editor Holyoke (Mass.) Transcript/Telegram, 1983-84; gen. mgr. Monday-Thursday Newspapers, Boca Raton, Fla., 1984-87; dir. editorial South Fla. Newspaper Network, Deerfield Beach, 1987-90; pub., editor York (Pa.) Newspapers, Inc., 1990-95; exec. editor Alameda Newspaper Group, Pleasanton, Calif., 1995—. Bd. dirs. Math.: Opportunities in Engring., Sci. and Tech.-Pa. State, York, 1991-95. Recipient writing awards, state newspaper assns. Mem. Am. Soc. Newspaper Editors, Soc. Profl. Journalists, Pa. Newspaper Pub. Assn. Office: Alameda Newspaper Group PO Box 10367 4770 Willow Rd Pleasanton CA 94588

CONWAY CAREY, ALLISON, banker; b. N.Y.C., May 4, 1957; d. Edmund Virgil and Audrey (Oehler) Conway; m. Richard Brian Carey, Mar. 7, 1987; 1 child, Edmund Bowering. BA, Bowdoin Coll., 1979; MBA, Columbia U., 1983. Credit analyst, asst. sec. Mfrs. Hanover Trust Co., N.Y.C., 1979-81, asst. v.p., 1983-85, v.p. investment banking, 1985-91; mng. dir. Chase Securities, Inc., N.Y.C., 1991—. Mem. Jr. League Bronxville. Office: Chase Securities Inc 270 Park Ave New York NY 10017-2014

CONWAY-GERVAIS, KATHLEEN MARIE, reading specialist, educational consultant; b. Bklyn., Apr. 18, 1942; d. John Joseph and Mary Josephine Conway; m. Stephen Paul Gervais, July 10, 1976; 1 child, John Joseph. BA, Coll. Mt. St. Vincent, 1970; MS, Hunter Coll. of N.Y.C., 1973, Reading Specialization, 1974. Cert. reading and social studies tchr., nursery and elem. ecuator, N.Y., N.J. Elem. tchr. Archdiocese of N.Y., N.Y.C., 1963-74; reading specialist Malverne (N.Y.) Union Free Sch. Dist., 1974-86, dist. reading, testing coord., 1986-91, reading specialist, 1992-95; reading specialist East Meadow (N.Y.) Union Free Sch. Dist., 1995-96; reading cons., tchr. trainer Uniondale (N.Y.) Union Free Sch. Dist., 1996—; adv. bd. mem. Newsday in Edn., Melville, 1982—; adj. prof. Nassau C.C., Garden City, N.Y., 1995—. Active Getting Out the vote presdl. election, N.Y., 1992. Recipient Ambassador in Edn. award Newsday, Melville, 1982, Congruence Model Project award N.Y. State Dept. Edn., Albany, 1988, Elizabeth Ann Seton award Office of Cathechesis and Worship, Long Island, 1991. Mem. ASCD, Internat. Reading Assn., N.Y. State Reading Assn., Orton Dyslexia Soc., Nassau Reading Coun. (bd. dirs.). Democrat. Roman Catholic. Home: 174 Nassau Blvd West Hempstead NY 11552-2218 Office: Uniondale Union Free Sch Dist 50 Lawrence Rd Hempstead NY 11550

CONWELL, ESTHER MARLY, physicist; b. N.Y.C., May 23, 1922; d. Charles and Ida (Korn) C.; m. Abraham A. Rothberg, Sept. 30, 1945; 1 son, Lewis J. B.A., Bklyn. Coll., 1942; M.S., U. Rochester, N.Y., 1945; Ph.D., U. Chgo., 1948; DSc, Bklyn. Coll., 1992. Lectr. Bklyn. Coll., 1946-51; mem. tech. staff Bell Telephone Labs., 1951-52; physicist GTE Labs., Bayside, N.Y., 1952-61; mgr. physics dept. GTE Labs., 1961-72; vis. prof. U. Paris, 1962-63; Abby Rockefeller Mauze prof. M.I.T., 1972; prin. scientist Xerox Corp., Webster, N.Y., 1972-80; research fellow Xerox Corp., 1981—; adj. prof. U. Rochester, 1990—; cons., mem. adv. com. engring. NSF, 1978-81. Author: High Field Transport in Semiconductors, 1967, also research papers; mem. editorial bd. Jour. Applied Physics; Proc. of IEEE; patentee in field. Fellow IEEE, Am. Phys. Soc. (sec.-treas. div. condensed matter physics 1977-82); mem. AAAS, Nat. Acad. Scis., Soc. Women Engrs. (Achievement award 1960), Nat. Acad. Engring. Office: 800 Phillips Rd Webster NY 14580-9720

CONWELL, THERESA GALLO, financial services representative; b. Utica, N.Y., Mar. 6, 1947; d. Ernest and Anna (Caiazzo) Gallo; m. Charles Ray Conwell, Aug. 19, 1978. BS in Edn., SUNY-Potsdam, 1968; MA in Edn., SUNY-Cortland, 1978; Cert. tchr., N.Y.; CLU; chartered fin. cons., registered rep.; ChFc. Tchr. pub. schs., Clinton, N.Y., 1969-78, Portland, Conn., 1978-80; supr. mktg. services Phoenix Home Life Ins. Co. (now Phoenix Home Life Ins. Co.), Hartford, Conn., 1980-82, assoc. mgr. agt. tng., 1982-84, mgr. agt. tng., 1984-85, dir. agt./mgmt. devel., 1985-88, fin. svcs. rep., 1988—; speaker to small bus. orgns., women's groups, N.Y., New Eng., 1986—. Mem. NAFE, NOW, Am. Soc. CLU, Nat. Assn. Life Underwriters, Internat. Assn. Fin. Planners, Hartford Assn. Life Underwriters, Conn. Assn. Life Underwriters, Nat. Assn. Securities Dealers, Nat. Assn. Profl. Saleswomen, Bus. and Profl. Women of Glastonbury (pres.), Pres. Club (assoc. 1991). Democrat. Avocations: tennis, golf, swimming, aerobics, reading. Home: 191 Knollwood Dr Glastonbury CT 06033-1821 Office: Phoenix Home Life Ins Co Commerce Ctr One 333 E River Dr East Hartford CT 06108-4201

COOEY, PAULA MARIA, religious studies educator; b. Hayes, Kans., Mar. 21, 1945; d. Edward Wilton Jr. and Paulina Vernett (Miller) C.; m. Philip Charles Nichols Jr., June 4, 1967; 1 child, Benjamin Charles. BA in Philosophy, U. Ga., 1968; MS in Theology, Harvard Divinity Sch., 1974; PhD in Religion, Harvard U., 1981. Rsch./resource assoc. in women's studies and religion Harvard Divinity Sch., Cambridge, Mass., 1980-81; asst. prof. religion Trinity U., San Antonio, 1981-87, assoc. prof., 1987-93, prof., 1993—. Author: Religious Imagination and the Body, 1994, Family, Freedom and Faith, 1996; co-editor: After Patriarchy, 1991; mem. editl. rev. bd. Jour. Feminist Studies in Religion, 1987—; mem. bd. contbg. editors: Spotlight on Teaching, 1992—; contbr. articles to profl. jours. Active Emily's List, Washington. Gretchen C. Northrup Jr. Faculty fellow Trinity U., 1985-87, Kent fellow Danforth Found., 1976-81. Mem. Am. Acad. Religion (bd. dirs. 1994-98, regional pres. 1990-91), Soc. for Scientific Study Religion, Soc. for Buddhist-Christian Studies (bd. dirs. 1991-95), S.W. Commn. on Religious Studies (pres. 1993-94), Am. Coun. Learned Socs. (AAR del. 1994-97), ACLU, AAUP, Ams. United for Separation of Religion and State. Democrat. Presbyterian. Office: Trinity U Dept Religion 715 Stadium Dr San Antonio TX 78212-7200

COOGAN, MELINDA ANN STRANK, chemistry educator; b. Davenport, Iowa, Mar. 29, 1955; d. Gale Benjamin and Margie Delene (Admire) Strank; m. James Daniel Coogan, July 10, 1976; children: James Benjamin, Jessica Ann. AA, Stephens Coll., Columbia, Mo., 1975; BS, E. Carolina U., Greenville, N.C., 1978. Biology, physical science educator York (Pa.) Catholic H.S., 1989-90; science adv. Bettendorf (Iowa) Children's Mus., 1993; gifted, chemistry and physics educator St. Katherine' Coll. Prep. Sch., Bettendorf, 1994; biology educator Lewisville (Tex.) H.S., 1995, chemistry educator, 1996; violinist Augustana Symphony Orchestra, Rock Island, Ill., 1993-94; pres. bd. dirs. Flower Mound (Tex.) Cmty. Orchestra, 1994-95; founder, instr. Northlakes Violin Acad., Flower Mound, 1994—; violinist Waterforde Women's String Ensemble, Lewisville, 1995—. Mem. Roanoke Art Mus. (docent 1983-86), Jr. Bd. of Quad City Symphony (chair promotion 1987-88), Jr. Svc. League Moline (Ill.) (chair Riverfest 1987-88), Jr. League of York (Pa.) (chair thrift shop spl. sales 1989-92), Jr. League of Quad Cities (nom./placement 1993-94), Jr. League of Dallas (sustaining 1995-96), Gamma Beta Phi, Chi Beta Phi, Phi Kappa Phi. Republican. Roman Catholic. Home: 2629 Bierstadt Dr Highland Village TX 75067

COOK, ANDA SUNA, civil rights advocate; b. Riga, Latvia, Mar. 15, 1935; came to U.S., 1952.; d. Janis Suna and Erna Alexandra (Kletnieks) Sirmais; m. William E. Cook, May 27, 1961; children: Lisa Inara Hamilton, Inta Marie Mitterbach, John William. Student, Augustana Coll., Sioux Falls, S.D., 1954-55, Cleve. State U., 1970-85; MS, Case Western Res. U., 1989. Lic. real estate agt. With Cuyahoga Plan of Ohio, Inc., Cleve., 1976-91, dir. resource devel., 1988-91; exec. dir. Living in Cleve. Ctr., 1992—; v.p. regional div. U.S. Orgn. Internat. Trade, Inc., Cleve., 1989—; price analyst U.S. Steel Corp., Cleve., 1955-62; pres. ASC Cons.-Orgn. Devel., Cleve., 1988; presenter World Latvian Sci. Congress, Riga, 1991. Writer 60 Years of Leage of Women Voters, 1980; writer, prodr. Vol. Affirmative Mktg. Agreement in Action, 1989. Bd. dirs. Dept. Human Svcs., Cuyahoga County, 1984-93, Cudell Sr. Adv. Coun., 1980-85; trustee Friends of Cleve. Met. Housing Authority, 1986-92; active Cuyahoga C.C. Adv. Bd., 1980—; bd. trustees Citizens League, Cleve., 1989-95, Housing Advocates, 1996—; chair Cleve. PTA, 1972-73; pres. Louisa May Alcott Elem. Sch. PTA, Cleve., 1971-72, LWV, Cleve., 1975-77. Recipient Dedicated Svc. award The Cuyahoga Plan, Cleve., 1985, Cleve. Leadership award United Way, 1976, Cleve. Area Bd. Realtors Fair Housing award, 1993. Mem. Am. Soc. Tng. and Devel. Democrat. Lutheran. Home: 9801 Lake Ave Cleveland OH 44102-1230 Office: US Orgn Internat Trade Inc 9801 Lake Ave 4d Cleveland OH 44102

COOK, ANGELA DENISE, business analyst; b. Chgo., Oct. 31, 1963; d. Mary Grey; m. Joseph Clinton Cook, Jan. 1, 1989; 1 child, Meaghan Mary. BS in Computer Sci., Northeastern U., Chgo., 1984; MBA, Northwestern U., Evanston, Ill., 1986. Quality assurance mgr. Quality Assurance Inst., Orlando, Fla., 1985—; guest speaker Harold Washington Womens Affairs com., Chgo., 1987. Counselor Rape Victim Adv., Chgo., 1984-88; bd. dirs. Rape Trauma Victim Assistance, Chgo., 1989; adv. at large Chgo. Com. on Homeless, 1988; dir. ministries homeless coun. United Meth. Ch., 1995-96. Democrat. Office: Va Power One James River Plz Richmond VA 23219

COOK, BECKY JO, small business owner, computer consultant; b. Hanover, N.H., May 6, 1952; d. Sidney L. and Ruth (Tyler) Cook; m. Fred S. Norful, July 19, 1975 (div. Feb. 1986); children: Jared D., Morgan R.S.; m. Theodore V. Boze, Dec. 19, 1989; stepchildren: Jeremy R., Kristen E. BS in Home Econs., U. Vt., 1975. Supr. acctg. dept. New Eng. Digital Corp., White River Junction, Vt., 1981-86; supr. client acctg. Bridgman Valiante Villard, Lebanon, N.H., 1987; computer cons. Bus. Automation Specialists, Hanover, 1988; owner, mgr. Cook Assocs., Norwich, Vt., 1986—; mem. loan bd. Connecticut Valley Revolving Loan Fund, White River Junction, 1995—. Mem. adv. coun. Vt. Gov.'s Commn. on Women, Montpelier, 1993—; mem. com., mgr. task force Vt. Gov.'s Com. for Gender Neutral Lang.. in Vt. Constn. Mem. NAFE, AAUW, NOW, Women Bus. Owners Network (treas. 1987—). Home: 673 Union Village Rd Norwich VT 05055

COOK, BETH MARIE, copy director; b. Griffin, Ga., Feb. 13, 1964; d. J. Milan and Betty M. (Foster) C. BA in Journalism in Advt., U. Ga., 1986. Typesetter Macy's South/Bullock's, Atlanta, 1986-88, copywriter, 1988-89, asst. copy dir., 1989-92; freelance writer Atlanta, 1992-94; sales promotion mgr. The Butler Group Inc., Marietta, Ga., 1993-94; copywriter 3 Score, Tucker, Ga., 1994-95, copy dir., 1995—. Vol. Arts Festival of Atlanta, 1987-94, High Mus. of Art, Atlanta, 1989-91; bd. trustees DeKalb Choral Guild, 1992-93, sec., 1992-93; vol. Cathedral Antiques Show; mem. Cathedral of St. Philip Cathedral & Evensong Choirs, 1991—, publicity chair, 1993-94, publicity com. 150th anniversary, 1994-97; mem. William O. Baker Singers, Capitol City Opera Co. Recipient ASTAR awards Retail Advt. Conf., 1990, 91. Episcopalian.

COOK, CATHERINE COGHLAN, lawyer; b. Chgo., Jan. 25, 1934; d. John Patrick and Catherine Marie (Lyons) Coghlan; m. Bruce A. Cook, Dec. 5, 1956 (div. 1982); children: Robert, Catherine, Cecilia. BA, Loyola U., Chgo., 1954, MA, 1960; JD, George Washington U., 1974; LLM, Georgetown U., 1975. Bar: Md. 1974, D.C. 1975, Ill. 1991. Instr., lectr. Loyola U., Chgo., 1960-67, George Washington U., Washington, 1968-71; trial atty. U.S. Consumer Product Safety Commn., Washington, 1975-83; asst. gen. counsel, dep. gen. counsel Dept. Energy, Washington, 1983-86; gen. counsel, spl. counsel Fed. Energy Regulatory Commn., Washington, 1986-91; gen. counsel U.S. Railroad Retirement Bd., Chgo., 1991—; instr. DePaul U. Law, Chgo., 1996—. Ford Found. fellow, 1974-75. Office: US Railroad Retirement Bd 844 N Rush St Chicago IL 60611-2031

COOK, CATHY WELLES, state legislator; b. New London, Conn.. BA, Conn. Coll.; postgrad., U. Mass. Mem. Groton Bd. of Edn., 1983-91; chmn. adv. coun. State Dept. Mental Retardation, Region 6, 1984—; mem. Eastern Conn. Long Island Sound Commn., 1990-92, Conn. State Senate, Hartford, 1993—; chmn. environ. com., tourism subcom.; vice-chmn. edn. com.; mem. commerce and exportation com. Republican. Office: Conn State Senate State Capitol Hartford CT 06106 Address: 8 W Mystic Ave Mystic CT 06355-2329

COOK, CHRISTI ROSE, mental health counselor, psychometrist; b. Jackson, Miss., Oct. 14, 1968; d. John Lucius and Elizabeth Carolyn (Burney) C. BA, Miss. Coll., Clinton, 1990; MS, U. So. Miss., Hattiesburg, 1992. Nat. cert. counselor. Rsch. asst. dept. psychiatry and human behavior U. Miss. Med. Ctr., Jackson, 1988-90; spl. edn. asst. 1st Bapt. Ch., Jackson, 1990-91; transition specialist, grad./rsch. asst. univ. affil. progs. U. So. Miss., Hattiesburg, 1991-92; vocat. placement coord. for handicapped individuals Miss. Employment Security Commn., Columbia, 1991-92; grad. asst. spl. edn. dept. severe/profound divsn. Hattiesburg H.S., 1992; grad. asst. Pine Belt Alcohol and Drug Clinic, Hattiesburg, 1992; counseling psychology extern dept. psychiatry/human behavior U. Miss. Med. Ctr., Jackson, 1992, mental health counselor, psychometrist, 1994—. Mem. 1st Bapt. Sanctuary Choir, 1993—, exec. com., sec., 1994-95, exec. com., membership chmn., 1995-96. Mem. ACA, Am. Mental Health Christian Counselors, Miss. Counselors Assn., Miss. Mental Health Counselors Assn., Student Governance Assn. (counseling psychology program U. So. Miss. 1992), Psi Chi (Miss. Coll. chpt., charter mem.). Republican. Baptist. Office: U Miss Med Ctr Dept Psychiatry 2500 N State St Jackson MS 39216-4505

COOK, CHRISTINE, elementary education educator; b. Phila., Jan. 24, 1964; d. James Joseph and Ann (Kolankiewicz) B.; m. Kenneth Mark Cook, June 9, 1990; children: Jennifer Lynn, Megan. B in elem. edn., West Chester U., 1985; M in elem. edn., Millersville U., 1992. Kindergarten tchr. Somerton Nursery Sch. and Kindergarten, Phila., 1985-86, Milton Hershey Sch., Hershey, Pa., 1986—; field hockey coach Milton Hershey Sch., 1986-92, softball coach, 1986-92, driver edn. instr., 1989-91. Mem. Assn. for Edn. of Young Children, Assn. for Childhood Edn. Internat. Democrat. Roman Catholic. Office: Milton Hershey Sch PO Box 830 Hershey PA 17033

COOK, CYNTHIA ANN, editor; b. New Rochelle, N.Y., Dec. 20, 1964; d. John Joseph and Maureen (McGinnis) C. BA, NYU, 1995. Adminstrv. asst. Sch. Law, NYU, 1990-93; prodn. asst. Hachette Filipacchi Mags., N.Y.C., 1993-94; editl. coord. Women's Day Mag., N.Y.C., 1994-96, editl. coord., asst. to exec. editor, 1996—; adv. newspaper Washington Irving H.S., N.Y.C., 1994—; freelance writer various publs. Founder Univ. Moderate Dems. NYU, 1992. Mem. LWV, Alpha Sigma Lambda. Democrat. Office: Womens Day Mag 1633 Broadway 42d Flr New York NY 10019

COOK, DEBORAH L., judge. Former judge Ohio Ct. Appeals (9th dist.), Columbus; justice Ohio Supreme Ct., Columbus, 1994—. Office: Ohio Supreme Ct 30 E Broad St 3rd Fl Columbus OH 43266-0419*

COOK, DIERDRE RUTH GOORMAN, school administrator, secondary education educator; b. Denver, Nov. 4, 1956; d. George Edward and Avis M. (Wilson) Goorman; m. Donald Robert Cook, Apr. 4, 1981; 1 child, Christen. BA in Theatre Arts, Colo. State U., 1980, MA in Adminstrn., MEd, 1995. Cert. secondary tchr. Tchr. Centennial High Sch., Ft. Collins, Colo., 1983-87; tchr., also dir. student activities Poudre H.S., Ft. Collins, 1987-95; asst. prin. Lesher Jr. H.S., Ft. Collins, 1995—; mem. curriculum devel. com. Poudre R-1 Sch. Dist., Ft. Collins, 1984, mem. instrnl. improvement com., 1985—, trainer positive power leadership, 1986-87, mem. profl. devel. com., 1994—; comm. cons. Woodward Gov. Com., Ft. Collins, 1991, 92, 95; mem. evaluation visitation team North Ctrl. Evaluation, Greeley, Colo., 1991. Campaign worker Rep. Party, Littleton, Colo., 1980, Ft. Collins, 1984, 88; mem. Colo. Juvenile Coun., Ft. Collins, 1986, 88, loaned exec., 1987; bd. dirs. Youth Unltd., 1994—; mem. Leadership Ft. Collins, 1992-93; troop leader Girl Scouts U.S., 1991-94. NEH scholar, 1992; named Disting. Tchr. 1993 Colo. Awards Coun.; recipient Tchr. Excellence award Poudre High Sch., 1992. Mem. NEA, ASCD, Colo. Edn. Assn., Poudre Edn. Assn. (rep. 1989-91), Nat. Speech Comm. Assn., Nat. Forensics League (degree for outstanding distinction 1992), Nat. Platform Soc., Kappa Kappa Gamma (pres. Epsilon Beta chpt. 1985-90, mem. corp. house bd., alumni pres. Ft. Collins 1996-97). Home: 1600 Burlington Ct Fort Collins CO 80525 Office: Poudre R-1 Sch Dist 1400 StoverRd Fort Collins CO 80524

COOK, DORIS ADELE, artist; b. Ligonier, Pa., Apr. 16, 1930; d. William Issac and Adele Henrietta (Siebert) Routch; m. David Glen Eckholm, Feb. 14, 1956 (div. 1969); 1 child, Melissa Marie Schoenberg; m. George E. Cook, Apr. 13, 1973 (dec. 1992). AB, U. Houston. Sec. to dean of men Clarion (Pa.) State Tchr. Coll., 1948-49; sec. dean of edn. U. Houston, 1951-57; sec., v.p. Napko Corp., Houston, 1959-62; adminstrv. sec. Ben Taub Hosp., Houston, 1968-73; victim/witness coord Cherokee County Dist. Atty., Rusk, Tex., 1992—; bd. child advocacy ctr. Crisis Ctr., Cherokee, Jacksonville, 1996—; lay rep., libr. Rusk Libr., 1994—; east Tex. handweaver guild, Nacogdocher, Tex., 1985-92. With USAF, 1949-51. Mem. Tyler Art League, Nat. Women's Mus., Cherokee County Art League (pres., sec., treas.). Home: Rt 1 Box 221 Rusk TX 75785 Office: Cherokee County PO 450 Rusk TX 75785

COOK, DORIS MARIE, accountant, educator; b. Fayetteville, Ark., June 11, 1924; d. Ira and Mettie Jewel (Dorman) C. BSBA, U. Ark., 1946, MS, 1949; PhD, U. Tex., 1968. CPA, Okla., Ark. Jr. acct. Haskins & Sells,

Tulsa, 1946-47; instr. acctg. U. Ark., Fayetteville, 1947-52, asst. prof., 1952-62, assoc. prof., 1962-69, prof., 1969-88, Univ. prof. and Nolan E. Williams lectr. in acctg., 1988—; mem. Ark. State Bd. Pub. Accountancy, 1987-92, treas., 1989-91, vice chmn. 1991-92; mem. Nat. Assn. State Bds. of Accountancy, 1987-92; appointed Nolan E. Williams lectureship in acctg., 1988—. Mem. rev. bd. Ark. Bus. Rev., Jour. Managerial Issues; contbr. articles to profl. jours. Named Outstanding Grad. acctg. dept. U. Ark., 1996. Mem. AICPA, Ark. Bus. Assn. (editor newsletter 1982-85), Am. Acctg. Assn. (chmn. nat. membership 1982-83, Arthur Carter scholarship com. 1984-85, membership Ark. 1985-87), Am. Women's Soc. CPAs., Ark. Soc. CPA's (v.p. 1975-76, pres. N.W. Ark. chpt. 1980-81; sec. Student Loan Found., 1981-84, treas. 1984-92, pres. 1992—; chmn. pub. rels. 1984-88, 93-95, Outstanding Acctg. Educator award 1991), Acad. Acctg. Historians (trustee 1985-87, rev. bd. of Working Papers Series 1984-92, sec. 1992-95, pres.-elect 1995, pres. 1996), Ark. Fedn. Bus. and Profl. Women's Clubs (treas. 1979-80), Fayetteville Bus. and Profl. Women's Clubs (pres. 1973-74, 75-76, Woman of Yr. award 1977) Mortar Bd., Beta Gamma Sigma, Beta Alpha Psi (editor nat. newsletter 1973-77, nat. pres. 1977-78), Phi Gamma Nu, Alpha Lambda Delta, Delta Kappa Gamma (sec. 1976-78, pres. 1978-80, treas. 1989—), Phi Kappa Phi. Home: 1115 N Leverett Ave Fayetteville AR 72703-1622 Office: U Ark Dept Acctg Fayetteville AR 72701

COOK, FRANCES D., diplomat; b. Charleston, W.Va., Sept. 7, 1945; d. Nash and Vivian Cook. B.A., Mary Washington Coll. of U. Va., 1967; M.P.A., Harvard U., 1978. Certificats d'Etudes, Université d'Aix-Marseille (France), 1966. Commd. fgn. svc. officer Dept. State, 1967; spl. asst. to R.S. Shriver amb. to France, Paris, 1968-69; mem. U.S. Del. Paris Peace Talks on Viet-Nam, 1970-71; cultural affairs officer, consul Am. Consul Gen., Sydney, Australia, 1971-73; cultural affairs officer, first sec. Am. Embassy, Dakar, Senegal, 1973-75; personnel officer for Africa USIA, Washington, 1975-77; dir. office public affairs African Bur. Dept. State, Washington, 1978-80; amb. to Republic of Burundi Dept. State, Bujumbura, 1980-83; consul gen. Dept. State, Alexandria, Egypt, 1983-86; dep. asst. sec. of state for refugees Dept. State, Washington, 1986-87, dir. Office of West African Affairs, 1987-89; amb. to Cameroon Dept. State, Yaoundé, 1989-93; U.S. coord. for Sudan Dept. State, 1993; dep. asst. sec. of state for political-military affairs Dept. of State, Washington, 1993-95; amb. to Oman Dept. of State, Muscat, 1996. Recipient various honor awards Dept. State. Mem. AAUW, Am. Fgn. Svc. Assn., Coun. of Fgn. Rels., Harvard Club of N.Y.C., Army-Navy Club/Washington, Phi Beta Kappa (alumni). Office: Am Embassy Muscat Dept of State Washington DC 20520-6220

COOK, JANICE ELEANOR NOLAN, elementary school educator; b. Middletown, Ohio, Nov. 22, 1936; d. Lloyd and Eleanor Lee (Caudill) Nolan; m. Kenneth J. Cook, May 16, 1980; children: Gerald W. Fultz Jr., Jana Linn Perkins, Jennylee Haines. BSEd, Miami U., 1971; MEd, reading specialist cert., Xavier U., 1982, rank 1 cert., 1987, spl. edn. cert., 1988. Tchr. pre-sch. and elem. Middletown (Ohio) Pub. Schs., 1957-58, 71-80; tchr. Boone County Schs., Florence, Ky., 1980—; resource tchr. Ky. Internship Program, 1985-95. Fellow ABI Rsch. Assn. (life); mem. NEA, Nat. Assn. Edn. Young Children, Internat. Reading Assn., Nat. Coun. Tchrs. English, Ky. Edn. Assn., Boone County Edn. Assn., Assn. Childhood Edn. Internat., Nat. Coun. Tchrs. Math. Home: 2028 W Horizon Dr Hebron KY 41048-9600 Office: New Haven Elem Sch 10854 US Hwy 42 Union KY 41091-9502

COOK, KAREN LYNNE, auditor; b. Carbondale, Pa., Jan. 4, 1968; d. Walter Andrew and Yolanda Ann (Gentile) Scotchlas; m. Michael Joseph Cook, Oct. 24, 1992; children: Kayleigh Michael, Abigail Christine. BS, Wilkes Coll., 1989. Cert. cmty. bank internal auditor. Internal auditor Honesdale (Pa.) Nat. Bank, 1989—. Leader Scranton-Pocono coun. Girl Scouts U.S.A., 1994—. Mem. Am. Inst. Banking, Inst. Internal Auditors (audit com. 1995—). Republican. Roman Catholic. Office: Honesdale Nat Bank 733 Main St Honesdale PA 18431

COOK, KARYN ELAINE, editor; b. Long Beach, Calif., Apr. 17, 1971; d. Foster George and Eleanor Regina (Bagnoli) C. B, Calif. State U., Long Beach, 1993. Editorial asst. Offcl. Calif. Apt. Jour., Long Beach, 1992-93, Jour. of The Am. Assn. Gynecologic Laparoscopists, Sant Fe Springs, Calif., 1993-95; sr. editor Curant Comms., Marina del Rey, Calif., 1995—S. Mem. program com. Orange County coun. Girl Scouts U.S., 1995-96. Mem. NAFE, Sos. Profl. Journalists, Internat. Assn. Bus. Communicators. Republican. Roman Catholic. Office: Curant Comms 4676 Admiralty Way Ste 202 Marina Del Rey CA 90292

COOK, LINDA WALTERS, primary education educator; b. Corning, N.Y., Dec. 11, 1947; d. Richard B. and Helen S. (Vandervort) Walters; m. John J. Cook, June 12, 1971 (div. July 1988). BA, Alderson-Broaddus Coll., 1971; postgrad., W.Va. U., 1972—. Cert. elem. tchr. with specialization in lang. arts, S.C. Tchr. Davis-Thomas (W.Va.) Elem. Sch., 1972-87; tchr. North Myrtle Beach (S.C.) Primary Sch., 1987—, chmn. sci. dept., 1991—, team leader strategic planning, 1994—, math. stds. pilot tchr., 1995—. Sci. mini grantee W.Va. Edn. Fund, 1985. Mem. ASCD, S.C. ASCD, S.C. Assn. Children's Sci., Palmetto State Tchrs. Orgn., S.C. Coun. Tchrs. Math., Delta Kappa Gamma (sec.). Office: North Myrtle Beach Primary Sch 901 11th Ave N North Myrtle Beach SC 29582-2509

COOK, LYNN J., nursing educator; b. Newark, Aug. 18, 1950; d. George Roy Cook and Jean Aileen (Wegner) Cook Ainsley; m. Troy Wagner Ray, Mar. 11, 1995. Diploma, Mass. Gen. Hosp. Sch. Nursing, 1971; BSN, U. Va., 1975; MPH, Boston U. Sch. Pub. Health, 1986. RN, Pa.; cert. neonatal nurse practitioner. From staff nurse newborn ICU to nursing dir. for neonatal transport and perinatal outreach edn. U. Va., Charlottesville, 1973-83, nat. coord. for the perinatal continuing edn. program, 1983—; coord. perinatal edn. for Poland/Project HOPE, Millwood, Va., Krakow, Poland, 1986-89; lectr., gen. faculty U. Va. Sch. Medicine, 1992—; staff NICU Hosp. U. Pa., Phila., 1991-93; mem. Va. Perinatal Svcs. Adv. Coun. to Va. Dept. Health, 1979-83; fellow Project HOPE, Hangzhou, China, 1985. Author: Perinatal Continuing Education Program, 1978—; contbr. articles to profl. jours. Recipient outstanding instrnl. devel. award Nat. Soc. Performance & Instrn., 1979. Mem. AWHONN, Nat. Assn. Neonatal Nurses, Nat. Perinatal Assn., Phila. Perinatal Soc., Pa. Perinatal Assn., Del. Valley Assn. Neonatal Nurses. Office: U Va Health Sci Ctr Dept Pediatrics Box 386 Perinatal Cont Edn Program Charlottesville VA 22908

COOK, MARCY LYNN, mathematics educator, consultant; b. Culver City, Calif., Mar. 5, 1943; d. Lloyd Everett and Theresa J. (Matusek) Rude; m. Robert Lee Cook, Aug. 26, 1968; children: Bob, Jim. BA, U. Calif., Santa Barbara, 1964; MA, Stanford U., 1968. Tchr. 5th and 6th grades Sunnyvale (Calif.) Sch. Dist., 1964-67; tchr. Thessaloniki (Greece) Internat. H.S., 1968-70; tchr. primary grades Carmel (Calif.) Unified Sch. Dist., 1970-72; faculty of edn. Calif. State U., Fullerton, 1973-80; tchr. gifted and talented Newport Mesa Unified Sch. Dist., Calif., 1980-85; math. cons. Newport Beach, Calif., 1985—; lectr. in field nationally and internationally. Author over 100 books including Act It Out, Assessing Math Understanding, Basic Games, Book A, Book B, Clues and Cues, Communicating with Tiles, Contrasting Facts, Coop Thinking, Crack The Code Book A, Book B, Do Math, Do Talk It Over, Duo Do Dominoes, Follow the Clues, I Have, Justify Your Thinking, Numbers Please! Questions Please!, Postitive Math at Home and School, I, II, Primary Today is the Day, Reason Together, Show Me and Stump Me, Talk It Over, Think in Color, Tile Awhile, many others. Stanford U. fellow, 1968. Mem. Calif. Assn. Gifted, Calif. Math. Coun., Nat. Coun. Tchrs. Math., Assn. for Advancement of Internat. Edn., Nat. Coun. Suprs. of Math. Home and Office: PO Box 5840 Newport Beach CA 92662-5840

COOK, MARILYN JANE, elementary school educator; b. Covington, Ky., Jan. 27, 1948; d. Ralph Benjamin and Jane Elizabeth (Doddy) C.; 1 child, Elisabeth Anne Brundrett-Cook. BA, St. Andrews Presbyn. Coll., 1970; MDiv, Austin Presbyn. Theol. Sem., 1974; MS in Curriculum and Instrn., Corpus Christi State U., 1992; MS in Ednl. Adminstrn., Tex. A&M, Corpus Christi, 1996. Cert. tchr., Tex.; master tchr. Nat. Tchr. Tng. Inst. Edn. dir. Northwood Presbyn. Ch., San Antonio, 1976-77; mgr. Summer Place, Port Aransas, Tex., 1977-78; adminstrv. asst. Crisis Intervention Svc., Corpus Christi, 1978-79; mgr. Nueces County Mental Health/Mental Retardation, Corpus Christi, 1979-81; educator Sacred Heart Sch., Rockport, Tex., 1982-83, Port Aransas Sch. Dist., 1983—; mem. leadership team Project 2061, Tex., 1989-95, Tex. Ctr. Sci., Math. & Tech., 1995—; mem. manuscript and rev. panel Sci. and Children jour., Arlington, Va., 1991—, dist. and campus site based decision making teams; insvc. facilitator Tex. Elem. Sci. program; Title I sch. support team ESC region 2; adj. Tex. Essential Knowledge & Skills English/Lang. Arts. Contbr. articles to profl. jours. Troop leader Jr. Girl Scouts, Girl Scouts USA, Port Aransas, 1992—; bd. dirs. Keep Port Aransas Beautiful, 1990-93, Dewey Dreyer Cmty. Day Care, Port Aransas, 1988-90; elder Cmty. Presbyn. Ch., Port Aransas; bd. dirs. Corpus Christi Ballet, 1996—. Recipient Sadie Ray Gaff award of merit Keep Tex. Beautiful, 1990, 92. Mem. NSTA (presch./elem. program rep. area conv. 1995), AAUW, Tex. ASCD, Tex. Assn. for Environ. Edn. (bd. dirs. 1991-93), Tex. Coun. for Elem. Sci. (area dir. 1993-94, bd. dirs. 1993—, Dorothy Lohman award 1994, Dillo Press editor jour. 1995—), Coun. for Elem. Sci. Internat., Sci. Tchrs. Assn. Tex., Tex. State Reading Assn., Nat. Project Wet Crew, Orton Dyslexia Soc., Coastal Bend Art Edn. Assn., Kappa Delta Pi. Office: Port Aransas Ind Sch Dist 100 S Station St Port Aransas TX 78373

COOK, MARTHA JANE, educator, counselor; b. Canton, Ohio, Feb. 23, 1926; d. Harry Alfred and Flossie Faye (Haynam) Barber; m. Marvin Lester Cook, June 5, 1949; 1 child, Mark Dennis. BS in Edn., Ohio State U., 1947; MEd, Kent State U., 1962; EdD, U. Akron, 1978. Cert. high sch. English and sci. tchr., high sch and elem. music tchr., prin.; lic. high sch. and elem. profl. counselor; nat. cert. counselor. Tchr. Fairhope Sch., Louisville, Ohio, 1947-49, Sandyville (Ohio) Elem. Sch., 1949-50, East Sparta (Ohio) Elem. Sch., 1950-54; comptometer operator Hoover Co., North Canton, Ohio, 1949-50; tchr., counselor Sandy Valley H.S., Magnolia, Ohio, 1958-62; counselor Canton South H.S., 1962-80; prof. grad. sch. profl. counseling Malone Coll., Canton, 1980—. Author: Bibliotherapy, 1978, Grammar for Professionals, 1981. Treas., tchr., dir. choir East Sparta Christian Ch., 1954-74; mem. Pike Twp. Zoning Bd. Appeals, 1985—; mem. Canton Loan Fund, 1988—; vice chmn. bd. dirs. Canton Christian Home, 1989—. Named Counselor of Yr., Ohio Sch. Counselors Assn., 1974, Citizen of Yr., KC, 1981, Outstanding Acad. Advisor, Am. Coll. Testing Svc., 1984, Outstanding Educator, Canton YWCA, 1990. Mem. ACA, Stark County Counselors Assn. (founder, pres.), Kappa Delta Pi, Phi Delta Kappa. Republican. Home: 8395 Maplehurst SE East Sparta OH 44626

COOK, MARY GOOCH, elementary school educator; b. Columbus, Ga., May 1, 1943; d. Joe Lee and Ella Mae (Crimes) Gooch; m. Robert James Cook Sr.; children: Robert James Jr., Kevin Scott. BS, Ala. State Coll., 1965, M in Edn., reading spl., 1973; cert. in elem. edn., Tuskegee U., summer 1968; cert. reading specialist, Ga. State U., 1973; cert. edn. specialist, Troy State U., 1991. Cert. tchr., Ga. Tchr. Fox Elem. Sch., Columbus, Ga., 1973-94, Gentian Elem. Sch., Columbus, Ga., 1994—. Arbitrator BBB, Columbus, 1989-95; cmty. leader tchr. Combined Cmty. South Columbus, 1988-91; mem. voter registration com. Bd. Registration, Columbus, 1990-95; mem. support youth activities com. Columbus Cmty. Ctr., 1994. Mem. AAUW, Nat. Coun. Tchrs. Math., Internat. Reading Assn., Muscogee Assn. Educators (faculty rep. Fox Elem. Sch. 1973-94, Gentian Elem. Sch. 1994-96), Sigma Rho Sigma (pres. Montgomery, Ala. chpt. 1964—), Kappa Delta Pi. Home: 4655 Illini Dr Columbus GA 31907-6613 Office: Gentian Elem Sch 4201 Primrose Rd Columbus GA 31907-1156

COOK, MARY MARGARET, steamfitter; b. Royal Oak, Mich., Apr. 28, 1944; d. John Patrick and Agnes Hannah (Anderson) McMahon; m. Barney Albert Cahill, Aug. 19, 1967 (div. Apr. 1971); m. Frank Melvin Cook, Jan. 26, 1974. BA in Elem. Edn., Ariz. State U., 1971; cert. United Assn. instr., Mich. State U., 1990; Cert., Ariz. Community Coll. Cert. elem. tchr., Ohio, Ariz.; lic. mech. journeyman. Tchr. St. Agnes Elem. Sch., Phoenix, 1967-71, Bevis Elem. Sch., Cin., 1971-73; GED instr. Scottsdale, Ariz., 1975-78; steamfitter United Assn. Local 469, Phoenix, 1978—; instr. apprentices Rio Salado C.C., Phoenix, 1984-90; math. cons. Ariz. Dept. Edn., 1988-90; state dir. AFL-CIO Apprenticeship Awareness Program, 1990-92. Chair State Con. Emerging Careers for Women, 1993—; mem. Apprenticeship Adv. Coun., 1990—, chair, 1995—; mem. Gov.'s Commn. on Nontraditional Employment for Women; Ariz. dir. Project Nontraditional Assistance and Info. Link, 1992—. Mem. Ariz. State U. Alumni Assn. (life), Internat. Tng. in Comm. Club (sec. 1988-89, pres. 1989-90, del. to coun. 1990-91, coun. v.p. 1992-93, coun. newsletter editor 1991-92, region newsletter editor 1994-95). Home: 15827 N 23rd Dr Phoenix AZ 85023-4136

COOK, NANCY W., state legislator; b. May 11, 1936. Ed. U. Del. Mem. Del. Senate from 15th Dist.; mem. Kent County Dem. Com. Democrat. Home: PO Box 127 Kenton DE 19955-0127 Office: Del State Senate Legislative Hall Dover DE 19901*

COOK, NORMA BAKER, consulting company executive; b. North Wilkesboro, N.C.; d. Charles Chauncey and Mildred Baker. BA in Bus. and Econs., Meredith Coll., 1963; postgrad., Alliance Francaise, N.Y.C., 1980-83, N.Y. Sch. Interior Design, 1983-84. Cert. tchr., N.C. Pres., owner John Robert Powers Sch. Fashion Careers, Raleigh, N.C., 1971-87, NBC of Raleigh, Inc., 1979—; mem. adv. commn. N.C. Pvt. Bus., Trade and Corr. Schs., 1986; exec. distbr. NuSkin Internat., 1988—; pvt. bus. broker, 1991-93; instr. continuing edn. Meredith Coll., Raleigh, 1994—; pres. Fast Forward Concepts tm, 1996—. Author articles on fashion and success motivation for women. Established Norma Baker Cook Art Scholarship at Meredith Coll., 1989; vice chmn. Meredith Coll. Bd. Assocs., 1991-92; charter mem. Meredith Coll. Heritage Soc., Raleigh. Recipient Svc. award Am. Cancer Soc., 1978. Mem. AFTRA, The Fashion Group, Inc., Greater Raleigh C. of C. (arts com.), North Raleigh Civitans. Office: 3725 National Dr Ste 118 Raleigh NC 27612

COOK, REBECCA MCDOWELL, state official; m. John Lakin Cook; children: Hunter, Morgan. BA with honors, U. O., 1972. Sec. of state State of Mo. Office: PO Box 778 Jefferson City MO 65102*

COOK, SUSAN FARWELL, alumni relations director; b. Boston, Apr. 28, 1953; d. Benjamin and Beverly (Brooks) Conant; m. James Samuel Cook Jr., Aug. 17, 1985; children: Emily Farwell, David McKendree. AB, Colby Coll., 1975. Bank teller Boston 5 Cent Savs. Bank, 1975-76; asst. technician plan cost John Hancock Mut. Life Ins. Co., Boston, 1976-77, technician plan cost, 1977-78, sr. technician plan cost, 1978-79, asst. mgr. group pension plan cost, 1979-81; assoc. dir. alumni rels. Colby Coll., Waterville, Maine, 1981-86; dir. alumni rels. Colby Coll., Waterville, 1986—; co-dir. adv. bd. women's studies Colby Coll., 1987-89, adv. women's group, 1987-89. Bd. dirs., newsletter sec. Literacy Vols. Maine, Waterville, 1986-89, 91-92, v.p., 1995—; bd. dirs. Congress Lake Assns., Yarmouth, Maine, 1988-92; treas. Pitcher Pond Improvement Assn., 1988-95; treas. Gagnon/100 Campaign, 1996. Mem. AAUW (sec. Waterville br. 1989-91, pres. 1991-93, co-pres. 1993-95), Coun. Advancement and Support of Edn., CASE Dist. I (exec. bd. dirs. 1994—, sec. 1996—). Home: 6 Pray Ave Waterville ME 04901-5359 Office: Colby Coll 4310 Mayflower Hill Waterville ME 04901

COOK, VIVIAN, state legislator; b. Rock Hill, S.C., May 23, 1937; d. McDonald Eaves and Eva Phillips; m. John Cook; 1 child, Reginald. Grad., DeFrans Bus. Inst. Mem. alcoholism and drug abuse, commerce, industry and econ. devel., corps., authorities and commns., housing, ins., majority steering coms. N.Y. State Assembly, Albany, 1991—; dist. leader, Queens County; founder Cmty. Edn. Resource Ctr.; chairwoman Queens County Dem. Com.; mem. Dem. Nat. Com., Queens County Exec. Com.; del. Dem. Nat. Conv., 1988, 92. Recipient Sojourner Truth award Nat. Assn. Negro Bus. and Profl. Women's Club, Inc., Sr. Citizens award 113th Precinct, Cmty. Svc. award 103 and 113th Precincts, Sutphin Blvd. Civic Assn. award, Cmty. Svc. award Citizens for Jenkins, 10-Yr. Cmty. Bd. Svc. award City of N.Y., Cmty. Svc. award Neighborhood Coun., Mother's Day award Springfield Gardens, Commn. Svc. & Leadership award NYS Martin Luther King, Jr. Inst., Polit. Action Com. award P.E.F., Little League award Rochdal Village. Mem. Allied Regular Dem. Club, Inc. (founder, exec.), South Ozone Park Women's Assn. (founder, chairperson bd. dirs.). Office: 14215 Rockaway Blvd South Ozone Park NY 11436 also: NY State Assembly State Capitol Albany NY 12224*

COOKE, CONSTANCE BLANDY, librarian; b. Woodbury, N.J., Mar. 7, 1935; d. John Chase and Josephine Spond (Black) Blandy; m. Len B. Cooke Jr., Jan. 7, 1978 (div. 1987). B.A., U. Pa., 1956; M.A., U. Denver, 1957. Adult cons. Onondaga Library System, Syracuse, N.Y., 1965-66; asst. dir. Mt. Vernon (N.Y.) Public Library, 1966-75; dep. dir. Queens Borough Public Library, Jamaica, N.Y., 1975-79; dir. Queens Borough Public Library, 1980-94; founder pres. Literacy Vols. Mt. Vernon, 1972-74. Trustee METRO, 1980-81, v.p., 1985-88, pres., 1988-91; mem. N.Y. State Libr. Svcs. and Constrn. Act Adv. Coun., 1982-88, chmn., 1986-87; bd. dirs. Queens Coun. on the Arts, 1988-94, v.p., 1989-93; bd. dirs. Queens Mus. of Art, 1988—, v.p., 1994-96, pres. 1996—. Mem. ALA, N.Y. Libr. Assn., Queens C. of C. (dir. 1982—), Circumnavigators Club. Democrat. Episcopalian. Home: 20920 18th Ave Flushing NY 11360-1452

COOKE, EILEEN DELORES, retired librarian; b. Mpls., Dec. 7, 1928; d. Walter William and Mary Frances C. BSLS, Coll. St. Catherine, 1952; extension courses, U. Minn. Bookmobile libr. Mpls. Pub. Libr., 1952-57; br. asst. Queensborough Pub. Libr., 1957-58; br. asst., hosp. libr., pub. rels. specialist Mpls. Pub. Libr., 1958-63; asst. dir. Washington office ALA, 1964-68, asso. dir., 1968-69, dep. dir., 1969-72, dir., 1972-94, ret., 1994; lectr. U. Mich., Ann Arbor; mem. steering com. White Conf. on Libr. and Info. Svcs. Task Force. Contbr. articles to profl. jours. Mem. bd. visitors Sch. Libr. and Info. Sci., Cath. U. Mem. ALA (hon.), Minn. Libr. Assn., D.C. Libr. Assn., Joint Coun. Ednl. Telecom. (past pres.), Higher Edn. Group Washington, World Future Soc., Women's Nat. Book Assn., Home and Sch. Inst., Nat. Adv. Coun., Minn. Ctr. for the Book (bd. dirs. 1995—).

COOKE, JOAN ELLEN, healthcare executive, consultant; b. Phila., Sept. 2, 1953; d. Joseph Thomas and Lillian Josephine (Tjarks) Cooke. AS, Columbus (Ohio) State U., 1973; BS, Franklin U., 1980. Supr. State Health Planing and Devel. Agy. Ohio Dept. Health, 1978-80; account exec. Nationwide Health Care, 1980-82; with HealthAm. Corp., 1982-86; exec. dir. HealthAm. Corp., Columbus, Ohio, 1984-85; v.p. ops. Health Am. Corp., Columbus, Ohio, 1985-86; sr. v.p. Vol. Health Plan, Nashville, 1986-87; exec. v.p. Managed Care Products, Inc., Columbus, 1987-89; regional strategic health planner Humana, Inc., Miami, Fla., 1989-90; assoc. exec. dir. S.W. Fla. market Humana, Inc., 1990-91, assoc. exec. dir. South Fla. region, 1991—. Author: The Development of an Efficient Health Care System, Planning Guidance to State and local Health Planning Agencies, Strategic Five-Year Health Plan for the State of Florida. Mem. NAFE, Group Health Assn. Am., Smithsonian Assocs. Office: Humana Med Plan 3400 Lakeside Dr Bldg 2B Miramar FL 33027-3238

COOKE, LYNNE CATHERINE, curator; b. Geelong, Victoria, Australia; came to U.S., 1989; d. Allan Stewart and Beryl Edith (Agg) C. BA with honors, U. Melbourne, Victoria, 1974; MA, London U., 1979; PhD, U. London, 1987. Lectr. dept. art history London U., 1979-88; co-curator Mus. Art Carnegie Internat./Carnegie Mus. of Art, Pitts., 1991; curator Dia Ctr. for Arts, N.Y.C., 1991—; artistic dir. Biennale of Sydney, Australia, 1995-96; mus./exhbn. panelist Nat. Endowment for Arts, Washington, 1996. Mem. editl. bd. Burlington Mag., London, 1990—; contbr. articles, essays to mags., numerous exhbn. catalogues. Recipient award Gt. Britain-Sasakawa Found., 1987; Smithsonian fellow Hirshhorn Mus./Smithsonian Inst., 1989. Mem. Internat. Coun. Mus., Art Table. Office: Dia Ctr for Arts 542 W 22d St New York NY 10012-3203

COOKE, SARA MULLIN GRAFF, daycare provider, kindergarten teacher, doctor's assistant; b. Phila., Dec. 29, 1935; d. Charles Henry and Elizabeth (Mullin) Brandt Graff; m. Peter Fischer Cooke, June 29, 1963 (div. July 1994); children: Anna Cooke Smith, Peter Fischer Jr., Elizabeth Cooke Haskins, Sara Reynolds, Laina Koerting. AA, Bennett Coll., 1955; BE in Child Edn., Westchester State Tchrs. Coll., 1956. Asst. to tchr. 1st grade The Woodlyn Sch., 1956-58; tchr. Sara Bircher's Kindergarten, Germantown, Pa., 1958-62, Chestnut Hill (Pa.) Acad., 1962-63, Tarleton Sch., Devon, Pa., 1963-64; with F.C.I. Mktg. Co-ordinators Inc., N.Y.C., New Canaan, Conn., 1980-86; fundraiser Children's Hosp., Phila., 1989-92, pres. women's com., 1987-88; coord., master of ceml. ceremonies Phila. Soc. for Preservation Landmarks, 1991-93; coord. Elderhostel Program Landmarks Soc., 1992-93; pvt. day caretaker Spl. Care, Inc., 1988—; pvt. daycare and dr.'s asst., 1994—. Mem. bd. aux. Children's Hosp. Phila., 1970-76, mem. women's bd., 1977—, pres., 1987-88; mem. commonwealth bd. Med. Coll. Pa., 1984—, mem. Gimbel award com., 1994; alt. del. Rep. Nat. Conv., 1992. Mem. Pa. Assn. Hosp. Auxs. (health rep.) Nat. Soc. Colonial Dames (garden com. 1988—), Ch. Women's Assn. (past pres.), Alumnae Assn. Madeira Sch. (class sec., class agt.), Phila. Cricket Club, Jr. League Garden Club. Republican. Episcopalian. Home and Office: 3421 Warden Dr Philadelphia PA 19129-1417

COOKE, SARAH BELLE, health care facility professional, farmer; b. Murfreesboro, Tenn., Sept. 14, 1910; d. Robert Jesse and Mattie (Neal) C. BS, Middle Tenn. State U., 1961. Cert. tchr., Tenn. Patient funds clk. VA Med. Ctr., Murfreesboro, 1943; voucher auditor VA Med. Supply Svc., Murfreesboro, 1945-46, purchasing agt., 1946-83, contracting officer, 1984-89; now ret. Pres. VA Fed. Employees Credit Union, Murfreesboro, 1965-86. Mem. AAUW (pres. Murfreesboro chpt. 1977-79), Tenn. Credit Union League (br. pres. 1973-79). Democrat. Mem. Church of Christ. Home: 5078 Sulphur Springs Rd Murfreesboro TN 37129-7206

COOKSON, LINDA MARIE, elementary education educator; b. Emporia, Kans., Feb. 15, 1944; d. Fred Rolum and Mary Lavern (Bennett) C. BS, Emporia State U., 1966, MS, 1970. Cert. tchr., Kans. Tchr. 2d grade Howard Wilson Sch., Leavenworth, Kans., 1966-67; tchr. 5th and intermediate Unified Sch. Dist. 253, Emporia, 1967-74; youth advisor Lyon County Youth Ctr., Emporia, summer 1975; lectr. in edn. Emporia State U., 1975-80; art tchr. K-8 Unified Sch. Dist. 251, Admire and Americus, Kans., 1980-81; art and title I tchr. K-8 Unified Sch. Dist. 251, Americus, 1981-82, tchr. 6th grade, 1982-84, art tchr. K-8, 1984-94, comms. tchr. mid. sch., 1994—. Mem. PTO, 1980—; pres., life mem. PTA, 1966-80. Mem. NEA, Kans. Nat. Edn. Assn. (Sunflower Uniserv region 1 adminstrv. bd. 1995—), Americus Site Based Coun. (sec. 1994-96). Republican. Methodist. Home: 645 Wilson St Emporia KS 66801-2452

COOL, KIM PATMORE, retail executive, needlework consultant; b. Cleve., Feb. 1, 1940; d. Herman Chester Earl and Eva (Geneau) Patmore; m. Kenneth Adams Cool Jr., Mar. 12, 1963; 1 child, Heidi Adams. BA in Econs., Sweet Briar Coll., 1962; postgrad., Case Western Reserve U., 1962-63. Test adminstr. Pradco, Cleve., 1962-63; pvt. needlework cons. Cleve., 1970-72; retail v.p., treas., custom designer And Sew On, Inc., Cleve., 1973-92, exec. v.p., treas., 1982-92; v.p. Shure Stiches Inc., 1991-92; owner Shure Stitches, Inc., Cleve., 1992-93, The Hare Necessities, Venice, Fla., Germany, 1994—, Hare Necessities Craft & Needlework Mfg., Venice, Fla.; lectr. bus. seminars Nat. Needlework Assn.; tchr. Wellesley Coll. Continuing Edn. Program, 1986; pub. Fredericktown Press, Md.; designer and mktg. assoc. Kappioe OriginalsLtd., 1988-93. Artist collector quality custom hand-painted canvases; co-author: How to Market Needlepoint--The Definitive Manual, 1988, Easy Macrame, 1990, Basic Macrame, 1990, Wearable Macrame, 1990, Playmate Dolls to Stitch, 1991, Pillows and Purses to Stitch, 1991, Needlepoint from Start to Finish, 1992, Pathway to Profit in the Needlework Industry, 1995; homes corr. Venice (Fla.) Gondolier, 1995—. Rep. committeeman Cuyahoga County, Shaker Heights, Ohio, 1964-72. Regional Curling champion, 1987-88. Mem. USFSA (competitions com., ea. vice chair precision, judges edn. tng. com., nat. vice chair for precision), Nat. Needlework Assn. (lectr. seminar on mktg. needlepoint, seminars on buying and merchandising, 1988—, charter assoc. retail), Embroiderers Guild of Cleve. (bd. dirs. 1980-82), Am. Profl. Needlework Retailers, S.E. Yarncrafters Guild (conductor merchandising seminars 1989—), Nat. Standards Coun. Am. Embroiderers, U.S. Figure Skating Assn. (nat. precision judge, sr. competition judge, gold test judge 1967—), Sweet Briar Coll. Alumnae Assn. (nat. bd. dirs., upper MW region, 1965-66, class sec. 1988-92), Cleve. Skating Club, Mayfield Country Club. Mem. United Ch. of Christ. Home and Office: The Hare Necessities 312 Shore Rd Venice FL 34285-1257

COOL, MARY L., elementary education educator; b. Buffalo, Dec. 7, 1954; d. Paul G. and Dorothy R. (O'Brien) Wailand; m. Ronald J. Cool, June 23, 1979; children: Logan Elizabeth, Colin Jeffery. BS in Elem. Edn. cum laude, SUNY, Fredonia, 1976. Cert. tchr., N.Y., Fla. Tchr. grade 1 Buffalo, N.Y., 1976-77; tchr. grade 5 Orange County, Orlando, Fla., 1979-85; tchr. grade 1, ESEA Title I head tchr. Manatee County, Myakka City, Fla., 1977-79; tchr. grade 5, media specialist Volusia County, Osteen, Fla., 1985-89; intermediate resource tchr. S.W. Volusia County, Fla., 1989-91; dist. elem. resource tchr., elem. tchr. specialist Volusia County Schs., Fla., 1991—; grade lever chair, sci. chair, reading chair, facilitative leader, coop. learning trainer, tchr. coach, tech. edn. coach, tchr. asst. coord., student success team coord. Volusia County Schs.; ednl. cons. Scholastic, Inc., Sports Illus. for Kids, Kids Discover, Marvel Comics, Miami Mus. Arts and Scis. Mem. ASCD, AAUW, Nat. Coalition for Sex Equity in Edn., Nat. Staff Devel. Coun., Kappa Delta Pi. Home: 1566 Gregory Dr Deltona FL 32738-6159 Office: PO Box 2410 Daytona Beach FL 32115-2410

COOLEY, FANNIE RICHARDSON, counselor educator, consultant; b. Tunnel Springs, Ala., July 4, 1924; d. Willie C. Richardson and Emma Jean (McCorvey) Stallworth. B.S., Tuskegee Inst., 1947, M.S., 1951; Ph.D., U. wis., 1969. Cert. counselor. Asst. instr. Tuskegee U., Ala., 1947-48, prof. counseling, 1969—; instr. Alcorn A&M Coll., Lorman, Miss., 1948-51; asst. prof. Ala. A&M Coll., Normal, 1951-62, assoc. prof., 1964-65; grad. fellow Purdue U., West Lafayette, Ind., 1962-64; house fellow U. Wis., Madison, 1965-69; cons. VA Med. Ctr. Tuskegee, 1969—. Mem. AAUW, AAUP, Am. Assn. Counseling and Devel. (Disting. Svc. award 1985, bd. dirs.), Ala. Assn. Counseling and Devel. (pres. 1976-77, Svc. award 1978-79), Ala. Assn. for Counselor Edn. (pres. 1985-86), Assn. Specialist in Group Work (pres. 1989-90), Internat. Platform Assn., Chi Sigma Iota. Episcopalian. Home: 802C Ave A Tuskegee Institute AL 36088-2496 Office: Tuskegee Inst Dept Counseling and Student Devel Thrasher Hall Tuskegee AL 36088

COOLEY, HILARY ELIZABETH, real estate manager; b. Leesburg, Va., May 8, 1953; d. Thomas McIntyre and Helen Strong (Stringham) C. BA in Econs., U. Pitts., 1976; postgrad. in bus. adminstrn., Hood Coll., Frederick, Md., 1985-90. Mgr. Montgomery Ward, Frederick, 1976-80, merchandiser, 1980-82; asst. bus. mgr. Arundel Communications, Leesburg, 1982-84; bus. mgr. Loudoun Country Day Sch., Leesburg, 1984-85, bd. trustees, 1989-93, sec. bd. trustees, 1989-90, v.p., 1990-92; contr. Foxcroft Sch., Middleburg, Va., 1984-86, 91-92; corr. Loudoun Times Mirror, Leesburg, 1985-87; estate mgr. Delta Farm Inc., Leesburg, 1988—. Area chmn. Keep Loudoun Beautiful, Middleburg, 1983-90, pres., bd. dirs. 1993-96; pres. Waterford (Va.) Citizens' Assn., 1985-86, Waterford Players, 1986-88; bd. dirs. Waterford Found., Inc., 1992-95, pres. 1995—; bd. dirs. Loudoun Hist. Soc., Leesburg, 1987, Mt. Zion Ch. Preservation Assn., 1996—. Mem. Penn Hall Alumnae Ann. (pres. 1987-92). Democrat. Episcopalian. Home and Office: Delta Farm PO Box 234 Philomont VA 22131-0234

COOLEY, LORALEE COLEMAN, professional storyteller; b. Charleston, Ill., Jan. 17, 1943; d. Leland Henry and Lorene Madge (Carpenter) C.; m. Edwin Mark Cooley, July 1, 1967; foster children: Jenni, Gail, Bridgette, Carla. BA, Ea. Ill. U., 1965; postgrad., So. Bapt. Theol. Sem., Ky., 1965-67, Ariz. State U., 1972-74; MA, Antioch U., 1994. Piano, music tchr. various schs., 1967-69; women's program dir. Sta. WDXB-AM, Chattanooga, 1969-70; tutoring svcs. coord. Newton Community Ctr., Chattanooga, 1969-71; asst. editor New Age mag., Washington, 1971-72; publicity coord. Firebird Lake/Watersports World, Phoenix, 1975; asst. libr. Casa Grande (Ariz.) Pub. Libr., 1975-77; profl. storyteller Casa Grande, 1977-78, Richmond, Va., 1978-79, Atlanta, 1979-88, Anderson, S.C., 1988-94; Pampa, Tex., 1994—; publicity dir. Callanwolde Fine Arts Ctr., Atlanta, 1987; toured Republic of Ga., Newly-Ind. States, started rsch. project on Georgian Folklore, 1989. Co-chmn. Casa Grande Bicentennial Com., 1974-76; bd. dirs. Genesis House, Pampa, M.K. Brown Mcpl. Auditorium, Pampa. Named Miss Louisville, 1966 (preliminary to Miss Am. pageant). Mem. AAUW, Nat. Storytelling Assn., So. Order Storytellers (founder 1982), Profl. Spkrs. Assn. of S.W., Pampa Fine Arts Assn. (bd., pres. 1996-97). Democrat. Presbyterian. Home and Studio: 410 Buckler Ave Pampa TX 79065-6207

COOLEY, NANCY JO, university administrator; b. Cadillac, Mich., June 28, 1952; d. Gordon and Frances Perry (Hiller) Berghorst; m. Jeffery Lynn, Aug. 25, 1973. BS in Edn., Ctrl. Mich. U., Mt. Pleasant, 1974; MA in Tchg., Oakland U., Rochester, Mich., 1977; PhD, U. Mich., 1988. Lic. tchr. grades K-8, ages 0-25 spl. edn. Tchr. Lapeer (Mich.) Pub. Schs., 1974-78; tchr. cons. Kearsley Schs., Flint, Mich., 1978-81; dir. Cooley Reading Clinic, Lapeer, Mich., 1981-88; faculty tchr. edn. Ctrl. Mich. U., Mt. Pleasant, 1989-93, dept. chair, 1993-95, spl. asst. to provost, 1995, asst. vice provost, 1995—; mem., past adv. bd. Mich. Coun. Presvc. Edn., Detroit, 1990-96;mem. Tchr. Edn. Admissions Bd., Mt. Pleasant, 1995-96. Vol. Forfar Biol. Field Sta., Andros Island, Bahamas, 1991, Playscape, Mt. Pleasant, 1994. Mem. Internat. Soc. Tech. Edn., Assn. Managing and Using Info. Tech. in Higher Edn., Mich. Assn. Computer Users in Learning, Internat. Reading Assn., Mich. Assn. for Colls. of Tchr. Edn. (treas. 1995—), Phi Beta Delta. Office: Ctrl Mich U Warriner 312 Mount Pleasant MI 48858

COOLEY, WENDY, judge, lawyer; b. Birmingham, Ala., Jan. 1, 1948. BS, Ea. Mich. U., 1968; MA, U. Mich., 1971; JD, U. Detroit, 1982. cert. spl. edn. tchr., Mich. Spl. edn. cons. Detroit Bd. Edn., 1971-80; assoc. Kirk & McCargo, Detroit, 1982-84; judge Mich. 36th Dist. Ct., Detroit, 1984—; host TV show Winning Ways CBS; instr. Wayne County C.C., Detroit, 1979-84. Contbr. articles to various publs. Bd. dirs. U.Detroit, Wayne County Cmty., Wayne County Econ. Growth; speaker various ch. and cmty. groups, Detroit area; radio hostess Sta. WNIC, Detroit; active Leadership Detroit, Second Ebeneezer Bapt. Ch.; mem. Mich. Martin L. Ling Holiday Commn.; apptd. to Mich. Correction Officer Tng. Coun., 1987. Mem. Mich. Dist. Judges Assn., Mich. State Bar Assn., Eastern Star, Delta Sigma Theta. Home: PO Box 32687 Detroit MI 48226 Office: Mich 36th Dist Ct 421 Madison St Detroit MI 48226-2358

COOLIDGE, LAETITIA KELLY, artist; b. Belair, Mo., Sept. 13, 1904; d. Howard Atwood Kelly and Laetitia Bredow; m. Winthrop Knowlton Coolidge, July 31, 1935 (div. 1945); children: Laetitia, Deborah Jean, Olga, Dexter, Carol. Attended, Bryn Mawr Sch., Balt., 1911-18, Oldfields, Glencoe, Md., 1918-19; MA, Master's Sch., Dobbs Ferry on Hudson, N.Y., 1919-21; degree, Gen. Design Ind. Inst., Balt., 1926. artist in charge Jr. League, Balt., 1925-35. Artist: (watercolor) Goldilocks, 1912 (Tuck prize 1912); exhbns. include Rancho Bernardo, San Diego, 1994, Presly Cmty. Ch., Rancho Bernardo, 1995, 96, Towson Md. Library. Active Seven Oaks Cmty. Ctr., 1980-95. Republican. Presbyn. Home: 12730 Monte Vista Rd Poway CA 92128

COOLIDGE, MARTHA, film director; b. New Haven, Aug. 17, 1946; m. Michael Backes. Ed. RISD, Columbia U. Dir. films: Valley Girl, 1983, The City Girl, 1983, Joy of Sex, 1984, Real Genius, 1985, Plain Clothes, 1988, Rambling Rose, 1991, Crazy in Love, 1991, Lost in Yonkers, 1993, Angie, 1994, Three Wishes, 1995; dir. TV shows and TV films Sledge Hammer pilot episode, 3 episodes The Twilight Zone, CBS miniseries The Winners, Roughhouse pilot episode, 1988, Trenchcoat in Paradise, 1989, Bare Essentials, 1991, Crazy in Love, 1992; dir. documentaries David: On and Off, 1972, More Than A School, 1973, Old Fashioned Woman, 1974, Not A Pretty Picture, 1976 (all winners Am. Film Festival awards). Office: care Beverly Magid Guttman Assoc 118 S Beverly Dr Ste 201 Beverly Hills CA 90212-3016

COOLIDGE, MARTHA HENDERSON, volunteer environmental and East Asian specialist; b. Cambridge, Mass., Jan. 26, 1925; d. Robert Graham and Lucy (Gregory) Henderson; m. Harold Jefferson Coolidge, May 26, 1972 (dec. Feb. 1985). Student, Smith Coll., 1942-43; BA, Radcliffe Coll., 1946; MA, Harvard U., 1956, postgrad., 1956-57, 58-60. Asst. sec. China Program Harvard U., Cambridge, Mass., 1948; adminstr. Fulbright Program Inst. Internat. Edn., N.Y.C., 1949-50, assoc. dir. GARIOA program, 1950-51; staff mem. Ctr. for Internat. Studies at MIT, Cambridge, 1953-54; exec. sec. The Japan Soc. of Boston, 1958-62; asst. to mng. dir., dir. film services Ednl. Devel. Inc., Watertown, Mass., 1963-65; program dir. for internat. exchanges Smithsonian Instn., Washington, 1965-66; edn. assoc. Cen. Atlantic Regional Edn. Labs., Washington, 1966-68; sr. assoc. for edn. The Conservation Found., Washington, 1968-70; ednl. assoc. Pub. Broadcasting Environ. Ctr., Washington, 1970-71; vol., bd. dirs. Coolidge Ctr. for Environ. Leadership, Cambridge, 1983-94, vice chmn., 1983-85; assoc. to prof. Harvard U., Cambridge, 1988-91, assoc in rsch. Fairbank Ctr. East Asian Rsch., 1992—; mem. temp. staff student adaption study MIT, 1962-63; cons. social studies curriculum project Harvard Grad. Sch. Edn., Cambridge, 1964-65. Author: (P.R.C. sect., bibliography for John K. Fairbank) China: A New History, 1992, (with John King Fairbank and Richard J. Smith) H.B. Morse, Customs Commissioner and Historian of China, 1995; contbg. author: Fairbank Remembered, 1992; author: (annotated bibliography) Prospects for Communist China, 1954; contbr. articles to publs. in field. Propr., Boston Athenaeum; affiliate Dudley House, Harvard U.; mem. coun. New Eng. Aquarium, Boston; active Quebec-Labrador Found. Corp., Ipswich, Mass. Grantee, Yenching Inst., 1958-59, Radcliffe Coll., 1955-57; Fulbright rsch. fellow Tokyo U., 1957-58. Fellow Royal Soc. Arts (London); mem. Fragment Soc., Assn. Asian Studies, Internat. House of Japan, Women's Travel Club, Squam Lake Assn., Squam Lakes Conservation Soc., Boston Mus. Fine Arts. Episcopalian. Home: 19 Brewster St Cambridge MA 02138-2203 also: Harvard U Fairbank Ctr for East Asian Rsch 1737 Cambridge St Cambridge MA 02138-3016

COOLIDGE, RITA, singer; b. Nashville, May 1, 1945; m. Kris Kristofferson, Aug. 19, 1973 (div. June 1980); 1 dau., Casey. Grad., Fla. State U. Singer with Delaney & Bonnie Bramlett, Joe Cocker, Leon Russell, Kris Kristofferson, also soloist; film appearance: Pat Garrett and Billy the Kid, 1973, A Star is Born, 1980; recordings include Anytime...Anywhere, 1978 (multi-platium), Love Me Again (recipient Grammy awards), Greatest Hits, Love Sessions, 1992, Out of the Blues, A&M Classics vol. 5, Cherokee, Music for the Native Americans; performed: title song All Time High in Octopussy, Love Came for Me in Splash; first female video jockey on Video Hits One (cable TV); rec. artist appearing regularly on MTV Networks; performed a tribute to Native Am. music and dance during the festivities of 1996 Atlanta Olympics. Office: care Shocorp Internat Ltd 11684 Ventura Blvd # 899 Studio City CA 91604-2613*

COOMBS, BETSY JEWETT, artist, conservationist; b. Spokane, Wash., Aug. 13, 1954; d. George Frederick and Lucille Winifred (McIntyre) Jewett; m. David Kemp Coombs, Dec. 8, 1984; children: Sarah Elizabeth, David Frederick. AB in Biology, Dartmouth Coll., 1976; MES, Yale U., 1982, MPPM, 1982; postgrad., Corcoran Sch. Art, 1982-83. Devel. field coord. Nature Conservancy, Arlington, Va., 1977-79; intern U.S. Nat. Pk. Svc., Rocky Mountain Nat. Pk., 1980; bus. analyst Weyerhauser Co., Tacoma, Wash., 1981; program dir. Am. Farmland Trust, Washington, 1982-83; cons. Calif. Acad. Scis., San Francisco, 1984; project coord. EPA, San Francisco, 1985-86; bd. v.p. Coombs Mfg. Co., 1996—. Bd. dirs. World Wildlife Fund, Washington, 1983-89, No. Lights Inst., Missoula, Mont., 1983-93; treas., bd. dirs. Inland Northwest Land Trust, Spokane, 1991—; mem. steering com. Conservation Futures, Spokane, 1995—. Mem. Spokane Club.

COOMBS, CASSANDRA RUNYON, geologist, educator; b. Elmira, N.Y., Jan. 19, 1960; d. John Marquis and Dorothy Jane (Hessenius) Runyon; m. Gregory Alton Coombs, June 21, 1985; children: Zoe, Zachary, Zane. AS, Corning (N.Y.) C.C., 1980; BS, SUNY, Fredonia, 1982; MS, So. Ill. U., Carbondale, 1984; PhD, U. Hawaii, 1989. Grad. rsch. asst. So. Ill. U., Carbondale, 1982-84, U. Hawaii, Honolulu, 1985-89; postdoctoral rsch. fellow NRC/NASA Johnson Space Ctr., Houston, 1989-91; staff scientist, program mgr. POD Assocs., Inc., Albuquerque, 1991-93; rsch. asoc. U. Hawaii, Honolulu, 1993-95; asst. prof. Coll. Charleston, S.C., 1995—; coord. NEAR-C, Albuquerque, 1992-93; mem. NASA adv. bd., Washington, 1992—; cons. Enrichment in Sci. Program, Honolulu, 1987-89; campus dir. NASA Space Grant Consortium, 1995—; summer faculty fellow NASA Johnson Space Ctr., 1995, 96. Author rsch. papers and rev. articles. Harold T. Stearns fellow U. Hawaii, 1989, Mary Manhoff Meml. Sci. Fund scholar, 1987; named Disting. Alumni Corning C.C., 1995. Mem. Geol. Soc. Am. (sec. 1993—), Assn. for Women Geoscientists, Am. Geophys. Union, Am. Assn. Petroleum Geologists, N.Mex. Hazardous Waste Soc. Home: 1948 Falling Creek Circle Mt Pleasant SC 29464 Office: Dept of Geology College of Charleston 66 George St Charleston SC 29424

COOMBS, JANET, advertising executive. Chmn. bd. dirs., CEO Chapman Direct Advt. (divsn. Young & Rubicam, Inc.), N.Y.C. Office: Chapman Direct Advertising divsn of Young & Rubicam Inc 230 Park Ave S New York NY 10003*

COOMBS, VANESSA MOODY, journalism educator, lawyer; b. Petersburg, Va., May 2, 1955; d. Theodore Washington Moody and Doretha Winifred (Edwards) Moody Raines; m. Cyril Francis Coombs, Mar. 14, 1992; 1 child, Taylor Lindsey. BA, Hampton U., 1977; MA, U. Mich., 1978; JD, Georgetown U., 1983. Bar: D.C., 1983. Reporter, rschr. Money Mag., N.Y.C., 1979-80; comm. atty Schwartz, Woods & Miller, Washington, D.C., 1982-84; gen. assignment reporter WSET-TV, Lynchburg, Roanoke, Va., 1984-85, WGHP-TV, High Point, Greensboro, N.C., 1985-86, WKRN-TV, Nashville, Tenn., 1986-87; reporter, anchor WTVT-TV, Tampa, Fla., 1987-89; nat. correspondent Inside Edition, N.Y.C., 1989-91; gen. assignment reporter WDIV-TV, Detroit, 1991-92; chair and assoc. prof. dept. mass media arts Hampton (Va.) U., 1992—; bd. dirs. Black Coll. Comm. Assn. Grantee: Freedom Forum, 1993, 95. Mem. Assn. for Edn. in Journalism and Mass Comm. (task force on alliances 1993, 96), Assn. of Schs. Journalism and Mass Comm., (secondary edn. com. 1995, 96). Office: Hampton U Dept Mass Media Arts Hampton VA 23668

COON, PENNY K., administrator; b. Penn Yan, N.Y., May 21, 1959; d. Wilfred Orval and Marilyn Estelle (Wells) Knapp; m. Thomas Allen Gray, Aug. 30, 1980 (div. July 1990); m. David Charles Coon, May 23, 1992; 1 child, Rachel Mariah. BSW, Keuka Coll., 1980. Residence counselor Cath. Charities Residential Program, Penn Yan, N.Y., 1981-82, residence mgr., 1982-92, residential supr., 1992—; bd. dirs. Yates County (N.Y.) ARC, Penn Yan, 1993—, mem. human rights com., 1989; co-chmn. Keuka Lake Conf. Com., Rochester, N.Y., 1986—; mem. Yates County Devel. Disabilities Subcom., 1990. Recipient Direct Care award, N.Y. State Assn. Community Residence Adminstrs., 1985. Mem. DAR, Daughters Am. Colonists. Republican. Home: 2599 Knapp Rd Dundee NY 14837-9730 Office: Cath Charities Residential Program 607 W Washington St Geneva NY 14456-1804

COONEY, JOAN GANZ, broadcasting executive; b. Phoenix, Nov. 30, 1929; d. Sylvan C. and Pauline (Reardan) Ganz; m. Timothy J. Cooney, 1964 (div. 1975); m. Peter G. Peterson, 1980. BA, U. Ariz., 1951; hon. degrees, Boston Coll., 1970, Hofstra U., Oberlin Coll., Ohio Wesleyan U., 1971, Princeton U., 1973, Russell Sage Coll., 1974, U. Ariz., Harvard U., 1975, Allegheny Coll., 1976, Georgetown U., 1978, U. Notre Dame, 1982, Smith Coll., 1986, Brown U., 1987, Columbia U., 1991, NYU, 1991. Reporter Ariz. Republic, Phoenix, 1953-54; publicist NBC, 1954-55, U.S. Steel Hour, 1955-62; producer Sta. WNET, Channel 13; pub. affairs documentaries Sta. WNET, Channel 13, N.Y.C., 1962-67; TV cons. Carnegie Corp. N.Y., N.Y.C., 1967-68; exec. dir. Children's TV Workshop (producers Sesame Street, Electric Company, others), N.Y.C., 1968-70, pres., trustee, 1970-88, chmn., chief exec. officer, 1988-90, chmn. exec. com., 1990—; trustee Channel 13/Ednl. Broadcasting Corp.; dir. Xerox Corp., Johnson & Johnson, Chase Manhattan Corp., Chase Manhattan Bank N.A., Met. Life Ins. Co. Mem. Pres.'s Commn. on Marijuana and Drug Abuse, 1971-73, Nat. News Council, 1973-81, Council Fgn. Relations, 1974—, Pres.'s Commn. for Agenda for 80's, 1980-81, Adv. Com. for Trade Negotiations, 1978-80; mem. Gov.'s Commn. on Internat. Yr. of the Child, 1979, Carnegie Found. Nat. Panel on High Sch., 1980-82. Recipient numerous awards for Sesame Street and other TV programs including Nat. Sch. Pub. Relations Assn. Gold Key 1971; Disting. Service medal Columbia Tchrs. Coll., 1971; Soc. Family Man award, 1971; Nat. Inst. Social Scis. Gold medal, 1971; Frederick Douglass award N.Y. Urban League, 1972; Silver Satellite award Am. Women in Radio and TV; Woman of Yr. in Edn. award Ladies Home Jour., 1975; Woman of Decade award, 1979; NEA Friends of Edn. award; Kiwanis Decency award; NAEB Disting. Service award; 5th Women's Achiever award Girl Scouts U.S.A.; Stephen S. Wise award, 1981; Harris Found. award, 1982; Ednl. Achievement award AAUW, 1984; Disting. Service to Children award Nat. Assn. Elem. Sch. Prins., 1985; DeWitt Carter Reddick award Coll. Communications, U. Tex.-Austin, 1986; Emmy Lifetime Achievement award Acad. TV Arts and Scis., 1989; named to Hall of Fame Acad. TV Arts and Scis., 1989. Mem. NOW, Nat. Acad. TV Arts and Scis., Nat. Inst. Social Scis., Internat. Radio and TV Soc., Am. Women in Radio and TV. Office: Children's TV Workshop 1 Lincoln Plz New York NY 10023-7129*

COONEY, PATRICIA RUTH, civic worker; b. Englewood, N.J.; d. Charles Aloysius and Ruth Jeannette (Foster) McEwen; m. J. Gordon Cooney, June 8, 1957; 1 child, J. Gordon, Jr. Student, Fordham U., 1950-51; DHL honoris causa, Phila. Theol. Sem. St. Charles Boromeo, 1991. Blood bank chmn. Strafford Village Civic Assn., 1968-69, sec., 1970-71; vice chmn. Spl. Gifts Com. Cath. Charities Appeal of Archdiocese of Phila., 1980—, chmn., 1985. Mem. Coun. of Mgrs. Archdiocese of Phila., 1982-88, sec., exec. com., 1983-88; bd. dirs. Cath. Charities of Archdiocese of Phila., 1984—, sec., exec. com., 1988-90, v.p., exec. com., 1991—; bd. dirs. Village of Divine Providence, Phila., 1982—, sec., 1983-85, v.p. exec. com., 1990—; bd. dirs. St. Edmond's Home for Crippled Children, Phila., 1984—, v.p. exec. com., 1990—; bd. dirs. Don Guanella Village of Archdiocese of Phila., 1984—, v.p. exec. com., 1990— ; mem. Archdiocesan Adv. Com. on Renewal, 1991—; mem. Women's Com. Wills Eye Hosp., 1973—, mem.-at-large, 1st v.p.; mem. Women's Aux. St. Francis Country House, Darby, Pa., 1976—, treas., 1978-82; exec. com. United Way of Southeastern Pa., 1984-90, sec., 1986-88; bd. dirs. Chapel of Four Chaplains, 1984-89, Phila. Criminal Justice Task Force, 1989-90. Decorated Cross Pro Ecclesia et Pontifice, 1982. Republican. Home: 320 Gatcombe Ln Bryn Mawr PA 19010-3628

COONLEY-HARTNETT, MICHEL LYNN, critical care nurse, nurse practitioner; b. Ridgewood, N.J., Apr. 10, 1952; d. P.W. and Mary Margaret (Hall) C.; m. Terrance Michael Hartnett, Oct. 20, 1979. Diploma, St. Francis Med. Ctr., 1974; BSN, Richard Stockton State Coll., 1991; MSN, U. Pa., 1994. RN, N.J., Pa., N.C.; CCRN; cert. adult cardiopulmonary RN practitioner, ACLS, cert. specialist adult nurse practitioner. Charge nurse, insvc. coord. Deborah Heart and Lung Ctr., Browns Mills, N.J., 1974-79; cardiovascular specialist Roche Med. Electronics, Inc. (now Arrow), Cranbury, N.J., 1979-80; staff nurse South Miami Hosp., Miami, Fla., 1980-84; asst. nurse mgr. So. N.J. Regional Trauma Ctr., Cooper Hosp./U. Med. Ctr., Camden, N.J., 1984-86; staff nurse Our Lady Lourdes Med. Ctr., Camden, N.J., 1986-94; transplant coord. Duke U. Med. Ctr., Durham, N.C., 1995—; instr. grad. program Duke U. Sch. Nursing, Durham, N.C., 1995—; instr. U. N.C. Sch. Nursing, Chapel Hill, 1996—; S.E. regional mgr. HomeTec, Inc., Englewood, Colo., 1981-83; pres., dir. edn. Counterpulsation, Inc. Pa., Phila. and Miami, 1981-84; cons. Oximetric, Inc., Mountain View, Calif., 1984; regional mgr. autotransfusion div. Clin. Perfusionists, Inc., Annapolis, Md., 1989-90; mem. faculty Episcopal Hosp. Sch. Perfusion Scis., Phila., 1989-90; nursing transfer counselor Richard Stockton State Coll. N.J., Pomona, 1991-93. Co-author: (manual) Counterpulsation's IABP Training Manual, 1981. Participant Atlantic County Health Fair, Richard Stockton State Coll. N.J., 1990. Recipient award for program distinction in nursing Stockton State Coll. Nursing Faculty, 1991. Mem. ANA (nurses strategic action team), AACN, Am. Heart Assn. (coun. on cardiovascular nursing), N.J. Nurses Assn. (Bernardine Hefferman Nursing Leadership award 1991), N.C. Nurses Assn. (mem. coun. primary care nurse practitioners), Soc. Critical Care Medicine, Sigma Theta Tau. Home and Office: 413 Emerywood Dr Raleigh NC 27615-1526

COONS, BARBARA LYNN, public relations executive, librarian; b. Peoria, Ill., June 1, 1948; d. Harold Leroy and Norma (Brauer) C. BA, Stephens Coll., Columbia, Mo., 1970; MA, U. N.C., 1972; MLS, Cath. U., 1982. Research asst.Am. Revolution Bicentennical Office Library of Congress, Washington, 1974-76, editorial asst., office of the Asst. Librarian, 1976-78; Ednl. Liaison Specialist Library of Congress, Washington, 1978-82; dir. research service Gray and Co., Washington, 1982-85, v.p., 1985-86; v.p., dir. rsch. svcs. Hill and Knowlton Pub. Affairs Worldwide, Washington, 1986-92, sr. v.p., 1992-95, sr. mng. dir., 1996—; pres. Library of Congress Profl. Assn., 1982. Mem. Spl. Libraries Assn., Am. Library Assn., Stephens Coll. Alumnae Club of Greater Washington (pres. 1987). Lutheran. Home: 532 N West St Alexandria VA 22314-2159 Office: Hill & Knowlton Pub Affairs Worldwide 7th Fl 600 New Hampshire Ave NW Washington DC 20037

COONTS, VIOLET GADD, retired business educator, retired art educator, artist; b. Charleston, W. Va., Sept. 23, 1913; d. Lundy John and Luvada (Cart) Gadd; m. Gilbert Gray Coonts, July 15, 1941; children: Stephen Paul, John Jacob. BS, W. Va. U., 1940; student, Mason Coll. Music and Fine Art, 1942-45. Bus. instr. East Bank (W. Va.) H.S., 1940-45, Charleston (W. Va.) H.S., 1945-46; bus. and art instr. Buckhannon-Upshur H.S., Buckhannon, W. Va., 1952-72; instr. journalism Buckhannon-Upshur H.S., 1959-69, art W.Va. Wesleyan Coll., Buckhannon, 1972-75, oil painting Upshur-County Adult Edn., 1980-82. Author: The Western Waters, 1991; group exhbns. include Hunington (W.Va.) Gallery, 1964, Hackett Gallery, Charleston, W.Va., 1965, Parkers Art Studio, Parkersburg, W.Va., 1967, Clarksburg (W.Va.) Art Ctr., 1993-95, Art Co. of Davis, W.Va., 1994; designed mural Ctrl. Nat. Bank, 1978. Mem. United Methodist Ch. Mem. NEA (life), Barbour County Hist. Soc. (life), Order of the Ea. Star, Literary Club, Nat. Mus. Women in the Arts (charter). Methodist. Home: 2 Highland Dr Buckhannon WV 26201

COOPER, CAROLINE ANN, hospitality faculty dean; b. Gardner, Mass., Oct. 16, 1943; d. Frank D. and Florence M. (O'Neil) Toohey; m. Paul Geoffrey Cooper, Apr. 16, 1972; children: Geoffrey Paul, Heather Ann. BS, Russell Sage Coll., 1966; MBA, Bryant Coll., 1983; postgrad., U. Mass., Boston. Adminstrv. dietitian Mass. Gen. Hosp., Boston, 1967-68; with rsch., devel., mktg. Mkt. Forge Co., Everett, Mass., 1968-71; food svc. administr. Jane Brown R.I. Hosp., Providence, 1971-74; self-employed pres., cons. pvt. practice, Attleboro, Mass.; from instr. to asst. prof. Johnson & Wales U., Providence, 1978-86, acad. coord., 1984-86, dept. chair HRI, Hospitality, Food Svc. mgmt. and tourism, 1986-91; asst. dean Hospitality Coll., 1991-94, dean, 1995—; del. White House Conf. on Travel and Tourism Implementation Team, 1995, mem. implementation team, 1995-96. Vol. Parent Orgn. for Sch., 1978-91, Pub. Sch. System, 1981-84, Cmty. Sports Program, 1989-95. Recipient Hon. Doctorate medallion N.Am. Foodsvc. Assn. Mfrs.; named Pacesetter Nat. Roundtable for Women, 1989. Mem. Am. Dietetic Assn., Am. Hotel Motel Assn. (trustee Ednl. Inst. 1990—, Outstanding Educator 1990), Am. Hotel and Motel Industry, Computer Application Food Svc. Edn. (pres. 1987-89), Internat. Coun. on Hotel Restaurant Inst. Edn. (bd. dirs., pres. N.E. chpt. 1992-93, pres. 1994-95, chmn. bd. 1995-96). Office: Johnson and Wales U Abbott Park Pl Providence RI 02903

COOPER, DORIS JEAN, market research executive; b. N.Y.C., Dec. 17, 1934; d. James N. and Georgina N. (Cassidy) Breslin; student Sch. of Commerce, N.Y. U., 1953-55, Hunter Coll., 1956-57; m. S. James Cooper, June 17, 1956; 1 son, David Austin. Asst. coding supr. Crossley S-D Surveys, N.Y.C., 1955-57; asst. field supr. Trendex, Inc., N.Y.C., 1957-59; coding dir. J. Walter Thompson Co., N.Y.C., 1960-63, Audits & Surveys, N.Y.C., 1964-65; pvt. practice cons., N.Y.C., 1965-73; pres. Cooper Svcs., Hastings-on-Hudson, N.Y., 1973—; pres., CEO computer tabulation and lang. manipulation Doris J. Cooper Assocs., Hastings-on-Hudson, N.Y., 1989—; cons. market rsch. Mem. Am. Mktg. Assn. (N.Y. chpt.), Nat. Bus. Women Owners Assn., Am. Assn. Pub. Opinion Researchers (N.Y. chpt.), Acad. Health Svcs. Mktg., Hastings C. of C. Republican. Episcopalian. Office: Doris J Cooper Assocs Ltd 1 North St Hastings On Hudson NY 10706-2308

COOPER, DOROTHY SUMMERS, real estate agent; b. Lee County, Ala., Aug. 8, 1918; d. Carl and Mattie Will (Thompson) Summers; m. Arthur Wiggins Cooper, July 20, 1940; children: Arthur Wiggins Jr., Mary Cooper Kitchen, Robert Wayne, Donald Summers. BS, Auburn U., 1939. Tchr. Columbus (Ga.) Jr. High Sch., 1939-40; grad. asst. Auburn (Ala.) U., 1941-42; tchr. Lee County Head Start, 1965-70; real estate agt. Stan Weber Real Estate, New Orleans, 1972-80, Shamrock and James Grant Realty, Auburn, 1981-88; real estate exec. A&D Properties, Opelika, 1989—; lectr. Nat. Gallery Art, Washington, 1971-72; New Orleans Mus. Art, 1973-78. Treas. Auburn United Meth. Women, 1987-89. Named Honor Roll Bus., Auburn C. of C., 1990. Mem. PEO, Home Econs. Club, Sangahatchee Country Club, Delta Kappa Gamma, Green Gardeners. Democrat. Methodist. Home: 2590 Windy Hill Pl Auburn AL 36830-6408

COOPER, GINNIE, library director; b. Worthington, Minn., 1945; d. Lawrence D. and Ione C.; m. Richard Bauman, Dec. 1995; 1 child, Daniel Jay. Student, Coll. St. Thomas, U. Wis., Parkside; BA, S.D. State U.; MA in Libr. Sci., U. Minn. Tchr. Flandreau (S.D.) Indian Sch., 1967-68, St. Paul Pub. Schs., 1968-69; br. libr. Wash. County Libr., Lake Elmo, Minn., 1970-71, asst. dir., 1971-75; assoc. adminstr., libr. U. Minn. Med. Sch., Mpls., 1975-77; dir. Kenosha (Wis.) Pub. Libr., 1977-81; county libr. Alameda County (Calif.) Libr., 1981-90; dir. librs. Multnomah County Libr., Portland, Oreg., 1990—. Chair County Mgr. Assn.; county adminstr. Mayor's Exec. Roundtable. Mem. ALA (mem. LAMA, PLA and RASD coms., elected to coun. 1987, 91, mem. legislation com. 1986-90, mem. orgn. com. 1990—),

Calif. Libr. Assn. (pres. CIL, 1985, elected to coun. 1986, pres. Calif. County Librs. 1986), Oreg. Libr. Assn. Office: Multnomah County Libr 205 NE Russell St Portland OR 97212-3708

COOPER, ILENE LINDA, magazine editor, author; b. Chgo., Mar. 10, 1948; d. Morris and Lillian (Friedman) C.; m. Robert Seid, May 28, 1972. BJ, U. Mo., 1969; MLS, Rosary Coll., 1973. Head of children's svcs. Winnetka (Ill.) Libr. Dist., 1974-80; editor children's books Booklist Mag., ALA, Chgo., 1981—. Author: Susan B. Anthony, 1983, Choosing Sides, 1990 (Internat. Reading Assn.-Children's Book Coun. choice 1990), Mean Streak, 1991, (series) Frances in the Fourth Grade, 1991, numerous others. Mem. Soc. Midland Authors, Soc. Children's Book Writers, Children's Reading Roundtable. Jewish. Office: Booklist Mag 50 E Huron St Chicago IL 60611-2729

COOPER, ISABEL SELMA, sculptor, writer, art historian; b. N.Y.C.; d. Benjamin and Beth (Trachtenberg) Blank; m. Stanley Bert Cooper, July 22, 1956; children: Bruce, Sharon, Vanessa, Douglas. MA, Queens Coll., 1987; BA with honors, SUNY, Purchase, 1983. Cons., asst. Art and Slide Libr. Queens Coll., Flushing, N.Y., 1984-85; editor, reviewer, writer Nat. Sculpture Rev., N.Y.C., 1985-86; art coord. Ch. St. Cmty. Gallery, White Plains, N.Y., 1990-92; lectr. art history Hadassah, 1989, Nat. League Am. Pen Women, 1995; juror art competition Rye Arts Ctr., 1988, Mamoroneck Women's Fedn., 1985, 92. Exhbns. include Bergdorf Goodman, White Plains, Ciba-Geigy Corp., Ardsley, N.Y., Larchmont (N.Y.) Pub. Libr., United Hosp., Pt. Chester, N.Y., Pt. Chester Pub. Libr., Bloomingdales, White Plains, 1980, Iona Coll., New Rochelle, N.Y., 1980, Bergen County (N.J.) Comty. Mus., 1980, Greenwich (Conn.) Art Barn, 1981, Ossining (N.Y.) Libr., 1981, Greenburgh Pub. Libr. Showcase, Elmsford, N.Y., 1983, Mamaroneck Artists Guild Gallery, Larchmont, 1984, Rye Art Ctr., 1984, Eastchester (N.Y.) Pub. Libr., 1984, Hurlbutt Gallery, 1985, Marsh and McLennon Corp., Greenwich, 1985, Pen and Brush, N.Y.C., 1986, Harbor Gallery, S.I., N.Y., 1991, Westchester C.C., 1991, Cork Gallery, 1993; Slides of "Grief" sculpture series included in permanent registry of U.S. Holocaust Meml. Mus., Washington; contbr. poetry to anthologies and articles to jours. Recipient 1sr prize Rye Women's Club, 1975, Beaux Arts Finale award Westchester Fedn. Women's Clubs, 1976, Most Popular Sculpture award Eastchester Women's Club, 1976, N.Am. Pempco Sculpture award Nat. Arts Club, 1983, IBM Sculpture award, 1987, 1st prize Women's Club Pocantico Hills, 1984, Sculpture award Marsh and McLennon award, 1985, Ruth Katay award Ridgewood Art Inst., 1992, 1st and 2d prizes for sculpture Art Soc. Old Greenwich, 1996. Mem. Nat. League Am. Pen Women, Nat. Mus. Women Arts, N.Y. Artists Equity Assn., Catharine Lorillard Wolfe Art Club (award 1990), Coll. Art Assn. Am., Coun. Arts Westchester, Internat. Soc. Poets, Mamoroneck Artists Guild, Pen and Brush. Home: 61 Country Ridge Cir Rye Brook NY 10573

COOPER, JANELLE LUNETTE, neurologist, educator; b. Ann Arbor, Mich., Dec. 11, 1955; d. Robert Marion and Madelyn (Leonard) C.; children: Lena Christine, Nicholas Dominic. BA in Chemistry, Reed Coll., 1978; MD, Vanderbilt U., 1986. Diplomate Nat. Bd. Med. Examiners; diplomate in neurology Am. Bd. Psychiatry and Neurology; registered med. technologist Am. Soc. Clin. Pathologists. Med. technologist Swedish Hosp. Med. Ctr., Seattle, 1978-80, U. Wash. Clin. Chemistry, Seattle, 1980-82, Vanderbilt U. Hosp., Nashville, 1983-84; intern medicine Vanderbilt U. Med. Ctr., Nashville, 1986-87, resident neurology, 1987-90; instr. neurology Med. Coll. Pa., Phila., 1990-91, asst. prof., clerkship dir., 1991—, mem. curriculum com., 1990-91, vis. asst. prof., 1991-95; neurologist Greater Ann Arbor Neurology Assocs., 1991-93; dir. neurological svcs., med. dir. Industrial Rehab. Program St. Francis Hosp., Escanaba, Mich., 1993—; founder, dir. No. Neuroscis., Escanaba, 1993—; physician MCP Neurology Assocs., Phila., 1990-91; emergency rm. physician Tenn. Christian Med. Ctr., 1989-90. Contbr. articles to Annals of Ophthalmology, Ophthalmic Surgery. Vol. Rape and Sexual Abuse Ctr., Nashville, 1988-90; mem. adminstrv. bd. Edgehill United Meth. Ch., Nashville, 1989-90; mem. editorial bd. Nashville Women's Alliance, 1989-90; bd. dirs. Upper Peninsula Physicians Network; mem. adv. bd. Perspective Adult Daycare Ctr., 1996—. Recipient Svc. award for outstanding contbns. Rape and Sexual Abuse Ctr., 1990; epilepsy minifellow Bowman Gray U., 1995. Mem. AMA (physician's Recognition award 1989-92), NOW, AAAS, NAFE, Am. Med. Women's Assn., Am. Acad. Neurology, Am. Psychol. Soc., Mich. State Med. Soc., N.Y. Acad. Scis., Upper Peninsula Physician Network (bd. dirs. 1995—), Aircraft Owners and Pilots Assn., Women in Aviation Internat. (charter). Democrat (mem. nat. com.). Methodist. Home: 519 S 8th St Escanaba MI 49829-3608 Office: Northern Neurosciences 3415 Ludington St Ste 201 Escanaba MI 49829-1300

COOPER, JANIS CAMPBELL, public relations executive; b. Laurel, Miss., July 26, 1947; d. Clifton B. and Hilna Mae (Welch) Campbell; m. William R. Cooper, Sept. 18, 1971; 1 child, Emily Susanne. BS, U. So. Miss., 1969. Certified home economist. Staff home economist Maytag Co., Newton, Iowa, 1969-73, supr. home econs., 1973-81, mgr. consumer edn., 1981-86; mgr. corp. pub. affairs Maytag Corp., Newton, Iowa, 1986-87, asst. dir. corp. pub. affairs, 1987-88, corp. dir. pub. affairs, 1988-89, corp. v.p. pub. affairs, 1989—; trustee Maytag Corp. Found., Newton, 1990-96, dir. found. programs, 1996—. Chmn. bd. trustees Newton Cmty. Edn. Found., 1992-95; campaign vice chmn. United Way, Newton, 1996. Mem. Assn. Family and Consumer Scis., Pub. Rels. Soc. Am., Home Economists in Bus. (nat. chmn. 1981-82, Disting. Svc. award 1986, Nat. Bus. Home Economist of Yr. 1991), Iowa Assn. Bus. and Industry (bd. dirs., mem. exec. com.), Assn. Home Appliance Mfrs. (treas. 1988-89, 1st vice chmn. 1989-90, chmn. 1990-92, chmn. Major Appliance Divsn. Bd. 1993-95), Maytag Mgmt. Club, Kiwanis Internat. Office: Maytag Corp 403 W 4th St N Newton IA 50208-3026

COOPER, JEAN SARALEE, judge; b. Huntington, N.Y., Mar. 7, 1946; d. Ralph and Henrietta (Halbreich) C.; stepchildren: Mitzi Concklin Prochnow, John Todd Concklin. B.A., Sophie Newcomb Coll. of Tulane U., 1968; J.D., Emory U., 1970. Bar: La. 1970, Ga. 1970, U.S. Dist. Ct. (ea. dist.) La. 1970, U.S. Ct. Appeals (5th cir.) 1972, U.S. Ct. Appeals (2d cir.) 1976, U.S. Ct. Appeals (4th cir.) 1979, U.S. Ct. Appeals (fed. cir.) 1982, U.S. Supreme Ct. 1974. Trial atty. Office of Solicitor, U.S. Dept. Labor, Washington, 1970-73, spl. projects asst., 1973, sr. trial atty., 1973-77; adminstrv. judge Bd. Contract Appeals, HUD, Washington, 1977—, acting chmn. and chief judge, 1980-81, vice chmn., 1983—; cons., lectr. Contbr. articles to profl. jours. Recipient Moot Court award Tulane Law Sch., 1968. Fellow ABA (standing com. on jud. selection, tenure and compensation 1992-95, jud. adminstrn. divsn. 1993—, sec. 1996-97, exec. com., chmn. edn. com., mem. editl. bd. Judges Jour., vice-chair debarment and suspension com. pub. contracts sect. 1992—, adminstrn. law sect.); mem. La. Bar Assn., Am. Law Inst., Am. Inns of Ct. Found. (trustee 1992—), Prettyman-Leventhal Am. Inn of Ct. (past pres., master of bench), Am. Judicature Soc., Inst. Jud. Adminstrn., Bd. Contract Appeals Judges Assn., Nat. Assn. Women Judges, Fed. Bar Assn., Am. Inst. Wine and Food, Bds. of Contract Appeals Bar Assn., L'Academie de Cuisine (tchr.), Rep. Women's Forum, Federalist Soc., Ind. Women's Forum. Republican. Address: HUD Bd Contract Appeals 451 7th St SW Ste 2131 Washington DC 20410-0001

COOPER, JO MARIE, elementary school administrative assistant; b. L.A., Oct. 13, 1947; d. Joseph M. Langham and Christina (Burton) Lister; m. Leonard Cooper Jr., May 13, 1967; children: Leonard Joseph, Jo-Lynne Louise, Layton Bishop. Grad., Chgo. State Coll., 1967; MA, Governor State U., University Park, Ill., 1976. Postal worker, mail handler Chgo. Post Office, 1966-67; tchr. Chgo. Bd. Edn., 1968-75, resource tchr., 1975-93, adminstrv. asst., 1993—; advisor Homewood (Ill.) Full Gospel Ch., 1992-94, Homewood Christian Acad., 1994—. Pres. South Ctrl. Women's Aglow, Chgo., 1983-85; chair women's ministries Homewood Full Gospel Ch., 1990-94; South Chicago area leader Marriage Ministries Internat., University Park, 1994—; advisor Human Rels. Commn., University Park, 1987-89. Mem. ASCD. Pentecostal. Office: Oglesby Elem Sch 7646 S Green St Chicago IL 60620-2854

COOPER, JOAN, marketing executive; b. Bklyn., Jan. 7, 1948; d. Bernard and Grace (Garfink) C.; m. Owen Chong Lang, Aug. 1, 1976; children: Gabrielle, Miriam. BA, U. Pa., 1968; edn. cert., CCNY, 1973; MA in Drama, San Francisco State, 1979. Cert. elem. tchr. Tchr. United Cerebral Palsy, Nadick, Mass., 1974-76; founder, exec. v.p. Biobottoms Inc., Petaluma, Calif., 1981-96; spkr. Direct Mail Assn. convs., N.Y., San Francisco, 1993-94, Bus. Social Responsibility, San Francisco, 1993. Founder Friends Petaluma, 1993-94. Named 1 of 100 Most Influential Direct Marketers Target Mktg., 1992. Home: 333 Pleasant St Petaluma CA 94952

COOPER, JOSEPHINE SMITH, trade association and public relations executive; b. Raleigh, N.C., Aug. 2, 1945; d. Joseph W. and Marie (Peele) S. BA in bus. and econs., Meredith Coll., Raleigh, 1967; MS in mgmt., Duke U., 1977. Program analyst Office of Air & Quality Planning and Standards EPA, Rsch., Triangle Park, N.C., 1968-78; environ. protection specialist Office of Rsch. and Devel., Washington, 1978-80; mem. profl. staff majority leader Howard H. Baker, Jr., U.S. Senate Com. on Environ. and Public Works, Washington, 1980-83; asst. adminstr. for external affairs EPA, Washington, 1983-85; asst. v.p. for environ. and health program Am. Paper Inst., Washington, 1985-86; sr. v.p. for policy Synthetic Organic Chem. Mfrs. Assn., Washington, 1986-88; sr. v.p., dir. environmental policy Hill & Knowlton, Inc., Washington, 1988-91; founder, dir. Capitoline Internat. Group, Ltd., Washington, 1991-92; v.p. environ. and regulatory affairs Am. Forest & Paper Assn., 1992—; treas. RTP Fed. Credit Union, 1969-72, pres., 1975; pres. Women's Coun. on Energy and Environ., 1986-88, Nat. Coun. on Clean Indoor Air, 1988—; mem. nat. adv. environ. health scis. coun. NIH, 1990-94; mem. adv. com. EPA Clean Air Act, 1994—; mem. trade and environ. policy adv. com. USTR, 1994—; mem. corp. coun. Nat. Pks. and Conservations Assn. Bd. visitors Duke U. Sch. Environ., 1994—. Congl. fellow, 1979-80. Mem. Federally Employed Women (treas., pres. 1972-77), Women in Govt. Rels., Tenley Sport and Health Club. Mem. Disciples of Christ. Office: Am Forest & Paper Assn 1111 19th St NW Ste 800 Washington DC 20036-3603

COOPER, KATHLEEN BELL, economist; b. Dallas, Feb. 3, 1945; d. Patrick Joseph and Ferne Elizabeth (McDougle) Bell; m. Ronald James Cooper, Feb. 6, 1965; children—Michael, Christopher. B.A. in Math. with honors, U. Tex., Arlington, 1970, M.A. in Econs, 1971; Ph.D. in Econs, U. Colo., 1980. Research asst. econs. dept. U. Tex., Arlington, 1970-71; corp. economist United Banks of Colo., Denver, 1971-79, chief economist, 1980-81; v.p., sr. fin. economist Security Pacific Nat. Bank, Los Angeles, 1981-83, 1st v.p., sr. economist, 1983-85, sr. v.p., economist, 1985-86, sr. v.p., chief economist, 1986-87, exec. v.p., chief economist, 1988-90; chief economist Exxon Corp., Irving, Tex., 1990—. Trustee Scripps Coll., Com. for Econ. Devel.; mem. Dallas Com. on Fgn. Rels., Internat. Women's Forum. Mem. Nat. Assn. Bus. Economists (past pres. Denver and L.A. chpts.; bd. dirs. 1975-78, pres. 1985-86), Nat. Bur. Econ. Rsch. (bd. dirs., exec. com.), Am. Bankers Assn. (econ. adv. com. 1979-81, 86-90, chmn. 1989-90), U.S. Assn. Energy Econs. (pres. 1996), Am. Econ. Assn., Conf. Bus. Economists (tech. cons. to bus. coun. 1993-94). Office: Exxon Corp 5959 Las Colinas Blvd Irving TX 75039-2298

COOPER, MAGGI FISK, accountant; b. Mpls., Dec. 13, 1947; d. Frank W. and Eleanor J. (Mielke) Fisk; m. Paul David Miller, Aug. 31, 1968 (div. Jan. 1973); m. Sam M. Cooper, May 17, 1980 (div. Oct. 1991). MusB, Capital U., 1970; postgrad. in Medieval Music History, Ohio State U., 1971-76; postgrad.in acctg. and taxation, several state and community schs., San Diego, 1980-91. Vocal music tchr. Licking Heights schs., Summit Station, Ohio, 1970-71; music tchr., performer Columbus, Ohio, 1972-73; head acctg., distbg. Arthur Treacher's Fish and Chips, Columbus, 1972-77; ptnr. Miller, White Assocs., Columbus, 1979-80; part owner Cooper Bus. Machines, Columbus, 1975-78; Ptnr. Brain Bank, Columbus, 1978-80; ptnr. Hamilton-Fisk Guild, Columbus, 1978-80; owner Margo Ltd. Bookkeeping Services, Columbus, 1978-80, Total Mgmt. Systems, San Diego, 1980-91; chmn. bd. Bauhaus, Ltd., San Diego, 1983-91; chmn. bd. dirs. M.F. Cooper Ltd., San Diego, 1988-91; chmn. bd. Maggi Fisk Cooper, Deland, Fla., 1991—; owner, CFO Triczar Mktg., Inc., Flatwoods Prodns, Inc., 1995—, Sackett, Cooper & Busse, Inc., 1995—; owner, Brunhilde, Ltd., 1995—. Author: The Monarchy Series, 1977, The Suicide Book, 1978; contbr. articles, short stories, poetry to numerous mags., 1976—. Program bd. mem. House Next Door, 1991-94; mem. fin. & endowment com. First Presbyn. Ch., Deland, 1991-93; fin. sec. First Congl. Ch., Lake Helen, 1993—. Mem. AAUW (local treas.), P.E.O. Internat. Sisterhood (Internat. scholar 1970), Am. Mensa Ltd., Phi Beta. Democrat.

COOPER, MARY BERRY, retired legal assistant, association executive; b. McDonough, Ga., July 27, 1923; d. Wilson Ray and Annie Vernis (Morgan) Berry; m. Raiford Wilson Cooper Sr, Feb. 18, 1944; children: Raiford Wilson Jr., Jack Glenn. Grad. H.S., Atlanta. Legal asst. Farris, Warfield, Kanaday Law Firm, Nashville, 1962-94; ret., 1994; exec. dir. Tenn. Feed and Grain Assn., Nashville, 1962—; pres. Tenn. Assn. Legal Assts., Nashville, 1978-80; bd. dirs. Tenn. Conf. Children's Svcs., Nashville, 1984—, chmn., 1994—. Active Davidson County Dem. Exec. Com., Nashville, 1966-74; bd. mem. ARC, Nashville, 1970—; bd. mem., organizer Serindipity House, Nashville, 1973—; commr. Davidson County Human Rels., Nashville, 1975-85; chair adminstrv. bd. Glendale Meth. Ch., Nashville, 1982-92, chair fin. com., 1992-95, pres. Meth. Women, 1994—. Recipient Mary Catherine Strobel award Serindipity House, Nashville, 1985. Mem. Nat. Assn. Legal Assts. (charter, chair 1982 workshop, state bar liaison 1982-86), Tenn. Paralegal Assn. (organizer, dir. 1981-84), Order Ea. Star. Home: 626 Gen George Patton Rd Nashville TN 37221

COOPER, MARY CAMPBELL, information services executive; b. Meadville, Pa., Aug. 14, 1940; d. Paul F. and Margaret (Webb) Campbell; m. James Nicoll Cooper, June 8, 1963; children: Alix, Jenny. BA, Mt. Holyoke Coll., 1961; MLS, Simmons Coll., 1963; MEd, Harvard U., 1965. Cert. museum adminstrn. With Harvard U. Libr., Cambridge, Mass., 1961-63, Carleton U. Libr., Ottawa, Can., 1965-85; archive cons. U.S., Can., 1985-86; info. mgr. Haley & Aldrich Inc., Cambridge, 1986-88, Tsoi/Kobus & Assocs., Cambridge, 1988-90; pres., founder Cooper Info., Cambridge, 1990—; bd. dirs. Mass. Com. for Preservation of Archtl. Records, Boston. Author: Records In Architectural Offices, 1992. Bd. dirs. Berkshire Hist. Soc., Pitts., Mass., Constrn. Specifications Inst., Boston. Travel grantee Nat. Hist. Pub. Records Commn., 1991. Mem. Spl. Librs. Assn., Am. Mus. Assn., Assn. Ind. Info. Profls., Assn. Moving Image Archivists, Assn. for Info. and Image Mgmt., Assn. Records Mgrs. and Adminstrs. (nat. com. 1991—), Constrn. Specification Inst. (bd. dirs. 1994—). Home and office: 5 Ellery Pl Cambridge MA 02138-4200

COOPER, MARY DARNELL, small business owner; b. St. Albans, N.Y., Oct. 5, 1940; d. John M. and Yvonne M. (Brindisi) Darnell; m. Robert P. Cooper, July 11, 1959; children: Robert, Catherine, James, Elizabeth. Grad. high sch., Webutuck, N.Y. Pres. Assoc. Lightning Rod Co. Inc., Millerton, N.Y., 1985—. Mem. Greater Millerton C. of C. (sec. 1991-94). Republican. Roman Catholic. Home and Office: Cooper Rd Box 329A Millerton NY 12546

COOPER, PAULA, art dealer; b. Mass., Mar. 14, 1938. Student, Pierce Coll., Athens, Greece, Sorbonne, Paris, Goucher Coll.; DFA (hon.), R.I. Sch. Design, 1995. Asst. World House Galleries, N.Y.C., 1959-61; pvt. dealer, 1962-63; with Paula Johnson Gallery, N.Y.C., 1964-65; dir. Park Place Gallery, N.Y.C., 1965-67, Paula Cooper Gallery, N.Y.C., 1968—; bd. chair Art Dealers Assn. Am., 1982-86, 88-90, The Kitchen Ctr., N.Y.C., 1985-95. Office: Paula Cooper Gallery 155 Wooster St New York NY 10012-3159

COOPER, PHYLLIS L., county official, educator; b. Kalamazoo, Mich., Dec. 15, 1943; d. Douglas M. and Dorris I. (McIntyre) Gainder; m. Lonnie E. Johncock, July 24, 1964 (dec. Feb. 1975); children: Lonnie Johncock Cooper, Elizabeth Dorton, Andrew Johncock Cooper; m. Charles L. Cooper, Aug. 7, 1976; children: Charles, Lenore Austin, Ross, Linda Mijangos. BS, Mich. State U., East Lansing, 1966, MA, 1988. Tchr. Greenville (S.C.) County Schs., 1966-70; extension home economist Mich. State U. Extension, Corunna, 1972-76; extension 4-H Mich. State U. Extension, East Lansing, 1976-78; tchr. Jackson (Mich.) Baptist Schs., 1978-82; coord. W.I.C. Jackson Co. Health Dept., 1982-85; extension home economist Mich. State U. Extension, Howell, 1985-92, county extension dir., 1992-96; mem. adv. bd. Head Start, 1988-96; sec. Livingston Co. Food Bank, 1985-93; sec. Livingston Child Care Coun., 1993-96. Author: (bulletin) After Death, 1975, (puppet show) Grand River Gang, 1992. Mem. Livingston 2001, 1988-94. Recipient Outstanding Alumni award Mich. State U., 1996. Mem. Am. Home Economics Assn., Nat. Extension Assn. For Family and Consumer Scis. (sec. 1988-90, pres.-elect, pres., past pres. 1993-95, Disting. Svc. award 1991, Continued Excellence award 1994, Doris Wetters Travel fellow 1995), Mich. Assn. Extension Home Economists (sec., pres.-elect, 1972-78, pres., past pres. 1984-96), Mich. Home Econs. Assn. (sec. 1974-78, v.p. 1985-96). Republican. Baptist. Home: 13820 Bancroft Rd Byron MI 48418

COOPER, RACHEL BREMER, accountant; b. Oak Park, Ill., Dec. 21, 1950; d. James Louis and Betty Charlene (Barfield) B.; m. Terry Linn Cooper, Aug. 14, 1981. BS in Acctg., Murray State U., 1982. CPA, Tenn. Gen. bookkeeper The Paducah (Ky.) Sun, 1975-80; staff acct. Kraft Bros., Esstman, Patton, & Harrell, CPAs, Nashville, 1983; acquisition analyst Freeman Cos., Nashville; asst. controller Surg. Care Affiliates, Nashville, 1984-86; sr. staff acct. O'Neill & Co. CPAs, Nashville, 1986, EQUICOR, Nashville, 1987; acctg. mgr. Times Pub. Co., DBA The St. Petersburg (Fla.) Times, 1987-93; pres. Eco Solutions, Inc., St. Petersburg Beach, 1993—; pres., owner The Cover Story, Inc., Clearwater, Fla., 1996—; pres., owner Lady Rachael Imports, Nashville, 1986-87. Officer Don Cesar Property Owners Corp., St. Petersburg Beach, 1988-90. Named to Dean's List Paducah Community Coll., 1978, 79, Murray State U., 1980-82. Mem. Tenn. Soc. CPAs, Fla. Inst. CPAs, AICPA. Republican. Home: 3616 Casablanca Ave Saint Petersburg Beach FL 33706

COOPER, REBECCA, art dealer; b. Phila., July 11, 1957; d. Frank N. Cooper and Bernice Silverstein; m. Michael J. Waldman, June 27, 1982. BA NYU, MA, postgrad. Cert. appraiser. Owner Gallery Rebecca Cooper, Washington; pres. Rebecca Cooper Fine Art, N.Y.C., 1980s-90s; hon. chairperson N.Y. Women Bus. Owners Art Roundtable, 1981; lectr. Resources Coun., 1983, N.Y. Mayor's com. on interior design and furnishings, 1983; sec. bd. assocs. Am. Craft Mus., lectr. Collectors Circle; nat. patron Am. Fed. Art., Ind. Curators Inc. Patron, Mus. Modern Art; benefactor New Mus. Dirs. Forum; exhbn. assoc. Whitney Mus. Mem. Am. Appraisers Assn. (assoc.), Nat. Women's Rep. Club, Women's Investment Club, Pvt. Art Dealers Assn., Nat. Arts Club, Guggenheim Mus. (internat. cir.).

COOPER, SHARON MARSHA, marketing, advertising executive; b. Chgo., Feb. 6, 1944; d. Ralph and Esther Lepack; m. Steven Jon Cooper; children: Robin Eve, Erik Scott. BA, Northeastern Ill. U., Chgo., 1974; MEd, Loyola U., Chgo., 1977. Adj. asst. prof. Chgo. Med. Sch., North Chicago, Ill., 1974-79; edn./media coordinator Humana Hosp., Aurora, Colo., 1980-82; v.p. Healthcare Mktg. Corp., Denver, 1982-84; pres. Sharon Cooper Assocs., Ltd., Englewood, Colo., 1984—; cons./speaker Jason Pharms., Balt., 1988—; cons. Am. Soc. Bariatric Physicians; lectr. in field; guest lectr. U. Denver, 1988—. Illustrator: A Manual of Radiographic Positioning, 1973; contbr. articles to profl. jours. Bd. dirs., v.p. The Barre Assn./Colo. Ballet, Denver, 1989—; bd. dirs. Am. Diabetes Assn., Denver, 1983—, Am. Cancer Soc., Denver, 1988—, Hospice of St. John, Denver, 1986-90. Named Co-Woman of the Yr., Lerner Newspapers, Chgo., 1973, Silver Microphone award, 1988, Golden Leaflet award, Colo. Hosp. Assn., 1981, 84. Mem. Am. Hosp. Assn., Assn. Healthcare Pub. Rels. and Mktg. (reg. rep. 1987—), Colo. Soc. Health Care Pub. Rels., Pub. Rels. Soc. Am., Zonta, Toastmasters (sec. 1972-84). Home: 8522 E Dry Creek Pl Englewood CO 80112-2701 Office: Sharon Cooper Assocs Ltd 9085 E Mineral Cir Ste 160 Englewood CO 80112-3418

COOPER, SIGNE SKOTT, retired nurse educator; b. Clinton County, Iowa, Jan. 29, 1921; d. Hans Edward and Clara Belle (Steen) Skott. BS, U. Wis., 1948; MEd, U. Minn., 1955. Head nurse U. Wis. Hosp., Madison, 1946-48; instr. U. Wis. Sch. Nursing, Madison, 1948-51, asst. prof., 1952-57, assoc. prof., 1957-62; prof., assoc. dean U. Wis. Sch. Nursing, 1948-83, prof. emeritus, 1983—; prof. U. Wis. Extension, 1955-83. Contbg. author: American Nursing: A Biographical Dictionary, Vol. 1, 1988, Vol. 2, 1992; contbr. articles to profl. jours. 1st Lt. U.S. Army Nurse Corps, 1943-46. Recipient NLN Linda Richards award, ANA Honorary Recognition award, Adult Edn. Assn. Pioneer award; named Fellow Am. Acad. Nursing. Mem. ANA, Am. Assn. for History Nursing, Wis. Nurses Assn. (pres.).

COOPER-LEWTER, MARCIA JEAN, fine arts educator, administrative assistant; b. Petersburg, Va., Nov. 2, 1959; d. Andrew Ezekiel and Lillian (Bonner) Wyatt; m. Nicholas Charles Cooper-Lewter, Nov. 29, 1986. BS in Elem. Edn., Va. State U., Ettrick, 1984; MEd in Spl. Edn., 1993. Lic. minister, 1987; ordained to clergy, 1990. Tchr. Marion (Ind.) Community Schs., 1985-86, Inglewood (Calif.) Unified Schs., 1986-87; office mgr. C.R.A.V.E. Christ Counseling, Tustin, Calif., 1986—; asst. minister New Garden of Gethsemane B.C., L.A., 1987-90; assoc. minister New Hope Bapt. Ch., St. Paul, 1990—; assoc. pastor New Garden of Gethsemane B.C., L.A., 1990—; assoc. minister New Hope Bapt. Ch., 1990—; pres. C.R.A.V.E. Christ Singers, L.A., 1987-90; adminstr. asst. Eldorado Bank, Orange, Calif., 1988-90; tchr. fine arts Mpls. Sch. Dist., 1990—; with Wyatt, Cooper-Lewter Consulting, Shoreview, Minn., 1986—; founder, dir. "Diversity in Motion" program for A.A. students, 1992—; stage dir. "Babu's Magic" with reknown dancer Chuck Davis, 1994. Mem. C.R.A.V.E. Christ Ministries (Relax in Christ, Affirm with Christ, Visualize Christ, Experience Christ); nominated to Pres.'s Commn., White House Fellowships, 1993. Imagination grant Star Tribune, 1994, 1995-96, Fulbright grant to Namibia Africa Curriculum Waiting, 1996, U. Wis.-Madison African Studies grant, 1995-96. Mem. NAFE, Alpha Kappa Alpha.

COOTE, SHARON MURPHY, secondary education educator; b. Wheeling, W.Va., May 7, 1947; d. Mark and Jeannette (Hamilton) Murphy; m. W.W. Harper Jr., June 18, 1972 (div. Oct. 1981); 1 child, Andrew; m. Richard J. Coote, June 17, 1995. BA, West Liberty State Coll., 1969; MA, W.Va. U., 1981. Tchr. Newport (Ky.) City Schs., 1970-72; substitute tchr. Knox County (Ohio) Schs., 1972-73; tchr. Brooke County Schs., Wellsburg, W.Va., 1973-95, ret., 1995. Founder Brooke Hills Playhouse, Wellsburg, 1972; pres. Brooke County Arts Coun., Wellsburg, 1981. Recipient Outstanding Achievement award Ashland Oil, 1993. Mem. NEA (mem. congl. contact team 1973-76), Nat. Coun. Tchrs. of English, Brooke County Edn. Assn. (pres. 1973-75), Wellsburg Shakespeare Club (pres. 1970-72). Democrat. United Methodist. Home: 15821 Rica Vista Way San Jose CA 95127

COOTS, LAURIE, advertising executive. COO TBWA Chiat/ Day L.A., Venice, Calif. Office: TBWA Chiat/Day LA 340 Main St Venice CA 90291*

COOVER, PAULA LOUISE HENRY See HENRY, PAULA LOUISE

COPAS, LINDA LOUISE, elementary education educator; b. Elmhurst, Ill., July 18, 1951; d. Edward F. and Florine W. (Steege) Brettmann; m. Michael Roy Copas, June 16, 1973; children: Michael Eric, Melissa Louise. BS in Elem. Edn., U. Wis., Stevens Point, 1973, MEd in Profl. Devel., 1982. Cert. elem. edn. 1-8. Tchr. 4th grade Tri-County Area Sch. Dist., Plainfield, Wis., 1973—, coord. K-12 gifted and talented, 1975-85, coord. K-12 microcomputer, 1982-85, block grant coord. chpt. 2, 1984—, head tchr. K-4, 1985-86; sec. Wis. Assn. Educators for Gifted and Talented, 1983-85. Music and drama leader, dir. 4-H, Waushara County, Wis., 1989-96; accompanist jr. choir United Meth. Ch., Plainfield, 1992-96. Recipient Sen. Kohl Tchr. Fellowship award, 1992, Disting. Svc. award Cen. Wis. UniServ Coun., 1993. Mem. Wis. Edn. Assn. Coun. (pub. rels. chair, com. mem. 1989-95), Tri-County Area Edn. Assn. (Uniserv bd. rep. 1991-96, past pres., sec., treas., pub. rels. com. 1973-96, Disting. Svc. award 1993), Wis. State Reading Assn., Gen. Fedn. of Women's Clubs (past pres. local chpt. 1984-86), Order Ea. Star (Zarah chpt., Worth Matron 1984-86, officer 1994-95), Delta Kappa Gamma (com. chair, music chair 1990-96), Phi Delta Kappa. Home: 9758 County Rd BB Plainfield WI 54966-9121 Office: Tri-County Area Sch Dist 407 West St Plainfield WI 54966

COPE, JEANNETTE NAYLOR, human resources consultant; b. Corpus Christi, Tex., Feb. 9, 1956; d. Glen R. and Jeannine (Withington) N.; m. John R. Cope, May 22, 1993. BA in Psychology and Sociology, Trinity U., 1978. Asst. fin. dir. Jim Baker for Atty. Gen. Campaign, Houston, 1978; fin. dir. Rep. Party of Tex., Austin, 1979-81; regional Eagle rep. Rep. Nat. Com., Washington, 1981-83; devel. officer Nat. Endowment for the Arts, Washington, 1983-87; sr. project mgr. Internat. Skye Assocs., Washington, 1988;

spl. asst. to Pres. of U.S. The White House, 1989-90, dep. asst. to Pres. of U.S., dep. dir. of presdl. pers., 1990-93; pres. J. Naylor Cope Co., Washington, 1994—; NEA liaison Pres.' Com. on Arts and Humanites, Washington, 1985-87; dir. Internat. Skye Advisor, Washington, 1988; bd. dirs. Bush/Quayle Alumni Assn., 1991—; mem. Officer Pers. Mgmt.'s Task Force on Exec. and Mgmt. Devel., Washington, 1990. Chmn. alumni admissions coun. Trinity U., Washington, 1986-87; bd. dirs. Coop. Urban Ministry Ctr., Washington, 1987-89, Pennsylvania Ave. Devel. Corp., 1993-96; vestrywoman St. John's Episcopal Ch., Washington, 1990-94, co-chmn. outreach com., 1991-94, chmn. search com. for 14th rector, jr. warden, 1994—. Tex. Coun. of Ch. Related Colls. scholar, 1974. Mem. The Pres.' Club, The 1925 F St. Club (Washington), Columbia Country Club (Chevy Chase, Md.), Tex. State Soc. (chmn. membership com. 1981), Nat. Trust for Hist. Preservation, Smithsonian Instn., Am. Film Inst., Mcpl. Art Soc. (N.Y.C.), Tex. Breakfast Club (Washington), Blue Key (sec. 1976-78), Chi Beta Epsilon (v.p. San Antonio coun. 1976). Republican. Episcopalian. Office: J Naylor Cope Co PO Box 40069 Washington DC 20016-0069

COPELAND, CAROLYN ABIGAIL, retired university dean; b. White Plains, N.Y., May 5, 1931; d. Robert Erford and Mary Terwilliger; B.A. (CEW scholar), U. Mich., 1973, M.A. (Rackham Grad. Student scholar), 1979, postgrad. 1992—; m. William E. Copeland, Aug. 16, 1964; children—Rob Cameron, Diana Elizabeth Bosworth. With dean's office Coll. Lit., Sci. and Arts, U. Mich., Ann Arbor, 1967-91, asst. dean, 1980-84, assoc. dean, 1984-91. Mem. Mortar Bd., Phi Beta Kappa (v.p. Alpha chpt. 1984-86, pres. Alpha chpt. 1986-88). Author: Tankas from the Koelz Collection, 1980; Walter Norman Koelz, A Biography, in progress. Research in Buddhist art history. Home: 520 Darwin Rd Pinckney MI 48169-8828 Office: U Mich Ann Arbor MI 48109

COPELAND, CAROLYN ROSSI, producer, director; b. N.Y.C., Feb. 1, 1954; d. Dante Robert and Margaret (Gallo) Rossi; m. James Masson Copeland, Apr. 24, 1982; children: Margaret T., Beatrice Jnowles, Marion Masson, Eugenia Dante. BA in Polit. Sci., Tulane U., 1976. Congl. asst. Congressman Peter W. Rodino Jr., Washington, 1976-79; founder, producing artistic dir. Lambs Theatre Co., N.Y.C., 1980—. Bd. trustees Garrison (N.Y.) Union Free Sch., 1996—. Recipient Richard Rodgers award, 1993, NEA Musical award, 1994. Mem. Nat. Alliance Musical Theatres, Women in Theatre, Off Broadway Assn. Republican. Episcopalian. Home: The Clumpse RiB4 Garrison NY 10524

COPELAND, JACQUELINE TURNER, music educator; b. Birmingham, Ala., Mar. 22, 1939; d. Charles Smith and Julia (Northrop) Turner; m. William Edward Copeland, Apr. 20, 1962; children: Denise Arlene, Dawn Alane. B in Music Edn., Birmingham-So. Coll., 1960; M in Music Edn., Wichita State U., 1977. Cert. music tchr. grades K-12, Ala., Ga., Kans., La., Va. Music tchr. Jefferson County Bd. Edn., Birmingham, 1960-62, 63-64, DeKalb County Bd. Edn., Decatur, Ga., 1965-68; choral music tchr. Fairfax (Va.) County Bd. Edn., 1968-69, Derby (Kans.) Unified Sch. Dist. #260, 1977-80, Maize (Kans.) Unified Sch. Dist. #266, 1980-84; music tchr. Montgomery (Ala.) County Pub. Schs., 1984-85; instr. voice and piano Acad. Performing Arts, Montgomery, 1985-95, Studio of Jacqueline T. Copeland, Montgomery, 1995—; accompanist County-Wide Music Festivals, Birmingham, 1960-65; sect. leader Dekalb Cmty. Chorus, Decatur, Ga., 1965-68; sect. leader, exec. bd. New Orleans Concert Choir, 1970-74; asst. dir., dir. chorale Wichita Choral Soc., 1974-84; dir. opening ceremony Bicentennial Fair, Wichita, 1976; mem. Montgomery (Ala.) Civic Chorale, 1984-87; musical dir. for theatre depts. Performing Arts Jr. High, Performing Arts H.S., Faulkner U., 1986—. Author: Music Teacher Handbook, 1967; editor, contbg. author: Teacher Advisement Handbook, 1980. Secret svc. wife White House Wives, Washington, 1968-70; leader, trainer, area chmn. Camp Fire Girls, New Orleans, 1970-74; leader, membership com., exec. bd. Camp Fire Girls, Wichita, 1974-82; elected ofcl. Citizens Participation Orgn., Wichita, 1984; area chmn. Am. Heart Assn., Montgomery, 1988-94; vol. DA Election, Montgomery, 1994. Recipient Groovey Tchr. award WQXI Radio, Atlanta, 1967, Gov.'s commendation Revolutionary Bicentennial Com., Wichita, 1976; named Outstanding Young Women of Am., New Orleans, 1971. Mem. Music Tchrs. Forum, Alpha Chi Omega (treas. 1995—), Alpha Chi Omega Alumnae (del. to 4 nat. convs., pres., v.p.). Democrat. Baptist. Home: 6121 Bell Road Manor Montgomery AL 36117

COPELAND, LOIS JACQUELINE (MRS. RICHARD A. SPERLING), physician; b. Malden, Mass., Sept. 16, 1943; d. Arnold Alan and Ann (Goldfarb) C.; BA magna cum laude with distinction in all subjects, Cornell U., 1964, MD, 1968; m. Richard A. Sperling, June 7, 1970; children: Mark Edward, Larissa Lynn, Lauren Anne, Lorraine Elizabeth. Intern N.Y. Hosp., N.Y.C., 1968-69, resident, 1969-70; resident Bellevue Hosp., NYU Med. Ctr., 1970-72; teaching asst. internal medicine NYU Med. Ctr., 1971—; attending physician Pascack Valley Hosp., Westwood, N.J., 1974—; courtesy staff Valley Hosp., Ridgewood, N.J., 1980—. Mem. secondary schs. com. Cornell U., 1978—; bd. dirs. Found. For Free Enterprise; steering com. physicians coun. Heritage Found., 1993—; pres. coun. Cornell Women, 1993-95. Mem. Bd. Assn. Am. Physicians and Surgeons, Assn. Am. Physicians and Surgeons (bd. dirs. 1991—, pres. 1995), Phi Beta Kappa, Phi Kappa Phi, Alpha Lambda Delta. Home: 25 Sparrowbush Rd Saddle River NJ 07458-1411 Office: 47 Central Ave Hillsdale NJ 07642-2118

COPELAND, M. SHAWN, theological educator, researcher; b. Detroit, Aug. 24, 1947; d. John L. Copeland and Geraldine (Billingslea) Williams. BA in English, Madonna Coll., 1969; PhD in Systematic Theology, Boston Coll., 1991. Assoc. prof. theology and Black studies Yale U., New Haven, Conn., 1989-94; assoc. prof. theology Marquette U., Milw., 1994—. Author, co-editor Concilium: Feminist Theology in Different Contexts jour., 1996; co-editor Concilium: Violence Against Women jour., 1994. Recipient Sojourner Truth award Black Women's Cmty. Devel. Foun., 1974, Christian Faith and Life Sabbatical grant The Louisville Inst., 1996. Fellow Soc. for Values in Higher Edn.; mem. Cath. Theol. Soc. Am. (bd. dirs. 1994-96), Am. Acad. Religion, Black Cath. Theol. Symposium (assoc. convenor 1990-96). Roman Catholic. Office: Marquette Univ Dept Theology Coughlin Hall PO Box 1881 Milwaukee WI 53201-1881

COPELAND, SUSAN JOAN, realtor; b. La Mesa, Calif., Sept. 23, 1951; d. Donnell Dean and Mary Ann (Simpson) Swenson; m. Steven Andrew Euthon, Aug. 21, 1971 (div. 1975); 1 child, Tyler; m. Cody Thomas Copeland, Feb. 11, 1977; children: Matthew, Jeremy. AA in Gen. Studies, Western Okla. State Coll., Altus, 1978; BSBA in Fin., Cameron U., 1982; MBA in Fin. & Econs., Avila Coll., 1986. Cert. paralegal. Paralegal Altus, 1977-80; asset/liability mgr. U.S. Ctrl., Overland Park, Kans., 1982-85; mgr. new product devel. U.S. Ctrl. Credit Union, Overland Park, Kans., 1985-87; v.p. instl. sales U.S. Ctrl. Credit Union Brokerage, Overland Park, Kans., 1985-87; asst. v.p. R & D U.S. Ctrl. Credit Union, Overland Park, Kans., 1987-88; v.p. investments UMB Kansas, Kansas City, 1988-90; cash mgr. Johnson County, Kans., 1990-92; chief investment officer State of Kans., Topeka, 1992-96; realtor Coldwell Banker Gill Agy., Lawrence, Kans., 1996—. Author: Using Quattro Pro, 1987; adv. editor Quattro Pro for Beginners, 1988. Mem. Kansas City Treasury Mgrs. Assn., Treasury Mgrs. Assn., Soroptimist Internat. (treas. 1995-96). Home: 3609 Riverview Rd Lawrence KS 66049 Office: Coldwell Banker Gill Agy 901 Tennessee Lawrence KS 66044

COPELAND, SUZANNE JOHNSON, real estate executive; b. Chgo., Aug. 1; d. John Berger and Eleanor (Dreger) Johnson; m. John Robert Copeland, Aug. 1, 1971 (div. June 1976). Assoc. French Lang. and Culture, Richland Coll., Dallas, 1974; BFA, Ill. Wesleyan U., Bloomington, 1965. Commercial artist Barney Donley Studio, Inc., Chgo., 1966-69; art dir. Levines Dept. Store, Dallas, 1970-74; creative dir. Titche-Goettinger, Inc., Dallas, 1974-78; catering mgr. Dunfey Hotel, Dallas, 1978-82; regional dir. corp. sales Lakeway/World of Tennis Resort, Austin, Tex., 1982-84; real estate sales assoc. Henry S. Miller, Dallas, 1984-86; v.p. Exclusive Properties Internat., Inc., Dallas, 1986—; cons. North Tex. Commn., Dallas, 1988. Acquisitions editor: Unser, An American Family Portrait, 1988. Mem. The Rep. Forum, Dallas, 1983-94; vol. Stars for Children, Dallas, 1988, Soc. for Prevention of Cruelty to Animals, Dallas, 1973-92, Preservation of Animal World Soc., 1986-92, Sedona Acad., 1996—, Sedona Human Soc., 1996—; charter mem. P.M. League Dallas Mus. Art. Mem. Nat. Assn. Realtors, Tex. Assn. Realtors, Greater Dallas Assn. Realtors (com. chmn., Summit award 1984, 85), North Tex. Arabian Horse Club (bd. dirs. 1975-76, Pres.'s award 1978), Dallas Zool. Soc., Humane Soc. Dallas County (v.p. 1973-74), Humane Soc. U.S./Gulf States Humane Edn. Assn. (bd. dirs. 1990-91), Am. Montessori Soc., Sedona Humane Soc., Sedona Acad., Delta Phi Delta, Phi Theta Kappa. Lutheran. Office: Exclusive Properties 5025 Capitol Ave Dallas TX 75206-6934

COPELAND, TATIANA BRANDT, accountant, tax executive; b. Dresden, Germany; came to U.S., 1959, naturalized, 1967; d. Cyril Alexander and Maria (von Satin) Brandt; m. Gerret van Sweringen Copeland, May 12, 1979. BS summa cum laude, UCLA, 1964; MBA, U. Calif.-Berkeley, 1966. Sr. tax cons. Price Waterhouse & Co., Los Angeles, 1966-72; asst. tax mgr. Whittaker Corp., L.A., 1972-75; mgr. internat. dept. E. I. Du Pont de Nemours, Wilmington, Del., 1975-80; pres. Tebec Assocs. Ltd., Wilmington, 1980—; co-owner, chief fin. officer Bouchaine Vineyards, Inc., Napa, Calif.; owner The Wine & Spirit Co., Greenville, Del.; co-owner and v.p. Rokeby Realty Co., Wilmington. Bd. dirs. Del. Symphony, Grand Opera House, Nat. Symphony Orch., Washington; presdl. appointee Adv. Com. for Trade Negotiations, 1982-87. Mem. Am. Inst. CPAs, Del. Soc. CPAs, Am. Woman's Soc. CPA's, Am. Soc. Women Accts., Internat. Fiscal Assn., Rodney Square Club (dir.), Phi Beta Kappa. Home: 175 Brecks Ln Wilmington DE 19807-3008 Office: PO Box 3662 Wilmington DE 19807-0662

COPENHAVER, MARION LAMSON, state legislator; b. Andover, Vt., Sept. 26, 1925; d. Joseph Fenwick and Christine (Forbes) Lamson; m. John H. Copenhaver, June 30, 1946; children: John III, Margaret, Christine, Eric, Lisa. Student, U. Vt., 1945-46. Legislator State of N.H., Concord, ranking Dem. health & human svcs. com., 1973—, mem. adminstrv. rules com., 1982—, mem. health & human svcs. oversight, 1990—. Chair Grafton County Dems., 1986-91; assoc. supr. Grafton County Soil Conservation Dist., 1980—; mem. Hanover (N.H.) Dem. Town Com., 1992; mem.-at-large Dem. State Com., Concord, 1992; bd. dirs. Dartmouth Hitchcock Found., Hanover, 1991—; bd. incorporators Dartmouth Hitchcock Med. Ctr., Lebanon, N.H., 1984—; bd. dirs. Grafton County Sr. Citizens Coun., Inc., 1995-96. Named N.H. Legislator of Yr. N.H. Nurses Assn., 1989; recipient Meritorious award N.H. Women's Lobby, 1996. Mem. NOW, Bus. and Profl. Women's Club (outstanding mem. 1990). Democrat. Unitarian. Home: 14 Woodcock Ln Etna NH 03750-4402

COPLEN, MOLLY ANN, financial analyst, accountant; b. Hutchinson, Kans., Feb. 8, 1964; d. Harold Edwin and Mary Jane (Webber) C. BBA, Wichita State U., 1986, M.Profl. Accountancy, 1994; MBA, U. Kans., 1989. Fin. analyst Union Nat. Bank, Wichita, 1989-93; budget analyst Commerce Bancshares, Kansas City, Mo., 1993-95; analyst Fed. Reserve Bank, Kansas City, 1996; auditor U. Kans., Lawrence, 1996—. Mem. Inst. Mgmt. Accts. Mormon. Home: 122 Carlton Rd Hutchinson KS 67502 Office: University of Kansas 351 Strong Hall Lawrence KS 66045

COPLEY, CYNTHIA SUE LOVE, insurance adjuster; b. Defiance, Ohio, Oct. 26, 1957; d. Thomas Lee and Pauline Ann (Brandt) Love, Jr.; m. James Earl Copley, Jr., Oct. 19, 1985. B.Criminal Justice, Ohio U., 1981, A. in Law Enforcement, 1979, A in Fire and Safety Tech., 1982. Cert. profl. ins. woman. With Spangler Candy Co., Bryan, Ohio, 1976-77; guard Juvenile Detention Ctr., Chillicothe, Ohio, 1978; security officer J.C. Penney Corp., Inc., Chillicothe, Ohio, 1979, Rink's Bargain City, Chillicothe, Ohio, 1979; with Rubbermaid Sales Corp., Chillicothe, Ohio, 1980; asst. dept. sec. and computer lab asst. Ohio U., Chillicothe, 1977-81; supr. collections and investigation Bur. of Support, Ross County, Chillicothe, 1981-82; asst. mgr. Tecumseh Claims Svc., Chillicothe, 1982—; owner Copley Adjusting, Chillicothe, 1982—. Poll worker Rep. Party, Chillicothe, 1983—. Mem. So. Ohio Claims Assn., Ohio Assn. Ind. Ins. Adjusters (sec.-treas. 1994, v.p. 1995, pres. 1996), Ohio Assn. Mut. Ins. Cos., Nat. Assn. Ins. Womne, Scioto Valley Assn. Ins. Women (auditor 1991, sec. 1989-90, Claims Woman of Yr. 1989-91), Nat. Soc. Profl. Ins. Investigators. Lutheran. Home and Office: Tecumseh Claims Svc PO Box 15 Chillicothe OH 45601-0015

COPLEY, HELEN KINNEY, newspaper publisher; b. Cedar Rapids, Iowa, Nov. 28, 1922; d. Fred Everett and Margaret (Casey) Kinney; m. James S. Copley, Aug. 16, 1965 (dec.); 1 child, David Casey. Attended, Hunter Coll., N.Y.C., 1945. Assoc. The Copley Press, Inc., 1952—, chmn. exec. com., chmn. corp., dir., 1973—, chief exec. officer, sr. mgmt. bd., 1974—; chmn. bd. Copley News Svc., San Diego, 1973—; chmn. editorial bd. Union-Tribune Pub. Co., 1976—; pub. The San Diego Union-Tribune, 1973—; bd. dirs. Fox Valley Press., Inc. Chmn. bd., trustee James S. Copley Found., 1973—; life mem. Friends of Internat. Ctr., La. Jolla, Mus. Contemporary Art, San Diego, San Diego Hall of Sci., Scripps Meml. Hosp. Aux., San Diego Opera Assn., Star of India Aux., Zool. Soc. San Diego; mem. La Jolla Town Coun. Inc., San Diego Soc. Natural History, YWCA, San Diego Symphony Assn.; life patroness Makua Aux.; hon. chmn., bd. dirs. Washington Crossing Found.; hon. chmn. San Diego Coun. Literacy. Mem. Inter-Am. Press Assn., Newspaper Assn. Am., Calif. Press Assn., Am. Press Inst., Calif. Newspaper Pubs. Assn., Calif. Press Inst., San Francisco Press Club, L.A. Press Club. Republican. Roman Catholic. Clubs: Aurora (Ill.) Country, Army and Navy (D.C.), Univ. Club San Diego, La Jolla Beach and Tennis, La Jolla Country. Office: Copley Press Inc 7776 Ivanhoe Ave La Jolla CA 92037-4520

COPPOLA, PATRICIA L. (SCHEFFEL), elementary school educator; b. Kingston, N.Y., Apr. 27, 1966; d. John J. and Barbara (Brennan) Scheffel; m. Paul A. Coppola, July 11, 1992. BS cum laude, SUNY, Brockport, 1989; MS, SUNY, New Paltz, 1993. Tchr. 1st grade Gov. George Clinton Elem. Sch., Poughkeepsie, N.Y., 1989-91, pre-kindergarten and kindergarten tchr., 1991—, tchr. gifted and talented C.O.M.E.T. program, 1990—. Mem. Jr. League of Kingston, 1996—. Mem. N.Y. State Reading Assn. (mid-Hudson reading com. 1995—), Kappa Delta Pi. Home: 51 Brookfield Rd Apt D-8 Wallkill NY 12589

COPPOLA, PHYLLIS GLORIA, special education educator; b. Bklyn., Apr. 20, 1930; d. Marie Cecire Manley; m. Ben J. Coppola, Nov. 4, 1950; children: Robert, Joseph, John, Karen. AAS, Nassau C.C., 1972; BA, St. Joseph's Coll., 1974; MS, L.I. Univ., 1978. Cert. tchr., spl. edn. tchr. Head bookkeeper Babylon (N.Y.) Nat. Bank (now Chem. Bank), 1948-54; homemaker, 1955-74; tchr. North Babylon (N.Y.) Schs., 1975-78; spl. edn. educator West Islip (N.Y.) Schs., 1978—; advisor Udall Rd. Student Coun., West Islip, Beautification, West Islip; mem. sch. adv. bd. Udall Rd. Sch., West Islip; mem. advisory homeroom com. West Islip Sch. Dist. Mem. AAUW, Orton Soc., Lions. Roman Catholic. Home: 71 Eaton Ln West Islip NY 11795-4501

COPPOLA, SARAH JANE, special education educator; b. Alton, Ill., Apr. 20, 1957; d. Howard Earl and Dorothy Elizabeth (Eads) Cox; m. Daniel Joseph Coppola Jr., June 26, 1977; children: Daniel Joseph III, Shawn Marie. BS, Trenton State Coll., 1979; M Counseling Edn., Kean Coll. of N.J., 1995. Cert. guidance counselor, substance abuse counselor, N.J. Substitute tchr. Dunellen (N.J.) Bd. Edn., 1979-87, Greenbrook (N.J.) Bd. Edn., 1979-87, Middlesex (N.J.) Bd. Edn., 1979-87, Bound Brook (N.J.) Bd. Edn., 1983-84; tchr. of handicapped Piscataway (N.J.) Bd. Edn., 1987—, prin. adv. bd., 1990-91. Youth group advisor Trinity Reformed Ch., North Plainfield, N.J., 1983-91, deacon, 1985-87. Mem. NEA, ASCD, N.J. Edn. Assn., Piscataway Edn. Assn., N.J. Counseling Assn., N.J. Sch. Counselor Assn., Kean Coll. Alumni Assn. Home: 334 Runyon Ave Middlesex NJ 08846 Office: Piscataway Bd Edn 100 Behmer Ave Piscataway NJ 08854

COPPS, SHEILA, Canadian government official; b. Hamilton, Ont., Can., Nov. 27, 1952; d. Victor Kennedy and Geraldine (Guthro) C.; 1 child, Danelle Lauran Copps. BA in French, English with hons., U. Western Ont., London; postgrad., U. Rouen, France, McMaster U., Hamilton. Reporter Ottawa Citizen, 1974-76, Hamilton Spectator, 1977; asst. to Ont. Liberal leader Stuart Smith, Hamilton, 1977-81; mem. Legis. Assembly Ont., Toronto, 1981-84, House of Commons, Ottawa, 1984-96; apptd. dep. leader Liberal Party Can., Ottawa, Ont., 1990—; dep. prime min., min. environment Govt. of Can., Ottawa, 1993—; dep. prime min., min. of Can. heritage, 1996. Author: Nobody's Baby, 1986. Mem. Liberal Party. Roman Catholic. Office: House of Commons Rm 509S, Ottawa, ON Canada K1A 0A6

CORASH, MICHELE B., lawyer; b. May 6, 1945. BA, Mt. Holyoke Coll., 1967; JD cum laude, NYU, 1970. Legal advisor to chmn. FTC, 1970-72; dep. gen. counsel U.S. Dept. Energy, 1979; gen. counsel EPA, 1979-81; ptnr. Morrison & Foerster, San Francisco and L.A. Bd. editors Toxics Law Reporter; bd. advisors Jour. Environ. Law and Corporate Practice; mem. nat. editl. adv. bd. Prop 65 News. Bd. dirs. Calif. Counsel on Environ. and Econ. Balance, 1991—; mem. blue ribbon commn. Calif. Environ. Protection Agy. Unified Environ. Statute; mem. V.P. Bush Regulatory Task Force, 1981. Mem. ABA (mem. standing com. on environ. 1988-91, chair com. environ. crimes 1990), Inter-Pacific Bar Assn. (chair environ. law com.). Office: Morrison & Foerster 555 W 5th St Ste 3500 Los Angeles CA 90013-1080 also: 345 California St San Francisco CA 94104-2635

CORBEIL, SUSAN MARIE, counselor, investigator; b. Bristol, Conn., Mar. 7, 1958; d. Edward Leo and Shirley Anne (Beliveau) C. BA in Polit. Sci., Colo. Women's Coll., Denver, 1980; cert., Denver Paralegal Inst., 1982; student, U. Denver, 1990. Libr. asst. Holme, Roberts & Owen, Denver, 1979-82; paralegal Sherman & Howard, Denver, 1982-83; mail carrier U.S. Postal Svc., Denver, 1983-96, counselor, investigator, 1996—. Author short stories (1st pl. Raices Mestizas Literary symposium 1995). Vol. Dem. Com., Denver, 1992. Mem. Rocky Mountain Fiction Writers. Democrat. Home: 1244 Monroe St Denver CO 80206

CORBETT, IDNA MARITZA, university program director; b. San Pedro Sula, Honduras, Oct. 26, 1960; arrived in U.S., 1986; d. Samuel and Adaljitza Julieta (Rivera) Castellon; m. Robert James Corbett, June 17, 1986. BA, Goshen Coll., 1980; MA, Mich. State U., 1983; EdD, Temple U., 1995. Cons. Mktg. Ctr., San Pedro Sula, Honduras, 1982; tchr. Summer Hill Sch., Tegucigalpa, Honduras, 1982-83; prof., dept. head U. Pedagógica Nat., Tegucigalpa, Honduras, 1982-86; guidance counselor Escuela Internat. Sampedrana, San Pedra Sula, Honduras, 1983-86; tchr. Westtown (Pa.) Sch., 1986-87; instr. Messiah Coll., Phila., 1987-89; counseling coord. Temple U., Phila., 1988-89, program dir., 1989-92; dir. tutorial svcs. West Chester (Pa.) U., 1992-94, dir. acad. programs and support svcs., 1994—; advisor L.Am. Student Orgn., West Chester U., 1992—. Youth comm. coord. Ptnrs. of Am., San Pedro Sula, 1985-86; bd. dirs. Big Sisters Phila., 1991-94; advisor Hispanic Students Assn. Temple U., 1991-92; bd. dirs. Chester County Migrant Ministry. Mem. ASCD, Nat. Assn. Women in Edn., Pa. Assn. Ednl. Opportunities Program (sec. 1990-92), Am. Ednl. Rsch. Assn., Nat. Assn. for Devel. Edn., Nat. Tutoring Assn., Rotary (West Chester Sunrise club). Methodist.

CORBETT, SUZANNE ELAINE, food writer, film producer, marketing executive, food historian; b. St. Louis, Jan. 23, 1953; d. George Edward and Opal Laverne (Duncan) Traxel; m. James Joseph Corbett, Jr., July 17, 1970; 1 child, James J. III. BA, Webster U., 1994, MA in Media Comm., 1995. Cert. culinary profl. Tchr. Inst. Continuing Edn. St. Louis C.C., 1976—; tchr. cmty. edn. Lindbergh Sch. Dist. Pub. Schs., St. Louis, 1983-89; confectioner/caterer Suzanne Corbett Seasonal Confections, St. Louis, 1977-84; test baker Fleishman's Yeast, St. Louis, 1983; food stylist St. Louis, 1980—, rsch. cons./food mktg. and rsch. food/product history, 1994; rsch. cons. PanCor Prodns., 1994—; food historian/folklorist St. Louis County Parks and Recreation, Mo. Hist. Soc., St. Louis Art Mus., Colonial Dames Am.; food media trainer Internat. Assn. Culinary Profls., 1990; ALHFAM lectr. in field. Author: Cowpuncher's Provision, 1988, River Fare, 1990, Pharoh's Pheast-Food from the Nile, 1991, Tips from Missouri Win Country, 1993; food writer, cookbook editor St. Louis Bugle food editor, 1991-96, columnist, 1991-96; columnist Sr. Circuit Newspaper; food writer, columnist News Weekly. Bd. dirs. St. Louis South sect. Am. Heart Assn., Historyonics Theatre Co.; mem. Mo. Grape and Wine Adv. Bd. Recipient Folklife Greentree grant award Ralston Purina, 1989, grant award Commerce Bank, 1990, grant award Wetterau Foods, 1991. Mem. Women in Communications (pres. St. Louis chpt. 1996—, Communication awards 1989, 90, 91, 92, 93, 94, 95, 96), Mo. Press Women (past pres., Communication award 1989, 96, Communicator of Yr. 1993), Victorian Soc. Am. (past pres. St. Louis chpt.), James Beard Found. (charter), Am. Inst. Wine and Food, Internat. Assn. Culinary Profls. (cert., culinary historian Boston and Ann Arbor, internat. conf. com. 1990), Assn. Ind. Video and Filmmakers, St. Louis Press Club (former co-editor Courier, Pres.' award, Press Club Charitable Fund pres. 1993-94), Nat. Fedn. Press Women (Communication and Writing awards), Nat. Trust for Hist. Preservation, St. Louis Culinary Soc. (sec., bd. dirs.), Order Eastern Star. Roman Catholic. Home and Office: 5850 Pebble Oak Dr Saint Louis MO 63128-1412

CORBIN, ALEXANDRA KRAELER, filmmaker, artist; b. N.Y.C., Mar. 8, 1951; d. Leonard and Madeleine Cecille (Kraeler) C.; m. Lawrence Stanley Mondschein; children: Anneliese Patra, Todd Kraeler. BA, Barnard Coll., 1973; MFA, Cornell U., 1975. Dir. Franklin Gallery, instr. drawing and painting Cornell U., Ithaca, N.Y., 1973-75; dir. rsch. N.Y. Hist. Soc., N.Y.C., 1976-78; artist in residence Guadalajara, Mex., 1979-82; pres., founder Kraeler Art Rsch., Washington, 1982-86; film specialist Nat. Gallery Art, Washington, 1984-86; curator Clark Art Inst., Williamstown, Mass., 1987; founder, pres. Native Films & Documents, N.Y.C., 1987—. Dir., writer, editor, producer: (films) The Star Program, 1993, The Italian Gardens of South Brooklyn, 1990, Can You See the Color Grey?, 1996; author, illustrator: (children's fiction) Montgomery Max, 1989, Sweet Dreams of Anda, 1993. Victorian Soc. fellow, 1977.

CORBIN, ROSEMARY MAC GOWAN, mayor; b. Santa Cruz, Calif., Apr. 3, 1940; d. Frederick Patrick and Lorena Maude (Parr) MacGowan; m. Douglas Tenny Corbin, Apr. 6, 1968; children: Jeffrey, Diana. BA, San Francisco State U., 1961; MLS, U. Calif., Berkeley, 1966. Libr. Stanford (Calif.) U., 1966-68, Richmond (Calif.) Pub. Libr., 1968-69, Kaiser Found. Health Plan, Oakland, Calif., 1976-81, San Francisco Pub. Libr., 1981-82, U. Calif., Berkeley, 1982-83; mem. coun. City of Richmond, 1985-93, vice mayor, 1986-87, mayor, 1993—; mem. Solid Waste Mgmt. Authority, 1985—, Contra Costa Hazardous Materials Commn., Martinez, Calif., 1987—, San Francisco Bay Conservation and Devel. Commn., 1987—; mem. League of Calif. Cities Environ. Affairs Com., 1994—; mem. energy and environ. com. U.S. Conf. Mayors and Nat. League of Cities, 1993—. Contbr. articles to profl. publs. Mem. Calif. Libr. Assn., Local Govt. Commn., League Calif. Cities, Nat. League Cities, LWV, NOW, Nat. Women's Polit. Caucus. Democrat. Home: 114 Crest Ave Richmond CA 94801-4031 Office: Richmond City Hall 2600 Barrett Ave Richmond CA 94804-1654

CORBINE ESPINOSA, JUANITA GRACE, cultural association administrator; b. Pine Ridge, S.D., Sept. 27, 1956; d. Melvin William and Philomene (Peltier) Corbine; m. Edward Paul Espinosa, Jan. 14, 1978 (div. 1979); children: Adonijah Edward Espinosa, Demetrius Paul Espinosa, Wastewin Margareta Patrice Gonzalez, Wakinyan Adelita Sandoval. AA, Mpls. C.C., 1985. dir. Native Arts Ctr.; program dir. Native Am. Cultural Arts Program, COMPAS, Inc.; organizer People of Phillips, Mpls.; team leader Career Assessment Ctr., Heart of the Earth Survival Sch.; cmty. educator N.Am. Water Office, cooperative organizer, office mgr. Womanswork Diversified Arts; cons. Alliance Cultural Democracy, 1988-89, Lerner Pubs., 1990, Minn. Hist. Soc., 1992. Interim editor The Cir.; co-prodr. Honor the Grandmothers, 1993. Bd. dirs. Mpls. Am. Indian Ctr., 1983—, Alley Newspaper, 1989-93, Alliance Cultural Democracy, 1992—; adv. mem. McKnight Neighborhood Self Help Initiatives Program Found., 1987-92; pres. In the City Arts, 1990—; mem. grants com. Headwater Fund, 1992—. Recipient McKnight Human Svc. award, 1985; Jerome Travel grantee, 1992. Home: 1433 E Franklin Minneapolis MN 55404 Office: Native Arts Cir 1433 E Franklin Minneapolis MN 55404

CORBITT, DORIS ORENE, real estate agent, dietitian; b. Warrior, Ala., Oct. 25, 1929; d. Olen J. and Begie Pernie (Motte) Florence; m. Wallace R. Cornett, Nov. 29, 1952 (div. 1980); children: Wallace R. Jr., Kris J., Brett T.; m. Weldon Plant Corbitt, Jr., Apr. 21, 1984. BS in Dietetics, Maryville Coll., 1950; postgrad., Duke U., 1950-51. Registered dietitian; lic. real estate agt., Fla. Asst. dir. dietary St. Mary's Hosp., Knoxville, 1952-53; dir. dietary Soldier and Sailor Sch. for Children, Bloomington, Ill., 1966-68; tchr. Nashville Area Vocat. Sch., 1971-73; dir. dietary Westside Hosp., Nashville, 1973-79, Meml. Hosp., Tampa, Fla., 1980-85, Ill. Soldier & Sailor Sch. Children, Bloomington, 1966-68, Ill. Soldier and Sailor Sch. for Children, Bloomington, 1966-68; tchr. Nashville Area Vocat. Sch., 1971-73; dir. dietary

Meml. Hosp., Tampa, 1980-85; realtor assoc. Coldwell Banker, Tampa, 1986—; asst. dir. dietary St. Mary's Hosp., Knoxville, 1952-53; Spkr. in field. Devel. original curriculum for Food Svc. Workers and Suprs., Tenn.; co-author first diet manual for Nashville Dietetic Assn.; pioneer in devel. of low-sodium programs for hypertensive patients at Westside Hosp. for outpatients, devel. of first pulmonary outpatient nutritional care program at Meml. Hosp., Tampa. Sec. Galleria Homeowners Assn., Tampa, 1986-87; Sunday sch. tchr. Recipient Internat. Citizenship award, 1995, and nobility status and title "The Honourable", 1996, both from Prince Kevin of Australia. Mem. Am. Dietetic Assn., Tampa Dietetic Assn., Tampa Bd. Realtors, Million Dollar Club. Republican. Mem. Ch. of Christ. Home: 11515 Galleria Dr Tampa FL 33624-4752 Office: Coldwell Banker Residential Real Estate Inc 14007 N Dale Mabry Hwy Tampa FL 33618-2401

CORCORAN, BARBARA ASENATH, author; b. Hamilton, Mass., Apr. 12, 1911; d. John Gilbert and Anna (Tuck) C. BA, Wellesley Coll., 1933; MA, U. Mont., 1955. Instr. English, U. Ky., No. Center, 1956-57; with story dept. CBS-TV, Hollywood, Calif., 1957-58; tchr. English, Marlborough Sch., Hollywood, 1958-59; instr. English, U. Colo., 1960-65; instr. Corr. Sch. Creative Writing, 1964-72; instr. English, Palomar Coll., San Marcos, Calif., 1965-69. Author numerous children's books, including Make No Sound, 1977, Hey, That's My Soul You're Stomping On, 1977, Me and You and a Dog Named Blue, 1979, Rising Damp, 1979, Strikel, 1983, Abigail, You Put Up With Me, I'll Put Up With You, 1987, The Hideaway, 1987, The Sky is Falling, 1988, The Potato Kid, 1989, Annie's Monster, 1990, Stay Tuned, 1991, Family Secrets, 1992, Wolf at the Door, 1993 (Western Writers Am. award 1994); other works under pen names of Paige Dixon and Gail Hamilton; contbr. stories to popular mags. Recipient William Allen White award, 1972, Nat. Sci. Tchrs.-Children's Book Coun. award, 1974, 77, Merriam award U. Mont., 1992. Mem. PEN, Authors League Am. Democrat. Episcopalian.

CORCORAN, EILEEN LYNCH, special education educator emerita; b. Newark, Mar. 12, 1917. A.B. in English, Montclair (N.J.) State Coll., 1938, Litt.D. (hon.), 1976; M.S. in Elem. Edn, SUNY, Brockport, 1953; spl. edn. cert., U. Rochester, 1958; Ed.D., SUNY, Buffalo, 1970. High sch. tchr. spl. edn., 1957-65; coordinator spl. edn. Bd. Coop. Ednl. Services, 2d Supervisory Dist., Monroe County, N.Y., 1965-67; asst. prof. to asso. prof. D'Youville Coll., Buffalo, 1967-72; dir. spl. edn. D'Youville Coll., 1969-72; dir. edn. Children's Psychiat. Centre, N.Y. State Dept. Mental Hygiene, 1970-71; mem. faculty SUNY, Brockport, 1972-81; prof. curriculum and instrn. SUNY, 1977-81, prof. emeritus, 1981—; bd. visitors Monroe Devel. Center, Rochester; mem. adv. council Commn. on Quality of Care for Mentally Disabled, State of N.Y.; cons. in field. Author curriculum materials, articles. Bd. dirs. Home Owner's Assn., Sun City, Ariz., Sun City Ambs. Fellow Am. Assn. Mental Deficiency; mem. AAUW, AAUP, Coun. for Exceptional Children (pres. N.Y. State 1971, Disting. Svc. award), Assn. for Children with Learning Disabilities, Sun City 79ers Lioness Club (sec.), Delta Kappa Gamma, Union Hills Country Club. Address: 10007 W Pineaire Dr Sun City AZ 85351-1259

CORCORAN, MAUREEN ELIZABETH, lawyer; b. Iowa City, Feb. 4, 1944; d. Joseph and Velma (Tobin) C. BA in English with honors, U. Iowa, 1966, MA in English, 1967; JD, Hastings Coll. of Law, San Francisco, 1979. Bar: Calif. 1979, D.C. 1988, U.S. Ct. Appeals (9th cir.), 1979, U.S. Dist. Ct. (no. dist.) Calif., 1979, U.S. Dist. Ct. (cen. dist.) Calif., 1979, US. Ct. Appeals (D.C. cir.) 1983. Assoc. Hassard Bonnington Rogers & Huber, San Francisco, 1979-81; spl. asst. to gen. counsel HHS, Washington, 1981-83; assoc. Weissburg & Aronson, San Francisco, 1983-84; gen. counsel U.S. Dept. Edn., Washington, 1984-86; of counsel Pillsbury, Madison & Sutro, San Francisco, 1987-; dir. Hastings Coll. Law U. Calif., San Francisco, 1993—; chmn. Managed Health Care Conf., 1989; mem. AIDS adv. com. Ctrs. for Disease Control, 1989-91; speaker health law mtgs. Author: (book) Managed Care Contracting: Advising the Managed Care Organization, 1996; contbr. articles on health law to profl. jours. Mem. U.S. delegation to 1985 World Conf. to Review and Appraise Achievements of UN Decade for Women, Nairobi, Kenya, 1985; mem. Adminstrv. Conf. U.S., Washington, 1985. Mem. ABA (Forum on Healthcare Law), Calif. State Bar Assn., Nat. Health Lawyers Assn. Office: Pillsbury Madison & Sutro 225 Bush St San Francisco CA 94104-4207

CORCORAN, NANCY HELEN, minister; b. Portsmouth, N.H., Dec. 19, 1944; d. Maurice Richard and Helen Clare (Warren) C. BA in govt., Regis Coll., Weston, 1966; M in theol. studies, Harvard Div. Sch., Cambridge, 1991. Tchr. St. Joseph's Sch., Waipahu, Hawaii, 1966-69, St. Agnes Sch., St. Louis, 1969-70, Holy Name Elem. Sch., St. Louis, 1971-77; tchr. art and sculpture Broome County (N.Y.) Cath. Schs., 1977-79; dir. ancillary svcs. Nazareth Home, St. Louis, 1979-82; dir. literacy ctr. Lowndes County Cath. Ctr., Hayneville, Ala., 1982-88, Excel, Okalona, Miss., 1988-89; campus minister Regina Dominican, Wilmette, Ill., 1991—; cons. anti-racism workshops; facilitator cultural diversity workshops; facilitator and presenter feminist spirituality/preaching retreats. Contbr. articles to profl. jours. Literacy trainer Laubach Literacy, 1986; leader Alternative Spring Break, Ozarks, 1995—. Mem. Am. Acad. of Religion. Roman Catholic.

CORDER, BILLIE FARMER, clinical psychologist, artist; b. Dundee, Miss., Sept. 12, 1934; d. Lee Kennith and Jimmy Louise (Hawkins) Farmer; B.S., Memphis State U., 1957; M.A., Vanderbilt U., 1959; Ed.D., U. Ky., 1966; student Memphis Acad. Art, 1959, Sch. Design, N.C. State U., 1971-75; m. Robert Floyd Corder, July 11, 1961. Intern, U. Tenn. Sch. Medicine, Memphis, 1959; staff psychologist Eastern State Hosp., Lexington, Ky., 1960-65, Child Guidance Clinic, Lexington, 1965-67; asst. prof. psychology Inter-Am. U., P.R., 1967-68; dir. psychology adolescent day care Area Community Mental Health Center, Washington, 1968-70; dir. psychol. services Alcoholic Rehab. Center, Butner, N.C., 1970-71; co-dir. psychol. services in child psychiatry Dix Hosp., Raleigh, N.C., 1971—; mem. adv. bd. Raleigh Developmental Evaluation Clinic, 1976-80; adj. faculty psychology dept. N.C. State U., Raleigh, 1975—, U. N.C. Sch. Medicine, 1975—. Mem. Wake County Youth Adv. Bd., 1979-80; mem. adv. com. Raleigh Arts Commn., 1980-82; bd. dirs. Haven House for Children, 1980-85, Nazareth House for Children, 1980-85. Recipient best research award N.C. Dept. Mental Health, 1965, cert. of appreciation Washington Tchrs. Assn., 1969, Outstanding Youth Svcs. award Wake Coun., 1991; numerous awards for art, including Purchase award N.C. Mus. Art, 1976, awards N.C. Watercolor Soc., 1978, 79; numerous research grants. Mem. Am. Psychol. Assn., Southeastern Psychol. Assn., N.C. Psychol. Assn., Am. Assn. Psychiat. Services for Children (program chmn. 1976-77), Raleigh Artists Guild (pres.), Raleigh Fine Arts Soc., N.C. Art Soc., Women's Equity Action League. N.C. Women's Polit. Caucus, Durham Artists Guild, N.C. Watercolor Soc. (v.p.), Wake Visual Artists Assn. (pres.), AAUW. Democrat. Baptist. Contbr. articles to profl. jours.; dir. editorial bd. N.C. Jour. Mental Health, 1974—; adj. editorial rev. bd. Hosp. and Community Psychiatry, Quar. Jour. Studies on Alcohol, Raleigh Acad. Women, 1993. Office: Child Psychiatry Clinic Dix Hospital Raleigh NC 27611

CORDINGLEY, MARY JEANETTE BOWLES (MRS. WILLIAM ANDREW CORDINGLEY), social worker, psychologist, artist, writer; b. Des Moines, Jan. 1, 1918; d. William David and Florence (Spurrier) Bowles; m. William Andrew Cordingley, Mar. 17, 1942; children: William Andrew, Thomas Kent, Constance Louise. Student, Stephens Coll., 1936; BA, Carleton Coll., 1939; postgrad. U. Denver, 1944-45; MA in Psychiat. Social Work, U. Minn., 1948; grad. art student, 1963; MA in Counseling Psychology Pepperdine U., 1985; Co-pub. Univ. News, 1939-40; with U.S.O. Travelers Aid Service, 1942-44; mem. Jr. League, Des Moines, 1943, bd. dirs., sec. Mpls., 1951-56; clinic psychiat. social worker U. Minn. Hosp., 1947-48; social worker community service project neuropediatrics U. Minn., 1964-65; med. dir. med. sch. svc. Mont. Deaconess Hosp., 1970-74; instigator, pres. Original Pioneer Prints Notepaper Co.; paintings in variety of galleries and traveling shows; exhibited in numerous one-woman shows including Chas. Russell Gallery, Mont., Student Union U. Minn., Nat. Biennial League Am. Pen Women, 1968, 70, U. Mont., 1974, Mont. Traveling Exhibit, 1966-67, Mus. of the Rockies hist. show, 1976, Bergen Art Guild, 1976, 78, U.S. Traveling Show, 1987-89, Russell Auction, 1977, 91, Kessel Long Gallery, Scottsdale, 1991, Great Falls Pub. Libr. hist. art show oil exhibit 1992—, Artist's Kaleidoscope, 1995; Ariz. terrain show, Mayo Clinic, Scottsdale, 1991—; illustrator: The Tobacco Route, Geol. Soc. Guide Book, 1992; Mon. Artist Exhibit-Gov.'s Mansion, 1990; graphic artist in metal etchings; therapist Mental Health Center, 1977-82. Organizer, Hazeltine Nat. Golf Club Womens Assn., 1962-64, I. & R. Ctr., 1967; pres. adv. bd. Mont. State U.; past mem. bd. dirs. United Way, mem. arts adv. bd. Sierra Nev. Coll.; former mem. Youth Guidance Home Bd. Recipient various awards. Mem. NASW, State Arts Coun. (art instr. Ariz.), Scottsdale Jr. League (sustainers 1986—), Am. Mus. Women in Arts (participating). Co-author: State Arts Coun. Series on Mont. Instns.; author: Speaking With a Brush. Home: Box 4674 Incline Village NV 89450 also (winter): 7878 E Gainey Ranch Rd Unit 47 Scottsdale AZ 85258-1770

CORDON, GLENDA SUE, college dean; b. Harlingen, Tex., Mar. 2, 1943; d. Nolan Edgar and Helen Doris (Hays) Wilborn; children: Matthew Chandler, Heather Joan. BS, U. Ill., 1965. Rsch. asst. Ill. Geol. Survey, Urbana, 1965-67; tchr. Arcola (Ill.) Jr. High Sch., 1967-69; geology text author O'Fallon (Ill.) High Sch., 1976-82; compliance officer St. Clair County Grants Dept., Belleville, Ill., 1983-87; dir. job tng. McKendree Coll., Lebanon, Ill., 1987-88, dean of admissions, 1988—. Co-author: (high sch. text) Geology Is, 1977. Bd. dirs. bootstrap program St. Clair County Housing Authority, 1991—. Mem. Nat. Assn. Coll. Admissions Counselors, Nat. Assn. Collegiate Registrars and Admissions Officers, Ill. Assn. Collegiate Registrars and Admissions Officers, Ill. Assn. Coll. Admissions Counselors,. Home: 107B W St Louis St Lebanon IL 62254 Office: McKendree Coll 701 College Rd Lebanon IL 62254-1212

CORDON, RAQUEL LYNN, marketing manager; b. Portsmouth, Va., Nov. 10, 1969; d. Ricardo and Angela Louise (Wilson) C. BS in Mktg., Winthrop U., 1992. Sales mgr. Palmetto Expo Ctr., Greenville, S.C., 1992—; monitor Bus. Edn. Partnership, Greenville, 1996. Site coord. Hands on Greenville, 1994—; com. mem. C. of C. membership drive, Greenville, 1996, Bus. After Hours, 1996; advisor Chi Omega Frat., Furman U., Greenville, 1995—. Mem. Women in Communications, Inc. (membership com. 1996). Office: Palmetto Expo Ctr One Exposition Ave Greenville SC 29607

CÓRDOVA, FRANCE ANNE-DOMINIC, astrophysics scientist, administrator; b. Paris, Aug. 5, 1947; came to U.S., 1953; d. Frederick Ben Jr. and Joan Francis (McGuinness) C.; m. Christian John Foster, Jan. 4, 1985; children: Anne-Catherine Cordova Foster, Stephen Cordova Foster. BA in English with distinction, Stanford U., 1969; PhD in Physics, Calif. Inst. Tech., 1979. Staff scientist earth and space sci. div. Los Alamos Nat. Lab., 1979-89, dep. group leader space astronomy and astrophysics group, 1989; prof., head dept. astronomy and astrophysics Pa. State U., University Park, 1989-93; chief scientist NASA, Washington, 1993-96; vice chancellor for rsch. U. Calif., Santa Barbara, 1996—; mem. Nat. Com. on Medal of Sci., 1991-94; mem. adv. com. for astron. scis. NSF, 1990-93, external adv. com. Particle Astrophysics Ctr., 1989-93; bd. dirs. Assn. Univs. for Rsch. in Astronomy, 1989-93; mem. Space Telescope Inst. Coun., 1990-93; mem. com. space astronomy and astrophysics Space Sci. Bd., 1987-90, internat. users com. Roentgen X-ray Obs., 1985-90, extreme ultraviolet explorer guest observer working group NASA, 1988-92, com. Space Sci. and Applications Group, NASA, 1991-93; mem. Hubble Telescope Adv. Camera Team, 1993; chair Hubble Fellow Selection Com., 1992. Author: The Women of Santo Domingo, 1969; guest editor Mademoiselle mag., 1969; editor: Multiwavelength Astrophysics, 1988, The Spectroscopic Survey Telescope, 1990; contbr. over 100 articles, abstracts and revs. to Astrophysics Jour., Nature, Astrophysics and Space Scis., Advanced Space Rsch., Astron. Astrophysics, Mon. Nat. Royal Astron. Soc., chpts. to books. Named One of Am.'s 100 Brightest Scientists under 40, Sci. Digest, 1986; numerous grants NASA, 1979—, recipient group achievement award, NASA, 1991. Mem. Internat. Astron. Union (U.S. nat. com. 1990-93), Am. Astron. Soc. (v.p. 1993-96, chair high energy astrophysics divsn. 1990, vice chair 1989), Sigma Xi. Office: NASA Code AS 300 E St SW Washington DC 20546

CÓRDOVA, MARIA ASUNCION, dentist; b. Punta Arenas, Magallanes, Chile, May 14, 1941; came to U.S., 1972; d. Miguel Cordova and Maria Asucion Requena; m. Carlos F. Salinas, July 27, 1963; children: Carlos M., Claudio A., Lola. DDS, U. Chile, Santiago, 1965; DMD, Med. U. S.C., 1986. From instr. to assoc. prof. medicine U. Chile Dept. Physiology, Valparaiso, 1965-72; postdoctoral fellow Johns Hopkins U., Balt., 1972-75; from instr. to asst. prof. M.U. S.C. Dept. Physiology, Charleston, 1975-86; pvt. practice Charleston, 1987—; vis. scientist N.Y. Med. Coll., 1975. Contbr. articles to profl. jours. Program coord. Circulo Hispanic Charleston; coord. Amnesty Internat. U.S.A., Spoleto, Neighborday, Charleston, S.C.; bd. dirs. YWCA; active NOW. Mem. Charleston Women's Network (pres. 1989-90). Roman Catholic. Office: 159 Wentworth St Charleston SC 29401-1731

CORE, MARY CAROLYN W. PARSONS, radiologic technologist; b. Valpariso, Fla., Dec. 8, 1949; d. Levi and Mary Etta (Elliott) Willey; m. Joel Kent Core, Aug. 3, 1979; 1 child, Candace W. Parsons. Student, Peninsula Gen. Hosp. Sch. Radiologic Tech., Salisbury, Md., 1969; student, U. Del., 1969-73, Del. Tech. Community Coll., 1973-79, St. Joseph's Coll., 1983-86; BSBA, St. Joseph's Coll., 1987; MGA, U. Md., 1995. Technologist Peninsula Gen. Hosp., Salisbury, 1967-72; tech. dir. edn. Sch. Radiologic Tech., Salisbury, 1973-75; technologist Johns Hopkins Hosp., Salisbury, 1972-73, Nanticoke Meml. Hosp., Seaford, Del., 1975-79; adminstrv. chief technologist, imaging depts. Shady Grove Adventist Hosp., Rockville, Md., 1979-81; dir. dept. radiol. scis. Anne Arundel Diagnostics, Inc., Annapolis, Md., 1981-92; COO Anne Arundel MRI (Magnetic Resonance Imaging, Annapolis, Md., 1981-92; CEO Anne Arundel Diagnostics, Inc. and Anne Arundel MRI, Annapolis, Md., 1981-92; v.p. corp. svcs. Anne Arundel Healthcare Systems, Inc., 1992—. Mem. Ctrl. Md. Coun. Girl Scouts Am., Pres.'s award svc. team, 1989; bd. mem. Anne Arundel Trade Coun., 1996—; adv. bd. YWCA Careers, 1994—. Recipient twin awards YWCA, 1988. Mem. NAFE, Md. Soc. Radiologic Technologists (pres. 1980-81, sr. bd. mem. 1982-83, various awards including 1st Pl. Essay awards 1974, 76, 84, 87), Am. Hosp. Radiology Adminstrs. (v.p. 1984-85, chmn. by-laws com. 1984-85, statis. resources com. 1985-86), Am. Mgmt. Assn., Radiology Bus. Mgrs. Assn., Ea. Shore Dist. Radiologic Technologists (pres. 1976-78), Md. Assn. Healthcare Execs., Project Mgrs. Inst., Phi Kappa Phi. Republican. Methodist. Home: 1907 Harcourt Ave Crofton MD 21114-2103 Office: 135 E 55th St New York NY 10022-4049

CORELLI, TERESA ANN, laboratory director; b. Far Rockaway, N.Y., Nov. 24, 1955; d. Vincent William and Rose Bella (D'Amato) C. AAS in Med. Lab. Tech., SUNY, Farmingdale, 1976; BS in Biology, SUNY, Geneseo, 1978; MBA, Tampa Coll., 1994. Lab. mgr. Meml. Hosp., Bunnell, Fla., 1990-91; lab. dir., coord. Total Quality Mgmt. program Sun Coast Hosp., Largo, Fla., 1991—. Mem. Am. Soc. Quality Control, Clin. Lab. Mgmt. Assn. Home: 1971 Whitney Way Clearwater FL 34620 Office: Sun Coast Hosp 2025 Indian Rocks Rd Largo FL 34644

COREN, LOIS MARTIN, artist, photographer; b. Chgo., Apr. 11, 1931; d. Oscar and Lillian (Lubliner) Kohn; m. John Bazil Martinez, Sept. 10, 1950 (div. 1952); children: Loel Phillip Martin, Keith David Martin; m. Clyde Ira Coren, May 8, 1971. Attended, Art Inst. Chgo., 1948-50, Evanston (Ill.) Art Ctr., 1970-80; studied with Richard Loving and Ruth Jennings. Office mgr. Coren Rod & Reel Svc., Chgo., 1970-82. Solo shows include Goldman-Kraft Gallery, Chgo., 1988, DeFalco Gallery, Chgo., 1996; two-person show No. Ind. Arts Assn., 1992, Blue Moon Gallery, Skokie, Ill., 1996; group shows include Art Sales and Rental Gallery-Art Inst. Chgo., 1978, Nina Owen Ltd. Gallery, Chgo., 1986, Ft. Wayne (Ind.) Mus., 1986-87, Chiaroscuro Gallery, Chgo., 1987, 90, Lakeview Mus. Sci. and Art, Peoria, Ill., 1987-88, White House Gallery, Lake Geneva, Wis., 1987, Charles Allis Art Mus., Milw., 1989, Riverwalk Gallery, Naperville, Ill., 1989, Goldman-Kraft Gallery, 1989, Crosscurrents Gallery, Chgo., 1990, Met. Gallery, Milw., 1991, Limner Gallery, N.Y.C., 1993, New Visions, Marshfield, Wis., 1993, Seebeck Gallery, Racine, Wis., 1993, Enid Oklahoma Gallery, Chgo., 1994, Gallery Centre, Indpls., 1994, Balzekas Mus. of Lithuanian Culture, 1996, others; permanent collections include Mus. U. So. Ill., Edwardsville, DuPage Libr. Art Collection, Wheaton, Ill., Amoco Oil Co., many others. Historian Green Sch. PTA, Chgo., 1956-59; mem. faculty com. Evanston Art Ctr., 1972-78; bd. publicity Co-op of the Evanston Art Ctr., 1978-84. Grantee Mid-Career Visual Artists Lester Cooke Found.; nominee Awards in the Visual Arts, 1990. Mem. Chgo. Artists Coalition (bd. mem.), Primitive Arts Soc. (membership chairwoman). Home and Studio: 1310 Wesley St Evanston IL 60201

COREY, KAY JANIS, business owner, designer, nurse; b. Detroit, Aug. 22, 1942; d. Alexander Michael Corey and Lillian Emiline (Stanley) Kilborn; divorced; children: Tonya Kay, William James, Jason Ronald. Student, C.S. Mott Community Coll., 1960-62, Mich. State U., 1962-64; AA, AS in Nursing, St. Petersburg Jr. Coll., 1978; student, U. South Fla., 1985-86. RN; cert. perioperative nurse; cert. varitypist. Mgr. display Lerner Shops, Flint, Mich., 1960-62; layout artist Abdulla Advt., Flint, 1966-67; varitypist, artist City Hall Print Shop, Flint, 1967-70; nurse Suncoast Hosp., Largo, Fla., 1976-78; nurse, coord. plastic surgery svc., perioperative staff nurse Largo Med. Ctr. Hosp., 1978-81, 84—; assoc. dir. nursing Roberts Home Health Svc., Pinellas Park, Fla., 1982-84; co-owner Sand Castle Resort, White Bay, Jost Van Dyke, Brit. Virgin Island, 1990-95; perioperative nurse Columbia Golf Coast Surgery Ctr., 1996—; designer, artist K.J. Originals clothing line, 1990-95; insvc. edn. instr., dir. video edn., team leader oncology dept. Largo Med. Ctr. Hosp., 1980-81, now part-time nurse. Editor, illustrator: (book) Some Questions and Answers About Chemotherapy, 1981, Thoughts for Today, 1981; illustrator (cookbooks) Spices and Spoons, 1982, Yom Tov Essen n' Fressen, 1983; various brochures and catalogues; art work in permanent collection of C.S. Mott Jr. Coll., Flint, 1962; artist, designer of casual and hand painted clothing for children and adults. Historian Am. Businesswomen's Assn., Flint, 1968-73 (scholarship 1976); outreach chmn. Temple B'nai Israel, Clearwater, Fla., 1981-85; regional outreach coord. Union of Am. Hebrew Congregations, N.Y.C., 1983-85. Mem. Assn. of Oper. Rm. Nurses, Phi Theta Kappa. Republican. Jewish. Office: Columbia Gulf Coast Surgery 411 2nd St E Bradenton FL 34208 also: 1500 53d Ave W Palmetto FL 34221-5510

COREY, MARCIA V., federal agency administrator; b. Rockville Ctr., N.Y., Dec. 29, 1948; d. Charles H. and Arlene M. (Vohringer) C.; m. Robert A. Wright, Sept. 19, 1986. BA, SUNY, Cortland, 1970, MS, 1973. Tchr., 1970-73, 75-76; bus. mgr. U.S. Forest Svc., Idaho, 1977-80; personnel mgmt. specialist U.S. Forest Svc., Mont., 1980-85; human resource specialist U.S. Customs Svc., Washington, 1985-87; human resource specialist FAA, Washington, 1987-88, various mgmt. positions, 1988—. Active BPW, 1980-82, Big Bros. and Sisters, 1980-82, Cmty. Intervention Women's Hotline, Hospice, 1982-85; vol. Nat. Gallery of Arts, 1986—; resident assoc. Smithsonian. Mem. NAFE, Nat. Mus. Am. Indian (charter), Women's Transp. Seminar (treas. 1992-94), Women in Aviation, Tech. Women's Orgn., Capitol Hill Restoration Soc.

CORK, HOLLY A., state legislator; b. Savannah, Ga., Mar. 8, 1966; d. William Neville II and Helen (Holloman) C. BA, U. S.C., 1988. Legis. asst. to Rep. Arthur Ravenel Jr., 1988-89; mem. S.C. Ho. Reps., dist. 123, 1989-92, S.C. Senate Dist 46, 1992—. Republican. Presbyterian. Home: 3 Rowboat Row Hilton Head Island SC 29928-3007 Office: PO Box 142 Columbia SC 29202-0142

CORKERY, MARTHA GALLAGHER, elementary education educator; b. Portland, Maine, Apr. 21, 1956; d. Martin Patrick and Laurette (Lauzon) Gallagher; m. David Robert Corkery, Aug. 12, 1989. BA in English & Theatre, U. Maine, 1978; MS in Edn., U. So. Maine, 1989. Tchr. English Massabesic High Sch., Waterboro, Maine, 1978-81, Gorham (Maine) High Sch., 1981-88, U. So. Maine, Gorham, 1989-92; assoc. cons. So. Maine Partnership, Gorham, 1992-94; tchr. 6th grade Gorham Village Sch., 1994—; speaker in field. Trustee Old Red Ch., Standish, Maine, 1983-86; chair common ground planning com. Maine Leadership Consortium, Augusta, 1993-94. Blaine House scholar, 1988-89. Mem. Nat. Coun. Tchrs. English, Maine Edn. Assn. (bd. dirs. 1992—), Maine. Coun. Tchrs. English/Lang. Arts, Maine Reading Assn., Gorham Tchrs. Assn. (pres. 1989—), Internat. Reading Assn. Home: RR 1 Box 6830 Sebago Lake ME 04075-9748 Office: Village Elem Sch 12 Robie St Gorham ME 04038-1710

CORKRAN, VIRGINIA BOWMAN, real estate associate; b. N.Y.C., Feb. 13, 1924. BA, Conn. Coll., 1945. Tchr. Low-Heywood Sch., Stamford, Conn., 1946-47; editor North Shore Calendar, Winnetka, Ill., 1955-59; real estate assoc. Premier Properties, Naples, Fla., 1969—. Elected mem. City Coun., Naples, 1974-78. Mem. Old Naples Assn. (pres. 1995—). Office: Premier Properties Inc 283 Broad Ave S Naples FL 33940

CORLESS, DOROTHY ALICE, nurse educator; b. Reno, Nev., May 28, 1943; d. John Ludwig and Vera Leach (Wilson) Adams; children: James Lawrence Jr., Dorothy Adele Carroll. RN, St. Luke's Sch. Nursing, 1964. Clinician, cons., educator, author, adminstr. Fresno County Mental Health Dept., 1970-94; pvt. practice mental health nurse Fresno, 1991-94; instr. police sci. State Ctr. Tng. Facility, 1991-94; pvt. practice, mental health con., educator Florence, Oreg., 1994—. Vol. ARC, Disaster Mental Health Svcs., 1993—. Maj. USAFR, 1972-94. Mem. NAFE, Forensic Mental Health Assn. Calif., Calif. Peace Officer's Assn., Critical Incident Stress Found. Home: 1580 Kalla Kalla Ct Florence OR 97439-8963

CORLEY, FLORENCE FLEMING, history educator; b. Augusta, Ga., Jan. 6, 1933; d. William Cornelius and Sarah Virginia (Sibley) Fleming; m. James Weaver Corley, Jr., Dec. 29, 1955; children: Florence Hart Corley Johnson, James Weaver Corley III, Mary Anne Corley Herbert, Sarah Virginia Corley, William Thomas Corley. BA, Agnes Scott Coll., 1954; MA, Emory U., 1955; PhD, Ga. State U., 1985. Cert. tchr., T-5, Ga. Alumnae rep. Agnes Scott Coll., Decatur, Ga., 1955; history tchr. The Westminster Schs., Atlanta, 1968-88, The Walker Sch., Marietta, Ga., 1989; history instr. Kennesaw State U., Marietta, Ga., 1989-91, asst. prof. history, 1991—; U.S. history cons. The Coll. Bd., N.Y.C., 1978—; reader, table leader Ednl. Testing Svc., Princeton, N.J., 1975—. Assoc. editor: American Presbyterians, Phila., 1984—, Ga. Jour. of So. Legal History, Atlanta, 1989; editor: The Landmarker, 1978-79; author: Confederate City: Augusta, Georgia 1860-65, 1960, 74, 95; contbr. articles to hist. jours.; compiler (slides/tape) Where Were the Women? 1979. Sixth grade and adult tchr. First Presbyn. Ch., Marietta, 1960—, elder, 1990—; active U.S. history contest DAR, Marietta, 1991—; cons. Girls club of Cobb/Marietta 1981; mem. Ga. Nat. Registry Rev. Bd., 1994—, chmn. 1996-97. Woodrow Wilson fellow Emory U., 1954-55; recipient fellowship in women's history NEH, Stanford U., Palo Alto, Calif., 1978-79, scholarship in classical studies, Vergilian Soc., Cumae, Italy, 1982, scholarships in medieval Eng. and Eng. today, English Speaking Union, U.K., 1979, 80. Mem. Cobb Landmarks and Hist. Soc. (charter bd. dirs., co-pres. 1985-86, 87-88), Atlanta Hist. Soc., Atlanta Civil War Round Table, Soc. Civil War Historians, Ga. Assn. Historians, Ga. Hist. Soc., So. Assn. Women Historians, So. Hist. Assn., So. Garden History Soc., Richmond County Hist. Assn., Presbyn. Hist. Soc., Phi Beta Kappa, Phi Alpha Theta. Democrat. Home: 285 Kennesaw Ave Marietta GA 30060-1671 Office: Kennesaw State Coll 1000 Chastian Rd Kennesaw GA 30144-5591

CORLEY, JEAN ARNETTE LEISTER, infosystems executive; b. Charleston, S.C., June 16, 1944; d. William Audley and Arnette (Mason) Leister; m. Fred G. Wix, Aug. 27, 1995; children: Arnette Elizabeth, Daniel Lee, Heather, Gretchen. BS, Med. Coll. Ga., 1970; MBA, M of Pub. Adminstrn., Southeastern U., 1980. Various positions health care orgns., Augusta, Ga., 1960-70; office mgr., counselor Info. Ctr. for Alcohol and Drug Abuse, Augusta, 1970-71; planner health care systems Nat. Med. Assn. Found., Washington, 1971-72; research assoc., systems analyst GEOMET, Inc., Gaithersburg, Md., 1972-74; dir. med. records Georgetown U. Hosp., Washington, 1974-80; dir. med. info. svcs. Lahey Clinic Med. Ctr., Burlington, Mass., 1980-84; nat. sales mgr. 3M Health Info. Systems, Boston and Atlanta, 1984-91; mktg. mgr. 3M Health Info. Systems, Salt Lake City, 1992—. Contbr. articles to profl. jours. Mem. adv. bd. various colls., 1973-96; grad. proctor U. Ala., U. Utah, Brigham Young U., Ohio State U.; active Habitat for Humanity, Leadership Utah. Mem. Am. Health Info. Mgmt. Assn. (program com. 1977-80, chmn. 1981-82, fed. health program adv. com. 1978-80, computerized health info. task force 1983-87, subcom. on edn. 1990-93, Workgroup on Electronic Data Interchange 1992-94), Computer-based Patient Record Inst., Women in Info. Processing, New Eng. Med. Records Conf. (exec. dir. 1984-88), LWV, Emily's List, Utah Women's Polit. Caucus. Democrat. Presbyterian. Home: 545 De Soto St Salt Lake City UT 84103-2134

CORLEY, JENNY LYND WERTHEIM, elementary education educator; b. Lincoln, Ill., June 18, 1937; d. Robert Glenn and Nancy Lynd (Hoblit) Wertheim; m. William Gene Corley, Aug. 9, 1959; children: Anne Lynd Corley Baum, Robert William, Scott Elson. BS in Music Edn., U. Ill., 1959, MS in Music Edn., 1961; postgrad., U. Ill., Loyola U., 1985—. Tchr. choral music Mahomet (Ill.)/Seymour K-12, 1959-61; supr. music Fairfax County (Va.), 1961-63; Tchr. music Highland Park (Ill.) 107, 1969, dir. gifted edn., 1969-70; tchr. music Glenview (Ill.) 34, 1981—; sec.-treas. Corley Agroleum Properties, 1993—; water safety instr./trainer ARC; lifeguard instr./trainer Cmty. First Aid, 1995. Dir. mid-Am. bd. ARC, Chgo., 1980-86. Recipient Heart of Gold United Way, 1992, Community Svc. award Ill. Park & Recreation Assn./Ill. Assn. Park Dists., 1994, Disting. Svc. award Boys and Girls Swimming Official, Ill. High Sch. Assn., 1994. Mem. Music Edn. Nat. Conf., North Shore Music Tchrs. Assn. (treas. 1987-90), Jr. League Chgo. (treas. 1978-81), Sigma Alpha Iota, Phi Delta Kappa (found. chmn. 1994—), U. Ill. Music Alumnae (pres. bd. dirs. 1995—). Presbyterian. Home: 744 Glenayre Dr Glenview IL 60025-4411 Office: Springman Sch 2701 Central Rd Glenview IL 60025-4134

CORLEY, M. DEBORAH, therapist; b. Lubbock, Tex., Nov. 22, 1949; d. Clifton D. and Marvel E. (Kelly) C.; m. Robert Casselman, Aug. 17, 1969 (div. 1976); 1 child, Stephanie Casselman; m. Gary N. Whiteside, Oct. 1, 1991. BA, U. Colo., Colorado Springs, 1977; MA in Psychology, Calif. Western U., 1979. Cert. addiction specialist. Dir. continuing edn. Rocky Mountain Planned Parenthood, Denver, 1980-83; dir. Human Svcs. Inc., Denver, 1983-87, Colo. Initiative Teen Pregnancy, Denver, 1987-90; CEO, adminstr. Diamond Mountain Ctr., Dallas, 1990—. Contbr. articles to profl. jours. Mem. Am. Assn. Marriage & Family Therapists, Nat. Couns. Sexual Addiction (sec., pres. bd. dirs. 1990-95), Tex. Abortion Rights Action League. Home: 3016 Leahy Dr Dallas TX 75229

CORLEY, ROSE ANN MCAFEE, weapon systems advisor; b. Lawton, Okla., Aug. 21, 1952; d. Claude James and Mary Margaret (Holman) McAfee; m. Gary Michael Griffin, Feb. 14, 1973 (div. Oct. 1984); m. Terry Joe Corley, July 31, 1988; stepson Troy Justin Corley. BS, Cameron U., Lawton, Okla., 1970; diploma, Army Command and Staff Coll., Ft. Leavenworth, Kans., 1989; MCJA, Oklahoma City U., 1990; cert., Army Mgmt. Staff Coll., Ft. Belvoir, Va., 1991. Cert. in Distbn. Mgt. Supply clk. Dept. of Army, Ft. Sill, Okla., 1972-80, supply mgmt. asst., 1980-82; supply systems analyst Dept. of Army, Ft. Lee, Va., 1982; supply tech. Dept. of Army, Ft. Sill, Okla., 1982-83, supr. inventory mgmt. specialist, 1983-86, manprint program mgr., 1986-91; weapon system advisor Def. Logistics Agy., San Antonio, 1991-96; customer svc. rep. Def. Logistics Agy., Robins AFB, Ga., 1996—; equal employment counselor USA Field Artillery Sch., Ft. Sill, Okla., 1976-82; mentor Fed. Women's Program, Kelly AFB, Tex., 1991-96. Recipient Cert. of Appreciation, Sec. of Def., Washington, 1984, Cert. of Appreciation, Directorate of Engring. and Housing, Ft. Sill, 1986; decorated Order of St. Barbara, U.S. Army Arty. Sch., Ft. Sill, 1991. Mem. Fed. Women's Program, Soc. Logistics Engrs., Fed. Mgrs. Assn., Kelly Mgmt. Assn., World Affairs Coun. of San Antonio, Internat. City Mgmt. Assn., Tex. Corvette Assn. Home: 325 Kibbee St Hawkinsville GA 31036 Office: Def Logistics Agy Bldg 301E 420 2nd St Robins AFB GA 31098

CORLISS, SANDRA IRENE, correctional health care professional; b. Nashua, N.H., June 9, 1949; d. Robert Henry Corliss and Elizabeth Juliette (Duffina) Knowles. Diploma in Nursing, Yoville Hosp., Cambridge, Mass., 1971; postgrad., Regents Coll., 1992—. LPN, Fla.; cert. BLS, cert. health profl., IV nurse, AIDS counselor, staff tng. officer. LPN staff nurse Yoville Hosp., Cambridge, Mass., 1972-73, Huntington Gen. Hosp., Brookline, Mass., 1973-76, Riverview Nursing Home, 1976-77, Cohassett Nursing Home, 1977-78, Rosary Hill, Hawthorne, N.Y., 1982-84, Humana Hosp. Pasco, Dade City, Fla., 1984-85, Pasco County Sheriff Office, Land-o-Lakes, Fla., 1985—. Cons. Sunrise of Pasco, Dade City, 1987—, sec. bd. dirs., 1990-92, pres. bd. dirs., 1992; cons. Oaks Royal Civic Assn., Zephyrhills, Fla., 1987—, social svcs. dir. subdivsn. III; bd. advisors Sunrise Domestic Violence Shelter, Dade City. Mem. Am. Jail Assn., Am. Correctional Health Svcs. Assn., Fla. Correctional Health Svcs. Assn., Nat. League of Nursing, Fla. Jail Assn., Cert. Correctional Health Profls. Republican. Roman Catholic. Home: 36440 Malibu Way Zephyrhills FL 33541-2060 Office: Pasco County Sheriff's Office 10200 Central Blvd Land O'Lakes FL 34639-7001

CORMAN, LINDA WILSON, librarian; b. Washington, Nov. 25, 1944; d. Earl and Elsie (Bex) Wilson; m. Brian Corman, Sept. 2, 1967; 1 child, Sarah Wilson Corman. AB magna cum laude, Vassar Coll., 1966; MA, U. Chgo., 1969; MLS, U. Toronto, Ont., Can., 1974. Libr. Ont. Inst. for Studies in Edn., Toronto, Can., 1974-80; head libr. U. Toronto Trinity Coll., Ont., Can., 1980—. Author, compiler: Community Education in Canada, 1975 (best of eric award 1975); contbr. articles to profl. jours.; mem. editl. bd. Papers of the Bibliographical Soc. of Can., 1986-90; consulting editor: Jour. of Religious and Theological Info., 1990—. Mem. exec. com. Friends of the Osborne Collection, Toronto, 1979-85. Recipient Nat. Merit scholarship, 1962-66; Ont. Libr. Assn. prize, 1974; Brit. Coun. grant, 1988. Mem. Am. Theological Libr. Assn. (bd. dirs. 1991—, pres. 1995-96), Can. Libr. Assn. (chair pubs. com. 1987-88), Bibliographical Soc. Can., Phi Beta Kappa, Beta Phi Mu. Home: 94 Mayfield Ave, Toronto, ON Canada M6S 1K8 Office: Trinity Coll, 6 Hoskin Ave, Toronto, ON Canada M5S 1H8

CORMANICK, ROSA-MARIA MORENO, academic program coordinator; b. Guatemala, Guatemala, Sept. 4, 1946; d. Armando and Lily (Cordon) Moreno; children: Liza Maria, Angie Michele, David William. Diploma, Liceo Bilingue, Guatemala, 1964; BA, Ohio State U., 1982, MA in Higher Edn. Adminstrn., 1995. Fgn. dept. asst. Banco del Agro, Guatemala, 1964-66; regional mgr. asst. gen. food div. Incasa, Guatemala, 1966-68; translator/asst. human rsch. ctr. Ohio State U., Columbus, 1968-69, dirs. asst. internat. program, 1969-71, acad. program coord. dept. Slavic and East European langs., 1971—; v.p./treas. St. Anthony Sch. Bd., Columbus, 1982-86; bd. dirs. St. Francis DeSales Sch., Columbus, 1991-95; liaison on the comms. and edn. team Adminstrv. Resource Mgmt. Sys. Project, 1996—. Mem. Dobro Slovo Slavic Honor Soc., Phi Kappa Phi. Office: Ohio State U Slavic Dept 232 Cunz Hall 1841 Millikin St Columbus OH 43210

CORMIER, CHERYL ANN, sales executive; b. Houston, Jan. 16, 1959; d. Calvin Jr. and Dorothy M. (Malveaux) Williams. BS, Patten Coll., 1996. Exec. asst. to exec. v.p. Cambridge Plan, Monterey, Calif., 1981-86, sales support coord., 1986-90, sales support mgr., 1990-91; resource mgr. Syntex Rsch., Palo Alto, Calif., 1992-95; mgr. nat. sales support svcs. PrimeQuest, Monterey, Calif., 1995—. Editor: Church of God in Christ Directory of Credential Holders, 1994. Campaign mgr. Seaside City Coun., Calif., 1990; vol. dir. computer ops. Ch. of God in Christ, Memphis, 1992—; vol. bus. mgr. Greater Victory Temple COGIC, Seaside, 1992—; vol. health forum com. Am. Heart Assn., 1995—.

CORMIER, MARY EALY, jewelry maker, sculptor; b. Salem, Iowa, Sept. 24, 1933; d. Elmer Russell and Stella Elizabeth (Fenn) Hodges; m. Wilbert Leroy Ealy, Oct. 12, 1952 (div. 1977); children: Sheri Luper, Lorita Heale, James Ealy, Gerald Ealy, Jeanne Zoschke; m. John Joseph Cormier, Aug. 6, 1979. Diploma, Paris Acad. of Beauty, Cedar Rapid, Iowa, 1950. Hairstylist Ga. Case Beauty Salon, Keokuk, Iowa, 1950-52; hairstylist, makeup artist Charles of the Ritz, Falls Church, Va., 1955-65; developer, cosmetic, perfume line Amarna XVIII, Ltd., Peotone, Ill., 1970-74; customer svc. Xerox Corp., Springfield, Ill., 1977-78; electronic bd. stuffer Tome Comdr., Inc., Redmond, Wash., 1979; porcelain doll artist, costumer Liza Jane Dolls, Coquitlam, B.C., Can., 1980-89; costume jewelry maker A.T. Storrs, Ltd., Vancouver, B.C., Can., 1990—. Home: 301-1315 7th Ave, New Westminster, BC Canada V3M 2J9

CORNAY, STACY SHELTON, public relations specialist; b. Laramie, Wyo., Oct. 18, 1961; d. Vern E. and Nancy A. (Reinhart) Shelton; m. Paul J. Cornay, Dec. 29, 1984; 1 child, Tanner. BS in Psychology, U. Wyo., 1984; MS in Comm., U. S.W. La., 1986. Panhellenic cons. U. S.W. La., Lafayette, 1984-86; account exec. Comm. Concepts, Lafayette, 1986-87; exec. dir. Vol. Ctr. of Lafayette, 1987-90; pub. rels. rep. ARC, Boulder, Colo., 1990-92; v.p. Longmont (Colo.) C. of C., 1992-94; pvt. cons., 1994—; pres., owner Comm. Concepts, Longmont, 1992-94. Editor newsletter The Leader, 1986-87; editor La. Crawfish Farmers Jour., 1986-87. Bd. dirs. Rape Crisis Ctr., Lafayette, 1988-90, Festival Internat. de Louisiane, Lafayette, 1993—, Longmont Coun. for the Arts, Tiny Tim Devel. Pre-sch.; mem. Existing Industry Task Force. Mem. Pub. Rels. Soc. Am. (newsletter, speakers com. 1990—), Twin Peaks Rotary Club (program chair 1992-93, vocat. chair 1995—, bd. dirs. 1996—), Boulder C. of C., Longmont C. of C., Econ. Devel. Assn. Longmont. Home: 1506 Frontier St Longmont CO 80501-2405

CORNELL, SARAH ASHLEY HAVILAND, controller; b. N.Y.C., June 22, 1971; d. John Russell and Sharon Forester (Salembier) C.; children: (Sarah) Dana, Tyler. BA in English, U. Va. Artist Rosenwald Studios, Cambridge, 1992, 93; fin. asst. Chancellor Capital Mgmt., N.Y.C., 1993; devel. officer San Francisco Symphony, 1994; landscape engr. Paesaggio Landscape Architects, San Francisco, 1994; fin. contr. London Antique, Inc., San Francisco, 1994—. Mem. Jefferson Literary and Debate Soc.

CORNELL, SHEILA, softball player; b. Feb. 26, 1962. Grad., UCLA; master's degree, U. So. Calif. Phys. therapist. Recipient Silver medal Pan Am. Games, 1983, Gold medal Pan. Am. Games, 1987, 91, 95, ISF Women's World Championship, 1990, 94, Intercontinental Cup, 1993, South Pacific Classic, 1994, Superball Classic, 1995, Atlanta Olympics, 1996. Office: Amateur Softball Assn 2801 NE 50th St Oklahoma City OK 73111-7203*

CORNELLA, JANET ANN, assistant principal; b. Boston, Nov. 13, 1948; d. James Joseph and Gertrude Phyllis (Arno) Cavalen; m. Robert Louis Cornella, July 16, 1972; children: Lauren, Jennifer. BA, Boston Coll., 1970; MA, Fla. Atlantic U., 1995. Cert. tchr., Mass., Fla. Tchr. St. Bridget Cath. Sch., South Boston, Mass., 1970-71, Broward County Pub. Sch., Hollywood, Fla., 1971-72, Watertown (Mass.) Pub. Schs., 1972-77; asst. prin. Wellington Christian Sch., West Palm Beach, Fla., 1983—. Co-author (handbook) Christian Schools of Florida Accreditation Handbook, 1994. Sch. bd. liason Wellington Edn. Found., West Palm Beach, 1991-94; alumni interviewer Boston Coll., West Palm Beach, 1975—; mem. Christian Sch. of Fla., 1993—,. Grantee NSF, 1976. Mem. Assn. of Curriculum Devel., Boston Coll. Alumni Club (treas. 1993—), N.T.C.M. Home: 12338 Old Country Rd West Palm Beach FL 33414 Office: Wellington Christian Sch 1000 Wellington Trace West Palm Beach FL 33414

CORNING, JOY COLE, state official; b. Bridgewater, Iowa, Sept. 7, 1932; d. Perry Aaron and Ethel Marie (Sullivan) Cole; m. Burton Eugene Corning, June 19, 1955; children: Carol, Claudia, Ann. BA, U. No. Iowa, 1954. Cert. elem. tchr., Iowa. Tchr. elem. sch. Greenfield (Iowa) Sch. Dist., 1951-53, Waterloo (Iowa) Community Sch. Dist., 1954-55; mem. Iowa Senate, Des Moines, 1984-90, asst. Rep. leader, 1989-90; lt. gov. State of Iowa, Des Moines, 1991—; bd. dirs. Iowa Nat. Bankshares Corp. Pres. Cedar Falls (Iowa) Sch. Bd., 1975-83; state pres. Iowa Talented and Gifted, 1975-77; mem. adv. bd. Waterloo Comty. Playhouse, Cedar Arts Forum; bd. dirs. Iowa Housing Fin. Authority, Des Moines, 1981-84, Iowa Assn. Sch. Bds., Des Moines, 1983-84, Iowa Peace Inst., 1987-91; mem. Edn. Commn. of States, 1987-90, The Caring Found., 1989—. Named Citizen of Yr., Cedar Falls C. of C., 1984; recipient ITAG Disting. Svc. to Iowa's Gifted and Talented Students award, 1991, Pub. Svc. award Iowa Home Econs. Assn., 1994, Friend of Math. award Iowa Coun. Tchrs. of Math., 1995, Iowa State Edn. Assn. Human Rels. award 1996; recognized for Extraordinary Advocacy for Children of Iowa chpt. Nat. Com. for Prevention of Child Abuse. Mem. AAUW, LWV, PEO, Nat. Assn. for Gifted Children (mem. adv. bd. 1991—), Delta Kappa Gamma, Alpha Delta Kappa. Republican. Mem. United Ch. of Christ. Office: State Capitol Office Of Lt Gov Des Moines IA 50319

CORNISH, ELIZABETH TURVEREY, stockbroker; b. Ionia, N.Y., Dec. 31, 1919; d. Clifford Dwight and Mildred Althea (Spicer) T.; m. Louis Joseph Cornish, June 21, 1941 (div. June 1955); 1 child, Carol Cornish Reeves. BS, Cornell U., 1941. Lic. stockbroker N.Y. Stock Exch., Prin. Reg. Options Prin., Commodity prin., Insur. prin. Teletype operator, sec. to mgr. Carl M. Loeb Rhoades & Co., Ithaca, N.Y., 1955-65; reg. rep. Carl M. Loeb Rhoades & Co., Ithaca, 1962-75; branch mgr. Loeb, Rhoades & Co., Ithaca, 1975-82; registered rep. Shearson Loeb Rhoades, Shearson Am. Express, Ithaca, 1982-86, Hutton, Shearson, Ithaca, 1986-88, First Albany Corp., Ithaca, 1988-91; registered rep., br. office mgr. A.G. Edwards & Sons, Inc., Ithaca, 1991—; charter mem. Nuveen Adv. Coun., 1984, 85, 86; instr. stock market and various br. office jobs for coll. interns. Mem. Planning Com. Downtown Mall, Ithaca, N.Y., 1972-75; chmn. campaign United Way Tompkins County, Ithaca, 1983, dir., 1983-89; bd. dirs. Ithaca Neighborhood Housing, Leadership Tompkins, 1986-88; pres. Friends of Ithaca Coll., 1985-86. Mem. Downtown Bus. Women (pres. 1971-72), Tompkins County C. of C. (bd. dirs. 1974-77, 83-86, v.p. 1980-81, pres.-elect 1989, pres. 1990), Ithaca Yacht Club (bd. dirs. 1988-90). Republican. Episcopalian. Office: A G Edwards & Sons Inc 107 N Aurora St Ithaca NY 14850-4301

CORNISH, JEANNETTE CARTER, lawyer; b. Steelton, Pa., Sept. 17, 1946; d. Ellis Pollard and Anna Elizabeth (Stannard) C.; m. Harry L. Cornish; children: Lee Jason, Geoffrey Charles. BA, Howard U., 1968, JD, 1971. Bar: N.J. 1976, U.S. Dist. Ct. N.J. 1976. Atty. Newark-Essex Law Reform, 1971-72; technician EEOC, Newark, 1972-73; atty., asst. sec. Inmont Corp., N.Y.C., 1974-82; sr. atty., asst. sec. Inmont Corp., Clifton, N.J., 1982-85; sr. atty. BASF Corp., Mt. Olive, N.J., 1986—; speaker on diversity in bus. Past mem., bd. dirs. YWCA, Paterson, N.J.; trustee Barnert Hosp., Paterson; bd. dirs. Lenni-Lenape coun. Girl Scouts Am. Mem. ABA (gen. practice sect., corp. counsel com., diversity vice chair), Nat. Bar Assn., Assn. Black Women Lawyers, Am. Corp. Counsel Assn., Internat. Trademark Assn. (past mem. editorial bd. The Trademark Reporter, mem. exec. commn. com.), N.J. Assn. Women Bus. Owners. Office: BASF Corp 3000 Continental Dr N Mount Olive NJ 07828-1234

CORNISH, LINDA SOWA YOUNG, children's books author and illustrator, educator; b. Woodburn, Oreg., May 14, 1943; d. Cecil Edward and Marian Regina (Nibler) Sowa; m. Edmund Y.W. Young, June 11, 1966 (div. July 1988); children: Laura Young Engelmann, Amy L.H. Young, Kimberly Young Brummund; m. H.T. Cornish, Oct. 6, 1991. BA, U. Portland, 1966; EdM, Temple U., 1968. Tchr. spl. edn. Phila. Sch. System, 1966-69; tchr. elem. and spl. edn. North Clackamas Dist. 12, Milwaukie, Oreg., 1974-92; author, illustrator Cornish Hen, Dahlia Pub. Co., Hillsboro, Oreg., 1994—. Author, illustrator: (juvenile) Pong's Visit, 1994, Pong's Ways, 1995. Mem. AAUW, ASCD, Assn. for Childhood Edn. Internt., Oreg. Coun. Tchrs. English, Northwest Assn. Book Publishers. Democrat. Methodist. Home: 1295 SW Brookwood Ave Hillsboro OR 97123-7593

CORNWALL, DEBORAH JOYCE, consulting firm executive, management consultant; b. Wilmington, Del., Dec. 9, 1946; d. Samuel and Norma (Bram) Handloff; m. Barry Newland Cornwall, June 22, 1968; 1 child, Deborah Leigh. BA, Mount Holyoke, 1968; MBA, Boston U., 1975. Editor Houghton Mifflin Co., Boston, 1967-69; editor Harbridge House, Inc., Boston, 1969-73, cons., 1973-74, assoc., 1974-75, sr. assoc., 1975-77, prin., 1977-79, v.p., 1979-81, v.p., div. mgr., 1981-83, sr. v.p., div. mgr., 1983-90; founder and mng. v.p. Korn/Ferry Organizational Cons., Boston, 1991-96; founder and mng. dir. The Corlund Group, 1996—; mem. mid. mgmt. excellence com. City of Boston, 1986. Bd. dirs. Mass. divsn. Am. Cancer Soc., 1994—. Mem. Human Resources Planning Soc., Phi Beta Kappa, Beta Gamma Sigma. Office: The Corlund Group 75 Federal St Boston MA 02110-1904

CORNWELL, ILENE JONES, writer, editor; b. Spartanburg, S.C., Sept. 27, 1942; d. Thurmond G. and Elizabeth (Furber) Jones; m. James H. Cornwell, Mar. 2, 1963 (div. 1977); children: James David, Robert Grant. Student, U. Tenn., 1975, Tenn. State U., 1987-88, Cumberland U., 1990—; Nashville Travel Inst., 1991. Pub. info. officer Tenn. Hist. Commn., Nashville, 1974-78; publs. editor, pub. info. officer Vanderbilt U. Med. Ctr., Nashville, 1978-81; writer, editor, owner So. Resources Unlimited, Nashville, 1981-92; copy editor, editorial cartoonist West Nashville Digest, 1993-94; contbg. editor and ptnr. New South Archtl. Press, Richmond, Va., 1993—; ptnr., contbg. writer/editor Serviceberry Press, Memphis, 1993—; adminstrv. asst. tchr. edn. and Pew retention program Fisk U., Nashville, 1995—; speaker, panelist Women in Media Com., Saginaw State U., Mich., 1990; speaker, workshop leader Elderhostel, 1990, Austin Peay State U., 1990; speaker to 40 civic, hist. and environ. groups; part-time asst. to coord. cmty. edn. Cohn Adult Learning Ctr., Nashville, 1992-93; mem. planning com. The Perfect 36 Exhibit Fisk U.; compiler spl. exhibit on 4 black suffragists; editor The Perfect 36 Exhbn. Catalogue, 1996. Author: Footsteps Along the Harpeth, 1970, 76, Travel Guide to the Natchez Trace Parkway, 1984; Natchez Trace Treasury and Travel Guide; Biographical Directory of the Tennessee General Assembly, (4 vols.) 1987, 88, 89, 90, Ruskin!, 1972; (with Jim Leeson) The Old Trace in Tennessee, 1972; (2 screenplays) Early Travels on the Natchez Trace, 1974, Natchez Trace: Pathway to Parkway, 1986 (nominated Nashville's Emmy 1988); compiler: (selected bibliography) The Legacy of Tenn. Women, 1995; editor various publs.; contbr. to publs. Charter mem. West Nashville Founders' Mus., Nashville, 1987, bd. dirs., 1989; chmn. Richland Creek Campaign, West Nashville Community Coun., 1989, 90; founder Bellevue-Harpeth Hist. Soc., 1970, 3-term pres.; Natchez Trace program presenter Internat. Conf. on Pkwys., Riverways, and Greenways Asheville, N.C., 1989; chair Natchez Trace Adv. Com., Tenn., 1990—; speaker and activist Natchez Trace Pky.: Doomed to Become an Interstate Hwy.?, 1990—; state judge Voice of Democracy student essay and scholarship contest, VFW, 1992, Tenn. Dept. Edn., Pencil student essay contest, 1994, history essay Tenn. students Tenn. Hist. Commn., 1989-97, others; program co-chmn. Tenn. women's history symposium com. Vanderbilt U. Women's Ctr., 1993-95. Recipient Vintage award Internat. Assn. Bus. Communicators, 1980, MacEachern award Am. Hosp. Assn., 1981, Pres. award Natchez Trace Pkwy. Assn., 1989, Outstanding Svc. and Leadership award West Nashville Cmty. Coun., 1989, Cert. of Merit, Unsung Am. Woman Essay competition Nat. Women's History Project, 1994; named Tenn. Outstanding Young Woman, 1975; Lawlor scholar Cumberland U., 1990-91. Mem. AAUW, Nat. League of Am. Pen Women (Nashville br., former pres., v.p., state conv. chairwoman), Tenn. Woman's Press and Authors Club (affiliate of Nat. Fedn. of Press Women, pres. 1978, former v.p. and chairwoman of state conv.), White Bridge Neighborhood Assn. (charter, bd. dirs.), Tenn. Environ. Coun., Am. Biog. Inst. Rsch. Assn. (selected assoc. and mem. adv. bd. 1990), Friends of Richland Creek (charter), Nat. Women's History Project, Nat. Mus. of Women in the Arts (charter), Tenn. Native Plant Soc. Home: 5632 Meadowcrest Ln Nashville TN 37209-4631

CORNWELL, PATRICIA DANIELS, author; b. 1956. Police reporter Charlotte (N.C.) Observer, 1979-81; computer analyst Office Chief Med. Examiner, Richmond, Va., 1985—. Author: (biography) A Time for Remembering, 1983, (novels) Postmortem, 1990, Body of Evidence, 1991, All that Remains, 1993, Cruel and Unusual, 1993, From Potter's Field, 1995 (One of Top 15 Bestsellers for 1995 Pubs. Weekly). Vol. police officer. Address: Don Congdon Assocs Inc care Michael Congdon 156 Fifth Ave Ste 625 New York NY 10010*

CORPUZ, SHEILA MAE, nurse; b. Honolulu, June 8, 1968; d. Antonio Abunan and Aida (Chan) C. BSN, Loma Linda U., 1990. RN, Calif; cert. neonatal intensive care nurse Nat. Cert. Corp. for Ob.-Gyn. and Neonatal Nursing Spltys. Nursing asst. Loma Linda (Calif.) U. Med. Ctr., 1988, unit sec., 1988-89, RN, 1989—; neonatal transport asst. Loma Linda U. Med. Ctr., 1993—. Mem. Nat. Assn. Neonatal Nurses. Home: 1487 Sycamore Ln San Bernardino CA 92408

CORRADINA, LINDA, broadcast executive. BS in Comm., Emerson Coll. Journalist CNN, Atlanta; assoc. prodr. ABC News; news prodr. MTV, sr. v.p., exec. prodr. news and spls.; sr. v.p. programming and prodn. VH1, N.Y.C., 1994—. Recipient Peabody awards (2), Ace awards (4). Office: MTV Networks 1515 Broadway 20th Fl New York NY 10036

CORRADINI, DEEDEE, mayor. Student, Drew U., 1961-63; BS, U. Utah, 1965, MS, 1967. Adminstrv. asst. for public info. Utah State Office Rehab. Svcs., 1967-69; cons. Utah State Dept. Community Affairs, 1971-72; media dir., press sec. Wayne Owens for Congress Campaign, 1972; press sec. Rep. Wayne Owens, 1973-74; spl. asst. to N.Y. Congl. Rep. Richard Ottinger, 1975; asst. to pres., dir. community rels. Snowbird Corp., 1975-77; exec. v.p. Bonneville Assocs., Inc., Salt Lake City, 1977-80; pres. Bonneville Assocs., Inc., 1980-89, chmn., CEO, 1989-91; mayor Salt Lake City, 1992—; mem. urban con. policy com. U.S. Conf. on Mayors, mem. unfunded fed. mandates task force, mem. crime and violence task force, chmn. adv. bd.; chair Mayor's Gang Task Force; mem. interngovtl. policy adv. com. U.S. Trade Rep., 1993-94; mem. transp. and comm. com. Nat. League of Cities, 1993-94. Bd. trustees Intermountain Health Care, 1980-92; bd. dirs., exec. com. Utah Symphony, 1983-92, vice chmn., 1985-88, chmn., 1988-92; dir. Utah chpt. Nat. Conf. Christians and Jews, Inc., 1988; bd. dirs. Salt Lake Olympic Bid Com., 1989—; chmn. image com. Utah Partnership for Edn. and Econ. Devel., 1989-92; co-chair United Way Success by 6 Program; pres. Shelter of the Homeless Com.; active Sundance Inst. Utah Com., 1990-92; disting. bd. fellow So. Utah U., 1991; active numerous other civic orgns. and coms. Mem. Salt Lake Area C. of C. (bd. govs. 1979-81, chmn. City/County/Govt. com. 1976-86). Office: Office of the Mayor City & County Bldg 451 S State St Rm 306 Salt Lake City UT 84111-3104

CORREA, SYLVIA I., federal agency administrator. BA in Polit. Sci. cum laude, Rutgers U.; JD, George Washington U., 1979. With Legal Svcs. Corp., N.Y.C., Vladeck, Elias, Vladeck and Engelhard, N.Y.C.; atty.-adv. office of mobile sources EPA, Washington, 1984-88, mgr. office internat. activities, 1988—. Recipient Latina Excellence Environment award, 1995. Office: EPA Office Internat Activities 401 M St SW 2620 Washington DC 20460*

CORRELL, HELEN BUTTS, botanist, researcher; b. Providence, R.I., Apr. 24, 1907; d. George Lyman and Albertine Louise (Christiansen) B.; m. Donovan Stewart Correll (dec. 1983); children: Louise, Stewart, Selena, Charles; m. William Merton Carter, Oct. 10, 1992. AB, Brown U., 1928, AM, 1929; PhD, Duke U., 1934. Instr. Smith Coll., Northampton, Mass., 1929-31, Wellesley (Mass.) Coll., 1934-39; assoc. prof. U. Md., Towson, 1956; research assoc. Tex. Research Found., Renner, 1959-65, co-investigator aquatic plant research, 1966-71; collaborator, adjunct staff Fairchild Tropical Garden, Miami, Fla., 1973-93. Co-author: Aquatic and Wetland Plants of the Southwestern United States, 1972, 2d edit. 1975, Flora of the Bahama Archipelago, 1982; editor: Wright Botanical Jour., 1959-63; contbr. articles to profl. jours. Chmn. Libr. Bd., Richardson, Tex., 1965-70; bd. dirs. East Ridge Retirement Village, 1992-94. Recipient disting. alumna citation Brown U., 1983, Marjory Stoneman Douglas award Fla. Native Plant Soc., 1985, medal for Individual Achievement in Horticulture award Fla. Fedn. Garden Clubs, Inc, 1992. Mem. Soc. Women Geographers, Friends of Fairchild (v.p. 1986-87, pres. 1987-89), Altrusa (officer 1964-71), Phi Beta Kappa, Sigma Xi. Congregationalist. Home: 216 E Ridge Village Dr Miami FL 33157-8090

CORRENTE, JUDITH ANN CHRISTINE, non profit volunteer; b. New Brunswick, N.J., Sept. 6, 1948; d. Thomas Joseph and Philomena Mary (Dalessio) C.; m. Willem Kooyker, Jan. 22, 1983; children: Noah Corrente Schankler, Corrente Ann Schankler, Terence Reece Kooyker. AB, Princeton U., 1970; MA, NYU, 1972; postgrad., Harvard U., 1973-80. Pres. The Monteforte Found., Far Hills, N.J., 1994—; pres. bd. trustees Far Hills (N.J.) Country Day Sch., 1990—, Philharm. Orch. N.J., Warren, 1991-95, Starfish Found. for Children with AIDS, Inc., Woodbridge, N.J., 1993—; bd. trustees The Delbarton Sch., Morristown, N.J., 1995—.

CORRICK, ANN MARJORIE, communications executive; b. Grosse Pointe, Mich; d. John A. and Mary (Nickell) C. B.J., U. Tex., 1943. Reporter Transradio Press Service, Washington, 1943-51; producer Am. Forum of the Air, Youth Wants to Know, NBC, Washington, 1951-52; Washington corr. and broadcaster Sta. WDSU-TV, New Orleans, 1954-58; asst. chief Washington News Bur.; also reporter-broadcaster Westinghouse Broadcasting Co., Washington, 1958-66; USIA congl. liason officer Expo '67, Montreal, Can., 1967; info. officer USIA Fgn. Service, Saigon, Vietnam, 1968-70; dir. promotion and communication Corrick Internat., Santa Cruz, Calif., 1980—. Recipient Sylvania citation for producing and moderating TV film Dateline Washington for WDSU-TV, 1955, Theta Sigma Phi Nat. Headliner award, 1962. Mem. Radio-TV Corrs. Assn. (pres. 1961-62). Home and Office: 3050 Dover Dr Apt 56 Santa Cruz CA 95065-1948

CORRIGAN, COLLEEN HELEN, city official; b. Cleve., Apr. 14, 1970; d. Patrick Joseph and Celia Anne (Ginley) C. BA in Rhetoric and Comm.,

Kent State U., 1993. Counter mgr. Lancôme Cosmetics, Cleve., 1993-94; mgr. conv. svcs. Conv. and Visitors Bur. Greater Cleve., 1994—. Coord. Youth Amb. Program, Cleve., 1993—; mem. vol. com. Ask Me about Cleve., Rock & Roll Hall of Fame and Mus., 1995; mem. conv. com. ARC, Cleve., 1996. Recipient Young Alumni Achievement award Kent State U., 1996. Mem. Women in Comm. Roman Catholic. Home: 5306 Archmere Ave Cleveland OH 44144 Office: Conv and Visitors Bur Greater Cleve 50 Public Sq Cleveland OH 44113

CORRIGAN, LYNDA DYANN, banker; b. Selmer, Tenn., Nov. 24, 1949; d. A. Sammuel and Eunice (Burks) Davis. BBA, Mid. Tenn. State U., 1978; MBA, U. Tenn., 1979; JD, Nashville Sch. Law, 1984. CPA, Tenn.; bar: Tenn. 1985. Sr. v.p. First Am. Corp., Nashville, 1980—; faculty Am. Inst. Banking, Nashville, 1982—; mem. Nat. Panel Consumer Arbitrators, Nashville, 1985-87. Pres. Buddies of Nashville, 1985, adv. bd., 1986—; treas. Mid.-East Tenn. Arthritis Found., Nashville, 1982-85, Floyd Cramer Celebrity Golf Tournament, Nashville, 1981-84; bd. dirs. Nashville, 1981-84; bd. dirs. Nashville Br. Arthritis Found., 1980-87. Named Instr. of Yr. Am. Inst. Banking, 1994; recipient Leadership award Mid.-East Tenn. Arthritis Found., 1985, Gold award Jr. Chamber, 1981. Mem. ABA (mem. tax com. 1987—), Nashville Bar Assn. (mem. tax com. 1986—, vice chmn. tax sect. 1989, chair tax sect. 1990), Tenn. Taxpayers and Mfrs. Assn. (mem. tax com. 1986—), Tenn. Soc. CPA's. Home: 806 Fountainhead Ct Brentwood TN 37027-5833

CORROTHERS, HELEN GLADYS, criminal justice official; b. Montrose, Ark., Mar. 19, 1937; d. Thomas and Christene (Farley) Curl; m. Edward Corrothers, Dec. 17, 1968 (div. Sept. 1983); 1 child, Michael Edward. AA in Liberal Arts magna cum laude, Ark. Bapt. Coll., 1955; BS in Bus. Adminstrn. Mgmt., Roosevelt U., 1965; grad. officer leadership sch., WAC Sch., 1965; grad, Inst. Criminal Justice, Exec. Ctr. Continuing Edn., U. Chgo., 1973; postgrad., Calif. Coast U., 1981—. Enlisted U.S. Army, 1956, advanced through grades to capt., 1969; chief mil. pers. U.S. Army, Ft. Meyer, Va., 1965-67; dir. for housing Giessen Support Ctr., Fed. Republic Germany, 1967-69; resigned, 1969; social interviewer Ark. Dept. Corrections, Grady, 1970-71; supt. women's unit Ark. Dept. Corrections, Pine Bluff, 1971-83; commr. U.S. Parole Commn., Burlingame, Calif., 1983-85, U.S. Sentencing Commn., Washington, 1985-91; fellow U.S. Dept. Justice, Washington, 1992-95; criminal justice cons., 1996—; instr. women & crime U. Md., College Park, 1994; instr. corrections U. Ark.-Pine Bluff, 1976-79; mem. bd. visitation Jefferson County Juvenile Ct., Pine Bluff, 1978-81; bd. dirs. Vols. in Cts., 1979-83, Vols. Am., 1985-94; mem. Am./Can. study team Mex. penal system Am. Correctional Assn., Islas Marias, Mex., 1981; mem. Ark. Commn. Crimes and Law Enforcement, 1975-78; mem. U.S. Atty. Gen.'s Correctional Policy Study Team, 1987; criminal justice cons., U.S. Dept. Justice, 1996—. Mem. Ark. Commn. on Status of Women, 1976-78; bd. dirs. Com. Against Spouse Abuse, 1982-83; mem. nat. adv. bd. dept. criminal justice Xavier U., Cin., 1993—; bd. dirs. Bapt. Mission Found. of Md./Del., Columbia, Md., 1993—. Recipient Ark, Woman of Achievement award Ark. Press Women's Assn., 1980, Human Rels. award Ark. Edn. Assn., 1980, Outstanding Woman of Achievement award Sta. KATV-TV, Little Rock, 1981, Correctional Svc. award Vols. Am., 1984, William H. Hastie award Nat. Assn. Blacks in Criminal Justice, 1986, Outstanding Victim Advocacy award Nat. Victim Ctr., 1991, Appreciation cert. Dept. Justice Office for Victims of Crime, 1994; recipient testimonial for svc. to fed. judiciary Adminstrv. Office of Cts., 1991. Mem. NAFE, Am. Correctional Assn. (treas. 1980-86, v.p. 1986-88, pres.-elect 1988-90, pres. 1990-92, E.R. Cass Correctional Achievement award 1993, mem. Del. Assembly 1993—), N.Am. Assn. Wardens and Supts., Ark. Law Enforcement Assn., Nat. Coun. on Crime and Delinquency, Am. Soc. Criminology, Ark. Sheriff's Assn. (hon.), Delta Sigma Theta (local sec. 1976-79, local parliamentarian 1983). Baptist. Office: Am Correctional Assn 4380 Forbes Blvd Lanham MD 20706

CORSAW, ARDITH, geriatrics nurse, administrator; b. Decatur, Ill., Sept. 10, 1950; d. Everette Eugene and Norma L. (Swarm) Kirkman; m. David Corsaw, Dec. 19, 1971; children: Adam, Tara, Karen. Diploma, Decatur Meml. Hosp., 1971. RN. Pvt. duty nursing, charge nurse med.-surg. unit Graham Hosp., Canton, Ill., 1972-82; nurse Hooper-Holmes Port-A-Medic, Peoria, Ill., 1982-83; office nurse family practice physician's office, Cuba, Ill., 1982-87; factory first-aid sta. relief nurse Caterpillar, Inc., Mapleton, Ill., 1986-88; nursing supr., insvc. dir. Heartland of Canton (Ill.) Health Care and Retirement Corp., 1988-91, DON, 1991-92; quality assurance coord., rehab. coord. Health Care and Retirement Corp., 1992; DON Sprucewood Health Care, 1992-96, Ill. River Correctional Ctr., 1996—; supr. nursing, clin. support br. chief ambulatory svcs. McDill AFB. Ill. Air N.G. Nurse Exec., 1971-95, MOS Comdr. 1995—. Mem. Assn. Air N.G. Nurses, Alliance Air N.G. Flight Surgeons, Assn. Mil. Surgeons U.S., N.G. Assn. U.S., N.G. Assn. Ill. Home: 8442 E Beaver Pass Rd Smithfield IL 61477-9716

CORTA, NANCY RUTH, nurse; b. Gorman, Tex., Feb. 15, 1957; d. Dale Newton and Perelene Ruth (Wright) Johnson; 1 child, Joseph Henry Johnson. BSN, Tex. Woman's U., Denton, 1980. Staff nurse Baylor U. Med. Ctr., Dallas, 1980-81; charge nurse ICU/CCU DeLeon Hosp., Tex., 1981-82; staff nurse MICU/CCU VA Med. Ctr., Phoenix, 1982-83; staff nurse Harris Hosp. Meth., Ft. Worth, 1983-84, Tex. Dept. Health, Stephenville, 1984-95; nurse Dublin Ind. Sch. Dist., 1995—. Mem. Tex. Women's U. Alumni Assn., Epsilon Sigma Alpha. Lodge: Order Eastern Star. Home: Rt 2 Box 192 De Leon TX 76444 Office: 701 Thomas Dublin TX 76446

CORTÉS-HWANG, ADRIANA, Spanish language educator; b. Valaraíso, Chile, Nov. 9, 1928; came to U.S., 1962; d. Luis Alberto Cortès and Sofía Garcès; m. Arturo Peralta-Vila; 1 child, Verónica Peralta. Lic. English, Inst. Chileno, 1963; BA in English, Portland State U., 1964; MA in Spanish Lit., U. Oreg., 1967; postgrad., U. N.C., 1970, U. Madrid, 1971, Duke U. Cert. secondary edn., Pa., Oreg. Liaison officer Chilean Inst. Culture and U. Chile, 1961-63; instr. Spanish Portland (Oreg.) State U., 1963-64, Grants Pass (Oreg.) Sr. H.S., 1964-65, U. Oreg., Eugene, 1965-67, Wilson Coll., Chambersburg, Pa., 1967-68; asst. prof. Shippensburg (Pa.) State Coll., 1968, coord. Latin Am. studies, 1970, chair com. internat. edn., 1971, fgn. student advisor, 1972; asst. prof. Bloomsburg (Pa.) State Coll., 1980, Kutztown (Pa.) U., 1981—; vis. instr. summer sch. U. Madrid, 1968; Fulbright rep. Shippensburg State Coll., 1972; spkr. on current polit. issues of Latin Am.; guest spkr. Inst. Pedagógico, U. Chile, Valparaíso, Sch. of Engring, U. Buenos Aires. Mem. MLA, AAUP, Latin Am. Studies Assn., Sigma Delta Pi. Democrat. Roman Catholic. Home: 337 E Main St Kutztown PA 19530 Office: Kutztown U De Francesco # 204 Kutztown PA 19530

CORTINAS, CYNTHIA ANN, community services coordinator; b. San Antonio, Tex., Mar. 24, 1971; d. Charlie and Rosie (Gonzalez) C. BA in comm., Trinity Univ., 1993. Communications officer San Antonio Area Found., San Antonio, Tex., 1993-94; cmty. svcs. coord. Trinity Univ. Office Pub. Rels., San Antonio, Tex., 1994—. Mem. VIA Met. Transit Pub. Opinion Com., San Antonio, 1995—; asst. troop leader San Antonio Area Coun. Girl Scouts, 1996—; greeter St Brigid's Catholic. Ch., 1990—, eucharistic minister, 1993—. Mem. San Antonio Profl. Chpt. Women in Communications (v.p. programs 1994-95, 96—), Assn. Conf. and Events Dirs. Internat. Roman Catholic. Office: Trinity Univ Office Pub Rel 715 Stadium Dr San Antonio TX 78212

CORTRIGHT, INGA ANN, accountant; b. Silver City, N.Mex., Sept. 30, 1949; d. Lester Richard and Claudia Marcella (Huckaby) Lee; m. Russell Joseph Cortright, June 25, 1987. BS in Acctg., Ariz. State U., 1976, MBA, 1978; postgrad., Walden U., 1991—. CPA, Ariz., Tex. Sole practice cert. pub. acctg. Ariz., 1981—; cons. in field. Mem. AICPA, Beta Alpha Psi. Republican. Episcopalian. Office: 9421 W Bell Rd Ste 108 Sun City AZ 85351-1361

CORTRIGHT, LOUISE VERA, retired medical technologist, small business owner; b. Buffalo, Apr. 22, 1938; d. Asa Lawrence and Mary Lois (Ward) C. BS with honors, Fairleigh Dickson U., 1960; postgrad., Rutgers U., 1965-67. Nationally registered med. technologist. Bacteriology supr. Middlesex Gen. Hosp., New Brunswick, N.J., 1963-64; hematology supr. Princeton Hosp., Princeton, N.J., 1964-65; teaching supr. Somerset Med. Ctr., Somerset, N.J., 1965-67; chief technologist Somerset Med. Ctr., 1966-79; owner, operator Aurora Kennel, Bridgewater, N.J., 1973-92; cons. N.J. State Dept. of Health, Trenton, 1979-80. Treas., v.p. Bridgewater Twp. Bd. of Health, 1974, 1975; chmn. Regional Animal Shelter, 1978-81. Mem. Morris Hills Dog Training Club (founding mem. 1961), North Jersey Shetland Sheepdog Club (founding mem. 1965).

CORUM, JANET MAUPIN, child development specialist, child care administrator; b. Pasco, Wash., Jan. 9, 1947; d. James Corbett and Mabel Ruth (Lewis) Maupin; m. Dallas Smith Corum, July 6, 1968; children: Dayana Smith, Mary Katherine. BS in Edn., Mo. State U., 1969; MEd, Baylor U., 1974. Cert. tchr., Mo., Tex.; cert. counselor Tex.; cert. spl. ednl. counselor, Tex. Tchr. Consol. Sch. Dist. # 1, Hickman Mills, Mo., 1970-71, Waco (Tex.) Ind. Sch. Dist., 1971-79; profl. counselor Family Abuse Ctr., Waco, 1982-84; exec. dir. Lakewood Christian Ch. Day Care Ctr., Waco, 1987—; substitute tchr., vol. 1st United Meth. Presch., St. Paul's Episc. Sch., Waco Ind. Sch. Dist., 1982-87, profl. in-svc. ednl. speaker, 1973; profl. ednl. cons. Region XII Svc. Ctr., Waco, 1978; adv. bd. McLennan Community Coll., Waco, 1989—. Chmn. comm. com. alumni bd. dirs., 1990-91, program devel. com., 1991—, bd. dirs. Leadership Waco, 1990—, Earle-Napier-Kinnard House Hist. Waco Found., 1986—, chmn. Brazos River Festival, 1987-88; selected for 1st inaugural class Lonestar Leadership sponsored by Assn. of Tex. Leadership Programs, bd. dirs., 1996—; elder, edn. com. bd. dirs. Lakewood Christian Ch., 1987—; bd. dirs. St. Paul's Episc. Ch. Parents and Friends Orgn., 1990-91, treas., 1990-91; bd. dirs. Waco-McLennan County Teen Pregnancy Coun., edn. com., 1987—; bd. dirs. McLennan County Mental Health Assn., 1991—; mem. early childhood adv. com. McLennan C.C., 1992-96; mem. McLennan County Youth Collaboration Task Force, 1994—; bd. dirs. YWCA, 1986—. Recipient Pathfinders award YMCA, 1995. Mem. AAUW (pres. 1984-86, chmn. bd. 1982-84, Woman of Yr. 1984, Gift Honoree 1985), Waco Assn. Edn. Young Children (v.p. 1991—, bd. dirs. 1990—, chmn. week of young children 1990), Leadership Waco Alumni Assn. (pres. 1995, Outstanding Alumna 1995), N.W. Waco Rotary Club (bd. dirs. 1994—, v.p. 1994-95, sec. 1996). Republican. Home: 10015 Shadowcrest Dr Waco TX 76712-3122 Office: Lakewood Christian Ch Day 6509 Bosque Blvd Waco TX 76710-4162

CORWELL, ANN ELIZABETH, public relations executive; b. Battle Creek, Mich.; d. James Albert Corwell and Marion Elizabeth (Petersen) Shertzer. BA, Mich. State U., 1971, MBA, 1981; cert. fin., Wharton Sch., 1986. Sr. publicist City of Dearborn, Mich., 1972-76; sr. assoc. Gen. Motors Corp., Detroit, 1976-77; media coord. Gen. Motors Corp., N.Y.C., 1977; mgr. community rels. Gen. Motors Corp., Pontiac, Mich., 1977-81; mgr. internal communications Gen. Motors Corp., Pontiac, 1981-82; dir. pub. rels. Pillsbury Co., Mpls., 1982-85, Avon Products Inc., N.Y.C., 1985-87; exec. v.p. MECA Internat., Flat Rock, Mich., 1987—. Dir. Mich. State U. Nat. Alumni Bd. Mem. Pub. Rels. Soc. Am., Women In Communications, Oakland County C. of C. (dir. 1988-91), Dearborn C. of C. (dir. 1989-91).

CORWIN, CAROLYN F., lawyer; b. Mpls., July 27, 1950. AB, Oberlin Coll., 1971; MSLS, Cath. U. of Am., 1972; JD, Yale U., 1977. Bar: D.C. 1977. Law clk. to Judge Caleb M. Wright U.S. Dist. Ct. Del., 1977-78; asst. to solicitor gen. U.S. Dept. Justice, Washington, 1982-85; ptnr. Covington & Burling, Washington. Mem. Am. Law Inst. Office: Covington & Burling PO Box 7566 1201 Pennsylvania Ave NW Washington DC 20044-7566*

CORWIN, ELIZABETH A., foreign service officer; b. Newark, N.J., Nov. 22, 1961; d. Edward Stanley and Patricia Goldman C. BA, Johns Hopkins U., Balt., 1983; attended, Columbia U., N.Y.C., 1985. Jr. officer U.S. Consulate Gen., Munich, 1986-87; asst. cultural attache Am. Embassy, Warsaw, 1988-92; country affairs officer U.S. Information Agy., Washington, D.C., 1992-94; cultural attache Am. Embassy, Athens, 1995—; mem. bd. dirs. Hellenic Am. Union, Athens, 1995—; exec. sec. Fulbright Program, Warsaw, 1990-92, dep. treas., Athens, 1995—. Office: Am Embassy PSC # 108 Box 48 APO AE 09842

CORWIN, JOYCE ELIZABETH STEDMAN, construction company executive; b. Chgo.; d. Cresswell Edward and Elizabeth Josephine (Kimbell) Stedman; m. William Corwin, May 1, 1965; children: Robert Edmund Newman, Jillanne Elizabeth McInnis. Pres. Am. Properties, Inc., Miami, Fla., 1966-72; v.p. Stedman Constrn. Co., Miami, 1971—; owner Joy-Win Horses, Gray lady ARC, 1969-70. Guidance worker Youth Hall, 1969-70; sponsor Para Med. Group of Coral Park High Sch., 1969-70; hostess, Rep. presdl. campaign, 1968; aide Rep. Nat. Conv., 1972. Mem. Dade County Med. Aux. (chmn. directory com. 1970), Marion County Med. Aux., Fla. Psychiat. Soc. Aux., Fla. Morgan Horse Assn., Fla. Thoroughbred Breeders Assn. Clubs: Coral Gables Jr. Women's (chmn. casework com.), Golden Hills Golf and Turf, Heritage, Royal Dames of Ocala. Home: Windrift Farm 8500 NW 120th St Reddick FL 32686-4513

CORWIN, VERA-ANNE VERSFELT, small business owner, consultant; b. Glen Ridge, NJ; d. Porter LaRoy and Vera Anna (Price) Versfelt; m. John M. Corwin, Apr. 9, 1955; children: Gail Elizabeth Corwin Bayne, Gregory John, Lynn B. Corwin Byers. BS, Upsala Coll., 1954; MEd, Wayne State U., 1972, PhD, 1977. Instr. Wayne (N.J.) Sch. Dist., 1954-55; engr., spec., analyst Chrysler Corp., Highland Park, Mich., 1955-56, 78-85; instr. Royal Oak (Mich.) Sch. Dist., 1968-78; sr. systems engr. Electronic Data Systems, Troy, Mich., 1985-87; pres. Unique Solutions, Inc., Royal Oak, 1987—; adj. prof. U. Mich., Dearborn, 1989, Wayne State U., 1989. Pres. Arlington Park Homeowners Assn., Royal Oak, 1984-85, road commr., 1984-90; trustee First Presbyn. Ch. of Royal Oak, 1990-93, sec. 1993, Presbys. sec. 1994; sec. bd. dirs. Cmty. Concert Assn. of Troy, 1996. Mem. Soc. Automotive Engrs. (trainer 1991—), Automotive Industry Action Group (chmn. design expts. subgroup 1988-94), Am. Soc. Quality Control (sr.), Soc. Mfg. Engrs. (sr., trainer 1987-91), Am. Statis. Assn. Office: Unique Solutions Inc PO Box 1711 Royal Oak MI 48068-1711

CORY, MIRIAM ELAINE, speech and language pathologist; b. South Bend, Ind., Sept. 4, 1935; d. Paul Wilson Sr. and Helen Marina (White) Bradfield; m. Delbert Jason Cory, June 23, 1956; children: Stephen, Nadine, Catherine, Karen. BS in Edn., Ball State U., 1957. Cert. speech and lang. pathologist. Speech and lang. pathologist Midview Sch. Dist., Elyria, Ohio, 1960-64, Beaufort (S.C.) Schs., 1969-70, N.E. Met. Intermediate Sch. Dist., White Bear Lake, Minn., 1973—. Group leader, bd. dirs., day camp dir., and other vol. adminstrv. offices Camp Fire Boys & Girls, Inc., St. Paul, Minn., 1971— (Luther Halsey Gulick award 1983); youth camping com. Minn. Dist. Reorganized Ch. of Jesus Christ of Latter Day Saints, 1981— (World Community Youth Svc. award 1981); bd. dirs., camp standards vis. Northland sect. Am Camping Assn., 1990—. Recipient Good Neighbor award WCCO Radio, St. Paul, 1981, Disting. Svc. award S. Communities Youth and Family Counseling Svcs., Cottage Grove, Minn., 1988. Mem. Am. Speech, Lang. and Hearing Assn., Minn. Speech, Lang. and Hearing Assn. Office: NMISD # 916 White Bear Lake HS S Campus 3551 Mcknight Rd N Saint Paul MN 55110

COSBY, CATHERINE, bank executive, lawyer. JD, U. Fla. Assoc. Mahoney, Adams and Criser, Jacksonville, Fla., until 1983; with Barnett Banks, Jacksonville, 1983—, sr. counsel, corp. sec., 1992—. Office: Barnett Banks Inc 50 N Laura St Jacksonville FL 32202-3664

COSGRIFF, JANE ERVIN, small business owner; b. Haydenville, Ohio; d. William and Lenora Ervin; m. Apr. 20, 1946; children: Robert Kevin, Brian Kurt, Alan Ervin. Diploma, Ohio State U., 1948. Legal asst. Carrington T. Marshall Law Firm, Columbus, Ohio, 1948-67; pres. Creative Tours, Lexington, Ky., 1986—. Mem. Stonewall PTA, Lexington, 1986, Rep. Women's Club, Lexington, 1996—. With USAR, 1977—. Mem. Bus. Women's Club (Lexington), Suburban Women's Club (Lexington). Office: USAR Officers Assn Univ of Kentucky 101 Barker Hall Lexington KY 40503

COSGROVE, ANNA MARIE BRADY, nursing educator, neonatal nurse; b. N.Y.C., Aug. 10, 1955; d. Michael J. and Mary A. (McAdam) Brady; m. Patrick Daniel Cosgrove, June 23, 1979; children: Patrick Brady, Colin Brady. BSN, Herbert H. Lehman Coll., 1980; MSN, Columbia U., 1993. Cert. neonatal nurse practitioner. Staff nurse Babies and Childrens Hosp. The Presbyn. Hosp. City of N.Y., 1980-94, ednl. coord., 1994—. Mem. ANA, AWHONN, Am. Acad. Nurse Practitioners, Nat. Assn. Neonatal Nurses, N.Y. State Nurses Assn. Roman Catholic. Home: 14 Scenic Pond Dr Warwick NY 10990 Office: Presbyn Hosp Babies and Children 12N 360 W 168th St New York NY 10032

COSSABOOM, JILL MUNDY, real estate accountant; b. Clark AFB, The Philippines, Dec. 1, 1964; d. Henry Francis and Alice Joan (Bergin) Mundy; m. Kim Scott Cossaboom, June 17, 1989; 1 child, Brooke Lauren. B of Sci. Bus., Monmouth U., 1986. Fin. acct. Realty Income Corp., Escondido, Calif., 1987—. Mem. Inst. Mgmt. Accts. (CMA). Office: Realty Income Corp 220 W Crest St Escondido CA 92025

COSTA, DONNA MARIE, secondary education educator; b. Peabody, Mass., Dec. 5, 1955; d. Antonio Sariva Costa and Lulu Rose (Silva) Costa-Smith; m. Brian Michael Phelan, Oct. 27, 1972 (div. 1982); children: Dawne Marie Phelan, Brian Michael Phelan II. AS, N. Shore Community Coll., Beverly, Mass., 1982; BA, U. Mass. at Boston, 1986; MEd in Sch. Adminstrn., Salem (Mass.) State Coll., 1988; cert. advanced studies, Harvard U., 1991; EdD candidate, 1992—. Cert. acad. and occpl. tchr., Mass. Instr./dept. head Peabody Sch. Dept., 1981—; tech. prep. site facilitator, 1993—; instr. North Shore C.C., Mass., 1994—; mem. Faculty Adv., Vocat. Adv., Electronics Adv., Ednl. Tech., Extended After Sch. Program bds., Peabody Sch. Dept., ednl. tech. com. Author, editor: 4 yr. electronics curriculum, 1990. Vol. ARC. Recipient Horace Mann grants, 1988, 89. Mem. ASCD, NAFE, Phi Delta Kappa (bd. dirs. Harvard chpt.). Roman Catholic. Home: 8 Munroe St Peabody MA 01960-4468

COSTA, LISA SUZANNE, artist, fine art and antiques appraiser; b. Modesto, Calif., Dec. 31, 1969; d. Larry M. and Carlyn I. Costa. BFA summa cum laude, U. San Francisco, Acad. of Art Coll., 1994. Intern in furniture and decorative arts Butterfield & Butterfield Fine Art Appraisers & Auctioneers, San Francisco, 1991-92, adminstrv. asst., 1992-95; rsch. asst., office mgr. Hobart Assoc., Inc. Fine and Decorative Art Appraisals, San Francisco, 1995—; gallery cons. Van Den Berg Gallery, San Francisco, 1994-95. Artist original artwork book: Art Life, 1992; contbr. poetry to Nat. Libr. of Poetry, 1996. mem. Ctr. for Visual Arts, Museo Italia of San Francisco, Nat. Mus. Women in the Arts. Roman Catholic.

COSTA, MARY, soprano; b. Knoxville, Tenn.; student Los Angeles Conservatory of Music. Film voice of Sleeping Beauty by Walt Disney; appeared TV commls., 1955-57; debut Los Angeles Opera, 1958, in La Boheme, San Francisco Opera, 1959, as Violetta in La Traviata at Met. Opera, N.Y.C., 1964; appeared Glyndebourne Opera House, Royal Opera House Covent Garden, Teatro Nacional de San Carlos, Grand Theatre de Geneve, Vancouver, Lisbon, Kiev, Leningrad, Tbilisi, Boston, Cin., Hartford, Newark, Phila., San Antonio, Seattle; toured U.S. with Bernstein's Candide; appeared English prodn. Candide; revival Bernstein's Candide at John F. Kennedy Center for Performing Arts, 1971; tour Soviet Union, 1970; Bolshoi debut in La Traviatta, 1970; starring role motion picture The Great Waltz, 1972; appeared internat. recitals, orchs.; v.p. Hawaiian Fragrances, Honolulu, 1972. Vice pres. Calif. Inst. Arts. Named Woman of yr., Los Angeles, 1959; recipient DAR Honor medal, 1974, Tenn. Hall of Fame award, 1987, Women of Achievement award Northwood Inst., Palm Beach, Fla., 1991, Woman of Achievement award So. Birmingham Coll., 1993; Mary Costa Scholarship established at U. Tenn., 1979. Address: 3340 Kingston Pike Unit 1 Knoxville TN 37919-4674

COSTA, ROBIN LEUEEN, psychologist, counselor; b. Hackensack, N.J., Dec. 9, 1948; d. Frank G. and Hazel L. (Brown) C. BA, Colby Coll., 1970; MA in Clin. Psychology, Fairleigh Dickinson U., 1973; MBA, Fla. Atlantic U., 1984. Lic. mental health counselor, sch. psychologist, Fla.; nat. cert. sch. psychologist. Sch. psychologist Broward County Sch. Bd., Ft. Lauderdale, Fla., 1973-91; pres., chief exec. officer Silver Linings Fin. Care, Ft. Lauderdale, 1986—; pvt. practice Ft. Lauderdale, 1991—. Mem. Jung Generations Soc. (founder). Home: 3750 Galt Ocean Dr Fort Lauderdale FL 33308-7656

COSTA, ROSANN, sociologist, educator; b. Bklyn., Sept. 1, 1967; d. Frank Anthony and Diane Grace (Lagiovani) C. BA, CUNY, Flushing, N.Y., 1990; MA, NYU, 1994. Cert. elem. educator, N.Y. Pvt. tutor, 1987—; rsch. asst., data analyst Helen Keller Ctr., Sands Point, N.Y., 1990, 91; edn. evaluator N.Y.C. Bd. Edn., Bklyn., 1991-95; staff assoc., sr. project coord., officer of rsch. Columbia U., N.Y.C., 1995—; mem. Com. of Hundreds, Futures in Edn. Found., Douglaston, N.Y., 1993, 94; exec. bd. mem. Am. Cancer Soc., N.Y.C., 1993—, CORE team mem., 1994—. Contbr. articles to profl. jours. Dean's list Queen's Coll., 1988-90. Mem. Am. Ednl. Rsch. Assn., Am. Sociol. Assn., Soc. for Study of Social Problems, Assn. Tchr. Edn., Eastern Sociol. Soc. Roman Catholic. Home: 69-20 Eliot Ave Middle Village NY 11379-1133 Office: Columbia U Sergievsky Ctr 630 W 168 St New York NY 10032

COSTANTINO, LORINE PROTZMAN, woodworking company executive; b. Chattanooga, Feb. 8, 1921; d. John Edgar and Rosa Jane (Ellis) McClelland; student U. Balt., U. Ill.; m. Conrad Protzman, 1937 (dec. 1958); children: Rosa Lorine, Charles Conrad, James Paul, Sharon Lee; m. 2d, Anthony A. Costantino, Feb. 27, 1960. With Conrad Protzman, Inc., Balt., 1954-94, pres., chief exec., 1958-95, ret. 1995; developer apprenticeship programs for woodworking industry. Mem. Archtl. Woodworking Inst. (dir.), Bldg. Congress and Exchange Balt., Am. Sub-Contractors Assn., Nat. Assn. Women Bus. Owners, Iota Lambda Sigma (hon. mem. Nu chpt.). Republican. Roman Catholic. Club: Hillendale Country.

COSTANZO, NANCI JOY, fine arts educator; b. New Britain, Conn., June 2, 1947; d. Edward Francis and Vivian Evelyn (Allen) Sarisley; m. Joseph Paul Costanzo, Apr. 10, 1974; 1 child, Ashley Allen Bailey. BA, Cen. Conn. State U., New Britain, 1973; MAE, R.I. Sch. Design, 1979. Assoc. prof. art Elms Coll., Chicopee, Mass., 1985—, also chair dept. visual arts; lectr. in field. Exhibited in shows at Western New Eng. Coll., 1977, Springfield Art League Show, 1978, Zone Gallery, 1981, Westfield State Coll., 1985, Valley Women Arts Show, 1980, 83, 85, 86, 87, 88, 89, New Britain Mus. Am. Art, 1987, 88, 89, 90, Borgia Gallery at Elms Coll., 1989, 90, 91, 92, Hampden Gallery at U. Mass., 1990, Sino-Am. Women's Conf., Beijing, People's Republic of China, 1990, numerous others; one woman shows include Thronja Art Gallery, 1979-80, Elms Coll., 1992; represented in pvt. collections in Mass., R.I., Wash., N.Y., Italy, corp. collections in R.I. and Conn.; contbr. articles to profl. jours.; lectr. Greece, Mex. and China. Recipient Outstanding Arts Educator in Mass. award Mass. Alliance for Arts Edn., 1985, New Britain Mus. Am. Art, 1987, 88; Nat. Endowment for Humanities grantee, 1987, 88; Faculty Devel. grantee, Beijing, 1989, 90. Mem. Nat. Art Edn. Assn., Valley Women Artists, Mass. Art Edn. Assn. (mem. coun. 1984-86, v.p. 1986-88), Nat. Mus. of Women in the Arts, Coll. Art Assn., Nat. Women's Studies Assn., Internat. Soc. for Edn. through Art, Women's Caucus for Art. Office: Elms Coll 291 Springfield St Chicopee MA 01013-2837

COSTA-ZALESSOW, NATALIA, foreign language educator; b. Kumanovo, Macedonia, Dec. 5, 1936; came to the U.S., 1951; d. Alexander P. and Katarina (Duric) Z.; m. Gustavo Costa, June 8, 1963; 1 child, Dora. BA in Italian, U. Calif., Berkeley, 1959, MA in Italian, 1961, PhD in Romance Langs. and Lits., 1967. Tchg. asst. U. Calif., Berkeley, 1959-63; instr. Mills Coll., Oakland, Calif., 1963; asst. prof. San Francisco (Calif.) State U., 1968-74, assoc. prof., 1974-79, prof., 1979—. Author: Scrittrici italiane dal XIII al XX secolo; Testi e critica, 1982; contbr. articles to profl publs. Sidney M. Ehrman scholar U. Calif., Berkeley, 1957-58, Gamma Phi Beta scholar U. Calif., Berkeley, 1958, Herbert H. Vaughan scholar U. Calif., Berkeley, 1959-60, Advanced Grad. Traveling fellow in romance lang. and lit. U. Calif., Berkeley, 1964-65. Mem. MLA, Am. Assn. Tchrs. Italian, Renaissance Soc. Am., Dante Soc. Am., Croatian Acad. Am. Roman Catholic. Office: Dept Fgn Lang & Lit San Francisco State Univ San Francisco CA 94132

COSTELLESE, LINDA E. GRACE, banker; b. Providence, Mar. 22, 1950; d. Lawrence A. and Lucy R. (Fiore) Grace; m. Dennis P. Costellese, May 8, 1971. AS in Bus. Adminstrn., Bryant Coll., 1981; cert., Sch. Bank Mktg., Colo., 1982; BS in Organizational Behavior, Lesley Coll., 1985, MS in Applied Mgmt., 1988. Sec. R.I. Hosp. Trust Nat. Bank div. Bank of Boston, Providence, 1969-78, adminstrv. asst., 1978-80, br. adminstrn. officer, 1980-81, community mktg. officer, 1981-82, retail sales officer, 1982-84, asst. v.p.

sales and telemarketing, 1984-85, v.p. sales and tng., 1985-87, regional mgr., 1986-87, 1st v.p., dept. mgr. retail brs., 1987-89, sr. v.p., dept. head retail banking, 1989-90, exec. v.p., dir. R.I. retail banking, 1990-94; dir. N.E. sales, svc. and telebanking devel. group Bank of Boston, Boston, 1994—; mem. regional bd. New Eng. Banking Inst., 1993-95. Vol. Spl. Olympics, Providence, United Way Southeastern R.I., Providence; mem. St. Frances de Sales Women's Guild, Save-the-Bay; grad. Leadership R.I., 1993, mem. Leadership R.I. Recruitment Com., 1994—; advisor City Yr.-Providence, 1993—; mem. R.I. City Yr. Adv. Coun., 1993-95. Named Woman of Yr., North Kingstown Bus. and Profl. Women's Assn., 1987. Mem. Internat. Inst. R.I. (bd. dirs. 1992-95), R.I. Bankers Assn. (pres. 1993-94), New Eng. Bank Mktg. Assn. (bd. dirs. 1985-87, 91-92, sec. 1987-88, 1st v.p. 1988-89, pres. 1990-92), Bank Mktg. Assn. (schs. adv. coun.). Office: Bank of Boston MA BOS 01-15-04 100 Federal St Boston MA 02110-1802

COSTELLO, MARCELLE WELLING, marketing consultant, arts program administrator; b. Dallas, July 20, 1964; d. Brent Carlson and Viki Lee (Norrish) Welling; m. Keith Conan Costello, Nov. 5, 1994. BA in English with honors, U. Calif., Berkeley, 1986, BA in Mass. Comm. with honors, 1986. Account exec. Murdoch Mags., N.Y.C., 1987-88; sr. account exec., launch team Calif. Mags. Inc., San Francisco, 1988-90; mktg. mgr., launch team Licensing Group Internat., San Francisco, 1990-92; mktg. dir. Barcelino Continental Corp., San Francisco, 1992-94; spl. asst. to dir. Art in Embassies program U.S. Dept. State, San Francisco/Washington, 1994—. Bd. dirs., pub. rels. mgr. San Francisco Children's Zoo's "Zoo 11," San Francisco, 1994-96; pub. rels. mgr. Grace Cathedral, San Francisco, 1993—; mem., bd. nominee San Francisco Opera's "Bravo" Club, 1995; mem. San Francisco Ballet's "Encore" Club, 1994—, Women Make a Difference, San Francisco, 1993-94. Mem. Internat. Assn. Bus. Communicators (mgr. membership directory 1994-96, v.p. nominee 1995), Women in Comms., San Francisco Young Collectors. Republican. Episcopalian. Home: 2945 Pacific Ave#4 San Francisco CA 94115 Office: 4th Fl 244 Kearny St San Francisco CA 94108

COSTILOW, SUSAN LYNN, education and conference coordinator; b. Morgantown, W.Va., Dec. 31, 1963; d. John Barton Costilow and Rita Irene (Dunn) Towns. BA, W.Va. U., 1986, MA, 1991. Staff writer W.Va. U., Morgantown, 1986-88, program mgr., 1988-93; instr. Fairmont (W.Va.) State Coll., 1992-93; coord. edn. and conf. ctr. Harbor Br. Oceanographic Instn., Ft. Pierce, Fla., 1993—. Contbr. articles to profl. jours. Coord., vol. W.Va. Pub. TV, 1992-93; facilitator, tchr. Learn to Read, Fla., 1996. Mem. MLA, Assn. Conf. and Event Dirs. Internat., Meeting Profls. Internat. Office: Oceanographic Instn Harbor Br 5600 US 1 North Fort Pierce FL 34946

COSTLEY, MONA JOYCE, elementary education educator; b. Houston, Aug. 31, 1936; d. John Newton and Erma Joyce (Casey) L.; m. Albert W. Costley Jr., June 15, 1957 (div. 1980); children: Leslie S., S. Casey, Wade H. BA, So. Meth. U., 1957; MA, U. Colo., Colorado Springs, 1984. Tchr. James Bowie Elem. Sch., Baytown, Tex., 1957-60, Skyway Park Elem. Sch., Colorado Springs, Colo., 1981—; tchr. rep. PTO, Colorado Springs, 1991—; grade level chair Cheyenne Mountain Schs., Colorado Springs, 1986-94. Mem. NEA, Colo. Edn. Assn., Colo. Coun. Internat. Reading Assn., Internat. Reading Assn., Cheyenne Mountain Edn. Assn. (treas. 1984-85), Phi Delta Kappa. Republican. Methodist. Home: 715 Orion Dr Colorado Springs CO 80906-1017 Office: Skyway Park Elem Sch 1100 Mercury Dr Colorado Springs CO 80906-1741

COSTNER, STEPHANIE, automation systems specialist; b. Sept. 16, 1969; d. Bobby Lee and Leslie Brenda (Sain) C. BSBA, Appalachian State U., 1991. Claim adjuster Carolina Freight, Cherryville, N.C., 1991-92; comml. acct. rep. Davis Inst. Svc., Winston-Salem, N.C., 1992-93, North State Ins., Lincolnton, N.C., 1993-95; bus. customer svc. rep. BB&T Cimmungs LeGrand Ins. Svc., Shelby, N.C., 1995-96; automation sys. specialist BB&T Ins. Svc., Shelby, N.C., 1996—. Child mentor Rock Springs Elem. Sch., Denver, N.C., 1994-95. Mem. Winston-Salem Assn. Ins. Women (safety chmn. 1992-93). Home: PO Box 323 Lincolnton NC 28093

COTE, DENISE LOUISE, federal judge; b. St. Cloud, Minn., Oct. 13, 1946; d. Donald Edward and Dorothy (Garberson) C.; m. Howard F. Maltby, Dec. 24, 1987. BA, St. Mary's Coll., 1968; MA, Columbia U., 1969, JD, 1975. Bar: N.Y. 1976, U.S. Dist. Ct. (so. and ea. dist.) N.Y. 1976, U.S. Ct. Appeals (2d cir.) 1984. Law clk. to Hon. Jack B. Weinstein U.S. Dist. Ct. (ea. dist.) N.Y., 1975-76; assoc. Curtis Mallet-Prevost, N.Y.C., 1976-77; asst. U.S. Attys. Office, N.Y.C., 1977-85, dep. chief criminal divsn. so. dist., 1983-85, chief criminal divsn. so. dist., 1991-94; atty. Kaye Scholer Fierman Hays & Handler, N.Y.C., 1985-88, ptnr., 1988-91; judge U.S. Dist. Ct. (so. dist.) N.Y., 1994—. Mem. Assn. of Bar of City of N.Y. (mem. fed. cts. com.). Office: 1040 US District Court 500 Pearl St New York NY 10007-1312

COTÉ, KATHRYN MARIE, psychotherapist, stress management educator; b. Oceanside, Calif., May 31, 1953; d. Richard Alfred Kauth and Carole Maxine Brue Potter; m. Dennis Malcolm Coté, Dec. 23, 1983; children: Claire Marie, Simone Gloria, Jesse Patrick. BA, St. Norbert Coll., DePere, Wis., 1975; MSSW, U. Wis., 1977. Lic. clin. social worker; cert. clin. social worker. Psychiat. social worker Napa (Calif.) State Hosp., 1977-79, team leader, 1979-80; supr. adolescent clin. svcs. Solano County Mental Health, Vallejo, Calif., 1980-83; sect. head of residential svcs. for children and adolescents London Borough of Camden, 1983-84; mental health program mgr. Solano County Mental Health, Fairfield, Calif., 1985-87; clin. social worker, county liaison West Ctrl. Cmty. Svc. Ctr., Montevideo, Minn., 1987-90; pvt. practice as psychotherapist and stress mgmt. educator Berlin, N.H., 1990—; profl. cons. North Bay Suicide Prevention and Stressline, Napa, 1985-87. Bd. dirs. Coos County Family Health, Berlin, 1990—. Recipient Cert. of Appreciation, Solano County Mental Health Adv. Bd., 1987. Democrat. Roman Catholic.

COTE, LOUISE ROSEANN, creative director, designer; b. Quincy, Mass., Sept. 16, 1959; d. John Anthony and Theresa Janet (Oriola) Burke; m. Robert Andrew Cote, Aug. 6, 1983. BA, Bridgewater State Coll., 1981. Advt. asst. Dunnington Super Drug, Brockton, Mass., 1978-81; bus. forms and graphic design artist Shawmut Bank of Boston, N.A., 1981-86; artist AlliedSignal Inc., East Providence, R.I., 1986-92, adminstr. creative svcs., 1992-94, supr. creative svcs., 1992-94, supr. computer graphics svcs., 1994-95; prin., designer Katmandu Studio, North Attleborough, Mass., 1995—. Mem. Women's Advt. Club R.I., North Attleborough and Plainville C. of C. Roman Catholic. Office: Katmandu Studio 885 Mount Hope St North Attleboro MA 02760

COTHERN, BARBARA SHICK, real estate investor; b. Okmulgee, Okla., Mar. 5, 1931; d. Roy and Irene Maude (Baldwin) Shick; m. George Albert Cothern, Mar. 21, 1954; children: Cynthia Lou, Deborah Sue, James Albert. BA in Human Resources, Seattle U., 1980, MBA, 1983. Owner Human Resource Svc., 1980-85; mem. Wash. Ho. of Reps., Olympia, 1992-94; chair Northshore Shoreline Health & Safety Network, 1995—; exec. dir. Northshore Pub. Edn. Found.; mem. Wash. State Pub. Disclosure Commn. Crisis counselor, 1979—; pres. Northshore Sch. Bd., Bothell, Wash., 1990-91, bd. dirs., 1987—, legis. rep., 1989-91; mem. resolutions com. Wash. State Sch. Dis. Assn., 1989—; pres. Shoreline Sch. Bd., 1974-75; chair Northshore Legis. Coalition, 1989-91; mem. Snohomish County Com. for Improved Transp., 1992; numerous other civic activities. Mem. NOW, AAUW, LWV, Nat. Women's Polit. Caucus. Mem. Reorganized Ch. of Jesus Christ of Latter Day Saints. Home: 20006 4th Ave SE Bothell WA 98012-9659

COTHRAN, PHYLLIS L., personal care industry executive; b. Charlottesville, Va., Feb. 12, 1947; d. James T. and Mary C. BS in Acctg., Va. Commonwealth U.; student, U. Va. sch. bus., Northwestern U., London Sch. Econs. Sr. acct. Blue Cross/Blue Shield Va., Richmond, 1972-74, systems acct., then sr. fin. analyst, 1974-75, adminstrv. asst. to v.p. fin., 1975-77, mgr. fin. planning and mgmt., 1977-78, corp. contr., 1978-81, v.p. fin., 1981-85, sr. v.p. fin. CHI, 1985-88, sr. v.p. fin. and planning HMC, 1988, chief. fin. officer, treas. BCBSVA, 1989, exec. v.p. ops., 1989-90, exec. v.p., chief oper. officer, then pres., chief oper. officer, 1990—; mem. audit com. Blue Cross/Blue Shield Assn., Chgo., 1990. Mem. cost rev. coun. VA Health Svcs., Richmond, 1990-91, Spl. Adv. Commn. on Mandated Health Ins. Benefits, Richmond, 1991; bd. dirs. Metro Richmond Drug Coalition, 1991, Va. Pub. Safety Found., Sci. Mus. Va. Found., Richmond Forum, Weed & Seed of Richmond, Nat. Mus. Health and Med. Found. Recipient Star award Va. Commonwealth U., 1990, YWCA Outstanding Women award. Mem. Fin. Execs. Inst., Soc. Internat. Bus. Fellows, Metro Richmond C. of C. (bd. dirs. 1991). Office: Trigon Blue Cross/Blue Shield 2015 Staples Mill Rd Richmond VA 23230-3108*

COTTEN, CATHERYN DEON, medical center international advisor; b. Erwin, N.C., Apr. 13, 1952; d. Ben Hur and Minnie Lee (Smith) C. BS in Anthropology, Duke U., 1975. Asst. internat. advisor Med. Ctr. Duke U., Durham, N.C., 1975-76; internat. advisor Med. Ctr. Duke U., Durham, 1976—. Editor and contbr. chpt. to Advisors Manual of Federal Regulations Affecting Foreign Students and Scholars. Key vol. City of Durham, 1990-91; pres. Durham County Lit. Coun., 1992-94. Recipient Cert. Recognition So. Regional Coun. Black Am. Affairs, Atlanta, 1985. Mem. Nat. Assn. Fgn. Student Affairs: Assn. Internat. Educators (gov. regulations adv. com. 1985-96, nat. chair 1991-94, chair Southeastern region 1989-90), Altrusa Club (pres. Durham chpt. 1987-89). Office: Duke U Med Ctr PO Box 3882 Durham NC 27710

COTTEN-HUSTON, ANNIE LAURA, psychologist, educator; b. Oxford, N.C., Nov. 18, 1923; d. Leonard F. and Laura Estelle (Spencer) Cotten; diploma Hardbarger Bus. Coll., 1944; AB, Duke U., 1945; MEd, U. Hartford, 1965; PhD, The Union Inst., 1979; children: Hollis W., Rebecca Ann, Laura Cotten. Diplomate Am. Bd. Sexology. Asst. to pres. So. Meth. U., 1953; rsch. asst. Duke U., 1947-49; exec. sec. Ohio Wesleyan U., 1955-56, Conn. Coun. Chs., 1958-60; adj. prof. U. Hartford, 1976-78; clin. pastoral counselor Hartford Hosp., 1962-65; asst., then asso. dir. social svcs. Hartford Conf. Chs., 1965-67; teaching fellow U. N.C., 1970-71; adj. prof. U. Hartford, 1976-78; assoc. prof. Cen. Conn. State U., New Britain, 1967-93, adj. prof. 1994—; adj. prof. St. Joseph Coll., 1986-96; clinical internship, Montefiore Med. Ctr., 1995; dir. elderhostel programs, Cen. Conn. State U., 1989—; organizer ctr. adult learners Cen. Conn. State U., 1991—; cons. Somers Correctional Ctr. (Conn.), 1980-81, instr./researcher, 1980-81; cons. Life Ins. Mktg. Rsch., 1981—; amb. to China, spring, 1986; presenter 3d Internat. Interdisciplinary Cong. on Women, 1987; vis. prof., scholar Duke U., 1989; vis. prof. Conn. Coll. New London, Conn., 1990; dir. Ctr. Adult Learners Cen. Conn. State U., 1991—, Sex Info. and Edn. Conn., 1995—(named Human Sexuality Educator of Yr. 1996); clin. faculty, supr. Am. Bd. Sexology, 1991, 94. Elder hostel dir. Cen. Conn. State U., 1987-93, organizer Elder Hostel Affiliate Network, 1991. Mem. AAUW, Am. Assn. Marriage and Family Therapists (cert.), Am. Psychol. Assn. (chair divsn. 1987—), Nat. Coun. Family Rels., Am. Assn. Sex Educators, Counselors and Therapists (cert., presenter conf. 1970—), Conn. Psychol. Assn., Conn. Council Chs. (dir.), Hartford Women's Network. Contbr. articles to profl. jours. Home: 193 Westland Ave West Hartford CT 06107-3057 Office: Ctrl Conn State U Dept Psychology New Britain CT 06050

COTTINGHAM, BETTY ANN, human services administrator, nurse; b. Cold Spring, Ky., Oct. 27, 1956; d. Ralph Louis and Marie Henrietta (Scharold) Kroger; m. Thomas Henry Cottingham, Oct. 27, 1956; children: Christopher, Laura, Thomas, Michael, Elizabeth, Matthew, Joseph. BSN, Coll. of Mt. St. Joseph, Cin., 1956. RN Ohio, Ky. Psychiatric staff nurse Good Samaritan Hosp., Cin., 1956-58; bookkeeper Cottingham Hardware, Alexandria, Ky., 1959-89; pediatric nurse St. Elizabeth Med. Ctr., Edgewood, Ky., 1981-87; dir. dept. human svcs. Campbell County Fiscal Ct., Newport, Ky., 1987—; adv. bd. Campbell County (Ky.) Health Bd., 1988—; adv. and policy coms. Tri-State White House Conf. on Aging, Cin., 1994-96; adv. bd. Gr. Cin. Coun. Geriatric Care, 1994—; instnl. rev. bd. St. Luke Hosp., Ft. Thomas, Ky., 1987-96. Contbr. articles to newsletters and reports. Chair MH-MR Tax Com., Campbell County, 1980-81; mem. bd. No. Ky. Children's Psychol. Hosp., Kenton County, 1985-95; chair, mem. bd. Alexandria (Ky.) Cmty. Orgn., 1987—; sec., v.p. 1978-86. Recipient Pres.' award for Outstanding Svc., No. Ky. MH-MR Regional Bd., 1978, 93, 94, 95, Outstanding Contbn. award No. Ky. Dist. Health Dept., 1993; named Outstanding Woman No. Ky., The Kentucky Post, Covington, 1996. Mem. Coun. of Aging (chair 1993-96), Assn. for Older Kentuckians (mem. bd., sec., vice-chair 1994-96), No. Ky. Area Devel. Dist. (com. chair 1993-96), No. Ky. Regional Human Svc. Coun. (mem. bd., planning com. 1995-96), Family Preservation Commn. (mem. bd. 1995-96). Roman Catholic. Office: Campbell County Fiscal Court 24 W 4th St Newport KY 41071

COTTINGHAM, JENNIFER JANE, city official; b. Salt Lake City, July 10, 1961; d. Miles Dixon and Ruth Eugenia (Skeen) Cottingham; m. Richard Frame Cavenaugh, July 23, 1983 (div. Apr. 1989); 1 child, John Douglas. BS in Civil Engring., So. Meth. U., 1984. Lic. profl. engr., Tex. Estimator Avery Mays Constrn., Dallas, 1981-83, project engr., 1984; owner, gen. contr. Dallas, 1985-89; asst. project mgr. Austin Comml., Dallas, 1989; ct. appointed receiver 14th Dist. Ct., State of Tex., Dallas, 1990-91; engr. asst. Dallas Water Utilities, 1990-91, project mgr., 1991-96; dir. CBC Investors, L.P., Dallas. Goodwill ambassador City of Dallas Water Utilities, 1990-92, 95-96, fin. strength com., 1991. Mem. CBC Investments (founding pres.), Dallas Symphony Orch. League, DAR (pres. jr. group 1989-92), Cotillion Book Club (founding mem.). Republican. Episcopalian. Office: City of Dallas Water Utilities 2121 Main St Ste 300 Dallas TX 75201

COTTINGHAM, MARY PATRICIA, vocational rehabilitation counselor; b. Seattle, May 9, 1930; d. Carl Frank and Frances Mary (Keon) Fox; m. Ken Cottingham, Sept. 15, 1951 (div. Sept. 1982); children: Cathy Ann, David Carl, Susan Mary, Keith Bryan, Patricia Frances. BA, U. Wash., 1974, MEd in Psychology, 1977. Diplomate Am. Bd. Vocat. Experts; cert. mental health counselor, Wash.; cert. vocat. rehab. counselor, cons. Counselor Mental Health North, Seattle, 1974-77; vocat. rehab. counselor Counseling Svcs. Northwest, Lynnwood, Wash., 1977-79; owner, cons. People Systems Inc., Seattle, 1979—. Bd. dirs. King County Mental Health Bd., Seattle, 1982-84; guardian ad litem King County Juvenile Ct., Seattle, 1981-84. Mem. AACD, Am. Mental Health Counselors Assn., Nat. Rehab. Assn., Pvt. Rehab. Orgns. Wash. (sec. 1986-89), Wash. Mental Health Counselors Assn. (sec. 1983-85). Home: 14727 42nd Ave W Lynnwood WA 98037-5511 Office: People Systems Inc 155 NE 100th St Ste 406 Seattle WA 98125-8012

COTTLE, GAIL ANN, retail executive; b. Yakima, Wash.. Student, U. Wash. With Nordstrom, Inc., 1972—, corp. mdse. mgr. Brass Plum Jr. Women's Apparel, 1982-85, v.p., officer Jr. Women's Apparel divsn., 1985-92; exec. v.p. product devel. Nordstrom, Inc., Seattle, 1992—. Ford Found. grantee. Mem. Columbia Tower Club, Fashion Group Internat. Office: Nordstrom Inc 1423 3rd Ave Seattle WA 98101*

COTTON, BARBARA LYNN, correctional health systems management consultant; b. St. Catharines, Ont., Can., Apr. 17, 1945; d. Ivan and Dorothy Rose (Manvil) Remely; m. Robert Lee Cotton, June 21, 1971 (div. Oct. 1979). ADN, Mont. State U., 1966, BSN, 1967; M of Health Svcs. Adminstrn., St. Marys Coll. of Calif., 1986. Instr. Bishop Clarkson Sch. Nursing, Omaha, 1971-74; discharge planning cons. Vis. Nurse Assn., Modesto, Calif., 1974-76; spl. projects officer Stanislaus County Med. Soc., Modesto, 1976-79; mgr. correctional programs Calif. Med. Assn., San Francisco, 1979-85; prin. Norman & Cotton Assocs., Lafayette, Calif., 1985-89; pres., owner The Cotton Group, Lafayette, 1989—; cons. Calif. Med. Assn., San Francisco, 1985—. Co-author, editor: Guidelines for Planning and Evaluating Jail Health Svcs., 1989. Capt. U.S. Army Nurse Corps, 1966-70. Mem. Am. Jail Assn., Am. Correctional Assn. (del. assembly 1989-91), Am. Correctional Health Svcs. Assn. (bd. dirs. 1981-93, v.p. 1985-87, pres. 1989-91, Disting. Svc. award 1994). Home: 669 Sky Hy Cir Lafayette CA 94549-5228 Office: The Cotton Group 3744 Mount Diablo Blvd Ste 200 Lafayette CA 94549-3602

COTTON, PATRICIA ALICE, psychology educator, counselor; b. N.Y.C., June 5, 1940; d. Earnest Patrick and Mary Amelia (Toich) Cotton; m. Frederick Lawton Cox, Nov. 7, 1959 (div. 1974); 1 child, Constance Saige. BA in Art Edn., English, U. Tex., El Paso, 1973, M. in Counseling Guidance, 1974; EdD in Psychology, U. Houston, 1985. Lic. profl. counselor; lic. marriage and family therapist; cert. tchr., nat. cert. clin. mental health counselor. Vocat. counselor, coord. group program U. Tex., El Paso, 1971-74; asst. dir. Cath. Counseling Svcs., El Paso, 1974-79; personnel rsch. specialist City of Houston, 1981-82; pvt. practice counselor Houston, 1983-88; teaching asst. U. Houston, 1979-85; instr. Houston Community Coll., 1980-88; asst. program dir., counselor Houston N.W. Med. Ctr., 1985-88; pvt. practice counselor Alamo Mental Health Group, San Antonio, 1989-92; instr. psychology St. Mary's U., San Antonio, 1990—; pvt. practice, Houston, 1985-87, San Antonio, 1992—. Artist sculpture "Rinocessoris", 1965 (Nat. Army Art/Craft award); contbr. articles to profl. jours. Active outreach seminars for jobless Exec.-Blue Collar North West Med. Ctr., Houston, 1986. Recipient Scholastic Achievement award Kappa Delta Pi, 1972; 2-yr. grantee outreach for work with elderly City of El Paso, 1975-77. Mem. Am. Psychol. Assn., Tex. Assn. for Counseling & Devel. Roman Catholic. Office: Box 31 3510 N St Marys St Ste 200 San Antonio TX 78212-3164

COTTRELL, JANET ANN, controller; b. Berea, Ohio, Dec. 2, 1943; d. Carmen and Hazel (French) Volpe; m. Melvin M. Cottrell, Mar. 2, 1963; children: Lori A., Gregory C. Student, Los Angeles State Coll., 1961-63. Lic. ins. agt., Calif. Loan processing Eastern Lenders, Covina, 1962-64; asst. bookkeeper Golden Rule Discount Stores, Rosemead, Calif., 1964-66; acctg. supr. Walter Carpet Mills, Industry, Calif., 1967-69; co-owner Motorcycle Specialties Co., Industry, 1969-78, Covina (Calif.) Kawasaki, 1978-84; v.p., contr. M.C. Specialties Inc., Covina, 1984—; v.p., controller Aviation Communications Inc., Covina, 1992—; active various coms. relating to promotion, safety and advancement of the recreational vehicle and auto industry, So. Calif., 1981—. Mem. com. Miss Covina Pageant, 1986—, presdl. task force, nat., 1982—, Rep. nat. com., 1986—. Mem. Covina C. of C., Calif. Motorcycle Dealers Assn., Nat. Auto Dealers Assn., Internat. Jet Ski Boating Assn. Republican. Office: Aviation Comm Inc 1025 W San Bernardino Rd Covina CA 91722-4106

COTTRELL, JEANNETTE ELIZABETH, retired librarian; b. Buffalo, Dec. 10, 1923; d. Benjamin Birch and Mary Jeannette (Ashdown) Milnes; m. William Barber Cottrell, Jan. 21, 1944 (dec.); children: Karen Jean, Susan Marie, William Milnes, Scott Barber, Stephen Ashdown. BA in Sociology, U. Tenn., 1970, MS, 1976; student, Alfred U., 1940-43. Cert. tchr. libr., Tenn. Nursery sch. tchr. Concord Meth. Ch., Knoxville, Tenn., 1964-65; libr. City Sch. System, Knoxville, Tenn., 1971-84, ret., 1984. Author: (with husband) An American Family in the 20th Century, 1987; recorder textbooks for the blind, 1983—. Libr. Concord United Meth. Ch., Knoxville, 1975—, curriculum chair spl. studies class, 1989—, reading chair Suzanna Wesley Circle. Mem. AAUW, Phi Kappa Phi, Beta Phi Mu. Republican. Methodist. Home: 308 Camelot Ct Knoxville TN 37922-2076

COTTRELL, MARY-PATRICIA TROSS, banker; b. Seattle, Apr. 24, 1934; d. Alfred Carl and Alice-Grace (O'Neal) Tross; m. Richard Smith Cottrell, May 17, 1969 (dec. 1995). BBA, U. Wash., 1955. Systems service rep. IBM, Seattle, also Endicott, N.Y., 1955-58, customer edn. instr., Endicott, 1958-60, 62-65, edn. planning rep., San Jose, Calif. and Endicott, N.Y., 1960-62; cons. data processing, Stamford, Conn., 1965-66; asst. treas. Union Trust Co., Stamford, 1967-68, asst. v.p., 1969-76, v.p., 1976-78, v.p., head corp. services, 1978-83; v.p. corp. fin. svcs. Citytrust, Bridgeport, Conn., 1983-90, sr. v.p. cash mgmt. svcs., 1990-91; v.p. cash mgmt. Chase Manhattan Bank of Conn., N.A., 1991-92, Centerbank, New Haven, 1992-95; v.p. corporate svcs. Lafayette Am. Bank, Bridgeport, 1995—. Bd. dirs. Family and Children's Aid of Greater Norwalk, Conn., chmn. 1986-87, Gaylord Hosp., 1986-92, vice chmn., 1991, chmn. devel. com., 1992—, Bridgeport Housing Svcs., 1985-91, New Eng. Network, Inc., Bank Mktg. Assn., 1988-91. Mem. Electronic Funds Transfer Assn. (vice chmn., bd. dirs., chmn. bd. dirs. 1983-84), Fairfield County Bankers Assn. (dir., pres. 1984-85), New Eng. Automated Clearing House Assn. (bd. dirs. 1995—), Phi Beta Kappa, Beta Gamma Sigma. Republican. Roman Catholic.

COTTRILL, MARGARET JOAN JODY, arts administrator; b. Columbus, Ohio, Oct. 25, 1951; d. Chester Curtin and Joan Marie (Miller) Dodd; m. Gary Lee Cottrill, Dec. 31, 1977; children: Justin Lee, Elizabeth Ellen, Anne Hathaway, Christopher Dodd. BA, Ohio Wesleyan U., 1973. Corr. sec. Office of the Gov., Charleston, W.Va., 1974-76; events coord. W.Va. Dept. Culture and History, Charleston, 1976-78; asst. dir. spl. events The Art Inst. Chgo., 1978-80; asst. to the dir. Sunrise Mus., Charleston, 1991-92; asst. to the commr. for devel. W.Va. Divsn. Culture and History, Charleston, 1994—; state rep. Am. Assn. Mus. Vols., 1996—; peer assistance network advisor Peer Assistance Network, W.Va., 1995—; advisor Capitol Market Promotion Com., Charleston, 1995—; mem. Leadership W.Va., 1996. Mem. U. Charleston Cmty. Chorus, 1981—, Parent Involvement Coun., Charleston, 1985—; troop leader Girl Scouts Am., Fla., Va., W.Va., 1989-93; den leader Boy Scouts Am., Charleston, 1995—; founding bd. dirs. Christ Ch. for Liturgical Arts, 1996. Mem. Nat. Soc. Fund Raising Execs. (bd. dirs. W.Va. chpt., chmn. Nat. Philanthropy Day Recognition Dinner 1996). Methodist. Office: The Cultural Ctr 1900 Kanawha Blvd E Charleston WV 25305

COUCH, JENNIE LEIGH, artist, educator; b. Huntsville, Ala., May 7, 1954; d. Austin Leigh and Nancy Jane (Moyers) Couch; m. Gary Louis Hasness, May 23, 1981; children: John Austin, Joshua Louis. BS in Art Edn., U. Ala., Tuscaloosa, 1977, MA in Painting/Printmaking, 1981; postgrad., U. Houston, 1990-92; MFA in Ceramics/Sculpture, Stephen F. Austin State U., 1993. Teaching asst. U. Ala., Tuscaloosa, 1980-81; teaching fellow U. Houston, 1981; art instr. Alief-Ind. Sch. Dist., Houston, 1986-88, 89-92, 1993-94; ceramic artist Houston, 1988-89; grad. teaching fellow Stephen F. Austin State U., Nacogdoches, Tex., 1992-93; art instr. Spring Br. Ind. Sch. Dist., Houston, 1994-95; asst. prof. art Concordia Coll., Moorhead, Minn., 1995—; juror Mus. of S.E. Tex., Beaumont, Houston C.C., 1995, Archies West Gallery, Moorhead, 1995. Solo exhbns. include ceramic sculpture at Forgotten Lang., Inman Gallery, 1991, Gateways, Mus. S.E. Tex., 1992, Vocabulary, Galveston (Tex.) Arts Ctr., 1995, Recent Work, Ala. A&M U., 1995. Recipient Grand prize 39th Ann. Delta Arts Exhbn., Little Rock, 1991, Juror's prize Houston Area Women's Ctr., 1992, Juror's Choice award Art League of Houston, 1993. Mem. Coll. Art Assn., Art League of Houston, Lawdale Art and Performance Ctr., Phi Kappa Phi. Office: Concordia Coll 901 8th St Moorhead MN 56562

COUCHARA, SISTER CAROL ANNE, education educator; b. Norristown, Pa., Dec. 21, 1951. BA, Immaculata Coll., 1977; MA, West Chester U., 1988; postgrad., Lehigh U., 1993—. Cert. instr. II elem. Spanish, Pa. Tchr. St. Patrick Sch., McAdoo, Pa., 1972-74, Sacred Heart Sch., Havertown, Pa., 1974-76, Annunciation Sch., Shenandoah, Pa., 1976-77, Escuela Inmaculado Corazon, Lima, Peru, 1977-82, Incarnation Sch., Phila., 1982-84; tchr. St. Joseph Sch., Downington, Pa., 1984-89, Athens, Ga., 1989-92; instr. Immaculata (Pa.) Coll., 1992—. Mem. Nat. Coun. Social Studies, Nat. Coun. Tchrs. of Math., Nat. Sci. Tchrs. Assn., Pa. Assn. Coll. Tchrs. of Edn. Roman Catholic. Office: Immaculata Coll PO Box 684 Immaculata PA 19345-0684

COUGHLIN, CAROLINE MARY, library consultant, educator; b. Bronx, N.Y., Dec. 6, 1944; d. Daniel Anthony and Antoinette (Aponte) C.; m. William Martin Weinberg, Oct. 3, 1981; 1 child, Nora Harie Weinberg. BA, Mercy Coll., 1966; MLS, Emory U., 1967; PhD, Rutgers U., 1976. Reference libr. First Nat. City Bank, N.Y.C., 1967-68; instr. Emory U., Atlanta, 1968-71; teaching asst. Rutgers U., New Brunswick, N.J., 1971-74; children's libr. Phillipsburg (N.J.) Pub. Libr., 1972-73; asst. prof. libr. sci. Simmons Coll., Boston, 1974-78; asst. dir. libr. Drew U., Madison, N.J., 1978-86, dir., 1986-94, assoc. prof. bibliography and rsch., 1986-94; vis. lectr. Further Edn. Cen., Tampere, Finland, 1994, 96; cons. to librs., 1974—; team membership for site visits Mid. State Assn., 1979—; chair libr. dir.'s group Assn. Ind. Colls. and Univs. of N.J., 1987-92; bd. dirs. Ctr. for Rsch. Librs., Chgo., 1987-92; vis. faculty mem. Rutgers U., 1988, 90, 93—; vis. prof. Internat. Libr. Sch. U. Coll. Wales, 1992; evaluator HEA Office of Edn., 1987—. Co-author: Lyle's Administration of College Library, 1992; editor: Recurring Library Issues, 1978; also articles. Bd. dirs. Women's Project of N.J., 1984—; mem. Women's Polit. Action Caucus, N.J., 1985—. Mem. ALA (councillor 1977-81), Assn. Libr. and Info. Sci. Educators (various coms.), Archons of Colophon, N.J. Libr. Assn. (pres. coll. and univs. librs. sect. 1974-75, Disting. Svc. award 1993, Rsch. award 1993), Soc. for History of Authorship, Reading and Publ. (treas. 1994—), Beta Phi Mu. Democrat. Home: 304 Grant Ave Highland Park NJ 08904-1828

COUGHLIN, KAREN A., health care company executive. Sr. v.p. Region II Humana Inc., Louisville. Office: Humana Inc 500 W Main St Louisville KY 40202*

COUGHLIN, MARGARET ANN, marketing communications executive; b. Muncie, Ind., Oct. 14, 1955; d. Thomas Francis and Mary Alice (Guffigan) C. BA, Skidmore Coll., 1977; MBA, Babson Coll., 1984. With Procter & Gamble, Cin., 1977-79; account exec. Hill Holiday Advt., Boston, 1979-81; account supr. HBM/WCRS Advt., Boston, 1982-84; sr. v.p. Ingalls Quinn & Johnson/BBDO, Boston, 1984-91; pres. Cone Coughlin Comms., Boston, 1991—; bd. dirs. Stuarts Dept. Stores. Bd. dirs. Boston Children's Svc. Assn., 1988-92, Faneuil Hall Trust. Mem. Women in Communications (pres. 1989-90), Ad Club Boston (bd. dirs.). Office: Cone Coughlin Communications 90 Canal St Boston MA 02114-2022*

COULSON, MARION CROSBEE, psychologist, educator; b. Newark, Oct. 7, 1918; d. Howard Thomas Crosbee and Elizabeth Weiner. BS, Newark State Tchrs. Coll., 1947; MEd, Rutgers U., 1953; student, Harvard U., 1985. Cert. tchr., N.J., sch. psychologist, N.J. Tchr. Union, N.J., Morristown, N.J.; sch. psychologist Hackensack, N.J.; assoc. prof. N.J. Dept. Edn.; prof. Glassboro State Coll., N.J.; prof. psychology Trenton State Coll.; staff psychologist Middlesex Gen. Hosp., N.J.; librarian, Denville, N.J., 1965. Contbr. articles to profl. jours. Sch. exec. Readiness for Sch., 1960; innovator Head Start program, Trenton. Grantee Grant Found., Trenton, President John F. Kennedy, 1959. Mem. Am. Psychol. Assn. (emeritus), Monmouth-Ocean County Psychol. Assn. Episcopalian. Home: Leisure Village 88B Dorchester Dr Lakewood NJ 08701

COULSON, ZOE ELIZABETH, retired consumer marketing executive; b. Sullivan, Ind., Sept. 22, 1932; d. Marion Allan and Mary Anne (Thompson) C. BS, Purdue U., 1954; AMP, Harvard Bus. Sch., 1983. Asst. dir. home econs. Am. Meat Inst., Chgo., 1954-57; account exec. J. Walter Thompson Co., Chgo., 1957-60; creative consumer dir. Leo Burnett Co., Chgo., 1960-64; mag. editor-in-chief Donnelley-Dun & Bradstreet, N.Y.C., 1964-68; food editor Good Housekeeping, N.Y.C., 1968-75, dir. G H Inst., 1975-81; corporate v.p. Campbell Soup Co., Camden, N.J., 1981-91; mktg. cons., 1991-96; mem. bd. dirs. Rubbermaid Inc., 1982-95. Author: Good Housekeeping Cookbook, 1972, Good Housekeeping Illustrated Cookbook, 1981 Trustee Cooper Hosp./Univ. Med. Ctr., 1982-91; elder Old Pine Presbyn. Ch., 1992-96. Named Disting. Alumni, Purdue U., 1971. Mem. Women's Econ. Bus. Alliance (bd. govs. 1987-91), Food and Drug Law Inst. (food bd. dir. 1979-81), Harvard Bus. Sch. Club (Phila. v.p. budget 1994-95), Kappa Alpha Theta House Corp. (pres. U. Pa. chpt. 1992—). Republican. Avocation: Meso-Am. archaeology. Home: 220 Locust St Apt 18-B Philadelphia PA 19106

COULTER, CATHERINE, writer; married. BA, U. Tex.; MA, Boston Coll. With human resources N.Y.C., San Francisco. Author: The Rebel Bride, 1979, 94, Lord Harry's Folly, 1980, rewritten as Lord Harry, 1995, Lord Deverill's Heir, 1980, rewritten as The Heir, 1996, The Generous Earl, 1981, rewritten as The Duke, 1995, Devil's Embrace, 1983, Sweet Surrender, 1984, Devil's Daughter, 1985, Chandra, 1985, Midnight Star, 1986, Wild Star, 1986, Midsummer Magic, 1987, Jade Star, 1987, Moonspun Magic, 1988, Calypso Magic, 1988, Night Shadow, 1989, Night Fire, 1989, An Intimate Deception, 1989, False Pretenses, 1989, Portrait of Indifference, 1989, Night Storm, 1990, Impulse, 1990, Fire Song, 1990, Earth Song, 1990, Secret Song, 1991, Season of the Sun, 1991, The Hillion Bride, 1992, Beyond Eden, 1992, The Heiress Bride, 1993, Lord of Hawk Fell Island, 1992, The Aristocrat, 1992, Aftershocks, 1992, Afterglow, 1993, The Wyndham Legacy, 1994, The Nightingale Legacy, 1994, Lord of Raven's Peak, 1994, Lord of Falcon Ridge, 1995, The Cove, 1996, Rosehaven, 1996, The Valentine Legacy, 1996. Recipient Romantic Times award for best historical romance author, 1989. Mem. Mystery Writers Am., Romance Writers Am. Address: PO Box 17 Mill Valley CA 94942*

COULTER, CYNTHIA JEAN, artist, educator; b. Lincoln, Nebr., Jan. 16, 1951; d. George Wallace and Arlene Jean (Winzenburg) C. Student, U. Tex., 1970-72; BFA in Sculpture, U. Colo., 1975; postgrad., U. Iowa, 1976-77; MFA in Sculpture, U. Okla., 1980. Instr. Arts Annex, Oklahoma City, 1977-78, Firehouse Art Ctr., Norman, Okla., 1979-80, Francis Parker Sch., Chgo., 1986-87, Express-Ways Children's Mus. Art, Chgo., 1987, Wai Sch., Hong Kong, 1987, Field Mus. Natural History, Chgo., 1987-88, Oklahoma City Pub. Schs., 1988-90, Fine Arts Inst. of Edmond, Okla., 1990-91, U. Okla. Mus. Art, 1991, Okla. Sch. Sci. and Math., Oklahoma City, 1992, St. Michael's Presch., Amagansett, L.I., 1994—, Country Sch., Amagansett, 1994—, Guild Hall, East Hampton, N.Y., 1994—; resident studio artist Inst. for Art and Urban Resources, N.Y.C., 1980-81; instr. SPARK Program for Inner City Children, Oklahoma City, 1989; instr., artist-in-residence State Arts Coun., Oklahoma City, 1989-92, City Arts Coun., Oklahoma City, 1977, 89-92, State Arts Coun. Colo., Denver, 1990-95, BOCES Program, Suffolk County, N.Y., 1994—; art dir. Hampton Day Sch. Summer Camp, Bridgehampton, N.Y., 1993; set designer Okla. Children's Theater, 1992; instr. adult art edn. City Coll., Chgo., 1992-94; vis. artist Sch. of Art Inst. Chgo., 1980; instr. art fundamentals program U. Okla., 1979-80. One-woman shows include Ctrl. Innovative Gallery, Oklahoma City, 1979, Alternative Space, Norman, Okla., 1979, U. Nev. Sheppard Fine Arts Gallery, Reno, 1981, Lenore Gray Gallery, Providence, 1981, Sch. of Art Inst. Chgo. Sculpture Gallery, 1981, ABC No Rio, N.Y.C., 1984, Gas Sta./Performance Space, N.Y.C., 1987, 1997 Gallery with Alvin Gallery, Hong Kong, 1988, Kirkpatrick Ctr., Mus., Oklahoma City, 1989, Helio Gallery, N.Y.C., 1989, Okla. State U. Gardiner Art Gallery, Stillwater, 1990, Oklahoma City Art Mus., 1991, City Arts Ctr., Oklahoma City, 1992, Brickhouse Gallery, Tulsa, 1992, Conscience Point Yacht Club, Southampton, N.Y., 1993, Ashawagh Hall, East Hampton, N.Y., 1994, TSL Warehouse, Hudson, N.Y., 1996; exhibited at group exhbns. at M.A. Doran Gallery, Tulsa, 1991, Individual Artists of Okla. Gallery, Oklahoma City, 1992, U. Ctrl. Okla. Mus. Art, Edmond, 1989-93, Brickhouse Gallery, Tulsa, 1992, Ea. N.Mex. U., Portales, 1992 (award 1992), Spazi Fine Art, Housatonic, Mass., 1992, 93, 94-95, Ashawagh Hall, 1994-95, Gallery North, Setauket, N.Y., 1994 (award), Danette Koke Fine Art/Ramscale Art Assocs., N.Y.C., 1995, others; represented in permanent collections at Oklahoma City Art Mus., U. Okla. Mus. Art, also pvt. collections. Bd. dirs. Renaissance Arts Found., Oklahoma City, 1977. Grantee Ill. Arts Coun., Chgo., 1983, 84, Artists Space Exhbn., N.Y.C., 1987, Columbia Coll., Chgo., 1988, Okla. Visual Arts Coalition, 1990, Pollack-Krasner Found., Inc., 1991, Eben Demarest Trust, 1995; recipient Individual Artists award Okla. Gallery, 1992.

COULTER, ELIZABETH JACKSON, biostatistician, educator; b. Balt., Nov. 2, 1919; d. Waddie Pennington and Bessie (Gills) Jackson; m. Norman Arthur Coulter Jr., June 23, 1951; 1 child, Robert Jackson. A.B., Swarthmore Coll., 1941; A.M., Radcliffe Coll., 1946, Ph.D., 1948. Asst. dir. health study Bur. Labor Stats., San Juan, P.R., 1946; research asst. Milbank Meml. Fund, N.Y.C., 1948-51; economist Office Def. Prodn., 1951-52; research analyst Children's Bur.-HEW, 1952-53; from statistician to chief statistician Ohio Dept. Health, 1954-65; lectr. econs., then clin. asst. prof. preventive medicine Ohio State U., 1954-65; asst. clin. prof. biostats. U. Pitts. Sch. Pub. Health, 1958-62; assoc. prof. biostats. U. N.C., Chapel Hill, 1965-72, assoc. prof. econs., 1965-78, biostats. prof., 1972-90; adj. assoc. prof., hosp. adminstr. Duke U., 1972-79; assoc. dean undergrad. pub. health studies U. N.C., Chapel Hill, 1979-86, prof. biostats. emerita, 1990—. Contbr. articles to profl. jours. Mem. AAAS, AAUP, APHA (governing coun. 1970-72), Am. Econ. Assn., Am. Statis. Assn., Am. Acad. Polit. and Social Sci., Biometric Soc., Am. Evaluation Assn., Assn. for Health Svcs. Rsch., Sigma Xi, Delta Omega. Methodist. Home: 1825 N Lakeshore Dr Chapel Hill NC 27514-6734

COULTER, JULIETTE D(ARUNI), public relations professional; b. Bangkok, Thailand, May 25, 1969; d. Arnold W. and Sasithorn Peters; m. Ross C. Coulter, May 21, 1994. BA, U. Calif., Daivs, 1991. Legis. aide Calif. State Assembly, Sacramento, 1991; acct. coord. Fleishman-Hilland, Inc., Washington & Dallas, 1992-94, Cox Communications, Dallas, 1994—. Vol. pub. rels. dir. The 500, Inc., 1995, pub. rels. advisor, 1995-96. Recipient Cmty. Svc. award ITAD/FW Area, Dallas, 1996. Mem. Women in Communications (bd. dirs. 1996—), Dallas Coun. World Affairs (bd. dirs. 1996), Dallas World Salute (bd. dirs. 1995-96), Internat. Profl. League (pres., v.p. 1994-96). Presbyterian.

COULTON, MARTHA JEAN GLASSCOE (MRS. MARTIN J. COULTON), library consultant; b. Dayton, Ohio; d. Lafayette Pierre and Gertrude Blanche (Miller) Glasscoe; m. Martin J. Coulton; children: Perry Jean, Martin John. student Dayton Art Inst., 1946-47. Dir., Milton (Ohio) Union Pub. Libr., 1968-89; libr. cons., Centerville, Ohio, 1989—. Named Outstanding Woman Jaycees, 1978-1979; recipient Spl. Recognition award Ohio Ho. Reps., 1989. Mem. ALA, Ohio Library Assn., Miami Valley Library Orgn. (sec. 1981, v.p. 1982, pres. 1983), Internat. Platform Assn., Puppeteers of Am., DAR, Union Internat. Marionnette, Amnesty Internat., Pub. Citizen Health. Home and Office: 6029 Buggywhip Ln Dayton OH 45459-2407

COUNIHAN, DARLYN JOYCE, mathematics educator; b. Cumberland, Md., May 1, 1948; d. Joseph Paul and Clara Kathryn (Miller) C.; m. Mark W. Chambré, Jan. 20, 1979. AB, Hood Coll., 1970, MA, 1982; postgrad., U. Md., 1971-73. Tchr. math. Cabin John Jr. High Sch., Montgomery County, Md., 1970-75, coach girls volleyball team, 1975; math. resource tchr. Takoma Park (Md.) Jr. High Sch., 1975-77, Ridgeview Jr. High Sch., Gaithersburg, Md., 1977-81; math. tchr. Kennedy High Sch., Silver Spring, Md., 1982-84; magnet math. tchr. Takoma Park Mid. Sch., 1984—, also math. team coach; mem. area 3 adv. coun. Montgomery County Pub. Schs., 1972-73; coach boys basketball team Montgomery County Recreation Assn., 1971; mem. Mathcounts Adv. Group, Md. Mathalon Com. Co-author geometry textbook. Recipient various acad. athletic award in high sch., coll., Presdl. award for Excellence in Sci. and Math. Teaching, 1990, Women in Edn. award, 1986, David W. Taylor award Sigma Xi, 1993, Albert Shanker award, 1993; NSF grantee, 1971-72, 90, 92. Mem. Am. Fedn. Tchrs., Montgomery County Math. Tchrs. Assn., Nat. Coun. Tchrs. Math., Math. Assn. Am. (Edyth May Sliffe award 1996), Mil. Order of the Cooties Aux., Capts. Cove Golf and Yacht Club, Lake Holiday County Club, VFW Aux., Phi Kappa Phi. Home: 13900 Zeigler Way Silver Spring MD 20904-1160 Office: Takoma Park Mid Sch 7611 Piney Branch Rd Silver Spring MD 20910-5102

COUNSELMAN, ANNE, librarian; b. Silas, Ala., Oct. 5, 1940; d. Chester Arthur and Elva (Daniels) Martin; m. Terry J. Counselman; children: Daphne, Bruce, Phillip. BS, U. Montevallo, Ala., 1961; MA, U. Ala., Birmingham, 1979; EdS, U. Ala., Tuscaloosa, 1988. Tchr. Clarke County Bd. Edn., Grove Hill, Ala., 1966-69; libr. asst. Birmingham Pub. Libr., 1971-72, head bookmobile, 1972-73; project dir. Appalachian Adult Edn. Ctr., Birmingham, 1974-75; libr. Birmingham City Bd. Edn., 1975-76, Wallace State C.C., Selma, Ala., 1980-83, Marengo County Bd. Edn., Linden, Ala., 1984—; reader rsch. and rev. team Libr. Rsch. and Demonstration Div. Libr. Programs, Washington, 1974. Mem. Thomaston (Ala.) Planning and Zoning Bd., 1992, 93; active Thomaston Bapt. Ch. Linly Heflin scholar, 1958-61, scholar Columbus Sch. Speech Correction, 1960, Pacers scholar Program for Rural Svcs. and Rsch., 1987; fellow Coun. for Basic Edn., 1992. Mem. NEA, Am. Edn. Assn., Ala. Edn. Assn., Thomaston Study Club. Home: 122 Lake Cir Thomaston AL 36783-3577 Office: AL Johnson High Sch Coates Ave Thomaston AL 36783

COUNTRYMAN, JOAN CANNADY, academic administrator; b. Phila., Mar. 16, 1940; d. William Patrick and Virginia Bayton (Banks) C.; m. Peter Jon Countryman, Aug. 27, 1963 (div. 1972); children: Matthew, Rachel; m. Edward Bernard Jakmauh, June 24, 1990. BA, Sarah Lawrence Coll., 1962; M in Urban Studies, Yale U., 1966; postgrad., Wesleyan U., 1963-64, London Sch. Econ., 1966-67. Dir. cmty. schs. Sch. Dist. Phila., 1967-69; dir. career planning U. Pa., Phila., 1969-70; from tchr., dept. head to asst. head sch. Germantown Friends Sch., Phila., 1970-93; head Lincoln Sch., Providence, 1993—; cons. Nat. S.E.E.D. (Seeking Ednl. Equity and Diversity), Wellesley, Mass., 1989—; master tchr. Woodrow Wilson Nat. Fellowship Found., Princeton, N.J., 1986-89, bd. dirs., 1993—; book reviewer N.Y. Times, 1986-94. Author: Writing to Learn Mathematics, 1992; editor: Black Images in American Literature, 1977. Bd. dirs. Cmty. Prep. Sch., Providence, 1994—, City Bridge, Concord, Mass., 1994—, Project AIDS, Providence, 1993-94; bd. mgrs. Haverford Coll., 1996—. Klingenstein fellow Tchrs. Coll., N.Y.C., 1988-89, Fulbright fellow London U., 1966-67. Mem. Assn. Ind. Schs. New Eng. (bd. dirs. 1995—), Ind. Sch. Assn. R.I. (bd. dirs. 1994—), Nat. Assn. Prin. Schs. for Girls (bd. dirs. 1995—), Nat. Coun. Tchrs. Math. Mem. Religious Soc. Friends. Office: Lincoln Sch 301 Butler Ave Providence RI 02906

COUNTS, CHRISTINE GAY, dental hygienist; b. Toledo, Dec. 31, 1951; d. Jack G. and Virginia Aileen (Doyle) Tornga; m. John Howard Mosher, May 11, 1974 (div. July 1990); children: Heather Kristen, Andrew Jacob; m. Robert Milton Counts, July 5, 1991 (dec. Mar. 1993). BS in Dental Hygiene, U. Mich., 1974. Registered dental hygienist, Nat. Bd. Dental Examiners, Ind. State Bd. Dentistry, Fla. State Bd. Dentistry, Mich. State Bd. Dentistry. Asst. supr. dental hygiene Ind. U., South Bend, Ind., 1974-75; expanded functions hygienist South Bend Dental Ctr., 1975; periodental hygienist Dr. John B. Lehman, South Bend, 1976-82, Dr. Cristene Maas, Longwood, Fla., 1983-84; periodontal hygienist Dr. Richard Altman, Orlando, Fla., 1984-85; dental hygienist Dr. H. Raymund Barcus, Winter Park, Fla., 1984—; adj. instr. So. Coll., Orlando, 1984. Med./dental mission Wekiva Presbyn. Ch., Honduras, 1987, 89, Diocese of Orlando, Dominican Republic, 1994, 95; deacon Presbyn. Ch., 1992. Mem. U. Mich. Club of Orlando, Greater Orlando Dental Hygiene Assn (sec. 1986-87), Alpha Chi Omega (Gamma Upsilon Gamma chpt., pres. 1995-97). Republican. Roman Catholic. Office: Dr H Raymund Barcuss Office 271 W Canton Ave Winter Park FL 32789

COUPEY, SUSAN MCGUIRE, pediatrician, educator; b. Montreal, Que., Can., June 29, 1942; came to U.S., 1978; d. Clarence Herbert and Paulette (Lefevre) McGuire; m. Pierre M.L. Coupey, July 1964 (div. 1981); children: Marc M.R., Ariane S.; m. James R. English III, Nov. 23, 1988. BA, Queen's U., Kingston, Ont., Can., 1962; postgrad., McGill U., Montreal, 1962-63; MD, U. B.C., Vancouver, Can., 1975. Diplomate Am. Bd. Pediatrics, subboard in adolescent medicine. Devel. chemist Merck, Sharp & Dohme, Ltd., Montreal, 1963-64; rotating intern Montreal Gen. Hosp., 1975-76; resident in pediatrics Montreal Children's Hosp., 1976-78; fellow in adolescent medicine Montefiore Med. Ctr., Bronx, N.Y., 1978-79, attending pediatrician, 1980—; rsch. asst. Cancer Rsch. Ctr., U. B.C., 1967-72; instr., asst. prof. pediatrics Albert Einstein Coll. Medicine, Bronx, 1979-85, assoc. prof., 1985-93, prof., 1993—, assoc. dir. div. adolescent medicine, 1984—, course dir. introduction to clin. medicine, 1989—, mem. faculty senate, 1983-84, 88-90; attending pediatrician North Ctrl. Bronx Hosp., 1979—; cons. in adolescent medicine Flushing (N.Y.) Hosp. and Med. Ctr., 1982—; Maricopa-Pima vis. prof. U. Ariz., 1989; vis. prof. Children's Hosp. Ea. Ont., U. Ottawa and Ea. Can. chpt. Soc. for Adolescent Medicine, 1990; chmn. health svcs. adv. com. Children's Aid Soc., 1985—, bd. trustees, 1993—; mem. adv. bd. Office Substance Abuse Ministry, Archdiocese of N.Y., 1983-85. Assoc. editor Adolescent Medicine: State of the Art Revs., 1990—, Jour. Devel. & Behavioral Pediatrics, 1992-96, Jour. Pediat. & Adolescent Gynecology, 1992—; contbr. articles to med. jours., also chpts. to books and monographs. Fellow Am. Acad. Pediatrics; mem. Soc. for Adolescent Medicine (nominations com. 1984-85, chmn. jour. adv. com. 1987—, program com. 1991-93, awards com. 1992-95), Ambulatory Pediatric Assn., Soc. for Behavioral Pediatrics, N.Am. Soc. Pediat. and Adolescent Gynecology (bd. dirs. 1993-96, sec. 1996—), Ea. Soc. Pediat. Rsch., Soc. Rsch. in Adolescence, Sex Info. and Edn. Coun. U.S., Am. Acad. Physicians & Patients, Albert Einstein Coll. Medicine Alumni Assn. (v.p. pediatrics 1983-84, pres. 1984-85). Office: Albert Einstein Coll Medicine Montefiore Med Ctr 111 E 210th St Bronx NY 10467-2490

COURIC, KATHERINE, broadcast journalist; b. Arlington, Va., 1957; m. Jay Monahan; 2 children, Elinor and Caroline. Grad., with Am. Studies major, U. Va. Began career with reporting and producing jobs NBC affiliates, Miami, Washington; joined NBC Network News, 1989; former nat. corr. Today, NBC, Washington; co-anchor Today, NBC, 1991—; co-host Now with Tom Brokaw and Katie Couric, NBC, 1993-94. Address: NBC TV Today Show 30 Rockefeller Plz New York NY 10112*

COURNOYEA, NELLIE J., Canadian government official; b. Aklavik, N.W.T., Canada, 1940; div.; 2 children: John, Maureen. Radio announcer, later regional mgr. CBC, Inuvik, N.W.T.; negotiator, Com. for Original People's Entitlement; mem. territorial legislature Yellowknife, 1984—; minister of renewable resources, and of culture and communications, 1983-85, minister various portfolios, from 1987, govt. leader, 1991—; now premier N.W.T. Yellowknife. Office: Office of the Premier, PO Box 1320, Yellowknife, NT Canada X1A 2L9

COURSON, MARNA B. P., public relations executive; b. Waynesboro, Pa., Feb. 22, 1951; d. Eugene Perry and Charlotte Mae (Sherman) Roschli; m. Sydney E. Courson, May 24, 1982; 1 child, Sydney Alexandra. BA, Franklin and Marshall Coll., 1973; postgrad., U. Kans., Kansas City. Reporter Beach Haven Times/The Beacon, Manahawkin, N.J., 1973-74, Dailey Observer Newspaper, Toms River, N.J., 1974-76; communications mgr. Frick India Ltd., New Delhi, 1976-77; reporter, dictationist UPI, Washington, 1978-80; reporter UPI, Richmond, Va.; reporter, editor AP, Balt., 1980-84; communications coord. St. Luke's Hosp. Found., Kansas City, Mo., 1986-88; exec. v.p. pub. rels. Spaw and Assocs., Inc., Overland Park, Kans., 1988-89; exec. v.p. CCI Pub. Rels. & Mktg. Comm., Inc., Shawnee Mission, Kans., 1990-92, pres., 1992—. Active adv. bd. Wonderscope Children's Mus., Vol. Leadership Coun.; vol. bd. dirs. Ctr. for Mgmt. Assist.; active MidAm. Planned Giving Coun., Greater Kansas City Coun. Philanthropy. Recipient Prism award for fund raising, numerous awards and honors for reporting, 1973-80; also pub. rels. awards, 1988-94. Mem. Internat. Assn. Bus. Communicators, Pub. Rels. Soc. of Am. (Pres.'s award with GKC), Nat. Soc. Fund Raising Execs., Silicon Prairie Tech. Assn., C. of C. Office: 5832 Grand Ave Kansas City MO 64113-2128

COURTNEY, CAROLYN ANN, school librarian; b. Plainview, Tex., Aug. 1, 1937; d. John Blanton and Geneva Louise (Stovall) Ross; m. Moyland Henry Courtney, Aug. 17, 1957; 1 child, Constance Elaine. BA summa cum laude, Wayland Bapt. Coll., 1969; MEd, W. Tex. State Coll., 1976; MLS, U. North Tex., 1990. Cert. elem., secondary, libr. tchr. 5th grade tchr. Hale Ctr. (Tex.) Ind. Sch. Dist., 1970-77, libr., 1977—. Mem. LWV (bd. mem. 1970-75), DAR (Good Citizen chair 1981-85), Tex. State Tchs. Assn. (life), Tex. Classroom Tchrs. Assn. (sec. 1983-85), Tex. Libr. Assn., Delta Kappa Gamma (rsch. chair 1975-77, publs. chair 1984-86, scholarship 1975). Methodist. Home: 209 S Floydada St Plainview TX 79072-6665 Office: Hale Center Ind Sch Dist Drawer M Hale Center TX 79041

COURTNEY, SARAH ANN, retail executive. BA in Lit., Dunbarton Coll., 1969. Asst. buyer Hechinger Co., Hyattsville, Md., 1969-70, housewares buyer, 1970-72, buyer housewares and paint, 1972-75, divsn. merch. mgr., 1976-80, gen. merchandise mgr., 1980-85, sr. v.p., gen. merchandise mgr., 1985-95, bd. dirs., 1985-92; sr. v.p., gen. merchandise mgr. Hechinger/Home Quarters Co., Hyattsville, 1995—; bd. dirs. Serex Corp., Youngstown, Ohio. Bd. trustees St. Joseph Coll., Renasselaer, Ind.; chairperson class of '69 Dunbarton Coll. Alumni. Named Merchandiser of Yr., Home Ctr. Industry, 1985. Office: Hechinger Co 1801 McCormick Dr Hyattsville MD 20785

COURVILLE, SUSAN KAY, secondary education educator; b. Port Arthur, Tex., Apr. 27, 1948; d. Robert Owen and Hazel Fae (McCardell) Barnard; children: Kenneth C., Amy Caroline. BS, Tex. Technol. U., 1969; postgrad., U. Houston, 1990. Vocat. Edn. for the Handicapped cert., Tex. Educator Stephen F. Austin H.S., Port Arthur, 1969-70, Sheldon Ind. Sch. Dist., Houston, 1980-84; exec. H. & W. Petroleum Sheldon Ind. Sch. Dist., 1985-90; educator C.E. King-Sheldon Ind. Sch. Dist., 1990—; mem. adv. bd. Vocat. Edn. for the Handicapped, Sheldon Ind. Sch. Dist., Houston, 1991-96. Mem. United Meth. Women, 1st Meth. Ch., Houston, 1971—; mem. Woodforest Women's Club, Houston, 1972-80, sec., 1976; pilot mem. Pilot Internat., Houston, 1989-91. Mem. Alpha Delta Kappa. Office: Channelview Ind Sch Dist 1100 Sheldon Rd Houston TX 77530

COUSINS, BERNICE BRIGANDO, minister, educator, consultant; b. Flushing, N.Y., Nov. 2, 1937; d. August and Olympia (Tortora) Brigando; BFA in Interior Design, Pratt Inst., 1955, postgrad. 1959; postgrad. City U. N.Y., 1966; children: David Bruce, Jason Bruce. Asst. to dir., tchr., Mus. Modern Art, Dept. Edn., N.Y.C., 1963-72; tchr. N.Y.C. Bd. Edn., 1966-73; with Am. Map Corp., N.Y.C., 1975-84, dir cartographic services, dir. mktg. services, also dir., 1979-81; co-dir. CW Assocs., Flushing, N.Y., 1982-86; mgr. ops. support svcs. Consol. Appraisal Co., Inc., N.Y.C., 1987—; dir. art and prodn. The Consolidated Appraisal Report; tchr. Adminstrv. Dir. Actualism Ctr., N.Y.C., 1980—; bd. trustees Actualism, Calif., 1990—, sec., 1990—, chair bd. dirs., 1991—, chair creative devel., 1991—; editor: Step by Step; lectr. in field; counselor and tchr. in areas of death and dying, grief release, stress reduction, trauma release, health and wellness, women's issues, family and personal relationships, enlightened business relationships. Curriculum Adv. Com., Pub. Sch. 85Q, 1976-77. Mem. NAFE, Assn. for Research and Enlightment, Women Bus. Owners N.Y., Am. Space Found., High Frontier Soc., Am. Fedn. Astrologers, Inst. of Noetic Scis., Inst. for Integrative Therapy. Contbr. articles to profl. jours.; researcher, compiler, editor: Nutritive Value of Common Foods, 1978; researcher, editor: Art Work: Schick-Colorprint Anatomy Charts, 1976-84; Internet. Ltd., 1976-; cons. in spiritual growth and devel. and metaphysics. Office: 41-19 23rd Ave Astoria NY 11105-1508

COUSINS, ELAINE, educational administrator; b. Bklyn., Apr. 15, 1946; d. Eli and Rose Barbara (Kessler) Buxbaum; m. Peter Hannon, Aug. 15, 1965 (div. 1972); 1 child, Monica Nicole. Student, Bennington Coll., 1962-65; BA, U. Calif., Berkeley, 1967; MA, Ea. Mich. U., 1976. Asst. to dir. orientation Youth for Understanding, Washington, 1977-79; program asst. Deutsches Youth for Understanding Komitee, Hamburg, Germany, 1979-82; computer sys. cons. info. tech. divsn. U. Mich., Ann Arbor, 1984-87, user svcs. mgr. for edn., 1987-95, edn. svcs. mgr., 1995—, lectr. in computer sci. dept. elec. engring., 1993—, lectr. comprehensive studies program, 1993—. Contbr. articles to profl. publs. Dem. candidate for Washtenaw County Commn., 1972; chair Washtenaw County Dem. County Conv., 1972. Home: 660 Peninsula Ct Ann Arbor MI 48105 Office: U Mich Info Tech Divsn 519 W William St Ann Arbor MI 48103-4943

COUSTÉ, STEPHANIE KNIGHT, elementary school assistant principal; b. Lake Charles, La., Apr. 25, 1949; d. Elray John and Susan Estelle (Chandler) Knight; m. Thomas Lawrence Cousté, Dec. 18, 1971; children: Thomas Lawrence Jr., Jeanne Estelle. BA, McNeese State U., 1971, MEd, 1978. Cert. kindergarten tchr., elem. tchr., prin., supr. of instrn., La. Tchr. Calcasieu Parish Sch. Bd., Lake Charles, La., 1971-81, 89—, Lafayette (La.) Parish Sch. Bd., 1981-85, Paradise Valley Unified Sch. Dist., Phoenix, 1985-86, Simi Valley (Calif.) Sch. Dist., 1986-87, Cath. Diocese of San Bernardino, Ontario, Calif., 1987-88, Vermilion Parish Sch. Bd., Abbeville, Ala., 1988-89. Mem. La. Fedn. Tchrs., Calcasieu Parish Reading Coun., La. Assn. Children Under Six, So. Early Childhood Assn., Delta Kappa Gamma, Phi Delta Kappa. Democrat. Roman Catholic. Home: 566 Rolling Hill Dr Lake Charles LA 70611-5012 Office: Gillis Elem Sch 916 Topsy Rd Lake Charles LA 70611

COUTO, NANCY VIEIRA, literary consultant; b. New Bedford, Mass., June 11, 1942; d. Edward and Angelina (Vieira) C.; m. Joseph Anthony Martin, Aug. 13, 1988. BS in Edn., Bridgewater State Coll., 1964; MFA, Cornell U., 1980. Secondary rights asst. Cornell U. Press, Ithaca, N.Y., 1981-82; subsidiary rights mgr. Cornell U. Press, Ithaca, 1982-94; cons., proprietor Leatherstocking Literary Svcs., Ithaca, 1994—; juror literature fellowship program Pa. Coun. Arts, Harrisburg, 1994; mem. selection com. fellowships Am. Antiquarian Soc., Worcester, Mass., 1995. Author: The Face in the Water, 1990 (award), various poems; assoc. editor Epoch, 1979-82, The Laurel Review, 1992—. Creative Artists Pub. Svc. fellow N.Y. State, 1982-83, NEA fellow, 1987, Creative Performing Artists and Writers fellow Am. Antiquarian Soc., 1995; recipient Gettysburg Review award, 1994. Mem. Associated Writing Programs. Democrat.

COUTURE, JOSIE BALABAN, foundation director, insurance executive; b. Chgo., Dec. 10, 1922; m. Louis Couture, May 20, 1945 (div. 1948); 1 child, Dan B. Student, Tobias Matthay Sch. Pianoforte, London, Eng., 1938-39; studied with, Tobias Matthay; student, Yale U., 1939-40, Manhattan Sch. Music, 1940-42. Debut concert pianist Civic Theatre Chgo. Opera House, 1941; concert pianist live performances, radio, TV, 1941-50; entertainer USO tours; stockbroker N.Y. Stock Exch., 1955-60; ins. agt., broker, cons. N.Y.C., 1956—; internat. pub. info. coord. Al-Anon Hdqs., N.Y.C., 1970-76; founder, pres. TOVA (The Other Victims of Alcoholism, Inc.), N.Y.C., 1976—; lectr., speaker in field. Editor: Domino Quar., 1977—; past mem.

editorial adv. bd. Alcoholism Digest, Labour-Mgmt. Alcoholism Jour.; contbr. articles to profl. jours. Liaison rep. nat. adv. coun. Nat. Inst. on Alcohol Abuse and Alcoholism U.S. Dept. Health and Human Svcs., Washington, 1977 ; testified at senate hearings Women and Alcoholism, 1976, Impact Alcohol and Drug Abuse on Family Life, 1977, Comprehensive Alcohol Abuse and Alcoholism Prevention, Treatment, and Rehab. Act Amendments, 1979. Recipient New Pioneer award Office Women and Alcoholism Nat. Coun. Alcoholism Inc. and Women's Inst. Am. Univ., 1977; recognized in Congl. Record for New Nat. Orgn. TOVA, 1976. Home: 100 W 57th St New York NY 10019-3327 Office: TOVA PO Box 1528 Radio City Sta New York NY 10101

COUZENS, JULIA, artist; b. Auburn, Calif., July 9, 1949; d. John Richard and Jean (Little) C.; m. Jay-Allen Eisen, Mar. 22, 1975. BA, Calif. State U., Chico, 1970; MA, Calif. State U., Sacramento, 1987; MFA, U. Calif., Davis, 1990. Vis. lectr. Scripps Coll., Claremont, Calif., 1990-91, U. Calif., Davis, 1993, 95, U. Calif., Santa Cruz, 1995; guest artist Coll. Creative Studies, U. Calif., Santa Barbara, 1995, Claremont Grad. Sch., 1995; guest curator Armory Ctr. for Arts, Pasadena, 1995-96. One-person shows include Christopher Grimes Gallery, Santa Monica, Calif., 1991, 93, 95, 96, Donna Beam Fine Art Gallery, U. Nev., Las Vegas, 1993; exhibited in group shows Am. Cultural Ctr., Brussels, 1992, Crocker Art Mus., Sacramento, 1995, L.A. Mcpl. Gallery, 1995, San Francisco Art Inst., 1995, P.P.O.W., N.Y.C., 1995, Ten in One Gallery, Chgo., 1996, Weatherspoon Art Gallery, Greensboro, N.C., 1996; represented in pub. collections M.H. de Young Mus., San Francisco, Oakland Mus. Calif., Univ. Art Mus., Berkeley, Yale U., New Haven. Art-in-pub. places project grantee Sacramento Met. Arts Commn., 1986, artist-in-residence grantee Roswell Mus. and Art Ctr., 1994-95, grantee Louis Comfort Tiffany Found., 1995; grad. rsch. fellow U. Calif., Davis, 1989, fellow Art Matters, Inc., 1995. Mem. Coll. Art Assn. Home and Studio: PO Box 2641 Sacramento CA 95812-2641

COVARRUBIAS, AMANDA, journalist; b. Santa Paula, Calif., Sept. 29, 1959; d. Charles Alan and Mary Theresa (Alvarez) Covarrubias; m. Xerro Paul Ryan, Jan. 4, 1989 (div. Jan. 1994); 1 child, Eva Ryan. BS, San Diego State U., 1982. News writer Palm Springs (Calif.) Desert Sun, 1982-84, Oakland (Calif.) Tribune, 1984-86, Rocky Mountain News, Denver, 1986-90; freelance prodr. L.A., 1990-94; newswoman AP, San Diego, 1994-95, corr., 1995—. Mem. Nat. Assn. Hispanic Journalists.

COVARRUBIAS, PATRICIA OLIVIA, small business owner, consultant, author, communications educator, public speaker; b. Mexico, Mex., Sept. 17, 1951; came to U.S., 1959; d. Alfredo Izaguirre and Carmen (Baillet) C.; m. Robert Elvin Smith, Sept. 11, 1982. BA in French, Calif. State U., Sacramento, 1973, MA in French, 1978; student, Clown Camp, LaCrosse, Wis., 1992; postgrad., U. Wash. Tchr. d'anglais High Sch., Albi, France, 1973-74; instr. French Calif. State U., Sacramento, 1974-75; videotape editor Sta. KCRA-TV, Sacramento, 1977, news asst. assignment editor, 1978, news reporter, 1978-82; founder, exec. dir., instr. OCELOTL OCELOTL, Stockton, Calif., 1984—; guest speaker OCELOTL Speakers Bur., 1984—, Stockton Speakers Bur., 1985—; instr. lifelong learning program U. Pacific, Stockton, 1985—; instr. in community edn. San Joaquin Delta Coll., 1989—; cert. tutor Laubach Literacy Program, Stockton, 1984—. Author: Speaking Up with Style, 1985, Marketing Your Professional Self, 1986, Getting Good Press, 1988, The Speech Planner. . .Ten Steps to Successful Speaking, 1990; author video programs: Gear Up for Speaking English, 1987, Conversational English Made Easy, 1988, Make Presentations Work for You, 1993; columnist Clearly Speaking, 1990—; columnist for news jours.; contbr. articles to profl. jours. Child sponsor Feed the Children, Oklahoma City, 1986—; bd. dirs. San Joaquin County Arts Coun., Stockton, 1985-88, v.p., 1987; mem. Leadership Stockton, 1991-92. Mem. NAFE, Internat. Tng. in Communication (instr. 1985—, Florence Van Gilder award 1985), Stockton Women's Network, Lodi Writers Assn., Calif. Reading Assn., Pacific Delta Area Trainers, Greater Stockton C. of C. (liaison com. 1989—), Calif. State U. Alumni Assn. (bd. dirs. 1988—, pres. 1991-92, Rookie of Yr. 1988-89, Alumni Honors award 1991), Nat. Speakers Assn., Pi Delta Phi, Phi Kappa Phi. Home: 3144 Sea Gull Ln Stockton CA 95219-4603 Office: OCELOTL 917 K St Davis CA 95616-2102

COVIN, CAROL LOUISE, computer consultant; b. Chgo., July 2, 1947; d. Raymond Lincoln and Elizabeth Day (Notley) Frederick; m. David William Covin, Jan. 24, 1968; children: David William Jr., Jonathan Michael. BA, George Washington U., 1972. Data base adminstr. USN, Alexandria, Va., 1973-77; cons. Data Base Mgmt., Inc., Springfield, Va., 1977-79, 82-87; pres. Covin Assocs., Falls Church, Va., 1987-90; cons. Electro-Tech. Internat., Annandale, Va., 1990-91, Abacus Tech., Chevy Chase, Md., 1991-93, Tech. Internat., Fairfax, Va., 1993-95; with Computer Products & Svcs., Inc., Fairfax, 1995—. Author: The Computer Professional's Job Guide to Washington, D.C., 1989, Covin's New England Computer Job Guide, 1991, Covin's Washington Computer Job Guide, 1993, Covin's Midwest Computer Job Guide, 1995, Covin's Southeast Computer Job Guide, 1996. Mem. Assn. Systems Mgmt. (pres. 1990-92, v.p. 1992-93, treas. 1993—), Data Adminstrn. Mgmt. Assn., Washington Apple Pi.

COVINGTON, ANN K., judge, lawyer; b. Fairmont, W.Va., Mar. 5, 1942; d. James R. and Elizabeth Ann (Hornor) Kettering; m. James E. Waddell, Aug. 17, 1963 (div. Aug. 1976); children: Mary Elizabeth Waddell, Paul Kettering Waddell; m. Joe E. Covington, May 14, 1977. B.A., Duke U., 1963; J.D., U. Mo., 1977. Bar: Mo. 1977, U.S. Dist. Ct. (we. dist.) Mo. 1977. Asst. atty. gen. State of Mo., Jefferson City, 1977-79; ptnr. Covington & Maier, Columbia, Mo., 1979-81, Butcher, Cline, Mallory & Covington, Columbia, Mo., 1981-87; justice Mo. Ct. Appeals (we. dist.), Kansas City, 1987-89; justice Mo. Supreme Ct., 1989-93, chief justice, 1993—; now judge; bd. dirs. Mid Mo. Legal Services Corp., Columbia, 1983-87; chmn. Juvenile Justice Adv. Bd., Columbia, 1984-87. Bd. dirs. Ellis Fischel State Cancer Hosp., Columbia, 1982-83; chmn. Columbia Indsl. Revenue Bond Authority, 1984-87; trustee United Meth. Ch., Columbia, 1983-86. Recipient Citation of Merit, U. Mo. Law Sch., 1993, Faculty-Alumni award U. Mo., 1993; Coun. of State Govt. Toll fellow, 1988. Fellow Am. Bar Found.; mem. ABA (jud. adminstrv. divsn., mem. adv. com. on Evidence Rules, U.S. Cts.), Mo. Bar Assn., Boone County Bar Assn. (sec. 1981-82), Acad. Mo. Squires, Order of Coif (hon.), Mortar Bd. (hon.), Phi Alpha Delta, Kappa Kappa Gamma. Home: 1201 Torrey Pines Dr Columbia MO 65203-4825 Office: Mo Supreme Ct PO Box 150 Jefferson City MO 65102-0150

COVINGTON, B(ATHILD) JUNE, business owner, advocate; b. Butte, Mont., June 21, 1950; d. Joe Talmage Covington Sr. and Betty Lou (Jones) Tomlinson; m. Mark Halsey Stephens, Aug. 2, 1969 (div. 1982); children: Mark Halsey Jr., Kimm Covington Stephens; m. James Bradford Hams, Feb. 20, 1987 (div. 1994); 1 stepchild, Brent Keir Mulvaney. Student, So. Utah State U., 1968-69, Indian Valley Colls., 1981-83. Advt. asst. McPhail's, Inc., San Rafael, Calif., 1973-75; mgr. Clothes Factory, San Francisco, 1976; graphic designer Press Rm. Printing, Redding, Calif., 1977; co-owner Player's Choice Retail Store, Redding, 1978-80; with advt. and in-house display dept. Indian Valley Colls. Book Store, Novato, Calif., 1981-82; advt. mgr. part-time Heritage Homes Realty, Novato, 1983-87; interior design asst., graphic designer, project coord. Ruth Livingston Interior Design, Tiburon, Calif., 1983-85, 87; project mgr., spl. needs design div. head Potter & Co. Builders, Richmond, Calif., 1987-88; owner, prin. CDT Assocs., Novato, 1988—; dir. ops. Tilia, Inc., San Francisco, 1989-92; master's candidate advisor Acad. Art Coll., San Francisco, 1989—; pvt. practice cons. sexual abuse, No. Calif., 1982—; instr. tng. seminars on social issues, internet. bus. ops. and procedures at colls., univs. and pub. agys., No. Calif., 1982—; prin. Friends Affecting Cohesive Efforts for Intervention and Treatment, Novato, 1991—; pub. rels. for Voices Unheard, San Francisco, 1994; mem. Action Against Sexual Violence, San Francisco, 1993. Co-producer video documentary Victims of Incest: The Price They Pay, 1983, Surviving Incest: A Path to the Future, 1988; producer video pilot program Straight From the Lip, 1985, We are 68, 1988; producer, editor photo essay and exhibit FACE IT, 1991—; contbr. articles to profl. jours. Mem. maj. gifts com. Novato Human Needs Ctr., 1988; foster parent Marin County Social Svcs., San Rafael, 1983-84; pub. speaker Ind. and Parents United, Calif., 1982—; sponsor Sexual Abuse Survivors, Marin County, 1988-89; mem. exec. com., adv. bd. and edn. com. Sexual Assault Prevention Agy., No. Calif., 1991—; bd. dirs. Survivorship, 1993—; co-founder Healing Kidz, Inc., San Francisco, 1992, v.p. bd. dirs.; co-producer Kicked-Up, an internat. portfolio featuring at-risk and homeless youth. Coll. of Marin Found. scholar, 1983; Marin Community Colls. grantee, 1983, 88. Mem. Hospitality Industry Assn. (co-chair philanthropy com. San Francisco chpt. 1988-89, chair, fundraiser San Francisco chpt. 1988-89), Parents United of Marin County (chair interior design com. 1987-89, bd. dirs., v.p., chair edn. com. 1989—). Democrat. Home: #D108-217 5932 W Bell Rd Glendale AZ 85308

COVINGTON, LYNN NORRIS, special education educator; b. Whiteville, N.C., Mar. 10, 1957; d. Carlston Rudolph and Patricia Ann (Wilson) Norris; m. H. Marshall Brown, Aug. 4, 1979 (div. Apr. 1990); m. Richard J. Covington, Nov. 20, 1994. BS in Spl. Edn., East Carolina U., 1979; MEd in Elem. Edn., Francis Marion U., Florence, S.C., 1988. Cert. tchr. in educable mental retardation and trainable mental retardation. Ednl. specialist Murdoch Ctr., Butner, N.C., 1980-81; resource tchr. Chatham County Schs., Pittsboro, N.C., 1979-80, tchr. trainable mentally handicapped, 1981-82; tchr. trainable mentally handicapped Richmond County Schs., Hamlet, N.C., 1982-85, Marlboro County Schs., Bennettsville, S.C., 1985-92, Sch. Dist. 5 of Lexington and Richland Counties, Ballentine, S.C., 1992-95, Hartsville (S.C.) H.S./Darlington County Schs., 1995—; mem. adv. bd. Parents and Profls. Active for Spl. Svcs./Dist. 5, 1992—; bd. dirs., sec. Cmty. Based Alternatives, Inc., Rockingham, N.C., 1985-91. Area 2 dir. S.C. Spl. Olympics, Bennettsville, 1985-90; pres. Marlboro County Assn. for Retarded Citizens, Bennettsville, 1988-90; advisor Hamlet N.C.) Juniorettes, 1990-91. Recipient Individual Incentive award Marlboro County Schs., 1989; Dist. Tchr. of Yr. award, 1994; Pee Dee Ednl. Found. grantee, 1990. Mem. Coun. for Exceptional Children, S.C. Edn. Assn., Am. Vocat. Assn., S.C. Vocat. Assn., Delta Kappa Gamma. Methodist. Home: 2026 Hebron-Dunbar Rd Clio SC 29525 Office: Hartsville High School 701 Lewellyn Ave Hartsville SC 29550

COVINGTON, PATRICIA ANN, university administrator; b. Mt. Vernon, Ill., June 21, 1946; d. Charles J. and Lois Ellen (Combs) C.; m. Burl Vance Beene, Aug. 10, 1968 (div. 1981). BA, U. N.Mex., 1968; MS in Ed., So. Ill. U., 1974, PhD, 1981. Teaching asst. So. Ill. U., Carbondale, 1971-74, prof. art, asst. dir., 1974-88, asst. dir. in admissions and records, 1988—; bd. dirs. Am. Coun. on Edn., Nat. Com. for Army.Am. Coun. on Edn. Registry Transcript; mem. tech. com. Ill. Articulation Initiative, Ill. Bd. Higher Edn.; vis. curator Mitchell Mus., Mt. Vernon, 1977-83, judge dept. conservation; mem. panel Ill. Arts Coun., Chgo., 1982; faculty advisor European Bus. Seminar, London, 1983; edn. cons. Ill. Dept. Aging, Springfield, 1978-81, Apple Computer, Cupertino, Calif., 1982-83; mem. adminstrv. profl. coun. Soc. Ill. U., 1989-92; presenter in field. Exhibited papercastings in nat. and internat. shows in Chgo., Fla., Calif., Tenn., N.Y. and others, 1974—; author: Diary of a Workshop, 1979, History of the School of Art at Southern Illinois University at Carbondale, 1981; reviewer Mayfield Pub., Random House, (with William C. Brown) Holt, Reinhart & Winston. Bd. dirs. Humanities Couns. John A. Logan Coll., Carterville, Ill., 1982-88; mem. Ill. Higher Edn. Art Assn., chmn. bd. dirs., 1978-88; mem. Post-Doctoral Acad., 1981-95; sec. adminstrv. profl. coun., 1989-90; lifetime mem. Girl Scouts U.S., 1988—, del. 1992, 93. Grantee Kresge Found., 1978, Nat. Endowment for the Arts, 1977, 81, Ill. Bd. Higher Edn. HECA grantee, 1994, 95; named Outstanding Young Woman of Yr. for Ill., 1981, Woman of Distinction Girl Scouts U.S.. Fellow Ill. Ozarks Craft Guild (bd. dirs. 1976-83); mem. Am. Assn. Coll. Registrars and Admissions Officers, Ill. Assn. Coll. Registrars and Admissions Officers (chair so. dist., exec. com. 1992-93, nominating com. 1993-94), Spinx (hon.), Phi Kappa Phi. Presbyterian. Home: 389 Lake Dr Murphysboro IL 62966-5955 Office: So Ill U Admissions and Records Carbondale IL 62901

COVINGTON, STEPHANIE STEWART, psychotherapist, writer, educator; b. Whittier, Calif., Nov. 5, 1942; d. William and Bette (Robertson) Stewart; children: Richard, Kim. BA cum laude, U. So. Calif., 1963; MSW, Columbia U., 1970; PhD, Union Inst., 1982. Pvt. practice psychotherapy, co-dir. Inst. for Relational Devel., La Jolla, Calif., 1981—; instr. U. Calif., San Diego, 1981—, Calif. Sch. Profl. Psychology, San Diego, 1982-88, San Diego State U., 1982-84, Southwestern Sch. Behavioral Health Studies, 1982-84, Profl. Sch. Humanistic Psychology, San Diego, 1983-84, U.S. Internat. U., San Diego, 1983-84, UCLA, 1983-84, U. So. Calif., L.A., 1983-84, U. Utah, Salt Lake City, 1983-84; co-dir. Inst. Relational Devel.; cons. L.A. County Sch. Dist., N.C. Dept. Mental Health, Nat. Ctrs. Substance Abuse Treatment and Prevention, Nat. Inst. Corrections, others; designer women's treatment, cons. Betty Ford Ctr.; presenter at profl. meetings; lectr. in field; addiction cons. criminal justice sys. Author: Leaving the Enchanted Forest: The Path from Relationship Addiction to Intimacy, 1988, Awakening Your Sexuality: A Guide for Recovering Women and Their Partners, 1991, A Woman's Way Through the Twelve Steps, 1994; contbr. articles to profl. jours. Mem. NASW (diplomate), Am. Assn. Sex Educators, Counselors and Therapists, Am. Bd. Med. Psychotherapists (diplomate), Am. Bd. Sexology (diplomate), Am. Pub. Health Assn., Am. Assn. Marriage and Family Therapy, Assn. Women in Psychology, Calif. Women's Commn. on Alcoholism (Achievement award), Ctr. for Study of the Person, Friends of Jung, Internat. Coun. on Alcoholism and Addictions (past chair women's com.), Kettil Brun Soc. (Finland), San Diego Soc. Sex Therapy and Edn., Soc. for Study of Addiction (Eng.). Office: 7946 Ivanhoe Ave Ste 201B La Jolla CA 92037-4517

COWAL, SALLY GROOMS, diplomat; b. Oak Park, Ill., Aug. 24, 1944; d. James Joseph and Virginia Richmond (Colborn) Smerz; m. Thomas B. Grooms, Aug. 26, 1967 (div. Jan. 1979); m. Anthony Charles Cowal, Nov. 26, 1987; stepchildren: Gregory, J. Kirsten, Alexandra. BA, De Pauw U., 1966; MA, George Washington U., 1969. Fgn. svc. USIA and State Dept., Washington, 1966-71; spl. asst. USIS, New Delhi, 1971-73; dir. Centro Colombo Americano, Bogota, Colombia, 1973-78; cultural attache U.S. Embassy, Tel Aviv, 1978-82; dir. internat. youth exchange USIS, Washington, 1982-83; polit. counselor U.S. Mission-UN, N.Y., 1983-85; min.-counselor U.S. Embassy, Mexico City, 1985-89; dep. asst. sec. State Dept., Washington, 1989-91; amb. U.S. Embassy, Port of Spain, Trinidad and Tobago, 1991—. Mem. Coun. on Fgn. Rels., Phi Beta Kappa. Office: US Embassy, PO Box 752, Port of Spain Trinidad and Tobago Office: Dept of State Port-of-Spain Embassy Washington DC 20521-3410*

COWCHOCK, FRANCES SUSAN, geneticist, endocrinologist; b. Lebanon, Pa., June 19, 1941; d. John Robert and Mae Elsie (Williams) Zengerle; m. Michael Justin Cowchock, July 1, 1969 (dec. 1977); m. Richard Byrd Stewart, May 24, 1978 (div. Dec. 1995). B.S., Pa. State U., 1962; M.A., Temple U., 1966; M.D., Jefferson Med. Coll., 1968; MBA Temple U., 1996. Diplomate Am. Bd. Internal Medicine, Am. Bd. Med. Genetics. Intern, Meth. Hosp., Phila., 1968-69; resident Jefferson Hosp., Phila., 1971-73; fellow Columbia Presbyn. Med. Ctr., N.Y.C., 1969-71; instr. medicine Jefferson Med. Coll., Phila., 1973-75, asst. prof. medicine, ob-gyn., 1975-81, assoc. prof., 1981-89, prof. medicine, ob-gyn., 1989—. Contbr. articles to profl. jours. Fellow ACP, Am. Coll. Med. Genetics; mem. Am. Soc. Human Genetics, Am. Fertility Soc., Am. Soc. Reproductive Immunology, Soc. Obstetric Medicine, Phila. Genetics Group, Phila. Endocrine Soc. Office: Jefferson Med Coll 1100 Walnut St Philadelphia PA 19107-5563

COWDIN, MARIA VITA, management consultant; b. Manila, May 17, 1961; came to U.S., 1976; d. Eldon Abad and Bituin Ongchangco Vita. BS in Engring., Calif. State U., Long Beach, 1982; MBA, Pepperdine U., 1989. Mfg. data analyst Datatape, Inc., Pasadena, Calif., 1982-84; indsl. engr. Whittaker Electronic Systems, Simi Valley, Calif., 1984-87; sr. cons. Deloitte & Touche, L.A., 1987-91; prin. Cowdin & Assocs., Simi Valley, 1991—. Sr. mem. Inst. Indsl. Engrs. (dir. elect electronics industry div. 1990, chairperson electronics industry task force 1991). Republican. Mem. Ch. of Christ. Home and Office: Cowdin & Assocs 737 Talbert Ave Simi Valley CA 93065-5142

COWELL, STEPHANIE AMY, writer; b. N.Y.C., July 25, 1943; d. James Albert and Dora (Abrams) Mathieu; m. Theodore Richard Cowell, July 1968 (div. Feb. 1981); children: James Nordstrom, Jesse Ronald; m. Russell O'Neal Clay, Dec. 5, 1995. Author: Nicholas Cooke, 1993, The Physician of London, 1995. Recipient Before Columbus Found. Am. Book award, 1996. Mem. English Speaking Union (sch. essay judge 1996, Oxford scholar 1987), Author's Guild. Democrat. Episcopalian. Home: 585 W End Ave New York NY 10024

COWGILL, MARY LU, psychologist; b. Newton, Kans., Nov. 20, 1932; d. George David and Marian Chase (Axtell) Hanna; m. F. Brooks Cowgill, Dec. 22, 1954; children: David B., Ann M. AB, Stanford U., 1954; MA, Tufts U., 1972. Lic. sch. psychologist, Mass. Psychologist Fernald Lang. Grant Study, Mass. Dept. Health, Waltham, 1972-75, Learning Disorders unit Mass. Gen. Hosp., Boston, 1976-80; cons. on women's psychol. issues Winchester, Mass., 1980—; lectr. in field; treas., v.p., founder Waterfield Investors, Winchester, 1980—. Contbr. articles to profl. jours. Author and book reviewer Winchester Pub. Libr., 1991—. Mem. Wellesley Ctr. for Women's Studies, APA, Colonial Dames of Am., Boston Com. on Fgn. Rels., Stanford Alumni Assn. Congregationalist Ch. Home and Office: 75 Lawson Rd Winchester MA 01890-3153

COWLING, RACHEL ELIZABETH, health facility administrator; b. Jackson, Miss., Dec. 2, 1943; d. James Anthony and Marion Ione (Greenwood) Curran; m. Roy Randolph Cowling, Aug. 31, 1961; children: Ronda Cowling Burton, Roslyn Cowling Acosta, Romy Cowling Aguilar. Student, Lamar U., 1961-62, LA State U., 1968, Hinds C. C., 1984-85. Acct. clerk U. Miss. Med. Ctr., Jackson, 1980-84, patient acct. supr., 1984-86, mgr. admissions, 1986-91; asst. dir. admissions Mobile (Ala.) Infirmary Med. Ctr., 1991-94; bus. office mgr. Am. Home Patient, Mobile, 1994-95; mem. Nat. Assoc. of Hosp. Admitting Mgr., 1986-91, chair U. Med. Ctr. emp. of the month com., Jackson, 1988, mem. U. Miss. Credit Union Credit Comm., Jackson, 1990. Vice chmn. Leaders and Sponsers Assoc. Camp Firs Girls, Baton Rouge, La., 1972, adult leader rec., 1973, pres. Parent Tchrs Organ., Florence, Miss., 1978-79, McLaurin Attendance Ctr., Star, Miss., 1982-83. Democrat. Methodist.

COWLISHAW, MARY LOU, state legislator; b. Rockford, Ill., Feb. 20, 1932; d. Donald George and Mildred Corinne (Hayes) Miller; m. Wayne Arnold Cowlishaw, July 24, 1954; children: Beth Cowlishaw McDaniel, John, Paula Cowlishaw Rader. BS in Journalism, U. Ill., 1954. Mem. editorial staff Naperville (Ill.) Sun newspaper, 1977-83; mem. Ill. Ho. of Reps., Springfield, 1983—, chmn. elem. and secondary edn. com., 1995—, vice-chmn. pub. utilities com., 1995—, mem. joint Ho.-Senate edn. reform oversight com., 1985—; mem. Ill. Task Force on Sch. Fin., 1990—; vice chmn. Ho. Rep. Campaign Com., 1990—; co-chair Ho. Rep. Policy Com., 1991—; chmn. edn. com. Nat. Conf. State Legislatures, 1993—; mem. Joint Com. Adminstrv. Rules, 1992—; commr. Edn. Commn. of the States, 1995—; chair, Ill. Women's Agenda Task Force, 1994—. Author: This Band's Been Here Quite a Spell, 1983. Mem. Naperville Dist. 203 Bd. Edn., 1972-83; co-chmn. Ill. Citizens Coun. on Sch. Problems, Springfield, 1985—. Recipient 1st pl. award Ill. Press Assn., 1981, commendation Naperville Jaycees, 1986, Golden Apple award Ill. Assn. Sch. Bds., 1988, 90, 92, 94, Outstanding Women Leaders of DuPage County award West Suburban YWCA, 1990, Activator award Ill. Farm Bur., 1996; named Best Legislator, Ill. Citizens for Better Care, 1985, Woman of Yr., Naperville AAUW, 1987, Best Legislator, Ill. Assn. Fire Chiefs, 1994, Outstanding Edn. Adv. Indian Prairie Sch. Dist. 204, 1994, Legislator of Yr., Ill. Assn. Pk. Dists., 1995; commr. Edn. Commn. of the States, 1994—. Mem. Am. Legis. Exchange Council, Conf. Women Legislators, Nat. Fedn. Rep. Women, DAR, Naperville Rep. Women's Club (pres. 1994—). Methodist. Home: 924 Merrimac Cir Naperville IL 60540-7107 Office: 552 S Washington St Ste 119 Naperville IL 60540-6669

COX, ANNA LEE, retired administrative assistant; b. Knoxville, Tenn., Feb. 18, 1931; d. Carter Calloway and Fairy Belle (Byers) Bayless; m. William Smith Cox, Sept. 4, 1952; 1 child, Catherine Anne Cox Faust. Grad. high sch., Knoxville. Sec. Am. Mut. Liability Ins. Co., Knoxville, 1948-53; flight procedures clk. FAA, Atlanta, 1963-66; legal sec., paralegal U.S. Atty.'s Office for Dist. S.C., Greenville, 1972-79; sec. criminal investigation div. IRS, Knoxville, 1981-84; sec., adminstrv. asst. CIA, Knoxville, 1984-88; adminstrv. asst. U.S. Dept. Def., Knoxville, 1988-91, ret., 1991. Tutor Greenville Literacy Assn., 1977-79; founder, dir. NATO Womens Chorus, Izmir, Turkey, 1969-71; choir dir., pres. United Meth. Women, Stephenson Meml. United Meth. Ch., Greenville, 1972-79; bd. dirs. Fountainhead Conservatory Music, Knoxville, 1983-85, 92-95, sec. of bd. dirs., 1994-95; singer Knoxville Choral Soc., 1955-56, Atlanta Symphony Chorus, 1971, Greenville Civic Chorale, 1973-79; vol. Ch. and Knoxville Mus. Art, 1992—. Republican. Home: 6724 Arapahoe Ln Knoxville TN 37918-9515

COX, CAROL THAYER, art therapist, educator; b. East Orange, N.J., Apr. 5, 1946; d. John Alden Thayer and Sylvia Jessen Ott; m. William Jerome Cox, Feb. 3, 1968; children: Christopher Lawrence, Kimberly Thayer. BA, Mary Washington Coll., 1968; postgrad., George Washington U., 1979-80, MA, 1984. Registered art therapist; lic. profl. art therapist. Co-owner The Limited Edition Art Gallery, Fredericksburg, Va., 1975-78; art therapy cons. Prince William (Va.) County Cmty. Health Ctr., 1981-84; art therapist Accotink Acad., Springfield, Va., 1984-88; art therapy cons. Md. Inst. for Individual and Family Therapy, College Park, 1984-92; asst. prof. George Washington U., Washington, 1994—; adj. prof. George Wash. U., Washington, 1988-93; adj. faculty summer sch. grad. art therapy program Vt. Coll. Norwich U., Montpelier, 1992—; faculty Ea. Regional Conf. on Abuse, Trauma, and Dissociation, Alexandria, Va., 1989—; advanced internship child and adolescent svc. dept. psychiatry Walter Reed Army Med. Ctr., Washington, 1982-83. Co-author: Telling Without Talking: Art As a Window Into Multiple Personality, 1995; contbr. articles to profl. jours. and chpts. to book. Recipient Diagnostic Drawing Series Rsch. award, 1991. Mem. Am. Art Therapy Assn. (nominating com. chair 1995-96, mem. editl. bd. Art Therapy: The Jour. of the Am. Art Assn. 1990—), Assn. for Tchrs. of Mandala Assessment (co-founder, dir., treas. 1990—), Va. Art Therapy Assn. (co-founder, treas. 1986-88), Va. Coalition of Arts Therapy Assns. (treas. 1987-93). Democrat. Home: 130 Spring Wood Dr Fredericksburg VA 22401-7026 Office: George Washington U Grad Art Therapy Program 2129 G St NW Bldg L Washington DC 20052

COX, COURTENEY, actress; b. Birmingham, Ala.; d. Richard Lewis and Courteney (Bass-Copland) C. Appearances include (music video) Bruce Springsteen's Dancing in the Dark, 1984; (TV series) Misfits of Science, 1985-86, Family Ties, 1987-88, The Trouble with Larry, 1993, Friends, 1994—; (TV pilots) Sylvan in Paradise, 1986; (TV movies) If It's Tuesday, It Still Must Be Belgium, 1987, A Rockport Christmas, 1988, Roxanne: The Prize Pulitzer, 1989, Judith Krantz's Till We Meet Again, 1989, Curiosity Kills, 1990, Morton and Hays, 1991, Topper, 1992, Sketch Artist II: Hands That See, 1995; (feature films) Down Twisted, 1986, Masters of the Universe, 1987, Cocoon: The Return, 1988, Mr. Destiny, 1990, Blue Desert, 1990, Shaking the Tree, 1992, The Opposite Sex (and How to Live with Them), 1993, Ace Ventura, Pet Detective, 1994. Office: Susan Culley & Assocs 150 S Rodeo Dr Ste 220 Beverly Hills CA 90212

COX, GLENDA JEWELL, elementary education educator; b. Caruthersville, Mo., Mar. 6, 1938; d. Gladys Lee and Vera Lee (Malugen) Malone; m. Samuel Joseph Cox, Sept. 3, 1958; children: Cassandra Ann, Leslie Alexandria, Jonathan Paul, Peter Matthew. BS in Elem. Edn., Charleston (S.C.) So. U., 1975; MA, Maryville U., St. Louis, 1990. Cert. tchr., gifted, elem. edn. K-12, prin. Tchr, 2nd/3rd grade combination Midland Park Elem., Charleston, 1975-76; tchr. 2nd grade Summerville (S.C.) Sch. Dist. II, 1978; tchr. 2nd grade, 5th grade math. Mascoutah (Ill.) Dist. 19, 1980-82; 6th grade tchr. Francis Howell Sch. Dist., St. Charles, Mo., 1985-91, gifted facilitator, 1991—; mem. curriculum com. Francis Howell Sch. Dist., St. Charles, 1989-90, pilot mentor/mentor, 1988—, dist. site support team, 1993—; cooperating tchr. Becky-David Elem., St. Charles, 1986-88; site based team chmn./co-chmn., 1992—, Odyssey of the Mind coord., 1991—, tech. com., 1993—, cluster tchr. instr., 1993—, prins. selection com., 1993. English conversation tchr. Bapt. Ch., Fuchu, Japan, 1969-71, vacation Bible sch. dir., 1970-71; PTA parent vol. chmn. Newington Elem., Summerville, 1977-78; chmn. Cystic Fibrosis Found., Summerville, 1977. Mem. NEA, Gifted Assn. Mo. (dist. A 1994—, co-dir. 1994—, dist. A registration chmn. 1992-94, state conf. registration chmn. 1995, 96), St. Louis Assn. Gifted Edn. Baptist. Home: 14344 Rainey Lake Dr Chesterfield MO 63017-2933 Office: Ctrl Elem Sch 4525 Central School Rd Saint Charles MO 63304-7113

COX, HILLERY LEE, primary school educator; b. Akron, Ohio, Nov. 2, 1946; d. Ellwood Lester Jr. and Leonide Juanita (Williams) Cosper; m. William R. Cox Jr., Apr. 2, 1966; 1 child, Geoffrey William. Student, Ohio U., 1964-65; BS in Edn., U. Akron, 1967, MS in Edn., 1980. Cert. tchr.,

Ohio; cert. reading specialist, Ohio. Tchr. Copley (Ohio) Fairlawn Schs., 1967-69; presch. tchr. Northminster Coop. Nursery Sch., Cuyahoga Falls, Ohio, 1974-75; ednl. math. aide Stow (Ohio) City Schs., 1975-76; grad. tchg. asst. U. Akron, 1976-77; tchr. Cloverleaf Local Schs., Lodi, Ohio, 1977—; adj. prof. workshop presenter Ashland (Ohio) U., 1992—; cons. The ABC's of Whole Lang., Copley, 1988—; insvc. presenter various sch. sys. in Ohio, 1988—. Contbr. articles to profl. jours. Vol. Doggie Brigade, Children's Med. Ctr. of Akron, 1992—; driver substitute Mobile Meals, Copley, 1981-84; sec. Copley All Sports Boosters, 1984-88. Named Medina County Tchr. of Yr., 1993; grantee Ohio Dept. Edn., 1978-79, 79-80; Martha Holden Jennings Found. scholar, 1994. Mem. NEA, ASCD, Ohio Edn. Assn., Internat. Reading Assn. (pres. Lizotte coun. 1994-95, spkr. Great Lakes conf. 1993), Ohio Coun. Tchrs. English and Lang. Arts (presenter 1987, 88, 89), Cloverleaf Edn. Assn. (bldg. rep. 1977—), Nat. Campers and Hikers and Family Rivers (sec. local chpt. 1991—), Order of Ea. Star (line officer Ellsworth chpt. 1991—, Worthy Matron 1996), Delta Kappa Gamma. Home: 649 S Medina Line Rd Copley OH 44321-1162 Office: Cloverleaf Local Schs Lodi Elem 301 Mill St Lodi OH 44254-1427

COX, JANE, writer; b. Hackensack, N.J., Oct. 29, 1917; d. Herbert Newton and Antoinette (Vogeley) C.; m. Max Schober, Apr. 7, 1945 (div. 1971); children: Bonni Schober, Brian Schober. Student, Columbia U., 1950s, Union Theol. Sem., 1960s, Cir. in Sq. Theater, N.Y.C., 1960s. Dir., actress Chancel Players, Bloomfield, N.J., 1959-64; dir., actress, technician Probe Theatre Inc., 1965-83; dir. N.J. Regional Theatre, 1960s and 1970s; tchr. theater arts Oak Knoll Sch., Summit, N.J., 1972-79; tchr. creative drama Student Devel. Programs, Livingston and Montclair, N.J., 1960s, Manhasset (N.Y.) After Sch. Program, 1980s; freelance writer, editor N.Y.C.; N.J. state drama judge Fed. Women's Clubs for Edn. Tuition, 1960s and 1970s. Actress: (film series) Face Facts, 1992, (video), 1995— Mt. Sinai Hospital Observation Theatre; contbr. essays to popular publs. including N.Y. Times, Exec. Female, The Lobby, Prime of Life. Mem. Newspaper Inst. Am. (cert.). Home: Apt 202 464 Main St Port Washington NY 11050

COX, KATHRYN CULLEN, laboratory executive; b. Sedalia, Mo., June 29, 1943; d. Bernard Joseph and Ann (Matthews) Cullen; m. Paul John Cox, Oct. 3, 1964 (div. Sept. 1980); children: Donna, Eric. Diploma, St. John's Mercy Med. Ctr., 1964; BS, Coll. St. Francis, 1986. Staff RN Bapt. Med. Ctr., Kansas City, Mo., 1969-80, staff RN surgery, 1980-84; oper. rm. supr. Ctr. Eye Surgery, Kansas City, 1984-86; dir. nursing Hunkeler Eye Clinic, Kansas City, 1986-93; staff nurse Glendale (Calif.) Eye Med. Group, 1993-94; consumer affairs supr. Alcon Labs., Irvine, Calif., 1994—; cons. ophthalmology, 1988—. Mem. Am. Soc. Ophthalmic Registered Nurses (pres. local chpt. 1984-86), Assn. Oper. Rm. Nurses, Am. Soc. Cataract & Refractive Surgery. Home: 23592 Windsong Apt 10H Aliso Viejo CA 92656-1324 Office: Alcon Labs 15800 Alton Pky Irvine CA 92718-3818

COX, LYNETTA FRANCES, neonatal intensive care nurse; b. Bethlehem, Pa., Oct. 11, 1945; d. LeRoy Evan and Gloria Essie (Lee) Sell; m. Henry George Fromhartz, June 4, 1967 (div. May 1984); 1 child, Deborah Suzanne; m. Steven David Cox, Sept. 10, 1989. BS in Chemistry, Moravian Coll., 1967; diploma, Pottsville Hosp. Sch. Nursing, 1981; BSN summa cum laude, Armstrong State Coll., 1992; M Nursing in Neonatal Nurse Practitioner summa cum laude, Emory U., 1994. RN, Ga.; cert. neonatal nurse practitioner; cert. instr. BCLS and neonatal resuscitation program; cert. RN in neonatal intensive care. Rsch. chemist Water Pollution Control Dept., City of Phila., 1967-70; quality control chemist Just Born Candy Co., Bethlehem, Pa., 1971-72; neonatal staff nurse Geisinger Med. Ctr., Danville, Pa., 1981-84, Meml. Med. Ctr., Savannah, Ga., 1984-96, Egleston Children's Hosp., Atlanta, 1993-94; neonatal nurse practitioner Savannah Neonatology PC, 1995-96, Phoebe Putney Meml. Hosp., Albany, Ga., 1996—. Mem. Nat. Perinatal Assn., Ga. Perinatal Assn., Nat. Assn. Neonatal Nurses, Chattahoochee Assn. Neonatal Nurses, Sigma Theta Tau. Home: 210 Hibiscus Rd Albany GA 31705 Office: Phoebe Putney Meml Hosp Neonatal ICU 417 3rd Ave Albany GA 31705

COX, MARGARET STEWART, photographer; b. Indpls., Jan. 9, 1948; d. Douglass Falconer and Margaret Geraldine (Gates) Stewart; m. Herbert Leo Cox Jr., Dec. 21, 1977 (dec. Nov. 1985); 1 child, Matthew Michael. Student, Butler U., 1965-67. Real estate agt. Don Asher & Assocs., Orlando, Fla., 1972-80; real estate agt., appraiser Mary P. Logvin Real Estate, Orlando, 1987-90; freelance photographer Orlando, 1990—. Exhibited photographs in group shows at Marie Selby Gardens, 1993, 94 (Merit awards), Orlando Artists Biennial Exhbn., 1992 (Merit award), Mt. Dora Ctr. for the Arts, 1994 (Merit award), others. Bd. dirs. Adult Literacy League, Inc., Orlando, 1987-95, pres., 1994; bd. dirs. Fla. Literacy Coalition, 1988—; vice chair Orange County Devel. Adv. Bd., Orlando, 1991-94; active United Way Spkrs. Bur., 1994; judge Chertok Nature Photo Contest, 1993, chairperson, 1995—. Recipient Spl. Mission Recognition award United Meth. Women, 1985. Mem. High Country Art and Craft Guild, Nat. Audubon Soc., Fla. Audubon Soc., Orange Audubon Soc. (bd. dirs. 1993-96, rec. sec. 1996—). Democrat. Office: 3912 Harbour Dr Orlando FL 32806-7449

COX, MARJORIE MILHAM, marketing manager; b. Hamlet, N.C., June 11, 1960; d. Seth Thomas and Claudia Ann (Milham) C. BS in Psychology, Duke U., 1981; MBA in Mktg., Vanderbilt U., 1985. Adminstr. Stanley H. Kaplan Edn. Ctr., Nashville, 1984-85; asst. brand mgr. Procter & Gamble, Cin., 1985-87; assoc. product mgr. Planters Lifesavers divsn. RJR Nabisco, Winston-Salem, N.C., 1987-90; promotions mgr. Holly Farms divsn. Tyson Foods, Wilkesboro, N.C., 1990; product mgr. Oscar Mayer divsn. Philip Morris, Madison, Wis., 1990-92; mktg. mgr. Hanes Hosiery Div. of Sara Lee Corp., Winston-Salem, 1992-93; sr. brand mgr. Brown & Williamson Tobacco Corp., Louisville, Ky., 1994—. Democrat. Episcopalian. Home: 7209 Deer Ridge Rd Louisville KY 40059-9376 Office: Brown & Williamson Tobacco PO Box 35090 Louisville KY 40232-5090

COX, TERI P., public relations executive; b. Pitts., May 21, 1952; d. Meyer and Faye Helen (Tischler) Polack; m. William R. Cox, Jan. 1, 1982. BA, U. Pitts., 1974; MBA in Mktg., NYU, 1989. Info. dir. United Mental Health; prodr., host weekly PA radio program; pub. rels. dir. Atlanta Merchandise Mart; mktg. rsch., pub. rels. cons. Pfizer Inc., NYU Stern Sch. Bus.; acct. supr. Burson-Marsteller, Coleman & Pellet; mng. ptnr. Cox Comms. Ptnrs., 1992—. Bd. dirs. Allergy and Asthma Network, Mothers of Asthmatics, Inc., Lupus Found. N.J., N.J. divsn. Am. Cancer Soc., chair Tobacco Control Task Force. Mem. Pub. Rels. Soc. Am., Am. Mktg. Assn., Healthcare Businesswomen's Assn. Office: Cox Comms Ptnrs 2 Roseberry Ct Lawrenceville NJ 08648-1058

COX, VIRGINIA PRICILLA, sculptor, educator; b. Detroit, Apr. 26; d. Wallace Jackson and Bessie Juanita (Watson) C. Student, Wayne State U., 1948-49, Soc. of Arts and Crafts, Detroit, 1949-50, Art Students League, N.Y.C., 1950-51, Bklyn. Mus. Art Sch., 1951-54. art cons. in field; artist model, 1981-88; adj. instr. sculpture Parsons Sch. Design, N.Y.C., 1989-96. Exhibited in group shows at Parsons Sch. of Design, 1992, 93, 95, Emerson Gallery, Hamilton Coll., 1983, Ctr. for Art and Culture, Bedford Slyvesant, 1983, Pump House Gallery, Bushnell Park, Hartford, Conn., 1987, Sindin Gallery, 1981, Condon Rielly Gallery, 1970, C.R.T.S. Craftery Gallery, 1982, Gallery 62, 1980. Grantee Pullock-Krasner Found., 1990, Adolph and Esther Gottlieb Found., 1992. Democrat. Episcopalian. Home: 90 Bedford St New York NY 10014

COX-BEAIRD, DIAN SANDERS, middle school educator; b. Murchison, Tex., Dec. 18, 1946; d. Jessie Jackson and Lola Mae (Burton) Sanders; m. Richard Lewis Cox, May 24, 1969 (div. Nov. 1993); 1 child, Stuart Scott; m. Charles A. Beaird, Dec. 1994. AA, Kilgore Jr. Coll., 1967; BA, Stephen F. Austin State U., 1969, MEd, 1983. Cert. provisional gen. elem. edn., provisional h.s. history, govt. and polit. sci. Tchr. 8th grade Am. history and 7th grade Tex. history Chapel Hill Ind. Sch. Dist., Tyler, Tex., 1970-79; tchr. 6th-7th grade regular, advanced, remedial reading Sabine Ind. Sch. Dist., Gladewater, Tex., 1981—; mem., tutor East Tex. Literacy Coun., Longview, 1992—; sec. Sabine Jr. High PTO, Gladewater, 1990-91; faculty sponsor cheerleaders Chapel Hill Ind. Sch. Dist., Tyler, 1970-73, rep. curriculum com., 1976, historian PTO, 1974; mem. anthology com. N.J. Writing Project in Tex., Kilgore, 1991; selected hostess Internat. Reading Conf., Tucson, 1992. Presenter: The Toothpaste Millionaire, 1992; contbr.: (short story) Vocies from the Heart, 1991. Leader Girl Scouts Am., Tyler, 1973; counselor Camp Natowa-Campfire Girls, Big Sandy, Tex., 1970; dir. Bible Sch., 1st Meth. Ch., Overton, Tex., 1980; sec. Young Dems., Kilgore, 1965-67; actress Gallery Theater, Jefferson, Tex.; mem. Opera House Theater and Galley Theater, 1992—. Named Outstanding Tchr. in Tex., Macmillan/McGraw Hill, 1991; Free Enterprise Forum scholar East Tex. Bapt. U., 1991. Mem. Internat. Reading Assn. (presenter 1992), Tex. Mid. Sch. Assn., Piney Woods Reading Coun., Tex. State Tchrs. Assn. (campus rep. 1990—, sec. Chapel Hill Ind. Sch. Dist. 1971-72), Laubach Literacy Action. Home: PO Box 1146 Hallsville TX 75650 Office: Sabine Jr H S RR 1 Box 189 Gladewater TX 75647-9723

COY, PATRICIA ANN, special education director, consultant; b. Beardstown, Ill., Apr. 2, 1952; d. Ben L. and Dorothy Lee (Hubbell) C. BS in Elem. and Spl. Edn., No. Ill. U., 1974; MS in Spl. Edn., Northeastern Ill. U., 1976, MA in Spl. Edn., 1978; MEd in Spl. Edn., Northeastern U., 1984; postgrad., No. Ill. U., 1988—. Cert. elem. and spl. edn. tchr.; cert. counselor. Mental health supr. Waukegan (Ill.) Devel. Ctr., 1974-77; ednl. therapist Grove Sch. and Residential Program, Lake Forest, Ill., 1977-78; dir. residential svcs. N.W. Suburban Aid for the Retarded, Park Ridge, Ill., 1978-83; exec. dir. The Learning Tree, Des Plaines, Ill., 1983—; dir. residential svcs. Augustanan Ctr. Luth. Social Svcs. of Ill., Chgo., 1984-86, dir. planning and evaluation, 1986-93, dir. community svc., 1993-95; exec. dir. Blare House Inc., Des Plaines, Ill., 1995—; behavior advisor Habilitative Systems, Inc., Chgo., 1985-88; program coord. Human Resource Devel. Inst., Chgo., 1986-89; project dir. Support Svcs. Ill., Inc., Chgo., 1987-91; dir. TranSteps Inc. Steps for Success for Adults with Learning Differences, 1991—. Contbr. articles to profl. jours. Mem. Coun. for Exceptional Children, Am. Assn. Mental Deficiency, Chgo. Assn. Behavioral Analysis, Behavior Analysis Soc. Ill., Assn. for Supervision and Curriculum Devel., Nat. Rehab. Assn., Coun. for Disability Rights, Assn. for Learning Disability, Profls. in Learning Disabilities, Cwens, Echoes, Mortar Bd., Kappa Delta Pi. Democrat. Mem. United Ch. of Christ. Home: 8936 N Parkside Ave Apt 118 Des Plaines IL 60016-5517 Office: TranSteps 7144 N Harlem Ave Ste 344 Chicago IL 60631-1017 also: Blare House 960 Rand Rd Ste 216 Des Plaines IL 60016

COYLE, DIANE R., artist, educator; b. Seattle, Jan. 25, 1933; d. Raymond E. and Dorothy H. (Larson) Manning; m. Jack G. Coyle, Feb. 7, 1953; children: Michael Gordon, Patrick Colin, William Scott, Linda Diane. Comml. art tech., Sinclair C.C., 1980. Instr. mixed media Riverbend Art Ctr., Dayton, Ohio, 1983-87; instr. watercolor Sinclair C.C., Dayton, Ohio, 1984—, Kettering Adult Sch., Ohio, 1986-93, Centerville Adult Sch., Ohio, 1988-92; chmn. Dayton Fine Art Expo, 1986, 89, 95, Art in the Park, Dayton, 1984; pres. Tri Art Club, Dayton, 1986-88. One-woman shows include Children's Med. Ctr. and Miami Valley Hosp., 1990-95, Gallery Ten, 1993, Benham's Grove, Centerville, 1994, 95, Thum'prints Gallery, Sea Pines Ctr., Hilton Head Island, S.C., 1994, Miami Valley Gallery, 1996, Lumpkins Gallery, Centerville, 1996, Preble County Art Ctr., Eaton, Ohio, 1996, numerous others; exhibited in group shows at Ohio State U., Columbus, 1991, Middletown Fine Arts Ctr., 1992, numerous others; represented in permanent collections Kettering Meml. Hosp., Miami Valley Hosp., Children's Med. Ctr., WHIO Radio/TV, Four Seasons Country Club, Sunrise Fed. Savs. and Loan, Pridgen Jewelers, Mattec Corp., Hospice of Dayton, Dayton Soc. Painters & Sculptors. Mem. Ohio Watercolor Soc. (assoc.), Western Ohio Watercolor Soc., Dayton Soc. Painters & Sculptors (pres. 1986-88). Republican. Roman Catholic. Studio: Coyle Studio 1610 Ambridge Rd Centerville OH 45459

COYLE, JEAN MARIE, gerontological educator; b. Evansville, Ind., Apr. 2, 1945; d. Russell Francis and Bertha Jeanette (Lay) C. BA, U. Evansville, 1967; MA, Ball State U., 1971; PhD, Tex. Woman's U., 1976; specialist in aging, U. Mich., 1978. Editor Russell (Kans.) Record, 1967; pub. rels. dir. U. Evansville, 1967-70; dir. ctr. on aging N.E. La. U., Monroe, 1976-80; assoc. prof. Ea. Ill. U., Charleston, 1980-85; program analyst U.S. SBA, Washington, 1983-85; pres. Jean Coyle Assocs., Alexandria, Va., 1985—; dir. Nat. Inst. Sr. Ctrs. Nat. Coun. on Aging, Washington, 1987-89; dir. TIGRE N.Mex. State U., Las Cruces, 1989-92; chair, prof., spl. asst. to dean Fort Hays (Kans.) State U., 1992-94; dir. Christian edn. Christ Ch., Alexandria, Va., 1996—. Author: Women and Aging, 1989, Families and Aging, 1991; reviewer, mem. editorial bd. numerous profl. jours. Rec. sec. Coalition Against Domestic Violence, Charleston, 1982-83; treas. N.E. United Campus Ministries, Monroe, 1978-79; elder Mt. Vernon Presbyn. Ch., Alexandria, Va., 1985-87, 1st Presbyn. Ch., Las Cruces, N.Mex., 1991-92. Fellow Gerontol. Soc. Am.; mem. NAFE, S.W. Soc. on Aging (pres. 1993, bd. dirs.), Assn. for Gerontology in Higher Edn. (sec. 1978-80), N.Mex. Assn. for Gerontol. Edn. (pres. 1990-92), Nat. Alliance Home-Based Businesswomen (pres. 1987-88), Mortar Board (chpt. founder 1982-83), Pi Gamma Mu, Pi Delta Epsilon (chpt. pres.), Alpha Kappa Delta, Sigma Phi Omega (nat. pres.), Phi Kappa Phi (chpt. sec.). Democrat. Home and Office: 1201 Belle View Blvd A2 Alexandria VA 22307

COYLE, MARIE BRIDGET, microbiology educator, laboratory director; b. Chgo., May 13, 1935; d. John and Bridget Veronica (Fitzpatrick) C.; m. Zheng Chen, 1995. BA, Mundelein Coll., 1957; MS, St. Louis U., 1963; PhD, Kans. State U., 1965. Diplomate Am. Bd. Med. Microbiology. Sci. instr. Sch. Nursing Columbus Hosp., Chgo., 1957-59; research assoc. U. Chgo., 1967-70; instr. U. Ill., Chgo., 1970-71; asst. prof. microbiology U. Wash., Seattle, 1973-80, assoc. prof., 1980-94, prof., 1994—; assoc. dir. microbiology labs Univ. Hosp., Seattle, 1973-76; dir. microbiology labs Harborview Med. Ctr., Univ. Wash., 1976—; co-dir. Postdoc Training Clinic Microbiology, Univ. Wash., 1978—. Contbr. articles to profl. jours. Fellow Am. Acad. Microbiology; mem. Acd. Clin. Lab. Physicians and Scientists (sec.-treas. 1980-83, exec. com. 1985-90), Am. Soc. Microbiology (chmn. clin. microbiology divsn. 1984-85, recipient bioMerieux Vitek Sonnenwirth Meml. award 1994), Kappa Gamma Pi. Office: Harborview Box 359743 325 9th Ave Seattle WA 98104-2499

COYLE-REES, MARGARET MARY, chemist; b. Rochester, N.Y., June 10, 1960; d. Hughbert James and Patricia Ann (Crocker) Coyle; m. Wayne M. Rees, July 13, 1985; children: Sarah, William, Anna. BS, U. Buffalo, 1982, PhD, 1988. Sr. rsch. scientist Procter & Gamble, Cin., 1988-94, SC Johnson Wax & Son, Racine, Wis., 1994—. Leader Girl Scouts U.S., 1992-94. Mem. AAAS, N.Y. Acad. Scis., Internat. Assn. Dental Rsch., Am. Chem. Soc. Roman Catholic. Home: 3153 Rudolph Dr Racine WI 53406 Office: SC Johnson Wax 1525 Howe St Racine WI 53403-2236

COYNE, JANINE VIRGINIA, photographer, educator; b. Bklyn., Dec. 13, 1949; d. John Anthony and Anne Louise (De Santis) Cortese; m. Edward Anthony Coyne, May 2, 1971; children: Janine, Edward, Christopher. AA, Kingsborough C.C., Bklyn., 1969; BA, Bklyn. Coll., 1971, MFA, 1977. Art and photography instr. Dist. 22 N.Y.C. Bd. Edn., Bklyn., 1971-77; art tchr. and coord. Cath. Diocese of Bklyn. and Queens Schs., 1971-81; art tchr. N.Y.C. Bd. Edn., Bklyn., 1974-75; photography and drawing instr. Sheepshead Bay H.S./Adult Edn., Bklyn., 1972-77; asst. prof. performing and creative arts dept. Coll. S.I., N.Y., 1994—; asst. prof. art dept. Kingsborough C.C., Bklyn., 1977—. Photography exhbns. include: Statue of Liberty, Am. Mus. of Immigration, 1990, The Henry Street Settlement, N.Y.C., 1993, Bklyn. Mus., Snug Harbor Cultural Ctr., S.I., others. Grantee CUNY, 1993.

COYNE, MARY JEANNE, state supreme court justice; b. Mpls., Dec. 7, 1926; d. Vincent Mathias and Mae Lucille (Steinmetz) C. BS in Law, U. Minn., 1955, JD, 1957. Bar: Minn. 1957, U.S. Dist. Ct. Minn. 1957, U.S. Ct. Appeals (8th cir.) 1958, U.S. Supreme Ct. 1964. Law clk. Minn. Supreme Ct., St. Paul, 1956-57; assoc. Meagher, Geer, Markham & Anderson, Mpls., 1957-70, ptnr., 1970-82; assoc. justice Minn. Supreme Ct., St. Paul, 1982—; mem. Am. Arbitration Assn., 1967-82; mem. bd. conciliation Archdiocese St. Paul and Mpls., 1981-82; instr. U. Minn. Law Sch., Mpls., 1964-68; mem. Lawyers Profl. Responsibility Bd., St. Paul, 1982; chmn. adv. com. rules of civil appellate procedure Minn. Supreme Ct., St. Paul, 1982—, chair adv. com. rules of civil procedure, 1984—. Editor: Women Lawyers Jour., 1971-72. Mem. ABA, Minn. State Bar Assn., Nat. Assn. Women Lawyers, Nat. Assn. Women Judges, Minn. Women Lawyers Assn., U. Minn. Law Alumni Assn. Office: Minn Supreme Ct 422 Minn Jud Ctr 25 Constitution Ave Saint Paul MN 55155-1500

COZ, MARY KATHLEEN, respiratory therapist; b. Ravenna, Ohio, Aug. 1, 1952; d. John and Kathleen (Bronson) C. A in Secretarial Sci., U. Akron, 1972, A in Respiratory therapy, 1979, BS, 1986, MS in Tech. Edn., 1990. Registered and lic. respiratory therapist. Sec. Kent (Ohio) Bd. Edn., 1970; exec. sec. Ernst & Ernst, Akron, Ohio, 1972-75; respiratory therapist, tech. support assoc. Akron City Hosp. Summa Health Syss., 1977—. Mem. Am. Assn. Respiratory Care, Ohio Soc. Respiratory Care, Nat. Bd. Respiratory Care. Roman Catholic. Home: 1236 Chelton Dr Kent OH 44240-3240 Office: Akron City Hosp 525 E Market St Akron OH 44304-1619

COZZENS, WENDY KAY, graphic designer; b. Muskegon, Mich., June 10, 1966; d. William Myron II and Virginia Lee (Horner) C. BFA, U. Wis., Milw., 1990. Graphic designer H. Haas Hausch Design, Milw., 1990-91, Design Group, Milw., 1991-92; graphic designer, owner Cir. Midwest, Inc., Milw., 1992—; mentor Wis. Women's Bus. Initiative Corp., Milw., 1994—. Active Nat. Abortion Rights Action League, Milw., 1993. Layton Art scholar, 1988; named one of 40 Under 40, Milw. Bus. Jour., 1995. Mem. Wis. Women Entrepreneurs (bd. dris. Western Milw. chpt. 1994—), Ind. Bus. Asns. Wis. Democrat. Home: 2244 N Prospect # 38 Milwaukee WI 53202 Office: Circle Midwest Inc 301 N Water St Milwaukee WI 53202

CRABB, BARBARA BRANDRIFF, federal judge; b. Green Bay, Wis., Mar. 17, 1939; d. Charles Edward and Mary (Forrest) Brandriff; m. Theodore E. Crabb, Jr., Aug. 29, 1959; children: Julia Forrest, Philip Elliott. A.B., U. Wis., 1960, J.D., 1962. Bar: Wis. 1963. Assoc. Roberts, Boardman, Suhr and Curry, Madison, Wis., 1962-64; legal rschr. Sch. Law, U. Wis., 1968-70, Am. Bar Assn., Madison, 1970-71; U.S. magistrate Madison, 1971-79; judge U.S. Dist. Ct. (we. dist.) Wis., Madison, 1979—, chief judge, 1980-96, dist. judge, 1996—; mem. Gov. Wis. Task Force Prison Reform, 1971-73. Membership chmn., v.p. Milw. LWV, 1966-68; mem. Milw. Jr. League, 1967-68. Mem. ABA, Nat. Assn. Women Judges, State Bar Wis., Dane County Bar Assn., U. Wis. Law Alumni Assn.(defender svcs. com. jud. conf.). Home: 741 Seneca Pl Madison WI 53711-2950 Office: US Dist Ct PO Box 591 120 N Henry St Madison WI 53701-0591

CRABTREE, BEVERLY JUNE, college dean; b. Lincoln, Nebr., June 22, 1937; d. Wayne Uniack and Frances Margaret (Wibbels) Deles Dernier; m. Robert Jewell Crabtree, June 1, 1958; children: Gregory, Karen. BS in Edn., U. Mo., 1959, MEd, 1962; PhD, Iowa State U., 1965. Tchr. home econs. area pub. schs., Pierce City and Sarcoxie, Mo., 1959-61; mem. faculty home econs. Mich. State U., East Lansing, 1964-67; assoc. prof. U. Mo., Columbia, 1967-72, coord. home econs. edn., 1967-73, prof., 1972-73; assoc. dean home econs., dir. home econs. extension programs U. Mo., 1973-75; dean Coll. Home Econs. Okla. State U., Stillwater, 1975-87; dean Coll. Family and Consumer Scis. Iowa State U., Ames, 1987—; mem. faculty Family Impact Seminar Inst. Ednl. Leadership, George Washington U., 1976-82, Cath. U. Am., 1982-87; mem. nat. panel cons. for Vocat. Ednl. Pers. Devel., 1969-70; mem. nat. com. on future of coop. extension USDA and Nat. Assn. State Univs. and Land Grant Colls., 1982; mem. joint coun. on food and agrl. scis., 1987-91. Contbr. articles in field to profl. jours. Gen. Foods fellow, 1963-64; recipient Centennial Alumni award Coll. Home Econs. Iowa State U., 1971, Alumni Citation of Merit, Coll. Home Econs. U. Mo., 1976, Profl. Achievement award Iow State U., 1983. Mem. Am. Home Econs. Assn. (pres. 1977-78, chmn. adv. coun. Ctr. for Family 1982-83, mem. coun. profl. devel. 1980-83, a leader to commemorate 75th anniversary 1984, pres. found. 1987-88, chair Coun. for Certification 1991-92, Disting. Svc. award 1993), Okla. Home Econs. Assn. (Profl. Achievement award 1983), Nat. Assn. State Univs. and Land Grant Colls. (mem. commn. home econs. 1981-84), Assn. Tchr. Educators, Home Econs. Edn. Assn., Nat. Council of Adminstrs. of Home Econs., Am. Ednl. Research Assn., Am. Assn. Higher Edn., Nat. Assn. Tchr. Educators for Home Econs. (pres. 1969), Nat. Council on Family Relations, Mortar Bd., Golden Key, Omicron Nu, Phi Upsilon Omicron, Phi Delta Kappa, Omicron Delta Kappa, Pi Lambda Theta, Phi Kappa Phi, Gamma Sigma Delta. Methodist. Home: 3113 Rosewood Cir Ames IA 50014-4589 Office: Iowa State U Coll Family Consumer Scis MacKay Hall Ames IA 50011

CRABTREE, DAVIDA FOY, minister; b. Waterbury, Conn., June 7, 1944; Alfred and Davida (Blakeslee) Foy; m. David T. Hindinger Jr., Aug. 28, 1982; stepchildren: Elizabeth Anne, David Todd. BS, Marietta Coll., 1967; MDiv, Andover Newton Theol. Sch., 1972; D of Ministry, Hartford Sem., 1989. Ordained to ministry United Ch. of Christ, 1972. Founder, exec. dir. Prudence Crandall Ctr. for Women, New Britain, Conn., 1973-76; min., dir. Greater Hartford (Conn.) Campus Ministry, 1976-80; sr. min. Colchester (Conn.) Federated Ch., 1980-91; bd. dirs. Conn. Conf. United Ch. of Christ, Hartford, 1982-90; conf. min. So. Calif. Conf., United Ch. of Christ, Pasadena, 1991-96, Conn. Conf., United Ch. of Christ, Hartford, 1996—; rsch. assoc. Harvard Div. Sch., Cambridge, Mass., 1975-76. Author: The Empowering Church, 1989 (named one of Top Ten Books of Yr. 1990); editorial advisor Alban Inst., 1990—. Bd. dirs. Hartford region YWCA, 1979-82; trustee Cragin Meml. Libr., Colchester, 1980-91, Hartford Sem., 1983-91; founder Youth Svcs. Bur., Colchester, 1984-89; pres. Creative Devel. for Colchester Inc., 1989-91; coun. Religious Leaders of L.A., 1991-96; v.p. Hope in Youth Campaign, 1992-96; trustee Sch. of Theology at Claremont, 1993-96; dir. UCC Ins. Adv. bd., 1993—. Recipient Antoinette Brown award Gen. Synod, United Ch. of Christ, 1977, Conf. Preacher award Conn. Conf. United Ch. of Christ, 1982, Woman in Leadership award Hartford region YWCA, 1987; named one of Outstanding Conn. Women, UN Assn., 1987, Somos Uno award United Neighborhood Orgn., 1995. Mem. Nat. Coun. Chs. (bd. dirs. 1969-81), Christians for Justice Action (exec. com. 1981-91).

CRABTREE, VALLERI JAYNE, real estate executive, lawyer; b. Columbus, Ohio, Feb. 22, 1957; d. Ralph Dale and Ida Mae (Call) C. BS in Bus. Adminstrn., Ohio State U., 1979; JD, Capital U., 1983. Bar: Ohio 1983; lic. real estate broker, Ohio, life, health & annuity ins., Ohio; CLU; FLMI. Various mgmt. positions Nationwide Life Ins. Co., Columbus, 1980-87, dir. group annuity underwriting, adminstr., 1987-91; atty. Columbus, 1991-95; real estate salesperson Metro II Realty, Henderson Realty, Columbus, 1991-94; pres., broker Onyx Real Estate Svcs., Inc., Columbus, 1994—; atty., owner Crabtree & Assocs., Attys. at Law, Columbus, 1995—; mem. adj. faculty Columbus State C.C., 1995—; mem. equal opportunity com. Columbus Bd. Realtors, 1996—. Bd. trustees Unity Ch. Christianity, Columbus, 1991-94, chair devel. com., 1996—. Mem. AAUW, ACLU, Nat. Assn. Realtors, Ohio Assn. Realtors, Ohio State Bar Assn., Columbus Bar Assn., Columbus Bd. Realtors. Democrat. Office: Onyx Real Estate Svcs Inc 1150 Morse Rd Sts 106/110 Columbus OH 43229

CRAFT, CHERYL MAE, neurobiologist, anatomist, researcher; b. Lynch, Ky., Apr. 15, 1947; d. Cecil Berton and Lillian Lovelle (Ellington) C.; m. Laney K. Cormney, Oct. 14, 1967 (div. Sept. 1980); children: Tyler Craft Cormney, Ryan Berton Cormney. BS in Biology/Chemistry/Math., Valdosta State Coll., 1969; Cert. in Tchg. Biol./Math., Ea. Ky. U., 1971; PhD in Human Anatomy/Neurosci., U. Tex., San Antonio, 1984. Undergrad. rsch. asst. Ea. Ky. U., Richmond, 1965-67; tchg. asst. dept. cell-structural biology U. Tex. Health Sci. Ctr., San Antonio, 1979-84; postdoctoral fellowship lab. devel. neurobiology NICHD and LMDB/NEI, Bethesda, Md., 1984-86; instr. dept. psychiatry U. Tex. Southwestern Med. Ctr., Dallas, 1986-87, asst. prof. dept. psychiatry, 1987-91; dir. lab. molecular neurogenetics Schizophrenia Rsch. Ctr. VA Med. Ctr., Dallas, 1988-94, Mental Health Clinic Rsch. Ctr., U. Tex. Southwestern Med. Ctr., Dallas, 1990-94; assoc. prof. dept. psychiatry U. Tex. Southwestern Med. Ctr., Dallas, 1991-94; Mary D. Allen prof. Doheny Eye Inst. U. So. Calif. Sch. Medicine, L.A., 1994—, chair dept. cell and neurobiology, 1994—; ad hoc reviewer NEI/NIH, Bethesda, 1993—; reviewer Molecular Biology, NSPB Fight for Sight Grants, 1991-94; STAR-sci. adv. bd. U. So. Calif./Bravo Magnet H.S., L.A., 1995—. Author: (chpt.) Melatonin: Biosyn., Physio. Effects, 1993; exec. editor Exptl. Eye Rsch. jour., 1993—. Recipient Merit award for rsch. VA Med. Ctr., 1992, 93, 94, nomination for Women in Sci. and Engring. award Dallas VA, 1992, 93; NEI fellow, 1986, NICHD/NIH fellow, 1986. Mem. AAAS, AAUW, Assn. for Rsch. in Vision and Ophthalmology (chair program planning com. 1991-94), Am. Soc. for Neurochemistry (Jordi Folch Pi Outstanding Young Investigator 1992), Sigma Xi (sec./treas. 1986-93, pres. 1993-94). Home: 1191 Brookmere Rd Pasadena CA 91105 Office: Univ So Calif Sch of Medicine 1333 San Pablo St BMT 401 Los Angeles CA 90033

CRAFT, KAY STARK, real estate broker; b. Yoakum, Tex., Oct. 15, 1945; d. Jesse James and Leona Charlotte (Manchen) Stark; m. Michael Joseph Grogan IV, May 31, 1969 (div. June 1974); 1 child, Michael Joseph V; m. Roger Dale Craft, Apr. 1, 1983. AA, Victoria (Tex.) Coll., 1964; BS, S.W. Tex. State U., 1966; Broadway Sch. Real Estate, Hot Springs, Ark., 1985. Lic. real estate broker, Ark. Tchr. Victoria Ind. Sch. Dist., 1966-68, Pasadena (Tex.) Ind. Sch. Dist., 1968-85; real estate agt. Coldwell Banker, Hot Springs Village, Ark., 1985-88; prin. broker-owner Cross Roads Realty, Inc., Hot Springs Village, Ark., 1988—, pres., bd. dirs., 1991—, v.p., 1988-91; sec., bd. dirs. Craft Classic Homes, Inc., Hot Springs Village, Ark., 1987—; v.p., bd. dirs. Coronado Homes, Inc., Hot Springs Village, Ark., 1992—. Mem. DAR, Colonial Dames of 17th Century, Nat. Soc. Magna Carta Dames, Nat. Assn. Realtors, Ark. Realtors Assn. (Million Dollar Club 1991—, Lifetime Million Dollar Prodr. award 1993, Multi Million Dollar Prodr. award 1993, 96, cert. Grad. Realtors Inst. 1992), N.W. Garland Bd. Realtors (treas. 1992, Million Dollar Prodr. award 1990, 95), Woman's Coun. Realtors, Residential Sales Coun. (cert. residential specialist 1993). Republican. Methodist. Home: 45 Gerona Way Hot Springs National Park AR 71909-2762 Office: Cross Roads Realty Inc 4136 N Highway 7 Hot Springs National Park AR 71909-9564

CRAFT, MARY FAYE, public relations consultant, television producer; b. Glennville, Ga., Jan. 20, 1936; d. James Levy Durrence and Mary Frances (Merritt) Thompson; widow; children: James P. Craft, Joseph A. Craft. DD, Calvary Grace Bible Inst., Rillton, Pa., 1975; cert. of journalism arts, CNS Internat., Willow Springs, Mo., 1991; D of Phil. in Film and Video, LaSalle U., Mandeville, La., 1995. Cert. tchr., Protocol Sch. of Washington, D.C., 1993. Dist. mgr. Family Record Plan, Honolulu, 1963-64; acct. exec. Heirloom Inc., Honolulu, 1964-65; pres. Durracraft Advt. and Photography, Cocoa Beach, Orlando, Fla., 1965-71; CEO Western American Corp., Orlando, 1971-73; pres. MF Craft & Assoc. Travel, Orlando, 1972-73, Mary Faye Craft & Assocs., Washington, 1977—; prodr., host FCAC Ch. 10, Fairfax, Va., 1990—; editor MFDC Rev., Springfield, Va., 1992—. Author: Poems of Perception, 1984, Gifts of Poetry, 1986, Poems by Mary Faye Craft, 1988; composer, performer music album Facets, 1989 (Mid Atlantic Contest winner 1990). Recipient three awards Civil Air Patrol, Maxwell AFB, Ala., 1982, 83, Golden Poets award, World of Poetry, Las Vegas, 1987. Mem. AAUW, Nat. Press Club, Nat. Space Club, Capitol Hill Club, Phi Theta Kappa. Republican. Roman Catholic. Office: Mary Faye Craft & Assocs PO Box 7817 Jacksonville FL 32238

CRAFT DAVIS, AUDREY ELLEN, writer, educator; b. Vanceburg, Ky., June 9, 1926; d. James Elmer and Lula Alice (Vance) Gilkison; m. Vernon Titus Craft, Nov. 5, 1943 (dec. Aug. 1979); children: James Vernon Craft, Alice Ann Craft Schuler; m. Louis Amzie Davis, Oct. 22, 1986. PhD, Ohio U., 1964; Dr. of Metaphysics, Coll. Divine Metaphysics, 1968; DD, Ohio U., 1971; postgrad., St. Petersburg Jr. Coll., 1975. Owner beauty salon Audrey Craft Enterprises, Tampa Bay, Fla., 1970-83; owner cosmetic co. Audrey Craft Enterprises, Portsmouth, Ohio, 1958-70; owner, distbr. Nightingale Motivation, Tampa Bay, 1960—; tchr., counselor Bus. Coll. U., Tampa Bay, 1965—; ins. staff Investors Heritage & Wabash, Portsmouth, 1967-70; ins. broker Jackson Nat. & Wabash, Tampa Bay, 1971-91; pres. The Gardens 107, Inc., Tampa Bay, 1987—; travel writer, counselor Cruises/Travel & Etc., Fla., 1981—. Author: (poetry) Pathways (1 Cert. awards), 1990, Metaphysical Techniques That Really Work, 1994, Metaphysical Encounters, 1992, How to Stay Secure in a Chaotic World, 1993, Metaphysics Encounters of a Fourth Kind, 1995, How to Safeguard Your World and Avoid Becoming a Target, 1996; contbr. articles to popular mags. Bd. dirs. The Gardens Domicurculums, Cmty. Coun., 1987—; bd. dirs. State Bd. Cosmetology, Columbus, Ohio, 1962-63, Bus. and Profl. Women, Portsmouth, 1967-69, Sci. Rsch., Portsmouth, 1965-69, Tampa Bay, 1972-74. Recipient Key to Miami, Office of Mayor Claude Kirk, 1969, Million Dollar trophy Lt. Gov. John Brown Ohio; commd. Ky. Col. by Gov. Edward T. Breathitt, 1968, Gov. Wendell Ford, 1969. Mem. AARP, S.E. Writers Assn., Christian Writers Guild, Writers Digest Book Club, Nat. Assn. Retired Fed. Employees (assoc.), Am. Heart Assn. (chmn. Seminole area 1994). Democrat. Home and Office: Audacious Prodn 8039 Garden Dr Apt 204 Largo FL 33777

CRAFTON-MASTERSON, ADRIENNE, real estate executive, writer, poet; b. Providence, Mar. 6, 1926; d. John Harold and Adrienne (Fitzgerald) Crafton; m. Francis T. Masterson, May 31, 1947 (div. Jan. 1977); children: Mary Victoria Masterson Bush, Kathleen Joan, John Andrew, Barbara Lynn. Student, No. Va. Community Coll., 1971-74; A in Biblical Studies, Christ to World Bible Inst., Jacksonville, Fla., 1992; A in Pastoral Leadership, Calvary Bible Inst., Jacksonville, Fla., 1993. Mem. staff Senator T.F. Green of R.I., Washington, 1944-47, 54-60; with U.S. Senate Com. on Campaign Expenditures Senator T.F. Green of R.I., 1944-45; asst. chief clk. Ho. Govt. Ops. Com., 1948-49; clk. Ho. Campaign Expenditures Com., 1950; asst. appointment sec. Office of Pres., 1951-53; with Hubbard Realty, Alexandria, Va., 1962-67; owner, mgr. Adrienne C. Masterson Real Estate, Alexandria, 1968-82; pres. Adrienne Investment Real Estate (AIRE) Ltd., Alexandria, 1982-91; devel. staff writer Calvary Internat., Jacksonville, Fla., 1992-93; Adrienne Crafton-Masterson Real Estate, Winchester, Va., 1993-94; owner, prin., broker Adrienne Crafton-Masterson Real Estate, Haymarket, Va., 1994—; pres. AIRE-Merkli developers, 1988-92; founder AIHRE USA, Inc., 1993—. Mem. adv. panel Fairfax County (Va.) Coun. on Arts, 1987-88; founder, pres. Mt. Vernon/Lee Cultural Ctr. Found., Inc. 1984-92; life patron, life dep. gov. Am. Biog. Inst. Fellow Internat. Biog. Ctr. (dep. dir. gen.); mem. Internat. Orgn. Real Estate Appraisers (sr.), Nat. Assn. Realtors, No. Va. Assn. Realtors (chmn. comml. and indsl. com. 1982-83, cmty. revitalization com. 1983-84, pres. land. comml. indsl. mems. 1985, v.p. land comml. and indsl. mems. 1989), Greater Piedmont Area Assn. Realtors, Fairfax Affordable Housing Inc. (sec. 1990-91), Haymarket-Gainesville (Va.) Busl. and Profl. Assn. (bd. dirs. 1996—), Alexandria C. of C., Mt. Vernon/Lee C. of C., Friends of Kennedy Ctr. (founder). Office: Haymarket Profl Ctr PO Box 499 6611 Jefferson St Haymarket VA 20168-0499

CRAFTS, HELEN PAULINE, health facility administrator, notary public; b. Dayton, Ohio, Oct. 27, 1950; d. Benjamin Franklin and Thelma Lee (Himes) LeMaster; m. Nelson Ernest Crafts (dec. Nov. 1995). AA in Acctg., Cleve. State, 1975, BS in Acctg., 1981, AA in Computer Sci., 1983; ADC, Marti Lindsey Cons., 1995. Cert. activity dir. Inventory control supr. Lesco Inc., Elyria, Ohio, 1976-83; cost analyst Invacare Corp., Elyria, Ohio, 1983-86; front end mgr. Wal-Mart, Sebring, Fla., 1986-92; activity dir. Integrated Health Sys. Skilled Nursing Facility, Sebring, 1992—; adv. bd. mem. Nu-Hope, Sebring, 1994—. Editor (newsletter) The Sunbeam, 1993—. Mem. Nat. Assn. for Activity Profls., Fla. Health Care Activity Coord. Assn. (Dist. III historian 1995-96, pres. 1996—), Am. Soc. Notaries, Nat. Notary Assn. Democrat. Roman Catholic. Office: IHS of Sebring 3011 Kenilworth Blvd Sebring FL 33825

CRAGNOLIN, KAREN ZAMBELLA, real estate developer, lawyer; b. Boston, May 19, 1949; d. John T. Zambella and Corrine M. (Feeney) Zenga; m. Robert Louis Cragnolin, Sept. 8, 1974; 1 child, Nikki Josephine. BA, Georgian Ct. Coll., 1971; JD, New Eng. Sch. Law, 1974. Bar: N.Y. 1974, D.C. 1981. Sr. tax editor Prentice-Hall, Englewood Cliffs, N.J., 1974-76; dir. pub. affairs Am.-Arab Affairs Coun., Washington, 1981-83; founder, dir. Am. Bus. Coun., Dubai, United Arab Emirates, 1983-86; dir. River Link, Inc., Asheville, N.C., 1987—. Pres. Young Dems., Georgian Court, N.J., 1970-71; chair Greenway Commn., Asheville, N.C., 1990—; pres., bd. dirs. Leadership Asheville, 1993—, Asheville Area C. of C., 1992-96; bd. dirs. Hand Made Am., Asheville, 1994—, Handi-Skills, Asheville, 1986-90, chmn., 1986-88. Recipient Downtown Hero award Asheville Downtown Assn., 1991, Cir. Excellence Leadership Asheville, 1995, Friend of River award Land Regional Coun., 1995. Mem. D.C. Bar Assn., N.Y. Bar Assn. Home: 7 Cedarcliff Rd Asheville NC 28803 Office: RiverLink Inc PO Box 15488 Asheville NC 28813

CRAIG, CAROL MILLS, marriage, family and child counselor; b. Berkeley, Calif.. BA in Psychology with honors, U. Calif., Santa Cruz, 1974; MA in Counseling Psychology, John F. Kennedy U., 1980; doctoral student, Calif. Sch. Profl. Psychology, Berkeley, 1980-87, Columbia Pacific U., San Rafael, Calif., 1987—. Psychology intern Fed. Correction Inst., Pleasanton, Calif., 1979-81, Letterman Army Med. Ctr., San Francisco, 1980-82; psychology intern VA Mental Hygiene Clinic, Oakland, Calif., 1981-82, Martinez, Calif., 1982-83; instr. Martinez Adult Sch., 1983, Piedmont Adult Edn., Oakland, 1986; biofeedback and stress mgmt. cons. Oakland, 1986—; child counselor Buddies-A Nonprofit, Counseling Svc. for Persons in the Arts, Lafayette, Calif., 1993—; founder Chesley Sch., 1994; rsch. asst. Irvington Pubs., N.Y.C., 1979, Little, Brown and Co., Boston, 1983. Mem. Calif. Assn. Marriage and Family Therapists (clin.), Musicians Union Local 424, Calif. Scholarship Fedn. (life).

CRAIG, CHERYL ANNE, psychologist; b. New Brunswick, N.J., May 11, 1962; d. Richard Howard and Marian Patricia (Farina) C. AA, Mercer County Coll., West Windsor, N.J., 1984; BA, Rowen Coll. N.J., 1987; MA, Rider U., 1991. Cert. Nat. Bd. Cert. Counselors. Dir. mental health managed care Mustard Seed, Inc., Ft. Washington, Pa., 1992-93, clin. dir. managed care, 1993-95; psychiat. emergency therapist Helene Fuld Med. Ctr., Trenton, N.J., 1987-91, program coord. psychiat. emergency dept., 1995—. Mem. ACA, Am. Assn. Forensic Counselors. Democrat. Roman Catholic. Office: Helene Fuld Med Ctr Psychiat Emergency Dept 750 Brunswick Ave Trenton NJ 08638

CRAIG, ELEANOR NAOMI, retired social worker; b. Providence, Apr. 6, 1917; d. John Johnson and Lucy (Snead) Jennings; m. Horace Hazard Craig, Oct. 22, 1943; children: David Hazard, Carol Naomi Brockington. AA magna cum laude, Roger Williams U., 1978; BSW magna cum laude, Barrington Coll., 1979-81. Ordained minister, 1996. Minority advisor Barrington (R.I.) Coll., 1981-85; counselor Dept. Employment Sec., Providence; chair Gov.'s Adv. Com., Providence; sec. Lt. Gov. Longterm Health Com., Providence; bd. dirs., pres. Bannister Nursing Care Ctr., Providence, 1987-89; sec. AAUW, Providence. Active ARC, Providence, 1963-73; life mem. PTA, Fox Point Sch., Providence, 1957-59; bd. dirs. Ret. Citizens, Providence, 1955—. Recipient plaque for cmty. svc. Providence Human Rels., 1985, Jefferson award for cmty. svc., 1989, plaque Bannister Nursing Care, plaque for civic endeavor Black Caucus R.I., 1994; featured with husband in Remarkable People, 1996. Mem. R.I. Black Social Workers (founder), NAACP (Joseph G. LeCount award for disting. svc. 1995), Alpha Kappa Alpha (pres. Theta Psi Omega chpt.). Democrat. Home: 86 John St Providence RI 02906

CRAIG, ELIZABETH JACKSON, artist; b. Lancaster, S.C., June 4, 1961; d. Ernest Caldwell Jackson and Clara Lee (Courtney) Sexton; m. Jack R. Pope, Apr. 12, 1981 (div. 1986); 1 child, Samantha Leanne Pope; m. Danny R. Craig, Aug. 31, 1986; 1 child, Victoria Noel. Student, U. S.C., Lancaster, 1991-93, Winthrop U., 1993—. Acct. Sears, Lancaster, 1980-84; microfilm rschr. Tech. Data Resources, Charlotte, N.C., 1984-86; freelance artist Lancaster, 1991—. Exhibited paintings at Taledaga Motorsport Hall of Fame, 1994—; artist (ltd. edit. prints) Dale Jarrett-Daytona's Reigning Star, (ltd. edit. prints) Homeward Bound, 1991; artist, sculptor Family Tree Houses (Martin Good award 1995); sculptor Reaching for Nurishment, 1996. Recipient Clara Barrett Strait scholarship Winthrop U., 1996. Democrat. Presbyterian. Home: 511 W Meeting St Lancaster SC 29720

CRAIG, JANE MARIE, career gudiance counselor; b. Cambridge, Minn., Aug. 26, 1958; d. George Frank and Virginia Phillis (Peterson) Schleicher; children: Jared Michael Craig, Garin Edward Craig. BA, U. Minn., Duluth, 1979. Registered Rainbows dir. Counselor Arrowhead Juvenile Detention Ctr., Duluth, 1978-79; resource planner Whatcom County Opportunity Counsel, Bellingham, Wash., 1979-80; judge's asst. Whatcom County Dist. Ct., Bellingham, Wash., 1980-81; servicing coord. Murray Investment Co., Dallas, 1981-84; adoption counselor Luth. Social Svcs., Midland, Tex., 1992-93; rainbows registered dir. Hospice of Midland, Tex., 1993-95; dir. Rainbows Internat., Chgo., 1993-95; cons. Hospice of Midland, 1993-95. Mem. Gifted and Talented Children's Advs., Midland, 1993-95. Mem. AAUW (bd. dirs. 1983-95, sec. 1991-93, charter mem. Midland chpt.), Women of Evang. Luth. Ch. Am. (pres. 1986-95). Home: 520 N Calhoun St Cambridge MN 55008

CRAIG, JOAN CARMEN, secondary school educator, drama teacher; b. Sacramento, Calif., July 13, 1932; d. Frank Hurtado and Enid Pearl (Hogan) Alcalde; m. Elmer Lee Craig, Aug. 14, 1955 (dec. Jan. 1981); children: Shelley, Wendy, Cathleen, Scott. BA, San Jose State U., 1954, gen. secondary cert., 1955; postgrad. studies, various univs., 1956—. Cert. tchr. (life), Calif. Drama tchr. Willow Glen High Sch. San Jose (Calif.) Unified Sch. Dist., 1955-58, Kennedy Jr. High Sch. Cupertino (Calif.) Sch. Dist., 1968-93; cons. Cupertino Unified Sch. Dist., 1990—; coord. program activiy Growth Leadership Ctr., Mountain View, Calif., 1993; presenter Computer Use in Edn., 1990-93. Author, coord.: Drama Curriculum, 1971-93, Musical Comedy Curriculum, 1985-93, (Golden Bell, Calif. 1992). Dir. Nat. Multiple Sclerosis Soc., Santa Clara County, 1983-86. Recipient Spl. Svc. award Nat. Multiple Sclerosis Soc., Santa Clara, Calif., 1986, Hon. Membership award Nat. Jr. Honor Soc., 1990, Hon. Svc. award Calif. Congress Parents, Tchrs. and Students, Inc., 1992; named Tchr. of Year, Kennedy Jr. High, Cupertino Union Sch. Dist., 1993. Mem. AAUW, NEA, Calif. Tchrs. Assn., Cupertino Edn. Assn. (rep. 1982). Home: 8121 Hyannisport Dr Cupertino CA 95014-4063 Office: Growth Leadership Ctr 1451 Grant Rd Ste 102 Mountain View CA 94040-3250

CRAIG, JUDITH, bishop; b. Lexington, Mo., June 5, 1937; d. Raymond Luther and Edna Amelia (Forsha) C. BA, William Jewell Coll., 1959; MA in Christian Edn., Eden Theol. Sem., 1961; MDiv, Union Theol. Sem., 1968; DD, Baldwin Wallace Coll., 1981; DHL, Adrian Coll., 1985, Otterbein Coll., 1993. Youth dir. Bellefontaine United Meth. Ch., St. Louis, 1959-61; intern children's work Nat. Coun. of Chs. of Christ, N.Y.C., 1961-62; dir. Christian edn. 1st United Meth. Ch., Stamford, Ct., 1962-66; inst. adult basic edn. N.Y.C. Schs., 1967; dir. Christian edn. Epworth Euclid United Meth. Ch., Cleve., 1969-72, assoc. pastor, 1972-76; pastor Pleasant Hills United Meth. Ch., Middleburg Heights, Ohio, 1976-80; conf. council dir. East Ohio Conf. United Meth. Ch., Canton, 1980-84; bishop United Meth. Ch., Mich. area, 1984-92, West Ohio area, 1992—; mem. Nat. Task Force on Itineracy, 1977-80; responder to World Coun. of Chs. (document on Baptism, Eucharist and Ministry 1975); gen. conf. del., 1980, 84; mem. United Meth. Publ. House Bd., 1992—; bd. dirs. U.S. Health Corp.; frequent lectr. and preacher; bd. trustees 27 institutions in West Ohio. Contbr. articles to ministry mags. Bd. dirs. YWCA, Middleburg Heights, 1976-80. Recipient Citation of Achievement William Jewell Coll., 1985, Woman of Achievement award YWCA, 1995. Office: 32 Wesley Blvd Worthington OH 43085

CRAIG, KARA LYNN, social service administrator; b. Portland, Oreg., Nov. 29, 1962; d. Raymond L. and Donna J. (Telford) Spencer. BA in Communication, Boise State U., 1985; MA in Psychology, Pepperdine U., 1990. Office mgr. Ustick Chiropractic Clinic, Boise, 1983-85; communications asst. First Interstate Bank of Idaho, Boise, 1985-87; dir. Golden Gate U., Irvine, Calif., 1988-91; adj. prof. Golden Gate U., Irvine, 1990-91; case mgr. Big Bros./Big Sisters of S.W. Idaho, Boise, 1992-94; exec. dir. Children's Home Soc. of Idaho, Boise, 1994—; adj. prof. Boise State U., 1992—. Pub. rels. com. Sounds of Music (community choir), Boise, 1987-88. Mem. APA, Psi Chi. Home: 7903 W Queen Ct Boise ID 83704-7100 Office: Children's Home Soc Idaho 740 Warm Springs Ave Boise ID 83712-6420

CRAIG, KAREN KAY, television producer; b. El Dorado, Ark., Oct. 8, 1965; d. Donald Richard and Charlotte Ann (Kilgore) C. BFA in Drama, U. Calgary, 1988; MFA in TV Prodn., U. New Orleans, 1996. TV prodn. instr. U. New Orleans, 1993-96; assoc. prodr. Sta. WYES-TV12, New Orleans, 1996; pres. UNO Video, New Orleans, 1994-96; com. mem. Prodn. Resource Com., New Orleans, 1995-96. Mem. Alpha Theta Epsilon.

CRAIG, KAREN LYNN, accountant; b. Detroit, Mar. 17, 1959; d. John and Corinne (Legel) C.; m. Robert A. Steshetz, May 3, 1986; 1 child, Kamden. A. in Commerce, Henry Ford Community Coll., 1980; BS in Bus. and Acctg., Wayne State U., 1982. CPA, Mich., Calif. Cost and staff acct. Wilson Dairy Co., Detroit, 1982-83, sr. acct., 1983-84, acting contr., 1984; staff acct. Coopers & Lybrand, Detroit, 1984-85, sr. acct., 1986-87, supr. acct., Newport Beach, Calif., 1987-89; asst. corp. contr. J.F. Shea Co., Inc., Walnut, Calif., 1989—. Mem. Mich. Assn. CPA's, Calif. Soc. CPA's. Avocations: music, hockey, photography, baseball. Office: JF Shea Co Inc PO Box 489 Walnut CA 91788-0489

CRAIG, SANDRA KAY, sales executive; b. Willoughby, Ohio, Nov. 21, 1962; d. Charles Soloman and Lacey Marie (Webb) Eggers; m. Robert Joseph Craig, June 28, 1986 (div. Jan. 1993); 1 child, Misty Marie Mangus; m. Robert David Del Tiempo, Feb. 14, 1995; stepchildren: Jaime Brandon, Joseph David Del Tiempo. AAB cum laude, Shawnee State U., 1985; BBA summa cum laude, Ohio U., 1987. Territory mgr. ARA Cory, San Diego, 1988-89, sales mgr., 1989-90; sales rep. Rsch. Inst. Am., Menifee, Calif., 1990-92; regional sales mgr. Rsch. Inst. Am., Menifee, 1992-96; dist. mgr. The Infortext Group (a divsn. of Equitrac), 1996—; leader's coun. Rsch. Inst. Am., Menifee, dist. mgr., 1996—; pres. The Infortext Group (divsn. Equitrac), Torrance, Calif., 1996, Rsch. Inst. Am., 1996—; cons. Video Ave., Paradise Pizza, Chillicothe, Ohio, 1987-88. Active Girl Scouts U.S., Menifee, 1988-92, Jr. All Am. Football. Mem. NAFE, NOW, PTA, Phi Kappa Phi, Phi Theta Kappa. Democrat. Home: 4888 Via De La Luna Yorba Linda CA 92886 Office: Rsch Inst Am Group 90 Fifth Ave New York NY 10011

CRAIG, SHEILA L., cosmetologist; b. New Castle, Pa., Sept. 19, 1937; d. Lawrence R. and Justine M. (Rankin) Weaver; m. Richard L. Craig, Oct. 14, 1960; children: Erna Leigh, Kelly, Christopher. BFA, Slippery Rock U., 1993. Lic. cosmetologist, Pa. Stylist Miller's Beauty Salon, New Castle, Pa., 1958-61; owner, mgr. stylist Sheila Craig's Style Shoppe, Mercer, Pa., 1961-68; stylist Miller Funeral Home, Mercer, 1968-75, Cunningham Funeral Home, Mercer, 1975—; part-time stylist Gay's Style Shoppe, Mercer, 1975—; art instr. State Regional Prison, Mercer, 1994—. Mem. commn. Civil Svc., Mercer, 1985-92; dir. Mercer County Arts Coun., 1995. Recipient 1st Pl. award Buhl Day Fine Arts Exhibit, 1987, Mercer County Fine Art Exhibit, 1990. Mem. Hoyt Inst. Fine Art, Chautauqua Art Assn. Republican. Home: PO Box 88 Maple St Ext Mercer PA 16137

CRAIG, SUSAN LYONS, library director; b. Barksdale Air Force Base, La., Feb. 23, 1948. BA, Trinity Coll., Washington, 1971; MSLS, Fla. State U., 1976; MBA, Rosary Coll., 1989. Pub. svcs. libr. St. Mary's Coll., Moraga, Calif., 1976-79; head pub. svcs. Hood Coll., Frederick, Md., 1979-85, Rosary Coll., River Forest, Ill., 1985-87; dir. libr. Aurora (Ill.) U., 1987—; adj. assoc. prof Rosary Coll. Grad. Sch. Libr. and Info. Sci., 1990—. Mem. ALA, Assn. Coll. and Rsch. Libr. (nat. adv. com., rep. Chgo. chpt. 1991-95), Pvt. Acad. Librs. of Ill. (pres. 1994-96), Ill. Libr. Assn. (del. pres.-White House Conf., Chgo., 1989-90), Beta Phi Mu, Phi Eta Sigma (hon.). Office: Aurora U 347 S Gladstone Ave Aurora IL 60506-4877

CRAIN, CHRISTINA MELTON, lawyer; b. Dallas, Mar. 18, 1966; d. William Allen Sr. and Sandra (Hays) Melton. BA in Govt., U. Tex., 1988; JD, Oklahoma City U., 1991. Bar: Tex. 1992, U.S. Dist. Ct. (no. dist.) Tex. 1992, U.S. Ct. Appeals (5th cir.) 1992, U.S. Dist. Ct. (ea. dist.) Tex. 1993, U.S. Dist. Ct. (so. and we. dists.) Tex. 1994. From law clk. to assoc. Nichols, Jackson, Dillard, Hager & Smith, LLP, Dallas, 1990-93; ptnr. Kirk, Griffin & Melton, LLP (now Christina Melton Crain PC), Dallas, 1994-96; sr. v.p., gen. counsel Shop On Line. Chmn. Tex. Young Reps. Fedn., 1993-95, 3d v.p.; dir., auditor Pub. Affairs Luncheon Club, Dallas, 1993—; patient navigator Bridge Breast Ctr., Dallas, 1994—. Recipient U.S. Congl. Silver Medal of Honor, U.S. Congress, 1987; named 40 Under 40, The Dalls (Tex.) Bus. Jour., 1993, Outstanding Young Rep. Woman of Yr., Tex. Young Reps. Fedn., 1994, 95. Mem. Dallas Bar Assn. (co-chair memls. history com.), Dallas Assn. Young Lawyers (co-chair legal aid to elderly com.). Baptist. Office: Christina Melton Crain PC # 104 -944 5521 Greenville Ave Dallas TX 75206

CRAIN, GAYLA CAMPBELL, lawyer; b. Cleburne, Tex., June 13, 1950; d. R. C. and Marilyn Ruth (McFadyen) Campbell; m. Howard Leo Crain, May 27, 1978; 1 child, Robert Leo. BA, Baylor U., 1972, JD, 1974. Bar: Tex. 1974, U.S. Dist. Ct. (no., ea., we., and so. dists.) Tex., U.S. ct. Appeals (5th cir.) 1988, U.S. Ct. Appeals (10th cir.) 1994. Asst. counsel Trailways, Inc., Dallas, 1975-79; counsel Schering Plough, Inc., Kenilworth, N.J., 1979-80, sr. counsel, 1980-81; assoc. Epstein Becker & Green, P.C., Ft. Worth, 1985-86; ptnr. Epstein Becker & Green, P.C., Dallas, 1986—. Contbg. author: State by State Guide to Human Resources Law, 1990, 91; editl. adv. bd. mem. Employee Rels. Law Jour. Trustee Dallas Bapt. U., 1989—. Office: Epstein Becker & Green PC 12750 Merit Dr Ste 1320 Dallas TX 75251-1246

CRAIN, GERTRUDE RAMSAY, publishing company executive; m. G.D. Crain Jr. (dec. Dec. 1973); children: Keith, Rance. D in Journalism (hon.), DePauw U., 1987; LHD (hon.), U. Detroit, 1988. Asst. treas. Crain Communications Inc., Chgo., 1942, sec., asst. treas., 1943-62, sec., treas., 1962-74, chmn. bd., 1974—; bd. dirs. Internat. Advt. Assn., Mag. Pubs. Am., Execs. Club of Chgo., The Nat. Press Found. of Wash., Advt. Coun. of N.Y. Trustee Lincoln Acad. of Ill., James Webb Young Scholarship U. of Ill.; founding mem. Com. of 200, 1982; bd. dirs. Mus. of Broadcast Comm. in Chgo., Northwestern Meml. Hosp. Corp.-Chgo., Mus. of Sci. and Industry. Named to Working Woman Hall of Fame, 1987; named Chicagoan of Yr. Boys and Girls Club of Chgo., 1987, One of Top 60 Women Bus. Owners Saavy Mag., 1987, One of Top 50 Businesswomen Mich. Womans Mag., 1987; recipient Magnificat medal Mundelein Coll., Chgo., 1988. Mem. Internat. Advt. Assn. (bd. dirs.), Mag. Pubs. Am. (bd. dirs.), Nat. Press Found. Washington, Advt. Club N.Y., Execs. Club Chgo. Office: Crain Communications Inc 740 N Rush St Chicago IL 60611-2525*

CRAIN, MARY TOM, volunteer; b. Vernon, Tex., Aug. 27, 1918; d. Samuel Asa Leland and Mary Verna (Johnson) Morgan; m. David Rasco, Dec. 24, 1941 (dec. Apr. 1955); children: Sarah M. Rasco Thomas, Mary Prudence Rasco Courtney; m. Sam H. Crain, Sept. 17, 1975 (dec. June 1980). Student, Stephens Coll., 1936-38, U. Tex., 1938-39; BS, U. Wis., 1941. Tchr. Williams Bay (Wis.) Schs., 1941; reporter Amarillo (Tex.) Globe News, 1957-65; exec. sec. Potter-Randall County Med. Soc., Amarillo, 1960-69; ret., 1969. Mem. lay adv. bd. St. Anthony's Hosp., Amarillo, 1957; mem. devel. bd. High Plains Hosp., 1995; coun. pres. Girl Scouts U.S., Amarillo, 1953-55; pres. Jr. League, Amarillo, 1956; bd. dirs. Amarillo Symphony, Art Mus., Panhandle Plains Hist. Soc., Amarillo Area Found., 1945—, Alano Cemetary; mem. City of Amarillo Park and Recreation Commn. Named Amarillo's Woman of yr., Beta Sigma Phi, 1955; named to Amarillo H.S. Hall of Fame, 1971. Methodist. Home: 2412 Travis Rd Amarillo TX 79109

CRAMER, BETTY F., life insurance company executive; b. Indpls., Dec. 9, 1920; d. Frank E. and Ethelyn L. (Jackson) C. B.A., Butler U., 1943. Sec. to v.p. and treas. Indpls. Life Ins. Co., 1951-69, supr. bond and stock acctg., 1969-75, securities asst., 1975-81, sec.-treas., 1981-89, ret., 1989. Advisor Jr. Achievement, Indpls., 1959-60; campaign chmn. United Way, 1980. Mem. Nat. Assn. Corp. Treas., Life Ins. Women's Assn. Indpls. (past v.p., pres.). Republican. Roman Catholic. Home: 5158 N Central Ave Indianapolis IN 46205-1060

CRAMER, ROXANNE HERRICK, gifted and talented education educator; b. Albion, Mich., Apr. 24; d. Donald F. and Kathryn L. (Beery) Herrick; m. James Loveday Hofford, Jan. 29, 1955 (div.); children: William Herrick, Dana Webster, Paul Christopher; m. Harold Leslie Cramer, Apr. 20, 1967. Student, U. Mich., 1952-55; BA, U. Toledo, 1956; EdM, Harvard U., 1967; EdD, Va. Poly. Inst. and State U., 1990. Tchr. Wayland (Mass.) Pub. Schs., 1966-70, Fairfax County (Va.) Pub. Schs., 1970—; tchr./team leader Gifted and Talented program, 1975—; coordinating instr. Trinity Coll., Washington, 1978; nat. coord. gifted children programs Am. Mensa, Ltd., 1981-84. Editor newletter Va. Assn. for the Edn. of Gifted, 1989-90; contbr. articles to profl. jours. Mem. NEA, Nat. Assn. Gifted Children, Fairfax County Assn. for the Gifted, Coalition for Advancement Gifted Edn. (bd. dirs. 1982-84), World Coun. Gifted and Talented Children, Intertel Found., Inc. (bd. dirs. 1986—), chmn. Hollingworth award com. 1984—, Fairfax County Assn. Gifted, Nat. Assn. Gifted Children, Va. Edn. Assn., Fairfax Edn. Assn., Mensa, Harvard Club, Phi Delta Kappa. Home: 4300 Sideburn Rd Fairfax VA 22030-3507 Office: Louise Archer Gifted Ctr 324 Nutley St NW Vienna VA 22180-4213

CRAMPTON, ESTHER LARSON, sociology and political science educator; b. Plainview, Nebr., Apr. 14, 1915; d. Charles W. and Anna Margrethe (Staugaard) Larson; m. Francis Asbury Crampton, Jan. 19, 1949 (dec.); children: Jacqueline, Edith. AB, Colo. Coll. of Edn., 1935; MA, U. Wis., 1937; PhD, Am. U., 1972. Observer, writer U.S. Weather Bur., Washington, 1942-48; interpreter Portuguese RFC Rubber Devel. Corp., Manaos, Brasil, 1943; tchr. Latin Glenn County High Sch., Willows, Calif., 1954-57;

tchr. Latin/German Scottsdale (Ariz.) High Sch., 1957-62; tchr. Latin Natrona County High Sch., Casper, Wyo., 1962-64; tchr. social studies Bourgade High Sch., Phoenix, 1964-65; substitute tchr. Phoenix High Sch., 1965-66; instr. supr. We. N.Mex. U. Lab. Sch., Silver City, 1966-67; prof. sociology and polit. sci. Cochise C.C., Douglas, Ariz., 1967-77. Sec., v.p., bd. dirs. Easter Seal Soc. of Santa Cruz, 1979-81; active Nat. Women's Polit. Caucus Br., Santa Cruz, 1979; tutor reading Literacy Coun., San Luis Obispo, 1988. Grantee Amazonia Rsch. Orgn. of Am. States, 1970, Am. Coun. of Learned Socs., 1941. Mem. AAUW (chair 1977-81, internat. rels. group Santa Cruz br. mem.-at-large 1981—), Am. Assn. Women in Cmty. and Jr. Colls. (charter mem.).

CRANBERG, MARCIA ANN, lawyer; b. Des Moines, Jan. 28, 1955. BA magna cum laude, Brandeis U., 1977; student, U. Nice, France; JD, U. Iowa, 1980. Bar: Iowa 1980, D.C. 1982, Colo. 1992. Spl. counsel Arnold & Porter, Washington; adj. prof. Columbus Sch. Law, Cath. U., 1987-91. Mem. ABA (co-editor Comms. Lawyer 1982-87). Office: Arnold & Porter 555 12th St NW Washington DC 20004*

CRANDALL, CHERYL HALL, special education resource educator; b. Richmond, Va., June 3, 1955; d. Garrison Thomas Sr. and Frances (Dameron) Hall; m. Thomas O. Crandall, Nov. 5, 1982; 1 child, LeNaya R. BS in Elem. Edn., Morgan State U., 1977; M of Spl. Edn., Western Md. Coll., 1987. Cert. elem. tchr., K-5 middle sch. graders, spl. edn. K-12. Classroom tchr. Balt. County Pub. Schs., Towson, Md., 1977-85; spl. edn. resource tchr. Balt. County Pub. Schs., Towson, 1985-89, Carroll County Pub. Schs., Westminster, Md., 1991-95; psycho educator Care Rehab, Inc., Balt., 1995-96; spl. edn. resource tchr. Prince George's County Pub. Schs., Upper Marlboro, Md., 1996—; diagnostician and ednl. therapist Think-Tank, Westminster, 1989—. Author: (children's booklet) I Dream A World: Children's Activity Booklet, 1991. 1st v.p. Nat. Coun. of Negro Women, Inc., Greater Balt. Sect., 1992-96; founding pres. Carroll County Women on the Move, Inc., Westminster, 1992—; supt. of Sunday sch. Union Street United Meth. Ch., 1994—. Recipient Achievement award for Life Membership Nat. Coun. of Negro Women, Inc., 1994, Citizen Citation City of Balt. Mayor Kurt Schmoke, 1992. Mem. NEA, Carroll County Edn. Assn. (com. chair 1992—), Md. State Tchr. Assn., Am. Bus. Women's Assn.

CRANDALL, RHONA, personnel manager; b. Rochester, N.Y., Sept. 13, 1947; d. Lawrence F. and Irene (Fowler) Bennett; m. John G. Crandall, 1994. BS, Mansfield (Pa.) State Coll., 1969; MS, Lesley Coll., 1992. Tchr. Randolph (Mass.) Pub. Schs., 1969-76, Hudson (N.H.) Pub. Schs., 1977-83; tng. officer Indian Head Banks Inc., Nashua, N.H., 1983-85; tng. specialist Fed. Res. Bank Boston, 1985-89; tng. adminstr. Fed. Res. Bank, Boston, 1990-95, pers. mgr., 1995—; tax preparer, planner, Epping, N.H., 1978-92. Mem. ASTD. Home: 15 Blake Rd Epping NH 03042-3006 Office: Fed Res Bank 600 Atlantic Ave Boston MA 02210-2211

CRANDALL, SONIA JANE, medical educator; b. Quincy, Ill., Sept. 2, 1952; d. Gerald Madison and Roselma Louise (Zeiger) Syrcle; m. Edward Young Crandall, June 28, 1975. Diploma, Michael Reese Med. Ctr., Chgo., 1974; BS, Western Ill. U., 1974; MED, U. Ill., 1980; PhD, U. Okla., 1989. Med. tech. U. Mo. Med. Ctr., Columbia, 1974-75; med. tech., clin. instr. St. Johns Hosp., Springfield, Ill., 1976-81; med. tech., supr. Okla. Teaching Hosp., 1982-85, tng. officer, 1985-87; Kellog fellow U. Okla., Norman, Okla., 1987-89; asst. prof., dir. faculty devel. and edn. resources, dept. family medicine U. Okla. Health Scis. Ctr., Oklahoma City, 1989-94; asst. prof., dept. family and community medicine Bowman Gray Sch. of Medicine, Wake Forest U., 1994—. Contbr. articles to prof jours. Named one of Outstanding Young Women in Am.; elected to Women's Inner Circle of Achievement, 1995, 500 Leaders of Influence, 1993, 2,000 Notable Am. Women, 1992. Mem. Am. Edn. Rsch. Assn., Am. Assn. for Adult and Continuing Edn., Am. Soc. Clin. Pathology, Soc. Tchrs. Family Medicine, Alliance for Continuing Med. Edn., World Found. of Successful Women (charter), Phi Kappa Phi. Home: 3969-E Valley Ct Winston Salem NC 27106-4379 Office: Dept Family & Cmty Medicine Bowman Gray Sch Medicine Wake Forest U Medical Center Blvd Winston Salem NC 27157

CRANE, BEVERLY ROSE, counselor; b. Clearfield, Pa., Oct. 9, 1924; d. Ralph Maynard and Clare Rose (Stewart) Pearce; m. Edward Crane (dec. Jan. 1970); children: Christine, Melissa Ann. AAS in Child Care, Niagara C.C., Sanbarn, N.Y., 1976; BA in English, Niagara U., 1981, MEd, 1985; PhD, U. Calif., Berkeley, 1990. Counselor Niagara County Cmty. Action Program, Niagara Falls, N.Y., 1980-86; pvt. practice counselor Niagara Falls, 1981-89, Gainesville, Fla., 1990-92; cmty. worker Gainesville, 1992—; cons. mem. bd. Niagara Falls (N.Y.) Schs., 1982-85, West Seneca (N.Y.) Hosp. for Retarded, 1985-87. Author of poetry. Treas. Dem. Party, Niagara Falls, 1976-81; ESL tchr. various schs., N.Y. and Fla., 1980-94. Mem. Basilian Soc. (sec. 1984-86), Our Lady of Angels. Presbyterian. Home: 2229 SW 39th Way Gainesville FL 32607

CRANE, ELIZABETH SUSAN, forester, government official; b. Pueblo, Colo., Sept. 11, 1962; d. Roland Frances and Edith Susan (Kuykendall) C. BS in Forest Mgmt., Clemson U., 1984; MF in Hydrology, N.C. State U., 1991. Registered forester, N.C. Vol. Peace Corps, La Fortuna de Bagaces, Costa Rica, 1985-86; forester N.C. Forest Svc., Rockingham, 1986-89, Lenoir, 1986-89; grad. asst. N.C. State U., Raleigh, 1989-91; watershed planner forest svc. USDA, Atlanta, 1991-92, rural devel. specialist, 1992—; firefighter N.C. Western Fire Crew, Big Cypress Swamp, Fla., 1986, Stanislaus Nat. Forest, Calif., 1987, asst. squad boss, Yellowstone-Jackson Hole, Wyo., 1988. Mem. Soc. Am. Foresters. Office: USDA Forest Svc Coop Forestry Ste 811 N 1720 Peachtree Rd NW Atlanta GA 30367

CRANE, GLENDA PAULETTE, private school educator; b. Orlando, Fla., June 29, 1946; d. James Author and Elizabeth Lorine (Johnson) C. AA in Edn., Orlando Jr. Coll., 1966; BA in Elem. Edn., U. S. Fla., 1967; postgrad. So. Bapt. Theol. Sem., 1970; MEd, Rollins Coll., 1985. Tchr., Orange County Schs., Orlando, 1967-70, 79-80, Lake Highland Prep. Sch., Orlando, 1981—; tchr. Belle Glade (Fla.) Christian Sch., 1970-79, asst. prin., 1970-74, prin., 1975-79. State treas. Fla. Rainbow Girls, 1964. Mem. NEA, Fla. Edn. Assn., Fla. Council Tchrs. English, Orange County Tchrs. Assn., Assn. Supervision and Curriculum Devel., Internat. Reading Assn., Orange County Reading Council of Internat. Reading Assn., Fla. Reading Assn., Nat. Council for the Social Studies, Alumni Assn. U. South Fla., Alumni Assn. So. Bapt. Theol. Sem., Fla. Coun. Tchrs. of Math, Kappa Delta Pi. Democrat. Baptist. Clubs: Winter Park Pilot, Eastern Star, Winter Park Rainbow Girls. Home: 1705 E Harding Ave Orlando FL 32806 Office: 1919 S Delaney Ave Orlando FL 32806

CRANE, JULIA GORHAM, anthropology educator; b. Mt. Kisco, N.Y., Nov. 8, 1925; d. Joseph Harold and Alma Evelyn (Reynolds) Crane. Student, Katharine Gibbs Sch., 1943-45; BS cum laude, Columbia U., 1959, PhD in Anthropology, 1966. Research asst. to Dr. Margaret Mead Am. Museum of Natural History, N.Y.C., 1956-59; asst. in anthropology Columbia U., N.Y.C., 1959-61; asst. prof. anthropology U. N.C., Chapel Hill, 1967-72; assoc. prof. U. N.C., 1972-76, prof., 1976-90. Author: Educated to Emigrate, 1971; co-author (with Michael Angrosino): Field Projects in Anthropology: A Student Handbook, 1974, 2d edit., 1984, 3d edit., 1992, Japanese edit., 1994, Saba Silhouettes, 1987. Recipient Prince Bernhard Fund award, The Netherlands, 1970; grantee NIH, 1961-66, U. N.C., 1970, 75, 85, 86, Cultural Cooperative Orgn. of Netherlands Antilles, 1985; Tanner award for teaching excellence, 1986. Mem. So. Anthropol. Soc., Phi Beta Kappa. Office: U NC Dept Anthropology Alumni Bldg 004A Chapel Hill NC 27514

CRANE, PATRICIA SUE, probation services administrator, social worker; b. Rockway, N.Y., Jan. 17, 1948; d. Herbert Milton and Miriam (Rosenblum) Brager; m. Marvin J. Crane, May 2, 1971; 1 child, Elizabeth A. BA, U. Wis., 1969; MS in Criminal Justice with honors, Wayne State U., 1984. Cert. social worker. Dir. probation svcs. 52d dist. ct. 1st div. State of Mich., Novi, 1979—. Jewish. Home: 5042 Meadowbrook Dr West Bloomfield MI 48322-1570 Office: 52nd Dist Ct 1st Divsn 48150 Grand River Ave Novi MI 48374-1222

CRANE, REGINA ANN, technical writer; b. Pine Bluff, Ark., Jan. 13, 1961; d. Lois Lynell and Lois Virginia (Martin) C. BA in Profl. & Tech. Writing, U. Ark. at Little Rock, 1983. Researcher, writer Ark. Women's History Inst., Little Rock, 1984; tech. writer UNISYS Corp., Nat. Ctr. for Toxicological Rsch., Jefferson, Ark., 1984-87; tech. editor CAE Link Corp., Jacksonville, Ark., 1988-93; assoc. tng. analyst CAE Link Corp., Jacksonville, 1993-95, Hughes Tng., Inc., Jacksonville, 1995—. Recipient Acad. Scholarship U. Ark. at Little Rock, 1979-80, Journalism Scholarship, 1982. Mem. U. Ark. at Little Rock Alumni Assn., Internat. Assn. Bus. Communicators. Office: Hughes Tng Inc PO Box 1282 Jacksonville AR 72078-1282

CRANIN, MARILYN SUNNERS, landscape designer; b. N.Y.C., Aug. 1, 1932; d. William And Rebecca (Yates) Sunners; m. A. Norman Cranin, June 14, 1953; children: Jonathan Blake, Andrew Ross, Elizabeth S. BA, Beaver Coll., Glenside, Pa., 1954, DHL, 1996; student, Harvard U., 1981-82; DHL, Beaver Coll., 1996. Landscape designer N.Y. Bot. Gardens, N.Y.C., 1974-76; hort. therapist Beth Abraham Hosp., 1975-85, N.Y. Bot. Gardens, N.Y.C., 1976-78; master gardener Nassau County Coop Extension Service, N.Y.C., 1976-80; landscape designer London Landscape, Massapequa, N.Y., 1984—. Columnist South Shore Record, 1980-82. V.p., bd. dirs. 5 Towns Music and Art Found., Woodmere, N.Y., 1962—; trustee, dep. mayor Village Hewlett Bay Park, N.Y., 1974-84; pres. bd. trustees Hewlett-Woodmere Pub. Library, 1977—; trustee Nassau Library System, Uniondale, N.Y., 1980-86, Waldorf Sch., Garden City, N.Y., 1985—, Am. Chamber Ensemble, 1981—, Beaver Coll. Alumni Bd., 1979-86, Beaver Coll., 1987—, sec. bd. trustees. Recipient Silver award for excellence in design L.I. Nurseryman's Assn., 1992, Alumni of Yr. Golden Disc award for meritorious svc. Beaver Coll., 1994; named Woman of Yr. Woodmere Merchants Assn., 1994. Mem. Am. Hort. Soc., Nassau County Coop Extension Service, N.Y. State Assn. Libr. Bds., N.Y. Bot. Garden, Wave Hill Hort. Soc. Clubs: Woodmere Bay Yacht, The Woodmere.

CRANNEY, MARILYN KANREK, lawyer; b. Bklyn., June 18, 1949; d. Sidney Paul and Aurelia (Valice) Kanrek; m. John William Cranney, Jan. 1, 1970 (div. June 1975); 1 child, David Julian. BA, Brandeis U., 1970; MA in History, Brigham Young U., 1975; JD, U. Utah, 1979; LLM in Tax Law, NYU, 1984. Bar: N.Y. 1980, U.S. Dist. Ct. (so. and ea. dists.) N.Y. 1992. Assoc. Cravath Swaine & Moore, N.Y.C., 1979-81; 1st v.p., asst. gen. counsel Dean Witter InterCapital Inc., N.Y.C., 1981—. Mem. Order of the Coif. Democrat. Jewish. Home: 1830 E 23rd St Brooklyn NY 11229-1529 Office: Dean Witter InterCapital Inc 2 World Trade Ctr New York NY 10048-0203

CRANS, ALICE M. SUTHERLAND, higher education administrator; b. Plainfield, N.J., Feb. 24, 1939; d. Hugh McCrea and Katherine (Connolly) Sutherland; m. Wayne J. Crans, June 27, 1959; children: Terrence, Scott, Brett. BA in Psychology, Douglass Coll., 1979; postgrad., Rutgers U. Field investigator U. Pa., Phila., 1978-80; rsch. asst. Reed & Carnick Pharm., Kenilworth, N.J., 1980-82; adminstrv. dir. biomed. careers Rutgers U., New Brunswick, N.J., 1982-87; asst. dir. MAP Rutgers U., New Brunswick, 1983-90; dir. challenge grant Coll. St. Elizabeth, Convent Station, N.J., 1990-92. Dir. music Spruce Run Ch., Glen Gardner, N.J., 1969-74; coach little league North Hunterdon, N.J. Mem. AAUW. Home: 306 Jeffrey Ln Glen Gardner NJ 08826

CRAPO, SHEILA ANNE, telecommunications company professional, artist; b. Elko, Nev., June 11, 1951; d. John Lewis and June Florene (Lani) C. BA, U. Nev., 1974. Various svc. positions Alltel-Nevada Inc. (now Citizens Telecom.), Elko, 1974-78, svc. rep., 1978-84, bus. office supr., 1984-87, bus. supr. Nev. office, 1987-94; bus. supr., state pub. rels. coord. Citizens Telecom, Elko, 1994—; active Citizens Ambassador program People to People Internat., 1995-96; writer, artist, 1974—; speaker in field. Officer, organizer Freedom Com., Elko, 1984. Mem. AAUW (editor newsletter Elko 1980-82, v.p. programs 1991-93, sec. 1995-96)m Northeastern Nev. Hist. Soc., Animal Relief Found., Soroptimists Internat. (treas. 1992-93, sec. 1993-94, v.p. 1995-96, pres.-elect 1995-96, pres. 1996—). Office: Citizens Telecom 111 W Front St Elko NV 89801-4163

CRAWFORD, BARBARA ANN CLELAND, federal official; b. San Antonio, Aug. 30, 1945; d. Gorden Edward Cleland and Aida Charlotte (Vazquez) Etier; m. Clyde Houston Crawford, May 27, 1966 (dec. 1984). BBA cum laude, Incarnate Word Coll., 1992. Notary public, 1989. Med. records technician Occupl. Medicine, Kelly AFB, Tex., 1984-85; med. clk. Kelly AFB, Tex., 1985-86; clk. Def. Contract Mgmt. Command, San Antonio, 1986-90; command support asst. DCMS, San Antonio, 1990-92, sec., 1992-94, mgmt. asst., 1994—. Mgr., trainer, recruiter, ticket taker U.S. Olympic Festival, San Antonio, 1993; Sunday sch. tchr., San Antonio, 1981-89; fundraiser Pub. TV, 1992—. Mem. AAUW, Nat. Trust Hist. Preservation, Libr. Congress, San Antonio Conservation Soc. (fundraiser 1994—, hist. tour leader 1994—), McNay Art Mus. Office: Def Contract Mgmt Command San Antonio 615 E Houston St San Antonio TX 78205

CRAWFORD, BETTY LEE, financial executive; b. Clarksburg, W.Va., May 16, 1925; d. William and Anna Marie (Wright) Wyatt; m. WIlliam D. Crawford, Feb. 27, 1942 (dec. 1980); children: Elizabeth Ann Bowman, Dorothea Crawford-Weaver, W. David II. Student, W.Va. U., 1969-71. Accounts payable bookkeeper Fountain and Grays Stores, Clarksburg, W.Va., 1950-55; sheriff's bookkeeper Harrison County Commn., Clarksburg, 1965-70; fin. sec. Harrison County Bd. Edn., Clarksburg, 1970-72, head fin. sec., 1972-79, dir. fin., 1979-92, treas., 1980-87, supr. fin. dept., 1980-92, ret.; acctg. com. W.Va. State Bd. Edn., 1984-92; fin. cons. Active Clarksburg Hist. Soc., 1991; active United Hosp. Ctr. Aux., Clarksburg, 1958. Mem. DAR, W.Va. Assn. Sch. Bus. Ofcls. (region chairperson 1982), Nat. Assn. Sch. Bus. Ofcls., Cath. Daus. Am. (regent). Republican. Home: 317 Grand Ave Bridgeport WV 26330-1831

CRAWFORD, CAROL ANNE, marketing executive; b. San Francisco, Jan. 17, 1945; d. Kenneth H. and Marcella (Schloesser) C. B.A., San Jose State U., 1967; M.B.A. in Mktg., Golden Gate U., 1985. Food publicist J. Walter Thompson, San Francisco 1967-70; asst. mktg and sales promotion dir. Eastridge Shopping Ctr., San Jose, Calif., 1970-72; consumer info. specialist Carl Byoir & Assocs., San Francisco, 1972-78; account supr. Ketchum Pub. Relations, San Francisco, 1978-80; v.p., dir. pub. relations Grey Advt., San Francisco, 1980-82; dir. corp. communications S&O Cons., San Francisco, 1982-84; mgr. mktg. and pub. relations GTE Sprint, 1984-86; dir. pub. relations U.S. Sprint, 1986; prin. Crawford Communications, 1986—; instr. pub. relations Golden Gate U., 1987-94; instr. pub. rels. U. Extension, U. Calif., Berkeley, 1994—; cons., lectr. in field, 1987—. Bd. mgrs. YMCA, Embarcadero, 1980-82. Mem. Pub. Relations Soc. Am. (past chpt. pres.), San Francisco Profl. Food Soc. (recording sec. 1992-94, com. svcs. chair 1995), Home Economists in Bus. (past chpt. chmn., past chmn. nat. pub. relations); Commonwealth Club. Office: Crawford Comms 423 Lansdale Ave San Francisco CA 94127-1616

CRAWFORD, CAROL I., opera company artistic director. Student, Julliard Sch., Mozarteum, Salzburg; PhD in music, Yale Univ. Assoc. condr. Memphis Symphony, Tenn.; condr. Memphis Youth Symphony, Tenn.; artistic dir. Tulsa Opera, Okla., 1993—; music dir. Houston Grand Opera's Tex. Opera Theater, San Francisco Opera's Western Opera Theater, Aslawn-Highland Festival, Charlottesville, Va.; assoc. music dir. Va. Opera. Condr.: (Tulsa Philharmonic) Madama Butterfly, 1991, Carmen, 1992; apprentice condr.: (documentary) Bernstein: Conductor, Teacher, Composer, 1984. Recipient first prize San Diego Opera Young American Opera Condrs. Competition, 1981. Office: Tulsa Opera Chapman Music Hall 1610 S Boulder Ave Tulsa OK 74119-4408

CRAWFORD, CAROL TALLMAN, government executive; b. Mt. Holly, N.J., Feb. 25, 1943; m. Ronald Crawford; children: Timothy, Jeffrey, Richard. BA, Mt. Holyoke Coll., 1965; JD magna cum laude, Washington Coll. Law, Am. U., 1978. Bar: Va. 1978, D.C. 1979. Legis. asst. to Senator Bob Packwood Washington, 1969-75; assoc. firm Collier, Shannon, Rill & Scott, Washington, 1979-81; exec. asst. to chmn. FTC, Washington, 1981-83, dir. bur. consumer protection, 1983-85; assoc. dir. Office of Mgmt. & Budget, Washington, 1985-89; asst. atty. gen. legis. affairs U.S. Dept. Justice, Washington, 1989-90; commr. U.S. Internat. Trade Commn., 1991—; sr. advisor Reagan-Bush Transition Team, 1981. Trustee Barry Goldwater Chair of Am. Instns., Ariz. State U., Phoenix, 1983—; mem. dean's adv. coun. Wash Coll. of Law, 1995—; adv. com. Ind. Women's Forum, 1996—; v.p. The Hist. Georgetown Club. Republican.

CRAWFORD, CHRISTINE ANN, lawyer; b. Washington, Aug. 3, 1951; d. Edward Thomas and Emma Jo (Sabo) C.; m. Robert N. Spinelli, Apr. 25, 1981. BA, U. Va., Fredericksburg, 1973; JD, Temple u., 1978. Bar: Pa., 1978, U.S. Dist. Ct. (ea. dist.) Pa., 1981, Ariz., 1982. Participant fin. mgmt. program Gen. Electric Co., Phila., 1973-75; asst. dist. atty. Phila. Dist. Atty.'s Office, 1978-82; assoc. corp. counsel Commodore Bus. Machines, Inc., West Chester, Pa., 1983-85; gen. counsel, sec., bd. dirs. Henkels & McCoy, Inc., Blue Bell, Pa., 1986—. Republican. Roman Catholic. Office: Henkels & McCoy Inc 985 Jolly Rd Blue Bell PA 19422-1903

CRAWFORD, JEAN ANDRE, clinical therapist; b. Chgo., Apr. 12, 1941; d. William Moses and Geneva Mae (Lacy) Jones; student Shimer Coll., 1959-60; BA, Carthage Coll., 1966; MEd, Loyola U., Chgo., 1971; postgrad. Nat. Coll. Edn., Evanston, Ill., 1971-77, Northwestern U., 1976-83; m. John N. Crawford, Jr., June 28, 1969; lic. profl. counselor; cert. sch. counselor Nat. Bd. Cert. Counselors, elem. edn., spl. edn. and pupil personnel services, Ill. Med. technologist, Chgo., 1960-62; primary and spl. edn. tchr. Chgo. Pub. Schs., 1966-71, counselor maladjusted children and their families, 1971-88; counselor juvenile first-offenders, 1968-88, post-secondary vocat. counselor, 1988-93; tchr., transition coord. Cook County Dept. Corrections Alternative High Sch., Chgo., 1993-94; clin. therapist St. Mary of Nazareth Hosp. Ctr., Chgo., 1994—. Vol. Sta. WTTW-TV; vol. counselor deaf children and their families; counselor post-secondary students; vol., mem. community devel. bd. New City YMCA, 1987-92. Mem. scholarship com. Chgo. Urban League. Mem. AACD, Ill. Assn. Counseling and Devel., Am. Sch. Counselors Assn., Ill. Sch. Counselors Assn., Ill. Vocat. Counselors Assn., Am. Mental Health Counselor Assn., Ill. Mental Health Counselor Assn., IIll. Assn. Advancement Black Ams. in Vocat. Edn., Coun. Exceptional Children, Coordinating Coun. Handicapped Children, Shimer Coll. Alumni Assn. (sec. 1982-84), Phi Delta Kappa. Home: 601 E 32nd St #1200 Chicago IL 60616-4054 Office: 2233 W Division St Chicago IL 60622-3043

CRAWFORD, LELA BURCH, school nurse; b. Fostoria, Ohio, Aug. 27, 1936; d. Jethro and Dorothy Leona (Brown) Burch; m. Roger A. Crawford Sr., Sept. 12, 1959; children: Regina Denise Crawford Kemp, Roger Alexander Jr. RN, St. Vincent's Sch. Nursing, 1957; BA in Elem. Edn., Mary Mause Coll., 1965; EdM in Guidance and Counseling, U. Toledo, 1976, Edn. Specialist Degree, 1977, M in Health Edn., 1982. Nurse St. Vincent's Hosp., St. Vincent's Med. Ctr., Toledo, 1957-60, St. Charles Hosp., Toledo, 1960-62, St. Teresa's Elem. Sch., Cath. Bd. Edn., Toledo, 1962-65; part-time staff nurse St. Luke's Hosp., Toledo, 1965-66; staff nurse, supr. Parkview Hosp., Toledo, 1966; sch. nurse Toledo Bd. Edn., 1966—; summer camp nurse Jewish Cmty. Ctr., Toledo, 1973; summer and part-time worker Toledo Hosp., 1974-76, Marigarde Nursing Home, Sylvania, Ohio, 1976-79; summer migrate workers program staff Toledo-Fed. Program, 1979-83; part-time instr. modeling Barbizon Modeling Sch., 1979-82. Mem. Dem. Bus. and Profl. Women's Club Lucas County, Toledo, 1996. Scholar St. Vincent Nursing Sch.-Grey Nuns, Toledo, 1954. Mem. Phi Kappa Phi. Baptist.

CRAWFORD, LINDA CAROLE, insurance executive; b. Wichita, Kans., July 14, 1944; d. Rodney Gene and Anna Lee (Rosenberger) Armour; m. Gary James Crawford, Oct. 14, 1966; children: Cheryl Lynn, Jennie Elizabeth. BS in Secondary Edn., Emporia State U., 1966; BBA, Washburn U., 1981, MBA, 1996. CPA, Kans.; master fellow Life Mgmt. Inst. Math. tchr. Unified Sch. Dist. 501, Topeka, 1966-69, substitute tchr., 1978-79; income tax asst. Sue Brandenburg, CPA, Topeka, 1982; acct. Victory Life Ins. Co., Topeka, 1982-83, mgr. fin. reporting, 1983-84, asst. contr., 1984-87, v.p., treas., 1987-90, asst. controller Am. Inv. Life Ins. Co., 1990—. Mem. Inst. Mgmt. Accts. (bd. dirs. 1989—, pres. 1996—), Kans. Soc. CPAs (cert.), Phi Kappa Phi. Republican. Office: Am Inv Life Ins Co 415 SW 8th Ave Topeka KS 66603

CRAWFORD, LINDA SIBERY, lawyer, educator; b. Ann Arbor, Mich., Apr. 27, 1947; d. Donald Eugene and Verla Lillian (Schenck) Sibery; m. Leland Allardice Crawford, Apr. 4, 1970; children: Christina, Lillian, Leland. Student, Keele U., 1969; BA, U. Mich., 1969; postgrad., SUNY, Potsdam, 1971; JD, U. Maine, 1977. Bar: Maine 1977, U.S. Dist. Ct. Maine 1982, U.S. Ct. Appeals (1st cir.) 1983. Tchr. Pub. Sch., Tupper Lake, N.Y., 1970-71; asst. dist. atty. State of Maine, Farmington, 1977-79; asst. atty. gen. State of Maine, Augusta, Maine, 1979-95; prin. Litigation Consulting Firm, N.Y.C. & Hallowell, Maine, 1986-, Linda Crawford and Assoc. Law Firm, Hallowell, Maine, 1988—; legal adv. U. Maine, Farmington, 1975; legal counsel Fire Marshall's Office, Maine, 1980-83, Warden Svc., Maine, 1981-83, Dept. Mental Health, 1983-90, litigation divsn. 1990-95; mem. tchg. team trial advocacy Law Sch., Harvard U., 1987-; lectr. Sch. Medicine Harvard U., 1991; counsel to Bd. of Registration in Medicine, 1994-95; chmn. editl. bd. Mental and Physical Disability Law Reporter, 1993-95; arbitrator Am. Arbitration Assn., 1995-; facilitator Nat. Constrn. Task Force, St. Louis, 1995. Mem. Natural Resources Coun., Maine, 1985-90; bd. dirs. Diocesan Human Rels. Coun., Maine, 1977-78, Arthritis Found., Maine, 1983-88; atty. expert commn. experts UN War Crime Investigation in the former Yugoslavia, 1994. Named one of Outstanding Young Women of Yr. Jaycees, 1981. Mem. ATLA, ABA (com. on disability 1992-95), Maine Bar Assn. (pub. affairs com.), Kennebec County Bar Assn., Nat. Assn. State Mental Health Attys. (treas. 1984-86, vice chmn. 1987-89, chmn. 1989-91), Nat. Health Lawyers Assn. Home: 25 Winthrop St Hallowell ME 04347-1150 Office: PO Box 268 Hallowell ME 04347 also: 20th Flr 45 Rockefeller Plz N.Y. NY 10111

CRAWFORD, MAMIE RUTH, elementary school educator; b. Jackson, Ga., May 24, 1950; d. Henry and Mamie (Cash) C. BS, Ga. State U., 1973, MEd, 1977. Cert. tchr., Ga. Tchr. Henderson Elem. Sch., Jackson, Ga., 1973-88, Henderson Middle Sch., Jackson, 1988-95; mem. Ga. Tchr. Evaluation Steering Com., 1987-89, Ga. Tchr. Evaluation Adv. Com., 1989-95, Ga. Profl. Standards Commn., 1989-92; mem. adv. bd. Macon Telegraph/Knight Rider Newspaper in Edn. Program. Sec. Zion Bapt. Ch., Jackson, 1967-95. Named Butts County Tchr. of Yr., Butts County Sch. System, Jackson, Ga., 1988-89, Atlanta Jour.-Constitution Honor Tchr., 1989, Honor Tchr. Exchange Club of Jackson, Ga., 1993, Woman of Influence, Zion Bapt. Ch., Jackson, 1993; recipient spl. recognition Ga. Ho. of Reps., Atlanta, 1990. Mem. NEA, Ga. Assn. for Edn., Butts County Assn. Educators (pres. 1981, 86, Tchr. of Yr. 1988-89), Flint River Reading Coun. (sec. 1993-95), Ga. Coun. Internat.Reading Assn., Zeta Phi Beta (fin. sec., v.p. 1986-95). Office: Henderson Mid Sch 820 N Mulberry St Jackson GA 30233

CRAWFORD, MARCELLA, migrant bilingual resource educator; b. Durango, Colo., Sept. 25, 1958; d. Antonio José and Antonia Rosa (Montaño) Martinez; m. James DeForest Crawford, Oct. 17, 1980; stepchildren: Jessie, Rheanna; children: Jamie, Sean. BA, So. Oreg. State Coll., Ashland, 1990. Migrant bilingual resource tchr. Klamath Falls (Oreg.) City Schs., 1990—, Mills Elem., Ponderosa Jr. H.S., Klamath Falls, 1990-93, Fairview Elem. Sch., Klamath Falls, 1993-94, Fairview Elem., Mills Elem., Klamath Falls, 1994-95, Mills Elem. Sch., Klamath Falls, 1995—; mem. 2d Lang. Com., 1994—. Troop leader Girl Scouts U.S., Klamath Falls, Oreg., 1986-91; bilingual translator, 1996—. Home: 1903 Crest St Klamath Falls OR 97603-4700 Office: Mills Elem Sch 520 E Main Klamath Falls OR 97601

CRAWFORD, MARY ELLEN, secondary education educator; b. Bklyn., Mar. 16, 1940; d. Robert P. and Kathryn C. (Guzzi) Graciano; m. Wheeler C. Crawford; children: Robert, Kathryn, Susan, Michael. BS, Marymount Manhattan Coll., N.Y.C., 1961; MA, Georgetown U., Washington, 1963. Tchr. math. Jr. H.S. # 278, Bklyn., 1963-65; adj. instr. North harris Coll., Houston, 1989—. Block capt. Ponderosa Forest Civic Assn., Houston. Mem. Madame Alexander Doll Club, Alpha Chi. Roman Catholic. Home: 17903 Canyon Creek Houston TX 77090

CRAWFORD, MARY LOUISE PERRI, naval officer; b. Grand Haven, Mich., Nov. 26, 1949; d. Louis and Helen Marie (Buckley) Perri; m. Keith Eugene Crawford, Feb. 23, 1974 (dec. Oct. 1986); children: Matthew Perri, Michael Kirk. AA, Muskegon County C.C., 1969; BA, U. Mich., 1971. Commd. ensign U.S. Navy, 1972, advanced through grades to capt., 1993; pub. affairs officer Naval Air Sta., Key West, Fla., 1974-77, adminstrv., personnel officer Naval Air Res. Detachment, Patuxent River, Md., 1977-78, adminstrn. br. head Strike Aircraft Test Directorate, Naval Air Test Ctr., Patuxent River, 1978-80, ops. watch officer Command Ctr., Comdr.-in-Chief Naval Forces Europe Staff, London, 1980-84, officer-in-charge Personnel Support Activity Detachment, Patuxent River, 1984-86; engring. officer Chief Test and Evaluation Div., Strategic C3 Systems Directorate, Ctr. for Command, Control, and Communications, Def. Communications Agy., Washington, 1986-89; mgr. ultra high frequency Joint Satellite Communications Ctr., Joints Chiefs Staff, Pentagon, Washington, 1989-91; comdr. N.Y. Mil. Entrance Processing Sta., 1991-94; dir. personal, family & cmy support divsn. Bur. Navy Pers., Washington, 1994-95; head surveillance & navigations programs Office of Chief Naval Ops., Washington, 1996—. Mem. AAUW, Armed Forces Comm. & Electronics Assn., Women's Overseas Svc. League, U. Mich. Alumni Assn. Roman Catholic. Avocations: painting, ballet. Office: Office of CNO-N633 2000 Navy Pentagon Washington DC 20350-2000

CRAWFORD, MURIEL LAURA, lawyer, author, educator; d. Mason Leland and Pauline Marie (DesIlets) Henderson; m. Barrett Matson Crawford, May 10, 1959; children: Laura Joanne, Janet Muriel, Barbara Elizabeth. Student, U. Calif., Berkeley, 1958-60, 67-69; B.A. with honors, U. Ill., 1973; J.D. with honors, Ill. Inst. Tech., 1977; cert. employee benefit specialist U. Pa., 1989. Bar: Ill. 1977, Calif. 1991, U.S. Dist. Ct. (no. dist.) Ill. 1977, U.S. Dist. Ct. (no. dist.) Calif. 1991, U.S. Ct. Appeals (7th cir.) 1977, U.S. Ct. Appeals (9th cir.) 1991; CLU; chartered fin. cons. Atty., Washington Nat. Ins. Co., Evanston, Ill., 1977-80, sr. atty., 1980-81, asst. counsel, 1982-83, asst. gen. counsel, 1984-87, assoc. gen. counsel, sec., 1987-89, cons. employee benefit specialist, 1989-91; assoc. Hancock, Rothert & Bunshoft, San Francisco, 1991-92. Author: (with Beadles) Law and the Life Insurance Contract, 1989, (sole author) 7th edit. 1994; co-author Legal Aspects of AIDS, 1990; contbr. articles to profl. jours. Recipient Am. Jurisprudence award Lawyer's Coop. Pub. Co., 1975, 2nd prize Internat. LeTourneau Student Med.-Legal Article contest, 1976, Bar and Gavel Soc. award Ill. Inst. Tech./Chgo.-Kent Student Bar Assn., 1977. Fellow Life Mgmt. Inst.; mem. Ill. Inst. Tech./Chgo.-Kent Alumni Assn. (bd. dir. 1983-89). Democrat. Congregationalist.

CRAWFORD, PATRICIA ALEXIS, healthcare and wildlife advocate, writer; b. N.Y.C., July 17, 1952; d. Alexander James and Dorothy Patricia (Mudzinski) C. BA in Polit. Sci., East Carolina U., 1974. With Naval Air Rework Facility, Dept. Navy, Norfolk, Va., 1973; news prodn. editor, fin. writer Media Gen. Fin. Weekly, Richmond, Va., 1974-75; editor, med. writer United Feature Syndicate, N.Y.C., 1975-79; asst. mng. editor United Feature Syndicate, Newspaper Enterprise Assn. and Ind. News Alliance, N.Y.C., 1979-86; bd. mem. Integrity/N.Y., 1996—. Recipient Spl. Achievement award Dept. of Navy, 1973. Mem. AAUW, APHA, Soc. Profl. Journalists, Civitas, Episcopal Pub. Policy Network, Cath. Fellowship of Episcopal Ch., Integrity/N.Y. (bd. dirs., comms. dir.), Empire State Pride Agenda-Human Rights Campaign, Anglican Soc., N.Y. Zool. Soc., Elephant Rsch. Found., Am. Mus. Natural History, Am. Scottish Found., African Wildlife Found., Nat. Assn. Investors, Disabled in Action, World Wildlife Fund, Born Free Found./Elephant Protection Group, Internat. Women's Writing Guild. Episcopalian. Home: 514 E 88th St Apt 4A New York NY 10128-7797

CRAWFORD, PEGGY SMITH, design educator; b. Christiansburg, Va., Dec. 27, 1943; d. Andrew Morgan Smith and Margie Smith (Hill) Blakeslee; m. John Linnie Crawford, Jan. 12, 1963 (div. May 1979); children: John Christopher, James Andrew. Sec. Draper's Meadow EGA, Blacksburg, Va., 1983-85; 2nd v.p. Draper's Meadow EGA, Blacksburg, 1989-90; com. mem. Smithfield Needlework Exhibit, Blacksburg, 1986-87, com. chairperson, 1987-88; pres. Blue Ridge Embroiderer's Guild, Roanoke, Va., 1989-90; regional rep. Brazilian Dimensional Embroidery Internat. Guild, Washington, 1991—, sec., 1996—; tchr. Nat. Embroiderer's Guild Am., Inc. seminar, Greensboro, N.C., 1991, Reynolds Homestead, Critz, Va., 1993, Nat. Embroiderer's Guild Nat. Seminar, Williamsburg, Va., 1994, Brazilian Dimensional Embroidery Internat. Guild, Inc. seminars, 1994-96. Author: Stitching the Wildflowers of Virginia., 1992. Mem. Am. Needlepoint Guild, Blue Ridge Embroiderer's Guild, Drapers' Meadow Embroiderer's Guild Am., Inc., Brazilian Dimensional Embroidery Internat. Guild. Home: 206 Upland Rd SE Blacksburg VA 24060 Office: Va Polytech and State U 1700 Pratt Dr Blacksburg VA 24060

CRAWFORD, ROBERTA, association administrator; b. Richmond, Ind.; d. Melvin Lee and Vida Ellen (Halstead) Smith; m. Melvin Barfield, Dec. 3, 1940 (div.); 1 child, Stephen; m. Charles Britt, Feb. 2, 1949 (div.); 1 child, Alan; m. Vernon Crawford, Aug. 29, 1970 (dec.). Radio engr. WLBC, Muncie, Ind., 1942; announcer, engr. WMAN, Mansfield, Ohio, 1943; dispatcher WPDH, Richmond, 1944; continuity dir. WPTW, Piqua, Ohio, 1945, WCAV, Norfolk, Va., 1947; writer, announcer WKBV, Richmond, 1950; continuity dir., announcer WSAL, Logansport, Ind., 1951; continuity dir. WAVE-TV, Louisville, Ky., 1953; sales-svc. mgr. WPTV, Palm Beach, Fla., 1954; copywriter WQXT, Palm Beach, 1962; city desk asst. Palm Beach Times, West Palm Beach, 1971; women's editor The Stuart (Fla.) News, 1973-77; founder, pres. Iron Overload Diseases, North Palm Beach, Fla., 1980—. Author: The Iron Elephant, 1995, "tick... tick ... tick...", 1995. Office: Iron Overload Diseases 433 Westwind Dr North Palm Beach FL 33408

CRAWFORD, SALLY SUE, nursing educator; b. LaGrange, Ga., Nov. 17, 1944; children from previous marriage: Patricia Anne, Elizabeth Sue, James Burton Jr. AA, DeKalb Coll. Nursing, 1973; BA, Ga. State U., Atlanta, 1971, MEd, 1978; EDS, U. Ga., 1987; BSN, Clayton State Coll., 1994. RN. Sr. health educator Ga. Dept. Human Resources, Lawrenceville, 1975-88; asst. dir. staff devel. ARC, Atlanta, 1988; with Atlanta Eye Screening, 1988-89; outreach coord. Cataract Inst., Atlanta, 1989-90; tng. coord. S.E. Regional Ctr. For Drug-Free Schs. & Communities, 1990; tng. planner Atlanta Community Prevention Coalition, 1991-92; sole propr. Health Lifestyles, 1992-95; nursing instr. Griffin Tech. Sch., 1992-93; sr. nurse Clayton Ctr., Jonesboro, Ga., 1993-95; adminstrv. supr. Peachtree Regional Hosp., 1994—; clin. nursing instr. Gordon Coll. Nursing Students, 1995—; supr. Healthways, Morrow, Ga., 1995; health svcs. adminstr. Correctional Healthcare Solutions, 1996—; chmn. bd. dirs. Canine Vision, Inc. Author: 6 manuals; contbr. articles to profl. jours. Mem. NAFE, ASTD, AAPHERD, UDC (state chmn. 1988-90, nat. chmn. of pages 1989), Ga. Fedn. Profl. Health Educators, Internat. Platform Assn., Daus. of 1812 (local officer 1989—, state officer 1992-94), Continental Soc., Daus. of Indian Wars (nat. officer, state officer 1990-94), DAR (organizing regent chpt. 1982-84, nat. spkrs. staff 1986-89), Daus. Am. Colonists (chpt. regent 1988-91, state officer 1991—), Colonial Dames of XVII Century (local registrar), Ga. Soc. Magna Charta Dames (state officer 1986—), First Families of Ga., Lions (1st female mem. Atlanta club, chmn. sight and vision 1989-90, officer 1990-91), Sigma Theta Tau. Episcopalian. Home: 2305 Luther Bailey Rd Senoia GA 30276-9218 Office: Griffin RYDC 105 Justice Blvd Griffin GA 30223

CRAWFORD, SANDRA KAY, lawyer; b. Henderson, Tex., Sept 23, 1934; d. Obie Lee and Zilpha Elizabeth (Ash) Stalcup; m. William Walsh Crawford, Dec. 21, 1968; children: Bill, Jonathan, Constance, Amelia, Patrick. BA, Wellesley Coll., 1957; LLB, U. Tex., 1960. Bar: Tex. 1960, U.S. Supreme Ct. 1965, Colo. 1967, Ill. 1974. Asst. v.p.-legal Hamilton Mgmt. Corp., Denver, 1966-68; v.p., gen. counsel, sec. Transamerica Fund Mgmt. Corp., L.A., 1968; cons. to law dept. Met. Life Ins. Co., N.Y.C., 1969-71; counsel Touche Ross & Co., Chgo., 1972-75; v.p., assoc. gen. counsel Continental Ill. Bank, Chgo., 1975-83; sr. div. counsel Motorola, Inc., Schaumburg, Ill., 1984; sr. counsel, asst. sec. Sears Roebuck & Co., 1985-90, cons., 1990—. Mem. ABA, Ill. State Bar Assn., Colo. Bar Assn., Tex. Bar Assn., Everglades Club, Beach Club (Palm Beach), River Club (N.Y.C.). Home: 100 Royal Palm Way Apt G5 Palm Beach FL 33480-4270

CRAWFORD, SARAH CARTER (SALLY CRAWFORD), broadcast executive; b. Glen Ridge, N.J., Oct. 3, 1938; d. Raymond Hitchings and Katherine Latta (Gribbel) Carter; m. Joseph Paul Crawford III, Sept. 10, 1960 (dec. 1966). BA, Smith Coll., 1960. Media dir. Kampmann & Bright, Phila., 1961-64; sr. media buyer Foote, Cone & Belding, N.Y.C., 1964-69; assoc. media dir. Grey Advt., Los Angeles, 1969-75; account exec., research dir. Sta. KHJ-TV, Los Angeles, 1975-76; mgr. local sales Sta. KCOP-TV, Los Angeles, 1977-82; gen. sales mgr. Sta. KTVF-TV, Fairbanks, Alaska, 1982—; bd. dirs. Vista Travel, Fairbanks; mem. adv. com. Golden Valley Electric Corp., Fairbanks, 1984-86; mem. coun. UAF Tanana County Campus, 1989-96, chair mktg. com. Chmn. Fairbanks Health and Social Svc. Commn., 1986-96; vice chmn. Fairbanks North Star Borough Health and Social Svc. Commn., 1993-96; pres. Fairbanks Meml. Hosp. Aux., 1988-90, creator trust fund, chmn. fin. com., 1990—; bd. dirs. Fairbanks Downtown Assn., 1984-87; mem. FBKS Health Ctr. Coalition; mem. search com. UAF Tanana Valley Campus dir.; bd. dirs. Interior Regional Health Corp.; mem. Tesoro (Alaska) Citizens Adv. Coun. Mem. Fairbanks Women's Softball Assn., Fairbanks Women's Hockey Assn.. Episcopalian. Home: 4171 E 20th D19 Anchorage AK 99508 Office: KTVF/KTVA 501 International Airport Anchorage AK 99518

CRAWFORD, SUSAN, library director, educator; b. Vancouver, B.C., Can.; d. James Y. and S. Young; m. James Weldon Crawford, July 5, 1955; 1 son, Robert James. B.A., U. B.C., 1948; M.A., U. Toronto, 1950, U. Chgo., 1954; Ph.D., U. Chgo., 1970. With bur. library and indexing service ADA, 1954-56; with office exec. v.p. AMA, Chgo., 1956-60; dir. div. library and archival services AMA, 1960-81; asso. prof. Sch. Library Sci., Columbia U., N.Y.C., 1972-75; prof., dir. Sch. Medicine Library and Biomed. Communications Ctr. Washington U., 1981-92; adj. prof. U. Ill., Chgo., 1994—. Author over 160 books and sci. papers; mem. editl. bd. Med. Socioecon. Rsch. Sources, Index to Sci. Revs., Jour. Am. Soc. Info. Sci., Med. Libr. Assn. News, Health Librs. Rev. (London), Health and Info. Librs. (Budapest); assoc. editor Jour. Am. Soc. Info. Sci., 1979-82; editor Med. Info. Systems, 1988-90; editor-in-chief Bull. of Med. Libr. Assn., 1982-88, 91-92. Bd. regents Nat. Library Medicine, NIH, 1971-75; mem. bd. overseers for univ. libraries Tufts U., 1988-89. Janet Doe hon. lectr., 1983; recipient Disting. Alumni award U. Toronto, 1987, Grad. medal U. Toronto, 1989. Fellow AAAS, Med. Libr. Assn. (life, Eliot award 1976, chmn. com. on surveys and stats. 1966-75, publs. panel 1977-80, chmn. consulting editors panel 1981-88, 91-92, spl. award to editor of bull. 1988, Noyes award 1992, pres.'s award 1992); mem. ALA, Soc. Social Studies of Sci., Assn., Acad. Health Scis. Libr. Dirs., Am. Soc. Info. Sci. (chmn. med. info. sys. 1987-88, outstanding specialty group award 1988, 89, bd. and program chair Chgo. chpt. 1984-95), Am. Med. Informatics Assn., Acad. Health Info. Profls. (disting. mem.), Sigma Xi (chmn. coms.).. Home: 2418 Lincoln St Evanston IL 60201-2151

CRAWFORD, SUSAN JEAN, federal judge, lawyer; b. Pitts., Apr. 22, 1947; d. William Elmer Jr. and Joan Ruth (Bielau) C.; m. Roger W. Higgins; 1 child, Kelley S. BA, Bucknell U., 1969; JD, New Eng. Sch. Law, 1977. Bar: Md. 1977, D.C. 1980, U.S. Ct. Appeals for Armed Forces 1985, U.S. Supreme Ct. 1993. Tchr. history, coach Radnor (Pa.) H.S., 1969-74; assoc. Burnett & Eiswert, Oakland, Md., 1977-79; ptnr. Burnett, Eiswert and Crawford, Oakland, 1979-81; prin. dep. gen. counsel U.S. Dept. Army, Washington, 1981-83, gen. counsel, 1983-89; insp. gen. U.S. Dept. Def., Arlington, Va., 1989-91; judge U.S. Ct. Appeals for the Armed Forces, Washington, 1991—; asst. states atty. Garrett County, Md., 1978-79; instr. Garrett County C.C., 1979-81. Del. Md. Forestry Adv. Commn., Garrett County, 1978-81, Md. Commn. for Women, Garrett County, 1980-83; chair Rep. State Cen. Com., Garrett County, 1978-81; trustee Bucknell U., 1988—, New England Sch. Law, 1989—. Mem. FBA, Md. Bar Assn., D.C. Bar Assn., Edward Bennett Williams Am. Inn of Ct. Presbyterian. Office: US Ct Appeals Armed Forces 450 E St NW Washington DC 20442-0001

CRAWFORD, VALERIE M., municipal official; b. Swedesboro, N.J., Nov. 7, 1947; d. William Chaplin and Edith Mae (White) Bragdon; m. Joseph Charles Crawford, Nov. 21, 1970 (div. Jan. 1977); 1 child, Michelle Diana Crawford Flicker. Registered pub. purchasing specialist. Adminstrn. sec. Glassboro (N.J.) State Coll., 1966-73; adminstrn. sec. City of Ocean City, N.J., 1980-86, purchasing asst., 1986—. Active breast cancer unit task force Am. Cancer Soc., Cape May County, N.J., 1995, 96; coord. Reach to Recovery, Cape May County, 1995-96; vestry mem., publicity chairperson Holy Trinity Episcopal Ch., Ocean City, 1996. Mem. Nat. Inst. Govtl. Purchasing. Office: 9th St & Asbury Ave Ocean City NJ 08226

CRAWFORD, VIRGINIA ANN, columnist; b. Amarillo, Tex., Jan. 23, 1939; d. William Wiley and Gladys Love (Roberts) Hibbetts; m. Henry A. Crawford, Aug. 7, 1958; children: Terrie Leigh, Cheryl Ann, Wendy Lynn, Mark Allen. Bus. sch. cert., U. Houston, 1959; student, Austin C.C., 1986-87. Co-owner, mgr. Crawford Sewing Ctr., Lubbock, Tex., 1966-72; co-owner, designer Charter House Interiors, Lake Jackson, Tex., 1976-86; corr., columnist Brazosport Facts, Clute, Tex., 1993—; corr. columnist Lake Charles (La.) Am. Press, The Brazorian, Lake Jackson, Tex. Vol., coord. Sick Baby Clinic 2nd Bapt. Ch., Lubbock, 1966-72; vol., pres. Brazosport Meml. Hosp. Aux., Freeport, Tex., 1972-77; chair dist. meeting Statewide Aux. and Adminstr., Lake Jackson, 1975. Recipient Cert. Appreciation Youth Choir, 2nd Bapt. Bd., Lubbock, 1968, Spl. Appreciation award 2nd Bapt. Clinic Bd., Lubbock, 1969, 2000 Hour Award pin Brazosport Hosp. Aux. Bd., Freeport, 1977. Home: 229 Wayne Dr Clute TX 77531 Office: Solutions Press PO Box 334 Clute TX 77531

CREADICK, ANNA GREENWOOD, English educator, researcher; b. Burlington, N.C., June 21, 1967; d. Robert Nowell Creadick and Susie (Boswell) Creadick Winters. BS in English Edn. summa cum laude, Appalachian State U., 1991; MA in Am. Studies, Boston Coll., 1994; postgrad., U. Mass., 1994—. Cert. tchr. secondary edn., N.C. Editl. asst. Appalachian Jour., Boone, N.C., 1990-92, assoc. editor, 1994-95; teaching fellow English Boston Coll., 1993-94; lectr. English Appalachian State U., Boone, 1994-95; teaching assoc. English U. Mass., Amherst, 1995—. Contbr. articles to profl. jours. Activist/lobbyist Watauga County Dem. Party, Boone, 1994; vol. tutor Watauga County Literacy Coun., Boone, 1991. Boston Coll. scholar, 1992-94, Jeni Gray Meml. scholar, 1991. Mem. NOW, Am. Studies Assn., Appalachian Studies Assn. Home: 16 Winter St North Brookfield MA 01535

CREAGER, REBECCA LYNN, middle school educator; b. Houston, Oct. 28, 1968; d. Edward Byers and Sandra Kay (Bridwell) C. BS in Edn., Baylor U., 1991, MS in Ednl. Psychology, 1992. Tchr. 5th grade Coppell (Tex.) Ind. Sch. Dist., 1992-93, tchr. 5th grade Austin Elem. Sch., 1993-94, tchr. 7th grade pre-algebra tchr. Coppell Middle Sch. East, 1994—; campus math. content area specialist Coppell Ind. Sch. Dist., 1992-94; tchr. rep. Tchr. Exch. Program. Mem. NEA, Assn. Coppell Educators, Nat. Coun. Tchrs. Math., Math. Assn. Am., Baylor Alumni Assn., Kappa Kappa Iota, Chi Omega Night Owls. Baptist. Home: 5937 Lodestone Dr Plano TX 75093-4653 Office: Coppell Mid Sch East 400 Mockingbird Ln Coppell TX 75019-4144

CREAMER, SHANNON JOAN, graphic design company executive; b. Weisbaden, Germany, Mar. 22, 1969; (parents Am. citizens); d. Peter W. and Joette (Haley) C.; m. Brad P. Pennock; 1 child, Asia Marcellus. Student, Moore Coll. Art and Design, Phila., 1988-89, Temple U., 1989-93. Claims svc. rep. Prudential Ins. Co., Ft. Washington, Pa., 1987-89, graphic designer, 1990-93; pres., creative dir. Odd Graphic Co., Phila., 1994—. Office: Odd Graphic Co 136 N Bread St Ste 103 Philadelphia PA 19106

CREAR, MILDRED CLEAREATHA, nursing administrator; b. Lorman, Miss., June 8, 1939; d. Luther James and Julia (Gordan) Green; m. Jeff Archie Crear, June 16, 1962; 1 child, Julia Ann. BS in Nursing, U. Calif., San Francisco, 1962; MA in Edn., San Francisco State U., 1970; MPH in Adminstrn., U. Calif., Berkeley, 1978. Cert. pub. health nurse, Calif. Psychol. nurse Langle Porter, San Francisco, 1962-63; pub. health nurse San Francisco Health Dept., 1963-71, pub. health nursing supr., 1971-82, dep. dir. children's med. svcs., 1982-94, maternal, children, adolescent health dir., 1994—. Co-prodr. (video) Parenting-African American Perspective, 1996. Chmn. Maternal, Child Health adv. bd., 1992-94, mem., 1982—; bd. dirs. Support for Parents, San Francisco, 1992—, Bridge (residential drug rehab.), Berkeley, 1980—. Recipient Svc. certification Mayor San Francisco, 1990; grantee Bay Area March Dimes, 1995. Mem. APHA, ANA, Nat. Black Nurses Assn., Bay Area Black Nurses Assn (pres. 1978-82, chair nursing and cmty. edn. com. 1984—). Democrat. Baptist. Home: 5845 Mendocino Ave Oakland CA 94618 Office: San Francisco Health Dept-MCAH 680 8th St Ste 200 San Francisco CA 94103

CREASMAN, VIRENA WELBORN (RENE CREASMAN), retired elementary and secondary school educator, genealogist, researcher; b. Lebanon, Nebr., Feb. 10, 1909; d. Lawrence Morgan and Auretta Iva (Daffer) Welborn; m. Sam Doran Creasman, May 8, 1929 (dec. Jan. 1982); children: Gary W., Lee-Ellen Creasman Matzke. AA, McCook Jr. Coll., 1928; B in Edn., U. Nebr., 1962; postgrad., Kearney State Coll., 1967, Creighton U., 1968. Cert. elem., secondary tchr. Tchr. Rural Sch. grades 1-8, Red Willow County, Nebr., 1928-29; elem. tchr. McCook (Nebr.) City Schs., 1949-67, tchr. jr. high reading, English, 1968-76; tchr. genealogy, rschr. McCook Coll. and Southwest Nebr. Genealogy Soc., 1976—; rschr. state and local genealogy confs., 1976—. Vol., mem. Nebr. Hist. Soc. and Mus., High Plains Hist. Soc. and Mus., 1980—. Recipient Plaque of Appreciation from High Plains Hist. Soc. and Mus., 1990, Cert. of Appreciation from Nebr. State Hist. Soc. and Mus., 1989, Genealogist of Yr. cert. Southwest Nebr. Genealogy Soc., 1984, Appreciation of Svc. award as thrift shop coord. Congl. Ch., 1984-90. Mem. AAUW (chpt. leader 1962—), DAR (chpt. regent and registrar 1976—), NOW, LWV, UN Assn. U.S.A., Sierra Club, Arbor Day Found., Humane Soc., Assn. Retired Tchrs. (local pres. 1976—, nat., state), Delta Kappa Gamma (publicity com.), Eastern Star, Daus. of the Nile, Shriners Auxilliary, Genealogy Socs. (nat., local, state, libr. local chpt.). Democrat. Home: 8 Parkview Dr Mc Cook NE 69001-2248

CREECH, KAREN, accountant; b. Elizabeth, N.J., Sept. 19, 1965; d. James Louis Sullivan and Diane (Batnia) Mulvey; m. James Stephen Prusarczyk, June 17, 1989 (div. Aug. 1995); 1 child, Jill Sara; m. Curtis Willard Creech, Nov. 25, 1995. BS, Montclair State Coll., 1987. CPA, cert. mgmt. acct., N.J. Staff auditor Coopers & Lybrand, Princeton, N.J., 1987-89; sr. acct. Personal Products Co. divsn. Johnson & Johnson Corp., Milltown, N.J., 1989-95; sr. acctg. supr. Johnson & Johnson Corp., New Brunswick, N.J., 1995, mgr. hdqrs. acctg., 1995—. Vol. for Vol. Income Tax Assistance, N.J., 1996. Mem. Inst. Mgmt. Accts. Office: Johnson & Johnson 1 J&J Plz WH # 6314 New Brunswick NJ 08933

CREECH, SHARON, children's author. BA, Hiram Coll.; MA, George Mason U. Editl. asst., indexer Congl. Quarterly, Washington; rschr. Libr. Congress. Author: The Recital, Nickel Malley, Walk Two Moons, 1994 (John Newbery medal 1995), Absolutely Normal Chaos, 1995, Pleasing The Ghost, 1996. Office: care HarperCollins Children's Bks 10 E 53rd St New York NY 10022-5244*

CREEDON, MARY ALICE, insurance company executive; b. Niagara Falls, N.Y., Apr. 1, 1950; d. Daniel Francis and Anne Walle (Moynihan) C. BA, Coll. New Rochelle, 1972. Dir. divns. ins. Fed. Savs. and Loan Ins. Corp., Washington, 1984-86, dep. exec. dir., 1987-88, exec. dir., 1989; assoc. dir. FDIC, Washington, 1989-91; COO Farm Credit System Ins. Co., McLean, Va., 1991—. Mem. Women in Housing and Fin. Home: 4315 31st St N Arlington VA 22207-4115 Office: Farm Credit System Ins Corp 1501 Farm Credit Dr Mc Lean VA 22102-5004

CREEK, KRISTIN ANN, special education educator; b. Topeka, Kans., Jan. 13, 1955; d. Edwin C. and E. Maxine (Nelson) Henry; m. Douglas E. Creek, Feb. 23, 1994; children: Dustin Grimm, Chris Creek, Brandon Grimm, Kristina Creek. AA, Hutchinson (Kans.) C.C., 1986; BS, McPherson (Kans.) Coll., 1989; MEd, Wichita State U., 1992. Cert. tchr. elem., gifted. Math/parenting tchr. Flint Hills Job Corps Ctr., Manhattan, Kans., 1992; gifted facilitator Unified Sch. Dist. 353, Wellington, Kans., 1993-95, Unified Sch. Dist. 260, Derby, Kans., 1995—; head injury counselor, life skills trainer Three Rivers Ind. Living Ctr., Wamego, Kans., 1992. Epiphany Festival prodr. Trinity Luth. Ch., McPherson, 1991, 93; CASA organizer McPherson Coll., 1988-89; vol. Coun. on Violence Against Persons, McPherson, 1990-92. Mem. ASCD, Kans. Gifted, Talented, Creative Assn., Derby Educator Assn., NEA, Kans. Edn. Assn. Office: Derby Middle Sch 801 E Madison Derby KS 67037

CREENAN, KATHERINE HERAS, lawyer; b. Elizabeth, N.J., Oct. 7, 1945; d. Victor Joseph and Katherine Regina (Lederer) Petervary; m. Edward James Creenan; 1 child, David Heras. BA, Newark State Coll., 1968; JD, Rutgers U., 1984. Bar: N.J. 1984, U.S. Dist. Ct. N.J. 1984. Various teaching positions including, Union and Stanhope, N.J., 1968-81; law clk. to presiding judge Superior Ct. of N.J. Appellate Div., Newark, 1984-85; assoc. Lowenstein, Sandler, Kohl, Fisher & Boylan, Roseland, N.J., 1985-88, Kirsten, Simon, Friedman, Allen, Cherin & Linken, Newark, 1988-89, Whitman & Ranson, Newark, 1989-93, Whitman Breed Abbott & Morgan, Newark, 1993—. Mem. ABA, N.J. State Bar Assn., Union County Bar Assn., Essex County Bar Assn. Office: Whitman Breed Abbott Morgan 1 Gateway Ctr Newark NJ 07102-5311

CREIGHTON, HARRIET BALDWIN, retired botany educator; b. Delavan, Ill., June 27, 1909; d. Cyrus Murray and Bertha (Baldwin) C. BA, Wellesley, 1929; PhD, Cornell U., 1933. Lab. asst. Cornell U., Ithaca, N.Y., 1929-33, instr. botany, 1933-34; instr. botany Conn. Coll., New London, 1934-39, asst. prof. botany, 1939-40; assoc. prof. botany Wellesley (Mass.) Coll., 1940-52, prof. botany, 1952-74, prof. emerita, 1974—; Fulbright lectr. in genetics U. Western Australia, Perth, 1952-53, U. Cuzco (Peru), 1959-60; genetics cons. NSF, Osmania U., Hyderabad, India, NSF, U. Allahabad (India). Contbr. articles to profl. jours. Fellow AAAS (v.p. sect. G 1964), Bot. Soc. Am. (pres. 1956), Phi Beta Kappa, Sigma Xi, Phi Kappa Phi.

CREIGHTON, JOANNE VANISH, academic administrator; b. Marinette, Wis., Feb. 21, 1942; d. William J. and Bernice Vanish; m. Thomas F. Creighton, Nov. 9, 1968; 1 child, William. BA with honors, U. Wis., 1964; MA, Harvard U., 1965; PhD, U. Mich., 1969. From instr. to prof. English Wayne State U., Detroit, 1968-85, assoc. dean liberal arts, 1983-85; dean arts and scis., prof. English U. N.C., Greensboro, 1985-90; v.p. acad. affairs, provost, prof. English Wesleyan U., Middletown, Conn., 1990—; now pres. Wesleyan U. Author: William Faulkner's Craft of Revision, 1977, Joyce Carol Oates, 1979, Margaret Drabble, 1985, Joyce Carol Oates: Novels of the Middle Years, 1992. Grantee Am. Coun. Learned Socs. Mem. Phi Beta Kappa, Phi Kappa Phi. Home: 164 Mt Vernon St Middletown CT 06457-3215 Office: Mount Holyoke Coll Office of the Pres South Hadley MA 01075-1414*

CRELL, ILENE ROBIN, marketing professional; b. White Plains, N.Y., Oct. 23, 1964; d. Jesse Donald and Barbara (Kleinman) C. BS, U. Md., 1986. Mgr. A & S, Whiteplains, 1986-88; fashion cons. Liz Claiborne Inc., N.Y.C, 1988-90, mgr. west coast, 1990-92, spl. events mgr., 1992-95, corp. mktg. mgr., 1995—. Democratic. Home: 100 Woodside Ave East White Plains NY 10604 Office: Liz Claiborne 1441 Broadway New York NY 10018

CRENSHAW, CORINNE BURROWES, kindergarten educator; b. Houston, Nov. 15, 1941; d. H. Clark and Corinne (Rue) Burrowes; m. James Leon Crenshaw Jr., June 2, 1963; children: Terri Lynn, James Alan. BS in Edn., Sam Houston State U., 1963; MEd, U. St. Thomas, Houston, 1991. Cert. tchr., Tex. 1st grade tchr. Lakeview Elem. Sch., Sugarland, Tex., 1963-64; kindergarten tchr. Calvery Episcopal Ch., Richmond, Tex., 1966-67, Holy Ghost Cath. Sch., Houston, 1978—. Co-author, prodr. sch. newsletter, 1984-87. Rep. Parish Coun., Holy Ghost Ch., Houston, 1981-84, 85-88; leader/co-leader Girl Scouts U.S., Houston, 1971-81, neighborhood jr. rep., 1982-84. Dyslexia awareness grantee Neuhaus Sch., 1990. Mem. Nat. Assn. for Edn. of Young Children, Tex. Assn. for Edn. of Young Children, Houston Area Assn. for Edn. of the Young Child (Educator of Young Children award 1993), Galveston-Houston Early Childhood Assn. (mem. evaluating achievment tests com. 1990-91, sec. 1992-95, kindergarten report card com. 1995, Galveston-Houston diocese accreditation com. 1992-93), Kindergarten Tchrs. of Tex., Kappa Delta Pi. Roman Catholic. Office: Holy Ghost Cath Sch 6920 Chimney Rock Rd Houston TX 77081-5614

CRENSHAW, DOROTHY W., public relations executive; b. Atlanta, July 29, 1955. BA in English and French, Wesleyan U., 1977. Copywriter, media specialist Simon & Schuster, N.Y.C., 1979-81; account exec. Dorf & Stanton Comm., N.Y.C., 1981-83, account supr., 1983-85, v.p., 1985-86, exec. v.p. and ptnr., 1988; sr. v.p. Edelman Pub. Rels. Worldwide, N.Y.C., 1988-93; exec. v.p. consumer mktg. GCI Group, N.Y.C., 1993—. Mem. Women Execs. in Pub. Rels., Women's Agenda. Office: GCI Group 777 3rd Ave New York NY 10017*

CRENSHAW, LORETTA ANN, elementary education educator; b. Youngstown, Ohio, Mar. 27, 1947; d. Thomas Lenzia and Ruth (Daniels) Hallman; m. Paul Leslie Crenshaw, June 17, 1972; 1 child, Paul Leslie II. BS in Edn., Youngstown State U., 1970. Cert. tchr. elem. edn. Tchr. Hubbard (Ohio) Exempted Village, 1970—; faculty adv. bd. mem. Roosevelt Elem. Sch., Hubbard, 1993-95. Mem. no. 2 Usher Bd. Triedstone Missionary Bapt. Ch., Youngstown, 1979—. Recipient Class Act award WFMJ-TV 21, 1991. Mem. NEA, Ohio Edn. Assn., Hubbard Edn. Assn. (exec. com. 1993-95). Home: 2730 Wardle Ave Youngstown OH 44505-4067

CRENSHAW, MARVA LOUISE, lawyer; b. DeFuniak Springs, Fla., Sept. 21, 1951; d. Lewis and Helen (Anderson) Crenshaw; m. Norman P. Campbell, Dec. 30, 1977; children: Kalinda I., Kamaria A. BS in Polit. Sci. with honors, Tuskegee Inst., Ala., 1973; JD, U. Fla., Gainesville, 1975. Bar: U.S. Dist. Ct. (mid. dist.) Fla., 1978, U.S. Ct. Appeals (11th cir.) 1978. Asst. state's atty. Dade County State's Atty. (Fla.), Miami, 1976-78; mng. atty. Bay Area Legal Services, Tampa, Fla., 1978-84, dep. dir., 1984-89; cons. tng. adv. com. Fla. Legal Service, Tallahassee, 1982-84; judge Hillsborough County Ct., 1989—. Vice pres. bd. dirs. Suicide and Crises Ctr., Tampa, 1983-84, pres., 1984-85, also mem. aux.; tutor Literacy Volunteers of Am. Mem. ABA, Hillsborough County Bar Assn. (chmn. county ct. civil rules com. 1984-85, mem. mock trial com. 1987-88, bulletin com. 1988-89, law week com. 1990, gender and ethnic bias implementation com. 1991—), Fla. Bar Assn., George Edgecomb Bar Assn., Nat. Inst. Trial Advocacy, Hillsborough Assn. for Women Lawyers (bd. dirs. 1991-92), William Glenn Terrell Inns of Ct. (pres. 1995-96), Fla. Bar Found. (mem. LAP com. 1991-92, bd. dirs. 1995—), Acad. Holy Names (mem. bd. trustees, 1995—), Delta Sigma Theta (legal advisor local chpt. 1988-89). Democrat. Baptist. Home: 14522 Wessex St Tampa FL 33625-6619

CRENSHAW, PATRICIA SHRYACK, sales executive, consultant; b. Kansas City, Mo., Oct. 7, 1941; d. George Randolf and Velma Irene (Carroll) Shryack; m. Paul Burton, Mar. 24, 1961 (div. 1971); m. Peter Frederick Schmidt, Jan. 21, 1989. Student, William Jewell Coll., 1959-60, S.W. Mo. State U., 1960-61; BEd, U. Mo., 1967; postgrad., Cen. Mo. State U., 1971-73. Cert. tchr. secondary edn. and history, Mo. Tchr. Lillis High Sch., Kansas City, 1967-69, Park Hill High Sch., Kansas City, 1969-73; terr. mgr. Hollister, Inc., Kansas City, 1973-75, field trainer, 1974-75; sales edn. mgr. Hollister, Inc., Chgo., 1975; dist. sales mgr. Detroit Mich., 1976-81; regional sales mgr. Chgo., 1981-84; dir. contract sales Chgo. Serta, Inc., 1984-86, nat. dir. contract sales div., 1987-89, v.p. nat. contract sales, 1989-90; area v.p. B G Industries, Northridge, Calif., 1990-91, v.p. sales, 1992-95, v.p. internat. sales, 1995—. Mem. women's com. Young Reps., Kansas City, 1962. Mem. NOW, NAFE, U.S. Golf Assn., Lake Barrington Shores (Ill.) Golf Club. Republican. Address: 101 E Ocean Dr Key Colony Beach FL 33051

CRENSHAW, TENA LULA, librarian; b. Coleman, Fla., Dec. 15, 1930; d. Herbert Joseph Crenshaw and Nellie (Wicker) Cox; BS, Fla. So. Coll., 1951; postgrad. U. Fla., 1952-55; MLS (Univ. scholar), U. Okla., 1960. Tchr. pub. schs., Coleman, Fla., 1952-55, St. Petersburg, Fla., 1955-57, Houston, 1957-59; tech. librarian Army Rocket & Guided Missile Agy., Redstone Arsenal, Huntsville, Ala., 1960-61; acquisitions librarian Martin Marietta Corp., Orlando, Fla., 1961-64; reader svcs. librarian John F. Kennedy Space Center, NASA, Fla., 1964-66; rsch. info. analyst, specialist, Lockheed Missiles and Space Co., Palo Alto, Calif., 1966-68; head svcs. to pub. A.W. Calhoun Med. Library, Emory U., Atlanta, 1969-78; dep. dir. Louis Calder Meml. Library, U. Miami (Fla.) Sch. Medicine, 1979-80; head edn. library U. Fla., Gainesville, 1980-84; librarian Westinghouse Electric Corp., Orlando, 1984-86; chief librarian tech info. ctr. U. Cen. Fla., Orlando, 1986-87, librarian contracts and grants, 1987-88; library cons. Coleman, Fla., 1988-89, sch. libr., 1989-90, libr. Kennedy Space Ctr., Fla., 1990-91, libr. Patrick Air Force Base, Fla., 1992-94; chmn. Fla. State adv. Council on Libraries. Mem. Spl. Libraries Assn. (treas. S. Atlantic chpt. 1970-72, chmn. membership com. 1973, v.p. 1973-74, pres. 1974-75, mem. resolutions com. 1975-76, nominating com. biol. scis. div. 1974-75, chmn. 1977-78), Med. Library Assn. (mem. conf. planning com. So. regional group 1973-74, membership com. 1977-79 by laws rev. com. 1979-80), Southeastern (mem. new directions com. 1972-74, chmn. spl. libraries sect. 1974), Ga. (careers in librarianship com. 1974-77), Fla. Library Assns., DAR, Alpha Delta Pi, Kappa Delta Pi. Democrat. Methodist. Home: PO Box 277 Coleman FL 33521-0277

CREQUE, LINDA ANN, non-profit educational and research executive, former education commissioner; b. N.Y.C.; arrived in V.I., 1967; d. Noel and Enid Louise (Schloss) DePass; m. Leonard J. Creque, July 29, 1967; children: Leah Michelle, Michael Gregory. BS, CUNY-Queens, 1963, MS, 1969; PhD, U. Ill., 1986. Tchr. 2d grade Bd. Edn., N.Y.C., 1963, tchr. demonstrations, team tchr., 1964-65, master tchr., 1965-66; elem. tchr. P.S. 69, Jackson Hgts., N.Y., 1963-67; tchr. English Cath. U., Ponce, P.R., 1967; cmty. exch. elem. tchr. grades K-6 Ponce, 1966-67; tchr. 4th grade Dept. Edn., V.I., 1967-69, tchr. remedial reading, master tchr., 1968-69; program coord. Project HeadStart, V.I., 1969-73, coord. Inst. Developmental Studies, 1970-71, acting dir., 1972-73; prin. Thomas Jefferson Annex Primary Sch., St. Thomas, V.I., 1973-80, Joseph Sibilly Elem. Sch., St. Thomas, 1980-87; commr. edn. Dept. Edn., St. Thomas, 1987-94; founder, pres. V.I. Inst. for Tchg. and Learning, St. Thomas, 1995—; cons. Edn. Devel. Ctr., Mass. Nat. SSI Project, 1992-93, Coll. V.I., 1978; mem. exec. com., bd. overseers Regional Lab. Ednl. Improvement NE and Islands, Andover, Mass.; bd. dirs. V.I. Pub. TV; mem. exec. bd. Leadership in Edn. Adminstrv. Devel., V.I., 1989—; presenter, keynote spkr. confs. in field. Contbr. articles to profl. jours. Trustee U. V.I., 1989—; mem. V.I. Residential Task Force for Human Svcs., 1989—, V.I. Labor Coun.; bd. dirs. Nat. Urban Alliance for Effective Edn. Tchrs. Coll. Columbia U., N.Y.C., 1993—, Cultural Inst. V.I., 1989-94; mem. cultural endowment bd., V.I., 1989-94; mem. governing bd. East End Health Ctr., 1979-80; mem. Gov.'s Conf. Librs., 1978. Grantee V.I. Coun. on Arts Ceramics for Primary Children, 1974-78, Comprehensive Employment and Tng. Act, 1977, NSF, 1989-93, Carnegie Found., 1988-90; recipient award NASA, award St. Thomas-St. John Counselors Assn., 1988, Ednl. Excellence award Harvard U. Prins. Ctr. and Ill. Edn. Svc. Ctr., 1975, Outstanding Leadership award FEMA, 1990, Disting. Svc. award Edn. Commn. of U.S., 1991, Outstanding Svc. award Coun. of Chief State Sch. Officers, 1995. Mem. LWV, St. Thomas Reading Coun., Nat. Assn. Tchrs. Math., Edn. Commn. of States (commr. 1987-93, steering com. 1988-92, internal audit com. 1988, policies priority com. 1991, exec. com. 1992, alt. steering com. 1991—), Coun. Chief of State Sch. Officers (chair extra jurisdictions com., bd. dirs., task force early childhood edn., ednl. equity com., restructuring edn. com.), Phi Kappa Phi, Kappa Delta Pi, Phi Delta Kappa. Office: VI Inst for Tchg and Learning PO Box 301954 Saint Thomas VI 00803

CRESS, CECILE COLLEEN, retired librarian; b. Colorado Springs, Colo., Feb. 26, 1914; d. John Leo and Elizabeth Veronica (Rouse) Haley; m. Arthur Henry Cress, May 8, 1937 (div. 1960); children: Ronnie Lou Kordick, Dan, Elaine. BA, Adams State Coll., 1936; MA in English, Colo. Coll., 1964; MLS, Denver U., 1970. 5th grade tchr. Westcliffe (Colo.) Elem., 1953-56; English tchr. Penrose (Colo.) High Sch., 1956-59; English-social studies tchr. Excelsior Jr. High, Sch. Dist. 70, Pueblo, Colo., 1959-64; libr. Pueblo County High, Sch. Dist. 70, Pueblo, 1964-80, Nat. Coll./Pueblo Br., 1980-91; cataloger in library Pueblo C.C., 1992—. Tutor adult literacy program South Cen. Bd. Coop. Svcs., 1991. Recipient Ace of Clubs award Am. Contract Bridge League, 1988, 89. Mem. AAUW, Pueblo Ret. Sch. Employees (v.p. 1990-92, pres. 1982-84, state bd. 1982-86, sec. 1995—), Colo. Libr. Assn., Unit 369 Am. Contract Bridge Assn., Irish Club Pueblo (pres. 1995—), Welsh Terrier Club Colo., Alpha Delta Kappa (Pueblo chpt., pres. 1976-78, state historian 1980-82, state bd. 1980-82, rec. sec. 1994—). Democrat. Roman Catholic. Home: 901 Jackson St Pueblo CO 81004-2425

CRESWELL, DOROTHY ANNE, computer consultant; b. Burlington, Iowa, Feb. 6, 1943; d. Robert Emerson and Agnes Imogene (Gardner) Mefford; m. John Lewis Creswell, Aug. 28, 1965. AA, Burlington C.C., 1963; BA in Math., U. Iowa, 1965; MS in Math., Western Ill. U., 1970; postgrad., Iowa State U., 1974—. Cert. netware engr., Novell Corp. Computer programmer Mason & Hanger, Silas Mason Co., Inc., Burlington, 1965-74; systems programmer Contractor's Hotline, Ft. Dodge, Iowa, 1974; dir. data processing Iowa Cen. C.C., Ft. Dodge, 1975-80; systems programming mgr. Norand Corp., Cedar Rapids, Iowa, 1980-82; spl. svcs. mgr. Pioneer Hi-Bred Internat., Inc., Cedar Rapids, 1982-87; owner, pres. D.C. Cons., Inc., Ankeny, Iowa, 1987—; computers-in-edn. del. to China, People to People Internat., Kansas City, Mo., 1987. Contbr. articles, papers to profl. publs. Mem. Data Processing Mgmt. Assn. (bd. dirs. 1986-87, v.p. 1988, 91-93, pres. 1993-94), Adminstrv. Mgmt. Soc. (sec. 1985-86, v.p. 1986-90, Merit award 1987), Assn. Computing Machinery, Hawkeye Pers. Computer Users, DEC Users Group (v.p. Ea. Iowa chpt. 1981-82), Ind. Computer Cons. Assn. (mem. editorial bd. 1989—, chpt. pres.-at-large 1993—), Systems Operator Computer Cons. Forum Computer Svc. Democrat. Methodist. Office: DC Cons Inc PO Box 195 Ankeny IA 50021-0195

CRESWICK, BETHANY KRISTIN, geriatrics, psychiatric nurse; b. Warwick, R.I., June 13, 1967; d. Paula Elaine (Clements) C. BSN, R.I. Coll., 1989. RN. Float nurse Eleanore Slater Hosp., Cranston, 1989—; mem. Eleanor Slater Hosp. QA & QI com. on Quality Drug Adminstrn., 1993-94, Eleanor Slater Hosp. Field Day Com., 1991—, vice chair 1992—. Epsicopalian.

CRETAN, DONNA, neonatal nurse; b. Mpls., May 18, 1939; d. Howard Robert and Frances E. (Warner) Bjerke; m. Nestor Nicholas Cretan, Jan. 24, 1959; children: Colette, John, Christopher, Bernadette. ADN, Contra Costa Coll., 1973; BSN, Sacred Heart U., Fairfield, Conn., 1986. RN, Conn. Nurse mgr., cons. St. Joseph Med. Ctr., Stamford, Conn., 1974-89; staff nurse Cmty. Hosp., Santa Rosa, Calif., 1989-93, Greenwich (Conn.) Hosp., 1993—. Host parent A Better Chance, New Canaan, Conn., 1982-84, Am. Field Svc., 1983-84, Calif., 1991-93, Cultural Homestay, Cohasset, Mass., 1991-95, People Link, Petaluma, Calif.; sec. Hist. Soc., Sebastopol, Calif., 1989-92; vol. nurse Americares Free Clinic Norwalk, 1994—. Mem. ANA, CCN, Assn. Women's Health, Obstetrics and Neonatal Nurses, Neonatal Network. Home: 126 Brushy Ridge Rd New Canaan CT 06840-4209 Office: Greenwich Hosp Perry Ridge Rd Greenwich CT 06840

CRIBBS, MAUREEN ANN, artist, educator; b. Marinette, Wis., Feb. 17, 1927; d. Roy Cecil Hubbard and Lillian Worner (Hubbard) Yeoman; m. James Milton Cribbs, Apr. 22, 1950; children: Cynthia, Valerie. BA, DePauw U., 1949; student, Sch. of Art Inst., Chgo., 1971-72, 79-81; MA, Govs. State U., 1973. Cert. secondary sch. tchr., Ill. Tchr. art Sch. Dist. 163, Park Forest, Ill., 1960-78; instr. humanities Sch. Dist. 227, Park Forest, 1978-79; artist, painter, printmaker Park Forest, 1979—; instr. painting Village Artists, Flossmoor, Ill., 1980-87; lectr. part-time Chgo. State U., 1980-81; adj. prof. Govs. State U., University Park, 1995; docent Nathan Manilow Sculpture Park, Govs. State U., 1996—; sec. Homewood-Flossmoor cmty. assocs. of woman's bd. Art Inst. Chgo., 1995-96, chair study group, 1989-95; artist-in-residence Ox Bow Sch. of Art. Exhbns. include Recent Work South Suburban Cmty. Coll., Thornton, Ill, 1983, Augsburg Coll., Mpls., 1988, Matrix Gallery Ltd., 1992, Personal Spaces, Matrix Gallery Ltd., 1992. Bd. dirs. Ill. Philaharm. Orch., Park Forest, 1981-83, Grace Migrant Day Care, Park Forest, 1981-85; adminstrv. chair Grace United Protestant Ch., Park Forest, 1984-94; lay mem. No.Ill. Ann. Conf. of United Meth. Ch., 1996, mem. commn. on christian unity and interreligious concerns, 1996. Monetary grantee to produce 15 works Freedom Hall, 1982; Artist-in-Residence Cmty. Arts Coun. Park Forest, 1983, Sch. of Art Inst. of Chgo., 1993. Mem. Mid-Am. Print Coun., Am. Print Alliance, Chgo. Artists Coalition. Methodist. Home: 74 Blackhawk Dr Park Forest IL 60466

CRIGER, NANCY S., professional society administrator; b. Ypsilanti, Mich., Apr. 16, 1951; d. Douglas D. and Edith (Nicoll) Smith; children: Amanda L. Denomme, William G. Denomme, Jr. Student, Mich. State U., 1969-71; BS in Elem. Edn., Wayne State U., 1973. Asst. v.p. Nat. Bank of Detroit, 1978-87; asst. v.p. Comerica Bank, Detroit, 1987-88, v.p. employee benefits, 1988-91; v.p. and mgr. trust adminstrn. and ops. Comerica Bank-Tex., Dallas, 1991-92; v.p. adminstrn., exec. v.p. Vis. Nurs Assn. Tex., 1992-94; pres. Continuum Healthcare Mgmt., Inc., Plano, Tex., 1994—. Asst. treas. Jr. League of Detroit, 1985-86, treas., 1986-87; treas. women's assn. Detroit Symphony Orch., 1987-89. Mem. Jr. League of Dallas, Rotary, The 500, Inc., Dallas Women's Found., Dallas Mus. of Art, DMA-PM Group, Dallas Hist. Soc., Dallas Symphony Assn., Dallas Arboretum, Dallas Zool. Soc., Dallas County Heritage Soc., Dallas Coun., Chi Omega. Home and Office: 2920 Haymeadow Ln Carrollton TX 75007

CRISMAN, MARY FRANCES BORDEN, librarian; b. Tacoma, Nov. 23, 1919; d. Lindon A. and Mary Cecelia (Donnelly) Borden; m. Fredric Lee Crisman, Apr. 12, 1975 (dec. Dec. 1975). BA in History, U. Wash., 1943, BA in Librarianship, 1944. Asst. br. librarian in charge work with children Mottet br. Tacoma Pub. Libr., 1944-45, br. librarian, 1945-49, br. librarian Moore br., 1950-55, asst. dir., 1955-70, dir., 1970-74, dir. emeritus, 1975—; mgr. corp. libr. Frank Russell Co., 1985—; chmn. Wash. Community Library Council, 1970-72. Hostess program Your Library and You, Sta. KTPS-TV, 1969-71. Mem. Highland Homeowners League, Tacoma, 1980—, incorporating dir. 1980, sec. and registered agt., 1980-82. Mem. ALA (chmn. mem. com. Wash. 1957-60, mem. nat. library week com. 1965, chmn. library adminstrn. div. nominating com. 1971, mem. ins. for libraries com. 1970-74, vice chmn. library adminstrn. div. personnel adminstrn. sect. 1972-73, chmn. 1973-74, mem. com. policy implementation 1973-74, mem. library orgn. and mgmt. sect. budgeting acctg. and costs com. 1974-75), Am. Library Trustee Assn. (legis. com. 1975-78, conf. program com. 1978-80 action devel. com. 1978-80), Pacific N.W. (trustee div. nominating com 1976-77), Wash. Library Assn. (exec. bd. 1957-59, state exec., dir. Nat. Library Week 1965, treas., exec. bd. 1969-71, 71-73), Urban Libraries Council (editorial sec. Newsletter 1972-73, exec. com. 1974-75), Ladies Aux. to United Transp. Union (past pres. Tacoma), Friends Tacoma Pub. Library (registered agt. 1975-83, sec. 1975-78, pres. 1978-80, bd. dirs. 1980-83), Smithsonian Assocs., Nat. Railway Hist. Soc., U. Wash. Alumni Assn., U. Wash. Sch. Librarianship Alumni Assn. Roman Catholic. Club: Quota Internat. (sec. 1957-58, 1st v.p. 1960-61, pres. 1961-62, treas. 1975-76, pres. 1979-80) (Tacoma). Home: 6501 N Burning Tree Ln Tacoma WA 98406-2108 Office: Frank Russell Co Russell Bldg 909 A St Tacoma WA 98402-5111

CRISMOND, LINDA FRY, public relations executive; b. Burbank, Calif., Mar. 1, 1943; d. Billy Chapin and Lois (Harding) Fry; m. Donald Burleigh Crismond, 1965 (dec.). B.S., U. Calif.-Santa Barbara, 1964; M.L.S., U. Calif.-Berkeley, 1965. Cert. county libr., Calif., assn. exec. Reference librarian, EDP coordinator San Francisco Pub. Library, 1965-72, head acquisition, 1972-74; asst. univ. librarian U. So. Calif., Los Angeles, 1974-80; chief dep. county librarian Los Angeles County Pub. Library, Los Angeles, 1980-81; county librarian Los Angeles County Pub. Library, Downey, 1981-89; exec. dir ALA, Chgo., 1989-92; v.p. public rels. Profl. Media Svc. Corp., Chgo., 1992—; Western rep. quality control council Ohio Coll. Library Ctr., Columbus, 1977-80; mem. Am. Nat. Standards Inst., N.Y.C., 1978-80; bd. councillors U. So. Calif. Sch. Library and Info. Mgmt., 1980-83; adv. bd. mem. UCLA Library Sch., 1981-89; chmn. bd. dirs. Los Angeles County Pub. Library Found., 1982-85; mem. OCLC Users Coun., 1988-89; mem. exec. com. L.A. County Mgmt. Coun., 1986-88, pres., 1988; cons. libr. Trinity Coll., 1995—; prin. The Charleston Group, Inc., 1996—. Author: Directory of San Francisco Bay Area, 1968, Against All Odds, 1994; editor: Urban Librs. Coun. Exch., 1994—, The Charleston Report, 1996—. Bd. dirs. So. Meth. U. Libr., 1992—. Named Staff Mem. of Year San Francisco Pub. Library, 1968. Mem. ALA , Calif. Library Assn. (council 1980-82), Calif. County Librarians Assn. (pres. 1984), L.A. County Mgmt. Assn. (pres. 1988). Home: 303 Mariner Dr Tarpon Springs FL 34689-6614 Office: Profl Media Svc Corp 19122 Vermont Ave Gardena CA 90248

CRISP, JENNIFER ANN CLAIR, neurosurgical nurse; b. Bangalore, India, Aug. 30, 1943; came to U.S., 1959; d. Arthur E. Cleland and Pamela M.N. Ottley Hemming; m. Fred R. Crisp; 1 child, Karyn. BSN, Greenville (Ill.) Coll., 1967. RN, Tex. Staff nurse Meth. Hosp., Ind. Sch. Nursing, Houston, 1978-80; asst. head nurse The Meth. Hosp., Houston, 1980-94, neurosurg. ICU nurse, 1994—. Home: Sea-lights PO Box 155 Gilchrist TX 77617 Office: Methodist Hosp 6565 Fannin St Houston TX 77030-2707

CRISP, LISA ANNE, banker; b. Bryson City, N.C., June 16, 1966; d. R.L. and Mary Elizabeth (Hobgood) C. BS in Fin., U. N.C., Greensboro, 1988. CFP. Consumer affairs specialist SEC, Washington, 1989; trust officer Wachovia Bank N.C., Winston-Salem, 1991-93, asst. v.p., 1993-95, v.p., 1995—. Bd. dirs. Sawtooth Ctr. for Visual Art, Winston-Salem, 1993-96; alumni trustee U. N.C., Greensboro, 1994.

CRISPELL, MARILYN B., jazz musician; b. Phila., Mar. 30, 1947; d. Milton Amber and Frances (Mall) Braune; m. Gareth Crispell, June 14, 1967 (div. 1972). BMus, New Eng. Conservatory, Boston, 1968. tchr. improvisation workshops; lectr. in field; performing artist New Eng. Found. Arts Touring Program, 1991-92. Pianist in collaboration with Anthony Braxton, 1978—, with his Quartet, 1983—, Creative Music Orch.; mem. Reggie Workman Ensemble, 1986—; featured performer N.Y.C. Opera in Anthony Davis's opera "X"; soloist London Jazz Composers Orch.; numerous appearances as soloist London Jazz Composers Orch.; recorder: (with Reggie Workman and Doug James) Gaia, 1987, (with others) Circles, 1991, (with Reggie Workman and Gerry Hemingway) Marilyn Crispell Trio, 1993, Stellar Pulsations/Three Composers, 1993, (with others) Santuerio, 1993, For Coltrane, 1993, Solo Concer '95/Mills College, Oakland, Calif., 1995, Contrasts, 1995, The Woodstock Concert, 1995; collaborator: (piano duo with Irene Schweizer) Overlapping Hands, 1991, (duo with Eddie Prevost) Band on the Wall, 1994, (with Fred Anderson and Hamid Drake) Destiny, 1994, (with Anders Jormin and Raymond Strid) Spring Tour, 1995, (with Barry Guy and Gerry Hemingway) Cascades, 1995, (with Peter Brotzmann and Hamid Drake) Hyperion, 1995, (duo with Tim Berne) Inference, 1995, (duo with Francois Houle) Any Terrain Tumultuous, 1995, (Greetje Bijma Trio with Marilyn Crispell and Mark Dresser) Barefoot, 1993. N.Y. Found. for the Arts fellow, 1988-89, 94-95; recipient Mary Flagler Cary Charitable Trust composition commn., 1988-89.

CRISPI, MICHELE MARIE, lawyer; b. Neptune, N.J., Mar. 10, 1962; d. Michael and Mary (Vaccaro) C.; m. Lawrence J. Moloney. BS in Accountancy magna cum laude, Villanova U., 1984, JD, 1987, LLM in Taxation, 1989. Bar: N.J. 1988, U.S. Dist. Ct. N.J. 1988, D.C. 1989, U.S. Tax Ct. 1989. Assoc. Lampf, Lipkind, Prupis & Petigrow, West Orange, N.J., 1987-88, Lautman, Henderson & Wight, Manasquan, N.J., 1990—. Mem. ABA (bus. law, real property, probate and trust law, taxation sects.), N.J. State Bar Assn. (corp. and bus. law, real property, probate and trust law, elder law and taxation sects.), D.C. Bar Assn. (taxation sect.), Monmouth County Bar Assn., Phi Kappa Phi, Beta Gamma Sigma, Gamma Phi. Republican. Roman Catholic. Home: 32 Hunters Pointe Rd Middletown NJ 07748-5148 Office: Lautman Henderson & Wight 52 Abe Voorhees Dr Manasquan NJ 08736-3545

CRISPIN, MILDRED SWIFT (MRS. FREDERICK EATON CRISPIN), civic worker, author; b. Branson, Mo.; d. Albert Duane and Anna (Harlan) Swift; m. Herbert William Kochs, Dec. 1, 1928 (div. Mar. 1955); children: Susan Kochs Judevine (dec.), Herbert William Jr., Judith Ann (Mrs. Nelson Shaw); m. George Walter King Snyder, Oct. 6, 1962 (dec. 1969); m. Frederick Eaton Crispin, May 20, 1972. Student, Galloway Woman's Coll., 1922-24. Bd. dirs. Travelers Aid Soc., Chgo., 1936-68, nat. dir., 1948-71; founding mem. U.S.O., Chgo., 1944-65, nat. dir., 1951-57; bd. dirs. John Howard Assn., 1958-67, Community Fund Chgo., 1950-56, Welfare Coun. Met. Chgo., 1950-56; chmn. woman's div. Crusade of Mercy, Chgo., 1964. Mem. U.S. Women's Curling Assn. (co-founder 1947, pres. 1950, founder Indian Hill Women's Curling Club, Winnetka, Ill., 1945, chmn. 1945-46), DAR, Daus. Am. Colonists, Town and Country Arts Club (pres. 1957-58, Chgo., Woman's Athletic Club Chgo., Everglades Club (Palm Beach, Fla.), Venice (Fla.) Yacht Club, Coral Ridge Yacht Club (Ft. Lauderdale, Fla.). Republican. Methodist. Home: 560 N Casey Key Rd PO Box 1098 Osprey FL 34229-1098

CRISS, SALLY RUTH JACOBSON, tax consultant; b. Pitts., Dec. 5, 1949; d. Robert Lawrence Jacobson and Shirley Rosalyn (Spiegel) Kleinman; m. Clifford Guy Deaner, Jan. 23, 1973 (div. May 1985); m. Gary William Criss, May 23, 1976; 1 child, Jessica Rose. BA, U. Mich., 1971; MBA, U. Colo., 1979. Owner Kalso Earth Shoes, Chapel Hill, N.C., 1972-74; fin. dir. Divine Light Dance Ensemble, Phila., 1974-76; owner The Stained Glass Studio, Boulder, Colo., 1976-79; asst. fund raiser Children's Home Soc., Miami, Fla., 1982-84; owner Sally Criss, MBA, EA, Sebastopol, Calif., 1985—; facilitator Women and Money Groups, Sebastopol, 1992-94, Interactive Bus. Planning, Sebastopol, 1995—. Advt. chairperson Women's Art Festival, Luther Burbank Ctr., 1994, Women's Arts Festival Women's Learning Ctr., Santa Rosa, cultural outreach chairperson, Santa Rosa, 1995. Mem. Nat. Assn. Enrolled Agts. Office: 154 Weeks Way Sebastopol CA 95472

CRIST, JUDITH, film and drama critic; b. N.Y.C., May 22, 1922; d. Solomon and Helen (Schoenberg) Klein; m. William B. Crist, July 3, 1947 (dec. Apr. 1993); 1 son, Steven Gordon. A.B., Hunter Coll., 1941; teaching fellow, State Coll. Wash., 1942-43; M.Sc. in Journalism, Columbia, 1945; DHL (hon.), SUNY, New Paltz, 1994. Civilian instr. 3081st Army AFB Unit, 1943-44; reporter N.Y. Herald Tribune, 1945-60, editor arts, 1960-63, assoc. theater critic, 1957-63, film critic, 1963-66; film, theater critic NBC-TV Today Show, 1963-73; film critic World Jour. Tribune, 1966-67; critic-at-large Ladies Home Jour., 1966-67; contbg. editor and film critic TV Guide, 1966-88; film critic N.Y. mag., 1968-75, The Washingtonian, 1970-72, Palm Springs Life, 1971-75; contbg. editor, film critic Saturday Rev., 1975-77, 80-84, N.Y. Post, 1977-78, MD/Mrs., 1977—, 50 Plus, 1978-83, L'Officiel/USA, 1979-80; arts critic Sta. WWOR-TV Channel 9 News, 1981-87; critical columnist for Coming Attractions, 1985-93; cons. editor Hollywood Mag., 1985-93; contbg. editor Columbia Mag., 1993-95; instr. journalism Hunter Coll., 1947, Sarah Lawrence Coll., 1958-59; assoc. journalism Columbia Grad. Sch. Journalism, 1959-62, lectr. journalism, 1962-64, adj. prof., 1964—. Author: The Private Eye, The Cowboy and the Very Naked Girl, 1968, Judith Crist's TV Guide to the Movies, 1974, Take 22: Moviemakers on Moviemaking, 1984, rev. edit., 1991; contbr. articles to nat. mags. Trustee Anne O'Hare McCormick Scholarship Fund. Recipient Page One award N.Y. Newspaper Guild, 1955; George Polk award, 1961; N.Y. Newspaper Women's Club award, 1955, 59, 63, 65, 67; Edn. Writers Assn. award, 1952; Columbia Grad. Sch. Journalism Alumni award, 1961; named to 50th Anniversary Honors List, 1963; Centennial Pres.'s medal Hunter Coll., 1970; named to Hunter Alumni Hall of Fame, 1973. Mem. Columbia Journalism Alumni (pres. 1967-70), N.Y. Film Critics Circle, Nat. Soc. Film Critics., Sigma Tau Delta. Office: 180 Riverside Dr New York NY 10024-1021

CRISTELLI, ROSEMARIE, occupational therapist; b. Galveston, Tex., Nov. 28, 1950; d. Bruno Peter and Mamie Teresa (Cantini) Sr. AS, Galveston Coll., 1971; BS, U. Tex. Sch. of Allied Health, Scis., 1973; MS, Southwest Tex. State, 1976. Cert. work adjustment and vocat. evaluation specialist, vocat. evaluator; cert. cardiopulmonary resuscitation instr., first aid instr.; EMT, Tex.; registered occupl. therapist. Occupl. therapist I, Adolescent Psychiatry Svc. U. Tex. Med. Br. Hosps. (UTMB), Galveston, 1973-75; instr. dept. occupl. therapy U. Tex. Sch. Allied Health Scis./U. Tex. Med. Br. Hosps., Galveston, 1976-79, asst. prof. dept. occupl. therapy, 1979-81, coord., asst. prof. dept. instl. scis., 1981-83; occupl. therapy cons. Logos Home Health and Personnel Svcs./St. Mary's Hosp., Galveston, 1984-85, 86-87; dir. occupl. therapy Transitional Learning Comm. for Head Injured Adults, Galveston, 1984-86; occupl. therapist II, clin. specialist home health programs U. Tex. Med. Br. Hosps., 1986-88, occupl. therapist II, clin. supr. Work Programs Divsn., 1988-92, occupl. therapist III, clin. supr. Work Programs Divsn., 1992—; mem. adv. bd. spl. edn. GISD, Galveston; mem. exec. bd. UTSAHS Alumni; mem. various C. of C. coms. Mem. edn. subcom. Galveston C. of C., 1993—, adv. com. for spl. population, Galveston Coll., 1992—; bd. dirs. Coalition for Barrier Free Living, 1991—; sec. Krewe of Hygeia, 1988-90; vol. cardiopulmonary resuscitation instr., ARC, Galveston, 1983-86, first aid instr.; mem. com. for Ball H.S. Class of 1969 Reunins, 1978—. Mem. Am. Occupl. Therapy Assn., Tex. Occupl. Therapy Assn., Phi Theta Kappa.

CRISWELL, KIMBERLY ANN, public relations executive, dancer; b. L.A., Dec. 6, 1957; d. Robert Burton and Carolyn Joyce (Semko) C. BA with honors, U. Calif.-Santa Cruz, 1980; postgrad. Stanford U., 1993—. Instr., English Lang. Services, Oakland, Calif., 1980-81; freelance writer Verbum mag., San Diego, Gambit mag., New Orleans, 1981; instr. Tulane U., New Orleans, 1981; instr., editor Haitian-English Lang. Program, New Orleans, 1981-82; instr. Delgado Coll., New Orleans, 1982-83; instr., program coord. Vietnamese Youth Ctr., San Francisco, 1984; dancer Khadra Internat. Folk Ballet, San Francisco, 1984-89; dir. mktg. comm. Centram Systems West, Inc., Berkeley, Calif., 1984-87; comm. coord. Safeway Stores, Inc., Oakland, 1985; dir. corp. comm. TOPS, div. Sun Microsystems, Inc, 1987-88; pres. Criswell Comm., 1988—; dir. Corp. Comm. CyberGold, Inc., Berkeley,

Calif., 1996—. Vol. coord. Friends of Haitians, 1981, editor, writer newsletter, 1981; dancer Komenka Ethnic Dance Ensemble, New Orleans, 1983; mem. Contemp. Art Ctr.'s Krewe of Clones, New Orleans, 1983, Americans for Nonsmokers Rights, Berkeley, 1985; active San Francisco Multimedia Developers Group, Artspan. Mem. Sci. Meets the Arts Soc. (founding), Oakland Mus. Assn., Mus. Soc. Democrat. Avocations: visual arts, travel, creative writing.

CRITELLI, NANCY BARBARA, music educator, retired cellist; b. Billings, Mont., Dec. 4, 1927; d. Frank S. and Inez Estell (MacDonald) C. MusB, Mont. State U., 1950, MusM, 1963; D of Mus. Arts, U. Mich., 1976. Orch. dir., tchr. Flathead County H.S., Kalispell, Mont., 1950-52; string instr. El Paso (Tex.) Pub. Schs., 1952-55; instrumental instr. Lansing (Mich.) Pub. Schs., 1957-62; instr. theory, cello, bass Wis. State U., Eau Claire, 1965-66; asst. prof. orch., chamber music theory, appreciation Rocky Mountain Coll., Billings, 1967-69; asst. prof. Western Ill. U., Macomb, 1972-73; asst. prof. cello, bass, chamber music, theory Appalachian State U., Boone, N.C., 1974-80; instr., adj. prof. Ea. Mont. Coll., Billings, 1987; adj. prof. Rocky Mountain Coll., Billings, 1988—; clinician N.W. Music Edn. Conv., Boise; workshop leader 7th Ann. Coulee region Festival of Arts, LaCrosse, Wis., 1966; organizer Solo and Small Ensemble Festival, Boone, N.C., 1977-78, Orch. Contest Festival, Winston-Salem, N.C., 1978, Mont. Music Tchrs. Dist. Festival, Billings, 1982; dir., founder Flathead County Symphony, Kalispell, 1951-52, Lansing Jr. Symphony, 1959, Red Lodge (Mont.) Music Festival, 1964-73; cellist Mont. Suzuki Inst., 1980-90, mem. faculty, 1985-95. Performed as cellist with U. Mont. Orch., Western Ill. Symphony, Appalachian State U. Symphony, Billings Symphony; also numerous recitals, Mont., Wis., Mich., N.C. Mem. Nat. Music Tchrs. Assn. (cert.), Music Educators Nat. Assn., Am. String Tchrs. Assn., Yellowstone Chamber Music Players, Suzuki Assn., Billings Music Tchrs. Assn.

CRITES, MARSHA SMITH, foundation officer, social worker; b. Greer, S.C., June 28, 1952; d. Donald Newton and Mildred Lou (Kelly) Smith; m. Lee Kern Crites, July 20, 1974; children: Savannah Noel, Emily Harrison, Lillian Walker. BS in Human Svcs., U. Tenn., 1974; MSW, San Diego State U., 1978. Social work dir. Golden Age Convalescent Ctr., Vista, Calif., 1974-75; med. social worker Home Health Svc. Agy., Sylva, N.C., 1978-80; instr. Southwestern C.C., Sylva, 1983-84; project dir. Ctr. for Improving Mountain Living Western Carolina U., Cullowhee, N.C., 1984-87, human resource dir. Ctr. for Improving Mountain Living, 1987-90; program dir. Save the Children, Asheville, N.C., 1990-92; sr. assoc. N.C. Comty. Found., Sylva, 1992—; cons. Western Carolina U., Cullowhee, 1979-83, Mountain View Manor, Bryson City, N.C., 1983-85. Co-author: Walking Up to Poverty in W. North Carolina, 1990; author: (book chpt.) Intergenerational Progams: Imperatives, Strategies, Trends, 1989. Bd. dirs. Region A Partnership for Children, Sylva, 1993—; pres. United Christian Ministries, Sylva, 1989-92; mem. Jackson County Coun. Aging, Sylva, 1988-90, Jackson Village Retirement Village, Sylva, 1988-90. Recipient Nancy Susan Reynolds award for personal svc. Z. Smith Reynolds Found., 1991, Best Practice Showcase winner Am. Soc. on Aging, 1987, Rural Aging award, 1987; named one of Outstanding Young Women of Am., 1987. Mem. Nat. Soc. Fund Raising, Western N.C. Funding and Devel. Orgn. Democrat. United Methodist. Office: NC Comty Found 7 Colonial Sq #200 Sylva NC 28779-2957

CRITTENDEN, MARY LYNNE, science educator; b. Detroit, Oct. 27, 1951; d. William and Marie (Ryall) C. BS, Wayne State U., 1974; MS, U. Detroit, 1984; postgrad., Wayne State U., 1991—. Tchr. sci. Detroit Bd. Edn., 1974-77, Highland Park (Mich.) C.C., 1980—; faculty rschr. Air Force program Wright Patterson AFB, Dayton, Ohio, 1991; speaker Mich. Ednl. Occupational Assn., 1989, Liberal Arts Network Devel., Lansing, Mich., 1990, 95; presider Qualities Edn. Minorities, Math., Sci. Engrng. Conf., Detroit, 1996. Author ednl. materials; contbr. to profl. publs. Mem. AAAS, Am. Chem. Soc. (outreach program 1992—), Civic Ctr. Optimist Club (bd. dirs. 1991-94, coord. scis. 1990-94), Mich. C.C. Biologists, Human Anatomy and Physiology Soc. Home: 15386 Alden St Detroit MI 48238-2104 Office: Highland Park C C Glendale at 3rd Highland Park MI 48203

CRITTENDEN, MARY RITA, clinical psychology educator; b. Binghamton, N.Y., Apr. 6, 1928; d. John Patrick and Anna Elizabeth (Griffin) Saxton; m. Rodney Whitman Crittenden, Aug. 6, 1955; children: John Whitman, Anne Catherine, Jean Patricia. BA, Cornell U., 1950; MA, Mills Coll., Oakland, Calif., 1952; PhD, Calif. Sch. Profl. Psychology, San Francisco, 1977. Cert. Nat. Sch. Psychologist; lic. clin. psychologist, ednl. psychologist, Calif. Psychologist numerous schs., N.Y., Calif., 1953-67; chief psychologist, asst. prof. dept. pediatrics U. Calif., San Francisco, 1967-93, clin. prof. dept. pediatrics, 1993—; lectr. Coll. Notre Dame, Belmont, Calif., 1963-66; coord. Child Assessment Svc., San Francisco Mental Health Svcs., 1993—. Contbg. editor Jour. Soc. Pediatric psychology, 1974-80; contbr. articles to profl. jours. Mem. bd. dirs. San Francisco Assn. for Gifted and Talented, 1972-81. Mills Coll. fellow, 1950-52; grantee U. Calif. San Francisco Acad. Senate, 1981. Mem. APA, NASP, Nat. Acad. Neuropsychology, Western Psychology Assn., Calif. Assn. Sch. Psychologists, Calif. Psychology Assn., Soc. Behavioral Pediatrics. Roman Catholic. Office: U Calif Dept Pediatrics A-203 Box 0314 400 Parnassus San Francisco CA 94143

CRITTENDEN, SOPHIE MARIE, communications executive; b. Mansfield, Ohio, Apr. 14, 1926; d. Joseph S. and Mary Ellen (Hagerman) Wojcik; m. Robert Eugene Crittenden, Aug. 24, 1946 (dec. 1987); children: Robert J., Mark A., Christopher E., Laura Ann. Student, Coll. St. Francis, 1944-45, Ohio U., 1945-46, North Cen. Tech. Coll., 1976-78. Substitute tchr. Mansfield City Schs., 1956-62; lab. technician The Ohio Brass Co., Mansfield, 1962-68, draftsman, 1968, mgr. internal publs., 1969-78, mgr. advt., 1978-83, mgr. communications, 1983-88; cons. communications EFE N.Am., Inc., Mansfield, 1989-90; account coord. D & S Creative Advt., Inc., Mansfield, 1990—. Creator and shower of quilts. Com. chmn. United Way Campaign, Mansfield and Richland, Ohio, 1978; pub. relations chmn. Tribute to Women and Industry Project, Mansfield, 1986 (award 1985). Named Mrs. Mansfield Mrs. Am. Contest, 1961. Mem. Mktg. Club North Cen. Ohio (bd. dirs., sec. 1987-90), Altrusa (pres. 1976, internat. chmn. mktg. and pub. rels. 1991-93). Republican. Roman Catholic. Home: 84 Wildwood Dr Mansfield OH 44907-1621 Office: 140 Park Ave E Mansfield OH 44902-1830

CRNIC, LINDA SMITH, psychobiologist, educator; b. Ft. Wayne, Ind., Mar. 29, 1948; d. Herman Edward and Patricia Ellen (Leeth) Smith; m. David Michael Crnic, June 21, 1969 (div. June 1976); m. Stanley Loyd Wilks, May 3, 1986; 1 child, Michael Smith Wilks. AB, U. Chgo., 1970; MA, U. Ill., Chgo., 1972, PhD, 1975. Postdoctoral fellow U. Colo. Sch. Medicine, Denver, 1975-77, prof., 1994—, asst. prof., 1979-85, assoc. prof., 1985-94; mem. psychobiol., biol. and neuroscis. subcoms. of the mental health AIDS rsch. rev. com. NIMH, 1989-92; mem. mental retardation rsch. com. NICHD. Contbr. articles to profl. jours. NIH grantee, 1975—; NIMH rsch. career devel. awardee, 1987-92. Mem. Internat. Soc. Devel. Psychobiology (sec.-treas. 1983-86, pres.-elect 1995), Internat. Soc. Devel. Neurosci., Soc. Neurosci. (chmn. Rocky Mountain region group 1983-86), Western Soc. Pediatric Rsch., Animal Behavior Soc. Home: 25 S Jasmine St Denver CO 80224-1028 Office: U Colo Sch Med 4200 E 9th Ave Denver CO 80262-3706

CROCE, ARLENE LOUISE, critic; b. Providence, May 5, 1934; d. Michael Daniel and Louise Natalie (Pensa) C. Student, Women's Coll., U. N.C., 1951-53; BA, Barnard Coll., 1955. Founder, editor Ballet Rev., 1965-78; dance critic New Yorker mag., 1973—; dance panelist Nat. Endowment for Arts, 1977-80. Author: The Fred Astaire & Ginger Rogers Book, 1972, Afterimages, 1977, Going to the Dance, 1982, Sight Lines, 1987. Recipient AAAL award 1979, award of Honor for Arts and Culture Mayor N.Y.C., 1979, Janeway prize Barnard Coll., 1955; Hodder fellow Princeton U., 1971; Guggenheim fellow, 1972, 86. NEH fellow 1992. Fellow AAAS. Office: New Yorker Mag 20 W 43rd St New York NY 10036-7400

CROCKER, BETTY CHARLOTTE, education educator; b. Jackson, Miss., Sept. 2, 1948; d. William Charlie and Virginia Frances (Cayson) C. BS, U. Tex., 1970; EdD, U. Ga., 1985. Cert. sci. edn., earth-life sci., elem. edn. Tchr. 5th grade Harlingen (Tex.) Ind. Schs., 1970-71, Am. Sch. Found., Monterrey, Mexico, 1971-74; tchr. grades 6-8, sci. chair Clear Creek Ind. Schs., Webster, Tex., 1974-83; asst. prof. edn. So. Oreg. State U., Ashland, 1985-88; asst. to assoc. prof. edn. U. North Tex., Denton, 1988—; adv. com. to state bd. edn. Tex. Environ. Edn. Adv. Com., Austin, 1991—; sci. spkr. The Edn. Ctr., Torrance, Calif., 1994-95. Author: Food for Thought, 1992, 93, 94, 95; editl. bd. mem. Jour. Elem. Sci. Edn., 1989-95; contbr. articles to profl. jours. Bd. dirs. hands-on mus. ScienceLand, Denton's (Tex.) Discovery Mus., 1994-95. Mem. S.W. Assn. Educators of Tchrs. of Sci. (sec.-treas. 1994-95, dir. elect 1995, dir. 1996-97), Sci. Tchrs. Assn. Tex. (v.p. 1990-91, pres. 1991-92, past pres. 1992-93, 94-95, Lawrence Buford award 1991), Phi Delta Kappa (sec.-treas. 1987-88, v.p. for programs 1989-90, pres. 1990-91). Office: Univ North Tex Coll Edn PO Box 13857 Denton TX 76203

CROCKER, JANE LOPES, library director; b. Mass., Sept. 19, 1946; d. Joseph Barros and Mary (Faria) Lopes; m. Lowell Steven Crocker, Feb. 14, 1976; children: Susan J., Jennifer L., Jacqueline M. BA in English, Bridgewater State Coll., 1968; MS in Libr. Sci., Simmons Coll., 1971. Cert. libr., Mass.; cert. secondary edn. tchr., Mass. Libr. New Bedford (Mass.) Pub. Libr., 1968-71; pub. svcs. libr. Simmons Coll. Libr., Boston, 1971-73; head libr. Boston City Hosp., 1973-76; libr. dir. Gloucester County Coll., Deptford, N.J., 1976—; pres. Libr. Network Rev. Bd., 1994—, vice-chmn., 1996—. Editor Bay State Libr., 1974-76; contbg. author: Reference and Information Service, 1978, N.J. Libraries, 1984, 89-90, 94, Vocat. and Tech. Resources for C.C. Librs., Laun, Mary Ann Assn. of Coll. and Rsch. Librs., ALA. Recipient Ray Murray award N.J. Assn. Libr. Assts., 1991. Mem. ALA (mem. chpt. rels. coun. 1995—), N.J. Libr. Assn. (pres.-elect 1991-92, pres. 1992-93), South Jersey Regional Libr. Coop. (pres. 1988-90, Resolution of Appreciation award 1990, Pres.'s award 1993). Roman Catholic. Office: Gloucester County Coll Tanyard Rd RR 4 Box 203 Sewell NJ 08080

CROCKER, JOY LAKSMI, concert pianist, composer; b. San Antonio, June 12, 1928; d. Hugo Peoples and Anna Kathryn (Ball) Rush; m. Richard Lincoln Crocker, July 24, 1948 (div. July 1977); children: Nathaniel Homer, Martha Wells, David Laramie. MusB, Yale U., 1950, MS, 1956; postgrad., Grad. Theol. Sem., 1978-81. Min. music First Congl. Ch., Branford, Conn., 1949-62; dir. music therapy West Haven (Conn.) VA Hosp.; min. music St. Stephen's Episcopal Ch./Sch., Orinda, Calif., 1963, First Bapt. Ch., Oakland, Calif., 1964-66, Greek Orthodox Cathedral, Oakland, 1969, San Quentin (Calif.) Protestant Chapel, 1976-78, Plymouth United Ch. of Christ, Oakland, 1977-84; pianist, assoc. dir. First Bapt. Ch., Managua, Nicaragua, 1984-94; organist, pianist Mills Grove Christian Ch., 1995; prof. organ San Francisco Conservatory Music, 1962-69; chmn. piano dept. Nicaraguan Nat. Conservatory Music, 1984-93; founder-dir., prof. Bapt. Conservatory of Music, Managua, 1989—; mem., adjudicator, instr. Yogalayam Yoga Ashram; creator, dir. diverse music edn. programs, 1969—; mem. adjudicator Nat. Guild Piano Tchrs. civic and legislation coord. Ch. Women United, Oakland, 1995—; pianist, organist Ch. Women United State Unit. Named Woman of Yr., Bus. and Profl. Women's Club, Inc., 1995. Mem. Am. Guild Organists, Am. Coll. Musicians, Music Tchrs. Assn., Nat. Guild Piano Tchrs. Democrat. Mem. United Ch. of Christ. Home: 3065 Monterey Blvd Oakland CA 94602

CROCKETT, FELICIA DODEE FROST, brokerage firm executive; b. Oklahoma City, Oct. 19, 1956; d. Carl S. Frost and Mikki (Matheny) Marcus; m. Billy Crockett. Student So. Meth. U., 1974-76. Gen. mgr. Keystone Readers Svc., Dallas, 1976-80; v.p. and sr. fin. cons. Merrill Lynch pvt. client, Dallas, 1980—. Bd. dirs. North Dallas Shared Ministries, 1988-91, Mental Health Assn, adv. bd. EXCAP Ctr. for the Prevention of Child Abuse, Ronald McDonald Children's Charities, 1992—; mem. investment com. Dallas Womens Found., 1991-94. Mem. Dallas Opera (bd. dirs. 1991—), Dallas Securities Dealers Assn., Nat. Assn. Securities Dealers (gen. securities prin., mcpl. securities rulemaking bd. prin., registered options prin., bd. arbitrators), NYSE (com. mem.), Merrill Lynch Chmns. Club, Park Cities Exch. Club (charter, bd. dirs. 1991—), Chief Executive Officers Club. Republican. Office: Merrill Lynch Pierce Fenner and Smith 2000 Premier Pl 5910 N Central Expy Ste 2000 Dallas TX 75206-5152

CROCKETT, PHYLLIS DARLENE, communications executive; b. Chgo., July 14, 1950; d. Leo F. Crockett and Mae (Corbin) Williams; divorced; 1 child, Adina Darlene Gittens. BA, U. Ill., Chgo., 1972; MS in Journalism, Northwestern U., 1979. Free-lance reporter AP and UPI, Raleigh and Durham, N.C., 1978-80; news writer Sta. WTTG-TV, Washington, 1981-82; free-lance writer Pacific News Svc., San Francisco, 1984; producer, reporter, anchorperson Sta. WSOC, Charlotte, N.C., 1978-79, Stas. WFNC/WQSM, Fayetteville, N.C., 1979-80; exec. editor, talk show moderator Sheridan Broadcasting Network, Washington, 1980-81; reporter gen. assignments Nat. Pub. Radio, Washington, 1981-89, White House corr., 1989-91, sr. corr., 1991-94; pres. Chronicle Communications, Johannesburg, South Africa, 1994—; panelist CNN & Co., CNN's Internat. Corrs., CNN's Inside Politics, 1992—, CNN's Both Sides with Jesse Jackson, Am.'s Black Forum, Washington, 1980-83; analyst C-Span Cable TV Network, Black Entertainment TV, Washington and Sta. WHMM-TV, Washington, 1987—, Am. Urban Radio News Network, others; cons. Clark-Atlanta U., others, 1982-94; vis. instr. Fayetteville State U., 1980, Johnson C. Smith U., Charlotte, 1979; guest lectr. Howard U., U. D.C., Fairfax (Va.) Pub. Schs., 1980-94; media cons. South African Broadcasting Co., Radio 702, others. Contbg. author: Split Image: African-Americans in the Mass Media, 1990, 93; contbr. book reviews to N.Y. Times, 1988, 92, L.A. Times, 1989, Washington Post, 1994; pub. The Crockett Chronicle, 1984—. John S. Knight fellow Stanford U., 1990-91; recipient NEA award, 1988, Robert F. Kennedy award, 1990. Mem. Nat. Assn. Black Journalists (Frederick Douglass award 1984), Washington Assn. Black Journalists (v.p. 1982), Sigma Delta Chi. Baptist. Office: PO Box 3257 Parklands, Johannesburg 2121, South Africa also: care Squire Padgett 1835 K St NW Ste 900 Washington DC 20006-1203

CROFFORD, BONNIE ANN, rehabilitation clinical specialist; b. Bryn Mawr, Pa., Nov. 28, 1944; d. James Howard and Anna Myrtle (Woodring) C. Diploma in nursing, Thomas Jefferson U. Hosp., Phila., 1966; BSN, Gwynedd Mercy Coll., 1976; MS in Nursing, Case Western Res. U., 1980. RN, Pa., Ohio, Va. Instr. Gwynedd Mercy Coll., Gwynedd Valley, Pa.; head nurse Bryn Mawr Rehab. Hosp., Malvern, Pa., clin. nurse specialist; clin. nurse specialist Piersol rehab. unit U. Pa.; staff nurse Bryn Mawr Rehab., Malvern; presenter profl. confs. Contbr. chpt. to: Rehabilitation Nursing: Concepts and Practice-A Core Curriculum, 1987. Mem. ANA (cert. gerontol. nurse), Assn. Rehab. Nurses (co-chairperson edn. com. Phila. chpt., Jeanne McGraw Achievement award, cert.), Nat. Gerontol. Nursing Assn., Pa. Nurses Assn., Sigma Theta Tau (Iota Kappa chpt.). Home: 45 Sullivan Rd Wayne PA 19087-1431

CROMER, MARY JOAN, community services director; b. Scottsbluff, Nebr., Aug. 21, 1932; d. Miltetus H. and Lillian V. (Yount) Ouderkirk; m. John Dale Cromer, June 19, 1953; children: Bradley Allen, Gregory D., Karen Kay Cromer Johnson. BS in Home Econ., Colo. State U., 1953; MSW, U. Nebr., Omaha, 1981; EdD, Nova Southeastern U., 1995. cert. social worker. High sch. instr. Mitchell (Nebr.) City Schs., 1953-56; substitute talk show host Sta. KSTF-TV, Scottsbluff, 1960-67; pre-sch. dir. Gering, Nebr., 1962-67; head start tchr. Panhandle Community Svcs., Gering, 1967-68, head start dir., 1968-73, dir. child and family devel. programs, 1973-81, exec. dir., 1981—; early childhood cons. Regions VII and VIII, Kansas City, Mo., 1970-78; evaluator and workshop presenter Office Child Devel. Health Human Svcs., 1970-78; early childhood adj. tchr. Western Nebr. C.C., Scottsbluff, 1980-90; social work adj. prof. Kearney (Nebr.) State Coll., 1986-87; with Scotts Bluff County Family Preservation Project, 1986—, pres., 1991-92; mem. Gov.'s Task Force on Homelessness and N.E. Jobs Tng. Coun., 1994—. Mem. adv. bd. Scottsbluff County Extension Svc., 1963-66; bd. dirs. United Way, Scottsbluff/Gering, 1985-88, Panhandle Substance Abuse Coun., Scottsbluff, 1985-90, YMCA, 1991—; conf. co-chair citizen amb. program U.S.-China Joint Conf. Women's Issues, 1995. Named Outstanding Nebr. 4-H alumnus Coop. Extension Svc., Lincoln, 1962, Lady of Yr., Beta Sigma Phi, Scottsbluff, 1981; recipient Trailblazer award Scottsbluff/Gering C. of C., 1995, Woman of Yr. N.E. Bus. Profl. Women, 1996. Mem. Nat. Assn. Edn. Young Children, Assn. Nebr. Comty. Action Agys. (chair 1987, 89), Soroptomists Internat. (gov. Rocky Mt. region 1990-92, pres. fedn. 1995-96), C. of C. (health and human svc. subcom. 1994—). Protestant. Home: 160750 Carter Canyon Rd Gering NE 69341-7306 Office: Panhandle Community Svcs 3350 10th St Gering NE 69341-1724

CROMWELL, ADELAIDE M., sociology educator; b. Washington, Nov. 27, 1919; d. John Wesley, Jr. and Yetta Elizabeth (Mavritte) C.; 1 son, Anthony C. Hill. AB, Smith Coll., 1940; MA, U. Pa., 1941; cert. social work, Bryn Mawr Coll., 1943; PhD, Radcliffe Coll., 1952; LHD (hon.), U. Southwestern Mass., 1972, George Washington U., 1989, Boston U., 1995. Mem. faculty Hunter Coll., 1942-44, Smith Coll., 1945-46; mem. faculty Boston U., 1951-85, prof. sociology, 1971-85, dir. Afro-Am. studies, 1969-88, prof. emerita sociology, 1985—; mem. adv. com. vol. fgn. aid AID, 1964-80; mem. NEH, 1968-70; adv. com. corrections Commonwealth Mass., 1955-68; mem. commn. instns. higher edn., 1973-74; adv. com. to dir. IRS, 1970-71, to dir. census, 1972-75. Bd. dirs. Wheelock Coll., 1971--74, Nat. Ctr. Afro-Am. Artists, 1971-80, African Am. Scholars Coun., 1971—, Nat. Fellowship Fund, 1974-75, Mass. Hist. Commn., 1993; bd. dirs. Sci. and Tech. for Internat. Devel., 1984-86; mem. exec. com. Am. Soc. African Culture, 1967. Mem. AAAS, African Studies Assn. (bd. dir. 1966-68), Am. Acad. of Arts and Scis., Am. Sociol. Assn., Council on Fgn. Affairs (bd. fgn. scholarships 1980-84), Phi Beta Kappa. Home: 51 Addington Rd Brookline MA 02146-4519 Office: Boston U 138 Mountfort St Brookline MA 02146-4039

CROMWELL, FLORENCE STEVENS, occupational therapist; b. Lewistown, Pa., May 14, 1922; d. William Andrew and Florence (Stevens) C. BS in Edn., Miami U., Oxford, Ohio, 1943; BS in Occupational Therapy, Washington U., St. Louis, 1949; MA, U. So. Calif., 1952; cert. in health facility adminstrn., UCLA, 1978. Mem. staff, then supervising therapist Los Angeles County Gen. Hosp., 1949-53; occupational therapist Goodwill Industries, L.A., 1954-55; staff therapist Vis. Nurse Assn., Phila., 1955-56; rsch. therapist United Cerebral Palsy Assn., L.A., 1956-60; dir. occupational therapy Orthopaedic Hosp., L.A., 1961-67; coordinator occupational therapy Rsch. and Tng. Ctr. U. So. Calif., L.A., 1967-70, assoc. prof., 1970-76, acting chmn. dept. occupational therapy, 1973-76, mem. adv. bd. project SEARCH, Sch. Medicine, 1969-72; founding editor Occupational Therapy in Health Care jour., 1984-88, editor emerita, 1988—; assoc. dir. L.A. Job Corps Ctr., 1977-78, cons. in edn. and program devel., 1976-95; free-lance editor, 1986—. Author: Manual for Basic Skills Assessment, 1960; also articles. Mem. scholarship com. Los Angeles March of Dimes, 1963-70; bd. dirs. Am. Occupational Therapy Found., 1965-69, v.p., 1966-69; bd. dirs. Nat. Health Council, 1975-78; mentor U. Tex. Class 1990 Occupational Therapy. Served to lt. (j.g.) WAVES, 1943-46. Recipient Disting. Alumni award Washington U., 1978, Disting. Lectr. Calif. Occupational Therapy Found., 1986. Fellow Am. Occupational Therapy Assn. (pres. 1967-73); mem. Inst. Medicine NAS (sr. 1989), So. Calif. Occupational Therapy Assn. (pres. 1950-51, 75-76), Coalition Ind. Health Professions (chmn. 1973-74), Assn. Schs. Allied Health Professions (dir. 1973-74), Cwen, Mortar Bd., Kappa Delta Pi, Kappa Kappa Gamma.

CRONE, MARCIA ANN, judge; b. Dallas, Dec. 12, 1952; d. Dan Moody and Marian Louise (Stewart) Cain; m. W. Seth Crone, Jr., Aug. 30, 1986; children: Kimball Montclair, Kirby Armitage. BA summa cum laude, Univ. of Tex., Austin, 1973; JD summa cum laude, Univ. of Houston, 1978. Bar: Tex. 1979, D.C. 1982. With Andrews & Kurth, 1978-92; magistrate judge U.S. Dist. Ct. (Tex. so. dist.), 5th circuit, Houston, 1992—. Methodist. Office: Federal Bldg Rm 7509 515 Rusk St Houston TX 77002

CRONENWORTH, GERI LYNN, artist; b. South Bend, Ind., Mar. 28, 1963; d. Lon David and Dora Jean (Goodman) Adams; m. Jeff Cronenworth, Mar. 19, 1984; children: Michael David, Sarah Ann. BFA, U. North Tex., 1996. art & craft coord. McKinney Meml. Bible Ch., Ft. Worth, Tex., 1992; dir. craft fair West Point Neighborhood Assn., Ft. Worth, 1994. Recipient 1st place Watercolor Granbury Art Coun., 1990, 2d place Painting Tarrent County Jr. Coll., 1990. Home: 505 Blue Haze Dr Fort Worth TX 76108

CRONIN, BONNIE KATHRYN LAMB, legislative staff executive; b. Mpls., Mar. 11, 1941; d. Edwin Rector and Maude Kathryn (MacPherson) Lamb; m. Barry Jay Cronin, Jan. 23, 1963 (div. Feb. 1972); 1 son, Philip Scott. B.A., U. Mo., 1963, B.S., 1964; M.S., Ill. State U., 1970. Copywriter Neds & Wardlow Advt., Columbia, Mo., 1962-64; tchr. Columbia Sch. System, 1964-68, Normal (Ill.) Sch. System, 1968-69; asst. gen. mgr. Sta. WGLT, Normal, 1969-70; dir. devel. Radio Sta. WBUR, Boston, 1970-71; program dir. Radio Sta. WBUR, 1971-75, gen. mgr., 1975-78; dir. public relations Joy of Movement Center, 1978-80; dep. scheduler Anderson for Pres., 1980; scheduler Spaulding for Gov., 1980-81; dir. scheduling John Kerry Campaign, 1982; dir. of scheduling Mass. Lt. Gov.'s Office, dir. ops., 1983-84; dep. campaign mgr. Kerry for Senate Com., 1984; dir. ops. Senator John Kerry, Washington, 1985-86; dir. constituency outreach Senator John Kerry, Boston, 1986-92, exec. asst., 1992-95; chief staff to Senator John Kerry Boston. Mem. Nat. Pub. Radio (dir. 1974-77, chairperson devel. com.), Mass. Broadcasters Assn. (dir. 1973-78, chairperson scholarship com., pub. service com., adminstrv. oversight com.). Office: 1 Bowdoin Sq 10th Fl Boston MA 02114-2919

CRONIN, ELLEN, journalist; b. Milton, Mass., Dec. 25, 1963; d. Cornelius Francis Jr. and Carol Ann (Boyle) C. BS in Comm., Lyndon State Coll., Lyndonville, Vt., 1986. Writer The Pioneer Group, Boston, 1986-90; news dir. Sta. WLTN, Littleton, N.H., 1990-93; reporter, regional editor The Caledonian-Record, St. Johnsbury, Vt., 1993—. Recipient hon. mention N.H. AP, 1992, 93. Roman Catholic.

CRONIN, PATTI ADRIENNE WRIGHT, state agency administrator; b. Chgo., May 25, 1943; d. Rodney Adrian and Dorothy Louise (Thiele) Wright; m. Kevin Brian Cronin, May 1, 1971; 1 child, Kevin. BA, Beloit (Wis.) Coll., 1965; JD with honors, U. Wis., 1983. Vol. Peace Corps, Turkey, 1965-67; recruiter Peace Corps, Washington, 1967-68; tchr. English Kamehameha III Sch., Lahaina, Hawaii, 1968-70, Evansville (Wis.) High Sch., 1972-77; tchr. math. and history Killian Sch., Hartford, Wis., 1977-78; tchr. English Kaiser High Sch., Honolulu, 1979-80; intern Wis Ct. Appeals, Madison, 1983; exec. dir. waste facility siting bd. State of Wis., Madison, 1983—; founder, v.p., bd. dirs. Justice Ctr. Honolulu, 1979-82; sec., treas. Cronin Constrn. Co., Inc., Madison, 1986—. Editor: Internat. Law Jour., 1982. Bd. dirs. Neighborhood Bd., Honolulu, 1979-82; chmn. United Way, 1989—; active Parent Citizens Adv. Coun. Recipient Mayor's award of outstanding achievement, City of Honolulu, 1980. Mem. Soc. Profls. in Dispute Resolution, ABA, State Bar Wis. Office: Waste Facility Siting Bd 101 E Wilson St Fl 5 Madison WI 53703-3422

CRONIN, SUSAN GAYLE, county official; b. Bayonne, N.J., June 10, 1949; m. Brian E. Cronin, Oct. 14, 1972; children: Jennifer, Bridget. Svc. rep. Social Security Adminstrn., Jackson Heights, N.Y., 1967-74; collection mgr. trainee Carroll County Hosp., Westminster, 1979-87; computer specialist Tandy Corp./Radio Shack, Westminster, 1987-88; county vol. program coord. Bur. of Aging, Westminster, 1989—; mem. Medigap nat. com. to preserve social security medicare State of Md. Area Office on Aging, Health Ins. Counseling, Balt., 1993. Mem. campaign Dem. Election, Westminster, 1990. Office: Bur of Aging 7 School House Ave Westminster MD 21157-4505

CROOKE, ROSANNE M., pharmacologist; b. Pittsfield, Mass., Oct. 30, 1955; d. Myron Michael and Marian Geneva (Russell) Muzyka; m. Stanley T. Crooke, Sept. 5, 1986. BA, Williams Coll., 1978; PhD, U. Pa., 1986. Rsch. asst. endocrine sec. dept. medicine U. Pa., Phila., 1978-81; fellow Wistar Inst. Anatomy and Biology, Phila., 1986-89; sr. scientist ISIS Pharms., Carlsbad, Calif., 1989—. Contbr. articles to profl. jours. Mem. AAAS, Soc. for In Vitro Biology. Home: 3211 Piragua St Carlsbad CA 92009-7840 Office: ISIS Pharms 2280 Faraday Ave Carlsbad CA 92008-7208

CROOKER, DIANE KAY, accountant; b. Elmira, N.Y., Nov. 19, 1945; d. John Woodrow and Katharine Eloise (Saunders) Wilson; m. Dennis H. Canfield, mar. 25, 1963 (div. June 1970); children: Douglas Arthur, Dennis John; m. Walter E. Crooker, Apr. 17, 1988. AAS in Computer Sci., Elmira Coll., 1987, BS in Acctg. summa cum laude, 1992. Assembler Westinghouse Elec. Corp., Horseheads, N.Y., 1979-81, traceability coord., 1981-87; buyer Imaging & Sensing Tech. Corp., Horseheads, 1987-89, acct., 1989-95; acct. Corning (N.Y.) Credit Union, 1995—. Bd. dirs. Spalding Found. for Injured Drivers, Owego, N.Y., 1988—. Recipient Scholastic Achievement award N.Y. State CPA Soc., 1992. Mem. Inst. Mgmt. Accts. (v.p. membership 1994), Alpha Sigma Lambda (sec. 1993-94, treas. 1994—).

CROOM, BEVERLY JO, social science educator; b. Coweta County, Ga., Jan. 31, 1937; d. Millard Houston and Grace Maureen (Watson) Eldson; m. Robert Edward Croom, Feb. 2, 1957; 1 child, Yashi Malenka Warner. BA, Ga. State U., Atlanta, 1964, MEd, 1974. Social studies tchr. Clayton County Bd. Edn., Jonesboro, Ga., 1965-87, instructional lead tchr., 1987-91; asst. prin. North Clayton High Sch., Jonesboro, 1991-94, prin., 1994—; rsch. in field. Contbr. articles to profl. jours. Vis. scholar to China, PRC, 1987; Asian Studies fellow U. Mich., 1986. Mem. ASCD, NEA, Nat. Coun. Social Studies, US-China People's Friendship Assn. (nat. coord. Teach-in-China program), Ga. Assn. Educators, Ga. Coun. Social Studies, Clayton County Assn. Educators. Home: PO Box 387 Union City GA 30291-0387

CROPPER, ROSEMARY MOXEY, special education educator; b. Cambridge, Md., Dec. 23, 1938; d. Thomas Nathaniel and Catherine Sophie (Davis) Moxey; m. Donald Andrew Cropper, Dec. 26, 1959; children: Kelly Marie, Christopher Michael, Kurt Matthew (dec.). BS, Salisbury State U., 1969, MEd, 1978, degree in spl. edn., 1980. Elem. edn. tchr. Wicomico County Bd. Edn., Salisbury, Md., 1969-78, spl. edn. tchr., 1978—.

CROPPER, SUSAN PEGGY, veterinarian; b. N.Y.C., Feb. 11, 1941; d. Eli and Ruth (Rader) Abrahams; divorced; 1 child, Tracy Lynn. BS, Kans. State U., 1962, DVM, 1964. Assoc. veterinarian Asbury Park (N.J.) Animal Hosp., 1964-65; instr. in Vet. Sci. Kans. State U., Manhattan, 1965-66; owner, veterinarian Markle (Ind.) Vet. Clinic, 1966-71, Meisels Animal Hosp. Clinic, Elmwood Park, N.J., 1971-73, Ridgewood (N.J.) Animal Hosp., 1973-75, Cropper House Call Practice, Wyckoff, N.J., 1975—; editor Nat. Assn. Women Vets., 1966-68; mem. Audibon Soc. Mus. Natural History. Co-author: Having and Losing a Pet; editor WJMA Jour., 1973; photographer: Best Diving Spots in Western Hemisphere, 1987. Leader Brownie troop Girl Scouts U.S., Glen Rock, N.J., 1976-77, Wyckoff, 1977-83; chairperson No. Jersey Tridents, Ridgefield, N.J., 1985-86. Mem. AVMA, Soc. Aquatic Vet. Medicine (treas.), No. N.J. Vet. Med. Assn. (pres. 1972-73), Met. Vet. Med. Assn., N.Y. Zool. Soc., Van Saun Zool. Soc., N.J. Acad., Ski and Scuba Club of Westwood, North Jersey Tridents Club (Ridgefield, chair 1985-86). Office: 310 Newtown Rd Wyckoff NJ 07481-2608

CRORY, ELIZABETH L., state legislator; b. Gardner, Mass., Sept. 12, 1932; d. James Quaiel and Mary (Reilly) Lupien; m. Frederick E. Crory, Aug. 21, 1954; children: Thomas, David, Ellen, Ann, Edward, Stephen. A.B., U. Mass., 1954; M.A.L.S., Dartmouth Coll., 1975. Tchr., Amherst (Mass.) Schs., 1954, Lyme (N.H.) Schs., 1972-76; mem. N.H. Ho. of Reps., 1977-87, 92-93, 94-95, mem. commerce/consumer affairs com., 1977-87, 93—, mem. spl. com. on med. malpractice, 1984; exec. dir. Children's Ctr. of Upper Valley, 1986-90; bd. incorporators Mascoma Savs. Bank; bd. overseers Mary Hitchcock Meml. Hosp.; mem. character and fitness com. N.H. Supreme Ct., 1987-96. Roman Catholic. Home: 40 Rip Rd Hanover NH 03755-1614

CROSBY, DAWN GEORGE, employment service company owner; b. Dover, Del., Dec. 18, 1940; d. Oscar and Grace Louise (Quillen) George; m. Warren Leo Crosby, Apr. 11, 1964 (dec. Apr. 1968); 1 child, Warren Leo Jr. AA in Sociology, Santa Barbara City Coll., Calif., 1977; BA in Social Psychology, Antioch U., Santa Barbara, 1979. Mgr. Hershey Chocolate Corp., Boston, 1984-86; writer Profl. Resume & Writing Svc., Wilmington, Del., 1986-87; owner Employment Network, Inc., Wilmington, 1987—. Author: Self-Marketing Techniques, 1994; artist collages art shows, N.Y., Calif., Mass., 1976. Mem. Del. State C. of C., Profl. Assn. Resume Writers. Office: Employment Network Inc 1601 Concord Pike Ste 38A Wilmington DE 19803

CROSBY, ELLEN LOUISE, counselor; b. Edenville, Mich., July 9, 1944; d. Donald Wellington and Gladys Leona (Fowler) Marsh; m. James A. Crosby, Mar. 15, 1964; children: Angela Louise, Andrew James, Allen Jackson, James Alvin, JoAnne Marie. BA, So. Coll., 1987; MEd, U. Tenn., Chattanooga, 1990. Cert. Nat. Bd. Cert. Counselors. Counselor Advent Youth Ranch, Calhoun, Tenn., 1989-92; dir., supr., founder Young Women's Prep. Home, Macon, Mo., 1992—; pres. Christian Family Learning Ctrs. Inc., McDonald, Tenn., 1992—. Mem. ACA, Am. Assn. Christian Counselors, Adventist-Laymen's Svcs. and Industires, Toastmasters Internat. (sec. 1992-94). Republican. Seventh-Day Adventist. Home: 6818 White Oak Cir McDonald TN 37353 Office: Christian Family Learning Ctrs Inc PO Box 2153 Collegedale TN 37315-2153

CROSBY, JACQUELINE GARTON, newspaper editor, journalist; b. Jacksonville, Fla., May 13, 1961; d. James Ellis and Marianne (Garton) C.; m. Robert Edward Legge, Jr., Oct. 19, 1985. ABJ, U. Ga., 1983; MBA, U. Cen. Fla., 1987. Staff writer Macon Telegraph & News, Ga., 1983-84; copy editor Orlando Sentinel, Fla., 1984-85; dir. spl. projects Ivanhoe Communications, Inc., Orlando, Fla., 1987-89; producer spl. projects Sta. KSTP-TV, Mpls., 1989-94; asst. news editor Star Tribune Online, Mpls., 1994—. Recipient award for best sports story Ga. Press Assn., 1982; award for best series of yr. AP, 1985, Pulitzer prize, 1985. Mem. Quill. Democrat. Episcopalian. Home: 5348 Drew Ave S Minneapolis MN 55410 Office: Star Tribune Online 425 Portland Ave Minneapolis MN 55488-0001

CROSBY, JANICE LEE, travel agency owner; b. Detroit, Nov. 5, 1951; d. William Francis Bellaire and Kathleen Margaret Lee; m. Charles David Crosby, Sept. 17, 1977. BBA, Western Mich. U., Kalamazoo, 1973; MBA, Wayne State U., Detroit, 1980. CMA. Internal auditor GM Truck & Bus. Divsn., Pontiac, Mich., 1973-76, mgmt. acctg. budgets, 1976-77, mgr. tax acctg., 1977-82, fin. analyst, 1982-88; fin. analyst Saturn Corp., Spring Hill, Tenn., 1988-89, team leader cost acctg., 1989-91, team leader dealer acctg., 1991-92; owner, mgr. Cruise Time Travel, Brentwood, Tenn., 1993—; pres. Am. Soc. Women Accts., Detroit, 1983. Mem. stewardship com. and adminstrv. bd. Brentwood (Tenn.) United Methodist Ch., 1991-93; mem. mixer com. Brentwood C. of C., 1993-96. Mem. Nat. Assn. Cruise Only Agys., Brentwood C. of C., Cruise Line Internat. Assn. (Richard Revnes award 1993, 94), Inst. Mgmt. Accts. (dir. spl. activites 1995-96). Methodist. Home: 8313 Alamo Rd Brentwood TN 37027 Office: Cruise Time 5115 Maryland Way Brentwood TN 37027

CROSHAL, KATHLEEN KLOTZ See HEARN, KATHLEEN K.

CROSLEY-MAYERS, DIANE, social worker; b. South Gate, Calif., June 22, 1954; d. Curtis and Olevia Frances (Boson) Richardson; m. Hilton Charles Crosley, May 28, 1977 (dec. Mar. 1986); 1 child, Hillary Calida Crosley; m. Robert Alonzo Mayers Jr., June 12, 1993. BA, Calif. State U., L.A., 1976; MPA, Pepperdine U., 1977; HROD, U. San Francisco, 1995. Supr., counselor L.A. Job Corps, 1976-77; program dir. Travis AFB, Calif., 1981-85; advocacy specialist Solano Napa Area Agy. Aging, Vallejo, Calif., 1984; group counselor Solano County Health & Social Svcs. Dept., Vallejo, Calif., 1984-85; sr. social worker Solano County Health & Social Svcs. Dept., Fairfield, Calif., 1985—; human resources generalist City of Vacaville, Calif., 1993—; cons. Mary Kay Cosmetics, Suisun, Calif., 1982-86; gust lectr. Solano C.C., Suisun, Calif., 1993—; affirmative action rep. Solano County, Fairfield, 1996; com. chair Black Adoption Fair, Countra Costa, Calif., 1994; core group adv. bd. Solano County Health & Social Svcs., Fairfield, 1995—. V.p. Local 535 State Calif., 1996; mem. Dem. Nat. Com., 1992—. Recipient Appreciation cert. USAF, 1995, Recognition cert. Calif. State Legislature, 1996. Mem. NOW, Pers. Testing Coun., No. Calif. Human Resources Coun., Delta Sigma Theta. Office: Solano County Health & Social Svcs PO Box 12000 Vallejo CA 94590-9000

CROSS, ALICE ELIZABETH, peer mediation and conflict resolution educator; b. S.I., N.Y., Oct. 19, 1942; d. John Thomas and Alice Gertrude (Johnson) O'Brien; m. Alexander Andrew Cross, Dec. 24, 1970; children: Alexander James, Jonathan Brien. BA, Mt. St. Vincent U., Halifax, N.S., Can., 1965; MA, Manhattan Coll., Riverdale, N.Y., 1970; EdD, Nova U., 1983. Cert. tchr. elem. edn., gifted, adminstr., early childhood edn., ESOL, Fla. Tchr. gen. edn. Job Corps of Am., Jersey City, 1967-68; tchr. elem. grades New Rochelle (N.Y.) Pub. Schs., 1968-70; tchr., curriculum specialist Orange County Pub. Schs., Orlando, Fla., 1970-84; tchr. gifted edn. Volusia County Pub. Schs., DeLand, Fla., 1984-95; coord. conflict resolution/peer mediation program Pine Ridge H.S., Deltona, Fla.; dir. Cross Edn. Svcs., Deltona, Fla., 1986—. Edn. editor EPOCH Mag., 1985. Bd. dirs. Mcpl. Svcs. Dist., Deltona, 1993—; mem. Children's Svcs. Coun., Volusia County, 1993-95; treas. Com. on Polit. Edn., Volusia County, 1992—; chmn. Deltona Youth Adv. Bd., 1994-95. Named Volusia County Tchr. of Yr., 1988, Woman of Change, AAUW, 1992, Environ. Tchr. of Yr., Volusia County Dept. Conservation, 1993; finalist Presdl. Award for Excellence in Sci and Maths. Tchg., 1995. Mem. Volusia County Coun. PTA (pres. 1990-92). Roman Catholic. Home: 1689 Gregory Dr Deltona FL 32738-6160 Office: Pine Ridge HS Howland Blvd Deltona FL 32738

CROSS, BETTY FELT, small business owner; b. Newcastle, Ind., Jan. 8, 1920; d. Frank Ernest and Olive (Shock) Felt; m. Paris O. Cross, July 14, 1939 (div.); children: Ernest, Betty J., Robert D., Paris, Toni, Frank; m. John B. Gatlin, 1976 (dec. Oct. 1995). Owner, mgr. Salon D'Or, Indpls., 1956-74; owner Bejon, Madison, Ind., 1974-78, Brass & Things, Madison, 1978-93; pres. Felts Mfg., Inc., 1966—, Silver City USA I, Madison, 1981—, Black Angus, Inc, 1991—, Silver City Video, Inc., Oak Grove, Ky., 1992—, Job Rock I and II, Inc., 1994—. Mem. Nashville C. of C. Avocation: collecting dolls, gold and silver coins, art objects, gold antique jewelry, silver sterling. Office: 928 Gallatin Rd S Madison TN 37115-4625

CROSS, CAROLE ANN, plastics engineer; b. Springfield, Mass., July 30, 1970; d. David Anthony and Linda Ann (Favreau) C. BS in engring. plastics, U. Lowell, 1992. Cost estimator engr. Solvay Automotive, Troy, Mich., 1993; mfg. engr. IBM Corp., Research Triangle Park, N.C., 1993-95; v.p. sales Carolina Jacobson, Sanford, N.C., 1995-96; application devel. engr. GE Plastics, Houston, 1996—. Contbr. article to profl. jours. Mem. Soc. Mfg. Engrs., Soc. Plastic Engrs., Soc. Automotive Engrs., Soc. Advancement of Materials. Roman Catholic. Home and Office: 17402 Valley Palms Dr Spring TX 77379

CROSS, CHARLOTTE LORD, social worker; b. Andalusia, Ala., Dec. 1, 1941; d. Roy Olice and Laura Emily (Smith) Lord; m. Jack Allen Cross, May 5, 1960; children: Jack Allen III, James Duane, Jeffrey Miles. BA in English, Auburn U., Montgomery, Ala., 1979, MS in Psychology, 1980, MS in Secondary Edn./English, 1993. Social worker dept. human resources State of Ala., Andalusia, 1980—; tchr. in English conversation to Nat. Cancer Inst. research scientists, Tokyo, 1965-66; adj. instr. psychology Lurleen B. Wallace State Jr. Coll, 1988-89, Troy State U., Fort Rucker, 1991. Recipient Dept. of Human Resources Commr.'s Merit award, 1989. Mem. United Coun. on Welfare Fraud (cert. welfare fraud investigator), Ala. Coun. on Welfare Fraud. Baptist.

CROSS, DOLORES EVELYN, university administrator, educator; b. Newark, Aug. 29, 1938; d. Charles and Ozie (Johnson) Tucker; children: Thomas E., Jane E. BA in Elem. Edn., Seton Hall U., 1963; MS, Hofstra U. 1968; PhD in Higher Edn. Adminstrn., U. Mich. 1971; hon. doctorates Marymount Coll., Skidmore Coll., Hofstra U., Elmhurst Coll. Asst. prof. edn. Northwestern U., Evanston, Ill. 1971-74; assoc. prof. Claremont Grad. Sch., Calif., 1974-78; vice chancellor CUNY, 1978-81; prof. Brooklyn Coll., 1978-81; pres. N.Y. State Higher Edn. Service Corp., Albany, 1981-88; assoc. provost, assoc. v.p. academic affairs U. Minn., Mpls., 1988-90; pres. Chgo. State U., 1990—; bd. dirs. Coll. Bd., Campus Compact, Assn. Black Women in Higher Edn., No. Trust Co.; sr. cons. South Africa's Historically Black Colls. Editor: Teaching in a Multicultural Society, 1978; bd. dirs. Field Mus., Chgo. Urban League, Leadership for Quality Edn., Chgo. Area Fulbright Scholars Program; Tosney award, Amer. Assn. of Univ. Admin., 1995. Mem. NAACP (life), Am. Edn. Research Assn., Am. Council on Edn. (bd. dirs.), Women Execs. in State Govt. (adv. bd.), Commercial Club (Chgo.). Avocations: running, hiking, bicycling, theater, writing. Office: Chgo State U Office of the President 95th St King Dr Chicago IL 60628

CROSS, DOROTHY ABIGAIL, retired librarian; b. Bangor, Mich., Sept. 9, 1924; d. John Laird and Alice Estelle (Wilcox) C.; B.A., Wayne State U., 1956; M.A. in Library Sci., U. Mich., 1957. Jr. librarian Detroit Public Library, 1957-59; adminstrv. librarian U.S. Army, Braconne, France, 1959-61, Poitiers, France, 1961-63; area library supr., 1963, asst. command librarian, Kaiserslautern, Germany, 1963-67, acquisitions librarian, Aschaffenburg, Germany, 1967, Munich, Germany, 1967-69, sr. staff library specialist, Munich, 1969-72, command librarian, Stuttgart, Germany, 1972-75, dep. staff librarian, Heidelberg, Germany, 1975-77; chief librarian 18th Airborne Corps and Ft. Bragg (N.C.), 1977-79; chief ADP sect. Pentagon Library, Washington, 1979-80, chief readers services br., 1980-83, dir., 1983-91. Mem. ALA, U. Mich. Alumni assn., Delta Omicron. Methodist. Home: 6511 Delia Dr Alexandria VA 22310-2609

CROSS, EILEEN KAY, school counselor; b. Houston, May 21, 1954; d. Robert Edward and Martha Agatha (Taylor) Johnson; m. James David Cross, June 3, 1978; children: Ezekial Robert Banjamin, Seth Jamison Taylor. BS in Edn., Tex. Tech. U., 1976; MS, U. Houston, 1992. Speech/hearing specialist Amarillo (Tex.) Speech & Hearing Ctr., 1976-78; instr. deaf edn. Denton (Tex.) Ind. Sch. Dist., 1978-80; instr. adult basic edn. Alvin (Tex.) C.C., 1982-85; instr. classroom/homebound Alvin Ind. Sch. Dist., 1982-88; devel. dir. Tex. Edn. Regions IV, I & VI, 1988-90; coord. LEAP Alvin C.C., 1990-92, compliance officer, 1992—, advisor students with disabilities, 1992—; cons. in field. Editor: Handbook for Students with Disabilities, 1995, Faculty Handbook, 1995, Staff Handbook, 1995. Bd. dirs. Home and Cmty. Svc., Alvin, 1993-95. Mem. Nat. AHEAD (treas.), Tex. AHEAD (treas.), Assn. Retarded Citizens (Recreation award 1991-92), Soroptimist. Home: PO Box 1165 Alvin TX 77512-1165

CROSS, LYNDA LEE, health facility administrator, nurse; b. L.A., June 18, 1943; d. Fredrick Lewis Heyle and Bonnie Verda (Fridell) Covey; m. Jim Carl Eckler, June 7, 1963 (div. Sept. 1972); children: Barry, Dennis, Shantel, Candace; m. Douglas William Cross, Apr. 10, 1981. Diploma, Paradise Valley Sch. Nursing, 1964; BSN, Sonoma State U., 1981. RN; cert. infusion therapist, 1987. Clin. coord. urology San Diego Urological Med. Group, 1965-71; relief head nurse nursery Grossmont Hosp., La Mesa, Calif., 1971-75; relief head nurse neonatal ICU Balboa Naval Hosp., San Diego, 1976-77; coord. IV therapy St. Helena Hosp. and Health Ctr., Deer Park, Calif., 1977-79; staff nurse, IV therapist Mass. Eye and Ear Infirmary, Boston, 1982-84; pres., owner, IV clinician I.V. Lifeline, Inc., Berkley, Mass., 1984—. Developer IV homecare module, 1984 (1st Nurse award), coop. extended IV therapy in physicians setting, 1993. Fellow New Eng. Intravenous Nurses Soc. (scholarship chmn. 1985-86); mem. Intravenous Nurses Soc. Home and Office: 15861 Hwy 101 South Brookings OR 97415

CROSS, RICHELLE VERONICA, English language educator; b. Ellsworth, Kans., Nov. 2, 1946; d. Richard Monroe and Lois Verona (Hodgson) C.; m. David Wilson Force, Feb. 14, 1993. BS in Journalism, Northwestern U., 1968; student, Colo. Coll., 1964-66. Newspaper reporter, photographer Courier & News-Champion, Gunnison, Colo., 1968-69; med. sec., transcriptionist, editor U. Colo. Health Scis. Ctr., Denver, 1980-94; instr. English Aims C.C., Ft. Lupton, Colo., 1991, Denver Inst. Tech., 1995—. Author: Pioneer Families of the South Platte Valley: Then and Now, 1995; writer (mag.) The Fence Post, 1991-94; (newspaper) His People, 1982-83; editor, writer (newsletter) Big Sisters of Colo., 1984-85; editor, prodn. supr.: History of the Department of Medicine, 1984-85. Mem. Am. Christian Writers, Am. Assn. Med. Transcriptionists, Nat. Writers Assn., Kappa Tau Alpha, Theta Sigma Phi. Home: 16569 Fillmore St Brighton CO 80601

CROSSLAND, ANN ELIZABETH, psychotherapist; b. Cambridge, Ohio, Apr. 24, 1940; d. H. Stewart and Laura Geraldine (Geese) Hastings; m. Eugene Joseph Szmuc, Nov. 30, 1963 (dec. Oct. 1976); m. Richard Ray Crossland, July 16, 1988; children: Rae Ann, Nancy, Carol. BS in Edn., Kent State U., 1965; MSEd in Counseling, U. Akron, 1981. Third grade tchr. Bertha Bradshaw Elem. Sch., Rootstown, Ohio, 1963-64; substitute tchr. Kent (Ohio) City Schs., 1967-84, Portage County Schs., Ravenna, Ohio, 1979-84; assoc. tchr. severely behaviorally handicapped Portage County Schs., Ravenna, 1984-88, H.S. tchr. severe behavior handicap, 1988-92; therapist Child & Adolescent Svc. Ctr., Canton, Ohio, 1992—. Bd. dirs., facilitator Oncology Support Group, Akron, 1977-81; bd. dirs., vol. trainer, counselor WomanShelter, Ravenna, 1980-87; organizer, group facilitator Portage County Cancer Group, Ravenna, 1982-83; mem. steering com. Portage County Adolescent Network, Ravenna, 1987-92. Mem. ACA, Am. Mental Health Counselors Assn., Delta Kappa Gamma (Theta chpt.). Democrat. Unitarian Universalist. Office: Child & Adolescent Svc Ctr 1226 Market Ave N Canton OH 44714-2604

CROSSLEY, ANN COOK, writer; b. Tampa, Fla., June 16, 1939; d. James Hugh and Anna Margaret (Frierson) Caldwell; m. Ross William Crossely, Jun. 7, 1960; 1 child, Georgia Dunagan. BSHE, U. Ga., 1962. Editor ABI Press, Sarasota, Fla., 1989—. Author: The Army Wife Handbook, 1990, 2d edit. 1994, The Air Force Wife Handbook, 1992. Recipient Cert. of Appreciation for Patriotic Civilian Svc., Dept. of Army, 1988. Mem. Phi Kappa Phi. Home: 7860 Estancia Way Sarasota FL 34238

CROSSLEY, HELEN MARTHA, public opinion analyst, research consultant; b. Phila., Sept. 8, 1921; d. Archibald Maddock and Dorothy (Fox) C. BA in Govt. cum laude, Harvard U., 1942; MA in Social Sci. and Pub. Opinion, U. Denver, 1948; postgrad., Heidelberg U., Germany, Am. U., Washington, George Washington U., Yonsei U., Korea. Jr. info. analyst Office War Info., Washington, 1942-43; rsch. specialist, bus. analyst War Food Adminstrn., Washington, 1943-45; data analyst, field supr. Crossley Inc., N.Y.C., 1945-47; from grad. rsch. asst. to sr. analyst Opinion Rsch. Ctr. U. Denver, 1947-49; from study dir. to chief attitude rsch. br. Dept. Def., Heidelberg, Germany, 1950-53; sec., treas., v.p., pres., project dir. ArchCross Assocs., Inc., Princeton, N.J., 1954-85; survey specialist U.S. Info. Agy., Washington, 1955-60, rsch. specialist, 1979-92, ret., 1992; tng. evaluation officer Internat. Coop. Admin., Seoul, 1960-63; ind. cons. Princeton, 1964-78; trustee Gallup Internat. Inst., Princeton, 1995—; co-organizer Korean Soc. for Social Sci. Rsch., 1961-62; technical dir. Nat. Coun. on Pub. Polls, 1969-71. Author: Highlights of Population Shifts, 1944, Evaluation Survey of Korea/U.S. Participant Training Program, 1955-60, 1963; co-author: (with Don Cahalan and Ira Cisin) American Drinking Practices, 1970; contbr. articles to profl. jours. Sec., treas., pres. Penzance Players, Woods Hole, Mass., 1939-45. Recipient Ann Radcliffe scholarship Radcliffe Coll., 1938, cert. of appreciation Korean Ministry of Pub. Info., 1962, cert. of merit Nat. Safety Coun., 1965. Mem. AAUW, NOW, Am. Assn. Pub. Opinion Rsch. (pres. Washington chpt. 1956, 77-78, councillor-at-large 1970-72, sec., treas. coun. 1973-75, mem. conf. com. 1994-95), Internat. Soc. Polit. Psychology, World Assn. Pub. Opinion Rsch. (sec., treas. v.p., conf. chmn., pres. 1960-62, historian 1993—), Washington Sociol. Soc., PC Users Group, Harvard Club at Nat. Press Club, Women's Coll. Club (scholarship prize 1938), Woods Hole Yacht Club. Home and Office: 21 Battle Rd Princeton NJ 08540

CROSSLEY, JODY LYNN, nursing educator; b. Fort Morgan, Colo., Oct. 25, 1960; d. Francis Douglas and Joan Marlene (Weimer) Jolliffe; m. Glenn Forrest Crossley; children: Katherine Lynn, Patrick Forrest. BSN, Fort Hays (Kans) State U., 1983; MSN, West Tex. A&M U., 1993. RN, Kans.; cert. CNS. Staff nurse Scott County Hosp., Scott City, Kans., 1985-86, dir. edn., 1986-87, DON, 1987-89; nursing educator Garden City (Kans.) C.C., 1989—; nursing cons. Nurse's Manual Lab. and Diagnostic Tests, 1995. Mem. ANA, Kans. State Nurses Assn., Kans. Edn. Assn., Am. Nat. Edn. Assn., Acad. of Nurse Practitioners, Sigma Theta Tau. Republican. Home: PO Box 603 Dighton KS 67839-0603

CROSSWHITE, JANE DEES, small business owner; b. Meridian, Miss., June 21, 1961; d. William H. Jr. and Peggy W. (Williams) Dees; m. Allen R. Crosswhite, June 4, 1983; children: Chadwick Dees, Clayton Russell. Cert. respiratory therapy tech., Meridian Jr. Coll., 1981; BS in Edn. Psychology, Miss. State U., 1983. Mgr., sec. Williams Bros. Inc., Philadelphia, Miss., 1983—. Home: 420 Pecan Ave Philadelphia MS 39350 Office: Williams Bros Inc Rt 5 Box 82 Philadelphia MS 39350-9299

CROTEAU, MAUREEN ELIZABETH, journalism educator; b. Hartford, Conn., Feb. 1, 1949; d. Maurice Joseph and Muriel Lucille (Follert) C.; m. Wayne Worcester. BA, U. Conn., 1971; MS, Columbia U., 1973. Reporter Hartford (Conn.) Times, 1971-72; editor Hartford (Conn.) Courant, 1973-76; reporter, editor Providence (R.I.) Jour., 1976-83; freelance journalist, 1983—; dept. head, prof. journalism dept. Univ. Conn., Storrs, 1983—; bd. dirs. Conn. Found. for Open Govt., Hartford, The New London Day newspaper. Co-author: Shipwrecked in the Tunnel of Love, 1983, The Essential Researcher, 1993. Mem. Assn. for Edn. in Journalism & Mass Communications, Soc. Profl. Journalists, Investigative Reporters and Editors. Office: Univ Conn Journalism Dept 337 Mansfield Rd Storrs Mansfield CT 06269

CROTHERS, MARTHA CYNTHIA, counselor, educator; b. Ft. Atkinson, Wis., May 18, 1951; d. James Whalen and Joyce Lavonne (Lindquist) C. BS, So. Ill. U., 1973, MS, 1980, postgrad. Cert. arts mgmt. Cons. Ky. Tng. Office, Frankford, Ky., 1974-75; clin. dir. Aeon Drug Treatment, Carbondale, Ill., 1976-81; pvt. cons. Carbondale, 1981-85; dir. Ill. Presenters Network, 1985-86; asst. coord. The Literacy Connection, Carterville, Ill., 1986—; adj. instr. dance So. Ill. U., 1981-85; cons. Ill. Arts Coun., Chgo., 1980-83, Shryock Auditorium, Carbondale. Active Friends of S.I. Dance. Recipient Rsch. award Assn. Counselor Edn. and Supervision. Mem. ACA, Nat. Sierra Club (chair wildlife com. Shawnee group 1988—, chair midwest wildlife com., Avery Fund grantee 1992). Home: RR 3 Box 84 Cobden IL 62920 Office: The Literacy Connection John A Logan Coll Carterville IL 62918

CROUCH, ALTHA MARIE, health educator, consultant; b. Belton, Tex., Aug. 23, 1933; d. Walter Loy and Nancy Elizabeth (Harrison) C. BS in Health, Phys. Edn. and Recreation, Sul Ross State U., 1966, MA in Health, Phys. Edn. and Recreation, 1967; EdD in Curriculum and Instrn., U. N.Mex., 1977; MA in Counseling Edn., Western N.Mex. U., 1992. Bookkeeper Midland (Tex.) Reporter Telegram, 1954-63; instr. physical edn. and health Our Lady of Peace Cath. Elem. Sch., Alpine, Tex., 1964-65; asst. prof., coord. Womens' Programs Wayland Baptist Coll., Palinview, Tex., 1966-71; vis. instr. Tex. Tech. U., Lubbock, 1971-72; teaching assoc., grad. rsch. asst. U. N.Mex., Alburquerque, 1972-75; asst. prof. health edn. and recreation U. N.Mex., Gallup, 1975-80; asst. prof., co-coord. health edn. program U. N.Mex., Alburquerque, 1980-83; coord. community edn., part-time tchr. U. N.Mex., Valencia, 1983-88; asst. prof., coord. health edn. program U. N.Mex., Gallup, 1988-93, assoc. prof., 1993—; v.p. Faculty Senate, U. N.Mex., Gallup, 1989, 90; exec. dir. Crouch and Assoc. Health Cons., Gallup, 1979—; presenter in field. Assoc. editor N.Mex. Jour. HPERD, 1993; contrb. articles to profl. jours. Bd. mem. Am. Lung Assn., Albuquerque, 1981-87, Am. Heart Assn., Valencia County, 1967-94, Nat. Inst. on Alcoholism, 1980-92, Optimist Club, Gallup, 1990—; cert. ARC, Albuquerque, 1967. Recipient Cert. of Appreciation Svc. award ARC, 1980, 1500 Hours Vol. Svc. in CPR and First Aid award, 1984, Ten Year Svc. Recognition award, 1987, Five Year Disting. Svc. award Wayland Bapt. Coll, 1971, Ella May Small award N.Mex. Sch. Health Assn., 1981, Disting. Svc. award Am. Sch. Health Assn., 1983, Six Yrs. Dist. Svc. Bd. Dirs. award Am. Lung Assn., 1987. Fellow Am. Sch. Health Assn. (internat. health coun. 1989—, rsch. coun. 1981—, budget and fin. com. 1983-85, sec. to study com. 1982, chair 2 coms. 1981-83, conducted surveys 1981, state constituents constitution and by-laws ad hoc com. chair 1981, acting chair resolutions com. 1981); mem. AAHPERD (S.W. dist. asst. registrar 1981, presenter 1981, 92-94, N.Mex. chpt. v.p. health sect. 1981-82, 92-94, tchr. accountability task force; developed AS degree in Cmty. Health 1994; developed AA degree in Sch. Health Edn. 1995), Am. Assn. Counseling and Devel., Am. Assn. Advancement Health Edn., N.Mex. Assn. Counseling & Devel., Coalition for Indian Edn. Office: U N Mex 220 College Rd Gallup NM 87301-5603

CROUSE, LINDSAY, actress; b. N.Y.C., May 12, 1948; d. Russel and Anna (Erskine) C. BA, Radcliffe Coll., 1970. Appearances include: (films) Slapshot, Between-the-Lines, All the President's Men, Prince of the City, The Verdict, Daniel, Iceman, Places in the Heart (Acad. award nomination 1985), House of Games, Communion, Desperate Hours, Being Human, Bye Bye Love, Indian in the Cupboard, The Juror, The Arrival, (TV movies) Out of Darkness, Parallel Lives, Final Appeal, Chantilly Lace, Between Mother and Daughter (Emmy award nomination), (TV series) Hill Street Blues, Murder She Wrote, Columbo, Law and Order, Lifestories, Civil Wars, L.A. Law, Traps, ER. Recipient Obie award for Reunion, 1980, Theater World award for The Homecoming, 1992.

CROW, ELIZABETH SMITH, publishing company executive; b. N.Y.C.; d. Harrison Venture and Marlis (deGreve) Smith; m. Charles P. Crow;

children: Samuel Harrison, Rachel Venture, Sarah Gibson. BA, Mills Coll., 1968; postgrad., Brown U., 1969-70. Editorial asst. New Yorker mag., N.Y.C., 1968-69; editorial asst., exec. editor New York mag., N.Y.C., 1970-78; editor in chief Parents mag., N.Y.C., 1978-88; pres., editorial dir., CEO Gruner & Jahr USA Pub., 1988-93; editor-in-chief Mademoiselle Mag., N.Y.C., 1993—; free-lance book reviewer N.Y. Times Book Rev.; screener, judge Nat. Mag. awards. Mem. Media adv. coun. March of Dimes; bd. advisors The Giraffe Project; trustee mills Coll., 1986-91; bd. dirs. YWCA N.Y. Peabody awards; bd. dirs., exec. com. Met. Opera Guild; mem. N.Y. steering com. Women's Studies in Religion Program, Harvard Divinity Sch.; advisor Ctr. for the Study of Women and Soc., CUNY Grad. Ctr.; with Intersch. Orchestras of N.Y. Recipient Nat. Mag. award for gen. excellence, 1988. Mem. Am. Soc. Mag. Editors (exec. bd. 1984-88), Mag. Pubs. Am. (bd. dirs. 1988-93), Cosmopolitan Club, Century Assn. Democrat. Office: Mademoiselle Mag Condé Nast Publs 350 Madison Ave New York NY 10017-3704

CROW, LYNNE CAMPBELL SMITH, insurance company representative; b. Buffalo, Oct. 13, 1942; d. Stephen Smith and Jean Campbell (Ruggles) Hall; m. William David Crow II, Apr. 16, 1966 (div. Dec. 1989); children: William David III, Alexander Fairbairn, Margaret Campbell. BA, Sweet Briar (Va.) Coll., 1964; postgrad., Am. Coll., 1986. CLU; ChFC. Claims rep. Liberty Mut. Ins. Co., Bklyn. and N.Y.C., 1964-66; with McGraw-Hill Corp., N.Y.C., 1966-67; claims rep. Liberty Mut. Ins. Co., East Orange, N.J., 1967-68; sales assoc. Realty World/Allsopp Realtors, Millburn, N.J., 1981-82; field rep. Guardian Life Ins. Co., 1982—. Bd. dirs. Jr. League Oranges and Short Hills, Millburn, 1979-80, 95-96, Millburn LWV, 1979-80; campaign chair, bus. chair, bd. dirs. United Way Millburn/Short Hills, 1981-88, 90-96, sec., 1990-91. Mem. Nat. Assn. Life Underwriters (Nat. Quality award 1988, 91, 95, Nat. Health Achievement award 1988, 90, Nat. Sales Achievement award 1988, 90), Am. Soc. CLUs and ChFCs (bd. dirs. 1994—), N.J. State Assn. Life Underwriters (dir. region II 1993-95, health chair 1995—), Newark Assn. Life Underwriters (pres. 1993-94, bd. dirs. 1986-94, 96—, sec. 1987-88, treas. 1988-89, 3d v.p. 1989-90, 2d v.p. 1990, pres.-elect 1991-92, pres. 1992-93, Life Underwriter of Yr. 1996), Million Dollar Round Table (qualifying mem.), Knight of Round Table, Internat. Platform Assn., Millburn Bus. and Profl. Women (bd. dirs. 1990-91), Assn. Health Ins. Agts., Nat. Assn. Security Dealers, Racquets Club Short Hills (bd. dirs. 1982-84), Chatham (Mass.) Beach and Tennis Club. Republican. Episcopalian. Home: 22 Winding Way Short Hills NJ 07078-2530 Office: 1150 Raritan Rd Cranford NJ 07016-3369

CROW, SHERYL, singer/songwriter, musician; b. Kennett, Mo., 1963. Degree in classical piano, U. Mo., 1984. Backup singer Bad tour Michael Jackson, 1987; backup singer The End of the Innocence tour Don Henley, 1989; also backup singer George Harrison, Joe Cocker, Stevie Wonder, Rod Stewart; singer, songwriter Tuesday Night Music Club, 1992—. Albums include Tuesday Night Music Club, 1993; singles include Leaving Las Vegas, All I Wanna Do (Grammy awards for Record of Year and Female Pop Vocal, 1995), Strong Enough. Recipient Grammy award for Best New Artist, 1995. Address: care A&M Records 1416 N La Brea Ave Hollywood CA 90028*

CROWDER, BARBARA LYNN, lawyer; b. Mattoon, Ill., Feb. 3, 1956; d. Robert Dale and Martha Elizabeth (Harrison) C.; m. Lawrence Owen Taliana, Apr. 17, 1982; children: Paul Joseph, Robert Lawrence, Benjamin Owen. BA, U. Ill., 1978, JD, 1981. Bar: Ill. 1981. Assoc. Louis E. Olivero, Peru, Ill., 1981-82; asst. state's atty. Madison County, Edwardsville, Ill., 1982-84; ptnr. Robbins & Crowder, Edwardsville, 1985-87, Robbins, Crowder & Bader, Edwardsville, 1987-88, Crowder & Taliana, 1988—. Co-editor ISBA Family Law Newsletter, 1993; co-author chpts. in ISBA Family Law Handbook, 1995; contbr. articles to profl. jours. Chmn. City of Edwardsville Zoning Bd. Appeals, 1986-87; committee woman Edwardsville De, Precinct 15, 1986—; mem. City of Edwardsville Planning Commn., 1985-87; bd. dirs. Madison-Bond County Workforce Devel. Bd., 1995-96. Named Best Oral Advocate, Moot Ct. Bd., 1979, Outstanding Young Career Woman, Dist. XIV, Ill. Bus. and Profl. Women, 1986; recipient Alice Paul award Alton-Edwardsville NOW, 1987, Outstanding Working Woman of Ill. Ill. Fed. of Bus. and Profl. Women, 1988-89, Woman of Achievement YWCA, 1996; recipient Athena award Edwardsville/Glen Carbon C. of C., 1991. Fellow Am. Acad. Matrimonial Lawyers; mem. ABA, Ill. Bar Assn. (assoc. mem. family law sect. coun. 1990-93, mem. 1994—, co-editor family law newsletter 1993, vice chair 1996—), Ill. Fedn. Bus. and Profl. Women (parliamentaria dist. XIV 1991-92), Women Lawyers Assn. Met. East (pres. 1986), Edwardsville Bus. and Profl Women's Club (pres. 1988-89, 95-96, treas. 1989-90, Woman of Achievement award 1985, Jr. Svc. award 1987), Ul Ill. Alumni Assn. (v.p. met.-east club 1994-95, bd. dirs. 1995—). Democrat. Home: 1409 Lantz Ct Edwardsville IL 62025 Office: Crowder & Taliana 216 N Main St Edwardsville IL 62025-1604

CROWDER, BONNIE WALTON, small business owner, composer; b. Lafayette, Tenn., Apr. 14, 1916; d. Edward Samuel Bailey and Nannie Elizabeth (Goad) Walton; m. Reggie Ray Crowder, Nov. 19, 1936; 1 child, Rita Faye. Grad., Nashville Beauty Coll. Owner, operator Bonnie's Beauty Salon, Tampa, Fla. Composer: A Man of Faith, 1988, This Miracle, 1988, (with Willard E. Walton) God Bless Our President, 1988, Awake, Arise America, 1989, Touching My Jesus, 1990, (with Willard E. Walton) Muscle Jerky Boogie, 1992. Mem. ch. choir, Tampa; mem. Bus. and Profl. Women's Chorus, 1960's and 70's, U. South Fla. Community Chorus, 1973-81. Mem. Beta Sigma Phi. Office: Bonnie's Beauty Salon 7230 Hwy 301 S Riverview FL 33569

CROWDER, ELISABETH See WADDINGTON, BETTE HOPE

CROWDER, JANE NELSON, middle school educator; b. Denver, Aug. 14, 1936; d. Arthur S. and Mildred E. (Bjornberg) Nelson; m. Paul A. Crowder, Dec. 27, 1956; children: Jennifer, Steffanie, Paul N., Douglas. BA in Chemistry, Biology, Edn., U. Colo., 1958; postgrad., Cornell U., 1960; MA in Sci. Edn., U. Wash., 1979; postgrad., Western Wash. U., 1981, U. Oreg., 1985. Tchr. sci. Pine Lake Mid. Sch., Issaquah, 1979—; curriculum developer U.S. Geol. Survey, K-12 Water Resources Sourcebook; adv. bd. Coalition for Earth Sci. Edn.; manuscript rev. panel Science Scope, 1991-94; creator, tchr. earth sci. workshops for tchrs. Co-author: Seismic Sleuths (tchr. and classroom manual), 1994, Earth: The Water Planet (tchr. classroom modules), 1989; author: The Quaternary Geology of the Issaquah Area, or How the Last Ice Sheet Shaped Our Land, 1987. Recipient Issaquah Supts. Award for Excellence, 1988, Golden Acorn award Pine Lake Parent-Tchr.-Student Assn., 1995; named Issaquah Tchr. of the Yr., 1988, Eastside Educator of the Yr., Bellevue, 1989; Issaquah Schs. Found. grantee, 1988-89. Mem. Nat. Sci. Tchrs. Assn. (bd. dirs., exec. com. 1993-95), Soc. for Mining, Metallurgy and Exploration (mem. edn. steering com.), Am. Geol. Inst. (adv. bd. 1989-91, adv. panels for earth sci. sourcebooks project), Wash. Sci. Tchrs. Assn. (Middle Level Tchr. of Yr. 1993). Office: Issaquah Sch Dist 565 NW HollyRd Issaquah WA 98027

CROWE, CAROLINE VON CANON, human resources executive; b. Chattanooga, Tenn., Sept. 30, 1949; d. Oliver Leon and Marion Graham (Yundt) Von Canon; m. Frank James Cobia, May 3, 1969 (div. Aug., 1975); 1 child, Frank Naylor Cobia; m. James Lamar Crowe, Nov. 7, 1987. Student in Art, U. Ga., 1966-70; BA in Bus., U. Tenn. at Chattanooga, 1981. Sec. II Clarke County Bd. Edn., Athens, Ga., 1970-73; adminstrv. asst. The Krystal Co., Chattanooga, Tenn., 1973-80; pers. officer TVA, Chattanooga, 1980-84; human resource officer, mgr. TVA, Spring City, Tenn., 1984—; human resource officer TVA, Soddy-Daisy, Tenn., 1995—. Mem. NAFE. Republican. Presbyterian. Office: Sequoyah Nuclear Plant TVA PO Box 2000 Soddy-Daisy TN 37379

CROWE, JUDITH ANN, technology educator; b. Willimantic, Conn., Oct. 7, 1940; d. James Emmett and Ethel Irene (Brown) C.; m. William Marvin Evarts, Aug. 15, 1963 (div. 1984); children: Jeffrey, Kimberly; m. Gary Wayne Talbot, June 28, 1986. BS, U. Conn., 1961; MA, Calif. Luth. U., 1987; EdD, U. Laverne, 1995. Tchr. Bolton (Conn.) Sch., 1962-65, Conejo Valley Unified Sch. Dist., Thousand Oaks, Calif., 1979-92; mem. edn. tech. faculty Calif. Luth. U., Thousand Oaks, 1987-92, coord. edn. tech., 1992—. Mem. Calif. Ednl. Rsch. Assn., Internat. Soc. for Tech. in Edn., Computer Using Educators, Delta Kappa Gamma (membership chair, pres. 1987—), Phi Delta Kappa. Home: 925 Birch Hill Thousand Oaks CA 91320 Office: Calif Luth U 60 West Olsen Thousand Oaks CA 91360

CROWE-HAGANS, NATONIA, manufacturing executive, engineer; b. Chgo., Feb. 10, 1955; d. Benjamin Kermit and Natalie (Williams) Crowe; m. Louis Fisher (div.); children: Sean Crowe, Tamara Fisher; m. William Hagans. AA, Vets. Hosp., Chgo., 1977; BSEE, U. Ill., Chgo., 1983; MS in Mgmt., Maryville U., 1988. Cert. mgr. ICPM. Intern Corning Glass Works, Bluffton, Ind., 1980, Corning (N.Y.) Glass Works, 1981-82; assoc. engr. McDonnell Douglas, St. Louis, 1983-84, engr., 1984-85, sr. engr., 1986-87, laser team leader, 1987-88; staff mgr. McDonnell Douglas, Huntington Beach, Calif., 1988-89; mgr. quick response ctr. Loral Electro-optical Sys., Pomona, Calif., 1989, mgr. mfg. svcs., 1989-91, mgr. material control svcs., 1991-92, program mgr., 1992-93; mgr. prodn. Loral Electro-optical Sys., Pomona, 1993-94; mgr. mfg. engr. Rockwell Automation, Allen Bradley, Milw., 1994-96, project mgr., 1994-95, dir. electro-mech. ops., 1995—; bd. dirs. Matarak Industries. Mem. Womens Aux., Yorba Linda, Calif., 1989, Illiteracy Com., St. Louis, 1984, PTA, Corona, Calif., 1991. Mem. NAFE, Nat. Soc. Black Engrs. (co-founding mem. Gateway chpt. 1987-88, Svc. award 1988), Nat. Mgmt. Assn. (sec., com. mem., numerous awards 1990), Profl. Dimensions, Assn. Mfg. Excellence. Home: PO Box 21792 Milwaukee WI 53221-0792

CROWELL, SHERRY DIEGEL, clinical psychologist; b. Colorado City, Tex., Oct. 19, 1951; d. Charles Ambrose and Jo Ellen (Elliot) Diegel; 1 child, Charles Michael. BA, Tex. Tech U., 1983, MA, 1985, PhD, 1992. Lic. psychologist, Tex. Sr. dir. Psychol. Clinic, Lubbock, Tex., 1987-89; psychometrist Med.-Surg. Neurology Clinic, Lubbock, 1987-89; assoc. clin. psychologist Big Spring (Tex.) State Hosp., 1987-89; psychology intern Austin (Tex.) State Hosp., 1989-90; pvt. practice psychotherapy Abilene, Tex., 1990-93; clin. psychologist Abilene Regional Mental Health Mental Retardation Ctr., 1991-93; pvt. practice psychology Abilene; cons. and chief psychologist Young County Family Resource & Advocacy Ctr., Child Advocacy of Tex., 1996—; adj. prof. psychology McMurry U., 1994—; chair symposium Tex. Assn. on Mental Retardation, 1992; presenter in field. Contbr. rsch. articles to profl. publs. Mem. adv. bd. Big Country AIDS Support Group, Abilene, 1992—; mem. Lubbock AIDS Health Care Planning Group, Lubbock, 1987-89; founding mem., trustee West Tex. AIDS Found., Lubbock, 1986-89, mentoring program, 1995—. Mem. APA, Tex. Psychol. Assn. (chair symposium 1987, 88, 92-93, Alexander award for Rsch. Excellence in Psychobiologic Field 1992), Abilene Philharmonic. Home: 1217 Ross Ave Abilene TX 79605-4230 Office: 3301 N 3rd St Ste 113 Abilene TX 79603-7033

CROWLEY, MARY ELIZABETH (MARY ELIZABETH CROWLEY-FARRELL), journalist, editor; b. Hackensack, N.J., Nov. 7, 1956; d. Jeremiah Christopher and Charlotte Mary (Keith) C.; m. William Christopher Farrell, Sept. 1, 1979; children: Eliza Carolyn Farrell, Luke Jeremiah Farrell. BA in Polit. Sci. & Comm. magna cum laude, Rutgers U., 1978; MA, U. Pa., 1980; postgrad., Trinity Coll., Dublin, Ireland. Reporter various local newspapers, 1974-77; regional corr. Capitol Hill News Svc., Washington, 1977; Washington corr. Thomson Newspapers, 1978-83; dep. mng. editor Comm. Daily, Washington, 1983-92; Washington bur. chief Stevens Pub. Corp., 1992; exec. editor, v.p. editl. Bus. Pubs., Inc., Silver Spring, Md., 1992-94; editl. dir. Phillips Bus. Info., Inc., Potomac, Md., 1995—; lectr., speaker in field. Contbr. articles to profl. publs., chpts. to books. Active many profl. and local civic orgns. Phila. Advertisers Soc. fellow, 1978, Annenberg fellow, 1978-80, Rotary Internat. fellow for profl. journalists, 1980-81, Found. Am. Comms. fellow, 1996; recipient Outstanding Newswriting award N.J. Press Assn., 1976, N.Y. Bldg. and Trades Assn. award, 1976. Mem. Am. Soc. Bus. Editors, Soc. Profl. Journalists (past pres. Washington chpt., Outstanding Newswriting award (2), Outstanding Profl. Chpt./Large award), Investigative Reporters and Editors, Soc. Environ. Journalists, Quill Big Inch Club, Nat. Press Club (v.p. speakers com., Outstanding Newsletter Journalism 1st Place award 1987), Newsletter Pub. Assn., Reporters Com. for Freedom of the Press (steering com.), D.C. On-Line Users Group, Pi Sigma Alpha, Sigma Delta Chi (vice chmn. Found.). Office: Phillips Bus Info 1201 Seven Locks Rd Potomac MD 20854

CROWLEY, MARY ROEMMELE, English and art educator; b. Camden, N.J., Apr. 6, 1937; d. Howard Carl and Anne (McDevitt) R.; m. Derick Foley Salls, Dec. 9, 1960 (div. Mar. 10, 1985); children: John Derick Salls, Katharine Crawford Salls; m. Arthur Edward Crowley, Jr., Feb. 21, 1987; stepchildren: Robert, David, Andrew, Christopher Crowley. BA, Middlebury Coll., 1958; MAE, Castleton State Coll., 1980. Cert. tchr. English 7-12, art K-12, elem. K-6, Vt. Tchr. English/art Stratford H.S., North Stratford, N.H., 1960-63; English tchr. Colebrook (N.H.) Acad., 1963-64; art tchr. Tupper Lake (N.Y.) Schs., 1966-70, Rutland (Vt.) Jr. H.S., 1973-76; tchr. sixth grade St. Peter's Sch., Rutland, 1976-77; tchr. fifth grade Lincoln Sch., Rutland, 1977-82; art tchr. Rutland Elem. Schs., 1982-93; English tchr. Rutland High Sch., 1993-94; tchr. English/art Rutland H.S., 1994-95, tchr. art, 1995-96; mem. Instrn. and Learning Coun., Rutland City Schs., 1991-92; mem. State of Vt. Arts Assessment and Design Team, 1991-93; chaperone Students Mtg. Students, Moscow, 1993. Artist water color, pastel, acrylic paintings. Class sec. and reunion chmn., Middlebury Coll. Class of 1958, Vt., 1988-93; bd. dirs. Crossroads Arts Coun., 1991-95. Mem. Phi Beta Kappa, Phi Delta Kappa. Republican. Mem. Ch. of Christ. Home: 24 Giorgetti Blvd Rutland VT 05701 Office: Rutland High Sch 22 Stratton Rd Rutland VT 05701

CROWN, NANCY ELIZABETH, lawyer; b. Bronx, N.Y., Mar. 27, 1955; d. Paul and Joanne Barbara (Newman) C.; children: Rebecca, Adam. BA, Barnard Coll., 1977, MA, 1978; MEd, Columbia U., 1983; JD cum laude, Nova Law Sch., 1992. Cert. tchr.; Bar: Fla. 1992. Tchr. Sachem Sch. Dist., Holbrook, N.Y., 1978-82; v.p. mail order dept. Haber-Klein, Inc., Hicksville, N.Y., 1984-88; mgr. mdse., dir. ops. Sure Card Inc., Pompano Beach, Fla., 1988-89; legal intern Office U.S. Trustee/Dept. Justice, 1992; assoc. John T. Kinsey, P.A., Boca Raton, Fla., 1993-95; pvt. practice Nancy E. Crown, P.A., Boca Raton, Fla., 1995—. Recipient West Pub. award for acad. achievement, 1992. Mem. ABA, NAFE, Fla. Bar Assn., South Palm Beach County Women's Exec. Club, Phi Alpha Delta. Democrat. Jewish.

CROWN, PATRICIA DAHLMAN, art history educator; b. Chgo., July 17, 1934; m. Keith Crown. PhD, UCLA, 1977. Prof. U. Mo., Columbia, 1977—; guest curator Huntington Art Gallery, San Marino, Calif., 1978, 95. Contbr. articles to profl. jours. Office: U Mo Art History Dept Columbia MO 65211

CROWTHER, ANN ROLLINS, dean, political science educator; b. Zanesville, Ohio, Aug. 29, 1950; d. Walter Edmund and Norma Lucille (Rollins) C. BA in English, Rollins Coll., 1972; M, EdS, U. Fla., 1975; D in Pub. Adminstrn., U. Ga., 1988. Dir. residence hall Ga. Southern U., Statesboro, 1975-78; asst. to head personnel and staff devel. dept. coop. ext. svc. U. Ga., 1978-80, acad. advisor Franklin Coll. Arts & Scis., 1980-81, grad. teaching asst. dept. polit. sci., 1981-84, instr. evening classes program, 1982-85, coord. acad. advising Franklin Coll. Arts & Scis., 1984-89, asst. dean, adj. asst. prof. polit. sci. Franklin Coll. Arts & Scis., 1989-93, assoc. dean, adj. asst. prof. polit. sci. Franklin Coll. Arts & Scis., 1993—. Mem. Am. Polit. Sci. Assn., Am. Soc. Pub. Adminstrn., Ga. Assn. Women in Edn., Nat. Acad. Advising Assn., Nat. Assn. Women in Edn., Nat. Assn. Acad. Affairs Afminstrs. Home: 270 Snapfinger Dr Athens GA 30605-4433 Office: Univ Ga Franklin Coll Arts & Scis 212 New College Athens GA 30601-1853

CROXFORD, LYNNE LOUISE, social services administrator; b. Schenectady, N.Y., Nov. 9, 1947; d. Frederick William and Elizabeth Elger (Irish) C.; BA, Kalamazoo Coll., 1969; MPA, Wayne State U., 1975; m. Daniel Roderick Talhelm; 2 children, Alan Frederick, Thomas Arthur. Caseworker dept. social svc. County of Calhoun, Battle Creek, Mich., 1969-70; caseworker, supr. County of Oakland, Pontiac, Mich., 1970-76; program specialist Mich. Dept. Social Svcs., Lansing, 1976-78; exec. coord. for programming Mich. State Planning Coun. for Devel. Disabilities, 1978-79; staff coord. Gov. Com. on Unification of Pub. Mental Health System, Lansing, 1979-80; dir. dept. social svc. County of Ingham, Lansing, 1980-90; dir. fin. control Mich. Dept. Social Svcs., 1990-91, dir. office payment systems, 1991—; adv. Mich. Assn. Non-Profit Residential Facilities, 1976-78; incorporating dir. Mich. Pub. Mgmt. Inst., 1990; co-chair Mich. Pub. Mgmt. Inst., 1992, chair, 1995-96. Trustee, Unitarian Universalist Ch. of Greater Lansing, 1979-82, v.p., 1980-82; bd. dirs. Coun. for Prevention Child Abuse and Neglect, 1980-83; mem. Lansing Tri-County Pvt. Industry Coun., 1980-90, chair Pvt. Industry Coun. Steering Com., 1987-90. Mem. ASPA (nat. coun. 1986-92, Mich. Pub. Svc. award, 1993), Am. Pub. Welfare Assn., Michigan County Social Svcs. Assn. Club: Zonta (charter Mich. Capitol area, v.p. 1991-92, pres. 1992-93). Recipient Disting. Alumnus award Wayne State U. Grad. Program in Pub. Adminstrn., 1988, Spl. Recognition award Mich. Pub. Mgmt. Inst., 1994. Contbr. in field. Home: 750 Pebblebrook Ln East Lansing MI 48823-2140 Office: 235 S Grand PO Box 30037 Lansing MI 48909-7537

CROYLE, BARBARA ANN, health care management executive; b. Knoxville, Tenn., Oct. 22, 1949; d. Charles Evans and Myrtle Elizabeth (Kellam) C. BA cum laude in Sociology, Coll. William and Mary, 1971; cert. corp. tax and securities law Inst. Paralegal Tng., 1971; JD, U. Colo., 1975; cert. program mgmt. devel. Colo. Women's Coll., 1980; MBA, U. Denver, 1983. Bar: Colo. 1976. Paralegal Holland & Hart, Denver, 1972-73; law clk. Colo. Ct. Appeals, Denver, summer 1976; assoc. firm Shaw Spangler & Roth, Denver, 1976-77; mgr. acquisitions/lands Petro-Lewis Corp., Denver, 1977-85; mgr. strategic planning Westinghouse, Transp. Div., 1985-87; mng. dir. Benefit Resource Mgmt. Group (subs. Blue Cross We. Pa.), 1987-92; COO and v.p. D.T. Watson Rehab. Hosp., 1992-93; regional dir. Franciscan Med. Ctr., Dayton campus, Ohio, 1994—; tchr. oil and gas law Colo. Paralegal Inst., 1978, 79; arbitrator Am. Arbitration Assn.; mediator Dayton Mediation Ctr. Mem. NAFE, ABA, Pa. Bar Assn., Inst. Noetic Scis., Am. Coll. Healthcare Execs. (ethics com., assoc.). Home: 330 Jones St Dayton OH 45410-1104 Office: Franciscan Med Ctr Dayton Campus 601 S Edwin C Moses Blvd Dayton OH 45408-1424

CROZIER, PRUDENCE SLITOR, economist; b. Boston, Oct. 27, 1940; d. Richard Eaton and Louise (Bean) S.; m. William Marshall Crozier, Jr., June 20, 1964; children: Matthew Eaton, Abigail Parsons, Patience Wells. BA with honors, Wellesley Coll., 1962; MA in Econs., Yale U., 1963; PhD in Econs., Harvard U., 1971. Research asst. Fed. Reserve Bank, Boston, 1963-64; teaching fellow-tutor Harvard U., Cambridge, Mass., 1966-69; instr. Wellesley Coll., Mass., 1969-70; sr. economist Data Resources Inc., Lexington, Mass., 1973-74; bd. dirs. Mass. Health and Ednl. Facilities Authority, 1985-93, Omega Fund, 1984-87, Boston Pub. Libr. Found., 1994—, vice chmn., 1996—; vis. com. Harvard Sch. Pub. Health, 1993—, Coll. des Conseillers French Libr. and Cultural Ctr., Boston, 1995—, trustee, 1996. Contbr. articles to profl. jours. Trustee Newton Wellesley Hosp., Mass., 1978-90; overseer Center Research on Women, Wellesley, 1982-83; trustee Wellesley Coll., 1980—. Mem. Am. Econ. Assn., Boston Econ. Club, Phi Beta Kappa. Home: Ridge Hill Farm Rd Wellesley MA 02181

CRUDDEN, ADELE LOUISE, social work research scientist, educator; b. New Orleans, Sept. 25, 1957; d. Edwin Francis and Eunice Louise (Courtault) C.; m. Curtis Edward Alford; children: Johnston, Amanda Louise. BS, Miss. State U., Starkville, 1979; MEd, Miss. State U., 1980; MSW, La. State U., 1989. Lic. social worker, profl. counselor; cert. rehab. counselor, ins. rehab. specialist. Vocat. therapist Developmental Ctr., Decatur, Ala., 1981-82; supr. New Orleans Assn. Retarded Citizens, 1982-84; rehab. specialist Sullivan Rehab., New Orleans, 1984-90; social worker Nat. Med. Care, New Orleans, 1990-91; adminstr., dir. Vocat. Rehab. for Blind, Jackson, Miss., 1991-94; rsch. sci. Miss. State U., Starkville, 1994—; counselor Children's Hosp., New Orleans, 1988, social work cons., 1989; social work cons. La. State U. Human Devel. Ctr., 1989. Active NOW, PTA, Coalition for Citizens with Disabilities, Miss., Parents for Pub. Schs., Starkville. Grantee Miss. Dept. Human Svcs., 1995-96. Mem. NASW, Nat. Assn. Rehab. Profls. in Pvt. Sector, Assn. Edn. and Rehab. Blind and Visually Impaired. Office: Miss State U RRTC PO Drawer 6189 Mississippi State MS 39762

CRUIKSHANK, MARGARET LOUISE, humanities educator, writer; b. Duluth, Minn., Apr. 26, 1940; d. George Patrick and Louise Wimmer C.; life ptnr. PhD, Loyola U., 1969; BA, Coll. St. Scholastica, Duluth, 1962; MA, San Fransisco State U., 1992. Prof. City Coll., San Francisco, 1981—; prof. U. Maine, Orono, summers 1994, 95. Author: Thomas Babington Macaulay, 1978, The Gay and Lesbian Liberation Movement, 1992 (award Myers Ctr. for Human Rights, 1993); editor: The Lesbian Path, 1980, Lesbian Studies, 1982, New Lesbian Writing, 1984, Fierce with Reality, 1995. Affiliate scholar U. Calif., Berkeley, 1996-97. Mem. Nat. Women's Studies Assn. Office: City Coll 50 Phelan Box A25 San Francisco CA 94112

CRUMBLEY, ESTHER HELEN KENDRICK, realtor, retired secondary education educator; b. Okeechobee, Fla., Oct. 3, 1928; d. James A. and Corrine (Burney) Kendrick; m. Chandler Jackson, Oct. 24, 1949; children: Pamela E., Chandler A., William J. BS in Math. Edn., Ga. So. Coll., 1966; M in Math., Jacksonville (Fla.) U., 1979. Cert. secondary edn. tchr., Ga. Secondary edn. tchr. Camden County Bd. Edn., St. Mary's, Ga., 1958-92, ret.; realtor Watson Realty, St. Mary's, 1985—; valedictorian H.S., 1946, dept. chairperson Camden H.S., St. Mary's, 1966-72; pres., sec., treas. Camden GMA, St. Mary's, 1976-78. Area contact person Max Cleand Sec. of State, Atlanta, 1982—; councilwoman City of St. Mary's, 1979-86, mayor pro tem, 1981-86. Named Star Tchr., 1972, Camden GMA, 1979-88. Mem. Camden Ga. Assn. Educators (pres. 1976, sec.-treas. 1977-78, star tchr. 1972), PAGE (biog. com. rep. 1984-92, 1992 retired, named outstanding 8th dist. bldg. rep.), Camden Gen. Mcpl. Assn. (pres., sec.-treas. 1979-88), fin. and budget coms.), Math. Assn., Internat. Platform Assn. Internat. Dictionary Ctr., ABI. Republican. Baptist. Home: RR 3 Box 810 Folkston GA 31537-9729

CRUMBLING, DEANA MARIE, environmental scientist; b. Moses Lake, Wash., Oct. 2, 1958; d. Dean Arthur and Fayalene Rae (Kunkel) C. AA in Life Scis., Harrisburg Area C.C., 1986; BA in Psychology, BS in Biochemistry, Lebanon Valley Coll., 1989; postgrad., Drexel U. Med. technologist several hosps., Pa. & Va., 1977-87; rsch. technician Weiss Ctr. Rsch./Geisinger Clinic, Danville, Pa., 1988-89; chemist United Tech. Assn., Hershey (Pa.) Foods, 1989-90; environ. chemist Pa. Dept. Environ. Resources, Harrisburg, 1990-91; rsch. asst. Drexel U., Phila., 1991-93; med. technologist West Jersey Health System, Voorhees, N.J., 1991—; asst. environ. scientist Woodward-Clyde Cons., Phila., 1995-96; lab. mgr., mem. adj. faculty Sch. Sci. and Health, Phila. Coll. Textiles and Sci., 1996—. Gay-rights activist, spokesperson Pa. Justice Campaign, Harrisburg, 1990, 91. Recipient Andrew Bender Meml. Chemistry award Lebanon Valley Coll., Annville, Pa., 1989, Jean O. Love Meml. award Psychology, 1989. Mem. AAAS, NOW, Am. Inst. Biol. Sci., Soc. Environ. Toxicology and Chemistry, Environ. Defense Fund, Natural Resources Defense Coun., Sierra Club. Democrat. Office: Phila Coll Textiles & Sci Sch Sci and Health School House Ln & Henry Ave Philadelphia PA 19144

CRUMLEY, MARTHA ANN, company executive; b. New Orleans, Aug. 8, 1910; d. Mark Oliver and Mary Elizabeth (Schroder) Carey; m. David Shiffer Crumley III, May 7, 1947; 1 child, David Oliver. Student, Tulane U., New Orleans, 1974. Pres., chief exec. officer Westbank Acad., Gretna, La., 1953-68; sr. v.p. The Social Directory Greater New Orleans, Inc., 1975-92, pres., 1992-94. Pres. Algiers Little Theatre, New Orleans, 1930; tchr. speech and drama YWCA, New Orleans, 1938-39, producer, dir. plays, 1938-39; prs. Krewe of Aparamest, New Orleans, 1938; chmn. fundraising New Orleans Philharmonic Symphony, New Orleans, 1967; mem. women's vol. com. New Orleans Mus. Art, 1967-68; dir. sr. and jr. choir Mt. Olivet Episcopal Ch., New Orleans, 1922-83, mem. altar guild, 1922-83; pres. Mt. Olivet's Women Aux., New Orleans, 1950; mem. women's guild New Orleans Philharmonic; pres. Social Directory of Greater Ne Orlenas, 1992-94. Mem. DAR, English Speaking Union, La. Landmark Soc., Friends of the Cabildo, Children of the Am. Revolution (sr. prs. 1969), Colonial Dames XVII Century (pres. La. chpt. 1977). Home: 4403 Maple Leaf Dr New Orleans LA 70131-7455

CRUMPLER-ROBERTS, SONIA MICHELLE, city administrator; b. N.Y.C., Oct. 6, 1956; d. Handson Charles Roberts and Catherine Ford-Roberts; married; children: Michelle, Samuel, Michael. Grad., CUNY, 1986; attended, Am. Hi-Tech Bus. Sch., N.Y.C., 1987-89, N.Y.C. Police Acad., 1977, 94; MA, ThD, St. Paul's Bible Coll., 1996. Cert. micro-computer specialist; ordained evangelist, 1977. Tchr. Regent Sch., N.Y.C., 1985-88; facilities property mgr. Binswanger Mgmt. Corp., N.Y., 1988-90; ctrl. mgmt.

housing asst. N.Y.C. Housing Authority, 1990—; police adminstrv. aide N.Y.C. Police Dept., 1977-85, 94-95; customer svc. agt. TWA, 1992-93; adminstrv. ct. clk. N.Y. State Unified Ct. Adminstrn., 1993-94. Active Salvation and Deliverance Ch., N.Y.C., 1975—, 2nd v.p. womens ministries, 1995—. Mem. NAFE, Nat. Assn. Housing and Redevelopment Ofcls., Nat. ARISTA Honor Soc. Office: NY Ctrl Housing Authority 1402 Webster Ave Bronx NY 10456

CRUMP-VOLCY, ANGELA RENÉE, policy analyst; b. Balt., Apr. 22, 1963; d. Izell and Elaine Marion (Smith) Crump; m. Guerdy Volcy, May 23, 1992. BA, U. Md., 1986; MPA, Syracuse U., 1987; postgrad., Georgetown U. Policy analyst U.S. Gen. Acctg. Office, Washington, 1987-90, sr. policy analyst, 1990—, recruiter, instr., 1993—; chair Profl. Devel. Inst., Capital Women's Network, Washington, 1993-94. Youth vol. Nat. Urban League, Washington, 1993; campaign vol., Balt., 1995. Recipient Citizenship award Mayor of Balt., 1985. Mem. Nat. Capital Spkrs. Assn. (speaking assoc. 1995—). Democrat. African Methodist Episcopalian. Office: US Gen Acctg Office 441 G St NW Washington DC 20548

CRUTE, DENISE ELAINE, neurosurgeon; b. Huntington, W.Va., May 26, 1961; d. Thomas and Jean (Tabor) C.; m. Michael James Keefe, Mar. 4, 1989. BS in Zoology, Duke U., 1983; MD, U. N.C., 1988, PhD in Neurobiology, 1996. Diplomate Am. Bd. Med. Examiners. Postdoctoral fellow U. N.C., Chapel Hill, 1988-90; housestaff physician, neurosurgery Northwestern U. Hosps., Chgo., 1990—; med. illustrator, webmaster, Northwestern U. Neurosurgery, Chgo., 1995-96. Mem. NOW, Found. for Internat. Edn. in Neurosurgery. Mem. Am. Assn. of Neurol. Surgeons, Congress of Neurol. Surgeons, Soc. for Neurosci., Chgo. Coun. on Fgn. Rels., Women in Neurosurgery, Am. Med. Women's Assn. Office: Northwestern U Divsn Neurosurgery Ste 614 233 E Erie St Chicago IL 60611

CRUVER, SUZANNE LEE, communications consultant, writer; b. Indpls., Mar. 24, 1942; d. William Edward and Margaret Rosetta (McArtor) Ozzard; m. Donald Richard Cruver, June 9, 1963 (div. Feb. 1989); children: Donald Scott, Kimberly Sue, Brian Richard. BA in English, Rutgers U., 1964; postgrad., Rice U., 1990—. Asst. dir. pub. rels. dept. Upsala Coll., East Orange, N.J., 1964-65; asst. planner, pub. editor N.J. Divsn. State & Regional Planning, Trenton, 1967-68; realtor Vonnie Cobb Realtors, Houston, 1979-81; owner Sugar Land Comm., 1980-94; exec. v.p., mktg. mgr. Photoflight Aviation Corp., Sugar Land, Tex., 1982; exec. v.p., artist mgr. H. McMillan Orgn., Inc., Sugar Land, 1983-85; account exec. Mel Anderson Comm., Inc., Houston, 1986; exec. dir. Ft. Bend Arts Coun., Sugar Land, 1986-87; dir. resource devel., vol. svcs., pub. info. Richmond (Tex.) State Sch., Tex. Dept. Mental Health/Mental Retardation, 1987-93; dir. corp. and found. giving Meml. Found., Meml. Healthcare Sys., Houston, 1993-94; owner SLC Comms., Houston, 1994—; mem. adv. bd. Ft. Bend Regional Coun. on Alcoholism and Drug Abuse, Rosenburg, Tex., 1989—. Writer, editor: PATCH Handbook: A Parent to Parent Guide to Texas Children's Hospital, 1983, Ft. Bend mag., 1985-86. Pres. Ft. Bend Arts Coun., Ft. Bend County, Tex., 1987-89; founding dir. PATCH, Tex. Children's Hosp., Houston, 1982; mem. adv. bd. Challenger Ctr. of Ft. Bend. Mem. NAFE, Nat. Soc. Fundraising Execs., Women in Comm., Ft. Bend Profl. Women, Pub. Rels. Soc. Am., Houston World Trade Assn., Ft. Bend C. of C., Rosenberg/Rich C. of C., Leadership Tex. Alumni Assn., Exch. Club of Sugar Land. Republican. Presbyterian.

CRUZ, WILHELMINA MANGAHAS, nephrologist, educator; b. Bulacan, Philippines, July 20, 1942; s. Rectorino Bernardo and Mercedes Correa (Mangahas) C.; A.A., U. Santo Tomas (Philippines), 1960, M.D., 1965; m. Antonio I. Lee, May 28, 1977; children: Richard Anthony, Alexander Victor. Intern, Meml. Hosp., Albany, N.Y., 1967-68; resident in internal medicine Coney Island Hosp., Bklyn., 1968-71; fellow in nephrology VA Hosp., Bronx, 1971-72, Downstate Med. Center, Bklyn., 1972-73; staff physician King's County Hosp. Center, Bklyn., 1973-76; coordinator in medicine Kingsbrook Jewish Med. Center, Bklyn., 1976—; assoc. medical dir. ICU, Doctor's Community Hosp., Lanham, Md., 1977—; clin. asst. prof. SUNY, Downstate Med. Center, Bklyn., 1977—. Diplomate Am. Bd. Internal Medicine, Am. Bd. Nephrology (spl. qualifications in critical care medicine). Mem. ACP, Med. and Chirurg. Soc. Md., Prince George's Med. Soc., Nat. Kidney Found., Internat. Soc. Nephrology, Am. Soc. Nephrology, Soc. Critical Care Medicine, Philippine Med. Assn. Washington. Roman Catholic. Office: 7700 Old Branch Ave Ste D205 Clinton MD 20735-1628

CRUZAN, CLARAH CATHERINE, dietitian; b. Cushing, Okla., Mar. 17, 1913; d. Ulysses Grant and Mamie Amanda (Montgomery) C. BS, Okla. State U., 1941; MS, U. Iowa, 1942. Lic. dietitian, Okla., 1984. Instr. household sci. Okla. State U., Stillwater, 1942-43, instr. home econs. edn., 1947-49; cons. dietitian Rest Haven Nursing Home, Cushing, Okla., 1967-91. Sec. Cushing Sr. Citizens Steering Coun., 1972-91; reporter Okla. Pioneer club, Cushing, 1973-85; precinct election judge, 1989-94. 1st lt. U.S. Army, 1943-46, ETO. Decorated Bronze Star. Mem. AAUW (life, treas. 1970-72, pres. 1974-75), Am. Dietetic Assn., Okla. Heritage Assn., Iris Garden Club (pres. 1971-73), Eastside Garden Club (reporter 1970-75), Omicron Nu, Phi Kappa Phi. Republican. Presbyterian. Home: RR 4 Box 2445 Cushing OK 74023-9123

CRUZ-ROMO, GILDA, soprano; b. Guadalajara, Jalisco, Mexico; came to U.S., 1967; d. Feliciano and Maria del Rosario (Diaz) C.; m. Robert B. Romo, June 10, 1967. Grad., Colegio Nueva Galicia, Guadalajara, 1958; student, Nat. Conservatory of Music of Mexico, Mexico City, 1962-64. Tchr. voice U. Tex., Austin, 1990—; asst. prof., coach, voice tchr. U. Tex., Austin, 1990—. With, Nat. and Internat. Opera, Mexico City, 1962-67, toured, Australia, N.Z., S.Am., with, Dallas Civic Opera, 1966-68, N.Y.C. Opera, 1969-72, Lyric Opera Chgo., 1975, Met. Opera debut as Madama Butterfly, 1970, leading soprano, 1970—, appeared in U.S. and abroad including, Covent Garden, La Scala, Vienna State Opera, Rome Opera, Paris Opera, Florence Opera, Torino Opera, Verona Opera, Portugal, Buenos Aires, others, concert appearances in, U.S., Can., Mexico; U.S. rep., World-Wide Madama Butterfly Competition, Tokyo, 1970; La Scala rep. in: Aida, USSR, 1974; appeared on radio, TV; filmed and recorded: Aida, with Orange Festival, France, 1976; roles include Aida, Madama Butterfly, Suor Angelica, Tosca, Odabella in Attila; Manon Lescaut, Leonora in Il Trovatore; Norma; Maddelena in Andrea Chenier; Desdemona in Otello; Donna Anna in Don Giovanni; Santuzza in Cavalleria Rusticana; (title role) La Gioconda; Adriana Lecouvreur; Luisa Miller; Elisabetta in Don Carlo; Margherite in Faust; Venus in Tannhauser; Giorgetta in Il Tabarro; also roles in Macbeth, Turnadot, Norma, Medea. Winner Met. Opera Nat. Auditions, 1970; recipient Critics award Union Mexicana de Cronistas de Teatro y Musica, 1973, Minerva al Arte award, Mexico, 1991, Ninerva al Arte, Mexico, 1991; named Best Singer, 1976-77; season Cronistas de Santiago de Chile, 1976.

CRYDER, SANDRA JEAN, secondary education educator; b. Delaware, Ohio, Jan. 29, 1955; d. George R. and Marilyn Jean (Moseley) C.; m. Ralph A. Slesinski, Sept. 8, 1979 (div. Aug. 1994); children: Anna J., Sandra Claire. BFA, Ohio Wesleyan U., 1976. Profl. tchg. cert., Md. Mgr. sales promotion, exec. asst. White-Rose Paper Co., Inc., Balt., 1977-81; print prodn. artist Van Sant Dugdale Advt., Balt., 1981-83; tchg. asst. Ednl. In-Roads, Inc., Balt., 1983-94; tchr. art and photography Milford Mill Acad., Baltimore County Pub. Schs., Balt., 1995—; owner, cons., condr. art workshops for children Artifex, Balt., 1994—; dir. arts and crafts Camp Umoja, Notre Dame Prep. Sch., Balt., summer 1994; ednl. cons. N. Woll & Co., Inc., San Jose, Ill., 1993—; presenter Ill. Acad. Sci., 1995, 96; tchr. arts and crafts Camp Holiday, Balt., summer 1996. Exhibited in group show Resurgam Gallery, Balt., 1993. Troop leader Ctrl. Md. coun. Girl Scouts U.S.A., 1991-93. Mem. Nat. Art Edn. Assn., Md. Art Edn. Assn., Balt. Folk Music Soc., Balt. Mus. Art, Walters Art Gallery, The Contemporary. Home: 3206 Tyndale Ave Baltimore MD 21214 Office: Milford Mill Acad 3800 Washington Ave Baltimore MD 21244

CSAPOSS, JEAN FOX, English and religion educator; b. N.Y.C., Mar. 13, 1931; d. John Edward and Elizabeth Marie (Lynch) Fox; m. James Csaposs, Apr. 25, 1981. BA, Manhattanville Coll., 1953, MA, 1971; MA, Columbia U., 1954. Tchr. English, history Acad. of the Holy Angels, Ft. Lee, N.J., 1954-57; asst. in pub. info. Manhattanville Coll., Purchase, N.Y., 1958-66, dir. pub. rels., 1966-69, dir. devel. svcs., 1969-72; editor, mgr. publs. AAUW, Washington, 1972-77; spl. asst. to asst. sec. for pub. affairs U.S. Dept. HHS, Washington, 1977-82; asst. prof. English Bergen C.C., Paramus, N.J., 1985—. Editor, contbr. mag. and newspaper of AAUW (annual awards from Ednl. Press Assn., 1973-77). Bd. trustees Manhattanville Coll., Purchase, 1987-90; bd. dirs. Bergen County coun. Girl Scouts U.S., 1989—; pres. N.J. Polio Network, 1995—. Recipient Disting. Alumni award Manhattanville Coll., 1978. Mem. Nat. Coun. Tchrs. English, Nat. Ctr. Learning Disabilities, Reading Reform Found., Heightened Independence and Progress (bd. dirs. 1988-95, pres. 1990-95), Nat. Soc. Fund Raising Execs., Columbia U. Alumni Club Bergen-Passaic Counties (v.p. 1989-91, pres. 1991-93). Democrat. Roman Catholic. Home: 644 Wyoming Ave Maywood NJ 07607-1544 Office: Bergen CC 400 Paramus Rd Paramus NJ 07652-1508

CSEJTEY, KAREN ELAINE, program administrator; b. Hollywood, Calif., Mar. 16, 1945; d. Roland Harry and Florence (Reiner) Schultz; 1 child, Julie Ann. AA in Sociology, Foothill C.C., Los Altos Hills, Calif., 1976; BS in Orgn. Devel., U. San Francisco, 1981; tng. cert., U. Calif., Santa Cruz, 1992. Vol. VISTA, Harlan County, Ky., 1965-67; program developer YWCA Mid-Peninsula, Palo Alto, Calif., 1970-74, City of Palo Alto, 1974-75; cons., co-founder Interface Applied Rsch. Corp., Palo Alto, 1975-76, Comm. Advocates, Palo Alto, 1976-82; vocat. rehab. counselor Dansker Assocs., Palo Alto, 1981-87; exec. dir. Touchstone Support Network, Palo Alto, 1982-91; dir. Women Entrepreneurs Program, YWCA Mid-Peninsula, 1991—; cons., facilitator, trainer, 1981—. Mem. steering com. Palo Alto Area Diversity Network, 1994—; bd. dirs. Calif. Assn. Microenterprise Opportunity, San Francisco, 1993—, Silicon Valley Small Bus. Devel. Ctr., Sunnyvale, Calif., 1995—, Mid-Peninsula Access Corp., Palo Alto, 1994-96. Recipient For Those Who Care award Sta. KRON-TV, 1985, Jefferson award Am. Inst. Pub. Svc., 1985. Office: YWCA Mid-Peninsula 4161 Alma St Palo Alto CA 94306

CUBA, NAN BRINDLEY, writer, administrator non-profit arts organization; b. Temple, Tex., Aug. 25, 1947; d. Hanes Hanby and Julia Martha (Barton) Brindley; m. Donald Lynn Cuba, July 10, 1967; children: Donald Lynn, Jr., Julia Nan. AA, Sullins Coll., Bristol, Va., 1965-67; BS, U. Tex., 1967-69; MFA, Warren Wilson Coll., 1989. Cert. tchr., Tex. Elem. sch. tchr. Parochial Schs., Dallas, San Antonio, 1970-81; freelance mag. writer San Antonio, Tex., 1982-87; fiction writer and poetess San Antonio, 1986—; host TV interview show Rogers Cablevision, San Antonio, 1984-88; writer in the schs. Tex. Commn. on Arts, San Antonio, 1986-91; faculty English dept. U. Tex, San Antonio, 1989-92; vis. writer Grad. dept. St. Mary's U., San Antonio, Spring 1992; co-creator of readers' theater and alternative sch. Gemini Ink- non-profit arts orgn., San Antonio, 1992—; co-creator and cons. Writers' Inst. at Our Lady of the Lake U., San Antonio, 1986—; vis. writer grad. dept., summer 1996; mem. Lit. Peer Rev. Panel, Tex. Commn. on the Arts, Austin, 1990-92; adv. bd. Guadalupe Cultural Ctr. Lit., San Antonio, 1990-92, Jefferson Arts and Humanities Magnet Sch., San Antonio, 1996; cons. Arts Teach Program San Antonio Arts and Cultural Affairs Dept., 1991; faculty advisor literary mag. U. Tex. at San Antonio, 1991-92. Author, poet: work appears in anthologies and literary reviews, 1992— including Descant, Inheritance of Light, Poets of the Lake, Bloomsbury Rev. and others; works of fiction in Quar. West, Columbia, Crosscurrents; contbr. popular articles to regional magazines including San Antonio Mag., San Antonio Monthly, D. Magazine, Third Coast; cons. for Life, 1984; co-author: (book) Henry Lee Lucas, 1991. Voting place official, Democrat, San Antonio, 1980's; panel mem. Discussion Censorship and the Arts, San Antonio Arts and Cultural Affairs Dept., Mus. of Art, 1990. Recipient 1st place fiction award San Antonio Writer's Guild, 1983, 1st place investigative article San Antonio chpt. Women in Comm., Inc., 1986; alt. Dobie Paisano fellowshp U. Tex. and Tex. Inst. Letters, 1989, 1st runner up Dobie Paisano, U. Tex., and Tex. Inst. Letters, 1991; honoree at Pen Party Friends of San Antonio Pub. Libr., 1984. Mem. NOW, Daedalus Fiction Writers. Episcopalian.

CUBBERLY, MARGARET THERESE, columnist, freelance writer; b. Troy, N.Y., Oct. 31, 1929; d. Joseph Francis and Alma Louise (Bechard) Cairns; m. Norman Graham Cubberly, Jan. 14, 1967; 1 child, Freya Morgan Cubberly. BA, U. R.I., 1951; MSLS, Cath. U., 1959. Head cataloguer Georgetown U., Washington, 1958-61; asst. libr. Calif. Acad. Scis., San Francisco, 1961-66; serials cataloguer U. Calif., Davis, 1966; head of serials Brown U., Providence, 1967-68; asst. head circulation U. Miami, Fla., 1969-72; head of circulation Fla. Internat. U., Miami, 1969-72; reporter, columnist York Town Crier, Yorktown, Va., 1978—; children's libr. Poquoson (Va.) Pub. Libr., 1990-92. Columnist (opinion column) York Town Crier (cert. merit Va. Press Assn. 1984), 1980—. Recipient Cert. of Merit Lifestyle, Va. Press Assn., 1982, Feature Story, 1983, Lifestyle writing 1989, I.D. Wilson award (reporting) Va. Vet. Medicine Assn., 1989. Mem. Friends of Tuva, Hampton Roads Sci. Fiction Assn. (co-founder). Democrat. Home: 115 Marine Cir Grafton VA 23692

CUBIN, BARBARA LYNN, congresswoman, former state legislator, public relations consultant; b. Salinas, Calif., Nov. 30; d. Russell G. and Barbara Lee (Howard) Sage; m. Frederick William Cubin, Aug. 1; children: William Russell, Frederick William III. BS in Chemistry, Creighton U., 1969. Chemist Wyo. Machinery Co., Casper, Wyo., 1973-75; social worker State of Wyo.; office mgr. Casper, Wyo.; mem. Wyo. Ho. Reps., 1987-92, Wyo. Senate, 1993-94; pres. Spectrum Promotions and Mgmt., Casper, 1993-94; congresswoman, Wyo., at large U.S. House Reps., Washington, 1995—; mem com. Nat. Coun. State Legislators, San Francisco, 1987—, Lexington, Ky., 1990—. Mem. steering com. Exptl. Program to Stimulate Competitive Rsch. (EPSCOR); mem. Coun. of State Govts.; active Gov.'s Com. on Preventive Medicine, 1992; vice chmn. Cleer Bd. Energy Coun., Irving, Tex., 1993—; chmn. Wyo. Senate Rep. Conf., Casper, 1993—; mem. Wyo. Rep. Party Exec. Com., 1993; pres. Southridge Elem. Sch. PTO, Casper, Wyo. Toll fellow Coun. State Govts., 1990, Wyo. Legislator of Yr. award for energy and environ. issues Edison Electric Inst., 1994. Mem. Am. Legis. Exch. Coun., Rep. Women. Episcopalian. *

CUCCO, JUDITH ELENE, international marketing professional; b. Summit, N.J., Aug. 9; d. Louis John and Patricia T. (Procaccini) C. BS in Internat. Rels. and Spanish, Am. U., 1973; MBA, U. Md., 1983. Prof. English Universidad Nacional Autonoma de Mex., Mexico City, 1971-72; tchr. Spanish, ESL Montgomery (Md.) County Pub. Schs., 1973-81; acct. exec., industry cons. AT&T Comms., Parsippany, N.J., 1983-87; mgr. internat. mktg. support ctr. AT&T, Morristown, N.J., 1987-89; dir. market devel. internat. ops. divsn. AT&T, Caracas, Venezuela, 1989-91; mgr. global product line Sch. Bus. AT&T, Somerset, N.J., 1991-93; regional mgr. market mgmt. Latin Am., Network Wireless Systems Bus. Unit AT&T, Whippany, N.J., 1994-95; bus. devel. dir. Asia/Pacific and Caribbean/L.Am. AT&T Global Bus. Multimedia Svcs., 1995-96; Ams. regional mgr. AT&T Internat. Product Mgmt., 1996—. Sponsor Child Reach, Warwick, R.I., 1984, Friends of India, 1995—; mem. Small Faith Cmty., Bridgewater, 1992—; vol. Interfaith Hospitality Network, Bridgewater, 1993—; mem. Womyn Included, 1994—. Mem. HISPA, U. Md. Alumni Assn., Am. U. Alumni Assn. Home: 308 Greenfield Rd Bridgewater NJ 08807-3714 Office: AT&T Internat Product Mgmt Rm 23A41 55 Corporate Dr Bridgewater NJ 08807

CUDAK, GAIL LINDA, lawyer; b. Bellville, Ill., July 13, 1952; d. Robert Joseph and Margaret Lucille (Martin) C.; m. Thomas Edward Young, Sept. 15, 1979. BA, Kenyon Coll., 1974; JD, Case Western Res. U., 1977, MBA, 1991. Bar: Ohio 1977, U.S. Dist. Ct. (no. dist.) Ohio 1977, U.S. Ct. Appeals (6th cir.) 1977, U.S. Ct. Appeals (fed. cir.) 1989. Assoc. Fuerst, Leidner, Dougherty & Kasdan, Cleve., 1977-79; staff atty. The B.F. Goodrich Co., Akron, Ohio, 1979-84; sr. corp. counsel The B.F. Goodrich Co., Independence, Ohio, 1985-89; divsn. counsel The B.F. Goodrich Co., Brecksville, Ohio, 1990—. Corp. fundraiser Great Lakes Theater Festival, 1990—, Ohio Found. Ind. Colls., 1993—. Mem. ABA, Ohio State Bar Assn., Cleve. Internat. Lawyers Group. Home: 12520 Edgewater Dr Apt 1405 Lakewood OH 44107-1639 Office: The BF Goodrich Co 9911 Brecksville Rd Cleveland OH 44141-3201

CUDDIHY, JUNE TUCK, pediatrics nurse; b. Buffalo, June 15, 1936; d. John R. Sr. and Monica A. (Donahue) Tuck; m. Robert V. Cuddihy, Aug. 24, 1957; children: Robert V., Timothy, Kathleen. BSN, D'Youville Coll., Buffalo, 1957; MA, Seton Hall U., 1972, MSN, 1979. Cert. primary care nurse practitioner. Pub. health nurse Monroe County, Rochester, N.Y.; health coord. Early Childhood Learning Ctrs. N.J., Morristown; asst. prof. Seton Hall U., South Orange, N.J., 1977-81, William Paterson Coll., Wayne, N.J., 1981-94; clin. assoc. Coll. Nursing Ohio State U., 1994—; cons. Berkeley BioMedical Group, Inc., 1991—. Contbr. articles to profl. jours. Named Outstanding Grad. Student, Seton Hall U., 1979. Mem. ANA (vice chmn. bd. examiners for cmty. health nursing practice, chmn. sch. nurse practice subcom.), N.J. State Nurses Assn., Nat. Child Abuse Assn., Nat. Burn Victim Found., Pub. Health Assn., Sigma Theta Tau. Home: 8798 Killie Ct Dublin OH 43017-8333 Office: Ohio State U Coll Nursing Dept Cmty Parent Child Psyc 1585 Neil Ave Columbus OH 43210-1289

CUDE, RHONDA MILDRED, corporate safety director; b. St. Louis, Aug. 28, 1956; d. James Bud and Edith L. (DeClue) Sly; m. Norman R. Schneider, Feb. 20, 1974 (div. Feb. 1980); children: Norman J., Joshua R.; m. Danny R. Cude, Apr. 10, 1995. Cert. safety supr., San Antonio Coll., 1992, chem. hygiene officer, 1992. Acctg. clk. Western Union, St. Louis, 1983-91; corp. safety dir. Newell Recycling of San Antonio, L.P., San Antonio, 1991—; safety/health cons. Newell Enterprises, San Antonio, 1991—, Newell Internat., San Antonio, 1994—, N.W. Scrap Metal, Houston, 1995—. Mem. Am. Soc. of Safety Engrs. (membership com. 1993-94), Greater San Antonio Safety Coun. Office: Newell Recycling of SA LP 726 Probandt St San Antonio TX 78204

CUGLER, CAROL MARIE MILLER, retired mental health services professional; b. Elizabeth, N.J., Dec. 25, 1942; d. Wilhelm Johannes Rudolph and Frances Caroline (Blank) Miller; m. Harry Clarke Cugler, Jan. 12, 1974; 2 stepchildren. Accredited records technician, Am. Med. Record Assn. Sec. Chris Craft Corporation, Salisbury, Md., 1960-64, Civil Def. Adminstrn., Salisbury, 1964-66; med. records libr. Pine Bluff State Hosp., Salisbury, 1966-74; dir. records/stats./quality assurance Holly Ctr., Salisbury, 1974-93, adminstrv. officer, 1993-95; ret., 1995. Vol. statistician Ea. Shore Hall of Fame, 1986; vol., sec. bd. Humane Soc. Wicomico County, Salisbury, 1988-95, capital campaign sec., 1990-95. Recipient numerous Appreciation awards United Charities Campaign, Appreciation award Ea. Shore Hall of Fame, 1986, Vol. of Yr. award Humane Soc. Wicamico County, 1992. Mem. Delmarva Peninsula Golf Assn. (sec. to adminstrv. asst. 1984-95). Republican. Methodist. Home: 402 E Chestnut St Delmar MD 21875-1711

CULBERTSON, JANET LYNN, artist; b. Greensburg, Pa., Mar. 15, 1932; d. Joseph F. and Helen C. (Moore) Culbertson; m. Douglas I. Kaften, Sept. 30, 1964. BFA, Carnegie Inst. Tech., 1953; MA, NYU, 1963. Instr. art Pace Coll., N.Y.C., 1964-68, Pratt Art Inst., Bklyn., 1973; assoc. prof. Southampton Coll., 1976; drawing instr. Parrish Art Mus., 1979. Exhibited one-woman shows 20th Century West Gallery, N.Y.C., 1967, Molly Barnes Gallery, L.A., 1970, Midtown Gallery, Atlanta, 1971, Lerner-Misrachi Gallery, N.Y.C., 1971, Lerner-Heller Gallery, N.Y.C., 1973, 75, 77, Tower Gallery, Southampton, N.Y., 1976, Benson Gallery, Bridgehampton, N.Y., 1978, 81, 89, Interart Gallery, N.Y.C., 1979, Harriman Coll., N.Y., 1980, Nardin Gallery, N.Y.C., 1981, Aronson Gallery, Atlanta, 1982, Harrisburg State Mus. Pa., 1988, Women Artists Series Rutgers U., N.J., 1988, Carnegie Mellon U., Pitts., 1991, Acme Art Co., Columbus, Ohio, 1992, Islip (N.Y.) Mus., 1992, Suffolk Coll., Riverhead, N.Y., 1996, Stone Quarry Art Park, Cazenovia, N.Y., 1996; two-women shows Women's Art Ctr., San Francisco, 1975; four-women show Heckscher Mus., Huntington, N.Y., 1980; group exhbns. include Carnegie Mus., Pitts., 1953, ann. drawing Bucknell U., 1966-68, Palos Verdes (Calif.) Mus., 1970, 16th ann. all Calif. purchase L.A. Art Assn., 1969-70, nat. drawing ann. San Francisco Mus., 1970, Princeton Gallery Fine Arts, 1972, drawing show Fleisher Meml., Phila., 1974, Am. Acad. Arts and Letters, N.Y.C., 1975, Kingpitcher Gallery, Pitts, 1976, West Broadway Galley, N.Y.C., 1976, Bronx Mus., 1976, Guild Hall, East Hampton, N.Y., 1976, 79, 82, 89, (invitational) 94 (Abstract award 1979, Mixed Media award 1992), Orgn. Ind. Artists, N.Y.C., 1978, Parrish Mus., Southampton, N.Y. Meml. Art Gallery, Rochester N.Y., 1979, Western Carolina U., Cullowhee, Phoenix Mus, Tucson Mus., 1980, The Arsenal, N.Y.C., 1981, 50 nat. women artists Edison Coll. Art Gallery, Ft. Myers, Fla., 1982, Norton Art Gallery, W. Palm Beach, Fla., 1985-86, Easthampton (N.Y.) Ctr. Contemporary Arts, 1988, Newport (R.I.) Art Mus., 1988, 91, Trabia Macafee Gallery, N.Y.C., 1988, Vered Gallery, Easthampton, 1989, 90, 92, Hillwood Mus., Brookville, N.Y., 1990, Islip Art Mus., N.Y., 1990, Ucross Wyo. (invitational), 1990, Women's Caucus for Art, Dallas, 1990, Wash., 1991, Benton Gallery, Southampton, N.Y., 1991, 92, 93, Ark. Arts Ctr. (invitational), Little Rock, 1991, Arlene Bujese Gallery, East Hampton, N.Y., 1994, Hillwood Art Mus., L.I. U., Brookville, N.Y., 1994, Hamilton Coll., Clinton, N.Y., 1995, Stony Brook (N.Y.) U., 1995, others; Babcock Gallery traveling exhibit, 1993-94, Art and the Law traveling exhbn., 1995, Anita Shapolsky Gallery, N.Y.C., 1995, Gerald Peters Gallery, 1996—; contbr. collage to Attica Book, 1972; contbr. articles to profl. jours., prodr. and contbr. Heresies #13 mag. Creative Artists Pub. Service grantee, 1979. Recipient Shirk Meml. award for oil painting Nat. Assn. Women Artists, Inc., 1993, first place award Notorious L.I. exhibit Hillwood Art Mus., Brookville, N.Y., 1994, Purchase award Hoyt Art Inst., 1995; fellow Ossabaw Found., 1981, Dorland, 1983, Ucross Found., 1989, Blue Mt. Found., 1991, 94, VCCA Ctr. Found., 1992. Home: PO Box 455 Heights Shelter Island NY 11965

CULBERTSON, JUDI C., writer, social worker; b. Norfolk, Va., Mar. 1, 1941; d. Hubert Roe and Charlotte Eleanor (Hess) Chaffee; m. Paul Culbertson, June 23, 1962 (div. Feb. 1971); 1 child, Andrew William; m. Thomas Randall, June 22, 1974. BA, Wheaton Coll., 1962; postgrad., Vt. Coll. Editorial asst. Eternity Mag., 1962-64; various teaching positions; sr. caseworker Suffolk County Dept. Social Svcs., Ronkonkoma, N.Y., 1970—. Author: Games Christians Play, 1967, Little White Book on Race, 1970, Permanent Parisians, 1985, Permanent New Yorkers, 1987 (named One of 25 Best Rsch. Books of 1988, N.Y. Pub. Libr. 1988), Permanent Californians, 1988, Permanent Londoners, 1991, Permanent Italians, 1996, The Nursery, 1996; also articles. Mem. AAUW. Democrat. Home: 211 Hawthorne St Port Jefferson NY 11777

CULBERTSON-STARK, MARY, art educator; b. Plainfield, N.J., June 2, 1953; d. Robert Warren and Betty Love (Macfarlane) Culbertson; m. Gary Stephen Stark, Dec. 10, 1977. BFA in Art Studio/Art Edn., U. S.C., Columbia, 1975; MEd in Art Edn., U. Pitts., 1979. Cert. instrnl. II, Pa. Art instr. Bethel Park (Pa.) Sch. Dist., 1975—, art dept. chmn. 6-12, 1992—; art instr. Peters Twp. Sch. Dist., McMurray, Pa., 1987-88; team leader/apprenticeships Assoc. Artists of Pitts., 1994—; ednl. cons. Carnegie Mus. of Art, 1994—, Pitts. Cultural Trust, 1993—, Pitts. Fund for Art Edn., 1990—, Western Pa. Hist. Soc., 1995—. Artist: (book illustration/cover) Pitts. Women's Yellow Pages, 1995, Expressions Theos Found., 1992; author: (ednl. guide) Carnegie Internat., 1995. Dir. visual art Nat. Student Coun. Conf., Pitts., 1985; co-chair edn. Master Visual Artist, Pitts., 1994—; vol. Greater Pitts. Commn. for Women, 1991, Hugh O'Brien Leadership Found., 1993; mem. edn. adv. com. Pitts. Cultural Trust, 1993-94; mem. steering com. Pitts. Artist Archives & Master Visual Artists of Pitts. Ednl. Outreach. Recipient Commendation award Pa. House of Reps., 1992, Pa. Senate, 1992, 1st Place award Mt. Lebanon Retailer's Assn., 1990, award of distinction for visual art, Hoyt Inst. Art. Mem. Nat. Assn. Tchrs. of the Yr., Assoc. Artists of Pitts. (bd. dirs. 1993-94, Juror's award 1989), Pitts. Watercolor Soc. (screening chair 1992, Jury award 1987, 89, 93), Pitts. Print Group, South Hills Art League (bd. dirs. 1988), Middle States Evaluation Team. Office: Bethel Park Sch Dist 309 Church Rd Bethel Park PA 15102

CULLEN, MARY LYNNE, artist; b. Camden, N.J., Nov. 2, 1962; d. Philip Anthony and Elizabeth (Townsend) Chiusano; m. James Francis Cullen; 1 child, Lynne Marie. Student, Santa Reparata Arts Studio, Florence, Italy, 1990; Cert., Pa. Acad. Fine Arts, 1992; BFA magna cum laude, U. Pa., Florence, Italy, 1993; MFA, Pa. Acad. Fine Arts, 1995. Artistic cons., adminstr. Chiusano, Inc., Marlton, N.J., 1985-93; shop asst. graphics dept. Pa. Acad. Fine Arts, Phila., 1991-96; owner, ptnr. Cullen and Howard Decorative Interior Finishes, Marlton, N.J., 1995—; residency, drawing instr. Inst. for Arts and Humanities Edn./Summer Arts Inst., Rider U., Lawrenceville, N.J. Exhibited in group shows at The Maitland (Fla.) Art Ctr., 1995, West Chester (Pa.) U., 1995, Artist House Gallery, Phila., 1994, Marketplace Design Ctr., Phila., 1993, Episcopal Acad., Merion, Pa., 1993, William Penn Charter Upper Sch., Phila., 1992, Art Ctr. Gallery, Westtown, Pa., 1992, The Plastic Club, Phila., 1993, The Painted Bride, Phila., 1995.

Recipient Edna Pennypacker Stauffer Meml. prize, 1991, spl. notice Traditional Media Print prize, 1990, John R. Conner Meml. prize in printmaking, 1991, Morris Blackburn Print prize, 1991. Fellow Pa. Acad. Fine Arts; mem. Phila. Print Club (prize 1990), Plastic Club Phila. (award 1992). Home and Office: 305 Blueberry Ct Marlton NJ 08053-1015

CULLEN, RUTH ENCK, reading specialist, elementary education educator; b. Freeport, N.Y., Mar. 13, 1937; d. Frederick Harold and Grace Bell (Morrow) Enck; m. Thomas J. Cullen, Aug. 22, 1959; children: Randall R., Lauren Cullen Radick, Amy A. BS, Coll. N.J., 1959; MA, Montclair State U., 1966; PhD, Fordham U., 1977. Cert. elem. edn., reading tchr., reading specialist, pupil pers. svcs., adminstr., supr., N.J. Tchr. Bergenfield (N.J.) Pub. Schs., 1959-61, Tenafly (N.J.) Pub. Schs., 1961-63; reading specialist Westwood (N.J.) Regional Schs., 1967—; rschr., conf. Rockaway Twp. (N.J.) Schs., 1978; spkr. N.Y. Reading Assn., 1980, N.J. Edn. Assn., Atlantic City, 1979, Fordham U., Lincoln Ctr., 1976, Montclair State Coll., 1974; instr. summer spl. edn. program Westwood Regional Schs., summers, 1980—; rschr., coord. childhood early excellence in reading program pilot, 1994—; mem. Pupil Assistance Coun. Westwood Regional Schs., mem. portfolio assessment com., 1995—. Mem. assessment com. Westwood Regional Schs., 1992-94, pupil assistance commn., 1985—. Mem. ASCD, NEA (editorial adv. com. 1980), Internat. Reading Assn., N.J. Edn. Assn., Kappa Delta Pi, Phi Delta Kappa. Home: 12 Shadow Rd Upper Saddle River NJ 07458-1918 Office: Westwood Regional Schs School St Westwood NJ 07675

CULLEN, VALERIE ADELIA, secondary education educator; b. Northampton, Mass., May 28, 1948; d. Stanley Walter and Wanda Mary (Rup) Helstowski; m. Lawrence Joseph Cullen, June 26, 1982; 1 child, Shanna Valerie. BA, Westfield (Mass.) State Coll., 1970; MALS, SUNY, Stony Brook, 1975. Cert. secondary math. tchr., N.Y., Mass. Tchr. math. Brentwood (N.Y.) Pub. Schs., 1970-71, Center Moriches (N.Y.) Jr.-Sr. High Sch., 1971-88, BOCES I, Alternative High Sch. and Adolescent Pregnancy Program, Riverhead, N.Y., 1988-90, Ctr. Moriches (N.Y.) Jr.-Sr. High Sch., 1990—. Mem. N.Y. State United Tchrs., N.Y. Math. Tchrs. Assn., Smithsonian Assocs. Home: 4 Keswick Dr East Islip NY 11730-2808 Office: Center Moriches Jr/Sr HS Frowein Rd Center Moriches NY 11934

CULLINGFORD, HATICE SADAN, chemical engineer; b. Konya, Turkey, June 10, 1945; came to U.S., 1966; d. Ahmet and Emine (Kadayifcioglu) Harmanci. Student, Mid. East Tech. U., 1962-66; BS in Chem. Engring. with high honors, N.C. State U., 1969, Engring. Honors Cert., 1969, PhD, 1974. Registered profl. engr., Tex.; cert. mgr. Statis. clk. Rsch. Triangle Inst., 1966; reactor engr. AEC, Washington, 1973-75; spl. asst. ERDA, Washington, 1975; mech. engr. U.S. Dept. Energy, Washington, 1975-78; staff mem. Los Alamos (N.Mex.) Nat. Lab., 1978-82; sci. cons. Houston, 1982-84; environ. control and life support systems test bed mgr. Johnson Space Ctr., NASA, Houston, 1984-85, sr. project engr. advanced tech. dept., 1985-86, sr. staff engr. divsn. solar system exploration, 1986-88, asst. divsn. advanced devel., 1988-90; sr. system engr. Exploration Programs Office NASA, Houston, 1990-92; engring. and mgmt. cons. Houston, 1992—; founder Peace U., 1993; mem. internal adv. com. Ctr. for Nonlinear Studies Los Alamos Nat. Lab., 1981; organizer tech. workshops, sessions at soc. meetings; lectr. in field; docent Mus. Fine Arts, Houston. Editor, author tech. reports; contbr. articles to profl. jours.; patentee in field. Mem. curriculum rev. com. U. N.Mex., Los Alamos, 1980. Recipient Woman's badge Tau Beta Pi, 1968, ERDA Spl. Achievement award, 1976, Inventor award Los Alamos Nat. Lab., 1982, Group Achievement award NASA Johnson Space Ctr., 1987, Outstanding Performance award NASA Johnson Space Ctr., 1987, 89, Superior Performance award NASA Johnson Space Ctr., 1987, 89, Cert. of Recognition for Inventions, NASA, 1988, 89, 90, 92, 93. Mem. AIAA (organizer, 1st chmn. human support com. Houston chpt. 1988-93), AIChE (organizer, 1st chmn. No. N.Mex. club 1980-81, organizer and chmn. low-pressure processes and tech. 1981-89), Am. Nuclear Soc. (sec.-treas. fusion energy divsn. 1982-84, vice chmn. South Tex. sect. 1984-86, mem. local sects. com. 1986-88), Am. Chem. Soc., Soc. for Risk Analysis (organizer, sec. Lone Star chpt. 1986-88, chmn. soc. publicity 1990-93), No. N.Mex. Chem. Engrs. Club, Engrs. Coun. Houston (councilor, sec. energy com.), Sierra Club, Houston Orienteering Club, Phi Kappa Phi, Pi Mu Epsilon.

CULNON, SHARON DARLENE, reading specialist, special education educator; b. Balt., Apr. 20, 1947; d. Clayton Claude and Ann (McIntyre) Legg; m. Allen William Culnon, July 9, 1975. BA in Elem. Edn., U. Mich., 1972; MAT in Reading Edn., Oakland U., 1980; Learning Disabilities Cert., Ariz. State U., 1983. Cert. K-8 edn., K-12 reading specialist, K-12 learning disabilities specialist. Tchr. Mt. Morris (Mich.) Consolidated Schs., 1972-77; reading specialist Paradise Valley Schs., Phoenix, 1978-87, learning disabilities specialist, 1987-90, tchr., 1990—. Mem. Kachina Jr. Women's Club, Phoenix, 1980-83, sec., 1981-82. Recipient Learning Leader/dist. award Paradise Valley Bd. of Edn., Phoenix, 1986. Mem. Phi Delta Kappa (historian 1987-88). Presbyterian. Home: 9035 N Concho Ln Phoenix AZ 85028-5318 Office: Hidden Hills Elem Sch 1919 E Sharon Dr Phoenix AZ 85022-5057

CULP, KRISTINE A., dean, theology educator. B in Gen. Studies with distinction, U. Iowa, 1978; MDiv, Princeton Theol. Sem., 1982; PhD in Religion, U. Chgo., 1989. Vis. instr. theology St. Paul Sch. Theology, 1985-86, instr. theology, 1986-89, asst. prof. theology, 1990-91; dean Disciples Div. House U. Chgo., 1991—, sr. lectr. theology Div. Sch., 1991—. Contbr. articles to profl. jours. Office: U Chgo Disciples Divinity House 1156 E 57th St Chicago IL 60637 also: The Divinity Sch-U Chgo Swift Hall 1025 E 58th St Chicago IL 60637

CULP, MILDRED LOUISE, corporate executive; b. Ft. Monroe, Va., Jan. 13, 1949; d. William W. and Winifred (Stilwell) C. BA in English, Knox Coll., 1971; AM in religion and literature, U. Chgo., 1974, PhD The Com. on History of Culture, 1976. Mem. faculty, adminstr. Coll., 1976-81; dir. Exec. Résumés, Seattle, 1981—; pres. Exec. Directions Internat., Inc., Seattle, 1985—; mem. MBA mgmt. skills adv. com. U. Wash. Sch. Bus. Adminstrn., 1993; spkr. in field. Author: Be WorkWise: Retooling Your Work for the 21st Century, 1994; columnist Seattle Daily Jour. Commerce, 1982-88; writer Singer Media Corp., 1991—, WorkWise syndicated column, 1994—; featured on TV and radio; contbr. articles and book revs. to profl. jours.; presenter WorkWise Report, KIRO Radio, 1991—, WorkWise Registered, 1992. Admissions counselor U. Chgo., 1981—; mem. Nat. Alliance Mentally Ill, 1984—, bd. dirs., 1987, mem. adv. bd., 1988; mem. A.M.I. Hamilton County, 1984—; founding mem. People Against Telephone Terrorism and Harassment, 1990. Recipient Alumni Achievement award Knox Coll., 1990, 8 other awards; named Hon. Army Recruiter. Mem. Nat. Assn. Radio Talk Show Hosts, U. Chgo. Puget Sound Alumni Club (bd. dirs. 1982-86), Knox Coll. Alumni Network. Office: Exec Directions Internat Inc 3313 39th Ave W Seattle WA 98199-2530

CULPEPPER, MABEL CLAIRE, artist; b. St. Louis, Mo., June 20, 1936; d. John Raymond and Mabel Lorene (Hardy) Bondurant; m. James William Culpepper, Dec. 24, 1957; children: Julie Ann, James Jeffrey, John William. AA, Columbia Coll., 1956; BS in Edn., Mo. U., 1958, MEd, 1965. Represented by Artel Gallery, Emmitsburg, Md., 1987-88, Nob Hill Artisans, Albuquerque, 1993-94, Amapola Gallery, Albuquerque, 1995-96; art tchr. Twinbrook BApt., Rockville, Md., 1972-75. One woman exhbn. Artel Gallery, 1987; group exhbns. Rockville (Md.) Art League, 1987, N. Mex. Watercolor Soc., 1989-96. Host parent, officer Am. Field Svc., Damascus, Md., 1978-80; program chmn. Albuquerque Newcomers, 1989-91; docent Albuquerque Mus., 1990-94. Recipient First Prize Rockville Art League, 1987. Mem. Nat. Mus. Women in the Arts, Nat. League Am. Penwomen, N. Mex. Watercolor Soc. (pres. 1992-93, First Prize 1990, Best of Show 1993), Frederick County Art Assn. (pres. 1988), Delta Gamma, Mortar Bd. Home: 3208 Casa Bonita NE Albuquerque NM 87111

CULTON, SARAH ALEXANDER, psychologist, writer; b. Burwell, Nebr., Nov. 12, 1927; d. James Claude and Frances Ann (Evans) Alexander;m. Verlen Ross Culton, June 19, 1949; children: James Verlen, Sarah Ann. BA in Edn., Ea. Wash. U., 1953, MA in Edn., 1956; EdD in Psychology, U. Idaho, 1966. Tchr. pub. schs. Kennewick, Northport, Wash., Potlatch, Idaho, 1946-56; prof. Lewis-Clark U. of Idaho, Lewiston, 1956-59, North Idaho Jr. Coll., Coeur d'Alene, 1961-66; sch. psychologist Sch. Dist. 81, Spokane, Wash., 1966-67; prof. psychology Spokane Falls Community Coll., 1967-88; author Colville, Wash., 1988—; sch. psychologist Adna (Wash.) Spl. Edn. Coop., 1994; mid. sch. counselor Soda Springs (Idaho) Sch. Dist., 1994—; sch. psychologist, sch. counselor vol. Northport Schs., 1989-92; presenter convs. in field. Author: Psychology of Stress and Nutrition, 1991. Doctoral fellow Wash. State U., 1959, U. Idaho, 1964; recipient Faculty Achievement award Burlington No. Found., 1988. Fellow Am. Inst. Stress; mem. NEA, APA, Internat. Coun. Psychologists, Internat. Stress Mgmt. Assn. (newsletter editor), Nat. Stroke Assn., Western Psychol. Assn., Am. Counseling Assn. (writer invitation 1992), Nat. Assn. Sch. Psychologists, Alpha Delta Kappa. Home and Office: 50 E Second S #5 Soda Springs ID 83276

CULVER, IRENE, writer; b. Sayre, Okla., Jan. 11, 1933; d. Joseph Carl and Thelma Veryl (Kirksey) C.; m. Allen L. Wray, Sept. 1, 1952 (div. 1974); children: Randall, Timothy, Christopher, Michelle. BA in English, Calif. State U., Sacramento, 1987. Freelance writer, Sacramento, 1968—; pub. relations cons. several non-profit orgns., Sacramento and Stockton, Calif., 1970-76. Contbr. numerous articles to various publs. With pub. relations dept. United Way, Sacramento, 1969-76; exec. dir. Go And Tell Everyone (G.A.T.E.) Inc., Sacramento, 1979-81.

CULVER, JOAN JOY JOHNSON, social worker, counselor; b. Yoakum, Tex., Nov. 15, 1934; d. William Carlton and Bess Louise (Baker) Johnson; m. Joseph Howard Culver, Aug. 14, 1953; children: Joseph Howard Jr. (Jay), Kendall Blake, Karen Louann Norman. BLS in Psychology summa cum laude, St. Edward's U., Austin, Tex., 1987; MSSW, U. Tex., 1995. Lic. master's social worker; cert. cognitive behavioral therapist. Counselor W-C Counseling Svcs., Austin, Tex., 1980—. Treas. Travis County Grand Jury Assn., Austin, Tex., 1974-75. Mem. NASW, Am. Counseling Assn., Nat. Assn. Cognitive Therapists. Home: 2620 Pecos Austin TX 78703 Office: W-C Counseling Svcs 720 W 34th St Austin TX 78705

CULVERWELL, ROSEMARY JEAN, principal, elementary education educator; b. Chgo., Jan. 15, 1934; d. August John and Marie Josephine (Westermeyer) Flashing; m. Paul Jerome Culverwell, Apr. 26, 1958; children: Joanne, Mary Frances, Janet, Nancy, Amy. BEd, Chgo. State U., 1955, MEd in Libr. Sci., 1958; postgrad., DePaul U., 1973. Cert. supr., tchr. Tchr. Otis Sch., Chgo., 1955-59; tchr., libr. Yates Sch., Chgo., 1960-61, Nash Sch., Chgo., 1962-63, Boys Chgo. Parental, 1969-72, Edgebrook and Reilly Schs., Chgo., 1965-67; counselor, libr. Reilly Sch., Chgo., 1968, tchr., libr., asst. prin., 1973, prin., 1974—. Pres. Infant Jesus Guild, Park Ridge, Ill., 1969-70; troop leader Girl Scouts U.S., Park Ridge, 1967-69; sec. Home Sch. Assn., Park Ridge, 1969, v.p. spl. projects, 1970; mem. Ill. Svc. Ctr. Six Governing Bd., 1994. Recipient Outstanding Prin. award Citizens Schs. Com., Chgo., 1987, For Character award, 1984-85, Whitman award for Excellence in Edn. Mgmt., 1990, Local Sch. Coun. award Ill. Bell Ameritech, 1991, Ill. Disting. Educator award Milken Family Found. Nat. Educators, 1991, Ill. Edn./Bus. Partnership award, 1994, 96. Mem. AAUW, LWV (chmn. speakers bur. 1969), Delta Kappa Gamma, Phi Delta Kappa. Home: 1929 S Ashland Ave Park Ridge IL 60068-5460 Office: FW Reilly Sch 3650 W School St Chicago IL 60618-5358

CUMING, PAMELA, marketing specialist, author; b. Denver, Oct. 13, 1944; d. John Gerald and Rosemary (Miller) C.; m. Terrence C. Shea, June 18, 1966 (div. 1973); m. William I. Bechard, June 23, 1974 (dec. July 1979); m. David Druetzer Gregory, Dec. 9, 1989; children: Monica Cuming, Melissa Cotter. BA, Smith Coll., 1966. Ins. underwriter Chubb & Son, N.Y.C., 1966-69; orgn. devel. specialist Am. Express, N.Y.C., 1969-71; orgn. devel. cons. Ednl. Systems & Designs, Westport, Conn., 1971-73; v.p. Dialectics Inc., Stamford, Conn., 1973-79; pres. Dialectics Inc., Stamford and Encinitas, Calif., 1979-93; sr. mng. dir., dir. mktg. Bear, Stearns & Co., Inc., N.Y.C., 1993—; developer computerized expert systems. Author: The Power Handbook, 1982, Turf and Other Corporate Power Plays, 1987; contbr. articles to profl. jours. Office: Bear Stearns & Co Inc 245 Park Ave New York NY 10167-0002

CUMMING, JANICE DOROTHY, clinical psychologist; b. Berkeley, Calif., Nov. 20, 1953; d. Gordon Robertson and Helen (Stanford) Cumming; 1 child, Shauna Cumming Keddy. BA, U. Calif., Davis, 1975; MA, Calif. State U., Sacramento, 1980; PhD, Calif. Sch. Profl. Psychology, Berkeley, 1985. Lic. psychologist, Calif. Counselor and instr. Serendipity Diagnostic/Treatment, Citrus Hts., Calif., 1978-79; reg. psychologist asst. John Gibbins, PhD, Castro Valley, Calif., 1984-87, Enrico Jones, PhD, Berkeley, Calif., 1985-86; asst. rsch. specialist U. Calif., Berkeley, 1985-90; clin. cons. Family Guidance, Children's Hosp., Oakland, Calif., 1987-90; clin. supr. psychiat. svcs. Children's Hosp., San Francisco, 1987-90; pvt. practice psychology Castro Valley, 1987-90, San Francisco, 1987-90, Oakland, Calif., 1990—; mem. rschr. San Francisco Psychotherapy Rsch. Group, 1987—, instr., 1991, conf. chair, 1992-93; conv. chair Calif. State Psychol. Assn., Sacramento, 1985, 86; asst. clin. prof. U. Calif., San Francisco, 1992—. Mem. APA, Calif. Psychol. Assn. (continuing edn. com. chair 1986, co-chair 1987), Psychologists for Social Responsibility (bd. dirs. 1984-87, chair 1987-89), No. Calif. Soc. Psychoanalytic Psychology, Alameda County Psychol. Assn., Phi Beta Kappa. Office: 5835 College Ave Ste C Oakland CA 94618-1653

CUMMING, MARILEE, apparel company executive; b. Columbus, Nebr.; m. Andrew Cumming; 1 child, Melissa. BA in Psychology, Rosemont Coll., 1969. Buyer trainee children's divsn. J.C. Penney, Inc., N.Y.C., 1975, asst. and assoc. buyer positions in children's and women's, 1975-82, catalog dress buyer, 1982-84, sr. buyer misses blouses, 1984-86, merchandise mgr. men's accessories and furnishings, 1986-87, merchandise mgr. women's, misses and updated apparel, 1987-90, dir. women's merchandise dept., 1990, dir. merchandising women's divsn., 1990-93, pres. home and leisure divsn., 1993-96, pres. women's apparel divsn., 1996—. Campaign vice chmn. Met. Dallas United Way Campaign, 1996—; mem. NWCA N.Y., Acad. Women Achievers. Office: JC Penney Co Inc 6501 Legacy Dr Plano TX 75024-3698

CUMMINGS, ANNE MARIE, production control manager; b. Cleve., Jan. 30, 1952; d. Eugene Patrick and Mary Agnes (Callahan) C. Student, Cleve. State U., 1970-72. Inventory ctrl. supr. Harris Calorific, Cleve., 1974-84; mgr. ADC Kentrox, Portland, Oreg., 1984—; vice chmn. Sunset Science Park Fed. Credit Union, Portland, 1989—. Mem. Am. Soc. of Prodn. & Inventory, Material Handling Soc. Democrat. Roman Catholic. Home: 3960 SW 203rd Ave Beaverton OR 97007 Office: ADC Kentrox 14375 NW Science Park Dr Portland OR 97229

CUMMINGS, CONSTANCE, actress; b. Seattle; d. Dallas Vernon and Kate Logan (Cummings) Halverstadt; m. Benn Wolfe Levy, 1933; children: Jonathan, Jemima. Chmn. Young People's Theatre Panel; mem. Arts Council, 1963-69. Broadway debut Treasure Girl, 1928; London debut Sour Grapes, Repertory Players, 1934; film debut Movie Crazy, 1932; appeared on radio, TV, films, theatre; joined Nat. Theatre Co., 1971; appeared in London stage prodns.: Madame Bovary, 1937, Romeo and Juliet, 1939, Saint Joan, 1939, The Petrified Forest, 1942, Return to Tyass, 1950, Lysistrata, 1957, The Rape of the Belt, 1957, Who's Afraid of Virginia Woolf?, 1964, Justice is a Woman, 1966, Fallen Angel, 1967, Nat. Theatre Co., A Long Day's Journey Into Night, 1972, The Cherry Orchard, 1973, The Circle, 1975, Mrs. Warren's Profession, Vienna, 1976, Wings, U.S., 1978, London, 1979 (Tony award 1979), Hay Fever, 1980, The Golden Age, 1981, The Chalk Garden, N.Y.C., 1982, The Glass Menagerie, N.Y.C., London, 1982, (one woman show) Fanny Kemble, 1986, Crown Matrimonial, 1987, Tête a Tête, Mass., 1989, The Chalk Garden, London, 1992, Uncle Vanya, Chichester Theatre, 1996, others; performed in Claudel-Honnegar oratorio St. John at the Stake, Albert Hall, London, 1949, Peter and the Wolf, Albert Hall, 1955, Wings on Am. pub. TV; dir. Royal Ct. Theatre. Recipient Obie award, 1979, Drama Desk award, 1979; decorated Comdr. Brit. Empire. Mem. Brit. Actors Equity (mem. council), Royal Soc. for Encouragement of Arts and Commerce. Mem. Labour Party. Club: Chelsea Arts.

CUMMINGS, DIANA CELESTE BAKER, accounting assistant; b. Savannah, Ga., May 30, 1956; d. Alfred Thomas and Nancy Caroline (Brodmann) Baker; m. William David Cummings, June 23, 1976; children: Christina Michelle, William Dean, John David. AA, Armstrong State Coll., 1994, postgrad., 1994—. Clk. Elliott's Drug Store, Savannah, 1974-75, McCrory's Dept. Store, Savanna, 1975-76; tchr. aide Bartlesville (Okla.) Sch. Sys., 1985-86; tchr. Bayou La Batre (Ala.) Childcare, 1987-88; clk. Armstrong State Coll., Savannah, 1988-92, acctg. asst., 1992—. Merit badge counselor Boy Scouts Am., 1993-95. Hope scholar, 1995-96. Mem. Nat. Mus. Women in Arts (charter), Phi Alpha Theta. Republican. Office: Armstrong State Coll 11935 Abercorn St Savannah GA 31419

CUMMINGS, EDITH EVELYN, special education educator; b. Brockton, Mass., May 21, 1944; d. E. Jane Murdoch; 1 child, David R. BA, Bridgewater State Coll., 1967; MEd, Boston U., 1978. Cert. English, social studies, and spl. edn. tchr., Mass. English tchr. Old Rochester Regional H.S., Mattapoisett, Mass., 1967-68; remedial reading tchr. Nathaniel Morton Sch., Plymouth, Mass., 1968-72; spl. edn. tchr. Plymouth-Carver Intermediate Sch., 1972-88, 95—; diagnostician, tchr. Plymouth North H.S., 1988-93, head dept. spl. edn., 1993-95; ind. tutor diagnostic testing specialist, Plymouth area. Author numerous plays for Priscilla Beach Theater, Manomet, Mass. (Geronimo award 1988). Organizer Baby Baskets project Marshfield (Mass.) Cmty. Christmas, 1992-94. Mem. NEA, Mass. Tchrs. Assn., Plymouth County Tchrs. Assn., Nat. Parks and Conservation Assn., Audubon Soc. Office: Plymouth Cmty Intermed Sch Long Pond Rd Plymouth MA 02360

CUMMINGS, ERIKA HELGA, business consultant; b. Offenbach, Germany; came to U.S., 1978; d. Erwin and Edith (Trunski) Maier; m. Robert H. Cummings, Dec. 1970; 1 child, Marisa Anne. BSBA, Calif. State U., Bakersfield; M in Internat. Mgmt., Am. Grad. Sch. Internat. Mgmt., Glendale, Ariz., 1983. Cert. fin. planner. Inflight supr. TWA, Paris; internat. ops. mgr. Cooper LaserSonics, Santa Clara, Calif.; bus. cons. Suncoast Bus. Industries, Sarasota, Fla., 1989—; fiin. planner Am. Express Fin. Advisors, Sarasota, 1989-94; bus. cons., 1994—; Peace Corps. vol. City Adminstrn. of Vladimir, Russia, 1994—. Mem. NAFE, Toastmasters, Beta Gamma Sigma.

CUMMINGS, JANE ANN, elementary educator; b. Elmira, N.Y., Mar. 21, 1948; d. James J. Sr. and Cecilia A. (Rush) C. BA in Elem. Edn., SUNY, Cortland, 1970; MS in Elem. Edn., Elmira Coll., 1973. Real estate salesperson Elliott R. Blauvelt Inc., Horseheads, N.Y., 1987-91; tchr. Elmira City Sch. Dist., 1970—; various dist. coms. Elmira City Schs., 1970—. Active Jr. League of Greater Elmira-Corning, Inc., 1987-95, sustainer, 1995—; bd. dirs. CASA of Chemung and Schuyler Counties, Elmira, 1993. Recipient Woman of Achievement Chemung County Coun. of Women, 1995. Mem. Am. Fedn. Tchrs., N.Y. State United Tchrs., Elmira Tchrs. Assn. Home: 957 Scio St Elmira NY 14901

CUMMINGS, JOAN E., health facility administrator, educator. BA, Trinity Coll., 1964; MD, Loyola U., 1968. Diplomate Am. Bd. Internal Medicine, Geriatric Medicine. Med. internship St. Vincent Hosp., Worcester, Mass., 1968-69; med. residency Hines VA Hosp., Hines, Ill., 1969-71; sr. residency Nephrology Hines VA Hosp., 1971-72, ambulatory care svc. chief gen. med. section, 1971-84, med. dir., hosp. based home care, 1972-87, chief, intermediate care svc., 1984-87, assoc. chief of staff, extended care and geriatrics, 1987-90, med. dir., extended care center, 1987-90, dir., 1990—; asst. prof. Clinical Medicine U. Ill., 1976-82; asst. prof. Clinical Medicine Loyola U., 1983-91, assoc. prof. Clinical Medicine, 1991—; mem. ad hoc com. on primary care U. Ill., 1980-82, coll. edn. policy com. U. Ill., 1980-82, State Ill. Emergency Med. Svc. Coun., 1981-83, Comprehensive Health Ins. Plan Bd. State Ill., 1990—, Med. Licensing Bd. State Ill., 1992—, exec. com. Chgo. Fed. Exec. Bd. State Ill., 1992—; program dir. Loyola/Hines Geriatric Fellowship Program, 1987-90. Contbr. to profl. mags. and jour. Recipient Disting. Svc. award Abraham Lincoln Sch. Med. Univ. Ill., 1979, 81, Leadership award VA, 1980, Certificate of Appreciation award VA, 1980, Laureate award Am. Coll. Physicians, 1990. Fellow Am. Coll. Physicians; mem. AMA (Ill. delegation 1985—, vice speaker ho. delegates 1987-89), Chgo. Med. Soc. (pres. Hines-Loyola Branch 1982-83), Ill. State Med. Soc. (trustee 1984—, chmn. com. on Ill. med., 1988—, speaker ho delegates 1989-91, exec. com., 1989-91, policy com., 1989—), Am. Coll. Physicians (councilor Ill. chpt. 1984—), Chgo. Geriatric Soc., Am. Geriatric Soc. Office: PO Box 5000 5th Ave & Roosevelt Rd Hines IL 60141-5000

CUMMINGS, JOSEPHINE ANNA, writer; b. Gainesville, Fla., July 12, 1949; d. Robert Jay and Marcella Dee (Mount) Cummings. A.B.J./Design cum laude, U. Ga., Athens, 1971. Copywriter William Cook, Jacksonville, Fla., 1971-73; creative dir. Leo Burnett, Chgo., 1973-76; sr. v.p., group creative dir. D. D. B. Needham, Chgo., 1976-84; sr. v.p., creative dir. Saatchi-Saatchi, N.Y.C., 1984; sr. v.p., sr. creative dir. Ted Bates, N.Y.C., 1984; exec. v.p., chief creative officer Tracy-Locke, Dallas, 1985-87; exec. v.p., exec. creative dir. Bozell, Chgo, 1989; exec. v.p., creative dir. Y&R, N.Y.C., 1990-92; pres. The Joey Co., N.Y.C., 1992—. Author: (play) Azaleas, 1988, (short story collection) Crimes of Passion, 1988, (childrens' book) The Hospital is a Funny Place, 1988, (short film) Night Magic, 1989. Named as creator One of Hundred Best TV Commls. Advt. Age, 1978-79, one of Advt. 100 Best Advt. Age, 1986, one of People to Watch Fortune mag., 1986, Ad Age one of Best and Brightest, N.Y. Mem. Amelia Earhard, Ninety Niners Club, N.Y. Women in Film. Office: The Joey Co 133 W 19th St Fl 5 New York NY 10011-4117

CUMMINGS, JUDY ANNETTE, secondary education educator; b. Denver, May 27, 1943; d. John Joseph and Garnett Edwana (Ferry) Leuthard; m. Ernest LeRoy Cummings, Aug. 6, 1965; 1 child, Scott Joseph. BS in Edn., Black Hills State U., Spearfish, S.D., 1971. Cert. tchr., Wyo. Clk. Workmen's Compensation, Denver, 1961-62, Woodo Product Co., Berkeley, Calif., 1962, Denver Pub. Sch. Sys., 1964-65; clk.-typist Martin Marietta Corp., Waterton, Colo., 1962-64; sec. Yardney Electric Corp., Pawcatuck, Conn., 1965; substitute tchr. Campbell County Sch. Dist., Gillette, Wyo., 1970-73, tchr. bus. edn., 1973—; dir. drug free sch. program Campbell County H.S., 1993—, quality sch. team, 1995-96, sch. improvement com., 1995-96; sec. CAMPCO Credit Union Bd.; alt. mem. Liaison Com. for Salaries and Benefits; mem. Elem. Sch. Keyboarding Task Force. Mem. adv. com. Juvenile Detention-Treatment Ctr., Gilette, 1993. Recipient plaque as outstanding bus. educator Campbell County H.S., 1991, named Tchr. of Yr., 1994. Mem. NEA, Am. Vocat. Assn. (life), Wyo. Edn. Assn., Wyo. Bus. Edn. Assn. (membership chmn. 1985), Wyo. Vocat. Assn. (membership chmn. 1985), Campbell County Edn. Assn. (membership chmn.), Nat. Bus. Edn. Assn., Campbell County Vocat. Assn. (sec.), Campbell County C. of C. (adv. bd. 1982-84), Wyo. Coaches Assn., Future Farmers Am. (hon., cert. of appreciation), Alpha Delta Kappa (past pres.). Republican. Methodist. Home: 1183 Country Club Rd Gillette WY 82718-5512 Office: Campbell County HS 1000 Camel Dr Gillette WY 82716-4950

CUMMINGS, LAURA LEE, anthropologist, educator; b. Torrance, Calif., Aug. 15, 1946; d. Donald McDonald and Evelyn Florence (Kennedy) C. BA, Sonoma State U., 1971; MA, San Diego State U., 1984; PhD, U. Ariz., 1994. Cons. for archaeology and site documentation Inst. Nat. Anthropologia e Historia, State of Baja Calif., Tijuana, Mex., 1979-84; rschr. Centro Fronterizo del Norte de Mex., Tijuana, 1984; rsch. asst. Bur. Applied Rsch. in Anthropology U. Ariz., Tucson, 1984-88, rschr., translator documentary Rels. of S.W., 1985-88, assoc. dir. women's studies, 1991-95, lectr. in anthropology, 1995; dir. Hopi visually impaired project Am. Found. for Blind, Kykotsmovi, Ariz., 1989-91; asst. prof. anthropology U. Tex., El Paso, 1995-96; linguistic cons. Hopi Tribe Health Dept., Kykotsmovi, Ariz., N.Y.C., 1987-88; rsch. assoc. Inst. Investigaciones Hist., U. Autónoma de Baja Calif., Tijuana, 1990—. Contbr. articles to profl. jours. Barbara Curran fellow, 1985; bilingual edn. fellow U.S. Dept. Edn., 1990-94. Mem. Am. Anthropol. Assn., Am. Ethnological Soc., Asociación Cultural de las Californias.

CUMMINGS, LESLIE EDWARDS, hospitality management educator; b. Modesto, Calif., Feb. 17, 1951; d. George Robert and Mary Lou (Bomberger) Edwards; m. William Theodore Cummings Jr., Mar. 12, 1977. BS in Home Econs., Ariz. State U., 1974, MS in Agriculture, 1977, D in Pub. Adminstrn., 1990. Intern General Mills, Inc., Golden Valley, Minn., summer 1968; diet technician Mesa (Ariz.) Luth. Hosp., 1972-73; salesperson Romney Products, Inc., 1974; pharm. ins. auditor Pharm. Card Sys., Inc., 1974-76; mem. chain hdqrs. staff Fry's Supermarkets, Inc., 1977; adj. instr. foodsvc. Auburn (Ala.) U., 1978-79, from asst. mgr. to mgr. Campus Ctr. Foodsvcs., 1979-80; customer support analyst WANG Labs., Inc., 1981-83; asst. prof. U. Nev., Coll. Hotel Adminstrn., Las Vegas, 1983-87, assoc. prof.,

1987-93, prof., 1993—; presenter Hotel-Motel Expo, 1985, So. Nev. Dietetics Assn. and So. Nev. Home Econs. Assn., Las Vegas, 1986, Inst. Food Technologists, Las Vegas, 1987, Universidad Madre y Maestra System, Santo Domingo, Dominican Republic, 1987, Internat. Assn. Hospitality Accts., Las Vegas, 1986, Foodsvc. and the Environment, Scottsdale, Ariz., 1990, State of Ariz. Dietetics Assn., Scottsdale, 1991, Assn. for the Study of Food and Soc., Tucson, 1991, ASPA, Las Vegas, 1991, Foodsvcs. Sys. Beyond 2000 Conf., Israel, 1992, Gaming Educator's Conf., Las Vegas, Hospitality Info. Tech. Assn., New Orleans, 1995, Environments for Tourism Conf., Las Vegas, 1996, Internat. Hospitality Tech. Conf., Nashville, 1996; panelist, spkr. in field of applied tech. and gaming trends. Author: (textbook) (with Lendal Kotschevar) Nutrition Management for Foodservices, 1989, Instructor's Manual for Nutrition Management for Foodservices, 1989; contbr. numerous articles to profl. jours. Vol. Women's Resource Network Career Event, Annual Nev. Gov.'s Conf. for Women. Recipient Nat. Assn. Schs. Pub. Adminstrn. dissertation award, 1990, Boyd Rsch. award, 1991, Ace Denken Disting. Rsch. award, 1996—; fellow Rotary Internat., 1978. Mem. ASPA, Am. Dietetic Assn. (treas. environ. nutrition dietetic practice group 1992-95, registered dietitian), Inst. Internal Auditors (cert.), Coun. on Hotel, Restaurant and Instnl. Edn., Phi Beta Kappa, Phi Kappa Phi, Pi Alpha Alpha. Office: WF Harrah Coll Hotel Adminstrn Food & Beverage Mgmt Dept 4505 Maryland Pkwy Las Vegas NV 89154-6022

CUMMINGS, MARIA TERESA, English as a second language educator; b. Jamaica, N.Y., Mar. 2, 1949; d. Daniel and Iris (Hernandez) Resto; m. John McGrew Cummings, III, May 30, 1970; children: Juan Carlos, Marissa Cristina. BA, Rutger's U., 1974; MS, U. Houston, 1987, U. Houston, 1992. Fixed assets account. RCA Corp., Camden, N.J., 1974-76; credit mgr., cost acct. Midland Ross Corp., Highland Park, N.J., 1977-79; gen. acct. supr. Joy Petroleum Co., Houston, 1979-80; bilingual elem. tchr. Goose Creek Ind. Sch. Dist., Baytown, Tex., 1986-90; v.p. Houston Ind. Sch. Dist., 1990-92; ESL educator Vallejo (Calif.) City Unified Sch. Dist., 1993—; lang. assessment comm. chair Goose Creek Ind. Sch. Dist., Baytown, 1987-90, sch. cmty. liaison Houston Ind. Sch. Dist., 1990-92, bd. dirs. Si Podemos Gen. Mills Grant, Vallejo, 1995—, Benicia Edn. Found., Benicia, 1993—. Bilingual Cmty. Liaison Dem. Party, Baytown, 1984, youth leader Girl Scout of Am., Baytown, 1986-92, bilingual liaison St. Vincent de Paul Soc., Benicia, 1992. Mem. Nat. Assn. of Bilingual educators, Am. Assn. of U. Women (v.p. 1994-95), Assn. for Supervision and Curriculum. Democrat. Roman Catholic. Home: 378 Allen Valley Benicia CA 94510-3905 Office: Valejo City Unified Sch Dist Franklin Jr High 501 Starr Ave Vallejo CA 94590

CUMMINGS, MARY VOIGT, counselor; b. Eagle Grove, Iowa, Sept. 23, 1937; d. Wilson Burns and Evelyn Louise (Allen) Voigt; m. William Grosvenor Cummings, Jr.; children: William Grosvenor III, Grace Ann, Mary Joan, Margaret Louise, Nancy Elizabeth. BS, Northwestern U., 1959; MA, U. South Fla., 1977. Counselor Pinellas Park H.S., Largo, Fla., 1977-84; guidance coord. Clearwater (Fla.) H.S., 1984—. Bd. dirs. Samaritan Counseling, Clearwater, 1984; bd. dirs., trustee MPM Health Systems, Clearwater, 1993—; pres. Jr. League, Clearwater, 1975; active in PTAs, sch. adv. bds., etc. Named Outstanding Young Woman, Jr. Woman's Club, Clearwater, 1975, Beautiful Activist, Burdines, Clearwater, 1977, Master Tchr., State of Fla., 1986. Mem. Am. Counselors Assn., Fla. Counselors Assn., Suncoast Counselors Assn., Pinellas County Counselors, Phi Kappa Phi. Episcopalian. Office: Clearwater HS 540 S Hercules Ave Clearwater FL 34624

CUMMINGS, PENELOPE DIRRIG, special education educator; b. Akron, Ohio, Sept. 16, 1944; d. Raymond Joseph and Pearl Penelope (Pantages) Dirrig; m. Ray Cummings, Jn. 21, 1967; children: Michael R., James E. BA in English, U. Akron, 1966; MS in Spl. Edn., U. Kans., 1992. Tchr. English Akron Pub. Schs., 1966-69; tutor learning disabled Delaware (Ohio) Pub. Schs., 1980-82; tutor homebound Trumbull (Conn.) Pub. Schs., 1982-87; tutor homebound, student support svcs. program Olathe (Kans.) Pub. Schs., 1987-91; tchr. English and learning disabled Penn Valley C.C., Kansas City, Mo., 1988-91; tchr. learning disabled Turner Pub. Schs. Unified Sch. Dist. # 202, Kansas City, Kansas, 1991—. Editor sorority mag. The Compass, 1976 78. Pres., sec. Officer's Wives' Club, Rickenbacher AFB, Columbus, Ohio, 1973-74; active Mortar Bd., Akron, 1965-66, PTA, 1976—. Scholar United Steelworkers Am., 1962-66, U. Akron, 1962-66, Theta Phi Alpha, 1992. Mem. NEA, Coun. for Learning Disabilities, (v.p. Mo.-Kans. chpt. 1992-93, pres. 1994-95), Coun. for Exceptional Children (pres. elect N.E. Kans. coun. 436), Kappa Delta Pi, Phi Sigma Alpha. Democrat. Roman Catholic. Home: 11014 W 126th Ter Overland Park KS 66213-2152 Office: Highland Middle Sch 3101 S 51st St Kansas City KS 66106

CUMMINGS, VIRGINIA (JEANNE), former real estate company executive; b. Greenwood, S.C., June 24, 1923; d. Samuel Barksdale and Alma Virginia (Davis) Jones; m. John W. Cummings, Nov. 7, 1938; children: John W., Martha Jean Wells. Student, U. Miami; PhD (hon.), Colo. State Christian Coll., 1973. Sec. Pine Crest Pvt. Sch., Ft. Lauderdale, Fla., 1956-59; real estate broker Am. Realty, Ft. Lauderdale, 1959-62; pres., founder Cummings Realty Inc., Ft. Lauderdale, 1962-85; v.p. Magic Carpet Travel, Ft. Lauderdale, 1975-89; pres. Women's Coun. Ft. Lauderdale Bd. Realtors, 1961; freelance writer. Feature writer Fla. Living Mag., 1969-74; contbr. articles to profl. jours. Bd. dirs., past chmn. Ch. of Religious Sci., Ft. Lauderdale. Mem. Nat. Bd. Realtors, Ft. Lauderdale Area Bd. realtors, DAR. Democrat. Home: 4300 N Ocean Blvd Apt 19A-B Fort Lauderdale FL 33308

CUMMINS, NANCYELLEN HECKEROTH, electronics engineer; b. Long Beach, Calif., May 22, 1948; d. George and Ruth May (Anderson) Heckeroth; m. Weldon Jay Cummins, Sept. 15, 1987; children: Tracy Lynn, John Scott, Darren Elliott. Student avionics, USMC, Memphis, 1966-67. Tech. publ. engr. Missile and Space divsn. Lockheed Corp., Sunnyvale, Calif., 1973-76, engring. instr., 1977; test engr. Gen. Dynamics, Pomona, Calif., 1980-83; quality assurance test engr. Interstate Electronics Co., Anaheim, Calif., 1983-84; quality engr., certification engr. Rockwell Internat., Anaheim, 1985-86; sr. quality assurance programmer Point 4 Data, Tustin, Calif., 1986-87; software quality assurance specialist Lawrence Livermore Nat. Lab., Yucca Mountain Project, Livermore, Calif., 1987-89, software quality mgr., 1989-90; sr. constrn. insp. EG&G Rocky Flats, Inc., Golden, Colo., 1990, sr. quality assurance engr., 1991, engr. IV software quality assurance, 1991-92, instr., developer environ. law and compliance, 1992-93; software, computer cons. CRI, Dabois, Wyo., 1993—; customer engr. IBM Gen. Sys., Orange, Calif., 1979; electronics engr. Exhibits divsn. LDS Ch., Salt Lake City, 1978; electronics repair specialist Weber State Coll., 1977-78. Author: Package Area Test Set, 6 vols., 1975, Software Quality Assurance Plan, 1989. Vol., instr. San Fernando (Calif.) Search and Rescue Team, 1967-70; instr. emergency preparedness and survival, Claremont, Calif., 1982-84, Modesto, Calif., 1989; mem. Lawrence Livermore nat. Lab. Employees Emergency Vols., 1987-90, EG&G Rocky Flats Bldg. Emergency Support Team, 1990-93, Dubois Search and Rescue, 1995—. Mem. NAFE, NRA, Nat. Muzzle Loading Rifle Assn., Am. Soc. Quality Control, Job's Daus. (majority mem.). Republican. Mem. LDS Ch. Home: PO Box 398 Dubois WY 82513 Office: CRI PO Box 398 Dubois WY 82513-0398

CUNNANE, PATRICIA S., medical facility administrator; b. Clinton, Iowa, Sept. 7, 1946; d. Cyril J. and Corinne Spain; m. Edward J. Cunnane, June 19, 1971. AA, Mt. St. Clare Coll., Clinton, Iowa, 1966. Mgr. Eye Med. Clinic of Santa Clara Valley, San Jose, Calif. Mem. Med. Adminstrs. Calif. Polit. Action Com., San Francisco, 1987. Mem. Med. Group Mgmt. Assn., Am. Coll. Med. Group Adminstrs. (nominee), Nat. Notary Assn., NAFE, Exec. Women Internat. (v.p. 1986-87, pres. 1987—), Profl. Secs. Internat. (sec. 1979-80), Am. Soc. Ophthalmic Adminstrs., Women Health Care Execs., Healthcare Human Resource Mgmt. Assn. Calif. Roman Catholic. Home: 232 Tolin Ct San Jose CA 95139-1445 Office: Eye Med Clinic of Santa Clara Valley 220 Meridian Ave San Jose CA 95126-2903

CUNNINGHAM, ANDREA LEE, public relations executive; b. Oak Park, Ill., Dec. 15, 1956; d. Ralph Edward and Barbara Ann C.; m. Rand Wyatt Siegfried, Sept. 24, 1983. BA, Northwestern U., 1979. Feature writer Irving-Cloud Pub. Co., Lincolnwood, Ill., 1979-81; account exec. Burson-Marsteller Inc., Chgo., 1981-83; group account mgr. Regis McKenna Inc., Palo Alto, Calif., 1983-85; founder, owner, pres. Cunningham Communication Inc., Santa Clara, Calif., 1985—. Mem. Am. Electronics Assn., U.S. C. of C. Republican. Office: Cunningham Communication Inc 3945 Freedom Cir Ste 900 Santa Clara CA 95054-1223

CUNNINGHAM, BILLIE M., accounting educator; b. Joliet, Ill., Apr. 2, 1946; d. William Morgan and Mildred Jane (Watson) Klett; m. Robert T. Cunningham, Feb. 27, 1971; 1 child, Dana Marie. BBA, North Tex. State U., 1968, MBA, 1975, PhD, 1980. Applications programmer Burroughs Corp., Dallas, 1969-71; software programmer USAA, San Antonio, 1971-72; asst. prof. Tex. Christian U., Ft. Worth, 1980-85; prof. Collin County C.C., Plano, Tex., 1986-93; Disting. lectr. U. North Tex., Denton, 1993-94; adj. asst. prof. U. Mo., Columbia, 1994—; mem. reaffirmation com. So. Assn. Colls. and Schs., West Palm Beach, Fla., 1991, DeKalb Coll., Decatur, Ga., 1992, Brevard C.C., Cocoa, Fla., 1993; mem. acctg. edn. workshop planning com. Tex. Tech U., Lubbock, 1992; mem. acctg. adv. bd. Brookhaven Coll., Dallas, 1993; ad hoc reviewer Issues in Acctg. Edn., Sarasota, Fla., 1993; breakout leader student lyceum Fedn. Schs. Accountancy/Ernst & Young, Vero Beach, Fla., 1993; grant reviewer KPMG Peat Marwick, Montvale, N.J., 1994. Author: (textbooks) Accounting: Principles and Applications, 5th edit., 1986, Financial Accounting, Principles and Applications, 5th edit., 1986, Accounting: Basic Principles, 5th edit., 1986; mem. editl. rev. bd. Acctg. Edn.: A Jour. of Theory Practice and Rsch., 1995—; contbr. articles to profl. jours.; speaker at numerous confs. Chair pedagogical resources subcom. on critical thinking Fedn. Schs. Accountancy, St. Louis, 1994, chair pedagogical resources com., 1995-96; com. mem. Second Century Breakfast Com., U. North Tex., 1991-92, mentor Cmty. Mentors Program, 1991-93. Recipient Nat. Teaching Excellence award Nat. Inst. for Staff and Orgnl. Devel., 1989, Exemplary Acctg. Educator award Mo. Assn. Acctg. Educators, 1995; Tex. Christian U. summer rsch. grantee, 1981, 82. Mem. Am. Acctg. Assn. (program adv. com. 1990-91, coun. 1991-92, acctg. edn. adv. com. 1992-94, v.p. 1994-96, sec.-editor 2-yr. coll. sect. 1989-90, vice-chair 2-yr. coll. sect. 1990-91, chair 2-yr. coll. sect. 1991-92, coord. regional reps./officer at large 2-yr. coll. sect. 1991-92, curriculum revision com. 2-yr. coll. sect. 1993-94, vice-chair tchg. and curriculum sect. 1996-97), Acad. Acctg. Historians (edn. com. 1990-94), Gamma Phi Beta, Phi Delta Kappa, Alpha Kappa Psi. Office: U Mo Columbia Sch Accountancy 328 Middlebush Hall Columbia MO 65211

CUNNINGHAM, CAROLYN AMY, counselor; b. Hempstead, N.Y., Apr. 3, 1966; d. Richard Otto and Anne Marie (Seidenschwang) Mann; m. Paul Richard Cunningham, June 29, 1991. BA in Psychology, Hartwick Coll., 1988; MS in Counseling Psychology, Villanova U., 1991; postgrad., U. Conn. Cert. counselor, Conn. Rehab. counselor Hall-Brooke Hosp., Westport, Conn., 1991-92; case mgr. liaison Cath. Family Svcs., Danbury, Conn., 1992-94; counselor Interlude, Inc., Danbury, 1994—. Mem. ACA, Am. Mental Health Counseling Assn., Nat. Bd. Cert. Counselors, Conn. Counseling Assn. Home: 1 Crest Ave Danbury CT 06811 Office: Interlude Inc 29B Grand St Danbury CT 06810

CUNNINGHAM, JACQUELINE LEMMÉ, psychologist, educator; b. Biddeford, Maine, Apr. 22, 1941; d. S. James and Alice (Fréchette) Lemmé; m. Seymour Cunningham II, Dec. 16, 1960 (dec. 1987); children: Macklin Todd, Danielle, Alyssa. BA in Psychology cum laude, U. Maine, Orono, 1963; MS in Psychology, U. South Ala., 1983; PhD, U. Tex., 1994. Tchr. Mobile (Ala.) Pub. Schs., 1976-81; intern Devereux Found., Devon, Pa., 1988-89; fellow in developmental disabilities Med. Sch. Harvard U., Cambridge, Mass., 1990; prof. U. S.D., Vermillion, 1994-95; fellow in pediat. neuropsychology Children's Nat. Med. Ctr., Washington, 1995—; cons. in field. Contbr. articles to profl. jours. Mem. APA (outstanding dissertation of yr. award divsn. 16 1994), Internat. Neuropsychol. Soc., Nat. Acad. Neuropsychology, Soc. History Behavioral Scis., Phi Kappa Phi.

CUNNINGHAM, KAREN JEAN, humanities educator; b. Woonsocket, R.I., Oct. 9, 1946; d. William Harvey and Ethel Mae (Graham) C.; m. Gary Jay Karasik. BA in English with honors, Sacramento State Coll., Calif., 1969; MA in English with honors, San Francisco State Coll., 1972; PhD in English, U. Calif., Santa Barbara, 1985. Cert. adult edn. tchr., Calif. Mgr. mgmt. achievement program Pacific Telephone, San Francisco, 1972-73; instr. ESL Berlitz Lang. Schs., San Francisco, 1973-74; libr. asst. City of Daly City, Calif., 1974-77; lectr. dept. of English U. Calif., Santa Barbara, 1985-86; asst. prof. English Fla. State U., Tallahassee, 1987-93, assoc. prof. English, 1993—. Contbr. articles to profl. jours. Income tax assistance vol. V.I.T.A., San Francisco, 1972-73; election precinct vol. City and County of San Francisco, 1973-76; commr. Fla. Commn. on the Status of Women, Tallahassee, 1995—. Rsch. fellowship S.C. Davis Ctr. for Hist. Rsch., Princeton U., 1993, U. Calif., 1981-82; grantee Folger, Shakespeare Inst. and NEH,. Mem. AAUW, MLA, Marlowe Soc. of Am., Renaissance Soc. of Am., Shakespeare Assn. of Am., Soc. for the Study of Early Modern Women, South Atlantic MLA (women's caucus). Democrat. Office: Fla State Univ English Dept Tallahassee FL 32306-1036

CUNNINGHAM, KAREN LEE, marketing professional; b. St. Louis, Sept. 23, 1949; d. Everett R. and Madelyn Marie (Restivo) Saddler; m. David G. Cunningham, May 4, 1970 (div. 1974). Attended, Ind. State U., 1967-69, Butler U., 1975. Cmty. affairs rep. Am. Fletcher Nat. Bank, Indpls., 1969-80; owner Corporate Art Cons., Indpls., 1980-83; dir. pub. rels. and spl. events L.S. Ayres & Co., Indpls., 1983-85; dir. pub. rels. and promotions Drum Corps Internat., Lombard, Ill., 1986; dir. bus. devel. Schmidt Assocs. Archs. Inc., Indpls., 1987-90; dir. mktg., bus. devel. and pub. rels. Eden Design Assocs., Inc., Carmel, Ind., 1990—. V.p. bd. dirs. Cathedral Arts, Inc., Indpls., 1978-86; mem. adv. coun. Humana Hosp., Indpls., 1983-85; mem. steering com. Eiteljorg Mus., Indpls., 1988-89; city govt. liaison Arts Coun. Indpls., 1989; mem. numerous coms. Meth. Hosp. Task Core, Indpls., 1987—, 500 Festival Assocs., Indpls., 1989—; bd. dirs. Ind. State Mus., Indpls., 1990—; mem. adv. bd. Ind. State U., Terre Haute, 1994—;. Mem. Pub. Rels. Soc. Am., Ind. Soc. Pub. Rels. Profls., Internat. Facility Mgmt. Assn. (bd. dirs., Affiliate Member of Yr. 1993), Soc. Mktg. Profl. Svcs. (bd. dirs.), Network Women in Bus. (bd. dirs. 1978-82, Networker of Yr. 1984). Home: 8516 Hague Rd Indianapolis IN 46256-3441 Office: Eden Design Assocs Inc 111 Congressional Blvd Ste 120 Carmel IN 46032-5652

CUNNINGHAM, LAURA, playwright, novelist; b. N.Y.C., Jan. 25, 1947; d. Laurence Moore and Rose Weiss. BA, NYU, 1967. Freelance playwright, novelist N.Y.C., 1967—; essayist New York Times. Playwright: Bang, 1986, Beautiful Bodies, 1987, Where She Went, What She Did, 1988; author: Sweet Nothings, 1977, Third Parties, 1980, Sleeping Arrangements (memoir), 1989. Recipient Best Profile award Standard Gravure, 1984, 85; fellow Yaddo, 1981, N.Y. Found. Arts, 1987, NEA fellow in playwritings, 1989, in lit., 1991, in non-fiction lit., 1991, theatre and lit., 1996. Mem. New Dramatists. Democrat. Office: care New Dramatists 424 W 44th St New York NY 10036-5205

CUNNINGHAM, MARCILE ELIZABETH, secondary education educator, musician; b. Mio, Mich., Feb. 23, 1938; d. Gleason Russell Smith and Mildred Florence (Speck) Smith-Foley; m. Edmund J. Cunningham, Jr., June 24, 1961; children: Elizabeth Anne, Edmund J. III. BME, Ctrl. Mich. U., 1959, MA in Edn., 1973. Cert. in secondary edn. for music, band, math.; cert. in elem. edn. for music. Tchr. band Clintondale Pub. Schs., Mt. Clemens, Mich., 1959-62; tchr. 6th grade CenterLine (Mich.) Pub. Schs., 1962-63; tchr. 6th grade Coleman (Mich.) Cmty. Schs., 1963-64, tchr. 7th and 8th grade math., 1964-81, tchr. elem. vocal music, 1981-85, tchr. math., computers and band, 1985-90; tchr. math., dir. honors program Mid Mich. C.C., Harrison, 1989—; organist St. Paul's Luth. Ch., Sanford, Mich., 1979—; clarinetist Eddy Concert Band, Saginaw, 1976—. Clarinetist Ctrl. Mich. Area Concert Band, Shepherd, 1973-90; clarinetist, libr. Midland Concert Band, 1990—; bass clarinetist, percussionist Midland Cmty. Orch., 1992—. Mem. Phi Theta Kappa (advisor 1993—). Roman Catholic. Home: 5031 W Shaffer Rd Coleman MI 48618-9368 Office: 1375 S Clare Ave Harrison MI 48625-9442

CUNNINGHAM, MARSHA LYNN, realtor; b. Tacoma, Wash., Apr. 25, 1947; d. Matt Antone and Sarah Esther (Luck) Vodanovich; m. John Stanley Cunningham, Sept. 28, 1968; children: Jonathan Todd, Bradley Stephen. Diploma in nursing, Tacoma Gen. Hosp. Sch. of Nursing, 1968. RN, Wash. Staff nurse Allenmore Hosp., Tacoma, 1968-70, RN, supr., 1973-79; dir. Staff Builders Health Care Svcs., Tacoma, 1979-83; assoc. exec. dir. Humana Hosp., Tacoma, 1983-88; sales asst. Hawkins Poe, Inc., Tacoma, 1988-92; sales assoc. Lyon & Brown Realtors, Tacoma, 1992-95, Coldwell Banker, Tacoma, 1995—. Chmn. ARC, Tacoma, 1995—; sec. Women in Networking, Tacoma, 1996—; bd. dirs. Corp. Devel., Tacoma, 1994—, Tacoma Youth Symphony Assoc., 1988-90; pres. club C. of C., 1980-92. Mem. Nat. & State Assoc. of Realtors, Nat. State & Local Assoc. of Cert. Residential Spl., Women in Networking. Home: 3408 N 35th St Tacoma WA 98407 Office: Coldwell Banker Hawkins-Poe Realtors 4001 N 26th Tacoma WA 98407

CUPP, MARILYN MARIE, sales executive; b. Coleman, Tex., Feb. 22, 1953; d. Kellum and Jean (Sheppard) Guthne: Johnson; m. David Allan Coyle (div. Aug. 1981); 1 child, Daniel Steven Jr. BBA, So. Meth. U., Dallas, 1976. Buyer Kelly's Childrens Shop, Dallas, 1982-90; saels rep. ATC, Addison, Tex., 1995—. Albums include I'm Walking On Sunshine; producer Nat. Dem. Conv., Stas. ABC, CBS and NBC, 1992. Mem. 500, Inc. Democrat. Methodist. Home: 5038 Airline Rd Dallas TX 75205-2930

CURETON, CLAUDETTE HAZEL CHAPMAN, biology educator; b. Greenville, S.C., May 3, 1932; d. John H. and Beatrice (Washington) Chapman; m. Stewart Cleveland, Dec. 27, 1954; children: Ruthye, Stewart II, S. Charles, Samuel. AB, Spelman Coll., 1951; MA, Fisk U., 1966; DHum (hon.), Morris Coll., Sumter, S.C., 1996. Tchr. North Warren High Sch., Wise, N.C., 1952-60; tchr. Sterling High Sch., Greenville, 1960-66, Wade Hampton High Sch., Greenville, 1967-73; instr. Greenville Tech. Coll., 1973-95, ret., 1995; bd. dirs. State Heritage Trust, 1978-91; commr. Basic Skills Adv. Program, Columbia, 1990—; mem. adv. bd. Am. Fed. Bank, NCNB Bank, Greenville, 1991—. Mem. Greenville Urban League, NAACP, S.C. Curriculum Congress; v.p. Bapt. E.& M. Conv. of S.C.; mem. S.C. Commn. on Higher Edn. Com. for Selection of the 1995 Gov.'s Prof. of the Yr. Recipient Presdl. award Morris Coll., 1987, 91, Svc. award S.C. Wildlife and Marine Dept., 1986, Outstanding Jack and Jill of Am. citation, 1986, Excellence in Tchg. award Nat. Inst. for Staff and Orgnl. Devel., U. Tex., Austin, 1992-93, Educator of Yr. award Greenville chpt. Am. Cancer Soc., 1994, Outstanding Svc. award Best Chance Network/Am. Cancer Soc., 1994, Citation S.C. House of Reps., 1995. Mem. AAAS, AAUW, Nat. Assn. Biology Tchrs., S.C. Curriculum Congress, Nat. Coun. Negro Women, Inc., Higher Edn. S.C. Com. for Selection Prof. of Yr. 1995, Delta Sigma Theta (past v.p. Greenville chpt. alumnae). Home: 501 Mary Knob Greenville SC 29607-5242

CURIE, EVE, writer, lecturer; b. Paris, Dec. 6, 1904; d. Pierre (Nobel prize winner for work in radium 1903) and Marie (Sklodowska) (Nobel prize winner in radio-active substances, 1903, in chemistry 1911) Curie; m. Henry Richardson Labouisse, Nov. 1954 (dec. 1987). B.S., Ph.B., Sevigne Coll.; D.H.L. (hon.), Mills Coll., 1939, Russell Sage Coll., 1941; Litt.D. (hon.), U. Rochester, 1941; Hartwick Coll., 1983. Took up study of music and gave first concert as pianist, Paris, 1925; later concerts in France and Belgium; mus. critic for Candide (weekly jour.) for several years; also wrote articles on motion pictures and the theater; made first visit to U.S. with mother, 1921; on 2d visit lectured in 10 U.S. cities (speaks English, French and Polish), 1939; witnessed fall of France, 1940, went to London to work for cause of Free France; came to U.S., 1941, lectured on war in France and Eng.; because of pro-ally activities deprived of French citizenship by Vichy Govt., 1941. Served in Europe with Fighting French as officer in Women's div. of army; one of pubs. Paris Presse (daily), resigned to return to ind. writing, 1949. Spl. adviser Sec. Gen., NATO, 1952-54. Decorated Chevalier Legion of Honor (France), 1939; Polonia Restituta (Poland), 1939; Croix de Guerre (France), 1944. Author: Madame Curie (selection of Lit. Guild, Jr. Guild, Book-of-the-Month Club, Scientific Book of the month; Nat. book award for non-fiction), 1937; Journey Among Warriors (Lit. Guild Selection), 1943. Home: 1 Sutton Pl S New York NY 10022-2471

CURKENDALL, BRENDA IRENE (BRENDA BURGETT), former financial planner, business owner; b. Mesa, Ariz., Dec. 20, 1954; d. Arthur Blatt and Dorothy June Goodnight; m. James Patrick Monagle (div.); m. Christopher Lee Curkendall; children: Robert, Chad, Jeremy, Sean. Student, Edison Jr. Coll., 1971-72; BA in History, Fla. State U., 1976; postgrad., Coll. for Fin. Planning, 1992. CFP. Realtor Harold A. Allen Co. Realtors, Tacoma, 1983; salesperson Computerland, Bellevue, Wash., 1983-84; systems analyst Boeing Computer Svcs., Seattle, 1985; stock broker Shearson Lehman Bros., Tacoma, 1985-87; fin. planner Curkendall Fin. Programs, Inc., Puyallup, Wash., 1988-95; instr. Pierce Coll., Tacoma; participant numerous acting tng. workshops and seminars. Contbr. articles to profl. jours; actress (cable TV) She's No Angel, (regional theater) It's A Mystery. Capt. U.S. Army, 1976-82, Korea. Mem. Apt. Assn. Pierce County (pres. 1988), Ft. Hood Flying Club (pres. 1980). Office: 12012 98th Ave E Ste B Puyallup WA 98373-5027

CURLE, ROBIN LEA, computer software industry executive; b. Denver, Feb. 23, 1950; d. Fred Warren and Claudia Jean (Harding) C.; m. Lucien Ray Reed, Feb. 23, 1981 (div. Oct. 1984). BS, U. Ky., 1972. Systems analyst 1st Nat. BAnk, Lexington, Ky., 1972-73, SW BancShares, Houston, 1973-77; sales rep. Software Internat., Houston, 1977-80; dist. mgr. Uccell, Dallas, 1980-82; v.p. Info. Sci., Atlanta, 1982-83; v.p. sales TesserAct, San Francisco, 1983-86, Foothill Rsch., San Francisco, 1986-89; pres., founder Curle Cons. Group, San Francisco, 1987-89; mgr. strategic mktg. MCC, Austin, Tex., 1989-90; founder, exec. v.p. Evolutionary Tech., Inc., Austin, 1991—. Mem. U. Ky. Alumni Assn., Delta Gamma (pres. 1969). Republican. Home: 7009 Quill Leaf Cove Austin TX 78750

CURME, ANN MARIE, lawyer; b. Sioux City, Iowa, Jan. 22, 1952; d. Lloyd Alden and Rosemary Connors Doescher; m. Ronald Lee Curme, June 7, 1975 (div.); children: Patrick, Daniel, Erin. BA, St. Mary's Coll., 1974; MSW, U. Ill., 1978; JD, Northwestern U., 1986. Assoc. Oppenheimer Wolff & Donnelly, Mpls., 1986-91; asst. gen. counsel Control Data Corp., Mpls., 1991-92; mng. counsel Ceridian Corp., Mpls., 1992-94, assoc. gen. counsel, dir. human resources, 1994—; adj. prof. William Mitchell Coll. Law, St. Paul, 1992—. Guardian ad Litem Hennepin County, Mpls. Office: Ceridian Corp 8100 34th Ave S Minneapolis MN 55425-1672

CURNS, EILEEN BOHAN, counselor, author, speaker; b. Chgo., May 22, 1927; d. Alvin Joseph and Lorraine Bohan; m. John R. Curns, July 1, 1950 (div. 1975); children: James Richard, Barbara Obrokta. BA in Sociology, DePaul U., Chgo.; MEd in Psychology and Edn., Loyola U., Chgo.; postgrad. in health edn., U. Wis. Cert. Gestalt therapist. Prin. ACCORD, Vernon Hills, Ill.; cons. in health care cost containment, stress researcher, inner healing; lectr. on the five stress signals leading to disease and how to reverse them. Recipient Golden Deeds award Exchange Club, 1965, commendation Queen Mary Vets. Hosp., Montreal, 1975. Mem. Am. Bd. Med. Psychotherapists (cert.), Nat. Wellness Assn., Midwest Satir Inst. Home: 825 Waterview Cir Vernon Hills IL 60061-2550

CUROL, HELEN RUTH, librarian, English language educator; b. Grayson, La., May 30, 1944; d. Alfred John and Ethel Lea (McDaniel) Broussard; m. Kenneth Arthur Curol, June 25, 1967 (div. 1988); children: Edward, Bryan. BA, McNeese State U., 1966; postgrad., L.I. U., 1969-70; MLS, La. State U., 1987. Tchr., libr. Cameron Parish Schs., Grand Lake, La., 1966-67; media specialist Brentwood (N.Y.) Sch. Dist., 1967-69; sch. libr. Patchogue (N.Y.) H.S., 1969-70;, 1976-95; reference libr., mgr. circulation dept. McNeese State U., Lake Charles, La., 1976-96; test adminstr. Edn. Testing Svc., Princeton, N.J., 1987-95; asst. prof. McNeese U., 1989-95; owner Creative Concepts Cons., Lake Charles, 1995—; head adult svcs. Laman Pub. Libr., North Little Rock, Ark., 1996—; rschr. Boise Cascade, DeRidder, La., 1987-88, Vidtron, Dallas, 1990-92, Nat. Archives, Washington, 1989; cons. Cmty. Housing Resource Bd., Lake Charles, 1988-93, Boyce Internat. Engrs., Houston, 1988-89, La. Pub. Broadcasting, Baton Rouge, 1989; devel. cons. Calcasieu Women's Shelter, 1988-92; reference cons. Calcasieu Parish Pub. Libr., 1990-95; presenter conf. at Tulane U., South Ctrl. Women's Assn., 1994. Sr. arbitrator Better Bus. Bur., Lake Charles, 1986-95; local facilitator La. Com. for Fiscal Reform, Lake Charles, 1988; state bd. dirs. PTA, Baton Rouge, 1981-83, LWV La., Baton Rouge, 1983-85; chairperson budget panel com. United Way S.W. La., Lake Charles, 1992-94, bd. dirs., 1995-96; judge La. region IV Social Studies Fair, 1979-89; program spkr. region IV tng. conf. HUD, El Paso, 1992. Named Citizen of the Day, Sta. KLOU, 1978; grantee La. Endowment for Humanities, 1987, La. Divsn. Arts, 1989, Fair Housing Initiative Program, 1990, HUD, 1992, La. Ctr.

Women and Govt. of Nicholls State U., 1993. Mem. ALA (sec. coun. 1988-90, chairperson coun. 1990-91), AAUW (chairperson intellectual freedom com. 1988-89), La. Libr. Assn. (chairperson reference group 1988-90), La. Assn. Coll. and Rsch. Librs. (chairperson 1995-96), Ark. Libr. Assn., McNeese U. Alumni Assn., S.W. La. C. of C. (mem. legis. com. 1992), Krewe du Feteurs (Mardi Gras Ct. Duchess 1992), Beta Sigma Phi (pres. Lake Charles chpt. 1983-84), Beta Phi Mu. Democrat. Lutheran. Office: Laman Pub Libr 2801 Orange St North Little Rock AR 72114

CURRAN, EMILY KATHERINE, museum director; b. Boston, Mar. 27, 1960; d. George Morton and Gloria Rose (Martino) C.; m. John Vincent Callahan, Oct. 8, 1989. AB in Fine Arts, Bard Coll., 1982; MS in Mus. Leadership, Bank Street Coll., 1992. Sr. developer The Children's Mus., Boston, 1982-88; dir. edn. The Old South Meeting House, Boston, 1988-92, exec. dir., 1992—; vis. community artist Great George's Project, Liverpool, Eng., 1983. Author: Science Sensations, 1989, An Architectural History of the Old South Meeting House, 1995. Bd. dirs. Freedom Trail Found., Boston, 1992—, Victorian Soc. Am.-New Eng. Chpt., 1996—; mem. cmty. adv. bd. WGBH, Boston, 1996—. Mus. edn. fellow Bank Street Coll., 1989-91. Mem. Am. Assn. Mus., Am. Assn. State and Local History, New Eng. Mus. Assn., Boston Mus. Educators' Roundtable (chair steering com. 1989-91). Office: Old South Meeting House 310 Washington St Boston MA 02108-4609

CURRAN-SMITH, ANITA STILES, public health medicine educator, dean; b. Northampton, Mass., 1929. BA, U. Conn., 1951; MD, N.Y. Med. Coll., 1955; MPH, Col. U., 1974. Diplomate Am. Bd. Preventive Medicine (bd. dirs.). Intern Mountainside Hosp., Montclair, N.J., 1955-56; house officer Maryview Hosp., Portsmouth, Va., 1960-63; pediat. clinic physician Met. Hosp., N.Y.C., 1963-65; med. dir. Newark Presch. Coun., 1965-70; child health physician N.J. Dept. Health, 1965-73; resident in pub. health N.Y.C. Dept. Health, 1974-75, dir. lead poisoning control program, 1974-78, dep. com., 1976-78; com. health Westchester County (N.Y.) Health Dept., 1978-89; prof. clin., environ. and cmty. medicine U. Medicine and Dentistry N.J. R.W. Johnson Med. Sch., New Brunswick, 1989—, assoc. dean cmty. health, 1992-96; chair RRC coun. ACGME, 1992-94; mem. exec. com. Am. Bd. Med. Specialists, 1995—. Fellow Am. Coll. Preventive Medicine, N.Y. Acad. Medcine, N.Y. Acad. Scis.

CURRENCE, GLENNDA KAY, elementary education educator; b. Davenport, Iowa, Feb. 4, 1954; d. Glenn Elston and Ethel Lucille (Watts) C. BME, Augustana Coll., 1976; M in Counseling, We. Ill. U., 1995. Tchr. elem. vocal music Clinton (Iowa) Cmty. Sch. Dist., 1976-77; tchr. elem. vocal music Davenport (Iowa) Cmty. Sch. Dist., 1977-95, elem. counselor, 1995—. Organist, pianist Faith United Meth.Ch., Davenport, 1968-77. Mem. NEA, ACA, Am. Sch. Counselors Assn., Internat. Assn. for Addictions and Offender Counselors, Iowa Music Educators Assn. Methodist. Home: 2032 N Ohio Ave Davenport IA 52804-2838 Office: Davenport Cmty Schs 1001 N Harrison St Davenport IA 52803-5025

CURRIE, BARBARA FLYNN, state legislator; b. LaCrosse, Wis., May 3, 1940; d. Frank T. and Elsie R. (Gobel) Flynn; AB cum laude, U. Chgo., 1968, AM, 1973; m. David P. Currie, Dec. 29, 1959; children: Stephen Francis, Margaret Rose. Asst. study dir. Nat. Opinion Rsch. Ctr., Chgo., 1973-77; part time instr. polit. sci. DePaul U., Chgo., 1973-74; mem. Ill. Ho. of Reps., 1979—, chmn. House Dem. Study Group, 1981-83, asst. majority leader, 1993, asst. minority leader, 1995. Mem. adv. bd. Harriet Harris YWCA; v.p. Chgo. LWV, 1965-69; mem. ACLU, Hyde Park-Kenwood Cmty. Conf., Ind. Voters of Ill.-Ind. Precinct Orgn., Hyde Park Coop. Soc., Ams. for Dem. Action. Named Best Legislator, Ind. Voters of Ill., 1980, 82, 84, 86, 88, 90, 92, 94, Best Legislator, Ill. Credit Union League, Outstanding Legislator, Ill. Hosp. Assn., 1987; recipient Ethel Parker award 1982, 86, 88, 90, 94, Leon Despres award, 1991, Ill. Environ. Coun. award, Ill. Cmty.Action Agys. award, Ill. Women's Polit. Caucus Lottie Holman O'Neill award, Susan B. Anthony award, honor award Nat. Trust Historic Preservation; awards Welfare Rights Coalition of Orgns., Ill. Pub. Action Coun., Chgo. Heart Assn.; named Legislator of Yr., Ill. Nurses Assn., 1984, Nat. Assn. Social Workers, 1984, Ill. Women's Substance Abuse Coalition, 1984; recipient BEST BETS award Nat. Ctr. For Policy Alternatives, 1988, Svc. award Nat. Ctr. For Freedom of Info. Studies, 1989, Beautiful Person award Chgo. Urban League, 1989, Friend of Labor award Ill. AFL-CIO, 1990, Ill. Maternal and Child Health Coalition award, 1990, Ill. Hunger Coalition award, 1991, Cert. of Appreciation SEIU Local 880, 1989, March of Dimes, 1988, Chgo. Tchrs. Union, Ill. Hosp. Assn., Ptnr. Vision award Families' and Children's AIDS Network. Mem. ACLU (bd. dirs. Ill.), Ill. Conf. Women Legislators, Nat. Order Women Legislators. Contbr. article to publ. Office: Ill Gen Assembly 300 State House Springfield IL 62704-1757

CURRIE, CONSTANCE MERSHON, consultant; b. Missoula, Mont., June 22, 1950; d. Alan Clark Van Horn and Saralee (Neumann) Visscher; m. R. Hector Currie, Aug. 14, 1986. BA in Art with highest hons., Mont. State U., 1977; MFA in Painting, U. Cin., 1981, MA in Arts Adminstrn., 1988; grad., Tsukuba Daigaku, Ibariki, Japan, 1977-78. Bus. mgr. Fort Peck Summer Theatre, Glasgow, Mont., 1983; asst. telemarketing mgr. Cin. Symphony Orchestra, 1984, telemarketing mgr., 1985; mem. coord. Cin. Mus. of Natural History, 1986-88; mktg. cons. Currie Consulting, Cin., 1988—; lectr., art Raymond Walters Coll./U. Cin., 1988—. Exhbns. include SUNY, Binghamton, 1983, Tangeman Gallery/U. Cin., 1981, Miami U., 1981, No. Rockies Regional Exhbn./Sheridan (Wyo.) Coll., 1981, Bell Art Competition, Cin., 1981 (Purchase award. 1981), Willmington Coll., 1979, Mont. State U., 1976, 77 (Printmaking Purchase award 1976, 77), Yellowstone Ehbn., Billings, Mont., 1977 (Printmaking Purchase award 1977), others. Trustee Good Harvest Cooperative, Middletown, Conn., 1974-75, Methuen & Gertrude Currie Found., 1986—; bd. dirs. Bozeman (Mont.) Film Festival, 1982-83; vol. Cin. Chamber Orchestra, 1985-87, Cin. Mus. Natural History, 1988-90. Mem. Beta Gamma Sigma, Tau Pi Phi, Phi Kappa Phi. Office: Currie Consulting 504 Mcalpin Ave Cincinnati OH 45220-1534

CURRIER, SUSAN ANNE, computer software company executive; b. Melbourne, Victoria, Australia, Nov. 20, 1949; d. David Eric and Irene Hazel (Baker) Bruce-Smith; m. Kenneth Palmer Currier, Feb. 16, 1974. Student, Melbourne U., 1967-70. Fashion model Eileen Ford Model Agy., N.Y.C., 1971-74, Wilhelmina Models, N.Y.C., 1974-82; owner Softsync Inc., N.Y.C., 1981-91; pres. Expert Software, Coral Gables, Fla., 1989—. Home: 201 Crandon Blvd Apt 1141 Key Biscayne FL 33149-1520 Office: Expert Software Exec Tower 800 Douglas Rd Coral Gables FL 33134

CURRIN, MARGARET PERSON, law educator; b. Oxford, N.C., June 17, 1950. AB, Meredith Coll., 1972; JD, Campbell U., 1979; attended, Georgetown U., 1980. Bar: N.C. 1979, U.S. Dist. Ct. (ea. dist.) N.C. 1982, U.S. Dist. Ct. (mid. dist.) N.C. 1996, U.S. Ct. Appeals (4th cir.) 1980, U.S. Supreme Ct. 1982. Legis. asst.to U.S. Senator John Tower, 1979-81; asst. dean, asst. prof. Sch. Law Campbell U., Buies Creek, N.C., 1981-88, prof. law, 1993-94, adj. prof. law, 1994—; U.S. atty. U.S. Dist. Ct. Ea. Dist. N.C., Raleigh, 1988-93; gen. counsel N.C. Rep. Party, 1981-83, treas., 1995-96. Mem. Phi Kappa Phi. Office: Currin Law Firm PO Box 269 333 Fayetteville St Mall Raleigh NC 27602-0269 also: Currin Law Firm 20 S 5th St Wilmington NC 28401-4539

CURRY, ANN, correspondent, anchor; b. Agana, Guam, Nov. 19, 1956; d. Robert Paul Hiroe (Nagase) C.; m. Brian Wilson Ross, Oct. 21, 1987; children: Anna McKenzie, William Walker. Student, U. Oreg. Journalism Sch., 1974-78. Reporter Sta. KTVL-TV, Medford, Oreg., 1978-81; reporter, weekend anchor Sta. KGW-TV, Portland, Oreg., 1981-84; reporter Sta. KCBS-TV, L.A., 1984-90; corr., anchor NBC News at Sunrise NBC News, N.Y.C., 1990—. Recipient Golden Mike award RTNA, 1986, 87, 89, Cert. Excellence award AP, 1987, 88, Cert. Excellence award Greater L.A. Press Club, 1987, Superior Reporting award NAACP, 1989, Emmy award Acad. TV Arts and Scis., 1987, 89, Emmy nominations, 1985, 86, 87, 88. Office: NBC News 30 Rockefeller Plz # 315 W New York NY 10112

CURRY, CYNTHIA J.R., geneticist; b. Cleve., July 20, 1941. MD, Yale U., 1957. Diplomate Am. Bd. Med. Genetics; Am. Bd. Pediatrics. Intern U. Wash., Seattle, 1967-68, resident, 1968-69; resident U. Minn., Mpls., 1969-70; fellow med. genetics U. Calif., San Francisco, 1975-76; med. faculty UCSF, Fresno, Calif.; med. dir. genetics Valley Children's Hosp., Fresno, Calif., 1976-96. Contbr. 15 chpt. to books, numerous articles to profl. jours. Office: Valley Children's Hosp 3151 N Millbrook Fresno CA 93703-1425

CURRY, KATHLEEN BRIDGET, retired librarian; b. Parnell, Iowa, May 19, 1931; d. John Michael and Ellen Theresa (Clear) C. BS in Libr. Sci., Marycrest Coll., 1953. Head libr. Moline (Ill.) Sr. High Sch., 1953-90; part-time libr. Moline Pub. Hosp. Sch. Nursing, 1957-66; mem. sch. nursing libr. St. Anthony's Hosp., Rock Island, Ill., 1955; hist. librarian Rock Island Hist. Libr., Moline, 1956-59; libr. Black Hawk Coll., Moline, 1958-59. Exec. bd. Miss Iowa Pageant, Davenport, Iowa, 1987—; bd. dirs. Miss Black Hawk Valley Pageant, Moline, 1986—, Quad City Arts Coun., Davenport, 1990; guild mem. Quad City Symphony Orch., Davenport, 1972—. Recipient Disting. Svc. award Marycrest Coll., 1987, Disting. Svc. award Moline High Sch. PTA, 1983. Mem. Ill. Edn. Assn., NEA, Ill. Sch. Libr. Assn., AAUW, Moline Edn. Assn., Iowa Libr. Assn., Zonta Internat., Delta Kappa Gamma. Democrat. Roman Catholic. Home: 1851 18th Ave Moline IL 61265

CURRY, TONI GRIFFIN, counseling center executive, consultant; b. Langdale, Ala., June 23, 1938; d. Robert Alton and Elsie (Dodson) Griffin; m. Ronald William Curry, June 13, 1959 (div. 1972); children: Christopher, Catherine, Angela. BA, Ga. State U., 1962; MSW, U. Ga., 1981. Lic. clin. therapist; cert. addictions counselor. Tchr. DeKalb County Bd. Edn., Atlanta, 1962-63; counselor Charter Peachford Hosp., Atlanta, 1974-79; dir. aftercare, 1976-79; dir. aftercare and occupational services Ridgeview Inst., Atlanta, 1979-82; owner, dir., adminstr., counselor Toni Curry and Assocs., Inc., Atlanta, 1982—; founder, bd. dirs. Anchor Hosp., 1985-93; cons., lectr. to numerous cos. and orgns.; mem. adv. bd. Peachford Hosp., Atlanta, 1982-87, Rockdale House, Conyers, Ga., 1981—, Outpatient Addictions Clinics Am., 1983-85; bd. dirs. Employee Assistance Programs Inst.; lectr. local, nat. and internat. confs. Cloud's House, Wilshire, Eng., 1986; founder Internat. Recovery Ctr., Cannes, France, 1990; seminars on addiction in Italy and Switzerland; pres., mem. exec. bd. Ga. Employee Assistance Programs Forum, Atlanta, 1981-86; appointed to Gov.'s Advisory Council on Mental Health, Mental Retardation and Substance Abuse, 1984, Commn. on Drug Awareness and Prevention, 1986; chairperson Driving under Influence of Alcohol Assessment Task Force; adv. bd. Hawthorne House; presenter European Conf. Drugs and Alcohol, Edinburgh, Scotland. Mem. Nat. Assn. Social Workers, Ga. Addiction Counselors Assn. (dir. 1982-86), Ga. Citizens Council Alcoholism, Employee Assistance Programs Assn., Assn. Behavioral Therapists, Nat. Assn. Alcoholism and Drug Abuse Counselors, Mems. Guild of High Mus. Art, Kappa Alpha Theta. Home: 7245 Chattahoochee Bluff Dr Atlanta GA 30350-1071 Office: 4546-D Barclay Dr Atlanta GA 30338

CURT, DENISE MORRIS, artist, limner, photographer; b. New Haven, Nov. 15, 1936; d. Bertrand and Anna Geraldine (Fiak) Rocheleau; m. John Morris, Oct. 4, 1954 (div. 1970); children: Tyler John, Cynthia Leigh Morris Bell; m. Albert A. Curt, 1973 (div. 1981). Student of Louis Crescenti, Orange, Conn., 1950-52; student, Whitney Sch. Art, New Haven, 1950, Luchetti Sch. Art, New Haven, 1951, Paier Sch. Art, Hamden, Conn., 1951. Dir. Meet The Artists and Artisans, Milford, Conn., 1962—; interior designer State of Conn., Hartford, 1972-75. One-woman shows Gull Gallery, Provincetown, Mass., Chapelle Jean Cocteau, Villefranche Sur Mer, France, Garfield Galleries, Orange, Conn., Yale U., Stratford Gallery, Stevenson (Md.) Galleries, also others; represented in numerous pvt. and pub. collections throughout world. Lectr. to numerous civic orgns.; mem. Vis. Artists in Schs., 1970—; commr. Conn. Commn. on Arts, 1974-79; photography chmn. Milford Fine Arts Coun., New Haven Arts Coun.; bd. dirs. Milford Hosp. Aux. Recipient award Mystic Art Festival, 1969, Sterling House Art Show, 1985, Glastonbury Art Guild, 1988. Mem. Guilford Art League (bd. dirs. 1975-80), Nat. Soc. Am. Pen Women (category painting), Conn. Classic Arts, Milford Hist. Soc., Yale U. Gallery, Met. Mus. Art. Republican. Congregationalist. Home and Studio: 41 Green St Milford CT 06460-4709

CURTIN, JANE THERESE, actress, writer; b. Cambridge, Mass., Sept. 6, 1947; d. John Joseph and Mary Constance (Farrell) C.; m. Patrick F. Lynch, Apr. 31, 1975. A.A., Elizabeth Seton Jr. Coll., 1967; student, Northeastern U., 1967-68. Appeared in plays The Proposition, Cambridge and N.Y.C., 1968-72, Last of the Red Hot Lovers touring co., 1973; Broadway debut in Candida, 1981; author, actress Off-Broadway mus. rev. Pretzels, 1974-75; star TV series NBC Saturday Night Live, 1975-79, Kate & Allie, 1984-88, Working It Out, 1990, 3rd Rock from the Sun, 1996—; appeared in films including Mr. Mike's Mondo Video, 1979, How to Beat the High Cost of Living, 1980, O.C. and Stiggs, 1987, Coneheads, 1993; TV films include Divorce Wars-A Love Story, 1982, Suspicion, 1988, Maybe Baby, 1988, Common Ground, 1990, Tad, 1995. Recipient Emmy nomination, 1977; Emmy awards for outstanding actress in comedy series, 1984, 85. Mem. Screen Actors Guild, Actors Equity, AFTRA. Office: ICM care Boaty Boatwright 40 W 57th St New York NY 10019*

CURTIN, KAREN LEA, adult nurse practitioner, educator; b. Newark, Jan. 31, 1960; d. John Abram and Sally Ann (Garrett) S.; m. Brian Joseph Curtin, July 1, 1995. BSN, Keuka Coll., 1982; MS, U. Rochester, 1988. RN, N.Y.; cert. adult nurse practitioner. Staff nurse dept. medicine Strong Meml. Hosp., Rochester, 1982-83, staff nurse skilled rehab. dept. medicine, 1983-88; dr. skilled nursing Clifton Springs (N.Y.) Hosp., 1988-89; adult nurse practitioner, dir. patient care svcs. St. Mary's Hosp., Rochester, 1989-94; adult nurse practitioner Strong Meml. Hosp., 1994—. Capt. USAR. Mem. Assn. Mil. Surgeons U.S., Genesee Valley Nurses Assn., Uniform Nurse Practitioner Assn., Sigma Theta Tau. Republican. Home: 233 Winona Blvd Rochester NY 14617

CURTIN, LEAH LOUISE, nurse, consultant, editor, author, ethician; b. Chgo., Mar. 8, 1942; d. Jean Wilson and Veronica Eloise (Dunst) Sutter; m. Peter Joseph Curtin, Apr. 15, 1966 (div. May 1990); children: Peter James, Rose Mary, Christopher Charles, Joseph Wilson. Diploma in nursing, Good Samaritan Hosp. Sch. Nursing, Cin., 1965; BS in Community Health Planning, U. Cin., 1976, MS in Health Planning and Adminstrn., 1977; MA in Philosophy, Athenaeum of Ohio, 1977; DSc (hon.), SUNY, Utica, 1990. RN, Ohio. Staff nurse Vets. Hosp., Cin., 1965-66, Vis. Nurses' Assn., Cin., 1966-67; instr. No. Ky. U., Highland Heights, 1974-76; asst. prof. Coll. Mt. St. Joseph-On-The-Ohio, Cin., 1976-80; editor Nursing Mgmt. Springhouse Corp., Phila., 1979—; ptnr. Metier Cons., Cin., 1990—; adj. faculty U. Cin., 1984—; organizational cons. Franciscan Sisters of Poor Health System, N.Y.C., 1987-96; cons. on nursing ethics Nurse Corps, USAF, Washington, 1991—. Author: Nursing Ethics: Theories and Pragmatics, 1982 (Am. Jour. Nursing Book of Yr. award 1982), DRGS: The Reorganization of Health, 1984, Curtin Calls, 1986, Cornerstones of Healthcare in the '90s, 1991; contbr. articles to profl. jours. Recipient Disting. Nurse award Virginia Mason Med. Ctr., 1986, recognition Med. Coll. Ohio, 1988, Mary Hammer Greenwood award Ohio Nurses Assn., 1990, Outstanding Svc. award Franciscan Sisters of Poor Health System, 1991; Am. Acad. Nursing fellow, 1983. Mem. ANA, Am. Nurses Assn., Internat. Acad. Nursing Editors, Nat. League for Nursing, Am. Acad. Polit. and Social Scis., Hastings Ctr., Sigma Theta Tau. Home: 5932 Rapid Run Rd Cincinnati OH 45233-4852 Office: Nursing Mgmt 672 Neeb Rd Cincinnati OH 45233

CURTIN, PHYLLIS, music educator, former dean, operatic singer; b. Clarksburg, W.Va.; d. E. Vernon and Betty R. (Robinson) Smith; m. Eugene Cook, May 6, 1956 (dec.); 1 child, Claudia Madeleine. BA, Wellesley Coll., 1943. Prof. Yale Sch. Music, New Haven, 1974-83; master Branford Coll. Yale U., New Haven, 1979-83; dean Sch. Arts, prof. music Boston U., 1983-91, prof. music, 1983—, dean emerita, prof. music, 1991—; artist-in-residence Tanglewood Music Ctr., Tanglewood, Lenox, Mass., 1965—; former mem. Nat. Coun. on the Arts; named Amb. for the Arts; tchr. master classes U.S., Can., Beijing, Moscow. Made recital debut Town Hall, N.Y.C., 1950, opera debut, N.Y.C. Opera in U.S. premiere of The Trial, 1953, recitals throughout, U.S. and fgn. countries; soprano soloist leading symphony orchestras; performer, tchr., Aspen Mus. Festival, 1953-57, appeared as Cressida in, Walton's Troilus and Cressida in, N.Y. premiere, 1955; title role in Floyd's: Susannah, world premiere, Tallahassee, 1955; title role in: Darius Milhaud's Medea, U.S. premiere, Brandeis U., 1955; world premiere Floyd's opera Wuthering Heights, 1958; leading soprano: Vienna Staatsoper, 1960-61; debut as Fiordiligi in Cosi Fan Tutte, Met. Opera Co., 1961; debut, La Scala Opera, Milan, 1962; U.S. premiere Benjamin Britten's War Requiem, 1963; world premiere of Darius Milhaud's opera La Mère Coupable, Geneva, 1966, U.S. premiere Dimitri Shostakovitch's Symphony No. 14, with, Phila. Orch., 1971. Home: 20 Chapel St Apt 801C Brookline MA 02146-5458 Office: Boston Univ Sch for the Arts 855 Commonwealth Ave Boston MA 02215-1303

CURTIS, ALVA MARSH, artist; b. N.Y.C., June 15, 1911; d. Charles Johan and Elizabeth (Hagstrom) Berg; m. Terrill Belknap Marsh, Nov. 3, 1932; children: Owen Thayer, Charles Ames, Ronald Belknap; m. Russell G. Curtis, Aug. 11, 1979; children: Russell G. Jr., William E. Student Art Students League, N.Y.C., 1928-29, Grand Central Art Sch., 1934-36, N.Y. Sch. Fine Arts, 1930-31, Nat. Acad., N.Y.C., 1934-35, Columbia U., 1943-44, Yale U., 1969-70. Ptnr., art dir. Terrill Belknap Marsh, Assocs., N.Y.C., 1934-69; lectr. in field. One-woman shows: Scranton Meml. Libr., Madison, Conn., 1969, Phippsburg (Maine) Libr., 1964, Town and County Club, Hartford, Conn., 1976, Conn. Bank & Trust Co., Madison, 1977, 1st Fed. Savs. & Loan, Madison, 1977; group shows include: The Mariner's Mus., Newport News, Va., Va. Salmagundi Club, N.Y.C., Smithsonian Instn., Washington, 1964, 66, Internat. Maritime Art Award Show (Sculpture award), 1981, Nat. League Am. Pen Women Art Show (Sculpture award), Atlanta, 1982, Arnold Gallery, Newport, R.I., 1984, Copley Gallery, Boston, 1986, Candlewood Gallery (Sculpture award 1986), New Milford, Conn., 1986, Lyme Acad. Fine Arts, Lyme, Conn.; represented in permanent collections: Swedish Club, Chgo., Conn. Bank & Trust Co., Windsor, Phippsburg Libr., Essex Meadows Retirement Cmty., Essex, Conn., also pvt. collections. Mem. Am. Soc. Marine Artists, New Eng. Sculpture Assn., Nat. League Am. Pen Women (pres. 1978—, Greenwich br. 1958), Conn. Soc. Sculptors, Soc. Conn. Sculptors, Garden Club of Madison (life mem.). Republican. Episcopalian. Clubs: Lyme Art Assn., Madison Winter, Garden Club of Madison (life mem.). Home: 319 Essex Mdws Essex CT 06426-1525

CURTIS, JAMIE LEE, actress; b. L.A., Nov. 22, 1958; d. Tony Curtis and Janet Leigh; m. Christopher Guest; 1 child. Student, U. of the Pacific. Actress: (films) Halloween, 1978, The Fog, 1980, Prom Night, 1980, Terror Train, 1980, Halloween II, 1981, Road Games, 1981, Love Letters, 1983, Trading Places, 1983, Grandview USA, 1984, Adventures of Buckaroo Banzai, 1984, Perfect, 1985, Amazing Grace and Chuck, 1987, Un Homme Amoreux, 1987, Dominick and Eugene, 1988, A Fish Called Wanda, 1988, Blue Steel, 1990, Queens Logic, 1991, My Girl, 1991, Forever Young, 1992, Mother's Boys, 1994, My Girl 2, 1994, True Lies, 1994 (Golden Globe award Best Actress - Musical or Comedy), House Arrest, 1996, Fierce Creatures, 1996; (TV pilots) Callahan, She's in the Army Now, 1981, Tall Tales, (TV series) Operation Petticoat, 1977-78, Anything but Love, 1990-93, (TV movies) Death of a Centerfold: The Dorothy Stratten Story, 1981, Money on the Side, 1982. As Summers Die, 1982, The Heidi Chronicles, 1995; author: When I Was Little, 1993. Office: care CAA 9830 Wilshire Blvd Beverly Hills CA 90212-1804*

CURTIS, JANET LYNN, elementary education educator; b. San Diego, Sept. 24, 1945; d. Kenneth E. and Jean L. (Clark) Brasier; m. Steven C. Curtis, Jan. 21, 1967; 1 child, Christopher. BS in Edn., SE Mo. State U., 1967, MEd, 1984. Elem. tchr. Ferguson-Florissant (Mo.) Pub. Schs., 1967-68, 69-74; 3d grade tchr. Rockwood Pub. Schs., Ellisville, 1968-69; tchr., dir. 1st Presbyn. Ch. Presch., Cape Girardeau, Mo., 1975-76; elem. tchr. Cape Girardeau Pub. Schs., 1976-77, 78-83; math. aide, tchr., gifted resource coord. Norman (Okla.) Pub. Schs., 1977-78, 85-96, tchr. 3d grade, 1996—; learning disabilities tchr. Moore (Okla.) Pub. Schs., 1984-85; gifted adv. bd. Norman Pub. Schs., 1992-96, computer adv. bd., 1990—, staff devel.com., 1994—, lang. arts adv. bd., 1985-92. Choir mem. 1st Christian Ch., Norman, 1985—; chmn. Christian Women's Fellowship, Norman, 1993-96; bell ringer Salvation Army, Norman, 1989—; vol. ARC, Norman, 1985—. Mem. NEA, Internat. Reading Assn., Okla. Assn. Gifted/Creative/Talented, Okla. Edn. Assn., Profl. Educators Norman (bldg. rep., treas., staff devel. com.), Alpha Delta Kappa. Democrat. Office: Truman Elem Sch 600 Parkside Rd Norman OK 73072-4200

CURTIS, JESSIE HUTCHISON, marketing professional; b. N.Y.C., Dec. 8, 1949; d. Edison Dent and Anna Paterson (Young) C.; m. Arne Stuart Pavis, May 11, 1971 (div. Mar. 1981); 1 child, Ian Joshua; m. Michael Daniel Roberts. BS summa cum laude, Jersey City (N.J.) State Coll., 1977. Photographer various orgns., N.Y.C., 1977-85; legal and internat. adminstr. ESPN, Inc., N.Y.C., 1985-88, internat. promotion coord., 1988-91, internat. promotion mgr., 1991-95; owner Two Prodns., Jersey City, N.J., 1996; participant start-up ESPN Internat. Distrbn. and Sports Network. Author, creative dir. (brochures) ESPN: One World One Sports Network and Others, 1994, 95, 96; photographs exhibited Hopoghan Gallery, 1983-84, Newark Gallery, 1984, Nat. Tour of Photography, 1985, New Age Gallery, 1995. Organizer, participant Hoboken (N.J.) Arts Festival, 1982-83; vol. Hoboken (N.J.) Polit. Action, 1988-90. Recipient Gold medallion Promax-BDA, L.A., 1994, Silver Work on Paper award James River Co., 1995. Mem. NOW, Am. Women in Radio and TV, Promax Broadcast Designers Assn. Home and Office: Two Prodns 63 Sherman Pl A-8 Jersey City NJ 07307

CURTIS, JOYCE MAE, physical education educator; b. Cleburne, Tex., Aug. 27, 1937; d. Robert Joyce and Maudie Mae C. BS, North Tex. State U., 1959, MS in Phys. Edn., 1960; D in Phys. Edn., Ind. U., 1970. Prof. Abilene (Tex.) Christian U., 1959—; grad. asst. Ind. U., 1967-70; treas. Tex. Assn. Intercollegiate Athletics for Women, 1971-79. Co-editor: (book) Physical Education Activities Handbook, 1971; author: (manual) Manual for Bowling Teachers at Abilene Christian University, 1982, Manual for Badminton Teachers at Abilene Christian University, 1985; author: (text) Pickle-Ball for Player and Teacher, 2d edit., 1988, Intermediate Bowling Notebook, 1993;contbr. articles to profl. jours. Named Bowler of Yr. Abilene Women's Bowling Assn., 1967, Outstanding Educator of Am., 1975; recipient Disting. Svc. award Tex. Assn. for Intercollegiate Athletics for Women, 1982, Faculty Devel. award Abilene Christian U., 1991. Mem. AAHPERD, Tex. Assn. for Health, Phys. Edn., Recreation and Dance, Delta Psi Kappa (life), Phi Lambda Theta. Mem. Ch. of Christ. Office: Abilene Christian U ACU Box 28084 Abilene TX 79699-8084

CURTIS, LORETTA O'ELLEN, construction executive; b. Washington, Pa., Apr. 5, 1937; d. Monroe and Mildred (Carr) Bogan; m. Joseph H. Dudley (div. Oct. 1964); children: Ronald S., Joseph T., Mildred M.; m. Wayne J. Curtis. AS, Franklin U., 1983, BS, 1989; Grad., Columbus Leadership Program, 1991; grad., Premier Sch. of Travel, 1996. With Bur. Employment Svcs., Columbus, Ohio, 1962-87, examiner, equal employment opportunity officer, 1983-87, ret., 1987; v.p. Aries Constrn., Inc., Columbus, 1988-91, pres., 1991—; mediator small claims divsn. Franklin County; tour leader GLAMER; chmn. Sch. of Ushering ICUA, Columbus. Mem. Interdenominational Ch. Ushers Assn. Columbus. Recipient Plaque ICUA of Dayton, 1989, ICUA of Columbus, 1991. Mem. NAFE, Nat. Assn. Parliamentarians, Nat. United Ch. Ushers Assn., Ohio Assn. Colored Women (treas. 1990-94), Ohio Assn. Parliamentarians (pres. 1989-90), ICUA of Columbus (pres. 1977-84), Mayme Moore Club (pres. 1990-93, cert. 1989). Home: 2257 Century Dr Columbus OH 43211-1919 Office: Aries Constrn Inc 983 E Main St # 7014 Columbus OH 43205-2342

CURTIS, MARY ELLEN (MARY CURTIS HOROWITZ), publishing company executive; b. Paragould, Ark., Oct. 24, 1946; d. Lloyd E. and Jean (Cain) C.; m. Irving Louis Horowitz, Oct. 30, 1979. AB cum laude, Washington U., St. Louis, 1968. Editorial dir. Transaction Pubs., New Brunswick, N.J., 1968-74, exec. v.p., 1987—, chmn. bd. dirs., 1994—; editor in chief Praeger Pubs. subs. CBS Edn1. Pub., N.Y.C., 1974-79; v.p., pub. periodicals John Wiley and Sons, N.Y.C., 1979-87; v.p. Scripta Techica subs. John Wiley and Sons, Washington, 1984-86; chair adv. com. Serials Industry Systems, 1985-88; dir. Transaction Pubs. (U.K.) Ltd.; mem. mktg. com. Coun. Biology Editors, 1989—; lectr. in field. Contbr. articles to profl. jours. Mem. Soc. Scholarly Pubs. (bd. dirs. 1984-88), Assn. Am. Pubs. (Freedom to Read com.). Jewish.

CURTIS, PAULA ANNETTE, elementary and secondary education educator; b. Natrona Heights, Pa., Apr. 16, 1953; d. Stephen John and Josephine Kathleen (Killian) C. BS in Edn., Geneva Coll., 1974; postgrad., U. Vt., 1975, Pa. State U., New Kensington, 1978. Cert. religious edn. tchr.,

Pitts. Diocese. Tchr. Transfiguration Sch., Russellton, Pa., 1979—, dir. relgious edn., 1995—; tchr. continuing edn. C.C. of Allegheny County, Pitts., 1992—, Pa. State U., New Kensington, 1988—; tchr. O'Mara Driving Sch., Lower Burrell, Pa., 1976—, Lenape Votech., 1990—; CCD tchr. Transfiguration Sch., Russellton, 1995—; chairperson vision and values in Pitts. Diocese, Transfiguration Sch., 1980—; CCD tchr. St. Clement Parish, Tarentum, Pa., 1986-92, dir. religious edn., 1987-92; dir. religious edn. St. Joseph Parish, Natrona, Pa., 1992-93; product tester Nat. Family Opinion Poll, 1987—; model Van Enterprises, Cranberry, Pa., 1989-92. Vol. Help Beautify the Cmty. with Art, Russellton. Mem. Nat. Cath. Educators Assn. Democrat. Roman Catholic. Home: 211 W Ninth Ave Tarentum PA 15084 Office: Transfiguration Sch CCD Office 100 McKrell Rd Russellton PA 15076

CURTIS, SUSAN M., lawyer; b. Nashville, 1956. BA, U. Tenn., Knoxville. Ptnr. Skadden, Arps, Slate, Meagher & Flom, N.Y.C. Office: Skadden Arps Slate Meagher & Flom 919 3rd Ave New York NY 10022*

CURTIS, VERNA P., reading educator; b. Jackson, Miss., Mar. 20, 1940; d. William Grady Polk and Mary Ann Gray; m. Edward L. Curtis, Apr. 12, 1968; 1 child, Vera. BS cum laude, Jackson State U., 1962; MEd, Boston U., 1968; EdS, Jackson State U., 1987; postgrad., Cornell U.; EdD, Jackson State U., 1991. Reading specialist/reading facilitator Jackson Pub. Schs., tchr.; reading instr. Jackson State U.; instr., advisor for second chance careers program Tougaloo Coll. Recipient fellowship. Mem. ASCD, Jackson Area Reading, IRA, MSCD, Miss. Reading Assn. Home: 114 Waylawn Ct Jackson MS 39206-2305

CURTISS, CAROL PERRY, nursing consultant; b. Worcester, Mass., Dec. 9, 1946; d. Joseph Anthony and Marjorie Ruth (Riedle) Perry; m. Jack Daniel Curtiss, Feb. 8, 1970; children: Paul Daniel, Jennifer Perry. Diploma in nursing, Mass. Gen. Hosp. Sch. Nursing, Boston, 1967; BS, Am. Internat. Coll., Springfield, Mass., 1978; MSN, Yale U., 1981. RN, Mass.; cert. Oncology Nursing Cert. Corp. Staff nurse Franklin Med. Ctr., Greenfield, Mass., 1970, Greenfield Ob-Gyn. Assocs., 1972-74, Greenfield Vis. Nurses, 1974-75; instr. Slim Living Program YMCA, Greenfield, 1977-78; instr. nursing Greenfield C.C., 1978; asst. prof. nursing Elms Coll., Chicopee, Mass., 1981-84; oncology program mgr. Franklin Med. Ctr, Greenfield, 1986-93; cancer care cons. Greenfield, 1981—; mem. faculty Greenfield C.C., 1985-87; vis. lectr., clin. instr. Fitchburg (Mass.) State Coll., 1985-86; vis. lectr. Elms Coll., Chicopee, Mass., 1984-85; mem. adj. faculty SUNY, 1987-90, U. Mass., Amherst, 1989—; mem. U.S. com. Internat. Union Against Cancer, NRC, 1992—, mem. nursing project, 1992-95; peer reviewer Agy. for Health Care Policy and Rsch., Cancer Pain Guidelines, Health & Human Svcs., 1993; presenter numerous instns., U.S. and fgn. countries, 1981—. Co-author: Cancer Doesn't Have to Hurt, 1996; guest editor Oncology Nursing Forum, 1993; contbr. articles to profl. jours. Bd. dirs. Franklin County, Am. Cancer Soc., Greenfield, 1979-95, mem. nurse and social work scholarship com., 1988—, nursing com. liaison, 1990—; mem. steering com. Mass. Cancer Pain Initiative, 1988-90, liaison, 1990—; trustee Oncology Nursing Found., 1995—. Mem. Oncology Nursing Soc. (mem. numerous sub coms. 1987—, bd. dirs. 1991—, pres. elect 1991-92, corp. adv. bd. 1991-93, Oncology Nursing Press pres. 1992-94, co-chair conf. on pain 1994, pres. 1993-94), Internat. Union Against Cancer (U.S. com. 1992—, nursing project 1992-94), Sigma Theta Tau. Home: 73 James St Greenfield MA 01301-3607

CUSACK, JOAN, actress; b. N.Y.C., Oct. 12, 1962; d. Richard and Nancy C. Student, U. Wis. Stage appearances include Road, 1988, Brilliant Traces, 1989, Cymbeline, 1989; TV appearances include (series) Saturday Night Live (regular 1985-86 season), (movies) The Mother, 1994; film appearances include My Bodyguard, 1990, Sixteen Candles, 1984, The Allnighter, 1987, Broadcast News, 1987, Married to the Mob, 1988, Working Girl, 1988 (Acad. award nominee best supporting actress 1989), Say Anything, 1989, Men Don't Leave, 1989, My Blue Heaven, 1990, The Cabinet of Dr. Ramirez, 1991, Hero, 1992, Toys, 1992, Addams Family Values, 1993, Corrina, Corrina, 1994, Nine Months, 1995. Office: Care Tracy Jacobs ICM 8942 Wilshire Blvd Beverly Hills CA 90211-1934*

CUSHING, SARAH LOUISE, crop consultant; b. St. Albans, Vt., Mar. 26, 1959; d. Morton Leonard Cushing and Colleen Shirley (Miller) Kissane; m. Daniel A. Brown, May 25, 1991. BS magna cum laude, U. Vt., 1989. Cert. crop advisor, N.Y., New England. Crop svc. coord. U. Vt., Burlington, 1990—; crop cons. Missisquoi Crop Mgmt. Assn., St. Albans, 1994—. Solid waste dist. supr. N.W. Solid Waste Mgmt. Dist., Franklin County, Vt., 1988-94. Office: U Vt Extension System 6 Valley Crossroads Saint Albans VT 05478

CUSHMAN, KAREN ANN, writer; b. Chgo.; married; 1 child, Leah. BA in English/Greek, Stanford U., 1963; MA in Human Behavior, USIU, 1977; MA in Mus. Studies, JFK U., 1987. Faculty mus. studies dept. John F. Kennedy U., San Francisco. Author: Catherine, Called Birdy, 1994, The Midwife's Apprentice, 1995 (John Newberry award 1996), The Ballad of Lucy Whipple, 1996. Office: Clarion Books 215 Park Ave South New York NY 10003

CUSIMANO, ADELINE MARY, educational administrator; b. Jamestown, N.Y., Apr. 18, 1939; d. Joseph and Rose (Bivona) Miletti; m. John Leo Cusimano, Sept. 24, 1960; children: Judith Ann Cusimano Pancio, John Anthony Cusimano. BS, Elmira Coll., 1961, MS, 1976. Cert. reading specialist, N.Y. Tchr. Horseheads (N.Y.) Sch. Dist., 1961-62; diagnostician, clinician Horseheads, 1962-76; reading specialist Elmira Heights Schs., N.Y., 1976-78; dir. Achievement Ctr., Horseheads, 1978-95; presenter ednl. N.Y. St. Reading Conf., Kiamesha Lake, N.Y., 1982, Bd. Coop. Ednl. Svcs. Tchrs. Tng., Horseheads, 1978-80; researcher learning disabilities, Horseheads, 1962—. Author: Achieve Visual Memory Teaching Material, 4 Vols., 1980. Mem. pub. affairs edn. home life Chemung Valley Jr. Women's Club, 1968-78, 1st v.p., 1971-72; asst. treas. Horseheads Women's Club, 1983-85. Recipient Outstanding Jr. Women's Club award, 1975. Mem. Nat. Assn. Learning Disabilities, N.Y. State Head Injury Assn., Chemung Valley Reading Assn., Horseheads Women's Club (asst. treas. 1983, corr. sec. 1990-91). Republican. Roman Catholic. Office: 1216 Scobee Dr Lansdale PA 19446

CUSIMANO, CHERYLL ANN, nursing administrator; b. New Orleans, Oct. 5, 1946; d. Raymond M. and Bernadette R. (Rich) Schroeder; m. Richard C. Cusimano, Aug. 27, 1967; children: Richard C. Jr., Beth Ann, Mark Allen. Diploma, Mercy Hosp. Sch. Nursing, New Orleans, 1967; cert. vocat. tchr., La. State U., 1979; student, U. New Orleans. RN, La.; cert. in ACLS, med. surg. nursing ANCC. Various nursing positions, 1967-76; asst. head nurse pediatric unit East Jefferson Hosp., 1976-77; instr. allied health field Jefferson Parish Vocat.-Tech. Sch., 1977-79; instr. med.-surg. nursing Charity Hosp., New Orleans, 1979-80; dir. operating room Marion County Gen. Hosp., Columbia, Miss., 1981; night house supr. Children's Hosp., New Orleans, 1984; asst. supr. progressive care unit Northshore Regional Med. Ctr., Slidell, La., 1985-87; pediatric staff nurse pediatric unit Touro Infirmary, New Orleans, 1982-85, charge nurse med.-surg. unit, 1987-91; nursing supr. Touro Infirmary Ctr. Chronic Pain, Rehab., New Orleans, 1992-94, program coord., 1994—. Mem. nursing com. East Jefferson chpt. ARC; ; former vol. classroom asst. Roudolph Matas Elem. Sch.; former mem. adv. bd. Project Head Start; guest speaker Am. Cancer Soc.; bd. dirs. Northshore Hospice, 1986-87, Charity Hosp. Sch. Surg. Tech., 1980. Nursing scholar Am. Legion. Mem. Am. Soc. Pain Mgmt. Nurses. Office: Touro Infirmary Chronic Pain Unit 1401 Foucher St New Orleans LA 70115-3515

CUSMANO, J. JOYCE, public relations executive. BA, Eastern Mich. U.; MA, U. Md., 1972. Asst. dir. Detroit Youtheatre Detroit Inst. Arts; spl. events dir. Detroit Renaissance; v.p. Franco Pub. Rels. Group, Detroit, 1985-90, sr. v.p., 1991—. Mem. Women's Econ. Club. Office: Franco Pub Rels Group 400 Renaissance Ctr Ste 600 Detroit MI 48243-1509*

CUSTIS, CATHERINE MARY, state agency supervisor; b. Columbus, Ohio, July 16, 1951; d. William Dalgarn and Charlotte Elizabeth (Gwynne) C.; m. Harry Raymond Condry, Jr., May 27, 1972 (div. Aug. 1983). BS in Acctg., Ohio State U., 1985. Billing clk. Med. Mgmt., Columbus, Ohio, 1967-69; retail clk. McLoughlin's Pharmacy, Columbus, 1969-70, F&R Lazarus Co., Columbus, 1970-71; billing clk./account clk. Hughes-Peters Inc., Columbus, 1970-72; electronic assembler MI 2, Columbus, 1972-75; account clk. Buckeye Union Ins., Columbus, 1975-80; sec. Ohio Bur. Employment Svcs., Columbus, 1980-83, field auditor, 1983-93, supr., 1993—. Episco-Buddhist.

CUSTODIO, BRENDA KAY, English language educator; b. Mansfield, Ohio, Dec. 27, 1948; d. Clifford C. and Geraldine (Payton) Mabry; m. Jerry K. Borden, Nov. 3, 1972 (div. Feb. 1983); children: Jeremy K., Vanessa K.; m. Heinz Orlando Custodio, Oct. 8, 1983. BA in English, History, Spring Arbor Coll., 1970; MA, Ohio State U., 1991, postgrad., 1995—. Tchr. English Knox County JVS, Mt. Vernon, Ohio, 1970-73; tchr. learning disabilities Newark (Ohio) City Schs., 1977-83; instr. ESL United Bus. Inst., N.Y.C., 1983-85; tchr. ESL Columbus (Ohio) Pub. Schs., 1985—; pres., owner Lotus House Publs., Columbus, 1992—; presenter workshop State Dept. Edn., Columbus, 1990—. Author: Pocket Guide to Columbus, 1992, study guides for: Children of the River, 1992, Shabanu, The Good Earth, A Woman of Her Tribe, Year of Impossible Goodbyes, 1993, New Kids in Town, Journey of the Sparrows, The Return, 1994, Shadow of the Dragon, 1995, Dragon's Gate, 1996. dir. Christian edn., bd. dirs. Dayspring (Ohio) Ch. of Nazarene, 1985—. Recipient Excellence in English award English-Spkg. Union, Columbus, 1990, Impact II Tchg. award Ameritech/Ohio Dept. Edn., Columbus, 1990, 91, 92, 93, 94, McKenzie Literacy Grant, 1996; White Castle/Ingram grantee, Columbus, 1994. Mem. Columbus Edn. Assn. (bldg. rep.), Columbus Christian Writers (founder, pres. 1989—), Tchr. of English as Second Lang., Star Trek Fan Club (capt. 1994—). Democrat. Home: 3069 Bocastle Ct Reynoldsburg OH 43068-5074 Office: Hilltonia Middle Sch 2345 W Mound St Columbus OH 43204-2901

CUTLER, LAUREL, advertising agency executive; b. N.Y.C., Dec. 8, 1926; d. A. Smith and Dorothy (Glaser) C.; m. Stanley Bernstein, July 3, 1952 (div. 1983); children—Jon Cutler, Amy Sarah, Seth Perry. B.A., Wellesley Coll., 1946. Reporter Washington Post, 1946—; copywriter J. Walter Thompson, N.Y.C., 1947-50; copy chief Wesley Assocs., 1950-56; v.p. Fletcher, Richard, Calkins & Holden, N.Y.C., 1956-63; sr. v.p., creative dir. McCann Erickson, N.Y.C., 1963-72; sr. v.p. Leber Katz Ptnrs., N.Y.C., 1972-80, exec. v.p., dir. mktg. planning, 1980-84, vice chmn., 1984—; vice chmn. FCB/Leber Katz Ptnrs., N.Y.C., 1986—; v.p. consumer affairs Chrysler Corp., Highland Park, Mich., 1988-91; global dir. mktg. and planning Foote Cone & Belding Comms., Chgo., 1991—; spkr. to orgns. including Assn. Nat. Advertisers, Am. Mktg. Assn., Produce Mktg. Assn., Grocery Mfrs. Am., Conf. Bd.; bd. dirs. True North Comms., Inc., Hannaford Bros. Co., Quaker State Corp., Domino's Mktg. Adv. Bd. Recipient Matrix award Women in Communications, 1985, Achievement award Wellesley Alumni Assn., 1990; named Ladies Home Jour. One of Am.'s Fifty Most Powerful Women, 1990, Advt. Industry Man of Yr., 1995. Mem. Fashion Group (bd. dirs.), N.Y.C. Partnership, Com. of 200, Cosmopolitan Club, Womens' Forum Inc. Home: 15 W 53rd St New York NY 10019-5410 also: 14 John St Sag Harbor NY 11963-2620 Office: Foote Cone & Belding Comms 150 E 42d St New York NY 10017

CUTLER, RONNIE, artist; b. N.Y.C.; d. Leo and Sarah (Saks) C.; m. Mar. 1, 1951 (dec. May 1990). Student, Columbia U., 1955-56, Bklyn. Mus. Art, 1958, Art Students League, N.Y.C., 1959-60. Exhibited in group shows Whitney Mus. Am. Art, N.Y.C., 1954, Delgado Mus. Art, New Orleans, 1955, Berkshire Mus. Art, Pittsfield, Mass., 1955, 56, Bklyn. Mus., 1956, 58, Riverside Mus. Art, N.Y.C., 1957, Springfield (Mass.) Mus. Art, 1957, Nat. Acad. Art, N.Y.C., 1958, Provincetown (Mass.) Art Assn. and Mus., 1993. Recipient Sherwood prize in oil Silvermine Guild Artists, 1955, 1st prize Riverside Mus. Art, 1957, alumni purchase award Art Students League, 1960, 1st prize in oil So. Berkshire Assn., 1979, 80, Painters and Sculptors Soc., 1955. Home and Studio: 175 W 12th St Apt 11J New York NY 10011-8213

CUTLER, SHERYL, electrical and software engineer; b. Orangeburg, S.C., Sept. 1, 1957; d. Louis Alfred and Virginia Vanessa (Austin) Single tary. BSEE magna cum laude, The Citadel, Charleston, 1995. Elec. tech. Charleston Naval Shipyard, Charleston, S.C., 1988-92; software engr. Scientific Rsch. Corp., Charleston, S.C., 1995—; tutor various high schs., Charleston, 1993-95. Recipient Writing Excellence award NCTE, 1976, 11th Annual Disting. Engring. Scholarship medal Citadel Tau Beta Pi, 1995. Mem. IEEE, NAFE, Phi Kappa Phi, Tau Beta Pi. Republican. Methodist. Home: 335 Hollywood Dr Charleston SC 29407 Office: Scientific Rsch Corp 3860 Farber Pl Dr North Charleston SC 29405

CUTNEY, BARBARA ANN, philosophy educator; b. N.Y.C., Aug. 28, 1941; d. Andrew and Josephine (Gondar) C.; 1 child, Justine. BA cum laude, Queens Coll., 1963; MA, Boston U., 1970; PhD, NYU, 1974. Assoc. prof. philosophy Coll. of New Rochelle, 1966—, dir. curriculum devel., 1994-95, asst. dean for acad. programs, 1995—. Contbg. editor Dance Pages, 1987; contbr. numerous articles and book reviews to profl. jours.; choreographer St. John's Eve, N.Y.C., 1987, numerous other ensemble dances, cons. for John Cage Retrospective Concert, N.Y.C., 1992. Bd. dirs. 782 W. End Ave. Coop., 1990-91, 94-96. NDEA fellow in philosophy of sci. Western Res., 1964, E. S. Brightman fellow Boston U., 1965-66, Walter A. Anderson fellow NYU, 1971-73; grantee NEH funds Coll. of New Rochelle, summers 1987, 89, 96. Mem. Am. Philos. Assn., Soc. for Women in Philosophy, Middle Atlantic States Philosophy Edn. Soc., Columbia U. Moral Edn. Seminar, Phi Beta Kappa. Home: 782 W End Ave New York NY 10025 Office: Coll of New Rochelle 29 Castle Pl New Rochelle NY 10805

CUTTER, DOROTHEA, medical nurse; b. New Hyde Park, N.Y., Feb. 10, 1953; d. John Wesley and Dorothea (Martin) C. BSN, Molloy Coll., 1974; postgrad., Adelphi U. BLS, CCRN; cert. PICC insertion. Staff nurse, head nurse South Nassau Cmty. Hosp., Oceanside, N.Y., 1974-81; staff nurse, asst. head nurse Winthrop U. Hosp., Mineola, N.Y., 1981-83; staff nurse St. Francis Hosp., Rosyln, N.Y., 1983-85; clin. nurse III North Shore U. Hosp., Manhasset, N.Y., 1985—. Mem. AACN (cert.), Am. Heart Assn. Republican. Roman Catholic. Home: 100 S 3rd St New Hyde Park NY 11040-4837 Office: North Shore Univ Hosp 300 Community Dr Manhasset NY 11030-3801

CUTTER, SUSAN LYNN, geography educator; b. Cin., Oct. 13, 1950. BA, Calif. State U., Hayward, 1973; MA, U. Chgo., 1974, PhD, 1976. Asst. prof. geography & human ecology Rutgers U., New Brunswick, N.J., 1977-83, assoc. prof. geography, 1983-93; prof., chair dept. geography U. S.C., Columbia, 1993—; vis. asst. prof. geography Inst. Environ. Studies U. Wash., Seattle, 1976-77. Author: Community Attitudes Toward Pollution, 1978, Rating Places: A Geographer's View of Quality of Life, 1985, Living with Risk, 1993; co-author: The Social Burdens of Environmental Pollution, 1977, Exploitation, Conservation, Preservation: A Geographic Perspective on Natural Resource Use, 2d edit., 1991; editor: Environmental Risks and Hazards, 1994; contbr. numerous articles to profl. jours. Grantee NSF, Nat. Geographic Soc. Office: U SC Dept Geography Columbia SC 29208

CUTTING, MARY DOROTHEA, audio and audio-visual communications company executive; b. N.Y.C., Feb. 20, 1943; d. Elliotte Robinson and Mary Dorothea (Clarke) Little; m. James H. B. Cutting, July 18, 1964; children—Gwendolyn Louise, Laura Elizabeth. Student Whitman Coll., 1960-62; B.A. in English Lit., U. Wash., 1964. Tchr. English, Severna Park High Sch., Md., 1965-66; remedial reading substitute tchr. St. Patrick's Day Sch., Washington, 1976-77; v.p. mktg. The Cutting Corp., Washington, 1978—; bd. dirs. Potomac Talking Book Svcs, Inc., 1990—; bd. dir. Editor children's cassettes: Fisher-Price Toys Spellbinder Series, 1983 (Consumer Com. of Ams. for Democratic Action award for being one of nation's 6 best toys for under $5 1983). Vol. chmn., bd. dirs. Washington Assn. for TV and Children, 1977. Mem. Internat. Assn. Bus. Communicators, Jr. League Washington (bd. dirs. 1977). Republican. Episcopalian. Office: 4940 Hampden Ln Ste 300 Bethesda MD 20814-2945

CUYKENDALL, CLYDIA JEAN, lawyer; b. Olympia, Wash., Apr. 19, 1949; d. Robert Charles and Clydia Vivian (Hall) C. BS in Math., Stanford U., 1971; JD, U. Wash., 1974. Bar: Calif. 1974, Wash. 1975, Tex. 1991. Assoc. Pillsbury, Madison and Sutro, San Francisco, 1974-78; corp. counsel Arabian Am. Oil Co., Dhahran, Saudi Arabia, 1979-88; gen. counsel Star Enterprise, Houston, 1989—. Contbr. articles to profl. jours. Dir. Bus. Arts Fund, Houston, 1992-96. Named one of Women Making a Difference, Houston Minority Bus. Coun., 1995; Nat. Merit. Presdl. scholar, 1967. Mem. Am. Corp. Counsel Assn., Marine Preservation Assn. (dir. 1994-96). Office: Star Enterprise 12700 N Borough Houston TX 77067

CYGANOWSKI, MELANIE L., bankruptcy judge; b. Chgo., June 8, 1952; d. Daniel F. and Sophia A. C.; married, 1989. AB in anthropology, Grinnell Coll., 1974; postgrad. in urban devel., Cornell U., 1975; JD magna cum laude, SUNY, Buffalo, 1981. Coord. program planning, planner, cons. dept. community devel. and human resources City of Buffalo, N.Y., 1974-78; dir. individual referral program Broadway-Filmore Area Coun., Inc., Buffalo, 1978-79; summer assoc. Hodgson, Russ, Andrews, Wood & Goodyear, Buffalo, 1980; law clerk to Hon. Charles L. Brieant U.S. Dist. Ct. (so. dist.) N.Y., 1981-82; litigation assoc. Sullivan & Cromwell, N.Y.C., 1982-89; sr. atty. Milbank, Tweed, Hadley & McCloy, 1989-93; judge U.S. Bankruptcy Ct. (ea. dist.) N.Y., Happauge, 1993—; Bar: N.Y. 1982, U.S. Supreme Ct., U.S. Ct. Appeals (2nd. cir.), U.S. Dist. Ct. (so., ea. and we. dists.) N.Y. Contbr. articles to legal jours. Mem. ABA, Fed. Bar Coun., N.Y. State Bar Assn. Roman Catholic. Office: US Bankruptcy Ct 601 Veterans Memorial Hwy Hauppauge NY 11788-2951

CYPRÈS, JENNIFER MITTS, advertising agency media specialist, copywriter; b. Chattanooga, Feb. 14, 1971; d. Rodrick Vaughn and Leslie Diana (Swafford) Mitts; m. Jean-Philippe Pierre Cyprès, Dec. 18, 1993. BA in English, U. Tenn., 1993. Tchr. English and typing Pvt. Industry Coun., Knoxville, Tenn., 1993; mng. editor Cast On, Sewing and Fine Needlework mags., Knoxville, 1993-94; media buyer, copywriter Lavidge & Assocs., Knoxville, 1995—. Author: (poetry) Remnants, 1993. Vol. George Bush for Pres., Chattanooga, 1988, Helen Hardin for State Rep., Chattanooga, 1988; asst. office mgr. Suzanne Bailey for Juvenile Judge, Chattanooga, 1990. Mem. Order of Ea. Star. Home: 3236 Fairmont Blvd Knoxville TN 37917

CZARNECKI, SELINA MICHELLE SNYDER, sales and marketing executive, artist; b. Trenton, N.J., Aug. 16, 1961; d. Thomas Donald and Theresa (Dulick) Snyder; m. Robert E. Czarnecki, Mar. 16, 1985. AA in Fine Arts with distinction, Mercer County C.C., Trenton, 1981; student, Md. Inst. Coll. Art; BA in Art and Art Edn., Trenton State Coll. Asst. banquet mgr. Cedar Garden, Trenton, 1978-85; office mgr. JC Tire Co., Trenton, 1984-85; English and history tchr. Mercer County C.C., 1979-81; sales exec. Aspen Data Graphics, Newtown, Pa., 1986-90; dir. mktg. and sales Mktg. Industries, Mount Prospect, Ill., 1990-92; dir. nat. mktg. and sales. Transnational, Boston, 1992-94; dir. mktg. and sales Quad/Graphics, N.Y.C., 1994—. Vol. arts and crafts YWCA, Trenton, 1980. Grantee Md. Inst. Coll. Art, 1981. Mem. Women's Direct Response Group, Humane Soc. of U.S., Save the Manatee, Phila. Direct Mktg. Assn., Nat. Humane Edn. Soc., People for the Ethical Treatment of Animals, Internat. Platform Assn., Direct Mktg. Club of N.Y. Office: Quad/Graphics NYC Sales Office 540 Madison Ave New York NY 10022

CZARNIECKI, HELENA JOY, federal investigator; b. Detroit, Feb. 21, 1948; d. Leonard John and Doris Ann (Noppert) C. BFA in Visual Arts, Fla. Internat. U., 1984; paralegal cert., U. Miami, 1987. Hearing clk. Office of Hearings and Appeals Social Security Adminstrn., Miami, 1979-84; legal sec. civil litigation U.S. Atty. U.S. Dept. Justice, Miami, 1984-87; sec., adminstrv. asst. to regional atty. U.S. EEOC, Miami, 1987-89, fed. investigator, 1989—. Legalman, yeoman, petty officer 2d class USNR, 1986—. Baptized Roman. Home: # C 6917 SW 115th Pl Unit C Miami FL 33173 Office: US EEOC 1 Biscayne Tower Ste 2700 2 S Biscayne Blvd Miami FL 33131

CZIN, FELICIA TEDESCHI, Italian language and literature educator, small business owner; b. Vallata, Avellino, Italy, Jan. 20, 1950; came to U.S., 1958; d. Pasquale Aurelio and Maria (Branca) Tedeschi; m. Peter Czin, Oct. 19, 1972; children: Jonathan, Michael. BA, Douglass Coll., Rutgers U., 1972; MA, NYU, 1978, ABD, 1981, postgrad. Assoc. producer RAI Corp. Italian TV, N.Y.C., 1973-77; teaching asst. dept. Italian NYU, 1977-79, adj. instr. dept. English, 1979-81; asst. prof. Vassar Coll., Poughkeepsie, N.Y., 1981-84; co-owner Czin Opticians, Teaneck, N.J., 1984—; coordinator Symposium on Italian Poetry, N.Y.C., 1978. Editor Out of London Press, N.Y.C., 1977-82, dir. pub. relations, 1977-82; editor jour. Yale Italian Studies, 1979-82; translator for jours. Home: 3 Horizon Rd Apt G1 Fort Lee NJ 07024-6703 Office: 489 Cedar Ln Teaneck NJ 07666-1710

CZNARTY, DONNA MAE, secondary education educator; b. Bridgeport, Conn., Aug. 17, 1950; d. Richard W. and Dorothy Mae (Kosturko (Oefinger); m. William C. Cole, Jr., July 11, 1970; 1 child, Michael William Cole; m. Thomas Robert Cznarty, Apr. 29, 1983. BS in Edn., So. Conn. State U., 1973, MS in Edn., 1977. Lang. arts tchr. Shelton Bd. Edn., Conn., 1973-82; English tchr. Millbrook Bd. Edn., N.Y., 1985-86; sec., bd. dirs. Hopewell Precision, Inc., Hopewell Junction, N.Y., 1986—; bd. dirs. Dutchess Arts Coun. Mem. Nat. Assn. Female Execs. Republican. Avocations: interior design, antiques, traveling, doll collecting. Home: Field Haven Stanfordville NY 12581 Office: Hopewell Precision Inc Ryan Dr Hopewell Junction NY 12533

CZUSZAK, JANIS MARIE, former credit company official, researcher; b. Greensburg, Pa., Aug. 3, 1956; d. Charles Clyde and Olga (Plica) C. BS, Indiana U. of Pa., 1978; MBA, U. Pitts., 1985, PhD, 1995. Supervising sr. acct., computer audit specialist KPMG Peat Marwick, Pitts., 1979-81; fin. analyst Westinghouse Credit Corp., Pitts., 1981-83, staff analyst, 1983-84, fin. and computer auditor, 1984-86, real estate financing rep., 1986-88, assoc. investment mgr., 1988-91, investment mgr., 1991-93; fin. analyst Mellon Bank, Pitts., 1993—. Mem. Greater Pitts. Commn. for Women, 1989—. Mem. Nat. Comml. Fin. Assn., NAFE. Office: Mellon Bank 1 Mellon Bank Ctr Pittsburgh PA 15258-0001

DAANE, DIANE MARY, criminal justice educator, lawyer; b. York, Pa., Oct. 23, 1953. BS in Psychology, Okla. State U., 1974; MS in Criminal Justice Adminstrn., Ctrl. Mo. State U., Warrensburg, 1977; JD, U. Mo., Kansas City, 1980. Bar: Mo. 1980, Nebr. 1985. Corrections caseworker Mo. Dept. of Corrections, Jefferson City, 1975-77; weekend supr. Ex-Change House, Inc., Kansas City, Mo., 1977-79; law clk. Fed. Bur. Prisons, Washington & Kansas City, 1979-80; staff atty. mcpl. ct. defense unit Legal Aid of Western Mo., Kansas City, 1980-84; asst. prof. Kearney (Nebr.) State Coll., 1984-85; spl. project editor Block Mgmt. Corp., Kansas City, Mo., 1986; asst. prof. Ball State U., Muncie, Ind., 1986-92; assoc. prof. criminal justice U. S.C., Spartanburg, 1992—; project dir. Grant to Study Adolescents Attitudes Toward Violence, Muncie, Ind., 1988-91; mem. adv. bd. Women's Resource Ctr., Spartanburg, 1995-96. Contbr. articles to profl. jours. Chairperson Mayor's Steering Com. on Domestic Violence, Muncie, 1990-92, pres., v.p., sec. bd. dirs. Aquarious House, Muncie, 1986-89. Recipient Liberty Bell award Muncie Bar Assn., 1992. Mem. Acad. Criminal Justice Scis., Am. Correctional Assn., So. Criminal Justice Assn. Office: U SC 800 University Way Spartanburg SC 29303

DAANSEN, JUDITH ANN, clinical therapist, medical social worker; b. San Francisco, Sept. 8, 1959; d. Adrian John and Patricia Margaret (Linney) D. AA in Liberal Arts, Coll. of San Mateo, 1979; BS in Therapeutic Recreation, Calif. State U., Fresno, 1983, MSW, 1990. Lic. clin. social worker, Calif. Rehab. therapist Atascadero (Calif.) State Hosp., 1983-87, Fresno County Mental Health, 1987-90; clin. therapist, coord. sexual abuse team Tulare (Calif.) Youth Svc. Bur., 1990—; med. social woker Valley Children's Hosp., Fresno, 1994—; presenter, spkr. Child Abuse Conf., Visalia, Calif., 1991—. Vol. Planned Parenthood, Fresno, 1994—, Fresno County Juvenile Hall, Big Bros. and Big Sisters, Fresno, 1996; pres. N.W. region Parents United, sexual abuse prevention and treatment, 1994—. Scholar Penisnula Hosp. Aux., Burlingame, Calif., 1978-79. Mem. NASW, NOW. Unitarian. Office: Tulare Youth Svc Bur 327 South K St Tulare CA 93274

D'ABATE, JANINA MONICA, library administrator; b. Providence, June 20, 1921; d. John Lawrence and Marya Ann (Swiatlowski) Barlowski; m. John D'Abate, Apr. 10, 1943; children: Marya Ann, John G., Janina V. BA, Brown U., 1943; MLS, U. R.I., 1977. Br. libr. Cranston (R.I.) Pub. Libr.,

1966-70; dir. North Scituate (R.I.) Pub. Libr., 1974—; mem. steering com. Gov. Conf. on Libr. and Info. Sci., 1977-79. Pres. bd. trustees Mohr Meml. Libr., Johnston, R.I., 1964-69; bd. dirs. R.I. Philharm., chmn. children's concert com., 1976-78; bd. dirs. Nickerson House, Providence, 1947—, sec., 1952-72; bd. dirs. Camp Fire Inc. R.I., 1980—, sec., 1980-86, pres., 1987; pres. First Unitarian Alliance, 1993—. Mem. R.I. Libr. Assn., Beta Phi Mu. Home: 28 Reservoir Ave Johnston RI 02919-2900 Office: Greenville Rd North Scituate RI 02857

DABBS, JEANNE MCCLUER KERNODLE, retired public relations executive; b. Corsicana, Tex., 1922; d. Robert and Anne (Forrest) McCluer; m. John David Kernodle, June 27, 1942 (div. 1968); 1 child, Elizabeth Kernodle Cabell; m. Jack Autrey Dabbs, Feb. 14, 1981 (dec. 1993). BS in Sociology, Tex. Woman's U., 1970. Supr., writer pub. rels. St. Paul's Hosp., Dallas, 1974-76; dir., v.p. mktg. svcs. Fidelity Union Life Ins. Co., Dallas, 1976-81, ret., 1981. Author poetry book and greeting cards. Mem. comm. com. Mental Health Assn., Austin, Tex., 1991—; pres. aux. Seton Med. Ctr., Austin, 1985-86; mem. Dallas Civic Chorus, Austin Choral Union. Recipient Editorial medal Freedoms Found. Valley Forge, 1973, Eddy award Internat. Assn. Bus. Communicators, 1974, 76, 79, Matrix award Women in Comm., Inc., 1975, Best of Show award Life Ins. Advts. Assn., 1980, Sr. Vol. award Retirees Coordinating Bd., 1989. Mem. Tex. Women's U. Alumnae Assn. (pres. Capital Area chpt. 1987-89), Tuesday Book Club Austin (pres. 1986), Austin Poetry Soc. Methodist. Home: 2301 Lawnmont Ave Apt 11 Austin TX 78756-1939

DACEK, JOANNE CAROLE, psychologist; b. Oceanside, N.Y., July 26, 1963; d. Gerald S. and Teresa E. (Iusi) Martinis; m. Stephen T. Dacek, Jan. 17, 1988; children: Stephen Thomas, Mark Brendan, Megan Michelle. BA, Adelphi U., 1984; MS, Syracuse U., 1987; MA, Seminary of the Immaculate Conception, 1995. Cert. sch. psychologist. Psychologist Greece (N.Y.) Ctrl. Schs., 1987-90, Bellmore (N.Y.) Union Free Sch. Dist., 1990-95; chair com. spl. edn. Bellmore (N.Y.) Unified Sch. Dist., 1995—. Office: Bellmore Unified Sch Dist 2750 South St Marks Ave Bellmore NY 11710

DACEY, EILEEN M., lawyer; b. N.Y.C., Dec. 15, 1948; d. Gabriel A. and Mary (Breen) D.; m. Kinchen C. Bizzell, Jan. 1, 1984. BA in Sociology, SUNY-Stony Brook, 1970; JD, St. John's U., 1975. Assoc. Mendes & Mount, N.Y.C., 1976-80, jr. ptnr., 1980-88; ptnr. Adams, Duque & Hazeltine, N.Y.C., 1988-94; ptnr. Morrison Mahoney & Miller, N.Y.C., 1994-96; ptnr. Querrey & Harrow, N.Y.C., 1996—. Mem. Vol. Lawyers for the Arts. Mem. ABA (chair subcom. fed. regulation of ins. co. investment sect.), N.Y. State Bar Assn., Assn. of Bar of City of N.Y. (com. profl. discipline class of 1996), Practicing Law Inst. (ins. law adv. bd.). Republican. Home: 71 Park Ave New York NY 10016-2507 Office: Querrey & Harrow 380 Lexington Ave Ste 1520 New York NY 10168

DADLEY, ARLENE JEANNE, sleep technologist; b. Cleve., Sept. 13, 1941; d. Bernard and Bernice Anne (Selleck) Davis; m. Charles Dadley, Sept. 15, 1967 (div. Oct. 1977); children: Anitra, Charles. BA in Bus., Ursuline Coll., 1980; postgrad., Case Western Res. U., 1983-85, Stanford U., 1988. Registered polysomnographic technologist. Jr. fund acct. Am. Univ., Washington, 1967-70; HTN and cancer rsch. asst. Case Western Res. U., Cleve., 1976-87, gastroent. rsch. assoc., 1984, sleep rsch. assoc., 1985-87; chief clin. sleep technologist Metrohealth Med. Ctr., Cleve., 1987-95; sleep diagnostics tchr./trainer Metrohealth Med. Ctr., 1987—, judge regional and state sci. fairs, 1984-86. Exhibited at Cleve. Mus. Art, Butler Inst. Art, Corcoran Gallery Art, Washington, Internat. Traveling Am. Artists Exhibit; contbr. articles to profl. jours. Pell grantee, 1976-80, Ohio Instnl. grantee, 1976-80; scholar Case Western Res. U., 1976-80, Yale U., 1982, Respironics, Inc., 1988; recipient presdl. lit. achievement citation League of Am. Pen Women, 1974, citation ARC, 1991. Mem. Internat. Platform Assn., Assn. Polysomnographic Technologists. Home: PO Box 894 Columbia Station OH 44028-0894 Office: Metrohealth Med Ctr 3395 Scranton Rd 100 Metro Health Dr Cleveland OH 44109

DAFFRON, MARYELLEN, librarian; b. Richmond, Va., Nov. 12, 1946; d. William Charles and Ellen (Ahern) D. BA, Coll. Mt. St. Joseph on Ohio, Cin., 1968; MLS, Drexel U., 1970. Libr. Richmond Pub. Libr., 1969-73, FMC, Washington, 1973-93; with U.S. Immigration and Naturalization Svc. Office of Gen. Counsel, Washington, 1993—. Vol. No. Va. Hotline, Arlington, 1974-79. City of Richmond fellow, 1968. Mem. Law Libr. Soc. Washington, Beta Phi Mu. Roman Catholic. Office: US Immigration Naturalization Svc Office Gen Counsel 425 I St NW Rm 6100 Washington DC 20536-0001

DAFFRON, MITZI LYNNAE, nurse educator; b. New Orleans, Sept. 27, 1965; d. Jerry Lee and Betty Jean (Dougherty) Need; m. Stanley William Daffron, Oct. 15, 1988; children: Lauren Alexandra, Joseph Duncan. BSN magna cum laude, U. Indpls., 1988. RN, Ind. Surg. nurse Meth. Hosp., Indpls., 1988-89; nurse telemetry unit Good Samaritan Hosp., Vincennes, Ind., 1989-91; home health care nurse, case mgr. Daviess County Hosp. Home Health, Washington, Ind., 1990-92; quality assurance nurse Meml. Hosp. Home Health Care, Jasper, Ind., 1992; nurse tng. and edn. project specialist Health Care Excel, Inc., Terre Haute, Ind., 1993—. Recipient Am. Legion scholarship, 1986. Mem. Sigma Theta Tau Internat. Home: 2201 S 9th St Terre Haute IN 47802-3119 Office: Health Care Ecel Inc 2901 Ohio Blvd Terre Haute IN 47803-2239

DAGAT, MA SOCORRO S., nurse; b. Cebu, The Philippines, Sept. 24, 1960; came to U.S., 1985; d. Serapio and Fidela (Suerte) D. BSN, Velez Coll. Nursing, 1981; MSN in Critical Care, Columbia U., 1995. RN, N.Y.; cert. ACLS. Staff nurse Velez Hosp., Cebu, 1982-85, L.I. Coll. Hosp., Bklyn., 1985—. Mem. AACN (CCRN), N.Y. State Nurses Assn. Roman Catholic. Home: 1537 68th St Apt 3C Brooklyn NY 11219-6322 Office: LI Coll Hosp 340 Henry St Brooklyn NY 11201-5525

D'AGATI, SUZANNE SNOOK, nursing educator, occupational therapist; b. Stamford, Conn., May 27, 1960; d. Stover H. and Marie (Rohrer) Snook; m. Dean P. D'Agati, Aug. 3, 1985; children: Dean S., Kristen M. BS in Occupl. Therapy, U. Fla., 1982, MHS in Occupl. Therapy, 1985; EdD in Exceptional Child Edn., Fla. Internat. U., 1995. Registered occupl. therapist, Fla. Staff therapist Assn. for Retarded Citizens Early Intervention Ctr., Gainesville, Fla., 1984-85; contract therapist United Cerebral Palsy Presch., Miami, Fla., 1986-87; rsch. and tng. cons. dept. occupl. therapy Mt. Sinai Med. Ctr., Miami Beach, Fla., 1989-95; asst. prof. occupl. therapy Fla. Internat. U., Miami, 1985—; rsch. affiliate dept. neonatology Mt. Sinai Med. Ctr., Miami Beach, 1996; faculty advisor Fla. Internat. U. chpt. Student Assn., Miami, 1994—, Pi Theta Epsilon, Miami, 1988-94; co-developer, co-dir. Profls. Educating Parents, Miami, 1986-92. Contbr. articles to profl. jours. Vol. art appreciation program Broward County Pub. Schs., 1995-96. Named one of Outstanding Young Woman of Am., 1987. Mem. Am. Occupl. Therapy Assn., Fla. Occupl. Therapy Assn. (spl. interest sect. liaison 1986-92), Phi Kappa Phi. Office: Fla Internat Univ Dept Occupl Therapy Miami FL 33199

DAGAVARIAN, DEBRA AGHAVNI, college administrator, consultant; b. N.Y.C., Oct. 26, 1952; d. Harry O. Dagavarian and Norma Siran (Cazanjian) Hansen; m. James B. Bonar, Dec. 26, 1988. BA, SUNY, New Paltz, 1973; MA, SUNY, Albany, 1975; EdD, Rutgers U., 1986. Transfer admissions counselor Mercy Coll., Dobbs Ferry, N.Y., 1976-79, asst. dir. spl. sessions, 1979-81, dir. evening programs, 1981-86, dir. acad. advising, 1986-87; asst. dean for assessment Empire State Coll., Hartsdale, N.Y., 1987-88; dir. testing assessment Thomas Edison State Coll., Trenton, N.J., 1988-96, dep. vice provost, 1996—; adj. prof. Empire State Coll., Mercy Coll., 1979-95; cons. various instns. and corps., 1987—. Author: Saying It Ain't So: American Values as Revealed in Children's Baseball Stories, 1987; author, editor: A Century of Children's Baseball Stories, 1990, (jour.) Jour. of the Nat. Inst. on Assessment of Experiential Learning, 1989—; contbr. articles to profl. jours., periodicals, books. Mem. NAFE, Nat. Assn. Women in Edn., Am. Sociol. Assn., Soc. for Am. Baseball Rsch., Coun. for Adult and Experiential Learning, Assn. for Continuing Higher Edn. Democrat. Office: Thomas Edison State Coll 101 W State St Trenton NJ 08608-1176

DAGGETT, BEVERLY CLARK, state legislator; b. Florence, S.C., Sept. 9, 1945; d. John and Beth Clark; m. Thomas A. Daggett, May 8, 1971; children: John, Page, Paul. BS in Biology, Hillsdale Coll., 1967. Mem. Maine Ho. of Reps., Augusta, 1987—; chair commn. to study biotech. and genetic engring., 1995—, house chair joint standing com. on state and local govt., 1995-96. Coun. State Govts. Toll fellow, 1990. Democrat. Home: 16 Pine St Augusta ME 04330-5340

DAGGETT, MARILYN PATRICIA, music educator; b. Phila., Mar. 17, 1947; d. Theodore Alfred and Mildred Marie (McCliment) Pettinicchi; m. William M. Daggett Jr., June 14, 1969 (div. Apr. 1982); children: William M. III, Brian A. BMus Edn., Temple U., 1969; MEd, George Mason U., 1989. Cert. tchr. music K-12, Va. String tchr., orch. dir. Fairfax County (Va.) Pub. Schs., 1969—, George C. Marshall H.S., Falls Church, 1977-82, 90—; founder, dir. Greater Tyson's Orch. Camp, Vienna, Va., 1987—. Mem. fine arts. adv. com. Arlington County Pub. Schs., 1989-91. Mem. Music Educators Nat. Conf., Nat. Sch. Orch. Assn., Am. String Tchrs. Assn., Fairfax County Fedn. Tchrs. (bldg. rep.), Sigma Alpha Iota. Home: 5725 25th St N Arlington VA 22207-1401 Office: George C Marshall HS 7731 Leesburg Pike Falls Church VA 22043

DAGGY, DARLENE A., materials manager; b. Richmond, Ind., Aug. 29, 1955; d. Stanley E. and Cecelia A. (McNaulty) Mozzer; m. Jack A. Dagg Jr., May 22, 1976; children: Mike A., Jamie R., Katie C. AS in Bus., Ind. U. E, Richmond, 1976; BS in Bus., Ind./Purdue U., Indpls., 1978. Jr. acct. Brady, Ware & Co. CPA, Richmond, 1978; acct. rep. Ins. Co. of N.Am., Richmond, 1974-78; acct. Belden Wire & Cable, Richmond, 1978, sr. acct., 1980, systems integrator, 1984, acctg. mgr., 1990; controller Belden Wire & Cable, Franklin, N.C., 1994, materials mgr., 1996—; mem. bd. dirs. Belde Credit Union, Ill. Mem. Am. Prodn. & Inventory Control Soc., Assn. Mgmt. Accts., Local Toasmasters (chpt. pres. 1981-82). Methodist. Office: Belden Wire & Cable 1281 Georgia Hwy Franklin NC 28734

D'AGNENICA, JILL MARIE, artist; b. Upland, Calif., June 30, 1964; d. Anthony Baron and Rosaria (Ruggeri) D'A.; m. John Michael Child, July 30, 1988. Student, U. Studi di Firenze, Florence, Italy, 1985-86; BA in History magna cum laude, UCLA, 1987; MFA in Visual Art, Claremont Grad. Sch., 1991. guest artist colls. and univs., So. Calif., 1993—. Works exhibited Margert Fowler Gardens, Claremont, Calif., 1990, Claremont Grad. Sch., 1991 (travel and rsch. grantee 1991), U. N.Mex., Portales, 1992 (Best of Show 1992), Calif State U., Northridge, 1992, throughout L.A., 1993-94 (L.A. Contemporary Exhbns. Artist's Project grantee 1994, City of L.A. Cultural Affairs grantee 1994-95), Robert Berman Gallery, Santa Monica, 1994, Lucky Nun Gallery, Silverlake, Calif., 1995, Rio Hondo Coll., L.A., 1995, Museo Civico, Padua, Italy, 1995, Ga. Mus. Art, Athens, 1995, Mt. San Antonio Coll., Walnut, Calif., 1996. Mem. NOW, So. Calif. Women's Caucus for Art (exec. bd. dirs. 1992-94), L.A. Contemporary Exhbns., Coll. Art Assn. Home: # 020 2020 N Main St Los Angeles CA 90031

D'AGNESE, HELEN JEAN, artist; b. N.Y.C.; d. Leonardo and Rose (Redavid) De Santis; m. John J. D'Agnese, Oct. 29, 1942; children: John, Linda, Diane, Michele, Helen, Gina, Paul. Student CUNY, 1940-42; student Atlanta Coll. Art, 1972-76. One-woman shows: Maude Sullivan Gallery, El Paso, 1964, John Wanamaker Gallery, Phila., 1966, U. N.Mex., 1967, Karo Manducci Gallery, San Francisco, 1968, Tuskegee Inst. Carver Mus., 1968, Lord & Taylor Gallery, N.Y.C., 1969, Harmon Gallery, Naples, Fla., 1970, Fountainbleau, Miami, 1970, Reflections Gallery, Atlanta, 1972, Williams Gallery, Atlanta, 1973, Atlanta Coll. of Art, 1976-80, Americana Gallery, Mineola, Tex., 1977, E. M. Howard Gallery, Amelia Island, Fla., 1978, Haitian Primitives Gallery, 1981, Highland Gallery, Atlanta, 1987, Edge of the World Gallery, 1996, others; donated painting to Fernandiana Beach High Sch., 1991; group shows: Musseo des Artes, Juárez, México, 1968, Benedictine Art Show, N.Y.C., 1967, Southeast Contemporary Art Show, Atlanta, 1968, Atlanta U., 1969, Red Piano Gallery, Hilton Head, S.C., Terrace Gallery, Atlanta, Ann. Bible Heritage Art Exhibit, Marietta, Ga., 1976, Nat. Judaic Theme Exhbn., Atlanta, 1976, Crystal Britton Gallery, Atlanta, Odyssey Collection Gallery, Mich., 1988, Artist Gallery, Atlanta, 1991, Pompono Beach, Fla., Ft. Lauderdale, 1992; represented in permanent collections: Carter Pres. Ctr., Atlanta, Juarez (Mexico) Art Mus., Vatican Mus., Rome, Nassau (Fla.) County Pub. Library. Judge art show Mt. Loretto Acad., El Paso, 1967; commd. sculptor of Bob Marley in Limestone, 1985; art demonstration and lectr. Margaret Harris Sch., Atlanta, 1970; artist-in-residence Montessori Sch., Atlanta, 1978-79. Recipient Gold medal Accademia Italia delle Arti, Italy, 1979, Calvatone, 1982, Golden Flame award, 1986; 1st place sculpture award Tybee Island Art Festival, 1982, Golden Flame award Parliamento U.S.A., 1987, Golden Palette award Academia Europea, 1986, 87, Gold medal Internat. Parliament for the Arts, 1982. Mem. Nat. Mus. of Women in the Arts (chartered), Arts Alliance Amelia Island. Home: 3240 S Fletcher Ave Apt 557 Fernandina Beach FL 32034-4321 Office: D'Agnese Studio & Fine Art Gallery 14 1/2 N 4th St Fernandina Beach FL 32034-4124

DAHL, ARLENE, actress, author, designer, cosmetic executive; b. Mpls., Aug. 11, 1928; d. Rudolph and Idelle (Swan) D.; m. Marc A. Rosen; children: Lorenzo Lamas, Carole Christine Holmes, Stephen Andreas Schaum. Student, U. Minn., 1943-44, Mpls. Inst. Art, 1945, Minn. Coll. Music, 1944, Minn. Bus. Coll., 1944. Pres. Arlene Dahl Enterprises, 1952-67; v.p. Kenyon & Eckhart, 1967-72; pres. Woman's World divsn. Kenyon & Eckhart Advt. Agy., 1967-72; nat. beauty and health advisor Sears Roebuck Co., 1970-75; internat. dir. Sales and Mktg. Execs. Internat., 1972-75; fashion dir. O.M.A., 1975-78; pres. Dahlia Parfums, Inc., 1975-80, Dahlia Prodns., Inc., 1978-81, Dahlmark Prodns., 1981—, Scandia Cosmetics, Ltd., 1978-80; pres., chmn. Lasting Beauty Ltd., 1986—. Author: Always Ask a Man, 1965, 12 Beautyscope books, 1968, rev. edit., 1978, Arlene Dahl's Secrets of Hair Care, 1969, Arlene Dahl's Secrets of Skin Care, 1972, Beyond Beauty, 1980, Arlene Dahl's Lovescopes, 1983, Arlene Dahl's Astro Forecast, 1991, 92, 93, 94, 95, 96, 97, Arlene Dahl's Hollywood Horoscope internat. syndicated weekly column, 1994—; actress: (Broadway plays) including Mr. Strauss Goes to Boston, Questionable Ladies, Cyrano de Bergerac, Applause (Tony award musical), (films) including (debut) My Wild Irish Rose, The Bride Goes Wild, Reign of Terror, A Southern Yankee, Ambush, The Outriders, Three Little Words, Watch the Birdie, Scene of the Crime, Inside Straight, No Questions Asked, Desert Legion, Slightly Scarlet, Sangaree, Caribbean Gold, Jamaica Run, Diamond Queen, Here Come the Girls, Bengal Brigade, Kisses for My President, Woman's World, Journey to the Center of the Earth, Wicked as They Come, She Played with Fire, Les Poneyettes, Du Blé Enliases, The Land Raiders, The Way to Kathmandu, Fortune Is a Woman, The Big Bank Roll, Who Killed Maxwell Thorn?, Midnight Warrior, 1991, (TV shows) Lux Video Theatre, 1952-53, guest starring appearances on The Love Boat, Renegade, Fantasy Island, Love American Style, One Life to Live, 1981-84, Night of 100 Stars, 1983, Happy Birthday Hollywood, 1987, All My Children, 1995, Renegade, 1995; hostess (TV series): Pepsi-Cola Theatre, 1954, Opening Night, 1958, Arlene Dahl's Beauty Spot, 1966, Arlene Dahl's Starscope, 1979-80, Arlene Dahl's Lovescope, 1980-82; played throughout U.S. in One Touch of Venus, The Camel Bell, Blithe Spirit, Liliom, The King and I, Roman Candle, I Married an Angel, Bell, Book and Candle, Applause, Marriage Go Round, Pal Joey, A Little Night Music, Forty Carats, Life with Father, Murder Among Friends, Dear Liar; nightclub acts Flamingo Hotel, Las Vegas, Latin Quarter, N.Y.C.; internat. syndicated beauty columnist Chgo. Tribune/ N.Y. News Syndicate, 1950-70, Arlene Dahl's Lucky Stars Column, Globe Communications, 1988-90, Arlene Dahl's Starscope Mag., 1991, 92, 93, 94, 95, 96, 97; designer sleepwear for A.N. Saab & Co., 1952-57, In Vogue with Arlene Dahl (Vogue Patterns), 1980-85, Arlene Dahl Pvt. Collection Jewelry, 1989-94, Arlene Dahl's Jewels of Fortune Home Shopping Network, 1996. Hon. life mem. Father Flannagan's Boys Town; internat. chair Pearl Buck Found.; bd. dirs. Hollywood Mus. Recipient 10 Laurel awards Box Office mag., Hollywood Walk of Fame Star, 1952, Coup de Chapeau Deaville Film Festival award, 1982, 92; named Best Coiffed, Heads of Fame awards, 1967-72, 80, Woman of the Yr., Advt. Club of N.Y.C., 1969, Mother of the Yr., 1982, Lifetime Achievement award WorldFest, 1994. Mem. NATAS (trustee), Acad. TV Arts and Scis. (bd. govs., v.p.), Acad. Motion Picture Arts and Scis. (N.Y. spl. events), Author's Guild, Commanderie de Bontemps du Medoc et Graves, Internat. Platform Assn., N.Y. Acad. TV Arts and Scis., Nat. Trust for Hist. Preservation, Sierra Club, Vesterheim Norwegian/Am. Found., Film Soc., Smithsonian Assocs., UNIFEM. Office: Dahlmark Prodns PO Box 116 Sparkill NY 10976-0116

DAHL, BREN BENNINGTON, screenwriter; b. Gary, Ind., Nov. 15, 1954; d. Paul Wayland and Shirley Ann (Havard) Bennington; m. Curtis Ray Dahl; children: Austin Brooks, Darren Curtis. Student Principia Coll., Elsah, Ill., 1972-74, Sch. of Art Inst. of Chgo., 1983; BA in English with honors, U. Hawaii, 1977. Tchr. English, Peace Corps, Mbuji-Mayi, Zaire, 1977-79, Asahi Cultural Ctr., Osaka, Japan, 1981-82, Osaka Inst. Fgn. Trade, Osaka, 1981-82, Kansai U. of Fgn. Studies, Osaka, 1980-82, Matsushita Electric, Osaka, 1982; pres., owner Video Enterprises, North Palm Beach, Fla., 1983-87; producer's asst. Casady Entertainment, Hollywood, Calif., 1989-91. Screenwriter Ties That Bink, 1991, The Spider Clock, 1993, Ticking Off Ryan, 1995. Mem. Palm Beach Opera Chorus, 1984-85. Fred Waring Scholar, 1972. Mem. Exec. Women of Palm Beaches, Fla. Motion Picture and TV Assn., Am. Film Inst., No. Palm Beach County C. of C. (co-chmn. spl. events 1985-86), Better Bus. Bur. Scriptwriters Network, Tourette Syndrome Assn.. Republican. Jewish. Avocation: calligraphy, tennis, singing, gourmet cooking, running.

DAHL, TERESE ROSE, elementary education educator; b. Mpls., Feb. 14, 1961; d. George Richard and Helen Ann (Shirley) Shimshock; children: Kevin, Sara. BA in Edn., St. Mary's Coll., 1983; MEd in Curriculum Instrn., U. St. Thomas, 1993. Cert. elem. tchr., Minn. 5th grade tchr. St. Peter Sch., Forest Lake, Minn., 1983-89; K-6, computer, phys. edn. tchr. St. Peter Sch., 1989-91, 2d grade tchr., 1991—; computer coord., St. Peter Sch., 1983—. Recipient full grad. sch. scholarship U. St. Thomas, 1990-93, Minn. Humanities Inst. weeklong fellowship, 1995. Mem. Minn. Sci. Tchrs., Elem. Mathematicians.

DAHLBERG, PATRICIA LEE, parochial school educator; b. Blue Island, Ill., Nov. 13, 1950; d. Frank George and Linda Frances (Burmeister) Toczek; m. Robert James Dahlberg, May 5, 1973. BA in English, Rosary Coll., River Forest, Ill., 1972, MS in Learning Disabilities, 1981. Cert. secondary school tchr., Ill., spl. K-12 tchr. social/emotional disorders, Ill. Tchr. lang. arts St. Nicholas/St. Louis Sch., Chgo., 1972-73; substitute tchr. St. John, St. Charles and St. Bernardine Schs., 1973; tchr. lang arts grades 7 and 8 St. Bernardine Sch., Forest Park, Ill., 1974-77; reading/English tchrs. grades 6-8 Our Lady of the Ridge, Chicago Ridge, Ill., 1977-79, tchr. reading grades 6-8, 1980-94, tchr. reading grades 5-8, 1994—. Mem. Internat. Reading Assn., West Suburban Reading Coun. Roman Catholic. Office: Our Lady of the Ridge 10859 Ridgeland Ave Chicago Ridge IL 60415-2154

DAHLING, SHELLEY JO, secondary education educator; b. Lake City, Minn., Dec. 18, 1970; d. Gerald Raymond and Roberta Jo (Ives) D. BS Social Studies, Math. Edn. cum laude, Mankato State U., 1993. Tchr. Morris (Minn.) H.S., 1993—; tutor Mankato (Minn.) State U., 1991-93, rsch. asst., 1992-93. Mem. Minn. Tchrs. Assn., Kappa Delta Pi. Lutheran. Office: Morris Area HS 201 S Columbia Ave Morris MN 56267

DAI, JING CHU LING, medical writer, researcher, consultant; b. Tacoma, Wash.; d. Yunan and Yet Sze Ling; m. Shenyu Dai (div.); children: Alexander M., Benjamin M. Student Temple U., 1960-63; BA in Journalism, Calif. State U., Long Beach, 1968; MPH, UCLA, 1977; CME, U. So. Calif., 1984. Mgr. med. order dept. J.B. Lippincott Co., Phila., 1956-62; copy editor Annals Internal Medicine, 1962; pub. rels. asst., editor Linton's Inc., Phila., 1962-64; exec. editor Bearing & Transmission Specialist, 1971-72; dir. publs. City of Hope Nat. Med. Ctr., Duarte, Calif., 1972-74; sr. proposal engr., writer, subcontractor for aerospace cos., 1965-66, 79-82, 86—; med. affairs rsch. cons., Gravity Guidance, Inc., Pasadena, Calif., 1982-84; freelance writer, cons.; rsch. cons. Musculo-Skeletal Clinic, Pasadena, 1982-84. Condr. study on Calif. marriage laws as preventative for congenital syphilis and congenital rubella, 1977; contbr. articles to profl. jours. Bd. dirs., v.p. Bougless-White Scholarship Found., Long Beach, 1967-71, mem., 1965—; publicity adviser Am. Cancer Soc., L.A., 1975; adv. Metric Cert. Specialist Bd., U.S. Metric Assn., 1981—. USPHS grantee, UCLA, 1975-77. Mem. Women in Comm. (chmn. careers conf., L.A., 1975, award 1975), Am. Med. Writers Assn., Am. Pub. Health Assn., Nat. Assn. Female Execs., Assn. Health Svc. Rsch., Soc. Tech. Comm. (chmn. ways/means, internat. tech. com. conf. 1978), Women's Internat. Friendship League (co-founder 1943), Coun. Biology Editors, U.S. Metric Assn. (planning com. ann. conf. 1987). Home: 320 S Gramercy Pl Los Angeles CA 90020-4543

DAIGLE, CANDACE JEAN, municipal services provider; b. Gilmanton, N.H., Jan. 25, 1953; d. Alfred Ephrem and Melba Jean (Clifford) LaRoche; m. Raymond Michael Daigle, Aug. 4, 1973. Student, N.H. Tech. Coll., 1994-95, Coll. for Lifelong Learning/, U. System of N.H., 1995—. Cert. paralegal. Adminstrv. sec. Laconia (N.H.) Fire Dept., 1971-86; adminstrv. clk. Laconia Zoning Bd. of Adjustment, 1984-92, Laconia Airport Authority, 1984-92; planning adminstr. Gilmanton (N.H.) Planning Bd., 1985-96; proprietor Acad. Village Bus. Svc., Gilmanton, 1987—; co-owner R.M. Daigle Constrn. Co., Gilmanton, 1975—; town auditor Town of Gilmanton, 1987-88, property mgmt. cons., 1989-93, interim dep. town clk./tax collector, 1993; method and systems cons. Belmont (N.H.) Planning Bd., 1991—; zoning cons. Belmont Zoning Bd. of Adjustment, 1993—. Mem. Am. Legion Aux., Gilmanton, 1958—; supr. Gilmanton Voter Checklist, 1988—; trustee Gilmanton Cemeteries, 1990—; sec., treas. Gilmanton 4th of July Assn., 1990—. Recipient Honorable Mention award for citizen planner of yr., N.H. Office of State Planning, 1994. Mem. Am. Planners Assn., Paralegal Assn. N.H., N.H. Planners Assn., Granite State Designers and Installers. Republican. Roman Catholic. Home: PO Box 56, State Rte 107 Gilmanton NH 03237 Office: Acad Village Bus Svc PO Box 56, State Rte 107 Gilmanton NH 03237

DAIKER, BARBARA LYNNE, occupational health nurse; b. Gary, Ind., Oct. 1, 1959; d. James Frederick Daiker and Donna Sue Butts Peterson; m. Andrean D. Lynch, Sept. 13, 1981. AS, North Hennepin Coll., Mpls., 1979; BS, Augsburg Coll., Mpls., 1984; MS, U. Minn., 1986, MA, 1992. Cert. occupl. health nurse. Chg. nurse ICU/CCU Fairview Hosp., Mpls., 1979-84; rehab. cons. Marg-Patton & Selting, St. Paul, 1984-85; mgr. NorthWorks North Meml. Med. Ctr., Mpls., 1985-90; preferred workcare mgr. PreferredOne, Inc., Mpls., 1990-93; dir. bus. devel. United Health Care Corp., Mpls., 1993-95; dir. network devel. Intracorp., Phila., 1995—; grant coord. North Meml. Med. Ctr., 1989-90. Dir. Block Nurse Program, Mpls., 1986-89. Named Disting. Alumna North Hennepin C.C., 1990. Mem. Am. Assn. Occupl. Health Nurses (author edn. update series 1994), Am. Pub. Health Assn., Am. Evaluation Assn., Minn. Assn. Occupl. Health Nurses (bd. dirs. 1991-93), Sigma Theta Tau (Zeta chpt. v.p. 1991-92).

DAIL, HILDA LEE, psychotherapist; b. Franklin Springs, Ga., Aug. 23, 1920; d. Ransom Harvey and Mattie (Gray) Lee; m. Francis Roderick Dail, Dec. 27, 1941; children: Janice Sylvia, Roderick Lee. BA, Piedmont Coll., 1941; PhD, The Union Inst., 1979. Cert. expressive therapist. Tchr. pub. schs. N.C., Tenn. and Ga., 1939-54; assoc. sec. Bd. of Missions, Methodist Ch., New York, 1954-60; dir. pub. rels. and tchr. Leonard Theol. Coll., Jabalpur, India, 1960-64; editor lit. Bd. of Missions, United Meth. Ch., N.Y.C., 1964-70; exec. dir. Int. Found. Ewha Women's Univ., Seoul, Republic of Korea, 1970-71; dir. devel. Ch. Women United, 1971-73; dir. resources cen. nat. bd. YWCA, 1973-75; pres. Hilda Lee Dail & Assoc. Internat., N.Y.C., 1975-83, Myrtle Beach, S.C., 1983—; mem. adj. faculty Coastal Carolina U., Conway, 1981-95, Webster U., Myrtle Beach, 1981—; bd. dirs. Enablement Inc., Boston, 1975-89, Assn. Coop. Agys. Asian Women's Coll., 1971-85; founder, pres. Internat. Ctr. for Creativity and Consciousness, 1989—; mem. Horry County Human Rels. Coun., 1994—. Author: Decision and Destiny, 1957, Encounters Extraordinary, 1969, Let's Try a Workshop With Teen Women, 1974, The Lotus and the Pool, 1983, How to Create Your Own Career, 1989. Dir. Citizens Against Spouse Abuse, Myrtle Beach, 1982-88, pres. Gotham Bus. and Prof. Women's Club, N.Y., 1978, dir. Green Chimney Sch., N.Y., 1978-83, v.p., Zonta Internat., N.Y., 1976-84. Fellow Nat. Expressive Therapy Assn. (speaker 1983-89); mem. ASTD (bd. dirs. 1972-89), Mental Health Assn. (bd. dirs., pres. 1988-89). Democrat. United Methodist. Home and Office: Briarcliffe Acres 154 Pine Tree Ln Myrtle Beach SC 29572-5641

DAILEY, COLEEN HALL, lawyer; b. East Liverpool, Ohio, Aug. 10, 1955; d. David Lawrence and Deloris Mae (Rosensteel) Hall; m. Donald W. Dailey

Jr., Aug. 16, 1980; children: Erin Elizabeth, Daniel Lester. Student, Wittenberg U., 1973-75; BA, Youngstown State U., 1977; JD, U. Cin., 1980. Bar: Ohio 1981, U.S. Dist. Ct. (no. dist.) Ohio 1981. Sr. library assoc. Marx Law Library, Cin., 1979-80; law clk. Kapp Law Office, East Liverpool, 1979, 1980-81, assoc., 1981-85; sole practice East Liverpool, 1985-95; magistrate Columbiana County, Ohio, 1995—; spl. counsel Atty. Gen. Ohio, 1985-92. Pres. Columbiana County Young Dems., 1985-87; bd. dirs. Big Bros./Big Sisters Columbiana County, Inc., Lisbon, Ohio, 1984-87, Planned Parenthood Mahoning Valley, Inc., 1993—; trustee Ohio Women Inc., 1991-95; mem. Columbiana County Progress Coun., Inc. Mem. ABA, Ohio Bar Assn. (Ohio Supreme Ct. Joint Task Force on Gender Fairness), Columbiana County Bar Assn., Assn. Trial Lawyers Am., Ohio Trial Lawyers Assn., Ohio Fedn. Bus. and Profl. Women (rec. sec. 1991-92), East Liverpool Bus. and Profl. Women's Assn. Democrat. Lutheran. Office: Columbana County Common Pleas Ct 105 S Market Lisbon OH 44432

DAILEY, IRENE ELEANOR, hospital volunteer services professional; b. Pitts., May 13, 1952; d. Russell Ford and Betty (Andra) D. BS in Secondary Edn., Slippery Rock U., 1974. Personnel cons. Liken Svcs., Inc., Pitts., 1974-76; asst. to regional campaign coord. John Heinz for Senate Com., Pitts., 1976; staff asst. community rels. H. John Heinz III H. John Heinz, U.S. Senate, Pitts., 1977-82; asst. dir. community and vol. svcs. Forbes Regional Health Ctr., Monroeville, Pa., 1983-88; dir. vol. svcs. Sewickley (Pa.) Valley Hosp., 1988—. Mem. Women's Polit. Caucus, Pitts., 1980, Minority Bus. Devel. Com., Pitts., 1982; bd. trainer United Way, Pitts., 1988—. Mem. NAFE, Soc. Dirs. Vol. Svcs. (legis. chair Pitts. unit 1984-85, 93, 94, membership chair 1990-92, state v.p. 1992-93), Zonta Three Rivers Pitts. East (bd. dirs. 1984-85, v.p. 1986-88, pres. 1988-89, del. to internat. conv. 1988), Alpha Sigma Alpha. Republican. Roman Catholic. Home: 1512 Cooper Ave Pittsburgh PA 15212-1835 Office: Sewickley Valley Hosp Blackburn Rd Sewickley PA 15143-8386

DAILEY, JANET, novelist; b. Storm Lake, Iowa, May 21, 1944; d. Boyd and Louise Haradon; m. William Dailey; 2 stepchildren. Student pub. schs., Independence, Iowa. Sec. Nebr., Iowa, 1963-74. Author: No Quarter Asked, 1976, After the Storm, 1976, Boss Man From Ogallala, 1976, Savage Land, 1976, Land of Enchantment, 1976, Fire and Ice, 1976, The Homeplace, 1976, Dangerous Masquerade, 1977, Night of the Cotillion, 1977, Valley of the Vapors, 1977, Fiesta San Antonio, 1977, Show Me, 1977, Bluegrass King, 1977, A Lyon's Share, 1977, The Widow and the Wastrel, 1977, Giant of Mesabi, 1978, The Ivory Cane, 1978, The Indy Man, 1978, Darling Jenny, 1978, Reilly's Woman, 1978, To Tell the Truth, 1978, Sonora Sundown, 1978, Big Sky Country, 1978, Something Extra, 1978, Master Fiddler, 1978, Beware of the Stranger, 1978, The Matchmakers, 1978, For Bitter or Worse, 1979, Green Mountain Man, 1979, Six White Horses, 1979, Summer Mahogany, 1979, Touch the Wind, 1979, Strange Bedfellow, 1979, Low Country Liars, 1979, Sweet Promise, 1979, For Mike's Sake, 1979, Sentimental Journey, 1979, A Land Called Deseret, 1979, The Bride of the Delta Queen, 1979, Tidewater Lover, 1979, Lord of the High Lonesome, 1980, Kona Winds, 1980, The Boston Man, 1980, The Rogue, 1980, Bed of Grass, 1980, The Thawing of Mara, 1980, The Mating Season, 1980, Southern Nights, 1980, Ride the Thunder, 1980, Enemy in Camp, 1980, Difficult Decision, 1980, Heart of Stone, 1980, One of the Boys, 1980, Wild and Wonderful, 1981, A Tradition of Pride, 1981, The Traveling Kind, 1981, The Hostage Bride, 1981, Dakota Dreamin', 1981, For the Love of God, 1981, Night Way, 1981, This Calder Sky, 1981, Lancaster Men, 1981, Terms of Surrender, 1982, With a Little Luck, 1982, Wildcatter's Woman, 1982, Northern Magic, 1982, That Carolina Summer, 1982, This Calder Range, 1982, Foxfire Light, 1982, The Second Time, 1982, Mistletoe and Holly, 1982, Stands a Calder Man, 1983, Separate Cabins, 1983, Western Man, 1983, Calder Born, Calder Bred, 1983, Best Way to Lose, 1983, Leftover Love, 1984, Silver Wings, Santiago Blue, 1984, The Pride of Hannah Wade, 1985, The Glory Game, 1985, The Great Alone, 1986, Heiress, 1987, Rivals, 1989, Masquerade, 1990, Aspen Gold, 1991, Tangled Vines, 1992, Riding High, 1994, The Proud and The Free, 1994, Touch the Wind, 1994, Summer Mahogany, 1995. Recipient Golden Heart award Romance Writers Am., 1981, Romantic Times Contemporary award, 1983. *

DAILY, ANNA WILKINS, science educator; b. Louisburg, N.C., Feb. 15, 1943; d. Ernest and Susie Anna (Collins) Wilkins; m. Albert James Daily, Jr., May 21, 1965; children: Albert J. III, Dwayne G., Letecia A. BS Biology, St. Augustine's Coll., 1965; EdM Urban Edn., Rutgers U., 1972. Tchr. Tri-County Headstart, Louisburg, N.C., 1966; lab. technician Perth Amboy (N.J.) Gen. Hosp., 1966-70, Med. Lab., Metuchen, N.J., 1970-71; tchr. Plainfield (N.J.) Bd. Edn., 1971-72, Perth Amboy Bd. Edn., 1972—; urban tchr. intern AT&T, Murray Hill, N.J., 1989; adviser Health Occupation Students of Am., Perth Amboy, 1976-83, Health Career Awarness Club, 1990-93; mentor/adviser Celebration of Tchg., Perth Amboy, 1986—; mentor tchr. Perth Amboy Afro-Am. Club, 1994—; adj. instr. Jersey City State Coll., 1989-91. Women's Day chmn. 2d Bapt. Ch., Perth Amboy, 1984-86, pres. edn. com., 1973-90, sec. usher bd., 1968-90, pastor aide com., 1994—; bd. trustees Perth Amboy Pub. Libr., 1994—; mem. exec. bd., com. chair Perth Amboy area NAACP, 1976—. Recipient N.J. Disting. H.S. Tchr. award Princeton U., 1983, Perth Amboy Tchr. of Yr., 1982, Middlesex Tchr. of Yr., 1982, N.J. Gov.'s Tchr. award, 1995. Mem. Nat. Sci. Tchrs. Assn. (Nat. Exemplary H.S. Sci. Tchr. award 1984), N.J. Edn. Assn. (local pres. 1994—), N.J. Biology Tchrs. Assn. Home: 1096 Rudyard Dr Perth Amboy NJ 08861 Office: Perth Amboy Bd Edn 178 Barracks St Perth Amboy NJ 08861

DAILY, ELLEN WILMOTH MATTHEWS, technical publications specialist; b. Marfa, Tex., Aug. 13, 1949; d. Lynn Henry Sr. and Wilmoth Hamilton (Cox) Matthews; m. John Scott Daily Sr., Mar. 21, 1970; children: John Scott Jr., Kristen Michelle. BS in Physics, U. Tex., El Paso, 1971; postgrad., George Mason U., Fairfax, Va., 1980; continuing edn., North Lake Coll., Irving, Tex., 1996—. House dir., activity counselor Southwestern Children's Home, El Paso, Tex., 1965-68; analyst Schellenger Research Found. Labs, El Paso, 1968-70; computer operator, supr. keypunch El Paso Nat. Bank, 1970-73; supr., progam analyst El Paso Sand Products, 1973-74; tech. rep. Xerox Corp., Jackson, Miss., 1975-77; product tech. specialist Xerox Corp., Jackson, 1977-79; tech. trainer Xerox Corp., Leesburg, Va., 1979-82; sr. tech. writer, tng. analyst Xerox Corp., Lewisville, Tex., 1982-95; technical publs. specialist RFMonolithics, Inc., Dallas, 1995—; group rep. Xerox Corp., various cities, 1975-90; co-owner Triple "D" Enterprises, 1994—; owner Daily Delight Cattery, Chantilly, Va. and Carrollton, Tex., 1979-89; co-owner J & M Answering Svc., Dallas, 1983-84. Co-author: (electronic Bible verse) Verse of the Day, 1987-92. Team and divsn. mgr. Chantilly Youth Assn., 1980-82; bd. dirs., swim team dir. Brookfield Swim Club, Chantilly, 1980-82; vol. Metrocrest Svc. Ctr., Carrollton, 1986-89; elder Nor'Kirk Presbyn. Ch., Carrollton, 1989-91; founding mem. United We Stand Am., 1993—; vol. Catherine the Great, 1992. Mem. Internat. Platform Assn., U. Tex. El Paso Cannoneers Club (sec.-treas. 1967-71), Xerox Bowling League (pres. 1988-89), Sigma Pi Sigma, Kappa Delta (social svc. dir. 1969-70). Home: 3701 Grassmere Dr Carrollton TX 75007-2616 Office: RF Monolithics Inc 4347 Sigma Rd Dallas TX 75244

DAILY, FAY KENOYER, retired botany educator; b. Indpls., Feb. 17, 1911; d. Fredrick and Camellia Thea (Neal) Kenoyer; A.B., Butler U., 1935, M.S., 1952; m. William Allen Daily, June 24, 1937. Lab. technician Eli Lilly & Co., Indpls., 1935-37, Abbott Labs., North Chicago, Ill., 1939, William S. Merrell & Co., Ohio, 1940-41; lubrication chemist Indpls. Propellor div. Curtiss-Wright Corp., 1945; lectr. botany Butler U., Indpls., 1947-49, instr. immunology and microbiology, 1957-58, lectr. microbiology, 1962-63, mem. herbarium staff, 1949-87, curator cryptogamic herbarium, 1987-95. Grantee Ind. Acad. Sci., 1961-62. Mem. Am. Inst. Biol. Sci., Bot. Soc. Am., Phycol. Soc. Am., Internat. Phycol. Soc., Ind. Acad. Sci., Torrey Bot. Club, Sigma Xi, Phi Kappa Phi, Sigma Delta Epsilon. Republican. Methodist. Co-author book on sci. history. Contbr. articles on fossil and extant charophytes (algae) to profl. jours. Home: 5884 Compton St Indianapolis IN 46220-2653

DAILY, JEAN A., marketing executive; b. Bloomington, Ill., Nov. 20, 1949; d. William H. and Niola N. (Thompson) D.; m. Ronald R. Willis, June 14, 1968 (div. 1972); m. Rodger D. Melick, Aug. 15, 1981. BS, Ill. State U., 1975. Sr. acctg. clk. Country Cos., Bloomington, 1976-78; owner, mgr. Danvers (Ill.) Motor Co., 1979-85; office mgr., ops. mgr. Goods Carpet, Bloomington, 1986-87; dir. mktg. Westminster Village Inc., Bloomington, 1987—. Chair Com. to Elect Judge Prall, Bloomington, 1996; publ. chair Danvers Days, 1982-85; bd. dirs., publ. rels. & devel. advisor Twin Cities Ballet, Bloomington, 1994-96; bd. dirs. ARC, 1991-94; pres. Chestnut Health Sys. Aux., 1995-96; vol. Arthritis Telethon, St. Jude's Golf Tournament. Mem. Women in Comms. Office: Westminster Village 2025 E Lincoln Bloomington IL 61701

DAIRAGHI, JEANNE EILEEN, therapist; b. St. Louis, Dec. 1, 1969. BA in Psychology and Internat. Rels., U. Wis., 1991; MS in Rehab. Psychology, Purdue U., 1995. Rsch. asst. Purdue U., Indpls., 1992-94; therapist A Woman's Choice Clinic, Indpls., 1993-95. Contbg. author: (textbook) Key Words in Psychosocial Rehabilitation, 1994. Mem. NOW, Nat. Abortion Rights Action League. Democrat. Roman Catholic. Home: 10901 Edgecliffe Dr Saint Louis MO 63123

DAJANI, MONA, lawyer; b. Auburn, Ala., Mar. 4, 1966. BA, U. Ill., 1988; MBA, U. St. Thomas, 1992; JD, Loyola U., 1996. Bar: Ill. 1996; CPA, Ill. With Edward T. Joyce Assocs., Chgo., 1996—. Home: Ste 3704 777 N Michigan Chicago IL 60611

DAJANI, VIRGINIA, arts administrator; b. Chgo., Jan. 19, 1936; d. Philip Linden Boddy and Lillian (McArdle) O'Brien; m. Majed Dajani (div. 1968); children: Magda, Tarek, Najeeb, Nadia. Student, Loyola U., Chgo., 1953-55, Am. U., Cairo, 1961, Am. U., Beirut, 1963-67; postgrad., Harvard U., 1980-81. News editor Archtl. Forum mag., N.Y.C., 1968-72, Architecture Plus mag., N.Y.C., 1972-74; asst. George Nelson, Architect, N.Y.C., 1975-76; editor The Livable City, quar. of Mcpl. Art Soc., N.Y.C., 1976-89; dir. spl. projects Mcpl. Art Soc., N.Y.C., 1977-89; exec. dir. Am. Acad. Arts and Letters, N.Y.C., 1990—; dir. archtl. competition Mcpl. Art Soc., N.Y.C., 1985, 87; competition advisor Bronx Mus. Arts, N.Y.C., 1989, Mcpl. Art Soc., N.Y.C., 1991—; lectr. Harvard U. Grad. Sch. Design, 1980-87. Author: Juror's Guide to Lower Manhattan, 1984, rev. edits., 1985, 87, 90; contbr. articles to profl. archtl. jours. Recipient Citation for editing design mus. catalogue Am. Inst. Graphic Artists, 1975, award for editing The Livable City, AIA, 1982; Loeb fellow Harvard U., 1980-81. Mem. Century Assn. Office: Am Acad Arts and Letters 633 W 155th St New York NY 10032-7599*

DAKIN, CHRISTINE WHITNEY, dancer, educator; b. New Haven, Aug. 25, 1949; d. James Irving, Jr. and Jean Evelyn (Coulter) Crump; m. Robert Ford Dakin, June 21, 1969 (div. Sept. 1982); m. Stephen J. Mauer, Aug. 1, 1985. Student, U. Mich., 1967-71; D of Arts (hon.), Shenandoah U., 1996. Performer, teacher Ann Arbor Dance Theater, Mich., 1965-71; tchr. Ann Arbor Pub. Schs., 1967-70, Lincoln Ctr. Inst., N.Y.C., 1978, Guanajuato U., Mex., 1982; vis. artist USIA Vladivastock, Vladivastock, Russia, 1992; Art-sLink grantee, vis. artist Vladivastock, 1996; tchr. Ballet Nacional de Mex., 1993—; vis. artist Ballet Contemporaneo, Buenos Aires, 1993; prin. dancer Martha Graham Dance Co., N.Y.C., 1976—; dancer, rehearsal dir. Pearl Lang. Dance Co., 1974-76, Kazuko Hirabayashi Dance Co., 1974-76; faculty Martha Graham Sch., 1972—, Julliard Sch., 1992—, Alvin Alley Am. Dance Ctr., 1989—. Appeared in: It's Hard to Be a Jew, 1972, The Dybuk, 1975; appeared (with Martha Graham Dance Co.) Covent Garden, London, 1976, Met. Opera, 1980, Sta. WNET Dance in Am. Series, 1979; Young Artist in Performance at The White House, Sta. WNET, 1982, (with Rudolph Nureyev) Paris Opera, Berlin Opera, 1984, N.Y. State Theater, 1985; NHK Film, Japan, 1990, Paris Opera Film, 1991, (documentary film) Les Printemps du Sacre, 1993; assoc. founder Buglisi/Foreman Dance. Scholar Am. Dance Festival, 1969; recipient award Dance Mag., 1994. Mem. Am. Guild Mus. Artists (life, bd. govs.). Office: Martha Graham Dance Co 316 E 63rd St New York NY 10021-7702

DAKOFSKY, LADONNA JUNG, radiation oncologist, educator; b. N.Y.C., Oct. 30, 1960; d. George S. and Kay (Han) Chung. BA magna cum laude, Columbia U., N.Y.C., 1982; MD, NYU, 1987. Bd. cert. radiation oncologist. Rsch. asst. dept. neurology UCLA, 1980-81, Harvard U., Boston, 1982; tchr. chemistry St. Ann's Sch., Brooklyn Heights, N.Y., 1982-83; resident in internal medicine Lenox Hill Hosp., N.Y.C., 1987-88; resident in radiation oncology Hosp. of U. Pa., Phila., 1988-91; instr. in radiation oncology New Eng. Med. Ctr., Boston, 1991-92; attending physician Norwalk (Conn.) Hosp., 1992—; clin. asst. prof. radiation oncology Yale U., 1994—; prin. investigator RTOG cancer rsch. Norwalk Hosp. Mem. jr. com. Boys Club N.Y.; sponsor Mus. City of N.Y.; mem. com. Vocat. Found., N.Y.c.; mem. Jr. League of Stamford-Norwalk. Marine Biol. Lab. scholar, 1981. Mem. AMA, Assn. Therapeutic Radiology and Oncology, Fairfield County Med. Assn., New Eng. Cancer Soc., Met. Breast Cancer Group. Presbyterian. Office: Norwalk Hosp Radiation Oncology Box 5050 Norwalk CT 06856

DALAL, MEENAKSHI NATH, economics educator, researcher; b. Calcutta, West Bengal, India, Mar. 3, 1950; Came to the U.S., 1972; d. Hemtosh Kumar and Jammuna Nath; m. Pabitra Kumar Dalal, Jan. 25, 1972 (div. Mar. 1989); children: Piyali, Pritam; m. Ram Prasad Bhattacharya, Jan. 18, 1996. BCom. with honors, Calcutta U., India, 1970; MA in Econs., Northeastern U., Boston, 1974, PhD in Econs., 1984. Instr. econs. Northeastern U., Boston, 1979-84, asst. prof. econs., 1994-95; co-dir. Ctr. for Econ. Edn. Wayne (Nebr.) State Coll., 1985—, asst. prof., 1985-87, assoc. prof. econs., 1988-96, prof. econs., 1996; vis. scholar Inst. East Asian Studies, U. Calif., Berkeley; v.p. Soc. Internat. Devel., Nebr., 1993, 94. Contbr. articles to profl. jours. Pres. Wayne Elem. Parent Tchr. Group, 1986-87; mem. steering com. START, 1990, 93; organizer and initiator Chautauqua Com., 1991-92; chair Multicultural Edn. Adv. Com., 1994. Recipient Workshop grantee Joint Coun. Econ. Edn., N.Y., 1988, Project grantee Nebr. Humanities Coun., 1990. Mem. AAUW (pres. Wayne branch 1992-94, v.p. membership Nebr., 1994, diversity resource team 1995—, Rsch. grantee 1987-88, 94-95. Hindu. Office: Wayne State Coll Wayne NE 68787

DALE, BRENDA STEPHENS, educator; b. Hickory, N.C., Sept. 24, 1942; d. John Doyle and Bertha (Barger) Stephens; m. James Darrell Dale, June 13, 1964; children: Ginger Leigh Rizoti, Jami Lynne. BS in English, Appalachian State U., 1964, MA in Reading Edn., 1977; cert. edn. academically gifted, Lenoir Rhyne, Hickory, N.C., 1982. High. sch. tchr. Moore County Schs., Carthage, N.C., 1964; high sch. tchr. Asheboro (N.C.) City Schs., 1964-65, 8th grade tchr. Davidson County Schs., Thomasville, N.C., 1967-68; reading specialist Randolph County Schs., Trinity, N.C., 1970-72; reading specialist Wilkes N.C. Schs., Wilkesboro, 1972-82, tchr. acad. gifted, 1982—; part-time tchr. Davidson County Community Coll., Lexington, N.C., 1965-68, Wilkes Community Coll., Wilkesboro, 1982-87, adult literary tutor. Edn. chmn., bd. dirs. Am. Cancer Soc., North Wilkesboro, N.C., 1985-90; mem. Wilkes Regional Med. Ctr. Aux., 1992—, YMCA. Tchr. scholar fellow N.C. Ctr. for Advancement of Teaching, Western Carolina U., 1990; recipient C. B. Eller Teaching award C.B. Eller Found., 1991. Mem. AAUW (charter, fundraiser 1977-78, bd. dirs., chmn. edn. found. 1992-96), NEA, N.C. Assn. Educators, Internat. Reading Assn. (sec. 1985-86), Internat. Platform Assn., Mary Hemphill Svc. Group, So. Appalachian Leadership on Cancer, Lynnwoode Recreation Club, United Meth. Women (dist. membership chair Western N.C. conf. 1996-97) Alpha Delta Kappa. Methodist. Home: 187 Laurel Mountain Rd North Wilkesboro NC 28659-8122 Office: Wilkes County Schs Main St Wilkesboro NC 28697

DALE, CYNTHIA LYNN ARPKE, educational administrator; b. Plymouth, Wis., Jan. 11, 1942; sd. BS, Wis. State U., Oshkosh, 1964; M degree, U. Ctrl. Fla. Cert. tchr., Wis., Fla. Tchr. Omro (Wis.) Sch. Sys., 1964-68, West Allis (Wis.) Sch. Sys., 1973-77; substitute tchr. Brevard County Sch. Sys., Melbourne, Fla., 1981-88; early edn. tchr. various schs. Melbourne, Fla., 1988-92; supr. site coord. for S. Brevard County Sch. Sys. Child Care Assn., Melbourne, Fla. Contbg. author: (poetry) A Far Out Place, 1994 (merit award), Forgetfulness, 1995 (merit award), Ickey Poo, A Special Birthday and Beth, 1996. Mem. PTA various schs. sys.; mem. choir, Christian edn. com., Sunday sch. tchr. Palmdale Presbyn. Ch., Melbourne; cub scout den mother Boy Scouts Am., Melbourne; soccer mother, coach, asst. Little League, Melbourne, swimming instr.; mem. homeowner's assn. Groveland Mobile Home Park, Melbourne. Mem. AARP, ASCD, Audubon Soc., Internat. Soc. Poets. Republican. Home: 4651 W Eau Gallie Blvd # 98 Melbourne FL 32934

DALE, EMILY DUNN, retired sociology and anthroplogy educator, poet; b. Normal, Ill., Oct. 19, 1924; d. Richard Francis and Clara Phoebe (Huxtable) Dunn; m. John R. Scott, Aug. 22, 1947 (div.); children: John, Elizabeth, Robert, Mary. Student, Swarthmore U., 1942-43; BA, BS, Western Reserve, 1946; MA, Ill. State Normal U.; postgrad., U. Ill., 1947-48, 61-62; PhD, Union Grad. Sch., 1963; postgrad., U. Minn., 1979-80. From. asst. prof. to prof. sociology Ill. Wesleyan U., Bloomington, 1958-90; vis. prof. London Sch. Econ., 1969; founder Ill. Sociology Assn., 1965, pres., 1975; Ill. rep. Midwest Sociology Assn., 1980. Co-author: The State of Marriage, 1985, Women as a Minotiry Focus on Family, 1986; contbr. poems to jours. Founder Countering Domestic Violence, McLean County, 1975, Bloomington-Normal Human Rels. Coun., McClean County, 1955, Religious Soc. Friends, 1955; bd. dirs. Planned Parenthood, McLean County, 1975-84. Recipient Martin Luther King Human Rels. award, 1990, citation Ill. House & Senate, 1990-91; named Woman of Distinction YWCA, 1989; grantee NSF, 1960, Lilly Found., 1980. Mem. PEO. Mem. Soc. of Friends. Home: 1 Brookshire Green Bloomington IL 61704

DALE, JUDY RIES, religious organization administrator; b. Memphis, Dec. 13, 1944; d. James Lorigan and Julia Marie (Schwinn) Ries; m. Eddie Melvin Ashmore, July 12, 1969 (div. Dec. 1983). BA, Rhodes Coll., 1966; M in Religious Edn., So. Bapt. Theol. Sem., 1969, Grad. Specialist in Religious Edn., 1969. Cert. tchr. educable mentally handicapped, secondary English, adminstrn. and supervision in spl. edn. EMH tchr., curriculum writer, tchr. trainer Jefferson County Bd. Edn., Louisville, 1969-88, ednl. cons., 1988-90; dist. coord. Gt. Lakes dist. Universal Fellowship Met. Community Chs., Louisville, 1990—; lectr. Jefferson C.C., Louisville, 1987-93, U. Louisville, 1976-77, 87-90; mem. faculty Samaritan Inst. for Religious Studies, 1992—; mem. program adv. com. Internat. Conf. Spl. Edn., Beijing, 1987-88. Editor, writer: (handbook) Handbook for Beginning Teachers, 1989, A Manual of Instructional Strategies, 1985; author: (kit) Math Activities Cards, 1978. Bd. sec. Com. of Ten, Inc., Louisville, 1987-91; active Greater Louisville Human Rights Commn., 1985-90, Ky. Civil Liberties Union, 1986—; v.p. GLUE, 1988-92, pres., 1992-94; mem. Universal Fellowship of Met. Cmty. Chs., programs and budget divsn., mem. gen. coun., 1990—, active Women's Secretariat steering com., 1991-95; mem. membership com. Cmty. Health Trust, 1991-94; trustee Samaritan Inst. Religious Studies, 1992—, chair acad. affairs com., 1996—. Recipient Honorable Order of Ky. Cols., 1976; named Outstanding Elem. Tchr. Am., 1975. Mem. AAUW, NOW, Coun. Exceptional Children (keynote speaker 1984-88, internat. pres. 1986-87, exec. com. 1984-88, bd. govs. 1981-88), Ky. Coun. Exceptional Children (bd. dirs. 1976-90, Mem. of Yr. 1987), Internat. Platform Assn., Women's Alliance, Phi Delta Kappa. Democrat. Home and Office: 1300 Ambridge Dr Louisville KY 40207-2410

D'ALENE, ALIXANDRIA FRANCES, human resources professional; b. Buffalo, Oct. 21, 1951; d. Fern (Hill) D'A.; BA, Canisius Coll., Buffalo, 1973, MS, 1975, MBA, 1980. Tchr., Buffalo pub. schs., 1973-76; pers. cons. Sanford Rose Assos., Williamsville, N.Y., 1976-78; mgr. benefits adminstrn. Svc. Sys. Corp., Clarence, N.Y., 1978-80; mgr. employee rels. Del Monte Corp., Walnut Creek, Calif., 1980-82; human resource mgmt. cons. H.R.S., Inc., Winston-Salem, N.C., 1982-87; corp. pers. specialist Advance Stores Co., Inc., Roanoke, Va., 1987-88; pers. dir. Alfred (N.Y.) U., 1988-94; dir. human resources Framtone Connectors USA, Inc., Norwalk, Conn., 1994—; adj. prof. bus., 1988-90; human resources mgr. Lord Corp., Shelton, Conn., 1990—. Mem. Assn. Pers. Adminstrs., Indsl. Pers. Soc., Coll. and U. Pers. Assn., Phi Alpha Theta. Episcopalian.

DALE RIIKONEN, CHARLENE BOOTHE, international health administrator; b. Washington, June 10, 1942; d. John Edward and Frances Elizabeth (Jett) Boothe; m. Esko Riikonen, 1989; children: Cynthia Lee, Anthony John, Jennifer Elizabeth. AA with high honors, Howard Community Coll., 1977; BA magna cum laude, U. Md., 1979. Asst. dir. univ. rels., alumni dir. U. Md., Catonsville, 1977-81; assoc. dir. univ. rels. and devel. U. Md., College Park, 1982-83; sr. devel. officer Internat. Ctr. Diarrhoeal Disease Rsch., Dhaka, Bangladesh, 1984-86; exec. v.p. Child Health Found. (formerly Internat. Child Health Found.), Columbia, Md., 1985—; cons. to organize symposium oral rehydration therapy Nat. Coun. Internat. Health, Washington, 1987; organizer internat. symposium on food-based oral rehydration therapy Aga Khan U., Pakistan, 1989; organizer consensus conf. cereal-based oral rehydration therapy, Columbia, Md., 1993. Author: (tng. manual) Prevention and Treatment of Childhood Diarrhea with Oral Rehydration Therapy, Nutrition and Breastfeeding, 1992; editor procs. Oral Rehydration Therapy Symposia, 1987, 89, 93, 94; editor Child Health News, 1993—; contbr. articles to profl. jours. Pub. affairs chmn. United Way, Washington Capital Area, Prince Georges County, 1981-83; v.p. Waterfowl Assn.; pres. Windstream Assn., 1988-89; v.p. Waterfowl Terrace Assn., 1994—; mem. pub. rels. com. Md., Del. Cable TV Assn., Balt., 1981-83. Mem. APHA (internat. maternal-child health com.), AAUW, Nat. Coun. Internat. Health Assn., U. Md. Balt. County Alumni Assn. (bd. dirs. 1979-83), Women's Internat. Pub. Health Network. Democrat. Club: Columbia Assn. Athletic (Md.) (capt. women's traveling racquetball team 1979-83).

D'ALESSIO, JACQUELINE ANN, middle school English language educator; b. Morristown, N.J., Jan. 26, 1943; d. Clifford Corbet and Helen Ann (Chrenko) Compton; m. Harold F. D'Alessio, Oct. 28, 1967. BA English, Coll. New Rochelle, 1964; MA English, Seton Hall U., 1969. Tchr. Bridgewater (N.J.)-Raritan Regional Sch. Dist., 1964—; advisor dramatics Bridgewater-Raritan Mid. Sch., Bridgewater, N.J., 1983—. Chmn. pub. rels. Mt. St. Mary Devel. Office, 1985—; bd. dirs. N.J. Legis Agenda for Women, Inc., 1993-94. Named Outstanding Elem. Tchr. U.S., 1971; Recipient Gov. Tchr. Recognition, N.J. Dept. Edn., Trenton, 1989. Mem. AAUW (N.J. pres. 1990-94, program v.p. 1988-90, rep. Women's Agenda 1989-94). Roman Catholic. Home: 30 Putnam St Somerville NJ 08876-2737

D'ALESSIO, NATALIE MARINO, artist; b. Elizabeth, N.J., July 4, 1951; d. John T. and Stefana (Sarullo) Marino; m. Anthony Paul D'Alessio, Aug. 28, 1968; 1 child, Stephanie Elsbeth. BA, NYU, 1969; postgrad., New Sch., N.Y.C., 1969-72; cert., N.J. Ctr. Visual Arts, 1977. One-woman shows include Exxon Corp., Linden, N.J., 1985, Florence Gallery, Dallas, 1985, Rosalyn Sailors, Phila., 1993, ART Insights, N.Y., Marino Galleries, Millburn, N.J., 1994, 96; exhibited in group shows at N.J. State Mus., 1979, Bergen Cmty. Mus., Paramus, N.J., 1980, Nat. Art Club, N.Y.C., 1981, Lincoln Ctr., N.Y.C., 1983, Cork Art Gallery, N.Y.C., 1983, Phila. Port of History Mus., 1984, numerous others; represented in permanent collections, including Rosalyn Sailor Gallery and Mus. Fine Art, Margate, N.J., Phila., Tom Weiner's Art Insights, N.Y.C., Marino Galleries, Inc., Millburn; contbr. illustrations to books; author: (screenplay) The Successor, 1989; illustrator: Art Lovers Cookbook, 1975; host cablecast series Art Forum; prodr., dir. video and TV programs. Vol. cons. N.J. Ctr. for Visual Arts, Summit, 1989; trustee TV 36, Communities on Cable, Summit, 1989; judge for sr. citizen art shows, Newark, 1989. Recipient Bee Co. award Pastel Soc. Am., 1981, European Banner of Arts, Accademia d'Europa, 1984, award-artists grant Union County Divsn. of Art and Cultural Affairs; N.J. state Coun. for Arts grantee Union County Cultural Commn., 1985-86, Ludwig Vogelstein Found. grantee, 1989. Fellow Artists Equity, Women's Caucus for Art, Riker Hill Art Park (exec. com.); mem. N.J. Ctr. Visual Art (award 1979). Home: PO Box 225 Springfield NJ 07081-0225

DALEY, BRIDGET, museum administrator; b. Princeton, N.J., Apr. 5, 1968; d. Robert Francis and Sharon Theresa (Howard) D. BA in Art History, Rutgers U., 1990. Mng. editor internat. divsn. Art Now Gallery Guide, Clinton, N.J., 1991-94; asst. dir. devel. The Morris Mus., Morristown, N.J., 1994—. Vol. Playwrights Theater N.J., Madison, 1994-95; founding mem. Michael Nunes Scholarship award 1996. Mem. Rutgers Alumni Assn., Golden Key Nat. Honor Soc. Office: The Morris Mus 6 Normandy Hgts Rd Morristown NJ 07960

DALEY, PAMELA, lawyer; b. Springfield, Mass., Oct. 1, 1952; d. Edward Murray and Elizabeth Bloom Daley; m. Randall Lee Phelps, Aug. 26, 1995. AB summa cum laude in Romance Langs. and Lit., Princeton U., 1974; JD magna cum laude, U. Pa., 1979. Bar: Pa. 1979, N.Y. 1991. Lectr. partnership taxation law U. Pa., Phila., 1982-89; assoc. tax sect. Morgan, Lewis & Bockius, Phila., 1979-86, ptnr., 1986-89; tax counsel GE, Fairfield, Conn., 1989-91, v.p., sr. counsel for transactions, 1991—; bd. outside advisor Va. Tax Review assn., 1982-92. Editor-in-chief U. Pa. Law Review; contbr.

articles to profl. jours. Trustee MacDuffie Sch., Springfield, 1986-92; bd. govs. Pa. Economy League, 1986-89. Teaching fellow Salzberg Seminar on Am. Law and Legal Instns., 1986; named to Acad. Women Achievers YWCA, 1992. Mem. Am. Corp. Counsel Assn., Order Coif, Phi Beta Kappa. Office: GE 3135 Easton Tpke W3A Fairfield CT 06431-0002

DALEY, ROSIE, cook, writer; b. South Seaville, N.J.; d. Fred and Joan Daley; 1 child, Marley. Chef's helper Cal-a-Vie, Vista, Calif., 1989-90, head cook, 1990-91; personal cook to Oprah Winfrey Chgo., 1991—. Author: (with Oprah Winfrey) In the Kitchen with Rosie: Oprah's Favorite Recipes, 1994. Office: care Harpo Prodns 110 N Carpenter St Chicago IL 60607-2101*

DALEY, SANDRA, retired artist, filmmaker, photographer; b. Fargo, N.D., Feb. 28, 1940; d. Cecil Raymond and Margaret (Anderson) D. AB cum laude, Oberlin Coll., 1961; MFA with high distinction, Calif. Coll. Arts and Crafts, 1965. Artist, photographer show (with Nicholas Quennell) Dwan Gallery, L.A., 1965; prodr., dir. film: (with Robert Mapplethorpe and Patti Smith) Robert Having His Nipple Pierced, 1970, (with Patti Smith, Sam Shepard and Vali) Patti Having Her Knee Tattooed, 1971. Home: 504 Marlborough Rd Brooklyn NY 11226

DALEY, VETA ADASSA, educational administrator; b. St. Elizabeth, Jamaica, Jan. 14, 1953; came to U.S., 1981; d. Waldemar and Princess (Bartley) Solomon; m. Vincent Daley, Jan. 27, 1973; children: Yuland, Angelo. Cert. in edn., U. W.I., Jamaica, 1978; BS, Westfield (Mass.) State Coll., 1987, MEd in Adminstrn., 1991. Tchr. Ministry Edn., Jamaica, 1972-81, Forest Park Jr.-Mid. Sch., Springfield, Mass., 1987-92; grad. asst. Westfield State Coll., 1988-90; asst. prin. Duggan Mid. Sch., Springfield, 1992-94; prin. John F. Kennedy Mid. Sch., Springfield, 1994—; Mem. Mass. Curriculum Adv. Commn., Malden, 1992—. Advisor Jamaica Festival Commn., Mandeville, 1973-80, Jamaica 4-H Clubs, 1970-76; vice chmn. adminstrv. bd. Wesley United Meth. Ch., Springfield, 1988—, pres. Meth. Women, 1991-93; chmn. Liberian Christian Fund, Springfield, 1990, New Eng. Conf. United Meth. Women, 1994; mem. African Task Force-R.I., 1991—. Recipient Outstanding Achievement award Jamaica 4-H Clubs, 1975, Outstanding Achievement in Edn. award Jamaican Cmty., Springfield, 1992, citation Mass. Ho. of Reps., 1992. Mem. New Eng. League Mid. Schs., Springfield Adminstrv. Assn., Jack and Jill Am. (pres. Springfield chpt. 1992—, Disting. Mother of Yr. award ea. region 1994). Home: 81 Embury St Springfield MA 01109-1847 Office: John F Kennedy Mid Sch 1385 Berkshire Ave Indian Orchard MA 01151-1360

DALIA, VESTA MAYO, artist; b. Atlanta, Aug. 14, 1932; d. Frank and Winnifred (Layton) Mayo; m. William Barber Macke, May 30, 1952 (div. 1971); children: William Barber Jr., Michael Mayo, Vesta Melissa, Mary Sue Macke Mullen; m. Joseph William Dalia, Aug. 31, 1973 (dec. 1990); stepchildren: Joseph W. Jr., Jeffrey Meade, Denise Marie Dalia Cooper, Nancy Dalia Cook. Student, U. Ga. Part owner Mayo Chem. Cos., other chem. cos., Smyrna and Dalton, Ga., chem. cos., Chattanooga; tchr. art Cen. Piedmont Coll., Charlotte, N.C. Exhibited art in shows in Charlotte and Atlanta. Mem. Nat. Tole and Decorative Painters (past pres. Dogwood chpt., recipient Golden Palet award 1990), Metropolitan Atlanta Better Films (v.p.), Weinman Mineral Mus., Salvation Army Womens Aux., Rabun Gap-Nacoochee Guild, Inc., Voters Guild of Met. Atlanta, Inc., Brookfield West Women's Club, Brookfield West Garden Club, West Fulton Owls Club, Frog Club, Zoo Atlanta, Friendship Force, Native Atlantans Club. Republican. Methodist. Home: 11635 Mountain Laurel Dr Roswell GA 30075-1393

DALIMONTE, JOSEPHINE ANN (JO-ANN DALIMONTE), school nurse practitioner; b. Boston, June 4, 1941; d. John and Jennie (Gangarossa) Frisoni; m. Anthony Dalimonte, Oct. 19, 1963; children: John Anthony, Denise Marie Schepper, Mark Andrew, Susan Ellen. RN, St. Elizabeth's Hosp., Brighton, Mass., 1962; lic. sch. nurse practitioner, pediatric nurse practitioner, U. Colo., 1985. Staff nurse Malden (Mass.) Hosp., 1962-63; pvt. duty nurse Ctrl. Registry, Boston, 1966-81; counselor Weight Loss Med. Ctr., Reading, 1979; nurse Student Health Svcs. Boston U., 1979-85; camp nurse Camp Rotary YMCA, Boxford, Mass., 1983; nurse practitioner Perkins Sch. for the Blind, Watertown, Mass., 1985-86, Fernald State Sch., Waltham, Mass., 1987-92; nurse practitioner Dept. Youth Svcs. Health Care of S.E. Mass., Abington, 1993-94; sch. nurse practitioner Somerville (Mass.) H.S., 1994—; health educator St. Patrick's Sch., Stoneham, Mass., 1985-86; ct. advocate in child custody cases, 1992; vis. resource Westboro State Hosp., 1992—. Contbr. articles to profl. jours. Mem. PTA Stoneham Sch. Sys., 1970-86; active Stoneham Red Cross, 1975-88; foster parent DSS, 1990-96; vol. food pantry, Malden, 1993, liturg. min. St. Patrick's Ch., Stoneham, 1993—; active Colonial Chorus, Reading, Mass., Reading Cmty. Singers, 1995-96; participant Bible study Blessed Sacramento Ch., Wakefield, Mass., 1993-96. Mem. North Shore Nurse Practitioner Assn., Mass. Sch. Nurse Assn., Stoneham Garden Club (v.p. 1992-94). Roman Catholic. Home: 21 Walsh Ave Stoneham MA 02180-1509 also: 19 Pinecrest Rd Raymond NH 03077

DALIS, IRENE, mezzo-soprano, opera company administrator, music educator; b. San Jose, Calif., Oct. 8, 1925; d. Peter Nicholas and Mamie Rose (Boitano) D.; m. George Loinaz, July 16, 1957; 1 child, Alida Mercedes. AB, San Jose State Coll., 1946; MA in Teaching, Columbia U., 1947; MMus (hon.), MS (hon.), San Jose State Coll., 1957; studied voice with, Edyth Walker, N.Y.C., 1947-50, Paul Althouse, 1950-51, Dr. Otto Mueller, Milan, Italy, 1952-72; MusD (hon.), Santa Clara U., 1987. Prin. artist Berlin Opera, 1955-65, Met. Opera, N.Y.C., 1957-77, San Francisco Opera, 1958-73, Hamburg (Fed. Republic Germany) Staatsoper, 1966-71; prof. music San Jose State U., Calif., 1977—; founder, gen. dir. Opera San Jose, 1984—; dir. Met. Opera Nat. Auditions, San Jose dist., 1980-88. Operatic debut as dramatic mezzo-soprano Oldenburgisches Staatstheater, 1953, Berlin Staedtische Opera, 1955; debut Met. Opera, N.Y.C., 1957, 1st Am.-born singer, Kundry Bayreuth Festival, 1961, opened, Bayreuth Festival, Parsifal, 1963; commemorative Wagner 150th Birth Anniversary; opened 1963 Met. Opera Season in Aida; premiered: Dello Joio's Blood Moon, 1961, Henderson's Medea, 1972; rec. artist Parsifal, 1964 (Grand Prix du Disque award); contbg. editor Opera Quarterly, 1983. Recipient Fulbright award for study in Italy, 1951, Woman of Achievement award Commn. on Status of Women, 1983, Pres.'s award Nat. Italian Am. Found., 1985, award of merit People of San Francisco, 1985, San Jose Renaissance award for sustained and outstanding artistic contbn., 1987, Medal of Achievement Acad. Vocal Arts, 1988; named Honored Citizen City of San Jose, 1986; inducted into Calif. Pub. Edn. Hall of Fame, 1985, others. Mem. Beethoven Soc. (mem. adv. bd. 1985—), San Jose Arts Round Table, San Jose Opera Guild, Am. Soc. Univ. Women, Arts Edn. Week Consortium, Phi Kappa Phi, Mu Phi Epsilon. Office: Opera San Jose 12 S 1st Ste 207 San Jose CA 95131

DALITZKY, MARTHA OKUN, interior designer; b. Springfield, Mass., Aug. 6, 1932; d. Morris and Esther (Chase) Okun; m. Milton Dalitzky, July 4, 1955; children: Scott David, Nancy Beth. BS, U. Mass., 1954. Pres. Studio East, East Longmeadow, Mass., 1963—; chmn. DataPix Pub. Inc., Raleigh, N.C., 1989-90. Designer Solo Showhouse, Am. Cancer Soc., Longmeadow, Mass., 1983; designs shown in various mags. Recipient 1st Prize for Residential Kitchen, DuPont Corian, 1989. Mem. Am. Soc. Interior Designers. Office: Studio East 15 Benton Dr East Longmeadow MA 01028-3153

DALLAS, NOELLE MARIE, financial analyst; b. Louisville, Sept. 24, 1959; d. Glenn Hoyle and Micheline Alice (Boudrias) Madison; m. Stephen Stavros Dallas Jr., Nov. 4, 1989; children: Dominique Marie, Stephen Stavros III. Student, Benjamin Franklin U., 1978-80; BS in Biology, George Mason U., 1984, postgrad, 1988; postgrad, Montgomery Coll., 1986-88. Mgr. Holly Enterprises, Alexandria, Va., 1975-81; gov. rels. intern TRW, Rosslyn, Va., 1984-85; med. asst. Cardiology and Internal Medicine, P.A., Chevy Chase, Md., 1985-86; sr. cons. Ernst & Young, Washington, 1986-90; sr. fin. analyst Community Energy Alternatives, Ridgewood, N.J., 1990-92; pvt. practice Downington, Pa., 1993—. Roman Catholic. Home and Office: 511 Buttonwood Dr Downingtown PA 19335-4121

DALLI, INALBYS R., accountant; b. Salma Spriano, Cuba, Jan. 27, 1946; d. Jose Roben and Aurelia (Natarro) Toro; m. Joseph Dalli, June 15, 1969, children: Jason, Erik. BS in Acctg., Hunter Coll., 1970. CPA, N.Y. Cost acct. H. Kohnstamm & Co., N.Y.C., 1970—; audit supr. Lucas, Tucker & Co., N.Y.C.; controller Consolidated Biscuit Co., Malta, Europe; internal auditor Ericcson, Inc., Greenwich, Conn., 1984-85; controller Fedn. Handicapped, N.Y.C., 1985—, City Vol. Corps., N.Y.C.; acct. pvt. practice, White Plains, N.Y., 1987—; controller Salesian Missions, New Rochelle, N.Y., 1995—. Home: 23 Old Mamaroneck Rd Apt 2L White Plains NY 10605-2015

DALPINO, IDA JANE, secondary education educator; b. Newhall, Calif., Oct. 20, 1936; d. Bernhardt Arthur and Wahneta May (Blyler) Melby; m. Gilbert Augustus, June 14, 1963 (div. 1976); 1 child, Nicolette Jane. BA, Calif. State U., Chico, 1960; postgrad., Sacramento State, 1961-65, Sonoma State, 1970-71; MA, U. San Francisco, 1978. Cert. community counselor, learning handicapped, community coll. instr., exceptional children, pupil pers. specialist, secondary tchr., resource specialist. Tchr. Chico High Sch., 1959-60; counselor Mira Loma High Sch., Sacramento, 1960-66; tchr. ESL Phoenix Ind. High Sch., 1968-69; resource specialist Yuba City (Calif.) High Sch., 1971—; English tchr. Rough Rock Demonstration Sch., summers, 1975, 76. Office sec. Job's Daus., North Bend, Oreg., 1953—; active Environ. Def. Fund, Centerville Hist. Assn., Chico, 1991—. Mem. NEA, Calif. Tchrs. Assn., Calif. State Alumni Assn., Sigma Kappa Alumni. Democrat. Mem. Science of the Mind Church. Home: 4676 Cable Bridge Dr Chico CA 95928-8840 Office: Yuba City Unified Sch Dist 850 B St Yuba City CA 95991-4926

DALRYMPLE, MARGARET FISHER, university press editor, writer; b. Calgary, Alta., Can.; d. Anton and Marie (Rusnak) Fisher. PhD, U. Wash., 1972. Instr. history La. State U., Baton Rouge, 1970-72; copy editor La. State U. Press, 1978-82, sr. editor, 1982-89, editor in chief, 1989-94, asst. dir., 1994-95; editor in chief U. Nev. Press, Reno, 1995—; lectr. history U. Paris I, 1972-73; translator, rschr., editor, Baton Rouge, 1975-89. Author essays; editor: The Merchant of Manchac: The Letterbooks of John Fitzpatrick, 1978. Office: U Nev Press Reno NV 89557-0076

DAL SANTO, DIANE, judge; b. East Chicago, Ind., Sept. 20, 1949; d. John Quentin Dal Santo and Helen (Koval) D.; m. Fred O'Cheskey, June 29, 1985. BA, U. N. Mex., 1971; cert. Inst. Internat. and Comparative Law, Guadalajara, Mex., 1978; JD, U. San Diego, 1980. Bar: N.Mex. 1980, U.S. Dist. Ct. N.Mex. 1980. Ct. planner Met. Criminal Justice Coordinating Coun., Albuquerque, 1973-75; planning coord. Dist. Atty.'s Office, Albuquerque, 1975-76, exec. asst. to dist. atty., 1976-77, asst dist. atty. for violent crimes, 1980-82; chief dep. city atty. City of Albuquerque, 1983; assoc. firm T.B. Keleher & Assocs., 1983-84; judge Met. Ct., 1985-89, chief judge, 1988-89; judge Dist. Ct., 1989—; mem. faculty Nat. Jud. Coll., 1990-95, bd. trustees, 1995-96. Bd. dirs. Nat. Coun. Alcoholism, 1984, S.W. Ballet Co., Albuquerque, 1982-83; mem. Mayor's Task Force on Alcoholism and Crime, 1987-88, N.Mex. Coun. Crime and Delinquency, 1987—, bd. dirs., 1992-94, Task Force Domestic Violence, 1987-94; pres. bench, bar, media com., 1987—, pres., 1992, rules of evidence com. Supreme Ct., 1993—. U. San Diego scholar, 1978-79; recipient Women on the Move award YWCA, 1989, Disting. Woman award U. N.Mex. Alumni Assn., 1994, Outstanding Alumnus Dept. Sociology U. N.Mex., 1995; named Woman of Yr. award Duke City Bus. and Profl. Women, 1985. Mem. ABA (Nat. Conf. State Trial Judges Jud. Excellence award 1996), LWV, AAUW, Am. Judicature Soc., N.Mex. Women's Found., N.Mex. Bar Assn., N.Mex. Women's Bar Assn. (bd. dirs. 1991-92), Albuquerque Bar Assn., Nat. Assn. Women Judges, Greater Albuquerque C. of C. (steering com. 1989), N.Mex. Magistrate Judges Assn. (v.p. 1985-89), Dist. Judges Assn. (pres. 1994-95). Democrat. Office: Dist Ct 415 Tijeras Ave NW Albuquerque NM 87102-3233

DAL SANTO, HELEN, artist; b. Miners Mill, Pa., Apr. 19, 1923; d. Adam and Dorothea (Litavic) Koval; m. John Quentin Dal Santo, June 5, 1948; children: Diane, Marlene, John Q. Jr., Paula. Diploma, St. Mary's Mercy Hosp, 1944. Docent Albuquerque Mus. Art History, 1991—. Lt. (j.g.) USN, 1945-51. Mem. Nat. League Am. Pen Women (corr. sec. 1989-92, stae treas. 1990-93), N.Mex. Watercolor Soc., Patsel Soc. N.Mex. (charter).

DALTCHEV, ANA RANGUEL, sculptor; b. Sofia, Bulgaria, Jan. 25, 1926; came to U.S., 1979; d. Ranguel and Struma Popov; m. Lubomir Daltchev, Jan. 23, 1949; 1 child, Lubomir. MA, Higher Inst. Visual Arts, Sofia, Bulgaria, 1952. Registered sculptor Europe, 1953-79; free-lance sculptor U.S.A., 1979—. Exhibited in group shows in U.S., Germany, Bulgaria, France, Yugoslavia, India, Greece, Rumania; prin. works include Motherhood, Fount, Weaver, Joy, Sophia, Youth, California Women, Dance; participation with sculptures in XIV World Biennial of Sculpture, Milan, European Biennial of Small Sculpture, Budapest, Hungary; rresented in pvt. collections. Mem. San Francisco Mus. Modern Arts, Women in Arts. East Orthodox. Office: PO Box 70054 Sunnyvale CA 94086

DALTON, CARYL, school psychologist; b. Mineral Wells, Tex., Aug. 8, 1949; d. Pat Francis Dalton and Yvonne (Ridings) Erwin. BA, U. Tex., 1970, MEd, 1977, PhD, 1987. Tchr. Brown Schs., Austin, San Marcos, Tex., 1971-73; homebound tchr. Rochester (N.Y.) City Schs., 1974-75; asst. dir. Big Buddies, Austin, Tex., 1975-77; ednl. cons. Edn. Svc. Ctr. XIII, Austin, Tex., 1978-79, pvt. practice, Austin, Tex., 1979-84; asst. instr. U. Tex., Austin, Tex., 1983-86; from doctoral intern to sch. psychologist Balcones Special Svcs. Coop., Austin, Tex., 1986-93; psychologist pvt. practice Austin, Tex., 1989—; cons. Edn. Svc. Ctr. XIII, Austin; adj. prof. U. Tex., Austin, 1990. Mem. YMCA, Austin, Tex., bd. dirs. Austin (Tex.) Rape Crisis Ctr. Mem. APA, Tex. Psychol. Assn. (pub. info. chmn. 1995-96), Audubon Soc. Office: 5750 Balcones Dr Ste 201 Austin TX 78731

DALTON, CLAUDETTE ELLIS HARLOE, anesthesiologist, educator, university official; b. Roanoke, Va., Jan. 18, 1947; d. John Pinckney and Dorothy Anne (Ellis) Harloe; m. Henry Tucker Dalton, May 17, 1973 (div. 1979); 1 child, Gordon Tucker. BA, Sweet Briar Coll., 1969; MD, U. Va., 1974. Resident in anesthesiology U. N.C., Chapel Hill, 1974-77; med. edn. Lenoir County Meml Hosp./East Carolina U., Kinston, N.C., 1978-80; med. edn. in intensive care Presbyn Hosp., Charlotte, N.C., 1981-82; practice anesthesiology Charlotte Eye, Ear, Nose and Throat Hosp., 1982-85, Medivision of Charlotte and Orthopedic Hosp. of Charlotte, 1985-89; asst. dean alumni affairs, 1989-92; asst. dean med. edn. U. Va. Health Scis. Ctr., Charlottesville, 1992—, cmty. preceptor coord., 1992-94; dir. Office of Cmty. Based Med. Edn., 1994—; bd. dirs. Kinston Bd. Health, 1979-81. Author developer patient edn. materials for illiterate patients, 1979—, emergency med. svc. tng. program, 1981. Bd. dirs. Charlottesville Family Svcs., Family Svcs. Albemarle County, 1992-93, Coun. on Aging, Lenoir County C.C., Am. Cancer Soc.; exec. dir. Cmty. Involvement Coun. Lenoir County, Kinston, 1979; county coord. Internat. Yr. of Child, Kinston, 1979; mem. women's task force U. Va. Med. Sch.; also others. Recipient Gov.'s award State of N.C., 1980, cert. of merit for svc. to children N.C. Dept. Human Resources, Outstanding Teaching award U. Va. Sch. Medicine, 1993; named Commencement speaker U. Va. Sch. Medicine Graduation, 1993. Mem. Va. Med. Soc. (editor med. news. Va. Med. Quar., mem. legis. com., mem. health acess com., bd. dirs. Va. Health Quality Coun. 1995—, chair ad hoc com. on telemedicine 1996—, del. to ann. meeting, reference com.), Albemarle County Med. Soc. (sec.-treas. 1995—), Va. Soc. Anesthesiology, U. Va. Med. Alumni Assn. (assoc. bd. dirs. 1989-92), Alpha Omega Alpha. Office: U Va Med Sch PO Box 325 Charlottesville VA 22902-0325

DALTON, HEIDI LYNN, financial analyst; b. Elko, Nev., Oct. 7, 1968; d. Ronald D. and Joan Aleece (Davis) Nelson; m. Doug W. Dalton, June 19, 1993. AAS, No. Nev. C.C., 1989; BBA, Boise State U., 1992. CPA, Idaho. Accounts receivable bookkeeper BriCo, Inc., Elko, 1987-88; office mgr. Builder's Mart, Elko, 1988-89; acctg. asst. Am. Bank of Commerce, Boise, Idaho, 1990-91; fin. analyst Hewlett Packard, Boise, 1992—; acctg. instr. Boise State U., 1996—. Top Ten scholar Boise State U., 1990-92. Mem. Inst. Mgmt. Accts. (cert.).

DALTON, MARY-MARGARET, lawyer; b. Hartford, Conn., May 21, 1959; d. E. Robert and Anne-Dillon C. (Curry) D. BA, St. Mary's Coll., 1981; JD, Gonzaga U., 1985. Bar: Conn. 1985, U.S. Dist. Ct. (fed. dist.) 1986. Assoc. Law Offices of Edward T. Dodd, Jr., Waterbury, Conn., 1985-90; ptnr. Dodd, Lessack, Ranando & Dalton, L.L.C., Cheshire, Conn., 1990—; instr. Nat. Acad. for Paralegal Studies, Inc., 1992—. Mem. Civitan. Roman Catholic. Home: 61 Gifford Rd West Hartford CT 06119-2207 Office: Dodd Lessack et al Ste 305 700 W Johnson Ave Cheshire CT 06119

DALTON, PHYLLIS IRENE, library consultant; b. Marietta, Kans., Sept. 25, 1909; d. Benjamin Reuben and Pearl (Travelute) Bull; m. Jack Mason Dalton, Feb. 13, 1950. BS, U. Nebr., 1931, MA, 1941; MA, U. Denver, 1942. Tchr. city schs., Marysville, Kans., 1931-40; reference libr. Lincoln Pub. Libr., Nebr.; libr. U. Nebr., Lincoln, 1941-48; libr. Calif. State Libr., Sacramento, 1948-57, asst. state libr., 1957-72; pvt. libr. cons., Scottsdale, Ariz., 1972—. Author: Library Services to the Deaf and Hearing Impaired Individuals, 1985, 91 (Pres.' Com. Employment of Handicapped award 1985); contbr. chpt., articles, reports to books and publs. in field. Mem. exec. bd. So. Nev. Hist. Soc., Las Vegas, 1983-84; mem. So. Nev. Com. on Employment of Handicapped, 1980-89, chairperson, 1988-89; mem. adv. com. Nat. Orgn. on Disability, 1982-94; mem., sec. resident coun. Forum Pueblo Norte Retirement Village, 1990-91, pres. resident coun., 1991-94; bd. dirs. Friends of So. Nev. Libraries; trustee Univ. Library Soc., U. Nev.-Las Vegas; mem. Allied Arts Council, Pres.' Com. on Employment of People with Disabilities, mem. emeritus 1989—, Ariz. Gov.'s Com. on Employment of People with Disabilities, 1990—, Scottsdale Mayor's Com. on Employment of People with Disabilities, 1990—, chmn. 1996—; mem.Scottsdale Pub. Libr. Ams. With Disabilities Com., 1994—. Recipient Libraria Sodalitas, U. So. Calif., 1972, Alumni Achievement award U. Denver, 1977, Alumni Achievement award U. Nebr., Lincoln, 1983; named Mover and Shaker Scottsdale Mag., 1994. Mem. LWV, ALA (councilor 1963-64, exceptional svc. award 1981, award com. O.C.L.C. Humphreys Forest Press award 1994), Am. Assn. U. Women, Assn. State Librs. (pres. 1964-65), Calif. Libr. Assn. (pres. 1969), Nev. Libr. Assn. (hon.), Internat. Fedn. Libr. Assns. and Instns. (chair working group on libr. svc. to prisons, mem. standing com. Sect. Librs. Serving Disadvantaged Persons 1981-95), Nat. League Am. Pen Women (Las Vegas chpt. 1988-94, mem. com. on qualifications for Letters membership 1994—, parliamentarian Scottsdale chpt. 1989-94, v.p. 1992-94, 96—, v.p. regional chpt. 1996—), Am. Correctional Assn. (libr. svcs. instns. com. 1994—), Pilot Internat. (mem.-at-large). Republican. Presbyterian. Home: 7090 E Mescal St Apt 261 Scottsdale AZ 85254-6125

DALY, CHERYL, broadcast executive; b. Providence, Apr. 20, 1947; d. Francis Patrick and Mary Ann (Wallis) D.; m. Arthur James Generas, July 18, 1970; 1 child, Caroline. BA, Rutgers U., 1969; postgrad., New Sch. for Social Rsch., 1975-78. Account exec. Phil Dean Assocs., N.Y.C., 1969-72; dir. pub. rels. Kirkland Coll., Clinton, N.Y., 1972-75; mgr. press svcs. CBS Radio, N.Y.C., 1976-80; assoc. dir. internal comm. CBS, Inc., N.Y.C., 1980-81, dir. corp. info., 1981-83; v.p. pub. rels. Group W Satellite Comm., N.Y.C., 1984-95; sr. v.p. pub. rels. Group W Satellite Comm., 1995—; examiner Westinghouse Quality Awards, Pitts., 1990. Recipient Best Co. Communication award Cable TV Bus., 1986, mktg. award Westinghouse Broadcasting Co., 1991. Mem. Cable TV Pub. Affairs Assn. (bd. dirs. 1985-87), Media Mommies (co-founder 1987). Democrat. Roman Catholic. Home: 1 W 67th St New York NY 10023-6200 Office: Group W Satellite Comm 685 3rd Ave New York NY 10017-4024

DALY, JANET MORGAN, home furnishings marketing consultant, editor; b. White Plains, N.Y., Jan. 14, 1937; d. William George and Laura Elizabeth (Josten) Russell; m. Hugh Thomas Morgan Jr. (div. Oct. 1976); 1 child, Hugh Thomas; m. Alan Frederic Daly, Oct. 4, 1985. Student, Washington Sq. Coll., N.Y.C., 1954-55. Ops. mgr. WISH-TV, Indpls., 1967-68; freelance writer various trade books and periodicals, 1969-72; assoc. pub. Earnshaw's Rev. and Small World, N.Y.C., 1972-75; sr. editor Men's Wear mag., N.Y.C., 1975-79, Chain Store Age, N.Y.C., 1979-80, HFD and Home Fashions Textiles, N.Y.C., 1980-84; v.p. Dan River Co., N.Y.C., 1984, Gear, Inc., N.Y.C., 1985; editor Floor Covering Weekly, Garden City, N.Y., 1985-94, Home Furnishings At Retail, 1994—, Signature, 1995—; editor, pub. Floor Covering Weekly, Garden City, N.Y., 1992-94; pres. A Daly Co., North Chatham, Mass., 1994—, Flooring Choices, 1996—; tchr. Parsons Buying Interior Furnishings, N.Y.C., 1986-87. Vol. fin. com. ARC, Westchester County, N.Y., 1988-94; com. Eldredge Pub. Libr. Endowment Campaign; adv. coun. C3TV. Mem. NAFE, Internat. Furnishings and Design Assn. (pres. N.Y. chpt. 1986, mem. career day com. 1987-90, program v.p. 1991, membership v.p. 1992). Home: 26 Rowland Dr North Chatham MA 02650-1049 Office: A Daly Co PO Box 407 North Chatham MA 02650-0407

DALY, JOE ANN GODOWN, publishing company executive; b. Galveston, Tex., Aug. 7, 1924; d. Elmer and Jessie Fee (Beck) Godown; m. William Jerome Daly, Jr., Jan. 25, 1958 (dec. 1965). BA in Journalism, U. Okla., 1945, BA in Piano, 1952. Asst. editor house organ Southwestern Bell Telephone, St. Louis, 1945-47; sec. to city mgr. Okla. Daily News, Oklahoma City, 1947-49; pvt. piano tchr. Alva, Okla., 1952-54; sec. to editor Prentice-Hall, Inc., N.Y.C., 1954-55, asst. to children's book editor, 1955-58; asst. editor children's books Dodd, Mead & Co., N.Y.C., 1963, dir. children's books, 1965-88, asst. v.p., assoc. pub. children's books, 1986-88; editorial dir. Cobblehill Books affiliate Dutton Children's Books, N.Y.C., 1988—; mem. Children's Book Council, N.Y.C., 1963, treas., 1969; mem. CBC/LA Com., N.Y.C., 1980, CBC/Prelude Com., N.Y.C., 1983. Active Bklyn. Heights Assn., 1976—; friend Carnegie Hall, N.Y. Philharm.; mem. Met. Opera Guild, Mus. Modern Art, Mus. Natural History. Mem. Phi Beta Kappa, Sigma Delta Chi, Theta Sigma Phi, Mu Phi Epsilon. Democrat. Methodist. Home: 80 Cranberry St Brooklyn NY 11201-1784 Office: Penguin USA 375 Hudson St New York NY 10014-3658

DALY, M. VIRGINIA, marketing executive; b. Washington, Sept. 10, 1945; d. John Jay and Mary Louise (Tinley) Daly; m. Garrett Sanderson, Nov. 1, 1982. BA, Coll. Saint Elizabeth, 1967. Copywriter, Doubleday Advt., N.Y.C., 1968-74; pres. Daly Direct Mktg., Washington, 1976— ; speaker, letcr. in writing; media spokesperson for catalog industry, 1994—. Author: (handbook) Expect The Unexpected, 1987. Mem. Direct Mktg. Assn. Washington (pres. 1982-83, Profl. of Year award 1985-86, ECHO award, bd. dirs. 1987-93, bd. dirs. Edn. Found., 1993—, advt. coun. direct mktg. com.), Am. News Womens Club (pres. 1986-88), Creative Guild, Womens Direct Response Group (Woman of Yr. 1990), Am. Women in Radio and Television (v.p. 1989-90), Rails to Trails Conservancy (bd. dirs. 1990—, chmn. bd. 1996—, 1st woman chair). Avocations: swimming, yoga, biking.

DALY, NANCY ELLEN, newspaper editor; b. San Francisco, June 14, 1954; d. Hugh Francis and Helen Margaret (Breen) D. BA, U. Ky., 1982. Freelance writer Lexington, Ky., 1979-82; reporter Lexington Leader, 1982; reporter Commonwealth-Jour., Somerset, Ky., 1985-86, Sunday news editor, 1986-88, news editor, 1988-89; news editor Hilltop Press & Northwest Press, Cin., 1990-92; mng. editor Press Cmty. Newspapers, Cin., 1992—; editor The Prime Edition, Cin., 1993—. Exec. com. mem., chair pub. rels. Tri-State White House Conf. on Aging, Cin., 1995. Recipient Award for Best Editl. Page, Suburban Newspapers of Am., 1992. Office: Press Community Newspapers 5552 Cheviot Rd Cincinnati OH 45247

DALY, TYNE, actress; b. Madison, Wis., 1947; d. James Daly and Hope Newell; m. Georg Stanford Brown (div.); children: Alyxandra, Kathryne, Alisabeth. Student, Brandeis U., Am. Music and Dramatic Acad. Performed at Am. Shakespeare Festival, Stratford, Conn.; appeared on Broadway in Gypsy, 1990, 91 revivals, The Seagull, 1992; films include Angel Unchained, 1970, The Enforcer, 1976, The Entertainer, 1976, Speed Trap, 1977, Telefon, 1977, Zoot Suit, 1982, The Aviator, 1985, Movers and Shakers, 1985; made TV debut in series The Virginian; guest appearances in various TV series, starring role in Cagney & Lacey, 1982-88 (Emmy awards 1982, 83, 84, 88); TV films include In Search of America, 1971, A Howling in the Woods, 1971, Heat of Anger, 1972, The Man Who Could Talk to Kids, 1973, Larry, 1974, Intimate Strangers, 1977, Better Late Than Never, 1979, The Women's Room, 1980, A Matter of Life and Death, 1981, The Great Gilly Hopkins, 1981, Your Place or Mine, 1983, Kids Like These, 1987, Stuck With Each Other, 1989, The Last to Go, 1990, Face of a Stranger, 1991, On the Town, 1993, Scattered Dreams, 1994, Christy, 1994 (Emmy award 1996), Colombo: Bird in the Hand, 1994, Columbo: Undercover, 1994, The Forget-Me-Not Murders, 1994, Cagney and Lacey: The Return, 1994, Cagney and Lacey: Together Again, 1995. Recipient Tony award for Mama Rose role in Gypsy, 1990. Address: The Blake Agy 415 N Camden Dr Ste 121 Beverly Hills CA 90210-4403*

DALY-MATTIO, BARBARA ANN, counselor, nurse; b. Erie, Pa., May 12, 1950; d. Frederick and June (Fanta) Salter; m. Karl D. Straub; children: Stephanie Anne Nobles, Elizabeth Marie; m. Gaylord N. Mattio (dec. Aug. 1995); children: Carisa Mattio, Mario Mattio. Cert. HIV counselor, Ohio; LPN. Nurses aide Extended Care Facility, Erie, Pa., 1978-79; charge nurse, medication nurse Erie Geriatric Ctr., Erie, Pa., 1979-87; counselor Preterm, Inc., Cleve., 1994—; donor health counselor Am. Red Cross, Cleve., 1994—; mem. Pa. Coalition Against Domestic Violence, 1982-90; domestic violence counselor, legal advocate Hospitality House Svcs. for Women, Inc., Erie, Pa., 1983-90, recording sec., chmn. property com., chmn. domestic violence awareness month coms., bd. trustees, 1985-90; bd. dirs. The Ctr. for the Prevention of Domestic Violence. Mem. Womens Polit. Caucus, Erie, Pa., 1986-87; recording sec., com. chmn., bd. trustees YWCA, Erie, 1988-90; vol. coord. Campaign Com. 1st Woman Judge for Common Pleas Ct., Erie. Mem. NOW (bd. mem., chmn. domestic violence taskforce Greater Cleve. chpt.), Nat. Mus. Women in the Arts (charter), Amnesty Internat., Women's Roundtable (founding bd. mem. 1987-90, past co-chmn. membership com.). Democrat. Home: 472 Fordham Pkwy Bay Village OH 44140

DALZELL, HELEN DEXTER, human resources professional; b. Cin., Jan. 13, 1941; d. Morris W. and Helen (Taylor) Dexter; m. Robert C. Dalzell, Sept. 16, 1978; 1 child, Elizabeth Louise. Student, Vassar Coll., 1959-62; BS, U. Miami, 1963; cert. in fin. planning, Coll. Fin. Planning, 1985. Cert. Personnel Cons., 1994. Mgmt. trainee Macy's, N.Y.C., 1963-64; adminstrv. asst. Tina Leser Internat., Bombay, India, 1964; asst. buyer Frederick Atkins, N.Y.C., 1964-65; counselor, mgr. Snelling & Snelling, N.Y.C., 1965-68; v.p., cons. Barnest & Boswell, N.Y.C., 1968-73; founder, pres. Taylor Assoc., N.Y.C., 1973-79; fin. planner IDS-Am. Express, Clearwater, Fla., 1984-87; pres., founder Taylor Assoc. Pers., Clearwater, Fla., 1987—. Tutor Pinellas County Schs., Clearwater, 1990-92; bd. dirs. Girls Clubs Pinellas County, Clearwater, 1983-92; mem. strategic planning Oak Grove Sch., Clearwater, 1991. Mem. Fla. Assn. Pers. Cons., Fine Arts Soc. (life), Clearwater C. of C., Clearwater Yacht Club, Rotary (Belleair chpt., bd. mem. 1994—). Republican. Presbyterian. Home: 1983 Belleair Rd Clearwater FL 34624-2536 Office: Taylor Assoc Pers Cons 612 Druid Rd E Clearwater FL 34616-3912

DAMASCHINO, ANN TOOTHMAN, development consultant; b. Oakland, Calif., Dec. 14, 1938; d. James Wesley and Aileen Elizabeth (Cox) Toothman; m. Douglas Alan Damaschino, Aug. 12, 1961; children: Lori Damaschino Berry, Ellen Damaschino Mellies, Gerald, Anthony. BA in English Lit. with honors, Holy Names Coll., 1962; MA in Philanthropy and Devel., St. Mary's U., Minn., 1994. Reader in English/social studies Acalanes Union H.S. Dist., Lafayette, Calif., 1964-77; interior designer, ptnr. Damaschino/Thurling, Lafayette, Calif., 1973-81; tech. writer, editor Shell Oil Co., Martinez, Calif., 1981-85; dir. devel. St. Mary's Coll. H.S., Berkeley, Calif., 1985-96; cons. devel. fund-raising, Lafayette. Pres., sec., treas. Walnut Creek (Calif.) Gallery Guild, 1968-76; mem. Contra Costa County Bd. "Project Second Chance" Adult Literacy Program, 1986-88. Mem. AAUW, Coun. for Advancement and Support of Edn., East Bay Devel. Dirs., Diocese of Oakland Devel. Dirs. Democrat. Roman Catholic.

D'AMATO, BARBARA STEKETEE, writer; b. Grand Rapids, Mich., Apr. 10, 1938; d. Harold Arthur and Yvonne (Watson) Steketee; m. Anthony Alfred D'Amato, Sept. 4, 1958; children: Brian Richard, Paul Steketee. BA, Northwestern U., 1971, MA, 1972. Author: Hardball, 1990, Hard Tack, 1991, The Doctor, The Murder, The Mystery (Anthony award 1992, Agatha award for best true crime), 1992, Hard Luck, 1992, Hard Women, 1993, Hard Case, 1994, Hard Christmas, 1995, (plays) Magic Man, 1975, The Magic of Houdini, 1976, RSVP Broadway, 1979. Mem. Mystery Writers Am. (nat. bd. dirs. 1994—, pres. Midwest chpt. 1985-87, 90-91), Sisters in Crime (pres. 1995), Phi Beta Kappa. Home and Office: 860 N Lake Shore Dr Chicago IL 60611

D'AMATO, FRANCES LOUISE, art and psychology educator; b. N.Y.C., Mar. 30, 1943; d. Louis and Frances Anna (O'Resto) D'Amato; m. Lewis M. Smoley, Sept. 17, 1977 (div. Mar. 1988). BS in Edn., SUNY, Oswego, 1964; MEd, Hofstra U., Hempstead, N.Y., 1969; MA in Orgnl. Psychology, Columbia U., 1986, MA in Art Edn., 1991. Cert. tchr. K-6, N.Y. Tchr. 5th grade Farmingdale (N.Y.) Pub. Schs., 1965-67; reading supr. Lynbrook (N.Y.) Pub. Schs., 1967-69; reading coord. Am. Cmty. Sch., Beirut, Lebanon, 1969-71; internal tng. cons. Chase Manhattan Bank, N.Y.C., 1971-73; asst. v.p. CIT Fin. Corp., N.Y.C., 1973-78; v.p. human resources Am. Mgmt. Assn., N.Y.C., 1978-81; cons. Tree Group, N.Y.C., 1981-87; prof. art Caldwell C.C., Hudson/Boone, N.C., 1988-95; prof. art and psychology Catawba Valley C.C., Hickory, N.C., 1991-95; cons., spkr. Women's Resource Ctr., Hickory, 1990-96; cons. exec. program Columbia U. Bus. Sch., 1981-82; cons. Frye Regional Hosp., Seminar on Assertiveness Tng., 1994; organizer Advent Retreat Cath. Conf. Ctr., Hickory, 1993-96; spkr. various seminars, 1994, 96; conf. leader Dreams Visions of the Night seminar Belmont Abbey Coll. Conf. Ctr., 1995, 96, Stress Reduction seminar, 1996. Author: Benjaman and the Tent, 1986; editor OD Network Newsletter, 1983-87, EIC Intelligence, 1987-90. Grassroots grant participant N.C. Arts Coun., Boone, 1988-90; participant Blue Ridge Leadership Challenge, Boone, 1990-91; organicer Visual Art Tchrs., Valle Crusis, N.C., 1991; alumni bd. dirs. SUNY-Oswego, 1974-84. Recipient Printmaking award Caldwell Arts Coun., Lenoir, N.C., 1989. Mem. ASTD (bd. dirs. 1975-77, mem. awards com. 1980-81), Nat. Art Edn. Assn. (conf. organizer 1991), OD Network (steering com. 1972-84), Kappa Delta Pi. Home: 1140 Knollwood Dr Claremont NC 28610 Office: 156 Olancha Peak Ave Boone NC 28607

DAMATO, KATHRYN LEATHEM, dental hygienist; b. Troy, N.Y., Nov. 30, 1948; d. James J. and Margurite (Judge) Leathem; m. Kenneth James Damato, May 7, 1977; children: Meaghan Leathem Damato, Kaitlyn Leathem Damato; 1 stepchild, Kenneth J. Damato. AS, Hudson Valley C.C.; BS, U. Bridgeport, 1972; MS, So. Conn. State U., 1976. Registered dental hygienist. Clin. dental hygienist pvt. practice, New Haven, Conn., 1975-85; instr. dept. dental hygiene U. Conn. Sch. Dental Medicine and Tunxis Coll., Farmington, Conn., 1985-89, asst. prof., 1989—; program developer, rschr. dept. oral diagnosis U. Conn. Sch. Dental Medicine, 1996—; course leader for clin. component of dental hygiene curriculum, 1989—, dir. clin. affairs, 1992—. Co-editor: Clinical Dental Hygiene Handbook. Adviser Student Am. Dental Hygienist Assn., Conn., 1985-90; cons. infection control and task force AIDS, 1988—; pres., founder Women and Children First, Inc.; oral health coord. spl. skills-spl. athletes Conn. State Olympics. Grantee AIDS Found. participation in Grant Edn., 1991, 92; recipient Conn. Higher Edn. Cmty. Svc. award, 1995. Mem. AAUP, Am. Dental Hygienist Assn., Internat. Assn. Dental Rsch., Am. Assn. Dental Rsch., Nat. Cancer Insts. Info. Assocs., Sigma Phi Alpha. Roman Catholic. Home: 1280 Durham Rd Wallingford CT 06492-2667 Office: U Conn Sch Dental Medicine Dept Dental Hygiene Mail Code 2105 Farmington CT 06509 also: Tunxis Coll RR 6 Woodbridge CT 06525

DAME, THERESA SUSAN, accountant; b. Albany, N.Y., Jan. 13, 1942; d. Kenneth and Doris Smith; m. Michael Dame, Apr. 4, 1971; children: Christine, Scott, Brian. BBA, SUNY, Albany, 1964, MBA, 1966. CPA, N.Y. Staff acct. Schmidt, Pfaffenbach & Cole CPAs, Green Island, N.Y., 1964-68, tax sr. staff acct., 1968-88; ptnr. Werik, Dame, Moore, Baxter & Assocs., CPAs, N.Y.C., 1989—. Mem. AICPA N.Y. Inst. CPAs. Office: Werik Dame Moore Baxter & Assocs 220 W 19th St Ste 2A New York NY 10011-4098

DAME-BRAYTON, LAUREEN EVA, nursing administrator; b. Framingham, Mass., Mar. 15, 1947; d. Irving Lawrence and Cora Justina (Wells) Dame; children: Daryl Lawrence, Jeffrey Lee. Diploma, Dartmouth-Hickock Med. Ctr., Hanover N.H., 1968; BSN, Clayton State Coll., Morrow, Ga., 1996; postgrad., Emory U., 1996—. RN, Ga. Staff nurse, charge nurse, team leader maternity and surgical nursing various hosps., N.H., Boston, St. Louis, 1968-69, 80-83; sch. nurse practitioner Dept. Pub. Health, Bedford, Mass., 1983-85; perioperative nurse, 1st asst. South Fulton Hosp., East Point, Ga., 1985-86; nurse, first asst., plastic surgery John Munna M.D., Atlanta, 1986-90; resource nurse, intake coord. Shallowford Hosp., Atlanta, 1989-91; staff educator, quality assurance coord. dept. surgical svcs. Shallowford Hosp., Atlanta, 1991-92; quality improvement coord., nursing South Fulton Med. Ctr., East Point, Ga., 1992; nurse coord. quality assurance Kaiser Permanente, Atlanta, 1992-93, dir. quality assurance, 1993-95; coord. care mgr. Egleston Children's Hosp., Emory U., Atlanta, 1995—. Mem. NAACOG (charter; chmn. steering com. 1972), AORN (chmn. hospitality com. 1992, mem. workshop and publicity coms. 1983), NAFE, Am. Soc. Plastic and Reconstructive Surg. Nurses, Nat. Assn. Quality Profls., Ga. Assn. Quality Profls., Ga. North Ctrl. Dsit. Quality Profls., Am. Acad. Disting. Students, Am. Needlepoint Guild and Embroiderers Guld of Am. (life), Sigma Theta Tau. Lutheran. Home: 8726 Twin Oaks Dr Jonesboro GA 30236-5152 Office: Egleston Children's Hosp 1405 Clifton Rd NE Atlanta GA 30322-1060

D'AMELIO, GEORGETTE CHESHIRE, artist, art educator, art therapist; b. Rockaway Beach, N.Y., Apr. 15, 1949; d. George Fleming and Janet marie (Bender) Cheshire; m. Kenneth Philip D'Amelio, Aug. 11, 1974. BS, Hofstra U., 1971; MS, Fla. State U., 1996. Cert. tchr., Fla., N.Y. Art tchr. Manatee County Schs., Bradenton, Fla., 1986—, Copiague (N.Y.) Pub. Schs., 1971-76. Recipient Ace awards Arts for a Complete Edn., Tallahassee, 1990-91, 91-92, edn. grantee Manatee County Pub. Schs., Bradenton, 1991-92. Mem. AAUW, Am. Assn. Art Therapists, Fla. Assn. Art Therapists, Fla. Art Edn. Assn., Manatee County Coun. for Arts, Digital Fine Artists Assn.

DAMES, JOAN FOSTER (MRS. URBAN L. DAMES), magazine editor, columnist; b. New Orleans, Sept. 29, 1934; d. Albert Steere and Lucia (Valdes) Foster; m. Urban Louis Dames, Feb. 10, 1959 (dec.); children: Alice Dames Whittaker, Lucia Ann Dames Byrns, Cecilia Dames Scherer, Madeline Sophie. Student, St. Louis U., 1953-56. Seismograph rec. librarian St. Louis U., 1954-55; feature writer St. Louis Globe Democrat, 1955-59; feature writer St. Louis Post-Dispatch, 1966-68, women's editor, 1968-79; editor Everyday mag., 1972-79, features editor, 1973-79, features dir., 1975-78, travel editor, 1979-91, columnist, 1979—; sr. feature writer St. Louis Post-Dispatch, 1991—; mem. pres.'s adv. coun. St. Louis U. High Sch., 1979-82; adv. Full Achievement, St. Louis U., 1982-84; v.p. St. Louis Bridal Bur., 1959—; bd. dirs. Southside Day Nursery, 1983-84; mem. pres. adv. coun. St. Louis area Girl Scouts Am., 1992-94. Radio personality: sta. KMOX-CBS, 1969-71; Author: Prelude, 1956. Bd. dirs. White House Retreat League Inc., 1993—. Recipient Mo. Press Women's Quest award, 1993, Media award, Mental Health Assn. St. Louis, 1993. Mem. Soc. Am. Social Scribes (bd. dirs. 1969-72), DAR (vice regent Ft. San Carlos chpt. 1992—), Nat. Soc. Colonial Dames of Am. Home: 7149 Lindell Blvd Saint Louis MO 63130-4404 Office: 900 N Tucker Blvd Saint Louis MO 63101-1069

DAMÉ-SHEPP, DIANE, art management administrator; b. Berkeley, Calif., Nov. 1, 1946; d. Paul David and Eleanor June Ingraham; m. Michael Joseph Damé (div.); children: Josette Laura, Criselle Lynn; m. Alan Martin Shepp; children: Castiel Armanda, Zia Felice. BA, U. Calif., Berkeley, 1977, cert. Mus. Mgmt. Inst. Am. Fedn. Arts, 1982; cert., Grantsmanship Tng. Ctr., San Francisco, 1984; cert. Leadership Inst., Calif. Arts Coun., Sacramento, 1988. Teaching asst., video co-prodr., writer art dept. Los Medanos Coll., Pittsburg, Calif., 1974-78; asst. security supt., spl. events coord. Univ. Art Mus., Berkeley, Calif., 1976-82, exec. dir. Univ. Art Mus. Coun., 1982-83; asst. devel. dir. Univ. Art Mus., U. Calif., Berkeley, 1983-85; exec. dir. Napa (Calif.) County Arts Coun., 1985-88, Solano County Arts Alliance, Fairfield, Calif., 1993-95; founding bd. dirs., past pres. Calif. Assembly Local Arts Agys., San Francisco, 1986-92; mem. leadership com. Nat. Assembly Local Arts Agys., Washington, 1987-91; art mgmt. cons. Calif. Arts Coun., Mono County Arts, Nevada County Arts, Napa Landmarks, Calif., River Sch., Napa, Calif., Magical Moonshine Theatre, Calif., 1988—; guest speaker Nat. Fedn. Flyfishers, Livingston, Mont., 1996. Artist/sculptor Sacramento Met. Arts Commn.-Light Rail Project Starfire Sta., 1984-87; exhibited in group shows at Weiss Gallery, San Francisco, 1984-85, Zaks Gallery,Chgo., 1982-87, San Francisco Airport, 1987-88, San Francisco Mus. Modern Art Coun. Auction, 1988, New Langston Arts, San Francisco, 1990, Headlands Art Ctr., Marin, Calif., 1993, Clos Pegase Winery, St. Helena, Calif., 1994, Sonoma State U., 1986, 88-91, 94, Oakland Mus. Collectors Gallery, 1994, Falkirk Cultural Ctr., San Rafael, Calif., 1995. Founding bd. dirs., v.p., fundraising sec./treas. Napa Valley Opera House, Inc., 1985—; mem. faculty Leadership Napa, 1986-90; founding bd. mem., sec. Napa Valley Film Festival; sight coord. Internat. Sculpture Conf., Oakland, 1982. Recipient Calif. State Scholarship, 1976, Scholarship AAUW, 1975-77, Mus.Mgmt. Inst. Scholarship Art Mus. Assn., Berkeley, 1982. Home and Office: PO Box 2398 Yountville CA 94599

DAMICO, DEBRA LYNN, college administrator, English educator; b. Passaic, N.J., Apr. 15, 1956; d. Nicholas Biagio and Eleanore Lorraine (Hugle) D. BA, Montclair State U., 1978, MA, 1989. Cert. tchr., N.J, reading specialist. Tchr. St. Francis Sch., Hackensack, N.J., 1978-79, Saddle Brook (N.J.) High Sch., 1979-80, St. Dominic Acad., Jersey City, 1980-84; adult basic edn./gen. edn devel. and ESL instr. Montclair State U., 1974—, coord. EXCEL program, 1993—; internat. student advisor Manhattan Coll., Bronx, N.Y., 1984—, ESL instr., 1986—; instr. Writing Inst. Adult Edn. Resource Ctr., Jersey City State Coll., 1987—; Outstanding Internat. Student advisor, 1989—. Mem. Dist. Wide Curriculum Council, Lodi, N.J., 1977-78; ch. cantor and musician. Nat. Assn. for Foreign Student Affairs grantee, 1985-86; named Outstanding Young Woman Am., 1986. Mem. Nat. Assn. Tchrs. of English as a Fgn. Lang., N.Y. Tchrs. of ESL, Nat. Assn. Fgn. Student Affairs-Assn. of Internat. Educators, Metro-Internat., Am. Assn. Tchrs. French, YMCA Internat. Student Svc., Kappa Delta Pi, Pi Delta Phi. Democrat. Roman Catholic. Office: Manhattan Coll 4513 Manhattan College Pky Bronx NY 10471-4098

DAMON, GENE See GRIER, BARBARA G.

DAMON, MARIANA LISA, secondary school educator; b. Wilmington, Del., Jan. 26, 1954; d. George W.F. and Adelaide Blessing (Corn) Simmons; m. John Edward Damon; children: Edward, William. BA in English and French magna cum laude, U. Ariz., 1990; postgrad., U. N.C., 1991. Cert. tchr., Ariz. Lit. grader U. Ariz., Tucson, 1989, writing tutor, 1990; student tchr. Amphitheater H.S., Tucson, 1990; substitute tchr. Carrboro City Schs., Chapel Hill, N.C., 1991; English and French tchr. Indian Oasis Baboquirari H.S., Sells, 1991-96. Recipient Silver Apple Tchg. award, 1994. Mem. NEA, Ariz. Reading Assn., Fgn. Lang. Assn., Golden Key Honor Soc. Home: 626 N Camino Miramonte Tucson AZ 85716-4632 Office: Baboquirari HS PO Box 248 Sells AZ 85634-0248

DAMSBO, ANN MARIE, psychologist; b. Cortland, N.Y., July 7, 1931; d. Jorgen Einer and Agatha Irene (Schenck) D. B.S., San Diego State Coll., 1952; M.A., U.S. Internat. U., 1974, Ph.D., 1975. Diplomate Am. Acad. Pain Mgmt. Commd. 2d lt. U.S. Army, 1952, advanced through grades to capt., 1957; staff therapist Letterman Army Hosp., San Francisco, 1953-54, 56-58, 61-62, Ft. Devers, Ft. Devens, Mass., 1955-56, Walter Reed Army Hosp., Washington, 1958-59, Tripler Army Hosp., Hawaii, 1959-61, Ft. Benning, Ga., 1962-64; chief therapist U.S. Army Hosp., Ft. McPherson, Ga., 1964-67; ret. U.S. Army, 1967; med. missionary So. Presbyterian Ch., Taiwan, 1968-70; psychology intern So. Naval Hosp., San Diego, 1975; predoctoral intern Naval Regional Med. Ctr., San Diego, 1975-76, postdoctoral intern, 1975-76, chief, founder pain clinic, 1977-86; chief pain clinic, 1977-86; adj. tchr. U. Calif. Med. Sch., San Diego; lectr., U.S., Can., Eng., France, Australia; cons. forensic hypnosis to law enforcement agys.; approved cons. in hypnosis. Contbr. articles to profl. publs., chpt. to book. Tchr. Sunday sch. United Meth. Ch., 1945—; Rep. Nat. Candidate Trust Presdl. adv. com., platform planning commn. at-large-del. Fellow Am. Soc. Clin. Hypnosis (psychology mem.-at-large, exec. bd. 1989-90), San Diego Soc. Clin. Hypnosis (pres. 1980); mem. AAUW, Am. Phys. Therapy Assn., Calif. Soc. Clin. and Hypnosis (bd. govs.), Am. Soc. Clin. Hypnosis Edn. Rsch. Found. (trustee 1992-94), Internat. Platform Assn., Am. Soc. Clin. Hypnosis (exec. bd.), Ret. Officers Am., Ret. Officers Assn. (rep. presdl. task force, pres. adv. com.), Toastmasters (local pres.), Job's Daus. Republican. Home and Office: 1062 W Fifth Ave Escondido CA 92025-3802

DAMSEY, JOAN, medical management consultant; b. Jamestown, N.Y., Sept. 12, 1931; d. Frederick Vincent and Sara (Caccamise) Landy; m. Lloyd Damsey, June 12, 1955 (dec. Oct. 1985); children: Eve, Laurie, Lloyd Jr., J. Landy. BA, Coll. St. Elizabeth, 1953; MA, Cath. U. Am., 1961. Founder, bd. dirs. First Nat. Bank Fla. Keys, Marathon, 1974-83; pres. Damsey & Assocs. Ltd., Portsmouth, Va., 1980—; dir. practice mgmt. Eastern Va. Med. Sch., Norfolk, 1982—; founder Resource Bank, Virginia Beach, Va. Author: Joan Damsey Mgmt. Semicars, 1986, (book) Increasing Referrals, 1993; mem. editorial adv. bd. Physicians Fin. News; contbr. chpts. to books and articles to mgmt. jours. Vice chmn. Dem. State Com., Fla., 1964-68; del. Dem. Nat. Conv., Atlantic City, 1964; bd. dirs., pres. St. Mary's Infant Home, 1994—. Fellow Am. Coll. Med. Practice Execs. (bd. dirs., devel. chmn. 1991—); mem. Med. Group Mgmt. Assn. (bd. dirs.), Tidewater Med. Group Mgmt. Assn., Soc. Med.-Dental Cons., Va. Med. Group Mgmt. Assn., Med. Soc. Va. (edn. com.), Chesapeake Bay Found. (chmn. bd. dirs. 1993—). Roman Catholic.

DANA-DAVIDSON, LAOMA COOK, English language educator; b. Herndon, W.Va., Nov. 23, 1925; d. Virgil A. and Latha (Shrewsbury) Cook; m. William J. Davidson, Apr. 1946 (div. 1971); 1 child, Deborah Davidson Bollom. BE, Marshall U., 1956; MA in Adminstrn., Azusa U., 1981. Cert. tchr., Calif. Tchr. Cajon Valley Union Sch. Dist., El Cajon, Calif., 1958—; master tchr. to 50 student tchrs. Author: Reading series used in dist., 1968. Former pres. El Cajon Rep. Women Federated; chaplin San Diego County Rep. Women; mem. El Cajon Hist. Assn.; v.p. Cajon Valley Union Sch. Bd. Recipient sabbatical to study British Schs. Cajon Valley Union Sch. Dist., 1977-78. Mem. Am. Assn. Univ. Women (pres. 1964-66, edn. com. 1993-94, policy com., women's issuees com.), League Women Voters, Grossmont Concert Assn., Delta Kappa Gamma. Office: 609 Ecken Rd El Cajon CA 92020-7312

DANAHER, MALLORY MILLETT (MALLORY JONES), actress, photographer, writer, poet; b. St. Paul, 1939; d. James Albert and Helen Rose (Feely) Millett m. Thomas C. Danaher, Mar. 1985; 1 child by previous marriage, Kristen Vigard. BA, U. Minn. Chief fin. officer Sheets & Co., N.Y.C. Active with N.Y. Theatre 1971-90; mem. original cos. of Annie and The Best Little Whorehouse in Texas, 1977; appeared in stage roles in Dodsworth, Berkshire Theatre Festival, Hedda Gabler, Kennedy's Children (dir. Olympia Dukakis), Edward Albee's Everything in the Garden (dir. Shelley Winters), House of Blue Leaves by John Guare, Berkshire Theatre Festival, Tornado, Lincoln Ctr. Libr. Theatre, Stella, Nat. Horn Theatre, N.Y.C., Cocteau's one-character play The Human Voice at Deutsches-Haus, NYU, Full Moon and High Tide (dir. Shelley Winters); off-Broadway prodn. Loose Connections, Judith Anderson Theatre; also (TV series) Love of Life, CBS-TV, Another World, NBC, Hunter, Thirtysomething, Superior Ct., Divorce Ct., The Judge, (NBC Movie of the Week) Eischied: Only the Pretty Girls Die, (motion picture) Tootsie, Columbia Pictures, Hell Hath No Fury with Barbara Eden, New Line Cinema: Alone in the Dark; exhibitor of photography: Third Eye Gallery, N.Y.C., 1974—, Modernage Discovery Gallery, N.Y.C., 1976-79, Gallery of St. Clement's, N.Y.C., 1979; performer own poetry; author: Fatherless Child; co-producer, subject of film Three Lives; contbr. poetry to mags. Mem. The Actors' Studio. Mem. The Creative Coalition. Mem. Nat. Assn. TV Programming Execs., Women in Theatre, Nat. Assn. for Self-Employed, Am. Women's Econ. Devel., The Friars Club.

DANBURG, DEBRA, state legislator; b. Houston, Sept. 25, 1951; d. Stanley and Barbara Jean (Walker) D. BA, U. Houston, 1974, JD, 1979. Asst. dir., lobbyist Texans for ERA, 1974-75; atty. pvt. practice, Houston, 1979—; mem. Tex. Ho. of Reps., 1981—, house com. on state affairs, 1991—, chmn. house coms. on elections, 1991—; mem. Appropriations Com.; chair Budget & Oversight for Cultural and Hist. Resources Com., Appropriations Subcom. on AIDS; mem. Appropriations Subcom. on the State Employee Classification System; Speaker's appointments Tex. Adv. Commn. on Intergov. Rels. and Tex. Health & Human Svcs. Coord. Coun., 1992; del. Dem. Nat. Convention, 1984; mayoral appointee City of Houston's Mcpl. Arts Commn., 1991—; hon. bd. dirs. S.W. region Am. Jewish Congress; mem. Leadership Am., Tex. coun. Family Violence; ex-officio dir. San Jacinto River Assn, 1992; speaker's appointments Elections Adv. Com., State Artist Com., Select Com. on Rules; mem. faculty in residence, new leadership program Ctr. Am. Women in Politics, Eagleton Inst., Rutgers, 1994; mem. 3rd Conf. Jewish Parliamentarians in Israel, 1993; speaker Jewish Women's Leadership Conf. in Israel, 1994. Named Outstanding feminist Now, 1975, best legislator Houston mag., 1981, Vol. of Yr. KS/AIDS Found., 1984, Outstanding Houston Profl. Woman by Fedn. of Houston Profl. Women, 1988, Tex. Recreation and Park Soc. Legislator of Yr., 1987, Friend of Psychology, Tex. Psychology Assn., 1992, Alumnae of Yr., U. Houston Coll. Social Scis., 1993; recipient Spl. Presdl. award Houston Apt. Assn., 1985, Environ. Def. award Sierra Club, 1987, Outstanding Legislator award Tex. Assn. of Symphony Orchs., 1990, Good Brick award Greater Houston Preservation Alliance, 1990, Mary Polk award Tex. Coun. Family Violence, Unsung Heroine award The Women's Advocacy Project, 1991, Women's Suffrage award Houston Area Women's Ctr., 1991, Hollyfield Polit. Svc. award Tex. Human Rights Campaign Fund, 1995, cert. of appreciation Common Cause, 1995, cert. recognition Tex. Mcpl. League, 1995, Good Gal award Tex. Women's Polit. Caucus, 1995. Mem. Harris County Criminal Lawyers Assn. (bd. dirs. 1982-83), Nat. Trust Hist. Preservation (hon.), Sierra Club. Office: Tex Ho Reps PO Box 2910 Austin TX 78768-2910

DANCYGER, RUTH, art historian; b. Cleve., Nov. 11, 1918; d. Henry and Nellie (Friedman) Steuer; married, Dec. 21, 1939; widowed, July 1968; children: Polly Sherard, Emily Edelstein. Student, Goucher Coll., 1936-38; BA, Case Western Res. U., 1942; MA, John Carroll U., 1966. Art historian John Carroll U., Cleve., 1987-93; art historian Cleve. Artists Found., 1986—, also bd. dirs.; art historian Cleve. Artists Now, 1993—; lectr. Midwest Art History Found., 1996—; catalogue rsch. asst. Cleve. Mus. Art and Ohio Univ. Press, 1996. Author monographs in field. Bd. dirs. Temple Mus., 1984—; mem. mayor's com. Adopt-A-Sculpture, 1993; women's coun. Cleve. Mus. Art, 1994—, Cleve. Ctr. for Contemporary Art, 1985—, docent coun. of Cleve., 1989—. Ohio Bell Telephone Co. grantee, 1987. Mem. Cleve. Soc. for Contemporary Art (program and travel planner 1989—), Cleve. Print Club. Home: 2632 S Green Rd Cleveland OH 44122-1536

DANDOY, MAXIMA ANTONIO, education educator emeritus; b. Santa Maria, Ilocos, Sur., Philippines; came to U.S., 1949, naturalized, 1951; d. Manuel and Isidra (Mendoza) Antonio. Teaching cert., Philippine Normal Coll., 1938; A.B., Nat. Tchrs. Coll., Manila, 1947; M.A., Arellano U., Manila, 1949; Ed.D. (John M. Switzer scholar, Newhouse Found. scholar), Stanford U., 1951, postgrad. (Calif. Fedn. Bus. and Profl. Women's Club scholar), 1952. Tchr. elem. sch. Philippines, 1927-37; lab. sch. tchr. Philippine Normal Coll., Manila, 1938-49; instr. Arellano U., Manila, 1947-49; lab. sch. prin. U. of East, Manila, 1953-54; assoc. prof. U. of East, 1952-55; prof. edn. Calif. State U., Fresno, 1956-82, prof. edn. emeritus, 1982—; curriculum writer, gen. office supr. Manila Dept. Edn., 1944-45; Mem. com. for the selection social studies textbooks for state adoption Calif., 1970-71; vis. prof. UCLA, 1956; Floro Crisologo Meml. lectr. U. No. Philippines, 1977. Author: Teaching Competencies, A Workbook and Log, 1985. Mem. Friends of the Stanford (Calif.) U. Sch. Edn., 1993, Sch. of Edn. and Human Devel. Alumni and Friends, Calif. State U., Fresno, 1992-93; mem. Calif. Gov.'s Conf. on Traffic Safety, 1962, Calif. Gov.'s Conf. Delinquency Prevention, 1963. Named Disting. Woman of Year, Fresno Bus. and Profl. Women's Club, 1957, Woman of Achievement, 1973, Outstanding Filipino, 1982; recipient Higher Edn. and Internat. Understanding award Philippine Normal Coll. Alumni Assn., 1986. Mem. AAUW (liaison Calif. State U. Fresno 1970-71, bridge gen. coord. 1995-96), Nat. Coun. Social Studies (chmn. sec. internat. understanding, nat. conv. 1966), Calif. Fedn. Bus. and Profl. Women's Clubs (state chmn. scholarships 1961-63, treas. Fresno), Calif. Tchrs. Assn., Orgn. Filipino-Am. Educators Fresno (pres. 1977-95), Filipino-Am. Women's Club (adv. 1969-74), Internat. Platform Assn., Phi Delta Kappa, Pi Lambda Theta, Kappa Delta Pi (counselor 1972-79, nat. com. attendance and credentials 1975, nat. com. regional confs. 1966). Home: 1419 W Bullard Ave Fresno CA 93711-2324

D'ANDREA, KIMBERLY SAWCHAK, retail executive; b. Kearny, N.J., Feb. 22, 1966; d. Thomas Walter and Mary Ann (Pronko) Sawchak; m. Jeffrey Paul D'Andrea, Nov. 9, 1991. Student, Chestnut Hill Coll., 1993-96. Profl. model N.Y.C., 1986-88; sales staff wholesale furs Louis Milona & Sons, N.Y.C., 1988-89; sales staff retail furs Revillon-Saks Fifth Ave., Bala Cynwyd, Pa., 1989-93; dir. Revillon-Saks Fifth Ave., Bala Cynwyd, 1993-96; dir. fur salon Saks Fifth Ave., Bala Cynwyd, 1996—. Mem. NOW, Alpha Sigma Lambda. Office: 2 Bala Plaza Bala Cynwyd PA 19004

DANELL, JANICE MAURINE, secondary school educator; b. Culver City, Calif., Sept. 1, 1940; d. John and Dorothy Maurine (Shepard) Krackenberger; m. Anthony Downham Kreider, Dec. 26, 1959 (div. Aug. 1972); children: Cynthia Maurine Kreider Craft, Vance Anthony; m. David Eugene Danell, Feb. 14, 1976. BA in Elem. Edn., Idaho State U., 1968; M Tchg., U. Ariz., 1977; MEd in Reading, San Diego State U., 1985. 2d grade tchr. Washington Elem. Dist., St. George, Utah, 1968-71; 1st grade tchr. Yuma (Ariz.) Elem. Dist., 1971-78, reading resource tchr., 1978-81; reading tchr. Sweetwater Union H.S., Chula Vista, Calif., 1985—; presenter workshops in field; leader, mem. study groups, San Diego, 1991-93; mem. summer exch. program U. Ariz.-New Zealand Reading Assn., 1977, NEA-Brit. N.U.T., 1979. Author curriculum materials in field. Mem. Keepers Club, San Diego Zoo, 1987; mem. sponsor San Diego Art Mus., 1990. Grantee Alpha Delta Kappa. Mem. NEA, Calif. Edn. Assn., Sweetwater Edn. Assn., Greater San Diego Reading Assn., Internat. Reading Assn., Calif. Reading Assn. Democrat. Home: 4307 Collwood Ln San Diego CA 92115-2012 Office: Montgomery HS 3250 Palm Ave San Diego CA 92154-1507

DANERI, SILVIA SARINANA, art educator; b. Mexico City, Aug. 12, 1954; came to U.S., 1989; d. Carlos and Sara Carmela (Flores) Sarinana; m. Edward Nicholas Daneri, Aug. 15, 1992. Interpreter, translator, Berlitz Sch. Langs., Mexico City, 1973; TESOL, U. Autonoma de Mexico, Mexico City, 1978; BA in Edn., Incarnate Word Coll., 1993; postgrad., Tex. Tech. U. Lic. art tchr. Interpretation and transl. instr. Berlitz Sch. Langs., Mexico City, 1973-74; H.S. English tchr. Ignacio L. Vallarta H.S., Mexico City, 1976-82; head elem. English dept. Colegio del Bosque, Mexico City, 1984-87, head jr. H.S. English/Spanish dept., 1987-89; tchr. art St. Luke's Episcopal Sch., San Antonio, 1993—. Roman Catholic. Home: 8211 Heritage Park San Antonio TX 78240 Office: St Lukes Episcopal Sch 11 Saint Lukes Ln San Antonio TX 78209-4445

DANFORD, ARDATH ANNE, retired librarian; b. Lima, Ohio, Feb. 11, 1930; d. Howard Gorby and Grace Rose (Klug) D. B.A., Fla. State U., 1951, M.A., 1952. Head tech. services Lima Pub. Library, 1956-60; librarian Way Pub. Library, Perrysburg, Ohio, 1960-70; asst. dir. Toledo-Lucas County Pub. Library, 1971-77, dir., 1977-85, ret.,, 1985. Author: The Perrysburg Story, 1966, Perrysburg Revisited, 1992. Bd. dirs. Toledo Cmty. Found., Sunset House, Way Libr. Found., Sisters of Mercy No. Health Found.; mem. adv. bd. St. Charles Hosp. Recipient Toledo Headliner award Women in Communication, 1978, Boss of Yr. award PerRoMa chpt. Am. Bus. Women's Assn., 1978. Mem. Ohio Libr. Assn. (Libr. of Yr. 1985, Hall of Fame 1993), Toledo Club, Perrysburg Garden Club, Zonta (pres. Toledo club 1975-76). Methodist. Home: 1075 Cherry St Perrysburg OH 43551-1615

D'ANGELO, BEVERLY, actress; b. Columbus, Ohio, Nov. 15, 1954. cartoonist Hanna-Barbera Studios, Hollywood, Calif., former singer with Rompin' Ronnie Hawkins. Performances include (feature films) The Sentinel, 1977, Annie Hall, 1977, First Love, 1977, Every Which Way but Loose, 1978, Hair, 1979, Coal Miner's Daughter, 1980, Honky Tonk Freeway, 1981, Paternity, 1981, National Lampoon's Vacation, 1983, Finders Keepers, 1984, National Lampoon's European Vacation, 1985, Big Trouble, 1986, Maid to Order, 1987, In the Mood, 1987, Aria, 1988, Trading Hearts, 1988, High Spirits, 1988, National Lampoon's Christmas Vacation, 1989, Daddy's Dying...Who's Got The Will?, 1990, Pacific Heights, 1990, The Miracle, 1991, The Pope Must Die, 1991, Man Trouble, 1992, Lonely Hearts, 1992, Lighting Jack, 1994, Widow's Kiss, 1994, Eye for an Eye, 1995, The Crazysitter, 1995; (stage prodns.) Rockabye Hamlet, Hey, Marilyn, The Zinger, Simpatico; (TV movies) A Streetcar Named Desire, 1984, Doubletake, 1985, Hands of a Stranger, 1987, Trial: The Price of Passion, 1992, A Child Lost Forever, 1992, Judgement Day: The John List Story, 1993, Menendez: A Killing in Beverly Hills, 1994, Jonathan Stone: Threat of Innocence, 1994, Sweet Temptation, 1996. Recipient CMA award 1981, Golden Globe award, 1981, Golden Reed award, 1981, Emmy award Nomination, 1985. Office: William Morris Agy 151 S El Camino Dr Beverly Hills CA 90212-2704*

DANIEL, BARBARA ANN, elementary and secondary education educator; b. LaCrosse, Wis., Mar. 22, 1938; d. Rudolph J. and Dorothy M. (Farnham) Beranek; m. David Daniel; children: Raychelle, Clarence, Bernadette, Brenda. BS in Edn. cum laude, Midwestern U., Wichita Falls, Tex., 1967; postgrad., U. Alaska, Fairbanks, Anchorage, Juneau, U. Alaska, Bethel. Cert. tchr., Alaska. Primary tchr. Bur. Indian Affairs, Nunapitchuk and Tuntutuliak, Alaska, 1967-70; tchr., generalist, English lang. devel. and ESL grades 6-12 Lower Kuskokwim Sch. Dist., Tuntutuliak, 1981—; mem. lang. arts curriculum revision task force Lower Kuskokwim Sch. Dist.; mem. state bd. Academic Pentathlon, Alaska; acad. decathlon, pentathlon coach. Rsch. video recording of elders in Alaskan village. Mem. NEA, Lower Kuskokwin Edn. Assn., Nat. Coun. Tchrs. English, Alaska Coun. Tchrs. English, Alaska Assn. Bilingual Tchr. Home: 25 West Circle PO Box WTL Tuntutuliak AK 99680-9998

DANIEL, BETH, professional golfer; b. Charleston, S.C., Oct. 14, 1956; d. Robert and Lucia D. Grad., Furman U., 1978. Profl. golfer Ladies Profl. Golf Assn. tour, 1979—; Winner U.S. Amateur Title, 1975, 77; youngest mem. S.C. Hall of Fame, 1979. Winner 31 LPGA events including Patty Berg Classic, 1979, World Ladies, Japan, 1979, World Series Women's Golf, 1980, 81, Columbia Savs. Classic, 1980, 82, Patty Berg Classic, 1980, Golden Lights, 1980, J.C. Penney Classic, 1981, 90 (with Davis Love III), Lady Citurs, 1981, Bent Tree Classic, 1982, Sun City Classic, 1982, Birmingham Classic, 1982, J & B Putting Championship, 1982, 85, WUI Classic, 1982, McDonald's Kids Classic, 1983, Kyocera Inamori Classic, 1985, Rail Charity Classic, 1989, 90, Konica San Jose Classic, 1989, Greater Washington Open, 1989, Safeco Classic, 1989, LPGA Championship, 1990, Orix Hawaiian Open, 1990, Kemper Open, 1990, Centel Classic, 1990, Northgate Classic, McDonald's Championship, Phar Mor Classic, 1990, 91, Corning Classic, 1994, Oldsmobile Classic, 1994, Big Apple Classic, 1994; Mazda Series winner, 1982; named Rookie of Yr., Ladies Profl. Golf Assn., 1979, Player of Yr., 1980, 94, Golfer of Yr., Seagrams Seven Crown Royal, 1981. Office: care Pros Inc PO Box 673 Richmond VA 23206-0673*

DANIEL, DEBORAH BLOOMFIELD, English language educator; b. Albuquerque, June 19, 1949; d. John Wesley and Susan (Wattoff) Bloomfield; m. Ernest Wayne Daniel, Aug. 22, 1968; 1 child, Audra Elizabeth. BA in English, Augusta Coll., 1971. Cert. tchr., grades 7-12 English tchr., Ga. Tchr. Richmond County Bd. of Edn., Augusta, Ga., 1971-72, Louisville H.S., Jefferson County (Ga.) Bd. of Edn., 1972-73, Glenn Hills H.S., Richmond County Bd. of Edn., 1975-78, Evans (Ga.) H.S., Columbia County Bd. of Edn., 1979—; workshop presenter, Evans, 1993—; free-lance destop pub., Evans, 1987—. Journalism advisor (student newspaper) Excalibur, 1989, 92-93 (Excellence award Augusta Chronicle 1989, Ga. Scholastic Press 1992); lit. cons. Nimbus mag., 1988-91. Mem. N.E. Presbyn., Ga., 1991, vol. Mission to Piedras Negras, Mex., 1991; mem. YMCA, Augusta, 1990—. Recipient Tchr. award Ga. Star Student/Tchr. Program, 1988. Mem. Profl. Assn. Ga. Educators, Ga. Assn. Educators, Savannah Waterways Assn., Augusta Coll. Alumni Assn. Home: 4394 Fernbrook Crossing Evans GA 30809

DANIEL, LISA ANN, journalist; b. Charleston, W.Va., Feb. 13, 1969; d. Gerald and Shirley (Wahl) D.; m. Steven Johnson, Sept. 4, 1993. BS in Journalism, W.Va. U., 1991. Newspaper reporter Shenandoah Publ. Co., Strasburg, Va., 1991-93, The Jour. Publ. Co., Fairfax, Va., 1993-95, Army Times Publ. Co., Springfield, Va., 1995—. Contbr. articles to newspapers. Mem. AAUW, Soc. Profl. Journalists, W.Va. U. Alumni Assn. Office: Federal Times 6883 Commercial Dr Springfield VA 22159

DANIEL, MARILYN S., lawyer; b. Tulsa, Okla., July 30, 1940; d. Basil M. and Kathryne (Shannon) Stewart; m. John A. Daniel, June 15, 1962; 1 child, John S. BA, Rhodes Coll., 1962; JD, U. Ky. Coll. of Law, 1976. Bar: Ky. Sec. math. tchr. Ky., N.J., 1962-71; legal clerk U.S. Dist. Judge, Lexington, Ky., 1977; asst. U.S. atty. U.S. Dept. Justice, Lexington, 1978-81; gen. counsel Mason & Hanger-Silas Mason Co., Inc., Lexington, 1982—, v.p. adminstrn., 1992—; dir. Mason Techs. Inc., 1988—, The Mason Co., Lexington, 1990—, Ky. Bar Assn. for Women, 1991-93. Mem. Fayette County Bd. Edn., 1985-88; trustee Transylvania Presbytery, 1985—; elder Maxwell St. Presbyn. Ch., 1993—. Recipient Women of Achievement award YWCA, 1993. Mem. ABA, KBA (CLE chair ann. conv. 1992), Fayette County Bar Assn. (Henry T. Duncan award 1994. Office: Mason & Hanger-Silas Mason Co 2355 Harrodsburg Rd Lexington KY 40504-3324

DANIEL-DREYFUS, SUSAN B. RUSSE, civic worker; b. St. Louis, May 30, 1940; d. Frederick William and Suzanne (Mackay) Russe; m. Don B. Faerber, Nov. 27, 1962 (div. Nov. 1968); 1 child, Suzanne Mackay; m. Marc Andre Daniel-Dreyfus, Aug. 9, 1969; 1 child, Cable Dunster. Student, Smith Coll., 1958-60, Corcoran Sch. Fine Arts, 1960-61, Washington U., St. Louis, 1961-62; MEd, Cambridge Coll., 1991. Mng. ptnr. Comm., Inc., 1980-82; asst. dir. Harvard Bus. Sch. Fund, Cambridge, 1982-86; pres. SCR Assocs. Corp., Cambridge, 1986—; mem. bd. advisors Odysseum, Inc.; bd. dirs. Future Mgmt. Systems. Mem. St. Louis-St. Louis County White House Conf. on Edn., 1966-68; mem. Mo. 1st Gov.'s Conf. on Edn., 1966, 2d Conf., 1968; bd. dirs. Tunbridge Sch., 1973-78, St. Louis Smith Coll.; hon. bd. dirs. New Music Circle; mem. woman's bd. dirs. Washington U., New Music Circle, 1963-67; mem. woman's bd. Mo. Hist. Soc.; bd. dirs. Non-Partisan Ct. Plan for Mo., Young Audiences Inc., 1967-69; bd. dirs. Childrens Art Bazaar, 1968-70; founder St. Louis Opera Theater; chmn. Art. Mus. Bond Issue election St. Louis, 1966; jr. bd. dirs. St. Louis Symphony, 1966-68, Opportunities Indsl. Center, Boston; legis. chmn. bd. dirs. Boston LWV, 1969-72; mem. coun., bd. dirs. Jr. League Boston, 1970-72, 74-76, v.p. Bd. of Family Counseling Services-Region West, Boston, 1979—; pres. Family Counseling Bd., Brookline, Mass.; trustee Chestnut Hill Sch., Boston, Brookline Friendly Soc.; mem. steering com. ann. fund Boston Children's Hosp. Med. Center, 1980-84; v.p. Nat. Friends Bd., Joslin Diabetes Found., 1980-83; mem. corp. bd. Joslin Diabetes Ctr.; v.p. bd. dirs. Boston Ctr. Internat. Visitors, 1979-82; Boston bd. dirs. Mass. Soc. Prevention of Cruelty to Children, 1980-84; exec. v.p. Ctr. for Middle East Bus., 1978-82; pres. bd. Brookline Community Fund, 1984—; overseer Old Sturbridge Village, 1987—. Mem. Colonial Dames, Soc. Art Historians. Clubs: Women's City (dir., Boston); Vincent (dir.). Home: 120 Middlesex Rd Chestnut Hill MA 02167-1800

DANIELS, ARLENE KAPLAN, sociology educator; b. N.Y.C., Dec. 10, 1930; d. Jacob and Elizabeth (Rathstein) Kaplan; m. Richard Rene Daniels, June 9, 1956. B.A. with honors in English, U. Calif., Berkeley, 1952; M.A. in Sociology, 1954, Ph.D. in Sociology, 1960. Instr. dept. speech U. Calif., Berkeley, 1959-61; rsch. assoc. Mental Rsch. Inst., Palo Alto, Calif., 1961-66; assoc. prof. sociology San Francisco State Coll., 1966-70; chief Center for Study Women in Soc., Inst. Sci. Analysis, San Francisco, 1970-80; mem. faculty Northwestern U., Evanston, Ill., 1975-95; prof. dept. sociology Northwestern U., 1975-95, dir. Women's Studies, 1992-94, prof. emerita; vis. prof. dept. sociology U. Calif., Berkeley, 1996; cons. NIMH, 1971-73, NEH, 1975-80, Nat. Inst. Edn., 1978-82. Editor: (with Rachel Kahn-Hut) Academics on the Line, 1970; co-editor: (with Gaye Tuchman and James Benét) Hearth and Home: Images of Women in the Mass Media, 1978, (with James Benét) Education: Straightjacket or Opportunity?, 1979, (with Rachel Kahn-Hut and Richard Colvard) Women and Work, 1982, (with Alice Cook and Val Lorwin) Women and Trade Unions in Eleven Industrialized Countries, (with Teresa Odendahl and Elizabeth Boris) Working in Foundations, 1985, Invisible Careers, 1988, (with Alice Cook and Val Lorwin) The Most Difficult Revolution: Women in the Trade Union Movement, 1992; editor: Jour. Social Problems, 1974-78; assoc. editor: Contemporary Sociology, 1980-82, Symbolic Interaction, 1979-84, Am. Sociol. Rev., 1987-90. Trustee Bus. and Profl. Women's Rsch. Found. Bd., 1980-85, Women's Equity Action League Legal and Ednl. Def. Fund, 1979-81; mem. Chgo. Rsch. Assoc. Bd., 1981-87. Recipient Social Sci. Rsch. Council Faculty Rsch. award, 1970-71; Ford Found. Faculty fellow, 1975-76; grantee Nat. Inst. Edn., 1978-79, 1979-80, NSF, 1974-75, NIMH, 1973-74. Mem. Inst. Medicine NAS, Sociologists Women in Soc. (pres. 1975-76), Am. Sociology Assn. (coun. 1979-81, chmn. occupations and orgns. 1987, chmn. pubs. com. 1985-87, sec. 1992-95, Jessie Bernard award 1995), Soc. Study Social Problems (v.p. 1981-82, pres. 1987 Lee Founders award 1988), Soc. Study Symbolic Inter-Action.

DANIELS, ASTAR, artist; b. Fostoria, Ohio, Nov. 27, 1920; d. Alfred Henry and Edna Mae (Roush) Shultz; m. Bert Franklin Daniels, May 17, 1942 (div. Sept. 1976); children: Larry Bert, Cheri Hogue-Daniels, N. Dana Rahbar-Daniels. Honor grad., Art Instrn., Inc., Mpls., 1952; student, Toledo Mus. Sch. Design, 1950-52; studied with, Emerson C. Burkhart, 1952-54; student, Thomas Moore Coll., 1971-73; grad. summa cum laude, U. Cin., 1977; student, Ohio U., 1984-85. Tchr. art pvt. adult and youth art classes Forest and Cin., Ohio, 1950-57; portrait demonstrator numerous galleries, colls., mus., TV nationwide, 1951-79; dir. art, tchr. Defiance (Ohio) Coll., 1956-57; tchr. art and drama Meth. Ch. Camp, Sabina, Ohio, 1960-64; lectr. on liturgical art Hyde Park Comty. Ch., Cin., 1960-79; tchr. art and drama Fairview Arts Ctr., Cin., 1977-78; judge, mem. jury art shows, 1956-70; gallery guide Contemporary Art Ctr., Cin., 1972-73; costume designer Girl Scout Symphony Music Hall, Cin., 1960, 62, 66; dir. art Ohio State Fair, Columbus, 1955-57; nat. art dir. Sr. Girl Scout Round-up, Button Bay, Vt., 1962; founder, chairperson Fine Arts Com. Ecclesia, Cin., 1960-79. Exhibited in one woman portrait shows mus., colls., galleries, 1954-72; exhibited glass sculpture Schaff Gallery, Cin., 1996; commns. include Richard Nixon, Dr. A. B. Graham, James Arness; author, illustrator: (book) Aiming in His Direction, 1971; illustrator: (book) Woman Spirit Bonding, 1983. Art therapist Christ Hosp. Psychiat. Ward, Cin., 1959-61; youth liturgical dance dir. Hyde Park Comty. Ch., Cin., 1959-66; citizen diplomat Soc. for Positive Future, 1986. Recipient Scouters award for tng. leadership Boy Scouts Am., Forest, 1957, Cert. of Achievement, Charlotte R. Schmidlapp Found., Cin., 1977, Exptl. Inst. for Human Devel. award Hyde Park Comty. Ch., 1976. Mem. Soc. for Universal Human (founding mem.). Home and Office: Daniels Portrait Studio 3740 Drakewood Dr Cincinnati OH 45209

DANIELS, AUDREY OCTAVIA, community development manager; b. Montclair, N.J., Aug. 25, 1932; d. Alexander Gordon and Elizabeth Ruth (Wilkerson) Trent; m. Jeff Daniels Jr., May 10, 1952; children: Bruce D. (dec.), Cheryl J. Washington, Michael G. BSBA, Del. State U., 1977. Input data contr. Del. State U., Dover, 1963-76; exec. dir. Kent County Head Start, Dover, 1977-88; cmty. devel. dir. City of Dover, 1988—. co-chair edn. Del. Housing Coalition, Dover, 1989—; govt. liason Del. Homeless Coalition, Dover, 1987—, Ctrl. Del. Habitat for Humanity, Dover, 1990—; pres., bd. dirs. Shepard Place for the Homeless, Dover, 1990-94; mem. Mifflin Rd. Civic Assn., Dover, 1988—. Recipient Presdl. Sports award Pres. of the U.S., 1990. Mem. Nat. Assn. Housing Rehab. Offcls., Kent County Head Start Dirs. Assn. (pres. 1982-87), Delta Sigma Theta (life, Dover alumnae chpt. asst. recording sec. 1985-89). Roman Catholic. Home: 238 Mifflin Rd Dover DE 19904

DANIELS, BARBARA GAYLE, state official, real estate broker; b. St. Paul, July 15, 1950; d. Edwin W. and Hedwig D. (Wiereke) Grossman; m. James R. Daniels, July 10, 1971 (div. 1983); 1 child, Robyn. Attended, U. Minn., 1968-70; BA in Social Work and Psychology, Avila, 1973. Caseworker Kansas City Divsn. Family Svcs., 1971-74, supr., 1974-76, agt. rep. hearing, 1976-77, staff devel. specialist, 1977-83, program devel. specialist, 1983—. Mem. NASW, NAFE, Women in Energy. Office: Divsn Family Svcs 615 E 13th St Kansas City MO 64106

DANIELS, CINDY LOU, space agency executive; b. Moline, Ill., Sept. 24, 1959; d. Ronald McCrae and Mary Lou (McLaughlin) Guthrie; m. Charles Burton Daniels, June 19, 1982. Student, Augustana Coll., Rock Island, Ill., 1977-78; BS cum laude, No. Mich. U., 1981. Field engr. Ford Aerospace, Houston, 1982-83; engr. flight ops. McDonnell Douglas Corp., Houston, 1983-85; electronics engr. Johnson Space Ctr. NASA, Houston, 1985-89; project mgr. multiple program control ctr. NASA, 1989-90; project mgr. NASA, Houston, 1989-91, mission control ctr. upgrade project mgr., 1990-91; mgr. program control office NASA, 1991-93; mgr. ground facilities Space Sta. Program Office NASA, Houston, 1993-94; engring. and ops. mgmt., space sta. program NASA Hdqrs., Washington, 1994-96; acquisition mgr., solar terrestrial probes NASA Langley Rsch. Ctr., Hampton, Va., 1996—; dynamics contr. NASA Johnson Space Ctr., 1982-83; payload data engr. NASA, 1983-84, earth radiation budget satellite joint ops. integration plan mgr., 1984; mem. payload assist module team NASA-McDonnell Douglas Corp., 1984-85. Home: 110 Spoon Ct Yorktown VA 23693 Office: NASA Langley Rsch Ctr 12 W Taylor St Hampton VA 23681

DANIELS, DIANA M., lawyer; b. Dillon, Mont., BA, Cornell U., 1971, JD, Harvard U., 1974; M of City Planning, MIT, 1974; diploma, U. Edinburgh, Scotland, 1976. Bar: N.Y. 1975, U.S. Dist. Ct. (ea. and so. dists.) N.Y. 1975, U.S. Ct. Appeals (2d cir.) 1975, D.C. 1978, U.S. Supreme Ct. 1988. Assoc. Cravath, Swaine & Moore, N.Y.C., 1975-78; asst. counsel Washington Post newspaper, 1978-79; gen. counsel Washington Post Co., 1988-89, v.p., gen. counsel, 1989-91, v.p., gen. counsel, sec., 1991—; v.p., counsel Newsweek, N.Y.C., 1979-85, v.p., gen. counsel, 1985-88. Office: Washington Post Co 1150 15th St NW Washington DC 20071-0001

DANIELS, ELIZABETH ADAMS, English language educator; b. Westport, Conn., May 8, 1920; d. Thomas Davies and Minnie Mae (Sherwood) Adams; m. John L. Daniels, Mar. 21, 1942; children: John L., Eleanor B. (dec.), Sherwood A., Ann S. A.B., Vassar Coll., 1941; A.M., U. Mich., 1942; Ph.D., N.Y. U., 1954. From instr. to prof. English Vassar Coll., Poughkeepsie, N.Y., 1948-85; dean freshmen Vassar Coll., 1955-58, dean studies, 1965-73, chmn. dept. English, 1974-76, 81-84, acting dean faculty, 1976-78, chmn. self-study, 1978-80, Vassar historian, 1985—. Author: Jessie White Mario, Risorgimento Revolutionary, 1972, Main to Mudd, Bridges to the World, 1994, Main to Madd, and More, 1996; also articles. Bd. dirs. Young Morse Hist. Site. Recipient Grad. award Alumnae Assn. N.Y. U., 1954; Vassar fellow, 1941; Nat. Endowment Humanities summer stipend, 1981. Mem. MLA, AAUP, N.E. Victorian Soc., Phi Beta Kappa. Democrat. Club: Poughkeepsie Tennis. Home: 129 College Ave Poughkeepsie NY 12603-2804 Office: Vassar Coll PO Box 74 Poughkeepsie NY 12602-0074

DANIELS, GLENNIE OVERMAN, family and consumer educator; b. Yadkinville, N.C., Mar. 27, 1945; d. Rex Thomas and Mary Blanche (Simmons) Overman; m. Michael Dean Daniels, Jan. 28, 1967. BSHE, U. N.C., Greensboro, 1967, MEd, 1972, PhD, 1996. Cert. tchr., N.C. Asst. dir. residence halls UNCG, Greensboro, 1967; tchr. Berlin-Am. Sch., Berlin, Germany, 1969, Guilford County Schs., Greensboro, N.C., 1970-83; sole proprietor Fibers and Frames, Statesville, N.C., 1983-93; family and consumer educator N.C. Cooperative Extension Svc., Newton, 1995—; mem. adv. bd. Children's Protection Coun., Hickory, N.C., 1995—, Longterm Care, 1995—, Project HEART, 1995—; v.p. Catawba County Interagency Coun., 1996—, vice chair. Author, presenter: (symposium) Am. Ednl. Studies Assn., 1994, N.C. Assn. for Rsch. in Edn., 1995. Mem. literacy and lifelong learning com. Statesville C. of C., N.C., 1991. Recipient Terry Sanford Creative Tchg. Local award N.C. Public Schs., Greensboro, 1977, Tchr. of the Yr. award Assn. Classroom Tchrs., 1979, Hammermill Paper Creative Design award Hammermill Paper, 1989, Science Tchg. Excellence award Guilford County, N.C., Greensboro, 1983. Mem. AAUW, Am. Assn. Family and Consumer Science, Am. Bus. Women's Assn. (v.p. 1995-96), Am. Ednl. Studies Assn., N.C. Assn. for Rsch. in Edn., Alpha Delta Kappa (past chpt. pres.), Kappa Omicron Nu. Office: NC Cooperative Extension Svc 1175 S Brady Ave Newton NC 28658

DANIELS, KATHERYN MARTINA, accountant; b. Kingston, Jamaica, West Indies, Apr. 16, 1967; arrived in U.S., 1979; d. Anthony Rushton and Beverley Evelyn (Lindo) Page; m. Aaron Novester Daniels, Mar. 16, 1990; 1 child, Sean Anthony. BS in Acctg., Orlando Coll., 1995. Acctg. clerk Strates Enterprises, Orlando, Fla., 1992-93; reconciliation specialist Darden Restaurants, Orlando, 1993-96, property tax coord., 1996—. With U.S. Army, 1988-91. AICPA scholar, 1994, Orlando Coll. scholar, 1994. Mem. Toastmasters, Inst. Mgmt. Accts. Democrat. Methodist. Home: 6344 Tidewave St Orlando FL 32822

DANIELS, LYDIA M., health care administrator; b. Louisville, Dec. 21, 1932; d. Effort and Gladys T. (Turner) Williams; student Calif. State U., Hayward, 1967, 69-72; BA, Golden Gate U., 1992, MS, 1993; cert. Samuel Merritt Hosp. Sch. Med. Record Adminstrs., 1959; student Cen. State Coll., Ohio, 1950-52; children by previous marriage: Danny Winston, Jeffrey Bruce, Anthony Wayne. Sec. chemistry dept. Cen. State Coll., Wilberforce, Ohio, 1950-52; co-dir. Indian Workcamp, Pala Indian Reservation, Pala, Calif., 1956-58; clk.-typist Camarillo (Calif.) State Hosp., 1956-58; student med. record adminstr. Samuel Merritt Hosp., Oakland, Calif., 1958-59, asst. med. record adminstr., 1962-63, asst. chief med. record adminstr., 1965, chief med. record adminstr., 1965-72; med. record adminstr. Albany (Calif.) Hosp., 1964-65; asst. med. record adminstr. Children's Hosp., San Francisco, 1960; co-dir. interns in community svc. Am. Friends Svc. Com., San Francisco, 1960-61; med. record adminstr. Pacific Hosp., Oakland, Calif., 1963-64; med. record cons. Tahoe Forest Hosp., Truckee, Calif., 1969-73; chief med. record adminstr. Highland Gen. Hosp., Oakland, 1972-74; dir. med. record svcs. U. Calif. San Francisco Hosps. and Clinics, 1975-82; mgr. patient appointments, reception and registration Kaiser-Permanente Med. Ctr., 1982-88; dir. ambulatory adminstrv. svcs., 1988-94, asst. dir. human resources, 1994-96, dir. human resources Brookside Hosp., San Pablo, Calif., 1996—; adj. prof. mgmt., labor mgmt. rels. Golden Gate U., 1978—; pres. Daniels Consultation Svcs., 1988—. Leader Girl Scouts Am. Oakland area council, 1960-62; sunday sch. tchr. Soc. of Friends, Berkeley, Calif., 1961-63, mem. edn. com., 1965-68; mem. policy and adv. bd. Far West Lab. Demonstration Sch., Oakland, 1973-75; bd. dirs. The Californians, Oakland, 1993—, Patrons of the Arts and Humanities, Oakland, 1994—, YWCA, Berkeley, 1995—. Recipient Mgmt. Fellowship award U. Calif., San Francisco, 1979-80. Mem. Am. Med. Record Assn., Calif. Med. Record Assn. (editorial bd. 1976-77, pres. 1974-75), East Bay Med. Record Assn. (chmn. edn. com. 1971-72, pres. 1969-70), Assn. Systems Mgmt., Am. Mgmt. Assn., San Francisco Med. Records Assn. (pres.-elect 1982-83, pres. 1983-84), Am. Assn. Tng. and Devel. (Golden Gate chpt., v.p. prof. devel. 1994—). Author: Health Record Documentation: A Look at Cost, 1981; Inservice Training as a Tool in Managing the Changing Environment in the Medical Record Department, 1983; the Budget as a Management Tool, 1983. Issues editor Topics in Health Record Management, Parts I and II, 1983. Home: 545 Pierce St Apt 1105 Albany CA 94706-1048 Office: Brookside Hosp 2000 Vale Rd San Pablo CA 94806

DANIELS, MARY IRENE, public health nurse, educator; b. Gooding, Idaho, Nov. 11, 1955; d. Arthur and Elizabeth Ann (Lenker) D. BSN, Idaho State U., 1978; MPH, Loma Linda U., 1989. RN, Calif.; cert. pub. health nurse, Calif.; cert. health edn. specialist. Staff mem. Campus Crusade for Christ Internat., San Bernardino, Calif., 1978-88; dir. health promotion Riverside-San Bernardino County Indian Health, Banning, Calif., 1989-93; health educator drug prevention San Bernardino (Calif.) County Pub. Health, 1994-95; nurse cons. L.A. City Immunization Program, 1995—. Mem. APHA, Job's Daus. (Honored Queen 1968), Order Ea. Star. Home: 1903 Roanoke St San Jacinto CA 92582

DANILOW, DEBORAH MARIE, rancher, musician, bondsman; b. Mineral Wells, Tex., Dec. 9, 1947; d. Stanton Byron and Irval Leona (Vanhoosier) D.; m. William Paul Cook Jr., June 1965 (div. Oct. 1967); m. Chance Gentry, Oct. 1971 (div. May 1974); m. Ellis Elmer Aldridge, Dec. 3, 1977 (div. Nov. 1984); children: Chandra Desiree, Anthony Ellis; m. Carl Graham Quisenberry, Feb. 7, 1992. Student, Brantley Draughon Bus. Coll., Ft. Worth, 1965-66, Tex. Christian U., 1965-67, U. Ariz., 1967-69. Asst. to pres. Hollywood Video Ctr., L.A., 1969-72; producer Western Inst. TV, L.A., 1972-77; owner Chanelde Ranch, Weatherford, Tex., 1977-84; band musician Bonnie Raitt, Malibu, Calif., 1984, Mick Fleetwood, Malibu, 1984; lead musician Jazz Talk, Ft. Worth, 1985—; owner Brazos Valley Ranch Inc., Seymour, Tex., 1987—, AAA Bail Bonds, Seymour, 1990—. Composer numerous pub. songs, 1969—. Active Sheriffs Assn. Tex., Seymour, 1991—, North Tex. Taxpayers League, Wichita Falls, Tex., 1991—, Tex. State Notary Bd., Austin, 1990—. Mem. NAFE, NRA, Okla. Game Breeders Assn., United Game Breeders Assn., Tex. Game Breeders Assn., Tex. Limousin Assn., Tex. Southwestern Cattle Raisers Assn., Tex. Cattlewomen's Assn., Am. Quarter Horse Assn. (life), Dallas-Ft. Worth Profl. Musicians Assn., Ft. Worth Jazz Soc. (sec. 1987-89), N.Am. Limousin Found. (life), Australian Shepherd Club Am., Internat. Platform Assn., Marchigiana Cattle Assn. (life), N.Am. Fishing Club. Baptist. Office: Brazos Valley Ranch Inc 111 S Main St Seymour TX 76380-2528

DANITZ, MARILYNN PATRICIA, choreographer, videographer; b. Buffalo. BS in Chemistry, Le Moyne Coll.; MS in Chem. Engring., Columbia U. Artistic dir. High Frequency Wavelengths/Danitz Dances, 1976—; assoc. prof. Tainan Cheng Chuan Coll., Taiwan, 1984; profl. dancer Ballet Mcpl.

Strasbourg, France, Ballet Mcpl. Geneva, Switzerland; choreography commns. performances include The 11th Internat. Ballet Comp. Varna, Bulgaria, 1983, Tbilisi Ballet co., USSR, Nat. Ballet of Colombia, Nat. Inst. Arts, Taiwan, Nanatsudera Theatre, Nagoya, Japan, Shanghai Ballet and Shanghai Jiao Tung U., People's Republic of China, Nat. Cheng Kung Dance Group, Taiwan, others; master choreography workshops include Chinese Cultural U., Taipei, Taiwan, Okuda Studio, Nagoya, Ballet Philippines, Manila, NSW Coll. Dance, Sydney, The Ballet Sch., Bogota, Colombia, others; video prodn. Real Art Ways Nat. Residency, funded by NEA, 1990; video art collaboration with Allen Ginsberg. Presentations include Internat. Conf. on Dance and Tech., 1993, Naropa Inst. 20th Anniversary Celebration, 1994; video work presented at Lincoln Ctr., N.Y.C., 1995; video work in permanent collection Lincoln Ctr. Dance Collection; TV prodns. of works include Nat. Broadcasting, Venezuela, Colombia, Pub. Broadcasting, Albany, N.Y.C., Mpls.; works performed by Nat. Ballet with the Nat. Philharm. Orch. of Colombia Gala Performance, 1984; co. tours include China, Japan, Taiwan, Europe, Hawaii. Recipient Outstanding Dance-Theater Work of 1986 award Dance Brew-ATV Cable Manhattan, award for disting. choreography Nat. Assn. Regional Ballet, 1982; Bessie Schoenberg Lab. for Experienced Choreographers Dance Theater Workshop; NIH fellow; Gold Medal scholar Conservatoire Geneve, N.Y. State Regents scholar, Le Moyne Coll. Chemistry scholar, others. Mem. Dance Theater Workshop, Am. Dance Guild (exec. com., editor Am. Dance, bd. dirs., nat. conf. planning com.). Address: 560 Riverside Dr Apt 16E New York NY 10027-3203 also: PO Box 216 Sand Lake NY 12153-0216 also: 3200 Holly Rd Apt 2 Virginia Bch VA 23451-2926

DANKO, PATRICIA ST. JOHN, visual artist, writer, educator; b. Orange, Tex., Aug. 7, 1944; d. George Milton and Rebecca Alice (McCoppin) Solomon; m. Jim Danko, Aug. 19, 1973 (dec. 1983). BA, Dominican Coll., Houston, 1965; postgrad. U. Ibero-Americana, Mexico, 1965, Mich. State U., 1965, Mus. Fine Arts Sch., Houston, 1972; BFA, U. Houston, 1979, MEd in Second Lang. Edn., 1992. Tchg. asst. Mich. State U., East Lansing, 1965; vol. Peace Corps, Chile, 1965-68; silkscreen apprentice, printer Atelier Zárate, Buenos Aires, 1969; tchr. h.s. Orange Ind. Sch. Dist. (Tex.), 1971, Houston Ind. Sch. Dist., 1973; instr. English, English Lang. Svcs., Houston, 1973-75; instr. English, Spanish, Inlingua Lang. Schs., 1976; instr. Art League Houston, 1978-81; performance art writer Houston Art Scene, 1979-84, editor, 1981-84, mng. editor, 1982-83, exec. editor, 1983-84; acting Tex. editor New Art Examiner, 1985-86; contbg. editor Tex. New Art Examiner, 1986-88; curriculum writer Houston Ind. Sch. Dist., 1990-91; tchr. Caminos Bilingües al Exito Fed. Title VII Grants program Burbank Middle Sch., Houston, 1996—; ind. art hist. rschr., writer; freelance writer, 1979-85; Visual artist, pub. collections: Nat. Mus. Women in Arts, Washington, Libr. and Rsch. Archives, Washington, N.Y. Feminist Art Inst., Equinox Theatre, Houston, Chomo Uri Collective, U. Mass., Memphis-Brooks Mus. Art, Several Dancers Core Sch., Atlanta, McGlothlin Ins. Agy., Houston, Cameron Petroleum Co., Houston, Emdyne, Inc., Women's Studio Workshop, N.Y. Designer numerous art therapeutic programs for children; designer and mask-maker numerous artistic and theatrical performances; exhbns. of artistic work to numerous museums and cultural instns. throughout U.S., Mex. and China; designer, writer Bilingual Sci. Curriculum Houston Zoo, 1994. Jesse H. Jones Found. scholar, 1961-65; recipient Presdl. Commendation by Pres. Johnson for Service to U.S. and Chile, 1968; named Outstanding Young Woman of Am., OYWA Press, Chgo., 1970; Sum Arts grantee for sculpture The Matriarch as Phoenix, 1981; Shell Found. grantee for performance of Thanatopsis, 1983, grantee Ruth Chevon Found., Inc., 1987, Change, Inc., N.Y.C., 1987, Adolph and Esther Gottlieb Found., 1988; Lamar Found. grantee, 1989; Impact II Developer grantee, 1990-91; Bus. Com. for Ednl. Excellence grantee, 1991-92, 94-96; Title VII Edn. Project grantee U. Houston, 1991-92; endowed chair to design and implement program for immigrant and refugee children, I Have a Dream Found., 1991-92, endowed chair to continue program for immigrant & refugee children Mid. Sch. Initiative Funds, Houston Ind. Sch. Dist., 1992-96. Mem. Artists Equity Assn., Contemporary Arts Mus. (Houston). Roman Catholic. Address: 2112 Dunlavy St Houston TX 77006-1704

DANKWORTH, MARGARET ANNE, management consultant; b. Bellaire, Ohio, July 22, 1920; d. Charles Henry and Annie Harvey (Parks) D. BA, Ohio Wesleyan U., 1942; MA, NYU, 1949; postgrad., Mich. State U., 1960. Cert. assn. mgr. Bus. mgr. Nat. Recreation Assn., N.Y.C., 1948-50; dist. rep. Nat. Recreation Assn., Toledo, Ohio, 1950-58; asst. exec. dir. Am. Inst. of Pk. Execs., Ogle Bay Park, W.Va., 1958-66; advt. mgr., pub. rels. dir. Nat. Recreation and Pks. Assn., Washington, 1966-71; exec. dir. Am. Assn. Zool. Pks. and Aquariums, Wheeling, W.Va., 1958-75; cons. Am. Inst. for Leisure, Wheeling, W.Va., 1985—; owner Historic Morristown, Ohio, 1975—; founder Nat. Sch. for Zool. Adminstrn., 1975—; bd. dirs. Buckeye Savs. Bank. Editor Parks and Recreation Mag., 1964-66; founder, editor AAZPA Newsletter, 1966-75. Bd. dirs. St. Clairsville Pub. Libr., 1988—. Lt. USNR, 1943-46, ret., 1980. Mem. Historic Morristown Pres. Assn. (sr. bd. 1988—), Questers Nat. Trail (bd. dirs.), Ohio Historic Soc., Nat. Trust for Historic Preservation, Tues. Night Club, Delta Gamma (pres. 1988-92). Republican. Methodist. Home: 145 Crisswill Rd Saint Clairsville OH 43950-1415 Office: Historic Morristown PO Box 335 Saint Clairsville OH 43950-0335

DANLEY, STEPHANIE A., television news operations manager; b. Jacksonville, Fla., June 5, 1961; d. Robert John Steven and Patricia Arianne (Twiggs) McGreevy; m. Edward William Danley, Oct. 6, 1986. BS, U. Fla., 1983. Promotion producer WVFT-TV 5, Gainesville, Fla., 1983; traffic and ops. dir. WFSV-TV 11, Tallahassee, Fla., 1983-84; video editor WJKS-TV 17, Jacksonville, Fla., 1984-87, assignment editor, 1987-89; sr. editor WTLV-TV 12, Jacksonville, Fla., 1989-94, news operation mgr., 1994—. Named Vol. of Yr., Museum of Sci. & History, Jacksonville, 1994. Home: 11021 Challeux Dr S Jacksonville FL 32225 Office: WTLV-TV 12 1070 E Adams St Jacksonville FL 32202

DANNA, JO J., publisher, author, anthropologist; b. N.Y.C.; d. Lucy (Macaluso) D.; m. David Pender (div. 1961). BA, Hunter Coll., 1948; MA, Columbia U., 1964, PhD, 1974. Elem. sch. tchr. N.Y.C. Bd. Edn., 1956-65; advisor to founder, asst. to dir. Villaggio Del Superdotato, Sicily, Italy, 1967-70; asst. prof. Hofstra U., 1970; asst. prof. anthropology Baldwin Wallace Coll., Berea, Ohio, 1971-73, No. Ill. U., 1974; dir., writer ethnic studies curriculum edn. dept. NYU, Albany, 1975-76; asst. prof. La Trobe U., Melbourne, Australia, 1976-79; author, 1982—; pub. Palomino Press, N.Y.C., 1983—; founder Network Ind. Pubs. Greater N.Y.; mem. Inst. of Immigration and Ethnic Studies, La Trobe U., Melbourne, Australia, 1978. Contbr. articles to profl. jours. Mem. Good Neighbour Coun. of Melbourne, Australia, 1977. Mem. Pubs. Mktg. Assn., Com. Sml. Mag. Editors and Pubs., MENSA, N.Y. Acad. Scis. Home and Office: 86-07 144th St Briarwood NY 11435-3119

DANNER, BLYTHE KATHARINE, actress; b. Phila., 1944; d. Harry Earl and Katharine D.; m. Bruce W. Paltrow, Dec. 14, 1969; children: Gwyneth Kate, Jake, Laura. B.A. in Drama, Bard Coll., 1965, D.F.A. (hon.), 1981; L.H.D. (hon.), Hobart-Smith Coll., 1981. Appeared as Laura in Glass Menagerie, 1965; repertory at Theatre Co. Boston, The Knack, and 7 new Am. Plays, 1965-66; appeared as Helena in repertory Midsummer Night's Dream, Trinity Sq. Playhouse, R.I.; appeared as Irena in repertory Three Sisters, Trinity Sq. Playhouse, R.I., 1967; with Lincoln Ctr. Repertory Co. in Summertree, 1968, Cyrano de Bergerac, 1968, Elise in the Miser, 1969 (Theatre World award); appeared on Broadway as Jill Tanner in Butterflies Are Free (Tony award 1971); also appeared in Major Barbara, 1971, Twelfth Night, 1972, The Seagull, 1974, Ring Around The Moon, 1975, Betrayal, 1980 (Tony award nominee), Blithe Spirit, 1987, A Streetcar Named Desire, 1988, Sylvia, 1995, Moonlight, 1995; TV appearances include To Confuse the Angel (with Lee J. Cobb), George M. (with Joel Grey), 1970, Doctor Cook's Garden (with Bing Crosby), To Be Young, Gifted and Black, 1971, F. Scott Fitzgerald and 'The Last of the Belles', 1974, The Seagull, 1975, Eccentricities of a Nightingale, 1976, The Scarecrow, Adam's Rib; TV movies include Dr Cook's Garden, 1971, F. Scott Fitzgerald and "The Last of the Belles", 1974, Sidekicks, 1974, A Love Affair: Eleanor and Lou Gehrig, 1978, Are You in the House Alone?, 1978, Roots: The Next Generations, 1979, Inside the Third Reich, 1982, In Defense of Kids, 1983, Helen Keller-The Miracle Continues, 1984, Guilty Conscience, 1985, A Streetcar Named Desire, 1988, Tattinger's, 1988, Judgment, 1990, Never Forget, 1991, Cruel Doubt, 1992, Getting Up and Going Home, 1992; motion picture appearances include 1776, 1972, To Kill a Clown, 1972, Lovin' Molly, 1974, Hearts of the West, 1975, Futureworld, 1976, The Great Santini, 1980, Too Far to Go, 1982, Man, Woman, And Child, 1983, Brighton Beach Memoirs, 1986, Another Woman, 1988, Mr. and Mrs. Bridge, 1990, Alice, 1990, The Prince of Tides, 1991, Husbands and Wives, 1992, To Wong Foo, Thanks for Everything, Julie Newmar, 1995. Recipient Theatre World award, 1969; Best Actress award Vevey Film Festival, Switzerland, 1982. *

DANNER, PATSY ANN (MRS. C. M. MEYER), congresswoman; b. Louisville, Ky., Jan. 13, 1934; d. Henry J. and Catherine M. (Shaheen) Berrer; m. Lavon Danner, Feb. 12, 1951 (div.); children: Stephen, Stephanie, Shane, Shavonne.; m. C.M. Meyer, Dec. 30, 1982. Student, Hannibal-LaGrange Coll., 1952; B.A. in Polit. Sci. cum laude, N.E. Mo. State U., 1972. Dist. asst. to Congressman Jerry Litton, Kansas City, Mo., 1973-76; fed. co-chmn. Ozarks Regional Commn., Washington, 1977-81; mem. Mo. State Senate, 1983-1992, 103rd Congress from 6th Mo. dist., 1993—; mem. internat. rels. com., transp. and infrastructure com. Roman Catholic. Home: 6 Nantucket Ct Smithville MO 64089-9605 Office: US House of Representatives Office of House Members 1323 Longworth Washington DC 20515*

D'ANNIBALLE, PRISCILLA LUCILLE, contracting company executive; b. Martins Ferry, Ohio, Oct. 28, 1950; d. James Louis and Smyrna Isabell (Prieto) D'A; m. Terrence E. Holdren. BE, U. Toledo, 1973. Credit mgr. Kabat Distbg. Co., Toledo, 1973-80; comml. ops. officer Ohio Citizens Bank, Toledo, 1980-81, credit officer, 1981-82, mktg. officer, 1982-83, mortgage banking officer, 1983-85; owner, pres. D'Ann Enterprises, Inc. dba Paul Davis Systems, Holland, Ohio, 1985—; pres. district V Paul Davis Systems, Toledo, 1992-95, mem. nat. exec. com., 1992-95, treas. nat. exec. com., 1994-95; chmn. arbitration com. Paul Davis Systems, 1991. Mem. fund drive United Way, Toledo, 1982, Jr. Achievement, Toledo, 1983; bd. dirs. Voluntary Action Ctr., Toledo, 1981-82. Mem. Nat. Assn. Credit Mgmt. (bd. dirs. 1981-87, bd. dirs. Ednl. Forum 1976-82, pres. 1980, Credit Person of Yr. award 1982, Credit Exec. of Yr. award 1987), Holland-Springfield C. of C. (exec. bd. dirs. 1990-95, v.p. 1991-92, pres. 1993), Paul Davis Systems Franchisee Assn. (pres. 1991). Roman Catholic. Home: 704 Oak Park Dr Toledo OH 43617-2024 Office: D'Ann Enterprises Inc 1049 S Mccord Rd Holland OH 43528-9596

DANOFF-KRAUS, PAMELA SUE, shopping center development executive; b. Gallup, N.Mex., Aug. 29, 1946; d. Isadore Harry and Armida Catherine (Ceccardi) Danoff; m. Milo Joseph Warner III, Dec. 28, 1968 (div. 1974); m. Robert Warren Kraus, Nov. 30, 1985; 1 child, Jillian Amaris. BA, U. N.Mex., 1968. Lic. in real estate, Calif. Real estate rep. Kaiser Aetna, Newport Beach, Calif., 1975-76; leasing agt. Alexander Haagen Co., Rolling Hills, Calif., 1976-77; dir. leasing Warren Kellogg & Assocs., Newport Beach, 1977-81, Center Devel. Co., Newport Beach, 1981-84; exec. v.p., ptnr. The Von Der Ahe Co., Newport Beach, 1984-86; ptnr. Marketplace Properties, Tustin, Calif., 1986-92; lectr. in field; panelist various convs., univs.; conductor seminars in field. Contbr. articles to profl. jours. Sponsor Californians Working Together to End Hunger and Homelessness, Los Angeles, 1988; mem. Orange County Performing Arts Ctr., 1983-85. Mem. Internat. Coun. Shopping Ctrs. (program chmn. 1987-89, small ctr. devel. com., state dir. pub. rels. and community affairs for Calif., 1989-92, chair pub. rels. and community svc. Western divsn. 1992-95), Calif. Bus. Properties Assn., Calif. Redevel. Assn., Women in Retail Real Estate, Chi Omega. Republican. Roman Catholic. Home: 10182 Brier Ln Santa Ana CA 92705-1531 Office: Danoff Kraus Enterprises 10182 Brier Ln Santa Ana CA 92705-1531

DANTE, HELENA, retired medical professional; b. Welsch Birke, Italy, May 2, 1923; Came to the U.S., 1969; d. Joseph and Helena D.; 1 child, Helena. lic. med. technologist. Founder, supr. Biochem. Procedure Labs., North Hollywood, Calif., 1969-76; histology technologist The Group of Pathologists, Inc., 1979-82; med. technologist Meml. Hosp., Las Vegas, Nev., 1982-83; supr. lab. dept. oncology clinic VA Med. Ctr., Washington, 1984—. Contbr. articles to profl. jours. Recipient Outstanding Rating Cert. award for work in Cancer Rsch., 1986, Best Poet Plaque award APA, 1988, Golden Poet award World of Poetry, 1992. Mem. Nat. Mus. Women in the Arts, Internat. Soc. of Poets (poetry of merit award), Planetary Soc.

D'ANTONIO, CYNTHIA MARIA, sales executive; b. Chgo., Sept. 12, 1956; d. Michael Patrick and Joan Marie (Funk) D'A. BS in Natural Resource Devel., Mich. State U., 1979. Chemist Aqualab, Streamwood, Ill., 1980-83; R&D specialist Seaquist Closures, Crystal Lake, Ill., 1983-87; internat. sales & mktg. exec. Seaquist-Valois Australia, Sydney, 1987-93; internat. sales exec. Pfeiffer Inc., Princeton, N.J., 1993—; speaker in field. Contbr. articles and photos to profl. jours. Mem. Nat. Assn. Female Execs., Plastic Inst. Australia. Republican. Roman Catholic. Home: 5 Bradway Ave Ewing NJ 08618

DANZIG, JOAN, newspaper editor; b. Elmira, N.Y., Mar. 3, 1929; d. George Hamilton and Estelle (Saqui) Danzig; m. Joseph Krasner; children: Susan, Karin. BA, Empire State Coll., 1975; student Elmira Coll., 1946-47; BA, Empire State Coll., 1975. Reporter, society editor Evening Times, Sayre, Pa., 1948-51; asst. feature editor Buffalo News, 1952-60; ; editor Lifestyles sect., Buffalo News, 1960-89; pubs. editor SUNY, Buffalo, 1989—. Mem. bd. Temple Beth Zion Sisterhood. Recipient Page One award Buffalo Newspaper Guild, 1957, 64, Pa. Women's Press Assn., 1949, Outstanding Woman award Cmty. Adv. Council, SUNY-Buffalo, 1984, Coun. for Advancement and Support of Edn., 1991, 92, 93, 94. Mem. Am. Newspaper Guild, Bus. and Profl. Women (charter pres. 1948-50), AAUW, Edn. Writers Am., Sigma Delta Chi.

DANZIG, SHEILA RING, marketing and direct mail executive; b. N.Y.C., Mar. 18, 1948; d. David and Yetta Ring; m. William Harold Danzig, Aug. 11, 1968; children: David Scott, Gregory Charles. BS, CUNY, 1968; PhD, Am. Coastline U., 1996. Tchr. N.Y.C. Bd. Edn., 1968-71; treas. Nat. Success Mktg. Inc., Sunrise, Fla., 1969—; pres. Innovative Comm. Market Cons., Plantation, Fla., 1984-87; cons. Crush Softball Team, Hollywood, Fla., 1986-87, The Eye Ctr., Sunrise, 1986-87, Bus. Expo., Plantation, 1987. Author: You Deserve to be Rich, 1972, A Free Press, 1990, A Better Medical Practice, 1986; author, pub.: Turn Your Computer Into A Money Machine, 1994; contbr. articles to profl. jours. Coord. Day Out program Mills Boys' Shelter, Ft. Lauderdale, Fla., 1985, 87, Put Seat Belts on Sch. Buses program Broward County Sch. Bd., 1986; vol. Miami Children's Hosp.; campaign dir. Help the Handicapped Keep Their Parking Spots, 1987. Mem. Mail Order Bus. Bd., Am. Med. Writers Assn., Plantation Bus. and Profl. Women's Assn., MADD, Speechcrafters. Office: Nat Success Mktg 2574 N University Dr Fort Lauderdale FL 33322-3045

DANZIGER, GERTRUDE SEELIG, metal fabricating executive; b. Chgo., Oct. 24, 1919; d. Isidor and Clara (Fuchs) Seelig; widowed; children: Robert, James. With Homak Mfg. Co., Inc., Chgo., 1966-79; pres. Homak Mfg. Co., Inc., 1979—. Patentee in field.

DANZIGER, PAULA, author; b. U.S., 1944. Tchr. jr. high sch. Author: The Cat Ate My Gymsuit, 1974 (N.J. Inst. of Tech. award 1976, Mass. Children's Book award Edn. Dept. of Salem State Coll. 1979, Nene award Hawaii Assn. of School Librs. and Hawaii Libr. Assn. 1980, Children's Choice award Internat. Reading Assn. and Children's Book Coun. 1980), The Pistachio Prescription, 1978 (Children's Book of Yr. citation Child Study Assn. 1978, Mass. Children's Book award Edn. Dept. of Salem State Coll. 1979, Children's Choice award Internat. Reading Assn. and Children's Book Coun. 1979, Nene award Hawaii Assn. of School Librs. and Hawaii Libr. Assn. 1980, Ariz. Young Reader award 1983), Can You Sue Your Parents for Malpractice?, 1979 (Children's Choice award Internat. Reading Assn. and Children's Book Coun. 1980, N.J. Inst. of Tech. award 1980, Land of Enchantment award N. Mex. Libr. Assn. 1982), There's a Bat in Bunk Five, 1980 (Children's Choice award Internat. Reading Assn. and Children's Book Coun. 1981, CRABbery award Prince George's County Meml. Librs. 1982, Young Reader's medal 1984), The Divorce Express, 1982 (Children's Choice award Internat. Reading Assn. and Children's Book Coun. 1983, Parents' Choice award for lit. Parents' Choice Found. 1982, Woodward Park School Annual Book award 1983, S.C. Young Adult Book award S.C. Assn. of School Librs. 1985), It's an Aardvark-Eat-Turtle World, 1985 (Parents' Choice award for lit. Parents' Choice Found. 1985, Children's Book of Yr. citation Child Study Assn. 1985), This Place Has No Atmosphere, 1986, Remember Me to Harold Square, 1987, Everyone Else's Parents Said Yes, 1989, Make Like a Tree and Leave, 1990, Not for a Billion Gazillion Dollars, 1992, Earth to Matthew, 1992, Thames Doesn't Rhyme with James, 1994, Amber Brown Is Not a Crayon, 1994, You Can't Eat Your Chicken Pox, Amber Brown, 1995. Address: care G.P. Putnam's Sons The Putnam & Grosset Group 200 Madison Ave New York NY 10016-3903*

DANZIGER, TERRY LEBLANG, public relations and marketing consultant; b. Jan. 20, 1933; d. Leon Leventhal and Dorothy Leblang; m. Arthur Lewis Danziger, Mar. 29, 1953; children: Robin Danziger-Ross, Stephen. Student, Syracuse U., 1950-52, C.W. Post Coll., 1962-66; BA in Psychology, Empire State Coll., 1974. Advt. copywriter, account exec. Grey Adv., Foote, Cone & Belding, Kaplan & Bruck, and others, N.Y.C., 1952-55; editorial writer Syosset (N.Y.) Tribune, 1956-62; pres. Mail Arts Co., Syosset, 1962-68; exec. dir. Nassau Easter Seal Soc., Crippled Children and Adults, Inc., Albertson, N.Y., 1968-74; pres. TLD Enterprises, Syosset, Bethpage, N.Y., 1974-77; regional dir. Telequin Ltd., N.Y.C., 1977-78; state pub. rels. dir., regional campaign dir. Arthritis Found. Fla., Miami, Ft. Lauderdale, 1978-79; pub. rels. dir. FPA Corp., Pompano Beach, Fla., 1979-81; pres. PR Mktg. Concepts, Boca Raton, Fla., 1980—. Adv. coun. NCCJ. Mem. Am. Mktg. Assn. (bd. dirs.), Pub. Rels. Soc. Am. (counselors acad.), Am. Bus. Women's Assn., Pub. Rels. Soc. Fla. (v.p.), Profl. Resource Network, Psi Chi. Office: PR Mktg Concepts 1280 S Powerline Rd Ste 120 Pompano Beach FL 33069

DANZIS, ROSE MARIE, emeritus college president; b. Adrian, Pa.; d. Paul A. and Josephine (Bugala) Manger; m. James Gordon Channing, Jan. 24, 1954 (dec. 1973); children: Rose Marie Buhrman, Lorraine Genieczko; m. Sidney Danzis, June 1, 1986. Diploma, Jersey City Hosp. Sch. Nursing, 1949; B.S., N.Y. U., 1954; M.A., Columbia U., 1961, M.Ed., 1971, Ed.D., 1973. Staff nurse, asst. supr. Public Health Nursing Service, Jersey City, 1949-55; dir. health and recreation, clin. coordinator, asso. dir. nursing edn. Charles E. Gregory Sch. Nursing, Perth Amboy (N.J.) Gen. Hosp., 1958-66; chmn. dept. nurse edn., dir. health techs., dean div. health techs. Middlesex County Coll., Edison, N.J., 1966-78; pres. Middlesex County Coll., 1978-86; ret.; Mem. Middlesex County Comprehensive Health Planning Council, 1973-75, N.Y. Com. Regents External Degree in Nursing, 1972-80, Council on Continuing Edn. for Allied Health Personnel, N.J.; Regional Med. Program, 1968-71; chmn. N.J. Health Professions Edn. Adv. Council, N.J. Dept. Higher Edn., 1979-82, chmn. nursing subcom., 1975-78; mem. health careers com. J.F. Kennedy Hosp., 1972-75; chmn. Middlesex County Coll. Assembly, 1975-77; mem. Pres.'s Adv. Com. Sch. Allied Health, Coll. Medicine and Dentistry of N.J., 1976-79; commr. Middle States Assn. of Colls. and Schs.; chmn. Commn. High Edn., 1984-85; mem. liaison com. Am. Assn. Community and Jr. Colls. and Nat. League for Nursing, 1978-82; chmn. acad. affairs com. N.J. Council of Community Coll., pres., 1978-82; trustee Nat. Bank of N.J., 1979-81; exec. com. Acad. Pres.'s, Am. Assn. Community and Jr. Colls.; also exec. com. Internat./Intercultural Consortium. Contbr. articles to profl. jours. Recipient Torch of Liberty award Anti-Defamation League, 1981, Disting. Service award U. Medicine and Dentistry of N.J. Sch. Health Related Professions, 1983; named to Hall of Fame, Perth Amboy High Sch., 1985. Mem. Council of County Coll. Presidents, Am. Nurses Assn., Nat. League for Nursing, Am. Soc. Allied Health Professions, Am. Council on Edn., Am. Assn. Community and Jr. Colls. (bd. dirs. 1984-86), Coll. Consortium for Internat. Studies., Jersey City Sch. Nursing Alumni Assn., N.Y. U. Alumni Assn., Tchrs. Coll., Columbia Alumni Assn., Kappa Delta Pi. Home: 32 Troy Dr Short Hills NJ 07078-1334

DARBY, BARBARA ANN-LOFTHOUSE, chemical technician; b. Phila., Sept. 15, 1961; d. Robert William and Lina Evelyn (James) Lofthouse; m. Joseph Francis Darby, Dec. 23, 1988; children: Robert Lofthouse, Joseph. GED, Phila., 1982. Cert. biocides operator; indsl. firefighter. Chem. operator Rohm & Haas, Phila., 1992-95; chem. technician Rohm & Haas, La Porte, Tex., 1995—. Active World Wildlife Fund, Washington, 1994-95, Clear Lake Ind. Sch. Dist. PTA, 1995, Nature Conservancy, Tex., 1995; vol. United Way Campaign, Rohm & Haas Plants, 1992-95. Lutheran. Home: 1749 Hialeah Seabrook TX 77586 Office: Rohm & Haas Bay Port Biocides 13300 Bay Area Blvd La Porte TX 77572

DARBY, JOANNE TYNDALE (JAYE DARBY), arts and humanities educator; b. Tucson, Sept. 22, 1948; d. Robert Porter Smith and Joanne Inloes Snow-Smith; stepchildren: Margaret Loutrel, David Michael. BA, U. Ariz., 1972; MEd, U. Calif., L.A., 1986, PhD, 1996. Cert. secondary tchr., gifted and talented tchr., Calif. Tchr. English, chmn. dept. Las Virgenes Unified Sch. Dist., Calabasas, Calif., 1979-82; tchr. English and gifted and talented edn. Las Virgenes Unified Sch.Dist., Calabasas, Calif., 1983-84; sch. improvement coord./lang. arts/social studies/drama tchr Las Virgenes Unified Sch. Dist., Calabasas, Calif., 1991-92; tchr. English and gifted and talented edn. Beverly Hills (Calif.) Unified Sch. Dist., 1982-83, 84-89, English and drama tchr., 1994; tchr., cons. Calif. Lit. Project, San Diego, 1985-87; cons., free lance editor L.A., 1977—; dir. Shakespeare edn. and festivals project Folger Libr., Washington, 1990-91; field work supr. tchr. edn. program Ctr. X, Grad. Sch. Edn. and Info. Studies, UCLA, 1992-96, Ctr. X postdoctoral scholar, tchr. edn. program, 1996—; cons. arts and edn., L.A., 1991—. Contbr. articles to profl. pubs. Mem. Am. Alliance for Theatre and Edn., Am. Ednl. Rsch. Assn., Nat. Coun. Tchrs. English, Phi Beta Kappa, Phi Beta Phi, Alpha Lambda Delta. Home: 972 Hilgard Ave Apt 310 Los Angeles CA 90024-3066

D'ARCANGELO, MARCIA DIANE, educational media producer; b. Meadville, Pa., May 16, 1945; d. Terrence Benjamin and Eileene Marie (Judy) Darcangelo; m. Thomas Brown Andrews V, Sept. 16, 1989. BS in Chemistry, Grove City Coll., 1967. Info. specialist Eastman Kodak Co., Rochester, N.Y., 1967-68; singer/dancer Kids Next Door-Young Ams. Orgn. (Katand Prodns.), L.A., 1968-69, Stand Up and Cheer TV Show, The Johnny Mann Singers, L.A., 1970-74; singer, dancer, actor John Brown's Body AEA Nat. Tour, Fitzgerald Prodns., L.A., 1975-76; singer, dancer The Perry Como Show-Roncom Prodns., 1977-82; med. news journalist Physicians Radio Network, N.Y.C., 1983-84; prodn. asst., prodn. coord. ASCD, Alexandria, Va., 1985-86, producer, sr. producer, 1987-88, mgr. media prodns., 1989—; cons. Holbrook & Kellogg, Falls Church, Va., 1990, Developmental Studies Ctr., San Ramon, Calif., 1991, Soc. for Preservation of Social Security and Medicare, Washington, 1991. Composer 4 mus. pieces (words and music); co-author 20 tng. manuals; author/co-author 41 video-based tchr. tng. programs, articles. Recipient award of merit VFW, 1971, Jack Kennedy Alumni Achievement award Grove City Coll. Alumni Assn., 1984, Clarion award Women in Comm., 1991, 6 Cine Golden Eagle awards Coun. on Internat. Nontheatrical Events, 1991, 92, 93, 94, Silver Apple award Nat. Ednl. Film and Video Festival, 1991, 93, Bronze Apple award, 1993, Silver Screen award and Cert. for Creative Excellence U.S. Internat. Film and Video Festival, 1993, Disting. Achievement award and Best of Category Ednl. Press Assn. Am., 1994. Mem. SAG, AFTRA, NAFE, AAUW, ASCD, ASTD, Am. Guild Variety Artists, Actors Equity Assn., Nat. Staff Devel. Coun., Internat. TV Assn., Internat. Interactive Comm. Soc., Women in Film and Video Internat.

DARCE, SHIRL JOHNSON, computer sales director; b. New Orleans, Feb. 11, 1964; d. Mervin L. and Virginia A. (Scandirato) Johnson; m. Ralph James Darce, Jr., July 16, 1983. A in Computer Programming, Phillips Jr. Coll., Metairie, La., 1983. Tech. support person Amann Bus. Machines, New Orleans, 1983-84; computer saleswoman Computer Terminal, New Orleans, 1984-85, Compumark, Metairie, 1985-86; v.p. Value Bus. Ctr., Metairie, 1986-94; gen. mgr. PC Warehouse, Metairie, 1994—; cons. City of New Orleans, 1992-95, State of La., 1988—. Office: PC Warehouse 2222 S Clearview Pky B2 Metairie LA 70001

DARDEN-SIMPSON, BARBARA L., library director; b. Cleve., Apr. 6, 1947; d. Curley and Cora (Chambliss) Brown; m. Joseph S. Darden; children: Michelle, Crystal, Twilla. BS, Ohio State U., 1967; MS in Ednl. Media, Kent. State U. (Ohio), 1971, MLS, 1971. Adminstrv. supr. Cleve. pub. schs., 1968-72; libr. Cuyahoga C.C., Cleve., 1972-75, coord., 1975-77, interim dir., 1977-78, asst. dean, 1978-80, dir., 1980-84; dir. libr. Kean Coll., Union, N.J., 1984—; cons. Dembsy Assocs., Boston, 1967-81; editl. cons. Max Pub. Co.,

N.Y.C., 1967-81; cons. reader U.S. Office Edn., Washington, 1979-80; editl. cons. Jossey-Bass Pub. Co., 1979, Cons. editor Probe, 1975, Sch. Media Ctr., 1968, Booklist, 1969; contbr. articles to profl. jours. Bd. dirs. N.J. Adv. Bd. on the Status of Women, 1988, Africana Studies, 1988, N.J. State Libr. Adv. Bd., 1996; bd. dirs. N.J. Ednl. Activities Task Force Libr. Com. Recipient Phillips award Kent State U., 1970. Mem. ALA (chmn. pay equity com. 1996), Higher Edn. Reps., N.J. Acad. Libr. Network (chmn. 1987, bd. dirs. 1995—), Coun. N.J. Coll. Librs. (pres. 1987—), N.J. Libr. Assn., Oral History Soc., N.J. Hist. Soc., Jr. League (Cleve. vice chmn. 1981, 83), Concerned Parents Club (pres. 1984), Women's City Club. Avocations: music, reading. Office: Kean Coll Libr Morris Ave Union NJ 07083

DARESTA, PAMELA BEAGLE, artist; b. Flint, Mich., Oct. 4, 1949; d. Harold Edward and Peggy Jean (Packer) Beagle; m. William Leroy Guest, Jan. 8, 1971 (div. Jan. 1979); m. Andrew Matteu Daresta, Feb. 14, 1982; 1 child, Christopher Kiel. Grad., Ringling Sch. of Art, Sarasota, Fla., 1970. Art instr. Hambrick Elem. Sch., Stone Mountain, Ga., 1986-90; artist instr. Chastain Art Ctr./City of Atlanta, 1975-90; mem. Fulton County Arts Coun., Atlanta, 1984-96; artist-in-residence Ga. Coun. for the Arts, Atlanta, 1984-96, St. Joseph Sch., Marietta, Ga., 1990-96; mem. mus. adv. bd. Marietta Cobb Mus. of Art, 1995. Artist: (hist. murals) McRae/Helena, Ga., 1995, Pineview, Ga., 1994, Dublin, Ga., 1995, Irwinton, Ga., 1996. Vol. YWCA Marietta, 1995, Atlanta Olympics, 1996; artists Art Papers Auction, Atlanta, 1993-95. Recipient Artist-Initiated Grant, Ga. Coun. for the Arts, Installation Fulton County Cen. Libr., 1984, Mural Grant Project, Fulton County Arts Coun. and Edn., 1996. Mem. Ga. Citizens for the Arts. Home: 1975 Clearwater Dr SE Marietta GA 30067

DARGER, JENNIFER W., lawyer; b. Salt Lake City, Nov. 1, 1960. BS magna cum laude, U. Utah, 1982; JD, Brigham Young U., 1984. Bar: Utah 1985, Ohio 1986, N.Y. 1989. Ptnr. Anderson, Kill, Olick, Oshinsky, P.C., N.Y.C. Mem. ABA, N.Y. State Bar Assn., Ohio State Bar Assn., Nat. Moot Ct. Team (bd. advocates), Phi Beta Kappa. Office: Anderson Kill Olick Oshinsky PC 1251 Avenue of the Americas New York NY 10020-1182*

DARKOVICH, SHARON MARIE, nurse administrator; b. Ft. Wayne, Ind., Dec. 10, 1949; d. Gerald Antone LaCanne and Ida Eileen (Bowman) LaCanne Cutler; m. Robert Eliot Ness, July 17, 1971 (dec. Aug. 1976); m. Paul Darkovich, Jan. 23, 1981 (div. May 1994); 1 child, Amy Elizabeth. BS in Nursing, Case Western Res. U., 1973, BA in Psychology, 1978; cert. in advanced bioethics, Cleve. State U., 1990, MA in Philosophy & Bioethics, 1994. RN, Ohio. Staff nurse Univ. Hosps., Cleve., 1973, asst. head nurse, 1973-76; quality improvement coord. St. Luke's Med. Ctr., Cleve., 1976-83, 84—, dir. nursing, 1983-84. cons. to long-term care facilities, 1986-92, pressure ulcer dressing devel. B.F. Goodrich Co., 1988-92; JCAHO coord., 1993—; cons. to long term care facilities, 1989-93, cons. to ambulatory faculty for JCAHO Accreditation, 1994; cons. to cmty. hosp. med. staff, bylaws and JCAHO, 1996; adj. instr. U. Akron, Northeast Ohio U. Coll. Medicine. Mem. ANA, Greater Cleve. Nurses Assn. (mem. dist. coun. on practice, 1982-84), Sigma Theta Tau. Avocations: reading, needlework, sewing, camping.

DARLING, LYNDA KAREN, secondary education educator; b. Portland, Oreg., Oct. 25, 1949; d. Howard Wayne and Ruth Eileen (Russell) D.; m. Scott Reagen Hannigan, Feb. 14, 1975. BS, Portland State U., 1971, MS, 1976. Cert. basic integrated sci., std. extreme learning problems, std. reading. Reading tchr. Vocat. Village H.S.-Portland (Oreg.) Pub. Schs., 1972—; mem. Vocat. Village H.S. Citizen Adv. Com., Portland, 1980—; co-founder Read-Rite Assocs., Portland, 1982—. Coach Jr. Bowlers, Portland, 1993—. Recipient Outstanding Support to Spl. Needs Students award Nat. Assn. Vocat. Edn. Spl. Needs Pers., Portland, 1982; named Secondary Alternative Educator of Yr., Oreg. Assn. for Alternatives in Edn., 1990. Mem. Internat. Reading Assn., Oreg. Assn. Learning Disabilities, Portland Assn. Tchrs. (mem. legis. com. 1983-86, bd. mem. tchrs. voice in politics bd. 1984-86), Phi Kappa Phi. Office: Vocat Village HS 8020 NE Tillamook St Portland OR 97213-6655

DARLINGTON, DIANA ATTARDO, psychologist, marketing specialist; b. Hartford, Conn., July 25, 1939; d. Salvatore Attardo and Salvatrice Cartelli; m. Joseph B. Darlington, III, Aug. 6, 1960 (div. 1974). BA in Psychology summa cum laude, CUNY, 1978, MA in Gen. Psychology, 1980, MPhil in Social and Personality Psychology, 1986, PhD in Social and Personality Psychology, 1995. Cons. psychologist Robert Linn Med. Assocs., N.Y.C., 1980-90; adj. lectr. Lehman Coll., CUNY, N.Y.C., 1980-90; adj. asst. prof. Iona Coll., New Rochelle, N.Y., 1986—; v.p. customer rels., human resource mgr. Jordan Intercom Systems Inc., Bronx, N.Y., 1984—. Lectr. on psychology topics cmty. orgns. and hosps., N.Y.C. and Westchester County, 1980—, including lectures on Women and Stress, St. John's Hosp., Yonkers, N.Y., 1995. Mem. Benjamin Franklin Democratic Club, Bronx, 1974—. Mem. APA, NAFE, N.Y. State Psychol. Assn. (sec., treas. acad. divsn. 1995—), N.Y. League Fortune 500 Bus. and Profl. Women, N.Y. Acad. Scis., Riverdale Mental Health Assn. (bd. dirs. 1995—). Home: 2575 Palisade Ave Apt 3J Bronx NY 10463 Office: Jordan Intercom Systems Inc 295 W 231 St Bronx NY 10463

DARLINGTON, JUDITH MABEL, clinical social worker, Christian counselor; b. Deckerville, Mich., Nov. 29, 1942; d. Wallace and Mabel Lillian (Rich) Cole; m. Clare Robert Darlington, Dec. 15, 1962; children: Debra Lynn, Dawn Elizabeth. BA, Mich. State U., 1962; MSW, U. Mich., 1983. Tchr. Limestone (Maine) Presque Isle Schs., 1963-64; substitute tchr. Crestwood Sch. Dist., Dearborn Heights, Mich., 1971-74; monitor, tchr. Renewing Life Ministries, Annandale, Va., 1976-82; clin. social worker Westland (Mich.) Counseling Svc., 1983-84; family therapist, counselor Family Svc. of Detroit and Wayne County, Wyandotte, Mich., 1984-86; specialist substance abuse Plymouth (Mich.) Family Svc., 1986-87; exec. dir. Christian Conciliation Svc. of S.E. Mich., Detroit, 1987-90; pvt. practice clin. social worker/family therapist Brighton, Mich., 1990—; speaker in field. Mem. NASW (cert.), Am. Assn. Christian Counselors (charter), Christian Women's Club (chmn. Livonia chpt. 1981—), Inst. for Christian Conciliation, Kappa Delta Pi. Presbyterian. Home: 7911 Debora Dr Brighton MI 48116-9462 Office: 8137 W Grand River Ave Ste C Brighton MI 48116

DARNELL, SUSAN LAURA BROWNE, career officer; b. Milw., Mar. 11, 1955; d. William George Jr. and Jean Marie (Gable) Browne; m. Kevin Scott Charles Darnell, Oct. 4, 1984; children: Emily Elizabeth Browne, Katherine Maureen Browne. BSN, U. Md., 1982; MS in sys. mgmt., U. So. Calif., Okinawa, Japan, 1988. Cert. RN, Aeronautical Rating of Navigator. Commd. 2d lt. USAF, 1982, advanced through grades to maj., 1995; Army spl. 7th Army Soldiers Chorus, Heidelberg, 1975-78; AWACS navigator 964 AWAC Sqaudron, Tinker AFB, Okal., 1983-85; instr. navigator 961 AWAC Squadron, Kadena, Japan, 1985-90; flight comdr. 451 Flying Training Squadron, Mather AFB, Calif., 1990-92; chief current ops. 12 Ops. Support Squadron, Randolph AFB, Tex., 1992-94; asst. ops. officer 12 Ops. Support Squadron, Randolph AFB, Tex., 1994-95; asst. chief comdr. Action Group 12 FTW, Randolph AFB, Tex., 1995; plans officer 612 ASOS, Howard AB, Panama, 1996—; pub. speaker Randolph Pub. Affairs, San Antonio, Tex., 1994-96. Asst. leader Girl Scouts U.S., 1992-96. Recipient Appreciation award Girl Scouts of U.S., San Antonio, 1996. Mem. Air Forces Assn. (life), Women Mil. Aviators, Inc., Women Mil. Svc. for Am.Meml. Home: PSC 1 Box 963 APO AA 34001 Office: Howard AB 612 ASOS APO AA 34001

DARNELL-ELLIS, SUE ELLEN, educational administrator; b. Frankfort, Ky., Feb. 6, 1958; d. James Edwin Williams and Wilma (Linderman) Cassibry; 1 child, Seth Michael Darnell Jr. BS in Math., Murray State U., 1980, MA in Teaching, 1984. Cert. in adminstrn. and supervision, supr. of instrn., sci. supervision, Ky. Tchr. math. and sci. Marshall County Schs., Calvert City, Ky., 1980-85; edn. specialist Marshall County Schs., Benton, Ky., 1985-87; tchr. math., space edn. specialist Paducah (Ky.) Ind. Schs., 1987-89; dir. statewide space edn. program Ky. Dept. Edn., Frankfort, 1989-91, cons. state sci. curriculum, 1991-93; specialist curriculum and staff devel. Nat. Aeronautics and Space Adminstrn. Hdqs., Washington, 1993—; nat. faculty Challenger Ctr., charter mem., 1986—. Named Woman of Yr. BPW, Benton, Ky., 1985, Christa McAuliffe Nat. Tchr. of Yr. Air Force Assn., 1990, Nat. Tchr. of Yr. Nat. Congress on Aviation & Space, 1991. Mem. Nat. Sci. Tchrs. Assn. (regional dir., program chair 1982—, Recognition 1992), Murray State Univ. Alumni Bd. (bd. dirs. 1992—), Alpha Delta Kappa (Recognition 1992). Home: 1033 Pueblo Trl Frankfort KY 40601-2528 Office: NASA Code FE 300 E St SW Washington DC 20546-0001

DA ROZA, VICTORIA CECILIA, human resources administrator; b. East Orange, N.J., Aug. 30, 1945; d. Victor and Cynthia Helen (Krupa) Hawkins; m. Thomas Howard Kaminski, Aug. 28, 1971 (div. 1977); 1 child, Sarah Hawkins; m. Robert Anthony da Roza, Nov. 25, 1983. BA, U. Mich., 1967; MA, U. Mo., 1968. Contract compliance mgr. City of San Diego, 1972-75; v.p. personnel Bank of Calif., San Francisco, 1975-77; with human resources Lawrence Livermore (Calif.) Nat. Lab., 1978-86; pvt. cons. Victoria Kaminski-da Roza & Assocs., 1986—; lectr. in field; videotape workshop program on mid-career planning used by IEEE. Contbr. numerous articles to profl. jours. Mem. social policy com. City of Livermore, 1982. Mem. Am. Soc. Tng. and Devel., Western Gerontol. Soc. (planning com. Older Worker Track 1983), Gerontol. Soc. Am. Home and Office: 385 Borica Dr Danville CA 94526-5457

DARR, CAROL C., lawyer; b. Apr. 24, 1951; d. Patt Marks and Justine (DeCorse) Darr; m. Albert Louis May III Dec. 19, 1992. BA, Memphis State U., 1973, JD, 1976; M.Litt, Christ's Coll., Cambridge U., 1995. Bar: Tenn. 1977, D.C. 1981. Atty. Fed. Election Commn., 1976-77; asst. counsel U.S. Senate Com. on Rules & Adminstrn., 1977-79; dep. gen counsel Carter/Mondale Presidential Com., 1979-81; in house counsel Dem. Nat. Com., 1981-82; assoc. Skadden, Arps, Slate, Meagher & Flom, 1983-85; chief counsel Dukakis/Bentsen Com., Inc., 1987-91; gen. counsel Dem. Nat. Com., 1991-92; with Clinton/Gore Transition Com., 1992-93; actg. gen. counsel, dep. gen. counsel U.S. Dept. Commerce, 1993-94; assoc. Adminstrn. Nat. Telecom. and Info. Agy., Office Internat. Affairs, 1994—. Author: Political Parties, Presidential Campaigns, and National Party Conventions, 1992; Contributions and Expenditures by National, State, and Local Party Conventions, 1990; Active Corporate Participation, 1993; Candidates and Parties 1982, Registration and Reporting, 1981. Recipient Memphis State U. Outstanding Young Alumnus award 1982. Mem. ABA, Fed. Bar Assn. (chair. com. on political campaigns and election laws 1983-85. Office: NTIA/Dept Commerce Rm 4720 14th & Constitution Ave NW Washington DC 20230

DARROW, JILL E(LLEN), lawyer; b. N.Y.C., Jan. 6, 1954; d. Milton and Elaine (Sklarin) D.; m. Michael V.P. Marks, May 14, 1987. AB in English, Barnard Coll., 1975; JD, U. Pa., 1978; LLM in Tax Law, NYU, 1983. Bar: Pa. 1978, N.Y. 1979, U.S. Tax Ct. 1982. Assoc. Shearman & Sterling, N.Y.C., 1978-79; assoc. Rosenman & Colin, N.Y.C., 1979-86, ptnr., 1987—. Mem. ABA, N.Y. State Bar Assn., Pa. Bar Assn., Phi Beta Kappa. Home: 860 Fifth Ave New York NY 10021-5856 Office: Rosenman & Colin 575 Madison Ave New York NY 10022-2511

DARROW, KATHARINE PRAGER, lawyer, publishing executive; b. Chgo., Dec. 26, 1943; d. Frank D. and Herta Prager; m. Peter H. Darrow, June 29, 1968; children: Alexander, Jessica, James. AB, U. Chgo., 1965; JD, Columbia U., 1969. Bar: N.Y. 1970. Assoc. N.Y. Times Co., N.Y.C., 1968, staff atty., 1970-71, 73-76, asst. gen. atty., 1976-80, gen. atty., 1980-81, gen. counsel, from 1981, v.p., now sr. v.p., from 1988, now v.p. broadcasting, info. svcs. and corp. devel.; assoc. Gottesman, Evans & Van Merkeanstein, 1971-73. Trustee U. Chgo., from 1982. Mem. ABA, Am. Newspaper Pubs. Assn. (mem. press/bar rels. com.), ABA/Am. Newspaper Pubs. Assn. Joint Task Force, Assn. of Bar of City of N.Y. Office: NY Times Co 229 W 43rd St New York NY 10036-3913*

DARROW, KATHLEEN MICHELLE, psychologist; b. New Brunswick, N.J., Jan. 6, 1949; d. James E. and Margaret M. McKenzie; 1 child, Lara Felicia Darrow. BA, Rutgers U., 1985; MSEd, Bucknell U., 1987. Cert. sch. psychologist. Programmer Salant Corp., N.Y.C., 1980-82; sch. psychologist Midd-West Sch. Dist., Middleburg, Pa., 1987—; therapist Susquehanna Valley Cmty. Care, Lewisburg, Pa., 1988—; cons. team mem. Snyder County Children's Clinic, Middleburg, 1987—. Bd. dirs. battered women's shelter Susquehanna Valley Women in Transition, Lewisburg; exec. com. Parents Anonymous, Snyder and Union Counties, Pa. Mem. APA (assoc.), NOW (state and nat. liaison Snyder, Union and Northumberland counties), Nat. Assn. Sch. Psychologists. Democrat. Presbyterian. Home: 1204 Washington Ave Lewisburg PA 17837-1776 Office: Midd-West Sch Dist 568 E Main St Middleburg PA 17842-1218

DARSALIA, SVETLANA MICHAEL, art curator; b. Shuamta, Soviet Georgia, June 5, 1946; came to the U.S., 1981; d. Michael Vassily and Iraida Feodor (Chernyshova) Tshvaradze; m. Vladimir Matvei Letuchii, May 16, 1966 (div. 1977); 1 child, Marina Vladimir. MA in English and English Lit., Moscow Inst. Fgn. Langs., 1971. Libr. asst. II catalog dept. Doheny Libr. U. So. Calif., L.A., 1981-91; art curator, photographer Gallery 1912 L.A., 1988-90; art dir. George Mayers Gallery, L.A., 1990-91, Sherry Frumkin Gallery, Santa Monica, Calif., 1991-94; art cons. Darsalia Fine Art, L.A., 1994—; art curator Atropia Art Gallery, Hollywood, Calif., 1995-96; Russian tchr. Poly-Langs. Inst., L.A., 1988-90; translator 4th Internationalist, N.Y.C., 1986-91. Contbr. photography to lit. jours. Co-organizer, curator Nonconformist Artists Movement, Moscow, 1975-80. Recipient 3d place award N.Am. Nat. Poetry Competition, 1995. Home: 1022 N Coronado Terr Los Angeles CA 90026

DART, DEBORAH GORDON, artist; b. Princeton, N.J., Oct. 1, 1951; d. Henry Ward and Joyce V. (Switzgable) Gordon; m. John McRae Dart, Dec. 1, 1973; children: Sara M., Alexandra G. Student, Phila. Coll. Art, 1968-69, U. Miami, 1970-71, Ringling Sch. Art, 1971-73. Freelance artist Sarasota, Fla., 1972-86, 95—; contractor Renovation/Rehab. of Hist. and Non-Hist. Homes, Sarasota, 1983-91; v.p. John Ringling Ctr. Found., Sarasota, 1991-95. Illustrations published in New Yorker Mag., Bon Appetit Mag., Yankee Mag. Bd. dirs. City of Sarasota Hist. Preservation Bd., 1989-95, chair, 1992; bd. dirs. Sarasota County Hist. Commn., 1991-93; mem. Sarasota Alliance for Hist. Preservation, v.p., 1987—; mem. Hist. Soc. Sarasota County, v.p., 1986—; mem. Rosemary Cemetery Project, chair, vice chair, 1986-90; mem. Fla. Trust for Hist. Preservation, 1990-96, Preservation Action, 1994-96, Nat. Trust Hist. Preservation, 1990-96.

DART, IRIS RAINER, novelist; m. Steve Wolf (div.); m. Steve Dart; 2 children. Attended, Carnegie-Mellon Inst., Columbia U. Author: The Boys in the Mail Room, 1980, Beaches, 1985, 'Til the Real Thing Comes Along, 1987, I'll Be There, 1991, The Stork Club, 1992, Show Business Kills, 1995; collaborated on episode of TV series That Girl. Office: Elaine Markson Lit Agy 44 Greenwich Ave New York NY 10011*

DART, JUDITH C(ANDELOR) LALKA, lawyer; b. Phila., Dec. 14, 1947; d. Samuel and Helen Margaret (DiVito) Candelor; m. Thomas J. Dart; children: Carolyn, Susan. BS, Drexel U., 1968; MS, Carnegie Mellon U., 1970; JD magna cum laude, Wayne State U., 1973. Bar: Mich. 1973. Assoc. Dickinson, Wright, Moon Van Dusen & Freeman, Detroit, 1973-81, ptnr., 1981-85; gen. counsel, sr. v.p., corp. sec. Comerica Inc., Detroit, 1985-92, gen. counsel, exec. v.p., corp. sec., 1992—. Mem. conf. bd. Coun. on Gen. Counsels; dir. Detroit Club, 1992—; trustee Detroit Bar Found., 1985-93. Fellow ABA (co-chairperson subcoms. secured trans., com. on Uniform Comml. Code, 1987-91), Mich. Bar. Assn., Detroit Bar Assn., Detroit Bar Found. (trustee 1985—, treas. 1985-87), Am. Coll. Comml. Fin. Lawyers, Am. Corp. Counsel Assn. (bd. dirs. Mich. chpt. 1985-88), Detroit Clearing House Assn. (sec.-treas. 1992), Coun. Gen. Counsels (conf. bd.). Office: Comerica Inc Comerica Tower Detroit Ctr 500 Woodward Ave Detroit MI 48226-3423

DARTING, EDITH ANNE, pharmaceutical company coordinator; b. Hillsboro, Kans., Jan. 1, 1945; d. Sammuel E. and Carrie (Swehla) Jewett; m. John Ronald Darting, Aug. 11, 1979; children: Theresa Michelle, Lloyd L., Hope Marie. Grad., Emporia State Tchrs. Coll., 1963-65. Materials insp. Sterling Drug Inc., McPherson, Kans., 1977-78, auditor, 1978-82, coordinator, 1982-94; coord. Sanofi Winthrop, McPherson, 1994—. Mem. NAFE, Am. Soc. Quality Control. Republican. Methodist. Home: 320 N Birch St Hillsboro KS 67063-1135 Office: Sanofi Winthrop Pharm Inc PO Box 1048 Mc Pherson KS 67460-1048

DARVAROVA, ELMIRA, violinist, concertmaster; came to U.S., 1986; MusB, State Conservatory, Sofia, Bulgaria, 1977, MusM, 1979; certificate, Guildhall Sch. Music, London, 1982; artist's diploma, Ind. U., 1987. Concertmaster Plovdiv (Bulgaria) Philharm. Orch., 1979-86, Owensboro (Ky.) Symphony Orch., 1986-88, Evansville (Ind.) Philharm., 1987-88; artistic dir., concertmaster Evansville Chamber Orch., 1987-88; assoc. instr. violin Ind. U. Sch. Music, Bloomington, 1986-88; acting concertmaster Rochester (N.Y.) Philharm., 1988; vis. lectr. Ind. U. Sch. Mus., 1988; guest concertmaster Columbus Symphony Orch., Columbus, Ohio; concermaster Met. Opera Orch., N.Y.C., 1989—, Chgo. Grant Park Symphony, 1990—; founding mem. New World Trio, 1991. Performer recitals and concerts throughout world. Recipient 1st medal internat. competition, Barcelona, Spain, 1979, hon. diploma, prize Tchaikovsky competition, Moscow, 1982, silver medal Viotti internat. competition, Vercelli, Italy, 1984, 3d prize internat. competition, Sion, Switzerland, 1985. Office: Met Opera Orch Lincoln Ctr New York NY 10023

DATCHER, JEWELL ANTOINETTE, health insurance company consultant; b. Detroit, Aug. 21, 1948; d. Mack A. Jr. and Julia Maria (Oliver) McCartha; m. William Jerome Datcher, Sept. 7, 1968; 1 child, Antonia Latrece. BRE cum laude, William Tyndale Coll., Farmington Hills, Mich., 1984; BA in Bus. Adminstrn., Marygrove Coll., Detroit, 1992; MEd in Instnl. Tech., Wayne State U., 1995; postgrad., Word of Faith Internat. Christian Ctr., 1995—. Dir. Christian edn. Detroit Inst. for Bibl. Studies, 1988-89; customer svc. rep. II Blue Cross-Blue Shield Mich., Detroit, 1966-85, sr. trainer, 1985-87, supr. tng. and quality, 1987-89, tech. writer, 1989-90, lead performance analyst, 1990-91, interim supr., team leader, 1992-93, team leader, instnl. developer, 1991-94; project coord. benefit delivery svcs., 1994—; cons., del. Afro-Am. Mennonite Assn., Detroit, 1979; rep. missions tour to Ecuador, S.Am., William Tyndale Coll., 1980. Mem. TMBC Pastor's Chorus. Grosse Pointe Women's Aux. scholar, William Tyndale Coll., 1983, Marygrove scholar Marygrove Coll., 1985-92. Mem. ASTD, NAACP, Nat. Mgmt. Assn., Marygrove Coll. Alumni Assn., William Tyndale Coll. Alumni Assn.

DATCU, IOANA, artist; b. Bucharest, Romania, Apr. 22, 1944; arrived in U.S., 1981; d. Marin and Niculina (Chitescu) D; m. Vasile Porcisanu, Aug. 5, 1967 (div. 1983); 1 child, Isabelle Ioana. BA, Pedagogical Inst., Bucharest, 1967; BFA summa cum laude, U. Minn., 1987, MFA, 1991. Tchr. biology high sch., Argova, Preasna, Romania, 1967-74; photography asst. U. Minn., St. Paul, 1985-86; photographer civil rights dept. City Hall, St. Paul, 1986-87; darkroom supervisor Film in the Cities, St. Paul, 1987-88; gallery asst., curator Paul Whitney Gallery, St. Paul, 1987-91; art instr. Minn. Mus. Am. Art, St. Paul, 1993-94; instr. drawing & painting U. Minn., Mpls., 1996—. One-person exhbns. include Flanders Contemporary Art, Mpls., 1994, Winona (Minn.) State U., 1995, Mont. State U., Billings, 1996, Ea. Washington U., Cheney, 1996, Indpls. Art Ctr., 1996; juried group shows include Historic Trinity, Detroit, 1993, 95, 96, Barrett House Galleries, Poughkeepsie, N.Y.C., 1996, Nash Gallery, Mpls., 1996, Focal Point Gallery, N.Y.C., 1996, New American Paintings Exhibit in Print, Open Studio Press, 1995, Images of the Spirit Traveling Exhibit, 1995—; works represented in CD-Rom collections of Art Comms. Internat., 1995, Artmax Internat., 1995. Grantee Pollock-Krasner Found., 1992, Minn. State Arts Bd., 1994; McKnight Photography fellow, 1992, fellow NEA, 1994-95. Mem. Christians in the Visual Arts. Mem. Eastern Orthodox Ch.

DAUBENAS, JEAN DOROTHY TENBRINCK, librarian, educator; b. N.Y.C.; d. Eduard J.A. and Margaret Dorothy (Schaffner) Tenbrinck; m. Joseph Anthony Daubenas, May 29, 1965. AB, Barnard Coll., 1962; grad. Am. Acad. Dramatic Arts, 1963; MA, N.Y. U., 1965; MLS, U. Ariz., 1972; PhD, U. Utah, 1986. Tchr., Beth Jacob Tchrs. Sem. Am., Bronx, 1965-66; caseworker, Dept. Social Services, N.Y.C., 1966-67; actress Boothbay (Maine) Playhouse, others, 1967-70; reference librarian Ariz. State U., Tempe, 1972-75; asst. librarian, asst. prof. library sci. Avila Coll., Kansas City, Mo., 1979-83; assoc. prof./librarian St. John's U., Jamaica, N.Y., 1983—; grad. asst. U. Utah, 1976-77. N.Y. State Regents scholar, 1958-62, U. Ariz. scholar, 1971-72. Mem. ALA, Actors Equity Assn., AAUP, Theatre Libr. Assn., Assn. Theatre in Higher Edn., Beta Phi Mu, Phi Kappa Phi. Roman Catholic. Office: St Johns U Library 8000 Utopia Pky Jamaica NY 11439-1335

DAUGHERTY, LINDA HAGAMAN, private school executive; b. Denver, Jan. 25, 1940; d. Charles B. and Agnes May (Wall) Hagaman; m. Thomas Daniel Daugherty, Nov. 20, 1965; children: Patrick, Christina Marie. BS in Bus., U. Colo., 1961; postgrad., Tulane U., 1963-64, U. St. Thomas, 1990-91. Sr. systems analyst Lockheed Electronics NASA, Houston, 1966-73; sr. systems cons. TRW Systems Internat., Caracas, Venezuela, 1973-74; sy. systems cons. TRW Systems, L.A., 1974-75; sr. systems analyst Intercomp, Houston, 1979-80; cons. Daugherty Fin. Svcs., Inc., Katy, Tex., 1980-82, pres., 1979-91; mng. ptnr. Motivated Child Learning Ctrs., Katy, 1976—; pres. Williamsburg Country Day Sch., Katy, 1983—, Nottingham Country Day Sch., Katy, 1977—. Pres. Mason Creek Women Reps. Club, Katy, 1980; treas. Nottingham Country Civic Club, Katy, 1979; mem. adv. bd. Nottingham Country Club, 1982-85; co-founder Friends of Archaeology U. St. Thomas, pres., 1991-93; mem. Epiphany Ch. Social Works Commn.; asst. curator Archaeology Gallery, U. St. Thomas. Mem. Houston Archeology Soc., Tex. Archeology Soc., Archaeology Inst. of Am. Roman Catholic. Office: Nottingham Country Day Sch 20303 Kingsland Blvd Katy TX 77450-3010

DAUGHTREY, MARTHA CRAIG, federal judge; b. Covington, Ky., July 21, 1942; d. Spence E. Kerkow and Martha E. (Craig) Piatt; m. Larry G. Daughtrey, Dec. 28, 1962; 1 child, Carran. BA, Vanderbilt U., 1964, JD, 1968. Bar: Tenn. 1968. Pvt. practice Nashville, 1968, asst. U.S. atty., 1968-69, asst. dist. atty., 1969-72; asst. prof. law Vanderbilt U., Nashville, 1972-75; judge Tenn. Ct. Appeals, Nashville, 1975-90; assoc. justice Tenn. Supreme Ct., Nashville, 1990-93; circuit judge U.S. Ct. Appeals (6th cir.), Nashville, 1993—; lectr. law Vanderbilt Law Sch., Nashville, 1975-82, adj. prof., 1988-90; mem. faculty NYU Appellate Judges Seminar, N.Y.C., 1977-90, 94—. Mem. bd. editors ABA Jour., 1995—; contbr. articles to profl. jours. Pres. Women Judges Fund for Justice, 1984-85, 1986-87; active various civic orgns. Recipient Athena award Nat. Athena Program, 1991. Mem. ABA (chmn. appellate judges conf. 1985-86, jud. adminstrv. div. 1989-90, ho. of dels. 1988-91, standing com. on continuing edn. of bar 1992-94, commn. on women in the profession 1994—, bd. editors ABA Jour. 1995—), Tenn. Bar Assn., Nashville Bar Assn. (bd. dirs. 1988-90), Am. Judicature Soc. (bd. dirs. 1988-92), Nat. Assn. Women Judges (pres. 1985-86), Lawyers Assn. for Women (pres. Nashville 1986-87). Office: US Ct Appeals 304 Customs House 701 Broadway Nashville TN 37203-3944

DAUS, VICTORIA LYNN, nurse midwife; b. Cleve.; m. Arthur Steven Daus; 2 children. RN, Luth. Med. Ctr., Cleve., 1975; BSN, St. Louis U., 1982; MSN, U. Ky., 1987; D of Nursing, Case Western Res. U., 1996; postgrad. in nursing, Francis Payne Bolton Sch. Nursing. RN, Mo., Ohio, Ky., NSW, Australia. Nurse newborn nursery, neonatal intensive care nurse, pediatrics nurse Fairview Gen. Hosp., Cleve., 1975-78; neonatal intensive care nurse, neonatal transport nurse Royal Alexandria Hosp. for Children, Sydney, NSW, Australia, 1978-79; midwife Crown Street Women's Hosp., Sydney, 1979-80; labor and delivery nurse, postpartum nurse Deaconess Hosp., Cleve., 1980; neonatal intensive care nurse Cardinal Glennon Meml. Hosp. for Children, St. Louis, 1981-82; labor and delivery nurse Chandler Med. Ctr. U. Ky., Lexington, 1982-83; labor and delivery nurse, tchr. childbirth edn., labor and delivery charge nurse Humana Hosp., Lexington, 1983-85; coord. quality assurance Prince of Wales Hosp. for Children, Sydney, 1986; hosp. floater for coronary care, neurosurg., orthopedics and med., surg. nurse Good Samaritan Hosp., Lexington, 1985-87; clin. instr. obstetrics and pediatrics Lexington C.C., 1988. Mem. Am. Assn. Neurosci. Nurses, Am. Coll. Nurse-Midwives (cert.), Nat. Assn. Nurse Practitioners in Reproductive Health, N.Am. Nursing Diagnosis Assn., Assn. Reproductive Health Profls., Assn. Women's Health, Obstet. and Neonatal Nurses, Sigma Theta Tau. Republican. Roman Catholic.

DAUSCH, LINDA SHERIDAN, librarian; b. Pittsfield, Mass., July 22, 1966; d. Stephen George and Ann Sheridan D. BA in Russian and French Langs., U. Calif., Santa Cruz, 1989; MA in Russian Studies, Ind. U., 1993, MLS, 1993. Bilingual career counselor Jewish Vocat. Svc., Boston, 1989-90;

Slavic cataloger Ctr. for Rsch. Librs., Chgo., 1993-94; reference libr. Chgo. Pub. Libr., 1994—. Mem. ALA, Intellectual Freedom Roundtable, Reference and Adult Svcs. Divsn., Phi Beta Kappa.

DAUSER, KIMBERLY ANN, physician assistant; b. Detroit, Nov. 20, 1947; d. George Leonard and Jeanne (Austin) Wilkie; m. Steven Kent Dauser, Nov. 10, 1983; 1 child, Aaron Thomas. AA, Pensacola Jr. Coll., 1971; BS in Medicine, physician's asst. cert. in medicine, U. Ala., Birmingham, 1976; cert. in mgmt., Am. Mgmt. Assn., 1989; postgrad., U. West Fla., 1995—. Cert. physician's asst. Asst. mgr. Christo's, Gulf Breeze, Fla., 1966-67; teller, bookkeeper loan dept. Bank Gulf Breeze, 1967-72; med. tech. aide USN Hosp., Pensacola, 1972, physician's asst., 1972-73; physician's asst. John Kingsley, MD, Pensacola, 1976, Mountain Comprehensive Health Corp., Whitesburg, Ky., 1976-78; physician's asst. N.W. Fla. Nephrology, Pensacola, 1978-87, med. adminstr., 1987-95; med. adminstr. Nephrology Ctr. of Pensacola, Fla., 1987-95; COO Nephrology Ctr. Inc., Crestview, Pensacola, 1995—, Nephrology Ctr., Inc., Crestview, Pensacola, 1995-96, Nephrology Ctr. Assocs., Pensacola, 1995-96; regional COO Renal Care Group Inc., Pensacola, Fla., 1996—; regional chief ops. ofcr Nephrology Ctr., Inc./Renal Care Group, Inc., Pensacola, 1996—. Fellow Am. Acad. Physician's Assts. (del. nat. mtg. 1978-95), Nat. Commn. on Cert. Physician's Assts., Fla. Acad. Physician's Assts. (mem. jud. com. 1979-80), Natural Wildlife Assn. Republican. Roman Catholic. Office: Nephrology Ctr Inc 1717 N E St Ste 501 Pensacola FL 32501-6334

DAUSMAN, LYNN GIBSON, educational consultant; b. Dayton, Ohio, Oct. 1, 1934; d. Frank Emil and Ida Mae (Gibson) Brown; m. George E. Dausman; 1 child, Amelia Lynn Schaaf. BS in Edn., Miami U., Oxford, Ohio, 1956; MEd in Early Childhood Edn., George Mason U., 1986. Cert. tchr., Ohio. Jr. h.s. tchr. Kettering (Ohio) Pub. Schs., 1956-58; tchr. Fairfax (Va.) Schs., 1968-72; tchr., dir. F.B. Meekins Pre-Sch., Vienna, Va., 1973-94; pvt. tutor Tutorial Svc. Children with Learning Disabilities, Oakton, Va., 1983-85; tchr., asst. to dir. George Mason U. Pre-Sch., Fairfax, 1983-90; summer evaluator Fairfax County, 1989-91; lectr. No. Va. C.C., Alexandria, 1990-94; student tchr. supr. marymount U., Arlington, Va., 1990-94; lectr. Mitchell C.C., Mooresville, N.C., 1995—; cons. Fairfax County Adult Edn., 1983-90, devel. workshops Fairfax County Adult Edn., Falls Church, 1989-90; organizer edn. conf. George Mason U. Day Care Ctr., 1993-94, edn. cons. group Early Childhood Devel. Assn., Oakton, 1992-95; mem. gov. bd. George Mason Pre-Sch., 1983-85, No. Va. Assn. Edn. Young Children, 1985-87; lectr. in field. Author workshop series Parents-Your Child's First Teacher, 1989-90. Vol. Head Start, Oakton, 1970-71, Girl Scouts, Oakton, 1972-73, Meals on Wheels, Oakton, 1975-95, Sr. Citizen League, Mooresville, 1996—; pres. Woman's Club, Fairfax. Named Childcare Profl. of Yr. Fairfax County Bd. Suprs., 1983, Tchr. of Yr. Va. Cooperative Pre Sch. Coun., 1994. Mem. Iredell County's Assn. Edn. Young Children. Home: 134 Yacht Cove Ln Mooresville NC 28115 also: RR 1, Wolfe Island, ON Canada K0H 2Y0

DAVENPORT, DEBORAH MORGAN, physician; b. Phila., May 21, 1948; d. Michel Kerop Mugurdichian and Gloria Anita (Kremens) M.; m. James Whitman Davenport, Jan. 27, 1968; children: Jesse, Christopher, Michael, Andrew. BA, Douglas Coll., 1971; MD, U. Pa., 1975. Diplomate Am. Bd. Ob-gyn. Asst. prof. Sch. Medicine SUNY, Stony Brook, 1983-86, asst. clin. prof. Sch. Medicine, 1986—; pvt. practice 3 Village Ob-Gyn, Setauket, NY, 1983—; mentor Dept. Ob-gyn. Credentials com., Stony Brook, N.Y., 1994—. Contbr. articles to profl. jours. Mem. bd. Suffolk Network of Adolescent Pregnancy, 1982-85; mem. Physicians for Social Responsibility; vol. Unitarian Universalist Svc. Com., Stony Brook, N.Y.; mem. bd. dirs. Planned Parenthood of Suffolk County. Fellow Am. Coll. Ob-Gyn.; mem. Am. Med. Women's Assn. (treas. branch 92, 1988—), N.Am. Menopause Soc. (charter), Phi Beta Kappa, Alpha Omega Alpha. Democrat. Office: 3 Village Ob-Gyn 100 S Jersey Ave East Setauket NY 11733

DAVENPORT, DONA LEE, telecommunications consultant; b. Toledo, May 17, 1931; d. Juston Burns and Opal Thelma (Raines) D. B.A., tchrs.'s cert., U. Mich., 1953; summer postgrad., U. N.C., 1957, N.C. State U., 1958, Queens Coll., 1969. Tchr. Grosse Pointe, Mich., 1953-54, Jr. High Sch., Charlotte, 1955-58; radio-TV coordinator Charlotte Sch. System, 1958-60; co-founder, tchr. Am. Assn. U. Women Spl. Sch. for Academically Talented Children, Charlotte, 1960; radio-TV dir. Charlotte-Mecklenburg Schs., 1960-62; founding mgr. Sta. WTVI, Charlotte, 1962-72, gen. mgr., 1972-77; exec. dir. Sta. WTVI, Inc., Charlotte, 1977-79; telecommunications mgmt. cons. Atlantic Research Corp., 1979—; Chmn. FCC Instructional TV Fixed Service Com. for N.C., 1968-71; Bd. dirs. Pub. Broadcasting Service, 1972-79. Chmn. media libr. and tape ministry Myers Park Bapt. Ch., 1989—, mem. bd. edn., 1989—, mem. sr. minister seach com., 1992-94, deacon 1994—; vol. Belk Heart Ctr., Presbyn. Hosp., 1989—. Named Charlotte's Outstanding Career Woman in Communications, Central Charlotte Assn., 1967; recipient Broadcast Preceptor award Broadcast Industry Conf, 1969; Regent's scholar U. Mich., 1949-53. Mem. AAUW, So. Ednl. Comm. Assn. (dir. 1968-78, treas. 1973-74, vice chmn. 1977-78), Nat. Assn. Ednl. Broadcasters, Am. Women in Radio and TV (recognized as 1st Woman Pub. TV Sta. Mgr. 1980), N.C. Adminstrv. Women in Edn., Delta Kappa Gamma, Alpha Xi Delta. Clubs: Business and Professional Women's (Charlotte); Charlotte-Mecklenburg Republican Women's. Home and Office: 1510 Exeter Rd Charlotte NC 28211-2233

DAVENPORT, DOROTHY DEAN, nurse; b. Grandview, Idaho, Sept. 29, 1924; d. William Christian and Frances Beatrice (Campbell) Forcher; m. Richard Ellis Davenport, May 26, 1946 (dec. May 1982); children: Robert Ray, William Lee, Gary Edward, James Ellis. Student, Walla Walla Coll., 1942-44; ADN, Loma Linda U., 1946, 49-50. RN, W.Va. Office nurse Corona, Calif., 1946-49; nursing educator Jengre (Nigeria) Hosp., 1956-58; home health nurse Appalachian OH-9, Bluefield, W.Va., 1984-86, clinic charge nurse, 1986-89, health edn. tchr., 1989-91, nutrition counselor WIC program, 1995—. Author: Who Found Klippy and Other Stories, 1960, His Guiding Hand, 1993. Trustee, mem. conf. com., mem. fin. com. Mountain View Conf. of Seventh-day Adventists, Parkersburg, W.Va., 1993—; bd. dirs. Valley View Seventh-day Adventist Ch., Bluefield, 1977—. Home: Rt 2 Box 383 BB Bluefield WV 24701 Office: Appalachian OH-9 Rt 2 Box 382 Bluefield WV 24701

DAVENPORT, JUDY LYNNE, property manager; b. Visalia, Calif., Jan. 11, 1951; d. Lillard D. Mills and Alice Louise Line Archer; children from a previous marriage: Eric St. Peter, Angela St. Peter, Adam St. Peter. Cert. in property mgmt., Profl. Sch. Real Estate, 1988. Property mgr. Burgundy Studios, Middletown, Conn., 1985-87; dir. catering Northwoods Atrium Inn, Charleston, S.C., 1987-91; property mgr. Newport Green Assocs., Newport, R.I., 1991—; sec. Newport Condominium Coun., 1991-93. Founder Mil. Families Support Network, Charleston, S.C., 1990-91; pres. Ombudsman Coun., 1984. Mem. NOW. Democrat. Home: 8 Newport Green # B-2 Newport RI 02840 Office: Newport Green 1205 Newport Green Newport RI 02840

DAVENPORT, LINDSAY, professional tennis player; b. Palos Verdes, Calif., June 8, 1976. Profl. tennis player, 1993—. Ranked 3d Doubles (with Chanda Rubin), 1993; recipient 3 career pro singles titles (1) Lucerne, 1993, (2) Brisbane, Lucerne, 1994, 95; named to Olympic Team, Atlanta, 1996, gold medalist women's singles, 1996. Office: US Tennis Assn 1212 Ave of the Americas New York NY 10036 Office: National Tennis Center Flushing Meadow Corona Park NY 11368*

DAVENPORT, NYRA J., social work administrator; b. Dayton, Ohio, Dec. 6, 1951; d. Robert Lee Sr. and Virginia Ruth (Middleton) Cartwright; m. Edgar Davenport, Jr.; children: Jarrod, Justin. AA, Sinclair Coll., 1973; BA, Wright State U., 1975, MS, 1991. Lic. social worker, Ohio. Clk. Wright Patterson AFB, Dayton, 1969; sec. Luth. Ch. Am., Dayton, 1971-74; rehab. specialist City of Dayton, 1976-78; employment specialist Ohio Bur. Employment, Dayton, 1978-79; social worker Dept. Human Svcs., Dayton, 1979-82, Sr. Ctr. of Greater Dayton, 1982; case mgmt. specialist State of Ohio, Columbus, 1982-85; asst. dir., case mgmt. svcs. Montgomery County Bd., Dayton, 1985—; owner, cons. NJO Cons., Dayton, 1988—. Evangelist Christ Temple Apostolic Ch., Dayton, 1987-93; mem. Gov. of Ohio Task Force, 1990; vol. Housing Now!, Dayton and Columbus, 1986, 89, 90, Issue One-Housing, Dayton, 1990, Dayton Mohawks Basketball Program, 1988—; pres. Bethesda Temple, 1993—; founder Davenport Ministries, 1993. Recipient Doer award Dayton Spl. Edn. Ctr., 1986, 90. Mem. AACD, Assn. Adult Devel./Aging, Minority Health and Social Welfare Coalition, Black Family Coalition of Dayton, Ministerial Alliance. Democrat. Home: PO Box 26066 Trotwood OH 45426-0066 Office: 8114 N Main St Dayton OH 45415-1702

DAVENPORT, PAMELA BEAVER, rancher, small business owner; b. Big Spring, Tex., Nov. 18, 1948; d. Frank Jones and Doris Glynn (Wills) Beaver; m. Robert Sampson Davenport, Feb. 2, 1982; 1 child, Danielle. BS in Mktg. and Textiles, Tex. Tech U., 1969, MS, 1970; cert. in spinal orthotics, Northwestern U., 1976. Adminstrv. asst. Tex-Togs, Inc., El Paso, 1971-75; dir. edn. Camp Internat., Jackson, Mich., 1975-79; realtor Tom Carpenter, Realtor, San Angelo, Tex., 1979-83; retailer Davenport Barber & Beauty, San Angelo, 1985-95; owner, mgr. The Little Gym, San Antonio, Tex., 1995—. Copntbr. articles to profl. jours. Vice chmn. adv. bd. San Angelo Recreation Dept., 1987-88; chmn. adv. bd. Recreation Dept., River Stage, 1990; chmn. Tom Green County Adult Literacy Coun., 1989-90; publicity chmn. San Angelo Cultural Affairs Coun., 1986; treas. San Angelo Commun. Hosp. Aux., 1980-82; publicity chmn. Christmas at Old Fort Concho, 1986; mem. Leadership San Angelo. Mem. AAUW (cultural chmn. Tex. bd. 1988-89, pres. 1986-88, chmn. conv. 1984-86). Methodist. Home: 107 Longsford San Antonio TX 78209

DAVID, BARBARA MARIE, medical, surgical nurse; b. Wisconsin Rapids, Wis., Mar. 3, 1935; d. Stanley Spencer and Olga Agatha (Bissig) Stark; m. Russell Paul David, Jan. 19, 1957; children: Dennis James, John Paul. Diploma, St. Joseph's Hosp. Sch. Nursing, Marshfield, Wis., 1956. Cert. med./surg. nurse, clin. nurse 3. Asst. to dir. nursing rsch. St. Joseph's Hosp., Marshfield, Wis., 1966-70, head nurse, ICU, 1964-67, 70-71, staff nurse, 1983—. Mem. ANA, Wis. Nurses Assn. (treas. dist. 18), Acad. Med.-Surg. Nurses, Nat. League Nurses. Home: 2007 S Maple Ave Marshfield WI 54449-4957 Office: St Joseph's Hosp 611 St Joseph Ave Marshfield WI 54449-1898

DAVID, CECILY MARY, pediatrician; b. Ootacumund, Tamilnadu, India, June 27, 1946; came to U.S., 1971; d. T. Samuel and Anne (Kunjamua) George; m. Winston Paul David, Feb. 18, 1973; 1 child, Dilip G. MD, Madras (India) Med. Coll., 1970. Diplomate Am. Bd. Pediatrics. Intern Westchester County Med. Ctr., Valhalla, N.Y., 1971-72, resident, 1972-74; physician Westchester County Dept. Health, White Plains, N.Y., 1974-78, Ossining (N.Y.) Med. Assocs., 1974-78; asst. attending/prof. N.Y. Med. Coll., Valhalla, 1974-78; commd. U.S. Army, 1978—, advanced through grades to col., 1990; staff pediatrician/chief pediat. Keller Army Hosp., West Point, N.Y., 1978-84; chief pediat. Nuernberg (Germany) Hosp., 1984-85, chief exceptional family mem., 1985-87; chief dept. medicine Moncrief Army Hosp., Ft. Jackson, S.C., 1987-88; chief dept. medicine Keller Army Hosp., 1988-90, chief dept. primary care, cmty. medicine, 1990-93; comdr. Kirk-U.S. Army Health Clinic, Aberdeen Proving Ground, Md., 1993—. Active Girl Scouts U.S. Decorated Army Commendation medal, Meritorious Svc. medal with 2 oak leaf clusters. Fellow Am. Acad. Pediats.; mem. Am. Women's Physicians Assn. Methodist. Office: Kirk US Army Health Clinic 2501 Oakington Rd Aberdeen Proving Grd MD 21005

DAVID, CHRISTINE A., artist, marketing consultant; b. Buffalo, N.Y., July 15, 1965. AS, Jamestown (N.Y.) C.C., 1986; BFA, Fredonia (N.Y.) State, 1989; MFA, RIT, Rochester, N.Y., 1991; MBA, St. Bonaventure (N.Y.), 1995. Art therapist The Resource Ctr., Jamestown, N.Y., 1989-90; visual arts dir. The Art Coun. for C.C., Jamestown, 1991-93; gallery owner Emanon Gallery, Jamestown, 1992-94; artist Sirianno Assocs., Jamestown, 1994—; pres. bd. dirs. Grad. Sch. Bd. St. Bonaventure, 1995—. Designer: (illustration) People Mag., 1995 (Pro Com award 1996), Esquire Mag., 1995 (Am. Advtg. award 1996), Rolling Stone Mag., 1996; exhbns. include Horizon Internat. Art Gallery, 1990, Mayor's Pick Show City of Jamestown, 1990, 92. Vol. N.Y. AIDS Col., Am. Assn. for Retarded Children. Recipient Art scholarship Nat. Honor Soc., 1989. Mem. Nat. Assn. Women Artists, Delta Mu Delta. Democrat. Office: Sirianno Assocs 310 Fairmount Ave Jamestown NY 14701

DAVID, LINDA ELLEN, municipal official, former secondary school educator; b. Bklyn., Apr. 7, 1945; d. Joseph and Hannah (Baum) Bergman; m. Barry Ralph Dvid, Nov. 25, 1965; children: Mitchell, Gregg. BA, Bklyn. Coll., 1965; MPA, Pace U., 1982. Dir. support svcs. City of Peekskill, N.Y., 1982-84, asst. to city mgr., 1985-89; exec. to city mgr. City of Yonkers, N.Y., 1989, dir. cmty. devel., 1990, mgr. adminstrn. fin., 1991-92, capital project adminstr., 1992-93; adminstr., clk. Village of North Tarrytown, N.Y., 1994—. Mem. Mcpl. Mgmt. Assn., Internat. City Mgrs. Assn. Office: Village North Tarrytown 28 Beekman Ave North Tarrytown NY 10591

DAVID, LISA D., banker. BA in Russian Studies, Beloit Coll.; MBA in Mktg. and Fin., Columbia U. Asst. v.p. Citibank-Citicorp, N.Y.C.; v.p., sr. group product mgr. Bankers Trust Co.; v.p. nat. electronic products and card svcs. CoreStates Bank, Phila., 1988-91; various positions to sr. v.p. CoreStates Phila. Nat. Bank, 1991—; exec. v.p. responsible for bus. segment mktg.-devel. group CoreStates Bank, Phila. Office: CoreStates Bank 1345 Chestnut St Philadelphia PA 19107

DAVID, MARILYN HATTIE, lawyer, retired military officer; b. Biloxi, Miss., May 22, 1953; d. Walter Edward and Irma Lee (Shattles) D. BS in Psychology cum laude, Duke U., 1975; MA in Criminal Justice, Webster Coll., 1979; JD with honors, Tulane U., 1982; LLM in Govt. Procurement and Acquisition Law, George Washington U., 1996. Bar: Miss. 1982. Commd. 2d lt. USAF, 1975, advanced through grades to lt. col., 1991; base dir. telecom. USAF Security Svc., San Antonio, 1976-77, chief presentations prodn. br., 1977-79; asst. staff judge adv. civil and labor law USAF Air Tng. Command, Biloxi, Miss., 1982-83; asst. staff judge adv. criminal law USAF Air Tng. Command, Biloxi, 1983-84; chief of claims, civilian pers. and fiscal law USAF Pacific Air Force, Kunsan Air Base, Republic of Korea, 1984; area def. counsel USAF Judiciary, Kunsan Air Base, Republic of Korea, 1984-85; staff atty. telecom. law and policy Office of the Chief Regulatory Counsel, Def. Comm. Agy., Washington, 1985-87; trial atty. civilian pers. Air Force Gen. Litigation Divsn., Washington, 1987-90; team leader constant quality improvement tng. USAF Judge Adv. Gen.'s Dept., Washington, 1991-92; trial atty. fed. contract litigation USAF Contract Law Divsn., Washington, 1992-94; dep. dir. acquisition law USAF Devel. and Test Ctr., Fort Walton Beach, Fla., 1994-96; ret., 1996. Decorated Meritorious Svc. medal, Air Force Meritorious Svc. medal with four oak leaf clusters, Air Force Commendation medal, Nat. Def. Svc. medal, Air Force Overseas Ribbon, Air Force Longevity Svc. ribbon with four oak leaf clusters, Air Force Small Arms Expert Marksmanship ribbon, Air Force Tng. ribbon. Mem. NAFE, AAUW, Miss. Bar Assn., Ret. Officers Assn.

DAVID, MARTHA LENA HUFFAKER, real estate agent, former educator; b. Susie, Ky., Feb. 7, 1925; d. Andrew Michael and Nora Marie (Cook) Huffaker; m. William Edward David, June 24, 1952 (div. Jan. 1986); children: Edward Garry, William Andrew, Carolyn Ann, Robert Cook. AB in Music magna cum laude, Georgetown (Ky.) Coll., 1947; postgrad., Vanderbilt U., 1957-58; Spanish cert., Lang. Sch., Costa Rica, 1959; MEd, U. Ga., 1972. Elem. tchr. Wayne County Bd. Edn., Spann, Ky., 1944-45; music tchr. Mason County, Mayslick, Ky., 1947-49, Hikes Grade Sch., Buechel, Ky., 1949-53; English and Spanish tchr. Jefferson (Ga.) High Sch., 1961-63; music and English tchr. Athens (Ga.) Acad., 1967-71; music tchr. Barrow County Bd. Edn., Winder, Ga., 1971-88; real estate agt. South Best Realty, Athens, 1986—; data collector Regional Ednl. Svcs. Agy., Athens and Winder, 19176-78; tchr. music Union Theol. Sem., Buenos Aires, 1957-60. Author: (poems) Parcels of Love, 1980; composer (music plays) The B.B.'s, The Missing Tune, A Dream Come True, The Stars Who Creep Out of Orbit, 1976-86. Active cultural affairs orgns., Athens, 1962—; entertainer nursing homes and civic orgns., Athens, 1962; chmn. cancer drives, heart fund drive United Way, March of Dimes, Athens, 1962—; elder, pianist Christian Ch. Winner regional piano competition Ky. Philharm. Orch., 1946; nominated Tchrs. Hall of Fame, Barrow County, 1981. Mem. Ret. Tchrs. Assn., Writer's Group, Ga. Music Tchrs., Nat. Music Tchrs. Assn., Athens Music Tchrs. Assn. (pres. recital chmn.), Ga. World Orgn. China Painters, Athens Area Porcelain Artists, Women's Mus. Arts (assoc.), Women's Mus. Art (Washington), Touchdown Club, Band Boosters, Alpha Delta Kappa, Delta Omicron (life, scholar 1944). Republican. Mem. Christian Ch. Home: 105 Nassau Ln Athens GA 30607-1456

DAVID, MICHELE MARIE ALINE, physician, researcher; b. Port-au-Prince, Haiti, Apr. 16, 1956; d. Odnell and Aline (Cantave) D. BS, Roosevelt U., 1978; MBA, U. Ill., Chgo., 1985; MD, U. Chgo., 1988; MPH, Harvard U., 1994. Diplomate in internal medicine, pulmonary disease and critical care medicine Am. Bd. Internal Medicine. Resident Columbia Presbyn. Hosp., N.Y.C., 1988-91; pulmonary & critical care fellow Brigham & Women's Hosp., Boston, 1991-95; asst. prof. medicine Sch. Medicine Boston U., 1995—; staff physician Boston City Hosp., 1995—; bd. dirs. Haitian Am. Pub. Health Initiative, Boston. Co-chair social action com. First Parish Brookline, Mass., 1995—. Fellow Am. Coll. Chest Physicians; mem. ATS, MMS, Alpha Omega Assn. Unitarian Universalist. Office: Boston Med Ctr 91 E Concord St 2d Fl Boston MA 02118

DAVIDOW, JENNY JEAN, counselor, writer; b. Santa Monica, Calif., Mar. 25, 1953; d. Ray M. Davidow and Caroline D. (Kos) Lackmann; m. Bret S. Lyon, June 10, 1988. BA, UCLA, 1974; MA, Internat. Coll., Santa Monica, 1981; D Clin. Hypnotherapy, Am. Inst. Hypnotherapy, Santa Ana, Calif., 1994. Cert. clin. hypnotherapist. Pvt. practice counseling, L.A., 1981-92, Santa Cruz, Calif., 1992—; seminar leader, L.A., 1981-92, Santa Cruz, 1992—; bd. dirs. Tidal Wave Press, Santa Cruz; featured guest various TV and radio shows, L.A., 1983-88; featured speaker Whole Life Expo, L.A., 1983-87; mem. Am. Bd. Hypnotherapy, 1989—. Author: Dream Therapy Workbook, 1983, Embracing Your Subconscious, 1996; contbr. articles to various publs.; creator, presenter audiotape collection Comfortable and Capable, 1994. Mem. World Wildlife Fund (ptnr. in conservation 1995), Sierra Club (life). Democrat.

DAVIDSON, ANNE STOWELL, lawyer; b. Rye, N.Y., Feb. 24, 1949; d. Robert Harold and Anne (Breeding) Davidson. B.A. magna cum laude, Smith Coll., 1971; J.D. cum laude, George Washington U., 1974. Bar: D.C. 1975, U.S. Dist. Ct. D.C. 1975, U.S. Ct. Appeals (D.C. cir.) 1975, U.S. Supreme Ct. 1980. Asst. gen. counsel FDA, Rockville, Md., 1974-78; counsel Abbott Labs., North Chicago, Ill., 1978-79; counsel U.S. Pharm. Ops. Schering-Plough Corp., Kenilworth, N.J., 1979-83; sr. counsel Sandoz Pharms. Corp., Inc., East Hanover, N.J., 1983-86, v.p., assoc. gen. counsel, 1987—. Trustee, N.J. Pops Orch. Recipient Dawes Prize Smith Coll., 1971. Mem. ABA, Pharm. Mfrs. Assn., Food and Drug Law Inst., Non-prescription Drug Mfrs. Assn. (govt. affairs com.). Republican. Presbyterian. Club: Smith Coll. (pres. 1981-82). Contbr. articles to profl. jours. Office: Sandoz Pharms Corp 59 State Route 10 East Hanover NJ 07936-1011

DAVIDSON, BETTY ANNE, computer programmer, systems analyst, consultant; b. Miami, Nov. 23, 1939; d. Ernest and Helen (Haisley) Kanrich; m. Donald S. Davidson, Apr. 17, 1966 (div. 1975). BA cum laude, U. Minn., 1960. Cert. in data processing; certified sys. profl. Project mgr. windfall profit tax Cities Svc., Tulsa, Okla., 1980-81, sr. sys. analyst, 1979-81; cons. Deloitte, Haskins & Sells, Tulsa, Okla., 1981-82; programmer, analyst Hillcrest Med. Ctr., Tulsa, Okla., 1982-88; sr. analyst, programmer Phillips Petroleum, Bartlesville, Okla., 1988-92; cons. Hi-Tech Resources, Tulsa, Okla., 1993; programmer Arrow Trucking Co., Tulsa, Okla., 1993—; spkr. on wp tax World Oil and Gas Conf., Dallas, 1981. Bd. dirs. League of Women Voters Metro Tulsa, Okla., 1995—, Hope Unitarian Ch., Tulsa, chair various coms., 1985-95; first pres. Cmty. Unitarian Universalist Congregation, Tulsa, 1996. Mem. Assn. Sys. Mgmt. (chair arrangements 1982-83, directory 1984-85, dir. chpt. svcs. 1986-87).

DAVIDSON, BONNIE JEAN, gymnastics educator, sports management consultant; b. Rockford, Ill., Nov. 19, 1941; d. Edward V. and Pauline Mae (Dubbs) Welliver; m. Glenn Duane Davidson, June 4, 1960 (dec. Oct. 1993); children: Lori Davidson Aamodt, Wendy Davidson Seerup. Student, Rockford Coll., 1965, Rock Valley Coll., Rockford, 1969-77. Founder, owner, dir. Gymnastic Acad. Rockford, 1977-95; pres., dir., owner Springbrook, Ltd., swim and tennis club, Rockford, 1986-95; rep. trampoline and tumbling com. AAU, 1989—; coach nat. and world champion athletes; mgr., judge, head del. U.S.A. gymnastics teams, 1980—; speaker, lectr., clinician in field.; mem. organizing coms. world championships, also others, 1982—. Contbr. World Book Ency. Bd. dirs. U.S. Olympic Com., 1995—, U.S.A. Gymnastics, 1991—; instr. ARC. Named One of Most Interesting People, Rockford mag., 1987; recipient YWCA Janet Lynn Sports award, 1996. Mem. Internat. Fedn. Trampoline and Tumbling (internat. judge, mem. tech. com. 1986—, del. to congress 1976-86), Internat. Fedn. Sports Acrobats (internat. judge), U.S.A. Trampoline and Tumbling Assn. (nat. tumbling chairperson 1980-88, advisor 1988—, Coach of Yr. award 1980, Outstanding Contbn. to the Sport award 1987, 96, Master of Sport award 1989), U.S. Sports Acrobatics Fedn. (v.p. 1984—), Nat. Judges Assn. (exec. dir.). Republican.

DAVIDSON, CATHY NOTARI, English language educator, writer; b. Chgo., June 21, 1949; d. Paul Celestino Notari and Leona (Behnke) Ripes; m. Arnold E. Davidson (div. 1994); 1 stepchild, Charles Russell. BA, Elmhurst Coll., 1970; MA, SUNY, Binghamton, 1973, PhD, 1974; postdoctoral study, U. Chgo., 1975-76; LHD (hon.), Elmhurst Coll., 1989. Instr. St. Bonaventure U., Olean, N.Y., 1974-75; from asst. to full prof. Mich. State U., East Lansing, 1976-89; prof. dept. English Duke U., Durham, N.C., 1989-96, Ruth F. de Varney prof. English, 1996—; vis. prof. Kobe (Japan) Coll., 1980-81, 87-88, Princeton U., 1988-89. Author: The Experimental Fictions of Ambrose Bierce, 1984, Revolution and the Word: The Rise of the Novel in America, 1986, Thirty-Six Views of Mt. Fuji: On Finding Myself in Japan, 1993; editor: The Book of Love: Writers and Their Love Letters, 1992; co-editor: The Lost Tradition: Mothers and Daughters in Literature, 1980, The Art of Margaret Atwood, 1982, The Oxford Book of Women's Writing in the United States, 1994; editor: Reading in America: Literature and Social History, 1989, Charlotte Temple, 1986, The Coquette, 1986; assoc. editor Am. Lit., 1990-91, editor, 1991—; also over 50 articles. Woodrow Wilson fellow, 1970, Woodrow Wilson Dissertation fellowship, 1972, Irving J. Lee Meml. award, 1973, Newberry Libr. Scholar-in-Residence award, 1976, Mich. State Disting. Tchr.-Scholar award, 1979, Mich. State Disting. Faculty award, 1987, Kate B. and Hall James Peterson fellowship, hon. mem. Am. Antiquarian Soc., Worcester, Mass., 1984, Am. Coun. of Learned Socs. grant-in-aid, N.Y., 1986, John Simon Guggenheim Meml. fellowship, N.Y., 1986. Fulbright Sr. fellow, Australia, 1994, Bellagio Ctr. Rockefeller fellow, 1993. Fellow Nat. Humanities Ctr., Am. Coun. Learned Socs.; mem. MLA (exec. com. divsn. late 19th century Am. lit. 1981-86, divsn. early Am. lit. 1987—, mem. del. assembly 1980-86), Am. Studies Assn. (pres. 1993). Office: Duke Univ Dept English 6697 College Station Durham NC 27708

DAVIDSON, EVELYNE MONIQUE, internist; b. Knoxville, Tenn., Apr. 5, 1961; d. Elvyn Verone and Esther M. (Johnson) D. BS, Vanderbilt U., 1983; MD, Ea. Tenn. State U., 1987. Intern New Hanover Meml. Hosp., Wilmington, N.C., 1987-88, resident in internal medicine, 1988-90; pvt. practice, Knoxville, 1990-94; physician Bapt. Primary Care System, 1994—; med. dir. east office Housecall Home Health, Knoxville, 1990—. Mem. AMA, Nat. Med. Assn., Am. Soc. Internal Medicine. Office: 710 N Cherry St Knoxville TN 37914

DAVIDSON, GAIL MARGARET, minister; b. Abilene, Tex., Dec. 27, 1966; d. Ralph Mason and Dorothy Ann (Ayres) D. Student, Tex. Tech. U., 1985-88; BA, U. Ctrl. Fla., 1993; postgrad., Phillips Theol. Sem., 1996. Lic. minister Disciples of Christ Ch. Program coord. Mental Health Assn. Ctrl. Fla., Orlando, 1991-93; youth min. 1st Christian Ch., Cherokee, Okla., 1993-94; intern Ctrl. Christian Ch., Orlando, 1994; chaplain Tampa (Fla.) Gen. Hosp., 1995; pastor Peckham Christian CH., New Kirk, Okla., 1994-96; dir. lay ministries Ctrl. Christian Ch., 1996—; mem. evang. commn. Christian Ch. Okla., Oklahoma City, 1995; deacon Winter Park (Fla.) Christian Ch., 1991-92; del. Gen. Assembly Christian Chs. in U.S. and Can., Pitts., 1995; vol. coord. Winter Park (Fla.) Pub. Libr., 1996—. Reader Clearer Vision Ministry Blind, Orlando, 1992-93. Recipient Bates prize Phillips Theol. Sem., 1994, Christian Bd. Publ. CBP award, 1995. Mem. ACPE, Nat. Intercollegiate Band, Chorister's Guild, Mu Phi Epsilon, Phi Kappa Phi. Democrat.

DAVIDSON, GRACE EVELYN, nursing educator, retired administrator; b. Wabash, Ind., Aug. 2, 1920; d. William Alexander and Jennie Lavinia (Baker) Davidson. Diploma, Columbia Presbyn. Sch. Nursing, 1942; BS, U. Minn., 1948; MA in Teaching, Columbia U., 1954, postgrad. 1961, 63-64. Instr. Sch. Nursing, Columbia U., N.Y.C., 1948-51; assoc. prof. Skidmore Coll., Saratoga Springs, N.Y., 1954-66; asst. adminstr., dir. nursing Univ. Hosp., NYU Med. Ctr., 1966-79, assoc. prof., 1977-79, prof. 1979—; cons. nursing svc. adminstrn., N.Y.C., 1980-88. Contbr. articles to profl. jours. Served to Maj. Army Nurse Corps, 1943-46, World War II, 51-53, Korea, Res., 53-60, Ret. Recipient Alumni Fedn. medal Columbia U., 1981, Plaque for leadership in nursing NYU Med. Ctr., 1983; Grace Davidson award established in her honor NYU, 1991. Mem. AAUW, Nursing Edn. Alumnae Assn. Tchrs. Coll. Columbia U. (achievement award 1977), Am. Nurses Assn., Nat. League Nursing, Columbia U.-Presbyn. Hosp. Sch. Nursing Alumnae Assn. (pres. 1970-76, edn. bd. 1985-93, bd. dirs. 1993—, Disting. Alumnae award 1981), Fedn. Alumni Assn. Columbia U., Ret. Officers Assn., Ret. Army Nurse Corps., The Woman's Club of Dumont, Republican Club of Dumont. Presbyterian. Home: 67 Chestnut St Dumont NJ 07628-3214

DAVIDSON, JEAN DAIL, psychologist; b. Greenville, N.C., May 31, 1930; d. Frank Clifton and Pauline (Fornes) Dail; m. Elmer Hayes Davidson, Sept. 14, 1957; children: Brenda Joy, David Franklin. BA magna cum laude (Nat. Meth. Scholar), Greensboro Coll., 1957; MS (rsch. grantee), Pa. State U., 1963, PhD cand. (Gen. Foods fellow), 1964-65. Cert. psychol. assoc., N.C. Sch. psychometrist Greensboro (N.C.) Pub. Schs., 1958-60; instr. Tex. Technol. U., Lubbock, 1965-66; dir. New World Sch., Oklahoma City, 1966-71; dir. psychol. svcs. Southeastern Mental Health Ctr., Wilmington, N.C., 1971-74; dir. children's outpatient svcs. Edgecombe-Nash Mental Health Ctr., Rocky Mt., N.C., 1974-80; sr. psychologist Franklin County Family Counseling & Mental Health Ctr., Louisburg, N.C., 1980-87; founder, dir., pres. Little People Ednl. Day Care, Chapel Hill, N.C., 1987—; part-time instr. Nash County Tech. Inst., Rocky Mt., 1977-79, Cen. Carolina Community Coll., Silver City, 1988-91, infant/pre-sch. lab sch. steering com. mem., 1991-92. Mem. Com. Early Childhood Degree programs State Dept. Edn., Okla., 1969-70; bd. dirs Heald Start program New Hanover County, Inc., Wilmington, N.C., 1972-74; mem. Pub. Pvt. Ptnrship. Day Care Task Force, Chapel Hill, N.C., 1989-92. Fellow Vanderbilt U., 1957, Gen. Foods Co. fellow Pa. State U., 1963-65, Early Childhood Leadership Devel. Program fellow U. N.C., Chapel Hill., 1994. Mem. Nat. Assn. for Edn. Young Children, N.C. Assn. for Edn. Young Children, N.C. Day Care Assn., Omicron Nu. Methodist. Home: 59 Dogwood Acres Dr Chapel Hill NC 27516-3111 Office: Little People Ednl Day Care 1740 Smith Level Rd Chapel Hill NC 27516-3249

DAVIDSON, JEANNIE, costume designer; b. San Francisco, Mar. 21, 1938; d. Willis H. and Dorothy J. (Starks) Rich; children from previous marriage: David L. Schultz, Mark P. Schultz, Seana Davidson, Michael Davidson; m. Bryan N. St. Germain, June 14, 1980. BA, Stanford (Calif.) U., 1961, postgrad., 1965-68. Resident costume designer Oreg. Shakespearean Festival, Ashland, 1969-91; owner, designer Ravenna Fabric Studio, Inc., Medford, Oreg., 1994—. Designer over 150 prodns. including all 37 of Shakespeare's plays. Recipient numerous awards for excellence in costume design. Mem. U.S. Inst. for Theatre Tech., Phi Beta Kappa.

DAVIDSON, JOAN GATHER, psychologist; b. Long Branch, N.J., Jan. 26, 1934; d. Ralph Paul and Hilde (Bresser) Gather; m. Harry Gene Davidson, Sept. 14, 1957; children: Guy, Marc, Kelly. BA, Shorter Coll., 1956; BA cum laude, U. South Fla., 1982; MS, Fla. Inst. Tech., 1986, PsyD, 1987. Lic. psychologist, Fla., RN, Ga. Clin. instr. Ga. Bapt. Sch. Nursing, Atlanta, 1956-59; dir. nurses Aidmore Hosp., Atlanta, 1959-60; dir. insvc. edn., asst. dir. nurses Bayfront Med. Ctr., St. Petersburg, Fla., 1960; instr. St. Petersburg Jr. Coll., 1971-76; pvt. practice St. Petersburg-Clearwater, 1987—. Mem. Am. Psychol. Assn., Fla. Psychol. Assn., Nat. Register Health Svc. Providers in Psychology, Assn. for Advancement Psychology, Am. Assn. Christian Counselors, Psi Chi, Phi Kappa Phi. Republican. Baptist. Home: 11600 87th Ave Largo FL 34642-3613 Office: 25400 US Highway 19 N Ste 105 Clearwater FL 34623-2143

DAVIDSON, JOY ELAINE, mezzo-soprano; b. Ft. Collins, Colo., Aug. 18, 1940; d. Clarence Wayne and Jessie Ellen (Bogue) Ferguson; m. Robert Scott Davidson, Aug. 9, 1959; children: Lisa Beth, Robert Scott II, Jeremy Fergus, Bonnie Kathleen, Jordan Christian. B.A., Occidental Coll., Los Angeles, 1959; postgrad., Fla. State U., 1961-64. dir. vocal/opera dept. New World Sch. of Arts Coll./Conservatory Divsn., Miami, Fla. 1992—. Debut 1965 with Miami Opera; has performed with Met. Opera, opera cos. throughout U.S. and Can., La Scala, Vienna State Opera, Bayerische State Opera, Lyons (France) Opera, Welsh Opera, Florence (Italy) Opera, Torino (Italy) Opera. (recipient Gold medal Internat. Competition Young Opera Singers, Sofia, Bulgaria 1969), Rio de Janeiro; performed with numerous orchs. including N.Y. Philharm., Los Angeles Philharm., Boston Orch., Pitts. Orch., Columbus (Ohio) Orch.; rec. artist. Named Outstanding Miami Artist at Orange Bowl. Mem. PEO, United Meth. Women, Sigma Alpha Iota, Zeta Tau Zeta. Methodist. Home: 5751 SW 74th Ave Miami FL 33143-1735 Office: Sardos Artist Mgmt Corp 180 W End Ave New York NY 10023-4902 also: Vocal Opera Dept New World Sch Coll Conservatory Divsn 300 NE 2nd Ave Miami FL 33132-2204

DAVIDSON, JULI, creativity consultant, publisher; b. Houston, Aug. 23, 1960; d. Martin J. Davidson and Ruth Marder. Diploma, Park Sch., Brooklandville, Md., 1978; Cert., Richmond Coll., Surrey, Eng., 1978; student, Austin Coll., U. N.Mex, others, 1978-84, Hollywood Film Inst., 1996. Cert. med. terminology and transcription, 1981. Pres. mail order co. Surrenderings, Inc., Albuquerque, 1989-93; owner, artist Juli Davidson Studio Gallery, Albuquerque, 1987-89; freelance writer, editor, photographer Albuquerque, 1985-86; pres., paper artist, writer SI: A Paperworks Gallery, Sante Fe, 1993; exec. adminstr. Albuquerque Art Bus. Assn., 1989; bd. sec. Albuquerque United Artists, 1988; media, entertainment and multimedia creativity cons.; cons. for visuals, aurals and comedy. Pub., editor MCN: Media Creativity Now; pub. creativity products for The Creative Process; cover story author Funny Fiction for Writers Connection, 1996; screenplay and teleplay contest critic S.W. Writers Workshop, 1996; market rsch. theatrical film reviwer Audience Response, 1995; sitcom bible and pilot writer Think Tank Ink Producs, 1995. Recipient 2d and 3d place photography awards Churches in New Mexico Exhibit, 1985, 4th place Colorfest Human Interest category, Colo., 1986; writing award for pub. handmade booklet on dividing and multiplying potted plants Garden Writers Assn. Am., 1993. Mem. Writers Connection. Studio: PO Box 21669-WW Albuquerque NM 87154-1669

DAVIDSON, NANCY ELAINE, county official; b. Ritzville, Wash., Dec. 5, 1946; d. Alfred and Ruby (Wahl) Sackmann; m. James A. Davidson, June 27, 1970; children: Jon Eric, Jeanette Marie. AA, Big Bend Community Coll., Moses Lake, Wash., 1967; BA, Cen. Wash. U., 1969. Cert. mcpl. clk. Recreation supr. City of Moses Lake, 1969-70; auto-tutorial ctr. coord. Big Bend Community Coll., Moses Lake, 1970-72; ch. sec. Bethany Presbyn. Ch., Grandview, Wash., 1978-80; city clk. City of Grandview, Wash., 1980-85; asst. county treas. Yakima (Wash.) County, 1985-91, county treas., 1991—. Pres. Ft. Simcoe coun. Boy Scouts Am., Yakima, 1990-93; mem. City Coun., Grandview, 1976-80. Mem. YWCA, Govt. Fin. Officers Assn., Wash. Assn. County Treas., Yakima Rep. Women's Club, Horizon Club. Presbyterian. Home: PO Box 56 Grandview WA 98930-0056 Office: Yakima County Treas Office PO Box 1408 Yakima WA 98907-1408

DAVIDSON, NOREEN HANNA, financial services company executive; b. Hartford, Conn., Sept. 13, 1950; d. Morris A. and Allene Sullivan (Gotis) Bezzini; m. Herbert L. Davidson, May 27, 1983 (div. 1991); 1 child, Stephanie Wells. BA, Stephens Coll., 1972. Senate intern U.S. Senator Thomas Dodd, Washington, 1970; legis. aide Mo. State Senate, Jefferson City, 1972; liaison econ. stabilization and White House Exec. Office of Pres., Washington, 1972-74; senate staff U.S. Senator Jacob Javitts, Washington, 1974; dir. legislation Nat. Assn. Plumbing, Heating and Cooling Contractors, Washington, 1975-77, Am. Aviation Found., Washington, 1977-81; mgr. nat. sales Nat. Standards, Bethesda, Md., 1981-84; v.p. Great Lakes Investment, Reston, Va., 1984-91; dir., v.p., br. mgr. Meyers, Pollack, Robbins, Inc., McLean, 1991—; mem. adv. bd. Heritage Fin. Corp., McLean, 1988-90. Author, editor Fixed Income newsletter Fin. Mgmt. Group, 1990, 91, Legislative News newsletter Nat. Assn. Plumbing, Heating and Cooling Contractors, 1976. Mem. exec. staff Presdl. Inaugral for Reagan, Washington, 1984, mem. staff, 1980, Presdl. Inaugral for Nixon, Washington, 1972; mem. PTA. Recipient Cert. of Appreciation, Presdl. Inaugral Com., 1984. Mem. Nat. Assn. Security Dealers (cert. series 7, 63, 24), Hunt Club Assn. (fin. advisor), Stephens Coll. Alumni, Hunt Club Girls Club (pres. 1988-89), Rotary Internat. Republican. Roman Catholic. Office: Meyers Pollock Robbins Inc 8280 Greensboro Dr Ste 100 Mc Lean VA 22102-3807

DAVIDSON, NORMA LEWIS, concert violinist, composer, music educator, psychologist; b. Provo, Utah, Oct. 12, 1929; d. Arthur and Mary (Mortimer) Lewis; m. William James Davidson, Dec. 29, 1949; children: Kevin James, Nathanael Arthur. Artist's diploma, Juilliard Sch., N.Y.C., 1950; BS, North Tex. State U., 1962, MS, 1965; MusM, So. Meth. U., 1970. Prof. violin and chamber music Mannes Coll. Music, N.Y.C., 1950-54; prof., artist-in-residence Tex. Womans U., Denton, 1961—; vis. prof. North Tex. State U., Denton, 1968-69; violinist Dallas Symphony Orch., 1955—; violinist, soloist Utah Symphony, Salt Lake City, Ft. Worth Symphony Orch., New Symphony Orch. of N.Y., Richardson Symphony, Wichita Falls Symphony, San Antonio Symphony; assoc. concertmaster Graz (Austria) Symphony, 1990—; soloist movie documentary, Eng., 1987. Numerous concert tours in U.S., Europe, Asia, Mex., Can., 1945—; composer numerous works for voice, violin, viola, string quartet, and chamber music; contbr. articles to profl. jours. Recipient cert. of merit Federated Music Clubs, 1978, 1st prize for composition, 1984; 1st prize for composition Tex. Composers Guild, 1980; rsch. grantee Tex. Womans U., 1979. Mem. APA (assoc.), Am. String Tchrs. Assn., Phi Kappa Phi (internat. rep. for arts, pres. Tex. Womans U. chpt. 1991-93), Sigma Alpha Iota (arts assoc. 1980—), Phi Kappa Phi (nat. rep. for arts 1989-91, editorial bd. Nat. Forum 1994—). Office: Tex Womans U Dept Performing Arts Denton TX 76204

DAVIDSON, RHONDA ELIZABETH, preschool educator; b. Phila., Nov. 26, 1954; d. Charles and Thelma Viola (Porter) Ash.; m. Carl Davidson, June 7, 1974 (div. June 1977). AAS, C.C. Phila., 1984. Market rsch. intern WUSL Radio, Phila., 1983-84; telemarketing rschr. Sears Roebuck Inc., Phila., 1984-86; presch. tchr. Sch. Dist. of Phila., 1986—; bus. cons. M & G Enterprises, Phila., 1984—. Active Girl Scouts U.S., Phila., 1994; majority inspector Dem. Party, Phila., 1993. Mem. ASCD, Assn. for Childhood Edn. Internat. Lutheran. Home: 4534 N Smedley St Philadelphia PA 19140-1145 Office: M & G Enterprises 4534 N Smedley St Philadelphia PA 19140-1145

DAVIDSON, SUZANNE MOURON, lawyer; b. Oxford, Miss., Aug. 5, 1963; d. Bertrand D. Jr. and Barbara Jean (Baca) Mouron; m. Garrison H. Davidson III, Dec. 12, 1987; children: Jane Harrington, Catherine Stender. AB in English Lit., U. Calif., 1985, JD, 1988. Assoc. Peterson, Ross, L.A., 1988-89; asst. litigation counsel Ticor Title Ins., Rosemead, Calif., 1989-91; corp. counsel Forest Lawn, Glendale, Calif., 1991-96. Chair nat. area rush info. Chi Omega, 1988-95; deacon San Marino Cmty. Ch., 1995-96; bd. dirs. San Marino Cmty. Ch. Nursery Sch., 1995-96; mem. Jr. League, Pasadena, Calif., 1989-96. Mem. Calif. State Bar Assn., L.A. County Bar Assn., Pasadena Athletic Club, Salt Air Club. Presbyn. Office: Forest Lawn Company Legal Dept 1712 S Glendale Ave Glendale CA 91205-3320

DAVIDSON, THYRA, artist, sculptor; b. Bklyn., Oct. 15, 1926; m. George Wexler, Jan. 4, 1947; children: Andrew, James, Daniel. Student, Bklyn. Coll., 1943-45, Nat. Acad. Art, 1943-45, Bklyn. Mus. Art Sch., 1946, New Sch. for Social Rsch., 1946. Adj. lectr. Bklyn. Coll., 1973-76, Dutchess C.C., Poughkeepsie, N.Y., 1974, SUNY, New Paltz, 1975-76; graphic artist Hudson Valley Newspapers, Highland, N.Y. One person shows include Schoelkopf Gallery, N.Y.C., 1967, Simon's Rock Coll., Great Barrington, Mass., 1972, Dutchess C.c., 1973, First St. Gallery, N.Y.C., 1972, 75, 79, 82, Mus. of Hudson Highlands, Cornwall, N.Y., 1982, Company Hill Gallery, Kingston, N.Y., 1986; exhibited in group shows at Davis-Long Gallery, N.Y.C., 1977, Schoelkopf Gallery, 1977, 86, Albany (N.Y.) Art Inst., 1973, 84, FAR Gallery, N.Y.C., 1974, SOHO Ctr., N.Y.C., 1976, First St. Gallery, 1984, Chesterwood, Stockbridge, Mass., 1989, Mountain Gallery, New Paltz, 1990, Knowles Gallery, La Jolla, Calif., 1991, 92, Connoisseur Gallery, Rhinebeck, N.Y., 1993, Park West Gallery, Kingston, N.Y., 1995, Watermark-Cargo Gallery, Kingston, N.Y., 1995; represented in permanent collections at Albany Inst. History and Art, SUNY, Albany Art Gallery. Home: 180 Portuese Ln New Paltz NY 12561

DAVIDSON-SHEPARD, GAY, secondary education educator; b. Long Beach, Calif., Dec. 15, 1951; d. Leyton Paul and Ruth Leona (Gritzmaker) Davidson; m. Daniel A. Shepard, June 24, 1983. BA, U. Calif., Irvine, 1972; MA, Columbia Pacific U., 1986. Cert. elem. and secondary edn. tchr. Tchr. mid. sch. Ocean View Sch. Dist., Huntington Beach, Calif., 1973—; team mem. Calif. learning assessment system State Dept. of Edn., Sacramento, 1987—; chief reader Orange County pentathlon and decathlon Orange County Dept. Edn., Costa Mesa, Calif., 1980—; sr. reader new standards State Dept. Edn., Sacramento, 1995—; lang. arts cons. various sch. dists., Calif., 1976—; chief reader Calif. Learning Assessment System, Sacramento, 1993—; sr. reader New Stds., 1995—. Author/cons.: Teacher's Guide for Direct Assessment Writing, 1990; test writer Acad. Pentathlon Test, 1984—, Dist. Lang. Art Proficiency Test, 1980—. Mem. NEA, AAUS, AAUW, Nat. Assn. Tchrs. of English, Calif. Reading Assn., Mensa, Calif. Tchrs. Assn., Ocean View Tchrs. Assn. Democrat. Home: 6782 Rook Dr Huntington Beach CA 92647-5641 Office: Mesa View Sch 17601 Avilla Ln Huntington Beach CA 92647-6612

DAVIES, ALMA (ALMA ROSITA), producer, playwright, lyricist, composer, designer, sculptor; b. Bloemfontein, South Africa; came to U.S., 1949; d. Walter David and Elizabeth (Van der Kar) D.; m. Lee Kaye, Dec. 9, 1956 (dec. 1967); children: Elena-Beth Kaye, Walter Ian Kaye; m. Edwin William Williams, June 22, 1985. Tchr., choreographer Spanish dance ballet Sch. Dance Arts, Carnegie Hall, N.Y.C., 1944-55. Toured with Manhattan Opera Co. in Desert Song, 1946; soloist Dances of Spain, Am. Mus. Natural History, N.Y.C., 1947, Jose Greco Dance Co., Washington, 1954; soloist, choreographer Jacobs Pillow Dance Festival, Mass., 1948, Am. Youth Ballet, N.Y.C., 1951, Radio City Music Hall, N.Y.C., 1953; guest artist, soloist, choreographer Syracuse (N.Y.) Philharm. Orch., 1950; soloist, dancer, actress Voice of Firestone NBC-TV, N.Y.C., 1953; guest artist Simmons Cruise Concert-S.S. Olympia, Caribbean Seas, 1954-55; exhbns. for sculpted 3-D pictures include Schumacher Fabrics, N.Y.C., Warner Bros., others; puppeteer Rose Rivero Charity Showcase, N.Y.C., 1974-80; jewelry designer, 1966-74; author, composer, dir., prodr. musicals: Princessa, 1963, Moon Holiday, 1983, Little Lord, 1985, Dorinmore, 1986, Little Lord Fauntleroy, 1996. Recipient First prize for costume design Beaux Arts Ball, N.Y., 1975, Internat. Beaux Arts Ball, N.Y., 1977. Mem. ASCAP, Dramatists Guild, The Drama League, Comml. Theatre Inst., Internat. Platform Assn., Internat. Soc. Poets (disting.). Office: Alma Davies Prodns 1756 Broadway New York NY 10019-3207

DAVIES, JANE B(ADGER) (MRS. LYN DAVIES), architectural historian; b. Amboy, Ill., Sept. 9, 1913; d. Henry Harold and Clara May (Heermans) Badger; m. Lyn Davies, July 18, 1942 (dec. 1994). BA, Wellesley Coll., 1935; MA, Columbia U., 1942, BLS with high honors, 1944; postgrad., U. Mich., 1936, U. Wis., 1937, 38. Tchr. Monticello Prep. Sch., Godfrey, Ill., 1935-37, Kent Sch. Girls, Denver, 1937-41; reference libr. Columbia Univ. Librs., 1944-50, rare book cataloger, 1951-77; cons. Nat. Trust for Hist. Preservation, 1965, 87-88, 91-94, Smithsonian Inst., 1967, Greensboro (N.C.) Preservation Soc., 1967-70, Historic Green Springs, 1970-73, 82, Llewellyn Park Hist. Dist., 1982-84, Hist. Hudson Valley, 1986-89, Met. Mus. Art, N.Y.C., 1988-92; guest curator, author catalog A.J. Davis and Am. Classicism, Fed. Hall Mus., N.Y.C., 1989; lectr. on Am. archtl. history. Author: intro. Houston Mus. Fine Arts: The Gothic Revival Style in America, 1830-1870, 1976; intro. Alexander Jackson Davis: Rural Residences (1837), 1980; contbr. to Prophet with Honor, A.J. Downing, 1989, Alexander Jackson Davis, American Architect, 1992; editorial asst. Jour. Soc. Archtl. Historians, 1964-65; contbr. articles on Am. archtl. history to mags., jours., symposiums and reference books. Am. Coun. Learned Socs. grantee, 1970, Am. Philos. Soc. grantee, 1970-71; NEH fellow, 1978. Mem. Soc. Archtl. Historians (sec.-treas. N.Y. chpt. 1959-67), Victorian Soc. Am. (adv. com. 1966-76), Nat. Trust Historic Preservation, Friends of Lyndhurst, N.Y. Hist. Soc., Preservation League N.Y. State, Greensboro Preservation Soc. (hon.), Phi Beta Kappa, Beta Phi Mu. Presbyterian. Home: 549 W 123rd St New York NY 10027-5026

DAVIES, JANET KEESE, volunteer; b. Chattanooga, Nov. 18, 1934; d. William Shelton and Peggy (Gosnell) Keese; m. Howard Morgan Smith III, Nov. 24, 1956 (div. Apr., 1969); 1 child, Susan Connally Morgan; m. Richard Blair Davies, Mar. 10, 1971; step children: Richard Blair Jr., Michael Nixon. Student, Goucher Coll., 1952-54; studente, Inst. Tech. y Estudies Super., Monterey, Mexico, 1954 summer; BA with honors, U. Chattanooga, 1956. Tchr. 2d grade John A. Patten Sch., Chattanooga, 1958-59; asst. safe deposit vault custodian Am. Nat. Bank and Trust Co., Chattanooga, 1960-61; welfare worker Hamilton County Dept. of Human Svcs., Chattanooga, 1968-69; computer programmer Provident Life and Accident Ins. Co., Chattanooga, 1969-71; asst. or substitute organist various churches, Chattanooga, Nashville, 1965-78; dir. jr. and middler choirs Christ Episc. Ch., Nashville, 1971-74, dir. jr. choir St. Paul's Episcopal Ch., Franklin, Tenn., 1980-84, dir. St. Dunstan's Children's Choir, St. George's Episcopal Ch., Nashville, 1995; bd. dirs. Nashville chpt. Am. Guild of Organists, 1973-76, mem. steering com. for regional conv., 1974; bd. dirs. Nashville chpt. Choristers Guild, 1980-84. Docent and vol. book keeper Historic Carter House, Franklin, Tenn., 1977-79; docent Travellers Rest Hist. House, Nashville, 1979-82; libr. vol. Harpeth Hall Sch., Nashville, 1977-79; mem. Nashville Symphony Guild, 1971—, regional coun. mem., 1979-83, support drive capt. 1982-83; altar guild mem., choir mem., bd. Episcopal church women, chpt. chair St. Paul's Episcopal Ch., Chattanooga, 1960's; bd. mem. Episcopal Church Women, chpt. chair, 1973-74, vestry 1976-79, jr. warden 1978-79, new mems. com. 1987-89, Christ Ch., Nashville; new mem. com. St. George's Episcopal Ch., Nashville, 1990-91, bd. mem. Episcopal Ch. Women, chpt. chair, 1992-94. Mem. AAUW (bd. dirs. 1992—, parliamentarian Nashville br. 1992-94, treas. 1994-96, pres. 1996—), Ladies Hermitage Assn. (regional hostess 1978-84), Nat. Soc. Colonial Dames Am. in Tenn. (rep. to intermus. coun. of Nashville 1981-82, treas. fin. com. chair, exec. com. mem. 1986-89, long range planning com., bylaws com. 1989-90, historian, exec. com. mem., 1995—), Embroiderers Guild of Am. (bd. dirs. Cheekwood chpt., parliamentarian, bylaws chmn., 1989-91), Iroquois Neighborhood Club (v.p. 1988-89, social co-chair 1990-91, pres. 1992-93, sec-treas. 1994—). Home: 5103 Williamsburg Rd Brentwood TN 37027

DAVILA, ELISA, Spanish language, literature educator; b. Libano, Tolima, Colombia, May 29, 1944; came to U.S., 1974; d. Rafael Antonio Davila and Amalia Parra; m. Bruce Roger Smith, Oct. 17, 1973 (div. 1981). BA, U. Pedagogica Nat., Bogota, Colombia, 1966; MA, U. Pacific, 1972; PhD, U. Calif., Santa Barbara, 1983. Asst. prof. U. Valle, Cali, Colombia, 1968-73; researcher Inst. Colombiano de Pedagogia, Bogota, 1973-73; assoc. U. Calif., Santa Barbara, 1974-78, 78-80; instr. W. Tex. State U., Canyon, Tex., 1978-80, Def. Lang. Inst., Calif., 1981-82; visiting lectr. U. Calif., Santa Cruz, 1982—; assoc. prof. SUNY, New Paltz, 1990—, chair fgn. langs., 1990-94, 96—, dir. Latin Am. studies, 1991—; reader, evaluator N.J. Dept. Higher Edn., Princeton, 1987-89; reader Ednl. Testing Svc., Princeton, 1987-89; acad. dir. Spanish Immersion Inst., Bd. Edn. and Office Mental Health, N.Y.C. and Albany, 1987-90. Received Disting. Tchr. award Alumni Assn., 1996; The Heloise Brainer scholar, 1964, LASPAU scholar, 1968. Mem. MLA, Am. Assn. Tchr. Spanish & Portuguese, Assn. Para la Ensenanza del Espanol, Latin-Am. Studies Assn. Home: 551 Mountain View Ave Hurley NY 12443-5621

DAVILA, NORMA, developmental psychologist and program evaluator; b. Rio Piedras, P.R., Dec. 17, 1962; d. Fernando and Ana (Maldonado) D. BA in Psychology, Yale U., 1985; MA in Behavioral Sci., U. Chgo., 1988, PhD in Psychology, 1991. Asst. edn. coord. Head Start, New Haven, 1984-85; rsch. asst. Disengagement of Talent Project, Chgo., 1985-86; rsch. asst. Chgo. Stress Project, 1986-87, project coord., 1987; sr. pro-analyst Rsch. Pros, Chgo., 1988-89; instr. dept. psychology St. Xavier Coll., Chgo., 1988-89, 90, Roosevelt U., Chgo., 1990-91; asst. prof. dept. psychology U. P.R., Rio Piedras, 1991-96; dir. evaluation PR-SSI Project, Rio Piedras, 1993-95, dir. evaln. and assessment, 1996—; career counselor and career devel. instr. Women Employed, Chgo., 1991. Recipient Trustee's Fellowship U. Chgo., 1985-86, Minority Grad. Incentive Program Fellowship, State of Ill., 1986-89, Dissertation of Yr. Fellowship, Dorothy Danforth Compton Found., 1990-91. Mem. APA, Psychol. Assn. of P.R., Am. Ednl. Rsch. Assn., Am. Evaluators Assn. Office: Dept Psychology U Puerto Rico Rio Piedras PR

DAVILLIER, BRENDA BOZANT, university administrator; b. New Orleans, Nov. 17, 1941; d. Francis Edwin Bozant and Thelma Laura (Laurent) Gath; m. Lloyd Joseph Davillier, June 17, 1961; children: Alisa, Darius (dec.), Gerard (dec.), Jeanne (dec.), Daniel, John. BA, U. New Orleans, 1974, M of Urban and REgional Planning, 1980. Tchr. New Orleans, 1974-76, 87-89; tng. officer Housing Authority of New Orleans, 1976-77; housing and employment counselor Associated Cath. Charities, New Orleans, 1977-79; housing coord. City of New Orleans, 1980-85, dep. dir. for housing, 1986, housing cons., 1981-93; exec. dir. Xavier Triangle NDC, New Orleans, 1993—. Author: Dini's Secret, 1986, (with others) Parachute Shop Blues and other works, 1973, State of Black New Orleans, 1986; author, prodr., dir. Shepherds of the Flock, The Good Witch, 1979-93. Bd. dirs. New Orleans, Police Found., 1996; mem. Mayor's Environ. Adv. Com., New Orleans, 1994—; mem. Overall Econ. Devel. Plan Com., New Orleans, 1994—; mem. Nat. Congress for Cmty. Econ. Devel., mem. pol. subcom., 1995—. Office: Xavier Triangle NDC Box 118-B 7325 Palmetto New Orleans LA 70125

DAVION, ETHEL JOHNSON, school system administrator, curriculum specialist; b. Raleigh, N.C., July 21, 1948; d. John Arthur and Ethel Mae (Morgan) Johnson; m. Joel Davion, Aug. 6, 1988, 1 child, Laura Christal. BA, Livingstone Coll., 1971; MA, Glassboro (N.J.) State U., 1983. Cert. tchr., prin., supr., N.J. Sr. English tchr. Camden (N.J.) Bd. Edn., 1977-81; tchr. of English Westfield (N.J.) Bd. Edn., 1982-85, Union County Regional Dist. 1, Berkeley Heights, N.J., 1981-82, Hillside (N.J.) Bd. Edn., 1985-87; supr. English, lang. arts Irvington (N.J.) Bd. Edn., 1987-92; vice prin. Frank H. Morrell H.S., Irvington, N.J., 1992-95; acting prin. Frank H. Morrell H.S., Irvington, 1996—; writer, researcher Collegiate Rsch. Systems, Camden, 1976-77; participant profl. devel. programs Harvard U., 1989, Notre Dame U., 1990. Author: A Tutorial Approach to Teaching English, 1983, Teachers' Resource Manual, 1987; contbr. articles to jours. Bd. dirs., sec. Emmanuel Tabernacle, Linden, N.J., 1988. Recipient Resolution Town Coun. Irvington, 1992. Fellow N.J. Edn. Assn., Nat. Coun. Tchrs. English; mem. Linden Scholarship Guild (sec. 1985—), Assn. for Supervision and Curriculum Devel., Prin. and Suprs. Assn., Irvington Adminstrs. Assn. (treas.), Internat. Platform Assn., Good Samaritans Club, Obsidian Civic Club (Westfield, historian 1985—). Democrat. Pentecostal.

DAVIS, ADA ROMAINE, nursing educator; b. Cumberland, Md., June 7, 1929; d. Louis Berge and Ethel Lucy (Johnson) Romaine; m. John Francis Davis, Aug. 1, 1953; children: Kevin Murray, Karen Evans-Romaine, William Romaine. Diploma in nursing, Kings County Hosp., Bklyn., 1949; BSN, U. Md., Balt., 1973, MS, 1974; PhD, U. Md., College Park, 1979, postdoctoral student, 1985-89. Cert. editor in life scis. Asst. prof. grad. program U. Md., Balt., 1974-79; chmn. dept. nursing Coll. of Notre Dame, Balt., 1979-82; assoc. dean grad. program Georgetown U. Sch. Nursing, Washington, 1982-87; nurse cons. Health Resources and Svcs. Adminstrn., Rockville, Md., 1987-93, HHS, USPHS, Bur. Health Profls., Rockville, 1987-93; assoc. prof. and dir. undergrad. program Johns Hopkins U. Sch. of Nursing, Balt., 1993—; reviewer Choice, ALA; evaluator methodology and findings for rsch. studies; hist./med. biographer. Editor: Ency. of Home Care for the Elderly, 1995; contbr. articles to nursing jours. Recipient excellent performance award HRSA; rsch. grantee U. Md. Grad. Sch. Mem. ANA (cert. adult nurse practitioner), Soc. for Neoplatonic Studies, Nat. Orgn. Nurse Practitioner Faculties, Am. Acad. Nurse Practitioners, Md. History of Medicine Soc., Soc, for the Social History of Medicine (Oxford U.), N.Y. Acad. Scis., Sigma Theta Tau. Office: 1830 E Monument St Baltimore MD 21205-2114

DAVIS, ANN CALDWELL, history educator; b. Alliance, Ohio, June 3, 1925; d. Arthur Trescott and Jane Caldwell D. BA, Western Reserve U., 1947; MA, Columbia U., 1955; PhD, Columbia Pacific U., 1987. Cert. tchr.,

Ill., Ohio. Pres. The Clio Found. Inc., St. Petersburg, Fla., 1955—; tchr. Supr. Child Enterprise, Evanston, Ill., 1956-60; human rels. coun. U. Chgo., 1957-58, asst., 1961; tchr., dept. chair Evanston Pub. Schs., 1961-85; project English Northwestern U., Evanston, 1963-64; cons. Dist. #65 Sch., Evanston, 1985-90. Presenter, author: (speech) Do-it-Yourself Help For The Top 10%, 1964, The Non-Graded School, 1976, Social Studies Reading & Reference Skills, 1979; author: (video) U.S. & Ill. Constn., 1986. Vol. Meals ON Wheels, Treasure Island, Fla., 1990-94, Pinellas County Schs., Fla., 1991, steering com. St. Petersburg, Fla., 1995, health care chair Older Women's League, St. Petersburg, 1995. Mem. Am. Assn. of U. Women, Orgn. of Am. Historians, Ill. & Nat. Edn. Assn. Office: The Clio Found Inc PO Box 7472 Saint Petersburg FL 33734

DAVIS, ANNALEE C., clinical social worker; b. Bentonville, Ark., July 8, 1944; d. Lloyd Milton and Jesse Alberta (Robe) Conyers; m. Rushton Eric Davis, Aug. 26, 1967 (div. Apr. 1980); children: Michelle Leigh, Rushton Kendrick. BA, Hendrix Coll., 1966; MSW, U. Okla., 1982. Internat. cert. alcohol and drug counselor; diplomate Internat. Acad. Behavioral Medicine, Counseling and Psychotherapy; lic. marriage and family therapist, Okla.; lic. clin. social worker, Okla.; diplomate in clin. social work. Psychiat. intern Tulsa Psychiat. Ctr., 1980-82, postgrad. intern, 1982-83; clin. social worker New Choice, Inc., Tulsa, 1983-85; pvt. practice Tulsa, 1985—; bd. dirs. Associated Ctrs. for Therapy. Head edn. com. Sunbelt Alliance, Tulsa, 1978-80; mem. Fgn. Policy Study Group, Tulsa, 1980-88, LWV, Tulsa, 1978—; mem., tchr. Meth. Ch., Tulsa, 1967-90; bd. dirs. Ctr. Christian Counseling, 1978-88. Mem. NASW (diplomate), Acad. Cert. Social Workers, Am. Assn. Marriage and Family Therapists, Okla. Assn. Social Workers, Okla. Assn. Profl. Counselors, Okla. Assn. Alcohol and Drug Abuse. Democrat. Methodist. Home: 6714 E 76th St Tulsa OK 74133-3422

DAVIS, BARBARA JEAN SIEMENS, service company executive; b. Louisville, Nov. 12, 1931; d. Gustav Adolph Siemens and Alberta Jeanette (McAdams) Simon; m. Donald Elmore Davis, Aug. 4, 1950; children: Dale Montgomery, Gale Sue Davis Beaty. Mktg. and personnel mgr. Kelly Svcs., Louisville, 1962-65; tchr. asst. TV English, Jefferson County Schs., Louisville, 1965-70; wedding and floral designer Wedding Ring, Louisville, 1971-73; owner, designer Nook Flowers and Gifts, Memphis, 1973-75; cons. pub. rels. Dixie Rents, Memphis, 1975-79; div. mgr. pres. Party Concepts, Inc., Memphis, 1980-88; pres. Siemens-Davis Assoc., Cordova, Tenn., 1989-91; cons. Leon Loard, 1992; ficilitator/trainer Motivational Concepts Internat. 1993; pres., CEO, Siemens-Davis Assoc., 1993-94; cons., INTERIM personnel, Montgomery, Ala., 1994-95; chmn. bd. dirs. sdb Greenscape, Fla., 1996—. Author: Wedding Workshop Brides Work Book, 1984., Wedding Party Consultants Certification Program, 1984, Wedding Directors & Party Consultant Program, 1995. Mem. Sales and Mktg. Execs., Am. Rental Assn. (mem. party coun. 1985-88), Nat. Assn. Wedding Cons. (pres. 1983-87); NAFE dir. (Memphis Network, mem. Internat. Platform Assn.). Republican. Presbyterian.

DAVIS, BARBARA JOYCE WIENER, accountant, investment manager, finance educator, consultant; b. Berkeley, Calif., Aug. 28, 1947; d. Milton and Kathryn Gertrude (Weiss) Wiener; 1 child, Scott Evan. BA in Psychology, U. Calif., Davis, 1970; MA in Psychology, San Jose State U., 1986; cert. lifetime teaching credential, U. Calif., Riverside, 1971. Investment mgr. Cupertino, Calif., 1968—; tchr. elem. edn. Santa Clara (Calif.) Unified Sch. Dist., 1971-83; acct. Owl Land Co., Inc., San Leandro, Calif., 1981—, pres.; rsch. and stats. cons. Cupertino, 1984—; tchr. Chabot Coll., Hayward, Calif., 1990-91; tutor stats. San Jose (Calif.) U., 1984-86. Mem. APA, AAUW, NAFE, NOW, Women's Am. Overseas Rehab. Tng., Calif. Psychol. Assn., Santa Clara Psychol. Assn., Mensa, Pacific Grad. Sch. Psychology Round Table. Office: 7608 Erin Way Cupertino CA 95014-4343

DAVIS, BARBARA M(AE), librarian; b. Cranston, R.I., Dec. 23, 1926; d. Harrie S. and Marguerite M. (Cameron) D.; SB in Chemistry, Brown U., 1948; MS in Library Sci., Simmons Coll., 1956. Asst. research librarian research and devel. dept. Cabot Corp., Cambridge, Mass., 1948-57, research librarian, 1957-61, research librarian Billerica (Mass.) Research Center, 1961-68, head tech. info. services, 1968-81, mgr. tech. info. center, 1981-87 . Dir. Cabot Boston Credit Union, 1956-59, 61-64, 72-78, clk., 1961-64, 72-77, v.p., 1977-78. Vol., Lexington Coun. on Aging, 1990—, Lexington Hist. Soc., 1991—; chmn. research com. Greater Boston Young Rep. Club, 1959-61; treas. Women's Rep. Club Lexington, 1988—; committeeperson Lexington Republican Town Com., 1993—. Mem. Am. Chem. Soc. (sec. div. chem. lit. 1961-65), Spl. Libraries Assn. (chmn. Boston chpt. 1965-66, chmn. chemistry div. 1971-72), Simmons Coll. Library Sch. Alumni (v.p. 1965-66). Home: 37 Drummer Boy Way Lexington MA 02173-1200

DAVIS, BEATRICE ANNA KIMSEY, educator, civic worker; b. Oklahoma City, June 23, 1917; d. Carl Cleveland and Beatrice Mary (Rudersdorf) Kimsey; grad. Ward-Belmont Coll., 1938; m. Bruce A. Davis, Jan. 22, 1942; children: Belinda Anne Davis Pillow, Beatrice Annette Davis Orynawka, Beverly Anne Davis Steckler. BA, Vanderbilt U., 1940; MEd, Lamar U., 1973. Personnel interviewer Ft. Sam Houston, San Antonio, 1942; advisor Jr. Achievement, 1974-80; asst. instr. drama Watkins Night Sch., Nashville, 1939-40; substitute tchr. Port Arthur (Tex.) Ind. Sch. Dist., 1950-64; high sch. English tchr. South Park Ind. Sch. Dist., 1964—, head English dept., 1982-85; tchr. Nederland (Tex.) Ind. Sch. Dist., 1948-50. Co-author: Curriculum Guides for Reading, 1973, 81, Curriculum Guides for English, 1980; contbr. articles to mags. Mem. adv. bd. Profl. Resource Group, Houston, 1990; pres. Port Arthur Family Svcs. Am., 1979-81, Women's Orgn. Presbyn. Ch. of Covenant, 1989; v.p. Jefferson High Sch. PTA; bd. dirs. Hughen Sch. for Crippled Children, Gates Meml. Library, PTA of Tyrell Elem. Sch., Port Arthur, Parliamentarians of Port Arthur, Story League of Port Arthur, Jefferson County Hist. Commn.; mem., docent SE Tex. Mus. Art, Beaumont, 1987-90; mem. Community Concert Assn. Port Arthur; pres. Vol. Svc. Coun.; docent McFaddin-Ward House Mus., Beaumont, 1990—, pres. vol. orgn., 1990; mem. Women's Commn. S.E. Tex., 1985-86, Women-Vols. Svc. USNR; bd. dirs. SE Tex. Hist. Commn. 1986-90, Tyrell Library Hist. Preservation, 1988-89; sec. Chpt. CP of P.E.O. Sisterhood, Port Arthur, 1987—, pres., 1993-94, also chaplin; mem. Beaumont Opera Buffs; trustee, membership com., tchr. Presbyn. Ch. of Covenant; bd. dirs. Tyrell Restoration Geneal. Soc., Beaumont, 1987—; vol., book reviewer and reader for civic, social orgns. With USNR, 1942-43. Recipient numerous awards for outstanding civic svc., various ednl. stipends and grants; named Tchr. of Yr. for South Park High Sch., Tex. Agrl. and Mech. U., 1981-82. Mem. NEA, All Tchrs. Assn. Beaumont, Nat. Council Reading Tchrs., S.E. Tex. Council Reading Tchrs., Tex. Assn. for Specialists in Group Work, Sabine-Neches Personnel and Guidance Assn., AAUW (past pres. Port Arthur chpt.), Federated Women's Club (past pres. bd. Port Arthur chpt.), Rosehill Bd. (past pres.), Panhellenic Assn. (past pres. Port Arthur chpt.), Women's Orgn. Symphony Club (past pres.). Choral Club (past pres.), Thalian Drama Group (past v.p.), Heritage Soc., Hist. Soc., Knights of Neches Aux., DAR (regent Col. George Moffett chpt. 1996—, regent 1996—), United Daus. Confederacy (chariperson nat. def., 2d. v.p.), English-Speaking Union U.S., Port Arthur Antique Study Club (pres.), Key Club, Reading Club, Port Arthur Country Club Women's Aux. (past pres.), Sigma Kappa Alumni, Phi Lambda Phi, Phi Delta Kappa. Republican. Home: 2816 35th St Port Arthur TX 77640-2650

DAVIS, CAROL JEANNE, public relations and marketing executive; b. Little Rock, Jan. 23, 1953; d. Harry A. and Rubye Jean (Ezell) Mooney; m. Chris R. Davis, Dec. 9, 1978 (div. May 1990); children: Aaron R., Jordan A. BA in Journalism, U. Ark., Little Rock, 1982. Info. asst. Ark. Farm Bur. Fedn., Little Rock, 1974-82; dir. pub. affairs ARC, Little Rock, 1982-84; dir. informational svcs. Pulaski County Spl. Schs., Little Rock, 1984-86; dir. pub. rels. Brooks-Pollard Co., Little Rock, 1986-88; dir. account svcs. Kirkpatrick-Williams & Assocs., Little Rock, 1988-90; co-owner Holmes Davis Hoffmann, Inc., Little Rock, 1990—. Pres. U. Ark. Little Rock Alumni Assn., 1987-88; chmn. Bryant Pks. Commn., 1991-94; instr. U. Ark. Little Rock Small Bus. Devel. Ctr., 1996. Recipient Cmty. Leadership award Leadership Greater Little Rock, 1992, Disting. Svc. award Ark. Advtg. Fedn., Little Rock, 1990. Mem. Pub. Rels. Soc. Am. (accredited, chmn. accreditation Ark. chpt. 1990—, counselor 1988—, Aluminum award Ark. chpt. 1993, pres. Ark. chpt. 1984—). Methodist. Home: 2011 Cedar Dr Bryant AR 72022 Office: Holmes Davis Hoffmann Inc 221 W 2d St Ste 201 Little Rock AR 72201

DAVIS, CAROL LYN, research consultant, office assistant; b. West Palm Beach, Fla., Oct. 22, 1953; d. Robert Lee and Barbara Jean (Collett) D. BFA, Tex. Christian U., Ft. Worth, 1975, MA in Am. Studies, 1977. R & D product line designer Am. Handicrafts/Merribee Needlearts, Ft. Worth, 1977-81; ceramics/china sales cons. Dillard's, Ft. Worth, 1981-82; dept. mgr. Stripling-Cox, Ft. Worth, 1982-83; freelance ceramic and string art designer, 1982-83; with phase III, IV, V hist. sites inventory of Tarrant County for Hist. Preservation Coun. for Tarrant County (Tex.) and Page, Anderson & Turnbull, Inc., San Francisco, 1983-86; rep. Tarrant County Greater Ft. Worth Housing Starts, Texas Update, Inc., 1987-94, M/PF Rsch., Inc., Dallas, 1989-94; sales office clk. Summer Creek-Hulen Bend subdivsns. Perry Homes, Inc., A Joint Venture, Ft. Worth, 1994—; Mem. mgmt. adv. panel Chem. Week, 1981; alternative precinct election judge Dem. Party, 1994—. Author Pamphlets in field. Mem. Royal Over-Seas League. Democrat. Episcopalian. Home: 7800 Garza Ave Fort Worth TX 76116-7717

DAVIS, CAROLYN ARMENTA, arts organization administrator, curator. BA in Math., Ind. U., 1970. Owner Carolyn Armenta Davis Comms., Chgo., 1974—; founder, pres., curator Design Diaspora, Inc., Chgo., 1990—; bus. comms. specialist to Motorola, Harris Trust & Savings, Baird & Warner, Environ, Inc., Earl L. Neal Assocs., French Govt. Cultural Svcs., Chgo., City of Chgo. Dept. Housing, Urban Getaways: The Ctr. for Arts in Edn., others; guest lectr. Oberlin Coll., Bowling Green State U., Ohio, Latin Sch. Chgo., Rotary Club Wilmette Harbor, Ill., Soc. Black Archs., internat. colloquium Ecole d'Architecture de Normandie, Rouen, France, congress and assembly African Union of Archs., Nairobi, Amerika Haus, Munich. Contbr. articles to Interiors & Sources. Bd. dirs. Art in Pub. Places, Inc., 1988—, Chgo. Athenaeum: Mus. Architecture & Deisgn, 1991-94; v.p. bd. dirs. Lincoln Park Renewal Co., 1987—; mem., docent Chgo Arch. Found. Mem. Old Town Triangle Assn. (bd. dirs. 1990-93), Architecture and Design Soc. of Art Inst. Chgo., Landmarks Preservation Coun. Ill., Internat. Viss. Ctr. Address: 235 W Eugenie St #M7 Chicago IL 60614

DAVIS, CAROLYNE KAHLE, health care consultant; b. Penn Yan, N.Y., Jan. 31, 1932; d. Paul Frederick Kahle and Alice Edgerton (Kahle) Cargill; m. Ott Howard Davis, June 28, 1953; 1 son, Richard Ott. BS in Nursing, Johns Hopkins U., 1954; MS in Nursing, Syracuse U., 1965, PhD in Higher Edn. Adminstrn., 1972; LittD (hon.), Georgetown U., 1982; DSc (hon.), U. Evansville, 1982, U. Medicine & Dentistry N.J., 1984; LLD (hon.), Adelphi U., 1985; LHD (hon.), Med. U. S.C., 1986; DSc (hon.), Eastern Mich. U., 1989; DHL (hon.), Med. Coll. of N.Y., 1992. Chmn. baccalaureate nursing program Syracuse U., 1969-73; dean sch. nursing U. Mich., Ann Arbor, 1973-75, prof. nursing and edn., 1973-81, assoc. v.p. acad. affairs, 1975-81; adminstr. Health Care Fin. Adminstrn. HHS, Washington, 1981-85; cons. Ernst & Whinney, Washington, 1985-89, Ernst & Young, Washington, 1989—; bd. dirs. Pharm. Mktg. Svcs., Inc., Scottsdale, Ariz., Beckman Inst., Irvine, Calif., Prudential Ins. Co. of Am., Newark, Merck, Rahway, N.J., Sci. Applications Internat. Corp., San Diego. Mem. editorial bd. Nursing Economics, Pitman, N.J.; contbr. more than 100 articles to profl. jours. Bd. dirs. ARC, 1988-94; trustee U. Pa. Med. Ctr., Phila., 1987—; vice chmn. bd. trustees Nat. Rehab. Hosp., 1993-96; mem. health adv. com. GAO, 1990—. Recipient Disting. Alumnus award Johns Hopkins U., 1981, Alumni award Syracuse U. Sch. Edn., 1983, Alumni award U. Mich., 1984, Spl. Recognition award Assn. Am. Med. Colls., 1986; named one of the Top Young Leaders in Am. Acad. Mag., 1978. Mem. NAS Inst. Medicine, Nat. League for Nursing (bd. dirs. 1979-81, chmn. Cmty. Health Accreditation Program 1987-92, Presdl. award 1993). Sigma Theta Tau, Phi Delta Kappa. Republican. Office: Ernst & Young 1225 Connecticut Ave NW Washington DC 20036-2604

DAVIS, CAROLYNE KOVAL, lawyer; b. Toronto, Ont., Can., July 23, 1967; came to U.S., 1981; d. Robert John and Yvonne B. (Dumas) Koval; m. Matthew O'Neal Davis, Apr. 17, 1993. BA, So. Meth. U., 1988; JD, U. of Houston, 1991. Assoc. Tyler, Pearson and Sanders, Houston, 1991; pvt. practice Humble, Tex., 1991—. Mem. ABA, State Bar Assn. Tex., Houston Bar Assn., Houston Young Alumni Bar Assn., So. Meth. U. Young Alumni Assn. Roman Catholic. Home: 7718 Par Five Drive Humble TX 77346

DAVIS, CHRISTINE JEANES, art educator; b. Greenville, S.C., Aug. 31, 1951; d. James Gregg and Bertha Joanne (Sawicz) Jeanes; m. Dennis Thomas Davis, Nov. 25, 1970. BA in Art Edn., U. S.C., 1972, MAT, 1978; EdD in Art Edn., U. Ga., 1992. Cert. art educator. Tchr. art Woodruff (S.C.) Jr. H.S., 1974-75, Fairforest (S.C.) Jr. H.S., 1975-77; tchr. art Paul M. Dorman H.S., Spartanburg, S.C., 1977—, chmn. dept., 1984-93; cons. The Coll. Bd., Atlanta, 1992—, S.C. Arts Commn., 1987—. Editor: Nat. Art Honor Soc. News, 1989-93; artist Juried Electronic Gallery, 1989-92 (Hon. Mention 1993, Best of Show 1994), Internat. Colored Pencil Soc., S.C. State Mus., 1992, 93 (2d Place 1992); exhibited in group shows at Greenville County Mus. Art, 1979, Spartanburg County Art Tchrs., 1989, 90, 91, Guild S.C. Artists, 1991, N.C. Nat. Bank, 1992, S.C. Dept. Edn., 1992, S.C. State Mus., 1992; contbr. artwork to The Best of Colored Pencil 2, 3 Creative Colored Pencil. Recipient Marie Walsh Sharpe Tchr.-Artist Program award, 1994; named S.C. Outstanding Tchr., 1988. Mem. NEA, ASCD, Nat. Art Edn. Assn. (S.E. Region Secondary Dir. 1988-93, award 1995), Upstate Visual Artists, Colored Pencil Soc. Am., S.C. Edn. Assn., Nat. Art Edn. Assn., S.C. Art Edn. Assn. (sec. 1986-90, secondary coord. 1983-84, Tchr. of Yr. 1986, 87, Outstanding Art Educator 1989), S.C. Alliance for Arts Edn., S.C. Arts Alliance. Presbyterian. Home: 1071 River Rd Greer SC 29651-8197 Office: Paul M Dorman H S 1491 Ezell Blvd Spartanburg SC 29301-1588

DAVIS, CLARICE MCDONALD, lawyer; b. New Orleans, Jan. 20, 1941; d. James A. and Helen J. (Ross) McDonald. BA, U. Tex., 1962, MA, 1964; JD, So. Meth. U., 1968. Bar: Tex. 1969, U.S. Dist. Ct. (no. dist.) Tex. 1970, U.S. Ct. Appeals (5th cir.) 1971, U.S. Supreme Ct. 1973. Law clk. to presiding justice U.S. Ct. Appeals (5th cir.), Dallas, 1969-71; from assoc. to ptnr. Akin, Gump, Strauss, Hauer & Feld, Dallas, 1971—; comments editor Southwestern Law Jour., 1967-68; instr. Southern Methodist Univ. Sch. of Law, 1968-69. Bd. visitors So. Meth. U., Dallas, 1979-82, v.p. Law Sch. Alumni Adv. Coun., 1992, pres. 1993-94, mem. bd. govs., 1995—. Home: 6317 Churchill Way Dallas TX 75230-1807 Office: Akin Gump Strauss Hauer & Feld 1700 Pacific Ave Ste 4100 Dallas TX 75201-4624

DAVIS, CLISS JOHNSON, musician; b. Richmond, Utah, Dec. 3, 1921; d. Osbourn and Edna (Hendricks) Johnson; m. Edwin Reese Davis Sr., Feb. 4, 1942; children: Klair, Edwin Reese Jr. Cert. music tchr., Brigham Young U., 1944; affiliated tchr. piano, Sherwood Music Sch. Ext., Chgo., 1947-56. Tchr. Downey (Idaho) H.S., 1948-51, Box Elder Jr. H.S., Brigham City, Utah, 1953-56; bank teller Bank of L.A., 1956-57; pianist Santa Monica (Calif.) Jr. H.S. and Coll., 1966-74; organist LDS Jordan River Temple, South Jordan, Utah, 1987—; bank teller Box Elder County Bank, Brigham City, 1951-52; sec. City Nat. Bank, Santa Monica, 1958-65; assoc. accompanist So. Calif. Mormon Choir, L.A., 1956-74; pianist Joseph Smith Bldg., Salt Lake City, 1993—; organist LDS Glenmore 4th Ward, South Glenmore Stake, South Jordan, 1987-96; fin. chmn. Santa Cruz (Calif.) Symphony Guild, 1974-87; dir. Drum and Bugle Corp, Brigham City, 1951-56; pianist, accompanist Ind. Bankers Assn. No. Calif., 1975-87. Author story and music road show Atnas Zurk, 1974; oil paintings, 1974-87. Mem. Am. West Symphony and Choir (accompanist). Republican. Home: 4418 W Skye Dr South Jordan UT 84095-9712

DAVIS, COLLEEN TERESA, educational administrator; b. Monroe, Wis., Aug. 28, 1946; d. Francis Benedict and Norma Irene Doherty; m. John Oswin Davis, Aug. 25, 1973; children: John Francis, Christine Elizabeth. BS in Elem. Edn., Marian Coll., Fond Du Lac, Wis., 1967; MS in Edn.-Reading, U. Wis., Whitewater, 1975; MS in Ednl. Adminstrn., Ariz. State U., Phoenix, 1994. Cert. K-12 adminstr., K-12 curriculum supr., K-12 reading specialist. Elem. tchr. Holy Trinity Sch., Kewaskum, Wis., 1967-69; reading tchr. Friendship Mid. Sch., Adams, Wis., 1970-71, Ozaukee Mid. Sch., Fredonia, Wis., 1971-73; reading tchr. Johnson Creek (Wis.) Mid. Sch., 1973-75, 78-84, reading specialist, 1978-84; adult reading tchr. Waukesha County Tech. Inst., Pewaukee, Wis., 1976-79; reading tchr.-specialist Royal Palm Mid. Sch., Phoenix, 1984-93, chpt. 1 coord./curriculum, 1993—; presenter Wis. State Reading, Oconomowoc, 1981-82, Ariz. Reading Assn., Tucson, 1988, Washington Sch. Dist., Phoenix Mid. Sch. Conf., 1995, 6-7-8 Grade Acad., 1996. Author: (programs) Arizona Quality Programs and Practices, 1987, WSD Promising Practices, 1988. Lit. Days vol. Phoenix West Reading Coun., 1992-93. Recipient Golden Apple award Washington Sch. Dist., 1989, Tchr. of Excellence Royal Palm, PTO, Phoenix, 1989, 92, Lit. award-Leadership in Profession, Internat. Reading Assn./Phoenix West Reading Coun., 1990. Mem. ASCD, Internat. Reading Assn., Ariz. Reading Assn. (conf. com. 1984—), Phoenix West Reading Coun. (rec. sec., v.p., pres., membership chair), Ariz. Assn. Sch. Adminstrs. Office: Royal Palm Mid Sch 8520 N 19th Ave Phoenix AZ 85021-4201

DAVIS, CYNTHIA A. (CYNDEE DAVIS), mental health counselor, parental assessment specialist; b. Danville, Ill., Aug. 20, 1953; d. Kenneth Ralph and Patricia Ann (George) Grider; m. Eugene Andrew, July 1, 1972; children: Adam Guy, Kelly Dawn. BA in Psychology cum laude, Ctrl. U. of Iowa, 1975; MA in Clin. Psychology, Ill. State U., 1979. Diplomate Am. Acad. Forensic Counselors; lic. mental health counselor; cert. cognitive behavioral therapist. Clin. psychologist Broadlawn Med. Ctr., Des Moines, 1980-95; pres., counselor, dir. Mental Health & Assessment Svcs., Inc., Des Moines, 1995—. Pres. Starbase 17, Des Moines, 1983—; lay leader Marquisville Meth. Ch., Des Moines, 1995—. Mem. Am. Mental Health Counselors. Home: 5954 NE 6 Des Moines IA 50313 Office: Mental Health & Assessment Svcs Park Fair Mall 100 E Euclid Ste 113 Des Moines IA 50313

DAVIS, DAISY SIDNEY, history educator; b. Bay City, Tex., Nov. 7, 1944; d. Alex. C. and Alice M. (Edison) Sidney; m. John Dee Davis, Apr. 17, 1968; children: Anaca Michelle, Lowell Kent. BS, Bishop Coll., 1966; MS, East Tex. State U., 1971; MEd, Prairie View A&M, 1980. Cert. profl. lifetime secondary tchr., Tex.; mid-mgmt. adminstr. Tchr., Dallas pub. schs., 1966—; instr. Am. History El Centro Coll., 1991—; adv. Am. history telecourse Dallas County C.C. dist. Coord. Get Out the Vote campaign , Dallas, 1972, 80, 84, 88, 92, 94, 96. Recipient Outstanding Tchr. award Dallas pub. schs., 1980, Jack Lowe award for ednl. excellence, 1982; Free Enterprise scholar So. Meth. U., 1987; Constl. fellow U. Dallas, 1988; named to Hall of Fame, Holmes Acad., 1979. Mem. NEA, Tex. State Tchrs. Assn., Classroom Tchrs. Dallas (faculty rep. 1971-77), Dallas County History Tchrs., Afro-Am. Daus. Republicof Tex. (founder), Zeta Phi Beta. Democrat. Baptist. Club: Jack & Jill, (Dallas) (rec. sec., v.p., chair Beautillion Ball, pres.). Home: 1302 Mill Stream Dr Dallas TX 75232-4604 Office: 3000 Martin Luther King Jr Dallas TX 75215-5525

DAVIS, DEBORAH CECILIA, auditor; b. Mt. Pleasant, Mich., Aug. 7, 1952; d. Arthur Francis Schaefer and Ninamae Ellen (Confer) Reber. BBA summa cum laude, Western Mich. U., 1974. CPA. Acct. Phoenix Optical, Bay City, Mich., 1968-70; analyst 2nd Nat. Bank, Saginaw, Mich., 1970-72; CPA Deloitte & Touche, Saginaw, Mich., 1975-77; cost acct. AC Sparkplug div. GM, Flint, Mich., 1977-78; corp. auditor GMC, Detroit, 1980; sr. statistician Detroit Diesel Allison div. GM, 1980-83; sr. budget, forecast analyst Cen. Foundry divsn. GM, Saginaw, 1983-91; fin. dir. City of Bay City, Mich., 1991-94; corp. supplier auditor GM, 1994—.

DAVIS, DEBRA ELIZABETH, artist; b. Chehalis, Wash., Mar. 20, 1960; d. Sidney Allen and Ann Louise (Mueller) Davis; m. Kenneth Riley Bevis, June 22, 1991. AAS, Wenatchee (Wash.) Valley Coll., 1982; BFA, U. Idaho, 1988; MFA, Ctrl. Wash. U., 1993. Forestry technician USDA Forest Svc., various locations, 1982-90, Cle Elum, Wash., summers 1991—; grad. teaching asst. Ctrl. Wash. U., Ellensburg, 1991-93, adj. lectr. art, 1994; pvt. instr./cons. on art and creativity Ellensburg, 1993—. Exhibited work in two-person show at Clatsop C.C., Astoria, Oreg., 1996, in group shows at Wash. State Conv. and Trade Ctr., Seattle, 1994, Larson Gallery/Yakima C.C., 1995, St. John's U., Jamaica, N.Y., 1996, others; work in collections for Wash. State Arts Commn., also in pvt. collections in Wash., Oreg., Idaho, Minn. and S.C. Recipient Phil Baechler Purchase award, 1994, Idaho Watercolor Soc. award, 1987; Mary Kirkwood scholar U. Idaho, 1986. Mem. Phi Kappa Phi (Fine Arts award 1991), Tau Sigma Delta.

DAVIS, DENISE WHITLOCK (DENISE LUCILLE WHITLOCK), accountant, financial analyst; b. Marietta, Ga., July 5, 1959; d. J. Winston and Martha Josephine (Phillips) Whitlock. BS in Bus. Adminstrn., Auburn U., 1981. CPA, Ga. Audit profl. KPMG Peat Marwick, Dallas, 1982-85; with exec. office KPMG Peat Marwick, N.Y., 1985-86; audit mgr. KPMG Peat Marwick, Atlanta, 1986-87; fin. analyst Columbian Chem. Co. div. Phelps Dodge Corp., Atlanta, 1987-90; asst. v.p. acctg. policy C&S/Sovran Corp., Atlanta, 1990-91, v.p. acctg. policy, 1991-92; controller CryoLife, Inc., Marietta, 1992-94; sr. analyst N.W. Airlines, Inc., Atlanta, 1994-96, mgr. fin. projects, 1996—. Treas., chmn. fundraising Atlanta Symphony Assn., 1987-89; bd. dirs., treas. Morningside Terrace Condominium Assn., Atlanta, 1987-90. Mem. AICPA (editorial advisor 1990—), Ga. Soc. CPAs (continuing profl. edn. com. 1990—, bd. dirs. 1994—), Auburn U. Alumni Assn., Atlanta Lawn Tennis Club, Delta Gamma.

DAVIS, DIANNE LOUISE, marketing professional; b. Fresno, Calif., Mar. 1, 1940; d. Edwin L. and Adeline (Irvin) Gribble; m. John R. Jansen, June 11, 1960 (dec. 1966); children: Anthony, Julia; m. Edward Kent Davis, May 13, 1967 (div. 1977); 1 child, Edward Kent Jr. AA cum laude, Colo. Woman's Coll., 1957; student, Minot State Coll., 1968, Ottawa State U., 1987—. Cert. real estate broker, Mo., Kans; cert. resdl. specialist. Co-ptnr. Key Realty, Warrensburg, Mo., 1973-77; residential broker, assoc. DeLozier Realty, Warrensburg, 1977-78; owner, broker Old Drum Realty, Warrensburg, 1978-81; comml. broker, assoc. Varnum-Armstrong-Deeter, Overland Pk., Kans., 1981-82; residential broker, assoc. Kroh Bros. Realty, Overland Pk., 1982-83, Re/Max-Overland Pk., 1983-87, J. D. Reece Real Estate, Overland Pk., 1987-89; dir. mktg. Riss Lake Realty, Parkville, Mo., 1989-92; broker-salesperson JC Nichols Real Estate, 1992-93, The Prudential Summerson-Burrows, Realtors, Overland Park, Kans., 1993—. Mem. Friends of Art Nelson Art Gallery, Kansas City, 1989-90, Friends of the Zoo, Kansas City, 1989-90. Mem. nat. Assn. Home Bldrs. (mem. Inst. Res. Mktg. designation), Met. Kansas City Home Bldrs. Assn. (sales and mktg. coun. 1989-92), Met. Kansas City Bd. Realtors (profl. standards com. 1990-92, chmn., 1992), Johnson County Bd. Realtors, Nat. Assn. Realtors (state del. 1991-92). Republican. Episcopal. Office: Prudential Summerson-Burrow Realtors 8101 College Blvd Ste 100 Overland Park KS 66210-2671

DAVIS, DONNA MARIE, school counselor; b. Ft. Worth, June 21, 1949; d. Roy Elton Jr. and Geneva Marie (Helton) Michener; m. Jerald Adams Davis Jr., Aug. 11, 1973; children: Beverly Marie, Elizabeth Kathleen. BA, Harding U., Searcy, Ark., 1971; MEd, U. North Tex., Denton, 1994. Cert. elem. sch. tchr., sch. counselor, Tex. Tchr. New Madrid (Mo.) Schs., 1971-72, Venus (Tex.) Sch., 1972-73, Abilene (Tex.) Ind. Sch. Dist., 1973-74; tchr. Ft. Worth Christian Sch., 1984-93, counselor, 1993—; coord. pre-sch. Richland Hills Ch. of Christ, Ft. Worth, 1982-93. Named Outstanding Alumnus, Ft. Worth Christian Sch., 1989. Mem. Tex. Counseling Assn., Tex. Sch. Counseling Assn., Assn. for Play Therapy, Assn. for Career Devel. Home: 7721 Deaver Dr Fort Worth TX 76180-6221 Office: Ft Worth Christian Sch 7517 Bogart Dr Fort Worth TX 76180-6225

DAVIS, DORINNE SUE TAYLOR LOVAS, audiologist; b. East Orange, N.J., Mar. 29, 1949; d. William Henry and Evelyn Doris (Thorp) Taylor; BA, Montclair State Coll., 1971, MA, 1973; children: Larissa Louise, Peter Alexander. Ednl. audiologist Kinnelon (N.J.) Bd. Edn., 1972-94, Inst. for Career Advancement, Inc., 1980-82, Dover Gen. Hosp., 1984-86; pres. Hear You Are, Inc., 1987—; kindergarten tchr. Kinnelon (N.J.) Bd. Edn., 1994—; adj. prof. Kean Coll., Union, N.J., 1993-95. Cert. tchr. of hearing impaired, speech correctionist, tchr. speech and drama, supr. nursery sch. endorsement N.J. Dept. Edn. Mem. NEA, Internat. Orgn. Educators Hearing Impaired, Am. Speech and Hearing Assn. (cert. of clin. competence in audiology), Am. Acad. Audiology, Alexander Graham Bell Assn., N.J. Speech and Hearing Assn., Morris County Speech and Hearing Assn., N.J. Edn. Assn., Morris County Edn. Assn., Kinnelon Edn. Assn., Self Help for the Hard of Hearing, Ednl. Audiology Assn. (past pres.). Methodist. Home: 4 Musconetcong Ave Stanhope NJ 07874-2936 Office: Kiel Sch Kiel Ave Kinnelon NJ 07405 also: Hear You Are Inc 125 Main St Netcong NJ 07857

DAVIS, DOROTHY SALISBURY, author; b. Chgo., Apr. 26, 1916; d. Alfred Joseph and Margaret Jane (Greer) Salisbury; m. Harry Davis, Apr.

25, 1946 (dec.). AB, Barat Coll., Lake Forest, Ill., 1938. Mystery and hist. novelist, short story writer. Author: A Gentle Murderer, 1951, A Town of Masks, 1952, Men of No Property, 1956, Death of an Old Sinner, 1957, A Gentleman Called, 1958, The Evening of the Good Samaritan, 1961, Black Sheep, White Lamb, 1963, The Pale Betrayer, 1965, Enemy and Brother, 1967, God Speed The Night, 1968, Where the Dark Streets Go, 1969, Shock Wave, 1972, The Little Brothers, 1973, A Death in the Life, 1976, Scarlet Night, 1980, A Lullaby of Murder, 1984, Tales for a Stormy Night, 1985, The Habit of Fear, 1987. Recipient Life Achievement award Bouchereon, 1989. Mem. Authors Guild, Mystery Writers of Am. (former pres., recipient Grand Master award 1985), Adams Roundtable. Home: PO Box 595 Palisades NY 10964

DAVIS, ELEANOR LAURIA, biology educator, volunteer, lecturer; b. Pitts., Aug. 29, 1923; d. Anthony Francis and Antonia Jennie (Bove) Lauria; m. Earle Richard Davis, May 7, 1946; children: Susan Davis Hickerson, Janice Davis Johnston, Lisa Davis Kulp, Elena Davis Smoulder, Amy Davis Gordon, Kent Earle, Eric J. BS, U. Pitts., 1944, M Letters in Biology, 1950. Grad. teaching asst. in physiology dept. biology U. Pitts., 1944-46; instr. in biology Pa. Coll. for Women (now Chatham Coll.), Pitts., 1946-53; libr. Carnegie Libr., Pitts., 1947-50; instr. Acad. Life Long Learning, Pitts., 1995-96. Co-author: Lab. Manual for Biology, 1948; contbr. editorials to profl. newsletter. Pres. St. Joseph's Hosp. Aux., Pitts., 1977-78, Allegheny County Med. Soc. Aux., 1981-83, chmn. legis. com., 1984—; mem. Coun. on Govt. Rels. and Pa. Med. Polit. Action Com., Harrisburg, 1987-94, Pa. Atty. Gens. Task Force Drugs, 1989-90, Pa. Task Force on Aging, 1988-90, Pa. Task Force on AIDS, 1988-90, Pa. Task Force on the Impaired Physician, 1988-90; committeewoman Dem. Party of O'Hara Twp., 1983—, by-laws com. Allegheny County Dems., 1986-88, chmn. Dem. Party of O'Hara Twp., 1990-95; bd. dirs. Parental Stress Ctr., 1977-94, Bright Beginnings, 1979-94, Am. Cancer Soc. Aux., 1984-86, Vocat. Rehab. Ctr., 1986-88, Injury Prevention Works; bd. dirs., 1992-95, mem. program devel. and pub. rels. coms. Self Help Group Network, 1989-95; chmn. pub. rels. Rx Coun., 1986-92, program com., 1993—; mem. S.W. region Pa. Assn. Hosp. Auxs., 1990—, bd. dirs., 2d v.p., 1995, legis. chmn., 1992-94, health chmn., 1992-94; pub. policy chmn. Alzheimers Disease and Related Disorders, 1987-94; mem. parish coun. St. Scholastica Ch., 1988-90, Grass Roots Intelligence Team, South Hills Health System, 1989-94, aux. chmn. legis. and health, 1986—, adv. bd. Allegheny County Safe Kids Coalition, 1990—, mem. bylaws com.; elected del. AMA Aux. Conv., 1979-93; mem. Allegheny County Health Dept. Smoke Detector Task Force, 1983—, Task Force on Scald and Burn Prevention, 1994—, task force on health care reform Pa. Med. Soc. Alliance, 1993—. Recipient honor scholarship U. Pitts., 1941-44, Benjamin Rush award Allegheny County Med. Soc., 1987, Person of Yr. award South Hills Health System and Found., Pitts., 1989. Mem. AAUW (Women's Agenda), Nat. Inst. Adult Day Care (stds. com.), Nat. Coun. Aging (task force for day care stds. 1989-90), Allegheny County Fedn. Women's Clubs (RX coun. bd. dirs. 1986—), Stanton Heights Garden Club (pres. 1974-89, program chmn. 1989—), Piccadilly Herb Club (pres. 1994-95, by laws com. 1996), Hosp. Assn. Pa. (grass roots intelligence team), Pa. Med. Soc. (legis. key contact), Pa. Med. Soc. Alliance (PAMPAC rep. western dist. 1991-95, bylaws com. 1990-94, pres. 1988-89, 92-93, pres. Past Pres.'s Gavel Club 1992-93), Pa. Assn. Hosp. Auxs. (spring conf. planning com. 1995-96), Theta Phi Alpha, Nu Sigma Nu. Home: 109 Woodshire Rd Pittsburgh PA 15215-1713

DAVIS, ELISE MILLER (MRS. LEO M. DAVIS), writer; b. Corsicana, Tex., Oct. 12, 1915; d. Moses Myre and Rachelle (Daniels) Miller; student U. Tex., 1930-31; m. Jay Albert Davis, June 27, 1937 (dec. June 1973); 1 dau., Rayna Miller (Mrs. Michael Edwin Loeb); m. 2d, Leo M. Davis, Aug. 23, 1974. Freelance writer, 1945—; merchandiser and dir. Jay Davis, Inc., Amarillo, Tex., 1956-73; instr. mag. writing U. Tex., Dallas, 1978; lectr. creative writing Baylor U., Waco, Tex., 1980, 81, 83. Mem. Am. Soc. Journalists and Authors (bd. dirs. 1985-91). Author: The Answer Is God: The Personal Story of Dale Evans and Roy Rogers, 1955; articles to periodicals including Reader's Digest, Woman's Day, Nation's Business, others. Home: 7838 Caruth Ct Dallas TX 75225-8123

DAVIS, ELIZABETH HAWK, English language educator; b. Ft. Smith, Ark., Sept. 6, 1945; d. Arthur Carlton and Lolitta (Poe) Hawk; m. Leo Carson Davis, Aug. 31, 1968. BA, U. Ark., 1967, BM, 1967, MA, 1969; EdD, East Tex. State U., 1989. Classroom tchr. Springdale (Ark.) Pub. Schs., 1967-68; lectr. U. Md., Heidelberg, Fed. Republic Germany, 1978-79; from instr. to asst. prof. performing arts So. Ark. U., Magnolia, 1981-92, assoc. prof., 1992-96, chair English and fgn. langs. dept., 1993—, prof., 1996—. Contbr. articles to profl. jours. Organist First Presbyn. Ch., Magnolia, 1984—. Mem. MLA, Nat. Coun. of Tchrs. of English, Ark. Tchrs. of Coll. English, Ark. Philol. Assn., Phi Beta Kappa. Office: So Ark U PO Box 1356 Magnolia AR 71753

DAVIS, ELLA DELORES, special education educator, elementary educator; b. Quitman, La., July 19, 1957; d. Gencie Lee and Bessie (J.) D. BA, La. Tech. U., 1979; MS, Grambling State U., 1989. Tchr. lang. arts, social studies and leisure time activities Jackson Parish Sch. Bd., Jonesboro, La., 1982—; mem. Spl. Edn. Coun. Jonesboro, 1991-93. Author: The Power of Jesus--An Enlightening Story of Incidences That Happened in My Life and How Jesus Interceded, 1989, Behavior Booklet, 1992, A Complete Guide to Setting Up a Special Education Program, 1992, Special Education Lesson Plan Booklet, 1992, My Math Fact Booklet, 1992, My Word Booklet, 1993; inventor health and beauty aid products, variety other products. Mem. exec. bd. NAACP, Jonesboro, 1992—; mem. 5th Dist. Black Caucus, Monroe, La., 1990—, Jonesboro Beautification Bd., 1993—. Mem. La. Assn. Educators. Democrat. Baptist. Home: 271 Sugar Creek Rd Quitman LA 71268-1313

DAVIS, EMMA LAURA, social services specialist; b. Bryn Mawr, Pa., June 26, 1940; d. Joseph Stanley and Mary Elizabeth (Emery) Landis; m. Robert Dunlap Davis, Dec. 11, 1965 (div. Jan. 1990); children: Andrew Michael, Jessica Laura Wilson, Rebekah Mary Elizabeth. BA, Geneva Coll., 1962; MS, Ea. Wash. U., 1975. Sch. social worker Chittenden Sch. Dist., Essex Junction, Vt., 1966-69; therapist Spokane Mental Health Ctr., 1974-78; dir. social svcs. Whitewood Rehab. Ctr., Waterbury, Conn., 1990, 3030 Park Fairfield (Conn.) Health Ctr., 1990-96; chair ethics com., dir. social svcs./admissions Waveny Care Ctr., New Canaan, Conn., 1996—. Paintings exhibited at U. Bridgeport, 1991-92. Soccer referee U.S. Soccer Fedn., Spokane, 1979-85; comty. educator 3030 Park Fairfield, 1995; chair scholarship com. St. Luke's Hosp., Spokane, 1976-77; rec. sec., v.p. bd. dirs. Rockwood Garden Club, Spokane, 1983. Fellow AAUW (rec. sec. Naples, Fla. br. 1970-71), Conn. Assn. Nonprofit Facilities for the Aged (co-chair social work dirs. 1993-95, sec. 1992-93), Penfield Investment Club; mem. Conn. Hosp. Assn. (mem. ethics conf. 1995—). Episcopalian. Office: Waveny Care Unit 3 Farm Rd New Canaan CT 06840

DAVIS, EMMA-JO LEVEY, retired government executive, publishing executive; b. Greensboro, N.C., June 5, 1932; d. Harry Nelson and Alma (Snellen) Levey; m. Andrew Jackson Davis Jr., July 3, 1957 (div. July 1977); children: Anne Stone, Kelsie Lee. Student, Mary Washington Coll., 1949-51; AB, U. N.C., 1953; MEd, Coll. William and Mary, 1969. Tchr. local pub. schs., Gloucester, Va., 1959-61; editor U.S. Army, Ft. Eustis, Va., 1961-63, historian, 1963-67, curator Transp. Mus., 1967-80; chief curator U.S. Army, Washington, 1980-91. Author: History of the U.S. Army Transportation Corps, 1967, History of the U.S. Army Transportation School, 1967. Mem. Nat. Geneal. Soc., Mensa, Army Hist. Found. (v.p.), DAR, Nat. Soc. Colonial Dames XVII Century. Episcopalian. Home: 1202 Conway Dr Apt 202 Williamsburg VA 23185-3847 Office: 117 Colony Sq Williamsburg VA 23185-3331

DAVIS, EVELYN CLEVELAND, academic training consultant; b. Seneca, S.C., Aug. 12, 1934; d. James Benjamin and Evelyn Rebecca (Reaves) Cleveland; m. Richard L. Davis, Aug. 19, 1958 (div. 1970); children: Mark, Stuart, Carolyn. BA cum laude, Furman U., 1956; MA in Teaching, Converse Coll., 1969; EdD, Auburn U., 1975. Tchr. high sch. Ky., N.C., Tex. and S.C., 1956-65; reading specialist Denver Pub. Schs., 1966-67; chairperson dept. reading Fulmer Jr. High Sch., West Columbia, S.C., 1967-70; head dept. adult edn., instructional svcs. Midlands TEC, Columbia, S.C., 1970-73; dir. master's program in adult edn. Memphis State U., 1975-77; dir. master's program in adult edn. and ednl. svcs. U. N.C. Charlotte, 1977-87; cons. adult edn., 1977-87; internat. tng. cons. Summer Inst. Linguistics, 1987—. Editor jour. Living for Learning Modules, 1977; contbr. articles to profl. jours. Auburn U. fellow. Mem. AAUP, Acad. Excellence Leadership Forum, Assn. Tchr. Educators, Adult Edn. Assn. Republican. Lutheran.

DAVIS, EVELYN JEAN, consultant; b. Miami, Fla., May 15, 1948; d. Richard Eugene and Esther Jean (Fiske) D.; m. Leona B. LeBlanc, Dec. 3, 1983; children: Christopher Lee Bailey, Michael David Bailey. Student, Salem Coll., Winston-Salem, N.C., 1966-69; BA in History, Fla. Atlantic U., 1970; PhD in Adult Edn., Fla. State U., 1983, postgrad. Analyst Fla. Legislature, Tallahassee, 1970-74, 89-94; project dir. Fla. Ctr. for Children and Youth, Tallahassee, 1976-78, Legis/50 The Ctr. for Legis. Improvement, Denver, 1979-82; auditor Auditor Gen., Tallahasse, 1983-88; sr. cons. MGT of Am., Inc., Tallahasse, 1995—. Author poetry and short stories. Alumnae rep. Salem Coll., 1983—; mem. Seminole Boosters, Tallahassee, 1983—; founder Everywoman's Coffeehouse, Tallahassee, 1983—. Home: 2031 Chowkeebin Nene Tallahassee FL 32301 Office: MGT of Am Inc 2425 Torreya Dr Tallahassee FL 32303

DAVIS, EVELYN MAE, bank officer; b. Vina, Ala., Jan. 17, 1948; d. Newman Taft and Grace Mae (Pannell) Renfroe; m. Harold Bradford Davis, Dec. 23, 1968; children: Bradford Lane, Kimberly Renee Davis Holland. Grad., Cmty. Bankers Assn. Ala., Birmingham, 1996. Cert. bank compliance officer Bank Adminstrn. Inst., 1995. Sec., clerk Charm Step, Inc., Fulton, Miss., 1968-75; bank officer Bank of Red Bay, Ala., 1978—. Sec. We Care Ministries, Inc., Red Bay, 1991-95. Office: Bank of Red Bay 200 4th Ave SW Red Bay AL 35582

DAVIS, EVELYN MARGUERITE BAILEY, artist, organist, pianist; b. Springfield, Mo.; d. Philip Edward and Della Jane (Morris) Bailey; student pub. schs., Springfield; student art Drury Coll.; piano , organ student of Charles Cordeal; m. James Harvey Davis, Sept. 22, 1946. Sec., Shea and Morris Monument Co., before 1946; past mem. sextet, soloist Sta. KGBX; past pianist, Sunday sch. tchr., mem. choir East Ave. Bapt. Ch.; tchr. Bible, organist, pianist, vocal soloist and dir. youth choir Bible Bapt. Ch., Maplewood, Mo., 1956-69, also executed 12 by 6 foot mural of Jordan River; pvt. instr. piano and organ, voice, Croma Harp, Affton, Mo., 1960-71, St. Charles, Mo., 1971-83; Bible instr. 3d Bapt. Ch., St. Louis, 1948-54; pianist, soloist, tchr. Bible, Temple Bapt. Ch., Kirkwood, Mo., 1969-71; asst. organist-pianist, vocal soloist, tchr. Bible, Bible Ch., Arnold, Mo., 1969; faculty St. Charles Bible Bapt. Christian Sch., 1976-77; organist for Dr. Jack Van Impe Crusades and Dr. Oliver B. Green Crusades; organist, pianist, soloist, Bible tchr., dir. youth orch., music arranger, floral arranger Bible Bapt. Ch., St. Charles, 1971-78; organist, vocal soloist, floral arranger Bible tchr. Faith Missionary Bapt. Ch., St. Charles, 1978-82; organist, floral arranger, vocal soloist Bellview Bapt. Ch., Springfield, Mo., 1984-90; tchr. piano, organ, voice, organist, Springfield, Mo., 1983—; pianist Golden Agers Pk. Crest Bapt. Ch., Springfield, Mo., 1991; interior decorator and floral arranger, also organist and vocal soloist for weddings and funerals. Fellow Internat. Biog. Assn. (life), Am. Biog. Inst. Rsch. Assn. (life); mem. Nat. Guild Organists, Nat. Guild Piano Tchr. Auditions, Internat. Platform Assn. Composer: I Will Sing Hallelujah, (cantata) I Am Alpha and Omega, Prelude to Prayer, My Shepherd, O Sing unto The Lord A New Song, O Come Let Us Sing unto The Lord, The King of Glory, The Lord Is My Light and My Salvation, O Worship the Lord in the Beauty of Holiness, The Greatest of These is Love, Prayer to the Lord Our God, We Will Sing Praises, His Name is Jesus, From Bethlehem's Manger to the Cross, also numerous hymn arrangements for organ and piano. Home: 5135 East Farm Rd 174 Rogersville MO 65742-9434

DAVIS, FLORENCE ANN, lawyer; b. Pitts., Feb. 22, 1955; d. Richard Davis and Charlotte (Saul) McGhee; m. Kevin J. O'Brien, May 28, 1978; children: Rebecca Davis, Sarah Davis. AB, Wellesley U., 1976; JD, NYU, 1979. Bar: N.Y. 1980, U.S. Dist. Ct. (ea. and so. dists.) N.Y., N.Y. Ct. Appeals (2d cir.), U.S. Tax Ct., U.S. Supreme Ct. Assoc. atty. Sullivan & Cromwell, N.Y.C., 1979-86; litigation counsel Morgan Stanley & Co., N.Y.C., 1986-88, v.p., 1988-90, dir. compliance, 1989-90, prin., 1990-95; v.p., gen. counsel Am. Internat. Group, N.Y.C., 1995—. Root-Tilden scholar NYU Law Sch., 1976-79. Mem. Securities Industry Assn. (v.p. edn. Compliance and Legal div. 1992, exec. com. Compliance and Legal div. 1990-92). Office: Stanley Morgan Co Inc 1251 Avenue Of The Americas New York NY 10020-1104*

DAVIS, FRANCES KAY, lawyer; b. Phila., Apr. 1, 1952; d. Francis Kaye and Ida May (Lamplugh) D. BA, Mount Holyoke Coll., 1974; MA, Duke U., 1976; JD, Villanova U., 1983-86. Legal asst. Cozen, Begier & O'Connor, Phila., 1982-83; summer assoc. Montgomery, McCracken, Walker & Roads, Phila., 1985, assoc., 1986-89; assoc. Cozen & O'Connor, Phila., 1989-95, Jackson/LeGros, 1996; ptnr. LeGros Law Ptnrs., Media and Berwyn, Pa., also Princeton, N.J., 1996—; gen. ptnr. April Racing Stables, 1991-95, Steel Fist Video Co., 1994—. Contbr. articles to profl. jours. Served to capt. USAF, 1977-82. Mem. ATLA (Trial Advocacy award Phila. chpt. 1986), Phila. Bar Assn., N.J. Bar Assn., Welsh Soc. Phila. (bd. stewards 1990-93, scholar 1984-85, chmn. scholarship com. 1990-92, counselor 1992-94, chmn. women's com. 1992-94).

DAVIS, GAIL HEATHER, university athletic administrator; b. Phila., July 27, 1941; d. Walter Fulton and Sarah Ruth (McQuade) D. BS, East Stroudsburg State U., 1963; MS, So. Conn. State U., 1970. Tchr. health, phys. edn. Phila. Pub. Schs., 1963-67; head coach, grad. asst. So. Conn. State U., New Haven, 1967-69, instr./head coach, 1969-76; assoc. athletic dir., head coach R.I. Coll., Providence, 1976-80, acting athletic dir., 1980-81, assoc. athletic dir., coach, 1981-92, interim athletic dir., 1992-95, assoc. athletic dir., 1995—; planner health, phys. edn., athletic complex R.I. Coll., 1992-95. Mem. Edgewood Neighborhood Assn., Cranston, R.I., 1985-96; active Big Sisters of Conn. and R.I., 1974-76; mem. Friends of Big Sisters of R.I., 1972-96. Mem. AAUW, R.I. Assn. Intercollegiate Athletics for Women (pres., sec.-treas.), U.S.A. Gymnastics (bd. dirs. 1985-96), Nat. Coll. Athletic Assn. (woman's gym com. 1982-89), Assn. Intercollegiate Athletics for Women (chmn. gymnastics com. 1977-81), R.I. Assn. Women in Edn. (v.p.), N.E. Colls. Gymnastic Coaches Assn., Women's Sports Found., Sweet Adelines. Home: 214 Armington St Cranston RI 02905-4117 Office: Rhode Island College 600 Mt Pleasant Ave Providence RI 02905

DAVIS, GAY RUTH, psychotherapist, social welfare educator, author, researcher, consultant; b. Bellingham, Wash., Sept. 19, 1935; d. Lee Laverne Wickersham and Altha (Lund) Wickersham Knight; m. Paul Cushing Davis, Dec. 20, 1956; children: Jeffrey Richards, Jennifer Lynn. Student, Brigham Young U., 1953-55; BA summa cum laude, Western Wash. U., 1976; MSW, U. Wash., 1978, PhD, 1985. Diplomate in clin. social work. Dir. Social Svcs. Sound Health Assn., Tacoma, 1977-78; social work profl. Harborview Med. Ctr., Seattle, 1979-81; instr. Sch. Social Work U. Wash., Seattle, 1984-85; pvt. practice cons. social work and psychotherapy Seattle, 1985—; prin. investigator NINCDS Rsch., 1980-81; coord. Adult Svcs. Tng. Project, U. Wash., 1983-84. Contbr. articles to profl. jours. Mem. adv. bd. LDS Social Svcs., 1990-91. Grantee Wash. Dept. Health and Human Services, 1981-82. Mem. NASW (qualified clin. social worker), Nat. Registry Clin. Social Work, Am. Profl. Soc. on Abuse of Children, Gerontol. Soc. Am., Wash. Assn. Social Workers, Wash. Profl. Soc. on Abuse of Children, Assn. Mormon Counselors and Psychotherapists. Democrat. Mormon.

DAVIS, GEENA (VIRGINIA DAVIS), actress; b. Wareham, Mass., Jan. 21, 1957; m. Richard Emmolo, 1981 (div. 1983); m. Jeff Goldblum, 1987 (div. 1990); m. Renny Harlin, 1993. BFA, Boston U., 1979; attended, New England Coll., Henniker, N.H. Founder Genial Pictures; mem. My. Washington (N.H.) Repertory Theatre Co. Motion picture appearances include Tootsie, 1982, Fletch, 1985, Transylvania 6-5000, 1985, The Fly, 1986, Beetlejuice, 1988, The Accidental Tourist, 1988 (Academy award Best Supporting Actress, 1989), Earth Girls Are Easy, 1989, Quick Change, 1990, Thelma and Louise, 1991 (Acad. award nominee Best Actress 1991, British Acad Film and TV Arts award Best Actress in leading role 1991, Golden Globe award nominee Best Actress 1991), A League of Their Own, 1992, Hero, 1992, Angie, 1994, Speechless, 1994, Cutthroat Island, 1995; TV series: Buffalo Bill, 1983-84, Sara, 1985; appeared in TV film Secret Weapons, 1985, episodes series Family Ties, 1984. Address: care CAA 9830 Wilshire Blvd Beverly Hills CA 90212-1804*

DAVIS, GERALDINE SAMPSON, special education educator; b. Tacoma, Wash., Aug. 18, 1919; d. Philip and Merta M. (Thomas) Sampson; m. John Allen Davis, Nov. 26 1942 (div. 1971); children: Denise, Karin, Glen (dec.), Grant (dec.), Page, Gail (dec.). BS with distinction, U. Minn., 1941; MEd, San Francisco State U., 1971. Cert. tchr., Calif., cert. adminstr., Calif. Art and English instr. White Bear Lake (Minn.) Jr. and Sr. High Sch., 1941-43; Am. club mobile operator ARC, Eng. and Europe, 1944-45; exec. dir. Lincoln County chpt. ARC, Newport, Oreg., 1947-48; substitute tchr. Santa Cruz (Calif.) County Dept. Edn., 1964-67; learning disabled instr. Live Oak Dist. Schs., Santa Cruz, 1967-89; peer tutor developer Live Oak Schs., 1970-73, reading program mgr., 1973-76; evaluation team mem. County of Santa Cruz, 1980-84. Exhibited paintings in numerous galleries shows including Los Gatos Art Cooperative, 1961-65, Santa Cruz Art Festival, 1962, San Juan Bautista Art Fair, 1963, Santa Cruz County Fair, 1965; paintings represented in several pvt. collections. Chpt. sec. March of Dimes, Lincoln County, 1949-51, Santa Cruz County; vol. tutor Vols. of Santa Cruz, 1978-83; fundraiser Boulder Creek (Calif.) Schs., 1963; scenic and prop designer Santa Cruz County Schs., 1964, Boulder Creek Theater Group, 1965. Mem. Calif. Assn. Neurol. Handicapped Children (chair 1964-66, scholarships 1968-71), Women's Dem. Club, AAUW (com. chair for women's issues 1990—), Reproductive Rights Network, Santa Cruz Reading Assn. (sec. 1980, rep. Asilomar reading conf. bd. 1981-82, Chpt. and Internat. Reading Assns. award 1985), Calif. Ret. Tchrs. Assn. (nominating com. 1985—), Assn. Ret. Persons, Sr. Citizens Santa Cruz County, Pub. Citizens, Pub. Broadcasting Network, Conservation of Am, Amnesty, Delta Phi Delta (life, pres. Mpls. chpt. 1939-41), Pi Lambda Theta (life). Home: 319 35th Ave Santa Cruz CA 95062-5514

DAVIS, GLENNA SUE, human resources director; b. Elk City, Okla.; d. Toney and Wilma (Jansson) Wilcox; m. Wayne Milton Davis, Apr. 15, 1962 (div. Jan. 1984); children: Jeffrey, Bradley, Scott. BABA, Adams State Coll., 1982. Registered ombudsman, Ill. Dept. on Aging. Acct. Louis Moffett, CPA, Amarillo, Tex., 1961-65, J.H. Cochran, CPA, Monte Vista, Colo., 1968-69, T&W Ranch, Inc., Monte Vista, Colo., 1969-79; quality control mgr. A.E. Staley mfg. Co., Monte Vista, 1979-93, prodn. planner, 1993-95; dir., human resources Adams State Coll., Alamosa, 1995—; pres. Liberty Cons., Alamosa, 1993—; presenter Nat. Con. on Adult Learning, 1995, other confs. in field. Co-dir. San Luis Valley Kids Against Drugs, Alamosa, 1990-92; mem./treas. Monte Vista Community hosp. Bd., 1989-93; dir. San Luis Valley Network, Monte Vista, 1984-93; vol. Am. Cancer Soc., 1992-96; mem. Colo. 12th Dist. Jud. Performance Rev. Bd., 1992-93. Mem. AAUW (dist. dir. 1996—, state sec. 1990-92), Boys and Girls Club (exec. bd. 1995—). Republican. Baptist. Home: 5810 Blue Spruce Ave Alamosa CO 81101

DAVIS, GWENDOLYN S., lobbyist; b. Wake Forest, N.C., Mar. 3, 1958; d. Saul A. Jr. and Mary E. Smith; m. Angelo C. Davis, Jr., Mar. 7, 1992. BA in Polit. Sci. magna cum laude, Hampton U., 1980, MBA. Adminstrv. analyst Office of City Mgr., City of Suffolk, Va., 1981-82; adminstrv. asst. mgmt. svcs. City of Portsmouth, Va., 1982-84, adminstrv. analyst mgmt. svcs., 1984-85, mgmt. analyst mgmt. svcs., 1985-90, interim asst. to city mgr., 1990, asst. to city mgr., 1990, dir. human svcs., 1990-91, lobbyist and prin. mgmt. analyst, 1991—. Staff liaison Citizens Adv. Commn., City of Portsmouth, Mayor's Handicapped Commn., Youth Adv. Commn., various other coms.; pres. Conf. of Minority Pub. Adminstrs., Hampton Roads chpt., 1994-95; mem. exec. bd. NAACP; active Effingham St. YMCA. Recipient Julian F. Hirst award for disting. svc. Hampton Rds., 1996. Mem. NAACP, Effrenghan St. YMCA (exec. bd., 1996—), mem. Internat. City Mgmt. Assn., Va. Analysts Network (past pres.), Am. Soc. Pub. Adminstrs. (Hampton Roads chpt. exec. bd. 1995-96), Delta Sigma Theta, Alpha Kappa Mu. Office: City of Portsmouth City Mgrs Office 801 Crawford St Portsmouth VA 23704-3822

DAVIS, HELEN GORDON, former state senator; b. N.Y.C., Dec. 25; m. Gene Davis; children: Stephanie, Karen, Gordon. BA, Bklyn. Coll.; postgrad., U. South Fla., 1967-70. Tchr., High Sch. Commerce, N.Y.C., Hillsborough High Sch., Tampa, Fla.; grad. asst. U. South Fla., 1968; mem. Fla. Ho. of Reps. (1st woman to be elected in 1974 from Hills Co., 1st woman to chair the legis. delegation), 1974-88, state senator, 1988-92; mem. Fla Supreme Ct. Commn. on Gender Bias in the Cts., 1988-90; mem. Fla. Supreme Ct. Commn. on Mediation and Arbitration, 1987—. chmn. senate appropriations subcom. human svcs., mem. rules com., internat. trade and econ. devel. com., health and rehab. svcs. com. Jud. chmn. Local Govt. Study Commn. Hillsborough County (Fla.), 1964; mem. Tampa Commn. on Juvenile Delinquency, 1966-69, Mayor's Citizens Adv. Com., 1966-69, Quality Edn. Commn., 1966-68, Gov.'s Citizen Com. for Ct. Reform, 1972, Hillsborough County Planning Commn., 1973-74; mem. Gov.'s Commn. on Jud. Reform, 1976; mem. employment com. Commn. Community Relations, 1966-69; by-laws chmn. Arts Coun. Tampa, 1971-74; 1st v.p. Tampa Symphony Guild, 1974; bd. dirs. U. South Fla. Found., 1968-74, Stop Rape, 1973-74; founder Ctr. for Women, Tampa, 1978; past pres. PTA; active adv. commn. Nat. Child Care Action Campaign, Nat. Ctr. for Crime and Delinquency; chair Hillsborough County Dem. Party. Recipient U. South Fla. Young Democrats Humanitarian award, 1974, Diana award NOW, 1975, Woman of Achievement in Arts award Tampa, 1975, Tampa Human Rels. award, 1976, Hannah G. Solomon Citizen of Yr. award, 1980, St. Petersburg Times/Fla. Civil Liberties award, 1980, Friend of Edn. award, 1981, Fla. Alliance for Responsible Parenting award, 1981, Humanitarian award Judeo-Christian Clinic, 1984, Fla. Network of Runaway Youth award, 1985, Ctr. for Women Leader-advocate Friend award, 1985, Nat. Assn. Juvenile Ct. Judges Appreciation award 1986, Legis. Leadership appreciation Centre for Women, 1986, Children's Crisis Ctr. Leadership award, 1987, AAUW leadership award, 1987, Hillsborough County Halfway House appreciation, 1988, Martin Luther King award City of Tampa, 1988, Nat. Fedn. Dem. Women appreciation, 1989, Dept. Legal Affairs appreciation, 1990, Superwoman award Mus. Sci. and Industry, 1990, Nat. Childcare Merit award Nat. Assn. Sch. Psychologists, 1992, Am. Judicature award Am. Judicature Assn., 1993; named. Fla. Motion Picture and TV Outstanding Legislator, 1990, others. Mem. LWV (pres. Hillsborough County 1966-69, lobbyist, Fla. adminstrn. of justice chmn. 1969-74), Temple Guild Sisterhood (past pres.), Am. Arbitration Assn. Home: 45 Adalia Ave Tampa FL 33606-3301

DAVIS, HOLLIE REBECCA, infection control practitioner, medical technologist; b. Hot Springs, Ark., June 21, 1956; d. William Mack Davis and Hollie Lee Neal. BS, Miss. U. Women; MBA, U. So. Miss. Cert. med. technologist Am. Soc. Clin. Pathologists. Lab supr. Hermann Hosp., Houston, 1986-89; lab dir. Tri-City Regional Hosp., Pasadena, Tex., 1990-93; infection control practitioner U. Tex. Med. Br., Galveston, 1994—. Named one of Outstanding Young Women of Am., 1983.

DAVIS, JACQUETTA ANDERSON, English language educator; b. Phila., Jan. 16, 1958; d. Jacob Jenkins and Mary Geneva Anderson Brown; m. Eddie Bennie Davis, Jan. 15, 1990; children: Mary Wehma, Decontee Johanna. B in Bible, Phila. Coll. of Bible, 1979; B in Elem. Edn., Trenton (N.J.) State Coll., 1981, MEd, 1985. Cert. elem. edn. tchr., English as second lang. tchr., N.J. Fgn. missionary Fiji Islands United Missionary Fellowship, Inc., Sacramento, Calif., 1978; missionary, evangelist various chs. in Pa. and N.J., 1975-90; curriculum writer in ESL East Windsor Regional Schs., Hightstown, N.J., 1981—; workshop presenter Nat. TESOL Conf. Miami & Chgo., 1985, 86, N.J. TESOL, 1986, 94, 95, Ctrl. Jersey Network of Black Women for Edn., 1993, 94. Co-author: (with other colls.) ESL Curriculum Management Manual--"English As A Second Language Management Program K-12", 1986. Sun. sch. tchr. various chs. in Trenton, N.J., 1991—; guest spkr. to women and children in various chs. in Pa. and N.J., 1978—. Action grant: software and material for Schoolwide Reading Program in English and Spanish, East Windsor Regional Sch. Dist., 1995. Mem. N.J. TESOL and Bilingual Edn., N.J. Edn. Assn., Kappa Delta Pi (hon. mention for disting. educator award Trenton State Coll. chpt. 1991). Office: E Windsor Regional Sch Dist 384 Stockton St Hightstown NJ 08520

DAVIS, JAN, former secondary school educator; b. Corpus Christi, Tex., June 29, 1943; d. Reuben T. and Ruby (Englert) Pattillo; AA, Del Mar Coll., 1963; BA, U. Houston, 1965; teaching cert. S.W. Tex. State U., 1971; cert. profl. catechist, spiritual dir.; MA St. Mary's U., 1992; children: William A., Wade. Tchr., Edna (Tex.) Jr. H.S., 1966-67, counselor, 1967-68; tchr. Pleasanton (Tex.) H.S., 1972-85; mem. supt.'s com. Pleasanton Pub.

Schs., 1975-77, 78-79; chmn. social studies dept., 1976-85; owner Crystal Rose Enterprises, 1988-92; case asst. Casey Family Program. Leader 4-H, 1978-89, 4-H youth coord. County of Atascosa, Tex., 1986-89. Recipient Meritorious Svc. award Vol. Leaders Assn. Tex., Mem. Tex. Classroom Tchrs. Assn. (Tchr. of Year 1979), Pleasanton Classroom Tchrs. Assn., Nat. Speakers Assn., Lay Preaching Guild, 4-H Vol. Leaders Assn. (pres. Dist. 13 1987-88), Pleasanton Jr. Woman's Club (1st v.p. 1976, pres. 1977), A&M Women's Club of Atascosa County (pres. 1978-80), Spiritual Dirs. Internat., Toastmasters. Roman Catholic.

DAVIS, JANE STRAUSS, business owner; b. Chgo., July 3, 1944; d. Joseph Loeb and Leanore (Purvin) Strauss; m. Muller Davis, Dec. 28, 1963; children: Melissa Davis Smith, Muller Jr., Joseph. BA with honors in Am. Culture, Northwestern U., 1980, postgrad. studies in Am. History, 1980-81. With residential sales Kenneth Friend Realty, Winnetka, Ill., 1971-74, J.H. Kahn Realty, Glencoe, Ill., 1974-77; v.p. personal trust dept. Harris Trust & Savs. Bank, Chgo., 1983-89; v.p. Bankers Trust Co. Pvt. Bank, Chgo., 1989-90; founder Jane Davis Connections, Chgo., 1991—, Connections Next Step, 1993—, Young Chgo. Authors, 1992-95, Charlotte.Com, Inc., Chgo., 1996—; founder Charlotte Com, Inc.; dir. Met. Family Svcs. Mem. woman's bd. Rush-Presbyn.-St. Luke's Med. Ctr., Chgo., 1978—; co-chmn. med. rsch. campaign Michael Reese Med. Ctr., Chgo., 1982-96; mem. costume com. Chgo. Hist. Soc., 1980-90; mem. campaign for gt. tchrs. Northwestern U., Evanston, Ill., 1988-90, mem. vis. com., 1989—, mem. coun. of 100; mem. Chgo. Symphony Orch. Woman's Assn., 1990—; mem. coun. Children's Meml. Hosp. Med. Rsch. Inst., 1991—; mem. Coun. of 100, The Chgo. Bd.; chmn. 50th anniversary day celebration Roosevelt U., Chgo., 1995, co-chmn. Itzhak Pearlman concert, 1996.

DAVIS, JOAN, general contractor, tax preparer, vocational business educator; b. Anderson, Ind., Nov. 24, 1947; d. Harold Brewer and Alice Marie (Doll) Hall; m. L.R. Collier Sr., May 19, 1967 (div. 1980); children: Missy JoAn Collier Basham, L.R. Jr.; m. Timothy G. Davis, Oct. 10, 1982; stepchildren: Geraldine Marie, Eugene Francis. Grad. high sch., Riverside, Calif. Sec. Svc. Electric, Inc., Riverside, 1966-68; pres. Power Electric, Inc., Norco, Calif., 1972-76; office mgr. Cutter Electric, Inc., Rialto, Calif., 1976-77; exec. asst., controller, corp. sec. Home & Country, Inc., Riverside, 1977—; owner, tax preparer Davis Bus. Svc., Riverside, 1978—. Republican. Home: 6981 Pacheco Ct Riverside CA 92509-6326 Office: Home & Country Inc 7265 Jurupa Ave Riverside CA 92504-1011

DAVIS, JOANNE FATSE, lawyer; b. Bridgeport, Conn., June 8, 1956; m. Thomas J. Davis, Jr. BS, Boston U., 1977; JD, U. Bridgeport, 1982. Bar: Conn. 1982, N.Y. 1983. Motions law clk. U.S. Ct. Appeals (2d cir.), N.Y.C., 1982-83; assoc. Debevoise & Plimpton, N.Y.C., 1983-89; sr. corp. counsel Uniroyal Chem. Co., Middlebury, Conn., 1989—; bd. dirs. Legal Ctr. Conn. Nonprofit Orgns. Inc. Mem. Am. Corp. Counsel Assn., Conn. Bar Assn. Soc. Farsarotul (officer). Eastern Orthodox. Office: Uniroyal Chem Co Inc Benson Rd Middlebury CT 06749

DAVIS, JOANNE MARY, advertsing executive; b. Jersey City, Jan. 13, 1953; d. Walter Alan and Ann Mary (Sieno) D. BA, Coll. New Rochelle, N.Y., 1974; MBA, NYU, 1980. Account exec. Doyle Dane Bernbach, N.Y.C., 1974-78; v.p., account supr. Needham Harper and Steers, N.Y.C., 1978-82; v.p., account supr. Wells, Rich, Greene, N.Y.C., 1982-83, v.p., mgmt. supr., 1985-86, v.p. account group, 1986-87, sr. v.p., gen. mgr., 1987-89; pres. Omon, N.Y.C., 1989—; mng. ptnr. bus. devel. Bozell Worldwide, N.Y.C. Democrat. Roman Catholic. Clubs: Advt., 4A's (N.Y.). *

DAVIS, JOLENE BRYANT, magazine publishing executive; b. Lehigh, Iowa, Dec. 11, 1942; d. Joseph Albert and Joyce (Olson) Bryant; m. Richard Alan Alper, Feb. 12, 1967 (dec. July 1975); m. Steven Andrew Davis, Apr. 16, 1979; children: Bryant David, Suzanne Joyce. BA, U. Iowa, 1964; MA, Calif. State U., San Jose, 1972. Registered dietitian, Ind. Home economist The Oregonian, newspaper, Portland, 1965-67; dietitian Ind. U. Sch. Medicine, Indpls., 1973-74; clin. dietitian U. Calif. Hosps. and Clins., San Francisco, 1974-75, chief clin. dietitian, 1975-78, chief rsch. dietitian Clin. Study Ctr., 1979-83; pub., chief exec. officer Our Kids mag. Branford Pub., Inc., San Antonio, 1984—, v.p., 1988—; ptnr. Serendipity Video Prodns., 1996—; also bd. dirs. Branford Pub., Inc., San Antonio; co-founder, ptnr. Serendipity Video Prodns.; sports nutritionist San Antonio Spurs, 1993—; sec., bd. govs. Parenting Publs. Am., San Antonio, 1988-89; v.p., bd. dirs. The Magik Theatre. Mem. San Antonio Conservation Soc., 1985—; bd. dirs. Jewish Family Svc. Assn., San Antonio, 1986-88, Family Resource Ctr., San Antonio; chmn. cultural arts PTA, San Antonio, 1988-94. Recipient Life Mem. award PTA, 1994, Supt.'s award N.E. Ind. Sch. Dist., 1995-96. Mem. Women in Comms. (editor Best Mag. Column and Mag. award of Merit 1988, 90), Am. Dietetic Assn., Soc. Nutrition Edn., San Antonio Dist. Dietetic Assn., Soc. Profl. Journalists, Pi Beta Phi. Home: 178 Country Ln San Antonio TX 78209-2228 Office: Branford Pub Inc 8400 Blanco Rd Ste 201 San Antonio TX 78216-3055

DAVIS, JOY LEE, English language educator; b. N.Y.C., Apr. 3, 1931; d. William Henry and Genevieve (Rhein) Belknap; m. Peter John King, Aug. 26, 1955 (div. Feb. 1985); children: William Belknap King, Russell Stuart King; m. John Bradford Davis, Jr., July 5, 1986. AB, Wellesley Coll., 1952, AM, 1953; PhD, Rutgers U., 1968; postgrad., Oxford (Eng.) U., 1978. Tchr. English Dana Hall Sch. for Girls, Wellesley, Mass., 1953-54; instr. English U. Mo., Columbia, 1954-55, Boston U., 1955-56; tchr. English Brookline (Mass.) High Sch., Spartanburg (S.C.) High Sch., 1956-60; prof. English Ohio Wesleyan U., Delaware, 1966-71, Hamline U., St. Paul, 1972-74, U. Minn., Mpls., 1974-77, Coll. St. Thomas, St. Paul, 1977-88; lectr., dir. Joy Davis Seminars, St. Paul, 1988—; prof. MA in Liberal Studies Program, Hamline U., 1993—. Pub. poetry in New World Writing and Crisp Pine Anthology; lit. criticism in Midwest Quar., 1993, Jour. Grad. Liberal Studies, 1996. Bd. trustees Ramsey County Arts and Sci. Coun., St. Paul, 1974-80. Wellesley Coll. scholar, 1952. Mem. AAUW (dd. dirs., chair ednl. equity com. 1991, Svc. awrd St. Paul br. 1983), Midwest MLA, Mpls. Inst. Fine Arts, Minn. Club (bd. dirs. 1982-88), New Century Club (bd. dirs., spl. subjects chmn.) Schubert Club (bd. dirs., chmn. mus. com.), Wellesley Coll. Club (regional campaign com.), Delta Kappa Gamma. Republican. Presbyterian. Home and Office: 4312 Pond View Dr Saint Paul MN 55110-4155

DAVIS, JUDY, actress; b. Perth, Australia, Apr. 23, 1955; m. Colin Friels, 1984; 1 child, Jack. Student, Nat. Inst. Dramatic Art, Sydney, Australia. Appearences include: (film) High Rolling, 1976, My Brilliant Career, 1979 (Best Actress Sammy award Australian Film and TV Awards 1979, Best Actress award Brit. Acad. Film and TV Arts 1981, Best Newcomer Brit. Acad. Film and TV Arts 1981), Hoodwink, 1981 (Best Supporting Actress Sammy award Australian Film and TV Awards 1981), Winter of Our Dreams, 1981 (Best Actress Sammy award Australian Film and TV Awards 1981), Heatwave, 1982, The Final Option, 1983, A Passage to India, 1984 (Acad. award nominee for best actress 1984), Kangaroo, 1986, High Tide, 1987, Georgia, 1988, Alice, 1990, Impromptu, 1991, Barton Fink, 1991, Naked Lunch, 1991 (Best Supporting Actress award N.Y. Critics Cir. 1991), Where Angels Fear to Tread, 1991, Husbands and Wives, 1992 (Acad. award nominee for best supporting actress 1992), The Ref, 1994, The New Age, 1994, Children of the Revolution, 1996, Absolute Power, 1996; (TV movies) A Woman Called Golda, 1982 (Emmy award nominee 1982), The Merry Wives of Windsor, 1982, Rocket to the Moon, 1986, One Against the Wind, 1991, Serving in Silence: The Margarethe Cammermeyer Story, 1995 (Emmy award); (TV miniseries) Water Under the Bridge, 1982; (stage) Lulu (Frank Wedekind), Piaf (Pam Gem), Insignificance (Terry Johnson), 1982. Office: care ICM 8942 Wilshire Blvd Beverly Hills CA 90211 also: care Colin Freils, Woollomooloo, Sydney NSW 2011, Australia*

DAVIS, JULIA MCBROOM, college dean, speech pathology and audiology educator; b. Alexandria, La., Sept. 29, 1930; d. Guy Clarence and Addie (McElroy) McBroom; m. Cecil Ponder Davis, Aug. 25, 1951 (div. 1981); children: Mark Holden, Paul Houston, Anne Hamilton; m. David G. Reynolds, Aug. 26, 1987. BA, Northwestern State U., Natchitoches, La., 1951; MS, U. So. Miss., 1965, PhD, 1966. Cert. in clin. competence in audiology. Asst. prof. U. So. Miss., Hattiesburg, 1966-69, assoc., 1969-71; assoc. prof. Southwestern State U., Hammond, 1971; faculty U. Iowa, Iowa City, 1971-87; prof., chmn. dept. speech pathology and audiology U. Iowa, 1980-85, assoc. dean Coll. Liberal Arts, 1985-87, dir. Speech and Hearing Ctr., 1979-80; dean Coll. Social and Behavioral Scis. U. South Fla., Tampa, 1987-90, assoc. provost, 1990-91; dean Coll. Liberal Arts, U. Minn., Mpls., 1991-96. Author: (with Edward J. Hardick) Rehabilitative Audiology for Children and Adults, 1981; editor: Our Forgotten Children, 1977; assoc. editor Jour. Speech Hearing Research, 1975-77, Jour. Speech Hearing Disorders, 1982-83. Fellow Am. Speech-Hearing-Lang. Assn. (chmn. program com. 1980-81), Iowa Speech and Hearing Assn. (v.p.-liaison 1972-73, honors 1985); mem. Acad. Rehabilitative Audiology (pres. 1979-80), Iowa Conf. for Hearing Impaired (pres. 1975-76), Sigma Xi. Democrat. Methodist. Office: Univ Minn Dept Comm Disord 115 Shevlin Hall Minneapolis MN 55455

DAVIS, KAREN PADGETT, fund executive; b. Blackwell, Okla., Nov. 14, 1942; d. Walter Dwight and Thelma Louise (Kohler) Padgett; 1 child, Kelly Denise Collins. BA, Rice U., 1965, PhD, 1969. Asst. prof. econs. Rice U., 1969-70; econ. policy fellow Social Security Adminstrn. Brookings Instn., Washington, 1970-71, rsch. assoc., 1971-74, sr. fellow, 1974-77; dep. asst. sec. for planning and evaluation, health HEW, Washington, 1977-80; adminstr. health resources adminstrn. USPHS, Washington, 1980-81; prof. Johns Hopkins U., Balt., 1981-92; chmn., 1983-92; exec. v.p. Commonwealth Fund, N.Y.C., 1992-94, pres., 1995—; bd. dirs. Somatix Therapy Corp.; bd. dirs. Mt. Sinai MEd. Ctr., 1995—; mem. Physican Payment Rev. Commn., 1986-94; dir. Commonwealth Health Fund Commn. on Elderly People Living Alone, 1985-91; vis. lectr. Harvard U., 1974-75. Author: National Health Insurance: Benefits, Costs and Consequences, 1975, Health and the War on Poverty, 1978, Medicare Policy: New Directions for Health and Long-Term Care, 1986, Health Care Cost Containment, 1990. Bd. dirs. Mt. Sinai Med. Ctr., 1995—. Mem. Inst. Medicine, Am. Econs. Assn., Phi Beta Kappa. Democrat. Methodist. Home: 176 E 77th St New York NY 10021-1908 Office: The Commonwealth Fund The Harkness House 1 E 75th St New York NY 10021-2601

DAVIS, KATHARINE ISABELLA, elementary school educator; b. Alexandria, Va., Feb. 28, 1967; d. Gordon Bell and Virginia Mary (Ritchie) D. BA in English, Randolph-Macon Coll., 1988; MEd in Reading, Va. Commonwealth U., 1991. Reading specialist Goochland (Va.) County Pub. Schs., 1991—. Mem. Internat. Reading Assn., Va. State Reading Assn., Richmond Area Reading Coun. (bd. dirs. 1992—). Episcopalian. Office: Byrd Elementary School 2704 Hadensville-Fife Rd Goochland VA 23063

DAVIS, KATHERINE SARAH, physical therapy educator; b. Landstuhl, Germany, Oct. 14, 1960; (parents Am. citizens); d. Quentin Duane and Jean Elizabeth (Marshall) D. BS in Health and Phys. Edn., West Chester U., 1982; MA in Phys. Edn., U. No. Colo., 1983; BS in Phys. Therapy, U. Md., Balt., 1991. Lic. phys. therapist, Colo., Md. Tchr. phys. edn. Baltimore County Pub. Schs., Essex, Md., 1983-85, St. Joseph Sch., Perry Hall, Md., 1985-89; phys. therapist Meml. Hosp., Colorado Springs, Colo., 1991-93; instr. phys. therapy, acad. coord. clin. edn. U. Md., Balt., 1993—; phys. therapist VA Med. Ctr., Balt., 1993—; chair faculty/staff/student affairs com. dept. phys. therapy U. Md., Balt. Mem. Am. Phys. Therapy Assn., Kappa Delta Pi. Office: U Md Dept Phys Therapy 100 Penn St Baltimore MD 20201

DAVIS, KATHLEEN A., lobbyist; b. Phila., Mar. 15, 1958; d. William D. and Laura M. (Colalongo) Badger; m. Mark J. Davis, Sept. 4, 1982; 1 child, Craig Mark. BA, Rowan Coll., 1981. Legis. aide Senator Raymond Zane, Woodbury, N.J., 1981-84; supr. govtl. affairs South Jersey Gas Co., Folsom, N.J., 1984-91; asst. to Gov. Jim Florio, Trenton, N.J., 1991-92; dir. govtl. affairs N.J.-Am. Water Co., Haddon Heights, 1992-95; v.p. South Jersey C. of C., Voorhees, N.J., 1995—. State chair Employer Legis. Com., N.J., 1994-96, so. regional chair, 1993-94; mem. Bus. Vols. for the Arts. Mem. N.J. Utilities Assn. (chair legis. affairs com. 1994-95), N.J. Bus. and Industry Assn. (mem. govt. affairs com.). Office: Kevon Office Ctr 2500 McClellan Ave Pennsauken NJ 08109

DAVIS, KATHRYN WARD, fundraising executive; b. Florence, S.C., Oct. 11, 1949; d. Richard Dixon Ward and Kathryn (McFarland) Duncan; m. Michael R. Bumgardner, Feb. 16, 1974 (div. Nov. 1982); children: Carolyn E., Christopher G.; m. David Addison Davis, May 28, 1983. BA in English, U. N.C., 1971. Dir. devel. WFAE Radio, U. N.C., Charlotte, 1980-82, WUNC Radio, U. N.C., Chapel Hill, 1982-84, U. N.C. Hosps. Med. Found., Chapel Hill, 1984-87, St. Joseph Med. Found., Balt., 1987-88; exec. dir. MCG Found., Mt. Clemens, Mich., 1989-95; dir. devel. Leader Dogs for the Blind, Rochester, Mich., 1995—; fundraising coun. Macomb County Lit. Coun., Mt. Clemens, 1991. Tutor Macomb County Reading Ptnrs., 1992; cons. Jr. Achievement, Detroit, 1991. Named Disting Svc. Toastmasters, Chapel Hill, 1986. Mem. Nat. Soc. Fundraising Execs., Mich. Assn. Hosp. Devel. (pres. 1990-92), Assn. Healthcare Philanthropy (cert., region VI dir. 1994-96), Kiwanis of Sterling Heights (bd. dirs. 1994—, pres. 1996-97), Women's Econ. Club. Republican. Episcopalian. Office: Leader Dogs for the Blind 1039 S Rochester Rd Rochester MI 48307

DAVIS, KATHY J., banker; b. Omaha, Nebr., Oct. 27, 1956; d. Richard L. and Janet Elaine (Evans) Rau; m. Charles W. Harper, Dec. 31, 1978 (div. June 1983); 1 child, Stacey L. Harper; m. Stephen Christopher Davis, May 20, 1989; children: Matthew C., Jennifer R., Rebecca E. Student, Calif. State U., Hayward, 1974-77. Teller, accts. rep. NAS Alameda (Calif.) Federal Credit Union, 1982 83; br. supervisor Bank of Walnut Creek, Calif., 1983-85; asst. ops. mgr. Alameda First Nat. Bank, 1985-92; teller supervisor Bank One, Arlington, Tex., 1992-95; operational compliance teller Southwest Bank, Ft. Worth, 1995—. Mem. Alameda Bank Employees Assn. (pres. 1989-90). Home: 480 Turner-Warnell Rd Mansfield TX 76063 Office: Southwest Bank 3737 SW Loop 820 Fort Worth TX 76133

DAVIS, KIM MCALISTER, real estate sales executive, real estate broker; b. Woodruff, S.C., Dec. 30, 1958; d. James Calhoun and Nancy (Caldwell) McAlister; m. Robert James Godfrey (div.); 1 child, Lindsey Paige; m. Don Brigham Davis, 1988. BA in Elem. Edn., U. S.C., 1982, MBA, 1983—. Cert. tchr., S.C.; lic. real estate, Fla. Adminstrv. asst. Dr. G.R. Shanbhag and Assocs., Woodruff, 1977-78; sales rep. Reimer's Dept. Store, Woodruff, 1978-80; tchr. Spartanburg County Sch. Dist., Woodruff, 1981-82; pres., owner Godfrey Carpets, Inc., Woodruff, 1983-88; pharm. sales rep. Parke-Davis Pharm. Co., Ponte Vedra Beach, Fla., 1989-90. Mem. decorating com. 1st Bapt. Ch., Woodruff, 1984-87; chmn. bd. dirs. Small Towns Program, Woodruff, 1987—; Rep. candidate for Spartanburg County Coun., 1987; mem. S.C. Rep. Com.; sustaining mem. S.C. Rep. Party; chmn. Nat. Bus. Women's Week, 1984; bd. dirs., pres. 1991-93, Ponte Vedra-Palm Valley Elem. Sch. Parent Tchr. Student Orgn.; sustaining mem. Fla. Rep. Party; bd. dirs. St. Johns Pub. Edn. Found., St. Johns County Edn. Found.; mem. human resources strategic planning com. St. Johns County Pub. Schs.; Rep. candidate St. Johns County Sch. Bd., 1994. Named Young Careerist of the Yr., Nat. Bus. and Profl. Women, 1984. Mem. NAFE, Nat. Fedn. Ind. Bus., Greater Woodruff Area C. of C. (pub. spkr., bd. dirs. 1985-87, pres. 1986), Bus. and Profl. Women (v.p. 1985), Woodruff Jr. Women's Club, Ponte Vedra Assn. Realtors, Disting. Million Dollar Club, St. John's County C. of C. (Ponte Vedra coun., exec. bd.). Home: 8160 Seven Mile Dr Ponte Vedra Beach FL 32082-3004 Office: 270 Solano Rd Ponte Vedra Beach FL 32082-2234

DAVIS, LAURA ARLENE, foundation administrator; b. Battle Creek, Mich., Apr. 14, 1935; d. Paul Bennett and Daisy E. (Coston) Borgard; m. John R. Davis, Aug. 7, 1955; children: Scott Judson, Cynthia Ann Davis Welker. BS, Cen. Mich. U., 1986. Sec., Mich. Loan Co., Battle Creek, 1952-56; legal sec. Ryan, Sullivan & Hamilton, Battle Creek, 1957-64; exec. sec. W.K. Kellogg Found., Battle Creek, 1965-76, adminstrn./program asst., 1976, fellowship dir., 1977, asst. v.p. adminstrn., asst. corp. sec., 1978-84, v.p. corp. affairs, corp. sec., 1984-95, spl. asst. to pres., CEO, 1996—. Pres. bd. dirs. Charitable Union, Battle Creek, 1983-85; mem. allocations panel United Way of Battle Creek, 1983, v.p. community rels., 1990-91, 1st v.p., 1994, pres. of bd. 1995—; bd. dirs. Battle Creek Gas Co., 1988—, Riding for the Handicapped Cheff Ctr., 1991—, sec., 1992—; trustee Binder Park Zoo; mem. adv. coun. Argubright Bus. Coll., 1989-90; mem. Visionquest 5000, 1989; mem. selection com. Community Leadership Acad.; bd. dirs. Coun. Mich. Founds., 1994—; mem. membership com. Recipient Athena award C. of C., Community Svc. award J.C. Penney. Mem. Adminstrv. Mgmt. Soc. (pres. chpt. 1982-83), Am. Mgmt. Assn., Battle Creek C. of C. Home: 124 Heather Hills Dr Battle Creek MI 49017-8307 Office: W K Kellogg Found One Michigan Ave E Battle Creek MI 49017

DAVIS, LAURA ROSLYN, economist, international marketing professional; b. Jersey City, N.J., Dec. 27, 1959; d. Paul Leo and Ruth (Hochheimer) Hoffman; m. Robert Michael Davis, May 12, 1984; children: Andrew Benjamin, Jonathan Daniel. BS, Rutgers U., 1980, MS, 1983. Mkgt. economist Purdue U., West Lafayette, Ind., 1983-84; mktg. rsch. mgr. Stephen K. Plasman & Assocs., Mpls., 1985; project analyst The Pillsbury Co., Mpls., 1985-87, materials control mgr., 1987-88; internat. agricultural economist fgn. agricultural svcs. USDA, Washington, 1988-92, internat. mktg. dir. fgn. agricultural svcs., 1992—; fgn. svc. officer fgn. agricultural svc. USDA, Washington, 1990-91. contbr. articles to profl. jours. Instr. Presidential Classroom, Washington, 1990; keyworker Combined Fed. Campaign, Washington, 1989; adv. Jr. Achievement, Mpls., 1986-87. Mem. Kenwood Isles Townhouse Assn. (pres. 1986-87). Address: USDA - FAS Ag Box 1049 Washington DC 20250-1049

DAVIS, LINDA JACOBS, chamber of commerce official; b. Miami, July 10, 1955; d. Martin Jacque and Doris Harriet (Stucker) Jacobs; m. John Joseph Mantos, Jan. 1, 1984 (dec. 1988); m. Perry Davis, June 4, 1989; children: Aaron, Jacob. Student, U. South Fla., 1977. Mgr., cons. Werner Erhard & Assocs., San Francisco, 1978-82, program leader, 1979-90; asst. exec. dir. The Breakthrough Found., San Francisco, 1982-88; owner Mantagaris Galleries, San Francisco, 1988-92; dir. mktg. devel. Marin Child Care Coun., San Rafael, Calif., 1992-94; dir. devel. and pub. affairs Planned Parenthood of Marin, Sonoma and Menodcino, Calif., 1994-96; ptnr. Women's Initiative for Leadership Devel., 1994-96; CEO Mill Valley C. of C., 1996—; profl. fund-raiser. Vol. The Hunger Project, Fla., 1977-78; bd. dirs. Marin Child Care Coun.; appointed commr. Marin Commn. on Women, 1994—. Recipient Outstanding Young Women Am. Mem. NOW (pres. local chpt.), Marin Women's Coalition. Democrat. Jewish. Home: 419 Karla Ct Novato CA 94949 Office: Mill Valley C of C 85 Throckmorton Mill Valley CA 94941

DAVIS, LINDA L., association executive; b. Balt., Mar. 6, 1954; m. Joseph K. Davis Jr., Jan. 13, 1973. AA, Dundalk C.C., Balt., 1996. Exec. dir. Survivors of Incest Anonymous World Svc. Office Inc., Balt., 1982—. Recipient Gov. Victim Assistance award State of Md., 1993. Office: Survivors of Incest Anonymous PO Box 21817 Baltimore MD 21222-6817*

DAVIS, LINDA LARSON, financial information systems executive; b. Pasadena, Calif., Aug. 24, 1956; d. Lawrence Wayne and Eleanor Georgejean (Thompson) Larson; m. Ward Wesley Davis, Aug. 29, 1987. BA, Mills Coll., 1978; postgrad., Golden Gate U., 1986-88. Teller, new accounts clk. Bank Am., Oakland, Calif., 1975-78; customer svcs. rep., asst. mgr. customer svc. Decimus Corp., San Francisco, 1978-83; AVP ops. and security officer Redwood Bank, San Francisco, 1984-85; programming and client svc. supr. Systematics, San Francisco, 1985-88, account exec., 1988-90, account mgr., 1990-92; sales support mgr. ALLTEL Info. Svcs. (formerly Systematics), Little Rock, 1992—. Pillars Club mem. United Way, Little Rock, 1993-96. Mem. NAFE. Lutheran.

DAVIS, LISA ANNE, language educator; b. El Paso, Dec. 3, 1955; d. William Arthur and Betty Lu (Hood) D. BS in Edn., Lock Haven (Pa.) State Coll., 1977; MA in French, Millersville U., 1991. French tchr. Girard (Pa.) High Sch., 1978; French/English tchr. Northeastern High Sch., Manchester, Pa., 1978-80, So. Huntingdon County High Sch., Three Springs, Pa., 1980—. Active Dem. County Com., Huntingdon, 1994—; mem. fin. com. Huntingdon County Arts Festival, Saltillo, Pa., 1990. Mem. So. Huntingdon County Educators' Assn. (pres. 1996—), Am. Assn. Tchrs. French, Nat. Coun. Tchrs. English, Am. Assn. Kidney Patients.

DAVIS, LISA CORINNE, artist; b. Balt., Jan. 22, 1958; d. Robert Clarke and Elaine C. (Carsley) D.; m. Colin Murray Cathcart, Oct. 25, 1986; children: G. Davis Cathcart, Corinne Davis Cathcart. BFA, Pratt Inst., 1980; MFA, CUNY, 1983. Solo exhbns. include Print Club, Phila., 1993, 2d St. Gallery, Charlottesville, Va., 1994, Mcpl. Gallery, Atlanta, 1994, Halsey Gallery, Charleston, S.C., 1994, Dell Pryor Galleries, Detroit, 1994, Project Room Bronx Coun. on the Arts, N.Y., 1996; group shows include Inroads Gallery, N.Y.C., 1984, U.S. Capitol Bldg., Washington, 1986, The Schenectady Mus., N.Y., 1986, Ridge St. Gallery, N.Y.C., 1987, 88, Christie's, N.Y.C., 1989, 90, Artist's Space, N.Y.C., 1990, 91, Okeanos Gallery, Berkeley, Calif., 1992, Pyramid Atlantic Workshop, Washington, 1992, Print Club, Phila., 1992, Granary Books, N.Y.C., 1993, Kenkeleba Gallery, N.Y.C., 1993, Orgn. Ind. Artists, N.Y.C., 1993, Art in General, N.Y.C., 1993, 94, The Bronx Mus. Arts, 1993, 96, Butters Gallery, Portland, Oreg., 1993, Barrett House Galleries, Poughkeepsie, N.Y., 1994, Gallery Annext, N.Y.C., 1994, City Without Walls, Newark, 1994, Papermill, N.Y.C., 1995, Ctr. Contemporary Art, Newark, 1996. NEA fellow, 1995-96. Studio: 321 Greenwich St Ste 4 New York NY 10013-3340

DAVIS, LUANE RUTH, theatrical director, performer; b. Binghamton, N.Y., Sept. 10, 1960; d. Paul Joseph and Ruth Hardin (Wheeler) D., m. Jonathan Allen Fluck, (div. Dec. 1994). BA, Hunter Coll., 1983; MA, Goddard Coll., 1992; stage interpretation in ASL cert., The Juilliard Sch., 1994. Performer Broadway, regional, stock prodns., 1979—, Delta Queen Steamboat Co.; dir., choreographer showcase, cruise lines, children's shows, 1986—; adminstr. Maverick Theatre, N.Y.C., 1986-88; artistic dir. Interborough Repertory Theatre, N.Y.C., 1986—; writer self help, children's musicals, 1990—; pub. edn. specialist Dept. Mental Retardation Devel. Disabilities, N.Y.C., 1990-95; Am. Sign Lang. interpreter; creator Del-Sign acting technique, Interborough Repertory Theatre, N.Y.C., 1992—, spkr. in field. Author: (self-help) Taking Stage, 1995; (musical) Women of the American Revolution, 1991, The World in Her Hands: The Story of Helen Keller, 1993; author, prodr.: (musical) The Little Matchgirl, 1995. Active many accessibility issues for the disabled, N.Y.C. Mem. AFTRA, DAR, Actor's Equity Assn., League of Prof. Theatre Women, Registry of Interpreters of the Deaf. Episcopalian. Home: 42 Kilmer Dr Belle Mead NJ 08502 Office: Interborough Theatre 154 Christopher St 3B New York NY 10014

DAVIS, LUANN RAELENE, fund raising executive; b. Jamestown, N.D., Apr. 15, 1960; d. Wilbert and Lualla (Kungel) W.; m. Lynn Alan Davis, Dec. 12, 1993. BS, Union Coll., 1982; MBA, U. Nebr., 1996. Cert. fund raising exec. Devel. assoc. Union Coll., Lincoln, 1982-86, v.p. for advancement, 1992—; assoc. dir. Philanthropic Svc. for Instns., Silver Spring, Md., 1986-92, also bd. dirs.; bd. dirs. Milton Murray Found. for Philanthropy, Fla.; chair Nebr. Ind. Coll. Fedn. Adv. Coun., Omaha, 1996—. Editor (manual) Schools That Are Ready to Undertake Philanthropy, 1991. Mem. Nat. Soc. of Fund Raising Execs., Kiwanis Club of Lincoln S.E. (bd. dirs. 1993-96). Mem. Seventh-day Adventist. Office: Union Coll 3800 S 48th Lincoln NE 68506

DAVIS, LYNN ETHERIDGE, political scientist, government official; b. Miami, Fla., Sept. 6, 1943; d. Earl DeWitt and Louise (Featherston) Etheridge. BA, Duke U., 1965; MA, Columbia U., 1967, PhD, 1971. Lectr. Miles Coll., Birmingham, Ala., 1966-67; asst. prof. polit. sci. Bernard Coll., Columbia U., N.Y.C., 1970-74; rsch. assoc. Internat. Inst. for Strategic Studies, London, 1973; program analysis staff Nat. Security Council, 1974; asst. prof., lectr. dept. polit. sci. Columbia U., 1974-76; prof., staff mem. Senate Select Com. on Intelligence, 1975-76; dep. asst. sec. of def. for policy plans and nat. security affairs Office of the Under Sec. for Policy, Dept. Def., Washington, 1977-79, asst. dep. under sec. for policy planning, 1979-81; rsch. Internat. Inst. Strategic Studies, London, 1981-82; prof. national security affairs National War Coll., Washington, 1982-85; dir. studies Internat. Inst. Strategic Studies, London, 1985-87; hon. sr. rsch. fellow, dept. war studies Kings Coll., London, 1988-90; rsch. fellow John Hopkins Fgn. Policy Inst, Paul H. Nitze Sch. Advanced Internat. Studies, 1988-91; v.p. army rsch. divsn., dir. Arroyo Ctr. RAND, Santa Monica, Calif, 1991-93; under sec. for arms control and internat. security affairs Dept. State, Washington, 1993—. Author: The Cold War Begins, Soviet American Conflict Over Eastern Europe, 1974. Woodrow Wilson fellow, 1965-66, 69-70, 81-82; Columbia U. fellow, 1965-66, 68-69; recipient David D. Lloyd prize Harry S. Truman Library, 1976. Mem. Coun. on Fgn. Rels., Phi Beta Kappa. Home: 827 S Lee St Alexandria VA 22314 Office: Dept State Under Sec Arms Control/ Intl Security 2201 C St NW Rm 7208 Washington DC 20520-0001

DAVIS, LYNN RUPE, accountant; b. Dallas, Nov. 14, 1950; d. W.L. and Dorothy Lynn (Cole) Rupe; m. Jeff L. Davis, Apr. 19, 1973; children: Brian Rupe, Meredith Lynn. BBA, U. North Tex., 1971, M of Bus. Edn., 1972. CPA Tex., 1987. Bus instr. Mountain View C.C., Dallas, 1972-74; br. recs. cons. Sperry Univac, Dallas, 1974-76; acct. exec. Automatic Data Processing, Dallas, 1978-79; cost acct. supr. TSI Holdings, Inc., Dallas, 1979-84; asst. controller Criswell Devel. Co., Dallas, 1984-87; regional controller The Lehndorff USA Group of Cos., Dallas, 1987-88; acct., cons. pvt. practice, Forney, Tex., 1988-91; sr. cons. mgr. Melson Techs., Inc., Dallas, 1990-96; mng. prin. Oracle Corp., Irving, Tex., 1996—. Tng. fellow U. North Tex., 1971. Mem. AICPA, Tex. Soc. CPAs, Dallas chpt. Tex. Soc. CPAs, Comml. Real Estate Women. Republican. Baptist. Office: Oracle Corp Ste 1000 North Tower 222 W Las Colinas Blvd Irving TX 75039

DAVIS, MARGARET BERGAN, arts administrator; b. Chgo., Nov. 22, 1958; d. John Jerome and Carolyn Elizabeth (Widener) Bergan; m. Andrew Bashaw Davis; children: Caroline Bashaw, Katharine Elizabeth. AB in Art History, Mount Holyoke Coll., 1980. Asst. dir. devel. Northwestern U., Evanston, Ill., 1980-82; exec. dir. The Corporate Project, Chgo., 1982-84; asst. v.p., cons. Charles R. Feldstein & Co., Chgo., 1986-91; dir. devel. Ravinia Festival Assn., Highland Park, Ill., 1991—; mem. adj. faculty Columbia Coll., Chgo., 1995—; panelist Evanston Arts Coun., 1995—. Bd. dirs. Chgo. Children's Mus., 1981—, Milton (Mass.) Acad., 1989—, Family Focus, Chgo., 1995—. Mem. Nat. Soc. Fund Raising Execs., Chgo. Yacht Club. Office: Ravinia Festival 400 Iris Ln Highland Park IL 60035

DAVIS, MARGARET BRYAN, paleoecology researcher, educator; b. Boston, Oct. 23, 1931. AB, Radcliffe Coll., 1953; PhD in Biology, Harvard U., 1957. NSF fellow dept. biology Harvard U., Cambridge, Mass., 1957-58, dept. geosci. Calif. Inst. Tech., Pasadena, 1959-60; research fellow dept. zoology Yale U., New Haven, 1960-61, prof. biology, 1973-76; research assoc. dept. botany U. Mich., Ann Arbor, 1961-64, assoc. research biologist Great Lakes Research div., 1964-70, research biologist, assoc. prof. dept. zoology, 1966-70, research biologist, prof. zoology, 1970-73; head dept. ecology and behavioral biology U. Minn., Mpls., 1976-81, prof. dept. ecology, evolution and behavior, 1976-82, Regents prof. ecology, 1982—; vis. prof. Quaternary Research Ctr., U. Wash., 1973; vis. investigator environ. studies program U. Calif., Santa Barbara, 1981-82; mem. adv. panel for ecology NSF, 1976-79, mem. sci. adv. com. for biology, behavior and social scis., 1989-91, mem. adv. panel for geol. record of global change, 1991-92; mem. planetary biology com. NRC, 1981-82, mem. global change com., 1987-90, mem. screening com. in plant scis., internat. exch. of persons com. 1972-75, mem. sci. and tech. edn. com., 1984-86; vis. rsch. scientist scholarly exch. com. NAS/Nat. Rsch. Coun., People's Republic of China; mem. U.S. nat. com. Internat. Union Quaternary Rsch., 1966-74. Mem. editorial bd. Quaternary Research, 1969-82, Trends in Ecology and Evolution, 1986-92. Recipient Sci. Achievement award Sci. Mus. Minn., 1988, Alumnae Recognition award Radcliffe Coll., 1988, Nevada medal, 1993. Fellow AAAS, Am. Acad. Arts and Scis, Geol. Soc. Am.; mem. NAS (nominations com. 1988), Ecol. Soc. Am. (pres. 1987-88, Eminent Ecologist award 1993)), Am. Quaternary Assn. (councillor 1969-70, 72-76, pres. 1978-80), Internat. Assn. Vegetation Sci., Internat. Assn. for Great Lakes Research (bd. dirs. 1970-73), Nature Conservancy (bd. dirs. Minn. chpt. 1979-85), Brit. Ecol. Soc. (hon.), Phi Beta Kappa, Sigma Xi. Office: U Minn Dept Ecology 100 Ecology Bldg 1987 Upper Buford Cir Saint Paul MN 55108-6097

DAVIS, MARIAN BLOODWORTH, secondary education educator; b. Decatur, Ala., Apr. 7, 1933; d. Benjamin McGowan and Marguerite Maud (Nelson) Bloodworth; m. Judson Ervill Davis, Jr., June 6, 1958; children: Katheryne, Judson Ervill III, James Alexander Bloodworth. BA, U. Ala., Tuscaloosa, 1957; MA, U. North Ala., 1989. Cert. tchr., Ala. Social worker State of Ala., Decatur, 1957-58; tchr. Decatur City Schs., 1979—. Treas., bd. dirs. Jr. League Morgan County, Decatur, 1966-72; area coord. The Close Up Found., Washington, 1990—; mem. Morgan County Reps., 1990—. Mem. NEA, Ala. Edn. Assn., Decatur Edn. Assn., Nat. Coun. Social Studies, Ala. Coun. Social Studies (dist. dir. 1990-94, pres. 1994-95), Nat. Trust Historic Preservation, Ala. Hist. Soc., Nat. Alumni Assn. U. Ala., Delta Kappa Gamma (sec. 1996—), Kappa Delta. Republican. Baptist. Home: 2326 Quince Dr SE Decatur AL 35601-6138 Office: Decatur High Sch 1011 Prospect Dr SE Decatur AL 35601-3229

DAVIS, MARILYNN A., housing agency administrator; b. Little Rock, Oct. 30, 1952; d. James Edward and Erma Lee (Glasco) D. BA in Econs., Smith Coll., 1973; MA in Econs., U. Mich., 1976, Washington U., St. Louis, 1980; MBA, Harvard U., 1982. Sr. credit analyst State Street Bank, Boston, 1981; fin. staff analyst GM, Detroit, 1982-83; sr. fin. analyst GM, N.Y.C., 1984, asst. to group v.p. and chief economist, 1984-86; dir., fin. analyst Am. Express Co., N.Y.C., 1986-87, v.p. risk financing, 1987-92; dep. gen. mgr. finance N.Y.C. Housing Authority, 1992-93; asst. sec. for adminstrn. U.S. Dept. HUD, Washington, 1993—. Former trustee Studio Mus. in Harlem, N.Y.C., ; former chmn. com. on residence, bd. counselors Smith Coll.; former bd. dirs. Queensboro Soc. for Prevention Cruelty to Children; former mem. mgmt. assistance com. Greater N.Y. Fund-United Way. Named One of 100 Top Black Bus. and Profl. Women, Dollars & Sense, 1988; recipient Black Achiever's award YMCA, N.Y.C., 1989. Office: Dept Housing & Urban Devel 451 7th St SW Rm 10110 Washington DC 20410-0001

DAVIS, MARJORIE ALICE, former city official; b. Newton, Mass., July 1, 1917; d. Herbert Francis and Harriet Cole (Dodge) Parmenter; AB, Wellesley Coll., 1939; spl. grad. student Radcliffe Coll., 1941; cert. Harvard U., 1940; spl. courses in social work Boston U., 1961-62; m. Charles William Davis, Aug. 31, 1940 (dec.); children: Harriet Parmenter, Charles Edwin II. Exec. dir. Mid-Essex Area coun. Girl Scouts U.S.A., South Hamilton, Mass., 1952-59, Greater Lynn coun., 1959-63, Merrimack River coun., Andover, Mass., 1963-80; mem. Wenham Bd. Selectmen, 1972-89, chmn., 1977-87. Mem. Met. Area Planning Coun., Boston, 1975—, sec., 1984—, v.p., 1990-92, pres., 1992-93, mem. Mass. Com. Criminal Justice, 1974; v.p. Mass. Assn. Reg. Planning Agys.; exec. dir. Essex County Greenbelt Assn., 1980; mem. Lynn (Mass.) Area Pvt. Industry Coun., 1972-92, bd. dirs. Healthquarters, 1981, treas., 1982-83; v.p., 1983-86, pres., 1986-89; mem. ct./Cmty. Rels. Com. for Essex County, 1975; pres. Hamilton-Wenham Cmty. Svc., 1970-80, bd. dirs., 1983-87; sec. United Fund of Central North Shore, (v.p. United Way of Mass, 1982-88) 1969-84; mem. exec. com. Essex County Adv. Bd., 1983-89, sec., 1984-89; pres. Bay Area Vis. Nurses Assn., 1963-73, Bay area dir., 1983—; v.p. Mass. chpt. Children Am. Revolution, 1944; mem., chmn. Republican Town Com.; corporator North Shore Music Theater, Beverly, Mass., 1992—. Mem. Mass. Selectmen's Assn., Mass. Regional Planning Assn. (v.p. 1995-96), Essex County Selectmen's Assn. (pres. 1984-85, bd. dirs.), Women Elected Mcpl. Ofcls., Mass. Mcpl. Assn. (bd. dirs.), Halibut Point State Park (Mass. chmn. adv. com. 1981—), Mass. Assn. Regional Planning Agys. (v.p.), Christ Ch. Women (pres. 1987-92), Singing Beach club (Manchester, Mass.), Myopia Hunt Club (Hamilton). Home: 143 Grapevine Rd Wenham MA 01984-1801

DAVIS, MARTHA ALGENITA SCOTT, lawyer; b. Houston, Oct. 1, 1950; d. C.B. Scott and Althea (Lewis) Scott Renfro; m. John Whittaker Davis, III, Aug. 21, 1976; children: Marthea, John IV. BBA, Howard U., 1971, JD, 1974. Bar: Tex. 1974, U.S. Dist. Ct. (so. dist.) Tex. 1975, U.S. Ct. Appeals (5th cir.) 1976, U.S. Supreme Ct. 1980. Tax atty. Shell Oil Co., Houston, 1974-79; counsel Port of Houston Authority, 1979-89; sr. v.p., community affairs officer Tex. Commerce Bancshares, 1989—; ptnr. Burney, Edwards, Hall, Hartsfield & Scott, Houston, 1975-78; bd. dirs. Unity Nat. Bank. Bd. dirs. Houston Citizens Chamber, 1980-90, Neighborhood Ednl. Ctr., Houston, 1983-87, Peoples' Workshop to Performing Arts; coordinator Operation Big Vote, Washington, 1984-85; mem. planning commn. City of Houston, 1987-91; founding chair Houston Downtown Mgmt. Corp., 1991-92; with Natural Parliamentarian Links, Inc., 1994—. Recipient Achievement award Greek Council, Houston, 1973; Houston's Most Influential Black Women award Black Experience Mag., Five Young Outstanding Houstonians award Houston Jr. C. of C., 1989; named one of Houston Ten Women of Distinction, Chrones and Colitis Found. and The Houston Press, 1993, one of Women on the Move, Houston Post, 1994. Mem. Nat. Bar Assn. (pres. 1990-91, sec. 1983-88, chmn. voter edn./registration com. 1985-86, pres. award 1993, 94), Black Women Lawyers Assn. (vice chair 1983-84, profl. achievement award 1984), Houston Lawyers Assn. (bd. dirs. 1977-78, 85-89, pres. 1988-89). Baptist. Club: Links (Nat. we. area parliamentarian, Houston parliamentarian). Office: Tex Commerce Bancshares MS 26 TCBE 45 PO Box 2558 Houston TX 77252

DAVIS, MARY HELEN, psychiatrist, psychoanalyst, educator; b. Kingsville, Tex., Dec. 2, 1949; d. Garnett Stant and Emogene (Campbell) D.; m. Timothy Krenke, Oct. 3, 1992. BA, U. Tex., 1970; MD, U. Tex., Galveston, 1975. Cert. Nat. Bd. Med. Examiners, Am. Bd. Psychiatry and Neurology, Child and Adolescent Psychiatry. Intern, then resident in psychiatry SUNY, Buffalo, 1975-78; fellow in child psychiatry U. Cin., 1978-80; tng. in adult and child psychoanalysis Inst. for Psychoanalysis, Chgo., 1982-92; asst. prof. Med. Coll. Wis., Milw., 1980-89, clin. assoc. prof., 1989-93; med. dir. adolescent treatment unit Milw. Psychiat. Hosp., 1981-86, Schroeder Child Ctr., 1986-89; pvt. practice, 1989-93; med. dir. Devereux-Victoria (Tex.) Psych. Residential Treatment Ctr., 1993-94; pvt. practice Lancaster, Pa., 1995—; cons. Milw. Mental Health Cons., 1980-93, Children's Svc. Soc., Milw., 1982-93. Bd. dirs. Next Generation Theatre, Milw., 1988-90, Next Act Theatre, Milw., 1990-92. Mem. Am. Psychiat. Assn., Am. Soc. Adolescent Psychiatry, Am. Med. Women's Assn., Assn. for Child Psychoanalysis. Baptist.

DAVIS, MARY JOE, psychotherapist; b. Grove City, Pa., Oct. 29, 1948; d. Joseph Russell and Theressa (Frisk) La Ritz; children: Mikel Lynn, Jonathan. BA in Psychology, Geneva Coll., 1980, MA in Profl. Psychology, 1992. Pvt. practice psychotherapist Ellwood City, Pa., 1980—; coord. singles ministry Meml. Park Presbyn. Ch., Pitts., 1993-94; site supr. Duquesne U., Pitts., 1995; instr. C.C. of Beaver County, Monaca, Pa., 1995; program designer for laity Chippewa Free Evang. Ch., 1993-94. Author: How to Conduct Successful Writing Workshop, 1989; co-prodr. audio tapes Agoraphobia, 1981. Bd. dirs. Lazarus Ctr., Ambridge, Pa., 1989-93. Home: 130 Jessie St Ellwood City PA 16117 Office: Rte 19 Cranberry Township PA 16066

DAVIS, MARY LOU, secondary education educator; b. Lansford, Pa., Aug. 25, 1943; d. Lester Earl and Susan (Depuy) Snyder; m. David Hugh Davis, June 29, 1968; children: Scott David, Sean Geoffrey. BA in Math., Susquehanna U., 1965; MEd in Math., West Chester Coll., 1969. Cert. tchr. N.Y., Pa. Math. tchr. Marple Newton Sch. Dist., Broomall, Pa., 1965-68, Arlington Ctrl.Sch. Dist., Poughkeepsie, N.Y., 1968-73, 77-79; math. tchr. Spackenkill Union Free Sch. Dist., Poughkeepsie, 1979—, dept. chmn., 1988-91; adj. math. tchr. Dutchess Community Coll., Poughkeepsie, 1973-77, Marist Coll., Poughkeepsie, 1983, 1992-93. Sustainer Jr. League of Poughkeepsie, 1979—; v.p. Arlington Sch. Bd., Poughkeepsie, 1993-94; budget com., past program chmn. Dutchess County Sch. Bd., Poughkeepsie, 1988-94; active Mid-Hudson Alumnae Panhellenic, 1988—; mem. pub. rels. com. Habitat for Humanity, 1995—. Recipient Vision award IBM-Semiconductor Rsch. Corp. Competitiveness Found. Edn. Alliance, 1991. Mem. AAUW, ASCD, Nat. Coun. Tchrs. of Math., N.Y. State Tchrs. Union (alt. retirement rep., mem. pub. rels. com. 1995), Assn. Math. Tchrs. of N.Y. State, Dutchess County Math. Tchrs. Assn., Advocacy for Gifted and Talented Edn. in N.Y. State, Dutchess-Ulster-Sullivan-Orange Math. League (pres. 1984—). Republican. Methodist. Home: 369 Andrews Rd Lagrangeville NY 12540 Office: Spackenkill High Sch 112 Spackenkill Rd Poughkeepsie NY 12603-5040

DAVIS, MARY LOUISE, exceptional education educator, artist; b. Richmond, Ky., Mar. 10, 1944; d. James Martin and Geraldine Marie (Hubble) Pigg; m. Thomas Scott Davis, Aug. 14, 1961 (div. 1992); children: Marie Kathryn DeLory, Jennifer Martin, Julie Louise. BA in Bus. Adminstrn., Eckerd Coll., 1988. Cert. profl. educator, Fla. Owner, mgr. Customs Interiors, Richmond, Ky., 1965-71; interior design instr. Pinellas County Schs., Fla., 1974-84; dist. mgr. Doorstores of Fla. Inc., Miami, 1985-86; exceptional edn. tchr. Hillsborough County Schs., Tampa, Fla., 1989—; interior designer guest lectr. Ky. U., Richmond, 1969-71; judge U.S. Home Corp., Clearwater, Fla., 1980-82; cons. Honeywell Industries, Clearwater, 1983. Columnist Ky. Found. for Women's Club mag., 1966-67, Clearwater Sun, 1982; paintings exhibited Anson Gallery, Inc., Tampa, Fla. Sec. Telford Cmty. Ctr., Richmond, 1968; mem. pageant com. Miss Ky., 1969-71; 6th dist. jr. dir. Ky. Fedn. Women's Clubs, Louisville, 1967-68; corr. sec. Richmond Jr. Womens Club, 1966, pres. 1967. Recipient Disting. Achievement award J. Clifford Macdonald Ctr., 1995; named Clubwoman of Yr., Richmond Jr. Women's Club, 1967. Mem. NEA, Fla. Vocat. Assn., Nat. Assn. Fine Artists, Nat. Mus. Women in Arts, Dunedin Fine Art Ctr. Baptist.

DAVIS, MARY PRITTCHETTE, French language educator, educational consultant; b. Selma, Ala., Aug. 1, 1941; d. Thomas Waldo and Mildred (Jones) D. BA in Englisn magna cum laude, U. So. Alabama, 1983, MA in English, 1985; MA in French, U. Miss., 1988; assistante etrangere French, Min. of Nat. Edn., Paris, 1986-87. Instr. French Tougaloo (Miss.) Coll., 1988-92, coord. modern langs., 1990-93, asst. prof. French, 1993-96; instr. English Jefferson Davis Jr. Coll., Gulfport, Miss., 1990-91; scholar-in-residence N.Y.U., 1993; co-dir. Study Abroad Program in Dijon, France, 1996; cons. in field. Editor: The Harambee Poetry/Photo journal Vol. I, 1995, When She Dances by You: The Harambee Poetry/Photo Journal Vol. II, 1996. Chair culture com. Ptnrs. Ams., Jackson, Miss., 1991-96; program dir. Multicultural Christmas program homeless children, Tougaloo Coll., 1989-95, coord. Thanksgiving & Christmas drive, 1989-95. Recipient Appreciation cert. Tougaloo Student Govt. Assn., 1990, 92, Outstanding Tchr. award Tougaloo Coll., 1990. Mem. AAUW, Nat. Assn. Women Arts, Ptnrs. Ams., Am. Coun. Teaching Fgn. Lang., Am. Assn. Tchrs. French, Miss. Fgn. Lang. Assn., Miss. Craftsmen Guild, Phi Kappa Phi, Alpha Chi, Pi Delta Phi, Sigma Tau Delta.

DAVIS, MATTIE BELLE EDWARDS, retired county judge; b. Ellabell, Ga., Feb. 28, 1910; d. Frank Pierce and Eddie (Morgan) Edwards; m. Troy Carson Davis, June 6, 1937 (dec. Aug. 1948); stepchildren: Jane (Mrs. Robert Gordon Potter), Betsy (Mrs. James W. Clark, Jr.). Student law in law office. Bar: Fla. 1936, U.S. Supreme Ct. 1950. Legal sec., 1927-36; practice with husband in Miami, 1936-48, pvt. practice, 1948-59; judge Met. Ct. County of Dade, Fla., 1959-72, judge County Ct., 1973-80, sr. judge County Ct., 1981—; mem. exec. com. Women's Conf. Nat. Safety Coun., 1960-80, chmn., 1968-70; bd. dirs. Nat. Safety Coun., 1972-80, v.p. women, 1973-80; mem. Fla. Gov.'s Hwy. Safety Com., 1970-81, Nat. Hwy. Safety Adv. Com., 1967-71; mem. registrants adv. bd. SSS, World War II. Pres. Dade County Tb Assn., 1960-62; exec. com. Fla. Tb and Respiratory Disease Assn., 1960-66; pres. Haven Sch. Mentally Retarded, 1958-60, sec., 1960-69; Trustee Andrew Coll., Cuthbert, Ga., 1960-81. Recipient Disting. Svc. to Safety award Nat. Safety Coun., 1988; first woman 50 yr. awardee Fellows of Am. Bar Found., 1987. Mem. Nat. Assn. Women Lawyers (treas. 1961-62, corr. sec. 1962-63, v.p. 1963-64, pres. 1965-66, Appreciation award 1989), Fla. Assn. Women Lawyers (pres. 1957-58), ABA (ho. of dels. 1967-75, 77-81, resolutions com. 1973-75, com. on constitution and by laws 1980-86), Dade County Bar Assn., Fla. Bar, Internat. Fedn. Women Lawyers, Nat. Assn. Women Judges (founder, life mem.), Miami Bus. and Profl. Women's Club (pres. 1952-54), Nat. Fedn. Bus. and Profl. Women's Clubs (dir. dist. Fla. 1956-57), Kappa Beta Pi. Democrat. Methodist (supt. Sunday sch. 1948-54, chmn. ofcl. bd. 1957-60, trustee 1952-67, adminstrv. bd. 1968-90). Club: Zonta Internat. Home: 402 Como Ave Coral Gables FL 33146-3508

DAVIS, MICHELE ANN, secondary school educator; b. Muncie, Ind., July 22, 1956; d. Earl Leroy and Lorraine (Enterkin) D. BS, Ball State U., 1978, MA, 1986. Tchr. social studies and phys. edn. Franklin County Cmty. Sch. Corp., Brookville, Ind., 1980—. Mem. AAHPERD, Eagles, Kiwanis. Home: 9076 Whitewater Dr Brookville IN 47012-9412 Office: Mount Carmel Sch 6178 Johnson Fork Rd Cedar Grove IN 47016-9789

DAVIS, MICHELLE MARIE, elementary education educator; b. Cleve., Jan. 7, 1956; d. Frank Charles and Rita Theresa (Zdrojewski) Koran; m. Gary Wayne Davis, Sept. 24, 1976; children: Benjamin, Zachary. BA, Ball State U., 1978, MA in Edn., 1989. Substitute tchr. Baugo Cmty. Schs., Elkhart, Ind., 1982-83, Middlebury (Ind.) Schs., 1982-84, Goshen (Ind.) Cmty. Schs., 1982-84, Elkhart (Ind.) Cmty. Schs., 1984-87; elem. tchr. Ft. Wayne Diocese, Elkhart at St. Thomas, 1987-91, Williamsburg County Schs., Kingstree, S.C., 1991—; lead tchr. homework ctr. Kingstree Elem. Sch., 1992-93; chair S.C. grammar and Composition textbook rev. com., 1996. Adminstr. food bank St. Ann's Ch., Kingstree, 1992-94, mem. pastoral coun., 1992—, sec. 1992-94, pres. 1995—; vol. outreach ctr., 1992—. Grantee S.C. Dept. Edn., 1994. Mem. S.C. Coun. Tchrs. Math., St. Ann's Women's Club. Home: 106 Gourdin St Kingstree SC 29556-2736 Office: Kingstree Elem Sch 500 Academy St Kingstree SC 29556

DAVIS, PATRICIA ANN, school system administrator; b. Indpls., Feb. 16, 1949; d. Henry Daniel and Freddie Bea (Davis) D.; m. Clarence Cuzette Davis Jr., Dec. 27, 1969; children: Clarence C. III, Chad Davis. BS, Bishop Coll., 1971; M in Ednl. Adminstrn., Dallas Bapt. U., 1994; postgrad., Tex. Women's U. Tchr. fourth grade Arlington (Tex.) Ind. Sch. Dist., 1971-92, asst. prin., 1993—; author Black History curriculum for Arlington Ind. Sch. Dist., 1989, lang. art curriculum, Arlington Ind. Sch. Dist., 1988; mem. Partners of Excellence AISD, 1992-94. Mem. NAACP, Assn. Tex. Profl. Educators, Tex. Alliance Black Sch. Educators, Alpha Kappa Alpha (Silver Star award 1993). Democrat. Baptist. Home: 3419 Kiesthill Dr Dallas TX 75233-2534

DAVIS, PATTI, writer; b. L.A., Oct. 22, 1952; d. Ronald Reagan (former U.S. pres.) and Nancy Davis Reagan; m. Paul Grilley, 1984 (div. 1990). Attended, Northwestern U., U. So. Calif. Hostess, singer Gt. Am. Food and Beverage Co., Santa Monica, Calif.; conducted seminars on dysfunctional families. Appeared in Vega$, Nero Wolfe, Trapper John, M.D.; author: Home Front, 1986, Deadfall, 1989, A House of Secrets, 1992, The Way I See It, 1992, Bondage, 1994; featured in Playboy Mag., June 1994. Office: Simon & Schuster 1230 Ave of Americas New York NY 10020*

DAVIS, PAULETTE MCMAHAN, shop owner; b. Bakersville, N.C., Aug. 25, 1952; d. Paul and Josephine (McKinney) McMahan; m. Michael H. Davis, Apr. 17, 1988; children: Lydia Ashley Jayne, Michaela Josie Lee. BA in Classical Langs., Berea (Ky.) Coll., 1977. Cert. elem. tchr., N.C. Tchr. St. Geneieve of The Pines, Asheville, N.C., 1984-87, Carolina Way Sch., Asheville, N.C., 1987-89; mgr., owner Profl. Bicycles, Asheville, N.C., 1989—. Memt. Altamount Cycling Fedn. (town coord. 1994—), Land of Sky Racing Team (v.p. 1989-93). Home and Office: Pro Bikes 793 Merrimon Ave Asheville NC 28804

DAVIS, REGINA CATHERINE (GINA DAVIS), advocate; b. Miami, Apr. 7, 1951; d. Leonard William and Elizabeth (Sirback) Bartish; m. James P. Davis, Jr., Feb. 1, 1974 (div. 1984); 1 child, Jesse Lee. Student, U. Md., 1993—. V.p. Davis Prodns., N.Y.C., 1974-84; exec. recruiter Cornell Comp Corp., N.Y.C., 1984-90; recruitment cons. Washington, 1990-91; v.p. Main-Frame Applications, Inc., Washington, 1991-92; pres. Assn. Rape & Assault Prevention, Silver Spring, Md., 1993—. Active PTA, N.Y.C., 1976-83; vol. Beth Israel Hosp., N.Y.C., 1976; den. leader Cub Scouts Am., N.Y.C., 1979-83; mem. steering com. Md. Commn. Women Legis. Agenda, 1994; active Legis. Agenda for Md. Women, 1994-95; outreach vol. Montgomery County Sexual Assault Program, 1995; mem. Md. Coalition Against Sexual Assault. Mem. Women's Leadership Conf. Va. Democrat. Office: Assn Rape & Assault Prevention PO Box 3307 Silver Spring MD 20918-3307

DAVIS, RISA F., lawyer; b. Bklyn., May 31, 1962. BA magna cum laude, Barnard Coll., 1984; JD, NYU, 1987. Bar: N.Y. 1988. Ptnr. Anderson Kill Olick & Oshinsky, N.Y.C. Office: Anderson Kill Olick & Oshinsky 1251 Ave of the Americas New York NY 10020-1182*

DAVIS, RUTH C., pharmacy educator; b. Wilkes-Barre, Pa., Oct. 27, 1943; d. Morris David Davis and Helen Jane Gillis. BS, Phila. Coll. Pharmacy and Sci., 1967. Cert. pharmacist, Pa., Md. Mgr. pharmacist Fairview Pharmacy, Etters, Pa.; mgr., pharmacist Neighborcare Pharmacy, Balt.; dir. ambulatory svcs. Rombro Health Svcs., Balt.; tchr., pharmacist Boothwyn Pharmacy, Phila.; pharm. cons. Nat. Rx Svcs. of Pa.; Eagle Managed Care, 1996. Republican. Baptist. Home and Office: 75 Lion Dr Hanover PA 17331-3849

DAVIS, SANDRA BERNICE, nurse anesthetist; b. Charleston, S.C., Apr. 15, 1946; d. Sanford Quinton and Bernice Mildred (DeLoach) D. Diploma, Spartanburg Gen. Hosp. Sch. Nursing, 1967; cert., Ga. Bapt. Hosp. Sch. Anesthesia, 1972; BA, Stephens Coll., 1985. RN; cert. RN anesthetist. Staff nurse Roper Hosp., Charleston, 1967-68; staff anesthetist Ga. Bapt. Hosp., Atlanta, 1973-76; freelance anesthetist Forsyth County Hosp., Cumming, Ga., 1976-80; anesthetist Med. U. S.C., Charleston, 1983-86, Humana Women's Hosp., Tampa, Fla., 1986-88, Tampa Outpatient Surgical Facility, 1988-90. Care group leader Met. Cmty. Ch., Tampa, 1993—, eucharistic minister, 1994—. Lt. USN, 1968-70, Vietnam. Decorated Nat. Def. medal, Unit Commendation medal, Vietnam Svc. medal; recipient Campaign medal Republic of Vietnam, 1969. Mem. Navy Nurse Corp Assn. Democrat.

DAVIS, SARA IMOGENE, nurse anesthetist; b. Franklin, Ga., Oct. 17, 1927; d. Troy Madison and Ora Thelma (Prince) Shellnutt; divorced; children: Pamela Regina, Benjamin Earl. RN, Ga.; cert. RN anesthetist, La. Nurse inpatient clinic Macon (Ga.) Clinic, 1948-52; nurse Providence Lying In Hosp., 1955-58; anesthetist U. Calif.-San Diego Med. Ctr., 1961-95; Pres. Nursing Sch., Savannah, Ga., 1947-48, treas. student body, 1947-48. Author: (book of verse) As I See It, 1955. Mem. Dem. Nominating Com., 1992-96. Lt. U.S. Army, 1953-54. Mem. Am. Assn. Nurse Anesthetists, State Anesthetists, Calif. Assn. Nurses. Democrat. Home: 4768 Allied Rd San Diego CA 92120

DAVIS, SARA LEA, pharmacist; b. Knoxville, Tenn., Aug. 1, 1951; d. Horace William and Margaret Jewel (Hill) D. BS in Liberal Arts, U. Tenn., 1973; BS in Pharmacy, U. Tenn., Memphis, 1976, PharmD, 1977. Asst. mgr. Pharmaco Nuclear, Inc., Chgo., 1977-79; nuclear pharmacist Kansas City, Mo., 1979, Bapt. Meml. Hosp., Memphis, 1979-83; asst. mgr. Syncor, Inc., Washington, 1983-84; staff pharmacist Rite Aid Corp., Knoxville, 1984-87, pharmacist-in-charge, 1987—; rep. 3d High Country Nuclear Medicine Conf., Vail, Colo., 1983; mem. adv. bd. V.I.P. Home Nursing & Rehab., Knoxville, 1985-86. Active Leconte Exec. Women's Coun. Mem. Am. Pharm. Assn., Acad. Pharm. Sci. (sect. nuclear pharmacy), Soc. Nuclear Medicine, Memphis Bus. and Profl. Women's Assn. (bd. dirs. 1982-83), Club Leconte, U. Tenn. Century Club, Mortar Bd., Phi Beta Kappa, Phi Kappa Phi, Rho Chi, Alpha Lambda Delta. Baptist. Office: Rite Aid Pharmacy 508-B E Tri-County Blvd Oliver Springs TN 37840-1436

DAVIS, SARAH IRWIN, retired English language educator; b. Louisburg, N.C., Nov. 17, 1923; d. M. Stuart and May Amanda (Holmes) D.; m. Charles B. Goodrich, Nov. 18, 1949 (div. 1953). AB, U. N.C., 1944, AM, 1945; PhD, NYU, 1953. Teaching asst. English dept. NYU, 1948-51; tchr. English Elizabeth Irwin High Sch., N.Y.C., 1951-53; editor coll. texts Henry Holt, N.Y.C., 1953-55; editor coll. texts, enclopedias McGraw-Hill, N.Y.C., Rome, 1953-60; asst. prof. English Louisburg (N.C.) Coll., 1960-63; asst. prof. English Randolph-Macon Woman's Coll., Lynchburg, Va., 1963-70, assoc. prof. English, 1970-75, chairperson Am. studies, 1971-87, prof. English and Am. studies, 1975-87, ret., 1987. Contbr. articles to profl. jours. Mem. MLA, Am. Studies Assn., N.C.-Va. Coll. English Assn. (various coms.), Franklin County Hist. Soc. (pres. 1989—). Home: PO Box 246 Louisburg NC 27549-0246 also: PO Box 998 Chapel Hill NC 27514-0998

DAVIS, SHEILA KAY, legal secretary; b. Elkins, W.Va., Dec. 18, 1966; d. Darl Timmie Sr. and Gloria Becky (Armstrong) Kelley; m. Howard William Davis Sr., Nov. 23, 1985; 1 child, Howard William Jr. Diploma, Randolph County Vo-Tech., 1985, Computer Tng. Ctr., 1992. Office mgr., legal sec. Carlton K. Rosencrance Law Office, Elkins, 1986—. Sec. Elkins Jaycees, 1989, v.p., 1990.

DAVIS, SUSAN GRAY, academic administrator; b. Providence, Apr. 28, 1949; d. Robert Joseph and Harriet Eleanor Gray. BA in English Lit., Regis Coll., 1971; EMBA, Claremont Grad. Sch., 1994. Libr. dept. econ. U. Rochester, 1971-73, sec. to grad. program, libr. dept. econ., 1974-76; rsch. asst. Calif. Inst. Tech., Pasadena, 1973-74, 76-77, sec. to grad. program in social scis., 1977-81, divsn. adminstr., divsn. humanities and social sci., 1981—; com. on the quality of life Calif. Inst. Tech., Pasadena, 1990, James Michelin seminar com., 1992—, faculty liason com. on reengring., 1995—; deans alumni adv. coun. Drucker Ctr., Claremont (Calif.) Grad. Sch., 1995—. Bd. govs. L.A. Urban League, Pasadena-Foothill, 1994, exec. com., 1995; bd. dirs. Pasadena Dance Theatre, 1994-95. Recipient Medal of Excellence, Women at Work, 1989. Mem. AAUW, Caltech Mgmt. Assn., Orgn. for Women at Caltech. Office: Calif Inst Tech Mail Code 228-77 1201 E California Blvd Pasadena CA 91125

DAVIS, SUSAN LYNN, public relations executive; b. Brooklyn, N.Y., Nov. 29, 1947; d. Morton J. and Eunice Patricia (bailey) D.; 1 child. BA, Finch Coll., 1969; MA, George Wash. U., 1979. Dir. public relations Girls Clubs of Am., N.Y., 1978-81; pres. Susan Davis Pub. Relations, N.Y., 1982-90; dir. comm. YWCA of City of N.Y., 1991-95; dir. pub. affairs Banjamin N. Cardozo Sch. of Law, Yeshiva U., 1995—. Contbr. article to Mag. Pres. Eye and Ear Theatre, 1980-90; mem. Pres. Commn. on the Arts and Humanities, Wash., 1983-90; advisor Alexander Julian Found., 1986—; bd. dirs. N.Y. Women's Found., 1996—; mem. adv. bd. fine arts dept. Fashion Inst. Tech., 1995—; mem. com. Elsa Mott Ives Gallery, YWCA, N.Y.C., 1995—. Mem. Pub. Rels. Soc. Am. Office: Benjamin N Cardozo Sch of Law 55 Fifth Avenue New York NY 10003

DAVIS, SUZANNE GOULD, temporary employment service executive; b. N.Y.C., Apr. 22, 1947; d. Lawrence Robert and Diana (Klotz) Gould; 2 children. Diploma in French Civilization Studies with honors, Sorbonne U., Paris, 1967; BA in French magna cum laude, Tufts U., 1968; MA in ESL Edn., Columbia U., 1975, MLS, 1984. Prodn. asst. James Garrett and Ptnrs., N.Y.C., 1969-70; adminstrv. asst. Alvin Toffler, N.Y.C., 1970-71; dir. mktg. Econ. Models Ltd., London, 1971; mgr. John Player Info. Bur., London, 1972-73; mgr. mktg. Berkey Film Processing, N.Y.C., 1974-75; freelance editor, translator N.Y.C., 1975-82; gen. mgr. Rosemary Scott Temps. Inc., N.Y.C., 1983-86; pres. Suzanne Davis Temps. Inc., N.Y.C., 1986—. Editor-translator: La Méthode Orange: Teacher's Manual, 1977. Mem. Arts and Bus. Coun., N.Y.C., 1984-86, Common Cents N.Y., 1991—. Mem. NAFE, Nat. Assn. Women Bus. Owners, Spl. Librs. Assn., N.Y. Assn. Temp. Svcs. (bd.dirs. 1986-87, co-chmn. program com.), Murray Hill Bus. and Profl. Women's Orgn. (scholar com. 1985, chair, Young Careerist award 1986-90), Gotham Bus. and Profl. Women's Orgn., Beta Phi Mu. Office: Suzanne Davis Temps Inc 20 E 46th St Ste 302 New York NY 10017-2417

DAVIS, SUZANNE SPIEGEL, retired information specialist; b. St. Louis, Sept. 27, 1935; d. Albert Louis Jr. and Dorothy Lydia (Grafeman) Spiegel; m. Glenn Guy Davis Jr., Sept. 23, 1961 (dic. Mar. 1986); 1 child, Wendy Sue. BA, U. Okla., 1957; MLS, U. Ill., 1958. Reference asst. Atlanta Pub. Libr., 1958-59, head adult dept. Ida Williams br., 1959-61, head Fulton County dept., 1961-62; pub. svcs. and documents libr. Queens Coll. Libr., Charlotte, 1969-83; info. specialist Pub. Libr. Charlotte and Mecklenburg, 1983—. Pres. Charlotte Panhellenic Congress, 1965-66, Charlotte Nature Mus. Guild, 1969-70; rec. chmn. ARC, Mecklenburg County Unit, Charlotte, 1968-69, tng. chmn., 1969-70. Mem. Southeastern Libr. Assn., N.C. Libr. Assn., Charity League, Beta Phi Mu, Phi Alpha Theta, Alpha Phi. (Michaelenean award 1984). Republican. Presbyterian.

DAVIS, TEDDI LEE, business administrator; b. Denver, Apr. 4, 1960; d. Vincent Clark and Judith A. (Schamp) Fisk; m. Gary Wayne Davis, June 10, 1978; children: Thea, James. BBA magna cum laude, U. Denver, 1988. Dep. tax assessor Iraan-Sheffield (Tex.) Independent Sch. Dist., 1978-80; exec. asst. Arthur Andersen, Denver, 1980-81; tax analyst ARCO, Denver, 1981-87; assoc. and bus. mgr. Klipp Partnership, P.C., Denver, 1987-91; owner Davis & Assocs., Broomfield, Colo., 1991—; cons. Gensler & Assocs., Denver, 1991, Associated Bus. Products, Denver, 1992-93, Accurate Carpentry and Construction, Arvada, Colo., 1993-94, Scott Bourn Assocs., Broomfield, 1994-95; instr., developer nine month seminar series Small Bus. Acad., 1995. Commr. Planning and Zoning Commn., Broomfield, 1991—; mayoral cand. City of Broomfield, 1994; pres. Amateur Swimmers Assn., Broomfield, 1994—; voting mem. strategic planning com. City of Broomfield, 1995—. Mem. Suburban League (pres. 1995—). Republican. Roman Catholic. Office: Davis & Assocs 13730 Silverton Dr Broomfield CO 80020-6033

DAVIS, TERRI ANN, administrator; b. Portales, N.Mex., July 1, 1941; d. Sylvester Steven and Winnie Mae (Creamer) Kos; m. Michael Dean Ware, June 9, 1961 (div. Feb. 1990); children: Don, David, Steve. Diploma, Glendale C.C., 1990. RN Ariz., 1990. Owner, broker New Beginnings Realty, Phoenix, 1969-96; nurse St. Joseph's Hosp., Phoenix, 1990-91; nurse, clin. mgr. GranCare, Inc., Phoenix, 1991-92, dir. case mgmt., 1992-96; corp. dir. bus. devel. Plaza Healthcare, Inc., Scottsdale, Ariz., 1996—. Find raiser Rep. Party, Phoenix, 1996. Mem. Case Mgmt. Soc. Am. (founder, nominating com. 1995, v.p. 1996—), Scottsdale C. of C. Home: 1126 E Cheryl Phoenix AZ 85020 Office: Plaza Healthcare Inc 1475 N Granite Reef Rd Scottsdale AZ 85257

DAVIS, VICKI LYNN, college public relations director; b. Worthington, Minn., Nov. 6, 1956. BS in Mass Comms., Mankato State U., 1980; MA in Comm., St. Louis U., 1994. Newspaper reporter Wheaton (Minn.) Gazette, 1980; mem. prodn. staff Daily News, Bowling Green, Ky., 1981-82; graphic artist Fort Worth (Tex.) News Tribune, 1984-86; office mgr. Geotechnical Assocs., Collinsville, Ill., 1987-90; pub. rels. specialist Parks Coll. St. Louis U., Cahokia, Ill., 1990-95; dir. pub. rels. and publs. St. Louis Coll. of Pharmacy, 1995—. Bd. dirs. Our World-Educare Daycare, Ofallon, Ill., 1994—; Spl. Olympics Agy. Coord. Mem. Internat. Assn. Bus. Communicators. Office: St Louis Coll Pharmacy 4588 Parkview Pl Saint Louis MO 63110

DAVIS, WANDA ROSE, lawyer; b. Lampasas, Tex., Oct. 4, 1937; d. Ellis DeWitt and Julia Doris (Rose) Cockrell; m. Richard Andrew Fulcher, May 9, 1959 (div. 1969); 1 child, Greg Ellis; m. Edwin Leon Davis, Jan. 14, 1973 (div. 1985). BBA, U. Tex., 1959, JD, 1971. Bar: Tex. 1971, Colo. 1981, U.S. Dist. Ct. (no. dist.) Tex. 1972, U.S. Dist. Ct. Colo. 1981, U.S. Ct. Appeals (10th cir. 1981, U.S. Supreme Ct. 1976. Atty. Atlantic Richfield Co., Dallas, 1971; assoc. firm Crocker & Murphy, Dallas, 1971-72; prin. Wanda Davis, Atty. at Law, Dallas, 1972-73; ptnr. firm Davis & Davis Inc., Dallas, 1973-75; atty. adviser HUD, Dallas, 1974-75, Air Force Acctg. and Fin. Ctr., Denver, 1976-92; co-chmn. regional Profl. Devel. Inst., Am. Soc. Mil. Comptrollers, Colorado Springs, Colo., 1982; chmn. Lowry AFB Noontime Edn. Program, Exercise Program, Denver, 1977-83; mem. speakers bur. Colo. Women's Bar, 1995—, Lowry AFB, 1981-83; mem. fed. ct. liaison com. U.S. Dist. Ct. Colo., 1983; mem. Leaders of the Fed. Bar Assn. People to People Del. to China, USSR and Finland, 1986. Contbr. numerous articles to profl. jours. Bd. dirs. Pres.'s Coun. Met. Denver, 1981-83; mem. Lowry AFB Alcohol Abuse Exec. Com., 1981-84. Recipient Spl. Achievement award USAF, 1978; Upward Mobility award Fed. Profl. and Adminstrv. Women, Denver, 1979, Internat. Humanitarian award CARE, 1994. Mem. Fed. Bar Assn. (pres. Colo. 1982-83, mem. nat. coun. 1984—, Earl W. Kintner Disting. Svc. award 1983, 1st v.p. 10th cir. 1986—, Internat. Humanitarian award CARE, 1994), Zach Found. for Burned Children (award 1995), Colo. Trial Lawyers Assn., Bus. and Profl. Women's Club (dist. IV East dir. 1983-84, Colo. pres. 1988-89), Am. Soc. Mil. Comptrollers (pres. 1984-85), Denver South Met. Bus. and Profl. Women's Club (pres. 1982-83), Denver Silver Spruce Am. Bus. Women's Assn. (pres. 1981-82; Woman of Yr. award 1982), Colo. Jud. Inst., Colo. Concerned Lawyers, Profl. Mgrs. Assn., Fed. Women's Program (v.p. Denver 1980), Colo. Woman News Community adv. bd. 1988—, Dallas Bar Assn., Tex. Bar Assn., Denver Bar Assn., Altrusa, Zonta, Denver Nancy Langhorn Federally Employed Women. (pres. 1979-80). Christian.

DAVIS, YVONNE D., public administrator; b. Orange, N.J., Sept. 21, 1947; d. William J. and Alice-Ruth Patterson; m. Royce Davis; children: Shannon K., Sarah K. BA in Spanish, Montclair State Coll., Upper Montclair, N.J., 1975; cert. pub. mgmt., Kean Coll., Union, N.J., 1982; cert. equal employment, Rutgers U., 1984. Bilingual family svc. worker Essex County Div. Welfare, Dept. Citizen Svcs., Newark, 1971-78, family svc. supr., 1978-81, adminstrv. analyst, 1981-83, prin. personnel technician, 1983-86; personnel mgr., supr. prin. personnel technician Essex County Dept. Citizen Svcs., Newark, N.J., 1984—; adminstrv. deputy dir. of Welfare Dept. of Citizen Svcs. Div. of Welfare, Newark, N.J., 1992-93; dir. Essex County Dept. Citizen Svcs., 1994—. Mem. exec. bd. Essex County Minority Employees Assn., Newark, 1984-85; mem. employment coun. Tng., Inc., Newark; mem. Essex County Adv. Bd. on Status of Women; mem. Coordinating Coun. for Social Svcs., Essex County, N.J.; mem. Essex County Ins. Commn.; active Epilepsy Found. Am., Trenton. Recipient Excellence in Personnel Mgmt. award Essex County Minority Employees Assn., 1986, Excellence in Spanish award Nat. Assn. Tchrs. Spanish, 1964, 65, Excellence in French award Nat. Assn. Tchrs. French, 1965, Recognition award United Way, 1984-88; cert. of appreciation U.S. Dept. Treas., 1984, tng. cert. N.J. Div. Civil Rights, 1988. Mem. NAFE, NAACP, Am. Mgmt. Assn., Am. Assn. Affirmative Action, Nat. Assn. Pub. Sector Equal Opportunity Officers, Mcpl. Career Women Newark Inc. Democrat. Baptist. Office: Essex County Dept Citizen Svcs Directors Office 18 Rector St Fl 9 Newark NJ 07102-4512

DAVIS-DURANT, ERLYNNE, social work educator; b. Cleve., Oct. 16, 1925; d. Earle Vernon and Margaret Ruth (Sanders) Poindexter; m. Charles E. Davis Sr. (dec.); 1 child, Charles E. Jr.; m. John H. Durant. AB, Oberlin Coll., 1947; MS in Social Adminstrn., Western Res. U., 1950. Case worker Cuyahoga County Welfare Dept., Cleve., 1947-48, Family Svc. Assn., Cleve., 1950-54; supr. Cuyahoga County Welfare Dept., Cleve., 1956-63; instr. Sch. Applied Social Scis. Case Western Res. U., Cleve., 1963-66, asst. prof., 1966-69, assoc. prof. Sch. Applied Social Scis., 1969-87, assoc. prof. emerita Mandel Sch. Applied Social Scis., 1987—; cons., staff devel. trainer, continuing edn. instr., speaker in field, 1957-96. Bd. trustees Project Friendship, Cleve., 1986-91, pres., 1987, Youth Visions, 1991-95; bd. dirs. Met. YWCA, Cleve., 1987-92; vol. Ret. Srs. Vol. Program, Cleve., 1989—; mem. St. James African Meth. Episc. Ch. (Disting. Svc. award 1983); mem. adv. coun. Coun. Ret. Srs. Vol. Program, Greater Cleve., 1991-94, 95—; assoc. Aldersgate United Meth. Ch.; active Cmty. Coun., 1993-95, Fairhill Exec. Coun. Fairhill Ctr. for Aging, 1996—; vol. Intergenerational Resource Ctr.; mem. adv. coun. on sr. and adult svcs. Cuyahoga County, 1996—, coun. on older persons Fedn. Cmty. Planning, 1996—. Recipient 20h Anniversary Founders Recognition, Ctr. for Human Svcs., Cleve., 1990, Ebony Rose Edn. award Murtis Taylor Multi-Svc. Ctr., Cleve., 1990, Ebony Rose Most Honored award, 1995, Disting. Alumni award Sch. Applied Social Scis. Case Western Res. U., 1987, Women of Distinction award Women's Missionary Soc. African Meth. Episcopal Ch., 1983. Mem. NAACP, Alpha Kappa Alpha (Achievement award Alpha Omega chpt. 1963, 74).

DAVIS-IMHOF, NANCY LOUISE, elementary school educator; b. Stamford, Conn., Feb. 17, 1940; d. Ernest A. and Margaret (Carlson) Davis; m. William A. Imhof, Nov. 17, 1962 (div. Dec. 1989); children: Samuel, Jacqueline, Susan. BA, Barnard Coll., 1962; MEd, George Mason U., 1975. Cert. tchr., Va. Tchr. Arlington (Va.) Pub. Schs., 1975—; freelance photographer. Mem. family life edn. com., Arlington Pub. Schs., 1990-91; mem. ad hoc com. on future of T.J. Community Ctr., 1991; mem. vestry St. Georges Episcopal Ch., Arlington, 1987-90. Arlington Sch. System grantee, 1988-89. Mem. NEA, Va. Edn. Assn., Arlington Edn. Assn. (sch. rep. 1989, 90). Democrat. Home: 894 N Ohio St Arlington VA 22205-1530 Office: Arlington Traditional Sch 855 N Edison St Arlington VA 22205

DAVIS-JEROME, EILEEN GEORGE, principal; b. N.Y.C., Nov. 10, 1946; d. Rennie and Flora May (Compton) George; m. Bruce Davis, Aug. 8, 1970 (div. 1978); m. Frantz Jerome, Sept. 7, 1982; 1 child, Thais Davis. BFA, Pratt Inst., 1968; MA, CUNY, 1971, PD, 1990. Lic. ednl. adminstr., prin., instrn. specialist, N.Y. Tchr. fine arts Herbert Lehman High Sch., Bronx, N.Y., 1971-75; tchr. English/fine arts Jr. High Sch. 131, Bronx, 1975-76; tchr. English Jr. High Sch. 22, Bronx, 1976-79; tchr. fine arts Andrew Jackson High Sch., Cambria Heights, N.Y., 1979-83, coord. art dept., 1986-92; admissions counselor Fashion Inst. Tech., SUNY, N.Y.C., 1983-85; coord. Queensborough Coll. Project Prize, Bayside, N.Y., 1991-92; project dir. Andrew Jackson Magnet High Sch., Cambria Heights, N.Y., 1993—, project dir. humanities and the arts, 1994—; ednl. adminstr. Queens High Sch. Office, N.Y.C. Pub. High Schs., Corona, N.Y., 1993-94; prin. humanities and the arts Magnet H.S., Cambria Heights, N.Y., 1994—; coord. internat. studies Friends of Jackson High Sch., Cambria Heights, 1986-93, equal opportunity coord., 1989-92; exam asst. N.Y. C. Bd. Edn., Bd. Examiners, Bklyn., 1983-87; curriculum/career cons. Fashion Inst., SUNY, Detroit, Washington, Phila., 1983-86. Curriculum writer N.Y. State Project ot Implement Career Edn., 1975, N.Y. State Futuring, 1984; proposal writer Magnet Sch. Funding, 1993; author: Resource Book, 1989. Mem., speaker Cambria Heights Civic Assn., 1983; mem. N.Y. Urban League, N.Y.C.; vol. Mayor's Vol. Action/Alpha Sr. Cr., Cambria Heights, 1984; vol. Black Spectrum Theatre Co., 1983-86. Recipient Recognition award Black Spectrum Theatre Co., 1983, Speakers award N.Y.C. Bd. Edn. Open Doors, 1983-84, Black Exec. Exch. Program Nat. Urban League, N.Y.C., 1984, Developer Grant award Impact II Grant, N.Y.C., 1989; named Educator of Yr. NAACP/ACT-50, N.Y.C., 1992. Mem. ASCD, N.Y. State Art Tchrs. Assn., N.Y.C. Art Tchrs. Assn. (v.p., sec. 1983-85, cert. 1983-86), Cultural Heritage Alliance (assoc., Recognition award 1986), Delta Sigma Theta (chair arts and letters 1991—, Golden Life award 1991), Phi Delta Kappa (Disting. Cert. 1994). Democrat. Episcopalian. Office: Magnet HS Humanities and the Arts 207-01 116th Ave Jamaica NY 11411-1038

DAVIS-MYERS, JESSICA KATHERINE, elementary education educator; b. N.Y.C., Aug. 29, 1948; d. Hugh Peter and Alice Clinton (Kydd) Davis; m. Daniel A. Myers III, June 30, 1974; children: Andrew, Christopher. BA in History, U. Bridgeport, 1970; MEd in Reading, U. Mass., 1975. Cert. English, history, social studies, reading, sci. and elem. edn. Tchr. grade 6 advanced placement, grade 7 English Boston (Mass.) Pub. Schs., 1971-81; tchr. adult edn. Odwin Learning Ctr, Dorchester, Mass., 1985-88; tchr. grade 7 social studies, lang. arts and reading Quincy (Mass.) Pub. Schs., 1988—; co-chairperson Accelerated Schs. Vision Celebration, Quincy, 1992; cadre mem. extra curricular Sterling Accelerated Sch., Quincy, 1993. Cub scout leader Boy Scouts Am., Quincy, 1985-87. Named Outstanding Tchr., Patriot Ledger Newspaper, Quincy, 1994. Mem. Internat. Reading Assn. Office: Sterling Middle Sch 444 Granite St Quincy MA 02169-6407

DAVISON, VICTORIA DILLON, real estate executive; b. Ada, Okla., Jan. 11, 1949; d. Wiliam Jackson Jr. and Helen Lucille (Cate) Dillon; m. Charles Alton Jewett, July 7, 1973 (div.); m. Denver Norris Davison, May 31 1985; stepchildren: Shaun, Malia, Denver II. BFA, Tulane U., 1970. Exec. sec. ITT Corp., Washington, 1970-71; adminstrv. asst. Berens Associated, Washington, 1972-73; real estate trainee Equitable Life Assurance Soc. Comml. Real Estate, Washington, 1974-75, real estate analyst, sr. appraiser, 1976-82; v.p. Am. Security Corp., Washington, 1983-85; exec. v.p. Ada Shopping Ctr., Inc., 1985—; pres. Victoria Properties, Ltd., Ada, 1989—; bd. dirs. W.J. Dillon Co., Inc., Ada, Ada Shopping Ctr. Inc. Jr. warden and vestry St. Luke's Episcopal Ch., Ada, 1990-91. Mem. Ada Area C. of C. (bd. dirs. 1990, co-chmn. area retail 1990-92), Appraisal Inst. (MAI), Edn. for Ministry (award 1992), Ada Music Club, Tanti, Leadership Ada. Republican. Home: 825 W Kings Rd Ada OK 74820-8045 Office: Victoria Properties Ltd 902 Arlington Ctr Ste 196 Ada OK 74820-2883

DAVY, HELEN A., secondary education educator; b. Benedict, N.D., July 8, 1924; d. Alexander and Sadie (Sukumlyn) Harchanko; m. Joel A. Davy, Apr. 22, 1945 (div. July 1972); children: Joel Jr., Susan, Carol, Connie, Calvin. BA, Minot State U., 1944, spl. edn. credential, 1962; postgrad., Portland State U., 1975. High sch. prin./tchr. Ambrose Pub. (N.D.) H.S., 1946-49; instr. phys. edn. Sacred Heart Acad. and Convent, 1962-64; work-study supr. with mentally retarded Minot, N.D., 1966; tchr. Minot H.S., 1967-69; head dept. lit. Shelton (Wash.) H.S., 1976-80; tchr. English dept. Surrey (N.D.) H.S., 1981-83; pvt. tutor, editor, proofreader Minot, 1984—; tchr./student liaison Minot H.S., PTA officer; Colo. state treas. Social Svcs. Tech. and Bus. Staff, 1972-74; head girls phys. edn. dept. Bishop Ryan Jr./Sr. High Sch., 1961. Bd. dirs. youth program YMCA, Minot, Trail Riders Horse Club, Minot; Cub Scout leader Boy Scouts Am., Minot; leader Girl Scouts Am., Minot, 4-H, Minot. Recipient Life Honorary award State PTA, Minot, 1962, Cert. of Appreciation, U.S. Army, 1977, Leadership award 4-H. Mem. ACLU, Minot Assn. of the Arts, Ret. Tchrs. Assn. N.D., Beta Theta. Home: 1825-15 1/2 St SW Minot ND 58701

DAW, ILONA K., accountant; b. Euclid, Ohio; children: David Jr., Christian, J. Erik. AA in Bus., Lakeland C.C., 1989; BA in Bus., Notre Dame Coll., Cleve., 1991. CPA, Ohio; CMA, Ohio. Jr. acct. Beachwood (Ohio) Pl. Ltd., 1989-90; accounts receivable acct. Mallnetwork Publs., Beachwood, 1991; staff acct. Ferro Corp., Cleve., 1992-95, sr. internat. acct., 1995-96, supr. internat. and MBU reporting, 1996—; pvt. practice acct., Chardon Twp., Ohio, 1991—. Mem. AICPAs, Am. Soc. Women Accts., Inst. Mgmt. Accts., Ohio Soc. CPAs, Notre Dame Coll. Alumnae Assn. (treas. 1996). Office: Ferro Corp 4150 E 56th PO Box 6550 Cleveland OH 44105

DAW, LENORE E., elementary school educator, librarian; b. Pitts.; d. James E. Owens and Lillian E. Gregory Owens; m. Rev. Matthew L. Daw, July 27, 1947 (dec.); children: Andrea, Matthew Jr., Alan. BA, Calif. State U., 1968; MA, U. San Francisco, 1977; postgrad., Pacific Coll., 1979, Columbia Pacific U., 1990—. Cert. tchr., libr., adminstr., Calif. Elem. tchr. 3d and 4th grades Alvina Sch. Dist., Caruthers, Calif.; elem. libr., secondary libr./career edn. coord. Fresno (Calif.) Unified Sch. Dist., dist. libr. K-12, ret.; libr. media specialist Balderas Elem. Sch.; instrnl. materials evaluation panelist Calif. State Dept. Edn. Min. of music, soloist Second Bapt. Ch. Recipient G.W. Hayden award Second Bapt. Ch., 1990, Gold Apple award United Black Men Fresno, 1990, cert. of recognition Calif. Legis. Assembly, 1990, cert. of honor City of Fresno, 1990. Mem. ASCD, Assn. Calif. Sch. Adminstr., ALA, Am. Assn. Sch. Librs., Calif. Reading Assn., Reading Initiative Coordinating Coun., Internat. Reading Assn., NEA, Fresno Boys and Girls Club (exec. bd.), Calif. Media and Libr. Assn., Alpha Kappa Alpha (Mildred L. Robinson Alumna Basileus award 1975, Outstanding Svc. award Iota Omicron Omega chpt. 1990), Phi Delta Kappa, Iota Phi Lambda.

DAWBER, PAM, actress; b. Detroit; d. Gene and Thelma D.; m. Mark Harmon, Mar. 21, 1987; 2 children. Ed., Oakland Community Coll. Worked as model and appeared in commls.; appearances include (TV series) ABC-TV's Mork and Mindy, 1978-82, CBS-TV My Sister Sam, 1986-88, (TV movies) The Girl the Gold Watch and Everything, Remembrance of Love, NBC, 1982, Last of the Great Survivors, 1983, Through Naked Eyes, 1983, This Wife for Hire, 1985, Wild Horses, 1985, American Geisha, 1986, Quiet Victory: The Charlie Wedemeyer Story, 1988, Do You Know the Muffin Man?, 1989, Face of Fear, 1990, The Man Who Had Three Wives, 1993, Web of Deception, 1994, A Child's Cry for Help, 1994, Trail of Tears, 1995, Journey Home, 1996, (films) The Wedding, Stay Tuned, (Broadway play) My Fair Lady: Joe Papp's L.A. prodn. Pirates of Penzance, L.A. prodn. Love Letters, 1991. Nat. spokeswoman Big Bros., Big Sisters of Am. Office: care Mimi Weber 9738 Arby Dr Beverly Hills CA 90210-1203

DAWDY, FAYE MARIE CATANIA, photographer, lecturer; b. San Mateo, Calif., Sept. 15, 1954; d. Frank Benjamin and Melba Rita (Arata) Catania; m. John Thomas Dawdy, May 5, 1974; children: Tracy Marie, John Franco. AA, Coll. of San Mateo, 1979; student, San Francisco State U., 1979—. With Proctor & Gamble Distbg. Co., San Mateo, 1973-78; ptnr. Dawdy Photography, Millbrae, Calif., 1978—; dir., sec.-treas. Millbrae Stamp Co., 1980—; instr. Winona Sch. Profl. Photography, Mt. Prospect, Ill.; lectr. to high schs., various clubs, photography convs. including Goteborg, Sweden, Idaho, Oreg., Colo., Tex., Ill., Fla., Mo., Kans., Nev., Iowa, N.J., Chile, S.A. Contbr. articles to profl. jours. Area chmn. Millbrae Am. Heart Assn. Ann. Fund Dr., 1977-82; mem. fund raising and nutrition coms. San Mateo County chpt. Am. Heart Assn., 1980-88; co-chmn. Miss Millbrae Pageant, 1981, Queen Isabella Columbus Day Festival, 1981; judge arts and crafts exhbns. Millbrae Art and Wine Festival; judge photography competition Marin County Fair Photography Exhibit; vol. photographer Rotoplast, La Serena, Chile, 1994; mem. sister city com. City of Millbrae; trustee Golden Gate Sch. Profl. Photographers, 1985-90. Recipient awards No. Calif. Coun. Camera Clubs, 1979, 81, Mktg. contest award Mktg. Today mag., 1988; photograph accepted for Profl. Photographers Am. loan collection and on exhibit at Epcot Ctr., Fla., 1995. Mem. Profl. Photographers Am. (photog. craftsman degree), Profl. Photographers Greater Bay Area, Profl. Photographers No. Calif., Profl. Photographers Calif., Wedding Photographers Assn., NAFE, Millbrae C. of C. (sec. women's divsn. 1979, bd. dirs. 1991), South San Francisco C. of C., Millbrae Art Assn. (pres. 1979-80), Portola Camera Club (nature chmn. 1978—), Millbrae Hist. Assn., Friends Millbrae Libr., Italian Cath. Fedn., Calif. Women in Profl. Photography, Fedn. Ind. Bus., St. Dunstan Women's Club, Soroptimist (sec. 1981-82). Democrat. Roman Catholic. Office: 449 Broadway Millbrae CA 94030-1905

DAWES, DOMINIQUE, gymnast, Olympic athlete; b. Silver Spring, Md., Nov. 20, 1976. Student, U. Md., 1995—. Mem. U.S. Olympic Team, Barcelona, Spain, 1992, Atlanta, 1996. Recipient Arch McDonald award Touchdown Club Washington, 1995, McDonald's Balancing It All award, 1995, Henry P. Iba Citizen Athlete award, 1995, Gold medal team competition Olympic Games, Atlanta, 1996, Bronze medal floor exercise Olympic Games, Atlanta, 1996; named USA Gymnastics' Athlete of Yr., 1993, Sportsperson of Yr. USA Gymnastics, 1994; placed 3rd for team Olympic Games, Barcelona, Spain, 1992, 2d in all around and floor exercise, 1st in vault and balance beam, 3rd uneven bars Coca-Cola Nat. Championships, Salt Lake City, 1993, 2d in uneven bars and balance beam World Gymnastics Championships, Birmingham, Eng., 1993, 1st in all around, vault, balance beam and floor exercise McDonald's Am. Cup, Orlando, 1994, 1st in all around, vault, uneven bars, balance beam and floor exercise Coca-Cola Nat. Championships, Nashville, 1994, 1st in all around NationsBank World Team Trials, Richmond, Va., 1994, 2d for team World Championships, Dortmund, Germany, 1994, 1st in uneven bars and floor exercise, 3rd in balance beam Coca-Cola Nat. Championships, New Orleans, 1995. Office: care USA Gymnastics Pan Am Plz 201 S Capitol Ave Ste 300 Indianapolis IN 46225*

DAWKINS, DEBRA, elementary school educator; b. Miami, Fla., Apr. 16, 1950; d. Edmond Rollins and Utha Felts White; m. William Dawkins, Apr. 5, 1975 (div. Nov. 1978); 1 child, Caleb Avery. AA, Miami-Dade Jr. Coll., 1970; BA, Fla. Atlantic U., 1972. Tchr. grade 6 J.W. Johnson Elem. Sch., Hialeah, Fla., 1973-75; tchr. grade 4 J.H. Bright Elem. Sch., Hialeah, 1975-77, tchr. grade 3, 1977-78, compensatory edn. tchr., 1978-80, tchr. grade 5, 1980-85, 89-90, chpt. I facilitator, 1985-89, chpt. I resource tchr., 1990—, dept. chmn., 1993-94; team writer sch. improvement plan, 1990—; contact person Parent Outreach Program, Hialeah, 1992—; mem. Sch. Adv. Coun., Hialeah, 1992—. Mem. Sch.-Based Mgmt. Shared Decision-Making Cadre, Hialeah, 1990-92; mem. and sec. matron's dept. Nat. Primitive Bapt. Conv. Inc., 1992—; sec. East Fla. Ch. Sch. Conv., 1986—, East Fla. Dist. Primitive Bapt. Assn., 1992—; active Nat. Coalition Title I/Chpt. I Parents. Recipient Appreciation award Dade County Pub. Sch. Chpt. I Program, 1992, Black History Com. of J.H. Bright Elem. Sch., 1991; named Tchr. of Yr., Bright/Johnson Elem. Schs., 1996. Mem. NAACP, Women in the NAACP, United Tchrs. of Dade, Nat. Coalition of Title I/Chpt. I Parents, Zeta Phi Beta. Democrat. Home: 1840 NW 49th St Miami FL 33142-4011

DAWKINS, MARVA PHYLLIS, psychologist; b. Jacksonville, Fla., Apr. 12, 1948; d. Ralph and Altamese (Padgett) D.; student U. Freiburg, Germany, 1969-70; BS, Stetson U., 1971; MS, Fla. State U., 1972, PhD, 1975. Rsch. asst. Fla. State U., Tallahassee, 1970-72; clin. intern, psychology dept. Presbyn.-St. Luke's Med. Ctr. and mental health dept. Mile Square Health Ctr., Chgo., 1973-74; staff psychologist, dir. aftercare treatment program, mental health dept. Mile Square Health Ctr., Chgo., 1974-75, staff psychologist, coordinator devel. disabilities program, 1976-79; asst. prof. psychology U. North Fla., Jacksonville, 1975-76, Rush U.-Presbyn. St. Luke's Med. Ctr., Chgo., 1976—; pvt. practice clin. psychology, 1977—; exec. dir. Inst. for Community Mental Health, 1979—; cons. safety evaluation program Isaac Ray Ctr., 1986-91; dir. Ctr. for Applied Psychology and Forensic Studies, 1991—; psychology cons. Disability Policy Br. Social Security Adminstrn., Chgo, 1980—. Registered psychologist, Ill. Mem. Am. Psychol. Assn., Assn. Black Psychologists.

DAWSON, CAROL GENE, former commissioner, writer, consultant; b. Indpls., Sept. 8, 1937; d. Ernest Eugene (dec.) and Hilda Lou (Carroll) D.; m. Robert Edmund Bauman, Nov. 19, 1960 (div. 1982); children: Edward Carroll, Eugenie Marie, Victoria Anne, James Shields; m. Franklin Dean Smith, Aug. 2, 1986. BA, Dunbarton Coll., Washington, 1959, Cath. U., Washington, 1960; MA in Internat. Transactions, George Mason U., 1994. Staff asst. Senator Kenneth B. Keating, Washington, 1959; exec. asst. Americans for Constl. Action, Washington, 1959; exec. sec. Youth for Nixon Lodge, Washington, 1959-60; legis. asst. Rep. Donald C. Bruce, Washington, 1961-63; dep. dir., pub. info. Goldwater for Pres. Campaign and Rep. Nat. Com., Washington, 1963-64; editor, assoc. editor The New Guard Mag., Washington, 1965-66; dir. info. Am. Conservative Union, Washington, 1966-67; publs. and news analyst White House, Washington, from 1969; staff reporter Easton (Md.) Star-Democrat, 1971-72; freelance writer Easton,

1972-77; real estate salesperson Latham Realtors, Easton, 1977-80; sr. staff asst. presdl. transition U.S. Office of Personnel Mgmt., Washington, 1980-81; dep. press sec. U.S. Dept. Energy, Washington, 1981-82, dep. spl. asst. to sec., 1982-84; commr. U.S. Consumer Product Safety Commn., Washington, 1984-93; editor Cath. Currents newsletter, Washington, 1969-70. Bd. visitors Inst. Polit. Journalism Georgetown U., 1985-89; mem. Nat. Policy Forum, Coun. of Free Individuals in a Free Soc., Coun. on Internat. Trade, 1994—; bd. dirs. Consumer Alert, 1995—; chmn. Lancaster County (Va.) Rep. Ctrl. Com., 196—. Recipient Award of Merit Young Americans for Freedom, 1970. Mem. The Charter 100, Reagan Appointees Alumni, The Fairfax Hunt Club (bd. govs. 1989-91). Roman Catholic. Home and office: PO Box 2 Morattico VA 22523-0002

DAWSON, CATHY JAYNE, elementary school educator; b. Corpus Christi, Tex., Apr. 2, 1959; d. Richard C. and Esther J. (Zinn) Nieman; m. George H. Dawson Jr., Aug. 14, 1982. A degree, Del Mar Jr. Coll., Corpus Christi, 1979; B degree, U. North Tex., 1981. Cert. elem. tchr., Tex. Elem. spl. edn. tchr. Gregory (Tex.) Portland Ind. Sch. Dist., 1981-85; 3d grade tchr. Lewisville (Tex.) Ind. Sch. Dist., 1985-87; elem. spl. edn. tchr. Woodsboro (Tex.) Ind. Sch. Dist., 1987-89; mid. sch. spl. edn. tchr. Refugio (Tex.) Ind. Sch. Dist., 1989-96, mem. dist. improvement team, 1992-95, mem. supts. adv. coun., 1991-92, sponsor student coun., 1991-95; content mastery tchr. Holleman Elem. Sch., Waller (Tex.) Ind. Sch. Dist., 1996—. Vol. ARC, Refugio, 1988-95, summer reading program Nancy Carol Roberts Meml. Libr., Brenham, Tex.; chmn. bd. Good Samaritan Ministries, Refugio, 1993-94; mem. choir 1st United Meth. Ch., Refugio, 1989-95, St. Peter's Episc. Ch., 1996—, EYC sponsor, 1996—; vol. dir. summer reading program Refugio County Libr., 1988-94; chmn. ptnrs. in ministry com. Ch. of Ascension Episcopal Ch., Refugio; mem. Refugio Cmty. Choir, 1994-95; mem. Leaping Libr. Lizards Band. Mem. Tex. State Tchrs. Assn. (pres. Refugio county chpt. 1988-93; v.p. dist. III chpt. 1988-90, pres. dist. III chpt. 1990-92), Refugio Woman's Club, Alpha Delta Kappa, Delta Kappa Gamma. Episcopalian. Home: 2870 Trey Ln Brenham TX 77833

DAWSON, DAWN PAIGE, publisher; b. Paradise, Calif., Nov. 10, 1956; d. Wayne Paul and Donna Jean (Peckham) D.; m. Justin Keith Anderson, Mar. 12, 1989; children: Christopher Wayne Dawson Anderson, Gwendolyn Paige Peckham Anderson. AB, Occidental Coll., 1979. Editorial asst. Salem Press Inc., Pasadena, Calif., 1979-80, copy editor, 1980-81, sr. editor, 1982-83, mgr. editor, 1984-87, v.p. editing and prodn., 1987—. Mem. Customer's Guild West. Mem. Soc. Scholarly Pub., Nat. Assn. Female Execs. Office: Salem Press Inc 131 N El Molino Ave Ste 350 Pasadena CA 91101-1878

DAWSON, DIANA STAR, lawyer; b. Washington, Apr. 1, 1945; d. Donald S. and Alva A. Dawson; m. Randolph S. Coyner, June 14, 1966; children: William James, Charles Christopher. BA, Fla. Atlantic U., 1985; JD, Nova U., 1993. Bar: Fla. 1993, U.S. Dist. Ct. (so. dist.) Fla. 1994, D.C. 1996. Rsch./writing cons. Bethesda, Md., 1970-79; orgn. mgmt. staff Ecosometrics, Inc., Bethesda, 1979-82; juvenile justice and delinquency prevention mediator Broward County, Fla., 1992-93; pvt. practice Boca Raton, Fla., 1993—. Chair, founder Fla. Women's Consortium, 1994-96; instr. Fla. Atlantic U.; state v.p. Fla. Women's Polit. Caucus, 1992-94; coord. pay equity subcom. Fla. Dem. Party, 1984-88, mem. affirmative action com., 1984-88; chair campaign com. Palm Beach (Fla.) Dem. Exec. Com., 1988; co-founder Martin Luther King Jr. Ann. Birthday Party, Delray Beach, Fla.; pres. South Palm Beach County NOW, 1985-87; organizer, founding mem. Palm Beach Count Women's Polit. Caucus. Recipient Svc. award NOW, Delray Beach Voters League. Mem. Nat. Lawyers Guild (founder U. Miami chpt.). Home and Office: 841 Park Dr E Boca Raton FL 33432

DAWSON, JOANNE B., telemarketing service agency executive-consultant; b. Chgo., Apr. 11, 1950; d. Joseph Thomas and Marcella Anna (Laska) Bastuga; m. Edward John Dawson, Aug. 15, 1971. BA, Ill. Benedictine, 1972. Communication svcs. mgr. Tech. Pub. Co., Barrington, Ill., 1982-84, telemktg. mgr., 1984-86; telemktg. mgr. CAhners Pub. Co., Des Plaines, Ill., 1986-88; pres. JBD Enterprises, Inc., Wauconda, Ill., 1988—. Mem. Am. Telemktg. Assn. (Midwest chpt., v.p. 1989, pres. 1990-91), Telemktg. Mgmt. Assn. (sec. 1986, pres. 1987-88). Office: JBD Enterprises Inc 611 Lake Shore Blvd Wauconda IL 60084-1525

DAWSON, MARTHA BROMLEY, administrative assistant, software developer; b. Whitewater, Wis., Feb. 25, 1940; d. Fred G. and Ruth O. (Hackett) Bromley; m. James R. Dawson, June 10, 1959; children: Heather Joy Dawson Cudworth, Jamie Ruth Dawson Strebing. Student, U. Wis.-Stout, Menomonie, 1957-59, Ind. U., 1977-78. Cert. computer profl. Inst. for Cert. Computing Profls. Sys. analyst, programmer Johnson Controls, Milw., 1963-69; software developer various orgns., Bloomington, Ind., 1969—; sys. analyst, programmer Westinghouse Electric, Bloomington, 1973-75; adminstrv. asst. Bloomington (Ind.) Twp., 1979—. Bd. mem. Youth For Christ, Bloomington, 1989-93. Presbyterian. Office: Bloomington Twp 2111 Vernal Pike Bloomington IN 47404

DAWSON, MARY RUTH, curator; b. Highland Park, Mich., Feb. 27, 1931; d. John Elson and Olga Josephine (Down) D. B.S., Mich. State Coll., 1952; postgrad., U. Edinburgh, 1952-53; Ph.D., U. Kans., 1957. Instr. zoology Smith Coll., 1958-61; asst. program dir. NSF, Washington, 1961-62; mem. staff Carnegie Mus., Pitts., 1962—, curator, 1971—, chmn. earth sci. div., 1973—, acting dir., 1982-83; adj. prof. earth scis. U. Pitts., 1971-85, prof., 1985—. Recipient Arnold Guyot award Nat. Geog. Soc., 1981, Woman in Sci. award Chatham Coll., 1983; named Disting. Dau. Pa., 1987; Fulbright scholar, 1952-53; fellow AAUW, 1958-59; research grantee NSF, 1961-62, 65—. Fellow Geol. Soc. Am., Arctic Inst. N.Am.; mem. Soc. Vertebrate Paleontology (v.p. 1972-73, pres. 1973-74), Paleontol. Soc., Paläontologische Gesellschaft, Bernese Mountain Dog Club Am., Am. Soc. Mammalogists, Phi Beta Kappa. Office: Carnegie Mus 4400 Forbes Ave Pittsburgh PA 15213-4007

DAWSON, MURIEL AMANDA, legislator; b. Ft. Lauderdale, Fla., July 18, 1956; d. Clifford and Altemease (Laws) Hardy; divorced; children: Shatress (Tibby), Colongie, Ashley. Degree in social work, Fla. Agrl. and Mech. U., 1980. Legis. asst. Fla. Ho. of Reps., Ft. Lauderdale, 1988-92, state legislator Dist. 93, 1992—. Chairperson Fla. Commn. Minority Health, 1993-95; mem. children, families and health com. Nat. Conf. State Legis., 1995-96; co-vice chair Fla. Women's Legis. Caucus, 1995-96, mem. select com. on telecom., 1994-95; assoc. trustee Bethune-Cookman Coll., 1994; mem. north area adv. bd. Sch. Bd. Broward County, 1992—; mem. health care task force Nat. Black Caucus of SAtate Legislators, 1993—; mem. Fla. Conf. Black State Legislators, 1992—; bd. dirs. Broward County Urban League, Ft. Lauderdale, 1994—, Friends of Children, Youth and Families, Ft. Lauderdale, 1994, Voice of Choice Adv. Bd., 1995, Ft. Lauderdale Children's Theatre, 1994-96, Healthy Mothers/Healthy Babies Coalition of Broward County, 1993—, Minority Bus. Enterprise, 1991-92; mem. exec. adv. bd. Nat. Black Police Assn., 1994; adv. bd. Child Care Connection, 1992—; founding mem. Multicultural Women's Issues Group, 1993; mem. Broward Healthy Start Coalition, 1993—, Women's Polit. Caucus, Gwen Cherry chpt., 1990—, Ctrl. Broward Dem. Club, 1990—, Boisey Waiters Black Caucus Dem. Club of Broward County, 1990—, Young Dems. of Broward County, 1990—, Greater Ft. Lauderdale Dem. Club. Recipient Merit award M.A.D.D., 1991, Woman of the Yr. award Fla. Fedn. Bus. and Profl. Women, 1992, Competitive Edge Program award Broward C.C., 1991-92, 92-93, Trailblazer award Young Dems., 1993, Margaret Roach Leadership award Broward County Urban League, 1993, Hon. McKnight Achiever award, 1993, award Sickle Cell Anemia Found., 1993, 94, With the Multitude of Her Being tribute African Am. Women of South Fla., 1993, Ashanti Cultural Arts Cmty. Svc. award, 1994, Woman of Distinction award Women's Polit. Caucus Gwen Cherry chpt., 1994, Impact award New Rep. Club of Broward County, 1994, Legis. Advocate award Fla. Assn. Cmty. Health Ctrs., Inc., 1994, Humanitarian of the Yr. award Sunshine Health Ctr., 1994, Legis. Roll Call award Fla. C. of C., 1993, 94, Legis. award Fla. Assn. C.C.'s, 1994, Legislator of the Yr. award Fla. Coll. Emergency Physicians, 1995, Commendation for Svc. award Ft. Lauderdale Mayor Jim Naugle and City Commrs., 1995. Mem. NOW, Bus. and Profl. Women (Woman of the Yr. 1995), Broward Assn. Black Social Workers (founding mem.), Optimists, Kiwanis, Order of Ea. Star. Democrat. Baptist. Office: Fla Legis 612 N Andrews Ave Fort Lauderdale FL 33311-7436

DAWSON, NANCY ANN, hematologist, oncologist; b. San Francisco, Nov. 21, 1953; d. Malcolm Bryon and Helen Dorothy (Jones) D.; m. Neal Thomas Baron, Aug. 22, 1981; children: Blake Bryon Baron, Drew Randall Baron. AB, U. Calif., Berkeley, 1975; MD, Georgetown U., 1979. Diplomate Am. Bd. Internal Medicine, Am. Bd. Internal Medicine-Hematology, Am. Bd. Internal Medicine-Oncology, Nat. Bd. Med. Examiners; lic. MD, Md., Va. Commd. 2nd lt. U.S. Army, 1976, advanced through grades to lt. col., 1991; intern in internal medicine Walter Reed Army Med. Ctr., Washington, 1979-80, residency internal medicine, 1980-82, fellowship hematology-oncology, 1982-85; teaching fellow, instr. dept. medicine Uniformed Svcs. U. of Health Scis., Bethesda, Md., 1980-82, 83-85, asst. prof. dept. medicine, 1985-92, assoc. prof. dept. medicine, 1992—; staff physician hematology-oncology svcs., asst. chief Walter Reed Army Med. Ctr., Washington, 1985—, 88-90, asst. dir. intern tng. and transitional year program, 1990-91, dir. intern tng. and transitional year program, 1991-94, transitional program advsor to chief grad. med. edn., 1992-94, chief hematology-oncology clinic, 1994-95, dir. clin. rsch., 1995—. Editor: Prostate Cancer, 1994; contbr. chpts. to books and articles to profl. jours. Recipient Am. Med. Women's Assn. Disting. Student citation, 1979. Fellow Am. Coll. Physicians; mem. AMA, Am. Soc. Clin. Oncology, Assn. Mil. Surgeons of U.S., Am. Soc. Hematology, Women in Cancer Rsch., Am. Urol. Assn. Democrat. Roman Catholic. Home: 7721 Curtis St Chevy Chase MD 20815-4913 Office: Walter Reed Army Med Ctr Hematology Oncology Cl Washington DC 20307

DAWSON, SUZANNE STOCKUS, lawyer; b. Chgo., Dec. 29, 1941; d. John Charles and Josephine (Zolpe) Stockus; m. Daniel P. Dawson Sr., Sept. 1, 1962; children: Daniel P. Jr., John Charles, Michael Sean. BA, Marquette U., 1963; JD cum laude, Loyola U., Chgo., 1965. Bar: Ill. 1965, U.S. Dist. Ct. (no. dist.) Ill. 1965. Assoc. Kirkland & Ellis, Chgo., 1965-71, ptnr., 1971-82; ptnr. Arnstein & Lehr, Chgo., 1982-89, Foley & Lardner, Chgo., 1989-94; spl. counsel publicly held corps. Glenview, Ill., 1995—. Mem. various coms. United Way Chgo.; corp. adv. bd. Sec. State of Ill., 1973; past mem. bd. advisors Loyola of Chgo. Law Sch.; trustee Lawrence Hall Youth Svcs., Chgo., 1983—, pres., 1991-93, chair 1993-96; mem. adv. bd. Cath. Charities Chgo., 1985—; mem. exec. com., bd. governance Notre Dame High Sch., Niles, Ill., 1990—. Recipient Founder's Day award Loyola U., 1980, St. Thomas More award Loyola of Chgo. Law Sch., 1983. Mem. ABA, Am. Arbitration Assn. (appointed mem. nat. panel of comml. arbitrators 1996—), Ill. Bar Assn., Chgo. Bar Assn. Roman Catholic. Home: 2113 Valley Lo Ln Glenview IL 60025-1724

DAWSON, VIRGINIA SUE, newspaper editor; b. Concordia, Kans., June 6, 1940; d. John Edward and Wilma Aileen (Thompson) Morgan; m. Neil S. Dawson, Nov. 28, 1964; children: Shelley Diane Dawson Sedwick, Lori Ann, Christy Lynn. BS in Home Econs. and Journalism, Kans. State U., 1962. Asst. publs. editor Ohio State U. Coop. Extension Svc., Columbus, 1962-64; home editor Ohio Farmer mag., Columbus, 1964-78; food editor Columbus Dispatch, 1978—. Recipient Commn. award Ohio Poultry Assn., 1980. Mem. Am. Assn. Family and Consumer Scis. (cert. home economist), Assn. Food Journalists, Home Economists in Bus. (past pres. Columbus chpt.), Ohio Newspaper Women's Assn. (several writing and newspaper design awards 1985-94). Office: Columbus Dispatch 34 S 3rd St Columbus OH 43215-4201

DAWSON-THOMPSON, MARY MARQUETTA, guidance counselor; b. Norwalk, Conn., July 13, 1960; d. John E. and Darlyn F. (Bonner) Dawson; m. Allen Cornelius Thompson, July 7, 1984; children: Joshua Allen Thompson, Jeremy Ashton Thompson. BS, U. Conn., 1983; MS, U. Bridgeport, 1986, 93, 6th yr. cert., 1995. Cert. sch. guidance. Family counseling dir. MDT Counseling, Belrin, Conn., 1991—; guidance counselor Berlin Bd. Edn., 1994; intensive guidance counselor Farmington (Conn.) Bd. Edn., 1995—. Chair, program com. YMCA, 1993—, bd. dirs. sr. programming Shiloh Bapt. Ch. Mem. Am. Counseling Assn., Conn. Counseling Assn., Alpha Kappa Alpha. Baptist. Office: Farmington HS 10 Montieth Farmington CT 06037

DAY, ANN ELIZABETH, artist, educator; b. Valetta, Malta, June 1, 1927; came to U.S., 1940; d. John Dwight and Joyce Elizabeth (Marett) Harvey; m. George Frederick Day, Oct. 23, 1948 (div. Oct. 1979); children: Georgianna Day Ludcke, John F., David S.; m. Donald Monturean Mintz, Dec. 30, 1980. BA, Mt. Holyoke Coll., 1948. Asst. to dir. advanced studies Nat. Ctr. Atmospheric Rsch., Boulder, Colo., 1962-67; edn. dir. Waterloo (Iowa) Recreation and Arts Ctr., 1967-76; curator edn. svcs. Utah Mus. Fine Arts, Salt Lake City, 1976-80; lectr. art history YMHA of No. N.J., Wayne, 1982—; RSVP, Paramus, N.J., 1994—, Art History Tours of France, Tour de France, Ltd.; freelance artist Ringwood, N.J., 1982—; represented by Nathans Gallery, West Paterson, N.J., Oasis Gallery, Savannah, Ga., Wilson Galleries, Nantucket, Mass.; vice chair, panelist Fed. State Ptnrship., NEA, Washington, 1972-77; mem. exec. com. Nat. Assn. Community Arts Agys., Washington, 1975-77. Author of poems; represented in permanent collections Utah Mus. Fine Arts, also U.S. and abroad. Recipient Silver medal Utah Watercolor Soc., Salt Lake City, 1976, Lake Mohawk Club award Sussex County Art Assn., Sparta, N.J., 1992, 93. Mem. Nat. Watercolor Soc., N.J. Watercolor Soc. (Heimrod award 1991), Phi Beta Kappa. Democrat. Home and Office: 117 Cedar Rd Ringwood NJ 07456-1800

DAY, ANNE WHITE, retired registered nurse; b. Cin., July 9, 1926; d. Pinkney McGill and Anna Pearl (Glendenning) White; m. Raymond Eric Parker, Mar. 6, 1948 (div. 1969); children: Douglas McGill, Stephanie Morse. Diploma, Christ Hosp. Sch. Nursing, Cin., 1947. RN, Ohio; cert. chem. dependency nurse Consol. Assn. Nurses in Substance Abuse. Staff nurse to asst. head nurse Holmes div. U. Cin., 1948-84; nursing supr. Villa Hope Extended Care Facility, Cin., 1970-72; staff nurse Hillenbrand Nursing Home, Cin., 1980-82, Emerson A. North Hosp., Cin., 1982-94. Vol. Group Against Smoke Pollution, Cin., 1989—; donor Zoo, Cin., 1989—, Voters for Choice, Ohio, 1989—, Ams. for Non-Smokers Rights, Calif., 1989—, Action on Smoking or Health, 1989—, Stop Teenage Addiction to Tobacco; tutor for adult literacy. Mem. DAR (life). Episcopalian.

DAY, BILLIE ANN, secondary education educator; b. Wichita, Kans., Feb. 26, 1939; d. William Alvin and Velma Frances (Grieder) D. BA, Southwestern Coll., 1960; MA, Howard U., 1969; PhD, NYU, 1986. Cert. tchr., Kans., D.C. Tchr. Francis L. Cardozo High Sch., Washington, 1969-81, Benjamin Banneker High Sch., Washington, 1981-95; cons. in field. Contbr. articles to profl. jours. Chairperson of bd. World Hunger Edn. Svc., Washington, 1990; internat. election observer Sierra Leone, 1996. Recipient Roselle Lecture award for Creative Communication in the Social Studies, 1986, Am. Women of Today award, 1991, YFU Internat. Edn. award, 1992; named Cafritz fellow, 1991, Woodrow Wilson fellow, 1993; Fulbright scholar, 1986, 93. Mem. Returned Peace Corps Vols. of Washington (pres. 1991-94), Nat. Coun. for Social Studies (mem. nat. bd. 1980-83), Middle States Coun. for Social Studies (pres. 1980-82), D.C. Coun. for Social Studies (pres. 1976-77), Nat. Peace Corps. Assn. (bd. dirs. 1994—). Office: Benjamin Banneker High Sch 800 Euclid St NW Washington DC 20001-2296

DAY, CORNELIA S., volunteer; b. Iowa City, May 7, 1919; d. Harold Francis and Cornelia Fitch (Prentiss) Shrauger; m. John Robert Day, July 28, 1940; children: Dennis, Edward. BA in Journalism, U. Iowa, 1940. Author: Presbyterian Church History, 1989, History of Washington YWCA, 1994. Former pres., v.p. Washington (Iowa) YWCA, chmn. membership com., chmn. program com., chmn. world mutual svc. com., sponsor girls club, sponsor club employed men and women, organizer various camps, sponsor softball and basketball teams, attendee numerous nat. confs., chair disarmament conf., co-chair speakers bur. Internat. Yr. Child; former pres. Iowa Town and Country YWCA; former mem. nat. bd. YWCA of U.S.A., mem. world rels. com., Milw. elimination of racism com.fin. devel. com., comm. com., nat. vol., annual fundraiser; accredited vis. World YWCA meeting, Accra, Ghana, 1972; state rep. U.S. com. UNICEF, participant numerous confs., mem. U.S. com. corp. bd.; mem. Gov. Commn. Children and Youth; del. Commn. to White House Conf. on Children and Youth, 1960; mem. sub-area project review com. Iowa Health Systems Agy., vice chair plan implementation com., state bd.; Rep. appointee Community Action Program; former vice pres., pres. Planned Parenthood S.E. Iowa; pres. sec. Washington coun.; former sec. Washington House; mem. choir United Presbyn. Ch.; mem. Ecumenical Peace Luncheon Com.; formerly active Grant Wood Ednl. Agy., exptl. anti-poverty program Kirkwood U., Washington Rec. Coun., Washington Community Chest Bd., Great Rivers Region Tourism Coun.; former fund chmn. Rep. Ctrl. Com.; former v.p., chmn. housing Am. Field Svc.; former pres. PTO Lincoln Sch. Recipient Community Svc. award Washington Rotary Club, 1972, Gold Feather award Washington Community Chest Bd., 1988, Svc. award S.E. Iowa Planned Parenthood, 1991; named to Iowa Vol. Hall of Fame, 1990. Mem. Mortar Bd. Home: PO Box 88 1005 S Iowa Ave Washington IA 52353-1126

DAY, JENNIE D., state legislator; b. Madera, Pa., Dec. 13, 1921; m. Marvin Day. Ed. Temple U. City councilwoman, Coventry, R.I., 1978-84; realtor; mem. R.I. Senate, 1985—. Mem. Coventry Hist. Soc. Democrat. Roman Catholic. Office: R I Senate House State House Providence RI 02903 also: 19 Beechwood St Coventry RI 02816-4334*

DAY, LUCILLE LANG, health facility administrator, educator, author; b. Oakland, Calif., Dec. 5, 1947; d. Richard Allen and Evelyn Marietta (Hazard) Lang; m. Frank Lawrence Day, Nov. 6, 1965 (div. 1970); 1 child, Liana Sherrine; m. 2nd, Theodore Herman Fleischman, June 23, 1974 (div. 1985); 1 child, Tamarind Channah. AB, U. Calif., Berkeley, 1971, MA, 1973, PhD, 1979. Teaching asst. U. Calif., Berkeley, 1971-72, 75-76, research asst., 1975, 77-78; tchr. sci. Magic Mountain Sch., Berkeley, 1977; specialist math. and sci. Novato (Calif.) Unified Sch. Dist., 1979-81; instr. sci. Project Bridge, Laney Coll., Oakland, Calif., 1984-86; sci. writer and mgr. precollege edn. programs, Lawrence Berkeley (Calif.) Nat. Lab., 1986-90, life scis. staff coord., 1990-92; mgr. Hall of Health, Berkeley, Calif., 1992—. Author numerous poems, articles and book reviews; author: (with Joan Skolnick and Carol Langbort) How to Encourage Girls in Math and Science: Strategies for Parents and Educators, 1982; Self-Portrait with Hand Microscope (poetry collection), 1982. NSF Grad. fellow, 1972-75; recipient Joseph Henry Jackson award in lit. San Francisco Found., 1982. Mem. No. Calif. Sci. Writers Assn., Nat. Assn. Sci. Writers, Math/Sci. Network, Phi Beta Kappa, Iota Sigma Pi. Home: 1057 Walker Ave Oakland CA 94610-1511 Office: Hall of Health 2230 Shattuck Ave Berkeley CA 94704-1424

DAY, MARY, artistic director, ballet company executive; b. Washington; trained by Lisa Gardinier. ArtsD (hon.) Shenandoah Conservatory, DHL (hon.) Mount Vernon Coll. Co-founder Washington Sch. of Ballet, 1944—; founder Washington Ballet, 1976—. Recipient Mayor's award, Woman of Achievement award WETA-TV, Met. Dance award, Founders award Cultural Alliance, Excellence in Teaching Chautauqua Dance award, sr. Svcs. Disting. award IONA.; named Washingtonian of Yr. Washingtonian mag. Office: Washington Ballet 3515 Wisconsin Ave NW Washington DC 20016-3010*

DAY, MARY JANE THOMAS, cartographer; b. Connors, New Brunswick, Can., Oct. 12, 1927; d. Angus and Delina (Michaud) Thomas; m. Howard M. Day, July 1, 1949; children: Laurie Anne Day Greene, Angus Howard. BS in Geography, U. Md., 1974, BS in Bus. & Mgmt., 1977. Meteorol. aide Hangar 8 Eastern Airlines, N.Y.C., 1946-47, U.S. Weather Bur., Washington, 1948-50; cartographic aide U.S. Navy Hydrographic Office, Suitland, Md., 1950-57, cartographer, 1957-62; cartographer U.S. Navy Oceanographic Office, Suitland, 1962-72, Def. Mapping Agy., Suitland/Brookmont, 1972-93; ret., 1994; cartographer USNS Harkness, 1978, Indonesian Naval Personnel, Jakarta, Indonesia, 1981-82. Compiled, wrote and published: The Descendants of John Thomas of Connors, N.B., 1988; author (poem) An Ode to A Dreamer, 1995. Mem. Andrews Officers Club (Md.). Home: 3532 28th Pky Temple Hills MD 20748-2922

DAY, MARYLOUISE MULDOON (MRS. RICHARD DAYTON DAY), appraiser; b. St. Louis; d. Joseph A. and Dorothy (Lang) Muldoon; A.B., Washington U., St. Louis, 1940; postgrad. Air U., 1958, George Washington U., 1963-64; grad. Real Estate Inst. Md., 1972; m. Richard Dayton Day, Aug. 15, 1959. Intelligence specialist U.S. Air Force, Washington, 1947-60; program officer, spl. asst. to dir. project devel. VISTA, OEO, 1965-67; with Joint Intelligence Bur., London, Eng., 1953; appraiser, cons. on antiques, fine arts, 1969—; pres. Agts. For Sales Ltd., 1974—, Marylouise M. Day, Inc., 1978—. Recipient citation U.S. Air Force, 1960. Fellow Inc. Soc. Valuers and Auctioneers (London), Am. Soc. Appraisers (chpt. 1st v.p. 1977-78, pres. 1978-79, chmn. fine arts forum 1976-78, gov. Region 3 1980-82, internat. sec. 1982-84, treas. ednl. found. 1986-91); mem. Appraisers Assn. Am., Irish Georgian Soc., Winterthur Guild, Assn. Former Intelligence Officers, Decorative Arts Trust, Delta Gamma. Club: Kenwood Golf and Country (Washington). Home: 4928 Sentinel Dr Bethesda MD 20816-3591

DAYHARSH, VIRGINIA FIENGO, educator; b. New Haven, Dec. 2, 1942; d. Edward Arthur and Rose (Giaquinto) Fiengo; m. George R. Dayharsh, Dec. 31, 1966 (div. Nov. 1983); children: Regina Lynn, Jennifer Allison. BA, Coll. of New Rochelle, N.Y., 1964; MA, So. Conn. State U., 1974, cert. advanced study, 1985. Cert. social studies tchr., Conn. Tchr. Troup Jr. High Sch., New Haven, 1964-65, East Haven (Conn.) Jr. High Sch., 1965-69; tchr., dept. chairperson Lauralton Hall, Milford, Conn., 1979-81; tchr. Nathan Hale Ray High Sch., East Haddam, Conn., 1981-85, Naugatuck (Conn.) High Sch., 1985—. Mem. Rep. Town Com., East Haven, 1968-72, Library Bd., East Haven, 1968-81, Bd. of Edn., East Haven, 1986-87. Mem. NEA, Conn. Coun. Social Studies, Conn. Edn. Assn., Naugatuck Tchrs.' League, Conn. Social Studies Coun., Conn. Cath. Women, New Eng. Assn. Schs. and Colls. (evaluation com. 1990, 91, 93, 94), Vietnam Vets. of Am. (assoc.). Home: 77 Highland St West Haven CT 06516

DAYHOFF, NANCY BELMONT, artist; b. West Depford Township, N.J., Apr. 30, 1922; d. Donald Johnston and Ann Catherine (Gorry) Mackinnon; m. Thomas Simon Belmont, Nov. 15, 1944 (dec. Aug. 1982); children: Paul Thomas, Ann Frances, Thomas Matthew, Matthew Peta; m. Edward Samuel Dayhoff, Dec. 8, 1987. Student, Douglas Coll., 1940-43, Art Students League, N.Y.C., 1943; BA summa cum laude, SUNY, Utica, 1981. Tchr. art Catskill Art Soc., Hurleyville, N.Y., 1972-78, dir. publicity, 1974-80, exec. dir., 1978-80; asst. designer dept. pub. rels. SUNY, Utica, 1980-81. One woman shows include Herkimer (N.Y.) County Libr., 1984, Cedar Lane Unitarian Ch., Bethesda, Md., 1993, European Art Cafe, Bethesda, 1995, Robert's Gallery on 10th Ave., N.Y.C., 1995; exhibited in group shows at Catskill Art Soc., Hurleyville, 1972-80, N.Y. State Legislature bldg., Albany, 1978, Middletown (N.Y.) Art Group, 1978, Woodstock (N.Y.) Art Soc., 1983, St. Nicholas Parish House, Washington, 1995; author: (children's play) Small World, Glad World, 1971. Mem. Rockville Arts Place, Strathmore Hall Art Ctr., Strathmore Hall Artists. Democrat. Unitarian. Home and Office: 7716 Bells Mill Rd Bethesda MD 20817

DAYNEY, APRIL LYNN, roller skater; b. Bayshore, N.Y., Aug. 12, 1975; d. Randall Lynn and Petra Marieanne (Hausler) D. Grad., Springfield H.S., 1993. Roller skater, 1980—, world team mem., 1990-95, Pan Am. team mem., 1991-95. Recipient Gold medal Pan Am. Games, Havana, Cuba, 1991, Mar Del Plata, Argentina, 1995; winner World Championships, Salsomaggiore, 1994, 2d Place award 1995 World Championships, Bucaramanga, Colombia;. Home: 5916 Walnut Cir #14 Toledo OH 43615

DAYS, RITA DENISE, state legislator; b. Minden, La., Oct. 16, 1950; d. Marion and Juliette (Mitchell) Heard; m. Frank S. Days, June 17, 1972; children: Elliott Charles, Natalie Rechelle, Evelyn Jeanine. BMus, Lincoln U., 1972. Tchr. Webster Parish Sch. Bd., Minden, La., 1972; clk. typist Urban League of St. Louis, 1973-74, asst. dir. pub. info., 1974, placement interviewer, 1974-76; office supr. Burroughs Corp., St. Louis, 1976-80; sec., admissions counselor Jewish Coll. of Nursing, St. Louis, 1989-93; mem. Mo. Ho. of Reps., St. Louis, 1993—; chair elections com. Mo. Ho. of Reps., St. Louis, treas. Mo. Legis. Black Caucus, mem. Supreme Ct. Task Force on Children and Families; mem. Interagy. Coordinating Coun. part H. Active Ptnrs. for Kids, 1993—, New Sunny Mount Bapt. Ch.; sec. Women Legislators Mo.; bd. mem. Project Respond.; past bd. dirs. Normandy Sch. Dist. Mem. Alpha Kappa Alpha. Democrat. Office: Mo Ho of Reps State Capitol Building Jefferson City MO 65101-1556

DAYTON, MARY LEE, community volunteer; b. Marshall, Mo., May 12, 1925; d. Arnold and Braddie Lowe; m. Wallace C. Dayton, Oct. 15, 1948; children: Sally, Ellen, Katherine, Elizabeth. BA in Child Study, Vassar

Coll., 1946; LHD (hon.), Macalester Coll., 1995. Tchr. kindergarten Northrop Collegiate Sch., Mpls., 1946-48. Troop leader Girl Scouts USA, 1955-58; chair YWCA Capital Campaign, 1973-79; co-chair major gifts Minn. Women's Fund, 1983-87, mem. capital campaign steering com.; mem. pastoral nominating com. Westminster Presbyn. Ch., Mpls.; trustee Breck Sch., Mpls., Macalester Coll., chmn. bd. dirs., 1989-92; trustee Vassar Coll., bd. dirs. 1980-81, 96—; past chmn. bd. trustees YWCA, Mpls., pres. bd. dirs., 1970-74; nat. bd. dirs. YWCA, chair World Svc. Coun.; chmn. bd. dirs. Ripley Meml. Found., 1968-70, Planned Parenthood of Minn., 1980-82. Recipient Woman of Yr. award Mpls. YWCA, 1974, Leader Lunch award YWCA, 1984, Vol. Svc. award Channel 11, 1985, vol. Fundraiser of Yr. award Minn. chpt. of Nat. Soc. of Fund Raising Execs., Ambassador award YWCA of the U.S.A., 1993. Home: 510 Ferndale Rd W Wayzata MN 55391-9626

DEADERICK, LUCILE, retired librarian; b. Knoxville, June 22, 1914; d. Paul Stuart and Josephie Lee (Galyon) D. BA, U. Tenn., 1934; BLS, U. Ill., 1937. Catalog asst. Lawson McGhee Libr., Knoxville, 1929-41; editor bull. ALA, Chgo., 1941-47; libr. Ft. Loudoun Regional Libr., Lenoir City, Tenn., 1947-51, Knox County Schs., Knoxville, 1951-68; assoc. prof. Libr. Sch. U. Tenn., Knoxville, 1968-69; dir. Knoxville-Knox County Pub. Libr., 1970-78. Editor: Heart of the Valley: A History of Knoxville, Tennessee, 1976. Pres., bd. dirs. Mabry-Hazen Mus., Knoxville, 1992-95; bd. dirs., sec. ARC, Knoxville, 1980-95. Mem. Assn. for Preservation of Tenn. Antiquities, East Tenn. Hist. Soc. (treas., pres.). Democrat. Roman Catholic. Home: 7458 Somerset Rd Knoxville TN 37909

DEAL, LISA GAY, designer; b. Salisbury, N.C., Aug. 13, 1962; d. George Ray and Margaret Ann (Davis) D. BS in Textiles, N.C. State U., 1985. Designer Chatham Mfg., Elkin, N.C., 1985; from stylist to design mgr. Mastercraft, Spindale, N.C., 1985-94, dir. design, 1994—. Mem. Color Mktg. Group (chair 1995—, Superior Design award 1992). Mem. Ch. of God. Home: 3101 Harmon Homestead Rd Shelby NC 28150 Office: Mastercraft 111 Oakland Rd Spindale NC 28160

DEAL, LUISA, management consultant, trainer, speaker, former elementary school educator; b. Naples, Italy, July 15, 1943; came to U.S., 1948; d. Elaine (DeMarino) Bonomo; children: Pamela, Mark, Paula. AA, Muskegon C.C., Mich., 1967; BA, Saginaw Valley State U., 1969; MA, Cen. Mich. U., 1973; Ednl. Specialist, Mich. State U., 1982. Tchr. Saginaw (Mich.) Twp. Cmty. Schs., 1969-72, reading cons., 1972-77, reading specialist, 1977-86; mgmt. devel. trainer Automobile Club of Mich., Dearborn, 1986; assoc. mgr. ops. Gen. Physics Corp., Troy, Mich., 1987; tng. analyst Ball Systems Engring., San Diego, 1988; pres. Tng. Support Network, La Jolla, Calif., 1989—. Active Nine-Nines Internat., Detroit and San Diego, 1988—. Mem. ASTD (Detroit chpt. bd. dirs. 1987-88, San Diego chpt. EFO 1989-90, sec. 1990-91), Am. Soc. for Quality Control (chair 1996-97), Nat. Speakers Assn., Deming User Group, La Jolla Sunrise Rotary. Office: Tng Support Network PO Box 207 La Jolla CA 92038-0207

DEAL, LYNN HOFFMANN, interior designer; b. Atlantic City, N.J., Nov. 7, 1953; d. Ralph and Helen P. Hoffmann; m. James A. Deal, Sept. 19, 1981; 1 child, Katherine M. Diploma in environ. and interior design, U. Calif., Irvine, 1989. Prin. Lynn Deal and Assocs., Newport Beach, Calif., 1982—; mem. adv. bd. U. Calif., Irvine, 1984—. Chmn. Philharm. Showcase House, 1992; mem. Orange County Philharm. Soc. Mem. Am. Soc. Interior Designers (recipient Chpt. award 1991, Pres.'s award 1992, author introductory video Orange County chpt.), Internat. Furnishings and Design Assn., Interior Educators Coun., Internat. Platform Assn. Republican. Episcopalian. Home and Studio: 218 Via Palermo Newport Beach CA 92663-5502

DEAL, PATRICIA MARIE, political activist; b. Boston, Mar. 6, 1943; d. Paul Albert and Esther Helen (Hines) D. BS, Boston U., 1964; MEd, Salem State Coll., 1972; MBA, Bentley Coll., 1984. Cert. tchr., Mass. Tchr. Boston Pub. Schs., 1966-67, Sts. Peter & Paul H.S., St. Thomas, V.I., 1967-68, Wakefield (Mass.) Pub. Schs., 1968-71, Gloucester (Mass.) Pub. Schs., 1972-74; tchr., adminstr. St. Anne's Sch., Arlington, Mass., 1975-79; customer support supr. Educators Cons. Svcs., Burlington, Mass., 1979-82; project mgr. SEI Corp., Cambridge, Mass., 1982-86; treasury sr. sys. specialist Bank of Boston, 1987—. Town meeting mem. Town of Arlington, 1988—; Dem. state committeewoman Mass. Dem. Party, 1988—, mem. exec. com., 1992—; libr. trustee Robbin Libr., Arlington, 1994—; active Mass. Women's Polit. Caucus, 1984—, Nat. Women's Polit. Caucus, 1985—, v.p., 1995—. Home: 9 Ronald Rd Arlington MA 02174

DEAL, THERRY NASH, college dean; b. Iredell County, N.C., Apr. 21, 1935; d. Stephen W. and Betty (Sherrill) Nash; m. J.B. Deal, July 10, 1954 (dec. 1990); children: Melaney Dawne, J. Bradley. BS in Home Econs., U. N.C., 1957, MS, 1961, PhD, 1965; postgrad., Harvard U., 1964, 87. Instr. pub. schs. Iredell County, N.C., 1959-61; instr. U. N.C., Greensboro, 1961-65; prof. U. Ga., Athens, 1965-72; dept. chair Ga. Coll., Milledgeville, 1972-82, dir. continuing edn. and pub. svcs., 1982-84, dean continuing edn. and pub. svcs., 1984-95, dean emeritus, 1996—; bd. dirs. Pvt. Industry Coun., Baldwin Co.; vis. prof. Lanzhou Comml. Coll., China, 1993; participant World Conf. on Women, Beijing, 1994. Author numerous poems; contbr. articles to profl. jours. Mem. Am. Home Econs. Assn., Nat. Coun. Adminstrs. of Home Econs., Nat. Assn. Edn. of Young Children, Milledgeville/Baldwin County C. of C., DAR. Democrat. Methodist. Office: Ga Coll Clark St Milledgeville GA 31061

DEAN, DEAREST (LORENE GLOSUP), songwriter; b. Volin, S.D., Oct. 4, 1911; d. John Henry and Bessie Marie Donnelly Peterson; m. Eddie Dean, Sept. 11, 1931; children: Donna Lee Knorr, Edgar Glosup II. Grad. high sch., Yankton, S.D. Bd. dirs. Acad. Country Music, Hollywood, 1960-62. Composer songs including: One Has My Name, 1948, The Lonely Hours, 1970, 1501 Miles of Heaven, 1970, Walk Beside Me, 1980. Sec. ARC, Burbank, Calif., 1943. Mem. ASCAP. Republican. Roman Catholic. Avocation: golf.

DEAN, DIANE D., youth service agency executive, fund development consultant; b. Detroit, Aug. 26, 1949; d. Edward Lesley and Ada V. (Spann) D. Student, Mich. State U., 1966-68; BS, N.C. Argl. and Tech. State U., 1971; MS, Ind. U., 1973; postgrad., Stanford U. Summer Inst., 1981, UCLA, 1982-83; cert. in non-profit mgmt., Case Western Res. U., 1991; grad., Harvard Grad. Sch. of Edn., 1995. Area coord. U. Miami, Coral Gables, 1973-75; dir. housing Occidental Coll., L.A., 1975-78; asst. dir. admissions assistance and sch. rels. U. So. Calif., L.A., 1978-80; from asst. dir. to assoc. dir. admissions, dir. ops. LEAD program UCLA, 1980-85; dir. incentive grants and scholarship programs Nat. Action Coun. Minorities in Engring., N.Y.C., 1985-90; mgmt. cons. Girl Scouts U.S., N.Y.C., 1990-95; fund devel. cons. Girl Scouts U.S.A., N.Y.C., 1995—; appointed rep. Grad. Mgmt. Admissions Coun., Santa Monica, Calif., 1981-85. Author and editor: Directory of Minority Pers. Associated with Admissions, 1979-85. Named to J & B Winners Circle, Paddington Corp., N.Y.C., 1984. Mem. ASTD, NAFE, Nat. Assn. Fund Raising Execs., Nat. Assn. Student Pers. Adminstrn. (regional co-chair 1985), Corp. Women's Network, Assn. Coll. and Univ. Housing Officers (chair regional membership com.), Assn. Girl Scout Exec. Staff (bd. dirs.), N.Y. Women's Agenda, N.Y. Coalition of 100 Black Women, Trans Africa, Black Women's Forum, Girl Scouts U.S.A. (life), Schomberg Soc. for Preservation of Black Culture, Nat. Urban League, UCLA Alumni Assn. (life), N.C. Agrl. and Tech. State U. Alumni Assn., Cass Tech H.S. Alumni Assn. (life), Alpha Kappa Alpha (v.p. 1969-71). Office: Girl Scouts USA 420 Fifth Ave New York NY 10018-2729

DEAN, DONNA JOYCE, biochemist, government agency administrator; b. Danville, Ky., Apr. 22, 1947; d. Joe Harvey and Anna Mae (Jarvis) D. AB in Chemistry, Berea (Ky.) Coll., 1969; PhD in Biochemistry, Duke U., 1974. Rsch. faculty Princeton (N.J.) U., 1974-77; consumer safety officer FDA, Washington, 1979-82; research biochemist NIH, Bethesda, Md., 1977-79, scientist adminstr., chmn. tng. com., 1982—, mem. women's health rsch. com., 1993—; cons. numerous profl. assns. Contbr. articles to profl. jours., 1971-85. Recipient post-doctoral fellowship Nat. Cancer Inst., 1974-77. Mem. AAAS, Am. Soc. Cell Biology, Am. Assn. Pathologists, Am. Inst. Nutrition, Am. Chem. Soc., Assn. Women in Sci., Sci. Fair Assn. (mem. exec. bd. 1986-88), Berea Coll. Alumni Assn. (mem. com. 1987—). Office: NIH DRG Rockledge 2 MSC-776 Bethesda MD 20892

DEAN, DOROTHY K., county official, educator; b. Grand Rapids, Mich., May 29, 1948. BA, Aquinas Coll., 1970; MS, U. Wis., Milw., 1973. Vol. ElderCare Line, Milw., 1974-75; rsch. tech. Dept. Aging, Milw., 1975-77; rsch. analyst Milw. County, Milw., 1977-79, county supr., 1979—; instr. Alverno Coll., Milw., 1984—. Prodr., editor (video): The Positive Evolution of Bongo Baker, 1993; prodr., dir., editor (video): Into the Water, 1993, When the State Kills, 1995; prodr. (video) Portrait of the Artist As a Woman, 1993. Chair comm. and tech. com. Wis. Dem. Party, 1995—; county liaison Milw. Womens Polit. Caucus, 1990—; trustee Milw. Art Mus., 1983-95, War Meml., Milw., 1991—; bd. dirs. Hillside Boys and Girls Club, Milw., 1988—, Girl Scouts Am., Milw., 1992—. Recipient Fair Housing award Metro Milw. Fair Housing Coun., 1992, Wis. Fair Housing Network, 1993, Disting. Advocacy award Full Citizenship Initiative, 1993. Mem. Profl. Dimensions, Milw. Access Telecomms. Auth. Democrat. Home: 1121 E Vienna Ave Milwaukee WI 53212 Office: Milw County Bd 901 N 9th Rm 201 Milwaukee WI 53233

DEAN, JEAN BEVERLY, artist; b. South Paris, Maine, Aug. 23, 1928; d. Henry Dyer and Doris Filena (Judd) Small; m. Samuel Lester Dean. AS, Becker Coll., Worcester, Mass., 1948; AA, Edison Coll., Ft. Myers, Fla., 1980. Artist Ft. Myers, 1963—. One person shows include Edison C.C. Gallery, Ft. Myers, Joan Ling Gallery, Gainesville, Fla., Berry Coll., Mt. Berry, Ga., Gallery 10, Asheville, N.C., Cape Coral (Fla.) Arts Studio, Barbara B. Mann Performing Arts Hall, Ft. Myers, 1992, Sanibel (Fla.) Gallery, 1993, Barrier Island Group for the Arts, Sanibel, 1994, 96, Sanibel Gallery, 1995, Gallery Mido, Belleview Mido Resort, Belleair, Fla., 1996, No. Trust Bank, Ft. Myers, 1996, Lee County Alliance of the Arts, Ft. Myers, 1996, Art League of Manatee County, Fla., 1996; exhibited in group shows at S.E. Painting and Sculpture Exhbn., Jacksonville, Fla., Southeastern Ctr. for Contemporary Art, Ybor City, Park Shore Gallery, Naples, Fla., 1991, S.W. Fla. Internat. Airport, 1991, 95, Ctr. Art Show, St. Petersburg, Fla., 1991, Lee County Alliance of Arts, Ft. Myers, 1991, Ridge Juried Art Show, Winter Haven, Fla., 1992, Fla. Artists Group, Sarasota, 1992, Women's Caucus for Art, Sarasota, 1993, Polk Mus., Lakeland, Fla., 1993, Barrier Island Group for Arts, Sanibel, 1994, Daytona (Fla.) Mus., 1994, Women's Caucus Art Nat. Show, San Antonio, 1995, Capitol Gallery, Tallahassee, Fla., 1995, Women's Caucus Art State Show, Sarasota, 1995 , Women's Caucus for Art, Miami, 1996, Lee County Alliance of the Arts, Fla., 1996, Fla. Artist Group, Winter Haven, 1996; represented in permanent collections U.S. Embassy, Madrid, Edison Coll., First Fed. Savs. and Loan, Ft. Myers and Naples, Fla., NCNB Bank, Tampa, HealthPark, Ft. Myers, Clara Barton House, Washington, Hirshhorn Collection. Mem. Lee County Alliance for Arts, 1994, 95, 96; chair invitational com. Barrier Island Group for Arts, Sanibel, 1994, 95, 96.; founder Open Doors Lee County Alliance of the Arts, Fla., 1990—. Recipient more than 100 awards. Mem. Nat. Mus. Women in the Arts (charter mem.), Maine Coast Artists, Women's Caucus for Art, Fla. Artists Group. Democrat. Unitarian. Home: 17643 Captiva Island Ln Fort Myers FL 33908-6115

DEAN, LEANN FAYE LINDQUIST, librarian; b. Benson, Minn., Oct. 25, 1948; d. Lawrence Axel and Leonora Olivia (Nybakke) Lindquist; m. James Allen Dean, Aug. 20, 1971; children: Sonja Leonore, Trevor Lawrence. BA, Concordia Coll., Moorhead, Minn., 1969; MA in Libr. Sci., U. Minn., 1976; MA in Polit. Sci., U. S.D., 1991. Libr. Litchfield (Minn.) Jr. High Sch., 1969-76; asst. dir. Buckham Meml. Libr., Faribault, Minn., 1976-83; libr. Black Hills State Coll., Spearfish, S.D., 1983-85; libr. Sch. Bus. U. S.D., Box Elder, 1985-87; dir. learning svcs. Nat. Coll., Rapid City, S.D., 1987-91; head of public svcs. Briggs Library, U. Minn., Morris, 1991—; ch. libr. Litchfield Zion Luth. Ch., Our Saviors Ch., Faribault, Our Saviors Ch., Spearfish, South Canyon Luth. Ch., Rapid City. Democrat. Lutheran. Home: 7 S Court St Morris MN 56267-1613

DEAN, LINDA MARTIN, mental health nurse. BSN, No. Ill. U., 1989. Psychiat. nurse intern McLean Hosp., Belmont, Mass., 1989-90; psychiat. nurse Elmhurst (Ill.) Hosp., 1990—; mem. acuity com. Elmhurst (Ill.) Hosp., 1992—, psychiat. rev. com., 1993—, continuous quality improvement com., 1993—. Recipient Psychiatric Nursing Excellence award, 1994. Mem. Sigma Theta Tau. Office: Elmhurst Hosp 200 Berteau Ave Elmhurst IL 60126-2966

DEAN, LORI LADAWN, financial executive; b. Chgo., Nov. 16, 1956; d. Earl William and Agnes Imogene (Benson) Johnson; m. John Charles Dean, Apr. 17, 1989; children: Christine Ann, Danielle Marie, Kathleen Ann. Contract asst. Loral EOS, Pasadena, Calif., 1979-83; pricing analyst Marquardt Industries, 1984-86; exec. asst. to CEO ADS, Arcadia, Calif., 1986-89; exec. asst. to CEO Chetco Fed. Credit Union, Brookings, Oreg., 1989-93, asst. v.p. ops., 1994-95, v.p. ops./compliance, 1995—. Bd. sec. Brookings-Harbor Scholarship Found., Brookings, Oreg., 1993—; bd. dirs. Oasis House, shelter for abused women and children, 1996—. Mem. Inst. Internal Auditors, Nat. Notarial Soc. Office: Chetco Fed Credit Union 16147 Hwy 101 S Harbor OR 97415

DEAN, LYDIA MARGARET CARTER (MRS. HALSEY ALBERT DEAN), nutrition coordinator, author, consultant; b. Bedford, Va., July 11, 1919; d. Christopher C. and Hettie (Gross) Carter; m. Halsey Albert Dean; children: Halsey Albert Jr., John Carter, Lydia Margerae. Grad., Averett Coll.; BS, Madison Coll., 1941; MS, Va. Poly. Inst. and State U., 1951; postgrad., U. Va., Mich. State U.; PhD, D Nutrition Sci., UCLA, 1985. Cert. nutrition specialist Am. Coll. Bd. Nutrition, 1994. Dietetic intern, clin. dietitian St. Vincent de Paul Hosp., Norfolk, Va., 1942; jr. physicist U.S. Naval Op. Base, Norfolk, 1943-45; clin. dietitian Roanoke Meml. Hosps., 1946-51; assoc. prof. Va. Poly. Inst. and State U., 1946-53; community nutritionist Roanoke, Va., 1953-60; dir. dept. nutrition and dietetics Southwestern Va. Med. Ctr., Roanoke, 1960-67; food and nutrition cons. Nat. Hdqs. ARC, Washington, 1967—; staff and vol. Nat. Hdqs. ARC, 1973—; nutrition scientist, cons. Dept. Army, Washington, 1973—, Dept. Agr., 1973—; pres. Dean Assocs.; cons., assoc. dir. Am. Dietetic Assn., 1975—; coord. new degree program U. Hawaii, 1974-75; dir., nutrition coord. pub. health HHS, Washington, 1973-95, vol., 1996; mem. task force White House Conf. Food and Nutrition, 1969—; chmn. fed. com. Interagy. Com. on Nutrition Edn., 1970-71; tech. rep. to AID and State Dept.; chmn. Crusade for Nutrition Edn., Washington, 1970—; participant, cons. Nat. Nutrition Policy Conf., 1974. Author: (with Virginia McMasters) Community Emergency Feeding, 1972, Help My Child How to Eat Right, 1963, rev. edit., 1978, The Complete Gourmet Nutrition Cookbook: The Joy of Eating Well and Right, 1978, rev. edit., 1982, The Stress Foodbook, 1980; contbr. articles to profl. jours. Trustee World U., 1987—; apptd. rsch. bd. advisors Am. Biog. Inst., 1990. Named Women's Inner Cir. of Achievement N.Am., 1990. Fellow APHA, Internat. Inst. Cmty. Svc.; mem. AAUW (Hall of Fame 1992), Am. Dietetic Assn., Bus. and Profl. Women's Club (cons. 1970—, pres. 1981-82), Am. Home Econs. Assn. (rep. and treas. joint congl. com.), Inst. Food Technologists (blue ribbon spkr. 1972). Home: 7816 Birnam Wood Dr Mc Lean VA 22102-2709

DEAN, MARY SUE, English language and literature educator; b. Ashland, W.Va., July 14, 1934; d. Robert Stephen and Mary Hazel (Hall) D. BA, Radford (Va.) Coll., 1956. Cert. tchr., Va. Tchr. Andrew Lewis H.S., Salem, Va., 1956-59, Highland Springs (Va.) H.S., 1959-65, Garden H.S., Oakwood, Va., 1965-68; tchr., chair English dept. Richlands (Va.) H.S., 1968—; evaluator lang. arts Va. Schs. Dept., Richmond, 1980, 83; mem. textbook adoption com. Tazewell County Schs., 1983; tech-prep steering com. S.W. Va. Consortium, Richlands, Va., 1990—. Mem. NEA, Va. Edn. Assn. Democrat. Methodist. Home: PO Box 588 Cedar Bluff VA 24609 Office: Richlands HS Richlands VA 24641

DEAN, PATRICIA ANN, lawyer; b. Washington, Apr. 11, 1949. BSBA cum laude, Georgetown U., 1975, JD cum laude, 1981. Bar: D.C. 1981. Law clk. to Hon. Edward A. Tamm D.C. Cir. Ct. Appeals, 1981-82; dep. clk. U.S. Supreme Ct., 1981, law clk. to Hon. Byron R. White, 1982-83; ptnr. Arnold & Porter, Washington. *

DEAN, PENNY LEE, physical education educator, coach; b. San Francisco, Mar. 21, 1955; d. Joseph Edward and Frances (Von Hermann) D. BA in History, Pomona Coll., Claremont, Calif., 1977; MS in Phys. Edn., Calif. Poly. Inst., Pomona, 1980; EdD, U.S. Sports Acad., Daphne, Ala., 1996. Promotional tng. Queen Mary, Long Beach, Calif., 1979; asst. girls' swim coach Chino (Calif.) H.S., 1977; nat. swim coach U.S. Swimming, Colorado Springs, Colo., 1979-91; asst. men's swim and water polo coach Pomona Coll., 1978-84, prof. phys. edn., women's swim and water polo coach, 1978—. Author: History of Catalina Swims, 1980, How to Swim a Marathon, 1985; cons. films Water Dancer, 1987, Penny Dean Story, 1990. Holder world record for swimming English Channel, 1978; named All Am. Coach, U.S. Swimming, 1984, 86, 89, recipient Hummer award, 1985; named Disting. Coach/Master, Coll. Swim Coaches, 1993; named to Swimming Hall of FAme, 1996. Mem. So. Calif. Intercoll. Athletics (chmn. 1993-96). Office: Pomona Coll 220 E 6th Rains Ctr Claremont CA 91711-6346

DEAN, REBECCA KAY, speech educator; b. Charleston, W.Va., Feb. 11, 1957; d. William Hughes and Bonnie Lee (Johnson) D. BA in Englsih, U. Pitts., 1980, MA in Comm., 1984, postgrad. TV host Sta. WXIX, Pitts., 1974-81; assoc. prof. speech Northampton Comm. Coll., Bethlehem, Pa., 1991—; vis. prof. speech & English Pasco-Hernando C.C., New Port Rickey, Fla., 1984-87, Hillsborough C.C., Tampa, Fla., 1984-87, Lafayette Coll., Easton, Pa., 1989-91. Speech text reviewer Houghton-Mifflin Pub. House, 1994-95/. Mem. AAUW, LWV (bd. dirs. 1991—). Office: Northampton CC 3835 Green Pond Rd Bethlehem PA 18017

DEAN, SHARON LOU, information consultant; b. Ithaca, N.Y., Nov. 4, 1943; d. Kermit Lewis and Lila Lee (Moravia) D.; m. Richard Stephen Chrappa. BA, Keuka Coll., 1964; MA, Syracuse U., 1965; MLS, U. Wash., 1978, cert. in bus. adminstrn., 1981. Cert. profl. librarian, Wash.; cert. secondary tchr., Wash., N.Y., Ariz. Supr. learning resource ctr. Mercer Island Sr. High Sch., Wash., 1975-77; head librarian John F. Kennedy High Sch., Seattle, 1977-81; sr. info. analyst Cigna Corp., Phila., 1982-83, mktg. cons., 1983-84, systems mgr., 1984-86, bus. cons., 1986-90; pres. Corp. Fact Finders, 1989—. Author: Winning Marketing Techniques for Information Professionals, 1990; contbr. articles to profl. and bus. jours. Bd. dirs. Unitarian Ch., West Chester, Pa., 1984-85. Recipient State of Wash. Commendation award Gov., Sec. of State, 1976, Profl. Achievement award Keuka Coll., 1991. Mem. ALA (com. mem. 1978-80), SLA, Assn. Ind. Info. Profls. Avocations: sewing, photography, reading, needlework, travel.

DEAN, SHERRY, news reporter, producer; b. New York, July 31, 1959. BA, NYU, 1980. Copyperson N.Y. Daily News, N.Y.C., 1980-81; newswriter, prodr., reporter WPIX-TV, N.Y.C., 1981-88; prodr., reporter Good Day New York Fox-TV, N.Y.C., 1988-89; freelance newswriter WCBS-TV, WNBC-TV, N.Y.C., 1989; reporter, prodr. entertainment news CNN, N.Y.C., 1990—. Office: CNN Showbiz Today 5 Penn Plz 20th Fl New York NY 10001*

DEAN, SUSAN THACH, librarian; b. Denver, Dec. 11, 1946; d. Henry Clyde and Dorothy (Groff) Thach. BA with honors, U. Wis., Parkside, 1970; MA in Libr. Sci., U. Wis., Milw., 1971. Libr. ref. and spl. collections U. Wis., Parkside, 1971-74; reading rm. supr. spl. collections divsn. Newberry Libr., Chgo., 1974-79, asst. curator spl. collections, 1979-83; guest curator Caxton Club, Chgo., 1983-84; libr. theater arts Chgo. Pub. Libr., Chgo., 1984-89; fundraising coord. Karme-Choling, Barnet, Vt., 1989-91; libr. spl. collections, archivist Ind. U., South Bend, 1991-92; head spl. collections dept. U. Colo. Librs., Boulder, 1992—. Mem. editl. bd. Union List of Victorian Serials, 1984; assoc. editor Victorian Periodicals Rev., 1993—; contbr. articles to profl. jours. Rep. Interfaith Coun. of Boulder, 1993—. Coun. on Libr. Resources fellow, 1974. Mem. ALA (exhibition catalog awards com. mem. 1993—), Rsch. Soc. for Victorian Periodicals (bd. dirs.), Midwest Victorian Studies Assn. (exec. bd. 1982-86, 92-96). Office: Spl Collection Univ Colo at Boulder Libr Box 184 Boulder CO 80309

DE ANDA, ALICIA, artist; b. L.A., Mar. 8, 1965; d. Simon and Alicia (Saenz) De A. AA, Brooks Coll., 1985. Sales assoc. The Broadway, Orange, Calif., 1985-86, Nordstrom, Cerritos, Calif., 1986-89; sec. The Reef Funds, Cerritos, 1989-90; model L.A., 1990-92; bus. mgr. Estee Lauder/Robinsons May, Canoga Park, 1992-95; make-up artist Lancome/Saks Fifth Ave., Beverly Hills, 1995—. Actress in theatrical prodns. in Woodland Hills and Calabasas, Calif. Mem. NAFE, L.A. County Mus. of Art, Nat. Mus. of Women in the Arts, Mus. Contemporary Art (L.A.). Democrat. Office: Saks Fifth Ave 9600 Wilshire Blvd Beverly Hills CA 90212

DEANE, ANGELA RAY, professional development specialist; b. Clarksville, Tenn., Apr. 9, 1966; d. Stephen and D. Marsha Ray; m. Silas Edward Deane II, Sept. 28, 1991. BA, U. Ky., 1988; MA, Am. U., 1990. Account exec. Artisan Advt., Lexington, Ky., 1988-89; asst. press sec. Subcom. for Telecom. and Fin., Washington, 1990; cons. Ernst & Young, Reston, Va., 1990-91; sr. assoc. Ernst & Young, Vienna, Va., 1991-94, mgr. info. comm. and entertainment industry, 1994—. Editor: (booklets) Valuing the Learning Organization, 1993, Exploring New Measures for the Knowledge Era, 1994. Mem. Jr. League of No. Va., Fairfax, 1995—; chmn. Univ. Art Gallery, Lexington, Ky., 1986, 88. Mem. ASTD, Women in Comm. (interim v.p. profl. devel. 1994—), Alpha Omicron Pi (leadership coun. 1986-88). Methodist. Office: Ernst and Young 8075 Leesburg Pike Vienna VA 22182

DEANE, DEBBE, psychologist, journalist, editor, consultant; b. Coatesville, Pa., July 30, 1950; d. George Edward and Dorothea Alice (Martin) Mays; widowed; children: Theo, Vonisha, Lorise, Voniece. AA in Psychology, Mesa Coll., 1989; BA Psychology, San Diego State U., 1993; MA in Psychology, Nat. U., 1995; postgrad., U.S. Internat. U., 1995—. News dir. Sta. KLDR, Denver, 1976-78; host, reporter Sta. KMGH-TV, Denver, 1978-81; news anchor, editor Sta. KHOW, Denver, 1978-79; news & pub. affairs dir. Sta. KLZ, Denver, 1979-80, Sta. KCBQ, San Diego, 1980-82; news anchor Sta. KOGO, San Diego, 1983-84; news anchor, reporter Sta. KCST-TV, San Diego, 1984-87; dir. comm. Omni Corp., San Diego, 1987—; news anchor Sta. KFI, L.A., 1990-91; sr. psychiat. therapist Behavioral Health Group, San Diego, 1993—; media liaison United Negro Coll. Fund, San Diego, 1990-92; dir. comm. United Chs. of Christ, San Diego, 1989-92; cons. San Diego Assn. Black Journalists, 1985-92, San Diego Coalition Black Journalists, 1985-92. Campaign fin. analyst San Diego County Registrar of Voters, San Diego, 1990; cons. San Diego County Office Disaster Preparedness, 1990-91, Nu Way Youth Ctr. & Neighborhood House, Inc., San Diego, 1991-92; counselor Project STARRT, San Diego, 1991-92. Recipient San Diego Black Achievement award Urban League, 1989, Best News Show & Spot News award San Diego Press Club, 1985, Golden Mike award So. Calif. Broadcast Assn., L.A., 1986; named one of Top 25 Businesswomen Essence Mag., 1978, Outstanding Humanitarian Worldvision, 1993, Outstanding Humanities Alumna Mesa Coll., 1993, Woman of the Year, 1996 American Biographical Inst. Mem. AFTRA, APA, Am. Women in Radio & TV, Women in Comm., Black Students Sci. Orgn. (sec. 1989-91), Africana Psychol. Soc. (media coord. 1990-92), Psi Chi. Democrat. Home: 3545 Valley Rd Bonita CA 91902

DEANE, JUDITH BAUER, marketing executive, learning disabilities consultant; b. Bklyn., May 13, 1945; d. Ted and Rose (Mayer) Bauer; m. Stuart Sneed Deane, Oct. 3, 1971; children: Kenneth, Richard, Lauren. BA in Edn. and Psychology, Bklyn. Coll., 1965; MS in Info. Sys., Pace U., 1992; MS in Learning Disabilities, Coll. New Rochelle, 1995. Sys. analyst Honeywell, N.Y.C., 1966-71; ind. contractor, 1972-73; v.p. The Deane Group, Somers, N.Y., 1993—; exec. dir., ind. assoc. Mannatech, Grand Prairie, Tex., 1994—. Mem. Bus. Network Internat., Westchester Assn. Women Bus. Owners, Entrepreneurial Women's Network. Home: 18 Young Rd Katonah NY 10536 Office: The Deane Group Box 416 Somers NY 10589

DEANE, SALLY JAN, health services administrator, consultant; b. Downey, Calif., Sept. 24, 1948; d. Virgil Eldred and Pearl Jan (Kettell) D. BA, Whittier Coll., 1970; MEd, Boston U., 1971, MPH, 1988. Mgr. community health Peter Bent Brigham Hosp., Boston, 1974-76; coord. WIC program Martha Eliot Health Ctr., 1976-78; dir. S.W. Boston WIC program Shattuck Hosp. Corp., 1978-80; exec. dir. Fenway Community Health Ctr., 1980-84; exec. asst. commr. Boston Dept. Health & Hosps., 1984-86; assoc. dir. spl. projects Health Policy Inst. Boston U., 1986-87; dir. ambulatory reimbursement Mass. Medicaid, 1987-88; assoc. Cambridge (Mass.) Mgmt. Group, 1989; ptnr. Integrated Health Strategies Inc., Cambridge, Mass., 1990-96; asst. prof. Pub. Health Boston U., 1994—; v.p. Chadwick Martin

Bailey, Boston, 1996—; cons. Mass. Dept. Pub. Health, Boston, 1978-80, Citicorp Corp. Hdqrs., N.Y.C., 1986. Mem. Mayor's Task Force on AIDS, Boston, 1983-86; v.p. Trustees Charitable Donations, Boston, 1984-88. Mem. Mass. Pub. Health Assn., Am. Pub. Health Assn., Women in Health Care Mgmt. Presbyterian. Home: 115 University Rd Brookline MA 02146-4545 Office: Chadwick Martin Bailey 179 South St Boston MA 02111

DEANGELIS, CATHERINE D., pediatrics educator; b. Scranton, Pa., Jan. 2, 1940; m. James C. Harris. BA, Wilkes Coll., 1965; MD, U. Pitts., 1969; MPH, Harvard U., 1973. RN, Pa., N.Y.; diplomate Nat. Bd. Med. Examiners, Am. Bd. Pediatrics. Intern in pediatrics Children's Hosp., Pitts., 1969-70; resident in pediatrics Johns Hopkins Hosp., Balt., 1970-72, teaching fellow pediatrics dept. internat. health Sch. Pub. Health, 1972; pediatrician Roxbury Comprehensive Health Clinic, Boston, 1972-73; asst. prof. pediatrics Coll. Physicians and Surgeons, asst. prof. health svc. adminstrn. Sch. Pub. Health Columbia U., 1973-75; mem. staff divsn. pediatric ambulatory care, dir. med. edn. Child Care Project Columbia Presbyn. Med. Ctr., 1973-75; asst. prof. pediatrics Sch. Medicine U. Wis., 1975-77, assoc. prof. pediatrics Sch. Medicine, 1977-78; dir. ambulatory pediatric svcs. U. Wis. Hosps., 1975-78; assoc. prof. pediatrics Johns Hopkins Sch. Medicine, 1978-85; dir. pediatric primary care and adolescent medicine Johns Hopkins Hosp., 1978-84, co-dir. adolescent pregnancy program, 1979-82; with dept. health svcs. adminstrn. and dept. internat. health Johns Hopkins Sch. Hygiene and Pub. Health, 1980-90; dir. residency tng. dept. pediatrics Johns Hopkins Hosp., 1983-90, dir. divsn. gen. pediatrics and adolescent medicine, 1984-90; deputy chmn. dept. pediatrics Johns Hopkins Sch. Medicine, 1983-90, prof. pediatrics, 1986—, assoc. dean acad. affairs, 1990-93, sr. assoc. dean acad. affairs and faculty, 1993-94; vice dean acad. affairs and faculty, 1994—; mem. Gov.'s Task Force to Evaluate Health Care in Wis. State Prisons, 1975-78; chmn. ambulatory care com. U. Wis. Hosp., 1976-78; mem. med. sch. admissions com. U. Wis. Sch. Medicine, 1976-78, chmn., 1977-78; mem. exec. coun. dept. pediatrics and Children's Ctr., Johns Hopkins U. Sch. Medicine, 1982-90, chmn. fin. com. dept. pediatrics, 1984-85, chmn. assoc. prof.'s promotion com., 1985-88; chmn. com. developing Women's Health Ctr. at Johns Hopkins Med. Instns., 1993—; mem. Gov.'s Task Force on Women's Health, Md., 1993—, chair 1994—; mem. search com. U. Wis., 1976, Johns Hopkins Sch. Medicine, 1984, 88, 92, 93; mem. nat. review com. for accreditation of nurse practitioners Am. Nurses' Assn., 1975-79, co-chmn., 1977; mem. peer review com. nurse practitioner programs divsn. nursing Health Resources Agy., Dept. Health, Edn. and Welfare, 1979-81; mem. Nat. Commn. on Nursing, 1985-86, Physician Consortium on Substance Abuse Edn., 1989—; mem. clin. scholar's adv. com. Robert Wood Johnson Found., 1992-94, Assn. Acad. Health Ctrs., 1993—; mem. Assn. Health Svcs. Rsch., 1993—; with immunization team, Nicaragua, 1969; subintern Harbel Hosp., Liberia, West Africa, 1969; organizer immunization program Peru, 1972, West Indies Sch. Nursing, 1977; mem. editorial bd. The Hosp. Med. Staff, 1982—, Pediatrician, 1984—, Jour. of Pediatrics, 1986—, Pediatric Annals, 1990—, Pediatrics in Review, 1990—, Archives of Pediatrics and Adolescent Medicine, 1993—; reviewer Acad. Medicine, Am. Jour. Diseases of Children, Am. Jour. Medicine, Clin. Pediatrics, Jour. Pediatrics, Med. Care, Pediatrics; writer weekly column Balt. Sun, 1987-90. Author: Basic Pediatrics for the Primary Care, 1984; editor: An Introduction to Clinical Research, 1990; editor: (with others) Principles and Practice of PEdiatrics, 1990, 2d edit., 1994; assoc. editor Pediatric Annals, 1990—; editor Archives of Pediatrics and Adolscent Medicine, 1993—. Mem. steering com. Rural Health Planning, Wis.; cons. Robert Wood Johnson Found., 1973—; mem. adv. group on improving outcomes for children Pew Charitable Trusts, 1991-92; mem. adv. panel medicine Pew Health Profession's Commn.; mem. nat. adv. com. Robert Wood Johnson Clin. Scholars Program, 1992—. NIH fellow, 1973; recipient George Armstrong award Ambulatory Pedicatric Assn., Acad. Adminstrn. and Health Policy scholarship Assn. Acad. Health Ctrs., 1993. Fellow APHA, Am. Acad. Pediatrics (govt. affairs com. 198uth com. N.Y. chpt. 1974-75, chmn. adolscent com. Md. chpt. 1981-84); mem. Am. Pediatr. Soc. (sec., treas. 1989—), Am. Bd. Pediatrics (examiner 1986—, long range planning com. 1990-91, chmn. ling range planning com. 1992—, bd. dirs. 1990—, fin. com. 1991—, sec., treas. 1993-95, chair-elect 1995-96, chair 1996, search com. 1990), Soc. Adolscent Medicine, Alpha Omega Alpha. Office: Johns Hopkins Sch Medicine 720 Rutland Ave Ste 106 Baltimore MD 21205-2109

DE ANGELIS, DEBORAH ANN AYARS, university athletics official; b. San Diego, July 2, 1948; d. Charles Orvil and Janet Isabel (Glithero) Ayars; m. David C. De Angelis, Sept. 29, 1984. B.A., U. Calif.-Santa Barbara, 1970, Certificate in Social Services, 1972; M.S., U. Mass., 1979. Eligibility worker County Welfare Dept., Santa Barbara, Calif., 1970-73; women's crew coach, U. Mass., 1978-79, Northeastern U., Boston, 1979-83, bus. mgr. women's athletics, 1983-87, asst. dir. bus., 1987-89; mgr. athletics bus. Calif. State U., Northridge, 1989-93, assoc. dir., 1993-96; assoc. athletic dir. for internal affairs, Towson State U., 1996—; com. mem. Women's Olympic Rowing Com., 1976-84; life trustee Nat. Rowing Found., 1984; life mem. selection com. Rowing Found. Hall of Fame, 1984—, bd. dirs., 1994—; rowing mgr. Women's Olympic Team, 1976, 80; head mgr. U.S. Olympic Festival, Syracuse, N.Y., 1981, coach, Indpls., 1982, Colorado Springs, Colo., 1983; mem. alcohol and drug awareness com. Northeastern U., 1983. Mem. Nat. Women's Rowing Assn. (pres. 1976-80, Woman of Yr. award 1983), Fedn. Sociétés d'Aviron (women's commn. 1978—, U.S. del. to ann. congress 1978, 80-88, 95), U.S. Rowing Assn. (del. 1988, bd. dirs. 1975-80, 85—, co-chmn. internat. div., co-chmn. events div. 1985-86, chmn. internat. div. 1986-88, women's v.p. 1985-88, mem. exec. com. 1985-89, exec. v.p. 1988-89, sec. 1995-96), Calif. State U. Northridge Intercollegiate Athletics Oversight Adv. Bd., Tri C. of C. July 4th Spectacular Com. Club: ZLAC Rowing. Home: 15 Kitzbuhel Rd Parkton MD 21120

DEANGELIS, MARGARET SCALZA, publishing executive; b. Jersey City, May 27, 1936; d. Louis Patrick and Josephine M. (Cleary) Scalza; m. David Jenkins, Sept. 30, 1951 (div. 1962); children: Alison Brittain, Cynthia Higgins, Ann Marie; m. Henry DeAngelis, Aug. 28, 1977; children: Valerie, Brenda DeAngelis Falato, Louise DeAngelis Brine, Henry Jr. Owner Towne House Restaurant, Hackettstown, N.J., 1963-65; pres. Kinsley Assocs., Inc., Hackettstown, N.J., 1966—; pub. purchasing guides, sch. directories, N.J., N.Y., Calif., Ill. Co-chmn. Northwestern N.J. divsn. U.S. Postal Customer Coun., 1978—. Mem. Nat. Assn. Sch. Bus. Ofcls., Warren County Bd. Realtors, Nat. Assn. Female Execs., Hackettstown Trade Assn. (sec.-treas., bd. dirs. 1963). Republican. Roman Catholic. Home: G4-B3 37 Osprey Hackettstown NJ 07840 Office: 8 Ridge Rd Hackettstown NJ 07840-4602

DEANGELIS, SUSAN PENNY, human resources professional; b. N.Y.C., Nov. 20, 1950; s. Milton Abraham and Anne Pearl (Fleischer) Zwilling; m. Ivo DeAngelis, July 25, 1971 (div. Feb. 1982); m. Benjamin H. Pfeffer, May 17, 1985. BA cum laude, Bklyn. Coll., 1971. Spl. projects coordinator, customer service rep. N.Y. Property Ins. Underwriting Assocs., N.Y.C., 1971-72; office mgr. Pyramid Personnel Agy., N.Y.C., 1972-73; v.p. human resources Feature Enterprises Inc., N.Y.C., 1973-92; cons. JWJ Enterprises, Inc., N.Y.C., 1984-85; dir. pers. Hebrew Immigrant Aid Soc. Inc., N.Y.C., 1992—; mem. bus. adv. com. RUSK Inst. of Rehab., 1993—. N.Y. State Bd. Regents scholar, 1967. Mem. N.Y. Assn. New Ams. (chairperson pvt. sector adv. com. 1985-93), Pers. Assn. of Non-Profit Orgns. (mem. exec. com. 1993—), U.S. Power Squadrons (lt. comdr.). Avocations: photography, calligraphy, painting, boating. Home: 2258 E 27th St Brooklyn NY 11229-5030 Office: Hebrew Immigrant Aid Soc Inc 333 7th Ave New York NY 10001-5004

DEAR, SANDRA RICHARDS, counselor; b. Ft. Worth, Tex., May 10, 1939; d. Robert Clyde and Mildred (Green) Richards; m. Homer Pete Dear, Aug. 18, 1963; children: Nick, Rich. BSEd, U. North Tex., 1961, MEd, 1978. Lic. profl. counselor, lic. marriage and family therapist, Tex.; cert. tchr., Tex. Elem. tchr. White Settlement Ind. Sch. Dist., Ft. Worth, 1962-64, h.s. drama/English tchr., 1964-67, 73-81, jr. high drama/English tchr., 1970-73, mid. sch. counselor, 1981-96; mem. Brewer Mid. Campus Plan Com., White Settlement, Tex., 1982-96. Contbr. articles to Voice of School Counselor jour., 1992-96. Chmn. alumni awards com., U. North Tex., Denton, 1994-95; mem. Tex. Dem. Women, Ft. Worth, 1993—. Mem. ACA, Am. Sch. Counselors Assn., Tex. Counseling Assn. (legis. com. 1995—), Tex. Sch. Counselors Assn. (v.p. 1991-96, legis. com. 1996), North Cen. Tex. Counseling Assn. (Outstanding Mid. Sch. Counselor award 1993, sec. 1992-94, pres.-elect 1996), White Settlers Adminstrs. Assn. (pres. 1992-93), U. North Tex. Alumni Assn. (bd. dirs. 1996—). Democrat. Greek Orthodox.

DEARBORN, LAURA, advertising agency executive. Former sr. v.p. Dancer Fitzerald & Sample (now Saatchi & Saatchi), San Francisco; now exec. v.p. Saatchi & Saatchi, San Francisco. Office: Saatchi & Saatchi 1010 Battery St San Francisco CA 94111-1202

DEARBORN, MAUREEN MARKT, speech and language clinician; b. Brockton, Mass., Jan. 19, 1948; d. Francis Joseph and Marjorie Agnes (White) M.; m. James Clement Bovin, Nov. 6, 1970 (div. June 1973); m. David C. Dearborn, Jan. 14, 1989. BA in Speech Pathology and Audiology, U. Mass., 1970; MA in Ednl. Psychology, Am. Internat. Coll., Springfield, Mass. Speech and lang. clinician Holyoke (Mass.) Pub. Schs., 1970—. Chmn. Holyoke Cancer Crusade, 1985; voter registration chmn. Holyoke Dem. Com., 1987; chmn. deaconesses 2d Congl. Ch. Holyoke. Mem. Hampden County Tchrs. Assn. (pres. 1981, 87, sec. 1982, v.p. 1984-86, treas. 1988—), Holyoke Tchrs. Assn. (treas. 1989, DAR historian), Am. Speech, Hearing and Langs. Assn. (continuing edn. adv. bd. 1988-91, congl. action contact continuing edn. adv. bd. 1988-90), Mass. Tchrs. Assn., Mass. Speech, Hearing and Langs. Assn., New England Hist. and Geneal. Soc., Friends of the Lib. Coun. (treas. 1992—), Mass. Genealogical Soc., Assn. for Gravestone Studies, DAR (historian Eunice Day 1984), Wrentham Hist Soc., Dorchester Hist. Soc. Home: 257 W Franklin St Holyoke MA 01040-2210 Office: Holyoke Pub Schs 57 Suffolk St Holyoke MA 01040-5015

DEARDORFF, ELEANOR FREEDMAN, public relations executive; b. Chgo., Mar. 1, 1962; d. Jerome Kenneth and Carol Ann (Rosenburg) Freedman; m. Craig Stephen Deardorff, Apr. 13, 1991; children: Peter, Serena. BA in Eng. Lit. cum laude, Wheaton Coll., 1983. Account exec. Edelman Pub. Rels., N.Y.C., 1985-86, The Equity Group, N.Y.C., 1986; sr. account exec. Ecom Cons., N.Y.C., 1986-87; v.p. Edelman Pub. Rels., N.Y.C., 1987-91; pres. Deardorff Pub. Rels., Princeton, N.J., 1991—; cons. Gillespie Pub. Rels., 1994—. Mem. Wheaton Club. Office: Deardorff Pub Rels 308 Gallup Rd Princeton NJ 08540-7308

DEARDORFF, KATHLEEN UMBECK, nursing educator, researcher; b. Chgo., June 26, 1944; d. Paul Frederick and Lois Margaret (Deiters) Umbeck; m. Bruce Phillip Deardorff, Dec. 23, 1979; children: Sarah Louise, Philip Paul. Diploma, Evangelical Sch. Nursing, Oaklawn, Ill., 1965; BSN, U. Pa. Sch. Nursing, Phila., 1969, MSN, 1974. RN Ill., Pa., Tex.; ACCE ASPO Lamaze. Staff nurse obstetrics Christ Community Hosp., Oaklawn, Ill., 1965-66; staff nurse obstetrics Hosp. of the U. Pa., Phila., 1966-68, asst. instr. obstetrics, 1968-72; obstetrics practitioner tchr., unit leader Rush U., Chgo., 1974-77; asst. prof. maternity Elmhurst Coll., Ill., 1977-78, 80-82; lectr. maternity Trinity Christian Coll., Palos Heights, Ill., 1984; obstetrics intake liaison Hinsdale Family Medicine Ctr., Hinsdale, Ill., 1988-91; facilitator of post partum depression group Good Samaritan Hosp., Downer Grove, Ill., 1989-91; instr. maternity U. Tex., Tyler, 1992—, rsch. asst., 1994—; cons. Burnham & Hammond, Inc., Chgo., 1979-80, Trinity Christian Coll., Palos Heights, Ill., 1983-84; mem. nat. bd. Depression after Delivery, 1991-94. Contbr. to profl. jours. Advisor Naperville YMCA, Ill., 1987-88; vol. nat. hotline Depression after Delivery, 1989-94; communty rels. com. United Way, Tyler, 1993-94. Mem. Am. Soc. Psychoprophylaxis in Obstetrics (exec. com. 1986-87, chair 1987-89), Ill. Region Depression After Delivery (coord. 1989-91), Tex. Region Depression After Delivery (coord. 1991-94), Assn. Women's Health Obstet. and Neonatal Nurses, Post Partum Support Internat., Sigma Theta Tau. Presbyterian. Office: U Tex 3900 University Blvd Tyler TX 75701

DEARE, JENNIFER LAURIE, marketing professional; b. N.Y.C., Jan. 2, 1952; d. Bruce L. and Maxine L. (Schachter) Schneider; m. Jeffrey Cahn. Student, New Eng. Coll., Arundel, Eng.; BA in Fine Arts, Montclair State. Account executive Al Carlisle & Assocs., N.Y.C., 1979-81; account supr. The Hanley Partnership, N.Y.C., 1981-83; v.p. Walter Coddington Assoc., N.Y.C., 1983-87; pres. Deare Mktg., Inc., N.Y.C., 1987—. Fund raiser ARC, N.Y.C., 1988; bd. dirs. N.Y. Exploring div. Boy Scouts Am. Mem. Promotion Mktg. Assn. Am., Women's Direct Response Group. Office: Deare Mktg Inc 149 Fifth Ave New York NY 10010

DEARLOVE, KAREN S., public administrator; b. Richmond, Ind., June 18, 1960; d. Max E. and Beverly R. (Kempton) Tucker; m. Kent E. Lewis, Dec. 23, 1978; 1 child, Sandra Tucker-Lewis Dearlove; m. Thomas J. Dearlove, June 7, 1986. AAS in Forest Tech., Southeastern Ill. Coll., 1983; BS in Forestry, So. Ill. U., 1986. Rsch. tech. US Forest Svc., Missoula, Mont., 1983; rsch. vol. US Forest Svc., Carbondale, Ill., 1984-86; rsch. forester Natural Land Inst., Belknap, Ill., 1986-88; environ. studies mgr. Donan Engring., Jasper, Ind., 1988-90; exec. dir. Ind. 15 Regional Planning Commn., Jasper, 1990—. Dir. Historic So. Ind., Evansville, 1994—, So. VI Corp., 1995—, incorporator. Recipient Nat. Innovation award So. VI Corp., 1995. Mem. AAUW, Nat. Assn. Devel. Orgns. (dir. 1995-96), Ind. Assn. Cmty. Econ. Devel. (dir. 1995-96), The Nature Conservancy, Bristow Cmty. Club, Nat. Trust for Hist. Preservation, Phi Kappa Phi, Xi Sigma Pi. Democrat. Presbyterian. Office: Ind 15 Regional Planning Commn 610 Main St Jasper IN 47546

DE ARTEAGA, AIDA JOSEPHINA, musican, educator, art administrator; b. San Turce, P.R., July 8, 1951; d. Diego de Arteaga and Aida Alicia Santana. AA, Bronx (N.Y.) C.C., 1975; BA, Sonoma State U., 1982. V.p. Flamingo Club, N.Y.C., 1975-78; assoc. N.Y. Life. Ins., Calif., 1982-86; prof. jazz San Quentin (Calif.) Prison Stanford U. Jazz Camp Inst., 1986-90; bilingual educator Richmond (Calif.) Sch. Dist., 1989-90; art adminstr. San Quentin State Prison, 1990—; bass player Napa Valley Symphony, Calif., 1984—; cons. in field. Composer The Music That's Inside of You. Grantee NEA, 1983, Calif. Arts Coun., 1987-90. Mem. Musician's Union. Office: San Quentin State Prison PO Box 206 San Quentin Village CA 95476

DEASY, JACQUELINE HILDEGARD, insurance consultant; b. Rotterdam, The Netherlands, Oct. 17, 1959; came to U.S., 1960; d. Fred and Joyce (Snell) Lamsfus; m. Thomas W. Deasy, Sept. 27, 1980; 1 child, Sara Y. AAS in Bus. Adminstrn., Niagara County C.C., Sanborn, N.Y., 1993; BS in Commerce, Niagara U., 1995. Lic. ins. agt., N.Y. Svc. analyst Specific Solutions, Inc., Williamsville, N.Y., 1982-84; cons. Comml. Union Life Ins. Co. N.Y., Buffalo, 1984—. Cert. tutor Literacy Vols. Am., North Tonawanda, N.Y., 1995; vol. speakers bur. Ronald McDonald House, Buffalo, 1995—; tchr. religious edn. St. Francis of Assisi, Tonawanda, 1995. Mem. AAUW, Am. Soc. CLU and ChFC, Buffalo Life Underwriters Assn. (pub. rels. media mgr. 1995), Niagara County C.C. Alumni Assn. (exec. officer, treas. 1994—), Phi Theta Kappa, Delta Epsilon Sigma. Democrat. Roman Catholic. Home: 1058 Thomas Fox Dr E North Tonawanda NY 14120-2957 Office: CU Life Ins Co NY 100 Corporate Pkwy Buffalo NY 14226

DEATON, BEVERLY JEAN, nursing administrator, educator; b. Plainview, Ill., Oct. 15, 1942; d. Charles Byron Kirby and Wilma Irene Crocker Kirby Novy; m. John H. Deaton, May 18, 1963; children: Mary Kathryn Deaton Lovejoy, Amy Christine Deaton Williams. Diploma, St John's Hosp. Sch. Nursing, Springfield, Ill., 1963; BSN, So. Ill. U., Edwardsville, 1986, MSN, 1994. RN, Ill.; cert. inpatient obstet. nursing, ACLS instr. Maternity staff nurse St. Francis Hosp., Litchfield, Ill., 1971-76, maternity supr., 1976-81, dir. maternity, 1981—; childbirth educator, 1975—; presenter at cmty. and profl. orgn. confs. Named Nurse of Yr., March of Dimes, Chgo., 1994. Fellow Am. Coll. Cert. Childbirth Educators; mem. AWHONN (vice chair Ill. sect. dist. VI 1995-96), Sigma Theta Tau. Christian. Home: PO Box 374 Litchfield IL 62056-0374 Office: St Francis Hosp PO Box 1215 Litchfield IL 62056-0999

DEATRICK, MICHELLE MARIE, technical writer, editor; b. Waukesha, Wis., Nov. 13, 1961; d. Don Eugene and Gail Marie (Anderson) D.; m. Steven Allan Przybylski; 1 child, Elizabeth Maria Przybylski. BA, Wesleyan U., 1983; EdM, Harvard U., 1987; postgrad., Stanford U., 1987-91. Civil svc. exam. writer City of San Francisco, 1986; instr. Haverhill (Mass.) C.C., 1986-87; rschr. Stanford (Calif.) U., 1987-91; cons. tech. writer, editor San Jose, 1991—. Co-author: New DRAM Technologies, 1995, 2d edit., 1996; contbg. author: Let's Go: California, 1988; contbr. poetry to mags. Vol. Peace Corps, Kenya, 1983-85; Sunday sch. tchr. Comty. Congl. Ch., Sunnyvale, Calif., 1995-96; Sunday sch. coord. Sunnyvale Presbyn. Ch., 1992-93; dir., founder Grad. Student Counseling Svc., Harvard U., 1986-87; class sec. Wesleyan U., Middletown, Conn., 1987—. Calif. state grad. fellow, 1987, PhD fellow Stanford U., 1987-90. Home: 3281 Lynn Oaks Dr San Jose CA 95117

DEATS, PATTIE RACHELLE DERVAES, girl scouts executive; b. Tampa, Fla., Mar. 2, 1952; d. Arthur Stephen and Pattie Page (Taylor) Dervaes; m. Mark Alan Deats, June 2, 1975; children: Sara, Elizabeth, Marshall Glenn. BA in Edn., U. Fla., 1976. Processor bank cards Branch Bank & Trust Co, Raleigh, N.C., 1980-83; elem. classroom tchr. Franklin County Pub. Schs., Louisburg, N.C., 1986-93; dir. adult devel. Pines of Carolina Girl Scout Coun., Raleigh, N.C., 1993-96; bd. dirs. Youngville (N.C.) Sch. PTO, 1990-96, Franklinton Sch. Parents, Tchrs.,Students Assn., 1995-96. Mem. AAUW, ASTD, Girl Scouts of the U.S. (cert. instr. of trainees and many other coms. and offices). Home: 129 Delterra Dr Youngsville NC 27596 Office: Pines of Carolina Girl Scout Coun Inc PO Box 52294 Raleigh NC 27612

DEBAETS, DONNA LEE, park ranger; b. Detroit, Sept. 11, 1950; d. Charles Morris and Adele Teresa (Cooke) DeB.; m. Theodore Joseph Laliberte (div. 1976). BA, Mich. State U., 1972; MAT, Oakland U., 1979. Tchr. Warren Consol. Sch., Warren, Mich., 1972-79; park ranger Sonoma County Regl. Parks, Santa Rosa, Calif., 1983-96. Mem. Park Rangers of Calif., Gualala Arts Photo Club (pres. 1993), Anchor Bay Amatuer Radio Club. Democrat. Home: PO Box 1424 Gualala CA 95445 Office: Sonoma County Reg Parks Ste A120 2300 County Center Dr Gualala CA 95445

DEBAKEY, LOIS, science communications educator, writer, editor; b. Lake Charles, La.; d. S. M. and Raheeja (Zorba) DeBakey. BA in Math., Tulane U., MA in Lit. and Linguistics, 1959, PhD in Lit. and Linguistics, 1963. Asst. prof. English Tulane U., 1963-64; asst. prof. sci. communication Tulane U. Med. Sch., 1963-65, assoc. prof. sci. communication, 1965-67, prof. sci. comm., 1967-68, lectr., 1968-80, adj. prof., 1981-92; prof. sci. comm. Baylor Coll. Medicine, Houston, 1968—; mem. biomed. libr. rev. com. Nat. Libr. Medicine, Bethesda, Md., 1973-77, bd. regents, 1981-86, cons., 1986—, co-chmn. permanent paper task force, 1987—, lit. selection tech. rev. com., 1988-93, chmn., 1992-93, outreach planning panel, 1988-89; dir. courses in med. comm. ACS and other orgns.; bd. trustees DeBakey Med. Found.; exec. coun. Commn. on Colls. So. Assn. Colls. and Schs., 1975-80; mem. nat. adv. coun. U. Soc. Calif. Ctr. Continuing Med. Edn., 1981, steering com. Plain English Forum, 1984, founding bd. dirs. Friends Nat. Libr. Medicine, 1985—, chmn. med. media award of excellence com. FNLM, 1992—, adv. com. Soc. for Preservation English Lang. Literature, 1986, Nat. Adv. Bd. John Muir Med. Film Festival, 1990-92, The Internat. Health and Med. Film Festival, Acad. of Judges, 1992-93; mem. adv. coun. U. Tex. at Austin Sch. Nursing Found., 1993—; cons. legal writing com. cons. ABA, 1983—; former cons. Nat. Assn. Std. Med. Vocabulary; pioneered instruction in sci. communication in meds. schs. Sr. author: The Scientific Journal: Editorial Policies and Practices, 1976; co-author: Medicine: Preserving the Passion, 1987; mem editorial bd.: Tulane Studies in English, 1966-68, Cardiovascular Research Center Bull., 1971-83, Health Communications and Informatics, 1975-80, Forum on Medicine, 1977-80, Grants Mag, 1978-81, Internat. Jour. Cardiology, 1981-86, Excerpta Medica's Core Jours. in Cardiology, 1981—, Health Comm. and Biopsychosocial Health, 1981-82, Internat. Angiology, 1985—, Jour. AMA, 1988—; mem. usage panel: Am. Heritage Dictionary, 1980—; cons. Webster's Medical Desk Dictionary, 1986; contbd. articles on biomed. communication and sci. writing, literacy, also other subjects to profl. jours., books, encys., and pub. press. Active Found. for Advanced Edn. in Sci., 1977—; trustee DeBakey Med. Found., 1995—. Recipient Disting. Svc. award Am. Med. Writers Assn., 1970, Bausch & Lomb Sci. award, 1st John P. McGovern award Med. Libr. Assn., 1983, Outstanding Alumna award Newcomb Coll., 1994; fellow Am. Coll. Med. Informatics, 1990, Royal Soc. for Encouragement of Arts Mfrs. and Commerce, 1991. Fellow Am. Coll. Med. Informatics; mem. Internat. Soc. Gen. Semantics, Med. Libr. Assn. (hon.), Coun. Biology Editors (dir. 1973-77, chmn. com. on editl. policy 1971-75), Coun. Basic Edn. (spl. com. writing 1977-79), Assn. Tchrs. Tech. Writing, Dictionary Soc. N.Am., Nat. Assn. Sci. Writers, Soc. for Health and Human Values, Com. of Thousand for Better Health Regulations, Golden Key, Phi Beta Kappa. Office: Baylor Coll Medicine One Baylor Plz Houston TX 77030-3498

DEBAKEY, SELMA, science communications educator, writer, editor, lecturer; b. Lake Charles, La.. BA, Newcomb Coll., Tulane U., New Orleans, postgrad. Dir. dept. med. communication Ochsner Clinic and Alton Ochsner Med. Found., New Orleans, 1942-68; prof. sci. communication Baylor Coll. Medicine, Houston, 1968—; editor Cardiovascular Research Ctr. Bull., 1970-84; mem. panel judges Internat. Health and Med. Film Festival, 1992. Author: (with A. Segaloff and K. Meyer) Current Concepts in Breast Cancer, 1967; past editor Ochsner Clinic Reports, Selected Writings from the Ochsner Clinic; contbr. numerous articles to sci. jours., chpts. to books. Mem. AAAS, Soc. Tech. Communication, Assn. Tchrs. Tech. Writing, Am. Med. Writers Assn. (past bd. dirs.; publ., nominating, fellowship, constn., bylaws, awards, and edn. coms.), Council Biol. Editors (past mem. trn. in sci. writing com.), Soc. Health and Human Values, Modern Med. Monograph Awards Com., Nat. Assn. Standard Med. Vocabulary (former cons.). Office: Baylor Coll Medicine 1 Baylor Plz Houston TX 77030-3498

DE BARBIERI, MARY ANN, nonprofit management consultant; b. Winston-Salem, N.C., May 1, 1945; d. Robert Carroll and Annie Louise (Neal) Hutcherson; m. Alfredo Emanuelle De B.; children: Maria Luisa, Riccardo Roberto. BA in Theatre Arts, Mary Washington Coll., 1967; student, Herbert Berghof Studio, 1967-69. With J. Walter Thompson, N.Y.C., 1967-68; asst. to producer Norman Twain Prodns., N.Y.C., 1968-69, Contemporary Theatre Co., N.Y.C., 1971-74; co. mgr. Folger Theatre Group, Washington, 1974-77, bus. mgr., 1977-80; mng. dir. Shakespeare Theatre at the Folger, Washington, 1980-90; performing arts cons. Alexandria, Va., 1990-92; dir. The Found. Ctr., Washington, 1992-94; pres. De Barbieri and Assocs., 1994—; adj. prof. arts mgmt. grad. program Am. U., 1994—; treas. League of Washington Theatres, 1983-86. Bd. dirs. Washington Area Lawyers for Arts, 1984-94, Cultural Alliance Greater Washington, 1986—, Nat. Soc. Fundraising Execs., 1993-96, v.p. edn., 1995, treas., 1996; chair Performing Arts Coun., Alexandria, Va., 1981-84; chair Alexandria Commn. for Arts, 1984-88, theatre commr., 1984-94; contbr. to study of downtown stages for new theatre in Washington, 1985; v.p., bd. dirs. Cultural Alliance Greater Washginton, 1990—; mem. panel Va. Commn. for the Arts, 1990—. Recipient Outstanding Svc. to Theatre Community award League of Washington Theatres, 1990. Home and Office: 3812 Ft Worth Ave Alexandria VA 22304-1709

DEBIAGI, ANNA LILLIAN, retired educator; b. N.Y.C., July 21, 1930; d. Giovanni-Battista and Michelina (Caramanna) Pollara; m. Giovanni DeBiagi, Nov. 19, 1955; children: Gianni Deo, Maria-Michelina Cologera. BA, CUNY, 1952; MA, Columbia U., 1957; postgrad., L.I. U., 1977. Tchr. Massapequa (N.Y.) Pub. Schs., 1953-87. Exhibited in Massapequa Pub. Libr.; group shows in Huntington, Babylon. Tchr. Ch. St. John the Bapt., Bronx, 1952-54, supt. 1954-56; instr. CPR, Am. Heart Assn., 1976-78; tchr. rep. PTA. Mem. AAUW (chmn. 1964-65, pres. 1977-79, chmn. 1981—, Commendation award 1982, Eleanor Roosevelt Found. name grant 1990), Am. Italian Hist. Soc., Hist. Soc. Massapequas, Massapequa Fedn. Ret. Tchrs., Art League of L.I., Pequa Art Assn., Wantagh Arts Coun. Home: 662 SW 159th Dr Pembroke Pines FL 33027

DEBLOCK, JENNIFER THERESA, art educator, artist; b. Detroit, June 16, 1956; d. Arthur Arnold Jr. and Veronica Wanda (Popiela) DeB.; m. Gregory Dennis Presley, May 21, 1982 (div. July 1995); children: Alison Mary Presley, Jacob Arthur Presley. Student, Banff Sch. Fine Arts, Alta., Can., 1974, U. No. Colo., 1974-75, U. Mich., 1977; BFA, Western Mich. U., 1978; MFA, U. Md., 1981. Mgr. Brush Gallery, Houston, 1981-82; adj. instr. North Harris Coll., Houston, 1982-84; program coord. art Kingwood (Tex.) Coll., 1984-94, divsn. chair, 1988-89, program coord. graphic design, 1992-93; assoc. prof. art U. Evansville, Ind., 1994—; tchg. asst. U. Md., College Park, 1979-81; adminstr. art after sch. program Kingwood Coll., 1984-86; owner DeBlock Design, Evansville, 1996—; counselor European trips Cultural Heritage Alliance, Phila., 1992—; represented by West End Gallery, Houston, 1993—, Artswatch, Louisville, 1977—; presenter in field. One-woman shows at Fine Arts of Houston, 1982, 83, Ten Brooks Gallery, N.Y.C., 1986, Learning Resource Ctr. Gallery, Kingwood Coll., 1992, The Houstonian, 1993, Artswatch, 1997; exhibited in group shows at Steers Gallery, Kalamazoo, Mich., 1978, Western Mich. U., Kalamazoo, 1978, Glen Oaks Country Club Auction, Birmingham, Mich., 1978, Fransic Scott Key Bldg., College Park, Md., 1980, U. Md. Gallery, 1981, Glassel Sch. Art, Houston, 1982, Ctr. for Art and Performance, Houston, 1982, Fine Arts of Houston Gallery, 1983, Chocolate Bayou Theater, Houston, 1983, McKowey Gallery, Houston, 1983, Cmty. Art Ctr, West Bend, Wis., 1985, Washington Ave. Gallery, N.Y.C., 1985, Diverse Works, Houston, 1988, Lawndale Annex, U. Houston, 1987, 88, 89, Rosenburg Gallery, Galveston, Tex., 1989, Archway Gallery, Houston, 1989, 90, North Harris Coll. Gallery, Houston, 1984, 85, 86, 89, 90, 91, 92, 93, Two Houston Ctr., 1987, 90, 91, 92, Sam Houston State U. Gallery, 1990, Baytown (Tex.) Civic Ctr., 1990, Transco Towers, Houston, 1991, Toni Jones Gallery, Houston, 1991, Brazosport (Tex.) Coll. Gallery, 1992, Art League Gallery, Houston, 1992, Shepherd Plz., Houston, 1993, Firehouse Gallery, Houston, 1993, West End Gallery, Houston, 1994, Dishman Gallery, Lamar U., Beaumont, Tex., 1994, 96, Krannert Gallery Art, U. Evansville, 1994, 95, San Francisco Women Artists Gallery, 1994, 96, Evansville Mus. Arts and Scis., 1994, 95, Thorns Gallery Art, Ft. Hays State U., Hays, Kans., 1995, L.A. Conv. Ctr., 1995, Indpls. Marriott, 1995, Sawtooth Bldg. Galleries, 1995, S.W. Ind. Artists Collaborative, 1995, others. U. Md. scholar, 1979-81; recipient Hon. Mention award Tri-State Exhbn., Beaumont, 1986, Galveston Art League, 1988, 89, Top Artist award 4th Ann. East End Show, Lawndale Annex, 1988, 2d Pl. award YMCA Corp. Challenge, 1995, Southwestern Ind. Artists Collaborative, 1995. Mem. Univ. and Coll. Designers Assn., Coll. Art Assn., Founds. of Art and Theory in Edn., Amazing Space, Diverse Works, Founds. of Art and Theory in Edn., Houston Apple Users' Group, Houston Area Women's Ctr., Southwestern Ind. Artists Collaborative, Women's Caucus for Arts, Visual Arts Alliance, Am. Inst. Graphic Arts. Home: 1714 E Mulberry St Evansville IN 47714 Office: U Evansville 1800 Lincoln Ave Evansville IN 47722

DEBOER, ANNABEL, English language educator; b. Toledo, Feb. 7, 1948; d. Stanley Arthur and Shirley Mae (Ackerman) Dolgin; m. Bruce Anthony DeBoer, Aug. 22, 1970; children: Allison Beth DeBoer, Tiffiny Lynn DeBoer. BA, U. Mich., 1970; MA, U. Toledo, 1973, specialist cert., 1976. Summer sch. tchr. Toledo Pub. Schs., 1969-70; tchr. Mt. Clemens (Mich.) Pub. Schs., 1970-71, Bedford Pub. Schs., Temperance, Mich., 1971-96; lang. arts chairperson, Bedford Pub. Schs., 1976-83, 93-96; dir. Young Authors Conf., U. Toledo, 1974-84. Mem. Toledo Jr. League, Kappa Delta Pi. Home: 3841 Indian Rd Toledo OH 43606-2339 Office: Bedford Pub Schs 8405 Jackman Rd Temperance MI 48182-9459

DEBOLD, CYNTHIA ANN, sculptor; b. Lexington, Ky., June 12, 1950; d. Louis Bryan and Consuelo (Lopez) Skaggs; m. William Frank Debold, Nov. 16, 1974 (div. July 1989); children: James Patrick, Casey Louis. AA, Orange Coast Coll., 1971, Art Ctr. Coll. of Design, 1973. instr. in field. Exhibited in numerous nat. juried art shows. Mem. Internat. Sculpture Ctr., Tex. Soc. Sculptors (chmn. Sculptfest 1993, pres. 1993-95), Tex. Sculpture Assn., Tex. Fine Arts Assn., Austin Visual Arts Assn., Austin C. of C. (bus. com. for the arts 1993-95). Studio: 1117 W 5th St # D Austin TX 78703-5301

DEBRITO, DIANA R., lawyer; b. N.Y.C., Nov. 16, 1957. BA cum laude, Yale U., 1979; JD, Georgetown U., 1983. Bar: N.Y. 1984, D.C. 1986. Ptnr., resident Washington, D.C. office Cadwalader, Wickersham & Taft, N.Y.C. Contbr. articles to profl. jours. Mem. ABA (mem. bus. law sect. 1987—), D.C. Bar, Assn. of Bar of City of N.Y. (mem. com. on copyright and lit. property 1986-88). Office: Cadwalader Wickersham & Taft 1333 New Hampshire Ave NW Washington DC 20036*

DE BRUN, SHAUNA DOYLE, investment banker, industrialist; b. Boston, June 3, 1956; d. John Justin and Marie Therese (Carey) Doyle; m. Seamus Christopher de Brun, July 24, 1982; children: Brendan Joseph, Kieran Christopher. Student U. Salzburg, 1974-75; BA, Mt. Holyoke Coll., 1978; postgrad. Harvard U., 1981-82; M in Internat. Fin. Columbia U., 1984. Cert. fin. analyst. Assoc., Salomon Brothers, N.Y.C., 1978; rsch. assoc. Kennedy Sch. Govt., Cambridge, Mass., 1979-80; faculty assoc. Harvard Bus. Sch., 1980-81; fgn. expert Beijing Normal U., Peoples Republic China, 1981-82; assoc. dir. N.Y. Capital Resources, N.Y.C., 1984-85; ptnr. Eppler & Co., Denver, 1985-87, pres., Teaneck, N.J., 1987-88, v.p. fin. Patten Corp., Stamford, Vt., 1988-91; pres. Serfimex USA, Inc., 1991-92; vice-chmn. bd. dirs., pres, CEO Texel S.A. de C.V., 1992—. Columbia U. Internat. fellow, 1982; Sarah Williston scholar Mt. Holyoke Coll., 1975. Mem. Mex. Soc. Security Analysts, Am. C. of C. (pres., dir.), Navy League of the U.S., Phi Beta Kappa. Club: Harvard. Avocations: piano, horseback riding. Office: Texel SA de CV, 346 Lamartine, Mexico City Mexico

DEBS, BARBARA KNOWLES, academic administrator; b. Eastham, Mass., Dec. 24, 1931; d. Stanley F. and Arline (Eugley) Knowles; m. Richard A. Debs, July 19, 1958; children: Elizabeth, Nicholas. BA, Vassar Coll., 1953; PhD, Harvard U., 1967; LLD, N.Y. Law Sch., 1979; LHD, Manhattanville Coll., 1985. Freelance translation editor Ency. of World Art divsn. McGraw-Hill Pub., N.Y.C., 1959-62; from asst. prof. to prof. Manhattanville Coll., Purchase, N.Y., 1968-86, pres., 1975-85; trustee, chmn. collections com. N.Y. Hist. Soc., 1985-87, pres., CEO, 1988-92; cons. non-profit orgns. pvt. practice, Greenwich, Conn., 1992—. Contbr. articles on Renaissance and contemporary art to profl. publs. Mem. N.Y. Council Humanities, 1978-85; mem. Westchester Med. Ctr. Hosp. Implementation Bd., 1978-84; mem. Westchester County Bd. Ethics, 1979-84; trustee N.Y. Law Sch., 1979-89; trustee Geraldine R. Dodge Found., 1985—; bd. dirs. Internat. Found. for Art Rsch., 1985-92; trustee Com. Econ. Devel., 1985-94; mem. Coun. Fgn. Rels., 1983—; mem. Commn. Ind. Colls. and Univs. of N.Y., 1977-79; mem. com. on higher edn., adv. council to Dems. N.Y. State Senate, 1979-85; mem. exec. bd. Bard Ctr. for Decorative Arts, 1995—; mem. adv. bd. Greenwich Hist. Soc., 1995—. AAUW Nat. fellow and Ann Radcliffe fellow, 1958-59; Am. Council Learned Socs. grantee, 1973; Fulbright fellow Scuola Normale, Pisa, Italy, 1953, U. Rome, 1954. Mem. Am. Coun. on Edn. (chmn. commn. acad. affairs 1977-79), Young Audiences (nat. dir. 1977-80), Hundred Club of Westchester (bd. dirs.), Renaissance Soc. of Am., Coll. Art Assn., Phi Beta Kappa. Club: Cosmpolitan, Century Assn.

DEBUS, ELEANOR VIOLA, retired business management company executive; b. Buffalo, May 19, 1920; d. Arthur Adam and Viola Charlotte (Pohl) D.; student Chown Bus. Sch., 1939. Sec., Buffalo Wire Works, 1939-45; home talent producer Empire Producing Co., Kansas City, Mo., sec. Owens Corning Fiberglass, Buffalo; pub. rels. and publicity Niagara Falls Theatre, Ont., Can.; pub. rels. dir. Woman's Internat. Bowling Congress, Columbus, Ohio, 1957-59; publicist, sec. Ice Capades, Hollywood, Calif., 1961-63; sec. to contr. Rexall Drug Co., L.A., 1963-67; bus. mgmt. acct. Samuel Berke & Co., Beverly Hills, Calif., 1967-75; Gadbois Mgmt. Co., Beverly Hills, 1975-76; sec., treas. Sasha Corp., L.A., 1976-92; former bus. mgr. Dean Martin, Debbie Reynolds, Shirley MacLaine. Mem. Am. Film Inst. Republican. Contbr. articles to various mags.

DECARLO, DEENA M., mortgage company executive; b. Greenwich, Conn., Aug. 26, 1967; d. James Vito and Grace Joyce (Chiappetta) DeC. BA, Fordham U., 1989. Closing coord. Lomas Mortgage USA, Stamford, Conn., 1989; closing coord. Fleet Mortgage Svcs., Stamford, 1990, corp. svcs. coord., 1990-91, mgr. ops., tng. mgr., 1991-92; sr. loan processor, asst. sec. Prudential Real Estate Fin. Svcs., Trumbull, Conn., 1992-94; mgr. ops., asst. sec. Prudential Real Estate Fin. Svcs., 5, 1994, Conn. Home Mortgage, Trumbull, 1994—; notary public, Conn., 1989—. Author: Processing Manual, 1992. Sponsor Christian Children's Fund, Va., 1989—. Roman Catholic. Home: 224 Berkeley Rd Fairfield CT 06432

DECARLO, ELISA LYONS, comedian, writer; b. Bronxville, N.Y., Nov. 1, 1956; d. Charles Raymond and Dorothy Jean (Barrett) DeC.; m. Jeffrey Alan Shames, Oct. 27, 1984. Student, Hunter Coll., 1986-87. Author: (novels) The Devil You Say, 1993 (Best 1st novel Sci. Fiction Chronicle 1993, Cab Mag. Spl. Achievement award 1994), Strong Spirits, 1994; contbr. to popular mags.; writer, performer one-woman show I Love Drugs, 1995 (one of 5 Best of the Fringe shows San Francisco Fringe Festival 1995); TV appearances include Saturday Night Live, Break a Leg, Ready, Set, Cook!; theatrical appearances include It's Good Enough For Me, Buddy 'n' Janice, Destructive Surgery; sketch comedy and solo performances at Joseph Papp Pub. Theatre, Caroline's Comedy Club, Surf Reality, Shock of the Funny, Dixon Pl., Catch a Rising Star, others; radio appearances include The Raven, Kelley in the Morning, All Things Considered. Mem. AFTRA, The Dramatists Guild, Tall Mountain Cir. Democrat.

DECESARE, DONNA MARIE, photographer; b. N.Y.C., Jan. 31, 1955; d. Felix Anthony and Catherine (Boyle) DeC. BA in Lit., SUNY, Buffalo, 1976; MPhil in Lit., Essex (Eng.) U., 1978. Assoc. mng. editor Penguin Books, N.Y.C., 1979-82; assoc. art dir. Viking Penguin Pubs., N.Y.C., 1982-84; freelance photographer N.Y.C., 1984—; videojournalist V.N.I.—A N.Y. Times Co., Phila., 1995—; photographer mem. Impact Visuals Photo Agy., N.Y.C., 1986—; ind. cons. to orgns. concerned about youth gangs, U.S. and El Salvador, 1993—. Author, artist: (slideshow, photo exhibit) A Tale of Two Cities: The Rise of L.A. Gangs in El Salvador, 1995 (Photoworks Jury prize 1996); artist contbr.: (photo exhibit) Points of Entry: A Nation of Strangers, 1995; videojournalist: (TV documentary) Killer Virus, 1996 (Emmy award), Transplant, 1996; contbr. photos to newspapers and mags. including N.Y. Times. Organizer, shop steward Dist. 65 UAW/Viking Penguin, 1982-84. Recipient Dorothea Lange prize Ctr. for Documentary Studies, Duke U., 1993, 1st prize Gordon Parks Photo Contest, Ft. Scott C.C., 1995, 3d prize Project Competition, Santa Fe Photographic Workshops, 1995, Photography Artist fellowship N.Y. Found. for the Arts, 1996; Yeats Poetry Workshop resident St. Patrick's Scholarship Fund, Buffalo N.Y., 1976. Mem. Assn. Am. Picture Profls. Democrat. Home: # 22 128 Thompson St New York NY 10012

DE CHAMPLAIN, VERA CHOPAK, artist, painter; b. Kulmbach, Germany, Jan. 26, 1928; Am. citizen; d. Nathaniel and Selma (Stiefel) Florsheim; m. Albert Chopak de Champlain, 1948. Student, Art Students League, N.Y.C., 1950-60; spl. studies with Edwin Dickinson, 1962-64. Art dir., tchr. Emanuel Ctr., N.Y.C., 1967—. One person show Consulate Fed. Republic of Germany, N.Y.C., 1986, Fusco Gallery, N.Y.C., 1969-70, B. Altman Gallery, N.Y.C., 1982; exhibited group shows including Munich, Fed. Republic of Germany, 1966, Rudolph Gallery, Woodstock, N.Y., 1967, Artists Equity Gallery, N.Y.C., 1970-77, Lever House, N.Y.C., 1974, 80, 85, 88; Avery Fisher Hall-Cork Gallery, N.Y.C., 1970, 82, 83, 84, 87, 89, Fontainebleau Gallery, N.Y.C., 1972, 73, 74, NYU, 1978, Met. Mus., 1979, Muriel Karasik Gallery, Westhampton Beach, N.Y., 1980, Lever House, N.Y.C., 1990, Broome St. Gallery, N.Y.C., 1991, 92, 93, 94, 95, Avery Fisher Hall-Cork Gallery, N.Y.C., 1994, Cornell U. Med. Libr., 1995; represented in permanent collections Butler Inst. Am. Art, Youngstown, Ohio, Ga. Mus. Art, Athens, Slater Mus., Norwich, Conn., Webster Coll., St. Louis, Evansville Mus. Arts and Sci. (Ind.), Smithsonian Instn., Archives Am. Art, Washington, Jacob Javits Fed. Bldg., N.Y., Permanent Mission of The Netherlands to UN; traveling exhbn. in U.S, 1988-89. Recipient award in portrait painting, Hainesfalls, N.Y., 1965, First Prize-World award, Acad. Italia, Parma, 1985, 87; subject of TV interview, 1984; presented to Queen Elizabeth of England, 1991. Fellow Royal Soc. Arts (London); mem. Artists Equity Assn. N.Y., Arts Students League (life), Nat. Soc. Arts and Letters (art chmn. 1969—), Kappa Pi (life). Clubs: Woman Pays, Liederkranz City of N.Y. (trustee 1979—). Home: 230 Riverside Dr New York NY 10025-6172

DECHARY, JENET LYNN, broadcaster, freelance writer, researcher; b. Plaquemine, La., Feb. 14, 1946; d. Paul Luke and Mary Poynter (Schwing) D.; divorced; 1 child, Paul Joseph. BA, U. Southwestern La., 1968. Script asst. Sta. WRC-TV, Washington, 1969-71, mem. on-air promotion staff, 1971-72, license coord., 1972-74, reports analyst, 1980-86, analyst, standards coord., 1986-88, adminstr. reports and broadcast standards, 1988-91, broadcast standards mgr., 1991—; mem. comml. standards staff Stas. WRC-TV, WKYS-FM, WRC-AM, Washington, 1974-80. Author: (play) Souvenirs, 1984; author essays and feature articles. Vol. The Women's Ctr. Mem. The Writer's Ctr., Washington Ind. Writers.

DECINA, LISA ANN, elementary education educator; b. Bronx, N.Y., June 10, 1971; d. Donato John and Grace Helena (Jaicks) D. BA, U. Albany, 1993; MS in Tchg., Fordham U., 1994. Cert. tchr., N.Y. Tchr. Holy Cross Sch., Bronx, N.Y., 1993-94, Queens (N.Y.) Bd. Edn., 1994-95, Yonkers (N.Y.) Pub. Schs., 1995, Elmsford (N.Y.) Pub. Schs., 1995—. Named Westchester County Vol. of Yr., 1989; scholar Fordham U., 1993-94. Mem. Kappa Delta Pi. Roman Catholic. Home: 18 Lookout Pl Ardsley NY 10502

DECK, JUDITH THERESE, elementary school educator; b. Chgo., Feb. 1, 1947; d. Jerry S. and Rose Christine (Bartik) Pojeta; H.H. Skipp Gergory (dec.); children: Kurt, Kevin, Kristina; m. Donald Paul Deck (div.); 1 child, Jennifer. BS in Elem. Edn., Ind. U., Ft. Wayne, 1988, MS in Elem. Edn., 1992, postgrad., 1994—. Cert. mid. sch. tchr. math., lang. arts, social studies, Ind. 6th grade tchr. Smith Green Cmty. Shcs., Churubusco, Ind., 1988—, mem. strategic planning com., tech. plan grant com., staff devel. com., home tutor, 1996—. Grantee Ind. and Mich. Power, 1993-94. Mem. Internat. Reading Assn., Sch. Improvement Planning Coun. (curriculum writing/textbook adoption com., student handbook com. 1988-94), Classroom Tchrs. Assn. (co-pres. 1993-94), Kappa Delta Pi. Roman Catholic. Office: Smith Green Cmty Schs 1 Eagle Dr Churubusco IN 46723-1414

DECKER, CAROL ARNE, magazine publishing consultant; b. Rochelle, Ill., Apr. 3, 1946; d. Irvin Norman Arne and Edna (Olsen) Stein; m. Charles Levitt Decker, Feb. 17, 1979; children: Katharine Elizabeth. BS, So. Ill. U., 1969. Advt. sales rep. Travel Agent mag., N.Y.C., 1971-74, Business Week mag., N.Y.C., 1974-80, Reader's Digest Publs., N.Y.C., 1980-82; assoc. pub. The Atlantic Monthly, N.Y.C., 1982-84; pub. Personal Investor, N.Y.C., 1984-86, Lear's Mag., 1992-93; pub. cons. C.A. Decker & Assocs., N.Y.C., 1986-94. Home and Office: 236 Nyac Ave Pelham NY 10803-1908

DECKER, FLORENCE W., language educator, consultant; b. Waltham, Mass., July 16, 1938; d. Stanley Page and Jeanie Creighton (Lees) Whitcomb; m. John Malcolm Stubbert, Apr. 1959 (div. July 1969); children: Mary, Birgitte, Deborah, Linda; m. John Allen Decker, July 11, 1969. BA in Elem. Edn., Glassboro State U., 1975; MEd, U. Tex., 1982. Tchr. elem. edn. Terrace Hills Sch., El Paso, Tex., 1975-79; tchr. reading Guillen Intermediate Sch., El Paso, Tex., 1979-82; tchr. ESOL Bowie H.S., El Paso, Tex., 1982-86, Spence Mid. Sch., Dallas, 1986-87; tchr. ESOL, dept. chair Wiggs Mid. Sch., El Paso, 1987-89, Bassett Mid. Sch., El Paso, 1989-93; program asst. El Paso Ind. Sch. Dist., 1993; tchr. U. Autonoma, Juarez, Mexico, 1985—; owner Decker Cons., El Paso, 1993—; cons. SEDL, Austin, Tex., 1994, Silver City (N.Mex.) City Sch. Dist., 1991-93, Socorro Ind. Sch. Dist., El Paso, 1990-94. Life mem. El Paso PTA, 1982—. Mem. TESOL (assoc. chair, chair 1986-88), Tex. TESOL (pres. 1989-92), Nat. & Local TAWL, ASCD, Nat., State & Local IRA, Nat. State & Local NCTE.

DECKER, JOSEPHINE I., clinic administrator; b. Barling, Ark., May 24, 1933; d. Ralph and Ada A. (Claborn) Snider; BS in Health Mgmt., Kennedy Western U., 1986, MS in Bus. Adminstrn., 1987; m. William Arlen Decker, Feb. 4, 1952; 1 son, Peter A. With Southwestern Bell Telephone Co., Ft. Smith, Ark., 1951-52; with Holt Krock Clinic, Ft. Smith, 1952—, bus. adminstr., 1970—. Bd. dirs. Sparks Credit Union, Adv. Council Northside and Southside high schs., Ft. Smith, Ft. Smith Girls Shelter, Ft. Smith Credit Bur. Mem. Credit Women Internat., Soc. Cert. Consumer Credit Execs. Office: Holt Krock Clinic 1500 Dodson Ave Fort Smith AR 72901-5128

DECKER, JUDITH ELAINE, land development company executive; b. Derry, N.H., Nov. 2, 1940; d. Clayton Kent and Ariel Almina (Palmer) Gillis; m. Marshall Norman Decker, Nov. 2, 1965 (div. 1994); children: Timothy, Jennifer, Amy, James, Wesley. Diploma, McIntosh Bus. Sch., 1958-59; BS magna cum laude, Franklin Pierce Coll., 1986. Treas. N.H. Electric, Inc., Salem, 1974-77; treas. J.E.D. Assocs., Inc., Danville, N.H., 1978-86, pres., chief exec. officer, 1986—; bd. dirs. J.E.D. Assocs., Inc., Danville, MarDec, Inc., Salem, Shalles Corp., Salem. Chmn. Thompson for Gov., Salem, 1970, Heart Fund, Salem, 1969, 70, 71; troop leader Girl Scouts of Am., Salem, 1969-72. Mem. Nat. Assn. Female Execs., Greater Haverhill C. of C., Nat. Assn. Self Employed. Republican. Home: 37 Chandler Dr Atkinson NH 03811-2100 Office: J E D Assocs Inc PO Box 690 East Hampstead NH 03826

DECKER, SHARYN LYNN, newspaper reporter; b. Santa Rosa, Calif., Nov. 6, 1960; d. Richard Lee and Vicki Catherine (Whearty) D. AA with honors, Shoreline C.C., Seattle, 1989; BA in Bus. Administrn. and Comm. magna cum laude, U. Wash., 1994. Groundskeeper Evergreen Washelli, Seattle, 1980-96; reporter news svcs. U. Wash., Seattle, 1994; reporter intern The Herald, Everett, Wash., 1995-96, freelance reporter, 1994-96; bus. reporter Valley Daily News, Kent, Wash., 1996. Mem. Nat. Soc. Profl. Journalists (sec. Western Wash. profl. chpt. 1995—, honorable mention Pacific Northwest Excellence Journalism comp. 1995), U. Wash. Comm. Alumni Assn., Golden Key Nat. Honor Soc., Beta Gamma Sigma, Phi Beta Kappa.

DECKERT, MYRNA JEAN, executive director; b. McPherson, Kans., Nov. 4, 1936; d. Francis J. and Grace (Killion) George; m. Ray A. Deckert, Sept. 29, 1957; children: Rachelle, Kimberly, Charles, Michael. AA, Coll. of Sequoias, 1956; BBA, U. Beverly Hills, 1983, MBA, 1984. Youth dir. Asbury Meth. Ch , El Paso, Tex., 1960-63; teen program dir. YWCA, El Paso, 1963-69, assoc. exec. dir., 1969-70, exec. dir., 1970—; chair strategic planning com. Tex. Dept. Pub. and Regulatory Svcs., 1994—. Exec. forum, pres., 1991-92; bd. dirs. Tex. Commerce Bank, El Paso; chmn. Tex. State Title XX DayCare Providers, 1987-89; commr. Housing Authority City of El Paso, 1989-92; chair bd. trustees Columbia Med. Ctr. East, Tex. Tech. Med. Found. Bd.; trustee Dues/High Tower Found.; chair Leadership EP, 1994-95; trustee Unite El Paso. Recipient Hannah Soloman Cmty. Svc. award Nat. Coun. Jewish Women, Sertoma Club award Svc. to Mankind, 1974, Cmty. Svc. award League United L.Am. Citizens, 1980, Humanitarian award, 1994, Vol. Svc. award Vol. Bur., 1984, Merit award Adalante Mujer, 1986, Social Svc. award KVIA/Sunturians, 1986, Excellence award Nat. Assn. YWCA Execs., 1990, Racial Justice award YWCA of the U.S.A., 1991; named Woman of Yr., AAUW, 1975, Dir. of Yr., United Way El Paso County, 1985, First Lady of El Paso, Beta Sigma Phi, 1991, One of 10 Most Influential Women, El Paso Times, 1995, Citizen of Yr., Mil. Order of World Wars, 1996; inducted into El Paso Women's Hall of Fame, 1990, El Paso Hist. Soc. Hall of Honor, 1995. Mem. Coun. of Agy. Execs., Rotary (Club of El Paso, v.p. 1990-93). Methodist. Home: 4276 Canterbury Dr El Paso TX 79902-1352

DECKOFF, JANE VANDERPLOEG, music management company executive; b. Little Rock, June 2, 1937; d. Jan Bert and Margaret Ann (Raak) Venderploeg; m. Marvin Joseph Deckoff, June 7, 1964; children: John, Anthony, Hilary. BS, Mannes Coll. Music, 1976. Registrar, ext. divsn. The Mannes Coll. Music, N.Y.C., 1976-78; prodn. mgr. Tribune Printing Co., N.Y.C., 1979-91; pres. Jane Music Mgmt., Inc., N.Y.C., 1991—; trustee Bennington (Vt.) Coll., 1988—; dir. Chamber Music Conf., Bennington, 1987—. Bd. dirs., sec., treas. pres. Com. for Creative Playground, N.Y.C., 1967-72; sec. Yorkville Dem. Club, N.Y.C., 1959-64. Mem. Nat. Assn. Performing Arts Mgrs. and Agts., Am. Symphony Orch. League, Chamber Music Am., Assn. Performing Arts Presenters, Western Alliance Arts Adminstrs., Bennington Coll. Alumni Assn. N.Y. (pres. 1990—). Home and Office: 1060 Park Ave New York NY 10128

DECOMO, LUCY SANCHEZ, mathematics educator; b. Cleve., Dec. 12, 1935; d. Fortunato and Luisa (Branca) Sanchez; m. Michael J. DeComo Jr., Aug. 16, 1958; children: Theresa Mikus, Michael J. IV, Dina Preston. BS in Edn., Kent State U., 1958, MA in Maths., 1968. Tchr. math. West Tech. High Sch., Cleve., 1958-60, Green High Sch., Greensburg, Ohio, 1961-64; tchr. math, dept. chair Lincoln High Sch., Canton, Ohio, 1966-76; tchr. math., dept. chair Timken Sr. High Sch., Canton, Ohio, 1976-83, Perry Sr. High Sch., Massillon, Ohio, 1983-93; adj. instr. Walsh U., Canton, 1993—; adj. instr. Malone Coll., Canton, 1986—. Martha Jennings Found. scholar, 1991-92. Mem. Nat. Coun. Tchrs. Math., Ohio Coun. Tchrs. Math., Delta Kappa Gamma, Phi Delta Kappa (Tchr. of Yr. award 1993). Home: 725 Mohawk Ave NW Canton OH 44708-3449

DECONCINI, BARBARA, association executive, religious studies educator; b. Phila., Feb. 15, 1944; d. Edwin Francis and Anne Marie (Farrell) DeC.; m. Walter James Lowe, June 30, 1979. AB in English, Rosemont Coll., 1968; MA in English, Bryn Mawr Coll., 1973; PhD in Humanities, Emory U., 1980. Assoc. dean Rosemont (Pa.) Coll., 1971-74; from lectr. to prof. Atlanta Coll. of Art, 1975-91, interim pres., 1985, acad. dean, 1986-91; prof. religion and culture Emory U., Atlanta, 1991—; exec. dir., treas. Am. Acad. Religion, Atlanta, 1991—; coord. long-range instnl. and ednl. planning Soc. of the Holy Child, 1973-75; treas. Southeastern Commn. for Study of Religion, 1989-91; chair various acad. sessions in field. Author: Narrative Remembering, 1990; contbr. numerous articles to profl. publs. Bd. dirs. Art Papers, Atlanta, 1988-91, Rosemont Coll., 1992—; trustee Scholars Press, Atlanta, 1991—, chmn. bd. trustees, 1994—; bd. dirs. Ga. Artists Internat. Exhibit Fund, 1988-92. Alliance of Ind. Colls. of Art grantee. Mem. Am. Coun. Learned Socs. (mem. exec. com. coun. adminstrv. officers 1995—, bd. dirs. 1996—), Am. Acad. Religion, ACLS (bd. dirs. 1996), (bd. dirs. 1989—, cons. for reorgn. arts, lit. and religion sect. 1990, mem. program com. 1986-89, pres. S.E. sect. 1984-85, program chair 1983-84, 84-85, exec. com. 1980-83), So. Assn. Colls. and Schs. (accreditation evaluator), Mid. States Assn. Colls. and Schs. (accreditation evaluator), Phi Beta Kappa, Omicron Delta Kappa. Office: Am Acad Religion Ste G5 1703 Clifton Rd NE Atlanta GA 30329-4075

DECOTIS, DEBORAH ANNE, investment company executive; b. Salem, Mass., Nov. 13, 1952; d. John and Marie (Mahoney) DeC.; m. Nicholas B. Zoullas, Aug. 15, 1987. BA, Smith Coll., 1974; MBA, Stanford U., 1978. Analyst, Morgan Stanley & Co., Inc., N.Y.C., 1974-76, assoc., 1978-81, v.p., London, 1982-84, prin., N.Y.C., 1985-87, mng. dir., 1988-95, adv. dir., 1996—; mem. exec. com. spl. projects com. Meml. Sloan Kettering Cancer Ctr. Trustee Morgan Stanley Found., Stanford Bus. Sch. Trust, Wharton Fin. Instns. Ctr. Miller scholar Stanford U., 1978. Home: 211 Central Park W New York NY 10024-6020 Office: Morgan Stanley & Co Inc 1251 Avenue Of The Americas New York NY 10020-1104

DECROSTA, SUSAN ELYSE, graphic designer; b. Cambridge, Mass., Aug. 28, 1956; d. Joseph Mario and Gertrude Ermelinda (Galligani) DeC. BFA, Mass. Coll. Art, 1980. certified art tchr., supr. Graphic artist Nixdorf Computer Corp., Burlington, Mass., 1981-86; lead artist, illustrator Raytheon Co., Andover, Mass., 1986-94; graphic designer Raytheon Co., Burlington, Mass., 1994—; lead artist, illustrator Rivers, Trainor, Doyle, Providence, 1987; freelance graphic artist, 1980—; guest speaker to design and illustration students Northeastern U., 1992. Vol. AIDS Action Com., Boston. Recipient Excellence award Soc. Tech. Communications & Art Direction, 1986. Mem. Arlington Ctr. Arts, Mass. Art Alumni Assn., The Boston Computer Soc. Office: Raytheon Svc Co 2 Wayside Rd Burlington MA 01803

DECROW, KAREN, lawyer, author, lecturer; b. Chgo., Dec. 18, 1937; d. Samuel Meyer and Juliette (Abt) Lipschultz; m. Alexander Allen Kolben, 1960 (div. 1965); m. Roger DeCrow, 1965 (div. 1972, dec. 1989). BS, Northwestern U., 1959; JD, Syracuse U., 1972; DHL (hon.), SUNY, Oswego, 1994. Bar: N.Y., U.S. Dist. Ct. (no. dist.) N.Y. Resorts editor Golf Digest mag., Evanston, Ill., 1959-60; editor Am. Soc. Planning Ofcls., Chgo., 1960-61; writer Ctr. for Study Liberal Edn. for Adults., Chgo., 1961-64; editor Holt, Rinehart, Winston, Inc., N.Y.C., 1965; textbook editor L.W. Singer, Syracuse, N.Y., 1965-66; writer Ea. Regional Inst. for Edn., Syracuse, 1967-69, Pub. Broadcasting System, 1977; tchr. women and law, 1972-74; nat. bd. mem. NOW, 1968-77, nat. pres., 1974-77, also nat. politics task force chair; cons. affirmative action; pvt. practice, Jamesville, N.Y.; lectr. topics including law, gender, internat. feminism to corps., polit. groups, colls. and univs., U.S., Can., Mex., Finland, China, Greece, former USSR; nat. coord. Women's Strike for Equality, 1970; N.Y. State del. Internat. Women's Yr., 1977; originator Schs. for Candidates; participant DeCrow-Schlafly ERA Debates, from 1975; founder (with Robert Seidenberg) World Woman Watch, 1988; gender issues advisor Nat. Congress for Men; mem. Task Force on Gender Bias. Author: (with Roger DeCrow) University Adult Education: A Selected Bibliography, 1967, American Council on Education, 1967, The Young Woman's Guide to Liberation, 1971, Sexist Justice, 1974, First Women's State of the Union Message, 1977, (with Robert Seidenberg) Women Who Marry Houses: Panic and Protest in Agoraphobia, 1983, Turkish edit., 1988, 2d Turkish edit., 1989, United States of America vs. Sex: How the Meese Commission Lied About Pornography, 1988, (with Jack Kammer) Good Will Toward Men: Women Talk Candidly About the Balance of Power Between the Sexes, 1994; editor: The Pregnant Teenager

(Howard Osofsky), 1968, Corporate Wives, Corporate Casualties (Robert Seidenberg), 1973; contbr. articles to USA Today, N.Y. Times, L.A. Times, Chgo. Tribune, Nat. Law Jour., Women Boston Globe, Vogue, Mademoiselle, Ingenue, Newsday, Chgo. Sun Times, Penthouse, Washington Post, L.A. Times Mag., Policy Review, Miami Herald, Internat. Herald Tribune, Social Problems, Houston Chronicle, Pitts. Press, Nat. NOW Times, Syracuse U. Mag., San Francisco Chronicle, Civil Rights Quar., Women Lawyers Jour., other newspapers, mags.; columnist: Syracuse New Times; recording: Opening Up Marriage, 1980. Hon. trustee Elizabeth Cady Stanton Found.; active Hon. Com. to Save Alice Paul's Birthplace; Liberal candidate for Mayor of Syracuse, 1969. Recipient Profl. Recognition award for best newspaper column Syracuse Press Club, 1990, Best Column award, 1994-95, Best Column award N.Y. Press Assn., 1991-92, 95. Mem. NOW, Onondaga County Bar Assn.(profl. ethics com.), N.Y. Women's Bar Assn. (ctrl. N.Y. chpt. pres. 1989-90), N.Y. Bar Assn., ACLU (Ralph E. Kharas Disting. Svc. in Civil Liberties award 1985), Elizabeth Cady Stanton Found. (bd. trustees), Working Women's Inst. (bd. advisors), Syracuse Friends Chamber Music, Atlantic States Legal Found., Yale Polit. Union (hon. life), Nat. Congress Men (gender issues advisor), Mariposa Edn. & Rsch. Found., Nat. Coun. Children's Rights (adv. panel), Wilderness Soc., Northwestern U. Alumni Assn., Women's Inst. Freedom Press, Art Inst. Chgo., Nat. Women's Polit. Caucus, Theta Sigma Phi. Address: 7599 Brown Gulf Rd Jamesville NY 13078-9636*

DEDERA, NANCY KOVEL, public relations executive; b. New Britain, Conn., Sept. 26, 1931; d. Walter Henry and Margaret Ellen (Sullivan) Kovel; m. Fredric C. Joy, Sept. 16, 1966 (div. Aug. 1976); m. Donald E. Dedera, Aug. 16, 1981. BS, U. Conn., 1953; postgrad., Case Western Res. U., 1956. Registered dietition, Ariz. Womens editor, food editor Boston Herald Newspaper, 1956-66; food dir. The Houston Club, 1966-78; owner, operator The PanJoy Gourmetware Cooking Sch., Oceanside, Calif., 1978-83; pub. rels. mgr. Armour Food Co., Phoenix, 1983-85; dir. pub. rels. The Dial Corp., Phoenix, 1985—. Contbr. articles to profl. jours. Bd. dirs. Friends of Libr., Phoenix, 1992-93; founder, Friends of Ariz. Hwys., Phoenix, 1983-84. Mem. IABC, Am. Dietetic Assn., Soap & Detergent Assn. (bd. dirs. 1987—), Cosmetology, Toiletries and Fragrance Assn. (bd. dirs. 1991—). Republican. Roman Catholic. Home: 6001 E Le Marche Ave Scottsdale AZ 85254

DE DIOS, ANNE GILLIS MANNING, curator; b. Cleve., Oct. 5, 1969; d. William Dudley and Carol Randolph (Gillis) Manning; m. Gonzalo de Dios, Aug. 17, 1967. Attestato de frequenza, U. per Stranieri, Italy, 1990; cert. of study, Studio Arts Ctr., Italy, 1990; BA, U. Richmond, 1992; cert. in appraising fine decorative arts, George Washington U., 1994. Intern Fondazione Thyssen-Bornemisza, Lugano, Switzerland, 1992; asst. dir. St. Luke's Gallery, Washington, 1993-94; dir. decorative arts C.G. Sloan & Co., Bethesda, Md., 1994; curator, registrar Guarisco Gallery, Washington, 1994—; auction asst. C.G. Sloan & Co., 1994—. Author: (catalogue) Guarisco Gallery Collection, 1995, 96, Edward Cucuel 1875-1951, 1996; editor: (catalogue) Thyssen-Bornemisza Collection, 1993, Khara-Khoto, 1993. Tchr. religious edn. Blessed Sacrament, Alexandria, Va., 1993—. Recipient Borsa di Studio U. per Stranieri, Perugia, Italy, 1990. Mem. Philips Gallery, Washington Performing Arts Soc., Christian Children's Fund. Roman Catholic. Office: Guarisco Gallery, Ltd 2828 Pennsylvania Ave NW Washington DC 20007

DEDO, DOROTHY JUNELL TURNER, real estate company executive, civic worker; b. Norway, Mich., Oct. 17, 1920; d. Raymond and Esther Elvira (Junell) Turner; m. Lewis Joseph Dedo, Dec. 24, 1945; children: Craig Turner, Drew Jonathan. Student, U. So. Calif., 1939-40; AB with honors, U. Mich., 1942; postgrad., U. N.D., 1942, Marquette U., 1942-43. Cert. tchr., Wis. Safety person Kearney & Trecker Corp., Milw., 1942-43; supr. Town of Shelby, La Crosse, Wis., 1973-77, clk., 1977-81, chmn., 1981-85; pres. Turner Lands, Inc., Milw., 1985—; supr. County of LaCrosse, 1990-94. Contbr. numerous articles to La Crosse Tribune. Prodr., dir., actor La Crosse Children's Theater, 1959-65; sales mgr., actor La Crosse Cmty. Theatre, 1965-69; sec. Western Wis. Health Planning Orgn., 1964-68; chmn. Christian edn., mem. coun. English Luth. Ch., 1969-72; nominations chmn. bd. advisors Viterbo Coll., 1971-92; bd. dirs. Luth. Hosp. Found., 1978-90; bd. dirs. Winding Rivers Libr. Sys., 1990-95, v.p., 1994-95; sec. Wis. Towns Assn., 1973-85; v.p. La Crosse Area Devel. Corp., 1981-85; mem. La Crosse Area Planning Com., 1981-85; pres. La Crosse County Rep. Women, 1976-78. Lt. comdr. USNR, 1943-55. Recipient Dionysos award in bus. La Crosse Community Theatre, 1965, Women of Yr. award La Crosse Bus. and Profl. Women, 1982, Tribute to Outstanding Woman award YWCA, La Crosse, 1983. Mem. AAUW (pres. LaCrosse 1974-76, Wis., 1981-83, named grant honoree 1977), AARP, Viterbo Coll. Pres.'s Club, Heritage Club, LaCrosse Country Club, Pearl Investment Club (pres. 1988-91), Earthwatch, Alpha Kappa Delta, Alpha Lambda Delta, Alpha Chi Omega. Home: 5870 W Cedar Rd La Crosse WI 54601

DEE, JOAN MCHUGH, associate dean, educator; b. Newton, Mass., Dec. 10, 1934; d. Joseph Patrick and Esther Mary (Walsh) McHugh; m. Norman Edward Dee, Aug. 17, 1957. BS in Edn., Framingham State Coll., 1956; EdM in Elem. Edn., Boston U., 1959, EdD in Edn. Admisntrn., 1973. Cert. tchr. and adminstrn., Mass. Tchr. Natick (Mass.) Pub. Schs., 1956-61, Concord (Mass.) Pub. Schs., 1961-70; isntr. Lowell (Mass.) State Coll., 1970-71; asst. dean, asst. prof. Boston U., 1973-78, assoc. dean, asst. prof., 1978—; mem. Mass. Com. on Edn. Pers., Mass., 1982-92; reviewer La. Bd. of Regents-Proposals, 1990, Radcliffe Coll. Bunting Inst. Fellowship, 1991-93. Mem. Am. Edn. Rsch. Assn., Mass. Assn. Sch. Supts., Phi Delta Kappa, Pi Lambda Theta. Home: 582 Old Bedford Rd Concord MA 01742-2741 Office: Boston U Sch Edn 605 Commonwealth Ave Boston MA 02215-1605

DEE, PAULINE MARIE, artist; b. Concord, N.H., Jan. 9, 1933; d. Arthur Joseph and Anna Marie (Marquis) Champagne; m. Edmond Francis Dee, July 2, 1955; children: James Francis, Diane Mary. Bus. Cert., Burdett Coll., Lynn, Mass. Membership chmn. Danvers (Mass.) Art Assn., 1986-92, v.p., 1990-92; v.p. Lynnfield (Mass.) Art Guild, 1991-93, pres., 1994-96; v.p. Saltbox Gallery, Topsfield, Mass., 1995—; demonstrator in field; cons. Kohinor Accent Program, Bloomsbury, N.J., 1995—. Exhibited in solo shows at Woman's Club of Boston, 1980, Naval Officers Club, Pearl Harbor, Hawaii, 1994. Cons. Peabody (Mass.) Internat. Festival, 1995; bd. dirs. North Shore Art Assn., Gloucester, Mass., 1996. Recipient achievement awards, 1985-95; Lynnfield Arts Lottery grantee, 1996. Mem. Our Lady Guadalupe Sodality (prefect 1966-68). Roman Catholic. Home: 16 Samoset Rd Peabody MA 01960

DEE, RUBY (RUBY DEE DAVIS), actress, writer, director; b. Cleve.; d. Marshall Edward and Emma (Benson) Wallace; m. Ossie Davis, Dec. 9, 1948; children: Nora, Guy, Hasna. BA, Hunter Coll., 1945; ArtsD (hon.), Fairfield U.; BA (hon. doctorate), Iona Coll., Va. State U.; apprentice, Am. Negro Theatre, 1941-44; LHD (hon.), SUNY, Old Westbury, 1990; DFA, Spelman Coll., 1991. Ind. actress, writer, dir., 1945—. Author: (poetry) Glowchild, 1972, (musical) Take It from the Top, (collected poetry, humor, short stories) My One Good Nerve; adaptor: (African folk tales) Two Ways to Count to Ten, The Tower to Heaven, (play) Books With Legs, 1993; contbr. column N.Y. Amsterdam News; co-writer (film) Uptight; dir., adaptor (stage prodn.) Zora is my Name!, 1983; stage appearances include Jeb, 1946, Raisin in the Sun, 1959, Purlie Victorious, 1961, The Imaginary Invalid, 1971, Wedding Band, 1972 (Drama Desk award 1972), Boesman and Lena, 1970 (Obie award 1971), Anna Lucasta, Taming of the Shrew, Checkmates, 1988, The Glass Menagerie, 1989, Flyin West, 1994, Two Hah-Hahs and a Homeboy, 1995; actress: (films) Gone are the Days, The Jackie Robinson Story, Take a Giant Step, St. Louis Blues, A Raisin in the Sun, Purlie Victorious, To Be Young, Gifted and Black, Buck and the Preacher, Countdown at Kusini, Cat People, 1982, Do the Right Thing, 1989 (NAACP Image award as best actress 1989), Jungle Fever, 1991; numerous TV appearances including It's Good to be Alive, 1974, Today Is Ours, 1974, The Defenders, Police Woman, Peyton Place, (TV films) To Be Young, Gifted and Black, All God's Children, The Nurses, Roots: The Next Generation, I Know Why the Caged Bird Sings, Wedding Band, It's Good to Be Alive, Decoration Day (Emmy award for Supporting Actress in a Miniseries or Special 1991), The Atlanta Child Murders, (TV spl. with Ossie Davis) Martin Luther King: The Dream and the Drum, The Winds of Change, Windmill of the Gods, TV miniseries Stephen King's The Stand, 1994, Tuesday Morning Ride, 1995; co-producer: (TV spl.) Today is Ours, The Ernest Green Story, 1993, (radio show) Ossie Davis and Ruby Dee Story Hour, 1974-78, (TV series) With Ossie and Ruby, 1981, (home videotape) Hands Upon The Heart, 1991, Middle Ages, 1992, Hands Upon The Heart II, 1993; rec. artist poems and stories; host (with Ossie Davis) African Heritage Movie Network. Recipient Martin Luther King Jr. award Operation PUSH, 1972, Drama Desk award, 1974, (with Ossie Davis) Frederick Douglass award N.Y. Urban League, 1970, (with Ossie Davis) NAACP Image award Hall of Fame, Master Innovator For Film award Sony, 1991. Mem. NAACP, CORE, Student Non-Violent Coordinating Com., SCLC. Address: The Artists Agy 10000 Santa Monica Blvd Los Angeles CA 90067-7007

DEE-BURNETT, RITA, management consultant, trainer, lecturer; b. Chgo., Feb. 15, 1941; d. Francis Xavier Dee and Martha Werner; m. Joe R. Burnett, Aug. 9, 1980. BA in Edn., St. Xavier U., Chgo., 1964; MA in Edn., U. Mo., Kansas City, 1971; PhD in Ednl. Adminstrn., Northwestern U., Evanston, Ill., 1980. Master tchr. Ctr. for Urban Edn. Archdiocese of Chgo. Tchr. Edn. and Resource Ctr., 1963-69; coord. human rels./organizational devel. Archdiocese of Chgo. Cath. Sch. Sys., 1970-74; dir. Urban and Ethnic Edn. Sect. Ill. State Bd. Edn., Chgo., 1974-80; assoc. dir. Indsl./Organizational Resources Inst. for Personality and Ability Testing, Inc., Savoy, Ill., 1980-85; program dir. Office of Continuing Edn. and Pub. Svc. U. Ill., Urbana-Champaign, 1987-88; instr. Redlands (Calif.) U., 1990-91; lectr. Calif. State Poly. U., San Luis Obispo, 1991-93, 95—; instr. Calif. Conservation Corps, San Luis Obispo, 1991—; lectr. numerous confs. in field; cons. state and local govts., other orgns. in field. Co-author: (with Norah Lex and P.J. Farrel) Systems Approach for Education: A Planned Change Course for Administrators, 1973, (with Edgar Johns and Samuel Krug) Law Enforcement Assessment and Development Report Manual, 1980, (with Raymond W. Kulhavy and Samuel E. Krug) Individualized Stree Management Program Manual, 1982, (with Mark Michaels) Performance Management: A Training Program in Personnel Selection and Performance Review, 1984, (with others) Interim Manual for the Human Resource Development Report, 1985. Chair Ctrl. Coast Natural History Assn., San Luis Obispo, 1994, 96; docent Calif. State Pks., 1990-96. Recipient citation for Exceptional Svc. Ill. Conf. on Ethnicity in Edn., Chgo., 1980; grantee Ednl. Professions Devel. Act, Coll. of the Nazarenes, Pasadena, Calif., 1965, U. Mo., Kansas City, 1969-70; Edn. Policy fellow George Washington U. Inst. for Ednl. Leadership, Washington, 1977-78, fellow Northwestern U. Coll. Edn., 1978-79. Home: 962 Felicia Way San Luis Obispo CA 93401

DEEDS, VIRGINIA WILLIAMS, volunteer; b. Newark, Ohio, June 28, 1934; d. Theodore Nelson and Nell Elizabeth (Hoover) Williams; m. Charles Lemoin Deeds, Aug. 7, 1955; children: Melinda, Jennifer Giesen, C. Jason, Stephanie. RN, White Cross Sch. Nursing, 1955. RN, Ohio. RN obstet. dept. Berea (Ohio) Cmty. Hosp., 1955-56; RN emergency dept. White Cross Hosp., Columbus, Ohio, 1956; RN med. & obstetrics Union Hosp., Dover, Ohio, 1961-62; vol. RN United Health Found. Sr. Ctr., Dover, Ohio, 1961—, Office Roy Geduldig, Dover, Ohio, 1967-68; co-founder, co-dir. Tuscarawas County Teen Pregnancy Prevention Taskforce, 1985-92. Co-editor The Chart newsletter, 1991—. Bd. dirs. United Health Found., New Philadelphia, YMCA, Dover, Union Hosp. Aux., Chestnut Soc. Kent State U., 1996—, Juvenile Ct. Citizens Review Bd., 1989—; pres. Jr. Clionian, 1996. Recipient Zeisberger award Tusc. County Hist. Soc., 1994.

DEEL, FRANCES QUINN, retired librarian; b. Pottsville, Pa., Mar. 9, 1939; d. Charles Joseph and Carrie Miriam (Ketner) Q.; m. Ronald Eugene Deel, Feb. 5, 1983. B.S., Millersville State Coll., 1960; M.L.S., Rutgers U., 1964; M.P.A., U. West Fla., 1981. Post librarian U.S. Army Armor (Desert Tng. Ctr.), Ft. Irwin, Calif., 1964-66; staff librarian Mil. Dist. of Washington, 1966-67; supervisory librarian 1st Logistical Command, APO San Francisco, 1967-68; tech. process specialist Naval Edn. and Tng. Supervisory Command, Washington, 1968-77, Pensacola, Fla., 1968-77; chief tech. library USAF Armament Lab., Eglin AFB, Fla., 1977-81; dir. command libraries Air Force Systems Command (Andrews AFB), Washington, 1981-92; mem. exec. adv. council Fed. Library and Info. Network, Washington, 1983-86; libr. Air Force Dist. of Washington(Bolling AFB), Washington, 1992-94; dir. Navy Dept. Libr., Washington, 1994; ret., 1994. Mem. ALA (dir.-at-large armed forces libraries sect. Chgo. 1983-86), Spl. Libraries Assn., D.C. Library Assn. Roman Catholic. Home: 9225 Forest Haven Dr Alexandria VA 22309-3216 Office: Navy Dept Libr Bldg 44 Washington Navy Yard Washington DC 20374-5060

DEELY, MAUREEN CECELIA, community health nurse; b. Washington, Feb. 8, 1960; d. Thomas Michael and Felice R. (Alvarez) D. AA, Montgomery Coll., 1984. Staff RN Phi Szabo PG Count/Detention Ctr., Upper Marlboro, Md., 1984-85, Sands Nursing Svcs. Inc., Silver Spring, Md., 1985-86, Windsor HomeCare Inc./Alliance Against AIDS, Washington, 1988-89; community health nurse Montgomery County Health Dept., Silver Spring, 1989—; mem. adv. bd. for cmty. programs for clin. rsch. on AIDS Washington Regional AIDS Program, 1990—; mem. AIDS adv. com. Montgomery Hospice Soc., 1993; panelist, field reviewer to develop treatment improvement protocol Ctr. Substance Abuse Treatment, 1993; mem. cmty. adv. bd. Nat. Women's Interagy. HIV Study, 1993; Washington Area Consortium alt. rep. Nat. Cmty. Adv. Bd. for Nat. WIHS, 1994, rep., cmty. adv. bd.; spkrs. bur. NAPWA-Nat. Assn. people with AIDS; nat. rep. Washington Area Consortium for Nat. WIHS; mem. Met. Washington Regional HIV Health Svcs. Planning Coun., 1995. V.p. Suburban Md. HIV/AIDS Alliance, 1996, sec., 1996. Recipient Cheryl D. Friedman award Montgomery County Dept. Health and Human Svcs., 1995, Outstanding Svc. award Montgomery County Dept. Correction and Rehab., 1996.

DEEMER, (NORMA) JEAN, artist; b. Cleve., Sept. 5, 1929; d. Harold Charles and Erma Marie (Kaiser) Daniels; m. Fred Orlo Deemer Jr., Apr. 20, 1957 (div. Aug. 1991); 1 child, Fred Webster. Master classes with, Glen Bradshaw. Co-owner art gallery and frame shop, 1987; tchr. OASIS; presenter, demonstrator, lectr. at workshops in field. One woman shows at Women's City Club of Akron, Ohio, Akron Jewish Ctr., Little Art Gallery, North Canton (Ohio) Libr., Akron Gen. Med. Ctr., Taylor Libr., Cuyahoga Falls, Ohio, Twinsburg (Ohio) Libr., North Hill Libr., Akron, Martel's, Akron, Rocky Knoll, Akron, O'Neil's Dept. Store, Akron, others; exhibited in many group exhbns. (22 awards, including 4 Best of Show and 3 First awards), including Nicolet Coll., Rhinelander, Wis., 1992, Soc. Layerists in Multi Media, Bradford, Mass., 1994, Ohio Dept. Mental Health, Columbus (semi-finalist "Percent for Art"), 1994, Johnson-Humrick House, Coshocton, Ohio, 1994, Sandusky (Ohio) Cultural Ctr., 1994, U. Ark. Art Galleries, Fayetteville, 1994, Stocker Ctr., Lorain C.C., Elyria, Ohio, 1995, Tubac (Ariz.) Ctr. for Arts, 1994, 95, Kirkpatrick Ctr. Mus. Complex, Oklahoma City, 1991, 92, 95; represented in permanent collections at FirstMerit Corp., Ohio, Akron-Summit County Pub. Libr., Portage Lakes, Ohio, Soc. Nat. Bank, Cleve., Colony Savs. Bank, Pitts., Columbia-Greene C.C., Hudson, N.Y., Anthony Cerny Archtl. Design Studios, Medina, Ohio, Ohio Arts and Crafts Found., Ohio Watercolor Soc., Riverside Sweets, Cuyahoga Falls; contbr. art to jours. cover and books in field. Mem. faculty, edn. chmn. Cuyahoga Valley Art Ctr., Cuyahoga Falls, 1986-88, also workshop chmn., v.p. Recipient Silver medal Watercolor Ohio, 1993, Merit award Watercolor Ohio, 1995, Juror's award Nat. Watercolor Okla., 1995, GE award Aqueous Nat., 1990. Mem. Nat. Watercolor Soc., Ohio Watercolor Soc. (corr. sec. 1983-84, exhbn. coord. ann. state juried exhbn. 1991, workshop coord. 1992, trustee 1991-94, 1st v.p. 1994-96, exhbn. liaison officer 1994-96, pres. 1996—, Bronze medal 1988, Award of Excellence 1991, Silver medal 1993, Hunt Mfg. award 1980, Merit 1995), Ky. Watercolor Soc., Soc. Layerists in Multi-Media, Pitts. Watercolor Soc. Home: 1537 Briarwood Cir Cuyahoga Falls OH 44221

DEEMS, SHERRAN ELLEN (SHERRY DEEMS), artist, educator, editor; b. Farmville, Va., Feb. 27, 1947; d. Donald and Laura Ellen (Stewart) D.; m. William Arthur Diamond; children: Jessica Lynn, Justin Stewart. BFA in Art History, Va. Commonwealth U., 1972, MFA in Painting and Printmaking, 1993. Dir. Life Drawing Studio, Roanoke, Va., 1977-78; mktg. rep. Nat. Retail Svcs., Georgetown, Conn., 1982-86; writer Commonwealth of Va. Parole Bd., Richmond, 1988; coord. Alumni Open Drawing Studio Va. Commonwealth U., Richmond, 1987-91, asst. to dir. Arts Libr., 1991, asst. dir. devel. Sch. Arts, 1993-94, grad. asst. painting and printmaking dept., 1991-93, adj. instr., 1991-93, 95—, editor VCU Arts alumni mag., 1994—; presenter in field; coord. art history program for elem. schs. Roanoke Fine Arts Mus., 1977-78; guest artist Richmond Pub. Schs., 1990, 91, 92, John Tyler C.C., Chester, Va., 1992, 95, Va. Union U., Richmond, 1992, Hanover County Pub. Schs., Hanover, Va., 1993, Richmond Montessori Sch., 1995; instr. drawing Petersburg (Va.) Area Art League, 1987-89, mem. adv. bd.; instr. printmaking Richmond Hand Workshop, 1995—; mem. curriculum rev. com. for reading programs Petersburg Pub. Schs.; guest artist Richmond Pub. Schs., 1990-93, John Tyler C.C., 1992-95. One-woman shows Old Colony Gallery, Williamsburg, Va., 1978, John Tyler C.C., 1988, Va. Commonwealth U., 1990, Anderson Gallery, Richmond, 1993, Interior Dynamics, Inc., Richmond, 1993, Clark Pollard Gallery, Richmond, 1993, ArtSpace Gallery, Richmond, 1994, Arts in Hosp., Richmond, 1995, Richmond Montessori Sch., 1995, U. Richmond, 1995; exhibited in group shows Petersburg Area Art League, 1988, 89, John Tyler C.C., 1988, Jewish Cmty. Ctr., Richmond, 1988, 90, 95, Gallery 24, Richmond, 1989, Va. Commonwealth U., 1989, 91, 92, 93, 95, Crestar Gallery, Richmond, 1990, Gallery 25, Richmond, 1990, Larrick Ctr., Richmond, 1990, James Ctr. Gallery, Richmond, 1991, 96, ArtSpace Gallery, Richmond, 1992, 96, Art in D.C., Washington, 1992, Rockville (Md.) Arts Place, 1992, Randolph-Macon Coll., Ashland, Va., 1993, Roanoke Coll., Salem, Va., 1993, Arts Coun. Richmond, 1994, longwood Coll., Farmville, 1994, Galerie Corti, Brussels, 1995, U. Richmond, 1995, also others; represented in permanent collections Va. Commonwealth U., Anderson Gallery, Va., Cabell Libr., Richmond, also pvt. and corp. collections; work reviewed in various publs.; author: (exhbn. catalog) Roger Baugh; contbr. articles to profl. publs. Mem. scholarship com. Richmond Women's Caucus for Art, also fundraising chmn., mem. adv. bd.; mem. Petersburg City Commn.-Day of Child; bd. dirs. Old Towne Mchts. Assn., Petersburg, Jr. Federated Women's Clubs, Va.; bd. dirs. Va. Commonwealth U. Alumni Assn., 1996-97. Recipient award of excellence Sherwood Forest Competition, Larrick Ctr. Painting Show; Jessie Hibbs scholar Va. Commonwealth U., Commonwealth of Va. fellow. Mem. Richmond Artists Assn., Richmond Women's Caucus for Art. Home: 9001 Patterson Ave Apt 87 Richmond VA 23229 Studio: 7 N 23d St Richmond VA 23223

DEER, ADA E., federal agency official, social worker, educator; b. Menominee Indian Reservation, Wis., Aug. 7, 1935; d. Joe and Constance (Wood) D. BA in Social Work, U. Wis., 1957, LDH (hon.), 1974; MSW, Columbia U., 1961; postgrad., U. N.Mex., 1971, U. Wis., 1971-72; D in Pub. Svc. (hon.), Northland Coll., 1974. Group worker Protestant Coun. N.Y., N.Y.C. Youth Bd., 1958-60; program dir. Edward F. Waite Neighborhood House, Mpls., 1961-64; community svc. coord. bur. Indian affairs Dept. of Interior, Mpls., 1964-67; coord. Indian affairs Tng. Ctr. Cmty. Programs U. Minn., Mpls., 1967-68; trainer Project Peace Pipe Peace Corps., Arecibo, P.R., 1968; sch. social worker Mpls. Pub. Schs., 1968-69; dir. Upward Bound U. Wis., Stevens Point, 1969-70, dir. Program Recognizing Individual Determination through Edn., 1970-71; v.p., lobbyist Nat. Com. Save Menominee People and Forest, Inc., Washington and State of Wis., 1972-73; chair Menominee Restoration Com., Wis., 1974-76; sr. lectr. Sch. Social Work, Am. Indians Studies Program U. Wis., Madison, 1977—; asst. sec. Indian Affairs U.S. Dept. Interior, Washington, 1993—; legis. liaison Native Am. Rights Fund, Washington, 1979-81; cons., trainer Nat. Women's Edn. Fund, Washington, 1979-85; founding mem. Am. Indian Scholarships, Inc., Albuquerque, 1973-85; apptd. Joint Commn. on Mental Health of Children, Inc., Washington, 1967-68, Youth for Understanding, Wis., 1985-90; mem. adv. panel Office Technology Assessment, Washington, 1984-86; mem. Nat. Indian Adv. Com., Washington, 1989-91, Milw., 1990—, numerous other coms.; spkr. in field. Vice chair Nat. Mondale/Ferraro Presdl. Campaign, Washington, 1984; del.-at-large Dem. Nat. Conv., San Francisco, 1984; mem. spl. com. minority presence Girls Scouts U.S.A., N.Y.C., 1975-77, mem., 1969-75; bd. dirs. Planned Parenthood, Mpls., 1965-66, Indian Cmty. Sch., Milw., 1989—, Native Am. Rights Fund, Boulder, 1984-90, chmn., 1989-90, chair nat. support com., 1990—; mem. bd. improving health Native Ams. Robert Wood Johnson Found., Princeton, N.J., 1988—; bd. dirs. Quincentenary Com. Smithsonian Instn., Washington, 1989—, Hunt Commn. Dem. Nat. Com., Washington, 1981-82, Ind. Sector, Washington, 1980-84, Rural Am., Washington, 1978-85, Ams. for Indian Oppty., 1970-83; apptd. Pres. Commn. White House Fellowships, 1977-83; active Common Cause, Washington, 1974-78, Wis. Women's Coun., Madison, 1983-84, Camp Miniwanca, Stony Lake, Mich., 1953-57, Coun. Founds., Washington, 1977-83, Madison Urban League; Dem. candidate Wis. Sec. State, 1982. Recipient White Buffalo Coun. Achievement award, 1974, Politzer award Ethical Culture Soc., 1975, Wonder Woman Found. award, 1982, Indian Coun. Fire Achievement award, 1984, Nat. Disting. Achievement award Am. Indian Resources Inst., 1991; named Woman of Yr. by Girl Scouts Am., 1982; honoree Nat. Women's History Month Poster, 1987, Heroine Calendar Nat. Women's Studies Assn., 1987; Harvard U. fellow, 1977-78, Delta Gamma Found. Meml. fellow, 1960, John Hay Whitney Found. Meml. fellow, 1960; Menominee Tribal scholar, 1953-55. Mem. ACLU, NOW, Nat. Women's Polit. Caucus, Nat. Congress Am. Indians, Nat. Assn. Social Workers (pres. Wis. chpt. 1988-90, nat. com. women's issues 1988-90, decision making task force 1988-90, minorities com. 1977-81), Assn. Am. Indians and Alaska Native Social Workers (pres. Wis. 1978-80), Common Cause, Nature Conservancy. Office: Indian Affairs 1849 C St NW Washington DC 20240-0001

DEERING, ANNE-LISE, artist, real estate salesperson; b. Oslo, June 20, 1935; d. Reidar Ingolf Dahlsrud and Dagny Elfrida (Grönneberg) Nilsen; m. Reginald Atwell Deering, Oct. 20, 1956 (div. July 1992); children: Eric, Mark, Linda, Norman. BA in Art, Pa. State U., 1977, postgrad., 1990-91. Lic. real estate salesperson, Pa. Rsch. asst. Yale U., New Haven, 1955-57; ceramic artist/potter State College, Pa., 1977—; real estate agt. Coldwell Banker Univ. Realty, State College, 1992-93, Century 21 Corman Assocs., State College, 1993—. Editor Ctrl. Pa. Guild of Craftsmen newsletter, 1994. Artist advisor Ctrl. Pa. Festival of the Arts, State College, 1991—; vol. Habitat for Humanity, 1992, mem., 1992—. Mem. Nat. Assn. Realtors, Pa. Assn. Realtors, Centre County Assn. Realtors, Pa. Guild Craftsmen (bd. dirs. 1980-83, 85—), Ctrl. Pa. Guild Craftsmen (pres. 1986-87, 93-94, v.p. 1985, 91, 92, coord., chair ann. Christmas sale), Am. Mus. Women in the Arts (charter), Am. Medallic Sculpture Assn. Home: 745 Westerly Pkwy State College PA 16801

DEERING, BRENDA FLORINE, secondary education educator; b. Porterville, Calif., July 25, 1953; d. Kenneth Henry Rogers and Barbara Oleta (Herron) Ledbetter; m. Robert Edward Deering, Feb. 14, 1975; children: David James, Duane Jason. BS in Psychology, Tex. Wesleyan U., 1989, MS in Edn., 1993. Lic. alcohol and drug abuse counselor. Substitute tchr. Birdville Ind. Sch. Dist., Haltom City, Tex., 1984-94; counselor pvt. practice, Bedford, Tex., 1991—, Residential Treatment Ctr., Bedford, Tex., 1990-91; tchr. secondary sch. Bridville Ind. Sch. Dist., 1994—; counseling affiliate Tarrant Bapt. Assn., Ft. Worth, 1992-94; tchr. ESOL Bedford Pub. Libr., 1993-94. Named Vol. of Yr. City of Bedford, 1993. Mem. NEA, Nat. Coun. Tchrs. English, Tex. Assn. Alcohol and Drug Abuse Counselors (edn. com. 1990—), Internat. Reading Assn., Sigma Tau Delta (Creative Writing award 1992), Pi Lambda Theta (corr. sec. 1993—), Kappa Delta Pi. Home: 3721 Windomere Dr Bedford TX 76021-2327 Office: Haltom Mid Sch 5000 Hires Ln Haltom City TX 76117

DEES, SANDRA KAY MARTIN, psychologist, research consultant; b. Omaha, Apr. 18, 1944; d. Leslie B. and Ruth Lillian (May) Martin; m. Doyce B. Dees; BA magna cum laude, Tex. Christian U., 1965, MA, 1972, PhD, 1989. Adminstrv. asst./rsch. coord. Hosp. Improvement Project, Wichita Falls (Tex.) State Hosp., 1968-69; caseworker adoptions Edna Gladney Home, Ft. Worth, Tex., 1970-71; psychologist Mexia (Tex.) State Sch., 1971-72; sch. psychologist Ft. Worth Ind. Sch. Dist., 1971-78, program evaluator, 1978-86; pvt. counselor, 1986-88; assoc. rsch. scientist Tex. Christian U., 1989—; mem. adj. faculty, 1991-92, grad. faculty, 1994—; bd. dirs Because We Care, Ft. Worth, 1988—, Hill Sch., 1994—. Dallas TCU Women's Club creative writing scholar, 1962-64, Virginia Alpha scholar, 1963; NASA research asst., 1965-67; USPHS trainee, 1967-68; cert. Am. Montessori Soc., 1977. Mem. APA, Am. Ednl. Rsch. Assn., Mental Health Assn., Mortar Bd., Mensa, Alpha Chi, Phi Alpha Theta, Psi Chi, Phi Delta Kappa. Contbr. articles to profl. publs. Home: 29 Bounty Rd W Fort Worth TX 76132-1003 Office: Tex Christian U Dept Psychology Fort Worth TX 76129

DEETER, JOAN G., church administrator; m. Allen Deeter; children: Michael, Daniel, David. BS in Elem. Edn., Manchester Coll.; MA in Ednl. Guidance, Northwestern U., 1953; M in Religious Edn., Bethany Sem., 1955,

MDiv, 1982. Adminstr. Northlake (Ill.) Pub. Schs., 1955-56; tchr. Princeton, N.J., 1957-58; interim rsch. libr. Manchester Coll., 1961-62; interim min. nurture Manchester Ch. of Brethren, 1964-65; resident dir. asst. Brethren Colls. Abroad in Marburg, Fed. Republic of Germany, 1965-66; exec. dir. Mental Health Assn., Wabash County, Ind., 1967-68, 69-80; interim youth min. Manchester Ch. of Brethren, 1973-74; pastor West Manchester Ch. of Brethren, 1982-88; adj. faculty mem. Bethany Theol. Sem., 1984-85; mem. exec. parish ministries commn. Ch. of Brethren, 1988-92; assoc. gen. sec. World Ministries, 1992—; v.p. Ind. Coun. Chs.; rep. on mental health awareness and edn. com. Ch. of Brethren; mem. Brethren Health and Welfare Bd.; mem. Ind. com. for Jewish, Cath., Protestant Coop.; bd. dirs. Bowen Ctr. for Human Svcs.; long range planning com. Camp Mack; mem. New Ch. Devel. Com., S/C Ind. Ch. of Brethren, Discipleship and Reconciliation Com., S/C Ind. Ch. of Brethren, Human Rights Com., Wabash County Coun. for Retarded Children and Vocationally Handicapped; mem. adv. bd. Mental Health Assn., Wabash County, Ind.; spkr. confs., retreats. Contbr. articles to profl. jours. Supervising pastor EFSM, Pleasant View Ch. of Brethrn, 1983-86, mem. standing com., standing com. nominating com., Bible hour messenger at Roanoke Ann. Conf., 1986; moderator Ch. of Brethren, South Ctrl. Ind. Dist., 1985; pres. Brethren Jour. Assn., 1979-85; pres. Coll. Woman's Club, 1984-85; pres. North Manchester Ministerium, 1985-86. Office: Church of The Brethren 1451 Dundee Ave Elgin IL 60120-1674

DEETHS, LENORE CLAIR, retired secondary education educator; b. Omaha, Oct. 27, 1940; d. Edward James and Bess Helen (Sabatka) Baburek; m. Harry Jeoffrey Deeths, June 15, 1963; children: Lisa Marie, Matthew Jeoffrey, Maria Lenore. BA in English, Coll. St. Mary, Omaha, 1962. Tchr. English Holy Name High Sch., Omaha, 1962-64, Berlitz Lang. Sch., Tokyo, 1969-72; substitute tchr. Tachikawa (Japan) USAF High Sch., 1969-72; chair Coll. St. Mary Alumnae Assn., Omaha, 1979-80, chmn. breakfast series, 1990-92. Editor: (newsletter) Pulse Beat, 1965-69; author/producer (TV show) Health Topics, 1985-91. Chaired Officers' Wives Scholarship Com., 1971; br. chmn. Am. Assn. of Univ. Women Quality of Life Study, 1976-78; chaired fundraiser St. Joseph Hosp. and Creighton Med. Sch., 1979; publicity chmn. Emergency Pregnancy Svc. Omaha, 1980-85. Mem. AAUW (pres. 1991-92, 1st v.p. 1981-83, 3d v.p. 1983-84, br. chmn. 1978-80, br. del. chmn. nat. conv. 1991, br. del. chmn. Nat. Centennial Conv. 1981), LWV, Omaha Symphony Guild, Omaha Comty. Playhouse Guild, Omaha News Bull., Met. Omaha Med. Alliance (Merit award 1991, bd. dirs. 1989-91, pub. rels. com. 1985-90, pres. 1993-94, advisor 1994-95), Nebr. Med. Assn. Alliance (bd. dirs. 1994-96, parliamentarian 1994-97), Friends of Children's Hosp., Girls Inc. (vice chair career devel. 1992-93, chair 1993-94). Home: 6729 Davenport St Omaha NE 68132-2737

DEFALCO, ANTOINETTE L. (ANN DEFALCO), artist; b. Irvington, N.J., Feb. 21, 1927; d. Salvatore and Nettie T. Lazzaro; m. Victor J. DeFalco, June 27, 1954 (dec. Nov. 1989); children: Marie, Dolores, Christopher, Loretta, Susanne, Patrick. Grad., Newark Sch. Fine & Indsl. Arts, 1948-52; student, Ben Kern Sch. Lettering, 1976. Owner Ann DeFalco Custom Made Signs, Chester, N.J., 1976—; program asst. Time Out Adult Care Ctr., Madison, N.J., 1990—; art tchr. Mount Olive Adult Sch., Flanders, N.J., 1991—; pvt. tchr. Chester, N.J.; census person Census Bur., Morristown, N.J., 1990. Girl Scout leader Chester Girl Scouts, N.J. Mem. Fifty Plus Club. Republican. Roman Catholic. Home and Office: Ann DeFalco Custom Made Signs 110 Fairmount Ave Chester NJ 07930

DEFAZIO, LYNETTE STEVENS, dancer, choreographer, educator, chiropractor, author, actress, violinist; b. Berkeley, Calif., Sept. 29; d. Honore and Mabel J. (Estavan) Stevens; children: J.H. Panganiban, Joanna Pang. student U. Calif., Berkeley, 1950-55, San Francisco State Coll., 1950-51, D. Chiropractic, Life-West Chiropractic Coll., San Lorenzo, Calif., 1983, cert. Techniques of Teaching U. Calif., 1985, BA in Humanities, New Coll. Calif., 1986; Lic. Chiropracter, Mich. Diplomate Nat. Sci. Bd.; eminence in dance edn., Calif. Community Colls. dance specialist, standard services, childrens ctrs. credentials Calif. Dept. Edn., 1986. Contract child dancer Monogram Movie Studio, Hollywood, Calif., 1938-40; dance instr. San Francisco Ballet, 1953-64; performer San Francisco Opera Ring, 1960-67; performer, choreographer Oakland (Calif.) Civic Light Opera, 1963-70; dir. Ballet Arts Studio, Oakland, Calif., 1960; teaching specialist Oakland Unified Sch. Dist., 1965-80; fgn. exchange dance dir. Academie de Danses-Salle Pleyel, Paris, France, 1966; instr. Peralta Community Coll. Dist., Oakland, 1971—, chmn. dance dept., 1985—; cons., instr. extension courses UCLA, Dirs. and Suprs. Assn., Pittsburg Unified Sch. Dist., 1971-73, Tulare (Calif.) Sch. Dist., 1971-73; researcher Ednl. Testing Services, HEW, Berkeley, 1974; resident choreographer San Francisco Childrens Opera, 1970—, Oakland Civic Theater; ballet mistress Dimensions Dance Theater, Oakland, 1977-80; cons. Gianchetta Sch. Dance, San Francisco, Robicheau Boston Ballet, TV series Patchwork Family, CBS, N.Y.C.; choreographer Ravel's Valses Nobles et Sentimentales, 1976. Recipient Foremost Women of 20th Century, 1985, Merit award San Francisco Children's Opera, 1985, 90. Author: Basic Music Outlines for Dance Classes, 1960, rev., 1968, Teaching Techniques and Choreography for Advanced Dancers, 1965, Basic Music Outlines for Dance Classes, 1965, Goals and Objectives in Improving Physical Capabilities, 1970, A Teacher's Guide for Ballet Techniques, 1970, Principle Procedures in Basic Curriculum, 1974, Objectives and Standards of Performance for Physical Development, 1975, Techniques of the Ballet School, 1970, rev., 1974, The Opera Ballets: A Choreographic Manual Vols. I-V, 1986. Assoc. music arranger Le Ballet du Cirque, 1964; assoc. composer, lyricist The Ballet of Mother Goose, 1968; choreographer: Valses Nobles Et Sentimentales (Ravel), Transitions (Kashevaroff), 1991, The New Wizard of Oz, 1991, San Francisco Children's Opera (Gingold); Canon in D for Strings and Continuo (Pachelbel), 1979; appeared in Flower Drum Song, 1993, Gigi, 1994, Fiddler on the Roof, 1996, The Music Man, 1996; violinist Oakland Cmty. Concert Orch., 1995—. Mem. Calif. State Teacher Assn., Bay Area Chiropractic Research Soc., Profl. Dance Teacher Assn., Home and Office: 4923 Harbord Dr Oakland CA 94618-2506

DE FERRARI, GABRIELLA, curator, writer; b. Tacna, Peru, June 3, 1941; came to U.S., 1959, naturalized, 1964; d. Armando and Delia De Ferrari; children: Nathaniel, Gabriella, Jeppson. BA, St. Louis U., 1962; MS, Tufts U., 1965; MA, Harvard U., 1981. Dir. Inst. Contemporary Art, Boston, 1975-77; acting curator Busch Reisinger Mus., Harvard U., Cambridge, Mass., 1978-79; asst. dir. for curatorial affairs and program Fogg Art Mus., 1979-82; cons. editor Travel Leisure and House and Garden Mag. Author: A Cloud on Sand, 1990, Gringa Latina A Woman of Two Worlds, 1995. Office: 10 Jay St New York NY 10013-2819

DEFEVER, SUSANNA ETHEL, English language educator; b. Manistee, Mich., May 11, 1934; d. Arthur Theodore and Florence Marie Christine (Larson) Mason; m. Charles J. Defever, Aug. 1, 1959; children: Keith S., Kristin E. AB, Cen. Mich. U., 1956; MA, Wayne State U., 1963; postgrad., Mich. State U., 1957, 58. Cert. secondary education tchr. 1959. Tchr. English, journalism, drama Lakeview High Sch., St. Clair Shores, Mich., 1956-65; tchr. English, composition St. Clair County C.C., Port Huron, 1965-70, part time tchr., 1971-77, prof. English, composition, 1977-95; conf. planning Liberal Arts Network Devel. (LAND) for Consortium of Mich. Cmty. Coll., 1990-93, v.p., conf. chmn. 1994-95, pres. 1995-96; dir. writing workshops for K-12 tchrs. Sanilac County Intermediate Sch. dist., 1987, 88, 92, Cheboygan Otsego Presque Isle Intermediate Sch. Dist., 1989, Port Huron Area Schs., 1991; mem. adv. com. Mich. Proficiency Exam, 1992-96, exec. com. Mich. Writing Projects, 1987-93. Editor: The Heritage of IRA, 1990, An Enduring Heritage, 1992; scholar, lectr. Let's Talk About It series, Mich. Libr. Assn., 1987-93, NEH/ Modern Poetry series, St. Clair County Libr., 1994; contbr. articles to profl. jours.; presenter workshops. Founding mem. Marge Boal Drama Festival. Recipient Disting. Faculty award, 1983, 89, Nat. Inst. Staff Orgn. Devel. Excellence award for Tchg., U. Austin, 1992; Beacon grantee, 1991-92, Sperry grant, 1994. Mem. NEA, ASCD, Internat. Reading Assn., Nat. Coun. Tchrs. English (assoc. chmn. local conv. arrangements 1984, judge 1983-96), Mich. Coll. English Assn. (newsletter chmn., editor 1989-91), Mich. Coun. Tchrs. English (regional coord. 1979-85, v.p. 1986-87), Cmty. Coll. Humanities Assn., Mich. Assn. for Higher Edn., Delta Kappa Gamma (sec. 1992-94), Phi Theta Kappa (hon.).

DEFILIPPO, LINDA KELLOGG, preschool educator; b. Troy, N.Y., Jan. 21, 1947; d. John E. and Dorothy A. (Knapp) Kellogg; children: Elizabeth, Mark. AS, Hudson Valley C.C., Troy, 1966; BS, Russell Sage Coll., 1968, MS, 1980. Substitute tchr. Capital Dist. Schs., 1968-72; dir./owner The Plaza Nursery Sch., Schenectady, N.Y., 1973—; tchr. Albany Sch., Schenectady, N.Y., 1980-81; life skills educator Washington Irving Sch., Schenectady, N.Y., 1981-82; mgr. Family Rental Property, Troy, 1982-84; dir./owner The Plaza Day Care Ctr., Niskayuna, N.Y., 1984—; tchr. adult basic edn. Schenectady County Jail, 1981-82. Vol. Am. Cancer Soc., Schenectady, 1968—, Am. Heart Assn., Schenectady, 1970—. Mem. AAUW, Soropomist Internat. Episcopalian. Home: 1154 Palmer Ave Niskayuna NY 12309-5813 Office: Plaza Day Care Ctr 1335 Balltown Rd Schenectady NY 12309-5317

DEFLEUR, LOIS B., university president, sociology educator; b. Aurora, Ill., June 25, 1936; d. Ralph Edward and Isabel Anna (Cornils) Begitske; m. Melvin L. DeFleur (div.). AB, Blackburn Coll., 1958; MA, Ind. U., 1961; PhD in Sociology, U. Ill., 1965. Asst. prof. sociology Transylvania Coll., Lexington, Ky., 1963-67; assoc. prof. Wash. State U., Pullman, 1967-74, prof., 1975-86, dean Coll. Liberal Arts, 1981-86; provost U. Mo., Columbia, 1986-90; pres. Binghamton U., SUNY, 1990—; disting. vis. prof. USAF Acad., 1976-77; vis. prof. U. Chgo., 1980-81; pres.'s commn. NCAA, 1996—; bd. dirs. N.Y. State Electric and Gas. Author: Delinquency in Argentina, 1965; (with others) Sociology: Human Society, 3d edit. 1981, 4th edit., 1984, The Integration of Women into All Male Air Force Units, 1982, The Edward R. Murrow Heritage: A Challenge for the Future, 1986; contbr. articles to profl. jours. Mem. Wash. State Bd. on Correctional Svcs. and Edn., 1974-77, State of N.Y. Edn. Dept. Curriculum and Assessment Coun., 1991-94, Trilateral Task for N.Am. Ednl. Collaboration, USIA, 1993-95. Recipient Disting. Alumni award Blackburn Coll., 1991; grantee NIMH, 1969-79, NSF, 1972-75, Air Force Office, 1978-81. Mem. Am. Sociol. Assn. (publs. com. 1979-82, nominations com. 1984-86, coun. mem. 1987-90), Pacific Sociol. Assn. (pres. 1980-82), Coun. Colls. of Arts and Scis. (bd. dirs. 1982-84, pres. 1985-87), Aircraft Owners and Pilots Assn., Internat. Comanche Soc., Nat. Assn. State U. and Land-grant Colls. (exec. com. 1990-93, chair coun. of pres. 1994-95, chair 1996-97), Am. Coun. Edn. (bd. dirs. 1994—), Consortium Social Sci. Assns. (bd. dirs. 1993—). Office: Binghamton U Office of Pres PO Box 6000 Binghamton NY 13902-6000

DEFLORIO, MARY LUCY, physician, psychiatrist; b. Chgo.; d. Anthony Ralph adn Bernice B. (Bounell) DeF.; m. Robert Y. Shapiro, Dec. 27, 1986. BA with distinction, U. Wis.; MD, MPH, U. Ill., Chgo., 1984; cert. writing program, Columbia U., 1988-91. Cert. emergency med. technician. Adjudicator Fed. Disability Program, Ill. and Mass.; vocat. counselor U. Ill., Chgo.; resident internal medicine Mercy Hosp., Chgo., 1984-85; med. examiner Dept. Pub. Aid State of Ill., Chgo., 1985-87; resident psychiatrist St. Vincent's Hosp., N.Y.C., 1987-90; fellow cons. liaison psychiatry Meml. Sloan Kettering/Cornell Med. Ctr., N.Y.C., 1991-93; chief fellow Meml. Sloan Kettering, N.Y.C., 1992-93; attending physician Div. Psychiatry/Dept. Neurology Meml. Sloan Kettering and Cornell Med. Ctr., N.Y.C., 1993-95; pvt. practice N.Y., 1996—. Recipient Med. Econs. Writing award, 1987; James scholar U. Ill., Gen. Assembly scholar. Mem. AMA (Nutritional scholar 1983-84), Am. Women's Assn., Nat. Rehab. Assn., Assn. Acad. Psychiatrists (Mead-Johnson fellow 1990), Am. Psychiat. Assn. (Br. Rsch. award 1990), Am. Psychiat. Arts Assn. (black and white photography award 1993, 96, poetry award 1993). Roman Catholic.

DEFORGE, KATHERINE ANN, secondary education educator; b. Syracuse, N.Y., Nov. 2, 1950; d. Edward Carroll and Genevieve (Pretko) Miles; m. Timothy Edward DeForge, June 26, 1976; 1 child, Tanya Emily. AA, Maria Regina Coll., Syracuse, 1969; BA, LeMoyne Coll., Syracuse, 1972; MS in Edn., SUNY, Cortland, 1978. Tchr., supr. social studies Assumption Cath. Acad., Syracuse, 1972-81, Bishop Grimes H.S., East Syracuse, N.Y., 1981-88, Marcellus (N.Y.) Ctrl. Schs., 1988—; test cons. N.Y. State Edn. Dept., Albany, 1984—; mem. testing and assessment com. N.Y. State Edn. Dept. NEH grantee, 1986, 94. Mem. ASCD, Nat. Coun. for Social Studies, N.Y. State Coun. for Social Studies, N.Y. State Social Studies Suprs. Assn., Ctrl. N.Y. Coun. for Social Studies (sec. 1986-88, treas. 1989-91, v.p. 1993-95, pres. 1995—, Outstanding Social Studies Educator award 1992). Republican. Roman Catholic. Home: 230 Malverne Dr Syracuse NY 13208-1841 Office: Marcellus Ctrl Schs Reed Pky Marcellus NY 13108

DEFORGE, MICHELE, foundation executive. Pres. Nat. Found. for Fibromyalgia, San Diego, 1993—, San Diego Nat. Orgn. for Women Outreach Fund. Mem. Calif. Women's Health Leadership Program. Office: Nat Found for Fibromyalgia PO Box 3429 San Diego CA 92163-1429

DEFRANCIS, SUELLEN MARIA, interior architect; b. Bklyn., Sept. 21, 1946; d. Joseph Agustino and Mary DeF.; m. James D. Block, Apr. 23, 1965 (div. 1983); children: Melissa, Louis, Maximillian. BS, CCNY, 1982; BArch, CUNY, 1982, MS in Urban Design, 1983. Designer, dir. interiors Peter Gisolfi Architects, Hastings-on-Hudson, N.Y., 1983-85; designer John Burgee Architects, N.Y.C., 1985-86; prin., owner Suellen DeFrancis Archtl. Interiors, Scarsdale, 1986—; lectr. Iona Coll., New Rochelle, N.Y. Prin. works include N.Y. Yacht Club, N.Y.C., Nippon Steel, N.Y.C., Mitsubishi Estate Housing, Ashiya, Japan, Asahi Brewery, Kobe, Japan, Genex Hdqs., N.Y.C., Berkshire Place Hotel, N.Y., The Castle Restaurant and Inn, Tarrytown, N.Y., and others; also, features in Asset Housing mag., Mitsubishi Home mag., N.Y. Times, Ku-Kan mag., Housing mag.; pvt. residences designed and built in Tokyo, Iwaki, Japan and N.Y.C. Trustee St. Christopher's-Jennie Clarkson Childcare Svcs., Inc. Recipient Del Gaudio award N.Y. Soc. Architects, 1982; AIA scholar, 1982. Mem. AIA (assoc., N.Y.C. AIA interiors com.), Internat. Interior Design Assn., Internat. House of Japan, Far East Assn. Architects and Engrs., Nippon Club. Office: PO Box 247 Scarsdale NY 10583-0247 also: 900 Park Ave Ste 21C New York NY 10021

DEGENERES, ELLEN, comedian, actress. TV appearances include: Duet, 1988-89, Open House, 1989, Laurie Hill, 1992, Ellen, 1994—; films include Coneheads, 1993. Office: UTA Inc 9560 Wilshire Blvd Fl 5 Beverly Hills CA 90212-2401*

DEGENSTEIN, CANDACE TRACY WYNNE, nurse practitioner; b. Calgary, Alta., Can., Nov. 6, 1961; Came to the U.S., 1989; d. Peter William and Ruth Elouise (Trousil) D. BSN, U. Alta., Edmonton, 1983; MSN, U. South Ala., 1993. RN, Minn., La.; cert. neonatal intensive care nurse; lic. La. advanced practice; cert. primary nurse assoc., clin. nurse specialist; cert. family nurse practitioner, ANCC. Traveling nurse Cross Country, Boca Raton, Fla., 1989-90; staff nurse neonatal ICU Humana Hosp., New Orleans, 1990-91; pediat./ambulatory rsch. nurse coord. Tulane U. Med. Ctr., New Orleans, 1991-92, pediat. rsch. nurse specialist, 1992-93, adolescent rsch. nurse specialist, 1993-94, adolescent nurse, 1994—; presenter in field. Recipient Excellence in Practice award Women Child Health Nursing, 1993; Profl. Nursing Traineeship grantee U. South Ala., 1992. Mem. ANA, Nat. Assn. Neonatal Nurses, Am. Assn. Reg. Nurses, New Orleans Nurses in AIDS Care,, Assn. Nurses AIDS Care, Am. Women's Health Obs. and Neonatal Nursing, La. Pub. Health Assn., La. Assn. Nurse Practitioners, Sigma Theta Tau. Office: Tulane U Med Ctr Dept Pediats Adol Health 1430 Tulane Ave New Orleans LA 70112-2699

DE GETTE, DIANA LOUISE, lawyer, state legislator; b. Tachikawa, Japan, July 29, 1957; came to U.S., 1957; d. Richard Louis and Patricia Anne (Rose) De G.; m. Lino Sigismondo Lipinsky de Orlov, Sept. 15, 1984; children: Raphaela Anne, Francesca Louise. BA magna cum laude, The Colo. Coll., 1979; JD, NYU, 1982. Bar: Colo. 1982, U.S. Dist. Ct. Colo. 1982, U.S. Ct. Appeals (10th cir.) 1984, U.S. Supreme Ct. 1989. Dep. state pub. defender Colo. State Pub. Defender, Denver, 1982-84; assoc. Coghill & Goodspeed, P.C., Denver, 1984-86; sole practice Denver, 1986-93; of counsel McDermott & Hansen, Denver, 1993—; mem. Colo. Ho. of Reps., 1992—, asst. minority leader, 1995-96, mem. judiciary, legal svcs., legis. coun. coms. Editor: (mag.) Trial Talk, 1989-92. Mem. Mayor's Mgmt. Rev. Com., Denver, 1983-84; resolutions chair Denver Dem. Party, 1986; bd. dirs. Root-Tilden Program, NYU Sch. Law, N.Y.C., 1986-92; bd. trustees, alumni trustee Colo. Coll., Colorado Springs, 1988-94. Recipient Root-Tilden scholar NYU Sch. Law, N.Y.C., 1979, Vanderbilt medal, 1982. Mem. Colo. Bar Assn. (bd. govs. 1989-91), Colo. Trial Lawyers Assn. (bd. dirs., exec. com. 1986-92), Colo. Women's Bar Assn., Denver Bar Assn., Phi Beta Kappa, Pi Gamma Mu. Office: McDermott & Hansen 1890 Gaylord St Denver CO 80206-1211

DE GOFF, VICTORIA JOAN, lawyer; b. San Francisco, Mar. 2, 1945; d. Sidney Francis and Jean Frances (Alexander) De G.; m. Peter D. Coppelman, May 2, 1971 (div. Dec. 1978); m. Richard Sherman, June 16, 1980. BA in Math. with great distinction, U. Calif., Berkeley, 1967, JD, 1972. Bar: Calif. 1972, U.S. Dist. Ct. (no. dist.) Calif. 1972, U.S. Ct. Appeals 1972, U.S. Supreme Ct. 1989; cert. appellate law specialist, 1996. Rsch. atty. Calif. Ct. Appeal, San Francisco, 1972-73; Reginald Heber Smith Found. fellow San Francisco Neighborhood Legal Assistance Found., 1973-74; assoc. Field, De Goff, Huppert & McGowan, San Francisco, 1974-77; pvt. practice Berkeley, Calif., 1977-80; ptnr. De Goff and Sherman, Berkeley, 1980—; lectr. continuing edn. of bar, Calif., 1987, 90-92, U. Calif. Boalt Hall Sch. Law, Berkeley, 1981-85, dir. appellate advocacy, 1992; cons. Calif. Civil Practice Procedure, Bancroft Whitney, 1992; mem. Appellate Law Adv. Commn., 1995; apptd. applicant evaluation and nomination com. for State Bar Ct. by Calif. Supreme Ct., 1995. Author: (with others) Matthew Bender's Treatise on California Torts, 1985. Apptd. to adv. com. Calif. Jud. Coun. on Implementing Proposition 32, 1984-85; mem. adv. bd. Hastings Coll. Trial and Appellate Adv., 1984-91; expert 20/20 vision project, commn. on future cts. Jud. Coun. Calif., 1993, apptd. to appellate standing adv. com., 1993-95; apptd. to Appellate Indigent Def. Oversight Adv. Com., State of Calif., 1995; com. on appellate standards of Am. Bar Assn. Appellate Judges Conf., 1995—; adv. bd. Witkin Legal Inst., Bancroft Whitney, 1996—; bd. dirs. Calif. Supreme Ct. Hist. Soc., State Bar Calif., Appellate Law Cons. Group, 1994-95. Fellow Woodrow Wilson Found., 1967-68. Mem. Calif. Trial Lawyers Assn. (bd. govs. 1980-88, amicus-curiae com. 1981-87, editor-in-chief assn. mag. 1980-81, Presdl. award of merit 1980, 81), Calif. Acad. Appellate Lawyers (sec.-treas. 1989-90, 2d v.p. 1990-91, 1st v.p. 1991-92, pres. 1992-93), Am. Acad. Appellate Lawyers, Edward J. McFetridge Am. Inn of Cts. (counsellor 1990-91, edn. chmn. 1991-92, social chmn. 1992-93, v.p. 1993-94, pres. 1994-95), Boalt Hall Sch. Law U. Calif. Alumni Assn. (bd. dirs. 1989-91), Order of Coif. Jewish. Office: 1916 Los Angeles Ave Berkeley CA 94707-2419

DEGONIA, MARY ELISE, government community relations executive, publisher; b. St. Louis, Sept. 23, 1954; d. Joseph Milton and Janice Doris (Walls) DeG. Student, Riverside Community Coll., 1971-73, Calif. State U., 1973-76. Dir., youth svcs. Los Padrinos, San Bernardino, Calif., 1975-78; chief, planning and evaluation Mayor's Office of Employment and Tng., San Bernardino, 1978-79; program mgr., v.p. Mondale Task Force on Youth, Washington, 1979-80; sr. policy analyst Nat. Youth Work Alliance, Washington, 1979-81; v.p. govt. rels. Youth Employment, Washington, 1981-88; pres. Capitol Perspectives, Washington, 1988—; pub. Capitol Perspectives Update; dir. pub. policy and legislation Nat. Youth Employment Ctr., N.Y.C., 1979-89; founding mem. Nat. Assn. for Community Base Orgn., Washington, 1979-83. Co-author: State Coordination Guide, 1987, Food for Thought, 1988, Stalking the Large Green Grant, 1979, Fund Diversification Guide, 1988. Founding chmn. Calif. Child, Youth and Family Coalition, Sacramento, 1976-78; nat. bd. dirs. Wider Opportunities for Women. Recipient Outstanding Performance award, U.S. Dept. Labor, Washington, 1980, Disting. Achievement award, U.S. Basics, Alexandria, Va., 1988. Mem. Nat. Youth Employment Coalition, State Issues Forum (exec. mem., bd. dirs.), Nat. Job. Tng. Partnership. Office: Capitol Perspectives 1915 17th St NW # 200 Washington DC 20009-6202

DE GRAZIA, LORETTA THERESA, oil company executive; b. Boston, May 17, 1955; d. Gaetano T.P. and Nancy R. (Serino) De G. A in Mgmt./Mktg. magna cum laude, Newbury Coll., 1986. V.p. mktg. and sales Grimes Oil Co., Boston, 1977-85; pres. East Coast Petroleum, Boston, 1985—. Fellow NAFE, New Eng. Women Bus. Owners, Nat. Assn. Women in Constrn., Greater Boston Women's Network; mem. Women's Bus. Enterprise Alliance, Boston Women's Network, South Shore C. of C., Quincy-2000. Office: East Coast Petroleum Corp 235 Atlantic St North Quincy MA 02171

DEGUIRE, KATHRYN SILBER, psychologist; b. Mankato, Minn., Nov. 16, 1932; d. Ernest Albert and Anna (John) Silber; 1 child, Lise Kathryn. MusB, Eastman Sch. Music U. Rochester, 1954; postgrad. Akademie für Musik und Darstellende Kunst, Vienna, 1954-55, Upsala Coll., 1966-69; MA, Fordham U., 1971, PhD, 1974. Pianist, organist, instr. piano, 1955-66; clin. asst. psychologist Meml. Sloan Kettering Cancer Center, N.Y.C., 1974-83; pvt. practice, N.Y.C., 1976-88, Fairfield, N.J., 1976-94, Morristown, N.J., 1988—, Blairstown, N.J., 1994—; lectr. Upsala Coll., East Orange, N.J., 1971-72, 78-81. Fulbright scholar, Vienna, 1954-55; USPHS grantee, 1969-71. Mem. APA, N.J. Psychol. Assn., Soc. Psychologists in Pvt. Practice (pres. 1986). Rec. artist: Orion. Home and Office: 55A Primrose Rd Blairstown NJ 07825-3304

DE HAAN-PULS, JOYCE ELAINE, sales account representative; b. Grand Rapids, Mich., Dec. 22, 1941; d. Harry Herman and Dorothy Elaine (Kikstra) DeHaan; student Calvin Coll., 1960-61; BS with honors, Grand Valley State Colls., 1978; postgrad. U. Sarajevo, Yugoslavia, 1978, Grad. Inst., Siedman Grad. Coll., 1979—; M in Speech Communications Wayne State U., 1986 ; children: Bruce Todd, Daniel Lane, Cristy-Ann Sara Elizabeth Puls. Owner, operator Joyce Elaine's Beauty Parlor, Grandville, Mich., 1960-64; asst. assessor City of Hudsonville, Mich., 1978; dir. displaced homemaker program Women's Resource Ctr., Grand Rapids, 1979-81; visual products rep. 3M Corp., Grand Rapids, 1982-85, sr. account rep., Detroit, 1985-89, regional sales mgr. S.E. Mich., 1989-93; v.p. mktg. TransContinental Traders, Ltd., Detroit, 1993—; mem. Ottawa County (Mich.) CETA Adv. Bd. Bd. dirs. Downtown Day Care Ctr., Grand Rapids, 1972. Recipient Cert. of Appreciation Bishop of Saigon, Vietnam, 1969; Top Sales rep. 3M/US, 1983, VIP, 1983, 84, 85, 86, 87, 88, 89; Phillip Morris scholar, 1975. Mem. Preservation Wayne, Detroit Internat. Vis. Coun. Mem. NAFE, Internat. Visitors Coun., Nat. Assn. Fgn. Students, Grand Rapids Coun. on World Affairs, Am. Soc. Pub. Adminstrn, Hist. Indian Village Assn. Republican. Home: 1060 Parker St Detroit MI 48214-2613 Office: Transcontinental Traders Ltd 1060 Parker St Ste 100 Detroit MI 48214-2613

DEHART, KAREN TRAUTMANN, artist, educator; b. Pitts., Nov. 11, 1953; d. Elmer Martin and Jane Anne (Hesse) T.; m. Shannon Dean DeHart, May 23, 1976; children: Allison Anne, Rebekah Ellen, Rachel Elisabeth. AA, Miami U., 1975; BFA summa cum laude, Wright State U., 1991. Art instr. Troy-Hayner Cultural Ctr., Troy, Ohio, 1991-94; artist Troy, Ohio, 1990—, art tchr., 1991—; drawing tchr. Troy Christian Schs., Troy, Ohio, 1991-92; teaching asst. Wright State Univ., Dayton, Ohio, 1993; exhibition comm. Troy-Hayner Cultural Ctr., 1991—; chmn. Through Our Eyes Exhibit, 1993-95; adj. instr. Wright State U., 1996. One woman exhbns. include Preble County Fine Arts Ctr., Eaton, Ohio, 1994, The Crandall Gallery Mount Union Coll., Alliance, Ohio, 1995; exhibited in group shows at Bowery Gallery, N.Y., 1992, Butler Inst., 1994, Trumbull Art Gallery, 1994, Dayton Visual Arts Ctr., 1992, Mus. of Contemporary Art, Wright State U., 1991, Dayton Visual Arts Ctr., 1992, Butler Inst. Am. Art, 1993, 94, 95, Pearl Conard Gallery, 1993, 94, Rosewood Art Ctr. Gallery, Kettering, Ohio, 1993, Olin Fine Arts Ctr. Gallery, Washington and Jeffrson Coll., Washington, Pa., 1994, Books & Co., Kettering, Ohio, 1994, Fine Arts Inst. San Bernardino County Mus., Redlands, Calif., 1994, Evansville (Ind.) Mus. Arts and Sci., 1994, Wichita (Kans.) Ctr. Arts, 1994, Stables Art Gallery, Taos, N. Mex., 1995; featured in Nexus Mag., 1990, Art Duck, 1989-91, Dayton Daily News, 1992, Alliance Review, 1995. Com. mem. Troy C. of C., 1993; ad hoc mem. Troy-Hayner Cultural Ctr., 1992, chamn. photography exhibit, 1993-95, chmn. sister-city art exchange Troy-Takahashi City, Japan, 1995-96, mem. exhib. com., 1991-96; curriculum com. Troy Christian Schs., 1992-94. Recipient Grumbacher Gold medallion 26th Nat. Painting Show, 1994, Winsor Newton award Fine Arts Inst., 1994, Evansville Mus. Contemporaries Purchase award, 1994, Jurors Choice award Butler Inst. Am. Art, 1994, Best of Show award Rosewood Art Ctr., 1992, Award of Excellence Edison State C.C., 1989; Spl. Talent scholar Wright State U., 1989-91. Mem. Dayton Visual Arts Ctr., Phi Kappa Phi, Chi Omega. Home: 1498 Cheshire Rd Troy OH 45373 Office: Karen Trautmann DeHart Studio 1144 Swailes Rd Troy OH 45373

DEHN, VIRGINIA, visual artist; b. Nevada, Mo.; d. Finis Ewing and Ruby Grayson (Lane) Engleman; m. Adolf Arthur Dehn, Nov. 12, 1947 (dec. May 1968). AA, Stephens Coll., 1941; student, Traphagen Sch Design, 1941-42, Art Students League, N.Y.C., 1953, 54. One-woman shows include Caravan Galleries, N.Y.C., 1974, Discovery Gallery, Montclair, N.J., 1977, Capicorn Gallery, Bethesda, Md., 1979, Washington Coll., Chestertown, Md., 1983, Carlin Gallery, Ft. Worth, Susan Teller Gallery, N.Y.C., 1989, Mus. Fine Arts, Santa Fe, N.Mex., 1995, Horwitch-Lew Allen Gallery, 1996, Richmond Art Ctr., Windsor, Conn., 1996; group shows include Fine Arts Am., Gallery, Richmond, Va., 1983, Hick St. Gallery, Bklyn., others; represented in permanent collections Herbert F. Johnson Mus., Ithaca, N.Y., Columbus Mus. Art, Ohio, Butler Inst. Am. Art, Youngstown, Ohio, U. Calif. Berkeley, Castellon Meml. Collection, Columbia U., N.Y.C., N.Y. Pub. Libr., N.Y.C., State of Minn. Hist. Soc., Vivian and Gordon Gilkey Graphic Art Collection, Portland Art Mus., Oreg., AmerWest Fin. Ctr., Albuquerque, Springfield (Mass.) Mus. Fine Art, Albuquerque Internat. Airport, others. MacDowell Colony fellow, Yaddo fellow, Ossabaw Island Project fellow. Mem. Soc. Layerists in Multi-Media (a founder). Home: 524 Camino Militar Santa Fe NM 87501

DE HOYOS, DEBORA M., lawyer; b. Monticello, N.Y., Aug. 10, 1953; d. Luis and Marion (Kinney) de H.; m. Walter C. Carlson, June 20, 1981; children: Amanda, Greta, Linnea. BA, Wellesley Coll., 1975; JD, Harvard U., 1978. Bar: Ill. 1978, U.S. Dist. Ct. (no. dist.) Ill. 1980. Assoc. Mayer, Brown & Platt, Chgo., 1978-84, ptnr., 1985—, mng. ptnr., 1991—; bd. dirs. Am. Paging, Inc., Evanston Hosp. Corp., Providence St. Mel. Sch. Contbr. chpt. to Securitization of Financial Assets, 1991. Chmn. strategic issues com. Econ. Devel. Commn., Chgo., 1992; bd. mgrs. YMCA of Met. Chgo.; asst. Chancellor The Episcopal Diocese of Chgo. Bd. dirs. Chicagoland C. of C. Office: Mayer Brown & Platt 190 S La Salle St Chicago IL 60603-3410*

DEIDAN, CECILIA THERESA, neuropsychologist; b. N.Y.C., Oct. 24, 1964. BA Biology, Spanish, Psychology, St. Louis U., 1985; MEd in Counseling Psychology, U. Mo., 1987, PhD in Counseling Psychology, 1992. Lic. psychologist, Fla., sch. psychol. examiner, Mo. Counselor, detoxification asst. McCambridge Ctr. for Women, Columbia, Mo., 1986-88; shc. psychol. examiner Columbia Pub. Schs., 1988-90; geriatric neuropsychology postdoctoral fellow U. Miami Sch. Med., 1992-93; pvt. practice Pembroke Pines, Fla., 1993—; adj. prof. Fla. Internat. U., Miami, 1993—. Mem. ACA, NAN, APA, Kappa Delta Pi, Psi Chi, Sigma Delta Pi, Alpha Sigma Nu, Beta Beta Beta.

DEIOTTE, MARGARET WILLIAMS TUKEY, nonprofit consultant, grants writer; b. Lafayette, Ind., Mar. 6, 1952; d. Ronald B. and Elizabeth A. (Williams) Tukey; m. Charles E. Deiotte, Sept. 11, 1971; children: Raymond, Karl, Ronald. Student, U. Wash., 1969-72, 77-79. V.p., treas. Logical Systems, Inc., Colorado Springs, 1982-86; v.p. CEDSYS, Inc., Colorado Springs, 1987-92; pres. Penrose Enrichment Program Found., Colorado Springs, Colo., 1988-89; free lance tech. and grant proposal writer, 1990—; dir. Rexall Showcase Internat., Boca Raton, Fla., 1994—; conf. coord. Colo. Assn. Ptnrs. in Edn., 1994; editor Am. Boarding Kennels Assn., 1995—; presenter seminar Pikes Peace Pace Conf., 1991, 92. Mem. adv. bd. gifted and talented Sch. Dist. 11, 1989—, mem. grant writing team; pres. Penrose Elem. PTA, 1989-91; 1st v.p. El Paso Coun. PTA, 1990-91, treas., 1991-92; mem. grants commn. Colo. State PTA, 1990-91; coach Odyssey of the Mind, 1990, 91-92, 95-96; bd. dirs. YMCA Youth Leadership Inst., 1990-92, 92-93; mem. dist. accountability com. Sch. Dist. 38, 1993-94; bd. dirs. Sch. Dist. 38 Found., 1994-95; accountability chmn. Lewis-Palmer Mid. Sch.; mem. gifted and talented com. Sch. Dist. # 38; mem. parent bd., internat. baccalaureate Palmer High Sch., Colorado Springs, Colo., 1994—, treas., 1995-96. Home and Office: 1915 E Van Buren # 9 Colorado Springs CO 80909

DEISSLER, MARY A., foundation executive; b. Oneanta, N.Y., Dec. 30, 1955; d. George W. and Carol (Zorda) Baker; m. James N. Deissler, Nov. 24, 1987; children: Benjamin, Eliza. BA, U. Mass., 1978; MBA, Babson Coll., 1982. Fin. analyst Digital Equipment Corporation, Maynard, Mass., 1978-82; devel. dir. Handel & Haydn Soc., Boston, 1984-89, gen. mgr., 1984-89, exec. dir., 1990—; pres., bd. dirs. Studebaker Movement Theatre Co., Boston, 1986-88. Bd. dirs. Early Music Am., N.Y.C., 1989—, v.p., 1991—, pres., 1994; bd. dirs. Babson Coll., 1990-94, Chorus Am., 1991—, v.p., 1992; mem. adv. bd. Arts/Boston, 1994—, assoc. bd. dirs.; bd. dirs. Boston Ptnrs. in Edn.; sec. Handel House of Am. Found. Mem. Am. Symphony Orch. League. Office: Handel & Haydn Soc 300 Massachusetts Ave Boston MA 02115-4544

DEITMAN, THERESA MCGOWAN, medical administrator, nurse; b. Scranton, Pa., Feb. 8, 1950; d. Robert Bell and Agnes (Butler) McGowan; 1 child, Jennifer Emilie Nicole Drescher. Diploma in nursing, Hosp. U. Pa., Phila., 1970. Cert. R.N., Case Mgr. Staff nurse, asst. head nurse Riddle Meml. Hosp., Media, Pa., 1971-80; rehab. nurse, mgr. Upjohn Rehab. Scvs., Phila. and Cin., 1980-85; cons., life care planner Occupl. Health Resources, Cin., 1985-87, Springfield, Va., 1987-88; dir. life care planning Rehab. Experts, Vienna, Va., 1988-89; program mgr., account exec. Comprehensive Rehab. Assocs., Cin., 1989-93; dir. managed care case mgmt. Sheakley Med. Mgmt. Sys., Cin., 1993-95; clin. program coord. Mayfield Clinic and Spine Inst., Cin., 1996—; mem. cmty. adv. bd. Rehab. Inst. of Ohio Miami Valley Hosp., Dayton, Ohio, 1987-93, Integra Group Profl. Adv. Bd. Com., Cin., 1996—. Mem. Assn. Rehab. Nurses, Individual Case Mgmt. Assn. Office: Mayfield Spine Inst 506 Oak St Cincinnati OH 45219-3701

DEITZ, PAULA, magazine editor; b. Trenton, N.J., Apr. 26, 1938; d. David and Rosalie (Nathanson) D.; m. (George) Frederick Morgan, Nov. 30, 1969. BA, Smith Coll., 1959; MA, Columbia U., 1969. Asst. editor Bollingen series Bollingen Found., N.Y.C., 1962-67; assoc. editor The Hudson Rev., N.Y.C., 1967-75, co-editor, 1975—; rsch. asst. Pakistan Mission to UN, N.Y.C., 1961; lectr. Columbia U., N.Y.C., 1962. Contbr. articles on art, architecture, landscape design to newspapers and mags. Bd. counselors Smith Coll., 1992-96. Mem. Cosmopolitan Club. Office: The Hudson Rev 684 Park Ave New York NY 10021-5043

DEITZ, SUSAN ROSE, newspaper advice columnist; b. Far Rockaway, N.Y., Mar. 21, 1934; d. Emanuel and Florence Jean (Goodstein) Davis; m. Morris J. Mandelker, Nov. 29, 1975; 1 son, Scott Richard; m. Richard Alan Deitz, Dec. 22, 1958 (dec. 1967). Student Smith Coll., Barnard Coll., N.Y.C., Art Students League, N.Y.C., Stella Adler Theater Studio. Syndicated advice columnist L.A. Times Syndicate, 1975—; mem. faculty New Sch., N.Y.C., 1977-79; radio personality, 1979; columnist Prodigy Svcs., White Plains, N.Y., 1987-93; speaker satellite conf. NAFE, 1990. Author: (novel) Valency Girl, 1976, Single File, 1989, paperback edit., 1990. Mem. Women in Communications (Outstanding Mem. award 1984), Authors Guild, Newspaper Features Assn., Overseas Press Club (elect), Smith Coll. Club.

DEITZ, TRINA ANNE, physical therapist; b. Albany, N.Y., Sept. 25, 1968; d. William J. and Lorinda P. Deitz. BS summa cum laude, Springfield (Mass.) Coll., 1990, MSPT, 1991. Phys. therapist in-patient Baystate Med. Ctr., Springfield, 1991-93, phys. therapist level III workers compensation coord., 1993-95; phys. therapist clin. supr. Baystate Rehab. in South Hadley, Mass., 1996—. Home: 35 Craig Dr N-3 West Springfield MA 01089

DEJARDIN, FIONA MARY, art historian, educator; b. Glasgow, Scotland, Mar. 22, 1947; d. L.A.E. and Constance Lorna (Musk) D.; m. Stanley Shrodo, July 1, 1967 (div.); children: Adrian, Matthew, Neil; m. Terry L.H. Slade, Apr. 25, 1987. BA in Art History, Douglass Coll., 1981; MA in Art History, U. Del., 1986, PhD in Art History, 1993. Curator Hartwick Coll., Oneonta, N.Y., 1985-90, asst. prof., 1985-95, assoc. prof., 1995—; mem. adv. bd. Upper Catskill Cmty. Coun. on Arts, Oneonta, 1988-90. Author catalogues. Luce grantee U. Del., 1989, Cole Travel grantee, 1990. Mem. AAUW, Am. Assn. Mus., Coll. Art Assn., Cooperstown Art Assn. (bd. dirs. 1994—), Gallery 53. Office: Hartwick Coll Art Dept Oneonta NY 13820

DEJEAN, ISABELLE, educator; b. Oullins, France, May 21, 1967; came to U.S., 1988; d. Alain Patrick and Nicole Michele (Perret) D. Deug culture and comm., U. Lyon, 1987. Cert. CPR. Libr. asst. Atochem, Pierre Benite, France, 1985, mailroom asst., 1986, acct. asst., 1987; au pair Tsoucalas Family, Alexandria, Va., 1988-89; waitress Pizza Hut, London, 1989; receptionist Share Tel Apts., Venice, Calif., 1990-92, sch. tchr., 1992—. Contbr. L.A. Planned Parenthood, 1995-96. Mem. ACLU, Libr. of Congress, Smithsonian Inst., Sierra Club. Office: Ecole Clairefontaine 226 Westminster Ave Venice CA 90291

DEJESUS-BURGOS, SYLVIA TERESA, information systems specialist; b. Rio Piedras, P.R., Puerto Rico, Jan. 13, 1941; came to U.S., 1961; d. Luis deJesus Correa and Maria Teresa (Burgos) deJesus. BA, Cen. U., Madrid, 1961. Sr. systems analyst H.D. Hudson Mfg. Co., Chgo., 1974-76; mgr. software engring. Morton Thiokol, Chgo., 1976-87; prodn. and dist. systems mgr. Kraft Gen. Foods divsn. Phillip Morris, Glenview, Ill., 1987-94; mgr. systems and client svcs. Union Carbide Corp., 1994—. Editor U. Minn. Mgmt. Info. Systems Jour., 1984—. Pres. Chgo. chpt. Nat. Conf. Puerto Rican Women, 1980-83, nat. v.p. 1981-82; bd. dirs. Midwest Women's Ctr., 1980-82, YWCA, Chgo., 1982-84, Gateway Found. Substance Abuse Prevention and Rehab., 1986-87; v.p. communications Hispanic Alliance for Career Enhancements, 1986-87, bd. dirs. 1982-84, 91-92, chmn. bd., 1991-93; 1st v.p. Campfire Met. Chgo., 1982, bd. dirs. 1980-82; appointed to Selective Svc. Bd. by Ill. Gov. James Thompson, 1982; alt. del. Dem. Nat. Conv., N.Y.C., 1980; rep. Women in Mil. Svc. for Am. Meml., 1990-92. Served with USN, 1961-64. Recipient Youth Motivation award Chgo. Assn. Commerce and Industry, 1978-82, 86, YWCA Leadership award, 1980, 84, H.L. Kroft Achievement award, 1994. Mem. Women in Computing, Info. Systems Planners Assn., Navy League, Am. Legion. Republican. Roman Catholic. Office: Union Carbide 1300 Hercules Dr Houston TX 77058 Address: 16835 Middle Forest Dr Houston TX 77059-4033

DE JONG-HAWLEY, CHERIE, reading and language arts educator; b. Boise, Idaho, Dec. 19, 1947; d. Jack McCartney Marley and Marilyn (Carlock) Cunningham; 1 child, Brienne. BS, San Diego State U., 1971; MA, U. Calif., Santa Barbara, 1979, PhD, 1989. Supr. tchr. edn. reading clinic U. Calif., Santa Barbara, 1982-88; asst. prof. Calif. State U., L.A., 1989-95, assoc. prof., 1995—, dir. Reading/Lang. Arts Clinic, 1989—. Contbr. articles to profl. jours. Bd. dirs. So. Calif. chpt., Reading is Fundamental, L.A., 1990—. Mem. ASCD, Internat. Reading Assn., Am. Ednl. Rsch. Assn., Calif. Reading Assn. (pres. Santa Barbara chpt. 1986-89), Kappa Delta Pi (counselor Iota Phi chpt. 1992—). Home: 401 Deep Hill Rd Diamond Bar CA 91765 Office: Calif State U LA Sch Edn 5151 State University Dr Los Angeles CA 90032

DEJOY, NANCY CECILE, English language educator; b. Rochester, N.Y., Jan. 15, 1958; d. Robert William and Cecilia Patricia (Bonjorno) DeJ. BA, Nazareth Coll., 1987; MA, Purdue U., 1989, PhD, 1992. Prof. English Nazareth Coll., Rochester, N.Y., 1992-96, Millikin U., Decatur, Ill., 1996—; dir. writing programs Nazareth Coll., Rochester, 1995-96, dir. Summer Seminar in Rhetoric and Composition, Rochester, 1993—. Rev. editor: Rhetorical Grammar, 1994, The Writer's Brief Handbook, 1994; reader (jour.) Cultural Studies, 1994; contbr. articles to profl. jours. Acad. Achievement grantee Purdue U., 1991, summer rsch. grantee Nazareth Coll., 1992, 93, 94. Mem. MLA, NOW, Nat. Coun. Tchrs. English. Office: Millikin Univ Decatur IL 62522

DE KANTER, ELLEN ANN, English language professional, educator; b. Spokane, Wash., Mar. 10, 1926; d. George L. and Alison P. (Christy) Tharp; m. Scipio de Kanter, Feb. 2, 1949 (dec.); children: Scipio, Georgette, Robert, Adriana. BA, Mexico City Coll.-U. of Ams., 1947; MEd, U. Houston, 1972, MA in Spanish, 1974, EdD, 1979. Dir. bilingual edn., prof. U. St. Thomas, Houston, dir. bilingual edn., 1979—. Contbr. articles to profl. jours. Title VII grantee, 1986-89, 88-91, 89-92, 92-93, 92-95, 94-97, 95-98. Mem. Nat. Assn. Bilingual Edn. (chmn. 1989 conf., program chair 1993 conf.), Houston Area Assn. Bilingual Edn. (pres. 1987-88), Inst. Hispanic Culture (bd. dirs. 1989-90). Home: 3015 Meadowview Dr Missouri City TX 77459-3308 Office: U St Thomas 3800 Montrose Blvd Houston TX 77006-4626

DE LA BANDERA, ELNA MARIE, interpreter, translator; b. Rahway, N.J., Apr. 30, 1936; d. Laertes Gardner and Clara (Hansen) Fortenbaugh; m. Jorge Luis de la Bandera, Dec. 13, 1963; children: Jorge Luis Jr., Cristina Renee. BA in Spanish with honors, Colby Coll., 1958; MA in Spanish translation, Rutgers U., 1991. Cert. Spanish interpreter U.S. Cts., 1987; accredited translator Am. Translators Assn. Spanish-English, 1987, English-Spanish, 1988. Sec., translator U.S. Fgn. Svc., Argentina, Uruguay, 1959-63; translator Inter-Am. Coun. Commerce and Prodn., Montevideo, Uruguay, 1966-67; freelance interpreter, translator U.S. and Peru, 1968-86; sr. editor Princeton (N.J.) Internat. Translations, 1980-83; sec. Wysoker, Glassner & Weingartner, New Brunswick, N.J., 1984-86; translator, interpreter, test adminstr. N.J. Judiciary, Trenton, 1986—; mem. temp. faculty Rutgers U., New Brunswick, 1986, 91; cons., coord. interpreting svcs. State of Mass., 1988; cons. on ct. interpreter cert. State of Wash., 1990; oral examiner Fed. Ct. Interpreter Cert. Project, 1989, 93; cons. Nat. Ctr. for State Cts., 1994, 95. Mem. Nat. Assn. Judiciary Interpreters and Translators, Am. Translators Assn., Phi Sigma Iota, Alpha Delta Pi. Republican. Presbyterian. Home: 103 Fairway Blvd Jamesburg NJ 08831-2716 Office: Adminstrv Office of Cts Cn # 988 Trenton NJ 08625

DE LAGUNA, FREDERICA, anthropology educator emeritus, author, consultant; b. Ann Arbor, Mich., Oct. 3, 1906; d. Theodore and Grace Mead (Andrus) de L. A.B., Bryn Mawr Coll., 1927; Ph.D., Columbia U., 1933; L.H.D. (hon.), U. Alaska, 1982. Asst., field dir. U. Pa. Mus., Phila., 1931-35; assoc. soil conservationist U.S. Soil Conservation Svc., 1936; lectr. anthropology Bryn Mawr (Pa.) Coll., 1938-41, asst. prof., 1941-42, 46-49, assoc. prof., 1949-55, prof. anthropology, 1955-75, prof. emeritus, 1975—; vis. lectr. or vis. prof. U. Pa., U. Calif.-Berkeley, Bryn Mawr Coll. Author: The Thousand March: Adventures of an American Boy with Garibaldi, 1930, The Archaeology of Cook Inlet, Alaska, 1934, reprinted, 1975, The Arrow Points to Murder, 1937, Fog on the Mountain, 1938, reprinted 1995; (with Kaj Birket-Smith) The Eyak Indians of the Copper River Delta, Alaska, 1938, Prehistory of Northern America as Seen From the Yukon, 1947, Chugach Prehistory: The Archaeology of Prince William Sound, 1956, reprinted 1967, The Story of a Tlingit Community, 1960; (with others) The Archeology of the Yakutat Bay Area, Alaska, 1964, Under Mount Saint Elias, 3 vols., 1972, Voyage to Greenland: A Personal Initiation into Anthropology, 1977, reprinted, 1995, Tales from the Dena, 1995; editor: Selected Papers from the American Anthropologist 1888-1920, 1960, reprinted 1976, The Tlingit Indians (George Thornton Emmons), 1991. Recipient Lindback award for Disting. Teaching, Bryn Mawr Coll., 1975, Rochester Mus. award and fellowship, 1941, numerous fellowships including: Columbia U., 1930-31, NRC, 1936-37, Rockefeller Found., 1945-46, Wenner-Gren Found., 1949-50, Social Sci. Research Council, 1962-63; grantee Am. Philos. Soc., Arctic Inst. of N.Am., Bryn Mawr Coll., NEH, NSF, U. Pa. Mus., Wenner-Gren Found. for Anthrop. Rsch. Fellow AAAS, Am. Anthrop. Assn. (pres. 1966-67, Disting. Svc. award 1986), Arctic Inst. N.Am. (hon. life); mem. NAS, Soc. for Am. Archaeology (1st v.p. 1949-50, 50th Ann. award 1986), No. Studies Assn. (internat. secretariat, hon. pres. 1991—), Phila. Anthropology Soc. (pres. 1939-40), Alaska Anthrop. Assn. (hon. life, award for lifetime contbn. to Alaskan anthropology 1993), Homer (Alaska) Natural History Soc. (hon. life, Silver Trowel award), Before Columbus Found. (Am. Lifetime Book award 1995). Democrat. Home and Office: 3300 Darby Rd # 1310 Haverford PA 19041-1067

DELAHANTY, REBECCA ANN, school system administrator; b. South Bend, Ind., Oct. 18, 1941; d. Raymond F. and Ann Marie (Batsleer) Paczesny; m. Edward Delahanty, June 22, 1963; children: David, Debbie. BA, Coll. of St. Catherine, Minn., 1977; MA, Coll. St. Thomas, Minn., 1983; PhD, Ga. State U., 1994. Cert. in adminstrn. and supervision, Ga. Initiator, tchr. gifted kindergarten Dist. 284 Sch., Wayzata, Minn., 1977-83; gifted kindergarten coord. St. Barts Sch., Wayzata, 1983-85; prin. Dabbs Loomis Sch., Dunwoody, Ga., 1987-91; asst. to supt. Buford (Ga.) City Schs., 1993—; mem. staff devel. adv. coun. Ga. Contbr. article to profl. publ. Mem. ASCD, Am. Ednl. Rsch. Assn., Nat. Assn. Gifted Children, Minn. Coun. Gifted and Talented, Phi Delta Kappa, Omicron Gamma.

DELAHAY, ANNETTE MARIA, advertising executive; b. Sulphur, Okla., July 20, 1950; d. Joseph Jeremiah and Maxine L. (Folsom) Stancampiano; married; children: Jessica Linn, David Meloy, Jr., Daniel McKee, Olivia Ashley. Student, Cen. State U., Edmond, Okla. Corp. pilot Redman Pipe & Supply, Tulsa, Okla., 1984-86; restaurant owner Delahays, Collinsville, Okla., 1984-85; corp. pilot Phillips Petroleum Co., Bartlesville, Okla., 1987-91; campaign mgr. State Sen. Jerry Pierce, Bartlesville, 1991-92; radio personality, sales KWON, Bartlesville, 1991-92; sales/conf. planner Marriott Mgmt., Bartlesville, 1992-94; ad exec. Donrey Media Group, Bartlesville, 1994—. Prodr., host TV show, 1995-96. Dir. concessions, fundraising, Am. Legion Baseball, Bartlesville, 1989-92. Mem. Nat. Bi-Plane Assn. (dir. hospitality 1992-96). Roman Catholic.

DELAINE, PATRICIA BARNES, social studies, reading and science educator; b. Birmingham, Ala., Feb. 5, 1954; d. Stanley Sr. and Nettie (Wilbur) Barnes; children: Rickey DeJuan, Asya Patrice. BA, Ala. A&M U., 1976; Cert., U. Ala., Birmingham, 1978. Cert. history and polit. sci. tchr., Ala. Tchr. St. Mary's Cath. Sch., Fairfield, Ala., 1980-95, Birmingham City Sch., 1995—; advisor Scholar's Bowl; sch. historian. Recipient grant U. Ala., Huntsville, 1993, grant U. Montevello, 1993. Mem. NEA, Nat. Coun. Social Studies. Baptist. Home: 1225 Wycliffe Rd Birmingham AL 35228 Office: St Marys Sch 6124 Myron Massey Blvd Fairfield AL 35064-2529

DELANEY, CINDY M., controller; b. Stockton, Calif., Dec. 1, 1964; d. Nathan Cameron Doyel and Charlotte Blanche (Epler) Gezi; m. Michael Paul Delaney, July 16, 1994; children: Lisa, Nichole, Kelly. Student, Calif. State U., Sacramento, 1982-83; AA, MTI Bus. Coll., Sacramento, 1984. Supr. mini storage All Am. Mini Storage, Sacramento, 1988-89; asst. contr. Longview Devel. Corp., Sacramento, 1989-90; mng. contr. The Royce Cos., Roseville, Calif., 1990-93; contr. Calif. Comml., Sacramento, 1993-95; gen. ptnr., operator Sierra Micro, Fair Oaks, Calif., 1995—. Mem. NOW, NAFE, Nat. Abortion and Reproductive Right Action League. Presbyterian. Office: Sierra Micro 8125 Sunset Ave Ste 101 Fair Oaks CA 95628

DELANEY, JANE ELLEN, elementary education educator; b. Chgo., Oct. 7, 1946; d. Francis Xavier and Eileen (Collins) O'Connell; m. Michael Dennis Delaney; children: Collin, Devin. BA, Marian Coll., Fond du Lac, Wis., 1968; MEd in Pub. Policy, U. Ill., Chgo., 1978, postgrad. Tchr./jr. h.s. coord. St. Benedict Sch./H.S., Chgo., 1974-78; analyst Mayor's Office of Budget and Mgmt., Chgo., 1978-80; budget dir. Chgo. Fire Dept., 1980, CFO, 1980-82; instr. Gymboree, Lafayette, Calif., 1985, Diablo Valley Montessori, Lafayette, 1985-88; project coord. Family Learning Ctrs./Project Head Start Chgo. United et al, 1992-93; tchr. St. John of the Cross, Western Springs, Ill., 1993—; trea. Diablo Valley Montessori Sch., 1983-85. Contbr. to edn. manual Family Learning Centers/Head Start, 1994. Mem. Irish Fellowship Club, Chgo., 1990—. Recipient Merit award disaster svc. ARC, Fond du Lac, 1970, Founder Day award for pub. svc. Marian Coll., 1994. Mem. ASCD, Nat. Coun. Tchrs. English, Ill. Club for Cath. Women, Phi Delta Kappa. Home: 603 E 1st St Hinsdale IL 60521-4702

DELANEY, JEAN MARIE, art educator; b. Jersey City, Nov. 14, 1931; d. John Francis and Genevieve Mary (Boulton) Reilly; m. Donald Kendall Delaney, Dec. 29, 1956; 1 child, Laura Marie. BA in Art Edn., Fairmont (W.Va.) State U., 1954; MA in Clin. Psychology, Loyola Coll., Balt., 1979; PhD in Art Edn., U. Wis., Milw., 1992. Cert. art tchr., prin., supr., Md. Tchr. English and social studies Reedurban Sch., Stark County, Ohio, 1954-56; art tchr. Perry Hall High Sch., Stark County, 1956-57, Margaret Brent High Sch., St. Mary's County, Md., 1957-59, Middle River Mid. Sch., Baltimore County, Md., 1959-62; home and hosp. tchr. Harford County (Md.) Bd. Edn., 1968-78; lectr. art appreciation U. Md. Extension, Harford County, 1971-76; art educator Baltimore County Bd. Edn., 1979-93; assoc. prof. art edn. S.W. Mo. State U., Springfield, 1993—; cons. Salisbury (Md.) State Coll., 1987; adj. prof. art edn. Md. Inst. Coll. Art, Balt., 1988-89; cons. bd. examiners and art edn. Nat. Tchr.'s Exam. test devel. com. ETS, Princeton, N.J., 1988-92. Author: Art Image, 6th Grade Units, 1988; editor: Art Scholarships, 1988; editor videotape Ernest Goldstein: Art Criticism, 1987; author, editor curriculum guide. Recipient Youth Art Month award of excellence Art and Craft Materials Inst., 1989, grant to coordinate Crayola Dreammakers program for Ctrl. Region U.S. and Can., 1994-96. Mem. Nat. Art Edn. Assn. (Eastern Region Art Educator award of yr, 1989, Nat. Secondary Art Educator award of yr. 1990), Md. Art Edn. Assn. (state coun. 1985—, v.p. arts advocacy 1988-89, pres.-elect 1992—, Md. Art Educator of Yr. 1988), Internat. Soc. for Edn. Through Art. Home: 634 S National Ave Apt 402 Springfield MO 65804-0065 Office: Southwest Missouri State U 901 S National Ave Springfield MO 65804-0027

DELANEY, KIM, actress; b. Phila., Nov. 29, 1961; 1 child, Jack. Appeared in (TV series) All My Children, 1981-84, 94, Tour of Duty, 1987, The Fifth Corner, 1992, NYPD Blue, 1995—, (TV movies) First Affair, 1983, Perry Mason: The Case of the Sinister Spirit, 1987, Cracked Up, 1987, Christmas Comes to Willow Creek, 1987, All My Darling Daughters, Please Take My Daughters, 1988, Something Is Out There, 1988, The Broken Cord, 1992, Lady Boss, 1992, Closer and Closer, The Disappearance of Christina, 1993, Tall, Dark, and Deadly, 1995, (films) That Was Then...This Is Now, 1985, The Delta Force, 1986, Hunter's Blood, 1987, Campus Man, 1987, The Drifter, 1988, Hangfire, 1991, Body Parts, 1991, The Force, 1994, Inferno, Darkman II: The Return of Durant, 1994, Dark Goddess, 1994, Serial Killer, 1995, Project: Metalbeast, 1995. Office: care The Gersh Agy 272 N Cannon Dr Beverly Hills CA 90210*

DELANEY, MARY ANNE, pastoral educator; b. Waltham, Mass., Feb. 15, 1926; d. Thomas Joseph and Mary Teresa (Berry) D. BA, Regis Coll., 1953; MEd, U. Mass., Boston, 1973; MDiv, Andover Newton Theol. Sch., Newton Ctr., Mass., 1978. Tchr. various primary schs., Mass., 1953-73; pastoral counselor Boston City Hosp., 1974-76; dir. pastoral care Cape Breton Hosp., Sydney River, N.S., Can., 1978-81, Nova Scotia Hosp., Dartmouth, 1981-86, Misericordia Hosp., Edmonton, Alta., Can., 1986-91; pastoral counselor Assn. Pastoral Edn., Waltham, Mass., 1992-96, Emmanuel Coll., Boston, 1996—; vice chair bioethics consultative svc. Misericordia Hosp., Edmonton, 1987-91; vis. scholar Andover Newton Theol. Sch., 1991-92. Trustee Inst. Pastoral Tng., Halifax, N.S., Can., 1981-86; mem. commn. on ecumenism Archdiocese of Halifax, 1982-86; pastoral counselor Cong. of Sisters of St. Joseph, Boston, 1945-96. Mem. Can. Assn. Pastoral Edn. (cert., cert. com. 1987-91), Assn. for Clin. Pastoral Edn. (accreditation com. 1993-96, cert. supr.). Roman Catholic. Home: 16 Cutter St Waltham MA 02154

DELANEY, NANCY JO, statistician, consultant; b. Buffalo, N.Y., Sept. 15, 1941; d. Howard Joseph and Josephine Laura (Garguiolo) Klein; m. Thomas James Delaney; 1 child, Kathleen Grace Delaney. BS in Math., SUNY, 1962, MS in Math., 1963; MS in Stats., Rensselaer Poly. Inst., 1975, PhD in Stats., 1979. Math. tchr. various high schs. and jr. coll., Albany, Schenectady, N.Y., 1966-74; data analyst Space Astronomy Lab., Albany, 1974-76; asst. prof. Union Coll. Inst. Adminstrn. and Mgmt., Schenectady, 1978-82, Northeastern U. Coll. Bus., Boston, 1982-88; statis. advisor Mobil Solar Energy Corp., Billerica, Mass., 1988-92; asst. prof. Suffolk U., Sch. Mgmt., Boston, 1993-96; cons. Gen. Foods Inc., Tarrytown, N.Y., 1978, Sterling Drugs, Albany, 1981, Bard Cardiosurgery, Billerica, 1985-86, Design Tech., Billerica, 1993. Contbr. articles to profl. jours. Mem. Am. Soc. for Quality Control, Ops. Rsch. Soc. Am., Am. Statis. Assn. (Boston chpt., program chmn., 1984-85, treas. 1986-95), Epsilon Delta Sigma.

DELANY, DANA, actress; b. N.Y.C., Mar. 13, 1956. Student, Wesleyan U. Appeared in TV series Love of Life, 1979-80, As the World Turns, 1981, Magnum PI, 1986-88, Sweet Surrender, 1987, China Beach, 1988-91 (Emmy award for best actress in a drama series 1989, 92), Good Housekeeping, 1995, in TV films Threesome, 1984, Liberty, 1986, A Winner Never Quits, 1986, A Promise to Keep, 1990, The Enemy Within, 1994, Choices of the Heart: The Margaret Sanger Story, 1995, (miniseries) Wild Palms, 1993; in films The Fan, 1981, Almost You, 1984, Where the River Runs Black, 1986, Masquerade, 1988, Patty Hearst, 1988, Moon over Parador, 1988, Housesitter, 1992, Light Sleeper, 1992, Tombstone, 1993, Exit to Eden, 1994, Live Nude Girls, 1995; on Broadway in Translations, 1995. Office: Internat Creative Mgmt 8942 Wilshire Blvd Beverly Hills CA 90211-1934

DELAPA, JUDITH ANNE, business owner; b. Bad Axe, Mich., Feb. 1, 1938; d. John Vincent and Ellen Agatha (Peters) McCormick; m. James Patrick DeLapa, Jan. 10, 1959; children: Joseph Anthony, James P. II, John M., Gina M. BS, Mich. State U., 1959, MA, 1985. Tchr. various schs., Mich., 1959-64; co-founder Saluto Foods Corp., Benton Harbor, Mich.,

1963-76; founder Earthtone Interiors, St. Joseph, Mich., 1977-82, High Impact Mktg. Svcs., Grand Rapids, Mich., 1987—; mktg. cons., writer various clients, nationwide. Author: High-Impact Business Strategies, 1993. Bd. dirs. Econ. Club Grand Rapids, Grand Rapids Symphony Orch. Judith A. DeLapa Perennial Garden named in her honor Michigan State U. Office: High Impact Mktg Svcs 2505 E Paris Ave SE Grand Rapids MI 49546-6100

DELAURENTIS, LOUISE BUDDE, author; b. Stafford, Kans., Oct. 5, 1920; d. Louis and Mary (Lichte) Budde; m. Mariano Anthony DeLaurentis, Mar. 26, 1948 (dec. Oct. 1991); 1 child, Delbert Louis. BA, Ottawa (Kans.) U., 1942. Airport traffic contr. FAA, various cities, 1943-55. Author: Etta Chipmunk, 1962, A Peculiarity of Direction, 1975, Traveling to the Goddess, 1994; editor: Gentle Sorcery by Bessie Jeffery, 1972; author more than 300 poems various periodicals; contbr. articles to profl. jours. Chairperson Tompkins County Liberal Party, Ithaca, N.Y., 1969-72. Mem. LWV, AAUW, Writers Assn. of Ithaca Area (pres. 1964-65, co-editor anthology 1967, 95). Home: 983 Cayuga Heights Rd Ithaca NY 14850

DELAURO, ROSA L., congresswoman. Student, London Sch. Econs. & Polit. Sci., 1962-63; BA in History and Polit Sci. cum laude, Marymount Coll., 1964; MA in Internat. Politics, Columbia U., 1966. Tng. assoc. Community Progress Inc., New Haven, Conn., 1967-69; instr. in internat. rels. Albertus Magnus Coll., 1967-68; adminstrv. asst. Nat. Urban Fellows, 1969-72, asst. dir., dir., 1972-75; city coord. Carter-Mondale Presdl. Campaign, New Haven, 1976; exec. asst. Mayor Frank Logue, New Haven, 1976-77, campaign mgr., 1977; exec. asst., devel. adminstr. City of New Haven, 1977-79; campaign mgr. Chris Dodd for U.S. Senate, 1979-80, 86; adminstrv. asst. U.S. Senator Christopher J. Dodd, Washington, 1981-87; state dir. Mondale-Ferraro Presdl. Campaign, N.J., 1986; ptnr. DeLauro-Geller, 1987-88; regional dir. Dukakis for Pres. Campaign, N.Y., N.J., Con., 1988; exec. dir. EMILY's List, 1989; first elected to U.S. Ho. of Reps., 1990; mem. 102nd-104th Congresses 3rd Conn. dist., 1991—; mem. Ho. nat. security com.; del. to Dem. Nat. Conv., 1984; bd. dirs. Pax Ams. Past pres. New Haven Arts Coun. Assoc. fellow Timothy Dwight Coll., Yale U.; recipient Leadership award Am. Com. on Italian Migration. Mem. Nat. Italian-Am. Found., Dem. Women for Progress. Office: US House of Reps 436 Cannon Washington DC 20515*

DELBALZO, GAIL, general counsel; b. N.Y.C.; d. William and Alice (Boye) Millar; m. Vincent Del Balzo, Sept. 17, 1988; children: Joseph Vincent, Jeanne Francis. Student, SUNY, Oswego, 1973-75; BA, SUNY, Buffalo, 1977, JD, 1980. Bar: N.Y. 1981, D.C. 1981. Counsel U.S. Senate Com. Budget, 1981-82, sr. counsel, 1983-84; asst. U.S. Senate parliamentarian, 1984-88; assoc. gen. counsel Congl. Budget Office, Washington, 1989-92, gen. counsel, 1992—. Office: Congressional Budget Office Ford House Bldg Rm 408 Washington DC 20515

DEL DUCA, RITA, educator; b. N.Y.C., Apr. 1, 1933; d. Joseph and Ermelinda (Buonaguro) Ferraro; m. Joseph Anthony Del Duca, Oct. 29, 1955; children: Lynn, Susan, Paul, Andrea. BA, CUNY, 1955. Elem. tchr. Yonkers (N.Y.) Pub. Schs., 1955-57; tchr. kindergarten Sacred Heart Sch., Yonkers, 1962-64; tchr. piano, Scarsdale, N.Y., 1973-79; asst. office mgr. Foot Clinic, Hartsdale, N.Y., 1977-85; tchr. ESL, Linguarama Exec. Sch., White Plains, N.Y., 1985-89; ESL tutor, Scarsdale, 1989—. Dist. leader Greenburgh (N.Y.) Rep. Com., 1991-92. Home and Office: 6 Paradise Dr Scarsdale NY 10583-1522

DELEO, PHYLLIS C., academic administrator. BA in English summa cum laude, So. Conn. State Coll.; MA in English, U. Conn., PhD. Prof. English Teikyo Post U. (formerly Post Coll.), Waterbury, Conn.; chair Coll. Liberal Arts and Scis. Divsn. Teikyo Post U. (formerly Post Coll.), Waterbury, dean arts and scis., dean acad. affairs, v.p. acad. affairs, 1987-93, pres., 1993—; developed Rose Traurig Scholars Program, Teikyo Post U., Waterbury. Vol. United Way; trustee, mem. fin. and pers. com. Waterbury Hosp.; grad. Leadership Waterbury, 1987. Named Woman of the Yr., Am. Bus. Assn., 1985; recipient Leadership award YWCA, 1992, Cert. of Merit, ABWA, 1992, Bus. Women's Forum award, 1993, award for excellence in equity AAUW, 1993, Humanitarian award Boys' Town of Italy, 1993, New Haven Bus. Women's Leadership award, 1994. Office: Teikyo Post U 800 Country Club Rd Waterbury CT 06708-3200

DE LEON, LIDIA MARIA, magazine editor; b. Havana, Cuba, Sept. 10, 1957; d. Leon J. and Lydia (Diaz Cruz) de L. B.A. in Communications cum laude, U. Miami, Coral Gables, Fla., 1979. Staff writer Miami Herald, Fla., 1978-79; editorial asst. Halsey Pub. Co., Miami, 1980-81, assoc. editor, 1981, editor, 1981—, editor Delta Sky mag., 1983-95. Mem. Am. Soc. Mag. Editors, Am. Assn. Travel Editors, Golden Key, Sigma Delta Chi. Democrat. Roman Catholic.

DE LEON, SYLVIA A., lawyer; b. Corpus Christi, Tex., Mar. 2, 1950. BA, Briarcliff Coll., 1972; JD, U. Tex., 1976. Bar: Tex. 1976, D.C. 1977. Ptnr. Akin, Gump, Strauss, Hauer & Feld LLP, Washington; adj. prof. law Georgetown U. law ctr., 1988-90; bd. dirs. Amtrak, Nat. Railroad Passenger Corp., 1994—, chair long range strategic planning com. Bd. dirs. U. Tex. Law Assn., 1985-89, 92—; coord. issues transp. cluster group Clinton-Gore Presdl. Transition Team, 1992; commr. Nat. Commn. Ensure Strong Competitive Airline Industry, 1993. Mem. Bar Assn. D.C., State Bar Tex. (chmn. fed. law and regulations com. 1984-87). Office: Akin Gump Strauss Hauer & Feld Ste 400 1333 New Hampshire Ave NW Washington DC 20036-1511

DELESIO, ALICE BURCH, retired elementary education educator; b. Lyons, N.Y., Mar. 31, 1924; d. Charles Hulsaver and Elnora Carrie (Matthews) Burch; m. Dominic Anthony DeLesio, July 4, 1964. BS in Edn. cum laude, Buffalo State Tchrs. Coll., 1945; MA in English Edn., Syracuse U., 1954. Cert. tchr. grades 1-8, jr. h.s. Tchr. United Meth. and Vacation Bible Sch., Clyde, N.Y., 1944-45; tchr. 4th grade Silver Springs, N.Y., 1945-46; tchr. jr. h.s. Clyde-Savannah Sch., Clyde and Savannah, N.Y., 1946-71; election inspector Town of Galen, Clyde, 1974-77; judge, mem. honors selection com. Nat. Women's Hall of Fame, Seneca Falls, N.Y., 1993; sec. Mission Work Area, Clyde, 1980-96. Historian Village of Clyde and Town of Galen, 1974-77; co-organizer The Galen Hist. Soc., Clyde and Town of Galen, 1975-76; Sun. sch. tchr. Clyde United Meth. Ch., 1946-64. Mem. AAUW, N.Y. State Ret. Tchrs. Assn. (friendly svc. chair ctrl. we. zone 1972-96, v.p. 1970-74, state historian 1982-96, Cert. of Recognition 1990), Wayne County Ret. Tchrs. Assn. (friendly svc. chair 1973-96, historian 1990-96), Clyde C. of C. (Achievement award 1979), Nat. Trust for Historic Preservation, Wayne County Hist. Soc., Yorker Club (organizer, sponsor 1964-71), Order Eastern Star, Clyde Rebekah Lodge (sec. 1980-96, Decoration of Chivalry 1972), Delta Kappa Gamma (pres. 1974-76), Kappa Delta Pi. Democrat. Home: 94 Galen St Clyde NY 14433-1224

DELGADO, JANE, human services executive; b. Havana, Cuba, June 17, 1953; d. Juan Lorenzo Delgado Borges and Lucila Aurora Navarro Delgado; m. Herbert Lustig, Feb. 14, 1981. BA, SUNY, New Paltz, 1973; MA, NYU, 1975; MS, W. Averell Harrimann Sch., 1981; PhD, SUNY, Stony Brook, 1981. Children's talent coord. Children's TV Workshop, 1973-75; rsch. asst. SUNY, Stony Brook, 1975-79; social sci. analyst U.S. Dept. Health and Human Svcs., 1979-83, health policy advisor, 1983-85; pres., CEO COSSMHO, 1985—; pvt. practice in psychology, 1979—; bd. dirs. Nat. Health Coun., 1986—, Carter Ctr. Mental Health Taskforce, 1991—; trustee Found. Child Devel., 1989—. W.K. Kellogg Found. Nat. fellow, 1988, NIMH fellow, 1975-79; recipient Surgeon Gen.'s award, 1992; recipient Health & Sci. Latina Excellence award, 1995; named SUNY Alumna of Yr., 1993. Office: COSSMHO 1501 16th St NW Washington DC 20036-1401*

DELGADO, LISA JAMES, elementary education educator; b. Murfreesboro, Tenn., May 8, 1960; d. J. Butler and JoAnn Ireta (Griswold) James; m. Mark Crawford Delgado, June 28, 1986. BS in Art Edn., U. Ga., 1982, MEd in Edml. Media, 1984. Cert. media specialist, art tchr., Ga. Media specialist South Jackson Elem. Sch., Athens, Ga., 1984—; sch., system TOTY, 1994-95; mem. sch. coun., Athens, 1991-94, chairperson, 1992-93. Co-author: (1 chpt.) Blue Highways: Literacy Reform, School Change and the Creation of Learning Communities; contbr. articles to profl. jours. Mem. Ga. Libr. Media Assn., Profl. Assn. Ga. Educators. Office: South Jackson Elem Sch 8144 Jefferson Rd Athens GA 30607-3261

DE LISI, JOANNE, communications executive, educator; b. Bklyn.; d. Louis Anthony and Maria Anna (Ferrantelli) De L. BA, Hunter Coll., 1972, MA, 1977; postgrad., N.Y.U. Cert. tchr., N.Y. Asst. instr. Hunter Coll., N.Y.C., 1974-75; instr. N.Y.U., 1974-78; instr. Bklyn. Coll., 1978-82, dir. forensics, 1981-82, asst. dir. acad. prep. program, 1980-82; adjunct lctr. City U. System, N.Y.C., 1983-91; cons. communication N.Y.C., 1976—; Faculty advisor Alpha Tau Omega, Blkyn. Coll., 1980-82. Contbr. articles to profl. jours. Judge Am. Legion Forensics Tournament, Queens, 1979, 95; pub. rels. officer Queens County Am. Legion Aux., 1991-93, 2d v.p., 1993-94, pres., N.Y. state dept. delegation chmn. 1994-95; dir. pub. rels. and newsletter editor Leonard Unit Am. Legion Aux., Queens County, 1991-93, sec. 1993-94; pub. rels. dir., jr. acting chmn. Nat. Security Chmn. Glendale Unit Am. Legion Aux., 1995-96, pres. Glendale Unit, 1996—; nat. conv. ALA del., 1996. Recipient nat. award USO and POW/MIA Am. Legion Aux., 1996. Mem. Speech Communication Assn. (conf. chair info. com. 1980), Internat. Soc. Gen. Semantics, N.Y. St. Speech Assn., Nat. Assn. Female Execs., Kappa Delta Pi, Phi Delta Kappa, Phi Beta Honor Soc. (publicity coordinator 1978—). Roman Catholic. Clubs: Hunter Alumni Orgn., Fencers Am. Office: Wyckoff Heights Sta PO Box 370029 Brooklyn NY 11237-0029

DELISIO, SHARON KAY, secondary education educator, school administrator; b. Kansas City, Kans., May 7, 1943; d. Bernard James and Bernice Marie (Hansen) Hansen; m. Louis Charles Delisio, 1963; children: Lisa, Annette, Louis. BA summa cum laude, SUNY, Albany, 1974, MS in Reading, 1975, MS in Spl. Edn., 1980. Cert. reading, English, ESOL, varying exceptionalities. English tchr. Charlton Sch., Burnt Hills, N.Y., 1975-78; dir. edn., sch. prin. Charlton Sch., Burnt Hills, 1978-89; English/reading tchr. Lyndon B. Johnson Jr. High Sch., Melbourne, Fla., 1989-95, tchr., asst. principal, 1995—; N.Y. del. Internat. Conf. on Spl. Edn., Beijing, Republic of China, 1988; bldg. rep., mem. Brevard Fedn. of Tchrs., 1993-94; coun. mem. Tchr. Edn. Ctr. Coun., 1994-96; mem. capital planning team Brevard County Schs., 1994; tchr. of yr. selection com. and mgmt. plan Devel. Team; mem. improvement com. Johnson Jr. H.S., 1992-96. Mem. Melbourne Civic Theatre, Melbourne, 1992-94; mem. supporter Brevard County Zoo, Melbourne, 1993-96. Mem. AAUW (book sale vol. 1992-94), Nat. Coun. of Tchrs. of English (presenter Nat. Conv. at Orlando 1994), Brevard Coun. of Tchrs. of English, Internat. Reading Assn., Secondary Reading Coun. of Fla., Delta Kappa Gamma. Roman Catholic. Office: Lyndon B Johnson Jr HS 2155 Croton Rd Melbourne FL 32935-3337

DELL, HELEN DAVIS, education educator, writer, consultant; b. Calmar, Iowa, Feb. 18, 1927; d. Lawrence Henry and Verna Leona (Suman) Davis; m. Daryl Lee Dell, June 7, 1950; children: Pamela Fitzgerald, Marcia Smith, Kent Dell. BA, U. No. Colo., 1952; MA, Ball State U., 1963, EdD, 1967; postgrad., Stanford U., 1979. Asst. prof. San Jose (Calif.) State U., 1966-67; rsch. scientist Am. Inst. for Rsch., Palo Alto, Calif., 1967-70; project officer, disseminator coord. Title IV-C projects Minn. State Dept. Edn., St. Paul, 1974-77; asst. supt. for curriculum Archdiocese of San Francisco, 1977-80; tech. writer, tng. support specialist Saga Corp., Menlo Park, Calif., 1983-86; cons. curriculum devel. and critical thinking, Palo Alto, 1970-74, 89-91; workshop leader individualized instrn., Palo Alto, 1970-74; edn. coord., docent Sonoma County chpt. San Francisco Opera Guild, mem. adv. bd., 1992—. Author: (novels) The Top of the Mountain, 1996, (nonfiction) Individualizing Instruction, 1972, Students' Rights and Responsibilities, 1977; editor 4 books including Behavioral Objectives, 1971. Mem., organizer candidate debates LWV, Muncie, Ind., 1959-63, San Mateo, Calif., 1985-88. Tchg. fellowship grantee Ball State U., 1963-64, 65-66; grantee NIH, 1979. Mem. AAUW (v.p. membership 1994-96), PEO. Unitarian.

DELLA MARNA, MARIANNE, probation officer, former educator; b. Duluth, Minn., Aug. 15, 1933; d. Joseph Francis and Anna Rose (Peach) Rendulich; m. Nov. 16, 1954; children: Anthony Francis, Loren Joseph, Robert Eugene. AA, Chaffey Coll., Alta Loma, Calif., 1972; BA, Calif. State U., San Bernardino, 1973; MA, Claremont Grad. Sch., 1978; MA in Pub. Policy, UCLA, 1985. Secondary level tchg. credential, Calif. Tchr. social scis. Chaffey H.S. Dist., Ontario, Calif., 1974-85; assoc. probation officer San Bernardino County Probation Dept., San Bernardino, Calif., 1992—; peer counselor for elderly San Bernardino County Dept. Mental Health, 1988-91. Office: Probation Dept 8303 Haven Ave 2d Fl Rancho Cucamonga CA 91730

DELLAPIETRA, LINDA G., accountant, insurance agent; b. Bronx, N.Y., Oct. 28, 1959; d. Philip J. and Rose A. (De Lucia) D. BBA in Mgmt. cum laude, Iona Coll., 1984. Cert. fin. planner; lic. property and casualty ins. broker, life accident and health ins. broker, N.Y. State Dept. Ins., 1994. Treas. Trinder & Norwood Inc., White Plains, N.Y., 1978—; cons. in field. Republican. Roman Catholic. Office: Trinder & Norwood Inc 106 Corp Park Dr White Plains NY 10604

DELL'AQUILA-GEYRA, FELICITY ANN, retired educator, performing arts consultant; b. New Haven, May 17, 1930; d. Dominic John and Mary Veronica (Santonocito) Dell-Aquila; m. Zvi Geyra, Jan. 1, 1952 (div. June 1954); 1 child, Don Alfred. Student, Manhattan Sch. Music, N.Y.C., 1949-51, 56-58; BA, NYU, 1956; MA, Columbia U., 1961. Cert. K-12 English and French tchr., N.Y. Asst. to dean Manhattan Sch. Music, 1956-60, dean Sexton Acad., 1985 88; tchr. jr. high sch. N.Y.C. Pub. Schs., 1961-62; tchr. Pelham (N.Y.) H.S., 1962-64, Rye (N.Y.) City Schs., 1964-67; tchr. English and French, Rye H.S., 1967-84; adj. prof. English, Pace U., White Plains, N.Y., 1986-89; now performing arts cons. Rye Arts Ctr,, 1989—; cons. on aesthetic edn. SUNY, Purchase, 1978-88; host Collage: Conversations ib the Arts, cable TV, Rye, 1994-96. Contbr. articles on art and travel to various publs. and newspapers. Cons. New Rochelle (N.Y.) Coun. on Arts, 1989-96; bd. dirs. Rye Arts Ctr., 1988-89. Recipient achievement award Am. Heart Assn., Westchester County, N.Y., 1994. Mem. Alumni Assn. Manhattan Sch. Music (pres. 1986-89). Roman Catholic. Home: 106 Sutton Manor New Rochelle NY 10805 Office: Rye Arts Ctr 51 Milton Rd Rye NY 10580

DELLAS, MARIE C., retired psychology educator and consultant; b. Buffalo; d. Theodore Andrew and Katherine (Callos) D. BS cum laude, State U. Coll., Buffalo, 1945; MEd, U. Buffalo, 1967; PhD, SUNY, Buffalo, 1970. Asst. editor Urban Edn. Jour., Buffalo, 1966-67; rsch. asst. SUNY, Buffalo, 1967-69; asst. prof. psychology Ea. Mich. U., Ypsilanti, 1969-73, assoc. prof., 1973-79, prof., 1979-93; mem. adv. bd. Inst. Study Children and Families, 1983-93. Author: Dellas Identity Status Inventory, 1979, 81, Creative Thinking Applied to Problem Solving Manual, 1993; contbr. articles to profl. jours.; mem. bd. editors Midwestern Ednl. Researcher, 1980-87, Urban Edn. Jour., 1977-94. Recipient Josephine N. Keal award Women's Commn., 1980, 85, 86; Grad. Rsch. grantee Ea. Mich. U., 1980-84. Mem. APA, Am. Ednl. Rsch. Assn., Nat. Assn. Gifted Children, Midwestern Ednl. Rsch. Assn., Midwestern Psychol. Assn., Mich. Acad. Gifted, Pi Lambda Theta. Home and Office: 2201 Acacia Park Dr # 312 Lyndhurst OH 44124

DELNICK, MARTHA JOYCE, elementary education educator; b. Muncie, Ind., July 17, 1939; d. Doyt Randall and Susan (Straley) Whiteman; m. Jerry Spencer, July 6, 1962 (div. 1967); children: Jay Dee, Todd Alan. BA, Ball State U., 1970, MA, 1975; postgrad., Mich. State U., U. Mich. Cert. tchr., Mich. Tchr. Bennett Elem. Sch., Marion, Ind., 1965-67; tchr. elem. sch. Grand Rapids (Mich.) Pub. Schs., 1970-77, reading cons., 1977-87, tchr. compensatory edn., 1987—; Acad. Summer Success Acad., 1991—; presenter Compensatory Edn. Parent Orgn., Grand Rapids, 1980-89, Jefferson Sch. Family Math. program, Grand Rapids, 1992; mem. Mich. Math. Insvc. Project K-2, 1991-92, 3-6, 1992-93; math. svc. trainer Compensatory Edn. Tchrs. and Paraprofls., 1991-93; in-svc. MEAP trainer Grand Rapids Pub. Sch. Tchrs., 1995—. Author curriculum materials. Mem. NEA, Mich. Edn. Assn., Grand Rapids Edn. Assn. (rep. 1985-90, sch. bd. contact 1986-88), Mich. Reading Assn., Mich. Coun. Tchrs. Math. Mem. United Ch. of Christ. Office: Grand Rapids Pub Schs 1331 Franklin SE PO Box 117 Grand Rapids MI 49501-0117

DELONY, PATTY LITTON, management consultant; b. Nashville, Oct. 12, 1948; d. Chase and Jane (Chadwell) D.; BA in Econs., Duke U., 1970; MBA in Fin., Ga. State U., 1976; postgrad., Harvard U., 1985. Chartered fin. analyst. V.p., economist C&S Nat. Bank, Atlanta, 1970-79; v.p. investor relations Sara Lee Corp., Chgo., 1979-85, v.p. planning and devel., 1985-87; cons. Delony Assocs., Chgo., 1987—. Treas. Three Arts Club Chgo., 1983—. Recipient Woman Who Make A Difference award Minorities and Women in Bus. mag., 1986. Mem. Inst. Chartered Fin. Analysts, Econ. Club Chgo., Inst. Women's Studies. Republican. Presbyterian. Home and Office: 20 E Cedar St Chicago IL 60611-1149*

DE LOPEZ, JAYNE KELLY, lawyer; b. N.Y.C., Sept. 30, 1945; d. William Frederick and Kathleen (Kelly) Mueller; m. Pablo Antonio de Lopez, Jan. 9, 1993; children: Chris, Karyn, Paul, Mark, Michael, Seth, Julianne, Anna-Marie, Christina. BA, U. Calif.-Berkeley, 1977; JD, U. San Francisco, 1980. Bar: Calif. 1981, U.S. Dist. Ct. 1981, N.Y. 1988, U.S. Supreme Ct. 1987. Assoc., Sandvick & Martin, Oakland, 1981; pvt. practice, San Francisco, 1981—. Bd. govs. Bard Coll., Annandale-on-Hudson, N.Y., 1982. Mem. Am. Assn. Trial Lawyers (family law adv. com.), Calif. Assn. Trial Lawyers, San Francisco Trial Lawyers (bd. dirs. 1986-91). Democrat. Office: 1701 Franklin St San Francisco CA 94109

DELOREY, PATRICIA ANN, dramatic arts educator; b. Boston, Jan. 16, 1962; d. Leonard Anthony and Patricia Ann (Wentworth) D. BA, Salem State Coll., 1985; M Liberal Arts, Harvard U., 1992. Vis. artist, lectr. Salem (Mass.) State Coll., 1993—; instr. in dramatic arts North Shore C.C., Beverly, Mass., 1995—; lectr. Beckett Festival, U. Victoria, B.C., Can., 1996. Mem. ACLU, NOW, Phi Kappa Phi.

DE LOS SANTOS, LISA ALISON, administrator; b. Erie, Pa., Nov. 11, 1957; d. John Chester and Alice Catherine (Gesler) Engel; m. Sergio Antonio De Los Santos, Apr. 5, 1980; children: Alicia, Ana. BA, Thiel Coll., 1978; Montessori Cert., Southwestern Montessori, Denton, Tex., 1987; MEd, Tex. Woman's U., 1990, Adminstrv. Cert., 1993. Cert. tchr. K-8, ESL endorsement, reading recovery, adminstr. Tchr., kindergarten Am. Sch. Saltillo, Coahuila, Mexico, 1978-80; tchr. English Alfa Industries, Monterrey, N.Mex., 1980-81; mgr. Donn Advt. Agy., Erie, Pa., 1981-83; sec./receptionist Coldwell Banker Golden, Denton, 1984-86; tchr. Eren Horn Montessori, Denton, 1986-88; tchr. ESL Borman Elem., Denton, 1988-92, tchr. reading recovery, 1992-93, asst. prin., 1993—; bilingual/ESL coord. Denton Ind. Schs. Dist., 1992-93. Mem. ASCD, TESOL, Internat. Reading Assn., Nat. Assn. Bilingual Edn., Tex. Elem. Prins. and Suprs. Assn., Phi Delta Kappa. Republican. Lutheran. Home: 400 Woodson Cir Denton TX 76201 Office: Borman Elem 1201 Parvin St Denton TX 76205

DEL PAPA, FRANKIE SUE, state attorney general; b. 1949. BA, U. Nev.; JD, George Washington U., 1974. Bar: Nev. 1974. Staff asst. U.S. Senator Alan Bible, Washington, 1971-74; assoc. Law Office of Leslie B. Grey, Reno, Nev., 1975-78; legis. asst. to U.S. Senator Howard Cannon, Washington, 1978-79; ptnr. Thornton & Del Papa, 1979-84; pvt. practice Reno, 1984-87; sec. of state State of Nev., Carson City, 1987-91; atty. gen. State of Nev., 1991—. Mem. Sierra Arts Found. (bd. dirs.), Trust for Pub. Land (adv. com.), Nev. Women's Fund. Democrat. Office: Office of Atty Gen Capitol Complex 198 S Carson St Carson City NV 89710*

DELPH, DONNA JEAN (MAROC), education educator, consultant, university administrator; b. Hammond, Ind., Mar. 7, 1931; d. Edward Joseph and Beatrice Catherine (Ethier) Maroc; m. Billy Keith Delph, May 30, 1953 (div. 1967); 1 child, James Eric. BS, Ball State U., 1953, MA, 1963, EdD, 1970. Cert. in ednl. adminstrn./supervision, reading specialist, Ind.; cert. elem. sch. tchr., Ind., Calif. Elem. tchr. Long Beach (Calif.) Community Schs., 1953-54; elem. tchr., reading specialist, asst. dir. elem. edn. Hammond Pub. Schs., 1954-70; prof. edn. Purdue U. Calumet, Hammond, 1970-84, 88-90, prof. emeritus, 1990—, head dept. edn., dir. tchr. edn., 1984-88; cons. pub. schs., Highland, Ind., 1970-88, Gary, Ind., 1983-88, East Chicago, Ind., 1987-88, Hammond, 1970-88; speaker/workshop presenter numerous profl. orgns., Hammond, 1964—; mem. exec. coun. Nat. Coun. Accreditation Tchr. Edn., 1991—. Author: (with others) Individualized Reading, 1967; contbr. articles, monographs to profl. jours. Bd. dirs. Bethany Child Care and Devel. Ctr., Hammond, 1972-77. Recipient Outstanding Teaching award Purdue U. Calumet, 1981. Mem. Assn. Tchr. Educators, Assn. for Supervision and Curriculum Devel. (rev. coun. 1987-91, bd. dirs. 1974-83), Internat. Reading Assn., Ind. Reading Profs. (pres. 1985-86), Pi Lambda Theta. Office: Purdue Univ Calumet Dept Education Hammond IN 46323

DELPH, SHIRLEY COX, artist, designer, illustrator, consultant; b. Pasadena, Tex., Aug. 5, 1942; d. W. O. and Eula (Howell) Cox; m. Charles Robert Cox, July 12, 1964 (div. 1976); children: Robin Cox Schippel, Amy Cox Ecklund; m. Fred Kevin Delph, Apr. 15, 1978; 1 child, Nicholas Kevin. Student, Washington U., St. Louis, 1960-62; BFA, Chouinard Art Inst., 1964. Asst. Paramount Studios, L.A., 1963, design dept. Catalina Swimwear, L.A., 1964; designer Georgia Bullock, Inc., Santa Monica, Calif., 1964-65; adj. prof. textural design classes Sch. Internat. Studies Stanford U., Calif., 1966-67; owner, designer Cockamamy Needleart, Reno, Nev., 1968-76; tchr. needleart design Anderson Ranch Arts Found., Aspen/Snomass, Colo., 1977; owner, designer Needlepoint Whimsies Mfg., Austin, Tex., 1977-85; owner, artist Shirley Delph Design Art Licensing, Dripping Springs, Tex., 1985—; creative cons. Johnson Creative Arts, Townsend, Mass., 1973-95, ThermoServ, Inc., Dallas, 1990-95; cons. design Royal Doulton USA, Somerset, N.J., 1993-95. Featured in Am. Home Crafts, Better Homes and Gardens mag.; contbr. article Better Homes and Gardens mag. Mem. adv. com. Paul Laxalt for US Senate, Reno, 1976, local Rep. candidates, Austin, 1985-89; del. Rep. leadership conf., Washington, 1976; spkr. enrichment programs Austin Area Schs., 1980-95. Recipient Tex. SesquiCentennial prize Austin Heritage Soc., 1986. Mem. Am. Quilters Soc., Lawyers Wives Assn. Stanford U. Law Sch. (program coord., Putting Husbands Through hon. law sch. degree). Republican. Methodist. Home: 606 Blue Hills Dr Dripping Springs TX 78620 Office: Shirley Delph Design Studio 606 Blue Hills Dr Dripping Springs TX 78620

DEL ROSARIO, FELICIANA S., business analyst, investor; b. Metro Manila, The Philippines, Oct. 15, 1954; came to U.S., 1980; d. Felix M. and Adriana (Sarinas) del R. BS in Math. magna cum laude, U. of the Philippines, Quezon City, 1975, M in Indsl. Engring., 1978; MS in Ops. Rsch., Stanford U., 1982; MBA in Fin., NYU, 1989; postgrad., Rutgers U., Newark, 1991—. Sys. analyst, programmer Filipinas Life Assurance Co., The Philippines, 1975-76; ops. rsch. analyst San Miguel Corp., The Philippines, 1978-80; lectr. U. of the Philippines, 1978-80, De La Salle U., The Philippines, 1978-80; sys. analyst, programmer Equitable Life Assurance Soc., N.Y.C., 1980-81, ITT Comms. Svcs., Secaucus, N.J., 1983-84; bus. analyst Am. Express, N.Y.C., 1985-87, AT&T, Short Hills, N.J., 1987—. Roman Catholic. Home: 72 Gregory Ln Franklin Park NJ 08823 Office: AT&T 101 JFK Pkwy Short Hills NJ 07078

DEL SARDO, HELEN ANN, financial analyst; b. Boston, Jan. 5, 1954; d. Nick James and Mary Florence (Marino) Falce; m. Anthony Robert Del Sardo, June 25, 1982. BA in Polit. Sci., Duquesne U., 1976. Lic. securities dealer, ins. salesperson, Pa. Sr. budget analyst Allegheny County Controller's Office, Pitts., 1979-84; rep. Equitable Life Assurance Soc., Pitts., 1985-86; registered rep. Lincoln Investment Planning, Inc., Pitts., 1986-87, Renaissance Fin. Group, Pitts., 1987—; budget analyst U. Surg. Assocs., Inc. Med. and Health Care div. U. Pitts., 1988-90; account supr. U. Surg. Assocs., Inc., 1990—. Vol. Frank J. Lucchino for State Auditor Gen., Pitts., 1984; mem. YWCA Greater Pitts. Mem. Nat. Assn. Life Underwriters, Nat. Assn. Female Execs., Duquesne U. Alumni Assn. Democrat. Roman Catholic. Home: 2711 Brentwood Ave Pittsburgh PA 15227-2523 Office: U Surg Assoc Inc 3501 Forbes Ave Ste 610 Pittsburgh PA 15213-3306

DEL SESTO, JANICE MANCINI, opera company executive. Gen. dir. Boston Lyric Opera Co., Boston, Mass. Office: Boston Lyric Opera Co 114 State St Boston MA 02109-2402*

DE LUCA, ANDREA (HELEN SIGLAIN), psychoanalyst; b. Bklyn., Apr. 4, 1950; d. Wilbur Louis and Helen (Hansen) Siglain; m. June 1, 1973; children: Helena, Antoinette. BS in Edn., Wagner Coll., 1972; MSW, Fordham U., 1979; cert. sch. adminstrn., Coll. of S.I., 1993. Diplomate Cert. Bd. Clin. Social Workers; cert. psychotherapist, psychoanalyst, N.Y.; lic. N-6 tchr., spl. edn. grade advisor, sch. social worker, sch. supr., adminstr., N.Y.; lic. marriage counselor, N.J.; lic. clin. social worker, N.J. Dir. spl. edn. svcs. Am. Inst. for Creative Living, S.I., N.Y., 1976—, co-exec. dir., 1976—; bd.

dirs. clin. svcs. Internat. Sch. for Mental Health Practitioners, S.I., N.Y., 1980—; cons. S.I. Community TV. Named Tchr. of Yr. McKee Vocat. and Tech. High Sch., 1991. Fellow N.Y. State Soc. Clin. Social Work Psychotherapists; mem. ACA, ASCD, Am. Assn. Marriage and Family Therapists, Am. Group Psychotherapy Assn., Assn. for Specialists in Group Work, Phi Delta Kappa. Office: 2295 Victory Blvd Staten Island NY 10314-6625

DELUCA, ANGELINE F., elementary education educator, reading specialist; b. Sewickley, Pa., May 7, 1949; d. Michael and Maria (Barone) DeL. BS in Edn., Point Park Coll., Pitts., 1971; MEd, Duquesne U., 1979; postgrad., Pa. State U. Cert. elem. tchr., reading specialist, lang. arts tchr. Reading specialist Laughlin Children's Ctr., Sewickley; tchr. St. Peter and Paul Sch., Ambridge, Pa., Our Lady of Fatima Sch., Hopewell, Pa.; reading specialist Ambridge Area Sch. Dist. Mem. ASCD, Internat. Reading Assn., Pa. State Reading Assn., Leotta C. Hawthorne Reading Coun. (treas.), Delta Kappa Gamma (rec. sec. 1994—).

DELUCCIA, PAULA, artist; b. Paterson, N.J., Sept. 9, 1953; d. Ralph Lincoln and Isabel Miriam (Santucci) DeLuccia; m. Larry Poons, Dec. 18, 1981. Student, Ridgewood (N.J.) Sch. Art, 1971-73, Kansas City (Mo.) Art Inst., 1973-74. Exhibited in group shows at Nelson Atkins Mus., Kansas City, 1974, Ridgewood Sch. Art, 1978, Soghor Leonard & Assocs., N.Y.C., 1985, Art & Design, Phila., 1985, Jerusalem Gallery, N.Y.C., 1986, Helander Gallery, Palm Beach, Fla., 1990, 91, 92, 93, Wetherholt Gallery, Washington, 1991, Perspectives, Ghent, N.Y., 1991, Schulte Galleries, South Orange, N.J., 1992, Greene County Coun. on the Arts, Catskill, N.Y., 1992-93, Lorraine Kessler Gallery, Poughkeepsie, N.Y., 1992-93, Philharmonic Ctr. for the Arts, Naples, Fla., 1993, Farah Damji Fine Art, N.Y.C., 1993, Mountaintop Gallery, Windham, N.Y., 1994, 95, Roger Smith Gallery, N.Y.C., 1994, Art/Omi Studios, Omi, N.Y., 1994, Planet Thailand, Bklyn., 1995; two-person exhbns. include Farah Damji Fine Art, 1993, LaCappelli, Cambridge, Mass., 1995; one-woman shows include The Bentley Inn, Bay Head, N.J., 1993, Hair Gallery, N.Y.C., 1995; represented in permanent collections of City of Barcelona, Art Omi, Leshanski, O'Sullivan & Maybaum, N.Y.C., and numerous private collections; drawing reproduced in Cover Mag., 1982; paintings reproduced in Long Shot, 1993. Recipient Art Triangle Barcelona, Spain, 1987, Inaugural Yr. award Art/Omi, 1992. Home and Studio: 831 Broadway New York NY 10003

DE LUNG, JANE SOLBERGER, independent sector executive; b. Anniston, Ala., July 9, 1944; d. Samuel and Margaret Polk (Oldham) S.; m. Harry Leonard De Lung, Apr. 23, 1965 (div. 1972). BA in History, Emory U., 1966; MA in Urban Planning, Roosevelt U., Chgo., 1972. Exec. asst. Cook County Legal Assistance, Chgo., 1967-69; asst. dir. family planning Am. Coll. Ob-Gyn, Chgo., 1969-71; v.p. Ill. Family Planning Coun., Chgo., 1971-80; asst. commr. Chgo. Dept. Pub. Health, 1981-82; pres. Pub. Solutions, Princeton, N.J., 1982-88, Population Resource Ctr., N.Y.C., 1988—. Bd. dirs. Princeton Area Cmty. Planning, 1983-85, Planned Parenthood Mercer County, Trenton, N.J., 1986-94, UN Assn. U.S.A.; mem. adv. bd. dept. sociology Princeton U., 1981—. Mem. APHA, AAUW, LWV, Nat. Family Planning and Reproductive Health (bd. dirs. 1975-81), Population Assn. Am. Democrat. Episcopalian. Office: Population Resource Ctr 15 Roszel Rd Princeton NJ 08540-6248

DEL VECCHIO, DAWN MARIE, theatre manager; b. Phila., Mar. 16, 1957; d. Alfred Frederick and Edna Florence (McCoy) Del V. BS in Bus. Adminstrn., U. La Verne, Calif., 1994. Theatre mgr. Cinamerica Theatres, L.P., Encino, Calif., 1978—. Office: 650 W Huntington Dr Monrovia CA 91016

DEMAIO, BARBARA PATRICIA, social worker; b. Bronx, N.Y., Oct. 29, 1940; d. Alphonse Joseph and Elizabeth Elsie (Vogel) DeM.; children: Antonio Joseph, Damon Luis. AAS in Human Svcs., Rockland C.C., 1971; BSW summa cum laude, Fairleigh Dickinson U., 1973; MSW, Yeshiva U., 1975, postgrad., 1981. Cert. social worker; qualified clin. social worker; diplomate. Counselor developmentally disabled ARC, Pomona, 1971-73; counselor foster care Abbott House, Tarrytown, N.Y., 1973743; psychiat. social worker Mental Health Outpatient Clinic, Pomona, 1974-75; dir. med. social work Dept. Hosps. Robert Yeager Health Ctr., Pomona, N.Y., 1975—; instr. Yeshiva U. Gerontol. Inst., 1981; cons. Skilled Nursing Facility, 1980; rape crisis counselor, 1983; adj. prof. Albany State U.; field instr. Fordham U., Dominican Coll., St. Thomas Aquinas Coll., Fairleigh Dickinson U., Rockland C.C., 1975—. Mem. NASW, Acad. Cert. Social Workers, Worcester-Rockland Health Care Social Work Assn., Phi Sigma Omicron, Phi Omega Epsilon. Office: Dr Robt L Yeager Health Ctr Dept Hosps Bldg A Pomona NY 10970

DE MAR, LEODA MILLER, fabric and wallcovering designer; b. N.Y.C., May 26, 1929; d. Benjamin and Malvina (Altman) Miller; m. Robert Mathis de Mar, Dec. 30, 1955 (div. Jan. 1985); children: Victoria, Miller Mathis, Charles David. Diploma, Parson's Sch. of Design, N.Y.C., 1946-49; postgrad., Parson's Sch. of Design, Eng., France, Italy, 1949, NYU, 1950-53. Designer Joseph B. Platt, Indsl. Design, N.Y.C., 1950-53; instr. textiles Parson's Sch. Design, N.Y.C., 1953-55; freelance designer various companies, N.Y.C., 1956-62; designer Leoda de Mar, Inc., N.Y.C., 1962-74; designer, advt. cons. Woodson Wallpapers, N.Y.C., 1975-85, Richard E. Thibaut, Inc., Irvington, N.J., 1985—. Designer 1st wallpaper collection Pippin Papers, N.Y.C., 1954, 1st wallpaper collection Woodson Wallpapers, 1955, own collections Richard E. Thibaut, Inc., 1985—. fabric and wallcovering designs featured in various popular mags.; contbr. articles to mags. Recipient Creativity award Art Direction mag., 1981. Home and Office: 350 Riversville Rd Greenwich CT 06831-3255

DEMARCO, ANNEMARIE BRIDGEMAN, telecommunications company manager; b. Long Beach, N.Y., July 27, 1960; d. Benet Eugene and Rosemarie Anne Bridgeman; m. James Thomas DeMarco, Feb. 22, 1987; 1 child, Katherine Deborah. BS, Cornell U., 1982. Writer Am. Re-Ins. Co., N.Y.C., 1983-85; systems analyst AT&T, East Brunswick, N.J., 1986-87, project mgr., 1987-89; product mgr. AT&T, Bridgewater, N.J., 1989-90; billing mgr. AT&T, Basking Ridge, N.J., 1990-92; comm. mgr. AT&T, Warren, N.J., 1992—; mktg. mgr. AT&T, Bridgewater, N.J., 1993-94; new bus. devel. coach AT&T Growth Svcs., Bridgewater, 1995—; freelance writer, speaker, 1991—; presenter philanthropic, mgmt. and career devel. workshops, 1991-95; participant AT&T Insight Program, 1993, leadership advisor, 1995. Mng. editor: (newsletter) BSM Today, 1991 (HARP award), BAISline (3 Effie awards 1994); author: (textbooks) Assessing and Improving Not for Profit Performance, 1991, First Step Career Development Workbook, 1991; columnist Westfield (N.J.) Leader newspaper. Ch. sch. dir. Cornell Cath. Ch., Ithaca, N.Y., 1981-82; capt./campaign AT&T United Way 1991-92, Somerset/Basking Ridge/East Brunswick, 1991; facilitator AT&T Adopt an Angel Program, Bridgewater, 1989; cons. trainer Good Counsel, Hoboken, N.J., 1990-92, bd. dirs., 1992-93, Support Ctr. of N.J., Newark, 1990, chairperson; mem. Westfield Rep. Women's Club, 1991. Recipient Comm. award United Way, 1992; named Alt. finalist for Ideal Am. Couple Contest, Family Circle Mag./Am. Greeting Cards, N.Y.C., 1989, Young Career Woman of Westfield, Bus. and Profl. Women's Club, 1990. Mem. Cornell Alumni Assn. (alumni admissions amb. 1990-93), Cornell Alumni Assn. no. N.J. Roman Catholic. Home: 354 W Dudley Ave Westfield NJ 07090-4021

DEMARINIS, NANCY A., state legislator, educator; b. Glen Ridge, N.J., Sept. 11, 1930; d. Edmund Theodore and Sara Antoinette (Rosewater) Nesbitt; m. James Robertson, Feb. 14, 1948 (div. 1976); children: Margaret, Elizabeth, Theodore, Carl; m. Anthony R. Demarinis, Mar. 9, 1979. AS, Mohegan C.C., Norwich, Conn., 1973; BS, U. Conn., 1975; MS, So. Conn. State U., 1981. Cert. guidance counselor. Tchr. Groton (Conn.) Pub. Schs., 1975-78, guidance counselor, 1978-95; ret.; pvt. practice psychotherapist Groton, 1981-87; mem. Conn. Ho. Reps., Hartford, 1992—. Vol., bd. dirs., mem. various commns. United Way Women's Ctr., 1975—; town counselor, Groton, 1987-89. Address: 898 Shennecossett Rd Groton CT 06340 Office: Conn Ho of Reps Legis Office Bldg Hartford CT 06106

DE MARNEFFE, BARBARA ROWE, volunteer; b. Boston, June 2, 1929; d. H.S. Payson and Florence Van Arnhem (Cassard) Rowe; m. James Hopkins, Oct. 9, 1954 (div. 1969); m. Francis de Marneffe; stepchildren: Peter, Daphne, Colette. BA, Vassar Coll., 1952; postgrad., Boston U., 1959. Tchr. Chapin Sch., N.Y.C., 1952-54; adminstrv. asst. to dean Sch. of Indsl. Mgmt. MIT, Cambridge, Mass., 1959-60; asst. pub. rels. dir. Peter Bent Brigham Hosp., Boston, 1960-61, pub. rels. dir., 1961-63; pub. rels. cons. Diabetes Found. and Joslin Clinic, Boston, 1963-64; pub. rels. dir. McLean Hosp., Belmont, Mass., 1964-68; mgr. pub. affairs Cambridge (Mass.) C. of C., 1975-78; pres. de Marneffe Selections, Cambridge, 1978-90. Contbr. articles to profl. jours. Trustee Archives of Am. Art of the Smithsonian Inst., Washington, D.C., 1983—; com. mem. Ellis Meml. Settlement House Antiques Show, 1968-89; bd. dirs. Friends of McLean Hosp., Belmont, Mass., 1967-89; officer, bd. dirs. Family Counseling Svc. of Cambridge, 1969-78; Mass. Rep. State Committeewoman, 1977-80; exec. sec. Cambridge Rep. City Com., 1956-57; pub. rels. dir. Peabody for Congress Campaign, Newton, Mass., 1968; bd. dirs. Nat. Com. on the Treatment of Intractable Pain, Washington, 1980-90; trustee Peterborough Players, N.H., 1983-89; docent N.C. Mus. of Art, Raleigh, 1992-93; chair Friends of the Pain Ctr. Mass. Gen. Hosp., Boston, 1995—; corporator Brookline (Mass.) Savings Bank, 1995—; mem. adv. coun. Farnsworth Art Mus., Rockland, Maine; vestry Emmanuel Episcopal Ch., Dublin, N.H, 1995—. Mem. Jewelers of Am., Inc., Vassar Club (pres. Boston chpt. 1989). Home: 126 Coolidge Hl Cambridge MA 02138-5522

DE MARR, MARY JEAN, English language educator; b. Champaign, Ill., Sept. 20, 1932; d. William Fleming and Laura Alice (Shauman) Bailey. B.A., Lawrence Coll., 1954; M.A., U. Ill., 1957, Ph.D., 1963; postgrad., Universitaet Tuebingen, 1954-55, Moscow State U., 1961-62. Asst. prof. English Willamette U., 1964-65; asst. prof. English Ind. State U., 1965-70, asso. prof., 1970-75, prof., 1975-95, prof. emerita, 1996—. Co-author: Adolescent Female Portraits in the American Novel, 1961-81: An Annotated Bibliography, 1983, The Adolescent in The American Novel Since 1960, 1986; Am. editor: Annual Bibliography of English Language and Literature, 1979-90; editor, contbr. In the Beginning: First Novels in Mystery Series, 1995. Recipient Fulbright assistantship, 1954-55. Mem. MLA, Modern Humanities Research Assn., AAUP, Nat. Council Tchrs. English, ACLU, Phi Beta Kappa, Phi Kappa Phi. Home: 594 Woodbine Terre Haute IN 47803-1760 Office: Ind State U Dept English Terre Haute IN 47809

DEMAR-SALAD, GERALDINE, real estate sales and development executive, management consultant; b. Schenectady, N.Y., June 19, 1929; d. Matthew Peter and Mary Theresa (Sullivan) Relihan; m. Neil Joseph Demar, Aug. 5, 1950 (dec.); 1 child, Maureen Ann Demar-Hall; m. Bernard Salad, June 27, 1987; stepchildren: Andrew, Jane Salad-Bingham. BS, SUNY, Albany, 1979; MS, Russell Sage Coll., 1982. Cert. real estate broker, appraiser, cons.; cert. residential specialist. Real estate sales, 1964-69; dir. Mcpl. Leased Housing Program, Schenectady, 1969-71; pres. Geraldine M. Demar Realty & Devel., Schenectady, 1971—; pres Demar-Salad & Assocs., Mgmt. Consultants, Schenectady, 1988—; panel mem. Housing for Elderly, Housing for Low Income Families, Housing and Devel. Capitol Dist Region, N.Y. Active Fla. West Coast Symphony League, Fla. Ballet Ambassadors, Selby (Fla.) Bot. Gardens League, Friends of Schenectady Mus., League Schenectady Symphony Orch., Saratoga (N.Y.) Performing Arts Ctr.; mem. Gov.'s Panel for Housing for the Elderly and Low Income Families in N.Y. State; mem. Com. for Housing and Devel. for the Capitol Dist. Region of N.Y. State. Mem. AAUW, Nat. Assn. Realtors (grad. realtors inst. 1973, cert. residential specialist 1980), Soc. Real Estate Appraisers, N.Y. State Assn. Realtors, N.Y. State Assn. Real Estate Appraisers, Grad. Realtors' Inst., Nat. Trust for Historic Preservation, Schenectady Bd. Realtors, Albany Inst. History and Art, New Coll. Libr. Assn., Nat. Mus. Racing, Mohawk Golf and Country Club, Country Club Sarasota. Unitarian. Home: 1149 Ruffner Rd Schenectady NY 12309 Home (winter): 4021 Via Mirada Sarasota FL 34238-2750

DE MASSA, JESSIE G., media specialist. BJ, Temple U.; MLS, San Jose State U., 1967; postgrad., U. Okla., U. So. Calif. Tchr. Palo Alto (Calif.) Unified Sch. Dist., 1966; librarian Antelope Valley Joint Union High Sch. Dist., Lancaster, Calif., 1966-68, ABC Unified Sch. Dist., Artesia, Calif., 1968-72; dist. librarian Tehachapi (Calif.) Unified Sch. Dist., 1972-81; media specialist, free lance writer, 1981—; assoc. Chris DeMassa & Assocs., 1988—. Contbr. articles to profl. jours. Mem. Statue of Liberty Ellis Island Found., Inc.; charter supporter U.S. Holocaust Meml. Mus., Washington; supporting mem. U.S. Holocaust Meml. Coun., Washington. Named to Nat. Women's Hall of Fame, 1995. Fellow Internat. Biog. Assn.; mem. Calif. Media and Libr. Educators Assn., Calif. Assn. Sch. Librs. (exec. coun.), AAUW (bull. editor chpt., assoc. editor state bull., chmn. publicity, 1955-68), Nat. Mus. Women in Arts (charter), Hon Fellows John F. Kennedy Libr. (founding mem.), Women's Roundtable of Orange County, Nat. Writer's Assn. (so. Calif. chpt.), Calif. Retired Tchrs. Assn. (Harbor Beach divsn. 77), The Heritage Found. Home: 9951 Garrett Cir Huntington Beach CA 92646-3604

DEMATTEO, GLORIA JEAN, insurance saleswoman; b. Perth Amboy, N.J., May 23, 1943; d. John J. and Helena (Elias) Kancz; m. Ronald D. DeMatteo, Feb. 20, 1965 (div. Nov. 1987); children: Douglas J., Keith G. Student, Berkeley Sch., 1961. CLU. Exec. sec. Rhodia Inc., New Brunswick, N.J., 1961-65; real estate saleswomen Mid-Jersey Realty, East Brunswick, N.J., 1974-79; pntr. Realty World Garden of Homes, East Brunswick, 1979-81; spl. agt. Prudential Ins. Co. Am., Iselin, N.J., 1981—. V.p. Belcourt Condo Assn., North Brunswick, N.J., 1987-88. Mem. Am. Soc. of CLU and ChFC, Nat. Assn. Life Underwriters (nat. sales achievement award 1988, nat. quality award 1987, 92), Prudential Leaders Club. Home: 1144 Schmidt Ln New Brunswick NJ 08902 Office: Prudential Ins Co Sutton Metro Park 33 Wood Ave S Iselin NJ 08830-2719

DE MAURO, KAREN T., artistic director; b. Bridgeport, Conn., Nov. 18, 1948; d. Elward Austin Thompson and Katherine Lennon Carney. BFA, Boston U., 1970. Casting asst. Manhattan Theatre Club, N.Y.C., 1978; asst. edn. dir. Theatreworks USA, N.Y.C., 1981-82; artist-in-residence N.Y. Found Arts, N.Y.C., 1980—; artistic dir. The Acting Ctr., N.Y.C.; guest artist single master classes Julliard Sch., Brandeis Univ., Univ. Md., NYU Musical Theatre Lab.; guest on various radio and television programs; with The Kongo Noh Theatre, Japan, 1984-86; off-broadway performer, casting dir.; storyteller. Featured in Nat. Storytelling Mag., 1993-96; co-creator over 70 original musicals. Recipient Mobil Econs. award 2d prize, 1985; grantee various organizations.

DEMAY, HELEN LOUISE, nursing services administrator; b. Pitts., July 9, 1927; d. Patrick J. and Ellen (Kennedy) Duffy; m. John A. DeMay, Sept. 2, 1950; children: John A. III, Patrick J., Ann L., Mary Ellen, Theresa, Michael, Elizabeth, Stephen, Paul, David, Maureen. Nursing diploma, Braddock Gen. Hosp., 1948; postgrad., Cook County Hosp., 1949. Staff nurse Homestead (Pa.) Hosp., 1948; asst. head nurse Children Hosp., U. Pitts., 1949-52; staff nurse Kane Hosp., Pitts., 1978; activity dir. Jefferson Hills Nursing Home, Pitts., 1979-82; founder, officer Concerned Care Inc., Pitts., 1983-92; ret., 1992. Bd. dirs. St. Germaine Roman Cath. 1st Parish Coun., Bethel Park, Pa.; founding mem. Sch. House Arts Ctr., Bethel Park; bd. dirs., sec. Germaine Harbor, Bethel Park, 1990—; mem. Allegheny County Bd. Assistance, 1981-87; bd. advisor Allegheny County Single Parent Program, Pitts., 1984-94. Mem. S.W. Pa. RN Club. Republican. Home: 7166 Keith Rd Bethel Park PA 15102-3741

DEMBER, JEAN WILKINS, civic worker, civil rights advocate; b. Bklyn., Jan. 29, 1930; d. William H. and Marie (Benson) Wilkins; m. Clarence R. Dember, Apr. 15, 1950; children: Clarence, Judith, Regina, Lila, Theresa, Zelie. M of Human Service, Lincoln U., Pa., 1988. Curator Dember-Webb African Am. Heritage Workshop, Copiague, N.Y., 1970—; advocate, chair L.I. Day Care Svcs., Inc., 1985-87; advocate of the poor, 1970—; adj. prof. Nassau Community Coll.; founder, trainer white racism mental health com. Suffolk Mental Health Div., 1973-85; mem. multicultural adv. com. N.Y. Dept. Mental Health, 1986-91; convenor Suffolk County multicultural adv. com., 1989-90. Author: Sex Isn't Strawberry Jam, 1975, Black Lines in Poetry, 1973, Growing Pains, 1978. Nat. del. Black Polit. Assembly, Gary, Ind., 1972-82, Rainbow Coalition, Washington, 1984-86, Coalition Against Prisons and Genocide, Chgo., 1978; advocate Suffolk County (N.Y.) Econ. Opportunity Council, 1968-85; candidate Suffolk County Legis., 1975-77, 79; mem. Nat. Black Lay Cath. Caucus, Suffolk County del., 1970—, sec.-treas., 1978-79, Evangelist award, 1982; Black Congl. Caucus organizer nat. hearings on police brutality; lobbyist Criminal Justice Braintrust; bd. dirs. Cath. Interracial Council, 1984-90, elected pres. Cath. Internat. coun., 1990-93; mem. N.Y. Dept. of Mental Health Multicultural Adv. Com., 1986-91; chair S.C. Office of Mental Health multicultural adv. com., 1990-91, organizer Nassau/Suffolk coms., 1989-90; founder, exec. dir. Africans United for Sanity Now!, 1990—. Recipient awards Service to Christ's Mission St. Martin of Tours, L.I., 1969, Meritorious Service Am. Legion, 1968, Outstanding Service Greenhaven Preson NAACP, 1974, 78, Outstanding Contribution S.C. Human Rights Commn., 1975-80, Community Service Nassau County Black History, 1977, Polit. Leadership Gordon Heights Cultural Assn., 1981, Kuumba Creativity Our Lady Charity Ch., 1975, Civic Activities Cen. L.I. NAACP, 1978, Outstanding Service Union Black Collegians, 1981, Poetess, Pub. Servant, Humanitarian Chi Rho chpt. Omega Psi Phi, 1982, Martin Luther King Lifers' Com. Auburn Prison, 1982, Jupiter Hammond, L.I. Black History Month, 1985, Dedicated Service Nat. Office Black Caths., 1982, Nat. Assoc. of Negro, Business and profl. Women's Clubs Nat. Sojourner Truth award, 1991, Auburn Prison Black Solidarity Day com. Svc. award, 1991, 92, L.I. Black Alcoholism and Addictions Coun. award 1992, N.Y. Coun. award, 1993; named Woman of Yr. Nat. Coun. Negro Women, Inc., 1996. Home and Office: 2612 Rosewood St Houston TX 77004-5338

DEMBOWSKI, FANNIE RUTH, real estate brokerage executive; b. Blue Springs, Miss., Feb. 4, 1927; d. Lonnie Ervin and Callie (Dye) Hitt. BA, Upper Iowa U., 1970; MA, Ctrl. Mich. U., 1976. Various positions to divsn. chief for chief staff U.S. Army, Washington, 1956-58; pres., broker Ruth's Residential Real Estate, Inc., Huntsville, Ala., 1980—; fed. women's program coord. Dept. Army, Washington, 1975. Mem. Nat. Assn. Realtors, Ala. Real Estate Commn., Huntsville Bd. Realtors (life mem. Million Dollar Club). Republican. Roman Catholic. Home: 412 Homewood Dr SW Huntsville AL 35801 Office: 816 Andrew Jackson Way NE Huntsville AL 35801

DEMCHIK, VIRGINIA CAROL, secondary education educator; b. Butte, Mont., Apr. 15, 1944; d. Carl A. and Mary V. (Rodriguez) Felosa; m. Michael J. Demchik, Feb. 8, 1969; children: Michael C., Stephanie J. BA in Sci. and Math., Fairmont (W.Va.) State Coll., 1966; MA in Natural Sci. and Math., W.Va. U., 1969, EdD in Tchr. Edn., 1986. Cert. chemistry, physics, math. and gen. sci. tchr., W.Va. Instr., rsch. asst. W.Va. U., Morgantown, 1984-86; tchr. chemistry, chmn. dept. Jefferson Bd. Edn., Shenandoah Junction, W.Va., 1986—; instr. math. Shepherd Coll., Shepherdstown, W.Va., 1990—. Contbr. articles to profl. jours. Fellow U.S. Dept. Energy, 1992, 93, AT&T, 1994. Mem. NSTA, NEA, Coun. Elem. Sci. Internat. Home: PO Box 1420 Shepherdstown WV 25443-1420

DE MEDEIROS, MELISSA BROWN, librarian, art researcher; b. Gadsden, Ala., Aug. 23, 1950; d. Arnold Armistead and Nancy Apley (Hood) Brown; m. Marcus Clemente De Medeiros, Mar. 3, 1986. Student, Harvard U., 1968-69, CUNY, 1984—. Asst. libr. Knoedler Gallery, N.Y.C., 1984-88, libr., rschr., 1988—. Mem. Art Librs. Soc. N.Am., Coll. Art Assn., Art Students League of N.Y. (life). Office: Knoedler Gallery 19 E 70th St New York NY 10021-4907

DE MENIL, LOIS PATTISON, historian, philanthropist; b. N.Y.C., May 15, 1938; d. Charles Krone and Julia Anne (Hasson) Pattison; m. Georges Francois Conrad de Menil, Aug. 3, 1968; children: John-Charles, Joy-Alexandra, Benjamin, Victoria. AB, Wellesley Coll., 1960; diploma, Inst. d'Etudes Politiques, Paris, 1962; Lic. in Law, U. Paris, 1962; PhD, Harvard U., 1972. Pres. D. M. Found., N.Y.C., 1986—; mem. Coun. Fgn. Rels., 1976—, Inst. for Strategic Studies, London, 1978—, French Inst. Internat. Rels., Paris, 1980—, U.S. Coun. on Germany, N.Y.C., 1978—. Author: Who Speaks for Europe?, 1978; editor, translator: The African Unity Movement, 1965, French Foreign Policy under De Gaulle, 1967. Mem. internat. coun. Mus. Modern Art, N.Y.C., 1975—; mem. vis. com. to art mus. Harvard U., Cambridge, Mass., 1977—; vice-chair bd. dirs. Dia Ctr. for Arts, N.Y.C., 1985-96; vice-chair trustees coun. Nat. Gallery Art, Washington, 1988—; bd. dirs. World Monuments Fund, N.Y.C., 1990—, Groton Sch., 1991—. Fulbright scholar, France, 1960-62; Ford Found. fellow, 1966-68. Mem. Univ. Club, River Club, Harvard Club, Fishers Island Country Club, Phi Beta Kappa. Episcopalian. Home: 120 E 70th St New York NY 10021-5007 Office: D M Found 149 E 63rd St New York NY 10021-7405

DEMENT, IRIS, vocalist, songwriter; b. Paragould, Ark., Jan. 5, 1961; d. Patric Shaw and Flora Mae DeM.; m. Elmer McCall, Nov. 16, 1991. Represented by Rounder/Philo, 1990-93, Warner Bros., 1993—; songwriter, 1986—; performer open mic. nights, Kansas City. Albums include Infamous Angel, 1992, rereleased 1993, My Life, 1994. Home: PO Box 28856 Gladstone MO 64188 Office: Warner Bros 3300 Warner Blvd Burbank CA 91505 also: Peter Asher Mgmt 644 N Doheny Dr Los Angeles CA 90069*

DEMENTO, KIRSTEN MARIE, school counselor; b. Troy, N.Y., Jan. 6, 1966; d. Michael Angelo and Patricia Ann (Bastiani) DeM.; m. James William Holmes, Aug. 21, 1994. BS in Comms., Ithaca (N.Y.) Coll., 1988; MS in Edn. Counseling, Coll. of St. Rose, Albany, N.Y., 1993. Cert. sch. counselor, N.Y. Sales dir. Student Travel Svc., Ithaca, N.Y., 1988-89; acct. exec. WRGB-TV6, Schenectady, N.Y., 1989-91; guidance counselor K-12 Hartford (N.Y.) Cen. Sch., 1992-93; middle sch. guidance counselor Middleburgh (N.Y.) Cen. Sch., 1993; H.S. guidance counselor Berne Knox Westerlo C. Sch., 1993-94; H.S. counselor Cambridge (N.Y.) Ctrl. Sch., 1994—; team leader Career Connection, Saratoga, N.Y., 1994—; founder, dir. Ptnrs. in Edn., Cambridge, 1995—; mem. AIDS Adv. Coun., Cambridge, 1994—, Drug Free Schs., Cambridge, 1995—; organizer Career Day, 1993-95, Health Day, 1993-96. Mem. ACA, Adirondack Counseling Assn., Coll. Admissions Counselors, 1993—, Sch. Counseling Assn. Home: 58 North St Saratoga Springs NY 12866

DE MERE-DWYER, LEONA, medical artist; b. Memphis, May 1, 1928; d. Clifton and Leona (McCarthy) De M. BA, Rhodes Coll., Memphis, 1949; MSc, U. Memphis, 1984; PhD, Kennedy-Western U., 1990. Lic. embalmer, funeral dir.; m. John Thomas Dwyer, May 10, 1952; children: John, DeMere, Patrice, Brian, Anne-Clifton DeMere Dwyer, McCarthy-DeMere Dwyer. Med. artist for McCarthy DeMere, Memphis, 1950-80; pres. Aesthetic Med. & Forensic Art, 1984—; speech therapist, Memphis, 1950-82; lectr. on med. art univs., conf., assns.; cons. in prostheses Vocat. Rehab. Svcs.; elected expert witness in funeralization Nat. Forensic Ctr. Author: AIDS; Care of Health Care Workers in the Workplace. Bereavement counselor, organizer Ladies of St. Jude, Memphis, 1960; active Brooks Art Gallery League of Memphis; mem. God's Unfinished Bus. com. Temple Israel; vice dir. Tellico Hist. Found., 1980-80; mem. exec. bd. Chickasaw council Boy Scouts Am.; active Rep. campaign coms.; mem. com. God's Unfinished Bus. Temple Israel Congregation. Recipient Disting. Svc. award Gupton-Jones Coll. Mortuary Sci., 1981, Silver medal Sons of the Am. Revolution medal, 1985, Martha Washington medal. Mem. Nat. Foresic Ctr. (expert witness funeralization 1991—), Fedn. Internat. de'Automobile (internat. car racing 1972, lic.), Assn. Med. Illustrators, Am. Assn. Med. Assts., Emergency Dept. Nurses Assn., Am. Physicians Nurses Assn., Am. Soc. Plastic and Reconstructive Surgeons Found. (guest mem., cons.), Women in Law (chmn. assocs.), Exec. Women Am., Brandeis U. Women, DAR (1st v.p. regent 1980), UDC (pres. Nathan Bedford Forrest chpt.), Cotton Carnival Assn. (chairperson children's ct. 1968-70), Pi Sigma Eta, Kappa Delta (adv.), Kappa Delta Pi. Clubs: Tenn., Royal Matron Amaranth (Faith Ct.), Sertoma (1st female mem. Memphis, elected pres. 1989-90) (Memphis). Author: Aids: Care of Healthcare Workers in the Workplace, 1990; contbr. articles to profl. jours. Home: 1000 Murray Hill Ln # 304 Memphis TN 38120-2665

DEMERS, JUDY LEE, state legislator, university dean; b. Grand Forks, N.D., June 27, 1944; d. Robert L. and V. Margaret (Harming) Prosser; m. Donald E. DeMers, Oct. 3, 1964 (div. Oct. 1971); 1 child, Robert M.; m. Joseph M. Murphy, Mar. 5, 1977 (div. Oct. 1983). BS in Nursing, U. N.D., 1966; MEd, U. Wash., 1973, postgrad., 1973-76. Pub. health nurse Govt. D.C., 1966-68, Combined Nursing Service, Mpls., 1968-69; instr. pub. health nursing U. N.D., Grand Forks, 1969-71, assoc. dir. Medex program, 1970-72, dir., family nurse practitioner program, 1977-82, assoc. dir. rural health, 1982-85, dir. undergrad. med. edn., 1982-83, assoc. dean, 1983—; rsch. assoc. U. Wash., Seattle, 1973-76; mem. N.D. Ho. of Reps., 1982-92; mem. N.D.

Senate, 1992—; cons. Health Manpower Devel. Staff, Honolulu, 1975-81, Assn. Physician Asst. Programs, Washington, 1979-82; site visitor, cons. AMA-Com. Allied Health Edn. Accreditation, Chgo., 1979-81. Author: Educating New Health Practitioners, 1976; mem. editorial bd.: P.A. Jour., 1976-78; contbr. articles to profl. jours. Sec., bd. dirs. Valley Family Planning and Edn. Ctr., Grand Forks, N.D., 1982—; exec. com., bd. dirs. Agassiz Health Systems Agy., Grand Forks, 1982-86; mem. N.D. State Daycare Adv. Com., 1983-93, Mayor's Adv. Com. on Police Policy, Grand Forks, 1983-85, N.D. State Foster Care Adv. Com., 1985-87, N.D. State Hypertension Adv. Com., 1983-85, Gov.'s Com. on DUI and Traffic Safety, 1985-91, Statewide Adv. Com. on AIDS, 1985-90; bd. dirs. Casey Found. Families First Initiative, 1988—, Comprehensive Health Assn. N.D., 1993—, United Health Found, 1990—, Northern Valley Mental Health Assn., 1994—; mem. adv. bd. Mountainbrooke (formerly Friendship Place), 1992—; adv. com. Ruth Meiers Adolescent Ctr., Grand Forks, 1988—; mem. Commn. on Future Structure of VA Health Care, 1990-91; bd. dirs. Quad County Community Action Agy, 1991—; mem. Resource and Referral Bd. Dirs., 1990—; mem. caring coun. N.D. Blue Cross and Blue Shields Caring Program for Children; coun. mem. N.D. Health Task Force, 1992-94. Recipient Alpha Lambda Delta award, 1963, Pub. Citizen of Yr. award N.D. chpt. Nat. Assn. Social Workers, 1986, Golden Grain award N.D. Dietitics Assn., 1988, Person of Yr. award U. N.D. Law Women Caucus, 1990, Legislator of Yr. award Northern Valley Labor Coun., 1990, N.D. Martin Luther King Jr. award, 1990, Legislator of Yr. award N.D. Mental Health Assn., 1993, Dick Shea award for contbn. to high edn. AAUP, 1995, Voices award N.D. Children's Caucus, 1995; U. Wash. regional med. program service fellow, 1972-73; Toll fellow, 1989, U. Wash. Kellogg Allied Health fellow, 1972. Mem. AAUW, NOW, ACLU, LWV, Am. Nurses Assn., N.D. Nurses Assn. (mem. cabinet on edn. and practice 1982-86, Nurse of Yr. 1983), Am. Pub. Health Assn., Am. Ednl. Research Assn., N.D. Pub. Health Assn., N.D. Mental Health Assn., The ARC (Assn. for Retarded Citizens), Pi Lambda Theta, Sigma Theta Tau. Democrat. Home: 1826 Lewis Blvd Grand Forks ND 58203-1642 Office: U ND Sch Medicine 501 N Columbia Rd Grand Forks ND 58203-2817

DEMERS, MARY ADELAIDE, psychotherapist, educator; b. San Mateo, Calif., Sept. 9, 1955; d. Joseph Edward and Patricia Marie (Coughlin) Stanton; m. Paul Jordan, Feb. 15, 1992 (dec. July 1994); children: Jennifer, Philip, Katherine. BS, Santa Clara U., 1983, MA, 1989. Lic. marriage, family and child therapist, bd. Behavioral Scis. Clin. staff therapist Santa Clara County Children Shelter, San Jose, Calif., 1989-95; clin. dir. Unity Care Group, Inc., San Jose, 1990-96; pvt. cons. Adolescent Clin. Svcs., San Jose, 1992—; instr. grad. divsn. Santa Clara U., 1995—; clin. dir. Gray's Adolescent Group Home, San Jose, 1995—; exec. dir. Adolescent Clin. Svcs., San Jose, 1995—. Featured in books Working Women Today, 1986, Women and Work, 1994. Vol. Kids Vote, San Jose, 1994—. Mem. NAFE, Am. Group Psychotherapy Assn., Calif. Assn. Marriage and Family Therapists. Democrat. Roman Catholic. Office: Adolescent Clin Svcs Ste 220 2130 The Alameda San Jose CA 95126

DEMERS, NANCY KAE, nursing educator; b. Manchester, N.H., Oct. 18, 1938; d. Paul E. and Nellie (Matijas) Watts; m. Raymond Joseph Demers, Feb. 13, 1960; children: Paula, John, Diane. RN, Elliot Hosp. Sch. Nursing, Manchester, N.H., 1959; BSN, St. Anselm Coll., 1969; MSN, Boston U., 1978; postgrad., Nova U., 1994—. Social and health educator N.H. Youth Devel. Ctr., Manchester, 1969-73; dir. nursing svcs. Hanover Hill Nursing Home, Manchester, 1973-74; asst. prof. St. Anselm Coll., Manchester, 1974-82; maternal and child health coord. Concord (N.H.) Hosp., 1982-83; assoc. prof. N.H. Tech. Coll., Manchester, 1983-86; prof. nursing N.H. Tech. Coll., Claremont, 1986—; participant spl. seminars, rsch., workshops, 1991-93; panel item writer Nat. Coun. Licensure Exam, 1993; developer evaluation component for an ongoing AIDS edn./prevention program for youths between the ages of 14 and 19, Claremont Coll. and Fed. U. Ceara, Brazil. Mem. N.H. Am. Diabetes Assn. (bd. mem. 1988-93, Disting. Svc. award 1993), N.H. Nurse Educators, N.H. Ptnrs. of Americas (corr. sec. 1992—, travel awards 1991, 93, 95), Transcultural Nursing. Home: 501 Route 101 Bedford NH 03110-4710 Office: NH Tech Coll 1 College Dr Claremont NH 03743-9707

DEMERY, DOROTHY JEAN, secondary school educator; b. Houston, Sept. 5, 1941; d. Floyd Hicks and Irene Elaine Burns Clay; m. Leroy W. Demery, Jan. 16, 1979; children: Steven Bradley, Rodney Bradley, Craig Bradley, Kimberly Bradley. AA, West L.A. Coll., Culver City, Calif., 1976; AS, Harbor Coll., Wilmington, Calif., 1983; BS in Pub. Adminstrn., Calif. State U., Carson, 1985; MS in Instructional Leadership, Nat. U., San Diego, 1991. Cert. real estate broker, tchr. math. and bus. edn., bilingual tchr., crosscultural lang. and acad. devel.; lang. devel. specialist. Eligibility social worker Dept. Pub. Social Svcs., L.A., 1967-74; real estate broker Dee Bradley & Assocs., Riverside, Calif., 1976—; tchr. math L.A. Unified Sch. Dist., 1985-91; math/computer sci. tchr. Pomona (Calif.) Unified Sch. Dist., 1991—; adj. lectr. Riverside C.C., 1992-93; mem. Dist. Curriculum Coun./Report Card Task Force, Pomona, 1994—. Chairperson Human Rights Com., Pomona, 1992—, sec. steering com., 1993—, adv. bd., 1993—; mem. polit. action com. Assoc. Pomona Tchrs., 1993-94. Recipient Outstanding Svc. award Baldwin Hills Little League Assn., L.A., 1972. Mem. Nat. Bus. Assn., Nat. Coun. Tchrs. Math., Aux. Nat. Med. Assn., Alpha Kappa Alpha. Home: 157 Gracefield Way Riverside CA 92506-6156 Office: Simons Middle School 900 E Franklin Ave Pomona CA 91766-5362

DE MESA, CHERYL TESS, accountant, auditor; b. Bklyn., July 22, 1972; d. Jorge S. and Vilma R. (Ravago) de M. BBA magna cum laude, CUNY, 1994. Bookkeeper Daley & Pollack esq., N.Y.C., 1993-94; auditor Coopers & Lybrand LLP, N.Y.C., 1994—. Baruch Coll. scholar, 1990-94. Mem. Beta Alpha Psi. Roman Catholic. Office: Coopers & Lybrand LLP 1301 Avenue of the Americas New York NY 10019

DEMETREON, DAIBOUNE ELAYNE, minister; b. Brunswick, Maine, Aug. 5, 1945; d. James Demetreon and Grace Lewis; m. James Allison Devine, Mar. 3, 1986; children from previous marriage: William Anthony Decker, James Steven Decker. Degree, Unity Sch. Practical Christianity & Ordination, 1975; postgrad., Rio Salado Coll., 1992; BA in Psychology, Ottawa U., 1994. Ordained min. Unity Ch., 1975; cert. practitioner Neuro-Linguistic Program. Sr. min. Unity of Ann Arbor, Mich., 1975-77, Unity of Boulder, Colo., 1977-78, Unity of Colorado Springs, 1980-86, Unity of Scottsdale, Ariz., 1989—; chmn. World of One Fellowship, Colorado Springs, 1986—, pastoral counselor, Scottsdale, 1989—; adv. bd. dirs. Boulder (Colo.) Psychiat. Inst., 1977-78; campus min. U. Mich., Ypsilanti, 1975-77; conductor workshops chaplains program U.S. Army, Ft. Carson. Author, narrator audio tape Transformations, 1985; host talk show God and You, 1983; contbr. articles to profl. pubs. Chem. dependency counselor St. Luke's Hosp., 1993-96; Am. Fgn. Svc. vol., 1996—. Office: World of One Fellowship 8556 E Via De Risa Scottsdale AZ 85258-3931

DEMILLION, JULIANNE, health and fitness specialist and personal trainer, rehabilitation consultant; b. Monessen, Pa., Dec. 20, 1955; d. William Vincent and Enise Mary (Tocci) DeM. BA, BS, U. Pitts., 1977; cert. massage therapist Phoenix Therapeutic Massage Coll., 1985. Mgr. program devel. Exclusively Women Spas, Scottsdale, 1977-81; pvt. exercise therapist, Scottsdale, 1981-83, ; cons. City of Phoenix, 1981-88; cons., pvt. personal trainer, Scottsdale, 1983—; instr. advanced techniques Phoenix Therapeutic Massage Coll., 1986-90. Mem. NAFE, Am. Massage Therapy Assn. (State Meritorious award 1989), Ariz. Massage Therapy Assn. (sec.-treas. 1986-90, Svc. award 1991), Internat. Dance and Exercise Assn., Circulo-Systems Ltd., Am. Coll. Sports Medicine.

DEMING, ALISON HAWTHORNE, writer, poet, academic administrator; b. Hartford, Conn., July 13, 1946; d. Benton Hawthorne and Travilla Bregny (Macnab) D.; 1 child, Lucinda Bliss. MFA, Vt. Coll., 1983; postgrad., Stanford U. Instr. U. So. Maine, Portland, 1983-87; coord. of writing fellowship program Fine Arts Work Ctr., Provincetown, Mass., 1988-90; dir. U. Ariz. Poetry Ctr., Tucson, 1990—; vis. lectr. in writing Vt. Coll., 1983-85; guest lectr. various locations Okla., Maine, Ariz., Alaska. Author: Science and Other Poems, 1994, Temporary Homelands, 1994; editor: Poems of the American West: A Columbia Anthology, 1995; contbr. poems and essays to jours. and anthologies. Recipient Pablo Neruda prize Nimrod and the Arts and Humanities Coun. of Tulsa, 1983, Gertrude B. Claytor Meml. award Poetry Soc. of Am., 1992, Pushcart prize Pushcart Press, 1993; literary fellowship Tucson/Pima Arts Coun., 1993, poetry fellowship Ariz. Commn. on the Arts, 1995, fellowship Fine Arts Work Ctr. of Provincetown, 1984-85, Wallace Stegner fellowship Stanford U., 1987-88, fellowship Nat. Endowment for the Arts, 1990, 95; profl. devel. grant Ariz. Commn. on the Arts, 1992. Mem. Acad. Am. Poets (Walt Whitman award 1993), Associated Writing Programs, Assn. for the Study of Lit. and the Environ. Office: U Ariz Poetry Ctr 1216 N Cherry Ave Tucson AZ 85719 also: care Jennifer McDonald 1431 Thousand Oaks Blvd Albany CA 94706*

DEMITCHELL, TERRI ANN, law educator; b. San Diego, Apr. 10, 1953; d. William Edward and Rose Annette (Carreras) Wheeler; m. Todd Allan DeMitchell, Aug. 14, 1982. AB in English with honors, San Diego State U., 1975; JD, U. San Diego, 1984; MA in Edn., U. Calif., Davis, 1990; doctoral study, Harvard U., 1989—. Bar: Calif. 1985, U.S. Dist. Ct. (so. dist.) Calif. 1985; cert. elem. tchr., Calif. Tchr. Fallbrook (Calif.) Union Elem. Sch. Dist., 1976-86; adminstrv. asst. gen. counsel San Diego Unified Sch. Dist., 1984; assoc. Biddle and Hamilton, Sacramento, 1986-88; instr. U. N.H., 1990-93; teaching asst. U. Calif., Davis, 1987. Author: The California Teacher and the Law, 1985, The Law in Relation to Teacher, Out of School Behavior. Mem. ABA, Calif. Bar Assn., Sacramento County Bar Assn., Women Lawyers Sacramento Assn., Internat. Reading Assn., Nat. Orgn. Legal Problems in Edn., Pi Lambda Theta.

DEMOREST, MARGARET ORAHOOD, humanities educator; b. Burdett, Kans., May 30, 1916; d. Fred Marvin Wynett and Louisa Belle (Allen) Orahood; m. Albert Louis Demorest, Oct. 28, 1938; children: Janet Lee, David Louis. BA in English, U. Mont., 1937; MA in English, U. Wyo.; postgrad., Boston U., 1973, Princeton U., 1983. Tchr. English, music, drama Judith Gap (Mont.) H.S., 1937-39, Jackson (Wyo.)-Wilson H.s., 1943, 56-57; tchr., head English dept. Star Valley H.S., Afton, Wyo., 1947-55; instr. English, humanities, honors program Casper (Wyo.) Coll., 1959-85, cons. spl. programs, 1985-86, mem. humanities com., 1986—; cons. editor Rocky Mountain MLA, Boise, presenter, panel chairwoman, 1975-85. Author: Name in the Window, 1996; contbr. poetry and essays to popular mags. Guest mem. Salt Lake Tabernacle Choir, Salt Lake City, 1935-38; organist Chapel of Transfiguration, Moose, Wyo., 1953-57; actress John Stark's Theatre from New York, Jackson, summer 1956. Ann. Margaret Demorest Lectr. in Humanities named in her honor Casper Coll., 1986—. Episcopalian. Home: 3760 Carmel Ave Casper WY 82604

DE MORNAY, REBECCA, actress; b. Santa Rosa, Calif., Aug. 29, 1962. Student, Lee Strasberg Theatre Inst., Los Angeles; also studied with Kristin Linklater. Apprentice with Francis Coppola's Zoetrope Studio, 1981. Actress: (films) Risky Business, 1983, Testament, 1983, The Slugger's Wife, 1985, The Trip to Bountiful, 1985, Runaway Train, 1985, Beauty and the Beast, 1986, And God Created Woman, 1987, Feds, 1988, Dealers, 1989, Backdraft, 1991, The Hand That Rocks the Cradle, 1992, Guilty as Sin, 1993, The Three Musketeers, 1993, Never Talk to Strangers, 1995; (plays) Born Yesterday, 1988, Marat/Sade, 1990; (TV) The Murders in the Rue Morgue, 1986, By Dawn's Early Light, 1990, An Inconvenient Woman, 1992, Blind Side, 1993, Getting Out, 1994, The Shining, 1996.

DE MOSS, ELISABETH JOY, legislative staff member; b. Bryn Mawr, Pa., Jan. 8, 1971. BA in English Lit., Coll. William & Mary, 1992; MA in Latin Am. Studies, Georgetown U., 1994. Legis. rschr. Fgn. Rels. Com. U.S. Senate, Washington, 1992-94, profl. staff mem., 1995—. Mem. Young Reps. Pa., 1990—, Compassion Internat., 1980—, Enough Is Enough, 1992—; sponsor Mukti Mission, 1980—. Office: US Senate Fgn Rels Com 450 Dirksen Senate Office Bldg Washington DC 20510

DEMPSEY, BARBARA MATTHEA, medical, surgical and critical care nurse; b. The Netherlands, July 27, 1943; d. Petrus Antonius and Hendrika Petronella (Kemp) Petersen; m. James D. Dempsey, June 13, 1981; children: Jennifer, Daniel. AA, Santa Monica (Calif.) Coll., 1970; cert. lactation educator, UCLA, 1982. Staff nurse med./surg. Santa Monica Hosp., 1967-72; surg. intensive care nurse VA Wadsworth Hosp., L.A., 1973-77; staff nurse med./surg. Community Hosp., Santa Rosa, Calif., 1988-90; staff nurse Redwood Nurses Registry, Santa Rosa, 1990-93, Norrell Healthcare, Santa Rosa, Calif., 1990-93; charge nurse Creekside Convalescent Hosp., 1994; ret., 1994

DEMPSEY, MARY ANN, library commissioner, lawyer; m. Philip Corboy, Sept. 4, 1992. BA with honors, St. Mary's Coll., Winona, Minn., 1975; MLS, U. Ill., 1976; JD, DePaul U., 1982. Bar: Ill. 1982. Libr. Hillside (Ill.) Pub. Libr., 1976-78; assoc. Reuben & Proctor, Chgo., 1982-85; assoc. gen. counsel Michael Reese Hosp. and Med. Ctr., Chgo., 1985-86; pvt. practice, Chgo., 1987-89; counsel Sidley & Austin, Chgo., 1990-93; commr. Chgo. Pub. Libr., 1994—; adj. prof. law DePaul U. Coll. Law and Health Inst., Chgo., 1986-90; spl. counsel Chgo. Bd. Edn., 1987-89; mem. adv. bd. Rosary Coll. Grad. Sch. Libr. and Info. Sci., River Forest, Ill. Mem. State Street Commn., Chgo.; mem. exec. com. Greater State Street Coun.; bd. dirs. Big Shoulders Fund (for inner city Cath. schs.); bd. govs. Cath. Extension Soc.; mem. women's bd. Misericordia. Libr. scholar State of Ill. Mem. ALA (chmn. local arrangements com. ann. conf. 1995), Ill. Libr. Assn. (pub. policy com.), Chgo. Bar Assn. Office: Chgo Pub Libr 400 S State St Chicago IL 60605

DEMROSE, DAWNAREE, marketing executive; b. Detroit, May 17, 1967; d. Eugene Edward and Rosemarie Margaret DeBoer; m. Guy Robert Demrose, Oct. 7, 1992. Student, L.Am. Inswt., Vienna, Austria, 1989; BS in Mktg., Oakland U., 1991. Cheerleading team coach Clarkston (Mich.) Mid. Sch., 1985-87; trust clk. First Fed. Savs. Bank and Trust, Pontiac, Mich., 1985-89, sectl. asst., 1989-90; account exec. Olympia Arenas, Inc., Detroit, 1990-91; mktg. rep. DeBoer EDP Svcs., Inc., Clarkston, 1991—. Mem. Am. Mktg. Assn. (bd. dirs. 1995—, v.p. programming 1993-95, conf. chmn. 1990-91), S.E. Mich. S/38-AS/400 Users Group (bd. dirs. 1993—). Republican. Roman Catholic. Office: DeBoer EDP Svcs Inc 8362 Deerwood Rd Clarkston MI 48348

DEMUS, RENÉE ELIZABETH, health center official; b. Pitts., Sept. 17, 1962; d. Clyde Alexander and Emma Jean (Turner) D.; children: Taisha Lashawn, Nina Marie. LPN, Connelly Trade Sch. LPN, Pa. Coord. health care Ursuline Ctr. Inc., Pitts., 1991-95; file clk. Mercy Health Sys., Pitts., 1995—. Mem. Elks (asst. dau. ruler 1995). Home: 514 Brownsville Rd Apt 2 Pittsburgh PA 15210

DEMUTH, VIVIENNE BLAKE MCCANDLESS, artist, illustrator; b. Nutley, N.J., Mar. 8, 1916; d. George Wilbur and Hazel Metcalfe Blake; m. Henry DeMuth, July 3, 1935 (div. Sept. 1957); children: Simon (dec.), Vivienne, Shelley, David; m. George Warren McCandless, May 12, 1984 (dec. May 1995). Diploma, Am. Sch. Design, 1932, 33. Designer, artist Norcross Pub. Co., N.Y.C. and West Chester, Pa., 1936-40, 50-75; designer, illustrator Fisher Price Toys, East Aurora, N.Y., 1957-80; freelance book illustrator many pub. cos., 1992-94; mem. newspaper panel cmty. newspapers Cape Cod, Mass.; artist, crafts tchr. presch. Cape Cod Mus. Natural History, Brewster, Mass., 1994—. Illustrator: Little Golden Book A to Z, 1945, Pre-School Science, 1996, many others. Mem. Nature Conservancy, Mass. Audubon Soc., Cape Cod Mus. Natural History (artist environ. posters). Home: 2300 Herringbrook Rd Box 983 North Eastham MA 02651

DENBROCK, KRISTIE ANN, state official; b. Coldwater, Mich., Aug. 10, 1963; d. John David and Wilma Ruth (Anderson) D.; 1 child, Katie Virginia Lopez. BS in Mass Comm., U. South Colo., 1990. Editl. asst. Denver Post, 1984-87, Pueblo (Colo.) Chieftain, 1991-93; host, announcer, news dir. Sta. KTSC-FM, Pueblo, 1989; exec. prodr., host Capitol Jour., Sta. KTSC-TV, Pueblo, 1989-93; dir. media rels. Colo. Senate, Denver, 1993—. Vol., writer state Rep. campaigns, 1993—; vol. St. Frances De Sales Sch., Denver, 1995—, Daisy Troop Girl Scouts U.S.A., Denver, 1995—. Mem. Am. Legion, Lincoln Club Denver. Republican.

DENE, LINDA JO, financial executive; b. L.A., Apr. 26, 1948; d. Hyman Chaim and Ruth (Goldstein) Bergman; m. Richard Eugene Dene, Feb. 16, 1967; children: Ronald, Anthony, Angela. Cost control specialist South Bend (Ind.) Range Co., 1972-75; accounts payable specialist Thrifty Drug Co., West Los Angeles, Calif., 1975-76; cost acct. Sun Litho, Inc., Sepulveda, Calif., 1976-77; lead cost acct. Products Rsch. & Chem., Glendale, Calif., 1977-84; acctg. mgr. PhotoSonics, Inc., Burbank, Calif., 1984—; CFO Instrumentation Mktg. Corp., Burbank, 1988—. Mem. NAFE. Republican. Jewish. Office: Instrumentation Mktg Corp 820 S Mariposa St Burbank CA 91506-3108

DENENBERG, KATHARINE W. HORNBERGER, artist, educator; b. Ann Arbor, Mich., Nov. 20, 1932; d. Theodore Roosevelt and Marrian Louise (Welles) Hornberger; m. Allan Neal Denenberg; children: Peter David, Thomas Andrew. Student, Brown U., 1950-51; BA, U. Minn., 1953; MAT, Harvard U., 1954. Intern tchr. art Concord (Mass.) H.S., 1954-55; tchr. art Bedford and Pound Ridge (N.Y.) Schs., 1955-56, New Lincoln Sch., N.Y.C., 1956-62, Mus. Modern Art, N.Y.C., 1964-71, Children's Art Workshop, Mamaroneck, N.Y., 1971-81, Pelham (N.Y.) Art Ctr., 1981, 96. Solo shows include Manhattanville Coll., Purchase, N.Y., 1975, Rye (N.Y.) Libr., 1975, 85, West Cornwall (Conn.) Gallery, 1978, 79, West Cornwall Libr., 1979, 84, Condeso Lawler Gallery, N.Y., 1982, 84, Moviehouse Gallery, Millerton, N.Y., 1987, Larchmont Libr., 1988, St. Peter's Ch., N.Y., 1990, Sacco Ristorante, Ridgefield, Conn., 1990, 91; exhibited in group shows at Duffy-Gibbs Gallery, N.Y., Nat. Mus. of Taiwan, Bridge Gallery, White Plains, N.Y., Westport-Weston Arts Coun., Manhattanville Coll., Wildcliff Craft Mus., New Britain (Conn.) Mus., Sarah Rentzler Gallery, Condeso-Lawler Gallery, Silvermine Gallery, The Castle Gallery, Coll. New Rochelle, N.Y., Chaiwalla, Salisbury, Conn.; represented in permanent collections at Credit Lyonais, Bank of Boston, Chermayeff and Geismar, Great Lakes Corp., Tex. Comml. Bank, Sohio Petroleum. N.Y.State Coun. for the Arts grantee, 1975. Mem. Phi Beta Kappa.

DENHAM, ROBIN RICHARDSON, secondary school art educator; b. New Haven, Feb. 17, 1946; d. Charles King and Sally Geldart (deFreest) Richardson; m. James Dexter Denham, June 24, 1978; children: Lisa Anne, Jeffrey Scott. BS in Art Edn., U. N.H., 1969. Cert. art educator, N.H. Tchr. art Southside Jr. H.S., Manchester, N.H., 1969-70, Merrimack Valley H.S., Penacook, N.H., 1971—; chairperson dept. art Marrimack Valley Sch. Dist., 1985—, advisor Nat. Art Honor Soc., 1991—, curator permanent juried art collection, 1993—, active coms.; mem. vis. com. New Eng. Assn. Schs. and Colls., Inc., 1992, 95; mem. advocate bd. Boston Globe Scholastic Art Awards, N.H., 1993—, judge, Mass., 1993—; mem. N.H. Excellence in Edn. Com., 1993; art educator, coord. children's staff Star Island Conf., Isle of Shoals, N.H., 1993—; panel mem. statewide initiatives N.H. State Coun.'s Arts in Edn., 1994, N.H. Alliance for Arts in Edn., 1995—; mem. steering com. N.H. Alliance in Arts Edn., 1995-96; panel mem. N.H. State Coun.'s Arts in Edn. Educators Panel for Arts in Edn., 1995. Writer testimony for inclusion of art edn. Goals 2000: Educator Am. Act, 1993, 94; exhibited in group shows at Manchester Inst. Arts and Scis., 1991—, Star Island Art Exhibit, 1993—, New Eng. Art Edn. Conf., 1993—, Nat. Art Edn. Conv., 1993—; represented in permanent juried art collection Merrimack Valley H.S., 1993—. Recipient plaque honoring her achievements Congressman Dick Swett, 1994, resolution in honor of her achievements Concord City Coun., 1993. Mem. NEA, Nat. Art Edn. Assn., N.H. Art Educators Assn. (v.p. reion 2 1990-92, pres. elect 1992-93, site coord. fall conf. 1993, chairperson gala and awards ceremony 1994, co-chairperson 1993, pres. 1993-94, past pres. 1994-95, active various coms., long-range planning coms. 1992—, Yourth Art Month, 1992—, Excellence in Edn.: Visual Arts Gold Ribbon 1994, chair 1995-96, Art Educator of Month Feb. 1992, Jan. 1994, Art Educator of Yr. 1992, 94, N.H. Outstanding Art Educator of Yr. 1995). Office: Merrimack Valley HS 163 S Main St Penacook NH 03303-1924

DE NIGRIS, ANNA MARIA THERESA, middle school educator; b. N.Y.C., Oct. 18, 1947; d. Salvatore and Rosaria (Colletti) Insalaco; m. Michael Peter De Nigris, July 12, 1969; children: Jenniffer Ann, Tamara Alicia. AA in Langs., Bronx C.C., 1968; BA in English and Langs., CCNY, 1969; MA in English Linguistics, George Mason U., 1988. Cert. lang. profl., secondary tchr., Va. Tchr. Spanish and core subjects St. John's, Rubidoux, Calif., 1969-70; ESL specialist Sunset Hills Elem. Sch., San Diego, 1980; tchr. Sunrise Acres Elem. Sch., Las Vegas, Nev., 1984-85; tchr. 1st grade Talent House Pvt. Elem. Sch., Fairfax, Va., 1987-88; tchr. ESL Hammond Jr. High Sch., Alexandria, Va., 1988-90, Washington Irving Intermediate Sch., Springfield, Va., 1990-91; tchr. ESL 6th grade Ellen Glassgow Mid. Sch., Alexandria, 1991-92; tchr. ESL and English 7th grade Cooper Mid. Sch., McLean, Va., 1992-93; tchr. ESL Poe Mid. Sch., Annandale, Va., 1993-94; tchr. ESL and social studies Longfellow Mid. Sch., Falls Church, Va., 1994-95; tchr. ESL Herndon (Va.) Mid. Sch., 1995—; tchr. adult ESL, George Mason H.S., Falls Church, Va., 1988-89; chmn. for multicultural forum Coun. for Applied R & D, George Mason U., 1990-94; mem. steering com., faculty adv. com. Herndon Mid. Sch., 1995—; presenter in field; mem. sch. adoption com. Va. Dept. Transp., 1991, human rels com., 1990-91, ESL Portfolio Assessment com., 1993—; sch.-based mem. for minority achievement in prin.'s cabinet F.C. Hammond Jr. H.S., Alexandria, 1989-90. Vol. Family Svcs., Wright Patterson AFB, Ohio, 1971-72, ARC, Ohio and S.C., 1971-73; leader Girl Scouts U.S., 1980-87. Mem. Va. Edn. Assn. (del. 1990—), Nat. Assn. Bilingual Edn., Southwestern Conf. Lang. Tchrs., ESL Multi-Cultural Conv. (presenter, facilitator 1989), Tchrs. ESL, Washington Tchrs. ESL, Calif. Tchrs. ESL, Va. Assn. Tchrs. English, Fairfax Edn. Assn. (sch. rep., del. Va. Edn. Assn. 1991—). Roman Catholic. Home: 8814 Hayload Ct Springfield VA 22153-1213

DENIOUS, SHARON MARIE, publisher; b. Rulo, Nebr., Jan. 27, 1941; d. Thomas Wayne and Alma (Murphy) Fee; m. Jon Parks Denious, June 17, 1963; children: Timothy Scot, Elizabeth Denious Cessna. Grad. high sch. Operator N.W. Pipeline co., Ignacio, Colo., 1975-90; pub. Silverton (Colo.) Standard & Miner, 1990—. Mem. Colo. Press Assn., Nat. Newspaper Assn. Office: Silverton Standard & Miner 1257 Greene St Silverton CO 81433

DENISON, SUSAN S., television executive; b. Waterbury, Conn., Apr. 12, 1946; d. David and Ruth (Lichter) Signal; m. Grant Denison (div.). BA in Psychology cum laude, Conn. Coll., 1969; MA in Psychology, U. Rochester, 1971; MBA, Harvard U., 1973. V.p. mktg. Showtime Network Inc., N.Y.C., 1979-84; sr. v.p. mktg. Revlon, N.Y.C., 1984-89; gen. mgr., exec. v.p. Showtime Satellite Network, N.Y.C., 1990—. Bd. dirs. Arts & Bus. Coun., N.Y.C., 1989—. Mem. Phi Beta Kappa. Home: 340 W 55th St Apt 40 New York NY 10019-3766 Office: Showtime Networks Inc 1633 Broadway Fl 37 New York NY 10019-6708*

DENKERT, DARCIE, film company executive. Exec. v.p. bus. affairs MGM Pictures, Santa Monica, Calif. Office: MGM Pictures 2500 Broadway St Santa Monica CA 90404*

DENKO, JOANNE D., psychiatrist, writer; b. Kalamazoo, Mich., Mar. 29, 1927; d. John S. and Marian Mildred (Boers) Decker; m. Charles Wasil Denko, June 17, 1950; children: Christopher Charles, Nicholas Charles, Timothy Charles. BA summa cum laude, Hope Coll., 1947; MD, Johns Hopkins U., 1951; MS in Psychiatry, U. Mich., 1963. Lic. psychiatrist Md., Ill, Mich., Ohio. Pvt. practice Columbus, Ohio, 1961-68; staff psychiatrist Fairview Gen. Hosp., Cleve., 1968—; pvt. practice Rocky River, Ohio, 1968—; cons. Juvenile Diagnostic Ctr., Columbus, 1967-68, VA Hosp., Cleve., 1968-72, Cmty. Mental Health Ctrs., Greater Cleve., 1974-80; clin. instr. Case Western Res. U., Cleve., 1981-83. Author: Through the Keyhole at Gifted Men and Women, 1977, (monograph) The Psychiatric Aspects of Hypoparathyroidism, 1962; contbr. articles to profl. jours.; author poetry, 1960—. Mem. AAAS (reviewer children's books), Cleve. Astron. Soc. (bd. dirs. 1984-86), Mensa (Cleve. area br. pres. 1986-87), Great Books Discussion Group (Rocky River, chmn. 1985-92, 94—), Kiwanis Internat. Russian Orthodox. Home and Office: 21160 Avalon Dr Cleveland OH 44116-1120

DENMARK, STEPHANIE, writer; b. L.A., July 26, 1963; d. Burton and Roberta (Fischer) D. BA, U. Calif., 1985; MPS, Cornell U., 1990. Contbr. articles to pop. publs. including GQ, N.Y. Times, Self, Woman's Day, American Health, Good Housekeeping, Ms. Mem. Nat. Coun. Rsch. on Women, Nat. Writer's Union.

DENMON, FRANCES, resource specialist educator; b. Detroit, Sept. 11, 1950; d. Andrew Miles Jr. and Loretta (Futch) Jones; m. Lee Andrew Denmon Jr., Mar. 10, 1973; children: Lisa Denise, Lee Andrew III. BA in English, Calif. State U., Northridge, 1972, postgrad., 1975; postgrad., Calif.

State U., Dominguez Hills, 1977-79, 81. Cert. resource specialist, Calif. Tchr. educationally handicapped Hathaway Children's Village, Lakeview Terrace, Calif., 1972-75; spl. edn. tchr. Los Angeles County Office of Edn., Downey, Calif., 1975-87, resource specialist teacher, 1987—; mem. adv. bd. Children's Enrichment Ctr., Inglewood, Calif., 1977-84; scotopic sensitivity screener Helen Irlen Inst., Long Beach, Calif., 1991—. Patentee Feelings Game, 1986. Recipient Mentor Tchr. award Calif. Supt. Instrn., 1986. Mem. Calif. Tchrs. Assn. (site rep. 1982-84), Calif. Assn. Resource Specialists (pres. Los Angeles County Ct. Schs. chpt. 1992-94, treas. 1994—, bd. dirs. 1995—, svc. award 1994, Very Important Person award 1994), Los Angeles County Alliance Black Sch. Educators (founding). Office: Los Angeles Co Office Edn 9300 Imperial Hwy Downey CA 90242-2813

DENN, ESTHER ALICE, residential manager; b. San Jose, Calif., Oct. 12, 1949; d. Jerome Sanchez Mendez and Lucille Hollingsworth; m. Bernard Ralph Denn (div. 1989); children: Angela O'Roark, Ben O'Roark, Dale Harris. AA in Journalism, Houston C.C., 1976. Apt. mgr. Oaktree Apts., Houston, 1976-81; tech. writer Brown & Root, Inc., Houston, 1981-83; account exec. Jones Intercable Co., Oxnard, Calif., 1985-88; tech. writer sys. devel. group Unisys Corp., Pt. Mugu, Calif., 1988-90; apt. mgr. Sycamore Apts., Oxnard, 1991-93, Camino Ruiz Sq. Apts., Camarillo, Calif., 1993—. Mem. LWV, Ventura, Calif., 1994, North Oxnard Neighborhood Watch Com., Oxnard, 1991-93. Mem. Inst. Real Estate Mgmt. (accredited residential mgr.), Apt. Assn. Office: Pardee Constrn Co # 21 105 Camino Ruiz Camarillo CA 93012

DENNEHY, LEISA JEANOTTA, company executive; b. Fairfield, Ohio, May 30, 1961; d. Will Robert and Rethel Jeanotta (Russell) Fights. BA in Chemistry, Miami U., Oxford, Ohio, 1982; BS in Med. Tech., Miami U., 1983; MBA, Duke U., 1991. Registered med. technologist. Med. technologist Mercy Hosp., Hamilton, Ohio, 1982-85; analytical chemist Procter & Gamble Co., Cin., 1985-87, products rsch. chemist, 1987-88; new products anlyst GlaxoWellcome, Research Triangle, N.C., 1988-90; internat. product mgr.-dermatology GlaxoWellcome, Research Triangle Park, N.C., 1990-91, mgr. new product market devel., 1991-95, sr. product mgr., 1995-96, internat. comml. strategy mgr., 1996—. Co-author: Supercritical Fluid Extraction and Chromatography, 1988; contbr. articles to profl. jours. Named Women of the Day, 1979; recipient many acad. scholarships, 1980-82. mem. Am. Soc. Med. Tech., Am. Soc. Clin. Pathology. Home: 130 Marquette Dr Cary NC 27513-3488

DENNER, KRISTEN E., medical secretary; b. Norwalk, Conn., Dec. 6, 1961; d. Edward Robert and Janet Elizabeth (Ericson) Allen; m. Jerome Patrick Denner, June 12, 1994; 1 child, Alex Tiarnan. AS, Norwalk State Cmty. Tech., 1992. Med. sec. Allergy & Asthma Assoc., Norwalk, 1993—; tchr. Tuesday's Child, Wilton, Conn., 1993—. Founding mem. Colony Theatre Co., N.Y.C., 1985—. Roman Catholic. Home: 24 Carlin St Norwalk CT 06851

DENNER, VALERIE LOUISE DAINO, nurse; b. N.Y.C., July 21, 1952; d. Albert and Violet Louise (Acanfora) Daino; m. Alan Matthew Denner, May 29, 1976; children: Tami Danielle, Robert Albert. Diploma in nursing YWCA/Bklyn.-Cumberland Med. Ctr., 1972; AS, Genesee Community Coll., 1975; BA, SUNY-Albany, 1980. Staff nurse Albany Med. Ctr., N.Y., 1972-73, Hosp. of St. Raphael, New Haven, 1976-77; nursing instr. Quinnipeac Coll., Hamden, Conn., 1977-79; nurse Med-Staff, Boston, 1979-81; br. adminstr. Nurse World, Inc./Home Care Am. div. of Cosmopolitan Care Corp. Amex, Orlando, 1981-88, corp. v.p., 1985-86; pres., founder Sun Shine Temporaries, 1988—; mgmt. cons. Cosmopolitan Care Corp./Norell Health Care, 1988—; mem. med. adv. bd. Hospice of Cen. Fla., Orlando, 1984-85, Kimberly Clark Corp., Balt., 1986—; lectr. LPN Assn. of Orlando, 1986; founder, ltd. ptnr. Home Med. Services, 1984; founder, v.p. B. Daino Constrn., 1983, Investiclaim, Inc., 1986; founder, pres. Respiratory Therapy Inc., 1985; cons. Orlando Physicians Network Inc., 1987-88; bd. dirs. Buena Vista Acad., Inc.; bd. trustee The Friends of Princeton Hosp. Found., 1994-96.; cons. Firstat Nursing Svcs., Inc., 1992-96, Nurse Ctrl., 1996; founder DMH Mgmt. Inc., 1993-95. Asst. producer CBS 60 Minutes program, Sharon, Mass., 1980-81; author: How to Choose Home Health Care Services, 1986. Founder Hosp. of St. Raphael Physician Spouse Assn., 1976-79; pres., founder Citizens Action Group for Protection of Buyers of Newly Constructed Homes, 1979-81. Mem. Orlando C. of C., Am. Nurses Assn., Fla. Nurses Assn. (del. 1983), Nat. Assn. Female Execs., Nat. Assn. for Notary Pubs., Orange County Med. Aux. Republican. Avocations: designing and building houses; numismatics; skiing; swimming. Home: 9162 Kilgore Rd Orlando FL 32836-5504

DENNIES, SANDRA LEE, city official; b. Buffalo, Dec. 26, 1951; d. Norman John and Shirley Edith (Dils) D.; m. Robert Francis Gilbane, Sept. 21, 1974 (div. Apr. 1987); children: Brandon Michael, Gianpatrick. AS in Dental Hygiene, U. Bridgeport, Conn., 1972, BS in Dental Hygiene Edn., 1973; MS in Health Scis., So. Conn. State U., 1979. Dental hygienist various orgns., New Haven, 1972-73, Leonard B. Zaslow, DDS, Westport, Conn., 1973-81; lectr. U. Bridgeport, 1973-76; planner City of Bridgeport, 1977-79, planning asst., 1979-81; grants dir. City of Stamford, Conn., 1981—; sec. Com. on Emergency Med. Disaster Planning, Bridgeport, 1978-79; dir., dep. dir. Stamford Coliseum Authority, 1982-91; dep. dir. Stamford Film Commn., 1986-88. Editor, chief: Hy-Light Jour., 1973-76. Mem. Stamford Youth Planning and Adv. Bd., 1981-91, Stamford Youth Svc. Bur., 1991-95, United Way Corp., Stamford, 1986-93; pres., sec. Alcohol and Drug Abuse Coun., 1987-92; mem. bd. Christian outreach North Stamford Congl. Ch., 1988-92, 95—; mem. Coun. Chs. and Synagogues Assembly, Stamford, 1989; pres. Stamford Mcpl. Supervisory Employees Union, 1991—. Democrat. Home: 171 Shadow Ridge Rd Stamford CT 06905-1813 Office: City of Stamford PO Box 2152 888 Washington Blvd Stamford CT 06904-2152

DENNIS, ANITA ANNA, journalist; b. N.Y.C., Nov. 2, 1958; d. Carl Lent and Frieda Marie (Reynolds) Dennis; m. Gerard William Yates, Oct. 20, 1984; 1 chld, Madeline Jane Dennis-Yates. BA, Sarah Lawrence Coll., 1980. Intern N.Y. Daily News, N.Y.C., 1977-78; photo editor House and Garden Mag., N.Y.C., 1980-82; news asst. The Wall St. Jour., N.Y.C., 1982-83; reporter Munifacts/The Bond Buyer Wire, N.Y.C., 1983-84; bus. reporter The N.Y. Post, N.Y.C., 1984-85; sr. copy editor Jour. of Accountancy, Jersey City, 1988-89, sr. editor, 1989-94, mng. editor, 1994—. Editor: Sylvia Porter's Guide to Mutual Funds, 1986, Sylvia Porter's Guide to the Finances of Divorce, 1986; contbr. articles to newspapers. Mem. Women in Comm. (publicity com. 1993—), Am. Soc. Bus. Press Editors. Office: AICPA Harborside Fin Ctr 201 Plaza 3 Jersey City NJ 07311

DENNIS, HELEN MARION, gerontologist, educator; b. Lansdale, Pa., Aug. 27, 1940; d. Eric and Hedy (Gruenberg) Gutman; m. Lloyd B. Dennis, Dec. 1, 1963; children: Lauren, Susan. BA, Pa. State U., 1962; MA, Calif. State U., Long Beach, 1976. Asst. coordinator data analysis George Washington U., Washington, 1965-69; project dir., research assoc., lctr. Andrus Gerontology Ctr. U. So. Calif., Los Angeles, 1976—; dir. Andrus Inst., Andrus Gerontology Ctr. U. So. Calif., 1995—; project dir. The Conf. Bd., N.Y.C., 1988-90. Bd. dirs. Temple Menorah, Redondo Beach, Calif., 1981-92, pres. 1992-95; mem. Los Angeles Council Careers Older Americans, 1985-90; mem. adv. bd. Project Reinvest, Coro Found., Los Angeles, 1985; pres. Career Encores, 1991-93. Mem. Internat. Soc. Pre-Retirement Planners (nat. pres. 1986-87, pres. So. Calif. chpt. 1983-85), Am. Soc. Aging, Gerontol. Soc. Am., Nat. Coun. on Aging. Home: 347 Via El Chico Redondo Beach CA 90277-6757 Office: U So Calif Andrus Gerontology Ctr Los Angeles CA 90089

DENNIS, PATRICIA LYON, librarian; b. Rockford, Tenn., June 13, 1933; d. Howard Stanton and Dora Hester (Maynard) Lyon; m. Norman Bryan Dennis Jr., Jan. 12, 1957 (dec. Jan. 1985); children: Sarah Dennis Banks, Rebecca Dennis Morrissey. BS, George Peabody Coll., 1955; MA, U. Mo., 1977; postgrad., Auburn U., 1972-73, U. Kans., 1982-92. Cert. tchr.; cert. libr. media specialist, Kan; elem. classroom tchr., N.C., Mich., Mo., Ala. 3d grade tchr. Ray Street Elem. Sch., High Point, N.C., 1955-56; kindergarten and 3d grade tchr. Wurtsmith Dependent Sch., Clark AFB, Philippines, 1957-59; spl. reading tchr., 1st grade tchr. McDonald Elem. Sch., K.I. Sawyer AFB, Mich., 1961-63; kindergarten tchr. Gladden Elem. Sch., Richards-Gebaur AFB, Mo., 1964-65; 2d grade tchr., libr. Goose AFB Dependent Sch., Labrador, 1965-67; 2d grade tchr. Edgewood Acad., Wetumpka, Ala., 1969-70; 1st and 4th grade tchr. Trinity Christian Day Sch., Montgomery, Ala., 1970-72; 2d and 3d grade tchr. Fairview Elem. Sch., Olathe, Kans., 1974-77; libr. media specialist Wash. Elem. Sch., Olathe, Kans., 1977—. Pres. Pre-Sch. Bd., Gunter AFB, 1968-69; children's choir dir. Leawood (Kans.) Bapt. Ch., 1979-84, Sunday sch. dept. dir., 1987-88, ch. libr., 1990-93; bd. dirs. Scholarship Pageant, Kansas City, 1988-94; chaperone, traveling companion Miss Am.-Kans. Scholarship Pageant, Pratt, Kans., 1989-95; commr., book rev. com. Kans. State Reading Cir. Commn., Topeka, 1985-91, 94-96. Mem. NEA, Kans. Assn. Sch. Librs. (presenter 1990—), ALA, Kans. Reading Assn., Alpha Delta Kappa, Sigma Alpha Iota (treas. 1954). Republican. Baptist. Home: 10525 Chesney Ln Olathe KS 66061-2775 Office: Wash Elem Sch 1202 N Ridgeview Rd Olathe KS 66061-2946

DENNISON, JANICE ANN MURRAY, elementary education educator; b. Houston, Aug. 14, 1948; d. Edwin Lowell and Betty Holden Murray; m. Bobby G. Dennison, Sept. 6, 1969; children: Betsy, Hal. BS in Elem. Edn., U. Tex., 1970; MEd, U. St. Thomas, 1992. Cert. elem. edn., gifted and talented edn., Tex., cert. master tchr., Tex. Tchr. fourth grade Waller (Tex.) Ind. Sch. Dist., 1980-87, tchr. third grade, 1988—, bldg. technology coord., 1992—; site coord. Tex. Edn. Collaborative at Tex. A&M U., College Station, Tex., 1992—; mentor tchr. Waller Ind. Sch. Dist., 1992—. Mem. Assn. Tex. Profl. Educators, Tex. Assn. Gifted and Talented, Tex. Computer Educators Assn. Baptist. Home: 16639 Warren Ranch Rd Hockley TX 77447-9121 Office: Roberts Rd Elem Sch 24920 Zube Rd Hockley TX 77447-7842

DENNISTON, MARJORIE MCGEORGE, retired elementary education educator; b. Coraopolis, Pa., Mar. 21, 1913; d. Chauncey Kirk and Elsie (George) McGeorge; m. Delbert Dicks Denniston, Dec. 25, 1942 (dec. 1973); 1 child, Robert Bruce. Student, Ohio U., 1931-33; BA, Westminster Coll., 1936; postgrad., U. Kans., 1959, Western Ill. U., 1962, 64. Elem. tchr. county schs. West Pittsburg, Pa., 1936-42, New Castle Sch. System, Pa., 1942, 51-78. Pres. Newcastle NEA, 1965-67; vol. aid Pa. Assn. Retarded Children, Jameson Hosp., Law County Home, 1984-96; trustee, elder Presbyn. Ch., New Castle, 1986-92, v.p. Ch. Women United, 1990-94. Named First Lady of New Castle, 1989, Outstanding Woman of Yr. for Community Svc. Jr. Woman's Club, 1990, Disting. Alumni Achievement Cmty. Svc. award Westminster Coll., 1990. Mem. AAUW, LWV (sec. New Castle chpt. 1986—), Coll. Club (parliamentarian), Woman's Club (parliamentarian Lawrence County fedn. 1984—, sec. 1986-88), Woman's Club of New Castle (parliamentarian 1990-94), Fedn. Jrs. (v.p. 1994-96), Pa. Assn. State Retirees (v.p. local chpt. 1994—), Cmty. Ch. Women Lawrence County (parliamentarian 1995—), Delta Kappa Gamma. Republican. Home: 331 Laurel Blvd New Castle PA 16101-2523

DENNY, JUDITH ANN, retired lawyer; b. Lamar, Mo., Sept. 18, 1946; d. Lee Livingston and Genevieve Adelpha (Falke) D.; m. Thomas M. Lenard, May 29, 1976; children: Julia Lee, Michael William. BA, La. Tech. U., 1968; JD, George Washington U., 1972. Bar: D.C. 1973. Asst. spl. prosecutor Watergate Spl. Prosecution Force, Washington, 1973-75; pros. atty. U.S. Dept. Justice, Washington, 1975-78; dir. div. compliance U.S. Office Edn. HEW, Washington, 1978-80; acting asst. insp. gen. for investigations U.S. Dept. Edn., Washington, 1980; dep. dir. policy and compliance, office of revenue sharing U.S. Dept. Treasury, Washington, 1980-83, counselor to gen. counsel, 1983-89; insp. gen. ACTION, Washington, 1989-94; cons. Fed. Quality Inst., 1994-95. Mem. D.C. Bar Assn. Home: 3214 Porter St NW Washington DC 20008-3211

DENNY, MARY CRAVER, state legislator, rancher; b. Houston, July 9, 1948; d. Kenneth and Lois (Skiles) Craver; m. Henry William Denny, Jan. 26, 1969 (div. Aug. 1990); 1 child, Bryan William. Student, U. Tex., 1966-70; BS in Elem. Edn. magna cum laude, U. North Tex., 1973. Cert. tchr., Tex. Owner, mgr. Craver Ranch, Aubrey, Tex., 1973—; mem. Tex. Ho. of Reps., Austin, 1993—. Vol. Tex. Rep. Com., 1964—; chmn. Denton County Rep. Com., Denton, Tex., 1983-91; bd. dirs. Tex. Com. for Humanities, 1990, YMCA, Denton, 1985—, Tex. Fedn. Rep. Women, 1988-92, 94-96; life mem. president's coun. U. North Tex., Denton, 1974—, chmn., 1983; del. state and nat. Rep. convs., 1972—; mem. Denton Benefit League, 1976—, Denton Arts Coun., 1986—; member numerous other civic orgns. Named Outstanding Rep. Vol., Denton County Rep. Com., 1985, One of 10 Outstanding Rep. Women, Tex. Fedn. Rep. Women, 1991, Outstanding Alumna in Edn., U. North Tex. Coll. Edn., 1993. Mem. Am. Legis. Exch. Coun., Nat. Conf. State Legislatures, Ariel Club, Delta Zeta. Episcopalian. Address: 6637 FM 2153 Aubrey TX 76227-8732 Office: PO Box 2910 Austin TX 78768-2910 also: 416 W University Dr Ste 200 Denton TX 76201-1842

DENSEN-GERBER, JUDIANNE, psychiatrist, lawyer, educator; b. N.Y.C., Nov. 13, 1934; d. Gustave A. and Beatrice D.; m. Michael M. Baden, June 14, 1958; children: Trissa Austin, Judson Michael, Lindsey Robert, Sarah Densen. A.B. cum laude, Bryn Mawr Coll., 1956; JD, Columbia U., 1959; MD, NYU, 1963. Bar: N.Y. 1961. Rotating intern French Hosp., N.Y.C., 1963-64; resident psychiatry Bellevue Hosp., N.Y.C., 1964-65, Met. Hosp., N.Y.C., 1965-67; mem. core staff Addiction Services Agy., N.Y.C., 1966-67; founder Odyssey House (psychiat. residence for rehab. narcotics addicts), N.Y.C., Mich., Maine, N.H., Utah, La., Australia, N.Z., 1967, clin. dir., 1967-69, exec. dir., 1967-74, pres. bd., 1974-82; pres., founder, chief exec. officer Odyssey Inst. Am., 1974-82; pres. Odyssey Inst. Australia, 1977-86, Odyssey Inst. Internat., Inc., 1978—; chairwoman Odyssey Inst. Corp. Conn., 1974—; attending physician Gracie Sq. Hosp., N.Y.C., 1982-93; attending physician Park City Hosp., Bridgeport, Conn., 1985—, mem. ethics com., 1988-93; mem. ethics com. Bridgeport Hosp., attending physician, 1985—; attending physician Northwest Gen. Hosp., Detroit, 1985-86; active staff St. Vincent's Hosp., Bridgeport, 1987—; courtesy staff Norwalk Hosp., 1993—; assoc. vis. prof. law U. Utah Law Sch., 1973-75; adj. prof. law N.Y. Law Sch., 1973-76; chairperson plenary session drug abuse Am. Acad. Forensic Scis., 1972, sec. psychiatry sect., 1973, chmn. sect., 1974—; founder, 1973, since pres. Inst. Women's Wrongs; founder, since pres. Odyssey Inst. (health care for socially disadvantaged), 1974—; bd. dirs. Simpson St. Devel. Assn., An Extraordinary Event (One to One for Mental Retardation), Bridge House; mem. Nat. Adv. Commn. Criminal Justice Standards and Goals, 1971-74, Pres.'s Commn. on White House Fellows, 1972-76; mem. drug experience adv. com. HEW, 1973-76; v.p. psychiat. sect. Internat. Forensic Medicine Conf., Budapest, 1967; pres. N.Y. Council Alcoholism, 1978—; co-chair com. on reproductive rights vs. best interest of the child Mich. State Senate, 1984-86; trustee Nat. Forensic Ctr., Princeton, N.J., 1985—, keynote speaker nat. conf., 1988, lectr., 1988; speaker Conf. for Multiple Personality Disorder, Chgo., 1985—; cons. to Mich. State Legislature to draft legislation on The Best Interests of the Child vs. the New Reproductive Techs., 1986; amicus curiae brief in Mary Beth Whitehead appeal Surrogate Mothering, 1987; sr. non-govt. psychiatrist L'Ambiance Plaza disaster, Bridgeport, 1987; guest lectr. narcotics addiction NYU Sch. Medicine, also Sch. Law.; in field dir. Daitch Shopwell, Inc.; cons. substance abuse device Insight Inc., Flint, Mich., 1987-88; guest speaker Cornell U., 1989, Internat. Hypnosis Soc. of Yale, 1989, Cumberland Law Sch., 1989, Sacred Heart U., 1994; founder, CEO, pres. The Family Maintenance Health Orgn., LLC; guest speaker Nat. Ctr. Forensic Scis. Author: (with Trissa Austin Baden) Drugs, Sex, Parents and You, 1972, We Mainline Dreams, The Odyssey House Story, 1973, Walk in My Shoes, 1976; (with David Sandberg) The Role of Child Abuse in Delinquency and Juvenile Court Decision-Making, 1984, Chronic Acting-Out Students and Child Abuse: A Handbook for Intervention, 1986, Shortened Forms: A Manual for Teachers On; (with John Dugan) Issues in Law and Psychiatry, 1988; contbr. articles to profl. jours.; editor: Jour. Corrective and Social Psychiatry, 1975; co-developer, co-inventor virocidal surface cleaner against AIDS, 1988. Mem. N.Y.C. Crime Control Commn., 1975-79, Gov.'s Task Force on Crime Control, Albany, N.Y., 1977-79, N.Y. State Crime Control Planning Bd., 1975-79; del. White House Conf. on Youth, 1971; bd. dirs. Nat. Coalition for Children's Justice, 1975—, Am. Soc. for Prevention of Cruelty to Children, 1979—, Mary E. Walker Found., 1978; psychiat. cons. Good Shepherd Home for Girls, 1989-90. Recipient Woman of Achievement award AAUW, 1970; Myrtle Wreath award Hadassah, 1970; B'nai B'rith Woman of Greatness award, 1971; Otty award for service to N.Y.C. Our Town Newspaper, 1977; named Dame of White Cross Australia, #1 Dame of Malta, Ky. Col., N.Y. State Hon. Fire Chief. Fellow Am. Coll. Legal Medicine (Congl. cert. merit 1990); mem. AMA, N.Y. State, N.Y. County Med. Socs., Soc. Med. Jurisprudence, Therapeutic Communities of Am. (founding mem., 1st v.p. 1975—), Am. Acad. Psychiatry and Law (mem. AIDS ad hoc com 1988—), Am. Psychiat. Assn., Women's Forum N.Y. (founding mem.), Nat. Women's Forum, Internat. Women's Forum, Internat. Soc. Multiple Personality and Dissociative States, Conn. Med. Assn., Am. Orthopsychiat. Assn., ABA, N.Y. State Bar Assn., N.Y. County Women's Bar Assn., N.Y. Assn. Vol. Agys. Narcotics Addiction and Substance Abuse (dir. 1968—), Am. Psychiat. Assn., N.Y. Med. Assn., Post Traumatic Stress Syndrome Soc., Fairfield County Med. Soc. (physicians health subcom. 1986-92). Republican. Unitarian. Club: Women's City (N.Y.C.). Office: Odyssey Inst Internat 5 Hedley Farms Rd Westport CT 06880-6335

DENSING, KELLY LYNN, elementary education educator; b. Rancho Cordova, Calif., Sept. 6, 1968; d. Dennis Wayne and Patty Rene (Kelly) Walker; m. Matthew Lawrence Densing, May 7, 1994. AA in elem. edn., Ricks Coll., 1988; B in elem. edn., Utah State Univ., 1991; MA in Edn., Chapman Univ., 1996. 2nd grad tchr. Westside Union Sch. Dist., Lancaster, Calif., 1991—. Mem. Calif. Tchrs. Assn., NEA. Mem. Ch. of Jesus Christ Latter Day Saints. Home: 1308 East Landsford Lancaster CA 93535 Office: Quartz Hill Elem Sch 41820 50th St E Quartz Hill CA 93536

DENSLOW, DEBORAH PIERSON, primary education educator; b. Phila., May 2, 1947; d. Merrill Tracy Jr. and Margaret (Aiman) D.; m. James Tracy Grey III, Nov. 24, 1972 (div. Dec. 1980); 1 child, Sarah Elizabeth. BS, Gwynedd Mercy Coll., 1971. Tchr. Willingboro (N.J.) Bd. Edn., 1971—; union rep. Burlington County Edn. Assn., Willingboro, 1981-82; mem. task force for reoganization Morrisville Sch. Dist., 1991-92. Committeewoman 1st ward Morrisville (Pa.) Rep. Com., 1986—; mem. Borough Coun., Morrisville, 1988—, pres. 1992-94, rep. candidate, 1986; borough chmn. Am. Cancer Soc., 1986-87; sec. bd. dirs. Morrisville Free Libr., 1988-90, bd. dirs. 1988—; mem. Morrisville Mcpl. Authority, chmn. 1994—, asst. sec., treas., 1996, chmn. 1994-96. Mem. NEA, N.J. Edn. Assn., Willingboro Edn. Assn. (union rep. 1981-82, alt. union rep. 1988-89), Parents without Ptnrs. (bd. dirs. Mercer County chpt. 1981-82, sec. 1982-84), Bucks County Boroughs Assn. (bd. dirs. 1989—, v.p. 1990-92, pres. 1992-93). Presbyterian. Home: 1206 Ohio Ave Morrisville PA 19067-2417

DENSMORE, ANN, speech pathologist, audiologist, writer; b. L.A., Nov. 24, 1941; d. Ray B. and Margaret M. (Walsh) D.; children: Kristin Ann, Jennifer Ann. BS cum laude, UCLA, 1963; MA in Communicative Disorders, Calif. State U., 1975; student Cape Cod Conservatory of Arts, 1977-79, Harvard U. graphics-architecture program, 1980—; EdM in Human Devel. and Psychology, Harvard U., 1991; postgrad. Clark U., Worcester, Mass. Lic. speech pathologist and audiologist. Tchr., Santa Monica (Calif.) Unified Sch. Dist., 1973-74; speech pathologist Kennedy Child Study Center, 1975-76, Framingham (Mass.) Pub. Schs., 1979, Weston (Mass.) Schs., 1993—, Eliot-Pearson Children's Sch., Tufts U., Medford, Mass., 1993—; audiologist VA Hosp. Sepulveda, Calif., 1976-77, New Eng. Rehab. Hosp., Woburn, Mass., 1978; audiology cons. Wellesley (Mass.) Public Schs., 1979; speech pathologist and audiologist The Learning Center for Deaf Children, Framingham, 1978-80; dir. ann. fund Babson Coll., 1981-83; asst. dir. devel. Lakey Clinic Med. Ctr., 1984-86; assoc. dir. corp. devel. Harvard Med. Sch., 1986—; rsch. asst. Presch. Learning Lab., Harvard U., 1989, Judge Baker Children's Ctr., 1991-93; pvt. practice, Lexington, Mass., 1993—; freelance photographer, 1979—; career counselor corp. execs. Mackenna/Jandl Assoc., Inc., 1983—; v.p. U.S. sales Boston Corp.. Exhibited photographs Copley Soc. of Boston, 1979-80. Contbr. articles to Boston Globe, 1986—. Mem. Am. Speech and Hearing Assn. (cert. clin. competence, speech pathologist-audiologist), Copley Soc. of Boston. Episcopalian. Office: 1628 Massachusetts Ave Lexington MA 02173-3802

DENSON, SHADELLE FULLER, school system administrator, physical therapist; b. Atlanta, Dec. 1, 1954; d. Roosevelt and Helen Elizabeth (Watson) Fuller; m. Joe Ree Denson, Sept. 2, 1978; 1 child, Jynelle. BS, Tuskegee U., 1977, MS, 1979; postgrad., Nova U., 1994—. Cert. spl. edn., adminstrn. and supervision, Ga. Phys. therapist VA Hosp., Tuskegee, Ala., 1977-79; tchr. Atlanta Bd. Edn., 1979-83; tchr., adminstr. Fulton County Bd. Edn., Atlanta, 1983—; tutor, cons. Denson Tutorial Svcs., Atlanta, 1983—. Mem. Delta Sigma Theta (officer East Point/College Park chpt. 1986). Home: 125 Briarlake Ct Fairburn GA 30213 Office: Fulton County Bd Edn 786 Cleveland Ave SW Atlanta GA 30315-7239

DENT, LEANNA GAIL, art educator; b. Manhattan, Kans., Oct. 21, 1949; d. William Charles and Maxine Madeline (Kackley) Payne; children: Laura Michelle, Jeffery Aaron. BS in Edn., U. Houston, 1973; postgrad., U. Tex., 1975-76; MS in Edn., Okla. State U., 1988. Cert. elementary and secondary art tchr., Okla., Tex. Tchr. art Popham Elem. Sch., Del Valle, Tex., 1973-77; graphic artist Conoco, Inc., Ponca City, Okla., 1987-88; tchr. art Garfiled Elem. Sch., Ponca City, Okla., 1988-91, Reed Elem. Sch., Houston, 1991-92, Copeland Elem. Sch., Houston, 1992-94, Campbell Jr. High Sch., Houston, 1994—; cons. and specialist in field. Author: Using Synectics to Enhance the Evaluation of Works of Art, 1988. Vol. 1st Luth. Day Sch., Ponca City, 1977-91, Ponca City Inds. Sch. Dist., 1987-91; work com. Cy-Fair Ind. Sch. Dist., Houston, 1991-94. Acad. and Mem. scholar Okla. State U., 1986-88; named Spotlight Tchr. Yr., 1992-93. Mem. Nat. Art Edn., Tex. Art Edn. Assn. (judges commendation 1993), Assn. Tex. Profl. Educators, Houston Art Edn. Assn. (v.p. 1992-93, pres.-elect 1993-95, pres. 1995—), Phi Delta Kappa, Phi Kappa Phi. Republican. Lutheran. Office: Campbell Jr High Sch 11415 Bobcat Rd Houston TX 77064-3001

DENT, SHARON PIERCE, transportation executive; b. Leachville, Ark., Jan. 24, 1948; d. Thomas Ralph and Margaret Evelyn (Scott) Pierce; m. Ronald R. Dent, Mar. 7, 1969; 1 child, Rachel. BA in Polit. Sci., Ark. State U., 1970; MPA, Memphis State U., 1973; postgrad., Northeastern, 1982. Intern, planning asst., assoc. planner, sr. planner Memphis Shelby County Planning Commn., 1972-78; asst. to adminstr., deputy dir. City of Phoeniz Pub. Transit Dept., 1978-90; exec. dir. Hillsborough Area Regional Transit Authority, Tampa, Fla., 1990; founding mem., pres. Phoenix chpt. Women's Transp. Seminar, 1985-90; pres. Tampa (Fla.) chpt. Women's Trans. Seminar, 1995-96. Citizen advisor The Samaritans, Phoenix, 1988-90; chmn. ways and means Soroptimist, Phoenix, 1982-90; mem. LWV, Tampa, 1990-93. Mem. Am. Pub. Transit Assn. (bd. dirs. 1990-93, v.p. human resources 1994-96, mem. exec. com.), Southwest Transit Assn. (v.p. 1989-90, bd. dirs. 1986-90), Am. Planning Assn. (pres. West Tenn. chpt. 1977). Home: 420 S Royal Poinciana Dr Tampa FL 33609-3636 Office: Hillsborough Area Regional Transit 4305 E 21st Ave Tampa FL 33605-2311

DENTLER, ANNE LILLIAN, artist; b. Pitts., Oct. 13, 1937; d. Bailey Kent and Anna Wilhelmina (White) Schaefer; m. Gary Morgan, July 13, 1957 (div. Mar. 1975); children: Gary, Sherree, Mitch; m. David Daniel Dentler, Aug. 14, 1976; stepchildren: David, Jr., Joseph Charles. Degree in journalism, Penn State U., 1974; postgrad., McNeese U., 1984, 85, 86. Clk.- typist Westinghouse Electric, Beaver, Pa., 1956, 57, 58; clk. (part time) J.C. Penney, Baden, Pa.; rschr. survey analysis Penn State U., University Park, Pa., 1973-74; dep. prothonotary Beaver County Govt., 1974-76; dep. magistrate Pa. State Govt., Baden, 1976-80; workshop instr., Pa., La.; with arts immersion program Calcasieu Arts & Humanities, Lake Charles, La., 1989; illustrator, conceptual artist Vol. Ctr. Southwest La., 1989-95; artist in residence Calcasieu Parish Schs., Lake Charles, 1990; assoc. mem. Women in the Arts, Washington, 1995. Illustrator: Jean Lafitte, Louisiana Buccaneer, 1990—, Rhythmic Alphabet; author: Portraiture...in Plain Language, 1993;. Bd. dirs. Associated La. Artists, 1984—, Gateway Found., Lake Charles, 1988, Martin Luther King Coalition, Lake Charles, 1993. Recipient Best of Show award Arts and Humanities Coun., Southwest La., 1986; named Artist of Yr., Gateway Found., 1988. Mem. Assoc. La. Artists (founder 1984, pres. 1984, sec. 1990, workshop instr. 1986-96), Beaumont Art League, New Orleans Art Assn., New Brighton Art Assn. Democrat. Baptist. Studio: Annie's Artworks 2331 21st St Lake Charles LA 70601

DENTON, BETTY, lawyer, state representative; b. Waco, Tex., Aug. 19, 1946; m. Lane Denton; 1 child, Deeann Denton. BA, Baylor U., MA, JD, 1980. Bar: Tex. 1977, U.S. Dist. Ct. (we. dist.), U.S. Ct. Appeals (5th cir.); cert. family law, litigation and personal injury. Pvt. practice Waco, 1977—; state rep. State of Tex., 1977-95, chair house jud. com., 1991-94, mem. judicial coun., 1991—, mem. appropriations com., 1994-95. Active Family Abuse Ctr., Parent Tchr. Assn., League of Women Voters, Tex. Dem. Women, McLennan County Women Elected Officials. Baptist. Home: 600

Columbus Ave Ste C Waco TX 76701-1348 Office: Denton Law Office 600 Columbus Ave Ste C Waco TX 76701-1348

DENTON, SANDY, vocalist, producer; 1 child. Prodr. Next Plateau Records, N.Y.C., 1985—; mem. Salt-N-Pepa. Recs. include Black's Magic, 1990, Very Necessary, 1994. Office: Very Necessary care Next Plateau Records 1650 Broadway New York NY 10019*

DENTON, VICTORIA ROBERTSON, marketing consultant; b. Omaha, May 29, 1969; d. William Robertson and Mary (Palmer) D. BA, U. St. Thomas, 1991, postgrad. in Internat. Mgmt. Sales planner, account coord. Carlson Mktg. Group, Travel, Mpls., 1991-95; cons. Pacific World Network/Bali Tours and Travel, Bali, Indonesia, 1995-96; tchr. ESL to S.E. Asians, 1996—. Mem. Minnetonka Yacht Club (vol. 1993—), Wayzata Yacht Club (vol. 1990-95). Republican. Home: 13531 Wentworth Tr Minnetonka MN 55305

DEPACKH, MARY FRASER CARTER, artist, retired educator; b. Arlington, Va., May 15, 1914; d. Herbert Pering and Frances Lee (Sickels) Carter; m. David Calvert dePackh, Dec. 1, 1949 (dec. Aug. 1990); 1 child, Selene Naomi. Voice instr. Washington Coll. of Music, 1936-39; pvt. voice, piano, art, theory tchr. Prin works include bas relief sculpture Margaret Brent Meml., 1983, bas relief bust Mathias de Sousa, 1986, Capt. Sydney Sherby, 1993, statuette horse "Trespasser, 1931, Royal Acad., London, 1932. Founding mem. North End Artists, Leonardtown, Md., 1986-94; conservationist St. County LWV, So. Md., 1980-95; vol. art tchr. Prince Georges County Pub. Schs., Oxon Hill, Md., 1972-77. Recipient award Prince George's County (Md.) Sch. Bd., 1977, St. Mary's Commn. for Women, 1980's, St. Clement's Island/Potomac River Mus., 1980's, St. Mary's LWV, 1988. Mem. Music Tchrs. Nat. Assn., Pa. Music Tchrs. Assn., Prince Georges Music Tchrs. Assn. Home: 5850 Centre Ave # 213 Pittsburgh PA 15206-3782

DE PALMA, NANCY MARIE, school counselor, educator, counselor educator; b. Floral Park, N.Y., Oct. 10, 1948; d. Frank and Catherine (Castrigno) De P.; m. Thomas William Kessler, Oct. 8, 1972 (div. 1990). MS, St. John's U., 1981, profl. diploma, 1985, EdD, 1993. Cert. tchr., N.Y., Conn.; cert. counselor, N.Y., Conn. Tchr. Immaculate Conception Sch., Jamaica Estates, N.Y., 1970-81; sch. counselor The Mary Louis Acad., Jamaica Estates, 1981-86, dir. guidance, 1986-87; sch. counselor William H. Hall H.S., West Hartford, Conn., 1987-90, 95—, King Philip Mid. Sch., West Hartford, 1990-94; adj. asst. prof. U. Conn., Storrs, 1994—. Recipient Outstanding Grad. Student Scholarship award Assn. Counselor Edn. and Supervision, 1987. Mem. Conn. Sch. Counselor Assn. (sec. 1994-95, pres. 1995-96, Mid. Sch. Counselor of Yr. 1992). Roman Catholic. Office: William H. Hall HS 975 N Main St West Hartford CT 06117

DEPAN, MARY ELIZABETH, civic volunteer, nurse; b. Boston, Oct. 5, 1927; d. Frank and Josephine Madeline (Lennon) Natter; m. Harry McCarthy Depan, Apr. 26, 1952 (div. Aug. 1981); children: Harry, Madeline, Mark, Andrew. Diploma in nursing, St. Elizabeth Hosp., Boston, 1948; student, Skidmore Coll., 1960—. RN, Mass. Oper. rm. supr. Gt. Lake Naval Sta., Chgo., 1949; staff nurse Beth Israel Hosp., Boston, 1949. Monitor, leader Gt. Books Found., Glens Falls, N.Y., 1960—, Adirondack C.C., Glens Falls, 1960—; vol., bd. dirs. Literacy Vols., Glens Falls, 1983—; vol. nurse ARC, Glens Falls, 1985—; active area sr. citizen's orgn., 1992—. Lt. (j.g.) USN, 1949-52. Recipient cert. for porcelain painting, 1991. Mem. Women in Arts (chartered), Porcelain Artists, Nat. Mus. Women in the Arts (charter), Women's Meml. (charter). Roman Catholic. Home: 43 Quade St Glens Falls NY 12801

DEPAOLI, GERI M., artist, art historian; b. June 8, 1941; m. Alexander DePaoli, July 4, 1961; children: Alexander Mark, Michael Alexander. BA, U. Md., 1974, MA, 1978; student, U. Calif., Davis, 1965-68. Art history educator, artist, curator slides and photos Nat. Mus., Bangkok, Thailand, 1968-71; art prof. Montgomery Coll., Rockville, Md., 1978-82; cons. oriental slide and photo collection Princeton U., 1983-84; lectr. Princeton Sch. Visual Arts, 1986-90; curator The Mus. Art, Ft. Lauderdale, Fla., 1986; dir. Coun. for Creative Projects, N.Y.C., 1989-91; faculty artworks Princeton Sch. Visual Arts, 1984-91; exec. dir. EducArt Projects Inc., Davis, Calif., 1991—; cons. in field. Editor exhbn. catalog Elvis & Marilyn: 2 X Immortal Rizzoli, 1994; author ednl. resource guide Elvis & Marilyn: 2 X Immortal, 1994; author ednl. program Images of Power, 1994, also video prodr. Images of Power: Balinese Paintings made for Gregory Bateson and Margaret Mead, 1994; editor/co-curator Exhbn. Catalog, Transcending Abstraction, 1986; reviewer ArtMatters Newspaper, Phila., 1987-90; author-curator The Trans Parent Thread: Asian Philosophy in Recent Am. Art 1950-90; contbr. author to Art of Calif. Mag.; on-person shows include E.W. Gallery, Bethesda, Md., 1978, Upstairs Gallery, Kingston, N.J., 1982, Gallery at the Purple Barge, N.Y.C., 1984, The Art Gallery, Kingston, 1985, Back Door Gallery, Princeton, 1986, Campion Gallery of Art, 1987, Prineton, 1986, AT&T Corp. Gallery, Princeton, 1989, Rider Coll. Gallery, LAwrenceville, N.J., 1990; also numerous group shows. Councilor Nat. Abortion Rights Action League, 1989—. Recipient award for excellence in pub., Office of Pres. of U.S., 1969. Fellow Soc. for Arts Religion and Contemporary Culture; mem. Assn. Ind. Historians of Art (v.p. 1988—), Coll. Art Assn., Princeton Rsch. Forum, Nat. Coalition of Ind. Scholars, Sierra Club, Greenpeace. Buddhist. Office: EducArt Projects Inc PO Box 267 Davis CA 95617-0267

DE PASQUALE, LAURA RENÉE, artist, educator; b. Buffalo, Nov. 30, 1961; d. Anthony Charles and Virginia Anne (Burks) De P.; m. Frank Foti, June 14, 1993. BA, Am. Univ., 1984. Project coord., artist, instr. children's art workshops Bakehouse Art Complex, Miami, Fla., 1992—. One woman shows include Subculture Gallery, Phila., 1996; exhibited in group shows at Ft. Lauderdale Mus. Art, 1995, Vero Beach Ctr. Fine Art, 1995. Visual Arts Individual fellow Fla. State Dept. Cultural Affairs, 1995-96. Home and Studio: 739 NE 72 Terrace Miami FL 33138

DEPEW, MARIE KATHRYN, retired secondary education educator; b. Sterling, Colo., Dec. 1, 1928; d. Amos Carl and Dorothy Emelyn (Whiteley) Mehl; m. Emil Carlton DePew, Aug. 30, 1952 (dec. 1973). BA, U. Colo., 1950, MA, 1953. Post grad. Harvard U., Cambridge, Mass., 1962; tchr. Jefferson County Pub. Schs., Arvada, 1953-73; mgr. Colo. Accountability Program, Denver, 1973-83; sr. cons. Colo. Dept. Edn., Denver, 1973-85, ret., 1985. Author: (pamphlet) History of Hammil, Georgetown, Colorado, 1967; contbr. articles to profl. jours. Chmn. Colo. State Accountability Com., Denver, 1971-75. Fellow IDEA Programs, 1976-77, 79-81. Mem. Colo. Hist. Assn., Jefferson County Edn. Assn. (pres. 1963-64), Colo. Edn. Assn. (bd. dirs. 1965-70), Ky. Colonels (hon. mem.), Phi Beta Kappa. Republican. Methodist. Home: 920 Pennsylvania St Denver CO 80203-3157

DE PINHO, CONNIE MARIA, psychologist; b. Angola, Africa, Dec. 27, 1959; came to U.S., 1976; d. Francisco De Pinho and Generosa de Jesus (Reis) Laranjeira; m. Gary Strowe, May 30, 1982 (div. June 1986). MA in Ednl. Psychology, Kean Coll., 1986; MA in Psychology, Adelphi U., 1988, PhD in Clin. Psychology, 1991. Staff psychologist Coney Island Hosp., Bklyn., 1990-92, Stony Lodge Hosp., Briarcliff Manor, N.Y., 1992—; psychologist (cons.) East Bronx (N.Y.) Day Care Ctr., 1992—; pvt. practice Briarcliff Manor, 1993—; workshop leader in field. Contbr. articles to Portuguese media. Mem. NOW, AAUW, APA (spkr. ann. conv. 1992, 94), Portuguese-Am. Health Profl. Assn. (treas., membership dir.), Westchester County Psychology Assn. (women's issues divsn.), Sierra Club. Democrat. Roman Catholic. Office: 144 N State Rd Briarcliff Manor NY 10510

DE PINHO, MARY VOEGELI, French and art history educator; b. Summit, N.J., June 2, 1942; d. Lester Maynard and Helen Virginia (Hay) Voegeli; m. Manuel de Pinho Jr., June 25, 1966; 1 child, Michael Carl. AB, Sarah Lawrence Coll., 1964; MA, Am. Univ., Washington, 1984; postgrad., Johns Hopkins U., 1991. Cert. art historian Smithsonian Instn.; cert. French tchr., Md. Tchr. French lang. & lit. St. Timothy's Sch., Stevenson, Md., 1964-66; tchr. French lang, culture & civilization Potomac Sch., McLean, Va., 1966-69; tchr. French lang. & lit. Holton-Arms Sch., Bethesda, Md., 1969—, chair fgn. lang. dept., 1986-87, 89-92, history art tchr., 1993—; adj. prof. French lang. Am. U., 1983-84. Vol. Holton-Arms Sch. chpt. Am. Field Svc. Internat., 1970-80. Mem. MLA, Am. Assn. Tchrs. French, Am. Coun. Teaching Fgn. Langs., Nat. Mus. Women Arts, Smithsonian Instn., Phillips Gallery. Home: 4721 River Rd Chevy Chase MD 20816

DE PLANQUE, E. GAIL, physicist; b. Orange, N.J., Jan. 15, 1945; d. Martin William and Edna (Gilroy) de P. AB, Immaculata Coll., 1967; MS, N.J. Inst. Tech., 1973; PhD, NYU, 1983. Physicist U.S. AEC, U.S. Dept. Energy, N.Y.C., 1967-82; dep. dir. environ. measurement lab. U.S. Dept. Energy, N.Y.C., 1982-87, dir. environ. measurement lab., 1987—; adj. prof. NYU, N.Y.C., 1986—; pres. Pacific Nuclear Coun., 1989—; mem. engring. sci. dept. adv. com., bd. trustees N.J. Inst. Tech., Newark, 1985—. Contbr. articles to profl. jours. Fellow Am. Nuclear Soc. (bd. dirs. 1977-80, 84-91, v.p. 1987-88, pres. 1988-89), Health Physics Soc., AAAS, Am. Phys. Soc., Assn. for Women in Sci. (v.p. N.Y. met. sect. 1980-82).

DEPUY, BRENDA JANE, personnel specialist; b. St. Louis, Nov. 25, 1946; d. Harry and Elsie Irene (Bilyeu) Anderson; m. Roger Dean King, Apr. 3, 1965 (div. 1978); children: Carol Ann Kinder, Christina King. Student, Drury Coll., U. Mo., Cen. Tex. Coll. Supr. mil. pers. Spl. Dept. of the Army, Ft. Leonard Wood, Mo., 1975-78; supervisory staffing specialist, affirmative employment Spl. Dept. of the Army, Ft. Lee, Va., 1978-91; DMA staffing policy, employment planning, affirmative action policy reductions-in-force/incentives Def. Agy., 1991-93; head employment/classification NSA, Naples, Italy, 1993—; guest instr. handicapped program mgr. course U.S. Dept. of Army, Washington, 1987; mem. U.S. Dept. of Army Mobilization Task Force, Ft. Monroe, Va., 1989; guest speaker EEO Conf., TRADOC. Contbr. article to profl. jour. Mem. Internat. Pers. Mgmt. Assn., Order of Rosicrucians. Home and Office: NSA Human Resource Office PSC 810 Box 29 FPO AE 09619

DERANGO, MARY LAURA KEUL, service occupation careers counselor; b. Racine, Wis., Nov. 13; d. Kelly DeRango and Filomena Covelli; m. Richard C. Keul, Sept. 12, 1953; 1 child, Susan Keul. BE, U. Wis., Parkside, 1972; MEd in Counseling and Pers., Marquette U., 1977; student, U. London, 1979. Elem. tchr. Kenosha Unified Sch. Dist., 1972-81; health careers counselor Gateway Tech. Coll., Kenosha, 1981-90; gen. counselor Gateway Tech. Coll., Racine, Wis., 1990—; cons. CHAMP/pre-coll. program U. Wis.-Parkside, Kenosha, 1982-84; moderator, mem. planning com. Woman to Woman Conf., Milw., 1985; mem. Wis. Gov.'s State Coun. on Affirmative Action, 1987. Active Racine Teen-Age Parent Self-Sufficiency Program, Kenosha Alcohol and Drug Abuse Coun.; mem. accreditation com. Am. Assn. Med. Assts.; sec. Cath. Jr. League; vol. counselor Planned Parenthood; vol. Kenosha Hospice Alliance, Am. Cancer Soc.; vol. reader for the blind Edn. and Reading Svc. Mem. ACCD, Am. Assn. Women in Community and Jr. Colls., Nat. Mgmt. Assn., Wis. Assn. for Counseling and Devel., S.E. Wis. Assn. for Counseling and Devel., Wis. Student Pers. Assn., Wis. Assn. for Vocat. and Adult Edn. Roman Catholic. Home: 23 Globe Heights Dr Racine WI 53406 Office: Gateway Tech Coll 1001 S Main St Racine WI 53403-1501

DERBES, MARY HOWE, multimedia developer, programmer analyst; b. New Orleans, June 18, 1942; d. James Johnston and Alberta (Curren) Howe; children: Monica Derbes Gibson, Joseph Derbes. BA, Maryville Coll., St. Louis, 1963; MA, Emory U., Atlanta, 1964. Programmer analyst and multimedia developer Sun Trust Svc. Corp., Atlanta, 1988—. Republican. Roman Catholic. Office: Sun Trust Svc Corp 250 Piedmont Ave Atlanta GA 30308

DERBY, CHERYL ANN, bookstore owner; b. Syracuse, N.Y., Apr. 2, 1954; d. Lawrence Manuel Brenner and Rose Bunis Bernhardt; m. Paul Harris Derby, Sept. 4, 1982. BA in Art and English, SUNY, Geneseo, 1979. Bookstore owner The Village Booksmith, Albany, N.Y., 1980-84, The Book Outlet, Troy, N.Y., 1984—; part-time dance tchr. Sch. for Music and Dance, Clifton Park, N.Y., 1989-90; part-time art tchr., Troy, N.Y., 1990—. Contbr. poetry to jours. Home: 28 Bolivar Ave Troy NY 12180 Office: The Book Outlet 403 Fulton St Troy NY 12180

DERCHIN, DARY BRET INGHAM, writer; b. Camden, N.J., Sept. 15, 1941; d. Charles and Dorothy Roberta (Ingham) Lambiase; m. Michael Wayne Derchin, Dec. 29, 1970; children: Taylor-Leigh, Danielle Lacey. BA, Montclair State Coll., 1962; postgrad., NYU, 1965, New Sch., 1966. Tchr. Randolph, N.J., 1962-64; rsch. asst. NYU, N.Y.C., 1965-67, Bolivian Peace Corps Project, N.Y.C., 1966; co-head rsch. Derchin Enterprises, N.Y.C., 1970-75. Author: Real Talk, 1992; playwright Blue No More; contbr. articles to the N.Y. Times, Harper's and book the Big Picture, others; talk show host Sta. WALE, 1995; spkr., guest talk shows. Mem. New Dramatists, Lincoln Ctr. Film Soc., Am. Film Inst., Friends of Poets and Writers, Univ. Club, Nat. Art Club (lit. com., film com., Joseph Kesselring Playwright award com.). Home: Laurel Cove PO Box 200 Fair Haven NJ 07704-0200

DE REINECK, MARIE, interior designer; b. Ellington, Mo.; d. Thomas Otto and Lessie (Deen) Buford; m. Baron Radu de Reineck, Mar. 30, 1933; 1 child, Claire; m. Radu Romanesco, Dec. 8, 1970. BS, Fordham U., 1941; grad., N.Y. Sch. Interior Design. Freelance interior designer, 1941—; tchr. interior design Finch Coll., N.Y.C., 1946 61, NYU, N.Y.C., 1949-54; founder Claymar Sch. Design, 1948-55. Author: How to Decorate Your Home, 1954. Mem. Am. Inst. Decorators, AIA/Am. Archl. Found. (allied mem.). Republican. Roman Catholic.

DE RESENDIZ, SUSAN B., lawyer; b. Athens, Ohio, July 6, 1947. BA in French cum laude, Ohio State U., 1968; JD cum laude, George Washington U., 1974. Bar: Ohio 1974, D.C. 1975, Fla. 1980. Ptnr. Baker & Hostetler, Cleve. Contbr. articles to profl. jours. Mem. ABA (chmn. subcom. on taxation and fed. claims, bus. bankruptcy com., sect. bus. law 1989—), Ohio State Bar Assn., Cleve. Bar Assn., Phi Beta Kappa. Office: Baker & Hostetler 3200 Nat City Ctr 1900 E 9th St Cleveland OH 44114-3985*

DERITTER, MARGARET CATHERINE, journalist; b. Paterson, N.J., May 14, 1957; d. Elmer and Lena (Soodsma) DeR. BA in Philosophy, Calvin Coll., 1979. Assoc. editor Ch. Herald, Grand Rapids, Mich., 1980-83; reporter, copy editor Advance Newspapers, Jenison, Mich., 1983-84, asst. editor, 1985-86, sr. news editor, 1986-88; state wire editor Kalamazoo (Mich.) Gazette, 1988-89, metro copy editor, 1989-91, Sunday arts and entertainment editor, health and sci. editor, 1991—. Mem. spkrs. bur. Dreaming Me, Kalamazoo, 1994-96. Recipient Sch. Bell award Mich. Edn. Assn., 1986, 87, 3d Pl. award Mich. Press Club, 1987, Hon. Mention award Mich. Press Assn., 1995, 2d Pl. award Mich. Press Assn., 1993, 2d Pl. award Penney-Mo. awards, 1992, 1st Pl. award Mich. Press Assn., 1993, Hon. Mention award Women in Comms., Inc., 1993. Mem. Nat. Lesbian and Gay Journalists Assn., Women in Comms., Inc. (West Mich. chpt. bd. dirs. 1993-94). Office: Kalamazoo Gazette 401 S Burdick Kalamazoo MI 49007

DE RIVAS, CARMELA FODERARO, psychiatrist, hospital administrator; b. Cortale, Italy, Nov. 25, 1920; came to U.S., 1935, naturalized, 1942; d. Salvatore and Mary (Vaiti) Foderaro; m. Aureliano Rivas, Oct. 30, 1948; children: Carmen, Norma, Sandra, David. Student, U. Pa., 1940-42; M.D., Women's Med. Coll. Pa., 1946. Diplomate: Am. Bd. Psychiatry and Neurology. Intern women's Med. Coll. Pa. Hosp., 1946; gen. practice Phila., 1947-49, Tex., 1947-49; mem. staff Norristown (Pa.) State Hosp., 1949-63, supt., 1963-70, dir. family planning, 1979-87, clin. dir. spl. assignments, 1979-82; assoc. psychiatry U. Pa., 1963-75; psychiatrist Penn Found. Mental Health, Sellersville, Pa., 1970-72; dir. intake coping svcs. Ctrl. Montgomery Mental Health/Mental Retardation Ctr., Norristown, Pa., 1972-77, med. dir., 1977-82, psychiatrist, 1980-82; cons. surveyor HEalth Care Fin. Administrn., 1987—; dir. program evaluation Norristown State Hosp., 1979-82, med. dir., 1982-87. Named to Hall of Fame S. Phila. H.S., 1968; recipient citation Women's Med. Coll. Pa., 1968, Amita achievement award, 1976, achievement award Grad. Club Phila., 1976; named Woman of Yr. Pa. Fedn. Bus. and Profl. Women, 1979. Fellow Am. Psychiat. Assn., Pa. Psychiat. Soc. (rep. assembly of dist. brs. 1979-88); mem. AMA, Phila. Psychiat. Soc. (councilor), Montgomery County Med. Soc. (bd. dirs., past pres.), Pa. Med. Soc. (chmn. adv. com. to aux. 1981-88, mem. ho. of dels., mem. commn. on med. edn. 1991-94, mem. com. on continuing med. edn. 1994—). Home: 700 Joseph Dr Wayne PA 19087-1021

DERKSEN, CHARLOTTE RUTH MEYNINK, librarian; b. Newberg, Oreg., Mar. 15, 1944; d. John Philip and Wanda Marie (Rohrbough) Meynink; m. Roy Arthur Derksen, Dec. 27, 1966; children: Kathryn Marie Lesedi, Elizabeth Charlotte. BS in Geology, Wheaton (Ill.) Coll., 1966; MA in Geology, U. Oreg., 1968, MLS, 1973. Faculty and librarian Moeding Coll., Ootse Botswana, 1968-70, head history dept., 1970-71; tchr. Jackson Pub. High Sch. (Minn.), 1975-77; sci. librarian U. Wis., Oshkosh, 1977-80; librarian and bibliographer Stanford (Calif.) U., 1980—, acting chief scis., 1985-86, head Sci. and Engring. Librs., 1992—. Contb. author: Union List of Geologic Field Trip Guidebooks of North America, contbr. articles to profl. publs. Mem. ALA (rep. 1983-85), Spl. Library Assn., Western Assn. Map Librarians, Geosci. Info. Soc. (rep. 1985), Cartographic Users Adv. Coun. (mem. GeoRef adv. bd. 1992—, chair 1988-90). Republican. Lutheran. Home: 128 Mission Dr Palo Alto CA 94303-2753 Office: Stanford U Branner Earth Scis Library Stanford CA 94305

DERN, LAURA, actress; b. Santa Monica, Calif., Feb. 10, 1967; d. Bruce Dern and Diane Ladd. Student, Lee Strasberg Inst., Royal Acad. Dramatic Art, London. Appeared in films Alice Doesn't Live Here Anymore, 1975, Foxes, 1980, Ladies and Gentlemen, The Fabulous Stains, 1982, Teachers, 1984, Mask, 1985, Smooth Talk, 1985, Blue Velvet, 1986, Haunted Summer, 1988, Fat Man & Little Boy, 1989, Wild At Heart, 1990, Rambling Rose, 1991 (Acad. award nomination for best actress, Golden Globe nomination for best actress in a drama), Jurassic Park, 1993, A Perfect World, 1993, Citizen Ruth, 1996; TV appearances include: Afterburn, 1992 (Golden Globe award for best actress in TV movie or mini series), Fallen Angels (Murder, Obliquely), 1993 (Emmy nomination, Best Actress - Drama, 1994), Ruby Ridge, 1996; stage appearances include The Palace of Amateurs (N.Y.), 1988, Brooklyn Laundry (L.A.); dir. The Gift. *

DE ROECK, L. MILLIE, educational administrator; b. Puerto Rico, Dec. 14, 1950; came to U.S., 1950; d. Basilio Perez-Lugo and Carmen Mary (Hernandez); m. Luke De Roeck, 1978 (div. 1983). BA, Northeastern Ill. U., 1973; MA, Roosevelt U., 1976. Counselor Roberto Clemente H.S., Chgo., 1973-78, acting asst. prin., 1978-86; guidance counselor evening program and adult H.S. program summer sch. City-Wide Colls., Chgo., 1988-91; counselor Lane Tech. H.S., Chgo., 1986-91, summer program mgr., 1987, 88, 89, spl. edn. case mgr., 1989-91; acting asst. prin. Ellis Middle Sch., Elgin, Ill., 1992; dean of students Elgin H.S., 1991-94, Hinsdale (Ill.) Ctrl. H.S., 1994—; mem. North Central Evaluations com. Chgo. Sch. System, 1978-86, mem. peer counseling implementation com., 1987, mem. sch. improvement com., 1990. mem. Adminstr. Educator Supr. Assn Ill. Prin. Assn.

DE ROSE, ANNA MARIA, psychotherapist, counselor; b. Highland Park, Ill., Mar. 31, 1965; d. John F. and Maria C. (Sorrentino) De R. LPN, Loyola U., 1987; BA, Nat. Louis U., 1992, MS in Counseling and Human Svcs., 1993. Cert. NBCC, LPC. Nursing supr. Highland Park (Ill.) Hosp., 1979-90; instr., advisor Nat. Louis U., Chgo., 1993—; psychotherapist, counselor Tomorrow's Hope, Inc., Northbrook, Ill., 1993—. Mem. APA, Am. Counselor Assn., Am. Assn. Marriage and Family Therapy, Acad. Family Mediators, Ill. Alcohol Drug Dependence Assn. Democrat. Roman Catholic. Office: Tomorrows Hope Inc 3710 Commercial # 7 Northbrook IL 60062

DE ROSE, SANDRA MICHELE, psychotherapist, educator, supervisor, administrator; b. Beacon, N.Y.; d. Michael Joseph Borrell and Mabel Adelaide Edic Sloane; m. James Joseph De Rose, June 28, 1964 (div. 1977); 1 child, Stacey Marie. Diploma in nursing, St. Luke's Hosp., 1964; BA in Child and Community Psychology, Albertus Magnus Coll., 1983; MS in Counseling Psychology with honors, Century U., 1986, PhD in Counseling Psychology with honors, 1987. Gen. duty float nurse St. Luke's Hosp., Newburgh, N.Y., 1964-65; pvt. practice New Haven, 1975—; supr. nurses Craig House Hosp., Beacon, N.Y., 1986-94; dir. staff devel., team dir. divsn. outpatient treatment svc. Conn. Mental Health Ctr., New Haven, 1986-94; dir. edn., 1994-95; clin. instr. Sch. Nursing Yale U., New Haven, 1979-84, clin. instr. dept. psychiatry, 1989-96; dir. edn. outpatient divsn. Conn. Mental Health Ctr., New Haven, 1994-95; pvt. practice Comprehensive Psychiat. Care, New Haven, 1996—; clin. dir. Comprehensive Psychiat. Care, Norwich, Colchester and Willimantic, Conn., 1994-96. Mem. AAUW, ANA (cert.), Conn. Nurses Assn., Conn. Soc. Psychoanalytic Psychologists, Conn. Soc. Nurse Psychotherapists, Assn. for Advancement Philosophy and Psychiatry, Ea. Conn. Psychiat. Assn. (exec. dir.), Sigma Theta Tau, Delta Mu, Alpha Sigma Lambda. Office: 203 Starro Rd Willimantic CT 06226 also: 210 Prospect St New Haven CT 06511-2186 also: 200 W Town St Norwich CT 06360 also: 188 Norwich Ave Colchester CT 06415

DERR, DEBRA HULSE, advertising executive, publisher, editor; b. Newark, May 19, 1955; d. Edgar William and Mary Carway Hulse; m. David Derr, Oct. 6, 1984. Student, Fordham U., 1973-76. Lic. employment agy. operator, N.J. Prodn. coord. Telepages, Inc., Parsippany, N.J., 1976-79; credit investigator Hertz Corp., Parsippany, 1979-82; employment counselor Baker Pers., Pine Brook, N.J., 1982-84; copywriter Creative Mktg., Fairfield, N.J., 1984-87; pers. cons. Career Line, Inc., Morris Plains, N.J., 1987-92; v.p. D2 Studios, Inc., Parsippany, 1992—. Contbg. author: Journeys Into Self-Acceptance, 1994; pub., editor Tiny Lion, 1995. Activist, spkr. Nat. Orgn. to Advance Fat Acceptance, No. N.J. chpt., 1990—. Mem. NOW. Office: D2 Studios Inc PO Box 8112 Parsippany NJ 07054

DERR, JEANNIE COMBS, bilingual educator, anthropology educator; b. L.A., May 17, 1954; d. Jack Vincent and Evelyn Mary (Weiss) Combs; m. Dennis Eugene Derr, Aug. 6, 1983; children: Natalie Winona, Jeremy Lloyd. AA in Anthropology, Pasadena City Coll., 1975; BA in Anthropology, Calif. State U., L.A., 1978, MA in Anthropology, 1979. Calif. C.C. credential anthropology; Calif. multiple subjects credential. Textbook adoptions western region corr. Bowmar Noble Pubs., Inc., Glendale, Calif., 1979-80; bilingual tchr. Pasadena (Calif.) Unified Sch. Dist., 1981-82; exch. tchr. bilingual L'ecole Aujourd'hui, Paris, 1982-83; migrant edn., bilingual tchr. Oxnard (Calif.) Sch. Dist., 1983—; instr. anthropology Oxnard Coll., 1989—; instr. humanities St. John's Seminary Coll., Camarillo, Calif., 1990—; instr. ethnic rels. U. LaVerne, Pt. Mugu, Calif., 1995—. Editor (resource booklet) Oxnard Migrant Education, 1987. Violinist Jr. Philharm. Orch. Calif., L.A., 1967—, Opus 1 Chamber Orch., L.A., 1976-79; soprano, officer San Marino (Calif.) Cmty. Ch., 1974-83. Mem. AAUW, Am. Mexican Am. Educators, Am. Soc. Anthropology, Soc. Am. Archeology, Soc. for the Study Evolution. Republican. Presbyterian. Home: 1650 Shoreline St Camarillo CA 93010

DERRICK, CARLA RANDALIN, school librarian; b. Millard, Mo., Oct. 11, 1932; d. Royal L. and Rosalie A. (Burns) Peterson; m. Neil Tipton Derrick, Nov. 26, 1952; children: Karen, Neil Jr., Laura. BS in Edn., No. Mo. State U., 1954, MA in Sch. Adminstrn., 1978; MLS, U. Mo., 1986. Libr. Clark County H.S., 1971—; instr. No. Mo. State U., Kirksville, 1988—; pres. NE Mo. Dist. Librs., 1974-76. Bd. dirs. Mo. divsn. Am. Cancer Soc., 1985-90, Clark County unit, 1970—; choir dir. St. Paul United Ch. of Christ, Kahoka, 1986-94; bd. dirs., leader Girl Scouts U.S., 1964-79. Named Kiwanis Tchr. of the Yr., 1994. Mem. Mo. Assn. Sch. Librs., Delta Kappa Gamma (comms. chair 1993—). Office: Clark County HS 427 W Chestnut St Kahoka MO 63445-1314

DERRICKSON, DENISE ANN, social studies educator; b. Seaford, Del., Sept. 20, 1956; d. William Hudson and Patricia Ann (Adkins) D. BS, James Madison U., 1978; MEd in Counseling and Human Devel., George Mason U., 1990, MEd in Curriculum & Instrn., 1994. Social studies instr. Brentsville Dist. High Sch., Nokesville, Va., 1978-91; Woodbridge (Va.) Sr. High Sch., 1991—; faculty liaison Parent-Tchr. Action Coun., 1990-91; prin.'s adv. coun., 1994-96. Vol. Childrens Hosp., Washington, 1983-86, Action in the Community through Svc., Inc.-Helpline, Manassas, Va., 1988-92. Recipient Cert. Appreciation Prince William County Sch. Bd., 1989, Outstanding Educator award Va. Govs. Sch., 1990, ACTS-Helpline Outstanding Vol. Svc. award, 1990. Mem. NEA, AAUW, ASCD, Am. Assn. Curriculum Devel., Nat. Soc. for Study of Edn., Va. Edn. Assn., Va. Assn. Supervision and Curriculum Devel., Prince William Edn. Assn., Internat. Platform Assn., Kappa Delta Phi, Phi Delta Kappa. Office: Woodbridge Sr High Sch 3001 Old Bridge Rd Lakeridge VA 22192-3221

DERRICKSON, SHIRLEY JEAN BALDWIN, elementary school educator; b. Balt., Aug. 7, 1943; d. James Francis and Dorothy Elizabeth (Jubb) Baldwin; m. Ernest Hughes Derrickson, Aug. 19, 1978. BA, Knox Coll., 1965; MEd, Goucher Coll., 1969; postgrad., Towson State U., 1970-77. Cert. profl. status elem. tchr., Del. Tchr. Howard Park Elem. Sch., Balt., 1969-70, Lida Lee Tall Learning Resource Ctr., Towson (Md.) State U., 1970-83, Selbyville (Del.) Middle Sch., 1983-84, East Millsboro (Del.) Elem. Sch., 1984—. Foreign affairs chmn. Dagsboro (Del.) Century Club, 1990—, sec., 1986-88; sec. Dagsboro Rep. Club, 1986-88; active Friends of Prince George's Chapel, 1994—. Recipient Washington Regional scholarship, 1961-64. Mem. NEA, Del. State Edn. Assn., Indian River Edn. Assn., PTO. Republican. Methodist. Office: East Millsboro Elem Sch 500 E State St Millsboro DE 19966-1109

DERRY, CONNIE SUSIE, psychogeriatrics nurse; b. Elmira, N.Y., Oct. 24, 1958; d. Robert G. and Phyllis B. (Duggan) Wilber; m. James Derry; children: Melissa, Elizabeth. AAS, Corning (N.Y.) Community Coll., 1983; BSN, Alfred (N.Y.) U., 1990; MSN, Syracuse U., 1994. Cert. clin. nurse specialist, geriatric nursing. Charge nurse Tioga Gen. Hosp., Waverly, N.Y., 1983-84; head nurse rehab. unit Elmira Psychiat. Ctr., 1984-89; charge nurse Arnot Ogden Meml. Hosp., Elmira, 1989-91; asst. unit mgr. Founder's Pavilion, Corning (N.Y.) Hosp., 1991-93; dir. nursing Three Rivers Health Care Ctr., Painted Post, N.Y., 1993-96, acting adminstr., 1994-95; staff nurse VAMC, Durham, N.C., 1996—. Mem. ANA (cert. gerontological nursing), Am. Psychiat. Nurses' Assn., N.C. Nurse's Assn. Home: 405 Indigo Dr Cory NY 27513

DERSH, RHODA E., management consultant, business executive; b. Phila., Sept. 10, 1934; civ; d. Maurice S. and Kay (Wiener) Eisman; m. Jerome Dersh, Dec. 23, 1956; children: Debra Lori, Jeffrey Jonathan. BA, U. Pa., 1955; MA, Tufts U., 1956; MBA, Manhattan Coll., 1980. Interpreter Consul of Chile, 1954-57; various teaching and staff positions Albright Coll., Mt. Holyoke Coll., Amherst Coll., Marple Newtown Sch., 1957-58; pres., chief exec. officer Profl. Practice Mgmt. Assocs., Reading, 1976—, Pace Inst., Reading, 1981—, Pace Mgmt., Inc., 1983—;, 1984-90; mem. regional adv. bd. Core States Bank, 1991—; mem., bd. dirs. Ctr. City Devel. Corp., 1992—. Author: The School Budget is Your Business, 1976, Business Management for Professional Offices, 1977, The School Budget: It's Your Money, It's Your Business, 1979, Improving Public School Management Practices, 1979, Part-Time Professional and Managerial Personnel: The Employers View, 1979; contbr. articles to profl. jours. Bd. dirs. Pa. State Bd. Pvt. Lic. Schs., 1987-93; cons. dir. pub. sch. budget study project City of Reading, 1967-78, chmn. comprehensive community plan task force, 1973-75; chmn. pub. svc. cons. project 1980-90; panel chmn. budget allocations United Way, 1974-76; del. White House Conf. on Children Youth, 1970; co-founder World Affairs Coun., Reading and Berks County, 1963-65; chmn. Berks County Com. for Children Youth, 1968-72; commr. Trial Ct. Nominating Commn. of Berks County (Pa.), 1982-84; bd. dirs. United Way of Berks County, 1984-89; chmn. programs Leadership Berks, 1986-87; bd. dirs. Reading Ctr. City Devel. Corp., Berks Bus.-Edn. Coalition Corp., 1991—. Recipient Trendsetter award YWCA, 1985. Mem. AAUW (edn1. found. grant.), LWV, Pa. Assn. Pvt. Sch. Bus. Adminstrs. (bd. dirs. 1985-89), Berks County C. of C. (bd. dirs. 1983-86, chmn. edn. com. 1983-85), Am. Acad. Ind. Cons. (pres. 1978-80), Reading and Berks C. of C (Entrepreneur of Yr. 1985), Rotary (bd. dirs. Reading, Pa., chpt. 1989-90). Office: 606 Court St Reading PA 19601-3542

DERUBERTIS, PATRICIA SANDRA, software company executive; b. Bayonne, N.J., July 10, 1950; d. George Joseph and Veronica (Lukaszewich) Uhl; m. Michael DeRubertis, 1986. BS, U. Md., 1972. Account rep. GE, San Francisco, 1975-77; tech. rep. Computer Scis. Corp., San Francisco, 1977-78; cons., pres. Uhl Assocs., Tiburon, Calif., 1978-81; cons. mgr. Ross Sys., Palo Alto, Calif., 1981-83; COO, exec. v.p. Distributed Planning Sys., Calabasas, Calif., 1983-92; pres. DeRubertis & Assocs., Thousand Oaks, Calif., 1992-94, DeRubertis Software Sys., Inc., Jensen Beach, Fla., 1995—. Author: Rose Gardening By Color, 1994. Troop leader San Francisco coun. Girl Scouts Am., 1974; participant Woman On Water, Marina Del Rey, Calif., 1983; vol. Martin County Coun. for the Arts, 1995. Mem. AAUW, NAFE, Delta Delta Delta. Democrat.

DERVILLE-TEER, HOLLY ELIZABETH, dancer; b. Cin., Feb. 1, 1970; d. William Cranston and Brenda Lee (Peterman) Derville; m. Eldon Nelson Teer, Nov. 12, 1993. BA in Edn. and English, Principia Coll., 1992. Dancer Marcells Prodns., San Juan, P.R., 1992, Allan Albert Prodns., Hershey, Pa., 1993; sillouhetted dancer Star Search Opening, L.A., 1994; dancer Yagi Planning, Sappao, Japan, 1994-95; work scholarship Steps on Broadway, N.Y.C., 1995—. Mem. NOW. Democrat.

DERVIN, BRENDA LOUISE, communications educator; b. Beverly, Mass., Nov. 20, 1938; d. Ermina Diluiso; adopted d. John Jordan and Marjorie (Sullivan) D. BS, Cornell U., 1960; MA, Mich. State U., 1968, PhD, 1972. Pub. info. asst. Am. Home Econ. Assn., Washington, 1960-62; pub. info. specialist Ctr. Consumer Affairs, U. Wis., Milw., 1962-65; instr., rsch. and teaching asst. dept. communications Mich. State U., E. Lansing, 1965-70; asst. prof., Sch. Info. Transfer Syracuse (N.Y.) U., 1970-72; asst. to assoc. prof. U. Wash., Seattle, 1972-85; prof. dept. communication Ohio State U., Columbus, 1985—. Co-author: The Mass Media Behavior of the Urban Poor, 1980; editor: Rethinking Communication, 1989; editor jour. Progress in Communication Sci., 1981-92; contbr. numerous articles to profl. publs. Grantee U.S. Office Edn., 1974-76, Calif. State Libr., 1974-84, Nat. Cancer Inst., 1984. Fellow Internat. Communication Assn. (pres. 1986-87); mem. Internat. Assn. Mass Communications Rsch. (governing coun. 1988—). Home: 4269 Kenridge Dr Columbus OH 43220-4157 Office: Ohio State U Dept Communications 154 N Oval Mall Columbus OH 43210-1330

DERWENSKUS, MARILYNN, artist, educator; b. Detroit, Dec. 23, 1937. BFA, Wayne State U., 1960, MA, 1962; MFA, U. Chgo., 1988. Assoc. prof. Ball State U., Mincie, Ind., 1988—; co-dir. Art in Italy Ball State U., Muncie, 1994-95. Represented by Cary Gallery, Rochester, Mich. Lilly fellow, 1995-96. Mem. Nat. Watercolor Soc., Midwest Watercolor Soc., Watercolor Soc. Ind., N.W. Watercolor Soc., Ala. Watercolor Soc., Ga. Watercolor Soc., Pa. Watercolor Soc., Mich. Watercolor Soc., Soc. Exptl. Artists, Ptnrs. of Ams., Penwomen. Home: 3716 Lakeside Muncie IN 47304 Office: Ball State U Dept of Art Muncie IN 47306

DERYCKE, KIMBERLEY ANN, accountant; b. Rochester, N.Y., Sept. 23, 1968; d. Douglas Charles and Gayle Ann (McMichael) DeRycke. BS in Acctg., SUNY, Oswego, 1990. Bus. Edn. Tchg. Certificate, Nazareth Coll. of Rochester, 1994. Cost acctg. clerk Comstock-Mich. Fruit, Rochester, 1990-91, cost acct., 1991-93; check request disbursement clerk Xerox Corp., Rochester, 1993-94, control svcs. analyst, 1994-95, disbursement analyst, 1995-96, acct., 1996—. Mem. Inst. Mgmt. Accts., Nat. Bus. Educators Assn., N.Y. Bus. Educators Assn., Monroe County Bus. Educators Assn. Republican. Home: 90 Selborne Chase Fairport NY 14450

DE SÁ E SILVA, ELIZABETH ANNE, secondary education educator; b. Edmonds, Wash., Mar. 17, 1931; d. Sven Yngve and Anna Laura Elizabeth (Dahlin) Erlandson; m. Claudio de Sá e Silva, Sept. 12, 1955 (div. July 1977); children: Lydia, Marco, Nelson. BA, U. Oreg., 1953; postgrad., Columbia U., 1954-56, Calif. State U., Fresno, 1990, U. No. Iowa, 1993; MEd, Mont. State U., 1978. Cert. tchr., Oreg., Mont. Med. sec., 1947-49; sec. Merced (Calif.) Sch. Dist., 1950-51; sec., asst. Simon and Schuster, Inc., N.Y.C., 1954-56; tchr. Casa Roosevelt-União Cultural, São Paulo, Brazil, 1957-59, Coquille (Oreg.) Sch. Dist., 1978-96; tchr. piano, 1967-78; instr. Spanish, Southwestern Oreg. C.C., Coos Bay, 1991-94; pianist/organist Faith Luth. Ch., North Bend, Oreg., 1995—. Chmn. publicity Music in Our Schs. Month, Oreg. Dist. VII, 1980-85; sec. Newcomer's Club, Bozeman, Mont., 1971. Quincentennial fellow U. Minn. and Found. José Ortega y Gasset, Madrid, 1991. Mem. AAUW (sec., scholarship chmn., co-pres., pres.), Nat. Trust Hist. Preservation, Am. Coun. on Tchg. Fgn. Langs., Am. Assn. Tchrs. Spanish and Portuguese, Nat. Coun. Tchrs. English, Music Educators Nat. Conf., Oreg. Music Educators Assn., Oreg. Coun. Tchrs. English, Confedn. Oreg. Fgn. Lang. Tchrs., VoiceCare Network. Republican. Home: 3486 Spruce St North Bend OR 97459-1130

DESAI, ANITA, writer; b. Mussoorie, India, June 24, 1937; came to U.S., 1987; d. D.N. and Toni (Nime) Mazumdar; m. Ashvin Desai, Dec. 13, 1958; children: Rahul, Tani, Arjun, Kiran. BA, Delhi U., 1957. Author: Cry, the Peacock, 1963, Voices in the City, 1965, Bye-Bye Blackbird, 1968, The Peacock Garden, 1974, Where Shall We Go This Summer?, 1975, Cat on a Houseboat, 1976, Fire on the Mountain, 1977, Games at Twilight and Other Stories, 1978, Clear Light of Day, 1980, The Village by the Sea, 1982, In Custody, 1985, Baumgartner's Bombay, 1989, Journey to Ithaca, 1995. Recipient Winifred Holtby prize Royal Soc. Lit., 1978, Sahitya Acad. award, 1979, Guardian award for children's book, 1982, Lit. Lion award N.Y. Pub. Libr., 1993, Neil Gunn fellowship Scottish Arts Coun., 1994; Girton Coll. and Clare Hall fellow Cambridge U., Eng. Fellow Am. Acad. Arts and Letters (hon.), Royal Soc. Lit. Eng. Office: MIT 14E-303 Prog Writing/ Humanist Ideas Cambridge MA 02139

DESAI, VEENA BALVANTRAI, obstetrician and gynecologist, educator; b. Karvan, Gujarat, India, Oct. 5, 1931; came to U.S., 1973; d. Balvantrai P. and Maniben (Vashi) Desai; m. Vinay D. Gandevia, Sept. 19, 1994. MBBS, Seth G.S. Med. Coll., Bombay, 1957, MD, 1961. Jr. resident Bombay U., 1957-59; home officer gyn. Chalmer's Hosp., Edinburgh, Scotland, 1962-63; registrar ob-gyn. Neath (U.K.) Gen. Hosp., 1962-63, Scunthorpe (U.K.) Gen. Hosp., 1963-64; chief resident ob-gyn. St. John (Can.) Gen. Hosp., 1973-74; attending ob-gyn. Portsmouth (N.H.) Hosp., 1975-84; assoc. prof. Boston U., 1985-86; sr. staff ob-gyn. Santa Clara (Calif.) Valley Med. Ctr., 1986-87; mem. sr. staff ob-gyn. West Anaheim (Calif.) Med. Ctr., 1988-94, chief dept. ob-gyn., 1991-93; assoc. clin. prof. ob-gyn. U. Calif., Irvine, 1990-96, vice chmn. med. staff, 1994, 95; pres. Desai Med. Corp., Anaheim, 1989—. Chmn.'s advisor Nat. Security Coun.; charter mem. Presdl. Task Force; mem. Rep. Party Inner Cir., 1984-94. Recipient Presdl. Medal of Merit, 1982, award Spl. Congl. Adv. Bd., 1984, Order of Liberty, U.S. Congress, 1993, Medal of Freedom, U.S. Senate, 1994, medal Ronal Wilson Reagan Eternal Flame of Freedom, 1995. Fellow ACS, Internat. Coll. Surgeons, Am. Coll. Ob-Gyn., Royal Coll. Ob-Gyn.; mem. Buena Park Rotary (pres. 1994, chair internat. svc. 1992-93). Home: 15632 Sunburst Ln Huntington Beach CA 92647 Office: Desai Med Corp 3010 W Orange Ave Ste 110 Anaheim CA 92804-3170

DESAI, VISHAKHA N., gallery executive, society administrator; b. Ahemedabad, Gujarat, India, May 1, 1949; came to U.S., 1966; m. Robert B. Oxnam, 1993. BA, Bombay U., Elphinstone Coll., 1970; MA in History of Art, U. Mich., 1975, PhD in History of Art, 1984. With edn. div. Bklyn. Mus., N.Y.C., 1972-74; head exhibit resource Mus. sect. edn. dept. Fine Arts, Boston, 1977-80; acting dir. edn. dept. Mus. Fine Arts, Boston, 1980-81, coord. acad. program, 1981-88, asst. curator, 1981-90; dir. The Asia Soc. Galleries, N.Y.C., 1990—; v.p. The Asia Soc., 1993—; adj. asst. prof. Boston U., 1982-87; assoc. prof. U. Mass., Boston, 1986-90; adj. prof. Columbia U.; bd. dirs. Am. Com. South/S.E. Asia Art; reviewer Bunting Inst., Radcliffe Coll., Boston, 1990—; bd. dirs. Art Table, N.Y.C., 1991-94. Contbr. articles to profl. jours. Pres. Mass. Found. for Humanities, 1989-91. Outstanding Teaching fellow U. Mich., 1977, Am. Inst. of Indian Studies fellow, 1978; grantee, Nat. Endowment for the Arts, NEM, 1979—, Mus. Sabbaticatal grantee Nat. Endowment for the Arts, 1982. Mem. Coll. Art Assn. (bd. dirs. 1995—), Am. Assn. Art Mus. Dirs. (bd. dirs. 1995—). Office: The Asia Soc Galleries 725 Park Ave New York NY 10021-5025

DESAUTELS, ANNE CATHERINE, communications executive; b. Balt., Sept. 9, 1956; d. Paul Ernest and Lenora Catherine (Brennan) Desautels. BA cum laude, U. Md., 1978; student Goucher Coll., 1974-75; artist-in-residence Wolftrap/Am. U. Summer Acad., 1973. Supr., mdse. adjustments Woodward & Lothrop, Washington, 1979-81; officer mgr., researcher Paul Stafford Assocs., Washington, 1981-82; grad. recruiting adminstr. Strategic Planning Assocs., Washington, 1982-84; contract adminstr. Citcom Systems, Inc., Herndon, Va., 1984-85, market communications mgr., 1985-87, market communications coord. Alcatel Network Systems/Transcom, 1987-88; pub. relations specialist Peabody Devel. Corp., Washington, 1985-87; mgr. market communications Telco Systems Network Access Corp., Fremont, Calif., 1988-90; sr. pub. rels. specialist 3COM Corp., Santa Clara, Calif., 1990-91; dir. mktg. and comms. Telebit Corp., 1991-92; prin., founder Sagresse Mktg., 1992-93; tech. strategist Blanc & Otus, San Francisco, 1993—. Com. mem. Internat. Trade Assn. No. Va., 1985-87; panelist U.S. Sml. Bus. Adminstrn. Mktg. Edn. Svc., 1986; officer ad litum Ct. Apptd. Child Advocate Progran, San Jose and San Mateo, Calif. By-lined columnist iWorld. Mem. Telegraph Hill Cmty. Assn., Internat. Network Women in Tech. (adv. bd. dirs.), C. of C. (com. mem.), The Churchill Club (Palo Alto, Calif., program com. mem.), Phi Beta Kappa, Phi Kappa Phi, Delta Phi Alpha. Republican. Roman Catholic. Avocations: cross country cycling, jazz, dancing, music. Office: Blanc & Otus 135 Main St Fl 12 San Francisco CA 94105

DESCANO-NELSON, LINDA, environmental affairs administrator; b. Phila., Aug. 1, 1960; d. Joseph Felix and Henrietta Angela (Pennachietti) Descano; m. Eric Lundy Nelson. BA in Geology, Temple U., 1982; postgrad. in Geophysics, Tex. A&M U., 1982-85, postgrad. in Pub. Policy, 1988-90. Devel. coord. Tex. Alliance for Sci., Tech. and Math. Edn., College Station, 1987-88; tech. editor dept. computer sci. Tex. A&M U., College Station, 1989; litigation svcs. mgr. KW Brown Environ. Svcs., College Station, 1989-90, dir. law and pub. policy, 1990; ops. dir. KW Brown Environ. Svcs., Phila. and Houston, 1991-93; sr. assoc. environ. affairs Salomon Inc., N.Y.C., 1994, v.p. environ. affairs, 1994—; chpt. leader N.Y., Recycled Paper Coalition, San Francisco, 1995—; mem. Conf. Bd. Coun. of EHS Officers, N.Y.C., 1994—; interim chair UN Environ. Programme Americas Fin. Adv. Group, 1996. Pub. rels. chair LWV, Brazos County, Tex., 1988-90; vol. Dem. Party, Phila., 1978-80, Painted Bride Art Ctr., Phila., 1979-82, Theater Ctr., Phila., 1980-82. Mem. NAFE, Nat. Assn. Environ. Mgmt., Nat. Assn. Environ. Profls. (chair regulatory process working group 1992—). Office: Salomon Inc 7 World Trade Ctr New York NY 10048

DESCHAINE, BARBARA RALPH, real estate broker; b. Syracuse, N.Y., Feb. 16, 1930; d. George John and Dora Belle (Manchester) Ralph; children by previous marriage: Olav Bernt Kollevoll, Kristan George Kollevoll, Eric John Kollevoll; m. Bernard Richard Deschaine, May 23, 1981 (dec. 1994). BA, St. Lawrence U., 1952; postgrad. Pa. State U., 1969-72; grad. Pa. Realtors Inst., 1973; student Realtors Nat. Mktg. Inst., 1974-75. Salesman Brose Realty, Easton, Pa., 1967-72, assoc. broker/mgr., 1973, broker, owner, 1974-85; broker, mgr. John W. Monaghan Corp. Realtors, 1985-91; assoc. broker The Prudential/Paul Ford Realtors, Easton, 1991—; mem. Pa. Real Estate Polit. Edn. Com. Bd. dirs. Easton Area C. of C., 1973-79, v.p. organizational improvement, 1975-76, v.p. econ. devel., 1976-77, pres., 1977-78; mem. Greater Easton Corp. Strategy Group, 1977-78; mem. Northampton County Revenue Appeals Bd., 1982—; co-chmn. 1994—; trustee Easton area YWCA, 1984-91; bd. dirs. State Theatre for the Arts, 1994—. Mem. NAFE, Nat. Assn. Realtors, Pa. Assn. Realtors, Bethlehem Bd. Realtors, Eastern Northampton County Bd. Realtors (bd. dirs. 1973-87, sec. 1977, v.p. 1980-81, Realtor of Yr. 1978), Ea. Northampton County Multiple Listing Svc. (bd. dirs. 1987-91), Realtors Nat. Mktg. Inst., Homes for Living Network (state chmn. 1980), Sales & Mktg. Execs. (bd. dirs. Easton area chpt. 1976-91; Disting. Sales award 1982), Phi Beta Kappa. Republican. Presbyterian. Home: 330 Paxinosa Rd W Easton PA 18040-1322 Office: 126 Bushkill St Easton PA 18040-1842

DES CHATELETS, CELINE CHABOT, printed music broker; b. Quebec Ile D'Orleans, Que., Can., Nov. 16, 1945; came to the U.S., 1986; d. Eugene and Bernadette (Plante) Chabot; m. Henri Nadeau, May 4, 1979 (div. Nov. 1983); children: Sylvie, Johanne, Julie; m. Jean R. Des Chatelets, Dec. 12, 1986. Student, Coll. Fx Garneau, Que., 1973-74, Coll. Ste-Foy, Que., 1975-76, U. Laval, Ste-Foy, 1978-81, U. Montreal, Que., 1982-83. Head purchaser music Proc. Generale de Musique, Quebec, 1964-86; pvt. practice printed music broker C. Chabot Printed Music, Newport, Vt., 1986—; sec. Can. Music Competitions, Quebec City, 1980-86; v.p. Assn. Musique Actuelle, Quebec City, 1983-84; reader, monitor La Magnetotheque, Ste-Foy, 1983-86. Active Vt. Symphonic Orch., Burlington, 1989, St. Mary's Choir, Newport, Vt., 1989, After Five Women's Club, Newport, 1990. U.S. Champion-Literature French Lang., Dictée des Amériques, Montreal, 1994. Democrat. Roman Catholic. Home and Office: PO Box 0849 Newport VT 05855

DESCHNER, JANE WAGGONER, collage artist, public relations consultant; b. Bellefont, Pa., Feb. 9, 1948; d. George Ruble and Helen Louise (Talbert) Waggoner; m. William Henry Deschner, July 26, 1969 (div. Dec. 1987); children: John William, Elisabeth Anne. BA in Geography, U. Kans., 1969; BA in Art, Mont. State U., Billings, 1987. Economist Mid-Am. Regional Coun., Kansas City, Mo., 1970-73; ptnr., owner Castle Art Gallery, Billings, Mont., 1982-88; asst. dir. client svcs. Mont. Inst. of Arts Found., Billings, 1988-89; account exec., artist, writer Exclamation Point Advt., Billings, 1989-94; artist Billings, 1981—, cons. pub. rels./graphic design, 1994—; pers. rep. Fred. J. Urbaska Investments, Billings. Exhibited at Toucan Gallery, Billings, Sutton West Gallery, Missoula, Mont., Art Mus. Missoula, Mont. State U., Billings, Holter Mus. Art, Helena, Mont., Broken Diamond Gallery, Billings, U. Mont., Missoula. Bd. dirs. Billings Mental Health Assn., 1988-92, v.p., 1989, 90; gallery dir., bd. dirs. The Women's Ctr., St. Vincent Hosp. and Health Ctr., Billings, 1991—; mem. Youth Ct. Conf. Com. 13th Jud. Dist. Mont., Billings, 1992—. Recipient 1st pl. award in non-comml. art Billings Advt. and Mktg. Assn., 1992, 93. Mem. Nat. Mus. of Women in Art, Paris Gibson Sq., Yellowstone Print Club (bd. dirs., pres. acquisitions chair), Yellowstone Art Ctr. (Auction Artist 1989—). Unitarian. Studio: 1313 Granite Ave Billings MT 59102-0069

DESCOTEAUX, CAROL J., academic administrator; b. Nashua, N.H., Apr. 5, 1948; d. Henry Louis and Therese (Arel) D. BA, Notre Dame Coll., 1970; MEd, Boston Coll., 1975; MA, U. Notre Dame, 1984, PhD, 1985. Jr. high sch. instr., dir. religious studies St. Joseph's Sch., North Grosvenordale, Conn., 1970-73; jr. high sch. tchr., dir. religious edn. Notre Dame Sch., North Adams, Mass., 1973-77; jr. high sch. instr. Sacred Heart Sch., Groton, Conn., 1977-78; chairperson religious studies discipline U. Notre Dame, Grad. Theol. Union, Notre Dame, Ind., 1982-83, 84-85; pres. Notre Dame Coll., Manchester, N.H., 1985—; trustee King's Coll., Wilkes-Barre, Pa., 1987—; pres. Fedn. of Holy Cross Colls., 1985—; mem. adv. bd. Manchester Christian Life Ctr., 1978-80; treas. N.H. Coll. and Univ. Council, Manchester, 1985—; trustee N.H. Higher Edn. Assistance Found., 1986—. Mem. Manchester United Way campaign, 1985—; bd. incorporators, mem. ethics com., instl. research com. Cath. Med. Ctr., Manchester, 1986—. Named Disting. Woman Leader of Yr., So. N.H. region YWCA, 1985. Mem. Am. Acad. Religion, Coll. Theology Soc. Am., N.H. Women's Forum, Soc. Christian Ethics, AAUW, N.H. Women in Higher Edn. Democrat. Roman Catholic. Office: Notre Dame Coll Office of the President 2321 Elm St Manchester NH 03104-2299*

DESFORGES, JANE FAY, medical educator, physician; b. Melrose, Mass., Dec. 18, 1921; d. Joseph Henry and Alice (Maher) Fay; m. Gerard Desforges, Sept. 11, 1948; children—Gerard Joseph, Jane Alice. BA cum laude (Durant scholar), Wellesley Coll., 1942; MD cum laude, Tufts U., 1945; ScD (hon.), Holy Cross Coll., 1990. Diplomate: Am. Bd. Internal Medicine, Am. Bd. Hematology. Intern in pathology Mt. Auburn Hosp., Cambridge, Mass., 1945-46; intern in medicine Boston City Hosp., 1946-47, resident in medicine, then chief resident, 1948-50; USPHS research fellow in hematology Salt Lake Gen. Hosp., Salt Lake City, 1946-47; research fellow in hematology hosp. Thorndike Lab., 1950-52; physician-in-charge RH lab., 1952-53; mem. faculty Tufts U. Med. Sch., 1952—, prof. medicine, from 1972, disting. prof., from 1992, prof. emerita, 1994; asst. dir. Tufts Med. Svc., Boston City Hosp., 1952-67; assoc. dir. Tufts Med. Svc., 1967-68; acting dir., physician in charge, 1968-73; dir. Tufts Med. Svc., 1968-69; assoc. dir. Tufts hematology lab., 1954-67, asst. dir. hosp. labs., 1958-67, acting dir. labs., 1967-68; sr. physician in hematology, rsch. assoc. blood rsch. lab. New Eng. Med. Ctr. Hosp., Boston, 1973—; attending physician VA Hosp., Jamaica Plain; cons. in hematology to various area hosps., 1955-72. Assoc. editor New Eng. Jour. Medicine, 1960-93; mem. editl. bd. Blood, 1976-79; contbr. numerous articles to med. jours. Bd. dirs. Med. Found., Inc., 1976-82; trustee Boston Med. Libr., 1977-81; chmn. automation in med. lab. scis. rev. com. Nat. Inst. Gen. Med. Scis., 1974-76; chmn. consensus com. of infectious disease testing for blood transfusions NIH, 1995—; mem. subcom. on hematology Am. Bd. Internal Medicine, 1976-82, bd. dirs., 1980-88, exec. com., 1984-88; chmn. blood diseases and resources adv. com. Nat. Heart, Lung and Blood Inst., 1978-81. Recipient Disting. Alumna award Wellesley Coll., 1981; NIH fellow, grantee, 1955-88. Fellow AAAS; mem. ACP (Master 1983, Disting. Tchr. award 1987, chmn. med. knowledge self assessment program IX 1989-92), Am. Fedn. Clin. Rsch., Am. Soc. Clin. Pathology, Am. Soc. Hematology (exec. com. 1975-78, adv. bd. 1980-82, v.p. 1982-83, pres. 1984-85), Internat. Soc. Hematology, Mass. Med. Assn., N.Y. Acad. Scis., Am. Assn. Physicians, Inst. Medicine, Phi Beta Kappa, Alpha Omega Alpha (Outstanding Tchr. award 1994). Home: 49 Lake Ave Melrose MA 02176-2701 Office: New England Med Ctr 750 Washington St Boston MA 02111-1533

DESHAZO, MARJORIE WHITE, occupational therapist; b. Syracuse, N.Y., Apr. 25, 1941; d. Rexford Everett and Joyce Winifred Ella (Brown) Young White; m. Del DeShazo, Dec. 22, 1966; stepchildren: Chad A., Karen A. Lynch. BS in Occupl. Therapy, U. Puget Sound, 1964. Lic. occupl. therapist, 1996. Occupl. therapist VA Med. Ctr., Roseburg, Oreg., 1965-70, Salisbury, N.C., 1970-78; occupl. therapist, co-chief VA Domiciliary, White City, Oreg., 1978-80; chief occupl. therapist VA Med. Ctr., Lexington, Ky., 1980-87; pvt. cons. occupl. therapy Camdenton, Mo., 1987—; coord. TV21 Art Collections, Springfield, Mo. inventor in field; exhibited at Lexington Art League, 1986-87, Laurie Fine Arts Show, 1993, Ozark Art and Palette, 1996, Artery Gallery, 1996, Lloyd's Art Ctr. & Gallery, 1996, Lisa Frick Gallery, 1996. Active Greater Lake Area Arts Coun., Osage Beach, Mo., 1987—. Kappa Kappa Gamma scholar U. Puget Sound. Mem. Laurie Fine Arts Club, Ozark Art and Pallette Club, Creative Artists Club. Democrat. Methodist. Home: RR 82 Box 6225 5-58X Camdenton MO 65020

DESHIELDS, ELIZABETH PEGGY BOWEN, retired educator, bookkeeper; b. Ada, Okla., Nov. 11, 1928; d. Simuel Archie and Etta Berthel (Flowers) Bowen; m. Amos Jack DeShields, Sept. 19, 1947; children: Dennis Jack, Sheila Beth. BSBA and English Edn., East Ctrl. Okla. U., 1947, MEd in Counseling, 1977. Bus. tchr. Bearden (Okla.) H.S., 1947-48; confidential sec. to prodn. supt. Phillips Chem. Co., Borger, Tex., 1949-53; English tchr. Borger H.S., 1954-55; asst. prin., tchr. Ctrl. Oak Elem. Sch., Oklahoma City, 1955-68; tchr. Will Roger's Sch., Shawnee, Okla., 1968-70, Butner Pub. Schs., Cromwell, Okla., 1970-74, Castle (Okla.) Pub. Schs., 1976-79; counselor Okemah (Okla.) Pub. Schs., 1979-85; co-owner, bookkeeper DeShields' Energy, Cromwell, 1970—, Jack DeShields' Bldg. Stone, Cromwell, 1970—, Rainbow Hills Ranch, Cromwell, 1970—; reporter Ada Times Democrat, 1947; news corr. Daily Oklahoman, Oklahoma City Times, 1947; abstracting asst. Pontotoc Co. Abstract Co., Ada, 1946; legal sec. C.F. Green Law Offices, Ada, 1944-46. Contbr. poems to profl. pubs.; artist, illustrator for books: The Silver Chord (SHeila DeShields). Mem. choir, Sunday sch. tchr. First Bapt. Ch., Cromwell, chmn. trustees, 1991. Scholar Nat. Sch. Bus., 1944, East Ctrl. U., 1944; recipient Spl. Recognition Appreciation of Svc. award Crooked Oak PTA, 1967, Yearbook Dedication, Crook Oak PTA, 1966, Svc. award, 1967, Leadership Svc. award Girl Scouts U.S., 1968, Golden Eagle award for outstanding contbn. to journalism, 1973, Silver award Columbia Scholastic Press Assn., Butner Yearbook Dedication, Appreciation Plaque Cromwell Headstart, 1985, FFA, 1985, Plaque, First Bapt. Ch., 1991, others. Mem. Okla. Ret. Tchrs., Okfuskee County Ret. Tchrs., Nat. Mus. Women in Arts (charter). Democrat. Home: Rt 2 Box 71 Okemah OK 74859

DESIMONE, ANGELA ROSE, controller, financial consultant; b. Boston, Sept. 19, 1947; d. Henry John and Rose Marie (Boschetto) DeS. Student, Bentley Coll., 1965-67. Acct. Raytheon Corp., Waltham, Mass., 1968-71; bookkeeper Fgn. Auto, Watertown, Mass., 1971-75; office mgr., bookkeeper Waltham Racquet Club, 1975-77; pvt. practice bookkeeping, fin. cons., Boston, 1977-94; contr., office mgr., corp. clk. C-Q Constrn. Corp., Watertown, 1979-93; pres., treas. Cousins Contracting, Watertown, 1992—. Treas. Al Anon, Belmont, Mass., 1981-83; big sister Friend to Friend Orgn., Watertown, 1985-86. Office: Cousins Contracting Inc 9 Chauncey St East Watertown MA 02172

DESISTO, ELIZABETH AGNES, medical records specialist; b. Medford, Mass., May 15, 1954; d. John Anthony and Josephine Loretta (Passero) DeS. AS cum laude, Mass. Bay Community Coll., 1974; BS magna cum laude, Northeastern U., 1979. Sr. med. record technician Children's Hosp. Med. Ctr., Boston, 1974-76; asst. dir. med. records dept. Glover Meml. Hosp., Needham, Mass., 1980-82; asst. dir. med. records dept. McLean Hosp., Belmont, Mass., 1982-83, acting dir. med. records dept., 1983-84, dir.

med. records dept., 1984-91; dir. med. records dept. New Eng. Meml. Hosp., Stoneham, Mass., 1991-95; project mgr. home health Vis. Nurse Assn., Inc., Haverhill and Andover, Mass., 1995-96; med. record coord. Harvard Pilgrim Health Care, Boston, 1996—. Vol. Big Sister Assn. Greater Boston, 1985-87, Greater Boston Walk for Hunger, 1983-94, nat. and local congl. campaigns; bd. dirs. New Eng. Meml. Hosp. Aux., 1992-95. Mem. Am. Health Info. Mgmt. Assn. (registered records adminstr., mental health record sect., bd. dirs. 1987-90, chmn. 1988-90), Mass. Health Info. Mgmt. Assn. (bd. dirs. 1985-96, sec. 1989-90, pres.-elect 1996—, del. 1994-96). Democrat. Roman Catholic. Home: 235 Winthrop St # 7701 Medford MA 02155 Office: Harvard Pilgrim Health Care 1 Fenway Plz Boston MA 02215

DESMOND, MABEL JEANNETTE, state legislator, educator; b. Lower Southampton, N.B., Can., Jan. 30, 1929; d. Charles Edward and Ada Gertrude (Ritchie) Lenentine; m. Jerry Russell Desmond, June 23, 1951; children: Jerry Russell Jr., Ronnee Beth, Jed Carey, Jennifer Shea. BS, Aroostock State Coll., 1964; MEd, U. Maine, 1975. Cert. prin., tchr., Maine. Tchr. Bridgewater (Maine) Elem. Sch., 1949-50, Gouldville Sch., Presque Isle, Maine, 1950-58, Mapleton H.S. and Mapleton Elem. Sch., Maine, 1958-63, 65-67, Gouldville Elem., Presque Isle, Maine, 1964-65, Ashland (Maine) Elem. Sch., 1969-70, Eva Hoyt Zippel Sch., Presque Isle, 1970-91; mem. adj. faculty U. Maine, Presque Isle, 1991—; rep. State of Maine, Augusta, 1995—; mem. tchr. edn. adv. com. U. Maine Presque Isle, 1995—. Contbr. editls. to newspapers and articles to profl. jours. Recipient Disting. Alumni award U. Maine, Presque Isle, 1995. Mem. U. Maine Presque Isle Alumni Assn. (exec. bd., pres. 1962-63, 74-75, sec. 1992-96), Delta Kappa Gamma (pres. 1984-86), Alpha Psi State (parliamentarian 1993-95). Democrat. Baptist. Home: Maine St Mapleton ME 04757

DESMOND, PATRICIA L., psychotherapist, writer, publisher; b. Boston, June 25, 1946; d. Francis X. and Mary L. (Donohue) D.; children: June, Timothy. AB, Stonehill Coll., 1968; MEd, U. Mass., Boston, 1994. Reporter The Patriot Ledger, Quincy, Mass., 1968-81; publisher Hingham (Mass.) Mariner, 1981-83, The Women's Jour., Hingham, 1985, Milton (Mass.) Times, 1995—; assoc. editor The Hingham Jour., 1985-86; copy editor Boston Herald, 1987-89; columnist Hull (Mass.) Times, 1988-94; editor Mariner Newspapers, Marshfield, Mass., 1989-91; pvt. practice Milton, Mass., 1993-95; pub. Milton (Mass.) Times, 1995—; outpatient therapist High Point, Plymouth, Mass., 1994—; case mgr. Harbor Light Ctr., Boston, 1995; columnist Tiny Town Gazette, Cohasset, Mass., 1993-96; publicist Share New Eng., Canton, Mass., 1993-95; therapist S. Mental Health Ctr., Weymouth, 1995; relapse prevention counselor Nazareth Residence, Roxbury, 1995-96. Author: Cinnamon, 1988; co-author: How to Heal Your Heart, 1988; editor On the Edge, 1992-93; counselor/case mgr. St. Elizabeth's Comprehensive Alcoholism and Addictions Program, 1994-95. Recipient Honorary Mention Mass. Womens Press Assn., 1971, New England Press Assn., 1983. Mem. NOW (state coord. 1973-74), Am. Counseling Assn., Nat. Writers Union, Mass. Assn. Alcoholism and Drug Abuse Counselors, The Women's Poetry Collective. Home: 39 Willoughby Rd Milton MA 02186

DE SOLA, ISABELLA MIRIAM, lawyer, poet. JD, Columbia U., 1982. Bar: N.Y. 1984, U.S. Dist. Ct. (so. dist., ea. dist.) N.Y. 1984. Law clk. to Hon. Irving R. Kaufman U.S. Ct. Appeals (2nd cir.), 1983-84; pvt. practice N.Y.C., 1984—; former fashion model; tchr. women's self-defense. Contbr. (anthologies) Something For Everyone, Poetic Voices of America, Sunrise, Sunset, American Poetry Annual, Visions, American Poetry Anthology, Of Diamonds and Rust, Vol. 2, Another Place in Time. Sec.-treas. Beyond Shelter Coalition for Permanent Housing, N.Y.C., 1989-91. Harlan Fiske Stone Scholar Columbia U., Harold P. Seligson scholarships in N.Y. Civil Practice, Bankruptcy Law, Securities Law, N.Y. Real Estate Practice, Immigration Law, Practising Law Inst., 1989. Mem. ABA (litigation, tort and ins. practice, family law, bus. law, antitrust law, criminal justice, natural resources, energy and environmental law, internat. law, law practice mgmt., and gen. practice sects.), Assn. Trial Lawyers Am. (membership com.; comml. litigation and ins. sects.), N.Y. State Bar Assn. (trial lawyers, comml. and fed. litigation, ins., negligence and compensation law, family law, bus. law, antitrust law, law office econs. and mgmt., gen. practice sects.), N.Y. State Trial Lawyers Assn., N.Y. County Lawyers' Assn. (apptd. to com. family ct. and child welfare), Assn. of Bar of City of N.Y., Columbia Law Sch. Assn. (life), Columbia Law Women's Assn., Trial Practice Inst., Pub. Interest Law Students Assn., Profl. Karate League, Pi Upsilon Delta Honor Soc.

DESOMBRE, NANCY COX, academic administrator, consultant; b. Lake City, Minn., Sept. 7, 1939; d. Ray Ronald and Marjorie Mae (Lipa) C.; m. Eugene DeSombre, Sept. 10, 1960; children: Elizabeth DeSombre, Michael DeSombre. BA, U. Chgo., 1961, MA, 1962. Prof. English dept. Wilbur Wright Coll., Chgo., 1962—, chair English dept., 1976—, dean vocat. program, 1981-82, dean of instrn., 1982-86, v.p. faculty, instr., 1987-94; pres. Harold Washington Coll., Chgo., 1994—; cons. evaluator North Cen. Assn. of Coll./Schs., Chgo., 1987—; dir. LaSalle Northwest Nat. Bank, Chgo., 1994—; mem. bd. dirs. Greater State St. Coun., Chgo., 1995—, State Univ. Retirement System, Champaign, Ill., 1995—. Mem. bd. dirs. Frank Lloyd Wright Found., Oak Park, 1987—. Recipient Inst. Ednl. Mgmt. award Harvard U., 1990, Project Enhance award Wright Coll., 1991, Woman of the Yr. award Exec. Leadership Inst.-League for Innovation, 1993, 94. Office: Harold Washington Coll 30 E Lake St Chicago IL 60601

DESOUZA, JOAN MELANIE, psychologist; b. Bombay, Sept. 17, 1956; came to U.S., 1987; d. Anthony Julius and Natalia Marie (Alvares) deS.; m. John Alec Krzewinski, Sept. 7, 1990. BA in Psychology with honors, U. Bombay, 1976; BS in Guidance and Counseling, Wayne State U., 1984, MA in Psychology, 1986, PhD in Ednl. Psychology, 1991. Lic. psychologist, Mich.; cert. sch. psychologist. Grad. asst. Wayne State U., Detroit, 1984-85; editor, mem. part-time faculty Inst. Gerontology, Detroit, 1985-87; extern St. Joseph Mercy Hosp., Pontiac, Mich., 1986; psychologist Huron Valley Mens' Facility, Ypsilanti, Mich., 1987-96, Huron Valley Ctr., 1996—; cons. Arab-Am. cmty., Detroit, 1988, Ctr. Behavior and Medicine, 1994—. Co-author: (handbook) Medicare Survey Project: Effectiveness of DRG's, 1987; editor (newsletter) Info. on Aging, 1985-87. Intern Parents and Children Together, Detroit, 1984; activist for Laotian community and immigrants Internat. Inst., Detroit, 1983; asst. soup kitchen Mother Theresa's order, Detroit. Grad. profl. scholar Wayne State U., 1985, Rumble fellow, 1986-87, 87-88; parenting skills grantee for low-functioning child abusers Mich. Dept. Edn., Lansing, 1989-90, Spl. Edn. grantee, 1995; recipient Bob Richardson Meml. award for excellence in correctional edn. and rsch., 1995. Mem. APA, Mich. Psychol. Assn., Mich. Assn. Sch. Psychologists, Pi Lambda Theta (Detroit chpt.). Roman Catholic. Home: 203 Russell St Saline MI 48176-1133 Office: Huron Valley Ctr 3511 Bemis Rd Ypsilanti MI 48197

DESPAIN, BECKY ANN, dental educator; b. Oklahoma City, July 14, 1948; children: Brian Thomas, Meredith Lynn. BS in Dental Hygiene, Baylor U., 1970; MEd, Cen. State U., Okla., 1982. Registered dental hygienist. Pvt. practice clin. dental hygienist Oklahoma City, 1970-73; instr. Coll. Dentistry, Okla. U. Health Scis. Ctr., Oklahoma City, 1973-82, asst. prof., 1982-85, acting chair dept. dental hygiene, 1984-85, clin. dental hygienist faculty practice, 1977-85; assoc. prof., dir. Caruth Sch. Dental Hygiene Baylor Coll. Dentistry, Dallas, 1985-93, assoc. prof. dept. pub. health scis., 1993—; clin. dental hygienist Drs. Israelson, Plemons & Jaynes, Richardson, Tex., 1995—; clin. instr. Rose Jr. Coll., Midwest City, Okla., 1972; mem. affil. staff Okla. Children's Meml. Hosp., Oklahoma City, 1977-85; clin. dental hygienist North Tex. Periodontal and Implant Assn., Richardson, 1988-91; clin. dental hygienist Drs. Hilton Israelson and Jacqueline Plemons, Richardson, Tex., 1995—; mem. test constrn. com. Nat. Bd. Dental Hygiene, ADA, Chgo., 1987-91, dental hygiene cons. Commn. on Dental Accreditation, 1989-96; investigator grants and contracts HHS, NIH. Editorial rev. bd.: Jour. Dental Hygiene, Chgo., 1982—; contbr. abstracts and articles to profl. jours. Spkr. Sch. Vols. Program, Oklahoma City Pub. Schs., 1976-85; project dir. Oral Healthlink: Dallas/Ft. Worth Coalition for Oral Health 2000; bd. dirs. Dallas chpt. ACLU of North Tex., pres., 1996; Tex. coord. Nat. Spit Tobacco Edn. Program, Oral Health Am., 1996. Recipient small grant award Rsch. Coun., OUHSC, Oklahoma City, 1985, Dental Hygiene Rsch. grant Oral-B Labs., Redwood City, Calif., 1985. Mem. ACLU (pres. Dallas chpt.), Am. Assn. Dental Schs., Am. Assn. Dental Rsch., Am. Dental Hygienists Assn. (del. 1980-84), Tex. Dental Hygienists Assn., Tex. Dental Hygiene Dirs. Assn. (sec. 1990-92), Dallas Dental Hygienists Soc. (v.p. 1994, pres.-elect 1995, pres. 1996), The Woman's Ctr. of Dallas (chair health care task force, bd. dirs. 1994-96, health com. Women's Coun. of Dallas County 1995—), Sigma Phi Alpha, Kappa Delta Pi. Office: Baylor Coll Dentistry PO Box 660677 Dallas TX 75266-0677

DES RIOUX, DEENA VICTORIA COTY, artist, graphics designer; b. Cambridge, Mass., Dec. 7, 1941; d. Sam and Sophina G. (Cohen) Coty; m. Philippe Roger Armand des Rioux de Messimy, Aug. 29, 1964. Student RISD, 1959-62, Brown U., 1960-62, Sorbonne, Paris, 1961, 63-64. Package designer, illustrator, pvt. tchr., free-lance artist, Boston, 1962-63, 64-70; guest lectr. Mass. Coll. Art, Boston, 1975, Harvard Grad. Sch. Design, Lesley Coll., Cambridge, Mass., 1976, 77, UN Photography Soc., N.Y.C., 1993; juror Heritage Plantation Mus., Cape Cod, Mass., 1977; exhbns. coord. Women Exhibiting in Boston, Inc., 1973-75; founder, dir. 7 at Large (artists collective), Boston, 1975-78; exhbns. coord. Assn. Artist-Run Galleries, N.Y.C., 1980-82, pub. relations dir., 1983-84. Solo exhbns.: Psychoanalytic Inst., Boston, 1974, Art Inst. of Boston, 1975, Mus. of Science, Boston, 1978, Ward-Nasse Gallery, N.Y.C., 1978, Helander Gallery, Palm Beach, Fla., 1985, Columbia U., N.Y., 1992, Maison Française of Columbia U., N.Y.C., 1992, RISD, Providence, 1993-94, U. Wyo. Art Mus., Laramie, 1994, Silicon Gallery, Phila., 1996; group shows include: Ward-Nasse Gallery, 1975-84, Helander Gallery, Palm Beach, Fla., 1984-86, Gallery Hirondelle, N.Y.C., 1985-87, Mokotoff Gallery, N.Y.C., 1986, Grace Harkin Gallery, N.Y.C., 1989, Laguna Gloria Art Mus., 1990-92, POLAND, Germany, 1991-92, Warwick Mus., 1991, Downey Mus. of Art, 1993, Alexandria Mus. of Art, 1993, LATVIA/Mus. Arsenāls, 1993, EGYPT/Nat. Ctr. of Fine Arts, 1994, Mus. Art, Rhode Island Sch. of Design, 1994, POLAND, 1994-95, Cartier/Fifth Ave., 1994, Fuller Mus. Art, 1995, Staten Island Inst. Arts & Scis., 1995, Palm Springs Desert Mus., 1995, JAPAN/Tama Art Univ. Mus., 1995, Silicon Gallery, 1995, NEXUS Found., 1996, Ea. Wash. U. USA Mus. Tour, 1994—; represented in permanent collections Ind. U. Art Mus., Internat. Print Triennale, Krakow, Poland, Boise (Idaho) State U., Mus. Art at RISD, Laguna Gloria Art Mus., Austin, Tex., Alexandria (La.) Mus. Art, Universal Graphic Mus., Cairo, Egypt, Downey (Calif.) Mus. Art, Austin Mus. Art, Downey Mus. Art, Ea. Washington U., Fuller Mus. Art, Brockton, Mass., Internat. Soc. Graphic Art, Krakow, Nat. Ctr. Fine Arts, Cairo, N.Y. Pub. Library, Palm Springs (Calif.) Desert Mus., Tama Art U. Mus., U. Ala. at Birmingham, U. Pa., Phila., U. Wyo. Art Mus., Laramie; coord., exhibitor Art Inst. Boston, 1975 (grant), Mus. Sci., Boston 1977-78 (grant); cons. spl. exhibit Mus. City of N.Y., 1983-84; guest exhibitor Danvers Art and Hist. Soc., Attleboro Mus., Mass., Nashua Arts and Sci. Ctr., (N.H.); competitive exhbns. include: 62d Newport Annual Nat., 1973, 45th Annual New Eng. Painting, Jordan Marsh, Boston, 1974, Past/Post/Future, Robert Atkins, N.Y.C., 1985, Photo-Derived, Joel-Peter Witkin, Ind. U., 1989, At The Edge II, Wendy Weitman, Laguna Gloria Art Mus., Austin, Tex., 1990, La Sierra U., Riverside, Calif., 1991, Seattle Ctr. Internat., 1991, Warwick Mus., R.I., 1991, Hill Country Arts Found. Nat., Ingram, Tex., 1991, Boise State U., Sun Valley Ctr. for the Arts, Idaho, 1991, ADOGI Barcelona, Tour, Cadaqués, and Cities of Japan Tour 1991-92, Juniper Gallery, Napa, Calif., 1991-92, Internat. Print Triennale, Krakow, Poland/Nuremberg, Germany, 1991-92, City Without Walls Gallery, Newark, 1992, L.A. Printmaking Soc. 12th Nat. Exhbn., Palos Verdes Art Ctr., Calif., 1993, The Boston Printmakers 44th N.Am. Exhbn., Boston U. Gallery, 1993, Lubbock (Tex.) Fine Arts Ctr., Illuminance '93, Alexandria (La.) Mus. Art 12th Ann. Sept. Exhbn., 1993, Soc. for Am. Graphic Artists 65th Nat. Print Exhbn., N.Y.C., 1993, Fine Arts Ctr./Giza, Egypt, 1st Egyptian Internat. Print Triennale, Cairo, 1994, Fla. Ctr. Contemporary Art, Tampa, 1994—, Eastern Washington U., 1994—, One West Art Ctr., Ft. Collins, Colo., 1994. Scholar RISD, 1959-61; named one of New York Outstanding Artists, Ethel Scull, N.Y.C., 1983; travel citation Mid-Am. Arts Alliance, 1990-92, recipient Juror/Roberta Waddell award Soc. Am. Graphic Artist, N.Y.C., 1993, Grantee Duggal Color Projects, Inc., N.Y., 1992; guest speaker UN Photography Soc., N.Y., 1993. Mem. Boston Visual Artists Union (coord. 1973-75), Art & Sci. Collaborations, Cambridge Art Assn. (juror 1973-74), RISD N.Y. Alumni Chpt., Art and Sci. Collaborations Inc. Democrat. Jewish. Avocations: psychology, yoga, jewelry design. Home and Studio: 251 W 19th St New York NY 10011-4039

DESROCHES, DIANE BLANCHE, English language educator, writer, director, actor, editor; b. Webster, Mass., Nov. 17, 1947; d. Victor Joseph and Rose Blanche Blouin; m. Roger John DesRoches, Aug. 27, 1966 (div. Apr. 16, 1974); 1 child, Bill. AA with high honors in French, Mesa Coll., 1976; BA in English magna cum laude, San Diego State U., 1979, MA, 1981. Cert. lang. arts, lit. and ABE:ESL instr., Calif. community colls. ESL instr. Coll. of English Lang., San Diego, 1982—; ESL instr. North City Ctr., Kearny Mesa campus San Diego Community Coll. Dist., 1982—; presenter in field. Author: (short story) Something Special, 1979, Cinderella of the 80s, 1980; (software) Basic Map Reading Skills, 1981; writer (video) The College of English Language, 1989, numerous recipes, word search puzzles, variety puzzles and ednl. puzzles., 1980—; writer, dir. (video) The Challenge Is Ours, 1989; co-writer (multimedia show) Holiday Sky Show, 1988, (screen adaptation) The Wind From the Sun, 1989; contbr. articles to mags.; contbr. (reading comprehension series) Comprehension Plus, 1982, (student assessment system) CASAS, 1982; editl. cons. (multimedia shows) Dimensions, 1987, Cycles, 1987, Star Tracks, 1988, Thundering Water, 1988, Flying Blue Marble, 1988, Night on Dream Mountain, 1988, Mars, 1988, From Here to Infinity, 1989, To Worlds Beyond, 1989, Stars Over China, 1989, Eclipse!, 1991; translator: ABC of Ecology, 1982; actor (photoplay) And the Winner Is...?, 1982, (film) Killer Tomatoes Eat France, 1991, Tainted Blood, 1993; writer, dir., co-prodr. (TV comml.) Mount Laguna Observatory. Recipient Gregg award Gregg Inst., 1965; fellow State of Calif., 1979; DB Williams scholar San Diego State U., 1979. Mem. TESOL, Calif. TESOL, Am. Fedn. Tchrs., Am. Film Inst., Phi Kappa Phi, Psi Chi, Pi Delta Phi. Democrat. Roman Catholic.

DESSASO, DEBORAH ANN, social welfare organization specialist, communication specialist; b. Washington, Feb. 6, 1952; d. Coleman and Virginia Beatrice (Taylor) D. AS in Bus. Adminstrn., Southeastern U., 1986, BSBA, 1988; postgrad. U. D.C., 1993—. Clk.-stenographer FTC, Washington, 1969-70; sec. NEA, Washington, 1970-72; sec. AARP, Washington, 1972-79, assoc. adminstrv. specialist, 1979-80, adminstrv. specialist, 1979-89, legis. specialist, 1989—; founding mem., sec. Andrus Fed. Credit Union, 1980. Mem. NAFE. Mem. Worldwide Ch. of God. Home: 3052 Stanton Rd SE Washington DC 20020-7883 Office: 601 E St NW Washington DC 20049-0001

DESSAUER, CARIN, journalist; b. Pottstown, Pa., Dec. 31, 1963; d. Ralph and Margot (Abrams) D.; m. Marc Richard Engel, May 29, 1988. BA cum laude, Bucknell U., 1985; postgrad., George Washington U., 1987. Reporter The Polit. Report, Washington, 1986-87; off-air reporter ABC News Polit. Unit, Washington, 1988; assoc. editor Congl. Quarterly's Politics in Am., Washington, 1989; contbg. editor Campaigns and Elections mag., Washington, 1989-91; head Washington polit. unit Cable News Network, 1990-91; assoc. polit. dir. CNN, Washington, 1991-95, dep. pol. dir., 1995—. Co-author: (monograph) Running to Win, 1988. Mem. recruiting com. for sports challenge Cystic Fibrosis of Washington, 1990; mem. devel. com. New Endeavors by Women, Washington; vol. Make a Wish Found., Doing Something, Washington. Mem. UJA Bus. and Profl. Women's Network, Phi Beta Kappa. Office: CNN 820 1st St NE Washington DC 20002-4243

DESSYLAS, ANN ATSAVES, human resources and office management executive; b. Bklyn., Jan. 28, 1927; d. Charles and Agnes (Cocoros) Atsaves; m. George Dessylas, Dec. 28, 1969. BA, Bklyn. Coll., 1957; MA, NYU, 1961, MBA, 1977. Exec. asst. W.R. Grace & Co., N.Y.C., 1950-70; asst. sec. St. Joe Minerals Corp., N.Y.C., 1970-81, asst. v.p., 1981-85; cons. Cyprus Minerals, Denver, 1985-91; pres. AAD Enterprises, Forest Hills, N.Y., 1992—; dir. Continental Owners Corp. Home and Office: 70-20 108th St Ste 8-p Forest Hills NY 11375-4449

DESTAFFANY, SANDRA RUSSELL, childbirth educator, author; b. Billings, Mont., Mar. 15, 1957; d. Alexander Emmett and Cleora Jean (Saunders) Russell; m. Joe Lee DeStaffany, Oct. 13, 1979; children: Naomi Jo, Andrea Renee, James Russell. BS, Mont. State U., 1979. cert. childbirth educator. Childbirth educator Conrad (Mont.) Childbirth Edn. Assn., 1983—; U.S. western dir. Inter Childbirth Edn. Assn., Mpls., 1990-92, pres. elect 1992-94, pres. 1994-95. Contbr. numerous articles to profl. jours.

D'ESTE, MARY ERNESTINE, health administration executive; b. Chgo., Apr. 1, 1941; d. Ernest Gregory and Mary (Turcich) D'E. Student, Mundelein Coll., 1958-61. Sec. MMM, Bedford Park, Ill., 1961-69, Michael Reese Med. Ctr., Chgo., 1969-73; adminstrv. asst. Thomas Jefferson U., Phila., 1973-85, divisional adminstr., 1985-86; adminstr. dept. cardiothoracic surgery Hahnemann U., Phila., 1986-94, Med. Coll. Pa.-Hahnemann U. Hosps., Phila., 1994-96, Allegheny U. Hosps.-Center City, 1996—; v.p. CTS Cardiac & Thoracic Surgeons PC, Phila., 1986—. V.p. archtl. review com. GTV Homeowners Assn., Marlton, N.J., 1979-85. Mem. Med. Group Mgmt. Assn., Am. Assn. Notaries, NAFE. Roman Catholic. Office: Allegheny U Hosp and Ctr City MS 111 Broad & Vine Sts Philadelphia PA 19102-1192

DETERMAN, SARA-ANN, lawyer; b. Palmerton, Pa., Aug. 17, 1938; d. Albert H. and Evelyn (Tucker) Heimbach; m. Dean W. Determan, July 28, 1957 (div. Nov. 1981); children: Dann, David; m. Gary Sellers, May 21, 1988. Student, Conn. Coll., 1956-57, Stanford U., 1958; AB, U. Del., 1960; LLB, George Washington U., 1967. Bar: U.S. Dist. Ct. D.C. 1968. Law clk. to sr. judge U.S. Ct. Appeals (D.C. cir.), Edgerton, 1967-68; assoc. Hogan & Hartson, Washington, 1968-75, ptnr., 1975—; trustee Lawyers Com. for Civil Rights Under Law, Washington, 1982-94, co-chmn., 1994—. Bd. dirs. Mex.-Am. Legal Def. and Ednl. Fund, 1983-88, Women's Legal Def. Fund, 1980—. Fellow Am. Bar Found.; mem. ABA (chmn. individual rights sect. 1985-86, commr. legal programs for elderly 1983-89, com. on delivery of legal svcs. 1989-93, mem. consortium on legal svcs.), ACLU (bd. dirs. 1975-92), D.C. Bar (pres. 1990-91). Democrat. Unitarian. Office: Hogan & Hartson Columbia Square 555 13th St NW Washington DC 20004-1109

DETERT, MIRIAM ANNE, chemical analyst; b. San Diego, Calif., Sept. 16, 1925; d. George Bernard and Margaret Theresa Zita (Lohre) D. BS, Dominican Coll., San Rafael, Calif., 1947. Chem. analyst Shell Devel. Co., Emeryville, Calif., 1947-72, Houston, 1972-86. Photo participant Wax Rsch.: Quest, 1981. Vol. Falkirk Cultural Ctr., San Rafael, 1987-91, M.D. Anderson Tumor Inst., Houston, 1978-86, Rep. Party, San Rafael, 1990, 94; mem. Jewish Comm. Ctr. Recipient Disting. Alumni award Dominican Coll., 1994. Mem. Marin Geneal. Soc. Republican. Roman Catholic.

DETERT-MORIARTY, JUDITH ANNE, graphic artist, civic activist; b. Portage, Wis., July 10, 1952; d. Duane Harlan and Ann Jane (Devine) Detert; m. Patrick Edward Moriarty, July 22, 1978; children: Colin Edward, Eleanor Grace, Dylan Joseph. Student U. Wis.-Madison, 1970-73; BA, U. Wis.-Green Bay, 1991. Cert. in no-fault grievance mediation, Minn. Legis. sec., messenger State of Wis. Assembly, Madison, 1972, 74-76; casualty-property div. clk. Capitol Indemnity Corp., Madison, 1976-77; sec./credit clk. comml. credit div. Affiliated Bank of Madison, 1977-78; word processor consumer protection div. Wis. Dept. Agr., Madison, 1978; graphics arts composing specialist Moraine Park Tech. Inst., Fond du Lac, Wis., 1978-79; free-lance artist Picas, Pictures and Promotion (formerly Detert Graphics), 1978-90; prodn. asst. West Bend News, 1980-83; devel. assoc. Riveredge Nature Ctr., Inc., Newburg, Wis., 1983-84; exec. dir. Voluntary Action Ctr. of Washington County, West Bend, 1984-86; devel. cons. West Bend Hospice Program, 1985; instr. community svcs. Austin (Minn.) Community Coll., 1988; art and promotional publs. dir. Michael G. & Co., Albert Lea, Minn., 1988-89; corp. art dir. Newco, Inc., Janesville, Wis., 1989-91; owner, artist Art Graphica, 1991—; bd. dirs. Health Net Janesville, Inc., 1993. Vol. activities include Austin Pub. Schs. Omnibus Program polit. cartooning instr. Dane County vol. Udall for Pres., 1976; student vol. McCarthy for Pres., U. Wis., Madison, 1968, coord. student residences McGovern for Pres., 1972; Washington County campaign coord. Nat. Unity Campaign for John Anderson for Pres., 1980; Washington County ward coord. Earl for Gov., 1982; Washington County campaign chmn. Peg Lautenschlager for Wis. state senate, Washington County ward coord. Mondale/Ferraro, 1984; vol. coord. Rock County Dukakis for Pres., 1988; campaign chair Lew Mittness for Wis. State Assembly, 1990; vol. Rock County Clinton For Pres., 1992, 96; sec., newsletter editor Dem. Party of Manitowoc County, Wis., 1986, Rock County, 1988—; local chair Women's Polit. Caucus, 1987-88; publicity coord. Wis. Intellectual Freedom Coalition, 1981; founding exec. bd. dirs., newsletter editor Moral Alternatives, Catholics for a Free Choice Wis. community contact, 1990-92; v.p., 1990-92, newsletter editor Rock County Voice for Choice, 1990-94; bd. dirs., v.p. Wis. Pro-Choice Conf., 1981-82; pres., founder People of Washington County United for Choice, 1981-83; mem. Rock County Citizens for Peace; bd. pres. Planned Parenthood of Washington County, 1984-85, newsletter editor, mem. coms., 1980-85; vol. newsletter editor Badger Coun. Girl Scouts, Inc., Roosevelt Elem. Sch. PTA; bd. mem. Montessori Children's House, West Bend, 1983-85, newsletter editor, com. chmn.; pres. Montessori Parents Assn., 1995-96; artist LWV Washington County, 1984-86; newsletter editor, artist Friends of Battered Women, West Bend, 1983-86; apptd. to Austin Human Rights Commn, 1987-88, Janesville Historic Commn., 1991-94, sec., 1992-94; founder, pres. Janesville Arts Alliance, 1996; fundraiser Victims Crisis Ctr., 1987; v.p., comm. officer Rock County Dem. Party, 1988—; cartooning instr., contbg. artist Janesville Pub. Schs., 1989-93, contbr. articles to profl. jours.; Mower County Dem. precinct chair, affirmative action officer, county sec. Dem. Party, 1988; artist LWV Rock County; vol., bd. dirs., chmn. advt. com. Janesville Concert Assn., 1994—; contbd. artist Spolight on Kids Theatre, 1995—. Recipient award of Excellence Bd. Report Graphic Artists, 1994, 95. Mem. ACLU, NAFE, NOW (newsletter editor Dane County 1977-78, Wis. state 1994—, coord. Wis. state reproductive rights task force 1982-84, coord. reproductive rights task force North Suburban Chpt., 1981-84, Minn. pub. rels. coord., 1987-88, Rock County chpt.), Nat. Assn. Desktop Pubs., Wis. Women Entrepreneurs, Montessori Children's House Parents Assn. (pres. 1995-96), Graphic Artists Guild, Forward Janesville (steering com. for Celebrate Janesville 1992, 93, 94). Quaker. Avocations: reading, hand spinning and knitting, world wide correspondence, antiques, gardening. Office: Art Graphica 23 S Atwood Ave Janesville WI 53545-4003

DETMAR-PINES, GINA LOUISE, business strategy and policy educator; b. S.I., N.Y., May 3, 1949; d. Joseph and Grace Vivian (Brown) Sargente; m. Michael B. Pines, Sept. 11, 1988. BS in Edn., Wagner Coll., 1971, MS, 1972; MA in Urban Affairs and Policy Analysis, New Sch. for Social Rsch., 1987; MPhil, CUNY, 1995; PhD in Bus./Orgn. and Policy Studies, CUNY-Baruch Coll., 1996. Cert. adminstr. and supr., sch. dist. adminstr. Tchr. pub. schs. N.Y.C., 1971-82; coord. spl. projects, pub. affairs N.Y.C. Bd. Edn., 1982, spl. asst. to exec. dir. pupil svcs., 1983, asst. to chancellor, 1983-84, dir. Tchr. Summer Bus. Industry Program, 1984-93; prof. pub. adminstrn. and mgmt. John Jay Coll. Criminal Justice CUNY, 1992-93; vis. prof. Hartford Grad. Ctr., 1993—; liaison for the Tech. Industry Program, N.Y.C. Partnership, 1985-93. Mem. com. to re-elect Borough pres. Lamberti, S.I., 1985-86; chairperson Crystal Ball event Greater Hartford Easter Seals Rehab. Ctr., 1994, trustee, 1994—; bd. dirs. Hartford Symphony, com. mem. 5th Anniversary Gala, 1993. Mayor's scholar City of N.Y., 1984-96. Mem. ASPA, Fgn. Lang. Instrs. Assn., U.S. Seaplane Pilot's Assn., Internat. Orgn. for Lic. Women Pilots, Chinese-Am Soc., Am. Mgmt. Assn., Acad. Mgmt., Strategic Mgmt. Soc., Ea. Acad. Mgmt., Cambridge Flying Group Club. Episcopalian. Office: Hartford Grad Ctr 275 Windsor St Hartford CT 06120-2910

DE TORNYAY, RHEBA, nurse, former university dean, educator; b. Petaluma, Calif., Apr. 17, 1926; d. Bernard and Ella Fradkin; m. Rudy de Tornyay, June 4, 1954. Student, U. Calif., Berkeley, 1944-46; diploma, Mt. Zion Hosp. Sch. Nursing, 1949; A.B., San Francisco State U., 1951, M.A., 1954; Ed.D., Stanford U., 1967; Sc.D. (hon.), Ill. Wesleyan U., 1974; LHD (hon.), U. Portland, 1974, Georgetown U., 1994. Mem. faculty San Francisco State U., 1957-67, prof. nursing, 1966-67, chmn. dept., 1959-67; assoc. prof. U. Calif. Sch. Nursing, San Francisco, 1968-71; prof. U. Calif. Sch. Nursing, 1971; dean, prof. Sch. Nursing UCLA, 1971-75; dean emeritus, prof. U. Wash., Seattle, 1986—. Author: Strategies for Teaching nursing, 1971, 3rd edit., 1987, Japanese transl., 1974, Spanish edit., 1986; co-author: (with Heather Young) Choices: Making a Good Move to a Retirement Community. Trustee Robert Wood Johnson Found. Mem. ANA, Am. Acad. Nursing (charter fellow, pres. 1973-75), Inst. Medicine (governing coun. 1979-81), Nat. League for Nursing. Home: Apt 1001 4540 8th Ave NE Seattle WA 98105-4739

DETUNCQ, KAREN RUTH, occupational health nurse; b. Virginia, Minn., Aug. 28, 1948; d. Oscar Everett and Lila Irene (Rauma) Lahti; m. Ronald James McCulloch, Feb. 26, 1972 (div. Oct. 1982); children: Shannon Leigh, Seth Allen, Erin Rhea; m. Thomas Jeffery DeTuncq, May 9, 1986; stepchildren: Tammy Lynn, Todd Jeffery. Diploma in Nursing, St. Luke's Sch. Nursing, Duluth, Minn., 1970. Cert. occupl. health nurse specialist. Staff nurse Abbott-Northwestern Hosp., Mpls., 1970-71, 74-78, Miller-Dwan Hosp., Duluth, 1971-73, Med. Pers. Pool, Mpls., 1973-74; occupl. health nurse Cornelius Co., Anoka, Minn., 1978-82, U.S. Postal Svc., Eagan, Minn., 1982; occupl. health adminstr. Fed. Res. Bank, Mpls., 1982—. Mem. cast for video: The Way We Work: A User's Guide to Office Ergonomics and Body Mechanics, 1991. Mem. Spkrs. Bur., United Way, Mpls., 1988—; Bloodmobile chmn. Meml. Blood Ctr. of Mpls., 1979—; spkr. Minn. State Svcs. for Blind, 1986; ann. conf. planning com. Minn. Safety Coun., 1985, 87; worksite forum com. Am. Cancer Soc., 1990-92; vol. Santa Anonymous, 1990-93; charter mem., bd. dirs. Fed. Employees Action Team, 1990-93; mem. Minn. FoodShare Dr., 1990-93; mem. Minn. Dept. Health Task Force on devel. of proposed rules for Minn. Infectious Waste Mgmt. Act, 1990-92, others. Recipient Good Neighbor award WCCO Radio, 1992, Respiratory Health and Wellness Vol. award Am. Lung Assn., 1986, Outstanding Cmty. Svc. award United Way, 1989, 90. Mem. Am. Assn. Occupational Health Nurses (bd. dirs. 1988-90, 94—, Medique Nat. Leadership award 1991), Minn. Assn. Occupational Health Nurses (past pres., treas., nominating com., awards com., bylaws com., membership com., edn. com., Nurse of the Yr. 1994). Home: 15164 Taylor St NE Ham Lake MN 55304-6132 Office: Fed Res Bank 250 Marquette Ave Minneapolis MN 55401-2171

DEUFEL, LAURA JOAN, elementary education educator; b. Caledonia, Minn., Feb. 3, 1946; d. Hilary Penwarren and Laura Ann (Bunge) Allen; m. Joseph Robert Deufel, July 3, 1974; children: Benjamin Joseph, Christopher Lawrence. BS in Elem. Edn., Winona State U., 1968, MS, 1976, postgrad., 1992-93; postgrad., U. Minn., 1986-89. 3d grade tchr. Burlington Area (Wis.) Sch. Dist., 1968-73; tchr. spl. learning/behavior problems Southland Ind. Schs., Rose Creek, Minn., 1974-77; cons. gifted and talented Southland Ind. Schs., Adams, Minn., 1978-84; 3d grade tchr. Southland Ind. Schs., Rose Creek, Minn., 1984—; substitute tchr. Southland Schs. and Lyle (Minn.) Sch., 1978-84. Recipient Cert. for Superior Art Instrn., Am. Automobile Assn., 1985-92, 95; nominee for Tchr. of Excellence, Minn. C. of C. Found., 1989. Mem. NEA, Minn. Edn. Assn., Southland Edn. Assn. (bldg. rep. 1990-92, chairperson staff devel. 1994—). Office: Southland Schs PO Box 157 Rose Creek MN 55970-0157

DEUTSCH, FLORENCE ELAYNE GOODILL, nursing and health care consultant; b. San Diego, Aug. 1, 1923; d. George Ehrlich and Beatrice Marie (Urick) Goodill; m. Edward Thomas Deutsch, June 27, 1953 (dec.); 1 son, George Edward. Student, San Diego State Coll., 1942-43; B.S.N., Villa Maria Coll., 1948; diploma in nursing Evanston Hosp., Northwestern U., 1947; M.Ed., Edinboro U., 1961. Staff nurse St. Vincent Hosp., Erie, Pa., 1947; clin. instr.-supr. Hamot Med. Ctr., Erie, 1948-58, dir. edn., 1958-62, dir. Sch. Nursing, 1962-66, asst. adminstr., dir. Sch. Nursing, 1969-73; exec. dir. Florence Crittenton Home, Erie, 1966-69; asst. adminstr., dir. nursing Capitol Hill Hosp., Washington, 1974-79; assoc. adminstr. profl. services Millcreek Community Hosp., 1980-82; v.p. nursing East Liverpool City Hosp. (Ohio), 1982-87; lectr., cons. on nursing and nursing law, 1988-89; lectr. Gannon U., Erie, Pa. Editor newsletter U.S. Brig Niagara, 1991-93. Past bd. dirs. Columbiana County Cancer Soc.; bd. dirs. Sarah A. Reed Retirement Ctr., Erie, 1991—, treas. 1992-95; treas. Spl. Purpose Fund, 1995—. Served with USNR, 1948-53. Recipient Vol. of the Year award U.S. Brig Niagara, 1993, Named Most Outstanding Nurse Erie County, 1969, Disting. Nursing Alumna Villa Maria Coll. Gannon U., 1989, Disting. Alumnus Gannon U., 1991. Mem. Nat. League Nursing, Am. Orgn. Nurse Execs., Svc. Corps Of Ret. Execs. (vice-chmn. Erie chpt. 193 1988-90, chmn. 1995—), Sigma Theta Tau, Delta Kappa Gamma. Republican. Presbyterian. Editor: Penn League News, 1968-70; contbr. articles to profl. jours. Address: 3207 Georgian Ct Erie PA 16506-1109

DEUTSCH, NINA, pianist; b. San Antonio, Mar. 15; d. Irvin and Freda (Smukler) D. BS, Juilliard Sch. Music, 1964; MMA, Yale U., 1973. Concert pianist internat. and U.S. tours, 1965-82; entertainer, solo pianist Holland Am. Cruise Lines, 1987, 89-90; freelance pianist, lectr. on music, 1990—; exec. v.p. Internat. Symphony, N.Y.C., 1978-82. Pianist: (records) Charles Ives, 1976, Vox Records; author: (book) Can You Afford Not to Be a Successful Private Teacher, 1994, (plays) Portrait of Liberace, 1995, Portrait of Clara Schumann, 1987; contbr. to mags. and newspapers. Tanglewood fellow Wulsin Fellowship, 1966. Mem. Music Critics Assn. (NEA grantee 1975), Yale Alumni Assn. Bergen County, Sigma Alpha Iota. Home: 410 Hazlitt Ave Leonia NJ 07605

DEUTZ, NATALIE RUBINSTEIN, actress, consultant; b. Plymouth, Mass., Sept. 26; d. Louis and Lillian Rubinstein; student Simmons Coll., Modern Sch. Applied Art; m. Nov. 29, 1947 (dec.). Fashion buyer Wm. Filene's Sons Co., Boston, 1940-47; asst. to corp. pres. Columbia Textiles, Inc., N.Y.C., 1956-68; dir. John Robert Powers Sch., N.Y.C., 1968-72; v.p., nat. dir. fashion merchandising, dir. advt. workshop Barbizon Internat., Inc., N.Y.C., 1972-83; cons., 1983—; modeling judge IMTA. Films include Arthur on the Rocks, Crocodile Dundee, Moonstruck, Six Degrees of Separation; appeared in Super Elderly People for Japanese TV. Mem. NATAS, SAG, AFTRA.

DEV, PARVATI, medical educator; b. New Delhi, India, Dec. 6, 1946. B Tech with hons., Indian Inst. Tech., Kharagpur, 1968; MSEE, Stanford U., 1969, PhD Elec. Engring., 1975. Rsch. assoc. VA, Palo Alto, Calif., 1979-82; v.p., rsch. and devel. Cemax, Inc., Mountain View, Calif., 1982-89; staff scientist neurosci. rsch. program MIT, Cambridge, 1972-77; asst. prof. Boston U., 1976-78; dir. summit Stanford (Calif.) U. Sch. Medicine, 1990—; speaker numerous scientific and comml. mtgs., 1982—; cons. Am. Bd. Family Practice, Lexington, Ky., 1991-93, Kaiser Family Found., Menlo Park, Calif., 1994. Editorial bd.: Jour. of the Am. Med. Informatics Assn., 1994—; adv. bd. Med. Nutrition Curriculum Initiative/U. N.C., Chapel Hill, 1992—; contbr. articles to profl. jours. Mem. Am. Med. Informatics Assn. (chmn. edn. group 1993—, mem. publs. 1991—, assoc. editor jour.). Office: 1215 Welch Rd Stanford CA 94305

DEVANEY, CAROL ANN, nurse; b. Nome, Alaska, Aug. 26, 1946; d. Lawrence and Virginia (Weoluk) Morris; m. Ronald Wieber, May 16, 1963 (div. 1970); m. Steven DeVaney, Apr. 30, 1971; children: Mitchell, Sean, Dorothy. Student, Anchorage C.C., 1968; ADN, Chemeketa C.C., Salem, Oreg., 1982; B of Profl. Arts, St. Joseph's Coll., Windham, Maine, 1990, postgrad. RN; cert. cmty. health nurse. Staff nurse Alaska Native Hosp., Anchorage, 1968-72; charge nurse Ridgeview Care Corp., Anchorage, 1972-75, Lynn Care Nursing Home, Albany, Oreg., 1976-77, Marion Home, Sublimity, Oreg., 1977-79, St. Timothy's Nursing Home, Salem, 1979-80; staff nurse Tuba City (Ariz.) Indian Health Svc., 1982-83; nursing supr. Taholah (Wash.) Indian Health Svc., 1983-88, N.W. Wash. Indian Health Svc., Bellingham, 1988-92; dir. ACN svcs. Yakama Indian Health Svc., Toppenish, Wash., 1992—; mem. Portland Area Nurses Ambulatory Com., 1987—, chair, 1990-94; mem. Yakima Valley Leadership Task Force, 1994—; chmn. Indian Edn. Com., Bellingham, 1989-91. Mem. Am. Holistic Nurses Assn. Home: 106 Mobile Home Ave Union Gap WA 98903 Office: Yakama Indian Health Svc 401 Buster Rd Toppenish WA 98948

DEVANEY, CYNTHIA ANN, real estate broker, educator; b. Gary, Ind., Feb. 6, 1947; d. Charles Barnard and Irene Mae (Nelson) Burner; m. Harold Verne DeVaney, Nov. 23, 1974 (dec. 1981). BS, Ball State U., 1970, MS, 1972; postgrad., Ind. U. and Purdue U., 1974-76. Cert. real estate broker, Ind. Real estate broker Century 21 McColly Realtors, Merrillville, Ind., 1979-86; real estate broker Better Homes and Gardens McColly Realtors, Merrillville, 1986—, with Pres.' Coun.; tchr. Merkley Elem. Sch., Highland, Ind., 1969—. Active Schubert Theater Guild, Chgo. Mem. N.W. Ind. Bd. Realtors (Million Dollar Club), Nat. Bd. Realtors, Jr. Ind Hist. Soc., Innsbrook Country Club, Match Point Tennis Club. Democrat. Methodist. Home: 607 E 78th Pl Merrillville IN 46410-5624 Office: McColly Better Homes & Gardens 9143 Indianapolis Blvd Hammond IN 46322-2504

DEVANY SERIO, CATHERINE, clinical psychologist; b. N.Y.C., July 27, 1964; d. Edward Heath and Mary Langley (Peebles) Devany; m. Vincent Joseph Serio, III, May 2, 1992. BA in Am. Studies magna cum laude, U. Tex., 1987; MS in Clin. Psychology, Va. Commonwealth U., 1990, PhD in Clin. Psychology, 1993. Rsch. assoc. Dept. Mental Health, Mental Retardation and Substance Abuse, Richmond, 1988-90; extern in family therapy Family Therapy Practice Ctr., Washington, 1993-94; postdoctoral fellow dept. phys. medicine and rehab. Med. Coll. Va., Richmond, 1993-94; clin. dir. Community Rehab. Svcs., Richmond, 1994—; invited lectr. in field. Contbr. articles to profl. jours. Rehab. Psychology fellow Nat. Inst. Disability and Rehab. Rsch., 1990-92; recipient Young Investigator award Nat. Head Injury Found., 1993. Mem. APA (divsn. family psychology). Office: Community Rehab Svcs 4128 Innslake Dr Glen Allen VA 23060-3344

DEVARIS, JEANNETTE MARY, psychologist; b. Burbank, Calif., Jan. 7, 1947; d. Nicholas Propper Klein and Elizabeth (Von Lichtenberg) Schaeffer; m. Robert Lee Blake, May 20, 1967 (div. 1979); 1 child: Brendon; m. Panayotis Eric DeVaris, Dec. 5, 1988. BA, Adelphi U., 1968; MA, Fairleigh Dickinson U., 1977; PhD, Seton Hall U., 1987. Lic. psychologist, N.J. Caseworker N.Y.C. Welfare Dept., 1968-72; alcohol and drug rehab. counselor U.S. Army, Ft. Monmouth, N.J., 1972-76; psychol. intern N.J. State Intern Program, Trenton, 1977-78; psychologist Greystone Psychiat. Hosp., Greystone Park, N.J., 1979; sr. psychologist R. Hall Community Mental Health Ctr., Bridgewater, N.J., 1979-90; pvt. practice South Orange and Somerset, N.J., 1988—; tng. supr. Grad. Sch. Applied and Profl. Psychology; adj. prof. Seton Hall U.; sponsor and participant in Cable TV program. Contbr. articles to profl. jours. Mem. APA, Nat. Register Health Svc. Providers, N.J. Psychol. Assn. (bd. dirs., interprofl. rels. com.), Soc. Psychologists in Pvt. Practice (bd. dirs., spkrs. bur. com.). Office: 2 Worlds Fair Dr Somerset NJ 08873-1377

DEVAUD, JUDITH ANNE See HALVORSON, JUDITH ANNE

DEVECCHIO, ANN MARIE, fundraiser; b. Hackensack, N.J., Oct. 29, 1970; d. Roy Lindley DeVecchio and Janet Marlene (Charles) Mansoldo. BA in Internat. Rels., Bucknell U., 1992. Asst. dir. ann. giving Rutgers U. Found., New Brunswick, N.J., 1992-94; devel. offficer N.Y. Philharm., N.Y.C., 1994-96, Columbia U., N.Y.C., 1996—. Editor: The Rutgers Parent newsletter, 1994 (Case award 1994), Developments newsletter, 1995. Mem. Bucknell Club of N.Y. (bd. dirs. 1995—). Home: 325 West 51st St New York NY 10019 Office: Columbia U 500 W 120th New York NY 10027

DEVENEY, SUSAN ELAINE, lawyer, state legislator; b. Worcester, Mass., Sept. 14, 1958. BA summa cum laude, U. Bridgeport, 1980; JD, Suffolk Law Sch., 1986. Bar: Mass. 1986, R.I. 1987, U.S. Dist. Ct. R.I. 1987, U.S. Dist. Ct. mass. 1986, U.S. Ct. Appeals (1st cir.) 1990; cert. mediator, Williams Univ., 1995. With sales and mktg. AT&T, Boston, 1981-88; atty. Wallick & Paolino, Providence, 1988-90; ptnr. Deveney & Hagopian, Cranston, R.I., 1990—; mem. R.I. Ho. of Reps., 1992—; pres., founder Mediators, Inc., Cranston, R.I., 1994—; mem. R.I. Ho. of Reps., 1992—; commr. Commn. on Jud. Tenure and Discipline, Providence, 1992—, Select Commn. to Study Airport Devel., 1993; bd. dirs. Warwick (R.I.) Econ. Devel. Corp.; founder, pres. Mediators, Inc. Officer Edgewood Waterfront Preservation Soc., Cranston, 1994—. Republican. Home: 11 Longmeadow Rd Lincoln RI 02865 Office: Deveney & Hagopian 1215 Reservoir Ave Cranston RI 02920 also: Mediators Inc 1215 Reservoir Ave Cranston RI 02920

DEVER, MELISSA MARY, computer consulting company executive; b. Portsmouth, Va., May 4, 1953; d. John allen and Patricia (Moore) D.; m. Craig Martin. BS in Edn., U. Vt., 1975, MS in Computer Sci., 1982. Cert. Microsoft instr., Windows NT, Windows NT Server; cert. Microsoft profl. Tchr. math. North Country Jr. H.S., Derby, Vt., 1976-80; mfg. sys. engr. Digital Equipment Corp., Burlington, Vt., 1982-85; tech. sys. arch. Digital Equipment Corp., Tewksbury, Mass., 1985-91; application engring. mgr. Digital Equipment Corp., Burlington, 1991-93; v.p. engring. Competitive Computing, Colchester, Vt., 1993—; cons. Competitive Computing, Colchester, 1993—, Digital Equipment Corp., Burlington, 1991-93, engr., 1985-90. Contbr. tech. papers to profl. jours. Mem. Nat. Ctr. for Mfg. Svcs., C. of C. Home: 21 Sunderland Rd Colchester VT 05446 Office: Competitive Computing Inc Ste 106 2000 Mountainview Dr Colchester VT 05446

DEVERS, GAIL, track and field athlete. Student, UCLA. Gold medalist, 100m Track and Field Barcelona Olympic Games, 1992; Gold medalist 100m, 100m Hurdles World Track and Field Championships, Stuttgart, Germany, 1993; Gold medalist, 100m Track and Field Atlanta Olympic Games, 1996, Gold medalist 4x100m relay, 1996. Address: Track and Field 1 Hoosier Dome Ste 140 PO Box 120 Indianapolis IN 46206*

DEVIGNE, KAREN COOKE, retired amateur athletics executive; b. Phila., July 31, 1943; d. Paul and Matilda (Rich) Cooke; m. Jules Lloyd Devigne, June 26, 1965; children: Jules Paul, Denise Paige, Paul Michael. AA, Centenary Coll., Hackettstown, 1963; student, Northwestern U., 1963-65; BA, Ramapo Coll., Mahwah, 1976; MA, Emory U., Atlanta, 1989. Founder GYMSET, Marietta, Ga., 1981—. Cons. Girls Club Am. Marietta, 1989; vol. Cobb County Gymnastic Ctr., Marietta, 1976-95, Ga. Youth Soccer Assn., Atlanta, 1976-95; fundraiser Scottish Rite Children's Hosp., Atlanta, 1989. Recipient recognition awards from various youth groups, Atlanta, 1976—; named Nominee Woman of Yr. ABC News, Atlanta, 1984. Home: 3701 Clubland Dr Marietta GA 30068-4006 also: 445 White Cloud Breckenridge CO 80424

DE VINCK, CATHERINE, poet; Came to the U.S., 1948; m. José de Vinck; six children. LittD honoris causa, St. Mary's Coll., Notre Dame, 1982; LHD (hon.), Coll. of St. Scholastica, Duluth, Minn., 1986; LittD honoris causa, Regis Coll., 1986. Author: News of the World in Fifteen Stations, 1988, A Book of Peace, A Passion Play, A Time to Gather, 1967, 3d edit. 1987, Readings: John at Patmos and A Book of Hours, 1978, The Book of Eve, 1979, A Book of Uncommon Prayers, 1977-78, Ikon, 1972-74, A Liturgy 1973, 74, 77, A Garland of Straw, 1981, Poems of the Hidden Way, 1991, God of a Thousand Names, 1993. Office: Alleluia Press 672 Franklin Tpk Allendale NJ 07401

DEVINE, BARBARA ARMSTRONG, purchasing agent; b. Lawrence, Kans., Mar. 2, 1965. BS in Microbiology, U. Ill., 1987; postgrad., Lake Forest (Ill.) Grad. Sch., 1994—. Cert. purchasing mgr. R & D technician Abbott Labs., Abbott Park, Ill., 1987-90, asst. scientist, 1990-91, assoc. biochemist, 1991-93, purchasing agt., 1993-95, sr. purchasing agt., 1995—. Patentee in field. Vol. Choices program Abbott Labs., 1994—. Named Outstanding Buyer, Chgo. Minority Bus. Devel. Coun., 1996. Mem. NAFE, AAUW, Am. Assn. Clin. Chemistry, Purchasing Mgmt. Assn. Chgo., Am. Mgmt. Assn., Am. Purchasing Soc. Office: Abbott Labs D-06D AP34 200 Abbott Park Rd Abbott Park IL 60064

DEVINE, KAREN AUDREY, pediatric home health nurse; b. Phila., Nov. 17, 1953; d. Richard Andreas and Irma Cecilia (Scott) Oerth; m. Robert William Devine, Jan. 2; children: Robert, Peter, Joseph. LPN, Montgomery County C.C., 1982; student, Gwynedd (Pa.) Mercy Coll., 1982—; AAS, Montgomery County C.C., 1991. RN, Pa.; cert. pediatric RN, ANCC. Staff nurse telemetry unit North Penn (Pa.) Hosp., 1983-85; psychiat. nurse Eagleville (Pa.) Hosp., 1983-86; gen. home health nurse Personal Care, Phoenixville, Pa., 1986-89; pediatric home health nurse Family Help, King of Prussia, Pa., 1989-90, Skilled Nurses Inc., Bethlehem, Pa., 1990-92; ind. contractor, 1993-96. Author: (program) Increase Self Esteem, 1985; contbr. articles to profl. publs. Mem. Nat. League Nursing, Alliance for Mentally Ill, Bible Assn. Friends (bd. dirs. 1989—), Tract Assn. Friends (bd. dirs. 1989—), St. Davids Christian Writers Assn. Home and Office: 175 Lodle St Graterford PA 19426

DEVINE, KATHERINE, environmental consultant, educator; b. Denver, Oct. 15, 1951. BS, Rutgers U., 1973, MS, 1980; postgrad., U. Md., 1981-82. Lab. technician Princeton (N.J.) U., 1974-76; econ. and regulatory affairs analyst, program mgr. U.S. EPA, Washington, 1979-81, 82-89, cons., 1989—; exec. dir. Applied BioTreatment Assn., Washington, 1990-91; pres. DEVO Enterprises, Inc., Washington, 1990—; chair adv. bd. Applied Bioremediation Conf., 1993; co-chair Environ. Biotech. Conf., 1996. Author: N.J. Agricultural Experiment Station of Rutgers Uniersity, 1980, Bioremediation Case Studies: An Analysis of Vendor Supplied Data, 1992, Bioremediation Case Studies: Abstracts, 1992; co-author: Biomediation: Field Experiences, 1994, Bioremediation, 1994; founder, pub., editor (mag.) Biotreatment News, 1990—; pub. The Gold Book; contbr. articles to profl. jours., chpts. to books. Mem. Women's Coun. on Energy and the Environment, 1991-93. Recipient numerous fed. govt. and non- govt. awards. Mem. Am. Chem. Soc., Met. Washington Environ. Profls., Futures for Children, Alpha Zeta. Office: DEVO Enterprises Inc 1003 K St NW Ste 570 Washington DC 20001-4425

DEVINE, KATHLEEN ANNE, elementary school educator; b. Phila., Nov. 30, 1963; d. James Raymond and Claire Anne (Merman) D. BFA in Photography, Moore Coll. of Art, 1986; MA in Art Edn., Univ. of Arts, 1992. Cert. art edn. Art instr. St. Dorothy Sch., Drexel Hill, Pa., 1987-90, Radnor (Pa.) Sch. Dist., 1988-89, Moore Coll. of Art/Young People's Art Workshop, Phila., 1988-91, Rose Tree Media (Pa.) Sch. Dist., 1989—. Chandler scholar Moore Coll. of Art, 1988-89; recipient Roberts prize Univ. of Arts, 1993. Mem. Nat. Art Edn. Assn., Pa. Coalition for Arts in Edn., Pa. State Edn. Assn., Phila. Mus. Art. Roman Catholic. Office: Indian Lane Elem Sch 309 S Old Middletown Rd Media PA 19063

DEVINE, NANCY, postmaster; b. Hyannis, Mass., Feb. 8, 1949; d. Joseph Peter and Rose (Almeida) Cabral; m. Michael G. Devine, Mar. 20, 1971 (div. 1975); 1 child, Paul. Student, U. Mass., 1967-70. Postal clk. U.S. Postal Svc., Centerville, Mass., 1977-80; postmaster U.S. Postal Svc., West Hyannisport, Mass., 1980—; Affirmative Action planner U.S. Postal Svc., Brockton, Mass., 1979-80, prin. rep./exec. bd., Providence, 1993. Painter in acrylics. Art and Humanities grantee Barnstable Arts Coun., Mass. Art Coun., Nat. Endowment for the Arts. Mem. Cape Cod Art Assn., Smithsonian Instn. Home: PO Box 361 West Hyannisport MA 02672-0361

DEVINE, SHARON JEAN, lawyer; b. Milw., Feb. 27, 1948; d. George John Devine and Ethel May (Langworthy) Devine Chase; m. Curtiss Coughlin; children: Devin Curtiss, Katharine Langworthy. BS in Linguistics magna cum laude, Georgetown U., 1970; JD, Boston U., 1975. Bar: Ohio, Colo. Staff atty. FTC, Cleve., 1975-79; asst. regional dir., Denver, 1979-82; atty. Mountain Bell, Denver, 1982-84, US West Direct, 1984-85; assoc. gen. counsel U.S. West Direct, 1985-87, Landmark Pub. Co., Denver, 1987-88; antitrust counsel US West, Denver, 1988-91, corp. counsel, 1991—; dir. Denver Consortium, 1982-83, Ctr. for Applied Prevention, Boulder, Colo., 1982-90; dir. Legal Aid Found. of Colo., 1990-96, Suzuki Assn. of Colo., 1990-94. Active mem. Jr. League, Denver, 1980-87. Contbr. article to law rev. Mem. Am. Corporate Counsel Assn. (dir. Colo. chpt. 1994—), Colo. Bar Assn., Denver Bar Assn., Colo. Women's Bar Assn. Home: 118 Pika Rd Boulder CO 80302 Office: US West 7800 E Orchard Ste 480 Denver CO 80111

DEVINEY, SUSAN KAY, mathematician, educator; b. Hardtner, Kans., July 29, 1956; d. Irvin Lee and Carol Maxine (Harbison) Silcott; m. David Alan Deviney, Aug. 28, 1971; children: David Wayne, Sheila Ann, Jack Lee. BS in Edn., E. Ctrl. U., 1982, MEd, 1992. Cert. tchr. math., social studies. Tchr. remedial lang. arts Paoli (Okla.) Pub. Schs., 1982; tchr. elem. Maysville (Okla.) Pub. Schs., 1982-92; tchr. math., sci. Wynnewood (Okla.) Pub. Schs., 1992—. Mem. Delta Kappa Gamma (scholarship 1992). Democrat. Roman Catholic. Home: Rt 2 Box 246 Maysville OK 73057 Office: Wynnewood Pub Schs 702 E Robert S Kerr Wynnewood OK 73098

DEVINS, JULIE C. NIECE, pharmaceutical executive; b. Monett, Mo., Sept. 23, 1945; d. Russell Allen and Julia Agnes (Gimbel) Cole; children: Ronald J. III, Julia Allyson, Ellen Michelle; m. George S. Devins, Sept. 1990. Grad., St. John's Mercy Sch. Nursing, Springfield, Mo., 1968. RN. Critical care nursing St. Luke's Hosp., Kansas City, Mo., 1968-71; staff devel. instr. Shawnee Mission Med. Ctr., Merriam, Kansas, 1971-76; dir. edn. & training Olathe Community Hosp., Kansas, 1976-79; cont. edn. editor Greater Kansas City Nursing Journal, Mo., 1979-81; dir. nursing & allied health cont. edn. Johnson County Community Coll., Overland Park, Kansas, 1981-83; pharmaceutical sales rep. Fisons Corp., Boston, 1983-88; product rep. Hoffman-La Roche, Kansas City, Mo., 1988-90; pharmaceutical study coord. Devins Clinic, Kansas City, Mo., 1990—; bd. mem. Kansas City Allergy & Asthma Found. Am., Kansas City 1983-; mktg. mgr. Internat. Med. Tech. Cons. Inc., Prairie Village Kansas 1988. Co-author: R.N. Mag., I.V. Antiobiotic Therapy 1974, Nursing Procedure. Nursing procedure instr. Am. Heart Assn., Olathe & Merriam, Kansas, 1973-81. Home: 9836 Ash Dr Overland Park KS 66207

DEVITT, PAMELA KRUSE, legislative staff member; b. Washington, May 31, 1964. BA, Wheaton Coll., 1986. Staff asst. Ho. subcom. Edn. and Labor, 1986-87; legis. asst. to Rep. Marge Roukema, 1987-89, legis. asst. to Sen. James Jeffords, 1989-92; majority staff dir. subcom. edn., arts and humanities Senate Labor and Human Resources, 1993—. Office: Subcom on Edn Arts & Humanities 608 Hart Senate Office Bldg Washington DC 20510

DEVITT, SUSAN B., lawyer; b. N.J., Sept. 15, 1956. BA with distinction, U. Mich., 1978; JD with high honors, U. Tenn., 1987. Bar: Ga. 1987, U.S. Dist. Ct. (mid. and no. dists.) Ga. 1988; U.S. Ct. Appeals (11th cir.) 1988. Ptnr. Alston & Bird, Atlanta. Mem. Tenn. Law Rev. Mem. ABA, Atlanta Bar Assn., State Bar of Ga., Order of the Coif, Phi Alpha Delta, Phi Kappa Phi. *

DEVIVO, ANGE, former small business owner; b. Bay Shore, N.Y., Oct. 20, 1925; d. Romeo Zanetti and Karolina (Hodapp) King; m. John Michael DeVivo, Dec. 30, 1950; 1 child, Michael. Student, Washington Sch. for Secs., N.Y.C., 1945-46. Sec. Am. Airlines, N.Y.C., 1946-51; exec. sec. W.C. Holzhauer, N.Y.C., 1951-52; dist. sales mgr. Emmons Jewelers, Inc., Bound Brook, N.J., 1952-53; exec. sec. N.J. Rep. State Com., 1960-64; adminstrv. sec. Mercy Hosp., Charlotte, N.C., 1973-81; pres. Secs., Plus, Convs., Plus, Charlotte, 1983-91; prin. Ange DeVivo & Assocs., Inc., Charlotte, 1991-92. Editor: The North Carolina Republican Woman, 1994, 3d edit., 1995. Mem. Human Svcs. Coun., Charlotte, 1984-88; mem. Emergency Med. Svc. Adv. Coun., Charlotte, 1981-92, chmn., 1988-90; mem. Charlotte Women's Polit. Caucus, 1972—, Mecklenburg Evening Rep. Women's Club, Charlotte, 1970—, pres., 1973-74, 93-94; mem. citizens adv. com. Conv. and Visitors Bur., 1986-90; coord. Women's Equality Day celebration Mecklenburg County Women's Commn., 1990, coord., fin. chair, 1991-92, co-chmn., fin. chair, 1993, chair, fin. chair, 1994-95, fin. chair, 1996, mem. adv. bd., 1993—, vice chair, 1995; exec. sec. N.J. Rep. State Com., 1960-64. Recipient Order of Long Leaf Pine award Gov. of N.C., 1974, Entrepreneur of Yr. award Women Bus. Owners, 1987, Spl. Recognition award for devotion, dedication and untiring efforts Mecklenburg County Women's Commn., 1996; honoree N.C. Fedn. Rep. Women, 1987; nominee for Cmty. Svc. award, 1994. Mem. Women's Roundtable. Roman Catholic.

DEVLIN, GAIL E., insurance company executive. Sr. v.p. fin., dir. investor rels. The Chubb Corp., Warren, N.J. Office: The Chubb Corp PO Box 1615 15 Mountain View Rd Warren NJ 07061-1615*

DEVLIN, JEAN THERESA, educator, storyteller; b. Jamaica, N.Y., Apr. 14, 1947; d. Edward Philip and Frances Margaret (Tillman) Creagh; children: Michael, Bernadette, Patrick. BA magna cum laude, Queens Coll., 1972, postgrad., 1994—; MA, St. John's U., Jamaica, 1987; PhD, So. Ill. U., 1991. Substitute tchr. Diocese of Bklyn., 1969-75; tchr. St. Gregory's Sch., Bellerose, N.Y., 1975-82; dist. mgr. Creative Expressions, Robesonia, Pa., 1980-83; asst. to dean, adj. instr. workshop supr. Spl. Univ. Program St. John's U., Jamaica, 1983-87, asst. prof. dept. English, 1992; asst. dean St. John's Coll. Liberal Arts, St. Johns U., 1993-94; owner Tara's Tees and Golden Hands Embroidery, 1984-87; from grad. asst. to doctoral fellow English dept. So. Ill. U., Carbondale, 1987-89, storytelling tchr. Continuing Edn., 1992; adj. asst. prof. St. John's U., Jamaica, 1992-94, Poly. U., N.Y., 1995-96, Bayside Acad., N.Y., 1995—, St. Anthony's H.S., Huntington, N.Y., 1996—; cons. Family Lit. Project; supr. workshops Popular Culture, 1991—, Children's Lit. Assn., 1990-92, Midwest Popular Culture, 1991, Wyo. Centennial, 1990; presenter poetry readings, dramatic interpretation, storytelling, including Internat. Rsch. Soc. in Children's Lit., Paris, 1991, Nat. Coun. Tchrs. English Conf., 1992, Ill. Assn. Tchrs. of English, 1990, 91,

92, South Atlantic MLA, 1992, Mid Atlantic Popular/Am. Culture, 1993; speaker Speak Easy Workshop, 1981; showcased Nat. Congress Storytelling, Children's Reading Roundtable, 1990; world-wide storyteller, 1991—. Author: Gabby Diego, 1992, repub. 1994; contbr. articles to profl. jours. and children's mags.; actress (videotape and audiocassette) Peter Kagan and the Wind, 1990, 91, played at White House, 1992, Sta. WKTS, 1992-94; performed as storyteller on 5 continents, 1991—. Den leader Boy Scouts Am., Bayside, N.Y., 1975-80; troop leader Girl Scouts U.S.A., Flushing, N.Y., 1976-78; vol. Elderwise Day Care, Carbondale, Ill., 1992, Alice Wright Day Care Ctr., Carbondale, 1989-92, ABC Quilts (A Pediatric AIDS group), 1991—; mem. The Stage Co., Cill Cais Players. Honored for outstanding svc. Boy Scouts Am., 1978; recipient Outstanding Cmty. Svc. award, named Most Admired Woman of the Decade Sta. WPSD-TV, 1991, Internat. Women of Yr., 1993; grantee So. Ill. Art Coun., 1992. Mem. MLA, ASCD, AAUW, AAUP, Nat. Coun. Tchrs. English, Nat. Assn. Preservation and Perpetuation of Storytelling, Children's Lit. Assn., Mid-Atlantic Popular Culture Assn., Popular Culture Assn., Ladies Ancient Order Hibernians (chpt. founder, pres. 1984-85), Beatrix Potter Soc., Skull & Circle Honor Soc. (St. John's U.), Alpha Sigma Lambda, Sigma Tau Delta, Phi Delta Kappa, others. Home: 54-23 151 St Flushing NY 11355

DEVLIN, WENDE DOROTHY, writer, artist; b. Buffalo, Apr. 27, 1918; d. Bernhardt Phillip Wende and Elizabeth May Buffington; m. Harry Devlin, Aug. 30, 1941; children: Harry, Wende, Jeffrey, Alexandra, Brian, Nicholas, David. BFA, Syracuse U., 1940. Author: (children's books) Old Black Witch, 1963, Old Witch and the Polkadot Ribbon, 1963, The Knobby Boys to the Rescue, 1965, Aunt Agatha, There is a Lion Under the Couch, 1968, How Fletcher was Hatched, 1970, (N.J. English Tchrs. award), A Kiss for a Warthog, 1970, Cranberry Thanksgiving, 1971, Old Witch Rescues Halloween, 1973 (Chgo. Book Fair award for excellence 1974), Cranberry Christmas, 1973, Cranberry Mystery, 1979, Hang on Hester, 1980, Cranberry Summer, 1991, Cranberry Valentine, 1986, Cranberry Autumn, 1994, The Trouble with Henriette, 1995; artist, painter comic strip Ragg Mopp, 1969-72; contbr. of many poems to Good Housekeeping mag.; one person show at Schering Plough, N.J.; represented in permanent collections at Midlantic Bank of N.J., Nat. Westminster Bank of N.J., also many private collections. Mem. Rutgers Adv. Coun. on Children's Lit., 1980—. Recipient Arents award Syracuse U., 1977; named to N.J. Literary Hall of Fame, 1989. Congregationalist. Home and Office: 443 Hillside Ave Mountainside NJ 07092 Office: Simon & Schuster 866 Third Ave New York NY 10022

DEVNEY, ANNE MARIE, nursing educator; b. Jackson Heights, N.Y., July 31, 1948; d. Edward James and Lillian Hazel (Ryan) D. BSN, U. R.I., 1970; BS, George Washington U., 1978; MSEd, Pepperdine U., 1981; MAEd, San Diego State U., 1985; EdD in Adult Edn., No. Ill. U., 1994. Cert. instructional tech. Commd. ens. Nurse Corps USN, 1968; charge nurse Naval Hosp., St. Albans, Queens, N.Y., 1970-72, Marine Corps Dispensary, Iwakuni, Japan, 1972-74; charge nurse intermediate ICU Naval Regional Med. Ctr., San Diego, 1974-76; advanced through grades to comdr. USN, 1989; nurse anesthetist U.S. Naval Hosp., Long Beach, Calif., 1978-81; ret. USN, 1989; coord. inservice U.S. Naval Hosp., Long Beach, Calif.; instr. Naval Sch. Health Scis. U.S. Naval Hosp., San Diego, 1981-84; edn. cons. No. Ill. U., DeKalb; dir. health svcs. Coll. of Lake County, Grayslake, Ill., former coord. allied health svcs.; staff nurse Condell Med. Ctr., Libertyville, Ill.; mem. nursing adv. faculty, dir. Health Ctr., Coll. of Lake County, Grayslake, Ill.; mem. adj. faculty Nat.-Louis U., Wheaton, Ill., Coll. of St. Francis, Joliet, Ill.; cons., pres. Devney Interactive Design. Contbr. articles to profl. jours., chpts. to books, rsch. on The Effectiveness of Interactive Video on Performance of Simple Nursing Procedure, Crisis Learning: Family Members of ICU Trauma Patients. With USN. San Diego Navy League finalist for Mil. Women of the Year award, 1983. Mem. ANA, Ill. State Nurses Assn., Nat. League for Nursing, Internat. Interactive Comms. Tech., Pi Lambda Theta (pres. Chgo. area chpt.). Home: 18670 W Old Plank Rd Grayslake IL 60030 Office: Coll Lake County 19351 W Washington St Grayslake IL 60030-1198

DEVON, MARJORIE LYNN, art administrator, educator; b. Jersey City, Dec. 2, 1945; m. Paul Gregory Baroacke, Dec. 16, 1965 (div. 1977); children: Julie, Brynn; m. W. Anthony Evanko, Sept. 3, 1994. BA, U. Calif., Berkeley, 1968. Asst. dir. Tamarind Inst., Albuquerque, 1980-84, assoc. dir., 1984-85, dir., 1985—; asst. prof. dept. art and art history U. N.Mex., Albuquerque, 1985—; curator various exhbns.; juror exhbns. in field. Bd. dirs. Art in the Schs., Albuquerque, 1995—. Office: Tamarind Inst 108 Cornell Dr SE Albuquerque NM 87106

DEVONE, DENISE, artist, educator; b. Newark, Sept. 13, 1953; d. William Joseph and Josephine Loretta (Miserendino) DeV. BFA cum laude, Temple U., 1975; MFA, U. Hawaii, 1978. Instr. Newark Mus., 1990—; art tchr. Holy Cross Sch., Harrison, N.J., 19956; adj. prof. County Coll. of Morris, Randolph, N.J., 1994—; cons. Donald B. Palmer Mus., Springfield, N.J., 1992-95. Executed murals Kaiser Hosp., Honolulu, 1985, Kaiser Pensacola Clinic, Honolulu, 1986, Distinctive Bodies Fitness, Warren, N.J., 1993, Ambulatory Pediatric Clinic, Overlook Hosp., Summit, N.J., 1994. Recipient Purchase awards Hawaii State Found. on Culture and the Arts, 1976, 78, 80, 86, award of merit City and County of Honolulu, 1988; N.J. State Coun. on Arts/Dept. State fellow, 1994-95. Mem. New Art Group/ Watchung Arts Ctr., City Without Walls, Artists Space. Home: 33 Kew Dr Springfield NJ 07081-2530

DEVORAH, RUTH, vocalist, cantor, artist; b. N.Y.C., Dec. 28, 1930; d. Albert and Gladys (Chayet) Cohen; m. Marvin Abraham Trelin, Dec. 1, 1951 (div. Aug. 1967); children: Jayne Susan, Steven Ira; m. Harold Israel Glick, June 6, 1976. Student, Fashion Inst. Tech., N.Y.C., 1982-83, Art Students League, N.Y.C., 1983-84, Parsons Sch. Design, N.Y.C., 1989-90; cantorial cert., Herzliah Hebrew Seminary, N.Y.C., 1978. Author: (collection of poems) Imagine That! A Fly-A Fish-A Tree...A Few Expressions of My Impressions, 1995; vocal performer various events. Mem. Am. Soc. for Jewish Music, Actors Equity Assn., Screen Actors Guild. Home: 240 Central Park South 5Q New York NY 10019-1413

DEVORE, BARBARA JANE EGAN, corporate finance executive; b. Harrisburg, Pa., Aug. 15, 1958; d. John Joseph and Pearl Catherine (Schaeffer) Egan; m. Timothy Dale DeVore, Oct. 22, 1983; children: Dale Vincent, Jessica Lynne. BS in Bus./Acctg., Wright State U., Dayton, Ohio, 1980. CPA, Ohio, CMA. Acctg. intern Delco Air divsn. GM, Dayton, 1979-80; auditor NCR Corp., Dayton, 1980-83, fin. specialist office systems divsn., 1983-86, analyst, sect. mgr. U.S. mktg., 1986-90; tax adminstr. NCR Corp. Taxes, Dayton, 1990-94; corp. analyst/planning office corp. controller NCR Corp., Dayton, 1994-95, fin. and adminstrv. tng. analyst office corp. controller, 1995; fin. mgr. sales and mktg. O-Cedar/Vining, Springfield, Ohio, 1996—. Fin. sec. Knob Prairie Ch., Enon, Ohio, 1990-91, choir dir., 1991—; song leader Enon Cmty. Hist. Soc., 1991—. Mem. Wright State Alumni Assn. Republican. Home: 560 Brunswick Dr Enon OH 45323-1802

DEVORE, JUDITH TRAVERS, executive recruiter; b. Detroit, Sept. 13, 1959; d. Thomas E. and Lillian A. (Appenzeller) DeV. BGS, Oakland U., Rochester, Mich., 1988. Personnel staff asst. Campbell-Ewald Co., Advt., Warren, Mich., 1979-86; sr. human resources rep. CIS/CMI Corp., Bloomfield Hills, Mich., 1986-89; sr. recruiting specialist Kelly Assisted Living, Troy, Mich., 1989-92; employment mgr. Ross Roy Advt., Warren, 1992-94; exec. recruiter human resources Blue Care Network, Southfield, Mich., 1995—. Mem. NAFE, Soc. Human Resource Mgmt., Human Resource Assn. of Detroit. Home: 12342 Canterbury Dr Warren MI 48093-1842

DEVORE, KIMBERLY K., sales executive; b. Louisville, June 19, 1947; d. Wendell O. and Shirley F. DeV.; student, Xavier U., 1972-76; AA, Coll. Mt. St. Joseph, 1979. Patient registration supr. St. Francis Hosp., Cin., 1974-76; cons., bus. mgr. Family Health Care Found., Cin., 1976-77; exec. dir. Hospice of Cin., Inc., 1977-80; pres. Micro Med, 1979-86; v.p. Sycamore Profl. Assn., 1979-86; ptnr. Enchanted House, 1979-86, sec., 1979-80, treas. 1980-83; dist. sales rep. Control-O-Fax, 1986, br. sales mgr., 1987, nat. dealer devel. rep., 1987—, computer specialist, 1987, nat. computer field sales trainer, 1987-90; pres. U.S. Exec. Leasing and U.S. Med. Leasing, Inc., 1991—, Accu Svcs., Inc., 1993—, U.S. Med. Mgmt., Inc., 1994—, U.S. Med. Mgmt. of Ga., Inc., 1994—; pres. Saddle Creek Homeowners Assn., Inc., 1992-95, parliamentarian, 1995-96; membership chairperson Smith Plantation City of Roswell, 1996—; pres. Roswell Citizen's Police Acad., Inc., 1994—; mem. North Fulton Civic League, Inc., 1995-96; bd. dirs. Nat. Hospice Orgn., 1979-82, chmn. long-term planning com., fin. com., ann. meeting com., 1979-82, sec., 1980-81. treas., 1981-82; bd. dirs. Hospice of Miami Valley, Inc., 1982-86, also chmn. pers. com., by-laws com.; mem. med. dist. com. City Roswell, 1995—; bd. dirs. Smith Plantation, 1996—. Mem. Greater Cin. Soc. Fund Raisers, Better Housing League; Mem. service and rehab. com. Hamilton County Unit, Am. Cancer Soc., 1977-78; chair road com. Saddle Creek Homeowners Assn., 1991-92. Mem. Ohio Hospice Assn. (co-founder, state chmn., pres., 1978-83), Nat. League for Nursing, Ohio Hosp. Assn., Nat. Fedn. Bus. and Profl. Women's Clubs, Ohio Fedn. Bus. and Profl. Women's Clubs, Cin. Bus. and Profl. Women's Clubs (pres. 1973-75).

DEVORE, SADIE DAVIDSON, art educator, artist; b. Wheaton, Mo., June 12, 1937; d. Noah Fred and Marion Ollie (Jones) Davidson; m. Harry L. DeVore III, Dec. 12, 1959 (dec.); children: Desa DeVore Buffum, H.L. DeVore IV, David Christopher DeVore. BS, Southwest Mo. State U., 1958; MAT, RIC, 1980; postgrad., N.Y.U., 1986. Cert. art K-12 tchr. Art tchr. grades K-12 Springfield (Mo.) Art Mus., 1956-58; comml. artist Springfield Utilities, 1958-59; jr. high art tchr. Jarrett, Pershing, Springfield, 1959-62; h.s. art tchr. Shawnee Mission (Kans.) North H.S., 1963-65; artist Stonington (Conn.) Cmty. Ctr., 1971; art tchr. Stonington Pub. Sch., Pawcatuck, Conn., 1972-96; art history tchr. Mitchell Coll., New London, Conn., 1989; art reader Coll. Bd. of N.J., Princeton, N.J., 1996. Exhibited in numerous art shows including Hoxie Gallery, Hat Shop, Conn. Com. of the Arts, Slater Mus., Marcus Gallery, Emporium Gallery, Conn. Coll., others. Skidmore Art fellow, 1989. Mem. Nat. Art Edn. Assn., Nat. Art Honor Soc. (sponsor), Lyme Art Assn., East Lyme Art Assn., Mystic Art Assn., Vangarde Artists, South County Art Assn., Monotypes Today, Art Ptnrs., Alpha Delta Pi. Democrat. Home and Studio: 137 High St Mystic CT 06355-2415 Office: Stonington Pub Schs 176 S Broad Pawcatuck CT 06379

DEVRIES, BRIGID LARKIN, educational association administrator; b. Lexington, Ky., July 27, 1949; d. Stuart Ralph and Helen Mary (Larkin) D. BA in Phys. Edn., Health and Recreation, U. Ky., 1971, MS in Edn., 1975. Phys. edn. tchr. Nicholas County Elem. Sch., Carlisle, Ky., 1971-73; grad. asst. dept. campus recreation U. Ky., 1973-75; coach women's intercollegiate swimming and track Ohio U., Athens, 1976-79; exec. asst. Ky. High Sch. Athletic Assn., Lexington, 1979—; coach men's and women's diving U. Ky., Lexington, 1980-90. Bd. dirs. Blue Grass State Games, 1984—. Named to Swimming and Diving Hall of Fame U. Ky., 1994. Mem. Citizens for Sports Equity (pres. 1993-96), Nat. Fedn. Rules Com. (gymnastics 1981-84, volleyball 1986-89, swimming and diving 1983-86). Democrat. Office: Ky High Sch Athletic Assn 2280 Executive Dr Lexington KY 40505

DE VRIES, CAROL N., performer, music educator; b. Fresno, Calif., Dec. 20, 1938; d. John and Georgia C. (Lofgren) de V. BA, Calif. State U., 1960, MA, 1988. Tchr. Madera (Calif.) Sch. Dist., 1960-61; music educator Fresno (Calif.) City Schs., 1963-68; voice faculty Calif. State U., Stanislaus, 1972-74, Fresno Pacific Coll., 1978-80, Clovis (Calif.) Unified Sch. Dist., 1985—; profl. singer, dancer and actress N.Y.C./L.A./San Francisco, 1962—; pvt. voice tchr., Fresno, 1969—; guest lectr. Calif. State U., Fresno, 1989-92. Mem. Am. Choral Dirs. Assn., Calif. Music Educators, Equity. Office: Cole Sch 615 Stuart Clovis CA 93612

DE VRIES, MARGARET GARRITSEN, economist; b. Detroit, Feb. 11, 1922; d. John Edward and Margaret Florence (Ruggles) Garritsen; m. Barend A. de Vries, Apr. 5, 1952; children: Christine, Barton. B.A. in Econs. with honors, U. Mich., 1943; Ph.D. in Econs., MIT, 1946. With IMF, Washington, 1946-87, sr. economist, 1949-52, asst. chief multiple currency pratices div., 1953-57, chief Far Eastern Div., 1957-59, econ. cons., 1963-73, historian, 1973-87; professorial lectr. econs. George Washington U., 1946-49, 58-63. Author: The International Monetary Fund, 1966-71, The System Under Stress, 2 vols., 1977, The International Monetary Fund, 1972-78, Cooperation on Trial, 3 vols., 1985, The IMF in a Changing World, 1945-85, transl. into Chinese, 1986, Balance of Payments, Adjustment: The IMF Experience, 1945-86, transl. into Chinese, 1989, (with I.S. Friedman) Foreign Economic Policy of the United States in the Postwar, 1947, (with J.K. Horsefield) The International Monetary Fund, 1945-65, Twenty Years of International Monetary Cooperation, 3 vols., 1969; contbr. articles to profl. jours. Recipient Disting. Alumni award U. Mich., 1980, Cert. of Appreciation George Washington U., 1987, Outstanding Washington Woman Economist award, 1987; AAUW scholar, 1939-42; U. Mich. Univ. scholar, 1942; MIT fellow, 1943-46; Ford Found. grantee, 1959-62. Mem. Am. Econ. Assn., U. Mich. Alumni Assn., MIT Alumnae Assn., Phi Beta Kappa, Phi Kappa Phi. Mem. United Church of Christ. Home: 10018 Woodhill Rd Bethesda MD 20817-1218

DE VRIES, ROBBIE RAY PARSONS, author, illustrator, international consultant; b. Idabel, Okla., Sept. 11, 1929; d. General Forrest Sr. and Jessie Demma (Burch-Oldham) Parsons; m. Douwe de Vries, Apr. 2, 1953; children: Jessica Joan de Vries Kij, Peter Douwe. BS in Bus. Adminstrn. and Journalism, Okla. State U., 1952; postgrad., U. Houston, 1987, 88, Rice U., 1988, 89. Sec. to mgr. drafting and survey Shell Oil Co., Houston, 1952-53; sub. tchr. Spring Br. Ind. Sch. Dist., Houston, 1989-92; pres., owner Robbie P. de Vries Interests, Houston, 1983—, author, illustrator, pub., 1989—; mem. governing bd. Oilfield Systems, Inc., Houston, 1981—; bd. dirs. Friends of Okla. State U. Libr., Stillwater; mem. Friends of U. Houston Libr., 1981—; bd. dirs., cons. Ctr. for Internat. Trade, Okla. State U., Stillwater, 1990—; invited guest Peoples Republic of China/U.S. State Dept., China, 1992. Columnist Conroe, Tex. Daily Courier, 1988-89; editor Idabel Warrior newspaper (Gold medal), 1947, Houston Symphony League newspaper, 1974-75; author, illustrator, pub.: A Cultural Exchange: American and Chinese Weddings, 1993, Chinese edit., 1995; author, pub.: Regional Study of Russian and the Eurasian States, 1996. Vol cultural and internat. areas, New Orleans, 1960-69, Houston, 1969—; bd. dirs. New Orleans C. of C., 1964-69; bd. dirs. Houston Symphony Soc. and League, 1972—, Inst. Internat. Edn., Houston, 1969—; home host internat. youth exch./The Netherlands, 1978; grand jury mem. Harris County Tex., 1986-87; patron Jr. League, Houston, 1970—; docent Mus. Fine Arts, Houston, 1974—; mem., yearbook cover designer Tuesday Music Club, Houston, 1975—; mem. Forum Club Houston, 1980—; co-chmn. Houston-Baku, Azerbaijan, USSR Sister City, 1979-89; bd. dirs. Boy Scouts, Houston, 1985—; bd. dirs., chair Internat. Conf. YWCA, Houston, 1986-87; mem. magic cir. Rep. Women of Houston, 1989—; mem. donor Baylor Med. Sch. Devel., 1990—. Recipient Ann. Fund Silver Tray award Houston Symphony League, 1972, Miss Ima Hogg Orchid award Houston Symphony Soc., 1975, Gen. Maurice Hirsch Leaf and Letter award Symphony Soc., 1980, 81, 82, Tex. Mother of Yr., Alpha Delta Pi, 1982, Mayor's award Baku, Azerbaijan USSR, 1979, 83, 87, 89, U.S. State Dept. pin, 1986, 10-Yr. Leadership award Mayor of Baku, 1988, U. Houston Ball Merit/Honor, 1991, Merit award Boy Scouts of Am., 1993, 10-Yr. Svc. award, 1995; named Acting First Lady of Houston for goodwill trip to Baku, Azerbaijan, USSR, by Mayor of Houston Jim McConn, 1979; named Hon. Dep. Sheriff, Harris County Sheriff Johnny Klevenhagen, 1986, Harris County Sheriff Tommy B. Thomas, 1996; feature Honor Villages mag., 1994. Mem. AAUW (past pres.), Tex. Fine Arts Assn., Inspirational Writers, Houston Coun. Writers, Nat. Women's Hall of Fame, Étoffe Littéraire (founder, Founder's award 1985), Tex.-Netherlands Bus. Assn., Nat. Mus. Women in the Arts (charter), Mu Kappa Tau. Republican. Presbyterian. Home and Office: Robbie P de Vries Interests 802 Piney Point Rd Houston TX 77024-2725

DEWALT, MARY E., bank executive. Sr. v.p. retail Calif. Fed. Bank, Orange. Office: Calif Fed Bank 4050 Metropolitan Dr Orange CA 92668*

DEWBERRY, BETTY BAUMAN, retired law librarian; b. Dallas, Jan. 18, 1930; d. William Allen Bauman and Julia Ella (Owen) Hurt; m. James A. Dewberry Jr., Mar. 22, 1952 (div. Apr. 1976); children: Mary Julienne, Jennifer Camille, Robert Bruce. BA, U. Tex., 1951; MLS, Tex. Women's U., 1982. Asst. librarian Johnson & Swanson, Dallas, 1979-85; dir. librs. Johnson & Gibbs, Dallas, 1985-94; retired, 1994. Mem. Am. Assn. Law Libraries, Dallas Assn. Law Librarians, Women's Nat. Book Assn., Lakeside Browning Club, Zeta Tau Alpha. Democrat. Methodist.

DEWEIL, DAWN SUSAN, lawyer; b. Passaic, N.J., July 1, 1957; d. Ralph Earl and Thelma Susan (Schwartz) DeW.; m. Jonathan Stuart Blausten, Oct. 12, 1989. BA, Rutgers U., 1979; JD, N.Y. Law Sch., 1987. Bar: N.J. 1987, N.Y. 1988, U.S. Dist. Ct. (so. and ea. dists.) N.Y. 1994, U.S. Dist. Ct. N.J. 1994. Asst. regional counsel U.S. Dept. Health and Human Svcs., N.Y.C., 1987-88; assoc. atty. N.Y.C. Police Dept., N.Y.C., 1988-89, Heidell Pittoni Murphy & Bach, N.Y.C., 1989-93; mng. atty. breast implant litigation unit Schneider Kleinick Weitz Damashek & Shoot, N.Y.C., 1993—; lectr. Prentice Hall Law and Bus., 1994; with Court TV, 1995. Mem. editl. bd. Medical and Legal Aspects of Breast Implant Litigation. Mem. Am. Trial Lawyers Assn., N.Y. Bar Assn., Metro. Women's Bar Assn., N.Y. State Trial Lawyers Assn. Office: Schneider Kleinick Weitz Damashek & Shoot 233 Broadway New York NY 10279-0001

DEWEY, ANNE ELIZABETH MARIE, lawyer; b. Balt., Mar. 16, 1951; d. George Daniel and Elizabeth Patricia (Mohan) D.; children: Brendan M., Andrew P., Meghan E. BA, Mich. State U., 1972; JD, U. Chgo., 1975; grad., Stonier Grad. Sch. Banking, East Brunswick, N.J., 1983. Bar: D.C. 1976. Legal clk. and atty. FTC, Washington, 1975-78; atty. and sr. atty. Comptr. of Currency, Dallas and Washington, 1978-86; assoc. gen. counsel, gen. counsel, spl. counsel Farm Credit Adminstrn., McLean, Va., 1986-92, FDIC counsel, closed bank litigation and policy sect., 1993-94; gen. counsel Office of Fed. Housing Enterprise Oversight, HUD, 1994—. Mem. ABA (bus. law sect., mem. banking law com.), FBA (bd. dirs. D.C. chpt. 1989-91, banking law com.), Women in Housing and Fin. (bd. dirs. 1982-83, gen. counsel 1991-93), D.C. Bar Assn., Exchequer Club. Roman Catholic.

DEWITT, EULA, accountant; b. Conway, S.C., Feb. 5, 1948; d. Joseph and Ethel Maude (Parmley) D.; m. John Ramos; children: Andre Carter, John Ramos III, David Carter. BS in Acctg., CUNY, 1981; cert., Bethlehem Missionary Bible Inst., 1990. Jr. acct. Kenneth Laventhol, CPA Firm, N.Y., 1981; agent IRS, N.Y., 1981—, staff pub. speakers bur., 1985—, instr. for revenue agents, 1986—. Author newsletter; contbr. numerous articles to profl. jours. Tutor York Coll. CUNY, Jamaica, 1991—; guest spkr. Hunter Coll. 6th Ann. Conv., 1991, Exploring Divsn. Greater N.Y., 1991, Cath. Charities Archdioces, N.Y., 1991; tchr. Sunday sch. Bethlehem Missionary Ch., 1979—, leader altar workers ministry, 1991—, missionary to Belize, 1991, to Eng., 1993, to Guyana, 1995. Mem. Inst. Mgmt. Accts. (bd. dirs. 1982—, v.p. profl. edn. 1994-95, pres.-elect 1996-97), Toastmaster's 21 Club (v.p., past pres., Able Toastmaster ATM 1996). Office: IRS 110 W 44th St New York NY 10036-4011

DEWITT, JUDY LYNN, accountant; b. Mt. Pleasant, Mich., May 18, 1957; d. Gerald Detweiler and Shirley Marilyn (Bontrager) Cassel; m. Kimber DeWitt, June 24, 1995; 1 child, Heather Victoria Cassel; stepchildren: Erin Leigh, Kevin Don, Jeffrey Karl. BSBA, Cen. Mich. U., 1992. CPA, Mich. Teller Isabella Bank and Trust, Mt. Pleasant, 1976-77; sec. Bergey Tires, Souderton, Pa., 1977-79; teller, sec. 1st of Am. Bank, Mt. Pleasant, 1980-81; sec. Yanmar Tractors, Chgo., 1981-82, TRW, Chgo., 1982-84, Xyvision, Inc., Chgo., 1984-85; ins. prodr. AVA Ins., Chgo., 1985-88; staff acct. Page, Olson and Co., CPAs, Mt Pleasant, 1992-94; chief acct. Isabella County, Mt Pleasant, 1994—. Treas. bd. deacons 1st Presbyn. Ch., Mt. Pleasant, 1992-95. Mem. AICPA, Inst. Mgmt. Accts., Mich. Assn. CPAs. Presbyterian. Office: Isabella County 200 N Main St Mount Pleasant MI 48858

DEWITT, KAREN LEE (KELLY DEWITT), computer information consultant; b. San Francisco, Apr. 13, 1963; d. Martin Johann and Dixie Lee (Mayhak) Whitted; m. Abel M.V. Garcia, Dec. 1, 1984 (div. Aug. 1986); m. Robert Martin DeWitt, Jan. 1, 1990. Student, Mills Coll., Oakland, Calif., 1981-82. Mgr. Video Outlet, Pitts., 1983-84; asst. mgr. ECX Computers, Walnut Creek, Calif., 1984-90; accounts payable mgr. Byte & Floppy Computers, San Diego, 1990 ; owner MicroByte, Concord, Calif., 1988-90, Pvt. Res. Products (now Berkshire Publishing), Lakeside, Calif., 1990—; cons. Svcs. Aiding Ind. Living, Concord, 1985-90, U.S. Submarine Vets. of W.W. II, Vallejo, Calif., 1985-90. Sponsor Save the Children, Mali, Africa, World Wildlife Fund, 1988, 91, Planned Parenthood, San Diego Zoo Soc. Mem. NAFE, Humane Soc. of U.S., Am. Inst. Profl. Bookkeepers.

DEWITT, MARY THERESE, private investigator; b. Chgo., Aug. 25, 1948; d. Robert Baldwin and Helen (Rossman) DeW.; m. Geoffrey M. Tait, Aug. 1, 1988. AA, Coll. of DuPage, 1968; BA in Edn., U. Wis., Whitewater, 1969; postgrad., U. North Tex., 1992-93, U. Tex., Arlington, 1993 ; BA in Anthropology, U. Tex. at Arlington, 1995. Dir. mktg. Homart Devel. Co., Florence, Ky., 1975-76, Melvin Simon & Assocs., Inc., Hurst, Tex., 1976-79; pres. Mary DeWitt Co., Ft. Worth, 1979-85; v.p. mktg. Southmark Comml. Mgmt., Dallas, 1986-87; prin. DeWitt Group and subs. Cat's-Eye Intelligence Svc., Dallas and Ft. Worth, 1988—; cons. logistics and documentation one team Internat. Group for Hist. Aircraft Recovery, The Phoenix Group South Pacific, 1989. Founder, co-dir. Svc. to Elist Resident Vols. in Euless, Tarrant County, Tex., 1989-91. Mem. Archaeoll. Inst. of Am., Internat. Assn. for Identification, Am. Assn. of Phys. Anthropologists, Lambda Alpha (v.p.). Episcopalian. Home: 1905 Cripple Creek Dr Euless TX 76039-2204

DEWITT, RITA MARIE, art educator; b. Whittier, Calif., Dec. 31, 1943; d. Walter Edward and Thelma Marie (Wilson) Taylor; m. Stanford P. DeWitt, Dec. 23, 1965 (div. Mar. 1995); children: Daren, Maria. BSEd, Mo. State U., 1964; M in Secondary Edn., Drury Coll., 1992. Cert. tchr., Mo. Home econ. tchr. Bourbon (Mo.) H.S., 1966; art and home econ. tchr. Marionville (Mo.) Jr. High and H.S., 1969-71; art tchr. Crane (Mo.) Sch., 1974—; demonstrator Arts Fest, Springfield, Mo., 1990—, Ozark Empire Fair, Springfield, 1990—. Elder Crane Presbyn. Ch., 1972—. Mem. Mo. State Tchrs. Assn., Springfield Fiber Artists (newsletter editor 1992—), S.W. Dist. Art Tchrs. (treas. 1991—), 4-State Fiber Guild, Crane Tchrs. Assn. Republican. Presbyterian. Home: PO Box 41 Crane MO 65633

DEWITT, SALLIE LEE, realtor; b. Ft. Smith, Ark., Oct. 11, 1923; d. Lee and Claudia Cordelia Victoria (Vest) DeW. BS, U. Tex., 1944; Cert. Profl. Sec., U. Houston, 1971; postgrad. in Computers, Del Mar Coll., 1989. Real estate broker, Tex.; cert. profl. sec. Layout artist, copywriter Corpus Christi (Tex.) Caller-Times, 1945-56; exec. sec. to chief geologist Exxon Co., Houston, 1956-73; adminstrv. asst. to gen. mgr. Valley Telephone Coop., Inc., Raymondville, Tex., 1976-89; owner, mgr. Sallie Lee DeWitt Real Estate, Raymondville, Tex., 1980-89; broker assoc. Alfred Edge Realtors, Corpus Christi, 1990—; property tax cons., Corpus Christi, 1992-94. Mem. Nueces County Hist. Soc., Corpus Christi, 1990—. Mem. AAUW, Women's Coun. Realtors, Corpus Christi Bd. Realtors, Civitan Internat., Tropical Trails Investment Club. Republican. Baptist.

DEWITT-MORETTE, CÉCILE, physicist; b. Paris, Dec. 21, 1922; came to U.S., 1948; d. André and Marie Louise (Ravaudet) Morette; m. Bryce S. DeWitt, Apr. 26, 1951; children—Nicolette, Jan, Chris, Abigail. B.S., U. Caen, 1943; Ph.D., U. Paris, 1947. With Centre Nat. de la Recherche Sci., 1944-65, Maitre de Confs. prof., 1965-88; mem. Inst. Advanced Studies in Dublin, 1946-47, Copenhagen, 1947-48, Princeton, 1948-50; lectr. U. Calif. at Berkeley, 1952-55, U. N.C., Chapel Hill, 1956-71; prof. U. Tex., 1972-93, Jane and Roland Blumberg Centennial prof. physics, 1993—; founder, dir. Ecole d'ete de Physique Theorique, Les Houches, France, 1951-72. Author: Particules Elementaires, 1951, (with Y. Choquet-Bruhat and M. Dillard-Bleick) Analysis, Manifolds and Physics, 1977, rev. edit., 1982, (with A. Maheshwari, B. Nelson) Path Integration in Non Relativistic Quantum Mechanics, 1979, (with Y. Choquet Bruhat) Analysis, Manifolds and Physics, Part II, 92 Applications, 1989, also articles. Decorated chevalier Ordre Nat. du Mérite, chevalier Ordre des Palmes Académiques; Rask-Oersted fellow, 1947-48, Prix des Sciences Physiques et Mathematiques (Comite du Rayonnement Français, 1992). Fellow Am. Phys. Soc.; mem. Internat. Astron. Union, European Phys. Soc. Home: 2411 Vista Ln Austin TX 78703-2343 Office: U Tex Dept Physics Austin TX 78712

DEWOLFE, MARTHA ROSE, singer, songwriter, publisher; b. Arlington, Tex., Nov. 30, 1959; d. Homer C. and Grace R. DeWolfe. Student, N. Tex. State U., 1978-79, Larimer County Vocat.-Tech., Ft. Collins, Colo., 1983; cert. peace officer, Tarrant County Jr. Coll., Euless, Tex., 1984; student, North Central Tex. Coun. Govts., 1984-94, Southwestern Law Enforcement Sch. of Police Supervision. Police officer Grand Prairie (Tex.) Police Dept., 1984-94, sgt., 1989-94, supr. crime prevention unit, 1991-92; mem. Police

Employee Rels. Bd., 1990-91; BMI assoc.; estabished Maui Records, 1992, Midnight Tiger Music, BMI, 1994. Albums include That Flame Keeps Burning, Take Good Care of My Heart; songs include Patsy Come Home, River of Tears, Take Good Care of My Heart, If You Don't Want Us, Insomniac in a Cadillac; acting credits include Paramount's "Denton County Massacre", 1993, and commercials. Sec. Grand Prairie Police Assn., 1985-86. Recipient 1st place Tex. Comml. Art Skill Speed Competition, 1977-78. Mem. NAFE, Nat. Assn. Women Police, Tex. Assn. Women Police, Tex. Police Assn., Fraternal Order Police, Grand Prairie Police Assn., Tex. Assn. Vet. Police Officers, Country Music Assn., Nashville Songwriter's Assn. Internat., Mensa, Leo Club (sec. 1976-78). Home: PO Box 2132 Hendersonville TN 37077

DEWS, JULIE, lawyer; b. Albany, Ga., Oct. 16, 1951; d. Thomas Milton and Virginia Glen (Tye) D.; m. James Frederick Brown, Aug. 15, 1970 (div. July 1987); m. Robert Wardlaw Warren, Aug. 11, 1987; children: Thomas Daniel Brown, Matthew Dews Brown. BA, U. N.C., 1974; JD, Northeastern U., 1990. Bar: N.C. 1990. Assoc. Goldsmith & Goldsmith, P.A., Marion, N.C., 1990-93; ptnr. Goldsmith, Goldsmith & Dews, P.A., Marion, 1993—; bd. dirs. West Carolinians for Criminal Justice, Asheville. Editor: (jour.) Trial Briefs, winter 1995; mem. editl. bd. N.C. Acad. Trial Lawyers, N.C., 1994—. Democrat. Episcopalian. Home: PO Box 851 Black Mountain NC 28711 Office: Goldsmith Goldsmith & Dews PA 25 S Main St Marion NC 28752

DEXHEIMER, MARION LOUISE (MARION LOUISE HINES), retired educator; b. Chgo., Dec. 31, 1920; d. Herbert Waldo and Helen (Gartside) Hines; m. Fred J. Dexheimer, Sept. 28, 1947; children: Gary Frederick, Helen Louise, William Henry. BS in Spanish, U. Ill., 1943; BS in Comml. Sci., Boston U., 1947; MS in Teaching, U. Wis., Whitewater, 1975. Sec. Fed. Civil Svc. AFB, Orlando, Fla., 1948, USDA, Madison, Wis., 1949; tchr. Spanish jr. and sr. high sch. Jefferson, Wis., 1963-65; tchr. Spanish and typing sr. high sch. Johnson Creek, Jefferson, Wis., 1965-80; ret., 1980. Treas. Women's Fellowship Congl. Ch., 1990-91; mem. bd. trustees, bd. deaconesses Union Congl. Ch., Tavares, Fla.; participant hosp. aux. Waterman Med. Ctr. Lt. (j.g.) USNR, 1944-46. Mem. AAUW (past treas. Ft. Akinson br., past membership v.p., past v.p. programs, past treas. Lake County br., spl. recognition award 1989, three terms as pres. Lake County br.), Lake Country Waves (publicity chmn. 1989-93), Lake Frances Estates Residents Assn. (bd. dirs., activities dir. 1986-95). Home: 1437 Apache Cir Tavares FL 32778-2519

DEXTER, DALLAS-LEE, education administrator; b. Rockville Center, N.Y., Nov. 30, 1950; d. David D. and Jane (Nesbitt) D.; m. Leonard Eugene Carter, Nov. 6, 1975 (div. 1982). Student numerous dance courses; BS, Mills Coll., 1972; MA, Tchrs. Coll. Columbia U., 1974; postgrad., Nat. U. Mex., 1974, Lesley Coll., 1974, Fgn. Service Inst., 1977, Johns Hopkins Sch. Advanced Internat. Studies, 1982, Middle East Inst., 1982-83, U. N.C., 1972, Bank St. Coll., 1989-92, Bklyn. Coll., 1989-90, U. Alaska, Fairbanks, 1994-95. Cert. sch. adminstr., sch. supr., sch. dist. adminstr., N.Y. Tchr. Am. Sch., Hawalli, Kuwait, 1975-76, Copenhagen (Denmark) Internat. Sch., 1978-80, Rygaards (Denmark) Internat. Sch., Denmark, 1980-82; mktg. contractor Nat. Right to Work Com., Springfield, Va., 1986-87, 21st Century Telemedial Mktg. Services, Inc., Roslyn, Va., 1986; sales mgr. Best Programs, Inc., Arlington, Va., 1987-88; cons. Success, Inc., Palm Beach, Fla., 1985-86, Resources Planning Sys., 1983-86, Mgmt. Engring. Affiliates, Calabasa, Calif., 1984, Aerojet Gen., Washington, 1983; ednl. cons. Mayors Program Summer Youth Employment, Washington, 1986; lectr. troop info. program USMC Hdqrs., Arlington, Va., 1983-84; sales rep. 1st Investors Corp., Arlington, 1983-86; assoc. Potomac Ins. and Fin. Planning Group, Rockville, Md., 1984-89; Am. adminstr., tchr. Kingdom Saudi Arabia, Islamic Saudi acad., Washington, 1986-87; mgr. telesales divsn. Best Programs, Inc., Arlington, 1987-88; dancer Twyla Tharp Dance Co., 1969-70, James Cunningham Co., 1970, others; dir. Head Start programs the Children's Aid Soc., N.Y.C., 1991-94; cons. to child devel. assoc. Nat. Credentialing Coun., Washington, 1994—; coord. Early Intervention/Infant Learning Program and Respite Program supr., North Slope borough, 1994—. Testified before Mayor's Commn. on Early Childhood and Child Care Programs, N.Y.C., 1991; mem. by-laws com. N.Y. State Head Start Assn.; charter mem., sponsor assn. for Friends of Art Mus. Ams.; bd. dirs. Tchrs. Coll., Columbia U., 1989-91, Kid Pac, 1996—. Mem. ASCD, NAFE (network dir. 1985-87), Mid. East Inst., Nat. Acad. TV Arts and Scis., Am. Def. Preparedness Assn., Nat. Assn. Edn. Young Children, Coun. for Exceptional Children (v.p. Alaska divsn. for early childhood 1995—, pres.- elect), Alaska Hist. Soc., Columbia U. Club, Phi Delta Kappa (bd. dirs.). Unitarian.

DEXTER, DEIRDRE O'NEIL ELIZABETH, lawyer; b. Stillwater, Okla., Apr. 15, 1956; d. Robert N. and Paula E. (Robinson) Maddox; m. Terry E. Dexter, May 14, 1977; children: Daniel M. II, David Maddox. Student, Okla. State U., 1974-77; BS cum laude, Phillips U., 1981; JD with highest honors, U. Okla., 1984. Bar: Okla., U.S. Dist. Ct. (no. and ea. dists.) Okla. 1985, U.S. Dist. Ct. (we. dist.) Okla. 1987, U.S. Ct. Appeals (10th cir.) 1987; grad. Nat. Inst. Trial Advocacy Advanced Trial seminar, 1990. Jud. intern Supreme Ct. Okla., Oklahoma City, summer 1983; assoc. Conner & Winters, Tulsa, 1984-90, ptnr., 1991, shareholder, 1991—. Article editor Okla. U. Law Rev., 1982-84. U. Okla. scholar, 1983. Mem. ABA, Okla. Bar Assn. (advising atty. state champion H.S. mock trial team competition 1992), Tulsa County Bar Assn., Order of Barristers, Order of Coif, Am. Inns of Ct. (barrister), Delta Theta Phi. Republican. Episcopalian. Office: Conner & Winters 2400 First Place Tower 15 E 5th St Tulsa OK 74103

DEZORT, JACQUELYN LOUISE LINK, bank executive; b. Woodriver, Ill., Sept. 12, 1950; d. Albert Frances and Margaret Josephine (Schafer) Link; m. Tom Edward Dezort, Nov. 24, 1973; children: Catherine Leigh, Josef Matthew, Amanda Blair. BS in acctg., U. Ill., 1972. CPA, Ill. Staff acct. Peat, Marwick, Mitchell, Chgo., 1972-73; sr. supr. Peat, Marwick, Mitchell, St. Louis, 1973-76; asst. auditor Boatmen's Bancshares, Inc., St. Louis, 1976, auditor, 1980-84, v.p. productivity, 1984-86, v.p. strategic planner, 1986-89; sr. v.p. Boatmen's Bancshares, Inc., 1989—. Office: Boatmen s Banchsares Inc LBP 3604 PO Box 236 Saint Louis MO 63166*

DE ZULUETA, CARMEN, writer; b. Madrid, Spain, Nov. 26, 1916; came to U.S., 1940; d. Luis and Amparo (Cebrián) de Zulueta; m. Richard Greenebaum (dec. Aug. 1990); children: Mary de Zulueta, John de Zulueta. PhD, Colegio del Rosario, Bogota, Colombia, 1939; MA, Radcliffe Coll., 1941; PhD, NYU, 1966. Instr. Wheaton Coll., Norton, Mass., 1941-43, Vassar Coll., Poughkeepsie, N.Y., 1943-44; asst. prof. CUNY, 1955-62; asst./assoc. prof. Lehman Coll., CUNY, Bronx, 1962-82, prof., 1982-84; bd. dirs. Spanish Inst., N.Y., 1975—; lectr. in field. Author: Navarro Ledesma Elhombre y su tiempo, 1968, Unamuno-Zulueta Cartas, 1972, Cartas sobre teatro (1893-1912) Benito Perez Galdos-José de Cubas Anejo 1982 Anales Goldosianos, 1983, Misioneras Feministas, Educatoras Historia del Instituto Internacional, 1984, Besteiro Cartas de la prisión, 1988, N. Convento ni College Historia de la residencia de Senortas, 1993; contbr. numerous articles to profl. jours. Mem. Dem. Party, N.Y., 1991—, Friend of the N.Y. Pub. Libr., friend of Ctrl. Park; vol. pub. schs., N.Y. Recipient Lazo de Dama de Isabel la Católica, King of Spain, 1989. Mem. Hispanic Soc. Am. (corr.).

DHOKIA, JOY, lawyer; b. Jinja, Uganda, Dec. 12, 1961; d. Kanji Bhimji and Maniben D. BS with honors, U. Salford, England, 1983; CPE/solicitor, U. Manchester, England, 1986. Bar: Calif. Assoc. Ladbroke Group, England, 1986-88, Beachcroft Stanley, England, 1988-90; assoc. atty. Fitzgerald & Assocs., Orange, Calif., 1994-95; owner Ladva & Assocs., Brea, Calif., 1995—; cons. Lions Club, L.A., 1995—; legal counsel Raksha Inc., L.A., 1995—. Recipient Duke of Edinburgh award, 1989. Mem. L.A. Toastmaster Club. Office: Ladva & Assocs 431 W Lambert Rd # 301 Brea CA 92621

DIACO, MARGARET, business administrator; b. White Plains, N.Y., Feb. 11, 1955; d. Edward John and Edwina Griffen (Secor) O'Keefe; m. Luigi Diaco, July 21, 1974; children: Filomena, Pasquale, Luigi Jr. Student, Westchester C.C., 1994—. Part-time sec. N.Y. Med. Coll., Valhalla, 1988-93, med. sec., 1993-94, divsn. coord., mgr. divsn. pulmonary/critical care medicine, 1994—. Contbr. articles to popular publs. Mem. Nat. Trust for Hist. Preservation, Alpha Beta Gamma. Republican. Home: 33 Virginia Ln Thornwood NY 10594 Office: NY Med Coll Divsn Pulm/Crit Care Med Pulmonary Lab 2-G WCMC Valhalla NY 10595

DIAKOS, MARIA LOUISE, lawyer; b. Buffalo, Jan. 31, 1959; d. Louis K. and Deanna (Doerr) D. BA in Polit. Sci., SUNY, Buffalo, 1979, JD, 1982. Bar: N.Y. 1983. Assoc. counsel divsn. corps. N.Y. Dept. of State, Albany, 1982-84; assoc. Sargent & Repka, P.C., Cheektowaga, N.Y., 1984-85; pvt. practice Amherst, N.Y., 1985—; hearing officer small claims assessment rev. 8th Jud. Dist. N.Y. Supreme Ct., Buffalo, 1986—; sr. closing atty. Pub. Abstract Corp., Buffalo, 1995—. Founding mem. joint pub. policy com. Hellenic Am. Women, Washington, 1993—; mem. parish coun. Hellenic Orthodox Ch. of Annunciation, Buffalo, 1985-88, 93-96, parish legal advisor, 1995-96, treas., 1995, interim treas., sec., 1996. Mem. Am. Hellenic Inst.-Bus. Network, Women's Philoptochos Com. (recording sec. 1984-85, corr. sec. 1995-97), Buffalo and Western N.Y. Women in Travel, Variety Club Women. Democrat. Eastern Orthodox.

DIAL, SARA GOERTZEN, state official; b. Seattle, Mar. 21, 1964; d. Don Phillip and Irma Edith (Rundstrom) Goertzen; m. Patrick Dial, Jan. 7, 1995. BA in Internat. Rels., Stanford U., 1986. Fin. analyst Rauscher, Pierce, Refsnes, Phoenix, 1986-88; assoc. Security Pacific Mcht., Phoenix, 1988-89; sr. assoc. Kemper Securities Group, Phoenix, 1989-91; dir. fin. svcs. and housing devel. Ariz. Dept. Commerce, Phoenix, 1991-93, dir., 1993—; mem. fin. com. Samaritan Health Sys.; bd. dirs. Ariz. Multibank C.D.C. Bd. chmn. Commerce Econ. Devel. Commn., Workforce Recruitment and Job Tng. Coun., Internat. Trade and Tourism Bd.; exec. bd. Gov. Strategic Partnership Econ. Devel.; bd. dirs. Ariz. Gov. Film and TV Adv.; chmn. Super Bowl XXX Bus. Devel. Com. Mem. Arizonans Cultural Devel., Assn. Corp. Growth (hon.). Republican. Lutheran. Office: Ariz Dept Commerce 3800 N Central Ave Ste 1500 Phoenix AZ 85012

DIAMOND, IRENE, foundation administrator; b. Pitts., May 7, 1910; d. Horace and Leah (Grekin) Levine; m. Aaron Diamond, 1942 (dec.); 1 child, Jean. Ed., Pitts. Pub. Schs.; LHD (hon.), City Coll., CUNY, 1989, The Juilliard Sch., 1992; LLD (hon.), Queens Coll., CUNY, 1990, New Sch. Social Rsch., N.Y.C., 1994. Asst. editor story div. Warner Bros., Hollywood, Calif., 1934-35, editor, 1937-40; supr. dept. lit. Leland Hayward, Hollywood, 1935-37; editor story and talent div. Samuel Goldwyn-MGM, Hollywood and N.Y.C., 1940-41; editor story div., head talent div. Hal Wallis-Paramount Pictures, Hollywood and N.Y.C., 1941-70; pres., bd. dirs. Aaron Diamond Found., Inc., N.Y.C., 1986—. Bd. dirs. Aaron Diamond AIDS Rsch. Ctr., 1989—. Recipient Pres.'s medal Bank St. Coll., 1989, Liberty award Lambda Legal Def. and Edn. Fund, 1990, Disting. Community Svc. award United Hosp. Fund, 1990, medal Correctional Assn. of N.Y./Osborne Assn., 1990, Sybil C. Simon Disting. Patron award Arts and Bus. Coun., 1994. Mem. Film Soc. of Lincoln Ctr., Sundance Inst., Young Concert Artists, Human Rights Watch. Office: Aaron Diamond Found Inc Ste 2624 1270 Avenue Of The Americas New York NY 10020-1801

DIAMOND, JESSICA, artist; b. Bronx, N.Y.. BFA, Sch. Visual Arts, N.Y.C., 1979; MFA, Columbia U., N.Y.C., 1981. One-woman shows include Standard Graphic, Cologne, Germany, 1990, Jablonka Gallery, Cologne, 1991, Gallery Fahnemann, Berlin, 1991, Gallery Massimo DeCarlo, Milan, 1993, Ynglingagatan 1, Stockholm, 1994, Rix, Linköping, Sweden, 1996; exhibited in group shows at Mus. van Hedendaagse Kunst Ghent, Belgium, 1993, Venice (Italy) Biennale, 1993, Vorarlberger Kunstverein, Bregenz, Austria, 1993, Corner House, Manchester, Eng., 1994, Deichtorhallen Hamburg, Germany, 1994, Mus. Contemporary Art, Sydney, Australia, 1994, Serpentine Gallery, London, 1994, Watari-um Mus., Tokyo, 1995, Kunsthalle Bern, Switzerland, 1995. Home and Studio: 289 3rd Ave # 2 Brooklyn NY 11215-1003

DIAMOND, MARIAN CLEEVES, anatomy educator; b. Glendale, Calif., Nov. 11, 1926; d. Montague and Rosa Marian (Wamphler) Cleeves; m. Richard M. Diamond, Dec. 20, 1950 (div.); m. Arnold B. Scheibel, Sept. 14, 1982; children: Catherine, Richard, Jeffrey, Ann. AB, U. Calif., Berkeley, 1948, MA, 1949, PhD, 1953. With Harvard U., Cambridge, 1952-54, Cornell U., Ithaca, N.Y., 1954-58, U. Calif., San Francisco, 1954-58; prof. anatomy U. Calif., Berkeley, 1962—; asst. dean U. Calif., Berkeley, 1967-70, assoc. dean, 1970-73, dir. The Lawrence Hall of Sci., 1990-95, dir. emeritus, 1995—; vis. scholar Australian Nat. U., 1978, Fudan U., Shanghai, China, 1985, U. Nairobi, Kenya, 1988. Author: Enriching Heredity, 1989; co-author: The Human Brain Coloring, 1985; editor: Contraceptive Hormones Estrogen and Human Welfare, 1978; contbr. articles to profl. jours. V.p. County Women Dems., Ithaca, 1957; bd. dirs. Unitarian Ch., Berkeley, 1969. Recipient Calif. Gifted award, 1989, C.A.S.E. Calif. Prof. of Yr. award, Nat. Gold medalist, 1990, Woman of Yr. award Zonta Internat., 1991, U. medal La. Universidad Del Zulia, Maricaibo, Venezuela, 1992, Alumna of the Yr. award U. Calif.-Berkeley, 1995; Calif. Acad. Scis. fellow, 1991. Fellow AAAS; mem. AAUW (fellowship chair 1970—), Am. Assn. Anatomists, Soc. Neurosci., Philos. Soc. Washington, The Faculty Club (Berkeley) (v.p. 1979-85, 90-95). Club: The Faculty (v.p. 1979-85, 90-95). Home: 2583 Virginia St Berkeley CA 94709-1108 Office: U Calif Dept Integrative Biology 3060 Valley Life Science Bldg Berkeley CA 94720

DIAMOND, MARY E(LIZABETH) B(ALDWIN), artist; b. Detroit, Sept. 2, 1951; d. Harold Barber and Evelyn (Glenn) Weaver; m. David Baldwin III, June 24, 1972 (div. Nov. 1982); 1 child, David Damar; m. Robert Proctor Diamond, Oct. 6, 1986; 1 child, Angelique Krista. Freelance artist, cartoonist, photographer Phase II Mag., Detroit, 1981-85; artist Montague Art Galleries Inc., Locust Valley, N.Y., 1989-96; adminstrv. asst. East End Arts and Humanities Coun., Riverhead, N.Y., 1996; guest spkr. and panelist "African-American Artists and Writers", Eastville Hist. Soc., Sag Harbor, N.Y., 1996; guest spkr. L.I. Univ., Southampton, N.Y., 1995, Jimmy Ernst Artists Alliance, East Hampton, N.Y., 1991, Southampton (N.Y.) Intermediate Sch., 1994, Galerie "Die Treppe", Stuttgart, Germany, "New York, New York" Exhibit, 1995, judge Parrish Art Mus., Southampton, 1993; vis. artist Southampton Adventures in Learning Southampton Elem. Sch., 1996. Sundance Gallery, Season Opening Invitational Exhbn., Havre De Grace, Md., 1995, Nat. Jr. Duck Stamp Competition, 1995; bd. dirs. Southampton Cultural and Civic Ctr., 1995. Exhbns. include Sundance Gallery, Season Oepning Invitational Exhbn., Bridgehampton, N.Y., 1996, Clayton & Liberatore Gallery 75th Anniversary Invitational Exhbn., Bridgehampton, N.Y., 1995, Landscape Today; East End Views Guild Hall Mus., East Hampton, N.Y., 1994, 39th Ann. L.I. Artists Juried Exhbn., Hecksher Mus., Huntington, N.Y., 1994, Landscape Observed, Landscape Transformed, Islip Art Mus., East Islip, N.Y., 1992, Nat. League Am. Pen Women, 12th Juried Exhibit, Vanderbilt Mus., Centerport, N.Y., 1992, Art Assn. Harrisburg (Pa.) 66th Ann. Exhibit, 1994, 1st Place award in oil painting L.I. Artists Open Juried Art Competition, Brookhaven Cultural Ctr., 1995, Hon. mention North Shore Art Guild Ann. Mems. Exhbn., Brookhaven, 1995. Bd. dirs. Cultural and Civic Ctr., Southampton, N.Y. Named Outstanding Woman of Eastern L.I., Hero award Southampton Ind. Newspaper, 1996; grantee N.Y. Found. for the Arts, 1994. Mem. Am. Soc. Portrait Artists, East End Arts Coun., Allied Artists of Am., Southampton Artists Assn. (organized life drawing workshop 1989-94, v.p. 1991, pres. 1992), The Onyx Group (founder, treas., pres. 1992-94), Jimmy Ernst Artists Alliance, North Shore Art Guild. Home and Studio: 83 Northside Dr Sag Harbor NY 11963-2003

DIAMOND, NANCY KAY, environmentalist, consultant; b. Detroit, July 16, 1956; d. Philip and Norma (Basof) D. BS in Forest Sci., Humboldt State U., 1980; MS in Agr., Calif. Poly State U., San Luis Obispo, 1988; PhD in Wildland Resource Sci., U. Calif., Berkeley, 1992. Agroforestry cons. Internat. Union for Conservation Nature & Natural Resources, Tanzania, 1988; social forestry advisor Office Economic & Internat. Devel. U.S. Agy. Intenat. Devel., Washington, 1991-93; gender & environ. advisor Office Women Devel. AID, Washington, 1993-96; rsch. & evaluation officer Acad. for Edn. Devel., Washington, 1996—; grad. student instr. U. Calif., Berkeley, 1986-91, rschr., Kenya, 1989-90. Vol. Doing Something, Washington, 1995-96; mem. adv. bd. Urban Creeks Coun., 1983-87. Recipient Doctoral Dissertation Rsch. award Fulbright-Hays, 1989-90; pre-dissertation rsch. fellow Social Sci. Rsch. Coun., 1987, dissertation fellow, 1990, Fgn. Lang. & Area Studies fellow U.S. Dept. Edn., 1987-88; Nat. Merit scholar, 1974-78. Mem. World Women in Devel. and Environment. Democrat. Jewish. Office: Acad for Edn Devel 1255 23rd St NW Washington DC 20037

DIAMOND, SARA ROSE, author, lecturer; b. 1958. BA in Spanish, U. Calif., Irvine, 1979; MA in Sociology, U. Calif., Berkeley, 1988, PhD in Sociology, 1993. Author: Spiritual Warfare: The Politics of the Christian Right, 1989, Roads to Dominion: Right-Wing Movements and Political Power in the United States, 1995, Facing the Wrath: Confronting the Right in Dangerous Times, 1996. Home: PO Box 2439 Berkeley CA 94702

DIAMOND, SUSAN R., lawyer; b. Mar. 19. BS with distinction, Stanford U., 1979; MCP, MIT, 1981; JD cum laude, Harvard U., 1983. Bar: Calif. 1983. Ptnr. Brobeck Phleger & Harrison, San Francisco; vis. lectr. U. Calif.-Berkeley Grad. Sch. Bus., 1985-89. Contbr. articles to profl. jours. Mem. Am. Planning Assn., Phi beta Kappa, Lambda Alpha. Office: Brobeck Phleger & Harrison Spear St Tower 1 Market Plz San Francisco CA 94105*

DIAMOND, SUSAN ZEE, management consultant; b. Okla., Aug. 20, 1949; d. Louis Edward and Henrietta (Wood) D.; m. Allan T. Devitt, July 27, 1974. AB (Nat. Merit scholar, GRTS scholar), U. Chgo., 1970; MBA, DePaul U., 1979; Cert. office automation profl. Dir. study guide prodn. Am. Sch. Co., Chgo., 1972-75; publs. supr. Allied Van Lines, Broadview, Ill., 1975-78, sr. account svcs. rep., 1978-79; pres. Diamond Assocs. Ltd., Melrose Park, Ill., 1978—; condr. seminars Am. Mgmt. Assn. Author: How to Talk More Effectively, 1972, Preparing Administrative Manuals, 1981, How to Manage Administrative Operations, 1981, How to be an Effective Secretary in the Modern Office, 1982, Records Management: A Practical Guide, 1983, 3d edit., 1995; co-author: Finance Without Fear, 1983; editor Mobility Trends, 1975-78; contbr. numerous articles to profl. jours. Mem. Inst. Mgmt. Accts., Assn. Records Mgrs. and Adminstrs., Am. Mgmt. Assn., Assn. Info. and Image Mgmt., Adventuresses of Sherlock Holmes, Delta Mu Delta. Office: 2851 Pearl Ave Melrose Park IL 60164-1421

DIAMONSTEIN-SPIELVOGEL, BARBARALEE, writer, television interviewer/ producer; b. N.Y.C.; d. Rubin Robert and Sally H. Simmons; m. Alan A. Diamonstein, July 22, 1956; m. Carl Spielvogel, Oct. 27, 1981. BA, BC, MA, doctorate, NYU, 1963; DHL (hon.), Md. Inst. Arts, 1990, Longwood Coll., 1995. Staff asst. The White House, 1963-66; 1st dir. dept. cultural affairs City of New York, 1966-67; dir. of Forums McCall Corp., 1967-69; editor spl. supplements, columnist Harper's Bazaar, 1969-71; spl. project dir., guest editor Art News, 1971-93; columnist Ladies Home Jour., 1979-84; contbr. to Saturday Rev., Vogue, Ms., Partisan Rev., N.Y. Times, Condé Nast, Traveller, others; mem. faculty Hunter Coll., CUNY, 1974-76, New Sch., 1976-84, Duke U. (Inst. Policy Scis.), 1978; arts cons. Sunday Morning CBS-TV, 1978-82; curator Buildings Reborn, Collaborations, Visions and Images, Remaking America, The Landmarks of N.Y. I and II (nat. travelling museum exhbns.), 1978—, and numerous others. TV interviewer, producer: About the Arts, WNYC-TV, 1975-79, ABC-TV Arts, 1980-88, A&E Network, 1980-89; videotape exhibitions Leo Castelli Gallery, 1978, 84, 88, 94; author: Open Secrets: 94 Women in Touch With Our Time, 1972, The World of Art, 1902-77, 75 Years of Art News, 1977, Buildings Reborn: New Uses, Old Places, 1978, Inside New York's Art World, 1979, American Architecture Now, 1980, Collaboration: Artists and Architects, 1981, Visions and Images: American Photographers on Photography, 1981, Interior Design: The New Freedom, 1982, Handmade in America, 1983, Fashion: The Inside Story, 1985, American Architecture Now, 1985, Remaking America, 1986, The Landmarks of New York, 1988, 18 Wonders of the New York World, 1992, The Landmarks of New York: Vol. II, 1993, Inside the Art World: Conversations with Barbaralee Diamonstein, 1994, Skills, Values, Dreams, 1995; editor: Our 200 Years: Tradition and Renewal, 1975, MOMA at 50, 1980, and numerous others. Commr. N.Y.C. Landmarks Preservation Commn., 1972-87, N.Y.C. Cultural Commn., 1975-86, N.Y.C. Arts Commn., 1991-94; bd. dirs. Mcpl. Art Soc., 1973-83, Am. Council Arts, 1982-89, N.Y.C. Bicentennial Commn., 1973-77, Bklyn. Acad. Music, 1969-74, N.Y. Landmarks Conservancy, 1973—, vice chmn., 1983-87; bd. advisors Film Anthology Archives, 1969—; mem. vis. com. Met. Mus. Art, 1982—, Fresh Air Fund, 1983—, Big Apple Circus, 1989-92, Whitney Mus. Am. Art, 1995—; chmn. N.Y. Landmarks Preservation Found., 1987-95; mem. Pres.' council Rockefeller U., 1987—; bd. visitors Pub. Policy Inst. Duke U., 1987-93; mem. U.S. Nat. Commn. on the Holocaust, 1987-93, chair Art Pub. Spaces com., Hist. Landmarks Preservation Ctr., 1995—, PEN Am. Ctr., 1990—; bd. dirs. Corcoran Gallery Art, Washington, 1992—, N.Y. State Archive's Trust, 1994—; trustee N.Y. Hist. Soc., 1993-95, Ctrl. Pk. Conservancy, 1993-95; bd. dirs. White House Endowment Fund, 1995—. Recipient Founder's Day award Pratt Inst., 1994. Home: 720 Park Ave New York NY 10021-4954

DIAZ, SHARON, education administrator; b. Bakersfield, Calif., July 29, 1946; d. Karl C. and Mildred (Lunn) Clark; m. Luis F. Diaz, Oct. 19, 1968; children: Daniel, David. BS, San Jose State U., 1969; MS, U. Calif., San Francisco, 1973. Nurse Kaiser Found. Hosp., Redwood City, Calif., 1969-73; lectr. San Jose (Calif.) State Coll., 1969-70; nurse San Mateo (Calif.) County, 1970-71; instr. St. Francis Meml. Hosp. Sch. Nursing, San Francisco, Calif., 1971-72, asst. dir., 1973-78; dir. Samuel Merritt Hosp. Sch. Nursing, Oakland, Calif., 1978-84; founding pres. Samuel Merritt Coll., Oakland, 1984—; v.p. East Bay Area Health Edn. Ctr., Oakland, 1980-87; mem. adv. com. Calif. Acad. Partnership Program, 1990; mem. nat. adv. com. Nursing Outcomes Project. Bd. dirs. Head Royce Sch., 1990—, vice chair, 1993-95, chair, 1995—; bd. dirs. Ladies Home Soc., 1992—, sec., 1994-95, treas., CFO, 1995—; active YWCA. Named Woman of Yr., Oakland YWCA, 1996. Mem. Nat. League for Nursing, Am. Assn. of Pres. Ind. Colls. and Univs., Sigma Theta Tau. Office: Samuel Merrritt Coll Office of Pres 370 Hawthorne Ave Oakland CA 94609-3108

DIAZ, VANESSA, school system administrator; b. Bklyn., Apr. 21, 1971; d. Dermis Diaz and Leticia (Gutierrez) Seamon. BA in English, Rutgers Coll., 1994. Cert. of eligibility elem. edn., N.J. Part time teller First Fidelity, North Brunswick, N.J., 1990-92, United Jersey Bank, Highland Park, N.J., 1992, Constellation Bank, Milltown, N.J., 1992-93; summer floater Sunshine Biscuits, Inc., Woodbridge, N.J., 1990-92; team asst. Automatic Data Processing, Inc., Princeton, N.J., 1993-94; teleservice rep. Automatic Data Processing, Inc., Princeton, 1994; new account coord., client svc. rep. Automatic Data Processing, Inc., Cleve., 1994-95; medicaid forms processor New Brunswick Bd. Edn., 1995—. Mem. NOW, Rutgers U. Alumni Assn. Home: 26 Mill Run West Hightstown NJ 08520 Office: New Brunswick Bd Edn 225 Comstock St New Brunswick NJ 08901

DÍAZ DE GONZALEZ, ANA MARÍA, psychologist, educator; b. San Juan, P.R., July 26, 1945; d. Esteban Díaz-González and Petra (Guadalupe) De Díaz; m. Jorge Gonzalez Monclova, Jan. 7, 1968; children: Ana Teresa, Jorge, Julio Esteban. BS, U. P.R., Río Piedras, 1965, MEd, 1973; MS, Caribbean Ctr. Advanced Study, San Juan, 1982, PhD, 1983. Lic. psychologist, P.R. Home economist U. P.R., Fajardo and San Juan, 1965-82; specialist in human devel. and gerontology U. P.R., San Juan, 1983—. Mem. APA, Assn. Economists Hogar (pres. 1965-92, Disting. Svc. award 1973), Assn. Specialists SEA (pres. 1982-93), Assn. Psychology P.R., Epsilon Sigma Phi (sec. 1970—), Gamma Sigma Delta. Roman Catholic. Home: 1325 Calle 23 San Juan PR 00924-5249 Office: U PR Svc Extension Agr Terrenos Estacion Exptl Río Piedras San Juan PR 00928

DIBATTISTE, CAROL A., lawyer; b. Phila., Dec. 28, 1951; d. Peter Martin DiBattiste and Hilda Yolanda (Battilana) Mignogna. BA, LaSalle U., 1976; JD, Temple U., 1981; LLM, Columbia U., 1986. Bar: Pa. 1982, N.Y. 1989, D.C. 1989, Fla. 1990, U.S. Ct. Mil. Appeals 1982, U.S. Supreme Ct. 1985. Commd. 2d lt. USAF, 1976, advanced through grades to maj., 1987, retired, 1991; acad. instr. USAF, Maxwell AFB, Ala., 1986-89; chief recruiting atty. Office of Judge Advocate Gen. USAF, Washington, 1989-91; asst. U.S. atty. So. Dist. Fla., Miami, 1991-93; prin. dep. gen. coun. Dept. of Navy, 1993-94; dir. Exec. Office for U.S. Attys., Washington, 1994—. Editor: The Reporter, 1986-87; mem. editorial bd. Air Force Law Rev., 1984, 85, 87; contbr. articles to profl. jours. Mem. ABA (chmn. standing com. on mil. law 1989-91), Pa. Bar Assn., Fed. Bar Assn. (Young Fed. Lawyer award 1985), Nat. Dist. Atty.'s Assn., Nat. Inst. for Trial Advocacy, USAF Assn., Phi Alpha Delta. Democrat. Roman Catholic. Home: 1300 Crystal Dr # 1201 Arlington VA 22202 Office: Exec Office for US Attorneys 10th St & Constitution Ave NW Washington DC 20530

DIBBLE, ELIZABETH JEANE, lawyer, educator; b. Hammond, Ind., May 26, 1958; d. Harold Richard and Janet Deliah (Lane) Elsey; m. John Taylor

Dibble, June 7, 1980; children: James Taylor, Katherine Elizabeth. BS in Learning Disabilities cum laude, MacMurray Coll., Jacksonville, Ill., 1979; JD, So. Ill. U., 1983. Bar: Ill. 1983. Tchr. learning disabilities Sedgwick (Kans.) Sch. System, 1979-80; atty. Powless & Brocking, Marion, Ill., 1984-85, Randy Patchett & Assoc., Marion, 1985-86; sole practice Marion, 1987-96; dir. paralegal studies program Belleville (Ill.) Area Coll., 1996—; part-time lectr. So. Ill. U., Carbondale, 1985—. Fundraiser Rep. Party, Williamson County, Ill, 1986; bd. dirs. So. Ill. Epilepsy Found., Mt. Vernon, 1984-86; mem. Episcopal Ch. Women; religious edn. dir. St. James Episcopal Ch., Marion, 1983-86. Cartwright scholar for women MacMurray Coll., 1976-79. Mem. Williamson County Bar Assn., Ill. State Bar Assn.. Republican. Home: 1513 N State St Marion IL 62959-2964 Office: 400 N Market St Marion IL 62959

DIBBLE, SUZANNE LOUISE, nurse, researcher; b. Pittsburg, Calif., June 3, 1947; d. Charles Stanley and Evelyn Virginia (Hansen) D.; m. Myron Bottsford Palmer III, June 12, 1971 (div. July 1974); life ptnr. Jeanne Flyntz DeJoseph, 1984. BSN, U. Del., 1969; MSN, U. Calif., San Francisco, 1971, D Nursing Sci., 1986. RN, Del., Calif. Staff nurse emergency room Stanford (Calif.) U. Hosp., 1969-71, rschr. dept. nursing rsch., 1986-88; instr. med. and surg. nursing Stanford U., 1971-72, renal transplant nurse coord., 1972-73, nurse rschr. dept. diagnostic radiology, 1987-88; staff, charge, head nurse, then supr. Children's Hosp.-Stanford U., 1973-86; mem. faculty stats. dept. U. Phoenix, San Jose, Calif., 1985-92; pres. Data Mgmt. Assocs., San Carlos, Calif., 1985—; investigator, project dir. U. Calif., 1988—; rsch. grant cons. NIH, Oakland, Calif., 1992-94, Loma Linda (Calif.) U., 1995—; manuscript reviewer Oncology Nursing Forum, Pitts., 1993—, Med.-Surg. Nursing, Pittmn, N.J., 1994—. Editor: Culture and Nursing Care, 1996; contbr. articles to nursing jours. Chmn. task force, mem. NOW, Palo Alto, Calif., 1978—; mem., chmn. Maternal, Child and Adolescent Health Bd., San Mateo County, Calif., 1987-90; mem. strategic planning com. San Mateo County Health Bd., 1989-90. Rsch. grantee Nat. Cancer Inst., 1992-97, Nat. Inst. for Nursing Rsch., 1994-99. Mem. ANA, Assn. for Care Children's Health (numerous offices), Oncology Nursing Soc. (numerous offices), Am. Statis. Assn. (numerous offices), Sigma ThetaTau (pres. Alpha Eta chpt.). Democrat. Office: U Calif Box 0610 N611Y 3d and Parnassus Aves San Francisco CA 94143-0610

DIBLE, ROSE HARPE MCFEE, special education educator; b. Phoenix, Apr. 28, 1927; d. Ambrose Jefferson and Laurel Mabel (Harpe) McFee; m. James Henry Dible, June 23, 1951 (div. Jan. 1965); 1 child, Michael James. BA in Speech Edn., Ariz. State U., Tempe, 1949; MA in Speech and Drama, U. So. Calif., L.A., 1950; fellow, Calif. State U., Fullerton, 1967. Cert. secondary tchr., spl. edn. tchr. English and drama tchr. Lynwood (Calif.) Sr. High Sch., 1950-51, Montebello (Calif.) Sr. High Sch., 1952-58; tchr. English and Social Studies Pioneer High Sch., Whittier, Calif., 1964-65; spl. edn. tchr. Bell Gardens (Calif.) High Sch., 1967-85, spl. edn. cons., 1985-90. Mem. DAR, Daus. Am. Colonists, Whittier Christian Woman Assn., La Habra Womans Club, Eastern Star Lodge, Kappa Delts, Phi Delta Gamma. Republican. Presbyterian. Home: 1201 Russell St La Habra CA 90631-2530 Office: Montebello Unified Sch Dist 123 Montebello Blvd Montebello CA 90640

DIBONA, LESLIE FAYE, librarian; b. Quincy, Mass., Sept. 7, 1953; d. Ferrer I.M. DiBona and Doris Louise (Mikkelsen) Boyes; m. Douglass Blake Payne, May 24, 1980 (div. Sept. 1987); m. Steven T. McGivern, July 31, 1993. AB, Boston U., 1975; MS in LIS, Simmons Coll., 1980. Serials libr. Tufts U.-Wessell Libr., Medford, Mass., 1980-84; head of tech. svcs. Harvard Grad. Sch. of Edn.-Libr., Cambridge, Mass., 1985-91, U.S. Dept. of Edn. Rsch. Libr., Washington, 1991-94; dir. libr. devel. U. Libr.-San Diego State U., 1994—; founding mem. Calif. State U. Libr. Devel. Dirs., 1994, Acad. Libr. Advancement and Devel. Network, 1995—. Mem. ALA, Calif. Assn. of Rsch. Libs., Phi Beta Kappa. Office: San Diego State U Libr 5500 Campanile Dr San Diego CA 92182

DIBONA, MARGARET ROSE, state official; b. Phila., Jan. 21, 1946; d. Peter Gerardo and Margaret E. (Moffett) DiB. BA, Cabrini Coll., Radnor, Pa., 1993. Inside sales rep. Arthur H. Thomas Co., Phila., 1965-69; sales corr. TRW Electronics, Villanova, Pa., 1969-71; pharmacy technician DiBona Pharmacy, Havertown, Pa., 1959-73; UC claims interviewer Upper Darby (Pa.) Job Ctr., 1973-76; UC claims examiner I Chester (Pa.) Job Ctr., 1976-87, employment svc. program supr. U.S. Dept. Labor, Commonwealth of Pa., Bur. Unemployment Compensation, Benefits, Allowances, Coatesville, Pa., 1987—. Employers adv. coun. Am. Lung Assn., West Chester, Pa., 1995—; facilitator of support group to redefine asthma, asthma educator Southeastern Pa., 1989—; cons., 1989—; primary educator Am. Lung Assn. Camp for Asthmatic Children, 1994—. Office: Bur Unemploy Compensation Benefits and Allowances 250 E Harmony St Coatesville PA

DIBOS, DIANNE LOUISE, financial analyst; b. Elyria, Ohio, May 17, 1968; d. Ronald Eugene and Jan Melody (Gorbach) Leshinski; m. George Merwin Dibos, Mar. 26, 1994. BS, U. Dayton, 1990, MBA, 1993. Cert. mgmt. acct. Fin. analyst Lexis/Nexis, Dayton, Ohio, 1990-95; cost analyst Miller Brewing Co., Trenton, Ohio, 1995-96; mgr. fin. reporting JewelWay Internat., Tucson, 1996—. Presdl. scholar U. Dayton, 1986. Mem. Inst. Mgmt. Accts.

DICARLO, SUSANNE HELEN, financial analyst; b. Greensburg, Pa., Nov. 24, 1956; d. Wayne Larry and Clara Emogene (Weaver) Gower; m. John Joseph DiCarlo, June 21, 1980; children: Sarah Rose, Kristen Marie. BS in Acctg., Va. Poly. Inst. and State U., 1978. Auditor U.S. Army Audit Agy., Ft. Monroe, Va., 1978-79; acct. technician Fleet Combat Tng. Ctr., Virginia Beach, Va., 1980-82, supervisory auditor, 1982-83; fin. analyst Comml. Activity Mgmt. Team, Norfolk, Va., 1983—; fed. women's program mgr. Fleet Combat Tng. Ctr., 1980-83. Creator newsletter Fed. Women's Program Manager, 1980-83. Mem. Am. Soc. Mil. Comptrollers. Club: Seaside Mountaineers (Va. Beach) (treas. 1986-88). Home: 4013 Dillaway Ct Virginia Beach VA 23456-1257

DICHTER, TOBEY GORDON, public relations executive; b. Phila., Apr. 16, 1944; d. Abraham David and Meelya (Slobodkin) Gordon; m. Mark S. Dichter; children: Aliza Beth, Melissa Eve. BS, Temple U., 1965, M in Indsl. Psychology, 1968. Assoc. editor Harvard U. Grad. Sch. of Edn., Cambridge, Mass., 1968-69; co-editor, co-prodr. SKF News, SmithKline & French, Phila., 1969-72, sr. employee comm. educator, 1972-74, educator corp. pubs., 1974-77, sr. comm. specialist, 1977-81, mgr. corp. TV and comm. programs, 1981-87; mgr. corp. comm. SmithKline Beecham, Phila., 1987-89; dir. comm. and pub. affairs SmithKline Beecham Clin. Labs., King of Prussia, Pa., 1989-93; v.p., dir. comm./pub. affairs SmithKline Beecham Healthcare Svcs., Collegeville, Pa., 1993—. Dir. bd. trustees The Children's Hosp. Phila., 1990—; mem. adv. bd. West Phila. Collaborative Program for Child Health, Phila.; dir. 21st Century League, Phila. Recipient Sarah award Women in Comm., 1978, Emmy award Nat. Acad. Film & TV, 1983, Chgo. Film Festival award. Mem. Am. Assn. Clin. Chemistry, Am. Clin. Lab. Assn. (comm. and legis. coms.), Internat. Assn. Bus. Communicators (Gold Quill award), Coun. Comm. Mgmt. Office: SmithKline Beecham Healthcare Svcs 1201 S Collegeville Rd Collegeville PA 19426-2998*

DICK, AURORA CLAUDETTE, insurance company executive; b. N.Y.C., Apr. 7, 1946; d. Emanuel Sr. and Josephine (Galanti) Palmieri; m. Douglas E. Tandberg, Oct. 17, 1965 (div. 1975); m. Frank Raymond Dick III, Sept. 4, 1984. CLU, chartered fin. cons.; cert. fin. planner; registered prin. Nat. Assn. Securities Dealers. Bank officer Garden State Nat. Bank, Hackensack, N.J., 1963-73; sales rep., gen. mgr., exec. N.Y. Life Ins. Co., N.Y.C., 1973-83; mng. dir. The Acacia Group, Washington, 1983-94; dir. fin. planning N.Y. Life Ins. Co., Bethesda, Md., 1994—. Mem. Salvation Army Women's Aux., Washington, 1988—. Fellow Am. Soc. CLU and ChFC; mem. Gen. Agts. and Mgrs. Assn. (bd. dirs., officer), D.C. Life Underwriters Assn., Suburban Md. Life Underwriters Assn., Inst. Cert. Fin. Planners, Internat. Assn. Fin. Planners, Capital Speakers Club (former bd. dirs.).

DICK, CAROL LYNNE, psychology educator; b. Ann Arbor, Mich., Oct. 26, 1942; d. C. H. and Lois M. (Wubbena) D. Student, Albion Coll., 1960-62; BA, U. Mich., 1965, MA in Edn., 1970. Rsch. asst. dept. psychology U. Mich., 1966-70; rsch. asst. High/Scope Ednl. Rsch. Found., Ypsilanti, Mich., 1971-72; counselor Cath. Social Svc., Ann Arbor, Mich., 1972-75; communications specialist Ann Arbor (Mich.) Schs., 1975-76; religious coord. U. Mich., Ann Arbor, 1976-77; office asst. U. Mich. Continuing Edn., Ann Arbor, 1977-78; bookkeeper Money Mgrs., Inc. (Debt Aid, Inc.), Ann Arbor, 1978-82; instr. psychology Holyoke (Mass.) Community Coll., 1985—; interviewer psychology dept. U. Mass., Amherst, 1992; mem. support staff Nat. Evaluation Systems, Amherst, 1992-94. Author: (poetry book) Transcendent Ways of God, 1976, (short book) Henry's Mother, 1990. Vol. Project Progress, Friends of the Earth and Ecology Ctr., Ann Arbor, 1976-82; forum coord. Unitarian Ch., Ann Arbor, 1978-79; vol. bd. dirs. LWV, Ann Arbor, 1978-82; active Action for Children's TV, Telecomm. Rsch. and Action Ctr., Coalition for Responsible Genetic Rsch., 1978-82; v.p. Lay Acad. Ecumenical Studies, Amherst, 1990-91, others.

DICK, PATRICIA A., counselor; b. Indpls., Mar. 31, 1929; d. Harold D. and Mary R. (Crockett) Barton; m. Richard D. Dick, Sr., June 21, 1947; children: G. Daniel, Richard D. Jr., Lynda S., Kevin D., Deborah D. AA, Wm. Rainey Harper Coll., Palatine, Ill., 1976; BA, Mundelein Coll., Chgo., 1978; MA, Northeastern Ill. U., Chgo., 1984; postgrad., Alfred Adler Inst., Chgo. Cert. sr. addiction counselor, clin. hypnotherapist; nat. cert. counselor. Counselor in pvt. practice Barrington, Ill., 1979—. Contbr. articles on alcoholism to local papers. Mem. Am. Mental Health Counselor Assn., Nat. Assn. Alcoholism and Drug Counseling, Nat. Assn. for Adult Children of Alcoholics, Am. Assn. for Counseling and Devel., Nat. Guild of Hypnotists, Internat. Assn. Marriage and Family Counseling. Roman Catholic. Office: 28662 W Northwest Hwy Barrington IL 60010-5928

DICKENS, DORIS LEE, psychiatrist; b. Roxboro, N.C., Oct. 12; d. Lee Edward and Delma Ernestine (Hester) D.; BS magna cum laude, Va. Union U., 1960; MD, Howard U., 1966; m. Austin LeCount Fickling, Oct. 15, 1975. Diplomate Nat. Bd. Med. Examiners. Intern, St. Elizabeth's Hosp., Washington, 1966-67, resident, 1967-70; staff psychiatrist, dir. Mental Health Program for Deaf, St. Elizabeth's Hosp., Washington, 1970-87; clin. prof. Howard U. Coll. Medicine, 1982—. Co-founder Nat. Health Care Found. for Deaf (named now Deaf Reach); med. officer Region 4 Cmty. Mental Health Ctr., Washington, Commn. on Mental Health, 1987—, now acting med. dir. Recipient Dorothea Lynde Dix award, 1980. Mem. Am. Psychiat. Assn. (achievement awards bd. 1988-89), Washington Psychiat. Soc., St. Elizabeth's Med. Soc. (mem. exec. com. 1993—), Alpha Kappa Mu, Beta Kappa Chi. Author: How and When Psychiatry Can Help You, 1972; You and Your Doctor; contbg. author: Hearing and Hearing Impairment, 1979, Counseling Deaf People, Research and Practice. Home: 12308 Surrey Circle Dr Fort Washington MD 20744-6244

DICKENS, SHEILA JEANNE, family preservation educator; b. Cleve., Sept. 15, 1958; d. Joseph David and Stella Maureen (Brown) Cogdell; children: Randy, Laura, Rebecca. AA, Lakeland C.C., Mentor, Ohio, 1985; BA magna cum laude, Walsh U., 1993, MA, 1995. Cert. counselor trainee, 1995. Tutor Lakeland Coll., Mentor, 1980-85; mgr. Wohl Shoe Co., St. Louis, 1985-89; merchandise asst. J.C. Penney, Kingsport, Tenn., 1989-91; grad. asst. Walsh U., North Canton, Ohio, 1994-96, instr., counselor-in-residence program coord., 1995-96, family preservation specialist, counseling coord., 1996—. Vol. Crisis Intervention Ctr., Canton, 1992-94; mem. disaster svc. team ARC, Canton, 1995—. Mem. Am. Counseling Assn., Assn. Specialists in Group Work, Chi Sigma Iota/Alpha Mu (liaison 1995-96). Office: PO Box 9432 Canton OH 44711-9432

DICKENSON, MICHELE LEIGH, counselor, educator; b. Memphis, Mar. 3, 1965; d. Ernest Grady and Marjorie (Cooley) Bogue; m. Keith Henry Dickenson, July 30, 1988. BA, U. Tenn., 1987; MA in Religious Edn., Southwestern Bapt. Theol. Sem., Ft. Worth, 1992, MA in Marriage and Family Counseling, 1992. Counselor Metroplex Counseling Ctr., Arlington, Tex., 1992-95; tchr. Sycamore Sch., Inc., Ft. Worth, 1993—. Mem. ACA, Alpha Kappa Delta. Republican. Baptist. Home: 808 Hodgson Fort Worth TX 76115

DICKERSON, AMY VIGILANTE, curator, educator; b. N.Y.C., Feb. 3, 1956; d. Joseph Louis and Florence Dennis (Wexler) V. BA, Hampshire Coll., 1977; MFA, Fla. State U., 1980, specialist in edn., 1985, PhD, 1989. Cert. tchr., adminstr., supr., Fla. Art tchr. Anneewakee Sch., Carrabelle, Fla., 1980-85, headmistress, 1983-85; tchr. Peachford Hosp., Atlanta, 1985-86; art tchr. Fulton County Schs., Atlanta, 1986-87; teaching asst. Fla. State U., Tallahassee, 1987-88, adj. prof., 1988-90; arts cons. Fla. Dept. of State, Tallahassee, 1989-90; mus. curator, educator Brevard Art Ctr. and Mus., Melbourne, Fla., 1991-94; dir. Art in Pub. Places City Hall & Airport Galleries, Tallahassee, 1994-95; curator Thomas Ctr. Galleries, Gainesville, Fla.; grant writer Marion County Pub. Schs. Found.; juror 40 art exhbns., 1990-96; art cons.; grant specialist Fla. UACAP Program. Author: booklets for AT RISK youth, 1989, 90, 91. Recipient Merit award Orlando Mus. of Art, 1990, Riverside Art Festival, 1991, Individual Artist fellowship in painting State of Fla., 1992. Mem. NEA, Nat. Art Educators Assn., Am. Assn. Mus., Fla. Assn. Mus.

DICKERSON, CLAIRE MOORE, lawyer, educator; b. Boston, Apr. 1, 1950; d. Roger Cleveland and Ines Idelette (Roullet) Moore; m. Thomas Pasquali Dickerson, May 22, 1976; children: Caroline Anne, Susannah Moore. AB, Wellesley Coll., 1971; JD, Columbia U., 1974; LLM in Taxation, NYU, 1981. Bar: N.Y. 1975, U.S. Dist. Ct. (ea. and so. dists.) N.Y. 1975, U.S. Ct. Appeals (2d cir.) 1975, U.S. Supreme Ct. 1980. Assoc. Coudert Brothers, N.Y., 1974-82, ptnr., 1983-86; ptnr. Schnader, Harrison, Segal & Lewis, N.Y., 1987-88, of counsel, 1988—; assoc. prof. law St. John's U., Jamaica, N.Y., 1986-88, prof., 1989—. Author: Partnership Law Adviser; contbr. articles to profl. jours. Trustee Rye (N.Y.) Presbyn. Nursery Sch., 1988-90. Mem. ABA, Assn. of Bar of City of N.Y., Union Internat. des Avocats, Shenorock Club. Democrat. Office: St John's U Sch Law Grand Central And Utopia Pky Jamaica NY 11439-0002

DICKERSON, COLLEEN BERNICE PATTON, artist, educator; b. Cleburne, Tex., Sept. 17, 1922; d. Jennings Bryan and Alma Bernice (Clark) Patton; m. Arthur F. Dickerson; children: Sherry M., Chrystal Charmine. BA, Calif. State U., Northridge, 1980; studied with John Pike. presenter demonstrations Cayucos Art Assn., Morro Bay Art Assn., El Camino Real Art Assn. One-woman shows include Morro Bay Cmty. Bldg., Amandas Interiors, Arroyo Grande, Calif., 1996; exhibited in group shows; represented in permanent collections, including Polk Ins. Co., San Luis Obispo, Med. Ctr. MDM Ins. Co., L.A. Mem. Ctrl. Coast Watercolor Soc. (pres. 1986-87), Art Ctr., Oil Acrylic Pastel Group (chmn., co-chmn. 1989—), Morro Bay Art Assn., San Luis Obispo Art Ctr., Mus. Women in Arts (assoc.). Home and Studio: 245 Hacienda Ave San Luis Obispo CA 93401-7967

DICKERSON, NANCY (WHITEHEAD), television producer, news correspondent; b. Milw.; d. Frederick R. and Florence (Conners) Hanschman; m. Claude Wyatt Dickerson, 1962 (div. 1983); children: Elizabeth, Ann, Jane, Michael, John; m. John C. Whitehead, Feb. 25, 1989. Student, Clarke Coll., Dubuque, Iowa, 1945-46; BS in Edn., U. Wis., 1948; HHD (hon.), Am. Internat. Coll., Springfield, Mass.; ArtsD (hon.), Pine Manor Coll., 1988. Sch. tchr. Milw.; staff asst. Senate Fgn. Relations Com., Washington; producer CBS News, 1956-60; 1st woman news corr. for CBS News, 1960-63; news corr. NBC, 1963-70; news analyst Inside Washington (syndicated nationally for TV stas.), 1971—; producer spl. syndicated TV programs, pres. Dickerson Co., 1971—; polit. commentator Newsweek Broadcasting Service; founder, exec. producer Television Corp. Am., 1980—; reporter Pres. Kennedy's funeral, Republican and Democratic convs., Civil Rights March on Washington, Kennedy, Johnson and Nixon inaugurations; represented Pub. Broadcasting Corp. (on all-network Conversation with Pres. Nixon), 1970; lectr.; commentator Fox TV News, 1986-91. Author: Among Those Present, 1976. Bd. trustees Covenant House, N.Y.C., Hosp. for Spl. Surgery, N.Y.C., Fgn. Policy Assn.; bd. dirs. N.Y. Pub. Libr., Nat. Fund U.S. Botanic Garden; mem. women's com. Cen. Park Conservancy. Recipient Collegian award LaSalle Coll., Phila; Spirit of Achievement award Albert Einstein Coll., Yeshiva U.; Sigma Delta Chi award Boston U.; Pioneer award New Eng. Women's Press Assn.; Assoc. fellow Pierson Coll., Yale, 1972—; Peabody award for 1982 TV program on Watergate; Silver Gavel award for 1982 TV program on Watergate ABA. Mem. Radio-TV News Analysts, Washington Press Club (past v.p.), The Century Club (N.Y.C.).

DICKERSON, RITA M., human resources professional; b. Phila., Oct. 7, 1946; d. Daniel Bryant Dickerson and Mary Rita (Dempsey) Moffa; m. Rocco John Albano, Jr., June 22, 1968 (div. Nov. 1990); children: Sharon Rita, Daniel Bryant. BS, La Salle U., 1994, MBA, 1995. Group claims examiner Aetna Ins. Co., Phila., 1965-69, Mass. Mut. Life Ins. Co., Phila., 1969-70; employee benefits coord. Nat. Liberty Corp., Phila., 1976; ins. plans claims examiner Guardian Life Ins. Co., Phila., 1979-80; group benefits examiner Bricklayers Benefit Plan, Phila., 1980-81; disability coord. and svcs. mgr. CIGNA Corp., Phila., 1981-91; benefits supr. Comcast Metrophone, Phila., 1993; cons. Lewis Co., Inc., Phila., 1994—; office mgr. Law Offices John W. Kormes, Phila., 1992-94. Creator: (pamphlet) Terminal Digit Filing System, 1993, reports in field. Coord. Tacony Civic Assn., Phila., 1978; mem. regional bd. St. Martin of Tours, Phila., 1974-76. Recipient Twentieth Century award for Achievement Internat. Biographical Ctr., 1995. Mem. Soc. Human Resource Mgmt., St. Jerome's Ch. Republican. Roman Catholic. Home: 8122 Lister St Philadelphia PA 19152-3108

DICKEY, JULIA EDWARDS, aviation consultant; b. Sioux Falls, S.D., Mar. 6, 1940; d. John Keith and Henrietta Barbara (Zerell) Edwards; m. Joseph E. Dickey, June 18, 1959; children: Joseph E., John Edwards. student DePauw U., 1958-59; AB, Ind. U., 1962, MLS, 1967, postgrad., 1967. Asst. acquisitions libr. Ind. U. Regional Campus Librs., 1965-67; head tech. svcs. Bartholomew County Libr., Columbus, Ind., 1967-74; dir. reference svcs. Southeastern Ind. Area Library Svc. Authority, Columbus, 1974-78, exec. dir., 1978-80; pres. Jedco Enterprises, 1981—; legis. strategy chmn. Ind. Library Coop. Devel., 1975; dir. Ind. Libr. Trustees Assn. Governance Project, 1982. Mem. Columbus exec. bd. Mayor's Task Force on Status of Women, 1973-76; del. Ind. Sch. Nominating Assembly, 1973-75, 75-77; bd. dirs. Human Svcs. Inc. (Bartholomew, Brown and Jackson Counties community action program), 1975-79, sec., 1975, v.p., 1979, pres., 1976-78; elder, mem. session, chair, personnel com. First Presbyterian Ch. of Aurora, Ind.; mem. adv. coun. Ind./Nat. Network Study, 1977-78; adv. coun. Salvation Army Local, 1984-88; bd. dirs. Columbus Women's Ctr.; precinct coord. Vols. For Bayh, 1974; sheriff Columbus 1st precinct, 1975, clk., 1976-77, insp., 1978, judge, 1980-83; treas. Hayes for State Rep. Com., 1978, 82—. Named Outstanding Young Woman Am., 1973. Mem. ALA, Ind. Library Assn. (dist. chmn. 1972-73, chmn. library edn. div. 1980-81, ad hoc com. on legis. effectiveness, 1982, various coms.), Library Assts. and Technicians Round Table (chmn. 1968-69), Tech. Services Round Table (chmn. 1971-72, sec. library planning com. 1969-72), AAUW (pres. 1973-75), Bartholomew County Library Staff Assn. (pres. 1975-76), Exptl. Aircraft Assn. (charter pres. chpt. 729, Inc. 1981, advisor 1982, sec. 1984-85, treas., 1990—; Ind. EAA Council (pres. 1982-88, advisor 1988—, internat. EAA conv. antique/classic mgmt. team 1988—), Internat. Expt. Aircraft Assn. (Major Achievement award 1983, Antique Airplane Assn., First Tuesday, Psi Iota Xi (thrift shop steering 1985-94, v.p. thrift shop chmn. 1986-87, Mem. of Yr. 1988-89, pres. elect 1991-92, pres. 1992-93, advisor 1993-94, mem. state assn. project com. 1992-93, constn./by-laws com. 1993-94). Review Club of Lawrenceburg, Ind. (corr. sec. 1996—), Zonta Club (newsletter editor Tel-Zon 1981-89, recording sec. 1984-85, treas. 1990-93, v.p. 1993-94). Home and Office: 55 Oakey Ave Lawrenceburg IN 47025-1538

DICKEY, LINDA ANN, learning center director; b. Chgo., Sept. 11, 1950; d. Edwin John and Bertha Melvina (Kryspin) Latos; m. Michael Dene Dickey, June 16, 1973; children: Beth Marie, Melissa Lynn, Jonathan Michael. BA in Secondary Edn., Social Scis., U. Ill., 1972, MLS, 1973. Media specialist Indian Trail Jr. H.S., Plainfield, Ill., 1973-77; dir learning resource ctr. St. Pius X Sch., Lombard, Ill., 1989-95; learning ctr. dir. Hinsdale (Ill.) Middle Sch., 1995-96; dir. Learning Resource Ctr. St. Pius X Sch., Lombard, 1996—. Pres. Pleasant Lane PTA, Lombard, Ill., 1987-89; trustee Helen Plum Meml. Libr., Lombard, 1987—, pres. bd. trustees, 1995—. Mem. Ill. Libr. Assn., Ill. Sch. Libr. Media Assn., Phi Beta Kappa. Roman Catholic.

DICKINSON, ELEANOR CREEKMORE, artist, educator; b. Knoxville, Tenn., Feb. 7, 1931; d. Robert Elmond and Evelyn Louise (Van Gilder) C.; m. Ben Wade Oakes Dickinson, June 12, 1952; children: Mark Wade, Katherine Van Gilder, Peter Somers. BA, U. Tenn., 1952; postgrad., San Francisco Art Inst., 1961-63, Académie de la Grande Chaumière, Paris, 1971; M.F.A., Calif. Coll. Arts and Crafts, 1982, Golden Gate U., 1984. Escrow officer Security Nat. Bank, Santa Monica, Calif., 1953-54; mem. faculty Calif. Coll. Arts and Crafts, Oakland, Calif., 1971—, assoc. prof. art, 1974-84, prof., 1984—, dir. galleries, 1975-85; artist-in-residence U. Tenn., 1969, Ark. State U., 1993; mem. faculty U. Calif., 1967-70; lectr. in field. Co-author, illustrator: Revival, 1974, That Old Time Religion, 1975; also mus. catalogs; illustrator: The Complete Fruit Cookbook, 1972, Human Sexuality: A Search for Understanding, 1984, Days Journey, 1985; commissions: University of San Francisco, 1990-92; one-person exhbns. include Corcoran Gallery Art, Washington, 1970, 74, San Francisco Mus. Modern Art, 1965, 68, Fine Arts Mus. San Francisco, 1969, 75, U. Tenn., Michael Himovitz Gallery, Sacramento, Calif., 1988, 89, 91, 93, 96; touring exhbns. include Smithsonian Inst., 1975-81, Oakland Mus., 1979, Interart Ctr., N.Y., 1980, Tenn. State Mus., 1981-82, Galeria de Arte y Libros, Monterrey, Mex., 1978, Hatley Martin Gallery, San Francisco, 1986, 89, Gallery 10, Washington, 1989, Himovitz Gallery, Sacramento, 1988, 89, 91, 93, 96, Diverse Works, Houston, 1990, Ewing Gallery, U. Tenn., 1991, G.T.U. Gallery, U. Calif., Berkeley, 1991, Mus. Contemporary Religious Art, St. Louis, 1995; represented in permanent collections Nat. Collection Fine Arts, Corcoran Gallery Art, Libr. of Congress, Smithsonian Instn., San Francisco Mus. Modern Art, Butler Inst. Art, Oakland Mus., Santa Barbara Mus.; prodr. (TV program) The Art of the Matter-Professional Practices in Fine Arts, 1986—. Bd. dirs. Calif. Confedn. of the Arts, 1983-88; bd. dirs., v.p. Calif. Lawyers for the Arts, 1986—; mem. coun. bd. San Francisco Art Inst., 1966-91, trustee, 1964-67; sec., bd. dirs. YWCA, 1955-62; treas., bd. Westminster Ctr., 1955-59; bd. dirs. Children's Theater Assn., 1956-60, 93-94, Internat. Child Art Ctr., 1958-68. Recipient Disting. Alumni award San Francisco Art Inst., 1983, Master Drawing award Nat. Soc. Arts and Letters, 1983, Cert. of Recognition, El Consejo Mundial de Artistas Plasticos 2d Internat. Conf., 1993, Pres.'s award Nat. Womens Caucus for Art, 1995; grantee Zellerbach Family Fund, 1975, Pa. Coll. Arts and Crafts, 1994, NEH, 1978, 80, 82-85, Thomas F. Stanley Found., 1985, Bay Area Video Coalition, 1988-92, PAS Graphics, 1988, San Francisco Cmty. TV Corp., 1990, Skaggs Found., 1991. Mem. Coalition of Women's Art Orgns. (dir., v.p. 1978-80), Coll. Art Assn., AAUP, Calif. Confederation of Arts (bd. dirs. 1983-89), Calif. Lawyers for Arts (v.p. 1986—), San Francisco Art Assn. (sec., dir. 1964-67), NOW, Artists Equity Assn. (nat. v.p., dir. 1978-92), Arts Advocates, Women's Caucus for Art (nat. Affirmative Action officer 1978-80). Democrat. Episcopalian. Office: Calif Coll Arts and Crafts 5212 Broadway Oakland CA 94618-1426

DICKINSON, JANE W., social services administrator; b. Kalamazoo, Sept. 27, 1919; d. Charles Herman and Rachel (Whaler) Wagner; student Hollins Coll., 1938-39; B.A., Duke U., 1941; M.Ed., Goucher Coll., 1965; m. E.F. Sherwood Dickinson, Oct. 23, 1943; children: Diane Jane Gray Clem, Carolyn Dickinson Vane. Exec. sec. Petroleum Industry Com., Balt., 1941-43; exec. sec. Sherwood Feed Mills Inc., Balt., 1943-79. Mem. exec. com. Children's Aid Md., 1960-61; mem. bd. women's aux. Balt. Symphony Orch., 1958-60; dist. chmn. Balt. Cancer Drive, 1958; dist. chmn. Balt. Mental Health Drive, 1957; co-chmn. Balt. United Appeal, 1968; bd. mgrs. Pickersgill Retirement Home. Mem. Alpha Delta Phi, Three Arts Club (Balt., sec. 1958-60, bd. govs. 1960-64, 67-70, pres. 1970-72), Women's Club of Roland Park (bd. govs. 1960-64, 86-88, 92-94), Cliff Dwellers Garden Club. Republican. Episcopalian. Home: 1708 Killington Rd Baltimore MD 21204-1807

DICKMAN, CATHERINE CROWE, retired human services administrator; b. Talladega, AL, Jan. 27, 1931; d. William and Catherine Elizabeth (Graeber) Crowe; m. Frederick Norton Dickman Jr., May 19, 1956 (div. July 1975); children: Frederick Norton Dickman III, Catherine Dickman Houghton, Elizabeth Dickman Blank, Janet Dickman Campbell. AB with honor, Agnes Scott Coll., 1952; MS, Cleve. State U. Coll. Urban Affairs, 1976. Pub. info. officer Cuyahoga County, Ohio, 1975-77; dir. Friends of Shaker Sq., Cleve., 1979-81; rsch. assoc. Frank Porter Graham Child Devel. Ctr., Chapel Hill, N.C., 1984; pres. Dickman Placement Svcs., Chapel Hill, N.C., 1988-91; dir. The Women's Ctr., Chapel Hill, N.C., 1991-96; ret. Author (newsletter) The Partnership Paper, 1986. Field dir. Girl Scout coun., Wilmington, N.C., 1952-53; dir. christian edn. St. Charles Ave.

Presbyn. Ch., New Orleans, 1956-57; co-founder, active Fair Housing, Inc., 1966-80; active Jr. League of Cleve. Inc., 1968—, pres. 1966-68, chair Assn. 12 Largest Jr. Leagues, 1967-68, Assn. Cmty. Agys., Chapel Hill, 1991-96, bd. dirs., 1995-96; chair nominating com., trustee The City Club of Cleve., 1979-82; trustee Health Mus. and Edn. Ctr., 1957-63, Karamu House, Cleve., 1968-70, Fedn. for Cmty. Planning, Cleve., 1979-82; adv. com. Health Profession Schs. in Svc. to the Nation, Chapel Hill, 1996—. Women's Ctr. established Catherine C. Dickman Ednl. fund in her honor, 1996. Mem. NOW (Chapel Hill chpt.), Nat. Audubon Soc (bd. dirs. 1986-88), Chapel Hill Preservation Soc. (v.p., trustee 1989-90). Democrat. Home: 409 North St Chapel Hill NC 27514

DICKSON, ELIZABETH ANNE MARGARET, realtor, caterer, consultant; b. Hinton, Va., Nov. 12, 1917; d. William Stuart and Hattie Susan (Kaiser) Harner; m. Robert H. Norcom (div. 1934); children: Robert Norcom, Ralph Norcom; m. Thomas Elton Dickson, 1966. Attended, James Madison U., 1937-38, Greensboro Coll., 1938. Lic. real estate. Caterer Greensboro, N.C., 1939—; real estate agt. Lowderonisk, Greensboro, 1955-58, Luper, Greensboro, 1958—; cons. Elizabeth Arden, Alexandria, Va., 1973-92, Eli Lily Pharmacial; supr. May Co., Washington, 1973-92. Tchr. First Presbyn. Ch., Greensboro, N.C., 1938; deacon Nat. Presbyn. Ch., Washington, 1992; active Nat. Com. to Preserve Social Security, AARP, Mary Knoll Soc., Beethoven Soc., Alexandria Symphony, Soc. Va. Mem. Nat. Mus. Women in Arts. Home: 425 The Plaza 805 N Howard St Alexandria VA 22304-5466

DICKSON, EVA MAE, credit manager; b. Clarion, Iowa, Jan. 16, 1922; d. James and Ivah Blanche (Breckenridge) D. Grad. Interstate Bus. Coll., Klamath Falls, Oreg., 1943. Reporter, Mchts. Credit Service, Klamath Falls, 1941; credit dept. Montgomery Ward, Klamath Falls, 1941-42; bookkeeper Heilbronner Fuel Co., Klamath Falls, 1942; stenographer City of Klamath Falls, 1943, bookkeeper, office mgr., 1943-52; owner, operator All Star Bus. Service, Klamath Falls, 1953-58, Ace Mimeo Service, Klamath Falls, 1958-73; mgr. Mchts. Credit Service, 1973-87; customer service rep. CBI/Credit N.W., 1987-91. Bd. dirs. United Way, Klamath Falls, 1980—; sec. Klamath Community Concert Assn., 1956—; treas., memls. chmn. Klamath County chpt. Am. Cancer Soc.; bd. dirs., treas. Hope in Crisis; mem. Klamath County Centennial Com., 1982, Unification for Progress Joint Planning Com., 1985; mem. nursing adv. com. Oreg. Inst. Tech., 1982—; mem. Klamath Employment Tng. Adv. Com., 1983-86; bd. dirs., sec., treas. Klamath Consumer Council; sec. Unified City for Progress Task Force, 1983-84, Snowflake Winter Festival, 1984—; sec. First Presbyn. Ch., 1992—. Recipient Bronze Leadership award Assoc. Credit Burs., Inc., 1976. Mem. Daughters of Am. Colonists (past regent local chpt.), Consumer Credit Assn. Oreg. (pres. 1984-85), Credit Profl. Internat. (treas. dist. 10 1984-85, 2d v.p. dist. 10 1987-88, 1st v.p. 1988-89, pres. 1989-90, internat. bull. chmn. 1990-91, 92—), Assoc. Credit Bur. Pacific N.W. (pres. 1981-82), Assoc. Credit Bur. Oreg. (pres. 1978-80), Klamath Basin Credit Women-Internat. (pres. 1976-78), Soc. Cert. Consumer Credit Exec., Internat. Consumer Credit Assn., Klamath County C. of C. (pres. 1979, ambs. com. 1980—, Nat. Fedn. Bus. and Profl. Women's Club (chmn. nat. fin. com. 1983-84, nat. fin. com. 1982-83), Oreg. Fedn. Bus. and Profl. Women's Club (state pres. 1971-72), Klamath Falls Bus. and Profl. Women's Club (pres. 1966-67, 76-77, 1996—). Republican. Presbyterian. Club: Quota (pres. 1958-59, dist. gov. 1969-70). Avocations: painting, traveling.

DICKSON, GERI LENZEN, nursing educator, researcher; b. Milw., Feb. 28, 1932; d. Gilbert Ernst and Lily (Rehbein) Morong; m. LeRoy L. Lenzen, Apr. 1, 1950 (div. Nov. 1971); children: Lynnda Lenzen, Kathie Lenzen; m. Carlisle H. Dickson, June 8, 1979; children: Joel, Robert. BSN, Alverno Coll., 1974; MSN, Marquette U., 1978; PhD, U. Wis., 1989. RN, N.Y., N.J., Wis. Various nursing positions Milw. County Med. Complex, 1970-79, nurse instr., 1979-89; asst. prof. U. Wis., Milw., 1984-90; asst. prof. divsn. nursing NYU, N.Y.C., 1990-94; asst. prof. coll. nursing Rutgers U., Newark, 1994—; pvt. practice as ind. generalist nurse, Milw., 1977-80; mem. health cabinet Ctrl. Presbyn. Ch., N.Y.C., 1993-94. Contbr. articles to profl. jours and nursing texts. Mem. Nat. League Nursing, N.Y. State Nurses Assn., Women's Health Network, Soc. Rogerian Scholars, Sigma Theta Tau, Phi Theta Kappa. Presbyterian. Home: 30 Ernst Ave Bloomfield NJ 07003-4509

DICKSON, SUZANNE ELIZABETH (SUE DICKSON), educational administrator; b. Dallas, Jan. 21, 1931; d. DeForest Zeller and Fay (Schmitz) Rathbone; m. Robert E. Dickson, Dec. 29, 1954 (div. 1984); children: Dianne Dickson Fix, Robert Jr., Franklin D. BS in Edn., James Madison U., 1952. Cert. tchr., N.J. Tchr. Arlington (Va.) Pub. Schs., 1952-56, Merrydowns Sch., Annandale, Va., 1962-64, Fairfax (Va.) Christian Sch., 1964-66, Mahwah (N.J.) Pub. Schs., 1966-83; cons. Edn. program/TV/CBN, Virginia Beach, Va., 1983-86; author/cons. Kelwynn Effective Schs. Group, 1986-89; pres. Internat. Learning Systems, Inc., Chesapeake, Va., 1988-94, St. Petersburg, Fla., 1994—; workshop provider to schs., 1972—. Author reading/lang. arts program: Sing, Spell, Read and Write, 1972-92, social studies program: Songs of America's Freedoms, 1987, Songs that Teach: U.S. Presidents, 1986, 91, Winning: The Race to Independent Reading Ability, 1989; author play: Pathway to Liberty, 1968, Musical Math Facts, 1992. Recipient George Washington Tchr's. Medal Freedom Found., Valley Forge, 1968. Mem. Internat. Reading Assn. (pres. North Jersey coun. 1979-80), Soc. Women Educators (past treas., past v.p.), Delta Kappa Gamma (chpt. pres. 1979-81). Office: Internat Learning Systems Inc 1000 112th Cir N Ste 100 Saint Petersburg FL 33716-2306

DICLAUDIO, JANET ALBERTA, health information administrator; b. Monroeville, Pa., June 17, 1940; d. Frank and Pearl Alberta (Wolfgang) DiC. Cert. in Med. Rsch. Libr. Sci., Luth Med. Ctr., 1962; BA, Thiel Coll., 1975; MS, SUNY, Buffalo, 1978. Registered record adminstr. Dir. med. records Bashline Hosp., Grove City, Pa., 1962, St. Clair Meml. Hosp., Pitts., 1963-73; asst. prof. Ill. State U., Normal, 1976-81; corp. dir. med. records Buffalo Gen. Hosp., 1981-85; dir. med. records Candler Hosp., Savannah, Ga., 1985-94, med. records analyst, 1994—; med. record cons. White Cliff Nursing Home, Greenville, Pa., 1973-75; mgmt. cons. Gifford W. Lorenz MD, Savannah, 1992-94. Contbr. articles to periodicals. Bd. dirs. Mid-Ill. Areawide Health Planning Corp., Normal, 1979-81. Mem. Am. Health Info. Mgmt. Assn., Ga. Health Info. Mgmt. Assn. Office: Candler Hosp 5353 Reynolds St Savannah GA 31405-6005

DICORPO-FULLER, DIANE, school system administrator; b. Lynwood, Calif., July 6, 1959; d. Nello Cesidio and Emilia Gilda (Morelli) DiCorpo; m. Glenn Evan Fuller, June 6, 1981; children: Brett, Brandon, Ashley, Brynne-Allyson. AA, Cerritos Coll., 1979; BA, Calif. Poly., 1978, MEd, 1980. Tchr. St. Thomas More, Alhambra, Calif., 1978-81, St. Catherines Sch., Laguna Beach, Calif., 1982-85, Laguna Beach Unified, 1987-88; mid. sch. dir. St. Johns Sch., Rancho Santa Margarita, Calif., 1988-94; asst. head of sch. St. Mary and All Angels, Aliso Viejo, Calif., 1994—, also bd. dirs.; cons. New Cath. Sch., Rancho Santa Margarita, 1994—. Bd. dirs., sec. Univ. of San Juan Capistrano, Calif., 1993-94. Recipient CTY award Johns Hopkins U., 1993. Mem. Nat. Assn. Mid. Schs., Calif. Math. Assn., Calif. Tchrs. Assn. Republican. Roman Catholic. Home: 15 Lindall St Laguna Niguel CA 92677-4738 Office: St Mary and All Angels 7 Pursuit Aliso Viejo CA 92656-4213

DICOSIMO, PATRICIA SHIELDS, art educator; b. Hartford, Conn., June 27, 1946; d. Richard Nichols and Rose Aimee (Roy) Shields; m. Joseph Anthony DiCosimo, Apr. 18, 1970. BFA in Art Edn./Printmaking, U. Hartford, 1969; MS in Edn./Art, Ctrl. Conn. State Coll., 1972; postgrad., Rochester Inst. Tech., 1986, 87. Cert. tchr., Conn. Tchr. art Simsbury (Conn.) High Sch., 1969—; tchr. Farmington Valley Art Ctr., Avon, Conn., 1989-95; supr. Nat. Art Honors Soc., Simsbury, 1989-95; mem. Conn. regional adv. bd. Scholastic Art Awards, 1991, 93—; mem. Conn. Scholastic Art Awards Com., 1989—, co-chair exhibit, 1994, prin.'s faculty adv. com., 1969—; guest lectr. secondary methods in art edn. Ctrl. Conn. State U.; presenter jewelry workshop; mem. Conn. Curriculum in Arts, 1995-96. One-woman shows include Farmington Woods, 1972, Ellsworth Gallery Simsbury, 1974, Annhurst Coll., 1976, Canaan Nat. Bank, 1991, Terryvill Libr., 1994; represented in group shows at Ctrl. Conn. State Coll., 1969-72 (Best in Show award 1972), Bristol Chrysanthemum Festival Art Show, 1973-84 (Non-objective award 1973, Graphic award 1975, Mixed Media award 1977, Tracy Driscoll Co. Inc. award 1981, Plymouth Spring award 1983, Dick Blick award 1984), Hartford Ins. Co. Art Educators Exhibit, 1990, Simsbury Libr. Gallery Art Educators Exhibit, 1991, 92, 93, Henry James Meml. Gallery, 1992, Riverview Gallery, 1993, Simsbury Dinner Theater, 1994—, Canton Gallery on the Green, 1996, Best of Conn. Mural Contest, 1996. Sec. Greater Bristol (Conn.) Condo Alliance, 1990-95; mem. Family Life & Marriage Enrichment, New Britain, Conn., 1970-77. Patricia Shields DiCosimo Day proclaimed by Town of Simsbury, 1993; recipient Book award Hartford Art Sch., 1969, Conn. B.E.S.T. Tchr. award, Conn. Alliance for Arts Edn. Sch. Dist. award, 1995-96. Mem. NEA, Nat. Art Edn. Assn., Conn. Art Edn. Assn. (H.S. rep. 1983-85, sec. 1985—, Conn. Art Educator 1993, Conn. Alliance for Arts Edn. award for Simsbury Art and Music 1995, presenter Fall conf. 1992, 93-94), Conn. Edn. Assn. (mem. Conn. 3-D curriculum project 1995-96), Conn. Craftsman, Farmington Art Guild (tchr. 1992-95). Independent. Roman Catholic. Home: 19 Hampton Ct Bristol CT 06010-4738 Office: Simsbury High Sch 34 Farms Village Rd Simsbury CT 06070-2320

DICOSTANZO, PAMELA S., science/mathematics educator; b. N.Y.C., July 8, 1941; d. William R. and Doris L. (Nigro) Siena; divorced; children: Jennifer Daile, John William. BS, Cen. Conn. State U., 1963; MS, U. Bridgeport, 1969. Cert. tchr. K-8, Conn. Tchr. grade five Columbus-Lincoln Sch., Norwalk, Conn., 1963-66; sci. tchr. Benjamin Franklin Mid. Sch., Norwalk, 1966-71, Brien McMahan H.S., Norwalk, 1972-73; sci. tchr. Roton Mid. Sch., Norwalk, 1973—, team leader, 1991—, sci. dept. head, 1989—; adj. supr. student tchrs. Fla. Inst. Tech., Melbourne, Fla., 1993; workshop presenter in field. Co-author: (curriculum) Project Connstruct, 1994. Publicity chmn. Norwalk Jr. Woman's Club, 1974-75, social chmn., 1973-74; vol. The Maritime Ctr. at Norwalk, 1988-91. Mem. Nat. Sci. Tchrs. Assn. (workshop presenter 1978, workshop evaluator 1977, 79), Nat. Fedn. Tchrs., Maritime Aquarium, Conn. Sci. Tchrs. Assn., Norwalk Fedn. Tchrs. (bldg. steward). Presbyterian. Home: 11 Chipmunk Ln West Norwalk CT 06850

DIDION, JOAN, author; b. Sacramento, Calif., Dec. 5, 1934; d. Frank Reese and Eduene (Jerrett) D.; m. John Gregory Dunne, Jan. 30, 1964; 1 child, Quintana Roo. BA, U. Calif., Berkeley, 1956. Assoc. feature editor Vogue mag., 1956-63; former columnist Saturday Evening Post, Life, Esquire; now contbr. The N.Y. Rev. of Books, The New Yorker. Novels include Run River, 1963, Play It As It Lays, 1970, A Book of Common Prayer, 1977, Democracy, 1984, The Last Thing He Wanted, 1996; books of essays: Slouching Towards Bethlehem, 1968, The White Album, 1979, After Henry, 1992; nonfiction Salvador, 1983, Miami, 1987; co-author: (with John Gregory Dunne) Screenplays for films The Panic in Needle Park, 1971, Play It As It Lays, 1972, A Star Is Born, 1976, True Confessions, 1981, Hills Like White Elephants, 1991, Broken Truet, 1995, Up Close and Personal, 1996. Recipient 1st prize Vogue's Prix de Paris, 1956, Morton Dauwen Zabel prize AAAL, 1978. Mem. Am. Acad. Arts and Letters, Am. Acad. Arts and Scis., Coun. Fgn. Rels. Office: care Janklow & Nesbit 598 Madison Ave New York NY 10022-1614

DIDOMENICO, MAUREEN ELLEN, art educator, muralist; b. Bridgeport, Conn., Aug. 25, 1957; d. Thomas Francis and Sallye Ann (Shaw) Devitt; m. Gary Anthony DiDomenico, June 30, 1979; children: Lynne Ann, Kaitlin Marie. BS in Art Edn., So. Conn. U., New Haven, 1979; M in Elem. Edn., Sacred Heart U., Fairfield, Conn., 1989. Cert. tchr., Conn. Classrm. tchr. grade 7 St. Charles Sch., Bridgeport, Conn., 1979-80, classrm. tchr. grade 3, 1982-85; substitute tchr. Stratford (Conn.) Bd. Edn., 1985-86; art educator Franklin and Nichols Elem. Schs., Stratford, 1986-94, Flood Mid. Sch., Stratford, 1994—. Mem. Dem. Town Party, Stratford, 1990-95; vol. Am. Heart Assn., New Haven, 1993-95; coord., creator of scenery Stratford Acad. Dance, 1986-92; judge of local art show Sterling House Cmty. Ctr., Stratford, 1994. Recipient Achievement award Kodak Co., 1993, others. Mem. NEA, Conn. Edn. Assn., Nat. Art Edn. Assn., Conn. Art Edn. Assn. Roman Catholic. Home: 4305 Main St Stratford CT 05497

DIE, ANN MARIE HAYES, college president, psychology educator; b. Baytown, Tex., Aug. 15, 1944; d. Robert L. and Dorothy Ann (Cooke) Hayes; m. Jerome Glynn Die, June 5, 1971; 1 child, Meredith Anne. BS with highest honors, Lamar U., 1966; MEd, U. Houston, 1969; PhD, Tex. A&M U., 1977. Lic. psychologist. Asst. prof. dept. psychology Lamar U., Beaumont, Tex., 1977-82, assoc. prof., dir. Psychol. Clinic, 1982-86, dir. grad. programs in psychology, 1981-86, Regents prof. psychology, 1986, pres. faculty senate, 1985-86; pvt. practice clin. psychology Beaumont, 1979-87; prof. Tulane U., New Orleans, 1988-92, dean Newcomb Coll., 1988-92, assoc. provost, 1991-92; pres., prof. psychology Hendrix Coll., Conway, Ark., 1992—; adminstr. adolescent residential unit Mental Health/Mental Retardation S.E. Tex., 1979-80, mem. cmty. adv. com., 1981-87; cons. in field; mem. coordinating bd. Tex. Coll. and Univ. Sys. Internship, 1986; bd. dirs. Nat. Merit Scholarship Corp., Acxiom Corp. Contbr. articles to profl. jours. Active cmty. adv. com. Beaumont State Ctr. Human Devel., 1981-88; participant Nat. Identification Program for Women, Am. Coun. on Edn., 1985; mem. govt. rels. commn., 1993—, chmn., 1994-96, chmn. coun. of fellow, 1995-96; bd. dirs. Beaumont Civic Opera, Lamar U. Wesley Found., Tulane U. Wesley Found.; bd. govs. Isidore Newman Sch., 1991-92; trustee Robert Morris Coll., 1990—, chmn. edn. com., 1990-94, chmn. pers. com., 1994—; mem. univ. senate United Meth. Ch., 1993—; 1st v.p. Nat. Assn. Schs. & Colls. United Meth. Ch., 1996; bd. dirs. Ouachita coun. girl Scouts U.S., 1996—; mem. Internat. Women's Forum, 1995—, Ark. Women's Leadership Forum, 1995—. Am. Coun. Edn. fellow Coll. William and Mary, 1986-87; recipient Regents Merit award, 1979, Coll. Health and Behavioral Sci. Merit award, 1982; named one of Top 100 Women in Ark., Ark. Bus., 1995-96. Mem. APA, Southwestern Psychol. Assn., Family Svcs. Assn. (bd. dirs. 1988-89), Tex. Psychol. Assn. (dir. div. acad. psychologists 1986), S.E. Tex. Psychol. Assn. (treas. 1978-80, pres. 1983), Nat. Coun. Family Rels., Mental Health Assn. Jefferson County, Nat. Register Health Svc. Providers in Psychology, Nat. Assn. Ind. Colls. and Univs. (bd. dirs. 1993—, vice chmn. 1995, chair bd. dirs. 1996). Home: 1256 Winfield St Conway AR 72032-2741 Office: Hendrix Coll 1600 Washington Ave Conway AR 72032-3001

DIEBOLT, JUDITH, newspaper editor; b. Atchison, Kans., Oct. 6, 1948; d. George Edward and Mary Lou (Hill) D.; m. John C. Aldrich, Oct. 25, 1985. BSJ, U. Kans., 1970. Reporter Detroit Free Press, 1970-80, columnist, 1980-82, asst. city editor, 1982-85; reporter Detroit News, 1986-88, asst city editor, 1988-89, suburban editor, 1989-91; mng. editor Burlington (Vt.) Free Press, 1991-94; city editor Detroit News, 1994—. Recipient Pub. Svc. award AP, 1978. Mem. AP Mng. Editors, Detroit Press Club (bd. govs., 1990-91), Univ. Club Detroit. Roman Catholic. Office: The Detroit News 615 W Lafayette Detroit MI 48236

DIEDERICH, ANNE MARIE, college president; b. Cleve., Apr. 8, 1943. BA in English, Ursuline Coll. for Women, 1966; MA in Ednl. Adminstrn., John Carroll U., 1975; PhD in Edn. Policy and Leadership, Ohio State U., 1988. Joined Order St. Ursula, Roman Cath. Ch., 1961. Tchr. Villa Angela Acad., Cleve., 1966-70, asst. prin., 1971-76, prin., 1976-82; tchr. Beaumont Sch. for Girls, 1982-84; pres. Ursuline Coll., Pepper Pike, Ohio, 1986—. Mem. Leadership Cleve. '89. Dan H. Eikenberry scholar Ohio State U., 1985; William R. and Marie A. Flesher fellow Ohio State U., 1986. Mem. Phi Kappa Phi. Office: Ursuline Coll Office of Pres 2550 Lander Rd Pepper Pike OH 44124-4398

DIEDERICHS, JANET WOOD, public relations executive; b. Libertyville, Ill.; d. J. Howard and Ruth (Hendrickson) Wood; m. John Kustings Diederichs, 1953. BA, Wellesley Coll., 1950; Sales agt. Pan Am. Airways, Chgo., 1951-52; regional mgr. pub. relations Braniff Internat., Chgo., 1953-69; pres. Janet Diederichs & Assocs., Inc., pub. relations cons., Chgo., 1970—; lectr. Harvard U.; mem. exec. com. World Trade Conf., 1983, 84. Com. mem. Nat. Trust for Historic Preservation, 1975-79, Marshall Scholars (Brit. Govt.), 1975-79; trustee Northwestern Meml. Hosp., 1985—, Fourth Presbyn. Ch., mem. bd. dirs. 1990-93; bd. dirs., mem. exec. com. Chgo. Conv. and Visitors Bur. 1978-87; bd. dirs. Internat. House, U. Chgo., 1978-84, Com. of 200, 1982—, Latino Inst., 1986-89, Chgo. Network, 1987—; com. mem. Art Inst. Chgo., 1980-83; mem. exec. com. Vatican Art Council Chgo., 1981-83; pres. Jr. League Chgo., 1968-69. Mem. Chgo. Assn. Commerce and Industry (bd. dirs. 1982-89, exec. com. 1985-88), Internat. Women's Forum, Pub. Relations Soc. Am., Pub. Relations Exch. Internat., Publicity Club Chgo., Chgo. Network, Econ. Club, Woman's Athletic Club of Chgo., Comml. Club of Chgo., The Casino Club (Chgo.), The River Club (N.Y.), The Exec. Svc. Corps. (mem. adv. com.). Office: Diederichs & Assocs 333 N Michigan Ave Ste 1205 Chicago IL 60601-3901*

DIEFFENBACH, ALICEJEAN, artist; b. Nashville, Dec. 18, 1931; d. Bailey Everette and Elizabeth R. (Vinson) Thompson; m. Otto Weaver Dieffenbach, June 14, 1952; children: Otto W. III, Linda Madeleine Harrison, Susanne Elizabeth Hume. AB in Art History, Duke U., 1952; MS in Edn. Adminstrn., Johns Hopkins U., 1974. Soprano Balt. Opera Co., 1956-58; starring roles Met. Mus. Theatre, Actors Theatre, Balt., 1958-75; head art dept., tchr. Cockeysville (Md.) H.S., 1965-79; owner, designer Design Plus, Balt., 1972-80; real estate salesperson Merrill-Lynch/Cousins, Miami, Fla., 1980-82, Dieffenbach Real Estate, Rancho Santa Fe, Calif., 1982-89; artist, painter Solana Beach, Calif., 1992—. Soprano soloist Towson (Md.) Presbyn. Ch., 1955-80, Plymouth Congl. Ch., Coconut Grove, Fla., 1980-82, The Village Ch. Presby., Rancho Santa Fe, 1982—, The Handel Choir Balt., The Bach Soc. Balt.; soloist, performer San Diego Chamber Orch., 1985, 86, 89, 90, 91; soloist Balt. Symphony Orch.; solo show Rancho Santa Fe Libr., 1996. Mem. Rancho Santa Fe Libr. Guild, 1982—, Rep. Women, Rancho Santa Fe. Recipient 1st, 2d, and 3d Hon. Mention awards various juried art exhbns., 1993—. Mem. Artists Equity Assn. (treas. 1994-96), San Diego Art Inst. (numerous ribbons), San Dieguito Art Guild (numerous ribbons), San Diego Mus. Art Guild, San Diego Mus. Contemporary Art, Rancho Santa Fe Garden Club. Presbyterian. Home: PO Box 261 Rancho Santa Fe CA 92067 Studio: 130 S Cedros Solana Beach CA 92067

DIEHL, DOLORES, communication arts director; b. Salina, Kans., Dec. 28, 1927; d. William Augustus and Martha (Frank) D. Student pub. schs., Kans., 1941-45. Bus. rep. Southwestern Bell Telephone Co., St. Louis and Kansas City, Mo., 1948-49, Mountain States Telephone Co., Denver, 1949-50; edn. coord. pub. rels. Pacific Telephone/AT&T, L.A. and San Diego, 1950-83; cons. Bus. Magnet High Sch., L.A. Unified Sch. Dist., 1977-79; pres. First Calif. Acad. Decathlon, 1979; owner Community Connection, L.A., 1983—; mgr., dir. DelMar Media Arts, Burbank, Calif., 1985-89; mgr. Susan Blu workshops Blupka Prodns., L.A., 1989—; dir. animation and commls. voiceover workshops Elaine Craig Voicecasting, Hollywood, Calif., 1989—; freelance performer, voiceover L.A., 1990—; mgr. Sounds Great Film Looping Workshops, L.A., 1992—; owner Voiceover Connection, L.A., 1994-95; pres. Voiceover Connection, Inc., L.A., 1995—; v.p. pub. rels. San Diego Inst. Creativity, 1965-67; mem. exec. com. San Diego's 200th Anniversary Celebration, 1967. Recipient Dedication to Edn. award Industry Edn. Coun., Calif., 1964. Mem. L.A. Area C. of C. (bd. dirs. women's coun.), Calif. Magnet Sch. Consortium of Cities (chairperson), Industry Edn. Coun. Calif., L.A. and San Diego (past pres.), Bus. and Profl. Women's Club, Delta Kappa Gamma (hon.). Republican. Methodist. Home and Office: 691 Irolo St Apt 212 Los Angeles CA 90005-4102

DIEHL, GERALDINE SHAFFER, reading specialist; b. Takoma Park, Md., Jan. 23, 1947; d. James Henry and Margaret (Kuzmich) Shaffer; m. Ronald Hayden Imbriale; Sept. 2, 1967 (div. July 1981); children: Ryan James, Scott Keith; m. William Clayton Diehl, Aug. 1, 1981; 1 child, Lindsay Kathleen. BS in Elem. Edn., U. Md., College Park, 1969; MEd in Human Devel., 1973. 3d, 5th and 6th grade tchr. Prince Georges County Bd. Edn., Upper Marlboro, Md., 1969-75, reading tutorial tchr. grade 9, 1978-80; elem. reading tchr. Glassmanor Elem. Sch., Woodmore Elem. Sch., Baden Elem. Sch., Brandywine, Md., 1981—. pres., bd. mem. Newport Estates Condo. Assn., Gaithersburg, Md., 1975-77; v.p. Peace Luth. Ch., Waldorf, Md., 1985-87. Mem. NEA, Md. State Tchrs. Assn., Prince Georges County Educators Assn., Price Georges County Internat. Reading Assn., Internat. Reading Assn. Lutheran. Office: Baden Elementary School 13601 Baden Westwood Rd Brandywine MD 20613-8422

DIEKMAN, DIANE JEAN, naval officer; b. Clear Lake, S.D., Sept. 18, 1950; d. John and Mildred (Hanson) D. BA in Elem. Edn., English and Spanish, Augustana Coll., Sioux Falls, S.D., 1972; MS in Aero. Sci., Embry-Riddle Aero. U., Norfolk, Va., 1988; MBA in Aviation, Embry-Riddle Aero. U., Jacksonville, Fla., 1992. Enlisted USN, 1972, commd. ensign, 1975, advanced through grades to capt., 1996; test control officer Armed Forces Enlistment Sta., Oklahoma City, 1975-78; aircraft div. officer Tng. Squadron 23, Kingsville, Tex., 1978-82; maintenance officer Patrol Squadron 16, Jacksonville, 1982-85; prodn. (ops.) officer Aircraft Maintenance Dept., Norfolk, 1985-88; dept. head Naval Air Sta., Agana, Guam, 1988-90, Jacksonville, 1990-93; maintenance liaison Naval Supply Sys. Command, Arlington, Va., 1993-96; asst. chief staff for material Fleet Air Western Pacific, 1996—. Columnist Clear Lake Courier, 1994—; contbr. articles to profl. publs. Organizer POW/MIA ceremonies Naval Air Sta., Jacksonville, 1991-93; vol. mail staff White House, Washington, 1994-96, Navy Meml., Washington, 1994-96; v.p. Springfield (Va.) Civic Assn., 1994-96, others. Mem. Naval Inst. (life), Tailhook Assn. (life), Ret. Officers Assn., Women in Mil. Svc. to Am. Meml. Found. (charter), Naval Aviation Mus. Found., USN Meml. Found. (charter). Lutheran. Office: Fleet Air Western Pacific (Code N42) PSC 477 Box 3 FPO AP 96036-2703

DIEKMANN, NANCY KASSAK, stage producer; b. Elizabeth, N.J., Oct. 22, 1952; d. Michael John and Eleanor Ruth (Wilson) Kassak; m. Mark Stefan Diekmann, Sept. 2, 1984; 1 child, Michael Kassak. BA, Clark U., 1974. Mng. dir. New Eng. Repertory Theatre, Worcester, Mass., 1973-79; adminstrv. dir. Theatre Communications Group, N.Y.C., 1979-84; mng. dir. N.Y. Theatre Workshop, N.Y.C., 1984—; chmn. theatre panel N.Y. State Coun. Arts, 1989-92; pres. N.Y. chpt. Assn. Non-Profit Theatre Cos., 1990—. Recipient OBIE award Village Voice, 1991. Office: NY Theatre Workshop 79 E 4th St New York NY 10003

DIENSTAG, ELEANOR FOA, corporate communications consultant; b. Naples, Italy; d. Bruno Garibaldi and Lisa (Haimann) Foa; m. Jerome Dienstag (div. 1978); children: Joshua Foa, Jesse Paul. BA, Smith Coll., Northampton, Mass. Asst. editor Random House/Harper & Row, N.Y.C.; editor/writer Monocle Mag., N.Y.C.; cultural columnist Genesee Valley Newspapers, Rochester, N.Y.; sr. mgr., speechwriter Am. Express, N.Y.C., 1978-83; freelance journalist, N.Y.C., 1983—; lit. resident Yaddo Y., 1980, Va. Ctr. for Creative Arts, 1990-91, 95; lectr., book pub. columnist and reviewer in field. Author: Whither Thou Goest, 1976, In Good Company: 125 Years at the Heinz Table, 1994; contbr. articles, essays and feature stories to N.Y. Times, Harper's, N.Y. Observer, McCalls; columnist New Choices Mag., 1994-96. Recipient Merit award for speechwriting Internat. Assn. Bus. Comm., N.Y., 1981-82, Merit award Am. Express Mgmt. Newsletter, 1981, Outstanding Mem. award Women in Comm., 1984. Mem. Am. Soc. Journalists and Authors, Nat. Writer's Union. Home and Office: Eleanor Foa Assocs 435 E 79th St New York NY 10021-1034

DIERSING, CAROLYN VIRGINIA, educational administrator; b. Rushville, Ohio, Sept. 13; d. Carl Emerson and Wilma Virginia (Neel) Deyo; m. Robert J. Diersing, Dec. 22, 1962; children: Robert, Timothy, Charles, Sheila, Christina. BA, Ohio State U., 1963; state cert., Ohio Dominican, 1985. Cert. tchr., Ohio. Libr. St. Mary's Sch., Delaware, Ohio, 1979-87; tech. svcs. asst. Beeghly Libr. Ohio Wesleyan U., Delaware, 1987-90, dir. curriculum resource dept. edn., 1990—. Contbr. poetry to Voices. Mem. ALA, Del. Area Recovery Resources (bd. dirs. 1994—, treas. 1995, sec. 1996), Acad. Libr. Assn. Ohio. Office: Ohio Wesleyan U Curriculum Resource Ctr Dept Edn Delaware OH 43015

DIESTELKAMP, DAWN LEA, systems analyst; b. Fresno, Calif., Apr. 23, 1954; d. Don and Joy LaVaughn (Davis) Diestelkamp. BS in Microbiology, Calif. State U.-Fresno, 1976, MS in Pub. Adminstrn., 1983, MBA, 1995, cert. in tng. design & mgmt., 1992. Lic. clin. lab. technologist, Calif.; cert. clin. lab. dir. Clin. lab. technologist Valley Med. Ctr., Fresno, 1977-82, info. systems coord., 1983-84, quality control coord. Valley Med. Ctr., Fresno, 1984-90, systems & procedures analyst, 1990-91; systems & procedures analyst Fresno County Cts., 1991—; instr. Fresno City Coll. Tng. Inst., 1993—; cons., instr. in field. Mem. ASTD, AAUW, Calif. Ct. Clks. Assn. (cert. com.), Fresno Women's Network (chair scholarship com., chair newsletter com., bd. dirs.), Fresno Met. Mus. Soc. Democrat. Office: 1100 Van Ness Ave Rm 200 Fresno CA 93724

DIETER, ALICE HUNT, journalist; b. Denver, Apr. 16, 1928; d. Thomas Addison and Alice (McCullough) Hunt; BA cum laude in English Lang., U. Colo., 1949; m. Leslie Louis Dieter, Sept. 10, 1948; children: Alice Dieter Crowley-Mize, Philip Leslie, Paul Wesley. Columnist, reporter, feature writer Intermountain Observer, Boise, Idaho, 1962-72, asst. editor, 1965-72, also TV news reporter Sta. KBOI, and news librarian, 1966-73; stringer Newsweek mag., 1970-73; editorial assoc. corp. communications Boise Cascade Corp., 1973-83; ret., 1983; weekly editorial columnist Idaho Daily Statesman, 1977-85. Chair, Idaho Assn. Humanities, 1972-78; bd. dirs. Idaho Farm Workers Svcs., Inc., 1963-69, pres., 1965-69; bd. dirs. "Friends of Four" (pub. TV sta. KAID), 1988-92; mem. Boise Com. Fgn. Rels.s, 1975—; mem. Idaho Gov.'s Commn. on Excellence in Edn., 1983; mem. Idaho Selection Com. for Rhodes Scholars, 1983-84; pres. Boise LWV, 1957-59; Idaho rep. UNICEF, 1963-65; mem. Boise Valley World Affairs Assn., 1956-65; mem. Boise City Park Bd., 1964-79; co-chair Idaho Johnson for Pres., 1964, Citizens for Andrus for Gov., 1966; del. Women's Conf., Houston, 1978; active YWCA, St. Michael's Episc. Parish, Boise Philharm., Friends of Boise Library, Idaho Hist. Soc.; press advisor Episc. Bishop Idaho, 1991—; bd. dirs. Episcopal Camp and Retreat Ctr., 1991— (chair 1996—). Recipient Idaho Press awards for feature writing and news photography, 1967, for gen. interest column, 1983. Mem. Idaho Press Club (bd. dirs.), Phi Beta Kappa. Home: 1563 E Holly St Boise ID 83712-8355

DIETRICH, JOYCE DIANE, librarian; b. Danville, Pa., Aug. 19, 1951; d. LeRoy Charles and Mae Elizabeth (Klinger) Smeltz; m. Lynn Allen, Sept. 2, 1972; children: Sarah Mae, Martha Ferne, David Lynn. BS in Libr. Sci., Millersville (Pa.) U., 1972; MS in Libr. Sci., Shippensburg (Pa.) U., 1974. Cert. in libr. sci., Pa.; cert. decorative artist. Middle sch. libr. Upper Dauphin Area Sch. Dist., 1972-73; high sch. libr. Shippensburg (Pa.) Area Sch. Dist., 1973-80; elem. libr. Greencastle-Antrim (Pa.) Sch. Dist., 1992—; adj. faculty libr. sci. Shippensburg (Pa.) U., 1982; painting instr. local craft shops, convs., etc., 1985-92. Designer: (painted object) Decorative Painter, 1992, Craftworks, 1992, Homestead Classics Christmas Crafts, 1993. Pianist for children Salem Luth. Ch., Marion, Pa., 1984—, Marion Cmty. Bible Sch., 1984—. Mem. ALA, Pa. Sch. Librs. Assn., Nat. Soc. Decorative Painters, Order of Eastern Star. Democrat. Lutheran. Home: 2798 Warm Spring Rd Chambersburg PA 17201-9269 Office: Greencastle-Antrim Sch Dist 500 E Leitersburg St Greencastle PA 17225-1138

DIETRICH, RENÉE LONG, educational foundation executive; b. Emerald, Pa., Oct. 10, 1937; d. Emmett A. and Arlene I. (Fenstermaker) Long; m. Bruce L. Dietrich, Nov. 25, 1959; children: Dodson, Katie. BS, Kutztown (Pa.) U., 1959; MLS, Rutgers U., 1966. Cert. fund raising exec., ednl. specialist. Tchr. history Reading (Pa.) Pub. Schs., 1959-65, libr., 1965-69; coord. coop. ed. Reading (Pa.) Area Community Coll., 1978-81, program adminstr. title III grant, 1982-92, coord. community and legis. rels., 1983-91, dir. institutional advancement, 1991—; exec. dir. Foundation for Reading Area Community Coll., 1986—; cons. Pa. Power and Light Co., Allentown, 1981—; U.S. Office of Edn., Washington, 1990—. Editor Reading Area Community Coll. newsletter, 1983—; contbr. articles to profl. jours. Bd. dirs. Kutztown U. Found., 1981-90; chmn. bd. trustees Kutztown U., 1976-81; mem. Berks County Commn. for Women, 1993—; pres. LWV Berks County, 1995—; mem. program com. Berks Cmty. TV, Reading, 1989—. Recipient Disting. Alumni award, Kutztown U., 1981; named to Pa. Honor Roll of Women, 1996. Mem. Coll.-Univ. Pub. Rels. Assn. Pa., Nat. Soc. Fundraising Execs., Delta Kappa Gamma (hon. edn. soc.). Mem. United Ch. of Christ. Home: 1546 Dauphin Ave Reading PA 19610-2118 Office: Reading Area C C 10 S 2nd St # 1706 Reading PA 19602-1014

DIETRICH, SUZANNE CLAIRE, instructional designer; b. Granite City, Ill.; d. Charles Daniel and Evelyn Blanche (Waters) D.; BS in Speech, Northwestern U.; MS in Pub. Communication, Boston U., 1967; postgrad. So. Ill. U., 1973-83. Intern, prodn. staff Sta. WGBH-TV, Boston, 1958-59, asst. dir., 1962-64, asst. dir. program Invitation to Art, 1958; cons. producer dir. dept. instructional TV radio Ill. Office Supt. Pub. Instruction, Springfield, 1969-70; dir. program prodn. and distbn., 1970-72; instr. faculty call staff, speech dept. Sch. Fine Arts So. Ill. U., Edwardsville, 1972-73, grad. asst. for doctoral program office of dean Sch. Edn., 1975-78; rsch. asst. Ill. public telecommunications study for Ill. Public Broadcasting Coun., 1979-80; cons. and rsch. in communications, 1980—; exec. producer, dir. TV programs Con-Con Countdown, 1970, The Flag Speaks, 1971. Mem. sch. bd. St. Mary's Cath. Sch., Edwardsville, 1991-92; cable TV adv. com. City of Edwardsville, 1994—, co-chair, 1996—; bd. dirs. Goshen Preservation Alliance, Edwardsville, 1992-94, pres., 1995—. Roman Catholic. Home: 1011 Minnesota St Edwardsville IL 62025-1424

DIETRICH, TAMARA SUE, newspaper editor, columnist; b. Heidelberg, Germany, Mar. 22, 1958; d. Daniel Flory Franklin Detrick and Betty Jean (Hartman) Phillips. BA in English and Creative Writing, U. N.Mex., 1982. Freelance writer Portland, Maine, 1982-83; project asst. Nat. Resources Defense Coun., Washington, 1983-87; city reporter The Independent, Gallup, N.Mex., 1987-90; features editor/columnist The Post-Star, Glens Falls, N.Y., 1990-93, Sunday editor/columnist, 1993—. Editor, contbr. lit. revs.: Conceptions Southwest, 1981, 82. Recipient awards for column writing, features, and news reporting, N.Mex. Press Women, Nat. Fedn. Press Women, AP, 1988-95; recipient Disting. Column Writing award of excellence, N.Y. Newspaper Publishers Assn., 1994-95. Mem. Nat. Soc. Newspaper Columnists, AP of N.Y. Deist. Home: 21 Mechanic St Hudson Falls NY 12839 Office: The Post-Star Lawrence & Cooper Sts Glens Falls NY 12801

DIETZ, CHERYL ANNE, artist; b. Edmonton, Alta., Can., Aug. 6, 1966; came to U.S., 1971; d. Arnold and Janet (Cripe) D. BFA in Painting, Ind. U./Purdue U., Indpls., 1996; postgrad., U. N.Mex., 1996—. Four color seperation technician Four Color Graphics Inc., Indpls., 1991-94; lab. asst. lithography dept. Herron Sch. Art, Ind. U./Purdue U., Indpls., 1994-95; decorative painter Blice Edwards, Indpls., 1995—. Exhibited in group shows at L.S. Ayres & Co. Gallery, Mishawaka, Ind., 1982, 83, 84, Midwest Mus. Am.Art, Elkhart, Ind., 1984, Herron Gallery, Indpls., 1993, 94, 95, 96. Recipient Scholastic Art award Northwestern Ind. Regional Exhbn., south Bend, 1982, hon. mention, 1983, Gold Key, 1984, Mildred Darby Menz award, 1996; Rotary woman's studies scholar, Indpls., 1995.

DIETZ, DEBORAH JEAN, paralegal; b. Honolulu, Apr. 26, 1958; d. John James Edwin and Josephine Y.M. (Chun) D. AA in Liberal Arts, Windward Community Coll., 1978; BA in Psychology, U. Hawaii, 1980. Substitute presch. tchr. Emmanuel's Presch. & Day Care, Kailua, Hawaii, 1981; supr. Cades Schutte Fleming & Wright, Honolulu, 1981-83, paralegal asst., 1983—, corp. paralegal, 1985—; spl. asst. sec. C T Corp. System, Honolulu, 1983—; bus. owner Pins 'N Things, 1992—. Sponsor Christian Childrens Fund, Inc., Va., 1985; active People for Ethical Treatment of Animals, Washington, 1986, Greenpeace, Washington, 1985. Republican. Roman Catholic. Office: Cades Schutte Fleming Wrigh 1000 Bishop St Fl 15 Honolulu HI 96813-4212

DIETZ, DOROTHY ELLEN, elementary education educator; b. Hanna, Wyo., Jan. 13, 1941; d. Laurence K. and Mary Elizabeth (Cummings) Cheesbrough; m. Gerald F. Gashler, Feb. 6, 1966 (dec. Sept. 1971); children: Courtney Gerald Gashler, Evelyn Diane Gashler Hagist; m. Arnold D. Dietz, July 7, 1973; children: Arnold L. Dietz, Martin D. Dietz, Kenneth W. Dietz. BA in Elem. Edn., U. Wyo., 1990; MA in Reading, U. No. Colo., 1992. Ins. clk. Mountain States Hwy Bur., Laramie, Wyo., 1959-66; sec. U. Wyo., Laramie, 1966-72, 86-88; realtor assoc. Century 21-Imperial Investments, Laramie, 1978-80; asst. mgr. family businesses, Laramie, 1980-86; reading tchr., tutor Northeastern Jr. Coll., Sterling, Colo., 1990-91; elem. tchr. Buffalo RE4J Sch. Dist., Merino, Colo., 1991—; mem. bus. edn. adv. bd. Laramie Sr. H.S., 1980-83. Mem. Laramie City Coun., 1973-77; mem. Laramie Planning Commn., 1973-80; leader Albany County 4-H Coun., Larmaie, 1973-81; bd. dirs., 1979-82, pres. 1981. Named Outstanding 4-H Leader; named to Outstanding Young Women of Am., 1973. Mem. ASCD, AAUW (v.p. programs 1993-94, treas. 1995-, co-pres. 1996—), Merino Edn. Assn. (pres. 1992-94), Internat. Reading Assn., Order Ea. Star (Worthy Grand Matron 1985-86, grand treas. 1986-88). Republican. Episcopalian. Home: 453 Plainview Ave Sterling CO 80751 Office: Merino Elem Sch PO Box 198 Merino CO 80741

DIETZ, JANIS CAMILLE, sales executive; b. Washington, May 26, 1950; d. Albert and Joan Mildred (MacMullen) Weinstein; m. John William Dietz, Apr. 10, 1981. BA, U. R.I., 1971; MBA, Calif. Poly. U., Pomona, 1984; postgrad. Claremont Grad. Sch., 1991—. Customer svc. trainer People's Bank, Providence, 1974-76; salesman, food broker Bradshaw Co., L.A., 1976-78; salesman Johnson & Johnson, L.A., 1978-79, GE Co., L.A., 1979-82; regional sales mgr. Leviton Co., L.A., 1982-85; nat. sales mgr. Jensen Gen. div. Nortek Co., L.A., 1985-86; retail sales mgr. Norris div. Masco, L.A., 1986-88; nat. sales mgr. Thermador Waste King div. Masco, L.A., 1988-91; nat. accts. mgr. Universal Flooring div. Masco, 1991-92; western regional mgr. Peerless Faucet div. Masco, 1992-95; performance devel. cons., Delta Faucet, div. Masco, 1995—; asst. prof. bus. adminstrn. U. LaVerne, 1995—; sales trainer, Upland, Calif., 1985—; instr. Calif. Poly. U., 1988—; lectr. Whittier Coll., 1994. Dir. pub. rels. Jr. Achievement, Providence, 1975-76; bd. trustees Nat. Multiple Sclerosis Soc., So. Calif. chpt. Recipient Sector Svc. award GE Co., Fairfield, Conn., 1980, Outstanding Achievement award, 1988. Mem. NAFE, Sales Profls. L.A. (v.p. 1984-86), Toastmasters (adminstrv. v.p. 1985). Unitarian.

DIETZ, KAREN PANTERMUEHL, early childhood education educator; b. Seguin, Tex., Aug. 14, 1941; d. Roland H. and Julia (Weigel) Pantermuehl; m. Frank H. Dietz, Aug. 17, 1963; children: Kevin Paul, Mark David. BA, Elmhurst Coll., 1963; MEd, U. Tex., 1987. Cert. elem. educator, ESL educator, gifted and talented educator, Tex. Tchr. elem. Lindbergh Sch. Dist., St. Louis, 1963-65; presch. tchr. Winnetka (Ill.) Pub. Sch., 1965-66; presch., daycare tchr. First Presbyn. Ch., Bryan, Tex., 1972-75; tchr. kindergarten Big Little Sch., Houston, 1978-82; tchr. elem. Austin (Tex.) Ind. Sch. Dist., 1989-95; kindergarten tchr. Cy-Fair Sch. Dist., Houston, 1995—. Homemaker, vol. ch., sch. and cmty. activities, 1966, 72, 75-78, 82-89; bd. dirs., officer Settegast Housing Village, Houston, 1977-82; chairperson, mem. Peace With Justice Conf., United Ch. of Christ, La., Tex., 1978-95, dir. bd. for world ministries, 1976-88, mem. Middle East policy panel, 1983; del. United Ch. of Christ Synod, St. Louis, 1994. Mem. Internat. Assn. Young Children (officer, bd. dirs. 1990—); workshop leader in field for various pubs. 1992-96). United Ch. of Christ. Home: 14422 Wynfield Dr Cypress TX 77429-1847

DIETZ, LINDA, hypnotherapist; b. Bedford, Ohio, May 15, 1950; d. Robert Llewellyn and Jytte Ernst (Hansen) Gardner; m. Stephen Paul Dietz, Nov. 22, 1988; 1 child, Gillian Arianna. Lic. med. asst., Career Acad., Toronto, Can., 1969; grad., Omni Hypnosis Tng. Ctr., Ft. Lauderdale, Fla., 1987. Cert. hypnotherapist. Dir. Sch. Metaphysics, 1978-85; adminstrv. asst. CSA Creative Design, Ft. Lauderdale, Fla., 1986-92; hypnotherapist, lectr., trainer Des Moines, 1992—; pres., founder Mindworks, Inc., Des Moines, 1995—; lectr. in field. Nat. coord. Clean Up Am. Mem. Assn. Past Life Rsch. and Therapy (life). Home: 1914 55th St Des Moines IA 50310

DIETZ, MARGARET JANE, retired public information official, tutor; b. Omaha, Apr. 15, 1924; d. Lawrence Louis and Jeanette Amalia (Meile) Neumann; m. Richard Henry Dietz, May 30, 1949 (dec. July 1971); children: Henry Louis, Frederick Richard, Susan Margaret, John Lawrence (dec.). BA, U. Nebr., 1946; MS, Columbia U., 1949. Wire editor Kearney (Nebr.) Daily Hub, 1946-47; state society editor Omaha World-Herald, 1947-48; library aide Akron (Ohio) Pub. Libr., 1963-66, publicity and display dir., 1966-74, editor Owlet, 1966-74; pub. info. officer Northeastern Ohio Univs. Coll. Medicine, Rootstown, 1974-85, dir. Office of Comm., 1985-87, ret. 1987; writer Ravenna (Ohio) Record-Courier, 1988-92; cons. Kent (Ohio) State U. Sch. Music, 1988-91. Mem. culture and entertainment com. Goals for Greater Akron, 1976; pres. bd. Weathervane Cmty. Playhouse, Akron, 1982-85, sec. to the bd., 1988-93, trustee, 1991-93, historian, 1993—, chair 60th anniversary season, 1994-95; trustee Family Svcs. Summit County, Ohio, 1980-94, dist. trustee, 1994—, Am. Heart Assn., Akron dist., 1986-91, Mobile Meals Found., Akron, 1988-91; v.p. Friends of Akron-Summit County Pub. Libr., 1988-94, pres., 1994-95; student tutor LEARN Literacy Coun., 1988-94, trustee 1988-95. Author: Akron's Library: Commemorating Twenty Five Years on Main Street. Recipient Trustee award Weathervane Community Playhouse, 1985, Family Svcs. Bernard W. Frazier award, 1994, John S. Knight award Soc. Profl. Journalists, 1995, Mary Kerrigal O'Neil award Women in Comm., 1995. Mem. Women in Comm., LWV (edn. fund. 1989-92, newsletter editor Akron 1957-60), College Club, Press Club, Akron Women's City Club. Home: 887 Canyon Trl Akron OH 44303-2401

DIETZ, PATRICIA ANN, engineering administrator; b. L.A., Nov. 30, 1958; m. Frank Raymond Dietz, July 1, 1978; children: Lindy K., Frank R. Jr. BA in Polit. Sci., U. Colo., 1983; MA in Psychology, Pepperdine U., 1993; Paralegal Cert., U. San Diego, 1988. Investment broker 1st Investors Corp., Colorado Springs, Colo., 1986-88; paralegal Law Offices of Ben Williams, Santa Monica, Calif., 1988-89; mgmt. analyst Bur. of Engring., City of L.A., 1989—; camp commandant Operation Safe Harbor-Haitian Humanitarian Relief Effort, 1992. Mem. Parent Tchr. Student Assn., Rosamond, Calif., 1992. With U.S. Army, 1983-86, capt. USAR, 1986—. Nat. Urban fellow, 1991. Mem. Civil Affairs Assn., Res. Officers Assn., Engrs. and Architects Assn. Republican.

DIFFILY, DEBORAH LYNN, early childhood education educator; b. San Bernardino, Calif., July 23, 1955; d. J.W. and Bobbye Dale (Funkhouser) Titsworth; m. David Thomas Hawkins, Feb. 1, 1983; 1 child, Michael Spear Hawkins; m. James Patrick Diffily, Aug. 3, 1991. BA, Oral Roberts U., 1976; MA, Tex. Wesleyan U., 1989; PhD, U. North Tex., 1994. Prekindergarten tchr. The White Lake Sch., Ft. Worth, 1988-90; kindergarten and 1st grade tchr. Ft. Worth Ind. Sch. Dist., 1990-96; faculty Tex. Wesleyan U., 1996—; teaching fellow U. North Tex., Denton, 1993; tchr., lectr. Tex. Christian U., Ft. Worth, 1993-95; adj. prof. Tex. Wesleyan U., Ft. Worth, 1995—. Co-author: Early Childhood Education: An Introduction, 1995; editor: Helping Parents Understand: Newsletter Articles on Early Childhood Issues, 1995; author articles. Trustee St. Luke's Episc. Sch., Ft. Worth, 1990-93; mem task force Ft. Worth Mus. Sci. and History, Ft. Worth, 1992; mem. alumni leadership coun. Tex. Wesleyan U., Ft. Worth, 1991-93; mem. renovation com. Fossil Rim Wildlife Ctr., Granbury, Tex., 1994. Community Fund grantee, 1993-94; Velma E. Schmidt scholar, 1993; Lauream Christian Robertson fellow, 1993. Mem. ASCD, Ft. Worth Area Assn. for Edn. of Young Children (pres. 1993-94), Tex. Assn. for Edn. of Young Children, So. Early Childhood Assn., Nat. Assn. for Edn. of Young Children, Phi Delta Kappa. Home: 3905 Sanguinet St Fort Worth TX 76107-7237

DI FRANCO, LORETTA ELIZABETH, lyric coloratura soprano; b. Bklyn., Oct. 28, 1942; d. Philip Carl and Lavinia (Russo) Di F.; m. Anthony Martin Pinto, June 15, 1968; 1 dau. Student, Hunter Coll., Julliard Sch. Music. Mem. chorus Met. Opera Assn., N.Y.C.; now soloist N.Y. Met. Opera, debut in Pique Dame, 1965; performances in Paris, also summer concerts, Lewisohn Stadium, 1966; mem. various choruses, festivals and concert series, including Empire State Music Festival, Mozart Opera Festival, Chautauqua, N.Y., 1964; also performed on radio and TV. (Recipient 1st prize Met. Opera Nat. Auditions 1965); major roles include Zerlina in Don Giovanni, Oscar in Un Ballo in Maschera, Lauretta in Gianni Schiechi, Marcellina in Le Nozze de Figaro, title role in Lucia di Lammermoor. Stuart and Irene Chambers award, 1965; Kathryn Turney Long scholar, 1965-66; Martha Baird-Rockefeller Fund for Music grantee, 1964. Mem. Am. Guild Mus. Artists. Office: care Met Opera Assn Inc Lincoln Ctr New York NY 10023*

DIGGS, LINDA STASER, human resource professional, speaker, writer; b. San Francisco, Nov. 10, 1955; d. Glenndon Staser and Josephine Marie (Katen) Smith. AA, Coll. of San Mateo (Calif.), 1976; BS, U. San Francisco, 1989; MS, Fordham U., 1995. Cert. internat. hospitality mgr. Dept. motor vehicles specialist The CTA Credit Union, Burlingame, Calif., 1976-79; asst. product adminstr. Itel Corp., San Francisco, 1979-81; adminstrv. asst. Main Hurdman, KMG, San Francisco, 1981-83; asst. mgr. Met. Club, San Francisco, 1983-88; human resource generalist The CIT Group, Livingston, N.J., 1990—. Recipient scholarships Lions, Brisbane, Calif., 1973, Masons, San Francisco, 1984. Mem. ASTD (v.p. profl. devel. No. N.J. 1993-94, bd. dirs. 1993-94), U. San Francisco (newsletter pub. N.Y. Chpt. Alumni 1990-92), Federated Women's Club of Brisbane (pres. 1987-88), Gen. Fedn. Women's Clubs (aide to dist. pres. Golden Gate dist. 1987-88). Roman Catholic. Home: 44 Center Grove Rd # E5 Randolph NJ 07869-4450 Office: The CIT Group 650 CIT Dr Livingston NJ 07039-5703

DIGIAMARINO, MARIAN ELEANOR, realty administrator; b. Camden, N.J., July 23, 1947; d. James and Concetta (Biancosino) DiG. BS in Mgmt., Rutgers U., 1978. Clk. stenographer transp. div. Dept. of Navy, Phila., 1965-70, sec., 1970-73, realty asst. Profl. Devel. Ctr.. program, 1973-75, realty specialist, 1975-81, supervisory realty specialist, head acquisition and ingrant sect., 1981-85, supervisory realty specialist, mgr. ops. br., 1985—; instr. USNR, Phila., 1983, 88. Contbr. articles to profl. jours. Mem. AAUW, Soc. Am. Mil. Engrs., Nat. Assn. Female Execs., Phi Chi Theta (pres. Del. Valley chpt. 1984-86, nat. councillor 1984, nat. fundraising com., pres. and corr. sec. (Alpha Omega chpt. 1976-78). Office: Dept Navy No Div Naval Facilities Engring Command Real Estate Div 10 Indsl Hwy Mail Stop # 82 Lester PA 19113-2090

DIGIOVANNA, EILEEN LANDENBERGER, osteopathic physician, educator; b. Columbus, Ohio, Nov. 24, 1933; d. Bernard Holman and Della Belle (Crabtree) Landenberger; m. Joseph Anthony DiGiovanna, Apr. 4, 1959; children: Michael, Mark, Gina, Geri, Vicki, Matthew, Kimberly. Student, Ohio State U., 1952-55; DO, Chgo. Coll. Osteopathy, 1959. Pvt. practice Massapequa Park, N.Y., 1960-81; asst. prof., assoc. prof. N.Y. Coll. Osteo. Medicine, Old Westbury, 1977-91, prof., asst. dean student affairs, 1991—. Author, editor: (textbook) Osteopathic Approach to Diagnosis and Treatment, 1991; contbr. articles to profl. jours. Lay speaker Meth. Ch., N.Y., 1988—, chmn. adminstrn. bd. 1993—. Fellow Am. Acad. Osteopathy (trustee 1992-94, pres. 1994-95); mem. Am. Osteo. Assn. (Educator of Yr. 1995), Am. Coll. Family Practice. Republican. Office: NY Coll Osteo Medicine Old Westbury NY 11568

DIGIOVANNI, ELEANOR ELMA, scaffold installation company executive; b. Long Island City, N.Y., May 14, 1944; d. Charles and Josephine (Laureni) DiG. Student Queensboro Coll. Collector Atlas/Re/Sun Ins. Co., N.Y.C., 1965-69; instr. Oak Manor Equitation, Weyers Cave, Va., 1970-76; dispatcher, salesperson Safway Steel Products, Long Island City, N.Y., 1977-83; ops. mgr. York Scaffold, Long Island City, 1983-95, scaffold sales rep. Safeway Steel Prod., Bklyn.; ptnr. E-Z Scholarship Data Svc., 1992—. Mem. Mus. Natural History, Nat. Assn. Female Execs., Women in Constrn., Internat. Platform Assn. Democrat. Roman Catholic. Avocations: reading, horseback riding, needlepoint. Home: 14-34 30th Rd Astoria NY 11102-3640

DIKE, MARGARET HOPCRAFT, retired education administrator; b. Prescott, Ariz., July 15, 1921; d. Walter Irving and Margaret Jennie (Lindsay) Hopcraft; m. Sheldon Holland Dike, Nov. 28, 1941 (div. 1971); children: Lawrence, Walter, Robert, Martin, Martha. BA, U. N.Mex., 1941, MA, 1975. Draftsman U. Calif., Los Alamos, N.Mex., 1943-45; coord. Albuquerque Pub. Schs., 1972-85; chmn. pub. adv. com. U. N.Mex., Albuquerque, 1973-74, chmn. search com. regional v.p., 1975. Co-editor: Bicentennial '76 - Albuquerque, 1977; editor booklet New Mexico Arts Resources Survey, 1957, rsch. papers in field. Trustee Albuquerque Mus., 1969-81; chmn. Albuquerque R.R. Centennial, 1979-80, Keep Albuquerque Beautiful Schs., 1984—; pres. Albuquerque Sister Cities Found., 1985-87, Albuquerque Hist. Soc., 1971-78, N.Mex. Assn. for Cmty. Edn. Devel., 1980-82; chair Albuquerque Sister Cities Bd., 1988-91, 96—; life mem. N.Mex. PTA, pres., 1977-79, 92-95; sec. Edn. Forum N.Mex., 1988-89. Recipient Lobo award U. N.Mex., 1968, Gov.'s award for outstanding N.Mex. women, Commn. on Status of Women, 1986, 90, N. Mex. Disting. Svc. award, 1996; named Woman on the Move for cmty. svc. YWCA, 1995, to Sr. Hall of Fame, 1995. Mem. AAUW (pres. N.Mex. 1989-93), Exec. Women Internat. (treas. 1983-85), Mortar Bd. (pres. alumni chpt. 1988-90, 96—, Nat. Cmty. Svc. award 1993), Phi Delta Kappa, Phi Kappa Phi, Phi Alpha Theta. Methodist.

DILEONE, CARMEL MONTANO, dental hygienist; b. New Haven, Aug. 24, 1926; d. Nicholas and Martha (Ercolano) M.; m. Eugene Francis Dileone, Jan. 28, 1948; children: Gina, Richard. Dental Hygienist, Temple U., 1945; AA, Albertus Magnus Coll., 1980; BS, U. Bridgeport, 1983; MS, So. Conn. State U., 1985. Registered dental hygienist. Dental hygiene practitioner George M. Montano, DDS, New Haven, 1946-50; George V. Montano, DDS, 1959—; dental hygiene practitioner Francis R. Mullen, DDS, West Haven, 1950-55; dental hygiene practioner Herbert Saunders, DDS, Orange, Conn., 1958-63; instr. Huntington Inst., North Haven, Conn., 1983; adj. assoc. prof. U. Bridgeport, Conn., Fones Sch. Dental Hygiene, 1985-96; adj. lectr. U. New Haven, 1994—. Mem. APHA, Am. Soc. Dentistry for Children, Am. Dental Hygienist Assn., Conn. Dental Hygienists Assn. (treas. 1986-88, v.p. 1988-89, pres.-elect 1989-90, pres. 1991, Mabel C. McCarthy award 1983, Pres. award 1994). Roman Catholic. Home: 348 Racebrook Rd Orange CT 06477-3109 Office: George V Montano DDS 436 Whalley Ave New Haven CT 06511-3012

DILL, JUDITH, education administrator; b. Newark, Sept. 30, 1940; d. David and Irene (Kryski) Tiber; m. James J. Dill, Apr. 30, 1962 (div. Sept. 1985); children: Cheryl I., Melissa A., Rebecca J., Joseph A. Student, Brookdale C.C., Lincroft, N.J., 1978-80; BA magna cum laude, Kean Coll., 1982; MEd, Rutgers U., 1984. Cert. ednl. supr., N.J. Spl. edn. tchr. Eden Inst., Princeton, N.J., 1982-83; spl. edn. tchr. High Point Adolescent Sch., Morganville, N.J., 1983-93, edn. supr., 1993—. Mem. N.J. Assn. Suprs. and Curriculum Devel. (exec. dir. 1996—). Home: 30 Ocean Blvd Leonardo NJ 07737 Office: High Point Adolescent Sch 1 High Point Center Way Morganville NJ 07751

DILL, SHERI, publishing executive. Assoc. pub. Wichita (Kans.) Eagle. Office: The Wichita Eagle PO Box 820 Wichita KS 67201*

DILLARD, ANNIE, author; b. Pitts., Apr. 30, 1945; d. Frank and Pam (Lambert) Doak; m. R.H.W. Dillard, 1965 (div.); m. Gary Clevidence, 1980 (div.); 1 child, Cody Rose; stepchildren: Carin, Shelly; m. Robert D. Richardson, Jr., 1988. B.A., Hollins Coll., 1967, M.A., 1968. Contbg. editor Harper's Mag., N.Y.C., 1974-81, 83-85; scholar-in-residence Western Wash. U., Bellingham, 1975-78; disting. vis. prof. Wesleyan U., 1979-83, adj. prof., 1983—, writer-in-residence, 1987—, bd. dirs. Writers Conf., 1984—, chmn., 1991—; Phi Beta Kappa orator Harvard-Radcliffe U., 1983; mem. U.S. writers del. UCLA US.-Chinese Writers Conf., 1982; mem. U.S. cultural del. to China, 1982; bd. dirs. The New Press; mem. usage panel Am. Heritage Dictionary; bd. dirs. Key West Writers Conf. Author: Tickets for a Prayer Wheel, 1974, Pilgrim at Tinker Creek, 1974 (Pulitzer prize for gen. non-fiction 1975), Holy the Firm, 1978, Living by Fiction, 1982, Teaching a Stone to Talk, 1982, Encounters with Chinese Writers, 1984, An American Childhood, 1987 (Nat. Book Critics award nomination 1987), The Writing Life, 1989 (English-speaking union Amb. Book award 1990), The Living, 1992, The Annie Dillard Reader, 1994, Mornings Like This, 1995; editor: (with Robert Atwan) Best Essays, 1988, (with Cort Conley) Modern American Memoirs, 1995. Mem. Nat. Com. on U.S.-China Rels., 1982—, Cath. Commn. Intellectual and Cultural Affairs; bd. dirs. Milton Ctr., Authors League Fund. Recipient N.Y. Presswomen's award for excellence, 1975, Wash. Gov.'s award for contbn. to lit., 1978, Appalachian Gold medallion U. Charleston, 1989, Found. award St. Botolph's Club, 1989, History Maker award Hist. Soc. Western Pa., 1993, Milton Ctr. prize, 1994, Campion award Am. Mag., 1994; grantee NEA, 1980-81, Guggenheim Found., 1985-86. Mem. NAACP, Soc. Am. Historians, Poetry Soc. Am., Authors Guild, Nat. Citizens for Pub. Librs., Century Assn., Phi Beta Kappa. Democrat. Address: care Timothy Seldes Russell & Volkening 50 W 29th St New York NY 10001-4227

DILLARD, LISA REICHERT, assistant superintendent; b. Ironton, Mo., Sept. 27, 1954; d. John Monroe and Darlene Elizabeth (Stirts) Reichert; m. David Warren Dillard, May 22, 1976. AA, Mineral Area Coll., 1975; BS in Elem. Edn., Southeast Mo. State U., 1977, MAT in Art, 1987, EdS, 1992. Cert. (life) elem. edn. tchr., art tchr., elem. prin. 6th grade tchr. South Iron RI, Annapolis, Mo., 1980-81; 2d grade tchr. Arcadia Valley R-2 Schs., Ironton, 1981-86, elem. art tchr., 1986-89, elem. prin., 1989-92, asst. supr., 1992-96, dir. spl. svcs. Mem. Mo. State Tchrs. Assn., Mineral Area Lase Assn., Phi Delta Kappa. Democrat. Roman Catholic. Office: Arcadia Valley R-2Sch Dist 750 Park Dr Ironton MO 63650

DILLARD, MARILYN DIANNE, property manager; b. Norfolk, Va., July 7, 1940; d. Thomas Ortman and Sally Ruth (Wallerich) D.; m. James Conner Coons, Nov. 6, 1965 (div. June 1988); 1 child, Adrienne Alexandra Dillard Coons (dec.). Studied with Russian prima ballerina, Alexandra Danilova, 1940's; student with honors at entrance, UCLA, 1958-59; BA in Bus. Adminstrn. with honors, U. Wash., 1962. Modeling-print work Harry Conover, N.Y.C., 1945; ballet instr. Ivan Novikoff Sch. Russian Ballet, 1955; model Elizabeth Leonard Agy., Seattle, 1955-68; mem. fashion bd., retail worker Frederick & Nelson, Seattle, 1962; retail worker I. Magnin & Co., Seattle, 1963-64; property mgr. Seattle, 1961—; antique and interior designer John J. Cunningham Antiques, Seattle, 1968-73; owner, interior designer Marilyn Dianne Dillard Interiors, 1973—; mem. rsch. bd. advisors Am. Biog. Inst., Inc., 1990—. Author: (poetry) Flutterby, 1951, Spring Flowers, 1951; contbr., asst. chmn. (with Jr. League of Seattle) Seattle Classic Cookbook, 1980-83. Charter mem., pres. Children's Med. Ctr., Maude Fox Guild, Seattle, 1965—, Jr. Women's Symphony Assn., 1967-73, Va. Mason Med. Ctr. Soc., 1990—, Nat. Mus. of the Am. Indian, Smithsonian Instn., Washington, 1992; mem. Seattle Jr. Club, 1962-65; bd. dirs. Patrons N.W. Civic, Cultural and Charitable Orgns. (chmn. various coms.), Seattle, 1976—, prodn. chmn., 1977-78, 84-85, auction party chmn., 1983-84, exec. com., 1984-85, chmn. bd. vols., 1990-91, adv. coun., 1991—; mem. U. Wash. Arboretum Found. Unit, 1966-73, pres., 1969; bd. dirs. Coun. for Prevention Child Abuse and Neglect, Seattle, 1974-75; mem. bd. dirs., v.p., mem. various coms. Seattle Children's Theatre, 1984-90, asst. in lighting main stage plays, 1987-93, mem. adv. coun., 1993—; asst. in lighting main stage plays Bathhouse Theatre, 1987-90; adv. bd. N.W. Asian Am. Theatre, 1987—, Co-Motion Dance Co., 1991—; organizer teen groups Episcopal Ch. of the Epiphany, 1965-67; provisional class pres. Jr. League Seattle, 1971-72, next to new shop asst. chmn., 1972-73, bd. dirs. admissions chmn., 1976-77, exec. v.p., exec. com., bd. dirs., 1978-79, sustaining mem., 1984—; charter mem. Jr. Women's Symphony Assn., 1967-73; mem. Seattle Art Mus., 1975-90, Landmark, 1990—, Corp. Coun. for the Arts, 1991—; founding dir. Adrienne Coons Meml. Fund, 1985, v.p., 1985-92, 95—, pres. 1992-95; mem. steering com. Heart Ball Am. Heart Assn., 1986, 87, auction chmn., 1986; mem. steering com. Bellevue Sch. Dist. Children's Theatre, 1983-85, pub. rels. chair, 1984, asst. stage mgr., 1985. Named Miss Greater Seattle, 1964. Mem. AFTRA, Am. Biographical Inst., U. Wash. Alumnae Assn. (life), Pacific N.W. Ballet Assn. (charter), Progressive Animal Welfare Soc., Associated Women (student coun. U. Wash. 1962), Profl. Rodeo Cowboys Assn. (assoc.), Seattle Tennis Club. Republican. Episcopalian. Home and Office: 2053 Minor Ave E Seattle WA 98102-3513

DILLARD, SUZANNE, interior designer; d. Jerome Wallace and Mary Mae (Price) Sorenson; m. Warren Marcus Dillard; 1 child, Jeremy Blake. Student, Tex. A&M U., 1961-64; BS, U. Tex., 1965; student, Pepperdine U., 1974, UCLA, 1977-78. Interior designer Pepperdine U., Malibu, Calif., 1982-95, exec. bd. dirs. Ctr. Arts, 1993-96; cons., interior design Neptune and Thomas, Architects, Pasadena, Calif., 1979-80; pres. Suzanne Dillard Interiors, Pacific Palisades, Calif., 1974—; prin. on camera designer TV pilot, Dream House, Forecast Group Prodns., 1983; speaker in field. Treas. Nat. Arts Assn., L.A., 1982-83, benefit chair, 1992; pres. Fine Arts aux., Assistance League So. Calif., L.A., 1984; patron, sponsor, prodn. chmn. The Footlighters, L.A., 1985-86, pres., 1992; pres. League for Children, 1991-93, Achievement Awards Coll. Scientists, 1994-96; benefit chair Freedoms Found., 1995. Mem. Delta Delta Delta (pres. L.A. chpt. 1970-72, pres. sleighbell 1993-94). Republican. Mem. Ch. of Christ. Home and Office: Suzanne Dillard Interiors 937 Chantilly Rd Los Angeles CA 90077-2615

DILLARD, TERESA MARY, school counselor; b. Columbus, Ga., May 12, 1956; d. Francis Joseph and Sadayo (Takabayashi) Luther; m. David Howard Dillard, July 22, 1978; children: Christine Marie, Justin David. BA, U. Md., 1977, MEd, 1981. Cert. guidance counselor, social studies tchr., modern fgn. lang. tchr., Mass., N.C. Asst. to supr. Bur. Govtl. Rsch., U. Md., College Park, 1977-78; tchr. high sch. Montgomery County Pub. Schs., Rockville, Md., 1978-80; substitute tchr. Anne Arundel Pub. Schs., Annapolis, Md., 1981, Bourne County Pub. Schs., Cape Cod, Mass., 1982-84; guidance counselor Camden County Pub. Schs., Camden, N.C., 1989-95; counselor, advisor U. Md. Relief Ctr., College Park, 1977, tutor Japanese lang., 1977, vol. substitute instr. Japanese lang. dept., 1977; cons. UCNC Radio Talk Show, Elizabeth City, N.C., 1991; program developer Grandy Primary Sch., Camden, N.C., 1989-95. Designer, creator children's clothing. Religious edn. tchr. Ft. Meade (Md.) Chapel Ctr., 1978, St. Bernadette Ch., Severn, Md., 1979-80; religious edn. tchr. Otis Chapel, Otis Air Nat. Guard Base, Mass., 1982-83, coord., dir. religious edn. program, 1983-84; bd. dirs., tchr. Holy Family Religious Edn. Program, Elizabeth City, N.C., 1989-91; asst. music ministry Holy Family Ch., Elizabeth City, 1991-95. Mem. ACA, Am. Sch. Counselors Assn., U. Md. Alumni Assn., Phi Beta Kappa, Phi Kappa Phi, Alpha Kappa Delta. Roman Catholic.

DILLASHAW, EULA CATHERINE, artist, graphic artist; b. Memphis, Feb. 19, 1947; d. John Clemons and Catheryn Livingston (Murdock) Ballew; m. Stanley Neil Williams, July 29, 1968 (div. Sept. 1982); children: John C., Eric N., Heather; m. William Alfred Dillashaw, Oct. 22, 1986. Student, Art Instrn. Sch., 1959-63, Memphis State U., 1965-66, Daytona Beach C.C., 1986-89. Exec. sec. Franklin Simon, N.Y.C., 1973-78, Benefit Providers for Local Unions, Memphis, 1979-82; tchr. Eula's Art Studio & Gallery, Lake Helen, 1993-95. One-person shows include Daytona Beach Airport, 1996; represented in pvt. collections Dr. Ravgvir Prabu, Bombay, Mr. Allen Turner, DeLand, Fla., Mrs. Tammy Askinazi, St. Louis, Mr. and Mrs. Ed Martin, DeLand, others. Supt. fine arts Volusia County Fair, Deland, 1995-96; pres. Lake Helen League of Artists & Crafters, 1994—. Mem. Lake Helen C. of C., Jaycees. Democrat. Home and Studio: 291 S Euclid Ave Lake Helen FL 32744

DILLBERGER-BEY, ROSE ALEXANDRA, artist; b. St. Louis, May 26, 1918; d. Louis Jerome and Katherine Elizabeth (Von Pozojevic) Mirjanich; m. Howard Bassford Bowen, May 24, 1946 (div. Jan. 1957); m. Hugo Dillberger, Jan. 30, 1958 (dec. 1983); 1 child, Alexandra Maria; m. Everett Edward Bey, Jan. 1, 1995. BFA, Washington U., St. Louis, 1941; postgrad., Pierce Coll., 1972-76, U. Calif., Northridge, 1986-87. Comml. artist Advertisers Artists, St. Louis, 1941-42; artist Wolf Printing Co., St. Louis, 1943-44, Gardner Advt. Co., St. Louis, 1944-46; advt. mgr. Kessler Fur Co., St. Louis, 1944; fine arts instr. Washington U., 1946-56; freelance artist, 1956—. One woman show at Sun Cities Art Mus., Sun City, Ariz., 1993; exhibited in group show at Sun City Art Mus., 1989. Art dir. Am. Women's Group, Teheran, Iran, 1976-79; treas. Advertising Artists, St. Louis, 1953-56. Mem. Ariz. Artists Guild, Vanguards (pres., treas.), Nat. Assn. Women in the Arts. Eastern Orthodox Catholic. Home and Studio: 10826 W Thunderbird Blvd Sun City AZ 85351-2646

DILLINGHAM, MARJORIE CARTER, foreign language educator; b. Bicknell, Ind., Aug. 20, 1915; m. William Pyrle Dillingham, (dec. 1981); children: William Pyrle (dec.), Robert Carter, Sharon Dillingham Martin. PhD in Spanish (Delta Kappa Gamma scholar and fellow), Fla. State U., 1970. High sch. tchr. Fla.; former instr. St. George's Sch., Havana; former mem. faculty Panama Canal Zone Coll., Fla. State U., Duke U., Univ. Ga.; dir. traveling Spanish conversation classes in Spain, Ctrl. and S. Am.; U.S. rep. (with husband) Hemispheric Conf. on Taxation, Rosario, Argentina. Named to Putnam County Hall of Fame, 1986. Mem. Am. Assn. Tchrs. Spanish and Portuguese (past pres. Fla. chpt.), Fla. Edn. Assn. (past pres. fgn. lang. div.), La Sociedad Honoraria Hispanica (past nat. pres.), Fgn. Lang. Tchrs. Leon County, Fla. (pres.), Delta Kappa Gamma (pres.), Phi Kappa Phi, Sigma Delta Pi (pres.), Beta Pi Theta, Kappa Delta Pi, Alpha Omicron Pi, Delta Kappa Gamma. Home: 2109 Trescott Dr Tallahassee FL 32312-3331

DILLMAN, KRISTIN WICKER, middle school educator, musician; b. Ft. Dodge, Iowa, Nov. 7, 1953; d. Winford Lee and Helen Caroline (Brown) Egli; m. Kirk Michael Wicker, Jan. 1, 1982 (dec. June 1982); m. David D. Dillman, Apr. 13, 1990; 1 child, Alek Joseph (adopted). AA, Iowa Cen. Coll., 1974; B in Music Edn., Morningside Coll., 1976; M in Mus., U. S.D., 1983. Cert. tchr., Iowa. Tchr. instrumental music Garrigan Affiliated Schs., Algona, Iowa, 1976-77, Sioux City (Iowa) Community Schs., 1977—. Asst. prin. bassist Sioux City Symphony, 1974-93, 95—, prin. bassist, 1993-95; freelance bassist Sioux City, 1976—. Named Tchr. of Yr. Sioux City Community Schs., 1988-89. Mem. NEA, Iowa Edn. Assn., Sioux city Edn. Assn., Iowa Bandmasters Assn., Sioux City Musicians Assn., Zeta Sigma, Mu Phi Epsilon. Republican. Lutheran. Office: Woodrow Wilson Mid Sch 1010 Iowa St Sioux City IA 51105-1711

DILLON, BARBARA LADENE, professional speaker, writer; b. Oklahoma City, Dec. 9, 1935; d. Leonard Paul and Ora Belle (Rogers) B.; m. Donald Dean Dillon, Mar. 21, 1954; children: Timothy Scott, Lisa Colleen. Student, Ctrl. State U., Edmond, Okla., 1960-64; B of Liberal Studies, U. Okla., 1977-79. Legis. lobbyist Okla. Tchrs. Wives, Oklahoma City, 1964-65; civil servant USAF, 1965, various office assignments, 1966-79; logistics officer Tinker AFB, Oklahoma City, 1979-81, prodn. mgmt. specialist, 1981-90, ret., 1990; Zig ziglar facilitator Tinker Mgmt. Assn., Tinker AFB, 1984-86; chair fund-raising E-3 divsn., Tinker AFB, 1988-90; guest lectr. Sch. Architecture U. Okla., 1993. Author: (with Donald Dean Dillon) Affirmations for a Successful Life (Or Things Your Momma Should Have Told You), 1995. Sponsor area K-3 Toastmasters Clubs, Tinker AFB, 1977-90; com. mem. constitution, deacon First Christian Ch., 1976; councilwoman City Coun. Edmond, Okla., 1969-73; bd. dirs. Hill Burton Hosp. Funds, Oklahoma City, 1973-74; trust fund mem. Edmond Utility Trust, 1972-73; deacon First Presbyn. Ch., Edmond, 1969-73. Tinker Mgmt. Assn. scholar, 1977, 78. Mem. Oklahoma City Profl. Spkrs. Toastmasters Club (pres. 1990), Look Who's Talking Toastmasters (mentor 1990, sec., treas. 1991-92), Sooner Toastmasters (sec., treas. 1991-92, Outstanding Toastmaster 1994), 3001 Toastmasters (pres., Outstanding Toastmaster 1984), Toastmasters Internat. Okla. (lt. gov. edn. and tng. 1991-92, adminstrv. lt. gov. 1990-91, gov. Dist. 16 1992-93, Disting. Dist. award 1993, Disting. Toastmaster 1984, Able Bronze and Silver award 1990, Outstanding Area Gov. Dist. 16), Tinker Mgmt. Club (4th v.p. 1984), Okla. Territorial Tellers, Oklahoma City Boomer Storytellers (pres. 1995-96, edn. v.p. 1994-95). Democrat. Southern Baptist. Homeand Office: 2308 Morgan Dr Norman OK 73069-6531

DILLON, DORIS (DORIS DILLON KENOFER), artist; b. Kansas City, Mo., Dec. 1, 1929; d. Joseph Patrick and Geraldine Elizabeth (Galligan) D.; m. Calvin Louis Kenofer, Aug. 25, 1950; children: Wendy Annette Kenofer Barnes, Bruce Patrick Kenofer. BA in Art, U. Denver, 1950, MA in Art History, 1965. Stewardess United Air Lines, 1950-51; founder, chmn. fine arts dept. Regis Coll., Denver, 1970-74; cons. Sarkisian's Oriental Imports, Denver, 1975-93; mus. curator Van Vechten-Lineberry Taos Art, Taos, N.Mex., 1995—; coord. Colo. Coun. on the Arts & Humanities, Denver, 1980, adv. panel, 1981; lectr. in field. One woman shows include Nelson Rockefeller Collection, N.Y.C., 1984, Amparo Gallery, Denver, 1985, Scottsdale, Veerhoff Gallery, Washington, 1986, Highland Gallery, Atlanta, 1988; exhibited in group shows including Cadme Gallery, Phila., 1987, Univ. Denver, 1970. Recipient 1st place drawing award 4 States Conf. Ctr., Colo., 1960. Mem. Soc. for the Arts, Religion and contemporary Culture, Fine Arts Guild (v.p. 1982), Asian Art Assn. (bd. dirs., treas. 1985), Mensa (scholarship juror 1993-94), Nat. Mus. for Women in the Arts (assoc.). Home and Office: Studio Gallery 561 Chapin Ln Estes Park CO 80517

DILLON, JEAN KATHERINE, executive secretary, small business owner; b. Birmingham, Ala., May 18, 1925; d. Andrew Crawford and Nell (Cook) Dillon; m. Roy Lerone Morris, June 12, 1946 (div. May 1969); children: Norma Jean, Elizabeth Annel. BA, Huntingdon Coll., 1950. Cert. tchr. secondary edn., Ala. Sec./bookkeeper H.T. Fitzpatrick CPA, Atty., Montgomery, Ala., 1948-50; sec., budget technician Dir. Budget, HQ Air Univ., Maxwell AFB, Ala., 1950-58; exec. sec., adminstrv. asst. Comptroller, HQ Air Univ., Maxwell AFB, Ala., 1958-86; adminstrv. asst. Family Violence Program, State Coalition, Montgomery, 1986; owner/operator The William Cook House, Nauvoo, Ala., 1989—. Pres. Nauvoo Hist. Soc., 1989—; sec., bd. dirs. Ala. Highland Games, Inc., Montgomery, 1992—, St. Andrew's Soc., Montgomery, 1995—; bd. dirs. Walker County Arts Coun., m1996. Mem. Huntingdon Coll. Alumni Assn. (life), C. of C. (sec.-treas., vice chair tourism task force), Capital City Rep. Women (treas. 1995—). Republican. Methodist. Home and Office: 929 Parkwood Dr Montgomery AL 36109

DILLON, PATRICIA ANNE, state legislator; b. Flushing, N.Y., July 9, 1948; d. Raymond Walter and Patricia Marie (Kuhlmann) D.; m. John Schley Hughes, July 5, 1977; 1 child, Patrick John. BA, Marymount U., 1970; MA, Ohio State U., 1974. Researcher Yale Sch. Medicine, New Haven, Conn., 1974-77; dir., founder New Haven Project Battered Women, 1977-80; devel. adminstr. City of Norwalk (Conn.), 1980-82; state legislator State of Conn., Hartford, 1984—; chmn. pub. health com. State of COnn., Hartford, 1990—; chmn. appropriations subcom. health and hosps. State of Conn., Hartford, 1992—, dep. majority leader, 1992—; adj. prof. Albertus Magnus Coll., New Haven, 1982-83; bd. dirs. Alcohol Svcs. Ctrl. Conn., New Haven, VA Hosp. Westhaven. Contbr. articles on family violence, health, taxation, solid waste and Irish issues to various publs. Ward chmn. Dem. Town Com., New Haven, 1976-86; alderwoman New Haven Bd. Alderman, 1979-85. Recipient Susan B. Anthony award Conn. NOW, 1987, Advocacy award Conn. Commn. Children, Hartford, 1991, Leadership award United Way Conn., Hartford, 1991. Mem. Nat. Acad. State Health Policy, Irish Am. Community Ctr. Roman Catholic. Home: 68 W Rock Ave New Haven CT 06515-2221 Office: Capitol Ave Hartford CT 06106*

DILLY, MARIAN JEANETTE, humanities educator; b. Vining, Minn., Nov. 7, 1921; d. John Fredolph and Mabel Josephine (Haagenson) Linder; m. Robert Lee Dily, June 22, 1946 (dec. Oct. 1987); children: Ronald Lee, Patricia Jeanette Dilly Vero. Grad., John R. Powers Finishing Sch., N.Y.C., 1957, Zell McC. Fashion Career Sch., Mpls., 1957, Estelle Compton Models Inst., Mpls., 1966, Nancy Taylor Charm Sch., N.Y.C., 1967, Patricia Stevens Career Sch., Mpls., 1968; BS in English cum laude, Black Hills State U., Spearfish, S.D., 1975. Instr. Nat. Coll., Rapid City, S.D., 1966-68; instr., dir. Nancy Taylor Charm Sch., 1966-68; hostess TV shows, 1966-74; lectr. in personality devel., dir., prodr. beauty and talent pageants, freelance coord. in fashion shows, judge beauty and talent pageants of local, state and nat. levels, 1966—. Actress bit parts Nauman Films Inc., 1970. Active ARC; dir., 1st v.p. Black Hills Girl Scout Coun., 1967-72; chmn. bd. dirs., pres. Luth. Social Svc. Aux., Western S.D. and Eastern Wyo., 1960-65; chmn. women's events Dakota Days and Nat. Premiere, 1968; bd. dirs. YMCA, 1976-81; mem. Dallas Symphony Orch. League, 1987-90, Dallas Mus. of Art League, 1987-90, Women's Club. Dallas County, Tex., Inc., 1987-90. Recipient award Rapid City C. of C., 1968, Fashion awards March of Dimes, 1967-72, Svc. award Black Hills Girl Scout Coun., award of appreciation Yellowstone Internat. Toastmistress Club. Mem. AAUW (sec., mem. exec.b d. 1988-90), Nu Tau Sigma (past advisor), Delta Tau Kappa, Singing Tribe of Wahoo. Home: 330 Agate St Broomfield CO 80020

DILUOFFO, SANTINA, chiropractor; b. Yonkers, N.Y., Aug. 29, 1958; d. Leone and Anna (Lanzara) DiL. BS in Biology, Mercy Coll., Dobbs Ferry, N.Y., 1980; D Chiropractic, N.Y. Chiropractic Coll., 1986. Pvt. practice Hempstead, N.Y., 1986—, Glen Cove, N.Y., 1988—; lectr. on chiropractic to pub. schs. and chs. Hempstead Police Dept., 1988—; promoter growing up drug free U.S. Dept. Edn., Washington, 1992—; apptd. to perform scoliosis screenings to Hempstead Pub. Schs.; Amway distbr. Active contbr. Father Flanagan's Boys' Home. Mem. MADD. Office: 33 Front St Hempstead NY 11550-3601

DIMAIO, VIRGINIA SUE, gallery owner; b. Houston, July 6, 1921; d. Jesse Lee and Gabriella Sue (Norris) Chambers; AB, U. Redlands, 1943; student U. So. Calif., 1943-45, Scripps Coll., 1943, Pomona Coll., 1945; m. James V. DiMaio, 1955 (div. 1968); children: Victoria, James V. Owner, dir. Galeria Capistrano, San Juan Capistrano and Santa Fe, N.Mex., 1979—; founder Mus. Women in Arts, Washington; cons., appraiser Southwestern and Am. Indian Handcrafts; lectr. Calif. State U., Long Beach; established ann. Helen Hardin Meml. scholarship for woman artist grad. Inst. Am. Indian Art, Santa Fe, also ann. Helen Hardin award for outstanding artist at Indian Market, S.W. Assn. on Indian Affairs, Santa Fe; bd. dirs. Mus. of Man, San Diego, 1989, Am. Diabetes Assn. Santa Fe, 1995; mem. Intertribal Coun. U. Calif., Irvine, 1990; founder Inst. Am. Indian Art, Santa Fe, 1993, bd. dirs., 1992—, chmn. devel. com., 1996; mem. task force San Juan Capistrano City, 1995; bd. dirs. Futures for Children, 1996. Author: (forward to Mus. of Man exhibit catalogue) Paths Beyond Tradition. Recipient Bronze Plaque Recognition award Navajo Tribal Mus., 1977. Mem. Indian Arts and Crafts Assn., S.W. Assn. Indian Affairs, Heard Mus., San Juan Capistrano C. of C. Republican. Roman Catholic. Office: PO Box 22868 Santa Fe NM 87502-2868

DIMANT, ROSE JEAROLMEN, personnel testing specialist, psychometrician; b. N.Y.C.; d. Bernard L. and Lillian (Herskowitz) Jearolmen; m. Jacob Dimant, Sept. 11, 1974; children: Kevin, Elliot. BA in Psychology magna cum laude, Bklyn. Coll., 1971; MA in Psychology, New Sch. for Social Rsch., N.Y.C., 1974; PhD in Psychology, CUNY, 1985. Rsch. assoc. CUNY Grad. Ctr. for Gerontological Studies, N.Y.C., 1978-80; from adj. lectr. to asst. prof. Kingsboro C.C., Bklyn., 1983-86; tests and measurement specialist N.Y.C. Dept. Personnel, 1985-88, adminstrv. tests and measurement specialist, 1988—; cons. The Rheumatology Ctr., Bklyn., 1980-83, Keenan Rsch. & Consulting, N.Y.C., 1984-85; bd. dirs. Crown Nursing Home Assocs., Inc., Bklyn., 1991—. Office: Dept Citywide Adminstrv Svcs Divsn Citywide Pers Svcs 2 Washington St New York NY 10004

DI MARCO, BARBARANNE YANUS, multiple handicapped special education educator; b. Jersey City, Nov. 16, 1946; d. Stanley Joseph and Anne Barbara (Dalack) Yanus; m. Charles Benjamin DiMarco, Mar. 15, 1986; 1 child, Charles Garrett. BA in Music Edn., Trenton State Coll., 1968; MA in Spl. Edn., Kean Coll., 1971, elem. edn. cert., 1974, adminstrv. cert., 1976. Cert. elem., music, adminstrn., spl. edn., N.J. Vocal music educator Roselle (N.J.) Bd. Edn., 1968-69, tchr. trainable mentally retarded, 1969-76, tchr. multiple handicapped, 1976—; color guard instr. Roselle Bd. Edn., 1973-88, elem. tutor, 1976-92, adminstrv. asst. to supt., 1980-85; program dir., sec., Expanded Dimensions in Gifted Edn., Westfield, N.J., 1978—. Vestryperson St. Luke's Ch., Roselle, 1989-91. Recipient Govs. Tchr. Recognition award, Gov. Florio, N.J., Trenton, 1992-93. Mem. NEA, N.J. Edn. Assn., Roselle Edn. Assn., N.J. Assn. for Retarded Children, Eastern Star (25-yr award 1991), Delta Omicron. Republican. Episcopalian. Home: 13 Gentore Ct Edison NJ 08820-1029 Office: Dr Charles C Polk Sch 1100 Warren St Roselle NJ 07203-2736

DI MARIA, VALERIE THERESA, public relations executive; b. Bronx, N.Y., Apr. 5, 1957; d. Victor Joseph and Vivian Roslyn (D'Amico) Di Maria. BA in Journalism, NYU, 1978. Asst. dir. U.S. Div. Sidonie S. Ltd., N.Y.C., 1978-79; acct. supr. The Rowland Co., N.Y.C., 1979-82, Ketchum Pub. Rels., N.Y.C., 1982-83; pub. rels. dir. Charles of the Ritz Group Ltd., N.Y.C., 1983-84; sr. v.p. Porter/Novelli Pub. Rels., N.Y.C., 1984-89; mng. dir. GCI Group, N.Y.C., 1989—, now pres., 1996. Mem. Pub. Rels. Soc. Am. (Silver Anvil award 1986), The Fashion Group, Am. Film Inst., Women Execs. in Pub. Rels. (bd. dirs.), Women in Comms., Advt. Women of N.Y., Women's Sports Found., Phi Beta Kappa. Office: GCI Group 777 3rd Ave New York NY 10017*

DI MARZO VERONESE, FULVIA, research scientist; b. Spilimbergo, Italy, Oct. 28, 1950; d. Annibale and Antonietta (Bertolini) Veronese; m. Marino di Marzo, June 11, 1986; children: Giulia Maria, Marina Antonia. Degree, Lyceum Sch., Milan, Italy, 1969; PhD in Pharmacology, U. Milan, 1976. Grad. rsch. asst. pharmacology inst. U. Milan, 1974-77, rsch. fellow tumor immunology lab., 1977-79, asst. prof. dept. pharmacology, 1981-83; vis. fellow lab. of cellular and molecular biology Nat. Cancer Inst., NIH, Bethesda, 1979-81; vis. fellow carcinogenesis mechanisms and control sect. Nat. Cancer Inst., NIH, Frederick, Md., 1981-82; cons. Litton Bionetics, Inc., Kensington, Md., 1983-85; sr. rsch. scientist, dept. cell biology Bionetics Rsch., Inc. (formerly Litton Bionetics, Inc.), Kensington, 1985-90; sr. rsch. scientist dept. cell biology Advanced BioSci. Labs. Inc. (formerly Bionetics Rsch. Inst.), Kensington, 1990-92; expert Lab. Tumor Cell Biology, Nat. Cancer Inst., NIH, Bethesda, 1992-96; health scientist advisor Strotoz, OAR, OD, 1996—. Contbr. articles to profl. jours.; patentee in field. Mem. AAAS. Home: 8405 Burdette Rd Bethesda MD 20817-2816 Office: NIH Office of AIDS Rsch (OAR) Bldg 31 Rm 4C06 Bethesda MD 20892

DIMASI, LINDA GRACE, epidemiologist; b. Trenton, N.J., Feb. 7, 1949; d. Nick and Pearl LaVerne (White) D. BS in Biology, Alderson-Broaddus Coll., 1970; MPA, Rutgers U., 1992. Cert. pub. mgr. Field rep. N.J. State Dept. of Health, Trenton, 1971-85, epidemiologist, 1985—. Contbr. articles to profl. jours. Mem. ASPA, APHA, Phi Alpha Alpha. Home: 35 Jennifer Ln Burlington NJ 08016-1144 Office: NJ State Dept of Health Divsn AIDS Prevention and Control CN 363 Trenton NJ 08625-0363

DIMINO, SYLVIA THERESA, elementary and secondary educator; b. N.Y.C., June 6, 1955; d. John Anthony and Elena (Berardesca) D. BA, St. John's U., 1977; MPA, NYU, 1980, MA in Elem. and Secondary Edn., 1982, cert. advance studies in ednl. adminstrn., 1986, cert. in advanced studies in mgmt., 1992; MA in Tchg. ESL, Adelphi U., 1984. Cert. elem. and secondary tchr., sch. adminstr., in mgmt. practices, social studies, math., N.Y. Traffic coord. Creamer Inc., N.Y.C., 1977-79; tchr. St. Patrick's Sch., N.Y.C., 1979-82; tchr. IS 131, Manhattan, N.Y.C., 1984-90, adminstr., coord., 1985-90, asst. prin., 1990—; 1985-90; tchr. h.s. ESL N.Y.C. Bd. Edn., 1995—. Named to 2000 Most Notable Women. Mem. NAFE, AAUW, Nat. Orgn. Women in Adminstrn., Bus. Cir. N.Y., Nat. Coun. Adminstrv. Women in Edn., Nat. Orgn. Italian-Am. Women (mentoring dir.). Roman Catholic. Office: John Bowne HS 63-25 Main St New York NY 11367

DIMM, SUSAN TYNER, artist, educator; b. Orange, N.J., Nov. 7, 1960; d. Wayne Foreman and Margaret Mitchell (Browne) D.; m. Michael Edward Fry, Sept. 9, 1995. AA, Simon's Rock Coll., 1980; student, Alfred U., 1982; BA, Bennington Coll., 1984. Student tchr. Early Learning Ctr., Stamford, Conn., 1981; asst. tchr. Cambridge Sch. Weston, Mass., 1993; tchr. Eng. Art Edn. Biennial Conf., Hyannis, Mass., 1993, Creative Arts Ctr., Chatham, Mass., 1992—, Truro (Mass.) Adult Edn., 1995—, Truro Elem. Sch., 1995—, Monomoy Youth Svcs., Chatham, 1996—; Pres. Cape Cod Potters, Chatham, 1995-96, sec., 1996—, v.p., 1994-95; bd. dirs. Creative Arts Ctr., Chatham. Mem. Nat. Coun. Edn. Ceramic Arts, Am. Craft Coun., Falmouth Artists Guild, Truro Ctr. Arts. Home: 46 Barn Hill Rd West Chatham MA 02669 Office: Cape House Pottery PO Box 238 West Chatham MA 02669

DIMMICK, CAROLYN REABER, federal judge; b. Seattle, Oct. 24, 1929; d. Maurice C. and Margaret T. (Taylor) Reaber; m. Cyrus Allen Dimmick, Sept. 10, 1955; children: Taylor, Dana. BA, U. Wash., 1951, JD, 1963; LLD, Gonzaga U., 1982, CUNY, 1987. Bar: Wash. Asst. atty. gen. State of Wash., Seattle, 1953-55; pros. atty. King County, Wash., 1955-59, 60-62; sole practice Seattle, 1959-60, 62-65; judge N.E. Dist. Ct. Wash., 1965-75, King County Superior Ct., 1976-80; justice Wash. Supreme Ct., 1981-85; judge U.S. Dist. Ct. (we. dist.) Wash., Seattle, 1985-94, chief judge, 1994—; chmn. Jud. Resources Com., 1991-95, active, 1987-95. Recipient Matrix Table award, 1981, World Plan Execs. Council award, 1981, others. Mem. ABA, Am. Judges Assn. (gov.), Nat. Assn. Women Judges, World Assn. Judges, Wash. Bar Assn., Am. Judicature Soc., Order of Coif (Wash. chpt.), Wash. Athletic Club, Wingpoint Golf and Country Club, Harbor Club. Office: US Dist Ct 911 US Courthouse 1010 5th Ave Seattle WA 98104-1130

DIMMITT, CORNELIA, psychologist, educator; b. Boston, Mar. 16, 1938; d. Harrison and Martha Fredericka (Read) D.; m. (div.); children: Colin Barclay Church, Jeffrey Harrison Church. BA, Harvard U., 1958; MA, Columbia U., 1966; PhD, Syracuse U., 1970; diplomate, C. G. Jung Inst., Zurich, Switzerland, 1985. Asst. prof. Am. U., Washington, 1970-71; from asst. to assoc. prof. (with tenure) Georgetown U., Washington, 1971-82; pvt. practice Boston, 1985—; Mem. admissions com. Coll. Arts and Scis., Georgetown U., Washington, 1974-76, mem. rank and tenure com., 1977-78; dir. admissions com. C. G. Jung Inst., Boston, 1986-89, pres. tng. bd., 1989-91; pres. NESJA, 1993—. Author: Classical Hindu Mythology, 1978. NEH fellow, 1979-80. Mem. Am. Oriental Soc., New England Soc. Jungian Analysts, Assn. Grads. in Analytical Psychology (Switzerland), Internat. Assn. for Analytical Psychology. Home and Office: 4 Otis Pl Boston MA 02108-1036

DI MUCCIO, MARY JO, retired librarian; b. Hanford, Calif., June 16, 1930; d. Vincent and Theresa (Yovino) DiMuccio. B.A., Immaculate Heart Coll., 1953, M.A., 1960; Ph.D., U.S. Internat. U., 1970. Tchr. parochial schs. Los Angeles, 1949-54, San Francisco, 1954-58; tchr. Govt. of Can., Victoria, B.C., 1959-60; asst. librarian Immaculate Heart Coll. Library, Los Angeles, 1960-62; head librarian Immaculate Heart Coll. Library, 1962-72; adminstrv. librarian City of Sunnyvale, Calif., 1972-88; ret., 1988; part-time instr. Foothill C.C., 1977-95. Exec. bd., past pres. Sunnyvale Community Services. Mem. ALA, ICF (past pres.), Spl. Libr. Assn., Cath. Libr. Assn. (past pres.), Calif. Libr. Assn., Sunnyvale Bus. and Profl. Women, Peninsula Dist. Bus. and Profl. Women (pres.). Home: 736 Muir Dr Mountain View CA 94041-2509

DINEEN, MADALYN HILLIS, marketing professional, astrologer, writer; b. Bklyn., June 23, 1951; d. Arthur and Agatha (Bartoletti) Botterio; m. Daniel Patrick Hillis, Sept. 6, 1971 (div. Aug. 1984); children: Mark Christopher, Katharine Zoe; m. Douglas W. Dineen, Sept. 29, 1996. BS, St. John's U., 1972. Fin. analyst Nat. Bank N.Am., N.Y.C., 1972-75; asst. dir. N.Y. State Chiropractic Assn., N.Y.C., 1975-77; vol. Nat. Coun. for Geocosmic Rsch., Ramsey, N.J., 1979-90, exec. dir., 1990-94; mktg. dir. Astrolabe, Inc., Brewster, Mass., 1994—; cons. Astrascope Corp., Melrose, Mass., 1991-93; cons., mgr. astrology product Malhotra and Assocs., Cranbury, N.J., 1992-93. Editor Urania, 1986-87; author, editor Nat. Coun. for Geocosmic Rsch. Memberletter, 1986-94; author Nat. Coun. for Geocosmic Rsch. Jour., 1991; monthly columnist Horoscope Guide, 1991-92. Pres. Village Sch. Parent Guild, Ridgewood, N.J., 1987-89; troop leader Girl Scouts U.S., 1991-94; dir. yearbook Ramsey Jr. Football Assn., 1991-93. Recipient Regulus award for cmty. svc. United Astrology Congress, 1995. Mem. Astrological Soc. Princeton, Assn. for Astrological Networking, Internat. Soc. Asrological Rsch., Nat. Coun. Geocosmic Rsch., B.P.W. Lower Cape Cod. Office: Astrolabe Inc P O Box 1750 Brewster MA 02631

DINGLE, MARGARET CONCETTA SPARGO, retired elementary reading director; b. New Haven, Conn., Apr. 2, 1918; d. Frank Curtlin and Clara (Eck) Spargo; m. Frederick Marvin Dingle, Sr., Aug. 23, 1941; children: Patricia, Frederick Jr., Marcia, Louise. EdB, New Haven State Tchr's. Coll., 1940; MS, So. Conn. State U., 1964. Elem. tchr. Clinton (Conn.) Grammar Sch., 1940-41, Ridge Rd. Sch., North Haven, Conn., 1949-50, Prince St. Sch., New Haven, 1950-55, Alice Peck Sch., Hamden, Conn., 1956-69; reading cons. elem. schs., Hamden, 1969-73; dir. reading grades kindergarten-12 Hamden, 1973-82. Author: (curriculum guide) Individualized Reading Program, 1975-80; contbr. Instructor mag., 1971. Literacy vol. and vol. tutor in cmty. Recipient Recognition of Svc. Plaque Internat. Reading Assn., 1972; federal grantee, 1976-79. Mem. Conn. Assn. Reading Rsch. (rsch. chairperson), Ret. Tchrs. Conn., Nutmeg Reading Coun. (charter mem., 1st pres.), Assoc. Reading Coun. Conn., Internat. Reading Assn., Delta Kappa Soc. Internat., Phi Delta Kappa. Republican. Mem. Congregational Ch. Home: Mill Pond Ln Apt 25A Durham CT 06422

DINGWERTH, JOAN H., religious organization administrator; b. Dallas, Apr. 7, 1933; d. Alfred August Holmberg and Reba Lilian Wells; m. Frank Sherrod Dingwerth, Aug. 14, 1954; children: Sherry Brown Dingwerth Kent, Susan Donnelly Dingwerth Paul, Carol Zipfel Dingwerth Mike, Cathy Sultze Dingwerth Stuart. BA, So. Meth. U., 1954; MA, Dallas Theol. Sem., 1986. Lic. bibl. counselor; cert. Christian counselor. Bd. dirs. Pioneer Ministries, Wheaton, Ill., 1980-85; camp dir. Piney Woods Camp Cherith, Athens, Tex., 1980-85; founding bd. mem., sec./treas. The Shepherd's Staff, Inc., Rexford, Kans., 1986—; with Shepherd of Womens Ministries divsn. Park Springs Bible Ch., Arlington, Tex., 1986-88, bibl. counselor, 1986—; guest instr. Tex. Sunday Sch. Convs., Arlington, 1984, Okla. Sunday Sch. Conv., Oklahoma City, 1984, Christian Camping Internat. Conv., French Lick, Ind., 1985, Dallas Theol. Sem., 1989-94. Contbr. articles to profl. jours. Pres. Arlington Meml. Hosp. Aux., 1960; v.p. Tex. Assn. Hosp. Auxs., 1962. Mem. Am. Assn. Christian Counselors, Christian Mgmt. Assn., Christian Camping Internat. Republican. Home: 14 Twin Springs Dr Arlington TX 76016

DINKINS, CAROL EGGERT, lawyer; b. Corpus Christi, Tex., Nov. 9, 1945; d. Edgar H. Jr. and Evelyn S. (Scheel) Eggert; children: Anne, Amy. BS, U. Tex., 1968; JD, U. Houston, 1971. Bar: Tex. 1971. Prin. assoc. Tex. Law Inst. Coastal and Marine Resources, Coll. Law U. Houston, Tex., 1971-73; assoc., ptnr. Vinson & Elkins, Houston, 1973-81, 83-84, 85—, mem. mgmt. com., 1991—; asst. atty. gen. environ. and natural resources Dept. Justice, 1981-83, U.S. dep. atty. gen., 1984-85; chmn. Pres.'s Task Force on Legal Equity for Women, 1981-83; mem. Hawaiian Native Study Commn., 1981-83; dir. Nat. Consumer Coop. Banks Bd., 1981. Author articles in field. Chmn. Tex. Gov.'s Flood Control Action Group, 1980-81; bd. dirs. The Nature Conservancy, 1996—, Orynx Energy Co., 1990-95, U. Houston Law Ctr. Found., 1985-89, 96—, Environ. and Energy Study Inst., 1986—, Houston Mus. Natural Sci.l, 1986—, Tex. Nature Conservancy, 1985—, chair, 1996—. Mem. ABA (ho. of dels., past chmn. state and local govt. sect., chair-elect sect. nat. resources, energy, and environ. law 1995-96), Fed. Bar Assn. (bd. dirs. Houston chpt. 1986), State Bar Tex., Houston Bar Assn., Tex. Water Conservation Assn., Houston Law Rev. Assn. (bd. dirs. 1978). Republican. Lutheran. Office: Vinson & Elkins 3300 First City Tower 1001 Fannin St Houston TX 77002

DINKLE, R. LYNN TUCKER, primary school educator; b. Reidsville, N.C., Dec. 21, 1958; d. Clifton Green and Rebecca Louise (Tudor) Tucker; m. Ronnie Lee Dinkle, June 13, 1993. BMus, U. N.C., Greensboro, 1981; MA in Spl. Edn., Appalachian State U., 1988. Cert. elem. and secondary tchr., N.C. Sales person Brodt Music Co., Charlotte, N.C., 1981-83; substitute tchr., tchr. asst. Rockingham County Sch. Dist., Madison, N.C., 1984-85; tchr. spl. edn. Ennichment Ct. Sch. Dist., Madison, 1985-86, Stokes County Sch. Dist., Danbury, N.C., 1986-87, Carroll County Sch. Dist., Hillsville, Va., 1987-88, Rockingham County Sch. Dist., Reidsville and Eden, N.C., 1988-94; tchr. kindermusik and musikgarden programs Danville, Va., 1994—. Recipient Vol. awards ARC, Madion-Mayodan Recreation Dept. Mem. Assn. for Retarded Citizens (ARC Tchr. of Yr. award), Coun. for Exceptional Children (pres.), Kindermusik Educators Assn., Early Childhood Music Assn. Home: 106 Lexington Ave Danville VA 24540-4917

DINOVI, DENISE, producer. Journalist, reporter, film critic Toronto, Can.; unit publicist, 1980; co-producer, assoc. producer, prodn. exec. Montreal's Film Plan; exec. v.p. prodn. New World Cinema; head Tim Burton Prodns., 1989-92. Movie prodns. include: Heathers, Edward Scissorhands, Meet the Applegates, Batman Returns, The Nightmare Before Christmas, Cabin Boy, Ed Wood. *

DINOWITZ, DEBRA, lawyer; b. Bklyn., Oct. 16, 1955; d. Sidney A. and Gloria (Spring) D. BA in Art History magna cum laude, Hofstra U., 1976, JD with distinction, 1979. Bar: U.S. Dist. Ct. (so. dist.) N.Y. 1980. Assoc. Cahill, Gordon & Reindel, N.Y.C., 1979-82, Colton, Weissberg et al, N.Y.C., 1982-83; v.p., gen. counsel Chemical Bank (formerly Mfrs. Hanover Corp.), N.Y.C., 1983—; vis. prof. Hofstra U. Sch. Law, Hempstead, N.Y., 1983. Mem. ABA, Phi Beta Kappa. *

DINSMORE, CLAIRE ALLAN, artist; b. Princeton, N.J., Oct. 16, 1961; d. Robert Braddock D. and Caroline Veronica (Luttman) Clancy. BFA, Parsons Sch. Design, 1985; MFA, Cranbrook Acad. Art, 1993. Artist-in-residence Am. Craft Mus., N.Y.C., 1984; asst. prof. Parsons Sch. Design, N.Y.C., 1986; founder, prin. Studio Cleo, Inc., Princeton, N.J., 1987—, Studio Cleo, N.Y.C., 1987—; prof. The New Sch. Social Rsch., N.Y.C., 1989-90; juror Cranbrook Acad. Art Mus., Bloomfield Hills, Mich., 1992-93; reviewer, critic Metalsmith Mag., Tampa, Fla., 1991—. Empire State Crafts Alliance grantee, Saratoga Springs, N.Y., 1988; Cranbrook Acad. Art scholar, 1992; recipient Merit award for Outstanding Achievement Parsons Sch. Design, N.Y.C., 1982-85. Mem. Am. Craft Coun., Soc. N.Am. Goldsmiths. Home and office: 5 Lincoln Ct Princeton NJ 08542-6908

DIOURI, MAGIDA, artist; b. Brussels, Aug. 10, 1966; came to U.S., 1989; d. Abdelouahhab dit Claude Diouri and Andréa Victorine Heerman. BA in Art, U. Ky., 1995. Freelance sign artist Lexington, Ky., 1991—. Sculptor, painter. Home and Office: 560 E High St #2 Lexington KY 40502

DIPAOLA, LUCY, education educator; b. N.Y.C., Nov. 27, 1949; d. Delfo and Francesca DiPaola. BA, S.I. Coll., 1971; MS in Edn., Fordham U., 1975, PhD, 1990. Cert. social studies tchr., sch. adminstr., supr., N.Y. Jr. H.S. tchr. St. Joseph Sch., N.Y.C., 1972-77; asst. prin., tchr. St. Joseph Sch., Millbrook, N.Y., 1980-82; curriculum coord. Happy House Presch. Ctr., Hopewell Junction, N.Y., 1977-80; prin. St. John the Evangelist Sch., Beacon, n.Y., 1982-86; prof. edn. Mt. St. Mary Coll., Newburgh, N.Y., 1986—, chair divsn. edn., 1989-95, coord. grad. edn., 1990—; dir. staff devel. Emergency Dept. Cons., Inc., Newburgh, 1992—; pres., dir. Profl. Devel. Cons., Chester, N.Y., 1995—; profl. cons. Orange/Dutchess/Sullivan County Sch. Dists., Mid Hudson Valley, N.Y., 1989—; cons. for health care facilities. Bd. dirs. Newburgh City Schs. Tchr. Ctr., 1989—; trustee Cheshire Acad., 1992—; adv. bd. Beacon Sch. Dist. Recipient Outstanding Contbn. to Emergency Medicine award Horton Med. Ctr., 1990, Spl. Contbn. to Team Devel. award Horton Med. Ctr., 1993, Spl. Recognition for Cmty. Svc. award, 1993. Mem. N.Y. State Assn. Colls. for Tchr. Edn. (bd. dirs. 1995—), Delta Kappa Gamma (pres. 1996—), Kappa Delta Pi (counselor). Home: 209 B Prospect Rd Chester NY 10918 Office: Mt St Mary Coll 330 Powell Ave Newburgh NY 12550

DIPASQUA, LUCY ANN, restaurant franchise executive; b. Norwalk, Conn., Feb. 12, 1927; d. Dominick Felix and Eva Renzulli Nardi; m. Peter M. Dipasqua, Oct. 4, 1947; (div. 1986); children: Gayle, Michael, Donna, Curtis, Lynn, Peter Jr. Sec. HCA, Norwalk, 1945--; sec., treas. Lucy Dipasqua, Inc., Maitland, Fla., 1977-86; pres. Dipasqua Enterprises, Maitland, 1986—; v.p. The Teaste of Ctrl. Fla.'s Best; pres. Perkit's Devel. Co. of Ctrl. Fla.; bd. dirs. ITT Tech. Inst., Mid Fla. Tech., Webber Coll. Mem. Franchise Advt. Fund (bd. dirs. 1981—, recipient Plaque), Fla. Restaurant Assn. (bd. dirs. 1986—, chmn. edn. com. 1989, sec. Chpt. 4, 1989, pres. elect 1990, pres. 1991, pres. elect 1992, pres. 1993—, chmn. 1994). Roman Catholic. Home: 411 Melanie Way Maitland FL 32751-3136 Office: Dipasqua Enterprises Inc 167 Lookout Pl Maitland FL 32751-4494

DIPERSIO, CATHERINE A., counselor, psychology educator, psychotherapist; b. Northampton, Mass., July 31, 1952; d. Francis G. and Emily R. (Hanley) Ciarfella; m. Richard D. DiPersio, June 30, 1974 (div.); children: Richard Jr., Edward, Mary Catherine. BS in Elem. Edn., U. Conn., 1974; MS in Counseling, So. Conn. State U., 1988; postmaster's sch. counseling cert., Cen. Conn. State U., 1992. Cert. K-12 counselor; cert. K-8 tchr., Conn. 1st grade tchr. Granby (Conn.) Pub. Schs., 1974-75; pvt. psychotherapist Meriden, Conn., 1988—; dir. counseling Paier Coll. Art, Hamden, Conn., 1988-90, 91—; h.s. counselor Sacred Heart H.S., Waterbury, Conn., 1990-91; personal devel. counselor U. Conn., Waterbury, 1991—; psychology instr. Paier Coll. Art, 1993—. Scout leader Cub Scouts Am., Meriden, 1984-86, Girl Scouts Am., 1986-87; hospitality chairperson PTA, Meriden, 1984-85; vol. Rep. Party, Meriden, 1988. Mem. NAFE, ACA, Am. Sch. Counseling Assn., Am. Assn. Christian Counselors, CT Ahead, Phi Kappa Phi. Roman Catholic. Home: 15 Spring Glen Dr Meriden CT 06451 Office: Paier Coll Art 20 Gorham Ave Hamden CT 06514

DIPIRRO, JONI MARIE, artist; b. Clarion, Pa., Jan. 7, 1940; d. Edmund Paul and Laura Geneva (Nietsche) DiP.; children: Paul Edmund Herman, Joni Maria Herman. Student, Acad. of Florence, Italy, 1969-71, U. Buffalo, 1977-78; studied with, Pietro Annigone, Florence, 1969-72. Dir. Sisti Gallery, Buffalo, 1974-76; curator Castellani Art Mus., Lewiston, N.Y., 1979-96. Restored statue at Niagara U., 1975; painted mural at House of Chauncey Stillman, 1979; represented in permanent collection at Castellani Mus., 1978. Mem. Amherst Soc. Artists, Kenmore Soc. Artists, Societa Delle Belle Arti, Casa ci Dante Florence. Home and Studio: 31 College St Buffalo NY 14201

DIPPO, JEANETTE FAYE, school health educator, nurse; b. Miami, Fla., Sept. 15, 1943; d. Llewellyn and Marie Elizabeth (Wanser) Potter; m. Walter Allen Dippo, June 27, 1964; children: Julie Lynn, Kimberly Michelle. RN, St Luke's Hosp., Newburgh, N.Y., 1964; BS in Health Edn., SUNY, Cortland, 1967, MS in Health Edn., 1969. Cert. tchr., N.Y. RN Cortland Meml. Hosp., 1964-66; health educator Cortland City Schs., 1966-73; health and drug edn. coord. Cortland-Madison Bd. Coop. Ednl. Svcs., 1973-75; health edn. and wellness coord. Cortland City Schs., 1975—; workshop conf. presenter various drug and health edn. confs., 1974—; cons., turnkey trainer N.Y. State Dept. Edn., Albany, 1968—; coop. master tchr. SUNY, Cortland, 1968—, Ithaca (N.Y.) Coll., 1968—; mentor tchr. Corland Jr./Sr. H.S., 1989-94; freedom from smoking clinic coord. Am. Lung Assn., Cortland, 1990-94; cons. feature TV segment on family dynamics course CBS 30 Minutes, 1978-79; grant co-dir. Healthy Me Project Met. Life Found., SUNY, Cortland, 1988-89. Editor: (newsletter) Health Instrnl. Resource Ctr., 1973-75; mem. editl. bd. Catalyst, 1979-81. Sun. sch. and confirmation tchr. First United Meth. Ch., Cortland, 1986—; original founder's com., mem. Seven Valleys Coun. on Alcohol and Substance Abuse, Cortland, 1987—; mem. Tri-County Tobacco Prevention Coalition, Tompkins, Cortland and Cayuga Counties, 1993—. Recipient commendation award Cortland County Legislature, 1989, Head Start Vol. award, 1995; Project Empathy grantee Zero Adolescent Pregnancy (ZAP), 1992; grantee Project Think It Over, 1995. Mem. NEA, Am. Sch. Health Assn., Cortland United Tchrs., N.Y. State United Tchrs., N.Y. State Fedn. Profl. Health Educators (life, regional chmn. 1974-75, pres. 1976, outstanding sch. health educator 1979, past pres. award 1990), Delta Kappa Gamma (internat. Beta chpt. 1991—). Republican. Methodist. Home: RR 1 2444 Ridge Rd Mc Graw NY 13101-9801 Office: Cortland City Schs 8 Valley View Dr Cortland NY 13045-3296

DI PRIMA, DIANE, writer; b. Bklyn., 1934; d. Francis Richard and Emma Sylvia (Mallozzi) Di P.; m. Alan Marlowe (div. 1969); m. Grant Fisher (div. 1975); children: Jeanne, Dominique, Alexander, Tara, Rudi. lectr. and reader in field. Author: This Kind of Bird Flies Backward, 1958, Dinners and Nightmares, 1961, The New Handbook of Heaven, 1962, The Man Condemned to Death, 1963, Poets' Vaudeville, 1964, Seven Love Poems from the Middle Latin, 1965, Haiku, 1966, New Mexico Poem, 1967, Earthsong, 1968, Hotel Albert, 1968, Memoirs of a Beatnik, 1969, L.A. Odyssey, 1969, The Book of Hours, 1970, Kerhonkson Journal, 1971, Revolutionary Letters, 1971, The Calculus of Variation, 1972, Loba, Part I, 1973, Freddie Poems, 1974, Selected poems 1956-1975, 1975, Loba, Part II, 1976, The Loba as Eve, 1977, Loba: Parts I-VIII, 1978, Wyoming Series, 1988, The Mysteries of Vision, 1988, Pieces of a Song, 1990, Seminary Poems, 1991, The Mask is the Path of the Star, 1993; editor: Various Fables from Various Places, 1960, War Poems, 1968, The Floating Bear, 1973; contbr. poems to over 300 mags. and newspapers. NEA grantee, 1966, 73, Lapis Found. grantee, 1978, 79, others; recipient Lifetime Achievement award Nat. Poetry Assn., 1993. Office: 584 Castro St 346 San Francisco CA 94114

DIRGO, MARGARET ROSE, accounting manager; b. Bridgeport, Conn., May 25, 1935; d. John Wasko and Margaret Emma Ritz; m. Edward John Dirgo, Jan. 19, 1957; children: Dawn Marie, Patricia Ann, Edward Robert, Margaret Mae, John Steven, Richard Michael. Student, Felt and Tarrart, Bridgeport, Conn., 1953. Std. cost clk. C Casco Products Corp., Bridgeport, 1954, std. cost clk. B, 1955-57; payroll clk. Carpenter Steel, Bridgeport, 1958-59; std. cost clk. A Casco Products Corp., Bridgeport, 1971-73, jr. std. cost acct., 1973-76, sr. std. cost acct., 1976-81, supr. cost acctg. and timekeeping, 1981-86, mgr. cost acctg. and timekeeping, 1986—. Recipient certs. Ask Man/Man H.P., 1985, 86, 87, Women Mgrs., 1987, Cert. of Achievement Avoiding Sexual Harrassment, 1996. Mem. Inst. Mgmt. Accts., Soc. Mfg. Engrs. (chpt. sec. 1992-94), Nat. Wildlife Fedn., Father Flaggens Boys Town. Office: Casco Products Corp 380 Horace St Bridgeport CT 06610-0241

DIRIENZO, MARGARET HELEN, nursing administrator; b. Tampa, Fla., May 17, 1962; d. Raymond Thomas and Helen Irene (Fortier) Connors; m. James Basilio Dirienzo, Sept. 21, 1984; children: James, Kaitlyn. AAS, Pace U., 1982, BSN, 1985. Cert. emergency nurse; ACLS, PALS; RN, Pa. From staff nurse to asst. mgr. emergency dept. Danbury (Conn.) Hosp., 1982-92; patient care mgr. asst. ER Geisinger Med. Ctr., Danville, Pa., 1992-94; triage supervisor Geisinger's Tel-A-Nurse Svc., Danville, 1994—; acting trauma coord. Danbury Hosp., 1991-92. Mem. Emergency Nurses Assn. Democrat. Roman Catholic. Home: 133 Mountain View Rd Lewisburg PA 17837 Office: Geisinger Tel-A-Nurse Svc Academy Dr Danville PA 17822-1518

DIRMEIER, GEORGIA GIDDINGS, school nurse; b. Dallas, Aug. 4, 1950; d. James Potter and georgia Audrey (Marsh) Giddings; m. Michael Dennis Dirmeier, Dec. 29, 1971; children: Lisa Marie, Kristen Elizabeth. BSN, Tex. Woman's U., 1972. RN, N.Y.; cert. sch. nurse. Staff nurse U. Chgo. Hosp. and Clinics, 1972-73, Providence Hosp., Southfield, Mich., 1974-75; nursing supr. Family Practice Ctr. of Providence Hosp., Southfield, Mich., 1975-76; head nurse Outpatient Dept. Mountainside Hosp., Montclair, N.J., 1976-80; clin. instr. BOCES, Yorktown Heights, N.Y., 1983-86; camp nurse, asst. camp dir. Westchester/Putnam coun. Girl Scouts U.S.A., Pleasantville, N.Y., 1990-93; sch. nurse Somers (N.Y.) Ctrl. Sch. Dist., 1991—; pediatric staff nurse Mt. Kisco (N.Y.) Med. Group, 1990—; instr. ARC, White Plains, N.Y., 1990—; instr. coord. first aid for coaches program Somers (N.Y.) Ctrl. Sch. Dist., 1994—; quartermaster Somers H.S. Marching Band Parents Assn., 1993—. Sunday Sch. tchr., Mt. Kisco, N.Y., 1980-86; choir mem., Chappaqua, N.Y., 1990-94; vestry, Chappaqua, N.Y., 1992-93, St. Mary's Ch. Mem. Nat. Assn. Sch. Nurses, N.Y. State Assn. Sch. Nurses. Episcopalian. Home: 135 Pines Bridge Rd Katonah NY 10536 Office: Somers Middle School Rt 202 Somers NY 10589

DISBROW, LYNN MARIE, communication educator; b. Chgo., Sept. 2, 1961; d. Ervin John and Patricia Ann (Grabarek) Lodyga; m. Michael Ray Disbrow, July 14, 1984; children: Matthew Ray, Nicole Marie. BA, Ind. U., South Bend, 1982; MA with distinction, Emerson Coll., Boston, 1986; PhD, Wayne State U., Detroit, 1989. High sch. program mgr. Jr. Achievement of Michiana, Inc., South Bend, 1982-84; account exec. AM The WNDU Stas., South Bend, 1984; instr. Emerson Coll., Boston, 1985-86; instr. Wayne State U., Detroit, 1986-87, grad. teaching asst., 1987; lectr. Ind. U., South Bend, 1988; lectr. I Sinclair C.C., Dayton, Ohio, 1989-90, asst. prof., 1993—; asst. prof. comm. U. Dayton, 1990-92. Author conv. papers Mass. Comm. Assn., 1985, Speech Comm. Assn., 1986-91, 94, 96, Ctrl. State Comm. Assn., 1989, 91-92, 94-96, others; mem. editl. bd. Ohio Speech Jour., 1993, N.D. Jour. Speech and Theatre, 1992. Rumble fellow, 1986-87. Mem. Speech Comm. Assn., Ctrl. States Comm. Assn., Speech Comm. Assn. Ohio (exec. bd. 1995-96). Republican. Roman Catholic.

DISMUKES, CAROL JAEHNE, county official; b. Giddings, Tex., July 17, 1938; d. Herbert Emil and Ruby (Alexander) Jaehne; m. Harold Charles Schumann, Feb. 7, 1959 (div. May 1970); children: Timothy, Michael, Keith, Gregory; m. Milton Brown Dismukes, Mar. 19, 1971. Student Tex. Lutheran Coll., 1958. Dep. Lee County Clk., Giddings, Tex., 1970-74, chief dep., 1975-77; accounts receivable clk. Invader Inc., Giddings, 1977-79; prodn. sec. Humble Exploration, Giddings, 1979-80; county clk. Lee County, Giddings, 1980—. Mem., Dime Box Ind. Sch. Dist. Trustees, Tex., 1972-80, pres., 1977-80; v.p. St. Johns Lutheran Ch. Council, 1982-84; chmn. Dime Box Homecoming and Mini-Marathon, 1978—; chmn. scholar com. Lee Co. Jr. Livestock Show, 1982—; sec. St. John's Luth. Ch., 1986, treas., 1987-89; chmn. St. John's Luth. Ch., 1991-93. Mem. County and Dist. Clks Assn. Tex. Democrat. Avocations: reading; sewing. Office: Lee County Clk PO Box 419 Giddings TX 78942-0419

DISMUKES, VALENA GRACE BROUSSARD, physical education educator; b. St. Louis, Feb. 22, 1938; d. Clobert Bernard and Mary Henrietta (Jones) Broussard; m. Martin Ramon Dismukes, June 26, 1965; 1 child, Michael Ramon. AA in Edn., Harris Tchrs. Coll., 1956; BS in Phys. Edn., Washington U., St. Louis, 1958; MA in Phys. Edn., Calif. State U., L.A., 1972; BA in TV and Film, Calif. State U., Northridge, 1981. Cert. phys. edn. tchr., standard svcs. supr. Phys. edn. tchr., coach St. Louis Pub. Schs., 1958-60; phys. edn. tchr., coach L.A. Unified Sch. Dist., 1960-84, health and sci. tchr., mentor tchr., 1984-93; coord. gifted and talented program 32d St./U.So. Calif. Magnet Sch., 1993-95, magnet coord., 1995; adminstrv. asst. Ednl. Consortium of Ctrl. L.A., Calif., 1993-95; owner, bus. cons. Grace Enterprises, 1994—; coord. Chpt. I, 1989-93; mem. sch. based mgmt. team, 1990-93. Author: (photography book) As Seen, 1995; editor parent newsletter, 1975-80; photographs exhibited in one-woman shows include The Olympic Spirit, 1984, L.A.-The Ethnic Place, 1986; contbr. articles to profl. jours. Mem. adv. com. Visual Comm., L.A., 1980; bd. dirs. NACHES Found., Inc., L.A., 1985-86; mem. Cmty. Consortium, L.A., 1986-87; mem. adv. com. L.A. Edn. Partnership, 1986-87; mem. adv. bd. Expo Sports Club, L.A., 1994. Marine Educators fellow, 1992; photography grantee L.A. Olympic Organizing Com., 1984, Teaching grantee L.A. Edn. Partnership, 1987-89, recipient Honor award L.A.-Calif. Assn. Health, Phys. Edn. and Recreation, 1971. Mem. ACLU, NAACP, Am. Fedn. Tchrs., United Tchrs. of L.A., Urban League, Sierra Club.

DISNEY, ANTHEA, publishing executive; b. Dunstable, Eng., Oct. 13, 1946; came to U.S., 1973; d. Alfred Leslie and Elsie (Wale) Disney; m. Peter Robert Howe, Jan. 28, 1984. Ed., Queen's Coll., Eng. Fgn. corr. London Daily Mail, N.Y.C., 1973-75; features editor London Daily Mail, London, 1975-77; bur. chief London Daily Mail, N.Y.C., 1977-79; columnist London Daily Express, N.Y.C., 1979-84; dep. mng. editor N.Y. Daily News, N.Y.C., 1984-87; editor Sunday Daily News, 1984-87, U.S. Mag., 1987-88; editor-in-chief Self mag., 1988-89; mag. developer Murdoch Mags., 1989-90; exec. producer Fox TV's A Current Affair, 1990-91; editor-in-chief TV Guide mag., N.Y.C., 1991-95; editorial dir. Murdoch Mags., 1994—; pres., CEO Harper Collins Publishers, 1996—. Office: Harper Collins Publishers 10 E. 53rd St. New York NY 10022*

DISON, CHARLOTTE ANNE, nursing administrator; b. Staunton, Va., July 26, 1931; d. Robert Clayton and Alice Clare (Eppard) Comer; m. Jack L. Dison, Nov. 6, 1954; 1 child, Jack Ross. Diploma, Lynchburg Gen. Hosp., 1953; BS in Nursing, Fla. State U., 1963; MA, Columbia U., 1966; postgrad., U. Pa. Wharton Sch. Bus., 1989. RN, Fla., Va.; cert. nursing adminstr., advanced. Staff nurse Norton (Va.) Community Hosp., 1953-55; asst. dir. nursing svcs. Miners Meml. Hosp. Assn., Wise, Va., 1956-64; nursing supr. Beekman-Downtown Hosp., N.Y.C., 1965-66; dir. nursing Bapt. Hosp. of Miami, 1966-79, assoc. adminstr. for patient care svcs., 1979-86, v.p. for patient care svcs., 1986—; mem. nursing coun. Sun Health Corp., 1992—. Contbr. articles to profl. jours. co-chair nursing manpower task force Commn. on Future of Nursing in Fla., 1988-91, nurse exec. rep. state commn., 1987-90, rec. sec., 1987-90; co-chiar FNA-FMA Task Force on Nursing Shortage, 1991—. Recipient Inaugural Leadership award Am. Orgn. Nurse Execs., 1995; Miami-Dade Coll. and Bapt. Hosp. grantee, 1987-88, 94. Mem. ACHE (diplomate, ad hoc com. on nurse execs.), Fla. Nurses Assn. (long-range planning com. 1988—, bd. dirs. dist. 5 1991—, mem. nursing adv. coun. 1991—, Employer of Yr. 1986, 87, 88, 90, Nurse Exec. of Yr. 1989, 90), Fla. Orgn. Nurse Execs. (pres. 1988-89, mktg. com. 1989—, chair search com. for exec. dir. 1989—), South Fla. Orgn. Nurse Execs. (pres. 1985-86, bd. dirs. 1980-82).

DISSETTE, ALYCE MARIE, television and multimedia producer, nonprofit foundation executive; b. Flint, Mich., Mar. 16, 1952; d. Leland Richard and Carol A.R. (Scott) D. Student, U. Mich., Flint, 1972-73, U. Wis., 1975-76. Personal asst. Gilbert V. Helmsly Jr., Madison, Wis., 1975-78; adminstrv. asst. Presentations, Met. Opera, N.Y.C., 1977-79; exec. dir. ODCI, San Francisco, 1983-86; producer, exec. dir. David Gordon/Pick Up Co., N.Y.C., 1986-89; founder/dir. 501C3 Inc., N.Y.C., 1994—; project co-dir. A Study of Choreographers, NEA, Washington, 1989-91; dir. computer art competitiion New Voices, New Visions, 1994. Exec. prodr. (PBS series) Alive TV/Alive from Off-Center, 1991-93; project work for Bklyn. Acad. Music, Performance Space 122, Pepsico Summerfun, MTV (Music TV Cable Ace award, 1994); producer websites. Office: 501C3 Inc 542 W 22nd St New York NY 10011

DITTUS, CAROLYN HELEN, special education educator, consultant, realtor; b. Plainfield, N.J., July 6, 1938; d. Joseph William and Catherine Margaret (Donehue) D. BA, Douglass Coll., 1960; EdD, Rutgers U., 1983; MA, Seton Hall U., 1968, Kean Coll., 1970. Cert. K-8 reading tchr., prin., supr., tchr. of handicapped, N.J., cert. paralegal. Tchr. Old Bridge (N.J.) Bd. Edn., 1960-65, reading tchr., 1965-66, supplemental instrn. tchr., 1972-81, learning cons., 1986—; tchr. Siderugica N.Am. Sch., Puerto Ordoz, Venezuela, 1965-66; spl. helps tchr. Dept. Health Edn. & Welfare, Ramey AFB, P.R., 1970-72; lectr. Inter Am. U., Ramey AFB, 1971-72. Mem. Learning Cons. Assn. (chmn. licensure 1990-95), Old Bridge Edn. Assn. (rep.), Kappa Delta Pi (past pres., sec. Delta Xi chpt. 1995-96), Alpha Delta Kappa (past pres.), Phi Delta Kappa. Roman Catholic. Office: Dept Spl Svcs Glenn Sch Cindy St Old Bridge NJ 08857

DITZEL, THELMA BRADFORD, small business owner, researcher; b. Charleston, Maine, Nov. 29, 1921; d. John Bearce and Maude Freelove

(Ewer) Bradford; m. Arthur Charles Ditzel (dec.); children: Arthur, Mary Ann, Thelma, Joseph, John, Jane, Ruth, James. BA, U. Maine, Orono, 1945; MA, Columbia U., N.Y.C., 1946. Cert. tchr. Maine, N.Y., N.J. Tchr. Berkeley Inst., Bklyn., 1946-47, John Marshall Coll., Jersey City, N.J., 1946-47, Mount Carmel Sch., Tenafly, N.J., 1963-88; founder, owner Ice-Out Co. Audio Tapes, Charleston, Maine, 1989—; speaker on Maine's history various groups and orgns., 1993—. Prodr. (audio tapes) Faces of Maine History, 1989—. Librarian Pub. Library, Charleston, 1989—; mem. comprehensive planning bd. Hist. Soc., 1990-93, v.p. 1995—. Recipient scholarship U. Maine, 1942, 43, 44, Columbia U., 1945. Mem. Retired Tchrs. Assn. (chaplain 1990—). Home: RR 1 Box 285 Charleston ME 04422 Office: Ice-Out Co PO Box 34 Charleston ME 04422

DIXON, IRMA MUSE, state commissioner, former state legislator, social worker; b. New Orleans, July 18, 1952; d. Joseph Sr. and Irma (White) Muse; m. Reuben Dixon, June 26, 1976. BA, So. U. of New Orleans, 1976; MSW, Tulane U., 1979; postgrad., Harvard U., 1985. Dir. community devel. New Orleans, 1980, bur. chief mgmt. svcs. Office of Employment and Tng., 1981-82, dir. dept. recreation, 1982-84; undersec. Dept. Culture, Recreation and Tourism Baton Rouge, 1984-86; dir. dept. property mgmt. New Orleans, 1987-88; state rep. Ho. of Reps., New Orleans, 1988-93; commr. La. Pub. Svc. Commn. Dist. III, 1993—; cons. Audubon Inst. Aquarium, New Orleans, 1985. Recipient Legislator of Yr. Alliance for Good Govt., 1988, Outstanding Svc. award City of New Orleans-Mayor's Office, 1988, Leadership award Earhart-Tulane Corridor Assn., 1989, Legis. Women's award La. Conf. Elected Women, 1989, Presidential award Nat. Caucus State Legislators, 1989. Mem. Am. Planning Soc., Am. Soc. Pub. Adminstrs., Nat. Orgn. Black Elected Legis. Women, Nat. Black Caucus State Legislators, Nat. Conf. State Legislators (bd. dirs.), Ind. Fee Appraisers, Young Leadership Coun., Harvard Club of La. Democrat. Baptist. Office: 4100 Touro St New Orleans LA 70122

DIXON, JEANE, writer, lecturer, realtor, columnist; b. Medford, Wis., Jan. 5, 1918; d. Gerhart and Emma (von Graffe) Pinckert; m. James L. Dixon, 1939. Founder, chmn. bd. Children to Children Inc., 1964—; pres. James L. Dixon & Co., Realtors, Washington. Author: My Life and Prophecies, 1969, Reincarnation and Prayers to Live By, 1970, The Call to Glory, 1972, Yesterday, Today and Forever, 1976, Jeane Dixon's Astrological Cookbook, 1976, Horoscopes for Dogs (Pets and Their Planets), 1979, The Riddle of Powderworks Road, 1980, A Gift of Prayer, 1995; syndicated columnist: Horoscope and Predictions, Universal Press Syndicate., featured in Star Mag.; exponent of extrasensory perception (subject of book A Gift of Prophecy), 1988. Chmn. Christmas Seal campaign, Washington, 1968; hon. chairperson, hostess Mystic Ball Cystic Fibrosis Found., 1990-94; pres. exec. adv. coun. United Cerebral Palsy of Washington and No. Va., 1992; mem. disting. citizen adv. bd., 1994. Recipient Loreto Internat. award Loreto Shrine, Italy, 1969; Internat. L'Enfant award Holy Family Adoption League, 1969; named Woman of Year Internat. Orphans, 1968; knight Internat. Order of St. Martin, Vienna; award Md. chpt. Cystic Fibrosis Found., hon. chairperson/hostess Mystic Carnival, 1992; St. John of Jerusalem Internat. Humanitarian Christian Chivalry award; knighted Dame of Humanity; Imperial Byzantine Order of St. Constantine the Great of St. George; Fall Gal award Nat. Saints and Sinners Conv.; Unsung Heroine award Ladies aux. VFW; Golden Lady Humanitarian award AMITA Internat.; Internat. Nostradamus award Internat. Platform Assn.; Leif Erikson Humanitarian award Sons of Norway; First Anglo hon. Navajo princess, 1968; Disting. Am. award (first female) Sales & Mktg. Execs. Met. Washington D.C., 1989; Rep. Senatorial medal of freedom, 1994, Am. Police Hall of Fame. Mem. ASCAP, Nat. League Am. Pen. Women, Internat. Platform Assn. Club: Internat. (Washington). Office: James L Dixon & Co 1765 N St NW Washington DC 20036-2802

DIXON, JOANNE ELAINE, music educator; b. Lancaster, Pa., July 3, 1944; d. William Russell and Anna Mary (Allen) D. B Music Edn., Westminster Choir Coll., Princeton, N.J., 1966; MEd, Trenton State Coll., 1982. Cert. music tchr., N.J. Music tchr. Warren (N.J.) Twp. Sch. Dist., 1966-67; vocal music tchr. Branchburg Twp. Sch. Dist., Somerville, N.J., 1967—, handbell dir., 1985—; music edn. handbell cons. Somerset County Dept. Edn., 1988-90; handbell dir., cons. Music Educator's Nat. Conf., Washington, 1990; N.J. rep. Com. for Handbells in Music Edn., Dayton, Ohio, 1990—. Handbell ringer First United Meth. Ch., Somerville, 1985—, mem. visions com., 1992-94, substitute handbell dir., 1992—; condr. N.J. Schs. Handbell Festival, 1995, 96. Recipient Excellence in Tchg. award State of N.J. Dept. Edn., 1988. Mem. Am. Guild English Handbell Ringers (area II N.J. rep. 1993—, N.J. state rep. 1993—, handbell workshop dir. 1993—), Branchburg Fedn. Tchrs. Democrat. Home: 977 Robin Rd Somerville NJ 08876-4440 Office: Stony Brook Sch 136 Cedar Grove Rd Somerville NJ 08876-3653

DIXON, JUDY E(ARLENE), management and marketing executive, consultant; b. Sweetwater, Tex., July 19, 1950; d. Robert E. Stewart and Verna May (Brown) Kirkpatrick; children: Tammy Taylor, Tara R. Taylor. Cert., U. Houston, 1986; BA in Mktg. and Mgmt. with honors, Ctr. Degree Study, Pa., 1992. Ops. mgr. Retail Investment Group, Odessa, Tex., 1981-82; sales cons. Rupert Advt., Odessa, Tex., 1982-83; dir. training Paisano Girl Scout Coun., Corpus Christi, Tex., 1979; owner Gingerbread Bakery, Odessa, 1981-83; exec. dir. Nat. Multiple Sclerosis Soc., Midland, Tex., 1983-86; mktg. dir. Melvin, Simin & Assocs., Midland, Tex., 1986-87; exec. dir. West Tex. Rural Health Edn. Ctr., Odessa, 1987-91; owner Creative Svcs., Odessa, 1991—; cons. small bus. mktg., 1984—. Editor, pub. West Tex. Health Prospective mag., 1989-90; contbr. articles to profl. jours. Recipient Writing grant Ector County Ind. Sch. Dist., 1990-91, Nat. Vice Chmn.'s award Nat. Multiple Sclerosis Soc., Cmty. Involvement award N.W. Civic League, 1979, Silver Appreciation award United Way, 1977. Republican. Home and Office: Creative Svcs 8418 NE 131st Pl Kirkland WA 98034

DIXON, LINDA, child, adolescent and adult therapist; b. Bronx, June 2, 1962; d. Joseph and Francine Marilyn (Rega) Incoronato; m. Charles Richard Dixon, Aug. 17, 1987 (div.); children: Joseph Anthony, Danielle Marie. AA, Dutchess C.C., Poughkeepsie, N.Y., 1979; BS, BA magna cum laude, Brockport Coll./SUNY, 1982; MA, Marist Coll., Poughkeepsie, 1986; postgrad., Fordham U., 1985. Behavioral edn. counselor Nutri-System Weight Loss Ctr., Fishkill, N.Y., 1983-85; nutrition/fitness cons. IBM/Mariott Corp., Poughkeepsie, 1985-86; psychol. specialist Eckerd Youth Developmental Found., Okeechobee, Fla., 1986-87; counseling cons. Child Protection Team/Children's Spl. Edn. Needs Team, Okeechobee, Fla., 1987-89; day treatment dir. West County Mental Health Ctr., Belle Glade, Fla., 1988-90; counseling cons. Counseling and Behavioral Assocs., Port St. Lucie, Fla., 1990-93; staff trainer/counseling cons. Calvary Assembly of God, Port St. Lucie, Fla., 1990-91; exec. dir. Network for Christian Counselors, Port St. Lucie, Fla., 1992-95; clin. dir. Renewed Hope Counseling Ctr., Fishkill, N.Y., 1995; mental health case mgr. Wellcare, Kingston, N.Y., 1996; mental health counselor, dir. Renewed Hope Counseling Ctr., Fishkill, N.Y., 1996—; EMT, Alamo Ambulance, Poughkeepsie, 1983-85; grad. asst. Office of Health Svcs., Psychology, Marist Coll., Poughkeepsie, 1984-86; cmty. rep. Sandypines Hosp., Tequesta, Fla., 1989-91; cons. Samaritan House for Boys, Stuart, Fla., 1993-94. Contbr. articles to profl. jours. Bd. dirs. Crisis Pregnancy Svcs., Port St. Lucie, 1992-93; vol. worker Heart Assn. Dutchess County, Poughkeepsie, 1980-81, March of Dimes, 1978-79, Muscular Dystrophy, 1978-79; mem. Congl. Campaign Com./Dutchess County Youth Adv. Com. to Legis, 1980-82. Day Treatment for adolescents Children's Svcs. Coun. grantee, 1988. Mem. Fla. Soc. Psychotherapists, Am. Assn. Christian Counselors, Am. Counseling Assn., Am. Mental Health Counselor Assn., Fla. Sheriff's Assn. Democrat. Home: 14 Ronsue Dr #W Wappingers Falls NY 12590-5312 Office: Renewed Hope Counseling 132 Main St Fishkill NY 12590

DIXON, LORI-RENEE, special education diagnostician; b. Chgo., Sept. 6, 1960; d. James Marshall and Alma (Taylor) Dixon. BEd, U. TEnn., 1982; MEd, Ga. State U., 1988. Cert. learning disabilities, interrelated spl. edn., curriculum and supervision, early childhood spl. edn. Behavior therapist Burwell Ctr., Carrollton, Ga., 1982-83; tchr. Atlanta Pub. Schs., 1983-89, diagnostician, 1989—; ednl. coord. Village of St. Joseph, Atlanta, 1994—; pres., cons. Something Spl. Ctr., Conley, Ga., 1987—; pres. Exceptional Ctr., Conley, 1991—. Author: Inclusion: Metamorphosis or Masquerade?, 1994. Chairperson Commn. on Missions, Ben Hill United Meth. Ch., Atlanta, 1991—; comm. organizer Cynthia McKinney Campaign, Ga., 1992; bd. mem. Genesis Shelter/Atlanta Urban Ministries, Ga., 1990, 94—. Recipient Svc. awards Ga. Fedn. Tchrs., Atlanta, 1994, Ben Hill United Meth. Ch., Atlanta, 1986, 88, 90. Mem. Coun. Exceptional Children (rec. sec. 1989—), Children's Def. Fund, Assn. Child Care Cons., Nat. Alliance Black Sch. Educators, Atlanta Fedn. Tchrs. (exec. com., rec. sec. 1983—, Svc. award 1992), Ben Hill Toastmasters (pres. 1994—). Home: 4130 Glad Morning Dr Atlanta GA 30349

DIXON, LUGENIA, psychology educator; b. Columbus, Ga., Jan. 20, 1949; d. Sam and Ola (Bowman) Dixon; m. Willie Cornelius Ladner, 1969 (div. Aug. 1973); children: Dexteralan Keith Ladner, Craig Jeffrey Ladner, Olivia Dara Young. Student, Harris Jr. Coll., Meridian, Miss., 1967-68, Columbus (Ga.) Coll., 1971-78; BA in Psychology, U. Ga., 1980, MEd in Early Childhood Edn., 1982, PhD in Ednl. Psychology, 1985; postgrad., Ft. Valley (Ga.) State Coll., 1989. Medicare claims approval clk. Blue Cross/Blue Shield, Columbus, 1969-71, Medicare unit leader, 1975-77; collector Sears, Columbus, 1971-75; substitute tchr. Clarke County Sch. Dist., Athens, Ga., 1981; instrnl. aide, substitute tchr. Clarke County Sch. Dist., Athens, 1984-85; work/study (rschr.) U. Ga., Athens, 1981-83; substitute tchr. Ga. Retardation Ctr., Athens, 1983-84; asst. prof. Psychology Gordon Coll., Barnesville, Ga., 1985-89; assoc. prof. Psychology Bainbridge (Ga.) Coll., 1989—; Social Sci. Fair judging coord. Bainbridge Coll., 1992—; Minority Achievement Program coord. Bainbridge Coll., 1992-94. Co-author: Living Psychology: An Introduction, 1995; co-author: (handbook) Handbook for Living Psychology: An Introduction, 1995. Sec. Decatur County Artist Guild, 1994; gender equity liaison AAUW, Bainbridge br., 1995-96. Recipient mini-grant Bainbridge Coll., 1996, Regents Minority scholarship U. Ga., 1983-84, Cmty. Svc. cert. Athens Recreation Dept., 1984, Internat. Scenario Writing Contest award 5th World Conf. on Children, Youth and Adults, Athens, 1984. Mem. Assn. of Women in Psychology, Coun. of Tchrs. of Undergrad. Psychology, Regents Acad. Adv. Com. on Psychology, Divsn. 2 Teaching of Psychology. Democrat. Roman Catholic. Home: 261 Dollar Dr Bainbridge GA 31717-6438 Office: Bainbridge College Hwy 84 Bainbridge GA 31717

DIXON, NANCY JEAN IOVANNI, physical therapist; b. Boston, Feb. 8, 1962; d. Anthony and Ann (Memmo) Iovanni; m. John A. Dixon, Aug. 10, 1996. BS in Phys. Therapy, Northeastern U., 1985. Registered phys. therapist, Mass., Ariz. Phys. therapist Walter E. Fernald State Sch., Waltham, Mass., 1985-91; phys. therapist Newell Home Health Svcs., Newton, Mass., 1991-93, Sundance Rehab. Corp., Phoenix, 1994—. Democrat. Roman Catholic. Home: 3240 E Wickieup Lane Phoenix AZ 85024

DIXON, NANCY POWELL, educational research administrator; b. Villa Rica, Ga., Oct. 22, 1943; d. Jack Wheeler and Myra (Lowry) Powell; children: Peter George, Susan Powell. BS in Edn., U. Ga., 1965, MEd, 1966; EdD, Okla. State U., 1975, postgrad., 1983-85. Spl. edn. tchr. Clarke County Pub. Schs., Athens, Ga., 1966-67, Putnam County Pub. Schs., Cookeville, Tenn., 1967-68; remedial reading tchr. Daniel Arthur Rehab. Ctr., Oak Ridge, Tenn., 1968-70, Morrison (Okla.) Pub. Schs., 1973-76; assoc. prof. spl. edn. Western Carolina U., Cullowhee, N.C., 1976-83; assoc. dir. exptl. program to stimulate competitive rsch. Okla. State Regents for Higher Edn., Stillwater, 1985—; mem. state adv. com. exptl. program to stimulate competitive rsch., 1991—; mem. Okla. Space Grant Consortium. Author: Children of Poverty With Handicapping Conditions: How Teachers Can Cope Humanistically, 1981. V.p. Friends of the Libr., Stillwater, 1988-92. Mem. Alliance for Invitational Edn., Nat. Coun. for Rsch. Adminstrs., Internat. Reading Assn., Coun. for Exceptional Children, Okla. State U. Women's Coun., Phi Kappa Phi, Phi Delta Kappa. Democrat. Baptist. Office: Okla EPSCoR Oklahoma State U 001B Life Sciences E Stillwater OK 74078

DIXON, ROBIN CHAMBERS, entrepreneur, consultant; b. Lynchburg, Va., Aug. 27, 1955; d. Raymond and Evelyn Marie Chambers; m. M. Ernest Dixon, Apr. 28, 1984. BA, Randolph-Macon Woman's Coll., 1978. Sales rep. Reynolds Metals Co., Richmond, Va., 1980-90; account mgr. Synectics Group, Inc., Allentown, Pa., 1990-91; sales rep. Pfizer Pharms., N.Y.C., 1991-94; prin. Chambers Consulting, Lansdale, Pa., 1994—. Trustee Randolph-Macon Woman's Coll., Lynchburg, 1996—; bd. dirs. Family Svcs., Montgomery County, Norristown, Pa., 1994—. Mem. Nat. Assn. Profl. Saleswomen. Office: Chambers Cons 5 Douglass Rd Lansdale PA 19446

DIXON, SHIRLEY JUANITA, restaurant owner; b. Canton, N.C., June 29, 1935; d. Willard Luther and Bessie Eugenia (Scroggs) Clark; m. Clinton Matthew Dixon, Jan. 3, 1953; children: Elizabeth Swanger, Hugh Monroe III, Cynthia Owen, Sharon Fouts. BS, Wayne State U., 1956; postgrad., Mary Baldwin Coll., 1958, U. N.C., 1977. Acct. Standard Oil Co., Detroit, 1955-57; asst. dining room mgr. Statler Hilton, Detroit, 1958-60; bookkeeper Osborne Lumber Co., Canton, N.C., 1960-61; bus. owner, pres. Dixon's Restaurant, Canton, 1961—; judge N.C. Assn. Distributive Edn. Assn., state and dist., 1982—; owner Halbert's Family Heritage Ctr., Canton. Past Pres. Haywood County Assn. Retarded Citizens Bd., 1985-94, past v.p., chmn. bd. dirs.; bd. commrs. Haywood Vocats. Opportunities, 1985-94, treas. bd. dirs.; Haywood Sr. Leadership Council; dist. dir. 11th Congl. Dist. Dem. Women, 1982-85; state Teen-Dem. advisor State Dem. party, 1985-90; del. 1988 Dem. Nat. Conv., Atlanta; alderwoman Town of Canton, N.C.; vice-chair Gov.'s. Adv. Coun. on Aging, State N.C., 1982-89; 1st v.p. crime prevention Community Watch Bd., State N.C., 1985, 86; mem. Criminal Justice Bd., N.C. Assembly on Women and the Economy; chair Western N.C. Epilepsy Assn., Haywood County N.C. Mus. History, 1987—; co-chair Haywood County Commn. on the Bi-Centennial of Constn., 1987-92; Haywood County Econ. Strategy Commn.; v.p., bd. dirs. Haywood County Retirement Coun., Region A Coun. on Aging; bd. dirs. Haywood County Sr. Housing, C.B.C. United Way (mem. chair); chair bd. Canton Sr. Citizen's Ctr.; mem. Haywood County Ease Retirement Com.; pres., chairwoman bd. Haywood County Assn. Retarded Citizens; pres. N.C. coun. Alzheimer's Disease and Related Disorders Assn.; bd. dirs. Canton Recreation Dept., Western N.C. Alzheimer's Disease and Related Disorders Assn., 1987-91, v.p., C.B; bd. dirs. Haywood Literary Coun., Haywood Sr. Leadership Coun., W.N.C. Econ. Devel. Com., United Way, 1991—, drive chmn.; mem. legis. subcom. Alzheimer's-State of N.C.; bd. dirs. N.C. Conf. for Social Svcs., 1987-91; v.p. bd. Western N.C. Alzheimer's Assn., 1987-91; pres. State Coun. on Alzheimer's; apptd. mem. Legis. Study Com. on Alzheimer's; apptd. mem. State of N.C. Adv. Bd. on Community Care and Health; mem. Habitat for Humanity Haywood County; bd. chair Pigeon Valley Optimist Club; apptd. by Senate Western N.C. Econ. Devel. Commn.; appointee Haywood County Econ. Devel. Commn., Canton Hist. Commn.; judge U.S. Olympic Torch Bearers. Recipient Outstanding Svc. award Crime Prevention from Gov., 1982, Gov.'s Spl. Vol. award, 1983, Outstanding Svc. award N.C. Cmty. Watch Assn., 1984, Cmty. Svc. award to Handicapped, 1983-84, Outstanding Svc. award ARC, 1988; named Employer of Yr. for Hiring Handicapped N.C. Assn. for Retarded Citizens, 1985, Cmty. Person of Yr. Kiwanis Club, 1991, Citizen of Yr. in Western N.C., 1995; Rec. Outstanding award Haywood Co. Sr. Games, 1992. Mem. AAUW, NAFE, Women's Polit. Caucus, Internat. Platform Assn., Women's Forum N.C., Nat. Bd. Alzheimers Assn. (regional del.), Canton Bus. and Profl. Assn. (pres. 1974-79, Woman of Yr. 1984), Altrusa (Woman of Yr. in N.C. 1989). Democrat. Episcopalian. Home: 104 Skyland Ter Canton NC 28716-3718 Office: Dixons Restaurant 30 N Main St Canton NC 28716-3805

DIXSON, DIANE ELIZABETH, acquisitions librarian, tax preparation business owner; b. Washington, Sept. 26, 1943; d. Charles Hanan and Doris (Cover) D. BA in English and German, George Mason U., 1978. Bibliographic technician Libr. Congress, Washington, 1966-68, preliminary cataloger, 1968-72, acquisitions libr., 1973—. Chair supervisory com. Libr. Congress Fed. Credit Union, 1982-90, bd. dirs., 1991-94, mem. credit com., 1994—. Recipient Edward A. Filene award Credit Union Nat. Assn., 1992. Roman Catholic. Home: 2914 Strathmeade St Falls Church VA 22042-1428 Office: Libr Congress 1st & Independence Ave SE Washington DC 20540

DIXSON, J. B., communications executive, columnist; b. Norwich, N.Y., Oct. 19, 1941; d. William Joseph and Ann Wanda (Teale) Barrett; BS, Syracuse U., 1963; postgrad. in bus. adminstrn. Wayne State U., 1979-81; MBA, Central Mich. U., 1984. Public relations editorial asst. Am. Mus. Natural History, N.Y.C., 1963-64; writer/producer Norman, Navan, Moore & Baird Advt., Grand Rapids, Mich., 1964-67; prin. J.B. Dixson Comm. Cons., Detroit, 1967-74; dir. Public Info. Services div. Mich. Employment Security Commn., Detroit, 1974-82; news relations mgr. Burroughs Corp., 1982-83, dir. creative services, 1983-85, dir. pub. relations, 1985-86; prin. Dixson Comm., Detroit, 1986-93, Durocher Dixson Werba, L.L.C., Detroit, 1994—; lectr., speaker in field at colls., univs., community orgns. Contbg. columnist Detroit News. Mem. Detroit Mayor's Transition Com. of 100, 1972; mem. bd. mgmt. Detroit YWCA, 1974; chmn. Detroit Women's Equality Day Com., 1975; bd. dirs., founding mem. Feminist Fed. Credit Union, Detroit, 1976; centennial chair Indian Village Assn., 1993-95; founding mem. Mich. Women's Campaign Fund, 1980; active Mich. Task Force on Sexual Harassment in Workplace, Mich. Women's Com. of 100, Mich. Women's Polit. Caucus, Mich. Women's Found. Named Outstanding Sr. Woman in Radio and TV, Syracuse U., 1963; recipient Five Watch award Am. Women in Radio and TV, Mich., 1969, cert. of recognition Detroit City Council, 1976, Feminist of Yr. award NOW, 1977, City of Detroit Human Rights Commn., 1988, Design in Mich. award Mich. Council of Arts/Gov. William G. Milliken, 1977, Achievement award U.S. Dept. Labor, 1979, Spirit of Detroit award Detroit City Council, 1980, PR Casebook, 1983, PR News case study, 1986; subject of Mich. Senate Resolution 412, 1979. Recipient Nat. Sch. Pub. Rels. Assn. award, 1992, Mich. Hosp. Pub. Rels. Assn. Pinnacle award, 1987. Fellow Public Relations Soc. Am. (accredited, pres. chpt. 1983-84, Dist. award and citation 1984, 86, 87, 93, exec. com. corp. sect. 1996), Internat. Assn. Bus. Communicators (Silver Quill award chpt., 1987, 88, 91, 93, dist., 1987, Renaissance award, 1988, 91, Mercury award, 1987), Nat. Assn. Govt. Communicators (Blue Pencil award 1977, Gold Screen award 1980), Econ. Club Detroit, Clubs: Maple Grove Gun, Detroit Press. Author: Guidelines for Non-Sexist Verbal and Written Communication, 1976; Sexual Harassment on The Job, 1979; The TV Interview: Good News or Bad?, 1981. Office: Durocher Dixson Werba 400 Renaissance Ctr Ste 2250 Detroit MI 48243-1602

DIXSON, JUDY SUE, elementary education educator; b. Bell, Calif., Dec. 30, 1944; d. Jack C. and Arlyne J. (Priddy) Parsons; m. Michael Dennis Dixson, Aug. 21, 1965; children: Tiffany Anne, Michael Bradley. BA in Life Sci., Fresno (Calif.) State U., 1966. Cert. tchr., Calif. Tchr. grades 3-5 Fresno Unified Sch. Dist., 1966—, mentor tchr., 1985-86; lead tchr. Calif. Sci. Implementarion Network, Fresno, 1993-94; tchr. leader Calif. Elem. Math. Initiative, Sacramento, 1994-95; tchr. Manchester G.A.T.E. Elem. Sch., Fresno, 1983—; mem. San Joaquin Valley Math. Project, Fresno, 1992; master tchr. Nat. Tchr. Tng. Inst., Fresno, 1994—. Writer ednl. materials. Mem. ASCD, AAUW, NEA, Calif. Tchrs. Assn., Nat. Coun. Tchrs. Math., Nat. Coun. Suprs. Math. Home: 4315 E Copper Ave Clovis CA 93611-9560 Office: Fresno Sch Dist Manchester GATE Elem Sch Tulare and M Sts Fresno CA 93721

DLUHY, DEBORAH HAIGH, college dean; b. Summit, N.J., Mar. 4, 1940; d. Richard Hartman Haigh and Elin Frederika Anderson Neumann; m. Robert George Dluhy, June 11, 1962; 1 child, Leonore Alexandra. BA, Wheaton Coll., 1962; postgrad., Boston U., 1962-63, U. Heidelberg, Germany, 1963-65; PhD, Harvard U., 1976. Instr. fine arts Wheaton Coll., Norton, Mass., 1975-76, Radcliffe Coll., Cambridge, Mass., 1977, Boston Coll., Newton, Mass., 1976-77, 78; devel. officer Mus. Fine Arts, Boston, 1978-84, asst. dir. devel., 1984-86; assoc. dean adminstrn. Sch. Mus. Fine Arts, Boston, 1986-87, dean acad. programs and adminstrn., 1987-93, dean, 1993—. Trustee Wheaton Coll., Norton, Mass., 1988-93, Cultural Edn. Collaborative Boston, 1987—; mem. commn. on rsch. Nat. Assn. Schs. Art & Design, Reston, Va., 1990—. Woodrow Wilson fellow, 1963. Mem. Wheaton Coll. Alumnae Assn. (pres. 1994—). Home: 104 Fletcher Rd Belmont MA 02178-2018 Office: Sch Mus of Fine Arts 230 Fenway Boston MA 02115-5534

DOAN, JANE ELIZABETH, elementary education educator, writer; b. Gettysburg, Pa., Dec. 13, 1943; d. George Henry and Sara Agnes (Stallsmith) Roth; m. Robert J. Doan, Mar. 19, 1966; children: Robert Michael, Kathryn Ann. BS, West Chester U., 1965; MA in edn., U. Maine, 1991. Tchr. Coatesville (Pa.) Area Sch. Dist., 1965-66, Waterville (Maine) Pub. Sch. System, 1972-76, West St. Sch., Fairfield, Maine, 1977-79, Sch. Adminstrn. Dist # 49, Fairfield, Maine, 1979—; adj. faculty U. Maine, Orono, 1991-93. Co-author: Full Circle: A New Look at Multiage Education, 1994. Recipient Publication award Maine Coun. Eng. Lang. Arts, 1994. Mem. Internat. Reading Assn., Nat. Coun. Tchrs. of Eng., Nat. Coun. of Tchrs. of Math., Maine Coun. Eng. Lang. Arts. Home: PO Box 192 Albion ME 04910-0192 Office: Benton Elem Sch 62 Old Benton Neck Rd Waterville ME 04901-3031

DOANE, EILEEN MALONEY, learning disabilities teacher consultant; b. Welcome, Md., Dec. 5, 1933; d. John Laurence and Lillian Marion (Posey) Maloney; m. Allan Hammond Doane, June 12, 1954; children: Kathleen, Sharon, Elizabeth. BA in Speech Arts, George Washington U., 1955; MA in Edn., Seton Hall U., 1983; postgrad. studies Learning Disabilities, Kean Coll., 1987. Cert. tchr. of handicapped, speech correction, prin., supr., learning cons., N.J. Mem. child study team Elizabeth (N.J.) Bd. Edn. Spl. Svcs., 1990-95; learning disability tchr. cons., instrnl. supr. Matheny Sch. and Hosp., Peapack, N.J., 1995—. Mem. Outreach Com. St. Peter's Episcopal Ch., Mountain Lakes, N.J., adult edn. com. Mountain Lakes. Recipient cert. appreciation Vol. Action Ctr., Morristown, N.J, Mental Health Players, Morris County Mental Health Assn., Madison, N.J., 1987, Benefactor award Rotary Found., Evanston, Ill., 1995; named Paul Harris fellow Rotary Found., 1984. Mem. AAUW, ASCD, N.J. Assn. Learning Cons., Kappa Delta Pi. Democrat. Home: 31 Rainbow Trail Mountain Lakes NJ 07046 Office: The Methany Sch & Hosp Main St Peapack NJ 07977

DOBBENGA, YVONNE AMY, women's health nurse; b. Paterson, N.J., July 20, 1966; d. John Henry and Joyce Amanda (Vander Horst) D. BSN, Calvin Coll., 1988; MS, U. Rochester, 1990. RN, Calif., N.Y. Staff nurse labor and delivery U. Rochester (N.Y.) Med. Ctr., 1988-91; shift mgr. perinatal svcs. Doctors Hosp. of Manteca, Calif., 1991-92; perinatal clin. nurse specialist San Joaguin Gen. Hosp., Stockton, Calif., 1992-94, Washington Hosp. Healthcare System, Fremont, Calif., 1994—; instr. neonatal resuscitation program Am. Acad. Pediatricians, 1992—; instr. BLS, Am. Heart Assn., 1994—. Mem. Assn. Women's Health, Obstetric and Neonatal Nurses, Nat. Perinatal Assn., Clin. Nurse Specialists of No. Calif., Sigma Theta Tau. Christian Reformed. Home: 34215 Kaspar Terr Fremont CA 94555-3804 Office: Washington Hosp Healthcare System 2000 Mowry Ave Fremont CA 94538-1716

DOBBINS, LORI ELLEN, composer, educator; b. Aberdeen, Md., May 10, 1958; d. Robert C. and Barbara Ellen (Park) D. BA, San Jose State U., 1980; MFA, Calif. Inst. for the Arts, 1982; PhD, U. Calif., Berkeley, 1990. Lectr. U. Calif., Berkeley, 1990-91, U. B.C., Vancouver, 1991-92; asst. prof. Lafayette Coll., Easton, Pa., 1992—. Composer (music) Fire and Ice, 1990, Percussion Quartet, 1991, Tres Recuerdos Del Cielo, 1989, Nova, 1995, Violin Concerto, 1996; commns. from The Koussevitzky Found. Libr. Congress, 1988, St. Paul Chamber Orchestra, 1990, Fromm Found., 1991. Goddard Lieberson fellowship Am. Acad. and Inst. of Arts and Letters, 1989; recipient Lili Boulanger award Nat. Woman Composers Resource Ctr., 1992, 1st prize composition contest Internat. League of Women Composers, 1989. Mem. Coll. Music Soc., Am. Music Ctr., Am. Soc. of Composers Authors and Publishers, Am. Composers Forum. Office: Lafayette Coll Dept of Music Easton PA 18042

DOBBS, EVANGELINA FRESCAS, lobbyist; b. El Paso, Tex., July 15, 1958; d. Manuel and Eva N. (Navarro) Frescas; m. Michael Keith Dobbs, Jan. 2, 1982; children: Keith M., Evan R. BA in Econs., Harvard U., 1980. Coord., exec. dir. El Paso (Tex.) Literacy Coalition, 1987-89; dist. dir. State Senator Peggy Rosson, El Paso, 1990-92; v.p. cmty. devel. Greater El Paso C. of C., 1992-93; mgr. pub. info, Washington rep. Ctrl. & South West Corp., Washington, 1993-96; mem. adv. bd. Mex. Am. Legal Def. and Edn. Fund, El Paso, 1991-95. Writer newspaper articles, columns El Paso Times, El Paso Herald Post, 1988, 91, 92. State bd. mem. Literacy Vols. Am., Austin, Tex., 1987-89; vice chairperson Convention & Visitors Bur., El Paso, 1992-94; bd. mem. Cmty. Justice Coun., El Paso, 1990-95; bd. mem. El Paso Symphony Orch., 1993-95, Jr. Achievement, El Paso, 1993-95, S.W. AIDS

Com., El Paso, 1994; co-chair, founding mem. Unite El Paso, 1993-94. Recipient Adelante Mujer Hispana Disting. Svc. award in politics Adelante Mujer Hispana, Inc., El Paso, 1993; named Outstanding Ex-Student Thomas Jefferson H.S., El Paso, 1994. Mem. Jr. League Washington, Exec. Forum El Paso, Women's Energy Resources Coun. Democrat. Roman Catholic. Home: 7710 Midday ln Alexandria VA 22306

DOBBS, HILARI BETH, public relations executive; b. Nov. 30, 1969; d. Duane and Rosalyn Ann (Rosenberg) D. BA in Englist lit. & rhetoric, SUNY, Binghamton, 1991. Sr. acct. exec. Kahn Travel Comm., N.Y.C., 1991—; mem. Caribbean Tourism Org., N.Y.C., 1996—. Mem. NAFE. Home: 2728 Henry Hudson Pkwy Riverdale NY 10463 Office: Kahn Trav Comm 100 N Village Ave Rockville Centre NY 11570

DOBECK, JOANN MARY, elementary education educator; b. Shamokin, Pa., Aug. 10, 1953; d. Joseph Naroleski and Catherine (Puceta) Engle; m. Edward W. Dobeck Jr., Aug. 9, 1975 (dec. Nov. 1994); children: Edward III, Lindsey. BS, Bloomsburg (Pa.) U., 1974, MA, 1977. Elem. tchr. Shamokin Sch. Dist., 1975—. Mem. NEA, Pa. Edn. Assn., Shamokin Edn. Assn. Republican. Roman Catholic. Home: 513 N 6th St Shamokin PA 17872

DOBELIS, INGE NACHMAN, editor; b. Würzburg, Germany, Nov. 16, 1933; came to U.S., 1938, naturalized, 1951; d. Rudolf Hugo and Resi (Hamburger) Nachman; BA in English, U. Ga., 1956; m. Miervaldis C. Dobelis, May 4, 1969; 1 son, Arthur N. Editorial positions Buttenheim Publs. and Crowell-Collier, 1956-64; copy editor Gen. Book div. Readers Digest, N.Y.C., 1965-72, assoc. editor, 1973-79, sr. editor, 1979-85, sr. staff editor, 1985—. Exec. bd., officer Murray Hill Democratic Club, 1968-74; exec. bd. Community Bd. No. 6, N.Y.C., 1973-78, sec., 1976, chmn. health and hosps. com., 1974-78; trustee, officer Brotherhood Synagogue, 1983—, pres. 1993-95; mem. N.Y. Dem. County Com., 1967-74. Mem. Phi Beta Kappa. Assoc. editor: Reader's Digest Family Encyclopedia of American History, 1975; Reader's Digest Family Health Guide and Medical Encyclopedia, 1976; Reader's Digest Illustrated Guide to Gardening, 1978; editor: Readers Digest Family Legal Guide, 1981; Quick and Thrifty Cooking, 1984; Magic and Medicine of Plants, 1986; Great Recipes for Good Health, 1988; America: Land of Beauty and Splendor, 1992, Legal Problem Solver, 1994, Know Your Rights, 1995. Club: Nat. Arts (N.Y.C.). Home: 201 E 17th St New York NY 10003-3607 Office: Reader's Digest Gen Books 260 Madison Ave New York NY 10016-2401

DOBIS, JOAN PAULINE, elementary education educator; b. S.I., N.Y., Sept. 11, 1944; d. Victor Raymond and Rosanna Elizabeth (Dandignac) Mazza; m. Robert Joseph Dobis, Dec. 21, 1968. BA in History, Notre Dame Coll., S.I., 1966; MS in Advanced Secondary Edn. and Social Studies, Wagner Coll., 1968; profl. diploma in ednl. adminstrn. supervision, Fordham U., 1979, postgrad. Cert. adminstr. and supr. K-12, social studies and math. tchr. K-12, elem., intermediate and jr. high sch. asst. prin., elem., intermediate and junior high sch. prin., N.Y. Tchr. Prall Intermediate Sch., Staten Island, 1966—, administrv. asst., 1977-82. Mem. S.I. Hist. Soc., 1966-78, Friends of Down's Syndrome Found., S.I., 1978—, Sister Helen Flynn Scholarship Com., S.I., 1981—, Friends Seaview Hosp. and Home, S.I., 1984—, Friends S.I. Coll., 1979—. Recipient St. John's U. Pietas medal, 1991; named Tchr. of Yr., Fordham U., 1993; scholar N.Y. State Bd. Regents, 1962, Can. Consulate St. Lawrence U., 1987, Internat. Brotherhood Teamsters U. Calif., 1988, Nat. Geographic Soc. Geography Edn. Program SUNY, Binghamton, 1989, Women in History Program, N.Y. State Coun. for the Humanities, Albany; Impact II grantee N.Y.C. Bd. Edn., 1992. Mem. ASCD, Nat. Coun. Social Studies, N.Y. State Coun. Social Studies, N.Y.C. Coun. Social Studies, S.I. Coun. Social Studies, United Fedn. Tchrs., Am. Fedn. Tchrs., N.Y. State Hist. Soc., Notre Dame Coll. Alumnae Assn. (regent 1978-80, pres. 1982-84), St. John's U. Alumni Fedn. (del. 1980-88, sec. exec. bd. 1988-90, chmn. bd. 1990-94), Phi Delta Kappa (co-founder S.I. chpt., pres. 1985-87, other offices, Tchr. of Yr. award Fordham U. 1993, named Disting. Kappan 1994). Republican. Roman Catholic. Home: 174 Bertha Pl Staten Island NY 10301-3807 Office: Prall Intermediate Sch 11 Clove Lake Pl Staten Island NY 10310-2712

DOBRIANSKY, PAULA JON, business and communications executive, consultant; b. Alexandria, Va., Sept. 14; d. Lev Eugene and Julia Kusy D. BS summa cum laude, Sch. Fgn. Service, Georgetown U., 1977; MA, Harvard U., 1980, PhD, 1991. Adminstrv. aide Dept. Army, Washington, 1973-76; staff asst. Am. embassy, Rome, 1976; rsch. asst. joint econ. com. U.S. Congress, Washington, 1977-78; NATO analyst Bur. Intelligence and Rsch., Dept. State, Washington, 1979; staff mem. NSC, White House, Washington, 1980-83, dep. dir. European and Soviet affairs, 1983-84, dir. European and Soviet affairs, 1984-87; dep. asst. sec. of state for Human Rights and Humanitarian Affairs, 1987-90; dep. head U.S. Del. to Conf. on Security and Cooperation in Europe, Copenhagen, 1990; assoc. dir. for policy and programs U.S. Info. Agy., 1990-93; co-chair internat. TV coun. Corp. Pub. Broadcasting, 1993-94; sr. internat. affairs and trade advisor Hunton and Williams, Washington, 1994—. Host Freedom's Challenge, Nat. Empowerment Television, 1994—. Bd. dirs. Congl. Human Rights Found., 1994-95, Western NIS Enterprise Fund, 1994—, Am. Com. for Aid to Poland, 1994-95; bd. vis. George Mason U., 1994—. Fulbright-Hays scholar, 1978; Rotary Found. fellow, 1979, Ford Found. fellow, 1980, adj. fellow, Hudson Inst., 1993—; named one of ten Most Outstanding Young Women in Am., 1982, one of ten Outstanding Working Women of 1990, Ethnic Woman of Yr., 1990; recipient Georgetown U. Alumni Achievement award, 1986, State Dept. Superior Honor award, 1990. Mem. Internat. Inst. Strategic Studies, Coun. Fgn. Rels., Am. Polit. Sci. Assn., Fulbright Assn., Phi Beta Kappa, Phi Alpha Theta, Pi Sigma Alpha, U.S. Environ. Tng. Inst. (bd. adv. 1992-93), Harvard Club (bd. dirs. 1982-85), Nat. Endowment for Democracy (bd. dirs. 1993—, vice chmn. 1995—), Am. Coun. of Young Polit. Leaders (trustee 1993—), University Club (Washington). Office: Hunton & Williams 11th Fl 1900 K Street NW Washington DC 20006

DOBRINSKY, SUSAN ELIZABETH, human resources director; b. Warren, N.J., Sept. 25, 1943; d. Samuel Henry Jr. and Janet Adeline (Ryder) Christie; m. Stanley Dobrinsky, Feb. 12, 1972; children: David Stanley, Mark Alan. BA, Lycoming Coll., 1965. Pers. asst. County of Somerset, Somerville, N.J., 1970-74, pers. mgr., 1974-82, pers. dir., 1982-90, dir. adminstrn. County of Somerset, Somerville, 1991-95, dir. human resources, 1995—; gov. apptd. Pub. Employees Occupl. Safety and Health Adv. bd. Dept. of Labor, Trenton, N.J., 1984—; bd. trustees, treas. NJPELA, Somerville, N.J., 1993—; mem. Soc. Human Resource Mgmt. Ctrl. Jersey, Somerset, 1978—; pres. Cmty. Indsl. Rels. Orgn., Somerset, 1990-92; apptd. senate pres., mem. Pension Commn., Trenton, 1992—. Mem., dep. mayor Green Brook Twp. Commn., 1987-88, mayor, 1989-93; v.p. Somerset County Governing Offcls., 1990, pres., 1991; sec. Rep. Club, Green Brook, 1977. Recipient N.J. Alumni award 4-H Youth Devel. Program, 1992. Mem. Pub. Employees Occupl. Safety (health adv. bd. 1994—), N.J. Pension and Health Commn., Cmty. Indsl. Rels. Orgn. (treas. 1988-90, pres. 1990-92), Pub. Pers. Orgn. (pres. 1990—). Republican. Methodist. Home: 11 Glenn Ave Green Brook NJ 08812 Office: County of Somerset 20 Grove St Somerville NJ 08876

DOBROF, ROSE WIESMAN, geriatrics services professional; b. Denver, Nov. 11, 1924; d. Jerome and Mildred (Hornbein) W.; m. Alfred Dobrof, June 8, 1948; children: Marilyn, Joan, Susan, Judy. BA, U. Colo., 1945; MSW, U. Pitts., 1948; DSW, Columbia U., 1976; DHL (hon.), SUNY, 1996. Lect. div. social svcs. Ind. U., Bloomington, 1952-60; dir. group svc. and vol. dept. The Hebrew Home for the Aged at Riverdale, Bronx, N.Y., 1961-63, project dir., 1963-66, asst. dir., 1966-70; assoc. prof. Hunter Coll. CUNY, 1975-78, prof. Hunter Coll., 1979-93; Brookdale prof. gerontology CUNY, N.Y.C., 1979—; exec. dir. Brookdale Ctr. on Aging Hunter Coll., N.Y.C., 1974-93, acting v.p., 1993-94; vis. lectr. Columbia U., 1963-70; adv. bd. Ctr. Psychological Studies of Dying, Death and Lethal Behavior, Wayne State U., U. Mich., 1968-83; coord. social policy sequence Hunter Coll., 1970-75, 79-80; grant proposal review team U.S. Adminstrn. on Aging, 1978, 88, 91, capt. 1975, 85, 90; doctoral faculty grad. ctr. CUNY, 1979—; cons. U. Pitts. Office of Dep. Chancellor, 1980; rev. team Fund for the Improvement of Secondary Edn., 1981; profl. lectr. in community medicine Mt. Sinai Sch. Medicine, 1982—, co-dir. long-term gerontological ctr., 1979-81, co-dir. geriatric edn. ctr., 1985—; com. on profl. practice, Vis. Nurse Svc. of N.Y., 1973-83, com. on tng. home health care workers, 1979-83; cons. N.Y. State Moreland Act Commn., 1975-76, VA, 1977, N.Y. Community Trust, 1979-80, Ark. Dept. Health and Social Svcs., 1976-80; task force of experts in svc. delivery and rsch. Ctr. Mental Health of Aging, 1976; adv. com. long term care evaluation study N.Y. State Dept. Health, 1978-82; adv. bd. Amalgamated Clothing and Textile Workers Union, 1979-82; nat. adv. com. Work in Am. Inst., Inc., 1979-80; nat. review team, adv. bd. Living at Home project, Commonwealth and other foundations, 1986, chair gov.'s task force on long term care in year 2000, 1986; mem. gov.'s task force on older women, 1986-87; needs assessment work group N.Y.C. AIDS task force, 1988; adv. com. sr. citizen affairs for Congresswoman Nita M. Lowey, 1990—; adj. prof. gerontology, Coll. of Optometry, SUNY, 1990—; mem. N.Y. State Pub. Health Coun., 1991—, Gov.'s Health Care Adv. Bd., 1991-94; mem. policy com. White Ho. Conf. Aging, 1995, Fed. Coun. on Aging, 1994—; trustee N.Y. Found.,. Editor-in-chief The Jour. of Gerontological Social Work, 1977—. Co-chmn. com. on aging Fedn. Jewish Philanthropies, 1979-81, mem. com. on aging, 1987-90; trustee Jewish Assn. for Svcs. of the Aged, N.Y.C., 1977-83; adv. bd. Found. Thanatology, 1968-78; rsch. utilization adv. com. Cmty. Coun. Greater N.Y., 1974-80; statewide adv. coun. N.Y. State Dept. Social Svcs., 1977-79; bd. dirs. N.Y.C. chpt. Nat. Caucus and Ctr. for the Black Aged, 1982—; adv. bd. N.Y.C. Dept. Aging, Alzheimer's Disease Resource Ctr., 1983—; exec. com., adv. bd. N.Y. Cmty. Trust Ctr. on Policy in Aging, 1985—, vice chmn., 1987—; nat. rev. team Project Hometown Am., Am. Express, 1986; bd. dirs. St. Margaret's House, 1987-90, New York Found., 1996—; mem. Fed. Coun. on Aging, 1995—; trustee N.Y. Found., 1996—; sr. fellow The Brookdale Found., 1985—. Named One of Five Outstanding Alumni, U. Pitts., 1979; recipient Outstanding Alumnus award for excellence in social work edn., U. Pitts., 1981, award for outstanding leadership in the field of social work, Nat. Assn. Soc. Workers, 1983, Robert Ray Parks award, 1986, Alice Brophy award, The Burden Ctr., 1987, The Gift of Life award, Parker Jewish Geriatric Inst., 1989, The Walter M. Beattie Jr. award N.Y. State Assn. Gerontol. Educators Inst., 1989, 1990 Social Worker in Aging award Nat. Assn. Social Workers, 1990, The Pres.'s medal Hunter Coll., 1991, Gerontology Educator Merit award, 1991, award of Merit Older Women's League Greater N.Y., 1993, Elinor Guggenheimer award Coun. Sr. Ctrs. and Svcs., 1995. Fellow N.Y. Acad. Medicine; mem. Vacations for the Aging and Sr. Citizen's Assn. (bd. dirs. 1974-77), Fres of the Institutionalized Aged (pres. 1976-80, bd. dirs. 1980-88), Acad. for the Humanities and Scis., Nat. Assn. Social Workers, Nat. Coun. on Aging, Am. Pub. Welfare Assn., N.Y. Acad. Sci., Am. Soc. in Aging, Gerontological Soc., Phi Beta Kappa, Delta Sigma Rho, Pi Gamma Mu. Democrat. Jewish. Office: Brookdale Ctr on Aging 425 E 25th St New York NY 10010-2547

DOBRONSKI, AGNES MARIE, state legislator; b. Detroit, Apr. 21, 1925; d. Clarence Robert and Agnes Frieda (Franz) Dobronski; m. James Z. Cichocki, June 27, 1987; stepchildren: Thomas, Jerry. BS, Detroit Coll. Bus., 1970; MA, Eastern Mich. U., 1975. Bus. mgr. Dearborn (Mich.) Pub. Schs., 1943-80; exec. dir. Retirement Coord. Coun., Lansing, Mich., 1980-85; mem. Mich. Ho. of Reps., 1987-88, 91—. Trustee Dearborn Bd. Edn., Henry Ford Community Coll., 1980-86. Recipient Disting. Alumna award Detroit Coll. Bus., 1974, Disting. Citizen award Henry Ford Cmty. Coll., 1987, Disting. Alumni award Henry Ford Cmty. Coll., 1989; named Sch. Adminstr. of Yr. Dearborn PTA Council, 1978. Democrat. Lutheran. Home: PO Box 1948 Dearborn MI 48121-1948 Office: House of Reps State Capitol Lansing MI 48909-7514

DOBRY, ALIKI CALIRROE, artist; b. Alexandria, Egypt, Sept. 11, 1929; came to U.S., 1953; d. Apostolos and Irene (Papassinessiou) Zafiriadis; m. Edward Adams Dobry, July 2, 1954 (dec. July 1985); children: Mary M., Dorothy Ann., Alice Elizabeth. BA in Arts, U. Alexandria, Egypt, 1950; M in Arts, U. Ga., 1953; BA in Fine Arts, St. Mary's Coll., St. Mary's City, Md., 1992. Mgr. mail dept. Ford Motor Co., Alexandria, Egypt, 1952; English tchr. Great Mills H.S., Md., 1954-55; mgr., co-owner St. Mary's Vet. Hosp., Lexington Park, Md., 1955-87. One woman shows include Gallery N. Psychico, Athens, Greece, 1995; exhibited in group shows at Internat. Bienale, Paris, 1993, Chapelle de la Sorbonne, Paris, 1994, Mattawoman Creek Art Ctr., Md., 1994 (supr. artist award 1994), Paris, 1994 (grand prix de Paris award 1994), Michael Stone Gallery, Washington, 1994, Gallery N. Psychico, Athens, Greece, 1995, Agora Gallery, 1996. Brownie leader Greek Girl Scouts, Alexandria, Egypt, 1949-50, hon. mem., 1990—; vol. March of Dimes, Leukemia Soc., Cancer Soc., Calif., Md., 1993—. Recipient scholarship Rotary Club Knights Templar, 1953; 2d prize Aurora Artists, 1995. Mem. Md. Fedn. Arts, Arts Alliance, Mattawoman Art Creek. Home: 721 Poplarwood Dr California MD 20619

DOBRZYN, JANET ELAINE, quality management professional; b. Allentown, Pa., Oct. 9, 1956; d. Frank John and Doris (Ross) D. Diploma, Pottsville Hosp. Sch. Nursing, 1977; AA, L.A. Valley Coll., 1984; BSN, Calif. State Coll., Long Beach, 1985; MSN, Azusa (Calif.) Pacific U., 1991. RN, Calif., Okla., Pa., Ky.; cert. profl. healthcare quality. Charge nurse evenings Allentown (Pa.) Osteo. hosp., 1977-80; charge nurse relief Encino (Calif.) Hosp., 1980-81; registry nurse Profl. Staffing, Northridge, Calif., 1981-82; clin. nurse II pediatric ICU Childrens Hosp. of L.A., 1982-86, clin. info. specialist, 1986-89; quality mgmt. specialist PacifiCare of Calif., Cypress, 1989-91, quality mgmt. spl. projects coord., 1991-92; mgr. quality mgmt. PacifiCare of Okla., Tulsa, 1992-93, sr. project specialist quality mgmt., 1993-95; accreditation facilitator Humana, Louisville, Ky., 1995-96; mgr. quality mgmt. Healthwise of Ky., Lexington, 1996—; cons., reviewer of prototype pub. Commerce Clearing House, Inc., Riverwoods, Ill., 1993; mem. ANA/GHAA task force to develop nursing curriculum in managed care for nursing students, 1994; speaker in field. Camp nurse vol. Forest Home Conf. Ctr., San Bernardino, Calif., 1988. Mem. Nat. Assn. for Healthcare Quality, Sigma Theta Tau (newsletter editor). Republican. Home: 207 Rolling Ridge Way Simpsonville KY 40067 Office: Healthwise of Kentucky 2409 Hamodsburg Rd Lexington KY 40504

DOBS, ADRIAN SANDRA, endocrinologist, educator; b. June 27, 1952; m. Martin Auster; children: Nina Auster, Becky Auster, Harry Auster, Paul Auster. BS in Nutrition Scis., Cornell U., 1973; MD, Albany Med. Coll., 1978; MHS in Cardiovascular Epidemiology, Johns Hopkins U., 1990. Diplomate Nat. Bd. Med. Examiners, Am. Bd. Internal Medicine, Am. Bd. Endocrinology and Metabolism. Resident in internal medicine Montefiore Hosp. Med. Ctr./Albert Einstein Coll. Medicine, Bronx, N.Y., 1978-81, chief resident, 1981-82; instr. medicine, physicians asst. program CCNY, N.Y.C., 1981-82; endocrinology fellow Johns Hopkins U., Balt., 1982-84, instr. divsn. endocrinology and metabolism, 1984-87, asst. prof. medicine, 1987-93, assoc. prof. medicine, 1993—, vice chair dept. medicine, clin. rsch., 1996—; mem. study sect., adv. com. Nat. Inst. Aging, 1992, NIH, 1993, 94; lectr. in field. Reviewer Am. Jour. Clin. Nutrition, Am. Jour. Medicine, Diabetes Care, Jour. AMA, Jour. Clin. Endocrinology and Metabolism, New Eng. Jour. Medicine; contbr. articles, abstracts to profl. jours., chpts. to books. Recipient Rsch. award Women Physicians Stetler Found., 1986-87; scholar Leopold Schepp Found., 1975, Vanderbilt U., 1976, Carnegie-Mellon Found., 1984-85, Robert Glassner Found. Diabetes Rsch., 1985-86; grantee Merck, Inc., 1991-93, TheraTech, Inc., 1991-94, NIH, 1992-93, 92—, Diabetes Rsch. and Edn. Found., 1992-93, Johns Hopkins Out-patient Clin. Rsch. Ctr., 1992-93. Mem. ACP, Am. Coll. Nutrition, Am. Diabetes Assn. (award Md. chpt. 1986-87), Am. Fedn. Clin. Rsch. (Johns Hopkins rep. 1990—, sch. coun. 1990—), Am. Heart Assn. (epidemiology coun. 1985, grantee 1990-94), Endocrine Soc. Home: 3510 Anton Farms Rd Baltimore MD 21208-1703 Office: Johns Hopkins Hosp 906B Blalock Bldg 600 N Wolfe St Baltimore MD 21205-2110

DOBSON, BRIDGET MCCOLL HURSLEY, television executive and writer; b. Milw., Sept. 1, 1938; d. Franklin McColl and Doris (Berger) Hursley; m. Jerome John Dobson, June 16, 1961; children: Mary McColl, Andrew Carmichael. BA, Stanford U., 1960, MA, 1964; CBA, Harvard U., 1961. Assoc. writer General Hospital ABC-TV, 1965-73, head writer General Hospital, 1973-75; producer Friendly Road Sta. KIXE-TV, Redding, Calif., 1972; head writer Guiding Light CBS-TV, 1975-80, head writer As the World Turns, 1980-83; creator, co-owner Santa Barbara NBC-TV, 1983—, head writer Santa Barbara, 1983-86, 91, exec. producer Santa Barbara, 1986-87, 91, creative prodn. exec. Santa Barbara, 1990-91; pres. Dobson Global Entertainment, L.A., 1994—. Author, co-lyricist: Slings and Eros, 1993; prodr. Confessions of a Nightingale, 1994. Recipient Emmy award, 1988. Mem. Nat. Acad. TV Arts and Scis. (com. on substance abuse 1986-88), Writers Guild Am. (award for Guiding Light 1977, for Santa Barbara 1991), Am. Film Inst. (mem. TV com. 1986-88). Office: 3490 Piedmont Rd NW Ste 1206 Atlanta GA 30305

DOBSON, PATRICIA ANN, educational promotions coordinator; b. Springfield, Mass., Jan. 9, 1962; d. Thomas III and Catherine Eileen (Beatrice) D.; m. Louis Donofrio Jr., Oct. 26, 1990. BS in Comm., Ea. N.Mex. U., 1989, postgrad., 1996—. Stringer Clovis (N.Mex.) News Jour., 1988-89, lifestyles editor, 1990-91; promotions coord. Coll. Fine Arts Ea. N.Mex. U., Portales, 1991—; adj. faculty Ea. N.Mex. U., Portales, 1994-95; mem. N.Mex. Press Assn., 1988-91. Pub.: Voices Christian Mag., 1994—; designer: (brochures) School of Music brochure, 1995 (1st pl. award 1995), Coll. Fine Arts newsletter, 1995 (1st pl. award 1995); author, designer: (dist. newsletter) Altru-News for District Ten, 1995-97. Bd. dirs. LifeSaver Food Bank, Clovis, 1993—; mem. Altrusa Internat. Clovis, 1990—. Gordon Greaves Meml. scholar Ea. N.Mex. U., 1989. Mem. Nat. Fedn. Press Women, N.Mex. Press Women Assn. (chair h.s. journalism contest 1991-92), Ea. N.Mex. Tourism Assn., Ea. N.Mex. Media Assn. (pres. 1990-91), Inspirational Writers Alive!, Altrusa Club Clovis (pres.-elect, pres. 1992-94), Epsilon Mu Beta. Home: 320 W Yucca Ave Clovis NM 88101 Office: Ea N Mex U Coll Fine Arts Station 16 Portales NM 88130

DOBY, KAREN ELAINE, data processing company executive; b. Amarillo, Tex., Nov. 1, 1955; d. Laurance Lee and Helen Marie (Davis) D. AS, Belleville (Ill.) Area Coll., 1976; BS, So. Ill. U., Edwardsville, Ill., 1977; MS, Georgetown U., 1978; MBA, Loyola U., New Orleans, 1984. Ops. researcher Dept. of Energy, Washington, 1977-78; geophysicist Naval Oceanographic Office, Bay St. Louis, Miss., 1978-82; engring. analyst Middle S. Utilities System, New Orleans, 1982; sr. systems analyst, mgr. Exploration and Devel. Systems CNG Producing Co., New Orleans, 1982-88; mgr. network security Sun Micro Systems, Inc., Mountain View, Calif., 1992-96; dir. enterprise svcs. Sun Microsystems, Inc., Mountain View, Ca., 1996—; cons. Macrobiotic Inst., New Orleans, 1987—. Mem. Nat. Computer Graphics Assn., IEEE Computer Soc., Am. Assn. Petroleum Geologists. Democrat. Home: 4546 B-10 El Camino Real # 321 Los Altos CA 94022-1041

DOCKTOR-SMITH, MARY ANN, employee benefits consultant; b. Indpls., Jan. 26, 1957; d. Leo Edward and Geraldine Marie (Staudt) Docktor; m. Randolph Davis Smith, July 11, 1981. Student, Loyola U., Chgo., 1988—. Cert. Qualified Pension Adminstr. Asst. dir. pension adminstrn. Indpls. Life, 1976-78; pres. Pen-Ad, Inc., Chgo., 1978-82; mgr. Aetna Life Ins. Co., Chgo., 1982-83; pres. Creative Pensions, Inc., Chgo., 1982-84, EBI Employee Benefits, Inc., Chgo., 1984—, The Flag Docktor Inc., Chgo., 1993—; treas. Adv. Flag Co., Inc., Chgo., 1983—. Co-author: The Only Tax-shelter You'll Ever Need, 1991; column author: Gene Balliett Report, 1984—; contbr. articles to profl. jour. Vol. adult reading tutor Literacy Chgo.; donor Ayn Rand Inst., Marina Del Rey, Calif., 1990—; mem. chmn.'s coun. Rep. Nat. Com. Acad. scholar Otto Lehman Found., Chgo., 1991-94. Mem. Am. Soc. Pension Actuaries, N.Am. Vexillogical Assn. (chmn. pub. rels. com., corr. sec. 1993—), Chgo. Coun. Fgn. Rels., Golden Key, Alpha Sigma Nu, Alpha Sigma Lamda, Pi Sigma Alpha. Republican. Office: EBI Employee Benefits Inc 4949 W Diversey Ave Chicago IL 60639-1705

DODD, DARLENE MAE, nurse, air force officer; b. Dowagiac, Mich., Oct. 11, 1935; d. Charles B. and Lila H. D.; diploma in nursing Borgess Hosp. Sch. Nursing, Kalamazoo, 1957; grad. U.S. Air Force Flight Nurse Course, 1959, U.S. Air Force Squadron Officers Sch., 1963, Air Command and Staff Coll., 1973; BS in Psychology and Gen. Studies, So. Oreg. State Coll., 1987, postgrad., 1987; Commd. 2d lt. U.S. Air Force, 1959, advanced through grades to lt. col., 1975; staff nurse, Randolph AFB, Tex., 1959-60, Ladd AFB, Alaska, 1960-62, Selfridge AFB, Mich., 1962-63; Cam Rahn Bay Air Base, Vietnam, 1966-67, Seymour Johnson AFB, N.C., 1967-69, Air Force Acad., 1971-72; flight nurse 22d Aeromed. Evacuation, Tex., 1963-66; chief nurse Danang AFB, Vietnam, 1967; flight nurse Yokotu AFB, Japan, 1969-71; clin. coordinator ob/gyn and flight nurse, Elmendorf AFB, Alaska, 1973-76; clin. nurse coordinator obstetrics-gynecology and pediatric services USAF Med. Center, Keesler AFB, Miss., 1976-79, ret., 1979. Decorated Bronze Star, Meritorious Service medal, Air Force Commendation medal (3). Mem. Soc. of Ret. Air Force Nurses, DAV, Ret. Officers Assn., Vietnam Vets. Am., VFW, Uniformed Services Disabled Retirees, Air Force Assn., Psy Chi, Phi Kappa Phi. Club: Women of Moose. Home: 712 1st St Phoenix OR 97535-9787

DODD, DEBORAH JANE, military contracting officer; b. Longmont, Colo., Oct. 11, 1947; d. John Jerome and Margaret Cora (Slee) D. BA, U. Colo., 1969; cert. teaching, Keane Coll., 1971; MS, San Jose State U., 1975. Vista vol. Palatka, Fla., 1969-70; tchr. N.J. Urban Edn. Corp., Newark, 1971-72, English Conversation Circle, Tokyo, Japan, 1972-73; camp dir. Baker Beach Golden Gate Nat. Recreation Area, San Francisco, 1975; recreation therapist Casa Grande (Ariz.) Rehab. Ctr., 1975-76; office mgr., counselor Tucson Rape Crisis Ctr., 1976-78; customs inspector U.S. Customs Service, Nogales, Ariz., 1978-81; elem. edn. tchr. Salome Show-Low Schs., Ariz., 1981-82; contract negotiator and contracting officer USAF, McClellan AFB, Calif., 1982—; gen. ptnr. Wymer and Assocs. Biol. Cons., Citrus Heights, Calif., 1986—. Mem. Calif. Native Plant Soc., McClellan Mgmt. Soc., Nat. Contract Mgmt. Assn., Federally Employed Women, Phi Beta Kappa. Democrat.

DODD, SYLVIA BLISS, special education educator; b. Ft. Worth, July 21, 1939; d. William Solomon and Sylvia Bliss (Means) Fisher; m. Melvin Joe Dodd, Sept. 4, 1959 (div. 1967); children: Lisa Dawn, Marcus Jay, Chadwick Scott. BA, Tex. Wesleyan Coll., Ft. Worth, 1960; MEd, Tex. Christian U., Ft. Worth, 1976. Tchr. Castleberry Ind. Sch. Dist., Ft. Worth, 1960-62; tchr. Hurst-Euless-Bedford (Tex.) Ind. Sch. Dist., 1967-69, dir. spl. edn., 1969-94; instr. Tex. Wesleyan Coll., Ft. Worth, 1978, 94—, Tex. Christian U., Ft. Worth, 1980. Bd. dirs. Mental Health Assn., Ft. Worth, 1983-88, 91-95, March of Dimes, Mid Cities, Tex., 1990, United Cmty. Ctrs., Ft. Worth, 1989—, pres., 1994-95; bd. dirs. So. Meth. U. Campus Ministry, 1992—; mem. adminstrv. bd. 1st United Meth. Ch., Ft. Worth, 1990-93, 95—; lay leader West Ft. Worth Dist. United Meth. Ch., 1992-96. Named Conf. Chairperson of Yr. Nat. Health and Welfare Ministries, 1981; recipient Outstanding Woman award Tex. Wesleyan U., 1991, Disting. Educator award, 1991. Mem. ASCD, Mental Health Assn. (pres. 1979-80), Nat. Coun. Exceptional Children, Tex. Coun. Adminstrs. Spl. Edn. (Hall of Honor award 1991, pres. 1975-76). Democrat. Methodist. Home and Office: 829 Timberhill Dr Hurst TX 76053-4240

DODDS, CLAUDETTE LA VONN, radio executive and consultant; b. Lenapah, Okla., Sept. 2, 1947; d. Willie Lee and Dora (Harrell) Davis; m. Donald Howard Dodds, Jan. 14, 1965 (div. June 1982); children: Clarence Adam, Donyielle Alana, Erin Michelle. AAS with honors, Kennedy-King Coll., 1984; BA, U. Ill., Chgo., 1989. Newscaster, newswriter Sta. WKKC-FM, Chgo., 1983-84, news dir., 1984-85, program and music dir., 1985, sta. mgr., 1985-87; research asst. Vernon Jarrett Chgo. Sun Times, 1988-89; exec. asst. to pres. Sta. WVON, Chgo., 1989; asst. sta. mgr. Sta. WYCA-FM, Crawford Broadcasting Co., Chgo., Hammond, Ind., 1989-90; mem. adv. com. Coll. Broadcasting, 1985-87; cons. Chgo. Nite Life, 1985-87, Hayes & Co., 1986—, Morning Show/Danny Jack Sta. KWEZ, Monroe, La., 1986—, Sta. WKKC-FM, Future Records, 1988—; music rschr. Let's Dance, Chgo., 1986-88; broadcast asst. Sta. WVON, Chgo., 1989, exec. bd. Young People's Network Sta. WKKC-FM, 1988—, Youth on the Move, 1994, facilitator YPN workshops, 1994. Producer: (TV special) Messiah, 1985, Youth on the Move, 1994; producer, writer (radio and TV specials) Dr. Martin Luther King, 1985-86; producer, hostess (radio specials) Englewood Parade, 1986, Bud Billiken Parade, 1986; mag. music reporter, 1987; editor current affairs newsletter, 1992. Mem. Dem. Student task force, Chgo., 1984, Student Disciplinary Bd., Chgo., 1986; coord. Concerned Studies for Broadcasting Equipment, 1984; mem. task force for AIDS Prevention, 1993—, cons. AIDS task force, mem. program evaluation com., 1994—; vol. Darrell Stingley Youth Found., 1994; bd. dirs. Midwest Ctr. for Comprehensive Svc.; active caring for patients with HIV/AIDS, providing med. svcs., housing and counseling. Recipient Alumni Recognition award Kennedy-King Coll., 1993. Mem. Coalition Labor Union Women, Families Advocating Injury Reduction, Ams. for Legal Reform, Order of Eastern Star (Cable chpt. # 108 Prince Hall), Sorority and Heroines of Jericho (Rahab Ct. # 61), Sigma

Gamma Rho (Delta Sigma chpt.). Home and Office: 305 W 69th St Chicago IL 60621-3720

DODDS, LINDA CAROL, insurance company executive; b. Tucson, June 2, 1957; d. George A. and Bette R. (Bell) D. AA, U. Md., 1979; BA, Tex. Tech U., 1982; MBA, Our Lady of the Lake U., 1986. Svc. rep. USAA, San Antonio, 1982-84, sr. mgr., 1985-86; asst. area mgr. USAA, Tampa, Fla., 1986-88, area mgr., 1988-92, dist. mgr., 1992—; portfolio asst. USAA-IMCO, San Antonio, 1984-85; spkr. in field. Treas. Forest Hills Homeowners Assn., Tampa, 1992-93; mem. Tex. Fedn. Rep. Women, San Antonio, 1985; co-chair United Way, Zero, 1995-96; active USAA Vol. Corp., Tampa, 1989—. Mem. Soc. CPCU, Delta Mu Delta, Sigma Iota Epsilon. Office: USAA SE Regional Office 17200 Commerce Park Blvd Tampa FL 33647

DODELES, ELISE, artist, illustrator; b. Freeport, N.Y., Jan. 4, 1964; d. Moses N. and Carole Colleen (Seiler) D. Student, Carnegie-Mellon U., 1981-83; BS, NYU, 1985; MFA, N.Y. Acad. Art, 1990; postgrad., Sch. Visual Arts, 1990-91. Asst. prodn. mgr. Miller Advt. Agy., N.Y.C., 1987-89; art tchr. St. Ignatius Loyola Parochial Sch., N.Y.C., 1990; freelance illustrator N.Y.C., 1991—; electronic art assoc. Visual Edn. Corp., Princeton, N.J., 1994—. Exhibited in exhibitions at Forbes Gallery, Carnegie-Mellon U., Pitts., 1983, Pitts Plan for Art, 1983, N.Y. Acad. Art Gallery, 1987, Ramapo (N.J.) Coll., 1988, Follow Your Art Gallery, Long Beach, N.Y., 1990, D.C. Arts Ctr., 1991, ABC No Rio, N.Y.C., 1991, Trial Balloon 2 Gallery, N.Y.C., 1992, Jack Hanley Gallery, San Francisco, 1994, U. Man. (Can.) Sch. of Art, 1994, Gallery Behemot, Prague, Czech Republic, 1994. N.Y. Acad. Art scholar, 1986. Mem. Coll. Art Assn. Home: 425 Huff Rd North Brunswick NJ 08902 Office: Visual Edn Corp 14 Washington Rd Princeton NJ 08543

DODERER, MINNETTE FRERICHS, state legislator; b. Holland, Iowa, May 16, 1923; d. John A. and Sophie S. Frerichs; BA, U. Iowa, 1948; m. Fred H. Doderer, Aug. 5, 1944 (dec. 1991); children: Dennis, Kay Lynn. Mem. Iowa Ho. of Reps. 1964-69, 80—, minority whip, 1967-68, chairperson ways and means com., 1983-88, chair commerce com., 1989-90, chair small bus., econ. devel. and trade com., 1991-92; mem. Iowa Senate, 1970-79, pres. pro tem, 1975-76; vis. prof. Stephens Coll., Iowa State Univ. (both 1979); vice-chairwoman Iowa Interstate Cooperation Commn., 1965-66; Vice-chairwoman Democratic Party Johnson County, 1957-60; vice chairperson com. on budget and taxation Nat. Conf. State Legislator's; mem. Dem. Nat. Com., 1968-70, Dem. Nat. Policy Council Elected Ofcls., 1973-76; chairwoman Iowa del. Internat. Women's Yr. Del. Bd. fellows Iowa Sch. Religion. Recipient Disting. Service award Iowa Edn. Assn., 1969, Wilson award Commn. on Status of Women, 1989, Gold Seal award Iowa Coalition Against Domestic Violence, 1995; named to Iowa Women's Hall of Fame, 1978; named Woman of Yr. Iowa City Sr. Ctr., 1995. Mem. LWV, Pioneer Lawmakers (pres. 1993-95), Delta Kappa Gamma (hon.). Democrat. Methodist.

DODGE, ELIZABETH LEYON, English educator; b. Newton, Mass., July 28, 1936; d. Renus Edward and Louise (Riblet) Leyon; m. David Sinclair Dodge, Aug. 22, 1959; children: Jennifer Dodge Eldredge, John Sinclair Dodge II, Andrew David. BA, Univ. New Hampshire, 1958, MEd, 1963. H.s. eng. tchr. Somersworth (N.H.) H.S., 1959-64; h.s. eng. tchr. Oyster River H.S., Durham, N.H., 1978—, dept. chair, 1980-88, 90-95; reader Eng. achievement Coll. Bd. ETS, Princeton, N.J., 1964-66, 82-86; reader advanced placement eng., 1965-66; presenter at numerous confs. Co-author: Weaving In The Women: Transforming The High School English Curriculum, 1993. Trustee Exeter Cong. Ch., 1983-85; mem. Brentwood Sch. Bd., 1975-84. Mem. Nat. Coun. Tchrs. of Eng., N.H. Assn. Tchrs. Eng. Home: 185 High St Exeter NH 03833 Office: Oyster River H S 55 Coe Dr Durham NH 03824

DODGE, KIRSTIN SUE, lawyer; b. N.Y.C., Apr. 23, 1966. BA in Polit. Sci., Yale U., 1988; postgrad. studies, U. Fribourg, Switzerland, 1988-89; JD, Harvard U., 1992. Bar: Wash., 1992. Law clk. Hon. Thomas S. Zilly U.S. Dist. Ct., Seattle, 1992-94; vis. lectr. Inst. for Civil Law U. Bern, Switzerland, 1994; assoc. Law Office Marilyn J. Endriss PS, Seattle, 1994-96, Perkins Coie, Bellevue, 1996—. Editor-in-chief Harvard Women's Law Jour., 1992; contbr. articles to profl. jours. Mem. exec. bd. Harvard Law Sch. Assn. Gay, Lesbian, and Bisexual Alumni/ae Com., 1994-96, nat. co-chair 1996—; membership com. N.W. Women's Law Ctr., Seattle, 1996. Recipient Grad. Fellow scholarship Rotary Internat. Found., 1988-89. Mem. Wash. State Bar Assn., King County Bar Assn. (bd. trustees young lawyers divsn. 1996—). Democrat. Office: Perkins Coie 411-108th Ave NE Ste 1800 Bellevue WA 98004-5584

DODOHARA, JEAN NOTON, music educator; b. Monroe, Wis., Feb. 21, 1934; d. Albert Henry and Eunice Elizabeth (Edgerton) Noton; BA, Monmouth (Ill.) Coll., 1955; MS, U. Ill., 1975, adminstrv. cert., 1980, EdD, 1985; m. Laurence G. Landers, June 7, 1955 (div.); children: Theodore Scott, Thomas Warren, Philip John; m. Edward R. Harris, Nov. 27, 1981 (dec.); stepchildren: Adrianne, Erica; m. Takashi Dodohara, Aug. 7, 1988; 1 stepchild, Eve D. Dodohara. Tchr. music schs. in Ill. and Fla., 1955-76; tchr. ch. music for children, 1957-72; tchr. music Dist. 54, Schaumburg, Ill., 1976-93; teaching asst. U. Ill., 1979. Named Outstanding Young Woman of Yr., Jaycee Wives, St. Charles, Mo., 1968; charter mem. Nat. Mus. Women in Arts. Mem. NEA (life), AAUW, Music Educators Nat. Conf. (life), Ill. Educators Assn. (life), Elgin Area Ret. Tchrs. Assn., U. Ill. Alumni Assn. (life), Mortar Bd., Mensa, Delta Kappa Pi. Mem. United Ch. of Christ. Home: 1068 Hampshire Ln Elgin IL 60120-4905

DODRILL, BARBARA RUTH, business educator; b. Miles City, Mont., Aug. 18, 1927; d. Loren Brownlee and Frances H. (Weiser) Brownlee Sommers; m. Donald L. Dodrill, Dec. 21, 1946; children: Nona June Scott, Walter Fred. BS cum laude, So. Oreg. State U., 1970; M of Bus. Edn., Oreg. State U., 1971. Various office positions Moore Mill and Lumber Co./Coquille Plywood, Bandon, Oreg., 1955-65; dist. clk., bus. mgr. Bandon Sch. Dist., 1965-68; tchr. Pacific H.S., Pt. Orford and Langlois, Oreg., 1970-72; prof., workshop leader Southwestern Oreg. C.C., Coos Bay, 1972—; coord. Am. Mgmt. Assn. adminstrv. asst. cert. program Southwestern Oreg. C.C. Bus. Devel. Ctr., Coos Bay, 1995-96. Author: (office simulation) Big Timber Lumber Company, 1975, (practice set acctg.) We Do Windows, 1980. Councilor City of Bandon, 1994—. Named Bus. Woman of Yr., Am. Bus. Women's Assn., 1981. Mem. Zonta Internat. Presbyterian. Home: PO Box 432 850 N Michigan Bandon OR 97411

DODSON, ALICEJEAN LEIGH, nursing administrator; b. S.I., N.Y., May 13, 1941; d. Wilbur Thomas Jr. and Beatrice Bertha (Beinert) Leigh; m. Robert Jean Olsen, Dec. 14, 1963 (div. Dec. 1969); 1 child, Aric Robert Olsen; m. Jonathan Boyd Dodson, June 1, 1988; stepchildren: Jacquelyn Nicole, Richard Lewis. BSN, Gustavus Adolphus Coll., 1963; postgrad., U. Puget Sound, 1977-78; M in Nursing, U. Wash., 1979. RN, Minn., Wash., Pa., Va., D.C., Ky., Md. Head nurse ICU, nursing instr. Mary Bridge Children's Hosp., Tacoma, 1967-74; instr. Tacoma C.C., 1974-76, 77-78; instnl. nursing cons. State of Wash., Olympia, 1980-81; head nurse ICU Good Samaritan Hosp., Puyallup, Wash., 1981-83; spl. projects mgr. Puget Sound Hosp., Tacoma, 1983-88; program mgr. Frankfurt (Germany) Mil. Cmty., 1988-90; survey team adminstr. Health Mgmt. Strategies, Alexandria, Va., 1990-92; clin. practice specialist Am. Health Care Assn., Washington, 1992-95; DON Continence Care, Inc., Vienna, Va., 1995—; ptnr. Owens-Moore Inc., Tacoma, 1987-88; reviewer on incontinence Agy. Health Care Policy & Rsch., Washington, 1994-95. Charter mem. Nat. Mus. Women in the Arts; mem. Tacoma Arts Commn., 1987-88; vice chairperson Pub. Arts Task Force, Tacoma, 1986. Mem. Soc Urologic Nurses and Assocs. Lutheran. Home: 6707 Kenmont Pl Springfield VA 22152 Office: Continence Care Inc 2110 B Gallows Rd Vienna VA 22182

DODSON, CLAUDIA LANE, athletic administrator; b. Washington, Aug. 31, 1941; d. Claude James and Edna Vera (Lane) D. BS in Phys. Edn., Westhampton Coll., 1963; MS in Phys. Edn., U. Tenn., 1965. Cert. tchr., Va. Tchr., coach Meadowbrook H.S., Chesterfield, Va., 1963-64, 65-71; grad. asst. U. Tenn., Knoxville, 1964-65; asst. dir. Va. H.S. League, Charlottesville, Va., 1971—; chmn. USOC Women's Basketball Com., Colorado Springs, Colo., 1976-80; mem. Nat. Basketball Rules Com., Elgin, Ill. and Kansas City, 1976-81; mem. U. Richmond (Va.) Athletic Coun., 1982-85; officials observer Atlantic Coast Conf., Greensboro, N.C., 1989—; spkr. in field. Mem. AAHPERD, Va. Assn. Health, Phys. Edn., Recreation and Dance, Nat. Interscholastic Athletic Adminstrs. Assn. (cert. adminstr.), Va. Interscholastic Athletic Adminstrs. Assn. (life), Women's Basketball Coaches' Assn., Westhampton Coll. Alumnae Assn. (chpt. pres. 1977-79), Delta Kappa Gamma (Rho chpt., pres. 1982-84), Phi Delta Kappa (treas. 1986—). Presbyterian. Home: 2540 Cedar Ridge Ln Charlottesville VA 22901 Office: Va H S League 1642 State Farm Blvd Charlottesville VA 22911

DODSWORTH, MARJORIE VAN SCOYOC, educator; b. Altoona, Pa., Dec. 30, 1935; d. Roger and Violet Marie (Dunn) Van Scoyoc; m. R.E. Kelly (dec. Jan. 1958); 1 child, Gregory D.; m. G.A. Dodsworth (div. Jan. 1977); dec. Jan. 1996. BS in Secondary Edn., Edinboro U., 1966; MS in English Edn., Syracuse U., 1971. Advt. asst. Erie (Pa.) Resistor Corp., 1954-62; tchr. North Syracuse (N.Y.) Sch. Dist., 1966-71, Girard (Pa.) Sch. Dist., 1971-72, Erie Sch. Dist., 1972—. Mem. NEA, ASCD, AAUW, Nat. Coun. Tchrs. English, Internat. Reading Assn. Office: Ctrl High Sch N 3325 Cherry St Erie PA 16508

DOEHLING, HELEN MARY, elementary education educator; b. Solihull, Eng., Feb. 26, 1962; came to U.S., 1988; d. Lawrence and Mary Gladys Rose (Pinfold) Andrew; m. Leslie Eugene Doehling, Aug. 12, 1988. BSc in Geography, Liverpool (Eng.) U., 1984; postgrad., Crewe and Alsagar Coll Edn., 1986; MEd, Lesley Coll., Boston, 1993. Cert. in elem. edn., Colo. Jr. sch. tchr. Redbridge Edn. Authority, London, 1986-88; substitute tchr. Mesa County Dist. 51, Grand Junction, Colo., 1988-90, tchr. 1st grade, 1990—. Contbr. poem to Nat. Library of Poetry, 1994. Mem. Internat. Reading Assn. Mem. Ch. of England. Home: 3124 Americana Dr Grand Junction CO 81504 Office: Nisley Elem Sch 543 28 3/4 Rd Grand Junction CO 81501

DOEHR-BLANCK, DENISE LOUISE, special education educator; b. Milw., Feb. 10, 1963; d. Dennis DeWayne and Mary Lou (Viola) Doehr; m. Timothy James Blanck, June 24, 1989. BA in Early Childhood Edn., Mt. Mary Coll., 1985; MA in Spl. Edn., Cardinal Stritch Coll., 1989. Tchr. grade 1 St. Jude the Apostle, Wauwatosa, Wis., 1985-89; pvt. practice edn. therapist Wauwatosa, 1986-90; edn. specialist Northbrooke Psychiat. Hosp., Brown Deer, Wis., 1989-91; instr. Waukesha County Tech. Coll., Pewaukee, Wis., 1990-91; edn. therapist Comprehensive Mental Health Svcs., Milw., 1990-92; pvt. practice ednl. therapist West Allis, Wis., 1991—; spkr., spl. ednl. therapist Northbrooke Hosp., Brown Deer, Wis., 1989-91; spl. edn. jr. h.s. tchr. St. Francis, Milw., 1993—; acad. coord. St. Francis Children's Ctr., 1994—. Columnist: Ask the Teacher, Chadd Tiddings, 1994—. Mem. Friends of the Milw. Symphony Orch., Zoo Pride. Theresa Ross scholar Mt. Mary Coll., 1983, 84. Mem. Coun. for Exceptional Children, Internat. Reading Assn., Wis. Reading Assn., Orton Dyslexia Soc. (sec. Wis. br. 1987-88), Learning Disabilities Assn. Wis., Children with Learning Disabilities, Nat. Assn. for Child and Adults with Learning Disabilities, Ch.A.D.D. of S.E. Wis. (sec. 1988-95). Republican. Roman Catholic. Home: 1109 S 90th St Milwaukee WI 53214-2838 Office: St Francis 6700 N Port Washington Rd Milwaukee WI 53217-3919

DOEPKE, KATHERINE LOUISE GULDBERG, choral director, former music educator; b. Suttons Bay, Mich., Dec. 18, 1921; d. Gottfred Johannes and Aasta Agnethe (Kalstad) Guldberg; m. Henry August Doepke, Aug. 13, 1944; children: Karen Sernett, Chris, Bruce, Barbara Potuck. BS, U. Minn., 1944, MA, 1967, postgrad. Tchr. music Mpls. Pub. Schs., 1963-83; choral dir. Trinity First Luth. Ch., Mpls., 1953-92; cons./mentor Mpls. Pub. Schs., 1984-87; organizer, producer 3 jr. high sch. honors choirs Am. Choral Dirs. Assn., 1986, 88, 89. Editor monograph; author curriculum materials; composer children's musicals for sch. and ch., 1966—; contbr. articles to profl. jours. Vol. Courage Ctr., Mpls., 1983-86, Food at Your Door, 1984-88; dir. Gray Aires Chorus, Mpls. 1986-95, Thursday Musical, 1984—. Named composer in residence Mpls. Pub. Schs., 1985. Mem. AAUW (chair coms.), Am. Choral Dirs. Assn. (state sec.-treas., historian), Music Educators Nat. Conf. (clinician 1976, 78, 80), Mu Phi Epsilon (internat. pres. 1992-95). Lutheran. Home: 2212 Mary Hills Dr Minneapolis MN 55422-4252

DOGANCAY, ANGELA, banker; b. Wetter/Marburg, Hesse, Germany, Jan. 9, 1950; Came to the U.S., 1969; d. Gerhard and Alice (Gruen) Hausmann; m. Burhan Dogancay, Dec. 11, 1978. BA, MA, CUNY, 1974; MA, U. Geneva, Switzerland, 1978. Public rels. officer UN, N.Y.C., 1974-76; sr. translator MHT Co., N.Y.C., 1976-78, credit analyst, 1978-80; credit analyst, asst. v.p. Christiania Bank, N.Y.C., 1986-89, v.p., head of loan adminstrn. dept., 1989—; treas. Whispering Walls, Inc., N.Y.C., 1994—. Home: 220 E 54th St New York NY 10022 Office: Christiania Bank 11 W 42d St New York NY 10036

DOGGETT, SHARON LYNN, insurance company executive; b. St. Charles, Mo., Oct. 19, 1953; d. Jesse Wayne and Aileen Ethel (Mertz) Daffron; m. Timothy Steven Oliver (div. Dec. 1979); m. Joseph James Doggett, Jan. 5, 1981; children: Natasha Rae, Tamara Lynn. Grad. high sch., Overland, Mo. Processor Shelter Ins. Co., Columbia, Mo., 1972-75, sec., 1975-76, spl. svc. asst., 1976-85, spl. svc. adminstr., 1985-90, supr. spl. svc., 1990-94; supr. assigned risk, errors and ommisions, spl. svcs. Mo. Joint Underwriters Assn., Columbia, Mo., 1995—. Mem. Ch. of Christ. Office: Shelter Ins Co 1817 W Broadway Columbia MO 65218

DOHERTY, SISTER BARBARA (ANN DOHERTY), academic administrator; b. Chgo., Dec. 2, 1931; d. Martin James and Margaret Eleanor (Noe) D. Student, Rosary Coll., 1949-51; BA in Latin, English and History, St. Mary-of-the-Woods Coll., 1953; MA in Theology, St. Mary's Coll., 1963; PhD in Theology, Fordham U., 1979; LittD (hon.), Ind. State U., 1990. Enter order of the Sisters of Providence. Tchr. Jr. and Sr. High Schs., Ind. and Ill., 1953-63; asst. prof. religion St. Mary-of-the-Woods Coll., Ind., 1963-67, 71-75, pres., 1984—; provincial supr. Chgo. Province of Sisters of Providence, 1975-83; summer faculty NCAIS-KCRCHE, Delhi, India, 1970. Author: I Am What I Do: Contemplation and Human Experience, 1981, Make Yourself an Ark: Beyond the Memorized Responses of Our Corporate Adolescence, 1984; editor: Providence: God's Face Towards the World, 1984; contbr. articles to New Cath. Ency. Vol. XVII, 1982, Dictionary of Catholic Spirituality, 1993. Pres. Leadership Terre Haute, Ind., 1985-86; bd. regents Ind. Acad., 1987—; bd. dirs. 8th Day Cen. for Justice, Chgo., 1978-83, Family Svcs., Swope Art Mus., Terre Haute, Ind., 1988—. Arthur J. Schmidt Found. grantee, 1967-71. Mem. Women's Coll. Coalition (nat. bd. dirs. 1984-90), Ind. Colls. Ind., Ind. Colls. Found. (exec. bd.), Ind. Conf. Higher Edn. (chair), Leadership Conf. Women Religious of USA (program chairperson nat. assembly 1982-83, chair Neylan commn. 1993—). Democrat. Roman Catholic. Home and Office: Office of the Pres St Mary of the Woods Saint Mary Of The Woods IN 47876

DOHERTY, COLLEEN ANN, critical care nurse; b. Cin., Mar. 22, 1961; d. William Martin and Marian Louise (Smith) D. Diploma in nursing, Jewish Hosp. Sch. Nursing, 1983; BSN, Xavier U., Cin., 1988; MSN, U. Cin., 1993. RN, Ohio. Staff nurse med./surg. oncology Jewish Hosp., Cin., 1983-85, asst. nurse mgr. cardiac med. surg. unit, 1985-87, clin. nurse I, mem. critical care float pool, 1987-91, clin. nurse III ICU, critical care unit, 1991-92, clin. nurse specialist in cardiology, 1992-94; clin. nurse specialist critical care St. Elizabeth Med. Ctr., Edgewood, Ky., 1994—. Mem. AACN, Ohio Nurses Assn., Sigma Theta Tau. Office: St Elizabeth Med Ctr One Med Village Dr Edgewood KY 41017

DOHERTY, EVELYN MARIE, data processing consultant; b. Phila., Sept. 26, 1941; d. James Robert and Virginia (Checkley) D. Diploma, RCA Tech. Inst., Cherry Hill, N.J., 1968. Freelance data processing programmer N.J., 1978-81; data processing cons. N.J., 1981—; cons. collection agy., brokerage, banking, med., edn., transp., pub., food wholesaleing, utility systems, mfg.; reseller of PC's and software; lectr. data processing Camden County (N.J.) Coll. Contbr. articles in field. Chairwoman Collingswood (N.J.) Dems., 1968; founder Babe Didrikson Collingswood Softball Team for Women; organizer Erlton South Town Watch (pub. cmty. notebook). Mem. Data Processing Mgmt. Assn. (chmn., mem. ednl. com., bd. dirs. N.J. chpt. 1980—). Roman Catholic. Office: PO Box 3780 Cherry Hill NJ 08034-0584

DOHERTY, KAREN ANN, corporate executive; b. Elizabeth, N.J., July 6, 1952; d. Eugene Nason Godfrey and Helen L. (Andersen) D.; m. Jonathan Kent Tillinghast, June 17, 1972 (div. Oct. 1978). Account exec. The John O'Donnell Co., N.Y., 1979-80; nat. conservation rep. Sierra Club, N.Y., 1980-81; dir. membership and top mgmt. programs Am. Mgmt. Assn., N.Y., 1981—; bd. dirs. Coop. Jamestown Tenants Assn., 1990—. Bd. dirs. Old Mill Landowners Assn. Mem. Trinity Coll. Alumnae Assn. (bd. dirs. Com. N.Y.C. group 1979-82), Direct Mktg. Assn., Internat. Coun., Women in Need (corp. adv. coun.). Democrat. Roman Catholic. Home: 138 71st St Apt Fl Brooklyn NY 11209-1141 Office: Am Mgmt Assn 1601 Broadway New York NY 10019

DOHERTY, REBECCA FEENEY, federal judge; b. Ft. Worth, June 3, 1952; d. Charles Edwin Feeney and Annabelle (Knight) Smith; divorced; 1 child, George Jason. BA, Northwestern State U., 1973, MA, 1975; JD, La. State U., 1981. Bar: La. 1981, U.S. Dist. Ct. (mid., ea. and we. dists.) La. 1981, U.S. Ct. Appeals (5th cir.) 1981, U.S. Dist. Ct. (so. dist.) Tex. 1986, U.S. Dist. Ct. (ea. dist.) Tex. 1989. Assoc. Onebane, Donohoe, Bernard, Torian, Diaz, McNamara & Abell, Lafayette, La., 1981-84, ptnr., 1985-91; U.S. dist. ct. judge We. Dist. La., Lafayette, 1991—; adj. instr. Northwestern State U., Natchitoches, La., 1975; co-dir. secondary level gifted and talented program Webster Parish, La., 1978. Contbr. articles to profl. jours.; mem. La. Law Rev., 1980, 81. Recipient Am. Jurisprudence award Lawyers Coop. Pub. Co., 1980, Career Achievement award 1991; inducted into La. State U. Law Ctr. Hall of Fame, 1987. Mem. ABA, La. Bar Assn., La. Assn. Def. Counsel, La. Assn. Trial Lawyers, Acadian Assn. Women Attys., Order of Coif. Office: US Dist Ct 705 Jefferson St Ste 200 Lafayette LA 70501-6936

DOHERTY, SHANNON, actress; b. Memphis, Apr. 12, 1971; d. Tom and Rosa D.; m. Ashley Hamilton, 1993 (div. 1994). TV series: Little House: A New Beginning, 1982-83, Our House, 1986-88, Beverly Hills, 90210, 1990-94; TV movies: The Other Lover, 1985, Robert Kennedy and His Times, 1985, Obsessed, 1992, Rebel Highway: Jailbreakers, Showtime, 1994, A Burning Passion: The Margaret Mitchell Story, 1994, Gone in the Night, 1996; films: Night Shift, 1982, (voice) The Secret of Nimh, 1982, Girls Just Want to Have Fun, 1985, Heathers, 1989, Blindfold: Acts of Obsession, 1993, Almost Dead, 1994, Mallrats, 1995. Baptist. Office: care ICM 8942 Wilshire Blvd Beverly Hills CA 90211*

DOHMEN, MARY HOLGATE, retired primary school educator; b. Gary, Ind., July 28, 1918; d. Clarence Gibson and Margaret Alexander (Kinnear) Holgate; m. Frederick Hoeger Dohmen, June 27, 1964; children: William Francis, Robert Charles. BS, Milw. State Tchrs. Coll., 1940; M of Philosophy, U. Wis., 1945. Cert. tchr., Wis. Tchr. primary grades Baraboo (Wis.) Pub. Schs., 1940-43, Whitefish Bay (Wis.) Pub. Schs., 1943-64. Contbr. articles, story, poems to various pubs. Bd. dirs. Homestead H.S. chpt. Am. Field Svc., Mequon, Wis., 1970-80; mem. Milw. Aux. VNA, 1975—, 2d v.p., 1983-85, Milw. Pub. Mus. Enrichment Club, 1975—, Boys and Girls Club of Greater Milw., 1986—; vol. Reading is Fun program, 1987—, Milw. Symphony Orch. League, 1960—, Ptnrs. in Conservation, World Wildlife Fund, Washington, 1991—, Milw. Art Mus. Garden Club, 1979—, com. chmn., 1981-86; mem. Chancellor's Soc. U. Wis.-Milw., 1991—; travel lectr. various orgns., 1980—. Mem. AAUW, Milw. Coll. Endowment Assn. (v.p. 1987-90, pres. 1991-93), Bascom Hill Soc. (U. Wis.), Woman's Club Wis., Alpha Phi (pres. Milw. alumnae 1962-64), Pi Lambda Theta (pres. Milw. alumnae 1962-64), Delta Kappa Gamma. Republican. Presbyterian. Home: 3903 W Mequon Rd Mequon WI 53092-2727

DOI, DOROTHY MITSUE, educator, consultant; b. Honolulu, Feb. 21, 1934; d. Tokuju Yano and Hisayo Kashiwabara; children: Ken Kenichi, Claire Emiko, Garret Seitoku. BS in Edn., Phillips U., Enid, Okla., 1956; postgrad., UCLA, 1958, U. Hawaii, Honolulu, 1966-67, 72-74, Chaminade Coll. Honolulu, 1972-74, 77, LaVerne (Calif.) Coll., 1970-71. Cert. tchr., Hawaii. Tchr. L.A. City Schs., 1957-58, Hawaii, 1956-57, 65, 70-71; account exec. Catering, ind. contractor, Honolulu; skin care, health and beauty cons. Honolulu, travel agt., ind. contractor; pres. Triple C Svcs., Honolulu, 1983—; researcher Manoa ethnic studies program U. Hawaii; account exec., cons. Royal Banquet, 1988-89; writer, researcher, editor, mng. editor Bulldogrowl. Active Kamuki Y-Teens, 1947-52; fund-raising co-chair Kaimuki High Sch., Hui O'Hauolani Y-Teens Jesters Ball, 1952; mem. World Wildlife Fund, 1991—, Hawaii Theatre Ctr., 1990—. Mem. NAFE, Nature Conservancy Local, Nat., Hawaii Fukuoka Kenjin Kai (gen. chairperson 35th anniversary and award ceremony, com. chair editor commemorative booklet, sec. 1988-91, 2d v.p. 1992-93, 1st v.p. 1993-94, 94-95, pres. 1996—), Smithsonian Instn., Kaimuki H.S. Alumni Assn. (charter, bd. dirs. 1988—, pub. rels. chairperson 1988-90), Okla. Sooners Club (Hon. Citizen of Okla. 1985), Japanese Cultural Ctr. of Hawaii (hon. lifetime charter), Future Tchrs. of Am. (treas. 1955-56), United Japanese Soc. of Hawaii (sec. 1991-92, 92-93, 93-94, youth com. chair 1992-93, 93-94, 94—, gen. chair 1st Ann. Youth Com. Picnic 1994, co-chair fundraising com. 1992-93, 95-96, emcee New Year luncheon 1993, 2d v.p. 1994-95, dir. 1995-96, 96-97), Internat. Platform Assn. Home: 2431 Yvonne Pl Honolulu HI 96816-3431

DOIG, BEVERLY IRENE, systems specialist; b. Bozeman, Mont., Oct. 21, 1936; d. James Stuart Doig and Elsie Florence (Andes) Doig Townsend. AA, Graceland Coll., 1956; BA, U. Kans., 1958; MS, U. Wis., 1970; cert. in Interior Design, UCLA, 1993. Aerodynamic technician II Ames Labs.-NACA, Moffett Field, Calif., 1957; real time systems specialist Dept. of Army, White Sands Missile Range, N.Mex., 1958-66; large systems specialist computing ctr. U. Wis., Madison, 1966-70; sr. systems analyst Burroughs, Ltd., Canberra, Australia, 1970-72; systems specialist Tech. Info. Office Burroughs Corp., Detroit, 1973-78; sr. systems specialist Burroughs Gmbh, Munich, 1978-79, Burroughs AB, Stockholm, 1979-80; networking cons. Midland Bank, Ltd., Sheffield, Eng., 1980-83; networking specialist Burroughs Corp. (now UNISYS), Mission Viejo, Calif., 1983—; teaching asst. Canberra (Australia) Coll., 1972; tchr. Wayne State U. Ext., Detroit, 1976-77; freelance interior designer, 1992—. Vol. youth groups and camps Reorganized LDS Ch., N.Mex., Wis., Australia, Mich., Calif., Germany, U.K.; inner youth worker, Detroit. Scholar Mitchell Math., 1956-58, Watkins Residential, 1956-58. Mem. Assn. Computing Machinery (local chpt. chmn. membership 1969), Lambda Delta Sigma. Republican. Office: UNISYS 25725 Jeronimo Rd Mission Viejo CA 92691-2711

DOKOUDOVSKY, NINA LUDMILA, dance educator; b. N.Y.C., Nov. 7, 1947; d. Vladimir Dokoudovsky and Nina Rigmor (Ström) Stroganova; m. Antoni Francis Zalewski. Student, Ballet Arts Carnegie Hall, 1954-78, Profl. Children's Sch., N.Y.C., 1959-66, Am. Acad. Dramatic Arts, 1960-62, Am. Ballet Theater Sch., 1968-70, N.Y. Conservatory of Dance, 1978-81. Faculty Ballet Arts Carnegie Hall, N.Y.C., 1964-70; tchr. dance Dokoudovsky Sch. of Classical Ballet, Englewood, N.J., 1964-70; head adminstr. Acad. Fine Arts Music and Dance, 1974-81; faculty Washington U., St. Louis, 1983-86; co-dir. Ballet Ctr. of St. Louis, 1984—; co-assoc. artistic dir. St. Louis Ballet (formerly Mo. Concert Ballet), 1981-84, co-artistic dir., 1984—; dir. Ballet Arts Lecture Demo Co., 1967-68; dancer, soloist with Ballet Arts Workshop, 1966-68, Marvin Gordon's Ballet Concepts, 1968, Empire State Ballet, 1969, Internat. Dance Competition, Varna, Bulgaria, 1970, Buffalo Ballet, 1970-72, Am. Classical Ballet, 1972, Wolf Trapp Co., 1972, L.I. Ballet Co., 1973, Festival Ballet of N.J., 1975-77, St. Louis Ballet (formerly Mo. Concert Ballet), 1982—; coach Am. dancers Internat. Dance Competition, Moscow, 1982. Choreographer: (ballets) Dance of the Hours, 1965, While the Cat's Away, 1966, Tchaikovsky Violin Concerto, 1967, In the Park, 1968, The Nyad, 1968, Adam Pas De Deux, 1969, Adam Pas de Cinq, 1974, 83, 86, 89, Weber Piano Concerto (complete), 1986-88, 93, Nutcracker, 1980, 81—, La Fille Mal Gardee, 1980, Une Petite Comedie, 1984, (staged ballets) Swan Lake, 1967, 69, 79, 80, 92, Les Sylphide, 1974, 79, 82, 84, 87, 93, Raymonda, 1972, Don Quixote, 1972, 84, 88, Sleeping Beauty, 1976, 79, 84, 91, 92, 94, La Bayadere 1989, 91, Bronislava Nijinska's Les Biches in collaboration with Irina Nijinska St. Louis Ballet, 1989, 90, 95, Tulsa Ballet Theatre, 1990, Paris Opera Ballet, 1991, Cinderella, 1995. Office: Ballet Ctr of St Louis 10 Kimler Dr Maryland Heights MO 63043 also: St Louis Ballet Co PO Box 2101 Saint Louis MO 63158-0101

DOLAK, ANNA ELIZABETH, lawyer; b. Ft. Monmouth, N.J., Apr. 18, 1957; d. George Albert and Charlotte Elizabeth (Robertson) D.; m. David Mark Wiener, Jan. 8, 1986. BA, Pa. State U., 1978; JD, Duquesne U., 1981. Bar: Pa. 1981, U.S. Dist. Ct. (we. dist.) Pa. 1981, Tex. 1987, U.S. Dist. Ct. (no. dist.) Tex. 1987. Assoc. counsel Brooks & Ewalt, P.C., Pitts., 1981-82;

gen. counsel, sr. v.p. Stockton Savs. Assn., Dallas, 1987-88, Commodore Savs. Assn., Dallas, 1988; gen. counsel, exec. v.p. Bluebonnet Savs. Bank, F.S.B., Dallas, 1988—. Contbr. chpt. in book. Capt. U.S. Army, 1982-86, Korea. Mem. Tex. Bar Assn., Dallas Bar Assn., Am. Corp. Counsel Assn., Am. Mgmt. Assn., Price Waterhouse Gen. Counsel Forum, Rotary Club of Dallas (chmn. recognition com., chmn. elect Salvation Army com.). Republican. Lutheran. Office: Bluebonnet Savs Bank FSB 3100 Monticello Ave Dallas TX 75205-3442*

DOLAN, GRACE FRANCES, elementary education educator; b. Nevada City, Calif., Apr. 16, 1939; d. Harold Still and Frances Gwendolen (Bigelow) Anderson; m. Edward Henry Beck, June 6, 1959 (div. 1971); chidren: Laura Frances Beck Whitacre, Reid Edward Beck, Connie Leigh Beck Hanle; m. Robert Michael Fitzpatrick, June 17, 1973 (dec. June 1986); m. Kenneth Burton Dolan, Jan. 20, 1992. BA in Edn., Chico (Calif.) State Coll., 1971; MS in Marriage, Family, and Child Counseling, Calif. State U., Sacramento, 1994. Cert. elem. tchr., sch. counselor, Calif.; registered marriage, family and child counselor-intern, Calif. Title I reading tchr. Hennessy Sch., Grass Valley, Calif., 1971-74; tchr. 3d grade Grass Valley Sch. Dist., 1974—, mentor tchr. in sci., 1985-88, also summer sch. tchr.; drama coach Children's Theater Co., Grass Valley, 1990; Odyssey of the Mind coach Hennessy Sch., 1986-96. Grant writer. Recipient Disting. Svc. in Edn. award Ptnrs. in Edn., Nevada County, 1990. Mem. NEA, ASCD, Calif. Tchrs. Assn., Grass Valley Tchrs. Assn. (pres. 1988-90), Calif. Sci. Tchr. Assn., Calif. Assn. Marriage and Family Therapists, Phi Kappa Phi. Episcopalian. Home: 101 Fiddick Ln Grass Valley CA 95945-7337 Office: Hennessy Sch 225 S Auburn St Grass Valley CA 95945-7229

DOLAN, JAN CLARK, state legislator; b. Akron, Ohio, Jan. 15, 1927; d. Herbert Spencer and Jean Risk (Morton) Clark; m. Walter John Dolan, Apr. 22, 1950 (dec. July 1986); children: Mark Raymond, Scott Spencer, Gary Clark, Todd Alvin. BA, U. Akron, 1949. Home svc. rep. East Ohio Gas Co., Akron, 1949-50; dietitian Akron City Hosp., 1950-51; tchr. Brecksville (Ohio) Sch. Dist., 1962-66; adminstr. Orchard Hills Adult Day Ctr., West Bloomfield, Mich., 1978-83; mem. Farmington Hills (Mich.) City Coun., 1975-88, Mich. Ho. of Reps., Lansing, 1989—. Mayor City of Farmington Hills, 1978, 85; elder Presbyn. Ch. Republican. Home: 22587 Gill Rd Farmington Hl MI 48335-4037 Office: Mich Ho of Reps State Capitol Bldg Lansing MI 48909

DOLAN, JUNE ANN, health facility administrator; b. Oakland, Calif., June 24, 1942; d. Edward Joseph and Pauline (McCune) D. AA, Orange Coast Coll., 1969; B of Religion and Philosophy, Loyola-Mary Mount U., Orange, Calif., 1965. MICN, ACLS. Asst. head nurse med./surg. ICU and neuro surg. ICU Riverside (Calif.) Gen. Hosp., head nurse med./surg. ICU, asst. dir. of nurses; care provider handicapped, 1987—. Vol. Spl. Olympics, 1987-91; mem. Inland AIDS project; adult advisory mem. Ability Counts Sheltered Workshop; Sister at St. Joseph of Orange, 1960-65. Mem. RGH Aux., Nursing Mgmt. Coun.

DOLAN, LOUISE ANN, physicist; b. Wilmington, Del., Apr. 5, 1950. BA, Wellesley Coll., 1971; PhD in Physics, MIT, 1976. Jr. fellow in physics Harvard U., 1976-79; asst. prof. physics Rockefeller U., N.Y.C., 1979-82, assoc. prof., 1983-90, lab. head, 1990; prof. physics U. N.C., Chapel Hill, 1990—; prof. dir. for theoretical physics NSF, 1995. John Simon Guggenheim fellow, 1988. Fellow Am. Phys. Soc. (Maria Goeppert-Mayer award 1987). Office: U NC Dept Physics Chapel Hill NC 27599-3255

DOLAN, MARYANNE MCLORN, small business owner, writer, educator, lecturer; b. N.Y.C., July 14, 1924; d. Frederick Joseph and Kathryn Cecilia (Carroll) McLorn; m. John Francis Dolan, Oct. 6, 1951 (dec.); children: John Carroll, James Francis McLorn, William Brennan. B.A., San Francisco State U., 1978, M.A., 1981. Tchr. classes and seminars in antiques and collectibles U. Calif., Berkeley, Davis, Santa Cruz, Coll. of Marin, Kentfield, Calif., Mills Coll., Oakland, St. Mary's Coll., Moraga, 1969-90, Solano C.C., 1990—; tch. writing Dolan Sch., 1969-90; owner antique shop, Benicia, Calif., 1970—; lectr. Nat. Assn. Jewelry Appraisers Symposium, Tucson; lectr. Vintage Fashion Expo., Oakland, Coll. for Appraisers, Placentia, Calif. Author: Vintage Clothing, 1880-1980, 3d edit., 1983, Collecting Rhinestone Jewelry, 3d edit., 1984, Old Lace and Linens, 1989, Commonsense Collecting, 1991, 300 Years of American Sterling Silver Flatware, 1992; weekly columnist The Collector, 1979-88; contbr. articles to profl. jours. Mem. AAUW, Antique Appraisal Assn. Am. Inc., Costume Soc. Am., New Eng. Appraisers Assn., Questers, Women's Nat. Book Assn. Inc., Nat. Assn. Jewelry Appraisers, Internat. Soc. Appraisers (lectr. ann. meeting), Internat. Platform Assn. Republican. Roman Catholic. Home and Office: 138 Belle Ave Pleasant Hill CA 94523-4640

DOLAN, REGINA, security firm executive. CFO, sr. v.p. Paine Webber Group Inc., N.Y.C. Office: Paine Webber Group Inc 1285 Ave of Americas New York NY 10019*

DOLE, ELIZABETH HANFORD, charitable organization administrator, former secretary of labor, former secretary of transportation; b. Salisbury, N.C., July 29, 1936; d. John Van and Mary Ella (Cathey) Hanford; m. Robert Joseph Dole (U.S. Senator from Kans.), Dec. 6, 1975. B.A. with honors in Polit. Sci., Duke, 1958; postgrad., Oxford (Eng.) U., summer 1959; MA in Edn. and Govt., Harvard U., 1960, J.D., 1965. Bar: D.C. 1966. Staff asst. to asst. sec. for edn. HEW, Washington, 1966-67; practiced law Washington, 1967-68; assoc. dir. legis. affairs, then exec. dir. Pres.'s Com. for Consumer Interests, Washington, 1968-71; dep. asst. to Pres. The White House, Washington, 1971-73; commr. FTC, Washington, 1973-79; chmn. Voters for Reagan-Bush, 1980; dir. Human Services Group, Office of Exec. Br. Mgmt., Office of Pres.-Elect, 1980; asst. to Pres. for pub. liaison, 1981-83; sec. U.S. Dept. Transp., 1983-87; with Robert Dole Presdl. Campaign, 1987-88; participant 1988 Presdl. and Congl. campaigns; sec. U.S. Dept. Labor, 1989-90; pres. American Red Cross, 1991—; mem. nominating com. Am. Stock Exchange, 1972, N.C. Consumer Council, 1972. Trustee Duke U., 1974-88; mem. coun. Harvard Law Sch. Assocs., vis. com. Harvard Sch. Pub. Health, 1992-95; bd. overseers Harvard U., 1989-95. Recipient Arthur S. Flemming award U.S. Govt., 1972, Humanitarian award Nat. Commn. Against Drunk Driving, 1988, Disting. Alumni award Duke U., 1988, N.C. award, 1991, Lifetime Achievement award (Breaking The Glass Ceiling) Women Execs. in State Govt., 1993, North Carolinian of the Yr. award N.C. Press Assn., 1993, Radcliffe medal, 1993, Leadership award LWV, 1994, Maxwell Finland award Nat. Found. Infectious Diseases, 1994, Disting. Svc. award Nat. Safety Coun., 1989, Raoul Wallenberg award for Humanitarian Svc., 1995; named one of Am.'s 200 Young Leaders, Time mag., 1974, one of World's 10 Most Admired Women, Gallup Pole, 1988; selected for Safety and Health Hall of Fame Internat., 1993; inducted into Nat. Women's Hall of Fame, 1995. Mem. Phi Beta Kappa, Pi Lambda Theta, Pi Sigma Alpha. Office: ARC care Roy Clason vp communication 430 17th St NW Washington DC 20006

DOLE, LINDA ANN INGOLS, lawyer; b. Meadville, Pa., Mar. 28, 1939; d. Robert Paul and Mary Catherine (Guiler) Ingols; m. Richard Fairfax Dole, Jr., Nov. 12, 1961; children: Richard Fairfax II, Robert Paul, Mary Grace. BA, Marietta Coll., 1960; JD, U. Iowa, 1978. Bar: Iowa 1978, Tex. 1979. Assoc. Baker & Botts, Houston, 1978-86; assoc. Andrews & Kurth L.L.P., Houston, 1986-90, ptnr., 1990—. Fellow Am. Coll. Investment Coun.; mem. ABA, Tex. Bar Assn., Phi Beta Kappa, Order of Coif. Office: Andrews & Kurth LLP 4200 Tex Commerce Houston TX 77002*

DOLE, PAMELA JEAN, nurse; b. Willimatic, Conn., Jan. 5, 1947; d. Roderick Almon and Shirley Jean (Moore) D. BSN, U. Conn., 1969; MHS, Inst. Advanced Study, San Francisco, 1982; student, Hunter Coll., N.Y.C., 1992—; DEd, 1996. RN, Conn., N.Y., Calif.; registered family nurse practitioner, Calif., N.Y.; HIV/AIDS clin. nurse specialist, comty. health nurse, women's health care, forensic nursing. Staff nurse U. Conn. McCook Hosp., Hartford, 1970-73; coord., founder women's health program U. Conn. Health Ctr., Storrs, 1975-79; asst. clin. prof. adolescent medicine U. Calif., San Francisco, 1981-84; cons. women's health care State of Conn., Mansfield, 1987-89; coord. edn. and outreach adolescent substance abuse program Elmcrest Hosp., Portland, Conn., 1988; medicolegal investigator office chief med. examiner City of N.Y., 1989-91; comty. health nurse, clin. care coord. Village Nursing Home, N.Y.C., 1991—; researcher cervical disease and HIV, Columbia U., N.Y.C.; nurse practitioner Planned Parenthood Fedn. Am., 1975-88; adj. faculty Columbia U. Sch. of Nursing, 1995. Author: (with others) Men's Reproductive Health, 1984, Parents, Key Players in Fight Against Drug Abuse, 1988; contbr. articles to profl. jours. Mem. ANA, Am. Acad. Forensic Scis., Am. Acad. Nurse Practitioners, Am. Coll. Sexology, Nat. Assn. Nurse Practitioners in Family Planning, N.Y. Coalition of Nurse Practitioners, Inc., Assn. Nurses in AIDS Care (nominations com. 1995-97), Internat. Assn. Forensic Nurses, Nurse Healers Profl. Assocs., Soc. Rogerian Scholars, Soc. Sci. Study Sexuality, Theosophical Soc., Audubon Soc., People for Ethical Treatment of Animals, Smithsonian Native Am. Mus., Mus. Natural History, Sigma Theta Tau, Inc. Office: Columbia U Coll Physicians & Surgeons 630 W 168th St New York NY 10032-3702

DOLEZAL, RUTH ELLEN, resort owner; b. Frence Camp, Calif., Feb. 14, 1937; d. Irwin Graham and Mary Elizabeth (Rathbun) Erickson; m. LAurence E. Dolezal, Feb. 14, 1955; children: Larry John, Gary Ron (dec.). Grad. high sch., Napa, Calif. Sec. Hinkley High Sch., Aurora, Colo.; owner, operator Sportsman's Resort, Ohio City, Colo. Sec., past pres. Quartz Greek Improvement Assn., Ohio City, 1973—; sec./treas. Cemetery Bd., Pitkin, Colo., 1991—, Vol. Fire Dept., Ohio City, 1976—; asst. coach Youth Bowling League, Gunnison, Colo., 1988—; election clk. Gunnison County. Mem. VFW (pres. 1995, Vol. of Yr. 1994), DAR, Am. Legion Aux., Top of the World Garden Club (v.p. 1994-96), Elks Ladies. Republican. Home: 116 County Rd 771 Ohio City CO 81237

DOLINSKY, REBECCA, artist, educator; b. N.Y.C., May 26, 1962; d. Hyman and Beverly (Leeds) D. BA magna cum laude, Amherst Coll., 1984; postgrad., L'École Normale Superieure, Paris, 1984-85; cert. in painting and sculpture, N.Y. Studio Sch., 1994. French tchr. The Dalton Sch., N.Y.C., 1989; art dir. New Art Ctr. in Andy Warhol's Factory, N.Y.C., 1995; art tchr. Brearey Sch., N.Y.C., 1996; curator art show Internat. Rescue Com., N.Y.C., 1996—. Translator: The Memoirs and Letters of Surrealist Painter Valentine Prax to her husband, Ossip Zadkine, 1989, The Work of Sideo Frombolutti, 1994; exhibited at N.Y. Studio Sch., 1996; represented in pvt. collections in Can., Europe, Mex. and U.S. Merit scholar in drawing and sculpture The Vera List Found., 1993-94. Mem. Young Assocs. of Morgan Libr., Phi Beta Kappa. Democrat. Home: 774 9th Ave New York NY 10019 Office: 427 W 14th St New York NY 10014

DOLL, ANNA LISA, municipal official; b. Stuttgart, Germany, May 21, 1955; d. Paul Napoleon and Akiko (Kinoshita) Cyr; m. John Thomas Doll, Sept. 6, 1980; children: Andrew Bryant, Lindsey Nicole. BA, Clark U., 1976; MPA, U. Mo., Kansas City, 1979. Health planning assoc. Tex. Area 5 Health Sys. Agy., Irving, 1980-81; sr. planning assoc. Harris Meth. Health Sys., Ft. Worth, 1981-83; adminstrv. asst. City of Grand Prairie, Tex., 1983-85, budget dir., 1985-92, dep. city mgr., 1993—; budget reviewer Govt. Fin. Officer Assn., Grand Prairie, 1986-92. Author, editor Budget Books for City of Grand Prairie, 1986-93. Deacon Emmanuel Presbyn. Ch., Bedford, Tex., 1993—, leader Girl Scouts of Am., Grand Prairie, 1994—. Conn. scholar, 1973-77, Jonas Clark scholar, 1973-77, HUD intern, 1977-79; recipient Disting. Budget Presentation award, Govt. Fin. Officers Assn., 1987-92. Mem. Internat. City Mgrs. Assn., Civic Orators Toastmasters (treas., sec.), Tex. City Mgrs. Assn., North Tex. City Mgrs. Assn. Home: 2310 Silver Horn Dr Grand Prairie TX 75050

DOLL, LYNNE MARIE, public relations agency executive; b. Glendale, Calif., Aug. 27, 1961; d. George William and Carol Ann (Kennedy) D.; m. David Jay Lans, Oct. 11, 1986. BA in Journalism, Calif. State U., Northridge, 1983. Freelance writer Austin Pub. Rels. Systems, Glendale, 1978-82; asst. account exec. Berkhemer & Kline, L.A., 1982-83; exec. v.p., ptnr. Rogers & Assocs., L.A., 1983—; exec. dir. Suzuki Automotive Found. for Life, Brea, Calif., 1986-91; mem. strategic planning com. Gateway to Indian Am. Corp. for Am. Indian Devel., San Francisco, 1988-90. Pub. rels. cons., Rape Treatment Ctr., L.A., 1986—. Mem. Ad Club L.A. (bd. dirs., pres. 1994-95), Pub. Rels. Soc. Am., So. Calif. Assn. Philanthropy, Coun. on Founds., Internat. Motor Press Assn., Nat. Conf. Christians and Jews (bd. dirs. 1996—). Democrat. Office: Rogers & Assocs 1875 Century Park E Ste 300 Los Angeles CA 90067-2504

DOLL, PATRICIA MARIE, marketing and public relations consultant; b. Bryn Mawr, Pa., Apr. 13, 1960; d. Otello Louis (dec.) and Eleanor Caroline (De Pasquale) De Grandis; m. John Russell Doll, Oct. 5, 1985. BS in Speech Comms., Millersville (Pa.) U., 1982. Lic. radio operator. News reporter, dj, writer, promotions coord. WIXQ and WLAN Radio, Lancaster, Pa., 1978-82; prodr., writer, researcher WGAL-TV 8, Lancaster, Pa., 1982; copywriter, advtsg.-mktg. coord. Strawbridge & Clothier, Phila., 1982-87; freelance writer, 1984—; mktg. dir. Rouse & Assocs., Internat. Developer, Phila., Pa., 1987-90; owner, pres. Publicity Works, Bowmansville, Pa., 1990—. Contbr. articles to local newspapers and trade mags.; producer TV documentary, 1982. Pub. rels. dir. Women's Bus. Com. of Berks County, other chambers, trade, local orgns. Recipient Small Bus. Woman of the Yr. award Athena, 1996, numerous regional and national awards for mktg. and cmty. work. Mem. Kappa Delta Phi. Roman Catholic.

DOLLARHIDE, COLETTE THERESA, college administrator, educator, consultant; b. Lancaster, Calif., Nov. 12, 1956; d. Charles Wesley and Kathleen Colette (Scherr) Reding; m. Jerry Glen Dollarhide, Mar. 24, 1975; 1 child, Shiloh Colette. BA in Polit. Sci., Calif. State U., 1980; MA in Counseling, U. Nevada-Reno, 1988, DEd in Counselor Edn., 1994; evening coll. dir. Reno Bus. Coll., 1982-85 , dean edn., 1985-88; dir. career devel. office U. Nev., Reno, 1988-95; asst. prof., coord. student personnel svcs. in higher edn. Emporia State U., 1995—. Author: The Better Sentence, 1984; contbr. articles to profl. jours. Dep. registrar of voters Washoe County Registry of Voters, Reno, 1982; bd. dirs. Reno Bus. Coll. Found., 1984. Mem. ACA, Am. Coll. Personnel Assn., Nat. Career Devel. Assn., Assn. Counselor Edn. and Supervision, Kans. Counseling Assn., Kans. Assn. for Counselor Edn. and Supervision, Kans. Coll. Student Personnel Assn. (pres. elect.), Am. Coun. Edn. (state coord. program for advancement of women in higher edn. 1996—). Roman Catholic. Office: Emporia State U Divsn Couns Edn Box 4036 1200 Commercial Emporia KS 66801

DOLLIVER, MARY GWEN, medical, surgical nurse; b. Mitchell, S.D., May 20, 1930; d. Barrett Prentiss and Emma Ethel (Close) D. Student, Meth. Hosp. Nursing Sch., 1949-52; grad. in Bible Studies, Chgo. Evangel. Inst., 1956; BSN, S.D. State U., 1958. RN, S.D. Staff nurse Platte (S.D.) Meml. Hosp., 1952-56, Mahaska Hosp., Oskaloosa, Iowa, 1952-56, Brookings (S.D.) Hosp., 1956-58, Redfield Community Hosp., 1958-60; pub. health nurse Todd County, S.D., 1960-63, S.D. Pub. Health Dept., Pierre; staff nurse Douglas County Hosp., Armour, S.D., 1963-72; staff nurse, surgery nurse Frontier Nursing Svcs., Wendover, Ky., 1972-76; nurse for children's home Bethany (Ky.) Christian Mission Ctr., 1976-89; night staff nurse Lakeandes (S.D.) Health Care Ctr., 1989-92; caregiver pvt. practice, Lakeandes, 1992-93. Home: PO Box 326 Lake Andes SD 57356

DOMAN, MARGARET HORN, land use planning consultant, civic official; b. Portland, Oreg., July 28, 1946; d. Richard Carl and Dorothy May (Teepe) Horn; m. Steve Hamilton Doman, July 12, 1969; children: Jennifer, Kristina, Kathryn. BA, Willamette U., 1968; postgrad., U. Wash., 1968-69, 72. Cert. tchr. Tchr. jr. high Bellevue (Wash.) Sch. Dist., 1969-70, subs. tchr., 1990-91; tchr. jr. high University City (Mo.) Sch. Dist., 1970-71; employment counselor employment security dept. State of Wash., Seattle, 1971; planning commn. mem. City of Redmond, Wash., 1980-83, chmn., 1982-83; city coun. mem. City of Redmond, 1983-91, pres., 1990-91; exec. dir. Eastside Human Svcs. Coun., Redmond, Wash., 1992; employment specialist Wash. State Dept. Employment Security, 1993; cons. land use planning & govt. process Redmond, 1993—; Redmond rep. Puget Sound. Coun. of Govt., Seattle, 1984-91, vice chmn., 1988, 90, chmn. transp., 1986-88, exec. bd., 1987, mem. standing com. on transp., 1986-91; bd. dirs., pres. Eastside Human Svcs. Coun., Bellevue, 1983-91, pres., 1990. Bd. dirs. Redmond YMCA, 1985-86; mem. state exec. com. Nat. History Day, Olympia, Wash., 1986; vol. Bellevue Sch. Dist., 1977-96; bd. dirs. Eastside br. Camp Fire, Bellevue, 1992-94. Mem. Redmond C. of C. (land use and transp. com. 1994—), Bellevue Rotary. Republican. Unitarian. Home: 2104 180th Ct NE Redmond WA 98052-6032

DOMBROSKI, KIMBERLY JO, critical care nurse; b. Medina, Ohio, Nov. 7, 1964; d. Walter Lewis Jr. and Judith Ann (Blair) D. A in Emergency Medicine, W.Va. No. U., 1992; Assoc., Belmont Tech. Coll., 1987. RN, Pa., Ohio, W.Va.; CCRN; trauma nurse core course; cert. ACLS and Pediat. Advanced Life Support instr., W.Va., BLS instr., Ohio, TLS instr., W.Va., firefighter, Ohio, EMT-P. Technician II paramedic Ohio Valley Med. Ctr.-Emstar, Wheeling, W.Va., 1986-92; staff nurse I East Ohio Regional-Emstar, Martins Ferry, Ohio, 1992-93; staff/charge nurse City Hosp. Bellaire, Ohio, 1993-94; field nurse Heritage Home Health, Tiltonsville, Ohio, 1994—; home IV infusion nurse Caremark Internat., Pitts., 1994—; cardiovasc. nurse I, ICU staff nurse Wheeling Med. Park, 1994—. EMS chief, tng. dir. Colerain (Ohio) Vol. Fire Co., 1990—. Home: 54139 Robinwood Dr Martins Ferry OH 43935

DOMBROWSKI, ANNE WESSELING, microbiologist, researcher; b. Cin., Jan. 26, 1948; d. Robert John and Margaret Mary (Bell) Wesseling; m. Allan Wayne Dombrowski, Apr. 17, 1982; children: Amy, Alicia. BA summa cum laude, Xavier U., 1970; MS, U. Cin., 1972, PhD, 1974. Fellow Scripps Clinic & Rsch. Found., La Jolla, Calif., 1974-76; sr. rsch. microbiologist Merck & Co., Inc., Rahway, N.J., 1976-87, rsch. fellow, 1987-96, sr. rsch. fellow, 1996—. Patentee in field; contbt. articles to profl. jours. Mem. AAAS, Soc. Indsl. Microbiology (sec. 1982-85), Am. Soc. Microbiology, Mycol. Soc. Home: 51 Landsdowne Rd East Brunswick NJ 08816-4156 Office: Merck & Co Inc PO Box 2000 Rahway NJ 07065-0900

DOMINGO, ESTRELLA TINA, fashion designer, consultant, paralegal; b. Bacarra, The Philippines, Sept. 26, 1965; came to U.S., 1969; d. Jaime Madrid and Estrella (Taganas) D. AA in Fashion Design, Brooks Coll., Long Beach, Calif., 1986; BA in Indsl. Psychology, San Francisco State U., 1989; postgrad, Sawyer Coll., 1994. Diploma paralegal. Sales assoc. J.C. Penney Co., Salinas, Calif., 1984; clk.-typist VA Med. Ctr., Palo Alto, Calif., 1987, sec. to chief anesthesiology svc., 1987-88; clk.-typist VA Med. Ctr., Menlo Park, Calif.; adminstr. dept. anesthesia Stanford (Calif.) U. Sch. Medicine, 1988-92; adminstrv. asst. Western Digital, 1992-93; from exec. asst. to v.p., sec., gen. counsel Robert Half Internat., Inc., Menlo Park, Calif., 1993—. Mem. rsch. adv. bd., editorial bd., dep. gov. ABI, adv. coun. IBC. Recipient Commemorative Medal of Honor, N.C. & Women of the Yr. award, 1991, Spl. Contbn. award VA Med. ctr., 1987, Superior Performance award, 1989; scholar Calif. Scholarship Assn., 1984. Mem. NAFE (hon. advisor, dep. gov. ABIRA & Women's Inner Circle of Achievement, The World Found. Successful Women, fellowship), Smithsonian Assocs., Calif. Honor Soc. Roman Catholic. Office: Robert Half Internat Inc 2884 Sand Hill Rd Ste 200 Menlo Park CA 94025

DOMINIC, MAGIE, writer, artist; b. Corner Brook, Nfld., Can., July 15, 1944; 1 child, Heather Rose. Diploma, Art Inst. of Pitts. Prodr./dir. Children's History Theatre, Woodstock, N.Y., 1978-84; freelance wardrobe asst. Met. Opera, N.Y.C., 1986—; freelance wardrobe asst. Broadway and TV N.Y.C., 1986—; assoc. curator Caffe Cino Exhibit, Lincoln Ctr. Libr. for the Performing Arts, Astor Gallery, N.Y.C., 1985. Editor, author: Belle Lettres/Beautiful Letters, 1995; author: (anthology) Outrage, 1993, Pushing the Limits, 1996, Countering the Myths, 1996; author words to final movement of "Symphony #2 - Visions of a Wounded Earth," Internat. Symphony Orch., 1996; art work in pvt. collection St. Vincent's Hosp., N.Y.C., The Malcolm Forbes Collection; created The Gown of Stillness installation, Toronto, 1995, N.Y.C., 1996. Recipient Langston Hughes award Clark Ctr., 1968; Children's History Theatre grantee Am. The Beautiful Fund, 1979, 80, Shaker Found., 1980, 81. Mem. League of Can. Poets.

DOMM, ALICE, lawyer; b. Phila., May 22, 1954; d. William Donald and Alice Frances (Day) D.; m. Richard Coles Grubb, Sept. 26, 1987; children: Stephanie Elizabeth, Samuel William. BA, Gettysburg Coll., 1976, JD, Rutgers U., 1981. Bar: N.J. 1981, Pa. 1981. Assoc. prof. Glassboro (N.J.) Coll., 1980-81; atty., juvenile sect. chief Office Pub. Defender, New Brunswick, N.J., 1982-92; sr. trial atty. Office of Pub. Defender, Belvidere, N.J., 1992-93, Trenton, N.J., 1993-95, New Brunswick, N.J., 1995—. Bd. dirs. Police Athletic League, New Brunswick, 1982-85; mem. Middlesex County Youth Services Commn., New Brunswick; steering com. treas. Middlesex County Women Lawyers Com.; mem. Gov.'s Council on Child Abuse and Neglect, Middlesex County, Gov.'s com. childrens Services Planning Juvenile Justice Subcom.; mem. Middlesex County Commn. Child Abuse and Missing Children, Criminal Justice Planning Com. Middlesex County. Mem. ABA, N.J. Bar Assn., Middlesex County Bar Assn. (trustee), Middlesex County Women's Bar Assn. (steering com., treas.), Assn. Criminal Def. Lawyers N.J. Office: Office Pub Defender 172 New St New Brunswick NJ 08901

DOMMEL, DARLENE HURST, writer; b. Charles City, Iowa, July 11, 1940; d. Roy and Elsie (Hopkes) Hurst; B.S. with high distinction, U. Minn., 1963; m. James H. Dommel, Oct. 15, 1961; children: Diann, Christine, David. MS, 1965, grad. exec. program Grad. Sch. Bus. Administrn., 1972; postgrad. So. Meth. U., 1976-77. Pub. health nurse Combined Nursing Service, Mpls., 1963-64; author: (book) Collector's Encyclopedia of the Dakota Potteries; contbr. articles on pottery to various collectors and antiques mags., 1967—; organizer, exhibitor of art pottery display touring fin. instns. in upper midwest, 1976-82; lectr. and cons. health care, antiques, journalism; health care specialist Health Services Research Center, St. Louis Park Med. Center, 1978-79; instr. Augsburg Coll., 1979-81. Mem. Minn. Adv. Task Force on Epilepsy, 1981-83, State Council for Handicapped, 1982-84, Dept. Pub. Welfare Adv. Council on Mental Retardation and Phys. Disabilities, 1982-84; mem. profl. adv. bd. Epilepsy Found. Minn., 1984-95. Mem. Mpls. Inst. Arts. USPHS trainee, 1964-65; Sigma Theta Tau scholar, 1962-63; Martha Ripley scholar, 1961-62: U. Minn. Sch. Nursing Found. scholar, 1962. Mem. U. Minn. Alumni Assn., Nat. Writers Club, Nat. League for Nursing (regional assembly constituent leagues for nursing. exec. com. 1985-87), Minn. League for Nursing (pres. 1983-85). Gethsemane Luth. Ch. Women, Am. Art Pottery Collectors Assn., Sigma Theta Tau, Delta Delta Delta. Lutheran. Home: 510 Westwood Dr N Minneapolis MN 55422-5266

DONAHOE, MAUREEN ALICE, accounting consultant; b. N.Y.C., June 9, 1959; d. William A. and Alice P. (O'Connor) D. BA in Acctg., Belmont Abbey Coll., 1982; MBA in Fin., Fordham U., 1992. CPA, N.Y. Staff acct. Bankers Trust Co., N.Y.C., 1982-85; sr. auditor Feldman Radin and Co., N.Y.C., 1985-87; valuation svcs. mgr. Ernst & Young, N.Y.C., 1987-91; mgr. cons. Policano and Manzo, Saddlebrook, N.J., 1991—; dir. 417 E. 90th St. Corp., N.Y.C., 1995—. Mem. alumni bd. Belmont Abbey Coll., 1994—. Mem. AICPA, Assn. Insolvency Accts., N.Y. State Soc. CPAs (mem. insolvency and reorgn. com. 1993-94). Republican. Roman Catholic. Home: 12 Upper Mountain Ave Montclair NJ 07042 Office: Policano and Manzo LLC Plz II Ste 200 Park 80 W Saddlebrook NJ 07663

DONAHUE, ELINOR, actress; b. Tacoma, Apr. 19, 1937; d. Thomas William and Doris Genevieve (Gelbaugh) D.; m. Harry Stephen Ackerman, Apr. 21, 1961 (dec. Feb. 1991); children: Brian Patrick, Peter Kyran, James Jay, Christopher Asher; m. Louis G. Genevrino, Feb. 29, 1992. AA, UCLA. Began show bus. career singing on Sta. KMO-Radio, Tacoma, 1939; with song and dance act Bert Levy Vaudeville Circuit, 1944-46; appeared in films Tenth Ave. Angel, Mr. Big, Unfinished Dance, Three Daring Daughters, Girls Town, Love is Better Than Ever, Going Beserk, 1983, Pretty Woman, 1990, Freddy's Dead, 1991, on TV series Father Knows Best, 1954-63, Andy Griffith Show, 1960-61, Many Happy Returns, 1964-65, Odd Couple, 1972-74, Mulligan's Stew, 1977, Please Stand By, 1978-79, Drs. Private Lives, New Adventures of Beans Baxter, 1987-88, Get a Life, 1990-92; numerous guest roles on TV including No Margin For Error on Police Story, 1978, Newhart, Golden Girls, 1989-91; television movies include In Name Only, 1969, Gidget Gets Married, 1972, Mulligan's Stew, 1977, Doctor's Private Lives, 1978, Condominium, 1980, High School U.S.A, 1983. Former 2d v.p. Share, Inc. (charitable orgn. for mentally retarded and developmentally disabled). *

DONAHUE, MARTHA, librarian, educator, retired; b. Danville, Ky., Jan. 5, 1936; d. Thomas E. and Mary Louise (Craig) D. BA, Centre Coll., 1958; MA, Ind. U., 1961; 6th Yr. Specialist's Cert., U. Wis., 1971. Tchr. Pompano Beach (Fla.) Jr. H.S., 1958-60; post libr. U.S. Army, Europe, Bad Tölz, Germany, 1961-65; instr. library Centre Coll., Danville, Ky., 1966-67, U. Wis., Whitewater, 1967-70; assoc. prof. library Mansfield (Pa.) U., 1971-93.

Bd. dirs. Centre Coll. Alumni, Danville, 1995—, Mansfield Free Pub. Libr., 1995—; vol. Area Agy. on Aging, Towanda, Pa., 1993—; mem. Parish Coun., Mansfield, 1994—. Recipient Higher Edn. Act fellowship U. Wis., 1960. Mem. ALA, Pa. Libr. Assn. (mem., chair various coms. 1971—), Friday Club of Wellsboro, Mansfield Garden Club, Columbia Lit. Exchange, The Book Group. Roman Catholic. Home: 146 S Main Mansfield PA 16933

DONAHUE, MARY ROSENBERG, psychologist; b. N.Y.C., Dec. 20, 1932; d. Lester and Ethel (Hyman) Rosenberg; children: Laurie, Rachel. BA, Adelphi U., 1954; MA, N.Y. U., 1958; PhD, St. John U., 1968. Tchr. Elmont, N.Y., 1954-57, sch. psychologist, 1957-63; cons. psychologist NIMH, 1964-65; sch. psychologist Mamaroneck, N.Y., 1966-67; pvt. practice psychology Bethesda, Md., 1971—; expert witness local jurisdictions regarding domestic issues, womens issues, abuse, 1974—; speaker on custody evaluations and expert witness considerations. Co-author: On Your Own, 1993. NIMH grantee, 1962-63, 64-65. Mem. Am. Psychol. Assn., Md. Psychol. Assn., D.C. Psychol. Assn., Am. Orthopsychiat. Assn., Assn. Pvt. Practitioners, Nat. Assn. Women Bus. Owners. Home: 12017 Edgepark Ct Potomac MD 20854-2138 Office: 5902 Hubbard Dr Rockville MD 20852-4823

DONAHUE, PATRICIA TOOTHAKER, retired social worker, administrator; b. Alamo, Tex., Sept. 6, 1922; d. Henry Tull and Minnie Elizabeth (Scott) Toothaker; m. Hayden Hackney Donahue, Feb. 22, 1947; children: Erin Kathleen, Kerry Shannon, Patricia Marie. BA, U. Okla., 1977, MSW, 1978. Lic. social worker with specialty in clin. social work, Okla. Clin. social worker Cen. Okla. Community Mental Health Ctr., Norman, 1979-91; participant VII World Congress Mental Health, Vienna, Austria, 1983; adj. asst. prof. U. Okla. Sch. Social Work, Norman, 1989—. Vol. counselor Woman's Resource Ctr., Norman, 1978-79; active Cleve. County Aging Svcs. Adv. Coun., 1988-91, pres., 1991. Mem. Nat. Alliance for Mentally Ill, Cleve. County Mental Health Assn., Cleve. County Med. Aux. (pres. 1970-71), Reviewers Club Norman (pres. 1970). Democrat. Methodist. Home: 1109 Westbrooke Ter Norman OK 73072-6308

DONAHUE-HOOKER, MARY KATHERINE, library director; b. Dallas, Jan. 14, 1942; d. Joseph W. and Ellen (Onan) D.; m. John Patrick Hooker, July 29, 1976. BA, Our Lady of the Lake U., 1963; MLS, U. Calif., Berkeley, 1965; MA, Tex. Agrl. and Mech. U., 1983. Librarian Dallas Pub. Library, 1963-64, 65; 1st asst. Lubbock (Tex.) City-County Librs., 1965-69, asst. dir., 1966-68; librarian U. Tex., Arlington, 1969; corp. librarian Univ. Computing Co., Dallas, 1969-72; sr. librarian Corpus Christi (Tex.) Pub. Librs., 1973-75, adminstrv. coord., 1975-76; coord. Hidalgo County (Tex.) Libr. Sys., McAllen, 1976-80; asst. prof. Tex. Agrl. and Mech. U., College Station, 1981-84; cons. Stone Child Coll. Libr., Box Elder, Mont., 1988—; dir librs. City of El Paso, 1994—. cons. in field. Recipient Disting. Svc. award Tex. Hist. Commn. Mem. ALA, Tex. Libr. Assn., Alpha Chi. Office: 501 N Oregon St El Paso TX 79901*

DONALD, AIDA DIPACE, publishing executive; b. Bklyn., Apr. 19, 1930; d. Victor E. and Bessie DiPace; m. David Herbert Donald; 1 child, Bruce Randall. AB cum laude, Barnard Coll., 1952; MA, Columbia U., 1953; PhD, U. Rochester, 1961. Instr. history dept. Columbia U., N.Y.C., 1955-56; editor Mass. Hist. Soc., Boston, 1960-64, Johns Hopkins U. Press, Balt., 1972-73; social sci. editor Harvard U. Press, Cambridge, Mass., 1973-79, exec. editor, 1979-89, editor in chief, 1989—, asst. dir., 1991. Editor: John F. Kennedy and the New Frontier, 1966, (with David Herbert Donald) Charles Frances Adams Diary, 2 vols., 1965. Columbia U. Dibblee fellow, 1952-53, U. Rochester fellow, 1953-55, 56-57, Oxford U. Fulbright fellow, 1959-60. Fellow AAUW; mem. Am. Hist. Assn., Orgn. Am. Historians, Polit. Sci. Assn. Am. Office: Harvard Univ Press 79 Garden St Cambridge MA 02138-1423

DONALD, BERNICE B., judge; b. Miss., Sept. 17, 1951; d. Perry and Willie Bell (Hall) Bowie; m. W. L. Donald, Oct. 9, 1973. BA in Sociology, Memphis State Univ., 1974, JD, 1979; student, Nat. Judicial Coll., 1983, 84. Bar: Tenn. 1979, U.S. Fed. Ct. 1979, U.S. Supreme Ct. 1989. Clk. South Central Bell Telephone Co., 1971-75, mgr., 1975-80; staff atty. Memphis Area Legal Svcs., 1980, Shelby County Public Defenders Office, 1980-82; judge Gen. Sessions Criminal Ct. of Shelby County, Tenn., 1982-88; bankruptcy judge U.S. Bankruptcy Ct. (we. dist.) Tenn., Memphis, 1988—; faculty mem. Fed. Judicial Ctr., 1991—, Nat. Judicial Coll., 1992—; adj. prof. Cecil C. Humphreys Sch. of Law. Recipient Cmty. Svcs. award Nat. Conf. on Christians and Jews, 1986, Martin Luther King Cmty. Svc. award, Young Careerist award State of Tenn. Raleigh Bureau of Profl. Women; named Citizen of Yr. Excelsior Chpt. of Eastern Star, Woman of Yr. Pentecostal Ch. of God in Christ. Mem. Nat. Assn. of Women Judges (pres. 1990-91), Am. Judges Assn., Nat. Ctr. for State Cts., Am. Bar Assn., Nat. Bar Assn., Tenn. Bar Assn., Memphis County Bar Assn., Shelby County Bar Assn., Am. Trial Lawyers Assn., Assn. of Women Attys. (pres. 1991, bd. dirs.), Nat. Conf. of Bankruptcy Judges (bd. dirs. 1993), Nat. Conf. of Women's Bar Assn. (bd. mem.), Nat. Conf. of Spl. Ct. Judges (sec.), Leadership Memphis (pres. 1987, bd. dirs.), Internat. Women's Forum.

DONALDSON, KATHARINE ELIZABETH, nurse practitioner; b. Teaneck, N.J., Dec. 5, 1962; d. Robert Brereton and Joan Elizabeth (Dixon) D. BSN, Valparaiso U., 1984; MSN, U. Pa., 1993. Asst. nurse mgr. Albert Einstein Med. Ctr., Phila., 1986-88, staff nurse, 1984-86, 88-90, nurse recruiter, 1990-92; staff RN Mercer Med. Ctr., Trenton, N.J., 1992-93; nurse practitioner Mercer Med. Ctr., Trenton, 1993—; bereavement counselor RTS Bereavement Svc., Trenton, 1994—, coord., 1995—. Mem. Pa. Nurses' Assn., Assn. of Women's Health, Obstetric and Neonatal Nurses, Am. Acad. Nurse Practitioners, Sigma Theta Tau. Home: 4010 Barry Ct Holland PA 18966

DONALDSON, LORETTA MARIE, librarian; b. Butler, Pa., Jan. 2, 1943; d. Harry Vernon and Anna Agnes (Lehnerd) Kidd; m. Raymond Benjamin Snyder Jr., June 6, 1964 (dec. Dec. 1985); children: Kenneth Scott Snyder, Timothy Patrick Snyder; m. Wilbert James Donaldson, Jr., Oct. 31, 1992. BS in Edn., Clarion U., 1964; MA in English, Slippery Rock (Pa.) U., 1989. Cert. tchr., Pa. Libr. Keystone Oaks High Sch., Dormont, Pa., 1964-66, Butler (Pa.) Area Sr. High Sch., 1966-67, Butler County Community Coll., 1967-68; substitute tchr. Butler Area Sch. Dist., 1971-83; English tchr. Moniteau Jr./Sr. High Sch., West Sunbury, Pa., 1983-89, libr., 1989—; English instr. Butler County Community Coll., 1988—; advisor Moniteau chpt. Nat. Honor Soc., West Sunbury, 1988—; libr. specialist Mid. States Evaluation Com., Punxsutawney, Pa., 1987. Editor (newsletter) The Good News, 1987-93. With pub. rels. LWV, Butler, 1989—; personnel mgr. Butler County Symphony, 1994—. Grantee NEH, Ind. U. of Pa., 1986. Mem. NEA, AAUW (Butler chpt. pres. 1990-92, v.p. 1988-90, treas. 1992—), Moniteau Edn. Assn. (negotiation team mem. 1989), Pa. State Edn. Assn. Republican. Methodist. Home: 104 Wild Wood Dr Butler PA 16001-3906 Office: Moniteau Jr-Sr High Sch 1810 W Sunbury Rd West Sunbury PA 16061-1220

DONALDSON, RUTH LOUISE, construction executive; b. Maryville, Mo., Nov. 16, 1909; d. Charles Adolph and Elva Bessie (McClurg) Jensen; m. John Clayton Donaldson, Jan. 3, 1931; children: Jacqueline, Elvalee, Patricia. BS in Edn., N.W. Mo. State U., 1930, AB, 1935. Prin. Hazen (Ark.) Jr. High Sch., 1930-31; engr., draftsman Sunflower Ordnance Plant, Eudora, Kans., 1941-43; elec. engr. Kaiser Shipyard, El Cerrito, Calif., 1943-45; tchr. Warwick High Sch., Providence, 1945-46; gen. contractor design and constrn. pub. utilities Donaldson Engrng. and Constrn. Co., Maryville, Mo., 1946—; county engr. Gentry County, Albany, Mo., 1950-52, asst. county engr., 1952-70. Bd. dirs. St. Francis Hosp., Maryville, 1974-88. Mem. AAUW. Democrat. Presbyterian. Home and Office: RR 1 Maryville MO 64468-9801

DONALDSON, SARAH SUSAN, radiologist; b. Portland, Oreg., 1939. BS, RN, U. Oreg., 1961; MD, Harvard U., 1968. Intern U. Wash., 1968-69; resident in radiol. therapy Stanford (Calif.) Med. Ctr., 1969-72; fellow in pediatric oncology Inst. Gustave-Roussy, 1972-73; prof. radiol. oncology Stanford U. Sch. Medicine., 1973—. Office: Stanford U Med Ctr Sch Medicine Stanford CA 94305

DONATH, JANET SUE, hospice and home health care nurse; b. Columbus, Ohio, Jan. 30, 1945; d. Samuel Joseph and Lola Mae (Marshall) Glines; m. Monroe Jefferson Donath, Jr., Dec. 10, 1966; children: Joseph Jefferson, James Monroe. Cert. vocat. nursing, Rosebud Sch. Vocat. Nursing, 1979; ADN, McLennan Community Coll., 1982; BSN, U. Tex., Arlington, 1990. RN, Tex. From nurse's aide to floor nurse Rosebud Community Hosp., 1977-81; patient care nurse Hillcrest Bapt. Med. Ctr., Waco, Tex., 1981-83; from charge nurse to home health dir. Rosebud Community Hosp., 1983-88; dir. hospice and home health svcs. Hillcrest Bapt. Med. Ctr., Waco, 1988-93; dir. home health, hospice and community outreach St. Joseph Hosp., 1993-95; dir. VNA Hospice, Vis. Nurse Assn. Houston, Inc., 1995—. With USN, 1963-66. Mem. ANA, Nat. Nurses Assn., Tex. Nurses Assn. (rec. sec. 1991-92, 92-93), Tex. Hospice Orgn. Home: 11326 Meadowchase Dr Houston TX 77065-4923

DONATH, THERESE, artist, author; b. Hammond, Ind.; student Monticello Coll., 1946-47; BFA, St. Joseph's Coll., 1975; additional study Oxbow Summer Sch. Painting, Immaculate Heart Coll., Hollywood, Calif., Penland, N.C., Haystack, Maine; radio/TV personality, 1978-92. Interviewer, producer Viewpoint, Sta. WLNR-FM, Lansing, Ill., 1963-64; reporter, columnist N.W. Ind. Sentinel, 1965; freelance writer Monterey Peninsula Herald, 1981-85; contbg. author Monterey Life mag. 1981-85; asst. dir. Michael Karolyi Meml. Found., Vence, France, 1979; one-woman shows include: Ill. Inst. Tech., Chgo., 1971; group shows include: Palos Verdes (Calif.) Mus., 1974, L.A. Inst. Contemporary Art, 1978, Mus. Contemporary Art, Chgo., 1975, Calif. State U., Fullerton, 1973, No. Ill. U., DeKalb, 1971, Bellevue (Wash.) Mus. Art, 1986-87; represented in permanent collections including Kennedy Gallery, N.Y.C., also pvt. collections; creative cons. Aslan Tours and Travel, 1983-85; instr., lectr. Penland, N.C., 1970, Haystack Mountain Sch., Deer Isle, Maine, 1974, Sheffield Poly., Eng., 1978. Bd. dirs., sec. Mental Health Soc. Greater Chgo., 1963-64; exec. dir. Lansing (Ill.) Mental Health Soc., 1963-64. Recipient awards No. Ind. Art Mus., 1966, 70, 71, 73; grantee Ragdale Found., Lake Forest, Ill., 1982. Represented in The Mirror Book, 1978; author: Screams and Laughter, 1992; author, illustrator: Before I Die, A Creative Legacy, 1989; contbr. articles to profl. jours., newspapers; illustrator: Run Computer Run, 1983.

DONDERO, GLORIA SERAFINA, urban planner, writer, musician; b. Reno, Nev., Oct. 8, 1954; d. Serafino Desiderio "Zedie" and Mary Louise (Bailo) D. BA, Vassar Coll., 1978; student, Columbia U., 1977-79, U. Nev., 1987—, McGeorge Sch. Law, 1991-92. Adminstrv. clk. City of Reno, Nev., 1984-86, planning technician, 1986-88, assoc. planner, 1988—; law lib. asst. McGeorge Sch. Law, Sacramento, 1991-92;. Contbr. articles to newsletters and mags. Co-founder St. John the Baptist Orthodox Mission and Bookstore, Reno, Nev., 1989—; organist Bethel A.M.E. Ch., Reno, Nev., 1984-87, V.A. Hosp. Chapel, 1987-89; organist Our Lady of the Blessed Sacrament Cath. Soc. St. Pius X, Silver Springs, Nev.; Nev. field rep. N. Am. Conf. Christianity and Ecology, 1987-91. Intermodal Surface Transp. Enhancement Act grantee on behalf of the City of Reno, U.S.D.O.T., 1994, 95. Mem. ABA (student divsn., planning and law divsn. 1991—, state and local govt. divsn. 1994—, natural resources law divsn. 1994—), Am. Planning Assn. (planning and law divsn. 1994—, state and local govt. law divsn. 1994—, natural resources law divsn. 1994—, Cert. of Achievement for Mcpl. Landscape Code 1995), Christian Soc. of the Green Cross, Mensa (asst. local sec. 1995), Toastmasters Internat. (pres. 1995). Republican. Home: 3250 Kingsview Ct Reno NV 89512-1457 Office: City of Reno 450 Sinclair St Reno NV 89505

DONDERO, GRACE MARIE, education educator; b. Bklyn., Feb. 28, 1949; d. Henry Angelo and Grace Veronica (Lagomarsino) D. BS, St. John's Univ., 1970, MS, 1971; MS, Pace Univ., 1975; EdD, Fordham Univ., 1993. Tchr. day elem. sch. Pub. Sch. 58 N.Y.C. Pub. Schs., 1970-91; asst. prof. St. John's Univ., S.I., N.Y., 1991—. Mem. ASCD, Doctorate Assn. of N.Y. (Laurel Wreath award), N.Y. Acad. of Pub. Edn., Phi Delta Kappa (Dissertation award 1992). Roman Catholic. Office: St Johns Univ 300 Howard Ave Staten Island NY 10301-4450

DONEHEW, PAMELA K., reading specialist; b. Fairmont, W.Va., Sept. 24, 1949; d. Walter Hal Donehew and Eldora Jean (Eddy) Van Tol; m. E. William Ball, Sr., June 1, 1968 (div. Oct. 1993); children: E. William, Jr., Jennifer Catena, Geoffrey J. AA, Ocean County Coll., Toms River, N.J., 1986; BA in English and Psychology, Monmouth U., 1989, MA, 1991, MSEd, 1992. Cert. reading specialist, tchr. psychology, English tchr., tchr. grades K-12, N.J. Dir. reading ctr. Monmouth U., West Long Branch, N.J., 1989-92; tchr. psychology Manasquan H.S., N.J., 1992-95; reading specialist West Ga. Tech., LaGrange, 1995—; learning cons. Georgian Ct. Coll., Lakewood, N.J., 1995; reader coll. bds. AP Psychology Exam, Clemson U., 1996; GRE, GMAT Test administr., 1990-94. Author: Library Handbook, 1996; co-author: Learn to Tutor, 1990. Mem. APA, NEA, Nat. Coun. English Tchrs., Internat. Reading Assn., Phi Delta Kappa. Office: West Ga Tech 303 Fort Dr La Grange GA 30240

DONELSON, LINDA TOURNEY, artist; b. Denver, Feb. 8, 1957; d. Dallas Wayne and Bessie Lucille (Ratliff) Tourney; m. Joseph Loren Johnston, Sept. 29, 1975 (div. Dec. 1985). BFA in Printmaking, U. Oreg., 1978; postgrad., U. Denver. Cert. graphoanalyst. One woman shows include: Gallery 141, Eugene, Oreg., 1978; group shows include: Gallery 141, 1978, Colo. AIDS project, Denver, 1992, 93, Genre Gallery, Denver, 1994; juried shows include: Greenwood Village (Colo.) Arts and Humanities Coun., 1981, El Dorado Gallery, Colorado Springs, 1982, Arte Gallery, Cherry Creek, Colo., 1994, Foothills Gallery, Golden, Colo., 1995, Soho Gallery, Pensacola, Fla., 1995. Mng. dir. Alternative Arts Alliance, Denver, 1995—; bd. dirs. City of Englewood Culturla Arts Commn., 1996—. Recipient Phillip Haley Johnson award, 1977, Greeley Nat. Show award, 1994, Foothills Art Ctr., 1995. Mem. Internat. Graphoanalysis Soc., Colo. Graphoanalysis Soc.

DONICA, CHERYL MARIE, elementary education educator; b. Greensburg, Ind., Aug. 26, 1953; d. Thurman Lloyd and Kathryn Lucille (Chadwell) D. BS in Edn., Ind. U., 1975, MS in Edn., 1979. Tchr. Decatur County Schs., Greensburg, Ind., 1975-81, Escola Americana de Brasilia, Brazil, 1981-85, Fontana (Calif.) Unified Schs., 1986—; mentor tchr. Fontana Unified Schs., 1989-92, 93-94, program specialist, 1990-92. Reading and Literacy Merit award Arrowhead Reading Coun., San Bernardino, Calif., 1989. Mem. NEA, Calif. Tchrs. Assn., Internat. Reading Assn., Assn. Childhood Edn. Internat. Calif. Kindergarten Assn., Nat. Assn. Edn. of Young Children. Republican. Methodist. Home: 1965 Coulston St Apt 6 Loma Linda CA 92354-1741 Office: Tokay Elem 7846 Tokay Ave Fontana CA 92335

DONIGER, IRENE G., psychologist, business owner; b. Bklyn., Sept. 29, 1944; m. Stanley Doniger, Aug. 27, 1967; children: Shawn Jason, Robin Jill. BS in Health Sci. & Edn., Bklyn. Coll., 1973; MS in Counseling and Human Rels., Villanova U., 1987. RN, Pa.; lic. psychologist, Pa. Maternity nurse, childbirth educator Bryn Mawr (Pa.) Hosp., 1973-76; addictions counselor Help Counseling, Westchester, Pa., 1987-89; psychology intern Psychol. Health Cons., Bryn Mawr, 1987-90; psychologist, addictions counselor Starting Point, Westmont, N.J., 1991—; psychologist, dir., founder Mind/Body Connection, Inc., King of Prussia, Pa., 1991—; co-founder, mediator Win/Win Negotiations, King of Prussia, Pa., 1995—; motivational spkr., trainer, bd. dirs. Parents Involved Network, Phila.; lectr. Huntington Found., 1996—; cons. in field. Author: (coloring book) Good Touch, Bad Touch, 1980; creator (audio tapes) Conquering Job Interview Anxiety, 1996, Conquering Test Anxiety, 1996, Mind/Body Communications, 1996. Mem. Multidisc. Team Montgomery County, Norristown; founder. Childwatch Block Parents Assn., King of Prussia, 1093-85. Mem. Pa. Psychol. Assn., Acad. Counseling Assocs., Women's Referral Network Montgomery County (sec. 1995-96). Office: Mind/Body Connection Inc 570 W DeKalb Pike Ste 102 King Of Prussia PA 19406

DONLEY, ROSEMARY, university official. Diploma in Nursing, Pitts. Hosp., 1961; BSN summa cum laude, St. Louis U., 1963; M in Nursing Edn., U. Pitts., 1965; postgrad. tng. in psychiatry, U. Pitts., Columbia U., 1967-69; PhD, U. Pitts., 1972; postgrad., Harvard U., 1986; LittD (hon.), Felician Coll., 1981, Villanova U., 1985; LLD (hon.), Loyola U., Chgo., 1988; HHD (hon.), Madonna Coll., 1988; Dr. Pub. Svc. (hon.), R.I. Coll., 1988, La Roche Coll., 1989. Staff nurse St. Mary's Hosp., St. Louis, 1961-63; instr. Pitts. Hosp. Sch. Nursing, 1963-71; cons. Vis. Nurses Assn. Allegheny County, Pitts., 1972; from instr. to assoc. prof. Sch. Nursing U. Pitts., 1971-79; dean and assoc. prof. Sch. Nursing Cath. U. Am., Washington, 1979-86, exec. v.p., 1986—; bd. dirs. Ea. Mercy Health Care System, Forbes Health Care System, Nursing Econs. Found.; cons. in field; advisor internat. programs, lectr. various colls. and univs. Contbr. articles to profl. jours.; mem. editorial bd. Ednl. Record, 1985—, Jour. Contemporary Health Law and Policy, 1985—. Bd. dirs. Seton Hill Coll., 1991—. Recipient Hon. Recognition award Pa. League for Nursing, 1978, Alumni Merit award St. Louis U., 1980, Woman of Yr. award Pres.'s Commn. on Women, Cath. U. Am., 1984, McGrady award, Cath. Youth Assn. of Pitts. Inc., 1987, Medal of Distinction. U. Pitts., 1987; fellow Robert Wood Johnson Found. and Inst. Medicine, Nat. Acad. Sci., 1977-78; Disting. scholar in nursing NYU, 1994; Alumni fellows award U. Pitts., 1995. Fellow Am. Acad. Nursing; mem. Inst. Medicine, Nat. League for Nursing (pres. 1987-89), Sigma Theta Tau (sr. editor Image Jour. Nursing, 1st v.p. 1971-74, pres. 1975-81). Home: 7004 Riggs Rd Hyattsville MD 20783-2933 Office: Cath U Am Office of Exec VP Washington DC 20064

DONNALLEY, MARY JANE, physical educational consultant, writer; b. Denver, July 11, 1922; d. Albert West and Anne Porter (Kolb) Metcalf; widowed; children: Kenneth Girard, James Edward (dec.). BA in Human Rels. with honors, Rollins Coll., Winter Park, Fla., 1943; MEd in Counselor Edn., U. Va., 1958, EdD, 1966; diploma, Harvard Grad. Bus. Sch., 1972. Lic. profl. counselor, psychotherapist, Va.; cert. tennis profl., sports psychologist, mgmt. cons., resdl. real estate broker. Asst. prof. mgmt. and counseling Pan Am U., Edinburg, Tex., 1980-84; v.p. human resources and pub. rels. Wooden Consol. Industries, Dallas, 1984-85; realtor/broker Ebby Halliday Realtors, Dallas, 1985-89; pres. The Behavioral Sci. Ctr., Dallas, 1985-89; spl. asst. Office Pub. Affairs Mgmt./Employe Tng. and Devel. Social Security Adminstrn., U.S. Dept. HHS, Washington, 1989-92; tennis and sports cons. Family Sports Ctr., Kerrville, 1993—; assoc. prof. health, phys. edn., recreation, tennis profl., dept. chmn. Mary Baldwin Coll., Staunton, Va., 1959-69; dean of students, adj. prof. ednl. psychology N.Mex. State U., Las Cruces, 1969-72; speaker in field; adj. prof. Dallas Bapt. U.; instr. Brookhaven, Northlake and Richlands Coll.; ednl. cons. Tch. Edn. Ctr., Rockville, Md., 1995; vis. prof. edn. and psychology Western N.Mex. U., Silver City, 1969, 82. Columnist Tennis Tips, Kerrville (Tex.) Daily Times, 1992-94, syndicated, 1995—; guest columnist Kerrville Times, 1994-95. Del. to state conv. Republican Party, Houston, 1988; mem. Northwood Rep. Women, Dallas, 1984-88; mem. Def. Adv. Com. for Women in the Svcs., 1973. Sloan Found. fellow, 1971-73; Presbyn. fellow, 1966. Mem. ACA, U.S. Profl. Tennis Assn. (cert.), U.S. Profl. Tennis Registry (cert.), Am. Assn. Health, Phys. Edn. and Recreation. Episcopalian. Home: 2300 Chalet Trl Kerrville TX 78028-2558

DONNAY, LOIS JOANN, marketing consulting company executive; b. Watkins, Minn., Feb. 18, 1956; d. Matthew Henry and Eleanor (Zutz) D.; m. Jeffrey Hamilton Zappa, Sept. 4, 1976. AA, Dunwoody Tech., 1986; BA, Metro. State U., 1994. Tchr. Dunwoody, Mpls., 1986-88; gen. mgr. MAICO, Edina, Minn., 1986-94; product, mktg. mgr. Madsen, Edina, Minn., 1994-95; pres. Donnay & Assocs., Mpls., 1995—. Contbr. article to profl. jour. Home: 7002 Cheyenne Tr Chanhassen MN 55317

DONNELLY, BARBARA ANN, artist, educator; b. Somerville, Mass.; d. Russell Winfield and Pearl Marie (Cameron) Chick; m. Robert Boag Donnelly, May 29, 1954; children: Kathleen, Sharon, Robert Jr., Patricia, Michael, Brian. AA, Boston U., 1954. Tchr. oil painting, watercolors Beverly (Mass.) Adult Edn., 1969-80, 83-90, tchr. basic drawing, 1970-90; tchr. Lakes Region Outdoor Painting, N.H., 1977-85; tchr. pen, ink No. Essex C. C., Newburyport, Mass., 1986-88; court rm. artist Channel 56, Boston, 1987—; tchr. watercolor Gloucester, Mass., 1993—. Illustrator: The Little Book Shop, 1989; cover artist: Palette Talk, 1990; contbr. articles to profl. jours. Asst. chmn. Beverly Bicentennial Arts Festival, 1975, chmn. 1976. Named Internat. Artist-in-Residence, Dinan, France, "Les Amis de La Grande Vigne" Mus., 1996. Mem. Am. Artists Profl. League, Acad. Artists Assn., North Shore Arts Assn., Rockport Art Assn., New England Watercolor Soc., Guild of Beverly Artists, Copley Soc. of Boston. Roman Catholic. Office: Barbara Donnelly Art Gallery 19 Harbor Loop Gloucester MA 01930

DONNELLY, BARBARA SCHETTLER, medical technologist; b. Sweetwater, Tenn., Dec. 2, 1933; d. Clarence G. and Irene Elizabeth (Brown) Schettler; A.A., Tenn. Wesleyan Coll., 1952; B.S., U. Tenn., 1954; cert. med. tech., Erlanger Hosp. Sch. Med. Tech., 1954; postgrad. So. Meth. U., 1980-81; children—Linda Ann, Richard Michael. Med. technologist Erlanger Hosp., Chattanooga, 1953-57, St. Luke's Episcopal Hosp., Tex. Med. Ctr., Houston, 1957-58, 1962; engrng. R &D SCI Systems Inc., Huntsville, Ala., 1974-76; cons. hematology systems Abbott Labs., Dallas, 1976-77, hematology specialist, Dallas, Irving, Tex., 1977-81, tech. specialist microbiology systems, Irving, 1981-83, coord. tech. svc. clin. chemistry systems, 1983-84, coord. customer tng. clin. chemistry systems, 1984-87, supr. clin. chemistry tech. svcs., 1987-88, supr. clin. chemistry customer support ctr., 1988-93, supr. clin. chemistry and x-systems customer support ctr., 1993—. Mem. Am. Soc. Clin. Pathologists (cert. med. technologist), Am. Soc. Microbiology, Nat. Assn. Female Execs., U. Tenn. Alumni Assn., Chi Omega. Contbr. articles on cytology to profl. jours. Republican. Methodist. Home: 204 Greenbriar Ln Bedford TX 76021-2006 Office: 1921 Hurd Dr Irving TX 75038-4313

DONNELLY, LYNNE CAROL, writer; b. Cin., Oct. 18, 1955; d. Francis Moreland and Marion Elizabeth (Yunkes) D.; m. Ronald John Donovan, Feb. 14, 1981; children: Marina Rose Donnelly Donovan, Keaton John Donnelly Donovan. BA in Linguistics summa cum laude, U. Cin., 1977. Editor Alaska Pub. Broadcasting, Anchorage, 1981-82; adj. faculty mem. Alaska Pacific U., Anchorage, 1982-85; columnist Anchorage Daily News, 1985-87; columnist, corr. Portsmouth (N.H.) Press, 1987-90; free-lance writer, editor Anchorage, Rollinsford, N.H. and Durham, N.H., 1982—. Editor Learning in Prime Time TV Guide mag., 1981-82; author over 170 articles on family, health, life styles. Bd. dirs. Tudor Community Sch., Anchorage, 1984-85. Mem. Phi Beta Kappa. Home and Office: 10 Carriage Way Durham NH 03824-4500

DONOGHUE, ANN RUTH, veterinarian, researcher; b. Ann Arbor, Mich., May 25, 1961; d. Wallace and Marlene (Speer) Donoghue; m. Steven Victor Radecki, Sept. 6, 1986. BS, Mich. State U., 1983, DVM, 1987, MS, 1992. Sect. chief parasitology Animal Health Diagnostic Lab. Mich. State U., East Lansing, 1989-90, specialist large animal clin. svcs. dept.; clin./rsch. veterinarian Hoechst-Roussel Agri-Vet Co., Somerville, N.J., 1990-96; product devel. and regulatory affairs Heska Corp., Ft. Collins, Colo., 1996—. Vol. reader/broadcaster WKAR Radio Talking Book, Mich. State U., 1988-90; 4-H resource person Somerset County 4-H, 1993—. Recipient Disting. Svc. award Ass. for Women Veterinarians, 1994, Ideal Veterinarian award Mich. Vet. Med. Assn., 1987, Leadership award student chpt. Am. Vet. Med. Assn., 1986. Mem. Am. Assn. Vet. Parasitologists (chair outreach/rsch. com. 1990-93), Am. Soc. Parasitologists, Am. Assn. Indsl. Veterinarians (bd. dirs. 1991-95, newsletter editor 1992—), N.J. Soc. Parasitology (sec.-treas. 1994—). Home: PO Box 272447 Fort Collins CO 80527 Office: Heska Corp 1825 Sharp Point Dr Fort Collins CO 80525

DONOGHUE, LINDA, nursing administrator, community health nurse; b. N.Y.C., Feb. 27, 1953; d. Raymond and Mary (McCormack) Carey; m. William Donoghue, June 7, 1975; children: William, Jamie. BSN, Villanova U., 1975; MPA, Am. Internat. Coll., Springfield, Mass., 1986. RN, Mass.; cert. nurse adminstr. Assoc. dir. nurses Noble Hosp., Westfield, Mass.; adminstr. Tech. Aid Corp., Newton, Mass., 1988-92; exec. dir. Spectrum Home Health, Longmeadow, Mass., 1994—; mem. bd. Home Care Risk Mgmt., New Eng. Healthcare Assembly; mem. nurse practice adv. com. to Mass. Bd. Registration in Nursing, 1991-93, chair substance abuse task force, 1994-96; mem. adv. task force Home and Health Work Force, 1989-90, home and health care mem. coms., 1989—, others; coord. publ. of standards of clin. practice in home health care; mem. profl. adv. bd. Bay Path Coll.; bd. registration in nursing, 1996. Mem. Am. Acad. Healthcare Adminstrs., Nat. Assn. Home Care, Home and Health Care Assn. Mass. (Mgr. of Yr. award for excellence/leadership 1989), Mass. Pub. Health Assn., Villanova U.

Nursing Alumni Assn. Home: 414 Inverness Ln Longmeadow MA 01106-2826

DONOGHUE, MILDRED RANSDORF, education educator; b. Cleve.; d. James and Caroline (Sychra) Ransdorf; m. Charles K. Donoghue (dec. 1982); children: Kathleen, James. Ed.D., UCLA, 1962; J.D., Western State U., 1979. Asst. prof. edn. Calif. State U.-Fullerton, 1962-66, assoc. prof., 1966-71; prof. Calif. State U., Fullerton, 1971—. Author: Foreign Languages and the Schools, 1967, Foreign Languages and the Elementary School Child, 1968, The Child and the English Language Arts, 1971, 75, 79, 85, 90; co-author: Second Languages in Primary Education, 1979; contbr. articles to profl. jours. and Ednl. Resources Info. Ctr. U.S. Dept. Edn. Mem. AAUP, AAUW, TESOL, Nat. Network for Early Lang. Learning, Nat. Coun. Tchrs. English, Am. Dialect Soc., Am. Ednl. Rsch. Assn., Nat. Soc. for Study of Edn., Am. Assn. Tchrs. Spanish and Portuguese, S.W. Conf. on Lang. Tchg., Internat. Reading Assn., Nat. Assn. Edn. Young Children, Orange County Med. Assn. Women's Aux., Authors Guild, Assn. for Childhood Edn. Internat., Phi Beta Kappa, Phi Kappa Phi, Pi Lambda Theta, Alpha Upsilon Alpha. Office: Calif State U Dept Elem Edn Fullerton CA 92634

DONOHUE, EDITH M., human resources specialist, consultant; b. Balt., Nov. 10, 1938; d. Edward Anthony and Beatrice (Jones) McParland; m. Salvatore R. Donohue, Aug. 23, 1960; children: Kathleen, Deborah. BA, Coll. Notre Dame, Balt., 1960; MS, Johns Hopkins U., 1981, CASE, 1985, PhD in Human Resources, 1990. Dir. pub. relations Coll. Notre Dame, Balt., 1970-71, asst. dir. continuing edn., 1978-81, dir. continuing edn., 1981-86; coord. program bus. and industry Catonsville C.C., Baltimore County, Md., 1986-88; mgr. tng. and devel. Sheppard Pratt Hosp., Balt., 1988-90; assoc. prof. Barry U., advisor grad. program, 1993—; adj. faculty Loyola Coll. Grad. Studies Program, Fla. Inst. Tech., Indian River C.C. Co-author: Communicate Like a Manager, 1989; co-editor, contbg. author career devel. workshop manual, 1985; contbr. articles to profl. jours. Pres. Cathedral Sch. Parents Assn., 1972-74; asst. treas., treas. Md. Gen. Hosp. Aux., 1975-78; dir. Homeland Assn., 1978-81; regional rep., leader Girl Scouts Cen. Md., 1975-76; dir. sect. Exec. Women's Network, Balt., 1983-85; adv. bd. Mayor's Com. on Aging, 1981-86; dir. Md. Assn. Higher Edn., 1985-88; vol. trainer United Way Martin County, co-chair campaign, 1994—; mem. steering com. Chautaugua South. Recipient Mayor's Citation, City of Balt. Council, 1985. Mem. Am. Assn. Tng. and Devel (bd. dirs.), Am. Counseling Assn., AAUW (dir., v.p. 1980-83), Soc. Human Resources Mgmt., Martin County Personnel Mgt. Assn. (edn. chmn. 1991-94), Martin County C. of C. (edn. com. 1991-94), Friends of Lyric (bd. dirs., chmn., strategic planning, pres.), Chi Sigma Iota (pres.), Phi Delta Kappa. Republican. Roman Catholic. Avocations: tennis, performing arts, reading, wellness. Home: Ste 3103 144 NE Edgewater Dr Apt 3103 Stuart FL 34996-4477 Office: Barry U 590 NW Peacock Loop Ste 5 Port Saint Lucie FL 34986-2213

DONOHUE, PATRICIA CAROL, academic administrator; b. St. Louis, Jan. 11, 1946; d. Carroll and Juanita Dohonue; m. James H. Stevens Jr., Aug. 27, 1966 (div. Mar. 1984); children: James H. III, Carol Janet. AB, Duke U., 1966; MA, U. Mo., 1974, PhD, 1982. Tchr. math, secondary schs. Balt., St. Louis and Shawnee Mission, Kans., 1966-71; lectr. U. Mo., Kansas City, 1975-76, rsch. asst. affirmative action, 1976-79, coord. affirmative action, 1979-82, instl. rsch. assoc., 1982-84, acting dir. affirmative action and acad. pers., 1984; dir. instl. rsch. Lakeland C.C., 1984-86; asst. dean acad. affairs, math., engring. and tech. Harrisburg Area C.C., 1986-89, dean sch. bus., engring., and tech., 1989—; dean Lebanon campus Pa. Coun. on Vocat. Edn., 1989-93, v.p. cmty. devel. and external affairs, 1993; vice chancellor edn. St. Louis C.C., 1993—; bd. dirs., v.p. St. Louis Sch. to Work, Inc., 1994—; chairperson Pa. Occupl. Deans, 1988-93. Bd. dirs., v.p. Am. Cancer Soc. Jackson County, 1975-84; mem. adv. coun. Ben Franklin Partnership, 1988-93; leader Hemlock coun. Girl Scouts U.S.A., bd, dirs. 1986-93; bd. dirs. PTA, 1975-77, Cmty. Lebanon Assocs.; mem. steering com. New Baldwin Corridor Coalition, 1991-93, chair edn. task force, 1992-93. Recipient Outstanding Service and Achievement award U. Mo. Kansas City, 1976; Jack C. Coffey grantee, 1978; named Outstanding Woman AAUW, 1989, one of Outstanding Leaders Nat. Inst. Leadership Devel., 1986, Exec. Leadership Inst., 1990. Mem. ASCD, Nat. Coun. Tchrs. of Math., Math. Assn. Am., Am. Vocat. Assn., Am. Assn. Cmty. Colls. (mem. coun. affiliated chairpersons 1994—, chairperson coun. 1996—, mem. commn. on cmty. and workforce devel. 1995—), Nat. Coun. for Occupl. Edn. (chairperson diversity task force 1991, chairperson job tng. 2000 task force 1992, bd. dirs. 1992—, v.p. programs 1992-93, v.p. membership 1993-94, pres. 1995—), Am. Assn. Women in Cmty. and Jr. Colls. (Pa. state coord. 1988, bd. dirs. Region 3 1989-91), Soc. Mfg. Engrs. (chmn. 1989-90), Women's Equity Project, Nat. Assn. Student Pers. Adminstrs., Women's Network, Assn. Inst. Rsch., Phi Delta Kappa (pres. 1975, Read fellow 1989), Phi Kappa Phi, Pi Lambda Theta, delta Gamma (past v.p., del. nat. conv. 1988, pres. 1989-91, Cream Rose Outstanding Svc. award 1970). Home: 6235 Washington Ave Saint Louis MO 63130-4847 Office: St Louis C C 300 S Broadway Saint Louis MO 63102-2800

DONOHUE, THERESE BRADY, artistic director, choreographer, designer; b. Washington, Jan. 13, 1937; d. John Bernard and Mary Catherine (Rupert) B.; m. Joseph W. Donohue Jr., June 13, 1959 (div. 1987); children: Sharon Marie, Maura Cathleen (dec.), Sheila Patricia. BA, Coll. of Notre Dame Md., 1958. Cert. tchr. ballet Royal Acad. Dance London. Advt. artist Kronstadt Advt. Agy., Washington, 1958; instr. art The Maret Sch., Washington, 1958-60, Princeton (N.J.) U., 1967-71; artist dir. Amherst (Mass.) Ballet Theatre Co., 1977—; founder, dir. Amherst Ballet Centre, 1971—; co-dir., founder Pioneer Valley Ballet, Northampton, Mass., 1972-77; dancer, tchr. Princeton Ballet, 1962-71; animal masks Charleston (S.C.) Ballet, 1985—; choreographer Roanoke (Va.) Ballet Theatre, 1983; chairperson N.E. Region Craft Choreography Conf., Amherst, 1979; artist/choreographer Nat. Gallery Art, 1986, 88, Guggenheim, 1986, Nat. Mus. Am. Art, 1989, Hirshhorn Mus. & Sculpture Garden, 1993. Choreographer (ballets for children) Peter & the Wolf, 1973, One Thousand Cranes, 1974, Punch & Judy, 1975, Amherst Poets, 1977, Uncle Wiggily & the Duck Pond, 1979, (Springfield Symphony) History of Dance, 1983, (Project Opera) Hansel & Gretel, 1983, Sea Study (included in Aberdeen Internat. Youth Festival in Scotland), 1994, Peter Pan Amherst Cmty. Theater, 1995, Aida Commonwealth Opera, 1996; rechoregraphed Matisse's Circus, Dancing with Dubuffet; toured Maui Hawaii Elem. Schs. (Amherst Ballet Theatre Co.), 1996. Mem. Amherst Arts Coun., 1983-89. Mem. Amherst Club. Home: 17 Juniper Ln Amherst MA 01002-1227 Office: Amherst Ballet Centre 29 Strong St Amherst MA 01002-1836

DONOVAN, CAROL, broadcast executive. V.p. music and spl. events MTV Networks, N.Y.C. Office: MTV Networks 1515 Broadway New York NY 10036*

DONOVAN, CAROL ANN, state legislator; b. Lynn, Mass., June 5, 1937; d. John Barrows and Virginia Mary (Pearce) D. AB, Regis Coll., Weston, Mass., 1959, MA, 1980. Tchr. home econs. Woburn (Mass.) Sch. System, 1959-74, spl. edn. tchr., 1974-84, spl. edn. liaison, 1984-90; mem. Mass. Ho. of Reps., Boston, 1991—; vice chair Post Audit and Oversight Com., Boston; polit. cons. Mass. Tchrs. Assn., Boston, 1985-89. Mem. Mass. Caucus of Women Legislators, 1991—; mem. Nat. Women's Polit. Caucus, 1989—; bd. dirs. Winchester (Mass.) Hosp., 1992—, New Horizons Woburn; bd. dirs. Ctrl. Middlesex Assn. Retarded Citizens, Woburn, 1984—, also past pres.; sec. Woburn Dem. City Com., 1984—. Recipient Elder Advocacy award Minuteman Home Care, Burlington, Mass., 1993, Disting. Citizen award ARC Mass., Waltham, 1993, Legislator of Yr. award Mass. Disabilities Coun. and ARC, 1994. Mem. Women's Legis. Lobby, Woburn Middlesex Lions Club. Roman Catholic. Office: State House Rm 146 Boston MA 02133

DONOVAN, HELEN W., newspaper editor. Exec. editor Boston Globe. Office: Globe Newspapers Co 135 Morrissey Blvd Boston MA 02125 Office: Globe Newspapers Co PO Box 2378 Boson MA 02107-2378*

DONOVAN, KIMBERLY STEGNER, nursing administrator; b. Belleville, N.J., June 27, 1961; d. Robert and Anna (Giza) Stegner; m. Richard Donovan, July 1, 1989 (div. July 1994); 1 child, Kaitlyn. Diploma, Muhlenberg Hosp. Sch. Nursing, 1983; ASN, Union County Coll., 1983; BSN, SUNY, Albany, 1990. RN, N.J.; cert. nurse administrator, emergency nurse, BLS, ACLS, TNCC. Med.-surg., oper. rm., emergency rm. staff nurse St. Clare's Hosp., Denville, N.J., 1983-87; emergency rm. patient care coord. St. Barnabas Med. Ctr., Livingston, N.J., 1987-90; adminstrv. coord. nursing dept. St. Mary's Hosp., Passaic, N.J., 1990-95, quality review coord., 1995—. Mem. AACN, Nat. Assn. Healthcare Quality, Muhlenberg Hosp. Sch. Nursing Alumnae Assn., Orgn. Nurse Execs., Sigma Theta Tau, Delta Phi Epsilon. Roman Catholic. Office: St Mary's Hosp 211 Pennington Ave Passaic NJ 07055-4617

DONOVAN, LOWAVA DENISE, data processing administrator; b. Galesburg, Ill., Mar. 27, 1958; d. Richard Eugene and Lowava Jeanine (Squire) Corbin; m. James Dean Rutledge, June 17, 1977 (div. May 1981); 1 child, Tiffany Michelle; m. Neal Edwin Donovan, July 9, 1983. Computer operator cert., Carl Sandburg Coll., 1977, student, 1976-86; student, IBM Edn., Chgo., 1979-87. Keypunch operator Fin. Industry Systems, Galesburg, Ill., 1977-79; computer operator Solution Assocs., Peoria, Ill., 1979-80; programmer, data processing mgr. May Co., Galesburg, 1980-81; programmer Kirkendall Gen. Offices, Galesburg, 1981-82; programmer, data processing mgr. Munson Transp., Monmouth, Ill., 1982-85, programmer/analyst, dir. data processing, 1985-87, dir. mgmt. info. systems, 1987-89; ind. contract programmer analyst Oklahoma City, Okla., 1989-92; product line mgr. Innovative Computing Corp., 1992-94; sr. programmer analyst, dir. info. resources Freymiller Trucking, Inc., Oklahoma City, 1994-96; ptnr. D&D Computers and Comm., 1996—. Mem. Ch. of God. Home: 1061 W North St Galesburg IL 61401

DONOVAN, MARGARET, consultant, investigator; b. Yankton, S.D., Jan. 1, 1950; d. Robert Bauerle and Norma Louise (Miller) D. BA in Psychology, Loretto Heights Coll., Denver, 1973; MS in Counseling and Pers., Drake U., 1986. Cert. substance abuse counselor II, Iowa. Svc. worker II div. youth svcs. State of Colo., Denver, 1976; youth svc. worker Woodbury County Juvenile Ct., Sioux City, Iowa; mental health, substance abuse advocate Woodbury County Ct., Sioux City, 1983-85; dir. chem. dependency treatment ctr. Winnebago Indian Reservation, 1984; residential dir. Intersect. United Advanced Planning Ctr., Des Moines, 1986-87; pvt. practice tng. and devel. Donovan & Assocs., Des Moines, 1987—; instr. devel. edn. Briar Cliff Coll., 1989-90; hospitalization adv. Woodbury County; coord. alcohol and edn. and disabled student svcs. Iowa State U., Ames, 1987-89; chair steering com. Univ. Without Walls, 1971; apptd. by gov. to State Vocat. Adv. Coun., 1993-94; owner mediation counseling and child custody investigation svc. Donovan Cons. and Rehab.-Expert Testimony, 1991—. Asst. editor: T'Akra, 1972-73; poet, author, 1970—. Mem. edn. com. Interfaith Resources, Sioux City, 1982-83. Mem. ACA, NOW.

DONOVAN, MARIE PHILLIPS, television executive; b. Detroit; m. Tom Donovan; children: Kathleen Marie, Kevin Thomas. Student, Wayne U., U. Mich. Profl. actress Actors Equity Assn., N.Y.C., AFTRA, N.Y.C.; bus. mgr. Dirs. Service Inc., N.Y.C., exec. v.p., treas. Mem. NAFE, Young Men's Philanthropic League, Am. Contract Bridge League (life master), Am. Bridge Tchr.'s Assn. (accredited tchr.), Cavendish Club.

DONOVAN, MEG, federal official; b. Rockville Centre, N.Y., Feb. 6, 1951; d. Daniel J. and Arline M. (Brassil) D.; m. Stephen C. Duffy, Sept. 21, 1974; children: Colin, Emma, Liam. Student, Emmanuel Coll., 1968-72. Legis. asst. Mass. State Legislature, Boston, 1972-74; adminstrv. asst. Nat. Conf. Soviet Jewry, Washington, 1975-76; mem. profl. staff Commn. Security and Cooperation in Europe U.S. Congress, 1976-84; staff cons. Ho. Com. Fgn. Affairs, 1985-93; sr. policy advisor Dept. State, Washington, 1993-94; dep. asst. sec. Dept. of State, Washington, 1995—; mem. Dept. State transition team Clinton-Gore Transition, 1992-93. Office: Dept of State 2201 C St NW Rm 7261 Washington DC 20520-0001

DONOVAN, RITA R., nurse anesthetist, trauma and critical care nurse, educator; b. Bklyn., May 19, 1957; d. Joseph and Antoinette (Burdo) Nigro. Student, Bklyn. Coll., 1975-77; BSN, SUNY, Bklyn., 1979. RN, N.Y. Sr. staff nurse med. surg. unit Maimonides Med. Ctr., Bklyn., 1979-81, staff nurse med. ICU, 1981-84, asst. head nurse pulmonary ICU, 1985-86; grad. nurse anesthetist Kings County Hosp., Bklyn., 1988-89, clin. and acad. instr., 1989-90; clin. specialist surg. ICU Maimonides Med. Ctr., Bklyn., 1990-91; quality improvement coord. dept. anesthesia Kings County Hosp., Bklyn., 1991—, clin., acad. instr., 1991—. Contbr. rsch. articles to profl. jours. and texts. Anesthetist, ICU Desert Storm Task Force, 1991. Recipient 5-Yr. Outstanding award Maimonides Med. Ctr., 1985, Agatha Hodgins Meml. award Outstanding Nurse Anesthetist, 1988, Cert. award Cardiac Anesthesia, Kings County Hosp., 1988, others; named Best All Around Sutdent, 1988. Mem. ACN, Am. Assn. Nurse Anesthetists, Soc. Critical Care Medicine, Soc. Trauma Nurses, Drs. Against Murder. Office: Kings County Hosp Ctr Dept Anesthesia 451 Clarkson Ave Rm B 2175 Brooklyn NY 11203

DONOVAN, SHARON ANN, educator; b. Balt., Feb. 17, 1944; d. Jesse F. and Ruth Elizabeth (Keller) D. BA, U. Md., Balt., 1969. Cert. profl. tchr. Assoc. Coppin-Hopkins Humanities Program, Balt., 1986-91; asst. dean arts and humanities UMBC, Catonsville, Md., 1973-76; asst. to dean fine arts Towson (Md.) State U., 1977-85; tchr. Balt. City Schs., 1986—. Contbr. articles to publs.; founding mem., bd. dirs. The Feminist Press; founder "Herstory" MS Mag., 1976. Grantee Fund for Endl. Excellence. Mem. NCTE, MCTELA, Md. State Conf. on Women's Studies (chairperson, Tchr. of Yr. 1994, 95). Home: 1122 S East Ave Baltimore MD 21224-5010 Office: 2555 Harford Rd Baltimore MD 21218-4837

DOODY, BARBARA PETTETT, computer specialist; b. Cin., Sept. 18, 1938; d. Philip Wayne and Virginia Bird (Handley) P.; 1 child, Daniel Frederick Reasor Jr. Attended Sinclair Coll., Tulane U., 1973-74. Owner, mgr. Honeysuckle Pet Shop, Tipp City, Ohio, 1970-76; office mgr. Doody & Doody, CPAs, New Orleans, 1976-77; computer ops. mgr. Doody & Doody, CPAs, 1979—; office mgr. San Diego Yacht Club, 1977-79; owner Hope Chest Linens, Ltd., 1994—. Mem. DAR, UDC, Jamestown Soc., Magna Charta, So. Dames, Colonial Dames of 17th Century, Nat. Soc. Daus. of 1812, Daus. Am. Colonists, Dames Ct. Honor, Colonial Order of the Crown, Societe Huguenot Nouvelle-Orleans, Huguenot Soc. Manakin, Soc. Knights of the Garter, Americans of Royal Descent, Plantaget Soc. Republican. Lutheran. Home: 36 Cypress Rd Covington LA 70433-4306 Office: 2525 Lakeway III 3838 N Causeway Blvd Metairie LA 70002-1767

DOODY, RACHELLE SMITH, neurologist; b. Pitts., Aug. 12, 1956; d. David and Audrey Margaret (Dixon) S.; m. Terrence Arthur Doody, Sept. 29, 1979; children: Clare, Robin. BA, Rice U., 1978; MD, Baylor Coll. Medicine, 1983; MA, PhD, Rice U., 1992. Diplomate Am. Bd. Psychology and Neurology. Intern in medicine McGill U., Montreal, Quebec, Can., 1983, 84; resident in neurology Baylor Coll. of Medicine, Houston, 1984-87, asst. prof., 1987-96, assoc. prof., 1996—; clin. dir. Alzheimer's Disease Ctr., Baylor Coll. Medicine, Houston, 1991—; mem. Tex. State Coun. on Alzheimers Disease, Austin, 1992—. Contbr. articles to profl. jours. including New Eng. Jour. Medicine, Jour. of Neuropsychiatry, Jour. of Neurology and Psychiatry, others. Recipient Harry E. Walker award for profl. excellence in Alzheimer's Disease, Greater Houston Chpt. Alzheimer's Disease Assn., 1992-94. Fellow Acad. of Aphasia, World Fedn. of Neurology (cognitive subgroup), Assn. of Women Faculty Mems. Baylor Coll. Medicine (pres. 1994-95). Office: Baylor Coll Medicine Neurology Dept 6550 Fannin Ste 1801 Houston TX 77030

DOOLEY, ANN ELIZABETH, freelance writers cooperative executive, editor; b. Mpls., Feb. 19, 1952; d. Merlyn James and Susan Marie (Hinze) Dooley; m. John M. Dodge, May 8, 1983; children: Christopher Dooley Dodge, Kathryn Dooley Dodge. BA in Journalism, U. Wis., 1974. Freelance journalist, 1974-75; photo editor C.W. Communications, Newton, Mass., 1975-77, writer, photographer, 1977-79; editor Computerworld O A, Framingham, Mass., 1979-83; editorial dir. Computerworld Focus, Framingham, 1983-92; pres. freelance writers coop. Dooley & Assocs., West Newbury, Mass., 1992—; speaker, chmn. mem. editorial adv. bd. various computer confs. Mem. Pub. Relations Soc. Am., Women in Communications (sec. 1982-84). Democrat. Home and Office: 1 Old Parish Way West Newbury MA 01985-1222

DOOLEY, ELIZABETH ARLENE, education educator, university official; b. Fairmont, W.Va., June 14, 1957; d. Fred Douglas and Juanita Ruth (Burks) D. BA, Alderson Broaddus Coll., 1979; MA, W.Va. U., 1986, EdD, 1989. Tchr. spl. edn. Harrison County Bd. Edn., Clarksburg, W.Va., 1981-86; asst. prof. Northeastern Ill. U., Chgo., 1989-91; lectr. W.Va. U., Morgantown, 1988-89, asst. prof. edn., 1991—, coord. Health Scis. Tech. Acad., 1993—, interim dir. Ctr. for Black Culture and Rsch., 1994-95; cons. on spl. edn. Chgo. City Schs.; field reader U.S. Dept. Edn., Washington. Assoc. editor Afrocentric Scholar, mng. editor, 1995-96; contbr. articles to profl. jours. Grantee HUD, 1993, Hughes Found., 1994, Kellogg Found., 1995. Mem. Coun. for Exceptional Children (tchr. edn. divsn., divsn. for learning disabilities), NAACP. Office: WVa U PO Box 6122 Morgantown WV 26505

DOOLEY, JO ANN CATHERINE, publishing company executive; b. Cin., Nov. 24, 1930; d. Joseph Frank and Margaret Mary (Flynn) D. Ed. U. Cin., 1966. Clk. Castellini Co., Cin., 1949-52; IBM operator Kroger Co., Cin., 1952; asst. acct. Gardner Publs., Inc., Cin., 1953-67, treas., sec., 1967-95, dir., 1983—, v.p. fin., 1986-95, also trustee employees profit sharing trust, trustee retirement trust, ret., 1995. Mem. Am. Soc. Women Accts. (advt. mgr. Woman CPA 1979-81, nat. pres. 1982-83, exec. com., achievement award). Roman Catholic. Office: 6600 Clough Pike Cincinnati OH 45244-4033

DOOLEY, SHARON L., obstetrician and gynecologist; b. 1947. MD, U. Va. Mem. faculty Prentice Womens Hosp. Northwestern U. Med. Sch., Chgo. Office: Northwestern U Med Sch Prentice Womens Hosp 333 E Superior St Rm 410 Chicago IL 60611

DOOLEY, SUE ANN, information systems specialist; b. Brockton, Mass.; d. Joseph Henry and May Isabelle (Card) Jessop; 1 child, Erika. BSBA, Northeastern U., Boston, 1993. Programmer, analyst Arthur D. Little Systems, Burlington, Mass., 1979-80, Wang Labs., Lowell, Mass., 1980-82; sr. programmer analyst Wang Labs., 1982-83, prin. programmer, analyst, 1983-84, project mgr., 1984-87, sr. project mgr., 1987-90, info. mgmt. cons., 1990—; sr. project mgr. Home: 139 N End Blvd Salisbury MA 01952-2209 Office: Wang Labs 836 North St Tewksbury MA 01876

DOOLEY-HANSON, BARBARA ANN, special education educator; b. Vici, Okla., Feb. 16, 1948; d. Loitz Eldon and Cora Lee (Morgan) Myers; m. Donald R. Hanson, Sept. 25, 1993; children: Lisa M. White, James B. Dooley. BS in Spl. Edn., Ctrl. State U., 1989, MEd in Spl. Edn., 1992. Cert. tchr., Okla. Tchr. Ctrl. City Bapt. Acad., Oklahoma City, 1975-76; spl. edn. tchr. Seminole (Okla.) Pub. Schs., 1977-78; tchr. Jones (Okla.) Pub. Schs., 1978-79; spl. edn. tchr. Midwest City-Del City Pub. Schs., 1979-95; spl. edn. coord. II State Dept. Edn., 1995—; adj. prof. U. Ctrl. Okla., fall 1995. Co-author: Doorway-Transition to the Real World, 1993. Mem. Citizens for a Safe Environ., Edmond, Okla., 1994; soccer coach Edmond Soccer Assn., 1985, 88. Mem. Learning Disabilities Assn., Kappa Delta Pi (v.p., pres., exec. bd. dirs. 1989—), Spl. Edn. Vocat. Edn. Assn. (mem. adv. bd. 1993, 95). Baptist. Home: 13205 Golden Eagle Dr Edmond OK 73013-7406 Office: State Dept Edn Spl Edn Sect 2500 N Lincoln Oklahoma City OK 73105

DOONE, MICHELE MARIE, chiropractor; b. Oak Park, Ill., Oct. 3, 1942; d. Robert Emmett and Tana Josephine (Alioto) D. Cert., Valley Coll. of Med. and Dental Careers, 1962; student, L.A. Valley Coll., 1960-63, Dallas County Community Coll., 1983-84; D in Chiropractic summa cum laude, Parker Coll. of Chiropractic, 1986. Lic. chiropractic, Calif., Tex.; cert. Nat. Bd. Chiropractic Examiners, impairment rater; diplomate Am. Acad. Pain Mgmt.; bd. eligible chiropractic orthopedist. Med. asst. William Orlando M.D., Edwin Crost, M.D., 1962-65; nursing supr., chief radiologic technologist Vanowen Med. Group, North Hollywood, Calif., 1965-76; radiologic technologist/purchasing agt. Lanier-Brown Clinic, Dallas, 1976-83; faculty mem./ chief radiologic technologist Parker Coll. of Chiropractic, Irving, Tex., 1983-85; exam and X-Ray doctor Margolies Chiropractic Ctr., Richardson, Tex., 1986; clinic staff doctor, assoc. prof. Parker Coll. of Chiropractic, Irving, Tex., 1986-87; doctor/ mgr. contractor Accident Ctrs. of Am., Garland, Tex., 1987; clinic dir. Back Pain Chiropractic, Carrollton, Tex., 1988-91; assoc. in group practice Mullican Chiropractic Ctr., Addison, Tex., 1991—; adviser health-related matters Inner Devel. Inst., Dallas, 1977—; seminar com. Back Pain Chiropractic, Inc., Metairie, La., 1989-91, clinic dir., 1988-91. Mem. Tex. Chiropractic Assn. (radiology com. chmn. 1990-94, practice protocols and parameters com. 1992-94), Metroplex Neurospinal Diagnostic Med. and Surg. Group (med. adv. com. 1989-95), Parker Chiropractic Rsch. Found., Parker Coll. Alumni Assn. (bd. dirs. 1988-90, 93-94, 95—, Dr. of Yr. 1990), Pi Tau Delta. Home: 4837 Cedar Springs Rd Apt 216 Dallas TX 75219-1280 Office: Mullican Chiropractic Ctr 4021 Belt Line Rd Ste 201 Dallas TX 75244-2330

DOORY, ANN MARIE, lawyer, legislator; b. Yonkers, N.Y., Aug. 19, 1954; d. Gerard R. and Patricia M. Lowe; m. Robert Leonard Doory Jr., Sept. 29, 1979; children: Brian Robert, Elizabeth Lowe. BA in Polit. Sci., Towson State U., 1976; JD, U. Balt., 1979. Bar: Md. Counsel to majority leader Md. State Senate, 1981; vol., arbitrator Better Bus. Bur., 1984-86; chm. bd. York Woodbourne Action Area and York Rd. Planning Com. Md. Ho. of Dels., 1982—, zoning chairperson Homeland Assn., 1984-86, v.p. Homeland Assn., 1987—. Mem. Dem. State Cen. Com. 43d Legis. Dist., Baltimore City, 1982—, 3d Dist. Cittizens for Good Govt., Baltimore City, issues and legis. com., Mayors Drug Abuse Adv. Council, Baltimore City, 1983-86. Mem. Women's Bar Assn., Md. Bar Assn. Democrat. Roman Catholic. Home: 112 Taplow Rd Baltimore MD 21212-3312 Office: Md Ho of Dels State Capitol Annapolis MD 21401*

DOPSON, ELIZABETH SCHULTZ, health system executive; b. Ancon, Panama, Jan. 8, 1951; d. Robert U. and Virginia (Richard) Schultz. BS, U. Southwestern La., 1975; postgrad., La. State U., 1981-82. Registered record administr. Dir. med. records, quality assurance, utilization rev. E.K. Long Hosp., Baton Rouge, 1975-81; dir. med. records Humana-Ft. Walton, Fla., 1984-86, Bay Med. Ctr., Panama City, Fla., 1986-88, HCA/L.W. Blake Hosp., Bradenton, Fla., 1988-91; cons., health info. mgmt. Ernst and Young, Tampa, Fla., 1991-92; corp. dir. health info. mgmt. Cmty. Health Sys., Seminole, Fla., 1992—; cons. HMO of Baton Rouge, 1978-80; nursing home cons. Greenwell Springs Hosp., 1976-81. With US Womens Army Corp., 1969-71. Mem. Am. Health Info. Mgmt. Assn., Am. Health Info. Clin. Coding Soc., Fla. Med. Record Assn., North Panhandle Fla. Assn. (v.p. 1986). Roman Catholic. Office: Cmty Health Sys 2111 88th St Ct NW Bradenton FL 34209

DORB, ALICE, library media specialist, technology information specialist; b. Bklyn., June 22, 1942; d. David and Sylvia (Wexler) Kantrowitz; m. Alan Dorb, Aug. 15, 1964; children: Madelyn Sheppard, Daniel Lawrence. BA, Hunter Coll., 1963; MLS, Queens Coll., 1967. Cert. sch. libr./media specialist, N.Y., pub. libr., N.Y. Elem. sch. tchr. Pub. Sch. 158, Bklyn., 1963-66, libr., media specialist, 1966-67; libr., media specialist Jamaica Ave. Sch., Plainview, N.Y., 1980-81; children's libr. Farmingdale Pub. Libr., 1982-83; libr., media specialist Clear Stream Ave. Sch., Valley Stream, N.Y., 1983—; facilitator Nassau Sch. Libr. Sys. Nassau County, N.Y., 1992—. Author: Voyage of the Miami Research Contract Package, 1989. Mem. Mid-Island Jewish Cmty. Ctr., Plainview, N.Y., 1981—; mem. Friends for L.I.'s Heritage, N.Y., 1992—. Recipient award for utilizing TV in edn., WNET-TV, 1989. Mem. Libr. Congress (charter), L.I. Sch. Media Assn. Democrat.

DORCHESTER, JANE ELIZABETH, historic researcher; b. Phila., July 29, 1956; d. John Edmund Carleton and Kathleen Margaret (Russell) D. BA in Theatre Arts, West Chester U., 1978. Contract historic rschr. Individual Property Owners, Pa., 1983—; records rschr. Chester County Office of Historic Preservation, West Chester, Pa., 1987; corr. Daily Local News, West Chester, 1987-88; prin. rschr. Ray H. Ott, Jr., Planner, West Chester, 1987—; survey coord. Chester County Hist. Soc., West Chester, 1988; prin. rschr. Willistown Hist. Commn., Willistown Twp., Pa., 1991—, Charlestown Hist. Commn., Charlestown Twp., Pa., 1994—; cons. nat. register Pa. Hist. and Mus. Commn., Harrisburg, 1993—; hist. preserviation cons. East Brandywine Hist. Commn., Gurthrieville, Pa., 1994-95. Archivist records mgmt. grant Pa. Hist. and Mus. Commn., 1994, 95. Mem. Pa. Fedn. of Mus. and Hist. Orgns., Friends of Pa. Mus. and Hist. Com., Preservation Pa., The Royal Oak Found., Nat. Trust for Historic Preservation, Chester

County Hist. Soc. (vol. curator's office 1984-90, chmn. edn. com. 1986-88), The Nature Conservancy (Pa. chpt.), The Cousteau Soc. (friend of calypso 1985-96), World Wildlife Fund, Nat. Wildlife Fedn. (assoc.). Home and Office: 217 S Walnut St 3rd Fl West Chester PA 19382

DORE, BETTY BROPHY, artist; b. Lexington, Ky., Oct. 2, 1937; d. William Anthony and Elizabeth Owens (Henry) Brophy; m. Joseph John McDade (div. 1963); children: Hallie Marie, Joan Elizabeth, Joseph William; m. Charley Richard Dore, Feb. 28, 1988. AA, Pasadena (Calif) City Coll., 1972; BA, Calif. State U., L.A., 1975, MA, 1976. Tchr. L.A. Theatre Works, Venice, Calif., 1993-95; painting advisor Chino (Calif.) H.S., 1995. Painter murals Pasadena (Calif.) City Coll., 1990, 92, Huntington Libr., 1992, Venice/Abbot Kinney Libr., 1995. Vol. Carecen, L.A., 1988-95, Cispes, L.A., 1990, Peta, 1990-95. Recipient R. Bissiri Meml. Scholarship award Pasadena City Coll., 1973, Video: Artlive award KPPC, Pasadena, 1989, Gottlieb Found. award N.Y.C., 1992. Mem. Mus. Contemporary Art, Mission West Art Group, Arrovo Arts Collective. Democrat. Home: 826 Winthrop Rd San Marino CA 91108

DORE, BONNY ELLEN, film and television production company executive; b. Cleve., Aug. 16, 1947; d. Reber Hutson and Ellen Elizabeth (McNamara) Barnes; m. Sanford Astor, May 22, 1987. BA, U. Mich., 1969, MA, 1975. Cert. tchr., Mich. Dir., tchr. Plymouth (Mich.) Community Schs., 1969-72; gen. mgr. Sta. WSDP-FM, Plymouth, 1970-72; prodn. supr. pub. TV N.Y. State Dept. Edn., 1972-74; producer TV series Hot Fudge Sta. WXYZ-TV, Detroit, 1974-75; mgr. children's programs ABC TV Network, L.A., 1975, dir. children's programs, 1975-76, dir. prime time variety programs, 1976-77; dir. devel. Hanna-Barbera, L.A., 1977; v.p. devel. and prodn. Krofft Entertainment, L.A., 1977-81, Centerpoint Prodn., L.A., 1981-82; pres., owner in assn. with Orion TV The Greif-Dore Co., L.A., 1983-87, Bonny Dore Prodns. Inc., L.A., 1988—; mem. Caucus of Writers, Producers and Dirs., 1989—; Marsh speaker Pres. Fund for Pres. Weekend U. Mich., 1989. Producer TV series The Krofft Superstar Hour, ABC, 1978 (2 Emmy awards 1979), comedy series The 1/2 Hour Comedy Hour (starring Arsenio Hall and Victoria Jackson), ABC, 1983-84, mini-series Sins (starring Joan Collins), CBS, 1986, comedy series First Impressions, CBS, 1987-88, mini-series Glory! Glory! (starring Ellen Greene, Richard Thomas and James Whitmore; 2 Ace cable awards), HBO, 1988-89, NBC movie Reason for Living, The Jill Ireland Story, 1990-91, ABC movie Captive!, 1991, The Sinking of the Rainbow Warrior, 1993, numerous others. Mem. fundraising com. U. Mich., 1990—; assoc. mem. Nat. Trust for Hist. Preservation, 1988—. Named Outstanding Young Tchr. of Yr., Cen. States Speech Assn., 1973; Cert. of Appreciation, Gov. of Mich., 1985, City of Beverly Hills, Calif., 1985, Coun. on Social Work Edn., 1990; recipient Action for Children's TV award, 1975, Gold medal Best TV Mini-series, Best TV Screenplay Silver medal Houston Internat. Film Festival, 1990, Best. TV Actress award, 1990, Best TV Supporting Actor, 1990, Best Music, 1990, Winner Best Mini Series Houston Film Festival, 1990. Mem. NATAS, Am. Film Inst. (corr. sec.), Women in Film (v.p. 1978-81, pres. 1980-81), Women in Film Found. (trustee 1981, chair 1994-96, exec. prodr. The Signature Series, co-chair 1994—), Nat. Cable TV Assn., Beverly Hills C. of C. (cons. 1985), Exec. Roundtable L.A. (trustee 1987—), Hollywood Radio and TV Soc., Acad. TV Arts and Scis. (caucus of writers, prodrs., dirs. 1991—, co-chair caucus writers, prodrs., and dirs. 1994-96). Office: Bonny Dore Prodns Inc 9454 Wilshire Blvd Ph Beverly Hills CA 90212

DORFMAN, ANDREA RANDALL, journalist; b. N.Y.C., Sept. 18, 1959; d. Irvin Sherrod Dorfman and Jane Randall. BS, Yale U., 1981. Prodn. editor Acad. Press, N.Y.C., 1981-82; asst. editor, assoc. editor to sr. writer Sci. Digest mag., N.Y.C., 1982-85; reporter to asst. editor, dept. head Time mag., N.Y.C., 1985—. Mem. Nat. Assn. Sci. Writers, Soc. Environ. Journalists, Yale Club. Office: Time Mag 1271 Avenue Of The Americas New York NY 10020

DORFMAN, ELISSA, artist; b. Bklyn., May 12, 1950. Student, Bklyn. Mus. Art Sch., 1969-72, CCNY, 1969-71, Art Students League, 1970-72, Pratt Graphic Ctr., 1972, New Sch. Social Rsch., 1972-76. Artist-in-Residence U.Md., 1980. Author: A Personal Journal, 1992, others; one woman shows at Collector's Gallery, N.Y., 1979, Galerie Raymond Duncan, Paris, 1979, U. Md., 1980, Art Space Gallery, Hyogo, Japan, 1982, Galler Fuji, Osaka, Japan, 1982; group exhbns. include Lever Bldg., 1961, Bklyn. Mus. Fence Show, 1969, Rafter House, L.I., 1970, The Brata Gallery, N.Y., 1973, CCNY, 1976, Art for Living Gallery, Henry St. Settlement, 1976, Ft. Lee (N.J.) Pub. Libr. Gallery, 1977, Orgn. Ind. Artists, Bologna, Italy, 1979, Pub. Sch. 1, L.I., 1979, Phillips Gallery, 1979, Village Gate, N.Y., 1979, Ny Carlsberg Glyptotek Mus., Copenhagen, 1979, Salon des Surindependents, Mus. Luxembourg, Paris, 1980, Sotheby Parke-Bernet, N.Y., 1980, Muse Gallery, Phila., 1980, Cork Gallery, Lincoln Ctr. Plz., 1981, Madison Sq. Garden, N.Y.C., 1981, Internat. Graphic Arts Exhbn., Bilbao, Spain, 1982, Komai Gallery, Tokyo, 1982, Tokyo Mus., 1983, Cabo Frio Internat. Print Biennial, Brazil, 1983, Gallery 124 Kemper Ctr., Kenosha, Wis., 1987, The Wedge Gallery, Rochester, N.Y., 1987, Gallery at Cox Arboretum, Dayton, Ohio, 1992, Paramount East Gallery, Peekskill, N.Y., 1994, Mills Pond House Gallery, St. James, N.Y., 1994. Mem. Visual Artists and Galleries Assn., Art Students League (life), Artists Equity. Home: 345 E 81st St New York NY 10028-4020

DORIA, MARILYN L., lawyer; b. Boston, Jan. 15, 1944. AB, Brandeis U., 1965; MPA, Syracuse U., 1967; JD, Temple U., 1974. Bar: Pa. 1974, U.S. Dist. Ct. (ea. dist.) Pa. 1974, Tex. 1986, U.S. Dist. Ct. (so. dist.) Tex. 1986, U.S. Ct. Appeals (5th cir.) 1986, U.S. Ct. Appeals (D.C. cir.) 1986, D.C. 1993. Dep. asst. to asst. gen. counsel for enforcement FERC, 1979-83; ptnr. Akin, Gump, Strauss, Hauer & Feld, L.L.P., Washington, 1983—. Office: Akin Gump Strauss Hauer & Feld Ste 400 1333 New Hampshire Ave NW Washington DC 20036-1511*

DORLAND, BYRL BROWN, civic worker; b. Greenwich, Utah, Apr. 25, 1915; d. David Alma and Ethel Myrle (Peterson) Brown; m. Jack Albert Dorland, June 11, 1944; children: Lynn Dorland Ballinger, Lee Allison. Cert. AA, Snow Jr. Coll., Ephraim, Utah, 1936; teaching cert. Brigham Young U., 1937; BS, Utah State Coll., Logan, 1940; grad.Family Inst. Vassar Coll., Poughkeepsie, N.Y., 1978; John Robert Powers Sch. Profl. Women, N.Y.C., 1980. Sch. tchr., Utah, 1937-39, 40-42; restored Washington Irving's graveplot in Sleepy Hollow Cemetery, North Tarrytown, N.Y. (named Nat. Hist. Landmark 1972); nat. dir. Washington Irving Graveplot Restoration Program, 1968—, designer landmark plaque for grave; mem. Nat. Coun. State Garden Clubs,1959—; pres. Potpourri Garden Club, Westchester, N.Y., 1966—; nat. chmn. for graveplot programs Washington Irving Bicentennial, 1983-84; dir. Dorland Family Graveyard Restoration, N.J. Hist. Landmark, 1983—. Recipient Disting. Alumni award for Community Svc. Snow Coll., 1989; Recipient May Duff Walters trophy Nat. Coun. State Garden Clubs, 1974; nat. trophy Nat. Historic Landmark Com., 1974; citation Keep Am. Beautiful, 1974. Mem. Nat. Trust for Historic Preservation (Pres.'s award 1977), Nat. Historic Soc. Am., Gen. Soc. Mayflower Desc., Internat. Washington Irving Soc. (founder, pres. 1981—), Nat. Assn. for Gravestone Studies (hon.), Herb Soc. Am., DAR, Internat. Platform Assn., Old Dutch Churchyard Restoration Assn. Home and Office: 10 Castle Heights Ave Tarrytown NY 10591-3702

DORLAND, HOLLY DEE, media buyer; b. Edmond, Okla., Aug. 5, 1964; d. Benny William and Kitty Faye (Hand) Wilson; m. William Henry Rowe, Mar. 19, 1983 (div. Aug. 1987); 1 child, William Chase; m. Shannon Lee Dorland, Apr. 9, 1994; 1 child, Loren Lee. BS, U. Tulsa, 1993. Owner In Shape Health Clubs, Marlow, Okla., 1985-87; salesperson Clinique Dillard's Dept. Store, Lawton and Tulsa, 1987-89; mgr. Fitness for Her, Tulsa, 1989-91; patient registrar St. John's Med. Ctr., Tulsa, 1991-93; account coord. J.L. Media, Inc., Tulsa, 1993—. Media chairperson Ctr. for Physically Ltd., Tulsa, 1996. Mem. Women in Comm., Scroll Honor Soc., Alpha Epsilon Delta. Home: 1603 W Gary Broken Arrow OK 74012 Office: J L Media 401 S Boston Ste 700 Tulsa OK 74103

DORMAN, ANGELIA HARDY, writer; b. Moncks Corner, S.C., July 6, 1963; d. Dallas Mewborn Hardy and Jule Ann (Wyndham) Spencer; m. David Parris Dorman, July 4, 1983. BA in History, U. S.C., 1983, MA in Tchg., 1990. Radio announcer Sta. WBER, Moncks Corner, 1980-81; radio announcer, writer WSCQ, Columbia, S.C., 1983; interlibr. loan libr. Thomas Cooper Libr., U. S.C., Columbia, 1989; asst. curator for edn. McKisick Mus., U. S.C., Columbia, 1989; tchr. Eau Claire H.S., Columbia, 1990, Alcorn Middle Sch., Columbia, 1990-92, Irving Jr. H.S., Pocatello, Idaho, 1992-96; adj. instr. Idaho State U., Pocatello, 1994-96, lead tchr. Moscow (Idaho) Alternative Sch. Ctr., 1996—; cons. in womens history Idaho State U., 1992-96; cons. in field. Author: 75th Anniversary History of Columbia YWCA, 1989, Martha Gellhorn and the Human Legacy of War, 1943-1945; contbr. articles to profl. jours. Mem. Martin Luther King Jr. Com., Pocatello, 1992—; com. mem. Women's Hist. Month com., Pocatello, 1992—; organizer Young women's Career Group, Pocatello, 1994—. Mem. AAUW, U. S.C. Alumni Assn., Minerva soc. for Study of Women in Mil., Phi Alpha Theta.

DORMAN, HATTIE LAWRENCE, management consultant, trainer, former government agency official; b. Cleve., July 22, 1932; d. J. Lyman and Claire A. (Lenoir) Lawrence; m. James L. Dorman, May 16, 1959; children—Lydia, Lynda, James Lawrence. Student Fenn Coll. (Cleve. State U.), part time 1950-58, D.C. Tchrs. Coll., 1960-64, Dept. Agr. Grad. Sch., 1968-69; BA, Howard U., 1987. Clk., tax specialist, mgmt. analyst, supr., staff advisor IRS, Washington, 1954-79; spl. asst. to dep. asst. sec. adminstrn. Dept. Treasury, Washington, 1978-79; dep. dir. Interagency Com. on Women's Bus. Enterprise, SBA; Task Force on EEO, Dept. Treasury 1978-79; mem. Pres.'s Task Force on Women Bus. Owners, 1979, now ret.; assoc. prof. continuing edn. U. D.C.; guest lectr. continuing edn. Howard U.; chief of staff for Dep. Dir. Presdl. Transition Team, 1992-93; bd. dirs. Wider Opportunities for Women, 1992-94; trainer and spkr. in field. Sec. Linton Hall Guild, 1978-80; chmn. trainer, cons., leader Girl Scout Service Unit, 1971-92; ofcl. observer Nat. Women's Conf., Houston, 1977; bd. dirs. YWCA, 1957-62; mem. planning com. Black Women's Summit, 1981; mem. Vestry Register, St. Paul's Episcopal Ch., 1981-86, Jr. Warden 1992-94. Recipient spl. achievement award Commr. IRS, 1978, thanks badge Girl Scout Nation's Capital, 1977, recognition cert. for work in Christian edn. St. Paul's Episcopal Ch., 1976, Mary McLeod Bethune Centennial award Nat. Council Negro Women, 1975, other awards and certs. of appreciation. Mem. ASTD, Am. Soc. Public Adminstrs., Fed. Exec. Inst. Alumni Assn., Assn. Psychol. Type Inc., Howard U. Alumni Assn. Club: Delta Sigma Theta. Journalist Neighbor's Inc., 1969-71.

DORMAN, JO-ANNE, elementary school educator; b. Greenville, Miss.; d. Joe Edward and Constance Bonita (Parks) D. BS, Delta State U., 1963. Cert. tchr., Fla. Tchr. Oakcrest Elem. Sch., Pensacola, Fla., 1963-93; ret., 1993; substitute tchr. Sch. Dist. Escambia County, Pensacola, Fla., 1993—. Sunday sch. tchr. Methodist Ch., Pensacola, Fla., 1963, 65, 68. Democrat. Methodist. Home: 188 Talladega Tr Pensacola FL 32506

DORN, VIRGINIA ALICE, art gallery director; b. Mpls., June 22, 1916; d. Raymond Edwin and Ruth Virginia (Nylander) Henneman; m. John Emil Dorn, Feb. 22, 1937 (dec. Sept. 1971); children: John Robert, Michael Raymond. BS, U. Minn., 1937. Mgr. med. lab. Orinda, Calif., 1955-61; instr. art Orinda Civic Ctr., 1980-81; mgr., tchr. San Francisco Women Artists Gallery, 1984—. One woman shows include Lucien LaBaudt Gallery, San Francisco, 1975, St. Paul's Towers, Oakland, Calif., 1976, Contemporary Arts, Berkeley, Calif., 1977, 80, Trinity Gallery, Berkeley, 1982, Valley Arts Gallery, Walnut Creek, Calif., 1982, Univ. Club, San Francisco, 1983, Holy Names Coll. Gallery, Oakland, 1987, Wellness Cmty. Gallery, Walnut Creek, 1991, Vincent's Ear Gallery, Orinda, Calif., 1994, also many juried and invitational shows in Calif. Recipient Lifetime Achievement award Women's Caucus for Art, 1996. Mem. San Francisco Women Artists (bd. dirs., fund raiser, mgr., instr., coord.), Oakland Art Assn., Valley Art Assn., Ctr. for the Visual Arts, Berkeley Art Ctr., East Bay Women Artists. Home: 95 Evergreen Dr Orinda CA 94563-3114

DORNER, BARBARA EMILIA, elementary school educator; b. Bronx, N.Y., Jan. 6, 1945; d. Helmut H. and Pierina E. (Gillio) D. BS, SUNY, New Paltz, 1967; MA, Hofstra U., 1971; AS in Bus. Adminstrn., Nassau Community Coll., 1979; postgrad., Adelphi U., 1988. Cert. fin. planner. Tchr. Merrick (N.Y.) Union Free Sch. Dist., 1967—. Vol. Internat. Games for Disabled, 1984; bd. dirs. 280 Guy Lombardo Owners' Assn., 1986-87. Mem. AAUW, Am. Fedn. Tchrs., N.Y. State United Tchrs., Merrick Faculty Assn. (sec. exec. bd. 1968-69, exec. bd. 1968-78, 79-82, 91—, treas. 1991—), Nat. Carousel Assn., Phi Theta Kappa. Home: 280 Guy Lombardo Ave Freeport NY 11520-4955 Office: Lakeside Sch Merrick Rd Merrick NY 11566

DORNER-ANDELORA, SHARON AGNES HADDON, computer technical consultant, educator; b. Morristown, N.J., Nov. 3, 1943; d. William P. and Eleanor (Dygert) Haddon: BA in Bus. Edn., Montclair State Coll., 1965, MA in Bus. Edn., 1970, MA in Guidance and Counseling, 1978; EdD in Vocat.-Tech. Edn., Adminstrn. and Supervision, Rutgers U., 1982; m. Robert Andelora, Feb. 17, 1985: children: Wendy, Meridith. Tchr., Morris Knolls High Sch., 1965-70; tchr. Katherine Gibbs Sec. Sch., Montclair, N.J., 1973-74; tchr. Leonia (N.J.) High Sch., 1974-75; tchr. bus. Woodcliff Sch., Woodcliff Lake, N.J., 1976—, adminstrv. intern to supt., 1980-82; computer tech. cons., 1992—; tchr. adult sch. Sussex Vocat. Sch., County Coll. Morris, Randolph, N.J. Judge, Election Bd., Montclair, 1972-82. Author: Southwestern Pub. Co., 1992—. Mem. ASCD, Am. Vocat. Assn., Am. Vocat. Research Assn., N.J. Vocat. Assn., NEA, N.J. Edn. Assn., Bergen County Edn. Assn., Woodcliff Lake Edn. Assn. (sec. 1976-84, treas. 1991—), N.J. Bus. Edn. Assn. (co-editor Observer 1988-90, historian/photographer 1990-92, sec. 1992-94, 1st v.p. 1994-95, pres.-elect 1995-96, pres. 1996—, educator of yr. award 1996), Internat. Soc. Bus. Edn., Nat. Bus. Edn. Assn. (mem. telecomm. com. 1995—), Ea. Bus. Edn. Assn., Consumers League (dir. 1979-85), N.J. Coll. Ednl. Leaders (v.p. 1985-89, treas. 1983-84, Northeastern regional rep. 1982-83, chairperson membership com. 1989-93), Northeast Coalition Ednl. Leaders, N.J. Assn. Ednl. Tech., N.J. Macintosh Users' Group, Delta Pi Epsilon (pres. Beta Phi chpt. 1979-80, v.p. 1978-79, sec. 1976-78, newsletter editor 1974-76, 89—, nat. com. 1980-84, nat. council rep. 1981-88, nat. historian 1987-89, chmn. nat. com. 1982-84, nat. pubs. com. 1996—), Sigma Kappa (nat. alumnae province officer 1977-81, nat. alumnae dist. dir. 1981-87, Nat. Colby award 1994), Phi Delta Kappa (pres. 1980-82 treas. 1975-79, 82-84, council del. 1977-80, 84-86, research rep. 1986-88, found. rep. 1988—), Omicron Tau Theta (pres. Delta chpt. 1987-88, v.p. 1986-87, nat. parliamentarian 1986-88). Lodges: Daus. of Nile, N.J. Eastern Star, Women of the Moose. Mem. adv. bd. Today's Sec., 1981-82. Home: 28 College Ave Montclair NJ 07043-1604 Office: 134 Woodcliff Ave Westwood NJ 07675-8245

DOROBEK, CARROLL FRANCES, secondary education educator; b. L.A., Sept. 30, 1939; d. Joseph Stanley and Gretchen Frances (Frock) D. BA, Immaculate Heart Coll., 1961; MS, Calif. Luth. Coll., 1981. Tchr. elem. L.A. Unified Sch. Dist., 1961-63, tchr. secondary, 1964—; therapist pvt. practice, L.A., 1981—. Mem. Coun. Exceptional Children, Assn. Ednl. Therapist (bd. dirs. 1989-91, treas. 1991—). Home: 821 N Catalina St Burbank CA 91505-3020

DOROFEE, MARY ANNE, education educator; b. Vineland, N.J., July 18, 1951; d. John and Margaret (Camp) D. BA, Marywood Coll., 1973; MA, Rowan State Coll., 1995. Math. tchr. John Carusi Sch., Cherry Hill, N.J., 1973-77; self-employed West Side Floral Gardens, Vineland, N.J., 1977-91; math. instr. Buena (N.J.) Regional H.S., 1978-80; long-term substitute Clearview Regional H.S., Mullica Hill, N.J., 1990; educator Cumberland County Coll., Vineland, 1990—; part-time instr. Glassboro (N.J.) Coll., 1974-77, Gloucester County Coll., Sewell, N.J., 1991-92; basic skills math. coord. Cumberland County Coll., Vineland, 1993—, math. adv. bd., 1990—. Author: (books) Geometry Learning Packet, 1994, Intro to College Math-Lab Booklet, 1994. Mini-grantee Cumberland County Coll., Vineland, 1993, 94, award, Kellogg Inst., 1995. Mem. AAUW, Am. Math. Assn., Tech. Assts.'s Assn. (treas. 1992-94), Nat. Assn. for Devel. Edn., N.J. Edn. Assn., Nat. Coun. Tchrs. Math. Home: 2000 Miller Ave Millville NJ 08332 Office: Cumberland County Coll PO Box 517 Vineland NJ 08360

DORON, MARY ELLEN, steel rule diemaker-executive; b. Pikesville, Ky., Dec. 5, 1946; d. Frank Day Marrs and Draxie Marie (Newsome) McKay; m. Robert Dale Doron, Oct. 18, 1969; 1 child, Christine. Office mgr. Steel Rule Die Co., Detroit, 1965-80; sales profl., estimator Advance Die Cutting, Warren, Mich., 1980-81; pres. Metro Trim Die & Rubber, Detroit, 1981—. Office: Metro Trim Die & Rubber Inc 6340 E Nevada St Detroit MI 48234-2825

DORR, STEPHANIE TILDEN, psychologist; b. Orlando, Fla., Sept. 21, 1950; d. Luther Willis Tilden II and Lillian Murfee (Grace) Owen; m. Darwin Dorr, May 21, 1986. AA, El Camino Coll., 1975; BA, U. N.C., 1985; MA, Western Carolina U., 1991. Cons. psychologist Sylva (N.C.) Psychol. Assocs., 1991-92; staff psychologist Park Ridge Hosp., Naples, N.C., 1992, Blue Ridge Ctr., Asheville, N.C., 1991-93; pvt. practice psychology Asheville, 1991-93; project mgr. Sedgwick County Dept. Mental Health, Wichita, Kans., 1993-95; pvt. practice psychotherapy and psychol. assessment Counseling and Mediation Ctr., Wichita, Kans., 1995—; adj. faculty Kans. Newman Coll., Wichita, 1995—, Butler County (Kans.) Cmty. Coll., 1996—; presenter in field. Contbr. articles to profl. publs. Mem. APA, Internat. Rorschach and Projective Techniques Soc., Soc. for Personality Assessment, Soc. for Psychologists in Mgmt., Psychoanalytic Study Group (sec. 1989-93, award 1993), Western N.C. Psychol. Assn. (mem.-at-large 1985-93, pres.-elect 1993), Psi Chi, Pi Gamma Mu. Episcopalian. Office: The Counseling and Mediation Ctr Inc 334 N Topeka Wichita KS 67202

DORRANCE, JEAN ELIZABETH, artist, educator; b. Oak Park, Ill., Sept. 22, 1960; d. Harold George and Patricia Loraine (O'Shea) D. BA, Adams State Coll., 1985; MA in Tchg., Nat. Lewis U., 1989. Cert. tchr., Ill. Activities coord. Americana Healthcare, Westmont, Ill., 1986-87; ESL tchr. Berkeley (Ill.) Sch. Dist., 1989-90; art tchr. Cicero (Ill.) Sch. Dist., 1990-93; art and health tchr. Lemont (Ill.)/Bromberek Sch. Dist., 1993—. Office: Lemont-Bromberek Sch Dist 1130 Kim Pl Lemont IL 60439

DORSA, CAROLINE, pharmaceuticals executive. Treas. Merck & Co., Whitehouse Station, N.J. Office: Merck & Co Inc 1 Merck Dr Whitehouse Station NJ 08889*

DORSEY, DOLORES FLORENCE, corporate treasurer, business executive; b. Buffalo, May 26, 1928; d. William G. and Florence R. D. B.S., Coll. St. Elizabeth, 1950. With Aerojet-Gen. Corp., 1953—; asst. to treas. Aerojet-Gen. Corp., El Monte, Calif., 1972-74; asst. treas. Aerojet-Gen. Corp., 1974-79, treas., 1979—. Mem. Cash Mgmt. Group San Diego (past pres.), Nat. Assn. Corp. Treas., Fin. Execs. Inst. (v.p.). Republican. Roman Catholic. Office: 10300 N Torrey Pines Rd La Jolla CA 92037-1020

DORSEY, DONNA BAGLEY, insurance agent; b. Macon, Ga., May 26, 1952; d. Clarence Henry and Sybil Audrey (Phillips) Bagley; m. David M. Lewis, June 14, 1969 (div. May 1979); children: Scott D., Jeffrey A.; m. J. Larry Dorsey, July 1, 1980. Grad. high sch., Macon, Ga. Cert. ins. counselor; cert. profl. ins. woman. Rating clk. Bibb Underwriters Ins., Macon, 1977-80; book-keeper Wilson Typewriter, Macon, 1980-85; customer svc. rep. Ga. Ins. Agy., Macon, 1985; agt., customer svc. rep. Johnson and Johnson Ins., Inc., Macon, 1985—. Recipient Outstanding Customer Svc. Rep. Ga. award Ind. Ins. Agts. Ga., 1993; Ruth Dupree Meml. scholar, 1987; Ins. Women of Macon Pres.'s Vol. award, 1994, Ins. Women of Macon Ins. Profl. award, 1995, Ins. Women of Macon Individual Edn. award, 1996. Mem. Profl. Ins. Agts. Ga. (bd. dirs. 1990-93, Eagle award 1989), Young Profl. Coun. Ga. (chmn. 1991-92), Ins. Women Macon (treas. 1991-92, v.p. 1992-93, pres. elect 1993-94, pres. 1994-95, Macon Ins. Woman of Yr. 1994, Ga. Ins. Woman of Yr. 1994, President's Vol. award 1994, Macon Ins. Profl. of Yr. 1995, Indivdual Edn. Achievement award 1996). Office: Johnson and Johnson Ins Inc 420 Rogers Ave Macon GA 31204-2042

DORSEY, HATTIE, community economic development executive; b. Teachey, N.C., May 31, 1939; d. Edward Henry and Gladys (Alderman) Dorsey; m. James F. Harlow, Nov. 1, 1979 (div.); m. Kenneth Samuel Hudson, Nov. 3, 1990 (div.); 1 child, Victoria Michelle Dorsey. Student, Clark Coll., 1957-61. Exec. dir. Stanford Mid-Peninsula Urban Coalition, Stanford, Calif., 1979-81; program officer Edna McConnell Clark Found., Calif., 1982-84; v.p. Atlanta Econ. Devel. Corp., 1985-91; pres. Atlanta Neighborhood Devel. Partnership, Inc., Atlanta, 1991—; cons. Spartanburg (N.C.) Devel. Coun., 1991, Econ. Devel. Alternatives, Washington, 1984. V.p. Young Dems., Washington, 1965-66; founding pres., organizer Metro Atlanta Coalition 100 Black Women, Atlanta, 1986-91; v.p. Nat. Coalition 100 Black Women, N.Y.C., 1987-92, pres., 1995—; dir. Nat. Assn. Housing Ptnr. Mem. Spelman Coll. Corp. Roundtable; exec. comm. and bd. mdm. of Nat. Housing Conf; mem. Buckhead/Cascade Chpt. of Links, Inc.; chair, GRAPEVINE (polit. action comm.). Democrat. Methodist. Office: Atlanta Neighborhood Devel Partnership 57 Forsyth St NW Ste 1250 Atlanta GA 30303-2210

DORSEY, MARY ELIZABETH, lawyer; b. Florissant, Mo., July 4, 1962; d. Richard Peter Jr. and Dolores Irene (McNamara) D. BA in Acctg., Benedictine Coll., 1984; JD, St. Louis U., 1987. Bar: Mo. 1989, U.S. Dist. Ct. (we. dist.) Mo. 1989, U.S. Dist. Ct. (ea. dist.) Mo. 1990, U.S. Supreme Ct. 1994. Researcher Ind. Legal Rsch., Florissant, 1987-89; atty. assoc. Deeba Sauter Herd, St. Louis, Mo., 1989—; bd. dirs. North County, Inc. Merit badge counselor St. Louis Area coun. Boy Scouts Am., 1988—, mem. com. Troop 748, mem. Order of the Arrow, 1992, Brotherhood, 1994; corr. sec. Florissant (Mo.) Twp. Open Dem. Club, 1989-91, sgt. at arms, 1991—; treas. Friends of Rick Dorsey, St. Louis, 1988, 90; mem. Dem. Com., Florissant Twp., 1996—. Mem. ABA, ATLA, Mo. Assn. Trial Attys., Bar Assn. Met. St. Louis (lectr. law related edn. com. 1988-91), St. Louis County Bar Assn., Florissant Valley Jaycees (dir. 1993-94, treas. 1994-95, state dir. 1995—). Democrat. Roman Catholic. Office: Deeba Sauter Herd 3415 Hampton Ave Saint Louis MO 63139-1916

DORSEY, RHODA MARY, retired academic administrator; b. Boston, Sept. 9, 1927; d. Thomas Francis and Hedwig (Hoge) D. BA magna cum laude, Smith Coll., 1949, LLD, 1979; BA, Cambridge (Eng.) U., 1951, MA, 1954; PhD, U. Minn., 1956; LLD, Nazareth Coll. Rochester, 1970, Goucher Coll., 1994; DHL (hon.), Mount St. Mary's Coll., 1976, Mount Vernon Coll., 1979, Coll. St. Catherine, 1983, Johns Hopkins U., 1986, Towson State U., 1987, Coll. Notre Dame of Md., 1995, Coll. of Notre Dame Md., 1995. Mem. faculty Goucher Coll., Balt., Md., 1954-94; prof. history Goucher Coll., 1965-68, dean, v.p., 1968-73, acting pres., 1973-74; pres. Goucher Coll., Balt., 1974-94, pres. emeritus, 1994—; lectr. history Loyola Coll., Balt., 1958-62, Johns Hopkins U., Balt., 1960-61; bd. dirs. Bell Atlantic-Md., First Nat. Bank Md.; bd. trustee Roland Park County Sch., 1995—. Bd. dirs. Friends of Cambridge U., 1978—, sec., 1989-93; bd. dirs. Gen. German Aged Peoples Home, Balt., 1984—, Greater Balt. Med. Ctr., 1990—, Balt. City Life Mus., 1993—, Baltimore County Cmty. Found., Md. Humanities Coun., Baltimore County Landmarks Preservation Commn., 1994—, bd. dirs., chair Hist. Hampton, Inc., 1992—; trustee Loyola, Notre Dame Libr., Balt., 1994—, Roland Park Country Sch., 1995—; chair Gov.'s Commn. Svc., 1994—. Named Outstanding Woman Mgr. of 1984 U. Balt. Women's Program in Mgmt. and WMAR-TV, Woman of Yr. Balt. County Commn. for Women, 1993; recipient Outstanding Achievement award U. Minn. Alumni Assn., 1984, Andrew White medal Loyola Coll., Balt., 1985; named in peer survey as one of 100 Most Effective Coll. and Univ. Pres. in U.S., Chronicle of Higher Edn., 1986. Mem. Internat. Women's forum, Smith Club, Hamilton St. Club (Balt.), Cosmopolitan Club (N.Y.C.).

DORST, HOLLY COMBES, counselor, educator; b. Cleve., Nov. 15, 1952; d. Richard Willard and Angela Katryn (Wright) Combes; m. John Darwin Dorst, Oct. 5, 1974; children: Jesse Clay, Emma Elizabeth. BA in Biology and Classics, Oberlin Coll., 1974; MS in Counselor Edn., U. Wyo., 1995. Cert. Nat. Bd. Cert. Counselors; lic. profl. counselor. Mgr. edn. consultation data processing Pa. Mut. Corp., Phila., 1977-80; mgr. staff svcs. CIGNA Corp., Phila., 1980-83; support advocacy edn. coord. SAFE Project, Laramie, Wyo., 1994-96; pvt. practice in trauma and incest, 1996—; support advocacy edn. coord. SAFE Project, Laramie, Wyo., 1994—; part-time lectr. U. Wyo., Laramie, 1996—. Bd. dirs. Open Sch., Laramie, 1988-90; den leader Cub Scouts, Laramie, 1991. Comty. Svc. Block grantee State of Wyo., 1995, Victims of Crime Act grantee U.S. Govt., 1995. Mem. ACA. Democrat. Home: 1320 Downey St Laramie WY 82070 Office: SAFE Project 901 South Third St Laramie WY 82070

DORTCH, MIMI TOY, religious organization administrator; b. Little Rock, Aug. 25, 1930; d. Frederick Gustave and Madalyn (Toy) Breitzke; m. William Pinkney Dortch, Sep. 16, 1950 (div. Aug. 1980); children: William Pinkney IV, Madalyn Dortch Johnson. Student, Mt. Vernon Jr. Coll., U. Ark. Dir. Ark. Interfaith Conf., Scott, 1989—. Active govs. commn. on Capital Punishment, 1970-72, The Handicapped, 1975-90, Kidney Transplant, 1970-90; co-chair new bldg. fund Our House Shelter. Recipient Rufus Young award Afro-Am. Ministerial Alliance, 1990, Top of the Rep. award Art Repertory Theater, 1990, Humanitarian award N.C.C.J., 1996; named Outstanding Sustainer of Yr., Jr. League of Little Rock, 1990, One of 100 Top Women, Ark. Bus. Mag., 1994. Mem. Nat. Mus. Women in Arts, Little Rock Country Club, Chi Omega (pres. 1960). Democrat. Roman Catholic. Office: Ark Interfaith Conf PO Box 151 Scott AR 72142

DORTON, LOUISE, library director; b. Oklahoma City, Mar. 6, 1936; d. Charles William Blatt and Beula O. (Williams) Nelson; m. Jack M. Dorton, Sept. 30, 1956 (div. 1985); children: Brenda, Kenneth, Janet, Dana. BA, Douglass Coll., 1973; MLS, Rutgers U., 1974. Dir. Pemberton (N.J.) Community Libr., 1974-79, Johnson City (Tenn.) Pub. Libr., 1979-89; br. dir. Chattanooga Libr.-Northgate, 1989-90; owner, mgr. Spoken Word Book Shop, Knoxville, Tenn., 1990-93; dir. Darlington County Libr., Darlington, S.C., 1991-96, Granville County Library System, Oxford, N.C., 1996—. Mem. North Johnson City Bus. Club, 1985-89; bd. dirs. Johnson City Girls' Club, 1986-89, pres., 1987-88. Grantee N.J. State Libr., 1975, 76, 77, N.J. Labor Dept., 1976, Tenn. State Libr., 1986, 87, U.S. Dept. Edn., 1987. Mem. AAUW (pres. 1984-85), C. of C. (Leadership 2000 1986-87). Office: Granville County Library System PO Box 339 210 Main St Oxford NC 27565

DORTON, TRUDA LOU, medical/surgical and geriatrics nurse; b. Elkhorn Creek, Ky., Aug. 26, 1949; d. Earl D. and Joyce (Kidd) Marshall; m. Eugene Anderson, Nov. 26, 1966 (dec. Apr. 1971); children: Gena Lynn, Richard Eugene; m. Leon Dorton, Dec. 15, 1972; children: Leondra Michelle, Jerald Thomas, Jonathan Layne. AS, Pikeville Coll., 1993, student, 1993. RN, Ky. Instr. computer usage Lookout (Ky.) Elem. Sch., 1983; water/sewage technician McCoy & McCoy Environ. Cons., Pikeville, Ky., 1984; owner Signs of the Times, Elkhorn City, Ky., 1979-89; sec.'s asst. humanities and social scis. divsns. Pikeville Coll., 1989-92; nurse aide Mud Creek Clinic, Grethel, Ky., 1992-93; charge nurse Jenkins (Ky.) Community Hosp., 1993-94; case mix coord. Parkview Manor Nursing Home, 1994-95, minimum data set and nursing care plan coord., 1995; staff nurse Harrison Meml. Hosp., Cynthiana, Ky., 1996—; vol. nurse aide Mud Creek Clinic, Grethel, 1989-92. Founder free blood pressure clinic H.E.L.P.S. Community Action Program, Hellier, Ky., 1983; co-founder H.E.L.P.S. Community Action Group, Hellier, 1983; mem. Ellis Island Centennial Commn., N.Y., 1986. Appalachian Honors scholar Pikeville Coll., 1989-92. Mem. Nat. Geog. Soc., Ky. Nursing Assn., Order Ky. Cols. (Honorable Ky. Col. 1989), Smithsonian Inst., Pikeville Coll. Alumni Assn. Democrat. Mem. Worldwide Ch. of God. Home: 503 W Pleasant St Cynthiana KY 41031-8950 Office: Harrison Meml Hosp South Wing 150 Millersburg Pike Cynthiana KY 41031

DORWARD, JUDITH A., association executive; b. Hazleton, Pa., Apr. 16, 1941; d. Eugene Joseph and Dorothy Cecelia (Shields) McNertney; m. Douglas Dean Owens, Apr. 15, 1961 (div. 1968); children: Kevin Patrick, Kelly Shawn; m. Clifford Neal Dorward, July 4, 1969 (div. 1974). AA, Lehigh County Community Coll., 1979; BA, Muhlenberg Coll., 1984; grad. in statis. process control, Process Mgmt. Inst., Inc., Mpls., 1986. Customer svc. clk. Pa. Power & Light Co., Allentown, 1959-61; mgr. Merle Norman Cosmetic Studios, Allentown and Bethlehem, Pa., 1968-70; adminstrv. clk. Pillsbury Co., East Greenville, Pa., 1970-85; ops. prodn. mgr. Pillsbury Co., East Greenville, 1985-87, mgr. distbn. and prodn. control, 1987-93, chair labor rels. com., 1987-91, customer svc., vender liaison mgr., 1993-94; Pillsbury customer svc. rep. Americold Corp., Fogelsville, Pa., 1994-95; exec. field rep. Better Bus. Bureau Ea. Pa., 1996—. Former voting machine operator Lehigh County, Slatington, Pa.; held various offices Gen. Fedn. of Women's Clubs. Mem. Exec. Women Internat. (dir. publs. 1991, dir. membership 1992-93, v.p., pres.-elect 1994, pres. 1995), Phi Beta Kappa. Democrat. Roman Catholic. Home: 2830 Linden St 3C Bethlehem PA 18017-3962 Office: BBB Lehigh Valley Divsn 528 N New St Bethlehem PA 18018

DORWART, BONNIE BRICE, internist, rheumatologist, educator; b. Petersburg, Va., Jan. 27, 1942; d. Gratien Bertrand and Myrtle Elizabeth (Houser) Brice; m. William Villee Dorwart, Jr., June 22, 1963; children: William Bertrand, Brice Burdan, Michael Walter. AB, Bryn Mawr Coll., 1964; MD, Temple U., 1968. Diplomate Am. Bd. Med. Examiners, Am. Bd. Internal Medicine, Am. Bd. Rheumatology. Intern, then resident in internal medicine Lankenau Hosp., Jefferson Med. Coll., Phila., 1968-72; instr. medicine Hosp. of U. Pa., Phila., 1972-74; fellow rheumatology U. Pa. Sch. Medicine, Phila., 1974; instr. medicine Jefferson Med. Coll., 1974-76, asst. prof., 1976-81, assoc. prof., 1981-95, clin. prof., 1995—; assoc. investigator div. rsch. Lankenau Hosp., 1978-88, chief arthritis clinic, 1982-86, chief connective tissue disorders, 1982—; assoc. dir. Greater Delaware Valley Arthritis Control Program, 1975; mem. Gov.'s adv. bd. on Systemic Lupus Erythematosus, Phila., 1981-88. Contbr. articles to med. jours., chpts. to books. Med. career advisor, active cells workshop Merion (Pa.) Elem. Sch., 1984—; fund raiser Arthritis Found., Am. Cancer Soc., Phila., 1974—; mem. resources com. Bryn Mawr Coll., 1985—. Named Physician of Yr., 32 Carat Club, Phila., 1986; Janet M. Glasgow scholar Temple U. Sch. Medicine, 1968. Fellow ACP; mem. AMA, Am. Coll. Rheumatology, Phila. Rheumatism Soc. (pres. 1981-82), Pa. Med. Soc., Philadelphia County Med. Soc. Lutheran. Home and Office: 124 Maple Ave Bala Cynwyd PA 19004-3031

DOSSICK, AUGUSTA, nurse, small business owner; b. N.Y.C., Sept. 24, 1926; d. Joseph Rubin and Mollie (Kean) Rubin-Wallack; m. Gerald L. Dossick; 1 child, Harrison Jon. Diploma in Nursing, Tampa (Fla.) Gen. Hosp., 1954; student, Hunter Coll., N.Y.C., 1951-54, Oneonta (N.Y.) State Coll., 1968; Cert., N.Y. Sch. Interior Design, 1981-83. RN, Calif. 1st surg. asst. Tampa, 1948-50; tchr. anatomy, chemistry, microbiology Bklyn. Jewish Hosp., 1951-54; operating room supr. Yonkers, N.Y., 1956-60; travel cons. Scarsdale (N.Y.) Travel Agy., 1963-65; sch. nurse/tchr. Ardsley (N.Y.) Sch. Dist., 1968-84; with interior design divsn. Dessick & Co., N.Y.C., 1984-88; peri-operative nurse Daniel Freeman Hosp., Marina Del Rey, Calif., 1992-95; designer, mfr., owner L.A., 1995—; tchr./leader meditation, N.Y.C., L.A., 1980—. Recipient Award for Outstanding Contbn., Am. Cancer Soc., Westchester County, 1974-83. Mem. Pacific Women's Investment Club (founder, pres. 1995—).

DOST, JANICE E.H. BURROWS, human resources director; b. Boston, Oct. 24, 1944; d. Lloyd F. and Bernice E. (Cross) Howard; m. Quentin C. Burrows, June 25, 1966 (div. Nov. 1986); children: Matthew Howard, Christopher Lynch; m. William A. Dost, Apr. 7, 1995. BA cum laude, Harvard U., 1966; MBA, U. Calif., Berkeley, 1987. Mgr. employment, tng. U.S. Govt., Boston, 1966-72, Washington, 1966-72, N.Y.C., 1966-72; personnel specialist City of Berkeley, 1974-76; asst. dir. personnel Alta Bates Hosp., Berkeley, 1976-79; personel dir. Alta Bates Med. Ctr., Berkeley, 1979-86; human resources cons. JHB Assocs., Berkeley, 1986—; human resources dir. U. Calif. Libr., Berkeley, 1988—; dir. Humanities West, San Francisco, 1991—. Co-author: Minority Recruitment and Retention in ARL Libraries, 1990; author: Training Student Workers in Academic Libraries, 1994, Onward or Upward? Getting Ahead in an Unfair World, 1994, The H.R. Balance Sheet, 1996. Docent Oakland Mus. Calif., 1992—; commr. personnel commn. Berkeley Unified Sch. Dist., chair, 1987-91. Nat. Merit scholar, 1962. Mem. Am. Libr. Assn., Nat. Forum Black Pub. Adminstrs., Indsl. Rels. Rsch. Assn., State Bar Calif. (assoc.). Home: PO Box 40073 Berkeley CA 94704-4073

DOSTER, ROSE ELEANOR WILHELM, artist; b. Balt., May 11, 1938; d. Lewis Milford and Leeanora A. (Naylore) Wilhelm; cert. illustration and design Art Instrn. Sch. Mpls., 1956; cert. design and painting Md. Inst. Coll. Art, 1960, postgrad., 1960-62; m. Jesse Alfred Doster, Feb. 22, 1958; children: Jeffrey Allen, Roxane Elana. Exhibited in one-woman shows: Hampstead Library Gallery, 1969, 70, Aurora Fed. Gallery, Balt., 1969, Goodman Gallery, Ellicott City, Md., 1971, Central Savs. Gallery, Towson, Md., 1971, Parkville (Md.) Library Gallery, 1972, Equitable Trust Bank Reisterstown Gallery, Balt., 1973, Hanover Art Guild, 1981, Md. Ctr. Pub. Broadcasting, 1982, Kent Island Fedn. of Art Gallery, 1990, others; exhibited in group shows: St. John's Coll., Johns Hopkins, Goodman Gallery, Slayton House, Columbia, Md., Paynter Gallery, Rehoboth, Del., Hilltop House, Harpers Ferry, W.Va., 1974-86, Balt. Mus. Art Downtown Gallery, 1976, Towsontowne Arts Festival, 1977-79, 82, 84, McDonough Sch.'s Cleve. Gallery, 1978, Unicorn Gallery, 1979, Canon Bldg. U.S. Ho. of Reps., Washington, 1981-82, Md. State NLAPW, Art Exhibit, Balt., 1983, Annapolis, 1985, Md. chpt. Nat. League Am. Penwomen, 1983, Easton Art Acad., 1987, 88, 89, 90, 91, 92, 93, 94, 95, 96, Invitational Craft Show, Cordova, 1988, Dorchester County Art Showcase, 1989, 90, 91, 92, 93, 94, 95, Salisbury-Wicomico Arts Festival, 1993, St. Michaels Maritime Mus. Show 1992-93, 94, 95, Chesapeake Coll. Art Show, 1987, 88, 89, 90, 91, 92, 93, 94, 95, Dorchester Educators Art Show, 1990, 91, 92, 94, 95, Working Artists Forum Juried Show, 1995; tchr. drawing, painting and ceramics, 1968—; craft supt. Carroll County 4H Fair, 1982, 83, 84, 85. Active Boy Scouts Am., Girl Scouts U.S.; leader Shiloh Clovers 4-H Club, Shiloh Clover's 4-H Club, 1983-84; trustee Balt. Mus. Art; pres. Carroll County Arts Coun., 1975-76, 94; v.p. Caroline County Arts Coun., 1993, pres. 1994; judge Montgomery County Fair, 1984, 86, 87, Howard County Fair, 1985, Balt. County 4-H Fair, Frederick County Fair, 1988, Caroline County Fair, 1989, 90, Easton Art Acad. Children's Exhibit, 1994, Federation Woman's Club of Denton Children's Competition, 1992-93, 94, Md. State Fair, 1993, 94, 95; mem. bd. Carroll County Farmers Market—crafts; elected mem. Working Artists Forum 1987-88, 89, 90, 91, 92, 93, sec., 1992-93, treas., 1993-94, 95, 96. Recipient numerous awards including George Peabody award, 1960, Judges Choice award Dorchester Educators Art Show, 1990, Best of Painters award Artisan's Fair Queen Anne Rotary Club, 1992, Nat. Potpourri Contest winner Floral and Nature Crafts Mags., 195, 96. Mem. Nat. League Am. Pen Women (br. art chmn. 1970-72, 1st v.p. 1972-74, pres. Carroll br. 1974-76, br. historian 1976-88, 89, 90, 91-94, 95, 96, branch achievement chmn., 1988-90, 92-94, br. newsletter editor 1992-93, 94, state historian 1982-84, 88-90, 93, chmn. tri-state miniature art show 1993, chmn. 50th Anniversary Show, 1995), Working Artist Forum (treas. 1994, 95, 96), Kent Island Fedn. of Art, Chestertown Art League, Rehoboth Art League, Md. Inst. Art Alumni Assns., Balt. Watercolor Soc. (assoc.), Carroll County Hist. Soc. (bd. dirs. 1986—), Caroline County Hist. Soc., Betsy Patterson Doll Club, Lady Baltimore Doll Club, Miss Carroll's Doll Study Club (founder, pres.), Ea. Shore Miniature Enthusiasts Club (founder, pres.), Ea. Shore Doll Study Club (historian 1993, libr. 1995, 96). Home: 9472 Quail Run Rd Denton MD 21629-1731

DOTSON, LINDA SUE, entertainment agent and manager; b. Richmond, Ky., Jan. 4, 1951; d. Mason and Ida Helen (Adams) Edington; m. Sheb F. Wooley, Dec. 30, 1985; 1 child, Shauna Michelle Dotson. AS in Nursing, U. Ky., 1978; BA in Nursing, U. Tenn., 1980. RN., Ky., Tenn. Talent buyer U.S. Govt.-Germany, Babenhausen, Fed. Republic of Germany, 1968-70; head writer Stars and Stripes, U.S. Govt., Frankfurt, Fed. Republic of Germany, 1969-70; die test, extruder Parker Hanifen, Berea, Ky., 1972-75; staff, head nurse Bapt. Hosp., Nashville, 1978-83; owner Pub. Relations/Talent Agy., Nashville, 1979—; co-owner Dotson-Wooley Entertainment Group (Film), Nashville, 1982—, Channel-Cordial Music Cos. (Pubs.), Nashville, 1982—; chief executive officer, owner Lito Internat. Inc. (Export/Import), Nashville, 1988—. Composer numerous songs; author: Elbows, 1979; assoc. TV Series, To Nashville, 1982, Cable TV show, Fandango, 1984. Named Top Ten Women in Entertainment, Performance Mag., 1988, finalist CBS Records/Am. Song Festival, 1982. Mem. ASCAP, Am. Fedn. Musicians, AFTRA, Internat. Country Music Buyers Assn., Nashville Assn. Talent Dirs. Office: Cir Rider Talent & Mgmt 123 Walton Ferry Rd 2nd Fl Hendersonville TN 37075

DOTSON, SUSAN MARY, accountant; b. Washington, May 16, 1961; d. Carlton and Peggy (O'Connell) Forsythe; m. Daniel M. Dotson, Dec. 29, 1990; children: Matthew Ryan, Timothy Sinclair. BS in Tech. and Mgmt., U. Md., 1993. Auditor Cen. Nat. Bank Md., Silver Spring, 1978-84; internal auditor Wash, Telephone Fed. Credit Union, Kensington, Md., 1984-85; acct. Svc. Employees Internat. Union, Washington, 1985-87, dir. acct., 1988-95, human resources mgr., 1995—. Mem. Howard County Dem. Women, Howard City, Md., 1995 96; chair legis. com. Spl. Edn. Adv. Com., Howard City, 1993-96; chair Howard County CP Parent Support Group, Howard City, 1993-96; grad. Ptnrs. in Policymaking, Md., 1995-96; mem. Howard County Arc Edn. Com., Howard County, 1996; del. Dem. Nat. Conv., 1996. Mem. Am. Soc. Assn. Execs., Assn. Mgmt. Accts. Democrat. Office: Svc Employees Intern Union 1313 L St NW Washington DC 20005

DOTT, NANCY ROBERTSON, geologist; b. Detroit, Sept. 20, 1929; d. James and Maud (Bignell) R.; m. Robert Henry Dott Jr., Feb. 1, 1951; children: James Robert, Karen Elizabeth, Eric Richard, Cynthia Elaine, Brian Russell. BS in Geology, U. Mich., 1951. Naturalist, guide U. Wis. Arboretum, Madison, 1972-94; naturalist Middleton (Wis.)/Cross Plains Sch. Dist., 1983—; presenter geology programs Rock Ladies of Madison, 1977—. Bd. dirs. Friends of Arboretum, Madison, 1993—; leader Girl Scouts Am., 1966-75; mem. LWV, Madison, 1965-80; pres. Unitarian Universalist Womens Alliance, Madison, 1984-85, 93-94. Mem. Wis. Assn. Environ. Edn., Wis. Soc. of Sci. Tchrs., Audubon Soc. Home: 231 Du Rose Terrace Madison WI 53705 Office: Middleton-Cross Plains Sch Dist 7106 South Ave Middleton WI 53562

DOTY, DELLA CORRINE, organization administrator; b. Marshalltown, Iowa, Apr. 12, 1945; d. Edwin Francis and Della Edna (Keller) Mack; BSBA in Acctg., Drake U., 1967; m. Philip Edward Doty, Dec. 23, 1967; children: Sarah Corrine, Anne Elizabeth. CPA, Colo. Audit staff Alexander Grant & Co., CPAs, Denver, 1967-71; controller Valley View Hosp. and Med. Ctr., Denver, 1971-75; rate rev. specialist Colo. Hosp. Assn., Denver, 1975-79; dir. Colo. Medicare Group Appeal Program, Littleton, Colo., 1979-91; assoc. dir. Communications Inst., 1992-94; lectr. in field. Dir., asst. treas. YWCA of Metro Denver, 1972-74; bd. dirs. Colo. Heart Assn., 1974-82; dir. Families First, Inc., 1987-89, chmn., bd. dirs., 1988-89; trustee Colo. Children's Chorale, 1988-94, 95—, chmn., 1992-94; pres. Denver Symphony Debs, 1996; mem. Jr. League of Denver, 1979—, v.p. mktg., 1985-86; sec. Littleton Pub. Schs. Bldg. Authority, 1983-86; active various charitable orgns.; v.p. fin. and housing Alpha Phi Internat., 1974-78, trustee, 1980-86; dir., treas. Alpha Phi Found., 1978-86. Recipient Founders Merit award Healthcare Fin. Mgmt. Assn., 1976, 83, Outstanding Vol. award Jr. League of Denver, 1984, Systainer Cmty. Svc. award, 1994. Mem. Alpha Phi (Ursa Major award 1980). Republican. Baptist. Contbr. articles to profl. jours. Address: 5981 S Coventry Ln W Littleton CO 80123-6706

DOUBLEDAY, OPAL PAULINE, small business owner; b. Moran, Kans., Aug. 25, 1924; d. George Washington and Artemesia Jane (Tinsley) Alumbaugh; m. Harlan Russell Boyer, June 29, 1942 (div. Dec. 1945); m. Russell Ralph Doubleday, Dec. 24, 1947 (dec. Apr. 1981); children: Jeffery Scott, Steven Craig. AA, Pierce Coll., 1958; BA, San Fernando Valley State Coll, 1962, MA, 1964. Tchr. L.A. City Sch. Sys., 1964-79; retailer Esto y Eso, Taos, N.Mex., 1982—; founder tchrs. aid program Sepulveda (Calif.) Jr. H.S., 1962-67, faculty pres., 1965-66; faculty pres. Chatsworth (Calif.) H.S., 1967-79; pres. L.A. Sci. Tchrs. Assn., 1969-70. Author: Whilst Thy Tower Crumbles, 1984. Mem. ACLU, Dem. Nat. Com., Taos C. of C. Home: PO Box 1556 Taos NM 87571 Office: Esto y Eso 110 Cruz Alta Road Taos NM 87571

DOUBLEDEE, DEANNA GAIL, software engineer, consultant; b. Akron, Ohio, July 29, 1958; d. John Wesley and Elizabeth (Nellis) Doubledee; m. Philip Henry Simons, Jan. 1, 1986. BSc in Computer Sci., Ohio State U., 1981; MSc in Software Engring., Nat. U., Inglewood, Calif., 1988. Cons. Ohio State U., Columbus, 1980-81; engr. Ocean Systems div. Gould, Inc., Cleve., 1981-82, Aircraft div. Northrop Corp., Hawthorne, Calif., 1982-83; tech. staff SEDD, TRW, Inc., Redondo Beach, Calif., 1983-85; staff engr. MEAD, TRW, Inc., Redondo Beach, Calif., 1985-88, subproject mgr., 1988-89; project engr. SDD, TRW, Inc., Redondo Beach, Calif., 1989-91; CEO, pres. Sequoia Bus. Solution, Redondo Beach, Calif., 1996—; dir. software engring. TWI Engring., Inglewood, Calif., 1991-92; cons. Microcosm, Inc., Torrance, Calif., 1990-91; sr. computer scientist IIT Rsch. Inst., 1993-94; cons. JAPA Sys. Engring.; chief architect Lockheed Martin Corp., 1996—; judge state sci. fair Ohio Acad. Sci., Columbus, 1988; active Orange County Venture forum, 1992, MIT Enterprises forum, Chgo., 1992-93. Chmn. bd. dirs. Fedn. of Presch. and Community Edn. Svcs. (Headstart), Carson, Calif., 1988-90, bd. dirs., 1990-91. Recipient award for outstanding vol. svc. Fedn. of Presch. and Community Edn. Ctrs., 1987; Exemplar Ohio Acad. Sci., 1987, 89, 90. Mem. IEEE, ACM, IEEE Computer Soc., Soc. Women Engrs. (awards chair 1987), Am. Astron. Soc.

DOUCETTE, MARY-ALYCE, computer company executive; b. Pitts., Feb. 12, 1924; d. Andrew George and Alice Jane (Sloan) Newland; m. Adrian Robert Doucette, Feb. 6, 1945 (dec. June 1983); children: David Robert, Regis Robert. BS cum laude, U. Pitts., 1945. Mgr. Newland Bros., Millvale, Pa., 1946-53; gen. mgr. Newland-Ludlo, Pitts., 1953-72; mgmt. cons. D3 Software, Garden City, N.Y., 1972-80, sec., corp. officer, 1980—. Fin. sec. Cerebral Palsy Assn., Garden City, Helen Keller Svcs. for Blind, Garden City; mem. Winthrop-U. Hosp. Aux., Mercy League, Friends of Adelphi Univ. Libr., Friends of Hist. St. George Ch. of Hempstead, N.Y., Adv. Coun. for Continuing Edn., Garden City Sch. Dist., 1988—. Mem. AAUW, L.I. Panhellenic, Univ. Club, Nassau County Hist. Soc. (life), Garden City Hist. Soc., Community Club Garden City-Hempstead, Woman's Club Garden City, Alpha Delta Pi, Pi Lambda Theta. Home: 146 Washington Ave Garden City NY 11530-3013 Office: D3 Software PO Box 8051 Garden City NY 11530-8051

DOUDS, VIRGINIA LEE, elementary education educator; b. Pitts., Jan. 17, 1943; d. Leland Ray and Virginia Helen (Dodds) Frazier; m. William Stewart Douds, June 20, 1964; children: William Stewart Douds, Michael Leland Douds. BA in Elem. Edn., Westminster Coll., New Wilmington, Pa., 1964; MA (Master's Equivalency), Dept. Edn., State of Pa., 1990. Cert. elem. tchr., Pa. Elem. tchr./non-graded Good Hope Elem. Sch., Glendale-Riverhills, Wis., 1964-65; elem. tchr./1st grade Carlisle Elem. Sch., Delaware, Ohio, 1965-66; elem. tchr./3rd grade Meml. Elem. Sch., Bethel Park, Pa., 1973-74; elem. tchr./1st and 3rd grades Logan Elem. Sch., Bethel Park, 1974-91; elem. tchr./3rd grade Neil Armstrong Elem. Sch., Bethel Park, 1991—; software cons. Coal Kids, U.S. Dept. Mines, 1993; mem. lang. arts, reading com. Bethel Park Schs., 1989—, SIP scholarship com. Bethel Park Fedn. Tcrhs., 1973—; cooperating tchr. Bethel Parks Schs., 1986—; mentor tchr. Bethel Park Schs., 1992-93, 95—; mem. instrnl. support team Bethel Park Schs., 1988-91; mem. Mid. States Accreditation com., 1993-94, strategic planning com., 1994-95. Mem. alumni coun. exec. bd. Westminster Coll., 1979-83; mem. exec. bd. Parents Assn., 1985-89. Recipient mini grant/writing, publishing ctr. Bethel Park Schs., 1989, Gift of Time tribute Am. Family Inst., 1990, 91, All Star Educator award U. Pitts./Pitts. Post Gazette, 1996. Mem. Nat. Coun. Tchrs. of English, Bethel Park Fedn. Tchrs., PTO. Republican. Presbyterian. Home: 2679 Burnsdale Dr Bethel Park PA 15102-2005

DOUGHERTY, BARBARA LEE, artist, writer; b. L.A., Apr. 25, 1949; d. Cliff and Muriel Tamarra (Rubin) Beck; m. Michael R. Dougherty, Feb. 10, 1970; children: Jessie, Luke, Elvi. BS in Fine Art, N.Y. State Coll., 1975. Staff writer South Coast Community Newspapers, Santa Barbara, Calif., 1988-90; contbg. editor Art Calendar, Upper Fairmont, Md., 1991—; dir. mktg. Art Calendar, Frenchtown, Md., 1993—; instr. art programs, 1975—; mem. City Adv. Bd. on Art, Santa Barbara, 1979-89, chmn., 1991-94; producer KCTV, Santa Barbara, 1990-94; CEO Harvest Am. Publs., 1992-93. Author, artist: In Search of a Sunflower, 1992, Harvest California, 1990, Getti ng the Word Out, 1996, Getting Exposure, 1996; prodr. 4 videos on art, 1990—; contbr. articles to Mktg. Art, 1991; exhibited in one-woman shows at Salisbury State U. Galleries, 1994. Fundraiser Boys and Girls Club of Am., Carpinteria, Calif., 1977-93. Recipient Best of Show award Hosp. Aux., Boulder, Nev., 1991, 1st place award Death Valley 49ers Club, 1989, 2d place award, 1990. Democrat. Roman Catholic. Home and Office: Dougherty Studios PO Box 170 Upper Fairmount MD 21867

DOUGHERTY, JUNE EILEEN, librarian; b. Union City, N.J., Mar. 27, 1929; d. Robert John and Jane Veronica (Smith) Beyrer; B.A. in Edn., Peterson State Coll., 1967; postgrad. Rutgers U. Sch. Library Sci., 1959-69; m. Donald E. Dougherty, Dec. 2, 1946; 1 son, Glen Allan. With A. B. Dumont, Paterson, N.J., 1950-54; sch. librarian St. Paul's Elementary Sch., Prospect Park, N.J., 1957—; dir. North Haledon (N.J.) Free Pub. Library, 1957—; sec.-treas. Dougherty & Dougherty, Inc., North Haledon, 1968—. Den mother Boy Scouts Am., 1954-57; mem. Gov. N.J.'s Tercentenary Com., 1962-64. Mem. Am., N.J., N. Haledon library assns., Cath. Library Assn., N.J. Libraries Roundtable, Bergen-Passaic Library Club, Friends N. Haledon Library. Roman Catholic. Club: St. Paul's Social. Home: 155 Westervelt Ave Haledon NJ 07508-3074 Office: 129 Overlook Ave North Haledon NJ 07508

DOUGHERTY, LEA M., social worker; b. Runnemede, N.J., Nov. 7, 1967; d. Michael J. and Nora M. (Smith) D. BSW, Marywood Coll., 1991, MSW, 1993. Lic. social worker, Pa. HIV case mgr. Cath. Social Svcs., Scranton, 1991-93; rsch. assoc. Mil. Family Inst., Scranton, 1993—; adj. faculty mem. Sch. Social Work Marywood Coll., Scranton, 1995—; presenter at confs. in field; group facilitator Cath. Social Svcs., Scranton, 1993-95; trainer HIV/AIDS Profl. Tng., Scranton, 1994. Bd. dirs. N.E. Regional HIV Planning Coalition, Pa., 1992-95; mem. health svcs. com. Scranton chpt. ARC, 1991-95. Mem. NASW (chair Scranton divsn. 1995—), NOW, Coun. Social Work Edn. Home: 1733 Dorothy St Scranton PA 18504 Office: Marywood Coll 2300 Adams Ave Scranton PA 18509

DOUGHERTY, MOLLY IRELAND, organization executive; b. Austin, Tex., Oct. 3, 1949; d. John Chrysostom and Mary Ireland (Graves) D. Student, Stanford U., 1968-71, Grad. Theol. Union, Berkeley, 1976; BA, Antioch U., 1980. Tchr., fundraiser Oakland Community Sch., Calif., 1973-77; assoc. producer, asst. editor film Nicaragua: These Same Hands, Palo Alto, Calif., 1980; free-lance journalist, translator, Nicaragua, 1981; assoc. producer, film: Short Circuit: Inside the Death Squads; exec. dir. Vecinos, A Tex. Inter-Am. Initiative, Austin, Tex., 1984—; cons. Magee & Magee Assocs., 1991—. Spanish lang. tutor St. Stephen's Episcopal Sch., Austin, 1988-89. Bd. dirs. Nat. Immigration Refugee and Citizenship Forum, Washington, 1985-88; speaker, fund-raiser Salvadoran Assn. for Rural Health, 1986—; lectr. St. Stephen's Episcopal Sch., 1989. Home: 1100 Claire Ave Austin TX 78703-2502 Office: Vecinos A Tex Inter-Am Initiative PO Box 4562 Austin TX 78765-4562

DOUGHERTY, PAMELA S., banker; b. Denver, Nov. 11, 1964; d. John Patrick and Marion Alexine (Denison) D. BS, Colo. State U., 1987. Dist. loan underwriting mgr. World Savs. & Loan, Melville, N.Y., 1981-89; asst. v.p. underwriting mgr. Citibank N.A., Bklyn., 1989-92; mgr. audit processing Mortgate Monitor, N.Y.C., 1992; ops. mgr. RPI Profl. Alternatives, N.Y.C., 1992-94; asst. v.p. vendor mgr. NatWest Home Mortgage, Wall Township, N.J., 1994—. Mem. Appraisal Found. Office: NatWest Home Mortgage 1415 Wyckoff Rd Wall Township NJ 07719

DOUGHERTY, URSEL THIELBEULE, communications and marketing executive; b. Rotenburg, W. Ger., July 30, 1942; naturalized U.S. citizen, 1965; d. Hugo and Margarete (Marquardt) Thielbeule; m. Erich A. Eichhorn, Jan. 3, 1979. BA summa cum laude in Polit. Sci., Cleve. State U., 1971; MA in Polit. Sci., U. Wis., 1972; MBA in Fin., Case Western Res., 1982. Journalist maj. daily, women's mag., Germany, 1962-66; assoc. editor Farm Chems., 1967; publs. mgr. Trabon Systems, 1967-68; rsch. analyst Legis. Coun., State of Wis., 1972; pub. rels. adminstr. to mgr. pub. info. Eaton Corp., Cleve., 1972-84; dir. pub. affairs Freightliner/Mercedes-Benz Truck Co., Portland, Oreg., 1984-87, v.p. chmn.'s office Daimler Benz N.A. Holding Co., Inc., Washington, 1987-90; v.p. bus. devel., corp. affairs Penske Corp., Cleve.; v.p. investor rels. Detroit Diesel Corp.; cons. small bus. Trustee, Lake Erie coun. Girl Scouts U.S., 1975-82, Sr. Citizen Resources, 1978-81; amb. Jr. Achievement, 1979; steering com. YWCA Career Women of Achievement, 1981; adv. bd. Women's Career Networking, 1980-84; trustee, chmn. fin. com. Young Audience Greater Cleve., 1982-84. Mem. Nat. Investor Rels. Inst., Pub. Rels. Soc. Am., Nat. Press Club. Home: 1510 Crest Rd Cleveland OH 44121-1722 Office: 13400 W Outer Dr Detroit MI 48239-1309

DOUGHTEN, MARY KATHERINE (MOLLY DOUGHTEN), retired secondary education educator; b. Belvidere, Ill., Apr. 26, 1923; d. Edwin Albert and Theora Teresa (Tefft) Loop; m. Philip Tedford Doughten, Oct. 15, 1947; children: Deborah Doughten Hellriegel, Susan Doughten Myers, Ann Doughten Fichenscher, Philip Tedford Jr., David, Sarah Doughten

Wiggins. BA, DePauw U., 1945; MS, Western Res. U., 1947. Social worker Children's Svcs., Cleve., 1947, San Antonio, 1948-49; tchr. English Indian Valley High Schs., Gradenhutten, Ohio, 1962-66; tchr. English and sociology New Philadelphia (Ohio) High Sch., 1966-86. Bd. dirs. Tuscarawas Valley (Ohio) Guidance Ctr., 1950-62, Cmty. Mental Health Care, Inc., formerly Mental Health Svcs. Cmty. Profl. Svcs., 1974-82, 84-92, pres., 1979-81, Alcohol, Drug and Mental Health Svcs. Bd., formerly Cmty. Mental Health Alcohol and Drug Svcs., Tuscarawas-Carroll County, 1992—, v.p. 1996—; mem. Tuscarawas County Juvenile Judges Citizens' Rev. Bd., Tuscarawas County United Way, 1960-67, ARC, PTA, 1955-58, coun. pres., 1960-62, mental health chmn. state bd., 1963-65, libr. chmn., 1966-68, Mobile Meals, 1986—, Dem. Women, 1986—, Hospice, 1987—, State C.C. Bd., 1965-68; founder, bd. dirs. Ohio Cmty. Mental Health Svcs., Columbus, 1970-80s; founding com. Kent State U. Tuscarawas campus, 1960s; bd. dirs. Tuscarawas County U. Found., 1994—, v.p., 1996—. Recipient Mental Health award Community and Profl. Svcs., 1978; Martha Holden Jennings scholar, 1975-76. Mem. AAUW (sec. 1962, v.p. 1996—), Ohio Ret. Tchrs. (sec. 1987-89), New Philadelphia Edn. Assn., Friends of Libr., Chestnut Soc. (bd. dirs. 1987-91), Tuscarawas County Med. Aux. (pres. 1959-60, state bd. 1960-64), Union Hosp. Aux. (bd. dirs. 1986—, editor 1986—), DAR, Coll. Club (scholarship chair 1989-91), Union County Club, Atwood Yacht Club, Lady Elks, Mortar Bd., Phi Beta Kappa, Alpha Chi Omega, Theta Sigma Phi. Democrat. Presbyterian. Home: 204 Gooding Ave NW New Philadelphia OH 44663

DOUGLAS, ANN, English literature educator; b. Morristown, N.J., 1942. BA in English Lit., Harvard U., 1964, PhD, 1970; postgrad., Linacre Coll., Oxford, 1964-66. Prof. English and comparative lit. Columbia U., N.Y.C., 1974—. Author: The Feminization of American Culture, 1977, Terrible Honesty: Mongrel Manhattan in the 1920s, 1994. Office: Columbia Univ 420 Lewisohn Hall Broadway 116th St New York NY 10027*

DOUGLAS, DIANE MIRIAM, museum director; b. Harrisburg, Pa., Mar. 25, 1957; d. David C. and Anna (Barron) D.; m. Steve I. Perlmutter, Jan. 23, 1983; 1 child, David Simon. BA, Brown U., 1979; MA, U. Del., 1982. Oral history editor Former Members of Congress, Washington, 1979-80; assoc. curator exhibitions John Michael Kohler Arts Ctr., Sheboygan, Wis., 1982-83; dir. arts ctr. Lill Street Gallery, Chgo., 1984-88; exec. dir. David Adler Cultural Ctr., Libertyville, Ill., 1988-91; dir. Bellevue (Wash.) Art Mus., 1992—; program chair, exec. bd. nat. Coun. for Edn. in Ceramic Arts, Bandon, Oreg., 1990-93; nat. adv. bd. Friends of Fiber Art, 1992; artists adv. com. Pilchuck Glass Sch., 1993—; mem. bd. dirs. Archic Bray Found., Helena, Mont., 1995—. Office: Bellevue Art Mus 301 Bellevue Sq Bellevue WA 98004-5000

DOUGLAS, DORIS FRANKS, primary education educator; b. Washington, Dec. 20, 1932; d. David Ransom and Lela Bectan (Duncan) Franks; m. Joseph Leon Douglas Jr., May 1, 1954; children: Wanda Thigpen, Patricia Jenkins, Susan Evans, Joseph L. Douglas III. BS cum laude, Miner Tchrs. Coll., Washington, 1954; MEd, U. Md., 1975. Tching. cert. Washington Bd. Edn., 1954. Classroom tchr. D.C. Pub. Schs., Washington, 1954-78, reading specialist, 1978-88; asst. prof. Dept. Edn. Univ. of the D.C., Washington, 1985-86. Mem. D.C. Reading Coun., 1978-88, counselor Adult Literacy Coun., Washington, 1987-89; mem. Southern Poverty Law Ctr., Montgomery, Ala., 1994—. Mem.; AAUW, Afro-Am. Caribbean Heritage Orgn. (membership com. 1990—), Palm Coast Civic Assn., Palm Coast Deck Bridge Club (sec. 1994—), Flagler County Taxpayers Assn., Delta Sigma Theta (sec. Flagler county chpt. 1995—). Presbyterian. Home: 2 Folson Lane Palm Coast FL 32137

DOUGLAS, EILEEN, news broadcaster, writer, television producer; b. Syracuse, N.Y., Sept. 17, 1946; d. Marvin and Shirley (Nadel) Bernstein; m. Jeffrey Stewart Zients, Dec. 17, 1967 (wid. Nov. 1975); 1 child, Rachel Susan; m. Stanley Israel, Aug. 24, 1985. BA with honors, Syracuse U., 1968. Reporter Sta. WNYS-TV, Syracuse, 1967-68, Herald Jour., Syracuse, 1969-70, Sta. WAKY Radio, Louisville, 1970; reporter, anchorman Sta. WKLO Radio, Louisville, 1970-74, news dir., 1974-76; producer, co-host show NOW Sta. WHAS-TV CBS, Louisville, 1974-75; writer, editor Sta. WINS Radio, N.Y.C., 1976-83, anchorwoman, reporter, 1983—; on-air corr. ABC-TV News Lifetime Mag., N.Y.C., 1993-94; ptnr. Douglas/Steinman Prodns., N.Y.C., 1994—. Author: New York Inflation Fighter's Guide, 1983, Rachel and the Upside Down Heart, 1990; creator Lets Make a Dream, 1985-90. Mem. AFTRA, Writers Guild Am. Jewish.

DOUGLAS, HOPE M., psychotherapist, forensic hypnotist; b. Marblehead, Mass., Jan. 14, 1947; d. W.I. and Beatrice B. Kenerson. BA in Psychology, Mich. State U., 1969, MA in Rehab. Counseling, 1970. Cert. mental health counselor, Fla.; cert. Ericksonian hypnotist. With Bur. Narcotics and Dangerous Drugs, U.S. Dept. Jusitce, Denver, 1971; with narcotics investigation, officer Glendale Police Dept., Denver, 1971-74; exec. dir., dir. edn., nat. speaker Child and Family Agy. of S.E. Conn., 1974-84; evidence technician, instr. homicide investigation Naples (Fla.) Police Dept., 1984-90; founder, exec. dir. wildlife rehab. svcs. and edn. Wind Over Wings, Inc., Clinton, Conn., 1990—; instr. wildlife rehab. Conn. Dept. Environ. Protection, 1991-92; adj. faculty Conn. Coll., Mitchell Coll. Contbr. articles to profl. jours. Mem. adv. bd. Child Welfare League Am. Recipient J. Edgar Hoover award for excellence, 1985. Mem. Conn. Wildlife Rehab. Assn. (pres. 1992), Internat. Wildlife Rehab. Coun. (v.p. 1993-94, acting exec. dir. 1995, bd. dirs. 1995-96, illustrator rehab. book series and disability book series 1995). Home: 22 Old Rd Clinton CT 06413-1855

DOUGLAS, JANICE GREEN, physician, educator; b. Nashville, July 11, 1943; d. Louis D. and Electa Green. BA magna cum laude, Fish U., 1964; MD, Meharry Med. Coll., 1968. Intern Meharry Med. Coll., 1968-71; NIH tng. fellow in endocrinology, instr. internal medicine Vanderbilt U., Nashville, 1971-73, sr. staff fellow sect. on hormonal regulation NIH, 1973-76; asst. prof. medicine Case Western Res. U. Sch. Medicine, Cleve., 1976-81, assoc. prof. medicine, 1981-84, prof. medicine, 1984—; dir. hypertension renal ambulatory care svc. Univ. Hosps. Cleve., 1976-80; dir. divsn. endocrinology and hypertension dept. medicine Univ. Hosps. Cleve. and Case Western Res. U., 1988-93, vice chair acad. affairs dept. medicine, 1991—, dir. divsn. hypertension dept. medicine, 1993—; mem. numerous grant rev. coms.; lectr., presenter in field; atteding physician in medicine and endicrinology U. Hosps., 1987; vis. prof. SUNY, Kings County Hosp. and Health Sci. Ctr., Bklyn., 1987, Med. U. S.C., 1989, Harlem Hosp., N.Y.C., 1993, N.Y. Med. Coll., Valhalla, 1994. mem. editl. rev. bd. Jour. Clin. Investigation, 1990—, Am. Jour. Physiology, Renal Fluid and Electrolytes, 1989-91; editl. bd. Hypertension, 1994—, Am. Soc. Clin. Investigation, 1990—, Ethnicity and Disease, 1990—, Circulation, 1993—; guest editor Jour. Clin. Investigation, U. Calif., San Diego, 1992—; assoc. editor Jour. Lab. and Clin. Medicine, 1986-90; reviewer numerous manuscripts and abstracts.; contbr. numerous articles, abstracts to profl. publs., chpts. to books. Fellow High Blood Pressure Coun., Am. Heart Assn., 1993—. Mem. Assn. Am. Physicians, Cleve. Med. Assn., Am. Soc. Hypertension, Kidney Found. Ohio, Women in Endocrinology, Inter-Am. Soc. Hypertension, Women in Nephrology, Assn. for Acad. Minority Physicians, Am. Physiology Soc., Endocrine Soc., Ctrl. Soc. for Clin. Rsch., Internat. Soc. Hypertension in Blacks, Inst. Medicine of NAS, Internat. Soc. Nephrology, Am. Soc. Nephrology, Am. Soc. Clin. Investigation, Am. Fedn. Clin. Rsch., Am. Heart Assn., Phi Beta Kappa, Alpha Omega Alpha (pres. Meharry chpt. 1968), Beta Kappa Chi. Office: Case Western U Sch Medicine Divsn Hypertension Rm W 165 10900 Euclid Ave Cleveland OH 44106-4982

DOUGLAS, MARION JOAN, proofreader, editor, labor negotiator; b. Jersey City, May 29, 1940; d. Walter Stanley and Sophie Frances (Zysk) Binaski; children: Jane Dee, Alex Jay. BA, Mich. State U., 1962; MSW, Sacramento State Coll., 1971; MPA, Calif. State U.-Sacramento, 1981. Owner, mgr. Linkletter-Totten Dance Studios, Sacramento, 1962-68, Young World of Discovery, Sacramento, 1965-68; welfare worker Sacramento County, 1964-67, welfare supr., 1968-72, child welfare supr., 1972-75, sr. personnel analyst, 1976-78, personnel program mgr., 1978-81, labor relations rep., 1981-89; cons. State Dept. Health, Sacramento, 1975-76; cons. in field. Author/editor: (newsletter) Thursday's Child, 1972-74. Presiding officer Cmty. Resource Orgn., Fair Oaks, Calif., 1970-72; exec. bd. Foster Parent's Assn., Sacramento, 1972-75; organizer Foster Care Sch. Dist. liaison programs, 1973-75; active Am. Lung Assn., 1983-87, 93-94; rep. Calif. Welfare Dirs. Assn., 1975-76; county staff advisor Joint Powers Authority, Sacramento, 1978-81; mem. Mgmt. Devel. Com., Sacramento, 1979-80; vol. auctioneer sta. KVIE Pub. TV, Sacramento, 1970-84, 88-90; adv. bd. Job and Info. Resource Ctr., 1976-77; spl. adv. task force coordinator Sacramento Employment and Tng. Adv. Council, 1980-81; vol. leader Am. Lung Assn., Sacramento, 1983-86, 94—, Calif. Dept. Social Welfare ednl. stipend, 1967-68, County of Sacramento ednl. stipend, 1969-70. Recipient Achievement award Nat. Assn. Counties, 1981. Mem. Mgmt. Women's Forum, Indsl. Relations Assn. No. Calif., Indsl. Relations Research Assn., Nat. Assn. Female Execs., Mensa. Republican. Avocations: real estate, nutrition. Home: 7812 Palmyra Dr Fair Oaks CA 95628-3423

DOUGLAS, PATRICIA PUMP, accounting and finance educator; b. Lewistown, Mont., Apr. 20, 1941; d. Henry F. Pump and Beatrice S. Skeel; m. Robert B. Bragg, June, 1958 (div. 1967); m. Charles E. Douglas, Aug. 23, 1968. BA, U. Mont., 1963; MBA, U. Calif., Berkeley, 1964, PhD, 1967. Grad. asst., assto to dean Sch. Bus. Adminstrn. U. Mont., 1961-63, rsch. assoc. Bur. Bus. & Econ. Rsch., 1966-72, asst. prof. Sch. Bus. Adminstrn., 1966-72, dir. continuing edn. & summer programs, asst. to pres., 1972-76, assoc. prof., 1972-74, prof., 1974—, asst. to pres., 1976-78, fiscal affairs v.p., 1978-82, prof. acctg. & fin. depts., 1983—; rsch. assoc. U. Calif., Berkeley, 1963-65; dir. state tch. svcs. State Mont., 1966-70; rschr. feasibility self-ins. state owned properties Mont. Legis. Coun., 1969-71; rschr. growth profitability Mont. Banks, Helena Br. Fed. Reserve Bank Mpls., 1970-71; vis. prof. U. Calif., Berkeley, 1972; dir. Continental Nat. Bank, Harlowton, Mont., 1980—, First Security Bank, Missoula, 1981-84; Ctrl. Feed Dir., 1987—; mem. bd. investments State Mont., 1977-80; chmn. Reserve Bank Minn. Helena Br., 1977-80, bd. trustees Missoula Cmty. Hosp., 1976-77; exec. com. Missoula Cmty. Med. Ctr., 1991—, treas. UM Fed. Credit Union, 1972-77, bd. dirs., 1972-77; mem. Bus. Sch. space com. U. Mont., 1994—, chair facilities svcs. evaluation oversight com., 1992-93, Sch. Bus. Internat. com., 1992-94, bond issuance com., 1992-94, bldg. fee com., 1990—, Sch. Bus. scholarship com., 1986-95, space com., 1978-83, campus devel. com., 1978-83, adv. bd. cmty. svc. program, 1974-77, faculty senate, 1970-72, sec. budget & policy com., 1967-68, ad hoc com. curriculum acctg. & fin. dept., 1967-68, ad hoc com. Sch. Bus. Adminstrn. space, 1994-95. Contbr. articles to profl. jours. Recipient Rsch. Achievement award Assn. Govtl. Accts. At-Large, 1992-93. Mem. Am. Inst. CPAs, Nat. Assn. Accts. (dir. Western Mont. chpt. 1970-73, 91, pres. Western Mont. chpt. 1972-73, nat. dir. 1975-77, v.p. nat. com. 1994-96, nat. fin. com. 1985-86, mgmt. acctg. practices com. 1985-86, MAP com. subcom. govt. 1985-95, Outstanding Educator award 1989), Fin. Acctg. Stds. Bd. (task force nonprofits 1989-94), Western Commn. Colls. (chair fin. & ops. com. 1992-94, commr. 1989-94), Mont. Soc. CPAs (ethics com. 1985—, com. to review procedures 1987-88, com. rels. with bar 1988-90, chmn. ethics com. 1985-89, bd. dirs. 1989—, ad-hoc com. pers. policies 1994-95, ad-hoc com. by-laws changes 1992-93, v.p. 1993-94, pres.-elect 1994-95, pres. 1995-96), Northwest Assn. Schs. Colls (accreditation pool), Data Processing Mgmt. Assn. Edn. Found. (bd. regents 1984-91, pres. 1990-91), Western Assn. Colls. & Univs. (commr. 1989-94, chair fin. com. 1991-94), Beta Alpha Psi (Outstanding Tchr. award 1985-86, 1992-93), Phi Kappa Phi. Home: Box 189 8200 Mormon Creek Rd Lolo MT 59847 Office: U Mont Acctg & Fin Dept Missoula MT 59812

DOUGLAS, ROXANNE GRACE, secondary school educator; b. Orange, N.J., Dec. 17, 1951; d. Joseph Samuel and Mary (Ferro) Battista; m. Richard Joseph Douglas, June 26, 1982; 1 child, Regina Grace. BA cum laude, Montclair State Coll., 1973; student, Sorbonne U., Paris. Cert. French, social studies and elem. sch. tchr., N.J. Tchr. social studies West Orange (N.J.) Bd. Edn., 1973-74, Orange (N.J.) Bd. Edn., 1974-75; substitute tchr. various schs. N.J., 1975-76; supplemental tchr. Irvington (N.J.) Bd. Edn., 1976-80, tchr. govtl. programs, 1980—; advisor 7th dist. NJSFWC-JM State Bd., 1991-93, membership chmn., 1994-96, pub. affairs chmn., 1996—. Mem. Montclair Hist. Soc., West Caldwell Hist. Soc., Montclair Mus., Newark Mus., Rahway Hist. Soc.; v.p., publicity chmn. West Caldwell Hist. Soc.; chmn. children's com. 1st Night, West Essex, 1994; troop leader Brownies, Girl Scout U.S.; vol. Family and Children's Svcs., North Essex; mem. ch. newsletter com., catechist Notre Dame Ch. Recipient Creative Writing awards NJSFWC-JM, Citizenship award Am. Legion. Mem. Victorian Soc., N.J. Edn. Assn., Nat. French Hon. Soc., Nat. Edn. Hon. Soc., Jr. Women's Club of West Essex (co-pres., liaison internat. affairs chmn., pub. affairs chmn.), Coll. Club Orange-Short Hills, West Essex Women's Club (liaison to jr. woman's club, chmn. internat. affairs and pub. affairs dept. 1st night com. mem., pres., parent adv. coun.-bd. edn., pres., 1994—, internat. affairs chmn., centennial chmn.), Verona Women's Club (membership chmn.). Roman Catholic.

DOUGLAS, SUSAN, data processing specialist, consultant; b. Chgo., Oct. 29, 1946; d. Lawrence and Phoebe Fern (Sibbald) D.; m. John D. Hauenstein, Dec. 21, 1972 (div. June 1975). BA, U. Iowa, 1972; postgrad., U. Wis., Whitewater, 1985, U. Wis., Madison, 1991—. Project coord. Westinghouse Learning Corp., Iowa City, Iowa, 1967-75; echocardiology technician Chgo. Osteo. Hosp., 1975-78; sys. programmer, analyst Household Fin. Corp., Prospect Heights, Ill., 1978-81; applications analyst Burdick Corp., Milton, Wis., 1981-84; cons. Edgerton, Wis., 1984—. Mem. Data Processing Mgmt. Assn. Episcopalian. Home and Office: 8203 N State Road 184 Edgerton WI 53534-8887

DOUGLAS GILL, JACQUELINE ANNICE, librarian, educator; b. N.Y.C., June 4, 1950; d. Nathan S. and Maude L. (Flanagan) Jones; 1 child, Christopher B. Aden. AA in Libr. Tech., Borough of Manhattan C.C., N.Y.C., 1976; BA in Sociology, Queens Coll., 1979; MLS, Pratt Inst., Bklyn., 1982; MS in Ednl. Adminstrn. and Supervision, CCNY, 1989. Libr. ast. Little Red Sch. House, N.Y.C., 1974-75; sr. libr. asst. Maritime Coll., Bronx, N.Y., 1976-79; asst. prof., serials libr. City Coll. Libr., N.Y.C., 1979—; rec. sec. N.Y. Black Librs. Caucus, 1992, corr. sec., 1991. COGNOTES reporter ALA, Chgo., 1989-90. Mem. Libr. Assn. CUNY. Office: City Coll Libr W 138th St and Convent Ave New York NY 10031

DOUGLASS, ENID HART, educational program director; b. L.A., Oct. 23, 1926; d. Frank Roland and Enid Yandell (Lewis) Hart; m. Malcolm P. Douglass, Aug. 28, 1948; children: Malcolm Paul Jr., John Aubrey, Susan Enid. BA, Pomona Coll., 1948; MA, Claremont (Calif.) Grad. Sch., 1959. Research asst. World Book Ency., Palo Alto, Calif., 1953-54; exec. sec., asst. dir. oral history program Claremont Grad. Sch., 1963-71, dir. oral history program, 1971—, history lectr., 1977—; mem. Calif. Heritage Preservation Commn., 1977-85, chmn. 1983-85. Contbr. articles to hist. jours. Mayor pro tem City of Claremont, 1980-82, mayor, 1982-86; mem. planning and rsch. adv. coun. State of Calif.; mem. city coun. City of Claremont, 1978-86; founder Claremont Heritage, Inc., 1977-80; bd. dirs., 1986-95; bd. dirs. Pilgrim Pla., Claremont; founder, steering com., founding bd. Claremont Cmty. Found., 1989-95, pres., 1990-94. Mem. Oral History Assn. (pres. 1979-80), Southwest Oral History Assn. (founding steering com. 1981, J.V. Mink award 1984), Nat. Council Pub. History, LWV (bd. dirs. 1957-59, Outstanding Svc. to Community award, 1986). Democrat. Home: 1195 N Berkeley Ave Claremont CA 91711-3842 Office: Claremont Grad Sch Oral History Program 710 N College Ave Claremont CA 91711-5530

DOUGLASS, MICHELLE JOAN, lawyer; b. Phila., Sept. 13, 1961; d. Roger Joseph and Vonna Jean (Riley) D. BS, Kutztown U., 1983; postgrad law studies, Marquette U., 1985-86; JD, Del. Law Sch., Wilmington, 1988. Bar: N.J. 1988, U.S. Dist. Ct. N.J. 1988. Judicial law clk. Cumberland County Superior Ct., Bridgeton, N.J., 1988-89; assoc. Horowitz, Perlow, Morris, Bridgeton, 1989-90, Horn, Kaplan & Goldberg, Atlantic City, N.J., 1990-91, Basile & Testa, Vineland, N.J., 1991—; personal counsel FamCare, Inc., Bridgeton, N.J. 1992—. Mem. NOW (co-founder Vineland chpt., ednl. speaker 1994, treas. 1995), ATLA (ednl. speaker People's Law Sch., Cumberland C.C. 1993, 94, boardwalk seminar Atlantic City, 1994, 95, bd. govs. 1994— co-chair civil practice com. 1995), ABA, AAUW, Women's Alliance for Job Equity, N.J. Bar Assn., Cumberland County Bar Assn. (trustee 1993, civil practice com. 1994—). Republican. Roman Catholic. Office: Basile & Testa 424 Landis Ave Vineland NJ 08360

DOUGLASS, NANCY URE, school social worker; b. Pitts., Nov. 14, 1953; d. Robert and Ruth (Jone) Ure; m. Melfard Douglass, Dec. 27, 1975 (dec. June 1994); children: Alexandra Ure, Baily A. BA in Sociology, U. Pitts., 1975, MSW, 1989. Lic. social worker, Pa.; cert. home and sch. visitor, Pa. Case worker Children and Youth, Pitts., 1975-78; spl. edn. social worker Allegheny Int. Unit, Pitts., 1989-91; sch. social worker Woodland Hills Sch., Pitts., 1991—; cons., spkr. Parental Stress Ctr., Pitts., 1994; keynote spkr. Allegheny Int. Unit., 1993, 94; spkr. in field. V.p. Edgewood (Pa.) Recreation Bd., 1992—; asst. coach Little League Baseball, Edgewood, 1994—; mem. adv. com. Children and Youth Allegheny County, 1994—, Rankin Christian Ctr., 1995—. Recipient Cmty. Svc. award Rankin Christian Ctr., Pitts., 1993. Presbyterian. Home: 307 Beech St Pittsburgh PA 15218 Office: Woodland Hills Sch Dist 241 Maple Ave Pittsburgh PA 15218

DOUGLASS, THELMA JEAN, educational administrator; b. Crockett, Tex.; d. Jesse and Rosa Douglass. BA, U. Houston, 1974, MA, 1977, EdD, 1992. Programming coord. U. Houston, 1982-83, conf. coord., 1982-84, recruitment coord., 1983-84, asst. mgr. housing, 1984-88, asst. to dean of campus life, 1988-89, mem. faculty, 1987-93, asst. dean students, 1989-93; lectr. Sam Houston State U., Huntsville, Tex., 1994—, assoc. v.p., 1993—; regional advisor Nat. Assn. Colls., Ark., La., Okla., Tex., 1985-88. Author: SWACHURH's Advisor's Handbook, 1986; co-author: Research of Regional Transit, 1988. Chair Camp Cougar, Houston, 1985-88. Recipient Young Black Achiever award City of Houston, 1992; two awards named in her honor U. Houston, 1988, 91. Mem. ASCD, Am. Coll. Pers. Assn., Nat. Assn. Colls. and Univs., Golden Key Honor Sco., C. of C. of Huntsville, Rotary. Home: PO Box 5464 Humble TX 77325-5464

DOUMLELE, RUTH HAILEY, communications company executive, broadcast accounting consultant; b. Charlotte County, Va., Nov. 6, 1925; d. Clarrie Robert Hailey and Virginia Susan (Slaughter) Ferguson; m. John Antony Doumlele, May 8, 1943; children: John Antony, Suzanne Denise Doumlele Owen. Cert. in commerce, U. Richmond, 1968; BA, Mary Baldwin Coll., 1982. Sta. acct. WLEE-Radio, Richmond, Va., 1965-67, bus. mgr., 1967-73; area bus. mgr. Nationwide Communications Inc., Richmond, 1973-75; corp. bus. mgr., Neighborhood Communications Corp., Inc., Richmond, 1978-86, asst. v.p., 1981-86; owner Broadcast Acctg. Cons., Midlothian, Va., 1986-95; treas., dir. Guests of Honor, Ltd., Richmond, 1984-89; sec., Inner Light, Inc., 1984—. Contbr. articles to profl. jours.; mem. editorial rev. bd. The Woman C.P.A., 1980—. Mem. Am. Soc. Women Accts. (chpt. pres. 1974-76, contbg. editor The Coord. 1990, Chgo., Woman of Achievement award 1991), Broadcast Fin. Mgmt. Assn., Nat. League Am. Pen Women (br. pres. 1984-86), Am. Fedn. Astrologers, Va. Assn. Amateur Athletic Union (records chmn. 1959-62), Women's Club of Powhatan, Selective Svc. System Local Bd., Powhatan Hist. Soc. Episcopalian. Avocations: salt water fishing, Civil War history, travel, astrology. Home and Office: 2510 Chastain Ln Midlothian VA 23113-9400

DOUSKEY, THERESA KATHRYN, health facility administrator; b. New Haven, Conn., Nov. 30, 1938; d. Stanley Anthony and Wadia (Mekdeci) D. RN, Grace New Haven Sch. Nursing, 1959; BS in Nursing, So. Conn. State U., 1962; MPA in Health Care, U. New Haven, 1979. Various positions Yale New Haven Hosp., 1959-80; asst. dir. nursing Meriden (Conn.) Wallingford Hosp., 1980-81; nurse Regional Visiting Nurse Agy., North Haven, Conn., 1983-87; home care coord. Milford (Conn.) Hosp., 1990-93; case mgr., nurse Community Care, Inc., New Haven, 1988-90, 93-96; med. br. supr. Priority Care, Inc., East Haven, Conn., 1996—. Mem. Am. Nurses Assn., Conn. Nurses Assn. (nominating com. 1972-74), Conn. Assn. Continuity of Care, Sigma Theta Tau. Republican. Home: 412 Narrow Ln Orange CT 06477-3315

DOUTHIT, PATRICIA ANN, counselor, secondary education educator; b. Rockingham, N.C., Jan. 2, 1942; d. Alton John and Alma (Adams) D. BS, Appalachian State U., Boone, N.C., 1964; MS, U. N.C., Charlotte, 1977, Winthrop U., Charlotte, 1985. Tchr. McClintock Jr. H.S., Charlotte, 1964-74, Myers Park H.S., Charlotte, 1976-86; tchr., counselor Harding U. H.S., Charlotte, 1986—, lead counselor, 1995—; mem. Coll. Bd., Charlotte, 1993—. Home: 6010 Coatbridge Ln Charlotte NC 28212 Office: Harding U HS 2001 Alleghany St Charlotte NC 28208

DOUTHITT, SHIRLEY ANN, insurance agent; b. Mexia, Tex., Feb. 21, 1947; d. Othello Young and Hazel Lorene (Corley) Thompson; m. A. Dwane Douthitt, Nov. 24, 1966; 1 child, Steven Dwane. Student, Leonard's Tng Sch., Houston, 1979; student Tex. local recording agts. licensing course, Austin, Tex., 1980; student farmers ins. group tng. program, Austin, 1980; student life underwriters trng course, Tyler, Tex., 1987. Lic. ins. agt. Sec. Lindsey & Newsom Ins. Adjusters, Palestine, Tex., 1965-73, J. Herrington Ins. Agy., Palestine, 1973-76, Ramsey Ins. Agy., Palestine, 1976-79; agt. Farmers Ins. Group, Palestine, 1979—. Recipient Bus. Woman of Yr. Palestine Profl. Bus. Women, 1983. Mem. NAFE, Women's Club. Office: Shirley Douthitt Ins Agy 101 7th St PO Box 7000 Palestine TX 75802

DOUVAN, ELIZABETH, social psychologist, educator; b. South Bend, Ind., Nov. 3, 1926; d. John and Janet F. (Powers) Malcolm; m. Eugene Victor Douvan, Dec. 27, 1947; children—Thomas Alexander, Catherine Des Ormiers. A.B., Vassar Coll., 1946; M.A., U. Mich., 1948, Ph.D., 1951. Study dir. Survey Research Center, U. Mich., Ann Arbor, 1950-58; lectr. dept. psychology Survey Research Center, U. Mich., 1951-61, asso. prof., 1961-65, Kellog prof. psychology, 1965—; also program dir. Inst. for Social Research, 1970—; assoc. dir. Inst. for Social Rsch., 1994—; dir. residential coll. U. Mich., 1985-88; cons. NIMH, NSF, various founds.; mem. Ann Arbor Bd. Health, 1972-76. Author: The Adolescent Experience, 1966, Feminine Personality and Conflict, 1970, The Inner American, 1981, Mental Health in America, 1981, Marital Instability, 1995; contbr. articles to profl. jours. Recipient various grants. Mem. AAAS, APA (pres. div. 35, 1970-71), Am. Psychol. Soc., Assn. for Women in Psychology, Nat. Women's Studies Assn. Democrat. Office: U Mich Dept Psychology 580 Union Dr Ann Arbor MI 48109-1346

DOUVILLE, PATRICIA, reading educator; b. Phila., Jan. 22, 1952; d. Charles Gregory Douville; m. Lawrence Milton Ricker, Apr. 11, 1980. BA, U. N.C., Wilmington, 1973; MA in Edn., East Carolina U., 1986; PhD, N.C. State U., 1996. Cert. K-12 reading tchr., K-4 early childhood edn. tchr., supr. Tchr. Onslow County Sch. System, Jacksonville, N.C., 1973-76, Dept. Def. Overseas Dependents' Schs., Kadena Air Base, Okinawa, Japan, 1976-80, Beeville (Tex.) Ind. Sch. Dist., 1980-83; tchr. New Bern (N.C.) Craven County Sch. System, 1983-86, reading specialist, 1986-88; instr. N.C. State U., Raleigh, 1990—. Contbg. author: Job Skills for the 21st Century. Recipient one of Top 20 Most Outstanding Grad. Student Instrs. award N.C. State U., 1991. Mem. Nat. Coun. Tchrs. English, Am. Edn. Rsch. Assn., Internat. Reading Assn., N.C. Assn. for Rsch. in Edn. (Twin Rivers coun. v.p. 1987—), Phi Kappa Phi. Office: NC State Univ Dept C&I Box 7801 Raleigh NC 27695-7801

DOVE, RITA FRANCES, poet, English language educator; b. Akron, Ohio, Aug. 28, 1952; d. Ray A. and Elvira E. (Hord) D.; m. Fred Viebahn, Mar. 23, 1979; 1 child, Aviva Chantal Tamu Dove-Viebahn. BA summa cum laude, Miami U., Oxford, Ohio, 1973; postgrad., Universität Tübingen, Fed. Republic Germany, 1974-75; MFA, U. Iowa, 1977; LLD (hon.), Miami U., Oxford, Ohio, 1988, Knox Coll., 1989, Tuskegee U., 1994, U. Miami, Fla., 1994, Washington U., St. Louis, 1994, Case Western Res. U., 1994, U. Akron, 1994, Ariz. State U., 1995, Boston Coll., 1995, Dartmouth Coll., 1995, Spelman Coll., 1996, U. Pa., 1996. Asst. prof. English Ariz. State U., Tempe, 1981-84, assoc. prof., 1984-87, prof., 1987-89; prof. U. Va., Charlottesville, 1989-93, Commonwealth prof. English, 1993—; U.S. poet laureate/cons. in poetry Libr. of Congress, Washington, 1993-95; writer-in-residence Tuskegee (Ala.) Inst., 1982; lit. panelist Nat. Endowment for Arts, Washington, 1984-86, chmn. poetry grants panel, 1985; judge Walt Whitman award Acad. Am. Poets, 1990, Pulitzer prize in poetry, 1991, Ruth Lilly prize 1991, Nat. Book award in poetry 1991, Anisfield-Wolf Book awards, 1992—. Author: (poetry) Ten Poems, 1977, The Only Dark Spot in the Sky, 1980, The Yellow House on the Corner, 1980, Mandolin, 1982, Museum, 1983, Thomas and the Beulah, 1986 (Pulitzer Prize in poetry 1987), The Other Side of the House, 1988, Grace Notes, 1989 (Ohioana award 1990), Selected Poems, 1993 (Ohioana award 1994), Lady Freedom Among Us, 1994, Mother Love, 1995; (verse drama) The Darker Face of the Earth, 1994; (novel) Through the Ivory Gate, 1992 (Va. Coll. Stores Book award 1993); (short stories) Fifth Sunday, 1985 (Callaloo award 1986); (essays) The Poet's World, 1995; mem. editorial bd. Nat. Forum, 1984—, Iris, 1989—; mem. adv. bd. Ploughshares, 1992—, N.C. Writers Network, 1992—, Civilization,

1994—; assoc. editor Callaloo, 1986—; adv. and contbg. editor Gettysburg Rev., 1987—, TriQuarterly, 1988—, Ga. Review, 1994—. Commr. The Schomburg Ctr. for Rsch. in Black Culture, N.Y. Pub. Libr., 1987—; mem. Renaissance Forum Folger Shakespeare Libr., 1993—, Coun. of Scholars Libr. of Congress, 1994—; mem. nat. launch com. AmeriCorps, 1994; mem. awards coun. Am. Acad. Achievement, 1994—. Presdl. scholar, 1970, Nat. Achievement scholar, 1970-73; Fulbright/Hays fellow, 1974-75, rsch. fellow U. Iowa, 1975, teaching/writing fellow U. Iowa, 1976-77, Guggenheim Found. fellow, 1983-84, Mellon sr. fellow Nat. Humanities Ctr., 1988-89, fellow Ctr. for Advanced Studies, U. Va., 1989-92; grantee NEA, 1978, 89; recipient Lavan Younger Poet award Acad. Am. Poets, 1986, GE Found. award, 1987, Bellagio (Italy) residency Rockefeller Found., 1988, Ohio Gov.'s award 1988, Literary Lion citation N.Y. Pub. Libr., 1991, Women of Yr. award Glamour Mag., 1993, NAACP Great Am. Artist award, 1993, Golden Plate award Am. Acad. Achievement, 1994, Disting. Achievement medal Miami U. Alumni Assn., 1994, Renaissance Forum award for leadership in the literary arts Folger Shakespeare Libr., 1994, Carl Sandburg award Internat. Platform Assn., 1994; inducted Ohio Women's Hall of Fame, 1991; named Phi Beta Kappa poet Harvard U., 1993. Mem. PEN, Poetry Soc. Am., Associated Writing Programs (bd. dirs. 1985-88, pres. 1986-87), Am. Acad. Achievement (mem. golden plate awards coun. 1994—), Phi Beta Kappa (senator 1994—), Phi Kappa Phi. Office: U Va Dept English Wilson Hall Charlottesville VA 22903

DOVRING, KARIN ELSA INGEBORG, author, poet, playwright, communication analyst; b. Stenstorp, Sweden, Dec. 5, 1919; came to U.S., 1953, naturalized, 1968; m. Folke Dovring, May 30, 1943. Grad., Coll. Commerce, Gothenburg, Sweden, 1936; MA, Lund (Sweden) U., 1943, PhD, 1951; Phil. Licentiate, Gothenburg U., 1947. Journalist several Swedish daily newspapers and weekly mags., 1940-60; tchr. Swedish colls.; rsch. assoc. of Harold Lasswell Yale U., New Haven, 1953-78; fgn. corr. Swedish newspapers, Italy, Switzerland, France and Germany, 1956-60; freelance writer, journalist, 1960—; represented by Joseph Nicoletti Hollywood, Calif., 1994—; vis. prof. Internat. U., The Vatican, Rome, 1958-60, Gottingen (W.Ger.) U., 1962; lectr. U.S. Army, Peace Corps, numerous univs. including Yale U., U. Wis., McGill U., U. Iowa, U. Warsaw, Poland; rsch. assoc. U. Ill., Urbana, 1968-69; invited contbr. Social Sci. Rsch. Coun., 1988; featured speaker Ann. Conf. Law and Policy, Yale U. Law Sch., 1992, 93; interviewee radio and TV programs; writer Ill. Alliance to Prevent Nuclear War, radio, theater; Hollywood songwriter; plays for TV movies. Author: Songs of Zion, 1951, Land Reform as a Propaganda Theme, 3d edit., 1965, Road of Propaganda, 1959, Optional Society, 1972, Frontiers of Communication, 1975 (short stories) No Parking This Side of Heaven, 1982, Harold D. Lasswell: His Communication with a Future, 1987, 2d edit., 1988, Forked Tongue? Body-Snatched English in Political Communications, 1989, (novel) Heart in Escrow, 1990, (collections of poems) Faces in a Mirror, 1995, Shadows on a Screen, 1996, Whispers on a Stage, 1996; contbr. numerous articles to mags. Recipient Swedish Nat. award for short stories Bonniers Pub. House Stockholm, 1951. Mem. NOW, Société Jean Jacques Rousseau of Geneva (hon. life), Inst. Freedom of Press (life asso.), Internat. Biog. Centre (Cambridge, England) (hon., adv. coun.). Democrat. Address: 613 W Vermont Ave Urbana IL 61801-4824 Office: care Creative Network Nicoletti Music Co PO Box 2818 Newport Beach CA 92659

DOW, CHRISTINE DETSCHER, school counselor; b. Wolfeboro, N.H., June 14, 1946; d. Richard William and Louise Hazel (Irish) Detscher; m. John Myrl Dow, Apr. 25, 1970; children: Matthew, Johanna, Bethany, Robin. BEd, Plymouth State Coll., 1968, MEd, 1993. Reality Therapy cert., Inst. for Choice Theory/ Reality Therapy & Quality Mgmt., 1992. 3d grade tchr. Hudson (N.H.) Sch. Dist., 1968-70; 2nd grade tchr. Inter-Lakes Sch. Dist., Meredith, N.H., 1972-73; tchr. Indian River Nursery Sch., Canaan, N.H., 1984-87, Cardigan Mt. Sch., Canaan, 1987-91; counselor Plymouth, N.H., 1993-94, Kearsarge Sch. Dist., Warner, N.H., 1994—; practicum supr. Inst. for Choice Theory/ Reality Therapy and Quality Mgmt., Chatsworth, Calif., 1994—. Chair ann. fund raising Dinner Friends of Mascoma Schs., West Canaan, N.H., 1979-83; charter bd. dirs. Indian River Nursery Sch., 1979-84; town rep. Mascoma Sch. Bd., West Canaan, 1980-87; vice chmn. SAU #43 Sch. Bd., Lebanon, N.H., 1985-87; rider, mem. com. Pemiquaney Riding Club, Plymouth, 1989—. Recipient 10 Yr. Leader award 4-H Grafton County, 1995. Mem. NEA, ACA, Northeast Reality Therapists, Pemiquaney Riding Club, Phi Delta Kappa. Home: Box C-2 Canaan NH 03741 Office: Kearsarge at Warner Church St Warner NH 03278

DOW, KAREN SUE, graphic designer, painter, sculptor; b. Port Arthur, Tex., Apr. 25, 1944; d. John Henry Jr. and Marcella Fredricka (Wetsel) Greenwood; m. Franklin Dennis Dow, May 29, 1965 (div. Nov. 1988). Student, RISD, 1962-63. Art dir. Mercury Publs., El Segundo, Calif., 1970-76; supr. Continental Graphics, Culver City, Calif., 1977-82; graphic designer TRW Inc., Redondo Beach, Calif., 1982—. Exhibited in group shows L.A., 1976, Pasadena (Calif.) Arts Coun., 1976, 77, RISD Alumni, L.A., 1978, 79, 80, El Segundo, 1995; graphic designer: (book) Foreer Yes, 1992; designer U.S. Acad. Decathlon Trophy, 1990—; represented in permanent collection Studio 218, El Segundo, also corp. and pvt. collections. Recipient purchase prize Los Angeles County Art Exhbn., 1976, 3d place for painting Pasadena Arts Coun., 1976. Home: 3603 Hidden Ln Apt 318 Palos Verdes CA 90274 Office: TRW Inc One Space Pk Redondo Beach CA 90278

DOW, LESLIE WRIGHT, communications company executive, photographer, writer; b. N.Y.C., Apr. 28, 1938; d. Charles Leslie Kerr and Margaret Scott (MacArthur) Wright; m. William Arthur Dow, 1987; 1 child, John M. Haywood. AA, Colby-Sawyer Coll., 1957; cert., Katharine Gibbs Sch., 1958. Prodn. asst. Time Inc., N.Y.C., 1958-60; exec. asst. Jefferson-Standard Broadcasting Co., Charlotte, N.C., 1960-68, G.B. Wilkins Inc., Charlotte, 1981-82; pres., pub. relations cons. Wright Comm., Inc., Charlotte, 1982—. Contbr. photography to mags. and profl. jours.; contbr. articles to mags. Bd. dirs. Charlotte Symphony Women's Assn., 1964-71, Charlotte Symphony Orch., 1965; mem. Aux. of the Mint Mus., Charlotte, 1965—. Mem. NAFE, Am. Soc. Interior Designers (dir. pub. rels. Carolinas chpt. 1984-88), Am. Bus. Women's Assn., Am. Soc. Mag. Photographers, Profl. Photographers N.C., Profl. Photographers Am. Home and Office: 3721 Pelham Ln Charlotte NC 28211-3723

DOW, MARY ALEXIS, auditor; b. South Amboy, N.J., Feb. 19, 1949; d. Alexander and Elizabeth Anne (Reilly) Pawlowski; m. Russell Alfred Dow, June 19, 1971. BS with honors, U. R.I., 1971. CPA, Oreg. Staff acct. Deloitte & Touche, Boston, 1971-74; sr. acct. Price Waterhouse, Portland, Oreg., 1974-77, mgr., 1977-81, sr. mgr., 1981-84; CFO Copeland Lumber Yards Inc., Portland, 1984-86; ind. cons. in field, 1986-94; elected auditor Metro, Portland, 1995—; bd. dirs. Longview Fibre Co. Bd. dirs., past treas. Oreg. Mus. Sci. and Industry; past chmn. bd., mem. exec. com. Oreg. Trails chpt. N.W. Regional Blood Svcs. ARC. Mem. AICPA, Am. Woman's Soc. CPAs, Oreg. Soc. CPAs (bd. dirs. edn. found.), Fin. Execs. Inst. (nat. bd. dirs., past pres. Portland chpt.). Roman Catholic. Clubs: City (bd. govs.), Multnomah Athletic. Contbr. articles to profl. publs. Office: Office of Auditor Metro 600 NE Grand Ave Portland OR 97232-2736

DOWBEN, CARLA LURIE, lawyer, educator; b. Chgo., Jan. 22, 1932; d. Harold H. and Gertrude (Geitner) Lurie; m. Robert Dowben, June 20, 1950; children: Peter Arnold, Jonathan Stuart, Susan Laurie. AB, U. Chgo., 1950; JD, Temple U., 1955; cert., Brandeis U., 1968. Bar: Ill. 1957, Mass. 1963, Tex. 1974, U.S. Supreme Ct., 1974. Assoc. Conrad and Verges, Chgo., 1957-62; exec. officer MIT, Cambridge, Mass., 1963-64; legal planner, Mass. Health Planning Project, Boston, 1964-69; assoc. prof. Life Scis. Inst., Brown U., Providence, 1970-72; asst. prof. health law U. Tex. Health Sci. Ctr., Dallas, 1973-78, assoc. prof., 1978-93; ptnr. Choate & Lilly, Dallas, 1989-92; head health law section Looper, Reed, Mark and McGraw, 1992—; adj. assoc. prof. health law U. Tex., 1993-95; cons. to bd. dirs. Mental Health Assn., 1958-86, Ft. Worth Assn. Retarded Citizens, 1980-90, Advocacy, Inc., 1981-85; dir. Nova Health Systems, 1975—. Contbr. articles to profl. jours.; active in drafting health and mental health legis., agy. regulations in several states and local govts. Mem. vis. com. sch. law Temple U., 1992—. Mem. ABA, Tex. Bar Assn., Dallas Bar Assn., Nat. Health Lawyers Assn., Hastings Inst. Ethics, Tex. Family Planning Assn. Soc. of Friends. Office: Looper Reed Mark & McGraw 1601 Elm St 4100 Thanksgiving Tower Dallas TX 75201

DOWD, FRANCES CONNELLY, librarian; b. Newburyport, Mass., Dec. 9, 1918; d. Martin Francis and Nelle Magdalen (Quinn) Connelly; m. James Reynolds Dowd, June 7, 1941 (dec. June 1944); children: James Reynolds Jr., Thomas Henry III. AB, Wellesley Coll., 1941; MLS, Columbia U., 1955. Cataloger Phillips Acad. Libr., Andover, Mass., 1955-57; asst. libr. Wheelock Coll. Libr., Boston, 1957-59; head of circulation U. R.I., Kingston, 1959-62; head libr. Ins. Libr., Boston, 1962-66; head bus. & sci. dept. Providence (R.I.) Pub. Libr., 1966-70; reference libr. Boston U. Libr., 1970-74; head libr. Mass. Horticulture Soc., Boston, 1974-79; reference libr. Haverhill (Mass.) Pub. Libr., 1979-89, Endicott Coll. Libr., Beverly, Mass., 1989—. Editor: Whittier, 1992. pres. Whittier Home Assn., Amesbury, Mass., 1989—; treas. Macy-Colby House, 1979; sec. Amesbury Carriage Mus., Amesbury, 1982—; reunion chmn. Wellesley Coll., 1971, 86. Mem. ALA, Abenaqui Country Club, Wellesley Coll. Club. Republican. Home: 3 Hillside Ave Amesbury MA 01913-2213

DOWD, JANICE LEE, foreign language educator; b. N.Y.C., Jan. 6, 1948; d. Edward H. and Mary A. (Vanek) D. BA, Marietta (Ohio) Coll., 1969; MA, Columbia U., 1971, MEd, 1979, EdD, 1984. Cons. tchr. Teaneck (N.J.) Bd. Edn., 1970—; adj. asst. prof. Queens Coll., CUNY, 1984-94, Columbia U., N.Y.C., spring 1988, 93—; asst. prof. MA TESOL program in China, Changsha, 1986, Shanghai, 1987; SAT program adminstr. Teaneck H.S., 1978-83, yearbook sponsor, 1975-79, newspaper sponsor, 1984-92, co-chair Global/Multicultural Mgmt. Team, 1992-95. Contbr. articles to profl. jours. Mem. program com. PEO, Teaneck, 1966—. Fellow Rockefeller Found., 1988. Mem. Am. Assn. Tchrs. of French, Tchrs. English to Speakers Other Langs., N.Y. State Tchrs. English to Speakers Other Langs., N.J. Tchrs. English to Speakers Other Langs., Am. Assn. Applied Linguists, Am. Coun. Tchrs. Fgn. Langs., Fgn. Lang. Educators N.J., Second Lang. Acquisition Circle N.Y., Nat. Assn. of Dept. Heads and Suprs. of Fgn. Langs. Home: 56 Boulevard New Milford NJ 07646-1602 Office: Teaneck High Sch 100 Elizabeth Ave Teaneck NJ 07666-4713

DOWD, KIM STEPHANIE, secondary education educator; b. Boston, July 5, 1969; d. Paul Ollenborger and Diane Marie (Roia) McKenney; m. Michael Andrew Dowd, Jan. 16, 1993. BA in English, Fitchburg State Coll., 1992. Cert. tchr., Mass. English tchr. Assabet Valley H.S., Marlborough, Mass., 1992-93, Keene (N.H.) H.S., 1993—; mem. English curriculum com. Keene H.S., 1993—, co-advisor Yearbook and Video Club, 1994—. Roman Catholic. Office: Keene HS 43 Arch St Keene NH 03431

DOWD, MAUREEN, columnist; b. Washington, 1952. Grad., Catholic U., 1972. Froml editl. asst. to feature writer The Washington Star, 1973-81; from corr. to writer Time mag., 1981-83; metro reporter N.Y. Times, 1983-86, D.C. reporter, 1986-95, opinion-editl. columnist, 1995—. Office: NY Times 229 W 43rd St New York NY 10036-3913*

DOWDY, DOROTHY WILLIAMS, political science educator; b. Limon, Colo., June 11, 1939; d. Thomas Edwin and Rachel Mae (Henry) Williams; m. Thomas William Dowdy, Feb. 28, 1963; children: Jessica, Laura, Thomas. AA, George Washington U., 1958; BA, George Washington U., 1961; MA in Polit. Sci., Tulane U., 1965. Cert. secondary educator in social studies and history, Va. Analyst CIA, Washington, 1961-62; govt. tchr. Fairfax (Va.) County Pub. Schs., 1964-69, 83-96; co-owner, mgr. Buckingham Springs Stables, Fairfax Station, Va., 1973-96; tchr. advanced placement U.S. govt. polit. and comparative politics Chantilly (Va.) H.S., 1987—; coach Nat. Acad. Decathlon, Chantilly, 1989-90, "Its Academci Team", Chantilly, 1985-96; del. Russian-Am. Joint Conf. on Edn., Moscow, 1994; presenter U.S.-Russian Educators Moscow COnf., 1994. Pres. Fairfax Lawyers Wives, 1976; co-founder Fairfax 4-H Therapeutic Riding Program, 1978; pres. Burke (Va.) Elem. Sch. PTA, 1982-84; mem. Fairfax Com. of 100, 1988-90, St. Georges United Meth. Ch., 1984-96. Named Tchr. of Yr., Chantilly High Sch., 1989, Tchr.-Leader, People to People Soviet Union Friendship Caravan, 1989; recipient Disting. Svc. award Fairfax 4-H Ext. Svc., 1988. Mem. Topical Symposia Nat. Def. U. Methodist. Office: Chantilly HS 4201 Stringfellow Rd Chantilly VA 22021-2600

DOWLING, DORIS ANDERSON, business owner, educator, consultant; b. Clover Valley, Minn., Sept. 24, 1917; d. Gustaf Axel and Amanda Sophia (Karlsson) Anderson; m. John Joseph Dowling, Jan. 8, 1943 (dec. Feb. 1953); 1 child, Mary Kathryn. Home econs. degree, U. Minn., Virginia, 1937. Fashion coord., lectr. Fair Store/Montgomery Ward, Chgo., 1939-65, Marshall Field's, Chgo., 1967-82; founder, owner Doris Anderson Sewing Schs., 1948—; cons. colls., textile industry, retail stores, 1948—; lectr. retail stores, 1954-94. Author: Simplified Systems of Sewing and Styling, 1948. Career counselor, trainer, Chgo., 1948-82. Recipient Future Farmers Am. award Duluth C. of C. Coun. Agr., 1934. Mem. Nat. Needlework Assn., Fashion Group Internat. Inc., Assn. Crafts & Creative Industries, Chgo. Apparel Ctr., Merchandise Mart. Home and Office: Doris Anderson Sewing Schs 222 E Pearson St #1108 Chicago IL 60611

DOWLING, MARY KATHLEEN, elementary education educator; b. Des Moines, July 22, 1950; d. Joseph Patrick and Sadie (Klein) D. BA in Elem. Edn., Avila Coll., 1972; MA in Reading, Clarke Coll., 1983. Joined Sisters of St. Joseph of Carondelet; cert. tchr., Ill., Mich., Mo. Tchr. St. Francis de Sales Sch., Denver, 1972-73, Holy Name Sch., St. Louis, 1975, St. Michael's Sch., Marquette, Mich., 1975-80; tchr., reading coord. Bishop Baraga Sch., Marquette, 1980-84; tchr. sci. Nativity of Our Lord Sch., Chgo., 1984-85; tchr., reading coord. St. Fidelis Sch., Chgo., 1985-90; tchr., primary coord. St. Philomena Sch., Chgo., 1990—. Donor United Blood Ctr., Chgo., 1984—; lector, eucharistic min. St. Fidelis Ch., Chgo., 1985—. Mem. Internat. Reading Assn., Nat. Cath. Edn. Assn., Ill. Reading Coun., Chgo. Area Reading Assn. Home: 2729 W Hirsch #3 Chicago IL 60622-1674 Office: Saint Philomena Sch 4131 Cortland Chicago IL 60639

DOWNEY, DEOBORAH ANN, systems specialist; b. Xenia, Ohio, July 22, 1958; d. Nathan Vernon and Patricia Jaunita (Ward) D. Assoc. in Applied Sci., Sinclair C.C., 1981, student, 1986-91; BA, Capital U., 1994. Jr. programmer, project mgr. Cole-Layer-Trumble Co., Dayton, Ohio, 1981-82; sr. programmer, analyst, project leader Systems Architects Inc., Dayton, 1982-84, Systems and Applied Sci. Corp. (now Computer Sci. Corp.), Dayton, 1984; analyst Unisys, Dayton, 1984-87; systems programmer Computer Sci. Corp., Fairborn, Ohio, 1987—; cons. computer software M&S Garage/Body Shop, Beavercreek, Ohio, 1986-87. Mem. NAFE, Am. Motorcyclist Assn., Sinclair C. C. Alumni Assn., Cherokee Nation Okla., Cherokee Nat. Hist. Soc. Democrat. Mem. United Ch. of Christ.

DOWNEY, JOHANNA ANASTASIA, elementary and primary education educator; b. Pitts., Nov. 26, 1958; d. Michael and Marie Amalia (Wanitschka) Labant; m. Michael Dean Downey, Aug. 26, 1989. BA in French, Duquesne U., 1980; cert. in elem. and primary edn., Sierra Nevada Coll., 1994. Cert. tchr. elem. and primary edn., Nev., Calif. Sous chef Hemingway's Cafe, Pitts., 1982-87; tchr., facilitator Carnegie Mus. Natural History, Pitts., 1984-87; instr., tchr. Sylvan Learning Ctrs., Carson City, Nev., 1994—; tchr. primary and elem. edn. Carson City Sch. Dist., 1994—; kindergarten tchr. St. Teresa Sch., Carson City, 1995—; substitute tchr. K-12 Carson City Sch. Dist., 1988-94; sole instr. The Picture Lady Program, Carson City, 1988—. Prodr., dir. Carson Access TV; actor Proscenium Players, Inc. Arts in the Comty. grantee Sierra Arts Found., 1991-92, 92-93. Mem. AAUW (v.p. Capital br. 1993-95), ASCD, Internat. Reading Assn. (Carson City br. 1993-94), Phi Sigma Iota. Republican. Methodist. Office: St Teresa Sch 567 S Richmond Ave Carson City NV 89703

DOWNEY, SCHEHERAZADE SHULA, academic administrator; b. Heidelberg, Germany, Aug. 19, 1952; came to U.S., 1954; d. Howard William and Dorothy Elizabeth (Mulliken) Rossow; m. John Harold Shula, Jan. 15, 1971 (div. Jan. 1976); m. Michael John Downey, July 29, 1989; 1 child, Joshua John. AA, Morgan C.C., 1979; BA magna cum laude, U. Denver, 1981, postgrad., 1988-90, 95-97. Libr. asst. Morgan C.C., Ft. Morgan, Colo., 1977-79; rsch. asst. dept. anthropology U. Denver, 1979-80, project coord. dept. anthropology, 1980-81, graduation evaluator registrar, 1981-85, functional coord. registration, 1985-89, dir. univ. registrations, 1989—; advisor, counselor U. Denver, 1986-92. Contbr. poetry to anthols. Advocate hotline Rape Awareness/Assistance Program, Denver, 1992-94; advisor Rape Awareness Counseling Edn., U. Dancer, 1991-93, S.P.E.A.K., 1993-95. Mem. Am. Assn. Collegiate Registrars and Admissions Officers (Best State Regional Profl. Activity award 1991), Colo. Collegiate Registrars Assn., Colo. Orgn. for Victims Assistance, Rocky Mountain Assn. Collegiate Registrars and Admissions Officers (com. mem. 1991—, Best State award 1991), Acad. Mgmt. Inst. (nominee Oustanding Svc. award 1996), Com. for Women on Campus (chair 1992—), Phi Beta Kappa (membership com. 1992—).

DOWNING, DANIELLE SANTANDER, brokerage house executive; b. N.Y.C., Sept. 17, 1964; d. Vincent and Pilar (Santander) D. Student, Taiwan Nat. U., Taiwan, 1984-85; BA, Princeton U., 1987; MBA, The Warton Sch., Phila., 1992; MA, The Lauder Inst., Phila., 1992. Terr. asst. Mfrs. Hanover, N.Y.C., 1987-88; dir. and advisor to bd. dir. Moscow Commodity Exchange, Moscow, Russia, 1990-91; pres. MOSGRAIN, Moscow, Russia, 1991; dir. Kouri Capital Group, Greenwich, Conn., 1992; ind. cons. KPMG, Moscow, Russia, 1993; dir. C.A. & Co. Russian Brokerage House, Moscow, Russia, 1994-95; mng. dir. Alliance-Menatep, Moscow, 1995—. Author: (with others) Guide to World Equity Markets: Chapter on Russia, 1991, 92, 93, 94. Princeton U. Rsch. grantee 1986; recipient Chinese Speech Competition prize Taiwan Rotary Club 1986. Home: 1060 Park Ave Apt 2E New York NY 10128-1033 Office: Alliance-Menatep, Kolpachny Peieillok No 6, 101000 Moscow Russia

DOWNING, HOLLY, artist, educator; b. San Francisco, Dec. 9, 1948; d. William and Lorraine (Chase) Downing; m. Michael John Zander, Mar. 12, 1977; children: Jessica Selene, Robin Peter. BA in Fine Art with honors, U. Calif., Santa Cruz, 1972; MFA, Goddard Coll., 1980. Lectr. art U. Calif., Santa Cruz, 1973, 81, 83; instr. art Haywards Heath Adult Edn., Eng., 1978-80; instr. printmaking Brighton (Eng.) Poly., 1978-80; lectr. art deYoung Mus. Art Sch., San Francisco, 1981-82, San Francisco State U., 1981-82; adj. faculty art Santa Rosa (Calif.) Jr. Coll., 1983—; hon. sec. The Printmakers Coun., London, 1978-79; exhbns. com. Calif. Mus. Art, Santa Rosa, 1994-95. Contbr.: (book) The Mezzotint: History and Technique, 1990; solo exhbns. include Craven Coll., Yorkshire, Eng., 1977, AIR Gallery, London, 1977, Connaught Gallery, Cranleigh, Surrey, Eng., 1978, Richard Demarco Gallery, Edinburgh, Scotland, 1978, S.E. Arts Traveling Exhbn., Eng., 1980, Luz Gallery, Manila, Philippines, 1980, Annex Galleries, Santa Rosa, 1984, Allport Gallery, San Francisco, 1986, Citadel Print Ctr., San Jose, 1989, Ebert Gallery, San Francisco, 1992, 93, On The Wall Gallery, Medford, Oreg., 1995; group shows include Allport Assocs. Gallery, San Francisco, 1985, L.A. Mcpl. Art Gallery, 1986, Sonoma State U. Gallery, Rohnert Park, Calif., 1987, World Print Coun., San Francisco, 1987, The Eloise Pickard Smith Gallery, Santa Cruz, 1989, Del. Ctr. for Contemporary Arts, Wilmington, 1990, Sylvan Cole Gallery, N.Y.C., 1990, Ebert Gallery, 1992, 93, Stanford U. Mus. Art, 1992, Claudia Chapline Gallery, Stinson Beach, Calif., 1993, Calif. Mus. Art, Santa Rosa, 1993, 94, Bradley U., Peoria, Ill., 1994, Patricia Stewart Gallery, Napa, Calif., 1994; works in pub. collections: Victoria and Albert Mus., London, U. Reading, Eng., U. Calif., Santa Cruz, U. Wash., Seattle, U. Calif., Santa Barbara, Stanford Mus. Art, Space Gallery, Seoul, Korea, Selkapet Kunst pa Arbeidsplassen, Norway, Scottish Nat. Gallery of Art, Edinburgh, Rheodyne, Cotati, Calif., Portland Art Mus., Luz Gallery, Manila, Dundee (Scotland) Art Gallery, City of Palo Alto, Calif., Ashmolean Mus., Oxford, Eng., others. Recipient Greenshields Found. award, Can., 1976-77, Intaglio prize Barcham Green Printmaking Competition Eng., Charles Brand Press prize The Print Club 59th competition, Phila., 1983, Phelan Art award for printmaking, 1983, Jacqueline and Jay Zemel Patron award Phila. Print Club 63d competition, 1987; Nat. Endowment for Arts fellow, 1975-76; S.E. Arts Assn. grantee, 1978. Home: 5929 Fredricks Rd Sebastopol CA 95472

DOWNING, JOAN FORMAN, editor; b. Mpls., Nov. 16, 1934; d. W. Chandler and Marie A. (Forster) Forman; children: Timothy Alan, Julie Marie Downing Giesen, Christopher Alan. BA, U. Wis., 1956. Editorial asst. Sci. Research Assocs., Chgo., 1960-61; asst. editor Sci. Research Assocs., 1961-63, Childrens Press, Chgo., 1963-66; assoc. editor Childrens Press, 1966-68, mng. editor, 1968-78, editor-in-chief, 1978-81, sr. editor, 1981-95; propr. Downing Pub. Svcs., Evanston, Ill., 1995—; dir. Chgo. Book Clinic, 1973-75, publicity chmn., 1973-74. Author: (with Eugene Baker) Workers Long Ago, 1968, Baseball Is Our Game, 1982, Junior CB Picture Dictionary, 1978; project editor: 15 vol. Young People's Story of Our Heritage, 1966 (Graphic Arts Council of Chgo. award), 20 vol. People of Destiny (Chgo. Book Clinic award 1967-68), 20 vol. Enchantment of South and Central America, 1968-70, 36 vol. Open Door Books, 1968, 42 vol. Enchantment of Africa, 1972-78, Hobbies for Everyone: Collecting Toy Trains, 1979 (Graphic Arts award Printing Industries Am.), (multi-vol.) World at War, 1980-87, (52 vol.) America the Beautiful, 1987-91, (52 vol.) From Sea to Shining Sea, 1991-95, (multi-vol.) Cities of the World, 1995—. Election judge, Cook County (Ill.), 1974—. Mem. Authors Guild, Authors League Am., Alpha Phi. Democrat. Home and Office: 2414 Brown Ave Evanston IL 60201-2526

DOWNING, JOANN ARLOWYN, non-profit association administrator; b. Detroit, Nov. 7, 1955; d. Kenneth Dale and Arlowyn Mary (Natche) D. BS with honors, Mich. State U., 1978. Program dir. level 1 YWCA of Metro Detroit, 1978, program dir. level 2, 1979; asst. camp dir. Fair Winds Girl Scout Coun., Flint, Mich., 1980, asst. camp dir. older girl program specialist, 1981-84, dir. The Timbers, 1985-94, dir. outdoor program and properties, 1995—. Prodr. radio show Sta. WFBE-FM, Flint, 1985—, Sta. WCBN-FM, Ann Arbor, Mich., 1994—. Mem. affirmative action leadership coun. Mich. Ho. of Reps., Lansing, 1995; vol. fundraiser Lana Pollack Campaign for U.S. Senate, Ann Arbor, 1994; bd. dirs. Washtenaw Rainbow Action Project, Ann Arbor, 1995; instr., instr. trainer ARC, 1975—. Named one of Outstanding Young Women Am., 1987. Mem. Am. Camping Assn. (sec. Mich. sect. 1986—, nominating com. 1983-84, v.p. for devel. com. 1984-85), NOW (sec. 1982-84, v.p. Flint chpt. 1991—), Kiwanis.

DOWNING, MARGARET MARY, newspaper editor; b. Altoona, Pa., June 3, 1952; d. Irvine William and Iva Ann (Regan) D.; m. Gary Beaver; children: Ian Downing-Beaver, Timothy Downing-Beaver, Abby Downing-Beaver. BA magna cum laude, Tex. Christian U., 1974. Reporting intern Corpus Christi Caller Times, 1973; reporter, bur. chief Beaumont Enterprise & Jour. (Tex.), 1974-76, Dallas Times Herald, 1976-80; from reporter, asst. city editor, asst. bus. and met. editor to mng. editor Houston Post, 1980-93; mng. editor Jackson (Miss.) Clarion-Ledger, 1993—; jurist Pulitzer Prize Awards 1992, 93; bd. dirs. News Media Credit Union, 1993, Santa's Helpers, 1992-93; respite foster parent vol. Harris County Children's Protective Svcs., 1993; chmn. landscape com. Windsor Hills Homeowners Assn.; active PTA Madison Sta. Elem., 1993—. Mem. AP Mng. Editor's Assn. (2d v.p. La./Miss. chpt. 1995—), YMCA (runners club 1994, activities adv bd. 1994, youth soccer & t-ball coach), Soc. Profl. Journalists, Press Club of Houston (pres. 1984, bd. dirs. 1982-85), Quota Club (bd. mem. 1996—), Leadership Jackson. Episcopalian. Home: 114 Windsor Hills Dr Madison MS 39110-8563 Office: The Clarion Ledger 311 E Pearl St Jackson MS 39201-3407

DOWNS, FLORELLA MCINTYRE, civic worker, pilot; b. Selmer, Tenn., Sept. 19, 1921; d. Edward N. and Ella Pearle (Byrd) McIntyre; m. James Harold Downs, May 27, 1946; children: Linda Downs Ulner, William Edward, James Patrick. BA, LaVerne U., 1969. Flight instr., comml. pilot FAA, Memphis, 1945-46; pilot flight examiner CAA, 1946; owner, mgr. Basic Tutoring Svc., Ventura, Calif., 1982-86; civil air patrol pilot, 1956-57. Pres. Naval Officer's Wives, Patuxent River, Md., 1957; active charitable orgns., Md., Italy, Ventura, Calif., 1946—; vol. Children's Home Soc., Ventura and Carpenteria, Calif., 1962-70. Ferry pilot WASP, USAF, 1943-44, 1st lt. USAFR, 1952-56. Mem. AAUW (area rep. community issues VTA 1980-82), Women's Air Force Svc. Pilots, Toastmistress (pres. Ventura 1982-83). Democrat. Home: 751 Montgomery Pl Ventura CA 93004-2169

DOWNS, JUDITH ANNE, city official; b. Oil City, Pa., Dec. 28, 1954; d. James Erwin and Isabelle Rose (Lauer) Stone; children: Heather Rose Stone, Kelly Faye Downs. BA in Geography, Slippery Rock State Coll., 1977; postgrad., Clarion U., 1984. Planning/zoning adminstr. Town of Harmony Colo., 1978-80; comm. operator City of La Habra, Calif., 1982-83; cmty. planner Venango County, Franklin, Pa., 1985-88; dir. planning/cmty. devel.

City of Oil City, 1988—. Sec. Venango Mus. Art, Sci. and Industry, Oil City, 1995—; mem. Oil City Arts Coun., 1992—, Preservation and Conservation, Franklin, 1994—, Pa. Downtown Ctr., N.W. Med. Ctr. Corp., Venango Econ. Devel. Corp. Mem. Pa. Planning Assn. Republican. Roman Catholic. Home: RD 5 Box 128J Titusville PA 16354 Office: City of Oil City 21 Seneca St Oil City PA 16301

DOWNS, KATHLEEN ANNE, healthcare consultant; b. Toledo, Sept. 20, 1951; d. Keith Landis and Cecelia Josephine (Wood) Babcock; m. Michael Brian Thomas, July 17, 1971 (dec. Oct. 1973); m. David Michael Downs, Aug. 8, 1981. Student, San Diego Mesa Coll., 1968-70; BS, Union Inst., 1989. Cert. med. staff coordinator. Sec. Travelodge Internat., Inc., El Cajon, Calif., 1970-73; intermediate stenographer City of El Cajon, 1973-77; adminstrv. asst. MacLellan & Assocs., El Cajon, 1977-78; sr. sec. WESTEC Services, Inc., San Diego, 1978; adminstrv. sec. El Cajon Valley Hosp., 1978-80; asst. med. staff Grossmont Dist. Hosp., La Mesa, Calif., 1980-83, coord. med. staff, 1983-87, mgr., 1987-94; mgr. med. staff Sharp Meml. Hosp., San Diego, 1994; dir. med. staff svcs. Sharp HealthCare, San Diego, 1994-96, sr. specialist med. staff svcs., 1996—; dir. med. staff svcs. Alvarado Hosp. Med. Ctr., San Diego, 1996—; tchr. The Vogel Inst., San Diego, 1986; mem. med. staff svcs. adv. com. San Diego Cmty. Dist.; adj. faculty Union Inst., 1991—, Chemeketa C.C., 1991-95; mem. credentials verification orgn. surveyor Nat. Com. Quality Assurance, Washington, 1996—. Mem. Nat. Assn. Med. Staff Svcs. (edn. coun. 1989-93, chmn. 1991-93, bd. dirs. 1991-93, editl. bd. Over View 1993-96, lectr., spkr.), Calif. Assn. Med. Staff Svcs. (treas. San Diego chpt. 1984-86, pres. 1986-87). Office: Alvarado Hosp Med Ctr 6655 Alvarado Rd San Diego CA 92120

DOYLE, CONSTANCE TALCOTT JOHNSTON, physician, educator; b. Mansfield, Ohio, July 8, 1945; d. Frederick Lyman IV and Nancy Jean Bushnell (Johnston) Talcott; m. Alan Jerome Demsky, June 13, 1976; children: Ian Frederick Demsky, Zachary Adam Demsky. BS, Ohio U., 1967; MD, Ohio State U., 1971. Diplomate Am. Bd. Emergency Medicine. Intern Riverside Hosp., Columbus, Ohio, 1971-72; resident in internal medicine Hurley Hosp., U. Mich., Flint, 1972-74; emergency physician Oakwood Hosp., Dearborn, Mich., 1974-76, Jackson County (Mich.) Emergency Svcs., 1975-95; core faculty St. Joseph Merch Hosp./U. Mich. Emergency Residency, Ann Arbor, 1995—; attending emergency physician St. Joseph Mercy Hosp., Ann Arbor, 1995—; cons. Region II EMS, 1978-79, disaster cons., 1983-95; St. Joseph Mercy Hosp., Ann Arbor, 1995—; survival flight physician helicopter rescue svc. U. Mich., 1983-91; course dir. advanced cardiac life support and chmn. advanced life support com. W.A. Foote Meml. Hosp., Jackson, 1979-85; clin. instr. emergency svcs., dept. surgery U. Mich., 1981—; faculty combined emergency medicine residency St. Joseph Mercy Hosp.-U. Mich., Ann Arbor, 1995—; instr. EMT refresher courses, Jackson County, Jackson C.C. Contbg. author: Clinical Approach to Poisoning and Toxicology, 1983, 89, May's Textbook of Emergency Medicine, 1991, Schwartz Principles and Practice of Emergency Medicine, 1992, Reisdorff Pediatric Emergency Medicine, 1993; contbr. articles to profl. jours. Fellow Am. Coll. Emergency Physicians (pres. Mich. disaster com. 1987-88, bd. dirs. Mich. 1979-88, chmn. Mich. disaster com. 1979-85, mem. nat. disaster med. svcs. com. 1983-85, chmn. 1987-88, cons. disaster mgmt. course Fed. Emergency Mgmt. Agy. 1982, treas. 1984-85, emergency med. svcs. com. 1985, pres. 1986-87, councillor 1986-87, chair steering com. policy sect., 1994—, mem. disaster sect., 1995—), Nat. Assn. Coll. Emergency Physicians (vice chair sect. of disaster med. svcs. 1990-92, nat. disaster subcom. 1989-90, chair subsection psychol. rehab. svcs., disaster med. svcs. 1992-94, chair policy and legis. 1994—, task force on hazardous materials 1993—, steering com. sect. disaster medicine 1994—, exec. com. sect. disaster medicine 1995—, sec. sect. careers in emergency medicine); mem. ACP, Am. Med. Women's Assn., Am. Assn. Women Emergency Physicians, Mich. Assn. Emergency Med. Technicians (bd. dirs. 1979-80), Mich. State Med. Soc., Washtenaw County Med. Soc., Sierra Club. Jewish. Home: 1665 Lansdowne Rd Ann Arbor MI 48105-1052 Office: St Joseph Mercy Hosp Dept Emergency Medicine Ann Arbor MI 48109

DOYLE, GLORIA THORPE, secondary education educator; b. St. Louis, Dec. 25, 1951; d. Earlie Endris and Martha Vivian (Branch) Thorpe; m. Jerry Nelson Doyle, Jan. 19, 1978; children: Keyar Jawaan, Jemauri George. BS, Hampton Inst., 1973, MA, 1975; cert. computer programmer, N.C. Ctrl. U., 1987. Jr. high math. tchr. Hampton (Va.) City Schs., 1973-80; computer edn. specialist Durham (N.C.) City Schs., 1980-84, high sch. math tchr., 1984-93; high sch. math tchr. Durham Pub. Schs., 1993-95; tech. coord. Hillside H.S., Durham, 1995-96; vis. prof. Hampton U., 1976, 77, 78, 79; workshop leader Durham City Schs., 1980-84. Editor: (brochure) Computer Programming in Basic & Math, 1980. Mem. Nat. Coun. Tchrs. of Math., Internat. Soc. Tech. in Edn. Democrat. Mem. United Ch. of Christ. Home: 1811 Primrose Pl Durham NC 27707 Office: Hillside HS 3727 Fayetteville St Durham NC 27707

DOYLE, IRENE ELIZABETH, electronic sales executive, nurse; b. West Point, Iowa, Oct. 5, 1920; d. Joseph Deidrich and Mary Adelaide (Groene) Schulte; m. William Joseph Doyle, Feb. 3, 1956. RN, Mercy Hosp., 1941. Courier nurse Santa Fe R.R., Chgo., 1947-50; indsl. nurse Montgomery Ward, Chgo., 1950-54; rep. Hornblower & Weeks, Chgo., 1954-56; v.p. William J. Doyle Co., Chgo., 1956-80, Ormond Beach, Fla., 1980-88. Served with M.C., U.S. Army, 1942-46. Mem. Electronic Reps. Assn. Republican. Roman Catholic. Club: Oceanside Country (Ormond Beach).

DOYLE, JENNIFER, surgical educator, scholar; b. Milw., Aug. 23, 1952; d. Sylvester Edward and Ethel Anna (Axmann) D. BA, Mt. Mary Coll., 1974; MA, U. Wis., Milw., 1979; postgrad., Brown U., 1979-84. Grad. tchg. asst. U. Wis., 1977-79; fellow Brown U., Providence, 1979-80, grad. teaching asst., 1981-84; adj. instr. Bryant Coll., Smithfield, R.I., 1985; adj. instr. history R.I. Coll., Providence, 1986-90; residency coord. dept. family medicine Brown U., Providence, 1986-87, edn. coord. dept. surgery, 1987-90; assoc. surgery Harvard Med. Sch., Boston, 1990-92, lectr. in surgery, 1992—; asst. dir. surg. edn. Deaconess Hosp., Boston, 1990—. Dem. committeeman, Wauwatosa, Wis., 1976-78; mem. Big Sisters of R.I., Providence, 1980-88; co-organizer Providence Freeze Coalition, 1982. Recipient Charles Edison Meml. fellowship, 1974, Lucetta Bissell Meml. fellowship, 1978, univ. fellowship Brown U., 1979, Wayland Collegium fellowship Brown U., 1988. Mem. Am. Ednl. Rsch. Assn., Assn. Am. Med. Colls., Assn. Surg. Edn., Assn. Program Dirs. in Surgery (assoc.), Assn. of Women Surgeons (assoc.), Assn. for Study of Med. Edn. (U.K.), Generalists in Med. Edn., Am. Evaluation Assn., AAUW, Mass. Consort. on Faculty Devel. Home: 219 Willow St West Roxbury MA 02132-1326 Office: Deaconess-Harvard Surg Svc 110 Francis St Ste 3A Boston MA 02215

DOYLE, JUDITH ANN, corporate executive, psychosocial consultant; b. L.A., Aug. 18, 1943; d. Raymond Ross Manley and Sarah Virginia (Pletcher) Manley Flint; life ptnr. Shelley Ann Doyle; children: Brennan Corey, Melody Rae. BA, Calif. State U.-Long Beach, 1975, MS, 1977. Registered hypnotherapist; ordained minister Universal Life Ch. Counselor Calif. State U., Long Beach, 1976-78; case mgmt. supr. Bridge/Boys Club, Wilmington, Calif., 1978-80, ElMonte Sr. Citizens Ctr., Calif., 1979-81; dir. counseling svcs. Gay/Lesbian Community Svc. Ctr., Orange County, Calif., 1985-88; owner, therapist Judith Doyle MFCC, Long Beach, 1978-90; cons. AIDS Response Program, Garden Grove, Calif., 1985-90; med. adv. bd. AIDS Svc. Found., Costa Mesa, Calif., 1985-88; exec. dir. One in Long Beach Inc., 1988-90; exec. dir. Marisol, Inc., 1990-92; with Doyle Enterprise, 1990—; exec. dir. Laguna Shanti, 1992-93; Golden mem. Long Beach Lambda Dem. Club, 1980—; chmn. So. Calif. Women for Understanding, L.A., 1981-85; active Orange County HIV Planning Adv. Coun., 1992-93; co-chair Orange County Regional LIFE Lobby, 1993; pres., bd. dirs., founder Long Beach Lesbian and Gay Pride, Inc., 1983-88; co-chair, founder AIDS Walk Long Beach, 1988-90; apptd. mem. Calif. State Commn. Econ. Devel. Task Force, 1984-85; trustee L. Diane Anderson Meml. Trust, 1984—. Recipient Woman of Yr. award Lambda Dem. Club, 1981, Christopher Street West, 1986, Disting. Community Leadership award, 1989, Spl. Person award Press/Telegram, 1985, Myra Riddell Svc. award So. Calif. Women for Understanding, 1985, Community Mentor award Orange County Blade Mag., 1993, Community Grand Marshal award 10th Annual Long Beach Lesbian & Gay Pride Parade, 1993. Mem. NAFE, ACLU, Calif. Assn. Marriage and Family Therapists (bd. dirs. 1981-85, pres. 1985-86, named Disting. Clin. Mem. 1988), Greenpeace, Human Right Campaign, Gay and Lesbian Assn. Against Defamation (mem. human rights campaign fund), Nat. Mus. of the Am. Indian, Smithsonian Instn., People for the Am. Way, Nat. Mus. Women in the Arts (charter). Avocations: dancing, theatre, volleyball, softball. Address: 11278 Los Alamito Blvd Ste 154 Los Alamitos CA 90720-3244

DOYLE, JUDITH STOVALL, real estate executive; b. Dothan, Ala., Apr. 19, 1940; d. E.H. and Justine (Knowles) Stovall; m. John P. Doyle Jr., Aug. 22, 1964; children: John Patrick III, Michael D., Julie A. Boedicker. BS, Miss. State Coll. for Women, 1961. Tchr. math., jr. high sch., Gulfport, Miss., 1961-62; asst. dir. dept. pub. rels. SUNY-Buffalo, 1962-64; tchr. math., jr. high schs., Alexandria, Va., 1964-65, Auburn, N.Y., 1970-71; realtor, assoc. Mosher Real Estate, Auburn, 1972-80, Doyle Real Estate, 1991—; owner real estate property, apt. units, Auburn. Active, past pres. Mercy Aux., Auburn; chairperson Owasco Bd. Assessment Rev., N.Y., 1976—; v.p. Sacred Heart Parish Council, Auburn, 1985-89; bd. dirs. Unity House, Auburn, 1985-87. Democrat. Roman Catholic. Lodge: Ancient Order Hibernians (charter mem. Ladies Aux. 2).

DOYLE, NANCY CAROLYN, writer; b. Taunton, Mass., Mar. 19, 1931; d. Herbert A. and Mildred (Sylvander) D. BA, Boston U., 1954; MA, Wellesley Coll., 1956. Rsch. and tng. asst. Wellesley (Mass.) Coll., 1954-56; press dir. United Fund Greater Boston, 1957-60; writer Mental Health Materials, N.Y.C., 1960-62, Nat. League Nursing, N.Y.C., 1962-65, Am. Lung Assn., N.Y.C., 1967-86; assoc. Am. Lung Assn. Greater Norfolk, Walpole, Mass., 1986-95. Author: The Dying Person and the Family, 1975, Smoking: A Habit to be Broken, 1979, Involuntary Smoking, 1987. Pres. Friends of Taunton (Mass.) Pub. Libr., 1993-95; bd. dirs. Star Players, Taunton, 1987-92. Mem. AAUW, Phi Beta Kappa, Sigma Xi. Home: 20 Fairview Ave Taunton MA 02780

DOYLE, NANCY HAZLETT, artist; b. Wilmington, Del., July 8, 1947; d. Theodore Jay and Catherine L. (Lynch) Hazlett; m. Michael Doyle, Nov. 20, 1982 (div. 1985). BS in Art Edn., Moore Coll. of Art, 1969; MFA in Painting, Pa. State U., 1975. Tchr. Chester County Juvenile Detention Home, Embreeville, Pa., 1972-73; instr. Pa. State U., State College, 1975-77; artist Chester County Art Assn., West Chester, Pa., 1977-78. One person shows include Pattee Meml. Libr., Pa. State U., University Park, 1974, Cygnet Framing Studio, West Chester, 1986, Va. Lippincott Gallery, Phoenixville, Pa., 1992, Agapè Gallery, Malvern, Pa., 1994; exhibited in group shows Coll. Arts and Arch., Zoller Gallery, Pa. State U., University Park, 1974-75, Erie (Pa.) Art Ctr., 1975, Corcoran Gallery, Washington, 1975, Juniata Coll., Huntingdon, Pa., 1976, Daisy Jamison Soroptomist Ann. Invitational Show, West Chester, 1979-82, Yellow Springs Ann. Art Show, Chester Springs, Pa., 1986—, Chester County Art Assn. Invitational, 1986-88, Artworks Gallery, Kennett Square, Pa., 1992—, Main Line Art Ctr., Haverford, Pa., 1994, 95, Jun Gallery, Phila., 1994, Leslie Eadeh Art Gallery, Devon, Pa., 1995. Recipient grad. assistantships Pa. State U., 1973-75. Mem. Main Line Art Ctr., Artists Equity. Democrat.

DOYLE, SALLY A., controller; b. Somerville, N.J., Jan. 19, 1956; d. Edward L. and Sarah M. (Wenrich) Padrazas; married. BA in Bus., Coll. of St. Elizabeth, Convent Station, N.J., 1989. CPA, Ga.; cert. mgmt. acct. Payroll clk. Ethicon, Somerville, 1974-78, asst. supr. payroll, 1978-81, payroll supr., 1981-86; payroll supr. J & J Advanced Materials Co., New Brunswick, N.J., 1986-89; gen. acctg. supr. J & J Advanced Materials Co., New Brunswick, 1989-90; sr. acct. J & J Advanced Materials Co., Gainesville, Ga., 1990-92, plant acctg. mgr., 1992-94; regional plant controller J & J Advanced Materials Co., Benson, N.C., 1994-95; regional contr. Chicopee, Inc., Benson, 1995-96; divsn. contr. PGI Non-Wovens/Chicopee Inc., Benson, 1996—. Mem. AICPA, Inst. Mgmt. Accts. Office: Chicopee Inc PO Box 308 Benson NC 27504-0308

DRAAYER, SHARI LYNN, sociologist; b. Clorinda, Iowa, Dec. 11, 1948; d. Gerald and Barbara (McGregor) D; children (adopted): Ryan, Randy, Rodney, Gregory, Halle, Marcy, George. BA cum laude, Eastern Coll., St. Davids, Pa., 1987; MA in Sociology summa cum laude, Temple U., 1989, postgrad. Hotline counselor, trainer Aware Shelter & Emergency Counseling Ctr., Inc., Jackson, Mich., 1978-83; adminstrv. assoc. Foote Hosp., Jackson, 1982-83; counselor, night mgr. Laurel House, Montgomery County, Pa., 1984-87; teaching asst. Temple U., Phila., 1987-92; rsch. intern Women's Ctr. Montgomery County, Norristown, Pa., 1987-92; lectr. in Sociology Chestnut Hill Coll., Phila., 1988-93; intern clin. and forensic sociology Walden Counseling and Therapy Ctr., Bryn Mawr, Pa., 1989; clin. sociologist, dir. McGregor Counseling and Therapy Assocs., King of Prussia, 1981—; foster care social worker and parent trainer Luth. Children and Family Svcs., Upper Darby, Pa., 1993-95; adj. prof. Ea. Coll., Pa., 1991-92; specialized foster parent adoption and foster care agys., Utah, Mich., Pa. Mem. Am. Sociol. Assn., Sociol. Practice Assn.(mem. sociology of children sect.), Eastern Sociol. Assn. Office: Defenders Assn Phila Child Advocate Unit 70 N 17th St Philadelphia PA 19103 also: McGregor Counseling & Therapy Assocs Valley Forge Towers N Ste 642 King Of Prussia PA 19406-1145

DRABEC, EMMA ANNA, retired human services administrator; b. Castro Valley, Calif., Mar. 8, 1934; d. Otto and Margaret (Habern) Jaegel; m. Charles L. Drabec, June 15, 1952 (div. 1971); children: Terese, Jeannette, Daniel, Nicholas. Attended, Personology Coll., 1969. Med. sec. Dr. Black, Hayward, 1969-70; patient svcs. technician II Alameda County, Oakland, Calif., 1971-93; ret. Insp. Alameda County Registrar of Voters, Oakland, 1993—; v.p. First Friday Club, Our Lady of Grace Ch., 1994; vol. usher various orgns., opera, little theatre; pres. San Lorenzo Singles, 1980-82. Republican. Home: 20169 Meadowlark Dr Castro Valley CA 94546-4452

DRAFTS, NORMA SHEALY, medical foundation executive; b. Leesville, S.C., Oct. 31, 1947; d. Carl Crosson and Carrie Ruth (Koon) Shealy; m. Milford Glenn Drafts, Jan. 26, 1973; 1 child, Carl Brian. Grad. high sch., Batesburg, S.C. Saleswoman, bookkeeper Economy Furniture Co., Leesville, 1965-68; quality control Saluda (S.C.) Mills, 1968-73; computer operator Southeastern Freight, West Columbia, S.C., 1973-78; owner, mgr. Green Hill Greenhouses, West Columbia, 1978-83; office mgr. S.C. chpt. Lupus Found. Am., Inc., West Columbia, 1989-95, exec. dir., 1995—, editor newsletter, 1996—; corr. S.C. Luth. mag., 1996; sec. Nat. Vol. Health Agys., Columbia, S.C., 1995-97. Editor, author: 2,000,000 Americans Have Lupus, 1996. Vol. S.C. chpt. Lupus Found. Am., Inc., 1983-89; sec. bd. dirs. Ann. Good Health Appeal, Columbia, 1995-97. Mem. Exec. Dirs. Assn. Lupus Found. Am., S.C. Assn. Vol. Adminstrs. Lutheran. Office: Lupus Found Am Inc SC Chpt PO Box 7511 Columbia SC 29202-7511

DRAKE, ELISABETH MERTZ, chemical engineer; b. N.Y.C., Dec. 20, 1936; d. John and Ruth (Johnson) Mertz; m. Alvin William Drake, July 31, 1957 (div. 1984); 1 child, Alan Lee. S.B. in Chem. Engring., MIT, 1958, Sc.D. in Chem. Engring., 1966. Registered profl. engr., Mass. Staff engr. Arthur D. Little Inc., Cambridge, Mass., 1958-64, sr. staff, 1966-76, mgr. risk analysis, 1977-82, v.p. tech. risk mgmt., 1980-82, 86-89, cons., 1990-94; assoc. dir. new tech. MIT Energy Lab., 1990—, dir., 1994-95; lectr. U. Calif., Berkeley, 1971; vis. prof. MIT, Cambridge, 1973-74; chmn. chem. engring. dept. Northeastern U., Boston, 1982-86; corp. mgr. MIT, 1981-86; mem. tech. pipeline safety stds. com. U.S. Dept. Transp., 1980-85; mem. mng. bd. Ctr. for Chem. Process Safety, 1988-90; vice chair com. on rev. and evaluation on army chem. stockpile disposal program NRC, 1993—. Contbr. articles to profl. jours.; inventor fractionation method and apparatus, 1972. Fellow AIChE (bd. dirs. 1987-90); mem. AAAS, NAE, Am. Chem. Soc., Sigma Xi. Home: 30F Inman St Cambridge MA 02139-2411

DRAKE, GRACE L., state senator; b. New London, Conn., May 25, 1926; d. Daniel Harvey and Marion Gertrude (Wiech) Driscoll; m. William Lee Drake (dec.), June 9, 1946; children—Sandra DeNobile Drake. With Am. Photographic Corp., N.Y.C., 1944-72; senator State of Ohio, Columbus, 1984—. Mem. Carmelite Guild of Cleve., 1973—, Tech. Leadership Coun., Leadership Cleve., Cleve. Music Sch. Settlement. Recipient Outstanding Woman award Nat. Fedn. Rep. Women, 1984; named Legislator of Yr. Nat. Rep. Legis's. Assn, 1988, Public Official of Yr Ohio chpt. Nat. Assn. Social Workers, 1989, Outstanding Legislator of Yr. Ohio Speech and Hearing Assn., 1989. Roman Catholic. Avocations: bridge, golf. Office: Ohio Senate Senate Bldg Rm 221 Columbus OH 43215-4276*

DRAKE, KAREN LORRAINE, beverage company executive; b. Kansas City, Mo., Oct. 6, 1964; d. Donald Arthur and Shirley Ann (Gibson) D. BS in Bus. Adminstrn., Ctrl. Mo. State U., 1987, MBA, 1992. Key account mgr. Ralston Purina Co., St. Louis, 1987-93; category specialist James River Corp., Dallas, 1993-95; mgr. micro mktg. & retail analysis Anheuser-Busch Inc., St. Louis, 1995—. Mem. Am. Mktg. Assn., Allied Food Club, Alpha Gamma Delta. Democrat. Methodist. Office: Anheuser-Busch One Busch Pl Saint Louis MO 63118

DRAKE, MIRIAM ANNA, librarian, educator; b. Boston, Dec. 20, 1936; d. Max Frederick and Beatrice Celia (Mitnick) Engleman; m. John Warren Drake, Dec. 19, 1960 (div. Dec. 1985); 1 child, Robert Warren. BS, Simmons Coll., Boston, 1958, MLS, 1971; postgrad., Harvard U., 1959-60; LittD (hon.), Ind. U., 1994, LHD (hon.), 1994. Assoc. United Research, Cambridge, Mass., 1958-61; with mktg. services Kenyon & Eckhardt, Boston, 1963-65; cons. Boston, 1965-72; head research unit libraries Purdue U., West Lafayette, Ind., 1972-76, asst. dir. libraries, prof. library sci., 1976-84; dean, dir. libraries, prof. Ga. Inst. Tech., Atlanta, 1984—; trustee Online Computer Libr. Ctr., Inc., 1978-84, chair, 1980-83; trustee Corp. for Rsch. and Edn. Networking, 1991-94, U.S. Depository Libr. Coun., 1991-94. Author: User Fees: A Practical Perspective, 1981; co-author: (with James Matarazzo) Information for Management, 1994; mem. editl. bd. Coll. and Rsch. Librs. Jour., 1985-90, Librs. and Microcomputers Jour., 1983—, Sci. and Tech. Librs., 1989—, Database, 1989—; contbr. chpts. to books, articles to profl. jours. Recipient Alumni Achievement award Simmons Coll. Sch. Libr. and Info. Sci., 1985, Kent Meckler Media award U. Pitts., 1994. Mem. ALA (councilor at large 1985-89, Hugh Atkinson Meml. award 1992), Am. Mgmt. Assn., Am. Soc. Info. Sci., Spl. Librs. Assn. (pres.-elect 1992-93, pres. 1993-94, H.W. Wilson award 1983). Office: Ga Inst Tech Lib Info Ctr Atlanta GA 30332

DRAKE, PATRICIA EVELYN, psychologist; b. Lewiston, Maine, Feb. 9, 1946; d. Lewis and Anita (Bilodeau) D.; m. Colin Matthew Fuller, May 13, 1973 (div. Aug. 1983); children: R. Matthew, Meaghan Merry. Diploma, St. Mary's Sch. Nursing, 1967; BS, U. Nev., 1985; MA, Calif. Sch. Profl. Psychology, 1987, PhD, 1989. RN. Nurse Maine Med. Ctr., Portland, 1967-73, U. Calif. Sacramento Med. Ctr., 1973-78, Ben Taub Hosp., Houston, 1978-79; psychology intern Shasta County Mental Health Ctr., Redding, Calif., 1988-89, clin. psychologist, 1989-91, tng. dir., chief psychology, 1991—; psychologist pvt. practice, Redding, Calif., 1991—. Mem. AAUW, APA, Calif. Psychol. Assn., Shasta-Cascade Psychol. Assn., Phi Kappa Phi. Democrat. Roman Catholic. Office: Shasta County Mental Health 2640 Breslauer Way Redding CA 96001-4246

DRAKE, SARAH FRANCES ASHFORD, electronic manufacturing company executive; b. Dallas, Jan. 31, 1943; d. Roger F. and Rosa M. (Hancock) Ashford; children: Sonja Mozelle Ayers, Monica Grace Harding. Student pub. schs., Odessa, Tex. Bookkeeper 1st State Bank, Odessa, 1963-64; pres. Magnum Mfg., Inc., Austin, 1974—. Recipient Outstanding Achievement for Entrepreneurship award Univ. YWCA, Austin, 1990; named Mfr. of Yr., Austin C. of C., 1990, Employer of Yr., Goodwill Industries Cen. Tex., 1990, Nat. Employer of Yr., Goodwill Industries of Am., 1991. Mem. Leadership Austin. Baptist. Office: Magnum Mfg Inc 1915 Kramer Ln Austin TX 78758-4009

DRAKE, SYLVIE (JURRAS DRAKE), theater critic; b. Alexandria, Egypt, Dec. 18, 1930; came to U.S., 1949, naturalized, 1952; d. Robert and Simonette (Barda) Franco; m. Kenneth K. Drake, Apr. 29, 1952 (div. Dec. 1972); children—Jessica, Robert I.; m. Ty Jurras, June 16, 1973. M. Theater Arts, Pasadena Playhouse, 1969. Free-lance TV writer, 1962-68; theater critic Canyon Crier, L.A., 1968-72; theater critic, columnist L.A. Times, 1971-91, theater critic, 1991-93, theatre critc emeritus, 1993—; lit. dir. Denver Ctr. Theatre Co., 1985; free lance travel writer, book reviewer, pres. L.A. Drama Critics Circle, 1979-81; mem. Pulitzer Prize Drama Jury, 1994; adv. bd. Nat. Arts Journalism Program. Dir. media rels. and publs. Denver Ctr. for the Performing Arts, 1994—; artistic assoc. for spl. projects Denver Ctr. Theatre Co., 1994—. Mem. Am. Theater Critics Assn. Office: Denver Ctr for Performing Arts 1245 Champa St Denver CO 80204-2104

DRANT, SANDRA ELIZABETH, court reporter, educator; b. L.A., July 18, 1939; d. Archie Delbert and Clara Mae (Sether) DeLane; m. Richard David Drant, Sept. 5, 1959 (div. 1965), m. Feb. 3, 1966; children: Stacey Allada, Ryan David. AA, Cypress Coll., 1989; BA in English, Chapman U., 1992; MA in Edn., Pepperdine U., 1995. Cert. shorthand reporter, cert. reporting instr. Freelance reporter Long Beach, Calif., 1960-65; state hearing reporter Calif. Unemployment Ins. Appeals Bd., Long Beach, Workers' Compensation Appeals Bd., Bell Gardens, 1972-82; cert. reporting instr. Cerritos Coll., Norwalk, Calif., 1990—; faculty advisor Ct. Reporting Club, 1995-96. Vol. chaperone Mammoth Mountain Ski Edn. Found., Mammoth Lakes, Calif., 1982-84; co-chair Grad-Night com. Mammoth High Sch., Mammoth Lakes, 1988; vol. archaeologist Cypress Coll., 1989—. Recipient Cert. of Recognition Calif. Legis. Assembly, 1993; named Parent of Yr., Mammoth Mountain Ski Edn. Found., 1983-84, Outstanding Curricular Advisor, 1995-96. Mem. AAUW, Nat. Ct. Reporters Assn., Calif. Ct. Reporters Assn., Faculty Assn. Calif. C.C.s, Pacific Coast Archaeol. Soc., Stanford Univ. Mothers Club (vol. contbr. 1988—). Home: 4109 Avenida Sevilla Cypress CA 90630-3413 Office: Cerritos Coll 11110 Alondra Blvd Norwalk CA 90650-6203

DRANTZ, VERONICA ELLEN, science educator and consultant; b. Chgo., Sept. 5, 1943; d. Albert William and Veronica Grace (Crowe) D. BS with high honors, U. Ill., Urbana, 1965, MS, 1969; PhD, De Paul U., Chgo., 1987. Biol. sci. forensic analytical chemist Chgo. Police Dept., Chgo., 1970-72, asst. head forensic analytical chemist, 1972-74; instr. Ravenswood Hosp. Sch. Anesthesia, Chgo., 1975—; instr. East-West Univ., Chgo., 1982-84, dir. biol. and phys. sciences, 1984—, asst. prof., 1987-88, assoc. prof., 1988-91, prof., 1991—, dir. electroneurodiagnostic technology program, 1988—; adj. prof. in MS of nursing DePaul U., Chgo., 1989—; spkr. Ill. Assn. Nurse Anesthetists, 1978-80, Ill. Soc. Electroneurodiagnostic Tech., 1986—, Am. Soc. Electroneurodiagnostic Tech., 1994—; sci. cons., spkr. Chgo. Tchrs. Ctr., 1989; instr. Chgo. Heart Assn., 1989—. Co-author: Population Genetics A BSCS Self Instructional Prog., 1969. Recipient Rsch. assistantship NSF, U. Ill., 1965-66, Rsch. Fellowship NSF, U. Ill., 1966-70, Schmidt Acad. fellowship Schmidt Found., DePaul U., 1975-80, Cardiopulmonary Resuscitation award Chgo. Heart Assn., 1990. Mem. Phi Beta Kappa. Office: 4942 W School St Chicago IL 60641-4340

DRAPALIK, BETTY RUTH, civic worker, artist; b. Cicero, Ill., July 4, 1932; d. Henry William and Jennie Margaret (Robbins) Degen; m. Joseph James Drapalik, Oct. 30, 1951; children: Betty Jennifer Drapalik Coryell, Joseph Henry. Grad. high sch., Cicero. Sec., clk. Gt. Lakes (Ill.) Naval Base, until 1982; sect. to asst. dir. Arden Shore Boys' Home, Lake Bluff, Ill., 1984-87. Group exhbns. include Anderson Art Ctr., Kenosha, Wis., 1994-96, Women's Works, Old Courthouse Art Ctr., Woodstock, Ill., 1994, 95, Cmty. Gallery of Art, Coll. of Lake County, Grayslake, Ill., 1993, 94, 96, David Adler Cultural Ctr., Libertyville, Ill., 1994, Layson Gallery, Waukegan, Ill., 1993, Hardy Gallery, Ephraim, Wis., 1996, Lake County Art League Fine Arts Festival at North Point Marina, Winthrop Harbor, Ill., 1996 (1st pl. watercolor 1996); two-person shows include Jack Benny Ctr. for the Arts, Waukegan, 1996; one-woman shows include Jack Benny Ctr. for the Arts, 1995. Former leader and mem. pub. rels. com. Girl Scouts U.S.A. Recipient purchase award Coll. of Lake County, Grayslake, Ill., 1994, numerous other courtesy awards. Mem. Lake County Art League (resource person, pres., various bd. positions), Lakes Region Watercolor Guild, Midwest Watercolor Soc., Deerpath Art League, Red River Watercolor Soc., Bloomin' Artists. Evangelical. Home and Studio: 2018 Grove Ave Waukegan IL 60085

DRAPER, MARY ELLEN LYTTON, writer; b. Staunton, Va., Nov. 30, 1940; m. David W. Draper, June 16, 1962; children: David W. Jr., Darryl L. BA, Coll. of William and Mary, Williamsburg, Va., 1962; MALS, Georgetown U., 1988, postgrad., 1989-91. Freelance writer; owner From the Heart, Stuarts Draft & Culpeper, Va., 1995—; editor-in-chief Colonial Echo, Coll. William and Mary. Mem. NAFE, AAUW, Am. Orchid Soc., Nat. Capital Orchid Soc., Hist. Staunton Found., Nat. Geographic Soc., Washington Opera Guild, Tamarack Civic Assn., Sierra Club, World Wildlife

Fund, Nat. Audubon Soc., Soc. of the Alumni Coll. William and Mary (Met. Washington area), Pi Delta Epsilon, Chi Delta Phi, Psi Chi. Baptist. Home and Office: 1602 Northcrest Dr Silver Spring MD 20904-1459 Home: 407 Alleghany Ave Staunton VA 24401

DRAUGHON, DEBORAH, writer; b. Atlanta, Apr. 23, 1949; d. Kerney Lee and Doris Aline (Snyder) Draughon; m. George Douglas Hosea, 1964 (div. 1981); children: Michael Douglas, David George; m. Marvin Charles Hirsh, June 21, 1984 (div. 1996). AA in Bus. Adminstrn., Gainesville Coll., 1988; BA in Internat. Affairs cum laude, Kennesaw State Coll., 1991. Free-lance writer, 1991—. Mem. Concerned Women for Am., Washington, 1991; instr. Am. Red Cross, Atlanta, 1991. Mem. Internat. Club, Blue Key, Golden Key. Republican. Home: 5180 Arbor View Way Sugar Hill GA 30518-6958

DRAY, DIANE, elementary education educator; b. Bluffton, Ohio; d. Charles Alex and Ola Ruth (Marshall) Conrad; widowed Jan. 1975. BS, Bowling Green (Ohio) State, 1969; MA, Ea. Mich., Ypsilanti, 1978. Tchr. Mich. Ctr. Sch., Mich., 1969-75, tchg. prin., 1976-80, tchr., 1981-84, prin., 1984—. mem. adv. bd. PTA, Michigan Ctr., 1984-96; mem. festival bd. Storyfest, Jackson, Mich., 1987-94; v.p. Rotary, Michigan Ctr., 1995, pres. 1996. Recipient Woman of the Yr. Am. Bus. Women Assn., 1990-91. Mem. Mich. Elem. Mid. Sch. Prins. Assn. (mem. curriculum coun. 1991, Elem. Prin. of the Yr. award 1989), Rotary Club (pres. Mich. Ctr.- East chpt. 1996), Delta Kappa Gamma. Methodist. Home: 388 Richard Spring Arbor MI 49283

DRAZIN, LISA, real estate and corporate investment banker, financial consultant; b. Washington, Nov. 26, 1953; d. Sidney and Bernice Ann (Jeweler) D. A.B. with honors, Wellesley Coll., 1976; M.B.A., George Washington U., 1980. Chartered Financial Analyst. Securities analyst Geico, Inc., Chevy Chase, Md., 1982; mng. prin. Jefferson Securities Ltd., Bethesda, Md., 1983; chmn., chief exec. officer Drazin & Co., Inc., Bethesda, 1983-89, Drazin Properties, Inc., Bethesda, 1985-89, Drazin Securities, Inc., Bethesda, 1985-88; chmn., chief exec. officer Woodmont Asset Mgmt., Inc., 1989—; affiliate Montgomery County Bd. Realtors; real estate investment banker Restructuring Fed. Deposit Ins. Corp. Founder, Ivy Connection, Washington, 1982; bd. dirs. Friends of Tel Aviv U., active planning com. Jewish Nat. Fund. Mem. Nat. Trust for Historic Preservation, UJA Fedn. of Greater Washington (young leadership divsn., Ruth Heritage Forum), Am. Friends Hebrew U., Nat. Kidney Found. Fellow Wexner Heritage Found., Friends for Life Benefit, Whitman Walker Clinic, Assn. for Investment Mgmt. and Rsch.; mem. Nat. Assn. Realtors, Comml. Investment Real Estate Council, Realtors Nat. Mktg. Inst., Wash. Soc. Investment Analysts, Inc., Beta Gamma Sigma. Club: Wellesley (interns coordinator, recent grads. rep. 1981-84) (Washington), Ben Gurion. Office: Woodmont Asset Mgmt Inc 4600 E West Hwy Ste 300 Bethesda MD 20814-3415

DREES, ELAINE HNATH, artist and educator; b. Orange, N.J., Aug. 20, 1929; d. John Anthony and Helen Louise (Godlesky) Hnath; m. Thomas Clayton Drees, Feb. 9, 1952; children: Danette, Clayton, Barry, Nancy. A.Comml. Art, Parsons Sch. Design, N.Y.C. Colorist and designer Hesse Wallpaper, N.Y.C., 1950-51; designer Lanz Wallpaper, N.Y.C., 1951-52; gallery asst. Longpre Gallery, La Canada, Calif., 1976-78; pvt. art tchr. La Canada, Calif., 1985—; pres. Elly's Originals, La Canada, 1980—. One-woman shows include La Canada, Calif., 1984, Barbara's Gallery, Agoura, Calif., 1989, Pasadena Livery Gallery, 1996; group shows include Hasenbein Gallery, Glendale, Calif., 1978, White's Gallery, Montrose, Calif., 1980, Graphic Showcase Gallery, Pas, Calif., 1985, Artistic Endeavors Gallery, Simi Valley, Calif., 1987, Mission West Gallery, South Pasadena, Calif., 1991; commns. include paintings for Alpha Therapeutic, Pasadena, 1980, Shannon Interiors, Pasadena, 1988-92; contbr. reproductions to Cal. Art Rev. 1989. Recipient Cert. of Honor, Centre Internat. D'Art Contemporain, Paris, 1984. Mem. Verdugo Hills Art Assn. (awards 1988-94). Republican. Roman Catholic. Home and Studio: 784 Saint Katherine Dr La Canada Flintridge CA 91011

DREHER, NANCY C., federal judge; b. 1942. BA, U. Wis., 1964, JD, 1967. Bar: Minn. 1967, U.S. Dist. Ct. Minn. 1969, U.S. Ct. Appeals (8th cir.) 1969, U.S. Supreme Ct. 1981. Law clk. to chief justice Calif. Supreme Ct., San Francisco, 1967-68; assoc. Leonard, Street & Deinard, 1968-72, ptnr., 1973-88; bankruptcy judge U.S. Bankruptcy Ct., Mpls., 1988—. Recipient Pres. Award for Profl. Excellence, Minn. State Bar Assn., 1985. Office: US Bankruptcy Ct Towle Bldg 330 2nd Ave S Ste 600 Minneapolis MN 55401-2225*

DREHOFF, DIANE WYBLE, electrical engineer, marketing manager; b. Amarillo, Tex., Oct. 11, 1950; d. James Stanley and Barbara Luella (Park) Wyble; m. John James Drehoff III, June 25, 1977; children: John, Brian, David. BSEE, Stanford U., 1972. Mktg. rep. Westinghouse, Jefferson City, Mo., 1972-74; sales engr. Westinghouse, Balt., 1974-75; Congl. fellow IEEE, Washington, 1976; govt. rep. Westinghouse, Washington, 1977-80; mktg. staff mgr. Westinghouse, Phila., 1980-81, regional mktg. mgr., 1981-82; regional mktg. mgr. Westinghouse, Orlando, Fla., 1982-84, projects mgr., 1986-89, sales staff mgr., 1989-91, total quality dir., 1991-95, mktg. mgr. power generation svc., 1995—. Contbr. tech. papers to profl. jours. Sun. sch. tchr. Community Alliance Ch., Orlando, 1989-93; participant Leadership Orlando C. of C., 1991-92. Recipient IEEE Congl. fellowship IEEE, 1976, Quality Achievement award Westinghouse, 1985, Corp. Controllers award Westinghouse, 1991. Mem. IEEE (spectrum editorial bd. 1980-81, Congl. fellows selection 1983, long-range planning com. 1989), Am. Soc. for Quality Control, IEEE/Power Engring. Soc. Office: Westinghouse Electric Corp The Quadrangle 4400 N Alafaya Trl Orlando FL 32826-2398

DREILING, DENISE JANE, accountant; b. Colby, Kans., May 13, 1958; d. Charles W. Schroeder and E. Jean (Eberle) D. Student, U. Kans., 1976-78; BS in Acctg., Emporia (Kans.) State U., 1980. Acct. Omnibancorp, Denver, 1981-83; acctg. clk. in mktg. Leprino Foods Co., Denver, 1983-84, acctg. systems and procedures, 1984-87, property acctg. supr., 1987-91, constrn. cost mgr., 1991-95; fin. controller Creos Inc., Englewood, Colo., 1995—. Mem. Inst. Mgmt. Accts. Democrat. Roman Catholic. Home: 20606 E Ida Cir Aurora CO 80015 Office: Creos Inc 7388 S Revere Pky #1003 Englewood CO 80112

DREISTADT, KRISTI N., insurance salesperson; b. Greensburg, Pa., Nov. 30, 1970; d. Philip C. and Joan N. (Macko) D. BS in Bus. Adminstrn., Lewis U., Romeoville, Ill., 1994. Lic. ins. producer, Ill. Agt. Allstate, Bolingbrook, Ill., 1988-91, sales mgr., 1991-94, exec. account agt., 1994—. Charter mem. Rep. Nat. Commn. of the Am. Agenda, Washington, 1992—. Mem. NAFE. Roman Catholic. Home: 147 Queenswood Rd Bolingbrook IL 60440 Office: Allstate 281 S Schmidt Rd Bolingbrook IL 60440

DRENNEN, EILEEN MOIRA, editor; b. Suffern, N.Y., May 27, 1956; d. D.A. and M. Eileen (Connolly) D.; m. Robert Wesley Townsend, Aug. 27, 1982. AA, Dutchess C.C., N.Y., 1978; BA in English, Fla. State U., 1983. Writer Fla. Flambeau, Tallahassee, 1980-84, editor, 1984-86; features editor Marietta (Ga.) Daily Jour., 1986-87; copy editor Atlanta Jour.-Constn., Atlanta, 1987-89, asst. arts editor, 1989-90, Leisure editor, 1990-93, Weekend Preview editor, asst. features editor, 1993—. Recipient Hon. Mention award Fla. Press Club, 1982, Spotlight award Women in Comm., 1986; AAUW scholar, 1978. Home: 304 Georgia Ave SE Atlanta GA 30312-3110 Office: Atlanta Jour-Constn Arts & Entertainment Desk 72 Marietta St NW Atlanta GA 30303-2804

DRERUP, PATRICIA MUSSNUG, intensive care nurse; b. New Orleans, Jan. 22, 1952; d. Robert Sigmund and Elizabeth Laverne (Mason) Mussnug; m. Karl Anthony Drerup, Nov. 24, 1979; children: Christopher Anthony, Scott Andrew. BSN, U. Md., 1974; M in Nursing, U. Wash., 1987. CCRN; cert. ACLS and BCLS. Commd. 1st lt. U.S. Army, advanced through grades to lt. col., 1990; staff nurse ICU/CCU Ft. Campbell (Ky.) Army Cmty. Hosp., 1974-75, Letterman Army Med. Ctr., San Francisco, 1976-78; asst. head nurse ICU/orthopedics and surgery ward Wuerzburg (Germany) Army Cmty. Hosp., 1978-80; sr. clin. nurse in MICU Walter Reed Army Med. Ctr., Washington, 1981-83, MICU clin. coord., 1983-84; evening/night supr. dept. nursing Ireland Army Cmty. Hosp., Ft. Knox, Ky., 1987, 88; head nurse ICU/CCU Ireland Army Cmty. Hosp., Ft. Knox, 1987-88, nursing project officer, ICU staff nurse, QA nurse, 1988-93; ret. U.S. Army, 1993; intensive care nurse CCU, ICU Alliant Health Systems, Louisville, 1993—. Contbg. author: Cardiac Nursing, 2d edit., 1989. Decorated Good Conduct medal, 1974, Nat. Def. medals, 1974, 90, Army Commendation medals, 1978, 80, Overseas Svc. medal, 1980, Army Svc. medal, 1980, Armed Forces Res. medal, 1980, Meritorious Svc. medal, 1992. Mem. AACN. Home: 1716 Lakewood Dr Elizabethtown KY 42701-5457

DRESBACH, MARY LOUISE, state higher education administrator; b. St. Paul, Feb. 17, 1950; d. Ernest Joseph and Kathryn Marion (Lauer) Mathes; m. David Philip Dresbach, Nov. 29, 1980. BA, Coll. St. Catherine, 1972; postgrad., U. St. Thomas, 1979-80; MA, Coll. of St. Catherine, 1995. Tchr. St. Paul Pub. Schs., 1974-78; mgr. contracts, budget and human resources Minn. Higher Edn. Svcs. Office, St. Paul, 1978—; speaker Minn. Quality Conf., 1994, chair, 1996. Contbg. author Leading Edge Newsletter. Mem. AAUW, Am. Bus. Womens Assn. (sec. 1979-80), Nat. Assn. Exec. Women, Mpls. Inst. Arts, Met. Mus. Art, Dakota County Leadership Initiative, Minn. Ctr. for Women in Govt., Minn. Coun. Mgrs., Phi Beta Kappa, Pi Gamma Mu.

DRESCHER, FRAN, actress; b. Flushing, N.Y., Sept. 30, 1957; d. Mort and Sylvia D.; m. Peter Marc Jacobson, 1978. Co-creator, writer, prodr., actress in TV series The Nanny; appeared in feature films: Saturday Night Fever, American Hot Wax (Five-Minute Oscar award Esquire mag.), This Is Spinal Tap, Cadillac Man, Serious Money, Dr. Detroit, Gorp; starred in TV series Princesses, What's Alan Watching?, WIOU, (TV film) Terror in the Towers; guest appearances on TV programs Civil Wars, Alf, Night Court, Nine to Five, Fame, The Tracy Ullman Show. Office: care CBS Television City 7800 Beverly Blvd Los Angeles CA 90036*

DRESCHER, JUDITH ALTMAN, library director; b. Greensburg, Pa., July 6, 1946; d. Joseph Grier and Sarah Margaret (Hewitt) Altman; m. Robert A. Drescher, Aug. 10, 1968 (div. 1980); m. David G. Lindstrom, Jan. 10, 1981. AB, Grove City Coll., 1968; MLS, U. Pitts., 1971. Tchr. Hempfield Sch. Dist., Greensburg, 1968-71; children's libr. Cin. Pub. Libr., 1971-72; br. mgr. Cin. Pub. LIbrary, 1972-74; dir. Rolling Meadows (Ill.) Pub. Libr., 1974-79, Champaign (Ill.) Pub. Libr., 1979-85, Memphis/Shelby County Pub. Libr. and Info. Ctr., 1985—; cons. Providence Assocs., Dallas, 1986-94; Tenn. del. White House Conf. on Librs. and Info. Svcs. Task Force, 1991-92; mem. Tenn. Sec. of State's Commn. on Tech. and Resource Sharing, 1991, 93, steering com. Tenn. Info. and Infrastructure, 1994—, nat. adv. panel for assessment of role of sch. and pub. librs. U.S. Dept. Edn., 1995—. Mem. Rhodes Coll. Commn. on 21st Century, Memphis, 1986-88, presdl. adv. com. Rhodes Coll., 1992—; mem. Leadership Memphis, 1987—, selection com., 1992-96; mem. Memphis Arts Coun., 1989-94; bd. dirs. Literacy Coun., 1986-91, Memphis NCCJ, 1989-93, Memphis Grants Info. Ctr., 1992—, sec., 1993—; bd. dirs. Memphis Literacy Found., 1988-92, v.p., 1989-90; bd. dirs. Goals for Memphis, 1988-93, chair edn. com., 1989-91, chair nominating com., 1992; mem. exec. adv. bd. Children's Mus., 1988-94, exec. adv. coun. U. Memphis, 1989—; mem. allocations subcom. United Way, 1989-91, allocations com. Memphis Arts Coun., 100 for the Arts, 1989-91, Libr. Self-study Com. U. Memphis; pres. adv. coun. Lemoyne Coll. Recipient Govt. Leader award U. Ill. YWCA, 1981; Communicator of Yr. award Pub. Rels. Soc. of Am., 1992. Mem. ALA (chmn. intellectual freedom com. 1986-87, coun. 1992—), Tenn. Libr. Assn., Memphis Libr. Coun., Pub. Libr. Assn. (v.p., pres. 1994-95), Rotary (bd. dirs. 1992-94, sec. 1993-94, chair mem. devel. com. 1994-95), Beta Phi Mu. Home: 1505 Vance Ave Memphis TN 38104-3810 Office: Memphis Shelby County Pub Libr & Info Ctr 1850 Peabody Ave Memphis TN 38104-4021

DRESSEL, DIANE LISETTE, dancer, choreographer, electrical designer; b. Las Cruces, N.Mex., Apr. 24, 1955; d. Ralph William Dressel and Elizabeth Tupper (Taylor) Dressel Hoobler; m. Arthur Stephen Bazan, Mar. 24, 1977 (div. June 1982). BFA in Dance, U. N.Mex., 1990; assoc. computer aided draft and design, ITT Tech. Inst., 1992. Journeyman's lic. N.Mex. Apprentice electrician Internat. Brotherhood Elec. Workers Local 611, Albuquerque, 1979-82, journey person electrician, 1982—; relay technician apprentice Plains Electric Generation and Transmission Coop., Albuquerque, 1983-85; dancer Elizabeth Waters Dance Workshop, Inc., Albuquerque, 1985-89; dancer, choreographer Albuquerque, 1983—; dancer, choreographer Mary Wang Sch. of Dance Benefit Prodns., Grants, N.Mex., 1982—; pres. U. N.Mex. Dance Club, Albuquerque, 1988-89; dance tchr. Devel. Dance, Albuquerque, 1988-89; mem., choreographer N.Mex. Dance Coalition, Santa Fe, 1989, 91; mem., pres. student prodn. adv. bd. U. N.Mex. Choreographer, dancer Wolf Eyes, 1982, Stages, 1985, A Little Plumbing Problem, 1988, Butch Babes Don't Wear Bras, 1989, Cypher Breaks the Original Spell, 1990, When I Don't Feel Celebration, 1992, That's How I Know, 1994. Mem. Parkland Hills Neighborhood Assn., Albuquerque, 1988-92. Recipient Elizabeth Waters scholarship U. N. Mex., 1987-90, Disting. Undergrad. scholarship, 1990. Mem. NAFE, NOW, Golden Key Honor Soc., Tech. Vocat. Honor Soc., Phi Kappa Phi. Home: 500 Val Verde Dr SE Albuquerque NM 87108-3464

DRESSELHAUS, MILDRED SPIEWAK, physics and engineering educator; b. Bklyn., Nov. 11, 1930; d. Meyer and Ethel (Teichteil) Spiewak; m. Gene F. Dresselhaus, May 25, 1958; children: Marianne Dresselhaus Cooper, Carl Eric, Paul David, Eliot Michael. BA, Hunter Coll., 1951, DSc (hon.), 1982; Fulbright fellow, Cambridge (Eng.) U., 1951-52; MA, Radcliffe Coll., 1953; PhD in Physics, U. Chgo., 1958; D Engring. (hon.), Worcester Poly. Inst., 1976; DSc (hon.), Smith Coll., 1980, N.J. Inst. Tech., 1984; Doctorat Honoris Causa, U. Catholique de Louvain, 1988; DSc (hon.), Rutgers U., 1989, U. Conn., 1992, U. Mass., Boston, 1992, Princeton U., 1992; DEngring, Colo. Sch. of Mines, 1993; D (hon.), Technion, Israel Inst. Tech., Haifa, 1994; dr honoris causa, Johannes Kepler U., Linz, Austria, 1993; DSc (hon.), Harvard U., 1995. NSF postdoctoral fellow Cornell U., 1958-60; mem. staff Lincoln Lab., MIT, Lexington, 1960-67; prof. elec. engring. MIT, Cambridge, 1967—, assoc. dept. head elec. engring., 1972-74, prof. physics, 1983—, Inst. prof., 1985—, Abby Rockefeller Mauze chair, 1973-85, dir. Ctr. for Materials Sci. and Engring., 1977-83; vis. prof. dept. physics U. Campinas, Brazil, summer 1971, Technion, Israel Inst. Tech., Haifa, 1972, 90, Nihon and Aoyama Gakuin Univs., Tokyo, 1973, IVIC, Caracas, Venezuela, 1977; vis. prof. dept. elec. engring. U. Calif., Berkeley, 1985; Graffin lectr. Am. Carbon Soc., 1982; chmn. steering com. on evaluation panels Nat. Bur. Stds., 1978-83; mem. Energy Rsch. Adv. Bd., 1984-90; bd. dirs. Rogers Corp. Contbr. articles to profl. jours. Bd. govs. Argonne Nat. Lab., 1986-89; mem. governing bd NRC, 1984-87, 89-90, 92-96; trustee Calif. Inst. of Tech., 1993—. Recipient Alumnae medal Radcliffe Coll., 1973, Killian Faculty Achievement award 1986-87, Nat. Medal of Sci., 1990; named to Hunter Coll. Hall of Fame, 1972. Fellow IEEE, AAAS (bd. dirs. 1985-89, pres.-elect 1996), Am. Phys. Soc. (pres. 1984), Am. Acad. Arts and Scis.; mem. Nat. Acad. Engring. (coun. 1981-87), Soc. Women Engrs. (Achievement award 1977), Nat. Acad. Scis. (coun. 1987-90, 92-96, chmn. engring. sect. 1987-90, chmn. class III 1990-93, treas. 1992-96), Brazilian Acad. Sci. (corr.), The Engring. Acad. Japan (fgn. asoc. 1993—), Am. Philos. Soc., 1995. Office: MIT Rm 13-3005 Cambridge MA 02139

DRESSLER, BRENDA JOYCE, health educator, consultant, book and film reviewer; b. N.Y.C., Jan. 30, 1943; d. Herbert and Betty (Kirshner) Dressler; m. Irving Kaufman, Dec. 30, 1961 (div. Dec. 1979); 1 child, Joshua Ari. BA, CCNY, 1964; MA, CUNY, 1969; PhD, NYU, 1986. Cert. health edn. specialist. CHES educator sex and health N.Y.C. Bd. Edn., 1964-75, 1979—; educator sex and health Sex Info. and Edn. Coun. U.S., N.Y.C., 1985-86; adj. asst. prof. health edn. N.Y. Inst. Tech., Hofstra, 1995—, Hofstra U., 1995—; health cons., 1996—; cons. PTA and curriculum adv. com. Steinway Jr. High Sch., N.Y.C., 1985-87, Bayside High Sch., 1987-90; regional coord. and cons. on family living, Queens, 1990—; comprehensive health coord. high sch. HIV/AIDS Edn., Queens, 1991—; adj. instr. C.W. Post, N.Y. Inst. Tech., 1992—. Columnist: Women Mean Business; contbr. numerous articles to profl. jours.; curriculum writer HIV/AIDS Edn. K-6; writer instrnl. tng. design on HIV/AIDS; tchr. tng. design HIV/AIDS Edn. 7-9; health counselor, instr. Bayside H.S., HIV/AIDS team leader; adj. instr. NYIT, CW POST. Mem. Am. Bd. Sexology, Soc. Phys. and Health Edn., Kappa Delta Pi. Home and Office: 16241 Powells Cove Blvd Whitestone NY 11357-1449

DREW, DIANE DENNEY, physician assistant; b. Lewiston, Maine, Mar. 31, 1947; d. Richard Vincent and Clarice Getchell (Parsons) Denney; m. Theodore S. Drew, Dec. 26, 1967; 1 child, Jennifer Jacquelyn. Cert., Dartmouth Med. Sch., 1975. Registered physician asst., N.H. Physician asst. Family Practice, New London, N.H., 1975-84, Primary Care-Internal Medicine, New London, N.H., 1984—. Contbr. articles to profl. jours. Mem. planning bd. Town of Washington, N.H., 1981; clk. Washington (N.H.) Sch. Dist., 1981-86; capt. Washington Rescue Squad, 1981-89. Recipient Award of Appreciation, Washington Rescue Squad, 1990. Fellow Am. Acad. Physician Assts., N.H. Soc. Physician Assts.; mem. Lake Sunapee Region Vis. Nurse Assn. (profl. adv. com. 1989—, bd. trustees 1989—), NOW, U.S. Golf Assn. Democrat.

DREW, ELIZABETH, television commentator, journalist, author; b. Cin., Nov. 16, 1935; d. William J. and Estelle (Jacobs) Brenner; m. J. Patterson Drew, Apr. 11, 1964 (dec. 1970); m. David Webster, Sept. 26, 1981. B.A., Wellesley Coll., 1957; LHD, Hood Coll., 1976, Yale U., 1976, Trinity Coll., 1978, Reed Coll., 1979, Williams Coll., 1981, Georgetown U., 1981, George Washington U., 1994. Writer editor Congl. Quar., 1959-64; free lance writer, 1964-67; Washington editor Atlantic Monthly, 1967-73; host TV interview program Thirty Minutes With, 1971-73; commentator TV program Agronsky and Company, 1973—; commentator syndicated TV program Inside Washington, 1973-92; Washington corr. New Yorker Mag., 1973-92; commentator Monitor Radio, 1992—. Author: Washington Journal, 1975, American Journal, 1977, Senator, 1979, Portrait of an Election, 1981, Politics and Money, 1983, Campaign Journal, 1985, Election Journal, 1989, On the Edge: The Clinton Presidency, 1994, Showdown: The Struggle Between the Gingrich Congress and the Clinton White House, 1996; contbg. Washington Post; contbg. author various mags. and jours. Recipient award for excellence Soc. Mag. Writers, 1971, Wellesley Alumnae Achievement award, 1973, DuPont award, 1973, Mo. medal, 1979, Sidney Hillman award, 1983, Ambassador of Honor award Books Across the Sea, 1984, Literary Lion award N.Y. Pub. Library, 1985, Edward Weintal prize, 1988. Home & Office: 3000 Woodland Dr NW Washington DC 20008-3543

DREW, ELIZABETH HEINEMAN, publishing executive; b. Evanston, Ill., Aug. 26, 1940; d. Ben Harlow and Marion Elizabeth (Heineman) D. BA, U. Wis., 1961. With Doubleday & Co., Inc., N.Y.C., 1961-84, prodn. asst., 1961-63, personal asst. to editor in chief, 1963-66, adminstrv. asst. to editor in chief, 1966-69, editorial asst. to editor in chief, 1969-71, assoc. editor, 1971-74, editor, 1974-77, sr. editor, 1977-79, exec. editor, editorial dir., 1979-84; v.p., sr. editor William Morrow and Co., N.Y.C., 1984-92; v.p., pub. Lisa Drew Books/Macmillan Pub. Co., N.Y.C., 1993-94; v.p. pub. Lisa Drew Books/Charles Scribner's Sons, N.Y.C., 1994—; tchr. NYU Sch. Continuing Edn., 1981-82. Bd. dirs. Barbara Bush Found. Family Literacy, 1995—. Mem. PEN (N.Y. chpt.), Women's Media Group (treas. 1982-84, pres. 1985-86), Nat. Press Club (Washington), Assn. Am. Pubs. (internat. freedom to pub. com. 1978—, chmn. 1990-93, freedom to read com. 1988—, chmn. 1994—), Century Assn. (N.Y.), First City Club (Savannah, Ga.). Democrat. Episcopalian.

DREW, K, financial advisor, management consultant; b. Freeport, N.Y.; d. Harry P. and Kathleen (Isdal) Barton; m. Peter Pantazes; children: Karen, Donna. BA, U. Ga., 1960; postgrad., U. Ill., 1961. Dir. YWCA, Corpus Christi, Tex., 1969-72, Dwoskin Nat. Wallcovering Co., Atlanta, 1974-76; dep. asst. fin. presdl. campaign, 1976-77; dir. fin. Presdl. Inaugural, Washington, 1976; dep. adv. for small bus. SBA, Washington, 1977-80, asst. to adminstr., 1980-82; v.p. Alpha Systems, Inc., Washington and Athens, Greece, 1980-85; human resource cons. MBA Mgmt., Inc., McLean, Va., 1982-84; bus. cons. Drew Cons., McLean, 1984—; cons. assoc. Walling, June & Assocs., Old Town Alexandria, Va., 1986-89; fin. advisor The Family Extended, Washington, 1990—; bus. rep. Nikken, Inc., Wshignton, 1996, KareMor Internat., Inc., Wshignton, 1996; fin. advisor SAKA, Inc., Merrifield, Va., 1991—, Warrenton, Va., 1991-92, DeLeo and Assocs., McLean, Va., 1991-92; fin. dir. Disting. Environments, Reston, Va., 1992-94. State rep. poverty program and suicide prevention bds. Corpus Christi Bus. Coun., 1969-71; bd. dirs. YWCA, Washington, 1983-85; head speaker's bur. Fairfax Symphony, 1979-85, mem. exec. devel. com., 1979-86; mem. Mental Health Exec. Bd. Dirs., Washington, 1983-88; deacon Nat. Presbyn. Ch., Washington, 1988-90; asst. to exec. dir. T. Monk Found., Jazzs Sch., Duke U., 1987-89; event dir. Easter Seal Soc., 1990-91; mem. Youth for Tomorrow devel. com. Joe Gibbs Charities, Washington, 1990-92; presdl. campaing team captain Va. and Ga. Inaugural Com., 1993; Ga. Ball host, Washington, 1993; host Presdl. Inaugural Gala, Washingotn, 1993; In Kind Svcs. to White House Advance Office of Pres., 1993—, In Kind Svcs., 1993-95, Washington Greetings Office, 1995; bus. cons. Bethany House for Battered Women, 1994. State rep. poverty program and suicide prevention bds. Corpus Christi Bus. Coun., 1969-71; bd. dirs. YWCA, Washington, 1983-85; head speaker's bur. Fairfax Symphony, 1979-85, mem. exec. devel. com., 1979-86; mem. Mental Health Exec. Bd. dirs., Washington, 1983-88; deacon Nat. Presbyn. Ch., Washington, 1988-90; asst. to exec. dir. T. Monk Found., Jazz Sch., Duke U., 1987-89; event dir. Easter Seal Soc., 1990-91; mem. Youth for Tomorrow devel. com. Joe Gibbs Charities, Washington, 1990-92; presdl. campaign team captain Va. and Ga. Inaugural Com., 1993; Ga. Ball host, Washington, 1993; host Presdl. Inaugural Gala, Washington, 1993; In Kind Svc. to White House Advance Office of Pres., 1993—; cons. advisor Battered Spouses & Their Children, Washington, 1995—. Mem. Nat. League Am. Pen Women (v.p., pres. Washington Capital chpt. 1987-89, nat. bd. dirs. 1987-90, nat. roster chmn. 1989—), Bus. and Profl. Women Washington, Nat. Platform Assn., Alpha Gamma Delta. Office: Ste 1-121 8350 Greensboro Dr Mc Lean VA 22102

DREW, KATHERINE FISCHER, history educator; b. Houston, Sept. 24, 1923; d. Herbert Herman and Martha (Holloway) Fischer; m. Ronald Farinton Drew, July 27, 1951. BA, Rice Inst., 1944, MA, 1945; PhD, Cornell U., 1950. Asst. history Cornell U., 1948-50; instr. history Rice U., 1946-48, mem. faculty, 1950—, prof. history, 1964—, Harris Masterson, Jr. prof. history, 1983-85, Lynette S. Autrey prof. history, 1985-96, prof. emeritus, 1996—, chmn. dept. history, 1970-80; editor Rice U. (Rice U. Studies), 1967-81, acting dean humanities and social scis., 1973, acting chmn. dept. art and art history, 1996-97. Author: The Burgundian Code, 1949, Studies in Lombard Institutions, 1956, The Lombard Laws, 1973, Law and Society in Early Medieval Europe, 1988, The Laws of the Salian Franks, 1991, also articles; editor: Perspective in Medieval History, 1963, The Barbarian Invasions, 1970; mem. bd. editors Am. Hist. Assn. Guide to Hist. Lit., 1987-94; contbr.: Life and Thought in the Middle Ages, 1967. Guggenheim fellow, 1959; Fulbright scholar, 1965; NEH fellow, 1974-75. Fellow Mediaeval Acad. Am. (coun. 1974-77, 2d v.p. to pres. 1985-87, del. to Am. Coun. Learned Socs. 1977-81); mem. Am. Hist. Assn. (coun. 1983-86), Am. Soc. Legal History, So. Hist. Assn. (vice chair, chair European sect. 1986-88, exec. com. 1989-91), Phi Beta Kappa. Home: 509 Buckingham Dr Houston TX 77024-5804 Office: Rice Univ Dept History 6100 South Main Houston TX 77005-1892

DREW, NANCY MCLAURIN SHANNON, counselor, consultant; b. Meridian, Miss., Apr. 29, 1934; d Julian Caldwell and Emma Katherine (Sanders) Shannon; m. Thomas Champion III, Feb. 11, 1956; children: Thomas Champion IV, Julian C. Shannon. BA, Furman U., 1956; MEd, N.C. State U., 1968. Cert. sch. counselor; cert. supr. curriculum and instrn., N.C. Rsch. asst. N.C. State U., Raleigh, 1957-59; tchr. English Raleigh City Schs., 1959-60; dir. guidance program Millbrook Sr. High/Wake County Schs., Raleigh, 1969-77; guidance chmn. Daniels Middle Sch./Wake County Schs., Raleigh, 1977-84, guidance info. specialist, 1984-85; guidance supr. Wake County Pub. Schs., Raleigh, 1985-88; coord. model dropout prevention program Wake County Pub. Sch./State Dept. Pub. Inst., Raleigh, 1985-88; counseling chmn. Garner Middle Sch., Raleigh, 1988-96; presenter, cons. 1st and 2d Nat. Dropout Prevention Confs., Winston-Salem, N.C., 1986-87, Raleigh, 1986-88, N.C. Sch. Counselors Conf., Raleigh, 1986-88, Am. Pers. and Guidance Assn., 1976; presenter career workshops ParentScope 1996, speakers' staff ParentScope 1995-96. Contbr. articles to profl. jours. Vice chmn. bd. trustees Crossnore (N.C.) Sch., 1977—; mem. adv. bd. Tamassee DAR Sch., 1994—; sec., bd. dirs. Wake Teen Med. Svcs., Raleigh, 1978-88, Garner Edn. Found., 1991-95; mem. Wake County Bus. and Edn. Leadership Coun., 1992-96. Mem. AACD, NEA, DAR (area rep. spkrs. staff N.C. 1975-78, chmn. state DAR sch. com. 1985-88, state editor DAR News 1989-91, 94—, chpt. regent 1992-95, nat. house com. 1992-94, nat. vice chmn. spl. svcs., state officer 1989-91, dir. dist. VI N.C. State DAR, N.C. Outstanding

Jr. Mem. 1970), N.C. Edn. Assn., Am. Sch. Counselors Assn., N.C. Sch. Counselors Assn., Phi Delta Kappa, Delta Kappa Gamma (pres. chpt. 1985-88, state chmn. 1991-93, state com. chmn. 1994—). Democrat. Methodist. Home: 6000 Winthrop Dr Raleigh NC 27612-2142

DREXLER, JOANNE LEE, art appraiser; b. Washington, Mar. 21, 1944; d. Elias J. and Beatrice Charlotte (Goldberg) D.; m. James R. Cohen, May 31, 1965; children: Terri I., Brett F. Student, Louvre, Paris, 1963-64; BA, Tufts U., 1965; Diamond and Pearl Cert., GIA, N.Y.C., 1974. Tchr. of French Stuyvesant High Sch., N.Y.C., 1965-66; decorator, art cons. Joanne Cohen Interiors, Mamaroneck, N.Y., 1967-69; assoc. prof. Hofstra U., L.I., N.Y., 1979-80; pres. Esquire Appraisals, N.Y.C. and Larchmont, N.Y., 1969—; numerous TV appearances including CNN, Sept. 1991; cons., lectr. in field; art judge various contests, art dealer. Organizer, curator N.C. in N.Y. art show Nat. Arts Club, 1993, African Am. art show Nat. Arts Club, 1994; weekly columnist Gannett chain newspapers, 1980-86. Mem. Am. Soc. Appraisers (sr.; v.p. White Plains chpt. 1989, bd. dirs. 1997, pres. 1991—), Appraisers' Assn. Am. (cert.), Nat. Arts Club N.Y. Home: 10 Normandy Rd Larchmont NY 10538-1910 Office: Esquire Appraisals Inc 45 East End Ave New York NY 10028-7953

DREXLER, MARY SANFORD, financial executive; b. Pontiac, Mich., Apr. 19, 1954; d. Arthur H. and Kathryn S. (Sherda) Sanford; m. Brian Day, 1975 (div. 1978); m. York Drexler, 1980. BS, Ea. Mich. U., Ypsilanti, 1976, MA, 1979; postgrad., Walsh Coll., Troy, Mich., 1983. CPA, Mich. Spl. edn. tchr. Oakland Schs., Pontiac, Mich., 1976-83; staff auditor Coopers & Lybrand, Det., 1983-84; sr. auditor Coopers & Lybrand, Det., Mich., 1984-86; asst. contr. Webasto Sunroofs Inc., Rochester Hills, 1986-88; contr. Inalfa Hollandia, Inc., Farmington Hills, Mich., 1988—, v.p. fin., controller, 1992-96, CFO, exec. v.p., 1996—; bd. dirs. Coun. for Exceptional Children, Oakland County 1976--83. Bd. Dirs. Neighborhood Civic Assn., Troy, 1986—. Mem. Inst. Mgmt. Accts., Oakland County, Mich. Assn. CPA Mich., Forest Lake Country Club. Office: Inalfa Hollandia Inc 26700 Haggerty Rd Farmington Hills MI 48331-5714

DREYER, LOIS H. GOODMAN, language arts educator, researcher; b. N.Y.C., Aug. 26, 1944; d. Mac and Lilyan (Shulman) Goodman; m. Neil P. Dreyer, June 26, 1965; children: Jonathan, Peter. BS in Spanish and Elem. Edn., NYU, 1965; MA in Ednl. Psychology, Columbia U., 1978, EdM in Learning Disabilities, 1980, PhD in Ednl. Psychology, 1989. Cert. reading cons., Conn.; cert. reading tchr. K-12, N.Y.; cert. tchr. common br. subjects K-8, N.Y. Classroom tchr. P.S. 87, N.Y.C., 1965-68; reading and lang. arts cons. The Long Ridge Sch., Stamford, Conn., 1978-80; asst. supr. reading clinic Columbia U. Tchrs. Coll., N.Y.C., 1980-82, coord. reading svcs., 1982-90, adj. asst. prof., 1989-91; rsch. assoc. Haskins Labs., New Haven, 1989-93; dir. reading ctr. So. Conn. State U., New Haven, 1989-93, assoc. prof. reading, 1991—. Contbr. articles to profl. jours., chpt. to book. Am. Ednl. Rsch. Assn., Internat. Reading Assn., Nat. Reading Conf., Orton Dyslexia Soc. (Outstanding Dissertation award 1990), Soc. for Scientific Study of Reading, Kappa Delta Pi. Home: 80 Sawmill Rd Stamford CT 06903 Office: So Conn State U 501 Crescent St New Haven CT 06903

DREYFUSS, PATRICIA, chemist, researcher; b. Reading, Pa., Apr. 28, 1932; d. Edmund T. and Anna J. (Oberc) Gajewski; m. M. Peter Dreyfuss, Jan. 30, 1954; children: David Daniel, Simeon Karl. BS Chemistry, U. Rochester, 1954; PhD, U. Akron, 1964. Postdoctoral fellow U. Liverpool (Eng.), 1963-65; rsch. chemist B.F. Goodrich, Brecksville, Ohio, 1965-71; rsch. assoc. Case Western Res. U., Cleve., 1971-73, sr. rsch. assoc., 1973-74; rsch. assoc. Inst. Polymers Sci., U. Akron, Ohio, 1974-84; sr. rsch. scientist, rsch. prof. Mich. Molecular Inst., Midland, 1984-90; vis. rsch. fellow U. Bristol, 1972; cons. in field, 1974—; vis. prof. Polish Acad. Scis., Poland, 1974; adj. prof. Cen. Mich. U., Mt. Pleasant, Mich. Tech U., Houghton, 1986-92, Mich. Molecular Inst., Midland, 1990-92. Author: Poly (Tetrahydrofuran), 1982; contbr. numerous articles to profl. jours.; co-author books. Flutist West Suburban Philharmonic Orch., Lakewood, Ohio, 1969-75, Midland (Mich.) Community Orch., 1990—; Explorer advisor Explorer post 2069 Boy Scouts Am., Akron, 1975-81; sec., bd. dirs. Adhesion Soc., 1976-88; treas. LWV, 1959-60; mem. ensemble Blessed Sacrament Ch., Midland; occasional flute soloist. Centennial scholar U. Rochester, 1950-54; Sohio fellow U. Akron, 1960, NSF Coop. Grad. fellow, 1961-63, Internat. fellow AAUW, 1964-65, NIH Spl. fellow, 1972-73. Mem. Am. Chem. Soc. (cen. region mtg. chmn. 1984-90, loc. sec. chmn., vice chmn., sec. and bd. dirs. Akron chpt. 1974-84, bd. dirs. Midland chpt. 1985-89, Outstanding Leadership Performance award 1981, Disting. Svc. award Akron chpt. 1985), AAUW (bd. dirs. Akron chpt.). Home: 3980 Old Pine Trl Midland MI 48642-8891

DRIES, COLLEEN PATRICIA, adult education educator; b. Lansing, Mich., Apr. 15, 1948; d. Peter C. and Mary Alice (Campion) D. BA, St. Louis U., 1971; postgrad., U. Ill.; MA, Bradley U., 1996. Cert. elem. edn., secondary edn., English as a 2nd lang. edn. Elem., mid. and jr. high sch. tchr. Holy Family Grade Sch., Peoria, Ill.; tchr. Peoria Pub. Schs., English as a 2nd lang. tchr., GED tchr.; tchr. adult basic edn., mem. Peoria Pub. Schs. Adult Edn. Task Force; mem. Commn. on Adult Basic Edn., region 4 rep., 1994-96, nominations and elections com., 1996. Mem. Gov.'s Parent Sch. Initiative Region 12 Adv. Com., 1993. Named Ill. Adult Edn. Tchr. of Yr., 1989. Mem. ASCD, Internat. Reading Assn., Am. Assn. Adult and Continuing Edn. (nominations and elections com. 1996), Nat. Coun. Tchrs. English, Ill. Adult and Continuing Educators Assn. (regional dir. 1987-91, pres. 1992-93, membership chair 1994-96, membership/legis. chair 1994—, pres. award outstanding contbns. to adult edn. in Ill. 1995). Home: PO Box 327 Peoria IL 61651-0327

DRIES, KATHLEEN MARIE, social worker; b. Beaver Dam, Wis., Feb. 21, 1946; d. Henry Frank and Eloise Marianne (Rake) D. BS in Sociology, No. Mich. U., 1969. Social worker Dept. Social Svcs., West Bend, Wis., 1969—; social work cons. Group Home Elderly, Slinger, Wis., 1972-75. Mem. Labor Assn. of Wis., Cath. Knights Ins. Soc. (bd. dirs. 1979-94), Alpha Xi Delta. Roman Catholic. Home: 601 Declark St Beaver Dam WI 53916-1309 Office: Dept Social Svcs 333 E Washington St Ste 3100 West Bend WI 53095-2585

DRISCOLL, SISTER BRIGID, college president; b. N.Y.C.; d. Daniel Driscoll and Delia Duffy. B in Math., Edn., Marymount Manhattan Coll., 1954; M in Math., Cath. U., 1957; PhD in Math., CUNY, 1967; EdD (hon.), Siena Coll. Joined Religious of Sacred Heart of Mary, Roman Cath. Ch., 1954. Prof. math., assoc. acad. dean, dir. continuing edn. Marymount Coll., Tarrytown, N.Y., founder Weekend Coll., 1975, pres., 1979—; mem. Commr. of Edn.'s Adv. Council on Post-Secondary Edn. in N.Y. State; trustee Commn. on Ind. Colls. and Univs. Bd. dirs. Girl Scouts U.S., Phelps Meml. Hosp. Ctr., North Tarrytown, N.Y., Axe-Houghton Funds; bd. dirs. Westchester/Putnam chpt. United Way, mem. nat. vol. involvement com. 2d Century Initiative; mem. Statue of Liberty/Ellis Island Commn.; trustee Marymount Sch., N.Y.C. Named Woman of Yr. Sleepy Hollow C. of C., 1982; honored for disting. service Westchester (N.Y.) chpt. NCCJ; NASA fellow, 1967. Mem. Assn. Cath. Colls. and Univs. (bd. dirs., chairwoman Neylan Commn.), Commn. on Ind. Colls. and Univs. (trustee). Office: Marymount Coll Office of the President 100 Marymount Ave Tarrytown NY 10591-3796*

DRISCOLL, CONSTANCE FITZGERALD, educator, writer; b. Lawrence, Mass., Mar. 29, 1926; d. John James and Mary Anne (Leecock) Fitzgerald; AB, Radcliffe Coll., 1946; postgrad. Harvard U., U. Hartford (Conn.), U. Bridgeport (Conn.), Worcester (Mass.) State Coll.; m. Francis George Driscoll, Aug. 21, 1948; children: Frances Mary, Martha Anne, Sara Helene, Maribeth Lee. Secondary sch. tchr., North Andover, Mass., 1946-48; book reviewer N.Y.C. and Boston pubs., 1955-64; asst. conf. edn. dir. U. Hartford, 1964-68; lectr. Pace U., N.Y.C., 1973-74; edn. commentary Radio WVOX, New Rochelle, N.Y., 1974-75; asst. ednl. adv. Nat. Girl Scouts, 1972-74; pres., owner, dir. Open Corridor Schs. Cons., Inc., Bronxville, N.Y., 1972-84, pres., dir. Open Corridor Schs., Inc., Oxford, Mass., 1984—; creator in-svc. edn. programs pub. schs., Norwalk, Conn., 1983-88; assoc. Worcester State Coll. (Mass.) 1984-85, Fitchburg State Coll., 1986-87; dir. grad. edn. programs for tchrs. Anna Maria Coll., Paxton, Mass., 1990-94; assoc. grad. tchr. edn. courses Fitchburg State Coll., 1995—, U. Bridgeport, Conn., 1995—; profl. devel. points provider Mass. State Dept. Edn., 1995—; tutor, cons. Worcester County sch. dists., 1989-95; CEU mgr. for Conn. Dept. Edn. O.C.S., Inc., Conn., 1989—, bi-lingual insti. for Indian and Vietnamese students in grades 5-12, 1988-91; freelance writer newspapers and small jours., 1991—. Author curriculum materials; contbr. poetry to The Patriot newspaper, 1991—. Recipient Educator award Nat. Coun. ARC, Washington, 1985, Edn. award Nipmuc Am. Indian Coun., Webster, Mass, 1985.

DRISCOLL, FRANCES MARIE, medical center administrator; b. Providence; d. Thomas D. and Frances M. Palumbo; m. Donald J. Driscoll, Aug. 18, 1964; children: Donald J. II, Christin, Deirdre. BEd, R.I. Coll., 1961; MA in English, U. R.I., 1968. Tchr. Ctrl. H.S. and Nathan Bishop Jr. H.S., Providence, 1961-64; asst. dir. admissions R.I. Coll., Providence, 1964-65; exec. dir., adult coord. R.I. Interagy. Coun. on Smoking, Pawtucket, R.I., 1972-79; dir. pub. info. and pub. rels. Bryant Coll., Smithfield, R.I., 1979-84; exec. asst. for comm. and pub. info. Office Gen. Treasurer, Providence, 1984-85; dir. pub. affairs and mktg. devel. RIGHA, Providence, 1984-89; v.p. pub. rels. and devel. R.I. Group Health Assn., Providence, 1989-94; sr. v.p. external affairs and corp. comm. and devel. Roger Williams Med. Ctr., Providence, 1994—; mktg. and advt. cons. R.I. Small Bus. Devel. Ctr., 1983-90. Mem. Statewide Health Svcs. Coun., Providence, 1993—; bd. dirs., co-chmn. governing com. Aging 2000, Providence, 1993—. Mem. Pub. Rels. Soc. Am. (accredited, Southeastern New Eng. chpt. treas. 1983-85, v.p. 1985-86, pres. 1986-87, bd. dirs. 1991—, nat. bd. dirs. 1991-94, Pres.'s award 1990). Home: 270 Snake Hill Rd North Scituate RI 02857 Office: Roger Williams Med Ctr 825 Chalkstone Ave Providence RI 02908-4728

DRISCOLL, GENEVIEVE BOSSON (JEANNE BOSSON DRISCOLL), management and organization development consultant; b. Pitts., Mar. 26, 1937; d. George August and Emma Haling Bleichner; B.S. cum laude, Fla. State U., 1959; postgrad. program for specialists in orgn. devel. Nat. Tng. Labs., 1970. m. John Edwin Bosson, June 17, 1959; 1 son, Matthew Edwin; m. 2d Frederick Driscoll, Oct. 7, 1972; stepchildren—Jennifer Locke, Cynthia Hall, Molly Davis, Julie Ann. Planning asst. Center for Planning and Innovation, Dept. Edn. State of N.Y., 1967-71, planning cons. So. Tier Regional Office for Ednl. Planning, Elmira, N.Y., 1971-72; tng. dir. Neusteters, Inc., Denver, 1973-74; orgn. devel. specialist CONNECT, Inc., N.Y.C., 1975-77; cons. Robert H. Schaffer & Assos., Stamford, Conn., 1977-80; partner Driscoll Cons. Group, Williamstown, Mass., 1980—; sales tng. mgr. Sheaffer Eaton, Pittsfield, Mass., 1983, mgr. human resources and orgn. devel., 1983-88; dir. human resources Canyon Ranch, Berkshires, 1989-95, ret., 1995; cons. in field. Office: 24 Lee Ter Williamstown MA 01267-2039

DRISCOLL, KAREN, advertising executive. Exec. v.p., acct. dir. Arnold, Fortuna, Lawner & Cabot, Boston. Office: Arnold Fortuna Lawner & Cabot 101 Arch St Boston MA 02110-1103*

DRISCOLL, KELLY COLLEEN, artist, printer; b. Houston, Sept. 17, 1964; d. James Fredrick and Anne Marie (Hens) D. BFA, U. Utah, 1987; postgrad., U. Plymouth (Eng.), 1984, Studio Art Ctr. Internat., Florence, Italy, 1990. Master printer The Printmaking Workshop, N.Y.C., 1993—, Am. Atelier, N.Y.C., 1995—; instr. The Printmaking Workshop, 1995; guest instr. printmaking workshop Scuola de Designo, Altos de Chavon, Dominican Republic, 1995; curator exhbn. Representing Women, N.G.O. Forum, China, 1995. Democrat. Office: The Printmaking Workshop 55 W 17th St New York NY 10011

DRISCOLL, KIMBERLEE MARIE, lawyer; b. Binghamton, N.Y., July 17, 1961; d. Patrick Donald and Diane Cecile (Richmond) Lake; m. Matthew Victor Driscoll, Aug. 6, 1983; 1 child, John Patrick. BA, Colgate U., 1983; JD, Union U., 1986. Bar: N.Y. 1987, Mass. 1988. Asst. gen. counsel Oxbow Corp., Dedham, Mass., 1987-90; corp. counsel, sec. Putnam, Hayes & Bartlett, Inc., Cambridge, Mass., 1990-92; v.p., gen. counsel Merrill Internat. Ltd., Cambridge, 1992—. Mem. ABA (vice chair spl. com. internat. energy law 1993—), Am. Corp. Counsel Assn., Mass. Bar Assn., N.Y. Bar Assn. Home: 22 Battle Flag Rd Bedford MA 01730 Office: Merrill Internat Ltd 20 University Rd Ste 510 Cambridge MA 02138-5756

DRISCOLL, LORRAINE EVA, obstetrician-gynecologist; b. Jersey City, Mar. 15, 1954; d. Anthony Edmunt and Albina Elizabeth (Kundracky) Zolnowski; m. Patrick Joseph Driscoll, Aug. 27, 1977; children: Kathrine Eva, Joseph Anthony Descours, Elizabeth Lucienne. BS in Biochemistry, St. Peter's Coll., Jersey City, 1976; MD, N.Y. Med. Coll., 1981. Diplomate Am. Bd. Obstetrics and Gynecology. Resident Lenox Hill Hosp., N.Y.C., 1981-85; pvt. practice N.Y.C., 1985-92, Rutherford, N.J., 1992—; staff physician Holy Name Hosp., Teaneck, N.J., St. Mary's Hosp., Passaic, N.J., Gen. Hosp. Ctr., Passaic, N.J., Beth Israel Hosp., Passaic, N.J.; lectr. in field. Troop leader Girl Scouts U.S., Rutherford, 1995—. Fellow Am. Coll. Obstetricians and Gynecologists; mem. AMA, N.J. Med. Assn., Bergen County Med. Assn., Am. Med. Women's Assn., N.J. Med. Women's Assn. Roman Catholic. Office: 9 Lincoln Ave Rutherford NJ 07070

DRIVER, JUDY ANNE, home health consultant; b. Bowdon, Ga., Sept. 2, 1946; d. Robert Eual and Verdie Louise (Whitman) Jeter; m. Louis Edward Driver, Mar. 7, 1965; children: Wendy Leigh-Anne, Stefanie Robyn. ADN, West Ga. Coll., 1978. Staff nurse to asst. dir. nursing Bowdon (Ga.) Area Hosp., 1978-82; edn. coord. Higgins Gen. Hosp., Bremen, Ga., 1982-91; standards surveyor Ga. Dept. Human Resources, Office of Regulatory Svcs., Atlanta, 1991; clin. dir. Liberty Home Health, Carrollton, Ga., 1992; cons. Family Home Health, Inc., Carrollton, 1992; regulatory cons. Cen. Health Svcs., Atlanta, 1992-96, Simione Ctrl., Inc., 1996—; PROBE chmn. for West Ga., Ga. Soc. Healthcare Edn. and Tng., 1988-89. Svc. and rehab. chmn. Am. Cancer Soc., Haralson County, Ga., 1986-91; profl. edn. chmn. Am. Heart Assn., Haralson County, 1987-91; dist. bd. dirs. Am. Lung Assn., 1982-85; coord. Lifeline Emergency Sys., Haralson County, 1983-91. Republican. Baptist. Home: 205 Hidden Lakes Dr Carrollton GA 30116

DRIVER, LOTTIE ELIZABETH, librarian; b. Newport News, Va., Dec. 6, 1918; d. James W. and Lottie (Williams) D. Student, Averett Coll., 1936-37; B.S., Mary Washington Coll. of U. Va., 1939; B.L.S., Coll. William and Mary, 1944. Band instr. Hampton (Va.) Sch. System, 1939-41; asst. librarian Newport News Pub. Library, 1941-47, librarian, 1947-69; asst. dir. Newport News Pub. Library System, 1969, dir., 1977-81; author book rev. column in Daily Press; library news reporter radio sta. WGH, 1959. Author articles for library supply house. Active United Fund. Recipient Community Service certificate Kiwanis Clubs Newport News, 1970; named Outstanding City Employee, 1970. Mem. ALA, Southeastern, Va. library assns., AAUW, P.E.O., DAR, Phi Theta Kappa, Alpha Phi Sigma. Baptist.

DRIVER, MARTHA WESTCOTT, English language educator, writer, researcher; b. N.Y.C., Oct. 24; d. Albert Westcott and Martha Louise (Miller) D. BA, Vassar Coll., 1974; MA, U. Pa., 1975, PhD, 1980. Lectr. English Vassar Coll., N.Y.C., 1980-81; from asst. prof. to assoc. prof. Pace U., N.Y.C., 1981-95, prof. English, 1995—; cons. N.Y. Pub. Libr., 1984; seminar participant Folger Inst., Folger Shakespeare Libr., 1994. Contbr. articles to profl. jours. Vestry mem. Ch. of the Incarnation, N.Y.C., 1995-96; mem., lectr. St. John the Divine, N.Y.C., 1995. Rsch. tools grantee NEH, 1995, travel grantee Am. Coun. Learned Socs., 1995. Mem. Early Book Soc. (chair 1988—), Coll. Art Assn., Medieval Acad. Am., Modern Humanities Rsch. Assn. (U.K.), Medieval Club of N.Y. (conf. coord. 1989-94. pres. 1987-89). Episcopalian. Office: Pace U English Dept 41 Park Row New York NY 10038

DRIVER, SHARON HUMPHREYS, marketing executive; b. Staten Island, N.Y., Jan. 5, 1949; d. William Edward and Gloria Patra (McCrave) Humphreys; m. William Weston Driver, Jr., June 3, 1972; children: Christopher John, Andrea Nicole. BA, Manhattanville Coll., Purchase, N.Y., 1970; MA, Coll. New Rochelle (N.Y.), 1973. Lic. tchr., N.Y. Tchr. Somers (N.Y.) Cen. Sch. Dist., 1970-76, Ossining (N.Y.) Village Recreation Dept., 1983-87; media coord./bookkeeper Equation Communications, White Plains, N.Y., 1986-89; media dir. Sims Freeman O'Brien, Elmsford, N.Y., 1989-90; project dir. Rsch. Advantage, Hawthorne, N.Y., 1990-92; asst. v.p. Merson/Greener Assocs., Tarrytown, N.Y., 1992-94; pres. Decision Drivers, Briarcliff, 1994—. Sec. tng. liason, Jr. League, Westchester-on-Hudson, 1982-88; sustainer, trainer-facilitator, Jr. League, Tarrytown, N.Y., 1988—; past pres. St. Theresa's Parish Coun., Briarcliff Manor, N.Y.; sec. bd. dirs. Ossining Open Door Health Clinic, 1985-89. Mem. NAFE, Am. Mktg. Assn., Women in Comm., Sleepy Hollow Toastmasters (charter, sec. exec. com.), Ad Club of Westchester. Roman Catholic. Home: 197 Macy Rd Briarcliff Manor NY 10510-1017

DRIVER, SUSANNAH AMBROSE, editor; b. N.Y.C., Dec. 28, 1957; d. Tom Faw Driver and Anne Llewelyn Barstow. BA, Wesleyan U., 1979. Accounts payable clk. NYU Book Ctrs., N.Y.C., 1980-83; editl. staff St. Martin's Press, N.Y.C., 1983-85, Inst. Internat. Edn., N.Y.C., 1985; pub.'s asst., editl. staff The Feminist Press, CUNY, N.Y.C., 1985-90, sr. editor, fgn. rights mgr., 1990-95; freelance feminist editor Accord, N.Y., 1996—. Mem. Women in Scholarly Pub., Editl. Freelancers' Assn., Orgn. for the Study of Comm., Lang. and Gender.

DRNJEVIC, NANCY ANN NORVILLE, home health services administrator; b. Taylorville, Ill., Oct. 20, 1956; d. Anthony Peter and Marian Ruth (Ream) Norville; m. Thomas Edward Drnjevic, Sept. 20, 1975. ADN, Lincoln Land community Coll., 1978; BSN, So. Ill. U., 1987. Staff nurse nephrology, kidney transplant and urology unit Meml Med. Ctr., Springfield, Ill., 1978-81; staff nurse Nephrology Clinic Meml Med. Ctr., Springfield, 1981-84; staff nurse home health St. John's Hosp., Springfield, 1984-88; supr. home care St. Vincent Meml. Hosp., Taylorville, 1988-89, exec. dir. home health svc. and bus. devel., 1989-94; pres. Ill. Emergency Responce Coop., Taylorville, 1990-94. Mem. NAFE, Ill. Home Care Coun., Ill. & West Ctrl. Region Continuity of Care Orgn. (sec. 1993-95, 95—). Home: 2112 S Walnut St Springfield IL 62704-4530 Office: St John's Hosp 800 E Carpenter Springfield IL 62769

DROKE, EDNA FAYE, elementary school educator; b. Sylvester, Tex., Dec. 4, 1932; d. Ira Selle and Faye Emily (Seckinger) Tucker; m. Louis Albert Droke, June 2, 1951; children: Sherman Ray, Lyndon Allen, Lona Faye Droke Cheairs. BEd, Tarleton State U., Stephenville, Tex., 1983. Cert. ESL and 3d-8th lang. arts tchr., Tex. Tchr. ESL in 3d-8th grades Wingate (Tex.) Ind. Sch. Dist., 1983-86; tchr. 2d grade and ESL Collidge (Tex.) Ind. Sch. Dist., 1986-88; tchr. 4th grade and ESL Peaster (Tex.) Ind. Sch. Dist., 1988-89; tchr. Chpt. I in 1st-6th grades, ESL in K-12th grades Ranger (Tex.) Ind. Sch. Dist., 1989—. Mem. ASCD, Kappa Delta Pi, Alpha Chi. Baptist. Home: PO Box 44 Comanche TX 76442-0044

DROST, MARIANNE, lawyer; b. Waterbury, Conn., Feb. 21, 1950; d. Albin Joseph and Henrietta Jean (Kremski) D. BA, Conn. Coll., 1972; JD, U. Conn., 1975. Bar: Conn. 1975. Assoc. Ritter, Tapper & Totten, Hartford, Conn., 1975-77; sr. atty. GTE Service Corp., Stamford, Conn., 1977-84, Chesebrough-Pond's Inc., Greenwich, Conn., 1984-85; corp. sec. GTE Corp., Stamford, 1985—; v.p., assoc. gen. counsel fin. GTE Svc. Corp., Stamford, 1991—. Tutor Lit. Vols., Stamford, 1985-90, bd. dirs. Lit. Vols. Am., 1988-94. Mem. ABA, Am. Soc. Corp. Secs. (former pres., bd. dirs. Fairfield-Westchester chpt.).

DROUKAS, ANN HANTIS, management executive; b. Boston, Aug. 27, 1923; d. Charles George and Paula (Kanaris) Hantis; m. Peter Droukas Jr., Sept. 28, 1941; children: P. Ronald, Paulette D., Roger C. Grad. high sch., Roxbury, Mass. With Droukas Cut Sole, Inc., Brockton, Mass., 1947—, pres., treas., 1985—; with DBA Drew Leather, Brockton, 1985-89; pres., treas. DBA Campello Tanning, Brockton, 1985—. Contbr. to translater textbooks from Spanish and Greek to English. Mem. adv. bd. Lincoln Trust; past adult participant Boy Scouts Am., Girl Scouts U.S.; active Two-Ten Nat. Found., Brockton Art Mus. 1st woman in U.S. to own and operate a cowhide tannery. Mem. Nat. Fedn. Ind. Bus., Assn. Industries Mass., Greek Ladies Philophotos Soc. (past. treas.), Brockton Hist. Soc., Nat. Trust for Historic Preservation, U.S. C. of C., New England Tanners Club, Shoe and Leather Club Cin., Rainbow Mothers Club, Order Ea. Star, Ten Times One Club (past pres.). Office: PO Box 4068 Brockton MA 02403-4068

DROUSE, LISA MICHELLE, health facility administrator; b. Buffalo, Oct. 6, 1964; d. Roderick Francis and Marjorie Joan (Rice) Bailey; m. Edward A. Drouse, Dec. 10, 1994; 1 child, Shannon Rose. BBA, St. Bonaventure U., 1986; MBA, Plymouth (N.H.) State Coll., 1993. Tech. coord., unit mgr., supr. rsch., customer svc. rep. Shawmut Bank N.Am., Worcester, Mass., 1986-89; fin. analyst Waterville Co. Inc., Waterville Valley, N.H., 1989-93, Healthsource, Hooksett, N.H., 1993-95; planning mgr. Optima Health, Manchester, N.H., 1995—. Mem. Inst. Mgmt. Accts. Republican. Roman Catholic. Office: Optima Health 100 McGregor St Manchester NH 03275

DRUCKER, JACQUELIN F., lawyer, arbitrator, author; b. Celina, Ohio, Oct. 15, 1954; d. Jack Burton and Dorothea (Eckenstein) Davis; m. John H. Drucker, Sept. 8, 1990. BA with distinction and honors, Ohio State U., 1977, JD with honors, 1981. Bar: Ohio 1981, N.Y. 1992, U.S. Supreme Ct. 1989. Legis. asst. Speaker of Ohio Ho. of Reps., Columbus, 1974-78; rsch. asst. United Auto Workers, Columbus, 1978-81; labor atty. Porter, Wright, Morris & Arthur, Columbus, 1981-84; gen. counsel Ohio Employment Rels. Bd., Columbus, 1984-86, exec. dir., 1986-88, vice chmn., 1988-90; pvt. practice arbitration and mediation N.Y.C., 1990—; dir. labor mgmt. programs sch. indsl. and labor rels. Cornell U., 1994—; adj. prof. Cornell U., 1994—; cons. on collective bargaining Ohio Dept. Adminstrv. Svcs., Columbus, 1983-84; adj. prof. law Franklin U. Columbus, 1988-89; mem. panel of arbitrators Fed. Mediation and Conciliation Svc., Am. Arbitration Assn., N.Y. State Employment Rels. Bd.; mem. roster of neutrals N.Y.C. Office of Collective Bargaining; mem. panel V.I. Pub. Employment Rels. Bd., N.J. Pub. Employment Rels. Commn., N.Y. Pub. Employment Rels. Bd.; mem. permanent arbitration panel United Mine Workers and Bituminous Coal Operators Assn., Am. Postal Workers Union, U.S. Postal Svc., Off-Track Betting Corp. and Local 32E, Consolidated Edison and Utility Workers Local 1-2; lectr., speaker in field. Author: Collective Bargaining Law in Ohio, 1993; editor L.I. Indsl. Rels. Quar.; contbg. editor Pub. Sector Law and Employment Law, 2d edit.; contbr. numerous articles to profl. jours. Mem. ABA, Ohio State Bar Assn., Assn. of Bar of City of N.Y., N.Y. State Bar Assn. (labor and employment law sect. sec.-elect), N.Y. County Lawyers Assn. (labor rels. com., sec.), Nassau County Bar Assn., Suffolk County Bar Assn., Indsl. Rels. Rsch. Assn. (N.Y. chpt., Cleve. chpt., L.I. chpt.), Soc. Fed. Labor Rels. Profls. Jewish. Office: 432 E 58th St # 2 New York NY 10022-2331

DRUCKER, JOHANNA RUTH, art historian, educator, research writer; b. Phila., May 30, 1952; d. Boris and Barbara Alice (Witmer) D.; m. Thomas Bradley Freeman, June 18, 1991. BFA in Printing, Calif. Coll. Arts & Crafts, 1973; MFA in Visual Studies, U. Calif., 1982, PhD in Ecriture, 1986. Teaching asst. U. Calif., Berkeley, 1982-84; vis. lectr. San Francisco State U., 1984; lectr. U. Calif., Berkeley, 1985-86; asst. prof. U. Tex. at Dallas, Richardson, 1986-88; Mellon faculty fellow Harvard U., Cambridge, Mass., 1988-89; asst. prof. Columbia U., N.Y., 1989-94; assoc. prof. Yale U., New Haven, Conn., 1994—; mem. editl. bd. Art Jour., N.Y., 1995—, Jour. of Artist's Books, New Haven, 1994—. Author: (book) The Visible World, 1994, Theorizing Modernism, 1994, Alphabetic Labyrinth, 1995, Dark Decade, 1995. Recipient Regent's fellow Regents of the U. Calif., 1980-82, Fulbright fellow Fulbright Com., 1984-85, Getty fellow Getty Ctr.', 1992-93. Mem. NOW, Coll. Art Assn. Office: Yale U Dept History of Art PO Box 208272 New Haven CT 06520

DRUEN, PERRI BETH, psychology educator, researcher; b. Albuquerque, N. Mex., Nov. 24, 1966; d. William M. and Mary O (Howell) Druen; m. Robert A. Krekel, May 20, 1994. BA in Psychology, U. Louisville, 1988, MA in Psychology, 1991, PhD in Social and Personality Psychology, 1995. Rsch. and stats. cons. Blue Cross & Blue Shield of Ky., Louisville, 1993-94; psychology instr. Irvine (Calif.) Valley Coll., 1994, Saddleback Coll., Mission Viejo, Calif., 1994, U. Louisville, 1991—. Contbr. articles to profl. jours. including Jour. of Social Issues, Jour. of Personality and Social Psychology; book reviewer Contemporary Psychology, 1992, 95—; jour. ad hoc reviewer, 1989-92, Jour. Social and Personal Rels. Mem. Am. Psychol. Assn. (affiliate, Student Presentation award 1992, Dissertation grant 1993), Internat. Network on Personal Relationships (grad. membership devel. com. 1992-93, Student Presentation award 1991, 93), Internat. Soc. for the Study of Personal Relationships. Home: 5485 Repecho Dr L-102 San Diego CA 92124 Office: U Louisville Dept Psychology Louisville KY 40292

DRUETT, JOAN, writer, historian; b. Nelson, New Zealand, Apr. 11, 1939; came to U.S., 1993; d. Ralph Totten Griffin and Colleen De La Hunt Butcher; m. Ronald John Druett; children: Lindsay, Alastair. BA, Victoria U., Wellington, New Zealand, 1960; tchg. diploma, Christchurch, New Zealand, 1961. Tchr. New Zealand Edn. Dept., 1961-63; actuary Mfrs. Life Ins., Toronto, Can., 1964-65; tchr. Waikato Diocese, New Zealand, 1974-84; freelance writer, 1984—; cons. historian Seafaring Women Project, 1994—; curriculum advisor L.I./Stony Brook (N.Y.) Schs., 1995—. Author: Exotic Intruders, 1984 (Pen award 1985, Hubert Ch. award 1985), Fulbright in New Zealand, 1988, Abigail, 1988, She Was a Sister Sailor, 1991 (best Book of Am. Maritime History 1992). Pres. Waikato Speech Therapy Assn., New Zealand, 1970-74.

DRULLINGER, LEONA PEARL, obstetrics nurse; b. Norton, Kans., Aug. 10, 1962; d. Floyd Allen and Frances Marie (Redfield) Blair; m. Richard Lee Drullinger, Aug. 2, 1981; children: Richard Jr., Charity, Kelsy, Brandon. AD in Practical Nursing, Colby (Kans.) C.C., 1985; ADN, Garden City (Kans.) C.C., 1987. RN; cert. BLS, ACLS, neonatal advanced lfie support, inpatient obstetrics. LPN, Citizens Med. Ctr., Colby, Kans., 1985-86; lic. practical nurse Nursing Home, Lakin, Kans., 1986-87; RN staff nurse St. Catherine's Hosp., Garden City, Kans., 1987-88; acting head nurse VA Med. Ctr., Lincoln, Nebr., 1988-90; telemetry nurse Bryan Meml. Hosp., Lincoln, 1990-92; staff nurse Nurse Finders, Omaha, 1990—; obstetric nurse Hunter Med. Inc., Offutt AFB Hosp., Bellvue, Nebr., 1992—, contract nurse, team leader, 1994-96; with Brodstone Meml. Nuckolls County Hosp., Superior, Nebr., 1996—. Democrat. Home: 457 Park Ave Superior NE 68978

DRUM, ALICE, college administrator; b. Gettysburg, Pa., June 22, 1935; d. David Wentz and Charlotte Rebecca (Kinzey) McDannell; m. D. Richard Guise, June 15, 1957 (div. Aug. 1975); children: Gregory, Brent, Richard, Robert, Clay; m. Ray Kenneth Drum, Mar. 2, 1979; 1 child, Trevor. BA magna cum laude, Wilson Coll., 1957; PhD, Am. U., 1976. Adj. prof. gen. studies Antioch U., Columbia, Md., 1976-78; adj. asst. prof. English Gettysburg (Pa.) Coll., 1977-80; lectr. in gen. studies Georgetown U., Washington, 1980-81; lectr. in gen. honors U. Md., College Park, 1980-83; asst. prof. English Hood Coll., Frederick, Md., 1981-85, coord. writing program, 1981-83, assoc. dean acad. affairs, 1983-85; dean of frehmen Franklin and Marshall Coll., Lancaster, Pa., 1985-88, v.p., 1988—; team mem. Mid. States Accreditation Assn., 1989-91; cons. in field. Co-author: Funding A College Education, 1996; contbr. chpts. to books, articles and book revs. to profl. jours. Chair Lancaster County DA Commn., Lancaster, 1990-91; mem. Lancaster County Commn. on Youth Violence, Lancaster, 1990-91. Mellon grantee, 1979, Davison Foreman fellow, 1975-76. Mem. MLA, N.E. MLA, Am. Assn. Higher Edn., Assn. Am. Colls., Eastern Assn. Coll. Deans (pres. 1988-89), Coll. English Assn., Phi Beta Kappa (pres. chpt. 1990-91), Phi Kappa Phi. Democrat. Episcopalian. Office: Franklin and Marshall Coll Lancaster PA 17604-3003

DRUM, JOAN MARIE MCFARLAND, federal agency administrator; b. Waseca, Minn., Mar. 31, 1932; d. Leo Joseph and Bergetthe (Anderson) McFarland; m. William Merritt Drum, June 13, 1954; children: Melissa, Eric. BA in Journalism, U. Minn., 1962; MEd, Coll. William and Mary, 1975, postgrad., 1984-85. Govt. ofcl. fgn. claims br. Social Security Administrn., Balt., 1962-64; freelance writer Polyndrum Publs., Newport News, Va., 1967-73; tchr. Newport News (Va.) Pub. Schs., 1975-79; writer, cons. Drum Enterprises, Williamsburg, Va., 1980-82; developer, trainer communicative skills U.S. Army Transp. Sch., Ft. Eustis, Va., 1982-86; govt. ofcl. test assistance div. U.S. Army Tng. Ctr., Ft. Eustis, 1986, course devel. coord. distributed tng. office, 1992; adj. faculty English dept. St. Leo Area Coll., Ft. Eustis, 1975-78; del. Communicative Skills Conf., Ft. Leavenworth, Kans., 1983; mem. Army Self-Devel. Test Task Force, 1991-92; task force mem. U.S. Army Tng. FAA; program developer multi-media electronic delivery prototype. Author: Ghosts of Fort Monroe, 1972, Travel for Children in Tidewater, 1974, Galaxy of Ghosts, 1992; editor: army newsletter for families, 1968-73, Social Services Resource Reference, 1970; contbr. articles to profl. jours. Chmn. Girl Scouts U.S., Tokyo, 1964-66, Army Cmty. Svc., Ft. Monroe, Va., 1967-68, chmn. publicity Hist. Home Tours, Ft. Monroe, 1971-73; chmn. adv. bd. James City County Social Svcs., 1989-95, chmn. adult svcs., 1989-90; mem. James City County Leadership Devel. Program Bd. Recipient numerous civic awards including North Shore Cmty. Svc. award, Hialeah, Hawaii, 1966, Home Bur. Svc. award, 1975, Svc. award Girl Scouts U.S., Tokyo, 1965, Comdrs. award for civilian svc., 1995. Mem. Nat. Soc. for Performance Instrn. (v.p. adminstrn. Tidewater chpt.), Va. Writers Club, Kappa Delta Pi. Home: 9 Bray Wood Rd Williamsburg VA 23185-5504 Office: Ind Tng Support Directorate US Army Tng Ctr Newport News VA 23604

DRUMMOND, CAROL ANN, artist; b. Bklyn., Aug. 13, 1947; d. Angelo and Gertrude (Scarbo) Mellano; m. Richard Alan Drummond, Nov. 12, 1966; children: Scott Richard, Troy David. Exhbns. include White House Christmas Tree, Washington, 1993, Red River Revel, Shreveport, La., 1994, Chasen Galleries, Sarasota, 1995, Fla. Craftsmen, St. Petersburg, 1995, Fine Arts Mus. of South, Mobile, Ala., 1993, Quitt Nat. Dairy Barn Southeastern Ohio, Cultural Arts Ctr., Athens, 1993, Fla. Nat., Tallahassee, 1994, Arrowmont Sch., Gatlinburg, Tenn., 1994, Fla. Craftsmen, Jacksonville, Fla., 1994, Bevier Gallery, Rochester (N.Y.) Inst. Tech., 1995, Scarfone Gallery, U. Tampa 1995, FAVA, Oberlin, Ohio, 1996, Mus. of Stephen F. Austin U., Nacogdoches, Tex., 1996, Zoller Gallery, 1996; traveling exhbn. at galleries and mus. throughout N.Am., 1993-95; contbr. artist: Art/Quilt mag., 1994, A Crafters Book of Angels, 1995, Fiberarts Design Book Five, 1995, Fiberarts mag., 1996. Recipient 1st prize Sarasota Visual Arts Ctr., 1989, Lee County Art Fair, 1990, award of merit 42d Fla. Craftsmen Exhbn., 1994, Mt. Dora Arts Festival, 1995, 1st Prize Tex. Nat., 1996; individual artist fellow Fla. Divsn. Cultural Affairs, 1995-96. Mem. Studio Art Quilt Assocs., Fla. Craftsmen, Am. Craft Coun. Studio: 4224 74th Ave E Sarasota FL 34243

DRUMMOND, CAROL CRAMER, voice educator, singer, artist, writer; b. Indpls., Mar. 5, 1933; adopted d. Burr Ostin and L. Ruth Welch; m. Roscoe Drummond, 1978 (dec. 1983). Student, Butler U., 1951-53; studied with Todd Duncan, Rosa Ponselle,, John Bullock and Dr. Peter, Herman Adler.; studied with, Frances Yeend, James Benner, W.Va.; studied drama with Adelaide Bishop, Adelaide Bishop, Washington. Original performer Starlite Musicals, Indpls., 1951; singer Am. Light Opera Co., Washington, Seagle Opera Colony, Schroon Lake, N.Y., 1963, 64, Noyes Flude, Lufkin, Tex., 1965; soloist 5th Ch. of Christ, Scientist, Washington, 1963-78, St. John's Episc. Ch., Washington; performer Concerts in Schs. Program, Washington Performing Arts Soc., 1967—; soloist with Luke AFB band ofcl. opening Boswell Meml. Hosp, Sun City, Ariz., 1970; painter, artist, 1980—; pvt. tchr. voice and speech Mt. Desert Island, Maine, 1986—; voice tchr. Mt. Desert Island High Sch., 1986—; soloist numerous oratorio socs., appearances with symphony orchs. including Nat. Symphony Orch., Fairfax (Va.) Symphony Orch., 1970, 71, Buffalo Philharm. Orch. Concerts in the Pk., Arlington Opera Co., Lake George Opera Co., Glen Falls, N.Y., Noyes Flood, Lufkin, ex., 1965, Washington Opera; voiceover radio and TV comml s., 1965-84, U.S. Govt. host The Sounding Bd., Sta. WGTS-FM, Washington, 1972-78; dir. ensembles, music/voice cons. Summer Festival of the Arts, S.W. Harbor, Maine, 1992-95; dir. Amahl and the Night Visitors, 1992; vocal solo concert, The Smithsonian Instn., 1980; soloist St. John's Episcopal Ch., Lafayette Sq., Washington. Former columnist Animal Crackers; writer newspaper and mag. articles and stories; exhibited in art group shows; one-woman shows in painting, oil and acrylics at Maine Med. Ctr., Bangor, 1995; one-woman shows Lemon Tree,, Bangor, 1995, 96, Grand Theater, Ellsworth, Maine, 1995, two-woman show The Cosmos Club, Washington, 1996. Bd. dirs. Washington Sch. Ballet, 1978; life bd. dirs. Internat. Soundex Reunion Registry, Carson City, Nev. Recipient 1st pl. women's divsn. Internat. Printers Ink Contest, 1951. Mem. Nat. League Am. Pen Women, Am. Art League, Nat. Press Club (Washington), Arts Club of Washington, Maine State Soc. (life), Kappa Kappa Gamma. Republican. Episcopalian. Home: Dream Come True 79 Clark Pt Rd PO Box 791 Southwest Harbor ME 04679 Office: 1350 Beverly Rd Ste 115-135 Mc Lean VA 22101-3924

DRUMMOND, DOROTHY WEITZ, geography education consultant, educator, author; b. San Diego, Dec. 19, 1928; d. Frederick W. and Dora (Weidenhofer) Weitz; m. Robert R. Drummond, Sept. 5, 1953 (dec. June 1982); children: Kathleen, Gael, Martha. AB, Valparaiso U., 1949; MA, Northwestern U., 1951. Cert. tchr., Ind. Social studies tchr. Woodrow Wilson Jr. High Sch., Oxnard, Calif., 1949-50; editorial asst. Am. Geog. Soc., N.Y.C., 1951-53; substitute tchr. Vigo County Sch. Corp., Terre Haute, Ind., 1960-67; social studies tchr. Ind. State U. Lab. Sch., Terre Haute, 1963-64; geog. edn. cons., author, workshop presenter, Terre Haute, 1953—; adj. asst. prof. geography Saint Mary-of-the-Woods (Ind.) Coll., 1967—, Ind. State U., Terre Haute, 1990—; dir. project GEO, Ind. State U., 1992-96; cons. McGraw-Hill, Scott-Foresman, Agy. for Instrnl. Tech., Hudson Inst.; bd. dirs. GIS for the Twenty-First Century, Ind. State u., 1996—. Author: The World Today, 3d edit., 1971, People on Earth, 3d edit., 1988, World Geography, 1989; contbr. numerous articles to profl. jours. Bd. dirs. Mental Health Assn. Wabash Valley, Terre Haute, 1984-93, Coun. on Domestic Abuse, Terre Haute, 1987-92, United Ministries Ctr., Terre Haute, 1991-94; organizer, leader ednl. tours to China, 1986, 88, Australia, 1993, 96. Fulbright scholar, Burma, 1957-58; grantee Geography Educators Network Ind., 1988-96, Ind. Commn. Higher Edn., 1990, 92, 94, NSF, 1993, 95, U.S. Dept. Edn., 1992-96. Mem. Ind. Coun. Social Studies, Geography Educators Network Ind. (bd. dirs.), Nat. Coun. Geog. Edn. (pres. 1990), Nat. Coun. Social Studies, Nat. Sci. Tchrs. Assn., Am. Geographers.

DRUMMOND-REEVES, SUSAN JANE, organizational trainer, consultant; b. Houston, Dec. 22, 1948; d. Charles Hanford and Frances G. (Burdick) Drummond; m. Harold Wade Clark, Aug. 15, 1971 (div. Apr. 1976); m. John Morris Reeves, Sept. 11, 1987; stepchildren: Crystal, Hannah, Dezerlee. BA in Comm., Boise State U., 1990, MA in Comm., 1996. Rschr., editor, sec. various companies, Moscow, Boise, Idaho, 1971-78; adminstrv. asst., dept. comm. Idaho Humanities Coun., Boise, 1978-87; adjunct faculty Boise State U., 1990—, Boise State U. Continuing Edn., Mountain Home, Idaho, 1991—; rschr./writer Parker Consulting, Boise, 1991—; prin. New Century Rsch. and Consulting, Boise, 1995—; leadership trainer, Idaho Dept. Correction, Boise, 1995, mentoring trainer Idaho Power Co., Inc., Boise, 1995. Recipient Pitman Comm. award, Boise State U., 1989, Sunrise award for creativity, 1995. Mem. NOW, AAUW, Am. Assn. Tng. and Devel., Am. Assn. Tng. and Devel. Treasure Valley (Idaho) Chpt. Home: 4720 Jewell St Boise ID 83706 Office: Boise State Univ Dept Communication 1910 University Dr Boise ID 83725

DRVAR, MARGARET ADAMS, vocational education educator; b. Morgantown, W.Va., Dec. 22, 1953; d. Lester Morris and Daun Collette (Benson) Adams; m. Marvin Lynn Drvar, July 29, 1978; children: Jacob Elias, Jared Nathaniel. BS in Family Resources, W.Va. U., 1977, MS in Family Resources, 1982. Cert. tchr., vocat. home econs. tchr., W.Va. Substitute tchr. Monongalia County Bd. Edn., Morgantown, 1983-86; tchr. vocat. home econs. Clay Battelle Jr.-Sr. H.S., Blacksville, W.Va., 1986-89, 91-92, South Jr. H.S., Morgantown, 1992—; instr. culinary arts Monongalia County Tech. Edn. Ctr., Morgantown, 1989-91; youth group adv. Future Homemakers of Am., 1986—. V.p. United Meth. Women, Brookhaven, W.Va., 1985-92; sec. bd. trustees Brookhaven United Meth. Ch., 1989—; bd. dirs., sec. Morgantown AES Fed. Credit Union, 1989—; vol. 4-H leader Brookhaven Bulls 4-H Club, 1992—; mem. Monongalia County 4-H Leaders Assn., sec., 1995—. Recipient FHA Master Advisor award, 1996, Golden Apple Achiever award Ashland Oil, 1996. Mem. NEA, Am. Assn. Family and Consumer Scis. (cert.), W.Va. Edn. Assn., Monongalia County Edn. Assn., W.Va. Assn. Family and Consumer Scis., Monongalia County Assn. of Family and Consumer Scis., Am. Vocat. Assn., W.Va. Vocat. Assn., W.Va. Vocat. Assn. (historian family and consumer sci. divsn.), Alpha Upsilon Omicron, Gamma Phi Beta. Home: 3307 Darrah Ave Morgantown WV 26505 Office: Monongalia County Schs South Jr High Sch 500 E Parkway St Morgantown WV 26505-6839

DRYDEN, MARY ELIZABETH, law librarian, writer, actress; b. Chgo., Oct. 18, 1952; d. James Heard and Hazel Anne (Potts) Rule; m. Ian Dryden, Nov. 22, 1975 (div. 1990); m. Stephen Quadros, Sept. 12, 1992. Student, U. London, 1969, Bath U., 1970; BA, Scripps Coll., 1971; postgrad. U. Edinburgh, 1971-74. Head librarian Hahn, Cazier & Leff, San Diego, 1980, Fredman, Silverberg & Lewis, San Diego, 1980-83, Riordan & McKinzie, L.A., 1983—; freelance photog. model, 1975—. Theatrical appearances include Antony and Cleopatra, McOwen Theatre, London, 1984, Table Manners, L.A., 1985, Julius Caesar, L.A., 1986, Witness for the Prosecution, L.A., 1987, Come and Go, L.A., 1988, The Actor's Nightmare, L.A., 1989, The Dresser, L.A., 1989, Absent Friends, Long Beach, Calif., 1990, Run For Your Wife!, Long Beach, 1991, The Hollow, Long Beach, 1992, Cock and Bull Story, Fountainhead Theatre, Hollywood, 1993, Towards Zero, Long Beach, 1993, Angel Street, L.A., 1994, Bedroom Farce, L.A., 1995; (film) Private Collections, 1989, Eye Opener, 1992, A Situation, 1994, Porn Queens of the Seventies, 1994, The Nutty Professor, 1996, The Sophia Replacement, 1996; also music videos and TV Commls.; book critic L.A. Times; contbr. articles to newspapers. Mem. ABA, Brit. Equity, So. Calif. Soc. Law Librs., Brit. Assn. Film and Television Arts, Screen Actor's Guild, Mensa, Phi Beta Kappa. Avocations: photography, wine, architecture, fine art, languages. Office: Riordan & McKinzie 300 S Grand Ave Fl 29 Los Angeles CA 90071-3109

DRYDEN, SUSAN MEREDITH, secondary education educator; b. Radford, Va., Aug. 4, 1968; d. John Frederick and Shirley Ann (Robbins) D. BS in sec. edn., Auburn U., 1991. English educator Hoover (Ala.) City Schs., 1991—; fac. honor coun. Hoover High Nat. Honor Soc., 1992-94, internat. baccalaureate fac. Hoover H.S., 1994—. Mem. adv. bd. Jr. High Ranch, Birmingham, Ala., 1994—, vol. Mountain Brook Cmty. Ch., Birmingham, 1994—. Mem. Assoc. of Am. Educators. Republican. Home: 2522 Beverly Dr Birmingham AL 35223 Office: Hoover H S 1000 Buccaneer Dr Birmingham AL 35244

DRYDEN, SUSANNAH, elementary school counselor; b. Salina, Kans., Jan. 8, 1944; d. Richard M. and Mary Louise (Gurley) Rodenberger; m. Phil Stanley Dryden, Aug. 23, 1964; adopted children: Edward, Victor Lafond, Ben, Laura. MusB, U. Ariz., 1966; MS, Ft. Hays State U., 1992. Tchr. music Sunnyside Schs., Tucson, 1966-69; tchr. orchestra music Winslow (Ariz.) Schs., 1969-72; tchr. music Unified Sch. Dist. 475, Junction City, Kans., 1972-74; sec. Western Kans. Bapt. Assn., Garden City, Kans., 1976-78; tchr. music Unified Sch. Dist. 457, Garden City, 1978-79, elem. counselor, 1993—; tchr. music Chetopa (Kans.) Schs., 1979-82; orchestra dir. Unified Sch. Dist. 443, Dodge City, Kans., 1982-92. Sunday sch. tchr. Bapt. Chs., Kans., 1972-92, ch. organist, 1979—. Mem. NEA, Am. Sch. Counselors Assn. Home: 1108 E Hamline Garden City KS 67846-3433 Office: Gertrude Walker Elem Sch Garden City KS 67846

DRYLIE, CHRISTINE MARIE, lawyer; b. Jacksonville, Fla., Jan. 10, 1966; d. James Todd and Constance Marie (Wallis) D. BA summa cum laude, U. Colo., 1987; JD cum laude, U. Mich., 1990. Bar: Colo. 1990, Ill. 1991, U.S. Dist. Ct. Colo. 1991, U.S. Dist. Ct. (no. dist.) Ill. 1991, U.S. Dist. Ct. (ctrl. dist.) Ill. 1994, U.S. Ct. Appeals (10th cir.) 1991, U.S. Ct. Appeals (7th cir.) 1993, U.S. Supreme Ct. 1995. Clk. to chief judge Sherman G. Finesilver U.S. Dist. Ct. Colo., Denver, 1990-91; income ptnr. McDermott, Will & Emery, Chgo., 1991-96; ops. atty. Corn Products divsn. of CPC Internat. Inc., Summit-Argo, Ill., 1996—; adminstr. Family Law Project, Ann Arbor, Mich., 1988-91; judge Julius H. Miner Moot Ct., Northwestern U. Sch. Law, 1993-95, Northwestern U. Sch. Law Negotiation Competition, 1992-94. Writer newspaper The Res Gestae, 1987-90; editor yearbook The Quadrangle, 1988-90; contbg. editor Jour. of Law Reform, 1988-90. Vol. Lincoln Park Homeless Shelter, Chgo., 1991-92, Chgo. Cares, 1993—; co. coord. Youth Motivation Program, 1991—. Recipient Negligence Sect. award Mich. Bar Assn., 1990; Carl B. Gussin Meml. prize U. Mich., 1991; scholar Elk's, 1983-84, faculty U. Colo., 1983-84; U. Colo. grantee, 1987. Mem. ABA, Colo. Bar Assn., Ill. Bar Assn., Denver Bar Assn. (vol. teen ct. 1991), Chgo. Bar Assn., Chgo. Coun. Laywers, Women Law Students Assn., U. Colo. Alumni Assn., U. Mich. Alumni Assn., Moot Ct., Mortar Bd., Phi Beta Kappa, Pi Sigma Alpha. Democrat. Presbyterian. Office: Corn Products divsn CPC Internat Inc Moffett Tech 6500 Archer Rd PO Box 345 Summit-Argo IL 60501-0345

DRYNAN, MARGARET ISOBEL, music teacher, retired consultant; b. Toronto, Ont., Can., Dec. 10, 1915; d. William James and Ellen (Rowney) Brown; MusB, U. Toronto, 1943; m. George Drynan, July 3, 1940; children: Judith, John, James. Mem. nat. exec. bd. Royal Can. Coll. Organists after 1951, nat. 1st v.p., 1980-82, nat. pres., 1982-84; charter mem. Oshawa Coun. for the Arts, Ont., Can., 1963, pres., 1972-74; founder, dir. Canterbury Singers, Oshawa, 1952-69; music supr., cons. Durham Bd. Edn., 1960-81; bd. dirs. Oshawa Symphony, 1957-96, 1st v.p., 1984-86, pres., 1986-96; percussionist. Dir. Oshawa Sr. Citizens Choir; adjudicator for piano and choral music Ontario Festivals. Recipient award Associateship Royal Conservatory Toronto, 1975, Lescarbot award Can. Govt., 1992, other awards; named Outstanding Women of Yr., YWCA, 1986. Fellow Royal Can. Coll. Organists (Honorary award 1986); mem. Fedn. Women Tchrs., Can. Fedn. Adjudicators, Registered Music Tchrs. (past pres.). Anglican. Clubs: Univ. Women's (past pres.); Heliconian of Toronto. Published compositions include: Songs for Judith, Why do the bells?, Including Me, Missa Brevis in F, The Fate of Gilbert Gim, The Canada Goose (operetta), British Columbia, Rainy Day Song, Superjogger, Roller-skating, November, To Mary and Joseph, Prelude and Fugue in C minor for organ; (arrangements) Little David, Bring a Torch, Lullaby for Judith, (4 part choral) Unto the Angels, 1996, When I Look Out on Canada, 1996. Home: 589 Pinewood St, Oshawa, ON Canada L1G 2S2

DRYSDALE, NANCY ALLENSWORTH, art dealer; b. Chgo., July 22, 1931; d. William Rolland and Frances Gertrude (Mason) Allensworth; m. Lloyd E. Hawkinson, Aug. 1, 1953 (dec. Apr. 1955); m. Robert C. McIntosh, Apr. 26, 1958 (div. 1969); 1 child, Amy Bennett; m. Douglas D. Drysdale, June 9, 1978. BS, Northwestern U., 1953. Owner, dir. Nancy Drysdale Gallery, Washington, 1977—, McIntosh/Drysdale Gallery, Washington and Houston, 1980-85. Chmn. bd. Cin. Cont. Art Ctr., 1974-75, pres., 1973-74. Named Woman of the Yr. Cin. Enquirer, 1968. Mem. Washington Art Dealers Assn. (v.p. 1991-93, pres. 1993—). Office: Nancy Drysdale Gallery 2103 O St NW Washington DC 20037-1008

DRYZGULA, SUSAN BISACKY, primary school educator; b. New Haven, Conn., May 25, 1952; d. Albert Steven and Barbara Ann (Gramm) Bisacky; m. Robert Edward Dryzgula Jr., Aug. 17, 1974; children: Robert Albert, Christine Susan, Daniel Robert. BS in Elem. Edn., Ctrl. Conn. State U., 1974; MS in Early Childhood Edn., So. Conn. State U., 1994. Cert. tchr., Conn. Substitute tchr. North Branford (Conn.) Bd. Edn., 1988-89, long-term substitute tchr., 1989, tchr. Jerome Harrison Sch., 1989—, mem. sci. com., 1993—; nat. trainer Talents Unltd., North Brandford, 1993—. Den leader Boy Scouts Am., 1982-86, com. chairperson, North Branford, 1988-93; den leader Girl Scouts USA, North Branford, 1985-89; mem. human rels. com. Town of North Branford, 1983-85; area capt. canvasser North Branford Scholarship Assn., 1987-92; mem. Jerome Harrison PTO, North Branford, 1991—; mem. Celebration of Excellence Adv. com. Recipient Svc. Recognition award No. Branford Little League, 1988, Branford Lions Club, 1990, 91, 92, 93, Celebration of Excellence award State of Conn. Dept. Edn., 1995. Mem. Am. Fedn. Tchrs., Conn. Sci. Tchrs. Assn., Conn. State Fedn. Tchrs., North Branford Fedn. Tchrs. Home: 26 Altieri Rd North Branford CT 06471-1424

DUARTE, PATRICIA M., real estate and insurance broker; b. Truro, Mass., Feb. 23, 1938; d. Antone Jr. and Marjorie (Beckley) Duarte. Grad. high sch., Provincetown, Mass. Lic. ins. and real estate broker; constrn. supt. Sec. various ins. agys., Amherst, Mass., 1957-60; ins. and real estate agt. Duarte Ins. & Real Estate, Truro, 1960-66, owner, prin. agt., 1966-78; ins. risk mgr. J.L. Marshall & Sons, Inc., Pawtucket, R.I., 1979-92; owner, mgr. Patricia-Duarte Real Estate, Rockport, Maine, 1988—; restorer antique homes New Eng., Mass., 1979—. Mem., sec. Truro Planning Bd., 1965-72, chmn., 1974-78; mem. exec. com. Cape Cod Planning and Econ. Devel. Com., 1971-76; mem. Reelect Brawn for Senate Com., Camden, Maine, 1988; mem. Rockport Planning Bd., 1991-94, Rockport Comprehensive Plan Implementation Com., 1991-94; co-chmn. Rockport Capital Improvement Com., 1991—; bd. dirs. Cape Cod chpt. Am. Heart Assn., 1963-70; mem. Opera House Commn., 1992-94. Mem. Penobscot Bay Bd. Realtors, Profl. Ins. Agts. New Eng. (bd. dirs. 1974-76), Gen. Fedn. Women's Clubs (2d v.p. Camden chpt. 1989), Hist. Preservation Assn. St. Thomas. Republican. Roman Catholic. Home and Office: 46 Pascal Ave Rockport ME 04856-5918 also: The Anchorage 6600 Estate Nazareth # 55 Saint Thomas VI 00802

DUBESA, ELAINE J., biotechnology company executive; b. Alton, Ill., July 26, 1943; m. Michael Dubesa, Oct. 28, 1967. BS in Med. Tech., Loyola U., New Orleans, 1966. Rsch. assoc. pesticides project U. Hawaii, Honolulu, 1968-69; field rep., pesticides project La. State U., New Orleans, 1970-71; lab. supr. Beaufort (S.C.) County Meml. Hosp., 1971-72; asst. supr. hematology Mayo Clinic, Rochester, Minn., 1973-75; edn. coord. Sherman Hosp., Elgin, Ill., 1975-78; sect. chief PCL (now Corning Clin. Labs.), Portland, Oreg., 1978-80; quality control supr. PCL-RIA, Inc., Portland, 1980-82; quality control mgr. Am. Bioclinical Inc., Portland, 1982-87; quality assurance mgr., regulatory affairs mgr. Epitope, Inc., Beaverton, Oreg., 1987-91, v.p. regulatory affairs, 1991-95, v.p. govt. affairs, 1995—. Active Troutdale (Oreg.) Hist. Soc. Mem. Am. Soc. Quality Control, Regulatory Affairs Profl. Soc., Am. Soc. Clinical Pathologists, Beta Epsilon Upsilon.

DUBEY, SONAL, division ergonomics simulation engineer; b. Kampala, Africa, Apr. 9, 1972; arrived in U.S., 1974; d. Bhupendra Motilal and Nalini Bhupendra (Barai) G. BS in industrial engring., GMI Engring. & Mgmt. Inst., 1994; postgrad., Rensselaer Poly. Inst., 1994—. Engr. Gen. Motors, Troy, Mich., 1990-94, divsn. ergonomics/simulation engr., 1994—; pres. Inst. Indsl. Engrs., 1994-95; tng. coord. Dale Carnegie classes, 1993; actress GMI Theatre, 1994. Recipient provost's honor award GMI-EMI, 1993, 94. Mem. Inst. Industrial Engrs. (pres. 1990-94), Soc. Women Engrs. (pres. 1990-94), Tech. Students of GM (pres. 1990-94), Toastmasters Internat. (mascot 1990-94), Sigma Phi Iota. Office: Delphi Gen Motors 1401 Crooks Rd MCT-24 Troy MI 48084

DUBIN, LUCY SARAH, management consultant; b. Urbana, Ill., Mar. 13, 1952; d. Robert and Elisabeth (Ruch) D. BA, U. Calif., Irvine, 1973; MA, Calif. State U., L.A., 1981; MS, Calif. Sch. Profl. Psychology, L.A., 1992, PhD, 1995. Mgr. Oak Media Corp., L.A., 1981-85; dir. Great Am. Comms. Co., L.A., 1985-89; cons. William M. Mercer, Inc., L.A., 1991-92; pvt. practice L.A., 1992—. Editor proceedings Family Firm Inst., 1991. Mem. APA, ASTD, Soc. of Indsl./Orgnl. Psychologists, Soc. of Psychologists in Mgmt., Acad. Mgmt.

DUBIN, SUSAN HELEN, private school educator, storyteller; b. L.A., Jan. 12, 1948; d. Hyman Benjamin and RoseAnne (Giser) Klane; m. Marc Jeffrey Dubin, June 5, 1969; children: Victor Matthew, Roseanne Danyelle. BA, UCLA, 1970; postgrad., Trenton State U., 1970-72, Hebrew Union Coll., L.A., 1982—. Cert. tchr., N.J., Calif. Tchr. Valley Campus Pres-Sch., North Hollywood, Calif., 1966-68; tchr., asst. dir. Storyland, North Hollywood, 1968-70; tchr. 2d grade Burlington Twp., N.J., 1970-72; pre-kindergarten tchr., dir. summer program Adat AriEl Pre-Sch., North Hollywood, 1972-75; substitute tchr. pvt. schs., L.A., 1975-78; owner, dir., tchr. Canby Hall, Reseda, Calif., 1978-80; pre-kindergarten tchr. Beth Kodesh Pre-Sch., Canoga Park, Calif., 1980-81; kindergarten tchr. Hillel Acad., L.A., 1981-82; libr. instr. Valley Beth Shalom Day Sch., Encino, Calif., 1982—; presenter seminars. Contbg. author: Starbright, 1986, Teaching Judaic Values in Literature Using Noah's Ark, 1985; author: (filmstrip and tchr.'s guide) The Tree, 1971. Mem. San Fernando Valley Arts Coun., 1992-93; mem. pers. practices com. Bur. Jewish Edn., Los Angeles County, 1993—. Mem. Nat. Coun. Tchrs. English, Assn. Jewish Librs. (co-chair conv. 1990-92, accreditation chair 1993—, parliamentarian 1994—, constitution com. chair 1995), Assn. Jewish Librs. of So. Calif. (program v.p. 1985-89, pres. 1989-93, Dorothy Schroeder award, western regional conv. chair 1996), Internat. Reading Assn., Calif. Assn. Ind. Schs. Libr. Network. Home: 18901 Marilla St Northridge CA 91324-1837 Office: Valley Beth Shalom Day Sch Day Sch Library 15739 Ventura Blvd Encino CA 91436-2903

DUBLIN, ELVIE WILSON, clinical psychologist; b. Athens, Greece, May 18, 1937; d. Anthony I. and Rosa (Protecdicos) Nicolopoulos; m. John Wilson, Oct. 29, 1958 (div. 1967); children: David Wilson, Toni Wilson; m. James Dublin, Dec. 21, 1973 (div. 1978). BA, Ind. U., 1966, PhD, 1972. Cons. Hospitality House Nursing Home, Bedford, Ind., 1972-73; psychotherapist Choice, Inc., 1973-79, sec.-treas., 1973-79; pres. Studentworld, Inc., 1978-81; pvt. practice psychology, Bloomington, Ind., 1979—; Arabian horse breeder, founder, owner Tall Oaks Arabians, 1980-86,

Dublin Racing Arabians, 1986—; bd. dirs. Midwestern Psychotherapy Inst., 1977. Trainee NSF, 1965-67, USPHS, 1967-70. Mem. Am. Psychol. Assn., Ind. Psychol. Assn., Assn. Advancement Psychology, Internat. Arabian Horse Assn., Arabian Horse Registry of Am. (assoc.), Arabian Racing Assn. Calif., Phi Beta Kappa. Clubs: Arabian Jockey, Ind. Horse Coun. Home: 9401 E State Rd 46 Bloomington IN 47401-9243 Office: 4151 E 3rd St Bloomington IN 47401-5539

DUBNER, FRANCES SEGALL, gifted/talented education educator; b. N.Y.C., Nov. 26, 1930; d. Jacob and Betty (Meyer) Segall; m. Raymond M. Dubner, Dec. 24, 1950; children: Steven, Jerrold, Nancy Dubner Teich. BA in Secondary Edn. Speech/English, CUNY, 1951, MA in Secondary Edn. Speech/English, 1953; PhD in Curriculum and Instrn., Ga. State U., 1979. D-7 life cert. secondary tchr., Ga. Tchr. N.Y.C. Maxwell Vocat. H.S., Bklyn., 1951-64; asst. prof. comm. Shaw U., Raleigh, N.C., 1965-71; English tchr. Jackson (Tenn.) Ctrl. Merry H.S., 1971-73; instr. speech Ga. State U., Atlanta, 1973-74; tchr. of gifted Chamblee (Ga.) H.S., 1974-89, Dunwoody (Ga.) H.S., 1989—; pres. Cinema, Inc., Raleigh, 1967-69, DeKalb Supporters of Gifted, Atlanta, 1984-86; pres.-elect N.C. Speech Assn., Raleigh, 1970-71. Contbr. articles to profl. jours. Del. N.C. Dem. Party, 1964. Fulbright-Hays fellow U.S. Edn. Dept., Israel and Egypt, 1991, Poland and Hungary, 1995. Mem. ACLU, Orgn. of Dekalb Educators, NEA, Ga. Edn. Assn., Common Cause, Amnesty Internat., Sierra Club. Jewish. Home: 5188 Charmant Pl Atlanta GA 30360-1455 Office: Dunwoody HS 5035 Vermack Rd Dunwoody GA 30338

DUBOIS, LOREE BETH, accountant; b. Fall River, Mass., Feb. 16, 1970; d. Joseph and Nancy E. (Gates) Fazzina. AA in Bus. Adminstrn., Bristol C.C., Fall River, 1990; BS in Acctg., U. Mass., North Dartmouth, 1992; postgrad., Bentley Coll., 1995—. CPA, Mass. Supr. Fall River (Mass.) Florist Supply, 1987-88; med. transcriber St. Anne's Hosp., Fall River, 1988-89; acct. John F. Doherty, CPA, Tiverton, R.I., 1989-92, Wolf & Co., P.C., Boston, 1992-95; prin. tax acct. Kendall Healthcare, Mansfield, Mass., 1995-96; tax supervisor Rosenfield, Holland & Raymon, P.C., New Bedford, Mass., 1996—. Recipient Nat. Bus. Merit award, 1990. Roman Catholic. Home: 15 Harvey Ln Somerset MA 02725 Office: Rosenfield Holland & Raymon PC 700 Pleasant St New Bedford MA 02740

DUBOIS, RUTH HARBERG, human service agency executive; b. Phila., Apr. 8, 1933; d. Sidney and Lenore (Abramson) Harberg; m. Jan E. DuBois, Aug. 9, 1956; children: Marc, Jon, Peter, Pamela. AB, Mt. Holyoke Coll., 1955. Prin. cons. N.Y. State Heroin and Alcohol Abuse Study, 1981; mem. Pa. Gov.'s Coun. on Drug and Alcohol Abuse, 1977-80; tech. asst. Nat. Inst. Drug Abuse/Pyramid Project, 1978-85; co-dir. DuBois and Rosenwald Assocs., 1982-87; with Children's Rsch. and Edn. Inst., 1984-87; exec. dir. Corp. Alliance for Drug Edn., Phila., 1987—; mem. com. on substance abuse The Mayor's Commn. on Health in the Eighties, Phila., 1983; tech. asst. Pa. Dept. Health, Office of Drug and Alcohol Program, 1981-85; rsch. asst. in cancer and endocrinology Yale U. Sch. of Medicine and Thomas Jefferson U., 1955-59. Contbr. articles to profl. jours. Mem. numerous bds. including chmn. bd. dirs. Albert Einstein Med. Ctr., Phila. Citizens for Children and Youth, Montgomery County Mental Health, 1982-85; bd. dirs. Abraxas Found., Inc., Pitts., 1981—; adv. coun. dept. pub. health Phila. Prevention Partnership, 1992-95; mem. Mayor's Pvt. Sector Task Force on Mgmt. and Productivity/Dept. Human Svcs. Study, Phila., 1992-93, others. Office: Alliance for Drug Edn Corp WCAU Bldg 393 City Ave Philadelphia PA 19131

DUBOUX, PATRICIA JANE, advertising agency and human resources executive; b. Chgo., Mar. 26, 1956; d. Carl Andrew and Rita Ann (Sullivan) Hulik; stepmother, Mercedes Elizabeth (Rusch) Hulik; m. Dennis Vincent DuBoux, May 17, 1986. BA in Advt., Mich. State U., 1978; MS in Indsl. Relations, Loyola U., Chgo., 1985. Media asst. Joint Commn. on Accreditation Health Care Orgns., Chgo., 1978-79, brochure asst., 1979-80, mktg. coord., 1980-81, recruitment/compensation coord., 1982-84, recruitment/employee relations mgr., 1984-86; human resources mgr. DDB Needham Worldwide, Chgo., 1986-87, dir. personnel adminstrn., 1987-89, dir. human resources, 1989-90, v.p., dir. human resources, 1990—. Mem. Human Resources Mgmt. Assn. Chgo., Soc. for Human Resource Mgmt. Home: 1025 Prairie Ave Park Ridge IL 60068-3939 Office: DDB Needham Worldwide 303 E Wacker Dr Chicago IL 60601-5212

DUBOVSKY, EVA VITKOVA, nuclear medicine physician, educator; b. Prague, Czechoslovakia, 1933. MD, Charles U. Faculty Medicine, Prague, Czech Republic, 1957. Diplomate Am. Bd. Nuclear Medicine. Intern U. Hosp., Charles U., Prague, 1956-57, chief resident, 1961-63, fellow divsn. endocrinology & metabolism, 1963-65; rsch. fellow divsn. endocrinology U. Ala., Birmingham, 1968-70; clin. assoc. VA Med. Ctr., Birmingham, 1970-72; from instr. to prof. U. Ala., Birmingham, 1954—; vis. prof. U. Cin., 1987, Cleve. CLinic, 1987, VA Med. Ctr., Portland, Oreg.,1988, Columbia Coll. Physicians & Surgeons, 1989, Dartmouth Med. Ctr., 1989, William Beaumont Hosp., 1992, 94, Charles U., 1994, Baptist Med. Ctr. Okla., 1994, U. Louisville, 1994. Editor: Nuclear Medicine Technology Continuing Education Review, 1976, 2d edit., 1981; co-editor: Nuclear Medicine in Clinical Urology and Nephrology, 1985, Atlas of Nuclear Medicine and Imagine; contbr. chpts. to books and articles to profl. jours. Mem. AMA, Am. Coll. Nuclear Physicians, Soc. Nuclear Medicine, SECSNIM. Office: U Ala Hosp Divsn Nuc Medicine 619 19th St S Birmingham AL 35233

DUBROVSKY, GERTRUDE WISHNICK, journalist, educator, independent scholar; b. N.Y.C., Mar. 10, 1926; d. Benjamin and Esther Raisa (Katz) Wishnick; m. Jack Dubrovsky, Feb. 24, 1946 (div. Sept. 1975); children: Richard, Steven, Benjamin; m. Sidney Gray, June 13, 1976. AB, Georgian Ct. Coll., 1956; MA, Rutgers U., 1959; EdD, Columbia U., 1974. Tchr. Keyport (N.J.) grammar sch., 1956-57, Point Pleasant (N.J.) H.S., 1959-61; asst. prof. Trenton (N.J.) State Coll., 1964-66; program dir. YIVO Inst. for Jewish Rsch., N.Y.C., 1975-81; freelance journalist, writer N Y Times, N.Y.C., 1979—; ind. scholar, rschr. Princeton, 1980—; rschr., writer, asst. to pres. Carnegie Found. for the Advancement of Tchg., Princeton, N.J., 1982-85; Yiddish instr. Ctr. Jewish Life Princeton U., 1974-95; pres. Documentary III, Princeton, 1980—; cons. in field. Editor newsletter: Rural Roots: Jewish Farm History, 1988-95; author: The Land Was Theirs: Jewish Farmers, 1992; translator: (poems) Kentucky, 1990 (Jewish Book Club selection); prodr., dir. documentary The Land Was Theirs, 1993. Mcpl. committeeperson Dem. Party, Princeton, 1980—, chair, 1982-84; mem. Commn. on Aging, Princeton, 1980—, chair, 1991-93;. Fellow Meml. Found. for Jewish Culture, 1975, Oxford (Eng.) Ctr. Hebrew & Jewish Studies, 1994; NEH grantee, 1976, 78. Mem. Assn. for Jewish Studies, Am. Jewish Hist. Soc., Am. Jewish Archives, Princeton Rsch. Forum. Home and Office: 244 Hawthorne Ave Princeton NJ 08540

DUBUC, MARY ELLEN, educational administrator; b. N.Y.C. July 20, 1950; d. Patrick Joseph and Catherine (McKenna) Reynolds; BA cum laude (scholar), Marymount Manhattan Coll., 1972; MA, Columbia U., 1973; cert. advanced grad. studies R.I. Coll., 1985; m. Leo Dennis Dubuc Jr., Sept. 9, 1978; children: Brian Robert, Kimberly Ann. Spl. edn. tchr. Cardinal Cushing Sch., Hanover, Mass., 1973-76, Ferncliff Manor Sch., Yonkers, N.Y., 1976-77; program coordinator Bronx Devel. Services, 1977-78; dir. edn. R.I. Assn. Retarded, Woonsocket, 1978-84, spl. edn. cons., 1984-92; qualified med. retardation profl. Seacliff, Inc., Cumberland, R.I., 1988-91; tchr. BICO Collaborative Program, North Attleboro, Mass., 1989; acting exec. dir. Seacliff, Inc., 1991-93; dir. quality assurance Avatar, Inc., 1992; dir. specialized svcs. The ARC of No. R.I., Woonsocket, 1992—. Fed. trainee, 1971, 72. Mem. North Smithfield PTA, 1986—; ednl. evaluator No. R.I. Collaborative, 1992. Mem. Assn. Severely Handicapped, R.I. Assn. Retarded Citizens, NAFE, R.I. Assn. Adult and Continuing Edn. (v.p. pub. rels. 1986-89, corr. sec. 1991-93), Alpha Chi. Democrat. Roman Catholic. Office: The ARC of No RI 80 Fabien St Woonsocket RI 02895-6277

DUCH, BECKY ANN, turbo jet engine mechanic; b. Fort Knot, Ky., Aug. 7, 1959; d. Doyle Eugene and Rachel (New) Barnett; m. José Manuel Duch, Febr. 15, 1957; children: Ryan Juan Carlos, Sarah Rachel. AS in Aircraft Powerplant Technology, Cmty. Coll. of Air Force, Eielson AFB, Alaska, 1992. Jet engine mechanic USAF 82d Field Maintenance, Williams AFB, Ariz., 1981-86, USAF 6th Strategic Wing, Eielson AFB, Alaska, 1986-90, Alaska Air Nat. Guard, Eielson AFB, 1990—. Mem. NOW. Democrat. Home: 3200 Monkshood Ln North Pole AK 99705 Office: 168th Air Refueling Wing-Alaska Air Nat Guard 1176 Flightline Ave Ste 101D Eielson AFB AK 99702

DUCKETT, BERNADINE JOHNAL, retired elementary principal; b. Flint, Mich., Aug. 7, 1939; d. John and Bernice (Robinson) Edwards: m. Ellis Duckett Jr., Apr. 15, 1963; children: Bruce Devlon, Janeen Jae; 1 stepchild, Ellis III; m. Charles Teaberry (div. June 1960). BS in Edn., Ctrl. Mich. U., 1962; MA in Ednl. Adminstrn., U. Mich., 1966; Reading Specialist, Mich. State U., 1970; postgrad., Flint (Mich.) C.C., 1989-92. Cert. elem. tchr., Mich. Classroom tchr. Dort Elem. Sch., Flint, 1959-65; reading tchr. Dort & Dewey Elem. Sch., Flint, 1965-67; instrnl. specialist Doyle and Dewey Elem. Sch., Flint, 1967-71; asst. prin. Dewey, Merrill & Cook Elem. Sch., Flint, 1971-74; prin. Garfield & Elem. M.L. King, Flint, 1974-96; ret., 1996; presenter, mem. Internat. Ednl. Symposium, Rome, 1988-92, Flint Schs. Employee of Month Program, 1985-92. Author: Diet on the Lighter Side, 1988, My Grandparents Said Go 4 It, 1989; author joint books: Bicentennial Sch. Cookbook, 1976, Tapestry, 1988, URA Winner, 1994; contbr. articles to mags. and newspapers. Fundraiser Walk-a-Thons, United Negro Coll. Fund, Children's Miracle, Flint, 1991, Crim Race for Spl. Children, Flint, 1989-96, Riverbend Striders, Flint, 1993-95; mem., presenter Consortium to Prevent Child Abuse, 1990; vol. St. Joseph Hosp. Aux., Flint, 1990-95; mem. Greater Flint Afro-Am. Sports Hall of Fame, 1992; mem. com. Aiding Hard of Hearing, Quota Club Internat., Flint, 1994. Recipient Outstanding Educator plaque NAACP, Flint Intern Plaque, 1986, Flint OBE Pioneer Plaque, 1993, Ednl. Contbns. as Family award, 1993, Walker medal Leukemia Soc., 1996; grantee Flint Cmty. Schs., 1990-93. Mem. Nat. Assn. Elem. Sch. Prins. (dir. founds. 1992-94, cons., student discipline Focus Group on Ethnic Minorities 1981, 92, 94, Outstanding Svc. Plaque 1993), Nat. Assn. Media Women (sec. Flint chpt. 1989-92, Media Woman of Yr. 1990), Mich. Assn. Elem. and Mid. Sch. Prins. (chairperson awards, mem. conf. planning and summer camp com., treas., membership chair, del., presenter 1977-92, certs. 1985, 87, 91, plaque 1990), Nat. Alliance Black Sch. Educators (presenter 1993), Internat. Platform Assn., Flint Assn. Elem. Prins. (sec., election chair, social chair 1980-93), Global Network of Schs., U. Mich. Alumni Assn., Nat. Leukemia Soc. (Alaskan marathon walker, medalist 1996). Home: 3720 Circle Dr Flint MI 48507-1879

DUCKETT, JOAN, law librarian; b. Bklyn., Oct. 21, 1934; d. Stephen and Mary (Wehrum) Kearney; m. Richard Duckett, Aug. 25, 1956; children: Richard, David, Daniel, Deirdre. BA, Kean Coll., 1974; MLS, Rutgers U., 1977; JD, Suffolk U., 1983; postgrad., Oxford (Eng.) U., 1986. Bar: Mass. 1983, U.S. Ct. Appeals (fed. cir.) 1984. Media specialist Oak Knoll Sch., Summit, N.J., 1976-80; law clk. Dist. Atty. Suffolk County, Boston, 1982; vol. atty. Cambridgeport Problem Ctr., Cambridge, Mass., 1984-85; reference libr. Harvard Law Sch. Libr., Cambridge, 1982-84, coord. The New Eng. Law Libr. Consortium, 1984-87, head reference svcs., 1987—, profl. devel. com., chmn. Bryant fellowship award panel, 1987—. Contbr. articles to profl. jours. Protocol hostess L.A. Olympic Com., 1984. Fellow Mass. Bar Found.; mem. Mass. Bar Assn., Boston Bar Assn., Am. Assn. Law Librs., Law Librs. New Eng., Assn. Boston Law Librs., Alpha Sigma Lambda, Beta Phi Mu. Office: Harvard Law Sch Libr Langdell Hall Cambridge MA 02138

DUCKLER, SELMA REGINA, retired actress, director, producer, educator; b. N.Y.C., Jan. 5, 1931; d. Solmon and Ida (Goodman) Linenberg; m. Lawrence Duckler, Mar. 6, 1950; children: Heidi, Merridawn, Geordie, Alysia, Garrick. Student, U. Wis., 1950. Actress Civic Theatre of Portland, 1950-65; actress Hilton Repertory Theater, Portland, 1965-73, prodr., 1977-83; tchr. Oreg. Artist in Residence, Portland, 1978-83; tchr. gifted and talented Pub. Schs., 1980-85; pres. Inst. Judaic Studies, Portland, 1989-92, Oreg. Psychoanalytic Inst., Portland, 1994-96; adminstr. Nat. Psychoanalytic Bd., Washington, 1994-96; dir. Metro. Arts Commn., Portland, 1981-85. Pres. World Without War Coun., Portland, 1977-80, Women's Alliance at Unitarian Ch., Portland, 1976-80, PTA Wilson H.S., Portland, 1980-92; v.p. Am. Jewish Com., Portland, 1989-91; dir. grants ACLU, Portland, 1977-82; docent Portland Art Mus., 1985-90; pres., chmn. Coun. Jewish Women, 1980-85; project dir. Neighborhood House, 1974-76; mem. bd., chmn. culture Mittleman Jewish Cmty. Ctr., 1980-90. Republican. Jewish. Home: 3137 SW Fairmount Blvd Portland OR 97201

DUCKWORTH, TARA ANN, insurance company executive; b. Seattle, June 7, 1956; d. Leonard Douglas and Audrey Lee (Limbeck) Hill; m. Mark L. Duckworth, May 16, 1981; children: Harrison Lee III, Andrew James, Kathryn Anne. AAS, Highline Community Coll., Seattle, 1976. Acctg. clk. SAFECO Ins. Co., Seattle, programmer analyst, 1977-80, programming supr., 1980-85, info. systems supr., 1985-90; rate systems mgr. mut. funds SAFECO Credit, SAFECO Trust, Seattle, 1990-94; systems mgr. PNMR, Seattle, 1994—; mem. tech adv. com. for the computer info. svcs. program North Seattle Community Coll., 1984—, chairperson tech. adv. com., 1988-90. Mem. Star Lake Improvement Club, 1988-94; mem. fellowship com. St. Lukes Luth. Ch., 1986—. Mem. NAFE, Nat. Assn. for Ins. Women, Soc. for State Filers, Nat. PTA. Office: SAFECO Ins Co SAFECO Plz Seattle WA 98185

DUCLOS, GLORIA SHAW, foreign language educator; b. Boston, Aug. 2, 1928; d. Shaw and Evelyn (Taylor) Livermore; m. Albert J. Duclos, Aug. 17, 1963 (div. June 1991); children: Catherine Shaw, Rebecca Taylor. BA, Radcliffe Coll., 1949, Oxford U., 1951; MA, Oxford U., 1955, Harvard U., 1953. Instr. Greek & Latin Wilson Coll., Chambersburg, Pa., 1954-55, Wellesley (Mass.) Coll., 1955-60; asst. prof. classics U. Maine, Orono, 1962-65; prof. classics U. So. Maine, Portland, 1965-92; vis. asst. prof. classics Bowdoin Coll., Brunswick, Maine, 1970, adj. lectr. classics, 1994; Fulbright prof. classics U. Malawi, Zomba, 1985-86; chmn. Latin achievement test com. Coll. Bd., Princeton, N.J., 1983-90. Contbr. articles to profl. jours. Mem., chair Maine Humanities Coun., Augusta, Maine, 1975-81; mem. Maine Hist. Soc., Portland, 1980-96, Maine Historic Preservation Commn., Augusta, 1972-76. AAUW fellow, 1953-54. Mem. Classical Assn. New England (pres., sec.-treas., Barlow-Beach award 1987), Vergilian Soc. (bd. trustees 1993-96), Phi Beta Kappa. Democrat. Episcopalian. Home: 13 Emerson St Apt 306 Portland ME 04101

DUCRAN, CLAUDETTE DELORIS, bank officer; b. Trinityville, St. Thomas, Jamaica, July 23, 1941; came to U.S., 1962; d. Wellesley Provan and Hilda Maude (Beckford) DuC. Student, Corcoran Sch. Art, Washington, 1967; cert. of diploma, USDA Grad. Sch., Washington, 1972; BBA, George Washington U., 1982. Adminstrv. asst. World Bank, Washington, 1964-75, fin. asst., 1975-85, ops. asst., 1985-88, disbursement asst., 1988-94, disbursement analyst, 1994-96; mem. adv. com. Very Spl. Arts Kennedy Ctr., Washington, 1990-93, Hands Across Hemisphere Craft Ctr., Washington, 1991; founder, pres. Let's Learn by Reading, Jamaica, 1990—; bd. dirs. Universal Investment Bank Ltd., Kingston, Jamaica. Author: (booklet) Exhibitors Guidelines, 1989, 90. Bd. dirs. Craft Ctr., Washington, 1991—; panelist Career Week George Washington U., Washington, 1991, Women's Ctr., McLean, Va., 1991; founder, chair The Claudette D. Ducran Found., Inc., Kingston, Jamaica, W.I., 1995—, The Eureka Alliance, Inc., Washington, 1995—. Recipient 1st prize Writer's League, Washington, 1967, Internat. Order of Merit, 1994; named Internat. Woman of Yr., 1993-94. Mem. World Affairs Coun., Soc. for Internat. Devel., The World Bank Art Soc. (v.p. 1986-88, pres. 1988-93), UN Assn./Nat. Capital Assn., 1818 Soc. Home: The Brighton 2123 California St NW # B-1 Washington DC 20008-1874

DUDASH, LINDA CHRISTINE, insurance executive; b. Pitts.; d. Andrew Daniel and Lillian (Reynolds) D. BA in English, Point Park Coll., 1969. Tech. writer Am. Insts. for Rsch., Pitts., 1968-69; claim svc. rep. Reliance Ins. Co., Pitts., 1969-70, claim rep., 1970-71; claim mgr. Reliance Ins. Co., Jacksonville, Fla., 1971-73, Harrisburg, Pa., 1973-80, Chgo., 1980-86; H.O. sr. claim supr. Zurich Ins. Co., Schaumburg, Ill., 1986-88; asst. v.p., mgr. liability claims Zurich-Am. Ins., Schaumburg, Ill., 1988-91, asst. v.p., mgr. claims continuous improvement, 1991-92, v.p. dir. field ops., 1992-95; v.p. claims Casualty Ins. Co., divsn. Fremont Compensation Ins. Co., Chgo., 1995—. Office: Casualty Insurance Co 321 N Clark St Chicago IL 60610-4789

DUDDEN, ROSALIND F., librarian; b. New Haven, Nov. 4, 1944; d. George B. and Mary Ellen (Forgan) Farnam; m. Fred I. Dudden, June 20, 1970 (div. July 1993); 1 child, Laura Melissa. BA, Finch Coll., 1966; MLS, U. Denver, 1970. Dir. libr. svcs. Mercy Med. Ctr., Denver, 1971-86; health scis. libr. Nat. Jewish Ctr. for Immunology & Respiratory Medicine, Denver, 1986—; web site adminstr., 1995—; pres. Colo. Coun. Med. Librs., Denver, 1975-77. Vol. St. Francis Ctr., Denver, 1993—. Mem. Acad. Health Info. Profs. (disting.), Med. Libr. Assn. (pres. hosp. librs. sect. 1987-88, Frank Bradway Rogers award 1995). Office: Nat Jewish Ctr 1400 Jackson St Denver CO 80206

DUDDY, MARIANNE TERESA, consultant; b. Englewood, N.J., Dec. 26, 1960; d. Joseph M. and Eunice Patricia (Scullion) D. BA, Wellesley Coll., 1982; MTS, Weston Sch. of Theology, 1986. Dir. Nursing Home Ombudsman Program, Lexington, Mass., 1983-85; exec. dir. Living is for the Elderly, Woburn, Mass., 1985-87; legis. dir., dir. planning AAA, Boston Elderly Commn., 1987-90; elder care program mgr., account mgr., sr. account exec. Work/Family Directions, Boston, 1990—. Pres. Dignity, Boston, 1987-89; v.p. Dignity USA, 1991-93, pres. 1993-97. Office: Dignity USA Ste 11 1500 Massachusetts Ave NW Washington DC 20005

DUDICS-DEAN, SUSAN ELAINE, interior designer; b. Perth Amboy, N.J., Oct. 22, 1950; d. Theodore W. and Joyce M. (Ryals) D.; m. Rick Dean, Apr. 30, 1989; 1 child, Merissa Joyce. BS in Sociology, W.Va. U., 1972; postgrad. Rutgers U., 1975-78, U. Calif., Irvine, 1979-81, Can. Coll., 1981-89. Programmer Prudential Life, Newark, 1972-73; sr. systems analyst Johnson & Johnson, New Brunswick, N.J., 1973-78, Sperry Univac, Irvine, Calif., 1978-80; sr. systems analyst, project leader Robert A. McNeil, San Mateo, Calif., 1981-83; dist. design dir. TransDesigns, Woodstock, Ga., 1982-93. lectr. in the field of interior design, 1994—, spkr. in field, 1994—. Contbr. articles to profl. jours.; writer (newspaper column) Design Lines, 1993—; guest (TV shows) House Doctor, Marketplace Sta. KGO-TV. High sch. mentor Directions, San Francisco, 1985-95. Mem. Women Entreprenuers (membership com., treas. 1983-87), Cen. N.J. Alumni Assn. Delta Gamma (assoc. sec., founder, pres.), San Francisco C. of C., Nat. Assn. of Profl. Saleswomen, Am. Soc. Interior Designers (allied mem. 1989-92), Profl. Bus. Women's Assn., Delta Gamma. Recipient awards TransDesigns, Woodstock, Ga., 1984, 85, 86, 87, 89, 90, 91. Avocations: skiing, sewing, scuba diving, ballet, hand crafts.

DUDLEY, BARBARA, environmental association administrator. Dir. Nat. Lawyers Guild, 1983-87, Veatch Program, N.Y.C., 1987-93; exec. dir. Greenpeace U.S.A., D.C., 1993—. Office: Greenpeace USA 1436 U St NW Washington DC 20009-3997*

DUDLEY, EDIE, social services administrator, artist; b. Laurinburg, N.C., Aug. 2, 1969; d. Francis Donald and Rebecca (Bundy) D. BS, U. S.C., 1991. Counselor S.C. Dept. Juvenile Justice, Bennettsville, S.C., 1992-95; adj. specialist S.C. Vocat. Rehab., Bennettsville, 1995—; rep. S.C. Gov.'s Commn. on Employment of People with Disabilities. Vol. U.S. Jaycees, Bennettsville, 1992-95. Congl. scholar U. S. Legis., 1991. Republican. Methodist.

DUDLEY, ELIZABETH HYMER, retired security executive; b. Hibbing, Minn., Mar. 12, 1937; d. Howard Golden and Esther Juliette (Wanner) Hymer; m. Richard Walter Dudley, 1962. BA Brown U., 1959; postgrad. U. Calif., Berkeley. With AT&T Bell Labs., Murray Hill, N.J., 1959-89, systems programmer, personnel info., 1965-67, systems analyst, personnel info., 1967-71, sr. systems analyst, mgmt. info. and adminstrv. systems, 1971-77, applications systems coordinator mgmt. info. and adminstrv. systems, 1977-78, group supr. affirmative action compliance and reports, 1978-81, group supr. service ops. system support group, 1982-84, mgr. security, 1984-85, mgr. govt. security, 1986-89; ret., 1989. Bd. dirs. Boca Ballet Theatre Co., 1994—; treas. Fla. Atlantic U. Vol. League, 1993-94; chmn. boutique Boca Ballet Guild, 1994, pres. 1994—. Mem. Humanitarian Society, Brown Nat. Alumni Sch. Program, Nat. Security Indsl. Assn., Women's Rights Assn. (treas. 1977, v.p. 1978), Am. Soc. Indsl. Security, Nat. Classification Mgmt. Soc., Brown Network, Royal Palm Improvement Assn. (bd. govs., chair. environ. inspection 1993-94, v.p., 1994, pres. 1994-96, chair security 1994), Friends of the Boca Pops (mem. governing coun.). Club: Pembroke Coll. of N.J. (publicity chmn. 1965-69, v.p. 1969-70).

DUDLEY, SUSAN D., psychologist, public policy advocate; b. Norfolk, Va., Apr. 8, 1949; d. William B. and Jean (Demaio) DeLoatch; m. James J. Franklin, Dec. 20, 1987. BS summa cum laude, Old Dominion U., 1973; MA, Coll. William and Mary, 1976; PhD, U. Mass., 1980. Asst. prof. Wheaton Coll., Norton, Mass., 1979-80; post-doctoral fellow Pa. State U. Med. Ctr., Hershey, 1980-82; lectr. U. Md. U. Coll., Heidleberg, West Germany, 1982-86, Seoul, Korea, 1986-87; asst. prof. Auburn U., Montgomery, Ala., 1987-90; asst. dir. Child Devel. Ctr., Torrejon Air Base, Spain, 1990-91; access initiative dir. Nat. Abortion Fedn., Washington, 1994—; founding mem. Ala. Forum, Montgomery, 1989-90; registered lobbyist Ala. State Legislature, Montgomery, 1989-90. Author: (with others) Back to School at My Age?, 1981; contbr. articles to profl. jours. and newspapers. Literacy tutor Ctrl. Ala. Laubach Literacy, Montgomery, 1987-88; active LWV, Montgomery, 1989-90; prin., media spkr. Ala. Pro-Choice Coalition, Montgomery, 1989-90; pres. NOW, Montgomery, 1989-90. Post-doctoral fellowship NIH, 1980-82. Mem. AAUW, APA, Jacobs Inst. Women's Health, Sigma Xi, Psi Chi. Democrat. Office: Nat Abortion Fedn 1436 U St NW Ste 103 Washington DC 20009

DUELL, MARIE O., human resources executive; b. N.Y.C., Sept. 26, 1962; d. Rocco Anthony and Dolores (Silva) DeCrescenzo; m. Christopher John Duell, June 3, 1984. BA in Biol. Scis., Smith Coll., 1983; MS in Human Resources, U of Ctrl. Tex., 1989. Human resources specialist Mason and Hanger-Silas Mason Co., Amarillo, Tex., 1992; asst. dir. human resources Rice U., Houston, 1992—. Mem. ASTD (Houston chpt.), Soc. of Human Resource Mgmt., Houston Human Resource Mgmt. Assn. Office: Rice University PO Box 2666 6100 S Main Houston TX 77005

DUENES, ELENA MARIE, speech/language pathologist; b. Inglewood, Calif., Dec. 8, 1967; d. Edward Manuel and Julia Ellen (Grehl) D. BA, U. Calif., Irvine, 1990; MA, Northwestern U., 1992. Cert. clin. competence; lic. speech/lang. pathology, Calif. Speech pathologist Gardner/Manzella Inc., Sherman Oaks, Calif., 1992-93, Pace Therapy Inc., Cypress, Calif., 1993-94, Beverly Enterprises, Seal Beach, Calif., 1994—. Mem. Am. Speech Lang. Hearing Assn. Home: 511 Electric Ave Seal Beach CA 90740-6177 Office: Beverly Manor Nursing Rehab 3000 Beverly Manor Dr Seal Beach CA 90740-2535

DUER, ELLEN ANN DAGON, anesthesiologist; b. Balt., Feb. 3, 1936; d. Emmett Paul and Annie (Sollers) Dagon; m. Lyle Jordan Millan IV, Dec. 21, 1963; children: Lyle Jordan V, Elizabeth Lyle, Ann Sheridan Worthington.; m. T. Marshall Duer, Jr., Aug. 23, 1985. AB, George Washington U., 1959; MD, U. Md., 1964; postgrad., Johns Hopkins U., 1965-68. Intern Union Meml. Hosp., Balt., 1964-65; resident anesthesiology Johns Hopkins Hosp., Balt., 1965-68, fellow in surgery, 1965-68; practice medicine specializing in anesthesiology Balt., 1968—; faculty Church Home and Hosp., Balt., 1969—; attending staff Union Meml. Hosp., Church Home and Hosp., Frankling Sq. Hosp., Children's Hosp., James Lawrence Kernan Hosp., Balt., 1982-94; co-chief anesthesiology James Kernan Hosp., 1983-94, med. dir. out-patient surgery dept., 1987-94; mem. med. exec. com. Kernan Hosp., 1988-94; affiliate cons. emergency room Church Home and Hosp., Balt., 1969—, mem. med. audit and utilizaions com., 1970-72, mem. emergency and ambulatory care com., 1973-74, chief emergency dept., 1973-74; cons. anesthesiologist Md. State Penitentiary, 1971; fellow in critical care medicine Md. Inst. Emergency Medicine, 1975-76; mem. infection control com. U. Md. Hosp., 1975—; instr. anesthesiology U. Md. Sch. Medicine, 1975—; staff anesthesiologist Mercy Hosp., 1978—, audit com., 1979-80, 82; asst. prof. anesthegiology U. Md. Med. Sch., 1989-94; mem. med. exec. com. Kernan Hosp., 1990-94, v.p. 1990, chief of staff, 1992—; mem. Tappahannock Family Practice, 1994-96, Rappahannock Gen. Hosp. Family Practice, 1996—; active staff Rappahannock Gen. Hosp., 1996—; med. examiner No. Neck of Va., 1996—; mem. Commonwealth of Va. Med. Bd. Mem. AMA, Am. Coll. Emergency Physicians, Met. Emergency Dept. Heads Am., Md. Soc. Anesthesiologists, Balt. County Med. Soc., Mid. Peninsula Med. Soc., No. Neck Med. Soc., Med. Soc. Va., Med. and Choir Faculty Med., Chirugical Soc., Internat. Congress Anaesthesiologists, Internat. Anesthesia Rsch. Soc., Am. L'Hirondelle Club, Annapolis Yacht Club, Chesapeake Bay

Yacht Racing Assn., Rappahannock River Yacht Club. Episcopalian. Address: Deep Creek Farm House RR 3 Box 463 Lancaster VA 22503-9803

DUERR, DIANNE MARIE, physical education educator, professional sports medicine consultant; b. Buffalo, July 14, 1945; d. Robert John and Aileen Louise (Scherer) D. BS in Health and Phys. Edn., SUNY, Brockport, 1967; cert., SUNY, Oswego, 1982; postgrad., Canisius Coll., 1970-71. Cert. tchr., N.Y. Tchr. North Syracuse (N.Y.) Sch. Dist., 1967—; tchr. dept. orthopedic surgery SUNY Health Sci. Ctr. at Syracuse, 1982—; creator Inst. for Sports Medicine and Human Performance SUNY Health Sci. Ctr., Syracuse, 1988; coord. scholastic sports injury reporting system project SUNY, 1985—; mem. com. on scholastic sports-related injuries NIH Inst. Arthritis, Musculoskeletal and Skin Diseases, 1993—. Author: SSIRS Pilot Study Report, 1987, SSIRS Fall Study Report, 1988, SHASIRS Report, 1991; creator Scholastic Sports Injury Reporting System, 1985, Scholastic Head and Spine Injury Reporting System, 1989. Co-chmn. sports medicine USA Amateur Athletic Union, Nat. Jr. Olympic Games, Syracuse, 1987; vol. sports medicine N.Y. State Sr. Games, 1990-94, sports medicine coord., 1990-95, U.S. Roller Skating Nat. Championships, 1995, N.Y. State Womens Lacrosse Championships; mem. com. sports injury surveillance Ctrs. for Disease Control, 1995; cons. N.Y. Sic., Tech. and Soc. Edn. Project, 1995. Mem. AAHPERD (N.Y. State chpt. pres. exercise sci. and sports medicine sect.), Am. Coll. Sports Medicine, United Univ. Profs., Women's Sports Fedn., Am. Fedn. Tchrs., N.Y. United Tchrs., North Syracuse Tchrs. Assn., Phi Kappa Phi. Home: 418 Buffington Rd Syracuse NY 13224-2208 Office: SUNY Dept Orthopedic Surgery 550 Harrison St Syracuse NY 13202-3096

DUERR, DONNA GRAHAM, designer; b. Hendersonville, N.C., Feb. 3, 1950; d. James and Jean Dixon Graham; children: Celeste, Keven, Erin. Student, U.N.C., 1987-90. Editor, layout designer Sch. News Svc., 1990-92; adminstrv. asst. Knightdale United Meth. Ch., 1993-94; advt. coord. The Great Atlantic and Pacific Tea Co., 1994-95; designer publs. and banners St. John's Episcopal Ch., N.C., 1992-93. Contbr. articles to profl. publs. Artist, art facilitator Episcopal Ch., 1979—. Mem. Sierra Club. Episcopalian.

DUFAULT, ROSEANNA LEWIS, humanities educator; b. Boulder, Colo., Jan. 29, 1954; d. Raymond Henry and Catherine Louise (Clair) Lewis. BA, Colo. Women's Coll., 1975; MA, Middlebury Coll., 1980; PhD, U. Colo., 1986. Instr. French U. Colo., Boulder, 1979-85; lectr. English U. Bordeaux, France, 1985-86; asst. prof. dept. fgn. langs. & lits. Colo. State U., Ft. Collins, 1986-89; assoc. prof. dept. fgn. langs. Ohio Northern U., Ada, 1992—; chair dept. fgn. langs. Ohio Northern U., Ada, 1996—. Author: Metaphors of Identity, 1991; editor: Women by Women, 1996; contbr. articles to profl. jours. and anthologies. Recipient rsch. grant Quebec Govt., 1985. Mem. MLA, AAUW, Am. Assn. Tchrs. of French, Am. Coun. for Quebec Studies, Conseil Internat. d'Etudes Francophones, Women in French. Office: Ohio Northern Univ 525 S Main St Ada OH 45810

DUFF, PATRICIA, foundation administrator; b. L.A., Apr. 12, 1954; d. Robert Orr and Mary Williamson; m. Ronald Perelman; 1 child, Caleigh Sophia Perelman. Student, Internat. Sch. Brussels, 1971, Barnard Coll.; BS in Internat. Econs., Georgetown U., 1976. Spl. asst. to chief counsel house select com. on assassinations U.S. Ho. of Reps., Washington, 1969; prodr., writer, researcher John McLaughlin Show-NBC Radio, Washington, 1979-80; asst. rsch. dir. Dem. Nat. Com., Washington, 1980; v.p. Patrick Caddell and Assocs., Washington, 1980-82, Squier, Eskew Assoc., 1982-84; with Communications Co., Washington, 1982-83, Mondale for Pres., L.A., 1984, Americans for Hart, L.A., 1984; ind. producer Columbia Pictures, Burbank, Calif.; pres. Revlon Found., 1995—; assoc. producer Dem. Nat. Conv., Atlanta, 1988; mem. nat. media adv. bd. Hart for Pres., L.A., 1988. contbg. editor Vogue Mag., 1989. Mem. platform com. Dem. Nat. Conv., 1984, 92; mem. Hollywood Women's Polit. Com, 1986; mem. bd. councilors Ascus sch. pub. policy and adminstrn. U. So. Calif.; founder, chair bd. dirs. Show Coalition The Common Good, L.A., 1988—; mem. bd. visitors Sch. Fgn. Svc., Georgetown U., 1988—; founder Am. Spirit Awards, 1992; bd. dirs. L.A. Colors United, Summer of Svc., Nat. Svc., 1993, L.A. Women on Status of Women, 1994-96, Women in Film, 1990—, Lincoln Ctr. Film Soc., 1995—, Poeple for the Am. Way, 1996; chair N.Y. Gov.'s Task Force on Teen Pregnancy, 1994-95; trustee Nat. Pub. Radio; mem. Presdl. Commn. on Libr. of Congress Trust Fund; mem. pvt. sector adv. bd. Inter Am. Devel. Bank; chair Women Vote Campaign of Emily's List, 1996. Named one of Rising Young Stars L.A. Times, 1989; named Dem. of Yr. L.A. County, 1989, recipient Women We Love award for polit. activism Esquire Mag., 1990. Office: 38 E 63rd St New York NY 10021-8034

DUFF, SHERYL KAY, parochial school educator; b. Frankenmuth, Mich., May 14, 1961; d. Eldon Earl and Ellen Christine (Rummel) D. BA, Concordia U., 1983. Tchr. 6th grade Lutheran Sch. Assn., Decatur, Ill., 1983-87; tchr. science St. John Lutheran, Wheaton, Ill., 1987—; tchr. Solid Waste Edn. U., Wheaton , Ill., 1995. Mem. Lutheran Edn. Assn. Lutheran.

DUFFIELD, ELEANOR MCALPIN, secondary education educator; b. Lexington, Va., May 5, 1942; d. Henry F. Jr. and Elizabeth Wilson (Jones) McAlpin; m. Joseph Hood Duffield, Aug. 21, 1971. BS, Madison Coll., 1964; MEd, U. Va., 1972. Tchr. social studies Fairfax (Va.) County Pub. Sch. Bd., 1964—; peer observer for performance evaluation of tchrs. Fairfax County, 1987—; clin. faculty George Mason U., 1989—; sponsor Students Involved in Volunteering; co-advisor Harvard Model Congress, 1990-92; co-coord. sch. renewal So. Assn. Colls. and Schs., 1994—. Co-author: Fairfax County Government: A Handbook for Teachers, 1975. Pres. Fairfax Com. of 100, 1988-90; bd. dirs. Fairfax-Falls Church United Way, 1986-88; v.p. Faxfair Corp., 1988-89; elder Fairfax Presbyn. Ch., mem. session, 1993-95. Recipient Ptnr. in Edn. award Vienna Optimist Club, 1988, citation of merit Washington Post, 1988; fellow Taft Inst., 1986. Mem. NEA, ASCD, Nat. Coun. Social Studies, Va. Coun. Social Studies (conf. presenter, Tchr. of Yr. award no. region 1983), Va. Edn. Assn., Fairfax Edn. Assn. Home: 909 Frederick St SW Vienna VA 22180-6451 Office: James Madison High Sch 2500 James Madison Dr Vienna VA 22181-5536

DUFFY, ERNA ANNAMARIE KROGER, retired elementary principal, educator; m. William N. Duffy; children: Kathleen, Karon, Marilynn, Kevin, Erin. BS in Edn., No. Ill., 1952, MS in Edn., 1962. Cert. elem. supervision and curriculum, Ill. Grad. asst. NIU, DeKalb, 1957-58; tchr. Sycamore (Ill.) schs., 1952-54; prin., tchr. Malta (Ill.) County. Schs., 1960-91; chmn. DeKalb County Film Com., 1970-80; mem. Schoolmasters Assn., De Kalb, 1965-70; dir. NIU Alumni Assn., DeKalb, 1965-72. Mem. DeKalb County Ret. Tchr.'s Assn.

DUFFY, MARY SMYTH, educator; b. Waltham, Mass., Dec. 8, 1955; d. John Lester and Katherine (Smyth) D.; m. David Haward Dain, June 6, 1981; children: Mimi Aitken, David Montrose. BA, Bard Coll., 1978; MFA, CUNY, 1985. Rights & permissions editor Dover Publs., N.Y.C., 1980-84; adminstrv. asst. E. Aleinikoff Atty., N.Y.C., 1984-85; curator Hunter Coll. Art Galleries, N.Y.C., 1985-87; legal sec. Sessions, Keiner & Dumont, Middlebury, Vt., 1987-89; vol. coord. Counseling Svcs. Addison County, Middlebury, Vt., 1992-94; acad. asst. Middlebury Coll., 1994—; instr. studio art C.C. Vt., Middlebury, 1988—. Co-editor: Whose Woods These Are, 1992. Mem. Coll. Art Assn. Office: Middlebury Coll Middlebury VT 05753

DUFFY, NANCY KEOGH, television broadcast professional; b. Washington, Nov. 24, 1947; d. William Francis and Gertrude K. (Keogh) D.; divorced; children: Peter Patrick, Matthew Michael. Student, St. Mary of the Woods Coll.; AB, Marywood Coll., 1967. News reporter Sta. WHEN TV and Radio, Syracuse, N.Y., 1967-70; city press sec. City of Syracuse, 1970; news reporter Sta. WTVH, Syracuse, 1971-77; news anchorperson Sta. WIXT-TV, Syracuse, 1977—; talk show host Syracuse New Channels, 1986-87; talk show host, producer Community Connections, 1987-89; instr. Syracuse U. Producer t.v. series Duffy's People. Founder Syracuse St. Patrick's Parade, 1983, pres., organizer 1983—; organizer Cooperstown 50th Ann. Baseball Hall of Fame Parade, 1989, opening ceremonies Empire State Games, 1990; co-organizer Save Our Syracuse Symphony, 1984—; organizer Bark-Out Against Rabies Paws Parade, 1995; bd. dirs. Syracuse Symphony, 1992-96, The Media Unit, 1977—; active Project children, Syracuse, YMCA; telethon hostess Muscular Dystrophy Assn.; organizer poetry workshops for children, 1995—; mem. Onondaga County Traffic Safety Bd., 1977-96, Le

Moyne Coll. Pres. Assocs.; cons. Jr. League, J. Dist. 4 Nurses. Recipient Nat. Angel award Best Spl. Religion in Media, Post Std. Woman of Achievement award, 1st Downtown award for excellence, 1986, Mayor's Achievement award, 1985, Humanitarian award Project Children, 1993, N.Y. State Senate commendation, 1995; named Woman of Achievement N.Y. State Fair, 1994. Mem. Am. Women in Radio and TV (nat. award 1973), Women in Comms. (Outstanding Communicator award 1985), Syracuse Press Club (bd. dirs. 1987—, v.p. 1990, pres. 1991-92, Bernard and Dorothy Newer Svc. award 1995), Syracuse Rotary (pub. rels. 1989-92). Roman Catholic. Office: Sta WIXT-TV 5904 Bridge St East Syracuse NY 13057

DUFFY-DURNIN, KAREN FRANCES, gerontological clinical nurse specialist; b. Phila., Nov. 8, 1955; d. Joseph Michael and Helen Frances (Sherin) Duffy; m. Stephen Durnin, Sept. 3, 1983; children: Brendan, Brian. AA, Endicott Jr. Coll., 1975; BSN, Keuka Coll., 1979; MSN, U. Rochester, 1984. RN, N.Y.; cert. clin. specialist in gerontol. nursing ANCC. Staff RN Strong Meml. Hosp., Rochester, 1979-83; nursing instr. Divsn. of Nursing, Keuka Coll., 1983-85, asst. prof. nursing, 1986-88; nursing edn. specialist Clifton Springs (N.Y.) Hosp., 1985-86; gerontol. clin. nurse specialist The Genessee Hosp., Rochester, 1988—; cons., educator Genesee Region Home Care, Rochester, 1992-95; adv. bd. mem. HCR home Care Assn., Rochester, 1990-92. Contbr. Political Action Handbook for Nurses, 1985; contbr. articles to profl. jours. Chairperson Community Coalition for Restraint Free Care, Rochester, 1993—; mem. spkrs. bur. Alzheimer's Assn., Rochester, 1986—, alzheimers support group facilitator, 1986-91; mentor Clara Barton Sch. Mentor Program, Rochester, 1995—. Mem. ANA, Gerontol. Soc. Am., N.Y. State Soc. Aging, N.Y. State Nurses for Polit. Action (chairperson 1986-88), N.Y. State Nurses for Polit. Action (bd. dirs. 1981-84), Sigma Theta Tau. Home: 5718 Allen Padgham Rd Farmington NY 14425 Office: Genesee Hosp care Nursing Office 224 Alexander St Rochester NY 14607-4002

DUFORD, CATHY ANN, elementary education educator; b. Boston, Jan. 8, 1951; d. James J. Burley and Dorothy J. Lane Lamont; m. Joseph F. Duford, Nov. 16, 1975; children: Thomas, Sarah. BS in Edn., Bridgewater State Coll., 1973; MEd, Cambridge (Mass.) Coll., 1995. Tchr. Brockton (Mass.) Pub. Schs., 1973—. Troop leader, treas., com. mem. Eight Feathers Dist. coun. Boy Scouts Am., 1986—; troop leader Plymouth Bay Girl Scouts, Brockton, 1988-94; CCD tchr. Our Lady of Lourdes Ch., Brockton, 1991—. Mem. ASCD, NEA, Mass. Tchrs. Assn., Brockton Edn. Assn. Home: 204 Torrey St Brockton MA 02401-4835

DUFRENE, ROXANE LUNK, psychological counselor; b. Raceland, La., Apr. 11, 1950; d. Joseph Lunk and Margaret Ruth Vicknair; m. Brian Alan Dufrene, July 4, 1968; children: Nicole, Brian, Natasha. BS, Nicholls State U., Thibodaux, La., 1991, MA in Psychol. Counseling, 1995. Supr. Otto Candies, Inc., Des Allemands, La., 1980, Ebasco-Waterford III, Taft, La., 1980-84; agt. Century 21, Houma, La., 1984-86; instr. Nicholls State U., 1992-95; psychol. assoc. Lafourche Mental Health Ctr., Raceland, 1995—. Tchr., tutor United Way Counseling on Aging, Lockport, La., 1992-95. Mem. ACA, Phi Chi. Office: Lafourche Mental Health Ctr PO Box B Raceland LA 70394

DUGAN, JEAN BRODSHAUG, public relations consultant; b. Fargo, N.D., Oct. 11, 1959; d. Robert L. and Jacqueline Adelle (Qualley) Brodshaug; m. Joseph Robert Dugan, Sept. 14, 1991; 1 child, Patrick Robert. BA, BS, U. N.D., 1981; MS, Boston U., 1984. Sr. copy editor Viewdata Corp., Miami, Fla., 1983-85; press sec. U.S. Senator Quentin Burdick, Washington, 1985-92, U.S. Senator Jocelyn Burdick, Washington, 1992-93; cons. Nat. Women's Polit. Caucus, Washington, 1993-96; comms. dir., dep. campaign mgr. Joan Kelly Horn for Congress, 1996— . Author: Campaigning to Win, 1993. Chair Capitol Hill Women's Polit. Caucus, Washington, 1991, sexual harrassment task force chair, 1991-92; legis. com. chair Nat. Women's Polit. Caucus, Washington, 1991-93, resolutions com. chair, 1994-95; comm. officer Metro St. Louis Women's Polit. Caucus, 1995. Mem. LWV. Democrat. Lutheran. Home and Office: 12006 Charter House Ln Saint Louis MO 63146

DUGAS, JOAN LINGARD, social services administrator; b. Manchester, Conn., Mar. 31, 1936; d. Ronald and Ellen J. (Knarr) Lingard; m. Richard P. Dugas, July 11, 1959 (div. Feb. 1984); children: Philip Richard, Paul Ronald, Mark Steven, Renée Marie. BS in Edn., Boston Coll., 1958; MA in Tchg., Bridgewater Coll., 1978. Social worker N.Y. Foundling Hosp., N.Y.C., 1958-59, Cath. Charities, Washington, 1960-61, Marian Manor Nursing Home, Boston, 1981-87; secondary tchr. English, Prince Georges County (Md.) Pub. Schs., 1959-60; social work supr. South Shore Elder Svcs., Braintree, Mass., 1987-95, program mgr., 1995—; coord., designer Elder Options, 1995. Mem. NOW, Older Women's League, South Shore Coalition Workers with Elderly. Home: 25 Highland Ter Apt 2514 Plymouth MA 02360 Office: South Shore Elder Svcs Inc 639 Granite St Braintree MA 02481

DUGGAN, CAROL COOK, research director; b. Conway, S.C., May 25, 1946; d. Pierce Embree and Lillian Watkins (Eller) Cook; m. Kevin Duggan, Dec. 29, 1973. BA. Columbia Coll., 1968; MS, U. Ky., 1970. Reference asst. Richland County Pub. Libr., Columbia, S.C., 1968-69, asst. to dir., 1970, chief adult svcs., 1971-82; dir. Maris Rsch., Columbia, 1982—; lectr., mem. Friends of Richland County Pub. Libr., 1977—, Greater Columbia (S.C.) Literacy Coun., 1973—; mem. worship com. Washington St. United Meth. Ch., Columbia, 1985-86, mem. staff-parish relations com., 1986-91, mem. history and archives com., 1988—, mem. adminstrv. bd., 1992—, chair staff-parish relations com., 1993, trustee 1995—; mem. exec. bd. United Meth. Women 1983—, treas. unit 7, 1989-91, pres. unit 7, 1992—. Recipient Sternheimer award, 1968; treas. Friends S.C. Elders. Mem. ALA (councilor 1980-82, chmn. state membership com. 1979-83), S.C. Libr. Assn. (sec. 1976, exec. bd. 1976, 78-82), S.C. Pub. Libr. Assn. (pres. 1980-81), Friends of S.C. Libr. (treas. 1995—), Columbia Coll. Alumnae Assn. Coun. (spl. events com. 1996—), Beta Phi Mu. Methodist. Club: PEO (pres. 1983-85, chmn. amendments and recommendations com. 1983-85, historian 1986-87, 90—), treas. State conv.-1987-88), Columbia Coll. Afternoon of S.C. Home: 2101 Woodmere Dr Columbia SC 29204-4341

DUHME, CAROL MCCARTHY, civic worker; b. St. Louis, Apr. 13, 1917; d. Eugene Ross and Louise (Roblee) McCarthy; m. Sheldon Ware, June 12, 1941 (dec. 1944); 1 child, Benton (dec.); m. H. Richard Duhme, Jr., Apr. 9, 1947; children: Benton (dec.), Ann, Warren (dec.). AB, Vassar Coll., 1939. Tchr. elem. sch., 1939-41, 42-44; moderator St. Louis Assn. Congl. Chs., 1952; dir. Christian edn. First Congl. Ch., St. Louis, 1959-62, trustee, 1964-66, mem. ch. coun., 1974-75, 84-85, 87-89, bd. deaconesses, 1978-81, bd. deacons, 1982-85, 92-95; chmn. bd. Christian Edn., 1987-88; former bd. dirs. Community Music Schs., St. Louis, Community Sch., Ch. Women United, John Burroughs Sch., St. Louis Bicentennial Women's Com., St. Louis Jr. League; pres. St. Louis Vassar Club; pres. bd. dirs. YWCA, St. Louis, 1973-76, chmn. ann. fund, 1989-90; bd. dirs. North Side Team Ministry, 1968-84, Chautauqua (N.Y.) Inst., 1977-79, mem. adv. coun. to bd., 1987—; adv. coun. Mo. Bapt. Hosp., 1973-89; exec. com. bd. dirs. Eden Theol. Sem., 1981-95, presdl. search com. 1986-87, 92-93, v.p. bd. dirs., 1991, chmn. 150th Anniversary com., 1996—; sec. bd. dirs. UN Assn., St. Louis, 1976-84, coun. of advisors, 1993—, nat. coun. mem., nat. coun. UN-USA, 1995—; pres. bd. dirs. Family and Children's Svc. Greater St. Louis, 1977-79; mem. chancellor's long-range planning com. Washington U., 1980-81, mem. Nat. Coun., Sch. Social Work, 1987—; chmn. Benton Roblee Duhme Scholarship Fund; trustee Joseph H. and Florence A. Roblee Found., St. Louis, 1984—, pres. 1984-90, bd. dirs.; chmn. Chautauqua Bell Tower Scholarship Fund, 1964—; bd. dirs. Nat. Inland Waterways Libr., St. Louis Merc. Libr. Mem. corp. assembly Blue Cross Hosp. Svc. of Mo., 1978-86. Recipient Mary Alice Messerley award for volunteerism Health and Welfare Coun. St. Louis, 1971; Vol. of Yr. award, YWCA, 1976; Woman of Achievement award St. Louis Globe Democrat, 1980; Outstanding Lay Woman nomination Mo. United Ch. of Christ, 1991; Outstanding Alumna award John Burroughs Sch., 1992. Home: 8 Edgewood Rd Saint Louis MO 63124-1817

DUING, EDNA IRENE, women's health nurse, nurse educator; b. Crystal City, Mo., July 11, 1959; d. Edwin Fred Duing and Ann Marie (Duro) Ems;

m. James Roger Davis, June 19, 1982; children: April Ann Rena Duing-Davis, Sarah Elizabeth Duing-Davis, Kenneth Alexander Duing-Davis. BA in History, S.E. Mo. State U., 1981, BSN, 1994; ADN, Jefferson Coll., 1989. RN, Mo.; cert. obstetric nurse, ACLS, pediat. ACLS. Ob/gyn staff nurse Jefferson Meml. Hosp., Crystal City, 1989-95; obstet. nursing instr. St. Louis Coll. Health Careers, 1995; home care nurse Washingtot County Meml. Hosp. Home Health Agy. Potosi, Md., 1996—; 1st aid, CPR instr. ARC, 1987—, flood shelter nurse, Festus and Crystal City, Mo., 1993. 1st lt. USAF, 1982-86. Mem. Mo. Perinatal Assn., La Leche League Internat. Amvets, Order of Ea. Star. Mem. Christian Ch. (Disciples of Christ). Home: PO Box 171 Buck Creek Rd Hematite MO 63047 Office: Washington County Meml Hosp Home Health Agy 300 Health Way Potosi MO 63664

DUITSMAN, HEIDI LYNN, management executive; b. Hinsdale, Ill., Aug. 18, 1964; d. Roger Lyle and Judith Lynn (Rieske) D. BS, Cornell U., 1987. Acct. mgr. Fleming Packaging, S. San Francisco, 1987-90; plant mgr. Fleming Packaging, Napa, Calif., 1990-92; project mgr. Heat & Control, S. San Francisco, 1992—. Republican. Presbyterian. Office: Heat & Control Inc 225 Shaw Rd South San Francisco CA 94080

DUKAKIS, OLYMPIA, actress; b. Lowell, Mass., June 20, 1931; d. Constantine S. and Alexandra (Christos) D.; m. Louis Zorich; children: Christina, Peter, Stefan. BS, Boston U., 1952, MFA, 1957. Co-founder, artistic dir. Whole Theatre, Montclair, N.J., 1970-90; co-founder Charles Playhouse, Boston; master tchr. NYU, 1970-85. Appeared in over 125 prodns. for regional theatres, N.Y. Shakespeare Theatre, Circle Repertory Theatre, American Place Theatre and numerous Off-Broadway theatres; appearances on stage include King of America, Social Security; appearances in film include Lilith, 1964, Twice a Man, 1964, John and Mary, 1969, Made for Each Other, 1971, Death Wish, 1974, Rich Kids, 1979, The Wanderers, 1979, The Idolmaker, 1980, National Lampoon Goes to the Movies, 1982, Flanagan, 1985, Moonstruck, 1988 (Golden Globe, Academy Award Supporting Actress), Working Girl, 1988, Steel Magnolias, 1988, Look Who's Talking, 1988, Dad, 1989, In the Spirit, 1990, Look Who's Talking II, 1990, Over the Hill, 1992, Look Who's Talking Now, 1993, The Cemetery Club, 1993, I Love Trouble, 1994, Digger, 1994, Jeffrey, 1995, Mighty Aphrodite, 1995, Mr. Holland's Opus, 1996, Dead Badge, 1995, Picture Perfect, 1996; (TV movies) Nicky's World, 1974, The Neighborhood, 1982, The Last Act is a Solo, 1990 (Ace award), Lucky Day, 1991, Fire in the Dark, 1991, Sinatra: The Mini-Series, 1992, Armistead Maupin's Tales of the City, 1994, A Century of Women, 1994, Young at Heart, 1995. Del. Dem. Nat. Convention, 1988. Recipient 2 Obie awards, Los Angeles Film Critics award, 1988. Mem. Actor's Equity Assn., Screen Actors Guild, Am. Fedn. TV and Radio Artists. Home: 222 Upper Mountain Ave Montclair NJ 07043-1016 Office: William Morris Agy Rm 1202 care Scott Henderson 1325 Avenue Of The Americas Fl 32 New York NY 10019-4702*

DUKE, ANNETTE IRONS, elementary education educator; b. Hartselle, Ala., Aug. 2, 1966; d. Bobby Gene and Mary Jane (Shugart) Irons. AS, Wallace State Coll., Hanceville, Ala., 1986; BA, Athens (Ala.) State Coll., 1988; MEd, U. Ala., Birmingham, 1990. Reading clinic coord. Athens State Coll., 1986-87; migrant asst. tchr. Cullman County Bd. Edn., Cullman, Ala., 1988-89, Chpt. 1 tchr., 1989—. Coord. Adopt-A-Sch. Program, Cullman, 1990-94. Mem. NEA, Ala. Edn. Assn. (state del. Welti Elem. Tchr. of Yr. nominee), Cullman County Edn. Assn. (publicity chair, membership chair 1992-94, bd. mem.), Internat. Reading Assn., Rainbow Reading Assn., Pilot Club, Welti PTO (sec. 1990-94), Kappa Delta Pi. Baptist. Home: 2013 Adelsheim Cir SW Cullman AL 35055-9315 Office: Welti Elem Sch 8545 County Road 747 Cullman AL 35055-9254

DUKE, ELLEN KAY, community activist, playground professional; b. Indpls., June 7, 1952; d. Richard Thomas and Ruby Mae (Wright) D. Student Chapman Coll., Orange, Calif., 1972; BS in Pub. Affairs, Ind. U.-Bloomington, 1975; postgrad. Portland State U., 1980-81. Cert. Dale Carnegie Pub. Speaking Instr. 1987-93; News reporter, Salem Statesman, Corvallis, Oreg., 1976-78; com. adminstr. Oreg. State Legislature, Salem, 1979-80; pub. involvement coord. Met. Regional Svc Dist., Portland, 1981-82; account mgr. Thunder & Visions, Portland, 1982-83; project asst. Amdahl Corp., Sunnyvale, Calif., 1983-84; spl. project coord. Computerland Corp., Hayward, Calif., 1984-89; prodr., lead facilitator Sage, Inc., Walnut Creek, Calif., 1990—; loan broker Capital Trust Mortgage, Campbell, Calif., 1994—; pub. rels. dir. local YMCA. Co-author: (edni. film) Communication Skills, 1975. Chairperson Corvallis Budget Commn., Oreg., 1978; commr. Hayward Library, Calif., 1985—, Alameda County Consumer Affairs, Oakland, 1985; rep. Nat. Democratic Conv., N.Y.C., 1982. Named Able Toastmaster Toastmasters Internat., 1981; grad. Leadership Oakland, 1991. Mem. NAFE, Pub. Rels. Soc. Am., Sierra Club (San Francisco). Office: We Build Playgrounds 1997 1st Ave Walnut Creek CA 94596

DUKE, MARGARET JOYCE, sound recordist; b. Baton Rouge, Nov. 18, 1945; d. James Henry and Joyce Olga (Boyd) D.; children: Diane Alana, Julie Rene, Richard Mark. BFA, La. State U., 1980. Sound recordist (films & TV) John Huston and the Dubliners, The Wild West, Comic Strip Live, Sledgehammer, Destined to Live, Diabetes Camp, Prisoners of Wedlock, It Was a Wonderful Life, Labours of Eve, Wise Women, Science, Math and Middleschool Girls, The Desert of No Lady, Far Out Man, Galaxies Is Colliding, Big Bang Theory, George Shdanoff and Hollywood. Mem. Women in Film, Cinewoman. Office: PO Box 5799 Beverly Hills CA 90209

DUKE, PATTY (ANNA MARIE DUKE), actress; b. N.Y.C., Dec. 14, 1946; d. John P. and Frances (McMahon) Duke; m. John Astin, 1973 (div. 1985); children: Sean, Mackenzie; m. Michael Pierce, March 15, 1986. Grad. Quintano's School for Young Profls. Pres. SAG, 1985-88, lectr. Am. Film Inst., 1988. TV appearances include Armstrong Circle Theatre, 1955, The SS Andrea Doria, The Prince and the Pauper, 1957, Wuthering Heights, 1958, U.S. Steel Hour, 1959, Meet Me in St. Louis, 1959, Swiss Family Robinson, 1958, The Power and the Glory, 1961, All's Fair, 1961-62; (series) The Brighter Day, 1957, Kitty Foyle, 1958, Patty Duke Show, 1963-66, It Takes Two, 1982-1983, Hail to the Chief, 1985, Karen's Song, 1987; (TV films) The Big Heist, 1957, My Sweet Charlie, 1970 (Emmy award 1970), Two on a Bench, If Tomorrow Comes, 1971, She Waits, Deadly Harvest, 1972, Nightmare, 1972, Look What's Happened to Rosemary's Baby, 1976, Fire!, 1976, Rosetti and Ryan: Men Who Love Women, Curse of the Black Widow, Killer on Board, The Storyteller, 1977, Having Babies III, Captain and the Kings, 1977 (Emmy award 1977), A Family Upside Down, 1978, Women in White, Hanging By A Thread, Before and After, The Miracle Worker, 1979 (Emmy award 1980), The Women's Room, Mom, The Wolfman and Me, The Babysitter, 1980, Violation of Sarah McDavid, Please, Don't Hit Me Mom, 1981, Something So Right 1982, September Gun, 1983, Best Kept Secrets, 1984, George Washington: The Forging of a Nation, 1984, A Time To Triumph, 1986, Fight for Life, 1987, Perry Mason: The Case of the Avenging Angel, Fatal Judgement, 1988, Everybody's Baby: The Rescue of Jessica McClure, Amityville: The Evil Escapes, 1989, Call Me Anna, 1990, Always Remember I Love You, 1990, Absolute Strangers, 1991, Last Wish, 1992, Grave Secrets: The Legacy of Hilltop Drive, 1992, A Killer Among Friends, 1992, A Family of Strangers, 1993, Cries From the Heart, 1994, One Woman's Courage, 1994; (theatre) The Miracle Worker, 1959-61, Isle of Children, 1962; motion picture appearances in I'll Cry Tomorrow, 1955, The Goddess, 1958, Happy Anniversary, The 4-D Man, 1959, The Miracle Worker, 1962 (Acad. award as best supporting actress 1962), Billie, 1965, Valley of the Dolls, 1967, Me, Natalie, 1969 (Golden Globe award as best actress 1970), The Swarm, 1978, Something Special, 1987, Prelude to a Kiss, 1992; co-author Surviving Sexual Assault, 1983, Call Me Anna, 1987, A Brilliant Madness: Living with Manic-Depressive Illness, 1992. Nat. coun. council Muscular Dystrophy Assns. Am. Recipient Emmy Awards, 1964, 69, 76, 79. Mem. AFTRA. Office: William Morris Agy 151 S El Camino Dr Beverly Hills CA 90212-2704*

DUKE, ROBIN CHANDLER TIPPETT, retired public relations executive; b. Balt., Oct. 13, 1923; d. Richard Edgar and Esther (Chandler) Tippett; m. Angier Biddle Duke, May 1962; children: Jeffrey R. Lynn, Letitia Lynn Valiunas, Angier Biddle Jr. Fashion editor N.Y. Jour. Am., N.Y., 1944-46; freelance writer N.Y.C., 1946-50; rep. Orvis Bros., N.Y.C., 1953-58; mem. pub. relations staff Pepsi Cola Co., Internat., N.Y.C., 1958-62; bd. dirs. Am. Home Products, N.Y.C., Internat. Flavors & Fragrances, N.Y.C., East River Bank, New Rochelle, N.Y. Vice-chmn., bd. dirs. Inst. Internat.

Edn., N.Y.C., 1975-96; chmn. Population Action Internat., Washington, 1972—, Met. Club Washington; bd. dirs. David Packard Found., U.S. Japan Found. Recipient Albert and Mary Lasker Social Svc. award, 1991, Margaret Sanger Woman of Yr. Valor award, 1995. Mem. Acad. Arts & Scis., Colony Club, River Club. Democrat. Home: 435 E 52nd St New York NY 10022-6445

DUKERT, BETTY COLE, television producer; b. Muskogee, Okla., May 9, 1927; d. Irvan Dill and Ione (Bowman) Cole; m. Joseph M. Dukert, May 19, 1968. Student, Lindenwood Coll., St. Charles, Mo., 1945-46, Drury Coll., Springfield, Mo., 1946-47; B.J., U. Mo., 1949. With Sta. KICK, Springfield, Mo., 1949-50; adminstrv. asst. Juvenile Office, Green County, Mo., 1950-52; with Sta. WRC-TV-NBC, Washington, 1952-56; assoc. producer Meet the Press, NBC, Washington, 1956-75; producer Meet the Press, NBC, 1975—; sr. producer Meet the Press, NBC News, 1992—; mem. Robert F. Kennedy Journalism Awards Com., 1978-82. Trustee Drury Coll., Springfield, Mo., 1984—. Recipient Disting. Alumna award Drury Coll., 1975, Disting. Alumni award U Mo., 1978, Ted Yates award Washington chpt. Nat. Acad. TV Arts and Scis., 1979, Pub. Rels. award for pub. svc. Am. Legion Nat. Comdrs., 1981, Internat. Disting. Svc. Journalism medal U. Mo. Sch. Journalism, 1993, Peter Hackes Meml. award Washington D.C. chpt. Radio/TV News Dirs. Assn., 1995. Mem. Am. Women in Radio and TV, Am. News Women's Club, Radio/TV Corrs. Assn., Women's Forum Washington, Soc. Profl. Journalists (dir. 1983-84, inducted into Hall of Fame 1991), Silver Circle Broadcasting, Nat. Acad. TV Arts and Scis., Nat. Press Club. Office: NBC News 4001 Nebraska Ave NW Washington DC 20016-2733

DUKES, REBECCA WEATHERS (BECKY DUKES), musician, singer, songwriter; b. Durham, N.C., Nov. 21, 1934; d. Elmer Dewey Weathers and Martha Rebecca (Kimbrough) Weathers-Hall; m. Charles Aubrey Dukes Jr., Dec. 20, 1955; children: Aurelia Ann, Charles Weathers, David Lloyd. BA, Duke U., 1956. Lic. elem. sch. tchr. Tchr. Durham City Schs., 1956-57; sec. USMC, Arlington, Va., 1957-58; tchr. Arlington County Schs., 1958-59; office mgr. Dukes and Kooken, Landover, Md., 1976; musical performer Washington and various locations, Va., Md., 1982—. Vocal student Todd Duncan; pianist, vocalist Back Alley Restaurant Lounge, 1982, also various hotels, lounges, 1982—; original program, A Life Cycle in Song, presented throughout mid-Atlantic states and Washington; full operatic solo recital, 1983; featured performer benefit for Nat. Symphony Orch.; frequent performer pvt. functions, athletic, civic, religious and cultural events including appearances at Capital Ctr., Cole Field House, George Washington U., Smith Ctr.; operatic solo concert with pianist Glenn Sales, 1985; benefit appearance U. Md. Concert Series, 1986, 87; holds copyrights for over 100 original songs including Between the Lovin' and the Leavin', Covers of My Mind, Gentle Thoughts (lead song Nat. Capitol Area Composers Series), Headin' Home Again, I Would Like to Be Reborn, Miss You, Tears, You Played a Part in My Life; songwriter, vocalist (album releases-12 songs) Alive, 1992, Rainbow, 1994, Borrow The Sun, 1995; author: (poems) Pottery, Canyons and Connections, Let the Trees of the Forest Rustle with Praise; contbr. poems to A Question of Balance, 1992, Treasured Poems of America, 1993, Distinguished Poets of 1994. Pres. Nat. Capitol Law League, Washington, 1976-77; pres. women's group, deacon, elder Riverdale Presbyn. Ch., Hyattsville, Md., 1968-94, elder, 1994; chmn. event honoring wives of Supreme Ct. justices, 1981; mem. women's com. nat. Symphony, 1980—; chmn. awards event Marian Anderson Internat. Vocal Arts Competition, 1991, 95; bd. dirs. Md. Coll. Art and Design, 1995. Recipient Friend of Yr. award Md. Summer Inst. for Creative and Performing Arts, U. Md., 1986, award for Vol. Svcs., Duke U., 1992; named Hon. trustee Prince George's (Md.) Arts Coun., 1984—, one of Women of Outstanding Achievement, Prince George's County, 1994. Mem. ASCAP (Popular Music award 1994, 95, 96), Songwriters Assn. Washington, William Preston Few Assn. of Duke U. (pres. couns., exec. bd. of ann. fund), Internat. Platform Assn., Pres.'s Club of U. Md., Univ. Club, Founders Club of Duke U. Republican. Home and Office: 7111 Pony Trail Ln Hyattsville MD 20782-1031

DULANY, ELIZABETH GJELSNESS, university press administrator; b. Charleston, S.C., Mar. 11, 1931; d. Rudolph Hjalmar and Ruth Elizabeth (Weaver) Gjelsness; m. Donelson Edwin Dulany, Mar. 19, 1955; 1 son, Christopher Daniel. BA, Bryn Mawr Coll., 1952. Editor, R.R. Bowker Co., 1948-52; med. editor U. Mich. Hosp., Ann Arbor, 1953-54; editorial asst. E.P. Dutton & Co., N.Y.C., 1954-55; editorial asst. U. Ill. Press, Champaign, 1956-59, asst. editor, 1959-67, assoc. editor, 1967-72, mng. editor, 1972-90, asst. dir., 1983-90, assoc. dir., 1990—. Democrat. Episcopalian. Home: 73 Greencroft Dr Champaign IL 61821-5112 Office: U Ill Press 1325 S Oak St Champaign IL 61820-6903

DULEY, MARGOT IRIS, administrator, history educator; b. St. John's, Can., Sept. 15, 1944; d. Cyril Chancey and Florence (Pitcher) D.; m. Lance Franz Morrow, Aug. 28, 1969 (div. Oct. 1986). BA with 1st class honors, Meml. U. of Newfoundland, 1966; MA, Duke U., 1968; PhD, U. London, 1977. Instr. dept. history St. Andrew's Presbyn. Coll., Laurinburg, N.C., 1970-71, Hiram (Ohio) Coll., 1973-75; dir., lectr. pilot program U. Mich., Ann Arbor, 1975-78, dir. law club, 1978-79, assoc. dir. honors program Coll. Lit. Sci. and the Arts, 1979-84; dir. women's studies program, assoc. prof. history Denison U., Granville, Ohio, 1984-89; dir. univ. honors program, assoc. prof. history U. Toledo, 1989-92; prof. head dept. of history and philosophy Ea. Mich. U., Ypsilanti, 1992—; adv. bd. Project on Equal Ednl. Rights, Mich., 1978-82. Editor/chief author: The Cross Cultural Study of Women, 1986; author: Where Once Our Mothers Stood We Stand, 1993. Recipient fellowship Duke U., 1966-67, Lord Rothermere fellowship Rothermere Trust, U. London, 1967-70, Can. Coun. fellowship, 1971-72, Robert Good Fellowship Denison U., 1989; grantee Nfld. Provincial Adv. Com. on the Status of Women, 1988. Mem. NOW (chair Mich. ERA task force 1978-80, pres. Mich. conf. 1980-82), Am. Hist. Assn., Can. Hist. Assn., Berkshire Conf. in Women's History, Phi Kappa Phi (hon.). Office: Dept History and Philosophy Eastern Mich U 701 Pray Harrold Hall Ypsilanti MI 48197-2210

DULIN, MAURINE STUART, volunteer; b. Lonerock, Iowa, Feb. 16, 1919; d. Frank Meagher and Fern Adrienne (Wetzel) Stuart; m. William Carter Dulin, Oct. 5, 1940; children: Jacquelyn Dulin Wilson, Patricia F., Stuart M. AB in Polit. Sci./Econs., The Coll. of William and Mary, 1939. Coll. cons. Woodward and Lothrop, Washington, 1939-40; adminstr. asst. Sightler and Cox, Washington, 1942-43; acctg. dept. asst. The Am. U., Washington, 1964-69; corp. sec. Bittinger and Dulin, Arlington, Va., 1949-73; ptnr. 41 Limited Partnership, Bethesda, Md., 1979—, Montrose-270 Ltd. Partnership, Bethesda, 1979—. Mem. Rock Creek Womens Rep. Club, Bethesda, 1951-57; sgt.-at-arms Montgomery County Fed. of Rep. Women, Bethesda, 1952-53, State Fedn. of Womens Rep. Club, 1953-54; charter mem., com. chmn. Nat. Mus. of Women in the Arts; mem. Women's Bd.Cathedral Choral Soc. 1975—, com. chmn., 1988-90; mem. Women's Bd. George Washington U. Hosp., 1970—, Save Our Seminary at Forest Glen, Md., 1989—. Mem. The Town Club (pres. 1958-59), Pi Beta Phi (nat. com. chmn. 1971-73, province officer 1967-71). Episcopalian. Home: 5612 Grove St Chevy Chase MD 20815

DUMAIS, ARLENE, psychiatric mental health and critical care nurse; b. Norwich, Conn., Nov. 27, 1939; d. Warren Frank and Harriett Woodward (Tracy) Norcross; m. Joseph D. Dumais, Aug. 24, 1970; children: Arlene Goodwin Starke, Wayne Goodwin. Diploma, Lynn Hosp. Sch. Nursing, Mass., 1961; BSN, U. Hartford, 1986; MS in Nursing, St. Joseph Coll., Hartford, Conn., 1989. RN, Conn.; cert. hypnotherapy practitioners, advanced practice RN. Nurse ICU, CCU, emergency rm. Lawrence & Meml. Hosp., New London, Conn., 1967-89; psychiat. nurse clinician Natchaug Hosp., Mansfield Center, Conn., 1989-92; dir. behavioral health dept. Mashantucket Pequot Health Dept. (Indian Reservation), Ledyard, Conn., 1995; managed disability nurse Benefit Mgmt. Svcs./ITT Hartford, Simsbury, Conn., 1995—. Mem. ANA, Conn. Nurses Assn., Sigma Theta Tau. Home: 14 Cove Rd Preston CT 06365-8301 Office: ITT Hartford 200 Hopemeadow St Simsbury CT 06089

DUMAS, RHETAUGH ETHELDRA GRAVES, university official; b. Natchez, Miss., Nov. 26, 1928; d. Rhetaugh Graves and Josephine (Clemmons) Graves Bell; m. A.W. Dumas, Jr., Dec. 25, 1950; 1 child, Adrienne. BS in Nursing, Dillard U., 1951; MS in Psychiat. Nursing, Yale U., 1961; PhD in Social Psychology, Union Grad. Sch., Union for Experimenting Colls. and Univs., Cinn., 1975; also various other courses; D Pub. Svc. (hon.), Simmons Coll., 1976, U. Cin., 1981; LHD (hon.), Yale U., 1989; LLD (hon.), Dillard U., 1990; LHD (hon.), U. San Diego, 1993, Georgetown U., 1996; DPub. Svc., Fla. Internat. U., Miami, 1996; DSc (hon.), Ind. U., Gary, 1996. Instr. Dillard U., 1957-59, 61; research asst., instr. Sch. Nursing Yale U., 1962-65, from asst. prof. nursing to assoc. prof., 1965-72, chmn. dept. psychiat. nursing, 1972; dir. nursing Conn. Mental Health Ctr., Yale-New Haven Med. Ctr., 1966-72; chief psychiat. nursing edn. br. Div. Manpower and Tng. Programs, NIMH, Rockville, Md., 1972-76; dep. dir. Div. Manpower and Tng. Programs NIMH, 1976-79, dep. dir., 1979-81; dean U. Mich. Sch. Nursing, 1981-94; vice provost health affairs, Cole prof. Sch. Nursing U. Mich., 1994—, cole prof. sch. nursing; dir. Group Rels. Confs. in Tavistock Model; cons., speaker, panelist in field; fellow Helen Hadley Hall, Yale U., 1972, Branford Coll., 1972; dir. Community Health Care Ctr. Plan, New Haven, 1969-72; mem. U.S. Assessment Team, cons. to Fed. Ministry Health, Nigeria, 1982; mem. adv. com. Health Policy Agenda for the Am. People, AMA, 1983-86; cons. NIH Task Force on Nursing Rsch., 1984; mem. Nat. Commn. on Unemployment and Mental Health, Nat. Mental Health Assn., 1984-85; mem. com. to plan maj. study of nat. long-term care policy Inst. Medicine, 1985; mem. adv. com. to dir. NIH, 1986-87; mem. Sec.'s Nat. Commn. on Future Structure of VA Health Care System, 1990-91; mem. coun. on grad. med. edn. Nat. Adv. Coun. on Nurse Edn. and Practice Workgroup on Primary Care Workforce Projection, Divsn. Nursing, 1994. Author profl. monographs; contbr. articles to profl. publs.; mem. editorial bd. Community Mental Health Rev., 1977-79, Jour. Personality and Social Systems, 1978-81, Advances in Psychiat. Mental Health Nursing, 1981. Bd. dirs. Afro Am. Ctr., Yale U., 1968-72; mem. New Haven Bd. Edn., 1968-71, New Haven City Demonstrations Agy., 1968-70, Human Rels. Coun. New Haven, 1961-63, Nat. Neural Circuitry Database Com., Inst. Medicine, Nat. Acad. Scis.; mem. commn. on future structure of vets. health care U.S. Dept. Vets. Affairs, 1990. Named Disting. Alumna, Dillard U., 1966; recipient various awards, including cert. Honor NAACP, 1970, Disting. Alumnae award Yale U. Sch. Nursing, 1976, award for outstanding achievement and service in field mental health D.C. chpt. Assn. Black Psychologists, 1980, Pres. 21st Century award The Nat. Women's Hall of Fame, 1994. Fellow A.K. Rice Inst., Am. Coll. Mental Health Adminstrs. (founding), Am. Acad. Nursing (charter, pres. 1987-89); mem. Inst. Medicine NAS, Am. Nurses Assn., Nat. Black Nurses Assn., Am. Assn. Colls. Nursing (govtl. affairs com. 1990-93), Am. Pub. Health Assn., Nat. League Nursing (pres.-elect 1995—), Sigma Theta Tau Internat. (mentor award 1989), Delta Sigma Theta. Office: U Mich 3088 Fleming Adminstrn Bldg Ann Arbor MI 48109-1340

DUMBLETON, SUSANNE P., university administrator, editor, publisher; b. N.Y.C., May 12, 1942; d. Vernon and Patricia (Leary) M.; m. William A. Dumbleton, Jan. 29, 1966; children: Kathleen, Timothy, Molia. BA, SUNY, Albany, 1964, MA, 1966, PhD, 1973. Assoc. prof., chair liberal arts Albany (N.Y.) Coll. Pharmacy, 1976-89; dean liberal arts Regent's Coll., Albany, 1989-94; v.p. acad. affairs Nat. U., San Diego, 1994-96; dean Sch. of New Leaning DePaul U., Chgo., 1996—; editor, v.p. Washington Park Press, Albany, 1983—; mng. editor Brit.-Am. Press, Albany, 1986-88. Author: Saving Union, 1988; In and Around Albany, Schenectady and Troy, 1990; editor: (books)O Albany, 1983 (Am. Book award 1993), Flashback, 1986. Pres., bd. govs. St. Margaret's Ctr. for Children, Albany, 1980-92. Mem. Assn. Am. Colls. and Univs., Coun. for Adult and Experiential Learning, Assn. of Continuing Higher Edn. Avocations: sailing, music, fiction. Home: 601 S LaSalle Bldg Box D456 Chicago IL 60605 Office: DePaul U Sch for New Learning 243 S Wabash Ave Chicago IL 60604-2302

DUMITRESCU, DOMNITA, Spanish language educator, researcher; b. Bucharest, Romania; came to U.S., 1984; d. Ion and Angela (Barzotescu) D. Diploma, U. Bucharest, 1966; MA, U. So. Calif., L.A., 1987, PhD, 1990. Asst. prof. U. Bucharest, 1966-74, assoc. prof., 1974-84; asst. prof. Spanish, U. So. Calif., 1985-89; assoc. prof. Calif. State U., L.A., 1990-94, prof., 1995—. Author: Gramatica Limbii Spaniole, 1976, Indreptar Pentru Traducerea Din Limba Romana in Limba Spaniola, 1980; translator from Spanish lit. to Romanian; assoc. editor: Hispania, 1996-98; contbr. articles to profl. jours. Fulbright scholar, 1993—. Mem. MLA, Am.-Romanian Acad. Arts and Scis., Linguistic Soc. Am., Internat. Assn. Hispanists, Assn. Linguistics and Philology L.Am., Am. Assn. Tchrs. Spanish and Portuguese (past pres. So. Calif. chpt.). Office: Calif State U 5151 State University Dr Los Angeles CA 90032-4221

DUMLER, PATRICIA ANN, critical care nurse; b. San Antonio, Feb. 16, 1960; d. Raymond Lee and Ann Dell (Comer) Dumler; m. David Hastings Smith, Dec. 28, 1985. BSN, U. Md., Balt., 1983; student, James Madison U., Harrisonburg, Va., 1978-81. Staff nurse Bon Secours Hosp., Balt., Rockingham Meml. Hosp., Harrisonburg, Va.; clin. nurse II Homewood Hosp. Ctr., Balt.; clin. nurse Johns Hopkins Hosp., Balt.

DUMMER, ROSEMARY JUNE, psychologist; b. St. Paul, Aug. 8, 1927; d. Clarence Martin and Evelyn May (McClusky) Dunn; m. Donald J. Dummer, June 18, 1949; children: Timothy, Michael, Daniel, Diana. BA, U. Minn., 1949, MA, 1972. Lic. psychologist, Minn., marriage and family therapist, Minn. Tchr. Springfield (Nebr.) H.S., 1949-50, Ralston (Nebr.) H.S., 1950-51; educator Cath. Ch., St. Paul, 1963-69; psychologist Silver Lake Clinic, Mpls., 1972—; psychologist Loring Family Clinic, Mpls., 1985—. Mem. Women Against Mil. Madness Commn., Mpls., 1968—. Recipient award New Brighton Human Rights Commn., 1972, Dreikurs award Adler Inst., 1983, Rosemary Dummer award Minn. Marriage and Family Inst., 1987. Mem. Nat. Assn. Marital and Family Therapists (cert. supr.), Minn. Assn. Marriage and Family Therapists (bd. dirs., past pres.), Minn. Psychologists Assn. Home: 781 Forest Dale Rd New Brighton MN 55112 Office: Silver Lake Clinic 3900 Stinson Blvd Minneapolis MN 55421

DUMOULIN, DIANA CRISTAUDO, marketing professional; b. Washington, Jan. 5, 1939; d. Emanuel A. and Angela E. (Cogliano) Cristaudo; m. Philip DuMoulin, May 30, 1964; children: Joanmarie Patricia, John Philip. MA, U. Wis., 1967; BA, Rosary Coll., 1961. Project mgr. IDC Cons. Group, Framingham, Mass., 1982-84; sr. market analyst Cullinet, Inc., Westwood, Mass., 1984-86; prof. assoc. Ledgeway Group, Lexington, Mass., 1987-89; prin. Customer Mktg. Specialist, Brookline, Mass., 1989-93; pres. Customer Solutions Int., Phoenix, 1994—; adj. faculty Ulster Count Community Coll., Stone Ridge, N.Y., 1967-74, Mass. Bay Community Coll., Wellesley Hills, Mass., 1983; lectr. Boston Coll., Chestnut Hill, Mass., 1976. Contbr. articles to profl. jours. Pres. League Women Voters, Kingston, N.Y., 1973-74. Recipient Svc. to Young Adults award 70001 Career Assn., 1977; faculty fellow U. Wis., 1964-66. Mem. Am. Field Svc. Mgrs. Internat. (software support spl. interest group, chmn. minuteman chpt. 1991-92), Nat. Assn. Women Bus. Owners. Office: Customer Solutions Internat 8441 N 1st Dr Phoenix AZ 85021-5515

DUMSICK, KAYE F., special education educator, consultant; b. Detroit, June 2, 1936; d. Samuel Edward and Frances Evelyn (Watson) Dukes; div. mar. 1976; children: Kathleen, Bryan, Kelly. A of Fine Arts, Schoolcraft C.C., 1971; BEd, U. Mich., 1992. Cert. secondary and English tchr., Mich. Tchr. spl. edn. Detroit Pub. Schs., 1993-94; pres., owner Fleetwood Diner, Inc., Ann Arbor, Mich., 1979-84. Author (poetry) Sparrowgrass, 1993, Internat. Soc. Poets, 1993 (Poet's award 1994). Recipient scholarship Schoolcraft C.C., 1971. Fellow Nat. Writing Project VIII; mem. Internat. Poetry Guild (mentor), Mich. Sci. Tchrs. Assn., Mich. Coun. for Tchrs. of English, Coun. for Exceptional Children, Phi Theta Kappa.

DUNAGAN, GWENDOLYN ANN, special education educator; b. Youngstown, Ohio, Sept. 27, 1941; d. Charles Jefferson and Emma Juanita (Alexander) Hicks; m. Willie Miles, 1966; 1 child, Byron Keith Miles; m. Kenneth Robert Dunagan, July 1, 1972. BS in Edn., Youngstown U., Ohio, 1963; postgrad., Ashland U., 1986-89. Cert. elem. tchr., Ohio, learning disabilities tchr., Ohio, tchr. to severe behavior disorder, Ohio. Elem. tchr. Youngstown Bd. Edn., 1963-67, 1968-72; adminstr., tchr. Free Kindergarten Assn., Youngstown, 1967-68; liaison home-sch. Alliance (Ohio) Bd. Edn., 1972-86, tchr. disadvantaged pupils, 1986-89, intervention tchr. learning disabilities, 1989-90, tchr. specific learning disabilities, 1990-94, tchr. spl. edn., 1990-96; contestant, winner TV show Price is Right; group leader Youngstown Detention Ctr. Contbr. articles to profl. mags., area newspapers. Pres. Domestic Violence Shelter, Alliance, 1990-92, hon. mem., 1992—; pres. John Slimack Homeless Shelter, Alliance, 1989-93; pres., founder Cmty. Civic Com., Alliance, 1987—; treas. Altrusic Civic Club, Alliance, 1988-91; mem. choir Holy Temple Ch. God in Christ, Alliance, 1972—, mem. usher bd. dirs., fin. sec., sec. Sunday sch., 1989—; chairperson Alliance Area Desert Storm Celebration, 1991; mem. Family Counseling Ctr., YWCA, Dr. King Birthday Celebration Com.; mem. Dr. Martin Luther King Jr. Steering Com., 1995; tchr. Prayer and Bible Band, 1990—; adv. bd. Salvation Army, 1994—. Honored for community svc. Stark County Community Action Agy., 1990. Mem. NAFE, AAUW, Alliance Edn. Assn. (Dowling scholarship com.), NAACP (2d v.p. 1990-93), McKinley Reading Assn., Quota Club, Alpha Kappa Alpha. Home: 1115 S Seneca Ave Alliance OH 44601-4068

DUNAWAY, CAROLYN BENNETT, sociology educator; b. Atlanta, Mar. 3, 1943; d. Clarence Rhodes and Gay (McKenzie) Bennett; m. William Preston Dunaway, Aug. 26, 1967; 1 child, Robert Bennett Dunaway. BS, Auburn U., 1966, EdD, 1983; MA, U. Ala., Tuscaloosa, 1967. Instr. sociology Jefferson State C.C., Birmingham, Ala., 1967-69; prof. Auburn U., Montgomery, Ala., 1970-71; prof. sociology and gerontology dept. Jacksonville (Ala.) State U., 1971—; student counselor Jacksonville State U., Ala., 1971—. Contbd. articles to profl. jours. Cons., trainer Calhoun County Hospice Anniston, Ala., 1983—; presenter Calhoun County Gerontology, Anniston, 1985—; officer Jacksonville Book Club, Ala., 1984; officer, tchr. St Luke's Episcopal Ch., Jacksonville, 1993. Recipient 100 Most Outstanding Women Alumna award Auburn U., 1991, U. Rsch. award Jacksonville State U., 1989. Mem. Ala.-Miss. Sociol. Assn. (v.p. 1975-76, ciology Club,Inter-Se Study Club, Ala. Fedn. Womens Club (dist. sect.), Phi Kappa Phi, Kappa Delta Pi, Delta Delta Delta, Phi Delta Kappa. Democrat. Episcopalian. Home: 902 11th St NE Jacksonville AL 36265-1230

DUNAWAY, (DOROTHY) FAYE, actress; b. Bascom, Fla., Jan. 14, 1941; d. John and Grace D.; m. Peter Wolf, Aug. 7, 1974 (div.); m. Terrence O'Neill; 1 son. Student, U. Fla., Boston U. Appearences include as original mem. Lincoln Ctr. Repertory Co., N.Y.C., off-Broadway in Hogan's Goat; also in (play) Curse of the Aching Heart, 1982; motion picture appearences include Bonnie in motion picture Bonnie and Clyde, 1967, Hurry Sundown, 1967, Puzzle of a Downfall Child, The Happening, 1967, The Thomas Crown Affair, 1968, A Place For Lovers, 1969, Little Big Man, 1970, Doc, 1971, La Maison Sous les Arbres, 1971, The Getaway, 1972, Oklahoma Crude, 1973, The Three Musketeers, 1973, Chinatown, 1974, The Towering Inferno, 1974, The Four Muscateers, 1975, Three Days of the Condor, 1975, Network, 1976 (Acad. award for Best Actress), The Voyage of the Damned, 1976, The Eyes of Laura Mars, 1978, The Champ, 1979, The First Deadly Sin, 1980, Mommie Dearest, 1981, The Wicked Lady, 1982, Ordeal by Innocence, 1985, Supergirl, 1984, Barfly, 1987, Burning Secret, 1988, La Partita, 1988, Midnight Crossing, 1988, The Gamble, 1989, In a Moonlit Night, 1989, Wait Until Spring, Bandini, 1989, The Handmaid's Tale, 1990, Three Weeks in Jerusalem, 1990, Scorchers, 1990, Arrowtooth Waltz, 1991, Double Edge, 1992, The Temp, 1993, Point of No Return, 1993, Even Cowgirls Get the Blues, 1994, Don Juan DeMarco, 1995, others; TV movies: After the Fall, 1974, The Disappearance of Aimee, 1976, Evita Peron, 1981, 13 at Dinner, 1985, Beverly Hills Madame, 1986, Casanova, 1987, Cold Sassy Tree, 1989, Silhouette, 1990 (co-exec. prodr.), Columbo: It's All in the Game (Emmy award for Guest Actress in Drama 1994), Mother Love, 1995, A Family Divided, 1995; TV miniseries: Ellis Island, 1984, Christopher Columbus, 1985; TV series: It Had To Be You, 1993. Recipient Most Promising Newcomer Award Brit. Film Acad., 1968. Address: c/o ICM 8942 Wilshire Blvd Beverly Hills CA 90211-1934*

DUNBAR, MARY ASMUNDSON, communications executive, investor and public relations consultant; b. Sacramento, Calif., Feb. 6, 1942; d. Vigfus Samundur and Aline Mary (McGrath) Asmundson; m. Robert Copeland Dunbar, June 21, 1969; children: Geoffrey Townsend, William Asmundson. BA in English Lit., Smith Coll., 1964; MA in Communications, Stanford, 1967; MBA in Fin., Case Western Res. U., 1985. Cert. pub. rels. profl. Tchr. Peace Corps, Cameroun, Africa, 1964-66; writer, editor Ednl. Devel. Corp., Palo Alto, Calif., 1967-68, Addison-Wesley, Menlo Park, Calif., 1969-70; free lance writer, editor various, Cleve., 1970-85; account exec. Edward Howard & Co., Cleve., 1985-87; account exec. Dix & Eaton, Inc., Cleve., 1987—, v.p., 1992—. Author publs. in field (Arthur Page award 1990, IABC award 1987, Women in Communications award 1987). Trustee Cleve. Coun. World Affiars, 1994—. Recipient scholarship Smith Coll., Northampton, Mass., 1960-64; fellowship Stanford Univ., Palo Alto, Calif., 1967. Mem. Smith Coll. Club Cleve., Pub. Rels. Soc. Am., Nat. Investor Rels. Inst. (membership Cleve.-Akron chpt.), Cleve. Soc. Security Analysts, Cleve. Com. Fgn. Rels. Republican. Episcopalian. Home: 2880 Fairfax Rd Cleveland OH 44118-4014 Office: Dix & Eaton Inc 1801 E 9th St Ste 1300 Cleveland OH 44114-3103

DUNBAR, SHARON KAY, controller, accountant; b. Terre Haute, Ind., Mar. 6, 1943; d. Thomas Shannon and Lillian Irene (Pipes) Parkhurst; m. Robert Michael Dunbar, Aug. 3, 1962; children: Robert Michael, Clinton Reece, Shannon Lynne. AA with honors, Modesto (Calif.) Jr. Coll., 1984; BS magna cum laude, Calif. State U., Turlock, 1987. CPA, Calif. Staff acct., auditor E. & J. Gallo Winery, Modesto, 1988-91; sr. acct. Dunker & Aced Accountancy Corp., Modesto, 1991-94, Korte & Co. CPAs, Modesto, 1994-95; asst. contr. Stanislaus Food Products, Modesto, 1995—; sole proprietor Sharon K. Dunbar, CPA, Modesto, 1995—. V.p., bd. dirs. Bravo Repertory Dance Theatre, Modesto, 1992—, pres., 1996—; bd. dirs. Downtown Arts Project, Modesto, 1993—. Modesto Jr. Coll. scholar, 1984, Women's Improvement Club scholar, 1984, Dept. Accountancy scholar Calif. State U., 1986, Bus. Adminstrn. scholar, 1985. Mem. Am. Inst. CPAs, Calif. Soc. CPAs, Inst. Mgmt. Accts. (bd. dirs., membership sec.). Home: 3201 Canterbury Ct Modesto CA 95350

DUNCAN, CAROL LYNN, English language and literature educator; b. Jellico, Tenn., June 15, 1948; d. Billy Gene and Vivian Alberta (Stanfill) Whited; m. Jackie Leland Duncan; children: Jennifer Lynn, Cresta Leigh, Jana Layne. BA, Cumberland Coll., 1971; MA in Edn., Eastern Ky. U., 1987. English tchr. Scott County Schs., Huntsville, Tenn., 1983-85; instr. English Alice Lloyd Coll., Pippa Passes, Ky., 1985-89; prof. English Jefferson C.C., Louisville, 1990—; coach, evaluator Carroll County Schs., Carrollton, Ky., 1994—, Owen County Schs., Owen, Ky., 1989-94. Mem. Nat. Coun. Tchrs. English, Libr. Congress. Home: 106 Delaware Way Carrollton KY 41008 Office: Jefferson CC 324 Main St Carrollton KY 41008

DUNCAN, CATHERINE THERESA, accountant; b. St. Louis, Mar. 5, 1955; d. Thomas Fred Busse and Peggy Lea (Jacobs) Martin; m. Thomas Arthur Duncan, Aug. 15, 1987; children: Theresa Lea, Thomas Edward, Stephanie Catherine. BBA, North Tex. State U., 1977. CPA, Tex.; cert. govt. fin. officer Govt. Fin. Officers Assn. Tex. Acct. Roerig & Lewellen, CPAs, Garden Grove, Calif., 1978-79, Fox, Byrd & Co., Dallas, 1979-84, City of Irving, Tex., 1984—. Mem. AICPA, Tex. Soc. CPA's, Govt. Fin. Officers Assn. Republican. Office: City of Irving 825 W Irving Blvd Irving TX 75060

DUNCAN, DEBORAH L., bank executive. Sr. v.p. corp. treas. Chase Manhattan, N.Y.C. Office: Chase Manhattan One Chase Manhattan Plz New York NY 10081*

DUNCAN, ELIZABETH CHARLOTTE, marriage and family therapist, educational therapist, educator; b. L.A., Mar. 10, 1919; d. Frederick John de St. Vrain and Nellie Mae (Goucher) Schwankovsky; m. William McConnell Duncan, Oct. 12, 1941 (div. 1949); 1 child, Susan Elizabeth Duncan St. Vrain. BA, Calif. U., Long Beach, 1953; MA, UCLA, 1962; PhD, Internat. Coll., 1984. Cert. marriage and family therapist, Wash. Dir. gifted program Palos Verdes Sch. Dist., Calif., 1958-64; TV tchr., participant ednl. films L.A. County, 1961-64; dir. U. So. Calif. Presch., L.A., 1965-69, Abraham Maslow rsch. assoc., 1962-69; pvt. practice family counselor, Malibu and Ventura, Calif., Eastsound, Wash., 1979—, also, Seattle, pvt. practice in psychotherapy, West Seattle, 1994—; pub. spkr., lectr. comm.; cons. in field; psychotherapist Mentor Program Eastsound, 1992; bd. dirs. Children's Program North Sound Regional Support Network, 1992; resident psychologist for film series Something Personal, 1987—; mem. Rsch. Inst. of Scripps

Clinic, La Jolla, Calif.; charter mem. Inst. Behav. Med., Santa Barbara, Calif.; TV performer: (documentary) The Other Side, 1985. Creator: Persephone's Child, 1988. Active Chryalis Ctr., L.A., 1984-86, Ventura County Mental Health Adv. Bd., Calif., 1985-86, United Way, L.A., 1985-92; mem. Menninger Found. San Juan County, Wash., 1992; adv. bd. North Sound Regional Support Network, 1992. Recipient Emmy award for best documentary Am. TV Arts and Scis., 1976, Child Adv. of Yr. Calif. Mental Health Adv. Bd., 1987. Mem. AACD (Disting. Svc. award 1990), Transpersonal Psychol. Assn., Calif. State Orgn. Gifted Edn. (sec. 1962-64), Internat. Platform Assn., Am. Assn. for Marriages and Family Therapy. Democrat. Avocations: swimming, plays, concerts, boating, political issues, especially women and child abuse. Office: 4505 44th Ave SW Seattle WA 98116

DUNCAN, FRANCES MURPHY, retired special education educator; b. Utica, N.Y., June 23, 1920; d. Edward Simon and Elizabeth Myers (Stack) Murphy; m. Lee C. Duncan, June 23, 1947 (div. June 1969); children: Lee C., Edward M., Paul H., Elizabeth B., Nancy R., Richard L. BA, Columbia U., 1942; MEd, Auburn U., 1963, EdD, 1969. Head sci. dept. Arnold Jr. H.S., Columbus, Ga., 1960-63; tchr. physiology, Spanish, Jordan H.S., Columbus, 1963-64; tchr. spl. edn. mentally retarded Muscogee County Sch. System, Columbus, 1964-65; instr. spl. edn. Auburn (Ala.) U., 1966-69; assoc. dir. Douglas Sch. for Learning Disabilities, Columbus, 1969-70; prof. edn. and spl. edn. Columbus Coll., 1970-85; ret., 1985. Past dir. Columbus Devel. Ctr.; dir. Columbus Regional Chartered Coun. Child Abuse-first steps/TRUST programs. Past sec. exec. bd. Muscular Dystrophy Assn., 1968-70; 73-74; mem. Gov.'s Commn. on Disabled Georgians; past trustee Listening Eyes Sch. for Deaf; past mem. Mayor's Com. on Handicapped; mem. team for evaluation and placement of exceptional children Columbus Pub. Schs. Fellow Am. Assn. Mental Retardation; mem. AAUP, AAUW (pres. 1973-75, div. rec. sec. 1975—), Council Exceptional Children (legis. chmn. 1973-74), Psi Chi, Phi Delta Kappa. Roman Catholic. Home: 1811 Alta Vista Dr Columbus GA 31907-3210

DUNCAN, GWENDOLYN MCCURRY, elementary education educator; b. Walhalla, S.C., Feb. 24, 1943; d. Benjamin Harrison and Lucy Rosa (Quarles) McCurry; m. Harold Edward Duncan, July 29, 1962; children: Gregory Scott, Michael Lane. BA in Elem. Edn., Clemson (S.C.) U., 1984. Tchr. Westminster (S.C.) Elem. Sch., 1984—. Sunday sch. tchr. Mountain View Bapt. Ch., Walhalla, 1968—; mem. Westminster Elem. PTA, 1984—. Mem. NEA, Oconee County Edn. Assn., S.C. Edn. Assn., S.C. Tchrs. of Math., Nat. Coun. of Tchrs. of Math., Kappa Delta Pi. Baptist. Home: 389 Fowler Rd West Union SC 29696-3122 Office: Westminster Elem Sch 206 Hamilton Dr Westminster SC 29693-1541

DUNCAN, JOYCE LOUISE, real estate broker; b. Canton, Ohio, Jan. 11, 1946; d. William Clayton and Virginia Ruth (Wilgus) Sommers; m. Daniel Bruce Duncan, Mar. 3, 1989 (dec. 1990); children: David Michael Calhoun, Traci Lyn Calhoun. Student, U. Chattanooga, 1963-65, Mansfield Bus. Coll., Canton, Ohio, 1992-93; Assoc in Bus. Adminstrn., Mansfield Bus. Coll., Canton, Ohio, 1993. Cert. property mgr. Property mgr. Niebel Realty, North Canton, Ohio, 1981-85, Century 21 Americana Properties, St. Petersburg, Fla., 1987, Royal Estate Mgmt. Corp., Canton, 1989-90; broker, pres. Greystone Group, Inc., Canton, 1989-94, Ostendorf-Morris Co., Canton, 1993—. Mem. Women's Coun. Realtors (phone chmn. 1982, publicity chmn. 1983, treas. 1984, pres.-elect 1985, phone com. 1990), Canton/Massilon-St. Petersburg Bd. Realtors (program com. 1982-85, bldg. com. 1985, equal opportunity in housing com. 1990), Inst. Real Estate Mgmt., Nazir Caldron # 27 (past Mighty Chosen One), Order Ea. Star (Delta chpt. # 539). Home: 2748 Deer Pass Dr SW Canton OH 44706-4305 Office: Ste 810 4450 Belden Village St NW Canton OH 44718-2540

DUNCAN, MARGARET CAROLINE, physician; b. Salt Lake City, June 9, 1930; d. Donald and Margaret Aileen (Eberts) D.; m. N. Paul Arceneaux, Dec. 26, 1958; children—David Paul, Eleanor Anne, Stephen Louis, Andre. B.A., U. Tex., 1952, M.D., 1955. Intern Kings County Hosp., Seattle, 1955-56; resident in pediatrics John Sealy Hosp., Galveston, Tex., 1956-58; resident in neurology Charity Hosp., New Orleans, 1958-60; fellow child neurology Johns Hopkins Hosp., 1960-61; mem. faculty La. State U. Med. Center, New Orleans, 1961—; prof. neurology and pediatrics La. State U. Med. Center, 1973—. Chmn. La. Com. Epilepsy and Cerebral Palsy, 1976-79. Fellow Am. Acad. Neurology, Am. Acad. Pediatrics; mem. Child Neurology Soc., Profs. Child Neurology, Alpha Omega Alpha. Episcopalian. Office: 1542 Tulane Ave New Orleans LA 70112-2825

DUNCAN, MARILYNN FRANCES, education educator; b. Muskogee, Okla., Dec. 7, 1951; d. Henry Vernard and Elizabeth (Bradley) D.; 1 child, Brenton V. Duncan. BA, Northeastern State U., Okla., 1973, MEd, 1974. Instr. psychology Eastern Okla. State Coll., Wiburton, 1975—, chair social sci. dept., 1984—, chairperson liberal arts divsn., 1986—. Named to Muskogee (Okla.) Svc. League Hall of Fame, 1985. Mem. AAUW, HEACO, Delta Sigma Theta, Phi Delta Kappa. Office: Eastern Okla State Coll 1301 W Main Wilburton OK 74578

DUNCAN, SANDY, actress; b. Henderson, Tex., Feb. 20, 1946; d. Mancil Ray and Sylvian Wynne (Scott) D.; m. Don Correia; children: Jeffrey, Michael. Studied dance at, Lon Morris Coll. Stage debut in The King and I at State Fair Music Hall, Dallas, 1958; N.Y. stage debut in The Music Man, 1965; stage appearances include The Boyfriend (Outer Critics Circle award, N.Y. Drama Desk award), Ceremony of Innocence, (Theater World award), Your Own Thing, The Music Box, Love Is a Time of Day, Peter Pan, My One and Only, 1984; starred in TV series Funny Face, 1971, The Sandy Duncan Show, 1972, Valerie's Family (title changed to The Hogan Family 1988), 1987-91; appeared in TV mini-series Roots, 1977; TV movies include My Boyfriend's Back, 1989, Miracle on I-880, 1993; other TV appearances include The Flip Wilson Show; film appearances include Million Dollar Duck, Star Spangled Girl, 1971, The Cat From Outer Space, 1978, (voice) Rock-a-Doodle, 1992, (voice) The Swan Princess, 1994; appeared in video Barney & Friends, 1988. Recipient Gold medal Photoplay, 1971, Golden Apple award, 1971. *

DUNDON, MARGO ELAINE, museum director; b. Cleve., July 3, 1950; d. Elmer Edward and Ruth Ann (Dreger) Buckeye. BS in Communications cum laude, Ohio U., 1972; postgrad. in Mus. Studies, U. Okla, 1987. Mem. gen. staff Grout Mus. History and Sci., Waterloo, Iowa, 1974-75; coordinator edn. Grout Mus. History and Sci., Waterloo, 1976-78, co-dir., 1979-87, dir., 1988-90; exec. dir. Mus. Sci. and History, Jacksonville, Fla., 1990—. Chairperson Waterloo Hist. Preservation Commn., 1987-88; cultural com. Visitors and Conv. Bur., Waterloo, 1988-90, My Waterloo Days, 1982, 93; mem. Jacksonville Women's Network, Non-Profit Execs. Round Table, 1990-95; bd. dirs. Resource Plus, Waterloo-Cedar Falls, Iowa, 1986-88; mem. Jacksonville C. of C., 1990—; bd. dirs. CJI; bd. dirs. Girls Inc. of Jacksonville, 1994-95. Am. Law Inst.-ABA scholar, 1979, 86; recipient Mayor's Vol. Performance award, Waterloo, 1983, Vol. award Gov. of Iowa, 1990. Mem. Am. Assn. Mus. (site surveyor ant. assessment program 1982—, site examiner ant. accreditation commn. 1987-90, regional councilor 1988-90), Midwest Mus. Conf. (pres. 1988-90), S.E. Mus. Conf., Fla. Assn. Mus. (pres. 1995—), Iowa Mus. Assn. (pres. 1984-86), Rotary, Quota Club (pres. 1982). Office: Mus Sci & History 1025 Museum Cir Jacksonville FL 32207-9006

DUNHAM, MARY HELEN, elementary education educator; b. Skiatook, Okla., Dec. 12, 1945; d. Walter and Anna Mae (Escue) Lonsinger; m. Roger Dale Dunham, May 13, 1967; children: Roger Lewis, Carl David. BS in Edn., Northeastern State U., Tahlequah, Okla., 1967. Tchr. elem. sch. Skiatook (Okla.) Marrs Elem. Sch., Vera (Okla.) Sch., Blue Sch., Locust Grove, Okla., St. Paul Sch., Memphis. Mem. Nat. Reading Assn., Okla. Reading Assn., Tulsa REading Assn., Sigma Epsilon Alpha. Home: 19300 N Harvard Ave Skiatook OK 74070-4135

DUNHAM, REBECCA BETTY BERES, school administrator; b. Cleve., Aug. 30, 1948; d. Michael Charles and Veda Mary (Vardian) Beres; m. William Grant Dunham, Mar. 15, 1969; children: Heidi Rebecca, Aaron William, Amanda Elisabeth (dec.), Meredith Lynne. BA, Kent State U., 1977. Rschr. Phillips Exeter (N.H.) Acad., 1977-84, dir. found. support, 1984-88, assoc. dir. capital giving, 1988-93; assoc. dir. alumni and alumnae affairs and devel. Groton (Mass.) Sch., 1993-95, dir. alumni and alumnae affairs and devel., 1995—; pres., v.p., bd. dirs. Richie McFarland Children's Ctr., Exeter, 1981-89; spkr., mem. Gov. Coun. Volunteerism, Concord, N.H., 1985-86; chair, vice chair Partnership Philanthropy, N.H., Maine, Vt., 1990-91. Trustee Mary Bartlett Meml. Libr., Brentwood, N.H., 1992-93; vol. Swasey Ctrl. Sch., Brentwood, 1978-85; bd. dirs., sec. bd., Montessori Sch. Creative Learning, North Hampton, 1976-78. Mem. Coun. Advancement and Support Edn., Coun. N.H. Fund Raising (pres. bd. 1989-92), Planned Giving Group New Eng., Assn. Ind. Schs. New Eng. (devel. com.).

DUNION, CELESTE MOGAB, township official, consultant; b. Atlantic City, Mar. 6, 1932; d. Cyril Joseph and Lavina Edna (Bolen) Mogab; m. John Joseph Dunion, May 8, 1954 (dec. Apr. 1978); children: Dana, John, Robert, Denise. Tech. degree, Am. Acad. Dramatic Arts, N.Y.C., 1951; grad. advanced govt. fin. inst., Georgetown U., 1986. Cert. govt. fin. mgr.; lic. notary pub., Pa. Asst. to bus. mgr. Rose Tree Media Sch. Dist., Media, Pa., 1969-78; dir. fin., tax collector, treas. Twp. of Middletown, Glen Riddle, Pa., 1978—; profl. model, N.Y.C., Phila., Atlantic City; mem. Christy Modeling Agy., Phila. Models Guild, Atlantic City Models Guild, Atlantic City Press Bur.; cons. in fin. mgmt. peer-to-peer program Pa. Dept. Cmty. Affairs, Harrisburg, 1988-96; treas., bd. dirs. Pa. Mcpl. Investment Program, 1990—. Mem. Delaware County Open Space Partnership Bd.; past sec. Wyncroft Civic Assn.; former committeewoman Middletown Twp. Recipient Dedicated Pumper award Lenni Fire Co., 1983, President's award Lima Fire Co., 1985, Outstanding Leadership award Pa. East Govt. Fin. Officers Assn., 1986. Mem. Govt. Fin. Officers Assn. (Pa. rep., nat. cash mgmt. com., women's fin. network, Mid-Atlantic rep.), Pa. Govt. Fin. Officers Assn. (past pres., sec., Southeast bd.), MidAtlantic Govt. Fin. Officers Assn. (Pa. rep., mem. legis. com.), Women's Fin. Officers Network (chmn. membership), Delaware County Tax Collectors Assn. (v.p. 1984-85, pres. 1986), Pa. Tax Collectors Assn., Pa. Assn. Notaries. Republican. Roman Catholic. Office: Twp of Middletown PO Box 157 27 N Pennell Rd Glen Riddle PA 19037

DUNKELMAN, LORETTA, artist; b. Paterson, N.J., June 29, 1937; d. Samuel and Rae (Gutkin) D. BA, Rutgers U., 1958; MA, Hunter Coll., 1966. Lectr. Hunter Coll., N.Y.C., 1966-67; vis. artist U. Cin., 1974; asst. prof. U. R.I., Kingston, 1974-75, Cornell U., Ithaca, N.Y., 1977-80; vis. artist Ohio State U., Columbus, 1984; asst. prof. Va. Commonwealth Univ., Richmond, 1986-88; vis. artist The Sch. of the Art Inst. of Chgo., 1990; vis. prof. art U. Calif., Berkeley, 1993-94; One woman shows include A.I.R. Gallery, N.Y., 1973-74, 78, 81, 83, 87, Douglass Coll., New Brunswick, 1973, U. Cin., 1974, U. R.I., Kingston, 1975, 1708 E. Main Gallery, Richmond, 1987; exhibited in group shows at Whitney Mus. Am. Art, N.Y., 1973, N.Y. Cultural Ctr., N.Y., 1973, Newark Mus., 1973, Cranbrook Acad. Art Mus., Bloomfield Hills, Mich., 1974, Grand Rapids (Mich.) Art Mus., 1974, Johnson Mus., Cornell U., Ithaca, N.Y., 1977, Inst. Art and Urban Resources, Pub. Sch. 1, N.Y.C., 1978, McIntosh/Drysdale Gallery, Washington, 1980, Douglass Coll., Rutgers U., New Brunswick, 1981, Kulturhuset, Stockholm and Lunds Konsthall, Sweden, 1981-82, Picker Art Gallery, Colgate U., Hamilton, N.Y., 1983, Hopkins Hall Gallery, The Ohio State U., 1984, Kenkeleba Gallery, N.Y., 1985, A.I.R. Gallery, 1985, 91, Bernice Steinbaum Gallery, N.Y., 1986, Anderson Gallery, Va. Commonwealth U., Richmond, Va., 1987, Rabbet Gallery, New Brunswick, N.J., 1989, Michael Walls Gallery, 1989, 148 Duane St., N.Y.C., 1992; represented in permanent collections Bellevue Med. Ctr., N.Y.C., The Chase Manhattan Bank, N.Y.C., City Univ. Grad. Ctr., N.Y.C., The Picker Art Gallery, Dana Art Ctr., Colgate U., Hamilton, N.Y., U. Cin., Gene Swenson Collection, U. Kansas Art Mus., Lawrence, Bristol-Myers, Squibb, Lawrenceville, N.J., Hunter Coll., N.Y.C. CAPS fellow N.Y. State Coun. Arts, 1975; Visual artist fellow Nat. Endowment for the Arts, 1975, 82, 93, AAUW fellow, 1976-77, Artist fellow N.Y. Found. for the Arts, 1991; grantee Adolph & Esther Gottlieb Found., 1991. Home and Office: 151 Canal St New York NY 10002

DUNKIS, PATRICIA B., principal. Prin. C.R. Streams Elem. Sch., Upper St. Clair, Pa. Recipient Elem. Sch. Recognition award U.S. Dept. Edn., 1989-90. Office: C R Streams Elem Sch 1560 Ashlawn Dr Upper Saint Clair PA 15241*

DUNKLE, JOAN OSBORN, artist; b. Boston, Aug. 13, 1931; d. John and Molly (Harding) Osborn; m. Robert Johnston Dunkle, June 6, 1953; children: Stephen, John, Joan, Robert. Student, Bradford Coll., 1950-52. Co=owner Needham (Mass.) Art Ctr., 1970-79; owner Art East, North Hampton, N.H., 1986—, SoHo South, Naples, Fla., 1994—; instr., Maine, N.H., Fla., Mass. Mem. Nat. Assn. Women Artists. Studio: 7 Pond Path North Hampton NH 03862 and: 3573 Enterprise Park Naples FL 33942

DUNLAP, ANGELA O., communications executive. Exec. v.p. corp. comm. MCI Comm. Corp., Washington. Office: MCI Comm Corp 1801 Pennsylvania Ave NW Washington DC 20006*

DUNLAP, CONNIE, librarian; b. Lansing, Mich., Sept. 9, 1924; d. Frederick Arthur and Laura May (Robinson) Robson; m. Robert Bruce Dunlap, Aug. 9, 1947. A.B., U. Mich., 1946, A.M. in Library Sci, 1952. Head acquisitions dept., then head grad. library U. Mich. Library, 1961-75, dep. asso. dir., 1972-75; univ. librarian Duke U., 1975-80; cons., 1981—. Authors articles in field, chpts. in books. Forewoman Grand Jury U.S. Dist. Ct. 13th Dist. Mich., 1967-68; bd. dirs. U. Mich. Libr. Friends, 1993—. Recipient Disting. Alumnus award U. Mich. Sch Library Sci., 1977. Mem. ALA (council 1974-83, exec. bd. 1978-83, pres. resources and tech. services div. 1972-73), Assn. Coll. and Research Libraries (pres. 1976-77), Assn. Research Libraries (bd. dirs. 1976-80, pres. 1979-80), AAUP. Address: 1570 Westfield Ave Ann Arbor MI 48103

DUNLAP, ELLEN S., library administrator; b. Nashville, Oct. 12, 1951; d. Arthur Wallace and Elizabeth (Majors) Smith; m. Arthur H. Dunlap, Jr., Dec. 27, 1972 (dec. 1977); m. Frank Armstrong, May 11, 1979; 1 child, Libbie Sarah. BA, U. Tex., Austin, 1972, MLS, 1974. Rsch. assoc. Humanities Rsch. Ctr. U. Tex., Austin, 1973-76, rsch. libr., 1976-83; exec. dir. Rosenbach Mus. and Library, Phila., 1983-92; dir. Conservation Ctr. for Art and Hist. Artifacts, Phila., 1985-92, Greater Phila. Cultural Alliance, 1985-92; mem. exec. com. Phila. Area Consortium Spl. Collections Librs., 1985-91; pres. Am. Antiquarian Soc., Worcester, Mass., 1992—; dir. Worcester (Mass.) Mcpl. Rsch. Bur., 1993—; chmn. archives manuscripts and spl. collections program com. Rsch. Librs. Group, Inc., Mountain View, Calif., 1989-91; dir. 18th Century Short Title Catalogue/N.Am., 1992—; corporator Alliance for Edn., Worcester, Mass., 1993—; mem. Worcester Bus. Devel. Corp., 1996—. Overseer Old Sturbridge Village, Mass., 1993—; mem. acad. affairs com. Winterthur Mus., 1995—; bd. dirs. Book Arts Press, U. Va., 1994—. Mem. Am. Antiquarian Soc., Colonial Soc. Mass., Grolier Club (N.Y.C.), Worcester Club. Office: Am Antiquarian Soc 185 Salisbury St Worcester MA 01609-1636

DUNLAP, PATRICIA PEARL, elementary school educator; b. Chgo., Jan. 16, 1951; d. Henry Law and Lucille Roberta (Singley) D. AA in Elem. Edn., Kennedy-King Coll., 1976; BS in Elem. Edn., Chgo. State U., 1978. Cert. intermediate/upper and primary tchr. with endorsements in computer sci., lang. arts, gen. sci. and social sci., Ill. Intermediate tchr. Wentworth Sch., Chgo., 1978-82; kindergarten tchr. Grimes/Fleming Sch., Chgo., 1982-83; intermediate/upper computer tchr. Harvard Sch., Chgo., 1983—; chorus music dir. Harvard Sch., Chgo., 1984—; computer cons. First Bapt. Ch., Chgo., 1989-93, Workshops R Us, Chgo., 1992—. Author, composer: Start With Me, 1993, Just Have Faith, 1994, Is It Me, 1994, We've Got The Power, 1994. Recipient Ella Flag Young award, Chgo., 1986. Mem. ASCD, Nat. Alliance of Black Sch. Educators, Kappa Delta Pi. Democrat. Office: Harvard Sch 7525 S Harvard Ave Chicago IL 60620-1616

DUNLAP, PATRICIA RILEY, history educator; b. Norfolk, Va., Mar. 25, 1943; d. Edward Miles and Annette (Powers) Riley; m. Steven James Dunlap, Dec. 26, 1964; children: Steven James Jr., Patricia Annette, Matthew Riley. BA in Philosophy, Coll. William & Mary, 1965; MA in Am. History, George Mason U., 1987, postgrad., 1996—. Tchr. geography York H.S., Yorktown, Va., 1965-67; tchr., curriculum coord. Green Valley Sch., Simi Valley, Calif., 1972-75; tchr., dept. chair, trainer Rippon Mid. Sch., Woodbridge, Va., 1979-87; coord. tng. & mktg. Koba Inst., Washington, 1987-88; dir. tng. & mktg. Info. Resources Tech., Falls Church, Va., 1988-89; pres., chief cons. Dunlap Communications, Dumfries, Va., 1989—; adj. instr. history No. Va. C.C., Alexandria, 1989—, Germanna C.C., Locust Grove, Va., 1991—, Park Coll., Quantico, Va., 1995—; dir. ednl. survey FAA, Washington, 1992; proposal writer, project mgr. MilVets Assocs., Landover, Md., 1989-94; tng. dir. Def. Sys. Mgmt. Coll., Ft. Belvoir, Va., 1989-96; regional dir. Am. Ctr. Cultural Exch., Alexandria, 1989-94. Author: Riding Astride: The Frontier in Women's History, 1995. Del. Dem. Com., Dumfries & Prince William County, Va., 1995—; chair bd. dirs. SAVAS Rape Crisis Ctr., Manassas, Va., 1990-91; chair edn. com. Commn. Bicentennial of Constitution, Manassas, 1987-88. Mem. Am. Assn. Historians, So. Hist. Assn., So. Women's Hist. Assn., Historic Dumfries, Inc. (v.p. 1990-93), Soroptimist Internat. (v.p. & pres. 1990, 92, 93), Phi Alpha Theta. Democrat. Home: 4701 Harmony Pl Dumfries VA 22026

DUNLAY, CATHERINE TELLES, lawyer; b. Cin., Apr. 5, 1958; d. Paul Albert and Donna Mae Telles; m. Thomas Vincent Dunlay, July 10, 1981; children: Christine Jennifer, Thomas Paul, Brian Patrick. Student, Ind. U., 1976-78; BA in English Lit. summa cum laude, U. Cin., 1981; JD summa cum laude, Ohio State U., 1984. Bar: Ohio 1984. Teaching asst., legal rsch. and writing Ohio State U. Coll. of Law, Columbus, 1982; law clk. Brownfield, Bowen & Bally, Columbus, 1983; assoc. Schottenstein, Zox & Dunn, LPA, Columbus, 1984-91, atty., principal, 1991—. Mng. editor Ohio State Law Jour., 1983-84; co-author Health Span, 1993, Akron Law Rev., Fall 1993; co-editor Health Law Jour. of Ohio, 1994-95. Grad. Columbus Leadership Program, 1991; mem. admissions/inclusiveness com. United Way of Franklin County, Columbus, 1991-94, 96—. Recipient C. Simeral Bunch award for Acad. Excellence, Ohio State U., 1984, Law Jour. Past Editors award, 1984. Mem. ABA, Ohio State Bar Assn., Columbus Bar Assn., Ohio Women's Bar Assn., Women Lawyers of Franklin County (trustee, treas. 1990-93, 91-92), Nat. Health Lawyers Assn., Soc. of Ohio Hosp. Attys., Order of the Coif. Roman Catholic. Office: Schottenstein Zox & Dunn 41 S High St Ste 2600 Columbus OH 43215

DUNLEAVY, MARY ANN, telecommunications company representative; b. N.Y.C., July 30, 1956; d. Anthony and Mary Frances (Glennon) D.; m. Terence Spillane, June 20, 1993. BA in Communication Arts, Iona Coll., 1978; MBA in Mktg., Fordham U., 1989. Asst. buyer Abraham and Straus, Bklyn., 1979-80; rep. NYNEX, N.Y.C., 1981—. Contbr. articles to profl. jours. Vol. Central Park Conservancy, N.Y.C., 1991. Mem. Manhattan Soc., Columba Soc., Fordham U. Aluni Assn., Iona Coll. Alumni Assn., St. Batholomews Community Club. Office: NYNEX 375 Pearl St New York NY 10038

DUNMEYER, SARAH LOUISE FISHER, health care consultant; b. Ft. Wayne, Ind., Apr. 13, 1935; d. Frederick Law and Jeanette Blose (Stults) Fisher; m. Herbert W. Dunmeyer, Sept. 9, 1967; children: Jodi, Lisa. BS, U. Mich., 1957; MS, Temple U., 1966; EdD, U. San Francisco, 1983. Lic. clin. lab. technologist, Calif. Instr. med. tech. U. Vt., Burlington, 1966-67; instr. med. tech. Northeastern U., Boston, 1967-68, instr. lab. asst. program, 1968-70; educator, coord. sch. med. tech. Children's Hosp., San Francisco, 1970-73; dir. continuing edn. program Pacific Presbyn. Med. Ctr., San Francisco, 1974-82; project mgr., cons. Peabody Mktg. Decisions, San Francisco, 1983-87; sr. rsch. assoc. Inst. for Health and Aging, U. Calif., San Francisco, 1986-89; rsch. analyst student acad. svcs. U. Calif., San Francisco, 1991-94; external cons. Health Care Consulting Svcs., San Francisco, 1986-96; clin. lab. technologist Kaiser Hosp., San Francisco, 1989-96; seminar presenter Am. Assn. Blood Banks, San Francisco, 1976, Am. Soc. Clin. Pathologists, Miami Beach, Fla., 1977, Ann. Meeting of Am. Soc. Med. Technology, Atlanta, 1977; site surveyor Nat. Accrediting Agy. for Clin. Lab. Scis., Chgo., 1974-80. Contbr. articles to profl. jours.

DUNN, BERNICE MARIE, retired women's health nurse; b. Danforth, Maine, Oct. 11, 1934; d. Henry Augustus Harding and Leah Orale (Gould) Crossman; m. Scott Andrew Dunn, Oct. 19, 1957 (div. Mar. 1984); children: Audrey M. Nutter, E. Lee Dunn Shirland, Janet L. Dunn Doucette, John E. II. Diploma in nursing, Ea. Maine Med. Ctr., Bangor, 1975. RN, Maine. Psychiat. aide to LPN, RN State of Maine, Bangor, 1953-76; aide, charge aide, charge LPN, med. nurse to supr. ob/gyn Ea. Maine Med. Ctr., 1976-95, ret., 1995. Vol. March of Dimes; organist, pianist, choir dir., Sunday Sch. tchr., Faith Bible Ch., Olarnon, Maine, 1957-82. Mem. ANA, AWHONN (cert.), Maine State Nurses Assn., Nat. Assn. ACOG. Democrat. Baptist.

DUNN, BONNIE BRILL, chemist; b. Bethesda, Md., Mar. 10, 1953; m. William H. Dunn, July 13, 1974 (div.); children: Daniel Brill, Vanessa Thompson; m. Ronald G. Manning, Aug. 4, 1996. AA, Montgomery Coll., 1972; BS in Food Sci., U. Md., 1974, MS in Food Chemistry and Statistics, 1978, PhD in Food Chemistry, 1982. Rsch. asst. U. Md., College Park, 1976-79, teaching asst., 1977-80; researcher div. chemistry and physics U.S. FDA, Washington, 1979; statistian USDA, Beltsville, Md., 1980, researcher, 1980-82; radiochemist Positron Emission Tomography; head quality assurance NIH, Bethesda, 1984-93; rev. chemist FDA, Rockville, Md., 1993-95, expert scientist, 1996, dep. dir. divsn. new drug chemistry, 1996—; mem. adv. bd. on intramural woman scientists NIH. Contbr. numerous articles to profl. jours. Sec., v.p. PTA, 1988-94; mem. PTA Forest Knolls Elem., Montgomery County, 1988-94; exec. bd. dirs. PTA Ea. Mid. Sch. Montgomery County, Md., 1992-94; leader Girl Scouts U.S., 1988-91. Recipient performance award NIH, 1987-92, USPHS, 1993-96. Mem. Am. Chem. Soc., Soc. Nuclear Medicine. Home: 18146 Windsor Hill Dr Olney MD 20832-3077 Office: FDA 5600 Fishers Ln HFD 160 Rockville MD 20857-0001

DUNN, DEBORAH DECHELLIS, special education educator; b. Plainfield, N.J., Jan. 16, 1960; d. Anthony and Joan Dora (Brown) DeChellis; m. Paul Michael Dunn, May 13, 1989; children: Joseph Daniel, Brian Jacob. BS in Elem. Spl. Edn., U. Hartford, 1982. Spl. edn. tchr. Hartford (Conn.) Pub. Schs., 1982-83, East Hartford (Conn.) Pub. Schs., 1983-84; individual retirement account ops. supr. Conn. Nat. Bank, Hartford, 1984-87; individual retirement account adminstr. Glastonbury (Conn.) Bank & Trust, 1987, mgr. fin. mgmt. svc. ops., 1987-91; asst. treas., FMS adminstr. Glastonbury (Conn.) Bank & Trust Co., 1988-94, investment rep., trust adminstr., asst. treas.; fin. cons. Mktg. One Inc., 1994-95, Dime Securities N.Y., Inc., 1995-96; tchr. of handicapped, 1996—; investment cons., 1994; ind. edn. cons. Democrat. Methodist.

DUNN, ERAINA BURKE, non-profit organization administrator, city official; b. Chgo., Oct. 4, 1945; d. Marion H. and Lolita D. (Ward) Moore; BA, Wilberforce U., 1968; m. James Dunn, July 23, 1981; children: Kyle T. (dec.), Jamison L. Programmer, analyst Blue Cross/Blue Shield, Chgo., 1968-74, membership cons. Blue Cross Assn., 1975; personnel, benefits specialist Kimberly-Clark Corp., Atlanta, 1976-78; exec. dir., sch. dist coord. Sch. Dist. 147, Harvey, Ill., 1980-88. Active community-based edn., tng. workshops, voter registration, mgmt. tng., crime prevention, adult literacy, effective parenting, environmental justice, 1971-88; coordinator Tchr. Corps. Project, Community Council, 1980—; exec. dir. The Human Action Cmty. Orgn., 1989—; cmty. liason for Met. Drug Enforcement Group of Cook County, 1993—; dir. human svcs. and devel. City of Harvey, 1995; vol. After sch. Tutorial Program, 1981—, United Family Found., 1981—, South Area Literacy Council, South Suburban Act-So, West Harvey Block Captains, South Suburban Citizen Patrol, 1994; chairperson PAC, 1983-88; v.p. human action community orgn. Minority Women's Devel.; chairperson adminstrv. council Wesley Meml. United Meth. Ch., 1987; chair Harvey Area Youth Devel. Task Force, 1990; mem. adv. bd. YWCA, 1990, Policy Rsch. Action Group, Loyola U., 1993-94. Fellow Leadership in Primary Care U. Ill. Sch. Nursing/Sch. Medicine, 1992-93; recipient Outstanding Vol. Service award B.U.I.L.D., 1971, Outstanding Community Service award Dist. 147, 1981, Vol. After Sch. Tutorial Program award, 1981, Image award Fred Hampton Found., 1994, Heart of Gold citation United Way, 1990. Mem. Nat. Community Edn. Assn., Ill. Community Edn. Assn., Delta Sigma Theta. Missionary Baptist. Home: 14746 Leavitt Ave Harvey IL 60426-1522 Office: HACO PO Box 1703 Harvey IL 60426-7703

DUNN, GAIL PEDERZOLI, English language educator; b. Springfield, Mass., July 28, 1947; d. Eugene A. and Ruth E. (Eaton) Pederzoli; m. John H. Dunn, Nov. 19, 1982. BA in English, Elmira Coll., 1969; MA in English, U. Wis., 1970; MEd in Guidance Psych. Svcs., Springfield Coll., 1976. Prof. English Springfield Tech. C.C., 1970—. Recipient Excellence in

Teaching award Nat. Inst. for Staff and Orgn. Devel., 1995-96. Mem. NEA, Nat. Coun. Tchrs. English, Nat. Mus Women in Arts (charter), Mass. Tchrs. Assn. Democrat. Roman Catholic. Home: 9 Pond View Dr Springfield MA 01118 Office: Springfield Tech CC 1 Armory Sq Springfield MA 01105

DUNN, GLENNIS MAE, writer, lyricist; b. Montevideo, Minn., Sept. 11, 1938; d. James Arnold and Mabel Helmina (Anderson) Haugernd; m. Edward Henry Roske, Mar. 19, 1956 (div. Mar. 1975); children: Daniel Edward, Deborrah Kay Roske Hawthorne, Judith Ann Roske Rinker, Kristine Jean Roske Harbeson, James William, William Benjamin; m. George Maurice Dunn, Sept. 1, 1984 (dec. Dec. 1992). Grad., Montevideo High Sch. Cert. pvt.-instrument pilot, basic ground flight instr. Comml.-instrument ground instr. Sawyer Aviation, Phoenix, 1976-78; pvt.-instrument pilot West Air Flight Club, Phoenix, 1976—; sales telemarketer Lone Star Performing Arts, 1994—, group sales rep., 1996; entrepreneur, 1996; security pub. adminstrn. officer Star of Tex., Galveston, 1994; flight program specialist Embery Riddle Aero. U., Daytona Beach, Fla., 1980-83. Author: You Never Need to Worry-If You Forget to Grow Up, 1985, Someday Darling, Under My Wings We'll Fly, 1993; author, lyricist (song) A Vet's Song, 1992, My Red, White and Blue, 1993, Little Crystal Town, 1993, Riverwalk Christmas, 1993, Santa Keeps an Eye on Me, 1993, One for the Duck, One for Mother, 1993, Texas Auction at the Wheel, 1993, Love your Irish Blue Eyes, 1994. Named to Tex. Hall of Fame, 1996. Mem. Nat. FAA Pilot Assn. (radio operator), Am. Legion Aux., Fraternal Order Eagles Aus. Republican. Home: PO Box 1643 12 Seadrift Rd Crystal Beach TX 77650

DUNN, GLORIA JEAN, artist; b. Detroit, Apr. 21, 1927; d. Donald Stanton and Etta Florence (Barber) Hopkins; m. Eugene Oliver Dunn, Dec. 28, 1944; children: Michael Eugene, Patricia Ann. Student, Wayne County C.C., Taylor, Mich., 1987-90. Instr. arts and crafts YWCA, Wyandotte, Mich., 1963-86; instr. painting and calligraphy, adult edn. Lincoln Park (Mich.) Sch. System, 1982-90; owner, mgr. Pen, Brush and Anvil Studio, Southgate, Mich., 1975-95, Gloria Hopkins Dunn Studio of Fine Art, Wyandotte, 1995—; mem. adv. bd. Wyandotte St. Art Fair, 1962—, organizer, co-chair, 1962-81. One woman shows include Taylor (Mich.) Cmty. Libr., Southgate (Mich.) City Hall, Swann Gallery, Detroit. Mem. Southgate Cultural Commn., 1974-82, 91—. Recipient Cmty. Svc. award City of Southgate, 1978, Hon. Tribute, City of Wyandotte, 1982, 20 Yrs. Dedication to Art award City of Wyandotte, 1991. Mem. Acanthus Art Soc. Wyandotte (pres. 1994—), Downriver Arts and Crafts Guild (exhibit chair 1995-96), Art Ambience (historian 1993—), Nat. Assn. Fine Arts. Office: 2930 Biddle Ave Wyandotte MI 48192

DUNN, GRACE VERONICA, retired executive secretary; b. Bklyn.; d. Richard William and Grace Veronica (Mason) D. BA, Our Lady of the Lake U., 1940; postgrad., Columbia U., 1958. Sec. Hunt Oil Co., Dallas, 1947-48, Standard Oil Co. (N.J.), N.Y.C., 1955-59, Pan Am. Health Orgn., Washington, 1964-76. Mem., Vol. Stephanie Roper Com., Upper Marlboro, Md., 1987-92, Friends of the Kennedy Ctr., Washington, 1991—; soprano soloist Holy Trinity Cath. Ch., Dallas, 1945-47, Ch. of the Incarnation Episcopal Ch., Dallas, 1945-47; soloist White House Christmas Tree, 1988. Grad. fellow Karl Schultz Found., 1940; pvt. scholar Elisabeth Schumann, N.Y.C., 1948-52. Roman Catholic.

DUNN, JANE ELIZABETH, elementary education educator; b. Lafayette, Ind., Oct. 25, 1946; d. Addison Gardner and Phyllis Jane (Dunnewold) D.; m. Russell John Harding, Jr., Aug. 20, 1966 (div. 1991); children: Carrie Lynn, Russell John III. BA, Purdue U., 1968; MA, Lesley Coll., 1985. Lic. tchr. Colo. Tchr. Academy Dist. #20, Colorado Springs, 1981—; tchr. leader communicator Acad. # 20, 1994-97; achieving excellence team Antelope Trails Sch., 1992—, tech. com., 1994—, dist. fgn. lang. com., 1995-98. Home: 2469 Hatch Cir Colorado Springs CO 80918-6025

DUNN, JENNIFER BLACKBURN, congresswoman; b. Seattle, Wash., July 29, 1941; d. John Charles and Helen (Gorton) Blackburn; div.; children: Bryant, Reagan. Student, U. Wash., 1960-62; BA, Stanford U., 1963. Former chmn. Rep. Party State of Wash.; now mem. 103rd Congress from 8th Wash. dist., Washington, D.C., 1993—; mem. house oversight com., mem. Ways and Means Com. Del. Rep. Nat. Conv., 1980, 84, 88; presdl. apptd. adv. coun. Historic Preservation; presdl. apptd. adv. coun. volunteerism SBA. Mem. Gamma Phi Beta. Office: US House of Reps 432 Cannon Washington DC 20515-4708*

DUNN, JUDITH LOUISE, secondary school educator; b. L.A., Jan. 6, 1945; d. Arthur B. and Lillian M. (Eyrich) D. BA, U. Calif., Santa Barbara, 1966; MA Edn., Pepperdine U., 1978; postgrad., U. Calif., Santa Barbara, 1967. Cert. secondary tchr., adminstr., Calif; cert. lay speaker United Meth. Ch. English tchr. Santa Maria (Calif.) Joint Union High Sch. Dist., mentor tchr., chmn. dept. English, 1991-94; mem. adv. coun. Student Age Parenting and Infant Devel. Program; dist. tchr. rep. Impact II Adv. Coun.; dist. rep. Ctrl. Coast Literacy Coun.; mem. del. tchrs. of English of People to People Citizen Amb. Program visitation to Gt. Britain, 1995. Assoc. lay leader Santa Barbara dist. Calif.-Pacific Annual Conf., 1986-89, United Meth. Ch., bd. Higher Edn. and Campus Ministry, 1982-90; English tchr. del. citizen amb. program People to People to Gt. Britain, 1995. Fellow South Coast Writing Project; Disseminator grantee, 1988, 89, 91. Mem. CTA, NEA, Nat. Coun. Tchrs. English, Local Faculty Assn. (profl. rels. chair 1986-88), Delta Kappa Gamma (immediate past pres. Eta Lambda chpt.). Office: Santa Maria High Sch 901 S Broadway Santa Maria CA 93454-6603

DUNN, KATHERINE ELIZABETH, kindergarten educator; b. Seattle, May 6, 1943; d. Elmer and Katherine S. (Welfare) Warner; m. David R. Dunn, July 12, 1969; children: Katy, David. BEd, Seattle U., 1965. Cert. tchr., Calif., Wash. Kindergarten tchr. Marina (Calif.) Sch. Dist., 1965-69, Bainbridge Island (Wash.) Sch. Dist., 1969—. Bd. dirs. Bainbridge Island Day Care, 1972. Mem. NEA, Wash. Edn. Assn., Bainbridge Island Edn. Assn. (bldg. rep. 1993-94). Home: 11510 Chatham Pl NE Bainbridge Island WA 98110-1221

DUNN, LINDA KAY, physician; b. Grand Rapids, Mich., Jan. 11, 1947; d. Roger John and Mary Kathryn (Bouwer) Kloote; m. Jeffrey Marc Dunn, June 3, 1972; children: David Alan, Kathryn Ann. AB in Chemistry, Hope Coll., 1968; MD, U. Mich., 1972. Diplomate Am. Bd. Ob-Gyn, Am. Bd. Maternal-Fetal Medicine, Am. Bd. Med. Genetics. Resident in Ob-Gyn. U. Mich., Ann Arbor, 1972-75, fellow in maternal-fetal medicine, 1975-77; hon. research registrar St. Mary's Hosp., London, 1977-78; dir. of perinatology Temple U. Sch. Medicine, Phila., 1978-79, assoc. prof. ob-gyn, 1991—; dir. subsect. on genetics Pa. Hosp., Phila., 1980-90; pres Medigen, Inc., Phila., 1987-90; dir. maternal-fetal medicine and genetics Abington (Pa.) Meml. Hosp., 1991—; med. dir. Comprehensive Maternal and Infant Svcs., Phila., 1987-90; pres. Abington Perinatal Assocs., P.C. Fellow Am. Coll. Ob-Gyn.; mem. AMA, Soc. of Perinatal Obstetricians, Am. Soc. Human Genetics, Am. Med. Women's Assn., Pa. State Med. Soc., Phila. Obstet. Soc., U. Mich. Med. Ctr. Alumni Soc. (chair), Norman Miller Gynecologic Soc. (pres.). Mem. Soc. of Friends. Office: Ste 119 Medical Plz 1235 Old York Rd Abington PA 19001-3800

DUNN, MARGARET ANN, religious studies educator, administrator, minister; b. Marshall, Mich., Nov. 18, 1953; d. Lee Donald and Hazel Lucille (Boehmer) D. BS cum laude, Alma Coll., 1975; MDiv, Asbury Theol. Sem., 1983; MA, Ball State U., 1989; EdD, U. Houston, 1995. Lic. minister Ch. of God (Anderson, Ind.), 1989, ordained, 1996. Tchr. Lydia Patterson Inst., El Paso, Tex., 1976-79; campus affiliate InterVarsity Christian Fellowship, Richmond, Ky., 1980-81; teaching asst. Asbury Theol. Sem., Wilmore, Ky., 1981-83; tchr. Southwood Christian Acad., Indpls., 1984-85, Liberty Christian Sch., Anderson, 1985-86; libr. clk. Anderson Sch. Theology, 1986-88; prof. religious studies, registrar, dir. admissions Bay Ridge Christian Coll., Kendleton, Tex., 1988—, registrar, 1993—; vis. lectr. Asbury Theol. Sem., 1983; min. Christian edn. Rosenberg (Tex.) 1st Ch. God, 1991-92, coord. women in ministry-mission Ch. of God, Anderson, Ind., 1992-94; dir. student ministries Bay Ridge Christian Coll., 1992-93, 94—; mem. Sunday Sch. TEAM Bd. of Christian Edn., Ch. of God. 1993—; adj. prof. U. Houston, Victoria, Tex., 1995—. Co-author: Framework of Our Faith, 1983. Chairperson South East Tex. Ministerial Assembly Christian Edn. Com. Mem. ASCD, Southwest Ednl. Rsch. Assn., Nat. Assn. Fgn. Student Advisors, Assn. Internat. Educators, Gamma Delta Alpha, Omicron Delta Kappa. Office: PO Box 58 East Bernard TX 77435-0058

DUNN, MÁRIA BACH, writer, researcher, translator; b. Kleinbettange, Luxembourg, Feb. 6, 1910; came to U.S., 1946; naturalized, 1950.; d. Dominique and Marie (Müller) Bach; m. James Taylor Dunn, Dec. 23, 1946. Student, Institut Ste Anne Soeurs du Sacré Coeur, Hougaerde, Belgium, 1926-28, Lycée Esch-Alzette, Luxembourg, 1922-26. interpreter, translator, negotiator hist. documents, 1967-71; translator ednl. program Voice Am., N.Y. State Hist. Assn., Cooperstown, 1953; initiator, sponsor Bibliotheque Luxemburgiana, St. Thomas U., St. Paul, 1993; active Mária Bach Dunn scholarship Miami U. European Ctr., Luxembourg Program, Oxford, Ohio, 1992. Contbg. editor: Luxembourg News Am., 1959—. Vol. Mary Imogene Bassett Hosp., Cooperstown, 1950-55; contbg. mem. Luxembourg Heritage Soc. Inc.; charter mem. U.S. Holocaust Mus.; sponsor Maria Bach Dunn scholarship Miami U. Dolibois European Ctr., Luxembourg, 1993—. Recipient Nat. Medal of Merit, Luxembourg Govt., 1993, award of merit regional chpt. Nat. Red Cross Am., 1950, 52. Mem. NOW, ACLU. Democrat. Roman Catholic.

DUNN, MARY DENISE, reading specialist, freelance editor; b. Brookline, Mass., Sept. 17, 1936; d. William Joseph and Mary Denise (McGillicuddy) O'Brien; m. William F. Dunn, Oct. 8, 1960; 1 child, Mary Denise. BS, Boston Coll., 1958; MEd in Reading and Lang., U. Mass., Lowell, 1981; postgrad., MIT, 1980-82, Simmons Coll., 1988-90. Cert. 7-12 English tchr., K-12 reading specialist, dir. reading, cons. in reading, Mass. Substitute tchr. secondary schs., 1974-78; tchr. English, Parker Jr. H.S. and Chelmsford (Mass.) H.S., 1978-84; tchr. ESL, Bartlett Sch., Lowell, Mass., 1990-91; reading specialist McCarthy Mid. Sch., Chelmsford, 1984-88, 92—. Editor: Life Insurance: Rate of Return (William D. Brownlie), 1993; also others. Vol. local nursing homes for elderly, 1975-92, Citizens for Mitt Romney for U.S. Senate, Boston, 1994; vol. tchr. ESL, S.E. Asia Comm. Ctr., Lowell, 1990-92; vol. driver Mass. Right-To-Life, Lawrence, Lowell, 1973-78; mem. St. John the Evangelist Parish, North Chelmsford, Mass., Cardinal's Guild Archdiocese of Boston, vol. dir. religious edn., 1967-76. Mem. ASCD, Mass. ASCD, Internat. Reading Assn., Nat. Coun. Tchrs. English, Assn. for Childhood Edn. Internat., U. Mass.-Lowell Alumni Assn., Boston Coll. Alumni Assn., Am. Fedn. Tchrs., Mass. Fedn. Tchrs., Chelmsford Fedn. Tchrs., Mass. Citizens for Life, Boston Eire Soc., Phi Lambda Theta (charter Gamma Eta chpt.). Roman Catholic. Office: Chelmsford McCarthy Mid Sch 250 North Rd Chelmsford MA 01824-1409

DUNN, MARY ELLEN, kindergarten educator; b. Perth Amboy, N.J., Aug. 10, 1956; d. Albert J. and Julia T. (Hearon) Graul; m. Gerard J. Dunn, Aug. 23, 1980; children: Erin Beth, Kyle Taylor. BS cum laude, U. Hartford, 1978; postgrad., U. Maine. Cert. elem. tchr., Mass., Vt., N.H., Maine. Self-contained tchr. Kolburne Sch., New Marlborough, Mass., 1978-80; resource room tchr. Stamford (Vt.) Elem. Sch., 1980-81; home day care provider Bedford, N.H., 1982-89; tchr. Forest Friends Nursery Sch., Montville, Maine, 1989-90; resource room tchr. Corina (Maine) Jr. High Sch., 1990-91; kindergarten tchr. Mt. Merici Sch., Waterville, Maine, 1991—; owner, operator Mount View Herb Farm, Thorndike, Maine, Bedford, N.H., 1983-89. Contbr. articles to profl. jours.; author: Pleasure of Herbs, 1989; speaker on ednl. perspectives of children, garden and plants. Organizer Unity Twp. (Maine) Alliance, 1992; mem. Regional Recycling Com., Unity, 1991; active several youth groups, Maine, 1989—. Grantee Ctrl. Maine Garden Club, 1994. Mem. Maine Math and Sci. Tchrs. Alliance. Home: RR 1 Box 104 Thorndike ME 04986-9705 Office: Mount Merici Sch 142 Western Ave Waterville ME 04901-4633

DUNN, MARY JARRATT, public relations executive; b. Clifton Forge, Va., Oct. 29, 1942; d. Robert Bell and Mary Louise (Wood) J. B.A., Mary Baldwin Coll., Staunton, Va., 1964; cert. bus., Katharine Gibbs Sch., Boston, 1965. Staff asst. com. on agr. U.S. Ho. of Reps., 1975-81; asst. sec. food and consumer services Dept. Agr., 1981-85; v.p. Wampler & Assocs. Inc., Washington, 1985-86; pres. Jarratt & Assocs., Inc., Washington, 1986-90. Editor various legis. reports. Republican. Episcopalian. Home: The Pines 6 Farmington Dr Charlottesville VA 22901-3241

DUNN, MARY MAPLES, library director; b. Sturgeon Bay, Wis., Apr. 6, 1931; d. Frederic Arthur and Eva (Moore) Maples; m. Richard S. Dunn, Sept. 3, 1960; children—Rebecca Cofrin, Cecilia Elizabeth. BA, Coll. William and Mary, 1954, LHD (hon.), 1989; MA, Bryn Mawr Coll., 1956, PhD, 1959; LLD (hon.), Marietta Coll., 1987, Amherst Coll., 1987, Brown U., 1989; LittD (hon.), Lafayette Coll., 1988, Haverford Coll., 1991; LHD (hon.), Transylvania U., 1991, U. Pa., 1995. Mem. faculty Bryn Mawr Coll., 1958-85, prof. history, 1974-85; acting dean Undergrad. Coll. Bryn Mawr (Pa.) Coll., 1978-79, dean, 1980-85; pres. Smith Coll., Northampton, Mass., 1985-95; Carl and Lily Pforzheimer Found. dir. Arthur and Elizabeth Libr. Radcliffe Coll., 1995—. Author: William Penn: Politics and Conscience, 1967; editor: Political Essay on the Kingdom of New Spain (Alexander von Humboldt), 1972, rev., 1988, (with Richard S. Dunn) Papers of William Penn, vols. I-IV, 1979-87. Trustee The Clark Sch. for the Deaf, 1988-95, Acad. Mus., 1985-95, Hist. Deerfield, Inc., 1986—, Bingham Fund for Teaching Excellence at Transylvania U., 1987—, John Carter Brown Libr., 1994. Recipient Lindbeck Found. award distinguished teaching, 1969; Fellow Inst. Advanced Study Princeton U., 1974. Mem. Berkshire Conf. Women Historians (pres. 1973-75), Coordinating Com. Women Hist. Profession (pres. 1975-77), Am. Hist. Assn., Inst. Early Am. History and Culture (chmn. adv. council 1977-80), Mass. Hist. Soc., Phi Beta Kappa. Office: Schlesinger Libr 10 Garden St Cambridge MA 02138

DUNN, MIRIAM D., legislative research firm executive; b. Lawrence, Mass., Oct. 17, 1927; d. Henry F. and Emilie W. (White) Dearborn; m. Vincent de Paul Dunn, July 28, 1951 (div. Jan. 1981); children: Mark, Jonathan (dec.), Vincent Jr. Student, Antioch Coll., 1945-48; BA, U. N.H., 1950; postgrad., Smith Sch. Psychiat. Soc. Work, 1950-51. Sch. social worker Derry and Concord, N.H., 1963-68; legal adminstr., rschr. Maynard, Dunn & Phillips Law Firm, Concord, 1968-78; pres. Capitol Eye of N.H., Inc., Concord, 1982—; state rep. N.H. Ho. of Reps., Concord, 1988—; mem. adv. bd. N.H. Small Bus. Devel. Ctrs., 1984—; del. White House Conf. on Small Bus., Washington, 1986. Contbr. articles to newspapers. Del. Dem. Nat. Conv., Miami, Fla., 1972, N.Y.C., 1992. Mem. Bus. & Profl. Women, Paralegals Assn., Greater Concord C. of C. Democrat. Home: 77 Pleasant St Concord NH 03301-3947 Office: Capitol Eye of NH Inc 77 Pleasant St Concord NH 03301-3947*

DUNN, PATRICIA ANN, school system administrator, English language educator; b. Englewood, N.J., Mar. 17, 1942; d. Thomas Joseph and Rosanna Valerie (Cummings) D.; m. James Edward Egan, 1963 (div. 1974); 1 child, Deirdre Tracy. BA in English Edn., William Paterson Coll., 1963, MA in Communication Arts, 1974; postgrad., Montclair (N.J.) State Coll., 1986—. Cert. tchr., N.J., N.Y.; cert. prin., supr., N.J. Tchr. English, Intermediate Sch. Dist. 218, Bklyn., 1965-66, tchr. English and humanities, 1966-67, co-chmn. dept. humanities, 1967-68; tchr. English Midland Park (N.J.) Schs., 1969-91, staff devel. coord., 1987—, dir. curriculum, instrn., staff devel., 1991—; coord. bus. workshops Women in Bus., 1983, Stress, 1983. Editor N.J. Staff Devel. Coun. Newsletter, 1988-91, 96—; contbr. articles to profl. pubs. Co-founder, coord. Ministry for Separated and Divorced Caths., Montclair, 1983-86. Recipient N.J. Woman of Distinction award World of People. Mem. ASCD, AAUW, N.J. Prins. and Suprs. Assn., Nat. Staff Devel. Coun., N.J. Staff Devel. Coun. (co-founder, dir. 1991-94, pres. 1995-96), N.J. Ctr. for Achievement of Sch. Excellence, N.J. Coalition Essential Schs. (del. to nat. congress 1996—), Nat. Coun. Tchrs. English, Le Terrace Club (Nutley, N.J.). Democrat. Roman Catholic. Office: Midland Park High Sch 250 Prospect St Midland Park NJ 07432-1332

DUNN-LANGOSCH, MICHELLE ELIZABETH, art educator, artist; b. Toronto, Sept. 1, 1951; came to U.S., 1982; d. Robert Nelson and Vincenza Maria (Bova) D.; m. Donald Robert Church, Jan. 8, 1972 (div. 1980); m. Paul Russel Langosch, July 2, 1982. Diploma Applied Arts and Scis., Sch. Crafts and Design, 1982; BFA, U. Arts, 1984; MFA, George Washington U., 1991. Instr. Mercersburg Acad., 1984-85; instr. ceramics Presbyn. Home of D.C., Washington, 1985-95; instr. Howard C.C., Columbia, Md., 1986, Prince Georges C.C., Largo, Md., 1986-87; prof. sculpture George Washington U., Washington, 1994, prof. 3-D design, handbuilding ceramics, 1995; lectr. ceramics Montgomery Coll., Takoma Park, Md., 1994; artist in residence Montpelier Cultural Arts Ctr., Laurel, Md., 1993-95, instr. 3-D design, 1995; gallery intern Janet Fleisher Gallery, Phila., Pa., 1983-84; artist in residence U. Md. Arts Ctr., College Park, 1984-87. Exhbns. include Nat. Coun. Edn. in the Ceramic Arts, 1986. Recipient Individual Artist award Md. State Arts Coun., 1992. Home: 200 Lexington Dr Silver Spring MD 20901 Office: George Washington U Art Dept 801 22nd NW Rm A101 Smith Hall Washington DC 20052

DUNPHY, MAUREEN ANN, educator; b. Springfield, Mass., Feb. 25, 1949; d. Donald J. and Mary C. (Tabb) Milbier; m. Terrence Michael Dunphy. BS in Edn., Westfield State Coll., 1971, MEd, 1975, Cert. Advanced Grad. Study, 1988; cert. paralegal, 1996. Tchr. Thornton Burgess Intermediate Sch., Hampden, Mass., 1971-75; reading specialist, dept. head West Springfield Jr. High Sch., 1975—; acting asst. prin. W. Springfield Jr. High Sch., 1989; cons. Nat. Evaluations Systems, Amherst, Mass. Mem. Long Range Bldg. Needs Com., Westfield, 1986-87. Mem. Pioneer Valley Reading Council (pres. 1977-79), Mass. Reading Assn. (dir. 1977-81), W. Springfield Edn. Assn. (negotiations sec.), Mass. Tchrs. Assn., Hampden Co. Tchrs. Assn. Home: 282 Steiger Dr Westfield MA 01085-4934 Office: West Springfield Jr High Sch 115 Southworth St West Springfield MA 01089-2724

DUNWICH, GERINA, author, magazine editor, astrologer; b. Chgo., Dec. 27, 1959; d. W.E. Novotny (dec.) and Teri Enies (LoMastro) D. Freelance writer, 1975—; editor, pub. Golden Isis mag., 1980—. Author: Candlelight Spells, 1988, The Magick of Candleburning, 1989, Circle of Shadows, 1990, The Concise Lexicon of the Occult, 1990, Wicca Craft, 1991, Secrets of Love Magick, 1992, The Wicca Spellbook, 1994, The Wicca Book of Days, 1995, The Wicca Garden, 1996, The Wicca Source Book, 1996; editor, pub. The Liberated Voice, 1987, Coven, 1987, Evil Genius Poetry Jour., 1987-88, Pagan Pride. High Priestess and founder Coven Mandragora; founder North Country Wicca, 1996; founder Wheel of Wisdom Sch. Mem. Wiccan Pagan Press Alliance, Pagan Poets Soc. (founder), Circle, The Fellowship of Isis, Author's Guild of Am., The Authors Guild, The Authors League Am. Office: Golden Isis Press PO Box 525 Fort Covington NY 12937

DUONG, ANH, artist, actress; b. Talence, Gironde, France, Oct. 25, 1988; came to U.S., 1988; d. Loi and Esther (Tejedor) D. BA, Lycee Evariste Galois, Yvelines, France, 1978; student, Ballet Sch. Acad. Nora Kiss, Paris, 1978-82, U. Beaux Arts, Paris, 1979. Ballet dancer various cos., France, 1978-82; Dir. documentary film: El Cuartel Del Carmen, 1988; appeared in films I Shot Andy Warhol, 30, Scent of a Woman, The Mambo Kings; paintings exhibited in one person show at Sperone Westwater, N.Y., 1990, Fukuoka, Japan, 1995, in group shows at Annina Nosei, N.Y., 1991, Daniel Blau, Munich, 1993; model for numerous mags. including Vogue, Harper's Bazaar, N.Y. Times Mag., Mirabella, Harpers and Queens, Glamour, Donna, Elle, also for numerous runways shows and campaigns for designers, including Donna Karan, Calvin Klein, The Gap, Banana Republic, Christian LaCroix, John Galliano, Isaac Mizrahi, others.

DUPEE, PAMELA ANNETTE, fisheries biologist, educator, trainer, consultant; b. Lemmon, S.D., Nov. 4, 1957; d. William Morrison and Dorothy Faith (Winkowitsch) D. BS in Fisheries with honors, Oreg. State U., 1982; MS in Zoology, U. Queensland, Brisbane, Australia, 1985. Cert. coxswains powerboat, Queensland; divemaster, rescue diver, advanced diver, open-water diver, Nat. Assn. Underwater Instructors. Fish culture asst. U.S. EPA, Corvallis, Oreg., 1978-80; fish and game cadet Oreg. State Police, Medford, 1981; U.S. fgn. fisheries biologist U. Wash., Seattle, 1979, 80, 82; edn. and rsch. specialist Reef Biosearch Pty. Ltd., Pt. Douglas, Australia, 1986-89; prof. naturalist Daintree (Australia) Reef and Rainforest Ctr., 1989; profl. photographer Pt. Douglas, 1987-90; rsch. fisheries habitat biologist Ea. Oreg. State Coll. Oreg. Dept. Fish and Wildlife, Hines and LaGrande, 1990-95; internat. bus. trainer, cons. Jewel Way Internat., Inc., Colorado Springs, 1995—, Champion Fishing Co., Ltd., Colorado Springs, 1995—, Startronix Inc., Colorado Springs, 1995—; cons., Champion Fishing Co. Ltd., Startronix Inc. Contbr. numerous articles, reports, and presentation to profl. confs. and pubs. Recipient 3 photographic awards for color prints and audiovisual, 1984-87, R.E. Chambers Meml. award for outstanding rsch. and writing in environ. and ecol. concerns, 1982, Albany Kiwanis Outstanding Achievement award, 1976; rsch. grantee (2) Gt. Barrier Reef Marine Park Authority, 1983-84; Milwaukie Rod and Gun Club scholar, 1979, Albany Altrusa scholar, 1976, Fulbright scholar U. Queensland, 1982-85. Mem. NAFE, Am. Fisheries Soc. (Oreg. State U. student rep. 1979, Cert. Recognition Oreg. chpt. 1995), Marine Edn. Soc. Australasia, The Nature Conservancy, Ocean Realm, Alpha Zeta (mortar bd.). Office: 2710 Warrenton Way Colorado Springs CO 80922-1386

DUPEY, MICHELE MARY, communications specialist; b. Bronx, N.Y., Feb. 26, 1953; d. William B. and Sandra Nancy (Raia) D.; m. Daniel Michael Gieser, July 14, 1980 (div. May 1991). BA, Montclair State Coll., 1975; cert. in Copywriting. NYU, 1988. Sec. DDB Needham Worldwide Inc. Advt. (formerly Doyle Dane Bernbach Advt. Co.) N.Y.C., 1985-88; asst. comm. dir. Hudson County, N.J., 1988—. Creator ann. Hudson County women's history month program and named athletic program Womansport; In-house planning chair 150th anniversary celebration of Hudson County; freelance copywriter Jersey City, 1988—; spkr. in field; ind. distbr. Km/Matol Botanical Internat. Comm. Gay Games IV, N.Y.C.; planning com., pub. rels. Hudson County Am. Heritage Festival, 1994, 95 (winner gov.'s award for best new cultural and heritage event 1995); program producer, pub. rels. 1996 Olympic Torch Relay Hudson County, 1996; developer Hudson County Adv. Commn. on Women; Fellow Leadership N.J., 1995. Contbr. articles to profl. publs. Democrat. Episcopalian. Home: 206 Washington St Apt 3A Jersey City NJ 07302-4557

DUPLANTIER, DAWN ELIZABETH, communications director; b. New Orleans, May 1, 1970; d. Dennis Paul and Judith Dawn (Hepburn) D. BBA, U. Tex., 1991, MA in Journalism/Pub. Rels., 1994. Pub. rels. asst. Nat. Wildflower Rsch. Ctr., Austin, Tex., 1993; comms. dir. Travis County Bar Assn., Austin, 1993-95, Tex. Bankers Assn., Austin, 1995—; mem. Austin Postal Customer Coun., 1992-95. Editor: (mags.) Austin Lawyer, 1993-95, Tex. Banking, 1995—. Vol. Am. Heart Assn., Austin, 1995, Goodwill Industries, Austin, 1995. Scholar Nat. Assn. Bar Execs. Mem. Women in Comms., Am. Soc. Assn. Execs., Soc. Profl. Journalists, Phi Kappa Phi. Office: Tex Bankers Assn 203 W 10th St Austin TX 78701

DUPRE, JUDITH ANN NEIL, real estate agent, interior decorator; b. Houma, La., May 7, 1945; d. Herbert Joseph and Doris Mae (LeBouef) Neil; m. Michael Anthony Dupre, Jan. 7, 1962 (div. Aug. 1987); children: Arienne Danielle, Travis Lance. BA in Psychology, Southeast Okla. State U., 1982. Fin. mgr., supr. Gen. Fin. Loan Co., La., Colo., 1960-69; exec. sec. Progressive Bank & Trust Co., Houma, La., 1973-74; health coordinator Spring Cypress Cultural & Recreation Ctr., 1974-75; bus. mgr., buyer June Morris Boutique, Ardmore, Okla., 1978-79; actress, model David Payne Agy., Dallas, 1985—; real estate agt. Vonnie Cobb Inc. Realtors, Sugar Land, Tex., 1986-91, Raymond Jepta Daniel, Jr., 1991—; nat. mktg. asst. North American Mortgage Co. (subs. MONY Mut. N.Y.), Houston, 1987-88; mgr., care coord. Sanus N.Y. Life, Inc., 1988-89; mgr. PPO Am. Health Network, 1989—; dir. admissions and bus. devel. The Transitional Learning Community, Galveston, Tex., 1990-92; owner Paradigm Health Care, 1993—; exec. dir. Rehab. Svcs. Network, Inc.; workers compensation cons. ETHIX S.E.; owner, pres. Summit Internat. Cons., Charlotte, N.C., Houston, 1991—, Ams. With Disabilities Act, Charlotte, 1991, JD Enterprises Internat., Inc., 1994—; adminstr. Ea. Carolina Med. Assn., Florence, S.C., 1995—, Coastal Physicians Org., LLC, Conway, S.W., 1995—. Active Strake Jesuit-Mothers' Club, Houston, 1985-87, St. Agnes Acad. Women's Club, Houston, 1985-87, Ft. Bend Republican Women, Sugar Land, 1985-86, Charlotte Philharm., 1994—, mem. CAST, 1994—; chmn. Texans War on Drugs, Sugar Land, 1985-86; bd. dirs. MUD (Dist. 6), Sugar Land, 1986-92. Mem. Cath. Daus. of the Americas, Nat. Assn. Realtors, Tex. Assn. Realtors, Bal Harbour Homeowners Assn., Assn. Profl. Mortgage Women, Lake Wylie Homeowners Assn., Sweetwater Ladies Golf Assn. Club, Sweetwater Country Club (Sugar Land), Assn. River Hills Country Club, Ladies Assn., Alpha Chi. Roman Catholic. Avocations: tennis, golf, fishing, boating, dancing. Home: 106 Timbelake Dr Florence SC 29501

DUPREE, SHERRY SHERROD, reference librarian, religion consultant, writer; b. Raleigh, N.C., Nov. 25, 1946; d. Matthew Needham and Mary Elouise (Heartley) Sherrod; m. Herbert Clarence DuPree, Jan. 11, 1975; children: Amil, André, Andrew. BS, N.C. Cen. U., 1968, MA, 1969; MLS, U. Mich., 1974, Cert. ednl. specialist, 1978. Media specialist Ann Arbor (Mich.) Pub. Schs., 1970-77; assoc. ref. libr. U. Fla. Librs., Gainesville, 1977-83; ref. libr. Santa Fe C.C. Libr., Gainesville, 1983—; project dir. Inst. Black Culture U. Fla., Gainesville, 1982—; vis. prof. Ea. Mich. U., Ypsilanti, 1975; prof. edn. Bethune Cookman Coll., Daytona Beach, Fla., 1984-88. Author: Displays for Schools: All Avenue of Communication, 1976, rev. edit., 1979, Busy Bookworm: Good Conduct, 1980, Mini Course in Library Skills, 1983, Bible Lessons for Youth, 1987, What You Always Wanted to Know About the Card Catalog But Was Afraid to Ask, 1988, Biographical Dictionary of African Americn Holiness--Pentacostals: 1880-1990, 1989, African American Pentecostals: Sourcebook, 1992, Exposed! Federal Bureau of Investigation (FBI) Unclassified Reports on Chruchs and Church Leaders, 1993, African-American Goods News (Gospel) Music, 1993, African-American Holiness Pentecostal Movement: An Annotated Bibiography, 1996. Chairperson Rosewood Massacre Forum. Vis. fellow Smithsonian Instn., 1987; recipient Gov.'s Achievement award State of Fla., 1986; rsch. grants Nat. Coun. Chs., 1983, Gatorade Found., 1987, 88, 90; travel grants NEH, 1983, So. Regional Edn. Bd., 1987, 88, 89, 90; grant-in-aid fellow Bd. Regents, State of Fla., 1980-81, Horace H. Rackham's Opportunity grant, 1975-76, OEG Libr. Sci. grant U. Mich., 1973-74, grad. fellow N.C. Cen. U., 1968-69; recipient Truth award Sojourner, 1995. Mem. ALA, NAACP, Soc. Pentacostal Studies, Soc. Am. Archivists, Alachua Libr. League, Fla. Libr. Assn. (chairperson resources to religious caucus 1994-96), Fla. C.C. Assn. Democrat. Mem. Ch. of God in Christ. Office: Santa Fe C C Libr 3000 NW 83rd St Rm 208 Gainesville FL 32606-6210

DUQUESNAY, ANN, actress, singer. Appeared in Broadway plays including Jelly's Last Jam, The Wiz, Blues in the Night; appeared in off-Broadway plays including Spunk; appeared in other plays including Ma Rainey's Black Bottom, House of Flowers, Porgy and Bess, The Outcast, Lady Day, Black Nativity, Bubbling Brown Sugar; appeared on TV shows including PBS' Reading Rainbow, Another World. Recipient AUDELCO, San Francisco's Bay Area Theatre Critics Circle award, Best Supporting Actress in a Musical Tony award Bring in Da Noise, Bring in Da Funk, 1996. Office: Pub Theater 425 Lafayette St New York NY 10003*

DUQUET, SUZANNE FRANCES, special education educator; b. Detroit, July 15, 1954; d. Nicholas John and Frances Catherine (Muscat) Calleja; m. Michael Patrick Duquet, Aug. 26, 1978; children: Michael II, James, Michelle, Christopher. AA, Siena Heights Coll., 1974, BA, 1976; continuing edn. & spl. edn. endorsement, Ea. Mich. U., 1980; MAT with LD Specialty, Madonna U., 1996. Sec. to dean of students Siena Heights Coll., Adrian, Mich., 1973-76; tchr. Boysville of Mich., Clinton, 1976-81, asst. prin., 1981-85; tchr. spl. edn., tchr. cons. Pinckney (Mich.) Comty. Schs., 1985—; cons. Livingston Pediat. Ctr., Brighton, Mich., 1990—; mem. adv. com. dept. student tchrs. Siena Heights Coll. Edn., Adrian, 1983-93. Author: (curriculum) Human Sexuality Program, 1983, K-12 Special Education Curriculum, 1991, Transition of Learning Disabled Students from High School to Adult Life: A Survey of Former Students, 1996. Eucharistic min., lector Holy Spirit Cath. Ch., Hamburg, Mich., 1986—; mem. MADD, Brighton, 1990—; faculty advisor Students Against Driving Drunk, Pinckney H.S., 1987—. Scholar Daus. of Korean Conflict, 1972, Walsh scholar Siena Heights Coll., 1973; tuition grantee State of Mich., 1972-76. Mem. Mich. Edn. Assn., Coun. for Exceptional Children, Mich. Reading Coun. Democrat. Home: 9456 Lakecrest Dr Whitmore Lake MI 48189-9388 Office: Pinckney Comty Schs Box 9 2100 E M-36 Pinckney MI 48169

DUQUETTE, DIANA MARIE, logistics service manager; b. Plattsburgh, N.Y., May 21, 1952; d. Clarence Elmer and Ruth Virginia (O'Connell) Duquette; 1 child, Marcelle Lynn. A in Humanities, Clinton C.C., Plattsburgh, N.Y., 1972; student, SUNY, Plattsburgh, 1982-87, Regents Coll., 1994—. Pers. asst. Georgia-Pacific Corp., Plattsburgh, 1973-85, asst. prodn. control mgr., 1985-87; allocation and inventory control mgr. Georgia-Pacific Corp., Atlanta, 1987-90, customer svc. mgr., 1990-93, nat. customer svc. mgr., 1993-95, logistics svcs. mgr., 1995—. Active Christian Action Ministry Program, St. Francis Table Ministry. Mem. Coun. Logistics Mgmt. Home: 4815 Hunters Trace Powder Springs GA 30073 Office: Georgia-Pacific Corp 233 Peachtree St Atlanta GA 30303

DUQUETTE, DIANE RHEA, library director; b. Springfield, Mass., Dec. 15, 1951; d. Gerard Lawrence and Helen Yvette (St. Marie) Morneau; m. Thomas Frederick Duquette Jr., Mar. 17, 1973. BS in Sociology, Springfield Coll., 1975; MLS, Simmons Coll., 1978. Libr. asst. Springfield City Libr., 1975-78; reference libr. U. Mass., Amherst, 1978-81; head libr. Hopkins Acad., Hadley, Mass., 1980; instr. Colo. Mountain Coll., Steamboat Springs, 1981-83; libr. dir. East Routt Libr. Dist., Steamboat Springs, 1981-84; agy. head Solono County Libr., Vallejo, Calif., 1984; dir. libr. svcs. Shasta County Libr., Redding, Calif., 1984-87; dir. librs. Kern County Libr., Bakersfield, Calif., 1987—; chmn. San Joaquin Valley Libr. System, 1988. Contbr. articles to profl. jours. Recipient John Cotton Dana Spl. Pub. Rels. award, H.W. Wilson and ALA, 1989. Mem. ALA, Calif. Libr. Assn. (mem. coun. 1987—), Calif. County Librs. Assn. (pres. 1990). Democrat. Roman Catholic. Home: PO Box 6595 Pine Mountain Club Frazier Park CA 93222 Office: Kern County Libr 701 Truxtun Ave Bakersfield CA 93301-4816

DURAN, KATHRYN A., federal agency administrator; b. Phila., June 7, 1954; d. Leonard Paul and Anna Theresa (Banach) Zarzecki; m. Clifford Ray Duran (div. Mar. 1985); children: Christopher Ray, Mercedes Kathryn. BS, U. So. Colo., 1990; postgrad., Chestnut Hill Coll. With U.S. Army-U. So. Colo., Pueblo, 1990, U.S. Army-LaSalle U., Phila., 1990-91, Resolution Trust Corp., Valley Forge, Pa., 1992-94, Fed. Emergency Mgmt. Agy., Phila., 1995—. Sgt. U.S. Army, 1973-79. Mem. Bus. and Profl. Women, VFW. Democrat. Roman Catholic. Home: 212 West First Ave # 13 Conshohocken PA 19428 Office: Fed Emergency Mgmt Agy 105 South 7th St Philadelphia PA 19106

DURAND, SYDNIE MAE M., state legislator; b. Lafayette, La., Apr. 30, 1934; d. Sidney August and Hattie Ann (Belaire) Maraist; m. Alcee J. Durand, Oct. 16, 1955; 1 child, Alcee J. (Chip). Student, U. Southwestern La., 1952-55. Landman Sohio Pet, Lafayette, 1955-60; acct. Austral Oil, Lafayette, 1960-79; environ. coord. Mobil Oil, Lafayette, 1979-91; mem. La. Ho. of Reps., Baton Rouge, 1991—. Police juror St. Martin Parish Govt., 1980-92. Recipient Conservation award Woodman of the World, 1988, Bishop's medal Diocese of Lafayette, 1989. Mem. Nat. Assn. Counties, La. Policy Jury Assn. (exec. bd. 1982-92), Evangeline Econ. Bd. (v.p. 1985-92). Democrat. Roman Catholic. Address: PO Box 2674 Saint Martinville LA 70582-2500 Office: 1010 Marie St Saint Martinville LA 70582-6619

DURBIN, KIRSTEN DAHLMAN, academic administrator; b. Boston, June 15, 1946; d. John Stanley and Lucille Elizabeth (Jacobson) Dahlman; m. William Applebee Durbin Jr., June 14, 1969; children: Alexandra, Adrian, Spencer. BA, U. Mass., 1969. Tchr. elem. sch. N.Y.C. Bd. Edn., 1970-72, Vt. Bd. Edn., Perkinsville, 1972-73; musician Lydian Consort, Needham, Mass., 1974-84; asst. dir. alumni affairs Wheaton Coll., Norton, Mass., 1990-94, major gifts officer, 1995—; jewelry designer, 1992—. Ambassador to Iowa Dukakis Presdl. Campaign, 1987, Ill., 1988; del. Mass. State Dem. Com., 1988-95; mem. town meeting Town of Needham, 1989-96; campaign mgr. several sch. com. races, Needham, 1986-92; campaign field dir. state rep. race, Needham, 1988, campaign mgr., 1994. Mem. LWV, Needham Edn. Found. (pres. 1992-94), Women Dems. Metro West (v.p. 1988-90), Women in Devel. Home: 301 Nehoiden St Needham MA 02192 Office: Wheaton Coll Norton MA 02766

DURBIN, (MARGARET) ROSAMOND, marketing executive; b. Shelbyville, Ind., Feb. 25, 1952; d. Willard Clyde and Irma Frances (Havens) Sandefur; m. Timothy Mark Durbin, Dec. 27, 1986. BA in English, Xavier U., 1974. Office mgr. Pryde, Inc., Cin., 1975-77; media mgr. Intermedia, Inc., Cin., 1977-80; media dir. Caldwell-Van Riper, Inc., Ft. Wayne, Ind., 1980-82; media supr. Jerrico/Abbott Advt., Lexington, Ky., 1982, Marsteller, Inc., Chgo., 1982-85; mgr. Midwest mktg. Pearle Vision Ctr., Chgo., 1985-86; v.p. Bonsib Inc. Mktg. Svcs., Indpls., 1986-94; pres. Durbin Mktg. Inc., 1994—; guest lectr. Ind. U.-Purdue U., Indpls. Pres. YWCA, Ft. Wayne, 1982; mem. local advt. rev. bd. Ctrl. Ind. BBB. Mem. Am. Mktg. Assn., Advt. Club Indpls., Nat. Wildlife Fedn., Xavier Alumni Assn. Republican. Roman Catholic.

DURDAHL, CAROL LAVAUN, psychiatric nurse; b. Crookston, Minn., Jan. 18, 1933; d. Elmer Oliver and Ovidia (Olson) Durdahl; m. Hans A. Dahl, May 22, 1956 (div. 1983); children: Hana Sorensen, Carla Pederson. RN, St. Lukes Hosp., Duluth, Minn., 1953; BA in Human Svcs., Met. State U., St. Paul, 1982. Staff nurse various hosps., Minn., 1953-59; human svcs. tech. Willmar (Minn.) State Hosp., 1970-74, supplemental tchr., 1974-83; staff nurse Rice Meml. Hosp., Willmar, 1983-86; utilization rev. various nursing homes, Willmar, 1985-86; tchr. Willmar Area Vocat. Tech. Inst., 1986; dir. nurses Glenmore Recovery Ctr., Crookston, Minn., 1986-88; shift supr. Golden Valley (Minn.) Health Ctr., 1988-92; with crisis dept. Hennepin County Med. Ctr., 1988—; managed care of psychiat. and substance abuse MCC Managed Behavioral Care, Mpls., 1992. Contbr. articles to profl. jours. Mem. AAUW, Bus. and Profl. Women, League Women Voters (pres. and state bd.), Federated Women, Does. Republican. Lutheran. Home: 6450 York Ave S Apt 403 Minneapolis MN 55435-2341 Office: Hennepin County Med Ctr 701 Park Ave Minneapolis MN 55415-1623

DURDIK, JEANNINE MARIE, immunologist, educator; b. Chgo., Feb. 11, 1954; d. Albert Anthony Durdik and Rose Marie (Jones) Petersen. BS, Purdue U., 1976; PhD, Johns Hopkins, 1981; rsch., Fred Hutchinson Cancer Ctr., 1979-81. Postdoctorial U. Wash., Seattle, 1981-83, Brandeis U., Waltham, Mass., 1984-89; asst. prof. U. Colo., Denver, 1989—, U. Ark.; organizer of transgenic facility U. Colo. Cancer Ctr., Denver, 1989—. Contbr. articles to profl. jours. Recipient Singleton award undergrad. rsch.; grantee Am. Cancer Soc., Arthritis Found., March of Dimes, NIH; Am. Cancer Soc. fellow, Cancer Rsch. Inst. fellow, Life Sci. Rsch. Found. fellow. Mem. AAAS, Am. Assn. Immunologists, Am. Assn. Cancer Rsch., Assn. Women in Sci., N.Y. Acad. Scis., U. Colo. Cancer Ctr. Office: U Arkansas 601 SCEN Fayetteville AR 72701

DUREGGER, KAREN MARIE, health facility administrator; b. Des Moines, Jan. 16, 1952; d. Francis William and Luella Marie (Smith) Moore; m. Michael Steven Duregger, Feb. 26, 1972; children: Chadwick Michael, Joshua William (dec.), Francis Steven. Secretarial diploma, Am. Inst. Bus., Des Moines, 1971; cert. health care adminstr., Des Moines Area Community Coll., 1985. Sec. Harry Rodine Co., Des Moines, 1970, Iowa State Assn. Secondary Sch. Prins., Des Moines, 1971-72; asst. adminstr. Hancock County Care Facility, Garner, 1973-74, adminstr., 1974-89; adminstr. Duncan Heights, Inc., Garner, 1989—, bd. dirs., recording sec., 1989—; mem., sec. Mental Health, Mental Retardation and Devel. Disabled Adv. Bd., Garner, 1983-93. Mem. Comty. Edn. Bd., Garner, 1989; mem. ch. choir, 1993—; music booster Garner-Hayfield Sch. Mem. County Care Facility Adminstrs. (dist. pres. 1985-87, treas. 1989-91), Human Svcs. Tng. Network, Tng. Planning Group Health Task Force. Republican. Lutheran. Home: 145 W Lyons St Garner IA 50438-1920 Office: 1465 Highway 18 Garner IA 50438-8621

DUREK, DOROTHY MARY, retired English language educator; b. Pitts., Jan. 23, 1926; d. Joseph Adam and Helen Barbara (Ondich) D. BS in Edn., Youngstown State U., 1962; MS in Edn., Westminster Coll., 1969. Cert. English tchr., Ohio, comprehensive English cert., Pa. Tchr. English Brookfield (Ohio) Schs., 1962-64, Sharon (Pa.) City Schs., 1964-88; mem., pres. Coll. Club Sharon, 1993-94. Charter mem., bd. dirs. LWV Mercer County, Pa., 1993-97; mem. docent Butler Inst. Am. Art, Youngstown, 1988—; mem. Shenango Valley Women's Interfaith Coun., Jewish-Christian Dialogue Group, Sharon, Youngstown Symphony Soc., Youngstown Opera Guild; charter mem. Mus. Women's Art, Washington; mem., bd. dirs. Christian Assocs. Shenango Valley. Mem. NEA, Pa. State Educators Assn., Sharon Tchrs. Assn., Cath. Collegiate Assn. (charter), Sharon Lifelong Learning Coun. (bd. dirs. 1995), Read and Discuss Group. Roman Catholic. Home: 1726 Ashton Ave Sharpsville PA 16150

DURETT, SUSAN DIANE, police officer; b. Elizabeth, N.J., Apr. 30, 1951; d. Paul J. and Eleanor F. (Trautman) D. BA, Georgian Ct. Coll., 1973; postgrad., Drew U., 1973-74, Rutgers U., 1992—. Cert. FBI def. tactics instr., law enforcement fitness instr., LoJack instr.; cert. police instr., N.Y.; PR 24 Baton instr. County investigator Union County Prosecutor's Office, 1974-79; from lt. to lt. commdg. officer ctrl. police res. unit Port Authority Police Dept., Jersey City, 1980—. Mem. Roselle Vol. Ambulance Corps, 1974-87. Mem. N.J. Honor Legion. Office: Pt Authority Police 1 Path Plaza Jersey City NJ 07306

DURGIN, DIANE, lawyer; b. Albany, N.Y., May 17, 1946; d. Leslie P. and Shirley A. (Albright) D. BA, Wellesley Coll., 1970; JD magna cum laude, Boston Coll., 1974. Assoc. Shearman & Sterling, N.Y.C., 1974-83; corp. sec. Ga.-Pacific Corp., Atlanta, 1983-92, v.p. law, dep. gen. counsel, 1986-89, sr. v.p. law, gen. counsel, 1989-93; arbitrator, mediator Atlanta, 1993—; dep. exec. dir. legal and non-profit affairs Atlanta Housing Authority, 1994—; bd. dirs. Am. Arbitration Assn. Bd. dirs. Atlanta Symphony Orch., 1991—, Met. Atlanta chpt. ARC, 1988-94; bd. dirs., mem. exec. com. Alliance Theatre Co., 1985—; mem. bd. sponsors Georgian Chamber Players, Inc., 1986-92. Mem. ABA, Am. Corp. Counsel Assn., N.Y. State Bar Assn., Ga. State Bar, Am. Law Inst., Nature Conservancy (bd. dirs. Ga. chpt. 1989-96), Order of Coif, Ga. Exec. Women's Network, Commerce Club Atlanta.

DURGIN, PATRICIA HARTE, college administrator, chemistry educator, counselor; b. Addison, Vt., Mar. 9, 1934; d. Patrick Francis and Helen (Cawley) Harte; m. Francis John Durgin, June 15, 1957; children: Ann Durgin Reese, Mary Durgin Allen. BS in Chemistry, Trinity Coll., 1954; MS in Counseling, Syracuse U., 1970. Cert. chemistry, earth sci., math. 7-12 tchr., guidance counselor. Rsch./tchg. asst. U. Vt., Burlington, 1954-58; tchr. chemistry Ctrl. Tech. H.S., Syracuse, N.Y., 1958-60; counselor Syracuse City Sch. Dist., 1972-74, Fayetteville-Manlius (N.Y.) Sch. Dist., 1974-76; dir. Career Ctr. Cazenovia (N.Y.) Coll., 1976—. Chair bd. dirs. Syracuse Peace Coun., 1966-71; convener local chpt. Women's Internat. League for Peace and Freedom, Syracuse, 1969-71. Recipient Unsung Heroine award NOW, Syracuse, 1995, Outstanding Alumna award for achievement, Trinity Coll., 1996. Mem. Nat. Assn. Women Educators, Ea. Coll. and Employers Network. Office: Cazenovia Coll Cazenovia NY 13035

DURHAM, BARBARA, state supreme court justice; b. 1942. BSBA, Georgetown U.; JD, Stanford U. Bar: Wash. 1968. Former judge Wash. Superior Ct., King County; judge Wash. Ct. Appeals; assoc. justice Wash. Supreme Ct., 1985—, chief justice, 1995—. Office: Wash Supreme Ct Temple of Justice PO Box 40929 Olympia WA 98504-0929

DURHAM, CHRISTINE MEADERS, state supreme court justice; b. L.A., Aug. 3, 1945; d. William Anderson and Louise (Christensen) Meaders; m. George Homer Durham II, Dec. 29, 1966; children: Jennifer, Meghan, Troy, Melinda, Isaac. A.B., Wellesley Coll., 1967; J.D., Duke U., 1971. Bar: N.C. 1971, Utah 1974. Sole practice law Durham, N.C., 1971-73; instr. legal medicine Duke U., Durham, 1971-73; adj. prof. law Brigham Young U., Provo, Utah, 1973-78; ptnr. Johnson, Durham & Moxley, Salt Lake City, 1974-78; judge Utah Dist. Ct., 1978-82; assoc. justice Utah Supreme Ct., 1982—. Pres. Women Judges Fund for Justice, 1987-88. Fellow Am. Bar Found.; mem. ABA (edn. com. appellate judges' conf.), Nat. Assn. Women Judges (pres. 1986-87), Utah Bar Assn., Am. Law Inst. (coun. mem.), Nat. Ctr. State Courts (bd. dirs.). Home: 1702 Yale Ave Salt Lake City UT 84108-1836 Office: Utah Supreme Ct 332 State Capitol Building Salt Lake City UT 84114-1202*

DURHAM, GUINEVERE MCCABE, educational administrator, writer, consultant; b. Elmira, N.Y., Apr. 24, 1937; d. John Francis and Carmelita (Fusare) McCabe; divorced; children: Susan Hendricks, John Scheithauer, Judy Velten, Elizabeth Price, Margaret Jarvis; m. H. Sarge Durham, June 20, 1986. AAS, Elmira Coll., 1957, BS, 1968, MS, 1971; EdD, Nova U., 1983. Cert. tchr., adminstr., Fla. Tchr. Horseheads (N.Y.) Cen. Schs., 1968-77, Fla. Youth Detention Home, Titusville, 1978; tchr. Brevard County Schs., Cocoa, Fla., 1978-79, primary specialist, 1979-85; asst. prin. Brevard County Schs., Melbourne, Fla., 1985-90; elem. prin. Lafayette Sch. Dist., Mayo, Fla., 1990-92, Gilchrist County Sch. Dist., Bell, Fla., 1992—; owner Automotive Svc. Ctr., Elmira, 1968-77, Merritt Island, Fla., 1977-83; tax prepared H & R Block, Melbourne, 1989-90; Gesell cadre trainer Brevard Sch. Bd., Melbourne, 1985. Author: (textbook) Test Taking Strategies K-4th Grade, 1985; contbr. articles to mags. Leader Boy Scouts Am., Horseheads, 1968-70, Girl Scouts U.S.A., Horseheads, 1968-72, 77-79. Ednl. grantee State of Fla., 1983-89. Mem. ASCD, Fla. Assn. Sch. Adminstrs., Fla. Reading Assn., Kiwanis. Democrat. Roman Catholic. Home: Adams St Bell FL 32619 Office: Bell Elem Sch Box 639 Bell FL 32619

DURHAM, LISA J., accountant; b. Manhattan, N.Y., Dec. 31, 1943; d. Gilbert S. and Constance S. (Carpp) Peters. BSBA, Hunter Coll., 1965. Bookkeeper Hans Eichler Motor Cars, N.Y.C., 1967-70, Cars of France, Inc., N.Y.C., 1970-78; asst. controller Diversion Mag., N.Y.C., 1978-83; controller Upland Holdings, N.Y.C., 1983-85, Haymarket Doyma Inc., N.Y.C., 1985-87; pres. Durham Assocs., Inc., Amagansett, N.Y., 1987—; adv. bd. Thursday's Child, Westhampton Beach, N.Y., 1993—; co-founder NOW Legal Referral Svc., Southampton, N.Y., 1994—. Co-author: The Working Wounding, 1996; editor-at-large Networking Newspaper, 1993—; contbg. editor The East Hampton Ind., 1995—; contbr. articles to popular publs. Mem. Suffolk County Rep. Women, 1995. Mem. L.I. Del. Profl. and Bus. Women, Zonta (co-chair svc. com. 1994—), Sons of Italy. Office: Durham Assocs Inc PO Box 2160 Amagansett NY 11930

DURHAM, MARY ANN, pharmacist, pharmacy owner; b. Bryan, Tex., Feb. 19, 1948; d. Philip Charles and Mable (Young) Hamlin; m. Harry Mahlon Durham, Sept. 20, 1975; children: Muriel Michelle, Darcie Ann. Student, Our Lady of the Lake, San Antonio, 1966-68; BS in Pharmacy, U. Houston, 1971. Pharmacist City Drug, Angleton, 1971-75, Meth. Hosp., Houston, 1971-75; pharmacist, owner Del Oro Pharmacy, Houston, 1975—, One Fannin Pharmacy, Houston, 1994—. Active Citizen Commn. Human Rights, Austin, 1980—; chmn. bd. dirs. Perfect Schooling, Inc., Houston, 1989—. Named Young Businesswoman of Yr., Bus. Women Am., 1974. Mem. Feingold Assn., Oak Forest Homeowners (chair 1993-96). Scientologist.

DURHAM, SUSAN B., state legislator; b. Portsmouth, Va., Nov. 15; d. J.C.G. Wilson and Irene Leona Jones; m. Frank Conrad Durham, July 26, 1958; children: Kimberly, Alison, Elizabeth, George. Student, U. Hawaii, 1957-58, U. Mich., 1963. Mem. N.H. Ho. of Reps., Concord; mem. edn. com. N.H. Ho. of Reps., 1991-94. Walk leader Beaver Brook Conservation Land, Hollis, N.H., 1980—; nature educator Soc. for Protection of N.H. Forest, Concord, 1985-90; mem. Hollis Sch. Bd., 1980-86, v.p., 1984-86; mem. Hollis Planning Bd., 1986-90; trustee Beaver Brook Assn., v.p. 1988-90, pres. 1990-91. Mem. LWV (bd. dirs. Milford area 1978-80). Republican. Unitarian-Universalist. Office: Rep's Hall State Capitol 33 N State St Concord NH 03301*

DURICKO, ERMA O., stage director, educator; b. Scranton, Pa., Sept. 3, 1947; d. Daniel and Nellie (Consagra) Fricchione; m. Allen John Duricko, June 28, 1969; children: Jeffrey Allen, Marissa Danielle. BA, Ariz. State U., 1969, MA, 1973. High sch. tchr. Phoenix, 1970-74; artistic dir. White Birch Theatre, Dalton, Pa., 1975-78; theatre arts dir. Tiffany Falls Performance Ctr., Pa., 1975-78; resident dir. women's project Ampitheatre Actors, N.Y.C., 1980-81; freelance dir.; founder, artistic dir. 4-Tenn Prodns., 1996—; mem. adj. faculty U. Scranton, 1977-78, guest artist-in-residence, 1993—; dir. Nat. Theatre Summer Inst., N.Y., 1988, 90; speaker at issue ceremony for Tennessee Williams postal stamp; asst. dir. Long Wharf Theatre, Conn.; prodn. "Robbers" by Lyle Kesseer. Dir. (Tennessee Williams festivals) Lady of Larkspur Lotion, New Orleans, 1991, Reflections of His Soul, Miss., 1993; dir., guest artist Camino Real, 1994; guest artist Strider; conceiver, dir. Tennessee and His Women, N.Y.C.; asst. dir. to Marshall Mason, Robbers, Long Wharf Theatre, Conn., 1995; appearing as Blanche in Streetcar, 1996; dir. Readings of Plays by M. O'Brien, N.Y.C., 1996. Mem. exec. coun. North Pocono PTA, Moscow, Pa., 1985-94; dist. cultural arts dir. Pa. PTA, 1989-94; bd. dirs. Community Concerts Assn., Scranton, 1982-84. M. Cervantes grantee Stage Dirs./Choreographers Found., 1990, Moscow Cultural Arts grantee, 1991, 92. Mem. Am. Theatre Wing, Soc. Stage Dirs./Choreographers. Home: Lake Watawga Gouldsboro PA 18424

DURKIN, CHERYL JEAN, nurse; b. Columbia, S.C., Sept. 22, 1950; d. Willard Lee and Hazel Marie (Clendening) Waisner; m. Thomas Lee Durkin, Feb. 2, 1974 (div. July 1994); children: Kathleen, Erin. ADN, Raymond Walters Gen. Tech., 1980; BSN, Xavier U., 1984. RN Ohio, Ill.; BLS Ill., ACLS Iowa. Staff nurse postpartum, newborn nursery U. Hosp., Cin., 1980-87, staff nurse ob-gyn., 1987-88, staff nurse rehab. unit, 1988-91, staff nurse IV therapy, 1991, staff nurse burn spl. care, 1991-92, staff nurse infectious diseases unit, 1992-93; staff nurse med. unit CGH Med. Ctr., Sterling, Ill., 1993—; mem. head injury task force Univ. Hosp., 1988, mem. spinal cord task force, 1989, diabetes resource nurse, 1989, safety rep., 199.5. Staff sgt. USAF, 1970-76. Mem. Am. Legion (exec. bd. 1989-92, fin. officer 1990-93, bingo worker 1990-93). Democrat. Presbyterian. Home: 1108 8th Ave Rock Falls IL 61071-2840 Office: CGH Med Ctr 100 E Le Fevre Rd Sterling IL 61081-1278

DURKIN, JOAN MARIE, lawyer, consultant; b. Bronx, N.Y., July 17, 1964; d. John Joseph and Anne Josephine (Mulholland) D.; m. Rick L. Powell, Dec. 24, 1982. BA in Political Science, U. Tex., Arlington, 1986; JD in Law, So. Methodist U., Dallas, 1989; Cert. in Mediation, Dispute Resolution Svcs., Fort Worth, 1991; MBA in Mgmt., U. North Tex., Denton, 1993. Bar: Tex. 1989; cert. mediator 1991, family law mediator 1992. Atty. Med. Designs, Azle, Tex., 1989-90, Baker Glast Middleton, Dallas, 1990-91, Fed. Labor Relations Authority, Dallas, 1991-94; hearing officer Tex. Workers Compensation Commn., Fort Worth, 1994-95; mng. atty. EBI/Orion, Dallas, 1995—. Mediator DRS, Fort Worth, 1991—; mem. Bedford (Tex.) Beautification Commn., 1991-95; big sister Big Brothers and Sisters, Tarrant County, 1992-95; mem. Metroplex Republican Women, Fort Worth, 1995—; dir. Hurst Euless Bedford C. of C., 1995—, Stars Theatre Group, 1996—; vol. Teen Court, 1996—. Mem. Dallas Bar Assn. (ethics com., coun. mem. employment law sect. 1993-94). Republican. Home: 38 Devonshire Dr Bedford TX 76021

DURO, MARCIA CULP, temporary employment agency official; b. Joliet, Ill., Mar. 13, 1954; d. Donald Elbert and Doloras Evon (Casper) Culp; m. Franklin James Duro, May 3, 1975; children: Amanda Marie, Jacob Culp. Student, Freeport (Ill.) C.C., 1972-74. Travel agt. Buehler Travel, Monroe, Wis., 1982-85; svc. rep. Manpower Internat. Inc., Monroe, 1985-87; svc. rep. Manpower Internat. Inc., Peru, Ill., 1987-88, mgr., 1988-89, dist. mgr. Chgo. South Western dist., 1991—; mem. adv. bd. 1st State Bank, Peru, 1992—, Illinois Valley C.C., Oglesby, 1991-93. Mem. Mendota (Ill.) Sch. Bd. 287, 1990-95; internat. rep. to Hanover (Germany) Indsl. Fair, Ctrl. Ill. Corridor Coun., 1992, 94, 95. Recipient Jaycette Project of Yr. award Wis. Jaycettes, 1980, Jaycette of Yr., 1981, Leadership Dynamics award 1985. Mem. Ill. Valley Pers. Assn. (pres. 1989-96), Ill. Valley Area C. of C. (pres. bd. 1994—, chmn. ann. auction 1992-93, internat. rep. to Hanover Indsl. Fair 1992, 93, 94, 95, 96). Office: Manpower Internat Inc 3941 Frontage Rd Peru IL 61354-1113

DUROCHER, FRANCES ANTOINETTE, physician, educator; b. Woonsocket, R.I., Mar. 11, 1943; d. Armand D. and Teresa (Leverone) DuRocher. BA (with honors), Trinity coll., 1964; MS, Brown U., 1966; postgrad., Woman's Med. Coll., 1970. Med. resident Phila. VA Hosp. and Med. Coll. Pa., 1971-73; assoc. in internal med. Guthrie Clinic Ltd., Sayre, Pa., 1973-79, Annandale (Va.) Group Health Assocs., 1979-87; assoc. chair internal med. Annandale Group Health Assoc., 1986-87; pvt. practice, Fairfax, Va., 1987—; clin. asst. prof. med. and health svcs. George Washington U. Med. Sch., Washington, 1994—. Bd. dirs. Fairways of Penderbrook Homeowners Assn., 1993—, sec., 1995-96, pres., 1996—. Mem. AMA, Am. Med. Women's Assn. (exec. bd. br. I, 1985-91, pres. 1987-88), Med. Soc. Va., Am. Soc. Internal Medicine, Fairfax County Med. Soc. Office: 9926 Main St Fairfax VA 22031-3901

DURR, MELISSA ANN, education consultant; b. Lafayette, Ind., July 3, 1952; d. Stephen Frank and Elizabeth Ann (Sullivan) May; m. Gregory Allen Durr, July 22, 1972; children: Kerensa Lea, Alexander Joseph. BS in Secondary Edn., Ind. U., Indpls., 1974, MS in Secondary Edn., 1977; cert. tng. cons., Ball State U., 1991. Social studies tchr. Taylor Cmty. Sch.,

Kokomo, Ind., 1974-77; co-owner Customer Keepers, Muncie, Ind., 1982-83; dir. religious edn. Unitarian Univarsalist Ch., Muncie, 1985-93; cons., owner Leadership Connection, Muncie, 1993—; adj. faculty mem. Ind. Inst. Tech., Indpls., 1993—, Ivy Tech. State Coll., Muncie, 1995—. Contbr. columns to newsletters, articles to profl. publs. Chair religious edn. com. Ohio Valley Unitarian Universalist Dist., Indpls., 1989-92; mem. commn. on lawyer discipline Ind. Bar, Indpls., 1993-95; mem. Citizens' Commn. on Cts., Indpls., 1994—; mem. Hoosier Forums Steering Com., Indpls., 1993-96. Recipient Anne Miller award for excellence in religious edn. Ohio Valley Unitarian Universalist Dist., 1992, Vivian Conley award for civic involvement Muncie Women's Coalition, 1993. Mem. NAFE, LWV (pres. Ind. 1991-95, v.p. Muncie chpt. 1995-96, chair nat. nominating com. 1996-98), Ind. Assn. Nonprofit Orgns. (bd. dirs. 1994—), Muncie-Delaware County C. of C. (mem. Gateways task force 1990-95), Liberal Religious Educators Assn., Optimist Club (pres. Muncie Hometown chpt. 1993-95, Growth award 1994). Office: Leadership Connection 8100 Oak Flat Rd Muncie IN 47303

DURRANCE, JOAN C., library science educator; b. Miami, Fla., Apr. 20, 1937; d. Benjamin Aldon and Elizabeth (Burkett) Coachman; m. Raymond E. Durrance, May 4, 1961; children: E. Brian, J. Katharine, Joseph R. BA, U. Fla., 1959; MSLS, U. N.C., 1960; Specialist Cert., U. Wis., 1975; PhD, U. Mich., 1980. Librarian Miami (Fla.) Pub. Library, 1960-62; internat. documents librarian U. N.C., Chapel Hill, 1962-65; community svcs. librarian Cen. Wis. Colony, Madison, Wis., 1972-73; instr. U. Toledo, 1975-76; asst. prof. Sch. Info. & Libr. Studies U. Mich., Ann Arbor, 1980-86, assoc. prof. Sch. Info., 1986-96, prof., 1996—, assoc. dean, 1986-88; mem. nat. adv. coun. Kellogg Edn. Info. Ctrs., 1987-90. Contbr. articles to profl. jours.; author: Armed for Action, 1984, Serving Job Seekers, 1993, Meeting Community Needs, 1994. Rackham fellow, 1977-78. Mem. ALA (mem. council 1978-82, Assn. Library Info. Sci. Edn. (bd. dirs. 1984-87, 95—, pres.-elect 1995-96, pres. 1996—), Mich. Library Assn., Beta Phi Mu. Democrat. Office: Univ of Mich 550 E University Ave Ann Arbor MI 48109-1092

DURST, CAROL GOLDSMITH, educator; b. Bklyn., Mar. 1, 1952; d. Hyman and Florence (Weisblatt) Goldsmith; m. Marvin Ira Durst, June 18, 1972 (div. Sept. 1977); m. Leslie Mark Wertheim, Apr. 1, 1984; 1 child, William David. BA, Hamilton Kirkland Coll., 1973; MA, Columbia U., 1974. Career counselor Hofstra U., Hempstead, N.Y., 1974-75, Ocean County C.C., Toms River, N.J., 1975-76; rsch. assoc. Catalyst, N.Y.C., 1975-77; coord. displaced homemakers program N.Y. State Dept. Labor, N.Y.C., 1977-79; dir. N.Y. restaurant sch. New Sch. Social Rsch., N.Y.C., 1979-83; pres., owner New Am. Catering Corp., N.Y.C., 1983—; tchr., career counselor Peter Kump's N.Y. Cooking Sch., N.Y.C., 1988—. Mem. AAUW, N.Y. Women's Culinary Alliance (new mem. chair 1995—), Internat. Assn. Culinary Profls., Internat. Assn. Women Chefs and Restaurateurs (job bank com. 1995—), Internat. Test Garden Soc., Older Women's League, Nat. Mus. Women in the Arts. Home and office: 210 W 70th St New York NY 10023

DURYEA, JAYNE ELLEN, artist, educator; b. Southampton, N.Y., July 15, 1954; d. Robert Martin and Helen (Broome) D. Student, Palm Beach Jr. Coll., Lake Worth, Fla., 1971-72, Suffolk County Community Coll., Farmingdale, N.Y., 1973-74; BFA in Architecture and Painting, East Carolina U., 1977; MS in Painting and Drawing, A&I U., Kingsville, Tex., 1988. Artist, illustrator, draftsman Bell Design Group, Raleigh, N.C., 1977-80, J.D. Latimer & Assocs., Durham, N.C., 1980-81; instr. architecture and drafting Bee County Coll., Beeville, Tex., 1981-87, instr. visual arts div., 1988—, chair visual arts div., 1988—; established glass blowing facilities Bee County Coll., 1989; lectr. on art and glass Jayne Duryea Studios, Beeville, 1981—; glassblowing demonstrations and workshops, 1989—. Exhibited in shows at Ariel Gallery, N.Y.C., 1988, San Antonio Art Mus., 1989, McAllen Internat. Mus., 1989, Art Mus. So. Tex., 1989, others; works in pvt. collections including Rockwell Found., Coca-Cola of San Antonio. Mem. Bee County Bd. Adjustments, Beeville, 1989-91; sponsor Bee County Coll. Art Assn., 1981—. Dougherty Found. grantee, 1989-92, Barnhart Found. grantee, 1992—. Mem. Nat. Mus. of Women in the Arts (charter mem. archives collection), Tex. Fine Arts Assn., Art Mus. South Texas (bd. mem.), Tex. Assn. Schs. of Art (bd. mem.), Art Mus. of San Antonio, Coll. Art Assn., AAUW (bd. dirs. 1981—), Tex. Jr. Coll. Tchrs. Assn., Art League Assn., Bus. and Profl. Women (bd. dirs. 1981—), Smithsonian Assn., Tex. Inst. Bldg. Design, ARS Glass Factory, Murano, Italy, 1996. Office: Bee County Coll 3800 Charco Rd Beeville TX 78102-2110

DUSA, JOAN ELIZABETH, history educator; b. Rochester, Pa., Sept. 4, 1949; d. Dan and Agnes (Kayden) D. BA, U. Pitts., 1971; MA, UCLA, 1974, PhD, 1988. Educator adult divsn. L.A. Unified Sch. Dist., 1988-96; educator juvenile ct. & cmty. schs. L.A. County Office Edn., 1994-96; mem. leadership coun. Washington Cmty. Adult Sch., L.A., 1990-92; co-chair leadership coun. Wilson-Lincoln Cmty. Adult Sch., L.A., 1995-96; mem. Team Leader, Central Juvenile Hall, 1996—, mem. law related edn. project Ctrl. Juvenile Hall, L.A., 1996. Author: Medieval Dalmatian Episcopal Cities, 1991. Mem. AMICA, L.A., 1996, Wildlife Waystation, L.A., 1991-96. Recipient Purrs of Praise award Wildlife Waystation, 1992, Outstanding Staff award Sylmar Juvenile Hall, 1995. Mem. Am. Hist. Assn., United Tchrs. L.A. (chpt. chair 1994-96), Western Assn. Women Historians, Orgn. History Tchrs., Haskins Soc., Sierra Club. Office: Ctrl Juvenile Hall 1605 Eastlake Ave Los Angeles CA 90033

DUSANEK, LINDA SUE, housing association administrator; b. Ottumwa, Iowa, Oct. 24, 1942; d. Walter Carol and Mildred Mozelle (Gharrett) Edmund; m. Donald Allen Carlson, Dec. 30, 1962 (div. May 1980); children: Lisa, John, Jeffrey; m. Robert John Dusanek, June 28, 1987; children: Michelle, Christine, Kendra, Andrea, Jonathan. Student, Black Hawk Coll., 1981, Marycrest U., 1988; cert. property mgmt., Inst. Real Estate Mgmt., 1989. Cert. property mgr., housing quality inspector. Asst. exec. dir. Housing Authority City of Rock Island, Ill., 1974-91; dir. of adminstrn. Housing Authority City Ft. Pierce, Fla., 1991-96, exec. dir., 1996—. Charter mem. Rock Island Clean and Beautiful, 1980-91; grad. St. Lucie County Leadership Bd., 1993, 94; campaign supporter Friends of Senator Bob Graham, Fla., 1992; mem. exec. bd., chair human resource com. Boys & Girls Club St. Lucie County. Mem. Nat. Assn. Housing and Redevel. Ofcls. (cert. pub. housing mgr. 1980), Adminstrn. Mgmt. Soc. (treas. Quad-Cities 1989-91), Bi-State Housing Assn. (pres., founder Iowa and Ill. chpts. 1987-91), No. Ill. Coun. Housing Assn. (sec.-treas. 1986-91), St. Lucie Pers. Assn. (sec. 1992, pres. 1994, 95, advisor program coord. com. 1993, advisor resident coun. 1993), Soc. Human Resource Mgmt. (mem. state coun. 1994, 95), Pub. Housing Dirs. Assn., SLC Exec. Round Table Shared Svcs. Network. Lutheran. Home: 4103 Smokey Pines Ct Fort Pierce FL 34951-3341 Office: Housing Authority Ft Pierce 707 N 7th St Fort Pierce FL 34950-3131

DUSENBURY, MARY MCCLINTOCK, arts scholar, farmer, rancher; b. N.Y.C., Aug. 22, 1942; d. John Thomas and Mary Bedinger (Mitchell) McClintock; m. Jerry Kenneth Dusenbury, July 25, 1964; 1 child, Kenneth Stuart. BA, Radcliffe Coll., 1964; MA, U. Kans., 1992, postgrad., 1992—. Ind. scholar, 1984—; instr. Wichita (Kans.) Ctr. for Arts, 1985-89; curatorial assoc. Spencer Mus. Art, Lawrence, Kans., 1992-95. Contbr. articles to jour., ency., catalog; contbr. chpts. to book. Pres., mem. exec. bd. Southcentral Coalition for Pub. Health, Kans., 1996; elder Presbyn. Ch. U.S.A., Freeport, Kans., 1994—. Mombusho fellow Japanese Ministry of Edn., Tokyo, 1974-76. Mem. AAUW, Coll. Art Assn., Textile Soc. Am. Democrat. Home: Rte 2 Box 158A Attica KS 67009 Office: Spencer Mus Art U Kans Lawrence KS 66045

DUSHANE, PHYLLIS MILLER, nurse; b. Portland, Oreg., June 3, 1924; d. Joseph Anton and Josephine Florence (Eicholtz) Miller; m. Frank Maurice Jacobson, Mar. 13, 1945 (dec. 1975); children: Karl, Kathleen, Kraig, Kirk, Karen, Kent, Krista, Kandis, Kris, Karlyn; m. Donald McLelland DuShane, July 21, 1979 (dec. 1989); stepchildren: Diane DuShane Bishop, Donald III. BS in Biology, U. Oreg., 1948; BS in Nursing, Oreg. Health Scis. U., 1968. R.N., Oreg. Pub. health nurse Marion County Health Dept., Salem, Oreg., 1968-77; pediatric nurse practitioner Marion County Health Dept., Salem, 1977-91, Allergy Assocs., Eugene, Oreg., 1979-89; mem. allied profl. staff Sacred Heart Gen. Hosp., Eugene, 1979—. Named Oreg. Pediatric Nurse Practitioner of Yr., 1991. Mem. P.E.O., P.E.O. Sisterhood, Oreg. Pediatric Nurse Practioners Assn. (v.p. Salem chpt. 1977-78), Am. Nurses Assn., Oreg. Nurses Assn., Nat. Assn. Pediatric Nurse Assocs. and Practitioners, Am. Acad. Nurse Practitioners, Nurse Practitioners Spl. Interest Group, Salem Med. Aux. (sec. 1968), Oreg. Republican Women, Delta Gamma Alumni (v.p. 1979). Presbyterian. Home: 965 E 23rd Ave Eugene OR 97405-3074 Office: Oakway Pediatrics P C 465 Oakway Rd Eugene OR 97401-5405 also: Eugene Pediatric Assocs 1680 Chambers St Eugene OR 97402-3655

DUSOLD, ELIZABETH LAUCH, lawyer; b. Cin., May 21, 1961. BA in Biology, U. Del., 1982; MS in Pub. Policy and Adminstrn., Purdue U., 1983; JD, Ind. U., Indpls., 1990. Bar: Ind. 1990. Rsch. assoc. Indpls. Ctr. for Advanced Rsch., 1984-86; policy analyst Ind. Dept. Environ. Mgmt., Indpls., 1987; law clk., assoc. Baker & Daniels, Indpls., 1988-90; attorney Eli Lilly & Co., Indpls., 1990—; 7. Mem. Ctrl. Ind. Tech. Soc. (chmn. 1990, program chair 1988-89), Ind. State Bar Assn. (treas./sec. environ. law sect. 1992-94, chmn. 1995-96).

DUSTAN, HARRIET PEARSON, former physician, educator; b. Craftsbury, Vt., Sept. 16, 1920; d. William Lyon and Helen Gordon (Paterson) D. BS, U. Vt., 1942, MD, 1944, DSc (hon.), 1977; DSc (hon.), Med. Coll. Wis., 1986. Diplomate Am. Bd. Internal Medicine. Intern Mary Fletcher Hosp. U. Vt., Burlington, 1944-45; asst. resident medicine Royal Victoria Hosp., Montreal, Que., Can., 1945-46; asst. prof. Coll. Medicine U. Vt., 1946-48; rsch. fellow Cleve. Clinic, 1948-51, mem. staff rsch. dir., 1951-77, asst. dir., 1971-77; prof. medicine Sch. Medicine U. Ala., Birmingham, 1977-90; VA disting. physician Birmingham VA Med. Ctr., 1987-90; emeritus prof. medicine Sch. Medicine U. Ala., Birmingham, 1990—; mem. adv. coun. Nat. Heart, Blood, Lung Inst., Bethesda, Md., 1972-76; bd. regents Am. Coll. Physicians, Phila., 1979-84; mem. Am. Bd. Internal Medicine, Phila., 1973-79. Recipient Sci. Achievement award AMA, 1988. Fellow Am. Heart Assn. (pres. 1976-77, Lifetime Achievement award 1991); mem. Am. Coll. Physicians (master, John Phillips Meml. award 1994), Assn. Am. Physicians, Inst. Medicine. Home: 34 Lang Dr Essex Junction VT 05452-3379

DUSTMAN, ELIZABETH, art educator, designer; b. Detroit, June 25, 1919; d. John Anthony and Frances (Brade) Kreuzer; m. Edward Anthony Matula, May 13, 1950 (dec. June 1976); children: Maura, Janet; m. Herman C. Dustman, Aug. 25, 1979; stepchildren: Herman, Karl. BFA, Mundelein Coll., 1940; MEd, Loyola U., Chgo., 1964. Artcraft instr. Chgo. Pk. Dist., 1941-44; art educator Mundelein Coll., Chgo., 1945-46, 1955-81, assoc. prof. emeritus, 1982—; package designer Walgreen Co., Chgo., 1946-51; instr. U.S. Mil. Recreation Pers. Ind. U., 1942. Mem. adv. bd. Northbrook (Ill.) Park Dist., 1983-85; bd. dirs. Northbrook Hist. Soc., 1983-90, North Shore Sr. Ctr., Northfield, 1990-92. Recipient Outstanding Educator award Outstanding Educators Am., 1972; Am. textiles rsch. grantee Kellogg Found., 1974-75.

DUSTON, ARLENE SUE, school board executive; b. Hays, Kans., Jan. 30, 1944; d. John J. and Nadine A. (Scott) Kastle; m. James Curtis Duston, Sept. 1, 1963; children: James Michael, Scott Christopher. BS in Home Econ., Kans. State U., 1967. Bank teller Valley Nat. Bank, Phoenix, 1967-68; sch. bd. mem. Deer Valley Sch. Dist., Phoenix, 1983—; field rsch. interviewer Westat, Inc., Rockville, Md., 1996—; bd. dirs. Ariz. Acad. Decathlon, Phoenix, 1987—. Author, editor: Bake Someone Happy, 1980. County coord. Kids Voting Ariz., Mesa, 1990; vol. March of Dimes, Phoenix, 1978-79, local schs., 1969—; active PTA; sr. mem. Deer Valley Sch. Bd., pres., 1990-95; bd. dirs. Maricopa County Sch. Bd., Phoenix, 1985-89, Ariz. Dept. Juvenile Corrections, Sch. Bd., Phoenix, 1996—; Sunday sch. tchr. First Christian Ch., Phoenix, 1970-75; pres., sec., vol. dir. Park Meadows PTA, Phoenix, 1978-82; reading tutor Mirage Hosts Program, Glendale, Ariz., 1993—. Named Outstanding Governing Bd. Mem., Ariz. Sch. Pub. Rels. Assn., 1995; Christian Womens fellow First Christian Ch., 1968-80. Mem. ASCD (com. mem. 1993-95), Ariz. Sch. Bds. Assn. (bd. dirs. 1987-89, legis. liaison, Boardmanship award 1994-95), Ariz. Sch. Adminstrs. Assn. (conf. planning com. 1995), Ariz. State Commn. for North Cen. Assn., North Cen. Assn. Exec. Bd. Office: Deer Valley Unified Sch 20402 N 15th Ave Phoenix AZ 85027

DUTCHER, JANICE JEAN PHILLIPS, oncologist; b. Bend, Oreg., Nov. 10, 1950; d. Charles Glen and MayBelle (Fluit) Phillips; m. John Dutcher, Sept. 8, 1971 (div. 1980). BA with honors, U. Utah, 1971; MD, U. Calif., Davis, 1975. Diplomate Am. Bd. Internal Medicine, Am. Bd. Med. Oncology. Intern Rush-Presbyn. St. Luke's Hosp., Chgo., 1975-76, resident, 1976-78; clin. assoc. Balt. Cancer Rsch., Nat. Cancer Inst., 1978-81, sr. investigator, 1981-82; asst. prof. U. Md., Balt., 1982; asst. prof. Albert Einstein Coll. Medicine, N.Y.C., 1983-86, assoc. prof., 1986-92, prof., 1992—; course co-dir. Advances in Cancer Treatment Rsch. Albert Einstein Coll. Medicine, Manhattan, 1984—; chmn. biol. response mod. com. Ea. Coop. Oncology Group, Madison, Wis., 1989-95, mem. exec. com., 1995—; mem. data safety com. Nat. Heart Lung Blood Inst., Bethesda, Md., 1990-95; mem. biologic response modifier study sect. Nat. Cancer Inst., Bethesda, 1988, 90, 94, 96; mem. NIH Consensus Panel on Early Melanoma, 1992; mem. FDA Oncology Drug Adv. Bd., 1995—, NCI subcom. D for program project rev., 1995—. Editor: Handbook of Hematology/Oncology Emergencies, 1987, Modern Transfusion Therapy, 1990; sect. editor: Neoplastic Diseases of the Blood, 1996; mem. editl. bd. Jour. Immunotherapy, Med. Oncology, Jour. Clin. Oncology; contbr. articles to Blood, Leukemia, Jour. Clin. Oncology. Recipient Beecham award in Hematology So. Blood Club, 1983, Henry C. Moses Clin. Rsch. award Montefiore Med. Ctr., 1989, Outstanding Alumnus award U. Calif., Davis, 1989; named Outstanding Young Investigator Ea. Coop. Oncology Group, 1993; recipient numerous grants. Fellow ACP; mem. Am. Soc. Clin. Oncology (program com. 1988), Am. Assn. Cancer Rsch., Am. Soc. Hematology, Soc. for Biol. Therapy, Am. Radium Soc. (chair Jane Way com. 1995-96), Phi Beta Kappa (Presdl. scholar 1968), Alpha Lambda Delta, Phi Kappa Phi, Alpha Omega Alpha. Office: Albert Einstein Coll Med Montefiore Med Ctr 111 E 210 St Bronx NY 10467

DUTT, KAMLA, medical educator; b. Lahore, Punjab, India; came to U.S., 1969; d. Gulzari Lal and Raj Bansi Dutt. BS with honors, Panjab U., Chandigarh, India, 1961, MS in Zoology with honors, 1962, PhD, 1970. Rsch. assoc. Harvard Med. Sch. Sidney Farber Cancer Ctr., Boston, Mass., 1972-76; rsch. assoc. Eye Inst. Retinal Fedn., Boston, 1977-80; sr. rsch. assoc. Yale Med. Ctr., New Haven, 1980-81, Emory U., Atlanta, 1981-82; asst. prof. Morehouse Sch. Medicine, Atlanta, 1983-89, assoc. prof., 1989—. Contbr. numerous articles to sci. jours.; author short stories (in Hindi); prodr., actor 3 maj. plays, Atlanta; actor 11 maj. plays, India. Bd. dirs. VSEI (vol. fundraising orgn. for edn. in India), 1973-78; v.p. Indian Am. Cultural Assn., 1985; podium spkr., participant King Week, 1990, 91, 93; spkr. Gandhi Day Celebration, 1984, 85; key participant Intercultural Conf., 1990; main participant joint document Women's Perspective; active human rights issues; stake holder Vision 20/20 Collaborative State of Ga., diversity and edn. coms., 1995. Hindu. Office: Morehouse Sch Medicine 720 Westview Dr SW Atlanta GA 30310-1458

DUTTON, DIANA CHERYL, lawyer; b. Sherman, Tex., June 27, 1944; d. Roy G. and Monett (Smith) D.; m. Anthony R. Grindl, July 8, 1974; children: Christopher, Bellamy. BS, Georgetown U., 1967; JD, U. Tex., 1971. Bar: Tex. 1971. Regional counsel U.S. EPA, Dallas, 1975-79, dir. enforcement div., 1979-81; ptnr., coord. firm-wide environ. sect., mem. Dallas practice com. Akin, Gump, Strauss, Hauer & Feld, L.L.P., Dallas, 1981—. Mem. ABA, Tex. Bar Assn. (chmn. environ. and natural resources law sect. 1985-86), Dallas Bar Assn. (chmn. environ. law sect. 1984). Episcopalian. Office: Akin Gump Strauss Hauer & Feld LLP 1700 Pacific Ave Dallas TX 75201-7322

DUTTON, DONNA MARIE, city clerk; b. Watertown, N.Y., Sept. 27, 1949; d. Robert W. Jr. and Doris S. (McDonald) Jackson; m. Mark E. Dutton, May 27, 1977; children: Kip, Kimberly, Robert, Jonathon. AA in Liberal Arts, Jefferson C.C., 1970; student, Syracuse U., 1994, 96. Cert. mcpl. clk. Dep. city clk. City of Watertown, 1986-90, city clk., 1990—; mem. regional adv. com. N.Y. State Dept. of Edn., Albany, 1994—. Mem. Internat. Inst. Mcpl. Clubs (records mgmt. com. 1992-94, 95—), N.Y. State Assn. of City and Village Clubs, Kiwanis (dir. Jefferson Breakfast Club 1993—). Lutheran. Office: City of Watertown 245 Washington St Watertown NY 13601

DUTTON, SHARON GAIL, elementary school educator; b. Greenville, S.C., Jan. 5, 1947; d. Melvin Thornton and Bessie Mae (Whitmire) B. BS in Elem. Edn., E. Tenn. State U., 1969; MA in Early Childhood Edn., Western Carolina U., 1976, EdS in Early Childhood Edn., 1983. Cert. tchr. N.C. elem, secondary, sch. adminstrn., early childhood. Tchr. grade 4 Brevard (N.C.) Elem. Sch., 1970; tchr. grade 3 Rosman (N.C.) Elem. Sch., 1970, tchr. grade 2, 1970-72, tchr. reading, 1972-73, tchr. grades 2, 3, 1973-87, tchr. grade 4, 1987-89; tchr. Headstart Rosman Elem. Sch. 1971, summer sch., 1972; lead tchr. Teacher Corps Grade 2 Western Carolina U., Cullowhee, N.C., Rosman, 1974-76; clin. practicum and reading conf. Western Carolina U., VA Ctr., Oteen, N.C., summer 1976. Organist, pianist, East Fork Bapt. Ch., Brevard, N.C. Mem. NEA, ASCD, Am. Fedn. Tchrs., N.C. Assn. Edn., Transylvania County Assn. Edn. Democrat. Home: PO Box 422 Rosman NC 28772-0422

DUVAL, KATHLEEN ANNE, legislative aide; b. Jonesboro, Ark., Jan. 10, 1970; d. John and Kay DuVal. BA, Stanford U., 1992. Legis. aide Calif. State Assemblyman Byron Sher, 1992—. Nat. Merit scholar, 1988. Mem. NOW, Nat. Women's Polit. Caucus. Democrat.

DUVALL, BERNICE BETTUM, artist, exhibit coordinator, jewelry designer; b. Washington, Mar. 17, 1948; d. William A. and Bergny (Farovig) Bettum; m. Donald Dunn Duvall, Oct. 5, 1968; children: Gregory Thomas, Peter Brian. Grad. high sch., Washington, 1966; art edn. pvt. study, 1970-74. Artist watercolor, acrylic, needlework design Chevy Chase, Md., 1972—; exhibit coord. Discovery Channel, Learning Channel, Discovery Comms., Inc., Bethesda, N.Y.C., 1993—, Your Choice TV, Bethesda, Md., 1995—; with pub. rels. and publicity Town Ctr. Gallery, Rockville, Md., 1986-89; banner designer St. Paul's Luth. Ch., Washington, 1985—. Exhbns. include Capricorn Gallery, Bethesda, 1982, Westmoreland Mus. Art, Greensburg, Pa., 1982, 87, Hull Gallery, Washington, 1983, 85, Butler Inst. Am. Art, Youngstown, Ohio, 1983, DeLand (Fla.) Mus., 1984, Springfield (Mo.) Art Mus., 1988, Newberry Gallery, Pa., 1989, Broadway Gallery, Va., 1989, Watergate Gallery, Washington, 1990, Fine Art Mus. of South, Mobile, Ala., 1990, Images Internat. Gallery, Bethesda, 1991, 92, 93, So. Watercolor Soc., 1993, Charles Sumner Sch. Mus., Washington, 1994, Sugar & Frichtl Gallery, Kensington, Md., 1994, Univ. Club, Washington, 1995, NIH, Bethesda, 1995, Margaret Smith Gallery, Ellicott City, Md., 1995, Univ. Club Washington, 1995, Office Gov. State of Md., Balt., 1996, Md. State House, Annapolis, 1996, Fine Arts Invitational, Oxford, Md., 1996, Hughes Network Sys., Germantown, Md., 1996, others; juried exhbns. include Internat. Artists in Watercolor, London, 1981; prin. works represented in many pub. and pvt. collections including Montgomery County Contemporary Art Acquisitions, New Eng. Life Ins. Co., Pelavin Assocs., Inc., Capricorn Gallery, Univ. Club Washington; contbr. articles to Am. Artist, Watercolor, The Artist mag. Vol. artist Nat. Zoo, Washington, 1985-91; art judge Art in Schs., Parks, Pub. Places, Montgomery County, Md., 1988-90; speaker various pub. schs., Montgomery County, 1988, 92. Recipient Award of High Commendation Internat. Artists in Water Colors, 1981, Arthur Alexander award So. Water Color Soc., 1981, Award of Merit Md. Fedn. Art, 1980, Liquitex award Adirondacks Am. Watercolorists, 1989, Bendann Gallery award Balt. Water Color Soc., 1990, Washington Water Color Assn. award, 1993, Patron's award Watercolor U.S.A., 1995, First Place award Fed. Reserve, 1995. Mem. Pa. Watercolor Soc., Art League (bd. dirs. 1982-86), Washington Water Color Assn. (bd. dirs. 1986-87, award 1993), Town Ctr. Gallery (bd. dirs. 1986-89), Potomac Valley Watercolorists (bd. dirs. 1993—), Artists Equity, Arts Coun. Montgomery County, So. Watercolor Soc. (co-chmn. ann. juried exhibit 1993), Balt. Watercolor Soc., Strathmore Arts Found., Women's Club Chevy Chase. Lutheran. Home and Studio: 3414 Taylor St Chevy Chase MD 20815-4024

DU VALL, BRENKA LYNN, telemetry nurse; b. Douglas, Ga., Oct. 31, 1953; d. Freddie La Vare and Ruby Lee (Walsh) Du V. BS in Elem. Edn., U. Ga., 1975; BSN, Ga. Coll., 1989, postgrad., 1990—. Cert. BLS, ACLS. Tchr. Laurens County Schs., East Laurens, Ga., 1975-76; supr. small display advt. Greensheet Advt. Paper, Houston, 1976-78; sec. BMC Software, Mobil Oil Corp., Houston, 1978-86; nurse USAFR, Warner Robins, Ga., 1989-92; telemetry nurse Oconee Regional Med. Ctr., 1992-93; gyn. nurse South Fulton Med. Ctr., Atlanta, 1993-95; psychiat. nurse Ga. Mental Health Inst., Atlanta, 1993-96. With USAFR, 1989-92. Whitehall scholar Whitehall Found., 1988-89; recipient Air Force Commendation medal. Mem. Nightingale Honor Soc., Sigma Theta Tau. Republican. Home: 3425-M North David Hills Rd Decatur GA 30033

DUVALL, LORRAINE, recreation center owner; b. Hamilton, Ohio, Jan. 31, 1925; d. Saul and Martha Jane (Huff) Baker; m. Ray DuVall, June 12, 1951; children: Sharon DuVall Keese, Deborah D. Velchoff, Steve, Annette. BA, U. Cin., 1951; MA, Tex. A&I U., 1963; postgrad. Miami U., Oxford, Ohio, 1958, U. Toledo, 1959, U. Tex.-Austin, 1968. Elem. tchr. Larkmoor, Lorain, Ohio, 1956-60; tchr. math. Incarnate Word High Sch., Corpus Christi, 1964-70; owner, instr. Aerobic Fitness, Corpus Christi, 1973-93; owner, coach Corpus Christi Marlin Swim Team, 1972—; mgr. Corpus Christi Country Club Pool, 1973-88; pres., mgr. Club Estates Pool Chems., Corpus Christi, 1980-89, Club Estates Recreation, Corpus Christi, 1977—. Vol. psychiat. ward Meml. Hosp., Corpus Christi, 1966-70, U.S. Swimming Club Devel., 1993—; harpist First Bapt. Ch. Orch., 1995—; bd. dirs. vol. YWCA, Corpus Christi, 1970-77; water safety trainer ARC, Corpus Christi, 1975-82; CPR instr. Am. Heart Assn., Corpus Christi, 1980-84; vol. children's choir dir. St. John Methodist Ch., Corpus Christi, 1966-78, Asbury United Meth. Ch., 1980-93; vol. harpist 1st Bapt. Ch., 1995. NSF grantee U. Tex.-Austin, 1968. Mem. Am. Swim Coaches Assn., Am. Harp Soc. Avocations: music, swimming, tennis, skiing, backpacking. Home: 6709 Pintail Dr Corpus Christi TX 78413-2337 Office: 4902 Snowgoose Dr Corpus Christi TX 78413-2328

DUVALL, SHELLEY, actress; b. Houston, Tex., July 7, 1949; d. Robert Duvall and Bobby Crawford. Founder Amarillo Prodns. Actress: films (debut) Brewster McCloud, 1970, McCabe and Mrs. Miller, 1971, Thieves Like Us, 1974, Nashville, 1975, Buffalo Bill and the Indians, 1976, Three Women, 1977 (Cannes Film Festival Best Actress award), Annie Hall, 1977, Popeye, 1979, The Shining, 1980, Time Bandits, 1981, Roxanne, 1987, Suburban Commando, 1991, (TV movies) Bernice Bobs Her Hair, 1977, Lily, 1986, (TV episode) Twilight Zone, 1986; exec. producer: Showtime pay TV series Faerie Tale Theatre, (Peabody award), Shelley Duvall's Bedtime Stories, Shelley Duvall's Tall Tales and Legends, The Strange Case of Dr. Jekyll and Mr. Hyde, Mrs. Piggle-Wiggle. Founder, Think Entertainment prodn. co., 1988. Mem. Nat. Acad. Cable Programming (bd. govs.). Office: c/o The Gersh Agency 232 N Canon Dr Beverly Hills CA 90210*

DUVALL-ITJEN, PHYLLIS, retail sales executive; b. Passaic, N.J., Oct. 13, 1951; d. August Richard and Joanne (Aquilina) D'Alessandro; m. Brian Alan Itjen, Apr. 1, 1979 (div.); 1 child, Shannon Alys. Office mgr. Servometer Corp., Cedar Grove, N.J., 1972-82; owner, mgr. Sweet Shoppe, Etc., Lyndhurst, N.J., 1979-82; adminstr.-pers. coord. Watson Machine Co., Paterson, N.J., 1982-88; pres. S.A.I. Personnel Svcs., West Paterson, N.J., 1988—, S.A.I. Expressions Unltd., Inc., West Paterson and Wayne, N.J., 1988—, Shannon Designs div. S.A.I. Expressions, 1991—, Kidtools Kidtapes, 1996—. Author children's lit. Fellow Am. Biog. Inst. (rsch. bd. advisors); mem. NAFE, Internat. Platform Assn., Am. Mgmt. Assn. Republican. Roman Catholic. Home: 220A Overmount Ave West Paterson NJ 07424-3247 Office: SAI Expressions Unltd PO Box 1233 Little Falls NJ 07424-8233

DUVEEN, ANNETA, artist; b. Bklyn., May 21, 1924; d. Julius and Shirley (Klugman) Applebaum; m. Charles J. Duveen Jr., Dec. 21, 1942 (div. 1954); children: Wendy, Charles III, Peter; m. Benjamin Duveen, Nov. 24, 1976. Student, U. Iowa, 1941, Adelphi Acad., 1941, Columbia U., 1941, 42, 56; HHD, St. Francis Coll., 1986. Founder, pres. Duveen Internat. Ltd., Port Chester, N.Y., 1987—; lectr. Westchester Arts Coun., White Plains, N.Y., 1993-94. Prin. works exhibited in group and retrospective and one-woman shows including Pacem in Terris Gallery, N.Y.C., 1970, The Signs of God in the World, Santa Croce Basilica Grand Cloister, Florence, Italy, 1985, Marymount Manhattan Coll., 1986, Artiste 86, Rome, 1986; commd. sculptures include heroic meml. busts of Ella T. Grasso, Robert F. Kennedy, St. Maximilian Kolbe and the Papal Family, The Child: Moments in Bronze, The Tabernacle: Mary and the Grain of Wheat, The Papal Family,

Tabernacle: Our Lady of the Grain of Wheat, many others; also 49 stained glass windows; also collage Alas, She Died in Childbirth; co-author: Essentials of Astronomy, 1976. Mem. exec. com. Franciscans Internat., Bklyn., 1989—; internat. rep. for justice, peace and ecology Internat. Secular Franciscan Order, Rome, 1990-92; tchr., dir., ednl. specialist, proposal designer, rschr., cons. Fellow Royal Astron. Soc.; mem. AAAS, AAUW, Societa Dante Alighieri, Sede di Dante, N.Y. Acad. Scis., Inst. for Theol. Encounter with Sci. and Tech., Nat. Fedn. Press Women, Cath. Press Assn., Greenwich Art Soc., Portchester Coun. for Arts, Westchester Arts Coun. Home and Office: Rye Rd Greyrock Park Port Chester NY 10573

DUVO, MECHELLE LOUISE, oil company executive, consultant; b. East Stroudsburg, Pa., Apr. 25, 1962; d. Nicholas and Arlene Birdie (Mack) D. AS, Lehigh County Community Coll., 1982. Rehab. counselor Phoenix Project, Bakersfield, Calif., 1982-84; nat. sales mgr. Olympia Advt., L.A., 1984-85; oil exploration cons. Cimmaron Mgmt., Nashville, 1985-86; exec. sec. Pueblo Resources Corp., Bowling Green, Ky., 1986-87; nat. oil cons. El Toro, Inc., Bowling Green, 1986-87; founder, pres. and CEO Majestic Mgmt. Corp., Albany, Ky., 1987—; nat. oil cons. Impact Oil, Inc., Bowling Green, 1987—; lease procurator El Toro, Inc., 1986-87; spkr. Nat. Investment Seminars, 1994—. Editor, pub.: (newsletter) The Majestic Field Copy, 1994—. Fundraiser Am. Cancer Soc., L.A., 1984-85; vol. Humane Soc., Nashville, 1985-86, Humane Soc., Bowling Green, 1986—; counselor Salvation Army, Bakersfield, 1982-84. Mem. NAFE (exec. program), AAUW, Internat. Platform Assn., Ky. Oil & Gas Assn. Home and Office: Majestic Mgmt Corp 1015 Tennessee Road Albany KY 42602-1065

DUZAN, MARY LOUISE, interior decorator; b. Charleston, Ill., Jan. 3, 1941; d. Kenneth Lee Sr. and Iola Fern (Baker) Staggs; m. Reese E. Duzan, Aug. 17, 1959; children: Kerry Lynn, Terry Lee, Sheri Rene Lydick. Sec. U.S.I., Tuscola, Ill., 1959-60, Reasor Corp., Charleston, 1961-64, Oakland (Ill.) H.S., 1964-65; owner, mgr. Duzan's Furniture & Carpet Ctr., Oakland, 1965—; sec. Oakland C. of C., 1970-76; bd. mem. Econ. Devel., Oakland, 1990-91. Recipient 1st place Ill. Classic D Class, 1995, 2d place Ladies Sporting Clays, 1994, 95, 8th place E Class U.S. Open Sportin Clays, 1995. Mem. NRA (10th place mega shoot 1995), Ducks Unlimited, Pheasants Forever. Home: PO Box 884 Oakland IL 61943 Office: Duzan's Furniture & Carpet Ctr 16 N Pike St Oakland IL 61943

DWORKIN, IRMA-THERESA, school system administrator, researcher; b. Busk, Galacia, Poland, May 1, 1942; d. Moses E. and Hedwig (Rappaport) Auerbach; m. Sidney Leonard Dworkin, Aug. 19, 1975 (dec. June 1984); children: Marc Elazar, Meyer Charles, Rebecca Joy. BS in Edn., CCNY, 1964, MS in Ednl. Psychology, 1966, cert. in clin. sch. psychology, 1968; EdD in Reading and Human Devel., Harvard U., 1971. Cert. tchr.; cert. reading cons.; cert. sch. psychologist; cert. sch. adminstr. Tchr. N.Y.C. Pub. Schs., 1964-66; rsch. asst., lectr. Bd. Higher Edn., N.Y.C., 1966-68; lectr., prof. Haifa (Israel) U., 1971-74; sr. investigator Baruch Coll. CUNY, N.Y.C., 1974-76; adminstr., evaluator, proposal and grant writer Bridgeport (Conn.) Pub. Schs., 1984—; asst. Edn. Clinic CCNY, 1964-66; endowed prof. chair Kunin-Lunenfeld Found., Haifa, 1973. Contbr. articles to profl. jours. Bd. dirs. Jewish Bd. Edn., Bridgeport, Jewish Fedn. Greater Bridgeport, chairperson Holocaust Edn. Com., 1986-89; mem., Rep. Town Com., Bridgeport, 1992-1996, vol. Cmty. Closet, Bridgeport, 1991—. Grolier fellow Harvard U., 1969-71. Mem. Conn. Testing Network (newsletter editor), Conn. Assn. Sch. Psychologists, Bridgeport Coun. Adminstrs. (editor, exec. bd. dirs. 1992, continuing edn. units mgr. 1993, v.p. 1994). Office: Bridgeport Pub Schs 45 Lyon Ter Bridgeport CT 06604-4023

DWORSKY, CLARA WEINER, merchandise brokerage executive, lawyer; b. N.Y.C., Apr. 28, 1918; d. Charles and Rebecca (Becker) Weiner; m. Bernard Ezra Dworsky, Jan. 2, 1944; 1 child, Barbara G. Goodman. BS, St. John's U., N.Y.C., 1937, LLB, 1939, JD, 1968. Bar: N.Y. 1939, U.S. Dist. Ct. (ea. dist.) N.Y. 1942, U.S. Dist. Ct. (so. dist.) Tex. 1993, U.S. Ct. Appeals (9th cir.), 1994. Pvt. practice, N.Y.C., 1939-51; assoc. Bessie Farberman, N.Y.C., 1942; clk., sec. U.S. Armed Forces, Camp Carson, Colo., Camp Claiborne, La., 1944-45; abstractor, dir. Realty Title, Rockville, Md., 1954-55; v.p. Kelley & Dworsky Inc., Houston, 1960—; appeals agt. Gasoline Rationing Apls. Bd., N.Y.C., 1942; bd. dir. Southlan Sales Assocs., Houston. Vol. ARC, N.Y.C.; vice chmn. War Bond pledge drive, Bklyn.; vol. Houston Legal Found., 1972-73; pres. Women's Aux. Washington Hebrew Acad., 1958-60, v.p. bd. trustees, 1959-60; co-founder, v.p. S. Tex. Hebrew Acad. (now Hebrew Acad.), Houston, 1970-75, hon. pres. women's div., 1973. Recipient Cert. award Treas. of U.S., 1943; Commendation Office of Chief Magistrate of City N.Y., 1948; Pietas medal St. Johns U., 1985. Mem. ABA (chmn. social security com., sr. lawyers divsn. 1989-93, 95—, chair subcom. 1993-95, mem. sr. lawyers divsn. coun. 1989-95), N.Y. State Bar Assn., Fed. Bar Assn. (vice-chair for programs, sr. lawyers divsn., 1994), Houston Bar Assn. (sec. social security sect. 1995—), Nat. Assn. Women Lawyers (chmn. organizer Juvenile Delinquency Clinic N.Y. 1948-51), St. Johns U. Alumni Assn. (coord. Houston chpt. 1983—, pres. 1986), Delphians Past Pres.'s Club, Amit Women Club, Hadassah. Jewish. Home: 9726 Cliffwood Dr Houston TX 77096-4406

DWYER, LAURAINE THERESA, ambulatory care administrator, rehabilitation nurse; b. Detroit, Feb. 29, 1948; d. Thomas Z. and Mary Alice (Parker) D. BSN, Ariz. State U., 1970, MS in Nursing, 1976; cert. nursing practitioner, Calif. State U., Long Beach, 1979. Cert. rehab. nurse. Staff and charge nurse Good Samaritan Hosp., Phoenix, 1970-75; staff nurse in neurology VA Med. Ctr., Phoenix, 1976-77, spinal cord injury nurse practitioner, 1980-85; rehab. clin. nurse specialist, 1977-85; assoc. chief nursing svc. spinal cord injury unit and ambulatory care VA Med. Ctr., San Diego, 1985-91, assoc. chief nursing svcs., ambulatory care, 1991—. Mem. editorial adv. bd. Rehab. Mgmt., 1992-94. Named Nurse of Yr., Dist. 18 Ariz. Nurses Assn., 1982. Mem. Assn. Rehab. Nurses (pres. Ariz. chpt. 1979-81, treas. San Diego chpt. 1990-94), Am. Assn. Spinal Cord Injury Nurses (bd. dirs. 1991-94, chmn. editl. bd. 1988-94, co-editor 1983-86, Disting. Svc. award 1994), Am. Acad. Ambulatory Care Nursing (sec. San Diego chpt. 1993—, chair VA spl. interest group 1995—), Sigma Theta Tau. Home: 8719 Ginger Snap Ln San Diego CA 92129-3715

DWYER, MARGARET ANN, university administrator; b. Syracuse, N.Y.; d. Edward P. and Margaret M. (O'Donnell) D. AB, Le Moyne Coll., 1954; MEd, Boston Coll., 1956; PhD (hon.), Le Moyne Coll., 1994. Tchr. Kingsford Park Pub. Schs., Oswego, N.Y., 1955-56; med. sch. worker St. Joseph's Hosp., Syracuse, 1956-60; registrar Le Moyne Coll., Syracuse, 1960-62, dean of women, 1962-71, asst. acad. dean, 1971-73; exec. asst. to pres. Boston Coll., 1973-75, v.p., asst. to pres., 1975—; mem. consumer's adv. bd. Dey Bros. Dept. Store, 1966-70; bd. dirs., dir. Bay Bank Newton Waltham (now Bay Banks Inc.), 1976-91. Sec. adv. bd. St. Mary's Hosp., Syracuse, 1965-70; trustee Cath. Charities Archdiocese Boston, Le Moyne Coll., Syracuse, 1987-93; mem. United Way, Mass.; chmn. bd. dirs. Syracuse chpt. ARC. Mem. AAUW. Home: 40 Carver Rd Wellesley MA 02181-5304 Office: Boston College Chestnut Hill MA 02167

DWYER, MARY ELIZABETH, nursery school director; b. N.Y.C., Sept. 23, 1928; d. Frank Stanton Burns and Eula Louise (Groenier) Gavin; m. Melvin Charles Christensen, Aug. 13, 1949 (dec. 1980); children: Mark, Alan, Paul; m. William Frederick Dwyer, Dec. 3, 1989. Student, Adelphi U., 1948, San Diego State U., 1949, SUNY, Farmingdale, 1980-86. Clk. Merrill Lynch, N.Y.C., 1946-47; sec. Ace Fence Co., Franklin Square, N.Y., 1949-50; switchboard operator Best & Co., Garden City, N.Y., 1950-51; dir. St. Francis Play Day Sch., Levittown, N.Y., 1978—. Active Levittown Rep. Club, 1960-89; mem. com. Inst. for Learning and Retirement, Farmingdale, N.Y., 1991-93. Recipient Bishop's Cross for Disting. Parochial Svc., Diocese of L.I., 1984. Mem. Amnesty Internat., Levittown Hist. Soc. (exec. dir. 1991—). Republican. Episcopalian. Home: 39 Old Oak Ln Levittown NY 11756

DY-ANG, ANITA C., pediatrician; b. Cavite, The Philippines, Feb. 21, 1943; came to U.S., 1970; m. Raymunso Ang., May 1, 1977; children: Aileen Ang, Audrey Ang. MD, U. East Ramon Magsaysay, Quezon City, Philippines, 1967. Diplomate Am. Bd. Pediatrics. Pediat. resident Tulane U. Charity Hosp. New Orleans, 1973; pvt. practice Warsaw, N.Y.; mem. attending staff Wyoming County Cmty. Hosp. Mem. Wyoming County Med. Soc. Office: 78 N Main St Warsaw NY 14569-1329

DYAR, KATHRYN WILKIN, pediatrician; b. Colquitt, Ga., Feb. 20, 1945; d. Patrick McWhorter and Virginia (Wilkin) Dyar; m. James Ansley Patten, Jan. 1, 1985. BS in Biology, Emory U., Decatur, Ga., 1966; MD, Med. Coll. Ga., Augusta, 1970. Resident in pediatrics Eugene Talmadge Meml. Hosp., Augusta, Ga., 1970-72, Georgetown U. Hosp., Washington, 1972-73; pediatrician Children's Clinic, Tifton, Ga., 1973-74; pediatrician Children and Youth Project, Norfolk, Va., 1974-83, 90-95, dir., 1990-94; pediatrician Hampton (Va.) Health Dept., 1983-90. Fellow Am. Acad. Pediatrics.

DYBELL, ELIZABETH ANNE SLEDDEN, clinical psychologist; b. Buffalo, Sept. 25, 1958; d. Richard Edward and Angela Brigid (Scimone) Sledden; m. David Joseph Dybell, Nov. 30, 1985. BA in Psychology summa cum laude, U. St. Thomas, Houston, 1980; PhD in Psychology, Tex. Tech. U., 1986. Lic. clinical psychologist, Tex. Rsch. asst. health sci. ctr. Tex. Tech. U., Lubbock, 1983-84, psychol. cons. health sci. ctr. neurology dept., 1982-84; psychology intern U. N.Mex. Med. Sch., Albuquerque, 1984-85; psychotherapist Katz & Assocs. P.C., Houston, 1985-88, Meyer Ctr. for Devel. Pediatrics Tex. Children's Hosp., Houston, 1988-92; pvt. practice Houston, 1990—. Author: (monograph) When Will Life Be Normal?, 1989; contbr. articles to numerous publs. choir mem. St. Thomas More Ch., Houston, 1974-87. Mem. Am. Psychol. Assn., Assn. for the Care of Childrens Health, Nat. Ctr. Clin. Infant Programs, Soc. Pediatric Psychology, Southwestern Psychol. Assn., Tex. Psychol. Assn., Houston Psychol. Assn., Am. Psychol. Soc. (charter). Roman Catholic. Office: 6001 Savoy Dr Ste 208 Houston TX 77036-3322

DYCHE, KATHIE LOUISE, secondary school educator; b. Waynoka, Okla., Sept. 8, 1949; d. Loren Neil and Bessie Louise (Wait) Callaway; m. Steven Lee Dyche, July 5, 1969; children: Cherilyn Nettie, Bradley Callaway. BA in Edn. in Art, Northwestern Okla. State U., 1972; postgrad., Southwestern Okla. State U., 1975, 78, Phillips U., 1981, 83-85; MEd, U. Cen. Okla., 1993. Cert. art, Am. history and democracy tchr., Okla. Tchr. art Fairview (Okla.) Pub. Schs., 1973-81, cons., 1973-76; asst. to handicapped Glenwood Elem. Sch., Enid, Okla., 1982-83; reading and math. asst. Longfellow Jr. High Sch., Enid, 1983-84; tchr. art Emerson Jr. High Sch., Enid, 1984—; freelance artist Gaslight Theater, Okla. Small Bus. Devel. Ctr., also others; represented by Dean Lively Gallery, Edmond, Okla. Exhibited in group shows Amarillo (Tex.) Artists' Studio, 1975, Kallistos Invitational Show, 1985, Dean Lively Gallery, Edmond, Okla., Art Educators as Artists exhibit Philbrook, Tulsa, 1994, 96. Pres., v.p., sec., historian, reporter Gamma Mother's Club, Fairview, 1973-80; co-chmn. Fairview Show of Arts, 1979, 80; art vol. Glenlwood Elem. Sch., 1981-82; pres., historian, parlimentarian Delta Child Study Club, Enid, 1981-84. Recipient Okla. Fall Arts Inst. Honor award, 1992, 94, 95; Northwestern Okla. State U. scholar, 1968. Mem. NEA, Nat. Art Edn. Assn., Okla. Art Edn. Assn., Okla. Edn. Assn., Cardinal Key, Kappa Delta Pi, Delta Kappa Gamma (sec. 1986-88, scholar 1993, 2d v.p. 1994-96), Phi Delta Kappa (historian 1995-96). Episcopalian. Office: Emerson Jr High Sch 700 W Elm Ave Enid OK 73701-3082

DYE, ELAINE GIBSON, home health nurse; b. Talladega, Ala., Aug. 23, 1944; d. John Lewis and Eunice (Vickers) Gibson; divorced; 1 child, Steven Dean Herring. Diploma, Sylacauga Hosp. Sch. Nursing, 1983. RN, Ala. ICU staff nurse Sylacauga (Ala.) Hosp., 1983-85; field staff nurse ABC Home Health Svcs., Talladega, 1985-88, quality appraisal coord., 1990-91, coord. adminstrn., 1991—; emergency rm. staff nurse Coosa Valley Med. Ctr., Sylacauga, 1988-89, Cooper Green Hosp., Birmingham, Ala., 1989-90; adminstr. Sylacauga (Ala.) Agy. of ABC Home Health Svcs., Inc., 1991—. Mem. Sylacauga C. of C., Bus. and Profl. Women (Sylacauga chpt.). Episcopalian. Office: First Am Home Care 401 W Third St Sylacauga AL 35150

DYE, NANCY SCHROM, academic administrator, history educator; b. Columbia, Mo., Mar. 11, 1947; d. Ned Stuart and Florence Andrea Elizabeth (Ahrens) Schrom; m. Griffith R. Dye, Aug. 21, 1972; children: Molly, Michael. AB, Vassar Coll., 1969; MA, U. Wis., 1971, PhD, 1974. Asst. prof. U. Ky., Lexington, 1974-80, assoc. prof., 1980-88, prof., 1988, assoc. dean arts and scis., 1984-88; dean faculty Vassar Coll., Poughkeepsie, N.Y., 1988-92; acting pres. Vassar Coll., 1992-94; pres. Oberlin Coll., Oberlin, Ohio, 1994—. Author: As Equals And As Sisters, 1981, contbr. articles to profl. jours. Mem. Coun. of Colls. of Arts and Scis. (bd. dirs. 1989—). Office: Oberlin Coll 70 N Professor Cox Bldg Oberlin OH 44074-1090*

DYER, ARLENE THELMA, retail company owner; b. Chgo., Oct. 23, 1942; d. Samuel Leo Sr. and Thelma Arlene (Israel) Lewis; m. Don Engle Dyer, July 3, 1965 (div. 1970); 1 child, Artel Terren. Cert. in mgmt. effectiveness, U. So. Calif., 1987. Community resource rep. Calif. State Employment Devel. Dept., Los Angeles, 1975-76, spl. projects rep., 1976; employment services rep. Culver City, Calif., 1977; contract writer L.A., 1976-80, employment program rep., 1980—; pres. Yabba and Co., L.A., 1981-83; pres., designer, cons. Spiritual Ties Custom Neckwear, L.A., 1985—; pres. Dyer Custom Shirts, Blouses and Suits, Beverly Hills, Calif., 1988—; founder self-evaluation seminar; radio presonality, 1995—. Author: Who Are You and What Are You All About?, 1994, Escaping to the Workplace, 1996; exhibited in fashion shows, Calif., 1984—; radio personality, 1995. Vol. Big Sister Gwen Bolden Found., L.A., 1986, Juvenile Hall, 1996; mem. Operation PUSH, Chgo., 1983, Mahogany Cowgirls & Co.; program chair Black Advs. in State Svc., 1987—; leader Girl Scouts U.S., L.A., 1982, L.A. Urban League; spirit team leader Calif. Special Olympics. Mem. Nat. Alliance Homebased Businesswomen (v.p., program chair 1987), Nat. Assn. Female Execs., Calif. State Employees Assn., U. So. Calif. Alumni Assn., L.A. Urban League, Black Women's Forum, NAACP (Beverly Hills-Hollywood chpt.). Democrat. Club: 92d St Block.

DYER, DORIS ANNE, nurse; b. Washington, Jan. 14, 1944; d. William Edward and Helen Gertrude (Smith) Swain; m. Robert Francis Dyer, Jr., June 27, 1970; children: Robert Francis, William Edward, Anne-Marie Helen Sallie, Scott Robertson McGavin. RN cum laude, Sibley Nursing Sch., Washington, 1964; BS, Am. U., 1966, MEd, 1969. Mem. staff emergency medicine dept. George Washington U. Hosp., 1960-69, emergency specialist protective svcs. clinic, 1967-70, adminstr. asst. to dir. clinic, 1970-78; nurse cons., 1987—. Author: Say Ah, 1971; also articles. Patron Sibley Meml. Hosp. Chapel, 1992. Trinity Coll. scholar, 1960; Lucy Webb Hayes scholar, 1964; recipient Martha Washington award Md. Soc. SAR, 1977, Community Leaders award, 1979, Washington medal, 1984, Disting. Women of Washington award 1987; decorated Comdr. Order of St. Lazarus, 1984, medal of Merit, 1989; created dame Order of Sovereign Mil. Order, 1980, dame comdr., 1992; named Dame Grand Officier, 1992. Mem. Am. Nurses Assn., D.C. Nurses Assns., Am. Acad. Ambulatory Nursing Adminstrs., Washington Med.-Surg. Soc. Aux. (pres.), Am. U. Grads. Assn., DAR, Washington Assembly, Washington Club, Annapolis Yacht Club, Kenwood Golf and Country Club. Address: 5608 Albia Rd Bethesda MD 20816-3303

DYER, GERALDINE ANN (GERI A. DYER), artist, poet; b. Bklyn., Nov. 4, 1921; d. Edward and Chattie (Holmes) Bingham; m. Ralph Dyer, Oct. 1956. Student, N.Y. Phoenix Sch. Design, N.Y.C., 1946-48, Bklyn. Mus. Art Sch., 1959, Bklyn. Coll., 1939; pvt. studies in voice with Julia Gille, 1947-50; reader poetry Bklyn. Poetry Circle, Bklyn., Moroccan Star, Bklyn., 1994. Commd. U.S. Army, 1941, ret. exec. USCG, 1979. One-woman shows include Henry Hicks Gallery, N.Y.C., 1978-79, 81, Womanart Gallery, N.Y.C., 1980, Keane Mason Gallery, N.Y.C., 1981, Esta Robinson Gallery, N.Y.C., 1983, Bklyn. Heights Br. Libr., Bklyn., 1986-89, St. Mary Star of the Sea, Bklyn., 1993; exhibited at numerous group shows; represented in permanent collection Samuel Schulman Inst., Bklyn.; author poetry in collections. Recipient numerous awards including Art Horizons Internat. Art Competition, 1988, Alma E. Wright Meml. poetry award, 1989, 90, BPC Critics Poetry award, 1991, 94, Editor's Choice award Nat. Libr. of Poetry, 1994, 95; named Internat. Woman of Yr., 1991-92. Mem. Poetry Soc. Am., Officers Club (Governors Island, N.Y.), Bklyn. Poetry Circle (v.p. 1990, 93, 1st prize Bklyn. Poetry Cir. Meml. Contest 1994), Mus. Modern Art. Avocation: writing poetry.

DYER, RITA FRANCES, medical/surgical and oncology nurse; b. Meridian, Miss., Sept. 14, 1947; d. Jesse E. and Frances A. (Nelson) Hahn; m. Lloyd D. Dyer, Mar. 9, 1985; children: Michelle Lee Belcourt, Michael Thomas Belcourt. Grad., Phillips Bus. Coll., Gulfport, Miss., 1966; lic. practical nurse, No. Mont. Coll., 1976; AS in Nursing, Miss. Gulf Coast Jr. Coll., Gulfport, 1985; student, St. Joseph's Coll., Windham, Maine; BSN, Elmira Coll., 1994. Cert. audiology tester. Staff nurse Gulfport Meml. Hosp., 1985-86; head nurse Coventry (R.I.) Health Ctr., 1987; charge nurse Biloxi (Miss.) Regional Med. Ctr., 1985-86; staff and charge nurse South County Hosp., Wakefield, R.I., 1987-90; staff nurse VA Hosp., Bath, N.Y., 1990—. With USAR Corp. Mem. ANA, N.Y. Nurses Assn.

DYER-COLE, PAULINE, school psychologist, educator; b. Methuen, Mass., Aug. 20, 1935; d. E. Dewey and Rose Alma (Des Jardins) Dyer; m. Richard Grey, Aug. 1, 1964 (dec. 1977); children: Douglas Richard, Christopher Lachlan, Heather Judith; m. Malcolm A. Cole, July 23, 1983. BS in Edn. and Music, Lowell State Coll., 1957; MEd, Boston State Coll., 1961; EdD, Clark U., 1991. Lic. psychologist; cert. sch. and ednl. psychologist. Supr. music and art Merrimac and W. Newburg (Mass.) Pub. Schs., 1957-59; music editor textbooks Allyn & Bacon, Inc., Boston, 1959-64; prof. music West Pines Coll., Chester, N.H., 1969-72; sch. psychologist Nashoba Regional H.S., Bolton, Mass., 1979—, chair SPED dept., 1995—; vis. lectr., then vis. prof. Framingham (Mass.) State Coll., 1980—; dir. psychol. testing Nashoba Regional Sch. Dist., Bolton, Mass., 1980—. Author: The Play Game Songbook, 1964. V.p., bd. dirs. Timberlane Devel. Ctr., Plaistow, N.H., 1970-73; founder Friends of Kimi Nichols Devel. Ctr., Plaistow, 1973; chmn. human svcs. St. Ann Parish, Southborough, Mass., 1974-77, active, 1973—; citizen amb. del. People to People, China, 1995; active The Regional Lab., Andover, Mass., 1993—. Frances L. Hyatt Sch. Psychology & Edn. fellow Clark U., 1977-79. Mem. NASP, Mass. Assn. Sch. Psychologists, Mass. Tchrs. Assn., CASE Sch. Psychologists Assn., People to People Internat. Roman Catholic. Home: 50 Framingham Rd Southborough MA 01772-1206 Office: Nashoba Regional Sch Dist 11 Green Rd Bolton MA 01740-1046

DYER-DAWSON, DIANE FAYE, educational administrator; b. Chgo., Feb. 16, 1941; d. Coy F. and Geraldine C. (Hardie) Smith; m. Nelson F. Dyer, Mar. 11, 1961 (div. 1983); children: Ouida F., Nelson F. Jr., Deidre M.; m. Bernarr E. Dawson, Apr. 9, 1988. BEd, Chgo. State U., 1970; MEd, U. Ill., 1976; EdD, Loyola U., Chgo., 1991. Tchr. Luella Elem. Sch., Chgo., 1970-74; learning disabilities tchr. Betsy Ross Elem. Sch., Chgo., 1974-76; asst. prin. Cather Elem. Sch., Chgo., 1976-84; prin. Park Manor Elem. Sch., Chgo., 1984-92, Proviso East High Sch., Maywood, Ill., 1992—; trainer Ill. Bd. Edn., Chgo., 1988—, mentor, 1989—, assoc., 1991—; instr. grad. sch. Chgo. State U., 1991-92, Loyola U., Chgo., 1992—. Mem. selection com. Golden Apple Found., Chgo., 1988—; bd. dirs. Salem House, Chgo., 1991—; sec. coun. Salem Luth. Ch., Chgo., 1992—. Named Prin. of Excellence, Chgo. Pub. Schs., 1992; grantee Chgo. Pub. Schs., 1991, Ill. Bd. Edn., 1991; recipient award of excellence Those Who Excel, 1995. Mem. ASCD, IASCD (H.S. com.), IHSA, NASSP, Ill. Prins. Assn., Chgo. Prins. Assn. (assoc.), Samuel B. Stratton Edn. Assn., Nat. Alliance of Black Sch. Educators, Innovators Serving Deprived Children (pres. 1984-88), Alpha Kappa Alpha, Phi Delta Kappa. Democrat. Home: 2561 Lake Shore Dr Lynwood IL 60411-1384

DYKEMAN, ALICE MARIE, public relations executive; b. Fremont, Nebr., May 18; d. Cecil Victor and Dorothy Lillian (Sillik) Jansen; divorced; children: David Clair, Cinda Cecille Dykeman Nordgren. Student, Nebr. Wesleyan U., 1949-50, So. Meth. U., 1960-70. Women's editor, feature writer Fremont (Nebr.) Guide and Tribune and Biloxi (Miss.) Daily Herald, 1950-55; adminstrv. asst. to v.p. sales promotion A. Harris & Co., Dallas, 1957-60; account exec. Contact Corp., Dallas, 1960-61; pub. relations dir. Meth. Hosp., Dallas, 1961-72; regional pub. info. officer Small Bus. Adminstrn., Dallas, 1972-74; owner Dykeman Assocs. Inc., Dallas, 1974—; adj. prof. U. Dallas Grad. Sch. Mgmt., Irving, Tex. 1972-78; guest lectr. numerous Univs., and seminars; mem. pub. relations com. Dallas/Ft. Worth Fed. Exec. Bd., 1973, mem. minority bus. opportunity com., 1974; mem. Gov.'s Council on Small Bus., Tex., 1980-81, 500, Inc., 1982-90; chmn. export council pub. affairs task force U.S. Dept. Commerce, 1980-83. Contbr. articles to health care and pub. relations jours. Mem. fgn. visitors com. Dallas Council on World Affairs, 1962—, North Tex. Commn., Dallas Pub. Health Bd., 1972-74, Dallas Urban Rehab. Standards Bd., 1981-83, Econ. Devel. Adv. Bd., City of Dallas, 1983-86, pres. Concerned Citizens for Cedar Springs, 1982—; bd. dirs. Oak Lawn Forum, 1983-92; mem. exec. com. Oak Lawn Com., 1983-95. Recipient Matrix award Women in Communications, Dallas, 1968, 88. Fellow Pub. Rels. Soc. Am. (chmn. S.W. dist. 1971-72, bd. dirs. North Tex. chpt. 1966-72, pres. 1969, assembly del. 1970-73, 91); mem. Internat. Pub. Rels. Assn., Internat. Trade Assn. Dallas, North Dallas Fin. Forum (pres. 1991), Nat. Assn. Women Bus. Owners, S.W. Venture Forum, North Dallas C. of C. (bd. dirs. 1980-82), Greater Dallas Chamber, Press Club Dallas (bd. dirs. 1981-83, headliner 4 times), SMU Mustang Club (bd. dirs. 1996), also others. Methodist. Office: Dykeman Assocs Inc 4115 Rawlins St Dallas TX 75219-3661

DYKEMAN, WILMA, writer, educator; b. Asheville, N.C., May 20, 1920; d. Willard J. and Bonnie (Cole) Dykeman; m. James R. Stokely Jr., Oct. 12, 1940; children: Dykeman Cole, James R. III. BS inSpeech, Northwestern U., 1940; LittD, Maryville Coll., 1974; LHD, Tenn. Wesleyan Coll., 1978. Lectr. English dept. U. Tenn., Knoxville, 1975-95, adj. prof., 1985—; columnist Knoxville News-Sentinel, 1962—; historian State of Tenn., 1980—; nat. lectr. in field; bd. dirs. First Union Bank. Author 16 books including: The French Broad: A Rivers of America Volume, 1955, The Tall Woman, 1962, Seeds of Southern Change, 1962, The Far Family, 1966, Return the Innocent Earth, 1973; co-author: Neither Black Nor White, 1957, Tennessee: A Bicentennial History, 1976, Tennessee Women: An Infinite Variety, 1993, Explorations, a collection of essays, 1984; contbr. articles to nat. mags. and Ency. Brit. Trustee Berea Coll., 1971—, Phelps Stokes Fund, 1981—, U. N.C.-Asheville, 1985—; active Friends of Great Smokies Nat. Park. Guggenheim fellow, 1956-57, NEH fellow, 1976-77; recipient Hillman award, 1957, Disting. So. Writers award So. Festival of Books, 1989; N.C. Gold medal for Contbn. to Am. letters, 1985. Mem. PEN, Authors Guild, So. Hist. Assn., Cosmos Club, Phi Beta Kappa, Delta Kappa Gamma. Home: 282 Clifton Heights Rd Newport TN 37821-2402 also: 189 Lynn Cove Rd Asheville NC 28804-1910

DYKES, TERESA JANE, primary school educator; b. Nashville, Sept. 9, 1944; d. John Alfred and Mary Evelyn Jackson; m. George H. Dykes, Jr., Aug. 9, 1963; children: Lana Patrice Dykes Leonard, Patricia D. Dykes Myers. BS, Belmont Coll., 1972; MEd, ETSU, 1985. Cert. Career Level III, Tenn. Kindergarten tchr. Pegram Elem. Sch., Cheatham County, Tenn., 1972-73, Nannie Berry Elem. Sch., Hendersonville, Tenn., 1973-78, Kingsport (Tenn.) City Sch., 1978—; cons. to Everyday Math. Corp., Chgo., 1993—. Sunday sch. tchr. St. Joseph's of Arimathea, Hendersonville, 1985-89. Mem. ASCD, NEA, Tenn. Edn. Assn., Kingsport Edn. Assn., Delta Kappa Gamma, Epsilon Sigma Alpha. Episcopalian. Home: 1612 Woodland Ave Johnson City TN 37601 Office: Jefferson Elem Sch Westmoreland Ave Kingsport TN 37664

DYKES, VIRGINIA CHANDLER, occupational therapist, educator; b. Evanston, Ill., Jan. 10, 1930; d. Daniel Guy and Helen (Schneider) Goodman; children: Ron Lee, Chuck Lee Chandler, James R. Jr. BA in Art and Psychology, So. Methodist U., 1951; postgrad. in occupational therapy Tex. Women's U., 1953. Occupational therapist Beverly Hills Sanitarium, Dallas, 1953-55; dir. occupational and recreational therapy Baylor U. Med. Ctr., Dallas, 1956-60, 68-89; pvt. practice, Dallas, 1989-92; dir. occupational and recreational therapy Fla. Hosp., Orlando, 1962-65; staff therapist Parkland Meml. Hosp., Dallas, 1965-68; cons. Arthritis Found., 1974-89, benefactor; Fanny B. Vanderkodi lectr. Tex. Women's U., 1993—. Mem. coordinating bd. allied health adv. com. Tex. Coll. and Univ. System, 1980-88; bd. dirs. Tex. Arthritis Found., chmn. patient svcs. com., 1985-89, exec. bd. sec.; sponsor Kimball Art Mus.; bd. dirs. Dallas Opera, also women's bd., CPA Wives, Theatre Ctr. Guild; women's bd. Dallas Arboretum; pres. Diana Dean Head Injury Guild, 1992-93. Named Tex. Occupational Therapist of Yr., 1985. Mem. Tex. Occupational Therapy Assn. (life mem. award), Am. Occupational Therapy Assn. (del. Fla. 1964, Tex. 1980-88), World Fedn. Occupational Therapists (participant 8th Internat. Congress, Hamburg, Germany, 1982, del. to 10th European Congress on Rheumatology, Moscow 1983), Chi Omega. Clubs: Boomerang (dir. 1971-88), Les Femmes du Monde, Pierian Lit. Club. Author: (manual) Lightcast II Splints, 1976; Adult Visual Perceptual Evaluation, 1981; contbr. articles to profl. jours. Home: 3203 Alderson St Dallas TX 75214-3059

DYKSTRA, EDIE M., human resource director; b. Gary, Ind., Nov. 9, 1954; d. Wayne H. and Edith P. (Christoff) D. BA in History, Ind. U., 1976; MPA in Urban, State, Fed. Gov. and Human Resources, Golden Gate U., 1986. Supr. internal acctg. KPMG Peat Marwick, San Francisco, 1980-87; asst. to dir. fin. City of Oakland, Calif., 1987; compensation and benefits analyst The Harper Group, San Francisco, 1987-89; mgr. internal svcs. Watson Wyatt Worldwide (formerly The Wyatt Co.), San Francisco, 1989-92; mgr. human resources The Wyatt Co., San Francisco, 1992-94, dir. human resources, 1994-95; mgr. human resources Graham & James, San Francisco, 1995—; adj. faculty U. San Francisco Coll. Profl. Studies/Pub. Mgmt. Program. Vol. Raphael House Shelter for Homeless Families, San Francisco, 1988—, vol., crisis counselor Woman Inc., 1988—. Mem. ASTD, Soc. for Human Resource Mgmt., Bay Area Personnel Assn. (pres. 1990-91), Bay Area Orgnl. Devel. Network, No. Calif. Human Resource Coun., Assn. Legal Adminstrs. Democrat. Office: Graham & James 3rd Fl One Maritime Plz San Francisco CA 94111

DYLAG, HELEN MARIE, healthcare administrator; b. Cleve., Oct. 14, 1950; d. Stanley John and Helen Agnes (Jarkiewicz) D. BSN, St. John Coll., Cleve., 1971; MS, Ohio State U., 1973. RN, Ohio. RN V.A. Adminstrn. Hosp., Brecksville, Ohio, 1971-72; clin. specialist, psychiat.-mental health nursing Marymount Hosp./Mental Health Ctr., Garfield Heights, Ohio, 1973-78, dir. consultation and edn. dept., 1978-84, dir. Ctr. for Health Styles, 1984-88; adminstrv. dir. Women's Healthcare Ctr./St. Luke's Hosp., Cleve., 1988-90; adminstrv. dir. dept. of psychiatry MetroHealth Med. Ctr., Cleve., 1990—. Contbg. author: Nursing of Families in Crisis, 1974, Distributive Nursing Practice: A Systems Approach to Community Health, 1977; producer and host "Health Styles" TV Talk Show, 1987-88; contbr. articles to profl. jours. Trustee The Stroke Assn. of Ohio, Cleve., 1990-91; mem. Women of Achievement com., Women's City Club, Cleve., 1989-91. Recipient award Greater Cleve. Hosp. Assn., 1981, Innovator award Am. Hosp. Assn./Ctr. for Health Promotion, 1985. Mem. Assn. Mental Health Adminstrs., Am. Coll. Healthcare Execs., Healthcare Adminstrs. Assn. of Northeast Ohio, Sigma Theta Tau. Home: 5709 Onaway Oval Cleveland OH 44130-1642 Office: Metro Health Med Ctr 2500 Metrohealth Dr Cleveland OH 44109-1900

DYMAN, KATHLEEN ELEANOR, medical association administrator; b. Port Jervis, N.Y., Aug. 16, 1950; d. Fred. J. and Gloria G. Murphy; m. Edward J. Dyman, Oct. 5, 1984; 1 child, Marc J. BS in Health Sys. Mgmt., SUNY, Utica, 1980. Pres. Profl. Career Sys., Utica, 1990-94; exec. dir. Med. Socs. Oneida, Herkimer, Madison, Chenango & Oswego Cos., New Hartford, N.Y., 1994—, Ctrl. N.Y. Acad. Medicine, 1994—, Med. Econs. Bur., 1994—; mem. adv. bd. Oneida County Medicaid Managed Care, Utica, 1990—; mem. Cmty. Alternative Placement Agy. of Oneida County, Utica, 1990—. Mem. budget panel United Way, 1990. Mem. Am. Assn. Med. Soc. Execs., Am. Coll. Health Care Adminstrs., N.Y. Assn. Long Term Care Adminstrs., Cosmopolitan Ctr. (bd. dirs. 1989—). Home: 10 The Hills Dr Utica NY 13501 Office: Med Socs 210 Clinton Rd PO Box 620 New Hartford NY 13413

DYRSTAD, JOANELL M., former lieutenant governor, consultant; b. St. James, Minn., Oct. 15, 1942; d. Arnold A. and Ruth (Berlin) Sletta; m. Marvin Dyrstad, 1965; children: Troy, Anika. BA, Gustavus Adolphus Coll., St. Peter, Minn., 1964; postgrad., Hamline U., 1988—. Mayor City of Red Wing, Minn., 1985-90; lt. gov. State of Minn., 1991-94; now independent bus. & govt. consultant; ptnr. Corner Drugstore, Red Wing, 1968—; v.p. League Minn. Cities, 1990-91, Minn. Mayors Assn., 1989-90. Trustee Gustavus Adolphus Coll., 1989—, U. Minn. Found., 1993—. Mem. AAUW (Citizen of yr. award 1985), League of Women Voters, Minn. Women Elected Ofcls. (chair nat. conf. lt. govs. 1993-94). •

DYSLIN, DIANNE MARIE, school communications coordinator; b. Chgo., Apr. 17, 1954; d. Robert Francis and Frances (Massias) D. BA in Religion and Psychology, Boston U., 1982; M Liberal Arts in Psychology, Harvard U., 1992. Publ. editor Harvard U./Harvard Real Estate, Inc., 1987-89, dir. comm., 1989-94; coord. comm. The Chapin Sch., N.Y.C., 1994—. Mem. N.Y. Women in Comm., Phi Beta Kappa. Office: The Chapin Sch 100 E End Ave 6th Fl New York NY 10028

DZAMBA, ANNE O., history and women's studies educator; b. N.Y.C., Oct. 18, 1938; d. Stephen Andrew and Barbara (Dressler) D.; m. Ronald Jay Miller, June 19, 1987. BA, Swarthmore Coll., 1960; PhD, U. Del., 1973. Instr. history Widener U., Chester, Pa., 1967-68; from asst. prof. to prof. history and women's studies West Chester (Pa.) U., 1968—, chairperson dept. history, 1995—. Author: Richard Wagner and the English, 1979; contbr. to books.

DZIEWANOWSKA, ZOFIA ELIZABETH, neuropsychiatrist, pharmaceutical executive, researcher, educator; b. Warsaw, Poland, Nov. 17, 1939; came to U.S., 1972; d. Stanislaw Kazimierz Dziewanowski and Zofia Danuta (Mieczkowska) Rudowska; m. Krzysztof A. Kunert, Sept. 1, 1961 (div. 1971); 1 child, Martin. MD, U. Warsaw, 1963; PhD, Polish Acad. Sci., 1970. MD recert. U.K., 1972, U.S., 1973. Asst. prof. of psychiatry U. Warsaw Med. Sch., 1969-71; sr. house officer St. George's Hosp., U. London, 1971-72; assoc. dir. Merck Sharp & Dohme, Rahway, N.J., 1972-76; vis. assoc. physician Rockefeller U. Hosp., N.Y.C., 1975-76; adj. asst. prof. of psychiatry Cornell U. Med. Ctr., N.Y.C., 1978—; v.p., global med. dir. Hoffmann-La Roche, Inc., Nutley, N.J., 1976-94; sr. v.p. and dir. global med. affairs Genta Inc., San Diego, 1994—; lectr. in field U.S. and internat. confs. Contbr. articles to profl. publs. Bd. dirs Royal Soc. Medicine Found.; mem. alumni coun. Cornell U. Med. Ctr. Recipient TWIN Honoree award for Outstanding Women in Mgmt., Ridgewood (N.J.) YWCA, 1984. Mem. AMA, AAAS, Am. Soc. Pharmacology and Therapeutics, Am. Coll. Neuropsychopharmacology, N.Y. Acad. Scis., PhRMA. (vice chmn. steering com. med. sect., chmn. internat. med. affairs com., head biotech. working group), Royal Soc. Medicine (U.K.), Drug Info. Assn. (Woman of Yr. award 1994), Am. Assn. Pharm. Physicians. Roman Catholic. Office: Genta Inc 3550 General Atomics Ct San Diego CA 92121

EADDY, PAULA JOHNSON, women's health nurse; b. Raleigh, N.C., June 9, 1965; d. Jack R. and Alice Faye (Paul) Johnson; m. Joseph Marion Eaddy III, June 3, 1995. Student, East Carolina U., Greenville, 1983-85; AAS, Ctrl. Carolina C.C., Sanford, 1987; AAS in Nursing, Wake Tech. C.C., Raleigh, 1990. RN, N.C.; BLS; cert. neonatal resusitation. Vet. med. technician N.C. State U., Raleigh, 1987-88; nurse technician II Wake Med. Ctr., Raleigh, 1988-90, maternal/child staff nurse II, staff nurse III, 1990—. Active United Way of N.C., Raleigh. Mem. Tarheel Triangle Cat Fanciers (past pres.). Baptist. Office: 3000 New Bern Ave Raleigh NC 27610-1215

EADIE, CYNTHIA, advertising executive. B, Boston Coll., 1980. Exec. dir. Subway Franchise Advt. Fund, Milford, Conn., 1990—. Office: Subway Franchise Advtg Fund 325 Bic Dr Milford CT 06460-3072*

EADS, LINDA LEE, financial manager; b. Ft. Thomas, Ky., Mar. 23, 1956; d. Malcolm and Eloise (DeJarnette) E. BA in Political Science with high distinction, Ea. Ky. U., 1977; M of Planning, U. Cin., 1983. Planner Kentuckiana Regional Planning and Devel. Agy., Louisville, 1979-86; sr. planner County of Polk, Bartow, Fla., 1986-87; program mgr. Va. Dept. Rail and Pub. Transp., Richmond, 1987-93, fin. mgr., 1993—; v.p. Downloading Users Orgn., Richmond, 1995—; chair Transp. Rsch. Bd. Adv. Panel, Washington, 1995. Mem. LWV (treas. 1992-94, voter svc. chair 1992), Women's Transp. Seminar, West of Blvd. Civic Assn.

EADS, M. ADELA, state legislator; b. Brooklyn, N.Y., Mar. 2, 1920. Ed. Sweet Briar Coll. Mem. Conn. Ho. of Reps., 1976-80; mem. Conn. Senate, from 1980; senate minority leader serving on legis. mgmt. com., exec. nominations com.; senate pres. pro tempore, 1995; mem. exec. nominations select com. children's regulations review; mem. adv. bd. New Milford Bank & Trust Co., Glenholm Devereux Sch. Trustee Marvelwood Sch., Kent, Conn.; bd. dirs. Drugs Don't Work, Easter Seals. Republican. Mem. Conn. Bd. Edn., 1972-76., Nat. Orgn. Women Legislators, Conn. Orgn. Women Legislators. Home: 160 Macedonia Rd Kent CT 06757-1306 Office: Conn State Senate State Capital Bldg Hartford CT 06106

EAGAN, MARIE T. (RIA EAGAN), chiropractor; b. Rockville Ctr., N.Y., June 17, 1952; d. John F. and Mary (Ebner) E. BA, Goddard Coll., 1975; D in Chiropractic Medicine, N.Y. Chiropractic Coll., 1983. Pvt. practice chiropractic medicine N.Y.C., 1983—; chiropractic examiner N.Y. State Bd. Chiropractic, 1995. Bd. dirs. Chalice Found., L.A., 1986. Fellow N.Y. Chiropractic Assn., Am. Chiropractic Assn., Internat. Chiropractic Assn. Democrat. Office: 231 W 21st St Apt B New York NY 10011-3119

EAGLY, ALICE HENDRICKSON, social psychology educator; b. L.A., Dec. 25, 1938; d. Harold Martin and Josara Alberta (Whyers) Hendrickson; m. Robert Victor Eagly, Sept. 8, 1962; children: Ingrid Victoria, Ursula Elizabeth. BA, Radcliffe Coll., 1960; MA, U. Mich., 1963, PhD, 1965. Asst. prof. Mich. State U., East Lansing, 1965-67; asst. to assoc. to full prof. U. Mass., Amherst, 1967-80; vis. asst. prof. U. Ill., Champaign, 1970-71; vis. assoc. prof. Harvard U., Cambridge, Mass., 1974-75; prof. social psychology Purdue U., West Lafayette, Ind., 1980-95, Northwestern U., Evanston, Ill., 1995—; MacEachern Meml. lectr. U. Alta., 1985; vis. prof. U. Tuebingen (Germany), 1991-92. Author: Sex Differences in Social Behavior: A Social Role Interpretation, 1987, (with Shelly Chaiken) The Psychology of Attitudes, 1993; cons. editor Jour. Personality and Social Psychology: Attitudes and Social Cognition, 1979—, mem. editorial bd., 1983—; cons. editor Psychology of Women Quar., 1978-86, also others; contbr. articles to profl. jours. Recipient Disting. Pub. award, Assn. for Women in Psychology, 1978, Gordon Allport Intergroup Rels. prize, Soc. Psychol. Study Social Issues, 1976; Nat. Merit scholar, 1956-60, Fulbright fellow, 1960-61, Woodrow Wilson fellow, 1961-62, NSF fellow, 1962-65; various rsch. grants. Mem. APA (citation as disting. leader for women in psychology com. on women in psychology), Soc. Personality and Social Psychology (pres. 1981), Donald Campbell award for disting. contbn. to social psychology 1994), Soc. for Exptl. Social Psychology (exec. com. 1973-76, 81-83), Midwestern Psychol. Assn., Phi Beta Kappa, Sigma Xi. Office: Northwestern U Dept Psychology Swift Hall 2029 Sheridan Rd Evanston IL 60208

EAKES, TERRI PARKER, town administrator; b. Edenton, N.C., Apr. 11, 1967; d. Percy Owen Jr. and Katherine (Starling) Parker; m. William Lee Eakes, May 6, 1995. BSP in Criminal Justice, Ea Carolina U., 1988. Cert. mcpl. adminstrn. Paralegal, intake worker Pamlico Sound Legal Svcs., Greenville, N.C., 1988-89; paralegal Dixon, Doub, & Conner, PA, Greenville, 1989, City of Greenville, 1989-95; town adminstr. Town of Bethel, N.C., 1995—. Guardian Ad Litem, Greenville, 1987—; loaned exec. United Way of Pitt County, 1991, mem. allocations com., 1993-95. Mem. N.C. Assn. City and County Mgmt., N.C. Fin. Officers Assn., County and Mcpl. Adminstrn. Alumni Assn. Methodist. Office: Town of Bethel 201 W Railroad St Bethel NC 27812-0337

EAKIN, MARGARETTA MORGAN, lawyer; b. Ft. Smith, Ark., Aug. 27, 1941; d. Ariel Thomas and Oma (Thomas) Morgan; m. Harry D. Eakin, June 7, 1959; 1 dau., Margaretta E. B.A. with honors, U. Oreg., 1969, J.D., 1971. Bar: Oreg. 1971, U.S. Dist. Ct. Oreg. 1973, U.S. Ct. Appeals (9th cir.) 1977. Law clk. to chief justice Oreg. Supreme Ct., 1971-72; Reginald Heber Smith Law Reform fellow, 1972-73; house counsel Hyster Co., 1973-75; assoc. N. Robert Stoll, 1975-77; mem. firm Margaretta Eakin, P.C., Portland, Oreg., 1977—; tchr. bus. law Portland State U., 1979-80; speaker; mem. state bd. profl. responsibility Oreg. State Bar, 1979-82. Mem. bd. visitors U. Oreg. Sch. of Law, 1986-93, vice chair, 1989-91, chair, 1992-93; mem. ann. fund com. Oreg. Episc. Sch., 1981, chmn. subcom. country fair, 1981; sec. Parent Club Bd., St. Mary's Acad., 1987; mem. Oreg. State. Bar Com. on Uniform State Laws, 1989-93. Paul Patterson fellow. Mem. ABA, Assn. Trial Lawyers Am., Oreg. Trial Lawyers Assn., Oreg. Bar Assn., Multnomah County Bar Assn. (jud. selection com. 1992-94), 1000 Friends of Oreg., City Club. Office: 30th Fl Pacwest Ctr 1211 SW 5th Ave Portland OR 97204-3713

EAMES, JUDY, English as second language educator; b. Christiansburg, Va.; m. George Grozdits. BS, Radford (Va.) U., 1966, MS, 1968; postgrad., U. Calif., Hayward, U. South Fla., Va. Poly. Inst., State U.; EdD in Higher Edn., Nova U., 1994. Instr. communication Upward Bound, Va. Poly. Inst. and STate U., Blacksburg, 1970; tchr. French Sch. Dist. 361, International Falls, Minn., 1971-74, Ottawa (Ont., Can.)-Carleton Schs., 1976-79; tchr. English, St. Petersburg (Fla.) Jr. Coll., 1987-90; instr. ESL and French Lindsey Wilson Coll., Columbia, Ky., 1990—; EdD. Fulbright Hayes Seminar grantee, Hungary and Poland, summer 1994. Mem. ASCD, TESOL, Nat. Coun. Tchrs. English, Am. Coun. Tchrs. Fgn. Langs., Ky. Coun. Internat. Edn. Office: Lindsey Wilson Coll 210 Lindsey Wilson St Columbia KY 42728-1223

EARHART, EILEEN MAGIE, retired child and family life educator; b. Hamilton, Ohio, Oct. 21, 1928; d. Andrew J. and Martha (Waldorf) Magie; m. Paul G. Earhart; children: Anthony G., Bruce P., Daniel T. B.S., Miami U., Oxford, Ohio, 1950; M.A. in Adminstrn. and Ednl. Services, Mich. State U., 1962, Ph.D. in Edn., 1969; H.H.D. (hon.), Miami U., Oxford, Ohio, 1980. Tchr. home econs. W. Alexandria (Ohio) Schs., 1950-51; elementary tchr. Waterford Twp. Schs., Pontiac, Mich., 1958-65; reading specialist Waterford Twp. Schs., 1965-67; prof., chmn. family and child ecology dept. Mich. State U., East Lansing, 1968-84; prof., head dept. home and family life Fla. State U., Tallahassee, 1984-89; ret., 1989. Author: Attention and Classification Training Curriculum; co-editor spl. issue of Family Relations, 1984; contbr. chpts. to profl. jours., books. Mem. adv. bd. Lansing Com. on Children's TV, Family/Sch./Cmty. Partnership Project, Tallahassee; bd. dirs. Women's Resource Ctr., Grand Rapids, Mich., Wesley Found., Fla. State U., 1989-96; mem. campus ministries bd. Fla. A&M U., 1995-96; mem. Mich. Gov.'s Task Force on Youth. Mem. Nat. Coun. on Family Rels. (pres. Assn. of Couns. 1987-88, bd. dirs. 1986-88, chair nat. meeting local arrangements 1992), Fla. Coun. on Family Rels. (pres. elect 1985-86, pres. 1986-87), Nat. Assn. Edn. Young Children, Assn. Childhood Edn. Internat., Am. Home Econs. Assn. (named an AHEA Leader at 75th Ann. of Assn. 1984), Internat. Fedn. Home Econs., Mich. Home Econs. Assn. (pres. 1980-82), Fla. Home Econs. Assn. (chmn. scholarship com. 1986-88, dist. chmn. 1990-91, chmn. nominating com. 1991-92, co-chair ann. meeting 1995), Ednl. Rsch. Assn., Phi Kappa Phi (pres. Fla. State U. chpt. 1988-89), Delta Kappa Gamma, Omicron Nu, others. Home: 4009 Brandon Hill Dr Tallahassee FL 32308-2653

EARL, DENISE MARIE, accountant, consultant; b. Lincoln, Nebr., May 4, 1962; d. Herbert Jean and Sandra Lee (Lehn) Grimes; m. Michael Leon Diedrich, May 20, 1983 (div. Dec. 1987); children: Jessica Lee, Veronica Janet; m. James Arthur Earl, Feb. 5, 1993; 1 child, Monica LaVeta-Juanita. AAS in Bus., Everett (Wash.) C.C., 1990; BS in Acctg., BS in Bus. Fin., Ctrl. Wash. U., 1992. CPA, Wash., CMA. Bookkeeper King Machine, Inc., Lynnwood, Wash., 1984-86, Clyde Revord Motors, Everett, 1986-87; contracts adminstr. Acro Tech, Inc., Everett, 1987-88; office mgr. Vector Industries, Inc., Everett, 1988-92; acct. Safeco Life Co., Redmond, Wash., 1993—; owner, mgr. Small Bus. Bookkeeping Svc., Snohomish, Wash., 1990—. Mem. Inst. Mgmt. Accts. (cert., scholar Bellevue chpt. 1992).

EARLE, BARBARA GAYLE, reading specialist; b. Phila., Nov. 1, 1930; d. David Thomas and Blanche Gertner (Kaplan) Jones; m. William C. Earle, Oct. 4, 1967. BA, Beaver Coll., 1952; cert. reading specialist, Pa. State U., King of Prussia, 1982. Tchr. Thomas Williams Jr. H.S., Cheltenham Twp. Schs., Wyncote, Pa., 1953-57; tchr. grade 10 Clay H.S., Oregon (Ohio) Pub. Schs., 1957-58; tchr. grades 9 and 10 DeVilbiss H.S., Toledo, 1958-61; tchr. grades 7 and 8 Ida (Mich.) Pub. Schs., 1961-64; tchr. grade 7 Lower Merion Sch. Sys., Ardmore, Pa., 1964-67; substitute tchr. Haverford Twp. Schs., Havertown, Pa., 1967-76; part-time tutor/reading specialist Main Line Project Learning, Havertown, 1976—. Contbr. several articles to area newspapers. Bd. dirs. ret. vol. program RSVP, Ardmore, 1968-70, Orton Dyslexia Soc., Bryn Mawr, Pa., 1990-93; fundraiser Sta. WHGY-Pub. TV, 1985V; campaign vol. M.M. Mezvinsky for U.S. Congress, 1990; class historian Beaver Coll., Glenside, Pa., 1952. Mem. AAUW, Internat. Reading Assn., Delaware Valley Reading Assn., Keystone Reading Assn., Phila. Rose Soc. (social/hospitality chairperson 1970-85). Unitarian. Home: 520 Twin Oaks Dr Wynnewood PA 19096-2623 Office: Main Line Project Learning Brookline Sch Earlington Rd Havertown PA 19083

EARLE, MARY MARGARET, marketing executive; b. Newberry, Mich., June 26, 1947; d. William Loren and Naida Theresa (Ward) E. Student, St. Mary's Coll., Notre Dame, Ind., 1965-67. Cert. employment cons. Receptionist Western Girl World, San Francisco, 1968-69; receptionist, sec. Advanced Memory Systems, Sunnyvale, Calif., 1969-71; career cons. Qualified Personnel, Madison, Wis., 1972-75; VIP asst. Summit Sports Arena Grand Open, Houston, 1975, S. Petroleum Gp/OTC, Houston, 1976, Astrodomain Assn., Houston, 1976-77; bus. mgr. Mobile Colo TV Prodn., Houston, 1977-80; broadcast bus. affairs dir. G.D.L. & W. Adv., Houston, 1980-90; broadcast talent cons. Willis, Tex., 1990-93; mktg. cons., pvt. practice Marquette, Mich., 1993-95; pres. IXL Creative-Mktg. Excellence, Marquette, Mich., 1996—; modeling judge Page Parks Sch. Modeling, Houston, 1988-91; cons. industry/union rels. AFTRA/SAG, Houston, 1985-92. Houston mem. Fashion Group, 1989-90; sec. Bluebell Estates Assn., Willis, 1991, pres. 1992; pub. rels. vol. Women's Ctr. seminars, Houston, 1984-85. Named Disting. Salesman of Yr. Sales and Mktg. Execs., Madison, 1973, 74. Mem. Adminstrv. Mgmt. Soc. (cons. ofcl. panel 1974), Pers. Adminstrs. Soc., Am. Assn. Advt. Agys. (so. broadcast policy com.), Lake Superior Art Assn. (bd. dirs. 1996—). Home and Office: 612 County Road 480 Marquette MI 49855-9411

EARLE, SYLVIA ALICE, research biologist, oceanographer; b. Gibbstown, N.J., Aug. 30, 1935; d. Lewis Reade and Alice Freas (Richie) E. BS, Fla. State U., 1955; MA, Duke U., 1956, PhD, 1966, PhD (hon.), 1993; PhD (hon.), Monterey Inst. Internat. Studies, 1990, Ball State U., 1991, George Washington U., 1992; U. R.I., 1996, Plymouth State Coll., 1996; DSc (hon.), Duke Univ., 1993, Ripon Coll., 1994, U. Conn., 1994. Resident dir. Cape Haze Marine Lab., Sarasota, Fla., 1966-67; research scholar Radcliffe Inst., 1967-69; research fellow Farlow Herbarium, Harvard U., 1967-75, researcher, 1975—; research assoc. in botany Natural History Mus. Los Angeles County, 1970-75; research biologist, curator Calif. Acad. Scis., San Francisco, from 1976; research assoc. U. Calif., Berkeley, 1969-75; fellow in botany Natural History Mus., 1989—; chief scientist U.S. NOAA, Washington, 1990-92, advisor to the adminstr., 1992-93; founder, pres., CEO, bd. dirs. Deep Ocean Tech., Inc., Oakland, Calif., 1981-90; founder, pres., CEO Deep Ocean Engring., Oakland, 1982-90, bd. dirs., 1992—; bd. dir. Dresser Industries. Author: Exploring the Deep Frontier, 1980, Sea Change, 1995; editor: Scientific Results of the Tektite II Project, 1972-75; forward to Photographs from the World's Greatest Underwater Photographers, 1993; contbr. 100 articles to profl. jours. Trustee World Wildlife Fund U.S., 1976-82, mem. coun., 1984—; trustee World Wildlife Fund Internat., 1979-81, mem. coun., 1981—; trustee Charles A. Lindbergh Fund, pres., 1990—; trustee Ctr. Marine Conservation, 1992—, Perry Found., chmn., 1993—; mem. coun. Internat. Union for Conservation of Nature, 1979-81; corp. mem. Woods Hole Oceanographic Inst.; mem. Nat. Adv. Com. on Oceans and Atmosphere, 1980-94. Recipient Conservation Svc. award U.S. Dept. Interior, 1970, Boston Sea Rovers award, 1972, 79, Nogi award Underwater Soc. Am., 1976, Conservation Svc. award Calif. Acad. Sci., 1979, Lowell Thomas award Explorer's Club, medal, 1996, Order of Golden Ark Prince Netherlands, 1980, David B. Stone medal New Eng. Aquarium, 1989, Gold medal Soc. Women Geographers, medal Radcliffe Coll., 1990, Pacon Internat. award, 1992, Dirs. award Natural Resources Coun. Am., 1992, Washburn award Boston Mus. Sci., 1995; named Woman of Yr. L.A. Times, 1970, Scientist of Yr., Calif. Mus. Sci. and Industry, 1981. Fellow AAAS, Marine Tech. Soc., Calif. Acad. Scis., Explorers Club, Calif. Acad. Sci.; mem. Internat. Phycological Soc. (sec. 1974-80), Phycological Soc. Am., Am. Soc. Ichthyologists and Herpetologists, Am. Inst. Biol. Scis., Brit. Phycological Soc., Ecol. Soc. Am., Internat. Soc. Plant Taxonomists, Explorers Club (fellow, bd. dirs. 1989—, hon.). Home: 12812 Skyline Blvd Oakland CA 94619-3125 Office: Deep Ocean Engring 1431 Doolittle Dr San Leandro CA 94577-2225*

EARLEY, KATHLEEN SANDERS, municipal official; b. Ortonville, Minn., Jan. 14, 1946; d. Robert E. and Shirley C. (Stansfield) Sanders; m. Jack L. Earley; children: Michael, Ralph. BA in English, Carroll Coll., Waukesha, Wis., 1975; student, Wright State U., 1974-75, 78-79; postgrad., Ariz. State U., 1985, 90. In accounts receivable Pickett Industries, Inc., Santa Barbara, Calif., 1969-71; in customer svc. Vernay Labs. Inc., Yellow Springs, Ohio, 1972-76; contracts adminstr. Western Gear, Flight Systems, Jamestown, N.D., 1977-78; adminstrv. asst. City of Fairborn, Ohio, 1978-79; new student coord. DeVry Inst. Tech., Phoenix, 1979-80; adminstrv. asst. City of Mesa, Ariz., 1980-90; asst. to city mgr. City of Big Bear Lake, Calif., 1990-92; budget & mgmt. analyst Coconino County, Flagstaff, Ariz., 1992-94; adminstrv. asst. Lockwood Greene Engrs., Cin., 1994-96; city adminstr. City of Indian Springs, Ohio, 1996—; mem. staff Big Bear Lake Film Commn., 1990-92. Editor: Earley Stop Smoking Plan, 1987, Earley Approach to Hatha Yoga, 1988, Earley's Customer Service, 1988; author: (poetry) Into the Night, 1967. Chair bd. dirs. Mesa Leadership Tng. and Devel. Alumni Assn., 1985; chair com. Mesa Community Coun., 1986; mem. Comty. Coun., Pleasant Ridge, Ohio, 1996. Mem. Internat. City/County Mgmt. Assn., League of Calif. Cities, Mcpl. Mgmt. Assts. So. Calif., Ariz. Mcpl. Mgmt. Assts. (sec. 1983), Calif. Assn. Pub. Info. Ofcls., Pub. Risk Mgmt. Assn., Gov. Fin. Officers Assn., Mesa Red Tape Toastmasters (charter mem., adminstrv. v.p. 1987, pres. 1989, 1st Place Area Speech Contest 1990). Home: 5881 Mindy Dr Indian Springs OH 45011 Office: City of Indian Springs 6032 Morris Rd Indian Springs OH 45011

EARLY, JUDITH K., program evaluation director; b. Evansville, Ind., 1954; d. Forrest M. and Dorothea E. Early. BA, Brescia Coll., 1976; MS, So. Ill. U., 1985, RhD, 1991. Cert. vocat. evaluator. Work activity supr. So. Ind. Rehab. Svcs., Inc., Boonville, 1976-78; vocat. evaluator Evansville Assn. for Retarded Citizens, 1978-85; vocat. evaluator Evaluation and Developmental Ctr., Carbondale, Ill., 1985-88; grad. asst., program evaluator So. Ill. U., Carbondale, 1988-90, rsch. and teaching asst., 1990-91; exec. dir. Albion Fellow Bacon Ctr., Evansville, Ind., 1991-93; family svcs. dir. Goodwill Family Ctr., Evansville, 1993-95, program evaluation dir., 1995-96, dir., 1996—. Contbr. articles to profl. publs. Bd. dirs. So. Ill. Ctr. for Ind. Living, Carbondale, 1990-91; bd. dirs., youth worker 1st United Meth. Ch., Carbondale, 1989-91; v.p. Altrusa of Evansville, 1993-94; bd. dirs. Youth as Resources, 1995—; chmn. Transitional Svcs., Inc., Human Rights Com., 1992—. Mem. ACA, AAUW, Nat. Rehab. Assn. (accessibility site surveyor 1990—), Vocat. Evaluation and Work Adjustment Assn. (chmn. student affairs com. 1988-90, Student Lit. award 1987), Ill. Rehab. Assn. (bd. dirs. 1989-91), Ill. Vocat. Evaluation and Work Adjustment Assn. (chmn. mem. 1989-91, pres. 1991—, Disting. Svc. award 1989), Am. Assn. Mental Retardation, Assn. Retarded Citizens, Kiwanis (sec. North Park chpt. 1993-94). Office: Goodwill Family Ctr 1351 W Buena Vista Rd Evansville IN 47710-3338

EARLY, LOUISE BEALL, physical education educator; b. Cumberland, Md., Dec. 27, 1950; d. Raymond and Louise (Cornachia) Beall; m. Tom Raymond Early, June 23, 1973; children: Christina, Patricia. AA, Allegany C.C., Cumberland, Md., 1970; BA, Fairmont (W.Va.) State Coll., 1972; MS in Edn., Va. Poly. Inst. and State U., 1977. Phys. edn. tchr. Woodberry, Stonewall, Bellview, Danville, Va., 1973-74, Taylor Middle Sch., Danville, 1974-81, 84-94; phys. edn. tchr. Bonner Jr. High Sch., Danville, 1981-84, health and phys. edn. instr., 1994—; boys and girls swim coach George Washington H.S., Danville, 1990—. Contbr. articles to profl. jours. Treas. PTA, Danville, 1989; beautification chair Taylor Sch., Danville, 1988-90; sponsor/dir. Jump Rope for Heart, Danville, 1974-94; dir. Children's Theatre, Danville, 1989-90; participant Am. Heart Assn., Danville, 1974-94; runner Chief of Police, Danville, 1991; participant/leader Adventurers, Danville, 1990-94, ARC, 1970-94; tchr. Ascension Luth. Ch., Danville, 1973-94; leader Va. Skyline Girl Scouts Coun., 1994. Named WBTM Woman of the Day, WBTM Radio Sta./Girl Scouts U.S., 1989-90; Academic Booster Club grantee, 1991; named Va. Secondary Health Educator of Yr., 1995, K-12 So. Dist. Health Educator of the Yr., 1995-96. Mem. AAHPERD, Va. Assn. Health, Phys. Edn., Recreation and Dance (dir. necrology com. 1992-94), Va. H.S. Coaches Assn., Danville Edn. Assn., U.S. Swimming Assn., Delta Kappa Gamma (dir. 1990-94, sec. 1994). Home: 195 Howeland Cir Danville VA 24541-3715 Office: Bonner Jr High Sch 300 Apollo Ave Danville VA 24540-4227

EARNEST, CARMELLA LYNN, art educator, artist; b. Welch, W.Va., Oct. 4, 1946; d. Melville McKinney and Irene Delores (Cardea) E. BA, Queens Coll., Charlotte, N.C., 1968; MFA, George Washington U., 1970. Social worker W.Va. Dept. Welfare, Welch, 1964-65; microscopic illustrator NSF Grants Queens Coll., Charlotte, 1966-68; art dept. asst. Queens Coll., Charlotte, 1967-68; biomed. abstractor Tracor, Washington, 1969-70; pvt.

practice artist Fine Arts Studio, Chgo., 1970-74; farm owner, operator Old Schoolhouse Hollow Farm, Griffithsville, W.Va., 1974—; prof. fine arts So. W.Va. C.C., Logan, 1974—, lead tchr. humanities dept., 1991-92; artist-in-residence Huntington (W.Va.) Galleries, 1970-74; guest faculty, lectr. W.Va. State Coll., 1970-74; workshop presenter Cabell County Bd. Edn., Huntington, W.Va., 1970-74; pub. awareness cons. W.Va. Dept. Culture and History, 1976; mem. editl. adv. bd. Collegiate Press, Alta Loma, Calif.; instr. and cons. Talented in Hamlin, W.Va. Sch. Sys.; lectr. Spkrs. Bur. of W.Va. Dept. of Humanities Inst.; resource cons. W.Va. U. Ext. Svc.; environ. design cons. Lincoln Sch. Design, Hamlin, W.Va.; resource cons. State of W.Va. Ednl. TV Networks; spkr./lectr. in field. Exhibitions include Charleston (W.Va.) Town Ctr. Gallery, Nat. Bank Commerce, Charleston, Huntington Gallery, Genesis, Huntington, Mary Washington Coll., Washington, Dimock Gallery, Washington, Caroll Hall Gallery, Charlotte, Lift Hand Gallery, Bluefield, W.Va., others. Mem. AAUW, ACLU, NOW. Home: Old Schoolhouse Hollow Farm Star Rt 1 Box 128 Griffithsville WV 25521 Office: SWVCC Box 2900 Mount Gay WV 25601

EARWOOD, BARBARA TIRRELL, artist; b. Quincy, Mass., July 18, 1920; d. Irving John and Vernice Estelle (Carraway) Tirrell; m. Armer Fred Earwood, May 30, 1942; children: Elsie E. Belk, Melinda E. Crain, Edward A. Student, Angelo State U., 1968-69; grad., Washington Sch. Art, 1974, North Light Art Sch., 1989; postgrad., Robert E. Wood Sch., 1978-80. 4th v.p. San Angelo (Tex.) Art Club, 1973-74; pres. Big Country Art Assn., Abilene, Tex.; pres. Region XVII Tex. Fine Arts Assn.; bd. dirs. West Tex. Art Guild, Sonora, 1992-95; tchr. Barbara Earwood Art Sch., Sonora, 1970-93. Permanent exhbts. include First Nat. Bank Sonora; artist Girl Scouts Am. pamphlet. Leader Girl Scouts Am., Sonora, 1952-53. Recipient State citation Tex. Fine Arts Assn., 1972, 76, Purchase prize, 1975, Best of Show award San Angelo Stock Show, 1973. Mem. Tex. Watercolor Soc. (signature mem., Purple Sage, Russell Rogers Purchase prize for transparent watercolor 1974), Southwestern Watercolor Soc. (signature), San Antonio Watercolor Group (signature). Episcopalian. Home: PO Box 1475 Hwy 277 S Country Rd 103 Sonora TX 76950

EASLEY, CHRISTA BIRGIT, nurse, researcher; b. Berlin, Apr. 30, 1941; came to U.S., 1966; d. Albert and Marianne (Uhlmann) Baldauf; m. Loyd Allen Easley, Oct. 23, 1964 (widowed Dec. 1993). Degree in nursing, Pawlow Coll. of Nursing, Aue, Fed. Republic of Germany, 1959; BS, NYU, Albany, 1978; MBA, Cen. Mich. U., 1979; EDS, Ctrl. Mo. U., 1983; PhD, Kensington U., Glensdale, Calif., 1983. With placement sect. Sembach, A.B., Fed. Republic of Germany, 1972-73, suggestion program mgr., 1973-74; adminstrv. clk. Lajes Field, A.B., Terceira, Acores, Portugal, 1975-78, incentive awards and suggestion program mgr., 1978-79; intern Cen. Mo. State U., Warrensburg, 1980-81; instr. in bus. overseas campus Cen. Tex. Coll../Yokota, A.B., Japan, 1983; instr. Tokyo Ctr. for Lang. and Culture, 1981-83; tchr. dept. of def. Yokota Dept. of Def., Yokota AFB, Japan, 1981-84; tax examiner IRS, Austin, Tex., 1984-86; clin. rsch. coord. HealthQuest Rsch., Austin, 1987-94; v.p. Austin Clin. Rsch., 1994—. Treas. Am. Sch. System PTA, Acores, 1978-79; precinct chmn. Austin Rep. Com., 1988—. Mem. Assocs. of Clin. Pharmacology, Am. Assn. Translators, AAUW, Sigma Tau Delta. Methodist. Home: 12422 Deer Trak Austin TX 78727-5746 Office: Austin Clin Rsch Inc Creek Plaza # 202 8705 Shoal Creek Austin TX 78757

EASLEY, JUNE ELLEN PRICE, genealogist; b. Chgo., June 7, 1924; d. Fred E. and Bernadette (Mailloux) Price; m. Raymond Dale Easley, Dec. 24, 1945. Student, McCormack Sch. Commerce, Englewood Jr. Coll., Chgo. Lic. genealogist Assn. Profl. Genealogists. Statis. clk. Arthur Andersen & Co., Chgo., 1968-74; corr. sec. ICG R.R., Chgo., 1974-86; self-employed genealogist-computers Arlington Heights, Ill., 1986-94, Mountain Home, Ark., 1994—. Contbr. religion articles to Daily Herald, 1991; editor romance stories, 1990—. Mem. DAR (auditor-treas. Chgo. chpt. 1981-82, rec. sec. Chgo. chpt. 1982-88, Mountain Home ROTC 1995 , publicity chmn. 1996—), Huguenot Soc., Nat. Soc. R.R. Bus. Women (newsletter editor 1991—), Northwest Suburban Coun. Genealogists (pres. 1988-90, corr. sec. 1990-94), Baxter County Hist. Soc., Daus. of War of 1812. Republican. Methodist. Home and Office: 1601 Franklin Ave Mountain Home AR 72653-2041

EASLEY, LOYCE ANNA, painter; b. Weatherford, Okla., June 28, 1918; d. Thomas Webster and Anna Laura (Sanders) Rogers; m. Mack Easley, Nov. 17, 1939; children: June Elizabeth, Roger. BFA, U. Okla., 1943; postgrad., 1947-49; student, Art Students League, N.Y.C., 1977; postgrad., Santa Fe Inst. Fine Arts, 1985. Tchr. Pub. Sch., Okmulgee, Okla., 1946-47, Hobbs, N.Mex., 1947-49; tchr. painting N.Mex. Jr. Coll., Hobbs, 1965-80; tchr. Art Workshops in N.Mex., Okla., Wyoming. Numerous one-woman shows and group exhbns. in mus., univs. and galleries, including Gov.'s Gallery, Santa Fe, Selected Artists, N.Y.C., Roswell (N.Mex.) Mus., N.Mex. State U., Las Cruces, West Tex. Mus., Tex. Tech U., Lubbock; represented in permanent collections USAF Acad., Colorado Springs, Colo., Roswell Mus., Carlsbad (N.Mex.) Mus., Coll. Santa Fe, N.Mex. Supreme Ct, also other pvt. and pub. collections; featured in S.W. Art and Santa Fe mag., 1981, 82. Named Disting. Former Student, U. Okla. Art Sch., 1963; nominated for Gov's. award in Art, N.Mex., 1988. Mem. N.Mex. Artists Equity (lifetime mem. 1963). Democrat. Presbyterian. Home: 10909 Country Club Dr NE Albuquerque NM 87111-6548

EASLEY, MARJORIE MAE, legal administrator; b. Fulton County, Ill., Mar. 6, 1935; d. Calvin Leo and Rita Jean (Henderson) Bainter; m. David L. Easley, Apr. 10, 1954 (dec. May 1992); children: James David, Joseph Leon, Julie Ann Easley Smick. Grad. high sch. Legal sec. Arthur D. Young, Atty., Lewistown, Ill., 1954-56, Martin M. Love, Atty., Lewistown, Ill., 1964-78; clk., recorder Fulton County, Lewistown, Ill., 1978-82; data processing cons. Fidlar Chambers Co., Moline, Ill., 1982-87; legal adminstr. Davis & Morgan Law Firm, Peoria, Ill., 1987-89, Husch & Eppenberger Law Firm, Peoria, Ill., 1989—. Mem. Ctrl. Ill. Legal Adminstrs. (treas. 1991-92, sec. 1995-96), Nat. Assn. Cert. Profl. Secs. (cert. profl. sec.). Republican. Presbyterian. Home: 14425 E Depler Springs Hwy Lewistown IL 61542-8435 Office: Husch & Eppenberger Law Firm 101 SW Adams St # 800 Peoria IL 61602-1335

EASON, ALYCE L., psychology educator; b. Huntsville, Ala., Oct. 14; d. Katie Eason. BS, Tenn. State U., 1977, EdD, 1996; MA, Ohio State U., 1979. Counselor, coord. Hazard (Ky.) C.C., 1979-85; asst. prof. psychology Austin Peay State U., Clarksville, Tenn., 1985—. Advisor African Am. Students, Clarksville, Tenn., 1989-91, Omega Psi Phi Fraternity, Clarksville, 1991-93; chair African Am. Planning Com., Clarksville, 1992; vol. various polit. campaigns, Nashville, 1990, 94; judge Tenn. Acad. Decathlon, Clarksville, 1992, Tenn. H.S. Speech/Drama Championship, Clarksville, 1992. Named Facilitator of Yr., Focus, 1992; recipient Citizenship award Omege Psi Phi, 1992, Unsing Hero award for perseverance The Time is Now, 1995. Mem. ACA, Internat. Black Women's Congress (life), Assn. Social/Behavioral Sci. Inc. (life, exec. bd. 1995—), Tenn. Counseling Assn., Tenn. Assn. Devel. Educator (Tenn. Developmental Educator of Yr. 1990), Phi Delta Kappa. Home: 3521 Geneva Cir Nashville TN 38209 Office: Austin Peay State U College St PO Box 4476 Clarksville TN 37044

EASON, BECKY JANE, university administrator; b. Excelsior Springs, Md., Nov. 6, 1965; d. Warren Dudley and Virgie Lee (Chiles) Alexander; m. Douglas Charles Eason, Dec. 31, 1988. BA in English, U. Kans., 1988, MA in English, 1990, postgrad., 1990-93. Adminstrv. asst. ot the chair English dept. U. Kans., Lawrence, 1990-93; asst. to the dean Sch. of Edn. U. Kans., Lawrence, 1994—; ex officio mem. Sch. of Edn. Nat. Adv. Bd., 1994—. Big sister Big Bros./Big Sisters, Lawrence, 1996; vol. Planned Parenthood, Lawrence, 1994. Mem. NOW, MLA, Humane Soc. of the U.S. Democrat. Methodist. Home: 3708 Overland Ct Lawrence KS 66049 Office: Sch of Edn U Kans 108 Bailey Hall Lawrence KS 66045-2330

EAST, NANCY MCKINLEY, private primary music educator; b. Harlan, Ky., Mar. 5, 1935; d. John H. and Nina (Howard) McKinley; children: Marie, Sandy, John, Nancy Elizabeth. BS, U. Ky., 1957, Kennesaw State Coll., 1984. Cert. piano tchr., Ga. Home svc. dir. Green River Rural Electric, Owensboro, Ky., 1972—; pvt. practice tchr. piano, kindermusik Marietta, Ga., 1989—. Past pres. Guild of the Cobb Symphony Orch., Hickory Walk Home Owners Assn.; pres. Episcopal Ch. women St. James Episcopal Ch.; Marietta convocation rep. Atlanta Diocese. Mem. Cobb County Music Tchrs. Assn. (past pres., program chmn.), Ga. Music Tchrs. Assn. (v.p.), Greater Atlanta Music Alliance (sec.), Am. Matthay Assn., Phi Upsilon Omicron, Sigma Alpha Iota (Outstanding Chpt. Mem. award). Home and Office: 360 Hickory Walk Marietta GA 30064-3090

EASTERLY, LINDA ROSE, health care administrator; b. Dayton, Ohio, Mar. 22, 1958; d. Richard George and Mary Ann (Schmid) W.; m. Glenn Charles Easterly, Aug. 1, 1984; 1 stepchild, Elizabeth. BSN, Wright State U., 1980; MS, Ga. Coll., 1988. RN, Ohio. Accounts dir. in mktg. Anchor Foods Ltd., Swindon, U.K., 1989-91; staff nurse labor and delivery East Montgomery (Ala.) Med. Ctr., 1991-92, dir. obstetrical svcs., 1992-94; DON Perry (Ga.) Hosp., 1994—. Chairperson Leadership Perry. Capt. USAF, 1981-88. Mem. NAFE, Nat. League Nursing, Healthcare Fin. Mgrs. Assn., Ga. Nursing Assn. (dist. 17 pres. 1994—), Rotary Internat., Am. Orgn. Nurse Execs., Perry C. of C. Office: Perry Hosp PO Box 1004 Perry GA 31069

EASTIN, CHRISTINA MARIE, elementary school educator; b. Dallas, May 1, 1969; d. Jerry Lynn and Cheryl Christina (Fox) Neel; m. Brian Patrick Eastin, May 23, 1992; 1 child, Benjamin Harrison. BA, U. Tex., Arlington, 1992. Cert. tchr., Tex., ESL. Nanny Dr. Ann Wildermann, Arlington, Tex., 1987-88; waitress Steak-N-Ale, Arlington, 1988-89, Atchafalaya River Cafe, Arlington, 1989-96; tchr. 4th grade, ESL tchr. Arlington Ind. Sch. Dist., 1992—; liason sci. Thornton Elem. Sch., Arlington, 1992; sponsor Student Coun., 1994-96. Vol. Meals on Wheels, Arlington, 1990-91; mem. Coll. Reps., U. Tex. Arlington, 1991-92. Mem. Assn. Tchrs. and Profl. Educators, Assn. for Childhood Edn. Internat., Tex. Reading Assn., Arlington Rep. Club. Baptist. Home: 1305 Sonora Ct Arlington TX 76012-1765 Office: Thornton Elem Sch 2301 E Park Row Dr Arlington TX 76010-4887

EASTMAN, CAROLYN ANN, microbiology company executive; b. Potsdam, N.Y., Sept. 8, 1946; d. Frank Orvis and Irene (Rheaume) Eastman. BS in Biology, Nazareth Coll., 1968; AAS in Photography, Rochester Inst. Tech., 1976. Technician U. Rochester, N.Y., 1968-69; chemist Castle/Sybron, Rochester, 1969-79; owner, v.p. Sterilization Tech. Svcs., Rush, N.Y., 1979—; owner Fairfield Cosmetics, Rush, 1986—; ptnr. EFC Properties, 1983—; owner Microdispersions, Inc., 1988—, Medisperse L.P., 1988—; owner STS Duotek Inc., 1991—, STS Particles Inc., 1991—, STS Biopolymers Inc., 1991—, STS Real Estate Co., LLC, 1995—. Contbr. articles to profl. jours.; patentee in field. Recipient various awards for photography, sculpture and painting. Mem. NOW, Assn. for Advancement of Med. Instrumentation, Sierra Club, Henrietta Art Club. Democrat. Roman Catholic. Home: 6 Genesee St Scottsville NY 14546-1310 Office: 7500 W Henrietta Rd Rush NY 14543-9790

EASTMAN, DONNA KELLY, composer, music educator; b. Denver, Sept. 26, 1945; d. Donald Lewis and Frances Marie (Smith) Kelly; m. John Bernard Eastman, July 1, 1973; children: Jonathan Kelly, James Alan; stepchildren: Barbara Kathleen, Sally Toye. B Music Edn., U. Colo., 1967; MA, U. Md., 1973, D Musical Arts, 1992. Pvt. studio tchr., coach, 1960—; choral dir. Dept. Def. Overseas Schs., Okinawa, Japan, 1970-72; dir. Choraleers Choral Ensemble, Stuttgart, Germany, 1974-76, Bangkok (Thailand) Music Soc. Ensemble and Madrigal Singers, 1982-84; instr. in music No. Va. C.C., Alexandria, 1986-89; creator, pianist, vocalist Am. Music Programs for U.S. Mission, Thailand, 1981-84; vis. asst. prof. Ill. Wesleyan U., Bloomington, 1994. Composer choral, orchestral, opera, vocal/instrumental solo and chamber, and electronic works; recs. include Soc. of Composers, Inc., Living Music Series; Piano Works on Contemporary American Eclectic Music for Piano; contbr. to jours. Fellow Charles Ives Ctr. for Am. Music, 1990, 93, Ragdale Found., 1991, Va. Ctr. for Creative Arts, 1991-96; recipient Internat. Composition award Composers' Guild, 1991, Internat. Piano Composition award Roodeport Internat. Eisteddfod, South Africa, 1991, Glad-Robinson-Youse Composition award Nat. Fedn. Music Clubs, 1992, Internat. Choral Composition award Florilège Vocal de Tours, France, 1995. Mem. Soc. for Electro-Acoustic Music in the U.S., Internat. Alliance for Women in Music, Soc. of Composers, Inc., Nat. Mus. Women in Arts (charter), Broadcast Music, Inc., Phi Kappa Phi, Pi Kappa Lambda, Sigma Alpha Iota. Home: 6812 Dina Leigh Ct Springfield VA 22153

EASTMAN, TAMARA JANE, private investigator; b. Ft. Lee, Va., Apr. 8, 1961; d. William Charles and Shirley Frances (Auen) E. Assoc. degree, Dominion Bus. Inst., Colonial Heights, Va., 1982; student, John Tyler Coll., Chester, Va., 1992—, Am. Coll., Marylebone, London, 1994. Registered pvt. investigator. Sec. Dept. Corrections, Richmond, Va., 1982-86; pvt. security cons. Richmond, Va., 1986-94; intern criminal rsch. Met. Police, London, 1994; pvt. investigator Dept. Criminal Justice, London, 1994—. Contbr. articles to profl. publs. Recipient S.G.A. Jefferson Cup, 1992; V.C.C. scholar, 1994. Mem. Nat. Assn. Profl. Investigators Internat., Union Students, Profl. Secs. Internat. Democrat. Baptist. Office: Quardian Pvt Investigations 2530 Profl Rd Richmond VA 23235

EASTMAN-ROAN, CYNTHIA, artist; b. Toronto, Ont., Can., Oct. 22, 1944; d. Alexander Coombs and Mary Ann (McKelvie) E.; m. Kenneth D. Roan, Dec. 28, 1961. Watercolor artist and miniature painter. Artist: (book) California Art Review, 1989, (mag.) Seafood Leader, 1990, Dolls House World, 1990, (book) Miniature Makers and Their Marks, 1996, Miniature Showcase mag., numerous others, Nutshell News mag. (cover 1996); one-woman shows include Sears Savs. Bank, Martinez, Calif., 1982, 84, Benecia Comm. Arts Gallery, Calif., 1987, Hammons Gallery of Fine Art, Kensington, Calif., 1988-90, Bayside Gallery, Benecia, 1991; group shows include A Little Gallery of Mont Alto, Pa., 1995, Marin Soc. of Artists Gallery, Ross, Calif., Miniature Art Soc. Fla. annuals. Recipient numerous awards Soc. Western Artists, Calif. Watercolor Assn., numerous juried invitation shows, including Best of Show Invitational award Calif. State Fair, 1993, merit award Calif. State Fair, 1996, Alameda County Fair, 1993, Nat. League Am. Pen Women, 1989, Wine Country Artists, 1995. Studio: 4355 Redwood Dr Oakley CA 94561

EASTWOOD, SUSAN, medical scientific editor; b. Glens Falls, N.Y., Jan. 2, 1943; d. John J. and Della Eastwood; m. Raymond A. Berry. BA, U. Colo., 1964. Diplomate Bd. Editors in Life Scis. Adminstr. rsch. assoc. Depts. Psychol., Psychiat., Stanford (Calif.) U., 1965-68; prin., tchr. Colegio Capitan Correa, Arecibo, P.R., 1968-70; sr. editor dept. lab. medicine U. Calif., San Francisco, 1971-77, prin. analyst sci. publs. dept. neurol. surgery and Brain Tumor Rsch. Ctr., 1977—; cons. March of Dimes Calif. Birth Defects Monitoring Program, Emeryville, 1988—; coord. Asilomar Working Group on Recommendations for Reporting Clinical Trials in Biomed. Lit., 1993-96. Collaborating editor: Current Neurosurgical Practice, 1984-91, Brain tumor biology and therapy, 1984; editor: Brain Tumors: A Guide, 1992; author: Guidelines on Research Data and Manuscripts, 1989. Recipient Pres. award Am. Med. Writers Assn., Bethesda, Md., 1989, Chancellors Outstanding Achievement award U. Calif., San Francisco, 1989, 94, Cert. of award Nat. Brain Tumor Found., 1992, Am. Soc. Journalists and Authors, 1992. Fellow Am. Med. Writers Assn.; mem. European Assn. Sci. Editors, Internat. Fedn. Sci. Editors, N.Y. Acad. Scis., Coun. Biology Educators (v.p. 1995-96, pres. 1996-97). Office: U Calif Dept Neurosurgery M-787 505 Parnassus Ave San Francisco CA 94143-0112

EATON, DOREL, elementary school educator; b. Atlantic City, N.J., Sept. 8; d. Ethel Donovan Joyce; divorced; 1 child, Melissa Elizabeth Eaton-Midgley. BA in Edn., U. Fla.; MS, Barry U., 1973; Design degree, Sch. for Interior Design, Miami Shores, Fla., 1976. Cert. guidance counseling, elem. educator, Fla. Elem. edn. tchr. Dade County Pub. Sch., Miami. Art displayed in numerous galleries including The Curzon Art Gallery of Boca Raton (Fla.) Country Club, Bill Nessen's Showroom/Design Ctr. of the Americas, Dania, Fla.; contbr. Book Nat. Coalition Against Pornography. Mem. MADD, Nat. Coalition for Protection of Children and Families, Concerned Women of Am., U.S. Holocaust Meml. Mus. (charter mem.), Morality in Media, Inc., Am. Fedn. for Decency, Prison Fellowship, Design Ctr. of the Ams., People for the Ethical Treatment of Animals, Enough is Enough, Physicians Com. for Responsible Medicine, Fla. Right to Life.

EATON, DORLA DEAN See KEMPER, DORLA DEAN

EATON, ELIZABETH SUSAN, middle school educator, jazz musician; b. Norfolk, Va., Apr. 13, 1947; d. Russell Samuel and Miriam Kathleen (Kindermann) E. BA, Marquette U., 1970; MS, U. Wis., Milw., 1973; PhD equivalency, Wis. Coll. Conservatory Music, 1979. Cert. tchr. grades 1-6, Wis., reading tchr. grades 1-8, Wis. Reading tchr. grades 1-6 Garfield Elem. Sch., Milw., 1973-77; reading tchr. grades 6-8 King Mid. Sch. Gifted & Talented, Milw., 1979-82; 2d grade tchr. Elm Creative Arts Elem. Sch., Milw., 1983-84; English & social studies tchr., jazz studies tchr. Roosevelt Mid. Sch. Creative Arts, Milw., 1984-89; reading tchr. grades 6-8 Morse Mid. Sch. Gifted & Talented, Milw., 1979-82, English tchr., 1990-94, yoga tchr., 1993-95, reading tchr., 1994-96; chmn., advisor Nat. Jr. Honor Soc., Milw., 1991-94; co-dir. Morse Drama Club, 1991-93, advisor, mem., performer Fin Arts Week Morse com., 1991-96. Prodr., vocalist, lyricist, arranger (CD and cassette recs.) It's Time Now, 1995. Bd. trustees Hist. Pabst Theatre, Milw., 1972-79; dir. asst., vol. Summerfest World Festivals, Inc., Milw., 1969-71; vol., fund raiser Sta. WYMS Jazz Radio, 1995. Mem. SYDA Yoga, Inc., Wis. Arts and Music, Inc., Pi Lambda Theta. Home: 1224 N Prospect Ave Milwaukee WI 53202-3001 Office: Morse Mid Sch Gifted & Talented 4601 N 84th St Milwaukee WI 53225-4990

EATON, NANCY RUTH LINTON, librarian, dean; b. Berkeley, Calif., May 2, 1943; d. Don Thomas and Lena Ruth (McClellan) Linton; m. Edward Arthur Eaton III, June 19, 1965 (div. 1980). AB, Stanford U., 1965; MLS, U. Tex., 1968, postgrad., 1969. Cataloger U. Tex. Library, Austin, 1968-71, head MARC unit, 1971-72, asst. to dir., 1972-74; automation librarian SUNY, Stony Brook, 1974-76; head tech. services Atlanta Pub. Library, 1976-82; dir. libraries U. Vt., Burlington, 1982-89; dean libr. svcs. Iowa State U., Ames, 1989—; bd. dirs. Ctr. for Rsch. Librs., 1988-92, chair, 1989-90; del. users' coun., mem. exec. com. Online Computer Libr. Ctr., Inc., Dublin, Ohio, 1980-82, 86-88, trustee, 1987—, chair bd. trustees 1992—; mgr. Nat. Agrl. Text Digitalizing Project, 1986-92; bd. dirs. New Eng. Libr. Network, 1987-89. Co-author: Optical Information Systems: Implementation Issues for Libraries, 1988.; co-editor: A Cataloging Sampler, 1971, Book Selection Policies in American Libraries, 1972; contbr. articles to profl. jours. U.S. Office of Edn. post-master's fellow, 1969; Dept. Edn. Title II-C grantee, 1985, 87, 88, Title II-D grantee, 1992-95. Mem. ALA, AAUW, Libr. and Info. Tech. Assn. (pres. 1984-85, bd. dirs. 1980-86), Assn. Rsch. Librs. (bd. dirs. 1994—), Iowa Libr. Assn. Democrat. Home: 3320 Kingman Rd Ames IA 50014-3943 Office: Iowa State Univ 302 Park Ames IA 50011-2140

EATON, PATRICIA P., performing company executive; m. Leonard Eaton; children: Leslie, Pamela, Alex. Water and sewer commr. City of Tulsa, 1980-86; mem. exec. com. Arts and Humanities Coun., Tulsa, Leadership Tulsa, Leadership Okla.; mem. exec. com. Tulsa Opera, exec. dir., 1995—; exec. dir. Okla. Water Resources Bd.; cabinet sec. for environ. State of Okla. Govt.; interim dir. Dept. Environ. Quality, Oklahoma City; creator of Ark.-Okla. Environ. Task Force, Gov.'s Ill. River Task Force. Office: Tulsa Opera Chapman Music Hall 1610 S Boulder Ave Tulsa OK 74119-4408

EATON, PAULINE, artist; b. Neptune, N.J., Mar. 20, 1935; d. Paul A. and Florence Elizabeth (Rogers) Friedrich; m. Charles Adams Eaton, June 15, 1957; children: Gregory, Eric, Paul, Joy. BA, Dickinson Coll., 1957; MA, Northwestern U., 1958. Lic. instr., Calif. Instr., Mira Costa Coll., Oceanside, Calif., 1980-82, Idyllwild Sch. Music and Arts, Calif., 1983—; juror, demonstrator numerous art socs. Recipient award Haywood (Calif.) Area Forum for the Arts, 1986. Exhibited one-woman shows Nat. Arts Club, N.Y.C., 1977, Designs Recycled Gallery, Fullerton, Calif., 1978, 80, 84, San Diego Art Inst., 1980, Spectrum Gallery, San Diego, 1981, San Diego Jung Ctr., 1983, Marin Civic Ctr. Gallery, 1984, R. Mondavi Winery, 1987; group shows include Am. Watercolor Soc., 1975, 77, Butler Inst. Am. Art, Youngstown, Ohio, 1977, 78, 79, 81, NAD, 1978, N.Mex. Arts and Crafts Fair, (Best in Show award) 1994, Corrales Bosque Gallery; represented in permanent collections including Butler Inst. Am. Art, St. Mary's Coll., Md., Mercy Hosp., San Diego, Sharp Hosp., San Diego, Redlands Hosp., Riverside, 1986; work featured in books: Watercolor, The Creative Experience, 1978, Creative Seascape Painting, 1980, Painting the Spirit in Nature, 1984, Exploring Painting (Gerald Brommer); author: Crawling to the Light, An Artist in Transition, 1987. Trustee San Diego Art Inst., 1977-78, San Diego Mus. Art, 1982-83. Recipient Best of Show award N.Mex. Arts and Crafts Fair, 1994, Grumbacher award Conf. 96 Hill Country Art Ctr. Mem. Nat. Watercolor Soc. (exhibited traveling shows 1978, 79, 83, 85), Rocky Mountain Watermedia Soc. (Golden award 1979, Mustard Seed award 1983), Nat. Soc. Painters in Acrylic and Casein (hon.), Watercolor West (Strathmore award 1979, Purchase award 1986), Soc. Experimental Artists (pres. 1989-92, Nautilus Merit award 1992), Marin Arts Guild (instr. 1984-87), San Diego Watercolor Soc. (pres. 1976-77, workshop dir. 1977-80), Artists Equity (v.p. San Diego 1979-81), San Diego Artists Guild (pres. 1982-83), N.Mex. Watercolor Soc. (Grumbacher award), Western Fedn. Watercolor Socs. (chmn. 1983, 3d prize 1982, Grumbacher Gold medal 1983), West Coast Watercolor Soc. (exhbns. chmn. 1983-86, pres. 1989-92), Eastbay Watercolor Soc. (v.p. 1988-90), Soc. Layerists in Multi-Media (bd. dirs. 1992—), Corrales Bosque Gallery (charter mem., pres. 1996). Democrat. Home: 68 Hop Tree Trl Corrales NM 87048-9613

EATON, SABRINA C. E., journalist; b. N.Y.C., Mar. 5, 1965; d. Barton Denis and Anne Elizabeth (Schaeffer) Eaton. BA, U. Pa., 1985. Correspondent The Record, Hackensack, N.J., 1985-87; reporter Daily Record, Morristown, N.J., 1987-88; Washington correspondent States News Svc., Washington, 1988-90; metro reporter The Plain Dealer, Cleve., 1990-94; Washington correspondent The Plain Dealer, Washington, 1994—. Nat. Press Club, Investigative Reporters and Editors. Episcopalian. Office: The Plain Dealer Wash Bur 930 National Press Bldg Washington DC 20045

EBERLEY, HELEN-KAY, opera singer, classical record company executive, poet; b. Sterling, Ill., Aug. 3, 1947; d. William Elliott and P. (Conneely) E. MusB, Northwestern U., 1970, MusM, 1971. Chmn., pres. Eberley-Skowronski, Inc., Evanston, Ill., 1973-92; founder H.K.E. Enterprises, 1993—, pres., 1993—; circulation libr. Evanston Pub. Libr., 1995—; artistic coord. Eberley-Skowronski, Inc., 1973-92; founder EB-SKO Prodns., 1976, tchr., coach, 1976—; exec. dir., performance cons. E-S Mgmt., 1985-92; featured artist Honors Concert, Northwestern U., 1970, Master Class and guest lectr. various colls. and univs.; music lectr. rep. Harvard Club, Chgo.; numerous TV and radio talk show appearances and interviews. Operatic debut in Peter Grimes, Lyric Opera, Chgo., 1974; starred in: Cosi Fan Tutte, Le Nozze Di Figaro, Dido and Aeneas, La Boheme, Faust, Tosca, La Traviata, Falstaff, Don Giovanni, Brigadoon, others; jazz appearances with Duke Ellington, Dave Brubeck; performing artist Oglebay Opera Inst., Wheeling, W.Va., 1968, WTTW TV/PBS, Chgo., 1968; solo star in: Continental Bank Concerts, 1981-89, United Airlines-Schubert, Schumann, Brahms, Mendelssohn, Faure, Mozart, Duparc/Worf, Supersta. WFMT Radio, Chgo., 1982-90; featured artist with North Shore Concert Band, 1989; starring artist South Bend Symphony, 1990, Mo. Symphony Soc., 1990, Milw. Symphony, 1990; spl. guest artist New Studios Gala Sta. WFMT, 1995; prodr.-annotator Gentlemen Gypsy, 1978, Strauss and Szymanowski, 1979, One Sonata Each: Franck and Szymanowski, 1982; starring artist-exec. prodr. Separate But Equal, 1976, All Brahms, 1977, Opera Lady, 1978, Eberley Sings Strauss, 1980, Helen-Kay Eberley: American Girl, 1983, Helen-Kay Eberley: Opera Lady II, 1984; performed Am. and Can. nat. anthems for Chgo. Cubs Baseball Team, 1977-83, Chgo. Bears Football, 1977; also starred in numerous concert recital and symphony appearances, Europe, Can., U.S.; author: Angel's Song, 1994, The Magdaleva Poems, 1995, ChapelHeart, 1996. Docent Art Inst. Chgo.; vol. Chgo. Christian Indsl. League, Evanston Shelter for Battered Women, Rape Victim Adv., St. Joseph's Table of St. Peter's in the Loop, Chgo., Chgo. Humanities Festival VII of Ill. Humanities Coun.; mem. Mayor's founding com. Evanston Arts Coun., 1974-75; judge Ice-Skating Competition, Wilmette (Ill.) Park Dist., 1974-77, bd. dirs., 1973-77; bd. dirs. Ctr. for Voice, Chgo., 1994—. Recipient Creative and Performing Arts award Ind. Jr. Miss and South Bend Jr. Miss, 1965, Milton J. Cross award Met. Opera Guild, 1968; prize winner Met. Opera. Nat. Auditions, 1968; F.K. Weyerhauser scholar Met. Opera, 1967. Mem. People for Ethical Treatment of Animals, Am. Soc. for Prevention of Cruelty to Animals, Am. Guild Mus. Artists, Internat. Platform Assn., Whale Adoption Project, Amnesty Internat., Environ. Def. Fund, Doris Day Animal Found., Humane Soc., Greenpeace (physicians com. for responsible medicine). Clubs: St. Mary's Acad. Alumnae Assn.,

Delta Gamma. Office: HKE Enterprises 1726 Sherman Ave Evanston IL 60201-3713

EBERSOLE, PATRICIA SUE, advertising executive, design educator; b. Poughkeepsie, N.Y., Nov. 6, 1952; d. Edward and Virginia Mae (Vanderof) E. AAS, Dutchess Community Coll., Poughkeepsie, 1974; student, Art Ctr. Coll. of Design, 1976-77; BS, SUNY, 1981; MA, Syracuse U., 1993. Graphic artist So. Dutchess News, Wappingers Falls, N.Y., 1974; asst. illustrator Jarvis Studio, Westwod, Calif., 1975-78; freelance illustrator Poughkeepsie, N.Y., 1978—; graphic dir. Ulster County Coun. for the Arts, Kingston, N.Y., 1979; art dir. Diversified Creative Svcs., Kingston, 1979; graphic designer Advertiser's Graphic Svcs., Poughkeepsie, 1981-82; pres. Ebersole Graphiks, Poughkeepsie, 1982—; adj. instr. Dutchess Community Coll., 1980-87. Recipient Recognition award IBM Corp., 1987, Cert. of Excellence Silver award Strathmore Graphics Gallery, 1988, 90, Desi award Graphic Design, 1984, 88, Excellence award Printing Industries of Am., 1988, Activities award Nat. Assn. for Campus Activities, 1985, Gold and Silver awards Hudson Valley Area Mktg. Assn., Inc., 1989, 94, 95, Merit awards, 1994, Nat. Calendar Bronze award, 1991, Bronze award 1995, award of Excellence Am. Econ. Devel. Coun., 1992, Notable Merit award FPG, Internat., 1992, Gold award Advt. Club of Westchester, 1994. Mem. Greater So. Dutchess C. of C. Office: Ebersole Graphiks 9 High Ridge Rd Hopewell Junction NY 12533-5560

EBERSOLE, PRISCILLA PIER, mental health nurse, geriatrics nurse; b. Salem, Oreg., Aug. 17, 1928; d. Joseph H. and Miriam E. (Holder) Pierre; m. Raymond V. Ebersole, May 14, 1948; children: Lorraine, Raymond, Randolph, Elisabeth. AA, Coll. San Mateo, 1965; BS, San Francisco State U., 1971; MS, U. Calif., San Francisco, 1973; PhD, Columbia Pacific U., 1986. RN, Calif.; BRN; VSC. Instr. Chabot Coll., Hayward, Calif., 1973, U. So. Calif., L.A., 1977-80; prof. nursing San Francisco State U., 1973—; vis. prof. Cellar Endowed Chair in Gerontology Case Western Res. U., Cleve. 1988. Editor Geriatric Nursing Jour. Named Alumni of Yr. San Francisco State U., 1987. Mem. ANA, ASA, GSA, AGHE, WIN. Home: 2790 Rollingwood Dr San Bruno CA 94066-2610 Office: San Francisco State U San Francisco CA 94132

EBEST, SALLY BARR, educator; b. Atlanta, Jan. 5, 1950; d. Charles Lee and Helen Lenore (Morris) Barr; m. Jack Warren Reagan, June 17, 1972 (div. Oct. 1977); children: Benjamin Joel Reagan, Jeffrey Jackson Reagan; m. Ronald John Ebest Jr., June 11, 1994. BA, Ball State U., 1972, MA, 1979; PhD, Ind. U., 1984. Assoc. instr. Ind.-Purdue U. at Indpls., 1979-81; asst. prof. Drake U., Des Moines, 1984-87; asst. prof. U. Mo., St. Louis, 1987-93, assoc. prof., 1993—; mem. adv. bd Gateway Writing Project, St. Louis, 1987—. Co-author: Writing from A to Z, 1994, Writing With: New Directions in Collaborative Teaching, Learning and Research, 1994; mem. editorial bd. Jour. of Teaching Writing, 1990—, Jour. of Advanced Composition, 1993—; contbr. articles to profl. jours. Rsch. grantee Women's Program Coun., St. Louis, 1996, Coun. of Writing Program Adminstrs., Oxford, Ohio, 1991, 95; U. Mo.-St. Louis summer rsch. grantee, 1988, 90; NEH grantee, Drake U. Mem. Nat. Coun. Tchrs. English, Coun. of Writing Program Adminstrs. Democrat. Home: 1407 Grant Rd Webster Groves MO 63119 Office: U Mo St Louis 8001 Natural Bridge Rd Saint Louis MO 63121

EBINGER, LINDA ANN, nurse; b. North Attleboro, Mass., Apr. 6, 1944; d. Donat Leo Deshetres and Muriel Francis Mumford; m. Carl R. Ebinger, Jr. (dec. Apr. 1994); children: Carl R. III, Eric Edward. Diploma in practical nursing, Lindsay Hopkins Nursing Sch., Miami, 1978. LPN, Fla.; cert. LPN IV therapy cert. ECG technician Sturdy Meml. Hosp., Attleboro, Mass., 1962-65, with radiology dept., 1968-69; stewardess TWA, 1965; clin. lab. technician Wrentham State Sch., Mass., 1965-71, EKG dept. mgr., 1965-70; rental property owner, mgr., 1973-96; orthopedic/med.-surg. unit nurse Bapt. Hosp. Miami, 1978-81, oncology unit nurse, 1981-82, ob/gyn. unit, 1982-84, with Joslin Diabetes Care Ctr., 1984-93, orthop./neurol. nurse, 1993—. Mem. LWV (sec. Dade County 1995—). Republican. Roman Catholic. Home: 11036 SW 139 Pl Miami FL 33186

EBINGER, MARY RITZMAN, pastoral counselor; b. Reading, Pa., Nov. 23, 1929; d. Michael Erwin and Daisy Mae (Shaeffer) R.; m. Warren Ralph Ebinger, Aug. 11, 1951; children: Lee, Lori, Jonathan. BA, North Cen. Coll., Naperville, Ill., 1951; MS, Loyola Coll., Balt., 1981; grad. student, Wesley Theol. Sem., 1976, Cath. U., 1977. Cert. nat. counselor Dept. of Md. Health and Mental Hygiene, cert. nat. counselor Am. Assn. Pastoral Counselors. Elem. tchr. Naperville Washington Sch., 1952-54; dir. adult work Millian Ch., Rockville, Md., 1974-76; pastoral counselor Washington Pastoral Counselors, 1976-81; assoc. dir. Balt. Washington Conf. Pastoral Care and Counseling, Balt., 1990—; mem. adj. faculty psychology Frederick (Md.) C.C., 1982-87, Anne Arnold (Md.) C.C., 1988-90; pres. Wesley Guild Wesley Theol. Seminary, Washington, 1987-89; del. gen. conf. U. Meth. Ch., 1988, 92. Author: I Was Sick and You Visited Me, 1976, 2d edit., 1995, enlarged and reprinted, 1996, Does Anybody Care, 1978. Pres. Ch. Women United, Springfield, Ill., 1969-71; chmn. Episcopacy com. United Meth. Ch., Balt., 1988-90; del. gen. and jurisdictional conf. United Meth. Ch., 1988, 92. Recipient Disting. Alumnus award North Cen. Coll., 1990, Loyola Coll., 1991, Two Thousand Women of Achievement award Dartmouth Eng. Mus., 1969. Mem. Am. Assn. Counseling and Devel., Am. Assn. Pastoral Counseling (cert., Atlantic region chmn. theol. and social concerns 1988-92). Home: 6 Saint Ives Dr Severna Park MD 21146-1430 Office: Balt-Wash Conf Pastoral Care and Counseling United Meth Ch 5124 Greenwich Ave Baltimore MD 21229-2393

EBISUZAKI, YUKIKO, chemistry educator; b. Mission City, B.C., Can., July 25, 1930; came to U.S., 1957; d. Masuzo and Shige (Kusumoto) E. BS with honors, U. Western Ont., London, Can., 1956, MS, 1957; PhD, Ind. U., 1962. Postdoctoral U. Pa., Phila., 1962-63; faculty rsch. assoc. Ariz. State U., Tempe, 1963-67; acting asst. prof. UCLA, 1967-75; assoc. prof. N.C. State U., Raleigh, 1975—. Contbr. articles to profl. jours. Ont. Rsch. Found. fellow Ont. Rsch. Coun., 1957-60, Gerry fellow Sigma Delta Epsilon, 1977-78. Mem. AAUW, Am. Chem. Soc., Am. Phys. Soc., Sigma Xi. Office: NC State Univ Dept Chemistry Clb # 8204 Raleigh NC 27695

EBITZ, ELIZABETH KELLY, lawyer; b. LaPorte, Ind., June 9, 1950; d. Joseph Monahan and Ann Mary (Barrett) Kelly; m. David MacKinnon Ebitz, Jan. 23, 1971 (div. 1981). AB with honors, Smith Coll., 1972; JD cum laude, Boston U., 1975. Bar: Maine 1979, Mass 1975, U.S. Supreme Ct 1982, U.S. Dist. Ct. Mass. 1976, U.S. Dist. Ct. Maine 1979, U.S. Ct. Appeals (1st cir.) 1976. Law clk. Boston Legal Assistance Project, 1973-75; law clk., assoc. Law Offices of John J. Thornton, Boston, 1974-76; ptnr. Ebitz & Zurn, Northampton, Mass., 1976-79; assoc. Gross, Minsky, Mogul & Singal, Bangor, Maine, 1979-80; pres. Elizabeth Kelly Ebitz, P.A., Bangor, 1980-92; pres. Ebitz & Thornton, P.A., 1993—. Pres. Greater Bangor Rape Crisis Bd., 1983-85; bd. dirs. Greater Bangor Area Shelter, 1985-92, 93—, Maine Women's Lobby, 1986-89, No. Maine Bread for the World, 1987-90; bd. dirs. Am. Heart Assn., Maine, 1989—, chair-elect, 1991-93, chair, 1993-95, past chair, 1995—; mem. various peace, feminist and hunger orgns., Bangor, 1982—. Named Young Career Woman of Hampshire County, Nat. Bus. and Profl. Women, Northampton, 1979. Mem. ABA, Assn. Trial Lawyers Am., Sigma Xi. Democrat. Roman Catholic. Home: 111 Maple St Bangor ME 04401-4031 Office: 15 Columbia St PO Box 641 Bangor ME 04402-0641

EBNER, CAROL DIANE, accountant, human resources manager; b. Detroit, Jan. 18, 1957; d. Fredrick Rupert and Joan Mary (Lowry) Glass; m. Patrick Joseph Ebner, Aug. 14, 1982. BS in Mgmt., Oakland U., 1980; MS in Taxation, Walsh Coll., 1996. CPA, CMA. Bookeeper Sierafor USA, Livonia, Mich., 1981-82; bookeeper McClelland & Co., Birmingham, Mich., 1982-84, contr., 1984-92; contr. Prodn. Rubber Prod. Co., Livonia, 1992-93; staff acct. Davis & Davis CPAs, P.C., Southfield, Mich., 1993-96. Vol. Mich. Humane Soc., Auburn Hills, Mich., 1982—; fundraiser Am. Diabetes Assn., 1995, Am. Cancer Soc., Detroit, 1990-95; sec., fundraiser Ch. & Soc. First United Meth. Ch., Northville, Mich., 1990-93. Mem. Am. Inst. CPAs, Inst. Mgmt. Accts. (newsletter dir. Oakland County chpt. 1990-92, dir. cmty. svc. 1994-95), Mich. Assn. CPAs. Republican. Home: 2927 Robina Berkley MI 48072

EBY, DONNA S., small business owner; b. Cin., Jan. 28, 1959; d. Vincent V. and Betty L. (Moore) E. BA, Coll. Mt. St. Joseph, 1981. Supervisor Hamilton County Auditor, Cin., 1981-90; ptnr. Sanger & Eby Design, Cin., 1990—. Bd. dirs. Coll. Mt. St. Joseph, Cin., 1992—; mentor Cin. Youth Collaborative, 1992. mem. Women in Comms. (bd. dirs. 1989-90), Internat. Assn. Bus. Communicators, Advt. Club. Cin (chmn. 1994-96), Cin. C. of C. Roman Catholic. Home: 1003 John St Cincinnati OH 45203 Office: Sanger & Eby Design 18 W 7th St Cincinnati OH 45202

EBY, LOIS, artist; b. Tulsa, May 5, 1940; d. Seth Gilman and Mary Nadine (Sample) E.; m. David W. Budbill; children: Gene, Nadine. BA, Duke U., 1962; MA, Columbia U., 1964. Instr. drawing Cmty. Coll. Vt., Morrisville, 1984-94; artist in residence Out and About, Morrisville, 1990—; adj. faculty art Vt. Coll. of Norwich U., Montpelier, 1994—. One-person show at Julian Scott Meml. Gallery, 1992; exhibited in group shows at Woodstock (Vt.) Gallery of Art, 1995-96, Peacock Collections Art Gallery, Durham, N.C., 1995-96, Chaffee Art Ctr., Rutland, Vt., 1995, Helen Day Art Ctr., Stowe, Vt., 1996, Trinity Coll., Burlington, Vt., 1996; drawings for numerous books of poems, 1977-87. Mem. Art Resource Assn.

EBY, MARLENE JEAN, secondary education educator; b. Montgomery County, Ohio, June 12, 1944; d. Emerson Leroy and Eileen Phyllis Eby. BS in Edn., Bowling Green State U., 1966, MA, 1970. Cert. tchr., Ohio. Grad. asst. Bowling Green (Ohio) State U., 1969-70; tchr. Gt. Valley Schs., Malvern, Pa., 1970-71; tchr. math. Huber Heights (Ohio) City Schs., 1966-69, 71—, head dept., 1992—, also condr. various insvc. workshops; charter mem. math. com. Alliance for Edn., Dayton, Ohio; renaissance tchr. Wayne H.S., Huber Heights, 1996. Vol. Good Samaritan Hosp., Dayton, Ohio, 1972-90, Victoria Theater, Dayton, 1991—. Mem. Nat. Coun. Tchrs. Math. (manuscript reader 1994—), Ohio Coun. Tchrs. Math. Office: Wayne HS 5400 Chambersburg Rd Huber Heights OH 45424

ECHOLS, MARY LOUISE BROWN, elementary school educator, secondary school educator; b. Milligan, Fla., Nov. 13, 1906; d. Edward Reese and Barbara Alabama Brown; m. Louie Samuel Echols Jr., June 18, 1932 (dec. Oct. 1984); 1 child, Louie Samuel III. AB, cert. in spoken English, Fla. State Coll. for Women, 1928; MEd, U. Fla., 1953, postgrad. Cert. elem. tchr., English tchr., biology tchr., sci. tchrs., Fla. (life); cert. jr. coll. instr. Tchr. Greenville (Fla.) H.S., 1928-29, Madison (Fla.) H.S., 1929-30, Dixie County H.S., Cross City, Fla., 1930-37, 41-43, Gainesville (Fla.) H.S., 1951-66; agronomist technician U. Fla., Gainesville, 1946; coord. lang. arts Alachua County Sch. Bd., Gainesville, 1966-67, reading specialist, 1967-68, 1969-71; reading coord., 1971-72; ret. Alachua County Sch. Bd., Gainesville, 1972; mem. leadership res. pool Bd. Pub. Instruction, Gainesville, 1969—; compiler curriculum guide 7-12 lang. arts Alachua County Sch. Bd., Gainesville, 1966; mem. team teaching unit; del. White House Conf. Edn. Vol. hospice Light Up a Life, Gainesville, 1989-90; active Friends of Libr. Alachua County; contbr., active Matheson Hist. Ctr., Gainesville. Recipient Fifty Yrs. Membership cert. Fla. Fedn. Women's Clubs, 1995. Mem. AAUW (telephone com.), Alachua County Ret. Tchrs., Fla. Ret. Educators, Gainesville Woman's Club, Nat. Ret. Tchrs. Assn., Gainesville Garden Club (assoc.), Matheson Hist. Soc., Fla. State U. Emeritus Club, Phi Kappa Phi, Delta Kappa Gamma. Democrat. Methodist. Home: 710 NE 11th Ave Gainesville FL 32601-4417

ECKER, BOBBI, small business owner; b. Waterloo, Iowa, Aug. 24, 1931; d. William H. and Elenora Elizabeth (Kurtt) Brunstein; m. Theodore John Ecker, Dec. 28, 1948 (div. May 1975); children: Lynn Diane, Cynthia Ellen, Theodore Bruce; m. Josiah Slaney Blatchford. Grad. high sch. Co-owner Eckers Flowers & Greenhouses, Waverly, Iowa, 1949—; dir. franchisee tng. Flowerama of Am., Inc., Waterloo, 1970-79; creative cons., owner The Flora Pros, Chgo., 1979—; pres. Advanced Floral Concepts, Shell Rock, Iowa, 1980-87; creative cons. The Brody Co., Cin., 1987—. Author: Symbolism in Flowers, 1960; columnist "Dear Bobbi" in Masterworks, 1980-85. Mem. Bd. of Edn., Waverly Shell Rock Schs., 1965-75. Recipient award Am. Inst. Floral Designers, 1977, Am. Acad. Florists, 1979, Profl. Floral Commentators Internat., 1980. Lutheran. Home: 1320 N State Pky Chicago IL 60610-2118

ECKER, SUSAN RUTH, mechanical engineer; b. Glen Cove, N.Y.; d. Adam and May Ecker. BSME, Lehigh U., 1984. Design engr. Leo A. Daly Co., Washington, 1985-88; staff engr. CUH2A, Princeton, N.J., 1988-90; sr. engr. Parsons Main, Inc., Boston, 1990—. Editorial adv. bd. Plumbing Engr. Mag., 1994—; contbr. articles to profl. publs. Mem. ASME, Am. Soc. Plumbing Engrs. Office: Parsons Main Inc Prudential Ctr Boston MA 02199

ECKERT, GERALDINE GONZALES, language professional, educator, entrepreneur; b. N.Y.C., Aug. 5, 1948; d. Albert and Mercedes (Martinez) Gonzales; m. Robert Alan Eckert, Apr. 1, 1972; children: Lauren Elaine, Alison Elizabeth. BA, Ladycliff Coll., Highland Falls, N.Y., 1970; student, U. Valencia, Spain, 1968; MA, N.Y.U., 1971; student, Instituto de Cultura Hispanica, Madrid, 1970-71. Tchr. Spanish Clarkstown High Sch. N. (N.Y.), 1971-73, Rambam Torah Inst., Beverly Hills, Calif., 1973-75; translator City of Beverly Hills, 1976-83; edn. cons. Los Angeles County of Calif. Dept. Forestry, Capistrano Beach, 1982-84; lang. services and protocol Los Angeles Olympic Organizing Com., 1983-84; pension adminstr. Pension Architects, Inc., Los Angeles, 1984-87; instr. El Camino Coll., Torrance, Calif., 1987-88, Santa Monica (Calif.) Coll., 1975—; owner, pres. Bilingual Pension Cons., L.A., 1987-89; bd. dirs. Institute for Hispanic Cultural Studies, Los Angeles; spl. asst. to Internat. Olympic Com., Lausanne, Switzerland, 1983—. V.p. Notre Dame Acad. Assoc., West L. A., 1987—; mem. L.A. March of Dimes Ambassadors Group, 1987; co-founder, pres. Blind Cleaning Express, L.A., 1989—; bd. dirs. Inst. Hispanic Cultural Studies, L.A., 1984-89; spl. asst. to pres. Internat. Olympic Com. Lausanne, Switzerland, 1983—. Democrat. Roman Catholic. Clubs: Five Ring, Los Angeles, Friends of Sport, Amateur Athletic Found., Los Angeles. Office: 8885 Venice Blvd Ste 103 Los Angeles CA 90034-3242

ECKERT, JEAN PATRICIA, elementary education educator; b. Pitts., July 22, 1935; d. Homer Michael and Berdena Leona (Kessler) Canel; m. William L. Eckert, June 13, 1959; 1 child, Suzanne Mary. BS, Indiana U. Pa., 1957; postgrad., U. Pitts., 1958-59, U. San Diego, 1981. Cert. pub. instrn., Pa. Elem. tchr. Pine-Richland Sch. Dist., Gibsonia, Pa., 1957-60; substitute tchr. Pine-Richland Sch. Dist., 1963-65; elem. tchr. Shaler Twp. Sch. Dist., Glenshaw, Pa., 1965-66; elem. tchr. St. Scholastica Sch., Diocese of Pitts., Aspinwall, Pa., 1966-91, substitute tchr., 1991—, tutor, 1991—. Judge election 4th dist. Rep. Party, Aspinwall, 1962-65, 91—. Mem. AAUW, Nat. Cath. Edn. Assn., Vols. in Teaching Alternatives, Ind. U. Pa. Alumni Assn., Delta Zeta (sec. 1955, pres. 1956, Gamma Phi chpt.). Roman Catholic. Home: 210 12th St Pittsburgh PA 15215

ECKERT, OPAL EFFIE CALVERT, retired journalism educator; b. Bolckow, Mo., Mar. 19, 1905; d. Price Wallingford and Mary Jane (Pittsenbarger) Calvert; m. Thomas H. Eckert, June 19, 1929 (dec.). BS in Edn., Northwest Mo. State U., 1928, AB, 1944, MS in Edn., 1963. Instr. prin. Butler, Bolckow & Pickering, Mo., 1928-44; instr., dir. pub. Maryville (Mo.) High Sch., 1944-65; freelance writer, feature writer, columnist, reporter Maryville Daily Forum, St. Joseph, News-Press Gazette, Mo., 1955-93; dir. journalism workshops N.W. Mo. State U., Maryville, 1963-74; instr. English, journalism, chmn. Northwest Mo. State Univ., Maryville, 1965-74; cons. Project Communicate, Northwest, Mo., 1964-67. Author: Grassroot Reflections, vols. I and II, Nodaway County Pictorial History, 1994; co-editor: Tales of Nodaway County; contbr. articles to profl. jours. Delegate, U.S. White House Conf. Aging, Wash., 1981; sec., treas. Mo. Divsn. AAUW; founder, pres. Nodaway County Heritage Collection Com., 1982-92; disting. svc. honoree First Christian Ch., Maryville, 1993. Named U.S. Journalism Tchr. of Yr. Newspaper Fund, Inc., 1963, One of Two Mo. Outstanding Vols., 1981, Mo. Pioneer Educator, 1979, Disting. Mo. Woman AAUW-Mo. div., 1990. Mem. Mo. Assn. tchrs. of English (pres., life mem.), Mo. Writers' Guild, Maryville C. of C. (Disting. Svc. award, 1975, Outstanding Woman of Maryville History, 1996). Democrat. Home: 610 W Halsey St # 5 Maryville MO 64468-2162

ECKHARDT, CAROLINE DAVIS, comparative literature educator; b. N.Y.C., Feb. 27, 1942; d. Joseph and Lilian (Lerner) Davis; m. Robert B. Eckhardt, Aug. 22, 1964; children—David, Naomi, Jonathan, Jennifer Ruth. BA, Drew U., 1963; MA, Ind. U., 1965; PhD, U. Mich., 1971. Lectr. U. Mich., Ann Arbor, 1971; asst. prof. Pa. State U., Univ. Park, 1971-76, assoc. prof., 1976-85, prof., 1985—, program head, grad. officer comparative lit. program, 1977-84, planning officer liberal arts, 1981-85, head dept. Comparative Lit., 1986—. Author: The Prophetia Merlini of Geoffrey of Monmouth, 1982; editor: Essays in the Numerical Criticism of Medieval Literature, 1980, Chaucer's General Prologue, 1990, Castleford's Chronicle, 1995; co-editor Jour. Gen. Edn., 1974-87; mem. editorial bd. Comparative Literature Studies, 1987—; contbr. articles to profl. jours., books. Mem. MLA (exec. com. medieval comparative sect. 1980-86), Am. Comparative Lit. Assn. (adv. bd. 1986-89), Assn. Depts. and Programs Comparative Lit. (nat. sec. 1994—), Medieval Acad., New Chaucer Soc. Jewish. Office: Pa State Univ Comparative Lit Dept Univ Park PA 16802

ECKHOFF, KRISTINE KAY, mental health therapist; b. Killen, Tex., Dec. 2, 1968; d. Dennis John Eckhoff and Patricia Marie (Cronin) Pearson. BS, U. S.D., 1991, MA in Counseling, 1994. Cert. AIDS counselor. Mental health counselor U. S.D., Vermillion, 1993-94; family therapist Luth. Social Svcs., Spearfish, S.D., 1994-95; therapist Turning Point, Sioux Falls, S.D., 1995—. Mem. ACA. Roman Catholic. Home: 4409 Valhalla Apt 9 Sioux Falls SD 57106 Office: Turning Point 1401 W 51st St Sioux Falls SD 57105

ECKLUND, CONSTANCE CRYER, French language educator; b. Chgo., Nov. 20, 1938; d. Gilbert and Electra (Papadopoulos) Cryer; m. Robert Lyons, June 18, 1966 (div. 1974); m. John E. Ecklund, Mar. 22, 1975. BA magna cum laude, Northwestern U., 1960; PhD, Yale U., 1965. Asst. prof. Ind. U., Bloomington, 1964-66; asst. prof. French Southern Conn. State U., New Haven, 1967-70, assoc. prof., 1970-76, prof., 1976—; speaker in field. Contbr. articles to profl. jours. Mem. AAUP, Am. Coun. Teaching Fgn. Langs., Am. Assn. Tchrs. French, Modern Lang. Assn., Phi Beta Kappa. Republican. Episcopalian. Home: 27 Cedar Rd Woodbridge CT 06525-1642

ECKSTEIN, MARLENE R., vascular radiologist; b. Poughkeepsie, N.Y., Sept. 6, 1948; d. Marc and Lola (Charm) E.; A.B., Vassar Coll., 1970; M.D., Albert Einstein Coll. Medicine, 1973. Diplomate Nat. Bd. Med. Examiners; cert. Am. Bd. Radiology. Intern in medicine Yale-New Haven Med. Center, 1973-74, resident in diagnostic radiology, 1974-77; asst. radiologist, chief vascular radiology sect. South Nassau Communities Hosp., Oceanside, N.Y., 1977-78, asso. radiologist, chief vascular radiology sect., 1978-81, asst. dir. dept. radiology, chief vascular radiology sect., 1981-83; asst. prof. clin. radiology SUNY-Stony Brook Med. Sch., 1980-83; instr. radiology, Harvard Med. Sch., 1983-84, asst. prof., 1984—; asst. radiologist Mass. Gen. Hosp., 1983-87, assoc. radiologist, 1987—. Mem. exec. com. and hosp. chmn. United Jewish Appeal of Physicians and Dentists of Nassau County (N.Y.), 1981-83. Fellow Am. Coll. Angiology, Soc. Cardiovascular and Interventional Radiology; mem. Am. Coll. Radiology, Am. Inst. Ultrasound in Medicine, Mass. Radiol. Soc., Am. Assn. Women Radiologists, Am. Med. Women's Assn., AMA, Mass. Med. Soc., New Eng. Soc. Cardiovascular and Interventional Radiology (pres. 1985-86), Radiol. Soc. N.Am., Designer and developer line of vascular catheters. Avocations: writing poetry, exercising, video and electronic equipment, musical keyboard, computer. Home: 141 Fulton Ave Apt 312 Poughkeepsie NY 12603-2841 Office: Mass Gen Hosp Vascular Radiology Sect Boston MA 02114

ECTON, DONNA R., business executive; b. Kansas City, Mo., May 10, 1947; d. Allen Howard and Marguerite (Page) E.; m. Victor H. Maragni, June 16, 1986; children: Mark, Gregory. BA (Durant Scholar), Wellesley Coll., 1969; MBA, Harvard U., 1971. V.p. Chem. Bank, N.Y.C., 1972-79, Citibank, N.A., N.Y.C., 1979-81; pres. MBA Resources, Inc., N.Y.C., 1981-83; v.p. adminstrn., officer Campbell Soup Co., Camden, N.J., 1983-89; chmn. Triangle Mfg. Corp. subs. Campbell Soup Co., Raleigh, N.C., 1984-87; sr. v.p., officer Nutri/System, Inc., Willow Grove, Pa., 1989-91; pres., CEO Van Houten N.Am., Delavan, Wis., 1991-94, Andes Candies Inc., Delavan, 1991-94; chmn., pres., CEO Bus. Mail Express, Inc., Reston, Va., 1995—; bd. dirs. Barnes Group Inc., Bristol, Conn., Vencor, Inc., Louisville, Ky. H&R Block, Kansas City, Mo., PETsMART, Inc., Phoenix, Ariz., Tandy Corp., Ft. Worth, Tex.; commencement speaker Pa. State U., 1987. Bd. Overseers Harvard U., 1984-90; mem. Coun. Fgn. Rels., N.Y.C., 1987—; trustee Inst. for Advancement of Health, 1988-92. Named One of 80 Women to Watch in the 80's, Ms. mag., 1980, One of All Time Top 10 of Last Decade, Glamour mag., 1984, One of 50 Women to Watch, Bus. Week mag., 1987, One of 100 Women to Watch, Bus. Month mag., 1989; recipient Wellesley Alumnae Achievement award, 1987; Fred Sheldon Fund fellow, 1971-72. Mem. Harvard Bus. Sch. Assn. (pres. exec. council 1983-84), N.Y.C. Harvard Bus. Sch. Club (pres. 1979-80), Wellesley Coll. Nat. Alumnae Assn. (bd. dirs., 1st v.p.).

EDDISON, ELIZABETH BOLE, entrepreneur, information specialist; b. Bronxville, N.Y., June 3, 1928; d. Hamilton Biggar and Elizabeth Owsley (Boyle) Bole; m. John Corbin Eddison, Feb. 10, 1951 (dec. Jan. 1993); children: Jonathan B., Elizabeth O., Martha C. AB, Vassar Coll., 1948; MS, Simmons Coll., 1973. Pres., bd. dirs. Lahore (Pakistan)-Am. Sch., 1959-61; chmn. evaluation com. Karachi (Pakistan)-Am. Sch., 1961-63; treas. bd. dirs. La Paz Coop. Sch., Bolivia, 1963-65; v.p. Assn. Am. Fgn. Svc. Women; coord. social svcs. Urban Svc. Corps, Washington Pub. Schs., 1965-69; sec. bd. dirs. Colegio Nueva Granada, Bogota, Colombia, 1969-71; chmn., treas. Warner-Eddison Assocs., Inc., Cambridge, Mass., 1973-88, pres., 1981-88; chmn., v.p. Inmagic Inc., Woburn, Mass., 1984—; mem. steering com. State House Conf. on Small Bus., Mass., 1986-88; mem. bd. advisors Internat. Sch. Info. Mgmt., Irvine, Calif., 1984—; mem. adv. con. Engring. Info., Inc., N.Y.C., 1989-93; computer applications com. Cary Meml. Libr., Lexington, Mass., 1986; mem. State Adv. Commn. on Librs., Boston, 1993-96. Compiler: Words that Mean Business, 1981; contbr. articles to profl. jours. Mem. adv. com. on internat. and tech. devel. U.S. Dept. State, 1980-83; mem. small bus. com. Mass. Gov.'s Bus. Adv. Coun., 1985-89; co-chmn. Lexington Dem. Town Com., 1990-92; active Mass. Bd. Libr. Commrs., 1990-91; mem. bd. corporators Symmes Hosp., Arlington, Mass., 1992-94; mem. Bd. Selectmen, Lexington, 1993—; mem. adv. bd. Babson Coll. Info. Tech. and Svcs. Divsn., 1996—. Recipient Alumni Achievement award Simmons Coll., 1986, Disclosure Achievement award Libr. Mgmt. Bus. and Fin. div. Spl. Librs. Assn., 1987. Mem. Am. Soc. Info. Scis., Info. Industry Assn. (chmn. emeriti com. 1983-88, small bus. forum 1986-89, entrepreneur award com. 1989-90, co-chmn. publs. com. 1984-87, Entrepreneur award 1989), Assoc. Info. Mgrs. (chmn. publs. com. 1984-86, bd. dirs. 1984-86, Knox award 1988), Spl. Librs. Assn. (chmn. program com. libr. mgmt. divsn. 1984-85, profl. devel. com. 1987-88, chmn.-elect 1988, chmn. 1989-90, bd. dirs. 1991-94, mem. consultation com. 1994—), Nat. Info. Stds. Orgn. (bd. dirs. 1994—), Beta Phi Mu. Democrat. Office: Inmagic Inc 800 W Cummings Park Woburn MA 01801-6372

EDDOWES, E(LIZABETH) ANNE, early childhood education specialist; b. Sandusky, Ohio, Nov. 23, 1931; d. Carl Emerson and Helen Ruth (Sutter) Evans; m. Edward Everett, June 17, 1956; children: Andrew Wayne, Scott Edward. BS, Ohio State U., Columbus, 1953; MEd, U. Mo., St. Louis, 1969; PhD, Ariz. State U., Tempe, 1977. Tchr. Sandusky (Ohio) Pub. Schs., 1954-56, Alachua County Pub. Schs., Gainesville, Fla., 1957-59; dir. Florissant (Mo.) Coop. Nursery Sch., 1967-70; instr. Florissant Valley Community Coll., Ferguson, Mo., 1970-73; grad. and faculty assoc. Ariz. State U., Tempe, 1974-78, coord. student teaching, 1979-84; child devel. assoc. rep. Coun. for Early Childhood Profl. Recognition, Washington, 1978—; asst. prof. U. Ala., Birmingham, 1985-91, assoc. prof., 1991—; validator Nat. Assn. Edn. Young Children, Washington, 1986—; cons. Southside Bapt. Child Devel. Ctr., Brookwood Forest Child Devel. Ctr., Mountain Brook, 1986-92. Contbr. articles to profl. jours. Pres., v.p. Family Resource Ctr., Tempe, 1977-79, children's ctr. bd. Desert Palm United Ch. of Christ, Tempe, 1978-84. Recipient Outstanding Svc. award Ariz. State U., 1984. Mem. Orgn. Mondiale pour Edn. Prescolaire, Ala. Assn. on Young Children (pres. 1989-90), Ala. Assn. Early Childhood Tchrs., Jefferson County Assn. Young Children, Phi Delta Kappa, Alpha Phi. Office: U Ala Dept Curriculum & Instrn University Sta Birmingham AL 35294

EDDY, COLETTE ANN, aerial photography studio owner, photographer; b. Sept. 14, 1950; d. William F. and Jeanne (Valeski) Trump; m. Robert K. Eddy, Aug. 21, 1976 (div. Sept. 1992). AA, St. Petersburg (Fla.) Jr. Coll., 1970; BA, U. South Fla., 1973; MS, Nova U., 1988. Yacht caretaker The Sundowner, St. Petersburg, 1972-73; mgr. Aunt Hattie's Restaurant, St.

Petersburg, 1973-79, Johnathan Jones, Inc., St. Petersburg, 1979-80; photographer, sales rep. Smith Aerial Photos, Tampa, Fla., 1980—; owner, aerial photographer Aerial Innovations, Inc., Tampa, 1987—; owner Havanna Connection Inc., Carribean. Mem. Tampa Mus. Art. Mem. Profl. Photographers Am. (30 Merit awards), Fla. Profl. Photographers (20 Merit awards 1987-90), Profl. Aerial Photographers Assn., Tampa C. of C. Republican. Home: 198 Ceylon Ave Tampa FL 33606-3330 Office: Aerial Innovations Inc 1413 S Howard Ave Ste 206 Tampa FL 33606-3176

EDDY, JULIA VERONICA, educator; b. Phila., May 25, 1950; d. Horace Charles and Pearl Marie (Houser) E. BA in Liberal Arts, Rutgers U., 1973; MA in History Edn., SUNY, Stonybrook, 1974, PhD in Latin Am. History, 1979. Cert. secondary tchr. Social studies dir. Community Voyage Sch., Phila., 1976-79; edn. mgr. Project 70001, Phila., 1979-82, Am. Bus. Inst., Phila., 1982-84; vis. lectr. C.C. Phila., 1984-87; mgr. Pvt. Industry Coun., Phila., 1988-92, Tradeswomen of Phila. in Non-Traditional Work, Inc., 1991-93; founder Eddy & Assocs., Phila., 1993—; cons. Jr. Achievement of Am., 1996—, WAWA Teen Parenting, Phila., 1995-96, Top/Win, Inc., Phila., 1991-92, Sch. for Exec. Secs., Newark, 1984, Voyage House, Inc., Phila., 1980. Editor, contbr: Women in Technology & Trades, 1992; contbg. editor: JTPA/PIC Case Management, 1991; editor: Unions/Apprenticeship in Pennsylvania, 1991. Bd. dirs. New Birth, Inc., Phila., 1993—; founder, pres. Mentor, Phila., 1993—; mem. Doris Day Animal League, Washington, 1989—. Recipient PIC Excellence award Pvt. Industry Coun., 1988; Samuel Robinson fellowship Lincoln U., 1970. Mem. Tutor Roundtable (treas. 1986), Am. Hist. Assn., Lamba Kappa Mu, Inc. (workshop presenter 1993, Community Svc. award 1993). Democrat. Roman Catholic. Home: 717 S Cobbscreek Pkwy Philadelphia PA 19143 Office: Eddy & Assocs 717 S Cobbs Creek Pky Philadelphia PA 19143-2210

EDELMAN, BARBARA J., cancer registrar; b. S.I., N.Y., June 18, 1943; d. Samuel J. and Edith Rose (Kovner) E. Sec. pathology dept. Richmond Meml. Hosp., S.I., 1961-62; pvt. sec. Nestle Le Mur Co., N.Y.C., 1962-65; tumor registrar Beekman Downtown Hosp., N.Y.C., 1965-68; exec. sec. UCLA Med. Ctr., 1968-70; office mgr. NYU Med. Ctr., 1971-74; exec. sec. S.I. Med. Group, 1974-77; tumor registrar J.F. Kennedy Med. Ctr., Edison, N.J., 1977-80; adminstrv. asst. UCLA Med. Ctr., 1980-83; exec. sec. Children's Hosp. L.A., 1984-88; tumor registrar Children's Hosp., L.A., 1989—. Vol. Westside Spl. Olympics, Santa Monica, Calif., 1981—, head bowling coach, 1983—, mem. adv. bd., 1984-89. Named Sec. of Month Profl. Sec. Internat., 1978. Mem. NAFE, Nat. Cancer Registrars Assn. (cert. 1990, founder pediat. group), Calif. Cancer Registrars Assn., So. Calif. Cancer Registrars Assn. Democrat. Jewish. Home: 15445 Cobalt St # 13 Sylmar CA 91342 Office: Childrens Hosp 4650 Sunset Blvd Los Angeles CA 90027

EDELMAN, IDA, independent school director; b. N.Y.C., Jan. 10, 1938; d. Max and Elizabeth (Nadel) E. BA, U. Rochester, 1959; MA, Trenton State U., 1977, EdS, 1980. Reading specialist Wordsworth Acad., Ft. Washington, N.J., 1971-73; supr. spl. learning Chapin Sch., Princeton, N.J., 1973-79; learning cons. South Brunswick (N.J.) Bd. Edn., 1979-83; coord. spl. svcs. Perth Amboy, N.J., 1983-85; dir. spl. svcs. Mariboro (N.J.) Twp., 1985-96; dir. Westbury Friends Sch., 1996—. Bd. dirs. Mental Health Assn., 1987-90. Grantee N.J. State Dept. Spl. Edn., 1985-86, 87-89. Mem. Nat. Assn. Legal Problems in Edn., Tri County Reading Assn. (pres. 1979-85). Home: 120 Mount Grey Rd Old Field NY 11733

EDELMAN, JUDITH H., architect; b. Bklyn., Sept. 16, 1923; d. Abraham and Frances (Israel) Hochberg; m. Harold Edelman, Dec. 26, 1947; children: Marc, Joshua. Student, Conn. Coll., 1940-41, NYU, 1941-42; BArch, Columbia U., 1946. Designer, drafter Huson Jackson, N.Y.C., 1948-58; Schermerhorn traveling fellow, 1950, pvt. practice architecture, 1958-60; ptnr. Edelman & Salzman, N.Y.C., 1960-79; partner Edelman Partnership (Architects), N.Y.C., 1979—; adj. prof. Sch. Architecture CUNY, 1972-76, vis. lectr. grad. program in environ. psychology, 1977, 77; vis. lectr. Washington U., St. Louis, 1974, U. Oreg., 1974, MIT, 1975, Pa. State U., 1977, Rensselaer Poly. Inst., 1977, Columbia U., 1979; First Claire Watson Forrest Meml. lectr. U. Oreg., U. Calif., Berkeley, U. So. Calif., 1982. Major archtl. works include Restoration of St. Mark's Ch. in the Bowery, N.Y.C., 1970-82, Two Bridges Urban Renewal Area Housing, 1970-96, Jennings Hall Sr. Citizens Housing, Bklyn., 1980, Goddard Riverside Elderly Housing and Cmty. Ctr., N.Y.C., 1983, Columbus Green Apartments, N.Y.C., 1987, Chung Pak Bldg., N.Y.C., 1992. Recipient Bard 1st honor award City Club N.Y., 1969, Bard award of merit, 1975, 82, award for design excellence HUD, 1970, 1st prize Nat. Trust for Hist. Preservation, 1983, award of merit Mcpl. Art Soc. N.Y., 1983, Pub. Svc. award Settlement Housing Fund, 1983, Women of Vision award NOW, 1989, 1st prize for design excellence C. of C., Borough of Queens, N.Y., 1989, Best in Srs.' Housing award Nat. Assn. Home Builders, 1993. Fellow AIA, dir. N.Y. chpt., chmn. commn. on archtl. edn. 1971-73, chmn. nat. task force on women in architecture 1974-75, v.p. N.Y. chpt. 1975-77, chmn. ethics com. 1975-77, Residential design award 1969, Pioneer in Housing award 1990, N.Y. State Assn. Architects-AIA Honor award 1975); mem. Alliance of Women in Architecture (founding, mem. steering com. 1972-74), Architects for Social Responsibility (mem. exec. com. 1982-85), Columbia Archtl. Alumni Assn. (bd. dirs. 1968-71). Home: 13 Bank St New York NY 10014-5252 Office: Edelman Partnership 434 6th Ave Fl 6 New York NY 10011-8411

EDELMAN, MARIAN WRIGHT (MRS. PETER B. EDELMAN), lawyer; b. Bennettsville, S.C., June 6, 1939; d. Arthur J. and Maggie (Bowen) Wright; m. Peter B. Edelman, July 14, 1968; children: Joshua, Jonah, Ezra. Merrill scholar, Univs. Paris, Geneva, 1958-59; BA, Spelman Coll., 1960; LLB (J.H. Whitney fellow 1960-61), Yale U., 1963, LLD (hon.); LLD (hon.), Smith Coll., 1969, Lowell Tech. U., 1975, Williams Coll., 1978, Columbia U., U. Pa., Amherst Coll., St. Joseph's Coll.; DHL (hon.), Lesley Coll., 1975, Trinity Coll., Washington, Russell Sage Coll., 1978, Syracuse U., Coll. New Rochelle, 1979, Swarthmore Coll., 1980, SUNY Old Westbury, Northeastern U., 1981, Bard Coll., 1982, U. Mass., 1983, Hunter Coll., U. So. Maine, SUNY, Albany, 1984, Columbia U., U. Pa., Yale U., 1985, Rutgers U., Bates Coll., Maryville Coll., Bank St., 1986, Claremont Grad Sch., Lincoln U., Georgetown U., Chgo. Theol. Coll., 1987, Wheaton Coll., Tulane U., Grinnell Coll. Brandeis U., Wheelock Coll., Dartmouth Coll., U. S.C., U. N.C., Grad. Ctr. CUNY, U. Wis. Milw., 1988, Interdenom. Theol. Ctr., Hofstra U., Tufts U., Borough Manhattan Community Coll., Wesleyan U., Calif. State U. L.A., Dillard U., U. Md., U. Miami, 1989, Howard U., Beloit Coll., Queens Coll., Am. U., New Sch. of Social Rsch., Coll. of Notre Dame, DePaul U., 1990, Beaver Coll., Fordham U., Simmons Coll., Hamline U., Clark U., Harvard U., Union Coll., 1991, Tuskegee U., Washington U. St. Louis, Hood Coll., Duke U., Mercy Coll., 1992, Princeton U., U. Ill., Calif. State U. San Francisco, Wittenberg (Ohio) Coll., Shaw U., So. Meth. U., 1993, Brown U., U. Balt., Ea. Conn. State U., U. Notre Dame, 1994. Bar: D.C., Miss., Mass. Staff atty. NAACP Legal Def. and Ednl. Fund, Inc., N.Y.C., 1963-64; dir. NAACP Legal Def. and Ednl. Fund, Inc., Jackson, Miss., 1964-68; Congl. and fed. liaison Poor People's Campaign, summer 1968; partner Washington Research Project of So. Center for Pub. Policy, 1968-73; dir. Harvard U. Center for Law and Edn., 1971-73; pres., founder Children's Def. Fund, 1973—. Author: The Measure of Our Success: A Letter To My Children and Yours, 1992, Families in Peril, 1987. Mem. exec. com. Student Non-Violent Coordinating Com., 1961-63; mem. adv. coun. Martin Luther King Jr. Meml. Libr.; mem. adv. bd. Hampshire Coll.; mem. Presdl. Commn. on Missing in Action, 1977, Presdl. Commn. on Internat. Yr. of Child, 1979, Presdl. Commn. on Agenda for 80's, 1980; bd. dirs. NAACP Legal Def. and Ednl. Fund; trustee Spelman Coll., Carnegie Coun. on Children, 1972-77, Martin Luther King Jr. Meml. Ctr.; mem. Yale U. Corp., 1971-77, Aetna Found., Nat. Commn. on Children, 1989—; bd. dirs. Aetna Life Casualty Found., Citizens for Constitutional Concerns, US. com. UNICEF, Robin Hood Found., Aaron Diamond Found., Nat. Alliance Business, City Lights, Leadership Conf. Civil Rights, Skadden Fellowship Found., Parents as Tchrs. Nat. Ctr., Inc.; U.S. rep. UNICEF; active U.S. Olympic Com. Named one of Outstanding Young Women of Am., 1966; recipient Mademoiselle mag. award, 1965, Louise Waterman Wise award, 1970, Washington of Yr. award, 1979, Whitney M. Young award, 1979, Profl. of Yr. award Black Ent., 1979, Leadership award Nat. Women's Polit. Caucus, 1980, Black Womens Forum award, 1980, medal Columbia Tchrs. Coll., Barnard Coll., 1984, Eliot award Am. Pub. Health Assn., John W. Gardner Leadership award of Ind. Sector, Pub. Svc. Achievement award Common Cause, Compostela award Cathedral St. James, 1987, MacArthur prize fellow, 1985, Albert Schweitzer Humanitarian prize Johns Hopkins U., 1987. Philip Hauge Ahelson award AAAS, 1988, Hubert Humphrey Civil Rights award, AFL-CIO award, 1989, Radcliffe Coll. medal, 1989, Fordham Stein prize, 1989, Gandhi Peace award, 1990, M. Carey Thomas award, Robie award for humanitarianism, Essence award, numerous others; hon. fellow U. Pa. Law Sch. Mem. Phi Beta Kappa (hon.). Address: Children's Def Fund 25 E St NW Washington DC 20001-1522*

EDELMANN, CAROLYN FOOTE, author, poet, editor; b. Toledo, Ohio. Pvt. studies with Theodore Weiss, Galway Kinnell, Stanley Plumly, Princeton U. Author: (poetry) Gatherings, 1987, Between the Dark and the Daylight, 1996; appearances include (TV) People are Talking, Phila., (radio) Pub. Radio, Manhattan; poetry readings: Encore Books and Music, Princeton, N.J., Mary Jacobs Libr., Rocky Hill, Beaver Pond Poetry Forum, New Hope, Pa. Recipient William Carlos Williams prize Paterson Pub. Libr., 1977, N.J. Poetry Monthly prize, 1978, Delaware Valley Poets prize, 1992. Mem. Acad. Am. Poets, Nat. League Am. Penwomen, Poetry Soc. Am., N.J. Penwomen, U.S. 1 Poet's Coop., Poets and Writers.

EDELSON, IRIS ROCHELLE, community health nurse; b. Bklyn., June 12, 1943; d. Louis and Anna (Cohen) Berman; m. Sanford Seth Edelson, July 1, 1967; 1 child, Stephen Mark. AAS Orange County C.C., Middletown, N.Y., 1966. Practical nurse, N.Y., 1961, RN, 1966. Nurse Unity Hosp., Bklyn., 1961-62, Mamonides Hosp., Bklyn., 1962-64, 66-67; nurse, supr. Whitestone (N.Y.) Gen. Hosp., 1968-75; sch. nurse Roslyn (N.Y.) Pub. Schs., 1988; coord. home care Imperial Surg. Supply Corp., Great Neck, N.Y., 1989—. Hebrew. Home: 21 Lake Dr Manhasset Hills NY 11040

EDELSON, MARY BETH, artist, educator; b. East Chicago, Ind.; d. Albert Melvin and Mary Lou (Young) Johnson; children: Lynn Switzman, Nick. Student, Art Inst. Chgo., 1953-54; BA, DePauw U., 1955; MA, NYU, 1959; DFA (hon.), DePauw U., 1993. Instr. Corcoran Sch. Art, Washington, 1970-75; artist in residence U. Ill., Chgo., 1982, 88, U. Tenn., Knoxville, 1983, Ohio U., Columbus, 1984, Md. Inst. Art, Balt., 1985, Kansas City Art Inst., Mo., 1986, Cleve. Art Inst., 1991, U. Colo., 1993, Clemson U., 1994; lectr. at various art gatherings. Solo exhbn. Creative Time, N.Y.C., 1994, Nicolai Wallner, Copenhagen, Denmark, 1996; group exhbns. include Internat. Feministiche Kunst, Stichting de Appel, Amsterdam, The Netherlands, 1980, Mendel Gallery, Mus. du Que., Phillips Gallery, Can., 1986-88, Queens (N.Y.) Mus., 1988, Corcoran Gallery Art, Washington, 1989, Mus. Modern Art, N.Y.C., 1988-89, Walker Art Ctr., Mpls., 1989, W.P.A., Washington, 1989, Dolan/Maxwell Gallery, N.Y.C., 1989, 90, Hillwood Mus., L.I., 1991, A.C. Project Room, N.Y.C., 1991—, Nicole Klagsburn Gallery, 1993, Phillippe Rizzo, Paris, 1992, P.P.O.W., N.Y.C., 1992, Fawbush Gallery, N.Y.C., 1992, Amy Lipton Gallery, N.Y.C., 1992, David Zwirner Gallery, N.Y.C., 1993, Turner/Krail Galleries, L.A., 1993, Mercer Union, Toronto, 1996, Velan Gallery, Torino, Italy, 1996, The Agency, London, 1995, Lombard/Freid, N.Y.C., 1995; represented in permanent collections: Walker Art Ctr., Nat. Mus. Am. Art, Washington, Nat. Collection, Washington, Nat. Mus. Women in the Arts, Washington, Guggenheim Mus. Art, N.Y.C., Mus. Contemporary Art, Chgo., Cleveland Inst. Art., 1993, and others; subject of 15-yr. retrospective travelling to numerous art and ednl. instns. throughout U.S., 1988-91; author: Seven Cycles: Public Rituals, 1981, To Dance: Painting with Performance in Mind, 1985, Seven Sites, 1988-90, Shape Shifter: Seven Mediums, 1990; author/photographer: Firsthand, 1993; contbr. articles to profl. jours.; included numerous books. Recipient Visual Arts grant NEA, 1981, Creative Artists Pub. Svc. grant State of N.Y., 1982. Mem. Conf. Women in Visual Arts (founding mem.), Women's Action Coalition, Heresies Mag. Collective (founding mem.). Home: 110 Mercer St New York NY 10012-3865

EDELSON, ZELDA SARAH TOLL, retired editor; b. Phila., Oct. 18, 1929; d. Louis David and Rose (Eisenstein) Toll; m. Marshall Edelson, Dec. 27, 1952; children: Jonathan Toll Edelson, Rebecca Jo Edelson, David Jan Tolchinsky. BA, U. Chgo., 1949, postgrad., 1949-52. Editor-writer Consol. Book Pubs., Chgo., 1953-56; social worker Balt. City Dept. Pub. Welfare, 1956-57; pub. relations writer Md. Dept. Employment Security, Balt., 1958-59; museum editor Yale Peabody Mus., New Haven, 1970-76, head publs., 1976-95, editor mus.'s Discovery mag., 1983-95; lectr. in sci. writing Yale U., 1983-84. Editor numerous publs. including: The Great Dinosaur Mural at Yale: The Age of Reptiles, 1990. U. Chgo. scholar, 1947-51.

EDELSTEIN, JEAN, artist, performance artist; b. N.Y.C., Mar. 18, 1927; d. Jack Silvers and Sarah Glassman; m. Seymour Edelstein, June 23, 1949, children: Bruce, Barbara. Cert., Pratt Inst., 1947; student, Art Students League, 1947-48, UCLA, 1952. One-person shows include Laguna Beach (Calif.) Mus. Art, 1973, Jacqueline Anhalt Gallery, L.A., 1974, Bird's Eye View Gallery, Newport Beach, Calif., 1978, Karl Bornstein Gallery, Santa Monica, Calif., 1981, Gallery Newz, Tokyo, 1985, Ruth Bachofner Gallery, Santa Monica, 1985, 87, 89, Sherry Frumkin Gallery, Santa Monica, 1992, U. Judaism, L.A., 1993, Nemiroff-Deutsch Gallery, Santa Monica, 1994; exhibited in group shows Otis Art Inst., L.A., 1967, Mt. St. Mary's Coll., L.A., 1975, L.A. County Mus. Art, Rental Gallery, 1978, LACE Gallery, L.A., 1980, Eason Gallery, Santa Fe, 1983, San Francisco Mus. Art, 1985, Korean Cultural Gallery, L.A., 1989, Sherry Frumkin Gallery, Santa Monica, 1991, Valerie Miller Gallery, Palm Desert, Calif., 1992, Art Space Gallery, N.Y.C., 1992; represented in pub. collections and commns. Robert Civitas Pub., Sao Paolo, Brazil, Sheraton Inner Harbor Hotel, Balt., Focus Lexington Hotel, Tulsa, Lloyds Bank, L.A., Toyota Corp., Torrance, Calif., Revoltella Mus., Trieste, Italy; performances at Ruth Bachofner Gallery, L.A., 1985, 93, Pacific Asian Mus., Pasadena, Calif., 1990, Exploratorium Mus., San Francisco, 1992, Revoltella Mus., Trieste, 1993, Nat. Mus. Women in Arts, Washington, 1994; works published in L.A. Times, Artweek, Images and Issues, ArtScene, Visions Mag., Flash Art. Recipient scholarship Art Students League, 1947, fellowship NEA Midatlantic, 1996. Home and Studio: # 5A 354 Broome St New York NY 10013

EDELSTEIN, TERI J., museum administrator, educator; b. Johnstown, Pa., June 23, 1951; d. Robert Morten and HuldaLois (Friedhoff) E. BA, U. Pa., 1972, MA, 1977, PhD, 1979; cert. NYU, 1984. Lectr., U. Guelph, Ont., Can., 1977-79; asst. dir. for acad. programs Yale Ctr. for Brit. Art, New Haven, 1979-83; dir. Mt. Holyoke Coll. Art Mus., South Hadley, Mass., 1983-90, dir. Skinner Mus., 1983-90, mem. faculty dept. art, 1983-90; dir. Smart Mus. Art, U. Chgo., 1990-92, sr. lectr. U. Chgo. dept. of art, 1990—; dep. dir. Art Inst. of Chgo., 1992—; mem. adv. bd. Sculpture Chgo., Mus. Loan Network, Knight and Pew Founds. Yale Ctr. Brit. Art fellow, NEA fellow; Penfield scholar U. Pa., 1975. Mem. Coll. Art Assn., Artable, Am. Assn. Museums, Am. Soc. 18th Century Studies, Chgo. Network, Walpole Soc. Office: Art Inst Chgo 111 S Michigan Ave Chicago IL 60603-6110

EDEN, F(LORENCE) BROWN, artist; b. Jericho Center, Vt., Oct. 10, 1916; d. Arthur Castle and Eva Merita (Lowrey) Brown; m. Edwin Winfield Eden, Sept. 4, 1937; children: Donna Jean, Sandra Elizabeth, Kathy Lynn. Student, U. Fla. Extension, 1955-59, U. Mich., 1963. Art instr. Ann Arbor (Mich.) City Club, 1962-63; tchr., oil painting, printmaking Jacksonville (Fla.) Art Mus., 1963-68; profl. artist pvt. practice Jacksonville, 1962—. One-woman shows include The Fox Galleries, Atlanta, 1986, Harmon Galleries, Sarasota, 1987, 89-90, 92-93, Gallery Contemporanea, Jacksonville, 1988, Artist Assocs. Gallery, Atlanta, 1990, The Donn Roll Galleries, Sarasota, 1994; corp. collections include Fed. Rs. Bank Atlanta, Bank Am., Coca-Cola Co., So. Bell, Sheraton Corp., AT&T, Trust Co. Ga., Shell Oil, Touche Ross, Cooper and Lybrand, Delta Airlines, 5th Dist. Ct. Appeals Bldg., Daytona Beach, Fla., Edwin and Ruth Kennedy Mus. Am. Art, U. Ohio, Athens; exhibited in group shows at Ala. Nat. Watercolors, Fla., Ga. Nat. Audubon Nat., Painters in Casein and Acrylics Nat., N.Y.C., Jacksonville Art Mus. Mem. Jacksonville Art Mus. Recipient First award Fla. Artist Group, 1971, 79, Fla. Artists, 1969, The Painting award Major Fla. Artists, 1979, numerous other 1st place awards. Mem. Am. Women Artists, Nat. Mus. of Women in the Arts (charter mem.), So. Watercolor Soc., Fla. Watercolor Soc., Ga. Watercolor Soc., Ala. Watercolor Soc., Jacksonville Coalition of Visual Artists, Fla. Artists, Fla. Crown Treasures. Home and Studio: 5375 Sanders Rd Jacksonville FL 32277-1333

EDEN-FETZER, DIANNE TONI, nurse, project coordinator; b. Washington, Mar. 1, 1946; d. Lawrence Antonio Laurenzi and Eleanor Charlotte (Sparrough) Watson; m. William Earle Eden, Aug. 5, 1967 (div. 1982); 1 child, Christopher Lance; m. John Thompson Fetzer, Sept. 2, 1987. AA in Nursing, SUNY, Farmingdale, 1978; BS in Nursing, Towson (Md.) State U., 1990. RN, N.Y., Md. Charge nurse dept. neurosurgery U. Md. Hosp., Balt., 1978-79, nurse clincian I, 1979-84, dept. nursing and neurology project coord. Nat. Stroke Data Bank, 1984-90, nursing edn. cons. dept. neurology and neurosurgery, 1984—, sr. ptnr. neuro intensive care unit, 1990—. Mem. AACN, Am. Heart Assn. (fellow stroke coun.), Sigma Theta Tau. Democrat. Roman Catholic. Office: Univ Md Hosp 22 S Greene St Baltimore MD 21201-1544

EDGAR, MARILYN RUTH, counselor; b. Springfield, Mo., Oct. 2, 1948; d. Donald LaVerne Sr. and Ruth Elenor (McClellan) Wilson; m. Robert Stephen Edgar, June 23, 1979; stepchildren: Terri, John, Shawna. BA in Psychology, Calif. State U., Sacramento, 1983, MS in Counseling, 1987. Lic. marriage, family, and child counselor, Calif. Counselor Sacramento Life Ctr., 1983-91; marriage and family therapist New Horizons Counseling Ctr., Carmichael, Calif., 1987—, exec. dir., supr. intern counselors, 1993—. Guest profl. therapist Faith in Crisis Group, Sacramento; mem. Warehouse Ministries of Sacramento, 1978—; mem. Arthritis Found., 1996. Mem. Calif. Assn. Marriage and Family Therapists (Valley chpt. 1992—), Capital City Motorcycle Club (pub. rels. officer 1994, sec., bd. mem. 1996). Republican. Office: New Horizons Counseling Ctr 3300 Walnut Ave Carmichael CA 95608-3240

EDGAR, RUTH R., retired educator; b. Great Falls, S.C., Jan. 7, 1930; d. Robert Hamer and Clara Elizabeth (Ellenberg) Rogers. AA, Stephens Coll., Columbia, Mo., 1949; BS, So. Meth. U., 1951; MA, Appalachian State U., Boone, N.C., 1977; postgrad., Limestone Coll., Gaffney, S.C., 1971. Lic. real estate salesman, broker. Home economist Lone Star Gas Co., Dallas, 1951-53, So. Union Gas Co., Austin, Tex., 1953-56, Southwestern Pub. Svc. Co., Amarillo, Tex., 1956-57; with Peeler Real Estate, 1970-71, Burns High Sch., Lawndale, N.C., 1971-73, Cen. Cleveland Mid. Sch., Lawndale, 1973-77, Burns Jr. High Sch., Lawndale, 1977-88; resource tchr. South Cleveland Elem. Sch., Shelby, N.C., 1988-90, Elizabeth Elem. Sch., Shelby, 1990-94, Washington Elem. Sch., Waco, N.C., 1990-92; ret., 1994. Mem. supts. adv. coun., Cleveland County, 1971-75, Cleveland County Art Soc., 1972-73, Cen. United Meth. Ch. Mem. N.C. Assn. Educators, NEA. Home: 401 Forest Hill Dr Shelby NC 28150-5520

EDGELL, KARIN JANE, reading specialist, special education educator; b. Rockford, Ill., July 17, 1937; d. Donald Rickard and Leona Marquerite (Villard) Williams; m. George Paul Edgell III, May 6, 1960; 1 child, Scott. Student, Rollins Coll., 1955-57; BS, U. Ill., 1960, MEd, 1966; MA, Roosevelt U., 1989. Tchr. Alexandria (Va.) City Pub. Schs., 1963-79; asst. to dir. Reading Ctr. George Washington U., Washington, 1979-80; tchr. Winnetka (Ill.) Pub. Schs., 1982-89, Arlington County (Va.) Pub. Schs., 1989—. Mem. NEA, ASCD, Nat. Coun. Tchrs. Eng., Internat. Reading Assn., Va. Edn. Assn., Va. Reading Assn., Greater Washington Reading Coun., Coun. Exceptional Children, Phi Delta Kappa. Home: 6275 Chaucer View Cir Alexandria VA 22304-3546

EDGERTON, ELIZABETH, artist, Shiatsu practitioner; b. N.Y.C., Apr. 24, 1947; d. Malcolm James and Adele Jeanne (Pleasance) E.; children: Wesley Elizabeth Cullen, Timothy Edgerton Cullen. BA, Sarah Lawrence Coll., 1970. Cert. art tchr. One-woman shows include Am. Lang. Ctr., Rabat, Morocco, 1983, U.S. Embassy, Rabat, 1983-84, Torreon de la Iglesia, Mojacar, Spain, 1985-86, U.S. nat. Arboretum, Washington, 1986, Entre a la Carte, 1988, Mus. Realty, Cambridge, Mass., 1988, Peter Christians, Hanover, N.H., 1989, Gallery Oshun, Lebanon, N.H., 1989, Upcountry Art, Gantham, N.H., 1989-90, Lightgate, Thetford, Vt., 1994, Batchelder Artist Studio, 1995; group exhibits include Silvermine Guild, A V A Gallery, Hanover, 1986, 88-90. Recipient 3d prize Art Show 88 Norwich U., 1988, 1st prize Expocician de Navidad Mojacar, Spain, 1985.

EDGREN, GRETCHEN GRONDAHL, magazine editor; b. Portland, Oreg., Mar. 17, 1931; d. Jack W. and Alice Belle (Wells) Grondahl; m. James McNeese, Oct. 22, 1955 (div. Nov. 1974); children: Amy, Terence James; m. Alvin H. Edgren, Dec. 14, 1984. BJ, U. Oreg., 1952. Staff writer The Oregonian, Portland, 1952-61; editor Sunday mag. The San Juan (P.R.) Star, 1963-65; inventory and info. specialist USAF and U.S. Army Recruiting Command, San Antonio and Chgo., 1965-67; assoc. editor VIP mag. (Playboy Clubs), Chgo., 1967-69, mng. editor, 1969-70; assoc. editor Playboy mag., Chgo., 1970-74, sr. editor, 1974-92, contbg. editor, 1992—. Author: The Playboy Book, 1994, The Playmate Book, 1996; editor: New Credit Rights for Women, 1976; contbr. articles to mags. Adv. bd. Old Oreg. Alumni mag., U. Oreg., Eugene, 1988—; pres. bd. dirs. Civic Arts Coun., Oak Park, Ill., 1976-84; bd. dirs. Village Players, Oak Park-River Forest (Ill.) Symphony Assn., Oak Park Concert Chorale, 1975-91; mem. Oak Park Cable TV commn., 1984-86. Mem. Confrerie des Vignerons de St. Vincent Mâcon (maitresse du chpt. 1988-92), Webfoot Soc. U. Oreg., Phi Beta Kappa, Delta Delta Delta. Episcopalian.

EDIGHOFFER-MURRAY, ANNA BARBEL, administrative officer, pharmacist, political scientist; b. Annweiler, Germany, Apr. 9, 1956; Came to the U.S., 1988; d. Kurt and Irmgard (J.) Edighoffer; m. Peter Ian Murray, Apr. 6, 1996. Diploma in Polit. Sci., Free Universität Berlin, 1985; Cert. in Internat. and European Law, Europa Inst. Der Universitaet Des Saarlandes, 1987. Cert. pharmacist asst. Germany. Pharmacist asst. Trifels-Apotheke, Berlin, 1973-75, Adler-Apotheke, Berlin, 1975-76, Dornier KG, Berlin, 1976-77; editl. asst. Der Tagesspiegel, Berlin, 1980-81; rsch. asst. Free U., Berlin, 1984-86; JPO UN, N.Y.C., 1988-89, procurement, adminstrv. officer, 1989—. Mem. NAFE, Nat. Assn. Procurement Mgmt., Gewerkschaft Oeffentlicher Transport und Verkeh. Office: UN 42d St & 21st Ave New York NY 10012

EDINBORO, CHARLOTTE HELENE, aerospace engineer; b. San Francisco, Aug. 26, 1955; d. Raoul Jose and Lieselotte H. (Werner) Fajardo; m. Terry William Edinboro, Mar. 18, 1978 (div. Dec. 1989). BS in Aero. and Astro. Engring., Purdue U., 1975, MS in Aero. and Astro. Engring., 1976; DVM, U. Calif., Davis, 1990. Engr. II and III, computing analyst III Jet Propulsion Lab., Pasadena, Calif., 1976-79; mem. tech. staff TRW Def. Sys. Group, Sunnyvale, Calif., 1979-82; staff engr. Ultrasys. Def. and Space Sys., Sunnyvale, 1982-84; sys. engr. Scitor Corp., Sunnyvale, 1984—; relief vet. various practices, San Francisco Bay area, 1990—. Bd. dirs. Ctr. for Animal Protection and Edn., Scotts Valley, Calif., 1996—. Recipient 2 group achievement awards NASA, 1981. Mem. AVMA, AIAA (Outstanding Student 1976), Peninsula Vet. Med. Assn. (treas., v.p. 1991—). Office: Scitor Corp 256 Gibraltar Dr Sunnyvale CA 94089

EDISON, DIANE, artist, educator; b. Plainfield, N.J., Sept. 3, 1950; d. Anthony Joseph and Davie Wilhelmina (Johnson) E. BFA, Sch. Visual Arts, N.Y.C., 1976; postgrad., Skowhegan Sch. Painting, 1984; MFA, U. Pa., 1986. Asst. prof. Savannah (Ga.) Coll. Art and Design, 1990-92, U. Ga., Athens, 1991—, U. Ga. Studies Abroad, Cortona, Italy, 1993; panelist Telfair Acad. Arts and Scis., Savannah, 1992, Ga. Mus. Art, Athens, 1993, Ga. Coun. for Arts, 1993—. Exhbns. include Marymount Manhattan Coll. Gallery, N.Y.C., 1989, Islip (N.Y.) Art Mus. Brookward Hall, 1989, The Bertha and Karl Leubsdorf Art Gallery, N.Y.C, 1990, Cork Gallery Lincoln Ctr., N.Y.C., 1990, Salena Gallery L.I. U., Bklyn., 1990, Savannah Coll. Art and Design, 1990, Rotunda Gallery, Bklyn., 1991, St. Louis Artist Guild, 1992, Frumkin/Adams Gallery, N.Y.C., 1992, 94, 95, Ark. Arts Ctr., Little Rock, 1992, 93, 94, 95, 96, Ga. Mus. Art, Athens, 1993, Ga. Artist Registry, Atlanta, 1994, Charles More Gallery, Phila., 1994, U. Mo., Kansas City, 1994, U. Ga., Athens, 1994, Southeastern Ctr. Contemporary Art, Winston-Salem, N.C., 1994, Chattahoochee Valley Art Mus., Lagrange, Ga., 1995, Nexus Contemporary Art Ctr., Atlanta, 1995; represented in permanent collections at Ark. Arts Ctr., also pvt. collections; represented by George Adams Gallery, 1995, 96. Artist grantee Ga. Coun. for Arts, 1993, Nat. Endowment for Arts, 1994, jr. faculty rsch. grantee U. Ga., 1994; Milton Avery Found fellow, N.Y.C., 1995; artist resident Millay Colony for Arts Inc., Austerlitz, N.Y., 1995, Blue Mountain Ctr., Blue Mountain Lake, N.Y., 1996. Mem. AAUP, Coll. Art Assn. Democrat. Episcopalian. Office: U Ga Visual Arts Bldg Jackson St Athens GA 30602

EDISON, JANIS DIANE, psychologist; b. Watertown, S.D., June 20, 1962; d. Elmer Louis and Lillian Mae (Wegner) Rogness; m. Tim Allen Edison, June 6, 1981 (div. Jan. 1990). Student, Concordia Coll., Moorhead, Minn., 1981; BS, Jacksonville State U., 1985; MS, U. Ga., 1988, PhD, 1990. Lic.

psychologist, Pa. Postdoctoral fellow Case Western Res. Sch. Medicine, Cleveland, OH, 1990-91; staff psychologist, coord. behavioral medicine VA Med. Ctr., Butler, Pa, 1991—. Mem. APA, Assn. for Advancement of Behavior Therapy (award for presentation, 1989), Phi Kappa Phi, Sigma Xi. Office: VA Med Ctr Psych (116B) 325 New Castle Rd Butler PA 16001

EDMANDS, SUSAN BANKS, consulting company executive; b. New Rochelle, N.Y., Oct. 7, 1944; d. George Dixon and Marian (Lepied) Banks; children: Whatleigh Winthrop, Benjamin Bruce II. BS, Boston U., 1966; cert. in libr. sci., Northeastern U., Boston, 1974. Tchr. project head start Office Econ. Opportunity, Washington, 1966; English tchr. Wattana Sch., Bangkok, 1969-71; market researcher Pauline Rendell Assocs., Somerville, Mass., 1971-72; food info. specialist FIND/SVP Inc., N.Y.C., 1977-80; mgr. tech. and indsl. group Find/SVP, Inc., N.Y.C., 1980-90, dir. consulting svcs. divsn., 1990—. Mem. Soc. Chimie Industrielle (v.p. Am. sect.), Chemists Club (trustee). Home: 24 Deming Ln Stamford CT 06903-4729 Office: Find/SVP Inc 625 Avenue Of The Americas New York NY 10011-2034

EDMISTON, MARILYN, clinical psychologist; b. Lewiston, Maine, Dec. 9, 1934; d. Lewis Walter and Anne Mary (Nezol) Burgess; m. John Laing Edmiston (div. May 1969); children: John Laing, Eric James. BA, Fla. Atlantic U., 1967, MA, 1969; PhD, U. Ga., 1973. Lic. ind. practice psychologist, Calif., Fla. Staff psychologist children and adolescent unit Cen. Ga. Regional Hosp., Milledgeville, 1973-74, chief psychologist, 1974-75; clin. psychologist South Fla. State Hosp., Pembroke Pines, 1976-77; state psychol. cons. Office Vocat. Rehab., Fla. Dept. Health and Rehab. Svcs., Tallahassese, 1977-83; sr. psychologist forensic svcs. Fla. State Hosp., Chattahoochee, 1983-96, pres.-elect, pres. profl. clin. staff, 1990-94; pvt. practice Tallahassee, 1996—; expert witness Fla. cts., 1983-96. Mem. APA, Am. Bd. Forensic Examiners (diplomate), Nat. Register Health Svc. Providers in Psychology, World Fedn. for Mental Health, Internat. Coun. Psychologists. Democrat. Home: 2161 Shangri La Ln Tallahassee FL 32303-2360

EDMONDS, ANNE CAREY, librarian; b. Penang, Malaysia, Dec. 19, 1924; d. William John and Nell (Carey) E. Student, U. Reading, Eng., 1942-44; BA, Barnard Coll., 1948; MSLS, Columbia U., 1950; MA, Johns Hopkins U., 1959; postgrad., Western Res. U., 1960-61; LHD Mount Holyoke Coll., 1994. With War Damage Commn., London, Eng., 1944-46; children's asst. Enoch Pratt Free Libr., Balt., 1948-49; reference libr. Sch. Bus. Adminstrn., CCNY, 1950-51; reference libr., then asst. libr. readers' services Goucher Coll., Balt., 1951-60; exchange reference libr. European svcs. libr. BBC, London, 1955; instr. Sch. L.S., Syracuse U., summer 1960; libr. Douglass Coll., Rutgers U., New Brunswick, N.J., 1961-64, instr., summer 1962, fall 1963; libr. Mt. Holyoke Coll., 1964-94; vis. librarian U. North, Turfloop, South Africa, 1976-77; mem. libr. vis. com. Wheaton Coll., Norton, Mass., 1978-92; mem. local systems adv. group Online Computer Libr. Ctr., Inc., 1984-87, mem. adv. com. on coll. and univ. librs., 1988-89. Author: A Memory Book: Mount Holyoke College, 1837-1987, 1988, (with Gai Carpenter and others) Computing Strategies in Liberal Arts Colleges, 1992. Mem. South Hadley (Mass.) Bicentennial Com., 1975-76; mem. accreditation teams Middle States Assn. Colls. and Secondary Schs., 1963-94, New Eng. Assn. Schs. and Colls., 1986-94; bd. dirs. U.S. Book Exchange, 1973-76, 80-83; exec. com. New Eng. Libr. Info. Network, 1974-76, 79-85, chmn., 1982-84; mem. Adv. Commn. Historic Deerfield, 1975-81, 86-94. Mem. ALA, Am. Hist. Assn., Assn. Coll. Rsch. Libraries (pres. 1970-71, chmn. constn. and bylaws com. New Eng. chpt. 1975-76, pres. New Eng. chpt. 1983-84).

EDMONDS, MARY PATRICIA, biological sciences educator; b. Racine, Wis., May 7, 1922; d. Millard Samuel and Sarah (Gibbons) E. BA, Milw.-Downer Coll., 1943; MA, Wellesley (Mass.) Coll., 1945; PhD, U. Pa., 1951; DSc (hon.), Lawrence U., 1983. Instr. Wellesley Coll., 1945-46; postdoctoral fellow U. Ill., Urbana, 1950-52; U. Wis., Madison, 1952-55; rsch. assoc. Montefiore Hosp., Pitts., 1955-65; asst. prof. U. Pitts., 1965-71, assoc. prof., 1971-76, prof., 1976—; mem. molecular biology study sect. NIH, Bethesda, Md., 1974-78. Contbr. articles to profl. jours. Recipient Woman of Yr. in Sci. award Chatham Coll., 1986; Rsch. Career Devel. award NIH, 1962-71, rsch. grantee, 1962-91. Mem. NAS, Am. Soc. Biol. Chemists, Am. Soc. for Cancer Rsch. Office: U Pitts Dept Biol Sci Pittsburgh PA 15260

EDMONDS, VELMA MCINNIS, nursing educator; b. N.Y.C., Feb. 17, 1940; d. Walter Lee and Eva Doris (Grant) McInnis; children: Stephen Clay, Michelle Louise. Diploma, Charity Hosp. Sch. Nursing, New Orleans, 1961; BSN, Med. Coll. Ga., 1968; MSN, U. Ala., Birmingham, 1980; postgrad. in doctoral nursing sci., La. State U., 1994—. Staff nurse Ochsner Found. Hosp., New Orleans, 1961-63, 1987—, clin. educator, 1987-89; staff nurse Suburban Hosp., Bethesda, Md., 1963-65; asst. DON svc., dir. staff devel. Providence Hosp., Mobile, Ala., 1967-70; staff nurse MICU U. So. Ala. Med. Ctr., Mobile, 1980-82, clin. nurse specialist, nutrition/metabolic support, 1982-84; instr., coord., BSN completion program Northwestern State Univ., Coll. Nursing, Natchitoches, La., 1984-86; head nurse So. Bapt. Hosp., New Orleans, 1986-87; instr. of nursing La. State U.Med. Ctr., New Orleans, 1989-91, asst. prof. nursing, 1991—; clin. coord. Transitional Hosp. Corp., 1994-95; gov.-apptd. mem. La. State Bd. Examiners in Dietetics and Nutrition, 1990—, sec.-treas. State Bd. of Examiners, 1996—. Gov.'s appointee La. State Bd. Examiners in Dietetics and Nutrtion, sec.-treas. Recipient Excellence in Nursing group award Ochsner Fedn. Hosp., New Orleans, 1987, cert. Merit Tuberculosis Assn. Greater New Orleans, 1961. Mem. ANA, Nat. Soc. Nutrition Edn., La. State Nurses' Assn. (dist. 7), Am. Soc. Parenteral and Enteral Nutrition, La. State Soc. Parenteral and Enteral Nutrition (program and edn. coms.), Assn. La. State Soc. Parenteral and Enteral Nutrition, Mobile Area Nonvolitional Nutrition Support Assn. (past pres.), Sigma Theta Tau.

EDMONDSON, LINDA LOUISE, optometrist; b. Wyandotte, Mich., Dec. 11, 1947; d. Richard Eugene and Mildred Louise (Horste) Weaver; m. William Edmondson II, June 1, 1969. BA, Ohio Wesleyan U., 1969; AM, Ind. U., 1971; BS, Pa. Coll. Optometry, 1975, OD, 1977. Assoc. instr. Ind. U., Bloomington, 1967-72; editor biol. abstracts Biosis Info. Svcs., Phila., 1972-73; optometrist pvt. practice, Bluefield, W.Va., 1977-84; prof. Northeastern State U. Coll. Optometry, Tahlequah, Okla., 1984—; jour. referee Jour. of Am. Optometric Assn., 1988—, Optometry and Vision Sci., 1990—. Editor: Eye and Vision Conditions in the American Indian, 1990; contbr. articles to profl. jours. Asst. dir. Heart O'The Hills Chpt., Sweet Adelines, Tahlequah, Okla., 1989—. Mem. AAUW, Am. Acad. Optometry, Am. Optometric Assn., Okla. Profl. Country Dance Assn., Cherokee County Soc. for Prevention of Cruelty to Animals, Beta Sigma Kappa. Home: PO Box 871 Tahlequah OK 74465-0871 Office: NSU Coll of Optometry Tahlequah OK 74464

EDMONDSON, MARY ELLEN, artist; b. McLean, Va., Nov. 8, 1919; d. William Grant and Mary Pauline (Neff) E. Student, George Washington Jr. Coll., Washington, 1938-39; degree in art, Abbott Art Sch., 1943. Artist, illustrator Fed. Govt. Petroleum Adminstrn. for War, 1942-46, Bur. Reclamation, 1946-49. Exhibited in group shows Art League, Alexandria, Va., 1972-87, Miniature Soc. Washington, 1974-96 (awards 1978, 89, 91), Royal Miniature Soc., London, 1995. Mem. Ga. Miniature Soc. (1st place graphics 1996), Miniature Soc. N.J. (2d place in fine prints, 1977, 3d place, 1994). Democrat. Home: 1927 Franklin Ave Mc Lean VA 22101

EDMUNDS, JANE CLARA, communications consultant; b. Chgo., Mar. 16, 1922; d. John Carson and Clara (Kummerow) Carrigan; m. William T. Dean, Aug. 30, 1947 (div. 1953; dec. July 1984); 1 son, John Charles; Edmund S. Kopacz, Sept. 24, 1955 (div. 1973); children: Christine Ellen, Jan Carson. Student in math., Northwestern U. Chemist Mars Inc., Oak Park, Ill., 1942-47; with Cons. Engr. Mag., Maujer Pub. Co., St. Joseph, Mich., 1953-58, 69-74; sr. editor Cons. Engr. Mag. Tech. Pub. Co., Barrington, Ill., 1975-77, exec. editor, 1977-82, editorial dir., 1983-86; asst. editor women's pages rewrite desk News-Palladium, Benton Harbor, Mich., 1967-68; free lance journalist St. Joseph, 1959-68; communications cons. Schaumburg, Ill., 1987—. Chmn. Berrien County (Mich.) Nat. Found. March of Dimes, 1968; mem. campaign com. Rep. Party, 1954. Recipient award Bausch & Lomb, 1940, award Nat. Found. Service, 1969, Silver Hat award Constrn. Writers Assn., 1986, Chmn.'s award Profl. Engrs. in Pvt. Practice div. NSPE, 1987; grantee AID, 1979. Assoc. fellow Soc. Tech. Communication (chmn. St. Joseph chpt. 1972 Disting. Tech. Communication awards); mem. Am. Soc. Bus. Press Editors (past bd. mem.), Constrn. Writers Assn. (past dir.), Smithsonian Instn., Chgo. Art Inst. Assocs., Field Mus. Assocs. Republican. Episcopalian. Office: 1404 Hampton Ln Schaumburg IL 60193-2531

EDMUNDS, NANCY GARLOCK, federal judge; b. Detroit, July 10, 1947; m. William C. Edmunds, 1977. BA cum laude, Cornell U., 1969; MA in Teaching, U. Chgo., 1971; JD summa cum laude, Wayne U., 1976. Bar: Mich. 1976. With Plymouth Canton Public Schools, 1971-73; law clk. Barris, Sott, Denn & Driker, 1973-75; law clk. to Hon. Ralph Freeman U.S. Dist. Ct. (ea. dist.) Mich., 1976-78; ptnr. litigation sect. Dykema Gossett, 1984-92, resident Oakland County, 1986-92; judge U.S. Dist. Ct. (ea. dist.) Mich., 1992—; trustee Hist. Soc. U.S. Dist Ct. (ea. dist.) Mich. Bd. trustees Temple Beth El; mem. bus. and profl. women's divsn., lawyers' divsn. Jewish Welfare Fedn./Allied Jewish Campaign; mem. Saginaw Valley State U. Bd. Control, 1991-92. Mem. ABA, Fed. Judges Assn., Nat. Assn. Women Judges, Federalist Soc., State Bar Mich. (chair U.S. cts. com. 1990-91). Office: US Dist Ct 211 US Courthouse Detroit MI 48226-2799

EDMUNDS, SHARON, artist; b. Waltham, Mass., Dec. 21, 1953; d. Aloysius Joseph and Clara Sylvia (Caia) Edmunds. Grad., Sch. of Mus. Fine Arts, Boston, 1979. Shows include AAO Gallery, Buffalo, N.Y., 1987, Newport Art Mus., R.I., 1987, Springville Mus. Art, Utah, 1987, 88, Galerie Triangle, Washington, D.C., 1988, Braithwaite Fine Arts Gallery, Cedar City, Utah, 1988, 89, Clary-Miner Gallery, Buffalo, N.Y., 1988, Currier Gallery Art Mus., Manchester, N.H., 1989, Galerie Art-Jeunesse, Montreal, Que., Can., 1990. Recipient 1st Pl. Watercolor Nepenthe Mundi Soc., Wichita, Kan., 1987, 3rd Pl. AAO Gallery, 1987, Award of Excellence, Braithwaite Fine Arts Gallery, 1988. Studio: 36 Prentice St Waltham MA 02154

EDSON, KAY LOUISE, equity trader; b. Montpelier, Vt., Apr. 9, 1946; d. Robert Robinson and Evelyn S. (Stowell) E. Student, Northeastern U., Boston, 1964-66, Johnson State Coll., 1984-85. Engring. aide Gen. Electric Co., Burlington, Vt., 1967-70; asst. equity trader Nat. Life Ins. Co., Montpelier, 1971-75, head equity trader, 1975-86; v.p., head equity trader Nat. Life Investment Mgmt. Co., Montpelier, 1986—. Membership chair Dist. One Altrusa Internat., East. Can., New Eng., Bermuda, 1986-88, fundraising coord., 1988-90. Mem. Vt. Women's Bowling Assn. (dir. 1985-93, v.p. 1993—), Twin City Women's Bowling Assn. (bd. dirs. 1967—), Altrusa Club of Barre (pres. 1986-88). Office: Nat Life Investment Mgmt Co One National Life Dr Montpelier VT 05604

EDSON, MARIAN LOUISE, communications executive; b. Sidney, Mont., Mar. 21, 1940; d. David Ira and Myrtle (Ewing) Drury; m. James Arthur Edson, Oct. 14, 1961; children: Nadine L. Mykins, Jeanine Clare Edson. Student, U. Wash., 1961-62; BS, Mont. State U., 1962; postgrad., SUNY, Binghamton, 1975-76. Cert. tchr. Mont., Wash., N.Y. Lead editor, flight data file Johnson Space Ctr., Houston, 1980-85, coordinator for payload reconfiguration data collection, 1985-86, supr. flight data file, 1986-87; lead technical editor Bell Aerospace/Textron, Buffalo, N.Y., 1987; prodn. mgr. ASYST Software Tech., Rochester, N.Y., 1987-88, publ. mgr., 1988-94; publ. mgr. Raymond Corp., Greene, N.Y., 1994—; project dir. Raymond Corp., Greene, N.Y., 1994—. Edn. com. Bay Area League Women Voters, Houston, 1984-85; assoc. Rochester Women's Network, 1987—; founding mem. Macedon (N.Y.) Reading Ctr., 1968—. Fellow Life Office Mgmt. Assn.; mem. AIAA, Soc. Tech. Communicators (pres.), Nat. Mgmt. Assn., Nat. Assn. Purchasing Mgrs., Women in Comm. Inc., Genesee Ornithol. Soc., Rochester Acad. Sci. Republican. Home: 4 Boulevard Pky Rochester NY 14612-5515

EDWARDS, BARBARA JEAN, secondary educator; b. Chgo., Mar. 22, 1962; d. Robert Casler and Karen Marina (Meister) E. BA in Spanish and Sociology, Gettysburg Coll., 1984; MA, Middlebury Coll., 1994. Cert. Spanish tchr., Pa. GED instr. Ctr. for Human Svcs., Gettysburg, Pa., 1984-86; Spanish tchr. Hempfield High Sch., Landisville, Pa., 1986-87; Spanish/ESL tchr. Gettysburg High Sch., 1987—. Chairperson missions com. Living Hope Presbyn. Ch., Gettysburg, 1989-94, sec. pastoral search com., 1994-95. Recipient Patriotism award VFW, 1980. Mem. Pa. State Edn. Assn., NEA, Am. Tchrs. Spanish and Portuguese, Phi Sigma Iota, Alpha Kappa Delta. Republican. Office: Gettysburg Area Sch Dist Lefever St Gettysburg PA 17325

EDWARDS, BRENDA FAYE, counselor; b. Hattiesburg, Miss., Apr. 3, 1945; d. Jack Howell and Annie C. (Sullivan) Zeigler; m. James A. Edwards Jr., June 5, 1962. BA, U. So. Miss., 1968; MEd, U. Ga., 1977. Registered catastropic rehab. supplier; lic. profl. counselor; cert. ins. rehab. specialist. Various positions Miss., 1968-70; tchr. Brunswick (Ga.) Coll., 1970-71; tng. coord. Coastal Ga. Regional Devel. Ctr., Brunswick, 1971-72; tchr. Glynn County Bd. Edn., Adult Edn. Ctr., Brunswick, 1972; social work tech. Gateway Ctr. for Human Devel., Brunswick, 1973; coord. consultation edn. and tng. Coastal Area Community Mental Health Ctr., Brunswick, 1979; rehab. counselor Div. Rehab. Svcs., Dept. Human Resources, Brunswick, 1973-78; supr. basic edn. dept. Brunswick Job Corp. Ctr., 1979-80; rehab. specialist Intracorp, Savannah, Ga., 1980-83; counselor, owner Southeastern Rehab. Svcs., St. Simons Island, Ga., 1983—. Pres. Citizens for Humane Animal Treatment, Brunswick, 1987-90, v.p. 1990-91; sec. Glynn County Animal Control Adv. Bd., Brunswick, 1987-88. Mem. ACA, Am. Mental Health Counselors Assn., Nat. Rehab. Assn., Ga. Rehab. Assn., Lic. Profl. Counselors Assn. Ga., Employee Assistance Profls. Assn., Brunswick Golden Isles C. of C. (chmn. drugs don't work com. 1995—), Internat. Coachmen Caravan, South Ga. Puddle Jumpers. Home: 135 Saint Clair Dr Saint Simons Island GA 31522-1036 Office: Southeastern Rehab Svcs 2483 Demere Rd Ste 103 Saint Simons Island GA 31522

EDWARDS, CAROLYN MULLENAX, public relations executive; b. French Camp, Calif., Dec. 3, 1943; d. Charles Harold and Jessie Jewel (Frost) Mullenax; m. Helton Pressley (div.); m. Dennis D. Edwards, May 29, 1993. BFA, U. Tulsa, 1967; MEd, Ea. N.Mex. U., 1976. Artist Wessels Agy., Spokane, Wash., 1968-70; pub. rels. dir. Spokane (Wash.) Symphony Soc., 1970-72; advt. coord. Crescent Dept. Store, Spokane, 1972-73; art dir., copywriter Sta. KMTY Radio, Clovis, N.Mex., 1976; news editor Clovis News Jour., Clovis, 1976-77; promotion and art dir. Sta. KENW-TV, Portales, N.Mex., 1977-78; coord. alumni affairs and pubs. Ea. N.Mex. U., Portales, 1978-80; dir. pubs., TV and pub. info. Ea. N.Mex. U., Clovis, 1985-90; dir. mktg. & pub. info. Clovis Community Coll. (formerly Ea. N.Mex. U.-Clovis), 1990—; producer pub. affairs program Sta. KMCC-TV, Clovis, 1981-84; devel. and pub. info. dir. Mental Health Resources Inc., Portales, N.Mex., 1980-85. Bd. dirs. N.Mex. Outdoor Drama Assn., San Jon, 1986-95, Univ. Symphony League, Clovis, 1984-88. Mem. N.Mex. Press Women (scholarship chair 1994-96, comm. awards 1981-96), Nat. Fedn. Press Women (comm. awards 1984-95), Am. Women in Radio and TV, Clovis C. of C. (bd. dirs. 1984-89), Jr. League (Lubbock, Tex.), Coun. for Advancement and Support Edn. (sec.-editor dist. IV 1990-92, design award 1991), Nat. Coun. for Mktg. and Pub. Rels. (dist. IV award 1989-91, 93-96, nat. award 1993-95), Altrusa Club. Republican. Episcopalian. Office: Clovis CC 417 Schepps Blvd Clovis NM 88101-8345

EDWARDS, DEBORAH TISCH, consumer products company executive; b. Orange, N.J., Feb. 17, 1947; d. Richard Tisch and Marjorie (Pierson) Farley; children: Christine, Harrison Eric. BA, U. S.C., 1969. Homemaker Chatham, 1969-78; fashion dir., buying mgmt. Sears Roebuck, Chgo., 1978-88; cons. Kellwood Co., N.Y.C., 1990-91; acct. exec. Mamiye Bros., N.Y.C., 1991-93; brand mgr. Healthtex (divsn. fo V.F. Corp.), Greenboro, N.C., 1993—; mem. cmty. scv. team Healthtex, Greensboro, N.C., 1993-94; lectr. U. N.C., Greensboro, 1993—. Chmn.'s soc. United Way, Greensboro, N.C., 1994, 95, city schs. panel, 1995; sponsor Christian Children's Fund, Va., 1984—. Home: 308 Tate St Greensboro NC 27403

EDWARDS, DEBRA ANNE DISOTELLE, foundation administration; b. Syracuse, N.Y., June 26, 1955; m. Donald Lee Edwards II, May 24, 1978; children: Brianne, Alexander. BS, U. Colo., 1979. Receptionist, registrar, program dir., dir. Colo. Mountain Coll., Breckenridge, 1979-85; exec. dir. The Summit Found., Breckenridge, 1985—. Mem. cmty. bd. Norwest Bank, Frisco, Colo., 1996; mem. adv. bd. Colo. Mountain Coll., 1990—, Colo. State U. Coop. Extension, Frisco, 1988—; initiating mem. Shaping our Summit, Summit County, Colo., 1995—. Mem. Nat. Soc. Fundraising Execs. (Colo. chpt.), Colo. Assn. Nonprofit Orgns., Colo. Assn. Founds., Summit County C. of C., Breckenridge Resort Chamber, Copper Mountain Resort Assn., Women of the Summit, Improve the Summit. Office: The Summit Found PO Box 4000 130 Ski Hill Rd Ste 225 Breckenridge CO 80424

EDWARDS, IRENE ELIZABETH (LIBBY EDWARDS), dermatologist, educator, researcher; b. Winston-Salem, N.C., Mar. 17, 1950; d. Robert Dixon Edwards and Irene Octavia (Temple) Fisher; m. Clayton Samuel Owens, Apr. 19, 1985; 1 child, Sarah Tay. BS magna cum laude, Wake Forest U., 1972; MD, Bowman Gray Sch. Medicine, 1976; postgrad., N.C. Bapt. Hosp., 1979, U. Ariz., 1981, 84. Diplomate Nat. Bd. Med. Examiners, Am. Bd. Internal Medicine, Am. Bd. Pediatrics, Am. Bd. Dermatology. Intern N.C. Bapt. Hosp., Winston-Salem, 1976-78, resident in pediatrics, 1978-79; resident in internal medicine U. Ariz. Health Scis. Ctr., Tucson, 1979-81, resident in dermatology, 1982-84; instr. dermatology U. Ariz. Coll. Medicine, Tucson, 1984-85, asst. prof. dermatology, 1985-90; chief section dermatology Tucson VA Med. Ctr., 1984-90; chief dermatology Carolinas Med. Ctr., Charlotte, N.C., 1990—; clin. assoc. prof. dermatology Bowman Gray Sch. Medicine, Winston-Salem, 1993—, U. N.C., Chapel Hill, 1993—; nat. lectr. in field. Co-author: Genital Dermatology, 1994; contbr. chpts. to books, numerous articles to profl. jours. Reynolds scholar, 1969-72. Fellow Am. Acad. Dermatology, Am. Acad. Pediatrics; mem. Soc. Pediatric Dermatology, Internat. Soc. Tropical Dermatology, Soc. Investigative Dermatology, Women's Dermatologic Soc., Internat. Soc. for Study of Vulvovaginal Disease (exec. coun.), Charlotte Dermatological Soc., Phi Beta Kappa, Alpha Epsilon Delta. Home: 2409 Cuthbertson Rd Waxhaw NC 28173-8110 Office: Carolinas Med Ctr 1000 Blythe Blvd Charlotte NC 28203-5812

EDWARDS, JOANN LOUISE, human resources executive; b. Lebanon, Pa., June 15, 1955; d. Harold Eugene and Kathryn Faye (Smith) E. AA in Human Svcs. with honors, Harrisburg Area Community Coll, 1975; BS with honors, Pa. State U., 1981; MA in Indsl. Rels./Human Resources Mgmt., St. Francis Coll., 1994. Residential program worker Pan Am. Corp., Hershey, Pa., 1975-80, residential program supr., 1981-82, intensive behavior shaping supr., 1982-83; program mgr. Devel. Resources, Inc., Harrisburg, Pa., 1983-85, dir. minimum supervision, 1985-86; dir. human resources New Directions for Progress, Inc. (formerly Devel. Resources, Inc.), Harrisburg, 1986—; faculty grad. program indsl. rels. St. Francis Coll., Harrisburg, 1991—; com. mem. New Directions for Progress Personnel Com., Harrisburg, 1988—. Com. mem. Christian Chs. United Personnel Com., Harrisburg, 1989-90. Mem. Harrisburg Area Personnel Assn., Soc. Human Resource Mgmt., Harrisburg Personnel Assn. Republican. Methodist. Home: 3022 N 3rd St Harrisburg PA 17110-2102 Office: New Directions for Progress 3544 N Progress Ave Harrisburg PA 17110-9638

EDWARDS, JUDITH ELIZABETH, advertising executive; b. St. Louis, May 22, 1933; d. Archie Earl and Ivy Elizabeth (Jones) Hector; m. George N. LaMont Jr., Jan. 9, 1960 (div. Oct. 1965); m. Gary W. Edwards, Nov. 25, 1966; stepchildren: Michael Brent, David Reed Edwards. Grad. high sch., St. Louis, 1951; student, Brown's Bus. Coll., St. Louis. Exec. sec., asst. to chmn. Rep. Nat. Com., Washington, 1958-60; dep. to county clk. Vandervurgh County, Evansville, Ind., 1972-76; sec.-treas. Edwards Outdoor Advtg., Carmi, Ill., 1979—; mem. Evansville Health Planning Coun., 1974-76. Pres. White County Rep. Women's Club, Carmi, 1989—, White County Hosp. Aux. Named Ky. Col. Mem. Carmi Bus. and Profl. Women's Club, Carmi C. of C., Kiwanis, Order Ea. Star, Sigma Alpha. Methodist. Office: PO Box 250 Carmi IL 62821-0250

EDWARDS, JULIE ANN, science researcher; b. Berea, Ohio, Jan. 31, 1945; d. Ralph Frederick and Elsie Marie (Koch) Schmiedlin; m. Donald E. Ellison (div.); m. O. James Edwards; children: J. Patrick, Tommie, Jami. BA in Biology, U. Detroit-Mercy, 1967; postgrad., Murray (Ky.) State U., 1985, Ea. Mich. U., Ypsilanti, 1988-89. Rschr. VA Hosp., Ann Arbor, Mich., 1969-72, U. Mich., Ann Arbor, 1967-69, 87—. Contbr. articles to profl. jours. Mem. Sci. Rsch. Club of U. Mich. (sec.), Sigma Xi. Office: U Mich M3311 MSI-0652 Ann Arbor MI 48109

EDWARDS, KATHRYN INEZ, educational technology consultant; b. L.A., Aug. 26, 1947; d. Lloyd and Geraldine E. (Smith) Price; 1 child, Bryan. BA in English, Calif. State U., L.A., 1969, supervision credential, 1974, adminstrn. credential, 1975; MEd in Curriculum, UCLA, 1971; PhD, Claremont Grad. Sch., 1979. Tchr., L.A. Pub. Schs., 1969-78, adv. specially funded programs, 1978-80, advisor librs. and learning-resources program, 1980-81, instructional specialist, 1981-84; cons. instructional media L.A. County Office of Edn., Downey, Calif., 1984-90; coord. ednl. media and tech. Pomona (Calif.) Unified Sch. Dist., 1990-92; cons. edn. tech. Apple Computer, Inc., 1992—; cons. Walt Disney Prodns., Alfred Higgins Prodns., others. Author guides and curriculum kits. Appointed by assembly speaker Willie Brown to Calif. Ednl. Tech. Com., 1990-92, Calif. State Assembly Resolution from Gwen Moore, 1988, Edn. Coun. for Tech. in Learning, 1993; mem. spl. com. Cable Access Corp. Cowners, 1991-92. Recipient cert. commendation Senator Diane Watson, 1988; Mabel Wilson Richards scholar, 1968, Calif. Congress Parents and Tchrs. scholar, 1968; UCLA fellow, 1968; named Outstanding Woman of Yr. L.A. Sentinel, 1987. Mem. Nat. Assn. Minority Polit. Women, Internat. Reading Assn. (speaker nat. conv. 1988), L.A. Reading Assn. (pres.), Calif. Assn. Tchrs. of English (conf. del. 1982), Assn. Supervision and Curriculum Devel., Calif. Media and Libr. Educators Assn. (state conf. co-chair 1989, v.p. legal divsn. 1992—), Nat. Assn. Media Women (Media Woman of Yr. 1987), Alpha Kappa Alpha. Democrat. Roman Catholic. Avocations: reading, gardening, travel. Office: Apple Computer Inc 2401 Colorado Ave Ste 325 Santa Monica CA 90404

EDWARDS, LOUISE WISEMAN, career counselor, educator; b. Greeley, Colo., Feb. 20, 1932; d. Hunter R. and Sarah L. (Spencer) Wiseman; m. Jasin W. Edwards (div. 1975); children: Mark Hunter, Kathleen Margaret. BA, U. Colo., 1953; MA, U. N.Mex., 1983. Lic. profl. clin. counselor. Asst. dir. pub. info. Mills Coll., Oakland, Calif., 1956-57; ESL tchr. Peace Corps, Santiago, Chile, 1963-64; career counselor U. N.Mex. Career Svcs., Albuquerque, 1980-84, supr. career counseling, 1984-87, asst. dir., 1987—, interim dir., 1992-93; presenter U. N.Mex. Law Sch., 1982-95, Nat. Assn. Med. Schs. Admissions and Registrations Conv., 1993; instr. Anderson Sch. Mgmt. U. N.Mex., 1983—; bd. dirs. YWCA Career Divsn., Albuquerque, 1992—;. Active Dem. Women of N.Mex., 1970-80. Mem. ACA, N.Mex. Career Devel. Assn., Rocky Mt. Placement Assn. (co-chair conf. 1980—). Home: 2821 Tennessee NE Albuquerque NM 87110

EDWARDS, LYDIA JUSTICE, state official; b. Carter County, Ky., July 9, 1937; d. Chead and Velva (Kinney) Justice; m. Frank B. Edwards, 1968; children: Mark, Alexandra, Margot. Student, San Francisco State U. Began career as acct., then Idaho state rep., 1982-86; treas. State of Idaho, 1987—; legis. asst. to Gov. Hickel, Alaska, 1967; conf. planner Rep. Gov.'s Assn., 1970-73; mem. Rep. Nat. Commn., 1972, del. to nat. conv., 1980. Mem. Rep. Womens Fedn. Congregationalist. Office: State Treas Office PO Box 83720 Boise ID 83720-0002

EDWARDS, MARGARET MCRAE, college administrator, lawyer; b. Wadesboro, N.C., July 2, 1931; d. Martin Alexander and Margaret Ashe (Redfearn) McRae; m. Sterling J. Edwards, June 30, 1953; children: Martin, Robert, Lee, Elizabeth. BA cum laude, Agnes Scott Coll., 1953; JD cum laude, Cumberland Law Sch., 1979. Bar: N.C. 1979, Ala. 1980, Fla. 1981. Asst. to alumnae dir. Mt. Vernon Coll., Washington, 1961-64; devel. staff S.E. Inst., Chapel Hill, N.C., 1973-75; law clk. U.S. Dist. Ct., Birmingham, 1979-80; atty. Carlton, Fields, Tampa, Fla., 1980-82; pvt. practice Birmingham, 1983-85; dir. planned giving Birmingham-So. Coll., 1985-90, assoc. v.p. for endowment and planned giving, 1991—; cons. Blackbaud Planned Giving Conf., Charleston, S.C., 1991—, Planned Giving, Philanthropic Action Coun., Tampa, 1980-82, Am. Philanthropy Group, Birmingham, 1983-88; prof. bus. law Samford U., Birmingham, 1984. Index editor: Manual for Complex Litigation, 1985. Bd. dirs. Girls Club, Birmingham, 1984-90, Ala. Planned Giving Coun., 1991-94, Ala. divsn. Am. Cancer Soc., co-chair major gifts, 1991—; speakers bur. Nat. Com. on Planned Giving. Recipient Achievement award in Planned Giving, Coun. for Achievement and Support of Edn., 1992, Will/Tax award Young Lawyers Assn., 1979, Estate Planning award Am. Jurisprudence, 1979. Mem. Am. Arbitration Assn. (arbitrator 1985—), Audubon Soc. (bd. dirs.), Agnes Scott

Alumnae (pres. Birmingham 1967-69, Charleston, S.C. 1954-55). Presbyterian. Home: 4239 Chickamauga Rd Birmingham AL 35213-1811 Office: Birmingham-So Coll Arkadelphia Rd Birmingham AL 35254

EDWARDS, MARGARET SALLY, retired educational administrator; b. Jones Fork, Ky., Mar. 1, 1937; d. Manis Casebolt and Mary (Slone) Layne; m. Cecil Edwards, Nov. 13, 1953; children: David, James. BS in Elem. Edn., Miami U., Oxford, Ohio, 1966, MEd in Ednl. Adminstrn., 1979, PhD in Ednl. Adminstrn. and Curriculum, 1991. Cert. supt., supr., prin., edn. specialist, tchr., Ohio. Tchr. elem. edn. Middletown (Ohio) City Schs., 1965-81, asst. prin., 1981-83, coord. elem. edn., 1983-85, coord. state and fed. programs, 1985-96; adj. prof. Miami U., Oxford, 1991-93; turnkey trainer Exemplary Ctr. for Reading Instrn., Salt Lake City, 1984-90. Bd. dirs. Sorg Opera Co., Middletown, 1991-93, Madison Twp. Life Squad, Middletown, 1993-94. Mem. Nat. Assn. for Edn. Young Children, Ohio Coun. Internat. Reading Assn. (membership dir. 1990-93), Ohio Assn. for Supervision and Curriculum Devel. (pres. 1993-94, Leadership Devel. award 1994), Middletown Artist-in-Residency (pres. 1987-91), Delta Kappa Gamma (legis. chair 1994-96), Phi Delta Kappa (pres. 1991-93, Svc. key 1994, Disting. award 1987, 92). Office: Middletown City Sch Dist 1515 Girard Ave Middletown OH 45044-4364

EDWARDS, MARIANNE, city clerk; b. Springfield, Ill., Mar. 20, 1936; d. Harry Benjamin and Louise Anna (Wolf) E. BS in Bus. Adminstrn., Ill. State U., 1986. Registered clk., Ill. Employment mgr. Horace Mann Ins., Springfield, Ill., 1956-67; employment counselor Piggott Personnel Agy., Springfield, Ill., 1967-68; city clk. City Hall, Normal, Ill., 1973—; chmn. Mcpl. Clks. Tng. Inst. Com., Ill., 1995—. Author: Municipal Clerks of Illinois Manual, 1984-86, Archives Primer Town of Normal, Illinois, 1992, Disaster Recovery Primer Town of Normal, Illinois, 1994; editor: Mcpl. Clks. Ill. Manual, 1989-90. Mem. Cen. Ill. Mcpl. Clks. Orgn. (charter), Internat. Inst. Mcpl. Clks. (chmn. membership com. for U.S. and Internat., mem. program rev./cert. com., chmn. internat. membership com. 1992, cert. mcpl. clk. 1982, Acad. for Advanced Edn. 1987), Quill award 1994), Mcpl. Clks. Ill. (dir. 1984-86, sec. 1986-87, v.p. 1987-88, pres. 1988-89, chmn. mcpl. clks. manual rewrite com., mem. of yr. 1987). Republican. Presbyterian. Office: City Hall 100 E Phoenix Ave Normal IL 61761

EDWARDS, MARIE BABARE, psychologist; b. Tacoma; d. Nick and Mary (Mardesich) Babare; B.A., Stanford, 1948, M.A., 1949; m. Tilden Hampton Edwards (div.); 1 son, Tilden Hampton Edwards Jr. Counselor guidance center U. So. Calif., Los Angeles, 1950-52; project coordinator So. Calif. Soc. Mental Hygiene, 1952-54; pub. speaker Welfare Fedn. Los Angeles, 1953-57; field rep. Los Angeles County Assn. Mental Health, 1957-58; intern psychologist UCLA, 1958-60; pvt. practice, human rels. tng., counselor tng. Mem. Calif., Am., Western, Los Angeles psychol. assns., AAAS, So. Calif. Soc. Clin. Hypnosis, Internat. Platform Assn. Author: (with Eleanor Hoover) The Challenge of Being Single, 1974, paperback edit., 1975. Office: 6100 Buckingham Pky Culver City CA 90230-7237

EDWARDS, MELBA SMITH, elementary educator; b. Shelby, N.C., Aug. 14, 1948; d. Ernest Marvin and Edna June Ferne (Atchley) Smith; m. Gordon Alexander Leslie Edwards, Sept. 8, 1979; children: Marta Irene Edwards, Mark Leslie Edwards. BA in Edn., Mars Hill Coll., 1970; MSEd, Hunter Coll., 1978. Cert. tchr. K-6, middle sch. 6-9 lang. arts, academically gifted edn., N.C.; cert. tchr. nursery, K-6, N.Y. Educator Fairfield County Schs., Winnsboro, S.C., 1970-71, Charlotte-Mecklenburg Schs., Charlotte, 1971-73; lead tchr. pre-internat. baccalaureate program, educator Charlotte-Mecklenburg Schs., 1979-89, 91—; substitute tchr. N.Y.C. Schs., 1974-75; educator St. Matthew Luth. Sch., N.Y.C., 1975-79; cons., educator Kings Mountain (N.C.) Dist. Schs., 1989-91; mem. effective schs. com. Charlotte-Mecklenburg Schs., 1992-94; mem. supt.'s advisory coun., Charlotte, 1981-88; coord. Interdisciplinary Thematic Instrn. Project, Reid Park Elem. Sch., Charlotte, 1994—. Devel. curriculum for acad. gifted program, Kings Mountain Sch. Dist., 1991. Chairperson family life com. St. John's Bapt. Ch., Charlotte, 1994-95, youth missions dir., 1989—; builder Habitat for Humanity, Charlotte, 1985-89; mem. LWV, Charlotte, 1993—. Recipient Outstanding Educator award N.C. Parent Tchr. Assn., 1989; grantee Arts and Sci. Coun., Charlotte, N.C., 1995. Mem. NEA, N.C. Assn. Educators, N.C. Assn. Gifted Educators, PTA of N.C. Democrat. Home: 10029 Withers Rd Charlotte NC 28278 Office: Reid Park Elem Charlotte-Mecklenburg Schs Charlotte NC 28278

EDWARDS, NANCY SMITH, special education educator; b. Roseboro, N.C., Nov. 16, 1949; d. Thomas Franklin Sr. and Alice Gray (Crumpler) Smith; m. Glenn Kyle Johnson, Jr., Apr. 15, 1971 (div. Aug. 1988); children: James Kyle, Timothy Glenn; m. Joseph Cullen Edwards, July 19, 1991. BS Elem. Edn., Pembroke State U., 1972; Early Childhood Cert., Meth. Coll., Fayetteville, N.C., 1984; MA Spl. Edn., Fayetteville State U., 1988, Sch. Adminstrn. Cert., 1994. Cert. tchr. elem. edn. 4-9, early childhood, sci., adminstrn., EMH, BEH, LD, N.C. Tchr. exceptional child East Arcadia Sch., Elizabethtown, N.C., 1987-90; tchr. emotionally handicapped East Bladen High, Elizabethtown, 1990-92; instr. psychology Bladen C.C., Dublin, N.C., 1991-95; tchr. emotionally handicapped Bladen Mid. Sch., Elizabethtown, 1992-93; tchr. EC cons. South View Sr. High, Fayetteville, 1993-95. Troop leader Girl Scouts U.S.. Mem. NEA, N.C. Assn. Educators, Cumberland County Assn. Educators (v.p. 1973, Citizen of Yr. 1974), Coun. for Exceptional Children, (v.p., pres. Bladen County chpt. 1991-93). Baptist. Home: Rte 5 Box 259 1/2 Fayetteville NC 28301 Office: South View Sr High Elk Rd Hope Mills NC 28348

EDWARDS, PATRICIA BURR, small business owner, counselor, consultant; b. Oakland, Calif., Feb. 19, 1918; d. Myron Carlos and Claire Idelle (Laingor) Burr; m. Jackson Edwards, Nov. 14, 1942; children: Jill Forman-Young, Jan Kurzweil. AB, U. So. Calif., 1939, MSEd, 1981. Prin. Constructive Leisure, L.A., 1968—; speaker, lectr. in field; writer, prodr. counseling materials for career, leisure and life planning including computer software, audio cassettes and assessment surveys. Author: You've Got to Find Happiness: It Won't Find You, 1971, Leisure Counseling Techniques: Individual and Group Counseling Step-by-Step, 1975, 3d edit., 1980; (computer software) Leisure PREF, 1986, Over 50: Needs, Values, Attitudes, 1988, Adapting to Change: The NVAB Program, 1996; contbr. articles to profl. jours., mags. and books. Chmn. L.A. County Foster Families 50th Anniversary, 1962-64, Hollywood Bowl Vols., L.A., 1952—. Mem. Am. Counseling Assn., Calif. Assn. for Counseling and Devel., Nat. Recreation and Park Assn., Assn. for Adult Devel. and Aging, Trojan League, Travellers Aid Soc., L.A., Jr. League L.A., First Century Families of L.A., Delta Gamma. Republican. Episcopalian.

EDWARDS, PHYLLIS MAE, accountant, graphologist; b. Wichita, Kans., June 25, 1921; d. William Noble and Nettie Mae (Riggs) Merry; m. Joseph Andrew Edwards, Sept. 19, 1945 (dec.); children: Joseph Noble (dec.), James Richard, Robert Andrew (dec.), Jacqueline Merry. Student, Bus. Preparatory Sch., Wichita, Kans., 1939; BA in Journalism, Wichita State U., 1944; grad. advanced graphologist, Sampson Inst. Graphology, 1967; cert. of proficiency, Tao Acupuncture, 1975; D of Graphology Sci., Rocky Mountain Graphology, 1978. Cert. profl. graphologist. Sec., bookkeeper Healy & Co., Wichita, 1939-42, Wichita State U., 1942-43; acct. Moberly & West, Pub. Accts., Wichita, 1943-45, McQuain, Edwards, & Teffs, Oakland, Calif., 1952-55; acct., graphologist Rocky Mountain Graphology Sch., Denver, 1972-81; prin. Multi-Pro Svcs., Denver, 1976—; acct. Indsl. Hard Chrome Plating Co., Denver, 1957-94; expert witness for all levels of ct., Colo., Wyo., 1976—; pub. and pvt. speaker Colo., Wyo., 1976—; sec., treas. Indsl. Hard Chrome Plating Co., Denver, 1990-94. Den mother Aurora (Colo.) Cub Scout Troop, 1956-59; asst. troop leader Girl Scouts U.S., Denver, 1960-64; charity fund raiser various churches, schs., and non-profit orgns., 1967—. Mem. AAUW (Denver br. treas. 1975-77, bull. editor 1980-81, 92-93, sec. 1986-88, roster/circulation editor, pres.-elect 1988-90, pres. 1990-92, chair interbr. coun. 1991-92), Am. Handwriting Analysts Found. (Rocky Mountain chpt.), Am. Assn. Handwriting Analysts, Coun. Graphological Socs., Rocky Mountain Graphology Assn. (treas. 1972-81), U. Denver Women's Libr. Assn. Home: 2986 S Fairfax St Denver CO 80222-6841 Office: Multi-Pro Svcs 2986 S Fairfax St Denver CO 80222-6841

EDWARDS, PRISCILLA ANN, litigation support business owner; b. Orlando, Fla., Sept. 28, 1947; d. William Granville and Bernice Roys-ter. Paralegal cert., U. Calif., Berkeley, 1994. Paralegal Charles R. Garry Esquire, San Francisco, Calif., 1989-90, Marvin Cahn Esquire, San Francisco, 1990-91; owner, mgr. Fed. Legal Resources, San Francisco, 1991—; speaker Sonoma State U., Santa Rosa, Calif., 1993. Publisher: (book) Zero Weather, 1981. Recipient Wiley W. Manuel award for pro bono legal svcs. Bd. Govs. State Bar of Calif., 1994, 95. Mem. ATLA, Bar Assn. San Francisco. Episcopalian. Office: Fed Legal Resources 345 Franklin St San Francisco CA 94102

EDWARDS, ROBIN MORSE, lawyer; b. Glens Falls, N.Y., Dec. 9, 1947; d. Daniel and Harriet Lois (Welpen) Morse; m. Richard Charles Edwards, Aug. 30, 1970; children: Michael Alan, Jonathan Philip. BA, Mt. Holyoke Coll., 1969; JD, U. Calif., Berkeley, 1972. Bar: Calif. 1972. Assoc. Donahue, Gallagher, Thomas & Woods, Oakland, Calif., 1972-77, ptnr., 1977-89; ptnr. Sonnenschein, Nath & Rosenthal, San Francisco, 1989—. Mem. ABA, Calif. Bar Assn., Alameda County Bar Assn. (bd. dirs. 1978-84, v.p. 1982, pres. 1983). Jewish. Office: Sonnenschein Nath Rosenthal 685 Market St 10th Fl San Francisco CA 94105

EDWARDS, SARAH ANNE, radio, cable television personality, clinical social worker; b. Tulsa, Jan. 7, 1943; d. Clyde Elton and Virginia Elizabeth Glandon; B.A. with distinction, U. Mo., Kansas City, 1965; M.S.W., U. Kans., 1974; m. Paul Robert Edwards, Apr. 24, 1965; 1 son, Jon Scott. Cmty. rep. OEO, Kansas City Regional Office, 1966-68; social service/parent involvement specialist, program rev. and resource specialist Office Child Devel., HEW, Kansas City, Kans., 1968-73; dir. tng. social services dept., children's rehab. unit U. Affiliated Facility, U. Kans. Med. Ctr., Kansas City, 1975-76; co-dir. Cathexis Inst. S., Glendale, Calif., 1976-77; pvt. practice psychotherapy, tng. and cons. personal, interpersonal, organizational behavior, Sierra Madre, Calif, 1973-80; systems operator working from home CompuServe Info. Svc., 1983—; prodr., co-host radio show Working From Home on the Business Radio Network, 1988—; co-host cable show Working From Home Scripp's Howard Home and Garden Cable TV Network, 1995—. Columnist for Home Office Computing Mag., 1988—; co-author: How to Make Money with Your Personal Computer, 1984, Getting Business to Come to You, 1991, Working From Home, rev. edit. 1994, Making it on Your Own, 1994, Finding Your Perfect Work, 1996. Address: 2607 2nd St Apt 3 Santa Monica CA 90405-4123

EDWARDS, TEENA ANN, community health nurse, educator; b. Denver, Mar. 16, 1951; d. Clifford Milton Delzell and Gratia Iola (Countryman) Hoffman; m. Richard Allison Edwards, June 16, 1973; children: Matthew, Wayne, Sarah Beth. BS, U. No. Colo., 1973; MS, Tex. Women's U., 1978; DPH, Loma Linda U., 1996. RN, Calif, Del. Asst. prof. Tex. Christian U., Ft. Worth, 1977; staff nurse Mont. Deaconess Med. Ctr., Great Falls, 1978-79, Tucson Med. ctr., 1982; instr. U. Ariz. Coll. Nursing, Tucson, 1982-84; clin. nurse specialist Penrose Community Hosp., Colorado Springs, Colo., 1984-85; pub. health nurse El Paso County Health Dept., Colorado Springs, 1986; nursing cons. SAFE/WITH Project, Honolulu, 1986; pub. health nurse SAFE Program, Honolulu, 1986; nursing supr. SAFE/WITH Program, Honolulu, 1987; dir. ASPECTS program Tripler Army Med. Ctr., Honolulu, 1988-92; mem. rsch. com. Tripler Army Med. Ctr., 1989-92; presenter at profl. confs.; outreach mgr. March AFB, 1992-95; nurse specialist David Grant Med. Ctr., Travis AFB, 1995-96. Active Girl Scouts U.S., 1988—. Recipient appreciation pin Hawaii coun. Girl Scouts U.S., 1992. Mem. NAACOG, NAFE, APHA, Am. Soc. Psychoprophylaxis in Obstetrics. Home: 3529 Hawthorne Dr Dover DE 19901

EDWARDS, TERESA, basketball player. Diploma, U. Ga., 1986. Profl. basketball player Vicenia, Magenta, Italy, 1987-88, Nagoya, Japan, 1989-93, Valencia, Spain, 1994, Tarbes, France, 1994. 1st Am. basketball player to compete in 4 Olympics; recipient bronze medal 1994 World Championship team, USA Olympic Team (co-capt.), 1992, Pan Am. Games, 1991, 2 gold medals World Championship and Goodwill Games, 1986, gold medal, 90, gold medal Olympics, 1984, 88, 96, bronze medal Olympics, 1992, Pan Am. Games, 1987, Jr. Pan Am. team, 1983; earned MVP honors Nat. Sports Festival; named USA Basketball's Female Athelete of Yr., 1987, 90, All-Am. Kodak Naismith Women's Basketball News Svc., Street & Smith's; selected All-SEC 1st team, 1984, 85, 86; one of only 3 Ga. women basketball players to have her number retired. Office: USA Basketball 5465 Mark Dabling Blvd Colorado Springs CO 80918-3842

EDWARDS, TONIA FAYE, building commissioner, architect; b. Coral Gables, Fla., Jan. 24, 1949; d. Donald Leon and Lola Faye (Patterson) E.; m. David Ramos, Sept. 4, 1971 (div. June 1977); m. Edward Rach, July 30, 1983; children: Hannah Lee, Samantha Faye. BArch, Pratt Inst., 1974. Registered arch. N.Y., Ohio; cert. bldg. ofcl. Coun. Am. Bldg. Ofcls.; cert. bldg. inspector Bldg. Ofcls. and Code Adminstrs. Sr. planner, urban designer Dept. City Planning, City of N.Y., Bronx, 1975-79; draftsperson The Stein Partnership, Archs., N.Y.C., 1979-80; designer, ptnr. Edwards-Saavedra, N.Y.C., 1980-81; project mgr. corp. facility asst. mgr. Citibank, UMFM, N.Y.C., 1981-84; project mgr. corp. facility mgr. Citibank, NAFG, N.Y.C., 1984-86; project arch. Bohm-NBBJ, Columbus, Ohio, 1986-88; arch., ptnr. Edwards/Rach, Archs./Planners, Hillsboro, Ohio, 1988-91; dep. bldg. commr. Dept. Bldg. Inspections Hamilton County, Cin., 1991-92, bldg. commr., 1993—; juror, profl. examiner IBC, NCIDQ, N.Y.C., 1984; mem. Hamilton County Unified Fire Code Com., Cin., 1993-94. Author, creator (quar. newsletter) Codeline, 1993, 94, 95, 96; art works exhibited Mus. Fine Arts, Houston, 1970. Womens Archtl. Aux. fellow and Pratt Inst. Scholastic grantee, Bklyn., 1971-73. Mem. AIA (chairperson fire and life safety task force group 1994-96), Nat. Coun. Archtl. Registration Bds., Nat. Fire Protection Assn., S.W. Ohio Bldg. Ofcls. Assn. (dir. 1996), Ohio Bldg. Ofcls. Assn. Home: 8326 W Prospect Rd Hillsboro OH 45133

EDWARDS, VIRGINIA DAVIS, music educator, concert pianist; b. Syracuse, N.Y., Jan. 8, 1927; d. Leslie Martz and Elsie (Gannon) Davis; m. William B. Edwards, Jan. 12, 1954. BA magna cum laude, Marshall U., 1948; MusB, Cin. Conservatory of Music, 1950, MusM, 1950; postgrad., U. Chgo., 1950-56, U. Calif., Berkeley, 1963. Pianist, young artists series Conservatory of Music, Cin., 1949-50; piano instr. Conservatory of Music, Evanston, Ill., 1955-56; music instr. Harvard Sch. for Boys, Chgo., 1954-55; pianist Opera Studios of Dimitri Onofrei/Bianca Saroya, Chgo., 1957-61; piano instr. Community Music Ctr., San Francisco, 1962-63; v.p. Gold Rush Gun Shop, Benet Arms Co. Imports, San Francisco, 1963-68, Afton, Va., 1968—; pvt. practice Afton, Va., 1978—; instr. piano Mary Baldwin Coll., Staunton, Va., 1988—. Soloist Marshall U. Symphony Orch., 1948, Chgo. Pops Concert Orch., Duluth, Minn., 1961; recitalist Curtis Hall, Chgo., 1961, Legion of Honor, San Francisco, 1966, Sta. WRFK-FM, Richmond, Va., 1979; prodr., performer Presbyn. Hunger Program series, 1984-87, St. John's Cath. Ch., Waynesboro, Va., 1985, Basic Meth. Ch., 1989, Augusta Hosp. Corp. Benefit, 1989; author: Conspiracy of 30 -- Their Misuse of Music from Aristotle to Onassis, 1994. Mem. AAUW, DAR, Va. Museum Soc. Unitarian. Home: PO Box 87 Waynesboro VA 22980-0066

EDWARDSON, SANDRA, dean, nursing educator. Dean Sch. Nursing, U. Minn., Mpls. Office: U Minn Twin CitiesSch Nursing 6-1001Weaver-Densford Hall 308 Harvard St Minneapolis MN 55455*

EDWIN, ELLEN OWENS, chief executive officer; b. Pensacola, Fla., Dec. 13, 1953; d. Ernest S. and Edna (Kell) Owens; m. James R. Edwin, Aug. 25, 1990; children: EJ, Emily, Jeremy. BS in Edn., Memphis State U., 1975; MA, U. West Fla., 1982; EdS in Leadership, U. Memphis, 1996. Instrnl. designer interactive media ManTech/Mathetics Divs., Alexandria, Va., 1985-88; design, asst. program mgr. Person-System Integration, Alexandria, Va., 1988-90; instr. U. Wyo., Laramie, 1990-91, rsch. asst., cons., 1991-92; chief exec. officer IntraTech Inc., Laramie, 1992—; sr. instrnl. multimedia designer DUAL, Inc., Arlington, Va., 1995-96; contract negotiator, curriculum cons. in field. Contbr. articles to profl. jours. and chpt. to book. Trustee, pianist Trinity Bapt. Ch., Laramie, 1992. Mem. NAFE, Nat. Assn. Govt. Communicators, Internat. Visual Literacy Assn., Assn. for Ednl. Comm. and Technology, Am. Ednl. Rsch. Assn., Fed. Ednl. Technology Assn., Soc. for Advancement of Learning Technologies, No. Rocky Mtn. Rsch. Assn. Republican. Baptist.

EFFEL, LAURA, lawyer; b. Dallas, May 9, 1945; d. Louis E. and Fay (Lee) Ray; m. Marc J. Patterson, Sept. 19, 1992; 1 child, Stephen. BA, U. Calif., Berkeley, 1971; JD, U. Md., 1975. Bar: N.Y. 1976, U.S. Dist. Ct. (so. and ea. dists.) N.Y. 1976, U.S. Ct. Appeals (2d cir.) 1980, U.S. Supreme Ct. 1980, D.C. 1993. Assoc. Burns Jackson Miller Summit & Jacoby, N.Y.C., 1975-78, Pincus Munzer Bizar & D'Alessandro, N.Y.C., 1978-80; v.p., sr. assoc. counsel Chase Manhattan Bank, N.A., N.Y.C., 1980—; bd. dirs. Bklyn. Legal Svcs. Corp. Mem. ABA (co-chair com. on banking and comml. litigation, litigation sect. 1992-95), Am. Corp. Counsel Assn. (com. chair 1992—, pro bono svc. award 1989), Assn. of Bar of City of N.Y. (com. on lectures and continuing edn. 1991-96). Office: Chase Manhattan Bank NA 1 Chase Manhattan Plz # 29th New York NY 10081-1000

EFFLER, FANNY PILLIOD, II, lawyer; b. Toledo, Ohio, July 11, 1952; d. Erwin Robert Effler and Edna King (Cook) Hammond; m. Robie Lloyd Cone, Jr., June 3, 1978 (div. Dec. 1986); 1 child, Taylor Pilliod. AA, Colby Jr. Coll., 1971; BA, Georgetown U., 1974; JD, U. Toledo Coll. Law, 1978. Bar: Ohio 1979. Atty. Toledo Legal Aid Soc., 1983-87; pvt. practice law Toledo, 1987-96. Bd. dirs. Options/Crittenton, Toledo, 1994-96, Toledo Olde Towne Cmty. Orgn., 1990-95, Aurora Project, Inc., Toledo, 1985-90, Housing Directions, Inc., Toledo, 1986-87; vol. Landmark Edn. Corp., 1995-96. Mem. Ohio Bar Assn., Toledo Bar Assn., Toledo Women's Bar Assn. Home and Office: 2830 Collingwood Dr Toledo OH 43610

EFFORD, JOY DAVIDSON, university administrator; b. Balt., July 30, 1961; d. Jack Allen Sr. and Irene Ellen (Pusey) Davidson; m. Edward Alan Williams Sr., Feb. 29, 1980 (div. June 1987); children: Edward Alan Williams Jr., Johnathon David Williams; m. David William Efford, Apr. 3, 1993; stepchildren: Allison Colleen, Ryan David. AA in Computer Programming, Wor-Wic C.C., Salisbury, Md., 1985. Mgr. Davidson's Market, Ocean City, Md., 1979-81; office mgr. Internat. Seafood, Inc., Ocean City, 1982-84; sys. analyst S. Lee Smith, Inc., Salisbury, 1984-86; regional account mgr. Delmarva Svcs. Group, Millsboro, Del., 1986; coord. clerical unit Go-Getters, Inc., Salisbury, 1987-89; asst. instr., acad. computer lab. supr. Wor-Wic C.C., Salisbury, 1989-94; owner, cons. Westside Computer Svcs., Nanticoke, Md., 1992—; network adminstr. Wor-Wic C.C., Salisbury, 1994—; advisor Wor-Wic C.C., Salisbury, 1991—, mem. adv. bd. program adv. com. computer, 1984—; cons. Go-Getters, Inc., Salisbury, 1989—. Participant Westside United Meth. Ch., Nanticoke, 1992—. Mem. NAFE. Republican. Office: Wor-Wic C C 32000 Campus Dr Salisbury MD 21804

EFIRD, BETTY RUTH, real estate appraiser, broker; b. Childress, Tex., Oct. 16, 1943; d. James Joseph Harcrow and Martha Mae (Greenhill) Fleming; children: Heather Cagle, LeAnna. Cert. gen. appraiser and real estate broker Tex., Okla. Broker, owner Efird Realty, Childress, Tex., 1980-82; broker, agent Mashburn Realty, Childress, Tex., 1982—; appraiser, owner Continental Appraisal, Childress, Tex., 1992—; v.p. BPW, Childress, 1994. Chmn. City of Childress Zoning Bd., 1991—, Childress Housing Authority, 1985—; bd. dirs. Girl Scouts USA, Wichita Falls, Tex., 1994—; pres. Childress Arts Coun., 1984-85. Mem. Nat. Assn. Realtors, Tex. Assn. Realtors, Nat. Assn. Master Appraisers, North Tex. Assn. Master Appraisers, Childress C. of C. (pres. women's coun. 1995-96). Office: Continental Appraisal 2806 Ave F NW PO Box 536 Childress TX 79201

EGAN, JANET LOUISE, software company executive; b. East St. Louis, Ill., June 28, 1950; d. James Andrew and Virginia Louise (McKenna) E.; m. Joseph O'Neill Unverferth, Sept. 10, 1977 (div. 1981); 1 child, Kyle Egan. BS in Elem. Edn., So. Ill. U., 1972, MBA, 1977. Tchr. math. Kinloch (Mo.) Schs., 1972-75; programmer First Nat. Bank, St. Louis, 1975-77, Mercantile Trust Co., St. Louis, 1977, Integrated Sys., Norfolk, Va., 1977-78; instr. Control Data, Norfolk, Va., 1978-79; mgr. sys. McDonnell Douglas, St. Louis, 1979-86, Ralston Purina, St. Louis, 1986-88; software engr. Boole & Babbage, Conyers, Ga., 1988-93; v.p. ops. Mitchem Techs., Madison, Ga., 1994—. Author, editor (newsletter) News From Mitchem Techs., 1994—. Ill. State Tchr. scholar, 1968. Mem. Beta Gamma Sigma. Office: Mitchem Techs 1462C Eatonton Rd Madison GA 30650

EGAN, KATHRYN SMOOT, communications educator; b. Salt Lake City, Mar. 11, 1942; d. Reed and Stella (Madsen) S.; m. David Edward Caldwell, Aug. 7, 1971 (div.); children: Jason Reed, Sherilyn Kathryn; m. Kenneth Wayne Egan, June 18, 1988. BS, U. Utah, Salt Lake City, 1964; MS, Northwestern U., 1965; PhD, U. So. Calif., 1972. Comm. coord. regional med. program UCLA, 1970-72, dir. instrl. design VA Experiments in Health Care, Denver, 1972-79; co-owner radio stas. KBLF-AM, KSNR, KNXN, Red Bluff, Quincy, Calif., 1981-85; rsch. coord. Bonneville Internat. Corp., Salt Lake City, 1985-87; prof. comm. Brigham Young U., Provo, Utah, 1987—; Rsch. cons. Salt Lake Tribune, Salt Lake City, 1994-95, Geneva Steel, Provo, 1994-95; guest lectr. UN Devel. Program, Lodz, Poland, 1995. Author: (books) Chandelle, Self-Propelled, 1993 (Utah Writers Competition award 1993), Spaces Between the Rocks, 1995 (2d place Utah Writers Competition 1995); columnist Salt Lake Tribune, 1992-95, Network Mag., Salt Lake City, 1995—; contbr. articles to jours. Mem. Am. Women in Radio and TV (v.p. programming 1991-92), Women in Comm. Mem. LDS Ch. Home: 5565 Hunt Rd Salt Lake City UT 84117 Office: Brigham Young U E 509 Harris Fine Arts Ctr Provo UT 84602

EGAN, SISTER M. SYLVIA, hospital administrator; b. Oshkosk, Wis., Sept. 15, 1930; d. Edward James and Dorothy Loretta (Loewen) E. BS in Nursing, Marquette U., 1956; postgrad., Wayne State U., 1969; MSA, Notre Dame U., 1981; LLD (hon.), Kans. Newman Coll., 1987. Rn., Kans.; joined Congregation of Sisters of Sorrowful Mother, Roman Cath. Ch., 1949. Nurse Mercy Hosp. Sch. Nursing, Oshkosh, 1952-54, night supr., 1954-55; med. supr. Mercy Hosp., Oshkosh, 1956-57; instr. St. John's Hosp. Sch. Nursing, Tulsa, 1975-63; dir. St. Mary's Hosp. Sch. Practical Nursing, Roswell, N.Mex., 1963-65; dir. novices, Tulsa Province Sisters of Sorrowful Mother, 1965-69, provinicial adminstr., 1970-78; pres. Franciscan Villa, Broken Arrow, Okla., 1978-79; pres., CEO St. Francis Regional Med. Ctr., Wichita, Kans., 1979—; del. renewal chpt. Sisters of Sorrowful Mother, Milw., 1967-68, 69, chmn. formation com., Tulsa Province, 1968, chpt. del. to Rome, 1970, 74, 78, internat. chmn. Centenary Com., Fed. Republic of Germany, 1980, internat. chpt. Brazil, 1992; bd. dirs. Union Nat. Bank; adj. prof. Health Adminstrn. and Geronotology, Wichita State U., 1988—; alternate del. Am. Hosp. Assn., 1988. Bd. dirs. ARC, 1981—, pres., 1991-93, Accent on Kids, Task Force for Kans. Econ. Devel., Cath. Charities, Wichita, Central States Cardiac Transplant Support Group, 1988-89, Gerard House Inc. (pres. 1988-90), United Way, 1987-89, Leadership 2000, Wichita, Sedgwick County Partnership for Econ. Growth, Wichita Downtown Adv. Com., 1989, Catholic Health Assn. Kans., Guadalupe Clinic, Kans. Hosp. Assn., Union Nat. Bank; adv. bd. YMCA, Wichita, adv. coun. YMCA, Wichita. Recipient Nursing Alumna award Marquette U., 1993. Fellow Am. Coll. Healthcare Execs.; mem. NCCJ (bd. dirs.), Am. Coll. Hosp. Adminstrs., Kans. Hosp. Assn. (bd. dirs. 1988), Cath. Health Assn. of Kans., Med. Edn. Assn., Kans. Forum for Women Healthcare Execs. (bd. dirs.), Kans. Community Svc. Orgn. (bd. dirs.), Kans. C. of C., Notre Dame Alumnae Assn., Rotary Club Witchita, Kans. Forum for Women Healthcare Execs., Sigma Theta Tau, Internat. Honor Soc. of Nursing, Epsilon Gamma. Republican. Home and Office: St Francis Regional Med Ctr 929 N Saint Francis St Wichita KS 67214-3821

EGAN, MARTHA AVALEEN, history educator, archivist; b. Kingsport, Tenn., Feb. 26, 1956; d. Jack E. and Opal (Pugh) E. BS in Comms., U. Tenn., 1978; MA in History, East Tenn. State U., 1986; postgrad., U. Ky., 1986-89, Milligan Coll., 1990. Cert. tchr., Tenn. News reporter, anchor WJCW-AM/WQUT-FM, Johnson City, Tenn., 1980-82; staff asst. 1st Dist. Office U.S. Senator Jim Sasser, Blountville, Tenn., 1982-84; instr. history East Tenn. State U., Johnson City, 1984-86; teaching asst. dept. history U. Ky., Lexington, 1986-89; teaching intern Dobyns-Bennett High Sch., Kingsport, Tenn., 1990; researcher history project Eastman Chem. Co., Kingsport, 1991; adj. faculty history Northeast State Tech. C.C., Blountville, 1992-93; archivist Kingsport Pub. Libr. and Archives, 1993—; adj. asst. prof. history King Coll., Bristol, Tenn., 1994—. Researcher: Eastman Chemical Company: Years of Glory, Times of Change, 1991. Vice chair Sullivan County Dem. Party, 1992-93; rec. sec. Sullivan County Dem. Women's Club, 1992, corr. sec., 1994; mem. Kingsport Tomorrow Exploritorium Task Force; mem. Kingsport Symphony Chorus, sec.-treas., 1994-95; mem. East Tenn. Camerata, Kingsport Cmty. Band. Mem. AAUW (Kingsport chpt.), Orgn. Am. Historians, Nat. Coun. Social Studies, Soc. Am. Archivists, Tenn. Archivists, Kingsport Music Club (corr. sec. 1995—), Phi Alpha Theta, Pi

Gamma Mu, Sigma Delta Chi. Episcopalian. Home: PO Box 481 Kingsport TN 37662-0481 Office: Kingsport Pub Libr/Archives 400 Broad St Kingsport TN 37660-4208

EGAN, SHIRLEY ANNE, retired nursing educator; b. Haverill, Mass.; d. Rush B. and Beatrice (Bengle) Willard. Diploma, St. Joseph's Hosp. Sch. Nursing, Nashua, N.H., 1945; B.S. in Nursing Edn., Boston U., 1949, M.S., 1954. Instr. sci. Sturdy Meml. Hosp. Sch. Nursing, Attleboro, Mass., 1949-51; instr. sci. Peter Bent Brigham Hosp. Sch. Nursing, Boston, 1951-53, ednl. dir., 1953-55, assoc. dir. Sch. Nursing, 1955-59, med. surg. coord., 1971-73, assoc. dir. Sch. Nursing, 1973-79, dir., 1979-85; cons. North Country Hosp., 1985-86; infection control practitioner, 1986-87; contract instr. Natchitoches Area Tech. Inst., 1988-90, Sabine Valley Tech Inst., 1990-91; coord. quality assurance Evangeline Health Care Ctr., 1991-92, asst. dir. nursing, 1992-93; coord. quality assurance Evangeline Health Care Ctr., Natchitoches, La., 1994-96; nurse edn. adviser AID (formerly ICA), Karachi, Pakistan, 1959-67; prin. Coll. Nursing, Karachi, 1959-67; dir. Vis. Nurse Service, Nashua, N.H., 1967-70; cons. nursing edn. Pakistan Ministry of Health, Labour and Social Welfare, 1959-67; adviser to editor Pakistan Nursing and Health Rev., 1959-67; exec. bd. Nat. Health Edn. Com., Pakistan; WHO short-term cons. U. W.I., Jamaica, 1970-71; mem. Greater Nashua Health Planning Council. Contbr. articles to profl. publs. Bd. dirs. Matthew Thornton health Ctr., Nashua, Nashua Child Care Ctr.; vol. ombudsman N.H. Council on Aging; mem. Nashua Service League. Served as 1st lt., Army Nurse Corps., 1945-47. Mem. Trained Nurses Assn. Pakistan, Nat. League for Nursing, Assn. for Preservation Hist. Natchitoches, St. Joseph's Sch. Nursing Alumnae Assn., Boston U. Alumnae Assn., Brit. Soc. Health Edn., Cath. Daus. Am. (vice regent ct. Bishop Malloy), Statis. Study Grads. Karachi Coll. Nursing, Sigma Theta Tau. Home: 729 Royal St Natchitoches LA 71457-5716

EGASHIRA, SUSAN LEA, elementary education educator; b. Spokane, Wash.; d. Masao Murphy and Ruby Kumi (Bunya) Iga; m. Jerry Egashira, June 21, 1970; children: Alicia, Scott, Derek. BA, Nat. Coll. Edn., 1970; MA, San Francisco State U., 1978. Cert. elem. and secondary edn., Wash. Human rels. aide San Mateo (Calif.) City Sch. Dist., 1971-73; tchr., prin. Woodland Sch., Redwood City, Calif., 1981-82; tchr. St. Thomas Sch., Medina, Wash., 1984-87; tchr., dir. Rainbow Sch., Issaquah, Wash., 1987-91; asst. dir. early childhood svcs. Jewish Cmty. Ctr., Mercer Island, Wash., 1991-93; tchr. North Creek Country Day Sch., Bothell, Wash., 1993—. Mem. Wash. State Social Studies Coun. Office: Keystone Sch 312 164th SE Lynnwood WA 98037

EGELSON, POLLY SELIGER, artist, educator; b. Balt., Aug. 6, 1928; d. Robert Victor Seliger and Beatrice Regina (Gordon) Summers; m. Louis I. Egelson, June 6, 1949; children: Robert, Betsy, David, Jane. BA, Radcliffe Coll., 1950. Sculptor, instr. Fuller Mus. Art, Brockton, Mass., 1976-93, Danforth Mus. Art, Framingham, Mass., 1976-79, Cape Mus. Art, Dennis, Mass., 1976-79, Falmouth (Mass.) Artist Guild, 1981—; bd. govs. Copley Soc., Boston, 1970-73; pres. New Eng. Sculptors Assn., Boston, 1972-74; chair Newton (Mass.) Cultural Com., 1974-76. Sculpture exhibits include Boston City Hall, 1976, Boston Art Festival, 1978, Ward-Nasse Gallery, N.Y.C., Lincoln Ctr., N.Y.C., 1977, Grand Prix Internat. Art Show, Monaco, 1977-78; represented in permanent collections Towson (Md.) State Coll., Cape Mus. Fine Arts, Dennis, Mass., Duxbury (Mass.) Mus. Complex; contbg. artist: (books) Falmouth, A Timeless Legacy, Women Artists in America. Assoc. mem. Nat. Mus. Women, Washington, 1995; panel mem., invited artist Cape Cod Women, Yarmouth, Mass., 1995-96. Recipient Best Sculpture award Attleboro Mus. Art, 1975, Cape Cod Art Assn., 1979, Curators Choice award. Mem. New Eng. Sculptors Assn., New Eng. Monotype Guild (bd. dirs. 1994-96), Falmouth Artists Guild (v.p. 1995), Crazy Quilters Guild (sec. 1990-96).

EGELSTON, ROBERTA RIETHMILLER, writer; b. Pitts., Nov. 20, 1946; d. Robert E. and Doris (Bauer) Riethmiller; m. David Michael Egelston, Oct. 10, 1975; 1 child, Brian David. BA in Bus. Administrn., Thiel Coll., 1968; MLS, U. Pitts., 1974. Bus. mgr. Pitts. Pastoral Inst., 1968-70; administrv. asst. Coun. Alcoholism and Drug Abuse, Lancaster, Pa., 1970-72; dir. career planning libr. U. Pitts., 1974-78; writer, 1978—; libr. Pitts. Inst. Mortuary Sci., 1991—, instr. bus. English, 1992—; part-time libr., part-time instr. bus. English, Pitts. Inst. Mortuary Sci., 1991—; instr. beginning genealogy, 1991—; book reviewer Coll. Placement Coun., Bethlehem, Pa., 1977-78; cons. State Affiliated Colls. and Univs., 1976; group leader Johns-Norris Assocs., Pitts., 1975-76. Author: Career Planning Materials, 1981, Credits and Careers for Adult Learners, 1985. Bd. dirs. Lauri Ann West Libr., Pitts., 1983-84; active PTA, 1985-88; mem. peace and justice com. Fox Chapel Presbyn. Ch., 1994—, deacon, 1995—. Mem. AAUW (bd. dirs. Fox Chapel Area br. 1980-91), Les Lauriers (sr. women's hon. at Thiel Coll.), Western Pa. Geneal. Soc. (libr. rsch. com. 1990-94, edn. com. 1992—), Beta Phi Mu.

EGGEBROTEN, ANNE MARIE, literature educator; b. Boulder, Aug. 19, 1948; d. Kermit Kenneth and Evelyn Frances (Gustafson) E.; m. John MacDonald Arthur, June 3, 1972; children: Rosamond Arthur, Ellen A.E., Marie A.E. BA, Stanford U., 1970; MA, U. Calif., Berkeley, 1973, PhD, 1979. Instr. Calif. State U., San Bernardino, Calif., 1981-82, City Coll. San Francisco, 1982-85; instr. Whittier (Calif.) Coll., 1987-89, Long Beach, 1990-91; assoc. prof. English, coord. women's studies program Mt. St. Mary's Coll., L.A., 1991—. Editor: Abortion: My Choice, God's Grace, Christian Women Tell Their Stories, 1994. Troop leader Girl Scouts U.S., Costa Mesa, Calif., 1989-90; elder Presbyn. Ch., Daly City, Calif., 1980-86. Mem. MLA (nat. steering com. 1975-78), NOW, Nat. Women's Studies Assn., Evangelical and Ecumenical Women's Caucus, Med. Acad. Am., Religious Coalition for Reproductive Choice. Episcopalian. Office: Mt St Mary's Coll 12001 Chalen Rd Los Angeles CA 90049

EGGERS, ANN, advertising executive. Sr. v.p., dir. ops. Earle Palmer Brown, Bethesda, Md. Office: Earle Palmer Brown 6935 Arlington Rd Bethesda MD 20814-5212*

EGGLAND, ELLEN THOMAS, community health nurse, consultant; b. Canton, Ohio, Nov. 2, 1947; d. John Marron and Mary Mernabelle (Miller) Thomas; m. Gregory Hugh Eggland, Sept. 9, 1972; children: Karen, Ryan. BSN, Georgetown U., 1969; MN, Emory U., 1972. Staff nurse Cleve. Clinic Hosp., 1969-71; nurse clinician Univ. Hosps., Cleve., 1972-73; dir. nursing Med. Personnel Pool, Cleve., 1975-83; v.p. Healthcare Pers., Inc., Naples, Fla., 1984—; nursing cons., Ohio, Fla., 1983—; v.p. MedPad, Atlanta, 1991-93; mem. adv. bd. Springhouse (Pa.) Skillbuilder Series, 1991-92; vis. lectr. symposium Fla. Gulf Coast U., 1996; vis. lectr. U. South Fla., 1996. Author: Nursing Documentation Resource Guide, 1993, Nursing Documentation: Charting, Reporting and Recording, 1994; contbg. author: Better Documentation, 1992, Managing the Nursing Shortage, 1989, Community and Home Health Care Plans, 1990; contbr. articles to profl. nursing jours.; inventor computerized clin. record. Chmn. St. William Respect Life/Sr. Citizens, Naples, 1985-86; mem. health com. Naples C. of C., 1985-86; sec. Pelican Bay Incorporation Study Com., Naples, 1990-91; bd. dirs. Prevent A Care, Naples, 1986-87; bd. dirs., sec. Pelican Bay Found., Naples, 1993-96; bd. vis. Georgetown U. Sch. Nursing, 1993-96. Fed. grantee for edn. U.S. Govt., 1971; recipient Involved Mem. of Yr. award Greater Cleve. Nurses Assn., 1978, 5th Ann. Author's award U. South Fla., 1995. Mem. ANA, Fla. Nurses Assn., Nat. League Nursing, Master's Group, Greater Cleve. Hosp. Assn. (info. tech. and nursing com. 1991-95), Sigma Theta Tau. Democrat. Roman Catholic. Office: Healthcare Personnel Inc Ste 407 2335 Tamiami Trl N Ste 407 Naples FL 34103

EHINGER, JENNIFER ANN, small business owner, consultant; b. Abington, Pa., Feb. 9, 1970; d. Wendell Charles and Elizabeth (Kidd) E. BA in internat. studies, Johns Hopkins, 1992. Mkgt. coord. Cert. Abstract Co., Blue Bell, Pa., 1993-95; pres. Clenair Products, Inc., Blue Bell, 1994—; sales cons. Pierce-Phelps, Inc., Phila., 1995—. Mem. Kiwanis Club (v.p. 1995-96). Lutheran. Offic: Deivce Phelps Inc 2000 N 59th St Philadelphia PA 19131-3099

EHLERS, EILEEN SPRATT, family therapist; b. Maynard, Mass., Feb. 28, 1948; d. Cyril J. and Irma A. (Wirkkanen) Spratt; m. Robert K. Ehlers, June 13, 1970; children: Robert (dec.), Edward, Erin, Katherine. BA, Boston Coll., 1970; MEd, Notre Dame Coll., Manchester, N.H., 1992. Social worker Cath. Med. Ctr., Manchester, 1991; grief counselor Hospice, Concord, N.H., 1992; program dir. Am. Cancer Soc., Bedford, N.H., 1992; pvt. practice family therapy Familystrength, Concord, 1993-96, coord. Worldwide Marriage Encounter, 1983-96; coord., supr. Mental Health Ctr. of Greater Manchester, N.H., 1996—; coord. Toward Marriage, Concord; regional dir., clin. supr. Family Strength, 1993-96; mem. Dist. Coun. for N.H. Health Care Reform; supr. Mental Health Ctr. Greater Manchester, 1996—. Mem. Mental Health Counseling Assn., Assn. for Counselor Edn. and Supervision, Internat. Assn. of Marriage and Family Counseling, Nat. Assn. for Family Based Svcs/. Democrat. Roman Catholic. Home: 14 Ardon Dr Hooksett NH 03106-1536 Office: Child and Adolescent Svcs 493 Beech St Manchester NH 03104-4209

EHLERS, ELEANOR MAY COLLIER (MRS. FREDERICK BURTON EHLERS), civic worker; b. Klamath Falls, Oreg., Apr. 23, 1920; d. Alfred Douglas and Ethel (Foster) Collier; BA, U. Oreg., 1941; secondary tchrs. credentials Stanford, 1942, master gardener cert. Oreg. State U., 1993; m. Frederick Burton Ehlers, June 26, 1943; children: Frederick Douglas, Charles Collier. Tchr., Salinas Union High Sch., 1942-43; piano tchr. pvt. lessons, Klamath Falls, 1958—. Mem. Child Guidance Adv. Coun., 1956-60; mem. adv. com. Boys and Girls Aid Soc., 1965-67; mem. Gov.'s Adv. Com. Arts and Humanities, 1966-67; bd. mem. PBS TV Sta. KSYS, 1988-92, Friends of Mus. U. Oreg., 1966-69, Arts in Oreg., 1966-68, Klamath County Colls. for Oreg.'s Future, 1968—; co-chmn. Friends of Collier Park, Collier Park Logging Mus., 1986-88, sec. 1988—; chpt. pres. Am. Field Svc., 1962-63; mem. Gov.'s Com. Governance of Community Colls., 1967; bd. dirs. Favell Mus. Western Art and Artifacts, 1971-80, Community Concert Assn., 1950—, pres., 1966-74; established Women's Guild at Merle West Med. Ctr., 1965, sec. bd. dirs, 1962-65, 76-90, bd. dirs., 1962—, mem. bldg. com. 1962-67, mem. planning com., chmn. edn. and rsch. com. hosp. bd., 1967—; pres., bd. dirs. Merle West Med. Ctr., 1990-92, vice chmn., 1992—. Named Woman of Month Klamath Herald News, 1965; named grant to Oreg. Endowed Fellowship Fund, AAUW, 1971; recipient greatest Svc. award Oreg. Tech. Inst., 1970-71, Internat. Woman of Achievement award Quota Club, 1981, U. Oreg. Pioneer award, 1981. Mem. AAUW (local pres. 1955-56), Oreg. Music Tchrs. Assn. (pres. Klamath Basin dist. 1979-81), P.E.O. (Oreg. dir. 1968-75, state pres. 1974-75, trustee internat. Continuing Edn. Fund 1977-83, chmn. 1981-83), Pi Beta Phi, Mu Phi Epsilon, Pi Lambda Theta. Presbyterian. Home: 1338 Pacific Ter Klamath Falls OR 97601-1833

EHLERS, PAMELA ICHORD, career services director; b. Salem, Mo., Sept. 2, 1955; d. Vera (Rodgers) Ichord-Pamperien; m. Kim Conrad Ehlers, Jan. 6, 1979; 1 child, Chase Conrad. BS, Okla. State U., 1977; MS, 1979; EdS in Counseling, Pitts. State U., 1993. Nat. Bd. Cert. Counselor. Art tchr. Hickman Mills Sch. Dist., Kansas City, 1979-80; Rockwood Sch. Dist., Eureka, Mo., 1981-83; employment cons. Deck and Decker Employment, Columbia, Mo., 1983-85; owner, mgr. Action Career Employment, Stillwater, Okla., 1985-87; instr. Art Edn. Okla. State U., Stillwater, 1987-88; art tchr. Lawson (Mo.) Sch. Dist., 1988-90; career counselor Cottey Coll., Nevada, Mo., 1991-93; coord. job devel. Pitts. State U., Kans., 1993-94; dir. Career Svcs., 1994—; bd. dirs., mem. Nevada, Mo. Learning Ctr., 1991-93; bus. industry coun. Pitts. (Kans.) C. of C., 1994—. Pres., v.p., treas. Beta Sigma Phi, 1979-91; pres. Grad. Student Coun., 1978-79; v.p. Cowboy Country Jaycees, 1985-90; mem. Pitts. Kiwanis, 1994—. Mem. Pittsburg Area C. of C. (bd. dirs.), Omicron Delta Kappa, Phi Delta Kappa, Kappa Delta Pi, Phi Kappa Phi. Office: Pittsburg State U Career Svcs 1701 S Broadway Pittsburg KS 66762

EHRENBURG, ANN ELEANOR, journalism educator; b. Ft. Monmouth, N.J., Jan. 14, 1943; d. Otto and Lois Huldah (Brakemeyer) E. BA in Journalism, U. Calif., Berkeley, 1965; MS in Communication, U. Southwestern La., 1984. Reporter various newspapers, Las Vegas, San Diego, Ft. Worth, 1971-82; tchr. Clark County Community Coll., Henderson, Nev., 1985-86; owner Calif. Pub. Rels. Co., Fresno, Calif., 1986-88; asst. prof. Journalism Ohio Wesleyan U., Delaware, Ohio, 1988-89; lectr. U. Nev., Las Vegas, 1989-90; TV writer Sta. KDL-TV, St. George, Utah, 1991-95; editl. writer The Spectrum, St. George, Utah, 1995—. Mem. Assn. for Edn. in Journalism and Mass Communication, Coll. Media Advisors Inc., Soc. Profl. Journalists. Democrat. Presbyterian. Home: PO Box 1633 Saint George UT 84771

EHRENZWEIG SINGER, RACHEL DEBRA, mental health counselor; b. Guelph, Ont., Can., Jan. 28, 1969; d. Joel and Vicki Phylis (Blaustein) E. BA in Psychology, Clark U., 1990; MA in Mental Health Counseling, Gallaudet U., 1992. Counselor for sexually abused disabled children Boys Town Rsch. Hosp., Omaha, 1992-93; counselor sch. team Lexington Sch. for the Deaf, Jackson Heights, N.Y., 1993—. Mem. Nat. Assn. for Deaf, Am. Mental Health Counselors Assn. Jewish. Office: Lexington Ctr 75th St and 30th Ave Jackson Heights NY 11370

EHRGOOD, SUSAN LEE, elementary school educator, counselor; b. Scranton, Pa., July 14, 1950; d. Robert P. and Lois E. (Thompson) E. BSE in Phys. Edn., Henderson State U., 1973, MSE in Phys. Edn., 1977, MSE in Elem. Counseling, 1988. Cert. tchr., Ark. Tchr. Magnet Cove Schs., Malvern, Ark., 1974—; cons. State Dept. Edn., Little Rock, 1977. Delivery person Meals on Wheels, Coun. on Aging, Arkadelphia, Ark., 1994; state coord. for jump rope for heart Am. Heart Assn., Little Rock, 1989—; vol. Nat. Multiple Sclerosis Soc., Little Rock, 1990, 91, 92, 93. Mem. AAHPERD (chair So. dist., jump rope for heart coun. 1993-94), NEA, Ark. Counseling Assn., Ark. Edn. Assn., Ark. Assn. for Health, Phys. Edn., Recreation and Dance (pres. 1989-90, Honor award 1981, Elem. Phys. Edn. award 1985, 89, Svc. award 1990). Methodist. Home: 1447 Welch St Arkadelphia AR 71923 Office: Magnet Cove Schs RR 7 Box 400 Malvern AR 72104-8740

EHRLICH, AVA, television executive producer; b. St. Louis, Aug. 14, 1950; d. Norman and Lillian (Gellman) Ehrlich; m. Barry K. Freedman, Mar. 31, 1979; children: Alexander Zev, Maxwell Samuel. BJ, Northwestern U., 1972, MJ, 1973; MA, Occidental Coll., 1976. Reporter, asst. mng. editor Lerner Newspapers, Chgo., 1974-75; reporter, news editor Sta. KMOX, St. Louis, 1976-79; producer Sta. WXYZ, Detroit, 1979-85; exec. producer Sta. KSDK-TV, St. Louis, 1985—; guest editor Mademoiselle mag., N.Y.C., 1971; freelance writer, coll. prof. Detroit, Chgo., St. Louis, 1987; adj. faculty mem. Washington U., St. Louis, 1994—. Trustee CORO Found., St. Louis, 1976-77, 86—; bd. dirs. Nat. Kidney Found., St. Louis, 1987. Named Outstanding Woman in Broadcasting, Am. Women in Radio & TV, 1983; recipient Journalism award Am. Chiropractic Assn., 1989, AP award Ill. UPI, 1989, Illuminator award AMC Cancer Rsch., 1994, Women in Comms. Nat. award, 1988, Emmy award, 1995; CORO Found. fellow in pub. affairs, 1975-76. Mem. NATAS (com. mem. 1986—, bd. dirs. 1994—, 13 local Emmy awards 1986—), Women in Comms., Inc. (sec. 1978-79, Clarion award 1989, Best in Midwest Feature award 1989), Soc. Profl. Journalists. Democrat. Jewish. Home: 8002 Walinca Dr Saint Louis MO 63105 Office: Sta KSDK-TV 1000 Market St Saint Louis MO 63101-2011

EHRLICH, GERALDINE ELIZABETH, food service management consultant; b. Phila., Nov. 28, 1939; d. Joseph Vincent and Agnes Barbara (Campbell) McKenna; m. S. Paul Ehrlich, Jr., June 20, 1959; children: Susan Patricia, Paula Jeanne, Jill Marie. BS, Drexel Inst. Tech. Nutrition cons., hypertension rsch. team U. Calif. Micronesia, 1970; regional sales dir. Marriott Corp., Bethesda, Md., 1976-78; dir. sales and profl. svcs. Coll. and Health Care div. Macke Co., Cheverly, Md., 1978, gen. mgr., 1978-79; v.p. ops., div., 1979-80, pres. Health Care div., 1980-81; regional v.p. Custom Mgmt. Corp., Alexandria, Va., 1981-83, v.p. mktg., 1983-87; v.p. mktg. and healthcare sales Morrison's Custom Mgmt., Mobile, Ala., 1987-88; v.p. sales ARA Svcs., Phila., 1988-93; v.p. bus. devel., ARAMARK, Phila., 1993-96; pres. Mktg. Matrix, 1996—; cons. mktg. The Green House, Tokyo, 1987-88; chmn. bd. Mktg. Matrix, Falls Church, Va., 1984—. Mem. Health Systems Agy. No. Va., 1976-77; chmn. Health Care Adv. Bd. Fairfax County Va., 1973-77; vice chmn. Fairfax County Cmty. Action Com., 1973-77; treas. Fairfax County Dem. Com., 1969-73; trustee Fairfax Hosp., 1973-77; bd. dirs. Tennis Patrons, Washington, 1984-88, Phila. Singers, 1993—, Physicians for Peace, 1994—. Mem. AAUW, Internat. Women's Assn., Am. Mgmt. Assn., Nat. Assn. Female Execs., Soc. Mktg. Profls. Home and Office: 6512 Lakeview Dr Falls Church VA 22041-1102

EHRLICH, MARGARET ISABELLA GORLEY, systems engineer, mathematics educator, consultant; b. Eatonton, Ga., Nov. 12, 1950; d. Frank Griffith and Edith Roy (Beall) Gorley; m. Jonathan Steven Ehrlich. BS in Math., U. Ga., 1972; MEd, Ga. State U., 1977, EdS, 1982, PhD, 1987; postgrad. Woodrow Wilson Coll. of Law, 1977-78. Cert. secondary tchr., Ga. Tchr. DeKalb County Bd. Edn., Decatur, Ga., 1972-83; chmn. dept. math. Columbia H.S., Decatur, 1978-83; with product devel. Chalkboard Co., Atlanta, 1983-84; math instr. Ga. State U., Atlanta, 1983-92; pres. Testing and Tech. Svcs., Atlanta, 1983—; course specialist Ga. Pacific Co., Atlanta, 1984-86; sys. engr. Lotus Devel. Corp., 1986-89; rsch. assoc. SUNY-Stony Brook, 1976; modeling instr. Barbizon Modeling Sch., Atlanta, 1991; instr. Ga. State Coll. for Kids, 1984-85; team leader guest svcs. ACOG; test-taking cons., hon. mem. Comm. Workers of Am. Local 3204, Atlanta, 1985—. Author: (software user manual) Micro Maestro, 1983, Music Math, 1984, (test manual) The Telephone Company Test, 1991, AMI Pro Advanced Courseware, 1992, A Study Guide for the Sales and Service Representative Test, 1993, A Study Guide for the Technical Services Test, 1995; mem. editl. bd. CPA Computer Report, Atlanta, 1984-85. Active Atlanta Preservation Soc., 1985, Planned Parenthood; tchr. St. Phillips Ch. Sch., Atlanta, 1981-88; vol. Joel Chandler Harris Assn., Atlanta, 1984-87; mem. St. Phillips welcome com., 1988-94, drug and alcohol counseling HOPE, 1988-94; sponsor Fair Test 1991—, Ctr. Fair and Open Testing; mem. parish choir St. Phillips Ch., 1995—; team leader guest svcs. Atlanta Com. Olympic Games. Named STAR Tchr. DeKalb County Bd. Edn., 1979, 80, 81, Most Outstanding Tchr., Barbizon Schs. of Modeling, 1980, Colo. Outward Bound, 1985, Disting. Educator, Ga. State U., 1987. Mem. LWV, Math. Assn. Am., Nat. Coun. Tchrs. Math., Ga. Coun. Tchrs. Math., Math. Assn. Am., Assn. Women in Math. (del. to China Sci. and Tech. Exch., 1989-90), Am. Soc. Tng. and Devel. Greater Atlanta, Ga. Hist. Soc., DeKalb Personal Computer Instr. Assn. (pres. 1984), Aux. Med. Assn. Ga., Daus. of Confederacy, Atlanta Track Club, N.Y.C. Track Club. Democrat. Episcopalian. Avocations: piano, jogging, fashion modeling, skiing, bonsai. Home: 240 Cliff Overlook Atlanta GA 30350-2601 Office: PO Box 500173 Atlanta GA 31150-0173

EHRMAN, MADELINE ELIZABETH, government administrator; b. N.Y.C., July 4, 1942; d. Donald McKinley and Marie Madeleine (Brandeis) Ehrman. BA summa cum laude Brown U., 1964, MA, 1965; M of Philosophy, Yale U., 1967; PhD, The Union Inst., 1989. Sci. linguist U.S. Dept. State, Washington, 1969-73, regional lang. supr. U.S. Embassy, Bangkok, Thailand, 1973-75, lang. tng. supr. U.S. Dept. State, Washington, 1975-84, curriculum and tng. specialist, 1984-85, acting chmn. dept. Asian and African Langs., 1985, chmn. dept. Asian and African Langs., 1986-88, acting assoc. dean Sch. Lang. Studies, 1987-88, dir. rsch., evaluation and devel., 1989—. Author: The Meanings of the Modals in Present Day American English, 1966, Contemporary Cambodian, 1975, Indonesian Fast Course, 1982, Communicative Japanese Materials, 1984, Ants and Grasshoppers, Badgers and Butterflies: Qualitative and Quantitative Exploration of Adult Language Learning Styles and Strategies, 1989, Understanding Second Language Learning Difficulties: Looking Beneath the Surface, 1996; mem. editorial bd. Jour. Psychol. Type, 1991—. Mem., ESOL/HILT Citizen's Adv. Coun., Arlington County, Va., 1985-89; psychotherapist Meyer Treatment Ctr. Washington Sch. Psychiatry, 1989-94. Woodrow Wilson Found. fellow, 1964; NSF fellow, 1964-69; recipient Meritorious Honor award U.S. Dept. State, 1972, 83. Mem. Am. Psychol. Assn., Tchrs. of English to Speakers of Other Langs., Am. Assn. Asian Studies, Assn. for Psychol. Type, Am. Orthopsychiat. Soc., Phi Beta Kappa, Psi Chi. Avocations: reading, bicycling, gardening. Office: Fgn Svc Inst 4000 Arlington Blvd Arlington VA 22204-1586

EICHHORST, GERDA IRENE, geriatrics nurse; b. Oranienburg, Germany, Feb. 24, 1944; came to the U.S., 1970; d. Artur Bernhard Bruno and Herta Ella Emma (Bräsicke) Ziemann; m. Peter Eichhorst, Dec. 29, 1967; 1 child, Stephanie. AS, South Ctrl. C.C., New Haven, 1991; LPN, W.F. Kaynor Regional Vo-Tech., Waterbury, Conn., 1993; student, Regents Coll., 1990—. CNA, Conn.; LPN, Conn. Auditor, tax cons. various acctg. offices, Berlin, Germany, 1963-68; bookkeeper, acct. Perfect Mfg., Montreal, Can., 1968-70; home health aide Vis. Nurse Assn., Derby, Conn., 1983-93; student nurse intern Milford (Conn.) Hosp., 1989-92; LPN Gardner Heights Nursing Home, Shelton, Conn., 1993—. Lutheran. Home: 24 Webster Dr Ansonia CT 06401-2553 Office: Gardner Heights Nursing Home 172 Rocky Rest Rd Shelton CT 06484-4234

EICHINGER, MARILYNNE H., museum administrator; m. Martin Eichinger; children: Ryan, Kara, Julia, Jessica, Talik. BA in Anthropology and Sociology magna cum laude, Boston U., 1965; MA, Mich. State U., 1971. With emergency and outpatient staff Ingham County Mental Health Ctr., 1972; founder, pres., exec. dir. Impression 5 Sci. and Art Mus., Lansing, Mich., 1973-85; pres. Oreg. Mus. Sci. and Industry, Portland, 1985-95; bd. dirs. Portland Visitors Assn., 1985-95; pres. Informal Edn. Products Ltd., 1995—, Portland, 1995—; bd. dirs. Portland Visitors Assn., 1994—, NW Regional Edn. Labs., 1991—; instr. Lansing (Mich.) C.C., 1978; ptnr. Eyrie Studio, 1982-85; bd. dirs. Assn. Sci. Tech. Ctrs., 1980-84, 88-93; mem. adv. bd. Portland State U.; condr. numerous workshops in interactive exhibit design, adminstrn. and fund devel. for schs., orgns., profl. socs. Author: (with Jane Mack) Lexington Montessori School Survey, 1969, Manual on the Five Senses, 1974; pub. Mich. edit. Boing mag. Founder Cambridge Montessori Sch., 1964; bd. dirs. Lexington Montessori Sch., 1969, Mid-Mich. South Health Sys. Agy., 1978-81, Cmty. Referral Ctr., 1981-85, Sta. WKAR-Radio, 1981-85; active Lansing "Riverfest" Lighted Boat Parade, 1980; mem. state Health Coordinating Coun., 1980-82; mem. pres.'s adv. coun. Portland State U., 1986—; mem. pres.' adv. bd. Portland State U., 1987-91. Recipient Diana Cert. Leadership, YWCA, 1976-77, Woman of Achievement award, 1991, Community Svc. award Portland State U., 1992. Mem. Am. Assn. Mus., Oreg. Mus. Assn., Assn. Sci. and Tech. Ctrs., Zonta Lodge (founder, bd. dirs. East Lansing club 1978), Internat. Women's Forum, Rotary Club Portland, City Club Portland, Portland C. of C. Office: Informal Edn Products Ltd 2520 SW Sherwood Dr Portland OR 97201-9999

EICHLER, EILEEN, tax accountant, educator; b. Bklyn., Sept. 5, 1949; d. Jack and Shirley E. (Hoffman) Milstein; m. Fred S. Eichler, June 13, 1970; Michelle Robyn, Mindy Paige. BS in Acctg., CUNY, 1971; MS in Taxation, Long Island U., 1986. Enrolled agt., IRS. Revenue agt. IRS, N.Y.C., 1971-74; tax preparer Eileen Eichler Enrolled Agt., Marblehead, Mass., 1974—; asst. prof. SUNY, Farmingdale, N.Y., 1986—. Mem. Am. Acctg. Assn., Inst. Mgmt. Accts. (v.p. membership 1993-94, 95-96, v.p. adminstrn. 1994-95. sec/ 1991-93). Office: Dept Bus & CIS SUNY Farmingdale NY 11735

EID, CYNTHIA ANN, metalsmith, jeweler, designer, educator; b. Madison, Wis., May 22, 1954; d. Richard O. and Ann E. (Henning) E.; m. David S. Reiner; children: Andrew Eid Reiner, Eric Eid Reiner. BS, U. Wis., 1977; MFA, Ind. U., 1980. Designer/goldsmith Joel Bagnal, Goldsmith, Concord and Wellesley, Mass., 1980-81; jewelry designer/goldsmith Neal Rosenblum, Goldsmith, Worcester, Mass., 1981; modelmaker, designer, supr. Verilyte, Inc., Brookline, Mass., 1982-85; tchr. metalsmithing Lexington (Mass.) Arts and Crafts Soc., 1992-94; instr. advanced silversmithing DeCordova Mus. Sch., Lincoln, Mass., 1995—; freelance metalsmith/jeweler Lexington, 1985—. Illustrator: Anthology of Fiddle Styles, 1976, Anthology of Jazz Violin Styles, 1981; metalwork featured: (Women in Design, Internat.) Compendium, 1981 (Outstanding Achievement award), (by Michael Wolk) Designing for the Table, 1992; exhibited at Soc. of Arts and Crafts, Boston, 1992—. Recipient Best in Show, Wis. Union Craft Exhbn., 1975, Metal award Beaux Arts Designer Craftsman, 1979, Flatware award Sterling Silver Design competition, 1980, Award winner SAVE Jewelry Design competition, 1996; Ford Found. fellow, 1978. Mem. Soc. Am. Silversmiths (artisan mem.), Soc. N.Am. Goldsmiths, Soc. Arts and Crafts (artist mem.).

EIDSON, COLLEEN FRANCES, special education educator; b. Auburn, N.Y., Apr. 9, 1958; d. Francis Charles and Valencia Alice (Nervina) Bellnier; m. Thomas Allen Eidson, Aug. 7, 1981; 1 child, Tyler James. AA, Cayuga County C.C., Auburn, N.Y., 1978; BS, Kent (Ohio) State U., 1981; MS, Canisius Coll., Buffalo, 1989. Cert. tchr. spl. edn. K-12, learning disabilities and behavior disorders, elem. edn. 1-8, counseling k-12. Specific learning disabilities tchr. Rootstown (Ohio) Mid. Sch., 1981-84; adapted phys. edn. instr./cons. Greenville (Tenn.) Sch. Dist., 1984-85; specific learning disabilities tchr. Build Acad., Buffalo, 1985-86, Mill Mid. Sch., Williamsville, N.Y.,

1986-88, Rootstown Elem. and H.S., 1988-95; elem. sch. counselor East Woods Sch., Hudson Sch. Dist., Hudson, Ohio, 1995—; girls' track coach Rootstown Local Schs., 1981-83, dir. internat. book project, 1983-84. Contbr. articles to profl. jours.; co-editor RTA Front Page News, 1992-94. Grantee Mid-Eastern Ohio Spl. Edn. Regional Coun., 1981, Buffalo Tchrs. Ctr., 1986, Maplewood Career Edn. Program, 1991, Kiwanis, 1991, Martha Holden Jennings, 1995. Mem. Rootstown Tchrs. Assn. (union rep. 1991—), Kappa Delta Phi. Republican. Roman Catholic. Home: 721 Fairchild Ave Kent OH 44240-2131 Office: East Woods Sch 120 N Hayden Pkwy Hudson OH 44236

EIDSON, DONNA STONE, elementary education educator; b. Aiken, S.C., June 7, 1946; d. Calvin Thomas Stone and Edith (Jordan) Carpenter; m. Edward Jackson Eidson, Sept. 9, 1966; children: Shawn Kisa, Edward Jackson II. ADN, Lander U., 1966; BA in Early Childhood Edn., U. S.C., Aiken, 1982; EdM in Elem. Edn., U. S.C., 1986. Cert. early childhood and elem. edn. Staff nurse Aiken (S.C.) County Hosp., 1966-67; office nurse Dr. R.O. Lipe, Aiken, 1967-68; RN, staff nurse Aiken (S.C.) Hosp., 1968-82, St. Joseph Hosp., Augusta, Ga., 1982-83, Augusta (Ga.) Regional Hosp., 1983; tchr. Jefferson Elem., Aiken (S.C.) County Sch. Dist., 1983—; com. mem. Ruth Patrick Sci. Ctr., Aiken, 1991—; adv. com. mem. Natural Resources Environ. Edn. Program, Savannah River Site, Aiken, 1993—. Recipient Hands-On Sci. award S.C. Dept. Edn., Columbia, 1989, Grocery Bag Recycling award S.C. Dept. Health and Environ. Control, Columbia, 1993, Sci./Litter Garden award Westinghouse-Savannah River Site, Aiken, 1993, Math. Manipulatives award Bechtel-Savannah River Site, Aiken, 1994. Mem. Nat. Sci. Tchrs. Baptist. Home: 10 Randall Dr PO Box 111 Graniteville SC 29829 Office: Jefferson Elem Sch Flynt Dr PO Box 340 Bath SC 29816

EIGEL, MARCIA DUFFY, editor; b. Denver, July 15, 1936; d. Eugene and Margaret (Foley) Duffy; m. Edwin G. Eigel Jr., May 30, 1959; children: Edwin III, Mary. BA, Webster U., 1958. Reg. rep. N.Y. Stock Exch. Dir. continuing edn. Mo. Soc. CPAs, St. Louis, 1978-79; dir. mktg. Greater Bridgeport (Conn.) Transp. Dist., 1979-81; security analyst Tucker, Anthony & R. L. Day, Stamford, Conn., 1981-84; fin. editor Evaluation Assoc., Westport, Conn., 1984-85; editor, writer corp. hdqrs. GE, Fairfield, Conn., 1985-92; dir. comms. Girl Scouts of Housatonic Coun., Bridgeport, Conn., 1994—; instr. in bus. writing So. Conn. State U., New Haven, 1986, U. Bridgeport, 1990. Writer, editor newsletter Customer Fin. Svcs. News, 1987-92, Woman Traveler, 1990—; contbr. articles and poetry to profl. jours. Bd. dirs. Friends McDonnell Planetarium, St. Louis, 1974-78, St. Louis U. Women's Club, 1975-79, YWCA, Bridgeport, 1980-83, Conf. Women, Bridgeport, 1981-83; founder, treas. St. Louis Free Lance Writers, 1977-79. Mem. NAFE. Home: 33 Pepperbush Ln Fairfield CT 06430-4036

EIKENBERRY, JILL, actress; b. New Haven, Jan. 21, 1947; m. Michael Tucker; 1 stepchild. Student, Yale U. Actress stage prodns. Saints, 1976, Uncommon Women and Others, 1977, Watch on the Rhine, 1980, Onward Victoria, 1980, Holiday, 1982, Porch, 1984, Fine Line, 1984, Life Under Water, 1985, feature film appearances include Between the Lines, 1977, An Unmarried Woman, 1977, The End of the World in Our Ususal Bed in a Night Full of Rain, 1978, Rich Kids, 1979, Butch and Sundance: The Early Days, 1979, Hide in Plain Sight, 1980, Arthur, 1981, Grace Quigley, 1985, The Manhattan Project, 1986; TV movie appearances include The Deadliest Season, 1977, Orphan Train, 1979, Swan Song, 1980, Sessions, 1983, Kane and Abel, 1985, Assault and Matrimony, 1987, Family Sins, 1987, A Stoning in Fulham County, 1988, My Boyfriend's Back, 1989, The Diane Martin Story, The Secret Life of Archie's Wife, 1990, An Inconvenient Woman, 1991, Living A Lie, 1991, Doc: The Dennis Littky Story, 1992, Chantilly Lace, 1993, Parallel Lives, 1994; teleplay Uncommon Women and Others, 1978, regular (TV series) L.A. Law, 1986-94 (Emmy nomination, Supporting Actress - Drama Series, 1994). Office: care William Morris Agency 151 S El Camino Dr Beverly Hills CA 90212-2704*

EILTS, SUSANNE ELIZABETH, physician; b. Council Bluffs, Iowa, Oct. 12, 1955; d. Ervin Edwin and Mary Margaret (Leonard) E. BS, Nebr. Wesleyan U., 1976; MD, U. Iowa, 1980. Diplomate Am. Bd. Internal Medicine. Intern, resident U. Nebr. Med. Ctr., Omaha, 1980-83; pvt. practice, Omaha, 1983—; clin. instr. internal medicine U. Nebr., Omaha, 1983—; med. dir. Amb. Nursing Home, Omaha, 1990-92; quality assurance reviewer Sunderbruch Corp. Nebr., Lincoln, 1990—, v.p. quality assurance Internal Med. Assocs., 1993-95; chmn. dept. medicine Clarkson Hosp., 1994-95, sec.-treas. med. staff, 1996-99, mem. staff exec. com., 1994—, med. outcomes coun., 1994-96. Med. columnist Omaha World Herald, 1986-88. Mem. ACP, Am. Geriatric Soc., Nebr. Med. Assn. (alt. del. 1990-91, del. 1992, young physician com. 1989-93, com. health care reform 1993-94, legis. com. 1993—, legis. subcom. for HMO/PPO policy statement 1995—), Am. Women's Med. Assn. Nebr. (sec. 1987), Nebr. Soc. Internal Medicine (bd. dirs. 1994—), Dundee-Meml. Park Neighborhood Assn., Beta Beta Beta, Phi Kappa Phi, Phi Lambda Upsilon. Office: Internal Medicine Assocs PC 4242 Farnam St Ste 650N Omaha NE 68131-2802

EIMERS, JERI ANNE, therapist; b. Berkeley, Calif., Jan. 20, 1951; d. Alfred D. Wallace and Marjorie E. (Nordheim) Stevens; m. Roy A. Neiman, June 12, 1969 (div. Aug. 1977); children: Lorien, Arwen; m. Richard A. Eimers, Mar. 2, 1996. AA, Palomar Jr. Coll., 1977; BA in Psychology with distinction, Calif. State U., Long Beach, 1979, MA in Psychology with distinction, 1981; postgrad. Human Sexuality Program, UCLA, 1991-92. Lic. marriage, family, child therapist, Calif.; cert. community coll. instr., counselor; cert. sex therapist. Rsch. asst. Calif. State U., 1978-82; tchr. Artesia (Calif.)-Bellflower-Cerritos Unified Sch. Dist., 1982-83; dir. Am. Learning Corp., Huntington Beach, Calif., 1983-85; social worker Los Angeles County Children's Protective Svcs., Long Beach, 1986-88; sr. social worker Orange County Social Svc. Agy., Orange, Calif., 1988-90; therapist Cypress Mental Health, Cypress, Calif., 1988—, cons., 1990—; cons., 1990—; group chair, leader Adults Abused as Children, Los Altos Hosp., Long Beach, 1991—, Coll. Hosp., Cerritos, 1993—; speaker, presenter in field. Mem. Child's Sexual Abuse Network, Orange, 1988—; mem. legis. com. Child Abuse Coun. of Orange County, 1988. Women's League scholar, 1980-81. Mem. AAUW, Am. Assn. Marriage, Family Therapists, Calif. Assn. Marriage, Family Therapists, Am. Profl. Soc. for Abused Children, Calif. Profl. Assn. for Abused Children, Phi Kappa Phi, Psi Chi. Republican. Methodist. Address: Huntington Group Ste 365 9191 Towne Centre Dr San Diego CA 92122

EINBINDER, SUSAN LESLIE, literature educator, rabbi; b. Ridgewood, N.J., Dec. 9, 1954; d. Seymour K. and Julia M. (Morrison) E. BA in Math. magna cum laude, Brown U., 1976; MHL, Hebrew Union Coll., 1983; MA in English and Comparative Lit., Columbia U., 1978, MPhil, 1986, PhD in Comparative Lit., 1991. Ordained rabbi, 1983. Vis. lectr., chaplain to Jewish students Colgate U., Hamilton, N.Y., 1987-88; adj. prof. gen. studies NYU, N.Y.C., 1990-92; adj. prof. Manhattan Sch. Music, N.Y.C., 1991-92; vis. lectr. U. Md., College Park, 1992-93; asst. prof. Hebrew lit. Hebrew Union Coll., Cin., 1993-96; assoc. prof. Hebrew Union Coll., 1996—. Translator: (novella) IYA (Shimon Ballas), 1995; contbr. articles to profl. jours. and confs. Bd. dirs. Prospect House, Cin., 1995—; spkr. at cmty. orgns. Fellow Fulbright Found., 1986-87, Nat. Found. for Jewish Culture, 1988-89. Mem. MLA, Cen. Conf. of Am. Rabbis, Nat. Assn. Profs. of Hebrew, Assn. for Jewish Studies. Office: Hebrew Union Coll Jewish Inst Religion 3101 Clifton Ave Cincinnati OH 45220

EINEKE, ALVINA MARIE, public health nurse; b. Elmhurst, Ill., Mar. 31, 1951; d. Herbert Fred and Gertrude (Gittings) E. BSN, Valparaiso U., 1973. Credentialed early intervention specialist. Staff nurse pediatrics Wyler Children's Hosp.-U. Chgo. Hosps. and Cinics, Chgo., 1973-78; pub. health nurse Tuscola County Health Dept., Caro, Mich., 1978-82, Saginaw County Health Dept., Saginaw, Mich., 1982-86; pub. health nurse, prenatal care program coord. Tuscola County Health Dept., Caro, 1986-87; staff pediatrics St. Josephs Hosp., Elgin, Ill., 1988; pub. health nurse Dupage County Health Dept., Wheaton, Ill., 1988; pub. health nurse DeKalb County Health Dept., DeKalb, Ill., 1988-92, coord. Maternal Child Health program, 1992-93, early intervention health specialist, mem. communicable disease staff, 1993—; co-founder, profl. cons. DeKalb County High Risk Parent to Parent Support Group, DeKalb, 1991-93. Bd. dirs. Assn. Care of Children's Health, Mich., 1979-81, family com. mem., Chgo., 1975-78; softball coach 7 to 10 yr. old girls Sch. Dist./Park Dist. Youth Softball, Caro, 1979; vol. Kane County Natural Area Vols., Geneva, Ill., 1989—; crisis vol. telephone and support Tuscola County, Caro, 1980-83. Mem. ANA, Ill. Nurses Assn. (dist. 2), No. Ill. Perinatal Regional (agy. rep. 1988-93). Lutheran. Office: 2337 Sycamore Rd De Kalb IL 60115

EINIGER, CAROL BLUM, foundation executive; b. Phila., Nov. 30, 1949; d. Bernard Michael and Bella (Karff) Blum; m. Roger William Einiger, Dec. 21, 1969; 1 child. BA, U. Pa., 1970; MBA, Columbia U., 1973. With Conde Nast Publs., N.Y.C., 1970-71, Goldman, Sachs & Co., N.Y.C., 1971-72; with 1st Boston Corp., N.Y.C., 1973-88, with corp. fin. dept., 1973-79, with capital markets dept., 1979-88, mng. dir., 1982-88, head short-term fin. dept., 1983-88, head capital markets dept., 1985-88; vis. prof., exec.-in-residence Columbia U. Bus. Sch., N.Y.C., 1988-89; mng. dir. Wasserstein Perella & Co. Inc., N.Y.C., 1989-92; v.p., chief fin. officer Edna McConnell Clark Found., N.Y.C., 1992—, acting pres., 1995-96. Trustee Horace Mann Sch., 1988-94, U. Pa., 1989—; bd. overseers Columbia U. Bus. Sch., 1988—; investment com. Mus. Modern Art, 1994—; mem. steering com. Wall Street div. UJA Fedn., 1989-93. Office: Edna McConnell Clark Found 250 Park Ave New York NY 10177

EINODER, CAMILLE ELIZABETH, secondary education educator; b. Chgo., June 15, 1937; d. Isadore and Elizabeth T. (Czerwinski) Popowski; student Fox Bus. Coll., 1954; BEd in Biology, Chgo. Tchrs. Coll., 1964; MA in Analytical Chemistry, Gov.'s State U., 1977; MA in Adminstrn. and Supervision, Roosevelt U., 1986; postgrad 1992—. m. Joseph X. Einoder, Aug. 5, 1978; children: Carl Frank, Mark Frank, Vivian Einoder, Joe Einoder, Tim Einoder, Sheila Einoder, Jude Einoder. Secretarial positions, Chgo., 1955-64; tchr. biology Chgo. Bd. Edn., 1964—, tchr. biology and agr., 1975-81, tchr. biology, agr. and chemistry, 1981—; human rels. coord. Morgan Park High Sch., Chgo., 1980—, tchr. biology Internat. Studies Sch., 1983—, mem. adv. bd., 1989—; career devel. cons. for agr. related curriculum. Bds. dirs., founding mem., author constn. Community Coun., 1970—; bd. dirs., edn. cons. Neighborhood Coun., 1974; rep. Chgo. Tchrs. Union, 1969; exec. bd. dir. The Lira Ensemble, 1996—. Mem. Phi Delta Kappa, Iota Sigma Pi. Home: 10637 S Claremont Ave Chicago IL 60643-3101 Office: 1744 W Pryor Ave Chicago IL 60643-3457

EIRIKSSON, SANDRA BURNS, biochemist, educator; b. Dover, Del., Mar. 16, 1956; d. James Ross and Barbara June (O'Neill) Burns; m. Dale Arman Eiriksson, June 9, 1984 (div. Jan. 1993); 1 child, Amanda Nicole. BS in Biology, S.W. Tex. State U., 1980; MS in Biology, U. West Fla., 1988; PhD in Sci. Edn., Fla. State U., 1995. Cert. chemistry, biology, math., gen. sci. tchr., Fla. Grad. asst., lab. instr., rsch. asst. S.W. Tex. State U., San Marcos, 1980-83; sci. tchr. 8th grade Ruckel Middle Sch., Okaloosa Dist., Fla., 1983-89; assoc. instr. gen. biology Okaloosa-Walton C. C., Niceville, Fla., 1989—; asst. prof. Coll. Edn. U. West Fla., Pensacola, 1995—; math. tchr. Ruckel Middle Sch., Niceville H.S., Okaloosa Dist., 1985-90; biology tchr. Niceville H.S., 1989-95; adj. prof. coll. edn. U. West Fla., 1995; environ. scis. tchr. Choctawhatchee H.S., Okaloosa Dist., 1995—; cons. dept. curriculum and instruction in biology Fla. State U., Fla. Panhandle Ctr. for Excellence in Sci. and Math., Fred Gannon State Park, Choctawhatchee H.S.; chairperson scientific rev. com., instl. rev. com. Walton and Okaloosa County Sci. and Engring. Fairs; presenter in field. Developer mentor program Eglin AFB, 1986—; facilitator U. Ala. Advanced Placement Biology Inst.; vol. Valparaiso Elem. Sch., Women's Detox Unit, Fort Walton Beach, St. Jude's Episcopal Ch.; judge sci. fair Okaloosa County Elem. and Middle Schs. Grantee Project CHILD Okaloosa County, DOE Eisenhower; Tandy Tech. scholar; named Tchr. of Yr.; recipient Outstanding Sci. Tchr. award Optical Soc. Am., Airlift award USAF Acad. Mem. Higher Edn. Consortium Math. and Scis. Region I, Am. Assn. Univ. Women, Nat. Assn. Rsch. Sci. Tchg., Qualitative Rsch. Interest Group, S.Ea. Assn. Edn. Tchrs. Sci., Assn. Edn. Tchrs. Sci., Nat. Biology Tchrs. Assn., Okaloosa County Edn. Assn, Fla. Tchg. Profession, Nat. Edn. Assn., Nat. Sci. Tchrs. Assn., Fla. Assn. Sci. Tchrs., County Okaloosa Assn. Sci. Tchrs., Bay County Sci. Coun., Pensacola Runner's Assn., N.W. Fla. Track Club, Phi Delta Kappa. Home: # 1 Hidden Cove Valparaiso FL 32580 Office: U West Fla Divsn Tchr Edn Bldg 85 Rm 196 11000 University Pky Pensacola FL 32514

EIS, RUTH SUSANNE, museum curator, artist; b. Mainz, Germany, Feb. 6, 1920; came to U.S., 1937; d. Sali and Margaret (Weissmann) Levi; m. Max Eis, Jan. 4, 1942 (dec. 1991); children: Regina, Steven. Student, Fashion Design Sch. Feige, Berlin, Fashion Design Sch. Traphagen, N.Y.; AA, Oakland Jr. Coll., 1956; BA, U. Calif., Berkeley, 1958; MA, Lone Mountain Coll., 1975. Curator ceremonial art J.L. Magnes Mus., Berkeley, 1960—. Author: (mus. catalogs) Hanukkah Lamps, 1977, Torah binders, 1979, Ornamented Bags, 1994, 25 Years Magnes Museum, 1987, (book) Poems of an Immigrant, 1995. Home: 5401 Belgrave Pl Oakland CA 94618-1743

EISEN, REBECCA DIANNE, lawyer; b. Pensacola, Fla., Oct. 13, 1949; d. Fred S. and Eva Marie (Plambeck) Strause; m. James Jonathan Eisen, Apr. 21, 1985; children: Samuel Jacob, Elias Gabriel. BA, U. Calif., Berkeley, 1971; MA, Calif. State U., 1973; JD, U. San Francisco, 1980. Bar: Calif. 1980, U.S. Dist. ct. (no., ea. and cen. dists.) Calif. 1983, U.S. Ct. Appeals (9th cir.) 1987. Assoc. Brobeck, Phleger & Harrison, San Francisco, 1980-88, ptnr., 1989—. Mem. Charles Lawrence Scholarship Com., San Francisco, 1986 . Mem. ABA, Calif. Bar Assn. Office: Brobeck Phleger & Harrison Spear St Tower 1 Market Plz San Francisco CA 94105*

EISENBERG, DOROTHY, federal judge; b. 1929. LLB, Bklyn. Law Sch., 1950. Bar: N.Y. 1951, U.S. Dist. Ct. (ea. and so. dists.) N.Y., U.S. Ct. Appeals (2nd cir.), U.S. Supreme Ct. Assoc. Otterbourg, Stiendler, Houston & Rosen, N.Y.C., 1950-51, Goldman, Horowitz & Cherno, Mineola, N.Y., 1970-80; pvt. practice Garden City, N.Y., 1981; ptnr. Shaw, Licitra, Eisenberg, Esernio & Schwartz, P.C., Garden City, 1981-89; bankruptcy judge U.S. Bankruptcy Ct. (ea. dist.) N.Y., 1989—; mem. Com. on Character and Fitness, Appellate divsn, 2nd Dept., 1983-89; panel trustee U.S. Bankruptcy Ct. (ea. dist.) N.Y., 1975-89, U.S. Bankruptcy Ct. (so. dist.) N.Y., 1979-89. Fellow Am. Bar Found.; mem. ABA, Nat. Assn. Women Judges, N.Y. State Assn. Women Judges, N.Y. County Lawyers Assn., N.Y. Women's Bar Assn., Bar Assn. Nassau County, Theodore Roosevelt Am. Inn Ct. Office: U S Bankruptcy Ct 1635 Privado Rd Westbury NY 11590-5241

EISENBERG, KAREN SUE BYER, nurse; b. Bklyn., Mar. 11, 1954; d. Marvin and Florence (Beck) Byer; m. Howard Eisenberg, May 11, 1974; children: Carly Beth, Mariel Bryn. Diploma, L.I. Coll. Hosp. Sch. Nursing, 1973; BS in Nursing, L.I. U., 1976, M in Profl. Studies, 1977. Nurse recovery room and surg. intensive care unit Downstate Med. Ctr., Bklyn., 1973-75; utilization rev. analyst Bezallel Health Related Facility, Far Rockaway, N.Y., 1975-76; utilization rev. analyst, R.N. supr. Seagirt Health Related Facility, Far Rockaway, 1976; staff nurse neurosurg. and rehab. nursing Downstate Med. Ctr., Bklyn., 1978, nurse intensive care unit, 1978-79; asst. nursing dir. pathology, clin. rsch. assoc. Rsch. Found., Bklyn., 1979-90; instrl. support specialist pathology Health Sci. Ctr. SUNY, Bklyn., 1990-92; nurse practitioner pathology SUNY Rsch. Found., Bklyn., 1992-95; nurse rsch. coord. surgery SUNY Health Sci. Ctr., Bklyn., 1995—. Contbr. articles to profl. jours. Mem. Oncology Nursing Soc., Am. Nurses Assn., N.Y. State Nurses Assn., N.Y. Acad. Scis., L.I. Coll. Hosp. Alumnae Assn. Office: 450 Clarkson Ave Brooklyn NY 11203-2012

EISENBERG, MARILYN, consultant; b. Chgo., Mar. 3, 1941; d. Frank and Rose (Kreisman) Spiegel; m. Jack Leo Eisenberg, Nov. 28, 1965; children: Erik, Amy Ilene. Exec. mgr. Knickerbocker Hotel, Chgo., 1966-70, Ambassador West Hotel, Chgo., 1976-85; tchr. hotel mgmt. City Coll. of Chgo., 1986-88. Co-founder, pres. Edn. Resource Ctr., Chgo., 1974-80; co-founder Chgo. Children's Mus., 1980, pres. 1983-86, bd. dirs., 1980—; vol. tchr. Nr. North High Sch., Chgo., 1983-90; bd. dirs. Personal PAC, 1992—; clinic escort Pro Choice Alliance, 1993—. Home: 3100 N Sheridan Rd Chicago IL 60657-4954

EISENBERG, PHYLLIS ROSE, author; b. Chgo., June 26, 1924; d. Lewis Rose and Frances (Remer) Rose Blossom; m. Emanuel M. Eisenberg; 1 child, Bart. BA, UCLA, 1946. Writing instr. L.A. Valley Coll., Van Nuys, Calif., 1975-78, L.A. Pierce Coll., Woodland Hills, Calif., 1983-85, UCLA, 1986, Calif. State U., Northridge, 1996—; jour. writing instr. Everywoman's Village, Van Nuys, 1987-92; lit. cons., 1975—. Author: A Mitzvah Is Something Special, 1978 (one of 12 outstanding works of fiction of yr. Yearbook Ency. 1979), Don't Tell Me A Ghost Story, 1982 (All Choice Book Internat. Children's Exhbn., Munich 1983), You're My Nikki (NCSS-CBC Notable 1992 Children's Trade Book award, Children's Book of Yr. Bank St. Coll.); contbr. fiction, poetry and non-fiction to numerous newspapers and periodicals. Exec. sec. Founder's Guild of San Fernando Valley Child Guidance Clinic, Studio City, Calif., 1985; writing instr. Sophia Myers Sch. for Visually Handicapped, Van Nuys, 1987; reading instr. remedial program for children YMCA, Van Nuys, 1990; exec. sec. Valley Jewish Cmty. Ctr., North Hollywood, Calif., 1982. Mem. PEN, Soc. Children's Book Writers and Illustrators, Soc. Children's and Young People's Literature.

EISENBERG, ROBIN LEDGIN, religious education administrator; b. Passaic, N.J., Jan. 10, 1951; d. Morris and Ruth (Miller) Ledgin. BS, West Chester State U., 1973; M Edn., Kutztown State U., 1977. Administrv. asst. Keneseth Israel, Allentown, Pa., 1973-77; dir. edn. Cong. Schaarai Zedek, Tampa, Fla., 1977-79, Kehilath Israel, Pacific Palisades, Calif., 1979-80, Temple Beth El, Boca Raton, Fla., 1980—. Contbr. Learning Together, 1987, Bar Bat Mizvah Education: A Sourcebook, 1993, The New Jewish Teachers Handbook, 1994. Chmn. edn. info., Planned Parenthood, Boca Raton Fla. 1989. Recipient Kamiker Camp award Nat. Assn. Temple Educators, Pres.'s award for adminstrn., 1990. Mem. Nat. Assn. Temple Educators (pres. 1990-92), Coalition Advancement of Jewish Edn. Home: 5692 Santiago Cir Boca Raton FL 33433-7297 Office: Temple Beth El 333 SW 4th Ave Boca Raton FL 33432-5709

EISENBERG, SONJA MIRIAM, artist; b. Berlin, June 10, 1926; came to U.S., 1938, naturalized, 1947; d. Adolf and Meta Cecilie (Bettauer) Weinberger; student Queens Coll., 1943-46, Middlebury Coll., 1945; NYU, 1952-54; BA, NYU, 1954; postgrad. Nat. Acad. Sch. Fine Arts, 1961; m. Jack Eisenberg, Mar. 31, 1946; children: Ralph, Lynn, Lauren. One-woman shows: Bodley Gallery, N.Y.C., 1970, 73, 75, 80, Galerie Art du Monde, Paris, 1973, Buyways Gallery, Sarasota, Fla., 1973, 74, 75, 78, Galerie de Sfinx, Amsterdam, Netherlands, 1974, Huntsville (Ala.) Mus. Art, 1974, Anglo-Am. Art Mus., Baton Rouge, 1974, Comara Gallery, L.A., 1974, Palm Spring (Calif.) Desert Mus., 1975, Fordham U., N.Y.C., 1976, Omega Inst., New Lebanon, N.Y., 1979, Am. Mus., Hayden Planetarium, N.Y.C., 1980, Avila Graphics, Ltd., 1981, YWCA, N.Y.C., 1981, Cathedral of St. John the Divine, N.Y.C., 1983, 85, The Millbrook Gallery, N.Y., 1989, 94, Christopher Leonard Gallery, N.Y.C., 1993, Park Hotel, Vitznau, Switzerland, 1994, The Burgenstock (Switzerland) Hotels, 1995; group shows include Mus. Fine Arts, St. Petersburg, Fla., 1973, Am. Watercolor Soc., 107th, 108th Exhbn., 1974, 75, Galerie Frederic Gollong, St. Paul de Vence, France, 1978, Betty Parson's Gallery, N.Y.C., 1981, Foster Harmon Galleries of Am. Art, Sarasota, Fla., 1988, Tokyo Met. Art Mus. 14th Internat. Art Friendship Exhbn., 1989, Galerie Herbert Leidel, Munich, Germany, 1991, Park Ave. Armory, N.Y.C., 1996, Akim-USA, N.Y.C., 1996; represented in permanent collections: Archives Am. Art, Smithsonian Inst., Jewish Mus., N.Y.C., Fordham U. Mus., N.Y.C., Palm Springs Desert Mus., Omega Inst., Cathedral of St. John the Divine; artist-in-residence Cathedral of St. John the Divine, N.Y.C.; designer WFUNA cachet for UN Water Power Conf., 1977, UN Internat. Yr. of Disabled Persons, 1981. Regent Cathedral of St. John the Divine, N.Y.C., 1990, commisioned painting to commemorate Crystal Night for Telecom Telefon Karte, Munich, 1993. Recipient gold medal for artistic merit Internat. Parliament for Safety and Peace, 1983, Palma D'Oro Europe, 1986. Mem. Accademia Italia delle Arti e del Lavoro (Gold medal 1981). Completed project Seeing the Gospel According to St. John (text and 41 paintings) for Cathedral of St. John, 1987; appointed art dir. Hermes Media B.V., Amsterdam, The Netherlands, 1992. Home and Office: 1020 Park Ave New York NY 10028-0913

EISENHAUER, ANITA LOUISE, appraiser; b. Amarillo, Tex., Feb. 27, 1942; d. Ora Calvin and Louise (Rorex) Holt; m. Gene Edmond Eisenhouer, Feb. 22, 1964; children: William Edmond, George Edward. BA in Geography, U. Tex., 1964; MA in History, Tex. A&M U., 1967. Tchr. Corpus Christi (Tex.) Ind. Sch. Dist., 1965-68; antiques dealer Attic Antiques, Corpus Christi, 1972-79; personal property appraiser Anita Eisenhauer Appraisers, Corpus Christi, 1979—. Mem. Landmark Commn., Corpus Christi, 1976-86; mem. Neuces County Hist. Commn., 1981—, chmn., 1986—. Recipient John Ben Shepherd award Tex. Hist. Commn., 1990. Mem. DAR, AAUW (pres. Corpus Christi br. 1980-82). Methodist.

EISENMAN, TRUDY FOX, dermatologist; b. Chgo., Oct. 14, 1940; d. Nathan Henry and Bernice (Greenberg) Fox; student U. Ill. at Navy Pier, Chgo., 1958-60; M.D., U. Ill., 1964; m. Theodore S. Eisenman, Aug. 19, 1962 (div. 1985); children: Lawrence, Robert. Rotating intern Milw. County Gen. Hosp., 1964-65, med. resident, 1965-66; resident in dermatology Northwestern U. Med. Sch., Chgo., 1970-73, instr., 1973—; practice medicine specializing in dermatology, Chgo., 1973—; attending dermatologist Louis A. Weiss Meml. Hosp., Chgo., 1973—. Diplomate Am. Bd. Dermatology. Fellow Am. Acad. Dermatology; mem. Chgo. Dermatol. Soc., Am. Med. Women's Assn., AMA, Chgo. Med. Soc., Alpha Omega Alpha. Office: 4640 N Marine Dr Chicago IL 60640-5719

EISENSTADT, PAULINE DOREEN BAUMAN, investment company executive, state legislator; b. N.Y.C., Dec. 31, 1938; d. Morris and Anne (Lautenberg) Bauman; BA, U. Fla., 1960; MS (NSF grantee), U. Ariz., 1965; postgrad. U. N.Mex.; m. Melvin M. Eisenstadt, Nov. 20, 1960; children: Todd Alan, Keith Mark. Tchr., Ariz., 1961-65, P.R., 1972-73; adminstrv. asst. Inst. Social Research U. N.Mex., 1973-74; founder, 1st exec. dir. Energy Consumers N.Mex., 1977-81; dir., host TV program Consumer Viewpoint, 1980-82; host TV program N.Mex. Today and Tomorrow, 1992—; asst. sec. energy Nat. Dept. Energy, 1993—; chmn. consumer affairs adv. com. Dept. Energy, 1979-80; v.p. tech. bd. Nat. Center Appropiate Tech., 1980—; pres. Eisenstadt Enterprises, investments, 1983—; mem. N.Mex. Ho. of Reps., 1985—, chairwoman majority caucus, chair rules com. N.Mex. House of Reps., 1987—, chair sub. com. on children and youth, 1987; mem. exec. com., vice chair pvt. coun. Nat. Conf. State Legislators, 1987; vice chmn. Sandoval County (N.Mex.) Democratic Party, 1981—, candidate for state senate, 1996; mem. N.Mex. Dem. State Central Com., 1981—; N.Mex. del. Dem. Nat. Platform Com., 1984, Dem. Nat. Conv., 1984; pres. Sandoval County Dem. Women's Assn., 1979-81; vice chmn. N. Mex. Dem. Platform Com., 1984—; mem. Sandoval County Redistricting Task Force, 1983-84; mem. Rio Rancho Ednl. Study Com., 1984—.; pres. Anti Defamation League, N. Mex., 1994-95; mem. N.Mex. First. Recipient Gov.'s award Outstanding N. Mex. Women, Commn. on the Status of Women and Gov. Bruce King, 1992. Mem. NEA, LWV, NOW. Author: Corrales, Portrait of a Changing Village, 1980. Mem. Kiwanis (1st woman mem. local club), Rio Rancho Rotary Club (pres. 1995—, Rotarian of the Year, 1995). Home: PO Box 658 Corrales NM 87048-0658

EISENSTEIN, ELIZABETH LEWISOHN, historian, educator; b. N.Y.C., Oct. 11, 1923; d. Sam A. and Margaret V. (Seligman) Lewisohn; m. Julian Calvert Eisenstein, May 30, 1948; children: Margaret, John (dec.), Edward. A.B., Vassar Coll., 1944; M.A., Radcliffe Coll., 1947, Ph.D., 1953; Litt. D. (hon.), Mt. Holyoke Coll., 1979. From lectr. to adj. prof history Am. U., Washington, 1959-74; Alice Freeman Palmer prof. history U. Mich., Ann Arbor, 1975-88, prof. emerita, 1988—; scholar-in-residence Rockefeller Found. Center, Bellagio, Italy, June 1977; mem. vis. com. dept. history Harvard U., 1975-81, vice-chmn., 1979-81; dir. Ecole des Hautes Etudes en Sciences Sociales, Paris, 1982; guest speaker, participant confs. and seminars; I. Beam vis. prof. U. Iowa, 1980; Mead-Swing lectr. Oberlin Coll., 1980; Stone lectr. U. Glasgow, 1984; Van Leer lectr. Van Leer Fedn., Jerusalem, 1984; Hanes lectr. U. N.C., Chapel Hill, 1985 first resident cons. Center for the Book, Library of Congress, Washington, 1979; mem. Coun. Scholars, 1980-88; pres.'s disting. visitor Vassar Coll., 1988; Pforzheimer lectr. N.Y. Pub. Libr., 1989, Lyell lectr. Bodleian Libr., Oxford, 1990, Merle Curti lectr. U. Wis., Madison, 1992; vis. fellow Wolfson Coll., Oxford, 1990. Author: The First Professional Revolutionist: F. M. Buonarroti, 1959, The Printing Press as an Agent of Change, 1979 , 2 vols. paperback edit., 1980 (Phi Beta Kappa Ralph Waldo Emerson prize 1980), The Printing Revolution in Early Modern Europe, 1983 (reissued as Canto Book, 1993), Grub Street Abroad, 1992; mem. editorial bd. Jour. Modern History, 1973-76, 83-86, Revs. in European History, 1973-86, Jour. Library History, 1979-82, Eighteenth

Century Studies, 1981-84; contbr. articles to profl. jours., chpts. to books. Belle Skinner fellow Vassar Coll., NEH fellow, 1977, Guggenheim fellow, 1982, fellow Ctr. Advanced Studies in Behavioral Scis., 1982-83, 92-93, Humanities Rsch. Ctr. fellow Australian Nat. U., 1988. Fellow Am. Acad. Arts and Scis., Royal Hist. Soc.; mem. Soc. French Hist. Studies (v.p. 1970, mem. program com. 1974), Am. Soc. 18th Century Studies (nominating com. 1971), Soc. 16th Century Studies, Am. Hist. Assn. (com. on coms. 1970-72, chmn. Modern European sect. 1981, council 1982-85), Renaissance Soc. Am. (council 1973-76, pres. 1986), Am. Antiquarian Soc. (exec. com., adv. bd. 1984-87), Phi Beta Kappa. Office: U Mich Dept History Ann Arbor MI 48109

EISLER, SUSAN KRAWETZ, advertising agency executive; b. N.Y.C., Aug. 18, 1946; d. Aaron and Bertha (Platt) Krawetz; m. Howard Irwin Eisler, June 8, 1980; 1 stepchild, Robin Joy, 1 adopted son, Joseph. BA, U. Pitts., 1967; MA, New Sch. for Social Rsch., 1971. Analyst, Marplan, Inc., N.Y.C., 1968-69; project dir. Market Facts, Inc., N.Y.C., 1969-70; assoc. rsch. mgr. Gen. Foods, Inc., White Plains, N.Y., 1970-75, product mgr., 1975-80; rsch. dir. Elizabeth Arden, N.Y.C., 1980-81; v.p., assoc. rsch. dir. Lintas: N.Y. (formerly SSC&B: Lintas Worldwide), N.Y.C., 1981-87, sr. v.p., assoc. rsch. dir., 1987-92, exec. v.p., dir. strategic planning and rsch., 1992-94; exec. v.p. dir. strategic planning & rsch., Gotham, Inc., 1995—. Named Woman of Yr. YWCA Acad. Women Achievers, 1989. Mem. Am. Mktg. Assn., Advt. Women N.Y., Advt. Rsch. Found. (copy rsch. coun.). Office: Gotham Inc 260 Madison Ave New York NY 10016

EISNER, DIANA, pediatrician; b. Houston, May 7, 1951; d. Elmer and Edith (Dubow) E. BA in Biology cum laude, Brandeis U., 1973; MD, Southwestern Med. Sch., 1977. Diplomate Am. Bd. Pediatrics. Intern, resident Baylor Coll. Medicine, Houston, 1977-80; pvt. practice Houston, 1981—; chmn. dept. pediatrics Meml. N.W. Hosp., Houston, 1990. Recipient Commendation award Children's Protection Com. Tex. Children's Hosp., 1978, Physician's Recognition award AMA, 1983. Mem. Am. Acad. Pediatrics, Tex. Med. Assn., Tex. Pediatric Soc., Houston Pediatric Soc., Harris County Med. Soc. Office: 1740 W 27th St Ste 170 Houston TX 77008-1435

EISNER, GAIL ANN, artist, educator; b. Detroit, Oct. 17, 1939; d. Rudolph and Florence (White) Leon; m. Marvin Michael Eisner, June 14, 1959 (dec. Feb. 1993); 1 child, Alan. Rsch. fellow, Art Inst. Chgo., Art Student League of N.Y.; BFA, Wayne State U. One-woman shows include Worthington Art Ctr., Ohio, OK Harris/David Klein Gallery, Birmingham, Mich., Sinclair Coll., LRC Gallery, Dayton, Ohio, U. Mich. Hosps., Ann Arbor; group shows include Islip Art Mus., East Islip, N.Y., Columbia (Mo.) Coll., Tubac (Ariz.) Ctr. of the Arts, Ft. Wayne (Ind.) Mus. of Art, C.W. Post Coll., Brookville, N.Y., NAWA, Jacob K. Kavits Ctr., N.Y.C., Schoharie County Coun. of the Arts, Cobbleskill, N.Y., ARC Gallery, Chgo., McPherson (Kans.) Coll., Med. Coll. Ga., Augusta, Heckscher Mus. Art, Huntington, Nassau County Mus. Art, Roslyn, N.Y., Guild Hall, East Hampton, N.Y., Castle Gould, Sands Point, N.Y., Pastel Soc. Am., N.Y.C., Carrier Found., Belle Meade, N.J., Hill Country Arts Found., Ingram, Tex., Cunningham Meml. Art Gallery, Bakersfield, Calif., Henry Hicks Gallery, Bklyn. Hgts., U. N.D., Grand Forks, Nassau C.C., Garden City, N.Y., Trenton (N.J.) State Coll., Wenatchee Valley (W.Va.) Coll., Del Mar Coll., Corpus Christi, Tex., Minot (N.D.) State U., Ctrl. Mo. State U., McNeese State U., Lake Charles, La., Worthington Art Ctr., Ohio, Art Ctr., Mt. Clemens, Mich., Oakland C.C., Mich., Krasl Art Ctr., St. Joseph, Mich., Fontana Concert Soc., Kalamazoo, Mich., Art Ctr. Battle Creek, Mich., Ctrl. Mich. U., Mt. Pleasant, Birmingham (Mich.) Bloomfield Art Assn., Cmty. House, Birmingham, Sch. of Art Inst., Chgo., Cheekwood Mus. Art, Nashville, Grand Rapids (Mich.) Mus. Art, Flint (Mich.) Inst. Arts, Ariana Gallery, Royal Oak, Mich., Judith Paul Gallery, Medford, Oreg., The Art Collector, San Diego, Gwenda Jay Gallery, Chgo., Columbia Greens Coll., Hudson, N.Y., Worthington (Ohio) Art Ctr.; permanent collections include Rabobank, Chgo., Resurrection Hosp., Kanai (Hawaii) Hotel, Jules Joyner Designs, Royal Oak, Mich., The Lumber Store, Chgo., others, also pvt. collections. Recipient Adriana Zahn award Pastel Soc. Am., Heckscher Mus. award, Our Visions: Women in Art award Oakland C.C., 1995. Mem. Nat. Assn. Women Artists (Sara Winston Meml. award 1992), N.Y. Artist Equity Assn., Art Student League N.Y. (Sidney Dickinson Meml. award), Birmingham Bloomfield Art Assn. Office: Gail Eisner Studio 104 W 4th St Ste 303 Royal Oak MI 48067-3808

EISNER, SISTER JANET MARGARET, college president; b. Boston, Oct. 10, 1940; d. Eldon and Ada (Martin) E. AB, Emmanuel Coll., 1963; MA, Boston Coll., 1969; PhD, U. Mich., 1975; LHD (hon.), Northeastern U. Joined Sisters of Notre Dame de Namur, Roman Cath. Ch. Dir. admissions Emmanuel Coll., 1967-71; lectr., teaching asst. U. Mich., Ann Arbor, 1971-73; dir. Emmanuel Coll. and City of Boston Pairings, 1976-78, asst. prof. English, 1976-78, chmn. dept., 1977-78, acting pres., 1978-79, pres., 1979—; mem. Mass. Bd. Regents, chmn. regents planning com., 1980-86; mem. adv. bd. Ctr. for Religious Devel., 1983—; mem. exec. com. Boston Higher Edn. Partnership, 1991—. Trustee Trinity Coll., 1979-85, mem. adv. coun. on enrollment planning, 1981-82; adv. coun. pres. Assn. Governing Bds., 1982-88; mem. commn. on women in higher edn. Am. Coun. on Edn., 1985-87; mem. adv. bd. Synod of Archdiocese of Boston, 1988, Anti-Defamation League Dinner Com., 1988-89; chair four-yr. coll. div. United Way Campaign, 1989; mem. NAICU/NIIC joint task force Minority Participation in Ind. Higher Edn., 1989; mem. govs. award com. Carballo Scholarships, 1989; bd. dirs. Med. Area Svc. Corp., 1989—; trustee Boston Cath. TV Ctr., 1990—. Rackham prize fellow, Ford Found. fellow, 1973-75. Mem. Nat. Assn. Ind. Colls. and Univs. (commn. on policy analysis 1991—), Assn. Ind. Colls. and Univs. in Mass. (chair 1991—), Women's Coll. Coalition (exec. com. 1991—). Office: Emmanuel Coll Office of the President 400 Fenway Boston MA 02115-5725*

EITELGEORGE, JANICE SUSAN WITCHEY, education educator; b. Dallas, Oct. 9, 1944; d. Leslie Eugene and Gerladine Loretta (Swigart) Witchey; m. John F. Eitelgeorge; children: Leslie, Derrick. MusB, Heidelberg Coll., 1966; MA, The Ohio State U., 1986, PhD, 1994. Cert. music educator, reading educator, reading supr., elem. educator. Coord. internships The Ohio State U., Mansfield, 1986-91; reading clinic The Ohio State U., Columbus, Ohio, 1991-92; instr. child lit. and literacy The Ohio State U., Newark, 1992-93; instr. kindergarten methods/reading The Ohio State U., Columbus, 1993-94, coord. early childhood edn., 1993-94; instr. corrective reading Ohio Wesleyan U., Delaware, 1994; asst. prof. Otterbein Coll., Westerville, Ohio, 1994-95, Mt. Vernon (Ohio) Nazarene Coll., 1995—. Pres. Nature Preservation League, Mansfield, 1976-94. Mem. Internat. Reading Assn., Nat. Coun. Tchrs. English. Baptist. Office: Mt Vernon Nazarene Coll 800 Martinsburg Rd Mount Vernon OH 43050

EIZENBERG, JULIE, architect. BArch, U. Melbourne, Australia, 1978; MArch II, UCLA, 1981. Lic. architect, Calif., reg. architect, Australia. Principal, architect Koning Eizenberg Architecture, Santa Monica, Calif., 1981—; instr. various courses UCLA, MIT, Harvard U.; lectr. in field; jury member P/A awards. Exhbns. incl. "House Rules" Wexner Ctr., 1994, "The Architect's Dream: Houses for the Next Millenium" The Contemporary Arts Ctr., 1993, "Angels & Franciscans" Gagosian Gallery, 1992, Santa Monica Mus. Art, 1993, "Broadening the Discourse" Calif. Women in Environmental Design, 1992, "Conceptional Drawings by Architects" Bannatyne Gallery, 1991, Exhbn. Koning Eizenberg Projects Grad. Sch. Architecture & Urban Planning UCLA, 1990; prin. works include Digital Domain Renovation and Screening Room, Santa Monica, Lightstorm Entertainment Office Renovation and Screening Room, Santa Monica, Gilmore Bank Addition and Remodel, L.A., 1548-1550 Studios, Santa Monica, (with RTA) Materials Rsch. Lab. at U. Calif., Santa Barbara, Ken Edwards Ctr. Cmty. Svcs., Santa Monica, Peck Park Cmty. Ctr. Gymnasium, San Pedro, Calif., Sepulveda Recreation Ctr., L.A. (Design award AIA San Fernando Valley 1995, Nat. Concrete and Masonry award 1996, AIA Calif. Coun. Honor award 1996, L.A. Bus. Coun. Beautification award 1996), PS # 1 Elem. Sch., Santa Monica, Farmers Market, L.A. Additions and Master Plan (Westside Urban Forum prize 1991), Stage Deli, L.A., Simone Hotel, L.A. (Nat. Honor award AIA 1994), Boyd Hotel, L.A., Cmty. Corp. Santa Monica Housing Projects, 5th St. Family Housing, Santa Monica, St. John's Hosp. Replacement Housing Program, Santa Monica, Liffman Ho., Santa Monica, (with Glenn Erikson) Electric Artblock, Venice (Beautification award L.A. Bus. Coun. 1993), 6th St. Condominiums, Santa Monica, Hollywood Duplex, Hollywood Hills (Record Houses Archtl. Record 1988), California Ave. Duplex, Santa Monica, Tarzana Ho. (Award of Merit L.A. chpt. AIA 1992, Sunset Western home Awards citation 1993-94), 909 Ho., Santa Monica (Award of Merit L.A. chpt. AIA 1991), 31st St. Ho., Santa Monica (Honor award AIACC 1994, Nat. AIA Honor award 1996), others. Recipient 1st award Progressive Architecture, 1987; named one of Domino's Top 30 Architects, 1989. Mem. L.A. County Mus. Art, Westside Urban Forum, Urban Land Inst., Architects and Designers for Social Responsibility, Mus. Contemporary Art, The Nature Conservancy, Sierra Club. Office: Koning Eizenberg Architecture 1548 18th St Santa Monica CA 90404-3404

EKANGER, LAURIE, state commissioner; b. Salt Lake City, Mar. 4, 1949; d. Bernard and Mary (Dearth) E.; m. William J. Shupe, Nov. 6, 1973; children: Ben, Robert. BA in English, U. Oreg., 1973. Various pos. Mont. State Employment & Tng. Divsn., Helena, 1975-80, dep. adminstr., 1980-82; adminstr. Mont. State Purchasing Divsn., Helena, 1982-85, Mont. State Personnel Divsn., Helena, 1985-93; labor commr. Mont. Dept. Labor & Ind., Helena, 1993—; council chair State Employee Group Benefits Coun., 1985-93; bd. dirs. Pub. Employee Retirement Bd., 1988. Home: 80 Pinecrest Rd Clancy MT 59634-9709 Office: Labor & Industry Dept 1315 E Lockey Helena MT 59624

EKMAN, PATRICIA, lawyer; b. Boston, Jan. 16, 1957; d. Robert and Charlotte (Grass) Schneider; m. Gerhson Ekman, Sept. 25, 1983. AB, Radcliffe Coll., 1978; JD, Stanford U., 1981. Bar: N.Y. 1982. Assoc. Seward & Kissel, N.Y.C., 1981-83, Thacher, Proffitt & Wood, N.Y.C., 1983-86; v.p., counsel, sec. finance Citicorp/Citibank NA, N.Y.C., 1986—. Mem. ABA. Democrat. Jewish. Clubs: Stanford (N.Y.), Stanford (N.J.). Office: Citicorp/Citibank 399 Park Ave New York NY 10022-4614*

EKONG, RUTH J., nursing administrator, author; b. St. Thomas, V.I.; d. Rufus and Ruby (Maduro) Norman; m. Eno A. Ekong. Commr. spl. edn., nurse cons., dir. nurses, nurse gerontology specialist; ethnic food cons.; developer Tantie Ruth Corp. Developer Original African Salad Dressings, Tantie Ruth Foods, Uzimi cooking, Serengeti Sauce and Dressing, (TV show) Tantie Ruth.

EKSTROM, KATINA BARTSOKAS, secondary education educator, artist; b. Springfield, Ill., Nov. 8, 1929; d. Tom A. and Elsie (Heinrich) Bartsokas; m. John Warren Ekstrom (div. Feb. 1978); children: John A., Kenneth M., Richard M., Timothy W., Christopher P. BFA, U. Ill., 1955, MAE, 1975. Tchr. art Urbana (Ill.) Jr. High Sch., 1974-89, Bronx (N.Y.) Sch. Dist., 1990-91, Astoria (N.Y.) Jr. High Sch., 1991—; tchr. adult edn., 1975-80, Urbana Pk. dist., 1977-88; artist Colwell Collection catalog, Champaign, Ill., 1985; juror Chgo. Ann. Met. History Fair, 1985, Cen. Ill. Scholastics High Sch., Springfield, 1988-89, also others; Fulbright cultural exch. tchr., 1986. Exhibited in group show Champaign Arts and Humanities Assn., 1983-84, Cen. Park Ranger 1990, Swoope Gallery, Ind., Lincoln Ctr., N.Y.C., 1994, Abney Gallery, N.Y.C., 1995. Artist Peace Coalition Concerts, Champaign, 1985-86, U. Ill. Sinfonia, Champaign, 1986-88. Recipient Award of Merit 1994 Manhattan Arts Internat. Cover Art Competition, 2d pl. award in painting Ill. 28th Ann. Art Exhbn. Mem. Urbana Educators Assn. (Outstanding Educator award 1986), Ind. Artists Ill., U. Ill. Alumni Assn., Kappa Delta, Phi Delta Kappa. Home: 30 W 96th St # 2D New York NY 10025-6555

EKSTROM, RUTH BURT, psychologist; b. Bennington, Vt., July 2, 1931; d. Ralph Amos and Bertha Paisley (Lambert) Burt; m. Lincoln Ekstrom, Nov. 9, 1957. AB, Brown U., 1953; EdM, Boston U., 1956; EdD, Rutgers U., 1967; LLD (hon.) Brown U., 1988. Pub. sch. tchr., Beverly, Mass., 1953-57; sr. rsch. asst. Ednl. Testing Svc., 1957-64; vis. lectr. Rutgers U., 1958-60; dir. documentation svcs. Ednl. Testing Svc., Princeton, N.J., 1964-68, rsch. scientist, 1968-80, sr. rsch. scientist, 1980-91, prin. rsch. scientist, 1991—, acting dir. edn. policy rsch. divsn., 1992-94. Co-author: Education and American Youth: The Impact of the High School Experience, 1988; co-editor: Kit of Factor-Referenced Cognitive Tests, 1976; editor: Measurement, Technology and Individuality in Education, 1983; mem. editorial bd. Psychology of Women Quar., 1978-86, Jour. Counseling & Devel., 1982-85, Measurement & Evaluation in Counseling & Devel., 1989-91; contbr. articles to profl. jours. Mem. corp. (governing bd.) Brown U., 1972-88, trustee, 1972-77, fellow, 1977-88, sec. corp., 1982-88. Fellow APA, AAAS, Am. Psychol. Soc.; mem. ACA (Rsch. award 1994, Extended Rsch. award 1996), Am. Ednl. Rsch. Assn. (chmn. rsch. on women and edn. 1984-85, publ. com., 1995—), Assn. For Study of Higher Edn. (program com. 1993), Assn. for Assesment in Counseling (chair com. on test use 1991-93, exec. coun. 1992-95), Nat. Coun. Measurement Edn. (mem. joint com. on testing practices 1994—, co-chair 1994—). Home: 78 Westerly Rd Princeton NJ 08540-2621 Office: Ednl Testing Svc Princeton NJ 08541

EKVALL, KARI, technical recruiter; b. Larvik, Norway, May 12, 1958; d. Kjell Kristian and Marit (Johnsen) E. BA in Econs., Copenhagen Bus. Sch., Denmark, 1981, diploma in mktg. statistics, 1984. Cons., programmer Andersen Consulting, Copenhagen, 1981-84, human resources, budgeting, 1984-89; controller Andersen Consulting, Stockholm, 1989; help desk support Andersen Consulting, Sophia Antipolis, France, 1989-91, human resources mgr., 1991-94; tech. recruiter Andersen Worldwide, Chgo., 1994—.

ELAM, ADA MARIA, education educator; b. Saxe, Va.; d. William H. and Mary (Price) E. BA in History, Va. State U., 1962, MS in Guidance and Counseling, 1964; EdD in Counselor Edn., Pa. State U., 1972. Nat. bd. cert. counselor; cert. counselor, Mo. Chair history dept. J.E.J. Moore H.S., Disputanta, Va., 1962-64; dean of students Bowie (Md.) State U., 1964-70, v.p. for student affairs, 1970-77, coord. and prof. counseling programs, 1977—; rschr. and study projects in Egypt, West Africa, India, 1975-93; cons. Nat. Assn. for Equal Opportunity in Higher Edn., Washington, 1980-94. Author: The Status of Blacks in Higher Education, 1988, Factbook on Blacks in Higher Education, 3 vols., 1993. Advanced study grantee Ford Found., Pa. State U., 1969-71; fellow program in acad. adminstr. Am. Coun. on Edn., George Washington U., 1972-73. Mem. Bowie/Crofton Bus. and Profl., Inc. Baptist. Office: Bowie State Univ Bowie MD 20715

ELBERRY, ZAINAB ABDELHALIEM, insurance company executive; b. Alexandria, Egypt, Sept. 30, 1948; came to U.S., 1973; d. Abelhaliem Elberry and Nazieha Ahmed (Ezzat) E.; m. Mohammed Nour Naciri, Aug. 7, 1975; 1 child, Nadeam El Shami. BA, Ain Shams U., Cairo, 1971; MA, Am. U., Cairo, 1975. Cataloger Vanderbilt Joint U. Librs., Nashville, 1976-77; sales rep. Equitable Life Assurance Soc., 1977-80; with Met. Life Ins., Nashville, 1980—, account rep., 1981—, mgr., 1984; mem. adv. bd. Parkview Surgery Ctr., 1983-84. Chmn. com., bd. dirs. Nashville Internat. Cultural Heritage, 1983—, also bd. dirs.; chmn. Internat. Women Nashville Fair, 1977-78; bd. dirs. YWCA, Coun. for Nat. Interest; fundraiser Peace Links, 1989, YMCA Internat. House, 1987-89, Nashville Animal Shelter, 1979, Nashville League Hearing Impaired, 1976-81; mem. adv. bd. Nashville celebration Internat. Yr. of Disabled Persons; pres. Internat. Women Nashville. Recipient Spl. Contbn. award U.S. Coun. Internat. Disabled Persons, 1981. Mem. Nat. Assn. Life Underwriters, Nat. Assn. Profl. Saleswomen (Recognition award 1986), Gen. Agy. Mgrs. Assn., UN Assn. (bd. dirs. Nashville chpt.), Altrusa Club. Islam. Home: 5600 Kendall Dr # B Nashville TN 37209-4548

ELBING, CAROL JEPPSON, business educator, administrator; b. West Ellis, Wis., Mar. 15, 1930; d. Ralph and Claire (Fredell) Jeppson.; m. Alvar O. Elbing, Aug. 3, 1950; children: Kristofer Erik, John Rolf. BA, U. Minn., 1951; MA, Calif. State U.-Sacramento, 1958; PhD, U. Wash., 1970. Instr. communication Am. River Coll., Sacramento, 1958-59, U. Wash., Seattle, 1959-62; lectr. Dartmouth Coll., Hanover, N.Y., 1962-66; rsch. fellow, cons. IMEDE, Lausanne, Switzerland, 1970-77; co-dir. Exec. and Environ. Ctr., Lausanne, Switzerland, 1977—; assoc. prof. Sch. Bus. and Accountancy, Wake Forest U., Winston-Salem, N.C., 1982-85. Author: (with Alvar Elbing) The Value Issue of Business, 1967, Do Agressive Managers Really Get High Performance?, 1991, Militant Managers, 1994. Mem. Phi Beta Kappa. Home and Office: Chalet Orphée, Domaine de la Residence, 1884 Villars sur Ollon Switzerland also: 4291 Boca Pointe Dr Sarasota FL 34238

ELDEFRAWI, AMIRA T., medical educator; b. Giza, Cairo, Egypt, Feb. 10, 1937; came to U.S., 1968; d. Hussein Khairy and Fadila Ibrahim (Aref) Toppozada; children: Mosen M., Mona D. Hoff, Mohab M. BS, U. Alexandria, Egypt, 1957; PhD, U. Calif., Berkeley, 1960. Asst. prof. U. Alexandria, 1960-68; rsch. assoc. prof. Cornell U., Ithaca, N.Y., 1968-76; from rsch. assoc. prof. to rsch. prof. U. Md., Balt., 1976-88, prof., 1988—; cons. U.S. State Dept., Washington, 1982-83, Nat. Inst. Environ. Health Sci. Rev. Com., Research Triangle Park, N.C., 1987-91; scholar-in-residence Queen's U. Sch. Medicine, Kingston, Ont., Can., 1985. Author: Resistance of Insects to Insecticides, 1966; editor: Myasthenia Gravis, 1983; assoc. editor Membr. Biochemistry, 1987-93; mem. editl. bd. Pestic. Biochem. Physiol. Jour. Tox. Environ. Health, 1987—, Environ. Rsch., 1995—; assoc. editor Membrane Biochemistry, 1987-93; mem. editorial bd. Pesticide Biochem. Physiology, 1987—, Jour. Toxicology and Environ. Health, 1987—, Environ. Rsch., 1995; publ. scientific papers in field. Grantee NIH, 1975—, NATO, 1986-89, U.S. Army, 1995—. Mem. Soc. of Toxicology (pres. neurotoxicology splty. sect. 1996—). Office: U Md Sch Medicine 655 W Baltimore St Baltimore MD 21201-1509

ELDENBURG, MARY JO CORLISS, mathematics educator; b. Tacoma, Wash., Mar. 5, 1942; d. John Ronald and Mary Margaret (Slater) Corliss; m. Paul Garth Eldenburg, Aug. 31, 1963; 1 child, Anthony Corliss. BA with honors, Wash. State U., 1964; MS, SUNY, Buffalo, 1971. Cert. secondary math. tchr. Tchr. math. Colton (Wash.) High Sch., 1964-65, Bellevue (Wash.) Jr. High Sch., 1965-68, Issaquah (Wash.) Jr. High Sch., 1968-75, Issaquah High Sch., 1975-77; tchr. math., dept. chair Liberty High Sch., Issaquah, 1977-93; tchr. math., dept. co-chair Holy Names Acad., Seattle, 1993—. Co-editor books: Cartesian Cartoons, 1980, Cartesian Cartoons, Holiday, 1990, Lil Gridders, 1977. Treas. Sch. Bd., Kirkland, Wash., 1987-90; pres. Bridle Trails/South Rose Hill Neighborhood Assn., Kirkland, 1987-93; precinct committee woman Issaquah Precinct, 1980-84. Mem. Issaquah Edn. Assn. (sec., negotiator 1969-75, 74-86), Wash. Edn. Assn. (dir. 1970-74), Math. Assn. Am., Oreg. State Coun. Tchrs. Math., Wash. State Coun. Tchrs. Math., Nat. Coun. Tchrs. Math., Phi Kappa Phi. Democrat. Roman Catholic. Office: Holy Names Acad 728 21st Ave E Seattle WA 98112-4022

ELDER, AMY HOPE, psychotherapist; b. Ann Arbor, Mich., June 16, 1970; d. Robert Gordon and Martha Key (Rock) Ause; m. Bobby Van Elder, Dec. 3, 1994. Student, Regensburg (Germany) U., 1990-91; BA in Psychology, Vanderbilt U., 1992; MA in Counseling, Denver Sem., 1995. Therapist InCare Inc., Knoxville, Tenn., 1996, Genesis Treatment Ctr., Kansas City, Mo., 1996—. Big sister Doulos Ministries/Shelterwood, Branson, Mo., 1992-93. Mem. Am. Counseling Assn., Am. Assn. Christian Counselors, Chi Omega, Psi Chi. Home: 6344 Hallet St Shawnee KS 66216 Office: Genesis Treatment Ctr 9237 Ward Pkwy Ste 305 Kansas City MO 64114-3365

ELDER, JENNIFER HOWARD, accounting educator; b. Morristown, N.J., Jan. 14, 1960; d. Brian Turner and Eunice Alexandra (Roy) Howard; m. Samuel Fletcher Elder III, Oct. 1, 1995. BA, U. Mass., 1981; A of Bus. Sci., McIntosh Coll., 1985; postgrad., Antioch New Eng., Keene, N.H., 1995. CPA, N.H., CMA, CIA. Mgr. James Baker & Co., North Andover, Mass., 1989, Stafford & Assoc., Portland, Maine, 1989; asst. prof. McIntosh Coll., Dover, N.H., 1989-90, dept. chair, acctg., 1990-92, dir. spl. acctg. programs, 1992—; pvt. practice, acct., cons. Portsmouth, N.H., 1990—. Author: (text) CPA Review Program, 1993. Recipient Outstanding Educator award N.H. Soc. of CPA's, Manchester, 1993. Mem. AICPA, Inst. Mgmt. Accts., Inst. Internal Auditors, Fibromyalgia Network. Office: McIntosh Coll 23 Cataract Ave Dover NH 03820

ELDERKIN, HELAINE GRACE, lawyer; b. New Rochelle, N.Y., Sept. 18, 1954; d. EllsworthJay and Madelyn A. (Roberts) E.; m. Stefan Shrier, Feb. 23, 1985. BA, Fla. Atlantic U., 1975; JD, George Mason U., 1985. Bar: Va. 1985, U.S. Ct. Appeals (4th cir.) 1985, U.S. Ct. Fed. Claims 1994. Aide Carter/Mondale Presdl. Campaign Com., Atlanta, 1976, Presdl. Transition Staff, Washington, 1976-77; spl. asst. Agy. Internat. Devel. U.S. Dept. State, Washington, 1977; spl. asst. U.S. Dept. Def., Washington, 1977-79; mem. tech. staff System Planning Corp., Arlington, Va., 1980-83; dir. corp. rsch. Analytics, Inc., McLean, Va., 1983-85; v.p., gen. counsel Analytics, Inc., Fairfax, Va., 1985-91; of counsel Feith and Zell, P.C., Washington, 1986-91; sr. counsel Computer Scis. Corp., 1991—; bd. dirs. Mil. Ops. Rsch. Soc., Alexandria (elected fellow 1990), Army Sci. Bd. Democrat. Home: 624A S Pitt St Alexandria VA 22314-4138 Office: Computer Scis Corp 3170 Fairview Park Dr Falls Church VA 22042-4528

ELDREDGE, LINDA GAILE, psychologist; b. Lubbock, Tex., Apr. 3, 1959; d. Jerry Greever and Madge (Harshbarger) Eldredge. BS, Howard Payne U., 1980; MA, Tex. Woman's U., 1981; EdD, Baylor U., 1989. Lic. psychologist, chem. dependency counselor, Tex.; cert. tchr. hearing impaired, sch. counselor, spl. edn. counselor, Tex.; lic. marriage and family therapist; cert. verbal self def. trainer; cert. eye movement desensitization and reprocessing. Tchr. hearing impaired Waco (Tex.) Ind. Sch. Dist., 1982-85, spl. edn. sch. counselor, cons. hearing impaired, 1986-87; doctoral teaching fellow Baylor U., Waco, 1985-87; dir. regional alcohol and drug abuse svcs. Heart of Tex. Coun. Govts., Waco, 1987; psychotherapist Houston, Tex., 1989-91; psychologist Houston, 1991-93; pvt. practice psychology Austin, 1993—; psychologist Tex. Sch. for the Deaf, Austin, 1993-95. Mem. APA, Nat. Assn. Alcoholism and Drug Abuse Counselors, Am. Deafness and Rehab. Assn., Am. Assn. of the Deaf-Blind, Gentle Art of Verbal Self-Defense Trainers Network, Tex. Assn. Alcoholism and Drug Abuse Counselors (sec.-treas. Waco chpt. 1988-89). Office: 5806 Mesa Ste 220 Austin TX 78731-3742

ELEAZAR, PAULA Y., health/medical products executive. Sr. v.p., chief info. officer Ornda Healthcorp, Nashville. Office: Ornda Healthcorp 3401 West End Ave Ste 700 Nashville TN 37203*

ELFAYER, GERALDINE JANICE, nursing administrator; b. Chgo., June 20, 1956; d. Edward and Lorraine (Berczynski) E.; children: Roger K. Lonak Jr., Danielle C. Lonak. AAS, Morton Coll., 1984; BS, Elmhurst Coll., 1993. Cert. alcohol drug counselor, Ill. Nurse, counselor Loretto Hosp., Chgo., 1984-86, Northwestern Meml. Hosp., Chgo., 1986-88; clin. nurse mgr. Riveredge Hosp., Forest Park, Ill., 1988-95, clin. nurse supr., 1995—; case mgmt. coord. MacNeal Hosp., Berwyn, Ill., 1995—. Mem. West Suburban Juvenile Assn., Berwyn, 1991, 92. Mem. Delta Mu Delta. Roman Catholic. Office: MacNeal Hospital 3249 S Oak Park Berwyn IL 60402

EL-FAYOUMY, JOANNE PATRICIA QUINN, writer, poet; b. L.I., N.Y., Oct. 7, 1930; d. Thomas Joseph and Helen Veronica (Foster) Quinn; m. Saad G.A. El-Fayoumy, Sept. 8, 1963 (dec. 1989). BA, Barnard Coll., 1952; MA, Columbia U., 1964. Copy trainee, sec. J. Walter Thompson & Co., N.Y.C., 1952-55; sec. BBDO, N.Y.C., 1956-57; pub. relations asst., writer Helena Rubenstein Inc., N.Y.C., 1957-59; asst., writer Bob Taplinger Assocs., N.Y.C., 1959-60; adminstrv. asst. Protestant Coun. of City of N.Y., 1964-67; instr. Norfolk (Va.) State U., 1967-74, asst. prof., 1974-88, ret., 1988; rsch. guest lectr. U. Jordan, Amman, 1986-87; numerous poetry readings. Author of poetry in various anthologies; editor: New Accounting Systems, 1984, New Budgeting Systems, 1984, (with Saad El-Fayoumy for Agrl. Bank of Sudan/World Bank) Agricultural and Commercial Banking, 1984. Founding mem. Coptic Orthodox Ch. N. Am., 1964; sec. Am. Arab Anti-Discrimination Commn., Hampton Roads, Va., 1990. Recipient award Tidewater Writers Conf., 1st prize Poetry Soc. Va., 1994; honoree Irene Leach Meml. Contest. Mem. AAUW (leader 1967-70), Arab Am. Assn. Va. (founding mem. 1973-80), World Affairs Coun. (dir. 1970-72), Poetry Soc. Va. (first prize 1993), Acad. Am. Poets, Nat. Mus. Women. Republican. Coptic Orthodox. Home: Apt 113A 700 Oriole Dr Virginia Beach VA 23451-4960 also: 170 Wianno Circle Osterville MA 02655 also: 8 Kasr El Nil St # 31, Cairo Egypt

ELGAVISH, ADA, molecular, cellular biologist; b. Cluj, Romania, Jan. 23, 1946; came to U.S. 1979; d. David and Malca (Neuman) Simchas; m. Gabriel A. Elgavish, Dec. 28, 1968; children: Rotem, Eynav. BSc, Tel-Aviv U., 1969, MSc, 1972; PhD, Weizmann Inst. Sci., Rehovot, Israel, 1978. Postdoctoral vis. fellow NIH, Balt., 1979-81; instr. U. Ala. Sch. Medicine, Birmingham, 1981-82, rsch. assoc., 1982-84, rsch. asst. prof., 1984-89, asst.

prof. comparative medicine, 1989-92, assoc. prof., 1992—; assoc. scientist Cystic Fibrosis Ctr., Birmingham, 1984-90; scientist Cell Adhesion and Matrix Rsch. Ctr., Birmingham, 1995—. Grantee Cystic Fibrosis Found., 1986-90, Am. Lung Assn., 1987-92, NIH, 1989—. Mem. AAAS, Am. Physiol. Soc., Am. Urol. Assn., Am. Urol. Assn., N.Y. Acad. Sci., Ala. Acad. Sci., Soc. for Basic Urol. Rsch., Am. Thoracic Soc., Sigma Xi. Home: 1737 Valpar Dr Birmingham AL 35226-2343 Office: U Ala Sch Medicine Dept Comparative Medicine Birmingham AL 35294

ELGIN, KATHLEEN, artist, painter, illustrator, writer; b. Trenton, N.J., Jan. 13, 1923; d. Charles Porter and Mary (Poore) E. Student, Dayton Art Inst., 1943. Illustrated 50 children's books; writer, illustrator of 20 children's books, 1950-70; one man shows in N.Y., 1976, Key West, 1985-93. Home: 1607 Johnson Key West FL 33040

ELIAS, ROSALIND, mezzo-soprano; b. Lowell, Mass., Mar. 13, 1931; d. Salem and Shelahuy Rose (Namy) E.; m. Zuhayr Moghrabi. Student, New Eng. Conservatory Music, Accademia di Santa Cecilia, Rome; studies with, Daniel Ferro, N.Y.C. Singer New Eng. Opera, 1948-52, Met. Opera, 1954—; artistic dir. Am. Lyric Theatre. Debut with Boris Goldowsky, Boston, 1948; appeared in numerous roles including Cherubino, Dorabella, Rosina, Hansel, Cenerentola, Carmen, Amneris and Azucena (Verdi), Charlotte and Giulietta (Massenet), Herodias, 1987; originated role of Erika in Vanessa (Samuel Barber) and Cleopatra in Antony and Cleopatra (Barber); also appeared with Scottish Opera, Vienna Staatsoper, Glynbourne Festival, many others; prodr. Carmen, Cin., 1988, Il Barbiere di Siviglia, Opera Pacific, Costa Mesa, Calif., 1989; recs. for RCA and Columbia records include La Gioconda, La Forza del Destno, Il Trovatore, Falstaff, Madama Butterfly, Rigoletto, Der fliegende Holländer. Mem. Sigma Alpha Iota. Office: care Robert Lombardo Associates One Harkness Plaza 61 W 62nd St/Ste 6F New York NY 10023*

ELIAS, SHEILA, artist; b. Chgo., June 30. MA, Calif. State U., Northridge, 1975; BFA, Columbus Coll. Art & Design, 1973; student, Art Inst. of Chgo., 1963-73. One-person shows include Alex Rosenberg, N.Y.C., 1987, U. N.C., Chapel Hill, 1987, Paula Allan Gallery, N.Y.C., 1987-89, Ratner Gallery, Chgo., 1990, Barnard Biderman & Worth Gallery, N.Y., 1996, Metro Dade Cultural Resource Ctr., Miami, Fla., 1994, others; group exhbns. include Louvre, Paris, 1987, Valerie Miller Fine Arts, Palm Springs, Calif., 1988, Otis Parsons Sch. of Design, L.A., 1988, Anne Jaffe Gallery, Bay Harbor, 1988-89, Ft. Lauderdale Mus., 1991, New Eng. Mus. of Contemporary Art, 1993; pub. collections include Bklyn. Mus. Art, Chase Manhattan Bank, N.Y.C., First L.A. Bank, Exec. Life Ins., L.A., Security Pacific Bank, L.A., Paramount Pictures, L.A., Laguna Beach Mus. Art, Kinsan Contemporary Mus., Korea, Capital Bank, L.A., Miami. Mailing Address: 9999 Collins Ave PH 1D Miami FL 33154

ELIASOPH, JOAN, radiologist, educator; b. N.Y.C.; d. Samuel and Martha (Coe) Freeman. AB, Hunter Coll., 1946; MD, NYU, 1949. Diplomate Am. Bd. Radiology. Intern Mt. Sinai Hosp., N.Y.C., 1949-50, resident in radiology, 1951-53, radiology Columbia U., N.Y.C., 1953-55; instr. Columbia U., N.Y.C., 1953-55; asst. attending radiologist Mt. Sinai Hosp., N.Y.C., 1955-70, attending radiologist, 1982-85, 90; clin. asst. prof. Mt. Sinai Med. Sch., N.Y.C., 1970-77; assoc. prof. radiology U. So. Calif., L.A., 1977-82, Columbia U., N.Y.C., 1982-85; assoc. prof. Mt. Sinai Med. Sch., N.Y.C., 1985-90, Dartmouth Med. Sch., Hanover, N.H., 1990-92; attending radiologist Dartmouth-Hitchcock Med. Ctr., 1990-92; attending radiologist gastrointestinal and critical care imaging Kingsbridge VA Med. Ctr., 1992—; cons. Silver Hill Found., Conn., 1965-77, Stamford Hosp., Conn., 1970-77. Contbr. articles to profl. jours. Mem. Friends of Ballona Wetlands, Los Angeles, 1977-82. Heineman Pathology fellow Mt. Sinai Hosp., 1950-51, Radiology fellow, 1955-56. Fellow Am. Coll. Radiology, Am. Coll. Gastroent.; mem. Am. Roentgen Ray Soc., Am. Gastroent. Soc., Radiol. Soc. N.Am., Soc. Gastrointestinal Radiologists, N.Y. Roentgen Soc., Assn. Univ. Radiologists, Am. Ukiyo-E Soc. Avocations: environment, birding, Japanese prints. Office: Kingsbridge Vets Adminstrv Med Ctr Dept Radiology 130 W Kingsbridge Rd Bronx NY 10468

ELION, GERTRUDE BELLE, research scientist, pharmacology educator; b. N.Y.C., Jan. 23, 1918; d. Robert and Bertha (Cohen) E. AB, Hunter Coll., 1937; MS, NYU, 1941; DSc (hon.), Hunter Coll., 1989, NYU, 1989; DMS (hon.), Brown U., 1969; DSc (hon.), U. Mich., 1983, N.C. State U., 1989, Ohio State U., 1989, Poly. U., 1989, U. N.C., Chapel Hill, 1990, Russell Sage Coll., 1990, Duke U., 1991, MacMaster U., 1992, SUNY, Stony Brook, 1992, George Washington U., 1969, Columbia U., 1992, Washington Coll., 1993, U. South Fla., 1993, U. Wis., 1993, East Carolina U., 1993, Wake Forest U., 1994, Utah State U., 1994; MD (hon.), U. Chieti, Italy, 1995; DHL (hon.), Rochester Inst. Tech., 1996; DSc (hon.), Phila. Coll. Pharmacy, 1996, Albany Coll. Pharmacy, 1996, Rensselaer Polytech. Inst., 1996. Lab. asst. biochemistry N.Y. Hosp. Sch. Nursing, 1937; rsch. asst. in organic chemistry Denver Chem. Mfg. Co., N.Y.C., 1938-39; tchr. chemistry and physics N.Y.C. secondary schs., 1940-42; food analyst Quaker Maid Co., Bklyn., 1942-43; rsch. asst. in organic synthesis Johnson & Johnson, New Brunswick, N.J., 1943-44; biochemist Wellcome Rsch. Labs., Tuckahoe, N.Y., 1944-50; sr. rsch. chemist Wellcome Rsch. Labs., 1950-55, asst. to assoc. rsch. dir., 1955-62, asst. to the rsch. dir., 1963-66, head exptl. therapy, 1966-83, sci. emeritus, 1983—; adj. prof. pharmacology and exptl. medicine Duke U., 1970, rsch. prof. pharmacology, 1983—; adj. prof. pharmacology U. N.C., Chapel Hill, 1973; chmn. Gordon Conf. on Coenzymes and Metabolic Pathways, 1966; mem. bd. sci. counselors Nat. Cancer Inst., 1980-84; mem. coun. Am. Cancer Soc., 1983-86; mem. Nat. Cancer Adv. Bd., 1984-91. Contbr. articles to profl. jours.; patentee in field. Recipient Garvan medal, 1968, Pres.'s medal Hunter Coll., 1970, Medal of Honor Am. Cancer Soc., 1990, Disting. Chemist award N.C. Inst. Chemists, 1981, Judd award Meml. Sloan-Kettering Cancer Ctr., 1983, Bertner award M.D. Anderson Hosp., 1989, Third Century award Fedn. for Creative Am., 1990, Discoverers award Pharm. Mfg. Assn., 1990, City of Medicine award Durham, N.C., 1990; co-recipient Nobel prize in medicine, 1988, Nat. Medal of Sci. NSF, 1991; inductee Hunter Coll. Hall of Fame, 1973, Nat. Inventors Hall of Fame, 1991, Nat. Women's Hall of Fame, 1991, Engring. and Sci. Hall of Fame, 1992; named Dame, Order of St. John of Jerusalem Ecumenical Found. (Knights of Malta) 1992. Fellow N.Y. Acad. Scis.; mem. AAAS, NAS (coun. 1994-97), Royal Soc. (fgn. mem.), Am. Chem. Soc., Am. Acad. Arts and Scis., Inst. of Medicine, Chem. Soc. London, Am. Soc. Biol. Chemists, Am. Assn. Cancer Rsch. (bd. dirs. 1981, 83, pres. 1983-84, Cain award 1984), Am. Soc. Hematology, Transplantation Soc., Am. Soc. Pharmacology and Exptl. Therapeutics. Home: 1 Banbury Ln Chapel Hill NC 27514-2504 Office: Glaxo Wellcome Inc 5 Moore Dr Research Triangle Park NC 27709

ELIOT, LUCY, artist; b. N.Y.C., May 8, 1913; d. Ellsworth and Lucy Carter (Byrd) E. B.A., Vassar Coll., 1935; postgrad., Art Students League, 1935-40. tchr. painting and drawing Red Cross Bronx Vets. Hosp., N.Y.C., 1950, 51. Exhibited one-woman shows, Rochester Meml. Art Gallery, 1946, Cazenovia Coll., 1942, 47, 62, Syracuse Mus. Fine Arts, 1947, Wells Coll., 1953, Ft. Schuyler Club, Utica, N.Y., 1971, Nat. Shows, Pa. Acad. Fine Arts, Phila., 1946, 48, 49, 50, 52, 54, Corcoran Biennial, Washington, 1947, 51, Va. Biennial, Richmond, 1948, NAD, N.Y.C., 1971, 78, 90, Butler Inst. Am. Art, 1965, 67, 69, 70, 72, 74, 81, Cooperstown Art Assn. ann. exhbn., 1978, 80, 90; represented in permanent collections: Rochester Meml. Art Gallery, Munson-Williams-Proctor Inst., also pvt. collections. Bd. dirs. Artists Tech. Research Inst., 1975-79. Recipient First prize Rochester Meml. Art Gallery, 1946, Purchase prize Munson-Williams-Proctor Inst., 1949, Painting of Industry award Silvermine Guild, 1957, 1st prize in oils Cooperstown Art Assn., 1978. Mem. Nat. Assn. Women Artists (Moore-Greenblatt Meml. award 1993), N.Y. Soc. Women Artists, N.Y. Artists Equity, Audubon Artists (bd. dirs. oil 1983-85, chmn. award 1986-88, Elaine and James Hewitt award 1991, Michael M. Engel Meml. award 1994, Robert Philipp Meml. award 1995), Am. Soc. Contemporary Artists, Pen and Brush Club N.Y.C. (Liquitex Art award spring oil exhbn. 1989, 90, Cecilia Cardman Meml. award 1991, Grumbacher Art award Pen and Brush 1993), Cazenovia Club, Cosmopolitan Club. Episcopalian. Home: 131 E 66th St Apt 11G New York NY 10021-6129 also: 70 Sullivan St Cazenovia NY 13035

ELKIN, LOIS SHANMAN, business systems company executive; b. Cin., Oct. 31, 1937; d. Jerome David and Mildred Louise (Bloch) Shanman; m. Alan I. Elkin, May 6, 1962; children: Karen A., Jeffrey R. BA in Math., Goucher Coll., 1959. Sys. engr. ea. region IBM, Balt. and Columbia, S.C., 1959-61, mgr. Computer Test Ctr. ea. region, 1961-64; exec. v.p. Advance Bus. Sys., Balt., 1964—, A&L Real Estate, Balt., 1970—; pres. Our World Gallery, Inc., Balt., 1995—; part owner, bd. dirs. ATMS, Balt., 1994—; mentor for math. and bus. Goucher Coll., Balt., 1982-86; guest lectr. MBA program Loyola Coll. Md., Balt., 1993-94; mem. steering com. Loyola Ctr. for Closely Held Cos., Balt., 1993—; bd. dirs. Hunt Valley Bus. Forum, Balt., 1993—. Vol. House of Ruth, Balt., 1990—, Image Recovery Ctr., Union Meml. Hosp., Balt., 1995—; exec. bd. dirs. Pride of Balt. II, 1994—. Mem. Nat. Assn. Women Bus. Owners (Woman of Yr. award Balt. chpt. 1985). Office: Advance Bus Sys 10755 York Rd Cockeysville MD 21030

ELKIND, CHARLOTTE WOODS, university dean; b. Evanston, Ill., May 6, 1926; d. John Hall and Rose Erskine (Heilman) Woods; m. Morton Digby Elkind, June 10, 1951; children: Elisabeth, Samuel, Margaret. BA, U. Rochester, 1947; MA, Columbia U., 1951; cert. in archival mgmt., NYU, 1991. Head publicity divsn. Inst. Internat. Edn., N.Y.C., 1952-56; tchr. Packer Collegiate Inst., Bklyn., 1968-76, Fieldston Sch., Riverdale, N.Y., 1976; asst. to grad. dean L.I. U., Bklyn., 1977-85, assoc. grad. dean arts and scis., 1985—. Trustee, recreation dir. Inc. Village of Saltaire, N.Y., 1977-81; br. chmn. LWV, N.Y.C., 1965-67, N.Y.C. bd. dirs., city coun., 1965-68. Mem. Archival Roundtable of Met. N.Y., Phi Beta Kappa. Democrat. Office: LI U 1 University Plz New York NY 11201

ELKINS, CAROLYN JOANNE, English language educator; b. Toledo, June 27, 1950; d. Robert Mathew and Phyllis (Jordan) E.; m. William Christopher Spencer, May 19, 1990; 1 child, Farzad Ali Sadjadi. BA, Wells Coll., 1973; MA, U. Tenn., 1981. Tchr. ESL Peace Corps, Cuiaba, Mato Grosso, Brazil, 1976-77; asst. prof. English Delta State U., Cleveland, Miss., 1989—. Author: (poetry) Psychopoetica, 1994, New Delta Review, 1995, Asheville Poetry Review, 1995, Tar River Poetry, 1996; editor Ruby Shoes Press, Cleveland, 1993—, Tapestry lit. jour., Cleveland, 1996. Poetry contest judge Girl Scouts U.S., Cleveland, 1995. Mem. Am. Acad. Poets, Assoc. Writing Programs, Miss. Poetry Soc., Miss. Philol. Assn., South Atlantic Modern Lang. Assn., N.C. Writers Network. Office: Delta State U Divsn Lang & Lit Cleveland MS 37833

ELKINS, TONI MARCUS, artist, art association administrator; b. Tifton, Ga., Feb. 22, 1946; m. Samuel M. Elkins, 1968; children: Stephanie Elkins Sims, Eric Marcus. Student, Boston U., 1965; ABJ, U. Ga., 1968; postgrad., Columbia (S.C.) Coll., Athens, 1980-82; postgrad. photography/silk screening, Columbia (S.C.) Coll. Owner, designer Designs by Elkins, Columbia, 1986—; water color artist, 1983—; supt. fine art S.C. State Fair Art Exhbn., 1987-96. Works include watercolors All American Things, And the Good Ones Look Alike, And the Good Ones with Lace. Auction chair The Elegant Egg McKissick Mus., Columbia, 1994; bd. dir. Trustus Theatre, 1994—. Recipient Best of Show award 18th Internat. Dogwood Festival, 1991, So. Water Color Assn. Pres.'s award, 1992, Purchase award Anderson County Arts Coun. 17th Ann. Exhibit, 1992, Meyer Hardware award Rocky Mountain National, 1992, Howard B. Smith award S.C. Watercolor Ann., 1992. Mem. Nat. Watercolor Soc., Watercolor U.S.A., S.C. Watercolor Soc., Nat. Watercolor Okla., Penn. Watercolor Soc., Ga. Watercolor Soc., Rocky Mountain Nat. Watercolor Soc., Cultural Coun. of Richland & Lexington Counties (exec. bd. sec. 1990-93), Southeastern Art and Craft Expn. (adv. bd. 1993-94). Home and Studio: 1511 Adger Rd Columbia SC 29205-1407

ELLEMAN, BARBARA, editor; b. Coloma, Wis., Oct. 20, 1934; d. Donald and Evelyn (Kissinger) Koplein; m. Don W. Elleman, Nov. 14, 1970. BS in Edn., Wis. State U., 1956; MA in Librarianship, U. Denver, 1964. Sch. libr. media specialist Port Washington (Wis.) High Sch., 1956-59, Homestead High Sch., Thiensville-Mequon, Wis., 1959-64; children's libr. Denver Pub. Libr., 1964-65; sch. libr. media specialist Cherry Creek Schs., Denver, 1965-70, Henry Clay Sch., Whitefish Bay, Wis., 1971-75; children's reviewer ALA, Chgo., 1975-82, children's editor, 1982-90, editor Book Links, 1990-96; vis. lectr. U. Wis., 1974-75, 81-82, U. Ill., Circle Campus, 1983-85; Disting. scholar children's lit., Marquette U., 1996—; cons. H.W. Wilson Co., 1969-75; mem. Libr. Congress Adv. Com. on selection for children's books for blind and physically handicapped, 1980-88, Caldecott Calendar Com., 1986; judge The Am. Book Awards, 1982, Golden Kite, 1987, Boston Globe/Horn Book, 1990; mem. faculty Highlights for Children Writers Conf., 1985-90; mem. orgn. com. MidWest Conf. Soc. Children's Books Writers, 1974-76; chair Hans Christian Andersen Com., 1987-88; advisor Reading Rainbow, 1986—, Ind. R.E.A.P. project, 1987-93; jury mem. VI Catalonia Premi Children's Book Exhbn., Barcelona, Spain, 1994; adv. bd. Parent's Choice, Cobblestone Publ., Georgia Pub. TV's 2000, The New Advocate mag.; speaker in field. Author: Reading in a Media Age, 1975, 20th Century Children's Writers, 1979, rev. edit., 1984, What Else Can You Do With A Library Degree?, 1980, Popular Reading for Children, 1981, Popular Reading II, 1986, Children's Books of International Interest, 1984; contbr. articles to profl. jours. Publicity chair Internat. Bd. Books for Young People Congress, Williamsburg, Va., 1990. Recipient Jeremiah Ludington award Ednl. Paperback Assn., 1996. Mem. ALA, Soc. Children's Book Writers (mem. orgn. com. MidWest Conf. 1974-76), Internat. Bd. Books for Young People (U.S. assoc. editor Bookbird 1978-86, chair nominating com., 1985, bd. dirs. 1990-92), Children's Reading Round Table Chgo. (award 1987), Nat. Coun. Tchrs. English (bd. dirs. children's lit. assembly 1986-88, mem. editl. adv. bd. CLA bull. 1989-91, mem. using nonfiction in classroom com. 1990-96), AAUW. Office: ALA 1884 Somerset Ln Northbrook IL 60062

ELLENBECKER, CATHERINE RIEDL, secondary art educator; b. Milw., July 16, 1950; d. Charles A. and Mary Wendt Riedl; m. Thomas L. Ellenbecker, Aug. 22, 1970; children: Mary Elizabeth, Thomas Jr., Timothy, Margaret, Kathleen, Colleen. BA in Art Edn. cum laude, Mt. Mary Coll., Milw., 1973; MS in Art Edn., U. Wis., Milw., 1982. Cert. tchr. grades K-12, Wis. Art specialist Mother of Good Counsel Sch., Milw., 1974-80; substitute tchr. Sch. Dist. Ripon and Green Lakes, Wis., 1982-84; art specialist grades 7-12 Sch. Dist. Montello, Wis., 1984—. Works appeared in group exhibits Kohler (Wis.) Art Ctr., 1986, 94, Wis. Edn. Assn. Showcase, Madison, 1989. Recipient tchr.'s citation Milw. Jour. Sentinel Student Calendar Art, 1991, 95, honors citation Nat. Scholastic Art Program, 1987, 89, 93, 94, 95. Mem. Nat. Art Edn. Assn., Wis. Art Edn. Assn., Wis. Edn. Assn., Wis. Designer Crafts Coun., Kappa Gamma Pi. Office: Sch Dist Montello 222 Forest Ln Montello WI 53949-9390

ELLENBERGER, DIANE MARIE, nurse, consultant; b. St. Louis, Oct. 5, 1946; d. Charles Ernst and Celeste Loraine (Neudecker) E.; RN, Barnes Hosp., St. Louis, 1970; BSN, St. Louis U., 1976; MSN, U. Colo., 1977. Staff nurse hosps., clin. nurse, St. Louis, 1973-76; nurse clinician, Sedalia, Mo., 1977-78; nurse clinician, educator Bothwell Hosp., Sedalia, 1977-78; clin. nurse specialist, coord. perinatal outreach edn. Cardinal Glennon Meml. Hosp. Children, St. Louis, 1978-80; instr. McKendree Coll., Lebanon, Ill., 1980; asst. prof. Maryville Coll., St. Louis, 1982-85; nurse cons. Carr, Korein, Tillery, Kunin, Montroy, & Glass, Attys. at Law, 1986—; owner, operator Diane Designs Needlepoint, St. Louis, 1981—. Served with Nurse Corps, USAF, 1970-72. Mem. Am. Nurses Assn., Nat. Perinatal Assn., Assn. Women's Health, Obstetric and Neonatal Nurses, Mo. Nurses Assn. (3d dist. sec. 1991-93, 1st v.p. 1993, pres. 1993-96, bd. dirs. 1995—, ANA del. 1996—), Mo. Perinatal Assn. (v.p. 1980), Sigma Theta Tau. Mem. Divine Sci. Ch. Contbr. articles profl. jours. Office: 412 Missouri Ave East Saint Louis IL 62201-3016

ELLENBOGEN, ELISABETH ALICE, accountant; b. Lemberg, Ukraine, Sept. 10, 1940; d. Joseph and Leah Karolina (Wiener) E. B in Humanities, cert. acctg., Pa. State U.; student, Elizabethtown Coll. Cert. civil servant. Buyer McCrory Corp., York, Pa., 1959-65; account mgr. WT Grant Co., York, Pa., 1965-70; various acctg. civil svc. positions Commonwealth of Pa., Harrisburg, 1970—; contract mgr. health and human svcs. Commonwealth of pa., 1989—. Author (bulletin) Out Cry!, 1975; author policies/procedures Constitutional Rights for Handicapped Citizens, 1975—. Bd. dirs. ACLU, Pa., 1978—, disability rights adv., 1978—; convenor Ecumenical Coalition to Abolish the Penalty of Death, Pa., 1985—; activist Harrisburg Rape Crisis, 1973-77; counselor Women's Ctr., Harrisburg, 1975-79. Mem. NOW, Prime Time Group (women's consciousness raising support 1973-77). Democrat. Jewish. Home and Office: 101 S Second St Harrisburg PA 17101

ELLENSOHN, KAROL KAYE, psychotherapist; b. Dubuque, Iowa, Sept. 14, 1942; d. Walter Alden and Winifred Mae (Putney) Roe; m. James Henry Mitchell, June 8, 1963 (div. 1984); 1 child, Jennifer Kaye; m. Edgar Ulrich Ellensohn, Sept. 27, 1989. AAS, RN, William Rainey Harper Coll., Palatine, Ill., 1977; BS, U. San Francisco, 1982; MS, U. La Verne, 1984; postgrad., Fielding Inst., Santa Barbara, Calif., 1984-86. RN, Calif., Ill.; MFCC; cert. community coll. tchr. Personnel dir. Mercy Hosp., Cedar Rapids, Iowa, 1963-64; personnel dir., exec. sec. to adminstr. Meml. Hosp., Colorado Springs, 1964-67; primary care and charge nurse oncology-hematology unit Evanston (Ill.) Hosp., 1977-78; adminstrv. asst. to interior designer Westlake Village, Calif., 1978-79; oncology nurse Vis. Nurses Assn., Ventura, Calif., 1979-81; contract therapist Caostal Radiation Oncology Med. Svcs., Inc., 1984—; art dealer, 1986—l contract chem. dependency therapy, 1983-84; pvt. practice as nurse therapist, Ventura County, Calif., 1979-83; quality assurance coord. Oxnard (Calif.) Cmty. Hosp., 1982, acting dir. nurses, 1982; part-time clin. instr. in psychology and neurology Ventura Coll., 1981-82; cons. in quality assurance Simi Valley (Calif.) Cmty. Hosp.; cons. Wellness Cmty., Westlake Village, 1988—, Palm Desert (Calif.) Art Assn., 1988—. Contbr. articles to local newspapers. Mem. lectr. staff Camarillo Women's Day.; vol., contbr. Bighorn Inst., Palm Desert, 1989—, AIDS Assistance Program, Palm Springs, 1993; contbr. McCallum Theatre for the Performing Arts, Palm Desert, 1993, Hospice of Valley, Scottsdale, 1996; vol. Phoenix Art Mus. Home Tour, 1996; counselor, developer Nat. Disting. Svc. Registry, 1989-90. Recipient award Danforth Found., 1956. Mem. AACD, Calif. Assn. Marriage and Family Therapists, Ill. Nurses Assn., ABA, Calif. Nurses Assn., So. Calif. Hospice Assn., Ventura County Hospice Assn. (lectr.), Ventura County Discharge Planners Assn., Nat. Assn. Quality Assurance Profls., Am. Cancer Soc. (vol. svc. and rehab. com., speaker's bur., facilitator coping with cancer therapy groups, co-facilitator understanding cancer course, bd. dirs., Midge Wilson award 1980, Order Golden Sword 1981, Outstanding Svc. 1983), Art Dealers Assn. Home: 55-801 Congressional La Quinta CA 92253-4754 Office: Le KAE Galleries 7175 E Main St Scottsdale AZ 85251

ELLER, LINDA SADLER, elementary school educator; b. Atlanta, Aug. 14, 1952; d. James Emmett and Mary Love (Dempsey) Sadler; m. David Warner Eller, Dec. 21, 1974; 1 child, Laura Marylove. BS in Elem. Edn., Tenn. Tech. U., 1974; MA in Curriculum and Instrn., Memphis State U., 1986. Cert. elem. tchr, 1-9, Tenn., cert. career ladder III. Tchr., tutor Jackson (Miss.) Tutorial Acad., 1974-75; tchr. DeSoto County Acad., Olive Branch, Miss., 1975-76, Glenmore Acad., Memphis, Tenn., 1976, Memphis City Schs., 1976—; instructional cons. Tchr. Ctr., Memphis, 1991-95; pres. Memphis City Schs. Tchr. Ctr. Adv. Bd., Memphis, 1993-95. Leader Girl Scouts of U.S., Memphis, 1987—; vol. Arts in the Park, Memphis, 1993. Named amb. to Edn. Ctr. N.C., 1993-94; grantee Memphis City Schs., 1984, Rotary, Memphis, 1987, Tenn. Dept. Edn., 1994; fellow Delta Tchrs. Acad., 1994-97. Mem. Internat. Reading Assn. (membership liaison 1994-95), West Tenn. Reading Assn., Kappa Delta Pi, Delta Kappa Gamma, Zeta Tau Alpha. Episcopalian. Home: 4436 Crescent Park Dr Memphis TN 38141-7214 Office: Idlewild Elem Sch 1950 Linden Ave Memphis TN 38104

ELLERBEE, INGRID CHINN, lawyer; b. Sulphur, La., Aug. 15, 1960; d. William David and Gerda A. (Maltzmueller) Chinn; life ptnr. T.L. Schroeder; 1 child, James Bart Ellerbee III. BS in Philosophy, U. So. Miss., 1983, MS in Criminal Justice, 1984; JD, U. Fla., 1991. Bar: Del. 1992, Tex. 1993. Grad. rsch. asst. dept. criminal justice U. So. Miss., Hattiesburg, 1984; life skills instr. Human Devel. Ctr., Seffner, Fla., 1984-86; group treatment leader Hillsborough alt. resideent program Fla. Dept. Human Svcs., Seffner, 1986-87, probation officer Fla. Dept. Corrections, Plant City, 1987-88; rsch. asst. Ctr. for Govtl. Responsibility, Gainesville, Fla., 1989-90; law clk. Atlanta (Ga.) Legal Aid, 1990; atty. Cmty. Legal Aid, Georgetown, Del., 1992; atty. Legal Aid of Ctrl. Tex., Belton, 1993-96, Austin, 1996—. Del., mem. credentials com. Tex. Dem. Conv., 1994, del., 1996; bd. dirs. Parents Friends and Families of Lesbians and Gays, Waco, Tex., 1995, Drug Abuse Info., Referral and Edn., Inc., Belton, 1995-96, Families in Crisis Spouse Abuse Shelter, Killeen, Tex., 1995; at-large rep. Tex. Gay and Lesbian Dems. Recipient Overall Achievement award U. Fla. Alumni Coun., Gainesville, 1991; Pub. Interest Rsch. fellow Fla. Bar Found., 1990. Mem. Tex. Women Lawyers, Travis County Women's Bar Assn., Tex. Young Lawyers Assn. (com. for prevention of domestic violence, com. for women in the profession, com. for low income Texans), Gay and Lesbian Alliance Ctrl. Tex. Unitarian. Home: 225 W Fm 93 Temple TX 76502 Office: Legal Aid Ctrl Tex 205 W 9th St Austin TX 78701

ELLERBEE, LINDA, broadcast journalist; b. Bryan, Tex., Aug. 15, 1944; children: Vanessa, Joshua. Ed., Vanderbilt U. Newscaster, disc jockey Sta. WVON, Chgo., 1964-67; program dir. Sta. KSJO, San Francisco, 1967-68; reporter Sta. KJNO and AP, Juneau, Alaska, 1969-72, Sta. KHOU-TV, Dallas, 1972-73, Sta. WCBS-TV, N.Y.C., 1973-76; Washington corr. NBC News, 1975-78; co-anchor Weekend, NBC News, NBC-TV, 1978-80; reporter NBC Nightly News, 1980-82; co-anchor NBC News Overnight, 1982-84; corr., reporter Today Show, NBC-TV; writer, anchor Our World, ABC-TV, 1986; founder, pres. Lucky Duck Prodns., N.Y.C., 1987—; commentator Cable News Network, 1989. Author: And So It Goes: Adventures in Television, 1986, Move On: Adventures in the Real World, 1991; exec. prod. (TV spls.) A Conversation with Magic (Cable ACE award 1992), It's Only Television (Peabody award 1992); exec. prod., writer, host (news/mag. program) Nick News (Columbia duPont award 1993, Parents' Choice Found. Gold TV award); writer, anchor Our World (Emmy for best writing 1986); weekly syndicated columnist King Features, New York. Office: Lucky Duck Prodns 96 Morton St Fl 6 New York NY 10014-3326*

ELLERT, MARTHA SCHWANDT, physiologist, educator; b. Jersey City, Nov. 27, 1940; d. Harry Richard and Emily (Brando) Schwandt; m. William Sam Hunter, Aug. 3, 1972; children: Anthony Martin, William Fritsche. B.S., Barry Coll., 1962; Ph.D., U. Miami, Fla., 1967. Instr. physiology St. Louis U. Sch. Medicine, 1967-70, asst. prof., 1970-75, dir. summer program, 1971-75; assoc. prof. physiology Sch. Medicine, So. Ill. U., Carbondale, 1975—, assoc. prof. med. edn., 1987—, asst. dean for curriculum, 1981-94, dir. univ. women's profl. advancement 1994—. Precinct committeeman Dem. Party, Makanda, Ill., 1978—; pres. exec. bd. Carbondale New Sch., 1983-85; mem. exec. bd. Makanda Cmty. Devel. Coun., 1980-83, First Christian Ch. of Carbondale; consumer adv. bd. Family Practice Ctr., Carbondale 1976-80; mem. steering com. Women's Coalition for So. Ill., 1990-91; bd. dirs. So. Ill. Chamber Music Soc. Mem. Am. Physiol. Soc., AAUP (nat. coun. 1976-79, chpt. pres. 1973-74, 79-80), AAUW (branch pres. 1994—), Sigma Xi. Avocations: singing, politics, raising dairy goats. Office: So Ill Univ Univ Women's Profl Advancement Carbondale IL 62901-4331

ELLIN, DOROTHY STOTTER, florist, sculptor; b. Chgo., July 26, 1917; d. Max and Lena Rose (Wolfson) Stotter; m. Frederick I. Ellin, Oct. 5, 1940; children: Leon Roland, Marlene B. Student, Wilson Jr. Coll., Chgo., 1936-37, Art Inst. of Chgo. Sec. Bus. Offices Comptometer, Chgo., 1938-41; salesperson Assn. Am. Artists, Chgo. and Fla., 1942-44; florist Designer Flower Shops and Stores, Chgo., 1963-95; wedding cons. Fla., 1965-77; docent Ringling Mus. of Art, Sarasota, Fla., 1975-95; founding pres., tchr. Art Guild, Skokie, Ill., 1960s; wedding cons., Chgo. Prin. works include Bronze Sculpture In the Beginning, 1964, Bright Future, 1970, Exercise Class, 1985. Bd. dirs. LWV, Skokie, 1960s; chair, organizer various art fairs, 1960s and 70s. Recipient Docent awards Ringling Mus., 1975-95, Sculpture award Longboat Key Art Ctr., 1990. Democrat.

ELLINGHAM, NANCY ELIZABETH, retired principal; b. Yakima, Wash., Oct. 4, 1931; d. Theodore Ottis and Frances Kathryn (Walker) E.; m. William Ewing Van Arsdel, Sept. 1956 (div. June 1972); children: Julia Ann, John Walker; m. George W. Pennell, July 14, 1990. AB magna cum laude, Whitman Coll., 1953; MA, Northwestern U., 1954. Tchg. cert., adminstrv. cert., Wash. Dir., co-founder CAMPI (Ctrl. Area Mothers for Peace and Improvement) Presch., Seattle, 1968-69; program mgr. CAMPI Seattle Preschs./Seattle Sch. Dist., 1970-76; asst. prin. Lowell Elem. Sch./Seattle Sch. Dist., 1977; prin. Rainier View Elem./Seattle Sch. Dist., 1978-80; asst. prin. Franklin H.S./Seattle Sch. Dist., 1981-87, West Seattle H.S./Seattle Sch. Dist., 1988-95; ret., 1995. Mem. NOW, Religious Coalition for

Reproductive Rights, Delta Kappa Gamma, Phi Beta Kappa. Democrat. Presbyterian.

ELLINGTON, CYNTHIA HEMPHILL, elementary education educator; b. Winder, Ga., Nov. 30, 1965; d. John Sylvan and Margaret Ann (Shore) Hemphill; m. Jerrel Keith Ellington, July 6, 1966. BS in Edn. cum laude, U. Ga., 1988, MEd, 1990; EdS, Brenau U., 1994. Tchr. South Jackson Elem. Sch., Jackson County, Ga., 1988-89, Kennedy Elem. Sch., Winder, Ga., 1989-90, County Line Elem. Sch., Winder, Ga., 1990-95, Bethlehem Elem., 1995—; tech. adv. bd. Brenau U., Gainesville, Ga., 1994—. Mem. Golden Key Honor Soc., Phi Delta Kappa,. Home: 389 Castle Ave Winder GA 30680-3403 Office: Bethlehem Elem 54 Star St W Bethlehem GA 30620

ELLIOT, ANN KOERBER, registered nurse, artist; b. Washington, Mar. 19, 1950; d. Allan Boynton and Mildred Elizabeth (Koerber) E.; m. Gilberto R. Jusino, June 1975 (div. 1986). A, Montgomery Coll., 1981. RN, Md. Hotline counselor Montgomery County Mental Health Assn., Kensington, Md., 1969-72; counselor Montgomery County Health Dept., Silver Spring, Md., 1969-71, Coll. Park (Md.) Youth Svcs., 1971-75; health asst. Montgomery County Health Dept., Rockville, Md., 1975-79; RN Providence Hosp., Washington, 1981-89, Mount Auburn Hosp., Cambridge, Mass., 1989—; artist Cambridge, Md., 1991—. Exhibited shows at Mystic Outdoor Art Festival, Scituate Art Festival, SONO Arts Festival, DeCordova Mus. Art in the Park Show, Cambridge Riverfest, Westfest Art Festival. Democrat. Home and Office: 224 Chestnut St Cambridge MA 02139

ELLIOT, DIANE ALYNN, dancer, choreographer, movement educator; b. Chgo., Apr. 25, 1949; d. Leonard and Florence (Asher) E. BA, U. Mich., 1971. Dancer, Phyllis Lamhut Dance Co., N.Y.C., 1974-77; master tchr. Centre Nat. de Danse Contemporaine, Angers, France, 1979-80; artist in residence U. Minn., Mpls., 1981-82; ind. dance artist N.Y.C., Mpls., 1974—, Body Arts Network, Mpls., 1982-87; choreographer Illusion Theatre, Mpls., Guthrie Theatre, Mpls., 1987-88; founding mem. Women's Performance Project, 1990-94. Choreographer Sweet Honey, 1984, Florence's Dress, 1984, Open Mind, 1985, Double Exposure, 1986, Arpeggios and Quiet Conversations, 1986, The Time Falling Bodies Take to Light, 1986, Yimani, 1988, Small Places have Deep Voices, 1990, Bloodroot, 1990; co-creator Fertile Crescent, 1991, Labyrinth, 1994, Bridge of Stones, 1996; contbr. articles to profl. jours. McKnight Found. fellow, 1983-91, Minn. State Arts Bd. fellow, 1983, 91, 95; Jerome Found. grantee, 1983, 86, 90, 94. Mem. Minn. Dance Alliance (bd. dirs. 1984-86), Body-Mind Centering Assn., Internat. Somatic Movement Edn. & Therapy Assn. Jewish. Avocations: reading, yoga, writing songs and poetry. Office: 2400 Blaisdell Ave S Minneapolis MN 55404

ELLIOT, PEGGY GORDON, academic administrator. BA, Transylvania U., LHD (hon.), 1993; MA, Northwestern U.; PhD, Ind. U. Faculty grad. sch. Ind. Univ., chancellor, CEO, 1984-92; pres. U. Akron, 1992—; chair com. on secondary/higher edn. Ohio Bd. Regents; chair Ohio Inter-Univ. Coun.; bd. dirs. Akron Regional Devel. Bd., Inventure Place, Akron Tomorrow, Lubizol Corp., A. Schulman, Inc., Ohio Aerospace Inst., Ohio Supercomputer Ctr., Cleve. Commn. on Higher Edn. Author: The Urban Campus: Preparing a New Majority for a New Century; contbr. articles to profl. jours. Recipient Disting. Alumni award Northwestern U. Mem. Am. Assn. State Colls. and Univs. (bd. dirs., chair spl. task force on the role of urban univs. in sch. and work life path, mem. new coordinating com. for urban and met. univs.), Am. Coun. on Edn. (bd. dirs., mem. nat. legis. commn.). Office: U Akron The Buchtel Commons Akron OH 44325

ELLIOTT, BETTY F., telecommunications industry executive. Formerly pres. Ameritech Credit Corp., Schaumburg, Ill.; v.p., comptr. Ameritech, Chgo., 1991—. Office: Ameritech 30 S Wacker Dr Chicago IL 60606-7402

ELLIOTT, CANDICE K., interior designer; b. Cedar Rapids, Iowa, Aug. 29, 1949; d. Charles H. and Eunice A. (Long) Goodrich; m. John William Jr. Elliott, Jan. 27, 1973; 1 child, Brandon Christian; 1 stepchild, John William III. BA, U. Iowa, 1971. Interior designer Dayton's, Mpls., 1971-76, Candice Interior Space Planning and Design, Guilford, Conn., 1981-87; owner, interior designer Sofa Works, King of Prussia, Pa., 1987-90; interior designer Jerrehians's Home Furnishings, West Chester, Pa., 1990-92; dir. sales and visual merchandising Sheffield Furniture, Malvern, Pa., 1992-95; owner Candice Interior Space Planning and Design, Wayne, Pa., 1996—. Bd. dirs. The Old Capitol Restoration Com., Iowa City, 1970-76; curator Guilford Keeping Soc., 1983-88; cons. Zion Episcopal Ch., North Branford, Conn., 1985-88. Mem. Am. Soc. Interior Designers (bd. dirs. Conn. chpt., profl. mem.). Republican. Home: 13 Windsor Cir Wayne PA 19087-5724

ELLIOTT, CORINNE ADELAIDE, retired copywriter; b. Chgo., Nov. 20, 1927; d. Bertram Otto and Lylia Arletta (Mansfield) Briscoe; m. William S. Elliott, June 18, 1947 (div. Nov. 1985); children: Patricia Frances, Christine Grace, Annie Lou. Cert., Famous Artists Schs., Conn., 1959; BA in English maxima cum laude, Carroll Coll., 1975. Advt. writer Sandy McPherson, Realtor, Helena, Mont., 1975-79; advt. copywriter KCAP Radio, Helena, 1979-83; Helena corr. Great Falls (Mont.) Tribune, 1981-83; radio copywriter Sta. KMTX-AM-FM, Helena, 1986-93; writer in field, 1994—; pres., owner The Funding Edge, Helena, 1991-95, Elliott Impress Silk Screen Works, Whitefish, Mont., 1960-70, Lotus Light Designs, Helena, 1988—; contbr. Salem Press, Pasadena, Calif. One-person show at Mont. Hist. Soc., 1956-59, Deer Lodge, Mont., 1994; exhibited in group shows at Electrum Fine Arts Show (Merit award), Hockaday Art Gallery, Kalispell, Mont., Ball State U., Mont. Inst. Arts, 1992, Art Chateau, Butte, Mont., 1992, New Eng. Fine Arts Inst., Boston, 1993, Mont. Interpretations, Butte, 1994 (Honorable mention); works represented in permanent collections Cason Gallery, Helena, also Utick and Grosfled Collection, Helena; contbr. articles to mags. and ref. books; ongoing contbr. Convergence Mag., Concord, N.H. Leader 5-8th grades Girl Scouts U.S., Stanford, Mont., 1955-59; tchr. Happy Medium Art Group, Whitefish, 1959-68; violinist Waukegan Philharm., 1945-47, Billings Symphony, 1951-55; donated art works for benefit auctions to Hockaday Gallery, 1970, Kalispell, 1971, Mont. Food Bank, 1991, 92, 93, Aids Found., 1990, Helena Area Habitat for Humanity, 1993. Mem. Mont. Inst. Arts, Mont. Watercolor Soc. (bd. mem. 1983), Nat. Writers Club.

ELLIOTT, DENI, ethics educator; b. Nanticoke, Pa., Nov. 16, 1953; d. Francis J. and Lottie (Peitrovich) Nitkowski; m. James P. Cramer; 1 child, James Wesley. BA, U. Md., 1974; MA, Wayne State U., 1982; DEd, Harvard U., 1984. Cert. secondary tchr., Mich. Journalism and English tchr. Plymouth (Mich.) Canton High Sch., 1979-81; assoc. prof. dept. communications Utah State U., Logan, 1985-88; rsch. assoc. prof. edn., adj. assoc. prof. dept. philosophy Dartmouth Coll., 1988-92; dir. Ethics Inst., Dartmouth, Hanover, N.H., 1988-92; Mansfield prof. ethics U. Mont., Missoula, 1992-96, dir. Practical Ethics Ctr., 1996—; reporter, ethics coach Sta. WCSH-TV, Portland, 1988, Louisville Courier-Jour., 1987, Phila. Inquirer, Phila., 1985. Co-author: Responsible Journalism, 1986, The Ethics of Asking, 1995; co-prodr. video documentary A Case of Need, 1989 (Silver Apple 1991), Buying Time, 1991 (Bronze Apple 1992), Burden of Knowledge: Moral Dilemnas in Prenatal Testing; columnist FineLine Mag., Louisville, 1989-91; contbr. articles to profl. jours., chpts. to books. Recipient Bronze Plaque Columbus Internat. Film Festival, 1990; Marion and Jasper Whiting Found. fellow Harvard U., 1983, Rockefeller fellow Dartmouth Coll., 1987. Mem. Soc. of Profl. Journalists, Am. Philosophical Assn., Assn. for Edn. in Journalism and Mass Communication, Assn. for Practical and Profl. Ethics (governing bd.). Home: PO Box 846 Lolo MT 59847 Office: U Mont Dept Philosophy Missoula MT 59812

ELLIOTT, DOLORES, disabilities advocate, film producer; b. N.Y.C., Nov. 13, 1950; d. Thomas Augustus Elliot and Vera A. Burll. BFA, NYU, 1972; MEd, Hunter Coll., 1996. Prodr. Ctr. for Study Music, N.Y.C., 1988—; assoc. prodr. Stanley Nelson Prodns., N.Y.C., 1990-93, SearchLight, San Francisco, 1993; tng. dir. Achilles Track Club, N.Y.C., 1994—; mentor Networking project, N.Y.C., 1993—. Mem. Soc. Disability Studies. Roman Catholic. Home: 535 W 110th St New York NY 10025

ELLIOTT, DOROTHY GAIL, music educator writer; b. Kennard, Ind., Oct. 23, 1918; d. Clyde Harrison and Hazel Uvah (Houk) Copeland; m. Robert E. Elliott, Aug. 22, 1948; children: R. Bruce, Marla Beth, John H. BS in Edn., Ball State Tchrs. Coll., 1940. Tchr. music and math. New Castle (Ind.) Jr. H.S., 1940-43; dir. religious edn. Bethany Union Ch., Chgo., 1945-47; dir. youth activities Hillfields Congl. Ch., Coventry, Eng., 1947-48; music tchr. grades 4, 5, 6 and 7 Silberstein Elem. Sch., Dallas, 1967-70; dir. H.S. choir Singapore Am. Sch., 1970-71; music tchr. grades 4, 5, 6 and 7 Degolyer Elem. Sch., Dallas, 1971-72; music edn. writer J. Weston Walch, Pub., Portland, Maine, 1973—; proprietor Noteman Press, Dallas, 1982—. Author (three books, two tapes) Harmonious Recorder, 1969-96, (book, worksheets, tapes) ZOUNDS!, 1973-94, (book, worksheets) Sight-Singing for Young Teens, 1981-96, (reproducible book) Rediscovered Songs, 1991, (historical musical) G.T.T. (Gone to Texas), 1984-96; author, editor: JUBILEE!, 1987; editor: Dancing with Cancer, 1995; contbg. author: Music and You, 1991. Named Music Alumni of Yr., Ball State U., Muncie, Ind., 1979. Mem. Am. Recorder Soc. Democrat. Home and Office: 2603 Andrea Ln Dallas TX 75228

ELLIOTT, INGER MCCABE, designer, textile company executive, consultant; b. Oslo, Feb. 23, 1933; came to U.S., 1941; naturalized, 1946; d. David and Lova (Katz) Abrahamsen; m. Osborn Elliott, Oct. 20, 1973; children by previous marriage: Kari McCabe, Alexander McCabe, Marit McCabe. AB in History with honors, Cornell U., 1954; postgrad., Harvard U., 1955; AM, Radcliffe Coll., 1957. Photographer Photo Rschrs. Rapho-Guillumette, U.S. and fgn. countries, 1960-94; pres. China Seas, Inc., N.Y.C., 1972-90, Gifted Textile Collection to L.A. County Mus. Art, 1991—; Textile Exhibit, L.A. County Mus. Art, 1996-97, cons. Sotheby's, Inc., 1992—; tchr. Newton (Mass.) Pub. Schs., 1955-56; mem. Coun. Fgn. Rels. Mem. East Asia vis. com. Harvard U. Jean Birdsall fellow Radcliffe Coll., 1957; trustee The Asia Soc.; recipient Roscoe awards, 1978, 79, 80, 82-88. Mem. Am. Soc. Mag. Photographers, Am. Women's Econ. Devel. Corp., Com. of 200, Nat. Home Fashions League, Cosmopolitan Club, Ellis Island Yacht Club (lt. comdr.), Phi Beta Kappa, Asia Soc. (trustee). Avocations: skiing, tennis. Author: Women Photographers, 1970, A Week in Amy's World, 1970, A Week in Henry's World, 1971, Batik: Fabled Cloth of Java, 1985, Exteriors, 1992; photographer, dir./prodr. Conversations at Sotheby's; contbr. photographic essays to Esquire, Vogue, Life, Newsweek, N.Y. Times, Infinity, House & Garden. Home: 36 E 72nd St New York NY 10021-4247 Office: IME Ltd 157 E 72nd St New York NY 10021-4331

ELLIOTT, JEAN ANN, library administrator; b. Martinsburg, W.Va., Jan. 18, 1933; d. Howard Hoffman and Dorothy Jean (Horn) E. AB in Edn., Shepherd Coll., Shepherdstown, W.Va., 1954; MS in Libr. Sci., Syracuse U., 1957; MS, Shippensburg (Pa.) U., 1974. Asst. libr. Fairmont (W.Va.) State Coll., 1957-60; reference asst. U. Pitts., 1960-61; acting libr. Shepherd Coll., 1961-62, coord. libr. sci., 1962—; compiler Jefferson County Hist. mag., 1990. Nat. treas. Palatines of Am., Columbus, Ohio, 1986-88. Mem. ALA, AAUW, DAR (W.Va. treas. 1980-83, 86-89, 95—), W.Va. Libr. Assn. (election chmn. 1988-90), W.Va. Edn. Media Assn., Va. Edn. Media Assn., Southeastern Libr. Assn. (continuing edn. com. 1991-95), Jefferson County Hist. Soc., Nat. Geneal. Soc., Nat. Soc. Daus. Am. Colonies (nat. libr. 1991-94), Nat. Soc. Daus. 1812 (nat. libr. 1994-96), W.Va. Soc. Daus. 1812 (state pres. 1991-94), Alpha Beta Alpha (nat. exec. sec. 1968-76). Presbyterian. Home: PO Box 239 Shepherdstown WV 25443-0239

ELLIOTT, JEANNE MARIE KORELTZ, transportation executive; b. Virginia, Minn., Mar. 9, 1943; d. John Andrew and Johanna Mae (Tehovnik) Koreltz; m. David Michael Elliott, Apr. 30, 1983. Student, Ariz. State U., 1967, U. So. Calif. Cert. aviation safety inspector. Tech. asst. Ariz. State U., Tempe, 1966-68; from supr. to mgr. inflight tng./in-svc. programs Northwest Airlines Inc. (formerly Republic Airlines, Hughes Airwest, Air West Inc.), Seattle, 1968—; air carrier cabin safety specialist Flight Standards Service, FAA, Washington, 1975-76; cons. Interaction Research Corp., Olympia, Wash., 1982—. Contbg. editor Cabin Crew Safety Bull., Flight Safety Found., 1978—. Recipient Annual Air Safety award Air Line Pilots Assn., Washington, 1971, Annual Safety award Ariz. Safety Council, Phoenix, 1972; first female to hold FAA cabin safety inspector's credential, 1976. Mem. Soc. Air Safety Investigators Internat., Survival and Flight Equipment Assn., Assn. Flight Attendants (tech. chmn. 1968-85), Soc. Automotive Engrs. (chmn. cabin safety provisions com. 1971—), Teamsters Local 2000 (chair nat. safety and health). Republican. Roman Catholic. Home: 16215 SE 31st St Bellevue WA 98008-5704 Office: NW Airlines Inc Inflight Svcs Dept Seattle-Tacoma Internat Airport Seattle WA 98158

ELLIOTT, LEE ANN, federal official. BA, U. Ill.; cert., Northwestern U. Cert. assn. exec. Commr. Fed. Election Commn., Washington, 1981—, chmn. commn., 1884, 90, 96; v.p. Bishop, Bryant amd Assocs., Inc., 1979-81; lectr., author and inventor in field. Bd. dirs., pres. Chgo. Area Pub. Affairs Group; bd. dirs. Kids Voting, USA. Mem. Am. Med. Polit. Action Com. (asst. dir. 1961-70, assoc. exec. dir. 1970-79), Am. Assn. Polit. Cons. (bd. dirs.), Nat. Assn. Mfrs. (award of excellence), U.S. C. of C. (pub. affairs com.). Office: Federal Election Commn 999 E St NW Washington DC 20463-0001

ELLIOTT, LINDA LUCILLE, writer, consultant; b. Birmingham, Ala., June 14, 1950; d. Bobby Milton and Rose (Gibilisco) E.; m. Bruce Stephen Bodner, Apr. 4, 1981 (div. Dec. 1995); 1 child. Student, U. Ala., Birmingham, 1979-80. Mgr. ins. and accounts receivable Cooper Green Hosp., Birmingham, 1978-82; CEO Personnel Mgmt. Cons., Birmingham, 1994—. Author: (poetry) With Rhyme and Reason, Part I, 1996, Part II, 1996; author, editor (periodical of book reviews) The Book Report, 1994-95. Mem. com. Rep. Nat. Com., 1989-96. Presbyterian. Home: PO Box 381701 Birmingham AL 35238

ELLIOTT, MARGARET ANN, fund-raising professional, writing consultant; b. Wantaugh, N.Y., Aug. 25, 1957; d. R. Duff and B. Irene (Zarr) Wilson; m. Dennis Robert Elliott, Apr. 9, 1988. AB in Art and Archaeology, Washington U., St. Louis, 1979, MBA, 1986. Asst. mgr. Nat. States Ins., St. Louis, 1981-84; devel. officer St. Louis Art Mus., 1985-90; dir. devel. Katherine Dunham Ctrs. for Arts and Humanities, St. Louis, 1990-92; owner, v.p. Non Profit Network Co., 1992—; owner, prin. The Write Focus, St. Louis, 1991—. Vol., Internat. Inst., St. Louis, 1989—, Washington U. Alumni Programs, 1985—. Mem. NAFE, Nat. Soc. Fund-Raising Execs. Presbyterian. Office: The Write Focus 3351-B Eminence Ave Saint Louis MO 63114

ELLIOTT, MARIE LOUISE, elementary school educator; b. Queens, N.Y., Jan. 19, 1955; d. Bernard J. and Ann Margaret (Pryor) L.; m. Peter James Elliott, Aug. 9, 1987. AS, Nassau C.C., Garden City, N.Y., 1975; BS, Adelphi U., 1978, M in Elem. Edn., 1980; cert. in staff devel., Coll. of New Rochelle, 1996. Elem. and secondary subsitute tchr. Valley Stream, Freeport Dist., N.Y., 1980; 4th grade tchr. St. Andrew Acad. on Sound, Whitestone, N.Y., 1980-81, 3-4th grade tchr., 1981-82; 3rd, 4th and 5th grade tchr. Whitestone (N.Y.) Acad., 1982-83, kindergarten tchr., 1983-84; jr. high tchr. St. Luke's Sch., Whitestone, 1984-87; remedial reading replacement tchr. Roslyn (N.Y.) Middle Sch., 1987-88; remedial reading 2nd and 3rd grade tchr. Centre Ave. Sch., East Rockaway, 1988-93, 6th grade tchr., 1994—; scorer State Edn. Dept., Albany, 1993. Mem. ASCD. Office: Centre Ave Elem Sch 55 Centre Ave East Rockaway NY 11518-1001

ELLIOTT, MARLENE BLANCHE, legislative staff member; b. Milford, Del., Aug. 4, 1959; d. Marshall Thomas and Blanche Dukes E. AAS in Bus. Adminstrn., Del. Tech. and Comml. Coll., Georgetown, Del., 1979; BS in Bus. Adminstrn., Salisbury State Coll., 1983. Jr. acct. David T. Boyce CPA, Seaford, Del., 1979-82; campaign coord. Sussex county Roth Senate Com., Del., 1982; asst. for Del. affairs U.S. Senator Wm. V. Roth, Jr., Georgetown, Del., 1983—. Mem. Rep. State Com., Sussex, Seaford and Kent County Rep. Women's Clubs; past treas. Rep. Com. Sussex County; pianist, choir dir. Trinity United Meth. Ch.; mem. Laurel Hist. Soc.; bd. dirs. Old Christ Ch. League. Named to Walk of Success Del. Tech. and C.C., 1993. Mem. AAUW, Bus. and Profl. Women's Club (past treas. Sussex County chpt., Del. Young Careerist 1985), Rotary Club (past sec. Georgetown-Millsboro). Republican. Methodist. Office: 12 The Circle Georgetown DE 19947

ELLIOTT, MYRA TURNER, nursing educator; b. Martin, Ky., Aug. 19, 1958; d. Langley and Violet (Sparkman) Turner; m. Olin Andrew Elliott II, June 10, 1978; 1 child, Myranda Grance Elliott. ADN, Prestonsburg (Ky.) C.C., 1978; BSN, U. Ky., 1981; postgrad., U. Tenn., 1985; MSN, U. Ky., 1993. Clin. I/nursing care mgr. St. Joseph's Hosp., Lexington, 1978-83; clin. I/nursing care mgr., office nurse Dr. Andy Elliott, Martin, Ky., 1983-84; assoc. prof. Prestonburg C.C., 1984—, senator, 1995—; chairperson devel. and implementation of a clin. ladder program, Prestonburg, 1990—. Mem. Floyd County Cmty. Com. for Edn., 1992—; bd. dirs. Hospice of Big Sandy, 1987-95; Sunday sch. tchr., mem. choir First Bapt. Ch., Prestonburg. Recipient NISOD Excellence award, 1996. Mem. ANA, Ky. Dental Aux. (state historian), Ky. Nurses Assn., Coun. on Critical Care, Ky. Mountain Dental Aux. (pres.), Ky. Dental Alliance (pres.-elect). Home: 1391 Abbott Creek Rd Prestonsburg KY 41653-8930 Office: Prestonsburg Cmty Coll One Bert Combo Dr Prestonsburg KY 41653

ELLIOTT, PEGGY GORDON, university president; b. Matewan, W.Va., May 27, 1937; d. Herbert Hunt and Mary Ann (Renfro) Gordon; children from previous marriage: Scott Vandling III, Anne Gordon. B.A., Transylvania Coll., 1959; M.A., Northwestern U., 1964; Ed.D., Ind. U., 1975. Tchr. Horace Mann High Sch., Gary, Ind., 1959-64; instr. English Ind. U. N.W., Gary, 1965-69, lectr. Edn., 1973-74, asst. prof. edn., 1975-78, assoc. prof., 1978-80, supr. secondary student teaching, 1973-74, dir. student teaching, 1975-77, dir. Office Field Experiences, 1977-78, dir. profl. devel., 1978-80, spl. asst. to chancellor, 1981-83, asst. to chancellor, 1983-84, acting chancellor, 1983-84, chancellor, 1984-92; instr. English Am. Inst. Banking, Gary, 1969-70; pres. U. Akron, Ohio, 1992—; vis. prof. U. Ark., 1979-80, U. Alaska, 1982; bd. dirs. Lubrizol Corp., A. Schulman Corp., Akron Tomorrow, Ohio Aerospace Consortium, Ohio Super Computer Com.; holder VA Harrington disting. chair edn., 1994—. Author: (with C. Smith) Reading Activities for Middle and Secondary Schools: A Handbook for Teachers, 1979, Reading Instruction for Secondary Schools, 1986, How to Improve Your Scores on Reading Competency Tests, 1981, (with C. Smith and G. Ingersoll) Trends in Educational Materials: Traditionals and the New Technologies, 1983, The Urban Campus: Educating a New Majority for a New Century, 1994, also numerous articles. Bd. dirs. Meth. Hosp., N.W. Ind. Forum, N.W. Ind. Symphony, Boys Club N.W. Ind., Akron Symphony, NBD Bank, John S. Knight Conv. Ctr., Inventure Pl., Akron Roundtable, Cleve. Com. Higher Edn. Recipient Disting. Alumni award Northwestern U., VA Disting. Alumni award, 1994, numerous grants; Am. Council on Edn. fellow in acad. adminstrn. Ind. U., Bloomington, 1980-81. Mem. Assn. Tchr. Educators (nat. pres. 1984-85, Disting. Mem. 1990), Nat. Acad. Tchrs. Edn. (bd. dirs. 1983—), Ind. Assn. Tchr. Educators (past pres.), North Ctrl. Assn. (commn. at large), Am. Assn. State Colls. and Univs. (bd. dirs.), Am. Coun. Edn. (bd. dirs.), Leadership Devel. Coun. ACE, Ohio Inter Univ. Coun. (chair), Internat. Reading Assn., Akron Urban League (bd. dirs.), P.E.O., Phi Delta Kappa (Outstanding Young Educator award), Delta Kappa Gamma (Leadership/Mgmt. fellow 1980), Pi Lambda Theta, Chi Omega. Episcopalian. Home: 856 Sunnyside Akron OH 44303 Office: U Akron Office of Pres Akron OH 44325-4702

ELLIOTT, SUSAN DONISE, substance abuse counselor, secondary educator; b. Newport Beach, Calif., Sept. 21, 1968. AAS in Bus. Adminstrn., Pima C.C., 1990; BA in Polit. Sci. and Comm., U. Ariz., 1994, tchr. cert., 1996. Cert. substance abuse counselor Ariz. Bd. Behavioral Health Examiners; cert. tchr. social studies. Behavioral health technician LaPaloma Family Svcs., Tucson, 1992-95; substance abuse counselor Gateway Found., Tucson, 1995, Project PPEP, Tucson, 1996; history tchr. Pueblo H.S./U. Ariz., Tucson, 1996. Author: Lyrical Poetry, 1991. Sec. Pima County Libertarian Party, Tucson, 1990. Mem. NEA, Nat. Coun. for Social Studies, Nat. Trust for Hist. Preservation, Smithsonian Inst., Libr. of Congress. Home: 520 E Agave Dr Tucson AZ 85704-5237 Office: 1548 S Euclid Ave # 100 Tucson AZ 85713

ELLIOTT, SUSAN SPOEHRER, information technology executive; b. St. Louis, May 4, 1937; d. Charles Henry and Jane Elizabeth (Baur) Spoehrer; m. Howard Elliott Jr., Sept. 2, 1961; children: Kathryn Elliott Love, Elizabeth Gray. AB, Smith Coll., 1958. Systems engr. IBM, St. Louis, 1958-66; pres., founder Sys. Svc. Enterprises, Inc., St. Louis, 1966—; systems analyst Mo. State Dept. Edn., Jefferson City, Mo., 1967-70; systems coord. Boatmen's Nat. Bank, St. Louis, 1979-83; bd. dirs., mem. exec. com. Mo. Automobile Club; class C dir., dep. chmn. Fed. Res. Bd., St. Louis, 1996—, St. Louis Zoo; bd. dirs. St. Louis Regional Commerce and Growth Assn., sec. bd. dirs., 1991-94. Trustee, vice chmn. Mary Inst., St. Louis, 1976-89, Webster U., 1987—; commr., vice chmn. St. Louis Civil Svc. Commn., 1985-86, Mo. Lottery Commn., Jefferson City, 1985-87; mem. corp. partnership coun. St. Louis Sci. Ctr.; mem. pres.'s adv. coun. area coun. Girl Scouts U.S.; class C dir., dep. chmn. Fed. Res. Bank St. Louis, 1996—. Mem. Internat. Women's Forum. Republican. Presbyterian. Office: Sys Svc Enterprises Inc 795 Office Pky Ste 101 Saint Louis MO 63141-7166

ELLIOTT-MOSKWA, ELAINE SALLY, psychologist, researcher; b. St. Louis; d. Walter Leonard and Helen (Krelo) E.; m. Alexander Moskwa Jr.; 1 child, Katherine. BA in Psychology, U. Mo., 1973; MA in Psychology, San Diego State U., 1977; PhD in Psychology, U. Ill., 1980. Vis. rsch. assoc. Lab. Human Devel., Harvard U., Cambridge, Mass., 1980-81; lectr. dept. psychology Brandeis U., Waltham, Mass., 1981; fellow Ctr. for Cognitive Therapy, U. Pa., Phila., 1982-83; cons. Presbyn. U. Pa. Med. Ctr., Phila., 1984-85; pvt. practice Newton Centre, Mass., 1985-92; dir. Ctr. for Cognitive Therapy Greater Boston, Newton Centre, 1988-92; pvt. practice Princeton, N.J., 1992—; instr. Med. Sch. Harvard U., 1989—; asst. dir. tng., cognitive therapy and rsch. program Mass. Gen. Hosp., 1991-92, cons. depression rsch. program, 1992—. Author: chpt. Carmichael's Handbook of Child Psychology, 1983, Advances in Psychology, 1989. Nat. Inst. on Aging grantee Brandeis U., 1988. Mem. Am. Psychol. Assn., Assn. for Advancement Behavior Therapy. Office: Ste 507 20 Nassau St Princeton NJ 08542-4509

ELLIOTT-WATSON, DORIS JEAN, psychiatric, mental health and gerontological nurse educator; b. Caney, Kans., Dec. 6, 1932; d. Alva Orr and Mary Amelia (Boyns) Elliott; children Marsha Jean Watson, Sherwood Elliott Watson. BE, U. Miami, Fla., 1952, MEd, 1954; EdD, Pacific Western U., 1982; BSN, U. Kans., 1985; AS in Psychology, Kansas City (Kans.) C.C., 1989; AA in Music, Kansas City C.C., 1994. RN, Kans., Mo.; cert. clin. specialist gerontology nurse, gerontology nurse generalist, psychiat.-mental health nurse, med.-surg. nurse, ANCC; cert. elem. to jr. coll. tchr., Kans., Mo.; lic. adult care home adminstr., Kans. Tchr. learning disabled, gifted, emotionally disturbed Shawnee Mission, Kans., 1961-76; instr. hospitalized psychiat. and med.-surg. children U. Kans. Med. Ctr., Kansas City, 1979-82; pvt. practice, gerontol. nurse educator Bonner Springs, Kans., 1985—; libr. U. Miami, 1952, Kans. U., 1978; nurse ARC, Kansas City, 1985—; nurse educator Am. Heart Assn., Kansas City, 1985—; program designer mainstreaming spl. needs children into regular classrooms, 1969; specialist geriatric sexuality nursing homes, 1986. Editor Park Stylus, Parkville, Mo., 1952; author, speaker Kansas City area, 1950—. Tutor-organizer Tutoring Vol.Orgn. for Inner City Children, 1965-68; sustaining mem. Rep. Nat. Com., Washington, 1978—, rep. Congl. Com., 1978—, Rep. Senatorial Com., 1978—; pres. Young Reps., Kansas City, 1960; mem. Rep. Nat. Conv. Platform Planning Com., 1995; patron, charter mem. Kaw Valley Cmty. Choir, 1990-92; mem. Kansas City Cmty. Choir, 1992—, mem. tour of cathedrals Christ Ch., Oxford and King's Coll., Eng., 1993; mem. Mid. Am. Nazarene Coll. Cmty. Choir, 1993—, Leavenworth Cmty. Carnegie Choir, 1994—. Recipient Coast to Coast 2810 miles award Am. Running and Fitness Assn., 1994; inducted Rep. Nat. Hall of Honor, Rep. Nat. Conv., 1992. Mem. ANA (coun. on gerontol. nurses, coun. for cmty., primary care and long term care nursing practice, coun. for nursing rsch.), NEA (life, del. state conv. 1980, nat. conv. 1973), Kans. Nurses Assn., U. Kans. Alumni Assn., Bus. and Profl. Women, Order Ea. Star (Electra 1982, Martha 1994, Marshal 1995, Assoc. Conductress 1996), Order Rainbow for Girls (worthy advisor 1950), Am. Volkssport Assn. (Tri-Athlete 1993, 94, 95, 4500 Km Walking award 1993, 5500Km 1994, Sunflower State Games Athlete 1993, 94, 95, Sooner State Games Athlete award 1994, 95, Mid-Am. Walking Marathon 1994, 6500 Km Walking award 1995), Tiblow Trailblazers Walking Club (pres. 1993—), Nat. Wildlife Fedn. (cert. backyard wildlife habitat 1994), Kappa Delta Pi, Pi Delta Epsilon, Phi Theta Kappa, Alpha Kappa Delta, Phi Alpha Theta. Home and Office: 231 Sheidley Ave Bonner Springs KS 66012-1410

ELLIOTT-ZAHORIK, BONNIE, nurse, administrator; b. Algona, Iowa. AAS, Coll. Lake County, Grayslake, Ill., 1979; student, U. Iowa; BS,

Coll. St. Francis, Joliet, Ill., 1988; MSM, Nat. Louis U., Evanston, Ill., 1989; doctoral fellow, Walden U., Mpls., 1995—. RN, Ill.; CCRN; cert. nurse adminstr.-advanced; cert. critical care preceptor and instr. Evening nurse dir. Victory Meml. Hosp., Waukegan, Ill., 1991—. Contbr. articles to profl. jours. Mem. AACN, Ill. Coun. Nurse Mgrs. (past pres. Region 2B), Ill. Orgn. Nurse Leaders (co-pres. region ZB).

ELLIS, ANNE ELIZABETH, fundraiser; b. Orngestad, Aruba, Aug. 21, 1945; d. Thomas Albert and Anne Elizabeth (Belis) Wolfe; m. Earl Edward Ellis, Feb. 14, 1970. BS, La. State U., 1967. Fashion coord. Baton Rouge, 1962-67; textile researcher La. State U., Baton Rouge, 1965-67; buyer I.H. Rubensteins., Baton Rouge, 1967-68; fashion distbr. J.C. Penney, Inc., Arlington, Tex., 1969-70; asst. buyer J.C. Penney, Inc., Dallas, 1970-73; exec. dir. Nassau County Mus. Fine Art Assn., Roslyn, N.Y., 1985-88; speaker C.W. Post U., Greenvale, N.Y., 1988—; cons. in field. Chmn., editor: (cookbook) Specialities of the House, 1981-83. Bd. dirs., com. chmn. Congregational Ch., Manhasset, N.Y., 1975—; exec. v.p., bd. dirs., com. chmn. Jr. League Internat.; benefit gala chmn., com. chmn. Grenville Baker Boys & Girls Club, Locust Valley, N.Y., 1983-91; pres. bd., vice-chmn. cmty. outreach, benefit gala chmn. Tilles Performing Art Ctr. L.I. U., Greenvale, N.Y., 1985—; bd. dirs., benefit co-chmn. Nassau County Family Assn. Svcs., Hempstead, 1988—; benefit vice-chmn. Glen Cove/North Shore Cmty. Hosp., 1989-93; mem. exec. bd., exec. v.p., trustee WLIW, L.I. Pub. TV, 1990—; trustee Cmty. Found. of Oyster Bay, 1991-94; trustee Dowling Coll., Oakdale, N.Y., 1993—; adv. bd. Westbury (N.Y.) Gardens, 1993—; chmn. adv. bd. Long Island chpt. Save the Children, 1995—. Recipient Vol. of Yr. award Jr. League L.I., 1984, 85, Outstanding Vol. Svcs. and Commitment award County of Nassau, 1989, Juliette Low award Nassau County Girl Scouts, L.I., 1991, Disting. Leadership award, L.I., 1991, Outstanding Community Vol. award Jr. League of L.I., 1991-92. Mem. P.E.O. (pres. 1985-87), The Creek Inc., Meadowbrook Club Inc., Lost Tree Club, Kappa Kappa Gamma (alumna pres. 1971-72). Republican. Congregationalist.

ELLIS, BERNICE, financial planning company executive, investment advisor; b. Bklyn.; d. Samuel and Clara (Schrier) H.; m. Seymour Scott Ellis; children: Michele, Wayne. BA, Bklyn. Coll.; MS, Queens Coll., 1970. Cert. fin. planner, N.Y. 1987, elem. educator, N.Y.C. Elem. tchr. L.I. Sch. Dists., Merrick, N.Y.; tchr. reading N.Y.C. Bd. of Edn., Bklyn., 1972-73; coordinator Reading is Fundamental, Lawrence, N.Y., 1973-75; pres., founder N.Y. State Assn. for the Gifted and Talented, Valley Stream, N.Y., 1974-87; pres. Ellis Planning, Valley Stream, N.Y., 1984—; cons. Nassau County Bd. Coop. Ednl. Svcs., Westbury, N.Y., 1973-74; adminstrv. intern region II U.S. Office Edn., 1977-78; adj. asst. prof. Nassau C.C., Garden City, N.Y., 1975-91, adj. assoc. prof., 1991-94, adj. full prof., 1995—; fin. commentator Money Talk radio program WHPC FM. Contbr. articles to profl. jours and fin. newsletters. Recipient Ednl. Professions Devel. Act fellow CUNY Inst. for Remediations Skills for Coll. Personnel, Queensborough Community Coll., 1970-73. Mem. AAUW (North Shore bd., chmn. Money Talk 1991—), Inst. for Cert. Fin. Planners, Inst. for Cert. Fin. Planners L.I. (bd. dirs.), Internat. Assn. Fin. Planners (legis. com. L.I. chpt. 1986-87), N.Y. State Reading Assn., Adj. Faculty Assn. Nassau Community Coll., Sales Exec. Club N.Y., L.I. C. of C. Office: Ellis Planning Inc 628 Golf Dr Valley Stream NY 11581-3550

ELLIS, BERNICE ALLRED, personnel executive; b. Lincoln, Ala., Mar. 15, 1932; d. Bernard Bobo and Lucille (Hogue) Allred; m. Marvin Leonard Ellis; 1 child, Jeffrey Craig. Student, Ala. A&M U., 1990, U. Ala., Huntsville, 1990, Gadsden State C.C., Ala., 1993. Personnel staffing specialist Bd. of U.S. Civil Svc. Examiners, Anniston, Ala., 1957-66; personnel mgmt. specialist Dept. of Army, Anniston, 1966-73; tech. svcs. officer Dept. of Army, 1973-74; personnel mgmt. specialist Dept. of Army, Redstone Arsenal, Ala., 1974-79; supervisory personnel mgmt. specialist U.S. Army Europe, Mannheim, Fed. Republic of Germany, 1979-83; tech. svcs. officer U.S. Army Europe, Darmstadt, Fed. Republic of Germany, 1983-86; supervisory personnel mgmt. specialist Dept. of Army, Fort Ritchie, Md., 1986-87; ret., 1987; tax preparer H&R Block, Gadsden, Ala., 1994, 95; tax preparer H&R Block, Gadsden, 1994-95, Etowah Chem., Gadsden, 1995-96. Vol. Huntsville Bot. Gardens, 1989-92; mem. local group Master Gardeners, Huntsville, 1990, Huntsville Wildflower Assn, 1990-92, State and Local Master Gardeners Assn., 1990-93. Mem. Huntsville Bot. Soc. (vol.), Ala. Master Gardeners Assn. (local and state vol.), Huntsville Wildflower Assn. Home: 82 Ty Pl Ohatchee AL 36271-9231

ELLIS, CAROLLYN, religious organization administrator; b. McPherson, Kans., Aug. 25, 1938; d. Joseph Hugh Reid and Lola Jean (Fairbairn Reid) Robinson; m. Raymond Wendel Ellis, Aug. 22, 1960; children: Timothy Ray, Wendel Joseph, Annette Jean, Janette Ruth. Diploma, Greenville Coll.; postgrad., U. Mich., Nova U. Pres. Women's Ministries Internat., 1989—; exec. v.p. Tykestown U.S.A., 1992-93; regional v.p. Free Meth. Found., Indpls., 1993—; now pres. Women's Ministries Internat. Home: 8531 Chapel Pines Dr Indianapolis IN 46234-2161 Office: Free Meth Ch of NA PO Box 535002 Indianapolis IN 46253-5002*

ELLIS, CAROLYN TERRY, lawyer; b. N.Y.C., Apr. 20, 1949; d. Francis Martin and Sarah Baker (Ames) Ellis; m. H. Lake Wise, Feb. 27, 1982; children: Carolyn Campbell Wise, Burke Ames. BA, U. Chgo., 1971; JD, NYU, 1974. Bar: N.Y. 1975. Rsch. analyst Dept. Justice, N.Y.C., 1973-74; assoc. Lord, Day & Lord, N.Y.C., 1974-84, ptnr., 1984-86; ptnr. Coudert Bros., N.Y.C., 1986—; instr. Bklyn. Law Sch., 1980-82. Mem. ABA, N.Y. State Bar Assn., Assn. of Bar of City of N.Y. (antitrust and trade regulation com. 1989-92, internat. trade com. 1993-95). Office: Coudert Bros 1114 Avenue Of The Americas New York NY 10036-7703

ELLIS, CYNTHIA ATKINSON, judge; b. Ft. Myers, Fla., Oct. 9, 1955; d. Thomas Harris and Alice Atkinson; m. Gerald Francis Ellis, Dec. 29, 1975. BA, U. Fla., 1976, JD, 1978. Bar: Fla. 1979, Collier County 1988. Asst. state's atty. State Atty's Office, Gainesville, Fla., 1978-86, Naples, Fla., 1986-89; county judge Collier County Courthouse, Naples, 1990—. Chairperson Naples Alliance for Children, 1990-92; bd. dirs. YMCA, pres., 1996—; bd. dirs. Naples, 1991, Consumer Credit Svcs. of S.W. Fla., 1991-92; adv. coun. Collier County Extension, Naples, 1990-94, chair, 1991-93; bd. trustees Big Cypress Wilderness Inst., 1996—. Recipient She Knows Where She's Going, Girls, Inc., 1991. Mem. Fla. Bar Assn., Collier County Bar Assn., Nat. Assn. of Women Judges, Fla. Ctr. for Children and Youth. Roman Catholic. Office: Collier County Courthouse Naples FL 34112

ELLIS, J. RENEE ELEY, special events administrator; b. Mobile, Ala., June 8, 1959; d. Howard and Barbara (Mallett) Eley; m. Larry Ellis, Mayy 28, 1994. BS in Leisure Svcs., U. South Ala., 1981, MPA, 1991. Activities therapist II Charter Hosp., Mobile, 1981-84; cmty. activities coord. Cmty. Activities Program, Mobile, 1984-86; program supr. City of Mobile Recreation Dept., 1986-91; spl. events mgr. City of Mobile, 1991—; sec. First Night Mobile, 1991—; bd. dirs. BayFest, Inc., Mobile; sec.,v.p., pres. Pub. Employees Tng. Coun., Mobile, 1988-90. Bd. dirs. U. South Ala. Leusire Svcs. Adv. Com., Mobile, 1986-87, Children's Musical Theatre, Mobile, 1987-91; mem. children's shopping spree Mobile Jaycees, 1988; mem. quality coun. City of Mobile, 1995—; mem. Leadership Mobile, 1996—. Recipient Recreation Program award Mobile Assn. for Retarded Citizens, 1989, Ala. Assn. for Retarded Citizens, 1990; named Career Woman of Yr., Gayfers Career Club, 1993, Jaycee of Month, Mobile, 1988. Mem. Nat. Soc. Fund Raising Execs., Internat. Festival Assn., Southeastern Festival and Events Assocs. (treas. 1995—), Art Patrons League. Republican.

ELLIS, JANE MARIE, real estate manager; b. Pittsfield, Mass., May 3, 1934; d. George and Delia Julia (Daly) Price; m. John LeRoy Waldron, Sept. 1, 1958 (dec. Jan. 1986); children: Jane Elizabeth Moser, John LeRoy Waldron III; m. Porter Duquette, Jan. 25, 1992. BS, Bryant Coll., 1955. Exec. sec. Pratt & Whitney Aircraft, East Hartford, Conn., 1955-57, GE, Pittsfield, 1957-58; real estate mgr. Milton, Pa., 1969—; dir. West Milton (Pa.) State Bank. Mem. AAUW (past treas. 1989—), Bucknell Golf Club, Willbrook Golf Club, Lithfield Golf Club. Republican. Roman Catholic. Home and Office: 21 Wilson Circle Milton PA 17847 also: 688 Tidewater Cir Pawleys Island SC 29585

ELLIS, KAY CROSBY, fundraiser; b. Dallas, Sept. 5, 1945; d. Albert S. and Frances B. (Rowland) Crosby; m. Frank C. Ellis, Jr., May 27, 1972; children: Sarah Elizabeth, Mary Katherine. BA, Tex. Christian U., 1967. Reporter, feature writer Dallas Morning News, 1967-74; free-lance writer/publicist Dallas, 1974-94; v.p. devel. Juliette Fowler Homes, Dallas, 1994—. Contbr. articles to mags. including Archtl. Digest, So. Accents, Dallas-Ft. Worth Home and Garden, Texas Homes. Bd. dirs. Greater Dallas Cmty. of Chs., 1991-93, v.p. bd. dirs., 1994. Recipient Matrix award Women in Comm., Dallas, 1974. Mem. Nat. Soc. Fund Raising Execs. Mem. Christian Ch. (Disciples of Christ). Office: Juliette Fowler Homes Inc 100 S Fulton Dallas TX 75214

ELLIS, MARY CATHERINE, secondary education educator; b. Anderson, S.C.; married; (div. July 1983). BA, Benedict Coll., 1960; MEd, Marygrove Coll., 1972. Cert. in emotional impairment. English tchr. Williston (S.C.) H.S., 1960-62, Bates H.S., Danville, Ky., 1962-64, Ctrl. H.S., Detroit, 1964-68, Webber Middle Sch., Detroit, 1968-80, Northwestern H.S., Detroit, 1980—; adv. bd. Northwestern Health Ctr., Detroit, 1989-92. Treas. 5200-5400 Pacific Block Club, Detroit, 1988-92. Mem. ASCD, Top Ladies Distinction, Alpha Kappa Alpha (parlimentarian), Phi Delta Kappa. Roman Catholic. Home: 5348 Pacific St Detroit MI 48204-4223 Office: Northwestern HS 2200 W Grand Blvd Detroit MI 48208-1178

ELLIS, MARY LOUISE HELGESON, insurance company executive; b. Albert Lea, Minn., May 29, 1943; d. Stanley Orville and Neoma Lois (Guthier) Helgeson; children: Christopher, Tracy; m. David Readinger, Nov. 5, 1994. BS in Pharmacy, U. Iowa, 1966; MA in Pub. Adminstrn., Iowa State U., 1982, postgrad., 1982-83. Faculty Duquesne U., Pitts., 1977; cons. in pharmacy, Colville, Wash., 1978-79; dir. pharmacy Mt. Carmel Hosp., Colville, 1978-79; clin. pharmacist Iowa Vets. Home, Marshalltown, Iowa, 1980-81; instr. Iowa Valley Community Coll., Marshalltown, 1981-83; dir. Iowa Dept. Substance Abuse, Des Moines, 1983-86; dir. State of Iowa Pub. Health, dir. Iowa Dept. Pub. Health, Des Moines, 1986-90; spl. cons. health affairs Blue Cross/Blue Shield of Iowa, 1990-91; v.p. Blue Cross/Blue Shield of Iowa and S.D., 1991—; chair Iowa Health Data Commn., Des Moines, 1986-90; bd. dirs. Health Policy Corp. Iowa, 1986-90; adj. asst. prof. U. Iowa, Iowa City, 1984—; comd. officer U.S. Food & Drug Adminstrn., 1989-90; mem. alumnae bd. dirs. U. Iowa Coll. of Pharmacy, 1989—; chair Nat. Commn. Accreditation of Ambulance Svcs., 1992—. Mem. Iowa State Bd. Health, 1981-83, v.p., 1982-83; mem. adv. council Iowa Valley Community Coll., 1983-85. Recipient Woman of Achievement award Des Moines YWCA, 1988. Mem. Iowa Pharmacists Assn., Am. Pub. Health Assn., Iowa Pub. Health Assn. (bd. dirs., Henry Albert award 1990), Alpha Xi Delta, Phi Kappa Phi, Pi Sigma Alpha. Republican. Home: 503 Hwy R57 Norwalk IA 50211 Office: Blue Cross and Blue Shield Iowa 636 Grand Ave Des Moines IA 50309-2502

ELLIS, NANCY KEMPTON, educator; b. Chgo., Nov. 3, 1943; d. Robert Lawrence and Mildred Elizabeth (Kitcher) Kempton; m. William Grenville Ellis, Dec. 30, 1963; children: William Grenville Jr., Bradford Graham. AA, Endicott Coll., 1963; BA, Castleton State Coll., 1970; MA, Marian Coll., 1989. Tutor remedial reading Waterville (Maine) Pub. Schs., 1975-79, migrant tutor, 1980, tchr. 1st grade, 1980-81; tchr. 4th grade Vassalboro (Maine) Pub. Schs., 1981-82; dir. study skills Wayland Acad., Beaver Dam, Wis., 1983-89, chair ednl. support, 1989-91, dir. spl. programs, 1993-95, co-pres., 1982-95; chair Wis. Ind. Sch. Educators, 1985-89, conf. co-chair, 1988; active Wis. Fellowship of Poets, 1993-95; wildlife presenter Beaver Dam Pub. Schs., 1994-95; presenter in field. Editor Marshland Monarch, 1984-88, Spouse News. Bd. dirs., festival dir. Beaver Dam Arts Assn., 1990-93; bd. dirs. AAUW Beaver Dam, 1992-95; coord. Beaver Dam Cmty. Forum on Health Care.

ELLIS, NANETTE C., home-based specialist; b. Georgetown, Tex., Aug. 1, 1943; d. Ernest Nelson and Gladys Beatrice (Anderson) Johnson; m. Howard Norman Ellis, July 18, 1970; children: Jay, Heidi, Kirsten. BS, Tex. Luth. Coll., Sequin, 1965; MEd, Lincoln U., Jefferson City, Mo., 1990. Rsch. technician Shrine Burns Hosp. for Crippled Children, Galveston, Tex., 1966-70, U. Tex. Med. Br., Galveston, 1965-66, 70-71; dir. family planning OEO, Galveston, 1971-72; in-sch. suspension supr. Dubuque (Iowa) Sr. High Sch., 1979-80; substitute tchr. Cheylin High Sch., Bird City, Kans., 1980-84; tchr. sci. Jefferson City High Sch., 1984-90; guidance counselor Russellville (Mo.) High Sch., 1990-95; home-based specialist Luth. Child and Family Svcs., Randolph County, Ill., 1996—. Contbr. articles to profl. jours. Primary election judge Rep. Party, Galveston, 1968-72; county sec., del. to Rep. State Confs., 1966, 70; v.p. Cheyenne County Com. on Alcohol and Drug Abuse, St. Francis, Kans., 1981-84; mem. subcom. Human Rels. Commn. for Prison Reform, Galveston, 1969-70; dir. Trinity Luth. Confirmation Choir, 1984-92; mem. com. on discipline Evang. Luth. Ch. in Am., 1991-97; multicultural change team Cen. States Synod, 1991-95, parish ministry Assoc. Cen. States Synod. Recipient various awards. Mem. Am. Assn. Christian Counselors. Home: Box 280 Campbell Hill IL 62916 Office: Lutheran Child & Family Svcs Ill 2408 Lebanon Ave Belleville IL 62221

ELLIS, PATRICIA JOAN, early childhood education educator; b. Louisville, Mar. 12, 1945; d. Bert Hale and Joan Hall (Casley) E. BS in Elem. Edn., U. Ga., 1967; MA in Early Childhood Edn., Oglethorpe U., 1985; Ednl. Specialist in Early Childhood Edn., Ga. State U., 1988, doctoral candidate, 1988—. Cert. early childhood educator, Ga., ednl. specialist, Ga. Tchr. Southland Acad., Americus, Ga., 1968 69, Cobb County Schs., Marietta, Ga., 1971-73, 84—; presenter in field of early childhood edn.; cons. Ga. Childcare Coun., Atlanta, 1993, Psychol. Corp., San Antonio, 1993; workshop presenter in field; mem. Ga. task force on remedial reading. Sec. Kappa Kappa Gamma, Atlanta, 1980-82; Bible sch. prin. Bapt. Ch., Roswell, Ga., 1980-82; den mother, leader Cub Scouts, Roswell, 1983-85; ways and means chmn. Roswell Woman's Club, 1985-86; mem. Cobb County sci. adoption com. Mem. ASCD, APA, NEA, Cobb County Assoc. Edn. (bldg. rep. 1994), Nat. Assn. for Edn. Young Children, Am. Ednl. Rsch. Assn., Assn. for Childhood Edn. Internat., Pi Lambda Theta, Kappa Delta Pi. Baptist. Office: Cobb County Schs 514 Glover St Marietta GA 30060-2706

ELLIS, SUSAN GOTTENBERG, psychologist; b. N.Y.C., Jan. 24, 1949; d. Sam and Sally (Hirschman) Gottenberg; B.S., Cornell U., 1970; M.A., Columbia U., 1971; M.A., Hofstra U., 1975, Ph.D., 1976; m. David Roy Ellis, July 23, 1972; children: Sharon Rachel, Dana Michelle. Instr. health edn. Nassau Community Coll., Garden City, N.Y., 1971-73; sch. psychologist public schs., Somerville, N.J., 1976-77; clin. psychologist Somerset County Community Mental Health Center, Somerville, 1976-77; sch. psychologist, Pinellas County, Fla., 1977-78; instr. St. Petersburg (Fla.) Jr. Coll., 1978; clin. psychologist, Largo, Fla., 1977—; cons. Fla. Dept. Health and Rehab. Services, Med. Center Hosp., Largo, Morton Plant Hosp., Clearwater, Fla., 1978-79, N.Y. State Regents scholar, 1966-71; adj. prof. Eckerd Coll. St. Petersburg, 1988. Author: Interpret Your Dreams, 1987, A Dream Primer, 1988, Make Sense of Your Dreams, 1988. Mem. Am. Psychol. Assn., Fla. Psychol. Assn., Pinellas Psychol. Assn. (treas. 1978, polit. action chmn. 1979), Kappa Delta Pi. Club: Universal U. Suncoast (v.p. 1979-80). Office: 3233 E Bay Dr Ste 100 Largo FL 34641-1900

ELLIS, TERRY, vocalist; b. Tex., 1967. Vocalist En Vogue, Acto/Eastwest Records, N.Y.C., 1988—. Albums include Born to Sing (Platinum 1990), Funky Dovas, Remix to Sing, Runaway Love. Recipient Soul Train Music award, 1991; nominated Grammy award. Office: care En Vogue Atco/Eastwest Records 75 Rockefeller Plz New York NY 10019-6908*

ELLISON-ROSENKILDE, WENDY MAUREEN, psychologist, educator; b. Meadville, Pa., July 6, 1941; d. Allen Vincent and Anna Winifred (Hickman) Ellison; m. Roy N. Bidwell, May 28, 1982 (div.); m. Carl Edward Rosenkilde, May 24, 1992; step-children: Karen Louise Rosenkilde, Paul Eric Rosenkilde. AB in English, Allegheny Coll., 1962; MS in Neurol. Learning Disabilities, U. Pacific, 1974; MS, Calif. State U., 1984; PhD, U. So. Calif., 1983. Learning specialist South Bay Psychiatric Med. Clinic, Campbell, Calif., 1971-81; registered psychol. asst. Santa Clara County Mental Health, Pleasanton, Calif., 1981-84; intern in psychology Santa Clara County Mental Health, San Jose, Calif., 1982-83; psychologist Family Svc. East Bay, Livermore, Calif., 1985-86; psychologist child devel. ctr. Children's Hosp., San Francisco, 1985-86; affiliate staff psychologist CPC Walnut Creek (Calif.) Hosp., 1985-94; pvt. practice Pleasanton, 1985—; affiliate staff psychologist Valleycare Hosp., Pleasanton, Calif., 1993—; part-time instr. child devel. Foothill Coll., Los Altos, Calif., 1976-77, Los Positas Coll., Livermore, Calif., 1984-92. Co-author: Student Guide for Teaching for Learning, 1981. Mem. APA, Calif. Psychol. Assn., Alameda County Psychol. Assn. (pres. 1989, pres-elect and chair program and nomination coms., chair info. and referral 1986), Soc. Personality Assessment, San Francisco Psychoanalytic Inst., Livermore Valley Tennis Club, Rorschach Internat., Amador Valley Alumni Assn. (pres. 1996), Livermore C. of C., Contra Costa Wind Symphony, Valley Choral Soc., Kappa Kappa Gamma (pres. Amador Valley Alumni Assn.). Democrat. Presbyterian. Home: 2604 Crater Rd Livermore CA 94550-6603 Office: 1882 Holmes St Livermore CA 94550-6014

ELLMAN, FAYE, photojournalist; b. N.Y.C., Apr. 13, 1953; d. Martin and Bertha (Reich) Horning; m. Dennis Ellman, June 18, 1973 (div. 1981); m. Teodors Ermansons, Oct. 16, 1991; 1 child, Maia Sage. Student, Boston U.; BFA, Parsons Sch. of Design. Freelance editl. and corp. photographer, 1978—; photojournalist N.Y. Law Jour.; tchr. New Sch. for Social Rsch., fall 1988, Post Grad. Ctr. for Mental Health, 1986—; tchr. artists-in-residence program N.Y. Found. for Arts, 1987-89. Exhibited at Am. Gathering of Holocaust Survivors, Phila., 1985, Tweed Gallery, N.Y.C., 1987, Midtown Y Photography Gallery, N.Y.C., 1988, Manhattan Borough President's Gallery, 1989, Ednl. Testing Svc., Princeton, N.J., 1990, Cardozo Law Sch. Gallery, 1990, Nikon House, N.Y.C., 1990, Tokyo, 1990; photographs published in various publs. Recipient Joseph Costa award for courtroom photography, 1991. Mem. Am. Soc. Mag. Photographers, Nat. Press Photographers. Home and Studio: 270 W 25th St New York NY 10001-7306

ELLMANN, SHEILA FRENKEL, investment company executive; b. Detroit, June 8, 1931; d. Joseph and Rose (Neback) Frenkel; BA in English, U. Mich., 1953; m. William M. Ellmann, Nov. 1, 1953; children: Douglas Stanley, Carol Elizabeth, Robert Lawrence. Dir. Advance Glove Mfg. Co., Detroit, 1954-78; v.p. Frome Investment Co., Detroit, 1980-96, pres., 1996—. Mem. U. Mich. Alumni Assn., Nat. Trust Hist. Preservation. Home: 28000 Weymouth Ct Farmington Hills MI 48334

ELLNER, JOSEPHINE HELENE, art educator; b. N.Y.C., Apr. 5, 1940; d. Angelo Edward and Ann (Ballentoni) Bilello; m. Michael William Ellner, Aug. 24, 1957; children: Eileen Lorraine, Deborah Lynn, Laurence Steven. AA in Art, San Jose City Coll., 1972; BA with great distinction, San Jose State U., 1974, MA, 1976, postgrad, 1976-77; postgrad, U. Calif., Santa Cruz, 1980-81, U. Calif., San Francisco, 1985. Cert. secondary art tchr., community coll. art tchr., Calif., learning handicapped life tchr., resource specialist life tchr., administrv. credential. Art and English tchr. John Muir Jr. High Sch., San Jose, 1975-80, tchr. art, humanities, gifted, 1981-82; spl. edn. tchr. Pioneer High Sch., San Jose, 1982-84, chair art dept., 1984-91; visual arts coord., dept. chair A. Lincoln AVPA Magnet High Sch., San Jose, 1991—; with A.P. Saturday Acad. San Jose Unified Sch. Dist., 1996—; mentor tchr. San Jose Unified Sch. Dist., 1984-88; cons. Coll. Bd., San Jose, 1989—; advisor Nat. Art Honor Soc., San Jose, 1984—; co-convenor Lincoln H.S. Magnet Curriculum Coun., San Jose, 1991—; intern advisor Casa Program, San Jose, 1991—; guest curator MACLA Gallery, San Jose, Genesis Gallery, San Jose, San Jose Art League; curator Egyptian Mus. Art Gallery, San Jose, New World Gallery, San Jose, Visions Gallery, San Jose, 1970—. Paintings included in numerous pub. collections including Coll. Bd., San Jose, Calif., Foot Mus., Long Beach, Calif. Recipient award San Jose Adminstrn. Assn., 1984, grant San Jose Found., 1985, grant Calif. Tchrs. Instrnl. Incentive Program, 1986, grant Nat. League Am. Pen Women, 1994, 95, 96. Mem. Nat. Art Edn. Assn., Calif. Tchrs. Assn., NEA, San Jose Tchrs. Assn., Artists Alliance Calif., Cmty. Partnership Santa Clara County, San Jose Inst. Contemporary Art, Phi Kappa Phi. Home: 1429 Scossa Ave San Jose CA 95118-2456

ELLSWORTH, LINDA VOLLMAR, nonprofit organization administrator; b. New Prague, Minn., Nov. 22, 1945; d. Roland Emil and Julie Ann (Pokladnik) Vollmar; m. Lucius Fuller Ellsworth, July 3, 1969 (div. 1987). BA, Macalester Coll., 1967; MA, U. Del., 1969. Historian, chief bur. of rsch. Hist. Pensacola (Fla.) Preservation Bd., 1969-84; dir. Historic Tallahassee Preservation Bd., 1984-87; dir. Mid-Atlantic regional office Nat. Trust for Hist. Preservation, Phila., 1987-90; exec. dir. Conservation Ctr. for Art and Hist. Artifacts, Phila., 1990—. Co-editor: The Cultural Legacy of the Gulf Coast, 1976, Ethnic Minorities in Gulf Coast Society, 1979; co-author: Pensacola: The Deep Water City, 1982. Bd. dirs. Fla. Hist. Soc., 1975-83, Phila. Hist. Preservation Corp., 1995—; mem. Fla. Nat. Register Rev. Com., 1982-87. Fellow Nat. Endowment for Arts, 1973, Royal Oak fellow Attingham Summer Sch., 1989, Brit. Coun. fellow, 1995. Mem. Am. Assn. for State and Local History (pres. bd. dirs. 1986-88), Am. Assn. Mus., Hist. Soc. Pa., Nat. Trust for Hist. Preservation, Mid-Atlantic Assn. Mus., Athenaeum of Phila. Office: Conservation Ctr Art & Hist Artifacts 264 S 23d St Philadelphia PA 19103

ELMAN, NAOMI GEIST, artist, producer; b. Chgo.; d. Harry and Rita (Goldstein) Geist; m. Murray Elman, May 29, 1946 (dec. Dec. 1965); 1 child, Margaret (Peggy) Gillespie. Student, Hamilton Inst. for Girls, Nat. Acad. of Design, Art Students League. Personal mgr. in performing arts, prodr. concerts in N.Y.C. and Hawaii, N.Y., Hawaii, 1968-80. One-woman show Churchill Gallery, 1962, Pen and Brush Club, 1986; exhibited in group shows. Vol. nurses aid pvt. and army hosps., ARC, 1939-45; v.p. N.Y. Diabetes Assn., 1955-58; mcpl. chmn. Dem. Club, Tenafly, N.J., 1958; Dem. com. woman, 1959-61; bd. dirs. Nat. Children's Cardiac Home, N.Y.C., 1940-49, Bergen County Dem. Club, 1958-60. Recipient Margareet Sussman award, 1985, Salamagundi award, 1987, Julia Lucille award, 1988. Mem. Internat. Platform Assn., Soc. Mil. Widows, Retired Officers Club (life), Disabled Am. Vets., Artists Equity. Democrat. Address: 500 E 77th St New York NY 10162-0025

ELMER, DORIS EILEEN, social worker, educator; b. Oshkosh, Wis., Mar. 14, 1936; d. Norman Edgar and Loretta Viola (Spooner) E. BS, U. Wis., 1957; MA, U. Chgo., 1960. Social worker Winnebago (Wis.) State Hosp., 1960-63; psychiat. social worker Fond du Lac (Wis.) Mental Health Clinic, 1963-68; sch. social worker Palm Beach County Schs., West Palm Beach, Fla., 1968-75; social worker Gold Coast Home Health, Pompano Beach, Fla., 1976-81; pvt. counselor Deerfield Beach, Fla., 1976-88; social worker Easter Seal Rehab. Ctr., Melbourne, Fla., 1988-90; residential supr. Youth Svc. Ctrs., Inc., Merrit Island, Fla., 1990—; adj. prof. Wilmington Coll., Boca Raton, Fla., 1976-81, Coll. of Boca Raton, 1976-81; bd. dirs. Paquette House, Fond du Lac; cons. police depts., South Fla., 1969-87. Publicity chair Altrusa Club, Fond du Lac, 1963-68; cons. Alzheimer's Group, Melbourne, 1989-90. Mem. Wis. Assn. Mental Health Clinics (bd. dirs. 1963-68), Stroke Club (cons. 1987-90). Home: 839 Angela Ave Apt B Rockledge FL 32955-2725 Office: Holmes Regional Hospice 1900 Dairy Rd Melbourne FL 32904-4046

ELOFSON, NANCY MEYER, retired office equipment company executive; b. Glencoe, Ill., Jan. 27, 1923; d. Bernard Francis and Agnes (Ulbrich) Meyer; m. Carl L. Elofson, Nov. 27, 1946 (dec. Dec. 1991); 1 child, Peter Carl. BA, Western Coll., 1944; postgrad., SUNY, Jamestown, 1960-80. Sales corr. Scott, Foresman Pub., Chgo., 1944-46; sec., treas. Office Machines and Equipment Co., Jamestown, 1948-86; ret., 1986—. Mem. coun. camp com. Girl Scouts U.S., Jamestown, 1962-66, mem. alumnae archives com., 1992—; candidate Chautauqua County Legis., 1979; mem. choir 1st congl. United Ch. of Christ, Jamestown, 1948—, moderator, 1978-79, ch. clk., 1995, mem. ch. coun., 1990-95, chmn. 175th anniversary com., 1990-91, mem. ch. growth com., mem. long range planning com., 1993-95, bd. trustees, 1996—; founder, pres. bd. dirs. Chautauqua Adult Day Care Ctrs., Inc., Jamestown, 1981-91; pres. bd. dirs. YWCA, Jamestown, 1983-85, trustee, 1987—; mem. exec. bd./com. United Way, Jamestown, 1991—, allocations chmn., 1991-95, chmn. planning com., 1996—; active Chautauqua County Domestic Violence Guidance Team, 1994. Named Chautauqua County Caregiver of Yr., Chautauqua County Office of Aging, 1988, Vol. of Yr., United Way, 1992; recipient Caregiver's award N.Y. State Office of Aging, 1988, Women Making a Difference award Jamestown Post Jour., 1991. Mem. AAUW (sec. 1958), Women's Polit. Caucus, Jamestown Audubon Soc., Jamestown Koinonia. Home: 81 Gordon St Jamestown NY 14701-1641

ELRICK, BILLY LEE, English language educator; b. Jackson, Miss., May 21, 1941; d. William Robert and Wesley James (Hall) Chambers; m. Donald Lee Elrick, June 29, 1965; children: Laura Katherine, John William. BA, Millsaps Coll., 1963; MA in Edn., U. Phoenix, 1992. Tchr. lang. arts North Arvada (Colo.) Jr. High, 1963-92, dept. chair, 1984-92; dean Wheat Ridge (Colo.) High Sch., 1993; tchr. English Arvada (Colo.) H.S., 1993-94, 95—, asst. prin., 1994-95; asst. prin. Chatfield Sr. H.S., 1995—, Chatfield H.S., 1995—; mentor tchr. Jefferson Couty Schs.-North; workshop presenter in field. Mem. ASCD, Phi Delta Kappa, Delta Kappa Gamma (sec. 1990-94, 2d v.p. 1994—), Sigma Lambda, Kappa Delta Epsilon. Democrat. Methodist. Home: 10615 Irving Ct Westminster CO 80030-2238 Office: Chatfield Sr H S 7227 So Simms Littleton CO 80127

ELROD, MARILYN A., legislative director; b. Indpls., Feb. 26, 1945; d. French M. and Burrlene (Holland) E. BA, Purdue U., 1967; postgrad., Am. U., 1967-69. Adminstrv. aide Rep. Allard K. Lowenstein, 1969-71; mem. legis. staff Rep. Ronald V. Dellums and Ho. Com. on D.C., 1971-83; mem. profl. staff Subcom. Mil. Installations and Facilities Ho. Armed Svcs. Com., 1983-89, mem. profl. staff Subcom. Rsch. and Devel., 1989-92; staff dir. Ho. Com. Armed Svcs., 1993-94; democratic staff dir. Ho. Nat. Sec. Com., 1996—. Mem. Pi Sigma Alpha, Kappa Sigma Phi. Office: Ho Nat Sec Coms Rm 2120 Rayburn House Office Bldg Washington DC 20515

ELROD, MIMI COBB MILNER, academic administrator; b. Atlanta, Jan. 30, 1944; d. Benjamin Charles and Eleanor Wuerpel (O'Beirne) Milner; m. John William Elrod, Jan. 21, 1940; children: Adam Milner, Joshua O'Beirne. BS, Oglethorpe U., 1966; MS, Iowa State U., 1977, PhD, 1980. Tchr. Cooper Jr. High N.Y.C. Pub. Schs., 1966-69, after sch. care provider, 1967-68; tchr. asst. Iowa State U., Ames, 1976-78, 79-80, instr., 1978-79, 80-81, asst. prof., 1982-84; asst. prof. Dabney Lancaster C.C., Clifton Forge, Va., 1985-86; asst. dir. admissions Washington and Lee U., Lexington, Va., 1986-90; asst. dir. spl. programs Washington and Lee U., Lexington, 1990-91, assoc. dir. spl. programs, dir. summer scholars, 1991—; child/family devel. cons., 1984-90. Contbr. articles to profl. jours. Vol./hotline adv. Project Horizon, Lexington, 1985—, bd. dirs., pres., 1989-97; vol. parent adv. com. Lylburn Downing Sch., Lexington, 1985-86; vol., adv. bd. mem. Total Action Against Poverty, Lexington, 1991—; bd. dirs., pres. Rockbridge Mental Health Assn., 1985-88; bd. dirs. Assn. for Retarded Citizens, 1985-88; bd. dirs., pres. Rockbridge Area Cmty. Svc. Bd., 1989-94; mem., elder Lexington Presbyn. Ch., 1991—. Recipient Women and Leadership award Washington and Lee U., 1996; Iowa Home Econs. Assn. scholar Iowa State U., Ames, 1977-78; Pearl Swanson Grad. fellow Iowa State U., Ames, 1978-79; grantee Home Econs. Rsch. Inst., 1980-81, 81-82, Iowa State U. Rsch. Found., 1982, others. Mem. Soc. for Rsch. in Child Devel., Nat. Assn. for the Edn. of Young Children, Va. Assn. for the Edn. of Young Children, Nat. Head Start Assn., So. Assn. on Children Under Six, Omicron Nu, Phi Kappa Nu, Phi Kappa Phi. Democrat. Home: 2 University Pl Lexington VA 24450 Office: Washington and Lee Univ Spl Programs 117 W Washington St Lexington VA 24450

ELSON, MARYGRACE, obstetrician and gynecologist; b. Champaign-Urbana, Ill., Nov. 2, 1956; d. James J. and Nancy (Popel) E.; m. Robert Uteg, Aug. 16, 1980; children: Charlotte Uteg, Gabriela Uteg. AB in Chemistry, Vassar Coll., 1978; MD, U. Ill. Coll. Medicine, Rockford, 1982. Diplomate Am. Bd. Ob-Gyn. Intern in ob-gyn. U. Wis. Hosp. and Clinics, Madison, 1982-83, resident in ob-gyn., 1982-86, asst. prof. ob-gyn., 1986-88; pvt. practice ob-gyn. Chico (Calif.) Med. Group, 1988-90, Glen Ellyn (Ill.) Clinic, 1990—; vol. cons. physician DuPage Cmty. Clinic, Wheaton, Ill., 1992—. Aux. mem. Sunny Pl. Family Ctr., Wheaton, 1990—; cantor St. Michael Ch., Wheaton, 1995—. Fellow ACOG; mem. Am. Med. Women's Assn., Am. Fertility Soc., Alumni Assn. Vassar Coll., Chgo. Vassar Club. Roman Catholic. Office: Glen Ellyn Clinic 454 Pennsylvania Ave Glen Ellyn IL 60137

ELSON, SARAH LEE, art historian; b. Valley Forge, Pa., Oct. 1, 1962; d. John Everett and Ione (Coker) Lee; m. Louis Goodman Elson, Aug. 26, 1989; 1 child, Isabel Coker Elson. BA, Princeton U., 1984; MA, Columbia U., 1990, MPhil in Art History, 1992. Prof. English Beijing Normal U., 1984-85; pub. affairs asst. Guggenheim Mus., N.Y.C., 1985-87; lectr. Met. Mus. Art, N.Y.C., 1990-92; freelance lectr. Nat. Gallery, London, 1994—; rschr. Tate Gallery, London, 1992-93; fellow The Frick Collection, N.Y.C., 1990—; rschr. Met. Mus., 1990-92. Author catalogs. Trustee Coker Coll., Hartsville, S.C., 1991—. Nat. Endowment for Arts fellow, 1988, Pres.'s fellow Columbia U., 1988-90, Luce Travel grantee, 1992. Mem. Woolnoth Soc. in the City of London, Jr. League of London. Democrat. Home: 2 Kensington Gate, London W8 5NA, England

ELSON, SUZANNE GOODMAN, community activist; b. Memphis, Oct. 17, 1937; d. Charles F. and Isabel (Ehrlich) Goodman; m. Edward Elliott Elson, Aug. 24, 1957; children: Charles Myer, Louis Goodman, Harry II. Student Randolph-Macon Women's Coll., Lynchburg, Va.; B.A., Agnes Scott Coll., 1959. Sec. Nat. Council Jewish Women, N.Y.C., 1977-79; pres., Nat. Mental Health Assn., 1980-82, pres., 1986-87; trustee, Randolph Macon Woman's Coll., 1986—, Am. Federation of Arts, 1992—; chmn. Am. Craft Coun., 1989-92, honorary chmn., 1992-94; bd. dirs. Rosalynn Carter Inst., Nat. Coun. Medicine Emory U., 1988—; bd. trustees Project Interconnections, Inc., Atlanta, 1989—, Va. Mus. of Fine Art., 1992—, High Mus. Fine Art, 1993—; bd. regents U. System of Ga., 1993—. Home: 65 Valley Rd NW Atlanta GA 30305-1115

ELWER, MARILYN ANN, counselor; b. Delphos, Ohio, Mar. 11, 1946; d. Joseph John and Anna Viola (Fischer) E. BA in Math., Coll. of St. Francis, Joliet, Ill., 1972; MA in Religious Studies, Seattle U., 1981; MA in Counseling, Heidelberg Coll., 1991; postgrad., U. Toledo, 1994—. Joined Sisters of St. Francis, 1964. Tchr. St. Bernard Sch., New Washington, Ohio, 1967-68, St. Mary Sch., Millersville, Ohio, 1968-69, Our Lady of Consolation Sch., Carey, Ohio, 1970-76, St. Francis H.S., Tiffin, Ohio, 1976-78; personel specialist Sisters of St. Francis, Tiffin, 1978-84; campus minister Heidelberg Coll., Tiffin, 1984-90, math. instr., 1987-90; counselor Cath. Charities, Fostoria, Ohio, 1990—. Vol. FISH, Tiffin, 1978-79, Women's Shelter, New Riegel, Ohio, 1980-81; youth moderator Cath. Youth Orgn., Carey, Ohio, 1971-76; co-leader Youth Elect Svc., Seneca County, Ohio, 1985-88. Mem. ACA, APA (student affiliate), Ohio Counseling Assn. Roman Catholic. Home: 3802 Watson Ave # 2 Toledo OH 43612 Office: Cath Charities 1933 Spielbusch Toledo OH 43697

ELY, JOANN DENICE, health science facility administrator; b. Bay City, Mich., Dec. 18, 1951; d. Phillip C. Maurer and Elsie (Etherington) McGowan. AS, Eas. Mich. U., 1979; BS in Pharmacy, Mercer U., 1982, PharmD, 1983. Registered Pharmacist, Ga., Fla. Pharmacy intern Drs. Meml. Hosp., Atlanta, 1979-82; pharmacist Egleston Hosp., Atlanta, 1982-84; clin. specialist Lee Meml. Hosp., Ft. Myers, Fla., 1984-90; asst. clin. prof. U. Fla., 1989-90; clin. mgr. Beyer Hosp., Ypsilanti, Mich., 1991—. Lectr. Arthritis Found., Ft. Myers, 1984-91. Mem. Am. Soc. Hosp. Pharmacists, So. Gulf Soc. Hosp. Pharmacists (pres. 1988), Fla. Soc. Hosp. Pharmacists, Am. Soc. Parenteral and Enteral Nutrition, Phi Theta Kappa. Republican. Episcopalian. Home: 185 E Shore Dr Whitmore Lake MI 48189-9441

ELY, LISA DORENE, newspaper managing editor; b. Akron, Ohio, Aug. 22, 1961; d. James T. and Ouida A. (DeSett) Ely-Pullin. BS in Polit. Sci./Pan African Studies, Kent State U., 1984. Police reporter Chgo. Daily Defender, 1986; editor/reporter Chatham-Southeast and Southend Citizen Newspaper, 1986-88; editor, acting mng. editor Hyde Park (Ill.) Citizen Newspaper, 1989-92; mng. editor Operation PUSH Mag., Chgo., 1994—, Chgo. Citizen Newspaper Group, 1993—; freelance photojournalist, 1986—; health-fitness editor Upscale mag., Atlanta, 1989; entertainment writer Jam Sessions mag., Chgo., 1986; moderator/panelist various forums, workshops, confs., secondary and elem. sch. career days and univ. forums; guest TV appearances include Oprah Winfrey Show, 1987, 91, Jerry Springer show, 1994; numerous radio and guest host spots, WVON, WBEZ, WVAZ, WBBM and WLIP; appear bi-weekly on local cable talk shows; media cons. Loyola U., Northwestern U., U. Chgo., Kent State U., DePaul U. Adv. bd. Cmty. Mental Health Coun., 1992—, Ill. Generations: African-Am. Travel Guide, 1994—, Woodson North Aiming Toward Success; publicity adv. bd. DuSable Mus.; bd. dirs. The Clifford Brown Golf Found., 1995—; mem. task force on African-Am. history and cultural affairs Ill. Sec. of State, 1994—. Named to Outstanding Young Women of Am., 1988, 91; recipient One Village award, 1992, 2 awards Ill. Press. Assn., Miller Brewing/A. Phillip Randolph Messenger award, 1996, Orchid award Top Ladies of Distinction, 1996; recipient 1st place award for best story Nat. Newspaper Pub. Assn., 1992, 2d place best news story, 1995, numerous second pl. awards. Mem. Nat. Assn. Black Journalists, Chgo. Assn. Black Journalists (bd. dirs. 1992-93), Internat. Press Club of Chgo. (bd. dirs. 1993—), Chgo. Film Critics Assn., Chgo. Press Photographers, Nat. Polit. Congress of Black Women (spl. award 1995), Delta Sigma Theta (alumnae charter mem. Chgo. Lakeshore chpt.).

ELY, MARICA MCCANN, interior designer; b. Pachuca, Mex., May 2, 1907 (parents Am. citizens); d. Warner and Mary Evans (Cook) McCann; m. Northcutt Ely, Dec. 2, 1931; children: Michael and Craig (twins), Parry Haines. B.A., U. Calif.-Berkeley, 1929; diploma Pratt Inst. of Art, N.Y.C., 1931. Free-lance interior designer, Washington and Redlands, Calif., 1931—; lectr. on flower arranging and fgn. travel, 1931—; prof. Sogetsu Ikebana Sch., Tokyo, 1972. Art editor (calendar) Nat. Capital Garden Club League, 1957-58. Pres. Kenwood Garden Club, Md.; bd. dirs. Nat. Libr. Blind, Washington; mem. adv. bd. George C. Marshall Home Preservation Fund, Inc. Leesburg, Va.; v.p. bd. dirs. Washington Hearing and Speech Soc., 1969; co-founder Delta Gamma Found. Pre-Sch. Blind Children, Order of Delta Gamma Rose. Finalist Nat. Silver Bowl Competition, Jackson-Perkins Co., 1966; garden shown on nat. tour Am. Hort. Soc., 1985. Mem. Calif. Arboretum Found., Redlands Hort. and Improvement Soc. (bd. dirs. 1982-94), Redlands Panhellenic Soc., Redlands Country Club, Chevy Chase Club (D.C.), Delta Gamma.

ELY-RAPHEL, NANCY, diplomat; b. N.Y.C, Feb. 4, 1937; d. Thomas Clarkson and Margaret (Merritt) Halliday; widowed; children: John Duff Ely, Robert Duff Ely, Stephanie Joyce Raphel. AB, Syracuse U., 1957; JD, U. San Diego, 1968. Bar: Calif. 1968, U.S. Supreme Ct. 1976. Dep. city atty. City San Diego, 1969-70; asst. U.S. atty. So. Dist. Calif., 1970-71; assoc. Tyler, Cooper, Grant, Bowerman and Keefe, New Haven, 1971-72; from asst. to assoc. dean Sch. Law Boston U., 1972-75; atty.-advisor U.S. Dept. State, Washington, 1975-77; spl. atty. Boston Strike Force U.S. Dept. Justice, 1977-78; asst. legal advisor African Affairs U.S. Dept. State, Washington, 1978-87, asst. legal advisor Nuclear Affairs, 1988-89; dep. asst. Sec. of State Bur. Democracy, Human Rights and Labor Affairs, Washington, 1989-93, prin. dep. asst., 1993-95; Bosnia coord. Bur. European and Can. Affairs, 1995—. Mem. Council on Fgn. Rels., 1988—, Obor Found., 1988—. Recipient Outstanding Alumni award U. San Diego Law Sch., 1979, Superior Honor award U.S. Dept. State, Washington, 1983, 84, Presdl. Meritorious Svc. award U.S. Govt., Washington, 1986, 94, Presdl. Disting. Svc. award, 1992. Home: 1304 30th St NW Washington DC 20007-3343 Office: Dept State European and Can Affairs 2201 C St NW Washington DC 20520-0001

ELZA, JANE LOUISE, political science educator; b. Knoxville, Tenn., Oct. 9, 1943; d. Karl Martin and Ruth Katherine (Morris) E. BS, U. Tenn., 1965, MA, 1966, PhD, 1974. Instr. Stephen F. Austin Coll., Nacodoches, Tex., 1967-69, U. Tenn., Knoxville, 1969-73; asst. Tuskegee (Ala.) Inst., 1973-74; assoc. Valdosta (Ga.) State Coll., 1974-92; mem. exec. com. Academic Alliance, 1991—. Pres. Nat. Women's Polit. Caucus, Valdosta, 1987-88. Mem. NOW, AAUP, So. Assn. Pre-law Advisors (pres. 1991). Office: Valdosta State Coll Dept Polit Sci Valdosta GA 31698

EMANUEL, BEVERLY S., geneticist; b. Phila., Aug. 16, 1941. PhD, U. Pa., 1972. Cert. PhD med. geneticist, clin. cytogeneticist. Geneticist Children's Hosp., Phila.; prof. pediatrics and genetics U. Pa., Phila., 1988—. Mem. AAAS, ABMG, ASHG, HUGO. Office: Children's Hosp Phila 10th Fl Abramson Rsch Ctr Philadelphia PA 19104

EMANUEL, EVELYN LOUISE, nurse; b. Curaçao, Netherlands Antilles, May 16, 1958; came to the U.S., 1980; d. Joshua George and Eileen Aurora (Phillip) E.; children: Jamal, Victor. AAS, Bronx (N.Y.) C.C., 1990; BSN, Coll. New Rochelle, 1994, postgrad., 1995—. RN, N.Y.; cert. med.-surg. nursing, ANCC.; chemotherapy cert.; respiratory cert., cardio pulmonary cert. Nursing asst. Our Lady of Mercy Med. Ctr., Bronx, 1987-89, LPN, 1989-90, RN oncology unit, 1990—. Tchr. Sunday Sch., Trinity Episcopal Ch., 1992—. Home: 4140 Carpenter Ave Apt 3D Bronx NY 10466-2633 Office: Our Lady Mercy Med Ctr 600 E 233rd St Bronx NY 10466-2697

EMANUEL-SMITH, ROBIN LESLEY, special education educator; m. Allen Weston Smith, Apr. 14, 1983; children: David, Ariel, Weston. BS in Engring., U.S. Mil. Acad., 1981; BS in Health-Phys. Edn. summa cum laude, Cameron U., Lawton, Okla., 1992; M Spl. Edn., Coll. of St. Rose, Albany, N.Y., 1995. Cert. spl. edn., health and phys. edn. tchr., N.Y. Enlisted U.S. Army, 1974-76, commd. 2d lt., 1981, advanced through grades to capt., 1984, resigned, 1990; tchr. spl. edn. Ulster County Bd. Coop. Ednl. Svcs., Port Ewen, N.Y., 1992—. Roman Catholic. Office: Ulster County Bd Coop Ednl Svs Rt 32 New Paltz NY 12561

EMBRY, KAREN THOMPSON, elementary education educator; b. Atlanta, Sept. 25, 1958; d. James Newton and Billie Reese (Cleveland) Thompson; m. Sterling Charters Embry, Aug. 14, 1982 (div. Jan. 1994); 1 child, Juliette Reese Embry; stepchildren: Hugh Cooper Embry III, Headen Davidson Embry. BA in Early Childhood Edn., LaGrange Coll., 1980; postgrad., North Ga. Coll., 1989-90, Lanier Tech. Inst., 1996—. Cert. EMT intermediate level, 1996. Kindergarten tchr. Hall County Bd. Edn., Gainesville, Ga., 1980-81; 1st grade tchr. Hall County Bd. Edn., 1981-90, ESOL tchr., 1990-95, 5th grade tchr., 1995—; mem. adv. com. on ESOL needs for Hall County, 1993—, curriculum devel. com. ESOL Tchrs. of Hall County, 1993—. Contbr. articles to newspapers. Vol. Gateway House for Battered Women, Gainesville, 1992, Meals on Wheels, Gainesville, 1993; vol. interpreter Good News at Noon Med. Clinic, Gainesville, 1994. Mem. Ga. Assn. Educators, Hall County Assn. Educators, Jr. League of Gainesville-Hall County. Democrat. Methodist. Home: 4588 Buckhorn Rd Gainesville GA 30506-3024 Office: Myers Elem Sch 2676 Candler Rd Gainesville GA 30507-8961

EMCH-DÉRIAZ, ANTOINETTE SUZANNE, historian, educator; b. Geneva, Nov. 9, 1935; came to U.S., 1964; d. Louis Georges and Renée Gabrielle (Bonnet) Dériaz; m. Gérard Gustav Emch, July 25, 1959; children: Florence Christiane, René-Didier Guillaume. PhD, U. Rochester, N.Y., 1984. Tech. asst. Am. Inst. of Physics, N.Y.C., 1968-70; vis. scholar U. Pa., Phila., 1981; rsch. assoc. U. Rochester, 1984; asst. prof. U. Miss., Oxford, 1985-92; mem. adj. faculty U. Fla., Gainesville, 1992—; vis. scholar U. Goettingen, Germany, 1985, Wellcome Inst., London, 1994, U. Vienna, 1994. Author: 18th Century Concept of Health, 1984, Tissot: Physician of the Enlightenment, 1992; contbr. chpt. to books, articles to profl. jours. Mem. AAUW, Am. Hist. Assn., Am. Assn. for History Medicine, Am. Soc. 18th-Century Studies. Presbyterian. Office: U Fla Gainesville FL 32611

EMEAGWALI, GLORIA THOMAS, humanities educator; b. Feb. 6, 1950; came to U.S., 1991; BA, U. W.I., 1973; edn. dipl., London U., 1975; MA, Toronto U., 1976; PhD, Ahmadu Bello U., Zaria, Nigeria, 1986. Asst. prof. Ahmadu Bello U., Zaria, Nigeria, 1979-86; assoc. prof. Nigerian Def. Acad., 1986, Ilorin U., Nigeria, 1986-89; vis. prof. U. W.I., Trinidad, 1989, Oxford U., U.K., 1990-91; assoc. prof. history and African studies Conn. State U., New Britain, 1991-96, prof. history and African studies, 1996—; mem. editorial bd. Review of African Political Economy, U.K., chief editor Africa Update, CCSU.; mem. adv. bd. Encyclopedia of the History of Science, Technology and Medicine, Hampshire Coll., Amherst. Editor: Historical Development of Science and Technology in Nigeria, 1992, Science and Technology in African History, 1992, African Systems of Science Technology and Art, 1993, Women Pay the Price: Structural Adjustment in Africa and the Caribbean, 1995. Fellow Oxford U., 1990; grantee Old Dominion U., 1986, 88, AAUP Conn. State award, 1992. Mem. Internat. Soc. for Study of Comp. Civilization (mem. governing body, exec. com. 1992—), World Anthrop. Soc., World Archeaol. Congress, Am. Hist. Assn., African Studies Assn. Home: 141 Francis St New Britain CT 06053-3245 Office: Cen Conn State U History/African Studies Dept New Britain CT 06050

EMEK, SHARON HELENE, business insurance and risk management specialist; b. Bklyn., Oct. 23, 1945; d. Hyman Sampson and Cynthia Gertrude (Roth) Rabinowitz; children: Aleeza Judith, Joshua Michael, Elana Yael. B.A., CCNY, 1967; M.A., Bklyn. Coll., 1970, Ed.D., Rutgers U., 1977; cert. ins. counselor. Dir. preliminary program for small coll. Bklyn. Coll., 1969-71, 73-74; dir. Am. Ctr. Reading Skills, Tel Aviv, 1972; asst. prof. Brookdale Community Coll., Lincroft, N.J., 1975-77, Rutgers U., New Brunswick, N.J., 1977-82; pres. The Emek Group, Inc., N.Y.C., 1980—; speaker profl. meetings. Author: Answers For Managers, 1986; Dealing Successfully with Key Management Issues, 1986. Contbr. articles to profl. jours. Recipient Promising Research award Nat. Council Tchrs. of English, 1978. Mem. Profl. Ins. Agents Assn., Ind. Ins. Agents Assn. Avocations: writing; reading; jogging; tennis; travel. Office: The Emek Group Inc 111 John St New York NY 10038

EMERSON, ALICE FREY, political scientist, educator emerita; b. Durham, N.C., Oct. 26, 1931; d. Alexander Hamilton and Alice (Hubbard) Frey; divorced; children: Rebecca, Peter. AB, Vassar Coll., 1953; PhD, Bryn Mawr Coll., 1964; LLD (hon.), Wheaton Coll., 1986; DHL (hon.), Trinity Coll., 1992. Tchr., Newton (Mass.) High Sch., 1956-58; mem. faculty Bryn Mawr (Pa.) Coll., 1961-64; mem. faculty U. Pa., Phila., 1966-75, asst. prof. polit. sci., 1966-75, dean of women, 1966-69, dean of students, 1969-75; pres. Wheaton Coll., Norton, Mass., 1975-91, pres. emerita, 1991—; sr. fellow Andrew Mellon Found., N.Y.C., 1991—; bd. dirs. AES Corp., Bank of Boston Corp., First Nat. Bank Boston, Champion Internat. Paper, Eastman Kodak Co.; trustee Penn Mut. Life Ins. Co., 1977-92; adv. bd. HERS Mid-Am. Chmn. bd. dirs. Corp. for Pub. and Pvt. Ventures; bd. dirs. World Resources Inst., Salzburg Seminar, Nantucket Hist. Assn. Mem. Coun. on Fgn. Rels. Home: PO Box 206 39 New St Siasconset MA 02564 Office: Andrew W Mellon Found 140 E 62nd St New York NY 10021-8142

EMERSON, ANDI (MRS. ANDI EMERSON WEEKS), sales and advertising executive; b. N.Y.C., Nov. 1, 1932; d. Willard Ingham and Ethel (Mole) E.; m. George G. Fawcett, Jr. (div.); children—Ann Fawcett Ambia, George Gifford III, Christopher Babcock; m. Kenneth E. Weeks (div.); 1 child, Electra Ingham. Student, Barnard Coll. Successively v.p. Eugene Stevens, Inc., N.Y.C.; pres., dir. Emerson Mktg. Agy., Inc., N.Y.C., 1960—; pres., dir. Mail Order Operating Co. Ltd., N.Y.C. and London, 1976-88, Ingham Hall, Ltd., 1977-83; chmn. bd. dirs. Sonal World Mktg. Ltd., N.Y.C. and Delhi, India, 1983-87; instr. NYU, 1960-65, 87—; internat. lectr., seminar conductor Buenos Aires, Argentina, 1995—, Manila, Philippines, 1996. Vol. children's ward Meml. Hosp., 1964-66, Hosp. for Spl. Surgery, 1967; mem. adv. com. African Students League, 1965-67; bd. dirs. Violet Oakley Meml. Found., Phila., 1964-81; founder, pres., chmn. John Caples Internat. Awards, 1977—; elected N.Y. State Del. to White House Conf. on Small Bus., 1986. Inducted into Silver Apple Hall of Fame, 1985. Mem. Direct Mktg. Assn. (Hall of Fame selection comn. 1989-91), Soc. Profl. Writers, Direct Mktg. Creative Guild (Andi Emerson award 1991, pres. 1975-81, bd. dirs. 1975-93), Direct Mktg. Club of N.Y. (treas. 1960-61). Home: 16 E 96th St New York NY 10128-0753 Office: Emerson Mktg Agy Inc 636 Broadway Ste 1000 New York NY 10012-2623

EMERSON, ANN PARKER, dietician, educator; b. Twin Lakes, Fla., Dec. 3, 1925; d. Charles Dendy and Gladys Agnes (Chalker) Parker; B.S., Fla. State U., 1947; M.S., U. Fla., 1968; m. Donald McGeachy Emerson, Sept. 22, 1950; children—Mary Ann, Donald McGeachy, Charles Parker, William John. Research dietitian U. Chgo., 1948-50; adminstrv. research dietitian U. Fla. Coll. Medicine, Gainesville, 1962-68, dir. dietetic edn., 1968-74, dir. dietetic internship program, 1968-75, dir. program in clin. and community dietetics, 1974-83; mem. Commn. on Dietetic Registration, 1974-77, Commn. on Accreditation, 1980-83. Pres., Gainesville chpt. Altrusa, Internat., 1977-78. VA Allied Health Manpower grantee, 1974-81; HEW Allied Health Manpower grantee, 1975-78, 78-81. Mem. Am., Fla. Dietetic Assns. Republican. Roman Catholic. Clubs: Jr. League, Altrusa.

EMERSON, ANNE DEVEREUX, university administrator; b. Boston, Oct. 6, 1946; d. Kendall and Margaret (Drew) E.; (div. 1980); children: Josephine, Hannah; m. Peter Alexander Altman, 1992. BA magna cum laude, Brown U., 1968; MA, Fletcher Sch. Law and Diplomacy, Tufts U., 1969; MBA, Boston U., 1990. Asst. to dir. Pathfinder Fund, Brookline, Mass., 1970-71; asst. to dir tech.adaptation project MIT, Cambridge, Mass., 1971-73; exec. asst. to v.p. adminstrn. Boston U., 1977-85, dir. adminstrn., program devel., 1985-88; exec. dir. Ctr. for Internat. Affairs Harvard U., Cambridge, 1988—, acting exec. dir. David Rockefeller Ctr. for L.Am. Studies, 1995—; cons. State Legis. Leaders Found., Boston, 1984-87. Panelist NEH, 1987; bd. dirs. Integrated Foster Care, Cambridge, 1985-89; trustee Winsor Sch., 1989-91, Internat. Honors Program, 1995—; bd. dirs. World Affairs Coun., Boston, 1991-94. Mem. Am. Polit. Sci. Assn., Women in Internat. Security, Phi Beta Kappa. Home: 200 Pond St Jamaica Plain MA 02130-2723 Office: Harvard U Ctr for Internat Affairs 1737 Cambridge St Cambridge MA 02138-3016

EMERSON, BRENDA ANN, radiology and emergency nurse; b. Kerrville, Tex., June 5, 1958; d. Ralph Wallace and Anna Frances (Hagelstein) E.; m. Robert Lewis Steinmetz, Jan. 8, 1982; children: Whitney Emerson Steinmetz, Alexandra Marie Steinmetz. LPN, Howard Coll., 1979; ADN, Ea. N.Mex. State U., Roswell, 1983; BSN with honors, N.Mex. State U., 1994. Cert. CEN, TNCC. Staff nurse Angelo Comty. Hosp., San Angelo, Tex., 1979-80; staff nurse, asst. head nurse ICU Lincoln County Med. Ctr., Ruidoso, N.Mex., 1980-86; staff nurse emergency dept. Meml. Med. Ctr., Las Cruces, N.Mex., 1987-95; staff nurse Imaging Svcs. Meml. Med. Ctr., 1996—; guest speaker Internat. Nursing conf. Accident and Emergency Assn. of Nursing, Wollongong, NSW, Australia, 1993. Mem. choir Calvary Bapt. Ch. Crimson scholar N.Mex. State U., 1993, acad. scholar Meml. Med. Ctr. Aux., 1994. Mem. ANA, Emergency Nurses Assn. (chpt. pres. 1992), Nursing Honor Soc. at N.Mex. State U. Home: 2031 Old Farm Rd Las Cruces NM 88005-3884

EMERSON, MIA DIANE, English language educator; b. Balt., June 20, 1969; d. Philip Henry and Constance Diane (Waesche) Scharper; m. Brian Matthew Emerson, 1993. BA, Coll. Notre Dame, Balt., 1991; MA, Johns Hopkins U., 1993. Adj. instr. Johns Hopkins U., Balt., 1993—, Coll. Notre Dame, Balt., 1993—, Goucher Coll., Balt., 1993—, Essex C.C., Balt., 1993—; freelance tutor and writer. Contbr. poetry to small jours. Mem. Delta Epsilon Sigma, Eta Sigma Phi, Sigma Tau Delta, Kappa Gamma Pi. Office: 4701 N Charles St Baltimore MD 21210

EMERSON, NANCY CHICKERING, professional surfer, film producer; b. L.A.; d. Donald E. and Betty Mae (Klein) E.; 1 child, Apache. BA, U. Hawaii, 1975. Cert. water safety instr.; lic. real estate salesperson, Hawaii. Lifeguard, swim instr. Barbers Point Air Navy, Oahu, Hawaii, 1970-71, Schofield Barracks Army, Oahu, 1970-72, City-County of Honolulu, 1971-72, County of Maui, Wailuku, 1973-74; pre-sch. tchr. Waianae Valley Sch., Makaha, Hawaii, 1972-73; beach, pool dir. Maui Surf Hotel, Lahaina, 1973-75; surfing instr. Nancy Emerson Sch. Surfing, various locations, 1973—; cost engr. Hawaiian Dredging and Constrn., Oahu, 1977-79; owner, prodr., location/prodn. mgr., dir. Island Vision Prodns., 1989—; writer surfing col. Maui News, Wailuku, 1977-82; stuntperson The New Gidget, L.A., 1986-87, Waterworld, 1995; stunt coord. ABC Eye on L.A., 1982-85; tech. advisor North Shore film, Sunset Beach, Hawaii, 1987-95; surf travel coord., Hawaii, Fiji, Australia, 1980—. Stuntsperson appearing in Woo Woo Kid, Night Dancer, Surrender, Slam Dance, Super Cross, Eye of the Tiger, North Shore, Water World; featured in Sports World, Wild World of Sports, Eye on L.A., KNBC, CBS, KABC, On the Tube, Downtown, CAgney & Lacey, Moonlighting, Am. Adventure, ESPN; surfer in comml. Bud Light Spuds; location mgr./prodn. coord. numerous commls. for Japan Airlines, G.Q. Mag., Dodge Neon, Nissan Pathfinder, Honda Accord, Winston Ultra Lights, Oldsmobile, Diet Coke, Evian, C&H Sugar, others; prodn. coord. TV shows including Double Kitchen, Super Dave Spl.; location mgr. China Beach, Eye on L.A.; stunt coord. Real Life Gidgets; location mgr. music videos: The Missing Pog, LaToya Jackson. Mem. Screen Actors Guild, Assn. of Surfing Profls., Am. Film Inst., Surfrider Found., Film and Video Assn. of Hawaii, Maui Boardriders Club, Surf Rider Found. Bah'ai Faith. Office: Nancy Emerson Sch Surfing Island Vision Prodns PO Box 463 Lahaina HI 96767

EMERSON, SUSAN, oil company executive; b. Bryan, Tex., Nov. 2, 1947; d. Joseph Nathanial and Lorraine Parks; m. John S. Emerson, June 5, 1970

(div. 1984); children: John H., Christopher P.; m. Gerald W. Parker, May 4, 1985. Owner Emerson Ins. Agy., San Antonio, 1970-84, Emerson Oil Co., San Antonio, 1970—; bd. dirs. Washington Hosp. Ctr. Mem. Washington Hosp. Ctr. Women's Aux., 1988—; mem. D.C. Rep. Com., 1991—, alt. del. Rep. Nat. Conv., Washington, 1992, 4th ward committeewoman, 1992; commr. Adv. Neighborhood Commn., Washington, 1990—; 2d v.p. 4D Commn., Washington, 1990—; founder Boarder Baby Project, 1991—; Rep. candidate for D.C. del. to Congress, 1992. Recipient Sr. Adv. Silver Fox award Wash. Hosp. Women's Aux., 1989, Vol. award, 1990. Mem. LWV, D.C. Hosp. Assn. (trustee 1989), Am. Hosp. Assn. (D.C. del. 1990-92), Vis. Nurses Assn. (bioethic com. 1991—), League Rep. Women, Tex. Breakfast Club. Lutheran. Home: 571 Rte 119 Rindge NH 03461

EMERY, CONSTANCE LOUISE, elementary school educator; b. Aurora, Ill., Sept. 18, 1948; d. George A. and Margaret L. (Pauly) Jares; m. Gerald D. Emery, Aug. 12, 1972; children: Jeff, David. BS, Ill. Wesleyan U., 1970; MEd, U. Ill., 1988. Cert. elem. tchr. Elem. tchr. Oswego (Ill.) Dist. 308, 1970—. Mem. NEA, Ill. Edn. Assn., Oswego Edn. Assn., Optimist Club, Alpha Gamma Delta. Presbyterian. Home: 335 Boulder Hill Pass Oswego IL 60543 Office: East View Sch Rt 71 Oswego IL 60543

EMERY, JANE DAILEY, English literature and language educator; b. Omaha, Aug. 27, 1917; d. Charles Edward and Alice Jane (Atkinson) Dailey; m. Tabor Robert Novak, Mar. 30, 1940 (dec. Jan. 1984); children: Nana Alice, Tabor Robert Jr., Kay Douglass, Clare Christine; m. Clark Mixon Emery, May 25, 1986. BA summa cum laude, Carleton Coll., 1934; MA in English, U. Miami, 1964; PhD in English Lang. and Letters, U. Chgo., 1970. Asst. editor Millar's Chgo. Letter, 1940-42; grad. asst. English dept. U. Miami, Coral Gables, Fla., 1962-64; instr., then asst. prof. U. Ill., Chgo., 1966-73; Leverhulme Found. vis. fellow U. East Anglia, Norwich, Eng., 1973-74; sr. lectr. U. Queensland, Brisbane, Australia, 1974-82, George Watson vis. fellow, 1986; vis. scholar Stanford (Calif.) U., 1982-84, lectr. dept. English, 1985—, mem. editl. bd. Notes in the Margins, 1993—. Author: (under name Jane Novak) The Razor Edge of Balance: Study of V. Woolf, 1975; Rose Macaulay: A Writer's Life, 1991. Vol. numerous orgns. Mem. MLA, Am. Assn. for Australian Lit. Studies, Virginia Woolf Soc., Phi Beta Kappa. Democrat. Episcopalian. Home: 3351 Alma St Apt 321 Palo Alto CA 94306 Office: Stanford U Dept English Stanford CA 94305

EMERY, MARGARET ROSS, educator; b. Columbus, Ohio, May 21, 1923; d. Galen Starr and Stella May (Albright) Ross; m. Richard Clayton Emery, Oct. 27, 1943 (dec. June 1988); children: Richard C. Jr., Margaret Elizabeth Chapman. BA in Edn., U. Mich., 1944; MS in Elem. Guidance, U. Notre Dame, 1967. Life lic. in edn., Ind. 1st grade tchr. Grosse Ile (Mich.) Schs., 1944-45; 2nd grade tchr. Rumson (N.J.) Pub. Schs., 1945-46; homebound tutor Schenectady (N.Y.) Pub. Schs., 1946-48; tutor Hinsdale (Ill.) Pub. Schs., 1948-50; substitute tchr. South Bend (Ind.) Pub. Schs., 1951-53, 93—; head lower sch., guidance couns., 1st grade tchr. The Stanley Clark Sch., South Bend, 1958-88. Mem. St. Joseph County Rep. Women, South Bend, 1958-96; election day clk. Election Bd., South Bend, 1986-96; docent No. Ind. Hist. Soc., South Bend, 1990—. Mem. AAUW, Panhellenic Assn. (pres. South Bend Mishawaka 1993-95), Zonta Internat. (historian, bd. mem. 1994—), Delta Kappa Gamma (pres. Nu chpt. 1992-94). Republican. Presbyterian. Home: 1601 E Colfax Ave South Bend IN 46617-2603

EMERY, NANCY BETH, lawyer; b. Shawnee, Okla., July 9, 1952; d. Paul Dodd Finefrock and Kathryn Jo (Saling) Hutchens; m. Lee Monroe Emery, May 18, 1974. BA with highest honors, U. Okla., 1974; JD, Harvard U., 1977. Bar: Okla. 1977, D.C. 1981. Atty. advisor Office Gen. Counsel, U.S. Dept. Agri., Washington, 1977-79; legal adv. to Fed. Energy Regulatory Commr. Matthew Holden, Jr., Washington, 1979-81; assoc. firm Pierson, Ball & Dowd, and predecessor Sullivan & Beauregard, Washington, 1981-83, Paul Hastings, Janofsky & Walker, Washington, 1983-87, ptnr., 1987-93; ptnr. Sutherland, Asbill & Brennan, Washington, 1993—. nat. adv. bd. USAID Tng. Program, 1994—. Bd. dirs., sec. Park Place Condominium Assn., Inc., Washington, 1982-84; page Continental Congress, DAR, 1978-82, chpt. del. Continental Congress, 1981, 84. Mem. ABA (natural resources energy & environ. law sect., bd. editors Natural Resources & Environ.), Fed. Energy Bar Assn., Soc. Profl. Journalists, Mortar Bd., Phi Beta Kappa. Democrat. Office: Sutherland Asbill & Brennan 1275 Pennsylvania Ave NW Washington DC 20004-2404

EMERY, SUSAN WOODRUFF, investment trust official; b. Salt Lake City, Jan. 13, 1923; d. Russell Kimball and Margaret Anglin (McIntyre) Woodruff; m. Terrence John Osborn, May 30, 1959 (div. Dec. 1963); 1 child, John Russell; m. Stephen Earnest Emery, Apr. 7, 1972 (dec. Apr. 1977). BA, U. Utah, 1944. Cashier Merrill Lynch, Pierce, Fenner & Beane, Portland, 1946-51; personal sec. to parents, Portland, 1951-71; co-trustee R.K.-M.M. Woodruff Trust, Portland, 1971—. Vol. driver ARC, Portland, 35 yrs.; mem. Rep. Nat. Com., 1944—, Oreg. Rep. Com., 1944—. Mem. AAUW (life), U. Utah Alumni Assn. (life), Univ. Club, Alpha Delta Pi. Episcopalian. Home and Office: 255 SW Harrison St Portland OR 97201-5338

EMERY, VICTORIA MILISAVA, English language educator; b. Rastište, Yugoslavia, Nov. 10, 1942; arrived in U.S., 1976; d. Milisav and Darinka (Simić) Djurić; divorced; 1 child, Audrey Lea. BA in Comparative Lit., U. Belgrade, Yugoslavia, 1975; BA in Russian Lang. Lit., U. Hawaii, 1981, MA in English Lang. and Lit., 1986. Lectr. in English U. Hawaii, Honolulu, 1986—. Author: (chap book of short stories) Indiana Review, 1987; contbr. poetry and short stories to anthologies and revs.; mem. editl. bd. Hawaii Rev., 1984-86. Mediator Campus Ctr., U. Hawaii, 1993, spkr. English Dept. Colloquium, 1994, poetry reader Hawaii Lit. Arts Coun., 1985, reader Women's Ctr., 1993. Recipient award Acad. of Am. Poets, 1985. Mem. NOW, Humane Soc. of U.S. Home: # 208 419-A Atkinson Dr Honolulu HI 96814 Office: U Hawaii English Dept 1733 Donaghho Rd Honolulu HI 96822

EMERY, VIRGINIA OLGA BEATTIE, psychologist, researcher; b. Cleve., Apr. 9, 1938; d. Joseph P. and Antoinette Pauline (Misja) Kennick; m. Paul Hamilton Beattie Sr., 1960 (div. 1975); children: Tamsan Beattie Tharin, Paul Hamilton Beattie Jr.; m. Paul E. Emery, 1979. BA, U. Chgo., 1962, PhD, 1982; MA, Ind. U., 1973. Lic. psychologist, N.H., Ohio. Adj., clin. asst. prof. psychiatry Dartmouth Med. Sch., Lebanon, N.H., 1983-85; asst. prof. psychology Case Western Res. U., Cleve., 1986-89, asst. clin. prof. psychiatry, 1986-89; sr. faculty assoc. Ctr. on Aging and Health, 1986-89; clin. assoc. prof. psychiatry Dartmouth Med. Sch., Lebanon, N.H., 1989—; dir. Ctr. on Aging, Health and Soc., Concord and Hanover, N.H., 1989—; mem. com. human devel. NIMH, Adult Devel. & Aging Traineeship, U. Chgo., 1974-76; sub-project dir. Case Western Res. U. Sch. Medicine, 1986-90; sec. women's faculty assn. Case Western Res. U., 1987-89; cons. Vets. Affairs Med. Ctr., Manchester, N.H., 1989—; sub-project dir. NIMH Mental Health Clin. Rsch. Ctr. Grant, Case Western Res. U. Sch. Medicine, 1986-90; mem. Dartmouth Coll. and Dartmouth Med. Sch. Neurosci. Group, 1990—. Author: Language and Aging, 1985, Pseudodementia: A Theoretical and Empirical Discussion, 1988; editor: Dementia: Presentations, Differential Diagnosis, and Nosology, 1994; contbr. articles to profl. jours. Bd. dirs. Frontiers of Knowledge Civic Trust, Concord, N.H., 1990—, pres. 1990-95. Recipient Adult Devel. and Aging grant/traineeship NIH/NIMH, 1974-76, Rsch. prize Am. Aging Assn., 1983, Havighurst prize for aging rsch. U. Chgo., 1984; named Frontiers of Knowledge Atlee Zellers lectr., 1994; rsch. grantee Western Res. Coll., 1986-87, NIMH Mental Health Clin. rsch. grantee, 1986-89. Fellow Gerontol. Soc. Am. (Disting creative contbn. award 1989), N.H. Psychol. Assn. (bd. dirs. 1991-93, chair com. acad. rsch. interests 1992-94, sec. 1994—, Riggs Disting. Contbn. award 1991); mem. AAAS, APA (student rsch. award 1984), AAUW, Internat. Psychiat. rsch. Soc., Internat. Psychogeriatric Assn. (2d place award for rsch. paper 1995, 2nd Pl. Rsch. award in psychogeriatrics for paper 1995, IPA/Bayer Rsch. award in psychogeriatrics 1995), Boston Soc. Gerontol. Psychiatry, Acad. Psychosomatic Medicine, N.Y. Acad. Scis. Home: 15 Buckingham Dr Bow NH 03304-5207 Office: Dept Psychiatry Box HB 7750 Dartmouth Med Sch Lebanon NH 03756

EMERZIAN, NATALIE BERNADETTE, graphic artist; b. New Haven, Conn., Dec. 25, 1921; d. Amadio and Rose (Zanni) Crescenzi; m. A.D. Joseph Emerzian, Aug. 21, 1948; 1 child, Joseph Paul Emerzian. BFA, Yale U., 1944; postgrad., Balt. Mus., 1962-63, U. Conn., 1973-74. Tech. support illustrator Conn. Telephone and Electric, Meriden, 1944-47; staff artist Silex Co., Hartford, Conn., 1947-53; asst. art dir. Post, Johnson and Livingston, Hartford, Conn., 1953-60; free lance graphic artist Conn., 1961-71; graphic arts designer IES Co., Stafford Springs, Conn., 1971-76; illustrator instructional and rsch. U. Conn., 1976-80; botanical illustrator, 1980—. Exhbns. include Conn. Mus. Natural History, 1991-92. Recipient award in Package Design Container Corp. Am., 1952, First prize Housewares Display Hudsons, 1953, award Creative Graphic Design Dynamics Graphics, Inc., 1980. Mem. Nat. Mus. Women in the Arts, Conn. State Mus. Natural History, New Eng. Wild Flower Soc.

EMIGH, AMANDA LYNNE, non-profit organization fundraiser; b. Framingham, Mass., July 12, 1971; d. Richard Chapman and Nellie Bunker (Revell) E. BA in Sociology, Villanova U., 1993. Pro bono project adminstr. Delaware County Legal Assistance, Chester, Pa., 1993-94; capital campaign coord. Polisar Cons., Phila., 1994-96, N.J. State Aquarium, Camden, N.J., 1996—; guest lectr. Rowan Coll., Glassboro, N.J., 1996; cons. Polisar Cons., 1994—. Child advocacy vol. Defenders' Assn., Phila., 1992-93; vol. big sister Rosemont (Pa.) Children's Village, 1993—; vis. vol. Little Bros. Friends of the Elderly, Phila., 1994—. Mem. Nat. Soc. Fundraising Execs., Young Friends of Art Mus. (event subcom. 1996—), Kappa Kappa Gamma (fraternity edn. com. 1991-93). Home: 115A Lincoln Ave Collingwood NJ 08108 Office: NJ State Aquarium 1 Riverside Dr Camden NJ 08013

EMMERICH, KAROL DENISE, former retail company executive, consultant; b. St. Louis, Nov. 21, 1948; d. George Robert and Dorothy (May) Van Houten; m. Richard James, Oct. 18, 1969; 1 son, James Andrew. B.A., Northwestern U., 1969; M.B.A., Stanford U., 1971. Nat. div. account officer Bank of Am., San Francisco, 1971-72; fin. analyst Dayton Hudson Corp., Mpls., 1972-73; sr. fin. analyst Dayton Hudson Corp., 1973-74, mgr. short term financing, 1974-76, asst. treas., 1976-79, treas., 1979—, v.p., 1980-93; exec. fellow U. St. Thomas Grad. Sch. Bus., 1993—; bd. dirs. Piper Funds Inc., Slumberland. Mem. nat. adv. coun. Ctr. for Applied Christian Ethics, Wheaton Coll.; bd. dirs. Women's Opportunity Fund, Minn. Hemerocallis Soc. Mem. Minn. Women's Econ. Roundtable, Minn. Women's Forum, Internat. Women's Forum, Mpls. Club, Trinity Forum, Women Venture (adv. bd.). Home and Office: 7302 Claredon Dr Edina MN 55439-1722

EMMERT, ROBERTA RITA, health facility administrator; b. Buffalo, Aug. 28, 1953; d. Robert George and Rita Rose (Lambert) E. Diploma, St. Elizabeth Hosp. Sch. Nsg., 1974; BSN magna cum laude, SUNY, Utica, 1989; MS, Syracuse U., 1993, postgrad., 1993—. RN, N.Y., Calif. Charge nurse, staff nurse pediatrics St. Joseph Hosp. Health Ctr., Syracuse, N.Y., 1974-83; charge nurse spl. care pediatrics St. Joseph Hosp. Health Ctr., 1983-89; adminstrv. supr., nurse educator St Joseph Hosp. Health Ctr., Syracuse, N.Y., 1989—; instr. Am. Heart Assn. Mem. ANA (cert. pediat. nurse), NAFE, AAUW, Am. Orgn. Nurse Execs., N.Y. State Nurses Assn., Soc. Pediat. Nurses, Sigma Theta Tau. Home: 4750 Woodard Way Apt 9K Liverpool NY 13088-4621

EMMETT, MARSHA A., executive secretary; b. Dallas, Feb. 14, 1944; d. William C. and Edna A. (Marshall) Klein; m. John S. Emmett, Aug. 16, 1963 (dec. Apr. 1996); children: Angella, John, Chet. Student, U. Tex. Dallas, Richardson. Adminstrv. sec. So. Meth. U., Dallas, 1985-87; adminstrv. asst. U. Tex. Dallas, Richardson, 1987-90; exec. sec. Dallas Citizens Coun., 1990-95; mem. adv. bd. Tex. Am. Bank Bd., Richardson, 1985-86, Leadership Richardson, Tex., 1985-86, Richardson Child Guidance, 1995-96. Bd. mem. Drug Task Force, Richardson, 1986-87; mem. student adv. bd. U. Tex. Dallas, Richardson, 1995-96. Mem. Exec. Women Internat. (scholarship and program chmn. 1990-96, Jr. League Richardson (treas., placement chair 1975-86, pres. 1985-86), Golden Key (scholarship award 1995). Republican. Roman Catholic.

EMMONS, JANET GALBREATH, secondary education educator; b. Columbus, Ohio; d. George Robert and Jean (Evans) G. BA in English, Sam Houston State U., 1972, MEd, 1985; postgrad., U. Houston. English tchr. Conroe (Tex.) H.S., 1973-77, 84-86, English and Creative Writing tchr., 1986-88; tchr. Reaves Intermediate Sch., 1981-84; English/Journalism tchr. The Woodlands (Tex.) High Sch., 1988—. Mem. NCTE, TCTE, AERA, ATPE, Phi Delta Kappa, Kappa Delta Pi, Delta Delta Delta . Home: 239 Tallahassee Park Conroe TX 77302-1069 Office: The Woodlands High Sch 6101 Research Forest Dr The Woodlands TX 77381-2732

EMMONS, JOANNE, state senator; b. Big Rapids, Mich., Feb. 8, 1934; d. Ray J. and Emma M. (Von Glahn) Gregory; m. John Francis Emmons, June 9, 1956; children: Sarah, Dorothy. BS, Mich. State U., 1956; degree in pub. svc. (hon.), Ferris State U., 1992. Tchr. Mecosta (Mich.) High Sch., 1956-58; treas. Big Rapids Twp., 1976-86; state rep. State of Mich., Lansing, 1987-91, state senator, 1991—. Chair Mecosta County Rep. Com., 1976-80; vice chair 10th dist. Rep. Com., 1984-86; bd. dirs. Luth. Child and Family Svcs., 1990—. Named Nat. Rep. Legislator of Yr., Nat. Assn. State Legislators, 1993, Legislator of Yr., Mich. Twp. Assn., 1993. Mem. Am. Legion Aux., Mich. Farm Bur. (legis. com. 1970—), Omicron Delta Kappa. Home: 13904 Northland Dr Big Rapids MI 49307 Office: Mich State Senate State Capitol Lansing MI 48909

EMPERADO, MERCEDES LOPEZ, librarian; b. Manila, Aug. 9, 1941; came to U.S., 1969; d. Evaristo Villasor and Marina (Gallardo) Lopez; m. Conrado Emperado, June 30, 1968; children: Joshua Caleb, Marita Eve. BS in Elem. Edn., Philippine Normal Coll., 1963; MLS, Cath. U. Am., 1974. Libr. math. and computation lab. Fed. Preparedness Agy., Washington, 1976-79; libr. Fed. Emergency Mgmt. Agy., Washington, 1979—. Mem. ALA, Am. Soc. Info. Sci., Spl. Librs. Assn., Nat. Coordinating Coun. on Emergency Mgmt. Baptist. Home: 6303 Elm Way Clinton MD 20735-3928 Office: Fed Emergency Mgmt Agy Libr 500 C St SW Washington DC 20472-0001

EMS, CHRISTINE MARIE, chiropractor; b. Phila., Dec. 25, 1965; d. Frank Vincent and Louise Grace (Pulignano) Spadafora; m. Joseph Gerad Ems (div. Nov. 1994); m. Larry Marc Moses; 1 child, Cody Lee. BA in Biology, Holy Family Coll., 1987; D of Chiropractic, Pa. Coll. Chiropractic, 1990. Assoc. doctor Torresdale Chiropractic, Phila., 1990-94; owner, pres. Mayfair Chiropractic Ctr., Inc., Phila., 1994—; owner Every-Wear Apparrel, 1996—; workman's compensation panel doctor Moss Rehab., Phila., 1993—, Coca-Cola, Phila., 1995—. Mem. Internat. Chiropractors Assn., Internat. Chiropractors Assn. Pediatric Assn., Pa. Chiropractic Fedn., Pa. Chiropractic Soc., Tacony Bus. Assn. (co-chair holiday dinner for needy sr. citizens 1990—), Mayfair Bus. Assn. Home: 4966 B Fitler St Philadelphia PA 19114 Office: Mayfair Chiropractic Ctr 7036 Frankford Ave Philadelphia PA 19135

ENAS, LENA MAE, research coordinator, consultant; b. Sells, Ariz., July 18, 1963; d. Floyd Michael and Lavina Mae (Segundo) Harris; m. Austin Enas, Jan. 19, 1990 (dec. Febr. 1994); children: Arlene Enas, Morris Enas. Detention officer Tohono O'Odham Nation, Sells, 1989-91, sec. I, 1990-93, rsch. coord., 1993—. Rep. Baboquivari Dist., Sells; sec. Choulic Cmty., Sells. Mem. Internat. Sonoran Desert Alliance (cons. 1995—). Home: PO Box 756 Sells AZ 85634 Office: Tohono O'Odham Nation Hia Ced O'odhani Program PO Box 837 Sells AZ 85634

ENDAHL, ETHELWYN MAE, elementary education educator, consultant; b. Duluth, Minn., May 27, 1922; d. Herman and Florence Jenny (Mattson) Johnson; m. John Charles Endahl Sr., Nov. 27, 1943; children: Merrilee Jean, Marsha Louise, John Charles Jr., Kimberly Ann. BS in Library Science, U. Minn., Mpls., 1943; MA in Edn., Fairfield U., 1978; attended, Elmhurst (Ill.) Coll., 1966-68, U. Bridgeport, Conn., 1981-83, Northeastern U., Martha's Vineyard, Mass., 1982-85, U. Conn., 1971. Cert. Tchr. Conn. Librarian children's hosp. Davenport (Iowa) Pub. Library, 1943-44; librarian Omaha (Nebr.) Pub. Library, 1944; tchr. 4th gr. Center Elem. Sch., New Canaan, Conn., 1968-81, writing coord., 1981-83; staff devel. Dept. Edn. State of Conn., 1986-88; writing coord. East Elem. Sch., New Canaan, 1986-88; instr. Grad. Sch. Edn. Simmons Coll., Boston, 1989; leader Reminiscence Writing Courtland Gardens Nursing Home, Stamford, Conn., 1985-86; leader adult writing group Charlotte Hobbs Library, Lovell, Maine, 1987-89; leader writing process-children's group Cmty. Ctr., Boca Grande, Fla., 1994; cons. writing process Banyan Elem. Sch., Sunrise, Fla., 1995-96. Mem. AAUW, Nat. League of Pen Women, Older Women's League. Democrat. Presbyterian. Home: 3101 NE 47 Ct # 206 Fort Lauderdale FL 33308

ENDE, ARLYN RUTH, textile artist, arts administrator; b. New Orleans, Oct. 6, 1932; d. Harry Gerhard Ende and Ruth Wilhelmina Anderson; m. J. William Lovett Jr., Aug. 8, 1952 (div. 1958); 1 child, Mark William Lovett; m. Jack B. Hastings, Sept. 17, 1987. Student, La. State U., 1949-51, Tulane U., 1951, The Art Inst. Chgo., 1951-52. Co-founder Dodge/Ende Assocs., N.Y.C., 1959-62; asst. dir. urban design Boston Redevel. Authority, 1961-64; co-owner, designer Fogeater Art Wearables, Tucson and Block Island, R.I., 1967-72; exec. dir. The Arts Ctr., Woodbury, Tenn., 1991-95; textile designer, 1972—; tchr., adj. instr. Mid. Tenn. State U., Murfreesboro, 1986; workshop instr. Appalachian Ctr. for Crafts, Smithville, Tenn., 1994—, Nat. Fiber Forum, Nashville, 1996; mem. adv. bd. Tenn. Assn. Craft Artists, 1995-97. Prin. works include 11 elevator lobby wall textiles Vanderbilt U. Med. Ctr., 1985 (Design Competition winner), atrium textile Provident Life and Accident Ins. Co., Chattanooga, 1990, 3 maj. textiles Mid. Tenn. State U. Recreation Ctr., Murfreesboro, 1995. Craft coord. Rural Area Devel. Com., Woodbury, Tenn., 1989-92. Recipient Grand Prize, Am. Craft Awards, 1989, Best of Show award Fiber Arts in the 90s, 1990. Mem. Am. Craft Coun., Surface Design Assn., Tenn. Assn. Craft Artists. Home: 464 Wildwood Ln Sewanee TN 37375

ENDERS, ANNA MARIA, art educator, business owner; b. New Kensington, Pa., Mar. 3, 1955; d. Anthony Louis and Elvira Sylvia (Longo) Ginocchi; m. Donald Edward Enders, Jr., Aug. 4, 1979; children: Andrew Michael, Emily Alexandra. BS in Art Edn., Ind. U. of Pa., 1977; MSED in Edn., Temple U., 1983; postgrad., Pa. State U. Cert. art edn. grades K-12. Interior designer Mountain View Interiors, Greensburg, Pa., 1977; substitute tchr. Various Pa. Sch. Dists., 1977-78; art educator Cumberland Valley Sch. Dist., 1978—; lead tchr. Cumberland Valley Sch. Dist., Mechanicsburg, Pa., 1993—; owner Bits O'Opulence, Harrisburg, Pa., 1984—; cons. Arts in Spl. Edn. Project of Pa., Harrisburg, 1980—; mem. exhibitions com. Susquehanna Art Mus., Harrisburg, Pa., 1985—. Art work contbr. Am. Cancer Soc., Leukemia Soc. Dir. Ind. U. Pa. Alumni Bd. Dirs. Recipient Tchr. of the Week award WHTM-TV, Harrisburg, Pa., 1981. Mem. ASCD, NEA, Nat. Art Edn. Assn., Pa. Art Edn. Assn. (Pa. Outstanding Art Educator award 1981), Pa. Edn. Assn. Democrat. Roman Catholic. Home: 2318 Fox Hollow Rd Harrisburg PA 17112 Office: Cumberland Valley Sch Dist 6746 Carlisle Pike Mechanicsburg PA 17055

ENDERS, ELIZABETH MCGUIRE, artist; b. New London, Conn., Feb. 18, 1939; d. Francis Foran and Helen Cuseck (Connolly) McGuire; m. Anthony Talcott Enders, June 9, 1962; children: Charles Talcott, Alexandra Eustis, Camilla, Ostrom II. BA, Conn. Coll., 1962; MA, NYU, 1987. Trustee Artists Space, N.Y.C., 1986-95, Conn. Coll., New London, 1988-93; assoc. dept. prints and illustrated books Mus. Modern Art, 1993, Lyman Allyn Art Mus., 1994. One woman shows include Paul Schuster Gallery, Cambridge, Mass., 1966, Ulysses Gallery, N.Y.C., 1992, 94, Lyman Allyn Art Mus., New London, Conn., 1994, Charles Cowles Gallery, N.Y.C., 1995; exhibited in group shows at Boston Symphony Orch., 1982, NYU, 1983, Conn. Coll., 1988, Bronx Coun. on Arts, 1990-91, Addison Gallery Am. Art, 1993, Angel Art, L.A., 1993, Lyman Allyn Art Mus., New London, Conn., 1994-95, So. Alleghenies Mus. Art, Loretto, Pa., 1994, Artists Space Multiple, 1995, New Mus. Contemporary Art, N.Y.C., 1995, Denise Bibro Fine Art, N.Y.C., 1995, N.Y. Studio Sch., N.Y.C., 1995, Divine Design '95, L.A., Spring Benefit Raffle, Sculpture Ctr., N.Y.C., 1996, Charles Cowles Gallery, N.Y.C., 1996; traveling group show Artists Space, 1992, 94, Southeastern Ctr. Contemporary Art, Winston-Salem, N.C., 1993, Allentown (Pa.) Art Mus., 1994, Cleve. Ctr. Contemporary Art, 1994, Kemper mus. Contemporary Art and Design, Kansas City, Mo., 1996; represented in permanent collections at Addison Gallery of Am. Art, Andover, Mass., Graham Gund, Cambridge, Daimler Benz Holding Co., Lyman Allyn Art Mus. Mem. nat. fin. coun. Dem. Nat. Com., Washington, 1988—. Recipient Citation of Appreciation, Conn. Coll., 1990, medal, 1993. Mem. The Drawing Soc., The Bklyn. Mus., Williams Coll. Mus. of Art, Mus. Modern Art (assoc.), Williams Club. Democrat. Roman Catholic. Home: 530 E 86th St New York NY 10028-7535

ENDICOTT, JENNIFER JANE, education educator; b. Oklahoma City, Oct. 17, 1947; d. M. Ector and Jessie Ruth (Carter) Reynolds; m. William George Endicott, June 2, 1975 (wid. Sept. 1975); 1 child, Andrea A. BA History, U. Okla., 1969, MEd Adminstrn., 1975, PhD, 1987. Cert. secondary edn. tchr.: history, govt., geography, econs., adminstr., Okla. Mid. sch. tchr. Norman (Okla.) Pub. Schs., 1970-77, adminstr. elem. edn., 1977-80; grad. asst. U. Okla., Norman, 1984-88; adj. lectr. U. Ctrl. Okla., Edmond, 1988-90, assoc. prof., 1990—; cons. Okla. Action Network, 1992—; sec. Mid-State chpt. Coop. Coun. Okla. Sch. Adminstrn., 1996—. Adv. bd. The Annual Editions Series, Guilford, Conn., 1994—; contbr. articles to profl. jours. Bd. dirs. Cleveland County Hist. Soc., Norman, 1980-88, Arts and Humanities Coun., Norman, 1982-88; bd. dirs. Jr. League, Inc., Norman, 1982-90; bd. dirs. Assistance League, Norman, 1982-90, pres. 1988-89. Recipient Harriet Harvey Meml. award U. Okla. Found., 1984; named Norman Community Family of the Yr. Finalist, LDS Ch., Norman, 1985. Mem. ASCD, Okla. Assn. Tchr. Educators (bd. dirs. 1994—, pres. 1966—), Am. Assn. Tchr. Educators, Soc. for Philosophy and History of Edn., Am. Assn. Teaching and Curriculum (charter mem. 1994—), Am. Ednl. Rsch. Assn., Kappa Delta Pi (univ. sponsor 1991-96), Phi Delta Kappa (found. rep. 1992—).

ENDICOTT, KATHERINE GRACE, author, columnist; b. Pasadena, Calif., June 16, 1954; d. Frank J. and Ruth Suzanne C.; children: Carolyn Mariko, Laurel Alexandria. BA, U. Calif., Berkeley, 1976. Columnist San Francisco Chronicle, 1986—. Author: Seasonal Expectations, 1990. Mem. Garden Writers Assn. of Am. (Quill and Trowel award of excellence 1991, 93). Office: c/o Belles Lettres Books PO Box 20405 Oakland CA 94620

ENDSLEY, JANE RUTH, nursing educator; b. Harrisburg, Ill., Oct. 14, 1942; d. Clifford B. Bond and Haroldene (Malone) Miller; m. William R. Endsley, June 6, 1964. Grad., Deaconess Hosp. Sch. Nursing, Evansville, Ind., 1963; student, So. Ill. U., 1968; BSN cum laude, U. Evansville, 1978. RN, Ind., Ill. Staff nurse Deaconess Hosp., 1963-64; psychiat. nurse med.-surg. emergency room and obstetrics Ferrell Hosp., Eldorado, Ill., 1964-68, DON, 1969-70; DON, Good Shepherd Nursing Home, Eldorado, 1971-72; instr. nursing Southeastern Ill. U., Harrisburg, 1973—; cons. parents too soon Egyptian Pub. Health Dept., Eldorado, 1985. Vice chmn. Pvt. Industry Coun., Harrisburg, 1983-91; precinct committeeperson Harrisburg Dem. Com., 1986-90; donor chmn. ARC, Harrisburg, 1970—; instr. CPR to civic orgns. and students, 1980-87; pres. Peartree Antiques, Inc., 1995. Mem. AAUW, Ill. Nurses Assn. (nominating com. 1975), Southeastern Ill. Coll. Edn. Assn. (pres. 1988-91), Faculty Wives and Women Southeastern Ill. Coll. (sec.-treas. 1974-75), Sigma Theta Tau. Home: PO Box 345 1075 Shawnee Hills Rd Harrisburg IL 62946-4943

ENG, CATHERINE, health care facility administrator, physician, medical educator; b. Hong Kong, May 20, 1950; came to U.S., 1953; d. Doi Kwong and Alice (Yee) E.; m. Daniel Charles Chan; 1 child, Michael B. BA, Wellesley Coll., 1972; MD, Columbia U., 1976. Diplomate Am. Bd. Internal Medicine, Am. Bd. Gastroenterology; cert. added qualifications geriatrics. Intern in internal medicine Presbyterian Hosp./Columbia, Presbyterian Med. Ctr., 1976-77, resident in internal medicine, 1977-79; fellow in gastroenterology/hepatology N.Y. Hosp./Cornell U. Med. Ctr., 1979-81; instr. medicine Cornell U. Coll. Medicine, N.Y.C., 1980-81; staff physician On Lok Sr. Health Svcs., San Francisco, 1981-86, supervising physician, 1986-91, med. dir., 1992—; asst. clin. prof. dept. family and cmty. medicine U. Calif., San Francisco, 1986—, asst. clin. prof. dept. medicine, 1992-95; assoc. clinical prof. dept. medicine, Univ. Calif., San Francisco, 1995—; primary care specialist Program of All-inclusive Care for the Elderly, San Francisco, 1987-94; asst. chief dept. medicine Chinese Hosp., San Francisco, 1993-94. Instr. BLS Am. Heart Assn., San Francisco, 1988-92; mem. nominating com. YWCA of Marin, San Francisco, San Mateo, 1991-95; mem. mgmt. com. YWCA-Chinatown/North Beach, San Francisco, 1989-95; bd. dirs. Chinatown Cmty. Children's Ctr., San Francisco, 1987-90. Durant scholar

Wellesley Coll., 1972. Mem. ACP, Am. Geriatrics Soc., Am. Soc. Aging, Am. Gastroent. Assn., Calif. Med. Assn. (assoc.), San Francisco Med. Soc. (assoc.), Sigma Xi, Alpha Omega Alpha. Office: On Lok Sr Health Services 1333 Bush St San Francisco CA 94109-5611

ENGEL, CATHERINE, chief deputy; b. Phila., Dec. 2, 1927; d. Samuel Walter and Olga (Frank) Douglass; m. Robert Francis Engel, Sr., June 14, 1947; children: Robert Francis, Jr., Catherine Eleanore. Grad. high sch., Phila., 1943. File clk. Phila. Credit Bur., Phila., 1943-44; order taker/typist Smith, Kline & French, Phila., 1945-54; toll ticket typist Bell Tele. of Penn., Phila., 1955-57; med. jour. editor Inst. Scientific Info., Phila., 1964-69; leasing agent Cmty. Mgmt. Realty, Ventnor, N.J., 1976-78; chief deputy Montgomery County Cts., Norristown, Penn., 1979—. Committeewoman Montgomery County Rep. Comm., Whitpain Twp., 1980—. Republican. Lutheran. Home: 3105 Aspen Cir Blue Bell PA 19422-3405

ENGEL, EMILY FLACHMEIER, school administrator, educator; b. Columbus, Tex., Sept. 15, 1938; d. William August and Jeanette D. (Hastedt) F.; m. Lars N. Engel, Dec. 28, 1957; children: Jan Kristin, Karen Gale. BSEd, U. Tex., 1959, MEd, 1966. Cert. tchr., counselor, adminstr., N.Mex. Sch. counselor, guidance team leader Los Alamos (N.Mex.) Pub. Schs., 1967-85, coord., fed. projects, 1985-87; asst. prin. Los Alamos Mid. Sch., 1987-89; prin. Mountain Elem. Sch., Los Alamos, 1989-95; ednl. cons., 1995—; presentor nat. confs. and convs. Bd. dirs. Los Alamos Family Coun., 1985-91, Family Strengths Network, 1994—, Self-Help, Inc., 1993—; mem. adv. com. Sci.-at-Home, 1994—. Mem. ASCD, NDEA (mem. counseling and guidance inst. U. Tex. Austin 1962-63), Nat. Assn. Elem. Sch. Prins., N.Mex. Assn. Elem. Sch. Prins. (pres.-elect 1992-93, pres. 1993-94), N.Mex. Assn. Sch. Adminstrs., Los Alamos Assn. Sch. Adminstrs. (pres. 1991-92), Delta Kappa Gamma (Rho chpt. sec.), Pi Lambda Theta. Methodist. Home: 192 Loma Del Escolar Los Alamos NM 87544-2525 Office: 192 Loma del Escolar Los Alamos NM 87544-2525

ENGEL, JOANNE BOYER, psychology educator; b. Meadville, Pa., Mar. 15, 1944; d. Edward Charles and Wanda Ann (Chasco) Boyer; m. Richard E. Hammer (dec.); 1 child, Cynthia; m. Harold N. Engel, Mar. 12, 1971; 1 child Keith Nichols. BS, Pa. State U., 1965; MEd, U. Sydney, Australia, 1972; MS, Iowa State U., 1978, PhD, 1979. Cert. elem. tchr., Pa., N.J., Ala., Australia. Tchr. Marple Newtown Sch. Dist., Broomall, Pa., 1965-67, Wallingford (Pa.) Sch. Dist., 1967-69, Sydney Pub. Schs., 1969-70; dir. child rsch. lab. Auburn (Ala.) U., 1971-75; instr. human devel. Coll. Home Econs. Iowa State U., Ames, 1975-79; asst. prof. Oreg. State U., Corvallis, 1979-80, assoc. prof., 1990—; from asst. prof. to prof., chair dept. Willamette U., Salem, Oreg., 1980-90. Contbr. articles to profl. jours. Commr. Tchr. Standards and Practice Commn.; mem. sch. reform com. Gov. of Oreg. Mem. Puget Sound English Setter Assn., Oreg. Responsible Dog Breeder Assn., Oreg. Brittany Club (sec., treas. newsletter 1988-91), Am. Kennel Club (dog show judge 1991—), Am. Brittany Club, Am. Whippet Club, N.W. Dog Judges Assn., Chintimini Kennel Club (pres. 1992-94), Pacific Rim Golden Retriever Club. Presbyterian. Home: 3336 NW Countryman Cir Albany OR 97321 Office: Oreg State U 202C Ed Hall Corvallis OR 97330

ENGEL, NANCY JUNE, actress, singer, director, coach; b. Detroit, Feb. 2, 1941; d. Walter C. and Beulah L. (McIntyre) E.; m. Walter L. Sacharczyk, Feb. 4, 1967 (div. 1982); 1 child, Walter Scott. Student, Henry Ford C.C., 1959-61; BA in Speech, Theatre and English, Ctrl. Mich. U., 1964; student, Macomb County C.C., Warren, Mich., 1976-77. Cert. tchr., Mich. Tchr. English Roseville (Mich.) Schs., 1964-66; employment counselor Detroit, 1966-67, 72-73; recruiter, counselor Nat. Edn. Ctr., East Detroit, Mich., 1982-87; artistic dir. Detroit Ctr. for Performing Arts, 1991-93; actress, singer, coach, dir. various theatres, Mich., 1964—; spkr. on women, spiritual, career and personal growth, Mich., 1982—. Author, performer (assemblies) Famous Historical Women, I, 1st Ladies, 1994—, Famous Historical Women, II, 1995, History of American Musical Theatre, 1995; performer, arranger (concert) one woman show, 1993—; co-author, dir. (plays) Sojourner Truth, 1991-92, Martin Luther King, 1991-92, Thomas Edison, 1991-92. Mem. Alpha Psi Omega. Democrat. Home: 720 Tidewater Cir Apt 14B Macon GA 31211

ENGEL, WALBURGA See VON RAFFLER-ENGEL, WALBURGA

ENGELBREIT, MARY, card company executive, illustrator; b. St. Louis, 1952. Freelance illustrator greeting card cos.; founder, head Mary Engelbreit Card Co., St. Louis; licensor Sunrise Pubs., 1986. Office: Mary Engelbreit Studios 6900 Delmar Blvd Saint Louis MO 63130*

ENGELMAN, MARJORIE JECKEL, retired higher education administrator; b. Delavan, Ill., Oct. 9, 1927; d. John B. and Reka M. (Hellman) Jeckel; m. Kenneth L. Engelman, Mar. 26, 1949; children: Ann K., Barth B. BA, Ill. Wesleyan U., 1945-49; MA, Northwestern U., 1953; MS, U. Wis., 1965, PhD, 1977. Dir. outreach/ext. U. Wis., Green Bay, 1973-85, dir. equal opportunity, 1974-79; asst. to chancellor affirmative action U. Wis. ext., Madison, 1985-89; part-time instr. U. Wis., Madison, 1991-93. Contbr. articles to ch. publs. Bd. trustees Garrett-Evangel. Sem., Northwestern U., Evanston, Ill., 1975-96; bd. Meriter Retirement Svcs., Meriter Health, Madison, 1985-96; bd. dirs. Madison Campus Ministry, 1994-96; del. to White House Conf. on Aging, 1995. Kramer Found. grantee, 1985, Wis. Humanities grantee, 1980. Mem. Alumni Assn., Assn. Aging Groups in Wis., Phi Delta Kappa, Phi Kappa Phi. Democrat. United Methodist. Home: 738 Seneca Pl Madison WI 53711

ENGELSGJERD, JANET LOUISE, gifted/talented educator; b. Slayton, Minn., Sept. 20, 1945; d. Ted Melvin and Norma Rudella (Nelson) Matson; m. Sander John Engelsgjerd, Dec. 25, 1945; children: Jon Michael, Kari Marie. BA, Augustana coll., 1967; MA, U. Wis., Eau Claire, 1988. Tchr. Anoka (Minn.) Hennepin Sch. Dist., 1967-71; substitute tchr. Beaver Dam (Wis.) Sch. Dist., 1972-75; tchr., coord. gifted/talented Altoona (Wis.) Pub. Schs., 1988—; v.p. Origin Investigators Assn., Inc., Chippewa Falls, Wis., 1978—. Co-author: Gifted Children in Small School Districts, 1988. Problem capt. Odyssey of the Mind, Eau Claire, Wis., 1991-95; mem. gifted adv. bd. U. Wis., Eau Claire, 1994—. Learning Assistance grantee Wis. Dept. Pub. Instruction, Madison, 1989-91, 91-93. Mem. Nat. Assn. Gifted Children, Wis. Edn. Assn. Wis. Assn. Gifted & Talented (Rookie of Yr. 1988-89), Area Assn. High Potential Children. Home: 17801 45th Ave Chippewa Falls WI 54729 Office: Altoona Pub Schs 1903 Bartlett Ave Altoona WI 54720

ENGERRAND, DORIS DIESKOW, business educator; b. Chgo., Aug. 7, 1925; d. William Jacob and Alma Willhelmina (Cords) Dieskow; BS in Bus. Adminstrn., N. Ga. Coll., 1958, BS in Elementary Edn., 1959; M Bus. Edn., Ga. State U., 1966, PhD, 1970; m. Gabriel H. Engerrand, Oct. 26, 1946 (dec. June 1987); children: Steven, Kenneth, Jeannine. Tchr., dept. chmn. Lumpkin County H.S., Dahlonega, Ga., 1960-63, 65-68; tchr., Gainesville, Ga., 1965; asst. prof. Troy (Ala.) State U., 1969-71; asst. prof. bus. Ga. Coll., Milledgeville, 1971-74, assoc. prof., 1974-78, prof., 1978-90, chmn. dept. info. systems and comms., 1978-89, ret., 1990; cons. Named Outstanding Tchr. Lumpkin County Pub. Schs., 1963, 66; Outstanding Educator bus. faculty Ga. Coll., 1975, Exec. of Yr. award, 1983. Fellow Assn. for Bus. Communication (v.p. S.E. 1978-80, 81-84, 89-92, bd. dirs.), Nat. Bus. Edn. Assn., Ga. Bus. Edn. Assn. (Postsecondary Tchr. of Yr. award 10th dist. 1983, Postsecondary Tchr. of Yr. award 1984), Am. Vocat. Assn., Ga. Vocat. Assn. (Educator of Yr. award 1984, Parker Liles award 1989), Profl. Secs. Internat. (pres. Milledgeville chpt. 1996—), Ninety-nines Internat. (chmn. N. Ga. chpt. 1975-76, named Pilot of Year N. Ga. chpt. 1973). Methodist. Contbr. articles on bus. edn. to profl. publs. Home: 1674 Pine Valley Rd Milledgeville GA 31061-2465 Office: Ga Coll Milledgeville GA 31061

ENGLAND, LYNNE LIPTON, lawyer, speech pathologist, audiologist; b. Youngstown, Ohio, Apr. 11, 1949; d. Sanford Y. and Sally (Kentor) Lipton; m. Richard E. England, Mar. 5, 1977. BA, U. Mich., 1970; MA, Temple U., 1972; JD, Tulane U., 1981. Bar: Fla. 1982, U.S. Dist. Ct. (mid. dist.) Fla. 1982, U.S. Ct. Appeals (11th cir.) 1982; cert. clin. competence in speech pathology and audiology. Speech pathologist Rockland Children's Hosp., N.Y., 1972-74, Jefferson Parish Sch., Gretna, La., 1977-81; audiologist Rehab. Inst. Chgo., 1974-76; assoc. Trenam, Simmons, Kemker, Scharf, Barkin, Frye & O'Neill, Tampa, Fla., 1981-84; asst. U.S. atty. for Middle Dist. Fla. Tampa, 1984-87; asst. U.S. trustee, 1987-91, ptnr. Stearns, Weaver, Miller, Weissler, Alhadeff & Sitterson, P.A., 1991-94, Prevatt, England, Ambler, Snyder & Taylor, Tampa, Fla., 1994—. Editor Fla. Bankruptcy Casenotes, 1983. Recipient clin. assistantship Temple U., 1972-74. Mem. ATLA, Comml. Law League, Am. Speech and Hearing Assn., Tampa Bay Bankruptcy Bar Assn. (dir. 1990-95), Am. Bankruptcy Inst., Fla. Bar Assn., Hillsborough County Bar Assn., Order of Coif. Jewish. Office: PO Box 2920 1 Tampa City Ctr Ste 2505 Tampa FL 33601-2920

ENGLE, CINDY, medical transcriptionist; b. Denver, Aug. 12, 1958; d. Wallace Clyde and Mary Margaret (Ingram) E. AA, Arapahoe C.C., 1979; BA in Kinesiology, U. No. Colo., 1992. Cert. paralegal; former cert. paramedic, Colo. EMT/paramedic Ambulance Svc. Co., Denver, 1978-80; pers. asst. payroll Burns Security Svc., Denver, 1980-82; part-time asst. mgr. Tokoyo Bowl Restaurant, Denver, 1982-85; paramedic Platte Valley Ambulance, 1982-85; part-time flight paramedic for Air Life North Colo. Med. Ctr., Greeley, Colo., 1986-91; paramedic Weld County Ambulance, Greeley, 1985-92; intern exercise svcs. Greeley (Colo.) Med. Clinic, 1992, med. transcriptionist, 1993-94; med. transcriptionist North Colo. Med. Ctr., Greeley, 1994—; part-time EMS/criminal justice instr. Aims C.C., Greeley, 1987—; founder The Human Factor, 1992—. Author ednl. game: The Reality Game, 1993. Office: The Human Factor 2626 23d Ave Greeley CO 80631

ENGLE, JEANNETTE CRANFILL, medical technologist; b. Davie County, N.C., July 7, 1941; d. Gurney Nathaniel and Versie Emmaline (Reavis) Cranfill; m. William Sherman Engle (div. 1970); children: Phillip William, Lisa Kaye. Diploma, Dell Sch. Med. Tech., 1960; BA, U. N.C., Asheville, 1976; postgrad., Marshall U., 1991—. Instr. Dell Sch. Med. Tech., Asheville, 1960-67; rotating technologist Meml. Mission Hosp., Asheville, 1967-68, asst. supr. hematology, 1968-71; supr. Damon Subs. Pvt. Clinic Lab., Asheville, 1971-73; chemistry technologist VA Med. Ctr., Durham, N.C., 1973-74, 75-76, supr., 1974-75; asst. supr. microbiology VA Med. Ctr., Salem, Va., 1976-79; supr. rsch. Med. Svc. Lab., Salem, 1979-90; flow cytometrist VA Med. Ctr., Huntington, W.Va., 1990-92, cons. to clin. lab. flow cytometry dept., 1992—; reviewer Jour. Club, Roanoke-Salem, Va., 1980-90. Author: (poem) Reflections on a Comet, 1984; contbr. numerous articles and abstracts on med. tech. to profl. jours., 1982—. Mem. The Acting Co. Ensemble. Democrat. Episcopalian. Home: 4775 Green Valley Rd Huntington WV 25701-9793

ENGLEHART, JOAN ANNE, trade association executive; b. Susquehanna, Pa., Sept. 15, 1940; d. George Louis and Muriel Elois (Washburn) Wanatt; m. Dale John Englehart, Nov. 24, 1958. AAS, Broome Community Coll., 1981; BS in Cultural Studies, Empire State Coll., 1984; postgrad., SUNY, Binghamton, 1984; PhD in Bus. Adminstrn., Century U., 1994. Office mgr., coord. sales Bush Transformer Corp., Endicott (N.Y.), Boston, 1959-65; mgr., cons. Snelling & Snelling, Binghamton, Endicott, 1965-71; mgr.-tchr. Can. Acad., Kobe, Japan, 1971-72; owner Typewriting, Endicott, 1980-85; exec. v.p. Tioga County C. of C., Owego, N.Y., 1985-87, pres., 1988—; exec. v.p. Chamber Found., 1987—. Mem. Broome C.C. Found., Binghamton, 1984-87; mem. scholarship com. Civic Club Binghamton, 1984-87; mem. Health Fair Adv. Bd., Broome and Tioga Counties, 1985-87; sec.-treas. Tioga County C. of C. Found., 1987—; chmn. sustaining membership com. Broome United Way, Binghamton, 1986-87; mem. planning process com. Broome-Delaware Tioga BOCES vocat. edn. coms., 1989, 92; bd. dirs. NYPENN Health Sys. Agy., 1989-91, Pvt. Industry Coun., 1994—, Tioga County Rural Ministry, 1992—, chmn., 1993—; pres. Tioga County divsn. Am. Heart Assn., 1994—; active Tioga County Tourism Coun., 1994—, County Comprehensive Plan, 1994—. Recipient award Boy Scouts Am., 1979, Evening Student Assn., 1991, Friends Binghamton Libr., 1982, ATHENA award C. of C., 1986; named Woman of Achievement Broome County Status of Women Coun., 1978. Mem. AAUW (life, pres. 1986-87), So. Tier World Commerce Assn. (bd. dirs. 1992—), Nat. Assn. Women in C. of C.'s (charter mem., Nat. Achievement award 1993, com. chmn. 1994-96), Am. C. of C. Execs., N.Y. State C. of C. Execs. (bd. dirs. 1991), Zonta (pres. Tioga County area club 1985-89, mem. internat. bd. dirs., gov. dist. II 1982-84, Woman of Achievement 1985-88). Republican. Baptist. Home: 4 Lancaster Dr Endicott NY 13760-4320 Office: Tioga County C of C 188 Front St Owego NY 13827-1521

ENGLER, RENATA J. M., allergist, internist, educator; b. Frankfurt, Germany, 1949. MD, Georgetown U., 1975. Diplomate Am. Bd. Internal Medicine, Am. Bd. Allergy and Immunology (bd. dirs.). Intern Nat. Naval Med. Ctr., Bethesda, Md., 1975-76, resident in internal medicine, 1976-80; fellow in allergy and immunology Walter Reed Army Med. Ctr., Washington, 1980-82, mem. staff, 1982—; asst. prof. internal medicine Uniformed Svcs. U. Health Sci., Bethesda; pvt. practice Silver Spring, Md. Mem. ACP, Am. Acad. Allergy and Immunology, Am. Coll. Allergy, Am. Fedn. Clin. Rsch. Office: Sair Hosp and Clinic 14536 Banquo Ter Silver Spring MD 20906-2678*

ENGLERT, HELEN WIGGS, writer; b. Nashville, June 1, 1927; d. Lawrence Raymond and Frances Eloise (Smith) Wiggs; m. Roy Theodore Englert Sr., Sept. 25, 1948; children: Lee Ann Englert Regan, Roy Theodore Jr. AA, Ward Belmont Coll., Nashville, 1948; AB, George Washington U., Washington, 1954, postgrad., 1969-71. Lectr. Weight Watchers, Washington & Va., 1972-84. Author: Hey, Wait a Minute! Dealing with Feelings and Weight Control, 1992; contbr. articles to profl. jours. Elder Old Presbyn. Meeting House, Alexandria, Va., 1982—; bd. mem. St. Citiques Employment Svcs. Inc., Alexandria, 1994—. Mem. George Washington U. Club, Campagna Ctr. (Alexandria), Nat. Mus. Women in Arts, Phi Theta Kappa. Home: 411 S Pitt St Alexandria VA 22314

ENGLERT, PHYLLIS ANN, psychology educator; b. Richmond, Calif., Oct. 15, 1961; d. Donald Carmen and Lenora Marie (Cardoza) McCrocklin; m. Paul Michael Englert, Mar. 20, 1985; 1 child, Ryan Paul. BA, U. Va., 1982; MA, U. Calif., Riverside, 1987, PhD, 1993. Mktg. coord. Am. Assn. Med. Transcription, Modesto, Calif., 1983-84; rsch. asst. U. Calif., Riverside, 1984-87, teaching asst., 1985-88; instr. Whittier (Calif.) Coll., 1989, Calif. State U., Fullerton, 1990, Chaffey Coll., Alta Loma, Calif., 1994—. Mem. Ontario (Calif.) PTA, 1994-95. Mem. AAUW (corr. sec. 1988-90), Am. Psychol. Assn., Western Psychol. Assn., Phi Beta Kappa. Roman Catholic. Home: 850 N Center Ave # 3-G Ontario CA 91764 Office: Chaffey Coll Dept Social Sc 5885 Haven Ave Alta Loma CA 91764

ENGLISH, DIANE, television producer, writer, communications executive; b. Buffalo, NY, 1948; d. Richard and Anne English; m. Joel Shukovsky. Grad., Buffalo State Coll., 1970. Tchr. high sch. English Buffalo, 1970-71; with Theatre In Am. series Sta. WNET-TV, N.Y.C., assoc. dir. TV lab.; TV columnist Vogue Mag., N.Y.C., 1977-80; creator, prodr., writer Foley Sq. CBS, 1985-86, exec. prodr., writer My Sister Sam, 1986-87; exec. prodr., ptnr. Shukovsky English Entertainment, 1988—; creator, exec. prodr. Murphy Brown CBS, 1988; creator, exec. prodr. Love & War CBS, N.Y.C., 1992-95; co-creator, exec. prodr. Double Rush CBS, 1995, exec. prod. The Louie Show, 1996. Co-author: (motion pictures-for-TV) The Lathe of Heaven, 1980 (Writers Guild award nomination), My Life as a Man, Classified Love. Recipient 3 Emmy awards, Golden Globe award, 1989, Outstanding Writing in a Comedy Series award Writers Guild, 1990, 92, Genie award Am. Women in Radio and TV, 1990, Commrs.' award Nat. Commn. on Working Women, Peabody award, 1991. Office: CBS Studio Ctr 4024 Radford Ave Studio City CA 91604-2101

ENGLISH, EILEEN MARY, artist, elementary education art educator; b. Norwood, Mass., May 14, 1955; d. Robert Edward and Evelyn Louise (McIntyre) E. B in Gen. Studies, Univ. Sys. N.H., 1993. Cert. tchr., N.H. Art tchr. Josiah Bartlett Elem. Sch., Bartlett, N.H., 1994-96, Edward Fenn Elem. Sch., Gorham, N.H., 1996—; instr. drawing Downtown Artworks, Plymouth, N.H., 1992—. Illustrator: Farmstead mag., 1980, The Maine Organic Farmer & Gardener, 1991, Ossipee Hist. Soc., 1991, Ossipee Crossings Child Care Ctr., 1993; one woman shows include Downtown Artworks Gallery, 1992-93, 95, Wolfeboro (N.H.) Pub. Libr., 1992, Conway (N.H.) Pub. Libr., 1994, Cook Meml. Libr., Tamworth, N.H., 1993, 96, Libby Mus., Wolfeboro, 1995; group exhbns. inlcude Gov. Wentworth Arts Coun., Wolfeboro, 1991-93, Group Exhibit Art Educators, Conway, 1994. Big sister Big Bros./Big Sisters No. N.H., Berlin, N.H., 1991—. Recipient People's Choice award Arts Rochester, 1990. Mem. N.H. Art Educators Assn., Mt. Washington Valley Arts Assn., Gov. Wentworth Arts Coun., Alumni-Learner Assn. (co-chairperson 1994—, bd. dirs. Coll. Lifelong Learning, Chair's Recognition of Extraordinary Vol. Effort award 1995). Office: Edward Fenn Elem Sch 169 Main St Gorham NH 03581

ENGLISH, ELIZABETH ANN, actress, educator, executive assistant; b. Bronx, N.Y., Jan. 18, 1962; d. Nicholas John and Jayne Ann (Matheson) E. BA in Theatre, Fordham U., 1984; MFA in Acting, U. Minn., 1986. Asst. instr. U. Minn., Mpls., 1985, assoc. instr., 1986; actress N.Y.C., 1986—; co-founder Lynx Prodns., 1993-95; head asst., exec. asst. to sr. v.p. and gen. mgr. FW Dodge divsn. McGraw Hill Corp., 1995; exec. asst. to sr. v.p. New Ventures, Alliances & Partnerships divsn. McGraw Hill Cos., 1996—; exec. asst. to mng. ptnr. Abernathy and MacGregor; co-founder The Sacred Clowns Theatre Co., N.Y.C., 1995; asst. to artistic dir. Irish Arts Ctr., N.Y.C., 1995. Co. actor The Children of the Salt, Belmont Italian Am. Playhouse; understudy for The Musical Comedy Murders, As Is, at Circle Repertory Co.; regional appearances include Barber of Seville, La Ronde, Much Ado About Nothing, Everyman, Riverwife's Daughters, The Music Man. U. Minn. fellow, 1984. Mem. NAFE, Am. Film and TV and Radio Artists, Actor's Equity Assn. Democrat. Roman Catholic.

ENGLISH, ELIZABETH ANN, communications executive; b. Berwyn, Ill., May 25, 1946; d. Albert Jackson and Florence Frances Leora (Bingley) E.; m. Robert Frank Eddy, Nov. 17, 1970 (div. Feb. 1979). BA, Boston U., 1969; postgrad., U. Ctrl. Fla., 1991—. Rsch. asst. Harvard Divinity Sch., Cambridge, Mass., 1965; survey asst. U. Durham (England), 1977-78; instr. Tunghai U., Taichung, Taiwan, 1978-81; computer operator Hydra Tool Corp., Greenwood, Miss., 1983-84; network adminstr., mgr. Saboungi Constrn., Ormond Beach, Fla., 1987—; pres. White Light Communications, Inc., Ormond Beach, Fla., 1990—. Author: Rainbow Path, 1991. Mem. Am. Counseling Assn., Am. Mental Health Counselors Assn., Mensa, Phi Theta Kappa, Chi Sigma Iota. Office: White Light Communications PO Box 1101 Ormond Beach FL 32175-1101

ENGLISH, EVONNE KLUDAS, artist; b. Cherokee, Iowa, Dec. 31, 1934; d. Earl Philip and Ruby Jacqueline (Whiting) Kludas; m. John Cammel English, July 29, 1966. BFA, Drake U., 1957; postgrad., U. No. Iowa, 1958-59; MFA, U. Iowa, 1962. Instr. h.s. & jr. h.s. art Sycamore Cmty. Unit Sch. Dist. 427, Sycamore, Ill., 1959-61; instr. art Wis. State U., Whitewater, 1962-63; asst. prof. art Stephen F. Austin State U., Nacogdoches, Tex., 1963-66; instr. adult edn. Lawrence (Kans.) Arts Ctr., 1976; presenter in field. One woman exhbns. include Sanford Mus., Cherokee, 1958, Cmty. Ctr., Cherokee, 1966, Baker U., Baldwin, Kans., 1971, 76, 7 East 7th Gallery, Lawrence, 1975-79, Unitarian Gallery, Kansas City, Mo., 1980, Kansas City Kans. Pub. Libr., 1984, Kans. U. Med. Ctr. Gallery of Art, Kansas City, Kansas, 1986, Lawrence Pub. Libr., 1986, 91, Baldwin State Bank, 1988, Lawrence C. of C., 1988, Galesburg (Ill.) Civic Art Ctr., 1988, Park Coll., Parkville, Mo., 1991; Sta. KSHB-TV, Kansas City, Mo., 1993; group exhbts. include Santa Fe Connection, Kansas City, 1979, Baker U., 1980, Kansas City Kansas Pub. Libr., 1995, Iowa Art Salon, 1957-59, 61-62, 65, Gallery Arkep, N.Y.C., 1965, George Walter Vincent Smith Art Mus., Springfield, Mass., 1965, Soc. Am. Graphic Artists, 1966, Galesburg Civic Art Ctr., 1983, Lawrence Arts Ctr., 1983, Carrier Fine Arts Show, Belle Mead, N.J., 1984-85, 88, 90, 92, Gallery Lawrence, 1986, Hays (Kans.) Arts Coun., 1990, Hunterdon Art Ctr., Clinton, N.J., 1991, Wis. State U., Whitewater, 1962, Park Ctrl. Gallery, Springfield, Mo., 1976, Crown Ctr., Kansas City, Mo., 1979, Kellas Gallery, Lawrence, 1980-82, 84, Santa Fe Depot Ctr., 1985, Baldwin City Pub. Libr., 1993-95, others; designer bicentennial plate Baldwin City Ofcl. seal, 1976. Panelist Spencer Mus. Art, Lawrence, 1978. Grantee State Wis. Bd. Regents State Colls., 1963; Lawrence Lithography Workshop grantee, 1988. Mem. AAUW (sec. Baldwin chpt. 1977-79, hospitality chair 1985—), Kansas City Artists Coalition, Baldwin Cmty. Arts Coun. (sec. 1988-90, exhibit com. chair 1988-90), Delta Phi Delta. Unitarian. Studio: PO Box 537 Baldwin City KS 66006-0537

ENGLISH, JOAN DIANE, artist, educator; b. Warren, Ohio, Apr. 5, 1942; d. John Maurice English and Madge (Olnhausen) Rosenbaum; m. John Christopher Newman, Aug. 21, 1966 (div. Dec. 1977); children: Aron English, Matthew John; m. Dennis Stanley Brown, June 9, 1984. Diploma, Cleve. Inst. Art, 1964; BFA, U. Pa., 1966, MFA, 1969. Instr. Otis-Parsons Sch. Design, L.A., 1984-85, Portland (Oreg.) State U., 1985, Bassist Coll., Portland, 1988, Oreg. State U., Corvallis, 1988-89, Linfield Coll. Sch. Nursing, Portland, 1992-96; co-pres. Blackfish Gallery, Portland, 1989-90. One-person shows include Avanti Galleries, N.Y.C., 1970, Mercer County Cmty. Coll., Trenton, N.J., 1975, Ariel Gallery, N.Y.C., 1987, Pacific U., Catherine Cawein Gallery, Forest Grove, Ill., 1988, Oreg. State U. Meml. Union, Corvallis, Oreg., 1989, Blackfish Gallery, 1989, 91, 93; exhibitor Art for Healing, San Francisco, 1984—. Mem. lay leadership com. First Presbyn. Ch., 1992—; mem. Com. on Ministry in Higher Edn., 1992-96. Grantee Oreg. Arts Commn., 1991, Peterson grantee for adj. faculty devel., Linfield Coll. Sch. Nursing, 1995. Democrat. Presbyterian. Home: 7511 SW 35th Ave Portland OR 97219

ENGLISH, JUJUAN BONDMAN, women's health nurse, educator; b. El Dorado, Ark., Dec. 16, 1947; d. Irvin Raymond and Ida Ruth (Payton) Bondman; m. Frederick J. English, Aug. 28, 1976; children: Michael, Christopher, Meagan. ADN, So. State Coll., Magnolia, Ark., 1970; BSN, U. Ark., 1988; MSN, U. Miss., 1992. Cert. childbirth educator. Charge nurse Union Med. Ctr., El Dorado; charge nurse Warner Brown Hosp., El Dorado, labor and delivery supr.; instr. nursing U. Ark., Monticello, asst. prof. nursing, 1993-95; dir. nursing edn. Area Health Edn. Ctr.-South Ark., 1995—; coord. Parenting Coalition of South Ark. Mem. ANA, Ark. State Nurses Assn. (strategic planning com., sec. 1994—, exec. com., Outstanding Dist. Pres. 1994), Ark. Nursing Coalition (steering com., Salute to Nursing com. chair), So. Nursing Rsch. Soc. (rsch. reviewer for D. Jean Wood award 1993), Nat. League Nursing, Ark. League Nursing, So. Regional Heidegerian Hermeneutrical Inst., So. Ark. Breast Feeding Coalition (chair edn. com.), Sigma Theta Tau.

ENGLISH, KARA LEE BUTLER, art educator; b. Denver, Feb. 18, 1958; d. Robert M. Sr. and V. Louise (Keenan) Butler; children: William P., Cassandra Joy. B of Edn., Ariz. State U., 1985; M of Visual Arts(hon), U. No. Colo., 1995. Tchr. St. Louis Sch., Englewood, Colo., 1986-87, Walsenburg (Colo.) Mid. Sch., 1987-88, Adams County Schs., Thornton, Colo., 1988-90, Cole Mid. Sch., Denver, 1990-91, Genoa Hugo Sch., Hugo, Colo., 1991-93; instr. Morgan C.C., Ft. Morgan, Colo., U. No. Colo., Greeley, 1993-95, Cook County Coll., Gainsville, Tex., 1996; tchr. Christ Our Savior L. Sch., Coppel, Tex., 1995—; participant Colo. State U. Creative Arts Symposium, 1995. Exhibited in group shows including U. No. Colo. (2d. pl. award for graphics), 1995, Student Fine Arts Gala, U. No. Colo., 1995. Mem. Delta Kappa Gamma.

ENGLISH, LAURA JANE, zoning coordinator; b. Berea, Ohio, Sept. 13, 1952; d. Donald Leo and Mary Jean (Vitek) Lamberton; m. Craig Scott English, Aug. 10, 1974. BA in Edn., Otterbein Coll., 1974. Agy. bookkeeper Lake County Cmty. Svcs. Coun., Mentor, Ohio, 1982-86; office mgr. Tartan Marine Co., Grand River, Ohio, 1986-90; adminstrv. sec. Concord (Ohio) Twp., 1990-92, zoning sec., 1992-95, zoning coord., 1995—. Mem. AAUW (treas. Painesville, Ohio br. 1991—), Benevolent Bear Soc. of Western Res. Office: Concord Twp 7229 Ravenna Rd Concord OH 44077

ENGLISH, MICHELLE DAWN, lighting technician; b. Mt. Lebanon, Pa., Mar. 9, 1970; d. Fred and Darlene Ann (DeLong) Exler-Kalimon; m. Dan Frederic English, Sept. 4, 1994. BFA, W.Va. U., Morgantown, 1992. Lighting technician Morpheus Lights Inc., San Jose, 1992—. Office: Morpheus Lights Inc 3021 Kenneth St Santa Clara CA 95054

ENGMAN, BONNIE JO, accountant; b. South Laguna Beach, Calif., July 9, 1963; d. David Robert and Jo Ann Betty (Vento) Bansemer; m. Arlyn Dean Engman, Apr. 6, 1985; children: Blake Anthony, Nicholas David. AA, U. Wis., Waukesha, 1983; BBA in Fin., U. Wis., Milw., 1984; MBA, Marquette U., Milw., 1992. Acctg. analyst I Kohler Co., Wis., 1985-87, acctg. analyst II, 1987-88, sr. acctg. analyst, 1988-92, mgr. corp. planning, 1992-94, mgr. treasury process re-engring., 1994, mgr. corp. sys. devel., 1995—; classroom cons. Jr. Achievement Project Bus., Sheboygan, 1993-95. Mem. Inst. Mgmt. Accts. Home: 1383 Spinnaker Dr Port Washington WI 53074 Office: Kohler co 444 Highland Dr Kohler WI 53044

ENNIS, ALANA MINETTE, protective services official, educator; b. Durham, N.C., June 17, 1950; d. Lee Warren Settle and Ruby Faye Hurt; m. Teen Whitfield Ennis, Jan. 16, 1979 (div. May 1991); 1 child, Taylor Kathleen. BA in English, Stratford Coll., 1971; advanced certification, N.C. Criminal Justice Edn. and Tng. Standards Commn., 1988; MA in Pub. Adminstrn., N.C. State U., 1989; student, Sr. Mgmt. Inst. for Police, 1993. Adminstrv. asst. Dallas (Tex.) County Sheriff's Dept., 1974-75; patrol officer Carrollton (Tex.) Police Dept., 1975-76; patrol officer uniform patrol Durham (N.C.) Police Dept., 1976-79, corporal uniform patrol, 1979-80, sgt. uniform patrol, 1981-84, lt. uniform patrol, 1984-85, lt., internal affairs divsn., 1985-88, lt., planning and fiscal svcs., 1988-89, lt., tng. dir., accreditation mgr., 1989, capt. uniform patrol bur., dist. comdr. N.W. quadrant of city, 1991-92; dir. pub. safety, CEO campus police dept. dept pub. safety U. N.C., Chapel Hill, 1992-95, Duke U., Durham, N.C., 1995—; tchr. basic and specialized law enforcement courses; cert. assessor, team leader commn. Accreditation for Law Enforcement Agys., Inc., nat. task force, 1993; vis. lectr. Inst. Govt. U. N.C., Chapel Hill, 1992—, co-dir. law enforcement exec. program, 1994-95, exec. bd. bridges program, 1996—; peer review, tech. assistance cons. Nat. Inst. Justice, 1993; adv. bd. adminstrv. officer mgmt. program N.C. State U., 1995-96, criminal justice program Durham Tech. C.C., 1994-96. Contbr. articles to profl. jours. Mem. Nat. Assn. Women Law Enforcement Execs. (chairperson, co-founder 1996—), Internat. Assn. Chiefs of Police (apptd. civil rights com. 1994), Police Exec. Rsch. Forum, N.C. Assn. Chiefs of Police, N.C. Assn. Police Execs., Internat. Assn. Campus Law Enforcement Adminstrs., N.C. Assn. Campus Law Enforcment Adminstrs., Rotary Internat. Democrat. Roman Catholic. Office: Duke U Police Dept 502 Oregon St Durham NC 27708-0425

ENOS, MINDY See PARSONS, MINDY

ENRIGHT, CYNTHIA LEE, illustrator; b. Denver, July 6, 1950; d. Darrel Lee and Iris Arlene (Flodquist) E. BA in Elem. Edn., U. No. Colo., 1972; student, Minn. Sch. Art and Design, Mpls., 1975-76. Tchr. 3d grade Littleton (Colo.) Sch. Dist., 1972-75; graphics artist Sta. KCNC TV, Denver, 1978-79; illustrator No Coast Graphics, Denver, 1979-87; editorial artist The Denver Post, 1987—. Illustrator (mag.) Sesame St., 1984, 85; illustrator, editor "Tiny Tales" The Denver Post, 1991-94. Recipient Print mag. Regional Design Ann. awards, 1984, 85, 87, Phoenix Art Mus. Biannual award, 1979. Mem. Mensa. Democrat. Home: 1210 Ivanhoe St Denver CO 80220-2640 Office: The Denver Post 1560 Broadway Denver CO 80202-5133

ENRIQUEZ, CAROLA RUPERT, museum director; b. Washington, Jan. 2, 1954; d. Jack Burns and Shirley Ann (Orcutt) Rupert; m. John Enriquez, Jr., Dec. 30, 1989. BA in history cum laude, Bryn Mawr Coll., 1976; MA, U. Del., 1978, cert. in mus. studies, 1978. Personnel mgmt. trainee Naval Material Command, Arlington, Va., 1972-76; teaching asst. dept. history, U. Del., Newark, 1976-77; asst. curator/exhibit specialist Hist. Soc. Del., Wilmington, 1977-78; dir. Macon County Mus. Complex, Decatur, Ill., 1978-81; dir. Kern County Mus., Bakersfield, Calif., 1981—; pres. Kern County Mus. Found., 1991—; advisor Kern County Heritage Commn., 1981-88; chmn. Historic Records Commn., 1981-88; sec.-treas. Arts Council of Kern, 1984-86, pres. 1986-88; county co-chmn. United Way, 1981, 82; chmn. steering com. Calif. State Bakersfield Co-op Program, 1982-83; mem. Community Adv. Bd. Calif. State Bakersfield, Anthrop. Soc., 1986-88; bd. dirs. Mgmt. Council, 1983-86, v.p., 1987, pres. 1988; bd. dirs. Calif. Council for Promotion of History, 1984-86, v.p., 1987-88. pres., 1988-90; mem. community adv. bd. Calif. State U.-Bakersfield Sociology Dept., 1986-88; mem. women's adv. com. Girl Scouts U.S., 1989-91; bd. dirs. Greater Bakersfield Conv. and Visitors Bur., 1993-95; co-chair 34th St. Neighborhood Partnership, 1994—. Hagley fellow Eleutherian Mills-Hagley Found., 1977-78; Bryn Mawr alumnae regional scholar, 1972-76. Mem. Calif. Assn. Mus. (regional rep. 1991—, v.p. legis. affairs 1992—), Am. Assn. for State and Local History (chair awards com. Calif. chpt. 1990—), Exces. Assn. Kern County. Unitarian Universalist. Office: Kern County Museum 3801 Chester Ave Bakersfield CA 93301-1345

ENRIQUEZ, NORA OLAGUE, artist, educator; b. El Paso, Tex., May 2, 1953; d. Rubén and Gloria (Castillo) Olague; m. Alfonso Enriquez, Dec. 26, 1976; 1 child, Alejandra. Student, Sch. Art and Design, London, 1970, U. de Cd Juarez, Mexico, 1979, U. Pa., Phila., 1988; BA in Art, U. Tex., El Paso, 1989, endorsement bilingual edn., 1989. Cert. art tchr., Tex. Lectr. U. Autonoma, Juarez, Mex., 1974-75; asst. editor Masca Jour., Mus. Phila., 1983-84; tchr. Ysleta Sch. Dist., El Paso, 1989-90, Socorro (Tex.) Ind. Sch., 1991-93. Author design Ann. Reunion Bilingual Program, 1991, logo design Socorro Mid. Sch., 1993. Vol. Nuns, Retirement Village, 1990. Recipient 1st pl. painting, 2nd place sculpture Socorro Sch. Dist., 1991, 1st pl. painting, 2nd pl. mixed media, 1st pl. sculpture Socorro Sch. Dist., 1992, 1st pl. ceramics, best of show print, 1st pl. print, hon. award painting Socorro Sch. Dist., 1993. Mem. Juntos Art Assn., Mus. Women in Arts. Roman Catholic.

ENSMINGER, AUDREY HELEN, writer, publishing company executive; b. Winnipeg, Manitoba, Can., Dec. 30, 1919; d. Ernest William and Helen Myra (Greaves) Watts; m. M.E. Ensminger,June 11, 1941; children: John Jacob, Janet Aileen (dec.). BSc, U. Manitoba, 1940; attended, U. Minn., Twin Cities, 1940-41; MSc, Wash. State U., 1943. Dietitian Wash. State U., Pullman, 1944-46; v.p. Ensminger Pub. Co., Pegus Press, Inc.; trustee Agrisvcs. Found., Clovis, Calif., 1962—. Co-author: China: The Impossible Dream, 1973; sr. author: Foods and Nutrition Encyclopedia, 1994; author: The Concise Encyclopedia of Food and Nutrition, 1995. Recipient Humanitarian award Acad. Destiny Internat., 1987, Disting. Svc. award AMA, 1993, Hon. Mention Am. Med. Writer's Assn., 1995. Republican. Office: Agrisvcs Found PO Box 429 Clovis CA 93613*

ENZ, PAMELA JOAN, film director, screenwriter, playwright; b. Queens, N.Y.; d. Peter Joseph and Florence Marie (Knapp) E.; 1 child, Aimee Alison Lutkin. Artistic dir. Bad Rep./Danziger Gallery, N.Y.C., 1993; resident Edward F. Albee Found., 1995; resident Cummington (Mass.) Cmty. of the Arts, 1992-93. Writer City Girls and Desperadoes, Circle Rep., Solo Subterranean Blues, Ensemble Studio Theater, N.Y.C., 1987, Limo Boots and Other Means of Locomotion, Open Eye Theater, N.Y.C., Gene Frankel Theater, N.Y.C., Met. Mus. of Art, N.Y.C., and Swedish Embassy, N.Y.C., 1980-86, Sushi Suicide, Ensemble Studio Theater, 1988, Fractured Hearts and Lurid Details, 1990 (Tennesee Williams One Act Play award), Are You My Kitchen Table?, Eugene O'Neill Theater Ctr., 1991, Heart on Fire Trilogy, Gallery One, N.Y.C., 1993, Plate on a Heart, Thread Waxing Space, N.Y.C., 1993; writer, dir. Didja Didja. . .didja Find A Gun?m 1996. Franklin Furnace Emerging Performance Artist grantee, N.Y.C., 1994, Lotta Thetrical Fund grantee, Boston, 1989; Robert Kaufman scholar N.Y. Film Acad., N.Y.C., 1994. Office: Music and Art/Stephen Cohen 245 W 14th St New York NY 10011

EPEL, LIDIA MARMUREK, dentist; b. Buenos Aires, Argentina, Sept. 30, 1941; came to U.S., 1966; d. Israel and Ita Rosa (Sonabend) Marmurek; children: Diana, Bryan. BS, Buenos Aires U., 1959, DDS, 1964. Lic. dentist, N.Y. Gen. practice dentistry Argentina, 1965-66, Long Beach, N.Y., 1967-70, Lynbrook, N.Y., 1970-73, Rockville Centre, N.Y., 1973—. Bd. dirs. Rosa Lee Young Childhood Ctr., Rockville Centre, 1982-94, Rockville Centre Edn. Found., 1990—; mem. adv. com. on HIV/AIDS Bd. Edn. Rockville Centre Pub. Schs., 1994—; past pres. Queens-L.I. Women's Dental Study Group. Mem. ADA, Am. Assn. Gen. Dentistry, Fedn. Dentaire Internat., Nassau County Dental Soc. (bd. dirs., chair com. on pub. and profl. rels. 1990—, chairperson com. on health. 1989-92, chair membership com. 1993, treas. exec. com. 1993, sec. exec. com. 1994, v.p. 1995, membership task force 1994-95, pres-elect 1996), Overseas Dentists Assn. (pres. N.Y. chpt. 1968-72), Dental Soc. of State of N.Y. (coun. for pub. and profl. rels. 1990—, chair children's dental health month campaign 1991, chair mem. recruitment and retention), Hadassah Club (bd. dirs. Rockville Ctr. 1983-84, 92-93). Democrat. Jewish. Office: 165 N Village Ave Rockville Centre NY 11570-3701

EPHRON, NORA, writer; b. N.Y.C., May 19, 1941; d. Henry and Phoebe (Wolkind) E.; m. Dan Greenburg (div.); m. Carl Bernstein (div.); children: Jacob, Max; m. Nicholas Pileggi. BA, Wellesley Coll., 1962. Reporter N.Y. Post, 1963-68; free-lance writer, 1968—; contbg. editor, columnist Esquire mag., 1972-73, sr. editor, columnist, 1974-78; contbg. editor N.Y. mag., 1973-74. Author: Wallflower at the Orgy, 1970, Crazy Salad, 1975, Scribble Scribble, 1978, Heartburn, 1983, Nora Ephron Collected, 1991; screenwriter: (with Alice Arlen) Silkwood (nominated Acad. award for best original screenplay), 1983, Heartburn, 1986, Cookie, 1989, When Harry Met Sally (nominated Acad. award, BAFTA award for best screenplay), 1989, My Blue Heaven, 1990; dir., screenwriter (with Delia Ephron) This Is My Life, 1992, Mixed Nuts, 1994; co-screenwriter, dir. Sleepless in Seattle (nominated Acad. award for best original screenplay), 1993. Mem. Writers Guild Am., Authors Guild, Dirs. Guild of Am., Acad. Motion Picture Arts and Scis. Office: care Sam Cohn ICM 40 W 57th St New York NY 10019-4001

EPPERSON, KATHLEEN MARIE, management consultant; b. L.A., May 9, 1943; d. George Burns and Helen Virginia (Mitchell) E.; m. William John Madden, Mar. 17, 1973 (div. 1995); children: Rose Mary Olinda Madden, William Sean O Madden, Margaret Kathleen Olinda Madden. BA in English, Dominican Coll. San Rafael, 1967; MA in Mgmt., John F. Kennedy U., 1995. Tchr. Notre Dame & Dominican Sisters, San Francisco, San Rafael, 1965-69, Lincoln Elem., Richmond, Calif., 1969-71; gen. mgr. Madblood Creations & Walrus Factory, San Rafael, 1971-79; fundraiser, area mgr. First Earth Run UNICEF, N.Y.C., 1986; dir. mktg. Wainwright House, Rye, N.Y., 1986-87; adminstrv. asst. Global Family, San Anselmo, Calif., 1988-89, PRJ+, Richmond, 1989-91; mgr. adminstrn. Tate Western, Sausalito, Calif., 1991-93; mgmt. cons. San Rafael, 1993—. Author: The Christmas Cook Book, 1969. Mem. Am. Soc. Devel. & Tng. (strategic planning com. 1994), Bay Area Orgn. Devel. Network (steering com. 1995-96), Orgn. Devel. Network (internet host 1996). Democrat.

EPPERSON, MARGARET FARRAR, civic worker; b. Hickman, Ky., Feb. 9, 1922; d. John Henry and Helen Margaret (Thompson) White; m. Liberty Weir Birmingham III, June 14, 1947 (dec. Feb. 1965); children: Margaret W., Elizabeth J., Richard L.; m. Ralph Cameron Epperson, Sept. 18, 1971. Student, Washington Sch. Art, 1940; BA magna cum laude, Judson Coll., Marion, Ala., 1945; postgrad., Lambuth Coll., Jackson, Tenn., 1964. Cert. secondary tchr., Ky. Tchr. biology and typing Robert L. Osborne High Sch., Marietta, Ga., 1945-46; tchr. typing Hickman High Sch., 1946-47; tchr. day care ctr. Southside Bapt. Ch., Jacksonville, Fla., 1972-73; sec. to min. of Edn. Jacksonville, Fla., 1973; file clk. Epperson Appraisers, Pensacola, Fla., 1986-87; formerly substitute tchr. various high schs. and jr. high schs., staff mem. Ridgecrest Bapt. Assembly, summer 1946, 1971. Exhibited in group shows, Jackson, Tenn., 1957, 58, West Tenn. Exec. Club, 1958-59. Pres. Alexander Sch. PTA, Jackson, 1959-60, devotional chmn., 1956-57, chmn. rm. mothers, 1957-58, 1st v.p., 1958-59; sec. Reelfoot Lake coun. Girl Scouts U.S.A., 1969-71, troop mother cookie chmn. 1958-65; PTA sec. Jackson, Tenn. H.S., 1967-68, 70-71; PTA 1st v.p. Jackson, Tenn. Ctrl. Coun., 1960-61; mem. aux. assn. Jackson-Madison County Bar, 1960-65; vol. ARC, Jackson, 1955, Meml. Med. Hosp. Aux., Jacksonville, 1978-86, Am. Heart Assn., 1987-90, Sacred Heart Hosp. Aux., Pensacola, 1986—; life mem. Jacksonville Children's Hosp. Aux., 1974—; hostess designer show house Symphony Guild, 1979-80; dir. Women's Missionary Union, Bapt. Ch., 1976-78, mission support chmn., 1992, 93, 94, sec., 1995; Newcomers Club Greater Pensacola Area, 1988-89, Bon Appetit Luncheon Group, 1986-87, sunshine chmn., 1987-88, sec., 1988-89, nom. com., 1993-94, scholarship com., 1993-94, newcomer's book club group program chmn., 1995-96; publicity chmn. MacDowell Music Club, Jackson, 1954-55, program chmn. 1957-58, social chmn. 1959-60, parliamentarian 1961; com. mem. Jackson Cmty. Concert Assn., 1958-64; mem. women's bd. Bapt. Health Care Found., 1993—, mem. invitations and tickets com. for Style Show, 1993-94, life mem., 1996—; active Friday Musicale of Jacksonville, Fla., 1979-86, Friends of Libr., 1993-94, Escambia Coun. on Aging, 1996. Mem. AAUW (sec. 1988-90, 2d v.p. 1990-92, tel. com. 1993—, br. area rep. cmty. problems Tenn. 1970-71, chmn. Tenn. divsn. cultural interests 1969-70, Fla. chmn. interest groups 1977-78), DAR (treas. 1981-82, chmn. Am. Heritage 1989-91, chmn. mag. 1991-93), UDC (sec. Jacksonville chpt. 1979-81, historian Jacksonville chpt. 1981-83, sec. Pensacola chpt. 1989-90, corr. sec. Pensacola chpt. 1992-94, mem. com. chmn. 1993-94, Christian Women's Club (prayer chmn. 1991—, book chmn. 1987, 88, 92-94, hostesses asst. chmn. 1994—), Pensacola Fedn. Garden Clubs (pres. Poinciana Circle 1989-91, pres. Bells of Ireland Circle 1978-80, civic chmn., 1991, sec. Alderman Park Cir., Jacksonville 1980-82), Judson Coll. Alumnae Assn. of Pensacola (pres. 1993—, exec. bd. 1993—), Tenn. Fedn. Garden Clubs (pres. Jackson Jr. 1958-60, 60-70, chmn. exec. bd. 1970-71, chmn. flower show 1968).

EPPERSON, STELLA MARIE, artist; b. Oakland, Calif., Nov. 6, 1920; d. Walter Peter and Martha Josephine (Schmitt) Ross; m. John Cray Epperson, May 10, 1941; children: Therese, John, Peter. Student, Calif. Coll. Arts & Crafts, 1939, 40-41, 56, Art Inst., San Miguel d'Allende, Mex., 1972. Portrait artist Oakland Art Assn., 1956—, San Francisco Women Artists, 1962—, Marin Soc. Artists, Ross, Calif., 1971—; art docent Oakland Mus., 1969-71, mem. women's bd., 1971—, art chmn. fund raiser, 1971-89, art guild chmn., 1965-69. One-woman shows include Oakland Mus. Auction, 1993, Univ. Club, San Francisco, 1994. Recipient San Francisco Women Artists award, 1989, Oakland Art Assn. award, 1991, Marin Soc. Artists award, 1992. Mem. U. Calif. Berkeley Faculty Club, Orinda Country Club. Republican. Roman Catholic. Home: 31 Valley View Rd Orinda CA 94563-1432

EPPLEY, FRANCES FIELDEN, retired secondary education educator, author; b. Knoxville, Tenn., July 18, 1921; d. Chester Earl and Beulah Magnolia (Wells) Fielden; m. Gordon Talmage Cougle, July 25, 1942; children:Russell Gordon Eppley, Carolyn Eppley Horseman; m. Fred Coan Eppley, Mar. 8, 1953; 1 child, Charlene Eppley Sellers. BA in English, Carson Newman Coll., 1942; MA, Winthrop Coll., 1963. Tchr., East Corinth (Maine) Acad., 1942-43; tchr. pub. schs., Charlotte, N.C., 1950-53, 59-83, Greenville, S.C., 1954-56, Spartanburg, S.C., 1957-58; head start tchr., summers 1964-68. Mem. hist. com. N.C. Bapt. Conv., 1985-88. Alpha Delta Kappa grantee, 1970. Mem. NEA, N.C. Social Studies Conf., Writers Assn., Alpha Delta Kappa, Pi Kappa Delta, Alpha Psi Omega. Baptist. Author: First Baptist Church of Charlotte, North Carolina: Its Heritage, 1981, History of Flint Hill, 1983, The First Astrologer, 1983, Sammy's Song, 1984, No Show Dog, 1985, Sun Signs for Christians, 1985, Astrology and Prophecy, 1987, Our Heavenly Home, 1987, Men Like-, 1987, A Hammer in the Land, 1988, Aunt Lillian's Seafoam Candy, 1988, Women's Lib in the Bible, 1988, William Penn, 1988, Columbus Was a Christian, 1988, Horoscopes of the Presidents, 1988, Messiah, 1989, 93, The Signs of Your Life, 1994; (musical drama): The Place To Be, 1982, Praise in the West, 1987; (musical show): Songs of The People, 1983; (song): Katie, 1985, (cantata) How Come, Jesus?, Stubborn Stella and The Sitting Stone, 1990, Columbus: The Race Home, 1990, Religion and Astrology, 1991, Astrology and Prophecy, 1991, The Ghosts of Elmwood, 1992, Full Circle, 1992, Sonnet to Charlotte, 1992, How Children Learn, 1992, Your Child and Astrology, 1992, Use Astrology to Help Your Child, 1992, Christmas Magnus, 1993, Ah, Jericho!, 1993, The Parthenon, U.S.A., 1993, The Shepherds Fields, 1993, Another Spring and World War II, 1994, The Mystery of the Laura K. Barnes, 1994, Contamination, 1994, First Landings, 1994, The Signs of Your Life, 1994, Teach the Children to Read, 1994, Hiawatha, 1995, The Stalker, 1995, Search for an Ancestor, 1995; editor: Chester's Letters, 1994, An Immediate Family, 1996, The Return, 1996. Home: 6611 Rolling Ridge Dr Charlotte NC 28211-5428

EPPS, ROSELYN ELIZABETH PAYNE, pediatrician, educator; b. Little Rock, Dec. 11, 1930; d. William Kenneth and Mattie Elizabeth (Beverly) Payne; m. Charles Harry Epps, Jr., June 25, 1955; children: Charles Harry III (dec.), Kenneth Carter, Roselyn Elizabeth, Howard Robert. BS, Howard U., 1951, MD, 1955; MPH, Johns Hopkins U., 1973; MA, Am. U., 1981. Intern Freedmen's Hosp., Howard U., Washington, 1955-56, pediatric resident, 1956-59, chief resident, 1958-59; practice medicine specializing in pediatrics Washington, 1960; med. officer, pediatrics D.C. Dept. Pub. Health, Washington, 1961-64, dir. Clinic for Retarded Children, 1964-67, chief Infant and Pre-Sch. div., 1967-71, dir. children and youth project, 1970-71, dir. maternal and crippled children services, 1971-75; chief Bur. Clin. Services D.C. Dept. Human Services, Washington, 1975-80, acting commr. pub. health, 1980; instr., asst. research investigator Howard U. Coll. Medicine, Washington, 1960-61, prof. Dept. Pediatrics and Child Health, 1980—, chief div. child devel., 1985-89, dir. Child Devel. Ctr., 1985-89; rsch. assoc., vis. scientist smoking tobacco and cancer program, div. cancer prevention and control Nat. Cancer Inst. NIH, Washington, 1989-91; expert Nat. Cancer Inst. NIH, Pub. Health Applications Br., Bethesda, Md., 1991—; chmn. task force to prepare comprehensive child care plan for D.C. Dept. Human Services, 1973-74; mem. nat. task force on pediatric hypertension Heart, Lung and Blood Inst., NIH, 1975; chmn. rsch. grants rev. com. maternal and child health and crippled children's svcs. HEW, Rockville, Md., 1978-80; sec. Commn. Licensure to Practice Healing Arts, Washington, 1980; trustee med. svc. D.C. Blue Shield Plan Nat. Capital Area, 1980; chmn. sec.'s adv. com. on rights and responsibilities of women HEW, Washington, 1981; dir. high-risk young people's project Howard U. Hosp., 1981-85; Washington coord. Know Your Body Program Am. Health Found., N.Y.C., 1982-91; mem. bd. advs. Coll. Home Econs. Ohio State U., Columbus, Ohio, 1983-87; adv. com. Nat. Ctr. for Edn. in Maternal and Child Health Georgetown U., Washington, 1983-89; nat. steering com., subcom. chmn. Healthy Mothers, Healthy Babies Coalition, Washington, 1983-90, mem. nominating com., 1991; cons. sickle cell disease NIH, 1984-88, Govt. Liberia and World Bank, 1984, UN Fund for Population Activities, N.Y. and Caribbean, 1984, filmstrip Miriam Berg Varian/Parents Mag. Films, 1978; bd. dirs. Vis. Nurse Assn., Inc., Washington, 1983-89; pres. bd. dirs. Hosp. for Sick Children, Washington, 1986-90, bd. dirs., 1984-94; frequent guest lectr. Weekly columnist Your Child's Health, Afro-Am. Newspaper, Washington, 1960-63; contbr. articles syndicated column Nat. Newspaper Pubs. Assn., 1982, Nat. Newspaper Assn., 1986-87; co-author audiocassettes; exhibitor sci. program; contbr. over 70 articles to profl. jours. Trustee nat. bd. Palmer Meml. Inst., Sedalia, N.C., 1969-71, Ford's Theatre, Washington, 1973-79; U.S. trustee Children's Internat. Summer Villages, Casstown, Ohio, 1969-76, pres., 1974-75; bd. mgrs. YWCA of D.C., 1970-76, 77-83, vice chmn., 1975-76; v.p. Jack and Jill of Am., Inc., Washington, 1970-71; nat. bd. dirs. Ctr. Population Options, Washington, 1980-86, Alexander Graham Bell Assn. for Deaf, Washington, 1974-78; bd. dirs. Washington Performing Arts Soc., 1971-81, v.p., 1979-81, hon. dir., 1981—; nat. bd. dirs. Meridian House Internat., Washington, 1974-81, counselor, 1981—; bd. dirs. YWCA Nat. Capital Area, 1975-76, United Negro Coll. Fund D.C., 1981-85; nat. bd. dirs. Girls Inc. (Formerly Girls Clubs Am., Inc.), N.Y.C., 1984-95, asst. sec., 1986-88, sec., 1988-90, pres., 1990-92; bd. dirs. Nat. Assembly Vol. Health and Welfare Agys., 1985-90, exec. bd., 1986-90, sec., 1988-90; bd. dirs. Mut. of Am., 1992—. Recipient Leadership and Meritorious Service in Medicine award Palmer Meml. Inst., 1968, 14th Ann. Fed. Women's award CSC, Washington, 1974, Superior Performance award D.C. Govt., 1975 Meritorious Cmty. Svc. award Howard U. Sch. Social Work Alumni Assns. and vis. com., 1980, Cert. Commendation Mayor of D.C., 1981, Roselyn Payne Epps M.D. Recognition Resolution of 1983 Council D.C., 1983, Disting. Vol. Leadership award March of Dimes Birth Defects Found., 1984, Community Svc. award D.C. Hosp. Assn., 1990, Physician of Yr. award Women's Med. Assn. N.Y.C., 1990, 91; named Outstanding Vol. in Leadership category YWCA Nat. Capital Area, 1983; inducted into D.C. Women's Hall of Fame D.C. Commn. for Women, 1990; grantee Robert Wood Johnson Found., Princeton, N.J., 1982, div. maternal and child health HHS, Rockville, Md., 1986; honored Tribute Resolution of 1981 declaring Feb. 14 Dr. Roselyn Payne Epps Day, Council of D.C., 1981; recipient Ophelia Settle Egypt award Planned Parenthood of Met. Washington, 1991, Advocacy award Soc. Advancement Women's Health, 1996. Fellow Am. Acad. Pediatrics (alt. state chmn. D.C. 1973-75, exec. com. D.C. chpt. 1983-94, pres. D.C. chpt. 1988-91, sec. cmty. pediatrics sect. 1973-75, cert. appreciation 1979, mem. coun. of child and adolescent health, cmty. and internat. health sect., charter mem., exec. com. 1992-94); mem. Acad. Medicine, AMA (alt. del. Nat. Med. Assn. 1983-85), Am. Med. Women's Assn. (chmn. pub. health com. 1973-75, pres. br. 1 1974-76, sec. 1988, v.p. 1989, pres-elect nat. 1990, pres. 1991, found. founding pres. 1992, bd. dirs. 1992—, chmn. nominating com. 1993, Physician of Yr. award 1991, Cmty. Svc. award 1990, Elizabeth Blackwell award 1992), Women's Forum Washington, Med. Soc. D.C. (exec. bd. 1990, sec. 1990, pres.-elect 1991, pres. 1992, chair exec. bd. 1993, ann. Cmty. Svc. award 1982), Am. Pediatric Soc., D.C. Hosp. Assn. (Cmty. Svc. award 1990), Am. Pub. Health Assn. (action bd. 1977-79, joint policy com. 1978-79, gov. council 1978-81), Met. Washington Pub. Health Assn. (gov. council 1975-78, 81-83, ann. award 1981), Nat. Med. Assn. (chmn. pediatric sect. 1977-79, Ross Labs. award 1979, Outstanding Svcs. to Children during Internat. Yr. of Child award 1979, Meritorious Service Appreciation award 1979, W.M. Cobb co-lectr. 1985, mem. Coun. on Maternal and Child Health, 1974-92, chmn. 1979-89, ann. Roselyn Payne Epps Symposium 1994—, Grace Marilyn James award for Disting svc. Pediatric sect. 1991, Achievement award 1993, ann. Roselyn Payne Epps symposium 1994—), Am. Hosp. Assn. (maternal and child health sect. governing coun. 1989, 1992-94, maternal and child health nominating com. 1991), Soc. for the Advancement of Women's Health Rsch. (award for advocacy 1991), The Women's Forum of Washington, Alpha Omega Alpha, Delta Omega, Alpha Kappa Alpha. Mem. United Ch. of Christ. Clubs: Pearls (pres. 1984-86), Carrousels (corr. sec. 1978-80), Links (pres. Met. chpt. 1986-89) (Washington), Cosmos. Lodge: Zonta. Home: 1775 N Portal Dr NW Washington DC 20012-1014 Office: Nat Cancer Inst NIH DCPC/CCSP/PHARB/EPN-241 6130 Executive Blvd MSC7333 Bethesda MD 20892-7333

EPSTEIN, BARBARA, editor; b. Boston, Aug. 30, 1929; d. Harry W. and Helen (Diamond) Zimmerman; children: Jacob, Helen. B.A., Radcliffe Coll., 1949. Editor N.Y. Rev. Books, N.Y.C., 1963—. Office: NY Rev of Books 250 W 57th St New York NY 10102-0158

EPSTEIN, CYNTHIA FUCHS, sociology educator, writer. B.A. in Polit. Sci., Antioch Coll., 1955; postgrad., U. Chgo. Law Sch., 1955-56; M.A. in Sociology, New Sch. Social Research, 1960; Ph.D., Columbia U., 1968. Instr. anthropology Finch Coll., 1961-62; assoc. in sociology Columbia U., 1964-65, instr. Barnard Coll., 1965; instr. sociology Queens Coll., N.Y.C., 1966-67, asst. prof., 1968-70, assoc. prof., 1971-74, prof., 1974-84; prof. grad. ctr. CUNY, 1974, Disting. prof. Grad. Ctr., 1990; resident scholar Russell Sage Found., 1982-88; co-dir. Program in Sex Roles and Social Change Ctr. Social Scis., Columbia U., 1977-82, co-dir. NIMH tng. grant on sociology and econs. of women and work Grad. Ctr., disting. prof. Grad. Ctr., 1990—; vis. prof. Health Sci. Ctr., SUNY-Stony Brook, 1975; vis. scholar Stanford U., 1991; Phi Beta Kappa vis. scholar, 1991-92; cons., lectr. and speaker in field; mem. com. on women's employment and related social issues NRC-Nat. Acad. Scis., 1981-88; adv. com. on econ. role of women Pres.' Council Econ. Advisers, 1973-74. Author: Woman's Place: Options and Limits in Professional Careers, 1970, Women in Law, 1981, 2d edit., 1993, Deceptive Distinctions: Sex, Gender and the Social Order, 1988; editor: (with William J. Goode) The Other Half: Roads to Women's Equality, 1971; (with Rose Laub Coser) Access to Power: Cross-National Studies of Women and Elites, 1981; mem. editorial bds.: Signs, Women's Studies, Internat. Jour. Work and Occupations, Sociol. Focus, Women 1974, Dissent, Am. Jour. Sociology, CUNY Mag., Gender and Soc.; contbr. chpts. to books, articles to profl. jours. Trustee Antioch U., 1984—. Recipient Award for Disting. Contb. to Study of Sex and Gender, ASAN, 1994; grantee Inst. Life Ins., 1974, Ford Found., 1975-77, Rsch. Found. City of N.Y., 1974-76, 90-93, Guggenheim Meml. Found., 1976-77, Ctr. Advanced Study in Behavioral Scis., 1977-78, Russell Sage Found., 1982-90, Sloan Found., 1995—; fellow NIH, 1963-66, MacDowell Colony, 1973, 74, 77, 80, Guggenheim Found., 1976-77, Ctr. Advanced Study in Behavioral Sci., 1977-78, Va. Ctr. Creative Arts, 1984. Mem. AAAS, Eastern Sociol. Soc. (v.p. 1977-79, exec. coun. 1973-74, pres. 1983-84, I Peter Gellman award), Am. Sociol. Assn. (coun. 1974-77, com. exec. office and budget 1978-81, chmn. sect. on orgns. and occupations, chmn. sect. on sociology of sex roles 1973-74), Social Rsch. Assn., Internat. Sci. Commn. on Family. Office: CUNY Grad Ctr 33 W 42nd St New York NY 10036-8003

EPSTEIN, JOAN OSBORN, music educator; b. St. Petersburg, Fla., June 14, 1953; d. Donald Newton and Marion Rita (Pangborn) Osborn; m. Daniel Mark Epstein, May 18, 1975; children: Ariel, Eve, Eliza. BA, Smith Coll., 1974; MusM, Yale U., 1976. Reading specialist Pinellas County Schs., Fla., 1979-81; music prof. Eckerd Coll., St. Petersburg, Fla., 1981—; part-time instr. humanities St. Petersburg Jr. Coll., 1978-81; pres. Tampa Bay Composer's Forum, Fla., 1991-93. Composer: (mus. compositions) Bond Revelations, 1992, Salamander Songs, 1993, Cumberland, 1994, Savannah, 1996. Pres. West Fla. Smith Coll. Club, 1989-92; chair adult edn. Congregation

B'nai Israel, St. Petersburg, 1981-83. Office: Eckerd Coll 4200 54th Ave S Saint Petersburg FL 33710

EPSTEIN, MARSHA ANN, public health administrator, physician; b. Chgo., Feb. 4, 1945; m. Syyed Tariq Mahmood, June 14, 1975; 1 child, Lee Rashad Mahmood. BA, Reed Coll., 1966; MD, U. Calif., San Francisco, 1969; MPH, U. Calif., Berkeley, 1971. Diplomate Am. Bd. Preventive Medicine. Intern French Hosp., San Francisco, 1969-70; resident in preventive medicine Sch. Pub. Health, U. Calif., Berkeley, 1971-73; fellow in family planning dept. ob-gyn. UCLA, 1973-74; med. dir. Herself Health Clinic, L.A., 1974-79; pvt. adult gen. practitioner L.A., 1978-82; dist. health officer L.A. County Pub. Health, Inglewood, Calif., 1982—; part-time physician U. Calif. Student Health, Berkeley, 1970-73; co-med. dir. Monsenior Oscar Romero Free Clinic, L.A., 1992-93. Mem. APHA, Am. Coll. Physician Execs., Am. Med. Women's Assn., So. Calif. Pub. Health Assn., L.A. County Med. Women's Assn., L.A. County Sr. Women Mgrs. Democrat. Jewish. Office: Tucker Health Ctr 123 W Manchester Blvd Inglewood CA 90301-1753

EPSTEIN, SANDRA GAIL, psychologist; b. Boston, July 19, 1939; d. Mischa and Frances (Greenfield) Schneiderman; 1 child, Suanne Charyl. AB, Boston U., 1962; MA, U. Conn., 1969, diploma, 1978, PhD, 1979. Sch. psychol. examiner various pub. schs., Conn., 1970-73, sch. psychologist, 1973—; staff psychologist Day Kimball Hosp. Mental Health Clinic, Putnam, Conn., 1971-74; psychologist Thompson (Conn.) Med. Ctr., 1973-80; staff psychiatry dept. Day Kimball Hosp., Putnam, 1983—; pvt. practice Woodstock, Conn., 1980-85, Farmington, 1983-93, Putnam, 1985—; instr. Annhurst Coll., Woodstock, Conn., 1971-76; cons. N.E. Area Regional Ednl. Svc., Wauregan, Conn., 1978-79, Capitol Region Ednl. Coun., West Hartford, Conn., 1980—, Ctr. for Interpersonal Rels., Putnam, 1985-88, Hebrew Acad. Greater Hartford, Bloomfield, Conn., 1983-89, Conn. Bur. Rehab. Svcs., Norwich, 1992—. Mem. Am. Psychol. Assn., Internat. Soc. Hypnosis, Internat. Psychosomatics Inst., N.Y. Acad. Sci., Conn. Psychol. Assn., Am. Soc. Clin. Hypnosis, Am. Acad. Pain Mgmt., N.Y. Acad. Sci. Office: PO Box 207 Woodstock CT 06281-0207

EPSTEIN, SUSAN, journalist; b. Clifton, N.J., July 25, 1952; d. Paul N. and Hannah (Pallay) E. BA Douglas Coll., Rutgers U., New Brunswick, N.J., 1974. Reporter Star Ledger, Newark, N.J., 1974—. Office: Star Ledger Monmouth County Courthouse Freehold NJ 07728

EPSTEIN, SUSAN BAERG, librarian, consultant; b. Chgo., Feb. 28, 1938; d. Philip William and Alice (Mackenzie) Ruppert; m. William Baerg, 1960 (div. 1971); children: Elisabeth, William Philip, Sara Margaret; m. A. H. Epstein, 1977 (div. 1981). BA in Econs., Wellesley Coll., 1960; MLS, Immaculate Heart Coll., 1972. Systems analyst IBM, San Jose, Calif., 1960-63, Control Data Corp., Palo Alto, Calif., 1963-64; dir. tech. and automation svcs. Huntington Beach (Calif.) Pub. Libr., 1972-74, asst. city libr., 1974-78; spl. asst. to county libr. L.A. County Pub. Libr., L.A., 1978-81, chief tech. svcs., 1979-81; pres. Susan Baerg Epstein, Ltd., Costa Mesa, Calif., 1981—. Columnist Libr. Jour., 1984—. Mem. ALA (chair com.), Calif. Libr. Assn. (councilor 1973-80), Am. Soc. Info. Sci. Office: 1992 Lemnos Dr Costa Mesa CA 92626

EPSTEIN-SHEPHERD, BEE J., professional speaker, consultant; b. Tubingen, Fed. Republic Germany, July 14, 1937; came to U.S., 1940, naturalized, 1945; d. Paul and Milly (Stern) Singer; student Reed Coll., 1954-57; m. Leonard Epstein, June 14, 1959 (div. 1982); children: Bettina, Nicole, Seth; m. Frank Shepherd, 1991 (dec. 1992). BA, U. Calif., Berkeley, 1958; MA, Goddard Coll., 1976; PhD, Internat. Coll., 1982. Bus. instr. Monterey Peninsula Coll., 1975-85; owner, mgr. Bee Epstein Assos., cons. to mgmt., Carmel, Calif., 1977—; pres. Success Tours Inc., Carmel, 1981—; founder, prin. Monterey Profl. Speakers, 1982; instr. Monterey Peninsula Coll., Golden Gate U., U. Calif., Santa Cruz, Am. Inst. Banking, Inst. Ednl. Leadership, Calif. State Fire Acad. Monterey Peninsula Coll., U. Calif., Berkeley, Foothill Coll., U. Alaska. Author: How to Create Balance at Work, at Home, in Your Life, 1988, Stress First Aid for the Working Woman, 1991, Free Yourself From Diets, 1994, Mental Management for Great Golf, 1996; contbr. articles to newspapers and trade mags. Research grantee, 1976. Mem. NAFE, Nat. Speakers' Assn., Peninsula Profl. Women's Network, Assn. for Advancement Applied Sports Psychology, Nat. Guild of Hypnotists. Democrat. Jewish. Office: PO Box 221383 Carmel CA 93922-1383

ERB, DORETTA LOUISE BARKER, polymer applications scientist; b. Upper Darby, Pa., June 21, 1932; d. Ralph Merton and Pauline Kaufman (Isenberg) B.; m. Robert Allan Erb, June 27, 1953; children: Sylvia Ann, Susan Doretta, Carolyn Joy. BS in Pharmacy, Phila. Coll. Pharmacy and Sci., 1954. Registered pharmacist, Pa. Pharmacist Borland's Pharmacy, Upland, Pa., 1954-65; assoc. scientist Franklin Rsch. Ctr., ATC div. Calspan Corp., Norristown, Pa., 1974-93; sole propr., pres. Siliclone Studio, Valley Forge, Pa., 1982—. Mem. Am. Anaplastology Assn., Sigma Xi (chpt. sec. 1990-93). Presbyterian. Home and Office: PO Box 86 Jug Hollow Rd Valley Forge PA 19481-0086

ERBACHER, KATHRYN ANNE, editor, art and design writer, marketing consultant; b. Kansas City, Mo., Dec. 11, 1947; d. Philip Joseph and Thelma Lillian (Hines) E. BS in English Edn., U. Kans., 1970; BA magna cum laude in Art, Metro State Coll., Denver, 1983. Reporter, Kansas City Star (Mo.), 1970-71; newswriter, publicist Washington U., St. Louis, 1972-76; copy editor Kansas City Star-Times (Mo.), 1976-79; corp. comm. mgr., editor Petro-Lewis Corp., Denver, 1979-82; assoc. Artours, Inc., Denver, 1983-84; assoc. editor arts and travel editor Denver Mag., 1984-86; owner Arts Internat., 1987—; internat. editor Gates Rubber Co., Denver, 1987-90. Creative dir. TV shorts for contemporary art collection Denver Art Mus., 1983. Bd. dirs. Metro State Coll. Alumni Assn., 1986-87, co-chair 1987 Metro State Coll. Alumni Awards Dinner, Denver; bd. govs. Metro State Coll. Found., 1986-87; mem. program com. Colo. Bus. Com. for the Arts, 1989-90; mem. pub. affairs com. Denver Ctr. for Performing Arts., 1989—; active Denver Art Mus. Alliance for Contemporary Art, 1984—. Recipient award for arts writing Denver Partnership, 1986, award for Artbeat column in Denver mag. Colo. MAC News, 1986, also award for spl. fashion sect. Dressing the Part; co-recipient award for Gates Rubber Co. Global Communications Bus./Profl. Advt. Assn., 1988. Mem. Denver Art Mus. (mem. design coun.), Museo de las Americas, Am. Assn. Museums, Mus. Modern Art. Avocations: visual art, theater, film, travel, Spanish language. Office: Arts Internat 1450 Wynkoop 3d Denver CO 80202

ERDEN, SYBIL ISOLDE, artist; b. N.Y.C., Nov. 30, 1950; d. Mark and Annelise (Stautner) E.; m. Philip M. Freund, July 7, 1970 (div. 1978); m. Jerry Buley, June 15, 1991. Student, Acad. of Art, San Francisco, 1970-71, San Francisco Art Inst., 1971-73, Ariz. State U., 1992-93. lectr. Calif. Coll. Arts and Crafts, 1978, Tempe Fine Art Ctr., 1985, Collins Gallery, San Francisco, 1986, Collage Art Appreciation Group, Colorado Springs, Colo., 1987, South Park Sch. Dist., Fairplay, Colo., 1987, Al Collins Sch. Graphic Design, 1989-90, Cerro Coso C.C., Calif., 1991, Chico State U., 1991; tchr. workshops City of Phoenix, 1991, Cerro Coso C.C., Calif., 1991, Chico State U., 1991; tchr. workshops City of Phoenix, 1991, Cerro Coso C.C., 1991, Phoenix Coll., 1992-94, Cochise Coll., 1993; guest speaker 6th ann. Tempe Art Ctr. Seminar for Artists, 1993, Mesa C.C., 1994—, Bird Talk, 1993-94, Caged Bird Hobbyest.1. Shows include San Francisco Art Inst., 1973, The Bush Street Gallery, San Francisco, 1977, The Top Floor Gallery, San Francisco, 1979, I-Beam, San Francisco, 1980, Diablo Valley Coll., Walnut Creek, Calif., 1980, The Stable, San Francisco, 1982, Tempe Fine Arts Ctr., 1985, Collins Gallery, San Francisco, 1986, 89, 90—, Berkeley (Calif.) Art Ctr., 1986, The Cave, San Francisco, 1981, Alwun House, Phoenix, 1985, 87-93 (award 1989), Grand Canyon Coll., Phoenix, 1988, N.Mex. Jr. Coll., 1988, 90 (award 1990), San Francisco State U., 1988, Pa. State U., 1989, Ohio State U., 1989, Mendocino Art Ctr., 1990, Jewish Cmty. Ctr., Denver, 1990, Cerro Coso Cmty. Coll., Kern County, Calif., 1990-91, Chico State U., 1991, Sierra Arts Found., 1991, Ea. N.Mex. U., 1992, Shemer Art Ctr., Phoenix, 1991, Chico (Calif.) State U., 1992, Sierra Arts Found., Reno, Nev., 1992, Movemiento Artistico del Rio Salado Artspace, 1993—, IOA Artspace, Oklahoma City, Okla., 1995; executed mural office of Dr. Peter Eckman, San Francisco, 1977, HandBall Express, San Francsico, 1981; archived by Smithsonian Mus. Archive Am. Art, Washington. Mem. Am. Surrealist Initiative, Ariz. Visionary Alternative (founder, dir. 1984-85, 87—), Movemiento Artistico del Rio Salado Artspace (artist mem.), LIC Rehabber for the Birdd Rehab.- Ilitation Found. Democrat. Jewish.

ERDLEY, SHIELA LYNN, rehabilitation nurse; b. Fairfax, Mo., Mar. 18, 1955; d. Harry Lee and Uldeen Merle (Underwood) Cooper; m. Scott Wayne Hall, June 20, 1976 (div. Jan. 1987); children: Brad, Clarence; m. Aaron Dean Erdley, Aug. 15, 1987; children: Mike, Aric. Dipl. nursing, Meth. Med. Ctr. Sch. Nursing, St. Joseph, Mo., 1976. Cert. med.-surg. nurse, Mo.; ACLS, Mo.; exercise specialist cert. Staff nurse Meth. Med. Ctr., St. Joseph, Mo., 1976-87; cardiac rehab. nurse Heartland Health Sys., St. Joseph, 1987—. Mem. Am. Assn. Cardiovascular and Pulmonary Rehab., Mo./Kans. Assn. Cardiovascular and Pulmonary Rehab. Lutheran. Home: 208 Lincoln Robinson KS 66532

ERDMAN, BARBARA, visual artist; b. N.Y.C., Jan. 30, 1936; d. Isidore and Julia (Burstein) E. Postgrad., Chinese Inst., 1959-60; BFA, Cornell U., 1956. Visual artist Santa Fe, 1977—; guest critic Studio Arte Centro Internat., Florence, Italy, 1986; guest lectr. Austin Coll. Sherman, Tex., 1986; mem. Oracle Conf. Polaroid Corp., nationwide, 1986-88. One-woman shows include Aspen Inst., Baca, Colo., 1981, Scottsdale (Ariz.) Ctr. for Arts, 1988, AAAS, Washington, 1994; exhibited in group shows, 1959—, including AAAS; represented in permanent collections N.Mex. Mus. Fine Arts, Santa Fe, IBM, N.Y.C.; author: New Mexico USA, 1985. Bd. dirs. N.Mex. Right to Choose, Santa Fe, 1981-87, Santa Fe Ctr. for Photography, 1983, pres. bd. 1985-89; mem. N.Mex. Mus. Found., Albuquerque Mus. Found. Mem. Art Student's League (life), Soc. for Photographic Edn. (guest lectr. 1987), Santa Fe Ctr. for Photography (pres., bd. dirs. 1984-89), Am. Coun. Arts. Home and Office: 1070 Calle Largo Santa Fe NM 87501-1090

ERDMAN, JEAN, dancer, choreographer; b. Honolulu, Feb. 20, 1916; d. John Pinney and Marion (Dillingham) Erdman; m. Joseph Campbell, May 5, 1938 (dec. Oct. 1987). Diploma, Sarah Lawrence Coll., 1936; DArts (hon.), Bard Coll., 1992. Organized Jean Erdman Dance Group, 1944, performer, choreographer, 1944-54; dir. dance dept. Bard Coll., Annandale-on-Hudson, N.Y., 1954-57; creator, producer, performer Jean Erdman Theater of Dance, 1957-72; co-founder Theater of the Open Eye, 1972; creator, head Dance Theater program NYU Sch. Arts, 1966-71; artist-in-residence arts festivals in Vancouver, Honolulu, Tokyo, L.A., San Francisco, Boulder; pres. Joseph Campbell Found., Honolulu; choreographer The Transformations of Medusa, 1942, Ophelia, 1946, The Perilous Chapel, 1949, The Coach with the Six Insides, 1960, Gauguin in Tahiti, 1972, Moon Mysteries, 1965, The Dream of Kitamura, 1978, The Minotaur Among Us, 1985. Recipient Obie award, 1963, Vernon Rice award Drama Desk, 1963, Drama Desk award, 1972, Heritage award Nat. Dance Assn., 1993, Manhattan award Manhattan Mag., 1994. Mem. Century Club, Outrigger Canoe Club, Am. Dance Guild, Sacred Dance Guild (hon.). Office: 136 Waverly Pl # 14D New York NY 10014

ERDMAN, TERRI SUE, pediatric and neonatal nurse, consultant; b. Casper, Wyo., June 27, 1954; d. Frederick Robert and Gretchen May (McCabe) Braunschweig; m. Steven H. Erdman, Oct. 2, 1982; 1 child, Samuel Cody. BS, U. Wyo., 1976; MS, U. Utah, 1981. RN, Calif.; cert. neonatal nurse practitioner. Staff nurse, charge nurse, transport nurse U. Utah Med. Ctr., Salt Lake City, 1976-80; neonatal nurse practitioner Primary Children's Med. Ctr., Salt Lake City, 1981-85; program coord. U. Utah Coll. Nursing, Salt Lake City, 1981-85; unit dir. med. transport svcs. dept. U. Nebr., Omaha, 1985-88, program dir. SKYMED, 1985-88; asst. prof. nursing, clin. instr. pediatrics Loma Linda (Calif.) U., 1988-90, acad. coord., 1988-90; cons. Tucson, Ariz., 1990—. Editl. cons., mem. rev. bd. Neonatal Network, 1985—, home study course reviewer, 1991—. Bd. dirs. Tucson Cmty. Sch., 1994-95, bd. trustees, 1995—. Mem. Nat. Assn. Neonatal Nurses (v.p. spl. interest group for advanced practice 1984-88, pres. 1989-91, bd. dirs. 1989-91, chair econ. task force 1992-95), Nat. Alliance Nurse Practitioners (bd. dirs., sec. 1992-95), Sigma Theta Tau Internat., Phi Kappa Phi. Democrat.

ERGEN, VIOLA S., accountant; b. Mpls., Sept. 10, 1915; d. Otto and Anna Katherine (Matikainen) Siebenthal; m. William Krasny Ergen, Feb. 5, 1944 (dec. Feb. 1971); children: Anne Katherine, John Arnold Krasny, Frederick Julien Krasny, Charles William Krasny, Mary Elizabeth. BBS, U. Minn., 1939. Sr. acct. U. Minn., Mpls., 1938-45; various duties Gallop Poll, Princeton, N.J., 1945-46; bus. mgr. Children's Mus. Oak Ridge, Tenn., 1973—. Bd. dirs., fin. chmn. Girl Scouts U.S., Knoxville, Tenn., 1972-84 (Thanks badge 1982); treas. U. Tenn. Arboretum Soc., Oak Ridge, 1984-91. Recipient Vol. Youth Svc. award Rotary Club Oak Ridge, 1984-85. Mem. AAUW (treas. 1990-92, 94—). Episcopalian. Home: 103 Orkney Rd Oak Ridge TN 37830 Office: Childrens Mus Oak Ridge 461 West Outer Dr Oak Ridge TN 37830

ERICHSEN-HUBBARD, ISABEL JANICE, music educator; b. LaCrosse, Wis., June 18, 1935; d. Frank Peter August and Janice May (Grutzmacher) Erichsen; m. Allan Paterson, Apr. 4, 1959; children: Janel Isabel, John Allan. BS with honors, U. Wis., Madison, 1957, MS, 1979, postgrad., 1980. Tchr., Kenosha (Wis.) Bd. Edn., 1957-60; tchr., supr. Madison (Wis.) Bd. Edn., 1968—; cooperating tchr. sr. program U. Wis. master tchr. seminars, 1978—; pvt. piano and vocal coach, 1950—; choir dir. St. Mary's Lutheran Ch., Kenosha, 1959-61; mem., soloist Madison Meth. Ch., Cath. Diocesan Choir, 1981-83, U. Wisc. Choral Union Choir. Author: Reading Techniques Using the Newspapers, Magazines, 1975, Spell It Again Sam, 1978, Hidden Curriculum, 1979, contbr. to Kenosha Kindergarten Teacher's Handbook, 1958. Program chair YWCA, 1961-65, bd. dirs., membership svcs., 1991—; chmn. UNICEF, 1960, Coop. Nursery Sch., 1960; info. chmn. Am. Cancer Soc., Dane County, 1960-68; bd. dirs., sec. Friends of Meth. Hosp., 1986-87, also vol. escort, info. desk, gift shop, chapel musician; bd. dirs., trustee Meriter Hosp.; R.S.V.P. Sch. Liaison Danc County, 1977-88; vocal & piano adjucator Wis. Assn. Music Schs., 1984—; vol. Am. Players Theatre, 1987—; bd. dirs. membership com. YMCA; active Methodist Women's Soc., United Ch. Women, Madison Civic Assn., U. Wis. Cooperating Mentor Program, 1987-91, Opera Buffs, Wis. Exec. Mansion Guides. Recipient Carol award Madison Jaycette Club, 1966, 3d grand prize Wis. State Jour. Cookbook, 1971, Golden Apple award Madison Met. Sch. Dist., 1988, Mature Lifetsyles winner, 1993-95, Firstar Recipe winner, 1995. Mem. NEA, Wis. Edn. Assn., Madison Tchrs., Inc. (grievance com. 1987-89), Lafollette Area Lang. Arts Cadre, Madison Met. Sch. Dist. Human Relations Cadre, Social Studies K-12 Cadre, U. Wis. Alumni Assn. (life, co-hostess chmn., mentor program-edn. adminstrn. cadre), Madison Metro Women's Club, Madison Civics Club, Cherokee Country Club, Jr. Golf Club (dir. 1974-75), Sigma Alpha Iota (Sword of Honor, past pres., sec., Patroness com. 1991—), Chi Omega (alumni sec. 1970-87), Pi Delta Kappa (life). Home: 6708 Clovernoon Rd Stonefield Village Madison WI 53562-3871 Office: Orchard Ridge Elem 5602 Russett Rd Madison WI 53711-3568

ERICK, MIRIAM ANNA, dietitian, medical writer; b. Norwich, Conn., Apr. 1, 1958; d. Eugene A. and Toini (Lampi) E. BS, U. Conn., Storrs, 1970; MS, U. Bridgeport, 1992. Morning sickness cons. Brigham and Women's Hosp., Boston, perinatal dietitian. Author: No More Morning Sickness: A Survival Guide for Pregnant Women, 1993, Take Two Crackers and Call Me in the Morning! A Real Life Guide for Surviving Morning Sickness, 1995; contbr. articles to profl. jours. Mem. Am. Dietetic Assn., Am. Coll. Nutrition, Assn. Chemoreception Scis., Am. Botanical Coun., Am. Coll. Ob/gyn. Home: 36 Winchester St # 8 Brookline MA 02146-2747 Office: Brigham and Women's Hosp 75 Francis St Brookline MA 02146-6638

ERICKSEN, ANNA MAE, retired nursing administrator; b. Moose Jaw, Sask., Can., Nov. 1, 1919; d. Eric Andrew and Evelyn (Kyle) E.; R.N., Deaconess Hosp., Spokane, Wash., 1943. Night charge nurse Deaconess Hosp., Spokane, 1943, pvt. duty nurse, 1946, staff nurse, 1947; head nurse emergency dept., outpatient dept., Spokane Poison Center, Deaconess Hosp., 1948-57, supr., 1957-70, asst. dir., 1970-73, assoc. dir. nursing service, 1973-78, adminstrv. asst. regional outreach services, physician liaison, 1978, asst. to adminstr., dir. outreach program, coordinator continuing edn., 1978-82, dir. Spokane Poison Center, dir. physician liaison, 1979-82; dir. outreach program Physician Liaison and Reg. Poison Ctr. Deaconess Med. Ctr., 1982-87, ret., 1987; chmn. disaster com., mem. safety com.; advisor to Wash. State Assn. Nursing Students, 1956-60; bd. dirs. Regional Emergency Med. Services Council, 1975—, 1st v.p., 1978-79, chmn., 1979—; mem. N.E. Hosp. Disaster Com., Gov.'s ad hoc com. Emergency Med. Svcs., Emergency Med. Ambulance Pier Com., Emergency Med. and Ambulance Review Com., Review Com. for Tng. Emergency Med. and Paramed. Technicians; bd. dirs. Nat. Poison Center Network; chmn. Govs. Emergency Med. Svcs. Commn., 1980-83; chmn. awards com. East Region Emergency Med. Svcs. Coun., 1990—; chmn. Citizens for Spokane County EMS Levy, 1993. Mem. Spokane Health Assn.; v.p. NE Heart Assn.; recruitment nurse for ARC in Inland Empire, 1960-68; bd. dirs. Spokane Area Safety Council, 1963-67, vice chmn., 1966-67; bd. govs. Home Safety Council Wash. State, 1966-69, v.p., 1969-70; bd. dirs. NE chpt. Wash. State Heart Assn., 1966—, v.p., 1974-75; polio fund com. Spokane County Med. Soc.; chmn. adv. bd. Rape Crisis Network 1978, 1980, 1982-84; program chmn. Spokane Youth Health Council; bd. dirs. Human Tng. Services Inst., Spokane, 1974-80, sec.-treas., 1976-77; bd. dirs. ARC, 1985-90, chmn. health svcs. com., 1989—, chmn. outlying svcs. area com., 1993, mem. disaster action team, 1993—, chmn. team and disaster health svcs. com., 1993—, lifetime mem. 1994; mem. panels United Crusade; panel mem. campaign com. United Way, 1978-81; founder Nat. Rural Nurse Orgn., 1989—, dir., 1989—, chmn. grants com., 1992—, lifetime mem., 1993; active Polio Program, 1962-69; adv. bd. Samaritan Ctr. of Inland Empire, 1981-85. Served to 1st lt. U.S. Army Nurse Corps, 1943-45. Named Spokane Woman of Achievement, Am. Bus. and Profl. Women, 1961, Theta Sigma Phi, 1968, Wash. State's Most Involved Nurse, 1970, Outstanding Lady of Year, Spokane, 1972; recipient Key award Inland Empire chpt. Safety Council, 1976, Disting. Citizen award Rotary Club of Spokane, 1982, 1st Ericksen award for emergency nursing, 1985, Appreciation award Am. Lupus Soc., 1985, Svc. to Future Farmers of Am. award, Sandpoint, Idaho, 1980, award of Appreciation People to People Citizen Ambassador Program, 1986, Wash. State EMS Outstanding Effort and Svc. award, 1991, Outstanding Citizen award Spokane City Coun., 1991, Ann Magnuson award Nat. ARC, 1991, Anna Mae Erickson award Indland N.W. chpt. ARC 1992, Inland Northwest Red Cross Clara Barton Honor award, 1995. Mem. Inland Empire Nurses Assn. (bd. 1956-60), Wash. State (bd. dirs. 1959-63, pres. 1960-64, chmn. careers com. 1970-72), ANA (del. 1960-62, 64), Emergency Nurses Assn. (life, founder Inland Empire chpt., pres. 1971, region X rep., 1970-77, asst. exec. dir. 1972, nat. pres. 1975-76, nat. bd. dirs. 1970-77), Spokane Greater Community Found., 1978—. Presbyterian. Clubs: Altrusa (pres. 1965-68), Epsilon Sigma Alpha (pres. Spokane chpt. 1960-62, treas. 1958-59, mem. state coms.). Home: 2311 W 16th Ave # 70 Spokane WA 99204-4467 Office: Deaconess Med Ctr-Spokane W 800 Fifth Ave PO Box 248 Spokane WA 00248

ERICKSON, CONSTANCE JUELKE, accountant; b. Mandan, N.D., Sept. 29, 1965; d. Conrad Orville and Gladys Irene (Goodrich) Juelke; m. Michael Blaine Erickson, Mar. 29, 1994; 1 child, Kallie Joan. B of Accountancy, U. N.D., 1987. CPA, N.D., 1989. Sr. auditor Arthur Andersen & Co., Mpls., 1987-92; JIT ops. specialist Graco, Inc., Mpls., 1992-95; dir. cost acctg. GNB Techs., Mendota Heights, Minn., 1995—. Bd. dirs. Feed My Starving Children, Mpls., 1992-94; vol., Jr. Achievement, Mpls., 1993. Mem. AICPA, Am. Women's Soc. of CPAs. Methodist.

ERICKSON, DONNA KAY, administrative assistant; b. Aurora, Ill., Oct. 5, 1938; d. Adam G. and Bernice C. (Poull) Pierce; m. Clifford Erickson, June 23, 1962; children: Kareen Kay, Katherine Louise. BA in Elem. Edn., Aurora Coll., 1960. Elem. tchr. Fourth St. Sch., Geneva, Ill., 1961-63; with various fin. instns. Aurora, 1963-68; adminstrv. asst. Ill. State Rep. from 42nd Dist., Aurora, 1979—. Pres. bd. dirs. Mutual Ground, Inc., 1996—. Mem. AAUW (1st v.p. Aurora br. 1992—, pub. policy chair Aurora br. 1993—, Named Gift recipient 1995, Spirit award 1995), PTA (life), Women Organizing Women for Aurora (v.p. 1996—). Lutheran. Home: 756 Duncan Dr Aurora IL 60506 Office: State Rep Suzanne Deuchler 1128 A Prairie St Aurora IL 60506

ERICKSON, LINDA RAE, educator; b. Huron, S.D., Aug. 17, 1948; d. Robert Emil and Esther (Schorzman) E. BS, U. Nebr., 1966; MA, U. No. Colo., Greeley, 1970; cert., U. Denver, 1990. Cert. elem. tchr., adminstr., prin. Spl. edn. resource tchr. Ignacio, Colo., 1983-85; elem. tchr. Woodland Park, Colo., 1985-86; tutor spl. edn. Am. Sch. London, 1987; elem. tchr. Borough of Brent, London, 1987, Internat. Sch. Hampstead, London, 1987-88; tchr. spl. edn. Carronhill Sch. for Handicapped, Stonehaven, Scotland, 1988-89; elem. tchr. Littleton (Colo.) Pub. Schs., 1970-83, 89—; enrichment program coord. Sandburg Sch., 1991-93; co-chair Alternative Authentic Assessment Com., 1991—, Sandburg Parent Adv. Com., 1993-96; facilitator Littleton Pub. Schs., 1977-83, 90—; workshop presenter Nat. Coun. Tchrs. English, Nat. Coun. Social Studies, WNET-TV Sta. Active Fawcett Soc., London, 1987-89, NEA-Colo. Edn. Assn. Women's Caucus, 1979—. Woman of Yr. nominee Littleton Jaycees, 1982; fed. grantee Use of Group Paperbacks in the Elem. Classroom, 1978. Mem. NEA (women's leadership tng. cadre 1978-85), NOW, Colo. Edn. Assn., Littleton Edn. Assn. (bd. dirs., chair unit-bargaining team 1976-85), Internat. Reading Assn. (chair Pikes Peak 1986, Colo. coun. children's books award com. 1993—, workshop presenter, reader meets writer com. co-coun. 1996—, tutor comitis crisis ctr. for homeless 1995—), Nat. Coun. Tchrs. English (co-lang. arts soc. exec. bd. dirs. 1995—), Colo. Assn. Sch. Execs., Sierra Club, Alpha Delta Kappa, Phi Delta Kappa. Democrat. Lutheran. Home: 439 Saddlewood Cir Hghlnds Ranch CO 80126-2284 Office: Sandburg Elem Sch 6900 S Elizabeth St Littleton CO 80122-1829

ERICKSON, MARGARET MARY PECHARICH, secondary education educator; b. Long Beach, Calif., July 4, 1944; d. Jasper C. and Mary (DeVaney) Pecharich; m. Russel R. Erickson Nov. 6, 1965 (div. Apr. 1990); m. Paul P. Freeburn, May 31, 1991. BA, U. Calif., Berkeley, 1966; MA, U. Colo., 1979, PhD, 1987. Tchr. Bret Harte Jr. High, Hayward, Calif., 1967-69, Sinclair Jr. High, Englewood, Colo., 1969-72, Flood Mid. Sch., Englewood, 1972—; adj. prof. U. Colo., Denver, 1989—. Recipient state scholarship, Calif., 1962-66; tchr. grantee, Colo. Mem. Nat. Coun. Tchrs. English. Office: Flood Mid Sch 3695 S Lincoln St Englewood CO 80110-3657

ERICKSON, MARIANNA CUANY, family physician; b. Washington, Iowa, Apr. 12, 1954; d. Robin Louis and Carolyn Ella (Brewer) Cuany; m. Kenton Lloyd Erickson, July 5, 1980; children: Matthew, Jeremy, Christopher. BS, Sterling Coll., 1975; MD, U. Kans., Kansas City, 1978. Diplomate Am. Bd. Family Practice. Resident in family practice Meth. Med. Ctr., Peoria, Ill., 1978-81; family physician Princeville (Ill.) Med. Ctr., 1981—. Mem. Am. Acad. Family Physicians. Home: 10721 N Sleepy Hollow Rd Peoria IL 61615-1123 Office: Princeville Med Ctr 223 E Main St Princeville IL 61559

ERICKSON, PHYLLIS TRAVER, marketing executive; b. N.Y.C., Mar. 31, 1952; d. Harold August and Barbara Lucille (Seifert) T.; m. C. Carl Muscari, June 30, 1979 (div. Nov. 1982); m. Roger C. Erickson, July 8, 1995. BA, Northwestern U., 1974; MBA, Harvard U., 1978. Dir. rsch. Staub, Warmbold and Assocs., N.Y.C., 1974-75; dir. rsch., assoc. cons. Coopers and Lybrand, N.Y.C., 1975-76; asst. product mgr. Nestle Food Corp., White Plains, N.Y., 1978-79, product mgr., mktg. mgr., 1979-83; bus. dir. Nestle Food Corp., Purchase, N.Y., 1983-90; pres. PT Ventures, 1990—, Barrier Systems, Inc., Greenwich, Conn., 1991-92; v.p. mktg. Homeview, Inc., Needham, Mass., 1992-94, Continental Cablevision, Inc., Boston, 1995—. Contbr. articles to mktg. jours. Named to Acad. Women Achievers YWCA. Mem. Harvard U. Bus. Sch. Club. Republican. Episcopalian. Home: 133 Washington St Duxbury MA 02332-4520

ERICKSON, SUSAN PHILLIANS, secondary education educator; b. Uniontown, Pa., July 31, 1947; d. John William and Louise (Grannell) P.; m. Philip Milton Erickson, July 1, 1972; 1 child, Spencer Philip. BA, Thiel Coll., 1969; student, W.Va. U., 1970-71, SUNY, Fredonia, 1974-92. Cert. tchr., N.Y. Tchr. Jamestown (N.Y.) Bd. Edn., 1969—; coord. German-Am. Partnership program Jamestown and Maximilian-Kolbe-Gymnasium, 1972-92, Lessing Gymnasium, 1993—. Mem. NEA, Am. Assn. Tchrs. German, Am. Assn. Tchrs. French, N.Y. Assn. Fgn. Lang. Tchrs., Nat. Edn. Assn. N.Y., N.Y. State Ret. Tchrs. Assn., Jamestown Tchrs. Assn. (dist. liasion com. 1976-79), DAR, Norden Women's Club, PTA, Delta Epsilon Phi. Republican. Methodist. Home: 4471 Bayview Rd Bemus Point NY 14712-9754 Office: Jamestown HS 350 E 2nd St Jamestown NY 14701-5623

ERICKSON-WEERTS, SALLY ANNETTE, dietetics educator; b. Phoenix, Oct. 18, 1952; d. Dennis Lee and Ann Marie (Conklin) E.; children: Matthew, Alexander, Kyle. BS, Mankato State U., 1973; MS, Kans. U., 1976. Registered dietitian, Minn. Clin. dietitian Saga Food Svc., Pitts., 1975-76; pub. health nutritionist Minn. Dept. of Health, Mpls., 1976-77; prof. Lakewood (Minn.) C.C., 1977-79; fed. nutritionist Indian Health Svcs./Pub. Health Svc., Anchorage, 1979-85; pvt. practice Mankato, Minn., 1986-89; pres. Dietary Care Systems, Inc., Mankato, Minn., 1989-92; asst. prof. Mankato State U., 1992—; cons. in field. Author: One Menu System, Nutritional Care System, Lite Weight, Diet Care Seminars, 1989-92. Mem. PEO, Am. Dietetic Assn. Office: Mankato State U Box 44/ PO Box 8400 Mankato MN 56002-0044

ERICSON, PHYLLIS JANE, psychologist, psychotherapist, consultant; b. Ft. Worth, Aug. 16, 1947; d. John H. and Charlotte Marie (Turner) E.; divorced; children: Colleen Nichole Murphy Pass, Sean Matthew Murphy Pass. B. Gen. Studies in Bus. Mgmt. and Advt., U. Tex., Arlington, 1981; MA in Psychology and Psychotherapy, Antioch U., 1990; Grad. in Psychology, Union Inst., Cin., 1995. Registered and cert. hypnotist, Calif.; cert. chem. dependency counselor, Tex.; lic. profl. counselor, marriage and family therapist, chem. dependency counselor, Tex.; cert. nat. and neuro-linguist programming master strategist. Clk.-typist Gen. Dynamics Corp., Ft. Worth, 1965-69; counselor Snelling & Snelling Pers., Ft. Worth, 1970-72; account exec. Ft. Worth Star Telegram, 1972-79; v.p., prin. Ericson Assocs., Inc., Hurst, Tex., 1979-83; account exec. L.A.Times, Times Mirror Corp., 1983; nat. advt. dir. Baker Comm., Beverly Hills, Calif., 1984; owner, prin., builder GE Rehabs, Ft. Worth, 1984-86; counselor Comprehensive Counseling (later Ctrl. Psychol. Svcs.), Hurst, 1988-91; dir., counselor, cons., awareness counseling of DFW Ctrl. Psychol. Svcs., St. Marteen, Ft. Lauderdale, Fla., 1988—; counselor J. Marszalek & Assoc., Dallas, 1984-87, Wynrose Outpatient Program, Arlington, Tex., 1988-89, HCA Richland Hosp., North Richland Hills, Tex., 1988-89; crisis intervention counselor Suicide and Crisis Ctr., Dallas, 1987-88; pvt. practice Ctr. for Counseling Devel. Svcs., Ft. Worth, 1987-88; group facilitator, clin. cons. Bedford Meadows Hosp., 1989-91; instr. psychology dept. Tex. Wesleyan U., 1989; mem. allied staff, group facilitator Charter Hosp.-Grapevine, Tex., 1991-92. Mem. ACA, Am. Assn. for Group Counseling, Nat. Assn. Alcohol and Drug Abuse Counselors, Tex. Assn. Alcohol and Drug Abuse Counselors, Internat. Soc. for Study Multiple Personality Disorders, North Tex. Assn. for Study Multiple Personality Disorders. Office: Ctrl Psychol Svcs PO Box 491938 Fort Lauderdale FL 33349

ERICSON, RUTH ANN, psychiatrist; b. Assaria, Kans., May 15; d. William Albert and Anna Mathilda (Almquist) E. Student, So. Meth. U., 1945-47; BS, Bethany Coll.; MD, U. Tex., 1951. Intern, Calif. Hosp., L.A., 1951-52; resident in psychiatry U. Tex. Med. Br., Galveston, 1952-55; psychiatrist Child Guidance Clinic, Dallas, 1955-63; clin. instr. Southwestern Med. Sch., Dallas, 1955-72; practice medicine specializing in psychiatry, Dallas, 1955—; cons. Dallas Intertribal Coun. Clinic, 1974-81, Dallas Ind. Sch. Dist., U.S. Army, Welfare Dept., Tribal Concerns, Alcoholism, Adv. Bd. Intertribal Coun. Fellow Am. Geriatrics Assn., Royal Soc. Medicine; mem. So. Med. Assn. (life), Tex. Med. Assn. (life), Dallas Med. Assns. (life), Am. Psychiat. Assn. (life), Tex. Psychiat. Assn., North Tex. Psychiat. Assn., Am. Med. Women's Assn., Dallas Area Women Psychiatrists, Alumni Assn. U. Tex. (Med. Br.), Navy League (life), Air Force Assn., Tex. Archaeol. Soc. (life mem.), Dallas Archaeol. Soc. (hon. life mem., pres. 1972-73, 82-84, 89-91, archival rschr.), South Tex. Archaeol. Soc., Tarrant County Archeol. Soc., El Paso Archeol. Soc., N.Mex. Archaeol. Soc., Paleopathology Soc., Internat. Psychogeriatric Assn. (Famous Women of the 20th Century), Alpha Omega Alpha, Delta Psi Omega, Alpha Psi Omega, Pi Gamma Mu, Lambda Sigma, Alpha Epsilon Iota, Mu Delta. Lutheran. Home: 4007 Shady Hill Dr Dallas TX 75229-2844 Office: 3026 Mockingbird Ln # 101 Dallas TX 75205-2323

ERICSON, VALLIE JEAN, middle school educator; b. Palmer, Alaska, July 15, 1948; d. Charles W. and and Gladys D. Peters; m. Timothy L. Ericson, July 15, 1970. BS, U. Wis., River Falls, 1971, MS in Edn., 1975. Cert. tchr. English, learning disabilities, reading specialist, dir. curriculum and instrn. Tchr. English Ellsworth (Wis.) Jr. H.S., 1970-74; reading/English tchr. River Falls Jr. H.S., 1974-75, 81-84; elem. learning disabilities tchr. New Richmond (Wis.) Elem. Sch., 1975-79; dist. reading specialist Prescott (Wis.) Schs., 1980-81; spl. edn. diagnostician Waisman Ctr., Madison, Wis., 1986-87; sr. high learning disabilities tchr. Northwestern Hosp., Chgo., 1987-88; tchr. English/learning disabilities Carl Sandburg and Andrew H.S., Orland Park, Ill., 1988-89; dist. reading specialist, English tchr. St. Francis (Wis.) Schs., 1989-92; reading specialist Horace Mann Mid. Sch., Sheboygan, Wis., 1992—; co-chair Site-based Mgmt. Team, Sheboygan, 1994—; coord. continuing edn. St. Francis and Sheboygan, 1991, 94. Mem. St. Croix Valley Adv. for Tchr. Edn., River Falls, 1982-84; vol. food delivery and transp. Milw. AIDS Project, 1995—; vol. homeless shelter Madison Urban Ministries, 1984-86, LaGrange (Ill.) United Ch. Christ, 1986-87; dir. ch. sch. River Falls United Ch. Christ/Madison United Ch. Christ, 1981-86. Sheboygan Area Schs. Chpt. II grantee, 1994. Mem. ASCD, Internat. Reading Assn., Nat. Coun. Tchrs. English, Wis. Reading Assn., PEO (recording sec. 1981-82). Home: 5148 N Lake Dr Milwaukee WI 53217-5750 Office: Sheboygan Area Sch Dist 2820 Union Ave Sheboygan WI 53081-5438

ERICSSON, SALLY CLAIRE, federal agency administrator; b. Madison, Wis., Jan. 16, 1953; d. William H. and JoAnn (Finnell) E.; m. Thomas A. Garwin, Oct. 7, 1979; children: Rachel, Benjamin. B in Urban and Regional Planning, U. Ill., 1976; M in Pub. Policy, Harvard U., 1980. Legis. analyst Dem. Steering and Policy Com, Washington, 1982-87; adminstr. asst. Rep. Sam Geidenson U.S. Ho. Reps., Washington, 1987-89; legis. asst. to Sen. John F. Kerry U.S. Senate, Washington, 1989-90; asst. to pres. for policy and rsch. Svc. Employees Internat. Union, Washington, 1990-93; assoc. under sec. for econ. affairs U.S. Dept. Commerce, Washington, 1993-96, dep. chief of staff, 1996—. Home: 1805 Monroe St NW Washington DC 20010-1014 Office: US Dept Commerce Office of the Sec 5858 Herbert C Hoover Bldg Washington DC 20230

ERIE, GRETCHEN ANN, cardiovascular clinician; b. Mason City, Iowa, June 18, 1945; d. Donald W. and Eloise M. Schultz; m. Thomas H. Erie, Aug. 19, 1990; stepchildren: Aaron, April. BSN, U. Iowa, 1967. RN; cert. basic life support, St. Paul. Staff nurse U. Iowa Hosp., Iowa City, 1967-68, Meth. Hosp., Houston, 1968-69; staff nurse cardiovascular surgery U. Minn. Hosp., Mpls., 1969-72, insvc. nurse cardiovascular surgery, 1972-75, head nurse cardiovascular surgery, 1975-81; nurse clinician Cardiac Surg. Assn., Mpls., 1981—; speaker U. Minn. Hosp. Community Edn. Dept., various cities in Minn., 1975-81, United Hosp., St. Paul, 1982, 87. Pianist Pleasant Hills Nursing Home, St. Paul, 1987-89; flutist North Heights Luth. Ch., St. Paul, 1987—; patterning exerciser Handicapped Toddler, St. Paul, 1987-88; leader singles group North Heights Luth. Ch., 1984-88. Mem. AACN, Am. Heart Assn. Republican. Lutheran. Home: 3220 Orchard Ct White Bear Lk MN 55110-5385 Office: Cardiac Surg Assn 920 E 28th St Ste 420 Minneapolis MN 55407-1139

ERIKSEN, BEVERLY MORGAN, primary education educator; b. Newark, Ohio, May 14, 1937; d. William Thomas and Geraldine Mae (Marsh) Morgan; m. Harold Eugene Eriksen, Nov. 11, 1961; children: Linda, Janet. BA, Wayne State U., 1959; postgrad., So. Conn. State U., 1969-71; cert. in elem. edn., Fla. So. Coll., 1985. Cert. elem. tchr., educator spkrs. of other langs. endorsement, Fla. Paraprofl. tchr. kindergarten Medulla Elem. Sch., Lakeland, Fla., 1979-85; tchr. kindergarten Scott Lake Elem. Sch., Lakeland, 1985-89, Sikes Elem. Sch., Lakeland, 1989-95, Walsingham Elem. Sch., Largo, Fla., 1995—. Mem. NEA. Fla. Tchrs. Assn., Pinellas County Tchrs. Assn., Heisey Collectors Am. (donator to Nat. Heisey Glass Mus.). Democrat. Home: 1575 Eunice Ln Clearwater FL 34616 Office: Walsingham Elem Sch 9099 Walsingham Rd Largo FL 33773

ERIKSSON, ANNE-MARIE, social services executive, educator; b. Dunkirk, N.Y., Mar. 30, 1932; d. J. Kenneth and Kate Findley; m. Erik A. Eriksson, Jan. 1, 1984; 3 children from prior marriage. BS, SUNY, Fredonia, 1955; postgrad., Hunter Coll. CUNY, 1960. Social worker N.Y. State Dept. Social Welfare, N.Y.C., 1960-64; probation officer N.Y., 1972-84; founder, pres. Incest Survivors Resource Network Internat. a Quaker witness ednl. resource, N.Y.C., 1983—; cons. mental health needs UN Hdqs., 1987; presenter 1st and 3d Internat. Conf. Incest and Related Problems, Zurich, 1987, London, 1989; founder first internat. incest tel. helpline, 1983; co-convenor Quaker Sexual Child Abuse Prevention Network. Mem. Quaker Studies Human Betterment, Internat. Soc. Traumatic Stress Studies (founding co-chair bldg. bridges between profls. and self-help interest area), World Fedn. Mental Health, others. Office: Incest Survivors Resource Network Internat PO Box 7375 Las Cruces NM 88006-7375

ERIKSSON, KIRSTEN M., lawyer; b. Manchester, Conn., Apr. 2, 1970. BA cum laude, Amherst Coll., 1992; JD magna cum laude, Georgetown U., 1995. Ptnr. Anderson, Kill, Olick, Oshinsky, P.C., N.Y.C. Assoc. editor: The Georgetown Law Jour., 1994-95. Mem. N.Y. State Bar Assn., Order of Coif. Office: Anderson Kill Olick Oshinsky PC 1251 Avenue of the Americas New York NY 10020-1182*

ERIKSSON, LINDA KAYE, elementary education educator; b. Taft, Calif., Dec. 31, 1946; d. Ellis E. and Eathel (West) Green; m. Henry Charles Eriksson, Oct. 25, 1975; 1 child, David Keith. AA in Edn., S.W. Bapt. Coll., 1966; BS in Edn., Ohio U., 1969; MEd, U. Mo., Columbia, 1990. Cert. elem. and reading tchr. 3d grade tchr. Athens (Ohio) City Schs., 1969-70; traffic contr., office mgr. U-Haul Co. of San Diego, 1970-75; substitute tchr. Tampa (Fla.) City Schs., 1977-83; substitute tchr. Camdenton (Mo.) R-III Schs., 1985-86, Chpt. I tchr.'s aide, 1986-89; Chpt. I tchr. Birmingham (Ala.) Pub. Schs., 1991-95, Title I tchr., 1995—. Mem. com. Boy Scouts Am., Birmingham, 1992—, sch. rep., 1994—; counselor Hugh O'Brian Youth Found., Birmingham, 1995—. Named Birmingham Pub. Schs. Tchr. of Yr., 1995-96. Mem. Internat. Reading Assn., Nat. Coun. Tchrs. Math., Ala. Reading Assn., Birmingham Area Reading Coun., Delta Kappa Gamma. Republican. Baptist. Home: 1363 Badham Dr Vestavia Hills AL 35216 Office: Wenonah Elem Sch 3008 Wilson Rd Birmingham AL 35221

ERION, CAROL ELIZABETH, music educator; b. Quincy, Ill., Jan. 16, 1943; d. Alva Eugene and Margaret Althea (Kaempfer) McKenney; m. David F. Erion, June 19, 1965; children: Elizabeth Celia Erion Brewer, Paul Frederick. MusB, Oberlin Coll., 1965; MusM, New England Conservatory Music, 1982; cert., U. Toronto, Ont., Can., 1978, Mozarteum Acad. Music, Salzburg, Austria, 1979. Music tchr. Montessori Sch. No. Va., Annandale, 1972-84, St. Agnes Episcopal Sch., Alexandria, Va., 1984-85, The Sidwell Friends Sch., Washington, 1985-87; music and fine arts tchr. Arlington (Va.) Pub. Schs., 1988—; music dir. All Saints Episcopal Ch., Alexandria, 1983-90; workshop clinician various music edn. orgns. in U.S., 1980—; adj. prof. George Mason U., Fairfax, Va., 1983—; cons. WETA-TV, Washington, 1987. Author: Tales to Tell, Tales to Play, 1982; contbr. articles to profl. jours. Humanities fellow Coun. Basic Edn., 1989. Mem. NEA, AAUW, ASCD, Am. Recorder Soc., Am. Orff Schulwerk Assn. (pres. 1993-95). Democrat. Episcopalian. Home: 19 W Linden St Alexandria VA 22301-2621

ERKKILA, BARBARA HOWELL LOUISE, writer, photographer; b. Boston, July 11, 1918; d. John William and Adelia Parsons (Jones) Howell; student Boston U. Evening Coll., 1959-62; m. Onni R. Erkkila, Apr. 27, 1941 (dec. 1981); children: John W., Kathleen L., Marjorie A. Corr., Gloucester (Mass.) Daily Times, 1936-53, feature writer, 1953—, women's editor, 1967-72, community news editor, 1972-74; freelance article writer for mags., 1953—; editor weekly mag. Essex County Newspapers, Gloucester, 1973, editorial asst., 1974-85, writer, photographer, 1970—; tchr. Russian, Ipswich (Mass.) Public Schs., evenings, 1962-63; jewelry designer; quarry historian. Mem. price panel Office Price Adminstrn., 1944-46; mem. ARC nurse's aide class Addison Gilbert Hosp., Gloucester, 1942-43; mem. Gloucester Hist. Commn. 1967-69, 93—; formerly active Girl Scouts U.S.A.; sec. Lanesville Community Ctr., 1957-94. Recipient 2d prize feature writing UPI, 1970; historian award Town of Rockport, 1978. Mem. Sandy Bay Hist. Soc., Ohio Geneal. Soc., Va. Geneal. Soc., Cape Ann Hist. Assn., North Shore Rock & Mineral (charter), Del. Geneal. Soc. Republican. Congregationalist. Club: North Shore Button. Author: Hammers on Stone, 1981, Village at Lane's Cove, 1989; editor: Lane's Cove Cook Book, 1954. Home: 31 Prospect St Gloucester MA 01930-3552

ERLANSON, DEBORAH MCFARLIN, state program administrator; b. Watertown, N.Y., Oct. 17, 1943; d. Raymond Thomas and Alberta Antoinette (Schultz) McF.; m. David Norman Erlanson, Sept. 10, 1966; 1 child, Joshua David. AA in Liberal Arts, Dutchess C.C., 1964; BA in Psychology, Am. Internat. Coll., 1966; MS in Edn., So. Ill. U., 1972. Coord. occupancy tng. Decatur (Ill.) Housing Authority, 1975-76, coord. target projects program, 1976-77, coord. spl. svcs., 1977-78, asst. dir. planning, 1978-82, dir. program devel., 1982—; speaker various convs., 1978—; cons. Piatt County Housing Authority, Monticello, Ill., 1985-89, Woodford Homes, Inc., Decatur, 1985-86. Mem. steering com. Near West Restoration and Preservation Soc., Decatur, 1985-86, bd. dirs., 1986—, v.p., 1992—; mem. steering com. Cmtys. in Partnership, 1991—, bd. dirs., 1993—; mem. Decatur Advantage 20/20, 1993, Macon County Literacy Coun., 1992-95; parent group counselor Macon County Parents Anonymous, Decatur, 1976-80; mem. health divsn. Decatur Coun. Cmty. Svcs., 1978-84; bd. dirs. YWCA, Decatur, 1992-95; mem. adv. bd. Ill. Housing Devel. Authority, 1993—. Mem. Nat. Assn. Housing/Redevel. Ofcls. (sr. v.p. 1995—, mem. nat. bd. govs. 1987—, mem. profl. devel. com. 1983-93, vice chariperson 1987-89, v.p. profl. devel. 1987-89, mem. task force on product devel. 1987, mem. task force on elderly housing issues 1990-91, profl. devel. trainer 1986—, mem. Award of Excellence jury 1991—, mem. task force on family self-sufficiency 1992-93, regional pres. 1993-95, Charles A. Thompson award 1991, mem. state exec. bd. 1983-93, state pres. 1984-87, William R. Hammond award 1993), Decatur Women's Network, Internat. City Mgmt. Assn. Home: 465 W Macon St Decatur IL 62522-3122 Office: Decatur Housing Authority 1808 E Locust St Decatur IL 62521-1565

ERLEBACHER, ARLENE CERNIK, lawyer; b. Chgo., Oct. 3, 1946; d. Laddie J. and Gertrude V. (Kurdys) Cernik; m. Albert Erlebacher, June 14, 1968; children: Annette Doherty, Jacqueline Erlebacher. B.A., Northwestern U., 1967, J.D., 1973. Bar: Ill. 1974, U.S. Dist. Ct. (no. dist.) Ill. 1974, U.S. Ct. Appeals (7th cir.) 1974, Fed. Trial Bar, 1983, U.S. Supreme Ct. 1985. Assoc. Sidley & Austin, Chgo., 1974-80, ptnr., 1980-95, of counsel, 1996—. Bd. dirs. Legal Assistance Found. Chgo. Fellow Am. Bar Found.; mem. ABA, Chgo. Bar Assn., Chgo. Council Lawyers, Order Coif. Office: Sidley & Austin 1 First Nat Plz Chicago IL 60603

ERLENMEYER-KIMLING, L., psychiatric and behavior genetics researcher, educator; b. Princeton, N.J.; d. Floyd M. and Dorothy F. (Dirst) Erlenmeyer; m. Carl F. E. Kimling. B.S. magna cum laude, Columbia U., 1957, Ph.D., 1961. Sr. research scientist N.Y. State Psychiat. Inst., N.Y.C., 1960-69; assoc. research scientist N.Y. State Psychiat. Inst., 1969-75, prin. research scientist, 1975-78, dir. div. devel. behavioral studies, 1978—, acting chief med. genetics, 1991—; asst. in psychiatry Columbia U., 1962-66, rsch. assoc., 1966-70, asst. prof., 1970-74, assoc. prof. psychiatry and genetics, 1974-78, prof., 1978—; vis. prof. psychology New Sch. Social Research, 1971—; mem. peer rev. group NIH, 1976-80; mem. work group on guidance and counseling Congl. Commn. on Huntington's Disease, 1976-77; mem. task force on intervention Pres.'s Commn. on Mental Health, 1977-78; mem. initial rev. group NIMH, 1981-85; mem. adv. bd. Croatian Inst. Brain Rsch., 1991-93. Editor: Life-Span Research in Psychopathology, 1986; issue editor: Differential Reproduction, Social Biology, 1971, Genetics and Mental Disorders, Internat. Jour. Mental Health, 1972, Genetics and Gene Expression in Mental Illness, Jour. Psychiat. Rsch., 1992, Measuring Liability to Schizophrenia: Progress Report 1994, Schizophrenia Bull., 1994; mem. editorial bd. Social Biology, 1970-79, Schizophrenia Bull., 1978—, Jour. Preventive Psychiatry, 1980-84, Croatian Med. Jour., 1991—, Neurology/Psychiatry/Brain Research, 1991—, Neuropsychiat. Genetics, Am. Jour. Med. Genetics, 1992—. Recipient Merit award NIMH, 1989-96, William K. Warren Schizophrenia Rsch. award Internat. Congress on Schizophrenia Rsch., 1995; grantee NIMH, 1966-69, 71-96, Scottish Rite Com. on Schizophrenia, 1970-74, 84-87, 89-94, W.T. Grand Found., 1978-86, MacArthur Found., 1981, Stanley Found., 1995-96, NARSAD, 1996-97. Fellow APA, Am. Psychopath. Assn., Am. Psychol. Soc.; mem. AAAS, Am. Soc. Human Genetics, Behavior Genetics Assn. (mem.-at-large 1972-74, Theodosius Dobzhansky award 1985), Internat. Soc. Psychiat. Genetics, Soc. Study Social Biology (bd. dirs. 1969-84, 92-95, sec. 1972-75, pres. 1975-78), Scientists Ctr. for Animal Welfare, Phi Beta Kappa, Sigma Xi.

ERLICHSON, MIRIAM, fundraiser; b. Bronx, N.Y., July 26, 1948; d. Jack and Bess (Hyatt) E.; m. Walter Forman, Sept. 26, 1970 (div. 1975); m. Victor Petrusewicz, July 17, 1980. BA in English, CCNY, 1969; postgrad., Hunter Coll., 1970-71; MA in English, CCNY, 1976; JD, Pace U., 1993. Cert. secondary tchr., N.Y. Tchr. English Intermediate Sch. 84, Bronx, 1972-78; coord. ann. giving N.Y. Hosp.-Cornell Med. Ctr., N.Y.C., 1979-90; bd. dirs. 77th Settler Corp. Mem. Jane Austen Soc. (Eng.), N.Y.S. Bar, Phi Beta Kappa.

ERMOIAN, DEBORAH SUE, mathematics educator; b. Phoenix, Nov. 22, 1956; d. Bill Richard and Mary Margaret (Taylor) Williams; m. Dan Edward Ermoian, Dec. 24, 1976; children: Matthew, Megan. BS, Grand Canyon U., 1979; MEd, Ariz. State U., 1988, doctoral studies, 1996—. Asst. prof. Grand Canyon U., Phoenix; math. educator, cons. Rio Salado Cmty. Coll., Phoenix Coll., 1993-96. Mem. Math. Assn. Am., Nat. Coun. Tchr. Math. Office: Grand Canyon U 3300 W Camelback Rd Phoenix AZ 85017

ERNEST, PAMELA KAY, government relations executive, lobbyist; b. St. Petersburg, Fla., Nov. 8, 1950; d. C.W. Bill and Marian June (Ford) Young; m. Harvey F. Ernest, Jr., Jan. 1, 1989. Grad. high sch., St. Petersburg. Press sec. to co-chmn. Rep. Nat. Com., Washington, 1971-74; sec., adminstrv. asst. to minority sgt.-at-arms U.S. Ho. of Reps., Washington, 1974-77; pub. affairs rep. NAM, Mpls., 1977-80; advanced person to Mrs. Bush, Reagan-Bush for Pres. Campaign, Washington, 1980; pub. affairs rep. Honeywell Inc., Washington, 1981-83, mgr. internat. policy, 1984-89, dir. fed. affairs, 1989-96; v.p. Rivergroup, Falls Church, Va., 1996—.

ERNST, MARY CHUMAS, elementary education educator; b. St. Paul, Aug. 15, 1931; d. Samuel Constantine and Athanasia (Strenglis) Chumas; children: Rosemary, John B. BA in Sociology and English, Macalester Coll., 1953, BS in Elem. Edn., 1957. Cert. tchr., Minn. Substitute tchr. St. Paul Schs., 1957-96; tchr. adult edn., St. Paul, 1980-89, Century Coll., U. St. Thomas. Author: (antique handbook) My Mother Had One Like That, 1995. Developer pilot for ESL, St. George Greek Orthodox Ch., St. Paul, 1991-92. Mem. Internat. Soc. Appraisers (assoc. mem.). Home and Office: Mary's Appraisers 2016 Yorkshire Ave Saint Paul MN 55116

ERNST BOGDAN, JANET LEE, interior designer; b. Winston-Salem, N.C., Apr. 16, 1955; d. William Lee Ernst and Marie Keith (Shouse) Snyder; m. Ivica Bogdan, Aug. 19, 1994; 1 child, Ivana Bogdan. BS in Home Econs., Interior Design, U. N.C., Greensboro, 1977. Instr. arts and crafts Craft Showcase, Winston-Salem, 1977-78; display design The Ltd., Inc., N.C. and S.C., 1978-79; designer ind. retail stores Winston-Salem, 1977-81; head design dept. Butler Enterprises, Inc., Winston-Salem, 1981-86; design prin. Carolina Contract Design, Winston-Salem, 1986—; pres. Triad Design Concepts, Inc., Winston-Salem and Greensboro, 1988-90; cons. design, catalog line drawings, photography contract furniture and lighting mfrs., N.C. and Ga.; mentor student interns U. N.C., Greensboro, 1983-84, 87-93; propr. Carolina Carpet Svcs., 1992. Vol. Humane Soc., Winston-Salem, 1977-78; bd. dirs. Jamestowne Homeowners Assn., 1991-94, treas., 1993, pres., 1994; invited participant citizen amb. program Comml. Interior Design Del. to People's Republic of China. Mem. Inst. Bus. Designers (affiliate, ednl. com. 1987), Nat. Trust Hist. Preservation., Internat. Interior Design Assn. (assoc.). Republican. Moravian. Office: Carolina Contract Design The Keystone 1386 Westgate Center Dr Ste F Winston Salem NC 27103-2948

ERRICKSON, BARBARA BAUER, electronic equipment company executive; b. Pitts., Apr. 5, 1944; d. Edward Ewing Bauer and Margaret J. McConnell; m. James Jay Burcham, June 30, 1966 (div. May 1972); children: James Jay II, Linda Lee; m. William Newel Errickson, Apr. 9, 1976 (div. Feb. 1987). BA, U. Ill., 1966; MBA, So. Meth. U., 1981. Programming trainee Allstate Ins. Co., Northbrook, Ill., 1973; programmer, team leader Motorola, Inc., Chgo., 1974-78; supr. systems Tex. Instruments, Dallas, 1978-81, product line mgr. worldwide shipping systems, 1981-83, product line mgr. shipping, inventory systems, 1983-84, mgr. mktg. info. systems, 1985, mgr. benefit systems, 1986-89, mgr. S.W. case cons. and edn., 1990-92, western area advanced practices mgr., 1992—; dir., billing and software developer Spring Park Home Owners, Garland-Richardson, Tex., 1984—, pres. and chmn. fin., 1985, v.p. legal, 1986. Active Dallas Women's Ctr., 1984—; mem. bus. adv. council So. Meth U. Bus. Adv. Program; mem. bus. adv. coun. El Centro Coll. Rehab. for Physically Challenged Through Data Processing, 1987—; chmn. control and adminstrn./mktg. United Way, 1986-89. Recipient Women in Leadership cert. YWCA Met. Chgo., 1977. Mem. Am. Mgmt. Assn., Am. Women in Computing (bd. dirs. 1987—, pres. 1989), Community Assns. Inst., So. Meth. U. MBA Soc., Spring Park Racquet Club, Beta Gamma Sigma. Republican. Presbyterian. Home: 6702 Lake Shore Dr Garland TX 75044-2044 Office: Tex Instruments Inc PO Box 869305 6620 Chase Oaks Blvd Plano TX 75086

ERSKINE, KATHARINE MUNSON HARDY, fundraiser; b. Ellsworth, Maine, June 27, 1962; d. Rodney Danforth and Katharine Townsend (Ducey) H.; m. James Stuart Erskine, Sept. 9, 1989; children: James Ducey, Andrew Hardy. BA, Denison U., 1984. Cert. fundraising exec. Office mgr. Pucker/Safrai Art Gallery, Boston, 1984-85; asst. dir. ann. fund Denison U., Granville, Ohio, 1985-87; dir. devel. Ashley Hall Sch., Charleston, S.C., 1987-90; from asst. to assoc. v.p. to assoc. dir. Wharton Ann. Fund U. Pa., Phila., 1990-94; assoc. dir. major gifts The Lawrenceville (N.J.) Sch., 1994-96; dir. maj. gifts Widener U., Chester, Pa., 1996—; cons. Perkins Art Ctr., Moorestown, N.J., 1990-91; decade chmn. & class agt., St. George's Sch., Newport, R.I., 1982-95. Pres. Interfaith Care Givers, Moorestown, N.J., 1992—. Mem. Am. Jr. League, Nat. Soc. Fund Raising Execs., Coun. for Advancement and Support of Edn. Episcopal. Home: 702 Cornwallis Dr Mount Laurel NJ 08054 Office: Widener University One University Pl Chester PA 19013

ERTEL, SUSAN LYNNE, writing educator; b. Lincoln, Nebr., Feb. 17, 1964; d. Oscar B. and Betty L. (Wright) McKinney; m. Philip R. Ertel, June 3, 1995; 1 child, Margaret Ann. AA, Westark C.C., Ft. Smith, Ark., 1983; BA, U. Ctrl. Ark., 1986, MA, 1991. Tchr. Greenwood (Ark.) Pub. Schs., 1987-88; substitute tchr. Leavenworth (Kans.) Pub. schs., 1988-89; instr. writing Westark C.C., Ft. Smith, 1989—. Accompanist, piano, clarinet First Bapt. Ch., Greenwood, 1979—; judge 4-H talent shows, Greenwood, 1990, 94; active PTO, North Main Elem. Sch., Greenwood, 1994—. Recipient Nat. Inst. for Staff and Orgnl. Devel. Excellence in Teaching award, 1995, Lucille Speakman Excellence in Tchg. award Westark Comm. Coll., 1993-94. Mem. Nat. Assn. for Developmental Edn. (nat. com. mem. 1996—), Ark. Assn. for Developmental Edn. (pres. 1995—), Nat. Coun. Tchrs. English, VFW Ladies Aux., Delta Kappa Gamma, Phi Delta Kappa. Office: Westark Community College PO Box 3649 5210 Grand Fort Smith AR 72913-3649

ERTL, RITA MAE, elementary education educator; b. Appleton, Wis., Dec. 22, 1939; d. Irving John and Bertha Helen (Van Ryte) Petrie; m. Andrew Philip Ertl, June 12, 1971; children: Kristyn Marie, Jessica Lynn. Student, Silver Lake Coll., 1961-71. Religious instr. for mentally handicapped Holy Name Parish, Sheboygan, Wis., 1965-69; tchr. grade 3 Holy Name Sch., Sheboygan, 1969-72; learning ctr. coord. Holy Name Sch., 1984—; tchr. grade 2 St. Mary's Sch., Sheboygan Falls, 1961-69; mem. CCD bd. Holy Name Sch. Co-founder Human Rights Assn., Sheboygan, 1960-69.

ERVIN, MARGARET HOWIE, elementary education educator, special education educator; b. L.A., May 13, 1924; d. James Stanley and Margaret (Goff) H.; m. E. Frank Ervin, Mar. 22, 1947 (div. 1957); children: Frank, Daniel, Charles. BA, Fresno (Calif.) State U., 1958; grad. student, Purdue U., 1965-66, San Francisco State U., 1974-75. Cert. elem. and spl. edn. tchr. Elem. tchr. Clovis (Calif.) Schs., 1958-60, Fremont (Calif.) Unified Schs., 1960-83; spl. tchr. in summers Dominican Coll., San Rafael, Calif., 1972-78; asst. dir., cons. Arena Sch. and Learning Ctr., San Rafael, 1974-75; dir. Ervin Sch. and Learning Ctr., San Rafael, 1983-88; researcher, tchr. Primaria Sch. #110 PRI9745, Celaya, Mex., 1988; elem., spl. tchr. Napa (Calif.) City/County Schs., 1989—; diagnosis cons. Ervin Learning Ctr., Napa, 1989—; spl. edn. guest speaker various cities, U.S., Can., 1974—; learning seminar Parents and Tchrs., Mexico, summer 1992, Psycho-motor Tgn. Don Bosco Home for Girls, Mexico, summer 1993. Vol. Option Inst. and Fellowship, "Sonrise" autism/devel. disabilities, Sheffield, Mass., summer 1994; pres. Children Handicapped Learning Devel., Calif., 1971-72, tchr. parents, 1970-80, 94—; bay area rep. Calif. Tchrs. Assn., Burlingame, 1970-74.

Recipient cert. of merit Calif. Tchrs. Assn., Burlingame, 1974, $5,000 gift to Ervin Sch. Calif. Assn. Neurol. Handicapped Children, Fremont, 1984. Mem. AAUW, NOW, Assn. Children With Learning Disabilities (trustee). Democrat. Unitarian. Home and Office: Ervin Learning Ctr 3361 Rohlffs Way Bldg 31 Napa CA 94558

ERVING-MENGEL, TAMMI, nursing administrator; b. Auburn, N.Y., July 28, 1959; d. John Lewis and Carolyn Mae (Farrell) Erving; m. Timothy Edward Mengel, May 23, 1987. BSN, Alfred U., 1981; MSN, U. N.C., Greensboro, 1995. CCRN. Staff LPN med./surg. State Univ. Hosp., Syracuse, N.Y., 1981-82, staff nurse pediat., 1982-84, 85, orientation insvc. coord., 1985-86; traveling nurse Traveling Nurse Corp., Worcester, Mass., 1984; staff nurse med. oncology Roswell Park Meml. Inst., Buffalo, 1984-85; staff nurse home health Upjohn Health Svcs., Greensboro, 1986-87; ICU nurse High Point (N.C.) Regional Hosp., 1987-88, patient/staff educator, 1988-90, nurse mgr. ICU, 1990-92, dir. critical care nursing, 1992—. Named to Great 100 of N.C., 1992; Sigma Theta Tau grantee, 1996. Mem. AACN, N.C. Nurses Assn. (Dist. 9 pres.-elect 1995-96, pres. 1996-97), Sigma Theta Tau. Roman Catholic. Office: High Point Regional Hosp 601 N Elm St High Point NC 27261

ERWIN, JUDITH ANN (JUDITH ANN PEACOCK), writer, photographer, lawyer; b. Decatur, Ga., Jan. 4, 1939; d. Milo Eugene and Lucy Isabelle (Simpson) Peacock; m. William Wofford Erwin, Sept. 5, 1959 (div. Mar. 1982); children: William Wofford Jr., Allison Sheridan (Norton). AA, Fla. C.C., 1987; BA summa cum laude, Jacksonville U., 1989; JD, U. Fla., 1993. Photography instr., freelance writer Jacksonville, Fla., 1986-91, freelance dance photographer, 1984-91; theater and dance critic Folio Weekly, Jacksonville, Fla., 1987-89; writer dance VUE mag.; founder On Our Own, 1991; lawyer Inman & Fernandez; pres. Ballet Guild, Jacksonville, 1973-75, Ballet Repertory Jacksonville, 1979-80; freelance costume designer, Jacksonville, 1981-86; mem. grand rev. dance panel Fla. Dept. Cultural Affairs, 1996; seminar spkr. in field. Mem. editorial staff Kalliope, Jour. Women's Art, 1989-91; editor-in-chief U. Fla. Jour. of Law and Pub. Policy, fall 1993. Mem. del.'s council Art's Assembly Jacksonville, 1979-80; grant rev. panelist Fla. Divsn. Cultural Affairs, 1996-97. Mem. AAUW, ATLA, Nat. Soc. Arts and Letters, Nat. League Am. Pen Women, Fla. Bar Assn., Jacksonville Bar Assn., Jacksonville Women Lawyers Assn., Phi Kappa Phi, Phi Theta Kappa. Democrat. Episcopalian.

ERWIN, SHELIA KAYE, newspaper publisher; b. Knoxville, Tenn., Feb. 5, 1946; d. Melton James Jr. and Ortha Lee (Phillips) Robbins; m. James Ray Erwin, June 23, 1995. BS, Tenn. Tech. U., 1970. Social worker Scott County Hosp., Oneida, Tenn., 1970-73; pub. Scott County News, Oneida, 1973—. Mem. Oneida Bus. and Profl. Club, Oneida C. of C. (ladies divsn.). Baptist. Office: Scott County News 224 Alberta Ave Oneida TN 37841

ESCHETE, MARY LOUISE, internist; b. Houma, La., Feb. 8, 1949; d. Marshall John and Louise Esther (Davis) E.; m. Lorphy Joseph Bourque, July 7, 1979. BS, La. State U., 1970; MD, La. State U. Med. Ctr., Shreveport, 1974. Diplomate, Am. Bd. Internal Medicine. Resident in internal medicine La. State U. Med. Ctr., Shreveport, 1974-77; staff instr. La. State U. Med. Ctr., 1979, fellow in infectious disease, 1979; pvt. practice Houma, 1980-83; staff, dept. internal medicine South La. Med. Assocs., Houma, 1983—; chmn. infection control, Terrebonne Gen. Hosp., 1981—, South La. Med. Ctr., 1983—. Contbr. articles to med. jours. Bd. dirs. Houma Battered Women's Shelter, 1983-87, Houma YWCA, 1987-94; mem. Roche Nat. AIDS Adv. Bd., 1993; Triparish vol. activist, 1994. Named Citizen of Yr. Regional and State Social Workers, 1992. Mem. ACP, AAAS, AMA, Infectious Disease Soc., Am. Soc. Microbiology, So. Med. Assn. (grantee 1978), N.Y. Acad. Sci., La. State Med. Soc., Terrebonne Parish Med. Soc. (sec. 1982-83, v.p. 1993-94, pres. 1994-95), Krewe of Hyachinthians (pres. 1989-90, 94-95, bd. dirs. 1990-96), Houma Jr. Women's Club (reporter 1988-89, rec. sec. 1989—, pres.-elect 1991-93, pres. 1993-95), Alpha Epsilon Delta. Democrat. Roman Catholic. Home: 3387 Little Bayou Black Dr Houma LA 70360-2840 Office: South La Med Ctr 1978 Industrial Blvd Houma LA 70363-7055

ESCOBAR, MARISOL See MARISOL

ESELY, MARY JANE, artist, vocational nurse; b. Borger, Tex., Aug. 14, 1949; d. Jack Edward and Joyce Marie (Townsend) E. AA in Liberal Arts, Frank Phillips Jr. Coll., Borger, 1969; AS, Amarillo (Tex.) Jr. Coll., 1971. Lic. vocat. nurse, Tex. Staff nurse Deaconess Gen. Hosp., Oklahoma City, 1972-76, High Plains Bapt. Hosp., Amarillo, 1976-92; charge nurse Ware Meml. Care Ctr., Amarillo, 1993—; tour nurse U. Nebr., Omaha, 1974. Illustrator (children's books): Shining Star, 1994, Oil Field Brats, 1995, Ghost of Castle Kilknockly, 1996. Mem. Amarillo Fine Arts Assn., Soc. Creative Anachronisms, Phi Theta Kappa.

ESFANDIARY, MARY S., physical scientist, operations consultant; b. Passaic, N.J., June 27, 1929; d. Peter J. and Veronica R. (Kida) Nieradka; m. Mohsen S. Esfandiary; children: Homayoun Austin, Dara S. BS in Chemistry, St. John's U., 1951; postgrad., Polytechnic Inst. N.Y., 1955-56. Research chemist Picatinny Arsenal, Dover, N.J., 1951-56; supr. phys. sci. Bur. Mines, Washington, 1956-61; asst. to dir. research Nat. Iranian Oil Co., Tehran, 1961-64; lectr. U. Tehran and Aryamehr Inst. Tech., Tehran, 1961-64, 69-73; dir. internat. affairs Acad. of Scis., Tehran, 1977-79; chief geog. names br. Def. Mapping Agy., Washington, 1981-86, chief prodn. mgmt. office, 1986-87, chief support div., chief inventory mgmt. div., 1987-90, chief product mgmt. dept., 1990-92, dep. dir. distbn. mgmt. ops. Combat Support Ctr., 1993, chief, co-prodn. mgmt. divsn., 1993-94, chief divsn. internat. ops. coprodn. mgmt., 1993-96; ops. mgmt., 1996—. Contbr. papers and articles to tech. jours., 1952-78. Pres. UN Delegations Women's Club, N.Y.C., 1967-69, v.p., program dir., 1964-67; pres. Diplomatic Corps. Com. for Red Cross, Bangkok, Thailand, 1974-76; v.p., bd. dirs. Found. for Blind of Thailand, Bangkok, 1973-77; mem. Edn. Working Group ARC, 1989-90. Recipient Badge of Honor for Social Service, Thailand, 1975, 1st Class medal Red Cross, Thailand, 1976. Democrat. Home: 4401 Sedgewick St NW Washington DC 20016-2713 Office: Exhibits Inc 4929 Wyaconda Rd Rockville MD 20852-2443

ESHOO, ANNA GEORGES, congresswoman; b. New Britain, Conn., Dec. 13, 1942; d. Fred and Alice Alexandre Georges; children: Karen Elizabeth, Paul Frederick. AA with honors, Canada Coll., 1975. Chmn. San Mateo County Dem. Ctrl. Com., Calif., 1978-82; chair Human Rels. Com., 79-82; mem. Congress from 14th Dist. Calif., 1993—; regional minority whip 5; chief of staff Calif. Assembly Spkr. Leo McCarthy, 1981; regional majority whip No. Calif., 1993-94. Co-founder Women's Hall of Fame; chair San Mateo County (Calif.) Dem. Party, 1980; active San Mateo County Bd. Suprs., 1982-92, pres., 1986; pres. Bay Area Air Quality Mgmt. Dist., 1982-92; mem. San Francisco Bay Conservation Devel. Commn., 1982-92; chair San Mateo County Gen. Hosp. Bd. Dirs. Roman Catholic. Office: US Ho of Reps Office Of House Mems Washington DC 20515

ESHOO, BARBARA ANNE RUDOLPH, academic official; b. Worcester, Mass., Sept. 27, 1946; d. Charles Leighton and Irene Isabella (Wheeler) Rudolph; divorced; 1 child, Melissa Clinton; m. Robert Pius Eshoo, July 11, 1981. Student, Morehead State U., 1964-66, U. N.H., 1974, 75; BA, New England Coll., 1976. Asst. to dir. Currier Gallery Art, Manchester, N.H., 1976-78, coord. pub. rels., 1979-82; dir. pub. rels. Daniel Webster Coll., Nashua, N.H., 1982-88, chief advancement officer, 1988-95; v.p. instnl. advancement Ea. Conn. State U., Willimantic, 1995—; mem. faculty Currier Art Ctr., Manchester, 1977-79; bd. advisers New Eng. Coll. Art Gallery, Henniker, N.H., 1989-91. Advisor on planned giving United Way, Nashua, 1989-90; com. mem. Manchester Mayor's Task force on Youth Affairs, 1986-88, Manchester Bd. of Sch. Commn., 1986-90; del. N.H. Sch. Bds. Assn., 1988-90; trustee, bd. sec. Manchester Hist. Assn., 1989-95; mem. Mayor's Com. on Leadership, Manchester, 1988-91; bd. dirs. Swiftwater coun. Girl Scouts U.S., 1990-95; chairperson parents com. Bennington Coll. Mem. Nat. Soc. Fundraising Execs. (bd. dirs., v.p. pub. affairs N.H./Vt. chpt. to 1995), Conn. Women in Higher Edn., Advt. Club N.H. (bd. dirs., v.p. 1980-82), Rotary (Nashua West chpt. 1990-95). Office: Ea Conn State U 83 Windham St Willimantic CT 06226

ESKENAZI, MAXINE SOLOMON, speech researcher; b. Pitts., Aug. 5, 1951; d. David E. and Clara (Knee) Solomon; 1 child, David Ryan. BA in Modern Langs., Carnegie-Mellon U., 1973; D.E.A. in Linguistics, U. Paris VII, 1981; D. in Computer Sci., U. Paris XI, 1984. Researcher Centre National de la Recherche Scientifique, Orsay, France, 1986—; systems scientist Carnegie Mellon U., 1996—; keynote spkr. Eurospeech '93; mem. rsch. bd. computer sci. dept. U. Paris XI, 1989-95. Mem. Acoustical Soc. Am., European Speech Communication Assn. (newsletter editor 1989-94), Soc. Française d'Acoustique (bd. dirs.). Office: Carnegie Mellon Univ 206 Cyert Hall 5000 Forbes Ave Pittsburgh PA 15213

ESKER-TOSCANO, PATRICIA MICHELE, psychological counselor; b. Newark, N.J.; d. Pasquale Peter and Megaline (Caporale) Toscano; m. Edward Vincent Esker; 1 child, Edward Vincent III. BA in Psychology, Montclair U., 1983; postgrad., William Paterson Coll., 1983-84; MA in Counseling Psychology, Rider U., 1996. Lic. elem. tchr., N.J. Spl. edn. tchr.-therapist The Children Inst., Livingston, N.J., 1981-83; elem. tchr. Holy Family Elem. Sch., 1983-84; tchr. Marlboro (N.J.) Bd. of Edn., 1984-88; psychoednl. group leader Monmouth Med. Ctr., Long Branch, N.J., 1992-94; therapist Dr. M. Reby, Lakewood, N.J., 1995; pvt. practice Manasquan, N.J., 1995—; sub. tchr. Ocean Twp. Bd. of Edn., 1993—, cons., 195—; adolescent counseling Ocean Twp. Spl. Svcs., 1996—. Designed and implemented psychoednl. workshop for primary grades, Ocean Twp. Elem. Schs., 1995. Vol. Patient Advocate Monmouth Med. Ctr., Long Branch, 1992-94, Rosa Mental Health Clinic Jersey Shore Med. Ctr., 1995. Mem. ACA, Am. Mental Health Counseling Agy., Assn. for Specialists in Groupwork, Am. Bd. Child Mental Health Svcs.

ESKIN, LISA YVONNE, secondary education educator; b. Rochester, N.Y., Aug. 15, 1961; d. Howard B. and Rosemarie D. Eskin. BS in English and Lang. Arts, Boston U., 1988; MS in Edn. Tech., L.I. U., 1992. Cert. tchr., N.Y. English tchr. Huntington (N.Y.) Schs., 1990—; spkr., presenter Families and Schs. Conf., Oakland, Calif., 1994. Editor Schs. of Thought, 1993-94. Vol. Cmty. Fund, Stony Brook, N.Y., 1990—; founder, advisor Multicultural Action Com., Huntington, 1991—; vol., trainer Spl. Olympics, Stony Brook, 1993-94. Mem. Am. Fedn. Tchrs. (local rep., local v.p.), Nat. Coun. Tchrs. English, Huntington Lang. Arts Coun., Associated Tchrs. Huntington (v.p. 1995—, presenter Spring conf. Melville, N.Y., 1996), L.I. Lang. Arts Coun., Internat. Soc. Poets (del., Internat. Poet Merit award 1995, Editor's Choice award 1996). Office: Finley Jr HS Greenlawn Rd Huntington NY 11743

ESKRIDGE, CAROLE FAY, artist; b. Port of Spain, Trinidad and Tobago, July 3, 1947; came to U.S., 1948; d. Woodrow Wilson and Lyda Mae (Blanchard) E.; m. Harold Sherman Frye, Aug. 6, 1966 (div. Aug. 1976); children: Sarah Mae Frye Maxon, Rebecca Jane Frye Coonrod. Grad. magna cum laude, Ala. A&M; photography cert., U. Ala., Huntsville, 1981. Found Visionary Artists Guild Mentally Ill, Huntsville, 1991—. Mural painter History of Mental Health, 1992. Recipient Disting. Svc. award Huntsville-Madison County Mental Health Bd., 1992, Consumer of Yr. award Ala. Alliance Mentally Ill, 1993, Creativity award Mental Health Consumers Ala., 1995, cert. Spl. Congrl. Recognition, 1996. Mem. Docents of Hunsville Mus. Art. Roman Catholic. Home: 115 Clinton Ave #801 Huntsville AL 35801 Office: Visionary Guild Mentally Ill Artists Huntsville AL 35801

ESKWITT ROSENBLUM, DONNA LYNN, audiologist; b. N.Y.C., Sept. 2, 1956; d. Herbert Melvin and Joyce Ann (Diamond) Eskwitt; m. Gary Robert Rosenblum, Sept. 12, 1982; children: Benjamin George, Jason Peter. BS, Ithaca Coll., 1978; MS, U. Ariz., 1980; PhD, NYU, 1988. Cert. clin. competence in audiology. Clin. audiologist House Ear Clinic, L.A., 1981-84; rsch. audiologist House Ear Inst., L.A., 1984-88; dispensing audiologist Cmty. Speech and Hearing Ctr., Canoga Park, Calif., 1989-93; account mgr. Qualitone Hearing Aids, Mpls., 1993-95; dir. audiology South Pacific Rehab. Svcs., Encino, Calif., 1995-96. Fellow Am. Acad. Audiology, Calif. Acad. of Audiology; mem. Am. Speech Lang. Hearing Assn. (Cert. of Appreciation 1987, Award for Continuing Edn. 1987, 91), Am. Auditory Soc., Internat. Hearing Soc., Hearing Health Care Providers of Calif. (v.p. dist. 6 1996). Home: 73061 Joshua Tree St Palm Desert CA 92260

ESPIN, OLIVA MARIA, psychology educator; b. Santiago, Cuba, Dec. 12, 1938; came to U.S., 1961; d. Oscar and Oliva (del Prado) E. BA in Psychology, U. Costa Rica, 1969; PhD, U. Fla., 1974; postgrad., Harvard U., 1981-83. Prof. St. Clare Coll., San Jose, Costa Rica, 1964-70, U. Costa Rica, San Jose, 1970; interin asst. prof. McGill U., Montreal, Can., 1974-75; asst. prof., assoc. prof. Boston U., 1975-86; assoc. prof. Tufts U., Medford, Mass., 1986-90; prof. San Diego State U., 1990—; psychologist pvt. practice, Boston, 1980-90, San Diego, 1992—. Mem. APA (Disting. Profl. 1991), Assn. Women in Psychology. Office: San Diego State U Dept Women's Studies San Diego CA 92182-8138

ESPOSITO, AMY SKLAR, lawyer; b. Bklyn., Nov. 9, 1955; d. Sidney and Rhoda (Weiner) Sklar; m. Francis Benedetto Esposito, May 4, 1985; children: Melissa, Anthony. BA, U. Vt., 1977; JD, Hofstra U., 1980. Bar: N.Y. 1981, Fla. 1983. Assoc. Herman & Natale, Esqs., Garden City, N.Y., 1980-81, Law Offices of Gabriel Kohn, Mineola, N.Y., 1981-84; ptnr. Ostor & Sklar, Esqs., Deer Park, N.Y., 1984-93; pvt. practice Deer Park, 1993-94, 95—; assoc. Naiburg & Rosenblum, Hauppauge, N.Y., 1994-95, Law Office of Lynne Adair Kramer, Commack, N.Y., 1994-95; pvt. practice Deer Park, N.Y., 1995—. Coach mock trials Nassau County (N.Y.) High Schs., 1984-86. Mem. N.Y. State Bar Assn., Nassau-Suffolk Women's Bar Assn. (assoc., speaker on matrimonial law). Jewish.

ESPOSITO, BONNIE LOU, marketing professional; b. Chgo., July 20, 1947; d. Ralph Edgar and Dorothy Mae (Groh) Myers; m. Frank Merle Esposito, Aug. 15, 1969 (div. Sept. 1985); children: Mario Henry, Elizabeth Ann. BA, George Williams Coll., 1969. Caseworker Little Bros. of the Poor, Chgo., 1969-72; dir. Little Bros.-Friends of the Elderly, Mpls., 1972-78; organizer Community Crime Prevention, Mpls., 1978-81; owner Espo Inc./Mario's Ristorante, Mpls., 1978-85; mktg. mgr. City of Mpls. Energy Office, 1981—; dir. mktg. and tng. The Energy Collaborative, 1987-93; dir. mktg. Ctr. for Energy and Environment, Mpls., 1989-95; dir. WINGS program Employment Action Ctr., Mpls., 1995—; v.p., bd. dirs. Resource Alternatives, Inc. Mem. NAFE (bd. dirs. Monday Night Network 1988), Midwest Direct Mktg. Assn., Minn. Multi-Housing Assn., Nat. Apt. Assn., Profl. Assn. for Consumer Energy Edn. (bd. dirs. 1993—, chmn. fin. com.). Office: WINGS Program Employment Action Ctr 1527 E Lake St 2d Fl Minneapolis MN 55407

ESSA, LISA BETH, elementary education educator; b. Modesto, Calif., Nov. 19, 1955; d. Mark Newyia and Elizabeth (Warda) E. BA, U. Pacific-Stockton, 1977, MA in Curriculum and Instrn. Reading, 1980. Cert. tchr. elem., multiple subject and reading specialist, Calif. Tchr. primary grades Delhi (Calif.) Elem. Sch. Dist., 1978-80; reading clinic tutor San Joaquin Delta Community Coll., Stockton, Calif., 1980; tchr. primary grades Hayward (Calif.) Unified Sch. Dist., Supr., San Francisco host com. Dem. Nat. Conv., 1984. Femmes Club scholar, 1973; U. Calif. Optometry Alumni Assn. scholar, 1973; Jobs Daughters scholar, 1974. Mem. Internat. Reading Assn., Calif. Tchrs. Assn., Hayward Unified Tchrs. Assn., San Francisco Jr. C. of C., Jr. League San Francisco. Democrat. Episcopalian. Home: 1960 Clay St Apt 109 San Francisco CA 94109-3435

ESSIG, KATHLEEN SUSAN, university official, consultant; b. Denver, July 5, 1956; d. Robert and Ethel (Sutherland) Essig. BS in BA, Colo. State U., 1979, MS, 1987. CPA, Colo. Personal fin. planner, v.p. fin. Successful Money Mgmt., Ft. Collins, Colo., 1987-88; accts. payable technician Colo. State U., Ft. Collins, 1980-81, supr. comml. accts. receivable, 1981-83, gen. acct. II, 1983-85, supr. student loans, 1985-87, supr. accts. receivable, acct. II, 1988-89, cost acct. III, 1989-94, univ. ofcl., contr., 1994; sr. cons. KPMG Peat Marwick, Denver, 1994—; univ. mgmt. cons. KPMG Peat Marwick, U.K., 1995—. Mem. Am. Bus. Women's Assn. (v.p. 1985, Woman of Yr. 1985), Nat. Assn. Accts.

ESSINGER, SUSAN JANE, special education educator; b. Paris, Ill., Oct. 7, 1952; d. Rex Milburn and Virginia Ellen (White) E. BS in Edn., Ea. Ill. U., Charleston, 1973; MS in Edn., Ind. State U., 1981, postgrad. Cert. learning disabilities, elem., educationally mentally handicapped with early childhood endorsement. Elem. tchr. Havana (Ill.) Sch. Dist., 1973-74; tchr. early childhood spl. edn. Paris Sch. Dist. 95, 1974—. Mem. NEA, Assn. for Edn. Young Children, Ill. Edn. Assn., Paris Tchrs. Assn., Coun. for Exceptional Children. Home: 1104 S Main St Paris IL 61944-2823 Office: Paris Sch Dist 95 S Main St Paris IL 61944

ESSLINGER, ANNA MAE LINTHICUM, realtor; b. Clifton, Tenn., May 29, 1912; d. Wallace Prather and Minnie P. (Bates) Linthicum; student Miss. State Coll. Women, La. State U.; m. William Francis Esslinger, Sept. 29, 1932; children—Ann Lynn (Mrs. James C. Wilcox), Susan Angie (Mrs. Heinz J. Selig). Founder, Esslinger-Wooten-Maxwell Inc., real estate, Coral Gables, Fla., 1968-85 . Pres. Coral Gables Bd. Realtors, 1975. Mem. Fla. (dir.) Assn. Realtors, Nat. Assn. Realtors, DAR, Assistance League of Eugene, Am. Contract Bridge League, Eugene Country Club, Eugene Symphony Guild, Chi Omega. Christian Scientist. Home: 759 Fairoaks Dr Eugene OR 97401-2392 Office: 1360 S Dixie Hwy Miami FL 33146-2904

ESSLINGER, NELL DANIEL, singer, choral director, writer; b. Huntsville, Ala., June 13, 1903; d. William Francis and Blanche (Russell) E.; m. Raymond G. Miller, Aug. 18, 1979. Vocal cert., Agnes Scott Coll., 1922; BA, U. Ala., 1954; MMus., U. Ill., 1962. Dir. Huntsville Music Study Club Chorus, 1938-39, 48-50, Male Chorus, 1948, Tri-Choral, 1950, Music Appreciation Club, 1950; dir., instr. voice Koch Sch. Music, Rocky River, Ohio, 1963-64; tchr. voice Baldwin Wallace Coll., Berea, Ohio, 1965-66; tchr. voice, choral dir. N.E. State Jr. Coll., Rainsville, Ala., 1966-69; owner, CEO The Notation Press, Ala., 1965—. Debut Carnegie Hall Chambers, N.Y., 1925; ch. and oratorio soloist, 1919-39, guest soloist Waldorf Astoria, N.Y., 1924, 25, Kenilworth Inn, Battery Park Inn, Ashveville, N.C., 1926; appeared in theatre prodns. ADrienne, 1924, Roxy's Gang, N.Y., 1925; radio shows Mr. Naftzeger's Morning Hour, N.Y., The House by the Side of the Road, others; author: (textbook) Revised Notation, 1965, 87 (award for Creative Achievement Ga. Sci. and Tech. Commn. 1968), The Variety of Voice, 1989; also poetry; composer (songs) Immortal, 1996, All for Alabama, 1996. Recipient awards Ala. Writers Conclave, Ala. State Poetry Soc., 1989-90. Mem. Ala. Assn. Inventors, Huntsville Music Study Club (hon. life), Bus. and Profl. Women's Club (charter Rainsville, Ala.), Alpha Epsilon Rho.

ESTABROOK, ALISON, breast surgeon, surgical oncologist, educator; b. N.Y.C., Oct. 29, 1951; d. Edwin Burke Estabrook and Shirley (Butler) Wood; m. William Neelis Harrington, June 13, 1981. BA cum laude, Barnard Coll., 1974; MD, NYU, 1978. Diplomate Am. Bd. Surgery. Resident in surgery Columbia-Presbyn. Med. Ctr., N.Y.C., 1978-81, 82-84, fellow in surg. oncology, 1981-82, asst. prof. surgery, 1984—, Florence Irving asst. prof., 1989-92; assoc. prof., 1992—; dir. Breast Clinic Columbia-Presbyn. Med. Ctr., N.Y.C., 1985—; chief breast surgery, 1991—. Contbr. articles to med. jours. Recipient Blakemore prize for rsch. Columbia-Presbyn. Med. Ctr., 1982, 84; Florence and Herbert Irving grantee, 1989-92. Fellow ACS; mem. AMA, Am. Med. Women's Assn., Am. Assn. Acad. Surgeons, Am. Fedn. Clin. Rsch., Am. Soc. Clin. Oncology, Nat. Surg. Advancement Breast Project, N.Y. Surg. Soc., N.Y. Met. Breast Cancer Group. Office: Columbia-Presbyn Med Ctr 161 Ft Washington Ave New York NY 10032-3713

ESTEFAN, GLORIA MARIA, singer, songwriter; b. Havana, Cuba, Sept. 1, 1957; came to U.S., 1959; d. Jose Manuel and Gloria G. (Garcia) Fajardo; m. Emilio Estefan, Jr., Sept. 1, 1979; children: Nayib Emil, Emily Marie. BA in Psychology, U. Miami, Fla., 1978, MusD (hon.), 1993. Composer: (popular songs) Anything for You, 1987, Live for Loving You, 1991, Can't Forget You, 1991, Coming Out of the Dark, 1991, Always Tomorrow, 1992, Go Away, 1993; performer songs for Olympics in Korea, 1987, World Series Baseball, St. Louis, 1987, Pan Am. Games, 1988, Superbowl Halftime, Mpls., 1992; albums: Primitive Love, 1986, Let It Loose, 1987, Cuts Both Ways, 1990, Coming Out Of The Dark, 1991, Greatest Hits, 1992, Mi Tierra, 1993 (Best Latin Tropical Album Grammy award, 1994), Christmas Through Your Eyes, 1993, Hold Me, Thrill Me, Kiss Me, 1994, Abriendo Puertas, 1995 (Best Latin Tropical Grammy award 1996), Destiny, 1996. Benefactress Children's Home Soc., Miami, 1991, Leukemia Soc., 1991, United Way, 1991, United Negro Coll. Fund, 1992, Community Alliance Against AIDS, Miami, 1992, Hurrican Relief Fund, So. Fla., 1992-93; pub. mem. U.S. Del. to 47th Gen. Assembly UN. Recipient Am. Music award, 1987, Victory award, 1991, Songwriter of Yr. award BMI, 1991, Humanitarian of Yr. award B'nai Brith, 1992, Casita Maria Gold Medal award, 1993, Hispanic Heritage award, 1993, Hearst Found. Gold Medal award, 1992, Ellis Island Congl. Medal of Honor, 1993.; named Billboard's Best New Pop Artist and Top Pop Singles Artist, 1986; also numerous Grammy award nominations, 1988-91, Musicares Person of Yr., 1994, Billboard Music Video of Yr. award Everlasting Love, 1995, also over 50 platinum albums worldwide. Office: Estefan Enterprises Inc 6205 Bird Rd Miami FL 33155-4823*

ESTELL, DORA LUCILE, retired educational administrator; b. Ft. Worth, Mar. 3, 1930; d. Hugh and Hattie Lucile (Poole) E. BA, East Tex. Bapt. U., 1951; MA, U. North Tex., 1959; EdD, East Tex. State U., 1988. Tchr. Mission (Tex.) Ind. Sch. Dist., 1951-53; tchr., adminstr. Marshall (Tex.) Ind. Sch. Dist., 1953-68; dep. dir. Region VII Edn. Svc. Ctr., Kilgore, Tex., 1968-94, ret., 1994. Contbr. articles to profl. jours. Mem. Phi Delta Kappa. Baptist. Home: 611 W Bell Ave Rockdale TX 76567-2809

ESTER, KAREN MARIE, nonprofit fundraiser; b. Rochester, N.Y., Oct. 16, 1950; d. William George and Leah (Ring) E.; div.; children: Brian James Nowak, Amber Leah Nowak. BA, SUNY, Brockport, 1993. Unit sec. Genesee Hosp., Rochester, N.Y., 1979-84; owner, mgr. Karen Nowak Pottery, Rochester, N.Y., 1979-94; dir. ann. campaign Rochester Philharmonic Orch., 1994—. Potter wheel thrown, hand painted pottery (award of merit Clothesline Art Show, 1982; named Mastercraftsman, Roycraft Artisans Guild, 1985). Bd. dirs. Temple Emanu-El, Rochester, 1985—, v.p. edn., 1987-89; chair artists' conf. Jewish Arts Festival, Rochester, 1991; daily ops. mgr. Montage, '93, Rochester, N.Y. Summer '93. Democrat. Office: Rochester Philharmonic Orch 108 East Ave Rochester NY 14604

ESTERLINE, SHIRLEY JEANNE, lithograph company executive; b. Paulding, Ohio, June 6, 1936; d. George Gary and Catherine Genevieve (Durbin) Sontchi; m. Meredith Esterline, Apr. 1, 1956; children: Gordon Alan, Amy Jeanne. Cert. med. technologist, Elkhart U., Ind., 1956. Lab technician, Fort Wayne, Ind., 1956-57; sec. Zollner Corp., Fort Wayne, 1957-58, Magnavox Corp., Fort Wayne, 1958-61; sales coord. Doty Lithograph Inc., Fort Wayne, 1975-77; sales mgr. Dot Line div. Dot Corp., Auburn, Ind., 1977-87, Midwest sales mgr. Falco/Sunbelt div. FL Co., Nashville, 1987-89; pvt. cons., 1989—. Recipient Top Sales award Dot Corp., 1985. Mem. Specialty Advt. Assn. Internat. (suppliers com. 1983—, cert. advt. specialist 1985, master advt. specialist 1986, chmn. 100 club 1983—, seminar facilitator calendar advt. coun. 1985-89, CAS Alumni 1985—, mgmt. awards 1984, 85, 86). Methodist. Avocations: reading, gardening.

ESTERLY, NANCY BURTON, physician; b. N.Y.C., Apr. 14, 1935; d. Paul R. and Tanya (Pasahow) Burton; m. John R. Esterly, June 16, 1957; children: Sarah Burton, Anne Beidler, John Snyder, II, Henry Clark, II. AB, Smith Coll., 1956; MD, Johns Hopkins U., 1960. Intern, then resident in pediatrics Johns Hopkins Hosp., 1960-63, resident in dermatology, 1964-67; instr. pediatrics Johns Hopkins U. Med. Sch., 1967-68; instr., trainee La Rabida U. Chgo. Inst.; also dept. pediatrics U. Chgo. Med. Sch., 1968-69; asst. prof. Pritzker Sch. Medicine, U. Chgo., 1969-70, asso. prof., 1973-78; asst. prof. dermatology Abraham Lincoln Sch. Medicine, U. Ill., 1970-72, asso. prof. dermatology and pediatrics, 1972-73; dir. div. dermatology, dept. pediatrics Michael Reese Hosp. and Med. Ctr., Chgo., 1973-78; prof. pediatrics and dermatology Northwestern U. Med. Sch., 1978; head div. dermatology, dept. pediatrics Children's Meml. Hosp., Chgo., 1978-87; prof. pediatrics and dermatology Med. Coll. Wis., Milw., 1987—; head div. dermatology, dept. pediatrics Children's Hosp. Wis., Milw., 1987—. Contbr. numberous articles to profl. jours. Mem. Internat. Soc. Pediatric Dermatology, Am. Acad. Dermatology, Am. Dermatol. Assn., Wis. Dermatol. Soc., Soc. Investigative Dermatology, Am. Acad. Pediatrics, Soc. Pediatric Rsch., Soc. Pediatric Dermatology, Women's Dermatol. Soc.,

Wis. Pediatric Soc., Sigma Xi. Office: 9200 W Wisconsin Ave Milwaukee WI 53226-3548

ESTERMANN, ROSEANNE ADELE, artist; b. Fond du Lac, Wis., Aug. 17, 1955; d. Rolland Oliver and Mary Jane (Gurber) Hebert; m. William Wagner, Mar. 25, 1974 (div. Mar. 1990); 1 child, Jay William Wagner; m. Joseph John Estermann, Oct. 25, 1992. Student, Northctrl. Tech. Coll., Wausau, Wis., 1988, U. Wis., Wausau, 1989-93, U. Wis., Steven's Point, 1992. Staff artist Seven Star Mktg., Manitowoc, Wis., 1973—; art dir. Custom Trophies, Inc., Two Rivers, Wis., 1974; comml. artist Fresno, Calif., 1980-85; pvt. art tchr. Wausau, Wis., 1990-92; owner, operator, fine artist Adele's Studio, Wausau, Wis., 1992—. Two-woman show Ctr. Visual Arts, Wausau, 1996; represented by The LandMark Frame and Gallery, Wausau, 1994-95; executed car mural featured on full-page QVO Car Mag.; represented in visual arts series Psychotherapy of Me, 1996. Activity coord. People's Ch., Fresno, Calif.; guest project tchr. James Monroe Elem. Sch., Fresno; instr. karate (1st degree black belt) Merrill (Wis.) Moose Lodge; vol. Liegh Yawkey Woodsen Art Mus., 1993. Recipient 1st premium and 2 2d premium ribbons Wis. Fair, Wausau, 1990. Mem. Ctr. Visual Arts. Home and Studio: 509 7th St Wausau WI 54403

ESTES, ELAINE ROSE GRAHAM, retired librarian; b. Springfield, Mo., Nov. 24, 1931; d. James McKinley and Zelma Mae (Smith) Graham; m. John Melvin Estes, Dec. 29, 1953. BSBA, Drake U., 1953, tchg. cert., 1956; MSLS, U. Ill., 1960. With Pub. Libr. Des Moines, 1956-95, coord. extension svcs., 1977-78, dir., 1978-95, ret., 1995; lectr. antiques, hist. architecture, libraries; mem. conservation planning com. for disaster preparedness for libraries. Author bibliographies of books on antiques; contbr. articles to profl. jours. Mem. State of Iowa Cultural Affairs Adv. Coun., 1986-94, Nat. Commn. on Future Drake U., 1987-88; chmn. Des moines Mayor's Hist. Dist. Commn.; bd. dirs. Des Moines Art Ctr., 1972-83, hon. mem., 1983—; bd. dirs. Friends of Libr. USA, 1986-92, Henry Wallace Housing Found.; mem. Iowa Libr. Centennial Com., 1990-91; nominations rev. com. Iowa State Nat. Hist. Register, 1983-89; chmn. hist. subcom. Des Moines Sesequecentennial com., 1993, Iowa Sister State Commn., 1993-95; mem. Sesequecentennial July 3 com.; mem. 45th anniversary com. Des Moines Art Ctr., 1993; mem. com. 40th anniversary Drake U. alumni weekend; mem. Iowa Sesequecentennial July 4 com., 1996. Recipient recognition for outstanding working women - leadership in econs. and civic life of Greater Des Moines, YWCA, 1975, Disting. Alumni award Drake U., 1979, Woman of Achievement award YWCA, 1989, City of Des Moines Excellence in Hist. Preservation award, 1994. Mem. ALA, Iowa Libr. Assn. (pres. 1978-79), Iowa Urban Pub. Libr. Assn., Libr. Assn. Greater Des Moines Metro Area (pres., chmn. 1992), Iowa Soc. Preservation Hist. Landmarks (bd. dirs. 1969—), Terrace (Gov.'s Mansion) Soc. (v.p. 1991-93, pres. 1993—), Links Club, Quester's, Inc. Club (pres. 1982, state 2nd v.p. 1984-86), Iowa Antique Assn., Proteus, Rotary.

ESTES, JULIE JOHNSTONE, elementary and secondary school educator; b. St. Petersburg, Fla., Nov. 4, 1942; d. James William and Enid Frances (Edgerly) Johnstone; m. Thomas Howard Estes, Oct. 26, 1973; 1 child, Jamie Lee. BA, Coll. of William & Mary, 1964; MEd, U. Va., 1969, EdD, 1973. Cert. elem., secondary tchr., Va. Tchr. Fairfax County Pub. Schs., Fairfax, Va., 1964-70; adj. prof. U. Va., Charlottesville, 1971-75, asst. prof., 1976-82; asst. to dir. of testing, Dept. Edn. State of Va., Richmond, 1986-89; coord. lang. arts, assessment Albemarle County Pub. Schs., Charlottesville, Va., 1989—, cons. 1973-86; mem. rev. bd. Va. State Reading Assn., 1990-92. Contbr. articles to profl. jours. Mem. Optimist Club of the Blue Ridge (historian 1993—), Phi Delta Kappa (mem. program com. 1990—). Democrat. Episcopalian. Home: 3619 Red Fox Ln Keswick VA 22947-0014 Office: Albemarle County Pub Schs 401 Mcintire Rd Charlottesville VA 22902-4579

ESTES, KAREN ANN, mathematics educator; b. Litchfield, Ill., Nov. 9, 1947; d. William Robert and Enice Estes. BS, Eastern Ill. Univ., 1969, MA, 1971, PhD, Univ. South Fla., 1990. Math. tchr. Bunker Hill (Ill.) H.S., 1969-70, Southwestern H.S., Piasa, Ill., 1971-83, St. Petersburg Jr. Coll., Tarpon Springs, Fla., 1983—. Recipient Nat. Excellence Teaching award Univ. Tex. Study, 1989. Mem. Am. Math. Assn. Two Yr. Colls. (TIME com. 1985-96), AAUW, Fla. Two Yr. Coll. Math. Assn. Roman Catholic. Office: St Petersburg Jr Coll 600 Klosterman Rd Palm Harbor FL 34683

ESTES, PAMELA JEAN, pastor; b. Topeka, Oct. 14, 1953; d. Jack E. and Bonita A. (Hatfield) E. BA, BME, Ouachita U., 1974, MME, 1976; MLS, Vanderbilt U., 1983; MDiv, Boston U., 1988, MST, 1989. Tchr. Thayer (Mo.) Schs., 1976-79; libr. Pochontas (Ark.) H.S., 1979-82; libr. intern Vanderbilt U., 1982-83, libr., 1983-85; cataloger Boston U. Sch. Theology, 1985-89; pastor Union Congl. Ch., Walpole, Mass., 1987-88; pianist East Walpole (Mass.) United Meth. Ch., 1988-89; pastor First United Meth. Ch., Camden, Ark., 1989-92, Stamps (Ark.) Charge, 1992-93, St. James United Meth., Little Rock, 1993—; pvt. musician, 1970—; cataloger Ouachita, summer, 1976-82; chair Commn. on the Status and Role of Women, 1989-95, Ark. Del. to White House Conf. on Librs., 1991, Sexual Harrassment Task Force United Meth. Ch., Ark., 1992-95. Editor: United Methodist Women's Day Reference, 1991; author of poetry. Debate moderator LWV, Camden, Ark., 1989-92; vol. Friends of the Libr., Little Rock, 1993-95. Oxnam scholar Boston U. Sch. Theology. Mem. Delta Kappa Gamma. Democrat. Home: 7002 Carrilon Little Rock AR 72205 Office: St James United Meth 321 Pleasant Valley Little Rock AR 72212

ESTES, VALERIE, independent consultant; b. Inglewood, Calif., Apr. 9, 1941; d. Warren Clough and Mary Katherine (Pray) E.; m. Robert Burns Morrill, May 26, 1963 (div. 1969). BS in Home Econs., U. Nev., 1962; AB in Anthropology, U. Calif., Berkeley, 1973, MA in Anthropology, 1975, PhD in Anthropology, 1984. Adminstrv. asst. Office of Sen. Howard W. Cannon, Washington, 1962-63; asst. pub. rels. Calif. Wine Inst., San Francisco, 1963-64; tutor English pvt. practice, Greece, Turkey, Libya, Italy, 1964-67; editorial asst. Grey Fox Press & Grove Press, San Francisco, 1968-75; dir. women, work & family project U. Calif., Berkeley, 1984-85; lectr. U. Calif., Hayward, 1985-86; dir. women & work and 3d world Am. Higher Edn. Consortium for Urban Affairs, Berkeley, 1986-88; co-dir. minority edn. project U. Calif., Berkeley, 1988-90; gender & socioeconomic analyst Devel. Strategies for Fragile Lands Project, Washington, 1991-93; sr. social analyst Gender in Social and Econ. Systems Project, Washington, 1993-94; creator, coord. Gender and Environ. Network, Washington, 1991-94; ind. cons. internat. devel. U.S. Agy. Internat. Devel. & Inter-Am. Devel. Bank, Washington, 1994—. Grad. fellow Danforth Found., U. Calif., 1974-80, rsch. fellow Inter-Am. Found., La Paz, Bolovia, 1977-80, Ford Found., 1981-83; Robert Lowie Grad. scholar U. Calif., 1983-84, vis. scholar, 1990-91. Mem. Am. Anthropology Assn., Consortium Women in Devel. Home and Office: 1600 N Oak St #1526 Arlington VA 22209

ESTEY, AUDREE PHIPPS, artistic director; b. Winnipeg, Man., Can., Jan. 7, 1910; d. Robert and Anna (Harrington) Phipps; student Immaculate Heart Coll., 1927-29, Ernest Belcher Ballet Sch., 1928-31, Robert Major Drama Sch., 1929-31, Koslov Ballet Sch., 1930-31; m. L. Wendell Estey, Sept. 18, 1933; children: Lawrence Mitchell, Carol.Dancer Ernest Belcher Ballet Co., L.A., 1930, Fanchon and Marco Co., L.A., 1930-31; actress-dancer Fox Studio, Hollywood, Calif., 1931-32; ballet tchr. Lawrenceville and Princeton, N.J., 1938-80, Perry Mansfield Camp, Steamboat Springs Colo., summers 1949-50; head dance dept. Les Chalets Francais, Deer Isle, Maine, 1951-73; founder non-profit Princeton (N.J.) Ballet Soc., 1954, dir., cons.; founder Princeton Regional Ballet Co., 1963; founder profl. co., Princeton Ballet, 1979, Am. Repertory Ballet Co. Host Northeast Regional Ballet Festival-Princeton, 1968; coordinator Northeast Regional Ballet Festival-Jacob's Pillow, 1970. Apptd. by gov. N.J. State Commn. to Study Arts, 1968, trustee N.J. Sch. of the Arts, 1980; bd. dirs. Sarasota Ballet of Fla., 1989-91, co-chair resource com., 1992-93, mem. artistic com., 1993—. Recipient Rutgers U. award for contbn. to arts in N.J., 1982. Mem. N.E. Regional Ballet Assn. (pres., 1967-68, exec. v.p., 1968-71), Sarasota-Manatee Dance Tchrs. Assn. (pres. 1990-93). Episcopalian. Choreographer over 20 ballets for children and young dancers including: Festival of the Gnomes, Pastels, Peter and the Wolf, Sleeping Beauty, Cinderella, Pied Piper, The Nutcracker (choreography for Act I currently used by Princeton Ballet), Chanson Innocente, Graduation Ball, Coppelia. Office: 262 Alexander St Princeton NJ 08540-7104

ESTIN-KLEIN, LIBBYADA, advertising executive, medical writer; b. Newark, July 13, 1937; d. Barney and Florence B. (Tenkin) Straver; m. Harvey M. Klein, Sept. 9, 1984. Student Syracuse U., 1955-57; BS, Columbia, 1960; RN, Columbia-Presbyn. Med. Ctr., 1960; cert., N.Y. Sch. Interior Design, 1962. Med. rsch. tech. writer, N.Y.C., 1960-62; pres. Libbyada Estin Interiors, N.Y.C., 1962-65; v.p. advt. and pub. relations Behrman/Estin Inc., N.Y.C., 1965-67; account exec., dir. pub. rels. J.S. Fullerton, Inc., N.Y.C., 1967-68; med. writer L.W. Frohlich & Co., Intercon Internat. Inc., N.Y.C., 1968-69, Kallir Philips Ross Inc., N.Y.C., 1969-71; copy supr. William Douglas McAdams Inc., N.Y.C., 1971-75, Sudler & Hennessey Inc., N.Y.C., 1975-80; v.p., exec. adminstr., creative dir. Grey Med. Advt. Inc., N.Y.C., 1980-84; founder, ptnr. Estin Sandler Comm. Inc., N.Y.C., 1984; v.p. Barnum Comm. Inc., N.Y.C., 1984-86; sr. v.p. ICE Comm., Inc., Rochester, N.Y., 1986-87; pres. Estin-Klein Comm. Inc., Rochester and Pittsford, N.Y., 1987—; dir. health group Roberts Comm., Inc., East Rochester, N.Y., 1993-95; bd. dirs. Grief Resource Info. Edn. Forum, Inc., Perinatal Network of Monroe County. Mem. Pub. Rels. Soc. Am., Advt. Women N.Y., Am. Advt. Fedn., Advt. Coun. of Rochester, Rochester Sales and Mktg. Execs. Club, Mktg. Communicators of Rochester, Am. Med. Writers Assn., Healthcare Mktg. and Comms. Coun., Healthcare Bus. Women's Assn., Am. Nurses Assn., Allied Bd. Trade, Columbia-Presbyn. Hosp. Alumnae Assn., Columbia U. Alumnae Assn., Syracuse U. Alumnae Assn., Sigma Theta Tau, Delta Phi Epsilon. Home and Office: 289 Garnsey Rd Pittsford NY 14534-4540

ESTRADA, YVONNE, artist, painter, sculptor; b. Bogota, Colombia, Dec. 7, 1960; came to the U.S., 1980; d. Jaime Estrada and Clara Rojas; m. Harrison C. Williams, June 26, 1987. Student, David Manzur Studio, Bogota, 1978-80, Art Students League, 1980-84; BA equivalent, Art Students League, 1986; postgrad., Skowhegan Sch. Paint/Sculpt., 1986. Selected exhbns. include Colombian Consulate, N.Y.C., 1983, Rayo Mus., Valle, Colombia, 1984, Mus. Modern Art, Bogota, 1985, Fed. Dist. Govt. Bldg., Caracas, Venezuela, 1985, Mus. Contemporary Hispanic Art, The Benjamin N. Cardozo Sch. Law, N.Y., 1986, Jadite Gallery, N.Y., 1986, 87, House of Culture, Bogota, 1986, Cork Gallery, Lincoln Ctr., N.Y., 1986, Mus. Contemporary Hispanic Art, N.Y., Museo de Arte Actual, Bogota, 1986, Art Students League, N.Y., 1987, The Rotunda Gallery, Bklyn., 1992, Colombian Consulate Gallery, N.Y.C., 1993, Carla Stellweg Gallery, N.Y.C., 1993, 80 Washington Square East Galleries, Dept. Art and Art Professions, NYU, 1996. Nessa Cohen grantee Art Students League, N.Y., 1984, 85, Edward McDowell Travel grantee Art Students League, Europe, 1986, Skowhegan Sch. for Painting and Sculpture. Home: 202 West 58 St New York NY 10019

ESTRELLA, JACQUELYN ANN, writer, newspaper; b. Bangor, Maine, Sept. 24, 1947; d. Richard Robert and Clara Ann (Turner) Ready; m. José Constanté Ferro Barros, May 11, 1966 (div. Feb. 1972); 1 child, Trina Mercedes Ferro Compton; m. Richard Cordero Estrella, Mar. 18, 1984; 1 child, Jacquelyn Kelly Ready Estrella. AA in Journalism, City Coll. of San Francisco, 1994; student, San Francisco State U., 1995—. Rsch. analyst Direct Lang. Pub., San Francisco, 1986-87; clerical asst. III San Francisco State U., 1987-88; freelance journalist San Francisco, 1992—; with The Guardsman, 1992-94; pub. rels. dir. dept. journalism City Coll. San Francisco, 1993; copy editor KIQI Newsletter, 1993-95, The City Voice, San Francisco, 1995-96; pres. Press Club, City Coll. San Francisco, 1993-94, pres. com. preservation of journalistic autonomy, 1993-94; participant in panel The Future of Journalism, San Francisco State U., 1994. Contbg. writer The San Francisco Examiner, The City Voice, El Tecolote, Inside Magazine, P.S. Bytes, Richmond Review, Sunset Beacon, The Guardsman, Vista Magazine, Baseball Weekly, The Golden Gator, 1993-95; contbr. articles to popular publs. Pres. Parents Advisory Coun., City Coll. San Francisco, 1992-93; mem. Glen Park Neighborhood Assn., San Francisco, 1993; vol. Am. Heart Assn., 1993. Recipient Outstanding Student Journalist award City Coll. San Francisco, 1992-93, Outstanding Achievement award City Coll. San Francisco Press Club, 1993-94, Chancellor's Plaque, City Coll. San Franciso, 1994, Cert. Appreciation, Clarendon Alternative Elem. Sch., San Francisco, 1995; Associated Students Coun. scholar City Coll. San Francisco, 1992. Mem. Women in Comm., Inc. (Leading Change award, scholar 1994), Soc. Profl. Journalists, Alpha Gamma Sigma (budget com. 1992—, scholar 1992). Democrat. Buddhist.

ESTRICH, SUSAN RACHEL, law educator; b. Lynn, Mass., Dec. 16, 1952; d. Irving Abraham and Helen Roslyn (Freedberg) E.; m. Martin Kaplan. BA, Wellesley Coll., 1974; JD, Harvard U., 1977. Law clk. to Hon. J. Skelly Wright U.S. Ct. Appeals, Washington, 1977-78; law clk. to Hon. John P. Stevens U.S. Supreme Ct., Washington, 1978-79; dep. nat. issues dir., spl. asst. Kennedy for Pres. campaign, Washington, 1979-80; sr. policy advisor Mondale-Ferraro campaign, 1984; of counsel Tuttle & Taylor, L.A., 1986-87; campaign mgr. Dukakis for Pres. campaign, Boston, 1987-88; asst. prof. law Harvard Law Sch., Cambridge, Mass., 1981-86, prof. law, 1986-90; Robert Kingsley prof. law and polit. sci. U. So. Calif., 1990—; host talk show Sta. KABC, L.A. Author: Real Rape, 1987; co-author: Dangerous Offenders, 1985; columnist L.A. Style mag.; weekly columnist USA Today; contbg. editor L.A. Times Opinion Sect.; pres. Harvard Law Rev.; contbr. articles to numerous jours. Mem. Dem. Nat. Com., Washington, 1984-88, ACLU (nat. bd.), pres. Boston chpt., 1985-86; mem. nat. governing bd. Common Cause, 1983-89. Mem. D.C. Bar, Calif. Bar, U.S. Supreme Ct. Bar. Jewish. Office: U So Calif Law Ctr Los Angeles CA 90089-0071

ESTRIDGE, TRUDY DONETTE, research scientist; b. Olney, Tex., Feb. 12, 1961; d. Donal Eugene and Johnnie Louise (York) E. BS, Tex. A&M U., 1983, MS, 1988; PhD, U. Ala., Birmingham, 1991. Rsch. scientist Collagen Corp., Palo Alto, Calif., 1991—. Mem. Soc. for Biomaterials. Office: Collagen Corp 2500 Faber Pl Palo Alto CA 94303

ETHERIDGE, MELISSA LOU, singer, songwriter; b. Leavenworth, Kans., 1962; d. John and Elizabeth Etheridge. Student, Berklee Coll. of Music, Boston, 1970. Wrote songs for the film, Weeds; albums include Melissa Etheridge, 1988, Brave and Crazy, 1989, Never Enough, 1992, Yes I Am, 1993. Named Entertainer of Year Can. Acad. Recording Arts and Scis., 1990; Grammy award, Best Female Rock Vocal for "Aint It Heavy," 1993, Female Rock Vocal Performance for "Come to My Window," 1994. *

ETHERINGTON, CAROL S., lawyer; b. Edmonton, Alta., Can., Dec. 21, 1949. BA with honors, U. Alta., 1971, LLB with honors, 1972. Bar: Alta. 1973, Calif. 1979. Ptnr. Brobeck, Phlegar & Harrison, San Francisco. Assoc. editor Alta. Law Rev., 1970-72. Office: Brobeck Phleger & Harrison Spear St Tower 1 Market Plz San Francisco CA 94105*

ETHERTON, JOAN ELAINE, real estate salesperson; b. Mpls., Sept. 10, 1945; d. Joseph Roman and Blanche Claudia (Hilst) Winter; m. Robert Gene Etherton, Sept. 6, 1980 (dec. Dec. 1988); 1 child, Mindy Anne McClean. Student, Western Wash. U., Bellingham, 1963-64, Seattle C.C., 1987-88. Notary Pub.; lic. real estate agt. Sec. to bank br. mgr. Key Bank-Wash., Seattle, 1979-80; owner Nat. Auction Svc., Seattle, 1980-89; sales assoc. Coldwell Banker, Seattle, 1993—. Bd. dirs. Swedish Hosp., Seattle, 1987-89; active Salvation Army, Seattle, 1988-89. Roman Catholic. Office: Coldwell Banker 122 SW 156th Seattle WA 98166

ETHRIDGE, VEREE KEPLEY, busines administration educator; b. Princeton, Ind., May 31, 1945; d. Vance Ivan and Georgia C. (Smith) Kepley; m. James I. Ethridge, Aug. 18, 1973; children: Kersten, Karee. BS, U. Ill., 1967, MS, 1971, PhD, 1978. Residential rep. Ill. Power Co., Danville, 1967-68; food svc. adminstrn. U. Ill., Urbana, 1968-71, asst. prof., 1978-81; instr. U. Nev., Reno, 1971-73; prof. bus. adminstrn. Coll. St. Francis, Joliet, Ill., 1984—. Contbr. articles to profl. jours. Pres. Troy Sch. Bd., Shorewood, Ill., 1982-86. Mem. Am. Econ. Assn., Midwest Bus. Econ. Assn. (v.p., pres. 1993-95), Delta Kappa Gamma (rsch. chair 1993, fin. chair 1994—). Office: College of St Francis 500 Wilcox Joliet IL 60435

ETTINGER, M(ARTHA) JEANNE, retired nurse; b. Granite City, Ill., July 11, 1924; d. John T. and Jennie Ethel (Bline) Liggett; m. Milton Gene Ettinger, June 26, 1957; children: Adrienne Sue Baranauskas, David Norman. Diploma, St. Luke's Sch. Nursing, 1946, U. Oreg., Portland, 1952. Surg. clin. instr. Providence Hosp. Sch. Nursing, Portland, Oreg., 1950-52; staff nurse VA Hosp., Long Beach, Calif., 1953-55; head bookkeeper Park Loan Co., Mpls., 1955-56; indsl. nurse Napco, Mpls., 1956-57; exec. sec. Tri Mut. Inc., Mpls., 1978-79, purchasing agt., 1980-81; project coord. Stroke study Mpls. Med. Rsch. Found., Mpls., 1982-87. Precinct chair Rep. party, Plymouth, Minn., 1977-79, vice chair, 1979-81, state del., 1978—; pres. Hennepin County Rep. Women, Mpls., 1978-80, Minn. Fedn. Ind. Rep. Women, Mpls., 1990-94; exec. bd. dirs. Hennepin County Med. Ctr. Svc. League, 1991—, treas., 1993—. Mem. Aux. to Am. Acad. Neurology (hon. mem., pres. 1971-73, newsletter editor 1962-68), Hadassah (life). Jewish. Home: 15545 17th Pl N Minneapolis MN 55447-2402

ETZ, LOIS KAPELSOHN, architectural company executive; b. Newark, Feb. 7, 1944; d. Sol D. and Matilda (Zlotnick) Kapelsohn; m. Leonard Etz, Dec. 4, 1967 (dec. May 1976); children: Rachel Jennie, Rebecca Sarah. BA, Mount Holyoke Coll., 1966; MA, Seton Hall U., 1968. Counselor N.J. Rehab. Commn., Trenton, 1966-68; pvt. antique dealer Princeton, N.J., 1968-78; pres. Nat. Code Cons., Princeton, 1971-78; dir. purchasing, aux. svcs. Mercer County Community Coll., Trenton, 1978-81; v.p. Hillier Group Architects, Princeton, 1981—. Bd. dirs. Vols. in Probation, Princeton, 1981, N.J. Printmaking Coun., Princeton Arts Coun., Mercer County Spl. Svc. Com., Hadassah; v.p. McCarter Theatre Assocs., Princeton, 1986-89; bd. dirs. McCarter Theatre Trustees, Princeton, 1989-91; past v.p., bd. dirs. Jewish Ctr. Commendation Chief Justice N.J. Supreme Ct., 1982. Commendation Chief Justice N.J. Supreme Ct., 1982. Mem. Mt. Holyoke Alumnae Assn. (past pres. Princeton chpt.), Record Mgmt. Assn. (founding officer), Princeton Pers. Assn. Democrat. Jewish. Home: 1038 Princeton Kingston Rd Princeton NJ 08540-4130 Office: The Hillier Group CN23 500 Alexander Pk Princeton NJ 08540

ETZEL, RUTH ANN, pediatrician, epidemiologist; b. Milw., Apr. 6, 1954; d. Raymond Arthur and Marian Dorothy (Neu) E. Student, St. Olaf Coll., 1972-73; BA in Biology summa cum laude, U. Minn., 1976; MD, U. Wis., 1980; PhD, U. N.C., 1985. Pediatrics resident N.C. Meml. Hosp., Chapel Hill, 1980-83; adj. asst. prof. pediatrics Emory U. Sch. Medicine, Atlanta, 1985-87; epidemic intelligence svc. officer Ctr. Environ. Health Ctrs. for Disease Control, Atlanta, 1985-87, med. epidemiologist Ctr. Environ. Health and Injury Control, 1987-90; chief air pollution and respiratory health br. Ctrs. for Disease Control and Prevention, Atlanta, 1991—; mem. preventive medicine and pub. health test com. Nat. Bd. Med. Examiners, 1992—; mem. U.S. Med. Licensing Exam. Step 2 Preventive Medicine and Pub. Health Test Material Devel. Com., 1992—; asst. dir. CDC Preventive Medicine Residency Program, 1992—. Contbr. articles to profl. publs. Robert Wood Johnson clin. scholar U. N.C., 1983-85, MacPherson scholar, 1972; recipient Arthur S. Flemming award D.C. Jaycees, 1991. Fellow Am. Acad. Pediatrics (com. on environ. hazards, CDC liaison 1986-92, chair sect. on epidemiology 1988-92, ex officio 1993—); mem. APHA, Ambulatory Pediatric Assn. (rsch. com. 1987—), Soc. for Pediatric Epidemiol. Rsch. (exec. com. 1988—), Physicians for Social Responsibility, Soc. for Pediatric Epidemiol. Rsch., Phi Beta Kappa, Delta Omega.

EU, MARCH FONG, ambassador, former California state official; b. Oakdale, Calif., Mar. 29, 1929; d. Yuen and Shiu (Shee) Kong; children by previous marriage: Matthew Kipling Fong, Marchesa Suyin Fong; m. Henry Eu, Aug. 31, 1973; stepchildren: Henry, Adeline, Yvonne, Conroy, Alaric. Student, Salinas Jr. Coll.; BS, U. Calif.-Berkeley, 1943; MEd, Mills Coll., 1947; EdD, Stanford U., 1956; postgrad., Columbia U., Calif. State Coll.-Hayward; LLD, Lincoln U., 1984; LLB (hon.), Western U., 1985, Pepperdine U., 1993. Chmn. div. dental hygiene U. Calif. Med. Center, San Francisco, 1948-56; dental hygienist Oakland (Calif.) Pub. Schs., 1948-56; supr. dental health edn. Alameda County (Calif.) Schs.; lectr. health edn. Mills Coll., Oakland; mem. Calif. Legislature, 1966-74, chmn. select com. on agr., foods and nutrition, 1973-74; mem. com. natural resources and conservation, com. commerce and pub. utilities, select com. med. malpractice; chief of protocol State of Calif., 1975-83, sec. of state, 1975-94; Ambassador to Federated States of Micronesia U.S. Dept. of State, Washington, 1994—; chmn. Calif. State World Trade Commn., 1983-87; ex officio mem. Calif. State World Trade Commn., 1987—; spl. cons. Bur. Intergroup Relations, Calif. Dept. Edn.; ednl., legis. cons. Sausalito (Calif.) Pub. Schs., Santa Clara County Office Edn., Jefferson Elementary Union Sch. Dist., Santa Clara High Sch. Dist., Santa Clara Elementary Sch. Dist., Live Oak Union High Sch. Dist.; mem. Alameda County Bd. Edn., 1956-66, pres., 1961-62, legis. adv., 1963, Assembly Retirement Com., Assembly Com. on Govtl. Quality Com., Assembly Com. on Pub. Health; pres. Alameda County Sch. Bds. Assn., others. Mem. budget panel Bay Area United Fund Crusade; mem. Oakland Econ. Devel. Council; mem. tourism devel. com. Calif. Econ. Devel. Commn.; mem. citizens com. on housing Council Social Planning; mem. Calif. Interagy. Council Family Planning; edn. chmn., mem. council social planning, dir. Oakland Area Baymont Dist. Community Council; charter pres., hon. life mem. Howard Elementary Sch. PTA; charter pres. Chinese Young Ladies Soc., Oakland; mem., vice chmn. adv. com. Youth Study Centers and Ford Found. Interagy. Project, 1962-63; chmn. Alameda County Mothers' March, 1971-72; bd. councillors U. So. Calif. Sch. Dentistry, 1976; mem. exec. com. Calif. Democratic Central Com., mem. central com., 1963-70, asst. sec.; del. Dem. Nat. Conv., 1968; dir. 8th Congl. Dist. Dem. Council, 1963; v.p. Dems. of 8th Congl. Dist., 1963; dir. Key Women for Kennedy, 1963; women's vice chmn. No. Calif. Johnson for Pres., 1964; bd. dirs. Oakland YWCA, 1965. Recipient ann. award for outstanding achievement Eastbay Intercultural Fellowship, 1959; Phoebe Apperson Hearst Disting. Bay Area Woman of Yr. award; Honor award Sacramento Dist. Dental Soc., award of Merit Calif. Chiropractic Assn. legis. dept., Lamplighter award for Outstanding Achievement in Crime Prevention Oakland Real Estate Bd. Lite-the-Night Com., Loyalty Day award VFW of U.S., Woman of Achievement award Golden Gate Chpt. Bus. and Profl. Women's Club, Woman of Yr. award Calif. Retail Liquor Dealers Inst., 1969; Merit citation Calif. Assn. Adult Edn. Adminstrs., 1970; Art Edn. award; Outstanding Woman award Nat. Women's Polit. Caucus, 1980; Person of Yr. award Miracle Mile Lions Club, 1980; Humanitarian award Milton Strong Hall of Fame, 1981; Outstanding Leadership award Ventura Young Dems., 1983; Woman of Achievement award Los Angeles Hadassah, 1983, Outstanding Leadership award Filipino-Am. C. of C., 1985, CARE award, 1985, Disting. Svc. award Republic of Honduras, 1987, Polit. Achievement award Calif Dem. Party Black Caucus, 1988, JFK Am. Leadership award Santa Ana Dem. Club, 1989, L.A. County Good Scout award, Boy Scouts Am., 1989; named Woman of Yr., Dems. United, San Bernadino, 1989, Woman of Distinction, Soroptimist Internat., Monterey Park, 1987, Woman of Achievement, Santa Barbara Legal Secs. Assn. and County Bar Assn., 1987, one of Am.'s 100 Most Important Women, Ladies Home Jour., 1988; recipient Community Leadership award Torat-Haijun Hebrew Acad., 1990, Special Appreciation U. Vietnamese Student Assns. So. Calif., 1990, Nat. Assn. Chinese-Am. Bankers, 1990, Orange County Buddhist Assn., 1990, Internat. Bus. award, West Coast U., 1992, others. Mem. Navy League (life), Am. Dental Hygienists Assn. (pres. 1956-57), No. Calif. Dental Hygienists Assn., Oakland LWV, AAUW (area rep. in edn. Oakland br.), Calif. Tchrs. Assn., Calif. Agrl. Aircraft Assn. (hon.), Calif. Sch. Bd. Assn., Alameda County Sch. Bd. Assn. (pres. 1965), Alameda County Mental Health Assn., Calif. Pub. Health Assn. Northern Divsn. (hon.), So. Calif. Dental Assn. (hon.), Bus. and Profl. Women's Club, Soroptimist (hon.), Hadassah (life), Ebell Club (L.A.), Chinese Retail Food Markets Assn. (hon.), Delta Kappa Gamma, Phi Alpha Delta (hon.), Phi Delta Gamma (hon.), others. Office: American Embassy PO Box 1286 Pohnpei FM 96941

EUBANKS, GLORIA BOLAND, elementary music educator; b. Prosperity, S.C., Nov. 14, 1934; d. Berley Euston and Eva Lucille (Dowd) Boland; m. George Edmund Eubanks, Jan. 29, 1965 (dec. July 1986); children: Laura E. Bullard, Mary E. Deal. BS in Music, Winthrop Coll., 1956; MA in Music Edn., Cola U., 1959. Cert. tchr., S.C. Piano tchr. Hampton (S.C.) Elem., 1956-59; gen. music and pvt. piano tchr. Summerton (S.C.) Sch., 1959-60; elem. and choral music tchr. Whitmire (S.C.) & Park St Schs., 1960-62; elem. music tchr. Rock Hill (S.C.) Schs., 1962-64, Newberry (S.C.) County, 1964-67; gen. music and English tchr. Jefferson Jr. High Sch., Bath, S.C., 1970-71; elem. music tchr. Aiken County Area, Langley, S.C., 1971-80; English and reading tchr. Newberry Jr. High Sch., 1980-81; elem. music tchr. Newberry County, 1981—; church pianist Chapin (S.C.) Bapt. Ch., 1983-90. Mem. Music Educators Nat. Conf., S.C. Music Educators Assn. Lutheran. Home: 167 Dana Pond Trl Prosperity SC 29127-8777 Office: Little Mountain Elem Sch 692 Mill St Little Mountain SC 29075

EUBANKS, PENNY LOUISE, school administrator; b. Leonard, Tex., Apr. 26, 1947; d. Horice Ivyl and Anna Marie (Vandagriff) Cunnyngham; m. Ronald Lee Eubanks, June 14, 1968; children: Gregory Ronald, Wendy René. BS, East Tex. State U., 1969, MEd, 1974. Cert. tchr., supt., Tex. Tchr. McKinney (Tex.) Ind. Sch. Dist., 1969-72, Greenville (Tex.) Ind. Sch. Dist., 1972-77; tchr., head dept. Rockwall (Tex.) Ind. Sch. Dist., 1977-89; tchr., head dept. Kaufman (Tex.) Ind. Sch. Dist., 1989-92, asst. prin., 1992-95, prin. Accelerated Learning Ctr., 1995—; univ. interscholastic league coord. Nash Elem. Sch., Kaufman, 1993, 94-95. Sunday sch. tchr. Ridgecrest Bapt. Ch., Greenville, 1975-77; tchr., dir., pianist First Bapt. Ch., Rockwall, 1979-83, Northside Bapt. Ch., Rockwall, 1983-87; tchr. First Bapt. Ch., Kaufman, 1990-92, 94—. Meadows Found. fellow, 1992-93. Mem. ASCD, Tex. Assn. Secondary Sch. Prins., Tex. Assn. Alternative Edn., Kaufman Garden Club, Phi Beta Kappa. Home: 6049 County Rd 152 Kaufman TX 75142

EUBANKS-POPE, SHARON G., real estate entrepreneur; b. Chgo., Aug. 26, 1943; d. Walter Franklyn and Thelma Octavia (Watkins) Gibson; m. Larry Hudson Eubanks, Dec. 20, 1970 (dec. Jan. 1976); children: Rebekah, Aimée; m. Otis Eliot Pope, June 7, 1977; children: O. Eliot Jr., Adrienne. BS in Edn., Chgo. Tchrs. Coll., 1965; postgrad., Ill. Inst. Tech., 1967, John Marshall Law Sch., 1970, Governor's State U., 1975-76. Educator, parent coord. Chgo. Bd. Edn., 1965-77; owner, ptnr. Redel Rentals, Chgo., 1977—; realtor ERA Diversified Real Estate, Hazel Crest, Ill., 1990—; bd. dirs. Jack and Jill of Am. Found. Adminstrv. bd. St. Mark United Meth. Ch., Chgo., 1967, bd. trustees, 1988; com. chair Englewood Urban Progress Ctr., Chgo., 1973; coord., educator League Women Voters, Chgo. (Outstanding Community Law Class award 1975), 1975-76. Named Outstanding Sch. Parent Vol., Chgo. Bd. Edn., 1977; recipient Christian Leadership award United Meth. Women, Chgo., 1985. Mem. NAFE, NAACP, Am. Soc. Profl. and Exec. Women, Nat. Assn. Realtors, Greater South Suburban Bd. Realtors, Jack and Jill Am., Inc. (Chgo. chpt. journalist 1989-91, Mid-western region sec./treas. 1993-95, Mid-western regional dir. 1995—, founder Parents for Parity in Edn. 1992, pres. Eubanks-Pope Devel. Co., Inc., 1993, parliamentarian of Parity 1991), Links, Inc., Jack & Jill of Am. Found. (bd. dirs. 1995—), Alpha Beta Gamma. Office: Redel Rentals 4338 S Drexel Blvd Chicago IL 60653-3536

EULER, ALINE, environmental center executive, naturalist; b. N.Y.C.; d. Henry and Alice (Revaz) E. BA, Queens Coll., 1960, MS, 1966, 77; EdD, St. John's U., 1988. Cert. permanent tchr., N.Y. Play street dir. Police Athletic League, Bklyn., 1960; elem. tchr. Bellew Pub. Sch., West Islip, N.Y., 1960-78; dir. edn. Alley Pond Environ. Ctr., Douglaston, N.Y., 1978—; instr. elem. edn. Adelphi U. Grad. Sch., Garden City, N.Y., 1981, 82, 91, 92, Queens Coll., 1982, 91, 92, 93,94; instr. continuing edn. Queensborough C.C., Bayside, N.Y., 1988-92. Contbr. articles to various publs. Sec. Orgn. Gen. Slocum Survivors, Queens Village, N.Y., 1984-95; v.p. Bayside Hist. Soc., 1985-87; chairperson Oakland Lake and Ravine Conservation Commn., Bayside, 1986—. Recipient Environ. Quality award U.S. EPA Region 2, 1970, 90. Mem. Nat. Assn. for Rsch. in Sci. Teaching, N.Am. Assn. Environ. Edn., Elem. Sch. Sci. Assn. (presnter), Environ. Ednl. Adv. Coun., Nat. Sci. Tchr. Assn., Queens County Bird Club (Flushing), Phi Delta Kappa. Home: 20405 43rd Ave Bayside NY 11361-2617 Office: Alley Pond Environ Ctr 22806 Northern Blvd Flushing NY 11363-1068

EURICH, NELL P., educator, author; b. Norwood, Ohio, July 28, 1919; d. Clayton W. and Adah (Palmer) Plopper; m. Alvin C. Eurich, Mar. 15, 1953 (dec. 1987); children: Juliet Ann, Donald Alan; m. Maurice Lazarus, 1988. AA, Stephens Coll., 1939; BA, Stanford U., 1941, MA, 1943; PhD, Columbia U., 1959. Dir. student union U. Tex., 1942-43; resident counselor Barnard Coll., 1944-46; asst. to pres. Woman's Found., 1947-49; officer charge pub. relations State U. N.Y., 1949- 52; acting pres. Stephens Coll., 1953-54; asst. prof. English NYU, 1959-64; academic dean New Coll., Sarasota, Fla., 1965; dir. project to reorganize curriculum Aspen (Colo.) Pub. High Sch., 1966; dean faculty, prof. English Vassar Coll., 1967-70; provost, dean faculty, prof. English, v.p. acad. affairs Manhattanville Coll., N.Y., 1971-75; sr. cons. Internat. Council for Ednl. Devel., 1975-82, Acad. for Ednl. Devel., 1982-88; mem. nat. selection com., chmn. Rocky Mountain regional com. Nat. Endowment Humanities, 1966-67, cons., 1970-71; mem. Middle States commn. Marshall Scholarships, 1967-68; chmn. Northeastern region, 1969-71; mem. U.S. Commn. on Ednl. Tech., HEW, 1968-69; mem. overseer's vis. com. on summer sch. and univ. extension Harvard, 1969-75; mem. panel of judge's Fed. Woman's award, 1969; cons. Acad. for Ednl. Devel., 1970-71; mem. career minister rev. bd. U.S. Dept. State, 1972; participant Ditchley Conf. V, 1973; mem. Rhodes Scholarship Selection Com., 1976; moderator exec. seminar Aspen Inst. for Humanistic Studies, 1977, 79, 80; dir. Adult Learning Project Carnegie Found. for Advancement Teaching, 1985-90; advisor Nat. Acad. of Engring., 1987-88; acad. advisor Cambridge Coll., 1990—; vis. com. Neuro Scis., Mass. Gen. Hosp. Author: Science in Utopia, 1967, Higher Education in Twelve Countries: A Comparative View, 1981, (with B. Schwenkmeyer) Great Britain's Open University, 1971, Corporate Classrooms, 1985, The Learning Industry, 1991; contbg. author: (Alvin Toffler) Learning for Tomorrow, 1974, From Parnassus: Essays for Jacques Barzun, 1976; contbr. articles to profl. jours. Past trustee Bank Street Coll., Salisbury Sch., Hudson Guild Neighborhood House, Colo. Rocky Mountain Sch., Bennington Coll., Carnegie Coun. on Policy Studies in Higher Edn., 1977-80, Carnegie Found. for Advancement Teaching, 1978-84; trustee New Coll. Found., Internat. Coun. for Edn. Devel. Mem. MLA, Am. Assn. Colls. (spl. com. on liberal studies 1966-70), World Soc. Ekistics, Nat. Coun. Women (hon.), Century Assn. N.Y.C. Home: 144 Brattle St Cambridge MA 02138-2202

EUSTER, JOANNE REED, librarian; b. Grants Pass, Oreg., Apr. 7, 1936; d. Robert Lewis and Mabel Louise (Jones) Reed; m. Stephen L. Gerhardt, May 14, 1977; children: Sharon L., Carol L., Lisa J. Student, Lewis and Clark Coll., 1953-56; B.A., Portland State Coll., 1965; M.Librarianship, U. Wash., 1968, M.B.A., 1977; Ph.D., U. Calif.-Berkeley, 1986. Asst. libr. Edmonds Community Coll., Lynnwood, Wash., 1968-73, dir. libr.-media ctr., 1973-77; univ. libr. Loyola U. of New Orleans, 1977-80; libr. dir. J. Paul Leonard Libr., San Francisco State U., 1980-86; univ. libr. Rutgers State U. N.J., New Brunswick, 1986-89, v.p. info. svcs., 1989-91, v.p. univ. librs., 1991-92; univ. libr. U. Calif., Irvine, 1992—; cons. Coll. S.I., Union Ejidal, La Penita, Nayarit, Mexico, 1973, Univ. D.C., 1988; co-cons. Office of Mgmt. Svcs. Assn. of Rsch. Librs., 1979—; bd. regents, Kansas; mem. adv. coun. Hong Kong U. Sci. and Tech. Librs., 1988—, Princeton U. Libr., 1988-92, U. B.C., Can., 1991—. Author: Changing Patterns of Internal Communication in Large Academic Libraries, 1981, The Academic Library Director, Management Activities and Effectiveness, 1987; columnist Wilson Libr. Bull., 1993-95; contbr. articles to profl. jours. Mem. ALA, Calif. Libr. Assn., Assn. Coll. and Rsch. Librs. (pres. 1987-88), Rsch. Librs. Group (chmn. bd. dirs. 1991-92). Office: Univ Calif Main Libr PO Box 19557 Irvine CA 92623-9557

EUSTIS, PAMELA JOAN, special events marketing executive; b. N.Y.C., Mar. 11, 1959; d. Richard Wood and Shirley Kendall (Tunison) E. AB, Smith Coll., 1981; cert. fund raising exec., NYU, 1994, cert. spl. event mktg., 1996. Assoc. for spl. events Met. Mus. Art, N.Y.C., 1981-87; assoc. for social events Mus. of City of N.Y., N.Y.C., 1987-88; merchandising svcs. mgr. Modern Bride mag., N.Y.C., 1988-89; dir. spl. events and fund raising coord. The Brit.-Am. C. of C., N.Y.C., 1989-95; spl. events coord. HSBC James Capel, 1995—. Bd. dirs. Coun. of Protocol Execs., 1991—; active The Blue Hill Troupe. Mem. Women in Fin. Devel. Republican. Episcopalian. Office: HSBC James Capel 250 Park Ave New York NY 10177

EUTSEY, RUTH ANNE MCGREE, office manager; b. Cecil, Ala., July 17, 1935; d. Wilie Dixie and Lula Mae (Allen) McGhee; m. Joseph W. Eutsey, July 31, 1956 (div. 1975); children: Dwight Adlwin, Heyward Leonardo, Tony McClester, Keith Otto, Victor Kerry, Joanne Bridgett. BS, Ala. State U., 1981, MS, 1982; postgrad., Troy Stat U., 1985-86. Beautician Montgomery, Ala., 1959-75; asst. intern coord. Ala. State U., Montgomery, 1979-81; sec. Ala. State Senate, Montgomery, 1981-823; office adminstr. Montgomery Pks. and Recreation, 1983-96; asst. dir. Drug Free Sch. Counselor Tng. Program, Ala. State U., 1993-94; substitute tchr. Montgomery County Bd. Edn., 1977-80; vol. probation officer Montgomery Family Ct., Montgomery, 1984-85. Dist. 11 counselor Pers. and Guidance Assn., 1994-96; pub. rels. chair Continental Soc., Montgomery, 1994-95. Democrat. Baptist. Home: 5349 Lola Ln Montgomery AL 36108 Office: Armory Learning Arts Ctr 1018 Madisen Ave Montgomery AL 36104

EUTSLER, THERESE ANNE, physical therapist; b. Jasper, Ind., Sept. 11, 1959; d. Joseph Martin and Viola Agnes (Rasche) Wagner; m. Mark Leslie Eutsler, Oct. 3, 1987. BS, Ind. U., 1982. Physicial therapist Reid Meml. Hosp., Richmond, Ind., 1982-84; physical therapist Cen. Convalescent Services, Crawfordsville, Ind., 1984-85, St. Elizabeth Hosp., Lafayette, Ind., 1985-86, 95—; clinical coord. St. Elizabeth Hosp., Lafayette, 1986-92; with Indsl. Rehab. of Crawfordville, 1992-94. Bd. dirs. Arthritis Found. Tippecanoe unit, Lafayette, 1986-89, John T. Conner Ctr. for U.S.-USSR Reconciliation, 1989—; del. Ind. State Dem. Conv., Indpls., 1988. Mem. Am. Phys. Therapy Assn. (Orthopedic sect., state ethics com. Ind. chpt.). Roman Catholic. Home: 207 Main St Linden IN 47955

EVAGUES, KATHERINE ANN, nurse; b. Bay Shore, N.Y., Apr. 18, 1948; d. ARthur Robert and Katherine (Weber) Kirchner; m. Jeffrey Evagues, Oct. 5, 1991. AAS in Nursing, Suffolk County Community Coll., 1968; BS in Nursing, C.W. Post Coll., 1976; MA in Health Care magna cum laude, SUNY, Stony Brook, 1986. RN, N.Y.; credentialed alcoholism counselor. Staff nurse Southside Hosp., Bay Shore, 1968-69, staff nurse oper. rm., 1974-76, 81-89; insvc. instr. Boston Hosp. for Women, Brookline, Mass., 1969-70; staff nurse med.-surg. Newton Wellesley Hosp., Newton Lower Falls, Mass., 1970-71; nurse-in-charge Univ. Hosp., Boston, 1970-74; nursing team leader Straub Hosp., Honolulu, 1976-80; alcoholism counselor Lighthouse Counseling Ctr., Riverhead, N.Y., 1989-92; nursing care coord. Eastern L.I. Hosp., Greenport, N.Y., 1989-91; pub. health nurse Suffolk County Riverhead (N.Y.) County Ctr. Bur. Pub. Health Nurses, 1991-93; nurse Dept. Social Svcs., Med. Assessment Bur., Hauppauge, N.Y., 1993—. Assn. Oper. Rm. Nurses scholar, 1974; HEW grantee, 1975. Mem. N.Y. State Nurses Assn., N.Y. Fedn. Alcoholism Counselors. Lutheran. Office: Dept Social Svcs Med Svcs Bur PO Box 2000 Hauppauge NY 11788

EVANCHYK, LINDA PATRICK, secondary school educator; b. Biloxi, Miss., Oct. 25, 1956; d. Morris A. and Alice M. (Wilkerson) Patrick. BA, U. W. Fla., 1979, MA, 1993. Cert. h.s. tchr., Fla. Tchr. Duval County Schs., Jacksonville, Fla., 1979-84, Okaloosa County Schs., Fort Walton Beach, Fla., 1984—; adv. journalism Okaloosa County Schs., Fort Walton Beach, Fla., 1984—, pub. rels., 1991—. Mem. Jr. League, Fort Walton Beach, Fla, 1986-89. Named one of Top Ten Journalism Advs. Dow Jones Newspaper Fund, 1995, Fla. Journalism Tchr. of Yr., 1995. Mem. Fla. Scholastic Press Assn. (Fla. Journalism Adv. of the Yr. 1995, Regional Journalism Adv. of the Year 1991, 95), Journalism Educators Assn. Home: 920 Roanoke Ct Fort Walton Beach FL 32547

EVANGELISTA, PAULA LEE, public policy and communications director; b. N.Y.C., Sept. 16, 1955; d. Frank Marino and Mary Louise (Denning) E. BA in History and Creative Writing, Carnegie Mellon U., 1977. Mgr. pub. policy and comm. Hoffmann-La Roche Inc., Nutley, N.J., 1986-90, asst. dir., 1990-92, dir. pub. affairs, 1992—. Bd. dirs. Soc. Progressive Supranuclear Palsy, Balt., 1990—; bd. dirs., trustee Boys and Girls Club, Clifton, N.J., 1991-92. Democrat. Roman Catholic.

EVANS, AMY A., artist, book designer; b. N.Y.C., Apr. 18, 1955; d. Gilbert and Anne Carolyn (Massa) E.; m. Michael McClure. BFA with hons., Calif. Coll. Arts and Crafts, Oakland, 1986; postgrad., San Francisco State U., 1987. Design and prodn. assoc. North Point Press, Berkeley, Calif., 1987-90; book designer Sierra Club Books, San Francisco, 1990—; artist Oakland, 1984—; artist and poet collaboration Visual Aids, San Francisco, 1994; lectr. artist, Calif. Coll. of Arts, Oakland, 1994, Oakland Mus., 1995. Artist: works exhibited in 2 1-person and 16 group art exhibitions since 1990, including: Field of Forms, Joan Roebuck Gallery, 1995 (one person show), The Figure (sculpture), Ohione Coll., 1995, (2-person show), Calif. Artists Juried Exhibition, Women Artists Gallery, 1995. Vol. Rainforest Action Network, San Francisco, 1991—; exhibitor 4th Ann. Artists for Amnesty Internat., 1991. Named hon. artist lectr. Calif. Conf. on Advancement of Ceramic Art, Davis, Calif., 1993. Mem. San Francisco Mus. Modern Art (artist, particpant rental gallery), Tom Marzloni Artist Cafe Soc., Sierra Club. Office: Sierra Club Books 85 Second St San Francisco CA 94104

EVANS, CAROL ROCKWELL, nursing administrator; b. New Orleans, Jan. 8, 1953; d. Daniel Raymond Sr. and Helen (Fischer) Rockwell; divorced; children: Nikki Elizabeth, Mimi Michelle. ADN, La. State Med. Ctr., 1990. RN, La.; cert. ACLS, BLS, cert. case mgr.; lic. life and health ins. agent. Life and health ins. agt. La. Ins. Agts. Assn., New Orleans, 1975-95; dir. case mgmt. and utilization rev. Associated Med. Rev. Svcs., Metairie, La., 1986-95; charge nurse med-surg. telemetry unit Elmwood Med. Ctr., Jefferson, La., 1990—; RN specialist III ICU St. Charles Gen. Hosp., New Orleans, 1993—; dir. med. mgmt. Nat. Health Resources, Inc., Metairie, La., 1995—. Lobby La. Health Care, Baton Rouge, 1991. Mem. ANA, Individual Case Mgmt. Assn., Assn. Rehab. Nurses Case Mgmt. Soc. Am., Assn. Respiratory Care, New Orleans Continuity Care, La. Managed Healthcare Assn., NAFE. Republican. Roman Catholic. Home: 6002 Mitchell Ave Metairie LA 70003-4254 Office: Nat Health Resources Inc Ste 800 3525 N Causeway Blvd Metairie LA 70002

EVANS, CHARLOTTE MORTIMER, communications consultant, writer; b. Newton, N.J., Nov. 26, 1933; d. Karl Otto and Wilhelmina (Otterbach) Pfau; student Douglass Coll., 1952-54; BS, RN, Columbia U. Presbyn. Hosp., 1957, postgrad., 1957-59; postgrad. NYU, 1959-60; MPA, Coll. of Notre Dame, 1979; m. John Atterbury Mortimer, Nov. 20, 1964; children: Meredith Elizabeth, Mandy Leigh; m. G. Robert Evans, Sept. 4, 1982. Spl. assignment nurse Columbia-Presbyn. Med. Center, N.Y.C., 1957-59; med. advt. copywriter Paul Klemtner & Co., N.Y.C., 1959-61, William Douglas McAdams Agy., N.Y.C., 1961-62; account exec. Arndt, Preston, Chapin, Lamb & Keen, N.Y.C., 1962-63; Rocky Mountain corr. Med. World News, Denver, 1963-64; owner Publicite, Denver; gen. mgr. Center Mktg. Assn., Palo Alto, Calif., 1964-66; freelance writer, pub. rels. and mgmt. cons., Woodside, Calif., 1966-85; pres. Communications for Youth, 1979—. Mem. Palo Alto-Stanford Hosp. Aux., 1968-72; pub. rels. assistance Peninsula Children's Ctr., Palo Alto, 1968-73, Triton Mus. Art, San Jose, Calif., 1966-70; chmn. citizens adv. com. San Mateo County Juvenile Social Svcs.; health component Early Childhood Com., Woodside Elem. Sch. Dist.; mem. adv. com. South County Youth and Family Svcs. Program; mem. Statewide Citizens Adv. Com. on Child Abuse and Neglect Ill. Dept. Children and Family Svcs., 1987—; past chair, mem., bd. dirs. ct.-apptd. spl. advocate program CASA-Kane County, 1989—; chair adv. com. to Congressman Dennis Hastert on Family and Child Legis., 1990—; bd. dirs. N.J. Jr. C. of C./UNICEF/African Project, 1960-61; mem. San Mateo County Mental Health Adv. Bd., Friends of Woodside Libr. Bd, 1983-85; mem. Rep. Senatorial Inner Circle, 1982—; vol. Nat. Com. for Prevention Child Abuse and Neglect, 1987—; acting chair, founder Chicagoland Media & Children Com., 1993—; adv. com. Our Children's Place, Kane County, 1995—. Home and Office: PO Box 710 Wayne IL 60184-0710

EVANS, ELIZABETH ANN WEST, real estate agent; b. Xenia, Ohio, Mar. 28, 1933; d. Millard Stanley and Elizabeth Denver (Johns) West. BA, Ohio U., 1966, MA, 1968. Cert. GRI, 1993. Sec. various orgns., Ohio, 1952-61; tchr. Ohio U., Athens, 1966-67, Zanesville, 1968-72; tchr. Collier County Pub. Schs., Naples, Fla., 1972-77; sales Helen's Hang Ups, Naples, 1978-79; mgr. pvt. practice Wilmington, Ohio, 1979-87; adminstrv. asst. Powell Assocs., Cambridge, Mass., 1987-90; real estate agt. Bill Evans Realty, Inc., Naples, 1989-90, Howard Hanna Real Estate Svcs., Naples, 1991-93, Downing-Frye Realty, Inc., Naples, Fla., 1993—. Mem. The Women's Network of Collier County. Mem. AAUW, Nat. Assn. Realtors, Greater Naples Alumnae Panhellenic (prs. 1984-86), Nat. Soc. DAR (chaplain 1988-90, chmn. Motion Picture, Radio and TV 1992-94, asst. chaplain 1994-96), Naples Marco Kappa Alpha Theta Alumnae Club (treas. 1990-92), Women's Network of Collier County, Phi Beta Kappa, Phi Kappa Phi, Phi Sigma Iota. Republican. Presbyterian. Home: Apt A200 15117 Royal Fern Ct Naples FL 34110-8081 Office: Downing-Frye Realty Inc 3411 Tamiami Trl N Naples FL 34102-3700

EVANS, G. ANNE, lawyer; b. Eastland, Tex., Feb. 24, 1954; d. Travis Clay and Maude Velma (DeMoss) E.; children: Courtney Faith, Alexandria Brooke. BA in Psychology, U. Nebr., Omaha, 1988; JD, U. Nebr., Lincoln, 1991. Bar: Nebr. 1991, U.S. Dist. Ct. Nebr. 1991, U.S. Ct. Appeals (8th cir.) 1992. Pvt. practice, Omaha, 1992—. Mem. ABA (vice chair solo practioners/small firm com.), Nat. Assn. Criminal Def. Attys., Nebr. Criminal Def. Attys. Assn., Am. Inns of Ct. (co-founder Omaha chpt.), Golden Key, Phi Alpha Delta, Psi Chi. Democrat. Roman Catholic. Home: 11926 Wakeley Plz Apt 11 Omaha NE 68154-2427 Office: Ste 730 105 S 17th St Omaha NE 68102

EVANS, GAIL HIRSCHORN, television news executive; b. N.Y.C., Dec. 17, 1941; d. David Louis and Violet Ideta (Burkart) Hirschorn; m. Robert Mayer Evans, Mar. 13, 1966; children: Jason, Jeffrey, Julianna. BA, Bennington Coll., 1963. Aide to rep. William Fitts Ryan U.S. Congress, Washington, 1960-63, aide to rep. James Roosevelt, 1963-64; exec. asst. senator Harrison Williams U.S. Senate, Washington, 1964-65; legis. asst. The White House, Washington, 1965-66; owner, ptnr. Global Rsch. Svcs., Atlanta, 1976-80; prodr. CNN, Atlanta, 1980-87, v.p., 1987-91, sr. v.p., 1991—; trustee Radio TV News Dirs. Found., Washington, 1993—; adj. faculty Emory U. Bus. Sch., Atlanta, 1994—; bd. advisors Ga. State U. Law Sch., Atlanta, 1995—. Bd. advisors Ga. State U. Law Sch., Atlanta, 1995—; participant Leadership Atlanta, 1978-79; bd. dirs. Atlanta Clean City Commn., 1976-79, Ga. Endowment for Humanities, Atlanta, 1976-80, chairperson, 1980-81; bd. govs. Atlanta Press Club, 1994—. Selected Mem. of 1995, YWCA Acad. Women Achievers. Mem. Am. Women in Radio and TV. Democrat. Jewish. Home: 4700 Paran Vly NW Atlanta GA 30327-3507 Office: CNN PO Box 105366 1 CNN Ctr 100 International Blvd Atlanta GA 30348-5366

EVANS, GERALDINE ANN, academic administrator; b. Zumbrota, Minn., Feb. 24, 1939; d. Wallace William and Elda Ida (Tiedemann) Whipple; m. John Lyle Evans, June 21, 1963; children: John David, Paul William. AA, Rochester Community Coll., 1958; BS, U. Minn., 1960, MA, 1963, PhD, 1968. Cert. tchr., counselor, prin. and supt., Minn. Tchr. Hopkins (Minn.) Pub. Schs., 1960-63; counselor Anoka (Minn.) Pub. Schs., 1963-66; cons. in edn. Mpls., 1966-78; policy analyst Minn. Dept. Edn., St. Paul, 1978-79; dir. personnel Minn. Community Coll. System, St. Paul, 1979-82; pres. Rochester (Minn.) Community Coll., 1982-92; chancellor Minn. C.C. System, St. Paul, 1992-94; exec. dir. Ill. C.C. Bd., Springfield, 1994-96; chancellor San Jose (Calif.) Evergreen C.C. Dist., 1994—. Vice chair, bd. dirs. Wayzata (Minn.) Sch. Bd., 1980-83; bd. dirs. Minn. Tech. Ctr., Rochester, 1991-92; sec.-treas. Coun. North Ctrl. Cmty. and Jr. Colls., 1990-92; moderator Mizpah United Ch. Christ, Hopkins, 1982; mem. Gov.'s Job Tng. Coun., St. Paul, 1983-94, chair, 1992-94; mem. ACE Commn. on Edn. Credit and Credentials, 1992-96. Inst. Ednl. Leadership fellow, Washington, 1978-79. Mem. Nat. League Nursing (bd. assoc. degree accreditation rev. 1990-93, exec. com. 1993-96), Am. Assn. Cmty. Jr. Colls. (bd. dirs. 1984-87), North Ctrl. Assn. Cmty. and Jr. Colls. (evaluator). Congregationalist.

EVANS, JANE KEEGAN, opera and music theatre producer; b. Milw., Oct. 24, 1956. BA in Econs., U. Wis., Milw., 1980. Dir. pub. rels. Milw. Symphony Orch., 1980-85; dir. mktg. Skylight Comic Opera, Milw., 1985-87; dir. communications Opera Am., Washington, 1987-89; gen. dir. Skylight Opera Theatre, Milw., 1989-92; mng. dir. Lyric Opera Cleve., 1993-95.

EVANS, JANET, Olympic athlete; b. Aug. 28, 1971. 3 time Gold medalist, 400m Freestyle, 800m Individual Medley Seoul Olympic Games, 1988; Gold medalist, 800m Freestyle Barcelona Olympic Games, 1992, Silver medalist, 400m Freestyle, 1992; wubber 40th nat. title-400m Freestyle Phillips 66 Nat. Swimming Championships, Indpls., 1994. Named U.S. Swimmer of Yr., 1987. Address: US Swimming Inc One Olympic Plaza Colorado Springs CO 80909-5724*

EVANS, JANET ANN, music educator; b. Muskegon, Mich., Aug. 26, 1936; d. Burt and Mildred (Gervers) Ruffner; 1 child, Eric Alan. BMus., U. Mich., 1958, MusM, 1959; cert., H & R Block, 1990. Permanent secondary teaching cert., Mich.; cert. completion H & R Block Tax Class, 1990. Vocal dir. South Redford (Mich.) Schs., 1959-63, orch., band and vocal dir., 1966-79; band dir. Detroit Pub. Schs., 1979-89, local sec., mem. sch. community rels. coun., 1988-89; band dir. Redford Union (Mich.) Schs., 1991—; mem. staff Nat. Music Camp, 1960-61; band dir. Fine Arts Honor Bands Detroit Pub. Schs., 1980-82, 84, 86, coord. Fine Arts Festival, 1986, ret., 1989; case contr. Raymond Berk Tax Cons., Bloomfield, Mich., 1989; music instr. Ward Presbyn. Ch., Sch. Sacred Arts, 1990-94. Author: (manual) Build Leadership NOW, 1983, Mich. NOW Policies and Guidelines, 1986; also articles. Mem. legis. liaison Older Women's League, Farmington Hills, Mich., 1981-86; del. Mich. Women's Assembly, Jackson, 1984, 86; precinct del. Mich. Dem. Party, 1984-90; state chair, treas. Mich. Women's Polit. Caucus, Roseville, 1985-88; vol. Botsford Hosp., Farmington, 1990—; bd. dirs. Dearborn Symphony Orch., 1991-94. Recipient Band Scholarship award U. Mich., 1957, 58, Cert. Achievement Metro-Detroit YWCA, 1985, Cert. Spl. Recognition Detroit Pub. Schs., 1985, 88, Cert. Appreciation Mich. Dem. Party, 1986, Cert. for Outstanding Leadership Detroit Pub. Schs., 1988. Mem. NOW (pres. N.W. Wayne County chpt. 1980-82, developer Mich. State chpt. 1982-84, adminstrv. v.p. 1984-86, Mich. Leadership award 1981, 82, Leadership plaque N.W. Wayne County 1982), ACLU (state bd. dirs. 1985-88), Coalition of labor Union Women (Metro Detroit chpt.), Mich. Osteo. Guild Assn. (treas. 1993-94, sec. 1994-95, pres. 1995—), Women Internat. League for Peace and Freedom, Mich. Women's Studies Assn., Women Band Dirs. Nat. Assn. (nat. historian 1985-87, nat. rec. sec. 1988-92), Am. Fedn. Tchrs., Mich. Fedn. Tchrs., Detroit Fedn. Tchrs., Mich. Sch. Band and Orch. Assn., Women in the Arts, Inc. (charter), Plymouth (Mich.) Oratorio Soc. (bd. dirs. 1995—), Martha Cook Bldg. Detroit Alumnae Assn. (bd. dirs. 1968-70, 86-91), Bus. and Profl. Women's Club (sec. Farmington Hills chpt. 1981-82, Leadership award pin 1982), Alpha Delta Kappa (chpt. pres. 1978-80, pres. dist. II 1980-82, pres. award pin 1980), Tau Beta Sigma (life), Sigma Alpha Iota. Democrat. Presbyterian. Office: Pearson Edn Ctr 19000 Beech Daly Rd Redford MI 48240

EVANS, JO BURT, communications executive, rancher; b. Kimble County, Tex., Dec. 18, 1928; d. John Fred and Sadie (Oliver) Burt; m. Charles Wayne Evans II, Apr. 17, 1949; children: Charles Wayne III, John Burt, Elizabeth Wisart. BA, Mary Hardin-Baylor Coll., 1948; MA, Trinity U., 1967. Owner, mgr. Sta. KMBL, Junction, Tex., 1959-61; real estate broker, Junction, 1965-74; staff economist, adv. on 21st Congl. Dist., polit. campaign Nelson Wolff, 1974-75; asst. mgr., bookkeeper family owned ranches and rent property, Junction, 1948—; gen. mgr. TV Translator Corp., Junction, 1968—, sec.-treas., 1980—. Treas., asst. to coordinator Citizens for Tex., 1972; historian Kimble Hist. Soc.; mem. Com. of Conservation Soc. to Save the Edwards Aquifer, San Antonio, 1973; homecoming chmn. Sesquicentennial Year, Junction; treas., asst. coordinator New Constitution, San Antonio, 1974; legis. chair Hill Country Women, Kimble County, 1990—. AAUW scholarship named in honor, 1973; named an outstanding Texan, Tex. Senate, 1973. Mem. Nat. Translator Assn., AAUW, Daus. Republic Tex., Tex. Sheriffs Assn., Nat. Cattlewomens Assn., Internat. Platform Assn., Bus. and Profl. Women (pres. 1981-82). Republican. Mem. Unity Ch. Home: PO Box 283 Junction TX 76849-0283 Office: 618 Main St Junction TX 76849-4635

EVANS, JOAN, mental health therapist; b. Toledo, Ohio, Oct. 30, 1944; d. Richard Joseph and Leona Agnes (Kuehlman) Moran; m. Terrence Joseph Evans, Apr. 15, 1967; children: Terrence J. Jr., Kelly Evans Koonce, Erin. BA in Sociology, Mary Manse Coll., Toledo, 1966. Social worker Toledo Cath. Charities, 1965-67; social worker/therapist Fallsview Mental Health Hosp., Cuyahoga Falls, Ohio, 1969-71; therapist Divine Providence Hosp., Williamsport, Pa., 1972-75; therapist Tressler Luth. Svcs., Williamsport, 1975-86, therapist primary grades initiative, 1992—; med. sales rep. Bristol Myers/Squibb, 1986-91; facilitator/educator Family Life Inst., Williamsport, 1992-94; trainer Assn. of Jr. Leagues, 1984-85; dist. sales trainer Bristol Myers/Squibb, 1989-91. Bd. dirs. Family and Children's Svcs. of Lycoming County, Williamsport, 1983-93; bd. dirs. Bishop Neumann Parents Orgn., Williamsport, 1983-85, 91-93, YWCA, Williamsport; adv. bd. Teen Parenting Program, Williamsport H.S., 1990-93; A Variety-inc. pres. Jr. League of Williamsport; co-founder West Branch Child Abuse Coun; pres. adminstrv. coun. Bishop Neumann H.S., 1995—. Mem. AAUW (bd. dirs.), ACA. Home: 700 Vallamont Dr Williamsport PA 17701

EVANS, JUDY ANNE, health center administrator; b. Elmira, N.Y., Mar. 29, 1940; d. Hugh Kenneth and Mary (Faul) Leach; m. Nolly Seymour

Evans, Feb. 18, 1965; children: Samantha, Meredydd, Clelia, Nolly III. BS, Cornell U., 1962; MBA, Syracuse U., 1992. Fin. analyst Morgan Guaranty Trust Co., N.Y.C., 1962-66; bus. adminstr. SUNY Health Sci. Ctr., Syracuse, 1983-89, adminstr. dept. pediatrics, 1990—. Mem. allocations com. Children Miracle Network, Syracuse, 1990—; children's hosp. steering com. Crouse Irving/Univ. Hosp., Syracuse, 1990—; bd. dirs. Syracuse Friends of Chamber Music, 1983-89, Syracuse Camerata, 1982-88. Mem. Assn. Adminstrs. of Acad. Pediatrics. Home: 26 Lyndon Rd Fayetteville NY 13066-1016 Office: SUNY Health Sci Ctr 750 E Adams St Syracuse NY 13210-2306

EVANS, JUDY KAY, furniture store executive; b. Morganton, N.C., May 6, 1946; d. Fred Anders and Olvia (Martin) E. Pres. Plaza Furniture Gallery, Inc., Granite Falls, N.C., 1988—; chmn. 20 Miles of Furniture, Lenoir, N.C., 1994-95. Republican. Baptist. Office: Plaza Furniture Gallery Inc 241 Timberbrook Ln Granite Falls NC 28630

EVANS, LINDA, actress; b. Hartford, Nov. 18, 1942; m. John Derek (div.); m. Stan Herman, 1976 (div.). Appearances include (films) Twilight of Honor, 1963, Those Calloways, 1964, Beach Blanket Bingo, 1965, The Klansman, 1974, Avalanche Express, 1979, Tom Horn, 1980, Dead Heat, 1988; (TV series) The Big Valley, 1965-69, Wonder Woman, Hunter, 1977, Dynasty, 1980-88 (Emmy award nominee 1983); (TV movies) Nakia, 1974, The Big Ripoff, 1975, Nowhere to Run, 1978, Standing Tall, 1978, Bare Essence, 1982, I'll Take Romance, 1983 (also exec. prodr.), Dynasty Reunion, 1991, The Gambler Returns: The Luck of the Draw, 1991; (TV mini-series) include Bare Essence, 1982, North and South Book II, 1986, The Last Frontier, 1986; sr. prodr.: Yanni in Concert: Live at the Acropolis, 1994; author: Linda Evans Beauty and Exercise Book, 1983. Office: William Morris Agy 151 S El Camino Dr Beverly Hills CA 90212-2704*

EVANS, LINDA KAY, publishing company executive; b. Tipton, Ind., June 16, 1945; d. Walter K. and Helen S. (Fakes) E. BA in English, Purdue U., 1968. Asst. to mng. editor Random House Pubs., N.Y.C., 1969-71; asst. to dir. editorial svcs. Sch. div. McGraw-Hill Book Co., N.Y.C., 1971-75, mgr. state contracts and inventory dept., 1975-88; bookstore owner, pres. The Literary Bookshop, N.Y.C., 1988-93; prodn. mgr. trade div. Simon & Schuster, N.Y.C., 1994—; pub. cons. for sch. textbooks Prentice-Hall Book Co., Englewood Cliffs, N.J., 1992-93. Recipient Holiday Window Display award to Lit. Bookshop, Greenwich Village C. of C., 1990. Office: Simon & Schuster Trade Div 1230 Avenue Of The Americas New York NY 10020-1513

EVANS, LOIS LOGAN, hotel/restaurant executive; b. Boston, Dec. 1, 1937; d. Harlan deBaun and Barbara (Rollins) Logan; m. Thomas W. Evans, Dec. 22, 1956; children: Heather, Logan, Paige. Student, Vassar Coll., 1954-55; BA, Barnard Coll., 1957. Alt. chief del. UN Commn. on Status Women, N.Y.C., 1972-74; bd. dirs. U.S. Commn. to UNESCO, Washington, 1974-78; pres. Acquisition Specialists, Inc., N.Y.C., 1975—, chmn. bd. dirs.; v.p. corp. and govt. rels. The Barrington Group, 1995—; chmn., mng. dir. Barrington Zagreb, Barrington/Sarajevo; asst. chief protocol U.S. State Dept., N.Y.C., 1981-83; chmn. bd. Fed. Home Bank, N.Y.C., 1986-88, mem. bd. dirs., 1984-88; mem. adv. bd. U.S. Export-Import Bank, 1988-90, Nat. Fin. Com.; mem. George Bush Nat. Fin. Com.; mem. Nat Policy Coun. Vice chair devel. council Williams Coll., N.Y., 1979-81; co-chair Reagan-Bush Campaign, N.Y., 1984; bd. dirs. Bklyn. Jr. League, 1968-72, mgmt. decision lab NYU, 1992—; U.S. rep. South Pacific Commn., 1990-92. Mem. Women's Forum (bd. dirs.), Econ. of N.Y. Club. Republican. Episcopalian. Office: Barrington Group 8966 SW 87th Ct Ste 22 Miami FL 33176

EVANS, MARGARET A., civic worker; b. N.Y.C., Jan. 20, 1924; d. Bernard J. and Katherine (Walsh) Markey; BA, Coll. Mt. St. Vincent, Mt. St. Vincent-on-Hudson, N.Y., 1944; postgrad. Columbia U.; m. John Cullen Evans, Jr., Nov. 24, 1951. Rep. N.Y. Telephone Co., 1944; pers. office Sak's 34th, N.Y.C., 1944-45, tng. supr., selling and non-selling depts., 1945-49, spl. assignment for store mgr. 1949-50, non-selling tng. supr. Gimbel Bros., 1950-51; rep. Gimbels and Sak's 34th at NCCJ Retail Group meeting, 1949-50. Instr. textile painting for ARC, Chelsea Navy Hosp., 1952-54, ARC vol., 1980-92; bd. dirs. Marblehead Hosp. Aid Assn., 1954, pres., 1955-58; sec. Mass. Hosp. Assn. Coun. of Hosp. Auxiliaries, 1957-59, chmn. North Shore region, 1959-61, chmn.-elect, 1961-62, state chmn., 1962-64, exofficio trustee Salem Hosp.; trustee Mary A. Alley Hosp., 1956-79, chmn. bd., 1974-79; mem. Welcome Wagon of Fairfield/Easton (Conn.), 1979-83; chmn. Fairfield/Easton Theater Group, Fifth Wheel Club of Fairfield, 1983-85 . Mem. Alumnae Assn. Coll. Mt. Saint Vincent, Arrangers of Marblehead (chmn. garden therapy 1967-79). Clubs: Marblehead Women's Newcomers (pres. 1953). Home: 108 Cedarwood Ln Fairfield CT 06432-1308

EVANS, MARGARET PATSOS, photographer, photography educator; b. Syracuse, N.Y., June 4, 1947; d. James George and Margaret Eileen (Jones) Patsos; m. Arnold Jay Berman, Aug. 12, 1989. BA, Goddard Coll., 1977; MFA, Rochester (N.Y.) Inst. Tech., 1989. Tchr. Seoul (Republic of Korea) Fgn. Sch., 1974-75; photographer Coop. Ext. Assn., Rochester, 1977-78; freelance photographer Rochester, 1978-84; asst. coord., acad. advisor Coll. Liberal Arts Rochester Inst. Tech., 1984-86, with scheduling & registration office Coll. Arts/Photograhy, 1986-87, coord. acad. advisors Ctr. for Imaging Sci., 1987-90, vis. mem. faculty, 1992-93; mem. faculty Mohawk Valley C.C., Utica, N.Y., 1990-92, Shippensburg (Pa.) U., 1995—; photographer Metro. Forum, Rochester, 1994; artist residency, Artists' Mus., Lodz, Poland. Exhibited in group shows including Upstairs Room, N.Y.C., 1994, others. Program dir. Returned Peace Corps Vols., Rochester, 1986; artist mem. artist adv. panel Pyramid Arts Ctr., Inc., Rochester, 1980-90; mem. edn. com. S.E. Area Coalition Vision 2000 Project, Rochester, 1994. Recipient Charles Rand Penny award Meml. Art Gallery, 1986, Best of Exhbn. award Digital Photography '94, Peoria (Ill.) Art Guild, 1994, Ernst Haas award Maine Photographic Workshop, 1995. Mem. Soc. Photographic Educators. Office: Dept Comm/Journalism Shippensburg U Shippensburg PA 17257

EVANS, MARSHA JOHNSON, naval officer; b. Springfield, Ill., Aug. 12, 1947; d. Walter Edward Johnson and Alice Anne (Field) Staffansson; m. Gerard Riendeau Evans, June 30, 1979. AB, Occidental Coll., 1968; MA, Fletcher Sch., 1977, MA in Law & Diplomacy, 1977; postgrad., Nat. War Coll., 1988-89. Commd. ensign USN, 1968, advanced through grades to real admiral, 1993; mideast policy officer Commander-in-Chief, U.S. Naval Forces, Europe, London, 1977-79; spl. asst. to sec. treasury U.S. Treasury Dept., Washington, 1979-80; staff analyst Office of Chief Naval Ops., Washington, 1980-81; dep. dir. Pres. Commn. on White House Fellowships, Washington, 1981-82; exec. officer Recruit Tng. Command, San Diego, 1982-84; commanding officer Naval Tech. Tng. Ctr., San Francisco, 1984-86; battalion officer, sr. lectr. polit. sci. U.S. Naval Acad., Annapolis, Md., 1986-88; chief of staff San Fransisco Naval Base, 1989-91, Naval Acad., Annapolis, Md., 1991-92; exec. dir. of the standing com. on mil. and civilian women Dept. of the Navy, 1992-93; comdr. Navy Recruiting Command, Washington, 1993-95; supt. Naval Postgrad. Sch., Monterey, CA, 1995—. White House fellow, 1979; Chief Naval Ops. scholar, 1976. Mem. Mortar Bd., Phi Beta Kappa.

EVANS, MARY JOHNSTON, transportation company director; b. Shawnee, Okla., Feb. 28, 1930; d. Paul Xenophon and Helen Elizabeth (Alford) Johnston; children by previous marriage: Marcy Benson, Paul Johnston Head, Eric Talbott Head; m. James H. Evans, 1984. Student, Wellesley Coll., 1947-48, U. Okla., 1949. Dir. Amtrak, 1974-80, vice chmn., 1975-79; bd. dirs. Household Internat., Inc., Saint-Gobain Corp., The Sun Co., Inc., Baxter Internat. Inc., Delta Air Lines, Inc., Dun and Bradstreet Corp.; mem. adv. bd. Morgan Stanley & Co. Pres. Jr. League Oklahoma City, 1968-69; trustee Nat. Council Crime and Delinquency, 1971-75, Presbyn. Med. Center, Oklahoma City, 1969-75, Brick Presbyn. Ch., 1985-89; bd. dirs. St. Anthony Hosp., 1973-75; bd. visitors U. Pitts. Grad. Sch. Bus., 1978-85; trustee Mary Baldwin Coll., Staunton, Va., 1976-83, Carnegie Hall, 1985-92. Recipient Law Day award-Liberty Bell award Oklahoma Bar Assn., 1971, Disting. Service award U. Okla., 1981; named one of Top 100 Corporate Women Bus. Week mag., 1976; named to Okla. Hall of Fame, 1978. Mem. Conf. Bd. (Sr.), Pi Beta Phi. Presbyterian (elder). Clubs: Colony, River; Maidstone (East Hampton, N.Y.). Address: 920 5th Ave New York NY 10021-4160 also: Windmill Ln PO Box 488 East Hampton NY 11937

EVANS, MELINDA DIANNE, educator; b. Lubbock, Tex., Nov. 28, 1967; d. Ernie DeWayne and Judith Kay (Shuler) Christie; m. John Robert Evans, June 3, 1989. BS in Edn., U. Mary Hardin Baylor, 1991. Tchr. 3d grade Abilene (Tex.) Ind. Sch. Dist., 1991-94, tchr. 4th grade, 1994-95; tchr. 3d grade Birdville Ind. Sch. Dist., Ft. worth, 1995—. Mem. Assn. Tec. profl. Educators, Tex. Coun. Tchrs. English, Big Country Coun. Tchrs. English (newsletter editor 1994-95). Republican. Mem. Ch. of Christ. Home: 6632 Ridgetop Dr Watauga TX 76148 Office: West Birdville Elementary 3001 Layton Ave Haltom City TX 76117

EVANS, MILLICENT LEVY, motivational company executive; b. Kansas City, Mo., Nov. 27, 1936; d. Joseph Sidney and Charlotte (Serkes) Levy; m. Robert M. Gordon, Aug. 2, 1958 (div. 1975); children: Amy J. Gordon Deutch, Jill E. Gordon, Jane H. Gordon. BS, Northwestern U., 1958. Dir. sales Travel Mgmt. Corp., Kansas City, 1969-75; v.p. Roundtrip Travel, Kansas City, 1975-82; v.p. group incentive divsn. Passport Travel, Overland Park, Kans., 1982-85; pres. Creative Incentives, Kansas City, 1985—. Recipient Richard E. Douglas Excellence award Corp. Meetings & Incentives Mag., 1993, Creative Planning, Performance & Achievement award Newton Mfg. Co., 1994. Mem. Soc. of Incentive Travel Execs. (chair Crystal awards banquet, chair Signet awards, Signet award 1993, SITE Crystal award for Outstanding Single Event 1994). Office: Creative Incentives 4225 Baltimore Kansas City MO 64111

EVANS, MONICA ELIZABETH (MONA EVANS), graphic designer, writer; b. Chgo., Apr. 16, 1936; d. John Richard and Florence Geraldine (Stelmaszek) Smoron; m. Rogers S. Evans, (div. 1972); children: Jan Evans Teichelmann, Robert, Jena. Student, U. Ill., 1954-56, Art Inst. Chgo., 1964; CLEP, Harper Jr. Coll., Rolling Meadows, Ill., 1972. Fine arts painter, writer, 1965-78; art dir., office mgr. Thomas Litho Printing Co., Fresno, Calif., 1976-79; graphic designer, writer Fresno, Seattle, 1980—; pubs. graphic design cons. Mental Health Assn. Greater Fresno, 1989-90; tchr. graphic design Clovis (Calif.) Sch. Dist. Adult Edn., 1992; publicity dir. Cultural Union Elgin, Ill., 1965-69. Script writer, creative dir.: (video) The Anniversary, 1986, Images: 19th Century Polish Painting, 1989 Charlie and Friends. Active books for kids, non-profit literacy program, Seattle, 1995—. Recipient Golden Oak awards Fresno Advt. Fedn., 1985; George M. Pullman Found. scholar, 1954-56. Home and Office: 7043 Beach Dr SW #1 Seattle WA 98136

EVANS, ORINDA D., federal judge; b. Savannah, Ga., Apr. 23, 1943; d. Thomas and Virginia Elizabeth (Grieco) E.; m. Roberts O. Bennett, Apr. 12, 1975; children: Wells Cooper, Elizabeth Thomas. B.A., Duke U., 1965; J.D. with distinction, Emory U., 1968. Bar: Ga. 1968. Assoc. Fisher & Phillips, Altanta, 1968-69; assoc. Alston, Miller & Gaines, Atlanta, 1969-74, ptnr., 1974-79; judge U.S. Dist Ct. (no. dist.) Ga., Atlanta, 1979—; adj. prof. Emory U. Law Sch., 1974-77; counsel Atlanta Crime Commn., 1970-71. Recipient Disting. award BBB, 1972. Mem. Atlanta Bar Assn. (dir. 1979). Democrat. Episcopalian. Office: US Dist Ct 1988 US Courthouse 75 Spring St SW Atlanta GA 30303-3309

EVANS, PAMELA R., marketing executive; b. Hoisington, Kans., Aug. 25, 1957; d. John Roy and Sarah Mace (Alder) E. BS in Bus., U. Kans., 1980. Sales rep. Home & Automotive Products div. Union Carbide Corp., Seattle, 1981; dist. sales mgr. Home & Automotive Products div. Union Carbide Corp., Syracuse, N.Y., 1981-82; mktg. assoc. Home & Automotive Products div. Union Carbide Corp., Danbury, Conn., 1982-84, assoc. product mgr., 1984; asst. product mgr. Grocery Products div. Ralston Purina, St. Louis, 1984-85, product mgr., 1985-86; product mgr. Eveready Battery Co. subs. Ralston Purina, St. Louis, 1986-88, group dir. mktg., 1988-90; dir. mktg. Consumer Products div. Esselte Pendaflex, 1990-91; dir. new bus. devel. Olympus Am., Inc., Woodbury, NY, 1991-92; v.p. mktg. consumer products group Olympus Am., Woodbury, NY, 1992-95; pres. blueprints, inc., New Hope, Pa., 1995—. Home and Office: 6803 Upper York Rd New Hope PA 18938-9511

EVANS, PATRICIA M., performing arts association administrator; m. Bill Johnson; 2 children. BA in Religious Edn. and Drama; postgrad., So. Meth. U. Ordained diaconal minister United Meth. Ch. Dir. music ministries Lake City (S.C.) United Meth. Ch.; exec. sec. Fellowship of United Methodists in Worship, Music; mem. music staff Highland Park United Meth. Ch., Dallas; adminstrv. asst. grad. music program sacred music Perkins Sch. Theology, So. Meth. U., Dallas, mem. adminstrv. staff; exec. dir., trustee Choristers Guild, Garland, Tex., 1987—; presenter workshops in field. Contbr. articles to mus. jours. Active Northaven United Meth. Ch. Office: 2834 W Kingsley Dr Garland TX 75041

EVANS, PAULINE D., physicist, educator; b. Bklyn., Mar. 24, 1922; d. John A. and Hannah (Brandt) Davidson; m. Melbourne Griffith Evans, Sept. 6, 1950; children: Lynn Janet Evans Hannemann, Brian Griffith. BA, Hofstra Coll., 1942; postgrad., NYU, 1943, 46-47, Cornell U., 1946, Syracuse U., 1947-50. Jr. physicist Signal Corps Ground Signal Svc., Eatontown, N.J., 1942-43, physicist Kellex Corp. (Manhattan Project), N.Y.C., 1944; faculty dept. physics Queens Coll., N.Y.C., 1944-47; teaching asst. Syracuse U., 1947-50; instr. Wheaton Coll., Norton, Mass., 1952; physicist Nat. Bur. Standards, Washington, 1954-55; instr. physics U. Ala., 1955, U. N.Mex., 1955, 57-58; staff mem. Sandia Corp., Albuquerque, 1956-57; physicist Naval Nuclear Ordnance Evaluation Unit, Kirtland AFB, N.Mex., 1958-60; programmer Teaching Machines, Inc., Albuquerque, 1961; mem. faculty dept. physics Coll. St. Joseph on the Rio Grande (name changed to U. Albuquerque 1966), 1961—, assoc. prof., 1965—, chmn. dept., 1961—. Mem. AAUP, Am. Phys. Soc., Am. Assn. Physics Tchrs., Fedn. Am. Scientists, Sigma Pi Sigma, Sigma Delta Epsilon. Achievements include patents on mechanical method of conical scanning (radar), fluorine trap and primary standard for humidity measurement Home: 730 Loma Alta Ct NW Albuquerque NM 87105-1220 Office: U Albuquerque Dept Physics Albuquerque NM 87140

EVANS, ROSEMARY HALL, civic worker; b. Lenox, Mass., Mar. 25, 1925; d. Alfred A. and Rosamond (Morse) Hall; m. Richard Morse Colgate, Jan. 1, 1949; children: Jessie Morse, Margaret Auchincloss, Pamela Morse; m. James H. Evans, July 1, 1972 (div. 1984). Trustee Menninger Found., Topeka, Princeton (N.J.) Theol. Sem., Nat. Recreation Found., N.Y.C., White Mountain Sch., Littleton, N.H.; founding mem., life trustee Nat. Recreation and Park Assn., Washington; past dir. Nat. Audubon Soc., N.Y.C., Joffrey Ballet, N.Y.C. and L.A., Simon's Rock of Bard Coll., Gt. Barrington, Mass., Westminster Choir Coll., Princeton; former mem. Green Acres Commn., N.J.; former mem. Equine Adv. Bd. N.J. Morgan Horse Assn.; former collaborator Nat. Park Svc. Mem. Colony Club (N.Y.C.), Tarratine Club (Dark Harbor, Maine), Birnam Wood Golf Club (Montecito, Calif.), Lenox (Mass.) Club, Profile Club (Sugar Hill, N.J.). Republican.

EVANS, SANDRA, clinical researcher; b. Jackson, Miss., Sept. 1, 1950; d. Alexander Grace and Marguerite (Turner) Henderson; m. Leslie Norman Evans, Aug. 2, 1975. BS, Howard U., 1972; MS, Seton Hall U., 1992; PhD, Walden U., 1996. Asst. scientist I Hoffman La Roche, Nutley, N.J., 1973-76, asst. scientist II, 1976-79, assoc. scientist, 1979-81, clin. rsch. assoc., 1981-87, sr. clin. rsch. assoc., 1987-90; clin. rsch. scientist Sandoz Pharms., East Hanover, N.J., 1990-92, sr. clin. rsch. scientist, 1992-94, asst. dir. CR&D mgmt., 1994-96, assoc. dir. CR&D mgmt., 1996—; clin. rsch. trainer Sandoz Pharms., East Hanover, 1991-93; participant various task forces Hoffman La Roche, Nutley, 1973-90. Co-author: (book chpt.) Advances in Biotechnology Processes, 1983; contbr. articles to profl. jours. Mentor Bloomfield (N.J.) Colls., 1989-91. Mem. AAUW, Am. Acad. Dermatology, Am. Coll. Healthcare Execs., Assocs. of Clin. Pharmacology, Drug Info. Assn., Sigma Xi. Office: Sandoz Pharms Inc 50 Rte 10 East Hanover NJ 07053

EVANS, SANDRA SUE, reporter, writer; b. St. Louis, Sept. 11, 1951; d. Alexander Edward and Mary Ruth Evans; m. Steven K. Hoffman, May 19, 1990; children: Zoë, Leah. Student, U. Mo., Columbia, 1969-73; BS in Journalism, U. Md., 1974. Press sec. to Sen. Ted Stevens, Washington, 1975-76; reporter BNA Publs., Washington, 1977-80; writer The Washington Post, Washington, 1980—. Recipient spl. award Am. Mental Health Fund, 1987, Washington dateline award Sigma Delta Chi, 1984. Mem. Investigative Reporters and Editors. Office: The Washington Post 1150 15th St NW Washington DC 20071-0001

EVANS, STARR F., elementary educator; b. Mineola, N.Y., Mar. 13, 1946; d. Harold and Stella (Ladehoff) Feuerstein; m. Noel John Evans, June 28, 1969. BS, SUNY, Oswego, 1968. Educator Full Year Head Start, Manhasset, N.Y., 1968-69, Hannibal (N.Y.) Pub. Schs., 1969-70, New Milford (Conn.) Pub. Schs., 1970—. Editor: (newsletter) The Drumbeat, 1980—. Mem. New Milford Edn. Assn., Conn. Edn. Assn., NEA, Internat. Reading Assn., Pontiac-Oakland Club (internat. dir. 1990-96). Office: New Milford Pub Schs 22 Hipp Rd New Milford CT 06776-2221

EVANS, TRELLANY VICTORIA THOMAS, entrepreneur; b. Georgetown, S.C., Apr. 18, 1959; d. Abraham Lincoln and Jannie Ruth (Brown) Thomas; m. Leroy Michael Evans, Sr., June 18, 1983; children: Leroy, Jr., Thomas, Trellany Janiece. BS, S.C. State U., 1980; MHA, MBA, Pfeiffer Coll., 1995. Instr. Horry-Georgetown (S.C.) Tech. Coll., 1982-83, Big Bend C.C., Bad Kreuznach, Germany, 1986-87; statistician U.S. Govt.-Europe, Bad Kreuznach, Germany, 1987-89; budget analyst U.S. Govt.-Europe, Baumholder, Germany, 1989-91; acct. U.S. Govt.-DeCA, Fort Lee, Va., 1991; pres., CEO Abraham & Evans Assocs., Huntersville, N.C., 1990—, DocuPrep, Charlotte, N.C., Info. Rsch., Inc., Huntersville, N.C., 1996—; cons. Abraham and Evans Assocs., Huntersville, 1990—; part-time computer applications instr. Mitchell C.C., Mooresville, N.C., 1994—; grad. rsch. asst. Pfeiffer Coll., 1994. Project dir. Charlotte (N.C.) Ctr. for Cmty. Self-Help, 1994—. Mem. Am. Soc. for Quality Control, Order of Eastern Star. Baptist. Office: Abraham and Evans Assocs 15312 Curling Ct-1020 Huntersville NC 28078

EVANS, VALERIE ELAINE, elementary education educator; b. Winston-Salem, N.C., July 12, 1971; d. Lindsay McRay an Beverly Kaye (Moser) E. BS in Edn., U. Ctrl. Fla., 1993, postgrad., 1996—. Vol. Pershing Elem. Sch., Orlando, Fla., 1991-92; intern Waterford Elem. Sch., Orlando, Fla., 1993; tchr. kindergarten Orange Ctr. Elem. Sch., Orlando, Fla., 1993-94, tchr. 4th grade, 1994-96; tchr. 4th grade Little River Elem. Sch., Orlando, Fla., 1996—; mem. computer tech. team, 1994, childcare team, 1994. Democrat. Methodist.

EVANSON, BARBARA JEAN, middle school education educator; b. Grand Forks, N.D., Aug. 15, 1944; d. Robert John and Jean Elizabeth (Lommen) Gibbons; m. Bruce Carlyle Evanson, Dec. 27, 1965; children: Tracey, John, Kelly. AA, Bismarck State Coll., 1964; BS in Spl. and Elem. Edn., U. N.D., 1966. Tchr. spl. edn. Winship Sch., Grand Forks, 1966-67, Simle Jr. High, Bismarck, 1967-70; tchr. Northridge Elem. sch., Bismarck, 1980-86, Wachter Middle Sch., Bismarck, 1986—; workshop facilitator Brass Found., Chgo., 1990-96, Dept. Pub. Instrn., Bismarck, 1988—, Chpt. I, Bismarck, 1989—, McRel for Drug Free Schs., Denver, 1990—. Co-founder The Big People, Bismarck, 1978—; mem. task force Children's Trust Fund, N.D., 1984; senator N.D. Legislature, Bismarck, 1989-94; mem. N.D. Bridges Adv. Bd., 1991—, DPI English Adv. Com., 1993—; co-facilitator Lead Mid. Sch. for Carnegie, 1994—; bd. dirs. Caring for Children, 1993-94, N.D. Art Edn. Task Force, 1992-93, N.D. Health Adv. Coun., 1993-94, N.D. Tchr.'s Fund for Retirement. Recipient Gold award Bismarck Norwest Bank, 1985; named Tchr. of Yr., N.D. Dept. Pub. Instrn., 1989, Legislator of Yr., Children's Caucus, 1991, Outstanding Alumnae, Bismarck State Coll., 1991, Milken Nat. Tchr. of Yr., 1995-96. Mem. N.O.R.A., N.C.T.E., Nat. Edn. Assn., N.D. Edn. Assn., Bismarck Edn. Assn., N.D. Reading Assn., Alpha Delta Kappa. Home: 723 N Washington St Bismarck ND 58501-3622 Office: Wachter Middle Sch 1107 S 7th St Bismarck ND 58504-6533

EVANSON, ELIZABETH MOSS, editor; b. Dallas, Oct. 13, 1934; d. Clifton Lowther and Virginia (Spence) M.; m. Jacob T. Evanson, Apr. 8, 1958; children: Evan A., Virginia M. BA with high honors, Swarthmore Coll., 1956; MA, Columbia U., 1957. Ency. and book editor Columbia U. Press, N.Y.C., 1957-61; adminstrv. asst. New Haven (Conn.) Redevel. Agy., 1961-63; freelance editor Yale U. Press, New Haven, 1964-69; editor Ctr. for Studies of John Dewey, Carbondale, Ill., 1971-72, U. Wis. Press, Madison, 1975-80; editor Inst. for Rsch. on Poverty U. Wis., Madison, 1980—, conf. organizer, 1984—; asst. dir. pub. info. Inst. for Rsch. on Poverty, Madison, 1989—, sr. editor, 1986—. Translator: The French Revolution, 1962; contbr. articles and essays on poverty rsch. Mem. Acad. Staff Pub. Representation Orgn., Phi Beta Kappa. Unitarian. Office: Inst for Rsch on Poverty 1180 Observatory Dr Madison WI 53706-1320

EVANS-PALMER, TERI ELLEN, art educator, art coordinator; b. Wichita, Kans., Sept. 24, 1953; d. Donald Krone and Evangeline Leora (Malott) Evans; m. Russell James Bennett, Aug. 7, 1977 (div. Mar. 1989); m. Lawrence Victor Palmer, April 18, 1992. BS in Art Edn., Kutztown (Pa.) U., 1975; MS in Art, Tex. A&M U., Kingsville, 1994. Cert. elem. tchr., Pa., Tex. Elem. classroom tchr. Harlingen (Tex.) Sch. Dist., 1986-88; elem./middle sch. art specialist Dept. of Defense, Wildflecken, Germany, 1988-90; elem. art specialist Edgewood Sch. Dist., San Antonio, Tex., 1990-91, dist. art specialist, 1991-94; dir. pub. info. Schertz-Cibolo-U.S. Dist., Schertz, Tex., 1994-95; visual arts coord. North East Sch. Dist., San Antonio, 1995—; graphic designer The Fountainhead Group, Inc., 1979-86; mime artist E. German Border Towns, 1988-89; del. Inst. for Fgn. Cultural Rels., Dilligen, Germany, 1988. Actress: (musical) Nunsense, Musical Wildflecken Theatre, Germany, 1989; exhibitor, artist: (watercolor paintings) Artists Who Teach Exhibit, 1994, 95 (Hon. Mention award 1994), Paint, Paste, Print-Artists Who Teach Young Children. Mem. bd. dirs. Students Help Art Reach Everyone (SHARE), 1994-96. Mem. ATPE, Nat. Art Edn. Assn., Tex. Art Edn. Assn., San Antonio Art Educator's Assn. Republican. Home: 19110 Red River Pass San Antonio TX 78259 Office: NE Ind Sch Dist 8961 Tesoro Dr San Antonio TX 78217

EVERETT, DIANA JEAN, educational association administrator, educator; b. Durant, Okla., Aug. 20, 1949; d. William Price and Francis Imogene (Harris) E. BA in Phys. Edn., U. Tex., Arlington, 1974; MS in Phys. Edn., Baylor U., 1978; PhD in Sports Adminstrn., Tex. Woman's U., 1995. Cert. tchr., Tex. Tchr., head coach Midlothian (Tex.) Ind. Sch. Dist., 1974-77; instr. Baylor U., Waco, Tex., 1977-78; tchr., head coach San Marcos (Tex.) Ind. Sch. Dist., 1978-80; owner retail and wholesale bus. Houston, 1980-85; tchr., head coach Clear Creek Ind. Sch. Dist., League City, Tex., 1985-91; asst. dir. athletics Tex. Woman's U., Denton, 1991-95; exec. dir. Nat. Assn. for Girls and Women in Sports, Reston, Va., 1995—; mem. host com. Dallas Internat. Sports Commn., 1994-95; tournament dir. Nat. Women's Wheelchair Basketball, Dallas, 1994; site dir. Tex. State Spl. Olympics, Denton, 1993; site facilitator Elk's Youth Basketball Shoot-Out, Denton, 1991-95. Mem. metroplex orgn. Nat. Girls and Women Sports Day, Denton and Dallas, 1991-95; sec. Exec. Women's Golf League, Denton, 1994-95; vol. Disabled Sports Assn. North Tex., Dallas, 1994-95. Mem. AAHPERD, AAUW, Nat. Assn. for Girls and Women in Sports, Nat. Assn. Coll. Women Athletic Adminstrs., Bay Area Women's Athletic Network (v.p. 1989-93), Delta Psi Kappa. Home: 1703 Wainwright Dr Reston VA 22090 Office: Nat Assn for Girls & Women in Sports 1900 Association Dr Reston VA 22091

EVERETT, DONNA RANEY, business educator; b. Corpus Christi, Tex., May 30, 1939; d. Donald Wayne and Zora Lee (Wynne) Raney; div.; 1 child, Donna Melinda. BA, Phillips U., Enid, Okla., 1961; MS, U. Houston, 1983, EdD, 1988. Various positions various orgns., Tex., 1965-80; adj. prof. U. Houston, 1983-88; asst. prof. bus. Tex. Tech U., Lubbock, 1988-89, Lamar U., Beaumont, Tex., 1989-90; asst. prof. bus. edn. Tex. Tech U., Lubbock, 1990-93; assoc. prof. bus. and mktg. edn. Ea. N.Mex. U., Portales, 1993-94; asst. prof. bus. edn. U. Mo., Columbia, 1994-96, Morehead State U., Morehead, Ky., 1996—; sponsor Zeta Kappa chpt. Pi Omega Pi; co-sponsor Gamma Chi, Delta Pi Epsilon; undergrad. mentor, 1996. Troop leader Girl Scouts U.S., Ft. Worth and Lake Jackson, Tex., 1964-80, dir. tng. Lake Jackson coun., 1980-82. Recipient curriculum devel. award Tex. Higher Edn. Coordinating Bd., 1987-88, outstanding article award Nat. Assn. Bus. Tchrs. Edn. Rev., 1992; named Outstanding Faculty Mem., Tex. Tech U., 1991. Mem. Am. Ednl. Rsch. Assn. (bus. edn. and inf. sys. spl. interest group), Internat. Soc. Tech. in Edn., Tex. Bus. Edn. Assn. (editor 1988-93, Collegiate Bus. Tchr. of Yr. dist. 4 1988, dist. 17 1992), Nat. Bus. Edn. Assn., Tex. Computer Edn. Assn., Mo. Bus. Edn. Assn., S.W. Fedn. Adminstrv. Disciplines (Disting. Paper award 1989, 93), Am. Vocat. Assn. (com. mem. 1990-95), Delta Pi Epsilon (pres. Alpha Gamma chpt. 1988-89), Phi Delta Kappa.

EVERETT, PAMELA IRENE, legal management company executive, educator; b. L.A., Dec. 31, 1947; d. Richard Weldon and Alta Irene (Tuttle) Bunnell; m. James E. Everett, Sept. 2, 1967 (div. 1973); 1 child, Richard Earl. Cert. Paralegal, Rancho Santago Coll., Santa Ana, Calif., 1977; BA, Calif. State U.-Long Beach, 1985; MA, U. Redlands, 1988. Owner, mgr. Orange County Paralegal Svc., Santa Ana, 1979-85; pres. Gem Legal Mgmt. Inc., Fullerton, Calif., 1986—; co-owner Bunnell Publs., Fullerton, Calif., 1992-96; instr. Rancho Santiago Coll., 1979—, chmn. adv. bd., 1980-85; instr. Fullerton Coll., 1989—, Rio Hondo Coll., Whittier, Calif., 1992-94; advisor Nat. Paralegal Assn., 1982—, Saddleback Coll., 1985—, North Orange County Regional Occupational Program, Fullerton, 1986—, Fullerton Coll. So. Calif. Coll. Bus. and Law; bd. dirs. Nat. Profl. Legal Assts. Inc., editor PLA News. Author: Legal Secretary Federal Litigation, 1986, Bankruptcy Courts and Procedure, 1987, Going Independent--Business Planning Guide, Fundamentals of Law Office Management, 1994. Republican. Office: 406 N Adams Ave Fullerton CA 92632-1605

EVERETT, VIRGINIA SAUERBRUN, counselor; b. Newark, N.J., Mar. 24, 1939; d. Arthur Gordon and Elwyna (Van Alen) Sauerbrun; m. Chandler H. Everett, Sept. 14, 1963 (div. Feb. 1986); children: Chandler P., Alexander U. BA, Coll. Wooster, 1961; MS in Gen. Counseling, Seattle Pacific U., 1990. Cert. chem. dependency counselor I. Counselor South King County Drug & Alcohol Recovery Ctrs., Seattle, 1990—; counselor Seattle Mental Health Inst., 1988-89, King County Perinatal Treatment Program, 1992-93, King County Pub. Health Dept., 1991—. Treas. Pacific N.W. Ballet League, Seattle, 1983; chmn. publicity Seattle Opera Guild, 1984; mem. work com. Washington State Coalition on Women's Substance Abuse Issues, 1990. Mem. ACA, Nat. Assn. Alchoholism and Drug Abuse Counselors, Chem. Dependency Profls. Wash. Republican. Episcopalian. Home: 8408 NE 19th Pl Bellevue WA 98004-3236 Office: South King County Recovery Ctrs 15025 4th Ave SW Seattle WA 98166-2301

EVERETT, VIRGINIA WOODS, director news research services; b. Jasper, Ala., Aug. 28, 1952; d. John Madison and Virginia Carolyn (Scott) Woods; m. Robert Burke Everett, Aug. 26, 1978. AB, Wesleyan Coll., 1974; MLS, U. Ala., 1978. Talking book libr. Mid. Ga. Regional Libr., Macon, 1978-80; asst. branch head Memphis-Shelby County Pub. Libr., 1980-87; asst. libr. dir. The Comml. Appeal, Memphis, 1987-88, libr. dir., 1988-94; dep. dir. news rsch. svcs. Atlanta Jour.-Constn., 1994-95, dir. news rsch. svcs., 1995—. Contbr. articles to profl. publs. Mem. DAR, Spl. Libraries Assn. (pres. Mid-South chpt. 1991-92, membership chmn. news divsn. 1994—), Memphis Libr. Coun., Investigative Reporters and Editors. Episcopalian. Office: The Atlanta Jour-Constn 72 Marietta St NW Atlanta GA 30303

EVERITT, ALICE LUBIN, labor arbitrator; b. Washington, Dec. 13, 1936; d. Isador and Alice (Berliner) Lubin; BA, Columbia U., 1968, JD, 1971. Assoc. firm Amen, Weisman & Butler, N.Y.C., 1971-78; spl. asst. to dir. Fed. Mediation and Conciliation Svc., Washington, 1978-81; editor Dept. Labor publ., 1979, pvt. practice labor arbitration, Washington, N.Y.C. and Petersburg, Va., 1981—; dean admissions Hofstra U. Sch. Law 1985-89; mem. various nat. mediation and arbitration panels including Fed. Mediation and Conciliation Svc., U.S. Steel and United Steelworkers. Mem. Am. Arbitration Assn., Soc. Profls. Dispute Resolution, Indsl. Rels. Rsch. Assn., Civil War Roundtable of Washington, N.Y.C. and Richmond. Office: 541 High St Petersburg VA 23803-3859

EVERIX, DONNA KATHLEEN, physical therapist; b. Milw., Feb. 18, 1966; d. Donald Joseph and Kathleen Dee (Siemann) E. BS in Phys. Therapy, Marquette U., 1988; MPA, Coll. Notre Dame, 1995. Phys. therapist Columbia Hosp., Milw., 1988-90; rehab. specialist Arthritis Ctr. at Mills Hosp., San Mateo, Calif., 1991-93; staff phys. therapist Brady Phys. Therapy, Foster City, Calif., 1993-95; sr. phys. therapist The Arthritis Ctr. Mills Hosp., San Mateo, 1995-96; physical therapy supervisor Mills Hosp., San Mateo, 1996—; mem. San Mateo Adv. Bd. for Arthritis Found., San Francisco; cons. and lectr. in field. Mem. Am. Phys. Therapy Assn., Assn. Rheumatology Health Profls. Roman Catholic. Home: 2007 Fairmont Dr San Mateo CA 94402 Office: Physical Therapy Dept Mills Hosp 100 S San Mateo Dr San Mateo CA 94401

EVERLY, JANE, gifted education educator; b. Corona, Calif., Nov. 13, 1964; d. John W. and Esther (Hubberstey) E. BS magna cum laude, Belhaven Coll., 1985; MS, MEd, Miss. Coll., Clinton, 1987, EdS, 1989. Cert. elem. edn., gifted edn., computer edn. and sch. adminstrn., Miss. Tchr. 6th grade Casey Elem., Jackson, Miss.; tchr. gifted Casey Elem., Jackson, Siwell Mid. Sch., Jackson; coord. Summer Challenge Camp. Author: Cavern's Quest, 1994. Coach 6 state champion teams Odessey of the Mind. Mem. Miss. Profl. Edn. Home: 4858 Maplewood Dr Jackson MS 39206-4817

EVERSOLE, VIVIAN L., bank executive. Exec. v.p. global investor svcs. Chase Manhattan, Bklyn. Office: Chase Manhattan 4 Metrotech Ctr Brooklyn NY 11245*

EVERSON, DIANE LOUISE, publishing executive; b. Edgerton, Wis., Mar. 27, 1953; d. Harland Everett and Helen Viola (Oliver) E. BS, Carroll Coll., 1975. Co-pub. Edgerton (Wis.) Reporter, 1976—; v.p. Silk Screen Creations, 1981—; bd. dirs. Inland Press. Pub. Career Directors newspaper, 1981—, Directions mag., 1981—, Career Waves Newsletter, 1989—, Coll. and Univs. Directories. Trustee Carroll Coll., 1987—; active ARC. Mem. Nat. Newspaper Assn. (regional bd. dirs.), Inland Press Assn. (bd. dirs. 1993—). Democrat. Lutheran. Home: 114 Kellog Rd Edgerton WI 53534-9352 Office: Directions Pub 21 N Henry St Edgerton WI 53534-1821

EVERS-WILLIAMS, MYRLIE, cultural organization administrator; b. Vicksburg, Miss., Mar. 17, 1933; m. Medgar Evers (dec. June 1963); m. Howard Williams; 3 children. Student, Alcorn State U.; BA in Sociology, Pomona Coll., 1968. Mem. staff, sec. NAACP; dir. planning Clarmont (Calif.) Colls., 1968-70; v.p. Seligman & Latz, N.Y.C.; dir. consumer affairs Atlantic Richfield Co.; commr. Pub. Works Bd., L.A., 1987-95; chairwoman NAACP, 1995—; civil rights leader. Author: For Us the Living, 1967. Candidate for Congress in Calif., 1970; candidate for L.A. City Coun., 1987. Office: NAACP 4805 Mount Hope Dr Baltimore MD 21215-3206*

EVERT, CHRISTINE MARIE (CHRIS EVERT), retired professional tennis player; b. Ft. Lauderdale, Fla., Dec. 21, 1954; d. James and Colette Evert; m. John Lloyd, Apr. 17, 1979 (div.); m. Andy Mill, July 30, 1988; children: Alexander James, Nicholas Joseph, Colton Jack. Amateur tennis player, until Dec. 1972, profl. tennis player, 1972-89, ret. from tennis, 1989; owner Evert Enterprises/IMG, Boca Raton, Fla., 1989—; Olympics commentator CBS Sports, 1992; commentator NBC Sports tennis events; winner numerous tournaments including U.S. Jr. Championship, 1970, 71, U.S. Open, 1975, 76, 77, 78, 80, 82, Wimbledon Singles, 1974, 76, 81, doubles, 1976, Australian Open, 1982, 84, French Open Singles, 1974, 75, 79, 80, 83, 85, 86, Virginia Slims, 1972, 73, 75, 77, 87, European Women's Open, Geneva, 1987, Eckerd Open, 1987; spl. advisor to U.S. Nat. Tennis Team by U.S. Tennis Assn.; bd. dirs. Internat. Tennis Hall of Fame; trustee Womens Sports Found. Star 3 vols. VCR instrnl. tennis tapes, 1991—; corp. spokesperson and rep., appearing in TV commls. and print advertisements; host and organizer Chris Evert Pro-Celebrity Tennis Classic, 1989, 90, 93, 94, 95, 96. Founder Chris Evert Charities, Inc., Healthy Start. Recipient Lebair Sportsmanship trophy, 1971; named Female Athlete of Yr. AP, 1974, 75, 77, 80, Athlete of Yr. Sports Illustrated, 1976, Greatest Woman Athlete of Last 25 Years Women's Sports Found., 1985, Flo Hyman award Women's Sports Found., 1990, Providencia award Palm Beach County Conv. and Visitors Bur., 1991; named one of Top 10 Romantic People of 1989, Korbel; inducted Madison Sq. Garden Walk of Fame, 1993, inductee, Internat. Tennis Hall of Fame, 1995. Mem. U.S. Lawn Tennis Assn. (Top Women's Singles Player award 1974), Nat. Honor Soc., Fla. Sports Found. (bd. dirs.), Women's Tennis Assn. (pres. 1982-91, exec. com., Sportmanship award 1979, Player Svc. awards 1981, 86, 87). Address: Evert Enterprises/IMG 7200 W Camino Real # 310 Boca Raton FL 33433-5511*

EVERT, SANDRA FLORENCE, medical/surgical nurse; b. Saginaw, Mich., Sept. 18, 1949; d. Charles William and Florence Arlene (Babcock) Wheeler; m. Raymond Clyde Evert, Jan. 20, 1968; children: Christine Michelle, Raymond Clyde II. AD cum laude, Lansing C.C., 1986. Med./surg. staff nurse E.W. Sparrow Hosp., Lansing, Mich., 1986—. Mem. Apostolic Ch. Home: 10 Willard Ct Grand Ledge MI 48837-1356

EVERTON, MARTA VE, ophthalmologist; b. Luling, Tex., Nov. 12, 1926; d. T.W. and Nora E. (Eckols) O'Leavy; B.A., Hardin-Simmons U., 1945; M.A., Stanford U., 1947; M.D., Baylor U., 1955; postgrad. N.Y.U.-Bellevue Hosp., 1956-57; m. Robert K. Graham, Oct. 15, 1960; children: Marcia, Christie, Leslie Fox. Intern, Meth. Hosp., Houston, 1955-56; resident in ophthalmology Baylor Affiliated Hosps., Houston, 1957-59; clin. instr. ophthalmology Baylor U., 1959-60; asst. clin. prof. ophthalmology Loma Linda U., 1962-73; practice medicine specializing in ophthalmology, Houston, 1959-60, Pasadena, Calif., 1961-74, Escondido, Calif., 1974—. Mem. Calif. Med. Assn., Am. Acad. Ophthalmology, Alpha Omega Alpha. Home: 3024 Sycamore Ln Escondido CA 92025-7433 Office: 820 E Ohio Ave Escondido CA 92025-3421

EVEY, LOIS REED, psychiatric nurse; b. Burgettstown, Pa., Aug. 23, 1925; d. Harry Lemoyne and Willa Blanche (Miller) Reed; diploma Presbyn. Hosp. Sch. Nursing, Pitts., 1946; B.Nursing Edn., U. Pitts., 1959, M.Nursing Edn., 1963, postgrad., 1978; m. Raymond Cuervo, Sept. 1946; 1 son, Craig Dale; m. 2d, Kenneth George Evey, Aug. 20, 1959. Successively staff nurse, relief head nurse Women's Hosp., Pitts., 1946-53; staff nurse, then head nurse, asst. bldg. supr. Woodville (Pa.) State Hosp., 1953-59; med.-surg. nursing instr. St. Margaret Meml. Hosp., Pitts., 1959-61; psychiat. staff nurse Council House, Inc., Pitts., 1962-66, acting exec. dir., 1966, exec. dir., 1966-80; exec. dir. VA Med. Center, Pitts., 1979-95, coordinator in-patient psychosocial rehab. program, 1984-85; lectr. community mental health workshops; mem. nurse adv. bd. Pitts. Planned Parenthood; mem. Task Force to Establish Domiciliary Care, Community Human Service Center, Pitts.; mem. Greater Pitts. Rehab. Council; mem. Pitts. chpt. Gov.'s Com. Employment of Handicapped; mem. citizens council bd. St. Francis Gen. Hosp., Western Psychiat. Inst. and Clinics; bd. dirs. continuing edn. for nurses U. Pitts., Indiana U. of Pa., Carlow Coll. Author: (with others) Rehabilitating the Mentally Ill in the Community. Served with Cadet Nurse Corps, U.S. Army, 1943-46. USPHS grantee, 1961-63. Mem. Am. Orthopsychiat. Assn., Internat. Assn. Psycho-Social Rehab. Services (co-founder, dir.), Pa. Assn. Mental Health and Mental Retardation Service Providers, Nat. Council Therapy and Rehab. Through Horticulture, Am. Nurses Assn. (legis. com.), Pa. Nurses Assn., Nat. Assn. Mental Health Adminstrs., Pa. Assn. Mental Health Adminstrs., Am. Public Health Assn., Pa. Public Health Assn., United Mental Health, Nat. Assn. Retarded Citizens, Pa. Assn. Retarded Citizens, Western Pa. Aftercare Assn., Health and Welfare Planning Assn., Pitts. Exec. Women's Council (charter), U. Pitts. Alumni Assn., Presbyn. U. Hosp. Alumni Assn. (past pres.; life), Sigma Theta Tau, Alpha Tau Delta. Republican. Mem. United Ch. of Christ. Club: East Hills Pitts. (life). Home: 305 Lougeay Rd Pittsburgh PA 15235-4502

EVRÉN, LISA ANN, director corporate treasury planning, tax attorney; b. Hoboken, N.J., June 14, 1955; d. Joseph William and Helen Minna (McCrossin) Tudisco; m. Robert Erik Evrén, Feb. 17, 1987; 1 child, Christopher Robert. BA in Philosophy, Pomona Coll., 1977; RN, Merritt Hosp. Nursing Coll., Oakland, Calif., 1982; JD, NYU, 1988, LLM in Taxation, 1993. Bar: N.Y., 1989; RN, N.Y., Calif. Pediatric RN U. Calif., San Francisco, 1982-84; pediatric ICU nurse Children's Hosp. of Buffalo, 1984-85; assoc. Debevoise & Plimpton, N.Y.C., 1987-91; tax atty. Pfizer Inc., N.Y.C., 1991-94; mgr. internat. fin. Pfizer Inc., 1994-95, dir. treasury planning, 1995—. Contbr. articles to profl. jours.; sr. editor NYU Law Rev., 1987-88. Bd. dirs. Pelham (N.Y.) Children's Ctr., 1992-94. Mem. NAFE, N.Y. State Bar Assn., Assn. of the Bar of City of N.Y. Democrat. Roman Catholic. Office: Pfizer Inc 235 E 42d St 235-30-9 New York NY 10017

EVSTATIEVA, STEFKA, opera singer; b. Rousse, Bulgaria, May 7, 1947; d. Evstati Bojanov Nedev and Maria Nikolai (Dencheva) Nedeva; m. Mladen Hristov Kovatchev, Oct. 28, 1973; 1 child, Valeria. Grad., State Conservatory, Sofia, Bulgaria, 1971. Spinto soprano Opera House-Rousse, 1971-79; dramatic soprano National Opera, Sofia, 1979—. Appeared in leading operatic roles at Met. Opera N.Y., San Francisco Opera, Washington Opera, Covent Garden, London, Grand Opera, Paris, La Scala, Milano, Stadts Opera, Vienna. Recipient 2d prize 5th Chaikovski Competition, Moscow, 1974, Grand Prix award Competition for Belcanto-Belgium Radio and TV, 1978, Competition for Young Opera Singers, Sofia, 1979, Giovanni Zanatello award Verona Festival, 1982.

EWALD, WENDY TAYLOR, photographer, writer, educator; b. Detroit, June 28, 1951; d. Henry Theodore and Carolyn Davison (Taylor) E.; m. Thomas Joseph McDonough, Oct. 21,1990; 1 child, Michael German. BA, Antioch Coll., 1974. Founder, dir. Camera Work, London, 1971-73, Mountain Photography Workshop, Whitesburg, Ky., 1975-81; tchr. photography Self-Employed Women's Assn., Raquira, Colombia, 1982-84, Gujarat, India, 1988-89; edn. cons. Fotofest, Houston, 1989-91; sr. rsch. assoc. Duke U., Durham, N.C., 1991—; vis. assoc. prof. photography Bard Coll., Annandale, N.Y., 1996; artist-in-residence Ky. Arts Coun., Whitesburg, 1976-80; asst. dir., scriptwriter Cine-Mujer, Bogota, 1986. Author, editor: Appalachia: A Self-Portrait, 1978; author: Portraits and Dreams, 1985, Magic Eyes, 1992, I Dreamed I Had A Girl In My Pocket, 1996. Recipient prize Lyndhurst Found., 1986; Fulbright fellow, fellow Nat. Endowment for Arts, 1988, non-fiction fellow N.Y. Found. for Arts, 1990, MacArthur fellow, 1992. Home: Box 582 Rhinebeck NY 12572

EWEN, PAMELA BINNINGS, lawyer; b. Phila., Mar. 22, 1944; d. Walter James and Barbara (Perkins) Binnings; m. Jerome Francis Ayers, Aug. 22, 1965 (div July 1974); 1 son, Scott Dylan; m. John Alexander Ewen, Dec. 13, 1974. B.A., Tulane U., 1977; J.D. cum laude, U. Houston, 1979. Bar: Tex. 1979, U.S. Dist. Ct. (so. dist.) Tex. 1981, U.S. Ct. Appeals (5th cir.) 1981. Law clk. firm Harris, Cook, Browning & Barker, Corpus Christi, Tex., 1977-79; assoc. firm Kleberg, Dyer, Redford & Weil, Corpus Christi, 1979-80; atty. law dept. Gulf Oil Corp., Houston, 1980-84; assoc. Baker & Botts, L.L.P., Houston, 1984-88, ptnr., 1988—. La. Legis. scholar, New Orleans, 1976-77. Mem. ABA (forum com. on franchising 1983-85, corp., banking, bus. law sect., 1984—, law practice mgmt. sect., subcom. Women Rainmakers Assn.), Am. Petroleum Inst. (spl. subcom. to gen. com. on law, com. on product liability 1982-85), Tex. State Bar (com. on uniform communal code 1988—), Tex. Assn. Bank Coun. (mem. bd. dirs. 1994), Order of Barons. Office: Baker & Botts 3000 1 Shell Plz Houston TX 77002

EWERS, ANNE, opera company director. Gen. dir. Boston Lyric Opera, 1984-89, Utah Opera, Salt Lake City, 1990—; panelist Nat. Endowment for Arts; freelance stage dir. San Francisco Opera, N.Y.C. Opera, Can. Opera Co., Minn. Opera, Vancouver Opera, numerous others. Dir. nearly fifty opera prodns. including La Giaconda, Un Ballo in Maschera, La Rondine, The Merry Widow, Ring Cycle, Salome, Dialogues des Carmelites, Eugene Onegin; dir. Dame Joan Sutherland's North American Farewell, Dallas Opera. Bd. dirs. Opera Am., 1993—. Office: Utah Opera 50 W 2d South Salt Lake City UT 84101

EWERS, PATRICIA O'DONNELL, university administrator; b. Chgo., July 22, 1935; d. Patrick Brenden and Johanna Marie (Galvin) O'D.; m. John Leonard Ewers, July 26, 1958; children: John P., Michele M. Ewers DeCesare. BA in English summa cum laude, Mundelein Coll., 1957; MA in English, Loyola U., Chgo., 1958, PhD in English, 1966. Instr. English Mundelein Coll., Chgo., 1964-66; asst. prof. English DePaul U., Chgo., 1966-69, assoc. prof. English, 1969-76, dir. humanities divsn. gen. edn. program, 1969-73, chair dept. English, 1973-76, prof. English, 1976-90, dean Coll. Liberal Arts and Scis., 1976-80, v.p., dean faculties, 1980-90; pres. Pace U., N.Y.C., 1990—; ptnr. N.Y.C. Ptnrs., 1990—; chmn., mem. North Ctrl. Assn. Accreditation Teams, 1977-90; mem. nat. identification program for women in higher edn. Ill. State Com. for Am. Coun. on Edn., 1983-86; commr.-at-large North Ctrl. Assn. Colls./Schs., 1984-87; mem. com. on study of undergrad. edn. State of Ill. Bd. Higher Edn., 1985-86, 1989-90; mem. Commn. Minorities in Higher Edn., Am. Coun. Edn., 1990-93; mem. N.Y.C. Workforce Devel. Commn., 1993; mem. human resources bd. AT&T Corp., Basking Ridge, N.J., 1994; mem. adv. coun. on postsecondary edn. State Dept. Edn., 1994—; mem. adv. com. on telecom., State Edn. Dept., Albany, N.Y., 1995—. Trustee Riverside (Ill.) Pub. Libr., 1980-86, Cath. Theol. Union, Chgo., 1985-90, sec., 1986-90, N.Y. Downtown Hosp., 1991—, Coun. Adult and Exptl. Learning, 1992-95, Our Lady of Mercy Med. Ctr., Bronx, N.Y., 1993—, El Museo del Barrion, N.Y.C., 1994—; chmn., bd. trustees Commn. Ind. Colls. and Univs./N.Y. State Commn. Ind. Colls. and Univs., 1992—; bd. dirs. Cath. Charities, 1984-90, Com. on Social Svc., 1986-90, subcom. on employer assistance programs, 1986-88, Am. Brands, 1991—, Phoenix Theatre, 1992—, Drama League, N.Y.C., 1993—, Richard Tucker Music Found., 1993—, Westchester County Assn., 1993—; mem. Chgo. Network, 1986-90, steering com. Assn. Colls. and Univs./N.Y. State Commn. Ind. Colls. and Univs., 1992—, individual investors adv. com. to bd. dirs. N.Y. Stock Exch., 1994—. Recipient Outstanding Alumna award Loyola U., Chgo., 1984. Mem. Nat. Assn. Ind. Colls. and Univs. (bd. dirs. 1995—), Am. Australian Assn. (bd. dirs. 1994—), Regional Plan Assn. (coun. for the region tomorrow 1990-93), Downtown Lower Manhattan Assn., Inc. (bd. dirs. 1991—), Women's Forum, Inc., Fin. Women's Assn., Econ. Club of N.Y., Univ. Club, Met. Club, St. Andrew's Golf Club, Phi Gamma Mu, Beta Gamma Sigma, Alpha Lambda Delta, Delta Epsilon Sigma. Roman Catholic. Office: Pace U Office of Pres Pace Plz New York NY 10038

EWERSEN, MARY VIRGINIA, retired secondary educator; b. Van Wert County, Ohio, June 7, 1922; B.S. in Elem. Edn., Bowling Green, 1966, Toledo and Ohio U. State U.; m. Herbert Ewersen (dec.); 2 children. Remedial reading tchr. Port Clinton (Ohio) City Schs., 1966-70, reading tchr. chpt. I/coord., 1970-94, ret. Cert. tchr. K-12, reading, Ohio. Mem. Internat. Reading Assn., Sandusky Choral Soc., Kappa Delta Pi. Author activity card set: From Hyperactive to Happy-Active in Limited Spaces, 1979; poet. Home: 1786 S Hickory Grove Rd Port Clinton OH 43452-9637 Office: 431 Portage Dr Port Clinton OH 43452-1724

EWIN, PAULA JEAN, actress, producer; b. Warwick, R.I., Dec. 6, 1955; d. Leon Roma Ewin and Lorraine Marie Potvin. Student, King's Coll., Wilkes-Barre, Pa., 1973-75; BA in Theater, R.I. Coll., 1978; studied at The William Esper Studio, N.Y.C., 1985-87. mem. newsletter com. Women in Theater, N.Y.C., 1981-84. Appeared in (plays) The Curate Shakespeare As You Like It, Necktie Breakfast, Between Friends, Dancing at Lughnasa, Visiting Oliver, Friends to the End, Cora Fry, I'm Getting My Act Together..., Fatal Attraction, Kiss Me, Kate, Chapter Two, Baptists/The Hand of God, Blue Window, The Wake of Jamey Foster, Bible Burlesque, The Mound Builders, (film and TV) The House of Mirth, Radio Days, Neon Passion, The Guiding Light, All My Children, As the World Turns; playwright, dir. Tuesday's Child, 1982 (The New Eng. Theater Conf. Excellence in Children's Theater award 1982); tour of Cora Fry, New Eng., N.Y., 1979-82; prodr., actress Visiting Oliver, 1993 (Samuel French Short Play Festival award 1993); dir. The 29th St. Repertory Theater, N.Y.C., 1988—. Recipient The Irene Ryan Alt. award The New Eng. Regional Competition, 1978, NEA grant, 1981. Democrat. Home: 99 Ave B Apt 2B New York NY 10009 Office: The 29th St Repertory Theater Inc 212 W 29th St New York NY 10001

EWING, GAIL HUMPHRIES, county official; b. Fort Leavenworth, Kans., June 19, 1945; d. Donald Harrison and Charlotte (Rose) Humphries; m. Robert John Ewing, July 22, 1967; children: Robert Wall Ewing, Michael Harrison Ewing. BA, U. Md., 1979. Confidential aide Montgomery County Coun., Rockville, Md., 1981-86, county coun. mem., 1990—, v.p., 1994-95, pres., 1995-96, chair health & human svcs., 1990—; lobbyist, pub. rels. dir. Alzheimer's Assn. Greater Washington, Bethesda, Md., 1986-90; chair human svcs. public safety com. Coun. Govts., Washington, 1993-94; mem. health steering com. Nat. Assn. Counties, Washington, 1990-95. Mem., past pres. Bethesda-Chevy Chase Bus. and Profl. women Orgn., 1986—, Fox Hills West Citizens Assn., Potomac, Md., 1981—. Recipient Key to County, Dade County, Fla., 1992, Disting. Svc. award Mobile Med. Inc., 1993, Reader's Choice award Potomac Almanac, 1994, Outstanding Elected Official award Washington Regional Alcohol Program, 1993, Commendation award Coun. Govts., 1993. Mem. AAUW, Bus. and Profl. Women, League Women Voters, North Bethesda Rotary. Democrat. Presbyterian. Office: Montgomery County Coun 100 Maryland Ave Rockville MD 20850

EXNER, JANE FRANCES, nursing administrator; b. Pitts., Nov. 20, 1958; d. Albert Francis and Jane Frances (Tweed) E. BSN, Wheeling (W.Va.) Jesuit Coll., 1980; MPH, Temple U., 1992. RN, W.Va., Pa. Staff nurse U. Pa. Hosp., Phila., 1980-83; vol. Peace Corps, Niger, West Africa, 1984-86; emergency dept. nurse Hahnemann U. Hosp., Phila., 1987-88; perioperative nurse Thomas Jefferson U. Hosp., Phila., 1989-92; coord. nursing Internat. Med. Corps., Baidoa, Somalia, 1992-93; country dir. Internat. Med. Corps., Burundi, 1996—; dir. health care CARE, Somalia/Tanzania, 1993-95; country dir. Burundi, Internat. Med. Corps, 1996—; guest lectr. nutrition Temple U., Phila., 1992; nutrition cons. Peace Corps, 1986. Nurse vol. Operation Smile, Liberia, West Africa, 1989, Romania, 1992. Recipient Disting. Alumni award Wheeling Jesuit Coll., 1994. Mem. Am. Pub. Health Assn., Emergency Nurses Assn., Maternity Care Coalition (program devel. and evaluation com. 1991-92). Roman Catholic.

EXRATI, SUSAN GRAHAM, pension investment strategist, economist; b. Denver, Dec. 29, 1945; d. Earl Ellis and Winona (Davidson) Graham; m. Milton Joseph Ezrati, June 19, 1976; 1 child, Isabel Diana. BA in Internat. Rels., Pomona Coll., 1968; MA in Internat. Rels., Denver U., 1970; MPhil in Econs., Columbia U., 1985. CFA. Econ. analyst Citibank, N.Y.C., 1970-73, economist, 1973-78; instr. econs. Hofstra U., Hempstead, N.Y., 1978-80, Rutgers U., Newark, 1980-81; sr. economist GM Corp., N.Y.C., 1982-88, mgr. internat. investments, 1988-95; dir. internat. strategy GM Investment Mgmt. Corp., N.Y.C., 1995—. Mem. Am. Econ. Assn., Assn. for Investment Mgmt. Rsch., N.Y. Soc. Security Analysts. Home: 12 Oakland Dr Port Washington NY 11050 Office: GM Investment Mgmt Corp 767 Fifth Ave New York NY 10153

EYRE, MARILEE YARDLEY, secondary school educator; b. Cedar City, Utah, Mar. 10, 1954; d. Ray and Mary (Joseph) Yardley; m. Chris Dale Eyre, June 2, 1972; children: Jason, Chris, Joshua, Kellee, Kiley, Daniel. BA, So. Utah U., 1989. Cert. secondary edn. educator in English, tchr. Utah, bus. edn., secretarial. Tchr. English Beaver (Utah) High Sch., 1990—; advanced placement coord. Beaver (Utah) High Sch., 1991—, Sterling scholar advisor, 1994, coach Academic Decathlon, 1992—, Girls' Athletic Assn. softball coach, 1992—. Editor: Literary Beaver High Sch., 1992—. Church organist, Beaver, 1989—. Mem. Utah Bus. Edn. Assn. (student rep. 1988-89), Beaver Betterment Club, Am. Legion Aux. LDS. Home: PO Box 1092 Beaver UT 84713-1092 Office: Beaver High Sch 170 N Main Beaver UT 84713

EYSTER, MARY ELAINE, hematologist, educator; b. York, Pa., Mar. 21, 1935; d. Charles Gable and March Viola (Schriver) E.; m. Robert E. Dye, Jan. 2, 1965; children: Robert E., Charles. AB, Duke U., 1956, MD, 1960. Intern. N.Y. Hosp.-Cornell Med. Coll., N.Y.C., 1960-61, resident in medicine, 1961-63, fellow in hematology, 1963-66, instr. medicine, 1966-67, asst. prof. medicine, 1967-70; asst. prof. medicine Milton S. Hershey Med. Ctr. Pa. State U., Hershey, 1970-73, assoc. prof. Milton S. Hershey Med. Ctr., 1973-82, prof. Milton S. Hershey Med. Ctr., 1982—, chief hematology div., dept. medicine Coll. Medicine, 1973—; bd. dirs. Hemophilia Ctr. Cen. Pa., 1973—, AIDS Clin. Trials Unit Pa. State U., 1987—; faculty rsch. assoc. Am. Cancer Soc., 1966-71; mem. State Hemophilia Adv. Com., 1973—, chmn., 1977-79, 1988-90; mem. policy bd. Coop. F VII inhibitor study Nat. Heart, Lung and Blood Inst., 1975-79; mem. med. and sci. adv. coun. Nat. Hemophilia Found., 1976-77, 82—, chmn. med. adv. com. Del. Valley chpt., 1979-82; co-investigator, mem. multi-agy. task force on AIDS HHS, 1982-83; mem. blood products adv. com. FDA, 1985-89; exec. com. NIH-NIAID Clin. Trials, 1988-90. USPHS grantee, 1976—. Fellow ACP; mem. Pa. Med. Soc., Am. Fedn. Clin. Rsch., World Fedn. Hemophilia, Am. Soc. Hematology, Am. Assn. Blood Banks, Internat. Soc. Thrombosis and Haemostasis, Insternat. Soc. Hematology, Pa. Soc. Hematology, Oncology (bd. dirs. 1982-85), Am. Heart Assn. Coun. on Thrombosis, Phi Beta Kappa,

Alpha Omega Alpha. Office: Milton S Hershey Med Ctr PO Box 850 Hershey PA 17033-0850

EZAKI-YAMAGUCHI, JOYCE YAYOI, renal dietitian; b. Kingsburg, Calif., Mar. 18, 1947; d. Toshikatsu and Aiko (Ogata) Ezaki; m. Kent Takao Yamaguchi, Oct. 28, 1972; children: Kent Takao, Jr., Toshia Ann. AA, Reedley Coll., 1967; BS in Foods and Nutrition, U. Calif., Davis, 1969. Dietetic intern Henry Ford Hosp., Detroit, 1969-70, staff dietitian, 1970-71; renal dietitian Sutter Meml. Hosp., Sacramento, 1971-72; therapeutic dietitian Mt. Sinai Hosp., Beverly Hills, Calif., 1972-73; clin. dietitian Pacific Hosp., Long Beach, Calif., 1973-77; consulting dietitian Doctor's Hosp., Lakewood, Calif., 1976-77; clin. dietitian Mass. Gen. Hosp., Boston, 1977-78, Winona Meml. Hosp., Indpls., 1978-80; renal dietitian Fresno (Calif.) Community Hosp., 1980—. Author: (computer program) Dialysis Tracker, 1987; author: (with others) Cultural Foods and Renal Diets for the Dietitian, 1988, Standards of Practice Guidlines for the Practice of Clinical Dietetics, 1991. Mem. Nat. Kidney Found. (exec. com. coun. renal nutrition 1992—, region V rep. 1992-93, chair elect 1994-95, chair 1995-96, immediate past chair 1996—), Am. Dietetic Assn. (bd. cert. renal nutrition specialist, renal practice group 1993—), No. Calif/No. Nev. chpt. Nat. Kidney Found. (disting. achievement award coun. on renal nutrition 1993, co-chair-elect 1993-94, co-chair 1994-95, co-past chair 1995-96, treas., corr. sec.). Buddhist. Office: Cmty Hosps Ctrl Calif Fresno & R Sts Fresno CA 93715-2094

EZELL, ANGIE FIELDS CANTRELL MERRITT DONELSON, real estate executive; b. Hermitage, Tenn., Dec. 2, 1914; d. Dempsey Weaver and Nora (Johnson) Cantrell; student public and pvt. schs., Hermitage, Nashville; m. Gilbert Stroud Merritt, Dec. 15, 1934 (dec.); 1 son, Gilbert Stroud; m. John Donelson, Jr., VII, Apr. 23, 1966 (dec.); step-children: John, Agnes Donelson Williams (dec.), William Stockley; m. DeWitt Ezell Sr., Mar. 5, 1996; stepchildren: DeWitt Jr., Camilla Ezell Martin, Dan. Pres., So. Woodenware Co., Nashville, 1955-61, So. Properties, Co., Hermitage, 1961—. Chmn. comml. flower exhibits Tenn. State Fair, 1951; committeewoman and v.p. Davidson County Agrl. Soil and Conservation Community Com., 1959-60; bd. mem. Nashville Symphony Assn., 1961-64, regional council mem., 1977-79; chmn. bd. Nashville Presbyn. Neighborhood Settlement House; elder Presbyn. Ch., 1989-92; founding bd. mem. Davidson County Cancer Soc.; bd. mem. Nashville Vis. Nurse Service; dist. chmn., speakers bur. Am. Red Cross. Proclaimed First Lady Donelson-Hermitage Community, 1986. Mem. Vanderbilt U. Aid, Peabody Coll. Aid, Tenn. Hist. Soc., Descs. of Ft. Nashboro Pioneers (bd. dirs. 1984-87), English Speaking Union. Clubs: Ladies Hermitage Assn. (dir. 1949-89), DAR, (chpt. regent 1941), Tenn. Pres.' Trust, Lebanon Rd. Garden Club (pres. 1947), Horticulture Soc. Davidson County (v.p. 1949). Clubs: Ravenwood Country, Centennial, Belle Meade. Contbr. to books and mags. on history of Tenn. Home and Office: Stone Hall 1014 Stones River Rd Hermitage TN 37076-2030

EZELL-GRIM, ANNETTE SCHRAM, business management educator, academic administrator; b. West Frankfort, Ill., June 19, 1940; d. Woodrow C. and Rosa (Franich) Schram; m. John R. Grim, III; BS U. Nev., 1962, MS in Physiology, 1967, postgrad., 1969; EdD in Pub. Adminstrn., Brigham Young U., 1977; children: Michael L., Rona Maria. Mem. staff Washoe Med. Ctr., Reno, 1962; teaching asst. U. Nev., Reno, 1962-63, instr., 1963-64, 1965-67, asst. prof., 1967-71; curriculum specialist U. Nev. Med. Sch., 1971-72, project mgr. Fed. Grant Intercampus Edn. Project, 1969-71, assoc. prof., curriculum specialist rural practitioner program, 1971-73, staff assoc. Mountain States Regional Med. Program, 1974-75; cons. Nev. Dept. Edn., 1975-77; asst. dean acad. affairs U. Utah, Salt Lake City, 1977-80; acting Dean, 1981, dir., prof. doctoral program Edn. Adminstrn.; prof., dept. head Coll. Human Development, Pa. State U., 1982-85; dean Coll. Profl. Studies, prof. bus. adminstrn. U. So. Colo., Pueblo, 1985-87; sr. asst. to pres. Towson State U., Balt., 1987-94, assoc. prof. mgmt. sch. bus., 1994-95; assoc. dean, prof. bus. mgmt. Wor Wic C.C., Salisbury, Md., 1995—; cons. higher edn., TV edn., research methology; adviser to various research, polit. and ednl. bds. Mem. Am. Ednl. Research Assn., AAAS, Am. Acad. Arts and Scis., AAUP, Am. Council on Edn., Am. Assn. Higher Edn., Soc. for Coll. & Univ. Planning, Decision Scis. Inst., Sigma Xi, Phi Kappa Phi, Delta Kappa Gamma. Home: 6536 Ocean Pines Berlin MD 21811 Office: Wor Wic CC 32000 Campus Dr Salisbury MD 21801

EZOLD, NANCY O'MARA, lawyer; b. Laconia, N.H., July 21, 1942; d. Francis L. and Edna Mae (Jackson) O'Mara; m. William L. Kennan; children: Christopher E., Matthew F. BA, U. Maine, 1964; JD, Villanova U., 1980. Bar: Pa. 1980, U.S. Supreme Ct. 1989, U.S. Ct. Appeals (3d and fed. cir.) 1982, U.S. Claims Ct. 1989, U.S. Dist. Ct. (ea. dist.) Pa. 1980, U.S. Dist. Ct. (mid. dist.) Pa. 1989, U.S. Dist. Ct. Ariz. 1991. Adminstrv. positions fed., state, and local govt. agys. fed., stage and local govt. agys., 1964-77; assoc. Kirschner, Walters & Willig, Phila., 1980-81, Phillips & Phelan, Phila., 1981-83, Wolf Block Schorr & Solis-Cohen, Phila., 1983-89, Rosenthal & Ganister, West Chester, Pa., 1990-94; chief counsel BES Environ. Specialists, Larksville, Pa., 1989-90; pvt. practice Bala Cynwyd, Pa., 1994—. Bd. dirs. Women's Law Project, Phila., 1995, 96. Named Feminist of Yr., Feminist Majority Found., 1993. Mem. ATLA, NAFE, Phila. Bar Assn., Nat. Assn. Women Lawyers (pres.' award 1991). Democrat. Office: 401 City Ave Ste 904 Bala Cynwyd PA 19004

FAATZ, JEANNE RYAN, state legislator; b. Cumberland, Md., July 30, 1941; d. Charles Keith and Myrtle Elizabeth (McIntyre) Ryan; B.S., U. Ill., 1962; postgrad. (Gates fellow) Harvard U. Program Sr. Execs. in state and local Govt., 1984; M.A., U. Colo.-Denver, 1985. children: Kristin, Susan. Instr. Speech Dept., Met. State Coll., Denver, 1985—; sec. to majority leader Colo. Senate, 1976-78; mem. Colo. Ho. Reps. from Dist. 1, 1978—, asst. majority leader. Past pres. Harvey Park (Colo.) Homeowners Assn., Southwest Denver YWCA Adult Edn. Club; Southwest met. coord. UN Children's Fund, 1969-74; mem. citizens adv. coun. Ft. Logan Mental Health Center; bd. mgrs. Southwest Denver YMCA. Mem. Bear Creek Rep. Women's Club. Home: 2903 S Quitman St Denver CO 80236-2208 Office: State Capitol Denver CO 80203

FABACHER, DIANE HAINS, psychiatric social worker; b. Baton Rouge, June 9, 1941; d. James Hubert and Frances (Gremillion) H.; m. Edward B. Fabacher, Jr., Feb. 9, 1963 (div. Feb. 1980); children: Edward B. III, Todd, Scott, Stacy, Julie. BS in Social Counseling, Our Lady of Holy Cross Coll., 1984; MSW, Tulane U., 1984. Outpatient and inpatient therapist, social worker Greenbriar Hosp., Covington, La., 1986—; dir. YWCA Parent Aide Program, New Orleans, 1985-86; pvt. practice Covington, 1988—. Mem. Nat. Assn. Social Workers, Northshore Social Workers Assn., La. Soc. Clin. Social Workers, Nat. Assn. Female Execs., NOW. Republican. Office: Greenbriar Hosp 204 W 15th Ave Covington LA 70433

FABARES, SHELLEY, actress; b. Santa Monica, Calif., Jan. 19, 1944; d. James Fabares; m. Mike Farrell, Dec. 1984; stepchildren: Mike, Erin. Began career as child model and actress; earned gold record for 1962 single Johnny Angel; early TV work includes adaptation of Our Town, Matinee Theatre, Playhouse 90; regular cast member The Donna Reed Show, 1958-63; appeared in TV movie Brian's Song, 1971, ABC, (other TV movies) Memorial Day, Run Till You Fall, Deadly Relations, 1993, ABC; other TV work includes (series) The Practice, The Little People, Forever Fernwood; co-star for five years One Day At A Time, CBS; co-star Coach, ABC, 1989— (Emmy nomination, Supporting Actress - Comedy, 1993, 94); (films) Never Say Goodbye, Rock Pretty Baby, Marjorie Morningstar, Summer Love, A Time to Sing, Hot Pursuit, Love or Money, Ride the Wild Surf, Hold On, Clambake, Spinout, Girl Happy. *

FABRICANT, GWEN, painter; b. Bklyn., Aug. 29, 1932; d. Max and Sarah (Genser) Offen; m. Donald Paul Fabricant, Dec. 28, 1952 (div. Oct. 1961); 1 child, Jonathan. BA cum laude, Bklyn. Coll., 1955. Faculty mem. Franconia (N.H.) Coll., 1977-78, Pacific N.W. Coll. Art, Portland, 1979-84, Smith Coll., Northampton, Mass., 1986-90, Bates Coll., Lewiston, Maine, 1990-91, Coe Coll., Cedar Rapids, Iowa, 1993, Md. Inst. Coll. Art, Balt., 1993-94, 96—, U. Hartford, Hartford Art Sch., West Hartford, Conn., 1995-96; vis. artist SUNY, Purchase, 1984, Vt. Coll., Montpelier, 1992, Ill. State U., Normal, 1994, Dartmouth Coll., Hanover, N.H., 1994. Exhbns. include Gruenebaum Gallery, 1977, 78, Portland Ctr. for Visual Arts, 1980, Blackfish Gallery, 1983, Orgn. Ind. Artists, 1984, Am. Acad., 1988, The Painting Ctr., 1996; costume designer The Open Theatre, N.Y.C., 1963-73. Yaddo Vincent Visual Artist grantee, 1986, Pollock-Krasner Found. grantee, 1986, Joan Mitchell Found. grantee, 1994, Elizabeth Foun. for Arts grantee, 1996; MacDowell Colony fellow, 1992. Mem. N.Y. Mycological Soc., The Painting Ctr. Jewish. Home: 463 West St D604 New York NY 10014

FABRICANT, MONA, mathematics and computer science educator; b. N.Y.C., Apr. 22, 1946. BA, Queens Coll., N.Y.C., 1966; MA, Queens Coll., 1967; EdD, Rutgers U., 1974. Editor Harcourt Brace Jovanovich, N.Y.C., 1970-72; asst. prof. math. LaGuardia C.C., Long Island City, N.Y., 1972-74; freelance author and editor, 1974-82; asst. prof. dept. math. and computer sci. Queensborough C.C., Bayside, N.Y., 1982-87, assoc. prof., 1987-90; prof. Queensborough C.C., Bayside, 1990—, chair dept. math. and computer sci., 1993—. Author: Algebra 2 with Trigonometry, 1990, Advanced Mathematics: A Precalculus Approach, 1993 (TAA Excellence award 1994); author articles. Mem. Nat. Coun. Tchrs. Math., N.Y. State Math. Assn. Two-Yr. Colls. (award for outstanding contbns. to math. edn. 1992), Math. Assn. Am. (vice chair for two-yr. colls. N.Y. Met. Region 1987-89), Phi Beta Kappa, Kappa Delta Pi. Office: Queensborough CC 56th Ave & Springfield Blvd Bayside NY 11364

FABRICK, OLGA, lawyer; b. Havana, Cuba, Dec. 14, 1949; came to U.S., 1960; d. Morris Kantoras and Sara Hochberg; m. Martin N. Fabrick, Sept. 12, 1970; children: Tess Sharie, Laura Michelle. BA, U. Calif., Davis, 1972; MS, Cal. State U., Fullerton, 1982; JD, LaVerne Coll. Law, 1988. Tchr. L.A.U.S.D., 1974-77; resource tchr. R.U.S.D., Rowland Heights, Calif., 1978-83; adminstr. O.M.U.S.D., Ontario, Calif., 1983-84; atty. pvt. practice, Upland, Calif., 1989—; pres. East West Family Law Coun., Claremont, Calif., 1994-96; minor's coun. L.A. County Superior Ct., 1992—, San Bernardino County Superior Ct., 1992-94. Chair, bd. dirs. pers. commn. Temple Beth Israel, Pomona, Calif., 1994-96. Recipient Boss of Yr. award Ontario Inland Valley Legal Sec. Assn., 1994. Mem. Phi Beta Kappa, Phi Kappa Phi. Democrat. Jewish. Office: Law Office Olga Fabrick 409B Central Ave Upland CA 91786

FACCIANO, PAULINE ROSE, publicist; b. Burbank, Calif., Aug. 31, 1959; d. Joseph John and Blanca Rosa (Portuguez) F. AB in English Lit., AB in Studio Art, U. Calif., Berkeley, 1985; MA in English Lit., Mills Coll., Oakland, Calif., 1994. Fellow Nat. Endowment for Arts, Washington, 1987; asst. dir. devel. Oakland Mus. Assn., 1988, dir. membership campaigns, 1988-89; dir. devel. and pub. rels. Internat. Visitors Ctr., San Francisco, 1990-91; dir. devel. and mktg. Planned Parenthood, Sunnyvale, Calif., 1991-92; freelance book publicist mktg. and spl. events, 1994—. Mem. No. Calif. Book Publicity and Mktg. Assn. Democrat.

FACKLER, NANCY GRAY, nursing administrator, military officer; b. Norfolk, Va., Jan. 24, 1941; d. Albert Edward and Rita Marie (Murray) Gray; m. Martin L. Fackler, Sept. 29, 1964. BSN, Fla. State U., 1962; postgrad., San Francisco State U., 1988, Golden Gate U., 1989-91; M of Adminstrn. and Health Svcs. Mgmt., Golden Gate U., 1991; postgrad., U. Fla., 1993-94. RN, Fla.; cert. gerontology; lic. pvt. and comml. pilot. Commd. ensign USNR, 1962, advanced through grades to rear adm. Nurses Corps, 1994; nurse Chelsea Naval Hosp., Boston, Yokosuka (Japan) Naval Hosp.; with N.W. Region, mem. navy med. command NW region policy bd. USNR, Oakland, Calif., 1986-89; readiness command nurse USNR, San Francisco, 1989-91; DON Univ. Nursing Care Ctr., Gainesville, Fla.; dep. dir. Navy Nurse Corps, 1995—; originator res. same day surgery program Naval Hosp. Jacksonville and Naval Hosp. Oakland. Mem. Sec. of Navy Nat. Navy Res. Policy Bd.; active Alachua County Health Coalition. Mem. ANA, Nat. Naval Res. (policy bd.), Nat. Gerontol. Nursing Assn., Naval Res. Assn., Am. Tennis Assn., Fla. Tennis Assn. Home: RR 4 Box 264 Hawthorne FL 32640-8043

FADER, SHIRLEY SLOAN, writer; b. Paterson, N.J.; d. Samuel Louis and Miriam (Marcus) Sloan; m. Seymour J. Fader; children: Susan Deborah, Steven Micah Kimchi. BS, MS, U. Pa. Writer, journalist, author Paramus, N.J., 1956—; chmn., coord. ann. writers seminar Bergen C.C., 1973-76. Author: (books) The Princess Who Grew Down, 1968, From Kitchen to Career, 1977, Jobmanship, 1978, Successfully Ever After, 1982 (Brit. edit. 1985), Wait a Minute: You Can Have It All, 1993, paperback edit., 1994; (columns) Jobmanship, People and You, Family Weekly mag., 1971-82, How to Get More From Your Job, Glamour mag., 1978-81, Start Here, Working Woman mag., 1980-88, Work Strategies, Working Mother mag., 1987-88, Women Getting Ahead, Ladies Home Jour., 1980-90, How Would You Handle It, New Idea mag., 1984—, Moving Up, Woman mag., 1989-90, Career Expert "Ask the Experts", Woman's World mag., 1992—; contbg. editor Family Weekly, 1971-82, Glamour mag., 1978-81, Working Woman mag., 1980-88, Working Mother mag., 1987-88, Ladies Home Jour., 1980-90, Woman mag., 1989-90; contbr. articles to mags. worldwide. Mem. Authors Guild, Am. Soc. Journalists and Authors (chmn.-moderator ann. writer's conf. 1971-96, nat. v.p. 1976-77, mem.-at-large nat. exec. coun. 1976-78, 83-86, nat. sec., mem. exec. coun. 1995-96), Nat. Press Club. Address: 377 Mckinley Blvd Paramus NJ 07652-4725

FADLEY, ANN MILLER, English language and literature educator, writer; b. Ft. Worden, Wash., Nov. 22, 1933; d. Albert Delmar and Helen Elizabeth (Bush) Miller; m. Mit Rowley White, June 19, 1953 (div. Apr. 1977); children: Don M., Sharon L. White Patterson, Barbara A. White Salzman, Brian A.; m. John Lewis Fadley, Oct. 13, 1979 (dec. Jan., 1996). Student, Denison U., 1951-53; BA cum laude, Ohio State U., 1974, MA, 1976, PhD, 1986. Lectr. Ohio State U., Columbus, 1981-84; instr. Ohio Dominican Coll., Columbus, 1984-87; asst. prof. English Marshall U., Huntington, W.Va., 1987-88, Fla. So. Coll., Lakeland, 1988—; adj. prof. Ohio U., Ironton, 1988; panelist pub. TV, Columbus, 1985; chmn. Nat. Poetry Day, 1991—; chmn. vis. creative writers Fla. So. Coll., Lakeland, 1994—. Author: (fiction and poetry) Onionhead, 1989, 95, (poetry) Birmingham Poetry Review, 1992, Heartbeat, 1994, also articles and lit. criticisms; asst. editor Ohio Jour., 1975-76; founder, editor Cantilever Jours., 1989-96. Organizer, pres. Tri-Village Jr. C. of C. Wives Club, Columbus, 1959-60; past awards chmn. Young Musician's competition; chair Ruth Flower Brown Scholarship, Huntington, 1988; contest supr., mem. com. SCORE, 1988; judge VFW Voice of Democracy contest, Lakeland, 1990, 91, Fla. state judge, 1992; trustee Christ United Meth. Ch., Lakeland, 1991—, sec. trustees, 1991-93, 95; mem. bldg. com., organ fund task force, 1993-94; judge short fiction contest Nat. League Am. Pen Women Fla. State Assn. 1995; judge creative writing Polk County Citrus Festival, 1993. Recipient Merit award Fla. Poets Competition, WORDART Soc., 1990, 96, Distinction award, 1991, hon mention for poems; recipient hon. mention Nat. League Am. Pen Women, Lakeland, 1993, 94; grantee Fla. Endowment for Humanities, 1991, award hanging poetry Arts in the Park, Lakeland, 1993, 94, hanging poetry display Lake Morton Libr., 1994. Mem. MLA, South Atlantic MLA, Southeastern Renaissance Conf., Renaissance Soc. Am., Nat. Coun. Tchrs. English (chair session 1990), Fla. State Poets Assn. (head Lakeland workshop 1991, 92), Popular Culture Assn. (chair session 1992), Delta Delta Delta. Republican. Office: Fla So Coll Dept English 111 Lake Hollingsworth Dr Lakeland FL 33801-5607

FAETH, JANICE KAYE, office manager; b. Denver, June 22, 1944; d. Clayton Harold and Betty Jane Floyd; children: Jennifer L., Jeffrey A. Office mgr. Ram Pattisapu, M.D., Irving, Tex., 1989—; sec./treas. Indus Aviation, Inc., Irving, Tex., 1994—.

FAGAN, ELLEN HACKL, artist; b. Morristown, N.J., June 13, 1960; d. Albert James and Christine Frances (Magruder) Hackl; m. Brendan Michael Fagan, Aug. 9, 1986; children: Christopher, Andrew, Thomas. BFA in Painting and Photography, St. mary's Coll., 1982. Artist Conn., 1982—; sales reps. Nystrom Co., Conn., 1983-89; art instr. Meriden (Conn.) Pub. Schs., 1994-95; lectr. Related to Exhbn., 1993—, curator various exhbn., 1991—. Recipient various awards for art. Mem. Arts & Crafts Assn. of Meriden, Women's Caucus For Art, Meriden Arts Coun., Women Mag., Paint & Clay Club. Roman Catholic. Home: 411 Weekeepeemee Rd Woodbury CT 06798

FAGBAYI, PATRICIA ANN, small business owner; b. Eleuthera, Bahamas, Dec. 31, 1955; came to U.S., 1974; d. Audley and Rachel (Martin) Russell; m. Mutiu O. Fagbayi, Dec. 31, 1977; children: Jumoke, Yinka. BSChemE, U. Dayton, 1977; MSChemE, U. Rochester, 1982. Product engr. Xerox Corp., Rochester, N.Y., 1977-82; product engr. Eastman Kodak Co., Rochester, 1982-90, supr., 1990-93; pres. The Russell Group, Rochester, 1993-95; pres., founder Bliss Unltd., Inc., Rochester, 1995-96; pres., bd. dirs. Network North Star, Inc., Rochester, 1990-93. Bd. dirs. Women's Forum of Kodak, Rochester, 1992-93. Nominee Pres. Bush's Vol.-Action award Adopt-A-Sch. Program, 1990, nominee Athena award Promoting Women in Bus., 1994; featured in mag. On Achieving Excellence, 1995. Mem. Nat. Orgn. Black Chemists and Chem. Engrs. (bd. dirs. 1990-91), Rochester Assn. UN (bd. dirs., v.p. 1994-95), Rochester Women's Network, Rochester C. of C. Home: 15 Old Westfall Dr Rochester NY 14625

FAGERSTEN, BARBARA JEANNE, special education educator; b. San Francisco, Feb. 29, 1924; d. Ernest Mauritz and Louise (Hopkins) F.; m. Harold Gurish, Feb. 7, 1950 (div. 1970); children: Michael, Matthew, Jonathon. BA, San Francisco State U., 1951; MS, Dominican U., 1973, degree in spl. edn., 1975; degree in adminstrn. and supervision, 1976, degree in community coll. instruction, 1981. Personnel sec. Arabian Am. Oil Co., San Francisco, 1944-45; union sec. Jeweler's Union, San Francisco, 1946-48; med. sec. Mt. Zion Hosp., San Francisco, 1949-50; spl. edn. tchr. Marin Office Edn., San Rafael, Calif., 1967-92; bd. dirs. DeWitt Learning Ctr., San Rafael, 1969. Bd. dirs. Marin Tchrs. Credit Union, San Rafael, 1978-93, Marinwood Cmty. Svcs., San Rafael, 1986-87; commr. Parks and Recreation Marinwood, San Rafael, 1983-86. Mem. Calif. Assn. Neurol. Handicapped Children (trustee 1973-74). Democrat. Home: 272 Blackstone Dr San Rafael CA 94903-1508

FAGIN, CLAIRE MINTZER, nursing educator, administrator; b. N.Y.C.; d. Harry and Mae (Slatin) Mintzer; m. Samuel Fagin, Feb. 17, 1952; children: Joshua, Charles. BS, Wagner Coll., 1948; MA, Tchrs. Coll. Columbia, 1951; PhD, N.Y. U., 1964; DSc (hon.), Lycoming Coll., 1983, Cedar Crest Coll., 1987, U. Rochester, 1987, Med. Coll. Pa., 1989, U. Md., 1993, Wagner Coll., 1993, Loyola U., 1996; DHL, Hunter Coll., 1993; LLD (hon.), U. Pa., 1994. Staff nurse, clin. instr. Sea View Hosp., S.I., N.Y.; clin. instr. Bellevue Hosp., N.Y.C.; psychiat. nurse cons. Nat. League for Nursing, N.Y.C.; asst. chief psychiat. nursing svc. clin. ctr. NIH; rsch. project coord. dept. psychiatry Children's Hosp., Washington; instr., assoc. prof. psychiat.-mental health nursing NYU, N.Y.C., dir. grad. programs in psychiat. mental health nursing, 1965-69; chmn. nursing dept., prof. Herbert H. Lehman Coll., CUNY, N.Y.C., 1969-77; dir. Health Professions Inst., Montefiore Hosp. and Med. Ctr., 1975-77; Margaret Bond Simon dean sch. of nursing U. Pa., Phila., 1977-92, Leadership chair prof., 1992-96, interim pres., 1993-94, dean emeritus, prof. emeritus, 1996—; cons. in health care and orgnl. leadership to state, nat. and internat. coms. and profl. bds.; dir. Provident Mut. Ins. Co., mem. audit com., 1978—, chmn., 1985—, mem. exec. com., 1986—; dir. Salomon Inc., 1994—; mem. audit com. CMAC, 1994—; mem. compensation com., investment com., cons. to many pub. and pvt. univs. and health care agys.; spkr. at profl. confs., on radio and TV. Contbr. articles to profl. publs. Recipient Achievement award Wagner Coll., 1956, Achievement award Tchrs. Coll., 1975, Disting. Alumna award NYU, 1979, Founders award Sigma Theta Tau, 1981, Hon. Recognition award ANA, 1988, Woman of Courage award Womens Way, 1990, Alumni Merit award U. Pa., 1991, Trustee Coun. Pa. Women First Leadership award, 1991, Caring award Vis. Nurses Assn., 1992—, Hildegard Peplau award outstanding contbn. psych-nursing, 1994; Am. Nurses Found. Disting. scholar, 1984, Disting. Dau. Pa., 1994. Mem. Inst. Medicine of NAS (governing coun. 1981-83, chmn. bd. health promotion and disease prevention 1991-94), Am. Acad. Nursing (governing coun. 1976-78), Am. Orthopsychiat. Assn. (bd. dirs. 1972-75, exec. com. bd. dirs. 1973-75, pres. 1985-86), Nat. League for Nursing (pres. 1991-93).

FAGUNDO, ANA MARIA, creative writing and Spanish literature educator; b. Santa Cruz de Tenerife, Spain, Mar. 13, 1938; came to U.S., 1958; d. Ramón Fagundo and Candelaria Guerra de Fagundo. BA in English and Spanish, U. Redlands, 1962; MA in Spanish, U. Wash., 1964, PhD in Comparative Lit., 1967. Prof. contemporary lit. of Spain and creative writing U. Calif., Riverside, 1967—; vis. lectr. Occidental Coll., Calif., 1967; vis. prof. Stanford U., 1984. Author 9 books of poetry including Invention de la Luz, 1977 (Carbala de Oro Poetry prize Barcelona 1977), Obra Poetica: 1965-90, 1990, Isla En Si., 1992, Antologia, 1994, La Miriada de Los Sonambulos, 1994; founder, editor Alaluz, 1969—. Grantee Creative Arts Inst., 1970-71, Humanities Inst., 1973-74; Summer faculty fellow U. Calif., 1968, 77; Humanities fellow, 1969. Mem. Am. Assn. Tchrs. Spanish and Portuguese, Sociedad Gen. de Autores de Espana. Roman Catholic. Home: 5110 Caldera Ct Riverside CA 92507-6002 Office: U Calif Spanish Dept Riverside CA 92521

FAHEY-WIDMAN, ANN MARIE, public relations executive; b. Suffield, Conn., Aug. 4, 1969; d. John Joseph Sr. and Kathleen Eleanor (Carroll) Fahey; m. Matthew Michael Widman, Sept. 2, 1995. BS, U. Fla., 1991; MBA, Fla. Atlantic U., 1996. Cmty. rels. asst. Shands Hosp., Gainesville, Fla., 1990, pub. rels. asst., 1990-91; pub. rels. coord. Women's Tennis Assn., St. Petersburg, Fla., 1991-92; dir. comms. Palm Glades Girl Scout Coun., Lake Worth, Fla., 1994—. Dir. devel. Am. Lung Assn. Southeast Fla. Recipient Rising Star award Women in Comm. in Palm Beach County, 1994-95, Nat. Clarion award Women in Comms., 1996; Fla. Pub. Rels. Assn. scholarship. Mem. NAFE, Pub. Rels. Soc. Am. (bd. dirs., conf. steering com.), Women in Comms., Inc., Internat. Assn. of Bus. Communicators, Fla. Pub. Rels. Assn., Lambda Chi Alpha (pres.), Pi Rho Sigma (pres.), Alpha Lambda Delta (pres.). Home: 1397 Fairfox Cir E Boynton Beach FL 33462 Office: 2701 N Australian Ave West Palm Beach FL 33407

FAHLBERG, SHEREE LYNN, special education educator; b. Moline, Ill., July 31, 1955; d. Richard Paul and Shirley Rae (Anderson) Rosenberg; m. Mark Randolph Fahlberg, Oct. 11, 1975; children: Zach, Todd. AA, Black Hawk Coll., 1975; BS, So. Ill. U., 1978. Cert. K-12 tchr., Ill. Phys. edn. tchr., coach Egyptian Unit Sch., Tamms, Ill., 1980; substitute tchr. various schs., Ill., 1978-84; adaptive phys. edn. tchr., coach Tri-County Edn. Ctr., Anna, Ill., 1985-87; tchr. learning disabilities resource, phys. edn., coach Anna-Jonesboro Cmty. H.S., 1988-92; 7-8th grade learning disabilities tchr. Cairo (Ill.) Jr. H.S., 1992-93; spl. edn. tchr. Goreville (Ill.) Unit Sch., 1993-94, Carbondale (Ill.) Cmty. H.S., 1994—; phys. edn., health, spl. edn. tchr., coach Anna Jr. H.S., 1983-84; GED instr. Shawnee Cmty. Coll., Ullin, Ill., 1984-87; cons. adaptive phys. edn. rehab. svcs. Alton (Ill.) Mental Health and Devel. Ctr., 1987. Assst. cub scout master Boy Scouts Am., Anna, 1991-92. Mem. Phi Theta Kappa. Home: 4185 Boyd Rd Anna IL 62906

FAHNESTOCK, JEAN HOWE, retired civil engineer; b. Pitts., May 22, 1930; d. James Murray and Hazel Margaret (Alberts) F. AA, Stephens, 1950; BS in Civil Engring., Carnegie-Mellon, 1955. Registered profl. engr., Ill., Mich., Iowa. Sr. project mgr. De Leuw, Cather & Co., Chgo., 1955-92; design mgr. De Leuw, Cather & Co., Kuwait, 1978-81, Abu Dhabi, 1981-85, Kennedy Expy. and Elgin-O'Hare Expy., Chgo., 1985-92. Recipient Outstanding Performance award De Leuw, Cather & Co., 1981. Fellow ASCE (life); mem. NSPE, Ill. Soc. Profl. Engrs. (life). Republican. Presbyterian. Home: 4606 W Bryn Mawr Ave Chicago IL 60646-6632

FAHR, LINDA MEYERS, radiologist, educator; b. N.Y.C., Sept. 20, 1942; d. Paul Tabor and Jessie V. (Jones) Meyers; B.A., Barnard Coll., 1964; M.D., U. Iowa, 1968; m. James Dwight Watson, Mar. 29, 1980; children—John Pearson Fahr, Bruce Tabor Fahr. Resident in radiology U. Iowa, Iowa City, 1971-74; staff radiologist VA Hosp., Houston, 1974-77, chief dept. radiology, 1977-79; chief radiologist MacGregor Med. Assocs., Houston, 1980-84, Loma Linda Radiology Group Inc., 1984—, asst. prof. Loma Linda (Calif.) U. Med. Ctr., 1987—; clin. asst. prof. Baylor Coll. Medicine, Houston, 1974-79. Mem. AMA, Am. Assn. Women Radiologists (pres. 1983, past pres. 1984), Am. Coll. Radiology, Radiol. Soc. N.Am., Tex. Radiol. Soc., Houston Barnard Club. Office: Baylor Coll Medicine One Baylor Plz Houston TX 77030

FAHRINGER, CATHERINE HEWSON, retired savings and loan association executive; b. Phila., Aug. 1, 1922; d. George Francis and Catherine Gertrude (Magee) Hewson; grad. diploma Inst. Fin. Edn., 1965; m. Edward F. Fahringer, July 8, 1961 (dec.); 1 child Francis George Beckett. With Centrust Bank (formerly Dade Savs. and Loan Assn.), Miami, 1958-85, v.p., 1967-74, sr. v.p., 1974-82, sec., 1975-79, head savs. personnel and mktg. div.,

1979-83, exec. v.p. office of chmn., 1984, dir., 1984-90, co-chmn. audit com. of bd. dirs., 1990; referral assoc. Referral Network Inc., subs. Coldwell Banker, 1990—. Trustee United Way of Dade County (Fla.) 1980-87, chmn. audit com. 1982-84; trustee Pub. Health Trust, Dade County, 1974-84, sec. 1976, vice chmn., 1977-78, chmn. bd., 1978-81; mem. adv. coun. Womens' Bus. Devel. Ctr., Fla. Internat. U., 1993-95; mem. spl. steering com. Breast Cancer Task Force, Jackson Meml. Hosp., 1991; hon. bd. govs. U. Miami, Soc. for Rsch. in Med. Edn.; trustee South Fla. Blood Svc., Miami, 1979-84, vice chmn., 1980, chmn., 1981-84; trustee Dade County Vocat. Found., 1977-81; trustee Fla. Internat. U. Found., 1976-90, trustee emeritus, 1990, v.p. bd., 1978-81, pres., 1982-84; bd. dirs. Sta. WPBT-TV, 1984—, founding lifetime dir. 1995, chmn. budget and fin com., 1986, mem. exec. com. 1985-92, sec. 1987, investment com., 1988-90, vice chmn. 1988-92, mem. fin. com., 1992, chmn. audit and control com., 1994; bd. dirs., mem. nominating com. Girl Scout Coun. Tropical Fla., 1985-89, chmn. 1988-89, mem. long range planning com., 1986-88; citizens oversight com. Dade County Pub. Sch. System, 1986-90, chmn. 1988-90; bd. dirs. New World Sch. of Arts, 1987-90, chmn. devel. com., 1987-90, mem. New World Sch. of Arts Found., 1989-90, chair New World Sch. of Arts Gala, 1990; mem. Disaster Relief Com., chair Hurricane Disaster Relief Distrbn. Ctr., 1992; mem. fin. commn., chmn. capital improvement fund com. Coral Gables Congrl. Ch., commd. Stephen min., 1995—; mem. grievance com. 11th Jud. Cir. Fla. Bar, 1988-92; bd. trustees United Protestant Appeal, 1994-96. Named Woman of Yr. in fin. Zonta Internat., 1975, amb. Air Def. Arty., U.S. Army Air Def. Command, 1970, Woman of Yr. in Sports, Links Club, 1986; recipient Trail Blazer award Women's Coun. of 100, 1977, Community Headliner award Women in Communication, 1983, Outstanding Citizen of Dade County award, 1984, Honors and Recognition award Golden Panthers Club of Fla. Internat. U., 1989, Disting. Svc. and Leadership award Fla. Internat. U., 1990, Woman of Yr. award Fla. Internat. U., 1991, appreciation New World Sch. of the Arts, 1990, Meritorious Pub. Svc. award Fla. Bar, 1991; hon. BA U. Hard Knocks Alderson-Broaddus Coll., 1987. Mem. Dade Bus. and Profl. Women's Club (past pres., Woman of Yr. 1974), LWV, Inst. Fin. Edn. (life, nat. dir., past pres. Local Greater Miami chpt.), Savs. and Loan Mktg. Soc. South Fla. (past pres.), Savs. and Loan Pers. Soc. South Fla., Internat. Women's Alliance, Fla. Women's Alliance (bd. dirs. 1983-91, pres. 1987-89), Women's Union of Russia (conf. del. 1992), Coral Gables Country Club (treas. women's golf assn. 1988-89, sec., bd. dirs. 1993, found. trustee 1993, v.p. bd. dir. 1994, pres. 1995, bd. advisor 1996), Links Fla. Internat. U. Club (bd. dirs., sec., v.p. 1992), Greenway Women's Golf Assn. (treas. 1988-89), Biltmore Women's Golf Assn., Greater Miami Women's Golf Assn., Golden Panther Club (bd. dirs. 1988—, v.p. 1991, pres. 1992-94), Fla. Internat. U. Athletics Club. Democrat. Contbr. articles to profl. jours.

FAHY, NANCY LEE, food products marketing executive; b. Schenectady, N.Y., Aug. 15, 1946; d. Christopher Mark and Frances (Lee) F.; m. Steven Neil Wohl, June 8, 1945 (div. Apr. 1978). BS cum laude, Miami (Ohio) U., 1968. Educator Palatine (Ill.) Pub. Schs., 1968-70, Glencoe (Ill.) Pub. Schs., 1970-78; sales rep. Keebler Co., Elmhurst, Ill., 1978-80, dist. mgr., 1980-82, account mgr., 1982-83, zone mgr., 1983-85, account mgr., 1985-89; regional mktg. mgr. Keebler Co., Morrow, Ga., 1989—. Vol. Lincoln Park Zool. Soc., Chgo., 1975-78. Mem. Food Products Club, Merchandising Execs. Club (bd. dirs. 1984-85), Grocery Mfgs. Sales Execs. Club (bd. dirs. 1984-85, asst. sec. 1987, treas. 1988, 1st v.p. 1989), Phi Beta Kappa. Office: Keebler Co 1135 Commerce Rd Morrow GA 30260-2913

FAIGEN, SUSAN LEE, business owner, sales and marketing professional; b. Pitts., May 20, 1954; d. Mark R. and Anne (Gussin) F. BA, U. Pa., 1976. Mgr. advt. and comm. Jessop Steel Co., Washington, Pa., 1978-81; acct. supr. Burson-Marstller, Pitts., 1981-87; v.p./ptnr. Allegro Graphics, Pitts., 1987-90; mgr. bus. devel. Burt Hill Kosar Rittelman Assoc., Pitts., 1990-91; dir. mktg. The Design Alliance Archs., Pitts., 1991-95; pres./owner Diversityworks, Pitts., 1995—; bd. dirs. Soc. for Mktg. Profl. Svcs., Pitts. Adv. bd. New Choices/New Options Program, Carlow Coll., Pitts.; mem. Mt. Washington Cmty. Devel. Coun., Pitts., 1993—. Mem. Nat. Assn. Women in Constrn., Pitts. Women in Comml. Real Estate (bd. dirs.). Office: Diversityworks 447 Sulgrave Rd Pittsburgh PA 15211

FAIN, CHERYL ANN, translator, editor; b. Providence, May 16, 1953; d. Harry and Pearl (Friedman) F. Student, U. Salzburg, Austria, 1973-74; BA with high distinction, U. R.I., 1975; MA, Monterey Inst. Internat. Studies, 1978, post graduate cert in translation English-German, 1978. Freelance German translator various govt. agys., burs., record co., others, Balt. and Monterey, Calif., 1976—; in-house German and French med. translator Social Security Adminstrn., Balt., 1984-94; German/French translator, asst. to counselor sci. and tech. Embassy of Switzerland, Washington, 1994—; mem. Swiss delegation to the European Space Agy. Internat. Space Sta. Working Group, Washington, D.C. Translator: Perspectives on Mozart, 1978, also various articles and liner notes. Mem. Am. Translators Assn. (accredited for translation from German-English, French-English), Phi Kappa Phi. Home: 2401 Calvert St NW Apt 421 Washington DC 20008-2646 Office: Embassy of Switzerland 2900 Cathedral Ave NW Washington DC 20008-3499

FAIN, KAREN KELLOGG, retired history and geography educator; b. Pueblo, Colo., Oct. 10, 1940; d. Howard Davis and Mary Lucille (Cole) Kellogg; m. Sept. 1, 1961; divorced; 1 child, Kristopher. Student, U. Ariz., 1958-61; BA, U. So. Colo., 1967; MA, U. No. Colo., 1977; postgrad., U. Denver, 1968, 72-93, Colo. State U., 1975, 91, U. No. Ill., 1977, 83, Ft. Hayes State Coll., 1979, U. Colo., 1979, 86-87, 92, Ind. U., 1988. Cert. secondary tchr., Colo. Tchr. history and geography Denver Pub. Schs., 1967-96; tchr. West H.S., Denver, 1992-96; area adminstr., tchr. coord. Close Up program, Washington, 1982-84; reviewer, cons. for book Geography, Our Changing World, 1990. Vol., chmn. young profls. Inst. Internat. Edn. and World Affairs Coun., Denver, 1980—; mem. state selection com. U.S. Senate and Japan Scholarship Com., Denver, 1981-89, Youth for Understanding, Denver; mem. Denver Art Mus., 1970—; vol. Denver Mus. Natural History, 1989—; bd. overseas Dept. Def. Dependents Sch., Guantanamo Bay, Cuba, 1990-91. Fulbright scholar Chadron State Coll., Pakistan, 1975; Geog. Soc. grantee U. Colo., 1986; recipient award for Project Prince, Colo. U./Denver Pub. Schs./Denver Police Dept., 1992. Mem. AAUW, Colo. Coun. Social Studies (sec. 1984-86), Nat. Coun. Social Studies (del. 1984), World History Assn., Fulbright Assn., Am. Forum for Global Edn., Rocky Mountain Regional World History Assn. (steering com. 1984-87), Colo. Geographic Alliance (steering com. 1986), Gamma Phi Beta, Kappa Kappa Iota. Democrat. Episcopalian. Home: 12643 E Bates Cir Aurora CO 80014-3315 Office: West High Sch 951 Elati St Denver CO 80204-3939

FAIN, KATHLEEN ANN, speech-language pathologist; b. Tyler, Tex., Aug. 7, 1953; d. Stanley N. Swift and Anne Gwendoline (Gale) Lennon; m. Gary Donald Fain, Jr., June 2, 1974; children: Jesse, Alison, Micah, Lacy, Caitlin. BSEd, Stephen F. Austin State U., 1974, MEd, 1991. Cert. speech-lang.-hearing profl. Speech therapist Vaughn Meml. Speech and Hearing Clinic, Tyler, 1975-76, Tyler Ind. Sch. Dist., 1976-78; speech pathologist Troup, Winona, Arp Spl. Edn. Co-op, Arp, Tex., 1988—; recording sec. East Tex. Speech and Hearing Assn., Tyler, 1990-92. Mem. East Tex. Speech and Hearing Assn., Tex. Speech and Hearing Assn., Am. Speech and Hearing Assn. Home: 19295 Jo Bar Dr Tyler TX 75703-9005 Office: Troup Winona Arp Spl Edn Co-op PO Drawer 70 Arp TX 75750

FAIR, ANNIE MAY, geological computer specialist; b. Coolidge, Ariz., Sept. 21, 1939; d. Jack C. and Birdie Geneva (Strickland) Cullins; m. Charles Leroy Fair, Sept. 12, 1964; children: Rex Lee Myers, Kathleen Ann, Rebecca Elizabeth. Student, Wichita State U., 1979-81, U. Colo., 1982-84, 94—, Met. State U., Denver, 1983-84. Cert. geol. engr. Pres., bd. dirs. Fresnal Minerals, Inc., Tucson, 1975-80; geol. technician Foxfire Exploration, Inc., Wichita, Kans., 1980-81, Coastal Oil & Gas Corp., Denver, 1981-93; stat. analyst fluid minerals Bur. Land Mgmt., Canon City, Colo., 1993—; geol. cons. C.L. Fair & Assocs., Littleton, Colo., 1984-93. Active adv. bd. Masonic-Rainbow Girls-Grand Cross of Color, Denver, 1983-84; vol.- helper United Way Campaign, Denver, 1990, 91; vol. Am. Cancer Soc., Littleton, 1991, 92; art judge Reflections Nat. Art Contest, Denver, 1992, 93, Skyline Elem. Sch., Canon City, 1993. Recipient Grand Cross of Color, Masons-Order Rainbow/Girls, 1957; Music scholar U. No. Ariz., 1957. Mem. Am. Assn. Petroleum Geologists, Geol. Soc. Am., Rocky Mountain Assn. Geologists, Computer Oriented Geol. Soc., Alpha Lambda Delta. Home: 2853 Melvina Canon City CO 81212

FAIR, MARY LOUISE, retired elementary school educator; b. Emporia, Kans., July 16, 1931; d. Dale Franklin Fair and Beulah Fair (Emma) Martin. BA, Marymount Coll., 1953. Bus. edn. tchr. Geneseo (Kans.) High Sch., 1953-55, St. John (Kans.) High Sch., 1955-56; sec. YMCA, Salina, Kans., 1956-57; alumna sec. Marymount Coll., Salina, Kans., 1957-58; bus. edn. tchr. Hayden High Sch., Topeka, Kans., 1958-59; sec. Mental Health Assn., Denver, 1959-60; sec., substitute tchr. Denver Pub. Schs., 1960-62, elem. tchr., 1962-86. 1st v.p. AARP, Heather Gardens, Aurora, Colo., 1988-90, pres. 1991, parliamentarian 1994, publication com. 1994—, Heather Gardens Restaurant Comm., 1995—; tutor Aurora and Cherry Creek elem. schs., 1987—. Mem. AAUW (Aurora br., historian 1993-94), Marymount Coll. Alumnae Assn. (pres. 1956-58), Luncheon Optomist Club, Altrusa Club Aurora, Alpha Delta Kappa (state sgt.-at-arms 1982-84, state pres. 1986-88, S.W. regional sgt.-at-arms 1989-91, internat. chmn. living meml. scholarship com. 1991-93, chpt. pres. 1994-96, chpt. pres. coun. (pres. 1994-96). Republican. Baptist. Home: 3022 S Wheeling Way Apt 311 Aurora CO 80014-5607

FAIRBAIRN, URSULA FARRELL, human resources executive; b. Newark, Feb. 5, 1943; d. Henry C. and Clara J. (Ziefle) Otte; m. William Todd Fairbairn III, May 14, 1978; children: W. Todd, Mary. BA, Upsala Coll., 1965; MA in Teaching, Harvard U., 1966. Instr., numerous mktg. positions IBM, N.Y.C., 1966-78; exec. asst. to sec., White House fellow U.S. Treasury Dept., Washington, 1973-74; exec. asst. to chmn. bd., group dir. IBM, Armonk, N.Y., 1978-80, v.p. mgmt. svcs., then v.p. mktg. ops. west, 1980-84, dir. pers. resources, 1984-87, dir. bus. and mgmt. edn., 1987, dir. edn., 1987-89, dir. edn. and mgmt. devel., 1989-90; sr. v.p. human resources Union Pacific Corp., Bethlehem, Pa., 1990—; bd. dirs. Armstrong World Industries, Lancaster, Pa., VF Corp., Wyomissing, Pa., Gen. Signal Corp., Stamford, Conn. Contbg. author: Managing Human Resources in the Information Age, 1991. Mem. Com. of 200, Catalyst, N.Y.C.; bd. assocs. Muhlenberg Coll., Allentown, Pa., 1991—; bd. dirs. Historic Bethlehem (Pa.) Inc., Lehigh Valley Bus. Conf. on Health Care, Bethlehem, 1990—. Mem. Bus. Roundtable (chair exec. com. employee rels. com.), Labor Policy Assn. (bd. dirs., mem. exec. com.), Cowdrick Group. Office: Union Pacific Corp Martin Tower 8th and Eaton Ave Bethlehem PA 18018

FAIRBROTHER, FAY PULLEN, photographer, educator; b. New Orleans, Aug. 25, 1947; d. Edward Bryant Pullen and Lillian Marie (LeBlanc) Lawhorn; m. Albert C. Fairbrother III, July 11, 1970; children: Aimee Cherie, Albert C. IV. BA in Art History and Studio Mgmt., Okla. State U., 1991; MA in Art History, U. Okla., 1993, MFA in Photography, 1994. Cert. arbitrator Nat. BBB; cert. Laubach reading method. Paralegal City of Jacksonville, Fla., 1966-76; property mgr. South Shore Assn. Unit Owners, Tulsa, 1978-82; grad. asst U. Okla., Norman, 1993, vis. asst. prof. photography, 1994-95; photographer, Norman, 1996—; artist-in-residence Norman Arts and Humanities Coun., 1995-96; conf. presenter in field. Exhibited in group shows North Lake Coll., Irving, Tex., 1994, Fred Jones Jr. Mus. Art, Norman, 1994, Fred Jones Jr. Art Ctr., U. Okla., 1995, Sheerar Mus. Art, Stillwater, Okla., 1995, Oklahoma City Art Mus., 1994, Hill County Arts Found., Ingram, Tex., 1994, Atlanta Gallery Photography, 1992, Spectrum Gallery, Rochester,N.Y., 1993, Orange County Ctr. for Contemporary Art, L.A., 1993, CEPA Gallery, Buffalo, 1994, Smithsonian Instn., 1995—, SFA Gallery, Nacodoches, Tex., 1996; permanent collections include Smithsonian Instn.; contbr. photographs to profl. jours., mags. and newspapers. Okla. enrichment program scholar, 1990, 92, Med. Heritage and Goldston scholar, 1990-91, Alliance for Visual Arts scholar, 1991, scholar Greater Okla. Antique Dealers Assn., 1991, Barnett scholar, 1991-94, Okla. Fall Arts Inst. scholar, 1992-96. Mem. Soc. for Photog. Edn., Ctr. for Exploratory and Perceptual Art, Okla. Conf. Art Historians, Golden Key. Roman Catholic. Home and Studio: 720 DeBarr Apt 2 Norman OK 73069

FAIRBROTHER, KATHRYN LOUISE, customer relations executive; b. Inglewood, Calif., Jan. 8, 1957; d. Edward McCullough Fairbrother and Carolyn (Howe) Stevens. BA in English Lit., UCLA, 1979; MBA, Calif. State U., Dominguez Hills, 1994. Asst. dept. mgr. Broadway, Westchester, Calif., 1978-79; customer svc. rep. Grand Rent A Car subs. First Gray Line Corp., L.A., 1979-82, supr. customer svc., 1982-84, mgr. charter sales, 1984-87, security investigator, 1987-88; mgr. charter sales Gray Line Tours subs. First Gray Line Corp., L.A., 1984-87; sr. supr. customer rels. Toyota Motor Sales, USA, Inc., Torrance, Calif., 1988-95, customer assistance ctr. mgr., 1995—. Mem. AIDS project L.A. Mem. NAFE, Soc. Consumer Affairs Profls., Am. Mgmt. Assn., Delta Mu Delta. Democrat. Presbyterian. Home: 5301 Knowlton St Apt B Los Angeles CA 90045-2041

FAIRCHILD, SUSAN S., nursing educator, consultant; b. Chattanooga, May 26, 1943; d. Richard G. and Helene (Cahn) Strassburger; m. Stephen G. Fairchild, Aug. 12, 1975; children: Mark D., Gabriel S. ASN, Miami Dade C.C., 1970; BS in Edn., Fla. Internat. U., 1972, MS in Edn., 1982, BSN, 1984; MSN, Barry U., 1992; EdD, Nova-Southeastern U., 1996. RN, Fla. Staff nurse Mt. Sinai Med. Ctr., Miami Beach, Fla., 1970—, cardiovasc. perfusionist, 1972—; staff nurse surgery Jackson Meml. Hosp., Miami, 1972-75; nursing educator, clin. nurse specialist Meml. Hosp., Hollywood, Fla., 1980-85; nursing educator CNS-surgery Broward Gen. Med. Ctr., Ft. Lauderdale, Fla., 1985-89; asst. prof. nursing Barry U., Miami Shores, Fla., 1989—; perioperative nursing, exec. dir., sr. nursing educator, cons. Ednl. Design Sys., Inc., Hollywood, 1985—. Author: Perioperative Nursing—Principles and Practice, 1993, Comprehensive Review for Perioperative Nursing, 1995. Mem. ANA (cert. med.-surg. nurse), AACN (cert.), Assn. Oper. Rm. Nurses (cert.), Fla. Coun. Oper. Rm. Nurses, Pi Kappa Alpha, Sigma Theta Tau (Lamda Chi). Office: Barry U Sch Nursing Miami FL 33161

FAIRFAX, TIFFANY ALISHA, astrologer, writer; b. Stamford, Conn., May 20, 1947; m. John Fairfax, May 22, 1981. Student, Loyola U., Rome, Italy, 1967-68; BA, U. Dayton, 1969. Pvt. art investor, 1970-75; mgr. of Hermès I. Magnin, San Francisco, 1975-79; pvt. practice astrologer and writer Ft. Lauderdale, Fla., 1980-92, Las Vegas, Nev., 1993—. Astrologer, writer (mags.) The Mountain Astrologer, Jan. 1994, Am. Astrology, Oct. 1995, The Ascendant, Oct. 1995 (Goldy's Seal award for excellence in astrol. writing), (column) Las Vegas Mag., Jan. 1996—. Mem. Nat. Coun. for Geocosmic Rsch., Las Vegas Stargazers, Am. Fedn. Astrologers (area leader for Las Vegas 1993—), Inst. of Noetic Scis. Republican. Home: 3950 Koval Ln #3083 Las Vegas NV 89109

FAIRLEIGH, MARGARET HILLS, lawyer; b. Atlanta, Apr. 11, 1912; d. Albert Lymanand Georgia Belle (Burns) Hills; m. George DuRelle Fairleigh, June 29, 1951 (dec. June 1978); children: Kathryn Fairleigh Allen, Henrietta Fairleigh Sparacino. LLB, Woodrow Wilson Coll. Law, Atlanta, 1939. Bar: Ga. 1940, U.S. Dist. Ct. (no. dist.) Ga. 1942, U.S. Ct. Appeals (5th cir.) 1949, U.S. Supreme Ct. 1954, U.S. Ct. Appeals (11th cir.) 1981. Assoc. Poole, Pearce & Graham, Atlanta, 1942-51; ptnr. Poole, Pearce & Hall (Poole, Pearce & Cooper), Atlanta, 1951-71; pvt. practice Decatur, Ga., 1971—. Pres. Atlanta Legal Aid Soc., 1966; vice-chmn. DeKalb County Salary Study Commn. for Statutory Pub. Employees, 1969; mem. Gov.'s Commn. on Status of Women, 1968-70; mem. Atlanta Estate Planning Coun.; treas. DeKalb Estate Planning Coun. Mem. Ga. Assn. Women Lawyers (pres. 1947-48), Ga. State Bar Assn., DeKalb County Bar Assn., DeKalb C.of C. (bd. dirs. 1976-78). Democrat. Presbyterian. Office: PO Box 15097 Atlanta GA 30333

FAISON, DOROTHY ANNE RIES, fine artist; b. Schenectady, N.Y., Sept. 15, 1955; d. Al Ries and Lois Harger (Parker) F.; m. Stephen E. Meder, June 29, 1990; children: Pualana, Moreau, Emile. Student, U. Edinburgh, Scotland, 1974-76, Edinburgh Coll. Art, 1974-76; BFA in Painting, U. Hawaii, Manoa, 1977; MFA in Intermedia, Otis Art Inst., L.A., 1979. Solo shows include Otis Art Inst., L.A., 1979, Croissanterie Gallery, Honolulu, 1984, Gallery on Pali, Honolulu, 1988, Kapiolani Coll., Honolulu, 1988, Honolulu Acad. Arts, 1990, Contemporary Mus. First Biennial, Honolulu, 1993; group shows include Rabbet Gallery, New Brunswick, N.J., 1995, Honolulu Acad. Arts, 1981-82, 86-96; collections include Honolulu Acad. Arts, State Found. Culture and Arts, Persis Collection, City and County of Honolulu. NEA Regional fellow in painting Western States Arts Fedn., 1994, Individual Artist Merit fellow Hawaii State Found. on Culture and Arts, 1995; recipient Catherine Cox award for excellence in visual arts Honolulu Acad. Arts, 1990, Melusine award for painting, 1993. Studio: 328A Oneawa St Kailua HI 96734

FAISON, HOLLY, communications professional; b. Sherman, Tex., Aug. 11, 1953; d. Ronald Miller and Ann (LaRoe) F. BA, Tex. A&M U., 1976. Dispatcher College Station (Tex.) Police Dept., 1976-77; police communications operator Tex. Dept. Pub. Safety, Bryan, 1977-83; supr. police communications facility Tex. Dept. Pub. Safety, Austin, 1983-85, Victoria, 1985-87; supr. police communications facility Tex. Dept. Pub. Safety, Bryan, 1987-92, regional supr. police communications, 1993—; mem. Brazos County Emergency Mgmt./Civil Def. Coun., Bryan, 1987-92. Producer video tng. tapes. Mem. Associated Pub. Safety Comms. Officers, Exec. Women in Tex. Govt. (chair-elect Houston chpt. 1996). Methodist. Home: 5500 De Soto St Apt 903 Houston TX 77091-3646 Office: Tex Dept Pub Safety 10110 Northwest Fwy Houston TX 77092-8603

FAJGIER, JOAN ADELAIDE, retired English educator; b. Bilston, Eng., May 11, 1920; came to U.S., 1946; d. Walter and Ethel Adelaide (Houchin) Emery; m. Joseph John Fajgier, Nov. 18, 1943; children: Ann Marie, Charles Joseph. AA, Burlington County (N.J.) Coll., 1975; BA, Thomas Edison State Coll., Trenton, N.J., 1978. Cert. profl. tutor, 1978. Program asst. YWCA, Mt. Holly, N.J., 1962-67; paste up artist Times Advertiser, Pemberton, N.J., 1968-72; asst. educator N.J. State Sch., New Lisbon, 1972-76; supr. writing lab. Burlington County Coll., New Lisbon, 1978-85; class leader, vol. Learning Inst. for Elders Burlington County Coll., 1990—; mem. coun. LIFE, Learning Inst. Elders, New Lisbon. Exhibited in group shows at Willingboro Art Festival, 1973 (1st prize), Burlington County Art Guild, 1975 (2nd Pl.), Allaire Village, 1976 (Honorable mention), Chatswoth Cranberry Festival, 1976 (1st Pl.), 1977 (3rd Pl.), Moorestown Mall Art Festival, 1977 (3rd Pl.). Life mem., advisor Burlington County Coun. Girl Scouts U.S.A., 1958—; past pres., orientation vice chair Soroptimist Internat., Rancocas Valley, 1975—; mem., founder Libr. Friends, Browns Mills, N.J., 1966—; mem. RSVP Doll Dressing for Retired Sr. Vol. Program, 1992—. Mem. Country Lakes Srs. (past pres.). Anglican. Home: 4 Etowah Trail Browns Mills NJ 08015

FALBO, NADINE LOIS, contractor; b. Swickley, Pa., Feb. 16, 1949; d. John Joseph and Bernadine (Juracko) F. Student, Riverside (Calif.) C.C., 1986-89, UCLA, 1987-88, Loyola Marymount U., 1987-89, Harvard U., 1993. Lic. gen. contractor, Calif.; cert. Calif. Coun. for Interior Design. Constrn. worker Calif., 1973-83; interior designer Nadine's Enterprises, Riverside, 1984—, gen. contractor, 1989—; thoroughbred horse trainer, Calif., N.Mex., 1973-83; mem. adv. bd. Serra Retreat, Malibu, Calif., 1994. Roman Catholic. Office: Nadines Enterprises 5590 46th St Riverside CA 92509-6578

FALCAO, VERONICA GRACE, midwife; b. Washington, July 12, 1957; d. John Moniz and Phyllis Margaret (Fleming) F. BA, Coll. of Holy Cross, 1979; MS, Stanford U., 1984; cert., Midwifery Inst. Calif., Windsor, 1995. Programmer Evans, Griffiths & Hart, Inc., Lexington, Mass., 1979-82; tchg. asst. Stanford U., Palo Alto, Calif., 1983-84; tech. staff mem. Acorn Rsch. Ctr., Palo Alto, 1984-86, Olivetti Rsch. Ctr., Menlo Park, Calif., 1987-90; sr. software engr. Metaphor, Inc., Mountain View, Calif., 1990-94; asst. midwife Tender Vigil Birthing Svc., East Palo Alto, Calif., 1995—. Stevens Creek Trail rep. Old Downtown Mountain View Neighborhood Assn., 1993—. Mem. Midwives Assn. N.Am., Calif. Assn. Midwives, Phi Beta Kappa, Pi Mu Epsilon. Home and Office: 286 Vincent Dr Mountain View CA 94041

FALCK, MARIA J., retail executive; b. Pitts., Jan. 16, 1962; d. Robert Charles and Penelope (Torlidas) F. BFA, SUNY, Purchase, 1984. Sales mgr. Macy's, N.Y.C., 1986-87, customer svc. mgr., 1987-88, budget mgr., 1988-89; assoc. mgr., ops. mgr. Banana Republic, N.Y.C., 1989-91; assoc. mgr. Tiffany & Co., N.Y.C., 1991-92; store mgr. Tiffany & Co., Troy, Mich., 1992-94; mgr. The Jr. League, 1993—; with Internat. Fashion Group, 1993-94; tng. mgr. Brooks Bros., N.Y.C., 1994-95; spl. projects coord., 1995-96, mgr. of labor rels. and compensation, 1996—. Capt. Macy's Thanksgiving Day Parade, N.Y.C., 1987; bd. dirs. Alumni Orgn., Purchase, 1989-91, rep. Coll. Coun., Purchase, 1989-91, 94-96. Mem. N.Y. Jr. League. Greek Orthodox. Home: 23-66 32nd St Astoria NY 11105-2416 Office: Brooks Bros 346 Madison Ave New York NY 10036-6700

FALK, AUDREY JANE, artist, educator; b. St. Paul, Apr. 14, 1935; d. Clarence Amos and Inga Ohleen (Stormo) Lee; m. Richard Verle Falk, Feb. 1, 1937; 1 child, Susan Lee. BS, U. Minn., 1958. Cert. art tchr. grades K-12. Art tchr. Willmar (Minn.) Sch. Dist. #347, 1958-61, Willmar (Minn.) C.C., 1964-67, Willmar (Minn.) Jr. H.S., 1967-91; pvt. practice artist Willmar, 1991—. Works exhibited Holiday Inn Conf. Ctr., Willmar, 1992, Rice Meml. Hosp., Willmar, 1993, 94, Ministry of Culture, Vitebsk, Belarus, 1994—, Land of Lakes Girl Scout Coun., St. Cloud, Minn., 1996; represented in permanent collections Chagall Mus., Vitebsk. Active LWV, Willmar, 1961-67, Curriculum Adv. Coun., Willmar, 1994—; chairwoman Kandiyohi County Dem. Farmer Labor Party, Willmar, 1962-64. Recipient Woman of the Yr. award Bus. and Profl. Women, Willmar, 1995; Artist Career grantee S.W. Minn. Arts and Humanities Coun., Marshall, Minn., 1994. Mem. AAUW, Willmar Fedn. Tchrs., Rural Arts Initiative Com. Democrat. Lutheran. Home: 624 Southwest 10 St Willmar MN 56201

FALK, DEAN, anthropology educator; b. Seattle, June 25, 1944; children: Sarah Falk Schofield, Adrienne Falk Dolen. Student, Antioch Coll., 1962-63, U. Wash., 1964-65; BA with honors, U. Ill., 1970, MA, 1972. Asst. prof. Rollins Coll., Winter Park, Fla., 1976-77, So. Ill. U., Carbondale, 1977-79; asst. prof. health scis. Boston U., 1979-80; investigator Caribbean Primate Rsch. Ctr., 1980-84, curator Cayo Santiago primate skeletal collection, 1982-86, assoc. researcher, 1984-86; asst. prof. anatomy Sch. of Medicine U. P.R., 1980-82, assoc. prof. anatomy Sch. of Medicine, 1982-86; assoc. prof. Purdue U., 1986-88; prof. SUNY, Albany, 1988—. Author: External Neuroanatomy of Old World Monkeys, Primate Brain Evolution: Methods and Concepts, 1982, Braindance: What New Findings Reveal About Human Origins and Brain Evolution, 1992; mem. panel referees Human Evolution; mem. editorial bd. Man, Advances in Human Evolution; contbr. articles to Jour. Neurosics., Jour. Neurosci. Methods, Am. Jour. Phys. Anthropology, Internat. Jour. Primatology. Antioch Alumni Assn. scholar, 1962, Ctr. for Continuing Edn. of Women scholar, 1975, Alice C. Lloyd scholar, 1975; grantee NSF, 1970-71, 71-72, 78, 82, 84-86, 90-92, U. Mich., 1976, So. Ill. U., 1979, NIH, 1986-90. Fellow Am. Anthropol. Assn. (elected, sec., treas. biol. anthropology sect. 1989-91); mem. AAAS, Am. Assn. Phys. Anthropologists, Lang. Origins Soc., Sigma Xi. Home: 173 S Main Ave Albany NY 12208-2411 Office: SUNY Dept Of Anthropology Albany NY 12222

FALK, DONNA TOMASELLO, art education educator; b. Oak Park, Ill., Apr. 7, 1955; d. Anthony Joseph and Gloria (Giammanco) Tomasello; m. Timothy James, Feb. 3, 1978; 1 child, Daniel Joseph. BA in Sociology, Rosary Coll., 1977; BFA in Painting, Sch. Art Inst., 1988; MA in Interdisciplinary Arts, Columbia Coll., 1995. Cert. art edn. grades K-12, social studies tchr. grades 6-12. Tchr. grade 6 Chgo. (Ill.) Cath. Sch., 1977-79, tchr. grade 8 social studies, 1979-80, tchr. grade 6 gifted, 1980-81; geographer rschr. Ency. Britannica, Chgo., 1981-83; archtl. rschr. Art Inst. Chgo., Ill., 1985-86; rschr., slide typist Art Inst. Chgo., 1989-91, grad. asst. in edn., 1990-91; art tchr. grades K-8 Chgo. (Ill.) Pub. Schs., 1991—; freelance designer/painter, Chgo., 1988-91; lectr. Sch. Art Inst., Chgo., 1990, Hinsdale (Ill.) South H.S., 1991, Chgo. (Ill.) Bd. Edn., 1994. Mem. local sch. coun. Chgo. (Ill.) Bd. Edn., 1991—. Recipient Nat. Collegiate Edn. award Sch. of the Art Inst., Chgo., 1991, Nat. Art Edn. Merit award Electronic Gallery, 1993; Smith Merit scholar Sch. of the Art Inst., Chgo., 1985-88, Weisman scholar Columbia Coll., Chgo., 1994. Mem. Ill. Art Edn. Assn., Coll. Art Assn., Chgo. Tchrs. Union, Chgo. Artists' Coalition, Around the Coyote. Home: 248 Elgin Ave Forest Park IL 60130-1306

FALK, JULIA S., linguist, educator; b. Englewood, N.J., Sept. 21, 1941; d. Charles Joseph and Stella (Sarafinovich) Sableski; m. Thomas Heinrich, Jan. 20, 1967; 1 child, Tatiana Prentice. BS, Georgetown U., 1963; MA, U. Wash., 1964, PhD, 1968. Instr. linguistics Mich. State U., East Lansing, 1966-68, asst. prof., 1968-71, assoc. prof., 1971-78, prof., 1978—, asst. dean Coll. of Arts and Letters, 1979-81, assoc. dean Coll. Arts and Letters, 1981-

86; cons. on lang. and law, lang. and gender, bias-free communication, East Lansing. Author: Linguistics and Language, 1973, 2d revised edit., 1978; contbr. articles on lang. acquisition, history of linguistics to profl. jours. Fellow Woodrow Wilson Found., 1963, NDEA Title IV, 1963-66, NSF, 1965; recipient Paul Varg Alumni award for Teaching, 1993. Mem. Linguistic Soc. Am., N.Am. Assn. History of Lang. Scis. Home: 2100 Holt Rd Williamston MI 48895-9747 Office: Mich State Univ Dept Linguistics A-614 Wells East Lansing MI 48824-1027

FALKENSTEIN, KARIN EDITH, elementary school principal; b. Michigan City, Ind., Feb. 12, 1950; d. Martin Victor and Helen Marion (Hedberg) Sandstrom; m. Chrles William Falkenstein Jr., July 13, 1985; 1 stepchild, Amanda Ann. BA in Elem. Edn., Spl. Edn., Mich. State U., 1972, MA in Reading Instrn., 1975. Spl. edn. tchr. Hesperia (Mich.) Pub. Schs., 1972-73; spl. edn. tchr. Buchanan (Mich.) Community Schs., 1973-79, elem. prin. Moccasin Sch., sch. farm coord., 1979-80; elem. prin. Ottawa Sch., Buchanan (Mich.) Community Schs., 1980—; dist. spl. edn. supr., 1980—; gifted and talented coord. Ottawa Sch., Buchanan (Mich.) Community Schs., 1980—, elem. coord., K-12 testing coord. and K-6 curriculum dir., 1993—; instr. Ind. U., South Bend, 1981—; presenter spl. edn. workshops. Mem. Big Bros./Big Sisters of Niles/Buchanan, Inc., 1982—, v.p., 1985, pres., 1986-87; mem. Mich. State U. Coll. Edn. Alumni Bd., 1982-94, v.p., 1987, pres., 1988; Sun. sch. tchr. First United Meth. Ch., 1982—, bd. trustees, 1986-91, Chrisian edn. chairperson, 1988-90; mem. Buchanan Fine Arts Coun., 1987—, treas., 1988-93; mem. Hospice Bereavement Care, 1987—; mem. Redbud Area Ministries LOVE, Inc., 1985-89, pres., 1988-89; bd. dirs. Berrien Coun. for Children, 1987—, mem. edn. com., 1984—; bd. dirs. Four Flags Samaritan Ctr., 1985—; mem. PTA, 1988—. Recipient Nat. Disting. Prin.'s award, 1989, Mich. Legis. recognition, 1989, Pres.'s award Mich. State U. Coll. Edn. Alumni Assn., 1987, Mich. State U. Nat. Alumni Assn. Svc. award 1995, Golden Nugget award for spl. edn., 1983, Milken Found. Family Educator award, 1993; named Mich. Outstanding Practicing Prin., 1988, Region 5 Prin. award, 1989. Mem. Mich. Elem. and Mid. Sch. Prins. Assn. (membership chair 1984-86, profl. devel. chairperson 1983-84, pres. 1987-88), ASCD, CEC, Tri-County Coun. of Women in Ednl. Adminstrn. (profl. devel. chair 1983-84, pres. 1985-87, historian 1987-92), Spl. Edn. Dirs. and Coords. for Berrien County, Internat. Reading Assn., Mich. Reading Assn., Mich. Alliance for Gifted Edn., Mich. Assn. Learning Disabilities Educators, Mich. State U. Alumni Assn. (nat. bd. v.p. 1992-93, treas. 1991-92, pres. 1993-94, Svc. award 1995), Phi Delta Kappa. Office: Buchanan Community Schs 109 Ottawa St Buchanan MI 49107-1136

FALL, DOROTHY, artist, art director, administrator; b. Rochester, N.Y., Apr. 7, 1930; d. Isadore and Esther Paula (Rudman) Winer; m. Bernard B. Fall, dec. Feb. 1967; children: Nicole Francoise, Elisabeth Anne, Patricia Madeleine Marcelle. BFA, Syracuse U., 1952; postgrad., Am. U., 1956-58, 66; student, Acad. de la Grande Chaumiere, Paris, 1961, Acad. Julian, Paris, 1965. Dep. art dir. AMERIKA Mag. U.S. Info. Agy., Washington, 1956-80; owner, art dir. Fall Design Comms., Washington, 1980-88; dir. Gallery 10, Washington, 1994—; pres., bd. dirs. Pyramid Atlantic, Riverdale, Md. Editor: Last Reflections on a War, 1967; art dir., designer Space Science Comes of Age, 1981; one-woman shows include Plum Gallery, Kensington, Md., 1989, O St. Studio, Washington, 1989, 92, AVA Gallery, Lebanon, N.H., 1990, Covington & Burling, Washington, 1990, Am. Horticultural Soc., Alexandria, Va., 1993, Gallery 10, Washington, 1996; represented in permanent collections and by Verve Art Gallery, Leuven, Belgiu, Gallery 10, Washington, AVA Gallery, Lebanon, N.H., Aries East, Brewster, Mass. Recipient gold medal award Art Dirs. Club of Met. Washington Exhibits, 1965, 66, 69, 79, distinctive merit Art Dirs. Club of N.Y. Exhibits, 1969, 74, 77, 78, 79, 81, 82, 83, silver medal N.Y. Soc. Illustrators, 1969. Mem. Women's Caucus on Arts, Washington Sculptors Group, Artists Equity, Cosmos Club. Home and Studio: 4535 31st St NW Washington DC 20008-2130

FALLETTA, JO ANN, musician; b. N.Y.C., Feb. 27, 1954; d. John Edward and Mary Lucy (Racioppo) F.; m. Robert Alemany, Aug. 24, 1986. BA in Music, Mannes Coll. Music, N.Y.C., 1976, MA in Music, Juilliard Sch., N.Y.C., 1982; PhD in Musical Arts, Juilliard Sch., 1989; Honorary Doctorate, Marian Coll., Wis., 1988. Music dir. Queens Philharmonic, N.Y.C., 1978-91, Den. Chamber Orch., Colo., 1983-92; assoc. condr. Milw. Symphony, Wis., 1985-88; music dir. Women's Philharmonic, San Francisco, 1986—, Long Beach Symphony, Calif., 1989—, Va. Symphony, Norfolk, 1991—. Stokowski Conducting Competition, Toscanini Conducting award. Office: ICM Artists LTD 40 W 57th St New York NY 10019-4001*

FALLIN, BARBARA MOORE, human resources director; b. Paducah, Ky., Nov. 12, 1939; d. James Perry Moore and Margaret Arminta (Winn) Kastner; m. Jon Ball, Jan. 21, 1961 (div. July 1963); m. Ralph Daniel Fallin, May 23, 1965; children: Wade, Cathi, Cindy Pergrim, Danielle. Student, Fla. Christian Coll., 1957-58. Cert. sr. profl. in human resource mgmt. Exec. asst. to contr. The Borden Co., Tampa, Fla., 1958-65; mktg. asst. Martin-Marietta Corp., Shalimar, Fla., 1965-71; asst. to pres. Browning-Marine, Ft. Walton Beach, Fla., 1973; pers. coord. Keltec Fla., Shalimar, 1974-78; pers. mgr. Metric Systems Corp., Ft. Walton Beach, 1979-87, pers. dir., 1987-92; dir. human resources Metric Sys. Corp., Ft. Walton Beach, 1992—; mem. Job Svc. Employer Com., Ft. Walton Beach, 1985—; adv. bd. Bay Area Vocat.-Tech. Ctr., Ft. Walton Beach, 1988-92, Okaloosa Applied Tech. Ctr. Sch., 1995—. First mistress Krewe of Bowlegs, Ft. Walton Beach, 1983-84, first lady to Cap'n Billy Bowlegs XXXII, 1986-87; mem. citizens adv. com. U. West Fla., Pensacola, 1991—; mem. funds distbn. com. Okaloosa County United Way, 1990-93; mem. BNA's Pers. Policies Forum, 1995-96; mem. Pacesetters fund raiser team Salvation Army Capital Campaign, 1996—. Mem. NAFE, Soc. Human Resource Mgmt., Emerald Coast Pers. Mgmt. Assn. (pres. 1986-88, bd. dirs. 1988-92), Nat. Mgmt. Assn., Ft. Walton Beach C. of C. (hosts com. 1991—), Sugar Beach Sertoma Club, Beta Sigma Phi. Republican. Presbyterian. Office: Metric Sys Corp 645 Anchors St NW Fort Walton Beach FL 32548-3803

FALLIN, MARY COPELAND, state official; b. Warrensburg, Mo., Dec. 9, 1954; d. Jospeh Newton and Mary (Duggan) Copeland; m. Joseph Price Fallin, Jr., Nov. 3, 1984; children: Christina, Price. BS, Okla. State U., 1977. Bus. mgr. Okla. Dept. Securities, Oklahoma City, 1979-81; state travel coord. Okla. Dept. of Tourism, Oklahoma City, 1981-82; sales rep. Associated Petroleum, Oklahoma City, 1982-83; mktg. dir. Brian Head (Utah) Hotel & Ski Resort, 1983-84; dir. sales Residence Inn Hotel, Oklahoma City, 1984-87; dist. mgr. Lexington Hotel Suites, Oklahoma City, 1988-90; real estate assoc. Pippin Properties, Inc., Oklahoma City, 1992-94; state rep. Okla. Ho. of Reps., Oklahoma City, 1990-94; lt. governor State of Okla., Oklahoma City, 1995—. Mem. Okla. Fedn. Rep. Women; mem. Am. Legis. Exch. Coun., Nat. Conf. State Legislatures. Mem., del. Okla. Fedn. Rep. Women; mem. Am. Legis. Exch. Coun., Nat. Conf. State Legislatures. Named Nat. Legislator of the Yr., Okla. Ladies in the News, Guardian of Small Bus. award. Presbyterian. Home: 2521 NW 59th St Oklahoma City OK 73112-7108 Office: State Capitol Rm 211 Office of Lt Governor Oklahoma City OK 73105

FALLON, RAE MARY, psychology educator, early childhood consultant; b. N.Y.C., Apr. 13, 1947; d. Frank J. and Santa A. (Lettera) Taccetta; m. John J. Fallon, 1972; children: Sean, Christopher. BA, CUNY, 1968, MA, 1971; postgrad., Fordham U., 1989—. Cert. N-6 tchr., spl. edn. tchr., N.Y. Elem. tchr. Pub. Sch. 1, Bronx, N.Y., 1968-72; pre-sch. tchr. Valley Nursery Sch., Walden, N.Y., 1972-73; tchr. spl. edn. Orange-Ulster Bd. Coop. Edn. Svcs., Goshen, N.Y., 1973-75, early childhood specialist, 1982-89; instr. edn. Mt. St. Mary Coll., Newburgh, N.Y., 1989-93, asst. prof., 1993—; early childhood cons., Montgomery, N.Y., 1989—; mem. early childhood com. Valley Ctrl. Sch. Sys., Montgomery, 1994. Mem. West Street Sch. Cmty. Sch. Bd., Newburgh, 1990—; mem. early intervention com. Orange County Health Dept., Goshen, 1993—; chmn. program com. Montgomery Rep. Club, 1990-94. Mem. ASCD, Coun. for Exceptional Children, Assn. for Edn. Young Children (regional coord. 1991-92), Kiwanis, Delta Kappa Gamma, Phi Delta Kappa. Roman Catholic. Office: Mt St Mary Coll 330 Powell Ave Newburgh NY 12550-3412

FALLS, KATHLEENE JOYCE, photographer; b. Detroit, July 3, 1949; d. Edgar John and Acelia Olive (Young) Haley; m. Donald David Falls, June 15, 1974; children: Daniel John, David James. Student, Oakland Community Coll., 1969-73, Winona Sch. Profl. Photography, 1973-80; degree in photography, 1988, 90. Lic. ham radio-technician class. Printer Guardian Photo, Novi, Mich., 1967-69; printer, supr. quality control N.Am. Photo, Livonia, Mich., 1969-76; free lance photographer Livonia, 1969-76; owner, pres. Kathy Falls, Inc., Carleton, Mich., 1976—; instr. digital imaging Monroe County (Mich.) C.C., 1994—; instr. Monroe County Community Coll. Continuing Edn., 1981-83; nat. artisan judge Congl. High Sch. Art Competition, 1985—; owner Picture Perfect, Carleton, 1987; co-owner Haleys Gift Shoppe, Dundee, Mich., 1989. Author: (booklet) Emergency Photo-Retouching for Photographers, 1988; contbr. articles to profl. jours. Represented in spl. categories in the Nat. Loan Collection, Profl. Photographers Am., 1980, 81, 83, 87; represented in permanent Collections Monroe County Hist. Mus., Archives Notre Dame. Catechist St. Parick's Ch., Carleton, 1984-87; active Big Bros. and Big Sisters, Monroe, 1986-87; corr. sec. Monroe Women's Ctr., 1986-88; bd mem. Heartbeat, 1995; mem. Amateur Radio Emergency Svc. Recipient Photographic Craftsman degree, 1989, numerous awards granted by profl. photographic orgns. Mem. NAFE, Am. Soc. Photographers, Detroit Profl. Photographers Assn. (bd. dirs. 1987—, artisan chmn. 1981-82, Best of Show award 1981, 83), Profl. Photographers Mich. (artisian chairperson 1982-83, Best of Show award 1976, 81, Artist of Yr. 1980, 91), Profl. Photographers Am. (cert. profl. photog. specialist, photographic specialist degree 1988), Am. Photographic Artisans Guild (council mem., bd. dirs. 1987—, pres. 1992, Photographic Artisan degree 1989, Artisan Laurel degree 1991), Monroe County Fine Arts Council, Monroe C. of C. (chmn. council women bus. owners), Nat. Orgn. Women Bus. Owners, Profl. Photographers Am. (Photographic Craftsman degree 1990), Monroe County Radio Communications Assn., Toastmasters, Internat. Club. Democrat. Roman Catholic. Club: Monroe Camera. Home and Office: 10779 Swan Creek Rd Carleton MI 48117-9324

FALUDI, SUSAN C., journalist, scholarly writer. Formerly with West Mag., San Jose, Calif., Mercury News; with San Francisco Bur., Wall St. Jour.; spkr. in field. Author: Backlash: The Undeclared War Against American Women, 1991 (National Book Critics Circle award for general nonfiction 1992); contbr. articles to mags. Recipient Pulitzer Prize for explanatory journalism, 1991. Office: care Sandra Dijkstra Sandra Dijkstra Literary Agency 1155 Camino Del Mar Ste 515 Del Mar CA 92014-2605*

FALZANO, COLLEEN, special education educator; b. Glens Falls, N.Y., Oct. 9, 1962; d. Richard Joseph and Patricia Anne (Sheridan) F. AA, Ulster County C.C.; BA in Psychology, SUNY, New Paltz; MS in Edn., SUNY, Brockport. Substitute tchr. Kendall (N.Y.) Ctrl. Sch. Dist., 1986-87, Holley (N.Y.) Ctrl. Sch. Dist., 1986-87, Albion (N.Y.) Sch. Dist., 1986-87; tchr. spl. edn. Children's Home Kingston, N.Y., 1987-90, New Paltz Ctrl. Sch. Dist., 1990-91, Saugerties (N.Y.) Ctrl. Sch. Dist., 1991-93; tchr. resource room, cons. Kingston City Sch. Dist., 1993—. Recipient Gappy Gurrison award, 1981, Girls Cmty. Club award, 1978. Mem. Nat. Coun. Tchrs. Math., Nat. Coun. Tchrs. English, Nat. Sci. Tchrs. Assn., Nat. Coaches Assn., Mid-Hudson Soccer Ofcls. Assn. (assoc.), Mid-Hudson Field Hockey Ofcls. Assn. (assoc.), Mid-Hudson Softball Ofcls. Assn. (assoc.). Home: 5 Boxwood Ct Saugerties NY 12477-2009

FAN, LINDA C., investment company executive; b. Princeton, N.J., Mar. 22, 1956; d. Chung-Teh and Mook-Lan (Mui) F.; m. William A. Schaefer, Aug. 9, 1985; children: Ralph, Fred. AB, Princeton U., 1978; MBA, U. Chgo., 1982. Assoc. Salomon Bros., N.Y.C., 1982-85; assoc. Morgan Stanley & Co., N.Y.C., 1985-87, v.p., 1987-91, prin., 1991—. Office: Morgan Stanley Co Inc 39th Fl 1585 Broadway New York NY 10036

FANCHER, CHRISTINE SUZANNE, photographer; b. Glendale, Calif., Aug. 9, 1951; d. John Carroll and Audrey Marie (Hoffman) F.; m. Joel Yancey Orr, July 23, 1975; 1 child, Shane Daniel Fancher Orr. BA in Profl. Photography, Brooks Inst., Santa Barbara, Calif., 1982. Graphic artist, tech. illustrator Santa Rosa, Calif., 1972-78; profl. photographer asst. L.A., 1982-84. Recipient Best of Show award Santa Barbara Advt. Club, 1985, 87. Office: Christine Fancher Photo PO Box 50347 Montecito CA 93150-0347

FANCY, BRENDA LEE, elementary education educator; b. Worcester, Mass., July 19, 1959; d. Robert Dana and Shirley Irene (Lloyd) F. BS in Edn., Worcester State Coll., 1981; MEd in Curriculum and Instrn., Lesley Coll., 1989. Cert. elem. tchr. grades K-8, secondary math. tchr. grades 7-12, supr. dir. prin. grades 5-9. Tchr. grade 8 math. Worcester (Mass.) East Middle Sch., 1981; tchr. grade 2 Calvin Coolidge Sch., Shrewsbury, Mass., 1982; tchr. grade 7 math. Nathaniel Morton Sch., Plymouth, Mass., 1982-86; tchr. grade 7 math. Plymouth (Mass.) Cmty. Intermediate Sch., 1987-95, housemaster, 1995—; mem. sch. coun. Plymouth (Mass.) Cmty. Intermediate Sch., 1994-95. Bd. dirs. Camp Fire Girls, Worcester, 1981-82. Recipient state level Presdl. award for excellence in sci. and math. NSF, Washington, 1994, 95. Mem. Nat. Coun. Tchrs. Math. Republican. Methodist. Home: 47 Jan Marie Dr Plymouth MA 02360 Office: PCIS Long Pond Rd Plymouth MA 02360

FANELLE, CARMELLA, dentist; b. Camden, N.J., Jan. 15, 1960; d. Joseph and Sylvia Catherine (Manganaro) F.; m. Frederick Matthew Rojek Jr., Nov. 15, 1986; 1 child, Eva Noel Rojek. BS, Chestnut Hill Coll., Phila., 1982; DDS, Temple U., 1986. Lic. dentist, Pa., N.J. Pvt. practice Phila., 1987-89, Barrington, N.J., 1990—; dentist, cons. Temple U., Phial, 1990; dir. gen. dentistry Temple Hosp., Phila., 1990. Mem. Barrington Bus. Assn. Recipient Am. Acad. Dental Radiology award, 1986. Fellow Acad. Gen. Dentistry; mem. ADA, Pa. Dental Assn., Phila. County Dental Assn., So. Dental N.J. Dental Assn. Roman Catholic. Office: 34 Clements Bridge Rd Barrington NJ 08007-1802

FANG, WEI LI, medical educator; b. Alexandria, Va., Mar. 20, 1953; d. Tien Chen and Siu Chung (Lai) F. BA in Psychology, U. Va., 1975, M in Health Edn., 1976, PhD in Edn. Evaluation, 1981. From instr. to asst. prof. med. edn. U. Va. Sch. Medicine, Charlottesville, 1981-90, assoc. prof. med. edn., 1990—, assoc. dir. student acad. support and strategic programs, 1993-95, dir., 1995—; curriculum editor Project SAGE, 1991; active Summer Inst. for Women in Higher Edn. Adminstrn., Bryn Mawr (Pa.) Coll., 1995. Bd. dirs. Children, Youth and Family Svcs., Charlottesville, 1990-93; mem. coun. Office Human Rights, Richmond, Va., 1987-91, chmn., 1989-91. Mem. Am. Evaluation Assn. (Robert B. Ingle Svc. award 1989), Am. Edn. Rsch. Assn., Internat. Visual Sociology Assn., Orgn. Chinese Americans, Asian Am. Arts & Media, Inc. Office: Univ Va Health Scis Ctr PO Box 382 Charlottesville VA 22902-0382

FANN, MARGARET ANN, counselor; b. Pasco, Wash., July 16, 1942; d. Joseph Albert David and Clarice Mable (Deaver) Rivard; m. Jerry Lee Fann, June 13, 1986; children: Brenda Heupel, Scott Sherman, Kristin Johnson, Robert Lack III. AA, Big Bend C.C., Moses Lake, Wash., 1976; BA in Applied Psychology magna cum laude, Ea. Wash. U., 1977, MS in Psychology, 1978. Cert. mental health counselor, Wash.; cert. chem. dependency counselor II, nat. cert. addictions counselor II, cert. in chronic psychiat. disability. Intern counselor Linker House Drug Rehab., Spokane, Wash., 1976-78; drug counselor The House drug program, Tacoma, Wash., 1978-80; exec. dir. Walla Walla (Wash.) Commn. Alcohol, 1980-82; dir. Cmty. Alcohol Svcs. Assn., Kennewick, Wash., 1982-86; primary care coord. Carondelet Psychiat. Care Ctr., Richland, Wash., 1986-90; part-time instr. Ea. Wash. U., Cheney, 1981-88; instr. Columbia Basin Coll., Pasco, 1990-93; adminstr. Action Chem. Dependency Ctr., Kennewick, 1993—; bd. dirs. Benton-Franklin County Substance Abuse Coalition, Pasco, Kennewick, Richland, 1990—. Vol. Pat Hale for Senator, Kennewick, 1994. Mem. Am. Counselors Assn., Nat. Mental Health Counselors Assn., Wash. State Mental Health Counselors Assn., Tri-Cities Counselors Assn., Phi Theta Kappa. Office: Action Chem Dependency Ctr 552 N Colorado Ste 5525 Kennewick WA 99336 also: Benton-Franklin County MICA Detoxification Ctr 1020 S 7th St Kennewick WA 99336

FANNIN, CAROLINE MATHER, library consultant; b. N.Y.C., July 22, 1959; d. Alfred Bruce and Marjorie Evelyn (Burns) Brown; m. John Paul Fannin, Jan. 12, 1991; stepchildren: Scott A., Brian W. BA, Wheaton Coll., 1982; MLS, Rutgers U., 1984; postgrad., NYU, 1996—. Profl. libr., N.J. Info. analyst Montclair (N.J.) Pub. Libr., 1979-85, br. supr., 1985-90; dir. Louis Bay 2d Libr., Hawthorne, N.J., 1990-92; exec. dir. Bergen-Passaic Regional Libr. Coop., Hawthorne, 1992-93; writer, 1993—; expansion coord. Montclair Pub. Libr., 1995—; prin. Caroline M. Fannin & Assocs., Inc., Hawthorne, 1996—; mayor's alt. bd. trustees Louis Bay 2d Libr., Hawthorne, 1995—. Co-author: (book chpts.) Abortion: Library in a Book, 1991, Capital Punishment: Library in a Book, 1991. Bd. dirs. Bergen-Passaic Regional Libr. Coop., Hawthorne, 1991-92; mem. Hawthorne Aux. Police, 1994—. Mem. ALA, Sisters in Crime. Republican. Episcopalian. Home: 44 Tuxedo Ave Hawthorne NJ 07506 Office: Montclair Pub Libr 50 S Fullerton Ave Montclair NJ 07042 also: Caroline M Fannin & Assocs 44 Tuxedo Ave Hawthorne NJ 07506

FANNING, KATHERINE WOODRUFF, editor, journalism educator; b. Chgo., Oct. 18, 1927; d. Frederick William and Katherine Bower (Miller) Woodruff; m. Marshall Field, Jr., May 12, 1950 (div. 1963); children: Frederick Woodruff, Katherine Woodruff Stephen, Barbara Woodruff; m. Lawrence S. Fanning, 1966 (dec. 1971); m. Amos Mathews, Jan. 6, 1984. BA, Smith Coll., 1949; LLD (hon.), Colby Coll., 1979; LittD (hon.), Pine Manor Jr. Coll., 1984; LHD (hon.), Northeastern U., 1984; hon. degree, Harvard U., 1988, Smith Coll., 1988, Babson Coll., 1988, U. Alaska, 1989, Govs. State U., Ill., 1989. With Anchorage Daily News, from 1965, editor, pub., 1972-83; editor The Christian Science Monitor, 1983-88; fall fellow Inst. of Politics Harvard U., Cambridge, Mass., 1989; adj. prof. journalism Boston U., 1991-93; dir. AP, 1988-89, Pulitzer prize bd., 1982-83, Boston Globe Newspaper Co., 1992—; mem. nat. adv. com. Freedom Forum Media Studies Ctr.; sr. adv. bd. Joan Shorenstein Ctr., Harvard U.; bd. dirs. Inst. for Global Ethics, Inst. for Journalism Edn., 1989-95. Med. editl. bd. PBS program Frontline. Trustee Kettering Found., Charles Stewart Mott Found.; bd. dirs. Internat. Ctr. Journalists, Boston Pub. Libr. Found.; bd. overseers Boston Symphony Orch. Recipient Elijah Parish Lovejoy award Colby Coll., 1979, Smith Coll. medal, 1980, Mo. medal of Honor, U. Mo. Journalism award, 1980. Mem. Am. Soc. Newspaper Editors (bd. dirs. 1981—, pres. 1987-88), Soc. Profl. Journalists, Coun. Fgn. Rels, Am. Acad. Arts and Scis., St. Botolph Club (Boston), Badminton and Tennis Club (Boston). Home and Office: 330 Beacon St Boston MA 02116-1153

FANNING, WANDA GAIL, elementary school educator; b. Chattanooga, Dec. 8, 1947; d. O' Knox and Hazel W. (McClendon) F.; stepmother E. Martha (O'Kelley) F. BEd, U. Ten., 1969; MEd, Trinity U., San Antonio, 1982. Elem. tchr. C.Z. Govt., Balboa, 1969-79, Dept. Def. Dependent Schs., Albrook, Panama, 1979-87; tchr. spl. edn. Dept. Def. Dependent Schs., Panama, 1982-84, ednl. prescriptionist, 1987-95; tchr. trainer, drug edn. trainer Dept. Def. Dependent Schs., Panama City, 1987-96, cooperative learning trainer, 1994-96, case mgr., 1995-96. Chmn. fine arts Ishmian Coll. Club, Balboa, 1985, fin. chmn., 1985; mem. Theatre Guild, Ancon, Panama, 1975-96; pres. Diablo Elem. Sch. Adv. Com., 1990-91; mem. orgnl. com. Spl. Games for Spl. People, Panama City, 1983-85. Recipient Just Cause cert. dept. nursing Gorgas Army Hosp., 1990, Spl. Act award Dept. Def. Dependents Sch., 1990. Mem. ASCD, Nat. Coun. Tchrs. Math., Coun. for Exceptional Children (treas. 1987—), Phi Delta Kappa (pres. 1990-91, Kappan of Yr. 1991, 94, v.p. 1991-92, del. 1992, 93), Kappa Delta Pi. Address: 813 Cherokee Ln Signal Mountain TN 37377-3014

FANOS, KATHLEEN HILAIRE, osteopathic physician, podiatrist; b. Bremerhaven, Germany, Aug. 18, 1956; came to U.S., 1957; d. Homer Dantangelo and Ilse Helmar (Ochs) F. AAS in Music, Nassau C.C., Garden City, N.Y., 1976; BS in Music Edn., Hofstra U., 1978, postgrad., 1978-79; D Podiatric Medicine, Coll. Podiatric Med. and Surg., Des Moines, 1987; DO, Coll. Osteo. Med. and Surg., Des Moines, 1994. Tchr. music McKenna Jr. High Sch. and Eastlake Elem. Sch., Massapequa, N.Y., 1978-79; musician numerous profl. orgns., N.Y., Iowa, 1979—; preceptorship in podiatry Bayshore, N.Y., 1987-88; pvt. practice podiatry Hyde Park, West Roxbury and Brookline, Mass., 1988-91; pvt. practice podiatry, Des Moines, 1991-92; resident in internal medicine Winthrop U. Hosp., Mineola, N.Y., 1994—; ins. med. examiner Portamedic, Burlington, Mass., 1988-91. Mem. AMA, Am. Coll. Physicians (assoc.), Am. Soc. Internal. Medicine, Am. Osteo. Assn., Am. Coll. Osteo. Family Physicians, N.Y. State Internal Medicine Soc., Phi Theta Kappa, Pi Kappa Lambda, Sigma Sigma Phi, Phi Delta Epsilon.

FANSLAU, CATHY ANN, chaplain, family care service administrator; b. Hammond, Ind., Oct. 15, 1952; d. Dayton Conrad and Mary Lou (Miner) Williams; m. Robert Davis Fanslau, May 15, 1971; children: Tausha, Michelle, Justin. BA cum laude, Concordia U., 1986; postgrad., U. N.C., Greensboro, Trinity Sem., Columbus, Ohio. Field worker St. Paul's Luth. Ch., 1983-84, Our Lady Mercy Hosp., 1985-86; field work supr. Concordia U., 1985-86; deaconess St. Paul's Evang. Luth. Ch., 1984-88; deaconess, workshop leader, resource liaison Mo. Synod, 1990; counselor Luth. Child and Family Svcs. Ind./Ky., 1990; care-link project asst. Shepherd's Ctr. Greensboro, 1991-92; dir. project Emmaus, deaconess Grace Luth. Ch., 1992-93; parish deaconess Macedonia Luth. Ch., 1992; dir. family care svcs., chaplain Twin Lakes Ctr., 1992—; past pres., bd. dirs., chmn., parliamentarian Chgo. Area Concordia Deaconess Conf. Past bd. dirs. Luth. Child and Family Svcs. Ill.; co-chair assembly Deaconess Cmty. ELCA. Named Miss Kirtland, 1970. Mem. Am. Counseling Assn., Luth. Women's Missionary League (local pres., Ohio dist. v.p., sec., treas.), Adam's Farm Women's Club (past v.p., past pres.). Home: 4 Swift Creek Ct Greensboro NC 27407 Office: Twin Lakes Ctr 100 Wade Coble Dr Burlington NC 27217

FANSLOW, KATHRYN MARIE (KAY FANSLOW), continuity writer, freelance journalist; b. Ames, Iowa, Jan. 10, 1962; d. Glenn Ellsworth and Alyce Ann (Muck) F. BA in Cinema/TV, U. So. Calif., 1984. Continuity writer Gelula & Co., Inc., L.A., 1985-91; rschr. WQED West, L.A., 1985; prodn. asst. At Close Range, L.A., 1985; rschr. Funny You Don't Look 200, L.A., 1987; continuity writer Masterwords, Santa Monica, Calif., 1991—; correspondent The Burbank (Calif.) Leader, 1988-90, Glendale (Calif.) News-Press, 1991-94. Contbr. to Runners World, L.A. Times Sunday Calendar, San Diego Union, Rochester Democrat, Pasadena Weekly, 1989—. Recipient Hon. Mention AeRo, 1981, award Ingersoll Publs., 1989, 1st pla. TV/Movie Script, Writer's Digest Mag., 1995.

FANUCCHI, CATHERINE ANN, lawyer; b. Bakersfield, Calif., Feb. 26, 1963; d. Charles A. and Charlotte Ann (Maranian) F. Student, Cambridge U., 1984; BA, U. So. Calif., 1985; JD, Santa Clara U., 1989. Bar: Calif. 1989. Intern Office of Congressman Bill Thomas, Washington, 1984; staff asst. Office of Congressman Bill Thomas, Bakersfield, Calif., 1985-86; recruiter Calif. Young Republicans, L.A., 1986; office mgr. Tri-Fanucchi Farms, Arvin, Calif., 1987; law clk. Santa Clara Pub. Defender, San Jose, Calif., 1988, Santa Clara Dist. Atty., San Jose, Calif., 1988; trial lawyer Borton, Petrini & Conron, Bakersfield, Calif., 1989-92, LeBeau, Thelen, Lampe, McIntosh & Crear, Bakersfield, Calif., 1992-95; lawyer Com. on House Oversight U.S. Ho. of Reps., Washington, 1995—. Mem. Calif. Young Republicans, Kern County, 1985—. Mem. Calif. Bar Assn., Republican Nat. Lawyers. Office: US Ho of Reps Com on House Oversight 1309 Longworth HOB Washington DC 20515

FANUS, PAULINE RIFE, librarian; b. New Oxford, Pa., Feb. 14, 1925; d. Maurice Diehl and Bernice Edna (Gable) Rife; m. William Edward Fanus, June 20, 1944; children: Irene Weaver, Larry William, Daniel Diehl. BS, Pa. State U., 1945; MLS, Villanova U., 1961; postgrad., Temple U., 1986—. Periodical librarian Tex. Coll. Arts Industries, Kingville, 1945; tchr. nursery sch. Studio Sch., Wayne, Pa., 1953-55; librarian circulation, reference Franklin Inst., Phila., 1963-66; asst. librarian Ursinus Coll., Collegeville, Pa., 1966; catalog librarian, instr. Eastern Coll., St. Davids, Pa., 1967-71; head libr. Agnes Irwin Sch., Rosemont, Pa., 1971-93, head libr. emeritus, 1993—. Book reviewer The Book Report. Mem. AAUP (chpt. sec. Eastern Coll. 1970-71), Pa. Library Assn. Home: Country Club Rd Phoenixville PA 19460

FARACE, VIRGINIA KAPES, librarian; b. Hazleton, Pa., July 10, 1945; d. Elmer Bernard and Elizabeth E. (Kuntz) Kapes; m. Frank John Farace, May 9, 1970. BA, Rider U., 1967; MLS, Rutgers U., 1968. Reference and govt. documents librarian Hazleton Area Pub. Libr., 1968-70; libr. dir. Boynton Beach (Fla.) City Libr., 1970—; bldg. cons. Boynton Beach City Libr., 1973-74, 85-89, Palm Springs (Fla.) Pub. Libr., 1976, 86. Editor: (directory) Library Resources in Palm Beach County, 1979; Centennial Book Com. Boynton Beach: The First 100 Years. Chair legis. com. Edn. Alliance, Palm Beach County, 1987-94; mem. strategic planning task force Palm Beach County Sch. Bd., 1990-91; chair job opportunity task force Project Mosaic,

Palm Beach County, 1990-93, transition team 1993; chair budget com. Book Fest! A Literary Festival, Palm Beach County, 1990-93, co-chair exhibitors com., 1994-95, chair steering com., 1995-96, chair bd. dirs., 1996—; edn. com. Govs. Initiative for Teens, 1992—, sec., 1993—; adv. coun. Santaluces H.S., 1991—, chair, 1994—; mem. Congress Mid. Sch. Adv. Coun., 1992—; mem. Palm Beach County Leadership Class of 1994, mem. pub. issues com., 1995—; mem. task force Boynton Beach Hist. Schs., Task Force, 1993; mem. cmty. network Palm Beach County Sch. Bd., 1993—, sch. bd. constrn. oversight and rev. com., 1996, chair pers. and tng. subcom., safe schs. task force; bd. dirs. Boynton Beach Hist. Soc., 1992—, chair by-laws com., 1993, chair nominating ocm., 1994-95, co-chair Hist. 1913 Schoolhouse Restoration Com., 1994—. Mem. ALA, AAUW (v.p. Boynton Beach br. 1989—, br. coord. 1995-96, br. pres. 1996—, state strategic planning com. 1990—, chair 1992, Woman of Change award 1991, state conv. planning com. 1992, chair credentials com. 1992, S.E. Fla. cluster rep. state bd. 1994-96, chair state nominating com. 1994-95, bylaws com. 1994-95, state parliamentarian 1996—), Southeastern Libr. Assn., Spl. Libr. Assn., Fla. Pub. Libr. Assn. (pres. 1989-90, chair libr. adminstrn. divsn. 1992-93, parliamentarian 1992-94, legis. com. 1993—, chair adult svcs. divsn. 1994-95), Palm Beach County Libr. Assn. (pres. 1979-80, citation for leadership and svc. 1980), Coop. Authority for Libr. Automation (treas. 1984-93, pres. 1993—), Boynton Beach C. of C. (chair edn. com. 1991—, bd. dirs. 1992—, vice chair 1994—, parliamentarian 1993—, chair nominating com. 1994, Outstanding Com. Chair award 1992, Dir. of Yr. 1993, 94), Alpha Xi Delta (pres. 1980-84). Roman Catholic. Home: Lake Clarke Shores 1841 Caribbean Rd West Palm Beach FL 33406-8606 Office: Boynton Beach City Libr 208 S Seacrest Blvd Boynton Beach FL 33435-4499

FARAH, CYNTHIA WEBER, photographer, publisher; b. Long Island, N.Y., June 2, 1949; d. Andrew John and Aria Emma (Jelnikova) Weber; m. James Clifton Farah, Jan. 12, 1974 (div. 1992); children: Elise, Alexa. BA in Communications, Stanford U., 1971; MA, U. Tex., El Paso, 1992. Mem. prodn. staff Sta. KDBC-TV, El Paso, Tex., 1971-73; v.p. Sanders Co. Advt., El Paso, 1973-74, film critic El Paso Times, 1972-77; lectr. film studies U. Tex., El Paso, 1995—; freelance photographer, El Paso, 1974—; pres. CM Pub., El Paso, 1981-89. Photographer, co-author: Country Music: A Look at the Men Who've Made It, 1982; author: Literature and Landscape: Writers of the Southwest, 1988; film critic Sta. KTEP, 1993—. Bd. dirs. N. Mex. State U. Mus. Adv. Bd., Las Cruces, 1982-90; dir., vice-chmn. Shelter for Battered Women, El Paso, 1981-86; active Jr. League, 1977-90, sustaining mem. 1990—, C. of C. Leadership El Paso Program, 1983-84; mem. El Paso County Hist. Comm., 1984-89, vice chmn., 1986, 87, El Paso County Hist. Alliance (v. chmn. 1986-88); trustee El Paso Community Found., 1984—; adv. bd. El Paso Arts Resources dept., 1987-93, chmn., 1991-93; mem. adv. bd. Tex. Film Alliance, 1991—, Tex. Ctr. for the Book, 1987—; mem. literary adv. panel Tex. Commn. on Arts, 1991-93; mem. adv. coun. El Paso Bus. Com. for Arts, 1988-90; mem. adv. coun. Harry Ransom Humanities Rsch. Ctr. U. Tex., Austin; mem. Tex. Com. Humanities Bd., 1993—; mem. lit. panel Cultural Arts Coun. Houston, 1993; mem. adv. com. Tex. Book Fair, 1996. Recipient J.C. Penny Golden Rule award, 1989, Vol. Svc. award El Paso Bur. United Way, 1989, Clara Barton Medallion ARC, 1979, Conquistador award City of El Paso, 1991; named Outstanding Active Mem. Jr. League, 1987-88, Outstanding Sustaining Mem., 1993-94; named to El Paso Women's Hall of Fame, 1992. Mem. Western Lit. Assn., U. Tex. at El Paso Libr. Assn. (v.p. 1987-88, pres. 1989-91), Modern Lang. Assn., Stanford U. Alumni Assn. Episcopalian.

FARBER, JACKIE, editor; b. Jersey City, Apr. 16, 1927; d. Herman B. and Pauline (Birnbaum) Levine; m. Samuel Farber, June 25, 1950 (div. 1981); children: Thomas Adam, John David; m. 2d Jay Topkis, Sept. 27, 1981. BA, Smith Coll., 1949. Editor Bernard Geis Assocs., N.Y.C., 1963-72; sr. editor Delacorte Press, N.Y.C., 1972-74, exec. editor, 1980-81, editor-in-chief, 1981-89, fiction editor, 1989—; sr. editor William Morrow, N.Y.C., 1974-78, Random House, N.Y.C., 1978-80; fiction editor Delacorte Press div. Bantam Doubleday Dell Pub. Group, 1980-91; v.p., fiction editor Delacorte Press divsn. Bantam Doubleday Dell Pub. Group, 1991—. Mem. Women's Media Group. Jewish. Home: 155 E 72nd St New York NY 10021-4371 Office: Bantam Doubleday Dell Pub Co 1540 Broadway New York NY 10036-4039

FARBER, LILLIAN, retired photography equipment company executive; b. N.Y.C., Aug. 4, 1920; d. Louis and Fannie (Disraeli) Bachrach; m. Leonard L. Farber, Nov. 3, 1940 (div. 1975); children: Lindy Linder, Robert D. (dec.), Peggy, Felicia Gervais. BA, NYU, 1940; MA, Sarah Lawrence Coll., 1966. Co-dir. Upward Bound Sarah Lawrence Coll., Bronxville, N.Y., 1966-70, dean student svcs., 1973-76; v.p., owner Zone VI Studios, Inc., Newfane, Vt., 1976-90, ret., 1990. One-woman photography shows include, Vt., N.Y. V.p. Greenburgh League Women Voters, Hartsdale, N.Y., 1955-63; state com. woman N.Y. State Dem. Com., 1968-70; family adv. Westchester Coun. of Social Agys., White Plains, N.Y., 1970-73; pres. bd. trustees Moore Free Libr., Newfane, 1977—; chmn. bd. trustees Marlboro (Vt.) Coll., 1978—; trustee Vt. Coun. on the Arts, 1992-96; mem. Vt. Bicentennial Commn., 1990-91. Mem. ACLU. Home: Maple Hollow PO Box 265 Newfane VT 05345

FARBER, VIOLA ANNA, dancer, choreographer, educator; b. Heidelberg, Germany, Feb. 25, 1931; came to U.S., 1938, naturalized, 1944; d. Eduard and Dora (Schmidt) F.; m. Jeffrey Clarke Slayton, June 14, 1971. Student, Am. U., 1949-51, Black Mountain Coll., 1951-52. Dancer Merce Cunningham Dance Co., N.Y.C., 1952-65; instr. dance Adelphia U., N.Y.C., 1959-67, Bennington (Vt.) Coll., 1967-68, NYU, 1971-73; dir., tchr. Viola Farber Dance Studio, N.Y.C., 1969-84; also artistic dir., choreographer, dancer Viola Farber Dance Co., N.Y.C., 1969-86; chair dance dept. Sarah Lawrence Coll., 1988—; artistic dir. Centre National de Danse Contemporaine, Angers, France, 1981-83; dir. Found. Contemproary Performance Arts; tchr. Am. Dance Festival, Durham, N.C., 1987, ADF, Seoul, Korea, 1990; guest tchr. throughout U.S., Asia and Europe including Holland, Germany, Denmark, others. Choreographer Viola Farber Dance Co. Théâtre contemporain d'Anders, France, Ballet Thèâtre Français, Repertory Dance Theatre, Utah, Manhattan Festival Ballet, Nancy Hauser Dance Co., Dance depts. Adelphi, NYU, Ohio State U. and U. Utah, Janet Gillespie and Present Co.; commd. by Heinz Found.; collaborated with Robert Rauschenberg and David Tudor on video tape Brazos River, 1976; choreographed Jeux Chorégraphique for Ballet Thèâtre Français de Nancy, 1980, Extemporary Dance co., London, Plymouth, Eng., 1984, London, 1986; performed Centre Poompidou, Paris, 1979; choreographer for Emlyn Claid, London, 1986, Pauline Daniels, London, 1986,, Nat. Youth Dance Co., Eng., 1986, New Dance Ensemble, Mpls., 1988; chroeographer Duet for Emmy and Karen, 1989; choregoraphed and performed Au Fil du Temps, Lyon, France, 1989, with Mathilde Monner Ainsi de Suite, Paris, 1992, Montpelier, 1994, Shipwreck, 1995, choreographed and performed at Joyce Theater, N.Y.C. with Ralph Lemon, 1995; guest tchr. London Contemporary Dance Sch., Richard Auston Dan Company, CNDC, Angers, France, 1996. Recipient Gold medal with Jeff Slayton, Paris Dance Festival, 1971; Guggenheim fellow, 1983-84; grantee NEA, 1975, 79, NEA, 1976, 81, N.Y. State Coun. on Arts, 1974-79, CAPS, 1974, 78, N.Y. Dept. Cultural Affairs, 1977. Office: Sarah Lawrence Coll Dept of Dance Bronxville NY 10708-5500

FARBMAN, RUTH ELLEN, lawyer; b. N.Y.C., July 1, 1935; d. Leon and Clara (Gersman) Shacknow; divorced; children: Leon Edward, Caroline Barbara, S. Peter. BA magna cum laude, Smith Coll., 1956; MA, Northwestern U., Evanston, Ill., 1972; JD, Northwestern U., Chgo., 1987. Claims rep., field rep. supr. Social Security Adminstrn., U.S. Dept. HEW, N.Y.C., 1957-63; assoc. Eich & Franklin, Chgo., 1987-95; cert. arbitrator Cook County Arbitration Bd., Chgo., 1993—; mem. social security disability project Northwestern U. Law Sch., Chgo., 1986-87. Pres. bd. dirs. Probation Support Sys., Evanston. Mem. AAUW, Chgo. Bar Assn., Woman's Bar Assn. Democrat. Jewish. Home: 2 E Oak St Unit 3604 Chicago IL 60611-1218

FARENTHOLD, FRANCES TARLTON, lawyer; b. Corpus Christi, Tex., Oct. 2, 1926; d. Benjamin Dudley and Catherine (Bluntzer) Tarlton; children: Dudley Tarlton, George Edward, Emilie, James Doughterty, Vincent Bluntzer (dec.). AB, Vassar Coll., 1946; JD, U. Tex., 1949; LLD, Hood Coll., 1973, Boston U., 1973, Regis Coll., 1976, Lake Erie Coll., 1979, Elmira Coll., 1981, Coll. of Santa Fe, 1985. Bar: Tex. 1949. Pvt. practice, 1949-65, 67-76, 80—; mem. Tex. Ho. of Reps., 1968-72; dir. legal aide Nueces County, 1965-67; asst. prof. law Tex. So. U., Houston; pres. Wells Coll., Aurora, N.Y., 1976-80; disting. vis. prof. Thurgood Marshall Tex. So. U., Houston, 1994-95. Mem. Human Relations Com., Corpus Christi, 1963-68, Corpus Christi Citizen's Com. Community Improvement, 1966-68; mem. Tex. adv. com. to U.S. Commn. on Civil Rights, 1968-76; mem. nat. adv. council ACLU; mem. Orgn. for Preservation Unblemished Shoreline, 1964—; Dem. candidate for Gov. of Tex., 1972; del. Dem. Nat. Conv., 1972, 1st woman nominated to be candidate v.p. U.S., 1972; nat. co-chmn. Citizens to Elect McGovern-Shriver, 1972; chmn. Nat. Women's Polit. Caucus, 1973-75; mem. Dem. platform com., 1988; trustee Vassar Coll., 1975-83; bd. dirs. Fund for Constl. Govt., Ctr. for Devel. Policy, 1983—, Mexican Am. Legal Def. and Ednl. Fund, 1980-83; chmn. Inst. for Policy Studies, 1986-91. Recipient Lyndon B. Johnson Woman of Year award, 1973. Mem. State Bar Tex. Office: 2929 Buffalo Speedway Apt 1813 Houston TX 77098-1710

FARFÁN, PATRICIA DEANNA, nursing administrator; b. Bogota, Colombia, Dec. 14, 1947; came to U.S., 1952; d. Jose Maria Farfán and Agnes Maxine (Foster) Lusk; m. Robert B. Neese, Aug. 17, 1990 (div. Feb. 1996). BSN, U. Tex., Austin, 1970; AA in Lang. and Lit., San Antonio Coll., 1992; postgrad., U. Tex., San Antonio. RN, Tex. Nurse recruiter Kansas City (Mo.) VA Hosp., 1980-83; tchr. ESL, El Colombo, Bogota, 1983-85; vis. nurse Upjohn Home Health, Pasadena, Tex., 1985-86; shift leader, preceptor Med. Ctr. Conroe, Tex., 1986-87; supr. patient care Vis. Nurse Assn., Houston, 1987-88; cons. Option Care, Houston, 1988-89; contract nurse Logos, Houston, 1989-91; home infusion specialist Caremark, San Antonio, 1994; evening nursing supr. Audie Murphy VA Hosp., San Antonio, 1994—; meme. caradiovasc. nursing com. Am. Heart Assn., San Antonio, 1994—. Contbr. articles to various mags. Vol. Today's Hospice, San Antonio, 1996. 1st lt. Nurse Corps, USAF, 1970-71. Mem. NOW, McNay Art Mus., Frinds Unitarian Universalists, Assn. for Rsch. and Enlightenment, Friends KLRN Pub. TV, Friends San Antonio Pub. Libr., Inst. Noetic Scis., Josephine Theater, Sigma Theta Tau. Home: 8101 Scottshill San Antonio TX 78209 Office: Audie Murphy Meml VA Hosp 740 Merton Minter San Antonio TX 78284

FARHAT, CAROL S., motion picture company executive; b. Santa Monica, Calif.; d. Annis Abraham Farhat; divorced; 1 child, Michael. Student, Santa Monica Coll., 1967; Assoc. degree, Inst. Audio Rsch., 1976-78; student, Otis Parsons Inst., 1980-84, UCLA, 1984-90; BA in Bus., Music, Antioch U., 1992. Recording studio mgr. The Village Recorder, L.A., 1972-78; audio engr. The Village Recorder Studio, L.A., 1978-79; music adminstr. 20th Century Fox Film Corp., Beverly Hills, Calif., 1980-82, music supr., 1983-86, music dir., 1986-92; supr. internat. music 20th Century Fox Film Corp., Tokyo, 1993; music prodr. Scopus Films, England, 1987-89; songwriter Music Experts Ltd., Santa Monica, Calif., 1989-90; v.p. music 20th Century Fox Film Corp., 1994-95; v.p. TV music and feature Am. Fedn. Musicians advisor 20th Century Fox Music, 1995-96. Author: China Diary, 1992; composer (music book) Children's Songbook, 1991; songwriter (for film) Rockin' Reindeer, 1990. Mem. BMI, NATAs, NARAS, Women in Film, Am. Film Inst., Pacific Composers Forum, Entertainment Industry Counsel. Office: 20th Century Fox Film Corp PO Box 900 Beverly Hills CA 90213-0900

FARINA, LAURA, lawyer; b. Trenton, N.J., Aug. 29, 1961; d. Charles Anthony and Regina Rose (Alvino) F. BA, Georgetown U., 1983; postgrad., NYU, 1985; JD, Rutgers U., 1988. Bar: N.J. 1988, N.Y. 1990, D.C. 1991, U.S. Dist. Ct. N.J. 1988, U.S. Dist. Ct. (so. and ea. dists.) N.Y. 1990. Law clk. to Hon. Justice Gary S. Stein N.J. Supreme Ct., Hackensack, 1988-89; assoc. Paul, Weiss, Rifkind, Wharton & Garrison, N.Y.C., 1989-91; dep. atty. gen. Office of N.J. Atty. Gen., Trenton, 1991-92; assoc. Crummy, Del Deo, Dolan, Griffinger & Vecchione, Newark, 1992-95; pvt. practice Princeton, N.J., 1995—; barrister Am. Inn. of Ct., New Brunswick, N.J., 1993-94. Articles editor Rutgers Law Rev., 1986-88. Sec.-treas. Princeton Day Sch. Alumni Bd., 1993—; alumni interviewer Alumni Admissions Program, Georgetown U., Princeton, 1984—. N.J. Bar Found. scholar, 1987-88. Mem. ABA, N.J. State Bar Assn., N.Y.C., Bar Assn., Sports Lawyers Assn. Home: 121 Rainier Ct # 10 Princeton NJ 08540 Office: 194 Nassau St Princeton NJ 08542

FARINELLI, JEAN L., public relations firm executive; b. Phila., July 26, 1946; d. Albert J. and Edith M. (Falini) F. BA, Am. U., Washington, 1968; MA, Ohio State U., Columbus, 1969. Asst. pub. relations dir. Dow Jones & Co., Inc., N.Y.C., 1969-71; account exec. Carl Byoir & Assocs., Inc., N.Y.C., 1972-74, v.p., 1974-80, sr. v.p., 1980-82; pres. Tracy-Locke/BBDO Pub. Relations, Dallas, 1982-87; pres. Creamer Dickson Basford, Inc., N.Y.C., 1987-88, chmn., chief exec. officer, 1988—; pres., chief exec. officer Eurocom Corp. & PR (U.S.), 1991, Corp. Graphics, Inc., 1992. Trustee Nat. Found. Infectious Diseases. Recipient PR CaseBook, PR Reporter, N.H., 1984, Silver Spur, Tex. Pub. Rels. Assn., Dallas, 1985, Matrix award Women in Comms., 1993. Mem. Pub. Rels. Soc. Am. (Silver Anvil award 1980-81, 85, Excalibur award Houston chpt. 1985, chmn. 1986, Silver Anvil awards chmn. 1987, honors and awards com. chmn. Spring Conf. Counselors Acad. 1989, acad. exec. bd. 1990-91, trustee found.), Women in Comms. (chmn. 1995, Matrix award 1993), Nat. Investor Rels. Inst., Internat. Pub. Rels. Assn. (pub. rels. seminar), Arthur W. Page Soc. (trustee, treas.), Nat. Found. for Infectious Disease (trustee), The Wisemen. Home: 20 Sutton Pl S New York NY 10022 Office: Creamer Dickson Basford 1633 Broadway New York NY 10019-6708

FARLEY, BARBARA SUZANNE, lawyer; b. Salt Lake City, Dec. 13, 1949; d. Ross Edward Farley and Barbara Ann (Edwards) Farley Swanson; m. Arthur Hoffman Ferris, Apr. 9, 1982 (div. 1995); children: Barbara Whitney, Taylor Edwards. BA with honors, Mills Coll., 1972; JD, U. Calif.-Hastings, San Francisco, 1976. Bar: Calif. 1976. Extern law clk. to justice Calif. Supreme Ct., San Francisco, 1975; assoc. Pillsbury, Madison & Sutro, San Francisco, 1976-78, Bronson, Bronson & McKinnon, San Francisco, 1978-80, Goldstein & Phillips, San Francisco, 1980-84; ptnr., head litigation, Rosen, Wachtell & Gilbert, San Francisco, 1984-89; of counsel Lempres & Wulfsberg, Oakland, Calif., 1989—; arbitrator U.S. Dist. Ct. (no. dist.) Calif., San Francisco, 1981—, Calif. Superior Ct., San Francisco, 1984-89; judge pro tem San Francisco Mcpl. Ct., 1983—; probation monitor Calif. State Bar, 1990—; speaker Nat. Bus. Inst. Estate Adminstrn. Contbg. author Calif. Continuing Edn. of the Bar; mng. editor Hastings Coll. of Law-U. Calif.-San Francisco Constl. Law Quarterly, 1975-76; civil litigation reporter. Mills Coll. scholar, 1970-72, U. Calif.-Hastings, San Francisco scholar, 1973-76. Mem. ATLA, San Francisco Bar Assn., Calif. Trial Lawyers Assn., San Francisco Trial Lawyers Assn., Alameda Bar Assn.

FARLEY, CAROLE, soprano; b. Le Mars, Iowa, Nov. 29, 1946; d. Melvin and Irene (Reid) F.; m. Jose Serebrier, Mar. 29, 1969; 1 dau., Lara Adriana Francesca. MusB, Ind. U., 1968. Fulbright scholar Hochschule für Musik, Munich, 1968-69. (Musician of Month, Musical Am./Hi Fidelity 1977), Am. debut at Town Hall, N.Y.C., 1969, Paris debut, Nat. Orch., 1975, London debut, Royal Philharmonic Soc., 1975, S.Am. debut, Teatro Colon, Philharmonic Orch., Buenos Aires, 1975; soloist with, major Am. and European symphony orchs., 1970—, soloist, Welsh Nat. Opera, 1971, 72, Cologne Opera, 1972-75, Phila. Lyric Opera, 1974, Brussels Opera, 1972, Lyon Opera, 1976, 77, Strasbourg Opera, 1975, Linz Opera, 1969, N.Y.C. Opera, 1976, New Orleans Opera, 1977, Cin. Opera, 1977, Met. Opera Co., N.Y.C., 1977—, Zurich Opera, 1979, Chgo. Lyric Opera, 1981, Can. Opera Co., 1980, Düsseldorf Opera, 1980, 81, 84, Palm Beach Opera, 1982, Theatre Mcpl. Paris, 1983, Theatre Royale dela Monnaie Brussels, 1983, Teatro Regio, Turin, Italy, 1983, Nice Opera (France), 1984, 86, 87, 88, Cologne Opera, 1985, Teatro Comunale, Florence, Italy, 1985, BBC Opera, 1987, TeatroColon, Buenos Aires, 1987, 88, 89, Opera de Montpellier (France), 1988, 94, Theatre des Champs Elysees, Paris, 1988, Helsinki Festival, 1989, Tchaikovsky Opera Arias Pickwick/IMP Records, 1993, Met. Opera Premiere Shostakovich Opera Lady Macbeth of Mzensk, 1994, Theatre Capitole de Toulouse Wozzeck, 1994; on New Zealand Broadcasting Commn. Orchestral Tour, 1986; TV film for ABC Australia La Voix Humaine, also co-producer compact disc and video for BBC, London, 1990; co-producer compact disc and video The Telephone, 1990; recorded compact disc Weill, 1992, Metro. Opera Shostakovich: "Lady Macbeth", 1994, Strausslieder with Czech Philharmonic, 1995, Les Soldats Morts, 1995 (Grand Prix du Disque); recorded for Deutsche Gramophone, Chandos, CBS, BBC, ASV, RCA, Ricercar and Varese-Sarabande records, London/Decca Records, IMP Masters, Pickwick. Recipient Abiati prize for her role as Lulu, Italy, 1984, Deutsche Schallplatten award for recording Carole Farley Sings French Songs, 1988; named Alumni of Year, U. Ind., 1976. Mem. Am. Guild Mus. Artists. Home: 270 Riverside Dr New York NY 10025-5209

FARLEY, JENNIE TIFFANY TOWLE, industrial and labor relations educator; b. Fanwood, N.J., Nov. 2, 1932; d. Howard Albert and Dorothy Jane (Van Wagner) Towle; m. Donald Thorn Farley Jr., June 16, 1956; children—Claire Hamlin, Anne Tiffany, Peter Towle. BA, Cornell U., 1954, MS, 1969, PhD, 1970. Mem. editorial staff Mademoiselle and Seventeen mags., N.Y.C., 1954-56; freelance writer, Eng., Sweden, Peru, 1956-67; lectr., research assoc., adj. asst. prof. Cornell U., Ithaca, N.Y., 1970-72, dir. women's studies, 1972-76, asst. prof. Sch. Indsl. and Labor Relations, 1976-82, assoc. prof., 1982-89, prof., 1989—, exec. bd. dirs. women's studies program, 1970—; vis. prof. Ctr. for Women Scholars and Research on Women Uppsala U., Sweden, 1985-86; trustee Cornell U., 1988-92. Author: Affirmative Action and the Woman Worker, 1979, Academic Women and Employment Discrimination, 1982; editor: Sex Discrimination in Higher Education, 1982, The Woman in Management, 1983, Women Workers in Fifteen Countries, 1985. Recipient Corinne Galvin award Tompkins County Human Rights Commn., 1987, Unsung Heroine award Cen. N.Y. NOW, 1991. Mem. AAUP, Ithaca AAUW (pres. 1980-82), Grad. Women in Sci., Sociologists for Women in Soc., Tompkins County NOW. Club: Cornell Women's of Tompkins County. Home: 711 Triphammer Rd Ithaca NY 14850-2504 Office: Cornell U Sch Indsl & Labor Rels Ithaca NY 14853

FARLEY, PEGGY ANN, finance company executive; b. Phila., Mar. 12, 1947; d. Harry E. and Ruth (Lloyd) F.; m. Reid McIntyre, Dec. 31, 1985 (div.); 1 child, Margaret Ruth Farley. AB, Barnard Coll., 1970; MA with high honors, Columbia U., 1972. Admissions officer Barnard Coll., N.Y.C., 1973-76; adminstr. Citibank NA, Athens, Greece, 1976-77; cons. Orgn. Resources Counselors, N.Y.C., 1977-78; sr. assoc. Morgan Stanley and Co. Inc., N.Y.C., 1978-84; mng. dir., chief exec. officer AMAS Securities Inc., N.Y.C., 1984—; also bd. dirs. AMAS Securities, Inc., N.Y.C.; bd. dirs. AMAS Group, London. Author: The Place Of The Yankee And Euro Bond Markets In A Financing Program For The People's Republic of China, 1982. Mem. Columbia U. Seminar on China-U.S. Bus., Rep. Senatorial Inner Circle, Fgn. Policy Assn. Mem. Asia Soc., China Inst., Met. Club, Econ. Club of N.Y. Republican. Presbyterian. Home: 1160 Fifth Ave New York NY 10029 also: 908 Owassa Rd Newton NJ 07860-4015 Office: AMAS Securities Inc 520 Madison Ave New York NY 10022-4213

FARMER, ANN DAHLSTROM, English language professor; b. South Gate, Calif., June 18, 1934; d. Merrill Xanthus and Marcia Hazel (Ross) Dahlstrom; m. Roger Lee Chandler, Aug. 19, 1956 (div. 1960); 1 child, Mark Walton Chandler; m. Malcolm French Farmer, Oct. 25, 1963. BA, Whittier Coll., 1956, MA, 1971; MA, Calif. State U., Fullerton, 1976. Prof.'s asst. Whittier (Calif.) Coll., 1960-62, gen. studies instr., 1963-70, English instr., 1970-72, dir. freshman English, 1972-87, dir. English language and lit. dept., 1978-86, asst. prof. English, 1983-95, assoc. prof. English, 1995—. Author: Jessamyn West, rev. edit., 1996; co-author: Creative Analysis, rev. edit., 1978. Mem. AAUW (gift honoree, 1995), Western Lit. Assn., Linguistic Soc., Delta Kappa Gamma (Star in Edn., 1990), Phi Kappa Phi. Democrat. Society of Friends. Office: Whittier Coll 13406 Philadelphia St Whittier CA 90608

FARMER, CATHY ANN, accountant; b. Tacoma, June 17, 1968; d. Carl Leroy and Carol Ann (Workman) F.; m. James Tobin Staley, Aug. 26, 1989 (div. July 1993). BBA in Fin. cum laude, Pacific Luth. U., 1994. Mail specialist Weyerhaeuser Co., Tacoma, 1987-88, adminstrv. asst., 1989, office support specialist, 1989-90, exec. sec., 1990-93, acct., 1993—. Mem., treas. ARC Tacoma Pierce County profls. club, 1996; vol. Habitat for Humanity. Mem. Inst. Mgmt. Accts. Office: Weyerhaeuser Co 501 S 336th St Ste 102 Tacoma WA 98477

FARMER, CHERYL CHRISTINE, internist, industrial hygienist; b. Detroit, Sept. 15, 1946; d. Donald Richard and Dorothy Ruth (Mattoon) F.; m. Dennis Michael Mukai, Aug. 3, 1968 (div. Sept. 1977). BA in Edn., Mich. State U., 1968, D of Medicine, 1982; BS in Biology, Wright State U., 1974; MS in Indsl. Health, U. Mich., 1978. Tchr. art Five Points Elem. Sch., Fairborn, Ohio, 1968-70; real estate saleswoman Dawson Realty, Fairborn, 1970; sanitarian trainee Dayton (Ohio) Health Dept., 1973; acting chief air pollution control southwest dist. Ohio EPA, Dayton, 1975; data analyst Columbus, Ohio, 1976; intern in medicine St. Joseph Mercy Hosp., Ann Arbor, Mich., 1982-83, resident in medicine, 1983-85; intern in medicine Winton Hills Med. Ctr., Cin., 1985-87; pvt. practice Ann Arbor, Mich., 1988—, Ann Arbor, 1988—; physician Cin. Health Dept., 1987-88; mem. peer rev. com. Magnacare Health Maintenance Orgn., Cin., 1988; mem. membership com. St. Joseph Mercy Hosp., 1990-94; mem. ethics com. Huron Valley Physicians Assn., 1996—; mem. bioethics com. Mich. State Med. Soc., 1994—; past com. mem. Washington Co. Med. Soc., 1992-94; commr. city charter City of Ypsilanti, 1993-94. Co-chmn. Citizens for Clean Air Com., Dayton, 1970-74, Miami Valley Citizens for Transfer, Fairborn, 1974; mayor of Ypsilanti, Mich., 1995—. Recipient Athena award, 1996, Ypsilanti area C. of C. Mem. AMA, ACP, Am. Soc. Internal Medicine, Am. Med. Womens' Assn., Acad. Medicine Cin. (mem. steering com. women in medicine 1986-88, co-chmn. networking and mentoring subcom. 1986-88), LWV, NOW, Sierra Club, Phi Kappa Phi, Kappa Delta Pi. Democrat. Office: 1950 Manchester Rd Ann Arbor MI 48104-4916

FARMER, DEBORAH KIRILUK, marketing professional; b. Richmond, Va., June 6, 1956; d. Curtis Wayne Kiriluk and Lilan Baltz Starford; m. Roger Paul Schatzel, Oct. 1993. Student, J. Sargeant Reynolds Community Coll., 1974-78, Va. Commonwealth U., 1978-79, John Tyler Community Coll., 1986. Paralegal asst. Hunton Willams, Richmond, 1974; coord. office svcs. Va. Housing Devel. Authority, Richmond, 1975-78; dist. adminstr. Lanier Bus. Products, 1978-80; exec. asst. Old Dominion Emergency Med. Svcs. Alliance, Richmond; asst program dir. Sta. WRVA-AM, Richmond, 1981-83; coord. local sales Stas. WRNL-AM and WRXL-FM, Richmond, 1983-84; sr. account exec. Sta. WTVR-FM, Richmond, 1984-85; mgr. nat. sales Sta. WQSF-FM, Richmond, 1985-88; nat. account exec. HNW&H, Atlanta, 1988-89; mgr. local sales Sta. WTKN/WHVE, St. Petersburg, Fla., 1989-90; gen. sales mgr. WFNS-AM, Tampa, Fla., 1990-91; sr. bus. devel. mgr. Staff Leasing Group, Tampa, 1991—; cons. mem., gov. adv. bd. EMS Pub. Info. Edn., Richmond, 1986; bd. dirs. Travelers Aid Soc. Va., 1987-88, sec., mem. exec. commn. Contbr. articles to profl. jours. CPR instr. ARC, Richmond, 1979-87, mem. VOAD com., 1994; emergency med. tech. Manchester Vol. Rescue Squad, Richmond, 1979-86, sec. bd. dirs., 1979-81, pub. rels. officer, 1985-86; dir. disaster relief Tampa Bay Bapt. Assn., 1993—; chair pub. rels. com. FBC Brandon, 1990-94. Am. Bus. Women's Assn. scholar, 1975. Mem. Am. Women in Radio and TV (charter, v.p. 1987-91, pres.). Republican. Baptist.

FARMER, ELAINE FRAZIER, state legislator; b. New Castle, Pa., Mar. 14, 1937; d. John R. and Pearle (McLure) Frazier; m. Sterling N. Farmer, Aug. 22, 1959; children: Heather, Drew. BBA, Case Western Reserve U., 1958, MEd, 1964. Employment supr. Stouffer Corp., Cleve., 1958-60; tchr. Lakewood Schs., Cleve., 1960-64; subs. tchr. North Allegheny Schs., Pitts., 1972-77; agt. Howard Hanna Real Estate Services, Pitts., 1977-86, mgr., 1983-86; elected mem. Ho. of Reps., Harrisburg, Pa., 1986—; state dir. Women in Govt. Councilman Town of McCandless, Pa., 1980-86; trustee Northland Libr., Pitts., 1980-85, North Hills Passavant Hosp., 1990-92; liaison McCandless Planning Commn., 1984-86; mem. comty. adv. bd. St. Barnabas Nursing Home, coun. Pitts. Cancer Inst., 1994—. Mem. Nat. Order Women Legislators, Am. Legis. Exch. Coun., Women in Govt. (state dir.), North Hills C. of C. Republican. Presbyterian. Office: House of Reps PO Box 202020 Harrisburg PA 17120-2020

FARMER, JANENE ELIZABETH, artist, educator; b. Albuquerque, Oct. 16, 1946; d. Charles John Watt and Regina M. (Brown) Kruger; m. Michael Hugh Bolton, Apr. 1965 (div.); m. Frank Urban Farmer, May, 1972 (div.). BA in Art, San Diego State U., 1969. Owner, operator Iron Walrus Pottery, 1972-79; designer ceramic and fabric murals, Coronado, Calif., 1979-

82; executed commns. for clients in U.S.A., Can., Japan and Mex., 1972—; designer fabric murals and bldg. interiors; painter rare and endangered animals, Coronado and La Jolla, Calif., 1982—; tchr. Catholic schs., San Diego, 1982-87, Ramona Unified Sch. Dist., 1988—, mentor tchr.; instr. U. Calif., San Diego, 1979-83, 92—. Mem. Coronado Arts and Humanities Coun., 1979-81. Grantee Calif. Arts Coun., 1980-81, resident artist U. Calif., San Diego; U. San Diego grad. fellow dept. edn., 1984; tchr. environ. art San Diego Natural History Mus. and San Diego Wild Animal Park, summer, 1996. Mem. edn. adv. com. La Jolla (Calif.) Playhouse, 1996. Mem. Am. Soc. Interior Designers (affiliate). Roman Catholic. Home: 4435 Nobel Dr Apt 35 San Diego CA 92122-1559

FARMER, MARTHA KNIGHT, academic administrator, executive; b. Roanoke, Ala., July 21, 1938; d. Edward Wilson Jr. and Bobbie (Neely) Knight; m. Claude William Farmer Jr., Oct. 10, 1958; children: Claude William III, Andrea Elizabeth. BS, U. Ala., 1960, MSc, 1965; PhD, U. S.C., 1977. CPA, Ga. Tchr. math. Aiken (S.C.) Jr. High Sch., 1964-66; from instr. to prof. Sch. of Bus. Adminstrn., Augusta (Ga.) Coll., 1966-94, coord. acctg., MIS and bus. law depts., 1982-85, acting assoc. dean, 1985-86, acting dean, 1986-88, dean, 1988-91, 93-94; acting pres. Augusta (Ga.) Coll., 1991-93; staff acct. Baird and Co., CPAs, Augusta, 1970-71; pres. Castleton State Coll., 1994—; mem. exec. com., treas. Vt. Higher Edn. Coun., 1995-96. editl. advisor Soc. for Advancement of Mgmt. Advanced Mgmt. Jour., North Dalmouth, Mass., 1990-92. Bd. dirs. Augusta chpt. ARC, 1992-94, Banker's First, Augusta, 1993-94, Rutland Econ. Devel. Corp., Vt., 1996—; mem. cmty. adv. bd. Jr. League Augusta, 1992-94. Mem. Am. Acctg. Assn. (com. rels. 2-yr. faculty), Ga. Soc. CPAs (sec.-treas., v.p., program chair Augusta chpt., pres. 1983-87), So. Bus. Adminstrn. Assn. (exec. com. 1988-94, sec.-treas. 1990-92, v.p. for programs 1993-94), Edn. Found. Ga. Soc. CPAs (bd. dirs. 1988-94), Augusta C. of C. (econ. devel. com. 1988-92, chair existing industry com. 1989-90, bd. dirs. 1989-91, 93-94, vice chmn. edn. com. 1991, exec. com. 1992-94, treas. 1994), Rotary, Phi Kappa Phi (editl. advisor Nat. Forum 1989-93). Home: PO Box 1425 Castleton VT 05735-1425 Office: Castleton State Coll Castleton VT 05735

FARMER, MARY BAUDER, small business owner; b. San Diego, Nov. 30, 1953; d. Chester Robert and Dixie (Cook) Bauder; m. L. Michael Dowling, July 1990. BS, Auburn U., 1986; postgrad., Ga. State U., 1992—. Exec. dir. Birmingham Woman's Med. Clinic, Ala., 1975-80; pres. Beacon Clinic, Montgomery, Ala., 1980-83; ptnr. Hill, Rose and Farmer, Atlanta, 1988-90; owner, mgr. Mary Farmer Fine Art, Atlanta, 1990—; creative dir., pres. Twin Studios, Inc., Atlanta, 1995—; v.p. Global Interests Inc., 1990—. Author, pub.: The Landlord's Primer for Georgia: A Self-Help Guide for Inexperienced Landlords. Mem. pub. rels. com. Project Open Hand, Ga. Citizens for Arts; mem. Bus. Com. for Arts. Mem. LWV, Ga. Women's Agenda (founder), Omicron Delta Kappa. Democrat. Office: Twin Studios Inc 312 N Highland Ave Atlanta GA 30307

FARMER, SUSAN BOMGARDNER, municipal official; b. Hershey, Pa., Nov. 11, 1964; d. William Earl and Jean Rupp (Ebersole) Bomgardner; m. Timothy Joel Farmer, May 7, 1988. BA, Lycoming Coll., Williamsport, Pa., 1986. Reporter Loudoun Times-Mirror, Leesburg, Va., 1986-87; copy editor DCI Pub., Reston, Va., 1987-89; pub. info. officer Town of Leesburg, 1989—. Bd. dirs. Loudoun Tourism Coun., Leesburg, 1995—; sec. Leesburg Cable Commn., 1989—; grad. Leadership Loudoun; charter mem. Friends of Balch Libr., 1995; publicity chmn. Arbor Day Com., Loudoun County, 1990—; co-founder Friends of Yellow Schoolhouse Rd., Round Hill, Va., 1995. Recipient Comm. award Va. Mcpl. League, 1995, Grand award for outstanding pub. periodical City Hall Digest, 1992, Conservation Group of Yr. Soil and Water Conservation Dist., 1995. Mem. City-County Comm. and Mktg. (sec. 1994—, Savvy award for mktg. 1995), Nat. Assn. Govt. Communicators, Va. Govt. Communicators, Nat. Assn. Telecom. Officers. Office: Town of Leesburg 25 W Market St Leesburg VA 20175

FARMER, SUSAN LAWSON, broadcasting executive, former secretary of state; b. Boston, May 29, 1942; d. Ralph and Margaret (Tyng) Lawson; m. Malcolm Farmer, III, Apr. 6, 1968; children: Heidi Benson, Stephanie Lawson. Student, Garland Jr. Coll., 1960-61, Brown U., 1961-62. Mem. Providence Home Rule Charter Commn., 1979-80; sec. of state State of R.I., Providence, 1983-87; pres., CEO, Sta. WSBE-TV, Providence, 1987—; spl. adv. R.I. Family Ct., 1978-83; mem. nat. voting stds. panel Fed. Election Commn. co-chmn. Nat. Voter Edn. Project; mem. electoral coll., 1984; chmn. Gov.'s Com. on Ethics in Govt., 1985-86; mem. teaching facility and adv. panel Internat. Ctr. on Election Law and Adminstrn.; mem. nat. edn. adv. com. Pub. Broadcasting System, 1987—; trustee Eastern Ednl. YV Network, 1987—; mem. R.I. Task Force on Tech., 1995—; bd. dirs. , exec. com. Program Resources Group, 1993—; mem. industry issues adv. com. Am.'s Pub. Television Stas., 1994—. Bd. dirs. Justice Resources Corp., Marathon House, Inc., R.I. Council Alcoholism, R.I. Hist. Soc., Planned Parenthood (R.I. chpt.), R.I. Rape Crisis Ctr., The Newport Inst.; mem. Mayor's Task Force on Child Abuse, R.I. Film Commn.; v.p. Miriam Hosp. Found.; mem. adv. com. Women in Polit. and Govtl. Careers Program, U. R.I., 1985—; mem. adv. bd. Com. for Study of Am. Electorate-Ford Found. Project-Efficacy in State Voting Laws, 1986; mem. Commn. to Study Length of Election Process, 1985—; steering com. Nat. Fund for America's Future, Project Vote R.I.; bd. dirs. Dawn for Children Tng. Thru Placement; pres. Channel 36 Found.; bd. dirs. R.I. Anti-Drug Coalition Exec. Com. Named Woman of Yr., Nat. Women's Polit. Caucus, 1980. Mem. LWV, N.E. Assn. Schs. and Colls. (com. on tech. and course instns.), So. Ednl. Comms. Assn. (bd. dirs. 1993—), R.I. Women's Polit. Caucus (Woman of Yr. 1980), Bus. and Profl. Women (Woman of Yr. 1984), Common Cause, Save the Bay, Women for Non-nuclear Future, Providence Preservation Soc., Orgn. State Broadcasting Execs, Agawam Hunt Club, Mill Reef Club (Antigua, West Indies). Home: 147 Lloyd Ave Providence RI 02906-1552 Office: Sta WSBE-TV 50 Park Ln Providence RI 02907-3124

FARNAN, JEANNE ANN, investment banker; b. Buffalo, N.Y., Feb. 27, 1940; d. Edward George and Rita Veronica (Malark) Senecal; 1 child, Christian Jon. BA in History, Rosary Hill Coll., Buffalo, 1962; postgrad. in polit. sci. and law, Canisius Coll., Buffalo, 1962-65; postgrad. in bus. adminstrn., U. Ga., 1968-69; postgrad. in trade and internat. fin., Georgetown U., 1987-89. Pub. rels. dir. Bowling Corps. of Am., Atlanta, 1965-68; real estate developer Phipps Land Co., Atlanta, 1968-70; cons. State of Ga. Industry and Trade Dept., Atlanta, 1971-74; dir. leasing fin. ops. Funding Sys. Inc., Washington, 1975-78; co-founder FSI Fin. Group of Va. Inc., 1978-84; dir. Suriel Fin. N.V., Vienna, Va., 1984-91; founder, dir. Sofitel Holdings, Inc., Annapolis, Md., 1991—. Active various charitable and non-profit projects in Md., including Sara House; active fundraiser for Talmudical Acad.; mem. fin. com. Holy Family Cath. Ch., Annapolis, 1995. KC scholar, Buffalo, 1958; recipient Eastman Kodak Sch. Photojournalism award, Rochester, N.Y., 1956, 57. Mem. Am. Women in the Arts, Smithsonian Assn., Washington Trade Assn., Annapolis Yacht Club, Phi Beta Kappa. Office: Sofitel Capital Corp 175 Admiral Cochrane Dr Annapolis MD 21401

FARNSWORTH, BARBARA, bookseller; b. N.Y.C., June 18, 1934; d. William A. and Margaret T. (Leczer) Blaha; m. Clyde H. Farnsworth, Sept. 8, 1956 (div. Oct. 1978); children: Andrew, Alexander. BA, Middlebury Coll., 1955. Editor McGraw Hill, N.Y.C., 1955-56; freelance writer London, Paris, 1963-78; owner Barbara Farnsworth Books, West Cornwall, Conn., 1978—. Treas. Hughes Meml. Libr., West Cornwall, 1995—, pres., 1984-95. Mem. Antiquarian Booksellers Assn. Am. Office: Rte 128 West Cornwall CT 06796

FARNUM, NANCY ALYSON, communications executive; b. Birmingham, Ala., Mar. 2, 1949; d. Leon Vernon and Martha Reeves (McGahee) F. BA, Rockford Coll., 1971; MSLS, Case We. Reserve U., 1972. cert. health information profl. Information specialist Merrell-Nat. Lab. Pharm. Co., Cin., 1973-78; dir. and comptroller U.S. ops. Applied Human Cybernetics, London, 1975-78; asst. prof. and online search analyst Coll. Medicine E. Tenn. State U., Johnson City, Tenn., 1982-84; assoc. dir. N.W. Area Health Edn. Ctr., Salisbury, N.C., 1984-88; asst. prof. Bowman Gray Sch. Medicine, Winston Salem, 1984-88; coord. multimedia svcs. U. Ala., Birmingham, 1989-92; cons. MRM Communications, Claremont, Calif., 1988—; cons. St. George's (Grenada) U. Sch. Medicine, 1989; dir. K-12 devel. U. of the World, La Jolla, Calif., 1989—; mem. Gov.'s Tech. Task Force on Edn. Reform, Montgomery, Ala., 1993—. Coord. Global Awareness Seminar Birmingham Pub. Schs., 1988-93, World Peace Day Friends of the City of Birmingham, 1988—. Recipient Grad. endowment Nat. Inst. Health, Bethesda, Md., 1971-72; scholarship Sch. Theology at Claremont (Calif.), 1993. Mem. NAFE, Med. Libr. Assn., Network Birmingham, Acad. Health Info. Profls. Methodist. Home: 1325 N College Ave Claremont CA 91711-3154

FARQUHAR, KAREN LEE, commercial printing company executive, consultant; b. Warwick, N.Y., May 27, 1958; d. Wesley Thomas and Margaret Anne (Storms) Kervatt; m. David W. Farquhar, July 17, 1982 (div. Feb. 1990); 1 child, Lauren Nichole. Assoc. Sci., Roger Williams Coll., 1978, BS cum laude, 1980. Office mgr. Price-Rite Printing Co., Dover, N.J., summer 1975-76; cons. SBA, Bristol, R.I., 1978-80; account exec. P.M. Press Inc., Dallas, 1980-90, sales trainer, 1984-85; v.p. KDF Bus. Forms Inc., Dallas, Tex., 1984-90; account exec. Jarvis Press, Dallas, 1990—; pres. Print Trends, Dallas, 1990—. Printer, Tex. Aux. Charity Auction Orgn., Dallas, 1985, Crescent Gala, Dallas, 1986, Cystic Fibrosis, Dallas, 1989-93, L.E.A.P. Found., 1992—, Dallas Soc. of Visual Comm., 1992, AIDS Resources Com., Dallas chpt. Cerebral Palsy, 1994, Lloyd-Paxton AIDS Benefit, 1994, Lloyd-Paxton AIDS Charity, Cerebal Palsy Charity, Yellow Rose Gala for Multiple Sclerosis, 1996. Recipient various awards Clampitt Paper Co., Dallas, 1982, P.M. Press Inc., 1983-89, Mead Paper Co., 1985-89. Mem. Printing Industry in Am. (recipient Judges Favorite award 1992, Best of Show Hon. Mention award 1994, gold award Best of Tex. 1996), Internat. Assn. Bus. Communicators, Nat. Bus. Forms Assn. Republican. Baptist. Avocations: piano, aerobics. Home: 2600 Raintree Dr Southlake TX 76092

FARQUHAR, MARILYN GIST, cell biology and pathology educator; b. Tulare, Calif., July 11, 1928; d. Brooks DeWitt and Alta (Green) Gist; m. John W. Farquhar, June 4, 1952; children: Bruce, Douglas (div. 1968); m. George Palade, June 7, 1970. AB, U. Calif., Berkeley, 1949, MA, 1952, PhD, 1955. Asst. rsch. pathologist Sch. Medicine U. Calif., San Francisco, 1956-58, assoc. rsch. pathologist, 1962-64, assoc. prof., 1964-68, prof. pathology, 1968-70; rsch. assoc. Rockefeller U., N.Y.C., 1958-62, prof. cell biology, 1970-73; prof. cell biology Sch. Medicine Yale U., New Haven, 1973-87, Sterling prof. cell biology and pathology, 1987-90; prof. pathology div. cell molecular medicine U. Calif., San Diego, 1990—, coord. div. cellular and molecular medicine, 1991—. Mem. editorial bd. numerous sci. jours.; contbr. articles to profl. jours. Recipient Career Devel. award NIH, 1968-73, Disting. Sci. medal Electron Microscope Soc., 1987. Mem. NAS, Am. Acad. Arts and Scis., Am. Soc. Cell Biology (pres. 1981-82, E.B. Wilson medal 1987), Am. Assn. Investigative Pathology, Am. Soc. Nephrology (Homer Smith award 1988). Home: 12894 Via Latina Del Mar CA 92014-3730

FARR, LONA MAE, non-profit executive, business owner; b. Phila., June 4, 1941; d. Alonzo Schroeder and Lillyan (Nickels) F.; m. Malcolm J. Gross, Aug. 24, 1963 (div. Mar. 1976); children: Andrea Lillyan, Stacey Jane, John Farr; m. David V. Voellinger, Sept. 27, 1981. AB in History and English, Muhlenberg Coll., 1962; MS in Edn., Temple U., 1968; PhD in Philanthropy, Union Inst., 1995. Advanced cert. in fund raising. Tchr. Swain Sch., Allentown, Pa., 1962-63, St. Monica's Sch., Berwyn, Pa., 1963-65, Hebrew Day Sch., Scranton, Pa., 1965-66; pub. rels. assoc. Muhlenberg Coll., Allentown, 1973-75, dir. alumni affairs, 1975-77; dir. devel. and pub. rels. Allentown Coll. St. Frances de Sales, Allentown, 1977-81; dir. pub. rels. Good Shepherd Home, Allentown, 1981-84, dir. devel., 1984-87, group exec., v.p. instnl. devel., 1987-92; v.p. instl. devel. Luth. Home at Topton, Pa., 1992-96; spl. adv. to pres. Luth. Home at Topton, 1996—; prin. Baxter, Farr, Thomas and Weinstein Ltd., 1996—. Prodr. (films) More Than a Name, 1983 (Golden Eagle award 1984), Venture of Faith, 1984 (silver medal N.Y. Film Festival 1985), Spirit of Good Shepherd Day, 1987, Aspects of Topton, 1993 (1st place PANPHA), Topton New Century, 1993 (1st place PANPHA), They Came to Topton, 1994, A Gift of Love, 1995, (video) The Best You Can Be, 1988. Bd. dirs. Muhlenberg Coll., Kids Peace, Allentown Symphony, Baum Sch. Art, Allentown; past bd. dirs. United Way Lehigh Valley; past adviser Lehigh County Human Svcs., Allentown, 1986-91. Recipient Disting. Sales award Sales and Mktg. Execs. Lehigh Valley, 1984, 1st place award in mktg. and pub. rels. Pa. Assn. Nonprofit Homes for Aging, 1994. Mem. Pub. Rels. Soc. Am., Nat. Soc. Hosp. Devel., Nat. Soc. Fund Raising Execs. (past chair cert. bd., rep. nat. bd. dirs. 1987—, founding pres. Ea. Pa. chpt. 1986-88, Girl Scout Disting Alumni award, Outstanding Exec. award 1988, Fund Raising Exec. of Yr. 1988), Appalachian Health Care Pub. Rels./Mktg. Assn. (pres. 1987), Ea. Pa. BBB (bd. dirs.), Muhlenberg Coll. Alumni Assn. (pres. 1981-85), Liberty Bell Rotary (Allentown, pres. 1993-94), Quota Club (pres. Allentown 1986-88). Home and Office: 2238 W Chew St Allentown PA 18104-5548

FARR, PATRICIA HUDAK, librarian; b. Youngstown, Ohio, Mar. 10, 1945; d. Frank Francis and Anna Frances (Tylka) Hudak; m. William Howard Farr, Aug. 28, 1971; children: Jennifer Anne, William Patrick. BA, Youngstown State U., 1970; MLS, U. Md., 1980. Children's libr. Pub. Libr. Youngstown and Mahoning (Ohio), 1970-71; asst. Fla. State U. Libr. Tallahassee, 1971-73; rsch. asst. John Hopkins U. Sch. Hygiene and Pub. Health, Balt., 1974-76; asst. Mary Washington Coll. Libr., Fredericksburg, Va., 1976-79; children's libr. Cen. Rappahannock Regional Libr., Fredericksburg, 1980-84, young adult svcs. coord., 1984-89, youth svcs. libr., 1989-91, young adult svcs. coord., 1991-94, children's libr., 1995—. Revision editor HEW pub. Thesaurus of Health Edn. Terminology, 1976; compiler Health Edn. Monographs, 1974-76. Youngstown State U. scholar, 1963-64; R.V. Lowery Meml. scholar, 1979-80. Mem. ALA, Va. Libr. Assn., Now and Then Doll Club. Democrat. Episcopalian. Club: Now and Then Doll. Home: 618 Kings Hwy Fredericksburg VA 22405-3156 Office: Cen Rappahannock Regional Library 1201 Caroline St Fredericksburg VA 22401-3701

FARR, REETA RAE, special education administrator; b. Edhube, Tex., Jan. 15, 1926; d. Paul Ray and Verna (Biggerstaff) Wright; m. Gerald Edward Self, June 1, 1946 (dec. Dec. 1977); children: Eddie, Lee; m. Barnie B. Farr Jr., Dec. 28, 1978. BS, Southeastern Okla. State U., 1959, MS, 1963. 1st grade tchr. Sherman (Tex.) Pub. Schs., 1959-61; 1st grade tchr. Denison (Tex.) Pub. Schs., 1961-64, spl. edn. tchr., 1964-72, spl. edn. counselor, 1972-76, spl. edn. diagnostician, 1976-85, dir. spl. edn., 1985-94. Named Educator of Yr. Denison Edn. Assn., 1991. Mem. NEA, AAUW (pres. 1981-83), Tex. State Tchrs. Assn. (local pres. 1971), Tex. Ednl. Diagnostician Assn., Tex. Assn. Counseling and Devel., Phi Delta Kappa (sec.-treas. 1983, del. 1978-96), Delta Kappa Gamma. Mem. Ch. of Christ. Home: PO Box 135 Denison TX 75021-0135

FARR, SIDNEY SAYLOR, editor, author; b. Stoney Fork, Ky., Oct. 30, 1932; d. Wilburn and Rachel (Saylor) S.; m. Leon Lawson, Feb. 23, 1947 (div. July 1967); children: Dennis Wayne, Bruce Alan; m. Grover V. Farr, Jan. 24, 1970. BA, Berea Coll., 1980. Assoc. editor Coun. of the So. Mountains, Berea, Ky., 1964-69; editor This Week in Asheville (N.C.) Daniels Graphics, 1970-71; editor Appalachian Heritage Berea Coll., 1985—. Author: (annotated bibliography) Appalachian Women, 1981, (poetry) Headwaters, 1995; (narrative cookbook) More Than Moonshine, 1983, Table Talk: Appalachian Meals and Memories, 1995; (biography of near-death experiencer) What Tom Sawyer Learned from Dying, 1993. Mem. AAUW, Kiwanis (pres. Berea club 1992-93). Democrat. Home: 109 High St Berea KY 40403-1520 Office: Berea Coll Berea KY 40403

FARRAR, ELAINE WILLARDSON, artist; b. L.A.; d. Eldon and Gladys Elsie (Larsen) Willardson; BA, Ariz. State U., 1967, MA, 1969, PhD, 1990; children: Steve, Mark, Gregory, JanLeslie, Monty, Susan. Tchr., Camelback Desert Sch., Paradise Valley, Ariz., 1966-69; mem. faculty Yavapai Coll., Prescott, Ariz., 1970-92, chmn. dept. art, 1973-78, instr. art in watercolor and oil and acrylic painting, intaglio, relief and monoprints, 1971-92; grad. advisor Prescott Coll. Master of Arts Program, 1993—. One-man shows include: R.P. Moffat's, Scottsdale, Ariz., 1969, Art Center, Battle Creek, Mich., 1969, The Woodpeddler, Costa Mesa, Calif., 1979; group show Prescott (Ariz.) Fine Arts Assn., 1982, 84, 86, 89, 90-95, 96, N.Y. Nat. Am. Watercolorists, 1982; Ariz. State U. Women Images Now, 1986, 87, 89, 90-92; works rep. local and state exhibits, pvt. nat. & internat. collections. Mem., curator Prescott Fine Arts Visual Arts com., 1992—; bd. dirs. Prescott Fine Arts Assn., 1995—, Friends Y.C. Art Gallery Bd., 1992—. Mem. Mountain Artists Guild (past pres.), Ariz. Art Edn. Assn., Ariz. Women's Caucus for Art, Women's Nat. Mus. (charter Washington chpt.), Kappa Delta Pi, Phi Delta Kappa (Yavapai chpt. v.p. mem., 1994-95; Ariz State U. chpt.).

FARRAR, GINGER ANN, safety and environmental specialist; b. Fairfield, Ala., July 6, 1960; d. Paul LeVoy and Ruby Mae (Thompson) Coble; m. Randy James Hollis, July 21, 1978 (div. Aug. 1984); m. Gary Wayne Farrar, July 19, 1985; children: Lindsey Brooke, Zachary Paul. Cert. in tech. data processing, Rogers Vocat. Ctr., 1978. Cert. EMT. Sec. to v.p. sales and mktg. Zurn Industries, Birmingham, Ala., 1985-87; safety specialist O'Neal Steel, Birmingham, 1987-91; safety and environ. mgr. Birmingham Steel Corp., 1991—. Mem. Nat. Safety Coun., Am. Soc. Safety Engrs., Assn. Women in Metals Industries (bd. dirs. 1993—). Home: 266 Flint Ave Gardendale AL 35071 Office: Birmingham Steel 2301 Shuttlesworth Dr Birmingham AL 35234

FARRAR, ROXANNE CLAIRE, humanities educator; b. Pompton Plains, N.J., July 30, 1958; d. William H. and Elise M. (Meima) F. BA, Fla. State U., 1986, MA, 1990, PhD, 1992. Instr. English Centro Ponte Vecchio, Florence, Italy, 1986; instr. art history City Coll. San Francisco, 1991-94, Acad. Art Coll., San Francisco, 1993—; lectr. humanities San Francisco State U., 1995—. Mem. AAUW, Nat. Mus. Women's Art, San Francisco Mus. Modern Art, Calif. Humanities Assn.

FARRAR, RUTH DORIS, reading and literacy educator; b. Freeport, N.Y., June 11, 1943; d. Frederick and Ruth Harriet (Pagington) F.; m. David Conrad Farrar. BA, Ea. Nazarene Coll., 1965; MS in Edn., Hofstra U., 1975, EdD, 1989. Cert. consulting tchr. of reading and supr. reading programs, tchr. English 7-12. Tchr. English Newport (R.I.) Pub. Schs., 1965-66; tchr. reading and English Norwin Pub. Schs., North Huntingdon, Pa., 1966-67; kindergarten tchr. USN Base, Somerset, Bermuda, 1967-68; clin. diagnostician Brookwood Child Care, Bklyn., 1972-76; instr. reading Nassau C.C., Garden City, N.Y., 1974-76; reading specialist Cambridge (Mass.) Sch. Dept., 1976-80; reading coord. Brookwood Sch., Manchester, Mass., 1980-90; asst. prof. Bridgewater (Mass.) State Coll., 1990-92, 93—, Rivier Coll., Nashua, N.H., 1992-93; dir. reading ctr. Bridgewater State Coll.; vis. lectr. Salem (Mass.) State Coll., 1987—;adj. prof. Hofstra U., Hepstead, N.Y., 1989—; mem. Mass. Consortium for Media Literacy Edn., 1994—; coord. grad. programs reading, curriculum leadership ctr., Bridgewater State Coll. Editor The Massachusetts Primer, 1991-94. Grantee Ctr. for Advancement Rsch. and Tchg., Bridgewater State Coll., 1993-94; fellow reading dept. Hofstra U., Hempstead, N.Y., 1985-86. Mem. Am. Edn. Rsch. Assn., Internat. Reading Assn. (presenter, chair publs. spl. interest group), Internat. Listening Assn. (presenter), Assn. Tchr. Edn. (presenter), Nat. Coun. Tchrs. English (presenter), Mass. Reading Assn. (bd. mem.), Mass. Assn. Coll./Univ. Reading Educators (bd. mem. 1993—). Home: 16 Herrick Street Ext Beverly MA 01915-2731 Office: Bridgewater State Coll Sch Edn 133 Hart Hall Bridgewater MA 02325

FARRAR, SUSAN LEE, special education educator, consultant; b. Princeton, Ind., Sept. 30, 1960; d. William Ellis and Mary Lee (Staley) Hinman; m. Francis Bruce Farrar, Mar. 30, 1985. BS in Edn., Ind. State U., 1982; MS in Edn., Ind. U. S.E., 1990. Tchr. emotionally handicapped New Albany (Ind.)-Floyd County Consol. Schs., 1983-90; tchr. learning disabled Spl. Svcs., Johnson County Schs., Franklin, Ind., 1990-91, cons. emotionally handicapped students, 1991—; mentor tchr. divsn. spl. edn. Ind. State Dept. of Edn., Indpls., 1992—. Mem. Coun. for Exceptional Children, Coun. for Children with Behavioral Disorders (Ind. chpt., Tchr. of Yr. award 1989), Ind. State Tchrs. Assn. (negotiations com. 1993—, discussions com. 1993). Anglican Catholic. Office: Johnson County Schs Spl Svcs 500 Earlywood Dr Franklin IN 46131-9711

FARRELL, ANNE VAN NESS, foundation executive; b. Peking, China, July 17, 1935; came to U.S. 1935; d. C. Peter and Virginia (Cheatham) Van Ness; m. E. Robert Farell, June 17, 1955; children: Virginia Farrell Day and Susan Farrell Johnson. BA, U. Wash., 1960. Dir. devel. Seattle Children's Home, 1978-80; exec. v.p. The Seattle Found., 1980-84, pres., chief. exec. officer, 1984—, dir. composite mutual funds, 1993—; bd. dirs. Washington Mut. Bank, Blue Cross of Wash. and Alaska, Composite GroupMut. Funds, Nat. Charities Info. Bur., N.Y.C., 1988—. Author: Puget Soundings, 1989. Regent Seattle U., 1986—; pres. bd. trustees Lakeside Sch., 1992-94; bd. dirs. Nature Conservancy, 1990-95, Ind. Sector, Wash., 1990-95, Girl Scouts U.S., N.Y.C., 1974-83. Recipient Community Svc. award YWCA, Seattle, 1984, Girl Scout of Yr. award, Seattle, 1986. Mem. Pacific N.W. Grantmakers Forum (pres. 1984-85), N.W. Devel. Officers Assn. (pres. 1983-84), Wash. Women's Forum, Seattle, Jr. League, Greater Seattle C. of C. (vice chair 1991-93). Republican. Episcopalian. Home: 1616 Lake Washington Blvd Seattle WA 98122-3540 Office: The Seattle Found 425 Pike St Ste 510 Seattle WA 98101-2334

FARRELL, EILEEN, soprano; b. Williamantic, Conn., Feb. 13, 1920; d. Michael John and Catherine (Kennedy) F.; m. Robert V. Reagan, Apr. 4, 1946; children: Robert V., Kathleen. Degrees hon., U. R.I., Loyola U., U. Hartford, Notre Dame Coll., N.H., Wagner Coll., Cin. Conservatory. Vis. prof. Hartford U. Made debut as singer, Columbia Broadcasting Co., 1941; singer own program, CBS, 6 yrs; made opera debut with San Francisco Opera in Il Trovatore, 1951; sang in film Interrupted Melody, 1955; singer with major symphony orchs. in, U.S.; toured throughout, U.S. and in S.Am.; performer pops, blues and jazz with symphony orchs.; rec. artist, ABC Dunhill, Columbia, RCA, London, Angel records; recordings include Eileen Farrell as Medea (Grammy award nomination 1958), I've Gotta Right to Sing the Blues (Grammy award nomination 1960), Arias in Great Tradition (Grammy award nomination 1960), Bach: Cantatas No. 58 and No. 202 (Grammy award nomination 1961), Wagner: Gotterdamerung, Brunnhilde's Immolation Scene; Wesendonck: Songs (Grammy award 1962); recent recs. include With Much Love, 1988, Eileen Farrel Sings Rodgers & Hart, 1989, Eileen Farrell Sings Harold Arlen, 1989, Eileen Farrell Sings Alec Wilder, 1990, This Time It's Love, 1991, Eileen Farrell Sings Johnny Mercer, 1992, It's Over, Robert Farrow and His Orchestra, 1992, Here, 1993, My Very Best, 1994. *

FARRELL, FRANCINE ANNETTE, psychotherapist, educator, author; b. Long Beach, Calif., Mar. 26, 1948; d. Thomas and Evelyn Marie (Lucente) F.; m. James Thomas Hanley, Dec. 5, 1968 (div. Dec. 1988); children: Melinda Lee Hanley, James Thomas Hanley Jr.; m. Robert Erich Haesche, June 3, 1995. BA in Psychology with honors, Calif. State U., Sacramento, 1985, MS in Counseling, 1986. Lic. marriage, family and child counselor, Calif.; nat. cert. addiction counselor. Marriage, family and child counselor intern Fulton Ct. Counseling, Sacramento, 1987-88; pvt. practice psychotherapist Sacramento, 1988—; instr. chem. dependency studies program, Calif. State U., Sacramento, 1985-94, acad. coord. chem. dependency studies program, 1988-90; trainee Sobriety Brings a Change, Sacramento, 1986-87; assoc. investigator, curriculum coord. Project S.A.F.E., Sacramento, 1990-91; presenter Sacramento Conf., ACA, 1986, 88, 89, 91, 92, Ann. Symposium on Chem. Dependency, 1993. Presenter (cable TV series) Trouble in River City: Charting a Course for Change, 1991. Mem. Nat. Coun. on Alcoholism, Calif. Assn. Marriage and Family Therapists, Calif. Assn. Alcoholism and Drug Abuse Counselors (bd. dirs. region 5, 1988-90), Phi Kappa Phi. Roman Catholic. Office: 2740 Fulton Ave # 100 Sacramento CA 95821-5108

FARRELL, JUNE ELEANOR, retired middle school educator; b. Ft. Atkinson, Wis., Dec. 31, 1916; d. Isaac Leslie and Thora Eleanor (Huppert) Winter; m. Martin Joseph Farrell, Sept. 21, 1946; children: Leslie June Kathryn, Robert Joseph. BA, DePauw U., Green Castle, Ind., 1939. Cert. secondary tchr. English, Latin, and drama, Fla. Tchr. English, Latin and drama Elmore (Ind.) Twp. High Sch., 1939-41; tchr. Latin and English Beach Grove High Sch., Indpls., 1941-46; v.p. Farrell Foods Inc., 1948-66; tchr. English Ft. Atkinson (Wis.) Jr. High Sch., 1966-67, Venice (Fla.) Jr. High Sch., 1967-82; tchr. sci. Venice Area Mid. Sch., 1982-89, ret., 1989. Contbr. articles to profl. jours. Bd. dirs. AARP, Venice, Fla., 1994—; pres. Friends of Venice Cmty. Ctr., 1984—. Mem. AAUW, Sarasota County Reading Coun. (pres. 1974-76), Sarasota County Tchrs. English (treas. 1975-79), Alpha Delta Kappa (pres. chpt. 1976-78, altruistic chmn. 1986-93), Delta Zeta. Republican. Methodist. Home: 640 W Venice Ave Venice FL 34285-2031 also: 603 Van Buren St Fort Atkinson WI 53538-1715

FARRELL, JUNE MARTINICK, public relations executive; b. New Brunswick, N.J., June 30, 1940; d. Ivan and Mary (Tomkovich) M.; B.S. in Journalism, Ohio U., 1962; M.S. in Public Relations, Am. U., Washington, 1977; m. Duncan G. Farrell, July 31, 1971. Public relations asst. Corning Glass Works, N.Y.C., 1963-65; assoc. beauty editor Good Housekeeping mag., N.Y.C., 1966; public relations specialist Gt. Am. Ins. Co., N.Y.C., 1967-68; assoc. editor Ea. Airlines, N.Y.C., 1968-82, regional public relations mgr., Washington, 1976-82; public relations dir. Nat. Captioning Inst., Falls Church, Va., 1982-83; dir. internat. pub. rels. Marriott Internat., 1984—; staff cons. Office of Public Liaison, White House, 1981-82. Creator, condr. spl. career awareness program for inner city youth, Washington, 1979-80; mem. public relations com. Jr. Achievement, 1979; motivational counselor for youth Nat. Alliance of Businessmen, 1979; adj. prof. tourism and pub. rels. George Washington U., 1992—; bd. dirs. Am. Mgmt. Svcs., 1985—; trustee, mem. devel. quality assurance coms. Nat. Hosp. Orthopedics and Rehab., 1984-92; mem. membership com. U.S. Travel Data Svc.; Mem. Soc. Am. Travel Writers, Am. Soc. Travel Agts., Travel Industry Assn. Am. (nat. conf. planning com., chair comm. com., Discover Am. task force), Women in Communication, Phi Mu. Republican. Club: Internat. Aviation. Home: 6630 Lybrook Ct Bethesda MD 20817-3029 Office: Marriott Internat One Marriott Dr Washington DC 20058

FARRELL, MEGAN SHAUGHNESSY, librarian; b. Pitts., 1960; d. William F. and Ava Shaughnessy; m. Robert Farrell, 1989. BA, Wayne State U., 1983, MA, 1984, MS, 1986. Editl. asst. Wayne State U. Press, Detroit, 1983-84; asst. visual resources libr. Ctr. for Creative Studies, 1984; libr. Chrysler Corp., Highland Park, Mich., 1985-86; bibliographer humanities & social scis. U. Southwestern La., Lafayette, 1987—; instr. art history U. Southwestern La., 1988; film programmer Bayou Bijou, Lafayette, 1991—; panelist, grants reviewer La. Divsn. Arts, Baton Rouge, 1992, 93, 96; cons. in field. Mem. ALA, Nat. Book Critics Cir., Jr. League, Pioneer Am. Soc. (book review editor 1991—), Soc. Archl. Historians, Daguerreian Soc. (book review editor 1994—). Office: U SW La Dupre Libr 302 E St Mary Blvd Lafayette LA 70503

FARRELL, PATRICIA ANN, psychologist, educator; b. N.Y.C., Mar. 11, 1945; d. Joseph Alexander and Pauline (Loth) F.; BA, Queens Coll., 1976; MA, N.Y.U., 1978, PhD, 1990. Lic. psychologist, N.J., Fla.Assoc. editor Pubs. Weekly Mag., N.Y.C., 1968-72; editor Bestsellers Mag., N.Y.C., 1972-73; assoc. editor King Features Syndicate, N.Y.C., 1973-78; staff psychologist, intake coord. Mid-Bergen Cmty. Mental Health Ctr., Paramus, N.J., 1978-84; instr. Bergen C.C., Paramus, 1978-94; adj. prof. The Union Inst., Cin., Walden U. cons. faculty. Thomas Edison State Coll.; resident clin. psychology Am. Inst. for Counseling, N.J., 1990-91; cons. Family Counseling Svc. of Ridgewood, N.J., 1984; clin. psychology intern Marlboro Psychiat. Hosp., N.J., 1984-85, staff psychologist, 1985-87; rsch. analyst Mt. Sinai Sch. of Medicine, 1987-88; account exec., sr. sci. writer Manning, Selvage and Lee, N.Y.C., 1988-90; sr. clin. psychologist, mem. med. staff Greystone Park (N.J.) Psychiat. Hosp., 1990-96; pvt. practice psychology, Englewood, N.J.; health sci. editor Time Warner Cable, Channel 10 News, 1995—; cons. Intensive Weight Loss Program, Cath. Med. Ctr. Bklyn. and Queens; cons. pharm. clin. protocols; cons. to Thomas Edison State Coll. Distance Learning program; guest radio and TV shows including Sta. WWDJ, Hackensack, N.J., Montel Williams, Good Day, New York, Mark Walberg, America After Hours, Dini, Camilla Scott, USA Alive and Wellness with Carol Martin, News Talk, Maury Povich TV Show, The Carnie Wilson Show, Judge For Yourself TV Show, N.Y.C. Ten O'Clock News, WPIX-TV, N.Y., WWOR-TV News, WNRR-TV, In Your Interest, LTV, Channel 10 News, On Campus, Sta. WTTM, WSNJ, WHSI-TV, Last Call, Common Concerns, WHSE-TV. Contbr. book chpt. to Innovations in Clinical Practice: A Source Book 15th edit., and articles to Writer's Digest, Real World, Postgrad. Medicine, Psychotherapy, New England Jour. Medicine, and newspapers, author manual Alzheimer's Disease Assessment Scale test. Mem. Bergen County Task Force on Crimes Against Children, Bergen County Task Force on Alcoholism and Drunken Driving, 1984; bd. dirs., chmn. med. liaison com. liaison to dept. psychiatry Bergen Pines County Hosp., Paramus, N.J., 1994-95. McDonald's rsch. grantee, 1994-95; recipient Good Citizen award DAR, Sci. award Rotary Club. Fellow Ab. Bd. Disability Analysts, Am. Coll. Forensic Examiners; mem. AAAS, APA, Assn. for Advancement Psychology, Assn. for Indep. Video and Filmmakers, Prescribing Psychologists Register, NYU/Bellevue Psychiatric Soc. Avocations: fitness, racquetball, kite-flying. Office: PO Box 1283 Englewood NJ 07632

FARRELL-LOGAN, VIVIAN, actress; b. N.Y.C.; m. Harvey Lewis, Aug. 5, 1979 (dec. Aug. 1980); m. Tracy Harrison Logan, June 3, 1984. BS in Edn., Syracuse U.; MA in Theatre, NYU. Tchr. elem. sch. Levittown (N.Y.) Schs., 1965-75; tchr. workshops Coll. of Cape Breton, N.S., Can., 1977-79. Appearences include (stage) Gateway Playhouse, Bellport, N.Y., Playhouse 3200, Richmond, Va., Bartke's Dinner Theatre, Tampa, Fla., (film) Impulse; narrator for Nutcracker, Eglevsky Ballet Co. with L.I. Symphony Orch., Nassau Coliseum, Uniondale, N.Y., 1978-79; appeared as The Musical Storyteller, Lincoln Ctr., N.Y.C., Carnegie Recital Hall, N.Y.C., 1978-80, also in various libraries and schs., N.Y. area; performer, 1978—, writer, performer (album) The Musical Storyteller, 1978; author: (children's book) Robert's Tall Friend: A Story of the Fire Island Lighthouse, Island-Metro Publs., Inc., 1987; appearing numerous schs., librs. in Author Narrates Her Book Robert's Tall Friend, 1989—; appearing N.Y.C schs. and on tour in one-woman play Amelia, My Courageous Sister, 1993—. Nassau County (N.Y.) Office Cultural Devel grantee, 1986—, N.Y. State Coun. on the Arts grantee, 1986—. Mem. Actors Equity Assn., Screen Actors Guild, AFTRA, Twelfth Night Club, Ninety-Nines, Alpha Psi Omega, Zeta Phi Eta. Office: PO Box 734 Lindenhurst NY 11757-0734

FARRELLY, DELPHINE JOHNS, guidance counselor, career education administrator, adult education career counselor; b. Bristol, Conn., Nov. 23, 1943; d. Edward Moncure and Frances Blair Johns; m. Francis Joseph Farrelly, Apr. 15, 1969; children: Sean Patrick, Meeghan Kathleen. BA in Spanish, St. Joseph Coll., 1965; MS in Edn., Ctrl. Conn. State U., 1969, MS in Counseling, 1991. Cert. K-12 counselor; cert. 9-12 Spanish, K-8 elem. tchr. Claim reviewer CIGNA, Bloomfield, Conn., 1965-66; elem. tchr. Wethersfield (Conn.) Bd. of Edn., 1966-72, career edn. coord., 1979—, guidance counselor, 1991—; cons. Alter and Assoc., Conn., 1986-94. Chairperson Youth Advisory Bd., Wethersfield, 1984-87; mem. State Advisory Sch. to Work Transition, Wethersfield, 1994-95. Named Educator of Yr. Wethersfield C. of C., 1996. Mem. NEA, Wethersfield Edn. Assn., Conn. Sch. Counselors, Conn. Career Counselors (past pres. 1991-94, pres. 1993-94), Conn. Counseling Assn. (sec.).

FARRER, CLAIRE ANNE RAFFERTY, anthropologist, folklorist, educator; b. N.Y.C., Dec. 26, 1936; d. Francis Michael and Clara Anna (Guerra) Rafferty; 1 child, Suzanne Claire. BA in Anthropology, U. Calif., Berkeley, 1970; MA in Anthropology and Folklore, U. Tex., 1974, PhD in Anthropology and Folklore, 1977. Various positions, 1953-73; fellow Whitney M. Young Jr. Meml. Found., N.Y.C., 1974-75; arts specialist, grant adminstr. Nat. Endowment for Arts, Washington, 1976-77; Weatherhead resident fellow Sch. Am. Research, Santa Fe, 1977-78; asst. prof. anthropology U. Ill., Urbana, 1978-85; assoc. prof., coord. applied anthropology Calif. State U., Chico, 1985-89, prof., 1989—; dir. Multicultural and Gender Studies, 1994; cons. in field, 1974—; mem. film and video adv. panel Ill. Arts Coun., 1980-82; mem. Ill. Humanities Coun., 1980-82; vis. prof. U. Ghent, Belgium, spring 1990. Author: Play and Inter-Ethnic Communication, 1990, Living Life's Circle: Mescalero Apache Cosmovision, 1991, Thunder Rides a Black Horse: Mescalero Apaches and the Mythic Present, 1994, 96; co-founder, co-editor Folklore Women's Commn., 1972; editor spl. issue Jour. Am. Folklore, 1975, 1st rev. edit., 1986; co-editor: Forms of Play of Native North Americans, 1979, Earth and Sky: Visions of the Cosmos in Native North American Folklore, 1992; contbr. numerous articles to profl. jours., mags. and newspapers, chpts. to books. Recipient numerous awards, fellowships and grants. Fellow Am. Anthrop. Assn., Royal Anthrop. Inst. (U.K.), Am. Astronomy Assn. (history divsn.); mem. Authors Guild, Am. Ethnol. Soc., Am. Folklore Soc., Am. Soc. Ethnohistory. Mem. Soc. of Friends. Office: Calif State U Dept Anthropology Butte 311 Chico CA 95929-0400

FARRIGAN, JULIA ANN, small business owner, educator b. Albany, N.Y., July 19, 1943; d. Charles Gerald and Julia Tryon (Shepherd) F. BS in Elem. Edn., SUNY, Plattsburgh, 1965; MS in Curriculum Planning and Devel., SUNY, Albany, and U. Manchester, Eng., 1973; postgrad. in adminstrv. svcs. Calif. State U., Fresno, 1976-78. With Monroe-Woodbury Ctrl. Sch. Dist., Monroe, N.Y., 1965-90; dist. coord. gifted programs The Pine Tree Sch., 1979-90; ptnr. Baskets Plain and Fancy, Jackson, Ga., 1994—; adj. prof. Gifted Edn. Contbr. articles to profl. jours. Officer United Meth. Women, Jackson United Meth. Ch.; bd. dirs., Butts County Hist. Soc., docent, editor newsletter; coord. blood drive ARC Butts County. Mem. DAR (vice regent William McIntosh chpt., state chmn.), AFT, ASCD, NYUFT, Nat. Assn. for Gifted Children, Coun. Exceptional Children, Monroe-Woodbury Tchr's. Assn., Hawthorne Garden Club (officer), Kiwanis (officer), Delta Kappa Gamma (officer Upsilon chpt., state officer). Democrat. Methodist.

FARRINGTON, BERTHA LOUISE, nursing administrator; b. Poteet, Tex., Jan. 20, 1937; d. Leonard Gilbert and Janie (Hernandez) Lozano; m. James Charles Farrington, Jan. 30, 1965; children: Mark Hiram, Robert Lee. BSN, Tex. Women's U., 1960; NP, U. Tex., 1984. RN, Tex. Charge nurse emergency rm. Parkland Meml. Hosp., Dallas; head nurse emergency rm./day surgery Bapt. Meml. Hosp., Pensacola, Fla.; asst. dir. health svcs. U. Tex. Southwestern Med. Ctr., Dallas, dir. student health svcs.

FARRINGTON, LISA EDITH, art historian, art educator; b. N.Y.C., June 11, 1956; d. Duane C. and Joan M. (Doyle) F. Regents grad., H.S. of Art & Design, N.Y.C., 1974; BFA, Howard U., 1978; MA, Am. U., Washington, 1980; postgrad., CUNY, 1989-96. Asst. to chief curator Mus. of Modern Art, N.Y.C., 1980-87; asst. to pres. Marlborough Gallery, N.Y.C., 1988-89; studio mgr. Anthony McCall Assocs., N.Y.C., 1989-94; adj. lectr. Hunter Coll., N.Y.C., 1990-91, Fashion Inst., N.Y.C., 1994-95, Manhattan C.C., N.Y.C., 1993—; faculty mem. The New Sch./Parsons, N.Y.C., 1993—; cons. Ednl. Testing Svc.-The Coll. Bd., Princeton, N.J., 1993—; ind. curator CUNY, 1994-95; freelance lectr. Howard U., SUNY, Washington, N.Y., 1996. Author: (brochure essays) 50 Years of Haitian Art, 1994, The Language of Color, 1994; contbg. editor Gilbert & George: Singing Sculpture, 1993. Pres. Dissertation fellow CUNY, 1995-96, Mellon Dissertaton fellow Andrew Mellon Found., 1995, travel fellow, CUNY, 1994; faculty devel. grantee The New School for Social Res., 1996-97. Mem. New Sch. for Social Res. (diversity com., adv. com., exhbn. com.), Coll. Art Assn., Studio Mus. in Harlem, Guggenheim Mus. Home: 160 West End Ave 16B New York NY 10023 Office: Parsons Sch of Design 65 5th Ave New York NY 10003

FARRINGTON-HOPF, SUSAN KAY, plumbing and heating contractor; b. Seattle, Dec. 17, 1940; d. Donald Robert and Dorothy May (Graf) Little; m. Edwin Terry Farrington, Sept. 4, 1959 (div. Apr. 1972); children: Cathe T., Jacqueline M.; m. William Desmond Hopf, Nov. 20, 1983. BA cum laude, U.S. Internat. U., 1975, MA, 1976. Program speaker AMR Internat., N.Y.C., 1977-82; pres. Dawson Plumbing & Heating Co., Seattle, 1979—; tng. cons. Fred Sherman, Inc., San Marcos, Calif., 1982—; cons. Pacific S.W. Airlines, San Diego, 1977, Dept. Labor Job Corps, Moses Lake, Wash., 1978. Developer assertive mgmt. workshop, 1976. Mem. Seattle Execs. Assn. (bd. dirs., treas., v.p., pres. 1993—), Am. Soc. Tng. and Devel., Nat. Assn. Plumbing Heating Cooling Contractors, Women Own Bus. Avocations: skiing, sailing, gardening. Home: 16419 261st Ave SE Issaquah WA 98027-8214 Office: Dawson Plumbing & Heating Co 1522 12th Ave Seattle WA 98122-3908

FARRIS, DIANE F., artist; b. Long Branch, N.J., Dec. 15, 1944; d. Hansford and Vera Farris; m. Ted Runions; 1 child, Andrew Uelsmann. BA, Carleton Coll., 1966; MA, U. Chgo., 1972, PhD, 1975. Author: Type Tales, 1991, In Dolphin Time, 1994; photographer for book: New Vegetarian Classics, Vol. I, 1993, Vol. II, 1994; represented in permanent collections at New Orleans Mus. Art, Mus. Contemporary Photography, Chgo., Mus. Fine Arts, Houston, Princeton U. Art Mus., The Polaroid Collection, Boston, Anwar Kamal Collection, High Mus., Atlanta, Jacksonville Art Mus., U. Fla., Gainesville, Maitlant Art Ctr., Orlando, Fla., Mus. Modern Art, So. Bell Tower Collection, Jacksonville, Haverford Coll., Cin. Art Mus. Grantee Polaroid Artists, 1988, Fine Arts Coun. of Fla., 1979-80. Office: Foxbridge II C-1 2630 NW 41st St Gainesville FL 32606

FARROW, MARGARET ANN, state legislator; b. Kenosha, Wis., Nov. 28, 1934; d. William Charles and Margaret Ann (Horan) Nemitz; m. John Harvey Farrow, Dec. 29, 1956; children—John, William, Peter, Paul, Mark. Student Rosary Coll., 1952-53; B.S. in Polit. Sci., Marquette U., 1956, postgrad., 1975-77. Tchr., Archiodese of Milw., 1956-57; trustee Elm Grove Village, Wis., 1976-81, pres., 1981-86; mem. Wis. State Assembly, 1986-89, State Senate, 1989—. asst. majority leader, 1993—; chair com. on govt. effectiveness, 1995—, mem. joint com. on audit, 1995—, mem. joint legislative coun., 1993—, mem. com. on environ. & energy, 1993—, mem. joint survey com. on tax exemptions, 1995—, mem. com. on orgn., 1993—, mem. commn. on state human resources reform, 1995—, chair Wis. women's coun., 1991—, mem. Wis. glass ceiling commn., 1993—, mem. gov.'s clean air task force, 1993—, mem. low level radioactive waste coun., 1991—. Home: 14905 Watertown Plank Rd Elm Grove WI 53122-2332 Office: Wis State Capitol Senate House Madison WI 53702

FASBINDER, MARCIA SUE, psychologist; b. Kansas City, Mo., July 28, 1948; d. Abe and Sylvia (Yukon) Oshry. Student, U. Tex., 1969-72; BA in Psychology with distinction, U. Mo., Kansas City, 1974; MS in Psychology, Avila Coll., 1995. Registered masters level psychologist, Kans.; cert. mental health rehab. specialist Santa Cruz County, Calif. Counselor, case mgr. Della C. Lamb Neighborhood House, Kansas City, 1973; aide Children's Spl. Edn. Ctr., Kansas City, 1973-74; rsch. asst. U. Mo., Kansas City, 1975; counseling intern psychiat. unit Vencor Hosp., Kansas City, 1994; counseling intern Rainbow Mental Health Facility, Kansas City, Kans., 1994; intern U. Kans., Kansas City, 1995-96; program dir. Front St. Residential Care, Santa Cruz, Calif., 1996—. Vol. Human Rescue, Kansas City, Mo., 1973-74. Grantee NSF, 1975. Mem. APA (affiliate), ACA, Psi Chi. Jewish. Home: 4971 Kenson Dr San Jose CA 95124-2446

FASCETTA, MICHELE ANNE, accountant; b. King of Prussia, Pa., Apr. 4, 1971; d. Maurice A. and Denise M. F. BS, St. Joseph's U., 1993, postgrad., 1993—. Corp. acct. SunGard Data Sys., Inc., Wayne, Pa., 1993—. Office: SunGard Data Sys Inc 1285 Drummers Ln Wayne PA 19087

FASKE, DONNA See KARAN, DONNA

FASSIHI, THERESA CARMELA, journalist; b. L.A., Sept. 12, 1959; d. John Harrison Simons and Sally Elisa Graham; m. Mohammad Reza Fassihi, July 14, 1984; children: Mansoor Reza, Samad Reza Donaciano. BA in Econs. and Journalism, Stanford U., 1981; postgrad., Tulsa U., 1992—. Copy editor, reporter Dallas Morning News, 1981-84; feature writer Tulsa Tribune, 1985-87; corr. Adweek mag., Dallas, 1986-90; co-editor Tulsa Women, 1990-91; editorial adviser S mag., Tulsa, 1985-86. pub. rels. cons. ARC, Tulsa, 1989. Mem. Women in Communications, Tulsa Exec. Exch. (v.p. 1987-88). Democrat.

FAST, BETTY BLOCKMAN, travel agency owner; b. Memphis, Oct. 12, 1929; d. Morris David Arthur and Sadie (Shefsky) Blockman; married, Dec. 1962. BA, Southwest Coll., 1952; MA, Memphis State U., 1960. Owner Betty Fast Travel Svc. Commr. Safety bd., Miami Beach, 1971. Mem. Am. Soc. Travel Agts., Women's Zionist Orgn. (pres. 1970-72), Cruise Line Industry Assn., Airline Reporting Corp.

FASTOOK, MARY ANN, school counselor; b. Bklyn., Sept. 29, 1944; d. Theodore Elias and Josephine Mildred (Mardany) F. BA in English, St. John's U., Bklyn., 1966; MA in English, St. John's U., Jamaica, 1968; MS in Reading, Fordham U., 1980, MS in Counseling, 1984; PD in Counseling, 1988. Lic. sch. counselor N.Y.; nat. cert. counselor. English tchr. All Saints High Sch., Bklyn., 1970-71, St. Andrew's Sch., Queens, N.Y., 1972-73, Boys High Sch., Bklyn., 1973-74, Jr. High Sch. 117, Bklyn., 1974-75, Prospect Hts. High Sch., Bklyn., 1974-75; English content specialist Hightstown (N.J.) High Sch., 1976-77; English tchr. Boys and Girls High Sch., Bklyn., 1977-83, Samuel Tilden High Sch., Bklyn., 1983-85; sch. counselor Seward Park High Sch., N.Y.C., 1985—. Driver Bklyn. Hts. Civilian Patrol, 1990-93. Mem. N.Y.C. Assn. for Counseling and Devel., N.Y. State Assn. for Counseling and Devel., Nat. Assn. for Counseling and Devel., Toastmasters (v.p. 1989). Home: 225 Adams St Apt 15F Brooklyn NY 11201-2834 Office: Seward Pk High Sch 350 Grand St New York NY 10002-4629

FATUM, DELORES RUTH, school counselor; b. Kingston, N.Y., Aug. 1, 1945; d. Robert and Dorothy Beatrice (Van Demark) F. BS, Winthrop U., 1968; MEd, Ga. Coll., Milledgeville, 1973; EdS, Ga. So. U. Cert. couselor, Ga.; practice tchr. supr. Sch. couselor Laurens County Bd. of Edn., Dublin, Ga.; EdS counseling educator Ga. So. U.; regional coordinator Outdoor Edn., Ga. Dept. of Natural Resources, Atlanta. Author: (manuals) Georgia Outdoor Education, Student Services for Lauren County. Mem. Am. Counseling Assn., Am. Sch. Counselors Assn., Nat. Mid. Sch. Assn., Profl. Assn. Ga. Educators. (v.p. Laurens county chpt.), Ga. Sch. Counselors Assn. (chair U.S. Congl. Dist. 8). Home: 573 Coleman Ln Dublin GA 31021-4417 Office: W Laurens Mid Sch 332 W Laurens School Rd Dublin GA 31021-1222

FAUGHNAN, MARGARET H., nurse; b. Dromod, Ireland, Aug. 3, 1941; d. Bernard and Catherine (Maguire) F. RN, St. Mary's Hosp., London, 1962; student, St. Gile's Hosp., London, 1962-64; cert., St. Paul's Hosp., Hemel Hempstead, England, 1964; student, Royal Coll. Nursing, London, 1965. Cert. midwife, Wash., community health nurse. Staff nurse Mt. Sinai Hosp., N.Y.C., Lenox Hill Hosp., N.Y.C., Group Health Co. Operative, Seattle; RN anesthetician Nancy Meadows Inc., Seattle; staff nurse Community Health Coop., Seattle. Mem. Am. Nurse's Assn. (polit. action com. coord. 1st Congl. dist.), Wash. Nurse's Assn. (bd. trustees), King County Nurse's Assn.

FAUGHT, STEPHANIE ROBIN, art educator; b. Indpls., Dec. 18, 1951; d. Edward Francis and Dorothy Marie (Teague) F. BFA, Montclair (N.J.) State U., 1973, postgrad., 1974-76. Substitute tchr. Woodbridge (N.J.) Twp. Bd. of Edn., 1971-73, elem. art tchr., 1973-84, 85-86; middle sch. art tchr. Colonia (N.J.) Middle Sch., 1984-85; high sch. art tchr. Woodridge High Sch., 1986-90; middle sch. art tchr. Avenel (N.J.) Middle Sch., 1990-94; art tchr. John F. Kennedy H.S., Iselin, N.J., 1994—; spkr. Woodbridge River Watch, 1991; pvt. art tchr., 1983-93; yearbook advisor Woodbridge H.S., 1989-90, Avenel Mid. Sch., 1991-94, John F. Kennedy H.S., 1995—; play set designer, 1989, 94—. Illustrator (book) Care of the Lower Back, 1975, Touching All the Bases, 1993. Campaign vol. Rep. Party, Woodbridge, 1992; sec. to the producer Fgn. Broadcast Svc. Dem./Rep. Nat. Convs., Miami, 1972. Recipient Gov.'s Tchr. Recognition award State Dept. of Edn., 1992, Excellence in Edn. award C. of C., 1992. Mem. Woodbridge Twp. Fedn. of Tchrs. (v.p. 1980-83, pres. 1983—, Cert. of Merit, 1982), Art Educators of N.J., Met. Mus. of Art, Ecology Club (advisor 1990-94). United Methodist. Home: 2702 Madaline Dr Avenel NJ 07001-1367 Office: John F Kennedy HS Washington Ave Iselin NJ 08830

FAUL, JUNE PATRICIA, education specialist; b. Detroit; d. John William and Shirley Olive (Block) Lynch; m. George Johnson Faul, Dec. 22, 1949; Robert M., Alison. BA, U. Calif., Berkeley, 1952. Cert. elem. tchr., Calif. Tchr. Tulare County (Calif.) Schs., 1945-46, Tulare City Schs., 1946-48, Visalia (Calif.) City Schs., 1948-49, Richmond (Calif.) City Schs., 1951-52, Pacific Grove (Calif.) Sch. Dist., 1965-85; designated English teaching specialist State of Calif., 1969—; edn. cons. Leo A. Meyer Assocs., Inc., Hayward, Calif., 1993—; prin. Group Four Assocs.; lectr. Calif. State U., Fresno, 1969, U. Calif., Santa Cruz, 1970. Co-author: The New Older Woman, 1996. Apptd. mem. first human relations commn. City of Richmond, 1962-64; mem. adv. bd. Family Resource Ctr.; founding mem., 1st pres. Monterey (Calif.) Peninsula Child Abuse Prevention Council, 1974; hon. life mem. Calif. PTA; bd. dirs. Carmel Cultural Commn., 1964-67, Harrison Meml. Library, Carmel, Calif., 1978-84; mem., chmn. bd. Monterey Peninsula Airport Dist., 1980—. Mem. Am. Assn. Airport Execs., Friends of Hopkins Marine Station (founder, bd. dirs.) Carmel Heritage (founder, bd. dirs.), Monterey NAACP (life), Monterey Mus. Art (life), Monterey Symphony Guild (life). Democrat. Avocation: writing. Home: PO Box 4365 Carmel CA 93921-4365

FAULKNER, ELLEN J., psychoanalyst; b. Fairview Park, Ohio, Apr. 17, 1958; d. Fredric George and Margaret Jean (Fray) Judd; m. L. Randall Faulkner, June 25, 1982; children: Laura Elizabeth, Judd Chapin, Samuel Caleb. BS in Music Edn., Elizabethtown Coll., 1980; MCAT, Hahnemann U., 1982; PhD in Psychoanalysis, Union Inst., 1991. Cert. psychoanalysis, Pa.; lic. psychoanalyst, Vt. Music therapist Warminster (Pa.) Hosp., 1982-87; individual therapist Stress Counseling Ctr., Horsham, Pa., 1987-89; pvt. practice Jamison, Pa., 1989—; faculty Phila. Sch. Psychoanalysis, 1993—, dir. clin. tng., 1991—, dir. admissions, 1995-96. Mem. NOW, Nat. Assn. for the Advancement Psychoanalysis. Unitarian. Office: 2581 York Rd Ste 600 Jamison PA 18929

FAULKNER, JANICE H., state official. BS in English, East Carolina U., MA in English. Postgrad. worker Breadloaf Sch. English, Vt.; English prof., dir. alumni affairs, dir. Regional Devel. Inst., assoc. vice-chancellor regional devel. East Carolina U.; revenue sec. State of N.C., Raleigh, 1993-96, sec. of state, 1996—. Dir. N.C. Dem. Party; mem. Univ. Found., chair bd. visitors East Carolina U.; former mem. Pitt County Indsl. Devel. Commn.; past pres. N.C. World Trade Assn.; past chair bd. dirs. N.C. Inst. Polit. Leadership; bd. trustees; Fedn. Tax Adminstrs. Recipient Disting. Alumnae award East Carolina U., 1993. Office: Office of Sec of State 300 N Salisbury St Raleigh NC 27603-5909*

FAULKNER, MARGARET ESTELLE, education educator, administrator; b. Springfield, Mo., Nov. 7, 1944; d. Clarence Roy and Margaret Estelle Martyn F. BS, Westchester State Coll., 1968; MA, Trenton State Coll., 1970; EdD, U. No. Colo., 1978; auditor in Theology, St. Mary's Sem. & Ecun. Inst, Balt., 1990—. Nat. umpire, U.S. Field Hockey Assn. Tchr. Westchester (Pa.) H.S., 1968-69; grad. asst. Trenton (N.J.) State Coll., 1969-70, U. No. Colo., Greeley, 1972-73; assoc. prof. psychology Towson (Md.) State U., 1970-72, assoc. prof. phys. edn., 1973-95; assoc. dean Coll. Liberal Arts Towson State U., 1995-96; chair Nat. Coll. Athletic Assn. Women's Lacrosse Com., 1981-87; v.p. umpiring U.S. Field Hockey Assn., 1988-92; vice chair Md. Spl. Olympics Bd. Dirs., Balt., 1992-94; presenter Lewis & Clark Coll. Gender Studies Symposium, Portland, Oreg., 1995. Author (book) Stress and Lifestyle, 1988. Named to U.S. Women's La Crosse Squad, 1969, U.S. Field Hockey Team, 1969, Touring Team To Zambia, Africa, 1970. Mem. Internat. Sport Psychology Assn. Office: Towson State U Coll Lib Art Psychology Dept Towson MD 21204

FAULKNER, MARY JAYE, special education educator; b. Paducah, Ky., July 28, 1955; d. Paul and Lora (Trovillion) Hunsaker; m. John Faulkner, Aug. 1, 1987. AA, Shawnee Coll., 1977; BS, So. Ill. U., 1979, MS, 1983. Cert. spl. edn. tchr., social studies tchr., Ill. Tchr. Vienna (Ill.) H.S., 1979-96, Lincoln Middle Sch., Carbondale, Ill., 1996—; fitness trainer Viginnano's Fitness Ctr., Herrin, Ill., 1994—; cons. Regular Edn. Initiative, Vienna, 1994—; conf. presenter U. Ill., St. Petersburg, Fla., 1995. Producer/writer: (video/documentary) The Berkeley Project, 1995. Mem. People for the Ethical Treatmetn of Animals, NEA (pres. local chpt. 1994-95), Greenpeace. Home: Rte 1 Box 42 Goreville IL 62939

FAULKNER, THERESA ANNE, psychologist; b. Cleve., July 21, 1964; d. Chester George and Shirley Marie (Krawczewicz) Laquatra; m. Kim Knox Faulkner, Aug. 13, 1993. BA, Miami U., Oxford, Ohio, 1986; MA, Tex. Tech. U., 1990, PhD, 1993. Staff psychologist, dir. clin. tng. The Wyo. State Hosp., Evanston, 1993—; dir. adult mental health svcs. Mountain Regional Svcs., Evanston, 1993—. Mem. APA (divsn. clin. psychology, divsn. psychoanalysis), Wyo. Psychol. Assn. Home: 98 Broken Circle Dr Evanston WY 82930 Office: Mountain Regional Svcs 50 Allegiance Cir Evanston WY 82930

FAULSTICH, JANET K., congressional worker; b. Washington, Dec. 17, 1942; d. Robert Charles and Ruth Virginia (Olson) F. BA in English, Coll. of William and Mary, 1964. Staff asst. Congressman James Roosevelt, Washington, 1965; office mgr. Congressman Thomas M.. Rees, Washington, 1966-76; chief of staff Congressman Anthony C. Beilenson, Washington, 1977—.

FAURIOL, SANDIE, nonprofit agency executive; b. Tokyo, Japan, June 19, 1949; d. William Arthur and Betsy Ross (Moore) Ellis; m. Georges Alfred Fauriol, Apr. 16, 1977 (div. 1993); m. Charles Stanley Thomason, Jr., Jan. 6, 1996. Student, U. N.C., 1967-69; BA, Ohio U., 1971; postgrad., Georgetown U., Wash., 1980. Resource devel. officer, exec. dir. Planned Parenthood of Met., Washington D.C., 1976-79; v.p. for devel. Martineau Corp., Washington D.C., 1979-80; campaign dir., dir. nat. salute Vietnam Vets. Meml. Fund, Washington D.C., 1980-83; dir. devel. Youth for Understanding, Washington D.C.; co-founder, exec. dir. Project on the Vietnam Generation, Washington D.C., 1985-87; founder, 1st pres. Ctr. for The New Leadership, 1987-90; campaign dir. Nat. Mus. Health and Medicine, 1990-91; fundraising cons., 1987-92, 96—; dir. devel. Asbury Methodist Village, 1992-94; exec. dir. Asbury Found., 1994-96; pres. Nat. Council Career Women, 1980-81, mem. adv. bd., Pub. Leadership Edn. Network, Wash., 1988--. Author: Enduring Legacies: Expressions from the Hearts and Minds of the Vietnam Generation, 1987. Mem. Nat. Soc. Fund Raising Execs. (pres. Greater Washington D.C. area chpt., 1988-90). Methodist. Office: Asbury Found 12126 Red Admiral Way Germantown MD 20876-2801

FAUST, NAOMI FLOWE, education educator, poet; b. Salisbury, N.C.; d. Christopher Leroy and Ada Luella (Graham) Flowe; AB, Bennett Coll.; MA, U. Mich., 1945; PhD, N.Y. U., 1963; m. Roy Malcolm Faust, Aug. 16, 1948. Elem. tchr. Pub. Schs. Gaffney (S.C.); tchr. English, French, phys. edn. Atkins High Sch., Winston-Salem; instr. English, Bennett Coll. and So. U., Scotlandville, La., 1944-46; prof. English, Morgan State Coll., Balt., 1946-48; tchr. English, Greensboro (N.C.) Pub. Schs., 1948-51, N.Y.C. Pub. Schs., 1954-63; prof. edn. Queens Coll. of City U. N.Y., Flushing, 1964-82; lectr. in field; writer, lectr., poetry readings, 1982—. Named Tchr.-Author of 1979, Tchr.-Writer; cert. of Merit for poem Cooper Hill Writers Conf., 1970; Achievement award L.I. br. AAUW, 1985. Mem. AAUP, Nat. Coun. Tchrs. English, Nat. Women's Book Assn., Nat. Assn. Univ. Women (L.I. br.), World Poetry Soc. Intercontinental, N.Y. Poetry Forum, NAACP, United Negro Coll. Fund, Alpha Kappa Alpha, Alpha Kappa Mu, Alpha Epsilon. Author: Discipline and the Classroom Teacher, 1977; (poetry) Speaking in Verse, 1974, All Beautiful Things, 1983, And I Travel by Rhythms and Words, 1990; contbr. poetry to jours. Home: 11201 175th St Jamaica NY 11433-4135

FAVREAU, SUSAN DEBRA, management consultant; b. Cleve., Dec. 15, 1955; d. Donald Francis and Helen Patricia (Rafferty) F. Cert., N.Y. State Police Acad., 1974; student, Cornell U., 1984, SUNY, 1986. Communications specialist N.Y. State Police, Loudonville, 1974-87; communications specialist div. hdqrs., 1987—; mgmt. cons., sec.-treas., dir. Don Favreau Assocs., Inc., Clifton Park, N.Y., 1983-86, v.p., 1986—; adj. faculty Internat. Assn. Chiefs of Police; NYSPIN coord. FBI/Nat. Crime Info. Ctr. cert. program, 1986—. Author: Teamwork in the Telecommunication Center, 1986, One More Time: How to be a Mature and Successful Telcommunications Manager, 1987, Law Enforcement Terminal Security, 1991; also NYSPIN cert. manuals. Recipient Dirs. commendation N.Y. State Police Acad., 1977, commendation N.Y. State Police, 1978, Supt.'s commendation, 1986. Mem. NAFE, N.Y. State Civil Svc. Assn., Emergency Communicators Profl. Assn. (adv. bd.), Colonie Police Benevolent Assn. (hon.), Am. Soc. Law Enforcement Trainers, Assoc. Pub. Safety Communications Officers (planning commn. Atlantic chpt. 1991, registration chair ann. NE conf. 1991), N.Y. State Troopers Police Benevolent Assn. (hon.), Nat. Bus. Women Am., Internat. Assn. Chiefs Police, Am. Horse Shows Assn., Am. Soc. Law Enforcement Trainers, Capital Dist. Hunter/Jumper Coun. Republican. Roman Catholic. Home: 45 Rapple Dr Albany NY 12205 Office: Hdqrs NY State Police State Office Bldg Campus Bldg # 22 Albany NY 12226

FAWCETT, FARRAH LENI, actress, model; b. Corpus Christi, Tex., Feb. 2, 1947; d. James William and Pauline Alice (Evans) F.; m. Lee Majors, July 28, 1973 (div. 1982); 1 son, Redmond James. Student, U. Tex. at Austin. Works as model. Movie debut in Myra Breckenridge, 1970; other film appearances include Love is a Funny Thing, 1970, Logan's Run, 1976, Somebody Killed Her Husband, 1978, Sunburn, 1979, Saturn 3, 1980, Cannonball Run, 1981, Extremities, 1986, See You in the Morning, 1989, Man ofthe House, 1995; TV movie appearances include Charlie's Angels, 1976, Murder in Texas, 1981, The Red Light Sting, 1984, The Burning Bed, 1984, Between Two Women, 1986, Nazi Hunter: The Beate Klarsfeld Story, 1986, Margaret Bourke-White, 1989, The Substitute Wife, 1994, Dalva, 1996; regular on TV series Charlie's Angels, 1976-77, Good Sports, 1991; other TV appearances include Harry O, McCloud, The Six Million Dollar Man, Marcus Welby, M.D., Apple's Way; N.Y.C. Stage debut (off-Broadway) Extremities, 1983; TV miniseries appearances include Poor Little Rich Girl: The Barbara Hutton Story, 1987, Small Sacrifices, 1989, Children of the Dust, 1995. Mem. Delta Delta Delta. *

FAWCETT, MARIE ANN FORMANEK (MRS. ROSCOE KENT FAWCETT), civic leader; b. Mpls., Mar. 6, 1914; d. Peter Paul and Mary (Stepanek) Formanek; m. Roscoe Kent Fawcett, Mar. 16, 1935; children: Roscoe Kent, Peter Formanek, Roger Knowlton II, Stephen Hart. Grad. high sch., Mpls.; cert. Harvard U., 1976-83. Chmn. of vols. Merry Go Round Club House and Mews, Greenwich, Conn., 1949-92, trustee, 1948-90, v.p., bd. dirs., 1949—, corr. sec., 1992—, chmn. entertainment, 1970-90; bd. dirs., vol. chmn., corr. sec. Nathaniel Witherell Hosp., Greenwich, 1952—, chmn. vols., 1956-89, corr. sec. aux. bd. 1956-94; bd. dirs., corr. sec. Nathaniel Witherell Auxiliary Hosp., 1952—; chmn. vols. Greenwich Hosp., 1953-54; dist. chmn. ARC, Community Chest, Mental Health, 1946-50; vol. mentally retarded children Milbank Sch., Greenwich, 1958-92. Bd. dirs. Cerebral Palsy, Greenwich Symphony, 1956—, Greenwich Symphony Guild, 1956—, Putnam Indianfield Sch.; bd. dirs., corr. sec. Merry Go Round Mews, 1949—; bd. dirs. Multiple Sclerosis Soc., 1948—, v.p., 1970, corr. sec., 1958—; active drives for ARC, Community Chest, Leukemia, Muscular Dystrophy, Mental Health, Mentally Retarded Children Milbank Sch.; bd. dirs. Merry-Go-Round News for the Elderly, 1948—, Nathaniel Whitherell Hosp. for Elderly, 1952—, Greenwich Symphony Guild, 1956—, Travel Club Greenwich, 1982—; participating mem. Huxley Inst. Biosocial Rsch.; mem. polo com. Susan Cancer Fund, Pegasus Therapeutic Riding and Rusk Inst. Rehab. Medicine. Named Woman of Year, Soroptomist Club, 1967; recipient Community Svc. award United Cerebral Palsy Assn. Fairfield County, 1972, Fund Drive award Cerebral Palsey, 1970, citations for 36 yrs. outstanding vol. svcs. Nathaniel Witherell Hosp. Aux., Conn. Dept. Health, 1977. Mem. Internat. Platform Assn., The Woman's Club of Greenwich, Travel Club of Greenwich (corr. sec., bd. dirs. 1982—). Address: 515 E Putnam Ave Greenwich CT 06830-4813

FAWELL, BEVERLY JEAN, state legislator; b. Oak Park, Ill., Sept. 17, 1930. BA, Elmhurst Coll., 1970; postgrad., No. Ill. U., 1974. Mem. Ill. Ho. of Reps., Springfield, 1981-83, Ill. Senate, Springfield, 1983—. Republican. Office: 213 Wesley Ste 105 Wheaton IL 60187

FAWSETT, PATRICIA COMBS, federal judge; b. 1943. BA, U. Fla., 1965, MAT, 1966, JD, 1973. Pvt. practice law Akerman, Senterfitt & Edison, Orlando, Fla., 1973-86; commr. 9th Cir. Jud. Nominating Commn, 1973-75, Greater Orlando Crime Prevention Assn., 1983-86; judge U.S. Dist. Ct. (mid. dist.) Fla., Orlando, 1986—. Trustee Loch Haven Art Ctr., Inc., Orlando, 1980-84; commr. Orlando Housing Authority, 1976-80, Winter Park (Fla.) Sidewalk Festival, 1973-75; bd. dirs. Greater Orlando Area C. of C., 1982-85. Mem. ABA (trial lawyers sect., real estate probate sect.), Am. Judicaturs Soc., Assn. Trial Lawyers Am., Fla. Bar Found. (bd. dirs. grants com.), Commn. on Access to Cts., Fla. Coun. Bar Assn. Pres.'s (pres., bd. dirs. 9th cir. grievance com.) Osceola County Bar Assn., Fla. Bar (bd. govs. 1983-86, budget com., disciplinary rev. com., integration rule and bylaws com., com. on access to legal system, bd. of cert., designation and advt., jud. adminstrn., selection and tenure com., jud. nominating procedures com., pub. rels. com., ann. meeting com., appellate rules com., spl. com. on judiciary-trial lawyer rels., chairperson midyr. conv. com., bd. dirs. trial lawyers sect.), Orange County Bar Assn. (exec. coun. 1977-83, pres. 1981-82, trustee Legal Aid Soc. 1977-81), Order of Coif, Phi Beta Kappa. Office: US Dist Ct Federal Bldg 80 N Hughey Ave Rm 611 Orlando FL 32801-2231*

FAY, NANCY ELIZABETH, nurse; b. Fulton, N.Y., May 10, 1943; d. Harold and Jean (Junker) Sant; m. Ronald George Fay, July 30, 1966; step children: Rory Patrick, Ronald George Jr. R.N., Genesee Hosp., Rochester, N.Y., 1964. Cert. gerontology nurse practitioner; cert. physician's asst., cert. diabetes educator. N.Y. Head maternity nurse St. Luke's Hosp., Utica, N.Y., 1975-78, diabetes clinician, 1978-82, co-dir. diabetes out-patient clinic, 1980-82; nurse practitioner, physician's asst. Slocum Dickson Med. Group, Utica, 1982-86; gerontol. nurse practitioner Masonic Home, Utica, 1988-96; diabetes educator Upstate N.Y. Spl. Profl. Pregram Eli Lilly and Co., 1988—. Chair ann. Gerontol. Teaching Day Masonic Home, 1988-96, N.Y. State Physicians Diabetes Teaching Day A.D.A., 1983-90. Recipient Extra Mile award St. Luke's Hosp., 1979, Outstanding Citizenship award Am. Legion, Utica, 1982; Diabetes research grantee Diabetes Project, Ctr. Disease Control Utica, 1980-82, 21st Ann. Scroll award Cen. N.Y. Acad. Medicine. Fellow Acad. Medicine Cent. N.Y.; mem. Am. Diabetes Assn. (pres. Utica chpt. 1983-85, Outstanding Vol. of Yr. 1978, bd. dirs. N.Y. State affiliate 1983-95, 1st v.p. 1986-87, Program award 1985-86, profl. edn. chmn. 1983-92, chair patient and pub. edn. Upstate Affiliate, 1987-92, 1st v.p., 1988-89, applicant nat. com. patient and pub. and profl. edn. 1988-89, pres.-elect N.Y. State Affiliate 1987-89, pres. 1990-92, immediate past pres. 1992-94, Sp. Svc. award N.Y. Upstate Affilliate Am. Diabetes Assn., 1994), Am. Acad. Physician's Assts., Am. Assn. Diabetes Educators, Womens Health and Edn. Referral Service St. Luke's Hosp. (bd. dirs. 1987—), N.Y. State Coalition Nurse Practitioners. Republican. Methodist. Avocations: doll collecting, dancing, poetry, bike riding. Home: Valley Rd PO Box J Oriskany NY 13424-0710 Office: Masonic Home 2150 Bleecker St Utica NY 13501-1714

FAY, TONI GEORGETTE, communications executive; b. N.Y.C., Apr. 25, 1947; d. George E. and Allie C. (Smith) Fay. BA, Duquesne U., Pitts., 1968; MSW (NIMH fellow 1970-72), U. Pitts., 1972, MEd, 1973; cert. Yale U. Drug Dependence Inst., 1973. Caseworker, N.Y.C. Dept. Welfare, 1968-70; regional commr. Gov. Pa. Coun. Drugs and Alcohol, 1973-76; dir. social services Pitts. Drug Abuse Ctr., 1972-73; dir. planning and devel. Nat. Council Negro Women, 1977-79; exec. v.p. D. Parke Gibson Assocs., 1979-82; mgr. community relations Time Inc. (name now Time-Warner Inc.), N.Y.C., 1982-83, dir. corp. community rels. and affirmative action Time Warner, Inc., 1983-93; v.p., corp. officer, Time Warner, Inc. 1993—. Bd. dirs. UNICEF, Congressional Black Caucas Found., NAACP Legal Def. Fund. Bd., Franklin and Eleanor Inst.; apptd. bd. advs. Nat. Inst. Literacy, 1996—. Named Woman of Yr., Pitts. YWCA, 1975, N.Y. Women's Forum; recipient Twin award YWCA of USA, 1987; named one 100 Top Women in Bus., Dollars and Sense Mag., 1986. Bd. dirs. Exec. Leadership Coun., Nat. Coun. Negro Women (v.p.), Alpha Kappa Alpha. Office: Time Warner Bldg 75 Rockefeller Plz New York NY 10019-6908

FAYNE, GWENDOLYN DAVIS, air force officer, English educator; b. Toledo, Dec. 8, 1951; d. Robert Louis and Marietta Beatrice (Sautter) Davis; m. Barry Dennis Fayne, Jan. 6, 1979; children: Ashleigh Elizabeth, Zachary Alexandur-John. BFA, So. Meth. U., 1972; MEd, U. North Tex., 1978; MA, U. Denver, 1987. Cert. tchr., Tex., Ala. Substitute tchr. Toledo and Dallas, 1972-73; film dir. Channel 39 Christian Broadcasting Network, Dallas, 1973-75; engr., air operator Channel 40 Trinity Broadcasting Network, Tustin, Calif., 1978; commd. 2d lt. USAF, 1978, advanced through grades to maj., 1989, ret., 1995; mgr. western area Hdqrs. USAFR Officers Tng. Corp., Norton AFB, Calif., 1979-81; chief tng. systems support Hdqrs. Air Force Manpower Pers. Pentagon, Washington, 1981-84; pers. policies officer J1, Orgn. of Joint Chiefs of Staff Pentagon, Washington, 1984-85; asst. prof. English, dir. forensics USAF Acad., Colorado Springs, Colo., 1987-92; adj. faculty mem. dept. English Auburn U., Montgomery, Ala., 1994-95; adj. faculty mem. dept. arts and scis. Troy State U., Montgomery, 1994—; dir. Bullock County HS Learning Ctr., Union Springs, Ala., 1995—; assoc. editor The Airpower Jour., Maxwell AFB, Ala., 1992-94, mil. doctrine analyst, 1994-95; dir. Bullock County H.S. Learning Ctr., Union Springs, Ala., 1995—; chair mil. affairs Jr. Officer's Coun., Norton AFB, 1981; invited spkr. in field; chmn. program devel. com. for nat. orgn. Cross Exam. Debate Assn., 1990-91. Assoc. editor The Airpower Jour., Maxwell AFB, 1992-94; contbr. articles to profl. jours. Teacher, mem. choir, soloist various chs., 1973; chair publicity com. Birthright, Inc., Woodbridge, Va., 1983. Named Command Jr. Officer of Yr., Hdqrs. USAFR Officers Tng. Corps, 1979. Mem. Speech Comm. Assn., Am. Forensics Assn., Nat. Parliamentary Debate Assn. (co-founder, editor Parliamentary Debate jour. 1992-95), Phi Upsilon Omicron. Republican. Methodist. Home: 8200 Harrogate Hl Montgomery AL 36117-5118 Office: Bullock County H S Union Springs AL 36089

FAY-SCHMIDT, PATRICIA ANN, paralegal; b. Waukegan, Ill., Dec. 25, 1941; d. John William and Agnes Alice (Semerad) Fay; m. Dennis A. Schmidt, Nov. 3, 1962 (div. Dec. 1987); children: Kristin Fay Schmidt, John Andrew Schmidt. Student, L.A. Pierce Coll., 1959-60, U. San Jose, 1960-62, Western State U. of Law, Fullerton, Calif., 1991-92. Cert. legal asst., Calif. Paralegal Rasner & Rasner, Costa Mesa, Calif., 1979-82; paralegal, adminstr. Law Offices of Manuel Ortega, Santa Ana, Calif., 1982-92; sabbatical, 1992-94; mem. editorial adv. bd. James Pub. Co., Costa Mesa, 1984-88. Contbg. author: Journal of the Citizen Ambassador Paralegal Delegation to the Soviet Union, 1990. Treas., Republican Women, Tustin, Calif., 1990-91; past regent, 1st vice regent, 2d vice regent NSDAR, Tustin, 1967—; docent Richard M. Nixon Libr. and Birthplace, 1993—, bd. dirs. Docent Guild, 1994—; docent Orange County Courthouse Mus., 1992-94. Mem. Orange County Paralegal Assn. (hospitality chair 1985-87). Roman Catholic. Home: 13571 Hewes Ave Santa Ana CA 92705-2215

FAZIO, EVELYN M., publisher; b. Hackensack, N.J.. BA in History, U. Bridgeport, 1975; MA in History, U. Conn., 1977. Cert. social studies tchr., N.J. Tchr. social studies Cedar Grove (N.J.) High Sch., 1977-79; prodn. editor Prentice-Hall, Inc., Englewood Cliffs, N.J., 1980-82, devel. editor, 1982-83, acquisitions editor, 1983-85; sr. acquisitions editor P-H/Simon & Schuster, Inc., Englewood Cliffs, 1985-88; mng. editor Random House, Inc., N.Y.C., 1988—; exec. editor polit. sci., internat. rels. and policy studies Paragon House Pubs., Inc., N.Y.C., 1989-91; editorial dir. Marshall Cavendish Pubs., N. Bellmore, N.Y., 1992-95; v.p., pub. M.E. Sharpe, Armonk, N.Y., 1995—; mktg. and editorial cons. The David M. Winfield Found., Ft. Lee, N.J., 1988-89; guest speaker Suncoast Young Author's Workshop, Clearwater, Fla., 1989—. Mem. Am. Polit. Sci. Assn., Am. Assn. for Advancement Slavic Studies.

FAZZINI, GEORGIA CAROL, corporate executive; b. Chicago Heights, Ill., Feb. 17, 1946; d. George and Corella A.T. (Roggeveen) Tjemmes; m. Dan Fazzini, Dec. 31, 1964; 1 child, Daniel Edward. Student, Ill. State U., Normal, 1963-64, Nat. Beauty Coll., 1979. Sec. Marshall Erdman & Assocs., Madison, Wis., 1972-73, U. Wis., Madison, 1973-74, Waukegan (Ill.) Devel. Ctr., 1974-75; br. adminstr. Universal Bus. Machines, Boise, Idaho, 1982-83; owner Substitute Sec. Typing Svc., Boise, 1983-87, Revisions Resume Writing Svc., 1987-90; chief exec. officer Diamond Devel. Ctr., Boise, 1988-96; cons. Nat. Multiple Sclerosis Soc., Boise, 1983-85; instr. resume writing Dept. Community Edn. Boise Schs., 1986-90, Caldwell Schs., 1989-90; resume cons. Tulsa Psychiat. Ctr., Corp. Assistance Program, 1988, Simplot Aquaculture, Caldwell, Idaho, 1991; lectr. resume writing, Tulsa, 1983, Boise, 1983—. Pres. New Neighbors' League, Canton, Ohio, 1978-79 (Rose of Month award 1979); vice chmn., bd. dirs., sec., cons. Nat. Multiple Sclerosis Soc., Boise, 1982-86; mem. Idaho Assn. Pvt. Devel. Disability Ctrs., 1989-91; guest speaker Miss Teen Pageant, Boise, 1983-84; lobbyist Boise Secretarial Svcs., 1985-86, Idaho Devel. Disability Ctrs., 1989. Mem. Idaho Assn. Pvt. Devel. Disability Ctrs., Nat. Fedn. Ind. Bus., People to People Internat, Citizen Amb. Delegation to China, Women in Mgmt. Home: 741 E State St K-104 Eagle ID 83616 Office: Diamond Devel Ctr 1119 Caldwell Blvd Nampa ID 83651-1719

FEARN, HEIDI, physicist, educator; b. Sutton-in-Ashfield, Eng., Aug. 21, 1965; came to U.S., 1989; d. Lawrence Leonard and Erika Hanna Elfreda (Kröger) F. BS in Theol. Physics with honors, Essex U., Colchester, Eng., 1986, PhD in Theol. Quantum Optics, 1989. Grad. lab. demonstrator Essex U., 1986-89; postdoctoral rsch. asst. Max Planck Inst. Quantum Optics, Garching, Germany, 1989; rsch. assoc. U. N.Mex., Albuquerque, 1989-91; lectr. physics Calif. State U., Fullerton, 1991-92, asst. prof. physics, 1992-95, assoc. prof. physics, 1995—; vis. scholar U. Ariz., Tucson, 1989-91; cons. Los Alamos (N.Mex.) Nat. Lab., 1994—. Mem. AAAS, Am. Phys. Soc. Office: Calif State U Physics Dept 800 N State College Blvd Fullerton CA 92631-3547

FEARRINGTON, ANN PEYTON, writer, illustrator, newspaper reporter; b. Winston-Salem, N.C., Aug. 25, 1945; d. James Cornelius Pass Fearrington and Florence Moore (McCanless-Fearrington) Blackwood; m. Hege Hill Russ, Sept. 1967 (div. 1984); children: James Pass Fearrington Russ, Joseph Peyton Fearrington Russ; m. Vance Edwin Cox, Jr., June 17, 1985; 1 stepson, Charles Jonathan Cox. BA in Secondary Edn. and English, U. N.C., 1967; MS in Life Scis., Botany & Horticulture, N.C. State U., 1972. Mid. sch. tchr. Wake County Sch. Sys., Raleigh, 1967-71; landscape designer pvt. practice N.Y.C., Winston-Salem, N.C., 1972-83; corr. Raleigh News & Observer, 1993—. Author, illustrator: Christmas Lights, 1996. Sch. libr. vol. Wake County Sch. Sys., Raleigh, 1985—; Sunday Sch. tchr. Highland United Meth. Ch., Raleigh, 1986—. Mem. Soc. Children's Book Writers & Illustrators, Raleigh Racquet Club.

FEARS, LOUISE MATHIS, educator; b. Washington, Ga., Dec. 31, 1935; d. Ambrose Powell Jr. and Sarah Louise (Moon) Mathis; m. Henry Beane Fears, June 22, 1958; children: Scott Powell, Douglas Edward, Leslie Fears Carter. BA, Shorter Coll., 1958; MEd, Ga. State U., 1977. Cert. Profl. Tchr., Ga. Evaluator Ga. State Dept. Ed., Atlanta, 1958-60; asst. Pers. Dept. City of Atlanta, 1960-61; tchr. DeKalb County Ga., Bd. Edn., Decatur, 1977-90; ednl. dir. Learning Solutions Gwinnett Pl. Ctr., Duluth, Ga., 1990-91; tchr. Christ the King Sch., Atlanta, 1991-95, Providence Christian Acad., Lilburn, Ga., 1995—. Author: A Limousine is a Magazine About Lemons, 1987. Trustee Shorter Coll., 1987-92, 94—; U.S. del. joint U.S./Chinese Early Childhood Edn. Conf., Beijing, 1993. Mem. Ga. Assn. Young Children, So. Early Childhood Assn., Nat. Assn. Edn. Young Children. Democrat. Baptist.

FEASTER, CHARLOTTE JOSEPHINE S., school administrator; b. Asheboro, N.C., Aug. 5, 1951; d. Earlie Lenan Staley and McCoy (Cheek) Staley Gathings; m. Jasper Nathaniel Feaster, July 23, 1983. BS in Intermediate Edn., Winston-Salem State U., 1973; MS in Intermediate Edn., N.C. Agrl. & Tech. State U., 1981, MS in Ednl. Leadership, 1993; Asst. Prin.'s Exec. Program, U. N.C., 1995-96. Cert. tchr., N.C., La. Dormitory asst. Winston-Salem (N.C.) State U., 1969-73; emergency rm. receptionist Reynolds Meml. Hosp., Winston-Salem, 1969-73; office asst. Employment Security Commn., Asheboro, 1969-71; cottage home parent asst. Guilford County Dept. Social Svcs., High Point, N.C., 1971-73; intermediate grade tchr. Randolph County Bd. Edn., Asheboro, 1973-94, summer sch. instr., 1987-91, 4th and 5th grade tchr., 1983-94; 4th and 5th grade tchr. Ramseur (N.C.) Sch., 1973-94; asst. prin. Randleman (N.C.) Elem. Sch., 1994-95, Liberty (N.C.) Sch., 1995—; enrichment camp instr. N.C. Agrl. & Tech. State U., Greensboro, 1982-87; Can. studies group leader Duke U., Durham, N.C., 1991-93; 4-H summer camp leader N.C. Randolph County, Asheboro, 1973-82; co-leader N.C. Tchr. Acad., Meredith Coll., Raleigh, N.C., 1993-94; site mgr. N.C. Tchr. Acad., Fayetteville (N.C.) State U., 1995, E. Carolina U., Greenville, 1996; mem. Asst. Prins. Exec. Program U. N.C., Chapel Hill, 1996—. 4-H leader Randolph County Agrl. Ext., Ramseur, 1983-85; Christian edn. dir. Deep River Assn. Bapt. Chs., Lee, Chatham and Randolph Counties, 1980-93; youth edn. resource person Oakland Bapt. Ch., Ramseur, 1983-93. Recipient Lay Leadership award Deep River Assn. Chs., 1990, Gold Clover award Randolph County Home Ext., 1989, Excellence First Project award Greensboro Area Math & Science Edn. Ctr., U. N.C. at Greensboro, 1991-93; grantee First Am. Bank, 1990; named one of Outstanding Young Educators Jaycees, 1990. Mem. N.C. Conf. Tchrs. Math. (workshop presenter 1988-93, Outstanding Math. Tchr. award 1992), N.C. Assn. Educators (county pres. 1992-95), Order Eastern Star (fin. sec. 1987-93), Gamma Omicron (award Eta Phi Beta chpt. 1991). Home: 361 Thornbrook Rd Ramseur NC 27316-9309 Office: Liberty Sch Asst Prin Exec Program 206 Fayetteville St Liberty NC 27298

FEASTER, SHARON ANNE, academic administrator; b. Spartanburg, S.C., Nov. 29, 1946; d. William Rice and Dorothy Mae (Stewart) F. BA, Furman U., 1969; MEd, Stephen F. Austin State U., 1977; EdD, East Tex. State U., 1985. Tchr. Lancaster (S.C.) Ind. Sch. Dist., 1969-70, Sea Island Acad., John's Island, S.C., 1970-72; bus. editor Charleston (S.C.) News & Courier, 1972-73; bus. mgr. Union (S.C.) Daily Times, 1974-76; tchr. Port Arthur (Tex.) Ind. Sch. Dist., 1977-78; coord. Curriculum Tree & Inst. Region 7 Edn. Svc. Ctr., Kilgore, Tex., 1978-90; dir. tchr. edn. LeTourneau U., Longview, Tex., 1990—; owner, writer Curriculum Tree, Longview, Tex., 1990—; cons. in field. Editor: History of First Baptist Church, 1992. Mem. ASCD, Tex. Assn. Colls. of Tchr. Edn., Phi Delta Kappa. Home: 603 Green Oak Dr Longview TX 75604-1808 Office: LeTourneau U PO Box 7001 Longview TX 75607-7001

FEATHERMAN, SANDRA, university president, political science educator; b. Phila., Apr. 14, 1934; d. Albert N. and Rebe (Burd) Green; m. Bernard Featherman, May 29, 1958; children: Andrew Charles, John James. BA, U. Pa., 1955, MA, 1978, PhD, 1978. Asst. prof. dept. polit. sci. Temple U., Phila., 1978-84, assoc. prof., 1984-91, asst. to pres., 1986-89, pres. faculty senate, 1985-86, dir. Ctr. for Pub. Policy, 1986-91; vice chancellor acad. adminstrn., prof. polit. sci. U. Minn., Duluth, 1991-95; pres. U. New Eng., Biddeford, Maine, 1995—. Author: Jews, Blacks and Ethnics, 1979; contbr. articles to profl. jours. Bd. dirs. Citizens Com. Pub. Edn. in Phila., 1977-89, pres., 1979-81; pres. Pa. Fedn. Community Coll.; trustee C.C. Phila., 1970-92, chmn. bd. trustees, 1984-86; life trustee, v.p. Samuel Fels Found., 1978 ; bd. dirs. United Way SE Pa., 1977-89, United Way Pa., 1981-84, Maine Civil Liberties Union, U. New Eng., Gulf of Maine Aquarium; pres. Girls Clubs Am., Phila., 1971-73, mem. nat. bd., 1971-74; mem. Pa. Coun. on Arts, 1979-83; nat. bd. dirs. Women and Founds.-Corp. Philanthropy, 1986-91; v.p. Jewish Community Rels. Coun., 1982-89; speaker Commonwealth of Pa. Humanities Coun., 1988, 90, 91; bd. govs. Am. Assn. Colls. Osteopathic Medicine; bd. dirs. Kennebec Girl Scout Coun. Recipient Brooks Graves award Pa. Polit. Sci. Assn., 1982, City of Phila. Community Svc. award, 1984, Women's Achievement award YWCA, 1989, Adminstr. of Yr. award Minn. Women in Higher Edn., 1994. Mem. AAUW (bd. dirs. Phila. chpt. 1975-78, 80-91, pres. 1984-86, nat. chair internat. fellowships panel 1987-91, Outstanding Woman award 1986, nat. bd. dirs. 1993—), Am. Polit. Sci. Assn. Office: U New Eng Hills Beach Rd Biddeford ME 04005-9526

FECTEAU, ROSEMARY LOUISE, educational administrator, educator, consultant; b. Niagara, Wis., Aug. 7, 1930; d. Andrew Raymond and Julianna Agnes (Wodenka) Waitrovich; m. Jack Richard Fecteau Sr. (dec. Dec. 1994), June 12, 1954; children: Michele, Julienne, Gervaise, Jack Jr., Andrew, Anne-Marie. BA with high distinction, U. R.I., 1974; MS in Edn., U. Maine, 1976; MS in Ednl. Adminstrn., U. So. Maine, 1979. Cert. supt. schs. K-12. Sec. A.O. Smith Corp., Milw., 1949-54, Judge Irving W. Smith, Niagara, 1954-55; asst. tchr. Regional Resource Rm., Yarmouth, Maine, 1974-75; prin. Breakwater Sch., Cape Elizabeth, Maine, 1975-78; tchr. grades 6-8 Wells (Maine) Jr. H.S., 1978-79; dir. spl. svcs. Maine Sch. Adminstrv. Dist. 75, Bowdoin, Bowdoinham, Harpswell, Topsham, Maine, 1979-84; ednl. cons. various states, 1984—; owner Serendipity Acres Sheep Farm; secondary handicapped task force State Dept. Edn., Augusta, 1980-81; chairperson nat. insvc. network U. Ind., Topsham, Maine, 1981-84. Mem. Friends of the Royal River, Friends of Prince Meml. Libr., Maine Spl. Edn. Rev. Team; founder Project Co-Step and Project S.E.A.R.C.H.; mem. focus group Casco Bay Estuary Project Maine; brownie leader, girl scout cons. Girl Scouts Am., Erie, Pa., 1965-66; dir. women's Cursillo Movement, Erie, 1967; co-chair publicity St. Vincent Hosp., Erie, 1966-67; chairperson conservation commn. Town of North Yarmouth, 1987; del. Dem. Conv., 1986. Mem. AAUW, LWV, U. So. Maine Alumni Assn., The Muskie Club, North Yarmouth Hist. Soc., Maine Organic Farmer and Gardener Assn., Maine Assn. Supervision and Curriculum Devel., Consumers for Affordable Health Care, Union of Concerned Scientists. Home: Serendipity Acres 29 W Pownal Rd North Yarmouth ME 04097-3725

FEDAK, BARBARA KINGRY, technical center administrator; b. Hazleton, Pa., Feb. 7, 1939; d. Marvin Frederick and Ruth Anna (Wheeler) Siebel; m. Raymond F. Fedak, Mar. 27, 1993; children: Sean M., James Goldey. BA, Trenton State Coll., 1961; MEd, Lesley Coll., Cambridge, Mass., 1986. Registered respiratory therapist. Dept. dir. North Platte (Nebr.) Community Hosp., 1974-75; newborn coord. Children's Hosp., Denver, 1975-79; edn. coord. Rose Med. Ctr., Denver, 1979-81; program dir. respiratory tech. program Pickens Tech., Aurora, Colo., 1981-86; mktg. rep. Foster Med. Corp., Denver, 1986-87; staff therapist Porter Meml. Hosp., Denver, 1987-

88; dir., br. mgr. Pediatric Svcs. Am., Denver, 1988-90; dir. clin. edn. Pickens Tech., Aurora, Colo., 1991—, divsn. chair health occupations, 1991—; site evaluator Joint Rev. Com. for Respiratory Therapy Edn., Euless, Tex. Met. coun. mem. Am. Lung Assn., 1987-91. Mem. Am. Assn. Respiratory Care (edn. sect. program com. 1992—, abstract rev. com. 1993—), Colo. Soc. Respiratory Care (dir. at large 1983-86, 90-92, sec. 1980-81, program com. 1982-92), Colo. Assn. Respiratory Educators (chair 1991-96). Methodist. Home: 11478 S Marlborough Dr Parker CO 80134-7318 Office: Pickens Tech 500 Airport Blvd Aurora CO 80011

FEDDERSEN, BARBARA R., secondary education educator; b. Moline, Ill., Jan. 3, 1953; d. Robert Paul and Marilyn Joyce (Dunlap) Vogt; m. Robert Lee Feddersen, April 21, 1979; 1 child, Paul Robert. BA, Western Ill. Univ., Macomb, 1975. Cert. tchr., Ill. Libr. North Boone H.S., Poplar Grove, Ill., 1986-93, social studies tchr., 1993—. Mem. North Boone Edn. Assn. (bldg. rep., pres. 1992-93). Home: 6982 Squaw Prairie Rd Belvidere IL 61008 Office: North Boone Cmty Dist 200 17641 Poplar Grove Rd Poplar Grove IL 61065

FEDERBUSH, MARCIA JOY, political and educational writer; b. Newark, May 25, 1934; d. Nathan and Esther Marion (Rubinstein) Rosenzweig; m. Paul Geraro Federbush (div. Sept. 1990); children: Jason, Laurel. BA, NYU, 1955; MEd, Rutgers U., 1958. Cert. elem. tchr., Mass. 5th grade tchr. West Windsor Twp. Pub. Schs., Dutch Neck, N.J., 1956-58; 6th grade tchr. Billerica (Mass.) Pub. Schs., 1958-59; lab. asst. biology, lab. instr. Brandeis U., Waltham, Mass., 1960-65; investigator, equal opportunity specialist U.S. EEOC, Detroit, 1978-93; cons. in sex discrimination edn., Ann Arbor, Mich., 1971-78; singer satirical songs for feminist groups, peace groups, civil rights groups and polit. candidates, 1969—; leader exch. trip to Soviet Union, 1960; mem. 4th World Conf. on Women, Beijing, 1995. Author, rschr. Let Them Aspire!, 1971; songwriter, singer audiotape: Songs Your Wouldn't Want to Hear (Especially your Holy Father), 1989. Active Habitat for Humanity; bd. dirs., vol. Student Advocacy Ctr., Ann Arbor, 1975—; co-chair equity audit com. Ann Arbor Pub. Schs., 1975—; bd. dirs. Ann Arbor Area 2000, 1988—; campaign worker various Dem. candidatesm 1969—. Named Feminist of Yr., U. Mich., 1973, prize Ctr. for Continuing Edn. of Women, U. Mich., 1988; named to Mich. Women's Hall of Fame, 1988. Mem. NEA, NOW (action v.p. 1975-77, Uppity Woman United award 1975), NAACP, Nat. Women's Polit. Caucus. Home: 2000 Anderson Ct Ann Arbor MI 48104

FEDERKIEWICZ, STEFANIE See POWERS, STEFANIE

FEDOROFF, NINA VSEVOLOD, research scientist, consultant; b. Cleve., Apr. 9, 1942; d. Vsevolod N. and Olga S. (Snegireff) Stacy; m. T. Patrick Gaganidze, June 18, 1966 (div. 1978); children: Natasha, Kyr; m. M. Broyles, 1990. B.S., Syracuse U., 1966; Ph.D., Rockefeller U., 1972. Asst. mgr. transl. bur. Biol. Abstracts, Phila., 1962-63; flutist Syracuse (N.Y.) Symphony Orch., 1964-66; acting asst. prof. UCLA, 1972-74; postdoctoral fellow UCLA and Carnegie Inst. Washington, Los Angeles and Balt., 1974-78; staff scientist Carnegie Inst. Washington, Balt., 1978-94; dir., biotechnol. inst. Pa. State U., 1995—, Willaman prof. of life scis., 1995—; prof. dept. biology Johns Hopkins U., 1979-94; mem. devel. biology panel NSF, Washington, 1979-80, sci. adv. panel Office of Tech. Assessment, Congress, Washington, 1979-80, recombinant DNA adv. com. NIH, Bethesda, Md., 1980-84, sci. adv. com. Japanese Human Frontier Sci., 1988; sci. adv. com. Competitive Rsch. Grants Office, USDA; mem. commn. on life scis., basic biology bd. NRC, NAS, Washington, 1984-90; bd. dirs. Genetics Soc. Am.; mem. bd. overseers Harvard U., 1988-91; trustee BIOSIS, Phila., 1990—; mem. NAS Coun., 1991-94; dir. Internat. Sci. Found., 1992-93; mem. adv. com. Directorate for Biol. Scis., 1994—. Editor: Gene, 1981-84; editor, bd. rev. editors Sci., 1985; mem. sci. adv. bd. The Plant Jour., 1991—; editor Perspectives in Biology and Medicine, 1991—, Procs. Nat. Acad. Sci., 1996—; book editor various publs.; contbr. chpts. to books, articles to profl. jours. Recipient Merit award NIH, 1990; grantee NSF and USDA, 1979-84, NIH, 1984—, NSF, 1992—. Mem. AAAS, NAS (editor procs. 1995—), Am. Acad. Arts and Scis., Phi Beta Kappa (vis. scholar 1984-85), Sigma Xi (Howard Taylor Ricketts award 1990). Home: 2398 Shagbark Ct State College PA 16803 Office: Biotechnol Inst Pa State U University Park PA 16802

FEDORUK, JOAN DIANE, accountant, nurse; b. Youngstown, Ohio, Feb. 20, 1956; d. Nicholas David and Elaine Francis (Kucher) F. BSBA, Youngstown State U., 1995. LPN, Ohio. Staff nurse South Side Hosp., Youngstown, 1980-83; pvt. duty nurse LPN Ofcl. Registry, Youngstown, 1983-90; staff nurse, counselor Physician's Weight Loss Ctr., Liberty, Ohio, 1990-93; acctg. intern Delphi Packard Electric Sys., Warren, Ohio, 1994-95; plant acct. U.S. Can Co., Columbiana, Ohio, 1995—; bus. owner, acct. Profl. Bus. Svcs., Austitown, Ohio, 1996. Univ. Found. scholar Youngstown State U., 1992-95, Dist. Dir.'s Tax Inst. scholar, 1995. Mem. Ohio Soc. CPAs, Inst. Mgmt. Accts., Phi Kappa Alpha, Alpha Tau Gamma. Republican. Roman Catholic.

FEE, VIRGINIA E., psychology educator; b. Burlington, N.C., Apr. 29, 1963; d. David A. Sr. and Evelyn Claire (Nester) F.; m. Guy L. Russell, July 24, 1993. BA, Hamline U., 1985; MA, La. State U., 1989, PhD, 1992. Lic. psychologist. Intern Child Devel. and Rehab. Ctr. Oreg. Health Scis. U., Portland, 1991-92; asst. prof. Miss. State U., Mississippi State, 1992—; supr. of psychology externs, Comm. Counseling Svcs., Starkville, Miss., 1993-94. Contbg. author: Handbook of Hyperactivity, 1992, Assessment, Analysis, and Treatment of Self-Injury, 1992. Grantee Found. for the Mid-South, 1993. Mem. Am. Psychol. Assn., Southeastern Psychol. Assn., Assn. for Advancement of Behavior Therapy. Office: Miss State Univ Dept Psychology PO Drawer 6161 Mississippi State MS 39762

FEEDER, GAIL ANNETTE, accountant; b. Colorado Springs, Colo., July 10, 1969; d. Wayne Oval and Sandra Elaine (Mitze) Naugle; m. David Warren Feeder II, Aug. 12, 1995. BSBA, U. Denver, 1992, M in Accountancy, 1992. CPA, Colo., Mo., Kans.; cert. mgmt. acct. Sr. acct. Deloitte & Touche LLP, Kansas City, Mo., 1992—. Mem. AICPA, Inst. Mgmt. Accts., Healthcare Fin. Mgmt. Assn., Kans. State Bd. Accountancy. Republican. Lutheran. Home: 3417 W 74th St Prairie Village KS 66208 Office: Deloitte & Touche LLP Ste 400 1010 Grand Ave Kansas City MO 64106

FEENEY, JOAN N., judge. BA in French and Govt., Conn. Coll., 1975; MA, Amherst Coll.; JD, Suffolk Univ. Law Sch., 1978. Law clk. to Judge Harold Lavien U.S. Bankruptcy Ct. Mass., 1978-79, law clk. to Judge James N. Gabriel, 1978-79, 82-86; assoc. Feeney & Feely, Boston, 1979-82; assoc., then ptnr. Hanify & King P.C., Boston, 1986-92; bankruptcy judge U.S. Bankruptcy Ct. Mass., Boston, 1992—; mem. Suffolk Univ. Law Review, 1976-78; editor Suffolk Transnational Journal, 1977-78, Suffolk Voluntary Defenders, 1977-78, Volunteer Lawyer's Project. Mem. Mass. Bar Assn., Boston Bar Assn., Mass. Assn. of Women Lawyers. Office: Thomas O'Neill Federal Bldg 10 Causeway St Rm 1101 Boston MA 02222-1047

FEENEY, MARY KATHERINE O'SHEA, retired public health nurse; b. Niagara Falls, N.Y., July 10, 1934; d. James T. and Mary Elizabeth (Woodside) O'Shea; m. Gerald E. Feeney, Apr. 27, 1957; children: Patricia, Elizabeth, Susan, Kathleen. BSN, Niagara U., 1956; MS in Mgmt., SUNY, Binghamton, 1981. RN, N.Y.; hypnotherapist; Assessment Modified Reflexology for Nurses. Pub. health nurse Herkimer County (N.Y.) Pub. Health Nursing Svc.; ret.; past coord. Herkimer County Long Term Health Care; bd. dirs. Oneida/Herkimer Coalition for Tobacco Control. Home: RR 3 Box 329 Little Falls NY 13365-9556

FEENEY, MARYANN MCHUGH, human resources professional; b. Bklyn., July 9, 1948; d. Michael Daniel and Mary Bridget (Hourican) McH.; m. Brian Francis Feeney, Sept. 21, 1974 (dec. Mar. 1992); 1 child, Michael. BA, Marymount Manhattan Coll., 1980. Human resources mgr. Mother Cornelius Moore, Inc., N.Y.C., 1977-84; human resources dir. Statue of Liberty-Ellis Island Found., N.Y.C., 1984-88; pres. The Taft Inst., N.Y.C., 1988—. Exec. producer Your Vote Video, 1991 (nominated ACE and Emmy awards 1991). Bd. dirs. Bklyn. Conservatory of Music, 1992-94, SFX-Prospect Park Baseball, Bklyn., 1988—. Recipient Cmty. Svc. award SFX-Prospect Park Baseball, 1992, 95. Mem. Am. Polit. Sci. Assn., Ireland House at NYU. Democrat. Roman Catholic. Office: The Taft Inst Queens Coll Powdermaker Hall # 186 Flushing NY 11367

FEFFERMAN, SUSAN KATHLEEN FINNEGAN, association executive; b. Detroit, Jan. 8, 1949; d. James Arthur and Jewel Judy Margaret (Platt) Finnegan; m. Dan Graydon Fefferman, Feb. 8, 1975; children: Donsu, Kaeleigh. M in Religious Edn., Unification Theol. Sem., Barrytown, N.Y., 1986; BFA, U. Mich., 1971. Art & religious edn. tchr. missions, Columbus, Ohio, Teheran, Istanbul, 1972-79; cons. Com. to Defend First Amendment Rsch. Assn., Washington, 1979-80; cons., photographer Collegiate Assn. Rsch. of Principle, Washington, 1980-83; cons. Am. Constitution Com., Washington, 1987-90; co-founder, vice prin. New Hope Acad., Landover Hills, Md., 1990-94; dir. Women's Fedn. for World Peace, Washington, 1994—; advisor True Family Values Ministry, Washington, 1996; coord. Internat. Women's Friendship Conf., Washington, 1995—. Active D.C. Commn. on Women, 1996. Mem. Wingate Homeowners Assn. (pres. 1994—). Home: 8018 Wingate Dr Glenn Dale MD 20769 Office: Women's Fedn World Peace 3600 New York Ave NE Washington DC 20002

FEHIR, KIM MICHELE, oncologist, hematologist; b. Chgo., Aug. 31, 1947; d. William Frank and Beatric Mae (Mc Glaughlin) Debelak; m. John Stephen Fehir, Dec. 24, 1974. BS, Mich. State U., 1969; MS, U. Ill., Chgo., 1973, PhD, 1975; MD, Rush Med. Sch., Chgo., 1978. Diplomate Am. Bd. Internal Medicine. Intern, resident John Hopkins Hosp., Balt., 1978-81; fellow in oncology Meml. Sloan Kettering Cancer Ctr., N.Y.C., 1981-83; dir. med. oncology Stehlin Oncology Clin., Houston, 1983—; asst. prof. medicine Bayler Coll., Houston, 1983—. Contbr. to profl. jours. Mem. AMA, Am. Med. Soc. Hematologist, Am. Med. Soc. Clin. Oncology. Republican. Office: 1315 Calhoun St Ste 1800 Houston TX 77002-8232

FEHLER, POLLY DIANE, neonatal nurse, educator; b. Harvard, Ill., Jan. 6, 1946; d. Arthur William and Charlotte (Stewart) Eggert; m. Gene L. Fehler, Dec. 26, 1964; children: Timothy, Andrew. AS, summa cum laude, Kishwaukee Coll., 1974; BSN, magna cum laude, No. Ill. U., DeKalb, 1977, MSN, summa cum laude, 1980. Cert. BLS, neonatal resuscitation instr. Obgyn. staff nurse Kishwaukee Hosp., 1977; community health nurse DeKalb County Health Dept., 1977-79; grad. teaching asst. No. Ill. Univ., 1978-80; adj. maternity instr. Auburn Univ., Montgomery, Ala., 1980-81; maternal/newborn nurse USAF Regional Hosp. Maxwell, Montgomery, Ala., 1980-81, nurse internship coord., 1981-83; edn. coord. USAF Hosp., Bergstrom, Austin, Tex., 1983-87; neonatal ICU & transport RN St. Mary's Hosp., Athens, Ga., 1988-90; nursing instr. Tri-County Tech. Coll., Pendleton, S.C., 1990—; EMT, course lectr. U. Tex., Austin, 1984-86; counselor, vol. Hospice, 1984-87; sec., v.p. Shared Resources for Nurses, Austin, 1984-87, high blood pressure instr.-trainer, 1986-87, home health staff nurse Interim Health Care, Anderson, S.C., 1991-94; expert witness St. Mary's Hosp., Athens, 1991-92; coord. NCLEX rev. course Health Edn. Systems, Inc., 1993—; lectr. on interculturalism in nursing, 1993—; mem. adv. bd. Tri-County Student Competencies, 1990—, mem. advising team, 1995—, mini grant sel. com., 1992-93, 95—. Nursing textbook reviewer Addison Wesley Pubs., 1993, Mosby Yearbook, 1995—. Nurse, med. evaluator Mass Casualty Exercises, Austin, 1984-87; tchr., sec. United Meth. Chs., Ill., Ala., Ga., S.C., 1970—; mem. alumni bd. No. Ill. Alumni, DeKalb, 1979-80; mem. Malta Dist. Bd. Edn., 1979-80; judge Austin Sch. Dist. Sci. and Math. Fair, Austin, 1983-84; S.C. Gov.'s Guardian ad Litem Vol., 1995—; vol. Oconee County Healthy Visions Task Force, 1996—, S.C. Good Health Appeal Coll. Campaign Mgr., 1996, Oconee County Humane Soc., 1996—. Capt. USAF, 1980-88. Decorated USAF Commendation medal with oak leaf cluster; recipient Sr. Nursing Class of Tri-County Tech. Coll. Instr. of the Yr. award, 1992, Nat. Inst. for Staff and Orgnl. Devel. Excellence award, 1995. Mem. AAUW, ANA, S.C. Nurses Assn., S.C. Assn. Perinatal Nurses, S.C. Tech. Edn. Assn., Nursing Faculty Orgn. (v.p. 1991-94), United Meth. Women, S.C. Internat. Ednl. Consortium, Delta Kappa Gamma, Sigma Theta Tau, Lambda Chi Nu. Meth. Home: 106 Laurel Ln Seneca SC 29678-2705 Office: Tri-County Tech Coll PO Box 587 Pendleton SC 29670-0587

FEHRMANN, CHERYL C. HAAS, reading specialist, elementary education educator; b. Belleville, Ill., July 6, 1950; d. Francis J. Haas and Estelle F. Terveer; m. Anthony Edward Fehrmann, June 11, 1971; children: Shannon Le, Matthew Anthony. BS in Elem. Edn., So. Ill. U., Edwardsville, 1972, postgrad., 1981, MS in Elem. Edn., 1990. direct distbr. environ. and ednl. products Nat. Safety Assn., Memphis, 1992—. Tchr. gifted Breese (Ill.) Dist. 12, 1980-86, tchr. 4th grade, 1980-81, Chpt. I tchr., 1982-86; tchr. gifted Aviston (Ill.) Elem. Sch., 1982-85; tchr. of autistic Ill. Ctr. for Autism, Fairview Heights, 1987-88; reading specialist Grant-Illini Dist. 110, Fairview Heights, 1990—; instr. parenting classes, Fairview Heights, 1993—. Bd. dirs. Am. Cancer Soc., Breese, 1991—. Recipient Gold Apple award St. Clair County, Ill., 1995. Mem. Lewis and Clark Reading Coun., Ill. Reading Coun., Young Authors. Roman Catholic. Home: 100 Westbrook Dr Breese IL 62230-1948

FEIG, REBECCA PAULINE, filmmaker, business executive; b. N.Y.C., Oct. 13, 1966; d. Werner and Judith (Kesselman) F. BFA in Film, SUNY, Purchase, 1990. Pres. Prolink Internat., N.Y.C., Paris, Moscow, 1993—, Persistence of Vision, N.Y.C., 1995—. Dir. film The Waiting, 1992 (various awards 1992), bye-bye Babushka, 1996.

FEIGIN, BARBARA SOMMER, advertising executive; b. Berlin, Germany, Nov. 16, 1937; came to U.S., 1940, naturalized, 1949; d. Eric Daniel and Charlotte Martha (Demmer) Sommer; m. James Feigin, Sept. 17, 1961; children: Michael, Peter, Daniel. BA in Polit. Sci., Whitman Coll., 1959; cert. of Bus. Adminstrn., Harvard-Radcliffe Program Bus. Adminstrn., 1960. Mktg. rsch. asst. Richardson-Vick Co., Wilton, Conn., 1960-61; market rsch. analyst SCM Corp., N.Y.C., 1961-62; group rsch. supr. Benton & Bowles, Inc., N.Y.C., 1963-67; assoc. rsch. dir. Marplan Rsch. Co., N.Y.C., 1968-69; exec. v.p. strategic svcs. Grey Advt. Inc., N.Y.C., 1969—, mem. agy. policy council; bd. dirs. VF Corp., Circuit City Stores, Inc. Contbr. articles to profl. jours. Bd. overseers Whitman Coll.; bd. advisors Catalyst. Recipient Women Achievers award YWCA, 1987. Mem. Advt. Rsch. Found. (bd. dirs. 1987, past chmn.). Office: Grey Advt Inc 777 3rd Ave 36th Fl New York NY 10017

FEIGL, THERESA JEAN, elementary education educator; b. Richland Center, Wis., May 20, 1958; d. Raleigh Gene and Eileen Josephine (Zacijek) Angle; m. Kevin Harvey Feigl, June 25, 1983; children: Rebecca Lynn, Aaron Andrew, Brittni Jean. BA, U. Wis., 1996. Mktg. dir. Valley Bank, Sauk City, Wis., 1976-85; elem. sch. sec. Sauk Prairie Schs., Sauk City, 1985—; asst. dir. sch. musicals Black Hawk Elem. Sch., Sauk City, 1985—, computer instr., 1991. Catechist St. Aloysius Ch., Sauk City, 1991-93. Mem. AAUW, Phi Kappa Phi. Roman Catholic. Home: S8857 Hwy C Plain WI 53577 Office: Black Hawk Elem E7995 School Rd Sauk City WI 53583

FEIGON, JUDITH TOVA, ophthalmologist, surgeon, educator; b. Galveston, Tex., Dec. 2, 1947; d. Louis and Ethel (Goldberg) F.; m. Nathan C. Goldman; children: Michael G., Miriam G. AB, Barnard Coll., Columbia U., 1970; postgrad., Rice U. and U. Houston, 1970-71; MD, U. Tex.-San Antonio, 1976. Diplomate Am. Bd. Ophthalmology. Intern Mt. Auburn Hosp., Cambridge, Mass. Intern and clin. teaching fellow, Harvard U. Med. Sch., 1976-77; resident in ophthalmology, Baylor Coll. Medicine, Houston, 1977-80, fellowship in retina, 1980-82, clin. instr., 1982—; asst. prof. ophthalmology U. Tex. Med. Br., Galveston, 1982-85, clin. asst. prof., 1985-91, clin. assoc. prof., 1992—; pvt. practice medicine specializing in ophthalmology, vitreoretinal diseases and surgery, Houston, 1983—; physician advisor to Houston br. Tex. Soc. to Prevent Blindness, 1987-89, also bd. dirs.; mem. staff Meth., St. Lukes, Tex. Children's, John Sealy, St. Joseph's Hosp., Park Plaza. Contbr. articles to profl. publs. Mem. AMA, Assn. Am. Physicians and Surgeons, Am. Acad. Ophthalmology, Tex. Med. Assn., Tex. Opthal. Soc., Houston Opthal. Soc., Harris County Med. Soc., U. Tex.-San Antonio Alumni Assn., Harvard Med. Sch. Alumni Assn., Vitreous Soc. Office: 7515 Main St Ste 650 Houston TX 77030-4519

FEIL, SANDRA ANN WEBER, retired elementary school educator; b. Detroit, Oct. 9, 1937; d. Don Louis and Stella Elizabeth Weber; m. Richard Holmstrom, Jan. 25, 1957 (dec. Aug. 1972); children: Holly, Laurie; m. Louis James Feil, Mar. 21, 1975. BA in Edn., Mich. State U., 1962. Tchr. 2nd and 3rd grades individualized reading program Horace Mann Elem. Sch., Schenectady, N.Y., 1963-64; tchr. 6th grade Chippewa Intermediate Sch., Port Huron, Mich., 1971-80; tchr. 4th grade Lee Britain Elem. Sch., Irving, Tex., 1987-88, Woodrow Wilson Elem. Sch., Port Huron, 1980-87; tchr. 4th grade Garfield Elem. Sch., Port Huron, 1988-95, ret., 1995. Chairperson ways and means com. Hudson Valley C.C. Women's Group, Troy, N.Y., 1967-68, v.p., 1968-69; vol. tutor; participant efforts to end Vietnam War, 1968-75; tchr. Sunday sch. area Luth. Ch., Schenectady, 1967-68, Christian Reformed Ch., Schenectady, 1968-69. Mem. AAUW (program chairperson 1975-76). Congregational. Home: 910 Vanderburgh Pl Port Huron MI 48060-6500

FEILER, JO ALISON, artist; b. Los Angeles, Ca., Apr. 16, 1951; d. Alfred Martin and Leatrice Lucille Feiler. Student, UCLA, 1969, Art Ctr. Coll. Design, L.A., 1970-72; BFA, Calif. Inst. Arts, 1973, MFA, 1975. Asst. dir. Frank Perls Gallery, Beverly Hills, Calif., 1969-70; photography editor Coast Environ. mag., L.A., 1970-72; art dir. Log/An Inc., L.A., 1975-82. One-woman shows Inst. Contemporary Art, London, 1975, Calif. Inst. Arts, Valencia, 1975, NUAGE, L.A., 1978, Susan Harder Gallery, N.Y.C., 1984; exhibited in numerous group shows, 1975—; represented in permanent collections including Nat. Portrait Gallery, London, Victoria and Albert Mus., London, Met. Mus. Art, N.Y.C., Mus. Modern Art, N.Y.C., Los Angeles County Mus. Art, Internat. Mus. Photography, Rochester, N.Y., Santa Barbara Mus. Art, Oakland Mus., Mus. Fine Arts, Houston, Bibliotheque Nat., Paris, Musee D'Art Moderne De La Ville De Paris, Fondation Vincent Van Gogh, Arles, France, others. Recipient cert. art excellence Los Angeles County Mus. Art, 1968, award Laguna Beach Mus. Art, 1976; Calif. Inst. Arts scholar, 1974. Mem. Royal Photog. Soc. Gt. Britain, Friends of Photography. Democrat. Office: 251 E 51st St Apt 19G New York NY 10022-6555 Office: 59 East 82nd St New York NY 10028

FEILER GOLDSTEIN, PAULETTE, secondary education educator, researcher; b. Paris, Mar. 27, 1933; came to U.S., 1949; d. Bernard Berel and Rachel Leja (Gimelsein) Feiler; widowed; children: Robert Bart Goldstein Feiler, Hillary Renee Goldstein. BA, Queens Coll., 1973; MA in Philosophy, CUNY, 1977, PhD in French, 1987. Cert. tchr. N.Y. Acct. Seligman & Latz, N.Y.C., 1950-58; dance tchr. Henry St. Playhouse, N.Y.C., 1959-65; tchr. Bd. Edn., N.Y.C., 1973-96; yearbook advisor Flushing H.S., 1992, 95. Mem. Nat. Assn. For the Children Of The Holocaust, N.Y.C., 1992. Mem. PhD Alumni Assn., Warthwatch, Smithsonian, Harvard Health Letter, Women's Health Watch, Temple Beth El of Great Neck, Earthwatch. Jewish. Home: 5 Brokaw Ln Great Neck NY 11023

FEIN, LINDA ANN, nurse anesthetist, consultant; b. Cin., Dec. 10, 1949; d. Joseph and Elizabeth P. (Kannady) Stofle; m. Thomas Paul Fein, Dec. 11, 1971. Nursing diploma, Miami Valley Hosp. Sch. Nursing, Dayton, Ohio, 1971, Wright State U., Dayton, 1969; postgrad. U. Cin. Med. Ctr., 1978. Nursing asst. Miami Valley Hosp., Dayton, 1969-71; staff nurse operating room Cin. Children's Hosp. and Med. Ctr., 1971, 73, Peninsula Hosp., Burlingame, Calif., 1972-73; staff nurse operating room and emergency room Doctors Hosp., San Diego, 1972; staff nurse emergency room Ohio State U. Hosps., Columbus, 1973-75, head nurse operating room, 1975-76; staff nurse anesthetist Bethesda Hosps., Cin., 1978-86; staff nurse anesthetist Mercy Hosp. of Fairfield, Cin., 1986-95; locum tenens anesthetist Good Samaritan Hosp., Dayton, Ohio, 1993—; staff nurse, anesthetist Fort Hamilton-Hughes Hosp., Hamilton, Ohio, 1995—. childbirth educator psychoprophylactic method, 1975—; critical care nursing cons. Med. Communicators & Assocs., Salt Lake City, 1985-89; ind. nursing cons., 1989—; co-owner Exec. Shops, Cin., 1982-85; speaker in field. Mem. search com. Cin. Gen. Hosp. Sch. of Anesthesia for Nurses, 1981-82; bd. dirs. YWCA, 1988-91, Children's Diagnostic Ctr., 1989-95, pres. bd. dirs., 1994, Planned Parenthood, 1992-95. Recipient Recognition of Profl. Excellence, First Nurse Anesthesia Faculty Assocs., 1982, Florence Nightengale awards, 1995. Mem. Miami Valley Hosp. Sch. of Nursing Alumni Assn., Cin. Gen. Hosp. Sch. Anesthesia for Nurses Alumni Assn., Nurse Anesthetists of Greater Cin., Ohio Assn. Nurse Anesthetists, Am. Assn. Nurse Anesthetists, Am. Assn. Operating Room Nurses, Am. Assn. Critical Care Nurses, Nat. Registry of Cert. Nurses in Advanced Practice (cert.), Ohio Coaliation of Nurses with Specialty Cert., Am. Soc. Critical Care Medicine, Am. Trauma Soc., NAFE, Altrusa Internat. (officer 1985-92). Republican. Methodist. Lodge: Eastern Star. Avocations: antiques, gourmet cooking, African violets, roses, swimming. Home: 650 History Bridge Ln Hamilton OH 45013-3659

FEINBERG, GLENDA JOYCE, restaurant chain executive; b. Louisville, Feb. 8, 1948; d. Harold and Winnie Esther (McIntosh) F.; divorced; 1 child, Anthony John. Student, Purdue U., 1967-68, Ind. U., 1977-79. Cert. in restaurant and personnel mgmt. Beverage mgr. Don Ce Sar Beach Hotel, St. Petersburg Beach, Fla., 1979-80; catering dir. Best Western-Skyway Inn, St. Petersburg, Fla., 1980-83; gen. mgr. Village, Inc., St. Petersburg Beach, 1983-86; banquet mgr. Tradewinds Resort Hotel, St. Petersburg Beach, 1986-87; exec. mgr. Ponderosa, Inc., Clearwater, Fla., 1987-90; food and beverage dir. Days Inn Island Beach Resort, St. Petersburg Beach, 1990-92; owner, mgmt. cons., pvt. caterer G.F. Sans, Marengo, Ind., 1992—. Bd. dirs. AIDS Coalitions Pinellas, 1990. Mem. NOW, World Wildlife Fedn., Nat. Geographic Soc., Greenpeace, Amnesty Internat., Environ. Def. Fund, Nat. Audubon Soc., Nat. Arbor Day Found. Democrat.

FEINBERG, GLORIA GRANDITER, psychologist; b. N.Y.C., Dec. 18, 1923; d. David and Ray (Davis) Granditer; B.A., U. Pa., 1944; M.A., N.Y. U., 1947; m. Mortimer R. Feinberg, June 22, 1947; children—Stuart Andrew, Todd E. Asst. psychologist Grasslands Hosp., Valhalla, N.Y., 1948-51; cons. BFS Psychol. Assos., N.Y.C., 1960-77, pres., 1977—. Mem. Am. Psychol. Assn., Phi Beta Kappa, Pi Gamma Mu. Author: Leavetaking, 1978. Home: 34 Brook Ln Cortlandt Mnr NY 10566-6502 Office: 666 Fifth Ave New York NY 10103-0001

FEINBERG, INA LEIGH, exhibit marketing manager; b. Langdale, Ala., Sept. 5, 1951; d. Morris and Norma Beryl (Goldstein) F. Student, U. Ga., 1969-70; AA in Fashion Merchandising, FIA/Massey Coll., Atlanta and London, 1971. Cert. mgr. of exhibits. Freelance fashion displayer various retail stores/apparel shows, Atlanta, 1971-73; show coord. GES/Manncraft Exhibitor Svcs., Atlanta, 1973-75; conv. svc. mgr. Sheraton Biltmore Hotel, Atlanta, 1975-77; account exec./conv. sales Shepard Conv. Svcs., Atlanta, 1977-80; mgr. exhibits and promotions So. Bell Telephone/AT&T Info. Systems, Atlanta, 1980-85; pub. rels. asst. to dir. The Peasant Restaurant Group, Atlanta, 1986-88; mgr. mktg. svcs. Telecom USA, Atlanta, 1988-90; sr. mgr. exhibits, mktg. MCI Comms., Washington, McLean, Va., 1990-95; exhibit mktg./cons. Bethesda, Md., 1995—; exhibit mgmt. and cons. Donna T. Tschiffely Assocs., Reston, Va., 1995—; exhibit mktg. cons. Ina L. Feinberg and Assocs., 1996—; mem. ICA exhibitor liaison coun. Internat. Comms. Assn., Dallas, 1990-95; mem. TCA conf. exhibit adv. bd. TeleComms. Assn., Covina, Calif., 1990-95; spkr. and seminar leader Internat. Exhibitors Assn. and Industry Workshops, Anaheim, Atlanta, Fairfax, Va., 1982, 89, 91. Editl. adv. bd.: Exhibitor Mag., Rochester, Minn., 1994; editor: (newsletter) MCI Trade Show News, 1994-95. Mem. Young Leadership Devel. Coun., Atlanta Jewish Comm. Ctr., 1982-83; vol. Carter Carter Campaign, Atlanta, 1980s. Recipient Exhibit Focus award AT&T Info. Systems, N.Y.C., 1983, Exhibit Focus award Trade Show Exhibitors Assn., 1996; named Most Valuable Performer, MCI/Nat. Accts. Mtkg., McLean, 1993. Mem. Internat. Exhibitors Assn., Ctr. for Exhibit Industry Rsch. Democrat. Jewish.

FEINBERG, MARY STANLEY, judge. AB, Mt. Holyoke Coll., 1970; JD, Univ. of Va., 1973. Bar: W. Va., U.S. Dist. Ct. (so. dist.) W. Va., U.S. Ct. Appeals (4th cir.). Atty. Columbia Gas Transmission Corp., 1973-76; law clk. to Judge Dennis R. Knapp, 1976-77; asst. U.S. atty. Charleston, W. Va., 1977-92; magistrate judge U.S. Dist. Ct. (so. dist.) W. Va., Bluefield, W. Va., 1992—. Mem. Am. Bar Assn., W. Va. Bar Assn., Kanawha County Bar Assn. Office: US Courthouse PO Box 4190 Bluefield WV 24701-1990

FEINEN, CYNTHIA LUCILLE, pediatric nurse; b. Pt. Pleasant, N.J., May 16, 1965; d. Lawrence Joseph and Lucille Carol F. Diploma in Nursing, Ann May Sch. Nursing. RN, N.J.; cert. pediatric advanced life support, BLS, ICC-PICC cen. cathether. Pediatric nurse Jersey Shore Med., Neptune, N.J., 1986—, Good Samaritan Hosp., West Palm Beach, Fla., 1990-91; nurse supr. Kimberely Quality Care, Eatontown, N.J., 1991-93; pediatric nurse cons. div. youth and family svcs. State of N.J., Asbury Park, 1993—, spl. home provider tng., foster parent tng.; owner Kidz First Consulting. Author: Task Sheet; co-author: (matrix) Medically Fragile, 1993, (guide) Medically Fragile, 1993. Mem. Perinatal Health Consortium, Monmouth County, 1993. Mem. ANA (cert. in pediatrics), N.J. League Nursing. Home: PO Box 762 Howell NJ 07731-0762

FEINER, ARLENE MARIE, librarian, researcher, consultant; b. Spring Green, Wis., Mar. 23, 1937; d. Herman Joseph and Cecelia Margaret (Meixelsperger) F. BA in History, Alverno Coll., 1959; MA in Libr. Sci., Rosary Coll., 1971; MA in Orgnl. Devel., Loyola U., Chgo., 1985. Gen. office worker USIA, Washington, 1959-60; adminstrv. sec. Nat. Coun. Cath. Women, Washington, 1960-62; asst. libr. Munich campus, U. Md., Fed. Republic Germany, 1962-64; preliminary cataloger, 1st editor MARC Pilot Project, Libr. of Congress, Washington, 1965-67; head libr. Acad. of the Holy Cross, Kensington, Md., 1967-70, Jesuit Sch. of Theology Libr., Chgo., 1971-79, coord. serial activities; women's studies bibliographer, Loyola U., Chgo., 1979-86; tech. svcs., collection devel. cons. DuPage Libr. System, 1986-91; contract adminstr. Wabash Nat. Fin., Arlington Heights, Ill., 1992—. Editor: (bibliography) Current Serials, 1980-85; compiler: (bibliography) Guide to Women's Studies Sources, 1985; author of poems; contbr. articles to profl. jours. Bd. dirs. Women's World Ctr., Chgo., 1985-88. Assn. of Theol. Schs. in U.S. and Can. grantee, 1976. Mem. ALA, NAFE, Nat. Mus. Women in Arts, C.G. Jung Inst. Chgo. Roman Catholic. Avocations: poetry, hiking, music. Home: 336 W Wellington Ave Apt 2102 Chicago IL 60657-5614

FEINN, BARBARA ANN, economist; b. Waterbury, Conn., Feb. 16, 1925; d. David Harris and Dora (Brandvein) F.; m. Steven L. Wissig, Jan. 10, 1991. AB magna cum laude, Smith Coll., 1946. MA (univ. scholar), Yale U., 1947, PhD (univ. fellow), 1952; cert. Oxford (Eng.) U., 1949. Rsch. economist First Nat. City Bank, N.Y.C., 1953-54; assoc. economist Office Messrs. Rockefeller, N.Y.C., 1954-61; asst. to dir. N.Y. State Office for Regional Devel., N.Y.C., 1961-62; cons. economist Nelson A. Rockefeller, N.Y.C., 1963-64; pvt. cons., 1965-68; sr. coun. economist N.Y. State Coun. Econ. Advisers, N.Y.C., 1969-72; chief economist Office S.C. Gov., Columbia, 1972-74; chief economist State of S.C., 1974—; mem. bd. econ. advisors, 1976-88 , sec. bd. econ. advisors, 1986-88, exec. dir. bd. econ. advisors, 1988— ; adj. prof. bus. adminstrn. U. S.C., Columbia, 1972-74. Ofcl. participant White House Conf. on Balanced Nat. Growth and Econ. Devel., 1978; del. meetings on nat. balanced growth Nat. Govs. Assn., Leesburg, Va., 1977; mem. S.C. Gov.'s Task Force on the Economy, 1980-84; mem. productivity measurement com. S.C. Coun. on Productivity, 1981-84. Dir. Smith Coll. Alumnae Fund Program, N.Y.C., 1965-66, mem. spl. gifts com., 1971, class v.p., 1986-91; del. assembly Assn. Yale Alumni, 1983-86, 91—. Recipient Wilbur Lucius Cross medal Yale U., 1987. Mem. Am. Econ. Assn., Nat. Assn. Bus. Econs., Soc. Govt. Economists, Downtown Economists Luncheon Group, Western Econ. Assn., N.Y. Assn. Bus. Economists, Atlanta Econ. Club, Carolinas Econ. Assn., Phi Beta Kappa. Clubs: Yale (N.Y.C. and cen. S.C.); Summit, Wildewood (Columbia, S.C.); Sea Pines (Hilton Head Island, S.C.); Smith Coll. (Columbia). Contbr. articles to profl. jours. Home: 50 Mallet Hill Ct Columbia SC 29223-3126 Office: Govs Office Columbia SC 29201

FEINSTEIN, ANITA A., management consultant; b. Rouro, Poland, Mar. 11, 1945; d. Alex and Sally (Krancberg) Edelman; m. Steven David Feinstein, Nov. 6, 1964; children: Jessica Opert, Joshua, Jordan. BA, McGill U., 1965; MBA, Adelphi U., 1979. V.p., internal cons. Citibank, N.Y.C., 1978-89; fin. cons. Shearson Lehman Hamilton, Manhasset, N.Y., 1989-90; mgmt. cons. pvt. practice, Frankfurt, Germany, 1992-94; sr. assoc. LoBue Assocs., Inc., Fairlawn, N.J., 1996—. Treas. Sanctuary Homeowners Assn., Arlington, Va., 1995—. Mem. Women in Tech. Home: 3810 M Richmond St Arlington VA 22207 Office: LoBue Assocs Inc 13-15 Broadway Fair Lawn NJ 07410

FEINSTEIN, DEBORAH, lawyer; b. Champaign, Ill., Dec. 30, 1960. BA with honors, U. Calif., Berkeley, 1983; JD cum laude, Harvard U., 1987. Bar: D.C. 1987. Asst. to the dir. Bur. of Competition, FTC, 1989-91; ptnr. Arnold & Porter, Washington. Office: Arnold & Porter 555 12th St NW Washington DC 20004-1202*

FEINSTEIN, DIANNE, senator; b. San Francisco, June 22, 1933; d. Leon and Betty (Rosenburg) Goldman; m. Bertram Feinstein, Nov. 11, 1962 (dec.); 1 child, Katherine Anne; m. Richard C. Blum, Jan. 20, 1980. BA History, Stanford U., 1955; LLB (hon.), Golden Gate U., 1977; D Pub. Adminstrn. (hon.), U. Manila, 1981; D Pub. Service (hon.), U. Santa Clara, 1981; JD (hon.), Antioch U., 1983, Mills Coll., 1985; LHD (hon.), U. San Francisco, 1988. Fellow Coro Found., San Francisco, 1955-56; with Calif. Women's Bd. Terms and Parole, 1960-66; mem. Mayor's com. on crime, chmn. adv. com. Adult Detention, 1967-69; mem. Bd. of Suprs., San Francisco, 1970-78, pres., 1970-71, 74-75, 78; mayor of San Francisco, 1978-88, U.S. senator from Calif., 1992—; mem. exec. com. U.S. Conf. of Mayors, 1983-88; Dem. nominee for Gov. of Calif., 1990; mem. Nat. Com. on U.S.-China Rels., mem. Judiciary Comm., Rukes & Adminstrn,, Senate Dem. Policy Com. Mem. Bay Area Conservation and Devel. Commn., 1973-78. Recipient Woman of Achievement award Bus. and Profl. Women's Clubs San Francisco, 1970, Disting. Woman award San Francisco Examiner, 1970, Coro Found. award, 1979, Coro Leadership award, 1988, Pres. medal U. Calif., San Francisco, 1988, Scopus award Am. Friends Hebrew U., 1981, Brotherhood/Sisterhood award NCCJ, 1986, Comdr.'s award U.S. Army, 1986, French Legion of Honor, 1984, Disting. Civilian award USN, 1987; named Number One Mayor All-Pro City Mgmt. Team City and State Mag., 1987. Mem. Trilateral Commn., Japan Soc. of No. Calif. (pres. 1988-89), Inter-Am. Dialogue, Nat. Com. on U.S.-China Rels. Office: US Senate 331 Senate Hart Office Bldg Washington DC 20510

FEINSTEIN, MARION FINKE, artistic director, dance instructor; b. Nov. 7, 1925; d. Charles and Anne (Krein) Finke; m. Seymour Feinstein, Apr. 2, 1944; children: Sandi, Sheree, Lori. Degree in sec. sci., U. S.C., 1944; student, Joffrey Ballet, N.Y.C., Am. Ballet Theatre, N.Y.C.; studied with Alvin Ailey, N.Y.C. Instr. dance Recreation Dept., Columbia, S.C., 1945; instr. ballet Furman Basketball Team, Greenville, S.C., 1950-55; instr. jazz U. S.C., Spartanburg, 1986-87; dance dir. Carolina Youth Dance Theatre, Spartanburg, 1980—; tchr. various pageant winners and profl. dancers, including Miss Black Am., Miss World, Miss Am. finalist, Jr. Miss Dance of S.C. Mem. USO troupe, Spartanburg, 1942-44; choreographer Spartanburg Little Theatre, 1955-62, Miss Spartanburg Pageant, 1963-72. Recipient Resolution award S.C. Ho. Reps. and Senate, 1988, Cert. Performance Appreciation, City New Orleans, Resolution of Appreciation award Spartanburg County Council, S.C., Cert. Performance Appreciation N.Y.C. com. for entertainment at the Statue of Liberty, Fund Raising award March of Dimes. Mem. Dance Educators Am. (regional dir.), Dance Masters Am., So. Coun. Dancemasters (v.p.), Cecchetti Coun. Am., Bus. and Profl. Women, Hadassah Club (Spartanburg), B'nai Israel Sisterhood Orgn. Democrat. Jewish. Address: 1206 Reidville Rd Spartanburg SC 29306-3930

FEIRSTEIN, JANICE, real estate executive; b. Binchester, Eng., Dec. 3, 1942; came to U.S., 1967; d. Edward Mons and Mary (Watson) Walmsley; m. Laurence Feirstein, Aug. 27, 1967; 1 child, Douglas. Grad. in bus., Christison U., Spennymoor, Eng., 1961; grad. in mgmt., Inst. Fin. Edn., Ft. Lauderdale, Fla., 1980. Mgr. gift and gourmet cookware store, Lauderhill, Fla., 1977-78; exec. asst. Werbel Roth Sec., Ft. Lauderdale, 1978-79; from teller to new accounts rep. to asst. br. mgr. to br. mgr. Broward Fed. Savs. and Loan, Ft. Lauderdale, 1979-82; v.p., resort mgr. Broward Ocean View Properties, Inc., Ft. Lauderdale, 1982-88; pres. Daily Mgmt. Inc., Ft. Lauderdale, 1988—; shareholder Daily Mgmt. Inc., Pompano Beach, Fla., 1990—; owner Light House Cove Resort Mgmt. Inc., Pompano Beach, 1988—; bd. dirs. Inst. Fin. Edn., 1981-83; mem. fin. com. Am. Resort and Recreational Devel. Assn., 1986. Vol. Gen. Hosp., Plantation, Fla., 1977-78; mem. adv. com. Broward County Sch. Bd., 1982; active Coop. Bus. Edn., Broward County, 1980-81, Nat. Adoption Ctr., 1986, Outreach Broward, 1986, Light House Condominium Community Assn., bd. dirs, v.p., sec. 1983-89. Mem. NAFE, Am. Bus. Women's Assn., Fla. Community Assn. Mgrs. Inc., Am. Resort Devel. Assn. (ednl. com. 1991—), Ft. Lauderdale C. of C., Pompano Beach C. of C. Office: 202 Bonaventure Blvd Fort Lauderdale FL 33326-1444

FEIR-STILLITANO, ELISABETH, gifted/talented education educator; b. N.Y.C., Feb. 27, 1971; d. Sherman Stuart and Olivia Terry (Gordon) F. BA, U. Buffalo, 1993; MEd, Lehigh U., 1994. Cert. elem. edn., secondary English edn., Pa., N.Y. Asst. kindergarten tchr. Allentown (Pa.) Jewish Cmty. Ctr., 1993-94; gifted and talented educator Island Park (N.Y.) Union Free Sch. Dist., 1994—. Mem. Nat. Coun. for Tchrs. English, Nat. Coun. for Tchrs. Math., Internat. Reading Assn., Assn. for Edn. Young Children, Nat. Assn. for Gifted Children. Democrat. Jewish. Home: 2103 Seneca Dr N Merrick NY 11566 Office: Island Park Union Sch Dist Trafalgar Blvd Island Park NY 11558

FEIST-FITE, BERNADETTE, international education consultant; b. Linton, N.D., Sept. 28, 1945; d. John K. and Cecilia (Nagel) F.; m. William H. Fite. BS in Dietetics, U. N.D., Grand Forks, 1967; MS in Edn., Troy (Ala.) State U., 1973; EdD U. So. Calif. Commd. officer USAF, 1965, advanced through grades to maj., 1983; prof. health and fitness Nat. Def. U., Ft. McNair, Washington, 1989—; pres. Feist Assocs., instr. internat.edn. programs, seminars and workshops. Mem. Alexandria Little Theatre. Decorated Air Force Commendation medal, Dept. Def. Meritorious Svc. medal. Mem. NAFE, VFW. Soc. Internat. Edn., Tng. and Rsch., Am. Dietetic Assn., Nat. Assn. Women Bus. Owners, Women in Defense, Japan-Am. Soc. Washington, Dieticians in Bus. and Industry, Sports and Cardiovascular Nutritionists, Nutritional Enterpreneurs, Andrews Officers Club. Home: 2442 Cerrillos Rd Ste 312 Santa Fe NM 87505-3262 Office: Feist Assocs PO Box 7105 Alexandria VA 22307-0105

FEITSMA, LAURINDA DAWN, business owner; b. Chipley, Fla., Sept. 4, 1968; d. David and Ethel LaMerle (Collins) F. BS, Troy (Ala.) State U., 1990; MBA cum laude, Orlando (Fla.) Coll., 1992. Sales assoc. J.c. Penney, Montgomery, Ala., 1989-90; sec. Olsen Staffing, Maitland, Fla., 1990-91; rental coord. Nat. Semi-Trailer Corp., Orlando, 1991-93; in sales Orlando Freightliner, Apopka, Fla., 1993-94; constrn. coord. Hallmark Builders, Longwood, Fla., 1994-95; owner D & J Mobile Repair Svc., Orlando, Fla., 1995—; mem. accreditation desk for Olympic Soccer, Orlando, 1996. Mem. Profl. Employment Network, Woodmen of the World (music coord. 1992—), Delta Sigma Pi (v.p. ops. 1988-90). Republican. Presbyterian. Office: D & J Mobile Repair Svc 1972 Lake Atriums Cir #195 Orlando FL 32839

FELBER, KAREN LEE, banker; b. Spokane, Wash., Dec. 5, 1941; d. Leroy Alfred and Ruth Elizabeth (Kakaris) Loeffler; m. Robert Stanley Felber Jr., July 12, 1959 (div. Aug. 1974); children: Timothy (dec.), Susan. AA, Spokane Falls C.C., 1985; BA, Ea. Wash. U., 1991. Teller Bank of Fairfield, Wash., 1965-81, br. mgr., 1981—. Treas. AIDS Life Link, Spokane, 1992-93, pres., 1994-95; chair person names project AIDS Meml., Spokane, 1993; fundraising chair Spokane AIDS Network, 1994-95. Home: 707 W 6th Ave # 23 Spokane WA 99204

FELD, KAREN IRMA, columnist, journalist, broadcaster, public speaker; b. Washington, Aug. 23, 1947; d. Irvin and Adele Ruth (Schwartz) F. Student, U. Pitts., 1965-67; BA, Am. U., 1969. Columnist, reporter Roll Call Newspaper, Washington, 1969-74; nat. pub. relations coordinator Ringling Bros./Barnum & Bailey Circus, Washington, 1971-74; publicist Twentieth Century Fox, Los Angeles, 1974-75; pub. relations account exec. Harshe, Rotman & Druck, Los Angeles, 1975; freelance writer, broadcaster, 1970—; corr. People mag., Washington, 1980-85; adj. instr. Kent State U. Pol. Campaign Mgmt. Inst., 1981; broadcaster Voice of Am., 1984; columnist, contributing editor Capitol Hill mag., Washington, 1980-89; columnist Washington Times, 1986-87, Universal Press Syndicate, 1988-89, Creators Syndicate, 1989-90, syndicated columnist Capital Connections, 1990—; Prodigy polit. columnist, 1990-93; radio/TV commentator, 1993—; lectr. in field, 1990—. Contbr. articles to Parade mag., People mag., Money mag., Time mag., Vogue mag., George, others. Recipient Health Journalism award Am. Chiropractic Assn., 1991. Mem. AFTRA/SAG, Nat. Fedn. Press Women (Excellence in Journalism awards 1984-96), Women in Comms., Capital Press Women (v.p. 1985-91, Excellence in Journalism awards 1984-96, Entrepreneur/Communicator of Yr. award 1995), Am. Soc. Journalists and Authors, Nat. Press Club, Capitol Hill Club, Woodmont Country Club (Rockville, Md.), U.S. Senate Press Gallery White House Corr. Assn., Am. Newswomen's Club, Sigma Delta Chi. Jewish. Office: 1698 32nd St NW Washington DC 20007-2969

FELD, KATHERINE PHOEBE, lawyer; b. Summit, N.J., June 9, 1958; d. Frank Kernan and Phoebe Elizabeth (Driscoll) Ward; m. Jeffrey Scott Feld, June 20, 1985; children: Deborah Phoebe, James Stuart. BA, U. Va., 1979; MBA, Cornell U., 1982, JD, 1983. Bar: N.Y. 1984, N.J. 1985. Assoc. Brown & Wood, N.Y.C., 1983-84; assoc. counsel Oppenheimer Funds, N.Y.C., 1984—, corp. sec., 1987—, v.p., 1990—. Mem. Phi Beta Kappa. Office: Oppenheimer Funds 2 World Trade Ctr New York NY 10048-0203

FELDHUSEN, HAZEL J., elementary education educator; b. Camp Douglas, Wis., Feb. 20, 1928; d. Vincent O. and Helen (Johnson) Artz; m. John F. Feldhusen, Dec. 18, 1954; children: Jeanne V., Anne M. B, U. Wis., 1965; M, Purdue U., 1968. Tchr. Suldal Sch., Mauston, Wis., 1947-50, Lake Geneva (Wis.) Schs., 1950-55, West Lafayette (Ind.) Schs., 1965-91, cons. World Conf., Hamburg, 1985, Juneau (Alaska) Schs., 1986, Connersville (Ind.) Schs., 1987, Vancouver (B.C., Can.) Schs., 1990, Norfolk (Va.) Schs., 1991, Taiwan Nat. U., 1992, U. New South Wales, Sydney, Australia, 1993, New Zealand Schs., Auckland, 1993; 2d Nat. Conf. Gifted, Taiwan, 1992. Author: Individualized Teaching of the Gifted, 1993. Mem. Tchr. of Yr. Com., West Lafayette, 1988. Recipient Outstanding Tchr. award Elem. Tchrs. Am., 1974, Appreciation award U. Stellenbosch, 1984, Appreciation award Australian Assn. for the Gifted, 1987; winner Golden Apple Tchg. award Greater Lafayette C. of C., 1989, Disting. Alumnus award Purdue U., 1996. Mem. NEA, Ind. State Tchrs. Assn., West Lafayette Edn. Assn. (Outstanding Achievement award 1984), Phi Delta Kappa, Delta Kappa Gamma (v.p 1983-85). Home: 2411 Trace 24 West Lafayette IN 47906-1887

FELDMAN, ARLENE BUTLER, aviation industry executive. BA cum laude in Polit. Sci., U. Colo., 1975; JD, Temple U. Sch. Law, 1978. Supervising atty. U.S. Railway Assn., Phila., 1977-82; dir. divsn. aeronautics N.J. Dept. Transp., Trenton, 1982-84; from acting dir. to dep. dir. tech. ctr. FAA, Atlantic City, N.J., 1984-86; dep. dir. Western-Pacific region FAA, L.A., 1986-88; regional adminstr. N.Eng. Region FAA, Burlington, Mass., 1988-94; eastern regional adminstr. FAA, Jamaica, N.Y., 1994—; panelist, guest spkr. Women in Aviation Conf., 1992, 93; vice-chair N.Y. Fed. Exec. Bd.; chairperson regional airport sys. planning adv. com. Delaware Valley Regional Planning Commn.; founder rotorcraft R&D forum FAA. Chairwoman Boston Federal Exec. Bd. Saving Bond, 1993; mem. adv. bd. U. So. Calif. Recipient Presdl. Meritorious Rank award Sr. Exec. Svc., Disting. Svc. award N.J. Aviation Hall of Fame, Amelia Earhart medal. Mem. ABA, Ninety-Nines Internat. Orgn., Lawyer/Pilot Bar Assn., Air Traffic Control Assn. (dir., exec. bd., conf. panel moderator 1993, 91, spkr. 1993), Am. Assn. Airport Execs., Am. Assn. State Hwy. and Transp. Ofcls., Am. Helicopter Soc., Helicopter Assn. Internat., Nat. Assn. State Aviation Ofcls., Nat. Coun. Women in Aviation Aerospce, Internat. Aviation Women's Assn., Profl. Women Controllers, Inc. (hon.), Pi Sigma Alpha. Office: FAA Fed Bldg # 111 JFK Internat Airport Jamaica NY 11430

FELDMAN, DEBORAH KARPOFF, nursing education consultant; b. Boston, Jan. 25, 1943; m. Samuel Feldman, 1961. AS, Miss. State Coll. for Women, 1973; BSN, Miss. U. for Women, 1975; M of Nursing, U. Miss., Jackson, 1976. Staff nurse, relief charge nurse Golden Triangle Regional Med. Ctr., Columbus, Miss., 1973-75; asst. prof. Sch. Nursing Miss. U. for Women, Columbus, 1975-77, Calif. State U., Chico, 1978; asst. prof., asst. dir. Sierra Coll., Rocklin, Calif., 1978-79; asst. prof. Coppin State Coll., Balt., 1979-80; nursing edn. cons. Md. Bd. Nursing, Balt., 1980—; cons. Allied Health programs Md. Higher Edn. Commn., Annapolis, 1989—. Contbg. author: (monograph) Collaboration for Articulation, 1987; editor: (newsletter) Communicator Board of Nursing Newsletter, 1986—. Presenter Am. Cancer Soc., Columbus, 1978-79; tchr. Hebrew sch. Temple Bnai Israel, Columbus, 1970-76; chair funds campaign Am. Cancer Soc., Balt., 1982; campaign worker Reelection of State Sen., Reisterstown, Md., 1994. Higher edn. scholar Miss. State Bd. Trustees of Instns. of Higher Learning, 1974-76, Harriet Hatcher scholar Miss. Nursing Assn. Dist. 17, 1973. Mem. Md. Nurses Assn., Md. League Nursing, Nat. Coun. State Bd. Nursing (chair com. to evaluate implementation of computer adaptive testing, mem. adminstr. of exam. com. 1989-94, com. on nominations 1996, exam. com. 1996—), Sigma Theta Tau. Office: Md Bd Nursing 4140 Patterson Ave Baltimore MD 21215-2254

FELDMAN, LILLIAN MALTZ, early childhood education consultant; b. N.Y.C.; d. Jacob and Ida (Burko) Maltz; m. Harry A. Feldman, June 14, 1939 (dec. Jan. 1985); children: Ronald, Donna Feldman Weisman, Jeffrey, Robert. AB, George Washington U., 1937, MA, 1939; EdD in Early Childhood Edn., Syracuse U., 1987; HLD (hon.), SUNY, 1993. Cert. tchr., guidance counselor, sch. adminstr., N.Y. Elem. sch. guidance counselor Syracuse (N.Y.) Sch. Dist., 1963-65, Kindergarten tchr., 1957-63, dir. early children edn., 1965-83; dir. Syracuse Head Start, summers 1968-70; cons. early childhood edn. Syracuse, 1985—; adj. instr. child, family and community studies Syracuse U., 1988-89, adj. prof. child and family studies, 1990-91. Author invited papers in early child devel. and care, 1988, 89, 95, 96. Adv. com. Dr. Martin Luther King Cmty. Sch., Syracuse, 1988—. Named Woman of Achievement in Edn., Post-Standard, Syracuse, 1969; recipient Hannah G. Solomon Award Nat. Coun. Jewish Women, Syracuse, 1979, Honoree Na'amat USA 1988, Friend of Children award Women's Commn. Task Force on Children, 1992. Mem. Syracuse Assn. for Edn. Young Children (Outstanding Early Childhood Educator award 1984), Consortium for Children's Svcs. (Silver Dove award 1985, Friend of Family award 1992), Onondaga County Child Care Coun. (Community Svc. award 1983, Friend of Children award 1992), Delta Kappa Gamma, Phi Delta Kappa. Democrat.

FELDMAN, MARTHA SUE, political scientist, educator; b. Oak Ridge, Tenn., Mar. 31, 1953; d. Melvin J. and Nancy Ann (McCarty) F.; m. Hobart Taylor III, Oct. 30, 1993; 1 child, Bruce Alexander Feldman Taylor. BA in Polit. Sci., U. Wash., 1976; MA in Polit. Sci., Stanford U., 1980, PhD in Polit. Sci., 1983. Asst. prof. dept. polit. sci., asst. rsch. sci. Inst. Pub. Policy Studies U. Mich., Ann Arbor, 1983-89, assoc. prof. dept. polit. sci., 1989—, assoc. prof. Sch. Pub. Policy, 1995—; health svcs. rschr. U. Wash., Seattle, 1975-76; cons. to Com. on Ability Testing NAS, Washington., 1980; regulatory impact analyst for fossil fuels Dept. Energy, Washington, 1980-81; vis. scholar Stanford (Calif.) U. Ctr. for Orgns. Rsch., 1990-91; vis. prof. Luigi Bocconi U., Milan, 1991, Swedish Sch. Econs., Helsinki, Finland, 1992. Author: Order Without Design: Information Production and Policy Making, 1989 Strategies for Interpreting Qualitative Data, 1994; co-author: Reconstructing Reality in the Courtroom, 1981; contbr. articles to profl. jours.; editorial bd. Info. Sys. Rsch. Ameritech fellow, 1986, Rachham Faculty Rsch. grantee, 1984-85, Brookings Instn. Rsch. fellow, 1979-80, NIMH fellow, 1978-79, others. Mem. Am. Polit. Sci. Assn. Office: U Mich Sch Pub Policy 454 Lorch Hall Ann Arbor MI 48109

FELDMAN, MIRIAM ELLIN, nursing home administrator, nurse; b. N.Y.C., Dec. 12, 1924; d. Charles and Ida (Novick) Ellin; m. Herbert Feldman, Mar. 23, 1958; children: Leslie Ellin, Peter Hilton, Madeleine Elyse. RN, N.Y. State U., 1965; AAS, Queens Coll., 1965; BS, SUNY, 1974. Asst. adminstr. Five Towns Nursing Home, Woodmere, N.Y., 1963-65; cons. nursing service, N.Y., 1967-73; adminstr., developer Cerebral Palsy Domiciliary Care Program, N.Y., 1973-79; adminstr. Woodmere Health Care Ctr., N.Y., 1979—; cons. gerontology and the handicapped. Producer ednl. video tapes Patient Abuse Series, 1979-81. Recipient Outstanding Service award United Cerebral Palsy Assn., 1981. Fellow Am. Coll. Health Care Adminstrs.; mem. Am. Nursing Assn., Assn. for Help of Retarded Children. Club: Hadassah. Office: 39 Burton Ave Woodmere NY 11598-1747

FELDMAN, SUSAN CAROL, neurobiologist, anatomy educator; b. Bklyn., Oct. 1, 1943; d. Saul Feldman and Ann Richmanl 2 children. BA, Hofstra U., Hempstead, N.Y., 1963; MS, Rutgers U., 1967; PhD, CUNY, 1976. Rsch. technician med. sch. Cornell U., N.Y.C., 1963-64; grad. teaching asst. CUNY, 1964-74; postdoctoral fellow Albert Einstein Coll. Medicine, Bronx, N.Y., 1975-77; postdoctoral fellow, instr. anatomy Columbia U., N.Y.C., 1977-79; asst. prof. anatomy N.J. Med. Sch., Newark, 1979-86, assoc. prof., 1986—. Contbr. articles to profl. jours. Mem. AAAS, Soc. Neurosci., Am. Assn. Anatomists, Am. Soc. Cell Biology, NOW. Office: U Med and Dentistry NJ NJ Med Sch 185 S Orange Ave Newark NJ 07103-2714

FELDMAN, VALERIE MICHELE, marketing professional; b. Chgo., Nov. 6, 1934; d. Bernard and Florence (Schwartzman) Berger; m. Leon, Mar. 25, 1956; 1 child, Suzanne Lynn. BA in Journalism magna cum laude, U. Wis., 1955. Copywriter Montgomery Ward & Co., Chgo., 1955-59; public rels. writer Am. Hosp. Assn., Chgo., 1959-60; advt. mgr. Maling Shoes, Inc., Chgo., 1960-65; free-lance copywriter Chgo., 1971-78; copy chief Clarkson Assocs., Wash., 1979-81; v.p. creative svcs. Levy/Zimberg Assocs., 1981-82; account exec. Pallace, Inc., Silver Spring, 1982-83; mktg./advt. cons. Chevy Chase, 1983-89; asst. mgr. comm. The Acacia Group, Washington, 1989-94; mgr. creative svcs. United Svcs. Life Ins., Arlington, Va., 1994-96; mktg. and advt. cons. Chevy Chase, Md., 1996—. Recipient Highest Readership Award Cons. Engr. Mag., Cons. Engr., Computer Decisions Mag., Awards of Excellence Employment Mgrs. Assn. Mem. Women Advt. and Mktg. (2d v.p., bd. dirs.), Wash. Ind. Writers, World Future Soc. (bd. dirs.). Office: 4620 N Park Ave Bethesda MD 20815-4549

FELDT, GLORIA A., social service administrator; b. Temple, Tex., Apr. 13, 1942; m. Alex Barbanell; 3 children; 3 stepchildren. BA in Sociology and Speech with honors, U. Tex. Permian Basin, 1974; postgrad., Ariz. State U., Western Behavioral Scis. Inst., La Jolla, Calif. Broadcast operator Sta. KOIP-FM, Odessa, Tex., 1965-67; substitute tchr. Ector County Ind. Sch. Dist., Odessa, Tex., 1967-68; tchr., spl. projects dir. head start Greater Opportunities of the Permian Basin, Odessa, Tex., 1968-73; exec. dir. Planned Parenthood of West Tex., Odessa, 1974-78; exec. dir., CEO Planned Parenthood Ctrl. and Northern Ariz., Phoenix, 1978-96; pres.-elect Planned Parenthood Fedn. Am., Planned Parenthood Action Fund, N.Y.C., 1996—; also bd. dirs. Planned Parenthood Fedn. Am.; mem. steering com. Pro-Choice Ariz.; founder Planned Parenthood Fedn. Am. Leadership Inst.; cons. in leadership and strategic planning for non-profit orgns. Spkr. in field. Mem. exec. bd. Ariz. Affordable Health Care Found.; bd. dirs. Pro-Choice Resource Ctr., Advances in Health Tech., Hospice of the Valley; mem. cmty. adv. bd. Jr. League of Phoenix; mem. adv. bd. UN Assn.; charter mem. Ariz. Women's Town Hall; active Charter 100, World Affairs Coun., Ariz. Acad. Town Halls. Recipient Women of Achievement award, 1987, Ruth Green award Nat. Exec. Dirs. Coun., 1990, award Women Helping Women, 1989, 94, Golden Apple award Sun City chpt. NOW, 1995, City of Phoenix Martin Luther King, Jr. Living the Dream award City of Phoenix Human Rels. Commn., 1996. Mem. APHA, Nat. Family Planning and Reproductive Health Assn., Ariz. Pub. Health Assn. Office: Planned Parenthood Fedn Am 810 7th Ave New York NY 10019*

FELENSTEIN, DIANE TERMAN, public relations executive; b. N.Y.C., Oct. 23, 1940; d. Joseph and Pearl (Scharfman) Terman; m. Robert Smiley, (div. Jan. 1970); 1 child, Deborah Smiley Kerner; m. Marshall Felenstein; 1 child, Deborah Kerner. lectr. Syracuse U. Sch. Comms., NYU, Cornell U. Founder DayLight; mem. bd. dirs. Samuel Waxman Cancer Rsch. Found. Mt. Sinai Hosp., Guggenheim Museum's Learning Through the Arts Program, The Children's Inst. Manhattan Eye & Ear Hosp., Fire Safety Edn., Inc. FDNY; co-founder Providence House; mem. adv. bd. Temple Emanu-El, Women's Health Inst. NYU; active vol. Lenox Hill Hosp.; founder, pres. 008 Women's Investment Club. Mem. Pub. Rels. Soc. Am., Women's Media Group, Women Execs. in Pub. Rels., The Fashion Group, Cosmetic Exec. Women. Home: 40 E 78th St New York NY 10021

FELESKY, CHRISTINE MISIVICH, elementary education educator; b. Sharon, Pa., Nov. 26, 1967; d. Joseph George and Patricia Marie (Hart) Misivich; m. Jeffrey Allan Felesky, June 16, 1990. BS Elem. Edn. cum laude, Youngstown State U., 1990; MEd Elem. Sch. Adminstrn., The Citadel, 1995. Cert. elem. edn. tchr., early childhood edn., reading K-12, elem. adminstrn., S.C. Tchr. first grade, reading recovery Mary Ford Elem. Sch., Charleston, S.C., 1990—. Youngstown State U. Found. scholar, 1985-90. Mem. Internat. Reading Assn., ASCD, Golden Key, Kappa Delta Pi. Democrat. Home: 5445 Ansley Trail Charleston SC 29418 Office: Mary Ford Elem Sch 3180 Azalea Dr Charleston SC 29405

FELICIJAN, JEAN MARIE, bilingual educator, special education educator; b. Prosser, Wash., June 28, 1960; d. Elmer Edward and Helga Marie (Rienhold) F. BA in Edn., Ea. Wash. U., Cheney, 1982; postgrad., Azuza Pacific, 1995-96. Cert. tchr., Calif. 4-6th grades tchr. Mapton (Wash.) Elem. Sch., 1983-84; 9th grade tchr. Mapton H.S., 1983-84; 4th-6th grades tchr. Gifford (Wash.) Elem. Sch., 1984-86; 4th grade Warden (Wash.) Elem., 1986-87; 3-6th grades tchr. Elsinore Elem. Sch., Lake Elsinore, Calif., 1987—. Mem. Lake Elsinore Tchrs. Assn. (site rep., leader exec. bd.). Home: 24385 Via Las Junitas Murrieta CA 92562

FELIX, PATRICIA JEAN, steel company purchasing professional; b. Baptistown, N.J., Dec. 13, 1941; d. Dmitri and Rosalia (Hryckowian) F. Student, Pratt Inst., 1960-61, Moravian Coll., Bethlehem, Pa., 1961-63. Cert. purchasing mgr. Pricing analyst Riegel Paper Corp., N.Y.C., 1966-69; placement mgr. Gardner Assocs., N.Y.C., 1969-72; buyer Bethlehem Steel Corp., 1973-78, buyer exempt, 1978-84, sr. buyer, 1984, purchasing supr., 1984-94, mem. raw materials team, 1994—. Sec. Coun. St.Nicholas Russian Orthodox Ch., Bethlehem, 1982-85, mem. coun., 1985-91, bldg. com., 1992-93, Bethlehem-Tondabayashi Sister City Commn., 1988-91, sec., 1989-90, chmn., 1991-93. Home: 1721 Millard St Bethlehem PA 18017-5142 Office: 1170 8th Ave Bethlehem PA 18016-7600

FELL, JENNIFER ANNE, technical writer; b. Columbus, Ohio, Nov. 6, 1968; d. James Frederick Fell and Mary Elizabeth Kelly McColl. BA in English, Santa Clara U., 1990. Pub. rels. asst. de Saisset Mus., Santa Clara, Calif., 1987-90; tech. writer Rational Software Corp., Santa Clara, 1990-94; sr. tech. writer ParcPlace-Digitalk, Inc., Sunnyvale, Calif., 1994—. Vol. Planned Parenthood, Calif. and Idaho, 1993—. Mem. NOW, Soc. for Tech. Comm., Alpha Sigma Nu, Sigma Tau Delta, Phi Sigma Tau.

FELLENSTEIN, CORA ELLEN MULLIKIN, retired credit union executive; b. Edwardsville, Ill., June 2, 1930; d. Russell K. and Elberta Mable (Rheude) Mullikin; m. Charles Frederick Fellenstein, Feb. 24, 1951; children: Keith David, Kimberly Diane. Student Community Coll., 1980-83. Cert. consumer credit exec. Teller, loan officer, office mgr. Credit Union of Johnson County, Lenexa, Kans., 1976-84, 1st v.p., supr. lending, collections and Mastercard depts., 1984-86, exec. v.p., 1987-94. Author: Moore Family History, 1987. Precinct committeewoman Johnson County Reps., Olathe, Kans., 1976-92; vol. Cerebral Palsey, 1957-66, Olathe Community Hosp., 1976-92, Shawnee Mission (Kans.) Med. Ctr., 1986-90. Mem. NAFE, Internat. Assn. Credit Card Investigators, Internat. Credit Assn., Kans. Credit Assn., Credit Profls. (dir. 1983-92), Exec. of Yr. Johnson County chpt.), DAR (treas. 1966-86), Daus. Am. Colonists (treas. 1976-86), Friends of Historic Mahaffie Farmstead, Soroptomist Internat., Beta Sigma Phi. Mem. Christian Ch. Avocations: genealogy, philately, numismatics, camping. Home: 2000 E Arrowhead Dr Olathe KS 66062-2467

FELLER, LORETTA ANNE, elementary education educator; b. Youngstown, Ohio, Dec. 13, 1946; d. Joseph and Julia Loretta (Bednar) Kolesar; m. Thomas Joseph Feller, Aug. 19, 1972; children: Jonathan Joseph, Jeffrey Thomas. BS in Elem. Edn., Youngstown U., 1964-69; postgrad., U. Ill., Champaign, 1982-84, Wright State U., 1990-94. Elem. tchr. St. Luke Sch., Boardman, Ohio, 1967-69, St. Nicholas Sch., Struthers, Ohio, 1969-70, Reed Middle Sch., Hubbard, Ohio, 1970-72, Reynoldsburg (Ohio) Middle Sch., 1972-73, St. Pius X Sch., Reynoldsburg, 1973-74, St. Alphonsus Sch., Grand Rapids, Mich., 1974-76; dir. rel. edn. Holy Redeemer, Jenison, Mich., 1976-78; elem. tchr. St. Matthew Sch., Champaign, Ill., 1982-90, St. Luke Sch., Beavercreek, Ohio, 1990—; com. mem. edn. commn. St. Luke Sch., Beavercreek, 1992-93; yearbook adv. St. Matthew Sch., Champaign, 1984-90; rep. edn. commn. Holy Redeemer Parish Coun., Jenison, 1976-78. Mem. Jr. Womens Club, Champaign, 1982-90, YMCA Wives Club, 1972-94; mem. Rotaryanns, Beavercreek, 1990-94. Named Outstanding Young Educator, Reynoldsburg Jaycees, 1974; recipient Contribution to Cath. Edn. award Peoria (Ill.) Diocese, 1987. Mem. Nat. Cath. Edn. Assn. (nominee Outstanding Tchr. 1993), Ohio Cath. Edn. Assn., Ohio Edn. Assn., Slovak Cath. Sokols. Roman Catholic. Home: 1378 Cowman Ct Beavercreek OH 45434-6714 Office: St Luke Sch 1442 N Fairfield Rd Beavercreek OH 45432-2638

FELLER, MIMI, newspaper publishing executive. BA cum laude, Creighton U.; JD, Georgetown U. Asst. dir. congl. rels. Gen. Svcs. Adminstrn., 1975-77; legis. asst. Environ. and Pub. Works Com. U.S. Senate, 1977-81; from legis. dir. to Washington chief of staff Sen. John Chafee (Rep.), R.I., 1981-83; dep. asst. sec. legis. affairs U.S. Dept. Treasury, 1983-85; from v.p. pub. rels. to sr. v.p. Gannett Co., 1985—; bd. advisors Nat. Ct. Apptd. Spl. Advocates Assn. Bd. dirs. Creighton U.; trustee Marymount U. Recipient Disting. Alumnus award Creighton U., 1987. Office: Gannett Co Inc 1100 Wilson Blvd Arlington VA 22209-2297

FELLIN, OCTAVIA ANTOINETTE, retired librarian; b. Santa Monica, Calif.; d. Otto P. and Librada (Montoya) F. Student U. N.Mex., 1937-39; BA, U. Denver, 1941; BA in L.S., Rosary Coll., 1942. Asst. libr., instr. libr. sci. St. Mary-of-Woods Coll., Terre Haute, Ind., 1942-44; libr. U.S. Army, Bruns Gen. Hosp., Santa Fe, 1944-46, Gallup (N.Mex.) Pub. Libr., 1947-90; post libr. Camp McQuaide, Calif., 1947; freelance writer mags., newspapers, 1950—; libr. cons.; N.Mex. del. White House Pre-Conf. on Librs. & Info. Svcs., 1978; dir. Nat. Libr. Week for N.Mex., 1959. Chmn. Red Mesa Art Ctr., 1984-88; pres. Gallup Area Arts Coun., 1988; mem. Western Health Found. Century Com., 1988, Gallup Multi-Model Cultural Com., 1988-95; v.p., publicity dir. Gallup Cmty. Concerts Assn., 1957-78, 85-95; organizer Gt. Decision Discussion groups, 1963-85; co-organizer, v.p. chair fund raising com. Gallup Pub. Radio Com., 1989-95; mem. McKinley County Recycling Com., 1990—; mem. local art selection com. N.Mex. Art Dirs., 1990; mem. Gallup St. Naming Com., 1958-59, Aging Com., 1964-68; chmn. Gallup Mus. Indian Arts and Crafts, 1964-78; mem. Eccles. Conciliation and Arbitration Bd., Province of Santa Fe, 1974; mem. publicity com. Gallup Inter-Tribal Indian Ceremonial Assn., 1966-68; mem. Gov's. Com. 100 on Aging, 1967-70; mem. U. N.Mex.-Gallup Campus Cmty. Edn. Adv. Coun., 1981-82; N.Mex. organizing chmn. Rehoboth McKinley Christian Hosp. Aux., pres., 1983, chmn. aux. scholarship com., 1989—, chmn. cmty. edn. loan selection com. 1990—, bd. dirs., corr. sec., 1991—; mem. N.Mex. Libr. Adv. Coun., 1971-75, vice chmn., 1974-75; chmn. adv. com. Gallup Sr. Citizens, 1971-73; mem. steering com. Gallup Diocese Bicentennial, 1975-78, chmn. hist. com., 1975; chmn. Trick or Treat for UNICEF, Gallup, 1972-77, Artists Coop, 1985-89; chmn. pledge campaign Rancho del Nino San Huberto, Empalme, Mex., 1975-80; active Nat. Cath. Social Justice Lobby; bd. dirs. Gallup Opera Guild, 1970-74; bd. dirs., sec., organizer Gallup Area Arts Council, 1970-78; mem. N.Mex. Humanities Council, 1979, Gallup Centennial Com., 1980-81; mem. Cathedral Parish Council, 1980-83, v.p., 1981, century com. Western Health Found., 1988-89; active N.Mex. Diamond Jubilee/U.S. Constn. Bicentennial Gallup Com., 1986-87, N.Mex. Gallup Campus 25 Silver Anniversary Com., 1994. Recipient Dorothy Canfield Fisher $1,000 Libr. award, 1961, Outstanding Community Service award for mus. service Gallup C. of C., 1969, 70, Outstanding Citizen award, 1974, Benemerenti medal Pope Paul VI, 1977, Celebrate Literary award Gallup Internat. Reading 8 Assn., 1983-84, Woman of Distinction award Soroptimists, 1985, N.Mex. Disting. Pub. Svc. award, 1987, finalist Gov's award Outstanding N.Mex. Women, 1988, Edgar L. Hewett award Hist. Soc. N.Mex., 1992; Octavia Fellin Pub. Libr. named in her honor, 1990. Mem. ALA, N.Mex. Library Assn. (hon. life, v.p., sec., chmn. hist. materials com. 1964-66, salary and tenure com., nat. coordinator N.Mex. legislative com., chmn. com. to extend library services 1969-73, Librar. of Yr. award 1975, chmn. local and regional history roundtable 1978, Community Achievement award 1983, Membership award 1994), AAUW (v.p., co-organizer Gallup br., N.Mex. nominating com. 1967-68, chmn. fellowships and centennial fund Gallup br., chmn. com. on women), Plateau Scis. Soc., N.Mex. Folklore Soc. (v.p. 1964-65, pres. 1965-66), N.Mex. Hist. Soc. (dir. 1979-85), Gallup Hist. Soc., Gallup Film Soc. (co-organizer, v.p. 1950-58), LWV (v.p. 1953-56), NAACP, Pax Christi U.S.A., Women's Ordination Conf. Network, Gallup C. of C. (organizing chmn. women's div. 1972, v.p. 1972-73), N.Mex. Women's Polit. Caucus, N.Mex. Mcpl. League (pres. libr.'s div. 1979), Alpha Delta Kappa (hon.). Roman Catholic (Cathedral Guild, Confraternity Christian Doctrine Bd. 1962-64, Cursillo in Christianity Movement, mem. of U.S. Cath. Bishop's Adv. Council 1969-74; corr. sec. Latin Am. Mission Program 1972-75, sec. Diocese of Gallup Pastoral Council 1972-73, corr. sec. liturgical commn. Diocese of Gallup 1977). Author: Yahweh The Voice that Beautifies, The Land, A Chronicle of Mileposts: A Brief History of the University of New Mexico Gallup Campus. Home and Office: 513 E Mesa Ave Gallup NM 87301-6021

FELLNER, MARY SOPHIA, speech-language pathologist; b. Elmire, N.Y., May 3, 1960; d. Kenneth Robert and Jessica Barbara (Kroczynski) Tuller; m. Daniel J. Fellner, Mar. 22, 1986 (div. June 1994). BBS, SUNY, Buffalo, 1982, MS, 1990. Cert. speech-lang. hearing profl. Speech-lang. pathologist Hendry County Schs., Clewiston, Fla., 1982-83, Buffalo Bd. Edn., 1983-94, Lee County Sch. Bd., Cape Coral, Fla., 1994—; mem. child-study team Buffalo, N.Y., 1993-94. Mem. Am. Speech-Lang.-Hearing Assn. (cert.). Roman Catholic.

FELLOWS, DIANE MCCAULEY, school system administrator, principal; b. N.Y.C., Aug. 1, 1946; d. Joseph and Virginia (McGuirk) McCauley; m. Albert Orlando (div.); children: Justin, Brian; m. George Fellows, Mar. 2, 1986; stepchildren: Julie Fellows Crow, Dana Fellows. Diplôme, La Sorbonne, Paris, 1968; BA in French, Fordham U., 1968, postgrad., 1996; MA in Orgnl. Psychology, Columbia U., 1988. French tchr. Pomona (N.Y.) Jr. High Sch., 1968-70; French tchr. Wandell Sch., Saddle River, N.J., 1978-92, asst. prin., 1992-94; prin. Woodside Avenue Sch., Franklin Lakes, N.J., 1994-95, 95-96; supr. curriculum and instrn. Franklin Lakes Sch. Dist., 1995—; affirmative action officer Wandell Sch., Saddle River, N.J., 1992-94, Franklin Lakes (N.J.) schs., 1994-96. Mem. Am. Isreal Pub. Affairs Com., N.Y.C., 1986. U.S. Adminstrn. on Aging fellow Columbia U., 1972; recipient N.J. Gov. Tchrs. Recognition award N.J. Univ., 1989, cert. d'honneur Prof. de Laureat, Am. Assn. Tchrs. of French, 1985-92. Mem. AAUW, Nat. Middle Sch. Assn., Women's Legal Def. Fund, Assn. for Supr. and Curriculum Devel., N.J. Assn. Sch. Adminstrs., N.J. Principals and Suprs. Assn., Kappa Delta Pi.

FELLOWS, VIRGINIA SUSAN, accountant; b. Santa Ana, Calif., Mar. 24, 1957; d. Donald Frank, Sr. and Sally Joan (Kraemer) Austin; m. Jeffrey michael Fellows, Sr., July 8, 1978; children: Jeffrey, Jr., Jessica Lynn, Christopher William. BBA, U. San Diego, 1978; MBA, Nat. U., 1983. CPA, Calif. Acct. County of San Diego, Calif., 1980-83; acct. Deloitte, Haskins & Sells, San Diego, 1983-86, sr. acct., 1986-87; contr. Gildred Devel. Co., San Diego, 1988-90, C.I. Holding Co., San Diego, 1990-94, Beacon Electric Supply, Inc., San Diego, 1993—; ind. CPA Alpine, Calif., 1990—; cons. Sunbelt Publs., El Cajon, Calif., 1993—, Alpine Sun Newspaper, 1993—, Womancare Clinic, Inc., San Diego, 1995—, El Cajon Machine, Inc., 1996—, Camp Pendleton Daycare Providers Assn., Oceanside, Calif., 1990—; mentor Nat. Univ. San Diego, 1983—; spkr. Mentor Week - Nat. U., 1985-89; spkr. various seminars. Vol. Queen of Angels Cath. Ch., 1994—, Alpine Comm. Ch., 1995—. Named Pres. of Yr., Jr. Achievementf, So. Calif., 1975. Mem. AICPA, Bus. Network Internat. (treas. San Diego chpt. 1994-96), Calif. Soc. CPAs (com. mem. 1985—), Inst. of Mgmt. Accts., Am. Soc. Women Accts. (various offices), Leaders Club (treas. San Diego chpt. 1994-95, 96, bd. dirs. 1995). Republican. Roman Catholic. Home: 4086 Via Palo Verde Lago Alpine CA 91901 Office: PO Box 1252 Alpine GA 91903-1252

FELSEN, CAROL ANN, human resources specialist; b. Albany, N.Y., Jan. 4, 1949; d. William Richard Terko and Katherine (Wagner) Fleischman; m. Joseph F. Laden, June 7, 1968 (div. 1974); m. Karl E. Felsen, June 17, 1978; children: Kristen Elizabeth, Alexander Karl. AA in Liberal Studies, SUNY, Albany, 1976, BA in Liberal Studies, 1978; human resources studies cert., Cornell U., 1995. Editl. clk. Knickerbocker News, Albany, 1968-72; pubs. editor St. WMHT-TV/FM, Schnectedy, N.Y., 1972-75; asst. dir. info. retrieval N.Y. State Assembly, Albany, 1975-76, editor, writer, 1976-78, sr. legis. assoc. judiciary com., 1979-87, chief staff ways & means com., 1987-92, dir. human resources, 1992—; bd. dirs. Empire State Performing Arts Corp., Albany, 1993—. Dep. bd. mem. Cornell U., Ithaca, N.Y., 1992-94; mem., former bd. chair Children's Corney Day Care Ctr., Albany, 1989-91; den leader Boy Scouts Am., Albany, 1993-96; troop leader Girl Scouts Am., Albany, 1991-94. Mem. Nat. Conf. State Legislators, Soc. Human Resource Mgmt., Ctr. Women Govt. Democrat. Roman Catholic. Office: NY State Assembly Albany NY 12248

FELSKI, RITA, language educator; b. Birmingham, Eng., Apr. 15, 1956. BA, Cambridge U., Eng., 1979; MA, Monash U., 1982, PhD, 1987. Asst. prof. Murdoch U., Perth, Australia, 1987-93; prof. U. Va., Charlottesville, 1994—. Author: Beyond Feminist Aesthetics, 1989, The Gender of Modernity, 1995. Fellow Soc. for Humanities, 1988-89, Commonwealth Ctr., 1991; grantee Australian Rsch. Coun., 1993. Office: U Va Dept English Bryan Hall Charlottesville VA 22903

FELSTED, CARLA MARTINDELL, librarian, travel writer; b. Barksdale Field, La., June 21, 1947; d. David Aldenderfer Martindell and Dorthe (Hetland) Horton; m. Robert Earl Luna, Aug. 24, 1968, (div. 1972); m. Hugh Herbert Felsted, Nov. 2, 1974. BA in English, So. Meth. U., 1968, MA in History, 1974; MLS, Tex. Woman's U., 1978. Cert. secondary tchr., Tex.; cert. learning resources specialist, Tex. Tchr. Bishop Lynch High Sch., Dallas, 1968-72, Lake Highlands Jr. High Sch., Richardson, Tex., 1973-75; instr. Richland Coll., Richardson, Tex., 1973-76; library asst. So. Meth. U., Dallas, 1977-78; librarian Tracy-Locke Advt., Dallas, 1978-79; corp. librarian Am. Airlines, Inc., Ft. Worth, 1979-84; research librarian McKinsey & Co., Dallas, 1984-85; reference librarian St. Edward's U., Austin, Tex., 1985—, assoc. prof., 1994—; ptnr. Southwind Info. Svcs. and Southwind Bed-Breakfast, Wimberley, Tex., 1985-92; bd. dirs. Women's S.W. Fed. Credit Union, 1978-81. Editor, compiler: Youth and Alcohol Abuse, 1986; co-editor Mexican Meanderings, 1991—; contbr. to Frommer's travel guides, 1991—. Mem. adv. bd. Sch. Libr. and Info. Scis., Tex. Women's U., Denton, 1982-84; mem. curriculum com. Wimberley Ind. Sch. Dist., 1986; bd. dirs. Hays-Caldwell Coun. on Alcohol and Drug Abuse, San Marcos, Tex., 1986-88, Inst. Cultures for Wimberley Valley, 1989-91, Tex. Alliance Human Needs, 1992—. Grantee St. Edward's U., 1986-89, 96. Mem. ALA, Tex. Libr. Assn. (dist. program com., membership com. 1986-88, Tex.-Mex. rels. com. 1992—), Wimberley C. of C. (bd. dirs. 1987-88). Unitarian. Home: PO Box 33057 Austin TX 78764-0057

FELT, JENNIFER RUTH, elementary physical education educator; b. Toledo, Ohio, Sept. 10, 1950; d. Albert Edward and Joyce Muriel (Haynes) Chiles; m. William Nickolas Felt, Dec. 30, 1983. BS, U. Iowa, 1972; MS in edn., Northern Ill. U., 1988. Cert. physical edn. tchr., Ill. Physical edn. tchr. C.U.S.D. # 303, St. Charles, Ill., 1972—; volleyball coach 8th grade C.U.S.D. # 303, track coach 8th grade, girls athletic dir., h.s. asst. volleyball coach; intramural dir. Munhall Elem. Sch., presenter creative drama Arts At Night, St. Charles, 1994; part edn. leadership conf., 1994-95; mem. state acad. stds. project Ill. State Bd. Edn., 1995-96, external team mem. for quality rev., 1996-97. Active Curriculum revision C.U.S.D. #303, 1991-96, Fine Arts curriculum work, 1993-94; mentor Golden Apple Scholars of Ill., 1994—. Recipient Tech. grant Ill. State Bd. Edn., 1994. Mem. IAHPERD (presenter state conv. 1995), AAHPERD, NEA, IEA, SCEA, IAAE. Office: Munhall Elem Sch 1400 S 13th Ave Saint Charles IL 60174-4405

FELTENSTEIN, MARTHA, lawyer; b. Kansas City, Mo., 1954. BA, Princeton U., 1975; MPhil, U. London, 1977; JD, Columbia U., 1981. Bar: N.Y. 1982. Ptnr. Skadden, Arps, Slate, Meagher & Flom, N.Y.C. Office: Skadden Arps Slate Meagher & Flom 919 3rd Ave New York NY 10022*

FELTEY, KATHRYN MARGARET, sociology educator; b. L.I., N.Y., Aug. 1, 1954; d. Donald Robert and Betty Jean (Monroe) F.; 1 child, Zachary Devlin Maher. BA in Sociology, Wright State U., Dayton, Ohio, 1978, MA in Applied Behavioral Scis., 1982; PhD in Sociology, Ohio State U., Columbus, 1988. Rsch. asst. dept. corrections State of Hawaii, Honolulu, 1974; asst. prof. sociology U. Akron, Ohio, 1988—; rsch. cons. Miami Valley Transit Authority, Dayton, 1981; rsch. cons. dept. black studies Ohio State U., Columbus, 1985, dept. ednl. policy, 1987; cons. Task Force on Homelessness, Akron, 1989—. Editor: (internat. newsletter) Network News, 1993—; contbr. articles to profl. jours. Bd. trustees Akron Citizen's Coalition for Emergency Shelter Svcs., Inc., 1990—. Ohio Bd. Regents grantee, 1988, N.E. Ohio Urban grantee, 1989, 90; Univ. Rsch. fellow, 1991. Mem. Am. Sociol. Assn., Sociol. for Women in Soc., Soc. for Applied Sociology, North Cen. Sociol. Assn., Project on Study of Gender and Edn. Office: U Akron Olin Hall Dept of Sociology Akron OH 44325-1905

FELTON, CYNTHIA, principal; b. Chgo., Apr. 1, 1950; d. Robert Lee Felton Sr. and Julia Mae (Cheton) Felton-Phillips. BA, Northeastern, 1970; MEd, National Coll., 1984; MA, DePaul U., 1988; PhD, Loyola U., Chgo., 1992. Cert. tchr, adminstrv., Ill. Tchr. Chgo. Pub. Schs., 1971-86, adminstr., 1986-89, asst. prin., 1989-92, prin., 1992—. Mem. ASCD, Nat. Coun. Tchrs. Math, Nat. Coun. Suprs. Math, Ill. Coun. Tchrs. Math (bd. dirs. 1992—). Office: Orr High Sch 730 N Pulaski Rd Chicago IL 60624-1063

FELTS, MARGARET DAVIS, librarian, bibliographer; b. Walla Walla, Wash., Jan. 26, 1917; d. Schuyler Ernest and Blanche Marie (Fischer) Davis; m. Wells Carter Felts, June 20, 1940 (div. 1966); children: Carol Margaret, Thomas William, Helen Elizabeth. StaBA, Stanford U., 1938; MLS, U. Calif., Berkeley, 1965. Libr. Mills Coll., Oakland, Calif., 1965-68; libr., bibliographer U. Calif., Santa Cruz, 1968-85; ret. Author: Archives of the South Pacific Commission and Related Papers, 1971; contbr. to Catalog of the South Pacific Collection, 1978; Selection of Library Materials for Area Studies, 1990, Part IV: The South Pacific: Polynesia, Micronesia, Melanesia, 1990. Address: 14 Sunset Dr Watsonville CA 95076-9651

FENDELL, SUSAN, lawyer; b. N.J., June 24, 1955. BA in Visual Comm., Am. U., 1976; BA in Media and SocioPolitical Change, Kirkland Coll., 1976; JD, Ohio State U., 1983. Bar: Tenn. 1983, Mass. 1986. Dir. Bergen County Energy Clinic, Hackensack, N.J., 1978-79; pub. info. officer, tech. specialist Divsn. Econ. Devel., Cleve., 1979-80; pub. advocacy coord., sr. planner County of Bergen, Hackensack, 1980; atty. Legal Svcs. of Upper East Tenn., Johnson City, 1983-86; asst. atty. gen. Dept. Atty. Gen., Boston, 1986-88; atty. Nat. Consumer Law Ctr., Boston, 1988-90, Greater Boston Legal Svcs., Boston, 1991-92; program coord. Interface, Cambridge, Mass., 1991-95; sr. atty. Mental Health Legal Advisors Com., Boston, 1992—. Contbr. articles to profl. jours. Mem. Ruby Rogers Human Rights Com., Somerville, Mass., 1995—; elected rep. Ward 6 Dem. Com., Somerville, 1995, 96. Recipient Scholastic Achievement award Am Jur Book Awards, 1981, Svc. to Cmty. award Alliance for the Mentally Ill, Boston, 1995. Mem. Nat. Lawyers Guild. Office: MHLAC Ste 320 294 Washington St Boston MA 02108

FENDERSON, CAROLINE HOUSTON, psychotherapist; b. East Orange, N.J., June 17, 1932; d. George Cochran and Mary Bullard (Saunders) Houston; m. Kendrick Elwell Fenderson, Jr.; 1 child, Karen Sibley. BA, Vassar Coll., 1954; MA, U. So. Fla., 1973. Lic. mental health counselor, Fla.; diplomate Am. Bd. Cert. Managed Care Providers; cert. Nat. Bd. for Cert. Clin. Hypnotherapists, Inc.; cert. trainer, devel. of human capacities Found. for Mind Rsch.; ordained to ministry of edn. Unitarian Universalist. Dir. of religious edn. Unitarian Universalist Ch., St. Petersburg, Fla., 1960-80; min. of religious edn. Unitarian Universalist Ch., Clearwater, Fla., 1981-83; counselor and staff devel. cons. Pinellas County (Fla.) Schools, 1973-83; pvt. practice Clearwater and Palm Harbor, Fla., 1983—. Author: Life Journey, 1988; (with Kendrick Fenderson Jr.) Magnets, 1961, Southern Shores, 1964; (with others) Man the Culture Builder, 1970, U.U. Identity, 1979; contbr. articles to profl. jours. Pub. affairs chmn. St. Petersburg Jr. League, 1960; founder Childbirth and Parent Edn. League of Pinellas County, 1960-70, pres., v.p., com. chair, tchr.; v.p. Child Guidance Clinic, St. Petersburg, 1960. Mem. ACA, Liberal Religious Edn. Dirs. Assn. (v.p. 1980-81), Assn. Transpersonal Psychology, Assn. Humanistic Psychology, Internat. Transpersonal Assn., Unitarian Universalist Assn. (com. mem. 1975-79), Phi Beta Kappa, Kappa Delta Pi. Home: 29 Freshwater Dr Palm Harbor FL 34684-1106 Office: 25 400 US 19 N Ste 172 Clearwater FL 34623

FENN, SANDRA ANN, programmer, analyst; b. Sugar Land, Tex., Oct. 31, 1953; d. William Charles and Helen Maxine (Kyle) F.; m. Jimmie Dan Watts, May 21, 1973 (div. June 1988); children: Gabriel Nathaniel Watts, Lindsay Nichelle Garza. A in Gen. Studies summa cum laude, Alvin (Tex.) C.C., 1994; student, U. Houston. Shampoo asst. LaVonne's Salon of Beauty, Houston, 1972-73; coding clk. Prudential Ins. Co., Houston, 1974-75; word processing operator MacGregor Med. Assn., Houston, 1983-85; computer applications analyst Computer Scis. Corp., Houston, 1987-92; program support adminstr. Sci. Applications Internat. Corp., Houston, 1992-95, programmer/analyst, 1995—. Mem. Am. Bus. Women's Assn. (newsletter chair), Phi Theta Kappa. Home: 107 Clearview Ave Apt 1206 Friendswood TX 77546-4058 Office: Sci Applications Internat Corp 16511 Space Center Blvd Houston TX 77058-2017

FENN, SHERILYN, actress; b. Detroit, Feb. 1, 1965. TV series: Twin Peaks, 1990 (Emmy award nomination best supporting actress in a drama series); TV movies Silence of the Heart, 1984, Dillinger, 1991, Spring Awakening, 1994; TV specials Divided We Stand, 1988, A Family Again, 1988; film appearances The Wild Life, 1984, Just One of the Guys, 1985, Out of Control, 1985, Thrashin', 1986, The Wraith, 1986, Zombie High, 1987, Two Moon Junction, 1988, Crime Zone, 1988, True Blood, 1989, Wild at Heart, 1990, Backstreet Dreams, 1990, Meridian: Kiss of the Beast, 1990, Ruby, 1992, Desire and Hell at Sunset Motel, 1992, Diary of a Hitman, 1992, Of Mice and Men, 1992, Twin Peaks: Fire Walk With Me, 1992, Three of Hearts, 1993, Boxing Helena, 1993, Fatal Instinct, 1993. *

FENNELL, DIANE MARIE, marketing executive, process engineer; b. Panama, Iowa, Dec. 11, 1944; d. Urban William and Marcella Mae (Leytham) Schechinger; m. Leonard E. Fennell, Aug. 19, 1967; children: David, Denise, Mark. BS, Creighton U., Omaha, 1966. Process engr. Tex. Instruments, Richardson, 1974-79; sr. process engr. Signetics Corp., Santa Clara, Calif., 1979-82; demo lab. mgr. Airco Temescal, Berkeley, Calif., 1982-84; field process engr. Applied Materials, Santa Clara, 1984-87; mgr. product mktg. Lam Rsch., Fremont, Calif., 1987-90; dir. sales and mktg. Ion & Plasma Equipment, Fremont, Calif., 1990-91; pres. FAI, Half Moon Bay, Calif., 1990—; founder, coord. chmn. Plasma Etch User's Group, Santa Clara, 1984-87; tchr. computer course Adult Edn., Half Moon Bay, Calif., 1982-83. Founder, bd. dirs. Birth to Three program Mental Retardation Ctr., Denison, Tex., 1974-75; fund raiser local sch. band, Half Moon Bay, 1981-89; community rep. local sch. bd., Half Moon Bay, 1982-83. Mem. Am. Vacuum Soc., Soc. Photo Instrumnentation Engrs., Soc. Women Engrs., Material Rsch. Soc. Home: 441 Alameda Ave Half Moon Bay CA 94019-1365

FENNELL, PATRICIA A., trauma specialist; b. Bridgeport, Conn., Feb. 8, 1956; d. Joseph Mortimer and Dorothy Theresa (Moriarty) F. BA magna cum laude, Coll. of St. Rose, 1979; MSW, SUNY, Albany, 1984. Cert. social worker, N.Y. Tchg. and rsch. asst. Sch. of Social Welfare SUNY, Albany, 1979-80, 82-84; policy analyst, devel. specialist N.Y. State Commn. on Quality of Care for Mentally Disabled, Albany, 1980-82; therapist St. Anne Inst., Albany, 1984-85; dir. vols. St. Peter's Hospice, Albany, 1985-87; therapist Forensic Mental Health Assn., Albany, 1984-87; designated agt.-liaison child abuse and neglect Rensselaer (N.Y.) City Sch. Dist., 1987-89; co-dir. Albany Health Counseling Assn., 1987-89; dir., founder Albany Health Mgmt. Assn., Inc., Latham, N.Y., 1987—; prin. investigator, sr. clin. cons. Capital Region Sleep/Wake Disorders Ctr., Albany, 1990—; lectr., cons. APA, Nat. Hospice Orgn., Rensselaer Poly., HMO-Value Behavioral Health, Dept. Social Svcs., 1987—; clin. supr. Brattleboro (Vt.) Psychiat. Hosp., 1995—. Contbr. articles to profl. jours. Cons., advisor Consultation Ctr., Roman Cath. Diocese of Albany, 1991—; activist, keynote spkr., lectr. Nat. Orgn. to Tell Truth-Sex Abuse Speakout, Albany, 1994-95; bd. dirs. Albany City Sex Abuse Task Force, 1993—, Rensellaer City Rape Crisis, Troy, N.Y., 1988-91; hospice bereavement vol. St. Peter's Hospice, Albany, 1984-85. Mem. NASW, N.E. Strategic Therapists Assn., Am. Assn. Chronic Fatigue Syndrome (clin.), Delta Epsilon, Kappa Gamma Pi. Office: Albany Health Mgmt Assocs 582 New London Rd Latham NY 12110

FENNELL ROBBINS, SALLY, writer; b. Greensburg, Pa., Feb. 17, 1950; d. Clifford Seanor and Charlotte Louise (Hoffman) Fennell; m. John W. Robbins, Sept. 22, 1984. BS in Journalism, cum laude, Ohio U., 1972; MA in Journalism, magna cum laude, Marshall U., 1974. Intern, reporter Tribune-Rev., Greensburg, Pa., 1972; prodn. asst. Harper's Bazaar, N.Y.C., 1972; reporter UPI, Birmingham, Ala., 1972-73; reporter, dept. editor HFD-Retailing Home Furnishings, Fairchild Pubs., N.Y.C., 1975-77; account exec. supr., client svc. mgr., v.p. Burson-Marsteller, N.Y.C., 1977-83; group mgr., v.p. pub. rels. div. Ketchum Communications, 1983-84; freelance writer, editor, 1984-89; dir. retail communications Deloitte & Touche Retail Svcs. Group, N.Y., 1989-93; writer, 1993—. grad. teaching asst. Sch. Journalism/

Reporting, Marshall U., Huntington, W.Va., 1973-74. Home and Office: 237 E 20th St New York NY 10003-1805

FENNIMORE, BEATRICE SCHNELLER, education educator; b. Plainfield, N.J., July 16, 1948; d. George Henry and Marjorie E. (Cooney) Schneller; m. Christian Joseph Fennimore, May 17, 1969 (div. Nov. 1993); children: Sharon Ellen, Maryann. BA, St. Joseph's Coll., Bklyn., 1970; MS, CUNY, Bklyn., 1977; MEd, Columbia U., 1983, EdD, 1986. Tchr. early childhood Park Pl. Ctr., Bklyn., 1971-73; ednl. dir. Union Presch., Bklyn., 1977-79; instr. Marymount Manhattan Coll., N.Y.C., 1981-83; instr. Tchrs. Coll., Columbia U., N.Y.C., 1984-85, adj. asst. prof., 1987-92, adj. assoc. prof., 1993—; asst. prof. Indiana U. Pa., 1987-92, assoc. prof., 1993-95, prof., 1995—; multicultural bd. visitors Pitts. Pub. Schs., 1991-93; cons., trainer Head Start Programs and Child Care Programs, Western Pa., 1993—; speaker/presentor various meetings/confs. Pa., 1987—; mem. multicultural edn. com. Am. Assn. Colls. Tchr. Edn., 1994-96; mem. commn. on preparing tchrs. for diverse populations Assn. Tchr. Educators, 1992—; mem. human rels. com. Pitts. Pub. Schs. Author: Child Advocacy for Early Childhood Educators, 1989, Student Centered Classroom Management, 1995; sect. editor, contbr. Ency. of Early Childhood Edn., 1992. Co-founder Parents United for Better Learning in Cmty. Schs., Bklyn., 1982; pres. Pitts. Coun. on Pub. Edn., 1988-90; convenor Reizenstein Sch. Consortium, Pitts., 1987-90. Named Outstanding Prof. Student Pa. State Edn. Assn., Indiana U. Pa., 1991. Mem. ASCD, Am. Ednl. Rsch. Assn., Assn. Childhood Edn. Internat., Nat. Assn. for Edn. Young Children. Democrat. Office: Indiana U Pa 203 Stouffer Hall Indiana PA 15705

FENNING, LISA HILL, federal judge; b. Chgo., Feb. 22, 1952; d. Ivan Byron and Joan (Hennigar) Hill; m. Alan Mark Fenning, Apr. 3, 1977; 4 children. BA with honors, Wellesley Coll., 1971; JD, Yale U., 1974. Bar: Ill. 1975, Calif. 1979, U.S. Dist. Ct. (no. dist.) Ill., U.S. Dist. Ct. (no., ea., so. & cen. dists.) Calif., U.S. Ct. Appeals (6th, 7th & 9th cirs.), U.S. Supreme Ct. 1989. Law clk. U.S. Ct. Appeals 7th cir., Chgo., 1974-75; assoc. Jenner and Block, Chgo., 1975-77, O'Melveny and Myers, Los Angeles, 1977-85; judge U.S. Bankruptcy Ct. Cen. Dist. Calif., Los Angeles, 1985—; bd. govs. Nat. Conf. Bankruptcy Judges, 1989-92; pres. Nat. Conf. of Women's Bar Assns., N.C., 1987-88, pres.-elect, 1986-87, v.p., 1985-86, bd. dirs.; lectr., program coord. in field; bd. govs. Nat. Conf. Bankruptcy Judges Endowment for Edn., 1992—, Am. Bankruptcy Inst., 1994—; mem., bd. advisors Nat. Jud. Edn. Program to Promote Equality for Women and Men in the Cts., 1994—. Mem., bd. advisors: Lawyer Hiring & Training Report, 1985-87; contbr. articles to profl. jours. Durant scholar Wellesley Coll., 1971; named one of Am's. 100 Most Important Women Ladies Home Jour., 1988. Fellow Am. Bar Found., Am. Coll. Bankruptcy (bd. regents 1995—); mem. ABA (standing com. on fed. jud. improvements 1995—, mem. commn. on women in the profession 1987-91, Women's Caucus 1987—, Individual Rights and Responsibilities sect. 1984—, bus. law sect. 1986—, bus. bankruptcy com.), Nat. Assn. Women Judges (nat. task force gender bias in the cts. 1986-87, 93-94), Nat. Conf. Bankruptcy Judges (chair endowment edn. bd.), Am. Bankruptcy Inst. (nominating com. 1994-95, bd. steering com. statis. project 1994—), Calif. State Bar Assn. (chair com. on women in law 1986-87), Women Lawyers' Assn. L.A. (ex officio mem., bd. dirs., chmn., founder com. on status of women lawyers 1984-85, officer nominating com. 1986, founder, mem. Do-It-Yourself Mentor Network 1986—), Phi Beta Kappa. Democrat. Office: US Bankruptcy Ct 255 E Temple St Rm 1682 Los Angeles CA 90012-3334

FENTON, SUSAN MEYER, artist; b. New Hartford, N.Y., Apr. 3, 1964; d. John Lawrence and Ann (Grace) Meyer; m. Martin Fenton III, Sept. 22, 1990. BS in Studio Art, Skidmore Coll., 1986; MFA in Visual Art, Tufts U./Boston Mus. Sch., 1991. Instr. in drawing, painting and photography Berkshire Sch., Sheffield, Mass., 1986-88; gallery coord. Weems Gallery, Boston Mus. Sch., 1989-90; instr. World Art Explorers, Denver, 1995-96; mem. artists-in-residence program Young Audiences, Denver, 1995; assoc. Rocky Mountain Women's Inst., Denver, 1995; gallery aide Schick Art Gallery, Skidmore Coll., Saratoga Springs, N.Y., 1985; mus. intern Children's Mus., Utica, N.Y., 1983, Munson Williams Proctor Art Inst., Utica, 1990; mus. intern Denver Art Mus., 1995-96; co-chair show design com. ann. print show Coll. Women's Assn. Japan, Tokyo, 1994, co-chair hospitality com. lecture series, 1994; assoc. Rocky Mountain Women's Inst., 1995-96. One-woman shows at Artyard, Denver, 1996; group exhbns. include Kingston Gallery, Boston, 1990, The Starr Gallery, Newton, Mass., 1990, Park Ctrl., Phoenix, 1992, Smash Culture Gallery, Phoenix, 1992, Mars Gallery, Phoenix, 1992, Jackson St. Studios, Phoenix, 1992, Art Ctr. No. N.J., New Milford, 1992, 11 E. Ashland, Phoenix, 1992, Lisa Sette Gallery, Scottsdale, Ariz., 1992, Alexandria (La.) Mus. of Art, 1992 (Juror's Merit award), Cooperstown (N.Y.) Art Assn., 1994, Schoharie County Arts Coun., Cobleskill, N.Y., 1994, Schemer Art Ctr. and Mus., Phoenix, 1994, Tokyo Met. Art Mus., 1994, Dinnerware Artists' Coop. Gallery, Phoenix, 1995, Holter Mus. of Art, Helena, Mont., 1995, Core New Art Space, Denver, 1995, Woman Made Gallery, Chgo., 1995, Singer Gallery, Denver, 1996, Eastern N.Mex. U., Portales, 1996, Mus. Fine Arts, Santa Fe (Friends of Contemporary Art award), 1996, San Francisco State U., 1996, Metro Ctr. Visual Arts, Denver, 1996, Tempe (Ariz.) Arts Ctr., 1996, Mariani & Michener Galleries, U. No. Colo., 1996, Boulder (Colo.) Mus. Contemporary Art, 1996. Vol. Art Link, Phoenix, 1992. Study grantee Berkshire Sch., 1987. Mem. Denver Art Mus., Alliance for Contemporary Art, Alternative Arts Alliance, Colo. Fedn. of Arts, Alternative Mus.

FENWICK, KATHLEEN E., lawyer; b. N.Y.C., 1937. AB cum laude, St. John's U., N.Y., 1958; JD, U. Houston, 1977. Bar: Tex. 1978, U.S. Supreme Ct. 1981. Of counsel Andrews & Kurth L.L.P., Houston; adj. prof. U. Houston Law Sch., 1980-82. Mem. State Bar Tex., Houston Bar Assn. Office: Andrews & Kurth LLP 600 Travis St Ste 4200 Houston TX 77002*

FERBER, LINDA S., museum curator; b. Suffern, N.Y., May 17, 1944. BA cum laude, Barnard Coll., 1966; MA, Columbia U., 1968, PhD in Art History, 1980. Curator Am. painting and sculpture The Bklyn. Mus., 1982—, chief curator, 1985—. Author: William Trost Richards (1833-1905): American Landscape and Marine Painter, 1980, Tokens of a Friendship: Miniature Watercolors by William T. Richards, 1982, (with others) The New Path: Ruskin and the American Pre-Raphaelites, 1985, Never at Fault: The Drawings of William T. Richards, 1986, (with others) Albert Bierstadt: Art and Enterprise, 1991; also articles on 19th and 20th century Am. art history. Wyeth Endowment for Am. Art fellow, 1976-77. Mem. Coll. Art Assn., Am. Assn. Mus., Phi Beta Kappa. Office: Brooklyn Mus 200 Eastern Pky Brooklyn NY 11238-6052

FERBERT, MARY LOU, artist; b. Cleve., Sept. 21, 1924; d. Czerny Edward and Gladys Helene (Monce) Mulligan; m. Frederick Winzer Ferbert, Nov. 22, 1947; children: Linda Ferbert Jonash, Frederick Winzer, Jr. BA, Duke U., 1941. Vol. tchr. Mus. of Natural History, Cleve., 1968-87, coord. environ. info. svc., 1969-87; profl. artist pvt. practice, Rocky River, Ohio, 1975—; instr. Inst. of Art, Cleve., 1989—. Author: (sci. enrichment curriculum) Nature in the City, 1979 (Nat. award 1984, 85; one-woman shows Bonfoey Co., Cleve., 1981, 89, 94, Cleve. Play House Gallery, 1985, Gallery Madison 90, N.Y.C., 1987, Butler Inst. Am. Art, Youngstown, Ohio, 1993; exhibited in group shows Butler Inst. Am. Art, 1974-78, 83, 89-91, Cleve. Mus. Art, 1975, 82-85, 87, 88, 93, So. Alleghenies Mus. Art, Loretto, Pa., 1978, Natural History Mus. Art, Cleve., 1988, 96, Columbus (Ohio) Mus. Art, 1988-89, NAD, N.Y.C., 1990, Nat. Assn. Women Artists, Athens, Greece, 1996; represented in permanent collections Avon Lake (Ohio) Pub. Libr., Cleve. Mus. Natural History, Cleve. State U., El Paso (Tex.) Mus. Art, Ella Carothers Dunnegan Gallery Art, Bolivar, Mo., 1984, Lakewood (Ohio) Hosp., Mus. of Beck Ctr. for Cultural Arts, Lakewood, Rocky River (Ohio) Pub. Libr., Univs. Hosps. Cleve. Trustee Mus. of Natural History, Cleve., 1978—, New Orgn./Visual Arts, Cleve, 1987-91; mem. adv. bd. Inst. of Art, Cleve., 1984—; mem. adv. com. WVIZ (pub. TV), Cleve., 1984-85. Recipient Mus. Purchase award, El Paso (Tex.) Mus. of Art, 1980, Spl. Mention Mus. of Art, Cleve., 1988, Harold Terry Clark medal, Mus. Nat. History, Cleve., 1994. Mem. Midwest Water Color Soc. (elected, Excellence award 1983), Watercolor USA Honor Soc. (charter), Am. Watercolor Soc. (elected, Bronze medal 1987), CatherineLorillard Wolfe Art Club (medal of honor 1993), Lakewood H.S. Alumni (Hall of Fame 1988), Nat. Assn. Women Artists, Knickerbocker Artists.

FERETIC, EILEEN SUSAN, editor; b. N.Y.C., Aug. 31, 1949; d. Joseph Anthony and Eileen Helen (Sohl) F.; m. William Kulakoski; 1 child, Shannon. B.A., Fordham U., 1971. Editor Manpower Edn. Inst., N.Y.C., 1970-72; editor UTP div. Hearst Bus. Communications, L.I., N.Y., 1972-90; editorial dir. FM Bus. Pub., Garden City, N.Y., 1990-92; editor Corporate Systems mag., 1975-80, Office Products News, 1972-82, Today's Office, 1982-92; also editorial dir. Office Group, 1978-92; editor in chief Beyond Computing mag., N.Y.C., 1992—; industry rep. U.S. Dept. Commerce, 1980, 83; mem. Pres.'s Pvt. Sector Survey on Cost Control/Office Automation Task Force, 1982. Co-author textbook on adminstrv. procedures in electronic office, 1979; co-producer, host (TV series) Office Automation; contbr. World Book Ency. Recipient N.Y. Daily News award journalism, 1970; Long Island Press Club Writing award. Mem. Am. Soc. Bus. Press Editors Assn. (writing award, Apex award for editorial writing, award for best new mag.). Home: 115 Rita Dr East Meadow NY 11554-1326 Office: Beyond Computing IBM Corp 590 Madison Ave New York NY 10022

FERETIC, GERALDINE ANN MARIE, program coordinator; b. Poughkeepsie, N.Y., Sept. 26, 1958; d. Nicholas Frank and Catherine (Cerrito) F. AAS, Farmingdale U., 1978; BA in Psychology, Adelphi U., 1982, MA in Psychology, 1984, MSW, 1991. Cert. social worker, ACSW. Psychologist Montefiore Hosp. Med. Ctr. Riker's Island Prison, East Elmhurst, N.Y., 1984-89; psychologist Suffolk Child Devel. Ctr., Smithtown, N.Y., 1989-91; program coord. Devel. Disabilities Inst., East Hills, N.Y., 1991—. Mem. APA, NASW, Assn. for Behavior Analysis. Office: Devel Disabilities Inst 210 Forest Dr Greenvale NY 11548-1206

FERGES, ROSE D., nursing educator; b. Balt., Feb. 8, 1930; d. Walker H. and Bessie E. (Dorsey) Dawson; m. Joseph H. Ferges Sr., Jan. 2, 1953; children: Frances, Toney, Joseph Jr., Paula. AA, Essex Community Coll., Balt., 1972; BS, U. Balt., 1979; MS, Coppin State U., 1991. Nursing supr. Highland Health Facility, Balt.; supr. Spring Grove Hosp., Balt.; supr. outpatient dept. & dialysis Veterans Adminstrn. Ft. Howard, Balt.; Instr. nursing edn., nursing informatic coord. Dept. Veterans Affairs, Balt. Chair Nurses Profl. Standards Bd.; equal employment opportunity counselor. Recipient Gov.'s citation for Outstanding Svc., Citizen citation for Dedication and Commitment from Mayor Kurt Schmoke, spl. contbn. award Dept. Vet. Affairs. Mem. Md. Nurses Assn., NAACP, Blacks in Govt. (rsch. com., sec. Ft. Howard br.), Toastmaster (charter; chair data validation com.).

FERGUS, PATRICIA MARGUERITA, English language educator emeritus, writer, editor; b. Mpls., Oct. 26, 1918; d. Golden Maughan and Mary Adella (Smith) F. B.S., U. Minn., 1939, M.A., 1941, Ph.D., 1960. Various pers. and editing positions U.S. Govt., 1943-59; mem. faculty U. Minn., Mpls., 1964-79, asst. prof. English, 1972-79, coord. writing program conf. on writing, 1975, dir. writing centre, 1975-77; prof. English and writing, dir. writing ctr., assoc. dean Coll. Mt. St. Mary's Coll., Emmitsburg, Md., 1979-81; dir. writing seminars Mack Truck, Inc., Hagerstown, Md., 1979-81; writer, 1964—; editorial asst. to pres. Met. State U., St. Paul, 1984-85; coord. creative writing, writer program notes for Coffee Concerts, The Kenwood, 1992-94; dir. Kenwood Scribes Presentation, 1994; speaker and cons. in field; dir. 510 Groveland Assocs.; bus. mgr. Eitel Hosp. Gift Shop. Author: Spelling Improvement, 5th edit., 1991; contbr. to Midwest Chaparral, Downtown Cath. Voice, Mpls., Mountaineer Briefing, ABI Digest; contbr. poems to Minn. English Jour., Mpls. Muse, The Moccasin, Heartsong and Northstar Gold, The Pen Woman, Midwest Chaparral, Rhyme Time; contbr. short stories to anthologies. Mem. spl. vocal octet St. Olaf Ch. Choir, St. Olaf Parish Adv. Bd., Windmore Found. for the Arts. Recipient Outstanding Contbn. award U. Minn. Twin Cities Student Assembly, 1975; Horace T. Morse-Amoco Found. award, 1976, Golden Poet award, World of Poetry, 1992; Ednl. Devel. grantee U. Minn., 1975-76; Mt. St. Mary's Coll. grantee, 1980; 3d prize vocal-choral category Nat. Music Composition Contest, Nat. League Am. Pen Women, speaker and Bronze Medalist, 13th Internat. Biographical Congress, 1986. Mem. AAUW, Am. Biog. Inst. (dep. gov.), Internat. Biog. Ctr. (hon. mem. adv. coun.), Nat. Coun. Tchrs. English (regional judge 1974, 76-77, state coord. 1977-79), Minn. Coun. Tchrs. English (chmn. career and job opportunities com., spl. com. tchr. licensure, sec. legis. com.), Nat. League Am. Pen Women (1st pl. Haiku nat. poetry contest 1992), World Lit. Acad., Mpls. Poetry Soc. (numerous poetry prizes), League Minn. Poets, Midwest Fedn. Chaparral Poets (numerous poetry prizes, 1st prize 1993), Poetry Soc. Va., Windmore Found. for the Arts, Va. Writers, Windmore Writers Group, Woman's Club of Culpepper, No. Dist. Woman's Club (2nd prize poetry 1996). Roman Catholic. Home and Office: 651B Southview Ct Culpeper VA 22701-3794

FERGUSON, AUDREY DIANE, elementary educator; b. St. Louis, June 28, 1946; d. Goldie Walter and Muriel Lee (Quarles) Buford; m. Chavis Edward Ferguson, Sr., Sept. 4, 1965; children: Chavis Edward II, Kevin, Robin. AB in Edn., Harris-Stowe Tchrs. Coll., St. Louis, 1968; MA in Teaching, Webster U., St. Louis, 1984. Cert. elem. edn., mid. schs., learning disabled, behavior disorders, emotionally handicapped, reading, Mo. Classroom tchr. St. Louis Pub. Schs., 1969-76, remedial math. tchr., 1976—, chpt. I supt. adv. com., 1984-85, elem. math. cons., 1982—. Chairperson INROADS Parent Support Group, St. Louis, 1992-93; mem. INROADS, 1989—. Recipient Parent of Yr. award INROADS, St. Louis, 1994. Mem. Nat. Coun. Tchrs. Math., Internat. Reading Assn., Harris-Stowe Alumni. Mem. Ch. of God. Home: 1864 Atmore Dr Saint Louis MO 63136

FERGUSON, JEAN KENNAN, psychotherapist; b. Maui, Hawaii, Sept. 22, 1940; d. Robert McCormack and Mary Violet (Judy) Kennan; m. Richard C. Ferguson, June 8, 1963; children: Kennan, Rona. BA cum laude, Whitman Coll., 1962; MA, UCLA, 1963; MS, U. So. Calif., 1985. Life gen. secondary tchg. and jr. coll. tchg. credentials, Calif.; lic. marriage, family and child counselor, Calif.; lic. profl. counselor, Wyo. Tchr. English secondary sch., Thousand Oaks, Calif., 1963-93, peer counseling tchr., 1990-95; pvt. practice psychotherapy, Westlake Village, Calif., 1985—; dir. Be Free substance abuse recovery program Woodland Hills (Calif.) Adult Group, 1983-88. Mem. planning group Celebrate Family Conf., Thousand Oaks, 1991-96; clk., mem. governing bd. Conejo United Ch. of Christ. Mem. AAUW, Am. Assn. Marriage and Family Therapists, Calif. Assn. Marriage and Family Therapists, Ventura County Marriage and Family Therapists, Phi Beta Kappa. Democrat. Home: 2062 Sapra St Thousand Oaks CA 91362 Office: 699 Hampshire Rd Ste 215 Westlake Village CA 91361

FERGUSON, MARGARET GENEVA, author, publisher, real estate broker; d. James B. and Dollie (McCloud) F. Student, Kansas City Jr. Coll., 1949, YMCA Real Estate Inst., 1960, Bryant and Stratton Bus. Coll., 1962, Ill. Inst. Tech., 1969. Sec. Cook County Grand Jury, 1979; acting mgr. internal svc. dept. Xerox Corp., 1985-86; tutor reading and math., 1988; host Black Image Prodn. Cable 19, 1989; interviewed on various TV shows, including PM Mag., 1983; active pub. rels. newspapers, Chgo., Detroit, Kansas City, St. Louis, 1970-91; conductor workshops in field, 1970-92; participant Pan Meth. Pilgrimage to Eng., 1984, World Meth. Conf., Nairobi, Kenya, 1986. Author, pub.: The History of St. Paul CME Church 1907-1988, 1989, Books in Print, 1989-90, This Is Your Life Dr. Owens, 1991. Co-chmn. fund raiser Citizens for Mayor Harold Washington, Chgo., 1987; treas. St. Paul Mortgage Fund, 1984; vol. Am. Cancer Soc., Salvation Army, Lighthouse for the Blind, Dem. Nat. Conv., 1996; dist. pres. Christian Methodist Episcopal Ch. Nat. Women's League, 1980-86, nat. fin. sec., 1980-92; officer St. Paul Christian Methodist Episcopal Ch., 1954—; v.p. lay ministry, 1987-92, pres. 1992—; v.p. Ann. Conf. Lay Ministry, 1996; sec. Christian Methodist Episcopal Long Range Planning Commn., 1982-86; mem. Chgo. State Street Women's Coun. Recipient History Writing award Christian Meth. Episcopal Ch., 1990, Gold Coaster Kiwanis Club award, 1983, Black on Black Love award, 1988; named to Cultural Citizens Found. Hall of Fame, 1990, Vol. of Yr. Chgo. Lighthouse, 1982, 1st Lady award V-103FM, 1991, Citizens award, 1994, Key to City, Ft. Smith, Ark., 1992, Bishop's award C.M.E. Ch., 1996; nominated Jefferson awards NBC, 1996, others. Mem. NAACP, Nat. Coun. Negro Women, People United to Serve Humanity (prison ministry award 1991), Chgo. Bd. Realtors, S.W. Suburban Bd. Realtors, Hyde Park Co-op Soc., Inc. (bd. dirs. 1994-95), Internat. Platform Assn. (met. pres., v.p. U.S.), Lambda Kappa Nu. Home: 727 E 60th St Apt 808 Chicago IL 60637-2539

FERGUSON, PAMELA ANDERSON, mathematics educator, educational administrator; b. Berwyn, Ill., May 5, 1943; d. Clarence Oscar and Ruth Anne (Stroner) Anderson; m. Donald Roger Ferguson, Dec. 18, 1965; children: Keith, Amanda. BA, Wellesley Coll., 1965; MS, U. Chgo., 1966, PhD, 1969. Asst. prof. Northwestern U., Evanston, Ill., 1969-70, U. Miami, Coral Gables, Fla., 1972-77; assoc. prof. U. Miami, 1978-81, prof. math., 1981-91, dir. honors program, 1985-87, assoc. provost, dean Grad. Sch., 1987-91; pres. Grinnell Coll., Iowa, 1991—. Contbr. over 50 articles to refereed jours. Mem. Iowa Rsch. Coun., 1993—. NSF grantee. Mem. Am. Math. Soc., Am. Women in Math., Wellesley Club, Sigma Xi, Phi Beta Kappa, Omicron Delta Chi. Lutheran. Office: Grinnell Coll Office of the Pres 1121 Park St PO Box 805 Grinnell IA 50112-0805

FERGUSON, SHARON C., community relations specialist; b. Little Rock, Oct. 17, 1942; d. Herman H. and Eleanor Beatrice (Fulmer) Scates; m. C. Anthony Ferguson, June 10, 1961; children: Lisa Ferguson Hirschman, Dana Ferguson Silaski, C. Anthony II. Student, U. Ark. Cert. meeting planner. Owner, exec. dir. North Little Rock (Ark.) Jr. Cotillion, 1969—; asst. to pres. Fed. Home Loan Bank, Little Rock, 1978-85; exec. asst. to pres., dir. cmty. rels. Fairfield Cmtys., Little Rock, 1988—. Staff mem. Ark. Ho. of Reps., 1974-81; mem. exec. com. Nat. Vol. Health Agys. Ark., Little Rock, 1988—; vol. Ark. Cancer Rsch., 1988—, F.L.A.M.E. Stewpot for the Homeless, 1980—, Alter Soc.-Cathedral of St. Andrew, 1980—; bd. dirs. United Way. Named Woman of Yr., North Little Rock C. of C., 1975, Ark. Outstanding Young Woman, 1976; recipient Outstanding Svc. to Youth award Mayor of North Little Rock, 1995. Mem. Ju. League of Little Rock (bd. dirs., chmn. 1994-95, Mem. of Yr. 1995). Roman Catholic.

FERGUSON, SUSAN KATHARINE STOVER, nurse, psychotherapist, consultant; b. Warsaw, Ind., Mar. 11, 1944; d. Robert Eugene and Barbara Louise (Swaney) Stover; m. Philip Charles Ferguson, Oct. 2, 1965 (div.); children: Scott Duane, Shawn Alaine, Erin Kirsten. Diploma in nursing, Meth. Hosp., 1966; BA in Psychology, Purdue U., 1988; MSW, Smith Coll., 1991; advanced cert. in Psychoanalytic Psychotherapy, Psychoanalytic Psychotheraphy Ctr., 1993-94. Staff nurse, health hazard appraiser Meth. Hosp. of Ind., Indpls., 1966-68; staff nurse USPHS, Bethel, Alaska, 1968-70; instr. childbirth preparation Wabash, Ind., 1973-83; nurse Family Physicians Associated, Wabash, 1976-83; rsch. asst. Purdue U., Ft. Wayne, Ind., 1986-88; staff nurse, self-awareness seminar coord. Charter Beacon Hosp., Ft. Wayne, Ind., 1988-89; intern clin. social work Clifford Beers Guidance Ctr., New Haven, Conn., 1990-91; psychiat. nurse Yale-New Haven Hosp., 1990-91; pvt. practice Citadel Psychiat. Clinic, Ft. Wayne, Ind., 1991-93; dir. social svcs. Charter Northridge Behavioral Health sys., Raleigh, N.C., 1993-94; dir. social svcs., clinician adult psychiatry Charter Northridge Hosp., Raleigh, 1993-94; pvt. practice Raleigh, 1993—. Bd. dirs. Hoosiers for Safety Belts, Indpls., 1987-88, Ind. Med. Pol. Action Com., Indpls., 1986-87; coordinator, founder Safe Start Infant Safety Seat Loan Program, Wabash, 1981-87; participant in leadership devel. com. Wabash County C. of C., 1983; workshop leader Wabash County Hosp. Stop Smoking Program, 1982-83. Mem. NASW (family rels. coun.), Charles F. Menniger Soc., N.C. Psychoanalytic Soc., Kappa Kappa Kappa. Republican. Office: Atlantic Behavioral Health Systems Inc 2501 Atrium Dr Ste 400 Raleigh NC 27607

FERGUSON, TAMARA, clinical sociologist; b. The Hague, Netherlands; came to U.S., 1955; d. Simon and Sonia (Pokrowska) Van den Bergh; m. John D.A. Ferguson, Sept. 12, 1958. MA in Sociology, Columbia U., 1962, PhD, 1970. Asst. prof. U. Detroit, 1960-71; asst. prof., then assoc. prof. U. Windsor, Ont., Can., 1971-78; adj. assoc. prof. sociology Wayne State U. Med. Sch., Detroit, 1978—; assoc. med. staff dept. psychiatry Harper Hosp., Detroit, 1982—. Co-author: The Young Widow: Conflict and Guidelines, 1981; contbg. author: Clinical Sociology in Mental Health Setting, 1991, Qualitative Analysis in Human Sciences: New Perspectives in Methodology, 1996. 2d lt. Free French armed forces, 1944-45, ETO. Mem. Am. Sociol. Assn., Found. Thanatology, Sociol. Practice Assn. (bd. dirs.). Office: Harper Hosp Neuropsych Day Treatment Prog 50 E Canfield St Detroit MI 48201-1804

FERGUSON KENNEDY, BARBARA GEARHART BROWNELL, reporter; b. Essex, Conn., June 27, 1951; d. Edward John Joseph and Virginia (Gearhart) F.; m. Eugene Timothy Kennedy, June 1, 1993. AA, Colo. Women's Coll., 1971; BA, U. Minn., 1974; postgrad., Sorbonne U., 1975-77. Tech. rschr. UNESCO, Paris, 1980-82; mng. editor, co-owner Internat. Mideast Tourist & Bus. Mag., Paris, 1984-88; corr. Saudi Gazette Newspaper, Paris, 1987-88, London, 1988-90; bur. chief Saudi Gazette Newspaper, Washington, 1990—; spkr. in field. Contbr. articles to profl. jours. Lay minister All Souls Episcopal Ch., Washington, 1992—. Recipient Tihama Pub. Co. award for journalistic excellence, Jeddah, Saudi Arabia, 1988, Outstanding Support award U.S. Intelligence and Threat Analysis Ctr. Pentagon, 1990. Mem. Nat. Press Club, Overseas Writers Assn., Fgn. Corrs. Assn. (v.p. 1990—, bd. dirs.), Fgn. Press Assn. London, Assn. de la Presse Etrangere (bd. dirs. 1985-88), Women's Fgn. Policy Coun., Anglo-Am. Press Assn. Paris, Women's Fgn. Policy Group, DAR, Alpha Phi. Independent. Office: Saudi Gazette Newspaper 1145 National Press Building Washington DC 20045-2101

FERGUSSON, FRANCES DALY, college president, educator; b. Boston, Oct. 3, 1944; d. Francis Joseph and Alice (Storrow) Daly. BA, Wellesley Coll., 1965; MA, Harvard U., 1966, PhD, 1973. Asst. prof. Newton Coll., Mass., 1969-75; assoc. prof. U. Mass., Boston, 1974-82, asst. chancellor, 1980-82; provost, prof. Bucknell U., Lewisburg, Pa., 1982-86; pres. Vassar Coll., Poughkeepsie, N.Y., 1986—; bd. dirs. Marine Midland Bank, Ctrl. Hudson Gas and Electric Corp. Trustee Mayo Found., 1988—, Ford Found., 1989—, Historic Hudson, 1990—; bd. dirs. Historic Hudson Valley. Recipient Founder's award Soc. Archtl. Historians, 1973. Office: Vassar Coll Office of the Pres Raymond Ave Poughkeepsie NY 12603-2312

FERHOLT, J. DEBORAH LOTT, pediatrician; b. New Rochelle, N.Y., Aug. 27, 1942; d. Sidney and Rose (Rubin) Lott; m. Julian Ferholt, June 19, 1963; children: Beth, Sarah. BS in Biology, U. Rochester, 1963, MD, 1967. Diplomate Am. Bd. Pediatrics. From instr. to assoc. prof. Yale Sch. Nursing, New Haven, Conn., 1969-90, lectr., 1990—, clin. assoc. prof. pediatrics, 1987—; pvt. practice pediatrics New Haven, Conn., 1982—. Author: (book) Health Assessment of Children, 1980 (Best Pediatric Book award 1981). Fellow Am. Acad. Pediatrics (mem. com. daycare State of Conn.). Office: 303 Whitney Ave New Haven CT 06511-7204

FERKINGSTAD, SUSANNE M., cosmetics executive; b. Red Wing, Minn., Aug. 19, 1955; m. Steve Ferkingstad, Oct. 19, 1991. Diploma Cosmetology, Ritter St. Paul Coll., 1974; grad., Bruno's, 1978. Instr. Ritter's St. Paul Coll., 1974-75; asst. mgr., mgr. Scot Lewis Inc., Bloomington, Minn., 1975-79; edn. dir. My Kind of Place, St. Paul, 1979-80; pres., co-owner Someone's Looking (formerly Charpentier's Inc.), St. Paul, 1980-86, owner, 1986—; styles dir. women's sect. Minn. Cosmetology Edn. Com. Fundraiser, chairperson Battered Women's Shelter, St. Paul, 1984, Children's Home Soc., St. Paul, 1985; vol. St. Paul Food Shelves Food Dr., 1985, 88; vol., model United Arts Fashion Show, 1986; vol. fundraiser pub. TV Action Auction, Ronald McDonald House, Food Shelf Drives Someone's Looking, St. Paul, MS Walkathon, 1988. Recipient numerous hairstyling awards. Mem. Nat. Cosmetologists Assn., Minn. Hairdressers and Cosmetologists Assn., St. Paul Cosmetologists Assn. (dir. 1981-83, pres. 1983-85), Hair Am., Minn. Hair Fashion Com. Home: 3111 Drew Ave N Robbinsdale MN 55422-3247 Office: Someone's Looking Inc 141 4th St E Ste 125 Saint Paul MN 55101-1620

FERLITA, THERESA ANN, clinical social worker; b. Pinar del Rio, Cuba, Sept. 8, 1944; came to U.S., 1945; d. Sam Marion and Maria (Garcia-Collia) F. AB in Sociology, Spalding Coll., Louisville, 1966; MS in Social Work, U. Louisville, 1972. Lic. clin. social worker, Fla. Various positions, 1966-70; sr. resource program developer Children's Bd. Hillsborough County, Tampa, Fla., 1990-92; supr. homefinding unit Ky. Dept. Child Welfare, Louisville, 1972-73; foster care worker Fla. Dept. Health and Rehabilitative Svcs., Tampa, 1974; homemaker supr. Family Counseling Ctr., Clearwater, Fla., 1974; sr. social worker, mem. intake team London Borough of Newham Social Svcs., 1976; clin. social worker Alcoholism Svcs. Hillsborough Community Mental Health Ctr., Tampa, 1977-78; clin. social worker The Children's Home, Inc., Tampa, 1978-80; case coord., coord. tng. and edn., supr.

teen mother program The Child Abuse Coun., Inc., Tampa, 1980-90, clin. supr. Rainbow Family Learning Ctrs., 1989-90; pvt. practice family therapy, adults abused as children, 1991; social worker med.-surg. and trauma Tampa (Fla.) Gen. Hosp., 1992-95; mgr. family svcs. Hillsborough County Headstart Dept., Tampa, 1995—; adj. instr. Hillsborough C.C., Tampa, 1988; cons. The Spring Battered Spouse Shelter, Tampa, 1984; coord. Parents Anonymous Children's Group, Tampa, 1980-85; mem. state health adv. com. Redlands Christian Migrant Assn., Immokalee, Fla., 1982—; mem. policy coun. Hillsborough County Headstart, Tampa, 1986-89; mem. Cmty. Action Bd., Hillsborough County. Editor, compiler manuals for child abuse and neglect investigations, 1986, 87. Pres. Fair Oaks Condominium Assn., Tampa, 1990-91; past pres. Child Abuse Com., Fla., Inc.; bd. dirs., v.p. Centro Tampa, 1989-90. Mem. NASW (sec. Tampa Bay unit 1981-83, vice-chmn. 1990-91, Social Worker of Yr. award 1988, sec. Fla. chpt. 1986-88, del. assembly 1986-91), Acad. Cert. Social Workers, Nat. Network Social Work Mgrs. Democrat. Roman Catholic. Home: 3810 N Oak Dr Apt N-31 Tampa FL 33611-2574 Office: Hillsborough Co Headstart Dept County Ctr 801 E Kennedy Blvd Fl 13 Tampa FL 33602-4144

FERM, LOIS ROUGHAN, religious organization administrator; b. Buffalo, Feb. 5, 1918; d. Laurence Francis and Bertha Margaret Lucy (Jopp) R.; m. Robert O. Ferm, June 28, 1941 (dec. Mar. 1994); children: Lois Esther, Rebecca Ann, Paul Robert, Stephen John. BA, Houghton Coll., 1939; MA, U. Mich., 1955; PhD, U. Minn., 1972. Cert. tchr., N.Y. Tchr. Rushford (N.Y.) Cen. Sch., 1939-41; instr. library, sociology John Brown U., Siloam Springs, Ark., 1949-51; librarian Cuba (N.Y.) Cen. Schs., 1953-55; chmn. dept. edn. Houghton (N.Y.) Coll., 1955-57; instr. edn. U. Minn., Mpls., 1959-61, mgr. Coll. Edn. Library, 1961-64; personal asst. rsch., resource coord. Billy Graham Evangel. Assn., Mpls., 1973—. Pres. Riceville Property Owners Assn., Asheville, N.C., 1982, 83, 87, 88; active N.C. Arboretum Bd., 1992-96. Mem. Soc. Am. Archivists, Oral History Assn., Christian Women's Clubs, Pi Lambda Theta, Pi Alpha Theta. Republican. Baptist. Home: 27 Patriots Dr Asheville NC 28805-9730 Office: Billy Graham Evang Assn 1300 Harmon Pl Minneapolis MN 55403-1925

FERN, CAROLE LYNN, lawyer; b. Freeport, N.Y., Sept. 2, 1958; m. Tariq Rafique. BA, Johns Hopkins U., 1980; JD, Harvard U., 1983. Bar: N.Y. 1983, Calif. 1987. Assoc. Donovan, Leisure, Newton & Irvine, N.Y.C., 1983-87, Shearman & Sterling, N.Y.C., 1987-91, Berlack, Israels & Liberman, LLP, N.Y.C., 1991-92; ptnr. Berlack, Israels & Liberman, N.Y.C., 1993—. Dep. counsel Dukakis for Pres. Mem. N.Y.C. Bar Assn., Am. Arbitration Assn. (panel of arbitrators), N.Y. County Lawyers Assn. (Supreme Ct. com.), Phi Beta Kappa. Democrat. Unitarian. Office: Berlack Israels & Liberman 120 W 45th St New York NY 10036-4041

FERN, YVONNE, writer, producer; b. Honolulu, Dec. 30, 1947; m. Herbert F. Solow; children: Christopher, Richard. BA, St. Mary's U., Halifax, N.S., Can., 1976; postgrad., Mills Coll. English instr. U. Calif., Berkeley, 1981-91, Mills Coll., Oakland, Calif., 1990-91; writing advisor to orgns.; spkr., lectr. in field. Author: Gene Roddenberry: The Last Conversation, The Star Trek Sketch Book. Mem. PEN, U. Calif. Women's Faculty Club, The Arts Club. Office: Solow Two PO Box 6504 Malibu CA 90264

FERNÁNDEZ, ANA M., rheumatologist; b. Rio Piedras, P.R., 1962; d. Manuel and Isis F. ; m. John Joseph; children: John Alexander, Chrisana. BA, U. Pa., 84; MD, U. P.R., 88. Diplomate Am. Bd. Internal Medicine, Am. Bd. Rheumatology. Rheumatologist Duluth Clinic, Minn., 1993—. Mem. AMA, Am. Coll. Rheumatology. Office: The Duluth Clinic 400 E Third St Duluth MN 55805

FERNANDEZ, EUGENIA, information systems educator; b. Bklyn., Aug. 29, 1957; d. José M. and Alma Mark M. BSME, Worcester Poly. Inst., 1979; MSE in Computer, Info. Control Engring., U. Mich., 1984; PhD in Mgmt. Info. Sys., Purdue U., 1988. Fire protection engr. Kemper Group, Southfield, Mich., 1979-82; grad. instr. Sch. Engring U. Mich., Ann Arbor, 1982-83; grad. instr. Krannert Grad. Sch. Mgmt., Purdue U., West Lafayette, Ind., 1985-86; asst. prof. Coll. William and Mary, Williamsburg, Va., 1987-90, Butler U., Indpls., 1990-94; asst. prof. info. sys. Pa. State U., Harrisburg, 1994—. Contbr. articles to profl. jours. Dir. Chisel Run Homeowners Assn., Williamsburg, 1988-90. IBM Doctoral fellow, 1983-84, GE Found. fellow, 1984-85, ICIS Doctoral fellow, 1985. Mem. Assn. for Computing Machinery, Internat. Assn. for Computer Info. sys., Beta Gamma Sigma. Office: Pa State Harrisburg Sch Bus Adminstrn 777 W Harrisburg Pike Middletown PA 17057-4846

FERNANDEZ, IRMA BECERRA, electrical engineer, researcher, educator; b. Havana, Cuba, Mar. 28, 1960; came to U.S., 1960; d. Daniel Ivan Becerra and Irma Maria Peiteado; m. Vicente L. Fernandez, June 29, 1985; children: Anthony John, Nicole Marie. BSEE, U. Miami, Coral Gables, Fla., 1982, MSEE, 1986; PhD in Elec. Engring., Fla. Internat. U., Miami, 1994. Cert. engr. in tng., Fla., 1982. Engr., corp. instr. Fla. Power and Light, Miami, 1983-90; rsch. assoc., adj. prof. Fla. Internat. U., Miami, 1990-94; dir. So. Tech. Application Ctr. Fla. Internat. U., 1994-96, dir. engring. mgmt. Coll. Engring. and Design, 1996—. Dir. Hands in Action, Miami, 1996. Scholar Nat. Hispanic Scholarship Fund, Miami, 1982, Unico Nat. Soc., Miami, 1978. Mem. IEEE, Assn. Cuban Engrs. (v.p. 1994-96, pres. 1996, Student of Yr. 1993), Soc. Women Engrs., Eta Kappa Nu (v.p. 1981-82, Most Valuable Mem. 1982), Tau Beta Pi, Phi Kappa Phi. Roman Catholic.

FERNANDEZ, ISABEL LIDIA, human resources specialist; b. Miami, Fla., Jan. 23, 1964; d. Rafael Juvencio and Lidia Rafaela (Morin) Fernandez. BBA, Fla. Internat. U., Miami, 1984, MS in Hospitality Mgmt., 1990. Personnel cons. Miami, 1984—; asst. dir. human resources Turnberry Isle Yacht & Country Club, Miami, 1985-87; dir. personnel Sheraton River House, Miami, 1987-88; program dir. hospitality mgmt. programs Miami-Dade Community Coll., 1988-89; dir. human resources Doubletree Hotel, Miami, 1989-91, Sky Chefs, Miami, 1991-93; tng. cons. Barnett Banks Inc., Miami, 1993—. Editor newspaper The Sunblazer, 1983-84; contbr. articles to profl. jours. Founder South Fla. Diversity Coun. Named Employee of the Month, Coconut Grove Hotel, Miami, 1985. Mem. NAFE, Am. Hotel and Motel Assn. (pres. Greater Miami chpt.), Young Reps. Club (pub. rels. com.). Republican. Lutheran. Home: 8510 NW 3rd Ln # 501 Miami FL 33126-3857

FERNANDEZ, LILLIAN, broadcast executive. Grad., Pa. Law Sch. Civil rights atty EEOC; staff dir., chief counsel subcom. on postal ops. and svcs. U.S. Ho. of Reps., dir. Congl. Hispanic Caucus, Inc.; dir. internat. affairs Pfizer, Inc.; spl. asst. to Pres. Clinton for legis. affairs Washington; sr. v.p. Hill & Knowlton; sr. v.p. govt. rels., gen. counsel, corp. sec. Corp. for Pub. Broadcasting, Washington; apptd. bd. mem. N.Y. State Job Tng. Partnership Coun., Bklyn. Navy Yard Devel. Corp. Co-chair N.Y.C. fundraiser for Bill Clinton, 1992; mem. N.Y. Electoral Coll. Clinton-Gore; candidate N.Y. State Senate, 1992; contbr., fundraiser and campaigner Dem. Party. Named one of the 100 Influential, Hispanic Bus. Mag. Office: Corp for Public Broadcasting 901 E St NW Washington DC 20047-2037

FERNANDEZ, LINDA FLAWN, entrepreneur, social worker; b. Tampa, Fla., Sept. 14, 1943; d. Frank and Rose (D'Amico) F.; 1 child, Marci. B.S., U. South Fla., 1965; M.S., U. Nev., 1976. Social worker Hillsborough County, Tampa, Fla., 1965-67; parole officer adult div. Fla. Parole Commn., Tampa, 1967-69; dir. social services Sunrise Hosp., Las Vegas, Nev., 1969-78; ind. real estate investor, Fla. and Nev., 1965—; pres. Las Vegas Color Separations, Inc., 1978—, Las Vegas Typesetting, Inc., 1983—; LMR Enterprises, Inc., Las Vegas, 1984—; sec.-treas. Sierra Color Graphics, Inc., Las Vegas, 1983—. Founder, organizer Human Relations, pet mascots for elderly; team ofcl. girls' softball, 1985; mem. Clark County Citizens Com. Efficiency and Cost Reduction, 1991; vice-chmn. Citizens Com. Efficiency and Cost Reduction, 1992. Recipient numerous awards Ad Club Fedn. Mem. Las Vegas C. of C. (congl. com.) Women's Las Vegas C. of C., Ad Club Fedn., Citizens for Pvt. Enterprise, U.S. C. of C. Avocations: tennis; water skiing. Office: 3351 S Highland Dr Ste 210 Las Vegas NV 89109-3430

FERNANDEZ, LISA, softball player. Student, UCLA. Recipient Gold medal Pan Am. Games, 1991, ISF Women's World CHampionship, 1990, 94, Women's World Challenger Cup, 1992, Intercontinental Cup, 1993, South Pacific Classic, 1994, Superball Classic, 1995, Atlanta Olympics, 1996, Honda award, 1991-93; named All-Am. Amateur Softball Assn., Sports Woman of Yr., 1991-92. Office: Amateur Softball Assn 2801 NE 50th St Oklahoma City OK 73111-7203*

FERNANDEZ, MARY JOE, professional tennis player; b. Dominican Republic, Aug. 19, 1971; d. Jose and Sylvia F. 3rd ranked woman USTA; winner women's doubles (with Patty Fendick) Australia Open, 1991; gold medalist women's doubles Olympic Games, Barcelona, Spain, 1992, Atlanta, 1996. Ranked # 8 World Tennis Assn. Tour, 1995, # 1 USA Women, 1995. *

FERNANDEZ, NANCY PAGE, history educator; b. Woodland, Calif., Feb. 10, 1957; d. Albert Lee and Shirley Lucille (Jessmore) P.; m. Raul Arnulfo Fernandez, Mar. 16, 1984. BA in Am. Studies, Stanford U., 1979; MA in Comparative Cultures, U. Calif., Irvine, 1983, PhD in Comparative Cultures, 1987. Lectr., social scis. U. Calif., Irvine, 1987-89; vis. lectr., Am. Civilization Brown U., Providence, 1989-90; asst. prof. history Calif. State U. Northridge, 1990-94, assoc. prof. history, 1995—; steering com. Huntington Libr. Women's Studies seminar, San Marino, Calif., 1992—, chair 1995—; proposal referee NEH, 1993, 96. Contbr. articles and revs. to profl. jours. Adv. com. Historic Preservation, Monrovia, Calif., 1992-94; docent, Monrovia Old House Preservation Group, 1990—. Hagley grantee, 1993; Winterthur Libr. fellow, 1993. Mem. Am. Studies Assn., Orgn. Am. Historians, Western Assn. Women Historians (nominating com. 1993, conf. local arrangements chair 1991-92), Costume Soc. of Am., Pasadena Pro Musica, Phi Kappa Phi. Office: CSU Northridge Dept History 18111 Nordhoff St Northridge CA 91330-8250

FERNANDEZ-POL, BLANCA DORA, psychiatrist, researcher; b. Buenos Aires, Mar. 5, 1932; came to U.S., 1967; d. Balbino Fernandez and Maria Remedios van Pol. MD, U. Buenos Aires, 1958. Diplomate Am. Bd. Psychiatry and Neurology. Intern N.Y. Polyclinic Med. Sch., 1967-68; resident in psychiatry UCLA/Brentwood Hosp., 1968-69, NYU/Bellevue Hosp., 1969-71; gen. practitioner Hosp. Espanol, Buenos Aires, 1959-62; forensic psychiatrist Criminoloy Inst., Buenos Aires, 1963-65; clin. attending psychiatrist Bellevue Psychiat. Hosp., N.Y.C., 1971-75; pvt. practice St. Petersburg, Fla., 1976-78; chief psychiat. svcs. USAF Hosp. Yokota, Tokyo, 1980, USAF Hosp., Homestead, Fla., 1981; chief continuing treatment program dept. psychiatry Bronx-Lebanon Hosp., Bronx, 1983—; prof. psychology U. Moran, Buenos Aires, 1962-67; asst. prof. psychiatry N.Y. Med. Coll., N.Y.C., 1972-74; clin. asst. prof. psychiatry Albert Einstein Coll. Medicine, Bronx, 1982—. Contbr. articles to profl. jours. Maj. USAF, 1978-81. Mem. Am. Psychiat. Assn., N.Y. Acad. Scis., Am. Acad. Psychiatrists in Alcoholism and Addictions, Res. Officers Assn. U.S., Assn. Mil. Surgeons U.S. Home: PO Box 21644 Brooklyn NY 11202-1644 Office: Bronx Lebanon Hosp 1285 Fulton Ave Bronx NY 10456-3401

FERNSTROM, DOROTHY BOND, former psychology educator; b. Dedham, Mass., Sept. 2; d. William Holden and Delia Henrietta (Hansen) Bond; m. Karl Dickson Fernstrom, May 1945 (dec. 1959); children: John Dickson, Henning II. A.B., Adelphi U., 1953; M.A., U. Houston, 1965; Ph.D., Nova U., 1976. Real estate salesman George Jarvis Co., Houston, 1955-58; counselor Houston Pub. Schs., 1958-67; asst. prof. edn., dean women C.W. Post Coll., Greenvale, LI., N.Y., 1967-71; prof. psychology Okaloosa-Walton Jr. Coll., Niceville, Fla., 1971-90. Bd. dirs. Okaloosa Community Concert, Niceville, 1973-93, chmn. publicity, 1981-85; chmn. publicity Okaloosa Symphony League, Ft. Walton Beach, Fla., 1983-84, bd. dirs., 1990-93; precinct chmn. Republican Party, Okaloosa County, Fla., 1972—; sec. Mattie M. Kelly Ctr. for Arts, 1981-84, pres., 1984-85; pres. N.W. Fla. Symphony Guild, 1988-90. Served to maj. USMCR, 1943-46. Mem. AAUW (chmn. advocacy 1981-85), LWV (bd. dirs.), Mental Health Assn. (bd. dirs.), Phi Delta Kappa, Delta Kappa Gamma. Episcopalian. Club: Ft. Walton Yacht. Avocations: tennis, extensive foreign travel, swimming, reading, music. Home: 928 Bay Shore Dr PO Box 95 Niceville FL 32578

FERRANTE, OLIVIA ANN, retired educator, consultant; b. Revere, Mass., Nov. 9, 1948; d. Guy and Mary Carmella (Prizio) F. BA, Regis Coll., 1970; MEd, Boston Coll., 1971, postgrad., 1977-81; postgrad., Middlebury Coll., 1974, Lesley Coll., 1982. Cert. history tchr., tchr. of blind. Chmn. Braille dept. Nat. Braille Press, Boston, 1971-74; tchr. of visually impaired, spl. needs dept. Revere High Sch., 1974-92; mem. Steven J. Rich scholarship com., 1993—; cons. Revere PTA, 1984—. Contbr. articles to profl. jours. Vol. Morgan Meml., Boston, 1983—, tchr. braille, 1993—, tchr. literacy program, 1993—; mem. Revere Com. for Handicapped Affairs, 1985—, Everett (Mass.) Chorus, 1974-76, Adult Music Ministry, 1989, Revere First Com., 1993, publicist; soloist Revere Music Makers, 1977-79; mem. partnership com. Internat. Year Disabled, 1980-81; mem. adult choir Immaculate Conception Ch., 1966—, lectr., 1995—; publicist Revere Commn. on Disabilities, 1985—, Revere Hist. Commn., 1996—, Cath. Daus., SHARE, 1995—, A Woman's Concern, 1996; mem. adv. bd. Mass. Commn. of Blind, 1988—, governing bd. on ind. living, 1989; access monitor Mass. Orgn. on Disability, 1988—; mem. adv. bd. Radio Reading Svc. for Blind, 1989; mentor Nat. Braille Literacy Project, 1992, Braille Lib., 1995—; mem. Friends of the Sick Children's Trust, 1992; vol. Birthright, 1992, ProLife Office, 1992; active Arts Coun. Coop, 1992—; mentor Vision Found., 1993—; friend Wang Ctr., 1993—, Boston Pub. Garden and Common, 1993—, Boston Pops, 1992—; mem. mobility adv. bd. Mass. Com. for Blind, 1994—; mem. Historic Mass., 1994—, Cath. League, 1994—; friend Paul Revere House, 1994—; mem. Peregrine Fund, 1994—, Ctr. for Marine Preservation, 1994—; sponsor Rite of Cath. Initiation for Adults, 1995—. Mem. NEA, Internat. Soc. for Endangered Cats, Mass. Tchrs. Assn. Revere Tchrs. Assn., Nat. Space Soc., Nat. Cath. Assn. for Persons with Visual Impairment, Cath. Daus. of Am. (publicist), Friends of Revere Pub. Libr., Friends of Librs. for Blind, Friends of Boston Symphony Orch., Nat. Writers Union, Amnesty Internat., Soc. Creative Anachronism, Women Affirming Life, Michael Crawford Internat. Fan Assn., Revere Soc. for Cultural and Hist. Preservation (publicist, life mem.), Chelsea Hist. Soc., Mass. Aviation Hist. Soc., Brian Boitano Fan Club. Democrat. Roman Catholic. Home: 115 Reservoir Ave Revere MA 02151-5825 Office: Revere High Sch Spl Needs Dept 101 School St Revere MA 02151-3001

FERRARA, RAMONA SHINN, computer engineer, consultant; b. Hancock, Mich., Apr. 15, 1962; d. Raymond James and Thelma Jean (Waldrop) Shinn; m. Anthony Frank Ferrara, Sept. 14, 1985; 1 child, Zakary Alexander. BA in Computer Sci., Ariz. State U., 1984. Database programmer Intel, Chandler, Ariz., 1982-83; sys. programmer Garrett Turbine Engine Co., Phoenix, 1983-85; mem. tech. staff Rockwell Internat., Downey, Calif., 1985-87, GTE Comms. Corp., Phoenix, 1987-89; sys. engr., industry cons. Teradata (now divsn. of AT&T), Phoenix, 1989-94; dir. ops., sr. cons. Sage Comms., Phoenix, 1994—. USAF Acad. scholar, 1980.

FERRARI, LINDA JOY, nurse; b. Wausau, Wis., Aug. 28, 1960; d. Joel Darwin and Sharron (Junghans) Walter; m. Louis A. Ferrari Jr., Oct. 28, 1989; 1 child, Louis A. III. ADN, Rochester (Minn.) C.C., 1982. Cert. BLS, ACLS, CCRN, Wis. RN Theda Clark Regional Med. Ctr., Neenah, Wis., 1982-88; RN Door County Meml. Hosp., Sturgeon Bay, Wis., 1988—, supr., 1992-95; supr. Dorchester Nursing Ctr., 1989—; staff nurse Baylake Outpatient Surgery Ctr., 1994—; entrepreneur LJ Mktg. and Promotions, 1996—; entrepreneur L.J. Mktg. and Promotions, 1996—.

FERRARI, NANCY, counselor; b. Long Branch, N.J., Sept. 29, 1946; d. Edward Anthony Jr. and Muriel Lois (Walling) F.; children: Jofie, Scott. BS in Spanish, Rosary Hill Coll., 1970; MS, W.Va. U., 1973. Nat. cert. counselor. Counselor Waynesburg (Pa.) Coll., 1981—, dept. chair, 1992-95, dir. counseling, 1993—, dir. Act 101, 1995—. Pres. MADD, Greene County, 1996—; bd. dirs. United Way, Southwestern Pa., 1994—; sec. WAM Investment Club, Waynesburg, 1995—. Named Outstanding Acad. Adviser, Nat. Acad. Advising Assn., 1993. Mem. ACA, Nat. Assn. Women in Edn. Democrat. Home: 341 Park Ave Waynesburg PA 15370 Office: Waynesburg Coll Waynesburg PA 15370

FERRARI-ROWLEY, SUSAN, artist, educator; b. Oceanside, N.Y., Aug. 28, 1950; d. Frank and Josephine (Pacelli) Ferrari; m. Michael E. Rowley, Feb. 12, 1972. BA, SUNY, Buffalo, 1972; MS in Tchg., Rochester Inst. Tech., 1976, MFA, 1981. Cert. art tchr., N.Y. Asst. prof. art Nazareth Coll. of Rochester, Rochester, N.Y., 1976-87; art tchr. Rochester (N.Y.) City Schs., 1987-91; vis. asst. prof. Rochester Inst. Tech., 1992-95; guest lectr. SUNY, Geneseo, 1992, Meml. Art Gallery Mus., Rochester, 1995, Chesterwood, Stockbridge, Mass., 1995. One-woman exhbns. include Genessee Cmty. Coll., Batavia, N.Y., 1992, Roberts Wesleyan Coll., Rochester, N.Y., 1991, SUNY Geneseo, 1990; group exhbns. include, among others, N.J. Ctr. for Visual Arts, 1994, Maubeuge Fine Arts Mus., France, 1992, Pitts. Ctr. for the Arts, 1989 (Meml. award for originality), Internat. Art Competition, N.Y.C., 1988 (cert. of excellence for outstanding achievement), Art Connections, Bethesda, Md., 1990, Wells Coll., Aurora, N.Y., 1990, Admas Meml. Gallery, Dunkirk, N.Y., 1990, Fota Gallery, Alexandria, Va., 1990, 55 Mercer St. Gallery, N.Y.C., 1991, Highland Park Outdoor Sculpture Exhbn., Rochester, 1991, No. Am. Sculpture Exhbn., Golden, Colo., 1992, Alexandria (Va.) Mus. Art, 1991, BASF Exhbn., Dalton, Ga., 1992, Ward-Nasse Gallery, N.Y.C., 1993, Cooperstown (N.Y.) Art Assn. Nat. Exhbn., 1993, Art Assn. of Harrisburg, Pa. 66th Juried Exhbn., 1994 (1st prize for sculpture),Meml. Art Gallery, Rochester, 1995, many others; major commns. include Gordon Black Inc. (office lobby), Rochester, 1984, Citibank Inc. (atrium), Bushnells Basin, N.Y., 1986, Kirstein Bldg. (atrium), Rochester, 1986, Kings Park Office Bldg. (entry hall), Rochester, 1987, United Ch. of Christ (reception area), Rochester, 1988, The Falls Bldg. (atrium/entry), Memphis, 1989, Genessee C.C., Albion, N.Y., Whyoming (N.Y. County Mental Health Clinic, 1994, Rochester (N.Y.) Internat. Airport (parking garage atrium), 1995; subject of PBS documentary The Artist and Her Works, 1986. Mem. Wheatland Tax Reform Party, 1993—, chair, 1996. Recipient First Sculpture prize Frank Gettings: Hirschorn Mus., 1994, Kraus Sikes Publishers award, N.Y.C., 1990, Ida Abrams Louis Meml. award, 1982 Finger Lakes Exhbn., Meml. Gallery, Rochester, and others. Mem. Internat. Sculpture Ctr. Home: 3892 North Rd Churchville NY 14428

FERRARO, BETTY ANN, corporate administrator, state senator; b. Newport, Vt., Mar. 3, 1925; d. Clarence John and Mauretta Rowena (Potter) Morse; m. Dominic Thomas Ferraro, Oct. 8, 1964; children: Deborah, David, Susan, Barbara. Student, Mary Hitchcock Hosp. Sch. Nursing, Coll. St. Joseph, Rutland, Vt. Exec. sec. to asst. treas. Ctrl. Vt. Pub. Svc. Corp., Rutland, 1943-44; sec. to dean N.Y. Med. Coll., N.Y.C., 1944-46; model G. Fox Co., Hartford, Conn., 1947; corp. sec., office mgr. John Russell Corp., Rutland, 1970-80; exec. dir. Rutland Area Coordinated Child Care Com., Washington, 1977-79; adminstrv. asst. Hilinex of Vt., Rutland, 1981-83; owner Classic Connection Gift Shop, Rutland, 1983-87; adminstr. Vicon Recovery Sys., Inc., Rutland, 1987-90; owner, operator nursery sch., 1973-77; mgr. Day Care Ctr., 1978-80; alderman City of Rutland, 1984-86; resource dir. Rutland City, Vt. Emergency Mgmt. Team for State of Vt., 1984-90; mem. Cmty. Devel. Commn., 1986; lectr. St. Peter's Parish, Rutland; office mgr. Circle Eye Cons. Chmn. Rutland City Rep. Com., 1991-93; state committeewoman State Rep. Com., 1991—, rep.; rep. Rutland County Rep. Com.; state del. Rep. Nat. Conv., 1992; Mem. Vt. Ho. Reps., 1990-92; mem. Vt. Senate, 1992-94, 95-97; mem. jud. nominating bd. Human Resource Investment Coun., Vt. Student Assistance Corp. Bd.; mem. Amtrack Study Commn., 1995-96; bd. dirs. Coll. St. Joseph, 1996—. Fleming Inst. fellow, 1995. Mem. Nat. Assn. Women in Constrn. (chartered, past pres.), Rutland County Rep. Women (founder). Republican. Roman Catholic. Home and Office: Condo 17 155 Dorr Dr Rutland VT 05701-3811

FERRARO, GERALDINE ANNE, lawyer, former congresswoman; b. Newburgh, N.Y., Aug. 26, 1935; d. Dominick and Antonetta L. (Corrieri) F.; m. John Zaccaro, 1960; children: Donna, John, Laura. B.A., Marymount Manhattan Coll., 1956, hon. degree, 1982; J.D., Fordham U., 1960; postgrad., N.Y. U. Law Sch., 1978, hon. degree, 1984; hon. degree, Hunter Coll., 1985, Plattsburgh Coll., 1985, Coll. Boca Raton, 1989, Va. State U., 1989, Muhlenberg Coll., 1990, Briarcliffe Coll. for Bus., 1990, Potsdam Coll., 1991. Bar: N.Y. 1961, U.S. Supreme Ct. 1978. Pvt. practice, N.Y.C., 1961-74; asst. dist. atty. Queens County, N.Y., 1974-78; chief spl. victims bur., 1977-78; mem. 96th-98th Congresses from 9th N.Y. Dist.; sec. House Democratic Caucus; first woman vice presdl. nominee on Democratic ticket, 1984; fellow Harvard Inst. of Politics, Cambridge, Mass., 1988; mng. ptnr. Keck Mahin Cate & Koether, N.Y., 1993-94; appointed Amb. to UN Human Rights Commn., 1994, 95; guest moderator CNN TV program Crossfire. Author: Ferraro, My Story, 1985, Changing History: Women, Power, and Politics, 1993. Chmn. Dem. Platform Com., 1984; bd. dirs. N.Y. Easter Seal Soc.; Dem. candidate U.S. Senate, 1992; U.S. President Clinton's appointee to UN Human Rights Commn. Conf., Geneva, 1993, World Conf., Vienna, Austria, 1993, 4th World Conf. on Women, 1995. Mem. Queens County Bar Assn., Queens County Women's Bar Assn. (past pres.), Nat. Dem. Inst. for International. Affairs (bd. dirs.), Coun. Fgn. Rels., Internat. Inst. Women's Polit. Leadership (former pres.). Roman Catholic. *

FERREE, CAROLYN RUTH, radiation oncologist, educator; b. Liberty, N.C., Jan. 29, 1944; d. Numer Floyd and Mary Isabel (Glass) Black; m. Bill K. Ferree, Aug. 17, 1968 (div. 1980). BA, U. N.C., Greensboro, 1966; MD, Bowman Gray Coll., Winston-Salem, 1970. Diplomate Am. Bd. Radiation Oncology. Intern medicine N.C. Bapt. Hosp., Winston-Salem, 1970-71, resident in radiation oncology, 1971-74; instr. radiation oncology Bowman Gray Sch. Medicine, Winston-Salem, 1974-75, asst. prof., 1975-80, assoc. prof., 1980-87, prof., 1987—. Contbr. articles to profl. jours. Mem., v.p. County Bd. of Pub. Health, Winston-Salem, 1985-92; bd. dirs. U. N.C.-Greensboro Excellence Found., 1988—; med. dir. Forsyth County chpt. Am. Cancer Soc., 1975—. Fellow Am. Coll. Radiology; mem. AMA (N.C. del. to AMA), Pediat. Oncology Group (radiotherapy coord.), N.C. Med. Soc. (2d v.p. 1990-91, sec.-treas. 1991-95, pres.-elect 1996), Am. Soc. Therapeutic Radiologists Orgn. Office: Bowman Gray Sch Medicine Med Center Blvd Winston Salem NC 27157

FERRELL, CONCHATA GALEN, actress, acting teacher and coach; b. Charleston, W.Va., Mar. 28, 1943; d. Luther Martin and Mescal Loraine (George) F.; m. Arnold A. Anderson; 1 dau., Samantha. Student, W.Va. U., 1961-64, Marshall U., 1967-68. N.Y. theater appearances The Hot L Baltimore, 1973, The Sea Horse, 1973-74 (OBIE award and Drama Desk award 1974), Battle of Angels, 1975; appeared in: Los Angeles plays Getting Out, 1978, Here Wait, 1980, Picnic, 1986; appeared in TV series: The Hot L Baltimore, 1975, B.J. and the Bear, 1979, McClain's Law, 1981, E.R., 1984, A Peaceable Kingdom, 1989, L.A. Law, 1991, Hearts Afire, 1993-94, Townies, 1996; appeared in movies: Network, 1975, Dangerous Hero, 1975, Heartland, 1981, Where the River Runs Black, 1986, For Keeps,1987, Mystic Pizza, 1987, Witches of Eastwick, 1987, Chains of Gold, 1990, Edward Sissorhands, 1990, Family Prayers, 1993, True Romance, 1993, Samurai Cowboy, 1993, Heaven and Earth, 1993, Freeway, 1995, Touch, 1996, My Fellow Americans, 1996; appeared in TV movies: A Girl Called Hatter Fox, 1977, A Death in Canaan, 1977, The Orchard Children, 1978, Before and After, 1979, Bliss, 1979, Reunion, 1980, The Rideout Case, 1980, The Great Gilley Hopkins, 1981, Life of the Party, 1982, Emergency Room, 1983, Nadia, 1984, Miss Lonely Hearts, 1985, Samaritan, 1986, Northbeach and Rawhide, 1986, Picnic, 1986, Eye on the Sparrow, 1987, Runaway Ralph, 1987, Goodbye Miss Liberty (Disney Channel), 1988, Running Mates, 1990, Deadly Intentions, Again, 1990, Back Field in Motion, 1991, 120 Volt Miracle, 1992, Forget Me Not, 1996, Sweetdreams, 1996. Recipient Wrangler award Nat. Cowboy Hall of Fame, 1981, Most Promising Newcomer award Theatre World, 1974, Emmy award nomination, 1991-92. Mem. AFTRA, ACLU, NOW, Actors Equity Assn., Screen Actors Guild, Women in Films. Democrat. Office: Paradigm 10100 Santa Monica Blvd Los Angeles CA 90067-4003

FERRELL, DARLA KAY, mental health counselor; b. Rockford, Ill., Oct. 27, 1967; d. Donald Darwin and Peggy Lou (Swenson) Grenke; m. Jeffrey Scott Ferrell, Dec. 31, 1993. BA, Augustana Coll., 1989; MS in Edn., U. Miami, 1992. Cmty. case mgr. Pioneer Ctr., Woodstock, Ill., 1989-90; therapeutic program coord. Fairview Plz., Rockford, Ill., 1992-95; program leader crisis program Decatur (Ill.) Mental Health Ctr., 1995; program mgr. Friendship House, Scranton, Pa., 1995—. Author: (poem) All Alone, 1991; composer (for quartet) Tears, 1987, (clarinet and oboe duet) Ode to Lord Culver, 1986, (for French horn and flute duet) Shadows, 1991 (flute solo with piano accompanist) Dreams, 1993. Mem. ACA. Lutheran. Home: Summit by the Lake 404 Woodside Manor Scranton PA 18505 Office: Friendship House Scranton PA 18505

FERRELL, PAULA MARIE, artist; b. Bristol, Conn., Apr. 20, 1963; d. Andrew C. and Eleanor M. (Musinski) Saturno; m. William Clark Ferrell, July 16, 1993; 1 child, Andrew Clark. Legal asst. program cert., Morse Sch. Bus., Hartford, Conn., 1991; student, Southampton (N.Y.) Coll., 1980-82. Cert. paralegal. Med. sec. Branford (Conn.) Pediatrics, 1988-89; account exec. Impressions Photography, Chester, Conn., 1988-90; paralegal Shluger & Shluger, Hartford, 1990-91; sr. paralegal Gansinger, Hinshaw & Buckley, L.A., 1991-92; legal sec., personalsec. Joseph Lorenzo, Esquire, Hartford, 1992-93; personal sec. Equitable, Atlanta, 1994; art tchr. Gibbes Mus. Art., Charleston, S.C., 1995—; tchr., docent High Mus. Art, Atlanta, 1994—. One-woman show Reflections of the Sea, 1995, Soho Art Dist., N.Y.C., 1996. Lead organizer Dem. Vols., Bristol, Conn., 1992. With CAP, 1976-77.

FERREN, EMILY HOLCHIN, public library director, consultant; b. Cleve., Mar. 30, 1949; d. Frank John and Emilie (Benko) Holchin; m. Bert James Ferren, May 27, 1989. BSE, Baldwin-Wallace Coll., 1971; MS in L.S., Case Western Res. U., 1973; LD/BD, U. Notre Dame, 1977. Tchr. 6th grade Cleve. Pub. Schs., 1971-72; head libr. Griswold Inst., 1972-73; head, children's room Lakewood (Ohio) Pub. Libr., 1973-76, Cuyahoga County Pub. Libr., 1976-81; libr. for physically impaired Queens Borough Pub. Libr., 1982-85; surp. outreach svcs. Lorain (Ohio) Pub. Libr., 1985-87; extension svcs. coord. Carroll County Pub. Libr., Westminster, Md., 1987-93; dir. Ruth Enlow Libr. of Garrett County, Oakland, Md., 1993—; adj. instr. Garrett C.C., 1995—; cons. Ams. with Disabilities Compliance. Book reviewer Libr. Jour. Sec. Children's Coun., Carroll County; bd. dirs., chair Literacy Providers of Carroll County; mem. adv. bd. Alternative Programs, Carroll County Bd. Edn. Recipient Winifred Fischer award N.Y. Adult Edn. Coun., 1983; grantee Bell Atlantic/ALA, 1992-93, Southland Corp., 1990, 92, Md. Assn. for Adult, Community and Continuing Literacy Edn., 1991. Mem. ALA (Caldecott com. 1984, exec. bd. Libr. Svcs. to the Deaf 1983, chair Libr. Svcs. to Deaf Forum), Quota Internat. (pres. Balt. chpt. 1990-92), lt. gov. Dist. 10), others. Lutheran. Office: Ruth Enlow Libr Garrett Co 6 N 2nd St Oakland MD 21550-1393

FERRER, MARIAN ANN, artist, art educator; b. South Bend, Ind., Oct. 18, 1942; d. Nathan and Esther Rosenfeld; divorced; children: Shawn, Mikka. BA, Univ. Mich., 1965. Tchr. Open Ctr., N.Y.; founder, tchr. Dobbs Ferry (N.Y.) Pottery, 1972—; tchr. Mercy Coll., N.Y., Elizabeth Seton Coll., N.Y. Author: Blue Sapphire, 1996; exhibited in numerous one-woman shows and group shows. Home: 191 N Broadway Dobbs Ferry NY 10522 Office: Dobbs Ferry Pottery 86 Main St Dobbs Ferry NY 10522

FERREY-LAUGHON, BARBARA ELOYCE, journalist, newspaper editor; b. Bishop, Calif., Oct. 28, 1964; d. Robert Hayes and Sandra Lee (Jensen) F.; m. Paul E. Laughon, May 16, 1992. BA, U. Nev., 1987. Staff writer Register Rev. Pub. Co., Bishop, 1987-88, sr. staff writer, 1988-89, community news editor, editor spl. issue, 1989, city editor, 1989-90, news editor, 1990-92, editor, 1992—. Co-recipient 1st place award for recreation publs. Calif. Newspaper Advt. Execs. Assn., 1989, 93; recipient Altrusa Outstanding Svc. award, 1991-2. Mem. Soc. Profl. Journalists, Altrusa Internat. of the Eastern Sierra (rec. sec. 1993-94, 1st v.p. 1994-95, pres. 1995-96, pub. rels. chair 1990-95, Altrusa Pres.'s award 1994-95, pub. rels. chair Altrusa Internat. Dist. 11 1995—), Calif. Soc. Newspaper Editors. Office: Chalfant Press Inc 450 E Line St Bishop CA 93514-3506

FERRI, ALESSANDRA MARIA, ballet dancer; b. Milan, Italy, May 6, 1963; came to U.S., 1985; d. Carlo and Gian-Carla (Ghelfi) F.; m. Mauricio Orbecchi, Nov. 10, 1990. Scuola media superiore, Teatro Alla Scala, Milan; Liceo Linguistico, Francesco Sforza, Milan; student, Scuola Di Ballo Teatro Alla Scala, Milan, Royal Ballet Sch., London. Mem. corps de ballet The Royal Ballet, 1980-83, solo dancer, 1983-84, prin. dancer, 1984-85; prin. dancer Am. Ballet Theatre, N.Y.C., 1985—; guest star Nat. Ballet Can., 1988, Ballet Nat.de Marseilles, 1989-90, Ater-Balletto, 1990-92, Teatro All Scala, 1991-92, Opéra de Paris, 1992. Created roles in L'Invitatino au Voyale, Valley of Shadows, Isadora, Consort Lessons, Different Drummer, Chanson; danced in Napoli Divertissements, Illuminations, Return to the Strange Land, The Sleeping Beauty, Afternoon of a Faun, The Two Pigeons, Swan Lake, Mayerling, Manon, Romeo and Juliet, Voluntaries, Konservatoriet, Cinderella, La Bayadere, Les Biches, Seven Deadly Sins, Carmen; roles with ABT include La Bayadere, Fall River Legend, Giselle, Manon, Other Dances, Pillar of Fire, Romeo and Juliet, Sinfonietta, The Sleeping Beauty, Some Assembly Required, La Sylphide, Les Sylphides, Bruch Violin Concerto No. 1; appeared with Ballet National de Marseill in Roland Petit's Le Diable Amoreux, 1989, with Ballet of Teatro alla Scala in Roland Petit's Suite Satie, 1994, with Nat. Ballet of Can. in Romeo and Juliet, with Paris Opera Ballet in Carmen. Recipient Prix De Lausanne, 1980, Sir Laurence Olivier award, London, 1984. Office: Am Ballet Theater 890 Broadway New York NY 10003-1211*

FERRILL, JUDITH ANN, nurse; b. Evanston, Ill., Mar. 16, 1946; d. Bernard Edwin and Mary Lucille (Killian) Harrison; m. Reed Willis Ferrill, May 25, 1968; children: Bonnie, Barbara, Jennifer, Christine. BSN, Loretto Heights Coll., Denver, 1968; postgrad., U. Colo., Denver, 1993—. RN, Colo. Staff nurse, team leader Natrona County Hosp., Casper, Wyo., 1968-72; charge nurse various nursing homes, Denver, 1973-77; staff nurse neurotrauma unit St. Anthony Hosp. Ctrl., Denver, 1988-89; vis. nurse Luth. Home Care, Wheat Ridge, Colo., 1989-96, asst. nursing supr., 1990-91; vis. nurse Dominican Sisters Homehealth, Denver, 1992—; tchr. family life and sex edn. Cath. Archdiocese of DEnver, 1980-84. Troop leader, coord. svc. unit Mile Hi coun. Girl Scouts U.S.A., 1975-85; instr. cmty. edn. classes, nurse blood pressure screeing and counseling clinic, nurse disaster shelter ARC, Jefferson County, Colo., 1978-82. Mem. ANA (Colo. del. 1976), ACA, Colo. Nurses Assn. (various coms. 1972—). Home: 3020 Joyce Way Golden CO 80401-1338

FERRIS, ANN T., volunteer; b. Newark, Oct. 18, 1931; d. Thomas Joseph Todarelli and Annie Franklin Hunt; widowed; children: Susan, Richard. Bachelor's degree, Vassar Coll., 1953; Master's degree, Fairfield U., 1978. Contbr. articles to newspapers. Vol. PTA, Jr. League; vol., sec. Darien (Conn.) Comty. Homes, 1978-95; sec. bd. Pilgrim Tower, Stamford, 1993—; bd. dirs. Greens Farms Pastoral Counseling Ctr.; pres. Darien LWV, 1984-87, 92-94, now fin. chair; bd. dirs. Social Svcs. Commn., Darien, 1993-94; v.p. Dem. Town Com., Darien, 1980s; mem. allocations com. Darien United Way. Democrat. Congregationalist. Home: 30 Hale Ln Darien CT 06820

FERRIS, EVELYN SCOTT, lawyer; b. Detroit, d. Ross Ansel and Irene Mabel (Bowser) Nafus; m. Roy Shorey Ferris, May 21, 1969 (div. Sept. 1982); children: Judith Ilene, Roy Sidney, Lorene Marjorie. J.D., Willamette U., 1961. Bar: Oreg. 1962, U.S. Dist. Ct. Oreg. 1962. Law clk. Oreg. Tax Ct., Salem, 1961-62; dep. dist. atty. Marion County, Salem, 1962-65; judge Mcpl. Ct., Stayton, Oreg., 1965-76; ptnr. Brand, Lee, Ferris & Embick, Salem, 1965-82; chmn. Oreg. Workers' Compensation Bd., Salem, 1982-89. Bd. dirs. Friends of Deepwood, Salem, 1979-82, Salem City Club, 1972-75, Marion County Civil Svc. Commn., 1970-75; com. mem. Polk County Hist. Commn., Dallas, Oreg., 1976-79; mem. Oreg. legis. com. Bus. Climate, 1967-69, Govs. Task Force on Liability, 1986. Recipient Outstanding Hist. Restoration of Comml. Property award Marion County Hist. Soc., 1982. Mem. Oreg. Mcpl. Judges Assn. (pres. 1967-69), Altrusa, Internat., Mary Leonard Law Soc., Western Assn. Workers Compensation Bds. (pres. 1987-89), Capitol Club (pres. 1977-79), Internat. Assn. Indsl. Accident Bds. and Commns. (pres. 1992-93), Phi Delta Delta. Republican. Episcopalian. Home: 747 Church St SE Salem OR 97301-3715

FERRIS, VIOLETTE IRENE, nursing educator; b. Mt. Holly, N.J., July 12, 1947; d. Charles R. and Violet F. (Brown) Gale; m. Seymour B. Ferris, Sept. 9, 1967; children: Dawn M., Gale I, Denise L., Charles S. RN, Trenton State Coll., 1968; BS in Health Care Adminstrn., St. Joseph Coll., Windham, Maine, 1988; edn. cert. nursing instr., Glassboro State Coll., 1988; D of Naturopathy, Clayton Sch. Natural Healing, 1994; DD, Univ. Life Ch., 1994; PhD, Am. Inst. Theology, 1995. Cert. administering sodium/bicarbonate to high risk infants, gentle therapeutic massage, edn. health occupations, health unit coord.; registered reflexologist, Internat. Inst. Reflexology. Charge nurse, staff nurse Toms River Hosp., N.J., 1968-70; med. charge nurse Burlington County Meml. Hosp., Mt. Holly, N.J., 1970-77; agy. nurse Upjohn Health Care, Marlton, N.J., 1973-75; charge nurse, supr. Jewish Geriatric, Cherry Hill, N.J., 1981-83; agy. nurse Med Staff, Cherry Hill, 1980-83; LPN instr. Burlington County Vo Tech., Medford, N.J., 1985-92; curriculum developer Burlington County Inst. Tech., Westampton, N.J., 1992-94; health occupation instr. Burlington County Inst. Tech., Medford, 1994—; instr. Nat. Cert. Licensing Exam-Practical Nurse Rev. Student Practical Nurse Assn., Maplewood, N.J., 1986-88. Author: Decubitus Prevention/Care, 1985, Biological and Physical Science Abstracts, 1995—. Organizer, pres. MADD of Burlington County, 1995—. Mem. Am. Assn. Med. Assts., Nat. Assn. Health Unit Coords. (cert. health unit coord.). Office: Burlington County Inst Tech Adult Edn Divsn 10 Hawkin Rd Medford NJ 08055-9412

FERRON, ROBERTA ANN, state administrator; b. Deadwood, S.D., Feb. 13, 1940; d. Robert Richard and Corinne Margaret (Bordeaux) Ferron; m. Thomas Lee Huddleston, July 5, 1960 (div. Nov. 1972); children: Richard, Jennifer, Danielle, Bryan. BA in Art Edn., U. Wash., 1970; MA in Counseling, U. S.D., 1973, JD, 1976. Bar: S.D. 1976. Tchr. Federal Way (Wash.) H.S., Project 80, Decatur H.S., Federal Way; dir. legal svcs. Rapid City (S.D.) Sch. Dist.; dir. Native Am. grad. fellowship program Mont. State U., Bozeman; coord. Am. Indian studies Eastern Mont. Coll., Billings; dir. Equal Opportunity-Affirmative Action U. Kans., Lawrence; Affirmative Action dir. City of Seattle; dir. human rights/Affirmative Action U. Wash., Seattle; sr. policy coord. Gov.'s Office, Olympia, Wash.; bd. dirs. N.W. Women's Law Ctr., Seattle. Bd. dirs. Haskell Found., Lawrence; trainee, participant Leadership Lawrence; mem. Human Rights Commn., Mont., 1979-83; mem. Indian Commn., S.D., 1976-79; mem. Mont. and S.D. Com. for the Humanities, 1975-83. Mem. Nat. Assn. Human Rights Workers. Democrat. Home: 324 NW Paget Dr Seattle WA 98177

FERRO-NYALKA, RUTH RUDYS, librarian; b. Chgo., June 2, 1930; d. Joseph F. and Anna (Serbenta) Rudys; BA, U. Chgo., 1950; MA in Library Sci., Rosary Coll., 1972; children: Keith A. Krisciunas, Kevin L. Krisciunas, Kenneth M. Krisciunas; stepchildren: Anita L. Abbate, Vincent A. Abbate. Tchr. elem. sch. Westmont, Ill., 1961-63; librarian Dist. 105 public schs., La Grange, Ill., 1972-95; mem. youth svcs. dept. Hinsdale Pub. Libr., 1995—; tchr. program for gifted children, 1979-81, 82-85, coordinator gifted program, 1981-82. Mem. ALA, NEA, Ill. Edn. Assn., Dist. 105 Tchrs. Assn. (pres. 1983-85, 91-93), AAUW. Roman Catholic. Home: 5800 Doe Cir Westmont IL 60559-2138 Office: Hinsdale Pub Libr 20 E Maple St Hinsdale IL 60521

FERRY, JOAN EVANS, school counselor; b. Summit, N.J., Aug. 20, 1941; d. John Stiger and Margaret Darling (Evans) F. BS, U. Pa., 1964; EdM, Temple U., 1967; postgrad., Villanova U., 1981. Cert. elem. sch. tchr., elem. sch. counselor. Indsl. photographer Bucksco Mfg. Co., Inc., Quakertown, Pa., 1958-59; math. and German tutor St. Lawrence U., Canton, N.Y., 1959-61; research asst. U. Pa., Phila., 1963; tchr. elem. sch. Pennridge Schs., Perkasie, Pa., 1964-74, 75-77, elem. sch. counselor, 1981—; pvt. practice counselor, real estate partnership Perkasie, 1981—; chair child study team Perkasie Elem. Sch., 1988-94; tutor math., German, St. Lawrence U., Canton, N.Y., 1959-61; supervisory tchr. East Stroudsburg U., Pennridge Schs., 1971-74; research asst. U. Pa., Phila., 1963; mem. acad. coms. for Pennridge Schs.; adj. faculty Bucks County Community Coll., 1983—; instr. Am. Inst. Banking, 1982—; notary pub., 1986—; mcpl. auditor, sec. bd. auditors, 1984-90, mcpl. auditor 1990—, chmn. bd. auditors 1990—; cons. in field. Author (with others) Life-Time Sports for the College Student: A Behavioral Objective Approach, 1971, 3d rev. edit. 1978, Elementary Social Studies as a Learning System, 1976. Vol. elem. sch. counselor Perkasie, 1979-81; mem. Hilltown Civic Assn., 1965-70, 92—; exec. com. chairperson Hilltown PTO, 1965-73; mem. soloist Good Shepherd Episcop. Ch. Choir, Hilltown, 1964-77; mem., steering com. Perkasie Sch., 1989-95; poll watcher, 1993; med. vol. 1996 Olympics, Atlanta. NSF grantee, Washington, 1972-73, Philanthropic Edn. Orgn. grantee, Doylestown, Pa., 1982; recipient Judith Netzky Meml. Fellowship award B'nai B'rith, Phila., 1979; Durning scholar Delta Delta Delta, Arlington, Tex., 1981, Am. Mgmt. Assns. scholar, N.Y.C., 1983, Statesman's award World Inst. Achievement, 1989, Achievement award Women's Inner Circle, 1990, Golden Acad. award for lifetime achievement, 1991; named to Internat. Tennis Hall of Fame, 2000 Notable Am. Women Hall of Fame, 1989, Cmty. Leaders of Am. Hall of Fame, 1990, Internat. Book of Honor Hall Of Fame, 1990, Internat. Bus. & Profl. Women's Hall of Fame, 1994, Lifetime Achievement Acad. Humane Soc. of U.S., Internat. Honor Soc. In Edn. Fellow Internat. Biog. Assn.; mem. AAUW, NEA, NAFE, Humane Soc. U.S., World Inst. Achievement, Pa. State Edn. Assn. (polit. action com. for edn., chair Pennridge Schs. 1986—, del. leadership conf. 1987, 89), Pennridge Edn. Assn. (faculty rep. 1986-88, exec. coun. 1986—, negotiations resource com. 1987-89, 1990-93, steering com. Perkasie Sch. 1989-95, chairperson Child Study Team, 1988-94, Instructional Support Team, 1992—, selection com. for asst. supt. Pennridge Schs. 1993, selection com. for prin. Perkasie Sch. 1994), Am. Inst. Banking (chairperson 1987), U.S. Tennis Assn. (hon. life), Pa. and Mid. States Tennis Assn. (hon. life), U.S. Profl. Tennis Registry, Mid. States Profl. Tennis Registry, Women's Internat. Tennis Assn., Nat. Ski Patrol (Svc. Recognition award 1994), Spring Mountain Ski Patrol (Outstanding Aux. 1993, MOM Dedication award 1995), Pa. Elected Women's Assn., Bucks County Assn. Twp. Ofcls., Pa. Sch. Counselors Assn., Pa. Assn. Notaries, Am. Soc. Notaries, Internat. Fedn. Univ. Women, Internat. Platform Assn., World Inst. Achievement, Am. Biog. Inst. Rsch. Assn. (rsch. bd. advisors, bd. govs. 1989—), World Inst. of Achievement, Lifetime Achievement Acad., Rails-to-Trails Conservancy, World Wildlife Fund, Highpoint Racquet Club, Pennridge Cmty. Rep. Club. (recording sec. 1986-91, publicity chmn. 1991-92, Pen care chmn. 1992—), Assn. Tennis Profls. Tour Tennis Ptnrs., Sierra Club, The Nature Conservancy, Nat. Wildlife Fedn., Mediterranean Club, Nockamixon Boat Club, Peace Valley Yacht Club, Kappa Delta Pi. Episcopalian. Home: 834 Rickert Rd Perkasie PA 18944-2661 Office: Pennridge Schs 601 N 7th St Perkasie PA 18944-1507

FERSHTMAN, JULIE ILENE, lawyer; b. Detroit, Apr. 3, 1961; d. Sidney and Judith Joyce (Stoll) F.; m. Robert S. Bick, Mar. 4, 1990. Student, Mich. State U., 1979-81, James Madison Coll., 1979-81; BA in Philosophy and Polit. Sci., Emory U., 1983, JD, 1986. Bar: Mich. 1986, U.S. Dist. Ct. (ea. dist.) Mich. 1986, U.S. Ct. Appeals (6th cir.) 1987, U.S. Dist. Ct. (we. dist.) Mich. 1993. Assoc. Miller, Canfield, Paddock and Stone, Detroit, 1986-89; assoc. Miro, Miro & Weiner P.C., Bloomfield Hills, Mich., 1989-92; pvt. practice, Bingham Farms, Mich., 1992—; adj. prof. Schoolcraft Coll., Livonia, Mich., 1994—; lectr. in field. Author: Equine Law & Horse Sense, 1996; contbr. article to Barrister Mag. Bd. dirs. Franklin Cmty. Assn., 1989-92, sec., 1991-92; mem. Franklin Planning Commn., 1993-94. Mem. ABA (planning bd. litigation sect. young lawyers divsn., honoree Barrister mag. 1995), FBA (courthouse tours com. Detroit chpt.), State Bar Mich. (exec. coun. young lawyers sect. 1989—, sec.-treas. bd. commrs. 1991-93, vice chmn. 1993-94, chmn. elect 1994-95, chmn. 1995—), Oakland County Bar Assn. (professionalism com. 1995—, Inns of Ct. com. 1995—), Markel Equestrian Safety Bd., Women Lawyers Assn. Mich., Soc. Coll. Journalists, Phi Alpha Delta, Omicron Delta Kappa, Phi Sigma Tau, Pi Sigma Alpha. Home: 31700 Briarcliff Rd Franklin MI 48025-1273 Office: 30700 Telegraph Rd Ste 3475 Bingham Farms MI 48025-4527

FESHBACH, NORMA DEITCH, psychologist, educator; b. N.Y.C., Sept. 5, 1926; m. Seymour Feshbach; children: Jonathan Stephan, Laura Elizabeth, Andrew David. BS in Psychology, CCNY, 1947, MS in Ednl. Psychology, 1949; PhD in Clin. Psychology, U. Pa., 1956. Diplomate Am. Bd. Prof. Psychology; cert. in clin. psychology, Phila.; lic. clin. and ednl. psychologist, Calif. Tchr. Betsy Ross Nursery Sch., Yale U., 1947-48; clin. psychologist Yale U. Med. Sch., 1948; teaching asst. dept. psychology Yale U., 1948-51; research asst. human resources research office George Washington U., Washington, 1951-52; psychology intern Phila. Gen. Hosp., 1955-56; research assoc. dept. psychology U. Pa., 1959-61; research assoc. Inst. Behavioral Sci. U. Colo., 1963-64; assoc. research psychologist dept. psychology UCLA, 1964-65; clin. psychologist II UCLA Neuropsychiat. Inst., 1965; prof. Grad. Sch. Edn. UCLA, 1965—, prof. psychology dept., 1975-92, chmn. dept. edn., 1985-90, interim dean Grad. Sch. Edn., 1991-92, acting dir. Corinne A. Seeds Univ. Elem. Sch., 1985-89; Fulbright sr. lectr./researcher U. Rome, 1988; lectr. Jr. Coll. Phys. Therapy, New Haven, Conn., 1948-49, dept. psychology, U. Pa., 1956-57, UCLA Neuropsychiat. Inst., Calif. Dept. Mental Hygiene, Los Angeles, 1966-69; vis. asst. prof. Stanford U. dept. psychology, 1961-62, U. Calif. Berkeley, 1962-63; vis. scholar dept. exptl. psychology Oxford U., 1980-81; co-prin. investigator various projects and programs; co-prin. dir. and investigator NIMH Tng. Program in Applied Human Devel., 1986-91, co-dir. tng. grant in applied human devel., 1991—; clin. and research cons. Youth Services, Inc., Phila., 1955-61; also cons. various media orgns.; head program in Early Childhood and Devel. Studies, 1968-80; dir. NIMH Tng. Prog. in Early Childhood and Devel. Studies, 1972-82; prog. dir. Ctr. for Study of Evaluation, UCLA Grad. Sch. Edn., 1966-69; co-dir. UCLA Bush Found. Tng. Prog. in Child Devel. and Social Policy, 1978-82; chair grad. faculty UCLA Grad. Sch. Edn., 1979-80. Editorial cons., mem. editorial bd. psychology and ednl. research revs., contbr. numerous articles on child psychology to profl. jours. Mem. adv. coun. of Women's Clinic, Los Angeles, 1974-76; mem. adv. bd. Nat. Com. to Abolish Corporal Punishment in Schs., 1972-80, Nat. Ctr. for Study of Corporal Punishment and Alternatives in the Schs., 1976—; mem. profl. adv. com. on Child Care, Los Angeles Unified Sch. Dist., 1978-80; trustee EVAN-G Com. to End Violence Against the Next Generation, 1972-80; exec. bd. Internat. Soc. for Research in Agression, 1982-84. Recipient James McKeen Cattell Fund Sabbatical award, 1980, 81, Townsend Harris Medal, Disting. Alumnus award CCNY, 1982, Disting. Sci. Achievement in Psychology award Calif. Psychol. Assn., 1983, Achievements in Psychology award CUNY, 1989, GSE Faculty award Harold A. and Lois Haytin Found., 1991; named Faculty Mem. Woman of Yr. Nat. Acad. Profl. Psychologists, Los Angeles, 1973; U.S. Pub. Health Tng. fellow, 1953-56; rsch. grantee NIMH, 1972-77 (co-principal with D. Stipek), 77-82, 1986—, Hilton Found., 1985-86, Spencer Found. 1984-85, Child Help, USA, 1982-84 (co-principal with C. Howes), UCLA Acad. Senate, 1981—, Bush Found., 1978-83, 79-80, 80-81, 81-82, 82-83 (co-dir. with J.I. Goodlad), Adminstrn. for Children, Youth and Families, 1981-82 (co-dir. with J.I. Goodlad), NSF, 1976-77, 77-78, 78-80 (co-prin. with S. Feshbach), Com. on Internat. and Comparative Studies, 1973-74, 77-78. Fellow Am. Psychol. Assn. (officer var. coms., Disting. Contbn. Psychology and Media, Divsn. 42, 1992); mem. Assn. Advancement Psychology, AAAS, AAUP, Am. Bd. Profl. Psychologists, Am. Ednl. Research Assn., Calif. Assn. for Edn. Young Children, Nat. Assn for Edn. Young Children, Internat. Assn. Applied Psychology, Internat. Soc. for Research on Aggression, Internat. Soc. Study of Behavioral Devel., Internat. Soc. Prevention Child Abuse and Neglect, Nat. Register of Health Services Providers in Psychology, Sor Research in Child Devel., Western Psychol. Assn. (pres. 1979-80); Sigma Xi, Delta Phi Upsilon.

FETNER, SUZANNE, small business owner; b. Fowlerville, Mich., May 4, 1929; d. Clayton Charles and Ferne Marie (Abbey) Fenton; m. William Clyde Peters, June 1950 (div. Aug. 1971); children: Randall Ray, Gregory Kim, Melinda Jane Peters Jones, Kelly Sue Peters Raymond; m. Eugene Macelee Fetner, Apr. 10, 1977. BS, Ea. Mich. U., 1967. Cert. early childhood edn., Fla. Tchr. kindergarten Fowlerville (Mich.) Pub. Schs., 1949-50, Horsebrook Sch., Lansing, Mich., 1950-51, Grand Ledge (Mich.) Pub. Schs., 1951-52, Manchester (Mich.) Pub. Schs., 1952-56, Holy Trinity Episcopal Sch., Melbourne, Fla., 1967-72; owner, tchr. Country Adventure, Inc., Melbourne, 1973-77; owner, dir. Woodlake Wonderland, Inc., Palm Bay, Fla., 1978-89, Country Beginnings, Inc., Palm Bay, 1985-93; mem. Presch. Adminstrv. Cons., Palm Bay, 1985—; mem. adv. bd. Dist. Interagy. Coun. for Early Childhood Svcs., Brevard County, 1990-96, South Brevard H.S. Child Care, Melbourne, 1980—. Author: (booklet) Stepping Stones, 1984. Founder, coord. Read to Your Child Week, Melbourne, Palm Bay, 1978-92. Named Unforgettable Lady of 80's Soroptomist Club, Melbourne, 1989. Mem. Nat. Assn. Child Care Profls., Brevard Assn. Children Under Six (pres. 1981-82), Fla. Assn. Children Under Six, So. Assn. Children Under Six. Republican. Methodist. Home and Office: 567 Birch St West Melbourne FL 32904-2541

FETRIDGE, BONNIE-JEAN CLARK (MRS. WILLIAM HARRISON FETRIDGE), civic volunteer; b. Chgo., Feb. 3, 1915; d. Sheldon and Bonnie (Carrington) Clark; m. William Harrison Fetridge, June 27, 1941; children: Blakely (Mrs. Harvey H. Bundy III), Clark Worthington. Student, Girls Latin Sch., Chgo., The Masters Sch., Dobbs Ferry, N.Y., Finch Coll., N.Y.C. Bd. dirs. region VII com. Girl Scouts U.S.A., 1939-43, nat. program com., 1966-69, nat. adv. bd., 1972-85, internat. commr.'s adv. panel, 1973-76, Nat. Juliette Low Birthplace Com., 1966-69; bd. dirs. Girl Scouts Chgo., 1936-51, 59-69, sec., 1936-38, v.p., 1946-49, 61-65, chmn. Juliette Low world friendship com., 1959-67, 71-72; mem. Friends Our Cabana Com. World Assn. Girl Guides and Girl Scouts, Cuernavaca, Mexico, 1969—, vice chmn., 1982-87; founder, pres. Olave Baden-Powell Soc. of World Assn. Girl Guides and Girl Scouts, London, 1984-93, bd. dirs., 1984—, hon. assoc., 1987; asst. sec. Dartnell Corp, Chgo., 1981-91, sec., 1991—, bd. dirs. 1989—; vice chmn. Dartnell Found., 1990—; bd. dirs. Jr. League of Chgo., 1937-40, Vis. Nurse Assn. Chgo., 1951-58, 61-63, asst. treas., 1962-63; women's bd. dirs. Children's meml. Hosp., 1946-50; v.p. parents coun. Latin Sch., 1952-54, bd. dirs. alumni assn., 1964-69; Fidelitas Soc., 1979; women's bd. U.S.O., 1965-75, treas., 1969-71, v.p., 1971-73; women's svc. bd. Chgo. Area coun. Boy Scouts Am., 1964-70, mem. nat. exploring com., 1973-76; staff aide and ARC Motor Corps, World War II. Recipient Citation of Merit Sta. WAIT, Chgo., 1971, Juliette Low World Friendship medal Girl Scouts U.S.A., 1989; 1st recipient Medal of Recognition World Assn.Girl Guides and Girl Scouts, 1993; Baden-Powell fellow World Scout Found., Geneva, 1983. Mem. Nat. Soc. Colonial Dames Am. (life, Ill. bd. mgrs. 1962-65, 69-76, 78-82, v.p. 1970-72, corr. sec. 1978-80, 1st v.p. 1980-84, state chmn. geneal. info. svcs. com. 1972-76, corr. sec. 1978-80, hist. activities com. 1979-83, mus. house com. 1980-83, house gov. 1981-83), Chgo. Dobbs Alumnae Assn. (past pres.), Nat. Soc. DAR, Chgo. Geneal. Soc., Conn. Soc. Genealogists, New Eng. Hist. Geneal. Soc., N.Y. Geneal. and Biog. Soc., Newberry Libr. Assocs., Chgo. Hist. Soc. Guild, Casino Club, The Racquet Club Chgo., Union League. Republican. Episcopalian. Home: 2430 N Lakeview Ave Chicago IL 60614-2720

FETTWEIS, YVONNE CACHÉ, archivist, historian; b. L.A., Nov. 28, 1935; d. Boyd Eugene and Georgette Louisa (Tilmann) Adams; m. Maurice Lee Caché, Jan. 8, 1955 (div. 1962); children: Maurice C.B. II, Michele-Yvonne (Mrs. Vernon Young Sr.); m. Rolland Phillip Fettweis, July 22, 1967. BA, Wagner Coll., 1954; postgrad, Am. U., 1973, Bentley Coll., 1981. Legal sec., asst. Judge, Davis, Stern, Orfinger & Tindall, Daytona Beach, Fla., 1961-66; head rec. sect., bd. dirs. 1st Ch. Christ Scientist, Boston, 1969-71, rsch. assoc., 1971-72, adminstrv. archivist, 1972-78, sr. assoc. archivist, 1979-84, records adminstr., 1984-91, div. mgr. records mgmt./orgnl. archives, 1991-92, divsn. mgr. ch. history, 1992—, divsn. mgr. ch. history and healing ministry, 1995; divsn. mgr. ch. history, 1995-96; ch. historian 1st Ch. Christ Scientist, Boston, 1996—. Trustee Ch. Hist. Trust, 1995—; exec. sec. Volusia County Goldwater campaign, Daytona Beach, 1964. Mem. Soc. Am. Archivists (editor The Archival Spirit), Automated Records and Techniques Task Force, Am. Mgmt. Assn., Orgn. Am. Historians, Ctr. for Study Presidency, Religious Pub. Rels. Coun., New Eng. Archivists, Assn. Records Mgrs. and Adminstrs. (bd. dirs. 1983—), Assn. Coll. and Rsch. Librs., Bay State Hist. League, Order Ea. Star, Order Rainbow (bd. dirs. 1972-77). Republican. Christian Scientist. Home: 42 Edgell Dr Framingham MA 01701-3181 Office: 1st Ch Christian Sci 175 Huntington Ave # A221 Boston MA 02115-3117

FEUER, MARGARET RODGERS, contractor; b. Bklyn., Mar. 24, 1943; d. Patrick and Catherine (Gorman) Rodgers; m. Michael Feuer, Aug. 14, 1965; children: Catherine Alexandra, Matthew Patrick. AB, Barnard Coll., 1964; MA, NYU, 1969; JD, Santa Clara U., 1987. Lic. gen. contractor, Calif. Mgmt. trainee AT&T, Oakland, Calif., 1965-66; H.S. tchr. North Cambridge (Mass.) Cath. Sch., 1966-67; parent/cmty. activist Poughkeepsie, N.Y., 1967-82, Palo Alto, Calif., 1982—; gen. contractor Palo Alto (Calif.) Constrn., 1990—. Author, editor Famous Women of Palo Alto, 1994. Mem. Poughkeepsie Zoning Bd., 1974-78; v.p., mem. Poughkeepsie Sch. Bd., 1978-82; vice chair Cmty Devel. Block Grant Com., Palo Alto, 1991-93; coord. Palo Alto NOW, 1992-95; chair Peninsula Bd. Women's Heritage Mus., Palo Alto, 1992-94; pres. Crescent Park Neighborhood Assn., 1992-95; bd. mem. Women's Club Palo Alto, 1992-95; co-chair Citizens for Affirmative Planning, 1994-95. Democrat. Roman Catholic. Home: 1310 University Ave Palo Alto CA 94301

FEUREY, CLAUDIA PACKER, not-for-profit executive; b. Pt. Hueneme, Calif., Apr. 24, 1949; d. Benjamin Ray and Phyllis Laura (McGrath) Packer; m. John J. Feurey Jr.; children: Matthew, Sarah, Nicholas. BA, Barnard Coll., 1970. V.p. comm. and corp. affairs Com. for Econ. Devel., N.Y.C., 1976—. Contbr: Wall St. Journal on Management, Successful Training

Strategies. Mem. Pub. Rels. Soc. Am. (exec. bd. dirs.), Mauweehoo Club. Republican. Presbyterian. Office: Com for Econ Devel 477 Madison Ave New York NY 10022-5802

FEUSS, LINDA ANNE UPSALL, lawyer; b. White Plains, N.Y., Dec. 9, 1956; d. Herbert Charles and Edna May (Hart) Upsall; m. Charles E. Feuss, Aug. 16, 1980; children: Charles Herbert, Anne Hart. BA, Colgate U., 1978; JD, Emory U., 1981. Bar: Ga. 1981, S.C. 1981. Assoc. Rainey, Britton, Gibbes & Clarkson, Greenville, S.C., 1981-83; counsel Siemens Energy & Automation, Atlanta, 1983-91; counsel Siemens Corp., Atlanta, 1991-93, sr. counsel, 1993-94, assoc. gen. counsel, 1994—; rep. law coun. II Mfr.'s Alliance Productivity and Innovation, Washington, 1995—; rep. law com. Nat. Elec. Mfr.'s Assn., Washington, 1995—. Bd. dirs. Am. Heart Assn., Greenville, 1981-93; mem. leadership com. Woodruff Arts Ctr. Campaign, Atlanta, 1985-90; vol. High Mus. Art, Atlanta, 1993—. Mem. ABA, Am. Corp. Coun. Assn. (dir. Ga. chpt. 1995, v.p. Ga. chpt. 1996), State Bar Ga., S.C. Bar, Atlanta Bar Assn., Colgate Club Atlanta (pres. 1986-88, bd. dirs. 1989—). Office: Siemens Corp 3333 Old Milton Pkwy Alpharetta GA 30202-4437

FEWELL, CHRISTINE HUFF, psychoanalyst, alchohol counselor; b. Ancon, Canal Zone, Oct. 12, 1942; d. Maenner B. and Antoinette (Baker) Huff; m. Charles K. Fewell, Jr., Jan. 23, 1971; children: Anna C., John M. BA, Antioch Coll., Yellow Springs, Ohio, 1965; MSW, U. Chgo., 1967. Cert. social worker; cert. psychoanalyst; credentialed alcoholism counselor. Social worker Ill. Children's Home and Aid Soc., Chgo., 1967-68, Bronx (N.Y.) State Hosp., 1968-70; field work instr. Columbia Sch. Social Work, 1973-75; social worker in alcoholism treatment ctr. St. Lukes/Roosevelt Hosp., N.Y.C., 1970-75; pvt. practice Hastings-on-Hudson, 1976—, N.Y.C., 1976—; alcoholism disability com. Ctrl. Westchester Area Mental Health Com. Westchester Dept. Cmty. Mental Health, 1981—; mem. N.Y. State Bd. Social Work, 1993—; adj. prof. Fordham Sch. Social Work, 1994—, NYU Sch. Social Work, 1995—; faculty advisor NYU Sch. of Social Work, 1996—. Editor: Social Work Treatment of Alcoholism 1984, Pychosocial Issues in the Treatment of Alcoholism, 1985, Alcoholism Treatment Quar., 1986; editorial adv. bd. Social Casework, 1978; contbr. articles to profl. jours. Mem. NASW (N.Y.C. chpt. alcoholism com. 1971—, chairperson 1975, editl. com. 1978-86, peer consultation com. for impaired social workers chairperson 1976—, cons. Com. on Inquiry), Internat. Psychoanalytical Assn., Inst. for Psychoanalytical Tng. and Rsch. (libr., adminstr. IPTAR clin. ctr.), Acad. Cert. Social Workers (diplomate), N.Y. State Soc. Clin. Social Workers (Westchester chpt. fellow 1981—, referral com. 1983-86), Employee Assistance Profls. Assn. (N.Y. and mid-Hudson chpt. 1983—). Home: 4 Nichols Dr Hastings On Hudson NY 10706-3525 Office: 1651 3rd Ave Ste 201 New York NY 10128-3679

FEYH, LEAH STUART, nurse anesthetist, educator; b. Charleston, W.Va., Mar. 20, 1953; d. Harry Ballard and Elizabeth Irene (McClung) Stuart; m. William Howard Feyh, May 23, 1987; children: Andrew, Elizabeth. BSN, U. Va., 1975; BS in Health Scis., George Washington U., 1983. Cert. RN Anesthetists, Coun. on Cert. Nurse Anesthetists. Commd. ensign USN, 1974, advanced through grades to comdr., 1992; staff nurse ICU Naval Hosp., Camp Lejeune, N.C., 1975-78, staff nurse anesthetist, 1983-85; p.m. charge nurse ICU Naval Hosp., Portsmouth, Va., 1978-81; head anesthesia dept. U.S. Naval Hosp., Guantanamo Bay, Cuba, 1985-86; sr. nurse anesthetist Nat. Naval Med. Ctr., Bethesda, Md., 1986-87; nurse anesthetist Riverside Hosp., Jacksonville, Fla., 1988-89; staff nurse anesthetist Naval Hosp., Jacksonville, 1989-91, Naval Med. Ctr., San Diego, 1991-92; asst. clin. coord., clin. instr. Navy Nurse Corps Anesthesia Program, San Diego, 1992-96; hosp. based instr. Neonatal Resuscitation Program, 1989—. Contbr. articles to profl. jours. Decorated Navy Commendation medal, 1985, 86, 92, Meritorious Svc. medal 1996. Mem. Am. Assn. Nurse Anesthetists (editorial adv. bd. jour. 1993-94), Nat. Soc. DAR, Sigma Theta Tau. Democrat. Presbyterian.

FIALA, DONNA L., public relations executive; b. Cleve., Apr. 13, 1938; d. Louis Beck and Violette Helen (Kish) Spencer; m. Ted Fiala (div.); children: Debbi, Bob, Sherri, T.J., Todd. Cert. travel counselor, Wellesley Inst., Mass., 1980-82. Dir. cmty. affairs Naples (Fla.) Cmty. Hosp., 1987—; nat. sales mgr. Provincetown Boston Airline (PBA), Naples, 1975-87; Mem. bd. govs. Naples Inst. of Mt.-IDA Coll., 1994—; mem. bd. dirs. Naples Area C. of C., 1988-93; exec. dir. Golden Gate C. of C., Naples, 1995. Pres. East Naples Civic Assn., 1994-95; mem. bd. dirs. Greater Naples Civic Assn., 1993—, Pres's. Coun., Naples, 1994—; mem. exec. bd. Focus-Visioning for Future of Collier County, Naples, 1995—. Mem. Pub. Rels. Assn. of Collier County (pres. 1995-96), Southwest Travel Ind. Assn. (pres. 1985-86), Kiwanis Club of Naples East (pres., bd. dirs. 1991—). Republican. Presbyn. Office: Naples Cmty Hosp PO Box 413029 Naples FL 33941

FICHTHORN, FONDA GAY, principal; b. Jamestown, Ohio, Sept. 4, 1949; d. Robert William and Evelyn Elizabeth (Schmitt) F. BS, Otterbein Coll., 1970; MEd, Wright State U., 1983. Cert. tchr., prin., supr., Ohio. Elem. tchr. Groveport (Ohio) Madison Schs., 1970-71; elem. tchr. Miami Trace Schs., Washington Court House, Ohio, 1971-92, prin., 1992—. Recipient Class Act award Sta. WDTN-TV, 1990. Republican. Home: 7313 State Route 729 NW Washington Court House OH 43160-9526 Office: Wilson Sch 1604 State Route 41 SW Washington Court House OH 43160-9789

FICKEN, MILLICENT SIGLER, zoology educator; b. Washington, July 27, 1933; d. Phares Oscar and Helen Elizabeth (Richards) Sigler; m. Robert William Ficken, June 25, 1955 (div. 1989); children: John William, Carolyn Marie Ficken Powers. BS, Cornell U., 1955, PhD, 1960. Postdoctoral fellow Cornell U., Ithaca, N.Y., 1960-62; rsch. assoc. dept. zoology U. Md., College Park, 1963-67; asst. prof. zoology U. Wis., Milw., 1967-69, assoc. prof. zoology, 1969-75, prof. dept. biol. scis., 1975—, acad. program dir. field sta., 1967—. Contbr. articles on ornithology and animal behavior to sci. publs. NSF grantee, 1967-80, 87, 88. Fellow Animal Behavior Soc., Am. Ornithologists' Union; mem. AAAS, Soc. for Study of Evolution, Cooper Ornithol. Soc., Wilson Ornithol. Soc. Home: 1623 16th Ave Grafton WI 53024-2019 Office: U Wis Dept Biol Scis Milwaukee WI 53201

FICKENSCHER, SUE, film company executive. CFO Castle Rock Entertainment, Beverly Hills, Calif. Office: Castle Rock Entertainment 335 N Maple Dr Ste 135 Beverly Hills CA 90210*

FIDDLE, LORRAINE ANNE, artist, art educator; b. N.Y.C., Sept. 21, 1956; d. Seymour and Adele (Gottdiener) F. BFA, Sch. Art Inst. Chgo., 1979, MFA, 1982. Cert. art tchr., N.Y. Artist-in-residence Studio in a Sch. Assn., N.Y.C., 1983-91, Bronx (N.Y.) Coun. for Arts, 1984, N.Y.C. Dept. Cultural Affairs, 1985, N.Y. Found. for Arts, N.Y.C., 1985; interdisciplinary art coord. Dodge Vocational H.S., Bronx, N.Y., 1993-94; art instr. Lehman Coll., South Bronx H.S., 1994—; tchr., advisor The Whitney Mus. Am. Art, 1993. Exhbns. include Bronx (N.Y.) Mus. of Arts, 1987, Sch. Art Inst. Chgo., 1991, Artists Space, 1995, Cork Gallery, Lincoln Ctr., N.Y.C., 1995, Sotheby's, N.Y.C., 1996, Queens (N.Y.) Theater in the Park, 1996. Grantee Ill. Arts Coun., 1983, Arts in Edn. grantee NEA, 1987. Office: South Bronx HS Art Dept 701 St Anne's Ave Bronx NY 10455

FIDLER, SHELLEY N., legislative director; b. Bklyn., Jan. 19, 1947; d. Jay William and Rhoda H. (Wander) F.; m. Curtis B. Gans, Sept. 23, 1979; 1 child, Aaron. BA, Brown U., 1968. Legis. asst. Rep. Philip Sharp, 1976-80; asst. to chmn. Subcom. Fossil and Synthetic Fuels Ho. Com. Energy and Commerce, 1980-86, asst. to chair Subcom. Energy and Power, 1987-94, staff dir., 1994-96; chief Staff Coun. on Environ. Quality, 1996—. Office: Old Executive Bldg Rm 360 Washington DC 20501*

FIEDLER, BOBBI, community agency director, former congresswoman; b. Santa Monica, Calif., Apr. 22, 1937; d. Jack and Sylvia (Levin) Horowitz; m. Paul Clarke, Feb. 15, 1987; children: Lisa, Randy. LLD (hon.), West Coast Coll. Law, 1978. Gen. office duties Miller & Co., 1955-60; owner, ptnr. 2 pharmacies, 1969-77; founder, exec. dir. BUSTOP, 1976-77; mem., chmn. com. of whole, chmn. bus. ops. com., bldg. com. L.A. Bd. of Edn., 1977-81; mem., house budget com., joint econ. com. U.S. Congress, 1981-87; bd. dirs., chmn. nominations com., vice chmn. audit com. United Edn. and Software, 1987-93; bd. commrs. L.A. Comty. Redevel. Agy., 1993—; lottery commn. Calif., 1993-94; advt. artist; 1955-60, interior decorater, 1957-60; polit. commentator Sta. KABC-TV, 1986-87; bd. commrs. Calif. State Lottery, 1993-94; cons. in pub. rels. and govt., 1987—. Vol. various comty. activities; mem. notification com. Reagan and Bush nominations, 1984; co-chair Wilson for Gov., San Fernando Valley, 1990, 94; Calif. vice-chair Bush for Pres., 1992; Calif. co-chair Bush for Pres., 1988; Calif. del. Rep. Nat. Conv., 1980, 84, 88, 92; mem. L.A. Citizen's Com. on Transit Solutions, 1987, Calif. Space and Def. Coun., 1981-87, Hadassah; statewide spokesperson Proposition 13, 1978, Proposition 1 & 4, 1979. Recipient Golden Bulldog award Watchdogs of the Treasury, 1981-87, Guardian of Small Bus. award Nat. Fedn. Ind. Bus., 1981-87, Golden Age award Nat. Alliance of Sr. Citizens, 1981-87, numerous commendations from city couns.; named Newsmaker of Yr., L.A. Daily News, 1977, 80, 84, one of Outstanding Women of So. Calif., L.A. Herald Examiner, 1978, Legislator of Yr., VFW, 1985, Outstanding Legislator, L.A. Jewish Fedn. Coun., 1982. Mem. Bus. and Profl. Women's Assn. (Woman of Yr.), Nat. Sch. Bds. Assn., Calif. State Soc. (bd. dirs.), San Fernando Valley Bus. & Profl. Assn., B'nai Brith Youth Orgn. (sponsor's bd., Anita S. Perlman award 1982).

FIEL, MAXINE LUCILLE, journalist, behavioral analyst, lecturer; b. N.Y.C.; d. William Jack and Rowena (Burton) Stempel; m. David H. Fiel; children: Meredith Susan, Lisa Beth. Student in psychology and humanities, NYU. Nat. columnist, contbg. editor Mademoiselle Mag., N.Y.C., 1972—; nat. columnist Womens World, Englewood, N.J., 1979-89; contbg. editor Overseas Promotions, N.Y.C., 1979—; articles and features editor Japanese Overseas Press, 1976—; feature editor N.Y. Now, N.Y.C., 1980-91; contbg. editor Woman's World mag., 1979-89, Bella mag., Eng., 1987-89; nat. columnist First mag. for women, 1989-91; founder Starcast Astrological Svcs., Floral Park, N.Y., 1993—; cons. legal profession jury selection, 1984—; mktg. cons. Imperial Enterprises, Tokyo and Princeton, N.J., 1983—; cons. spokesperson Rowland Co., N.Y.C., 1972-81, Allied Chem. Co., N.Y.C., 1972-75; lectr., cons. Atlanta and Fla. Bar Assns., 1986—; creator Touch Game Parker Bros., Salem, Mass., 1971-76; behavior analystand communications advisor multi-nat. bus. corps.; cons. Chesebrough-Ponds, Footwear Coun., Grand Marnier Liquor; founder Starcast Astrological Svcs., 1993. Pioneer field of polit. body lang., 1969; contbr. articles to News Am., L.A. Times, Newhouse News Svc., Newspaper Entertainment Assocs., King Features, Borderland Mag.; TV appearances on morning and afternoon shows, including A Current Affair, The Regis Philbin Show, Eyewitness News, Cable News Network, Tonight Show, Today Show, Good Morning Am., Joan Rivers Show, Jenny Jones, Entertainment Tonight, Merv Griffin Show, BBC Breakfast Show, Good Morning Japan, many others; appeared in daily segment Good Morning Japan. Active Sister Cities, Tokyo and N.Y.C.; charter mem. Elem. Sch. Cultural Exchange, Toyko and N.Y.C., Ctr. Environ. Edn.; bd. dirs. Periwinkle Prodns. Anti-Drug Abuse, N.Y.C. Recipient Achievement award field behavioral sci. and photojournalism, Tokyo, 1974, Outstanding Rsch. award field psychology of gesture, Tokyo, 1976, Outstanding Achievement award Internat. Conf. Soc. Para-Psychology, 1974-75; honored guest at award dinner for involvement and support in the merging of Eye Rsch. Inst. Boston and Harvard Med. Sch., 1991. Mem. AFTRA, Internat. Found. Behavioral Rsch. (past v.p.), Nat. Writers Assn. (profl.), Authors Guild, Authors League, World Wildlife Fund, Whale Protection Fund, Cousteau Soc., Nature Conservancy, Greenpeace, People for Ethical Treatment Animals, Humane Assn. U.S., Guiding Eyes for Blind, Braille Camps for Blind Children, Save the Children, Lotos Club (N.Y.C.), East End Yacht Club (Freeport, N.Y.). Office: 338 Northern Blvd Ste 3 Great Neck NY 11021-4808

FIELD, ANDREA BEAR, lawyer; b. New London, Conn., Nov. 30, 1949; d Geurson Donald and Lorraine (Solomon) Silverberg; m. Thornton Withers Field, May 17, 1984; children: Benjamin, Geoffrey. Student, Wellesley Coll., 1967-69; BA, Yale U., 1971; JD, U. Va., 1974. Bar: Va. 1974, D.C. 1978, U.S. Ct. Appeals (3d, 4th, 5th, 7th, 8th and D.C. cirs.). Assoc. Hunton & Williams, Washington and Richmond, Va., 1974-81; ptnr. Hunton & Williams, Washington, 1981—. Mem. ABA (chair sect. natural resources, energy and environ. law 1989-90, coun. 1984-87, 90-91, chair com. air quality 1982-84, vice chair teleconf. com. 1990—, environ. controls bus. law sect. 1990-91, vice chair com. environ. law, real property, probate and trust law sect. 1990-91; chair standing com. on natural conf. groups 1993-94, nat. conf. lawyers and scientists 1990-93, sect. ad hoc com. nat. insts. 1989-90, coun. sect. sci. and tech. 1991-92). Office: Hunton & Williams Ste 9000 2000 Pennsylvania Ave NW Washington DC 20006-1812

FIELD, CAROL HART, writer, journalist, foreign correspondent; b. San Francisco, Mar. 27, 1940; d. James D. and Ruth (Arnstein) Hart; m. John L. Field, July 23, 1961; children: Matthew, Alison. BA, Wellesley Coll., 1961. Contbg. editor, assoc. editor, asst. editor City Mag., San Francisco, 1974-76; contbg. editor New West/Calif. Mag., San Francisco, L.A., 1975-80, San Francisco Mag., 1980-82; fgn. corr. La Gola, Milan, Italy, 1990—; lectr. Smithsonian Inst., Washington, 1991, 95, Schlesinger Libr., Radcliffe Coll., 1995; television appearance with Julia Child, 1995; bd. dirs. Lyra Corp. Author: The Hill Towns of Italy, 1983 (Commonwealth Club award 1984), The Italian Baker, 1985 (Internat. Assn. Culinary Profls. award 1986), Celebrating Italy, 1990 (Commonwealth Club award Internat. Assn. Culinary Profls. award 1991), Italy in Small Bites, 1993 (James Beard award), Focaccia: Simple Breads from the Italian Oven, 1994; contbr. articles to profl. jours. Mem. lit. jury Commonwealth Club Calif., San Francisco, 1987, 88, 92; bd. dirs. Women's Forum West, San Francisco, 1990-92, Bancroft Libr. U. Calif. Berkeley, 1991—, The Headlands Inst., San Francisco, 1992-93; bd. dirs. The Mechanics' Inst., San Francisco, 1987-92, pres., 1990-92. Recipient Internat. Journalism prize Maria Luigia Duchessa di Parma, Italy, 1987, Barbi Colombini prize Tuscany, 1991; named Alumna of Yr. Head Royce Sch, Oakland, Calif., 1991. Mem. Accademia Italia della Cucina, Authors Guild, Am. Inst. Wine and Food, Les Dames d'Escoffier, Internat. Assn. Culinary Profls. Home and Office: 2561 Washington St San Francisco CA 94115-1818

FIELD, JULIA ALLEN, futurist, conceptual planner; b. Boston, Jan. 5, 1937; d. Howard Locke and Julia Wright (Field) Allen. BA cum laude, Harvard U. 1960, Harvard Grad. Sch. Design, 1964-65; postgrad. Pius XII Grad. Art Inst., Florence, Italy, 1961; postgrad. Walden U. Inst. for Advanced Studies, 1983-89. Cons. to archtl. and environ. firms, 1964-69; cons. Forestry Dept. of Simla (India), 1969-70; founder, v.p. Black Grove, Inc., Miami, Fla., 1970-80; founder, pres. Amazonia 2000, Bogotá, Colombia, 1970-72; leader Task Force Amazonia 2000, DAINCO, 1977-78; elected pres. Foundation Amazonia 2000 in Gen. Assembly, Leticia, Colombia, 1979—; pres. Acad. Arts and Scis. of the Ams., Miami, Fla., 1979—; mem. Presdl. Adv. Com. on tech. devel. Group of Yr. 2000, Colombia, 1971-74; mem. Man and Biosphere Com. UNESCO, Colombia, 1972-78; mem. Task Force on Colonization Report to President of Colombia, 1973; cons. Amazon Unified Command, Republic of Colombia 1981-86; hon. nat. insp. resources and environment Republic of Colombia, 1982—; bd. visitors Duke U. Primate Ctr., 1979-82; prin. speaker various seminars, congresses. Mem. City of Miami Bicentennial com., 1975-76; coord. Cmty. of Man Task Force, Miami, 1975-76; mem. Blueprint for Miami 2000, 1982-85; adv. Tech. Jour., Delhi, India, 1985-86; participant Only One Earth Forum, UN Environ. Program/Rene Dubos Ctr., N.Y.C., 1987, 15 Internat. Human Unity Conf., New Delhi, 1988; founder Amacayacu National Park, Amazonia, Colombia, 1975; creator, builder with other scientists Villa Ciencia , Rio Cotuhé, Colombia, 1975; signed 3d Amazon World Model Accord with IGAC and DAINCO, Colombia, 1988-93. Author: Amazonia 2000, 1978, Amazonia as a World Model, 1972. Fellow Royal Geog. Soc. (London); mem. World Future Soc., Internat. Assn. Hydrogen Energy, UN Assn. U.S., Planetary Citizens, The Friends of Worldwatch.

FIELD, KAREN ANN, real estate broker; b. New Haven, Jan. 27, 1936; d. Abraham Terry and Ida (Smith) Rogovin; m. Barry S. Crown, June 29, 1954 (div. 1969); children: Laurie Jayne, Donna Lynn, Bruce Alan, Bradley David; m. Michael Lehmann Field, Aug. 10, 1969 (div. 1977). Student Vassar Coll., 1953-54, Harrington Inst. Interior Design, 1973-74, Roosevelt U., 1987—. Cert. residential specialist. Owner Karen Field Interiors, Chgo., 1970-86, Karen Field & Assocs., Chgo., 1980-81; pres., ptnr. Field-Pels & Assocs., Chgo., 1981-86; with top sales volume Sudler-Marling, Inc., 1989; sales broker Koenig & Strey, Inc., Chgo., 1992—; elected to Pres.'s Club, Koenig & Strey, Inc., 1996. Mem. Women's Coun. Camp Henry Horner, Chgo., 1960; bd. dirs., treas. Winnetka Pub. Sch. Nursery (Ill.), 1961-63; pres. Jr. Aux. U. Chgo. Cancer Rsch. Found., 1960-66, mem. exec. com. woman's bd., 1965-66; bd. dirs., sec. United Charities, Chgo., 1966-68, Victory Gardens Theatre, Chgo., 1979; co-founder, pres. Re Entry Ctr., Wilmette, Ill., 1978-80; mem. br. Child Abuse Svcs., Chgo., 1981-89, Stop AIDS Real Estate Div., 1988, AIDS Walkathon Com., 1990; bd. dirs. The Chicago Ctr. for Self-Taught Art. Recipient Servian award Jr. Aux. of U. Chgo. Cancer Rsch. Found., 1966, Margarite Wolf award Women's Bd., U. Chgo. Cancer Rsch. Found., 1967, Founder's award, WAIT Woman of Day. Mem. Internat. Real Estate Fedn. (chmn. membership Chgo. chpt. 1994, bd. dirs. 1996), Chgo. Real Estate Bd., Chgo. Assn. Realtors, Chgo. Coun. Fgn. Rels., English Speaking Union (jr. bd. 1958-59), Carlton Club, Art Inst. Chgo., Field Mus., Chgo. Architecture Found., Presidents Club, Founders Club. Office: Koenig & Strey Inc 900 N Michigan Ave Chicago IL 60611-1542

FIELD, LAURA KATHRYN, health educator, consultant; b. Houston, Jan. 6, 1964; d. Linda Wheat (Steinhauser) Walcowich. Carin English, U. Tex., 1987, MA in Kinesiology and Health Edn., 1990; grad. student, John F. Kennedy U., 1994—. Cert. trainer. Secondary sch. tchr. English Am. Inst. Learning, Austin, 1987-88; exercise physiologist Lake Austin Resort, Austin, 1989-91; health promotion specialist Chevron Corp., Concord, Calif., 1991-96; wellness and promotional event planner Kaiser Permanente, Oakland, Calif., 1996—; Presenter, spkr. in field. Contbr. articles to profl. jours. Advocate, vol. Ct. Appointed Spl. Advocates, Oakland, Calif., 1993—. Mem. Nat. Wellness Assn., Calif. Assn. Marriage and Family Counseling. Democrat. Office: Kaiser Permanente 1800 Harrison St 13th Fl Oakland CA 94612

FIELD, PHYLIS SHARON, consulting director; b. Huntington, N.Y., Apr. 28, 1960; d. Richard Del and Jean (Sharp) F. BA, BS, U. Pa., 1981; MBA, UCLA, 1990. Bus. adminstr. TRW, San Diego and L.A., 1984-88; mem. staff UCLA, 1989-90; sr. cons. Deloitte & Touche Consulting, L.A., 1990-92, mgr., 1992-94; consulting dir. Deloitte & Touche Consulting Group, Santa Ana, Calif., 1995—. Office: Deloitte & Touche consulting-ICS Ste 600 3 Imperial Promenade Santa Ana CA 92707-0511

FIELD, SALLY, actress; b. Pasadena, Calif., Nov. 6, 1946; m. Steve Craig, Sept. 1968 (div. 1975); children: Peter, Eli; m. Alan Greisman, Dec. 1984 (div. 1994); 1 son, Samuel. Student, Actor's Studio, 1973-75. Starred in TV series Gidget, 1965, The Flying Nun, 1967-69, The Girl With Something Extra, 1973; film appearances include The Way West, 1967, Stay Hungry, 1976, Heroes, 1977, Smokey and the Bandit, 1977, Hooper, 1978, The End, 1978, Norma Rae, 1979 (Cannes Film Festival Best Actress award 1979, Acad. award 1980), Beyond the Poseidon Adventure, 1979, Smokey and the Bandit II, 1980, Back Roads, 1981, Absence of Malice, 1981, Kiss Me Goodbye, 1982, Places in the Heart, 1984 (Acad. award for best actress 1984), Murphy's Romance (also exec. producer), 1985, Surrender, 1987, Punchline, 1987 (also prodr.), Steel Magnolias, 1989, Soapdish, 1991, Not Without My Daughter, 1991, Homeward Bound: The Incredible Journey, 1993 (voice only), Mrs. Doubtfire, 1993, Forrest Gump, 1994; TV movies include Maybe I'll Come Home In the Spring, 1971, Marriage: Year One, 1971, Home for the Holidays, 1972, Bridges, 1976, Sybil, 1976 (Emmy award 1977), A Woman of Independent Means, 1994; prodr. Dying Young, 1991, Eye for an Eye, 1995, Homeward Bound II: Lost in San Francisco, 1996. •

FIELDER, DOROTHY SCOTT, postmaster; b. Detroit, Apr. 20, 1943; d. William Lacy and Gertrude Elizabeth (Coddington) Davis; m. Douglas Stratton Fielder, July 13, 1968; 1 child, William Todd. AB, Randolph-Macon Woman's Coll., 1965; MA, Kent State U., 1968. Lab. instr. Mary Baldwin Coll., Staunton, Va., 1965-66, Hartwick Coll., Oneonta, N.Y., 1969-70; rsch. and teaching asst. Kent (Ohio) State U., 1966-68; high sch. tchr. biology Fairfax County Pub. Schs., Va., 1968-69; postal clk. U.S. Postal Svc., Maryland, N.Y., 1978-80, rural carrier, 1980-81; postmaster U.S. Postal Svc., Schenevus, N.Y., 1981—; coord. Benjamin Franklin Stamp Club, U.S. Postal Svc., Albany, N.Y., 1982-93. Author: Pictorial History of the Town of Maryland, N.Y., 1990, Otsego County Postal History, 1994. Vice chmn. Town of Maryland Planning Bd., 1989-93, chmn., 1993—. Mem. AAUW, Nat. Assn. Postmasters U.S., Town of Md. Hist. Assn. (pres. 1982—), Tri-County Postmasters Assn. (pres. 1990-94), Empire State Postal History Soc., Am. Philatelic Soc., Rotary. Methodist. Home: RR 1 Box 1038 Maryland NY 12116-9769 Office: US Postal Svc 62 Main St Schenevus NY 12155

FIELDS, ANITA, dean; b. Amarillo, Tex., Oct. 29, 1940; d. Dera and Mamie Maureen (Craig) Bates; 1 child, William Kyle. Grad. nursing, Jefferson Davis Hosp., 1962; BSN, Tex. Christian U., 1966; MSN, Northwestern State U. La., 1974; PhD, Tex. Women's U., 1980. C.E. coord., asst. prof. Northwestern State U., Shreveport; prof., dean McNeese State U., Lake Charles, La.; gov.'s appointee Southwest La. Hosp. Dist. Commn., 1989-91, chmn., 1989-91. Mem. allocations com. and loaned exec. United Way, 1991-92, Am. Heart Assn., Am. Cancer Soc., ARC. Recipient Ben Taub award, 1962, Ann Magnussen award ARC, 1977. Mem. ANA (del.), La. Nurses Assn. (past pres. and 1st v.p., spl. recognition award 1993), Lake Charles Dist. Nurses Assn. (bd. dirs., Nurse of Yr. award 1972, 80), Nat. League Nursing (agy. mem.), Sigma Theta Tau (Image of Nursing award 1993), Delta Kappa Gamma, Phi Kappa Phi. Home: 1723 Fox Run Dr Lake Charles LA 70605-6404

FIELDS, DAISY BRESLEY, human resources development consultant; b. Bklyn.; student Hunter Coll., 1932-35, Am. U., 1949-53; m. Victor Fields, Aug. 2, 1936; 1 child, Barbara Fields Ochsman. Pers. officer USAF Base, Norfolk, Va., 1942-45; asst. pers. officer Dept. Agr., Phila., 1945-47; asst. dir. pers. Smithsonian Instn., Washington, 1954-60; chief spl. programs NASA, Washington, 1960-67; spl. asst. Fed. Women's Program, VA, Washington, 1967-70; sr. program assoc. Nat. Civil Svc. League, 1971-72; cons. Equal Employment Opportunity/Affirmative Action, 1972-75, 78—; exec. dir. Federally Employed Women, Washington, 1975-77; pres. Fields Assocs., Silver Spring, Md., 1978—; exec. dir. The Women's Inst., Am. U.; instr. Mt. Vernon Coll., 1979-80, Am. U., 1982; cons. USAID, 1990, 91, 92, 93. Author: A Woman's Guide to Moving Up in Business and Government, 1983; editor: Winds of Change: Korean Women in America, 1991; contbr. articles to profl. jours. Chmn., Montgomery County (Md.) Pers. Bd., 1972-78; chmn. legis. com. Comm. for Women in Pub. Adminstrn., 1976-79; commr. Md. Commn. for Women, 1973-77; commr. Montgomery County Commn. for Women, 1979-82; editor newsletter, past pres. Clearinghouse on Women's Issues; v.p., mng. editor Women's Inst. Press; bd. dirs. Nat. Woman's Party, 1989—. Recipient award UN Assn. U.S.A., 1980. Mem. NAFE, Nat. Coun. Career Women, Women's Equity Action League (pres. Md. 1972-74; award 1978), Federally Employed Women (pres. 1969-71, editor newsletter 1972-77, recipient award 1974, 78), Nat. Press Club, Am. News Women's Club, Internat. Women's Writing Guild, Washington Ind. Writers, Capital Press Women, Fedn. Orgns. Profl. Women (exec. coun. 1976-77, 80-82), Nat. Assn. Women Bus. Owners. Home and Office: 13905 N Gate Dr Silver Spring MD 20906-2218

FIELDS, HARRIET GARDIN, counselor, educator, consultant; b. Pasco, Wash., Feb. 25, 1944; d. Harry C. and Ethel Jenell (Rochelle) Gardin; m. Avery C. Fields; 1 child, Avery C. BS in Edn., S.C. State U., Orangeburg, 1966; MEd, U. S.C., 1974. Lic. profl. counselor and supr.; nat. bd. cert. counselor and career counselor. Tchr. Richaldn Sch. Dist., Columbia, S.C., 1966-67 73-76; counselor supr. S.C. Dept. Corrections, Columbia, 1971-73; counselor Techinal Edn. System, West Columbia, S.C., 1967-70; exec. dir. Bethlehem Community Ctr., Columbia, 1976-79; human rels. cons. Calhoun County Schs., St. Matthews, S.C., 1979-82; admission counselor Allen U., Columbia, 1982-83; pres., cons. H.G. Fields Assn., Columbia, 1973—; exec. dir. Big Bros./Big Sisters, Columbia, 1984-87. Mem. Richland County Coun., Columbia, 1989-92, chair, 1993, 94, 95, 96; 2d vice chair Richland County Dem. Party, Columbia, 1984-88; sec. Statewide Reapportionment Com., 1990—. Recipient inaugural Woodrow Wilson award Greater Columbus C. of C., 1994, Pres.'s Disting. Svc. award Nat. Orgn. Black County Ofcls., 1996, numerous human rels. and outstanding svc. awards. Mem. ACA (resolutions chair So. br. 1993-94), S.C. Assn. Counselors (chair govt. rels. 1985—, pres. 1982-83), Assn. Multicultural Counseling Devel., S.C. Coalition Pub. Health, Nat. Assn. Counties, S.C. Assn. Counties (employment and tng. steering com., taxation and fin. com. 1994), Am. Bus. Women's Assn. Democrat. Methodist. Office: Richland County Coun PO Box 192 2020 Hampton St Columbia SC 29202

FIELDS, JENNIE, advertising executive, writer; b. Chgo., July 25, 1953; d. Ira Samuel and Belle Harriet (Springer) F.; m. Steven W. Kroeter, Aug. 28, 1983; 1 child, Chloe Melinda. BFA, U. Ill., 1974; MFA, U. Iowa, 1976. Copywriter Foote Cone & Belding, Chgo., 1977-79; v.p., copy supr. Needham Harper & Steers, Chgo., 1979-82, Young & Rubicam, N.Y.C., 1982-85; v.p., creative dir. J. Walter Thompson, Chgo., 1985-86; assoc. creative dir. Leo Burnett, Chgo., 1986-89; sr. v.p., group creative dir. Young & Rubicam, N.Y.C., 1989-93; sr. v.p. Lowe & Ptnrs., SMS, N.Y.C., 1993-95; sr. ptnr., creative dir. Bozell Worldwide, N.Y.C., 1995—; ptnr. Steven Fields Design Assoc., Chgo., 1983—. Author: Lily Beach, 1993, paperback edit., 1994 (Featured Alternate, Book of Month Club 1993). Recipient 2 Lions Cannes Internat. Festival, Clio award, Nat. Addy award, Effie award, Chgo. Addy Gold award. Home: 452 8th St Brooklyn NY 11215-3616 Office: Bozell Worldwide 40 W 23d St New York NY 10010

FIELDS, KAREN KEYSE, physician; b. Berea, Ohio, Apr. 24, 1956; d. Dale Russell and Barbara Mae (Offenberg) Keyse; m. Paul Henry Fields III, Sept. 4, 1982; 1 child, Michael Fisher. BA, Ohio No. U., 1978; MD, Ohio State U., 1981. Diplomate Am. Bd. Internal Medicine, Am. Bd. Med. Oncology, Am. Bd. Hematology, Nat. Bd. Medicine. Intern and resident Jewish Hosp. Cin., 1981-84; fellow in hematology and oncology Coll. Medicine U. Cin., 1986-88; fellow in hematology and oncology Health Sci. Ctr. U. Fla., Jacksonville, 1988-89; asst. prof. internal medicine U. South Fla., Tampa, 1989-94, assoc. prof., 1994—; asst. chief Bone Marrow Transplant Svc. H. Lee Moffitt Cancer Ctr. and Rsch. Inst., Tampa, 1992—, assoc. dir. div. bone marrow transplantation, dept. medicine, 1996—, interim program leader bone marrow transplant program, 1996—; lectr., presenter in field. Contbr. 100 articles and abstracts to profl. jours. Mem. Keel Club, United Way, Tampa, Fla., 1992—. Named one of Outstanding Young Women of Am., 1985; grantee U. South Fla., 1990, H. Lee Moffitt Cancer Ctr. and Rsch. Inst., 1991, Lederle Labs., 1992, Bristol Myers, 1993. Mem. Am. Soc. Clin. Oncology, Am. Soc. Hematology, Am. Soc. Bone Marrow Transplantation, Internat. Soc. for Exptl. Hematology, N.Am. Assn. Bone Marrow Transplantation (breast cancer subcom.), Phi Alpha Kappa, Phi Kappa Phi, Beta Beta Beta, Tau Beta Sigma. Office: H Lee Moffitt Cancer Ctr Bone Marrow Transplant Svc 12902 Magnolia Dr Tampa FL 33612-9416

FIELDS, KATHY ANN, dermatologist; b. Waukegan, Ill., May 14, 1958; d. Maynard Bernard and Blanche (Telson) F.; m. Garry Rayant, Aug. 10, 1991; 1 child, Richard. Student, Northwestern U., 1975-76; BS, U. Fla., 1979; MD, U. Miami, Fla., 1983. Diplomate Am. Bd. Dermatology. Intern in ob-gyn. Jackson Meml. Hosp., 1983-84; resident in dermatology Stanford (Calif.) U. Med. Ctr., 1984-87; laser specialist Sydney, Australia, 1987; pvt. practice San Francisco, 1988—; skin and beauty cons. major mags. and dept. store including Glamour, Self, McCalls, Family Circle, Nordstroms/No. Calif.; co-owner K-R Dermatologics, Inc.; creator Proactiv Solution, nat. acne skin care line. Fundraiser Am. Cancer Soc., San Francisco, 1988—, Child Abuse Prevention, United Jewish Appeal, Women's Young Leadership Cabinet, 1991—, mosaic counsel. Fellow Am. Acad. Dermatology; mem. AMA, Calif. Med. Assn., San Francisco Med. Soc., San Mateo Med. Soc. Office: 350 Parnassus Ave San Francisco CA 94117-3608

FIELDS, WENDY LYNN, lawyer; b. N.Y.C., Sept. 22, 1946; d. Sidney and Helen (Silverstein) F. BA, George Washington U., 1968, JD, 1976. Bar: D.C. 1976. Assoc. Arent, Fox, Kintner, Plotkin & Kahn, Washington, 1976-78; ptnr. Weissbard & Fields, Washington, 1978-83, Wilkes, Artis, Hedrick & Lane, Washington, 1983-86, Foley & Lardner, Washington, 1986—. Mem. Geroge Washington Law Rev., 1973-75. Mem. D.C. Bar. Assn. Office: Foley & Lardner 3000 K St NW Ste 500 Washington DC 20007-5109

FIELO, MURIEL BRYANT, space engineer, interior designer; b. Bklyn., Dec. 11, 1921; d. Harry and Minnie (Dick) Bryant; m. Julius Fielo, June 17; 1 child, Michael Kenneth. Student, CCNY, 1938-41, Rutgers U., 1965-69; cert. N.Y. Sch. Interior Design, 1970. Gen. mgr. Fidelity Discount Corp., Irvington, N.J., adv. supr. Lincoln Loan Cos., Essex County, N.J., 1941-49; interior designer Alex Fielo Interior Decorators, Newark, 1942-49, prin., 1949-69, owner, 1969—; designer, cons. space engr. MUDGE Interior Design Studios, East Orange, N.J., 1969—. Mem. adv. panel Interior Design Mag, 1977—. Essex County freeholder clk. Bd. Freeholders, 1972-76; commr. East Orange Bus. Devel. Authority, 1977-86; mem. U.S. adv. coun. SBA-Region II, 1980-81; active LWV, 1950-55; organizer, 1st pres. South Orange chpt. Women's Am. ORT, 1952-54, mem. nat. speakers bur., 1952-65, parliamentarian No. N.J. coun., 1955-65; pres. Amity chpt. B'nai B'rith, Newark, 1946-48, v.p. No. N.J. coun., 1948-49, various nat. and state positions, 1948-80; mem. nat. com. on sect. fund raising Nat. Coun. Jewish Women, 1979-81, nat. tour. chmn., 1979-81; trustee cmty. svcs. coun. Oranges and Maplewood, United Way of Essex and West Hudson, 1981-83; bd. dirs. East Orange Central Ave. Mall Assn., 1979-83, chmn. new voter registration drive East Orange 2d Ward, 1955—, entire city, 1969; pres. East Orange Dem. Club, 1957-58, campaign coord. for Dem. mayoral candidate, 1969, calendar coord. Essex County Dem. Party, 1970-76; mem. N.J. Bipartisan Coalition for Women's Appts., 1981—. Named Outstanding Entrepreneur of 1984 N.J. Gov., Outstanding Orgn. Pres. Kean Coll. Profl. Women's Assn., 1985, Wonder Woman of 1986, Bus. Jour. of N.J., One of 8 Women to Watch in 1987 Jersey Woman Mag., 1987; also recipient various awards for civic svc.; named Bus. Person of Yr. East Orange C. of C., 1988. Mem. Internat. Soc. Interior Designers (bd. dir. 1981-85), Nat. Home Fashions League (N.J. membership chmn. N.Y. chpt. 1981-82), Interior Design Soc., Internat. Interior Design Assn. (charter mem.), N.J. Assn. Women Bus. Owners (state bd. 1979-82), Women Entrepreneurs N.J. (pres. 1981-85, chief exec. officer 1987—), N.J. Home Furnishings Assn. (bd. dirs. 1981-84, 86—), Constrn. Specifications Inst., N.J. Soc. AIA (profl. affiliate), Guild Designer Woodworkers, Women Bus. Ownership Ednl. Coalition (N.J. State pres. 1985-87, chief exec. officer 1987—, mem. steering com. interior designers for licensing in N.Y. 1985—), East Orange C. of C. (bd. dir. 1977—, v.p. 1981-85), Bus. and Profl. Women's Club of Oranges (bd. dir. 1958-66). Jewish. Home and Office: MUDGE Interior Design Studio 185 S Clinton St East Orange NJ 07018-3039

FIENUP-RIORDAN, ANN, writer, anthropologist, curator; b. Oct. 13, 1948; d. Kenneth L. and Beth (Fiske) Fienup; m. Dick Riordan, 1972; children: Frances, Jimmy, Nick. BA, U. Mich., 1971, MA, 1973; PhD, U. Ill., 1980. Instr. anthropology U. Alaska, Anchorage, 1973-74, asst. prof. anthropology, 1983-84; owner, operator Mud, Inc., 1974; rschr., pub. designer Nelson Island (Alaska) Sch. Design, 1975; instr. Alaska State Coun. on Arts, Anchorage, 1978; interviewer, rsch. cons. Yukon Kuskokwim Health Corp., Bethel, Alaska, 1978-80; asst. prof. social science Alaska Pacific U., Bethel, 1980-83; specialist village econs. rural Alaska Minerals Mgmt. Svc. U.S. Dept. Interior, Yukon Delta, 1986-88; cons. anthropologist Yupiit Nation, 1988-89; curator Agaiyuliyrallput: The Living Tradition Yuy'ik Masks Anchorage Mus. History and Art, 1994-96. Author: Maraiurivik Nunakauiami: The History and Development of Pottery at Toksook Bay, 1975, Shape Up with Baby: Games for the New Parent and Child, 1980, The Nelson Island Eskimo: Social Structure and Ritual Distribution, 1983, The Yup'ik Eskimos as Described in the Travel Journals and Thnographic accounts of John and Edith Kilbuck, 1885-1900, 1988, Eskimo Essays: Yup'ik Eskimo Encounter with Moravian Missionaries John and Edith Kilbuck, 1991, Boundaries and Passages: Rule and Ritual in Yup'ik Eskimo Oral Tradition, 1994, Freeze Frame: Alaska Eskimos in the Movies, 1995; contbg. author: Alaska's Future, 1986, Crossrads of Continentents, 1988, Russian America: The Forgotten Frontier, 1990; assoc. editor: Arctic Anthropology; mem. editl. bd.: Etudes/Inuit/Studies; contbr. over 50 articles and revs. to profl. jours., regional mags. Named Alaska Historian of Yr., 1991, Alaska Humanist of Yr. Humanities Forum, 1991; grantee U.S. Dept. Interior, 1980-81, Alaska Coun. Sci. and Tech., 1981-83, NEH, 1985-86, 89-91, 94-96, Adminstrn. Native Ams., 1988-89, Am. Assn. State and Local History, 1989, Alaska Humanites Forum, 1989, Nat. Hist. Pubs. and Records Commn., 1992-94, Rockefeller Found., 1994-96. Mem. Am. Ethnol. Soc., Am. Anthropol. Assn., Alaska Anthropol. Assn., Alaska Hist. Soc. (Alaska History award 1988). *

FIFE, BETTY H., librarian; b. Indpls., Mar. 31, 1925; d. Otho Cova and Mae Craddock (Paxton) Hay; m. James A. Fife, Aug. 30, 1945; children: Andrew, Marlie, John, Laurie. BS, Boston U., 1967, MS, 1969; student, Northeastern U. Classroom tchr., libr. Town of Hanover (Mass.); elem. libr. Town of Newburgh (N.Y.). Fellow Northeastern U. Mem. NCTE. Home: 174 Cedar Acres Rd Marshfield MA 02050-6036 Office: PO Box 115 Vails Gate NY 12584-0115

FIFER CANBY, SUSAN MELINDA, library administrator; b. Stockton, Calif., Jan. 23, 1948; d. Reginald Dekovan and Shirley Rae (Canaday) Fifer; m. Thomas Yellott Canby, Oct. 9, 1982. BS, U. Nebr., 1970; MLS, U. Md., 1974. Circulation libr. Nat. Geog. Soc., Washington, 1975-81, asst. librarian, 1981-83, dir. Libr., 1983-94, dir. libr. and indexing, 1994—; bd. dirs. tech. com. D.C. Council Govts., 1985-88; bd. dirs. Capital Area Lib. Network, 1989—, chair, 1994—. Lay reader St. Luke's Ch., Brighton, Md., 1985—, mem. vestry, 1994—. Mem. ALA (John Cotton Dana award 1985, 89), Spl. Librs. Assn. (chmn. geography and map div. 1978, 85), D.C. Libr. Assn. (pres. 1991-92, v.p. 1990-91, sec. 1981-83, Disting. Svc. award 1993, chmn. publs. com. 1993-94), Assn. Am. Geographers, Hort. Soc. Sandy Spring (v.p. 1987-88), Delta Delta Delta. Republican. Episcopalian. Avocations: gardening, reading. Home: 6855 Haviland Mill Rd Clarksville MD 21029-1308 Office: Nat Geog Soc Library 1145 17th St Washington DC 20036

FIGARD, WENDI AMOS, lawyer; b. McKeesport, Pa., June 4, 1968; d. James T. Amos and Bobbie G. (Jenkins) Voit; m. Gary Wade Figard, Oct. 12, 1991. BS in Indsl. Mgmt./Graphic Comml. Mgmt., Carnegie Mellon U., 1990; JD, Wake Forest U., 1996. Assoc. Shumaker, Loop & Kendrick, Charlotte, N.C., 1996—; legal writing tutor Wake Forest U., Winston-Salem, N.C., 1994-95. Notes and comments editor Wake Forest U. Law Sch. Rev., 1995-96. Disaster vol. ARC, Pa. and Eng., 1988-93, bd. dirs., Pitts., 1985-90; vol. U.S. Voter Registration, Eng., 1990-93, Boy Scouts Am., Bentwaters, Eng., 1991-92; student practicing lawyer Domestic Violence Advocacy Ctr., Winston-Salem, 1995-96. 1st lt. USAF, 1990-93. Recipient award World Affairs Coun., 1985, Haplan Humanitarian award Pitts. Jewish Assn., 1986, Excellence award Am. Legion, 1986, 10 Vol. Pin, ARC, 1991, Am. Jurisprudence award Lawyers Coop. Pub. Co., 1994, Intellectual Property Law award Computer-Assisted Legal Instrn., 1996; Charles L. Little scholar, 1994-96. Mem. ABA, Am. Judicature Soc., Criminal Law Roundtable, Kappa Kappa Gamma (social chmn. 1987-88). Home: 13608 Harvest Point Dr Huntersville NC 28078 Office: Shumaker Loop & Kendrick 227 W Trade St Ste 2150 Charlotte NC 28202

FIGGE, JUDY M., home health care corporation administrator; b. St. Louis, Oct. 29, 1948; d. William E. and Helen M. (Scheer) Austin; m. Kenneth J. Figge, June 23, 1978; children: Lori Grubb, Ron Figge. RN, Jewish Hosp. Sch. Nursing, 1970. Cert. RN. With Potamedic, St. Louis, Competent Nursing Svcs., Mpls.; owner, pres., CEO In Home Health, Inc., Minnetonka, Minn., 1981—, also, dir., 1983—. Mem. host family Fgn. Exchg. Students, 1988, 89, 93. Named Entrepreneur of the Yr. (woman-owned bus.) Ernst & Young. Mem. Nat. Assn. for Home Care, The Com. of 200. Office: In Home Health Inc 601 Lakeshore Pky Ste 500 Hopkins MN 55305-5214*

FIGLAR, ANITA WISE, banker; b. Camas, Wash., Oct. 7, 1950; d. William Hulon and Mary Wise (Adkisson) Ward; m. Richard Bould Figlar, Aug. 7, 1976; children: Richard Bould II, David Wise. Student, U. Wash., 1968-70; BA in Intercultural Studies, Ramapo Coll., 1974. Mktg. coord. power and control ops. Gen. Cable Corp., Union, N.J., 1975-76, mktg. analyst power and control ops., 1976-78; various positions Potters Industries, Inc., Hasbrouck Heights, N.J., 1971-75; with highway safety programs dept. Potters Industries, Inc., Parsippany, N.J., 1981-82, mgr. highway safety programs dept., 1982-84, mgr. bus. devel., 1985-86, industry mgr. Highway Products div., 1986-89; with customer svc. United Jersey Bank, Hackensack, N.J., 1989; fin. svc. rep. United Jersey Bank, 1989-90, asst. br. mgr., bank officer, 1990-91; bank officer retail sales United Jersey Bank, Hackensack, N.J., 1991-92, bank officer retail sales mgr., 1992-94; v.p., mgr. retail sales Summit Bank (formerly United Jersey Bank), Hackensack, N.J., 1994—. Contbr. articles to many profl. and govtl. pubs. Notary pub.

FILCHOCK, ETHEL, education educator, poet. BS in Edn., Kent State U. Tchr. Clevc. Pub. Schs.; with EFC Creations, Solon, Ohio. Author: Voices in Poetics: Vol. 1, 1985 (Merit award), Hall of Fame: Ethel Filchock, Vol. 1, 1991 (book of poetry) Softer Memories Across a Lifetime, 1989, (poetryu chapbook) A Glimpse of Love, 1991; composer: Praise God, The Lord is Coming; lyricist: (songs) He Is Born, 1991, An Old-Fashioned Christmas, Let's Wave the Stars and Stripes Forever, 1991, Be There for Me Music of America, 1993, Christmas Joy, Happy Holidays, 1993, Beautiful Lady of Medugorje, 1993 (Harmonious Honor award), Christmas Joy, There is a Story, 1994, Hilltop Country, Love is Not a Game, 1994, High Country, Loving is Caring, 1995. Chmn. sch. United Way, 1985-86. Recipient Cert. of Achievement N.Y. Profl./Amateur Song Jubilee, 1986, Editor's Choice award Disting. Poets of Am., Outstanding Achievement in Poetry, Nat. Libr. of Poetry, 1993, Outstanding Poets of 1994, Interregnum Nat. Libr. of Poetry, Best Poets of 1995, Transformation, Nat. Libr. of Poetry, Editor's Choice award Outstanding Achievement in Poetry, Nat. Libr. of Poetry, 1995. Mem. NAFE, Am. Fedn. Tchrs. Roman Catholic. Club: Akron Manuscript.

FILIPI, JOAN LEAHY (JODY FILIPI), medical association executive, speech pathologist; b. Park Falls, Wis., Nov. 29, 1950; d. James Joseph and Katherine A. (Lillestrand) Leahy; m. David H. Filipi, Nov. 28, 1975; children: Kristin Brita, James Bohdan. BS in Speech Pathology Edn., U. Nebr., Omaha, 1972, MS in Speech Pathology, 1974; Cert. of Clin. Competence in Speech/Lang. Pathology, The Am. Speech and Hearing Assn. Cert. speech pathologist, Nebr. Speech lang. pathologist Ednl. Svc. Unit #4, Auburn, Nebr., 1975, Ralston (Nebr.) Pub. Schs., 1975-78; adminstrv. asst. Nebr. Acad. Family Physicians, Omaha, 1987-89, interim exec. dir., 1989, exec. dir., 1989—; mng. editor Cornhusker Family Physician mag., 1990—; sec., exec. dir. Family Health Found. Nebr., 1990-93; exec. dir. Nebr. Acad. Family Physicians Found., Omaha, 1993—. Pres. Nebr. Children's Chorus, Omaha, 1985-90, designer T-shirt, 1985; bd. dirs. Nebr. Alliance for Arts Edn., Fremont, 1989-91, dir. vacation ch. sch. Dundee Presbyn. Ch., Omaha, 1985-87; asst. dir. LOGOS Program, 1993-94, dir., 1994—; mem. Christian Edn. Council, 1995; mem. class 14 Leadership Omaha, 1991-92; mem. Leadership Omaha Community Boardmanship Course, YWCA Women of Distinction, Nebr. Safety Ctr. Adv. Coun., 1992—. Mem. Profl. Convention Mgmt. Assn., Am. Soc. Assn. Execs., Am. Assn. Med. Soc. Execs., Nebr. Soc. Assn. Execs., Nebr. Choral Arts Soc. (bd. dirs. 1987-91, outstanding svc. award Nebr. Children's Chorus 1988), The Great Navy of the State of Nebr. (admiral 1994), Leadership Omaha Alumni Assn. Office: Nebr Acad Family Physicians 7101 Newport Ave Ste 201 Omaha NE 68152-2153

FILIPOWICZ, DIANE HELEN, architectural designer; b. Manchester, N.H., Jan. 4, 1953; d. Leo and Dorianne Bernadette (Demers) F. BA, Wellesley Coll., 1975; MA, Cornell U., 1986; MArch, N.C. State U., 1990. Cert. archtl. historian. Arch. historian Lakeshore Assn. for Arts, Fredonia, N.Y., 1976, S.D. Dept. Edn., Vermillion, 1978-79, State Hist. Soc. Wis., Madison, 1979-84; preservation planner N.C. Dept. Cultural Resources, Raleigh, N.C., 1984-86; editl. asst. N.C. State U., Raleigh, 1986-90; asst. prof. East Carolina U., Greenville, N.C., 1990-95; cons. Orion Designs, Greenville, 1992—, Willoughby Park Home Owners Assn., Greenville, 1991—; preservation officer Wis. Soc. Archtl. Historians, Madison, 1982-84; instr. continuing edn. Wake C.C., Raleigh, 1985. Co-author: Frank Lloyd Wright and Madison, 1990. Grantee Nat. Trust for Hist. Preservation, N.C., 1986. Mem. AIA (assoc.), Soc. Archtl. Historians, Assn. Collegiate Schs. Arch. Office: Stephens & Francis Architects PO Box 1387 New Bern NC 28560

FILIPPELLI, ALICE MARIE, special education educator; b. Paterson, N.J., Feb. 24, 1962; d. William Carl Jr. and Donna Marie (Altavilla) F. BA in Psychology, William Paterson Coll., Wayne, N.J., 1985, postgrad., 1985-88, 91—. Cert. tchr. of handicapped, N.J. Substitute tchr. United Cerebral Palsy League, Union, N.J., 1985; grad. asst. infant psychology program William Paterson Coll., 1985-87; classroom tchr. St. Patricks Spl. Classes Sch., Newark, 1985-88; spl. edn. tchr. Paterson Pub. Sch. # 27, 1988—; mem. ann. conv. Assn. Schs. and Agys. for Handicapped, Atlantic City, 1985-88. Vol. helper, fund raiser Eva's Kitchen/Homeless Shelter, Paterson, 1986—; polit. worker, poll worker Young. Dems. (Riverside) Assn., Paterson, 1978—. Recipient Sponsor Appreciation award Paterson PASS-PLAN Orgn., 1991. Mem. NEA, N.J. Edn. Assn., Passaic County Edn. Assn., Paterson Edn. Assn. (bldg. del. 1989—). Democrat. Roman Catholic. Home: 1036 E 24th St 2nd Flr Paterson NJ 07513-1028 Office: Paterson Pub Schs No 27 250 Richmond Ave Paterson NJ 07502-1332

FILLEMAN, TERESA ELLEN, technical writer; b. Columbus, Ohio, Aug. 19, 1952; d. Marion Denver and Doris Audrey (Freeland) Grow; m. John Jay Filleman, June 4, 1977; children: John Wesley, Scott Ashley. AA in Geology, Glendale C.C., 1973; BS in Geology, No. Ariz. U., 1975, postgrad., 1975-77. Hydrologist Ariz. Dept. Water Resources, Phoenix, 1977-82, 84-85; computer cons., bd. dirs. Cross Roads Presch., Ltd., Phoenix, 1984-89; computer cons. Geraghty & Miller, Inc., Phoenix, 1987-88; tech. writer Digital Equipment Corp., Phoenix, 1989-92; documentation designer ASI Solution Integrators, Phoenix, 1994-95, pres., 1994—; tech. writer, cons. Mt. Shadows Elem. Sch., Glendale, 1987-91, Desert Sage Elem. Sch., 1991-94. Co-author: A Study of Global Sand Seas, 1979, also various sci. studies and publs.; performer mus. CD and taps Wings Like Eagles, 1994; newsletter editor Mt. Shadows and Desert Sage Elem. Schs., 1987-94. Edn. coord. Dove of the Desert United Meth. Ch., Glendale, Ariz., 1990-94, dir. steel band, 1991—; parent rep. Deer Valley Unified Sch. Dist., Phoenix, 1993. Recipient Giant Slayer award Dove of the Desert United Meth. Ch., 1991, 93, Chmn.'s award City of Phoenix Electric Light Parade, 1993, Judges award for Best Theme Entry, City of Phoenix Electric Light Parade, 1994. Mem. Percussive Arts Soc., Phi Theta Kappa. Republican.

FILLER, MARY ANN, librarian; b. Altoona, Pa., Aug. 6, 1940; d. James Arthur and Mary DeLellis (Hopple) Sides; m. Richard Anthony Filler; children: Tracy Anne, Christopher Anthony. BS in Med. Tech., St. Francis Coll., 1962; MLS, U. Pitts., 1968; postgrad., Shippensburg U., 1975-77. Cert. med. tech. Rsch. asst. U. Pitts. Med. Sch. of Pub. Health, 1963-68; asst. tech. asst. prgm Pa. State U., 1968-70; asst. librarian Sheperstown (W.Va.) U., 1971-72; sr. reference librarian Pa. State U., Middletown, 1979-86; mgr. info. ctr. Armstrong World Ind., Inc., Lancaster, Pa., 1986—. Author: Acid Rain: A Pennsylvania Problem?, 1983. Mem. AAAS, Spl. Librs. Assn. (bus. mgr. 1987-88, nominating com. 1989, dir. 1990), Beta Phi Mu. Democrat. Roman Catholic. Home: 127 Maple Ave Hershey PA 17033-1547 Office: Armstrong World Industries 2500 Columbia Ave Lancaster PA 17603-4117

FILLEY, DOROTHY MCCRACKEN, museum consultant, antique costume restorer; b. St. Augustine, Fla., Mar. 22, 1915; d. Fred Wellman and Rozella May (Leith) McCracken; m. Marcus Lucius Filley IV, Sept. 11, 1937; children—Leith Child Filley Colen, Linda Derrick Filley Laguerre. BS in Fine Arts, Skidmore Coll. 1936; MA in Museology, SUNY-Oneonta, 1974. Founder, dir. Rensselaer County Jr. Mus., Troy, N.Y., 1954-59; exhibits cons. to N.Y. State historian N.Y. State Edn. Dept., Albany, 1956-57; mus. cons. Hist. Soc., Saratoga Springs, N.Y.-Park Casino, 1971-74; curator, coord. Rockefeller Empire State Mall Art Collection, Albany, 1978-80; curator exhibits and collections Albany Inst. History and Art, 1974-81, mus. cons., 1981-87; mem. N.Y. State Coun. on the Arts Mus. Adv. Bd., N.Y.C., 1974-75; cons. compiling history Town of Colonie, Newtonville, N.Y., 1975; mem. adv. bd. Shaker Heritage Soc., Albany, 1981-88; cons. textiles and costumes Albany Inst. History and Art, 1983-89; cons. Troy Savs. Bank Oil Painting Collection of bank presidents from 1823 to 1987 for conservation, 1988; spl. rsch. cons. History of SUNY Univ. Plaza Bldg., 1986; historian Village Improvement Soc., Yarmouth, Maine, 1992-96. Author: Recapturing Wisdom's Valley, 1975. Mem. Cooperstown Grad. Assn., Jr. League Troy (pres. 1950-51). Avocations: gardening, tennis, swimming, wildlife preservation. Home: RR 1 Box 136B Yarmouth ME 04096-9713

FILLIP, CHRISTINE, public relations executive. BJ, Ohio U. Account service rep. Hanes & Assocs., 1987-89; v.p. Edelman Worldwide, 1989-90; v.p. Kamber Group, Washington, 1990-94, sr. v.p., 1994—. Press sec. 2 congl. campaigns. Office: Kamber Group 1920 L St NW Ste 700 Washington DC 20036-5004*

FILLOY, BEVERLEE ANN HOWE, clinical social worker; b. Ogden, Utah, Mar. 11, 1926; d. Albert Herman Howe and Bernice Anna (Ewing) Howe Routt; m. Jose Antonio Filloy-Alvarez, Feb. 4, 1945 (dec. 1988); children: Richard Anthony, Emily Ann. BA with honors, U. Calif., Berkeley, 1947, MSW, 1954; PhD, Calif. Inst. Clin. Social Work, Berkeley, 1980. Bd. cert. diplomate clin. social work, sex therapist, clin. supr. Social caseworker Family Svc. Agy., Sacramento, Calif., 1959-63; cons. Stanford Lathrop Meml. Home, Sacramento, 1964-69; cons., supr. Arnold Homes for Children, Sacramento, 1968-71; pvt. practice social work Sacramento, 1963—; faculty Calif. Soc. Clin. Social Work, Sacramento, 1979—, Calif. State U., Sacramento, 1956-58, 90; sec. Nat. Registry Providers of Health Care in Clin. Social Work, 1983-85, bd. dirs., 1980-86, treas. Nat. Fedn. for Socs. for Clin. Social Work, 1981-86. Founder, bd. Planned Parenthood of Sacramento, 1964. Fellow Calif. Soc. for Clin. Social Work (pres. 1983-85, bd. dirs. 1969-87, Mem. of Yr. award 1990), Calif. Inst. for Clin. Social Worker (bd. trustees, sec.-treas. 1976-88, v.p. 1989-94); mem. Soc. for Sci. Study Sex, Amnesty Internat., Older Women's League, Am. Assn. Sex. Educators, Counselors, Therapists, Phi Beta Kappa. Democrat. Office: 3525 Watt Ave Ste 1 Sacramento CA 95821-2617

FILSHIE, MICHELE ANN, editor; b. Hartford, Conn., Mar. 5, 1964; d. Joseph James Fitzgibbons and Judith Ann (Bennett) Small; m. Glenn Filshie, May 24, 1986. BA in English, U. Western Ont., London, 1986. Asst. to the pub. Black Sparrow Press, Santa Rosa, Calif., 1991—. Bd. dirs. Sonoma County People for Econ. Opportunity, Santa Rosa, Calif., 1995—. Recipient Write Women Back into History award Nat. Women's History Project, Windsor, Calif., 1995. Mem. NOW (pres. Sonoma County, Santa Rosa chpt. 1994—), Am. Motorcycle Assn. Democrat. Office: Black Sparrow Press 24 Tenth St Santa Rosa CA 95401

FILTER, EUNICE M., business equipment manufacturing executive; b. Teaneck, N.J., Sept. 19, 1940. BA in Econs., CCNY, 1966. Security analyst Morgan Guaranty Trust Co. N.Y., 1966-70; sr. tech. analyst G.A. Saxton & Co., N.Y.C., 1970-73; mgr. Xerox Corp., Stamford, Conn., 1973-79, dir. investor rels., 1979-84, v.p., corp. sec., 1984—, treas., 1990—; dir. Baker Hughes, Inc., Houston, 1992—. Trustee Wells Colls., Aurora, N.Y., 1990—; bd. dirs. United Way Tri-State, N.Y.C., 1989-93, Westport-Weston (Conn.) United Way, 1989-93. Recipient Graham & Dodd award Fin. Analysts Fedn., N.Y.C., 1971; named to Acad. of Women Achievers YWCA of N.Y.C., 1981. Mem. Investor Rels. Assn. of N.Y. (pres. 1984-85), Nat. Investor Rels. Inst., Nat. Assn. Corp. Treas., Am. Soc. Corp. Secs., Fin. Women Assn. of N.Y., Nat. Assn. Corp. Treas., Coun. of Corp. Treas. (conf. bd. 1994—), Fin. Execs. Inst. (com. on corp. fin. 1994—). Office: Xerox Corp 800 Long Ridge Rd Stamford CT 06902-1227

FINARELLI, MARGARET G., federal government administrator; b. Phila., Apr. 14, 1946; d. Benjamin Fessenden Jr. and Margaret (Taliaferro) Griffith; m. John David Finarelli, July 8, 1966; children: John Albert, Matthew Brian. BA magna cum laude with distinction, U. Pa., 1967; MS, Drexel U., 1969. Sci. analyst CIA, Langley, Va., 1969-77; physical sci. officer U.S. Arms Control and Disarmament Agy., Washington, 1977-79; sr. policy analyst Office Sci. Tech. Policy, Washington, 1979-81; chief internat. planning and program NASA, Washington, 1981-86, dir. policy div. office space sta., 1986-88, dep. assoc. adminstr. external rels., 1988-91, assoc. adminstr. policy coordination and internat. rels., 1991-93; asst. for strategic planning NASA, 1993-94; asst. dir. internat. programs GLOBE Program, Washington, 1994-95, dep. dir., 1995—; bd. trustees Internat. Space U. Recipient Exceptional Svc. medal NASA, 1985, Exceptional Achievement medal, 1991, Presdl. Meritorious Rank U.S. Pres., Washington, 1988, Outstanding Achievement award Women in Aerospace, 1989. Mem. Am. Inst. Aeronautics and Astronautics (exec. coun. nat. capitol sect. 1988-89), Phi Beta Kappa. Office: The GLOBE Program 744 Jackson Pl NW Washington DC 20503

FINBERG, BARBARA DENNING, foundation executive; b. Pueblo, Colo., Feb. 26, 1929; d. Rufus Raymond and Velma Aileen (Hopper) Denning; m. Alan R. Finberg, June 21, 1953 (dec. 1995). B.A., Stanford U., 1949; M.A., Am. U. of Beirut, Lebanon, 1951. Intern U.S. Dept. State, Washington, 1949-50, fgn. affairs officer, Tech Coop. Adminstrn., 1952-53; program specialist, area chief Inst. Internat. Edn., N.Y.C., 1953-59; editorial assoc., program officer Carnegie Corp. N.Y., N.Y.C., 1959-80, v.p. program, 1980-88, exec. v.p., 1988—. Trustee Stanford U., 1976-86, v.p. bd. dirs., 1982-85; trustee N.Y. Found., 1979-91, vice chmn. bd. dirs., 1983-85, chmn., 1985-89; mem. accreditation com. Assn. Am. Law Schs., 1986-88; adv. com. Henry A. Murray Rsch. Ctr. for Study of Lives, Radcliffe Coll., 1986—; bd. dirs. The Hole in the Wall Gang Fund, Inc., 1987—, Investor Responsibility Rsch. Ctr. Inc., 1989—, vice chmn. bd. dirs., 1992-94, Ind. Sector, 1990—, chmn. mgmt. com., 1994-96, chmn. bd., 1995—, Consortium for Advancement of Pvt. Higher Edn., 1992; bd. dirs. Bard Musical Festival, 1995—. Rotary Found. fellow, 1950-51; recipient Women of Vision award N.Y. Women's Found., 1995. Mem. Am. Ednl. Research Assn., Soc. for Research in Child Devel., Council on Fgn. Relations. Club: Cosmopolitan of N.Y. Home: 165 E 72nd St Apt 19L New York NY 10021-4351 Office: Carnegie Corp NY 437 Madison Ave New York NY 10022-7001

FINCH, BRIDGETTE MARIE, airlines company executive; b. Cilmer, Tex., Aug. 13, 1962; d. Willie D. and Mattie Lou (Webb) F. AS, Southwestern Christian Coll., 1982; BA, U. Tex., Arlington, 1987. With Am. Airlines SABRE.

FINCH, CAROLYN BOGART, speech and language pathologist, kinesiologist; b. Mineola, N.Y., June 24, 1938; d. Harold Edwin and Ruth (Waring) Bogart; m. Gordon M. Finch (div. Oct. 1982); children: David Harold, Martha Louise; m. Donald Hall Hulme; children: Wendy Harriet Hulme, Allison Elizabeth Hulme. BS, Elmira Coll., 1965; MS, Western Conn. State U., 1972; postgrad., Nova U., 1982. Cert. speech and lang. pathologist, early childhood edn., elem. edn. and communication; cert. applied kinesiologist. Speech therapist Elmira (N.Y.) City Schs., 1963-65; supervision therapist Speech and Hearing Clinic Elmira Coll., 1966-67; speech therapist Greenshire Residential Sch., Cheshire, Conn., 1968-69; speech pathologist Danbury (Conn.) City Schs., 1970-73; owner, dir. Peter Piper Sch. and Learning ctr., Brookfield Center, Conn., 1973-88, Speech Pathology Assocs., Danbury, 1974-87; mem. adj. faculty Western Conn. State U., Danbury, 1974-86, prof., 1986-87; pres. Apples and Oranges; profl. spkr. Dunn & Brastreet Bus. Edn. Svcs.; organizer, chmn. bd. Liberty Nat. Bank, Danbury; freelance lectr., 1986-88; pres. nat. spkr. Bogart comm., Inc., Danbury; acct. exec. V.R. Bus. Brokers, R. Zemper Assocs.; pres. comm. Fitness Internat. divsn. Bogart Comm.; founder, dir. Candlewood Lake Seminars, 1995; nat. gender intercultural understanding; spkr. on body lang. and elctromagnetic. Author: (multisensory articulation program) Portraits of Sounds, 1969, (book and posters) Survival Sign System, 1982, Universal Handtalk, 1988, Socks Says!, 1993, Be Electrific. Dem. nominee Danbury Town Com., 1985; mem. adv. com. Fairfield County 4-H. Recipient Mayoral Proclamation for Survival Sign System, City of Danbury, 1986, Golden Apple Tchr. award, Danbury News Times; named Woman of Yr. Bus. and Prof. Women, 1990. Mem. Women in Comm., New Eng. Speakers Assn., Nat. Speakers Assn., Women in Comm., John Cosentino Singers. Home and Office: Bogart Communications Inc 51 Cedar Dr Danbury CT 06811-3302 Office: Treatment Office and Candlewood Lake Seminars 18 Old Rte 7 Brookfield CT 06804

FINCH, DIANE SHIELDS, retail sales administrator; b. Detroit, Aug. 25, 1947; d. Earl Arthur and Carrie (Steele) Shields; m. Glenn A. Finch III, Oct. 5, 1968; 1 child, Jennifer Lynn. AA, U. Houston, 1969; student, U. St. Thomas, 1970-73, Rice U., 1980. Apt. mgr. Moonmist Manor, Houston, 1972-75; sales merchandiser Mattel Toys, Houston, 1975-77; sales merchandiser Plough Sales, Houston, 1977-79, ter. mgr., 1979-80, area mdse. mgr., 1980-84, dist. sales mgr., 1984-86; dist. mdse. mgr. Schering-Plough Healthcare Product, Houston, 1986-92; dist. retail merchandising mgr. McNeil Consumer Products, Houston, 1992-95; dist. sales mgr. Walt Disney Home Video, Houston, 1995—. Area chmn. Assn. Cmty. TV, Houston, 1985-87; mem. Friends of Ronald McDonald House; mem. Citizens Animal Protection. Mem. Nat. Assn. Female Execs., Am. Mgmt. Assn., Tex. Exec. Women (bd. dirs.), Houston Fedn. Profl. Women. Office: Walt Disney Home Video 5020 Longmont Dr Houston TX 77056-2420

FINCH, EDITH GRAHAM, accountant, financial analyst; b. Marietta, Ga., Oct. 23, 1950; d. Camillus L'Engle and Susan (Darlington) Graham; m. Kenneth William Finch, Aug. 2, 1968 (div. Feb. 1987); children: Kenneth William Jr., Carrie Madeleine. AS in Acctg., Wake Tech. Coll., Raleigh, N.C., 1983; BA in Bus. Adminstrn. summa cum laude, N.C. Wesleyan Coll., 1985. Gen. mgr. acctg. Adams Products Co., Morrisvlle, N.C., 1985-89; fin. analyst Cooper Tools, Raleigh, 1989—. Elder 1st Presbyn. Ch., Garner, N.C., 1987-90; mem. Garner Bd. Adjustments, 1988-90, Garner Appearance Commn., 1990-93; election ofcl. Wake County Rep. Com., 1991-93. Mem. Inst. Mgmt. Accts. (dir. acad. rels. 1989—). Home: 119 Towne View Trail Garner NC 27529

FINCH, EVELYN VORISE, financial planner; b. Marietta, Ohio, Jan. 20, 1930; d. Richard Raymon Juantzee and Oreatha Fay (Carnes) Metcalf; m. Herman Frederick Ahrens, May 13, 1948 (div. Nov. 1957); children: Erick K.F., Hilda Kate (dec.), Nicole Schwartz; m. James Derwood Finch, June 29, 1973 (dec. Oct. 1993). BS in Music Edn., Concord Coll., 1961. Registered health underwriter, 1990. Music tchr. Prince George's County (Md.) pub. schs., 1961-72; pvt. piano tchr. Washington, 1961-73; china and crystal sales rep. Quality Products Co., Washington, 1973-80; ins. agt. Mut. of Omaha Cos., Washington, 1980-92, Memphis, 1992-94; pvt. practice fin. planner Alamo, Tenn., 1994—; registered mem. Internat. Fin. Exch., Inc., Memphis, 1996—; affiliate Tri-Ocean Internat., LLC, Emeryville, Calif., 1995—; registered mem. Internat. Fin. Exch., Inc., Memphis, 1996—; mem. internat. mktg. and investments divsn. TriOcean Internat., LLC, Emeryville, Calif., 1995—. Pianist for Sunday sch. class; supporting mem. Nat. Mus. Women in the Arts, Washington, 1990—, Women's Philharm., San Francisco, 1993—. Mem. NAFE, AAUW (br. pres. 1994-96, Tenn. chair ednl. found. 1996—), Nat. Assn. Health Underwriters, Internat. Assn. for Fin. Planning, Jackson (Tenn.) Assn. Life Underwriters (publicity dir.), Nat. Boating Fedn. (pres. 1985-87), Internat. Order of Blue Gavel, Chesapeake Commodores Club, Potomac River Yacht Clubs Assn. (legis. chair 1978-87), Chesapeake Bay Yacht Clubs Assn. (commodore 1982), Corinthian Yacht Club, Prince George's Yacht Club (commodore 1978), Pi Mu, Kappa Delta Pi. Home: Finch Rd Box 226A Alamo TN 38001-9734 Office: Finch Fin Svcs Finch Rd Box 226A Alamo TN 38001

FINDER, JOAN BORNHOLDT, academic administrator; b. St. Louis, Feb. 19, 1954; d. Michael and Charlotte E. (Barisic) Bornholdt; m. Kevin Gerard Finder, Oct. 6, 1984; children: Elizabeth Mara, Julia Katherine. BA in Theatre summa cum laude, Fontbonne Coll., 1976; MA in Media Communication, Webster U., 1987. Cert. secondary speech tchr., drama tchr., English tchr., Mo. Drama and English tchr. Valle High Sch., Ste. Genevieve, Mo., 1976-79; asst. dir. admission Fontbonne Coll., St. Louis, 1979-83; assoc. dir. Webster U., St. Louis, 1983—; presenter at internat. convs.; freelance theatre dir., St. Louis, 1976-85. Vol. theatrical cons. Borgia High Sch., Washington, Mo., 1990—; producer, dir. The Company Theatre, St. Louis, 1978-86; chairperson liturgy commn. Seven Holy Founders Ch., 1993—, commr. parish coun., 1993—. Mem. Mo. Assn. Coll. Admission Counselors, Mo. Assn. Collegiate Registrars and Admission Counselors, Mo. Assn. Cmty. and Jr. Colls. Roman Catholic. Home: 7213 General Sherman Ln Saint Louis MO 63123-2317 Office: Webster U 470 E Lockwood Ave Saint Louis MO 63119-3141

FINDER-STONE, PATRICIA ANN, registered nurse, nursing educator; b. Platteville, Wis., Jan. 27, 1929; d. Arthur Charles and Marcella Mary (Roseliep) Finder; m. Mark Henry Stone, Dec. 28, 1953; children: Teresa Kay Stone Gulyas, Susan Elizabeth Stone Crane, Mark Henry Jr., Matthew Riley. Grad., Columbia Sch. Nursing, 1950; BS, U. Wis., Green Bay, 1973; MS, U. Wis., Madison, 1975. RN; cert. in pub. health, Wis. Staff and adminstrv. nurse various hosps., 1980-95; dir. nurses San Luis Manor, Green Bay, 1967-68; asst. head nurse Bellin Meml. Hosp., Green Bay, 1968-69; instr. nursing Bellin Sch. Nursing, Green Bay, 1969-79; dir. Bellin Hospice Program, Green Bay, 1979-80; nursing cons. local law firms, Green Bay, 1984-87; instr. ADN program N.E. Wis. Tech. Coll., Green Bay, 1980—; vice chairperson Brown County Bd. of Health; mem. ethics com. St. Mary's Hosp., Green Bay, 1987—; mem. Wis. ethics com. network Med. Coll. Wis., Milw., 1988—; assoc. mem. Hastings Ctr. Inst. Soc., Ethics and Life Scis., N.Y., 1975—; assoc. mem. Wis. Health Decisions, Inc., 1991. Chairperson bd. dirs., sec., pub. affairs chair Wis. divsn. Am. Cancer Soc., 1978—, bd. dirs., pres., pub. affairs chair Brown County unit, 1976—; bd. dirs. Greater Green Bay Cmty. Found., 1991—, Bay Area Cmty. Coun., 1992—; mem. adv. bd. Brown County Planning Commn., 1992—; mem. planning bd. United Way, 1992—; past bd. dirs. Northeastern Wis. Health Systems Agys., Wis. Health Policy Coun. Named Woman of the Yr. Green Bay YWCA, 1977; recipient Tchr. of the Yr. award Wis. Vocat. Assn., 1983, Nurses Leadership award Green Bay Nurses. Mem. LWV (bd. dirs. Greater Green Bay chpt. 1984—, pres. 1989-92, bd. dirs. Wis. 1992-94, action chairperson), AAUW (pres.-elect 1996), Wis. Nurses Assn. (chairperson legis. commn. 1985-94, ethics commr. 1994—, pub. policy commr. 1995—), Green Bay Dist. Nurses Assn. (bd. dirs., pres. 1992-94, co-chairperson legis. com. 1994—), Nat. League for Nursing, Wis. League for Nursing, Pi Lambda Theta, Sigma Theta Tau (v.p.), Phi Delta Kappa. Home: Crow's Nest No 57 985 N Broadway De Pere WI 54115-2659

FINDLEY, MARY GODBEE, practical nurse; b. Savannah, Ga., Apr. 27, 1972; d. Harry Jay and Victoria Katrine (Davis) Godbee; m. Billy Findley, June 11, 1994. Diploma in Nursing, Savannah Tech. Inst., 1994. LPN. LPN Dr. Greer Gadsden Larned, Savannah, 1994, Chandler Med. Group, Savannah, 1994—. Methodist. Home: PO Box 239 Ellabell GA 31308-0239

FINDLING, KATHARINE RITMAN, retired educator, child studies consultant; b. Chgo., Dec. 23, 1919; d. Hyman Benjamin and Rose (Heda) Ritman; m. Seymour Leonard Lustman, June 10, 1941 (dec. 1971); children: Jeffrey, Susan; m. Ned Findling. BS, Northwestern U., 1941; MEd, Chgo. Tchrs. Coll., 1943. Cert. Chgo. Bd. Edn. Nursery sch. tchr. Yale U. Child Study Ctr., New Haven, Conn., 1959-75, nursery sch. dir., 1964-75, master, Davenport Coll., 1971-73, lectr., 1975-87; ret.; ednl. cons. Calvin Hill Day Care, New Haven, 1969—, Kitty Lustman-Findling Kindergarten (affiliated with Yale U.), New Haven, Phyllis-Bodel Day Care, New Haven, 1975—. Bd. dirs. Urban Improvement Corps (pres. 1980-95), Youth Together, New Haven Assn. for Edn. of Young Children, Calvin Hill Day Care Ctr., E.B.J. Family Day Care (all New Haven). Named first woman Master of a Yale U. Coll., 1971-73. Democrat. Jewish. Home: 22 North Lake Dr Apt A1 Hamden CT 06517 Office: Yale Univ Child Study Ctr 333 Cedar St New Haven CT 06520

FINE, JO RENÉE, management executive; b. Norfolk, Va., June 19, 1943; d. Ruby Arthur and Tillie Fern (Goldman) F.; BA, Smith Coll., 1965; MA, NYU, 1968, PhD, 1973; m. Edward Trieber, Apr. 12, 1981; 1 child, Jessica Fine Trieber. Probation officer N.Y.C. Office Probation, 1966; res. asst. N.Y.U., N.Y.C., 1966-68, assoc. res. scientist Inst. Devel. Studies, 1968-73, res. scientist, 1973-77, adj. asst. prof. dept. ednl. psychology, 1973-76; program analyst N.Y. State Dept. Mental Hygiene, N.Y.C., 1977-78; pvt. practice psychotherapy, N.Y.C., 1978-81; pres. CVM Prodns., Inc., N.Y.C., 1978-92; dir. Ctr. for Diversity and Quality Mgmt., Cicatelli Assocs., N.Y.C., 1992-96; dir. tng. Harris Rothenberg Internat., N.Y.C., 1996—; adj. asst. prof. ednl. communication and tech. NYU, 1988-95; cons. to bds. edn., N.Y.C., also greater met. area, 1973-92, tng. cons., 1990-96. Mem. APA, ASTD, Am. Jewish Com. (v.p.). Co-author: The Synagogues of New York's Lower East Side, 1978. Home: 55 W 16th St New York NY 10011-6305 Office: Cicatelli Assocs 505 8th Ave Fl 20 New York NY 10018-6505

FINE, MARJORIE LYNN, lawyer; b. Bklyn., Aug. 14, 1950; d. Percy and Sylvia (Bernstein) F.; m. John Kent Markley, May 6, 1979; children: Jessica Paige Markley, Laura Anne Markley. BA, Smith Coll., 1972; JD, U. Calif., 1977. Bar: Calif. 1977. Assoc. to ptnr. Donahue Gallagher Thomas & Woods, Oakland, Calif., 1977-87; sr. counsel Bank of Am., San Francisco, 1987-89; assoc., gen. counsel Shaklee Corp., San Francisco, 1989-90; gen. counsel, v.p. Shaklee U.S., Inc., San Francisco, 1990-94; gen. cousnel, v.p. Skahlee U.S. and Skahlee Technica, 1995—; judge pro tem Oakland Piedmont Emeryville Mcpl. Ct., 1982—; fee arbitrator Alameda Co. Bar Assn., 1980-87. Mem. ABA, Calif. Bar Assn., Calif. Employment Law Coun. (bd. dirs. 1993—). Jewish. Office: Shaklee Corp 444 Market St San Francisco CA 94111-5325

FINE, MIRIAM BROWN, artist, educator, poet, writer; b. Vineland, N.J., Mar. 8, 1913; d. Abraham and Katie (Walidarsky) Brown; m. Irvin Fine, Nov. 3, 1935; children: Ruth Eileen Fine, Adele Aviva Fine Gross. BFA, The U. Arts (formerly Indsl. Sch. Arts) and U. Pa., 1935; postgrad., Cheltenham (Pa.) Art Sch., 1968-77, Temple U., 1976-91. Tchr. art and watercolor painting Phila. Pub. Schs., 1953-60; lectr., watercolor tchr. Assn. Ret. Profls. Temple U., 1976-92; pvt. tchr. art, Phila., 1952-77; geriatric poster contest judge and program cover design Pa. Podiatric Med. Assn., 1984-95; tchr., vis. artist Abington Friends Com., 1989-90; tchr. watercolor N.E. Cultural Art Coun. Phila.1, 1987-90; tchr. watercolor, speaker poetry forum David G. Neuman Sr. Ctr., Jewish Community Ctr. Phila., 1991—. Executed 7 murals at Spruance Elem. Sch., Phila., 1951, Holocaust oils and watercolors displayed in Temple Sholom Synagogue, Oxford Cir. Synagogue, UN Women's Conf., Nairobi, Kenya, 1985—, Libr. Nat. Mus. Women in Arts, Washington, 1992—; 16 one-person exhbns. John Wanamaker's Fine Art Gallery, The Hahn Gallery, Cida Art Gallery, First Pa. Bank, Revsin Art Gallery, Frankford Trust Co., Temple U. Ctr. City, Northeast Regional Libr., Phila., 1996; group shows include: U.N. Women's Conference, Kenya, Phila. Art Show, Provident Nat. Bank, Cheltenham Art Ctr., Art Alliance, Pa. Acad. Fine Arts, Philda. Mus. Art, Camden County Hist. Soc., Rutgers Coll., Frankford Women's Art League, Pennock Art & Flower Show, Nat. Coun. Jewish Women, Immaculata Coll., Ocean City Art League, Artist Equity, Cape May Art Ctr.; author: (poetry and illustrations) Word and Drawings, 1984, (in braille) 1996, Mom I Didn't Know It Was Like That, Family History, 1984, The Full Moon Energises My Creativity, 1988, You Are in My Galaxy, 1990, That's Life, 1992, Flowers I, 1993 (Nat. Mus. Women in Arts, Washington), Treasures of Miriam Brown Fine for You, 1993; author, illustrator: My Bible, 1994; contbr. watercolor paintings on boxes and book covers Continental Box Co., 1995, Flower Book VII, 1996. Did benefit for St. Christopher's Children's Hosp., Phila., 1984-87; mem. Torch of Life chpt. City of Hope, Phila., 1935—, mem. Herman chpt., 1992—; vol. Overbrook Sch. for the Blind, Phila., 1991—. Recipient Phila. Art Tchrs. award, 1956, Chapel of Four Chaplains Humanitarian award Torch of Life chpt. City of Hope, 1964, Nat. Synagogue Women's League award, Frankford Women's League award, 50 Yr. Svc. award 1981, 60 Yr. Svc. award 1991, Solomon Schector Illustrated Book award, City Coun. Citizen award City of Phila., 1996, award City of Hope, 1996; Bd. Edn. Art scholar, 1931; Citation in honor of Miriam Brown Fine for her artistic and literary contbn. to the life of the city City of Phila. and N.E. Regional Libr., 1996. Mem. NOW, Artists Equity Inc., Phila. Watercolor Club (hon.), Women's Caucus for Art, Univ. Arts Alumni Assn., Acad. Am. Poets, Nat. Fedn. State Poetry Socs., Writers Cadence Crafters, Poets Study Group, Nat. Mus. of Women in Arts (charter mem.), Temple U. Assn. Ret. Profls. (pres. emeritus, award), Pa. State Poetry Socs., Fight for Sight. Democrat. Jewish. Home and Studio: 1438 Devereaux Ave Philadelphia PA 19149-2701

FINE, RANA ARNOLD, chemical, physical oceanographer; b. N.Y.C., Apr. 17, 1944; d. Joseph and Etta (Kreisman) Arnold; m. Shalle Stephen Fine, June 20, 1965 (div. 1979); m. James Stewart Mattson, Jan. 5, 1983. BA, NYU, 1965; MA, U. Miami, 1973, PhD, 1975. Systems analyst Svc. Bur. Corp. subs. IBM, Miami, 1965-69; postdoctoral rsch. assoc. Rosenstiel Sch. U. Miami, 1976-77, rsch. asst. prof., 1977-80, rsch. assoc. prof., 1980-84, assoc. prof., 1984-90, prof. of marine and atmospheric chemistry, 1990—, chair divsn. marine and atmospheric chemistry, 1990-94; assoc. program dir. NSF, Washington, 1981-83; mem. div. polar programs adv. com. NSF, Washington, 1987-90; mem. geophys. study com. NAS, Washington, 1989-92, mem. ocean studies bd., 1992—; mem. adv. panel Tropical Ocean/Global Atmosphere Program, 1990-93. Contbr. articles to profl. jours. Vol. guide Vizcaya Mus., Miami, 1967-78. Grantee NSF, 1977—, NOAA, 1986—, Office of Naval Rsch., 1983-88, NASA, 1990—. Fellow Am. Geophys. Union (sec. oceanography sect. 1986-88, pres.-elect oceanography sect. 1994-96, pres. 1996—); mem. AAAS (nominating com. atmosphere and hydrology sect.), Am. Meterol. Soc., Oceanography Soc. Office: RSMAS/MAC/U Miami 4600 Rickenbacker Cswy Miami FL 33149-1031

FINE, SALLY SOLFISBURG, artist, educator; b. Aurora, Ill., July 20, 1948; d. Roy John Jr. and Edith Warrick (Squires) Solfisburg; m. Philip Clark Fine, May 5, 1973 (div. 1996); children: Alexander, Arielle. BFA, Ohio U., 1970; postgrad., Boston U., 1978-82, MFA, 1984. Graphic designer Mus. of Sci., Boston, 1970-72; teaching fellow Boston U., 1980-81; instr., lectr. Bradford (Mass.) Coll., 1982-85; lectr. Art Inst., Boston, 1985, Wellesley (Mass.) Coll., 1984; instr., lectr. U. Mass., North Dartmouth, 1993-95; vis. artist Art New Eng., Bennington (Vt.) Coll., 1995; sr. lectr. Bradford Coll., 1995-96, asst. prof., 1996—; prin. S.S. Fine Design, Boston, 1970—; curator The Theatrical Image, Kendall Ctr. for the Arts, Belmont, Mass., 1990; vis. artist/tchr. Truro (Mass.) Ctr. for the Arts, 1991-96. Solo shows include Viridian Gallery, N.Y.C., Bradford Coll.; also exhibited in numerous group shows. Bd. dirs. Kendall Ctr. for the Arts, 1983-86; curator, author of map Cape Cod Nat. Seashore, North Eastham, Mass., 1992. Visual Artists grantee Mass. Coun. for the Arts, 1995, Sculpture fellow New Eng., Found. for the Arts, 1995, others. Mem. Women's Caucus for the Arts (program com.), A.I.R. Gallery, Coll. Art Assn., Internat. Sculpture Ctr. Unitarian. Office: Bradford Coll South Main St Bradford MA 01835

FINE, SARA F., information science educator; b. Pitts., Mar. 23, 1931; d. Joseph and Rose (Murovitz) F.; m. Milton Fine, June 15, 1952 (div. May 1970); children: Carolyn Frances, Sibyl Ann King, David Jeremy. BA, U. Pitts., 1952, MA, 1969, PhD, 1975. Psychologist Shadyside Hosp., Pitts., 1970-73; faculty U. Pitts., 1975-85, prof., 1985—; cons. Allegheny County, Pitts., 1970-75, Psychol. Measurements, Pitts., 1970-80; vis. prof. Tex. Womens U., Denton, 1980, Hebrew U., Jerusalem, 1986; vis. lectr. Hungarian Acad. Sci., Budapest, 1986, City Polytechnic Hong Kong, 1992; lectr. U. Cairo, 1987, Peking U., Beijing, 1992, Chula Longkorn U., Bangkok, 1992. Author: Career Information Centers, 1980; co-author: Group Dynamics and Individual Development, 1974, The First Interview, 1996. Fulbright scholar, Israel, 1986; Rsch. grantee U.D. Dept. Edn., 1978-80; recipient Lectr. award U.S. Info. Svc., Turkey and Nigeria, 1987. Mem. ALA, Am. Counseling Assn., Pitts. Psychol. Assn., Friends of Carnegie Libr. Democrat. Jewish. Office: Univ Pitts 135 N Bellefield Pittsburgh PA 15266

FINE, VIRGINIA O., psychologist; b. Great Falls, Mont., Apr. 18, 1921; d. Jesse Thomas and Helen (Hanner) Owens; m. Robert D. Kemble, Oct. 29, 1944 (div. 1968); children: Stephen B. Kemble; Brian S. Kemble, David B. Kemble, Maricia J. Kemble, Janet Kemble Onopa; m. Jules Fine, July 6, 1969 (dec. 1983). BA, Okla. A & M, 1943; postgrad., Columbia U., 1945; MEd, U. Hawaii, 1964, PhD, 1975. Lic. psychologist, Hawaii. Psychologist U. Hawaii, Honolulu, 1964-74; pvt. practice Honolulu, 1974—, Kailua, Hawaii, 1994—; cons. Family Ct., Honolulu, 1978-85, Dept. of Edn., Honolulu, 1994-95. Mem. APA, Hawaii Psychol. Assn., Assn. Humanistic Psychology, Assn. for Transpersonal Psychology, Assn. for Advancement of Psychology. Democrat. Unitarian. Home: 1042 Maunawili Loop Kailua HI 96734-4621

FINEBERG, ROBERTA, writer, photographer; b. Boston, Dec. 25, 1959; d. Robert G. Woolf and Joan Glick; adopted d. David and Elsie (Glass) Fineberg; 1 child, Paris Kent Fineberg-Heymann. BA in Social Theory and Polit. Economy, U. Mass., 1982. Tchr. Paris and London, 1983-90; instr. Am. Ctr., Paris, 1984-86; rschr. including Brit. documentary film on Jacqueline Kennedy, 1995, biography Liz, 1995, Genet, 1993, Madonna, 1991, Shakespeare's Sister, Bklyn., 1996, others. One-woman shows include 7th and 2d Photo Gallery, N.Y.C., 1991, La Nef des Fous Bookstore/gallery, Paris, 1990; exhibited in group shows at Union of Photography Russia, 1991, Maison des Ecrivains, Paris, 1989, childrens House, La Villette, Paris, 1988; represented in permanent collections La Bibliotheque Nat., La Bibliotheque Marguerite Durand; photos have appeared in publs. including Icarus, Soviet Photo Mag., Le Monde, L'Officiel Femme, Ms.; contbr. articles to popular publs. including Afrique Antilles, Art Monthly, Art Times, Saturday Rev., others. Address: 118 3rd Pl Brooklyn NY 11231

FINELLO, TERRY LEE, communications educator; b. Trenton, N.J., Nov. 1, 1947; d. Curtis Gillikin and Joy (Urban) Rooy; m. Dennis John, June 23, 1973 (div. July 1985); 1 child, Elaine Marie. BS in Communications, Psychology, Edn., Murray State U., 1970, MS in Communications, 1971; postgrad., Cen. Conn. State U., New Britain, 1972. Tchr. Tchr., teaching asst. Murray State U., Murray, Ky., 1970-71; instr. adult edn. Wincester Bd. of Edn., Winsted, Conn., 1973-76; special lectr. Central Conn. State U., New Britain, Conn., 1975-85; lectr. communications dept. Tunxis Community Coll., Farmington, Conn., 1986—; communications lectr. U. Conn., Waterbury, 1986, Torrington, 1986—; English educator Wincester Bd. of Edn., Conn., 1971—; cons., lectr. Vets. Hosp. Nursing Staff, Meridan, 1981, Bus. and Profl. Women, 1982; faculty cons. Conn. State Conf. Emergency Med. Techs., Hartford, 1988-96; cons. Pvt. Individuals Pub. Speaking Coach, 1976—; comms. lectr. gender comms. and sexual harassment United Techs., E. Hartford, Conn., 1995; presenter in field. Mem. editl. rev. bd. Elements of Speech Comm., 3rd edit., 1995. Mem. AAUP, NEA, Conn. Edn. Assn., Winsted Edn. Assn., Nat. Coun. Tchrs. English, New Eng. League Mid. Schs., Litchfield County Women's Network. Home: 51 Pythian Ave Torrington CT 06790-3712 Office: Univ of Conn University Dr Torrington CT 06790

FINERMAN, WENDY, film producer. prodr.: Hot to Trot, 1988, Forrest Gump, 1994 (Academy Award for Best Picture 1995); exec. prodr.: I Like It Like That, 1994; The Fan, 1996. Office: Paramount Pictures 5555 Melrose Ave Los Angeles CA 90038-3149*

FINGERHUT, MARILYN ANN, federal agency administrator; b. Bklyn., Oct. 3, 1940; d. Robert Vincent and Marion (Carroll) F.; m. David W. Haartz, May 14, 1988; children: Margot, D. Bradley. BS in Cell Biology, Coll. of St. Elizabeth, Convent Station, N.J., 1964; PhD in Cell Biology, Cath. U. Am., 1970; MS in Occupational Health, Harvard U., Boston, 1981. Tchr. elem. schs., Jersey City, 1961-62, East Orange, N.J., 1964-65; instr. Coll. of St. Elizabeth, 1970-71; rsch. assoc. N.J. Coll. Medicine and Dentistry, Newark, 1971-72; asst. prof. to assoc. prof. St. Peter's Coll., Jersey City, 1973-80; researcher St. Joseph Med. Ctr., Paterson, N.J., 1977-80; predoctoral fellow USPHS, 1966-69, commd. capt., 1989; epidemiologist Nat. Inst. for Occupational Safety and Health, Cin., 1981-88, br. chief, 1988-94; sr. scientist office of dir. Nat. Inst. for Occupational Safety and Health, Washington, 1994-95, asst. dir. ops., 1995—. Contbr. articles to sci. jours. Founding mem. Women's R&D Ctr., Cin., 1987-95. Recipient commendation medal USPHS, 1989, 92. Mem. APHA, Soc. for Epidemioligic Rsch. Democrat. Roman Catholic. Office: Nat Inst Occupl Safety Hlth Rm 317B 200 Independence Ave SW Washington DC 20201

FINGERSH, JULIE JO, community organization executive; b. Kansas City, Mo., Oct. 29, 1966; d. Jack Neal and Pella (Ben Josef) F.; m. David Mark Rudnick, Sept. 10, 1994. Degree in journalism, U. London, 1987; degree in French lang. and culture, U. Paris, 1989; BA in Lit., Arts-Sci. with high honors, U. Mich., 1989. Editl. asst. Assets, N.Y.C., 1989-90; fin. writer Bus. Week, N.Y.C., 1990-91; reporter for music industry East Coast and Europe, Billboard Publs., N.Y.C., 1992-94; exec. dir. Boston Cares, 1994—. Vol. N.Y. Cares, 1990-94; mem. Jewish Nat. Fund, Boston, 1994—. Mem. Golden Key. Home: 403 Marlborough # 4 Boston MA 02115 Office: Boston Cares PO Box 406 Boston MA 02102

FINIZZI, MARGUERITE H(ELENE), secondary education educator; b. Allentown, Pa., Nov. 16, 1934; d. John Michael and Margaret Mary (Havrilla) Martin; BS in Secondary Edn., Kutztown State Coll., 1956; MA in English, Lehigh U., 1973; m. Joseph Anthony Finizzi, Nov. 19, 1954. Tchr. English, Harrison-Morton Jr. H.S., Allentown, 1956-64, Louis E. Dieruff High Sch., Allentown, 1964-76, Allen H.S., Allentown, 1976—, instr. health/sci. & fitness acad., 1996; adviser pubs. Allen High Sch., 1978—, Quill and Scroll chpt., 1978, intramural bowling, 1992; instr. to develop. drug edn. competency for tchrs., Pa. dept. edn. Student Assistance Program and Intervention Team Tng., 1987, Lehigh U. Gifted Summer Inst., 1989—; mem. in-svc. coun. Allentown Sch. Dist., 1973-93; discussion leader for jr. classes Jewish Day Sch., 1969-71, peer coaching, 1989-90; v.p. Fearless Ladies Bowling League, 1986-89, Mountainville Bowling League, 1995-96, champion, 1996; coord. peer Leadership workshop, 1989, Traveling Ladies League, 1993-94, judge numerous acad. contests, Holistic Scorer SAT II Achievement Essay, 1995, Tchr. Expectations and Student Achievement (TESA), 1987-90, Allentown Sch. Dist. coord. for TESA Program, 1988, coord., 1989, lead tchr., 1990; leader workshops Kutztown U., 1993; workshop instr. Pa. State U. Summer Literary Mag., 1992; lectr., speaker in field; seminar discussion leader Council of Youth, 1980; adviser Student Newspaper Adv. Program; pres. Lehigh County (Pa.) Coordinating Coun., 1967-

71; mem. steering com. Allentown Sch. Dist., 1984. Recipient Meritorious award Kutztown State Coll., 1956; Newspaper Fund fellow, 1981; Commonwealth Partnerships fellow for lit. Inst. Secondary Tchrs., 1985. Mem. NEA, AAUW (membership com. 1993—, rep. Pa. 1993-94), Nat. Council Tchrs. English (co-chmn. conf. 1985, judge nat. writing contest 1987-93), Pa. Council Tchrs. English (judge state writing advancement 1994), Pa. State Edn. Assn. (editor eastern region constn.), Allentown Edn. Assn. (social chairperson 1964-79, exec. sec. 1964-69), Allentown Women Tchrs. Club (editor constn. and by-laws, welfare chmn. 1986-89, pres.-elect 1990—, pres. 1994, past pres. 1994—, scholarship chair 1996—), Lehigh U. Alumni, Kutztown U. Alumni (pres. Lehigh County 1969-72), Columbia Sch. Press Assn. (adviser Reflector Sci. newsletter 1978-90, conf. workshops 1992, student oratorical judge 1992), Pa. Sch. Press Assn., Pa. Shakespeare Festival (sustaining), Media Coalition. Home: 3025 Pearl Ave Allentown PA 18103-6424

FINK, BONNIE LEE, language educator; b. Brantford, Ont., Can., Mar. 28, 1948; came to U.S., 1958; d. John Charles and Isabelle Milburn (Scott) Burger; m. David Jeffrey Fink, Dec. 27, 1969; 1 child, Jennifer Leslie. BS, Bowling Green State U., 1969, MA in English, 1988. Tchr. English, Speech Port Clinton (Ohio) City Schs., 1969-70, Maple Heights (Ohio) City Schs., 1970-74, Otsego Local Schs., Tontogany, Ohio, 1975-87; instr. Bowling Green (Ohio) State U., 1989-92, lectr., acad. advisor, 1992—; cons. Perry House, Bowling Green, 1988-92. Writer, editor BG Chair Co., Bowling Green; presenter panel or workshops in field. Jennings scholar Martha Holden Jennings Found., 1982-83. Mem. Soc. for Tech. Comm., Women in Comm. Office: Bowling Green State Univ Bowling Green OH 43403

FINK, DIANE JOANNE, physician; b. Chgo., July 27, 1936; d. Roman John and Mary Frances (Obrzut) Paluszek; (widow); children—Laura, Janice. B.S., Stanford U., 1957, M.D., 1960. Rotating intern, then resident in internal medicine Kaiser Found. Hosp., San Francisco, 1960-63; resident in internal medicine, then research asso. immunohematology VA Hosp., San Francisco, 1963-66; chief oncology sect. VA Hosp., 1969-71, staff physician charge cancer chemotherapy sect., 1966-69, chmn. tumor bd., 1967-71; exec. sec., prin. investigator cancer chemotherapy group Pacific VA, 1966-71; program dir. chemotherapy, div. cancer research resources and centers Nat. Inst. Cancer, NIH, HEW, 1971-73, chief treatment br., then asso. dir. cancer control, cancer control program, 1973-74; dir. div. cancer control and rehab., 1974-79; asso. dir. Nat. Cancer Inst., 1979-81; v.p. Am. Cancer Soc., 1981—; mem. faculty U. Calif. Med. Center, San Francisco, 1967-71, asst. clin. prof. medicine, 1969-71; chmn. U.S. del. U.S.-USSR Exchange Cancer Control/Cancer Centers; mem. expert adv. panel on cancer WHO, 1977—; chmn. DES task force HEW, 1978; chmn. asbestos edn. task force HEW, 1978. Contbr. to med. jours. Recipient Gerard B. Lambert award Lambert Found., 1975; Superior Service Honor award NIH, 1975. Mem. Am. Assn. Cancer Research, Am. Assn. Cancer Edn., AMA, Am. Med. Women's Assn., Am. Soc. Clin. Oncology, Am. Soc. Hematology. Office: Am Cancer Soc 1710 Webster St Oakland CA 94612-3412

FINK, JANET, lawyer; b. N.Y.C., May 10, 1950; d. Karl K. and Sona (Holman) F. AB cum laude in Polit. Sci., Bryn Mawr (Pa.) Coll., 1971; JD, Georgetown U., Washington, 1974. Bar: N.Y. 1975, U.S. Dist. Ct. (so. and ea. dists.) N.Y. 1977, U.S. Ct. Appeals (2d cir.) 1978, U.S. Supreme Ct. 1980. Staff atty. family ct. and spl. litigation Legal Aid Soc. Juvenile Rights Divsn., N.Y.C., 1974-78, dir spl. litigation unit, 1978-84, asst. atty. in charge, 1984-90; sr. counsel codes com. N.Y. State Assembly, N.Y.C. and Albany, 1991-94; dep. counsel family law N.Y. State Unified Ct. Sys., N.Y.C., 1994—; adj. prof. Cardozo Law Sch., Yeshiva U., N.Y.C., 1995—; cons. N.Y. State Jud. Commn. on Justice for Children, N.Y.C., 1994, juvenile justiceexec. sessions Harvard U., JFK Sch. Govt., Cambridge, Mass., 1983-85; coord. Children's Rights Found., 1990—; mem. Citizens Com. for Children, 1989; mem Ct. Appellate divsn. Family Ct. Adv. Com., 1986—. Chair editl. bd. Criminal Justice Mag., ABA, 1995—; contbr. chpts. to books. Mem. ABA (chair juvenile justice com. criminal justice sect. 1988-92), Assn. Bar City N.Y. (ch. and law, family ct. and juvenile justice com. 1980—). Office: NY State Office Ct Adminstr 270 Broadway # 1401 New York NY 10007

FINK, LOIS MARIE, art historian; b. Michigan City, Ind., Dec. 30, 1927; d. George Edward and Marie Helen (Hensz) F. B.A., Capital U., 1951; M.A., U. Chgo., 1955, Ph.D., 1970; H.H.D. (hon.), Capital U., 1982. Instr. Lenoir Rhyne Coll., Hickory, N.C., 1955-56; instr. Midland Coll., Fremont, Nebr., 1956-58; asst. prof. Roosevelt U., Chgo., 1958-70; curator Nat. Mus. of Am. Art, Smithsonian Instn., Washington, 1970-93; curator emeritus, 1993—; adv. com. Washington area Archives Am. Art, 1979—. Co-author: Academy: The Academic Tradition in American Art, 1975; contbg. author: Elizabeth Nourse: A Salon Career, 1983; author: American Art at the Nineteenth-Century Paris Salons, 1990; contbr. articles to profl. jours. Fellow The Soc. for the Arts, Religion, and Contemporary Culture; mem. Coll. Art Assn., Am. Studies Assn. Home: 10401 Grosvenor Pl Apt 1306 Rockville MD 20852-4640 Office: Nat Mus of Am Art Smithsonian Instn Washington DC 20560

FINK, MARY, elementary school educator, administrator; b. Springfield, Mass.; d. Robert Balk and Helen (Hoppe) Elwell; m. Gary M. Fink, Mar. 26, 1959; children: Lisa, Jeffrey, Karen, Kristen. AA, Stephens Coll., 1956; BA, Mont. State U., 1959; MA, U. Mo., 1965. Cert. tchr. elem. k-8. Tchr. 5th grade Roosvelt Elem. Sch., Missoula, Mont., 1959-60; tchr. 2d grade Lewis & Clark Elem. Sch., Astoria, Oreg., 1960-63; tchr. grades 4,5,6,7 St. Thomas More Sch., Decatur, Ga., 1982—. Co-chair person divsn. Druid Hills Civic Assn., 1992—.

FINKEL, MARION JUDITH, physician, pharmaceutical company administrator; b. N.Y.C., Nov. 2, 1929; d. Israel and Bella (Stillman) F.; premed. student L.I. U., 1945-48; M.D. (Howard Sloan Meml. scholar), Chgo. Med. Sch., 1952; m. Simon V. Manson, Sept. 12, 1954. Intern, Jersey City Med. Center, 1952-53; resident in internal medicine Bellevue Hosp., N.Y.C., 1954-56; med. editor Merck and Co., 1957-61; pvt. practice specializing in internal medicine, N.Y.C., 1956-57, N.J., 1961-63; with FDA, 1963-85, dir. div. metabolic and endocrine drugs, 1966-70, dep. dir. bur. drugs, 1970-71, 72-74, dir. office new drug eval., 1971-72, 74-82, dir. office orphan products devel., 1982-85; exec. dir. research and devel. Berlex Labs., Inc., 1985-88, v.p. drug registration and regulatory affairs Sandoz Pharms., Inc., 1988-94, v.p. corp. regulatory compliance, 1994-95, cons. clin. rsch. & devel., 1995—. Recipient award of merit FDA, 1974; Superior Service award USPHS, 1976, 84; Fed. Woman's award Fed. Govt., 1976, Meritorious Exec. award, 1980; named Disting. Alumnus, Chgo. Med. Sch., 1977, L.I. U., 1980. Mem. Am. Soc. Clin. Pharmacology and Therapeutics, Drug Info. Assn. Contbr. chpts., numerous articles to profl. publs. Office: Sandoz Pharm Corp RR 10 East Hanover NJ 07936

FINKEL, SHEILA BERG, marketing professional; b. Houston, Sept. 13, 1947; d. Phillip Raymond and Anna (Roth) Berg; m. Steven M. Finkel (div. June 1979). BA, Washington U., St. Louis, 1969; MBA, Keller Grad. Sch. Mgmt., 1991. Lab. technician Jewish Hosp., St. Louis, 1969-70, Peoria (Ill.) Sanitary Dist., 1970-73; asst. to gen. mgr. Consol. Office Supply, Chgo., 1974, purchasing mgr., 1974-83; with Wilson Jones Co., Chgo., 1984-91, mktg. info. mgr., 1988-89, promotions and telesales mgr., 1989-90, sales promotion mgr., 1990-91; with Esselte Pendaflex Corp., Garden City, N.Y., 1990-91, dir. mktg., 1992-93; cons. Neiman Marcus Fashion, 1994-95; specialist Ellen Tracy, 1996—. Pres. Pattington Condominium Assn., Chgo., 1986, 90, sec., 1989. Mem. NAFE, Chgo. Assn. Direct Mktg. Home: 709 W Bittersweet Pl # K4 Chicago IL 60613-2309

FINKELSTEIN, CLAUDIA MARCELLE, school psychological examiner, jazz vocalist; b. Montreal, Can., Feb. 16, 1944; came to the U.S., 1944; adopted d. Marcel A. and Jeannette C. (Beauchamp) Fugere; d. Juliette Laplante Jobin; m. Martin R. Finkelstein, June 9, 1968; children: Beth, Leah. BA, Colby Coll., 1966; MA, U. Maine, 1973. Cert. psychol. examiner, sch. psychol. examiner. Sch. psychologist Tenn. Sch. for the Deaf, Knoxville, 1968-69; pvt. practice psychol. examiner Portland, Maine, 1976-94; sch. psychol. examiner Portland (Maine) Pub. Schs., 1994—. Vocalist with various jazz ensembles, 1979—. Vol. Dem. Party, Maine, 1964—; chairperson Cape Elizabeth (Maine) Arts Commn., 1992-95. Mem. Maine Psychol. Assn. Jewish. Office: Portland Pub Schs 331 Veranda St Portland ME 04103

FINKELSTEIN, MARJORIE SUE, social worker; b. N.Y.C., Sept. 29, 1952; d. Edward and Judith (Paskin) F. BA, NYU, 1973; MSW, Adelphi Sch. Social Work, 1975. Cert. social worker, N.Y. Social worker Creedmoor Psychiat. Ctr., 1977-82; social worker, psychotherapist A Comprehensive Counseling Ctr., 1983—; sch. social worker N.Y. Bd. Edn., 1985—. Mem. NASW, Am. Orthopsychiatric Soc., Calif. Sch. Profl. Psychology, Assn. for Play Therapy, Inc., Coalition of Mental Health Profls. and Consumers, Inc. Office: Comprehensive Counseling 98-120 Queeens Blvd Rego Park NY 11374

FINKLE, NANCY SINGER, elementary guidance counselor; b. Pitts., Apr. 9, 1967; d. Sidney William and Barbara (Felser) Singer. BA, U. Pitts., 1989; MA, Trenton State Coll., 1994. Cert. nat. counselor; cert. elem. and secondary counselor, Pa.; cert. in student pers. svcs., N.J.; cert. tchr. English, Pa., N.J. Tchr. English No. Burlington County Regional Sch. Dist., Columbus, N.J., 1989-90; benefits specialist Princeton (N.J.) U., 1990-94; guidance counselor Ewing (N.J.) Township Sch. Dist., 1994-95, Pemberton (N.J) Township Sch. Dist., 1995—. Mem. Newtown Arts Co., Playful Repertory Co. Mem. AAUW (interbr. coun. rep. 1994—), Am. Counselors Assn., Am. Sch. Counselors Assn., N.J. Edn. Assn., Chi Sigma Iota Hon. Counselor Soc. (treas. 1994—). Home: 4107 Waltham Ct Yardley PA 19067 Office: Howard Emmons Elem Sch 14 Scrapetown Rd Pemberton NJ 08068

FINLAND, CHRISTINE ELAINE, counselor; b. Sturgis, Mich., Oct. 23, 1948; d. Charles Hartford and JoAnn Eloise (Grady) Cross; m. Thomas Francis Finland, Jr., Dec. 19, 1986; children: Teresa, Jason, Javon, Jaime and Jennifer. BS in Edn., Ind. U., Ft. Wayne, 1973; MS in Edn., St. Francis Coll., Ft. Wayne, 1975; postgrad., Valdosta (Ga.) State U., 1978—, MS in Counseling and Guidance, 1993. Cert. T-5 social studies and interrelated spl. edn. tchr., Ga. Hosp. and homebound tchr. Marion County Schs., Buena Vista, Ga., 1978-79; tchr. spl. edn. Ochlocknee (Ga.) Children's Ctr., 1979-80, Comprhensive Psychoednl. Ctr., Valdosta, 1985-86; tchr. self-contained behavioral disorders Valdosta Jr. High Sch., 1986-88; tchr. behavioral disorders edn. Valdosta City Schs., 1980-85, tchr. emotional behavioral disorders edn., 1988-94; guidance counselor S.L. Mason Elem. Sch., Valdosta, 1994—. Named Tchr. of Yr., Valdosta City Schs., 1982. Mem. ACA, Coun. for Exceptional Children, Ga. Assn. Sch. Counselors. Democrat. Lutheran. Home: 3807 Cambridge Dr Valdosta GA 31602-6448

FINLAYSON-PITTS, BARBARA JEAN, chemistry educator; b. Ottawa, Ont., Can., Apr. 4, 1948; d. James Colin and Jean Burwell (Moore) Finlayson; m. James N. Pitts Jr., May 27, 1976. BSc (Hons.) in Chemistry, Trent U., Ont., Can., 1970; MS in Chemistry, U. Calif., Riverside, 1971, PhD in Chemistry, 1973. Rsch. asst., then postdoctoral rsch. chemist U. Calif., Riverside, 1970-74; asst. prof. chemistry Calif. State U., Fullerton, 1974-77, assoc. prof., 1977-81, prof. chemistry, 1981-94; prof. U. Calif., Irvine, 1994—; mem. grants rev. panel EPA, 1980-86; mem. adv. bd. series on photochemistry and photophysics CRC Press, 1986—; mem. editorial bd. Revista Internacional de Contaminacion Ambientel; mem. com. on tropospheric ozone NAS, 1989-91, com. atmospheric chemistry, 1989-92; mem. awards program adv. com. Rsch. Corp., 1993-95. Author: Atmospheric Chemistry: Fundamentals and Experimental Techniques, 1986; mem. editl. bd. Rsch. on Chem. Intermediates, 1995—, Atmos. Environ., 1996—, Internat. Jour. Chem. Kinet., 1996—, Jour. Environ. Sci. Health, 1996—; contbr. numerous articles to refereed jours. Mem. AAAS, Am. Chem. Soc., Am. Geophys. Union, Am. Women in Sci., Iota Sigma Pi. Episcopalian. Office: U Calif Dept Chemistry Irvine CA 92697-2025

FINLEY, DEBRA LYNN, elementary educator; b. Lancaster, Ohio, Feb. 8, 1954; d. Roger G. Minerd and Mary Ann (Kee) Minerd-Wallace; m. Joseph Robert Finley, Apr. 10, 1976; 1 child, Alexandra Jolyn. BS in Edn., Ohio State U., 1976; MEd, Ohio U., 1983. Cert. elem. tchr., Ohio. Dental hygienist Drs. Miller, Poole, and Griffith, Belpre, Ohio, 1976-79; elem. tchr. Warren Local Schs., Little Hocking, Ohio, 1980—. Active Pioneer Presbyn. Ch., Belpre, 1984—. Martha Holden Jennings scholar, 1995. Mem. NEA, Ohio Edn. Assn., Belpre Woman's Club. Democrat. Home: Rt 2 Box 349-B Ridgewood Ht Belpre OH 45714 Office: Little Hocking Sch Rt 1 Box 0 Little Hocking OH 45742

FINLEY, SARA CREWS, medical geneticist, educator; b. Lineville, Ala., Feb. 26, 1930; m. Wayne H. Finley; children: Randall Wayne, Sara Jane. B.S. in Biology, U. Ala., 1951, M.D., 1955. Diplomate Am. Bd. Med. Genetics; cert. clin. geneticist; cert. clin. cytogeneticist. Intern Lloyd Noland Hosp., Fairfield, Ala., 1955-56; NIH fellow in pediatrics U. Ala. Med. Sch., Birmingham, 1956-60; NIH trainee in med. genetics Inst. Med. Genetics, U. Uppsala, Sweden, 1961-62; mem. faculty U. Ala. Med. Sch., 1960—, co-dir. lab. med. genetics, 1966—, prof. pediatrics, 1975—, occupant Wayne H. and Sara Crews Finley chair med. genetics, 1986—; Disting. Faculty lectr. Med. Ctr., U. Ala. at Birmingham, 1983; mem. staff Univ., Children's hosps.; mem. ad hoc com. genetic counseling Children's Bur., HEW, 1966; mem. ad hoc rev. panel for genetic disease and sickle cell testing and counseling programs, 1980; mem. genetic diseases program objective rev. panel Bur. Maternal and Child Health and Resources Div., HHS, 1989, mem. adv. group on lab. quality assurance, 1989; Birmingham bd. dirs. Compass Bank. Author papers on clin. cytogenetics, human congenital malformations, human growth and devel. Mem. White House Conf. Health, 1965; mem. rsch. manpower rev. com. Nat. Cancer Inst., 1977-81; mem. Sickle Cell Disease Adv. Com., NIH, 1983-87; chairperson physician's campaign bd. dirs. United Way, 1993-95. Recipient Disting. Alumna award U. Ala. Sch. Medicine Alumni Assn., 1989, Med. award Ala. Assn. for Retarded Children, 1969, Turlington award Planned Parenthood of Ala., 1982, Nat. Outstanding Alumnae award Zeta Tau Alpha, 1992, Disting. Alumna award U. Ala. Nat. Alumni Assn., 1994; named Top Ten Women in Birmingham, 1989, Top 31 Most Outstanding Alumnae U. Ala., Tuscaloosa, 1993. Fellow AMA (founding), Am. Coll. Med. Genetics; mem. Am. Soc. Human Genetics, Am. Fedn. Clin. Rsch., Soc. Exptl. Biology and Medicine, N.Y. Acad. Scis., So. Soc. Pediatric Rsch., Med. Assn. Ala., Ala. Assn. Retarded Children (Ann. Med. award 1969), Ala. Acad. Sci., Jefferson County Med. Soc. (pres. 1990), Jefferson County Pediatric Soc., The Harrison Soc., Rotary Club of Birmingham, Phi Beta Kappa, Sigma Xi, Alpha Omega Alpha, Alpha Epsilon Delta, Omicron Delta Kappa, Phi Kappa Phi, Zeta Tau Alpha. Home: 3412 Brookwood Rd Birmingham AL 35223-2023 Office: U Ala UAB Station Birmingham AL 35294

FINLEY, SARAH MAUDE MERRITT, social worker; b. Atlanta, Nov. 19, 1946; d. Genius and Willie Maude (Wright) Merritt; m. Craig Wayne Finley, Aug. 10, 1968; children: Craig Wayne Jr., Jarret Lee. BA, Spelman Coll., 1968; postgrad., Atlanta U., 1968-69. Job placement advisor Marsh Draughton Bus. Coll., Atlanta, 1971-72; child attendant Fulton County Juvenile Ct., Atlanta, 1972; social worker Fulton County Dept. Family and Children Svcs., Atlanta, 1972—, casework suprs., 1976—, Title VI customer svc. coord. Ctrl. City/North Area office, 1990—. Mem. Am. Pub. Welfare Assn., Ga. County Welfare Assn., Ga. Conf. on Social Welfare, Atlanta Pub. Schs. PTSA, Nat. Assn. Counties, Nat. Alumnae Assn. Spelman Coll., Womens Aux. Ga. VFW, Atlanta Urban League. Baptist. Office: Fulton County Dept Family and Children Svcs 84 Walton St NW Atlanta GA 30303-2125

FINN, FRANCES MARY, biochemistry researcher; b. Pitts., May 6, 1937; d. Stephen B. and Geraldine H. (Weber) F.; m. Klaus Hofmann, Feb. 26, 1965. BS in Chemistry, U. Pitts., 1959, MS in Biochemistry, 1961, PhD in Biochemistry, 1964. Asst. rsch. prof. biochemistry U. Pitts., 1969-73, assoc. rsch. prof., 1973-80, assoc. prof. medicine, 1980-88, prof., 1988—. Mem. Am. Chem. Soc., Endocrine Soc., Am. Soc. for Biochemistry and Molecular Biology, Am. Peptide Soc., Protein Soc. Home: 1467 Mohican Dr Pittsburgh PA 15228-1613 Office: U Pitts Protein Rsch Lab 3550 Terrace St Pittsburgh PA 15213-2500

FINN, LINDA LEE, company official; b. Ware, Mass., Dec. 17, 1961; d. Alfred Thomas and Patricia Mae (Granger) Morris; m. Bradley Elliott Finn, Dec. 24, 1988. AA in English, U. Mass., 1984, AA in Classics, 1984, BA in History, 1984; MBA, Clemson U., 1994. Mgr. Cumberland Farms, Sunderland, Mass., 1984-86, U.S. Postal Svc., Amherst, Mass., 1986-93; adminstr. Avery Dennison Co., Clinton, S.C., 1995—. Recipient numerous letters of appreciation Cmty. Groups, Amherst, 1986-93. Mem. Nat. History Soc., Nat. Classics Soc., Kiwanis (second v.p. 1992-93). Office: Avery Dennison Hwy 76 East Clinton SC 29325

FINN, MARY RALPHE, artist; b. St. Paul, Nov. 13, 1933; d. Wendell W. and Rose Marie (Arendt) Ralphe; m. H. Roger Finn, June 15, 1957; children: Mark W., Shelly, Scott R. BS, U. Ark., 1955; MS, U. Iowa, 1957. Workshop demonstrator and cons. in field. Exhibited in solo shows at Art Mart Gallery, 1973, 76, Brown's Gallery, Boise, 1977, 80, 85, 89, 94, St. Lukes Regional Med. Ctr., Boise, 1982, Piper Jaffray Hopwood, Boise, 1979, 85, St. Alphonsus Med. Ctr., Boise, 1981, 90, Bank of Idaho, Boise, 1975, 79, Morrison Knudson, Boise, 1978; group shows include Browns Galleries, 1975-96, St. Lukes Regional Med. Ctr., 1976-90, Idaho State Capitol, 1978, Idaho Watercolor Soc., 1987, St. Alphonsus Hosp., 1990, Albertson Coll. Idaho, 1988-96, Boise State U., 1991; represented in permanent collections Morrison-Knudsen Corp., West One Bancorp, 1st Security Bank Idaho, Inc., St. Lukes Regional Med. Ctr., 1st Interstate Bank, Am.-Hydro Corp. Mem. Boise Gallery of Art, Phi Upsilon Omicron, Zeta Tau Alpha, Omicron Nu.

FINN, SARA SHIELS, public relations executive; b. Cin., July 12; d. Paul Vincent and Freda K. Shiels; m. Thomas Finn. BA in English, Maryville Coll., 1950. Reporter La Jolla (Calif.) Jour.; advt. and pub. rels. rep. San Diego Mag., 1964-71; dir. pub. rels. U. San Diego, 1971-87; owner Sara Finn Pub. Rels., San Diego, 1987—; pres. Finn/Hannaford (a divsn. of The Hannaford Co., Washington), San Diego, 1987-96; affiliate The Franklin Firm, Washington, 1996—; lectr. and cons. Bd. dirs. Ptnrs. for Livable Places; active Internat. Affairs Bd. City of San Diego, San Diego Hist. Soc., All Hallows Cath. Ch., La Jolla, Calif., Sister City Assn. San Diego/Tijuana; pres. Nat. Assn. Alumnae of Sacred Heart, 1979-81. Inducted into Papal Order Holy Sepulchre, Rome, 1982, elevated, 1985, honored, 1989. Mem. Pub. Rels. Soc. Am. (accredited), Inst. Latin Profls., Pub. Rels. Soc. Am. Counselors Acad., San Diego Press Club (charter star), San Diego C. of C. Roman Catholic. Office: 7817 Ivanhoe Ave Ste 300 La Jolla CA 92037-4542

FINNBERG, ELAINE AGNES, psychologist, editor; b. Bklyn., Mar. 2, 1948; d. Benjamin and Agnes Montgomery (Evans) F.; m. Rodney Lee Herndon, Mar. 1, 1981; 1 child, Andrew Marshal. BA in Psychology, L.I. U., 1969; MA in Psychology, New Sch. for Social Rsch., 1973; PhD in Psychology, Calif. Sch. Profl. Psychology, 1981. Diplomate Am. Bd. Forensic Examiners, Am. Bd. Forensic Medicine, Am. Bd. Med. Psychotherapists and Psychodiagnosticians, Am. Bd. Disability Analysts; lic. psychologist, Calif. Rsch. asst. in med. sociology Med. Coll. Cornell U., N.Y.C., 1969-70; med. abstractor USV Pharm. Corp., Tuckahoe, N.Y., 1970-71, Coun. for Tobacco Rsch., N.Y.C., 1971-77; editor, writer Found. of Thanatology Columbia U., N.Y.C., 1971-76, cons. family studies program cancer ctr. Coll. Physicians &Surgeons, 1973-74; dir. grief psychology and bereavement counseling San Francisco Coll. Mortuary Scis., 1977-81; rsch. assoc. dept. epidemiology and internat. health U. Calif., San Francisco, 1979-81, asst. clin. prof. dept. family and community medicine, 1985-93, assoc. clin. prof., dept. family and community medicine, 1993—; chief psychologist Natividad Med. Ctr., Salinas, Calif., 1984—; profl. adv. coun. Am. Bd. Disability Analysts; asst. chief psychiatry svc. Natividad Med. Ctr., 1985—, acting chief psychiatry, 1988-89, vice-chair medicine dept., 1991-93, sec.-treas. med. staff, 1992-94; cons. med. staff Salinas Valley Meml. Hosp., 1991—, Mee Meml. Hosp., 1996—. Editor: The California Psychologist, 1988-95; editor Jour. of Thanatology, 1972-76, Cathexis, 1976-81. Mem. govs. adv. bd. Agnews Devel. Ctr., San Jose, Calif., 1988-96, chair, 1989-91, 94-95. Fellow Am. Bd. Med. Psychotherapists and Psychodiagnosticians (diplomate); mem. APA, Nat. Register Health Svc. Providers in Psychology, Calif. Psychol. Assn. (Disting. Svc. award 1989), Soc. Behavioral Medicine, Mid-Coast Psychol. Assn. (sec. 1985, treas. 1986, pres. 1987, Disting. Svc. to Psychology award 1993). Office: Natividad Med Ctr PO Box 81611 1330 Natividad Rd Salinas CA 93912-1611

FINNEGAN, SARA ANNE, publisher; b. Balt., Aug. 1, 1939; d. Lawrence Winfield and Rosina Elva (Huber) F.; m. Isaac C. Lycett, Jr., Aug. 31, 1974. B.A., Sweet Briar Coll., 1961; M.L.A., Johns Hopkins U., 1965; exec. program, U. Va. Grad. Sch. Bus., 1977. Tchr., chmn. history dept. Hannah More Acad., Reisterstown, Md., 1961-65; redactor Williams & Wilkins Co., Balt., 1965-66, asst. head redactory, 1966-71, editor book div., 1971-75, assoc. editor-in-chief, 1975-77, v.p., editor-in-chief, 1977-81, pres. book div., 1981-88, group pres., 1988-94; editor Kalends, 1973-78, 89-92; exec. sponsor jour. Histochemistry and Cytochemistry, 1973-77; dir. Passano Found., 1979-91. Trustee St. Timothy's Sch., Stevenson, Md., 1974-83; mem. adv. bd. Balt. Ind. Schs. Scholarship Fund, 1977-81, mem. adv. coun. grad. study Coll. Notre Dame of Md., 1983; bd. overseers Sweet Briar Coll., 1987-88, bd. dirs. 1988—, chmn.-elect, 1994, chmn., 1995—; docent The Walters Art Gallery, 1994—. Mem. Assn. Am. Pubs. (exec. coun. profl. and scholarly pub. div. 1984-85), Internat. Sci., Tech. and Med. Pubs. Assn. (group exec. 1986-93, chmn.-elect 1988, chmn. 1989-92). Republican. Lutheran.

FINNERTY, FRANCES MARTIN, medical administrator; b. Asheville, N.C., Dec. 23, 1936; d. Robert James and Elizabeth Howerton (Babbitt) Martin; m. Richard Phillip Caputo, Sept. 23, 1961 (div. 1974); m. Frank A. Finnerty Jr., July 26, 1975; children: Jonathan, Robert, Richard. Student, Mary Washington Coll., 1954-55, Croft Coll., 1955-57. Dist. mgr. Bus. Census Dept. Commerce, Suitland, Md., 1969-71; program coord. Georgetown U. D.C. Gen. Hosp., Washington, 1972-76; clin. mgr. Hypertension Ctr. Washington, 1976-82; project dir. PharmaKinetic Clin. Rsch. Labs., Balt., 1983; dir. mktg. Classic Glass, Alexandra, Va., 1984-86; office adminstr. Frank A. Finnerty Jr., M.D., Washington, 1987—; cons. U.S. Census, U.S. Army, The Pentagon, Washington, 1969-70; cons. mapping ops. U.S. Census, Prince Georges County, Md., 1970; cons. paramedics pers. Merck Sharpe & Dohme, West Point, Pa., 1974. Contbr. articles to profl. jours. Recipient Cmty. Svc. award Dist. of Columbia, 1980. Mem. Am. Art League (Disting. Artist award 1993), Nat. Assn. Women in Arts, Dist. Med. Soc. Wives. Home: 519 E Front St New Bern NC 28560

FINNERTY, LOUISE HOPPE, beverage and food company executive; b. Alexandria, Va., Jan. 19, 1949; d. William G. and Ruth A. (Ehren) Hoppe; m. John D. Finnerty, May 21, 1988; 1 child, William Patrick Taylor. BA, Va. Commonwealth U., 1971; postgrad., Am. U., 1972-73. Staff asst. to Dr. Henry Kissinger NSC, Washington, 1971-73; adminstrv. asst. Nat. Petroleum Coun., Washington, 1973-75; profl. staff mem. Senate Armed Svc. Com., Washington, 1976-81; spl. asst. Office Legis. Affairs, U.S. Dept. State, Washington, 1981-84, dep. asst. sec. of state, 1984-88; mgr. govt. affairs PepsiCo, Inc., Purchase, N.Y., 1988-91; dir. govt. affairs Pepsico Foods and Beverages Internat., Somers, N.Y., 1991-95; v.p. internat. govt. affairs Pepsi-Cola Co., Purchase, N.Y., 1995—. Mem. Nat. Fgn. Trade Coun. (bd. dirs. 1991—), Spring Lake Bath and Tennis Club. Republican. Lutheran. Home: 400 Park Ave Rye NY 10580-1213 also: 506 2nd Ave Spring Lake NJ 07762-1107 Office: Pepsi-Cola Co Pepsico Foods & Beverage Internat Purchase NY 10577

FINNEY, LEE, negotiator, social worker; b. Balt., Feb. 25, 1943; d. E. William and Mildred Lee (Refo) Carr; m. James Nathaniel Finney, Feb. 25, 1967 (div. Aug. 1970); 1 child, Karen Elizabeth. Student, Sweet Briar Coll., 1961-63; BA in Govt., George Washington U., 1965; MS in Counseling, Calif. State U., Hayward, 1986. Caseworker N.Y.C. Welfare Dept., 1966-68; probation officer N.Y.C. Probation Dept., 1968-74; dep. probation officer Alameda County Probation Dept., Oakland, Calif., 1974-78, child welfare social worker, 1979-80; children's svcs. social worker Contra Costa County Dept. Social Svcs., Richmond, Calif., 1980-87; social work supr. Contra Costa County Dept. Social Svcs., Antioch, Calif., 1987-88; dir. staff devel. Contra Costa County Dept. Social Svcs., Martinez, Calif., 1989-90; pay equity analyst Contra Costa County Pers. Dept., Martinez, 1988-89; labor rels. cons. Indsl. Employers and Distributors Assn., Emeryville, Calif., 1990—; instr. edn. psychology dept. Calif. State U., Hayward, 1987-89; mem. exec. bd. Contra Costa Ctrl. Labor Coun., Martinez, 1987-89; no. v.p., chief negotiator Svc. Employees Internat. Union Local 535, Oakland, 1983-88; chair Coalition for Children and Families, Richmond, Calif., 1986-88. Author booklet: First Steps to Identifying Sex and Race Based Inequities in a workplace: A Guide to Achieving Pay Equity, 1989. Bd. dirs. YWCA, Contra Costa County, 1989-91; pres., acting dir. Comparable Worth Project, Inc., Oakland, 1984-87; mem. Adv. Com. on Employment and Econ. Status for Women Contra Costa, 1984-89, chair, 1987-89. Recipient Cmty. Svc. award Vocare Found., 1976, Golden Nike award Emeryville Bus. and Profl. Women, 1986, Woman of Yr. award Todos Santos Bus. and Profl. Women, 1989, Women Who Have Made a Difference award Coalition of Labor Union Women, 1989. Democrat. Home: 6 Commodre Dr C336 Emeryville CA 94608 Office: IDEA 2200 Powell St Ste 1000 Emeryville CA 94608

FINNEY, PATRICIA ANN, elementary education educator; b. Ft. Worth, Aug. 7, 1936; d. Thomas Lee and Mary Myrtle (Austin) Carleton; m. Roy Jack Finney, Nov. 9, 1957; children: Roy Jack Finney III, Thomas Lee Finney. BS in Edn., North Tex. State U., 1957. Cert. tchr., Tex. Tchr. art Ft. Worth Ind. Sch. Dist., Ft. Worth, 1957-67; tchr. Ft. Bend Ind. Sch. Dist., Sugar Land, Tex., 1979-85, tchr. elem. art, 1985—. One-woman gallery shows, 1972—; illustrator children's books, 1991, 92, 93. Vol. artist Audubon Soc. newsletter, Houston, 1991—; vol. Houston Mus. Natural Sci., 1994—. Mem. Tex. Art Edn. Assn., Nat. Art Edn. Assn., Soc. Children's Book Writers, PTA. Methodist. Home: 10019 Towne Brook Ln Sugar Land TX 77478-1642

FINNEY, WANDA J., archivist; b. Mechanicsburg, Pa., Feb. 5, 1956; d. John Henry and Mary Alice (Good) F. AB, Randolph-Macon Woman's Coll., 1978; MA, U. Cin., 1981, PhD, 1985; MLS, U. Md., 1995. Asst. prof. classics Ball State U., Muncie, Ind., 1983-90; asst. reference dept. Handley Regional Libr., Winchester, Va., 1992-93; intern Corcoran Gallery and Sch. of Art Archives, Washington, 1994; student asst. Nat. Pub. Broadcasting Archives, College Park, Md., 1994-95; asst. prof. libr. adminstrn. U. Ill. Archives, Urbana-Champaign, 1995—. Louise Taft Semple fellow U. Cin., 1978-83. Mem. Soc. Am. Archivists, Midwest Archives Conf., Am. Philol. Assn., Phi Beta Kappa, Beta Phi Mu. Home: 1515 Lincolnshire Dr Champaign IL 61821 Office: U Ill Archives 1408 W Gregory Dr Urbana IL 61801

FINNIE, DORIS GOULD, investment company executive; b. Mpls., Sept. 2, 1919; d. Earl Chester and Marie Ethelee (McGulpin) Gould; m. Donald Johnstone Finnie, May 23, 1939; children: Dianne Elaine Finnie Boggess, Denise Eileen. BA in Journalism, U. Denver, 1941. Office mgr. K&P, Inc., Golden, Colo., 1965-82; exec. dir. Rocky Mountain Coal Mining Inst., Lakewood, 1982—. Editor Procs. of Rocky Mountain Coal Mining Inst., 1982—. Founder City of Lakewood, 1968; dir. Alzheimer and Kidney Found., Denver, 1970-72. Recipient Ernest Thompson Seton award Camp Fire, Inc., 1963; named Woman of Yr. Denver Area Panhellenic, 1977. Mem. Colo. Soc. Assn. Execs., Rocky Mountain Assn. Meeting Planners (Humanitarian award 1992), Profl. Conv. Mgmt. Assn., Kappa Delta (Outstanding Alumnae Assn. award 1959, 74, Order of Emerald 1987). Office: Rocky Mountain Coal Mining Inst 3000 Youngfield St Ste 324 Lakewood CO 80215-6553

FINNIGAN, CLAIRE MARIE, media specialist, librarian; b. Putnam Valley, N.Y., Sept. 4, 1923; d. William Edward and Rose Ann (Crowell) F. BS, SUNY, Geneseo, 1945; MS, Columbia U., N.Y.C., 1952; postgrad., Columbia U., 1963, Westchester C.C., 1994-95. Sch. libr. Eden (N.Y.) Cen. Sch., 1945-47, New Paltz (N.Y.) High Sch., 1947-48; sch. libr. Peekskill (N.Y.) Elem. Schs., 1948-90, ret.; libr. U.S. Naval Air Sta., Atlantic City, N.J., summer 1948; assoc. prof. Queens Coll., Flushing, N.Y., summer 1955; cons. N.Y. State Edn. Dept., Albany, 1953-57, Franciscan H.S., Lake Mohegan, N.Y., 1984-86. Contbr. articles to profl. jours. Dir. RIF program, Peekskill, 1972-87; sec., bd. dirs. City Libr., Peekskill, 1991-95, sec., 1993-95; bd. dirs. City Mus., Peekskill, 1982-87, sec., 1984-85; vol. Westchester Lighthouse for the Blind, 1992-95, Peekskill Paramount Ctr. for the Arts, 1993-95. Recipient Svc. award Home-Sch. Coun., 1984, Leadership award Bd. of Edn., 1987. Mem. Internat. Reading Assn. (award 1982), Women's Club of Peekskill (sec., treas., bd. dirs. 1962-87), Delta Kappa Gamma, Alpha Omicron (v.p. No. Westchester, N.Y. chpt. 1988-90, pres. 1990-92, treas. 1994-95, comms. state com. 1991-93, travel and study state com. 1993-95). Home: 1 Lakeview Dr Apt 6L Peekskill NY 10566-2238

FIOCK, SHARI LEE, design entrepreneur, researcher; b. Weed, Calif., Oct. 25, 1941; d. Webster Bruce and Olevia May (Pruett) F.; m. June 6, 1966 (div. 1974); children—Webster Clinton Pfingsten, Sterling Curtis. Cert. Art Instrn. Sch., Mpls., 1964; pvt. student. Copywriter Darron Assocs., Eugene, Oreg., 1964-66; staff artist Oreg. Holidays, Springfield, 1966-69, part-time 1971; co-owner, designer Artre Enterprises, Eugene, 1969-74; design entrepreneur Shari & Assocs., Yreka, Calif., 1974— (retained as cons., devel. sec. Cascade World Four Season Resort, Siskiyou County, Calif., 1980-86); part time adminstrv. asst., coord. of regional catalog Great Northern Corp./U.S. Dept. Commerce and Econ. Devel., 1994—; cons., pres. Reunions, Family, Yreka, 1984—. Designer 5 ton chain saw sculpture, Oreg. Beaver, 1967; author: Goose Gabble, 1992; illustrator: Holiday Fun Book, 1978; author, illustrator Blue Goose Legend, 1995; co-creator Klamath Nat. Forest Interpretive Mus., 1979-91; owner Coyote Pub. Author, illustrator Family Reunions and Clan Gatherings, 1991. Residential capt. United Way, Eugene, 1972; researcher Beaver Ofcl. State Animal, Eugene, 1965-71; counselor Boy Scouts, 1983-91. Mem. Nat. Writers Assn. (founder, pres. Siskiyou chpt., past v.p. State of Jefferson chpt., N.W. rep.). Avocations: family activities; outdoor recreation; travel; theater; music. Home: 406 Walters Ln # 1854 Yreka CA 96097-9704

FIOLA, JANET SUE, human resources professional; b. Portsmouth, Ohio, June 20, 1942. B in Edn. and Social Sci., Coll. St. Theresa, Winona, Minn.; postgrad., U. Mich. Human resource mgmt. staff Target Divsn. of Dayton/Hudson Corp.; with Medtronic, Mpls., 1980—, v.p. corp. human resources, 1988-92, corp. v.p. human resources, 1993-94, sr. v.p. human resources, 1994—; former chair bd. dirs. The Medtronic Found., Mpls.; mem. Minn. Ctr. for Corp. Responsibility. Former bd. mem. ARC, Health Futures Inst.; former exec. com. ARC-Mpls. Br.; bd. mem. Courage Ctr., AAA Auto Club of Mpls., Working Opportunities for Women. Mem. ASTD (former v.p.), Human Resource Exec. Coun., Minn. Women's Econ. Roundtable. Office: Medtronic Inc 7000 Central Ave NE Minneapolis MN 55432-3576

FIORE, MARY, magazine editor. Former editor Photoplay mag.; mng. editor Good Housekeeping mag. Office: Good Housekeeping 959 8th Ave New York NY 10019-3767*

FIORELLA, BEVERLY JEAN, medical technologist, educator; b. Owensboro, Ky., Oct. 29, 1930; d. Gabriel and Agnes Loretta (Kurz) F. BS, Webster Coll./St. Louis U., 1952; MA, Cen. Mich. U., 1976. Chief microbiology and blood bank St. Mary's Hosp., Kansas City, Mo., 1956-67; instr., asst. prof. med. lab. scis. dept. Coll. Assoc. Health Professions, U. Ill., Chgo., 1967-74, assoc. prof., 1974-80, prof., 1980-95, prof. emerita, 1995—, assoc. head dept. med. lab. scis., 1977-90, acting dept. head, 1980-81, head, 1990-94, grad. program coord., 1977-81, dir. grad. studies, 1990-93; mem. adv. panel on health ins. Subcom. Health of Com. on Ways and Means, Ho. of Reps., 1975-80; cons. lab. improvement sect. immunohematology divs. labs. Dept. Pub. Health State of Ill., 1975-85; cons. editor Clin. Lab. Scis., 1987-90; mem. U. Ill. Pres.'s Coun., 1996—. Mem. bd. editors Med. Tech.-A Series, 1970-74. Recipient Lifetime Achievement award Chgo. Soc. Clin. Lab. Sci., 1996; named Med. Technologist of Yr., Mo. Soc. Med. Technologists, 1967. Mem. Am. Soc. Clin. Lab. Sci. (pres. 1976-77), Am. Assn. Blood Banks, Ill. Clin. Lab. Sci. Assn. (exec. sec. 1987—, named Ill. Med. Technologist of Yr. 1976), Chgo. Soc. Med. Technologists (treas., dir. 1969-70), Chicagoland Blood Bank Soc. (v.p. 1975-76), Internat. Assn. Med. Lab. Technologists (coun. 1988-96), Acad. Clin. Lab. Physicians and Scientists, Clin. Lab. Mgrs. Assn., Am. Soc. Allied Health Professions, Internat. Soc. Blood Transfusion, Alpha Mu Tau. Home: 950 Washington Blvd #103 Oak Park IL 60302-7305

FIORELLI, KAREN LYNN, nurse; b. Milw., Jan. 8, 1954; d. Enzo and Lydia Ann (Naspini) Fiorelli; children: Anthony P., Jack R. BS in Nursing, U. Wis., Milw., 1978. RN, Wis. Nursing asst. St. Luke's Hosp., Milw., 1974-75, nursing unit sec., 1975-79, staff nurse IV, orthopedics, 1979-85, chmn. unit based quality assurance, 1984-85; employee health supervisor Aurora Health Care Inc., Milw., 1986-91; quality mgmt. coord., 1991—. Roman Catholic. Avocations: music, art, theatre, sports. Home: 17406 W Cleveland Ave New Berlin WI 53146 Office: St Luke's Med Ctr PO Box 2901 2900 W Oklahoma Ave Milwaukee WI 53215-4330

FIORENTINO, LINDA, actress; b. Phila., 1958. Student, Rosemont Coll., 1980, Cir. on Sq. Theatre Sch. Appeared in films Vision Quest, 1985, Gotcha!, 1985, After Hours, 1985, The Moderns, 1988, Queens Logic, 1991, Shout, 1991, Wildfire, 1992, Chain of Desire, 1993, The Desperate Trail, 1994, The Last Seduction, 1994, Bodily Harm, Jade, 1995, Unforgettable; appeared in TV movies The Neon Empire, 1989, The Last Game, 1992, Action on Impulse, 1993, Beyond the Law, 1994. Mem. Cir. in Sq. Performing Workshops. Office: care United Talent Agy 9560 Wilshire Blvd 5th Fl Beverly Hills CA 90212*

FIPPINGER, GRACE J., retired telecommunications company executive; b. N.Y.C., Nov. 24, 1927; d. Fred Herman and Johanna Rose (Tesio) F. BA, St. Lawrence U., 1948; LLD (hon.), Marymount Manhattan Coll., 1980; DCS (hon.), Molloy Coll., 1982; DHL, St. Lawrence U., 1990. Dist. mgr. N.Y. Tel. Co., South Nassau, 1957-65, div. mgr., 1965-71; gen. comml. mgr. N.Y. Tel. Co., Queens, Bklyn., 1971-74; v.p., sec., treas. N.Y. Tel. Co., 1974-82; v.p., treas., sec. NYNEX Corp., N.Y.C., 1982-90; ret., 1990; bd. dirs. Bear Stearns Co., Pfizer, Inc. Former mem. Gov.'s Econ. Devel. Adv. Coun.; past bd. dirs. Consumer Credit Counseling Svc. Greater N.Y., 1972—, YMCA Greater N.Y., 1975—; former dir. A.R.C., L.I., Nassau County Health and Welfare Coun.; trustee Citizens Budget Commn., 1974—; former dir. exec. bd. Nassau County Fedn. Rep. Women; trustee emeritus Citizens Budget Com. Named Woman of Yr., Bus. and Profl. Women Nassau County, 1969, Woman of Achievement, Flatbush Bus. and Profl. Women's Assn., 1974, Woman of Yr., Soroptimist Club Nassau County; hon. mem. Soroptimist Club Nassau County, 1974; recipient John Peter Zenger award Nassau County Press Assn., 1975, Outstanding Bus. Women of 1977 award Marymount Manhattan Coll., 1978; honoree Catalyst Inc., 1977, Women's Equity Action League, 1978, Republican Women in Bus. and Industry, Cath. Med. Ctr. Bklyn./Queens, 1983, Girl Scouts, 1984, Clark Garden, L.I., 1985. Mem. LPGA (hon.), St. Lawrence Club L.I. (N.Y.C.).

FIRCHAK, BARBARA PARKS, secondary education educator; b. Waltham, Mass., Nov. 23, 1949; d. Norman George and Vesta Lenora (Rich) Parks; m. Edward John Firchak, Jr., Aug. 14, 1971; children: Kristen Michelle, Carolyn Renee. BA in English, U. Del., 1971. Cert. secondary English tchr., Del. Secondary tchr. English, Newark Sch. Dist., 1972-75; presch. tchr., Newark, 1980-88; secondary tchr. English, Christina Sch. Dist., Newark, 1976-78, 88—. Mem. NEA, Del. Assn. Tchrs. English (Shue Tchr. of Yr. award 1992, 95, Shue English Tchr. of Yr. award 1994, 95).

FIRE, NANCY ANN, elementary education educator; b. Bradford, Pa., Feb. 22, 1951; d. Francis John and Christine Ann (Ross) F. BS in Elem. Edn., Clarion (Pa.) State U., 1973; MEd in Acad. Curriculum and Instrn., Pa. State U., 1976. 3rd grade tchr. West Br. Sch. - Bradford Area Schs., 1973—, 2nd grade tchr., 1984-86; adj. instr. U. Pitts./Bradford Elem. Edn. Program, 1991—; cooperating tchr. Student Tchrs. for U. Pitts., Bradford, 1992; free-lance agt., project coord. Erie Area Fund for the Arts, 1996. Prodr., dir. vocalist (dinner theatre) Broadway Revue, 1989; novelty song lyricist, 1992; soloist A Musical Tribute to Ray Evans, 1993; prodr. Amahl and the Night Visitors Enchanted Mountain Players, 1993; vocalist TV show Nashville Starseek, 1995, Warren Festival of Arts, 1995. Congrl. internship Congressman William F. Clinger Jr., Washington, 1985, campaign vol. to re-elect William Clinger, Bradford, 1986. Mem. AAUW (v.p. 1980-82, pres. 1988-90), NEA, Pa. State Edn. Assn. Roman Catholic. Office: West Branch Elem Sch 645 W Washington St Bradford PA 16701-2634

FIRESTONE, JUANITA MARLIES, sociology educator; b. Wurzburg, Germany, Jan. 30, 1947; d. Harrison and Marlies (Breit) Gillette; m. Kenneth Todd Firestone, Aug. 31, 1968 (div. Oct. 1993); children: Jason Dean, Krystillin Elisabeth. BS in Sociology cum laude, Black Hills State U., 1979; MA in Sociology, U. Tex., 1982, PhD in Sociology, 1984. Office mgr. Silver Wings Aviation, Rapid City, S.D., 1975-76; pub. rels. mgr. Pacer Mining Co., Custer, S.D., 1976-79; lectr. sociology U. Tex., Austin, 1980-87; asst. prof. sociology U. Tex., San Antonio, 1987-94, assoc. prof., 1994—; cons. in field; attendee Nat. Security Forum, 1994; mem. Chancellor's Faculty Adv. Coun., U. Tex. Sys., 1994-96. Contbr. articles to profl. jours. Mem. spkrs. bur. Rape Crisis Ctr., Austin and San Antonio, 1984-94; bd. dirs. AIDS Found., San Antonio, 1992; coord. workshop Expanding Your Horizons, San Antonio, 1992-96; mem. Task Force on Crime and Violence, San Antonio, 1990. Recipient Rsch. award U. Tex. Sys., Austin, 1991, 95; Congrl. fellow, Washington, 1983. Mem. Internat. Sociol. Assn., Am. Sociol. Assn., S.W. Soc. Social Sci. (pres. women's caucus 1994-95), Golden Key (faculty advisor 1990-96), Alpha Kappa Delta. Office: U Tex at San Antonio Divsn Social and Policy Sci San Antonio TX 78249

FIRESTONE, NANCY B., lawyer; b. Manchester, N.H., Oct. 17, 1952; d. Albert and Bernice (Brown) F. BA, Washington U., St. Louis, 1973; JD, U. Mo., 1977. Bar: Mo. 1977, U.S. Ct. Appeals (2d, 4th, 5th, 6th, 8th and 10th cirs.). Trial atty. U.S. Dept. Justice, Washington, 1977-84; asst. chief U.S. Dept. Justice, 1984-85, dep. chief environ. enforcement, 1985-89; assoc. dep. adminstr. EPA, 1989-92, adminstrv. judge, 1992-95, dept. asst. atty. gen., 1995—; adj. prof. Georgetown U. Law Ctr., 1986—. Mem. ABA. Home: 3438 Mansfield Rd Falls Church VA 22041-1401

FIRESTONE, SUSAN PAUL, artist; b. Madison, Wis., Nov. 13, 1946; d. John Robertson and Sue Hadaway Paul; m. John D. Firestone, Nov. 30, 1943; children: Mary, Lucy. BA, Mary Baldwin Coll., 1968; MFA, Am. U., 1972. mem. Art Table, N.Y.C., Mus. sch. bd. Corcoran Gallery, Washington, collectors com. Nat. Gallery, Washington; trustee Skowhegan Sch., N.Y.C.; bd. dirs. Internat. Sculpture Ctr., N.Y. Artist/author: Armour-Amour, 1992; solo exhbns. include Gallery K, Washington, 1992, 95, Harmony Hall, Washington, Md., 1993, NIH, Bethesda, Md., 1992, Peat Marwick Inaugural Show, Washington, 1988, Covington and Burling, Washington, 1985, others; group exhbns. Inst. of Contemporary Art, Boston, 1995, San Diego Art Inst., 1995, Nat. Mus. of Women in Arts, 1994, Drawing Ctr., N.Y., 1993, Ctr. for Visual Arts, U. Toledo, 1993, Coll. of Notre Dame, Md., 1993, Minot (N.D.) Art Gallery, 1993, Art Works Gallery, Green Bay, Wis., 1993, others; various pub. and pvt. collections. Resident Pyramid Atlantic, Riverdale, Md., 1993; cultural exch. student USIS/Morocco, 1994. Office: Rubilite 2424 18th St NW Washington DC 20009-2024

FIRSTENBERG, JEAN PICKER, film institute executive; b. N.Y.C., Mar. 13, 1936; d. Eugene and Sylvia (Moses) Picker; m. Paul Firstenberg, Aug. 9, 1956 (div. July 1980); children—Debra, Douglas. BS summa cum laude, Boston U., 1958. Asst. producer Altman Prodns., Washington, 1965-66; media advisor J. Walter Thompson, N.Y.C., 1969-72; asst. for spl. projects Princeton (N.J.) U., 1972-74, dir. publs., 1974-76; program officer Markle Found., N.Y.C., 1976-80; dir. Am. Film Inst., L.A., Washington, 1980—; mem. com. L.A. Task Force on Arts; former chmn. nat. adv. bd. Peabody Broadcasting Awards; bd. dirs. Trans-Lux Corp. Trustee Boston U.; mem. adv. bd. Will Rogers Inst., N.Y.C., Big Sisters of Los Angeles; bd. dirs. Variety Club of Calif., Los Angeles; chmn., bd. advisors Film Dept. N.C. Sch. of Arts. Recipient Alumni award for disting. service to profession Boston U., 1982; seminar and prodn. chairs at directing workshop for women named in her honor Am. Film Inst., 1986. Mem. Women in Film (Los Angeles and Washington, Crystal award 1990), Trusteeship for Betterment of Women, Acad. Motion Picture Arts and Scis. Office: Am Film Inst 2021 N Western Ave PO Box 27999 Los Angeles CA 90027 also: Am Film Inst Kennedy Ctr Performing Washington DC 20056*

FISCHBARG, ZULEMA F., pediatrician, educator; b. Buenos Aires, Mar. 22, 1937; came to U.S., 1962; d. Naun and Esther (Pollner) Fridman; m. Jorge Fischbarg; children: Gabriel Julian, Victor Ernesto. MD, U. Buenos Aires, 1960. Pediatric intern Children's Hosp., Louisville, 1962-63, resident in pediatrics, 1963, chief resident in pediatrics, 1964; fellow hematology Michael Reese Med. Ctr., Chgo., 1964-66, Presbyn. St. Lukes Hosp., Chgo., 1966-67; fellow pediatric hematology Children's Meml. Hosp., Chgo., 1967-68; asst. clin. pediatrician U. Chgo., 1968-69; instr. in pediatrics Cornell U. Med. Sch., N.Y.C., 1970-72, asst. prof. in pediatrics, 1972-76, assoc. prof. pediatrics, 1978—; assoc. attending pediatrician N.Y. Hosp., 1979—; attending in pediatrics St. John's Hosp./Cath. Med. Ctr., N.Y.C.; med. specialist, sch. physician Bur. of Sch. Children and Adolescent Health, N.Y.C., 1994—; instr. in medicine Ill. U., Chgo., 1967-68; assoc. attending pediatrician, N.Y. Hosp., N.Y.C., 1972-76. Fellow Am. Acad. of Pediatrics, Queens Pediatric Soc. Democrat. Jewish. Home: 175 E 62nd St # 6D New York NY 10021-7626 Office: 125 Worth St Box 25 Rm 347 New York NY 10013

FISCHER, DALE SUSAN, lawyer; b. East Orange, N.J., Oct. 17, 1951; d. Edward L. and Audrey (Tenner) F. Student Dickinson Coll., 1969-70; BA magna cum laude, U. So. Fla., 1977; JD, Harvard U., 1980. Bar: Calif. 1980. Ptnr. law firm Kindel & Anderson, L.L.P., L.A., 1986—; judge pro tem L.A. Mcpl. Ct.; faculty Nat. Inst. Trial Advocacy; lawyer in classroom Constl. Rights Found.; moderator, panelist How to Win Your Case with Depositions. Mem. ABA, Am. Arbitration Assn. (mem. panel arbitrators), L.A. County Bar Assn., L.A. Complex Litigation Inn of Ct. (pres. elect). Home: 3695 Hampton Rd Pasadena CA 91107-3004 Office: Kindel and Anderson 555 S Flower St Los Angeles CA 90071-2300

FISCHER, FRANCES ARNETTE, school psychological examiner, counselor; b. Hot Springs, Ark., Aug. 25, 1935; d. Seldon Cooper and Lola (Doster) Thomas; m. Charles Adam Fisher, Sept. 10, 1957; children: Robin, Thomas Adam. BS in Elem. Edn., U. Ark., 1957; MS in Elem. Counseling, Ctrl. Mo. State U., 1975. Cert. sch. psychol. examiner. Kindergarten tchr. Bakersfield (Calif.) Sch. Dist., 1957, Columbia (Mo.) Sch. Dist., 1957-59, Ft. Osage Sch. Dist., Independence, Mo., 1967-69; kindergarten tchr. Blue Springs (Mo.) Sch. Dist., 1969-75, elem. counselor, 1975-85, sch. psychol. examiner, 1985—. Mem. Coun. for Exceptional Children (sec. 1992-94), Mo. State Tchrs. Assn., Blue Springs Cmty. Educators Assn. (v.p., treas. 1986-92), Delta Kappa Gamma (social chmn., chairperson calling com. 1992—). Office: Blue Springs Sch Dist 205 NW 16th St Blue Springs MO 64015

FISCHER, IRENE KAMINKA, retired research geodesist, mathematician; b. Vienna, Austria, July 27, 1907; came to U.S., 1941; d. Armand and Clara (Loewy) Kaminka; m. Eric Fischer, Dec. 21, 1930; children: Gay A., Michael M.J. MA, U. Vienna, 1931; postgrad., U. Va., Georgetown U., 1950-57; D. in Engring., U. Karlsruhe, Karlsruhe, Fed. Republic Germany, 1975. Tchr. secondary schs. Vienna, 1931-38; tchr. secondary schs. and colls. Washington, D.C., Mass., N.Y., Mass, 1941-45; researcher MIT, Cambridge, Mass., 1942-44; rsch. geodesist Army Map Svc., Def. Mapping Agy., Washington, 1952-77. Author: Geometry, 1965, Basic Geodesy, The Geoid--What's That?, 1973; contbr. hundreds of articles to profl. jours. Recipient medals Dept. Army, 1957, 66, 67, Dept. Def., 1967, Def. Mapping Agy., 1971, Nat. Civil Svc. League Career award, 1976; named Fed. Retiree of Yr. Nat. Assn. Retired Fed. Employees, 1978. Fellow Am. Geophys. Union, Internat. Assn. Geodesy (sec. sect. V 1963-71, chmn. study groups 1963-75); mem. Nat. Acad. Engring. Home: 6060 California Cir Apt 210 Rockville MD 20852-4835

FISCHER, MARSHA LEIGH, civil engineer; b. San Antonio, May 9, 1955; d. Joe Henry and Ellen Joyce (Flake) F. BSCE, Tex. A&M U., 1977. Engring. asst. Tex. Dept. Hwys. and Transp., Dallas, 1977-79; outside plant engr. Southwestern Bell Telephone Co., Dallas, 1979-82, staff mgr. for budgets, 1982-84; area mgr., engring. design Southwestern Bell Telephone Co., Wichita Falls, Tex., 1984-86; area mgr. Southwestern Bell Telephone Co., Ft. Worth, 1986-88; dist. mgr., local provisioning application Bell Communications Rsch., Piscataway, N.J., 1988-91; dist. mgr. engring. Southwestern Bell Telephone, Ft. Worth, Tex., 1992-94, dir. customer svcs., 1994-95, dir. network engring., 1996—. Named one of Outstanding Women of Am., 1987. Mem. NSPE, Tex. Soc. Profl. Engrs., Tex. Soc. Civil Engrs., Profl. Engrs. in Industry, Tex. A&M Assn. Former Students. Republican. Home: 6724 Johns Ct Arlington TX 76016-3622 Office: Southwestern Bell Telephone 1 Bell Plz Rm 1870 Dallas TX 75218-4053

FISCHER, PAMELA SHADEL, public relations executive; b. Harrisburg, Pa., Feb. 28, 1959; d. Richard Lee and Pauline Louise (Nies) S.; m. Charles J. Fischer Jr., June 11, 1983; 1 child, Zachary Joseph. BA in English, Lebanon Valley Coll., Annville, Pa., 1981. Pub. relations coordinator Pa. Optometric Assn., Harrisburg, 1981-83; pub. relations dir. Morris Center YMCA, Cedar Knolls, N.J., 1983-85; pub. relations coordinator Delta Dental Plan of N.J., Parsippany, 1985-86; pub. relations mgr. AAA N.J. Automobile Club, Florham Park, N.J., 1986-91, mgr. mem. svcs. and pub. affairs, 1991-94, asst. v.p. pub. rels. & safety, 1994—, asst. v.p. pub. and govt. rels. and fin. svcs., 1996—. Corp. capt. United Way of Morris County, Cedar Knolls, 1985-90, chmn. publs. com., 1989-90, chmn. mktg. com., 1991-95; career counselor Lebanon Valley Coll., 1983—, bd. dirs. of exec. com., vol. v.p., mktg., 1996—; bd. dirs. Morris Ctr. YMCA, 1992-94. Rotary Found. scholar, 1981; recipient Gold award United Way of Morris County, 1988. Mem. Pub. Rels. Soc. Am. (bd. dirs. 1995), N.J. Press Assn., Internat. Assn. Bus. Communicators, Y's Club of Cedar Knolls (pres. 1986-91). Democrat. Roman Catholic. Office: AAA NJ Automobile Club 1 Hanover Rd Florham Park NJ 07932-1807

FISCHER, TESSA R., geriatrics physician; b. L.A., Feb. 7, 1950; d. Benno and Anna (Lipcysz) F.; m. Murry A. Bass, Oct. 24, 76 (div. Nov. 1985); children: Leah, Gabriel. BA, U. Calif., Santa Cruz, 1971; MD, Georgetown U., 1975. Resident in family practice Cook County Hosp., Chgo., 1975-78; pub. health officer U.S. Pub. Health Svc., Brawley, Calif., 1978-81; staff Rush Anchor HMO, Chgo., 1981-93, chief geriat., 1991-93; staff Lutheran Gen. Hosp., Park Ridge, Ill., 1993-95; pvt. practice Chgo., 1995—. Mem. Jewish Reconstructionist Cong., Evanston, Ill., 1981—; mem. PTA bd. Nichols Middle Sch., Evanston, 1990, 95. Mem. Physicians For Social Responsibility, Am. Medical Womens Assn., APHA, NOW. Democrat. Home: 1219 Oak Ave Evanston IL 60202 Office: Ste 309 1325 W Howard Ave Evanston IL 60202

FISCHER, VIOLETA PÈREZ CUBILLAS, Spanish literature and linguistics educator; b. Havana, Cuba, Nov. 20, 1923; came to U.S., 1959; d. Josè M. and Carmen (Reyes Pizey) Pèrez Cubillas; m. Rolando F. Fischer, Dec. 27, 1947; 1 child, Violet Fischer Pack. PhD in Law, U. Havana, 1949; postgrad., U. N.C., 1967-68, MA in Romance Langs., 1975. Prin. Spl. Ctr. for English Teaching, Havana, 1945-59; lawyer Havana, 1949-59; asst. prof. East Carolina U., Greenville, 1962-66; prof. Spanish lit. and linguistics Coastal Carolina Community Coll., Jacksonville, N.C., 1970-96; speaker various civic, mil., ednl. assns., and community colls., 1963—. Bd. dirs. Onslow County Community Concerts, Jacksonville, N.C., 1987; chmn. CCCC Women's Assn., 1972-73. Recipient Josè de la Luz y Caballero award Cruzada Educativa Cubana Assn., 1987, Juan J. Remos award Cruzada Educativa Cubana, 1987, N.C. State Svc. award for 30 yrs. of svc., 1994; Paul Harris fellow Rotary Internat., 1996. Mem. MLA, Nat. Assn. Cuban Lawyers, Havana Bar Assn. in Exile, Nat. Cuban Tchrs. Assn., Nat. Assn. Cuban-Am. Educators, Count of Galvez Hist. Soc., Sigma Delta Mu (co-founder, state rep.), Delta Kappa Gamma (chmn. world fellowship com. 1982-84, 96—, Wreath of Excellence ednl. award 1989, 2d v.p. Upsilon chpt. Jacksonville 1994-96). Roman Catholic. Home: 2107 Perry Dr Jacksonville NC 28546-1642

FISCHLER, BARBARA BRAND, librarian; b. Pitts., May 24, 1930; d. Carl Frederick and Emma Georgia (Piltz) Brand; m. Drake Anthony Fischler, June 3, 1961 (div., Oct. 1995); 1 child, Owen Wesley. AB cum laude, Wilson Coll., Chambersburg, Pa., 1952; MM with distinction, Ind. U., 1954, AMLS, 1964. Asst. reference librarian Ind. U., Bloomington, 1958-61, asst. librarian undergrad. library, 1961-63, acting librarian, 1963; circulation librarian Ind. U.-Purdue U., Indpls., 1970-76, pub. services librarian Univ. Library, sci., engring. and tech. unit, 1976-81, acting dir. univ. libraries, 1981-82, dir. univ. libraries, 1982-95; retired, 1995; dir. Sch. Libr. and Info. Sci. Ind. U.-Purdue U., Indpls., 1995—; vis. and assoc. prof. (part-time) Sch. Libr. and Info. Sci. Ind. U., Bloomington, 1972-95, counselor-coord., Indpls., 1974-82, dir. sch. libr. and info. sci. campus Ind. U.-Purdue U., Indpls., 1995—; resource aide adv. com. Ind. Voc. Tech. Coll., Indpls., 1974-86; adv. com. Area Libr. Svcs. Authority, Indpls., 1976-79; mem. core com., chmn. program com. Ind. Gov.'s Conf. on Librs. and Info. Svcs., Indpls., 1976-78, mem. governance com., del. to conf., 1990; mem. Ind. State Libr. Adv. Coun., 1985-91; cons. in field. Contbr. articles to profl. jours. Fund-raiser Indpls. Mus. Art, 1971, Am. Cancer Soc., Indpls., 1975; vol. tchr. St. Thomas Aquinas Sch., Indpls., 1974-75; fund-raiser Am. Heart Assn., Indpls., 1985; bd. dirs., treas. Historic Amusement Found., Inc., Indpls., 1984-91; bd. advisors N.Am. Wildlife Park Found., Inc., Battle Ground, Ind., 1985-91, bd. dirs., 1991—; mem. adv. bd. Ind. U. Ctr. on Philanthropy, 1987-90. Recipient Outstanding Svc. award Ctrl. Ind. Area Libr. Svc. Authority, 1979, Outstanding Libr. award

Ind. Libr.-Ind. Libr. Trustee Assn., 1988, Louise Maxwell award for Outstanding Achievement, 1989, William Jenkins award for Outstanding Svc. to Ind. U. Libr. and the Libr. Profession, 1996. Mem. ALA, Libr. Adminstrn. and Mgmt. Assn. (vice chair and chair elect fund raising and fin. devel. sect. 1991-92), Ind. State Libr. Adv. Coun., Midwest Fedn. Libr. Assns. (chmn. local arrangements for conf. 1986-87, sec. 1987—, bd. dirs. 1987-91), Ind. Libr. Assn. (chmn. coll. and univ. div. 1977-78, chmn. libr. edn. div. 1981-82, treas. 1984-86), German Shepherd Dog Club of Cen. Ind. (pres. 1978-79, treas. 1988-89, v.p. 1989-90, pres. 1990-93, bd. dirs. 1993—), Wabash Valley German Shepherd Dog Club (pres. 1982-83), Cen. Ind. Kennel Club (bd. dirs. 1984-86), Pi Kappa Lambda, Beta Phi Mu. Republican. Presbyterian. Home: 735 Lexington Ave Apt 3 Indianapolis IN 46203-1000 Office: Ind-Purdue U 755 W Michigan St Indianapolis IN 46202-5195

FISCHLER, SHIRLEY BALTER, lawyer; b. Bklyn., Oct. 9, 1926; d. David and Rose (Shapiro) Balter; m. Abraham Saul Fischler, Apr. 9, 1949; children: Bruce Evan, Michael Alan, Lori Faye. BA, Bklyn. Coll., 1947, MA, 1951; JD, Nova U., Ft. Lauderdale, Fla., 1977. Bar: Fla. 1977, D.C. 1980, U.S. Ct. Appeals (D.C. cir.) 1980. Tchr., N.Y.C. Bd. Edn., 1948-50, Richmond (Calif.) Pub. Schs., 1965-66; assoc. Panza, Maurer, Maynard, Platow & Neel, Ft. Lauderdale, 1977-95; pro bono atty. Broward Lawyers Care, 1982-86. V.p. Gold Circle Nova Southeastern U., 1995—; bd. govs. Nova. U. Law Ctr., 1982—; mem. Commn. on Status of Women, Broward County, Fla., 1982-87, vice chair, 1983-84, PACERS Broward County Ctr. for Performing Arts. Mem. Fla. Bar Assn., D.C. Bar Assn., Broward County Bar Assn. Home: 5000 Taylor St Hollywood FL 33021-5839

FISCINA, ELIZABETH GLADYS, hotel industry administrator; b. Kew Gardens, N.Y., Mar. 27, 1944; d. Elizabeth C. Gaddis; m. Peter J. Fiscina (dec.); children: Vincent P. Musac, Elizabeth D. Musac Metz. Grad., L.I. Beauty Sch., Hempstead, N.Y., 1978. Lic. hairdresser. Cosmetologist, 1978; adminstrv. asst. I.W. Industries, Melville, N.Y., 1983-85; exec. housekeeper Woodcrest Club, Syosset, N.Y., 1986-87; head housekeeper Seawanhaka Corinthian Yacht Club, Centre Island, N.Y., 1987-88; exec. housekeeper Royal Inn Motor Lodge, Manhasset, N.Y., 1989-92; housekeeping mgr., 1992—. Home: 48-20 207th St Bayside NY 11364

FISCUS, KATHLEEN ELLEN, television station administrator; b. Council Bluffs, Iowa, Nov. 21, 1949; d. Ulyses Henry and Evelyn (Campbell) Spencer; m. Gary Lee Fiscus, June 23, 1979; children: Valerie Laura, Matthew Lee. BA, Iowa State U., 1972. Copy writer, sales exec. Sta. KTVO, Ottumwa, Iowa, 1972-75; prodn. asst. Sta. WFRV, Green Bay, Wis., 1976; print mgr., asst. acct. exec. Winslow Advt., Omaha, 1977-78; program asst., traffic mgr., sys. coord. Sta. KETV, Omaha, 1978—; cons. Pulitzer Broadcasting Co., St. Louis, 1992—. Vol. Jr. League, Council Bluffs, 1992—; founder C.B. Buddies for Low Income Presch. Children, Council Bluffs, 1989—. Named Friend of Young Children Iowa Assn. Edn. Young Children, 1994. Mem. Am. Women Radio & TV (pres. Nebr. chpt., pres. Omaha chpt., chair North Ctrl. Area conf. 1993, mem. converging tech. taskforce), Optimist Internat. (pres., bd. dirs.). Presbyterian. Home: 104 Golden Circle Dr Council Bluffs IA 51503 Office: Sta KETV 2665 Douglas Omaha NE 68131

FISH, BARBARA, psychiatrist, educator; b. N.Y.C., July 31, 1920; d. Edward R. and Ida (Citrin) F.; m. Max Saltzman, Dec. 12, 1953; children: Mark, Ruth Saltzman Deutsch. B.A. summa cum laude, Barnard Coll., Columbia U., 1942; M.D., NYU, 1945. Diplomate Am. Bd. Psychiatry and Neurology, Am. Bd. child psychiatry. Intern Bellevue Hosp., N.Y.C., 1945-47, resident in pediatrics, 1948-49, resident in psychiatry, 1949-52; resident in pediatrics N.Y. Hosp., N.Y.C., 1947-48; practice medicine specializing in child psychiatry N.Y.C., 1952-65; instr. psychiatry Med. Coll Cornell U., N.Y.C., 1955-60; instr. pediatrics Cornell U., 1955-56, asst. prof. clin. pediatrics, 1956-60; child psychiatrist dept. pediatrics N.Y. Hosp.-Cornell Med. Center, 1955-60; mem. faculty William A. White Inst. Psychoanalysis, N.Y.C., 1957-66; assoc. prof. psychiatry sch. medicine N.Y. U., N.Y.C., 1960-70; prof. N.Y. U., 1970-72, adj. prof., 1972—, dir. child psychiatry med. ctr., 1960-72; prof. psychiatry and behavioral sci. UCLA, 1972-89, Della Martin prof. psychiatry and behavioral sci., 1989-91, Della Martin prof. psychiatry and behavioral sci. emeritus, 1991—; mem. advisory com. mental health services for children N.Y.C. Community Mental Health Bd., 1963-72; mem. profl. advisory com. on children N.Y. State Dept. Mental Hygiene, 1966-72; mem. com. cert. child psychiatry Am. Bd. Psychiatry and Neurology, 1969-77; mem. clin. program projects research rev. com. NIMH, 1976-78. Contbr. articles on the antecedents of schizophrenia and other severe mental disorders, and on the psychiat. diagnosis and treatment of children; mem. editorial bd.: Jour. Am. Acad. Child Psychiatry, 1966-71, Jour. Autism and Childhood Schizophrenia, 1971-74, Child Devel. Abstracts and Bibliography, 1974-82, Archives Gen. Psychiatry, 1975-84. Recipient Woman of Sci. award UCLA, 1978; NIMH grantee, 1961-72, 78-88, Harriett A. Ames Charitable Trust grantee, 1961-66, William T. Grant Found. grantee, 1977-83, Scottish Rite schizophrenia rsch. grantee, 1979-87. Fellow Am. Psychiat. Assn. (Agnes McGavin award 1987), Am. Acad. Child Psychiatry, Am. Coll. Neuropsychopharmacology (charter); mem. Am. Psychopath. Assn. (v.p. 1967-68), Assn. for Research in Nervous and Mental Diseases, Soc. Research in Child Devel., Psychiat. Research Soc. Home: 16428 Sloan Dr Los Angeles CA 90049-1157 Office: UCLA Neuropsychiat Inst 760 Westwood Plz Los Angeles CA 90024-8300

FISH, HELEN THERESE, educator, author; b. Mpls., Mar. 17, 1944; d. John Howard and Helen Therese (Ochs) Berg; m. Ronald Bruce Fish, Oct. 13, 1967 (div. May 1994); children: Eric James, Angela Diane, Christine Ann. BS, U. Minn., Mpls., 1966; postgrad., U. Minn., Mankato, 1969-70, U. Wis., Whitewater, 1970-72; MEd, Brenau Coll., 1986; EdS U. Ga in Admnistrn., U. Ga., 1992, postdoctoral, 1994. Cert. elem. tchr., Minn., Wis., Ill., Kans., Ga. Tchr. kindergarten Lincoln Hills Sch., Mpls., 1966-68, Mapleton (Minn.) Pub. Schs., 1968-69; tchr. 1st grade Hoover Sch., Mankato, 1969-70; kindergarten tchr. Todd Sch., Beloit, Wis., 1970-73; tchr. presch., K-1 Wilson Sch., Janesville, Wis., 1973-75; tchr. gifted and reading specialist (remedial) Lakewood Sch., Park Forest, Ill., 1975-77; tchr. kindergarten, 1st and 3d grades Sibley Sch., Albert Lea, Minn., 1977-82; tchr. kindergarten Most Pure Heart Sch., Topeka, 1983-85; tchr. kindergarten Enota Sch., Gainesville, Ga., 1985-88, chronicler Danforth grant, 1988-91; tchr. kindergarten Centennial Sch., Gainesville, Ga., 1992—; adj. asst. prof. Brenau U., Gainesville, Ga., 1988—, U. Ga., 1990, 94—; cons. and field test tchr. Rsch. and Devel. Ctr. U. Wis., Madison, 1970-79, Ency. Britannica Edn. Corp.; workshop leader for adminstrs. and tchrs. in Pre-Reading Skills; demonstration tchr. Internat. Reading Assn. Conv., New Orleans, 1975. Author: Starting Out Well: A Parent's Approach to Exercise and Nutrition, 1989; editor Y's Menettes newsletter, 1971-75. Sec., treas. PTA, Mpls, Mankato, Albert Lea, Beloit, Janesville, Park Forest, Topeka, Gainesville; leader Girl Scouts U.S., Blue Birds, Topeka; softball coach, Gainesville. Recipient award for contbns. to edn. and participation in Tchr. in Space Program NASA, 1986; Cert. of World Leadership, Cambridge, Eng., 1990. Mem. Ga. Edn. Assn., Assn. for Supervision and Curriculum Devel., Ga. Presch. Assn., Internat. Platform Assn., Pi Lamda Theta (Hon. Teaching Soc. award). Roman Catholic. Home: 3650 Brown Well Ct Gainesville GA 30504-5774 Office: Enota Sch Gainesville GA 30501

FISH, MARGO EVANS, artist; b. Erie, Pa., May 4, 1929; d. Frederick Brandon and Mary (MacLeod) Evans; m. Howard Macfarland Fish, Jan. 27, 1951; children: Katherine, Farland, Howard, Peter. BA, Pa. State U., 1951; MA, NYU, 1996. Free-lance artist Princeton, N.J., 1976—, Union Theol. Sem., N.Y.C., 1978—; lectr. Lawrenceville Sch. Fellow ARC. Democrat.

FISH, MICHELE LOYD, retailer; b. Belleville, Ill., Jan. 5, 1952; d. Delmer Edward and Patricia Ann (Marshall) Munie; m. Robert Wendelin Fish, May 25, 1973 (div. Feb. 1981). BS cum laude, U. Mo., 1973. Asst. buyer Famous-Barr, St. Louis, 1974-75, dept. mgr., 1975-76, buyer, 1976-81, store mgr., 1981-82; buyer Venture Stores, St. Louis, 1982-84, divsn. merchandise mgr., 1984-85, divsn. v.p., 1985-93; sr. v.p. Roman Co., St. Louis, 1993-94; sr. dir. frame buying LensCrafters, Cin., 1995; market rep. May Co., St. Louis, 1996—; adv. bd. dept. textile and apparel mgmt. U. Mo., Columbia, 1987-96, chair, 1988-90. Spl. venue mgr. Athlete's Village, U.S. Olympic Festival, 1994; dir. AMC Cancer Rsch. Ctr., 1986-96, also v.p., sec.; chair gifts Women's Event, 1988-94, chair gifts golf tournament, 1989-93, co-chair St. Louis Walks for Women, 1994, Together a Day of Caring, 1995; vol. Reach to Recovery, 1992-94; vol. coord. First Night St. Louis, 1994-96, bd. dirs. 1996—; bd. dirs. Talking Tapes for the Blind, 1996—. Recipient Torch of Liberty award Anti-Defamation League, 1990, Citation of Merit, U. Mo., 1992. Republican. Roman Catholic. Home: 82 E Sherwood Dr Saint Louis MO 63114

FISHBURN, JANET FORSYTHE, university dean; m. Peter Clingerman Fishburn, 1958; children: Susan, Katherine, Sally. BA magna cum laude, Monmouth Coll., 1958, LHD (hon.), 1984; PhD, Pa. State U., 1978. Ordained to ministry Presbyn. Ch., U.S.A., 1988. Dir. Christian edn. 1st United Presbyn. Ch., Cleveland Heights, Ohio, 1958-60; lectr. Pa. State U., 1977-78; asst. prof. Christian edn. Theol. Sch., Drew U., Madison, N.J., 1978-83, assoc. prof., 1983-90, asst. prof. Am. ch. history, 1982-83, assoc. prof., 1983-95, prof. tchg. ministry, 1990-95, prof. emeritus, 1995—, acting dean Theol. Sch., 1994-95; parish assoc. Mt. Freedom Presbyn. Ch., 1991-94; manuscript reviewer Scholars Press, Fairleigh Dickinson Press, George Washington U. Press, U. Pa. Press; lectr. in field, 1982—; participant profl. confs. and religious orgns.; cons. books for Pastors Series, Abingdon Press, 1987; also others; mem. social justice com. Newton Presbytery, 1989-95, mem. coun., 1995—. Author: The Fatherhood of God and the Victorian Family: The Social Gospel in America, 1982; Confronting the Idolatry of Family: A New Vision for the Household of God, 1991; editor Drew Gateway, 1989-93; contbr. articles and revs. to profl. jours. and encys. Leader weekly Bible study Madison Presbyn. Ch., 1985-89, mem. chancel choir, 1982-90; mem. chancel choir Morristown United Meth. Ch., 1992-96, co-leader spiritual growth group, 1990-92. Mem. Assn. Profs. and Rschrs. in Religious Edn., United Meth. Assn. Scholars Christian Edn. (chmn. rsch. com. 1995—), Presbyn. Profs. Social Witness Policy (panel coord. 1994). Office: Drew U Theol Sch 36 Madison Ave Madison NJ 07940

FISHER, ADA MARKITA, physician, health services administrator; b. Durham, N.C., Oct. 21, 1947; d. Miles Mark and Ada Virginia (Foster) Fisher; adopted children: Shevin Michael, Charles Malvern. BA, U. N.C., Greensboro, 1970; MD, U. Wis., 1975; MPH, Johns Hopkins U., 1981. Resident in family medicine U. Rochester (N.Y.), Highland Hosp., 1975-78; chief med. officer, med. dir. Plain View Health Svcs., Inc., Greenevers, N.C., 1978-80; residency supr., employee health supr., physician, program dir. Alcohol Detoxification Unit John Umstead Hosp., Butner, N.C., 1981-85; indsl. physician Martin Marietta Energy Sts., Inc., Oak Ridge, Tenn., 1985-89; dir. occupl. medicine, med. dir., mgr. med. policies and practices Amoco Corp., Chgo., 1989-95; assoc. program dir. occupl. and environ. medicine program Healthline Corp. Health Svcs., St. Louis, 1995-96; occupl. health physician VA Hosp., Salisbury, N.C., 1996—; participant, med. rep. Am. Petroleum Inst.; lectr. in field. Life mem. NAACP, Oak Ridge, 1988—; mem sch. reform/local sch. coun. Chgo. Pub. Schs., 1989-94; treas. Alliance of Black Jews, 1995—. Named one of Ten Outstanding Young Women in Am., 1984, Outstanding Alumni, Hillside High Sch.; named to Hall of Fame, Durham, N.C.; recipient Alumni Disting. Svc. award U. N.C. Greensboro Alumni Assn., 1985. Mem. APA (occupl. heath psychology adv. bd.), AAUW, NAFE, AMA, APHA, Am. Coll. Occupl. and Environ. Medicine (back com.), Soc. Occupl. and Environ. Health. Jewish. Home: PO Box 777 Salisbury NC 28144 Office: VA Hosp Salisbury NC 28144

FISHER, ANITA JEANNE, English language educator; b. Atlanta, Oct. 22, 1937; d. Paul Benjamin and Cora Ozella (Wadsworth) Chappelear; m. Kirby Lynn Fisher, Aug. 6, 1983; 1 child by previous marriage, Tracy Ann. BA, Bob Jones U., 1959; postgrad., Stetson U., 1961, 87, U. Fla., 1963; MAT, Rollins Coll., 1969; PhD in Am. Lit., Fla. State U., 1975; postgrad., Writing Inst., U. Ctrl. Fla., 1978, NEH Inst., 1979, U. Ctrl. Fla., 1987, Stetson U., 1987, U. Fla., 1987, 90, Disney U./U. Ctrl. Fla., 1996. Cert. English, gifted and adminstn. supr.; cert. in ESOL. Chairperson basic learning improvement program, secondary sch. Orange County, Orlando, Fla., 1964-65; chmn. composition Winter Park H.S., Fla., 1978-80; chmn. English depts. Orange County Pub. Schs., Fla., 1962, 71; reading tchr. Woodland Hall Acad., Reading Rsch. Inst., Tallahassee, 1976; instr. edn., journalism, reading, Spanish, thesis writing Bapt. Bible Coll., Springfield, Mo., 1976-77; prof. English, S.W. Mo. State U., Springfield, 1980-84, instr. continuing edn., courses in music and creative writing, 1981-82, editor LAD Leaf; tchr. Volusia County Schs., Fla., 1984-88, 95—, gifted students, 1986-88; tchr. Lee County Schs., 1988-95; adj. prof. Edison C.C., 1989-95, U. So. Fla., 1990-95, Barry U., 1993; mem. steering com. So. Assn. Colls. and Schs., 1989-90; speaker in field. Contbr. writings to publs. in field, papers to nat. profl. confs. Vol. Greene County Action Com., 1977, Heart Fund, 1982; book reviewer Voice of Youth Advs. Writing Program fellow U. Cen. Fla., 1978. Named Lee County Tchr. of Distinction 1994-95. Mem. Volusia County Coun. Tchrs. English/Fla. Coun. Tchrs. English, Kappa Delta Pi, Phi Delta Kappa. Republican. Presbyterian.

FISHER, ANN L., pro tem judge; b. Reading, Pa., Mar. 31, 1948; d. William E. and Florence (Makowiecki) Lewis; m. Donald E. Fisher, Dec. 27, 1965 (div. July 1986); children: Caroline E., Catherine E.; m. David H. DeBlasio, May 28, 1988; 1 child, Michael Joseph DeBlasio. BS in Liberal Studies, Oreg. State U., 1975; JD, Willamette U., 1983. Bar: Oreg. 1984, U.S. Dist. Ct. Oreg. 1984, U.S. Ct. Appeals (9th cir.) 1984, Wash. 1987, U.S. Dist. Ct. (we. and ea. dists.) Wash. 1987. Atty. Spears, Lubersky, Portland, Oreg., 1983-85, Greene & Markley, Portland, Oreg., 1985-89; asst. gen. counsel Portland GE, 1989-94; atty. Schwabe, Williamson & Wyatt, Portland, 1994—; protem judge Multnomah County Ct., Portland, 1995—. Contbg. author: (treatise) ABA Year in Review, 1994, 95. Mem. ABA, Wash. State Bar Assn., Oreg. State Bar Assn. (ins. and bar sponsored program com. 1985-87, sec. 1986-87, chmn. 1987-88, MCLE bd. 1991-94, sec. 1992-93, chmn. 1993-94, Disciplinary Bd. Region 5 1991-96, chair 1995-96), Multnomah Bar Assn. (membership com. 1987-91, The Multnomah Lawyer publ. com. 1995-96, chair 1995-96, profl. com. 1996—), Fed. Energy Bar Assn. (electric utility regulation com. 1996—), Fed. Bar Assn., Sect. of Nat. Resources, Energy and Environ. Law (vice chair electric power com., vice chair gas pipelines com.). Office: Schwabe Williamson & Wyatt 1211 SW 5th Ste 1700 Portland OR 97204

FISHER, BARBARA TURK, school psychologist; b. Bklyn., Feb. 21, 1940; d. Jack and Reva (Miller) Turk; m. Ronnie Herbert Fisher, Aug. 15, 1961; children: Sylvia Kay, Mark Lee. BA, Fla. State U., 1961; MS, Barry U., 1966, EdS, 1977; EdD, Nova U., 1989. Coord. of counseling Immaculate La Salle High Sch., Miami, Fla., 1966-69; rehab. counselor Miami Adult Tng. Ctr., 1969-70; sch. psychologist Dade County Sch. Sys., Miami, 1970—; instr. Miami Dade C.C., 1991; presenter at profl. assn. meetings and social sci. seminars, 1993, 94, 95. Fellow AAUW; mem. Dade County Asns. Sch. Psychologists. Republican. Jewish. Home: 234 Antiquera Ave Apt 3 Miami FL 33134-2914 Office: Dade County BPI Region I Office 733 E 57th St Hialeah FL 33013-1357

FISHER, CARLYN FELDMAN, artist, writer; b. Atlanta, Nov. 5, 1923; d. Abrom Lewis and Jennie (Saul) Feldman; m. Ted V. Fisher, 1944 (div. 1972); m. Morris Berthold Abram, Jan. 22, 1975 (div. May 1987); 1 child, Eve Fisher Shulmister. BS in Fine Art, Skidmore Coll., 1945; postgrad., Atelier 17, Paris, 1964, Pembroke Coll., Oxford, Eng., 1984. Founder, pub. Abstract Arts Festival of Atlanta, 1955-67; art editor Atlanta Mag., 1966-72; dir., writer, rschr. NEA, 1967-68; writer, dir. TV documentaries PBS, Channel 8, 1974-75; exec. prodr. Cape Cod/Sta. WGBH, Cape Cod, Boston, 1986-87; co-founder, exec. Arts Festival Atlanta, 1953-62; chair bd. Hambidge Ctr., Rabun Gap, Ga., 1992-96; trustee adv. bd. Mus. Art, U. Ga., Athens, 1983—; artist-in-residence Hambidge Ctr. for Arts and Scis., Rabun Gap, 1987, 92-95, Mishkenot Sha'ananim, Jerusalem, 1987. One-person shows include Alexander Gallery, Atlanta, 1965, Heath Gallery, Atlanta, 1971, 88, Oglethorpe Gallery, Atlanta, 1973, Elaine Starkman Gallery, N.Y.C., 1982, Signature Shop Gallery, 1990, Dorothy Berge Gallery of Contemporary Art, Stillwater, Minn., 1993, Studio Exhbn., Atlanta, 1995; exhibited in group shows Atlanta High Mus. Art Shop, 1962, Ga. Artists Exhbn., 1967, Skidmore Coll., Saratoga Springs, N.Y., 1970, Lighting Assocs., Inc., N.Y.C., 1977, Ga. Artists Working in N.Y., N.Y.C., 1982, Cape Mus. Fine Arts, Dennis, Mass., 1985, Sen. Wyche Fowler Jr. Ga. Exhbn., Washington, 1991, Trinity Gallery, Atlanta, 1992; commd. murals installed Cobb Galleria Conv. Ctr., Atlanta, 1994; included in Exhbn. of Ga. Artists, Washington, 1992-93; commd. sculpture installed in front of The Jewish Comty. Ctr., Atlanta, 1989; designer, executor commemorative poster for Piedmont Park Centennial Celebration, 1995; rschr., author: The Arts in Georgia, 1967-68; writer, co-dir. (TV documentaries) The Image Makers, 1974 (Emmy award); exec. prodr. (TV documentary) Art In Its Soul, 1987 (Silver Apple award). Bd. dirs. Richard Allen Ctr., N.Y.C., 1977-79; bd. dirs., exec. com. Ga. chpt. Nat. Mus. Women, Washington, 1987-95. Mem. Mensa. Jewish. Home: 62 Forrest Pl Atlanta GA 30328

FISHER, CARRIE FRANCES, actress, writer; b. Oct. 21, 1956; d. Eddie Fisher and Debbie Reynolds; m. Paul Simon, 1983 (div. 1984); 1 child, Billie Catherine. Ed. high sch., Beverly Hills, Calif.; student, London Cen. Sch. Speech and Drama. Mem. chorus in Broadway musical Irene, 1972, also in Broadway prodn. Censored Scenes from King Kong; appeared in films Shampoo, 1975, Star Wars, 1977, Mr. Mike's Mondo Video, 1979, The Blues Brothers, 1980, The Empire Strikes Back, 1980, Under the Rainbow, 1981, Return of the Jedi, 1983, Garbo Talks, 1984, The Man with One Red Shoe, 1985, Hannah and Her Sisters, 1986, Hollywood Vice Squad, 1986, Amazon Women on the Moon, 1987, Appointment With Death, 1988, When Harry Met Sally..., 1989, The 'Burbs, 1989, Loverboy, 1989, She's Back, 1989, Sibling Rivalry, 1990, Drop Dead Fred, 1991, Soapdish, 1991, This Is My Life, 1992; TV movies include Come Back, Little Sheba, (spl.) 1977, Leave Yesterday Behind, 1978, Liberty, Sunday Drive, 1986, Sweet Revenge, 1990; author: Postcards from the Edge, 1987, (also screenplay, 1990), Surrender the Pink, 1990, Delusions of Grandma, 1994. Office: Creative Artists Agency 9830 Wilshire Blvd Beverly Hills CA 90212*

FISHER, DENISE BUTTERFIELD, marketing executive; b. San Diego; d. Wyartt Grant and Therese Marie (Hoffman) Butterfield; m. Paul Elliott Fisher, June 15, 1985. BS, Old Dominion U., 1978; MA, U. Va., 1984. Environ. planner Rappahannock Area Devel. Commn., Fredericksburg, Va., 1978-80; grants coord. Va. State Water Control Bd., Richmond, 1980-81, project mgr., 1981-83; mgmt. analyst City of Newport News, Va., 1984-88; intergovtl. rels. mgr. City of Newport News, 1988-91; mktg. mgr. Malcolm Pirnie, Inc., Newport News, 1991—; cons. Va. State Water Control Bd., Virginia Beach, 1984. Contbr. articles to profl. jours. Chmn. United Way Campaign, Newport News, 1985, 86, 87; v.p. North Suffolk Cir. Children's Hosp. of King's Daus., Suffolk, Va., 1989, 90. Recipient Betty Crocker Homemaker of Am. award Gen. Mills, 1972; tuition scholar Old Dominion U., 1973, Wallerstein scholar Va. Mcpl. League, U. Va., 1983. Mem. Internat. City Mgmt. Assn., Soc. Mktg. Profl. Svcs., Am. Soc. Pub. Adminstrn. (pres. Hampton Rds. chpt. 1992). Office: Malcolm Pirnie Inc 11832 Rock Landing Rd Ste 400 Newport News VA 23606-4278

FISHER, DIERDRE DENISE, mental health nurse, administrator, educator; b. N.Y.C., Mar. 13, 1945; d. Horace Anderton and Alma (Ames) Taylor; m. Robert Fisher, Oct. 29, 1962 (dec. 1978); children: Sevareid, Pheon (dec.). AAS, Mercer County Coll., 1972; BS, Trenton State Coll., 1979; MSN, U. Pa., 1982. Cert. clin. nurse specialist, nursing adminstr. Supr. Nursing Svcs. Trenton (N.J.) Psychiat. Hosp., 1979-81, program coord., 1981-84; cons. Pub. Health N.J. State Dept. Health, Trenton, 1984-87; psychiat. nurse cons. Div. Mental Health and Hosps., Princeton, N.J., 1987-89; asst. complex adminstr. Trenton Psychiat. Hosp., 1989-91; dir. edn. and practice N.J. State Nurses Assn., Trenton, 1991-96; dir. continuing edn. U. Tex. Health Sci. Ctr., San Antonio, 1996—; educator Ocean County Coll., Toms River, N.J., 1985-96; clin. instr. nursing Burlington County Coll., Pemberton, N.J., 1988-91; cons., educator Lake Area Health Edn. Ctr., Erie, Pa., 1988-96. Author nursing publs. Bd. dirs. Trenton YWCA, 1989-95. Recipient Care Givers award Delta Sigma Theta, 1991. Mem. Am. Acad. Cert. Pub. Mgrs., Trenton YWCA (bd. dirs. 1990-95), Psychiat. Mental Health Divsn. N.J. Nurses Assn., Soc. Cert. Clin. Specialists in Psychiat., Sigma Theta Tau, Delta Sigma Theta. Home: 14554 Indian Woods San Antonio TX 78249

FISHER, ELLENA ALLMOND, librarian; b. Windsor, Va.; d. Calvin Percy and Oretha Mae (Eley) Allmond; m. Eddie Lee Fisher; children: Ellena II, Melba. BA cum laude, Va. Union U.; MS, Atlanta U.; PhD (hon.), London Inst. Applied Rsch., Third World Coll., Paris. Lang. asst. Va. Union U., Richmond, tutor; libr. assoc. Atlanta U.; rsch. asst. Econ. Opportunity Atlanta; clk. typist West Employment Svc., River Forest, Ill.; monitor testing Pasadena (Calif.) Coll. Skills Ctr.; reference libr. L.A. Pub. Libr.; young adult libr. Mark Twain Libr., L.A.; mem. book com. L.A. Pub. Libr., 1990; founder teen writing club; founder Roger Williams Libr.; pres., CEO Ellena Calvin Enterprises; mem. adv. bd. Am. Biog. Inst. Mem. Castle Heights Sch. PTA, L.A., 1985-86; Doug Wilder supporter, Va. Named World Intellectual of 1993; named to Women's Inner Circle of Achievement, the 1st 500. Mem. NAFE, Am. Investors Network, Calif. Librs., Our Authors Study Club, Young Adult Reviewers. Baptist. Home: 3507 S Clyde Ave Los Angeles CA 90016-5043 Office: Mark Twain Libr 9621 S Figueroa St Los Angeles CA 90003-3928

FISHER, JANET WARNER, secondary school educator; b. San Angelo, Tex., July 7, 1929; d. Robert Montell and Louise (Buckley) Warner; m. Jarek Prochazka Fisher, Oct. 17, 1956 (div. May 1974); children: Barbara Zlata Harper, Lev Prochazka, Monte Prochazka. BA, So. Meth. U., 1950, M of Liberal Arts, 1982; student various including, Columbia U., U. Dallas,, U. Colo., U. London and others. Cert. English, German and ESL tchr., K-12, Tex., N.Y. Bd. dirs., sec. Masaryk Inst., N.Y.C., 1968-71; with orphan sect. Displaced Persons Commn., Washington, 1950; fgn. editor Current Digest of the Soviet Press, N.Y.C., 1953-55; cable desk clk. Time, Inc., N.Y.C., 1955-56; tchr. of English and reading, langs. Houston Ind. Sch. Dist., 1975-80; tchr. Carmine Ind. Sch. Dist., Round Top, Tex., 1980-82; instr. English Houston Community Coll., 1983-88; adj. prof. English U. Houston, 1983-87; tchr. Royal Ind. Sch. Dist., Brookshire, Tex., 1989-92, Hempstead Ind. Sch. Dist., Waller County, Tex., 1992-94; adj. prof. English, U. Houston, Houston C.C., 1983-87; tchr. Amnesty Program, Houston, 1988-90; adj. prof. English Blinn Coll., Brenham, Tex., 1995—. Candidate sch. bd., South Orangetown, N.Y., 1962, state rep., Houston, 1980; del. Dem. State Conv., 1996, Houston Tchrs. Assn., 1975-80; officer LWV, Nyack, N.Y., 1960-62; trustee Shepherd Drive United Meth. Ch., Houston; del. Tex. ann. conf. United Meth. Ch., 1996; del. Tex. State Dem. Conv., 1996. Recipient award for Svc. to Missions, United Meth. Ch., Houston, 1985. Mem. AAUW, NOW, WILPF, Harris County Women's Polit. Caucus. Home: PO Box 66067 Houston TX 77266-6067

FISHER, (MARY) JEWEL TANNER, retired construction company executive; b. Port Lavaca, Tex., Oct. 31, 1918; d. Thomas M. and Minnie Frances (Dunks) Tanner; grad. Tex. Luth. Coll., 1937; m. King Fisher, Aug. 13, 1937; children: Ann Fisher Boyd, Linda Fisher LaQuay. Sec. treas. King Fisher Marine Svc., Inc., Port Lavaca, 1959-82; dir., cons. King Fisher Marine Svc.; artist, poet. Trustee Meml. Med. Ctr., 1976-81, 90-94, pres. bd. trustees, 1992-93; trustee Golden Crescent Coun. Govts., 1980-81, Crisis Hotline Calhoun County, 1985-93. Lic. pvt. pilot. Mem. DAR (regent Guadalupe Victoria chpt. 1986-88), Daus. Republic Tex., 99's, Internat. Orgn. Women Pilots, Calhoun County Hist. Commn. Home: PO Box 166 Port Lavaca TX 77979-0166 Office: PO Box 108 Port Lavaca TX 77979-0108

FISHER, JIMMIE LOU, state official; b. Delight, Ark., Dec. 31, 1941. Student, Ark. State U.; grad. John F. Kennedy Sch. Govt., Harvard U., 1985. Treas. Greene County, Ark., 1971-78; auditor State of Ark., Little Rock, 1979, treas., 1981—; sec. Ark. State Bd. Fin. Trustee, ex-offico mem. Ark. Pub. Employees Retirement System, Ark. Tchr. Retirement System; trustee Ark. State Hwy. Retirement System; former vice chair Dem. State Com.; former mem. Dem. Nat. Com.; del. Dem. Nat. Conv., 1988; past pres. Ark. Dem. Women's Club; mem. Ark. Devel. Fin. Authority. Mem. State Bd. Fin. (sec.), State Bd. Election Commrs., Nat. Assn. State Treas. (pres.). Office: Treasury Dept 220 State Capitol Bldg Little Rock AR 72201-1059*

FISHER, JO ANN, television technical director; b. Mpls., Sept. 14, 1957; d. Philip and Rita Blossom (Joss) F.; m. Steven William Koeln, Oct. 29, 1983; children: Nathan Ross Fisher-Koeln, Gertrude Rose Fisher-Koeln. BA, U. Minn., 1981. Floor dir. KSTP-TV, Mpls., 1979-82, duty dir., 1982-85, tech. dir., 1985-88, occasional dir., 1987-88; freelance dir., tech. dir. IDS/Amex Fin. Advisors, Mpls., 1987—, Met. Sports Commn., Mpls., 1989—, IVL Post, Mpls., 1990—, KTCA Pub. TV, St. Paul, 1990—, ESPN, 1993—, N.W. Mobile TV, 1992—. Mem. com. J.C.C. Childcare, St. Paul, 1989-93; vol. St. Paul Pub. Schs., 1991—; mem. com. Shir Tikvah Synagogue, Mpls., 1992-93, chair com., 1994-95. Recipient I.D.E.A. award, 1993. Democrat. Jewish.

FISHER, LINDA ALICE, physician; b. Plainfield, N.J., Dec. 27, 1947; d. Alvin Edwin and Bertha Sophie (Steigmann) F. BA, Douglass Coll., New

Brunswick, N.J., 1970; M in Med. Sci., Rutgers U., 1972; MD, Harvard U., 1975; MPH, St. Louis U., 1996. Diplomate Am. Bd. Internal Medicine. Intern, then resident Jewish Hosp. St. Louis, 1975-78; dir. ambulatory care St. Luke's Hosp., St. Louis, 1978-84; chief med. officer St. Louis County Dept. Health, Clayton, 1984—; chief physician St. Louis Met. Police Dept., 1978-88; clin. instr. medicine Washington U., St. Louis, 1978-94, asst. prof., 1994—; asst. clin. prof. medicine St. Louis U., 1979-95, assoc. clin. prof., 1996—; adj. faculty health svcs. mgmt. U. Mo., Columbia, 1996; bd. overseers St. Louis Regional Med. Ctr., 1985-95; cons. Ill. Local Govtl. Law Enforcement Officers Tng. Bd., 1988. Contbr. articles to profl. jours.; author of short stories. Chmn. licensure com. Mo. Bd. Registration for Healing Arts, 1983-86; adv. coun. Girl Scouts U.S., 1986—. Recipient Disting. Alumni award Douglass Coll., 1992, Publ. award Mo. Pub. Health Assn., 1994, St. Louis Woman of Achievement award Sta. KMOX Radio and Suburban Jours., 1995. Fellow ACP; mem. AMA, APHA, Am. Med. Women's Assn. (chpt. pres. 1982-85, Cmty. Svc. award 1992), Am. Med. Writers Assn., Nat. Assn. Physician Broadcasters, St. Louis Met. Med. Soc. (councilor 1982-84, sec. 1986, editor 1989-90), Mo. Women's Forum. Lutheran.

FISHER, M. JANICE, hospital administrator; b. Phila., Dec. 16, 1937; d. Joseph John and Phyllis R. (Catarro) Ronollo; 1 child, Mary Phillips Talbutt. AS, Delaware County C.C., 1987. Dir. vol. resources Haverford (Pa.) State Hosp., 1971-95; liaison Friends of Haverford State Hosp., 1986-88. Pres. Local 2347 Am. Fedn. State, County, Mcpl. Employees Cheney U., 1976-83, Local 2346, Haverford State Hosp., 1987-88. Mem. Am. Hosp. Assn., Assn. Dirs. Vol. Svcs., Lioness Club Aston Twp., Delt. Valley Assn. Dirs. Vol. Programs, M.L.B. Club (v.p.). Home: 635 E 19th St Chester PA 19013

FISHER, MARSHA L., sales executive; b. East Liverpool, Ohio, Feb. 19, 1942; d. Benjamin Clark and Mildred Bessie (Coleman) Franklin; children: Guy Matthew, Wade Nelson, Kelly Erin, Shannon Leigh. BS in Edn., Baldwin Wallace Coll., 1964. Cert. elem. tchr., Ohio. Tchr. kindergarten Randolph (Ohio) City Sch. Sys.; program dir. Cleve. YMCA, Goodrich Social Settlement, Cleve.; owner, profl. skin care and color cons. Mary Kay cosmetics, Strongsville, Ohio, 1974—, exec. sr. sales dir.; image and fashion cons. to local bus. orgns., Cleve., 1980—. Home and Office: Terrace Woods 11495 Pearl Rd Strongsville OH 44136

FISHER, MARY, artist, photographer, health organization founder; b. Louisville, Apr. 6, 1948; d. Max and Marjorie S. (Switow) F.; divorced; children: Max Campbell, Zachary Campbell. Student, U. Mich., Wayne State U. Tapestry weaver, 1968-70, TV prodr., 1968-74, asst. to Pres. Gerald Ford, 1974-76, designer, mfr. signature line of boutique items, 1980-84. Author: Sleep with the Angels: A Mother Challenges AIDS, 1994, I'll Not Go Quietly, 1995, My Name Is Mary, 1996; one woman exhbns. include Linda Hayman Gallery, Detroit, 1991, Town and Country Sun Gallery, N.Y., 1992, Helander Gallery, Palm Beach, Fla. and N.Y., 1994; group exhbns. include Robertson Gallery, Beverly Hills, Calif., 1986, Harrison Gallery, Boca Raton, Fla., 1990, Helander Gallery, Plam Beach, 1993, Gallery 28, Boston, 1994. Founder Family AIDS Network, Inc., N.Y.C., 1992—; mem., former commr. Nat. Commn. AIDS; mem. chmn.'s coun. Betty Ford Ctr.; mem. Mich. AIDS fund com. Coun. Mich. Founds.; spkr. AIDS awareness in TV news, health forums, convs., Rep. nat. Conv., Houston, 1992, 96. Address: A James Heynen The Greystone Group Inc 678 Front St NW Grand Rapids MI 49504*

FISHER, MARY BUCHER, technical editor; b. Columbus, Ohio, Jan. 9, 1937; d. Paul and Florence Hale (Burington) Bucher; m. J.R. Fisher, Mar. 22, 1991 (div. Mar. 1993); 1 stepchild, Patricia Diane Fisher Anderson. BA cum laude, Ohio State U., 1958, MA, 1973. Sec. Ohio State U., Columbus, 1958-60; editorial asst. Ohio State U. Press, Columbus, 1960-68; asst. editor Jour. Higher Edn., Columbus, 1968-72; pub. info. specialist Transp. Rsch. Ctr., East Liberty, Ohio, 1974; editor Apropos Nat. Ctr. on Ednl. Media and Materials for Handicapped, Columbus, 1974-77; sr. tech. writer-editor Battelle, Columbus, 1978-89; freelance tech. editor Columbus, 1990—; rep. Columbus Tech. Coun., 1987-88; mem. tech. comms. adv. bd. Columbus State C.C., 1991—. Contbr. feature articles to various nationwide mags. and Ohio newspapers. Co-founder Buckeye Singles Coun., Columbus, 1981, originator Nat. Singles Week, 1984; mem., treas., group rep., publicity chair various Twelve-Step Groups, Columbus, 1988—; sewing guild vol. Riverside Meth. Hosp., Columbus, 1994—. Mem. Soc. for Tech. Comm. (sr., editing awards 1981-90), Women in Comm., Inc. (Excellent Book Editing award 1984), Soc. for Profl. Journalists, Am. Mensa (membership chair Columbus area), Phi Beta Kappa, Zeta Tau Alpha. Methodist. Office: 100 Glenmont Ave Columbus OH 43214

FISHER, MARY DEE, pediatric clinical nurse specialist; b. Pitts., Sept. 15, 1959; d. Thomas Patrick and Jane Francis (Naughton) O'Toole; m. Allen Lee Fisher, Oct. 30, 1993; 1 child, Michelle Fisher. ASN, Alleg County C.C., 1981; BSN, La Roche Coll., 1985; MSN, U. Pitts., 1989. RN Pa., BLS, PALS, CCRN. Staff nurse NICU Magee Women's Hosp., Pitts., 1981-82; staff nurse PICU Children's Hosp. Pitts., 1982-87, utilization review nurse, 1987-90, pediatric clin. nurse specialist, 1990—; adv. group mem. critical pathway project AACN, 1994—. Contbr. articles to profl. jours. Counselor Camp Huff 'n' Puff Am. Lung Assn., 1991—. Mem. AACN, Assn. Clin. Nurse Specialists (bd. dirs. 1994—). Home: 209 Bon Air Ave Pittsburgh PA 15210-3203 Office: Children's Hosp Pitts 1 Children's Way Pittsburgh PA 15212-5250

FISHER, NANCY, writer, producer, director; d. Seymour and Tema Fisher; 1 child, Sarah Olivia. BA, Barnard Coll. Creative group head Benton & Bowles Advt., London, 1970-74, McCann Erickson Advt., N.Y.C., 1974-75; creative dir. Norman, Craig & Kummel Advt., N.Y.C., 1975-78; pres. Nancy Fisher Inc., N.Y.C., 1978—, pres. Creative Programming, Inc., N.Y.C., 1981-89. Author: Vital Parts, 1993, Side Effects, 1994, Special Treatment, 1996. Creator, writer, producer TV series Womanwatch, 1982-89, Celebrity Chefs, 1983-89; numerous home video cassettes including Look Mom, I'm Fishing (Parents Choice award), The Annapolis Book of Seamanship Video Series (Cindy award), The Christmas Carol Video, Video Dog, Video Cat, Video Baby. Recipient 5 broadcast awards Network Documentary Series. Mem. Dirs. Guild of Am., Authors Guild. Office: 200 E 84th St New York NY 10028-2906

FISHER, NANCY LOUISE, pediatrician, medical geneticist, former nurse; b. Cleve., July 4, 1944; d. Nelson Leopold and Catherine (Harris) F.; m. Larry William Larson, May 30, 1976; 1 child, Jonathan Raymond. Student, Notre Dame Coll., Cleve., 1962-64; BSN, Wayne State U., 1967; postgrad., Calif. State U., Hayward, 1971-72; MD, Baylor Coll. of Medicine, 1976; M in Pub. Health, U. Wash., 1982, certificate in ethics, 1993. Diplomate Am. Bd. Pediatrics, Am. Bd. Med. Genetics. RN coronary care unit and med. intensive care unit Highland Gen. Hosp., Oakland, Calif., 1970-72; RN coronary care unit Alameda (Calif.) Hosp., 1972-73; intern in pediatrics Baylor Coll. of Medicine, Houston, 1976-77, resident in pediatrics, 1977-78; attending physician, pediatric clinic Harborview Med. Ctr., Seattle, 1980-81; staff physician children and adolescent health care clinic Columbia Health Ctr., Seattle, 1981-87, founder, dir. of med. genetics clinic, 1984-89; maternal child health policy cons. King County div. Seattle King County Dept Pub. Health, 1983-85; dir. genetic svcs. Va. Mason Clinic, 1986-89; dir. med. genetic svcs. Swedish Hosp., 1989-94; pvt. practice Seattle, 1994—; med. cons. supr. office of managed care Wash. State Dept. Social and Health Svcs., Olympia, 1996—; nurses aide psychiatry Sinai Hosp., Detroit, 1966-67; charge nurse Women's Hosp., Cleve., 1967; research asst. to Dr. Shelly Liss, 1976; with Baylor Housestaff Assn., Baylor Coll. Medicine, 1980-81; clin. asst. prof. grad. sch. nursing, U. Wash., Seattle, 1981-85, clin. asst. prof. dept. pediatrics, 1982—; com. appointments include Seattle CCS Cleft Palate Panel, 1984—; bd. dirs., first v.p. King County Assn. Sickle Cell Disease 1985-86, acting pres. 1986, pres. 1986-87; hosp. affiliation include Childrens Orthopedic Hosp. and Med. Ctr., Seattle, 1981-89, Virginia Mason Hosp., Seattle, 1985—, Harborview Hosp., Seattle, 1986—. Contbr. articles to profl. jours. Active Seattle Urban League, 1982—, 101 Black Women, 1986—; bd. dirs. Seattle Sickle Cell Affected Family Assn., 1984-85; mem. People to People Citizen Ambassador Group. Served to lt. USN Nurse Corps, 1966-70. Fellow Am. Coll. Medicine Genetics (founder); mem. Student Governing Body and Graduating Policy Com. Baylor Coll. Medicine (founding mem. 1973-76), Loans and Scholarship Com. Baylor Coll. Medicine (voting mem. 1973-76), Am. Med. Student Assn., Student Nat. Med. Assn., Admission Com. Baylor Coll. Medicine (voting mem. 1974-76), AMA, Am. Med. Women's Assn., Am. Acad. Pediatrics, Am. Pub. Health Assn. (co-chmn. genetic subsect. Mat. Child Health), Am. Soc. Human Genetics, Nat. Speakers Assn., Birth Defects and Clin. Genetics Soc., Wash. State Assn. Black Providers of Health Care, Northwest Chpt. Soc. Adolescent Medicine, Wash. State Soc. Pediatrics, Seattle C. of C. (mem. Leadership Tomorrow 1988—), Sigma Gamma Rho, Phi Delta Epsilon. Office: Mail Stop 45506 805 Plum St SE Olympia WA 98504

FISHER, PAULINE POSTILOFF, movement and stress management consultant; b. Phila., Dec. 16, 1935; d. Nathan and Bertha (Koltun) Postiloff; m. Martin Fisher, June 21, 1953 (div. Dec. 1976); children: Jeffrey Scott, Russ T., Kevin Todd. BA in Dance Edn., Temple U., 1975; MA in Dance Edn., George Washington U., 1978. Founder A Moving Experience, Washington; presenter, trainer, teacher in fields of therapeutic movement, stress reduction mgmt., special populations, intergenerational programming, and elderhostel programs; conducts numerous workshops in field, as well as staff training and consulting. Author: Creative Movement for Older Adults, 1989, More than Movement, 1995; dir., creator (videotape) More than Movement, 1996, (audiotape) Relaxation and Imagery, 1982; contbr. articles to profl. jours. Vol. trainer So Others Might Eat, Washington, 1996, Ctr. for Body/Mind Medicine, Washington, 1996. Recipient grants Ga. Coun. for the Arts, 1981, D.C. Commn. on the Arts, 1982-3, 84, 87, 88, 89, 94. Mem. GROWS. Home and Office: A Moving Experience 1884 Columbia Rd NW Washington DC 20009

FISHER, SALLIE ANN, chemist; b. Green Bay, Wis., Sept. 10, 1923. BS in Chemistry, U. Wis., 1945, MS, 1946, PhD, 1949. Instr. Mt. Holyoke Coll., South Hadley, Mass., 1949-50; asst. prof. U. Minn., Duluth, 1950-51; group leader Rohm & Haas Co., Phila., 1951-60; assoc. dir. rsch. Robinette Rsch. Labs., Berwyn, Pa., 1960-72; v.p. Puricons, Inc., Malvern, Pa., 1972-76; pres. Puricons, Inc., Malvern, 1976—; mem. adv. bd. Internat. Water Conf., Pitts., 1976-91, Reactive Polymers, Netherlands, 1982-88. Contbr. chpts. to books and over 100 articles to profl. jours. Recipient award of merit Engring. Soc. Western Pa., Pitts., 1984. Fellow ASTM (vice-chmn. D-19 1972-78, award of merit 1974, Max Hecht award con. D-19 1975); mem. Soc. Chem. Industry, Am. Chem. Soc., Am. Waterworks Assn., Nat. Assn. Corrosion Engrs. Office: Puricons Inc 101 Quaker Ln Malvern PA 19355-2480

FISHER, SHARON MARY, musician; b. Orange, N.J., Sept. 29, 1944; d. Stanley and Veronica Shirley (Conway) Cozza; m. Andrew Fisher IV, Aug. 16, 1969. B Music Edn., Westminster Choir Coll., 1966; postgrad., Acad. Vocal Arts, 1966-67, Temple U., 1967-69. Cert. music tchr., N.J. Chorister Westminster Choir, Princeton, N.J., 1964-66; music tchr. Phila. Pub. Schs., 1967-69; sect. leader Phila. Boys' Choir, 1969; performer Manhattan Light Opera Co., N.Y., 1969-70; soprano soloist St. Peter's Ch., Morristown, N.J., 1975-79; organist Ch. of the Saviour, Denville, N.J., 1981-84; performer, lectr., 1986—; guest performer, lectr. at chs., schs., librs. and benefits in N.J., N.Y., Conn., Pa., Fla.; feature performer ann. Scottish Games, Millington, N.J. Performer for recording Concert Memories, 1991. Grand marshal Holiday Parade, Denville C. of C., 1991. Recipient Marietta MacLeod award An Comunn Gaidhealach, 1989, Scots award Scottish Club of Twin-states, 1988-89, Harp/Voice trophy O'Carolan Harp Festival, Keadue, Ireland, 1988, award of merit Passaic County Irish Am. Cultural Soc., 1995. Mem. Clarsach Soc. (Edinburgh), Scottish Harp Soc. Am. (Ellice MacDonald grantee 1987), Am. Harp Soc., Nat. Assn. Tchrs. of Singing, Internat. Soc. Folk Harpers and Craftsmen, Comhaltas Ceoltoiri Eireann. Home: 46 W Shore Rd Denville NJ 07834-1520

FISHER, TINA LOUISE, training and developmeny consultant; b. Harrodsburg, Ky., Dec. 5, 1962; d. George H. and Pauline O. (Lyons) F. A in Data Processing, Lexington (Ky.) C.C., 1986; BA, Wright State U., 1992, MA, 1994. Credit specialist Monarch Marking Systems, Dayton, Ohio, 1987-90; new mem. acquisitioner Dayton, Ohio, 1992-95, corp. collections cons., 1995-96; tng. and devel. cons. Mascotech Tng. and Visual Svcs., Cin., 1996—. Democrat.

FISHER, VICTORIA ANN, program director; b. Chester, Pa., Mar. 19, 1938; d. John Joseph and Victoria Mary (Roscoe) Rutkowski; m. T. Forrest Fisher; children: Victoria Leigh, Geoffrey Joseph. BA in Communications, Chatham Coll., 1982; MA in Adult and Cmty. Edn., Ind. U. Pa., 1986, Columbia U., 1989; EdD, Columbia U., 1991. Dir. gateway program Chatham Coll., Pitts., 1983-87; dir. continuing edn. Neumann Coll., Aston, Pa., 1987-95, chair divsn. liberal studies degree program, 1995—; mem. adv. bd. Am. Assn. Colls. Pharmacy, Washington, 1994—; participant mgmt. lifelong edn. Harvard U., Cambridge, Mass., 1987. Mem. adv. bd. cmty. svc. United Way, Phila., 1982—; founding bd. mem. Vol. Ctr. Chester, Del. and Montgomery Counties, Phila., 1989-92; vol. Point of Light Found., 1995. Recipient Comm. Excellence award Point of Light Found., 1995. Mem. Pa. Assn. for Adult and Continuing Edn. (past pres. 1995, pres. 1994, 1st and 2d v.p. 1992-93, Eastern rep. 1987-92, Pres.' award 1994), Adult and Continuing Higher Edn. Roman Catholic. Office: Neumann Coll Concord Rd Aston PA 19014

FISHER, WENDY ASTLEY-BELL, marketing executive; b. London, Jan. 23, 1944; came to U.S., 1947; d. Leonard Astley and Rita (Duis) Astley-Bell; m. Richard Van Mell, Mar. 21, 1970 (div. May 1980); m. Lester Emil Fisher, Jan. 23, 1981. Student, Hood Coll., 1961-63, U. Alta., Can., summer 1963; BA honors, Northwestern U., 1965; postgrad., U. Chgo., 1965-66. Lab. technician Northwestern U. Med. Sch., Chgo., 1966-67; designer Okamoto/London Studio, Chgo., 1967-71, Communications Internat., Chgo., 1971-72; freelance artist K&S Photographics, Chgo., 1972-76; dir. spl. projects Lincoln Park Zool. Soc., Chgo., 1976-81; mem. pub. rels. staff Field Enterprises, Chgo., 1981; pres., creative dir. Mailworks, Inc., Chgo., 1981—; speaker in field. Co-author: The First Hundred Years, 1975; contbr. articles to profl. jours. Bd. dirs. Jr. League Chgo., 1965-74, Vis. Nurse Assn. Chgo., 1978-82; mem. women's bd. Lincoln Park Zool. Soc., 1981-84; trustee Crow Canyon Archeol. Ctr., 1994—. Recipient Gold Cert. Chgo. Savs. and Loan Assn., 1973, Award of Merit Splty. Advt. Assn., 1979; named Outstanding Women Entrepreneur Chgo. chpt. Women in Communications, 1983. Mem. Nat. Soc. Fundraising Execs. (bd. dirs. Chgo. chpt. 1982-88, Pres.'s award 1987, cert. in fundraising), Chgo. Assn. Direct Mktg. (bd. dirs. 1982-87, bd. dirs. edn. found. 1985-87), Assn. Direct Response Fundraising Counsel, Direct Mktg. Assn. (Leadership award 1978), Am. Assn. Mus., Am. Assn. Zool. Parks and Aquariums, Econ. Club Chgo. Office: Mailworks Inc 230 N Michigan Ave Chicago IL 60601-5910

FISHERMAN, NINA YARLOVSKY, nursing administrator; b. Flin Flon, Man., Can., Oct. 5, 1955; d. Vasyl Nicolov and Milka Georgi (Krehtinkoff) Yarlovsky; m. Jay Richard Fisherman, June 26, 1983 (separated 1991). BS, Roanoke Coll., 1977; postgrad., Autonomous U. Guadalajara, 1977-79; MS, Pace U. Grad. Sch. Nursing, 1982. Staff nurse oncology Yonkers (N.Y.) Gen. Hosp., 1982-83, Montefiore Med. Ctr., Bronx, N.Y., 1984-85; br. mgr., nursing supr. Staff Builders, Health Care Svcs., Inc., Flushing, N.Y., 1985-88; inpatient nurse mgr. Ritter-Scheuer Hospice, Bronx, 1988-90; supr. home care Jacob Perlow Hospice, Beth Israel Med. Ctr., N.Y.C., 1990; patient care mgr. Westmoreland Hospice, Greensburg, Pa., 1992-93; dir. clin. svcs. Olsten Kimberly Quality Care, Inc., White Plains, N.Y., 1993-94; utilization review supr. Staff Builders, Health Care Svcs., Inc., Washington, 1994-95; utilization rev. nurse ADP Integrated Med. Solutions, Bethesda, Md., 1996—; presenter AIDS conf. Mem. Nat. Hospice Orgn.

FISHER PRUTZ, MARY LOUISE, coronary care nurse; b. Brownsville, Pa., Sept. 5, 1954; d. Hilden Fredick and Bertha Elizabeth (Radek) Fisher; m. Thomas Prutz; children: Kristie, Farrah, Kelley, Tommy, Timmy. Diploma, Washington Hosp. Sch. Nursing, 1988; BSN, California (Pa.) U., 1995. RN, Pa.; cert. ACLS, BLS. Staff nurse Washington (Pa.) Hosp., 1989—, Monongahela Valley Hosp., Monongahela, Pa., 1991—; co-sponsor Program of Profl. Sharing, Washington, 1991—; sponsor AICD Support Group, Monongahela, 1991—; facilitator Heart to Heart Cardiac Rehab. Support Group. Vol., Am. Cancer Soc., 1985—. Named Nurse of Hope, Am. Cancer Soc., Washington County, 1985-86; recipient Anna Mae Fox pub. edn. award; Dr. Norman Golomb scholarship, 1996. Mem. AACN, Nurses Christian Fellowship, Washington Hosp. Sch. Nursing Alumni Assn. (ways and means com. 1990—). Democrat. Lutheran. Home: 307 Madison Heights Rd PO Box 122 Madison PA 15663 Office: Country Club Rd Monongahela PA 15063

FISHMAN, DONNA, school administrator; b. Providence, Feb. 15, 1942; d. Harry and Ruth (Schechter) F. BEd, R.I. Coll., 1963; MA, NYU, 1965. Cert. tchr. elem. edn., secondary prin., reading coord., sch. psychologist. Title I/Chpt. I tchr. Pawtucket (R.I.) Sch. Dist., 1965-75; Title I specialist East Greenwich (R.I.) Sch. Dist., 1975-92; dir. edn. divsn. Fortune Software, Boston, 1989-92; gender equity specialist Attleboro (Mass.) Pub. Schs., 1992-94; gender equity coord. Woonsocket (R.I.) Pub. Schs., 1994—; dir., coord. No. R.I. Regional Equity Ctr., 1995—; ednl. cons., Jamestown, R.I., 1993—; co-chair R.I. Coalition of Affirmative Action, 1995—. Author: (tchr.'s manuals) Words of Fortune, 1990, Numbers of Fortune, 1990. Negotiator, NEA/R.I./East Greenwich, 1990-91; mem. Dem. Town Com., Jamestown, 1970s. Named Bay St. Tchr. of the Yr., Schweitzer Internat. Ctr., Framingham State Coll., 1994. Mem. AAUW (R.I. Com. on Women), NEA, Am. Fedn. Tchrs., Internat. Reading Assn., Bost Computer Soc., Mass. Computer Using Educators. Democrat. Jewish. Home: 38 Top O Mark Dr Jamestown RI 02835-2438 Office: Woonsocket Sch Dept High St Woonsocket RI 02895

FISHTEIN, ELIZABETH (MARY BETH STONE), writer; b. N.Y.C., May 24, 1947; d. Oscar and Ruth (Cohen) F. Student, NYU, 1965-66, Baruch Coll., 1980-81. Lic. real estate salesperson, N.Y., tourguide, N.Y.C.; notary pub., N.Y. Owner Do the Write Thing!, N.Y.C.; co-owner Signature Tours, N.Y.C.; owner Big Mama Music, N.Y.C. Composer/lyricist: (song) Phoenix, 1989 (winner Billboard Ann. Songwriter's Contest). Mem. ASCAP, Songwriters Guild, Women in Music, Nashville Songwriters Assn. Internat., Nat. Acad. Popular Music. Democrat. Jewish. Home: 56 W 70th St New York NY 10023-4620 Office: Do The Write Thing! 56 W 70th St New York NY 10023-4620

FISKE, SANDRA RAPPAPORT, psychologist, educator; b. Syracuse, N.Y., Sept. 25, 1946; d. Sidney Saul and Helen (Lapides) Rappaport; B.S., Cornell U., 1968; M.Ed., Tufts U., 1969; M.A., Columbia U., 1971, Ph.D., 1974; m. Jordan J. Fiske, June 22, 1974. Supervising sch. psychologist St. Elizabeth's Sch., N.Y.C., 1971-76; instr. clin. psychology Tchrs. Coll., Columbia, N.Y.C., 1973, clin. asst. dept. psychology, 1975-76; adj. prof. Syracuse U., 1976; sch. psychologist Syracuse Bd. Edn., 1976-77; prof. psychology Onondaga Community Coll., Syracuse, 1976-87, prof. 1988—, chair social sci. dept., 1993—; pvt. practice psychology, Syracuse, 1976—. NIMH fellow, 1969-72. Mem. Am. Psychol. Assn., Psychologists of Central N.Y., Am. Orthopsychiat. Assn., Sigma Xi, Psi Chi. Home: 2 Signal Hill Rd Fayetteville NY 13066-9674 Office: Onondaga Community Coll Dept Psychology Syracuse NY 13215

FISKIN, JUDITH ANNE, artist, educator; b. Chgo., Apr. 1, 1945; d. Fred Albert and Cecile (Citron) Bartman; m. Jeffrey Allen Fiskin, Jan. 1, 1967 (div. Apr. 1975); m. Jonathan Marc Wiener, Jan. 17, 1987. BA, Pomona Coll., 1966; postgrad., U. Calif., Berkeley, 1966-67; MA, UCLA, 1969. Assoc. dean sch. art Calif. Inst. of Arts, Valencia, 1977-84, art faculty, 1977—. One-woman shows include Castelli Graphics, N.Y.C., 1976, Asher-Faure, L.A., 1991, Mus. Contemproary Art, L.A., 1992, Curt Marcus Gallery, N.Y.C., 1994, Patricia Faure Gallery, Sant Monica, Calif., 1994; exhibited in group shows at Luasanne, Switzerland, Vancouver, B.C., Internat. Ctr. for Photography, N.Y.C., San Francisco Mus. Modern Art, Corcoran Gallery Art, Washington, LaJolla (Calif.) Mus. Art and mus. in Richmond, Va., Miami, Fla., Chgo., Akron, Ohio. Cmty. funding bd. mem. Liberty Hill Found., L.A., 1994. Recipient Lifetime Achievement award in photography L.A. Ctr. for Photographic Studies, 1995; grantee Nat. Endowment for Arts, 1979, 90, Logan, 1986. Office: Calif Inst of Arts McBean Pkwy Valencia CA 91355

FISMER, ROBERTA D., nursing administrator; b. Nanticoke, Pa., Dec. 30, 1947; d. Robert D. and Violet Myrtle (Garey) Benscoter; m. Carl Edward Fismer, Nov. 8, 1974; children: Lee Alan, Diana Lynn. AA, Manatee Jr. Coll., 1967. RN, Fla.; CCRN; cert. BLS, ACLS, PALS. Staff nurse telemetry Sarasota (Fla.) Meml. Hosp., 1967-68, staff nurse ICU, 1968-80; paramedic instr. Sarasota County Vocat. Sch., 1973-78; nurse mgr., co-founder cardiac rehab. Sarasota County YMCA, 1977-80; staff nurse SICU South Miami Hosp., Miami, Fla., 1981-86; staff nurse ICU Mariners Hosp., Tavernier, Fla., 1986-88, supr. ICU, 1988-94, nursing quality assurance mgr., 1990—, nurse mgr. ICU and emergency dept., 1994—. Pres. Am. Heart Assn., Sarasota County, 1975-76; mem. Pride, Tavernier, 1989-91. Mem. AACN, Fla. Assn. Quality Assurance Profls. Republican. Home: 179 Azalea St Tavernier FL 33070-2201 Office: Mariners Hosp 50 High Point Rd Tavernier FL 33070-2006

FISZER-SZAFARZ, BERTA (BERTA SAFARS), research scientist; b. Wilno, Poland, Feb. 1, 1928; m. David Safars; children: Martine, Michel. MS, U. Buenos Aires, 1955, PhD, 1956. Lab. chief Cancer Inst. Villejuif, France, 1961-67; vis. scientist Nat. Cancer Inst., Bethesda, Md., 1967-68; lab. chief Institut Curie, Orsay, France, 1969—; vis. scientist Inst. Applied Biochemistry, Mitake, Gifu, Japan, 1986; gen. sec. dep. French-Israel Assn. Sci. Rsch. and Tech., 1994. Contbr. articles to profl. jours. Mem. European Assn. Cancer Research, Am. Assn. Cancer Research (corres. mem.), European Cell Biology Orgn., French Soc. Cell Biology. Office: Institut Curie-Biologie, Bat 110 Centre Universitaire, 91405 Orsay France

FITCH, LINDA BAUMAN, computer coordinator, educator; b. Elmira, N.Y., Jan. 6, 1947; d. Floyd Theodore Bauman and Wilma Mildred Rennie; m. H. Taylor Fitch, Feb. 15, 1969; children: Trevor Andrew, Matthew Taylor. BS, Keuka Coll., Keuka Park, 1969. Elem. tchr. Penn Yan Cen. Sch. Dist., Penn Yan, N.Y., 1972-73; computer coord. Fitch Auto Supply, Penn Yan, 1973—. Com. chmn. troop 48 Boy Scouts Am., Branchport, N.Y., 1986-92; v.p. Penn Yan Cen. Sch. Bd., 1984-92, 95—, pres., 1992-95; chmn. pub. rels. Yates Day Care Ctr., Penn Yan, 1980-82; mem. Bd. Coop. Ednl. Svcs., 1992—. Mem. AAUW, Nat. Sch. Bds. Assn. (fed. rels. network 1988—), N.Y. State Sch. Bds. Assn. (state legis. network 1991—), Four County Sch. Bds. Assn. (legis. chmn., 2d v.p., 1st v.p., pres., mem. commr.'s adv. coun. sch. bd. mems. 1995). Republican. Presbyterian. Home: 3120 Kinneys Corners Rd Bluff Point NY 14478-9752 Office: Fitch Auto Supply F&W Parts 211 Clinton St Penn Yan NY 14527-1704

FITCH, MARY KILLEEN, salary design and workers compensation specialist; b. Carroll, Iowa, July 15, 1949; d. Michael Francis and Mildred (Pauley) Killeen; m. David Paul Fitch, July 3, 1971; one child, Emily Grace. BS, Iowa State U., 1971, MS, 1975; postgrad. U. Minn., 1982—. Pers. adminstr. Control Data Corp., Roseville, Minn., 1976-77; sr. compensation analyst/employee rels. rep. Honeywell, Inc., Mpls., 1977-80; human resource mgr./compensation and benefits mgr. No. Telecom, Inc., Minnetonka, Minn., 1980-82; adj. instr., teaching asst. Lakewood Community Coll./U. Minn., Mpls., 1982-84; compensation cons. Gen. Mills, Wayzata, Minn., 1984-85; mgr. compensation Northwestern Nat. Life Ins., Mpls., 1985-87; prin. compensation specialist Comml. Bldgs. Group, Honeywell, Inc., Mpls., 1987-89; dir. compensation, HRIS, workers compensation, incentive design, Nat. Car Rental System, Inc., Mpls., 1989—; cons. exec. compensation Honeywell Inc., Mpls., 1984; cons. human resources Les Kraus & Assocs., Edina, Minn., 1984; pres. Personnel Mgmt. Services of Twin Cities, St. Paul, 1983—. Author: (with Paul Muchinsky) Organization Behavior and Human Performance, 1975; (with John Fossum) Personnel Psychology, 1985. Former chmn., bd. dirs. Kathadin, United Way Agy., Mpls., 1985—; curriculum com. U. Minn., 1983-84. George Catt Iowa State U. scholar, 1970. Mem. AAUW, Assn. Human Resources Systems Profls., Am. Compensation Assn., Psi Chi, Phi Kappa Phi. Avocations: dressage, karate. Home: 1188 90th St E Inver Grove MN 55077-4206 Office: HR Nat Car Rental Systems Inc 7700 France Ave S Minneapolis MN 55435-5228

FITCH, NANCY ELIZABETH, historian; b. White Plains, N.Y., June 17, 1947; d. Robert Franklin and Nancy Elizabeth (Harvey) F. BA in Polit. Sci./English Lit., Oakland U., Rochester, Mich., 1969; MA in History, U. Mich., 1971, PhD in History, 1981. Danforth teaching intern dept. history U. Mich., Ann Arbor, 1970; asst. prof. history and lit. Sangamon State U., Springfield, Ill., 1972-74; sr. social sci. rsch. analyst The Congl. Rsch. Svc. of

Libr. of Congress, Washington, 1975-78; asst. to the chmn./historian U.S. EEO Commn., Washington, 1982-89; asst. prof. history Lynchburg Coll. of Va., 1989-91; asst. prof. African Am. studies Temple U., Phila., 1991-92; Jesse Ball Dupont vis. scholar Randolph-Macon Woman's Coll., Lynchburg, Va., 1992-93; assoc. prof. history U. N.C. at Asheville, 1993-95; assoc. prof. English Coll. New Rochelle, N.Y., 1995—; chmn.'s rep. White House Inst. on Hist. Black Colls. and Univs., U.S. Dept. Edn., 1985-89; pub. rels. vol. S. Africa Exhibit Project, Washington, 1986-88; mem. adv. com. DuPont Vis. Scholars Project, Va. Found. Ind. Colls., 1990-91; adj. prof. in history Shaw U., Asheville, 1994. Editl. assoc.: Jour. S. Asian Lit., 1969-79; co-editor: Diversity: A Jour. of Multicultural Issues; mem. editl. adv. bd. Kente Cloth: African Am. Voices in Tex.; book reviewer Jour. S. Asian Lit., Lit. East and West, The Historian, Jour. Asian Studies; author: (series) Essays on Liberty, 1988; contbr. articles to profl. jours. Organizer, producer Ann. Dr. Martin Luther King Jr. Celebration prog., Washington, 1986-88; guest lectr. on history of Am. music Blue Ridge Music Festival, Lynchburg, 1991; participant Radio America African-Am. contbrs. to art and lit., 1990; vol./cons. The Holiday Project, Washington, 1986-88; mem. Widening Horizons Prog. of D.C. Pub. Schs., 1986-88. Recipient Achievement award Mt. Vernon Day Care Ctr., 1983, Spl. Commendation, U.S. EEO Commn., 1985-89, Ft. Drum Sgt. Maj.'s medal for svc. 10th Mountain div. Light Inf., Ft. Drum, N.Y., 1992; fellow Ford Found., 1971-72, Nat. Def. Fgn. Lagn., 1970, U. Mich., 1970-71, 78-79, John Hay Whitney Found., 1969-70; Faculty summer sr. fellowship Nat. Endowment for the Humanities, 1996. Mem. Assn. for Advancement of Core Curricula, Afro-Am. Archeology Network, Friends of Benjamin Banneker Hist. Pk., Phi Alpha Theta (faculty advisor 1990-91). Republican. Episcopalian/Buddhist. Office: Coll New Rochelle 267 Bedford Ave Mount Vernon NY 10553-1517

FITTING-GIFFORD, MARJORIE ANN, mathematician, educator, consultant; b. Detroit, Nov. 29, 1933; d. Ellis John and Dorothy Jennie Premo; m. George R. Pickering, Dec. 16, 1954 (div. 1964); children: William Russell, David Ellis, John Lawrence; m. Frederick N. Fitting, Feb. 25, 1972 (dec. 1985); m. Forrest W. Gifford, May 28, 1988. BS in Math., Mich. State U., 1954, PhD, 1968; MEd, Wayne State U., 1958; AM in Math., U. Mich., 1966. Cert. tchr., Mich., Calif. Tchr. math. secondary schs., Mich., 1954-61; instr. Lawrence Inst. Tech., Southfield, Mich., 1961-68; grad. asst. Mich. State U., East Lansing, 1966-68; prof. emeritus math. and computer sci. San Jose State U., Calif., 1968-92; instr. math U. Nev., Las Vegas, 1993-95; v.p. fin. Metra Instruments, San Jose, 1972-82; pres. Metier, Henderson, Nev., 1982—; cons. San Jose (Calif.) Unified Sch., 1969-71. Author: (software) Math Test Generation, 1983; co-author: (book series) Computer Literacy Series, 1983-85, (book) Introduction to Geometry, 1996. Recipient Dean's award for teaching excellence San Jose State U., 1982; J.C. Plant scholar Mich. State U., 1954; NSF fellow, 1965-66, Fulbright sr. lectr./rsch. grantee, Portugal, 1985-86. Mem. Math. Assn. Am., Am. Math. Soc., Nat. Coun. Tchrs. Math. (review panel 1954—), Computer Using Educators, So. Nev. Tchrs. Math, Calif. Math. Coun., Zeta Tau Alpha. Democrat. Roman Catholic. Avocations: gardening, rafting, kayaking.

FITTS, C. AUSTIN, investment banker, former federal agency administrator; b. Phila., Dec. 24, 1950; d. William Thomas Jr. and Barbara Kinsey (Willits) F. AA, Bennett Coll., 1970; student, Chinese U., Hong Kong, 1971; BA, U. Pa., 1974, MBA, 1978; postgrad., MIT. With Dillon, Read & Co., Inc., N.Y.C., 1978-89, sr. v.p., 1984-86, mng. dir., mem. bd. dirs., 1986-89; asst. sec. for housing, urban devel. and fed. housing commr. HUD, Washington, 1989-90; pres. The Hamilton Securities Group, Inc., Washington, 1990-94; bd. dirs. Student Loan Mktg. Assn. Sallie Mae; adv. bd. Fedn. Nat. Mortgage Assn. Fannie Mae, 1992-93; mem. emerging mkts. adv. com. SEC, 1990-93. Mem. grad. adv. bd. Wharton Sch., 1986-95. Mem. Urban Land Inst., Nat. Multi-Housing Coun. (bd. dirs.), Coun. for Excellence in Govt. (prin. 1991—), Econ. Club N.Y., Wharton Sch. Club Washington (adv. bd. 1991—). Office: The Hamilton Securities Group 7 Dupont Cir NW Washington DC 20036

FITZGERALD, ETHEL, lawyer; b. N.Y.C.; d. Sandy and Effie (Hargett) Brown; 1 child, Kim Saul Fitzgerald. BS, Hunter Coll., N.Y.C., 1954, MA, 1957, profl. cert., 1965; JD, Bklyn. Law Sch., 1981. Bar: N.Y. 1982, U.S. Dist. Ct. (no. dist.) N.Y. 1982, U.S. Dist. Ct. (ea. and so. dists.) N.Y. 1983, U.S. Ct. Appeals (2nd cir.) 1991, U.S. Supreme Ct. 1991. Chmn. bd. examiners Bd. Edn., Bklyn., 1974-91; pvt. practice Bklyn., 1991—; mem. com. on character and fitness appellate divsn. 2nd Dept., Bklyn., 1992—;mem. pro bono panel U.S. Dist. Ct. (ea. dist.) N.Y., Bklyn., 1983—. Mem. Moot Ct. Honor Soc. (sec. 1979-91, cert. 1991), Nat. Order of Barristers. Office: 16 Court St Ste 714 Brooklyn NY 11241

FITZGERALD, GERALDINE, actress; b. Dublin, Ireland, Nov. 24, 1913; came to U.S. 1938, naturalized, 1954; d. William and Mary (Richards) F.; m. Stuart Scheftel, Sept. 10, 1946; children: Michael Lindsay-Hogg, Susan Scheftel. Student, Queens Coll., London. Appeared in numerous motion pictures, 1936—, including Wuthering Heights (Acad. award nomination), 1939, Dark Victory, 1939, Wilson, 1944, Three Strangers, 1946, 10 North Frederick, 1958, The Pawnbroker, 1964, The Mango Tree, 1977, Arthur, 1980, Easy Money, 1983, Pope of Greenwich Village, 1984, Poltergeist II, 1986, Arthur II, 1988; appeared on stage as Mary Tyrone in Long Days Journey into Night (Variety Critics award), 1971, The Lunch Girl; appeared in Broadway prodn. Touch of the Poet, 1980; directed play Mass Appeal, 1980; TV film appearance Do You Remember Love?, 1985, The Best of Everything, Dixie: Changing Habits, 1983, Kennedy, 1983, Street Songs, Circle of Violence, 1986, Night of Courage, 1986, Bump in the Night, 1991. Active N.Y. State Council Arts. Recipient Handel medallion N.Y.C., 1974. Mem. AFTRA, Screen Actors Guild, Actors Equity. *

FITZGERALD, SISTER JANET ANNE, college president; b. Woodside, N.Y., Sept. 4, 1935; d. Robert W. and Lillian H. (Shannon) F. BA magna cum laude, St. John's U., 1965, MA, 1967, PhD, 1971, LLD (hon.), 1982. Joined Sisters of St. Dominic of Amityville, Roman Catholic Ch., 1953; NSF postdoctoral fellow Cath. U. Am., summer 1971; prof. philosophy Molloy Coll., Rockville Centre, N.Y., 1969—; pres. Molloy Coll., 1972-96; Trustee L.I. Regional Adv. Coun. on Higher Edn., 1972—, chmn., 1981-84; trustee Commn. on Ind. Colls. and Univs., 1981-84, 89-92, Fellowship of Cath. Scholars, 1977—, v.p., 1977-80; trustee Cath. Charities, Diocese of Rockville Centre, 1979-82; invited expert peritus Vatican Internat. Conf. on Cath. Higher Edn., Rome, 1989. Author: Alfred North Whitehead's Early Philosophy of Space and Time, 1979. Mem. bd. advisors Sem. of Immaculate Conception, 1975-80; mem. adv. bd. pre-theology program Dunwoodie Sem., Archdiocese of N.Y.; mem. pub. policy com. N.Y. State Cath. Conf., 1992-94; mem. N.Y. State Edn. Dept.-Blue Ribbon Panel on Cath. Schs., 1992-93; 1st woman grand marshal St. Patrick's Day Parade, Glen cove, 1992. Recipient Disting. Leadership award L.I. Bus. News, 1988, plaque of recognition L.I. Women's Coun. for Equal Edn. Tng. and Employment, 1989, Pathfinder award Town of Hempstead, 1990, Disting. Long Islander in Edn. award Epilepsy Found. L.I., 1991, Educator of Yr. award Assn. Tchrs. N.Y., 1980, Spl. award for arts in edn. L.I. Arts Coun., 1994; honored by L.I. Cath. League for Religious and Civil Rights, 1989; named L.I.'s 100 Influentials, L.I. Bus. News, 1992, 93, 94, 95. Mem. Soc. Cath. Social Scis. (bd. advisors). Office: Molloy College Philosophy Dept 1000 Hempstead Ave Rockville Centre NY 11571-5002

FITZGERALD, JANICE S., public relations executive, academic administrator; b. Poughkeepsie, N.Y., Nov. 2, 1948; d. Lloyd Raymond and Emily Mae (Anderson) Spinner. BA magna cum laude, Cheyney U. Pa., 1972, MEd, 1973; MA, Villanova U., 1980; postgrad., Carnegie Mellon U., 1979, Harvard U., 1992. Prof. Cheyney U. Pa., 1972-74; dir. pub. rels. Cheyney U. Pa., Cheyney, 1974-83; dir. pub. rels. Pa. State System of Higher Edn., Harrisburg, 1983—, exec. assoc. to chancellor, dir. communications, 1985-90, exec. deputy, 1990—; reader Nat. Edn. Assn.; pres. Correct Correspondence; free lance writer. Bd. mem. Allied Arts Fund; vol. radio reader, Tri-County Assn. of Blind, Suburban Guild, Community Gen. Osteo. Hosp.; pub. rels. coun. State System of Higher Edn. Named one of Outstanding Women in Am., 1981, named Alumnus of Yr. Nat. Assn. Equal Opportunity, 1985; recipient award Chapel of Four Chaplains, 1982, Valedictory and Alumni Key award Cheyney U. Pa., 1972. Mem. Am. Coun. Edn. (mem. nat. identification program for advancement of women, state planning com.), Coll. and Univ. Pub. Rels. Assn. of Pa., Pub. Rels. Soc. of Am., Edn. Writers Assn., Nat. Assn. Women in Edn. Office: Office of Chancellor Pa State Sys Higher Edn 2986 N 2nd St Harrisburg PA 17110-1201

FITZGERALD, JUDITH KLASWICK, federal judge; b. Spangler, Pa., May 10, 1948; d. Julius Francis and Regina Marie (Pregno) Klaswick; m. June 5, 1971 (div. Dec. 1982); 1 child; m. Barry Robert Fitzgerald, Sept. 20, 1986; 1 child. BSBA, U. Pitts., 1970, JD, 1973. Legal researcher Assocs. Fin., Pitts., 1972-73; law clk. to pres. judge Beaver County (Pa.) Ct. Common Pleas, 1973-74; law clk. to judge Pa. Superior Ct., Pitts., 1974-75; asst. U.S. atty. U.S. Dist. Ct. (we. dist.) Pa., Pitts. and Erie, 1976-87; U.S. bankruptcy judge U.S. Dist. Ct. (we. dist.) Pa., Pitts., Erie and Johnstown, 1987—. Co-author: Bankruptcy and Divorce, Support and Property Division, 1991; editor: Pennsylvania Law of Juvenile Delinquency and Deprivation, 1976; contbr. articles to legal jours. Mem. Pitts. Camerata, 1978-80, Allegheny County Polit.-Legal Edn. Project, 1980, West Pa. Conservancy, 1990—, Mendelssohn Choir Pitts., 1982—; mem. coun. Program to Aid Citizen Enterprise, 1985-87. Recipient Spl. Achievement awards Dept. Justice, Spl. Recognition award Pittsburgh mag., Operation Exodus Outstanding Performance award Dept. Commerce, 1986. Mem. Allegheny County Bar Assn., Women's Bar Assn. of Western Pa., Nat. Conf. Bankruptcy Judges, Am. Bankruptcy Inst., Nat. Conf. Bankruptcy Clks., Comml. Law League of Am., Fed. Criminal Investigators Assn. (Spl. Svc. award 1988), Zonta. Republican. Lutheran. Office: US Bankruptcy Ct 1000 Liberty Ave Pittsburgh PA 15222-4004

FITZGERALD, LAURINE ELISABETH, university dean, educator; b. New London, Wis., Aug. 24, 1930; d. Thomas F. and Laurine (Branchflower) F. B.S., Northwestern U., 1952, M.A., 1953; Ph.D., Mich. State U., 1959. Instr. English, dir. devel. reading lab., head resident-dir. Wis. State Coll., Whitewater, 1953-55; area dir. residence and counseling Ind. U., 1955-57; teaching grad. asst. guidance and counseling, then instr., counselor Mich. State U., East Lansing, 1957-59; asst. prof. psychology and edn., assoc. dean students U. Denver, 1959-62; asst. prof. counseling psychology, staff counselor for Carnegie Found. project U. Minn., 1962-63; assoc. dean, assoc. prof. Mich. State U., 1963-70, assoc. dean students prof. adminstrn. and higher edn., dir. div. edn. and rsch., 1970-74; dean Grad. Sch., prof. counselor edn., dir. N.E. Wis. Coop. Regional Grad. Ctr. U. Wis.-Oshkosh, 1974-85; dean/dir. Ohio State U.-Mansfield, 1986-87, prof. edn. policy and leadership, 1985-93, dir. student pers. asst. program, edn. policy and leadership, 1989-92; adj. prof. edn. policy and leadership Ohio State U., 1992-93; vis. lectr. U. Okla., Norman, 1961; vis. prof. Oreg. State U., 1977; cons. in field; vocat. expertwitness, 1962-95. Contbr. numerous articles to profl. jours.; co-author monographs, texts. Adv. bd. Mansfield Gen. Hosp., 1986-94; bd. dirs. Renaissance Theatre, 1986-87, New Beginnings, 1986-94; exec. com. Ohio Consortium on Tng. and Planning, 1985-87; trustee Mt. Carmel Coll. Nursing, chmn. acad. affairs com., 1988-96. Recipient Higher Edn. Rocky Mountain coun. Girl Scouts U.S., 1961, Evelyn Hosmer U. Denver, 1962, Merit award Northwestern Alumni Assn., 1993; named Old Master Purdue U., 1979, Most Disting. Women in Edn., Mich., 1973; Elin Wagner Found. fellow, 1963-64. Mem. AAUW, AAUP (chpt. treas. 1955-56), NEA, Am. Psychol. Assn., Mich. Psychol. Assn., Am. Pers. and Guidance Assn., Am. Coll. Pers. Assn. (sec. 1965-67, exec. bd. 1968-70, chmn. women's task force 1970-71, editor jour. 1976-82, Disting. Scholar award 1985, sr. scholars com. 1985-90, historian 1982-95, chmn. scholars com. 1986-87, sr. scholars diplomate 1990, awards and commendations com. 1988-89, pres.-elect 1989-90, pres. 1990-91, past pres. 1991-92), Assn. Counselor Edn. and Supervision, Am. Assn. Higher Edn., Nat. Assn. Women Deans, Adminstrs. and Counselors (rsch., ednl. by-laws programs, publs., univ. coms. 1959-72, v.p. 1972-74, KSP Trust Commn. 1979-81, pres. 1980-81, editorial bd. 1991—), Mich. Assn. Women Deans, Adminstrs. and Counselors (pres. 1967-69), Ohio Assn. Women Deans, Adminstrs. and Counselors, Mich. Coll. Pers. Assn., Wis. Coll. Pers. Assn., Midwest Assn. Grad. Schs. (pres. 1980-82), Intercollegiate Assn. Women Students (editorial bd., nat. advisor), Women's Equity Action League (past pres. Mich., nat. sec.-treas. legal and edn. def. fund), Bus. and Profl. Women's Club (chpt. pres. 1980, state officer 1981, Lena Lake Forest fellow 1966-67), Wis. Soc. for Higher Edn. (Achievement award 1985, Pres. award 1982), Altrusa Internat. (mem. bd. dirs. 1986-94), Mortar Bd., Shi-Ai, Beta Beta Beta, Psi Chi, Alpha Lambda Delta, Delta Kappa Gamma, Zonta (pres. Lansing club, chmn. internat. status of women com. 1960-85). Home: 812 Wyman St New London WI 54961-1771

FITZGERALD, LYNNE MARIE LESLIE, family therapist; b. Berea, Ohio, Aug. 21, 1946; d. Glenn Willis and Blanche Marie (Monkosky) Leslie; m. J. Michael Fitzgerald, May 3, 1974; children: Joseph Glenn, Leslie Marie. BA, U. Miami, 1968; MS, St. Thomas U., 1983; PhD, Nova Univ., 1994. Lic. marriage and family therapist, Fla. Sml. group facilitator U. Miami Med. Sch., 1988; family therapist Family Life Ctr. of Fla., Inc., Coral Gables, 1985—; facilitator stress, depression and suicide prevention program Mental Health Assn., Charlottesville, Va., 1995—; facilitator Dade County Pub. Schs./Depression and Suicide Prevention, Miami, 1985-92, Mental Health Assn. Charlottesville/Albemarle/Depression and Suicide Prevention Program for Schs., 1996—; cons. Mediation Ministries, Miami, 1990—, Counseling Ctr., St. Louis Cath. Ch., Miami, 1990-92. Mem. Jr. League, Va., St. Anne's-Belfield Sch. parents aux. bd.; bd. dirs. The Vizcayans, Miami, 1979-83, Party Parade, Charlottesville, 1995, gen. chmn. 1995-96, pres. 1996—; active Marian Ctr. Aux., Miami. Named Woman of Yr., Kappa Kappa Gamma Alumnae Assn., Miami, 1973. Mem. Am. Assn. Marriage and Family Therapists (approved supr.), Am. Orthopsychiat. Assn., Am. Assn. Christian Counselors, Mental Health Assn Charlottesville (profl. bd. dirs. 1995—), Kappa Kappa Gamma (U. Va. house bd., 1995—, alumnae exec. bd. 1994—, Woman of Yr. 1973). Roman Catholic. Home: 888 Tanglewood Rd Charlottesville VA 22901-7817 Office: Family Life Ctr of Fla Inc 1550 Madruga Ave Miami FL 33146-3039

FITZGERALD, SUSAN HELENA, elementary educator; b. Ft. Washington, Pa., Sept. 28, 1953; d. John Robert and Helen Eda (Groscost) Payne; m. Richard Michael Fitzgerald, June 8, 1974; children: Kevin Michael, Gregory Thomas, Wendy Elaine. BS in Edn., West Chester (Pa.) U., 1975, M, Reading Specialist, 1992. Cert. reading specialist, elem., spl. edn. tchr. Head start tchr. Chester County IU, Coatesville, Pa., 1987-89; intermediate spl. edn. tchr. Coatesville Sch. Dist., 1989-91, 5th grade tchr., 1991-92, 1st grade tchr., 1992—; coach Spl. Olympics, Coatesville Sch. Dist., 1989-91, mem. instrn. support team, 1994—; summer sch. tchr. Youth Writing Project, 1995, 96. Tchr. Penningtonville Presbyn. Ch., Atglen, Pa., 1992-93. Grantee Coatesville Sch. Dist., 1990, 92. Republican. Presbyterian. Home: 175 Upper Valley Rd Christiana PA 17509-9771 Office: Rainbow Elem Sch 50 Country Club Rd Coatesville PA 19320-1813

FITZGERALD-HUBER, LOUISE G., education educator; b. Balt., July 17, 1940; d. Charles Galt and Ida (Noon) Fitzgerald; m Horst Wolfram Huber, July 11, 1969. BA, Goucher Coll., 1962; MA, Harvard U., 1965, PhD, 1974. Asst. prof. Harvard U., Cambridge, Mass., 1975-80; lectr. Harvart Ext., Cambridge, Mass., 1987-91, Wellesley (Mass.) Coll., 1995—; vis. prof. U. Heidelberg, Germany, 1981-82, 87; assoc. rsch. Fairbank Ctr./Harvard U., Cambridge, 1984—. Contbr. articles to profl. jours. Woodrow Wilson fellow, 1962-63. Mem. Phi Beta Kappa. Home: 20 Prescott St Cambridge MA 02138 Office: Fairbank Ctr Harvard Univ 1737 Cambridge St Cambridge MA 02138

FITZGERALD-VERBONITZ, DIANNE ELIZABETH, nursing educator; b. Tampa, Fla., July 11, 1943; d. James Gerald and Bernice Elizabeth (Creel) F.; children: Deborah Elizabeth Guilbault, Fred Anthony Guilbault Jr. AA, Montgomery Coll., 1979; BS in Health Svcs., No. Ariz. U., 1984, MEd, 1987. Clin. specialist M.D. Willard, MD, Phoenix; pvt. practice counselor Hatcher Family Physicians Inc., Phoenix; mem. faculty C.V. Mosby Co., Hanover, Md.; clin. specialist in orthopedics Ctr. for Orthopaedic Disorders; mgr. orthopedic program Kimberly Quality Care; adminstr. Cypress Health Care Svcs., Phoenix, 1996—. Bd. dirs. Valley of Sun Sch. and Rehab. Ctr., Arthritis Found. Mem. ANA, Nat. Assn. Orthopedic Nurses (pres. 1989-90), Ariz. Nurses Assn., Assn. Rehab. Nurses, Phi Kappa Phi. Office: Cypress Health Care Svcs Cyprus Home Health Svcs 5225 N Central Ave Phoenix AZ 85012

FITZPATRICK, ELLEN, economist, consultant; b. Newark, June 22, 1957; d. Robert and Joan M. (Tampany) F. BA, Rutgers U., 1979; MS, Poly. U., White Plains, N.Y. Asst. staff mgr. N.Y. Telephone, N.Y.C., 1980-82, staff specialist, 1982-84, staff mgr., 1984-86, assoc. dir., 1986-87; sr. cons. KPMG Peat Marwick, Short Hills, N.J., 1987-89, mgr., 1989-91, sr. mgr., 1991-93; sr. mgr. Arthur Andersen & Co., Chgo., 1993—; dir. Fin. Mgmt. CP&M Ameritech Network Svcs. Mem. Am. Econ. Assn., Nat. Assn. Bus. Economists, N.Y. Assn. Bus. Economists. Home: 415 W Aldine Ave # 15-a Chicago IL 60657-3653 Office: Ameritech Rm 2F06 2000 W Ameritech Ctr Dr Hoffman Estates IL 60196

FITZPATRICK, GAYLE DANIEL, human resources professional; b. Sylvester, Ga., Feb. 5, 1941; d. Howard Alton and Gladys (Little) Daniel; m. Henry Harris Fitzpatrick, July 27, 1963; 1 child, Beth. BSBA, North Ga. Coll., 1964; MBA, George Washington U., 1974. Chief clk. spl. com nat. emergencies del. emergency power U.S. Senate, Washington, 1975-76, staff asst. temporary com. to study Senate com. system, 1976-77; office and personnel mgr. Resources for the Future, Washington, 1977-78; personnel mgr. Brookings Instn., Washington, 1978-81; employee devel. specialist U.S. Army Europe, Kaiserslautern, Germany, 1981-84; dir. for personnel and adminstrn. Clean Sites, Inc., Alexandria, Va., 1984-87; chief non-appropriated funds div. civilian personnel office U.S. Army South, Republic of Panama, 1987-89; mgr. dist. office U.S. Census Bur., Alexandria, 1989-90; sr. v.p. human resources Prison Fellowship, Reston, Va., 1991—. Mem. ASTD, Soc. Human Resources Mgmt. Methodist.

FITZPATRICK, LOIS ANN, library administrator; b. Yonkers, N.Y., Mar. 27, 1952; d. Thomas Joseph and Dorothy Ann (Nealy) Sullivan; m. William George Fitzpatrick, Jr., Dec. 1, 1973; children: Jennifer Ann, Amy Ann. BS in Sociology, Mercy Coll., 1974; MLS, Pratt Inst., 1975. Clk. Yonkers (N.Y.) Pub. Library, 1970-73, librarian trainee, 1973-75, librarian I, 1975-76; reference librarian Carroll Coll. Library, Helena, Mont., 1976-79, acting dir., 1979, asst. prof., 1979-89, dir., 1980—, assoc. prof., 1989—; chmn. arrangements Mont. Gov.'s Pre White House Conf. on Libraries, Helena, 1977-78; mem. steering com. Reference Point coop. program for librs., 1991; mem. adv. com. Helena Coll. of Tech. Libr., 1994—. Pres. elect Helena Area Health Sci. Libraries Cons., 1979-84, pres., 1984-88; bd. dirs. Mont. FAXNET; co-chmn. interest group OCLC; chmn. local arrangements Mont. Gov.'s Pre White House Conf.; mem. adv. bd. Helena Coll. of Tech. Mem. Mont. Library Assn. task force for White House conf. 1991). Democrat. Roman Catholic. Club: Soroptimist Internat. of Helena (2d v.p. 1984-85, pres. 1986-87). Home: 1308 Shirley Rd Helena MT 59601-6635 Office: Carroll Coll Jack and Sallie Corette Libr Helena MT 59625-0099

FITZPATRICK, NANCY S., advertising executive; b. 1930. V.p., sec., ptnr. J. Walter Thompson Co., N.Y.C. Office: J Walter Thompson Co 466 Lexington Ave New York NY 10017-3140*

FITZPATRICK, PHYLLIS ANN, university administrator; b. Dayton, Ohio, Dec. 24, 1949; d. William A. and Patricia Ann Rogge; m. James D. Fitzpatrick; children: James, Katelyn. BS, U. Dayton, 1971, MS, 1976. Tchr. lang. arts Corpus Christi Sch., Dayton, 1971-73; tchr. English Melbourne (Fla.) H.S., 1973-74, Wayne H.S., Wayne Township, Ohio, 1974-75; co-dir. Marycrest Hall U. Dayton, 1975-76; dir. residence life Fairfield (Conn.) U., 1976-84, dir. mgmt. info., 1984—. Treas. PTA Coun., Fairfield, 1995—; treas. Riverfield PTA, Fairfield, 1992-94, sec., 1991-92. Mem. N.E. Assn. for Instnl. Rsch. (sec. 1994-96), Conn. Assn. for Instnl. Rsch. (steering com., pres. 1993-94, sec. 1991-92). Office: Fairfield U N Benson Rd Fairfield CT 06430-5195

FITZSIMMONS, SHARON, tobacco and food products company executive. Treas. Philip Morris Internat., Port Chester, N.Y. Office: Philip Morris Internat 800 Westchester Ave Port Chester NY 10573-1322

FITZSIMMONS, SOPHIE SONIA, interior designer; d. Oleg and Sophie (Ovsianico-Koulikovsky) Yadoff; m. J. Heath Fitzsimmons; children: Gregory James, Raymond Heath, Douglas Paul. AAS with honors, Fashion Inst. Tech., N.Y.C., 1964; student, NYU Wagner Sch., 1994. Design intern Euster Assocs., Inc., Armonk, N.Y., 1964; prin. Sophie Y. Fitzsimmons Interior Design, N.Y.C., Conn, 1964-77; co-owner Avon (Conn.), Interiors, Inc., 1977-89; prin. Sophie Fitzsimmons Interior Design, N.Y.C., 1989—; pres. Fitz Family Enterprises, 1996, Designers Discoverys, 1996; guest exhibitor Fashion Inst. Tech. Symposium, 184. Author: A Salute, 1996. Chair ann. show Hope Benefit, Hartford, Conn., 1975; mem. Rep. Women's Club Conn., 1978-89; bd. dirs. Friends of Hartford Ballet, 1986-88; vol. N.Y. Commn. UN, Consular Corps and Internat. Bus., 1992—; vol. tchr. East Internat. Community Ctr., 1993—; pres., bd. dirs. Squadron Line PTAA 1976; bd. dirs. Simsbury chpt. Federated Women's Club, 1976. Decorated Medal of Recognition, French Resistance Movement, World War II; recipient Award Edn. Civique Chevalier. Mem. Nat. Soc. Interior Designers (adv. panel 1967), World Affairs Coun., Bamm Hollow Women's Golf Assn. (pres. 1995). Office: Sophie Fitzsimmons Interior 55 Liberty St New York NY 10005

FIVE, CORA LEE, elementary education educator; b. N.Y.C.; d. Helge and Lena Five. BS in Edn., Bucknell U.; MEd, Harvard U.; MA in Writing, Northeastern U., 1988. Cert. tchr. grades K-6. Tchr. Brookline (Mass.) Pub. Schs., Scarsdale (N.Y.) Pub. Schs.; spkr. and presenter in field. Author: Special Voices, 1992, Bridging the Gap, 1996; contbr. chpts. to books and articles to profl. jours. Vol. Achilles Track Club, N.Y.C., 1986—. Recipient Profl. Best Leadership award Learning Mag. 90, Pa., 1990. Mem. Internat. Reading Assn., Nat. Coun. Tchrs. English (com to evaluate curriculum guides 1988-93, nominating com. 1992, tchr. prep. com. 1994—, internat. consortium 1994—, elem. sect. rep. 1994—). Home: 400 E 85th St Apt 5C New York NY 10028-6321 Office: Scarsdale Pub Schs Edgewood Sch Roosevelt Pl Scarsdale NY 10583

FIX, CAROLYN ELIZABETH, geologist, sanitarian; b. Utica, N.Y., Nov. 28, 1922; d. William Anthony and Evelina Marie (Gray) F. BA in Biology cum laude, Utica Coll. of Syracuse U., 1951, MS in Geology, 1953. Registered radiology technician, N.Y.; registered pub. health sanitarian, Va. Geologist U.S. Geol. Survey, Denver, 1953-58, Washington, 1958-60; writer, editor U.S. Army and Navy, Washington, 1960-63; reporter, editor Free Press Newspapers, Falls Church, Va., 1964; pub. health sanatarian Fairfax (Va.) County Health Dept., 1971-77; indexer, editor (database) Am. Geol. Inst., Alexandria, Va., 1980—. Author: (U.S. Geol. Survey Book) Annotated Bibliography of Uranium in Marine Black Shales in the U.S., 1958; artist wood carving, painting,. Vol. demonstrator Fairfax Park Authority, 1980—; hist. demonstrator U.S. Nat. Park Svc., Jamestown (N.Y.) Festival, 1990 (awd. 1990), Mt. Vernon, Va., 1993; bd. dirs. Vienna (Va.) Comty. Band, 1993—; mem. at large Mayor's Adv. Com., Vienna, 1993—. Staff sgt, WAC, 1943-51. Recipient Fulbright scholarship U.S. Govt. Fulbright Program, U. Queensland, Australia, 1954; recipient many awards for photography. Mem. AAUW, Fairfax Am. Antique Arts Assn., (membership com. chmn. 1994—), Organ Hist. Soc. (sec.-treas. Hilbus chpt. 1971-77), Am. Guild of Organists, Nat. Geneal. Soc.

FIX, TOBIE LYNN, special education educator; b. L.A., Aug. 25, 1961; d. Howard Jacob and Pearl (Bram) Berger; m. Thomas Fix, Aug. 25, 1985. AA, Nat. U., L.A., 1992, student, 1992—. Substitute tchr. asst. of trainable mentally handicapped Los Angeles County, Calif., 1980-85, tchr. asst. trainable mentally handicapped, 1985—; substitute preschool tchr. Los Angeles County, Los Angeles County, Calif., 1996—; coaching asst. Spl. Olympic State Games, Los Angeles County. Recipient Vol. awards in spl. edn. Mem. Mus. of Tolerance, Huntington Libr./Gardens, L.A. Zool. Found. Democrat. Jewish. Home: 1628 Carlson Ln Redondo Beach CA 90278-4711

FIX-ROMLOW, JEANNE KAY, hair care products company executive; b. Madison, Wis., June 29, 1947; d. Glen H. and Violet M. (Bohnsack) Fix; m. Paul James Romlow, Nov. 7, 1985. Student, Madison Area Tech. Sch., 1966. Mgr. Fashion Fabrics, Madison, 1973-74; promotion dir. Livesey Enterprises, Madison, 1976-77; sales assoc. First Realty Group, Madison, 1977-79; territory mgr. Aerial Beauty and Barber Supply, Madison, 1979-83; regional dir. John Paul Mitchell Systems, Santa Clarita, Calif., 1983-85, v.p., 1986-87, sr. v.p., 1987-91, exec. v.p., 1991—. Home: 11344W Bay Dr Lodi WI 53555 Office: John Paul Mitchell Systems 26455 Golden Valley Rd Santa Clarita CA 91350-2621

FIZER, MARILYN DAHLE, elementary education educator; b. San Antonio, Tex., Dec. 12, 1947; d. Richard Ivy and Marjory Blanche (Rookstool) Gold; m. Lawrence Franklin Fizer, Aug. 31, 1968; 1 child, Lawrence Scott. BS, Southwest Tex. State U., San Marcos, 1969. Tchr. Tex., 1969. Tchr. Northeast Ind. Sch. Dist., San Antonio, 1969-74, Katy (Tex.) Ind. Sch. Dist., 1979—. Mem. NEA, Nat. Coun. Tchrs. Math., Tex. State Reading Assn., Tex. State Tchrs. Assn., Greater Houston Area Reading Coun., Katy Edn. Assn., Bear Creek Elem. PTA, Internat. Reading Assn. Home: 15810 Echo Canyon Dr Houston TX 77084 Office: Bear Creek Elem Sch 4815 Hickory Downs Houston TX 77084

FJORTOFT, NANCY FAY, univeristy administrator, educator; b. Osseo, Wis., Sept. 20, 1953; d. Willard c. and Rachel M. (Hubbard) Schmidt; m. Jon M. Fjortoft, May 10, 1986. BA, Blackburn Coll., 1975; MA, DePaul U., 1980; PhD, U. Ill., Chgo., 1994. Circulation mgr. DePaul U., Chgo., 1977-84; registrar, bus. mgr. Chgo. Sch. of Profl. Psychology, 1984-88; asst. to dean U. Ill., Chgo., 1988-93, asst. dean, 1993—. Lay leader First United Meth. Ch., Oak Park, Ill., 1993—. Recipient Lyman award Am. Assn. of Colls. of Pharmacy, 1994. Office: Univ Ill Chgo 833 S Wood St # MC 874 Chicago IL 60612-7229

FLACK, MIGNON SCOTT-PALMER, elementary educator; b. Silver Spring, Md., July 9; d. Lawrence Henry and Dorothy Elizabeth (Still) Scott; m. Harley Eugene Flack; children: Oliver S. Palmer II, Michael Scott Palmer; stepchildren: Harley E. II, Christopher F. BS, D.C. Tchrs. Coll., 1966; MS, Johns Hopkins U., 1977. Cert. tchr., Md. Elem. tchr. D.C. Pub. Schs., Washington, 1968-71; dir. Home Day Care Ctr., Columbia, Md., 1973-77; from elem. tchr. to resource tchr. gifted and talented Howard County Pub. Schs., Columbia, Md., 1977-90; elem. tchr. Cherry Hill (N.J.) Pub. Schs., 1990-94; lang. arts rep. Howard County Pub. Schs., Columbia, 1977-86, student tchr. coord., 1984-90, tchr. recruiter, 1986-90; cons., tutor Village Reading Ctr., Columbia, 1986-90. Bd. trustees Children's Mus. Dayton, Ohio, 1995—, Opera Guild Dayton, 1995—, Muse Machine, Dayton, 1995—, Dayton Mus. Natural History, 1996; planning com. Centennial Flight-Yr. 2003, 1995—; first lady of Wright State U., Dayton. Recipient Cmty. Svc. award United Way Ctrl. Md., 1982; named Outstanding Supt., Breath of Life Ch., 1981. Mem. AAUW, Nat. Assn. State U. and Land Grant Colls., Am. Assn. State Colls. and U., Wright State Orgn. for Women, Phi Delta Kappa, Alpha Lambda Delta. Home: Rockafield House 1 Circle Dr Dayton OH 45435

FLAGG, JEANNE BODIN, editor; b. N.Y.C., July 13, 1925; d. G. William and Joan (Lippoth) Bergquist; m. Allen Elias Flagg, Apr. 15, 1955 (div. 1967); children—Jennifer Andrea, Christopher Trevor. B.A., Barnard Coll., 1947; M.A., Columbia U., 1950. Tech. editor Reinhold Pub. Corp., N.Y.C., 1951-57; editor Barnes & Noble, Inc., N.Y.C., 1967-71, Harper & Row Pubs., N.Y.C., 1971-88; sponsoring editor McGraw-Hill Pub. Co., N.Y.C., 1989-95. Home: 1015 Old Post Rd Mamaroneck NY 10543-3901

FLAHERTY, SISTER MARY JEAN, dean, nursing educator. Dean, assoc. prof. Sch. Nursing, Cath. U. Am., Washington. Office: Cath U Am Sch of Nursing 620 Michigan Ave NE Washington DC 20064-0001*

FLAHERTY, PATRICIA, investment company executive; b. Boston, Dec. 1, 1946; d. Matthew Joseph and Elizabeth P. (Donovan) F. BS in Mgmt., U. Mass., Boston, 1981; MBA, Northeastern U., Boston, 1991. Mgr. of facilities Houghton Mifflin Co., Boston, 1981-84; sr. v.p., dir. gen. svcs. Putnam Investments, Boston, 1984-93; sr. v.p. The Putnam Funds, Boston, 1993—; mem. alumni adv. bd. Coll. Mgmt. U. Mass., Boston, 1993—. Office: The Putnam Funds 1 Post Office Sq Boston MA 02109-2103

FLAHERTY, SERGINA MARIA, ophthalmic medical technologist; b. Düsseldorf, Germany, Nov. 22, 1958; came to U.S., 1962; d. Austin W. and Evelyn (Kähl) F. Cert. ophthalmic med. technologist. Ophthalmic asst. U.S. Army, Ft. Rucker, Ala., 1978-82; ophthalmic technician Wiregrass Total Eye Care Clinic, Enterprise, Ala., 1983-86, Straub Hosp. and Clinic, Honolulu, 1986-90; ophthalmic technologist Eye Cons. of San Antonio, San Antonio, 1993-96, Stone Oak Ophthalmology, San Antonio, 1996—. Mem. Assn. Tech. Pers. in Ophthalmology, Ophthalmic Photographer Soc., Hawaii Ophthalmic Assts. Soc. (founding mem., sec. 1987-89, pres. 1989-90), Ophthalmic Pers. Soc. San Antonio (program dir. 1994-95, pres. 1996—). Home: 5650 Grissom Rd Apt 807 San Antonio TX 78238-2251 Office: Stone Oak Ophthalmology Ste 450 540 Stone Oak Med Bldg San Antonio TX 78258

FLAHERTY, TINA SANTI, corporate communications executive; b. Memphis; d. Clement Alexander and Dale (Pendergrast) Santi; m. William Edward Flaherty, Feb. 22, 1975. B.A., Memphis State U., 1961; hon. doctorate, St. John's U., 1979. Commentator host interview program Sta. WMC-TV, Memphis, 1960-61; newscaster, commentator Sta. WHER, Memphis, 1961-62; community rels. specialist Western Electric Co., N.Y.C., 1964-66; v.p. pub. rels. div. Grey Advt., N.Y.C., 1966-72; dep. dir. corp. rels. Colgate-Palmolive Co., N.Y.C., 1972-75; dir. corp. rels. Colgate-Palmolive Co., 1975-76, corp. v.p., v.p. in charge of communications, 1976-84; v.p. pub. affairs GTE Corp., Stamford, Conn., 1984-86; pres., chief exec. officer Image Mktg. Internat., N.Y.C., 1986—. Former chmn. Bus. Coun. of UN Decade for Women; bd. dirs. Nat. Jr. Achievement, 1978—, Hugh O'Brian Youth Found.; mem. adv. bd. Santa Fe Chamber Music Festival; mem. The White House Pub. Affairs Advisors; nat. bd. dirs. Animal Med. Ctr. Recipient Jr. Achievement Meml. award, 1984; Named One of N.Y.C.'s Outstanding Women of Achievement NCCJ, 1978; One of 100 Top Corp. Women Bus. Week, 1976, One of 73 Women Ready to Run Corp. Am., Working Woman, 1985; named Woman of Distinction Birmingham So. Coll., 1991. Mem. Com. of 200, Internat. Women's Forum. Home and Office: Image Mktg Internat 1040 Fifth Ave New York NY 10028-0137

FLAKE, LEONE ELIZABETH, special education educator; b. New Orleans, Jan. 12, 1938; d. Alfred Charles and Ione (Mills) Ittmann; m. Allen Oliver Flake, July 25, 1959; children: Diana Lee, Alan Mark, Wendy Lynn. BA, St. Mary's Dominican, New Orleans, 1973; MEd, U. New Orleans, 1979, postgrad., 1980. Cert. elem. tchr., learning disabled, social maladjusted, emotionally disturbed, kindergarten, mild moderate, severe profound, computer literacy, La. Tchr. grade 2 Jefferson Parish Sch. Board, Metairie, La., 1973-74, tchr. grade 3, 1974-75, tchr. grade 1, 1975-79, spl. edn. tchr. emotionally disturbed, 1979-87, generic tchr., spl. edn., 1987—, spl. edn. tchr., exptl. tchr., 1991—; substitute prin. Marie Riviere Elem., Metairie, 1992—. Spl. edn. chair, Marie Riviere Elem., 1987—, sch. rep., 1987—, sch. dir. very spl. arts., 1987—, spl. needs tchr., 1991—, elem. discipline com., 1987—, sch. bld. level com. for project read, 1992—, elem. safety com., 1987—, sch. effectiveness action plan com., 1987—, sch. bldg. level com., 1987—, spl. program to upgrade reading task force, 1984-85; counselor, At Risk Students for Project Charlie, 1991—. Recipient cert. of Merit Jefferson Parish Coun. Of Charitable Involvement, 1985, Jefferson Parish key to the City, 1985, Appreciation cert. Coun. for Exceptional Children, 1991, Outstanding Tchr. award Am. Petroleum Inst., 1992-93. Mem. The Orton Dyslecic Soc., Internat. Reading Assn., La. Reading Assn., Coun. for Exceptional Children, Children Adults with Attention Deficit Disorders, J.C. Ellis Coop. Club (v.p. 1984-84), Phi Delta Kappa, Kappa Delta Pi, Beta Sigma Phi (internat. mem, preceptor 1973—),. Home: 3701 Wanda Lynn Dr Metairie LA 70002-4523

FLAKES, SUSAN, playwright, director; b. San Diego, July 9, 1943; d. Herbert Franklyn and Dorothy Jean (Loafman) Barrows; m. Donald Lewis Flakes, Dec. 31, 1964; 1 child, Daniel Keith. BA, U. N.Mex., 1965; MA, San Diego State U., 1969; PhD, U. Minn., 1973. Asst., then assoc. prof. Tisch Sch. Arts NYU, 1973-76, dept. chair Tisch Sch. Arts, 1973-76; founder, artistic dir. Blue Tower Theatre, Stockholm, 1977-80, Strindberg's Intima Teater, Stockholm, 1981-83, Source Prodns., N.Y.C., 1984-90; instr. U.S. Internat. Univ., San Diego, 1972-73; founder, artistic dir. 1st Strindberg Festival, Stockholm, 1977; mem. Women's Project and Prodns., N.Y.C., 1984-90; v.p. Ibsen Soc. Am., N.Y.C., 1986—; coord. writers unit W. Coast Ensemble Theatre, Hollywood, Calif., 1991-93. Author plays, 1977, 92, The Woman Will Play Strindberg's Christina, Silent Star, And Immortality, Portrait of the Pysche, My Daddy's Eyes, To Take Arms; (libretto) Take It Higher; (screenplay) Angel in the Attic, Hometown, Inc.; dir. Mother Love, 1994; contbr. articles to profl. jours.; creator Exptl. Theatre Wing U.G. Drama Tisch Sch. Arts, NYU, 1975-76. Ensign USN, 1965-67. Fellow Am. Film Inst., 1990; grantee Nat. Endowment for Arts, 1972; travel grantee Am. Scandinavian Found., Norwegian and Swedish Govts., 1985, 86, 89, 94. Mem. Dramatists Guild, Phi Beta Kappa. Home and Office: 13513 Murphy Hill Dr Whittier CA 90601

FLAMIK, JUDY ANN, art educator; b. Cleve.; d. Carl and Jeanne (Furjanic) Onysyk; m. George John Flamik, June 21, 1968; children: George Gary, Glenn Carl. BA, Lake Erie Coll., Painesville, Ohio; postgrad., Baldwin Wallace Coll., Berea, Ohio, Fla. State U., Ashland (Ohio) Coll. Draftsperson Ohio Bell Telephone Co., Cleve., 1968-69; art dir. Shop 220 on the Square, Cleve., 1970-74, A.T.C., Lakewood, Ohio, 1974—; tchr. vocat. comml. art Willoughby-Eastlake (Ohio) Schs., 1980—; artist Am. Greetings, Cleve., 1976-77, Pitt Studios, Cleve., 1975-77, Nutron Nameplate, North Olmsted, Ohio, 1977-78; art dir. Lakewood H.S., 1979-80; tchr. swimming Kodak Cameras in the Curriculum, 1982. Artist book cover: Electronic Color Separation, 1989; illustrator Christmas cards for Rocky River Jr. Women's Club, 1984, 85, 89; designer 1995 Easter Seal; illustrator E.P.I.C. series for Econs. Am., 1994—. Adv. bd. Cleve. Ballet, 1989—, Lakewood H.S. Comm. Art, 1984—, East Ohio Gas Co., Cleve., 1984-95, Coun. Cleve. Children's Mus., 1990, Graphic Arts Coun. in Charge Student Seminars, 1994—; artist Rocky River Cmty. Theater, 1991-94; mem. Cleve. Mus. Art, 1990—, Rock & Roll Hall of Fame Mus., 1996—. Recipient Samuel H. Elliott award Harvard Bus. Sch. Club, 1993, Excellence in Econ. Edn. 1st place SOHIO/BP Am., 1984, 90; Jennings scholar, 1993-94. Mem. NEA, Nat. Art Edn. Assn., Ohio Art Edn. Assn., Am. Vocat. Assn., Ohio Edn. Assn., Vocat. Indsl. Clubs Am., Graphic Arts Coun. (class v.p Parma Sr. High), Parma Alumni Assn. (mem. in charge class reunions).

FLAMMING, MARTHA LOUISE, educator; b. Custer, S.D., Jan. 30, 1942; d. Clair Eugene and Verna Louise (Parsons) Goins; m. Jon Douglas Flamming, Apr. 9, 1966 (dec. Jun. 1994); children: Steven, James, Janet. BS in Edn., S.D. State U., 1964. Ext. agent Bon Homme Co., Tyndall, S.D., 1964—. Lay leader, 1989-93; youth leader United Meth. Ch., Tyndall, S.D., 1988—. Mem. Nat. Ext. Home Econs. Assn., S.D. Ext. Home Econs. Assn. (v.p. 1970, treas. 1990-92, disting. svc. 1982). Methodist. Home: PO Box 48 Tyndall SD 57066 Office: Bon Homme Co Ext Office 104 Pearl St Tyndall SD 57066

FLANAGAN, ANITA MARIE, public relations professional, environmentalist; b. South Charleston, W.Va., Sept. 25, 1940; d. Henry August and Mary Margaret (Hodge) Thormahlen; m. Shaun Michael Flanagan; children: Michael Lawrence, Sheilah Mary Catherine. AB, Northeastern U., 1963; BS, Southeastern Mass. U., 1977; MS in Environ. Health Mgmt., Harvard U., 1983. Planning cons. Town of Duxbury (Mass.), 1983; hazardous waste coord., mem. oil spill response team Town of Duxbury, 1980-85; mgr. Pub. Participation Program Mass. Dept. Environ. Mgmt., Boston, 1984-86; community relations dir. Clean Harbors Inc., Braintree, Mass., 1986-88, Flanagan-Thompson Assocs., Plymouth, 1988-89; sr. pub. info. rep. Boston Edison Co., Plymouth, Mass., 1989-95; asst. to pres. Bridgewater (Mass.) State Coll., 1995—; presenter pub. info. mgrs.' conf. European Nuclear Soc., Annecy, France, 1992. Mem. Internat. Teleconferencing Assn. (v.p. Boston-Hartford chpt. 1996-97).

FLANAGAN, ANNE PATRICIA, art educator, artist; b. Methuen, Mass., Jan. 26, 1927; d. John Joseph and Kathryn Josephine (Conley) Kane; m. Robert William Flanagan, Dec. 27, 1951; children: Robert W. Jr., Kathryn A., Joan Marie. B in Music Edn., Boston U., 1948; BFA, U. N.H., 1982. Cert. tchr. Mass. Supr. music Town of Middetown, R.I., 1948-50; asst. supr. music Towns of Littleton, Harvard and Stow, Mass., 1951-52; adj. therapist music Bayberry Psychiat. Hosp., Hampton, Va., 1973-74; relief mgr. Fidelity House, Lawrence, Mass., 1979-82; asst. mgr. Fidelity House, Lawrence, 1982; instr. oil painting Adult Edn. Program, Derry, N.H., 1984-86; art tchr., dept. chair St. Joseph's Regional Sch., Salem, N.H., 1989—; charter mem. Alley Art Gallery, Portsmouth, N.H., 1982-84; mem. Art Group Gallery, Manchester, N.H., 1988-91. Exhibited works in numerous one-woman and group shows including Art Group Gallery, 1989, 88, Newburyport (Mass.) Art Assn., 1987 (1st prize), St. Matthew's Art Show, Windham, N.H., 1985 (1st prize), Alley Gallery, 1983-84, U. N.H., 1982. Vol. art tchr. St. Joseph's Regional Sch., Salem, 1989-91; vol. Korean Orphange, Seoul, 1966-67; vol. tchr. artistically gifted children after sch. program St. Joseph Regional Sch., 1991-94; tchr. art sr. citizens group Royal Crest, Andover, Mass., 1983-84; tchr. developmentally retarded adults Fidelity House, 1979-82. Recipient cert. of achievement Republic of Korea, Seoul, 1967, cert. of appreciation U.S. Army, 1976. Roman Catholic. Home: 138 Shadow Lake Rd Salem NH 03079-1438 Office: St Josephs Regional Sch 40 Main St Salem NH 03079-1923

FLANAGAN, BARBARA, journalist; b. Des Moines; d. John Merrill and Marie (Barnes) F.; m. Earl S. Sanford, 1966. Student, Drake U., 1942-43. With promotion dept. Mpls. Times, 1945-47; reporter Mpls. Tribune, 1947-58; women's editor, spl. writer Mpls. Star and Tribune, 1958-65; columnist Mpls. Star, 1965—. Author: Ovation, Minneapolis. Active Junior League Mpls., Womans Club Mpls.; bd. dirs. Minn. Opera., Friends of Mpls. Pub. Libr. Mem. Mpls. Soc. Fine Arts (life), Mpls. Inst. Arts (founding mem. Minn. Arts Forum), Kappa Alpha Theta, Sigma Delta Chi. Episcopalian. Home: 3200 W Calhoun Pky Apt 301 Minneapolis MN 55416-4650 Office: Mpls Star Tribune 5th and Portland Sts Minneapolis MN 55488

FLANAGAN, DEBORAH MARY, lawyer; b. Hackensack, N.J., Sept. 17, 1956; d. Joseph Francis and Mary Agnes (Fitzsimmons) F.; m. Glen H. Koch, Aug. 27, 1983. BA summa cum laude, Fordham U., 1978, JD, 1981; LLM in Taxation, NYU, 1987. Bar: N.Y. 1982 and U.S. Dist. Ct. 1988. V.p., assoc. tax counsel McGraw-Hill Inc., N.Y.C., 1981—. Mem. Assn. Bar City N.Y., Fordham U. Law Alumni Assn., NYU Law Alumni Assn. Home: 201 Chestnut Ridge Rd Saddle River NJ 07458-2818 Office: McGraw-Hill Inc 1221 Ave Of The Americas New York NY 10020-1001

FLANAGAN, JUDITH ANN, marketing and entertainment specialist; b. Lubbock, Tex., Apr. 28, 1950; d. James Joseph II and Jean (Breckenridge) F. BS in Edn., Memphis State U., 1972; postgrad., Valencia C.C., Rollins Coll., Rollins Coll.; postgrad. in theme park mgmt., Disney Univ. Area/parade supr. Entertainment div. Walt Disney World, Orlando, Fla., 1972-81; parade dir. Gatlinburg (Tenn.) C. of C., 1981-85; entertainment prodn. mgr. The 1982 World's Fair, Knoxville, 1982; cons. Judy Flanagan Prodns./Spl. Events, Gatlinburg, 1982—, Miss U.S.A. Pageant, Knoxville, 1983; prodn. coord. Nashville Network, 1983; dir. sales River Terr. Resort, Gatlinburg, 1985-86; account exec. Park Vista Hotel, Gatlinburg, 1986-88; project coord. Universal Studios, Fla., 1988-90; dir. spl. events in univ. rels. U. Tenn., Knoxville, 1990—; prodn. mgr. 1984 World's Fair Parades and Spl. Events, New Orleans, Neil Sedaka rock video, Days of Our Lives daytime soap opera. Named One of Outstanding Young Women Am., 1981; recipient Gatlinburg Homecoming award, 1986, World Lifetime Achievement award, 1993. Mem. ASPCA, Human Soc. U.S., Internat. Spl. Events Soc., Defenders of Wildlife, U. Tenn. Pres. Club, Doris Day Animal League. Roman Catholic. Home: 350 Bruce Rd Gatlinburg TN 37738-5612

FLANAGAN, MARY HALEY, nursing administrator, mental health nurse; b. Nevada, Mo., Feb. 13, 1937; d. William Martin and Ethel (Lacy) Haley; (div.); children: Timothy, Thomas, Kathleen, Karen. BSN, U. Kans., Kansas City, 1980, MSN, 1984. RN, La. CEO Three Rivers Hosp., Covington, La., 1993-95; dir. clin. syss. CPC Meadow Wood Hosp., Baton Rouge, 1995—; mem. adj. faculty U. Kans. Sch. Nursing; cons. Health Care Financing Adminstrn.; mem. bd. advisors Mo. So. State Coll. Grantee NIMH. Mem. ANA (cert. clin. specialist child-adolescent psychiat. nurse), La. Nurses Assn., Sigma Theta Tau.

FLANAGAN, NATALIE SMITH, state representative; b. Bradford, Mass., Aug. 6, 1913; d. Forrest Van Zandt and Blanche (Robbins) Smith; m. John Frances Flanagan, Sept. 20, 1944 (dec.). Grad. high sch., Vassalboro, Maine. Mem. N.H. Ho. of Reps., Concord, 1973—, chmn. constl. and statutory com., 1987—. Pres. Mass. chpt. Young Reps., 1930—; pres. bd. dirs. Haverhill (Mass.) Girls Club, 1940—; founder Rockingham (N.H.) Nutrition Program, 1979; mem. N.H. Bicentennial Commn., 1983—. Recipient Meritorious Pub. Svc. medal Sec. State, 1990. Congregationalist. Home: 132 Maple Ave Atkinson NH 03811-2245 Office: NH State Legis Legis Office Bldg Rm 302 Concord NH 03301

FLANAGAN, THERESE ANN, real estate, roofing and construction executive; b. Chgo., Sept. 23, 1955; d. William Joseph and Margaret Eileen (McNellis) F. BA, U. Fla., 1984, MA, 1987. With First Fed. of Lake Worth, Fla., 1973-74, Fla. Nat. Bank, Palm Beach, Fla., 1974-75, 77-79; salesman Irish Realty, Inc., Lake Worth, 1979-81; asst. mgr. Sun Bay Apts., Gainesville, Fla., 1982; with Library Systems, U. Fla., Gainesville, 1982-86; pres. Flanagan & Assocs. Realty, Lake Worth, 1986—, The Flanagan Cos., Lake Worth, 1992—. Producer, dir.: (video) Zora Neale Hurston, 1986. Vol. Textbook Reading for the Blind, Gainesville, 1987, The Children's Pl., West Palm Beach, Fla., 1988-89, Project Literacy, West Palm Beach, 1988-89, Reading Tutor, 1991—. Mem. BBB, Am. Cmty. Assn. Mgrs., Real Estate Brokerage Mgrs. Coun., West Palm Beach C. of C., Russian Club (treas. 1983-84), Phi Kappa Phi. Democrat. Roman Catholic. Office: The Flanagan Cos 3939 S Congress Ave Lake Worth FL 33461-4107

FLANARY, KATHY VENITA MOORE, librarian; b. Amherst, Tex., Jan. 15, 1946; d. Charles Edward and Jean (Willman) Moore; children: Suzanne Flanary, Charles Flanary. BA, U. Ill., 1972, MLS, 1974. Cert. profl. libr., N.Mex.; cert. tchr., N.Mex. Dir. children's libr. Hayner Pub. Libr., Alton, Ill., 1974-76; dir. Ruidoso (N.Mex.) Pub. Libr., 1978-80; libr. media specialist Horgan Libr., N.Mex. Mil. Inst., Roswell, 1985-93; libr. N.Mex. Sch. Visually Handicapped, Alamogordo, 1993—; workshop presenter Lewis & Clark Regional Libr. Systems, Ill., 1975; outreach programer Hayner Pub. Libr., 1974-76; del. Pre-White Ho. Conf., State of N.Mex., 1991. Contbr. articles to newspapers and profl. jours. Bd. dirs. Alton Symphony, 1975; mem. Altrusa, Ruidoso, 1979-84, Friend of Roswell Pub. Libr.; sec. Ruidoso Summer Festival, 1979; bd. dirs. Supts. Adv. Bd., Roswell, N.Mex., 1987-89; pres. Friends of Libr., Ruidoso, 1980-83, Parent Advocacy for Gifted Edn., 1990-92; v.p. Sunset PTA; bd. dirs. N.Mex. Libr. Found., 1992—. Recipient Svc. award Altrusa, 1979, Sunset PTA, 1989. Mem. N.Mex. Libr. Assn. (libr. devel. com., ednl. tech. roundtable vice chair 1991, chair elect 1992, co-chair state conv. local arrangements 1990-91, 2d v.p. 1993-94, 1st v.p. 1994-95, pres. 1995-96), N.Mex. Acad. and Rsch. Librs. (vice chair 1992, pres. 1993), Kiwanis (bd. dirs. 1990-92).

FLANIGAN, ANNETTE LIPSCOMB, secondary education educator; b. Gainesville, Ga., Apr. 22, 1945; d. Demory Sr. and Willie Mae (Jackson) Lipscomb; m. Everett Flanigan, Aug. 31, 1968; children: Kyle Yusef, Ryan Llyn, Asa Karl, Erika. BS, Howard U., 1968; MA in Edn., Olivet Nazarene U., 1987. Cert. chemistry, physics and gen. sci. tchr. grades 6-12, middle sch. phys. sci. and social sci. tchr., Ill. Rsch. scientist Washington U., St. Louis, 1968-69, Jewish Hosp./Children, St. Louis, 1969-70, Brookhaven Nat. Labs., L.I., 1971-72; educator, counselor sci. Title 7 Alternative Sch., Kankakee, Ill., 1974-76; dir. alternative sch. Cmty. Action Program, Kankakee, 1975-77; mgr. sales Mid-Hudson Tupperware, Peekskill, N.Y., 1981-83; educator biology and gen. sci. Kankakee (Ill.) Sch. Dist., 1987-88; educator Riverside Med. Ctr./Partial Hospitalization Program, Kankakee, 1988-90; life sci. educator/tchr. Kankakee (Ill.) Sch. Dist. 111 Jr. H.S., 1990—. Mem. Urban Rural Sch. Devel., Kankakee, 1976-77; leadership trainer Boy Scouts Am., Westchester-Putnam, N.Y., 1980-83; bd. dirs. Kankakee Pub. Libr., 1994—; Kankakee area cmty. adv. panel Henkel/Rohm & Haas, 1995—. Grantee traineeship program Ill. State Bd. Edn., Springfield, Ill., 1985. Mem. ASCD, Am. Assn. for the Advancement Sci., Nat. Sci. Tchrs. Assn., Nat. Middle Sch. Assn., Ill. Sci. Tchrs. Assn., Assn. Ill. Middle-Level Schs., Sigma Pi Sigma. Lutheran. Home: 1290 S Lincoln Ave Kankakee IL 60901 Office: Kankakee Jr HS 2250 East Crestwood Kankakee IL 60901

FLANIGEN, EDITH MARIE, materials scientist, consultant. Sr. rsch. fellow materials sci. UOP Tarrytown (N.Y.) Tech. Ctr., ret.; cons. White Plains, N.Y. Recipient Perkin medal Am. Chem. Soc., 1992, Francis P. Garvan-John M. Olin medal Am. Chem. Soc., 1993. Home: 502 Woodland Hills Rd White Plains NY 10603-3136

FLANNELLY, LAURA T., mental health nurse, nursing educator, researcher; b. Bklyn., Nov. 7, 1952; d. George A. Adams and Eleanor (Barragry) Mulhearn; m. Kevin J. Flannelly, Jan. 10, 1981. BS in Nursing, Hunter Coll., 1974; MSN, U. Hawaii, 1984, PhD, 1996. RN, N.Y., Hawaii. Psychiat. nurse Bellevue Hosp., N.Y.C., 1975, asst. head nurse, 1975-77; psychiat. nurse White Plains (N.Y.) Med. Ctr., 1978-79; community mental health nurse South Beach Psychiat. Ctr., N.Y.C., 1979-81; psychiat. nurse The Queen's Med. Ctr., Honolulu, 1981-83; crisis worker Crisis Response Systems Project, Honolulu, 1983-86; instr. nursing U. Hawaii, Honolulu, 1985-92, asst. prof., 1992—; adj. instr. nursing Hawaii Loa Coll., Honolulu, 1988, Am. Samoa Community Coll., Honolulu, 1987, 89, 90; mem. adv. bd., planning com. Psychiat. Day Hosp. of The Queen's Med. Ctr., Honolulu, 1981-82; program coord. Premenstrual Tension Syndrome Conf., Honolulu, 1984; dir. Ctr. Psychosocial Rsch., Honolulu, 1987—; program moderator 1st U.S-Japan Health Behavioral Conf., Honolulu, 1988; faculty Ctr. for Asia-Pacific Exch., Internat. Conf. on Transcultural Nursing, Honolulu, 1990; mem. bd. dirs. U. Hawaii Profl. Assembly, 1994—. Contbr. articles to profl. jours. N.Y. State Bd. Regents scholar, 1970-74; NIH nursing trainee, 1983-84; grantee U. Hawaii, 1986, 91, Hawaii Dept. Health, 1990. Fellow Internat. Soc. Rsch. on Aggression; mem. AAAS, Am. Edni. Rsch. Assn., Am. Psychol. Soc., Am. Statis. Assn., Nat. League for Nursing, N.Y. Acad. Scis., Pacific and Asian Affairs Coun., Sigma Theta Tau. Home: 445 Kaiolu St Apt 1006 Honolulu HI 96815-2239 Office: U Hawaii Sch Nursing Webster Hall Honolulu HI 96822

FLANNERY, ELLEN JOANNE, lawyer; b. Bklyn., Dec. 13, 1951; d. William Rowan and Mary Jane (Hamilla) Flannery. AB cum laude, Mount Holyoke Coll., 1973; JD cum laude, Boston U., 1978. Bar: Mass. 1978, D.C. 1979, U.S. Ct. Appeals (D.C. cir.) 1979, U.S. Ct. Appeals (4th cir.) 1981, U.S. Ct. Appeals (6th cir.) 1983, U.S. Ct. Appeals (3d cir.) 1987, U.S. Dist. Ct. D.C. 1980, U.S. Dist. Ct. Md. 1985, U.S. Supreme Ct. 1983. Spl. asst. to commr. of health Mass. Dept. Pub. Health, Boston, 1973-75; law clk. U.S. Ct. Appeals D.C. cir., Washington, 1978-79; assoc. Covington & Burling, Washington, 1979-86, ptnr., 1986—; lectr. ins. U. Va. Sch. Law, 1984-90, Boston U. Sch. Law, 1993, U. Md. Sch. Law, 1994; mem. Nat. Conf. Lawyers and Scientists, AAAS-ABA, 1989-92. Contbr. to articles to profl. jours. Mem. ABA (chmn. com. med. practice 1987-88, chmn. life scis div. 1982-84, 88-91, vice chair food and drug law com. 1991—, chmn. sect. sci. and tech. 1992-93, del. of sci. and tech. sect. to ho. of dels. 1993—). Office: Covington & Burling PO Box 7566 1201 Pennsylvania Ave NW Washington DC 20044

FLANNERY, SUSAN MARIE, library administrator; b. Newark, Feb. 18, 1953; d. John Patrick Flannery and Assunta (Lardieri) Ege; m. Stephen A. Coren, Oct. 6, 1984. BA in History of Art, U. Pa., 1974; MLS, Simmons Coll., 1975. Dir. of libr. Newton Country Day, 1975-77, Am. Sch. in Switzerland, Montagnola, 1977-78; young adult libr. Somerville (Mass.) Pub. Libr., 1979-81; reference libr. Cary Meml. Libr., Lexington, Mass., 1981-83; asst. dir. Lucius Beebe Libr., Wakefield, Mass., 1983-87; dir. Reading (Mass.) Pub. Libr., 1987-91; assoc. dir. Cambridge (Mass.) Pub. Libr., 1991-1993, dir., 1993—; steering com. Mass. delegation to White Ho. Conf. on Librs., 1990. Reviewer Sch. Libr. Jour.; contbr. articles to profl. jours. incorporator Cambridge Family YMCA, Cambridge, 1991—; corporator East Cambridge Savs. Bank. Mem. ALA (Mass. councilor 1993—), ACLU Mass. (adv. bd. 1994-96, bd. dirs. 1996—), Mass. Libr. Assn. (pres. 1985-87, v.p. 1983-85), Rotary Club (bd. dirs. Cambridge club 1993—, v.p. 1995-96, pres. elect 1996—, pres. Reading club 1990-91), Cambridge Mental Health Assn. (bd. dirs. 1994—). Office: Cambridge Pub Libr 449 Broadway Cambridge MA 02138-4125

FLECHNER, ROBERTA FAY, graphic designer; b. N.Y.C., June 7, 1949; d. Abraham Julius and Evelyn (Medwin) F. BA, CCNY, 1970; MA, NYU, 1972; cert. Printing Industries Met. N.Y., N.Y.C., 1974, 75, 79. Researcher, asst. editor Arno Press, N.Y.C., 1970-73; free-lance editor Random House, N.Y.C., 1973-74, graphic designer/compositor coll. dept., 1984-88; graphic designer Core Communications in Health, N.Y.C., 1974-76; prodn. mgr. Heights-Inwood News, N.Y.C., 1976-77; art dir., graphic designer Jour. Advt. Research, N.Y.C., 1976-81; prin., graphic designer/compositor Roberta Flechner Graphics, N.Y.C., 1976—; graphic designer/compositor

W. W. Norton & Co., Inc., 1977—, McGraw Hill, Inc., 1990-94; mech. artist Fawcett, N.Y.C., 1979-80; graphic designer Avon Internat., N.Y.C., 1982; art dir., compositor, layout artist Source: Notes in the History of Art, N.Y.C., 1982—; graphic designer John Wiley & Sons, Inc., N.Y.C., 1985. Designer stationery, 1979 (Art Direction mag., Creativity-cert. distinction 1979). Art dir. enviroNews, N.Y. State Atty. Gen.'s Environ. Protection Bur., N.Y.C., 1977-78. Mem. Graphic Artists Guild, NOW, Women's Nat. Book Assn. (cons.), Nat. Assn. Female Execs., Women's Caucus for Art, Am. Inst. Graphic Arts, CCNY Alumni, NYU Alumni. Office: 10615 Queens Blvd Flushing NY 11375-4365

FLEEZANIS, JORJA KAY, violinist, educator; b. Detroit, Mar. 19, 1952; d. Parios Nicholas and Kaliope (Karageorge) F.; m. Michael Steinberg, July 3, 1983. Student, Cleve. Inst. Music, 1969-72, Cin. Coll.-Conservatory Music, 1972-75. Violinist Chgo. Symphony Orch., 1975-76; concertmaster Cin. Chamber Orch., 1976-80; violinist Trio D'Accordo, Cin., 1976-80; asst. prin. 2d violinist San Francisco Symphony Orch., 1980-81; assoc. concertmaster San Francisco Sympony Orch., 1980-89; acting concertmaster Minn. Orch., Mpls., 1988-89, concertmaster, 1989—; violinist Fleezanis-Ohlsson-Grebanier Piano Trio, San Francisco, 1984—; faculty mem. San Francisco Conservatory of Music, 1983-89, U. Minn., 1990-93, 95—; founder Chamber Music Sundaes, San Francisco, 1980-89. Performer World Premiere John Adams Violin Concerto with Minn. Orch., 1994; rec. artist CRI and Koch Classical Records. Democrat. Office: Minn Orch 1111 Nicollet Mall Minneapolis MN 55403-2406

FLEISCHAUER, BARBARA EVANS, lawyer; b. Homestead, Pa., Sept. 1; d. Fred J. and Eleanor Lee (Evans) F.; m. Robert Milton Bastress, Dec. 6, 1987; 1 child, Sarah Eleanor Evans Bastress. BA, Allegheny Coll., 1975; JD, W.Va. U., 1982. Bar: Pa. 1982, U.S. Dist. Ct. (no. and so. dists.) W.Va., U.S. Ct. Appeals (4th, 6th, D.C. cirs.) W.Va. Investigator Pa. Human Rels. Commn., Pitts., 1976-78; cons. Swedish State Pers. Adminstrn., Stockholm, 1978, Swedish Equality Commn., Stockholm, 1979; legal intern Swedish Occupational Safety and Health Adminstrn., Falun, Sweden, 1980; cons. Swedish Nat. Bd. Occupational Safety and Health, Stockholm, 1982-83; spl. asst. atty. gen. civil rights divsn. Office of Atty. Gen., State of W.Va., 1985-89; gen. counsel dist. 31 United Mine Workers of Am., Fairmont, W.Va., 1987-91; pvt. practice Morgantown, W.Va., 1983—; guest lectr. W.Va. U., Morgantown, 1990—. Contbr. articles and reports to profl. publs. Mem. judiciary com., constnl. revision com., health and human svcs. com., select com. on workers compensation W.Va. Ho. of Dels., 1994—; 1st female pres. Oakmont H.S. Student Coun., 1971; del., mem. implementation com. White House Conf. on Youth, 1971-72; nat. mem. Order of Barristers, 1982; adv. com. W.Va. Bar Inst.'s Intestate Succession and Spouse's Elective Share Project, 1989-90; mem. Monongalia County Dep. Sheriff's Civil Svc. Commn., 1991-94; civil justice reform act adv. com. U.S. Dist. Ct. (no. dist.) W.Va., 1992-95. Winner best brief Nat. Energy Law Competition, 1981; named Outstanding Am. Student, 1971. Mem. AAUW, NOW (pres. W.Va. chpt., former exec. v.p. and action v.p, W.Va. chpt., former chpt. pres., former chpt. v.p., chair W.Va. equality polit. action com.), LWV, NAACP, Bus. and Profl. Women of Am. (former chair Morgantown polit. action com., Cert. of Achievement for women breaking barriers in their careers 1993), Amnesty Internat., W.Va. State Bar, W.Va. U. Alliance for Women's Studies, Habitat for Humanity, Sierra Club. Democrat. Home: Rte 4 Box 362 Morgantown WV 26505

FLEISCHER, DOROTHY ANN, administrative assistant; b. N.Y.C., Mar. 1, 1957; d. Lester and Rose (Schwartz) F. BS in Speech, Emerson Coll., 1979. Asst. to pub. info. dir. Community Devel. Agy. N.Y., N.Y.C., 1977; asst. to pub. rels. dir. The Real Paper, Cambridge, Mass., 1979; copy editor Design & Printing Assocs., Boston, 1980; adminstrv. asst., database mgr. CEIP Fund, Boston, 1980-85; adminstrv. asst. to dir. Rsch. Lab. Electronics, MIT, Cambridge, 1985—. Editor, writer brochure, newsletters, booklets, 1980—; editor, staff writer RLE currents and undercurrents newsletters, 1987—. Mem. Nat. Assn. Sci. Writers (assoc.). Office: MIT Rsch Lab Electronics 50 Vassar St # 36-417 Cambridge MA 02139-4309

FLEISCHER, ELIZABETH LEE, materials science editor; b. Schenectady, N.Y., Aug. 27, 1963; d. Robert L. and Barbara S. Fleischer. BS in Materials Sci., U. Pa., 1985; MS in Materials Sci., Cornell U., 1988, PhD in Materials Sci., 1991. Rsch. asst. U. Pa. Tandem Accelerator Ltd., Phila., 1983; tech. assoc. AT&T Bell Labs., Murray Hill, N.J., 1984; prodn. mgr. writer Community Ink, Ithaca, N.Y., 1988-90; sci. reporter writer The Oregonian, Portland, 1989; tech. editor MRS Bull. Materials Rsch. Soc., Pitts., 1991-93, editor MRS Bull., 1994—. Contbr. articles to profl. jours. Mem. AAAS (Mass Media Sci. and Engring. fellow 1989), Am. Phys. Soc., Materials Rsch. Soc., Böhmische Phys. Soc. Home: 3528 Beechwood Blvd 2d Fl Pittsburgh PA 15217 Office: Materials Rsch Soc 9800 McKnight Rd Pittsburgh PA 15237

FLEISCHER, ELLEN LEE, real estate agent; b. Cin., Dec. 15, 1945; d. Leo Simon and Janet F. BA in Mgmt. Econs., U. Cin., 1968. Pub. rels. Cin. Gas and Electric CO., 1968-71; campaign coord. Taft for Senate, Cin., 1971-72; new bus. devel. profl. Fifth Third Bank N.A., Cin., 1973-77; mktg. mgr. Williamsburg Mgmt., Cin., 1984-86; real estate agt. Sibcy Cline Realtors, Ft. Mitchell, Ky., 1986-91, Re/Max Affiliates, Ft. Mitchell, 1992—; artist, Cin., 1978-85; mem. Kenton Boone Bd. Realtors, Northern Ky. Exhibitor watercolor abstracts various galleries in Cin., Naples and Coral Gables, Fla., N.Y.C.; author essay, Congl. Record, 1st pl. award, 1968. Mem. Ky. Assn. Realtors, Nat. Assn. Realtors, Million Dollar Club, Friends of Covington, No. Ky. Heritage League, Cin. Art Mus., Cin. Symphony Com., Omicron Delta Epsilon. Home: 100 Riverside Dr Covington KY 41011-1724

FLEISCHER, MARTHA HESTER, lawyer, English educator; b. Portland, Maine; d. Carl Everett and Ruth (Jordan) Hester; m. Bruce Golden, 1962 (div. 1967); m. Stefan Fleischer, June 15, 1968; children: Katharine Anne, Victor Everett. BA, Duke U., 1958; MA, Columbia U., 1959, PhD, 1964; JD, SUNY, Buffalo, 1982. Bar: N.Y. 1983, U.S. Dist. Ct. (we. dist.) N.Y. 1983, Fla. 1983. Assoc. Nixon Hargrave Devans & Doyle, Rochester, N.Y., 1982-86, Lacy, Katzen, Mittleman & Ryen, Rochester, N.Y., 1986-87; v.p., assoc. counsel Mfrs. and Traders Trust Co., Buffalo, 1987—. Home: 114 Windsor Ave Buffalo NY 14209-1019 Office: Mfrs and Traders Trust Co One M & T Plaza Buffalo NY 14240*

FLEISCHMAN, BARBARA GREENBERG, public relations consultant; b. Detroit, Mar. 20, 1924; d. Samuel J. and Theresa (Keil) Greenberg; BA, U. Mich., 1944; m. Lawrence A. Fleischman, Dec. 18, 1948; children: Rebecca, Arthur, Martha. Tchr., Detroit Public Schs., 1944-45, psychoanalyst's sec., Detroit, 1947-49; sec. Greenberg Ins. Agy., Detroit, 1947-49; customer/public relations cons. Kennedy Galleries, N.Y.C., 1976—. Bd. dirs. Detroit Artists Market, 1958-66; mem. women's com. Detroit Inst. Arts, 1957-66, founder, pres. vol. com., 1961-66; bd. dirs. Friends of Channel 13, 1968-80, pres., N.Y.C., 1975-79, chmn. auction, 1975, trustee, 1975-84; pres. Friends of N.Y. Pub. Library, 1979-84, trustee, 1980—, v.p. bd., 1987—; bd. dir. Am. Craft Coun., 1980-83; trustee The Acting Co., 1986-89, pres. 1988-89; governing bd. Off the Record Luncheons, Fgn. Policy Assn., 1978-85; assoc. producer Channel 13 Auction, 1978-80; trustee Mus. TV and Radio, 1988-92; mem. vis. com. Greek and Roman Dept. Boston Mus. Fine Arts, 1990—, Met. Mus., 1991—; bd. dirs. Planned Parenthood N.Y.C., 1990-96; commr. Art Commn. of the City of N.Y., 1995—. Mem. Cosmopolitan Club, Art Table. Office: Kennedy Galleries 730 Fifth Ave New York NY 10019-4001

FLEISHMAN, WENDY RUTH, lawyer; b. Phila., Dec. 28, 1954; d. Harry and Sylvia (Laub) F. B.A., Sarah Lawrence Coll., 1974; J.D., Temple U., 1977; postgrad. U. Pa., 1981-83. Bar: Pa. 1977, U.S. Dist. Ct. (ea. dist.) Pa. 1984, N.Y. 1992, U.S. Dist. Ct. (so. dist. N.Y.), 1994. Asst. dist. atty. City of Phila., 1977-84; assoc. Ballard, Spahr, Andrews & Ingersoll, Phila., 1984-86; ptnr. Fox, Rothschild, O'Brien & Frankel, 1987-93; assoc. Skadden, Arps, Slate, Meagher & Flom, N.Y.C., 1993-95; counsel Skadden, Arps, Slate, Meagher & Flom, 1995—. Bd. dirs. Women Organized Against Rape, Phila., 1986-89, Women's Way, Phila., 1986-89. Mem. ABA (editor torts and ins. practice Trial Techniques Newsletter 1993-94, vice chair torts and ins. practice, 1994—, mem. adv. bd. on products liability Practicing Law Inst., mem. faculty Nat. Inst. Trial Advocacy, mem. criminal justice com.), Fed. Bar Assn., Am. Arbitration Assn. (arbitrator), Pa. Bar Assn. (mem. prof. responsibility com., vice chair, atty. adv. com.), N.Y. Womens Bar Assn. Democrat. Jewish. Office: Skadden Arps et al 919 3rd Ave New York NY 10022

FLEMING, ALICE CAREW MULCAHEY (MRS. THOMAS J. FLEMING), author; b. New Haven, Dec. 21, 1928; d. Albert Leo and Agnes (Foley) Mulcahey ; m. Thomas J. Fleming, Jan. 19, 1951; children: Alice, Thomas, David, Richard. AB, Trinity Coll., 1950; MA, Columbia U., 1951. Author: The Key to New York, 1960, Wheels, 1960, A Son of Liberty, 1961, Doctors in Petticoats, 1964, Great Women Teachers, 1965, The Senator from Maine: Margaret Chase Smith, 1969, Alice Freeman Palmer: Pioneer College President, 1970, Reporters At War, 1970, General's Lady, 1971, Highways into History, 1971, Pioneers in Print, 1971, Ida Tarbell, The First of the Muckrakers, 1971, Nine Months, 1972, Psychiatry, What's it All About?, 1972, The Moviemakers, 1973, Trials that Made Headlines, 1974, Contraception, Abortion, Pregnancy, 1974, New on the Beat, 1975, Alcohol: The Delightful Poison, 1975, Something for Nothing, 1978, The Mysteries of ESP, 1980, What to Say When You Don't Know What to Say, 1982, The King of Prussia and a Peanut Butter Sandwich, 1988, George Washington Wasn't Always Old, 1991, What, Me Worry?, 1992, P.T. Barnum: The World's Greatest Showman, 1993; editor: Hosannah the Home Run!, 1972, America Is Not All Traffic Lights, 1976; contbr. articles to mags. Nat. bd. dirs., mem. bd. dirs. N.Y. region Medic Alert Found. U.S., past. chmn. N.Y. regional bd.; mem. pres.'s coun. United Hosp. Fund. Recipient Nat. Media award Family Svc. Assn. Am., 1973, Alumnae Achievement award Trinity Coll., 1979, Nat. Vol. of Yr. award Medic Alert Found., 1991, 93. Mem. PEN, Authors Guild. Address: 315 E 72nd St New York NY 10021-4625

FLEMING, BARBARA JOAN, university administrator; b. Chgo., July 23, 1936; d. Otto Albert and Mildred Edith (Coltman) Boehlke; m. Moray Leonard Fleming; children: Patricia Deane, Ian Moray. BS, U. State of N.Y., 1993. Market rsch. asst. Am. Oil Co., Chgo., 1960-64; computer programmer Ins. Co. of N.Am., Phila., 1966-68; libr. reference asst. The Coll. of Wooster, Ohio, 1981-84, dir. rsch. and records, 1984-89; dir. devel. rsch. St. Lawrence U., Canton, N.Y., 1989-93, dir. devel. svcs., 1993—; bd. dirs., nat. sec. Am. Prospect Rsch. Assn., 1990-94; dir. habitat for humanity St. Lawrence U. Chpt., 1990-94. Chair Borough Charter Commn., Ringwood, N.J., 1979-80; pres. LWV, Ringwood, 1976-78; mem. Grasse River Players, 1990—, bd. dirs. 1993—. Recipient Spotlight award for Excellence in Community Theatre Coll.-Community Theatre Com., 1989. Mem. Assn. Profl. Rschrs. for Advancement (Upstate N.Y. chpt. founder, bd. dirs., nat. sec. 1990-94), Ohio Prospect Rsch. Network (founder). Office: St Lawrence U Canton NY 13617

FLEMING, CHRISTINA SAMUSSON, special education educator; b. Ft. Belvoir, Va., Dec. 20, 1950; d. Lewis Frew and Gayle Virginia (Pribnow) Samusson; m. Hal Alex Fleming, July 16, 1977; children: Hilary Anne, Alex Andrew. BS, Tex. Woman's U., 1972, MEd, 1974. Cert. tchr., Tex. Spl. edn. tchr. Richardson (Tex.) Ind. Sch. Dist., 1972-81; ednl. diagnostician Mental Health Mental Retardation, Plano, Tex., 1985-90; pre-kindergarten tchr. U. Gymnastics, Plano, 1987-90; spl. edn. tchr. Plano Ind. Sch. Dist., 1990—; mem. spl. edn. task force Plano Ind. Sch. Dist., 1994—; ednl. diagnostician Collin County Mental Health Mental Retardation, Plano, 1985-90. Author: (manual) Self Concept in the Primary Years, 1974, (booklet) Heart to Heart: A Parent's Guide to Congenital Heart Disease, 1981. Mem. exec. bd. Child Guidance Clinic, Plano, 1984-91; mem. exec. bd. Shepard Elem. Sch. PTA, Plano, 1985-89, pres., 1987; mem. exec. bd., founding mem. Heart to Heart, Dallas, 1980-86; leader Girl Scouts U.S.A., Tex., 1985-94. Mem. Tex. Assn. Gifted and Talented, Richardson Learning Disabilities Assn. (exec. bd. 1974-87), Assn. Tex. Profl. Educators, Parent Tchr. Student Assn. Republican. Methodist. Home: 1217 Monterey Cir Plano TX 75075-7315 Office: Plano ISD Weatherford Elem 2941 Mollimar Dr Plano TX 75075-6306

FLEMING, JEAN ANDERSON, adult education educator, consultant; b. Cleve., May 17, 1952; d. Evert Ludwig Walter and Martha Fay (Oehling) A. BA, Colo. State U., 1973, MEd, 1977; EdD, U. No. Colo., 1996. Coord. adult basic edn. Poudre Valley Schs. and Vols. Clearinghouse, Ft. Collins, Colo., 1975-80; tchr. trainer Colo. Dept. Edn., Denver, 1981-83, cons. spl. projects, 1993-95; instnl. mgr., exec. dir. Cmty. Tech. Skills Ctr., Denver, 1987-91; dir. workplace edn. program Arapahoe C.C., Denver, 1991-92. Mem. Colo. Assn. for Continuing Adult Edn. (treas., bd. dirs., pres. 1989-90, Disting. Leadership award 1983, 90, 94), Mountain Plains Adult Edn. Assn. (bd. dirs. 1988—, pres. 1996, cert. of appreciation 1990), Colo. Alliance for Lifelong Learning (chair 1994-96), Am. Assn. for Adult and Continuing Edn.

FLEMING, LAURA CHRISTINE, software engineer; b. Oakland, Calif., May 8, 1953; d. Glen Thomas and Maxine B. (Stracner) F.; m. John Ignacio Cruz, Sept. 17, 1972 (div. 1979); m. Mark Paul von Gnechten, May 3, 1981; children: Paul, Thomas von Gnechten, Martin von Gnechten. BS in Computer Sci., Calif. State U., Hayward, 1989. Sys. design engr. Amdahl, Sunnyvale, Calif., 1978-85; sr. mem. tech. staff Cadence Design Sys., San Jose, 1985-94; sr. software engr. Dow Jones Telerate, Palo Alto, Calif., 1994-95; sr. engr. J. Frank Consulting, Palo Alto, 1995—. Sec. Citizen Action Com. for Spl. Edn., Fremont, Calif., 1988, Parent Faculty Assn., Fremont, 1992-93. Mem. IEEE, Soc. Women Engrs. Democrat. Home: 40010 Dolerita Ave Fremont CA 94539 Office: J Frank Consulting 1810 Embarcadero Rd Palo Alto CA 94303

FLEMING, LISA L., lawyer; b. Louisville, Nov. 14, 1961; d. Joseph D. Ware. BA cum laude, Hanover (Ind.) Coll., 1982; JD, U. Louisville, 1985. Bar: Ind., U.S. Dist. Ct. (so. and no. dists.) Ind.; cert. mediator pursuant to Ind. Trial Rules. V.p., chief legal officer Am-Ar Internat., Ltd., Louisville, Ky.; career cons. Hanover Coll. Mem. Leadership So. Ind., 1990—, bd. dirs. 1992—, v.p. programming, 1996-97; bd. dirs. Comty. Youth Leadership Collaborative, 1995—. Mem. NAFE, ABA (admiralty and corp. counsel coms.), Ind. State Bar Assn. (articles and by-laws com.), Clark County Bar Assn., Am. Corp. Counsel Assn. (bd. dirs., chpt. treas. 1992—), Environ. Law Inst., Jefferson County Pub. Sch. System Speakers Bur., River City Bus. and Profl. Women, Ky. Women Advs., Focus Louisville, Hanover Coll. Alumni Assn. (bd. dirs. 1990—, pres. elect 1991-92, pres. bd. dirs. 1992-93, past pres. 1993-94), So. Ind. C. of C. (chair govt. affairs debate subcom. 1991-95, women's bus. coun., 1991—, chair political skill workshop subcom. 1993—), Phi Mu (alumnae pres. Louisville chpt. 1985-91, advisor Rho chpt., Sigma area collegiate dir. 1996—). Office: Am Ar Internat Ltd 9721 Ormsby Station Rd Louisville KY

FLEMING, LOUISE ELAINE, education educator; b. Akron, Ohio, Aug. 22, 1948; d. Richard E. and Marian E. (Griffiths) Conn; m. William C. Fleming Jr., July 26, 1978; children: Emma, Anne, Melissa. BS in Edn., Bowling Green State U., 1970; MS in Edn., U. Akron, 1977, PhD in Secondary Edn., 1990. Cert. high sch. English and speech, counseling, Ohio. Tchr. English Revere H.S., Richfield, Ohio, 1972-75; tchg. asst. U. Akron, 1985-88, adj. prof., 1988-90; assoc. prof. edn. Ashland (Ohio) U., 1990—; bd. dirs., sec. Cooperative Market, Akron, 1992-93; mem. student health ctr. adv. bd. Ashland U., 1994—. Guest editor, contbr. profl. jours. Girl scout leader Girl Scouts Am., Akron, 1989-91, 93-95; vol. River Day, Akron, 1991. Mem. ASCD, Am. Ednl. Rsch. Assn., Midwestern Ednl. Rsch. Assn. (chairperson divsn. F), Am. Ednl. Studies Assn., Midwest History Edn. Soc., Internat. Soc. for Ednl. Biography, Audubon Soc. (bird counter 1992—, bd. dirs. 1995—), Kappa Delta Pi. Office: Ashland U Ashland OH 44805

FLEMING, PATRICIA STUBBS, federal official; b. Phila., Mar. 17, 1936; d. Fredrick Douglass Stubbs and Marion Turner Stubbs Thomas; m. Harold S. Fleming, June 1958 (div. Feb. 1971); children: Douglass, Craig, Gordon. BA, Vassar Coll., 1957; postgrad., NYU, 1958-60, U. Pa., 1957-58, Phila. Acad. Fine Arts, 1957-58. Legis. asst. to reps. U.S. Ho. of Reps., Washington, 1971-77; asst. to sec. HEW, Washington, 1977-78, dir. intergovtl. and legis. affairs Office Civil Rights, 1979-80; asst. to sec. U.S. Dept. Edn., Washington, 1979-80, dep. asst. sec. legis., 1980-81; sr. pub. policy assoc. James H. Lowry & Assocs., Washington, 1981-83; chief staff Rep. Ted Weiss U.S. Ho. of Reps., Washington, 1983-86, profl. staff mem. subcom. human resources & intergovtl. rels, 1986-93; spl. asst. to sec. HHS, Washington, 1993-94; dir. Office Nat. AIDS Policy The White House, Washington, 1994—. One-person show NYU; exhibited in group shows in N.Y.C. and Washington. Democrat. Episcopalian. Home: 6009 Massachusetts Ave Bethesda MD 20816-2041 Office: Office of Nat AIDS Policy 750 17th St NW Washington DC 20500

FLEMING, RENÉE L., opera singer; b. Indiana, Pa., Feb. 14, 1959; d. Edwin Davis Fleming and Patricia (Seymour) Alexander; m. Richard Lee Ross, Sept. 23, 1989. BM in Edn., Potsdam State U., 1981; MM, Eastman Sch. Music, 1983; student, Juilliard Am. Opera Ctr., N.Y.C., 1983-84, 85-87. Debut engagements include Spoleto Festival, Charleston and Italy, 1986-90, Houston Grand Opera & N.Y.C. Opera, 1988, 89, San Francisco Opera, 1991, Met. Opera, Paris Opera at the Bastille, 1991, Covent Garden, London, 1989, Teatro Colon Buenos Aires, 1991, La Scala, 1993, Lyric Opera of Chgo., 1993. Winner Met. Opera Nat. Auditions, 1988; recipient George London prize, 1988, Richard Tucker award, 1990; Fulbright scholar, Frankfurt, Germany, 1984-85. Office: care ML Falcone Pub Rels 155 W 68th St Ste 1114 New York NY 10023-3881

FLEMING, RHONDA NELL, elementary school educator, artist; b. Jacksonville, Fla., Feb. 8, 1955; d. Robert Bertram and Nellie Mae (Entrekin) F.; m. Dana Wayne Long, Feb. 14, 1980 (div. Mar. 1991); 1 child, Matthew Wayne; m. John Boyd Smith, Apr. 1, 1994. BFA in Drawing and Painting cum laude, U. Ga., 1978. Cert. tchg., Ga. Art tchr. Savannah (Ga.) Chatham County Pub. Schs., 1988—; co-designer, co-owner Decorative Metal Arts, Savannah, 1992-94, Smith Forge Gallery, Savannah, 1995—. Mem. Nat. Art Edn. Assn. Savannah Art Assn. (1st pl. award 1983, 84, Best of Show award 1992, 95), Delta Kappa Gamma. Home: 315 E 51st St Savannah GA 31405-2240

FLEMING, ROBYN MARIE, architect; b. Ann Arbor, Mich., Nov. 23, 1961; d. Arthur Wallace Fleming and Doris Marie (Watkins) Leverett; 1 child, Hasan Shariff. BArch, Howard U., 1984; postgrad., Bklyn. Law Sch. Registered arch., N.Y. Rsch. asst. Howard U., Washington, 1983; office asst. Bob Mackie & Assocs., Washington, 1983; project and practice mgr. Simmons Archs., Bklyn., 1985-89, 91-93; design cons. W.E. Salley & Assocs., Plainfield, N.J., 1988; detailer The Callison Partnership, Seattle, 1990-91; owner, prin. RMF Bryant Archs., Bklyn., 1992—. Active vol. program N.Y.C. Pub. Schs., 1988. Mem. AIA, ABA, NAFE, AAUW, N.Y. State Bar Assn., African Am. Archs. Roundtable for Entrepreneurs. Home and Office: 436 7th Ave Apt 1 Brooklyn NY 11215

FLEMING, SUZANNE MARIE, university official, chemistry educator; b. Detroit, Feb. 4, 1927; d. Albert Thomas and Rose E. (Smiley) F. BS, Marygrove Coll., 1957; MS, U. Mich., 1960, PhD, 1963. Joined Congregation of Sisters Servants of Immaculate Heart of Mary, Roman Catholic Ch., 1945. Chmn. natural sci. div. Marygrove Coll., Detroit, 1970-75, v.p., dean, 1975-78, acad. v.p., 1978-80; asst. v.p. acad. affairs Eastern Mich. U., Ypsilanti, 1980-82, acting assoc. v.p. acad. affairs, 1982-83; provost, acad. v.p. Western Ill. U., Macomb, 1983-86; vice chancellor U. Wis., Eau Claire, 1986-89; freelance writer, 1989—; vis. scholar U. Mich., 1989—; pres. Mich. Coll. Chemistry Tchrs. Assn., 1975; councilor Mich. Inst. Chemists, 1973-77; bd. dirs. Nat. Ctr. for Rsch. to Improve Postsecondary Teaching and Learning, 1988-90. Contbr. articles to profl. publs. NIH research grantee, 1966-69. Fellow Am. Inst. Chemists; mem. Am. Chem. Soc. (councilor, Detroit 1980-83, Petroleum Research Fund grantee, 1962-88), Am. Assn. Higher Edn., Sigma Xi. Home and Office: 2888 Cascade Dr Ann Arbor MI 48104-6659

FLENORL, ROSE JACKSON, corporate communications executive; b. Clarksdale, Miss., Oct. 14, 1957; d. Louis Alexander and Mertha (Lockett) Jackson; m. Richard Lee Flenorl, June 27, 1981; 1 child, Lillie Clarissa. BAE in Journalism and English, U. Miss., 1979. Asst. dir. student activities U. Miss., University, 1979-81; sys. engr. IBM, Memphis, 1981-88, mktg. rep., 1988-94; tng. mgr. Memphis Diversity Inst., 1994-95; mgr. corp. comm. Internat. Paper, Memphis, 1995—. Mem. adv. bd. Sarah Isom Ctr., University, Miss., Dept. Journalism, University, Black Alumni Coun., University, 1994—; trustee Hutchison Sch., Memphis, 1995—; bd. dirs. Leadership Memphis, 1994—, Memphis Zool. Soc., 1994—, United Way, Memphis, 1992—, Tenn. Leadership, Nashville, 1993-95. Mem. NAACP, The Links (chair arts com. 1994—), Alpha Kappa Alpha (chair membership 1994—). Methodist. Home: 8727 Stablemill Ln Cordova TN 38018 Office: Internat Paper 6400 Poplar Ave Memphis TN 38197

FLESHER, MARGARET COVINGTON, corporate communications executive; b. San Angelo, Tex., July 29, 1944; d. Charles C. and Helen Irene (Little) F.; m. Alexander Ribaroff, Dec. 11, 1976 (div. June 1988). BA in Polit. Sci., Vassar Coll., 1966. Asst. editor Harcourt Brace Inc., N.Y.C., 1966-74; prodr. Guidance Assocs. subsidiary of Harcourt Brace, N.Y.C., 1974-76; freelance writer, editor London, 1976-81; sr. editor Franklin Watts, Inc., N.Y.C., 1981-85; pres. The Westport (Conn.) Pub. Group, 1985-89; coord. cmty. rels. Texaco Inc., White Plains, N.Y., 1989-91; sr. coord. media rels. Texaco, Inc., White Plains, N.Y., 1991-93; contbg. editor Texaco, Inc., White Plains, 1993—. Author: Mexico and the United States Today: Issues Between Neighbors, 1985, New Leaves: A Journal for the Suddenly Single, 1987. Mem. Women in Comm., Inc. (Westchester chpt. bd. dirs., v.p. profl. devel. 1994-95, Clarion award 1995, Fairfield County chpt. pres. 1986-88), Fairfield County Pub. Rels. Assn. (bd. dirs. 1991-92). Republican. Home: 4 Fragrant Pines Westport CT 06880 Office: Texaco Inc 2000 Westchester Ave White Plains NY 10650

FLESHMAN, LINDA EILENE SCALF, private investigator, writer, columnist, consultant, communications and marketing executive; b. Oklahoma City, Sept. 17, 1950; d. James Truman and Dortcha Virginia (Stiles) Scalf; children: Leatha Michele, Misty Dawn. AA, Tarrant County Jr. Coll., 1977; BA, North Tex. State U., 1979. Copywriter, Advt., Graphics & Mktg., Ft. Worth, 1978-80; editor Ft. Worth mag. Ft. Worth C. of C., 1980-81; mktg. prodn. coord. City of Fort Worth, 1981-83; dir. pub. rels. Circle T coun. Girl Scouts U.S., Ft. Worth, 1983-85; mgr. corp. tng. Am. Airlines Direct Mktg., 1984-87; dir. corp. communications LeasPak Internat., 1987-89; mgr. background svcs. AMR Svcs. (div. Am. Airlines), 1989-94; owner The Private Investigators, Ft. Worth, Tex. Mem. Internat. Bus. Communicators, Am. Women in Radio and TV, Women in Communication. Democrat. Roman Catholic. Office: The Private Investigators PO Box 14807 Fort Worth TX 76117-0807

FLETCHER, BETTY B., federal judge; b. Tacoma, Mar. 29, 1923. B.A., Stanford U., 1943; LL.B., U. Wash., 1956. Bar: Wash. 1956. Mem. firm Preston, Thorgrimson, Ellis, Holman & Fletcher, Seattle, 1956-1979; judge U.S. Ct. Appeals (9th cir.), Seattle, 1979—. Mem. ABA (Margaret Brent award 1992), Wash. State Bar Assn., Am. Law Inst., Fed. Judges Assn. (past pres.), Order of Coif, Phi Beta Kappa. Office: US Ct Appeals 9th Cir 1010 5th Ave Seattle WA 98104-1130

FLETCHER, CATHY ANN, auditor; b. Barnesville, Ga., Aug. 23, 1949; d. John James and Dorothy Lee (Banks) Fletcher; 1 child, Lisa Faye. Student, Ohio State U., 1969-70; AS, Mass. Bay Community Coll., 1982; AS, Northeastern U., Boston, 1984, BS, 1984; MA in HumanResources Mgmt. Emmanuel Coll., Boston, 1993. Mail clk. Fed. Reserve Bank, Boston, 1971-72; office mgr. Breckenridge Sportswear, Boston, 1973-74; asst. dir. Whittier Street Health Ctr., Boston, 1974-81; sec. to dir. Northeastern U., 1981-84; auditor Def. Contract Audit Agy. N.E. Region, Boston, 1984—; sec., bd. dirs. Boston Tenant Policy Coun., 1977-79; mgr. northeastern region Fed. Women's Program, 1989—; mem. adv. bd. DCAA EEO, 1989—. Author: Softball Team Book, 1975. V.p., bd. dirs. Bromley Health Tenant Mgmt. Corp., Jamaica Plain, Mass., 1976-91; mem. fund-raising com. Com. to Elect Jesse Jackson Pres., Boston, 1984; apptd. fed. women program coordinator State of Mass., 1988; mem. women's opportunity com. Boston Fed. Exec. Bd., 1990—, mem. women's coun., 1994—; active Women's Ednl. Indsl. Union, 1993—; active NAACP. Mem. AAUW, NAFE, Profl. Coun., Nat. Tenants Orgn., Assn. Govt. Accts. (cert. govt. fin. mgr.), Federally Employed Women (treas. Greater Boston chpt. 1992-93, pres. 1994—), Hawkettes Social (pres., past mem. profl. coun. 1989), Elks, Sigma Epsilon Rho. Avocations: reading, swimming, cooking, walking, travel. Office: Def Contract Audit Agy Boston Br Office 101 Merrimac St Fl 8 Ste 820A Boston MA 02114

FLETCHER, DENISE KOEN, strategic and financial consultant; b. Istanbul, Turkey, Aug. 31, 1948; came to U.S., 1967, naturalized, 1976; d. Moris and Kety (Barkey) Koen; m. Robert B. Fletcher, Nov. 11, 1969; children—David, Kate. A.B. (Coll. scholar), Wellesley Coll., 1969; M.City Planning, Harvard U., 1972. Analyst Ea. div. Getty Oil Co., N.Y.C., 1972-73; sr. analyst Ea. div. Getty Oil Co., 1973-74, cash mgmt. and bldg. supr., 1974-76; cash mgmt. and bldg. supr. Getty Oil Co. (Eastern), 1976; asst. treas. N.Y. Times Co., N.Y.C., 1976-80; treas. N.Y. Times Co., 1980-88; pres. Fletcher Assocs. Inc., Larchmont, N.Y., 1988—; chief exec. officer Communication Venture Group, Ltd., N.Y.C., N.Y., 1989-90; bd. dirs. Software, Etx. Stores, Inc., 1991-94. Bd. dirs. Overseas Edn. Found. Internat., 1989-90, Boy Scouts Am., Exploring, 1991-93; bd. dirs., trustee and v.p. bd. dirs., exec. com. YWCA, N.Y., 1987—; mem. budget com. City of Larchmont, N.Y., 1981-83, chmn. zoning bd. appeals, 1987—, mem. selection com., 1985-87; mem. alumni exec. coun. Harvard U. Sch. Govt., 1982-87. Mellon scholar, 1970. Mem. Fin. Execs. Inst., Fin. Women's Assn., Treasurers Club N.Y., Phi Beta Kappa. Club: Harvard (N.Y.C.). Office: Fletcher Assocs Inc 154 E Boston Post Rd Mamaroneck NY 10543

FLETCHER, KATHERINE ANN PATRICK, pediatrics, emergency nurse; b. Rotan, Tex., Sept. 9, 1950; d. John Andrew and Elsie Louise (Moore) Patrick; m. James Lawson Fletcher, Dec. 23, 1971; children: James Jr., Janice, Carol. ADN, Nicholls State U., 1988. CEN, La.; cert. ACLS, pediatric advanced life support, trauma nursing. Staff nurse med. surg. South La. Med. Ctr., Houma, 1988-89, staff nurse pediat. emergency rm., 1990-92, charge nurse emergency rm., 1992-94; head nurse pediat. Chabert Med. Ctr., Houma, 1994—. Fellow Emergency Nursing Assn. Democrat. Baptist. Home: PO Box 42 Raceland LA 70394-0042

FLETCHER, LOUISE, actress; b. Birmingham, Ala., 1936; d. Robert Capers F. BA, U. N.C., 1957; student acting with Jeff Corey; LHD (hon.), Gallaudet U., 1982, Western Md. Coll., 1986. Films include Thieves Like Us, 1973, Russian Roulette, 1974, One Flew Over the Cuckoo's Nest, 1975 (Acad. award as best actress), Exorcist II: The Heretic, 1976, The Cheap Detective, 1977, The Magician, 1978, Natural Enemies, 1979, The Lucky Star, 1979, The Lady in Red, 1979, Strange Behavior, 1980, Brainstorm, 1981, Strange Invaders, 1982, Once Upon a Time in America, 1982, Firestarter, 1983, Overnight Sensation, 1983, Invaders from Mars, 1985, The Boy Who Could Fly, 1985, Nobody's Fool, 1986, Flowers in the Attic, 1987, Two Moon Junction, 1987, Blue Steel, 1988, Best of the Best, 1989, Shadowzone, 1989, Blind Vision, 1990, The Player, 1991, Return to Two Moon Junction, 1993, Tollbooth, 1993, Virtuosity, 1995, Mulholland Falls, 1995, 2 Days in the Valley, 1995, Edie & Pen, 1995, High School High, 1995; TV appearances include Maverick, Wagon Train, The Law-Man, Playhouse 90, The Millionaire, Alfred Hitchcock, Thou Shalt Not Commit Adultery, 1978, A Summer To Remember, 1984, Island, 1984, Second Serve, 1985, Hoover, 1986, The Karen Carpenter Story, 1988, Nightmare on the 13th Floor, 1988, Twilight Zone, 1988, Final Notice, 1989, The Hitchhiker, 1990, Tales from the Crypt, 1991, In a Child's Name, 1991, Boys of Twilight, 1991, The Fire Next Time, 1992, Civil Wars, 1993, Deep Space Nine, 1994, 95, The Haunting of Cliff House, Dream On, 1994, Someone Else's Child, 1994, VR5, 1994, 95. Bd. dirs. Deafness Rsch. Found., 1980—. Mem. Nat. Inst. Deafness and Other Communicable Disorders (adv. bd.).

FLETCHER, MARJORIE AMOS, librarian; b. Easton, Pa., July 10, 1923; d. Alexander Robert and Margaret Ashton (Arnold) Amos; A.B., Bryn Mawr Coll., 1946; m. Charles Mann Fletcher, May 14, 1949; children: Robert Amos, Elizabeth Ashton, Anne Kennard. Asst. to dir. rsch., then rsch. asst. to pres. Penn Mut. Life Ins. Co., 1946-49; officer A.R. Amos Co., Phila., 1949-66; part-time tchr., 1965-68; librarian Am. Coll., Bryn Mawr, Pa., 1968-77, archivist, 1973—, dir. oral history collection, 1975—, lectr. on archives, 1975—, asst. prof. edn., 1973-87, dir. archives and oral history, 1977—; pres. pub. rels. MAF Enterprises, 1987—. Author articles in field. Recipient awards Phila. Flower Show, 1965—. Mem. Spl. Librs. Assn. (pres. Phila. 1977-78), Soc. Am. Archivists (chairperson oral history sect. 1981-87, award of merit 1987), Oral History Assn., Hist. Soc. Pa., U.S. Pony Club, D.A.R., Nat. Soc. Colonial Dames in Commonwealth of Pa., Emergency Aid Pa. Found., Phila. Skating Club, Davis Creek Yacht Club, Bridlewild Pony Club (sponsor), Bridlewild Trails Club (Gladwyne). Republican. Episcopalian. Home: 1135 Norsam Rd Gladwyne PA 19035-1419 Office: Am Coll Bryn Mawr PA 19010

FLETCHER, MARY ANN, immunologist, educator; b. Little Rock; d. William T. and Myrtle P. (Jernigan) Sharp; divorced; 1 son, William T. B.S., Tex. Tech. Coll., 1959; M.A., U. Tex., 1961; Ph.D., Baylor U., 1966. Diplomate Am Bd. Bioanalysts. Asst. prof. Northwestern U., Evanston, Ill., 1968-69; adj. asst. prof. Ill. Inst. Tech., Chgo., 1970-71; asst. prof. U. Miami (Fla.) Sch. Medicine, 1972-75, assoc. prof., 1975-80, prof. medicine, microbiology/immunology and psychology, 1980—, dir. clin. immunology lab. NIH grantee, 1971—. Fellow Assn. Behavioral Medicine Rsch.; mem. AAAS, Am. Assn. Immunologists, Am. Assn. Microbiologists, NOW, Psychoneuroimmunology Rsch. Soc., Clin. Immunology Soc. Democrat. Contbr. articles to sci. jours.; holder 2 patents.

FLETCHER, MARY H., English language educator; b. Tehran, Iran, May 25, 1927; d. Ralph Cooper and Harriet T. (Thompson) Hutchison; m. Robert Fletcher (dec.); children: Edward John Clark, Elizabeth Clark Kendall, Lynn Clark Barbieri, Lori Clark Corrochano, Ralph Hutchison Clark; m. Wesley Moses Smith, 1969 (dec. 1993). BA, Wilson Coll., 1948; postgrad., U. Pa., 1948-49, Rollins Coll., 1963-65, Stetson U., 1973-74. Cert. tchr., Fla. Tchr. Leesburg (Fla.) Sr. H.S., 1963-68, 85-86, 90-91, Carver Heights Mid. Sch., 1968-84; English tutor Learning Lab. Lake Sumter C.C., 1991—. Co-author: (with Ann Meador) Saving Our Schools From the Religious Right The Lake County Florida Story, 1995. Dir. Fla. Fedn. Womens Clubs Dist. 5, 1955-57, 2d v.p., 1958; women's dir. Dale Carson Campaign Sheriff Duval County, 1956; elder New Life Presbyn. Ch., 1980-95; mem. Conservation Coun. Lake County, 1991-93, People for Mainstream Values, 1994-95; pres. LWV, 1991-93l; grad. Leadership Lake County, 1996. Mem. Phi Delta Kappa. Republican. Home: 32423 Mabel Ln Leesburg FL 34788 Office: Lake Sumter CC Learning Ctr Leesburg FL 34788

FLETCHER, MARY LEE, business executive; b. Farnborough, Eng.; d. Dugald Angus and Mary Lee (Thurman) F.; B.A., Pembroke Coll., Brown U., 1951. Ops. officer C.I.A., Washington, 1951-53; exec. trainee Gimbels, N.Y.C., 1953-54; head researcher Ed Byron TV Prodns., N.Y.C., 1954; copywriter Benton & Bowles, Inc., N.Y.C., 1955-63; creative dir. Alberto-Culver Co., Melrose Park, Ill., 1964-66; v.p. advt. and publicity Christian Dior Perfumes, N.Y.C., 1967-71; v.p. Christian Dior-N.Y., N.Y.C., 1972-78, exec. v.p., dir., 1978-85. Home: 12 Beekman Pl New York NY 10022-8059

FLETCHER, SHERRYL ANN, higher education administrator; b. Wyandotte, Mich., July 1, 1956; d. Richard Charles and Pauline L. (Fisher) Seavitt; m. Alan Morris Fletcher, July 26, 1980; children: Christopher Richard, Cameron Morris. BA summa cum laude, Albion Coll., 1978; MA with honors, U. Mich., 1986. Elem. art tchr. East Grand Rapids (Mich.) Schs., 1978-80; asst. dean students, dir. student activities Northwood U., Midland, Mich., 1981-83; admissions counselor Office of Undergrad. Admissions, U. Mich., Ann Arbor, 1983-84, sr. admissions counselor, 1984-88, asst. dir. admissions, 1988-93, assoc. dir. admissions, 1993-95; exec. dir., founder Coll. Access for Rural Am., 1995—; spl. asst. to the dir. Office of Undergrad. Admissions Johns Hopkins U., 1996—; guest faculty Annapolis (Md.) Edn. Inst. Inc., 1993-94; adminstrv. univ. liaison Cook Family Found., Mich., 1986—; speaker in field. Chair future planning Jr. League Ann Arbor, 1993-94, chair pub. rels., 1990-93; sustainer Jr. League Annapolis, 1995—; mem. David Hallissey scholarship com. Mem. Nat. Assn. Coll. Admissions Counselors (nat. presdl. com. 1993), Mich. Assn. Coll. Admissions Counselors (state sec. 1992—), Potomac Chesapeake Assn. Coll. Admissions Counselors, Albion Coll. Shield Club, Annapolis Club, U. Mich. Alumni Club of Washington, Alumnae Club Annapolis, Alpha Chi Omega. Methodist. Office: Johns Hopkins Univ Office Undergrad Admissions 140 Garland Hall 3400 N Charles St Baltimore MD 21218

FLETCHER, SUZANNE WRIGHT, physician, educator; b. Jacksonville, Fla., Nov. 14, 1940; d. Robert Dean and Helen (Selmer) Wright; m. Robert H. Fletcher; children: John Wright, Grant Selmer. BA, Swarthmore Coll., 1962; MD, Harvard Med. Sch., 1966; MSc, Johns Hopkins U., 1973. Diplomate Nat. Bd. Med. Examiners, Am. Bd. Internal Medicine. Intern Stanford (Calif.) U. Med. Ctr., 1966-67, resident, 1967-68, physician 22nd med. detachment U.S. Army, New Ulm, Germany, 1969-70; asst. prof. epidemiology and health Mc Gill U., Montreal, Can., 1974-77, assoc. prof., 1977-78, asst. prof. medicine, 1973-78; dir. med. clinic dept. medicine N.C. Meml. Hosp., 1978-82; assoc. prof. medicine U. N.C., 1978-83, co-chief divsn. gen. medicine and clin. epidemiology dept. medicine, 1978-86, rsch. assoc. health svcs. rsch. ctr., 1978-90, vice chmn. clin. svcs., 1981-84, prof. medicine, clin. prof. epidemiology, 1983-90, program dir. faculty devel. gen. medicine and gen. pediatrics, 1985-90, co-dir. internat. clin. epidemiology network program Rockefeller Found., 1986-90; editor Annals of Internal Medicine, Phila., 1990-93; adj. prof. medicine U. Pa., Phila., 1990-93, Jefferson Med. Coll., 1991-93, U. N.C., 1994—; prof. ambulatory care and prevention Harvard Med. Sch.; chmn. NIH Tech. Assessment Conf., 1992, Nat. Cancer Inst. Internat. Workshop, 1993; active World Bank Seminar on Preventive Strategies in Med. edn., Hangzhou, China, 1986, Ad Hoc NCI Com. on BSE Cancer Detection Rsch. and Applications, 1986. Author: Clinical Epidemiology—The Essentials, 1982, 2nd edit., 1988; contbr. chpts. to books; contbr. articles to profl. jours. Rsch. grantee Conseil de la Recherche en Sante du Quebec, 1975-77; grantee Health and Welfare Can., 1976-78, Robert Wood Johnson Teaching Hosp. Gen. Medicine Group Practice Program, 1980-84, Nat. Ctr. Health Scis. Rsch. and Health Tech., 1985-89, Rockefeller Found. Clin. Epidemiology Resource and Tng. Ctr., 1986-90, NIH, 1987-90; recipient Can. Nat. Health Rsch. Scholar award Can. Govt., 1975-78. Fellow Am. Coll. Physicians (mem. med. knowledge self assessment program 1984-85, mem. clin. practice subcom. 1987, mem. pub. policy subcom. 1988-89), Am. Coll. Epidemiology (chairperson pub. com. 1992-94, bd. dirs. 1990-93), Coll. Physicians Phila.; mem. Soc. Gen. Internal Medicine (counsellor 1978-81, pres.-elect 1982-83, pres. 1983-84, mem. pub. com. 1990—, chair Glaser Award com. 1991, co-editor Jour. Gen. Internal Medicine, 1984-89), Inst. Medicine (mem. coun. 1993—, mem. exec. com. 1993—), So. Soc. Clin. Investigation, Am. Pub. Health Assn., Sydenham Soc., Phila. Epidemiology Soc., Phila. Med. Soc. Democrat. Unitarian. Office: Harvard Med Sch Ambulatory Care/Prevention Dept 126 Brookline Ave Ste 200 Boston MA 02215-3920*

FLETTNER, MARIANNE, opera administrator; b. Frankfurt, Germany, Aug. 9, 1933; d. Bernhard J. and Kaethe E. (Halbritter) F. Bus. diploma, Hessel Bus. Coll., 1953. Sec. various cos., 1953-61, Pontiac Motor Div., Burlingame, Calif., 1961-63; sec. Met. Opera, N.Y., 1963-74, asst. co. mgr., 1974-79; artistic adminstr. San Diego Opera, 1979—. Home: 4015 Crown Point Dr San Diego CA 92109-6211 Office: San Diego Opera PO Box 988 San Diego CA 92112-0988

FLING, JACQUELINE ANN, library administrator; b. Bethesda, Md., Aug. 13, 1947; d. Esther (Lanza) F. BS in Edn., Kent State U., 1970; MLS, U. Pitts., 1984. Sch. libr. Crestwood Pub. Schs., Manuta, Ohio, 1971-74; asst. libr. Urban Inst., Washington, 1977-82; dir. tech. svcs. Pitts. Pub. Schs., 1985-87; dir. census bur. libr. Census Bur., Washington, 1987-92; dir. libr. and records mgmt. Garcia Cons., Inc., 1992—. U. Pitts. scholar, 1984. Mem. ALA, Spl. Libr. Assn., Beta Phi Mu. Office: Garcia Cons Inc Ste 400 7927 Jones Branch Dr Mc Lean VA 22102

FLINK, JANE DUNCAN, publisher; b. Atlanta, Feb. 17, 1929; d. James Archibald and Frances (Watkins) Duncan; m. Richard Albert Flink, Nov. 20, 1954; children: Jennifer, Elizabeth, Caroline, Charles Albert, James Duncan. Student Carleton Coll., U. Mo., Columbia Coll. Reporter, Tri-Town News, Greendale, Wis., 1958-61; reporter, photographer, feature writer, editor Cen. Mo. Rural and Farm Life mag., Centralia (Mo.) Fireside Guard, 1973-78, asst. editor, 1982-83; editor Bus. Briefs, MFA Oil Co., Columbia, 1977; editor Lifestyles, Kingdom Daily News, Fulton, Mo., 1978-82; assoc. editor Mo. Ruralist, Columbia; dir. external rels. Winston Churchill Meml. and Libr., Westminster Coll., Fulton, 1985-89, dir., 1989-90; owner, pub. Boone County Jour., Ashland, Mo., 1986—. Rep. committeewoman Ward I, Centralia, 1972, 74, 76; mem. exec. bd. Friends of Churchill Meml., Fulton; mem. Boone County Commn. on Child Abuse, 1978-81, Boone County Hist. Soc.; bd. dirs., mem. pub. rels., devel., Maplewood coms., now 1st v.p. Walters-Boone County Mus. and Visitors Ctr., 1995—; mem. Boone County Govt. Rev. Task Force, 1991; chair So. Boone County Sch. Budget Rev. Task Force, 1991-92; pres. Lake Champetra Homeowners Assn., 1994-95, v.p., 1995-96; vice chair Boone County Constn. Commn. Recipient numerous editorial awards. Mem. Nat. Fedn. Press Women (nat. achievement award 1982, bd. dirs. 1991-93, 21st century com. 1992-93), Mo. Press Women (dist. v.p. 1978-79, v.p. 1985-87, pres. 1991-93, chmn. honors, awards 1979-81, Woman of Achievement award 1988 Communicator award 1995), Mo. Press Assn., Mo. Soc. Newspaper Editors. Home: 7230 S Shore Dr Hartsburg MO 65039-9202 Office: Boone County Jour 104 W Broadway Ashland MO 65010-9779

FLINN, MARY AGNES, artist, educator; b. Balt., July 31, 1962; d. Eugene Aloyisious and Rose Flora (Maranto) F. BFA, Swain Sch. Design, New Bedford, Mass., 1985; MFA, CUNY, 1991. Bartender Santa Fe Restaurant, Bklyn., 1991-95; art handler, conservation technician NAD Mus., N.Y.C., 1992—; tchr. art Melrose Cmty. Ctr., Bronx, N.Y., 1993, Saraswati Prodns., Bklyn., 1996; vis. artist Fairleigh Dickinson Coll., N.J., 1994. One-woman show Prince St. Gallery, N.Y.C., 1995; group shows Balt. City Hall, 1995, Prince St. Gallery, 1996; also pvt. collections. Vol. Meth. Hosp., Bklyn., 1995-96. Fellow Vt. Studio Ctr., 1987. Mem. Women's Mus., Amnesty Internat.

FLINN, ROBERTA JEANNE, management and computer applications consultant; b. Twin Falls, Idaho, Dec. 19, 1947; d. Richard H. and Ruth (Johnson) F. Student Colo. State U., 1966-67. Cert. Novell netware engr. Ptnr., Aqua-Star Pools & Spas, Boise, Idaho, 1978—, mng. ptnr., 1981-83; ops. mgr. Polly Pools, Inc., Canby, Oreg., 1983-84, br. mgr. Polly Pools, Inc., A-One Distributing, 1984-85; comptr., Beaverton Printing, Inc., 1986-89; mng. ptnr. Invisible Ink, Canby, Oreg., 1989—. Mem. NAFE, Nat. Appaloosa Horse Club, Oreg. Dressage Soc. (pres. North Willamette Valley chpt.). Home: 24687 S Central Point Rd Canby OR 97013-9743

FLINNER, BEATRICE EILEEN, library and media sciences educator; b. Uledi, Pa., Feb. 8, 1924; d. Charles Robert and Esther Marjorie (Sickles) Jeffreys; m. Donald Allayaud, May 18, 1944 (killed in action World War II); m. Lyle P. Flinner, June 27, 1947; children: Donald Allayaud, Carol Jean Flinner Dorough. AB summa cum laude, Southern Nazarene U., 1974; MLS, U. Okla., 1977; MA in Social Studies, Southern Nazarene U., 1978, MA in Early Childhood, 1981. Cataloging dept. Asbury Theol. Sem., Wilmore, Ky., 1949-52; aquisitions Geneva Coll., Beaver Falls, Pa., 1959-62, audio visual coord., 1965-68; assoc. prof., head pub. svcs. Southern Nazarene U., Bethany, Okla., 1968—, assoc. prof. Libr. Scis., 1978—, adj. prof.grad. edn., 1981—; mem. adv. bd. Bethany Libr., rep. to Bd. Trustees, 1986-87. Book reviewer The Christian Librarian, 1980—; indexer Christian Periodical Index, 1988—; contbr. articles to profl. jours. Mem. AAUW, Okla. Libr. Assn., Assn. Christian Librs. (v.p. 1991-93, program chair internat. conf. 1992), Okla. Assn. Coll. and Rsch. Librs., Univ. Women's Club, U. Okla. Sch. Libr. Info. Sci. Alumni Assn., Assn. Christian Librs. (conf. coord. 1992-95), Phi Delta Lambda, Delta Kappa Gamma. Republican. Nazarene.

FLINT, BETTY RUTH, elementary education educator; b. Cin., Jan. 14, 1943; d. Clarence Lovelle Weaver and Dorothy Regina (Haynes) Copeland; m. Virgil Eugene Flint, Apr. 2, 1994; children: Cassandra Ellis, Aaron Ellis. BS in Elem. Edn., U. Cin., 1972, MA in Reading, 1978. Tchr. Cin. Bd. of Edn., 1973-76; tchr. Oceanside (Calif.) Unified Sch. Dist., 1976-96, Chpt. I reading tchr., 1996—; presenter workshops Calif. Math. Coun., Palm Springs, 1993, 94, San Diego Assn. for the Edn. of Young Children, 1994. Mem. Internat. Reading Assn., Greater San Diego Reading Assn., Calif. Reading Assn., Calif. Math. Coun., Whole Lang. Coun. of San Diego, San Diego Assn. for Edn. of Young Children. Democrat. Home: PO Box 527613 Flushing NY 11352-7613 Office: Benjamin Banneker Sch PS 156 750 Concourse Village W Bronx NY

FLOCK, ROBERTA RAE, real estate executive; b. Seattle, Nov. 14, 1937; d. Boyd Wilbur and Pearl C. (Hanson) Anderson; m. Larry Jay Flock, Apr. 4, 1964; children: Tony J., Shane M. Grad., Lincoln H.S., Seattle. Owner Real Estate Investments, Seattle, 1970—, Flock Apts., Seattle, 1970—; ins. agt. Seattle, 1968-73. Vol. Seattle Art Mus., Rental/Sales Gallery, Seattle, 1989-96, vol. chmn., 1991-92. Mem. Apt. Assn. Seattle and King County, Fremont C. of C., Laguna Art Mus., Seattle Art Mus., Tacoma Art Mus., Mus. of Northwest Art. Republican. Lutheran. Office: PO Box 60065 Seattle WA 98160

FLOM, ELENA MARIE, academic administrator; b. Allentown, Pa., July 15, 1941; d. Paul Henry and Anna M. (Zelrick) Koch; m. Mark Flom, June 29, 1963; children: Mark, Doug. BS in Psychology and Math., Pa. State U., 1963; MEd in Guidance, Stetson U., 1971, cert. in sch. psychology, 1976; EdD, Nova U., 1979. Math. instr. Longwood Jr. and Sr. H.S., L.I., 1963-67; counselor, coord. guidance svcs. Monroe Adult/Cmty. Ctr., Cocoa, Fla., 1972-76; sch. psychologist Ctrl. Area Brevard County Sch. Bd., Rockledge, Fla., 1976-77; from spl. asst. to pres., equal access opportunity coord. Brevard Cmty. Coll., Cocoa, 1977-82, assoc. v.p. instrn., provost Melbourne campus, 1987-89, provost, dean instrn. Melbourne campus, 1983-91, assoc. v.p. for instrnl. advancement Dist. Adminstrn., 1991—; mem. proposal evaluation panel New Am. Schs. Devel., Denver, 1991; mem. team Statewide Pub. Broadcasting Task Force, 1990; mem. Nat. Tech. Assistance Corps, 1979; ednl. cons. Dept. Def., Dept. Navy, Caribbean, 1991; project dir. Mgmt. Inst. for Surinamese Educators, 1981; project dir. for Far East program Innovative Profl. Study Abroad Program, China, India, Hong Kong, and Nepal, 1985, Africa program, Egypt, Ethiopia, Kenya, Zimbabwe, and South Africa, 1983. Exec. bd. dirs. Fla. Gov.'s Commn. on the Status of Women, 1978; state commr. Fla. Commn. on Human Rels., 1977-78, 82-92; co-chair Congressman Jim Bacchus' Commn. on Higher Edn., Fla.; bd. trustees Dept. Def. Equal Opportunity Mgmt. Inst. Found., Brevard County Civilian Mil. Rels. Coun.; bd. dirs. Brevard Arts Ctr. and Mus. Found., King Ctr. for Performing Arts, Melbourne, Space Coast Tiger Bay Club; mem. cmty. adv. bd. Jr. League of South Brevard, Inc. Recipient Disting. Educator award Kettering Found., 1976, State of Fla. Outstanding Contbn. in Quality Edn. award, 1990; Fulbright scholar, 1991; grantee Dept. Edn., 1991-96. Mem. Am. Assn. Women in Cmty. and Jr. Colls., Fla. Assn. C.C.'s (instrn. advancement consortium), Internat. Fulbright Assn., Assn. for Ednl. Comm. and Tech., Ctrl. Fla. Edn. Consortium for Women (founder bd. dirs.), South Brevard Area C. of C. (exec. bd. v.p. 1987-88, 90-92, chmn. bus. edn. com. 1990-91), Rotary (dir. internat. svc. 1995-96), Psi Chi, Pi Gamma Mu, Phi Delta Kappa. Home: 483 Barrello Ln Cocoa Beach FL 32931-3628 Office: Brevard CC 1519 Clearlake Rd Cocoa FL 32922-6503

FLOMENHAFT, ELEANOR, art curator; b. Bklyn., Aug. 21, 1933; d. Hirsch and Estelle (Landau) Wolf; m. Leonard Flomenhaft, Nov. 18, 1951; children: Michael, Fern, Ted. Degree, Willsey Inst. Interior Design, 1969; BA, Hofstra U., 1976; MA, Queens Coll., 1983; degree, N.Y. Inst. Finance, 1994. Curator of art Emily Lowe Gallery Hofstra U., Hempstead, N.Y., 1977-79; dir., chief curator contemporary art Fine Arts mus. L.I., Hempstead, 1981-92; ind. curator, art cons., writer, lectr. Hewlett, N.Y., 1992—; U.S. judge Ctrl. Am. Art Biennial, San Jose, Costa Rica, 1992; mem. adv. bd. Kutztown U. Coll. Visual Arts, Anne Frank Found. U.S.A., N.Y.C. Author: Roots and Development of CoBrA Art, 1985, Beyond Time/Art of Alfred Van Loen, 1993. Mem. adv. bd. Hewlett Woodmere Pub. Libr., 1993-95. Recipient Presdl. award for outstanding contbn. to arts Pres. Ronald Reagan, 1984, Pathfinder award Town of Hempstead, 1990; named Woman of Yr. Hempstead C. of C., 1989. Mem. Am. Assn. Mus., Art Table, Coll. Art Assn. Home: 1294 Seawane Dr Hewlett NY 11557

FLOOD, DIANE LUCY, marketing communications specialist; b. Plainfield, N.J., June 13, 1937; d. William Edward and Lucy (Dycker) Flood. B.A., Vassar Coll., 1959; postgrad. Fontainebleau Sch. Fine Arts (France), 1961. Advt. prodn. aide indsl. chem. div. Am. Cyanamid Co., Wayne, N.J., 1959-62, prodn. supr., 1962-64, creative coord. organic chems. div. advt., 1964-66, design art and copy mgr., 1966-70, advt. rep., 1970-72, advt. rep. paper, process chems. and resins, indsl. chem. div., 1972-77, advt. coord. water treating, mining, paper and enhanced oil recovery chems., 1977-83, mgr. mktg. communications indsl. products div., 1983—, mgr. mktg. communications Venture Chems. div., 1986-87; Chem. Products and Indsl. Products divs., 1987-89, mgr. mktg. communications Chem. Products, Indsl. Products and Internat. Chems. div., 1989-90, mgr. mktg. communications Chem. Group, 1990-93, Cytec Industries, Inc., 1993—. Past dir., v.p., past pres. 103 Gedney St. Owners Co-op, 1985-92. Mem. Vassar Coll. Alumni Assn. Mem. Consistory of Reformed Ch. Club: Vassar of N.Y.C. Home: 103 Gedney St Apt 3C Nyack NY 10960-2226 Office: Cytec Industries Inc West Paterson NJ 07424

FLOOD, DOROTHY GARNETT, neuroscientist; b. Sayre, Pa., Oct. 7, 1951; d. James Murlin and Dorothy Garnett (Dietrich) F.; m. Paul David Coleman, Feb. 26, 1983. BA cum laude, Lawrence U., 1973; student, U. Ill., 1972-73; MS, PhD, U. Rochester, N.Y., 1980. Sr. instr. in anatomy U. Rochester, 1980-83, asst. prof. neurology, neurobiology and anatomy, 1984-90, assoc. prof. neurology, neurobiology and anatomy, 1990-94; sr. sci. Cephalon, Inc., West Chester, Pa., 1994—. Contbr. to book chpts. and articles in field; editorial bd. Neurobiology of Aging, 1989—. Recipient Fenn award U. Rochester, 1980; grantee NSF, NIH, Office of Naval Rsch., 1979-94. Mem. Soc. Neurosci. Office: Cephalon Inc 145 Brandywine Pky West Chester PA 19380-4245

FLOOD, (HULDA) GAY, editor, consultant; b. Plainfield, N.J., Aug. 14, 1935; d. William Edward and Lucy (Dycker) F.; BA, Smith Coll., 1957. Picture dept. Sports Illustrated, Time Inc., N.Y.C. 1957-58, letters dept., 1958-59, reporter, 1959-60, writer-reporter, 1960-71, assoc. editor, 1971-85, sr. editor, 1985-90; editor, cons., 1990—. Mem. Alumnae Assn. Smith Coll., Smith Coll. Students Aid Soc., Smith Coll. Club N.Y., Garden Club of Nyack. Elder, chair fin. com. 1st Reformed Ch., Nyack, N.Y. Office: 103 Gedney St Apt 3C Nyack NY 10960-2226

FLOOD, JOAN MOORE, paralegal; b. Hampton, Va., Oct. 10, 1941; d. Harold W. and Estalena (Fancher) M.; 1 child by former marriage, Angelique. B.Mus., North Tex. State U., 1963, postgrad., 1977; postgrad. So. Meth. U., 1967-68, Tex. Women's U., 1978-79, U. Dallas, 1985-86. Clk. Criminal Dist. Ct. Number 2, Dallas County, Tex., 1972-75; reins. libr. Scor Reins. Co., Dallas, 1975-80; corp. ins. paralegal Assocs. Ins. Group, 1980-83; corp. securities paralegal Akin, Gump, Strauss, Hauer & Feld, 1983-89; asst. sec. Knoll Internat. Holdings Inc., Saddle Brook, N.J., 1989-90, 21 Internat. Holdings, Inc., N.Y.C., 1990-92; dir. compliance Am. Svc. Life Ins. Co., Ft. Worth., 1992-93; v.p., sec. Express Comm., Inc., Dallas, 1993-94; fin. transactions paralegal Thompson & Knight, Dallas, 1994-96; corp. transactions paralegal Jones, Day, Reavis & Pogue, Dallas, 1996—. Mem. ABA, Tex. Bar Assn. Home: PO Box 190165 Dallas TX 75219-0165

FLOOD-MORROW, ELIZABETH, news service company executive; b. Albany, N.Y., Apr. 6, 1936; d. Bernard Relf Gaucas and Mary Ann Reid; m. John J. Flood, June 29, 1963 (div. July 1971). Student, Russell Sage Coll. Legis. corr. Cuyler News Svc., Albany, N.Y., 1957-67, pres., 1969—; dir. pub. rels. to Gov. Nelson A. Rockefeller Albany, N.Y., 1967-68; sports writer N.Y. Turf Writers Assn., 1993. Bd. dirs., bd. trustees Vis. Nurses Found., 1980—; bd. dirs. Capital Dist. Cmty. Loan Fund, 1988—, Acad. of the Holy Names, Albany, 1990—; chmn. Ten Broeck Mansion Restoration, Albany, 1982. Recipient Alumni of Yr. award Acad. of the Holy Names, 1982, Cmty. Svc. award Kiwanis, 1990; N.Y. State Parks and Recreation grant for Ten Broeck Mansion Restoration, 1988. Mem. N.Y. State Legis. Corr. Assn. Alumni Assn., Women's Press Club of N.Y. State, Inc. (founder, 1st pres. 1966-68, 78-88, editor, pub. rels. Woman of Yr. award 1980), Women's Assn. Wolfert's Roost Country Club (bd. dirs. 1995-96), Paper Weight Collectors of Am. Office: Cuyler News Svc State Capitol PO Box 7205 Rm 358 Albany NY 12224

FLORA, CORNELIA BUTLER, sociologist, educator; b. Santa Monica, Calif., Aug. 5, 1943; d. Carroll Woodward and May Fleming (Darnall) Butler; m. Jan Leighton Flora, Aug. 22, 1967; children: Gabriela Catalina, Natasha Pilar. BA, U. Calif., Berkeley, 1965; MS, Cornell U., 1966, PhD, 1970. Asst. to full prof. Kans. State U., Manhattan, 1970-89, dir. population rsch. lab., 1970-78, univ. disting. prof., 1988-89; program adviser Ford Found., Bogota, Colombia, 1978-80; prof., head dept. sociology Va. Poly. Inst. and State U., Blacksburg, 1989-94; dir. north ctrl. regional ctr. for rural devel. Iowa State U., Ames, 1994—; cons. USAID, 1981-91, Inter Am. Devel. Bank, 1992, United Nations, 1992. Author: Rural Communities: Legacy and Change; editor: Sustainable Agriculture, 1990, Rural Policy for the 1990s; contbr. articles to sociol. publs. Chair bd. dirs. Cooper House, Blacksburg, 1990-92; bd. dirs. Henry A. Wallace Inst. for Alternative Agr., 1994—. Recipient Outstanding Alumni award Coll. Agrl. & Life Scis., Cornell U., 1994. Mem. Rural Sociol. Soc. (pres. 1988-89, Outstanding Rsch. award 1987), Latin Am. Studies Assn. (bd. dirs. 1982-84, pres. Midwest sect. 1989-90), Am. Sociol. Assn. Mem. Church of Brethren. Office: Iowa State U N Ctrl Regional Ctr Rural Devels 317 East Hall Ames IA 50011-1070

FLORA, JEANNE ANN, artist; b. Saginaw, Mich., Aug. 10, 1952; d. Leonard Dwight and Joan Leonilla (Davis) Thomas; m. Robert David Gilliland, Aug. 21, 1971 (div. May 1980); 1 child, Ian Jason Gilliland; m. Kenneth Lee Flora, June 27, 1986. Grad., high sch., 1970. Mktg. clk. Mich. Bell Telephone Co., Saginaw, 1971-73; phone supr. Women's Ob-Gyn., P.C., Saginaw, 1980-85; office mgr. Kenneth Mattson, DDS, Findlay, Ohio, 1986-91; artist Argostar Prodns., Findlay, 1991—; freelance artist Baghdad Express, Arnold, Mo., 1988-93. Illustrator: (booklets) Your Rottweiler Puppy, 1990, The Illustratard Standard of the Rottweiler, 1991, The Illustrated Standard of the Cardigan Welsh Corgi, 1993; illustrator logos Am. Rottweiler Club, 1993, Nat. Splty., 1994. Mem. Doberman Pinscher Club Am., Am. Rottweiler Club (award of recognition 1992, 93), Lima Kennel Club (sec. 1993—). Democrat. Roman Catholic. Home: 14982 State Rte 568 Findlay OH 45830 Office: Argostar Prodns 14982 State Rte 568 Findlay OH 45840

FLORENCE, VERENA MAGDALENA, small business owner; b. Interlaken, Switzerland, Nov. 4, 1946; came to U.S., 1967; d. Paul Robert and Marie (Raess) Demuth; m. Kenneth James Florence, Dec. 10, 1967. BA, U. Calif., Berkeley, 1974; MS, UCLA, 1979, PhD, 1982. Research scientist Procter & Gamble, Cin., 1983; adminstr. Swerdlow & Florence, Beverly Hills, Calif., 1984-89; pres., chief exec. officer, chmn. of bd. Böl Designs, Inc., L.A., 1989—. Contbr. articles to profl. jours. Mem. L.A. Computer Soc. (SIG leader). Democrat. Home and Office: 1063 Stradella Rd Los Angeles CA 90077-2607

FLORES, CHRISTINA ROSALIE, elementary education art educator; b. Tamuning, Guam, Nov. 17, 1947; d. George Pangelinan Franquez; m. Larry Blas Flores, June 20, 1970 (div. Nov. 1974); children: Tanisha, Briana. AA, Sacred Heart Coll., 1967; BA, San Diego State U., 1970; MA, Long Beach State U., 1979. Cert. art tchr., Guam. 5th grade tchr. Price Elem. Sch., Mangilao, Guam, 1970-80; 6th grade tchr. Harmon (Guam) Loop Elem. Sch., 1980-82; 6th and 7th grade art tchr. Agueda Johnston Mid. Sch., Ordot, Guam, 1982—; gifted and talented edn. art tchr. various elem. schs., Guam, summers, 1984—; art instr. Fun in the Sun camp for handicapped children, summers 1975-82, Parks and Recreation Summer Camp, 1983-85; instr., tchr. workshops in art Simon Sanchez H.S., Yigo, Guam, 1988-92; mem. adv. bd. Coun. Arts and Humanities, Maite, Guam, 1991-94, bd. dirs., 1995—; chief advisor Crime Stoppers Agueda Mid. Sch., 1992—; advisor Nat. Jr. Honor Soc. Agueda Johnston Mid. Sch., 1987—. Chief advisor Students Against Drunk Driving, Agueda Johnston Mid. Sch., 1987—; mem. Driver's Edn. Consortium, Guam, 1993-94; vol. Spl. Olympics, Guam, 1974—, ARC, Guam, 1992—; instr. Pacific Region Ednl. Lab., 1993—. Tchr. Inst. scholar Nat. Art Gallery, Washington, 1991. Mem. ASCD, Nat. Art Edn. Assn., Nat. Assn. Student Activity Advisers. Home: PO Box 1654 Agana GU 96910-1654

FLORES, LYDIA, Spanish educator; b. L.A., Sept. 1, 1929; d. Francisco Gomez and Anita Guadalupe (Perez) F.; children: William Francis, naomi Lynn, Stephanie, Carl Christopher, Kristin, Gretchen. BA, Immaculate Heart Coll., 1951; MEd, Long Beach State U., 1970. Cert. secondary, gen. elem., bilingual edn. tchr., Calif.; cert. lang. devel. specialist. Primary tchr. St. Eugene's Elem. Sch., L.A., 1952-53; primary tchr. Torrance (Calif.) Unified Sch. Dist., 1953-60, mid. grade tchr., 1965-68; bilingual resource tchr. Madera (Calif.) Unified Sch. Dist., 1979-89; Spanish tchr., limited English proficient resource tchr. Fresno (Calif.) Unified Sch. Dist., 1992-95; mem. bilingual adv. com., Madera, 1989-89, Fresno, 1992-95. Unitarian Universalist. Home: 8316 N Raisina Ave Fresno CA 93720

FLORES, ROBIN ANN, social worker, social services administrator; b. Allentown, Pa., Oct. 6, 1949; d. Norman Henry and Ann May (Huff) Flores. BS in Edn., Kutztown U., 1971; MS in Adminstrn., U. Scranton, 1983. With Lehigh County (Pa.) Area Agy. on Aging, 1973-75, info. referral outreach coord., 1975-78, supr. cmty. svcs., 1979-95, exec. dir., 1996—; lectr. cmty. svcs., family care giving and on aging process, 1978—; utilization cmty. resources, Lehigh County. Mem. adv. bd. Cmty. Action Com. of Lehigh Valley, 1979-82, Elder Well, 1987-90; Pa. del. White House Conf. on Aging, Hershey, Pa., 1981; bd. dirs. Vis. Nurse Assn. of Lehigh County, 1982—, Women Inc., 1983-87; adv. bd. Homecare, Inc., 1982—, Geriatric Edn. Modules, Allentown Osteo. Hosp., 1979; mem. profl. adv. com. Lehigh Valley Hospice, 1984—; mem. utilization and rev. bd. Vis. Nurse Assn., 1979—; consumer rep. Pa. Power and Light Co.; co-chmn. Human Svcs. Tng. Coop., 1975-81. Mem. NAFE, Am. Soc. on Aging, Allentown Art Mus., Old Allentown Preservation Assn., Quota Internat. Home: 1255 Forest Rd Whitehall PA 18052-6217 Office: Lehigh County Area Agy on Aging PO Box 1548 930 W Hamilton St Allentown PA 18105

FLORES, VERA JACOBSON, theater arts educator; b. San Francisco, Jan. 14, 1952; d. Leo David and Doris Bush (Mulford) Jacobson; m. Paul Vasiliy Kopeikin, Nov. 27, 1975 (div. Feb. 1990); 1 child, Katie Elizabeth Kopeikin; m. Leonard Flores, Jr., Dec. 29, 1993. BA in Theatre Arts, Calif. State U., Hayward, 1992; postgrad., San Francisco State U., 1993-94, 96. Cert. tchr., Calif. Realtor Trotter Realty, Burlingame, Calif., 1977-79; bookkeeper Vorsatz & Vorsatz, Burlingame, Calif., 1981-86; med. transcriptionist Mills Meml. Hosp., San Mateo, Calif., 1986-94, 94-96; tchr. Visitacion Valley Sch., San Francisco, 1994-96; drama tchr. Potrero Hill Mid. Sch., San Francisco, 1996—; mem. leadership team Visitacion Valley Sch., 1995-96; judge Shakespeare Festival, Calif. State U., Hayward, 1994-95. Dir. (musical theatre) The Wiz, 1995, Little Shop of Horrors, 1996. Mem. AAUW, Autism Soc. Am., San Francisco Mus. Modern Art, Calif. Ednl. Theatre, Epilepsy Soc. Am., Women in Arts, Performing Arts Libr. Mus., Nat. Urban Alliance, Calif. Ednl. Theatre Assn. Democrat. Episcopalian. Office: Potrero Hill Mid Sch 655 DeHane Stt San Francisco CA 94107

FLORESTANO, PATRICIA SHERER, university educator; b. Washington, Mar. 15, 1936; d. Wilbur L. and Virginia M. (Moriconi) F.; B.A. in Am. Civilization, U. Md., 1958, M.A. in Govt. and Politics, 1970, Ph.D. in Pub. Adminstrn. and Am. Govt., 1974; m. Thomas Florestano, Nov. 29, 1959; children—Leslie C., Thomas. Research staff State Legis. Commn. on Intergovt. Coop., 1972-75, State Gov.'s Commn. on Functions of Govt., 1973-75; staff asst. to pres. Md. Senate, 1975-78; asst. prof. Inst. Urban Studies, U. Md., College Park, 1974-79, dir. Inst. Govtl. Service, 1979-85, vice-chancellor govtl. relations, 1985-91; prof. govt. Schaefer Ctr. Pub. Policy U. Balt., 1991-95, pub. adminstr., sr. fellow; sec. Md. Higher Edn. Commn., Annapolis, 1995—; cons. ednl. evaluation, mgmt. and survey research. Lector St. Elizabeth Ann Seton Ch., 1970-92; dir. Crofton (Md.) Gymnastics Program, 1972-74; vice chmn. Anne Arundel County (Md.) Commn. on Women, 1975; mem. Transition Exec. Com. for Gov. Elect. State Md., Dec. 1994- Jan. 1995; mem. Anne Arundel County Schs. Adv. Forum, 1975-76, chmn. nominations com., 1976-78; sec. higher edn. Md. Commn. Higher Edn. Recipient Outstanding Teaching award Students Assn. of U. Md., 1979. Mem. Am. Soc. Pub. Adminstrn. (pres. 1983-84, conf. fellow), Am. Polit. Sci. Assn., So. Polit. Sci. Assn., Urban Affairs Assn. (past chmn. governing bd.), So. Consortium Univ., Pub. Service Orgns. (former editor). Democrat. Roman Catholic. Author: (with other) The States and Metropolitan Areas, 1981; Attitudes of Special Interest Groups and the Public on Chesapeake Bay Areas, 1980; also articles. Home: 1516 Farlow Ave Crofton MD 21114-1516 Office: Md Higher Edn Commn 16 Francis St Annapolis MD 21401

FLORI, ANNA MARIE DIBLASI, nurse anesthetist, educational administrator; b. Amsterdam, N.Y., Oct. 29, 1940; d. Tony and Maria (Macario) DiBlasi; children: Tammy, Tina, Toni; m. Gilberto Flori, May 24, 1986. Grad., Albany Med. Ctr. Sch. Nursing, 1962, Fairfax Hosp. Sch. Nurse Anesthetists, Va., 1972; BS in Anesthesia, George Washington U., 1979; M. in Bus. and Pub. Adminstrn., Southeastern U., Washington, 1982; PhD, Columbia Pacific U., 1983. Cert. registered nurse anesthetist. Staff nurse West Seattle Gen. Hosp., 1962-64; office nurse Filmore Buckner, M.D., Seattle, 1964-66; staff nurse anesthetist Fairfax Hosp., 1972-73; staff nurse anesthetist Potomac Hosp., Woodbridge, Va., 1973, chief nurse anesthetist, 1973—; dir. Potomac Hosp. Sch. for Nurse Anesthetists and Sch. for Nurse Anesthesia; faculty mem. Columbia Pacific U., 1973-90; chief nurse anesthetist No. Va. Anesthesia Assn., 1988—; guest lectr. No. Va. Community Coll., Inservice Potomac Hosp., George Washington U.; coord. Free Clinic Prince William County, Woodbridge, Va. Contbr. books on anesthesia. Mem. Am. Assn. Nurse Anesthetists, Va. Nurse Anesthesia Assn., Nat. Italian Am. Found. Home: 12954 Pintail Rd Woodbridge VA 22192-3831

FLORIAN, MARIANNA BOLOGNESI, civic leader; b. Chgo.; d. Giulio and Rose (Garibaldi) Bolognesi; BA cum laude, Barat Coll., 1940; postgrad. Moser Bus. Sch., 1941-42; m. Paul A. Florian III, June 4, 1949; children—Paul, Marina, Peter, Mark. Asst. credit mgr. Stella Cheese Co., Chgo., 1942-45; With ARC ETO Clubmobile Unit, 1945-47; mgr. Passavant Hosp. Gift Shop, 1947-49; pres., Jr. League Chgo., Inc., 1957-59; pres. woman's bd. Passavant Hosp., 1966-68; bd. dirs. Northwestern Meml. Hosp., 1974-81, mem. exec. com., 1974-79; pres. Women's Assn., Chgo. Symphony Orch., 1974-77, founder WFMT/CSO Radiothon, 1976; chmn. Guild Chgo. Hist. Soc., 1981-84, trustee Chgo. Hist. Soc., 1981-84; life trustee Orchestral Assn., v.p. 1978-82, vice chmn. 1982-86, mem. exec. com. 1978-87; mem. women's bd. U. Chgo.; mem. vis. com. dept. music U. Chgo., 1980-90; pres. bd. dirs. Antiquarian Soc. of Art Inst., 1989-91. Recipient Citizen Fellowship, Inst. Medicine Chgo., 1975, Presdl. Commendation for leadership and svc. Barat Coll., 1990. Clubs: Friday (pres. 1972-74), Contemporary; Winnetka Garden.

FLORIO, LUANN F., medical management and research consultant; b. Bklyn., Oct. 20, 1954; d. F. Anthony and Barbara Ann (Fehlker) Florio. Student, CUNY, Bklyn., 1972-77, Columbia U., 1974, 75, Pace U., 1977. Cert. tchr. pvt. vocat. schs., N.Y. Rsch. assoc. Meml. Sloan-Kettering Cancer Ctr., N.Y.C., 1977-79; with Med. Practice Adminstrn., N.Y.C., 1979-85; clin. trials coord. pharm. industry, 1985-87; regional dir. Dorex, Inc., Calif., 1988-91; owner Venturemedicus, Inc., N.Y.C., 1987-91; cons. to gen. counsel Columbia Presbyn. Med. Ctr., N.Y.C., 1988-90; cons. Dreyfus Found., 1988-90. Bd. govs. Dressage Found., 1990-91. Social Sci. scholar Bklyn. Coll. Sch. Social Scis., CUNY, 1975-77. Office: 27 W 72nd St Ste 212 New York NY 10023-3498

FLOURNOY, NANCY, statistician, educator; b. Long Beach, Calif., May 4, 1947; d. Carr Irvine and Elizabeth (Blincoe) F.; m. Leonard B. Hearne, Aug. 28, 1978. BS, UCLA, 1969, MS, 1971; PhD, U. Wash., 1982. Dir. clin. stats. Fred Hutchinson Cancer Rsch. Ctr., Seattle, 1974-86; dir. stats. and probability NSF, Washington, 1986-88; prof. stats. The Am. U., Washington, 1988—, chair dept. math. and stats., 1993-95; mem. of corp. Nat. Inst. Statis. Scis., Research Triangle Park, N.C., 1990—. Editor Multiple Stats. Integration, 1991, Adaptive Designs, 1995. Mem. leadership com. Nat. Abortion Rights Action League, Washington, 1990—, Emily's List, 1993—, Nat. Mus. for Women in the Arts, 1996—; grant reviewer AAUW, NSF, NIH, Nat. Security Agy.; faculty sponsor Students Against Sexual Violence. USPHS fellow, 1969-71; Nat. Cancer Inst. grantee, 1975-86, NSF grantee, 1989-90, 96-2001, Am. Math. Soc./Inst. of Math. Stats./Soc. of Indsl. Applied Math. grantee, 1989, 92, EPA grantee, 1994—. Fellow AAAS (mem. nom. com.), Inst. Math. Stats., Am. Statis. Assn. (chair coun. sects. 1994), World Acad. Art & Sci., Washington Acad. Sci.; mem. AAUW, Caucus for Women in Stats., Internat. Stats. Inst., Biometric Soc., Internat. Assn. for Statis. Computing, Assn. Women in Math., Washington Statis. Soc. Democrat. Presbyterian. Office: Am U Dept Math and Stats 4400 Massachusetts Ave NW Washington DC 20016-8050

FLOWE, CAROL CONNOR, lawyer; b. Owensboro, Ky., Jan. 3, 1950; d. Marvin C. Connor and Ethel Marie (Thorn) Smith; children: Samantha Kathleen, Andrew Benjamin. BME magna cum laude, Murray State U., 1972; JD summa cum laude, Ind. U., 1976. Bar: Ohio 1977, D.C. 1981, U.S. Dist. Ct. (so. dist.) Ohio 1977, U.S. Dist. Ct. Md. 1983, U.S. Dist. Ct. D.C. 1981, U.S. Supreme Ct. 1987, U.S. Ct. Appeals (2d, 4th, 5th, 7th and D.C. cirs.). Assoc. Baker & Hostetler, Columbus, Ohio, 1976-80, Arent Fox Kintner Plotkin & Kahn, Washington, 1980-87; deputy gen. counsel Pension Benefit Guaranty Corp., Washington, 1987-89, gen. counsel, 1989-95; ptnr. Arent, Fox, Kintner, Plotkin & Kahn, 1995—. Co-author: EEO Handbook, 1986. Trustee, The Newport Schs., Kensington, Md., 1986-88. Mem. ABA, D.C. Bar Assn., Order of Coif, Alpha Chi, Phi Alpha Delta. Home: 8608 Aqueduct Rd Potomac MD 20854-6249 Office: Arent Fox Kintner Plotkin & Kahn 1050 Connecticut Ave NW Washington DC 20036-5339

FLOWER, JEAN FRANCES, art educator; b. Schenectady, N.Y., Apr. 12, 1936; d. Francis Tunis and Marjorie (Colcord) Fort; m. Wesley Allen Flower, Aug. 23, 1958; children: Kimberly Lynn, Kristina Kathleen. BA, Syracuse U., 1958; BFA cum laude, Western Mich. U., 1984, MFA magne cum laude, 1989. Free-lance artist, 1981-86; tech. grad. asst. Western Mich. U., Kalamazoo, 1988, grad. asst. early mgmt., 1989, instr. art, 1989-93; instr. art Kalamazoo Inst. Art, 1993—. One-woman shows include Peoples Ch., Kalamazoo, Mich., 1991, Kalamazoo Area Art Show, 1992, 94 95, Nat. Art Show, Dallas, 1993, Libr., Parchment, Mich., 1993, EAA Aviation Internat. Art Show, 1992, 95; permanent works include murals Kalamazoo Valley Pub. Mus., 1995. Pres., mem. Anna Cir. 1st United Meth. Ch., Kalamazoo, 1980—, mem. communications commn., 1994—, sec.-treas. Airward, Plainwell, Mich., 1986—. Mem. Am. Assn. Aviation Artists, Plainwell Pilots Assn., Kalamazoo Aviatrix Assn. (past v.p.). Home and Studio: 8745 Marsh Rd Plainwell MI 49080-8818

FLOWERS, ANNA, writer; b. Dorchester County, Md., Oct. 8, 1930; d. Wilbur and Mildred Irene (Tall) F.; m. David Clinton Brotemarkle, June 25, 1955; children: Belle Brotemarkle Turner, Benjamin David. Student, U. Md., 1948-49, Washington Coll., Chestertown, Md., 1949-50, Trenton State U., 1962-63, U. Nebr., 1966-68. Reporter Sunday Star Newspaper, Wilmington, Del., 1950-51, State News Bur., Sta. WERE, Cleve., 1951-52; announcer/reporter Sta. WCEM, Cambridge, Md., 1952-53; art dir., writer Skipper Mag., Annapolis, Md., 1953-55; editor The Supply Line, Guam, 1956-57; family editor Base Newspaper, Anderson AFB, Guam, 1957-58; editor, prodr. mags. McGuire AFB, Wrightstown, N.J., 1962-63, Offutt AFB, Omaha, 1967-68, March AFB, Riverside, Calif., 1969-70, Greenhill Country Club, Salisbury, Md., 1975-77. Editor bicentennial Patriot, 1976; author: Blind Fury, 1993, Bound To Die, 1995. Performer mus. rev. March AFB, 1969; show dir. Cornhusker Mus. Rev., Offutt AFB, 1971; dir. The Ward Found., Salisbury, 1974; mem. Wicomico Bicentennial Com., Salisbury, 1975-76. Mem. Mystery Writers of Am. (Fla. chpt. bd. dirs. 1996—), Sisters-In-Crime, Nat. League Am. Penwomen (membership chmn. Fla. chpt. 1995).

FLOWERS, CYNTHIA, investment company executive; b. N.Y.C., May 29, 1951; d. Bernard and Pearl (Davis) Heller; m. Robert Flowers, June 3, 1973; children: Perry, Lindsey. BS summa cum laude, Boston U., 1973; MBA with honors, NYU, 1976. Sr. mgr. portfolios Citibank NA, N.Y.C., 1973-82; v.p. Nat. Securities Corp., N.Y.C., 1982-87; pres. Stillrock Mgmt. Inc., N.Y.C., 1987-90; founder, pres. Flowers Capital Mgmt. Inc., N.Y.C., 1990—. Mem. N.Y. Soc. Security Analysts, Westside Tennis Club, Beta Gamma Sigma. Office: Flowers Capital Mgmt Inc 97 Groton St Forest Hills NY 11375-5956

FLOWERS, JUDITH ANN, marketing and public relations director; b. Oxford, Miss., Feb. 21, 1944; d. Woodrow Coleman and Ola Marie (Harding) Haynes; m. Sayles L. Brown Jr., Apr. 20, 1963 (div. Apr. 1974); children: Sayles L. III, Gregory A., Matthew C., Stephen W.; m. Taylor Graydon Flowers Jr., Apr. 27, 1979. Grad. high sch., Clarksdale, Miss. Office mgr. The KBH Corp., Clarksdale, 1964-69; office mgr., estimator Willis & Ellis Constrn., Clarksdale, 1969-75; with advt. prodn. Farm Press Pub., Clarksdale, 1975-79, advt. mgr., 1979-86, dir. advt. svcs., 1986-93; dir. mktg. and pub. rels. Cotton Club Casino, Greenville, Miss., 1992-95; dir. spl. projects C. of C., Clarksdale, Miss., 1996—. Counselor County Youth Ct., Clarksdale, 1985—; sec. Keep Clarksdale Beautiful, 1990-92; bd. dirs. Delta Arts Coun., 1994-95, Miss. Tourism Promotion Assn., 1996—, Miss. Delta Arts Coun., 1996—; co-chair Tennessee Williams Festival, 1996. Mem. NAFE, Bus. and Profl. Women (corr. sec. 1987-88, 2d v.p. 1988-89, 1st v.p. 1989-90, pres. 1992-93), Agri-Women Am., Nat. Agri-Mktg. Assn. (v.p. mid-south chpt. 1989-90, pres. 1990-91, nat. dir. 1991-93), Clarksdale C. of C. (chmn. agri-bus. commn. 1989-92, bd. dirs. 1989-92), Greenville Hospitality Assn. (bd. dirs. 1993-95), So. Garden History Soc. (bd. dirs. 1992-95), The Garden Conservancy (city beatification 1996—). Republican. Baptist. Home: PO Box 3126 Dublin MS 38739-0126 Office: C of C PO Box 160 Clarksdale MS 38614

FLOWERS, VIRGINIA ANNE, academic administrator emerita; b. Dothan, Ala., Aug. 29, 1928; d. Kyrie Neal and Annie Laurie (Stewart) F. BA, Fla. State U., 1949; MEd, Auburn U., 1958; EdD, Duke U., 1963. Teaching asst. Duke U., Durham, N.C., 1963; elem. and secondary sch. tchr., adminstr. Dothan and Dalton, Ga., 1949-61; asst. prof., then prof. edn., head dept. Columbia (S.C.) Coll., 1963-68, assoc. dean, then dean, 1969-72; prof. edn. Va. Commonwealth U., 1968-69; teaching asst. Duke U., 1963; assoc. dean, asst. provost, acting dean, vice provost Trinity Coll. Arts and Scis., Duke U., 1972-74, prof. edn., chmn. dept., asst. provost ednl. program devel., 1974-80; dean Sch. Edn., Ga. So. Coll., Statesboro, 1980-85; asst. vice chancellor acad. affairs Univ. System of Ga., Atlanta, 1985-88, vice chancellor, 1988-90, vice chancellor emerita, 1990—; ind. ednl. cons. Co-author: Law and Pupil Control, 1964, Readings in Survival in Today's Society, 2 vols, 1978; editorial bd.: Jour. Tchr. Edn, 1980-82, Ednl. Gerontology, 1979—; contbr. articles to profl. jours. Bd. dirs., mem. exec. com. Learning Inst. N.C., 1976-80; mem. bd. visitors Charleston So. U., 1992-93; adv. trustee Queens Coll., Charlotte, N.C., 1976-78; vice chmn. continuing commn. on study of black colls. related to United Meth. Ch., 1973-76. Delta Kappa Gamma scholar Duke U., 1963, State of Fla. scholar Fla. State U., 1949. Mem. NEA, Am. Ednl. Rsch. Assn., So. Assn. Colls. and Schs. (mem. commn. on colls.), Am. Assn. Higher Edn., Am. Assn. Colls. of Tchr. Edn. (pres. 1983-84, bd. dirs., mem. exec. com. 1979-84), Nat. Orgn. Legal Problems in Edn., Kappa Delta Pi, Phi Delta Kappa. Home and Office: PO Box 1603 Marianna FL 32447-5603

FLOYD, SUSAN KEMPTON, artist; b. Miami, Fla., Apr. 3, 1956; d. Louis Thomas and Jane Fulton (Harney) Kempton; m. William Robert Floyd, Aug. 8, 1945. AA, Edison C.C., 1976; BFA, Fla. State U., 1978, MFA, 1980. Represented in permanent collection of Morris Mus. of Art; one-woman show includes Tallahassee City Hall, 1994. Recipient fellowship grant in visual art painting State of Fla. Divsn. Cultural Affairs, 1995-96. Office: PO Box 2 Lamont FL 32344

FLOYD-TENIYA, KATHLEEN, business services executive; b. Berwyn, Ill., June 23, 1953; d. David James and Phyllis L. (Lyons) Floyd; m. Robert Don Teniya, June 20, 1982 (div. Oct. 1991); 1 child: James David. Cert. credit and fin. analyst, lic. realtor, Ill. Indsl. specialist Technicon Instrument Corp., Elmhurst, Ill., 1971-74, service contract adminstr., 1974-76; asst. to pres. Elmed, Inc., Addison, Ill., 1976-77; credit rep. mgr. Memorex Corp., Lombard, Ill., 1977-79; nat. sales rep. Midcontinent Adjustment Co., Glenview, Ill., 1979-83, asst. v.p. sales, 1983-86; pres., chief exec. officer, (Inteletek) Innovative Telemktg. Techniques Inc., Itasca, Ill., 1986—. Newspaper editor, publicity chmn. Dupage County chpt. Young Ams. for Freedom, 1969-70, pres.; mem. bd. edn. Trinity Luth. Sch., Lombard, Ill, 1989—; appointed mem. legal and fin., citizen advisor Village Bd., Bloomingdale, Ill., 1989—. Mem. Nat. Assn. Female Execs., Am. Soc. Profl. and Exec. Women. Lutheran. Clubs: Lombard Women's Rep., Ill. Fedn. Rep. Women. Home: 263 Evergreen Ln Bloomingdale IL 60108-1815 Office: Inteletek Innovative Telemktg Techniques Inc PO Box 163 Itasca IL 60143-0163

FLUCK, MICHELE M(ARGUERITE), biology educator; b. Geneva, Aug. 5, 1940; came to U.S., 1972; d. Wilhelm and Henriette Alice (Delaloye) F. MS, U. Geneva, 1964, 66, PhD, 1972. Rsch. assoc. N.Y. Pub. Health Rsch. Inst., N.Y.C., 1972-73; instr. Harvard Med. Sch., Boston, 1973-78, asst. prof., 1978-79; assoc. prof. Mich. State U., East Lansing, 1979-86, prof., 1986-90, disting. prof., 1990—. Contbr. articles to profl. jours. Recipient Young Investigator's award, Nat. Cancer Inst.; grantee Nat. Cancer Inst., 1979—, Am. Cancer Soc. grantee, 1987—. Fellow Leukemia Soc. Am. (scholar 1979-85); mem. AAAS, Am. Assn. virologists. Office: Mich State U Microbiology Dept Giltner Hall East Lansing MI 48824-1101

FLUGGER, PENELOPE ANN, banker; b. Chgo., June 26, 1942; d. William and Florence Bernadette (Brongiel) Grabos; B.S., U. Ill., 1964; M.B.A., Baruch Coll., 1971; CPA, N.Y., Ill.; m. Robert John Flugger, July 11, 1970. Sr. mgr. Price Waterhouse Co., N.Y.C., 1964-75; with Morgan Guaranty Trust Co., 1975—, auditor, 1982-94, sr. v.p., 1982-94, mng. dir., 1994—; trustee Coun. Execs. in Econs., 1996; active N.Y.C. Audit Com., Fin. Exec. Inst., Coun. for Ethics in Econs. Mem. AICPAs, Inst. Mgmt. Accts., Fin. Execs. Inst., N.Y. State Soc. CPAs, Ill. State Soc. CPAs. Office: JP Morgan & Co 60 Wall St New York NY 10005-2807

FLYNN, BARBARA LOIS, developer; b. Hartford, Conn., May 5, 1937; d. Owen Leo and Grayce Josephine (Kearns) Quinn; m. Daniel Francis Flynn, June 12, 1965; children: Daniel Cauley, Garrett Scott, Laura Diane. BA, Conn. Coll., 1959; MS in Mgmt., Rensselaer Poly. Inst., 1987. Marketer The Insider's Guide to Greater Hartford, 1985-88, An Insider's Guide to Teenage Tennis, 1985-88; grants coord. Hartford Coll. Women, 1988-89; dir. devel. Open Hearth Assn., Hartford, 1989—; class agt. Conn. Coll. for Women; decade chmn. Loomis Chaffee Sch.; solicitor Major Grants for Youth Tennis, 1989; mem. auction com. New Eng. Lawn Tennis Assn., 1989. Co-author: The Insider's Guide to Greater Hartford, 1985, The Insider's Guide to Teenage Tennis, 1986. Bd. dirs. Women's Aux. of the Inst. of the Living, Hartford, 1980-86; vol. New England Lawn Tennis Assn., 1983-90, dir., 1985-90; dir. vols. Sectional Tennis Championship, 1985-86, tournament dir., 1986-88; sec., mem. exec. com. Hartford Golf Club, 1988-91; dir. Riverfront Recapture, Inc., 1990—; mem. United Way Cabinet, 1991-92; corporator The Inst. of Living, 1992—; elector Wadsworth Atheneum, 1993—. Home: 237 Westmont West Hartford CT 06117 Office: Open Hearth Assn 437 Sheldon St Hartford CT 06106

FLYNN, CAROL, state legislator; b. Aug. 7, 1933; m. Richard L. Flynn; 2 children. Mem. Minn. State Senate, 1990—. Mem. Democratic Farm Labor Party. Office: Minn State Senate State Capital Building Saint Paul MN 55155-1606*

FLYNN, CHERYL DIXON, accountant; b. Hartsville, S.C., Feb. 3, 1952; d. J. Leslie and Peggy E. Dixon; m. Mark A. Thompson, Aug. 17, 1974 (div. 1987); m. Daniel W. Flynn, Apr. 13, 1991; stepchildren: Kimberly, Chris. BS in Acctg., Furman U., 1992. CPA, S.C. Adminstrv. asst. Yeargin Properties, Inc., Greenville, S.C., 1976-89; staff acct. Crisp, Hughes & Assoc., Greenville, 1989-93, Farris, Cooke & Assoc., Charlotte, N.C., 1993-94, Hughes, Boan & Assoc., Columbia, S.C., 1994-95, Ouzts, Ouzts & Varn, PC, Columbia, 1995—. Mem. AAUW, AICPA, S.C. Assn. CPAs, Alpha Sigma Lambda. Presbyterian. Home: 24 Polo Ridge Cir Columbia SC 29223 Office: Ouzts Ouzts & Varn PC 115 Atrium Way Ste 110 Columbia SC 29223

FLYNN, DONNA STEELE, legislative staff director; b. Washington, Sept. 2, 1953. BS, U. Md., 1985; JD, George Mason U., 1991. Personal sec. Rep. Bill Archer, 1977-84, legis. dir., tax counsel, 1988—; legis. asst. Patton, Boggs & Blow, 1984-88, now dir. oversight com. Office: 1136 Longworth House Office Bldg Washington DC 20515*

FLYNN, ELIZABETH ANNE, advertising and public relations company executive; b. Washington, Aug. 21, 1951; d. John William and Elizabeth Goodwin (Mahoney) F. AA, Montgomery Coll., Rockville, Md., 1972; BS in Journalism, U. Md., 1976; postgrad. San Diego State U., 1976. Writer, researcher, Sea World, Inc., San Diego, 1977-79; sr. writer Lane & Huff Advt., San Diego, 1979-80; account exec. Kaufman, Lansky, Baker Advt., San Diego, 1980-82; mng. dir. Excelsior Enterprises, Beverly Hills, Calif., 1983-84; sr. account exec. Berkhemer & Kline, Inc., L.A., 1985; pres. Flynn Advt. & Pub. Rels., L.A., 1985—; cons. Coca-Cola Bottling Co. L.A., 1982-84; U.S. corr. Aeronovum mag., 1990—; v.p. mktg. Graffiti Prevention Systems, L.A., 1990-91; dir. new bus. devel. BBDO Hispanica, L.A., 1992-93; pub. rels. dir. Regional Organ Procurement Agy. So. Calif., L.A., 1994—. Bd. dirs. Friends of Reconstructive Surgery, Beverly Hills, 1983-89, Nat. Kidney Found., 1994, So. Calif. Coalition on Donation, 1994—, also mem. steering com., 1995-97; sec. Nat. Coun. Local Coalitions, 1995—; comms.

com. Assn. Organ Procurement Orgns. Address: Flynn Advt & Pub Rels 1440 Reeves St Apt 104 Los Angeles CA 90035-2950

FLYNN, FAYE WILLIAMS, elementary school educator; b. Wellington, Tex., Sept. 13, 1913; d. Benjamin Franklin and Willie (Tibbets) Williams; m. Alton Lavoy Flynn Sr., Sept. 25, 1934 (dec. 1940); children: Alton Lavoy Jr., Nelda Louise Flynn Willis. Student, Tex. Women's U., 1933-34; BA, West Tex. State U., 1943, cert. in lang. and learning, 1973. Tchr. 1st and 2d grades Hopkins Elem. Sch., Pampa, Tex., 1943-47; tchr. 1st grade Sam Houston Elem. Sch., Pampa, 1947-58; resource tchr. 1st grade Sanborn Elem. Sch., Amarillo, Tex., 1960-62; tchr. 1st grade Cononado Elem. Sch., Amarillo, 1962-70; reading specialist Avondale Elem. Sch., Amarillo, 1970-76; tchr. 2d grade Whittier Elem. Sch., Amarillo, 1976-78, ret., 1978. Mem. AAUW (leader internat. rels. interest group Amarillo chpt. 1991-92), Amarillo Ret. Tchrs. Assn., Panhandle Plains Hist. Soc., Tex. Ret. Tchrs. Assn., Amarillo Fedn. Women's Club, Amarillo Internat. Club, Amarillo Art League (program dir. 1989-91). Democrat. Methodist. Home: 1111 Buena Vista St Amarillo TX 79106-4310

FLYNN, JOAN MAYHEW, librarian; b. Mpls., Sept. 13, 1927; d. Oscar Koehler and Mabel Victoria (Stein) Mayhew; m. Elliot Colter Dick, Jr., Aug. 19, 1950 (div. May 1966); children: Emily Diane Dick Tuttle, Elliot Mayhew Dick; m. Paul James Flynn, Nov. 4, 1967. BMus, U. Minn., 1950; MLS, U. Hawaii, 1972, cert. in advanced libr. and info. studies, 1986. Circulation clk., 1972-75, reference libr., 1975-85; dir. acad. support svcs., head Sullivan Libr. Chaminade U. of Honolulu, 1986—; mem. Interlibr. Cooperation Coun., 1990, 91; supr. vocal music Forest Lake (Minn.) Pub. Schs. Asst. dir. races Norman Tamanaha Meml., 1982, dir. 1983; bd. dirs. Hawaii Kai Fun Runners. Mem. ALA, Hawaii Libr. Assn., MidPac Road Runners Assn. (bd. dirs.), Hawaii Masters Track Club, Beta Phi Mu, Pi Lambda Theta, Sigma Alpha Iota. Home: 130 Opihikao Way Honolulu HI 96825-1125 Office: Chaminade U 3140 Waialae Ave Honolulu HI 96816-1510

FLYNN, MARIE COSGROVE, portfolio manager; b. Honolulu, Jan. 1, 1945; d. John Aloysius and Emeline Frances Cosgrove; m. John Thomas Flynn, Jr., June 3, 1968; children: Jamie Marie, Jacqueline Elizabeth. BA., Trinity Coll., 1966. CFP. Analyst U.S. Govt., Washington, 1967-70; coord. nat. reading coun. F.X. Doherty Assocs., N.Y.C., 1970-71; security analyst Corinthian Capital Co., N.Y.C., 1971-73; portfolio mgr. Clark Mgmt. Co., Inc., N.Y.C., 1973-78; v.p., sr. portfolio mgr. Lexington Mgmt. Corp., Saddle Brook, N.J., 1978-96; pres. Corinthian Capital Mgmt. Co., Inc., Morristown, N.J., 1996—. Elected mem. Somerset County Rep. Com., 1994—, Bernardsville (N.J.) Environ. Commn., 1996—, Treas Bernardsville Repulblican com., 1996, Bernardsville Planning bd., 1996, bd. dir First call for help; bd. trustees N.J. Pension and Annuity Fund, 1996—, N.J. Retirement Fund TPAF. Mem. Fin. Analysts Fedn., Inst. Chartered Fin. Analysts, Fin. Women's Assn., N.Y. Soc. Security Analysts, Home: 50 Pickle Brook Rd Bernardsville NJ 07924-1909 Office: N Tower 14th Fl 89 Headquarters Plz Morristown NJ 07960

FLYNN, PAMELA, artist, educator; b. Bellmore, N.Y., Dec. 24, 1948; d. Robert S. and Amalie M. (Debler) Williams; m. Dennis M. Flynn, Aug. 7, 1971; children: Matthew, Amalie. BA, Monmouth U., West Long Branch, N.J., 1971; MA, Kean Coll, Union, N.J., 1995; MFA, Jersey City (N.J.) State Coll., 1996. Tchr. Freehold (N.J.) Regional Continuing Edn., 1978-95, St. Leo the Great Sch., Lincroft, N.J., 1985—; adj. instr. Jersey City State Coll., 1996—, Holy Family Coll., Phila., 1996—. Solo exhbns. include Monmouth U., 1995, Abney Gallery, N.Y.C., 1994, Art Space, Jersey City State Coll., 1996; group shows include Aijira Gallery, Newark, N.J., 1994, 5th Biennial Art Exhibit N.J. State Mus., Newark, 1985, 4th Biennial Art Exhibit N.J. State Mus., Trenton, 1983. Mem. Coll. Art Assn., Phi Kappa Phi. Home: 13 Dogwood Ln Freehold NJ 07728

FLYNN, PATRICIA MARIE, economics educator; b. Lynn, Mass.. BA in Econs., Emmanuel Coll., 1972; MA in Econs., Boston U., 1973, PhD in Econs., 1980. Rsch. assoc. Inst. for Employment Policy, Boston U., 1975-83; prof. econs. Bentley Coll., Waltham, Mass., 1976—; sr. rsch. fellow New Eng. Bd. Higher Edn., Boston, 1980-82; vis. sch. Fed. Res. Bd., Boston, 1983-84; exec. dir. Inst. for Rsch. & Faculty Devel., Bentley Coll., Waltham, 1986-90; assoc. dean faculty Bentley Coll., Waltham, Mass., 1991-92, dean grad. sch., 1992—; mem. faculty Inst. in Employment and Tng. Adminstrn. Harvard U., Cambridge, Mass., summers, 1979-81; cons. U. Mo., Columbia, 1983-84, First Security Svcs. Corp., Boston, 1985, Devel. Alternatives, Inc., Jakarta, Indonesia, summer, 1987, ABT Assocs., Cambridge, 1987-89; bd. dirs. Fed. Savs. Bank, Waltham, Mass. Author: Technology Life Cycles and Human Resources, 1993; co-author: Turbulence in the American Workplace, 1991; contbr. articles to profl. jours. Adv. panel mem. Office Tech. Assessment, U.S. Congress, Washington, 1989-91; accreditation team mem. New Eng. Assn. Schs. and Colls., 1985—; mem. Newton (Mass.) Econ. Devel. Commn., 1984-87. Grantee Dept. Labor, 1982-84, 88-89, Nat. Inst. Edn., 1982-83, NSF, 1990-93, Sloan Found., 1995—; recipient Gregory H. Adamian award for tchg. excellence Bentley Coll., 1986, Scholar of Yr., 1991. Mem. Am. Econ. Assn., Com. on the Status of Women in Econs. Professions, The Boston Club, The Boston Econ. Club. Office: Bentley Coll 175 Forest St Waltham MA 02154-4713

FLYNN, SHERYL MAUREEN, physical therapist; b. Miami, Fla., Jan. 17, 1967; d. William Kevin and Jayne LaBruce (Sherrill) F. AS, Tallahassee C.C., 1989; BS in Phys. Therapy, NYU, 1991. Lic. phys. therapist, N.Y. Phys. therapist N.Y.C. Bd. of Edn., 1991-92, Vis. Nurses Svc., N.Y.C., 1991-92; tchr. asst. NYU, 1992-93; phys. therapist Beth Israel Med. Ctr., NYC, 1992-—; mentor Beth Israel Mentor Program, 1994. Recipient Ida Bedman Svc./Leadership award NYU, 1990,1991, Arthur J. Nelson Electrotherapy award, 1991. Mem. Am. Phys. Therapy Assn., Phi Theta Kappa. Office: Beth Israel Medical Center 16th and 1st Ave New York NY 10003

FOARD, SUSAN LEE, editor; b. Asheville, N.C., Aug. 1, 1938; d. Carson Cowan and Anne (Brown) F. A.B., Salem Coll., 1960; M.A., William and Mary Coll., 1966. Asst. editor Inst. Early Am. Hist. and Culture, Williamsburg, Va., 1961-66; asso. editor Inst. Early Am. Hist. and Culture, 1966; editor U. Press of Va., Charlottesville, 1966—. Mem. Women Faculty and Profl. Assn. (U. Va.), Women in Scholarly Publishing of AAUP. Office: PO Box 3608 University Sta Charlottesville VA 22903-0608

FOCH, NINA, actress, creative consultant, educator; b. Leyden, The Netherlands, Apr. 20, 1924; came to U.S. 1927; d. Dirk and Consuelo (Flowerton) F.; m. James Lipton, June 6, 1954; m. Dennis de Brito, Nov. 27, 1959; 1 child, Dirk de Brito; m. Michael Dewell, Oct. 31, 1967 (div.). Grad., Lincoln Sch., 1939; studies with Stella Adler. Adj. prof. drama U. So. Calif., 1966-68, 78-80, adj. prof. film, 1987—; creative cons. to dirs., writers, prodrs. of all media; artist-in-residence U. N.C., 1966, Ohio State U., 1967, Calif. Inst. Tech., 1969-70; mem. sr. faculty Am. Film Inst., 1974-77; founder, tchr. Nina Foch Studio, Hollywood, Calif., 1973—; founder, actress Los Angeles Theatre Group, 1960-65; bd. dirs. Nat. Repertory Theatre, 1967-75. Motion picture appearances include Nine Girls, 1944, Return of the Vampire, 1944, Shadows in the Night, 1944, Cry of the Werewolf, 1944, Escape in the Fog, 1945, A Song to Remember, 1945, My Name Is Julia Ross, 1945, I Love a Mystery, 1945, Johnny O'Clock, 1947, The Guilt of Janet Ames, 1947, The Dark Past, 1948, The Undercover Man, 1949, Johnny Allegro, 1949, An American in Paris, 1951, Scaramouche, 1952, Young Man with Ideas, 1952, Sombrero, 1953, Fast Company, 1953, Executive Suite, 1954 (Oscar award nominee), Four Guns to the Border, 1954, You're Never Too Young, 1955, Illegal, 1955, The Ten Commandments, 1956, Three Brave Men, 1957, Cash McCall, 1959, Spartacus, 1960, Such Good Friends, 1971, Salty, 1973, Mahogany, 1976, Jennifer, 1978, Rich and Famous, 1981, Skin Deep, 1988, Sliver, 1993, Morning Glory, 1993, 'Til There Was You, 1996; appeared in Broadway plays including John Loves Mary, 1947, Twelfth Night, 1949, A Phoenix Too Frequent, 1950, King Lear, 1950, Second String, 1960; appeared with Am. Shakespeare Festival in Taming of the Shrew, Measure for Measure, 1956, San Francisco Ballet and Opera in The Seven Deadly Sins, 1966; also many regional theater appearances including Seattle Repertory Theatre (All Over, 1972 and The Seagull, 1973); actress on TV, 1947—, including Playhouse 90, Studio One, Pulitzer Playhouse, Playwrights 56, Producers Showcase, Lou Grant (Emmy nominee 1980), Mike Hammer; series star: Shadow Chasers, 1985, War and Remembrance, 1988, LA Law, 1990, Hunter, 1990, Dear John, 1990, 91, Tales of the City, 1993; many other series, network spls. and TV films; TV panelist and guest on The Dinah Shore Show, Merv Griffin Show, The Today Show, Dick Cavett, The Tonight Show; TV moderator: Let's Take Sides, 1957-59; assoc. dir. (film) The Diary of Anne Frank, 1959; dir. (nat. tour and on-Broadway) Tonight at 8:30, 1966-67; assoc. producer re-opening of Ford's Theatre, Washington, 1968. Hon. chmn. Los Angeles chpt. Am. Cancer Soc., 1970. Recipient Film Daily award, 1949, 53. Mem. AAUP, Acad. Motion Picture Arts and Scis. (co-chair exec. com. fgn. film award, membership com.), Hollywood Acad. TV Arts and Scis. (bd. govs. 1976-77). Office: PO Box 1884 Beverly Hills CA 90213-1884

FODREA, CAROLYN WROBEL, educational researcher, publisher, consultant; b. Hammond, Ind., Feb. 1, 1943; d. Stanley Jacob and Margaret Caroline (Stupeck) Wrobel; m. Howard Frederick Fodrea, June 17, 1967 (div. Jan. 1987); children: Gregory Kirk, Lynn Renee. BA in Elem. Edn., Purdue U., 1966; MA in Edn., U. Chgo., 1973; postgrad., U. Colo., Denver, 1986-87. Cert. elem. tchr., Ind., Ill. Tchr. various schs., Ind., Colo., 1966-87; founder, supr., clinician Reading Clinic, Children's Hosp., Denver, 1969-73; pvt. practice in reading rsch. clinic Denver, 1973-87, Deerfield, Ill., 1973—; creator of pilot presch.-kindergarten lang. devel. program Gary, Ind. Diocese Schs., 1987—, therapist lang. and reading disabilities, 1987—; pvt. practice Reading Clinic, Highland, Ind., 1987—, Deerfield, Ill., 1988—; founder Ctr. for Rsch. in Ednl. Ecology, Deerfield, Ill., 1989—; conducted Lang. Devel. Workshop, Gary, Ind. 1988; pres. Lang. Comm. Strategies for the 21st Century Corp. Cons. Firm; tchr. adult basic edn. Dawson Tech. Sch., 1990, Coll. Lake County, 1991, Prairie State Coll., 1991—, Chgo. City Colls., 1991, R.J. Daley Coll., 1991, Coll. DuPage, 1991—; condr. adult basic edn. workshops for Coll. of DuPage, R.J. Daley Coll., 1992, Ill. Lang. Devel. Literacy Program; tchr. Korean English Lang. Inst., Chgo., 1996. Author: Language Development Program, 1985, Presch. Kindergarten Lang. Devel. Program, 1988, A Multi-Sensory Stimulation Program for the Premature Baby in Its Incubator to Reduce Medical Costs and Academic Failure, 1986, Predicting At-Risk Babies for First Grade Reading Failure Before Birth, Oral Language Development Program, Grades 1 to Adult, 1988, 92; editor, pub.: ESL For Native Spanish Speakers, 1996, ESL for Native Korean Speakers, 1996. Active Graland Country Day Sch., Denver, 1981-83, N.W. Ind. Children's Chorale, 1988—. Mem. NEA, Am. Ednl. Rsch. Assn., Internat. Reading Assn., Am. Coun. for Children with Learning Disabilities, Assn. for Childhood Edn. Internat., Colo. Assn. for Edn. of Young Children, Infant Stimulation Edn. Assn., AAUW, NAFE, Nat. Assn. for Women in Career-North Shore, Art Inst. Chgo., Smithsonian Instn., Cousteau Soc., U. Chgo. Alumni Club (Chgo. area ann. fund, Pres. fund com. 1988—, numerous positions Denver area chpt. 1974-87). Roman Catholic. Office: Lang Comm Strategy 280 Crestwood Village Northfield IL 60093-3402

FOEGE, ROSE ANN SCUDIERO, human resources professional; b. Bklyn., Aug. 22, 1941; d. Thomas Edward and Catherine Mary (Demarsico) Scudiero; m. William Henry Foege, Apr. 19, 1975. BA, Queens Coll., 1973; MS cum laude, Iona Coll., 1981. Cert. Am. Registry Radiologic Technologists. X-ray technician St. Clare's Hosp., N.Y.C., 196-61; supr. x-ray N.Y. Internat. Longshoremen's Assn. Med. Ctr., N.Y.C., 1960-67, Life Extension Inst., N.Y.C., 1967-73; radiologic technologist Exxon Corp., N.Y.C., 1973-81, coordinator systems and records, 1981-86; staff human resources specialist Exxon Rsch. & Engrs., Linden, N.J., 1986-93; sect. supr. human resources Exxon Chem. Co., Linden, N.J., 1994—. Pres. Wykagyl Neighborhood Assn., New Rochelle, N.Y. Mem. NAFE, Soc. Human Resources Mgmt., Am. Mgmt. Assn., Am. Acad. Med. Adminstr., Am. Soc. Radiologic Technologists, Mensa, Iona Coll. Alumni Assn., Iona Coll. Pres.'s Club. Home: 149 Wykagyl Ter New Rochelle NY 10804-3124 Office: Exxon Chem Co Park and Brunswick Area Linden NJ 07036

FOISY, RENÉE THÉRÈSE, financial analyst; b. Nashville, Sept. 5, 1966; d. Hector Bernard and Joanne Theresa (Fleury) F. AB in French Lit., Dartmouth Coll., 1988; postgrad., U. Paris V, 1988-89; MBA, So. Meth. U., 1994, postgrad., 1995-96. English asst. Lycée Victor Duruy, Paris, 1988-89; tchr. French and Spanish, Greenhill Sch., Dallas, 1989-91; tchr. French, Spanish and German, Hurst Tex.)-Euless-Bedford Ind. Sch. Dist., 1992; grad. asst. So. Meth. U., Dallas, 1992; fin. analyst AMR Corp., Dallas-Fort Worth Airport, 1994-95, sr. fin. analyst corp. devel., 1995-96, assoc. treasury, 1996—. Vol. Girls' Inc. Met. Dallas, 1994—. Dean's scholar Southern Meth. U., 1992-94, Tate scholar, 1993-94, Tex. KT scholar, 1993-94. Mem. AMR Mgmt. Club, Dallas Sports and Social Club, Dartmouth Club Dallas (interviewer 1989—), Dallas-Ft. Worth Cox Alumni Club (v.p. 1994-96), AA Running Club. Unitarian.

FOK, AGNES KWAN, cell biologist, educator; b. Hong Kong, Dec. 11, 1940; came to U.S., 1962; d. Sun and Yau (Ng) Kwan; m. Fok, June 8, 1965; children: Licie Chiu-Jane, Edna Chiu-Joan. BA in Chemistry, U. Great Falls, 1965; MS in Plant Nutrition and Biochemistry, Utah State U., 1966; PhD in Biochemistry, U. Tex., Austin, 1971. Asst. rsch. prof. pathology U. Hawaii, 1973-74; Ford Found. postdoctoral fellow, anatomy dept. U. Hawaii, Honolulu, 1975, asst. rsch. prof. Pacific Biomed. Rsch. Ctr., 1975-82, assoc. rsch. prof., 1982-88, assoc. rsch. prof. biology program, 1985, rsch. prof., 1988-96, grad. faculty, dept. microbiology, 1977—; dir. biology program Pacific Biomed. Rsch. Ctr., 1994-96; prof., dir. biology program U. Hawaii, Honolulu, 1006—. Contbr. articles to profl. jours. Mem. Am. Soc. for Cell Biology, Soc. for Protozoologists, Sigma Xi (treas. Hawaii chpt. 1979—). Office: U Hawaii Biology Program Honolulu HI 96822

FOLCH-PI, WILLA BABCOCK, romance language educator; b. Milw., June 22, 1925; d. Charles Whitney and Helen Gertrude (Robinson) Babcock; m. Jordi Folch-Pi, June 23, 1945 (dec. Oct. 1979); children: Raphael, Diana, Frederic. BA, Barnard Coll., 1945; MA, Harvard U., 1963, PhD, 1969. Lectr. in English Pembroke, Brown U., Providence, 1945-46; teaching fellow Harvard U., Cambridge, Mass., 1968-69; curator of manuscripts Harvard Med. Sch., Boston, 1971-75; assoc. acad. dean, asst. prof. romance langs. Tufts U., Medford, Mass., 1975-85, assoc. dean, asst. prof. emerita, 1985—; vis. lectr. Mass. Inst. Tech., Cambridge, fall 1973; seminar lectr. Radcliffe U., fall 1975; coord. program abroad Tufts U., 1975-82, prelaw advisor, 1975-85. Author rsch. papers in field. Pres. Sandwich Woman's Club, Center Sandwich, N.H., 1990-92, N.E. Assn. Pre-law Advisors, 1984; mem. Squaw Lakes Assn., Holderness, N.H., 1962—, Friends of Sandwich Libr., Center Sandwich, 1985—, Sandwich Hist. Soc., Center Sandwich, 1985—. Travel grantee Am. Philos. Soc., 1967, Tufts Mellon Found., 1982; fellow Bunting Inst., Radcliffe, 1969-71. Mem. MLA, Medieval Acad. Am., Societe Internationale Arthurienne, Societe Rencesvals, N.Am. Catalan Soc., Harvard Club. Home: 909 Holderness Rd Center Sandwich NH 03227-0079

FOLEY, ANN, broadcast executive. Sr. v.p. programming and creative ops. Showtime Networks, Inc., N.Y.C. Office: Showtime Networks Inc 1633 Broadway 17th Fl New York NY 10019*

FOLEY, CORNELIA MACINTYRE, artist; b. Honolulu, Jan. 31, 1909; d. Malcolm and Florence (Hall) M.; m. Paul Foley Jr., June 4, 1936 (dec. July 1990); children: Jean Drake, John Malcolm, Mark Lincoln. Student, U. Hawaii, 1926-27, Slade Art Sch., London, 1929-31; BA in Fine Arts, U. Wash., Seattle, 1932. One-woman shows at Honolulu Art Acad., Long Beach (Calif.) Pub. Libr., Army-Navy Club, Long Beach, Newport (R.I.) Art Assn., Hofstra U. Libr., Mallette Gallery, Garden City, N.Y., also 6 banks in L.I.; 3 woman show at Manhasset Pub. Libr.; exhibited in numerous group shows, including Hofstra U., L.I. Fedn. Women Artists, Rockefeller Center, N.Y., Seattle Art Mus., Corcoran Gallery of Art, Washington, Nat. Art Gallery of NSW, Australia, Honolulu Acad. Arts, Mfrs. Hanover Trust, N.Y.C., Glen Cove Boy's Club, Lever House, N.Y.C., Equitable Life Assurance, N.Y.C., Nassau F.A. Mus., Manhasset Libr., Great Neck Libr., Post Coll., Great Neck House, others; represented in permenent collections at Libr. of Congress, Washington, Honolulu Printmakers Assn., Castle Collection, Honolulu, Harold Mertz Collection, L.I., Whitney Mus. of Am. Art, N.Y.C., Honolulu Acad. of Arts, Mitchell Wolfson Collection, Miami, Fla., also many pvt. collections; works reproduced in Islands, Discover Am. travel book, Island Home. Recipient Purchase prizes and Best in Show award Honolulu Printmakers, 1st and 2d prize Jr. League Regional Shows, 1st prize Nat. Jr. League Frontespiece Contest, Grand prize and Hon. Mention award Honolulu Artists, 4th prize L.I. Fedn. Women Artists, numerous 1st, 2d, 3d, and hon. mention awards Manhasset Art Assn., 1st prize Nassau County Cerebral Palsy, Molly M. Canaday Meml. prize Nat. Assn. Women Artists, Grumbacher Gold medal Nat. Assn. Women Artists, award of excellence Ind. Art Soc., Hon. Mention award Suburban Art League. Mem. Manhasset Art Assn. (past pres.), Nat. Assn. Women Artists. Home: 141 Chapel Rd Manhasset NY 11030

FOLEY, HELEN CLAIBORNE, university administrator; b. Columbia, S.C., June 8, 1945; d. David Bartholemew and Helen Irving (DuBose) F. BS magna cum laude, U. S.C., 1984; MEd, Vanderbilt U., 1986. Staff asst. U. S.C., Columbia, 1971-77; assoc. dir. U. S.C. Alumni Assn., Columbia, 1977-80; dir. devel. coll. pharmacy U. S.C., Columbia, 1980-85; dir. devel. Va. Poly. Inst., Blacksburg, 1987-90; v.p. devel. Tenn. Performing Arts Ctr., Nashville, 1991-92, fundraising cons., 1992; dir. spl. gifts La. State U. Found., Baton Rouge, 1992—. Vol. Richland Meml. Hosp., Columbia, 1970-75, Spl. Olympics, Columbia, 1976-78; tchr. Literacy Coun., Columbia, 1987. Named one of Disting. Alumni U. S.C., 1988. Mem. Rotary (chmn. mentor com. Blacksburg-Christiansburg chpt. 1989), Blacksburg C. of C. (chmn. legis. com. 1989). Episcopalian. Home: 9024 Fox Run Ave Baton Rouge LA 70808-8103

FOLEY, JANE DEBORAH, educational administrator; b. Chgo., May 30, 1952; d. Colin Gray Stevenson and Bette Jane (Cullenbine) Coleman; m. George Edward Foley, Jan. 29, 1972; 1 son, Sy Curtis. BA, Purdue U., 1973, MS, 1977, PhD, 1992. Cert. elem. adminstr., Ind., cert. elem. adminstrn. and supervision. Tchr. phys. edn. and health Lafayette (Ind.) Jefferson High Sch., 1973-74; tchr. music and phys. edn. Valparaiso (Ind.) Cmty. Schs., 1974-79, tchr. elem. phys. edn., 1979-90; prin. South Ctrl. Elem. sch., Union Mills, Ind., 1990-93, Flint Lake Elem. Sch., Valparaiso, 1993—; presenter state and nat. confs. Contbr. articles to profl. jours. Recipient Hoosier Sch. award, 1992, Ind. 2000 Designation award 1994, Outstanding Dissertation award Internat. Soc. Ednl. Planning, 1993, Nat. Educator award, Milken Family Found., 1994, Ind. Bell Ringer award Ind. Dept. Edn., 1994, Ind. 4 Star Sch. award, 1995, 96, Internat. Tech. Edn. Assn. award, 1995; grantee in field. Mem. ASCD (assoc.), Am. Assn. Sch. Adminstrs., Nat. Assn. Elem. Sch. Prins., Ind. Assn. Sch. Prins., Valparaiso Tchrs. Assn. (treas. 1989-90), Valparaiso Sch. Sys. PTA (exec. bd. 1993—), Phi Kappa Phi. Office: Flint Lake Elem Sch 4106 Calumet Ave Valparaiso IN 46383-2242

FOLEY, KATHLEEN M., neurologist, educator, researcher; b. Flushing, N.Y., Jan. 28, 1944; d. Joseph Cyril and Catherine (Cribbin) Maher; m. Charles Thomas Foley, Aug. 10, 1968; children: Fritz, David. BA in Biology magna cum laude, St. John's U., N.Y.C., 1965, DSc (hon.), 1992; MD, Cornell U., 1969. Diplomate Am. Bd. Psychiatry and Neurology (examiner 1980—); lic. physician, N.Y. Intern, then resident in neurology The N.Y. Hosp., N.Y.C., 1969-74; asst. attending neurologist, neuology dept. Meml. Sloan-Kettering Cancer Ctr., N.Y.C., 1974-79, assoc. attending neurologist, 1979-88, chief-pain svc., 1982—, attending neurologist, 1988—; attending neurologist Manhattan (N.Y.) Eye & Ear Hosp., 1974-83; instr. in neurology, Med. Coll. Cornell U., N.Y.C., 1974-75, asst. prof., 1975-79, assoc. prof., 1979-89, assoc. prof. pharmacology, 1979-89, prof. neurology and neuroscience, 1989—, prof. clin. pharmacology, 1990—; rsch. assoc. lab. neuro-oncology Sloan-Kettering Inst. Cancer Rsch., N.Y.C., 1981-84; vis. asst. physician, cons. in neurology Rockefeller U. Hosp., 1975-79, vis. assoc. physician, 1979—; cons. Calvery Hosp., 1982—; assoc. mem. Meml. Sloan-Kettering Cancer Ctr., 1985-88, mem. 1988—. Editor Clinical Jour. Pain, 1985-87, Jour. Pain and Symptom Mgmt., 1987—, Palliative Medicine Jour., 1993—. Patient Svcs. Adv. Group, Am. Cancer Soc. Genetic Training grant NIH, 1970-71, Program for Pain Rsch. grant Bristol-Myers, 1988-92; Neuro-Oncology spl. fellow Meml. Sloan-Kettering Cancer Ctr., 1975-78; recipient Jr. Faculty award Am. Cancer Soc., 1975-78, Disting. Svc. award, 1992, Nat. Bd. award The Med. Coll. Pa., 1986, Willaim M. Witter award U. Calif. San Francisco, 1987, Annie Blount Storrs award Calvery Hosp., 1988, Balfour M. Mount award Am. Jour. Hospice Care, 1988, Disting. Oncologist award Dayton Oncology Soc., 1990, Tenth Barbara Bohen Pfeifer award Am. Italian Found. for Cancer Rsch., 1993; named Outstanding Women Scientist Women in Sci. Met. N.Y. Chpt., 1987, A. Soriano Jr. Meml. Lectr. The Andres Soriano Cancer Rsch. Found. Inc., 1992. Mem. AAAS, AMA (ad hoc adv. panel mgmt. chronic pain, DATTA reference panel), NAS (Inst. Medicine), Acad. Hospice Physicians, Am. Acad. Neurology (chmn. long range planning com. 1990—, scientific program com. 1990, and other coms.), Am. Fedn. Clin. Rsch., Am. Med. Womens Assn., Am. Neurological Assn. (mem. com. 1984-85, councilor 1984, 94), Am. Pain Soc. (bd. dirs. 1980-82, pres. 1984-85, bylaws com. 1986-87 long range planning task force 1989—), Am. Soc. Clin. Onocology (program com. 1991-92, com. on care at the end of life 1993—, and other coms.), Am. Soc. Clin. Pharmacology and Therapeutics, Assn. Rsch. in Nervous and Mental Diseases, Children's Hospice, Children's Hospice Internat., Cornell U. Med. Coll. Alumni Assn. (bd. dirs., nominating com.), Eastern Pain Assn. (John J. Bonica award 1986), Harvey Soc., Internat. Assn. Study Pain (councilor 1984-90, edn. com. 1986-93, and various coms.), N.Y. Acad. Scis. (USP adv. panel on neurology 1990—), Soc. for Neuroscience, Alpha Omega Alpha. Office: Meml Sloan-Kettering Cancer Ctr 1275 York Ave New York NY 10021-6007

FOLEY, PATRICIA JEAN, accountant; b. Bridgeport, Conn., Jan. 12, 1956; d. John Edward and Louise (Caselli) F. AA, Housantonic Community Coll., 1978; BS, Cen. Conn. State Coll., 1980; MBA, U. Hartford, 1996. CPA, Conn. Staff acct. Spitz, Sullivan, Wachtel & Falcetta, Hartford, Conn., 1981-82, client acct., 1982-85, sr. acct., 1985-87, supr., mgr., 1987—; mem. Acctg. Del. to Russia, Ukraine & Estonia Citizens Amb., 1993. Pres. Woodsedge Condominium Assn., Newington, Conn., 1989-92, treas., 1985-92. Mem. AICPA (mgmt. adv. svs. com. 1987-95, info. tech. divs., 1992—), Conn. Soc. CPAs, Am. Women Soc. CPAs, Community Assn. Inst. (membership chair Conn. chpt. 1991-92). Home: 35 Woodsedge Dr Apt 1B Newington CT 06111-4271

FOLEY, TRACY YEVONNE LICHTENFELS, special education educator; b. Cheecktowaga, N.Y., May 3, 1966; d. Vaughn Glen and Georgia Zoanne (Carroll) Lichtenfels; m. Duane Paul Foley, Aug. 4, 1990. Student, Hiram Coll., 1984-85, U. S.C., Conway, 1985-88; BS in Edn., Kent State U., 1989; postgrad., U. S.C., Columbia, 1992-95, Kent State U., 1995—. Cert. elem. tchr., spl. edn. tchr., tchr. of emotionally disabled, S.C. Pvt. tutor Cuyahoga Falls, Ohio, 1988-90; spl. edn. tchr. Pinecrest Elem. Sch., Aiken, S.C., 1991-93, North Aiken Elem. Sch., Aiken, 1993-95, Newcomerstown (Ohio) Middle Sch., 1995—; cons. North Aiken County Textbook Adoption Coun., 1992-93; mentor Aiken County Pub. Schs., 1992-93; spkr. in field. V.p. North Aiken Sch. Improvement Coun., 1993—; pres. Pinecrest Sch. Improvement Coun., Aiken, 1991-93. Recipient EIA Tchr. grant State of S.C., Coun. for Exceptional Children chpt. 165 grant, 1994-95, Cert. of Honor Kidz Express Pub. Program, 1993-94; Martha Jennings Scholarship Series lectr., 1996-97. Mem. S.C. Edn. Assn., Ohio Edn. Assn. (profl. rights and responsibility com. 1988-90, Cert. of Honor 1988-89), Coun. for Exceptional Children, S.C. Curriculum Congress, Healthy People 2000 Coalition (tobacco awareness com.), Newcomerstown Edn. Assn. (exec. com.) 1995—. Democrat. Roman Catholic. Home: 2411 Post Boy Rd Newcomerstown OH 43832 Office: Newcomerstown Middle Sch 325 West State St Newcomerstown OH 43832

FOLEY, VIRGINIA SUE LASHLEY, counselor, international training consultant; b. Richmond, Ind., May 1, 1942; d. Robert E. and Flora Rose (Johnson) Lashley; m. Laurence Michael Foley Sr., Jan. 28, 1968; children: Megan Leigh, Jeremie Beth, L. Michael Jr. BA, Hanover Coll., 1964; MS, San Francisco State U., 1969. Cert. profl. counselor. Vol. Peace Corps, Danao City, The Philippines, 1964-66; counselor, tng. cons. In Touch Found., U.S. Peace Corps., Asian Devel. Bank, Manila, Internat. Sch., 1981-85; counselor, tng. cons. to Overseas Briefing Ctr. U.S. Dept. of State, Washington, 1988-90; counselor, mental health cons. U.S. Peace Corps/U.S. Peace Corps, La Paz, Bolivia, 1990-92; mental health cons. U.S. Embassy, Lima, Peru, 1992-95; counselor, mental health tng. cons. Action/HAI Designated EAP, Lima, Peru, 1994—. Author: Leisure Time Activities for Families in Manila, 1983; (manuals) Career Development Manual, 1984; writer mags. What's On in Manila, 1983-85, Off Duty Mag., 1985, USAID Frontlines, 1991-94, Lima Times, 1994, Fgn. Svc. Jour., 1996. Mem. U.S. Embassy Mental Health Com. Recipient award of recognition Bukidnon State Coll., The Philippines, 1985. Mem. Am. Counseling Assn., Am. Mental Health Counselors Assn., Assn. Boliviana de Psicologia Humanista (founding mem.), Padres Assn. Home and Office: US Dept State Harari (ID) Washington DC 20521-2180

FOLGATE, CYNTHIA A., domestic violence services intervention coordinator, educator; b. Chgo., Jan. 27, 1950; d. William C. and Cassie Edna (Sisemore) F. BA, No. Ill. U., 1974, MA, 1983. Sec. No. Ill. U., DeKalb, 1974-80, 83-84, instr., 1984-92; outreach coord. Safe Passage, DeKalb, 1992-96, crisis intervention/outreach coord., 1996—; instr. Waubonsee C.C., Sugar Grove, Ill., 1990—; mem. DeKalb County Domestic Violence Forum, 1990-91. Mem., bd. deacons 1st Congregational United Ch. of Christ, DeKalb, 1989-92; speech cons. for various election campaigns, DeKalb County, 1988-90. Mem. Friends of Barb City Manor. Democrat. Office: Safe Passage PO Box 621 De Kalb IL 60115

FOLLMER, HELENE GREENE, retired museum administrator, civic worker; b. Mitchell, S.D., Apr. 13, 1931; d. Walter Thomas and Frances Ellen (Spangler) Greene; m. Hugh Crawford Follmer, Aug. 27, 1954; children: Anne Frances Follmer DeMartini, Walter Crawford, Bruce Spangler. Student, Colo. Coll., 1949-51; BA, U. Nebr., Lincoln, 1953. Tech. artist U. Nebr. Coll. Medicine, Omaha, 1953-55; project dir. Discovery, The Children's Mus., Las Vegas, Nev., 1984-86, asst. dir., 1986-88; acting dir. Lied Discovery Mus., Las Vegas, 1991, mktg. and membership assoc., 1992-94, mem. adv. bd., 1994—; ret., 1994. Mem. com. City Spirit Project, Las Vegas, 1979-80; mem. Allied Arts Coun. So. Nev., 1975—, also past pres.; mem. adv. com. Las Vegas Master Plan, 1983; mem., sec. Nev. Coun. on Arts, 1981-89; mem. adv. coms. Clark County (Nev.) Sch. Dist., 1980, 81, 83; mem. steering com. Las Vegas Valley Cultural Plan, 1993; com. chmn. Jr. League Las Vegas, 1972—, Assistance League Las Vegas, 1985—; vestrywoman All Saints Episcopal Ch., 1996—. Recipient Carnation Cmty. Svc. award Vol. Action Ctr., 1979, gov.'s arts award State of Nev., 1981. Mem. PEO (past pres.), Kappa Alpha Theta (past pres. alumna club). Republican.

FOLMSBEE, PATRICIA HURLEY, reading consultant; b. Malden, Mass., Jan. 13, 1939; d. Patrick Francis and Maura Eileen (Earls) Hurley; m. Calvin Coolidge Folmsbee, June 29, 1968; 1 child, John Stephen. AB, Albertus Magnus Coll., 1960; MEd, U. Mass., 1962, postgrad., 1969; cert. in reading and lang. arts, Ctrl. Conn. State U., 1974. Cert. reading and lang. arts cons. Tchr. Chicopee (Mass.) Bd. Edn., 1960-62, 64-69, Air Force Deps. Sch., Toul-Rosieres, France, 1962-64; reading and lang. arts cons. East Windsor (Conn.) Bd. of Edn., 1970—, English ESL coord., 1990—. Town meeting mem. Town of So. Hadley Mass., 1961-67; treas. Enfield (Conn.) Cultural Arts Commn., 1989—; reading edn. del. to China Citizen Amb. Program of People to People Internat., 1993. Mem. NEA, East Windsor Edn. Assn., Internat. Reading Assn., Conn. Assn. Reading Rsch. Democrat. Home: 9 Martin Ter Enfield CT 06082-4528 Office: East Windsor Sr High Sch 76 S Main St East Windsor CT 06088-9741

FOLSOM, HYTA PRINE, educational grant writer, consultant; b. Day, Fla., Jan. 6, 1948; d. John Wesley and Estelle Melissa (Weaver) Prine; m. Terrence Franklin Folsom, Aug. 25, 1968 (div. 1995); children: Heather V., Laura E., Teresa A., Tyson F. AA, North Fla. Jr. Coll., Madison, 1967; BS in Elem. Edn., Fla. State U., 1969, cert. in early childhood edn., 1981; MS in Ednl. Leadership, Nova U., 1991. Tchr. Gladys Morse Elem. Sch., Perry, Fla., 1969-72, 73-74; owner, operator Hyta's Presch. and Nursery, Mayo, Fla., 1979; tchr. Lafayette Elem. Sch., Mayo, 1975-77, 81-93; grants writer Lafayette County Sch. Dist., Mayo, 1990-93; cons. Grant Writers Directory, Jostens Learning Corp., 1991—; dir. alt. resources Coun. of Govts., Odessa, Tex., 1993—; owner, CEO Devel. Strategies, Inc.; mem. tchr. edn. coun. Layafette County Sch. Dist., 1983-85, coord. pre-kindergarten program, 1989-93; rep. Nat. Child Devel. Assocs., 1992; mem. Lafayette Dist. Adv. Coun., 1990-93, Schoolyear 2000 Pub. Schs. Coun., 1991-93; chairperson Lafayette County Early Childhood Coun., 1989-92. Co-author: Rainbows of Readiness, 1990. Leader Brownie troop Girl Scouts U.S., 1984-85; mem.-at-large Suwannee River Resource Conservation Devel., 1991, sec., 1992-93; nursery coord., tchr. Sunday sch., leader children's ch. Brewer Lake Bapt. Ch., 1984-85. Named Master Tchr., State of Fla., 1986. Mem. Nat. Soc. Fund Raising Execs., Lafayette Edn. Assn. (v.p. 1976-77, 87-89, pres. 1990), Kiwanis (sec. Mayo chpt. 1992), Alpha Delta Kappa. Democrat. Home: 1513 Custer Ave Odessa TX 79761 Office: Coun of Govts City Municipal Plz 119 W 4th Odessa TX 79761-4502

FOLSOM, WYNELLE STOUGH, retired wood products manufacturing executive; b. Bankston, Ala., July 19, 1924; d. Richard Carey and Ora Beatrice (Fowler) Stough; m. Eugene Bragg Folsom, Sept. 3, 1944; children: Don Wayne, Dana L. Student U. Ala., Livingston U., 1962-63, Draughan Bus. Coll., Montgomery, Ala., 1941-42, Alexander State Coll., Alexander City, Ala., 1967-68, Chilton Vocat. & Tech. Sch., Clanton, Ala., 1969-70. Sec., Ala. Power Co., Birmingham, 1942-44; med. librarian Santa Rosa Hosp., San Antonio, 1944-46; payroll clk. Dow Chem. Co., Freeport, Tex., 1946-48; with audit dept. Sears, Roebuck & Co., Selma, Ala., 1956-66; sec.-treas. Oakline Chair Co., Inc., Selma, 1967-83, pres., 1983-86. Chmn. publicity Cahaba Regional Libr. (Friends of the Libr.), Clanton, Ala., 1979; mem. Selma-Dallas County Historic Preservation Soc., 1982-87. Mem. Selma C. of C., Hemorcallis Garden Club (pres. 1979), Woman's Study Club (chmn. publicity 1967-69). Republican. Mem. Ch. of Christ. Avocations: needlework, fishing, reading, painting, gardening. Home: 803 Lay Dam Rd Clanton AL 35045-2923 Office: Oakline Chair Co Inc Hwy 31 N PO Box 1698 Clanton AL 35045-1698

FONDA, BRIDGET, actress; b. Jan. 27, 1964; d. Peter and Susan Fonda. Films: Aria, 1987, You Can't Hurry Love, 1988, Shag, 1988, Scandal, 1989, Strapless, 1989, Frankenstein Unbound, 1990, The Godfather, Part III, 1990, Doc Hollywood, 1991, Out of the Rain, (also known as Remains), 1991, Single White Female, 1992, Singles, 1992, Bodies Rest and Motion, 1993, Point of No Return, 1993, Little Buddha, 1994, It Could Happen To You, 1994, Camilla, 1994, The Road to Wellville, 1994, Rough Magic, 1995, Balto (voice), 1995, Grace of My Heart, 1996, City Hall, 1996; TV appearances: (series) 21 Jump Street, 1989, Jacob Have I Loved, WonderWorks episode, 1989, (made for cable movie) Leather Jackets, 1991. Office: United Talent Agency 9560 Wilshire Blvd 5th Floor Beverly Hills CA 90212*

FONDA, JANE, actress; b. N.Y.C., Dec. 21, 1937; d. Henry and Frances (Seymour) F.; m. Roger Vadim (div.); 1 child, Vanessa; m. Tom Hayden, Jan. 20, 1973 (div.); 1 child, Troy; m. Ted Turner, Dec. 21, 1991. Student, Vassar Coll. Appeared on Broadway stage in There Was a Little Girl, 1960, The Fun Couple, 1962; appeared in Actor's Studio prodn. Strange Interlude, 1963; appeared in films Tall Story, 1960, A Walk on the Wild Side, 1962, Period of Adjustment, 1962, Sunday in New York, 1963, In the Cool of the Day, 1963, The Love Cage, 1963, La Ronde, 1964, Cat Ballou, 1965, The Chase, 1966, Any Wednesday, 1966, The Game Is Over, 1967, Hurry Sundown, 1967, Barefoot in the Park, 1967, Barbarella, 1968, Spirits of the Dead, 1969, They Shoot Horses, Don't They?, 1969, Klute, 1970 (Acad. award best actress), Steelyard Blues, 1973, A Doll's House, 1973, The Blue Bird, 1976, Fun with Dick and Jane, 1976, Julia, 1977, also producer Coming Home, 1978 (Acad. award best actress), California Suite, 1978, Comes a Horseman, 1978, also producer The China Syndrome, 1979, Electric Horseman, 1979, Nine to Five, 1980, On Golden Pond, 1981, Rollover, 1981, The Dollmaker, 1984 (ABC-TV, Emmy award best actress), Agnes of God, 1985, The Morning After, 1986 (Acad. award nomination best actress), Old Gringo, 1988, Stanley and Iris, 1990, producer Lakota Woman, 1994; author: Jane Fonda's Workout Book, 1981, Women Coming of Age, 1984, Jane Fonda's New Workout & Weight-Loss Program, 1986, Jane Fonda's New Pregnancy Workout & Total Birth Program, 1989, Jane Fonda Workout Video, 12 additional videos. Recipient Golden Apple prize for female star of yr. Hollywood Women's Press Club, 1977, Golden Globe award, 1978; rated no. 1 heroine of young Ams., U.S. News Roper Poll., 1985, 4th most admired woman in Am., Ladies Home Jour. Roper Poll, 1985. Office: CAA 9830 Wilshire Blvd Beverly Hills CA 90212*

FONER, JANET BRAUNSTEIN, coalition executive; b. Pitts., Sept. 9, 1945; d. Leonard and Florence (Hiller) Braunstein; m. Mayer Foner, Aug. 16, 1969; chldren: Joseph Mendel, Carl. BFA, Carnegie-Mellon U., 1968; MPSSc, Pa. State U., Harrisburg, 1986. Cert. re-evaluation counselor, tchr. Substitute and part-time art tchr., 1968-83, re-evaluation counseling tchr., 1976-77, 81—; leader 1-day and weekend Re-evaluation Counseling Workshops, 1981—; self-employed cons./trainer in advocacy and peer support Leadership Exch. Listening, 1989—; co-coord., co-exec. dir. Support Coalition Internat., Eugene, Oreg.; mem. Pa. Mental Health Planning Coun., 1990-91; internat. liberation reference person for mental health system survivors for Internat. Re-evaluation Counseling Comtys., 1992—. Co-author: (pamphlet) What's Wrong with the Mental Health System and What Can Be Done About It, 1991; contbr. chpts. to books. Recipient award for disting. svc. in cmty. psychology Pa. State U. at Harrisburg, 1992. Democrat. Jewish. Home and Office: 920 Brandt Ave New Cumberland PA 17070

FONG, MARGARET, counseling educator; b. Conneaut, Ohio, Oct. 16, 1946; d. William Erwin and Rachael M. (McGoun) Loomis; m. Yameen Fong, June 14, 1969 (div. Nov. 1978); 1 child, Heather Yue-Ling. BSN, SUNY, Buffalo, 1968; MS in Psychiat. Nursing, U. Calif., San Francisco, 1969; MEd in Counseling, U. Hawaii, 1977; PhD in Counseling Psychology, Ariz. State U., 1981. Lic. psychologist, Fla. Asst. prof. U. Hawaii, Honolulu, 1969-78; from asst. prof. to assoc. prof. U. Fla., Gainesville, 1981-90; prof. counseling, chair dept. U. Memphis (formerly Memphis State U.), 1990—; vis. assoc. prof. Boston U. Overseas, Mannheim, Germany, 1987-88; pvt. practice cons., Gainesville, 1985-90. Editor jour. Counselor Edn. and Supervision, 1991-94; contbr. over 25 articles to profl. jours., chpts. to books. Named Researcher of Yr., Am. Mental Health Counselors Assn., 1992. Mem. APA (chairperson continuing edn. com. 1991-94), ACA, Am. Assn. Counselor Edn. and Supervision (pres. elect 1996). Office: U Memphis 100 Education Bldg Memphis TN 38152

FONT, ANA MARGARITA, import/export company executive; b. Havana, Cuba, June 3, 1965; came to U.S., 1969; d. Armando Jesus and Hildelisa (Gonzalez) Arias; m. Eugene Santiago Font, Jan. 20, 1989; 1 child, Ariana Elysse. BBA, U. Miami, Fla., 1987; MBA, Nova Southeastern U., 1993. Lic. stockbroker, Fla. Customer svc. officer AmeriFirst Savings Bank, Miami, Fla., 1988-90; internat. private banking officer First Union Nat. Bank, Miami, Fla., 1990-94; pres. Starlight Trading Inc., Miami, Fla., 1994—. Mem. World Trade Ctr. Home: 6601 SW 44th St Miami FL 33155

FONTAINE, DEBORAH ANN, geriatrics nurse practitioner; b. Passaiac, N.J., Dec. 5, 1956; d. Daniel and Dorothy Elizabeth (Reif) Olasin; m. Laurence Roger Fontaine, Oct. 10, 1992. BSN, Cedar Crest Coll., 1979; MS in Gerontology, Boston U., 1983. RN, Pa., Mass., Calif. Staff nurse Hosp. U. Pa., Phila., 1979-81; evening supervisor Sherrill House, Inc., Boston, 1982-83; gerontol. nurse practitioner Sherrill House, Inc., 1983-91; neurol. rsch. U. Calif., San Diego, 1991—; coord. clin. drug trials for Alzheimers and Parkinsons Disease U. Calif., San Diego, 1992—; lectr. Alzheimers Assn., San Diego, 1992—. Mem. Calif. Nurses Assn., Calif. Coalition Nurse Practitioners, Gerontol. Soc. Am., Sigma Theta Tau. Episcopal. Office: U Calif Alzheimers Rsch Ctr 9500 Gilman Dr La Jolla CA 92093-0948

FONTAINE, LAURA ANN, social worker; b. Elmhurst, Ill., Oct. 4, 1965; d. Lawrence Arthur and Lenita Ann (Marak) F. AA in Psychology, Ctrl. Fla. C.C., Ocala, 1994; BSW, BA in Psychology, U. South Fla., 1996. Sec., receptionist Comml. Structures, Ocala, Fla., 1987-90, Frank Maio Gen. Contractor, Inc., Ocala, 1990-94; team mgr. asst. R.G.I.S. Inventory Specialist, Ocala, 1989-95. Vol. Rape Crisis, Domestic Violence, Ocala, 1996. Recipient Outstanding Svc. award Univ. S. Fla. Village Coun., Tampa, 1994-95. Mem. NOW, NASW, Psi Chi, Phi Alpha. Democrat. Home: 1746 SE 12th Ave Ocala FL 34471

FONTANA, SHARON MARIE, early childhood education educator; b. Pitts., Feb. 3, 1951; d. Tony and Thelma (Pereira) Simarro; m. Ernest J. Fontana, Aug. 26, 1973; children: Alison, Santino. BS, Calif. State U., Chico, 1973. Cert. secondary tchr., Calif., vocat. tchr., Wash. Home econs. tchr. Antioch (Calif.) Unified Schs., 1973-78, Lodi (Calif.) Unified Schs., 1989-92; early childhood edn. tchr. Kennewick (Wash.) Sch. Dist., 1992—; mem. GATE adv. bd. Lodi Unified Schs., 1986-92; cons. Home and Family Life Adv. Com., Kennewick, Wash., 1992-94. Master food preserver Coop. Extension, Davis, Calif., 1988-92; mem. Triaeyc, PTA. Mem. ASCD, Wash. Vocat. Assn., Nat. Assn. Edn. of Young Children. Democrat. Roman Catholic. Home: 205 Pacific Ct Richland WA 99352-8700 Office: Tri Tech Skills Ctr 5929 W Meta Line Kennewick WA 99336

FONTANAZZA, BARBARA ANN, women's health nurse, educator; b. Pottsville, Pa., June 9, 1953; d. John Joseph and Aldona Helen (Kasputis) Williams; m. Frank E. Fontanazza, July 11, 1986; children: Frank James, Patricia Louise. BSN, Va. Commonwealth U., 1975; MS, U. Del., 1980; postgrad., Widener U. Head nurse, labor and delivery Sinai Hosp., Balt., 1984-85; clin. nurse specialist, maternal-child health Mercy Hosp., Balt., 1985-86; perinatal nurse coord. Md. Inst. for Emergency Med. Svcs. Sys., Balt., 1986-95; parent edn. isntr. Greater Balt. Med. Ctr., 1987-90; asst. prof. nursing Morningside Coll., Sioux City, 1980-81, Iowa, U. Nebr. Coll. Nursing, Lincoln, 1981-82; cons., spkr. on high risk obstetrics; asst. prof. of nursing York Coll. Pa. Contbg. author: Women's Health Nursing Examination Review, 1985. U. Del. trainee, 1978-80. Mem. NAACOG (sec.-treas. Md. sect. 1982-84), Sigma Theta Tau. Home: 99 Far Corners Loop Sparks Glencoe MD 21152-9259 Office: York Coll 313 B Life Sciences York PA 17403

FOO, JENNIFER PING-NGOH, finance educator; b. Kuala Lumpur, Malaysia, Feb. 16, 1955. BA, Smith Coll., 1981; MA, Northeastern U., 1983, PhD, 1990. Asst. prof. Slippery Rock (Pa.) U., 1986-90; asst. prof. Stetson U., DeLand, Fla., 1990-96, assoc. prof. fin., 1996—. Contbr. articles to profl. publs. Mem. coun. Women in Ch., Immanuel Presbyn. Ch., DeLand, 1996—; apptd. to County Commn. on Status of Women, Volusia County, fla., 1994—. Fulbright scholar USIA, 1990; Freiburg Faculty Exch. fellow, Germany, 1996. Mem Am. Fin. Assn., Am. Acad. Acctg. and Fin., Chinese Fin. Assn. Internat. Office: Stetson U Fin Dept Deland FL 32720

FOOTE, BARBARA AUSTIN, civic foundation executive; b. Seattle, Mar. 26, 1918; d. Edwin Charles and Marion (Roberts) A.; m. Robert Lake Foote, June 14, 1941; children: Markell Foote Kaiser, Marion Roberts, Helen Foote Schloerb. AB, Vassar Coll., 1940. Tchr. Shady Hill Sch., Cambridge, Mass., 1942-43, Madeira Sch., Greenway, Va., 1943-44, North Shore Country Day Sch., Winnetka, Ill., 1960-71; mem. exec. com. Chgo. Community Trust, 1970-85, chmn. exec. com., 1978-85; bd. dirs. Harris Bank, Glencoe and Northbrook, Ill., The New Eng. (name formerly New Eng. Mut. Life Ins. Co.), Boston. Author book of verse, 1948. Pres. Jr. League Chgo., 1947-49, Assn. Jr. Leagues Am., 1954-56, Glencoe Bd. Edn., 1957-63; trustee Vassar Coll., 1966-74; bd. dirs. Presbyn. Home, Evanston, Ill. Mem. Vassar Alumni Assn. (nat. pres. 1975-78), Phi Beta Kappa. Congregationalist. Clubs: Fortnightly of Chgo.; Cosmopolitan (N.Y.C.). Home: 587 Longwood Ave Glencoe IL 60022-1736 also: Wausaukee Club Box 8-A HCR Hwy 1 Athelstane WI 54104

FOOTE, EVELYN PATRICIA, retired army officer, consultant; b. Durham, N.C., May 19, 1930; d. Henry Alexander and Evelyn Sevena (Womack) F. BA summa cum laude, Wake Forest U., 1953; student, U.S. Army Command & Gen. Staff Coll., Leavenworth, Kans., 1971-72, U.S. Army War Coll., Carlisle, Pa., 1976-77; MS in Govt. and Pub. Affairs, Shippensburg State U., 1977; student, U. Va. Sch. Bus. Adminstrn., 1980; LLD (hon.), Wake Forest U., 1989. Commd. 1st lt. U.S. Army, 1960, advanced through grades to brig. gen., 1986; platoon officer WAC U.S. Army, Ft. McClellan, Ala., 1960-61; officer selection officer 6th recruiting dist. U.S. Army, Portland, Oreg., 1961-64; comdr. WAC Co. U.S. Army Engr. Brigade, Ft. Belvoir, Va., 1964-66; student Adj. Gen. Officer Advanced Course, Ft. Benjamin Harrison, Ind., 1966; exec. officer, chief adminstrv. div. pub. affairs office U.S. Army, Vietnam, 1967; exec. officer, office personnel ops. WAC, Washington, 1968-71, plans and programs officer OFC, dir., 1972-74; personnel mgmt. officer U.S. Army Forces Command, Ft. McPherson, Ga., 1974-76; comdr. 2d basic tng. bn. U.S. Army Tng. Brigade and Military Police Sch., Ft. McClellan, Ala., 1977-79; faculty mem. U.S. Army War Coll., 1979-82; student Fgn. Service Inst., Dept. of State, Washington, 1982-83; comdr. 42d Mil. Police Group, Mannheim, Fed. Republic of Germany, 1983-85; spl. asst. to comdg. gen. 32d Army Air Def. Command Hdqrs., Darmstadt, Fed. Republic of Germany, 1985-86; dep. insp. gen. for inspections Hdqrs. Dept. of the Army, Washington, 1986-88; dep. comdg. gen. Mil. Dist. Washington, comdr. Ft. Belvoir, Va., 1988-89; ret. U.S. Army, 1989; free-lance lectr., cons. in def. pers. and leadership, mem. or advisor numerous bds.; lectr. various U.S. Army and civilian groups. Contbr. articles to military jours. Bd. visitors Wake Forest U.; trustee U.S. Army War Coll.; mem. Am. Battle Monuments Commn., 1994—; Disting. Fellows Hall of Fame, U.S. Army War Coll., 1996. Decorated D.S.M., Legion of Merit with oak leaf cluster, Bronze star, Meritorious Svc. medal with two oak leaf clusters, German Cross of Svc. 1st class; recipient Dist. Pub. Svc. award Wake Forest U., 1987. Mem. Army and Air Force Mut. Aid Assn. (bd. dirs.), Exec. Women in Govt., Zonta. Democrat. Lutheran.

FOOTE, FRANCES CATHERINE, association executive, living trust consultant; b. Chgo., Apr. 3, 1935; d. Peter and Ellen Gertrude (Quinn) F. BS in Edn., Cardinal Stritch Coll., 1957; MS in Edn., Ill. State U., 1966. Cert. tchr., Ill. Tchr. Sch. Dist. 123, Oak Lawn, Ill., 1959-84; asst. prin. Sch. Dist. 123, Oak Lawn, 1971-80; pres. Am. Now, St. Petersburg, Fla., 1985—; instr. geography workshops for tchrs., 1967-70, use of newspaper in classroom workshops, 1973-75; co-chair social Studies Curriculum Revision; living trust cons. Accurate Bus. Assocs., Inc., St. Petersburg; ind. rep. Watkins Products. Officer PTA, Oak Lawn, 1973-76; mem. Rep. Nat. Com., Washington, vol. State of Fla. Guardian ad litem, St. Vincent de Paul Soc. Mem. Am. Fedn. Tchrs. Roman Catholic. Home: 280 126th Ave E Apt 203 Treasure Island FL 33706-4442

FOOTE, JILL ARLENE, sculptor, English language educator; b. Kansas City, Mo., Sept. 21, 1970; d. Leo Layton and Jane Elizabeth (Wood) Sander. BFA, Webster U., 1994. Visual display coord., retail mgr. Frick & Frack, Lake Ozark, Mo., 1990-95; sculptor St. Louis, 1993—; tchr. English Hong Kong, 1995—; illustrator, Lake Ozark, 1995. Prin. works include sculpture Laumeier Sculpture Park, prop design for performance art; illustrator: We Bees, 1995. Organizer, pres. Aurora (Ill.) U. Amnesty Internat., 1990; asst. organizer Warehouse Ch. Benefit Concert, Aurora, 1991; active Habitat for Humanity, Chgo., 1991; artist Operation Brightside, St. Louis, 1994. Recipient Cert. of Appreciation, Echo Children's Home, St. Louis, 1992. Democrat. Mem. Christian Ch. (Disciples of Christ). Home: PO Box 1416 Lake Ozark MO 65049

FOOTE, LINDA GASS, property management executive; b. Livingston County, Ky., Sept. 12, 1939; d. Norman W. and Ruby (Sunderland) Gass.; m. Phillip L. Foote, Nov. 13, 1959 (div. Aug. 1976); children: Phillip L. Jr., Gerard Stuart. BA cum laude, Western Ky. U., 1960, postgrad., 1970—. Tchr. English lang., Latin, history, speech Marshall County High Sch., Benton, Ky., 1961-62, Murray (Ky.) High Sch., 1962-66, Paducah (Ky.) Tilghman High Sch., 1966-68, Hardinsburg (Ky.) High Sch., 1970-71, Glasgow (Ky.) High Sch., 1971-72, Ea. High Sch., Louisville, 1972-78; real estate broker Louisville, 1972—, gen. contractor, 1976—; property mgr. Thompson Properties Inc., Louisville, 1981-85, I.R.E. Fin. Svcs., Louisville, 1985-92; owner, mgr. Foote Property Mgmt., Louisville, 1985—; real estate broker, Ohio, 1986—; owner, mgr. Linda Foote Constrn., Inc. Women's Bus. Enterprise, Louisville, 1993—; instr., conductor seminars Continuing Edn. Ctr. U. Louisville, 1988—. Vol. fundraiser Sta. KET-TV, 1988. Named Bldg Mgr. of Yr., Bldg. Owners and Mgrs., 1990. Mem. AARP, Bldg. Owners and Mgr. Inst. (instr. 1990). Democrat.

FOOTE, RUTH ANNETTE, business official, land developer; b. Riverside, Calif., Nov. 2, 1925; d. Edgar Wallace and Murrel (Sibrell) Thomas; m. Harold Dale Borregard, July 15, 1945 (div.); children: Linda Gail, Valerie Louise, Jennifer; m. Robert Earl Foote, June 24, 1951; children: Robin David, James Wayne. Student pub. schs., San Bernardino, Calif. Comml. closer M.P. Crum Co., Dallas, 1964-67, Trammel Crow Co., Dallas, 1967-69; developer Hidden Valley Airpark, Denton, Tex., 1969-70, exec. sec., 1969-73; escrow officer, mgr. Southwest Land Title, Denton, 1970-75; exec. v.p. Lawyers Title Co., Denton, 1975-80, Attorneys Title Co., Dallas, 1984; legal sec. Ray & Gilchrist, Lewisville, Tex., 1984-86; founder, co-owner Am. Title Co. Dallas, Lewisville, Tex., 1986—; ins. agt. Alliance for Affordable Health Care, Dallas; assoc. Starcom, Inc.; owner, developer Whitehawk Valley, Denton, 1977—, Rainbow Valley, Denton, 1979—, Home Opportunities Made Easy, 1990; owner branch office Safeco Land Title Co., North Richland Hills, Tex., 1976-81; exec. v.p. Inpact Mortgage, Inc., 1993—; antiaging specialist Sterling Health Mktg. Group. Mem. fund raising com., historian, bd. dirs. Habitat for Humanity of Denton. Author: And the Truth Shall Set You Free, 1980. Mem. Women's Forum Dallas. Republican. Mem. LDS Ch. Pioneered (with Robert Foote) earth sheltered home communities which provide their own electricity, fuel and water. Home: RR 2 Box 1049 Sanger TX 76266-9525

FOOTE, SHERRILL LYNNE, retired manufacturing company technician; b. Marshalltown, Iowa, Apr. 19, 1940; d. Howard Raymond Ellis and Lois Ellen (Cooper) F.; m. Terry D. Downey, July 27, 1958 (div. 1978); children: Patrick L., Holly L. Harrelson; m. Frank H. Foote, Nov. 17, 1979 (div. 1989); stepchildren: Lauri K., Christopher R. Student, Marshalltown C.C., 1981—. Receptionist Drs. Long & Clawson, Marshalltown, 1958-59; clk. Fisher Controls, Marshalltown, 1963-73, cost estimating analyst, 1974-82, sr. cost estimator, 1982-95. Contbr. limericks Des Moines Register (Contest Winner), 1976, Marshalltown Times Rep., 1986. Mem. Mensa (contbr. Bull. Wordplay 1981—, limerick editor M-Pressions Ctrl. Iowa newsletter 1989-91, local sec. 1991-93). Democrat. Methodist. Home: 702 Ratcliffe Dr Marshalltown IA 50158-3453

FORAKER-THOMPSON, JANE, criminology educator, researcher; b. Alhambra, Calif., Oct. 23, 1937; d. Field and Margaret Hall (Foraker) Thompson; m. Laurence E. Lynn, Aug. 24, 1958 (div. 1972); m. Edwin W. Stockly, July 22, 1979; children: Stephen, Daniel, Diana, Julia; stepchildren: Sue, Ann, Leigh, Ned, Cynthia. Student U. N.Mex., 1955-56; BA, U. Calif.-Berkeley, 1959, MA, 1965; PhD, Stanford U., 1985; postgrad. U. Leiden (Netherlands), summer 1973; student Ch. Divinity Sch. Pacific, 1994—. A founder, active Stanford/Soledad Teaching Project, 1971-74; criminal justice specialist Bernalillo County Mental Health Ctr., Albuquerque, 1974-75; chief planner N.Mex. State Police, Santa Fe, 1975-78; project mgr. N.Mex. restitution project N.Mex. Criminal Justice Dept., Santa Fe, 1978-80; pres. Analysis, Innovation, Devel., Inc., human svcs. cons., Santa Fe, 1980-81; asst. prof. criminal justice Boise State U., 1981-86, assoc. prof., 1986-93, prof., 1993-94; mem. N.Mex. Task Force on Victims of Sex Crimes, 1974-81, pres., 1978-80; chairwoman N.Mex. Gov.'s Task Force on Family Policy, 1979-80; first pres., chairwoman bd. Alternatives, Inc., treatment program for offenders, 1974-75; appear as expert witness in ct. on prison conditions, victims of crime, juvenile justice system, correctional system, offender classification, substance abuse and addiction problems; mem. ABA Jail Incapacitation and Prisons Com., 1982-83; lectr. in field. Contbr. articles to profl. jours. Mem. planning com. workshop leader N.W. Regional New Call to Peacemaking Conf., 1983; mem. N.Mex. Council Community Mental Health Svcs., 1974-81, mem. exec. com., 1979-80; mem. adv. bd. Albuquerque Rape Crisis Ctr., 1974-75; mem. adv. bd. N.Mex. Bar Assn. Community Corrections, 1975; pres. Citizens for Prison Change, Inc., N.Mex., 1980-81; co-organizer Victims' Rights Week, Boise, 1982—; pres. Vanguard Victims Advocate Program, 1985-86, Victims Rights Bill in Idaho, 1985; clk. Santa Fe Religious Soc. Friends, 1976-78, N. Mex. quar. meetings, 1978-80, clk. Boise Valley Friends Worship Group, 1982-83; co-chair peace and justice com. Idaho Diocese Episcopal Ch., 1983—; mem. Ada County Citizens for Peace (Idaho); bd. dirs. Boise Stepping Stone Ministries Halfway House for Offenders, 1987-89; mem. state bd. Idaho Conservation League, 1986-88; mem., trainer community mediation conciliation program The Sounding Board, 1986—; mem. Fgn. Rels. Coun., Idaho Natural Resources Legal Found. Canadian govt. grantee, 1986; rsch. sabbatical leave, Republic of South Africa, 1990; recipient Woman of Yr. award Sante Fe, N.Mex., 1981. Mem. Western Assn. Sociologists and Anthropologists (pres. 1986-87), Am. Polit. Sci. Assn., Am. Soc. Pub. Adminstrn., ABA (mem. criminal justice sect. juvenile justice com.), Nat. Orgn. Victim Assistance, Acad. Criminal Justice Scis., Am. Soc. Criminology, Internat. Peace Rsch. Assn., Nat. Assn. Mediation in Edn. , Nat. Conf. Peacemaking and Conflict Resolution, Consortium for Peace Rsch. Edn. and Devel., Soc. Profls. in Dispute Resolution, South African Assn. Conflict Intervention, Idaho Mediation Assn. (bd. dirs. 1986-88), C. of C. (com. on state and fed. legislation), Snake River Alliance. Contbr. articles to profl. jours. Office: Boise State U Dept Criminal Justice Boise ID 83725

FORBES, CYNTHIA ANN, small business owner, marketing educator; b. Richmond, Calif., Dec. 27, 1951; d. James Martin and Mary Jane (Clafferty) Forbes; m. Larry Charles Osofsky, Mar. 20, 1970 (div. 1980); 1 child, Anna; m. William Charles Ham, Aug. 30, 1986. BA, U. Calif., 1977; MS, Golden Gate U., 1981. Research asst. U. Calif., Berkeley, 1975-77, Chevron Research, Richmond, 1977-79; specialist dealer affairs Chevron USA, San Francisco, 1979-80, sales rep., San Fafael, Calif., 1981-84, adminstrv. supr., San Ramon, Calif.; 1984-85, advt. mgr. Chevron Chem. Co., San Francisco, 1986-88; assoc. prof. Golden Gate U., San Francisco, 1981-92. Vol., lectr. child abuse prevention; bd. mem. Sierra Nev. Children's Svcs. Mem. ASTD. Democrat. Avocations: mountaineering, bicycling. Home: PO Box 427 Downieville CA 95936-0165 Office: PO Box 2348 Nevada City CA 95959-1946

FORBES, GEORGINA, artist, psychotherapist; b. Boston, Jan. 18, 1943; d. G. Donald and Faith (Fisher) F.; m. John Jacob Karol, Oct. 19, 1963 (div. Apr. 1977); children: Angelisse Forbes Karol, Christopher Hale Karol; m. Lesley P. Bracker, Dec. 15, 1993. Student, Regis Coll., 1962; MA in Counseling Psychology, Antioch U., 1978. Exec. officer Ministry of External Affairs Govt. Malawi, Zomba, 1965-67; interviewer, soundtechnician, asst. editor Apertura Films, Orford, N.H., 1968-74; nursing asst. Hanover (N.H.) Ter. Healthcare, 1974-75, social worker, 1975-76; psychotherapist outpatient svcs. Community Counseling Svcs., Lebanon, N.H., 1976-77; pvt. practice Boston, 1978-79, Thetford, Vt., 1979-89; outpatient psychotherapist Calvin Turley Assocs., Newton, Mass., 1979-81; dir. career counseling Women's Info. Svcs., Lebanon, 1987-89; outpatient clinician Healthcare and Rehab. Svcs., White River Junction, Vt., 1989-93. Exhibited paintings in solo and group shows, U.S. and Carribean, 1972—; dir., creator installation sculpture Peace Hunger Kitchen, Project East Coast Tour, 1986-88. Del. Ind. Party, Thetford, 1988. Mem. NOW, Nat. Mus. Women Arts, So. Vt. Art Ctr., Vt. Arts Coun., Fleming Mus. Chaffee Art Ctr., Alliance Visual Arts, Women's Peace and Freedom Project (co-chair 1992-93), Women's Caucus for Art, Women of Vision and Action, Artemis' Bow (co-dir.), Greenpeace, Nat. Resources Def. Coun., World Wildlife Fedn. Home: Artemis Bow RR 1 Box 624 Windsor VT 05089-9719

FORBES, MARJORIE WEBSTER, counselor; b. Providence, July 25, 1930; d. George Wickliffe and Kathryn Craig (Annable) Webster; m. Richard Daniel Forbes, Aug. 4, 1951; 1 child, Richard Bruce. BA in Psychology, U. R.I., 1988; MA in Counseling, R.I. Coll., 1992. Vol. pres. Get Out and Live Successfully, Warwick, R.I., 1984—. Vocal tape Panic Disorder, 1987. Chairperson adv. coun. John A. Ferris Health Ctr., 1988—; vol. Samaritans, Providence, 1988. Recipient Jefferson award Am. Inst. for Pub. Svc., 1989, Community Svc. award U. R.I., 1989. Mem. Phobia Soc. R.I. (treas. 1987-91).

FORBES, MARY GLADYS, educator; b. Bend, Oreg., June 19, 1929; d. Percy Lloyd and Bertha May (Gettman) F. BA in Edn. magna cum laude, Cascade Coll., 1951; BS in Edn., Western Oreg. State Coll., Monmouth, 1951, MS in Edn., 1968. Cert. tchr., Oreg. Tchr. Christian & Missionary Alliance, Mamou, Guinea, West Africa, 1952-54, Bend (Oreg.)-Redmond Christian Day Sch., 1954-56, Dalat Sch., Asia, 1956-76; tchr. Bend-LaPine Sch. Dist. 1, Bend, 1976—, adminstr., tchr., 1981-87, tchr. kindergarten, 1989—; cons. Chpt. I Program in Spl. Edn., 1976-88; supt. Sunday sch. Christian and Missionary Alliance, 1976-80, Faith Fellowship Four Sq., Madras, Oreg., 1981-88. Mem. Citizens for the Republic, Washington, 1989; mem. Rep. Nat. Com., 1990—. Recipient cert. of appreciation Hale Found., 1986, 87, Skyhook II Project, 1987, Concerned Women Am., 1987, Nat. Law Enforcement Officer Meml., 1991, Am. Indian Relief Coun., 1992. Mem. Am. Def. Inst., Nat. Right to Life Com., Coun. for Inter-Am. Security, Nat. Assn. for Uniformed Svcs., Concerned Women for Am., Capitol Hill Women's Club, Christian Coalition, Am. Ctr. for Law and Justice, Am. Life League, Oreg. Citizens Alliance, Heritage Found. Home: PO Box 107 Bend OR 97709-0257 Office: Bend LaPine Sch Dist 1 520 NW Wall St Bend OR 97701-2608

FORBES-RICHARDSON, HELEN HILDA, state agency administrator; b. Detroit, July 26, 1950; d. Henry and Trunette (Adams) Forbes; m. Leon Richardson (div.); 1 child, Leon Ronald Jr. BA in Edn. and Human Svcs., U. Detroit, 1972; MPA, Harvard U., 1989. Cert. tchr. Mich. Substitute tchr. Detroit Bd. Edn., 1972-75; assistance payment worker State Dept. Social Svcs., Detroit, 1975-79, supr. assistance payment, 1979-85, section mgr., 1985—; adminstrv. asst. to chief dep. dir. Wayne County Dept. Social Svcs., Detroit, 1989-90; mem. case rev. com. Mich. Dept. Social Svcs. Gen. Assistance, 1985, 87, labor rels. subcom., quality initiative task force tng. com., 1985; co-chairperson quality initiative error reduction com. and conf. planning com.; mem. tng. com. quality initiative task force Mich. Dept. Social Svcs., 1984, client svc. subcom., 1989—, coord. employee recognition program, 1989-90, chmn. procedure com., Grand River Warren local office, 1990—, coord. state employee recognition program, Wayne County, 1980-90; chair security plan com. client info. system County of Wayne, 1989, mem. UAW Secondary Contract Negotiations Team, 1988; mem. conf. planning com. Mich. County Social Svcs. Assn., 1988; chairperson Grand River/Warren Procedures Com., 1990, employee recognition awards program level 1 Grand River/Warren Dept. Social Svcs., 1990; pres. Forbes-Richardson Ltd., 1990—, mgmt. cons., 1990; owner, editor Adams-Forbes Pub. Co., Detroit. Coordinator Social Svc. United Found. Dr., Lafayette local office 1985, Social Svc. Black United Fund Dr. 1987, speaker Nat. Polit. Congress Black Women, 1986; student project coord. Wayne County Community Coll., Wayne County Dept. Social Svcs., 1989; coord. scholarship project Mary Holmes Coll. Spirit of Detroit Leadership award, 1985. Mem. Am. Pub. Welfare Assn. (planning com. 1986), Am. Legion Aux. Office: Mich Dept Social Svcs 1200 6th St Detroit MI 48226

FORCE, CRYSTAL ANN, school counselor; b. Atlanta, Jan. 4, 1947; d. Raymond Ralph and Mary Ellen (Sticher) Bennett; m. Edward James Force, June 26, 1971; children: Lane Bennett, Patrick Brendan. BA, Carson-Newman Coll., 1969; MEd, Fla. Atlantic U., 1971. Cert. sch. counselor, Ga. Tchr. English Clewiston (Fla.) High Sch., 1969-71, sch. counselor, 1971-72; sch. counselor Greenport (N.Y.) Sch., 1972-75; dir. after sch. program LaBelle Elem. Sch., Marietta, Ga., 1985-89; sch. counselor LaBelle and Fair Oaks Elem. Schs., Marietta, 1989-90, LaBelle and King Springs Elem. Schs., Marietta, Smyrna, Ga., 1990-91; sch. counselor King Springs Elem. Sch., Smyrna, 1991—, creator Peacewalk and Peacegardens; co-dir. Smart Kids Orgn., Smyrna, 1992—. Chair parent edn. com. Griffin Mid. Sch. Parent Teacher Student Assn., Smyrna, 1993-94, exec. bd. sec. 1988; chmn. celebrating differences multicultural com. King Springs Elem., chmn. parent edn. com. PTA; mem. Citizens Adv. Coun., Smyrna, 1984-85, 93-94; mentor Campbell High Sch., Smyrna, 1992-93; mem. nat. adv. coun. Inst. Human Resource Devel., Building Esteem in Students Today Program. Recipient Am. Hero in Edn. award Reader's Digest Assn., 1993, Today's Kids award Brawner Hosp., 1993, Elem. Sch. Counselor of Yr. for Cobb County, Ga., 1994. Mem. AAUW, Am. Counseling Assn., Am. Sch. Counselor Assn., Ga. Sch. Counselor Assn., Nat. Sch. Age Child Care Alliance, Ga. Sch. Age Child Care Assn., Cobb County Sch. Counselor Assn. (program chmn. 1995-96, profl. recognition com. 1994-95), Campbell High Sch. Booster Club. Republican. Baptist. Home: 4227 Deerwood Pky Smyrna GA 30082-3929 Office: King Springs Elem Sch 1041 Reed Rd Smyrna GA 30082-4230

FORCE, ELIZABETH ELMA, retired pharmaceutical executive, consultant; b. Phila., Sept. 6, 1930; d. Harry Elgin and Loretta G. (Werner) F. BA, Temple U., 1952; postgrad., U. Pa., 1965-67; MPh, George Washington U., 1972, PhD, 1973. Cons. sr. scientist Booz-Allen Hamilton, Bethesda, Md., 1967-68; rsch. cons. scientist GEOMET, Inc., Rockville, Md., 1968-70; profl. assoc. div. med. scis. NAS-NRC, Washington, 1970-74; mgr. clin. adminstrn. dept. clin. rsch. and devel. Wyeth Labs., Radnor, Pa., 1974-77; exec. dir. regulatory affairs Merck Sharp and Dohme Rsch. Labs., West Point, Pa., 1977-88; cons. Clin. Regulatory Systems, Sarasota, Fla., 1988-91; asst. professorial lectr. epidemiology and environ. health Sch. Medicine George Washington U., Washington, 1972-74; vis. assoc. prof. cmty. health and preventive medicine Med. Coll. Jefferson U., Phila., 1981-83. Editor Clin. Rsch. Practice and Drug Regulatory Affairs, 1983-85, Drug Info. Jour., 1984-88; contbr. 60 articles to profl. jours. Pres. Sterling Lakes Owners Assn., Boynton Beach, 1996—, Women's Resource Ctr., Sarasota, 1992-94; pres., bd. dirs. Siesta Tower Condominium Assn., Sarasota, 1990-92; vice chmn. Com. for Minority Contracts, Sarasota County, 1991; chmn. adv. coun. bd. trustees Ringling Mus. of Art, 1991-95, Coun. on Violence, Sarasota County, 1994. Ruhland Pub. Health fellow George Washington U. Sch. Medicine, 1971-73. Mem. Drug Info. Assn. (pres. 1986-87, Outstanding Dir. award 1985). Office: 7555 Northport Dr Boynton Beach FL 33437

FORD, ANN SUTER, family nurse practitioner, health planner; b. Mineola, N.Y., Oct. 31, 1943; d. Robert M. and Jennette (Van Derzee) Suter; m. W. Scott Ford, 1964; children: Tracey, Karin, Stuart. RN, White Plains Hosp. Sch. Nursing (N.Y.), 1964; BS in Nursing with high distinction, U. Ky., 1967; MS in Health Planning, Fla. State U., 1971, PhD, 1975; MSN, Fla. State U., 1992. Nurse, U. Ky. Med. Ctr., 1964-65, Tallahassee Meml. Hosp., 1968-69; guest lectr. health planning dept. urban and regional planning Fla. State U., Tallahassee, 1973-76, health planner and research assoc., 1974-76, vis. asst. prof., 1976-77, asst. prof. and dir. health planning splty., 1977-83, assoc. prof., 1982-83; health care analyst and policy cons., 1983-86; med., health program analyst Aging and Adult Svcs. for State of Fla., 1986-90; coordinator Fla. Alzheimer's Disease Initiative, 1986-90; family nurse practitioner Capital Area Physicians' Svcs., 1993-94; assoc. prof. nursing Fla. A&M U., 1994—; bd. dirs. Regional Fla. Lung Assn., 1986-91; mem. exec. com. human services and social planning tech. dept. Am. Inst. Planners, 1977-83. Author: The Physician's Assistant: A National and Local Analysis, 1975; contbr. numerous articles on health edn. and health planning to profl. jours.; contbr. chpts. to books; author rsch. reports. USPHS grantee, 1965-67; HEW grantee, 1978; Univ. fellow Fla. State U., 1971-72; recipient Am. Inst. Planners' Student award, 1975. Mem. Am. Planning Assn. (charter mem. human services and social planning tech. dept. 1976-83, chmn. health planning session Oct. 1978, 79, health policy liaison 1979-83, author assn. health policy statement), Am. Health Planning Assn., Fla. Nurses Assn., Phi Kappa Phi, Sigma Theta Tau. Address: 2602 Cline St Tallahassee FL 32312-3110

FORD, BARBARA JEAN, library studies educator; b. Dixon, Ill., Dec. 5, 1946. BA magna cum laude with honors, Ill. Wesleyan U., 1968; MA in Internat. Rels., Tufts U., 1969; MS in Libr. Sci., U. Ill., 1973. Dir. Soybean Insect Rsch. Info. Ctr. Ill. Natural History Survey, Urbana, 1973-75; from asst. to assoc. prof. U. Ill., Chgo., 1975-84, asst. documents libr., 1975-79, documents libr., dept. head, 1979-84, acting audiovisual libr., 1983-84; asst. dir. pub. svcs. Trinity U., San Antonio, 1984-86, assoc. prof., assoc. dir., 1986-91, acting dir. librs., 1989, 91; prof., dir. univ. libr. svcs. Va. Commonwealth U., Richmond, 1991—; mem. women's re-entry adv. bd. U. Ill., Chgo., 1980-82, student affairs com., 1978-80, student admissions, records, coll. rels. com., 1981-84, univ. senate, 1976-78, 82-84, chancellor's libr. coun. svcs. com. 1984, campus lectrs. com. 1982-83; admissions interviewer for prospective students Trinity U., 1987-91, reader for internat. affairs theses, 1985-91, libr. self-study com., 1985-86, internat. affairs com., 1986-91, inter-Am. studies com., 1986-91, faculty senate, 1987-90; with libr. working group U.S./Mex. Commn. Cultural Coop., 1990. Contbr. articles to profl. publs., papers to presentations. Bd. dirs. Friends of San Antonio Pub. Libr., 1989-91; adv. com. chair Office for Libr. Pers. Resources, 1994-95; mem. steering com. Virtual Libr. Va., 1994—, chair user svcs. com., 1995—. Celia M. Howard fellow Tufts U., 1969; sr. fellow UCLA Grad. Sch. Libr. and Info. Sci., 1993. Mem. ALA (conf. program com. 1985-91, libr. edn. assembly 1983-84, membership com. 1978-79, status of women in librarianship com. 1983-85, pres. elect, 1996—, exec bd., 1996—, Lippincott Award Jury 1979-80, Shirley Olofson Meml. award 1977), ALA Coun. (at-large councilor 1985-89, chpt. councilor Ill. Libr. Assn. 1980-84, com. on coms. 1987-88, spl. coun. orientation com. 1982-83), Assn. Coll. and Rsch. Librs. (bd. dirs. 1989-92, pres.-elect 1989-90, pres. 1990-91, publs. com. 1990-91, conf. program planning 1990-91), Nat. Assn. State Univs. and Land Grant Colls. (commn. info. tech. 1992-94), Internat. Fedn. Libr. Assns. and Instns. (sec. official pubs. sect., gen. info. com. 1985 conf., moderator Latin Am. seminar on official pubs. 1991), Med. Libr. Assn., Mid. Atlantic Libr. Assn., Spl. Librs. Assn. (program com. 1976-77, 80-82, publicity com. 1977-79, chair 1978-79, chair spl. projects com. 1981-82, sec./treas. divsn. social sci. internat. affairs sect. 1984-86), Assn. Libr. Info. Sci. Edn. (chair local arrangements conf. planning com. 1988, 92), Ill. Libr. Assn. (chair election com. 1976-77, exec. bd. 1978-79, 80-84, bd. govt. documents round table 1976-79, chair 1978-79, long range planning com. 1980-84), Tex. Libr. Assn. (pubs. com. 1985-87, legis. com. 1986-87, judge best of exhibits award 1987, task force Amigos Fellowship 1990, del. conf. on librs. and info. svcs., 1991, Va. Libr. Assn. (ad hoc. com. distance learning 1992), Va. State Libr. and Archives (Va. libr. and info. svcs. task force 1991-93, steering com. Arbuthnot lecture 1992-93, coop. continuing edn. adv. com. 1992-94), VIVA (steering com. 1994—), Va. Assn. Fund Raising Execs., Chgo. Libr. Club (2d v.p. 1983-84), Richmond Acad. Libr. Consortium (v.p. 1991-92, pres. 1992-93), Beta Phi Mu, Phi Kappa Phi, Phi Alpha Theta, Kappa Delta Pi. Office: Va Commonwealth U Box 2033 901 Park Ave Richmond VA 23284-2033

FORD, BETTY BLOOMER (ELIZABETH FORD), health facility executive, wife of former President of United States; b. Chgo., Apr. 8, 1918; d. William Stephenson and Hortence (Neahr) Bloomer; m. Gerald R. Ford (38th Pres. U.S.), Oct. 15, 1948; children: Michael Gerald, John Gardner, Steven Meigs, Susan Elizabeth. Student, Sch. Dance Bennington Coll., 1936, 37; LL.D. (hon.), U. Mich., 1976. Dancer Martha Graham Concert Group, N.Y.C., 1939-41; fashion dir. Herpolscheimer's Dept. Store, Grand Rapids, Mich., 1943-48; dance instr. Grand Rapids, 1932-48; chmn. bd. dirs. The Betty Ford Ctr., Rancho Mirage, Calif. Author: autobiography The Times of My Life, 1979, Betty: A Glad Awakening, 1987. Bd. dirs. Nat. Arthritis Found. (hon.); trustee Martha Graham Dance Ctr., Eisenhower Med. Ctr., Rancho Mirage; hon. chmn. Palm Springs Desert Mus.; nat. trustee Nat. Symphony Orch.; bd. dirs. The Lambs, Libertyville, Ill. Episcopalian. Home: PO Box 927 Rancho Mirage CA 92270-0927

FORD, EILEEN OTTE (MRS. GERARD W. FORD), modeling agency executive; b. N.Y.C., Mar. 25, 1922; d. Nathaniel and Loretta Marie (Laine) Otte; m. Gerard William Ford, Nov. 20, 1944; children: Margaret (Mrs. Robert Craft), Gerard William, M. Katie, A. Lacey. B.S., Barnard Coll., 1943. Stylist Elliot Clarke Studio, N.Y.C., 1943-44, William Becker Studio, 1945; copywriter Arnold Constable, N.Y.C., 1945-46; reporter Tobe Coburn, 1946; co-founder Ford Model Agy., N.Y.C., 1946—, now chmn. bd. Author: Eileen Ford's Model Beauty, Secrets of the Model's World, A More Beautiful You in 21 Days, Beauty Now and Forever, 1977. Bd. dirs. London Philharmonic, 1948—. Recipient Harpers Bazaar award for promotion internat. understanding., Woman of Yr. in Advt. award, 1983. Office: Ford Modeling Agy 344 E 59th St New York NY 10022-1570

FORD, E(MMA) JANE, public relations executive; b. Anderson, Ind., Mar. 25, 1918; d. Kenneth E. and Emma (Thomas) Griffith. BGS, Ind. U.-Purdue U. at Indianapolis, 1982. Advt. dir. Farm Bur. Ins., Indpls., 1956-73; pub. relations dir. Brulin & Co., Indpls., 1973-76; pub. info. dir. Ind. Arts Commn., Indpls., 1976-79, Indpls. Art League, Indpls., 1982-84; ret., 1984—; talent coord., moderator Indy Internat. Cable TV, Indpls.; past vice chmn. Svc. Corps of Retired Execs. Author: (play) An Evening With Zane Gray, 1985; sculpture Indpls. Mus. Art. Guide Eiteljorg Mus. Am. Indian and Western Art; nat. chmn. ann. conv. Women's Overseas Svc. League, 1994, pres., Ind. chpt. Named Ad Woman of Yr. Ad Club of Ind., 1961. Mem. AAUW (assoc. editor), Nat. Soc. Arts and Letters (pres. Indpls. chpt. 1996-97, Indpls. schs. poetry chair), Women in Comms. (past sec.), Women's Press Club Ind. (past sec.), Pub. Rels. Soc. Am. (accredited). Republican. Episcopal.

FORD, JEAN ELIZABETH, former English language educator; b. Branson, Mo., Oct. 5, 1923; d. Mitchell Melton and Annie Estella (Wyer) F.; m. J.C. Wingo, 1942 (div. 1946; m. E. Syd Vineyard, 1952 (div. 1956); m. Vincent Michel Wessling, Feb. 14, 1983 (div. Dec. 1989). AA in English, L.A. City Coll., 1957; BA in English, Calif. State U., 1959; MA in Higher Edn., U. Mo., 1965. Cert. English tchr. Dance instr. Arthur Murray Studios, L.A., 1948-51; office mgr. Western Globe Products, L.A., 1951-55; pvt. dance tchr., various office jobs L.A., 1955-59; social dir. S.S. Matsonia, 1959; social worker L.A. County, 1959-61; 7th grade instr. Carmenita Sch. Dist., Norwalk, Calif., 1961-62; English instr. Leadwood (Mo.) High Sch., 1962-63; dance instr. U. Mo., 1963-66, SW Mo. State U., 1966-68, NW Mo. State U., 1970-76, Johnson County Community Coll., 1976-77; tax examiner IRS, Kansas City, Mo., 1978-80; tax acct. Baird, Kurtz & Dobson, Kansas City, Mo., 1981; substitute tchr. various sch. dists., 1976-85; dance chmn. Mo. Assn. Health, Phys. Edn. and Recreation, 1965-66, 68-69, ctrl. dist. AAHPER, 1972-73; vis. author Young Author's Conf., Ctrl. Mo. State U., 1987, 88, 89; speaker Am. Reading Assn., Grandview, Mo., 1990; real estate sales agt., Kansas City, 1980-84; real estate sales broker, Mo. and Kans., 1990—; pvt. practice tax acct., dance tchr., 1984—. Author, pub.: Fish Tails and Scales, 1982, 2d edit., 1988. Mem. Village Presbyn. Ch., Prairie Village, Kans. Mem. Am. Contract Bridge League, Kansas City Ski Club. Democrat. Presbyterian. Home and Office: 9528 Manning Ave Kansas City MO 64134-2229

FORD, JO ANNE, artist, educator; b. Mill Valley, Calif., May 17, 1958; d. Robert Emett and Eunice Peay (McDowell) F.; m. Blaise Smith, May 17, 1989. AA in Dramatic Arts, Coll. of Marin, 1980, AA in Humanities, 1980; BFA, San Francisco Art Inst., 1987. Arts educator Lycee Francais, San Francisco, 1993-95, Bay Area Discovery Mus., Sausalito, Calif., 1994—; Youth in Arts '94, San Francisco Art Edn. Project, 1996—; lectr. facilitator San Francisco Artist's Com., 1994-95; mem. Alaline Kent Award com. San Francisco Artist Com., 1995. Recipient award of Honor Matrix Gallery, 1993, award of Excellence, Calif. State Fair, 1994, award of Merit, Calif. State Fair, 1995.

FORD, JO-ANN, food products company executive. V.p., corp. sec. RJR Nabisco Holdings Corp., N.Y.C. Office: RJR Nabisco Inc 1301 Avenue Of The Americas New York NY 10019-6022*

FORD, JUDITH ANN, retired natural gas distribution company executive; b. Martinsville, Ind., May 11, 1935; d. Glenn Leyburn and Dorotha Mae (Parks) Tudor; m. Walter L. Ford, July 25, 1954 (dec. 1962); children: John Corbin, Christi Sue. Student, Wichita State U., 1953-55; student, U. Nev.-Las Vegas. Legal sec. S.W. Gas Corp., Las Vegas, 1963-69, asst. corp. sec., 1969-72, corp. sec., 1972-82, v.p., 1977-82, sr. v.p., 1982-88, also bd. dirs., dir. 7 subs. Bd. dirs. NBA Svcs., Nev., residence for handicapped, 1989—, treas., 1990-91, chmn., 1994—; trustee Nev. Sch. Arts, Las Vegas, 1979-90, chmn. bd. dirs., 1985-86; trustee Disciples Sem. Found., Claremont Sch. Theology and Pacific Sch. Religion, San Francisco, 1985-91, 92—, vice chmn., 1993-94, chmn., 1994—; mem. Ariz. Acad., Ariz. Town Halls, 1986-92. Mem. Am. Soc. Corp. Secs., Greater Las Vegas C. of C. (bd. dirs. 1979-85), Pacific Coast Gas Assn. (bd. dirs. 1984-88), Ariz. Bus. Women Owners (exec. com. 1985-88). Democrat. Mem. Christian Ch. (Disciples of Christ).

FORD, KATHLEEN MARIE, home health nurse, trainer; b. N.Y., May 3, 1937; d. Gregory Henry and Mary Rose (Spinella) Kanellos; m. William Henry Ford, Jan. 8, 1958; children: William Henry Jr., Theresa Marie. AAS, Nassau C.C. RN N.Y., N.Mex., Tex. Staff nurse ICU, CCU North Shore U. Hosp., Manhassett, N.Y., 1973; LIJ Hillside Med. Ctr., New Hyde Park, N.Y., 1974-75; utilization rev. coord., med. auditing asst. Terrace Heights Hosp., Jamaica, N.Y., 1975-76; utilization review coord., supr. Belen area, freelance discharge planning coord., key nurse for quality assurance program in N.Mex. Hosp. Home Health Care, 1976-78; utilization review coord. Huguley Meml. Hosp., Fort Worth, Tex., 1981-82; admissions nurse, acting supr., field RN Upjohn Healthcare Svcs., 1983-84; field nurse Med. Plz. Home Health Care, Fort Worth, 1984-86, PMI, Fort Worth, 1986-88, Fort Worth Osteopathic Med. Ctr., 1989; supr. Home Health of Tarrant County, 1989-91; patient care coord. Family Svc. Inc., Fort Worth, 1991-94; home health field trainer Total Home Health Svcs., Fort Worth, 1994-95; field supr. Vis. Nurse Assn., Ft. Worth, 1995—. Host parent fgn. exch. student Aspect Found., San Francisco, 1989-90, 94-95. Roman Catholic. Home: 7525 Nutwood Pl Fort Worth TX 76133-7512 Office: Vis Nurse Assn 1300 S University Fort Worth TX 76107

FORD, KAY LOUISE, innovation consulting executive; b. Pontiac, Mich., Aug. 2, 1944; d. Norman Avery and Elsa Katherine (Wahlsten) F.; m. Billy Wayne Reed, Aug. 20, 1965 (div. Jan. 1979); children: Matthew Wayne Reed, Bradley Ford Reed. AB, U. Mich., 1965; MA, SUNY, Brockport, 1983. Speech therapist Community Treatment Ctr., Bath, Maine, 1966-68; continuing edn. coord. SUNY, Brockport, 1974-78, grad. asst., 1978-79; contract tng. dir. Monroe Community Coll., Rochester, N.Y., 1979-86; exec. dir. Livingston Washtenaw Pvt. Industry Coun., Ann Arbor, Mich., 1986-91; dir. devel. McKinley Found., Ann Arbor, 1991-92; v.p. community rels. Regional Coun. Aging, Inc., Rochester, 1992-93; v.p. Drake Beam Morin, Inc., Rochester, 1993-96; cons. KLF Personal PR Assocs., 1993—; sr. cons. Idea Connection System, Inc., Rochester, 1996—; contract trainer Cornell U., Rochester, N.Y., 1983-86, Learning Internat., Buffalo, 1984-87, Jannotta, Bray and Assocs., Chgo., 1992; field instr. U. Mich., 1988-92; adj. instr. SUNY, Brockport, N.Y., 1993—. Co-chmn. Internat. Spl. Olympics Ceremonies Com., Brockport, 1979-80, Washtenaw United Way Comm., Ann Arbor, 1987-91, Mich. Theatre Fund Raising, Ann Arbor, 1987-90; bd. dirs. Jazz for Life--On Stage for Kids, Ann Arbor, 1987-90, Peace Neighborhood Ctr., 1991-92; mem. bus. and labor leaders adv. com. Washtenaw C.C.; fund drive and career svcs. coms. Rochester YWCA, 1996—. Mem. ASTD, SHRM, Finger Lakes SHRM (strategic adv. bd.), Finger Lakes ASTD, Nat. Soc. Fund Raising Execs., Planned Giving Coun. Upstate N.Y., Ann Arbor Pers. Assn., Univ. Club Rochester, Rochester Women's Network.

FORD, LISA ARLENE, insurance sales executive; b. Chinon, France, Dec. 17, 1959; came to U.S., 1960.; d. Francis John and Rita Marie (Berrigan) F.; m. William D. Scheuerman, June 15, 1985; children: Jacob Thomas, Kevin Michael Francis, Derek James. BS in Human Devel. Family Studies, Colo. State U., 1982. Salesperson Farm Bur., Denver, 1983-88, ITT Hartford, Denver, 1989—. Author sales lit. Peer counselor for young mothers Comty. Caring Project, Denver, 1991-95; pub. spkr. Sertoma Orgn., Denver, 1995-96. Republican. Home: 12226 N Spring Creek Rd Parker CO 80134 Office: ITT Hartford # 800 4643 S Ulster St Denver CO 80234

FORD, LIZ, community organization administrator; b. N.Y.C.; Children: Almetha, Marcelle, Loresa. BS in Acctg., Boston U., 1976; MS in Bus. Mgmt., Western New England Coll., Springfield, Mass., 1980. Cert. paralegal, notary public, ct. mediator. Acctg. prodn. supr. Digital Equipment Corp., Maynard, Mass., 1974-80; prodn. supr. Burroughs Corp. (UNISYS), 1980-82; dir., founder Ind. Cmty. Assistance Network, Pa., 1983—. Mem. adv. bd. Phila. Gas Works; sec. urban leadership coun. GPUAC, Delaware Valley Housing Coalition; del. Citizens Assembly, Phila.; sec. Urban Leadership Coun., 1990-96. Mem. PACDC, Soroptimist Internat.

FORD, LORETTA C., retired university dean, nurse, educator; b. N.Y.C., Dec. 28, 1920; d. Joseph F. and Nellie A. (Williams) Pfingstel; R.N., Middlesex Gen. Hosp., New Brunswick, N.J., 1941; BS in Nursing, U. Colo., 1949, MS, 1951, EdD, 1961; DSc (hon.), Ohio State Med Coll.; LLD (hon.) U. Md., 1990; m. William J. Ford, May 2, 1947; 1 dau., Valerie. Staff nurse New Brunswick Vis. Nurse Service, 1941-42; supr., dir. Boulder County (Colo.) Health Dept., 1947-58; asst. prof., then prof. U. Colo. Sch. Nursing, 1960-72; dean Sch. Nursing, dir. nursing, prof. U. Rochester (N.Y.), 1972-86, acting dean Grad. Sch. Edn. & Human Devel., 1988-89; vis. prof. U. Fla., summer 1968, U. Wash., Seattle, 1974; mem. educators adv. panel GAO; dir. Security Trust Co., Rochester, Rochester Telephone Co.; internat. cons. in field. Bd. dirs. Threshold Alternative Youth Svcs., Easter Seal Soc., ARC, Monroe Community Hosp.; mem. adv. com. Commonwealth Fund Exec. Nurse Fellowship Program. Served with Nurse Corps, USAAF, 1942-46. Recipient N.Y. State Gov.'s award for women in sci., medicine and nursing, Modern Healthcare Hall of Fame award, 1994, Lillian D. Wald Spirit of Nursing award N.Y. Vis. Nurse Svc., 1994; named Colo. Nurse of Yr. Fellow Am. Acad. Nursing; mem. ANA, APHA (Ruth B. Freeman award), Nat. League Nursing (fellowship, Linda Richards award), Am. Coll. Health Assn. (Boynton award), NAS Inst. Medicine (Gustav O. Leinhard award, 1990). Author articles in field, chpts. in books. Office: U Rochester Med Ctr 601 Elmwood Ave Box SON Rochester NY 14642

FORD, LUCILLE GARBER, economist, educator; b. Ashland, Ohio, Dec. 31, 1921; d. Ora Myers and Edna Lucille (Armstrong) Garber; m. Laurence Wesley Ford, Sept. 1, 1946; children: Karen Elizabeth, JoAnn Christine. AA, Stephens Coll., 1942; BS in Commerce, Northwestern U., 1944, MBA, 1945; PhD in Econs., Case Western Res. U., 1967; PhD (hon.), Tarkio Coll., 1991, Ashland U., 1995. Cert. fin. planner. Instr. Allegheny Coll., Meadville, Pa., 1945-46, U. Ala., Tuscaloosa, 1946-47; personnel dir., asst. sec. A.L. Garber Co., Ashland, Ohio, 1947-67; prof. econs. Ashland U., 1967—, chmn. dept. econs., 1970-75; dir. Gill Ctr. for Econ. Edn. Ashland

Coll., 1975-86, v.p., dean Sch. Bus., Adminstrn. and Econs., 1980-86, v.p. acad. affairs, 1986-90, provost, 1990-92; exec. asst. to pres., 1993-95; pres. Ashland Comm. Found., 1995—; bd. dirs. Speciality Corp., Western Res. Econ. Devel. Coun., Morgan Freeport Corp., Ohio Coun. Econ. Edn.; lectr. in field. Author: University Economics-Guide for Education Majors, 1979, Economics: Learning and Instruction, 1981, 91; contbr. articles to profl. jours. Mem. Ohio Gov.'s Commn. on Ednl. Choice, 1992; candidate for lt. gov. of Ohio, 1978; trustee Stephens Coll., 1977-80; dir. Ashland U., Mary Holmes Coll.; elder Presbyn. Ch.; bd. dirs. Presbyn. Found., 1982-88; trustee Synod-Presbyn. Ch., 1994—; active ARC. Recipient Outstanding Alumni award Stephens Coll., 1977, Outstanding Prof. award Ashland U., 1971, 75, Roman F. Warmke award, 1981. Mem. Am. Econs. Assn., Nat. Indsl. Research Soc., Am. Arbitration Assn. (profl. arbitrator), Assn. Pvt. Enterprise Edn. (pres. 1983-84), North Ctrl. Assn. Colls. & Schs. (commr.), Omicron Delta Epsilon, Alpha Delta Kappa. Republican. Office: Ashland U Box 733 Ashland OH 44805-3702

FORD, MARCIA ANN, speech, language pathologist; b. Ozark, Ark., June 26, 1958; d. James Ray and Ouida Ann (Boggs) Whitaker; children: Jonathan Matthew, Andrew Lee; m. Ronald Allen Ford, July 31, 1987; stepchildren: Joseph Lane, Ashley Ann. BS in Edn. with honors, U. Ark., Fayetteville, 1982, MS in Speech Pathology, 1993. Democrat. Baptist. Office: Mag Pub Schs 351 E Priddy Magazine AR 72943

FORD, MARCYANNE ROSE, computer consultant; b. New Britain, Conn., July 17, 1941; m. John E. Ford, Jr., Aug. 3, 1991; children: William, Todd, Christopher, Kerilee, Alyssa, Derrick. BA in Math., St. Joseph Coll., West Hartford, Conn., 1963; MS in Computer Sci., Rensselaer Poly. Inst. Tchr. math. St. Paul High Sch., Bristol, Conn., 1980-81; analyst telecommunications Hartford (Conn.) Ins. Group, 1981-95; cons. Computer Profls. Inc., Cary, N.C., 1995—. mem. mentoring program St. Joseph Coll., 1992. Republican. Roman Catholic. Home: 6925-16 Spring Creek Cove Raleigh NC 27513 Office: Computer Profls Inc 2000 Regency Pkwy Cary NC 27511

FORD, MAUREEN MORRISSEY, civic worker; b. St. Joseph, Mo., July 1, 1936; d. Albert Joseph and Rosemary Kathryne (FitzSimons) Morrissey; student U. N.Mex., 1953-54, U. Bridgeport (Conn.), 1966-68; BS, Fairfield U., 1986, postgrad. in Applied Ethics, 1986—; m. James Henry Lee Ford, Jr., Feb. 12, 1954; children: Kathryne Elizabeth, Maryellen, James Henry Lee III, William Charles, Maureen Lee. Charity and sch. vol., 1959—; fundraiser for community causes, mus., agys., 1964—; active presdl. campaign Barry Goldwater, 1963-64, congressional campaign Senator Lowell Weiker, 1968; pre-sch. tchr. Nature Ctr. Environ. Activities, 1966-68, trustee, v.p. bd. dirs., 1968-75; assoc. program in applied ethics, Fairfield U., 1986—. Author: (with Lisa H. Newton) Taking Sides: Controversial Issues in Business Ethics, 3d edit., 1994—, 4th edit., 1996. V.p. Women's League, 1966-70; mem. exec. com. Republican Women's Club, Westport, 1967-68; leader, trainer Troops on Fgn. Soil br. Girl Scouts US, Caracas, Venezuela, 1971-72; founding trustee, treas. Kara Mus., Norwalk, Conn.; mem. adv. council Fairfield County (Conn.) for spl. edn. Staples High Sch.; bd. dirs. CLASP; mem. exec. com. Group Home Search; pres. Ind. Assocs. Cons. Firm, 1991—; cons., facilitator life planning workshops Merideth Assocs., Westport; v.p., bd. dirs. Isaiah 61:1, Inc., 1989—; active grants com. Bridgeport Pub. Edn. Fund and Devel. Commn.; mem. 1st selectmen's com. on recycling, 1974-75; bd. dirs. PTA, 1976-79; mem. YWCA of Bridgeport Com. of 100 and Task Force; v.p. bd. dirs. YWCA, 1980-87, pres., 1984-85; v.p. Conf. Women's Orgns., Bridgeport; founding mem. Concerned Women Colleagues of Bridgeport; pres. Jr. League Eastern Fairfield County, Inc., 1977-78; v.p., sec. J.H.L.F. Inc., Westport. Mem. Assn. Jr. League Am., Westport Tennis Assn. Roman Catholic. Home: 299 Sturges Hwy Westport CT 06880-1723

FORD, NANCY LOUISE, composer, scriptwriter; b. Kalamazoo, Oct. 1, 1935; d. Henry Ford III and Mildred Wotring; m. Robert D. Currie, June 7, 1957 (div. 1962); m. Keith W. Charles, May 23, 1964. BA, DePauw U., 1957; D of Arts (hon.), Eastern Mich. U., 1986. Composer: off-Broadway musicals (in collaboration with Gretchen Cryer) Now is the Time for All Good Men, 1967, The Last Sweet Days of Isaac, 1970, I'm Getting My Act Together and Taking It On the Road, 1978, (Broadway musical) Shelter, 1972; performer stage and TV prodns., scriptwriter: (TV daytime serials) Love of Life, 1971-74, Ryan's Hope, 1975, Search for Tomorrow, 1981-82, Guiding Light, 1977-78, As the World Turns, 1978-80, 87-95. Trustee DePauw U. Recipient Emmy awards, 1983, 84. Mem. Dramatists Guild, Writers Guild Am. East, AFTRA, Actors Equity, Am. Fedn. Musicians, League Profl. Theatre Women N.Y.

FORD, REBECCA LAURIE, film company executive. Sr. v.p., dep. gen. counsel Metro-Goldwyn-Mayer, Santa Monica, Calif. Office: Metro-Goldwyn-Mayer 2500 Broadway St Santa Monica CA 90404-3061*

FORD, SHERI LYNN, optical technician; b. Johnson City, Tenn., Dec. 11, 1964; d. Billy Joe and Reba Joyce (Reed) F.; m. Chris Thorkildsen, July 1, 1989 (div. Mar. 1994). Grad., Ganiel Goone H.S., 1983. Lic. optical technician. Optical technician Pearle Vision, Columbia, S.C., 1989-90, Sansbery, Columbia, 1990-92, H. Rubin, Columbia, 1992-93, Dr. Craig Culinski, Columbia, 1993—. Lutheran.

FORD, YVONNE ARDELLA, barber stylist, entrepreneur; b. Depew, Okla., May 7, 1942; d. Jessie Ardell and Wava Lee (Montgomery) F.;. Student, Draughon Bus. Sch., Oklahoma City, 1963. Registered cosmetologist and barber stylist. Manicurist Zella Bristol Salon, Oklahoma City, 1960-65; barber stylist DJ's Beauty Salon, Oklahoma City, 1965-75; svc. rep. Telephone Co., Oklahoma City, 1975-81; barber stylist Panache Salon, Oklahoma City, 1984—; pres., CEO Treasures and Pleasures, Inc., Oklahoma City, 1991—. Inventor JessVon hair and skin products. Republican. Baptist. Home: 10001 Carnie Cir Yukon OK 73099

FORDE, MARY MARGARET, foundation executive; b. Saginaw, Mich., Sept. 30, 1943; d. Frederick Theodore and Margaret Alberta (Rabie) Wegner; m. Vincent James Forde, June 8, 1968 (dec. Dec. 1993); children: Heather, Lara, Vincent James III, John. BA, U. Detroit-Mercy, 1965; postgrad., U. Detroit, 1966-67. Cert. tchr., Mich., N.C., Mass. Group chief operator Mich. Bell Tel. Co., Detroit, 1962-68; tchr. Grafton (Mass.) H.S., 1968-69, Shrewsbury (Mass.) H.S., 1984-85; legal asst. Fred Homan, Marlboro, Mass., 1985-87; events coord., asst. dir. Mass. Head Injury Found., Worcester, 1989-95; asst. dir. devel. St. Vincent Devel. Found., Worcester, 1995—. Editor brochures and promotional materials; contbr. articles to newsletter. Pres., chmn. St. Mary's Parent Group and St. John's Parent Group, Shrewsbury, 1978-92; chmn. Oktoberfest, Town of Shrewsbury, 1979, 81, 83; chmn. 500 Club, St. Mary Sch., 1979-89; bd. dirs., donor devel. golf tournaments, cancer walk-a-thon. Mem. Assn. for Healthcare Philanthropy, Shrewsbury Women's Club. Roman Catholic. Home: 16 Colonial Dr Shrewsbury MA 01545 Office: St Vincent Hosp 25 Winthrop St Worcester MA 01604

FORDHAM, SHARON ANN, food company executive; b. Somerset, N.J., Jan. 30, 1952; d. Thomas Anthony and Gladys Maryann (Hagaman) F. BA in History with honors, Rutgers U., 1975; MBA in Mktg., U. Pa., 1977. Asst. product mgr. Bristol-Myers (Drackett Co.), Cin., 1977-78, product mgr., 1979; product mgr. Borden, Inc., Columbus, Ohio, 1979-81, Nabisco Brands Inc., East Hanover, N.J., 1981-82; group product mgr. Nabisco Brands, Inc., East Hanover, N.J., 1982-84, dir. mktg., 1984-86; sr. dir. new bus. Nabisco, Brands Inc., East Hanover, N.J., 1986-91, v.p. new bus., 1991-94; v.p., gen. mgr. Life Savers Co., 1994—. Originator, dir. Almost Home (Cookie Wars), 1983, Low Salt Nabisco Crackers, 1987, Teddy Grahams, 1988, Mr. Phipps, 1991, Snack Wells, 1992, Nabisco Breakfast Snack Line, 1994. Mem. Woodbridge (N.J.) Wind Ensemble, 1982-83, Hillsborough Wind Ensemble, Somerset, N.J., 1984-87. Recipient award Point of Purchase Advt. Inst., 1983, 89, Gold Effie award Assn. Nat. Advertisers, 1986, 89, 92, New Product of Yr. award Bus. Week, 1988, Food and Beverage Mktg., 1988, 91, 93, New Snack Product of Yr. award Consumer Network, 1988, Gorman Pub., 1988, 91, Am. Mktg. Assn., 1989, 91, 92, 94. Mem. Mensa, Wharton Club N.Y. (bd. dirs.). Republican. Roman Catholic. Office: The Life Savers Co 1100 Reynolds Blvd Winston Salem NC 27105

FORD SOLLIMO, KAY LORAYNE, secondary education mathematics and science educator; b. Albany, Ind., Apr. 18, 1940; d. Garnet Roy and Donna Lorayne (Hammitt) Ford; m. Vincent James Sollimo, June 24, 1967 (div. Apr., 1982); children: Peter James, Paul John. BS, Ball State U., 1962; MS, U. Tenn., 1966; postgrad., Rutgers U., 1976—, Colo. State U., 1976—; Cert. Higher Edn., Rutgers, 1978. Cert. math., chemistry, physics tchr., Colo.; cert. math. tchr., N.J. Tchr. math. and sci. Littleton (Colo.) Jr. H.S., 1962-64; tchr. math., chemistry and physics. Kinnick H.S., Yokohama, Japan, 1964-65; instr. math., chemistry and phys. sci. St. Francis Coll., Ft. Wayne, Ind., 1966-67; tchr. math. Plymouth-Whitemarsh H.S., Plymouth Meeting, Pa., 1967; instr. math., chemistry, physics Eastern Coll., St. Davids, Pa., 1967-68; instr. math. Burlington County Coll., Pemberton, N.J., 1974-83; tchr. math. Ea. Sr. H.S., Voorhees, N.J., 1980—. Recipient Acad. Yr. fellowship NSF, Oak Ridge Inst. Nuclear Studies, 1965-66; grantee several summer workshop grants for math. and computer sci. Mem. NEA, Ea. Edn. Assn., Nat. Coun. Tchrs. of Math. Lutheran. Office: Ea Sr HS PO Box 2500 Voorhees NJ 08043-0995

FORD-WERNTZ, DONNA IRENE, herbarium curator, educator; b. Cin., Nov. 6, 1959; d. Charles Allison and Marlyn Mae (Griffith) Ford; m. Charles Livingston Werntz III, June 8, 1996. BS, Miami U., Oxford, Ohio, 1982; MS, U. Mich., 1985; PhD, Washington U., St. Louis, 1992. Curator, asst. prof. N.E. Mo. State U., Kirksville, 1991-94; curator, asst. prof. biology dept. W.Va. U., Morgantown, 1995—. Mem. Internat. Assn. Plant Taxonomy, Am. Soc. Plant Taxonomists, W.Va. Native Plant Soc. (treas. 1996). Lutheran. Office: W Va U Biology Dept Box 6057 Morgantown WV 26506

FOREHAND, JENNIE MEADOR, state legislator; b. Nashville; d. James T. and Estelle (Woodall) Meador; student Woman's Coll. of U. N.C., Greensboro; B.S. in Indsl. Relations, U. N.C., Chapel Hill; m. William E. Forehand, Jr.; children: Virginia, John Bentley. Reporter, Charlotte (N.C.) News, 1954-56; probation counselor Juvenile Ct., Charlotte, 1958; tchr. Anne Arundel County (Md.), 1958-60; statis. analyst NIH, Bethesda, Md., 1961-62; interior designer, owner Forehand Antiques and Interiors, Rockville, Md., 1971—; state rep. Md. Gen. Assembly, 1978-94; mem. Md. State Senate, 1995—. mem. appropriations com., joint capital budget com., health and environ. subcom., chair Montgomery County delegation transp. com., co-chair com. on mgmt. of pub. funds; mem. Senate Judicial Proceedings Com., Exec. Nominations Com., vice-chmn. Montgomery County Senate Delegation; mem. Small Mus. Com., Rekgulatory Review Com., NIH Bio-Safety Com.; vice chair Econ. and Culture Devel. Com. of So. Legis. Conf., 1994—; Planning bd. Montgomery County Health Systems; consumer rep. Rockville Econ. Devel. Council, Md. Community Mental Health Adv. Bd.; pres. local civic assn., Girl Scout Adv. Coun.; bd. dirs. Lung Assn., Montgomery County Hist. Soc.; mem. Peerless Rockville Hist. Preservation, Ltd.; bd. dirs. Md. Coll. Art and Design, Rockville Arts Place, Asbury Meth. Homes. Recipient Bus. Leadership award Suburban Md. Tech. Coun.; named Outstanding Legislator Montgomery County Med. Soc. Mem. Women's Caucus of Md. Gen. Assembly (pres.), AAUW, Women's Polit. Caucus. Democrat. Methodist. Office: State Senate 214 Senate Office Bldg Annapolis MD 21401

FOREHAND STILLMAN, MARGARET P., library director; b. Nov. 12, 1951; m. Peter R. Stlliman, Feb. 11, 1995; children: Lindsay Howell, Walker Harrison. BA in Edn., U. Richmond, 1973; MA in Edn., Va. Commonwealth U., 1974; MLS, U. Md., 1977. Libr. hdqrs. Chesapeake Libr. Systems, 1979-85, dir. librs. and rsch. svcs., 1985—. Bd. dirs. Tidewater ARC, 1980-83, Western Tidewater Area Health Edn. Ctr., 1980—, exec. coun. 1982—; v.p. Va. Stage Co., 1981-82, bd. dirs., 1979-85; bd. dirs. the Planning Coun. Cultural Alliance of Greater Hampton Roads, 1985—, exec. coun. 1986-88; bd. dirs. Am. Cancer Soc. Portsmouth-Chesapeake Bds., 1987—, pres., 1991—; mem. Mayor's Com. on Protocol, 1987, Mayor's Commn. on Bicentennial Constitution, 1987; co-chmn. Mayor's Task Force on Libr., 1989—, Gov.'s Rural Econ. Devel. Task Force, 1990-91. Named Outstanding Young Career Woman Va. Fedn. Bus. and Profl. Women's Clubs, 1978, Outstanding Bus. and Profl. Woman, 1993. Mem. ALA (Va. chair nat. libr. week 1985-86), Va. Libr. Assn. (coun.mem. 1978-86, chair Va. Pub. Libr. sect. 1978-79), Va. State Libr. Bd. (vice chmn. 9186-87, chmn. 1987-88, chmn. bldg. com. 1988—), State Adult Literacy Com. (chmn. 1989—), Chesapeake C. of C. (chmn. pub. rels. com. 1989—, planning coun., bd. dirs., UVA adv. bd., Hampton Roads Bd.), DAR (bd. dirs. Chesapeake chpt. 1983—). Office: Chesapeake Pub Libr 298 Cedar Rd Chesapeake VA 23320-5512

FORELLE, HELEN (GRACE JANET LEIH), publishing executive, writer, poet; b. Canton, S.D., Jan. 27, 1936; d. Geurt and Ruth Victoria (Hall) Leih; m. John Maxwell Jeffords, Dec. 2, 1955 (div. 1968); children: Ruthanne Sheperd, John Maxwell Jeffords, Pamela Leih Meder. BA, Memphis State U., 1967, postgrad., 1967-69; postgrad., U. Wuerzburg, Munich, 1970, Technische Hochschule, Munich, 1971. Computer programmer, analyst various cos., San Francisco, 1972-77; instr. computer sci. Augustana Coll., Sioux Falls, S.D., 1978-79; project dir. S.D. State Poetry Soc., Sioux Falls, 1984-87; temp. jobs various agencies, Sioux Falls, 1978-88; enumerator U.S. Census Bureau, Sioux Falls, 1989; owner Tesseract Pub., Fairview, S.D., 1989—; lectr. in field. Author: (pseudonym Mario Edlosi) (trilogy) Which Way the Wind Blows, 1978, Shouting to the Wind, 1996, The Windmill, 1996, (children's story) The Adventures of Mortimer Troll, 1981, If Men Got Pregnant, Abortion Would Be A Sacrament, 1982, (pamphlets) Conversations in a Clinic, 1980, Publication Indexing, a Writers' Guide to Inventory, 1989, (poems) Pearls Among the Swine, 1990, (musical comedy) The Tea-Totalers, 1982; editor: South Dakota Authors' Catalog, 1982, 83, 85, 87, The Wash Rag Newsletter; mng. editor, project dir. for S.D. State Poetry Soc.-A Sixty Year Comprehensive Index of Pasque Petals, 1926-1986), 1987; contbr. poetry to popular mags. and newsletters, and cartoons to Broomstick mag. Dir. Women Against Sexual Harassment, Fairview, S.D., 1992-96; recorder Valley of Many Winds S.D. State Libr. Talking Books; judge contests Nat. Fedn. State Socs., 1985, 88. With USN, 1954-56. Recipient Poet of the Year S.D. State Poetry Soc., Sioux Falls,, 1982, 2d place Denver Am. Pen Women contest, 1978, S.D. State Poetry Soc., 1980, best of show S.D. State Fair, 1980, 84, Hon. Mention award Nat. Assn. State Poetry Soc., 1980, 81, also numerous poetry awards. Mem. AAUW, WAVES, Nat. Assn. Atomic Vets., S.D. State Poetry Soc. (pres. 1985-86), Bardic Round Table (treas. 1988, pres. 1989-91). Office: Tesseract Pubs PO Box 164 Canton SD 57013

FOREMAN, CAROL LEE TUCKER, business executive; b. Little Rock, May 3, 1938; d. James Guy and Willie Maude (White) Tucker; A.A., William Woods Coll., Fulton, Mo., 1958; A.B., Washington U., St. Louis, 1960; postgrad. Am. U.; LL.D. (hon.), William Woods Coll., Fulton, Mo., 1976; m. Jay Howell Foreman, June 13, 1964; children: Guy Tucker, Rachel Marian. Rsch. asst. Com. on Govt. Ops., U.S. Senate, 1961; assoc. Fed. Counsel Assocs., 1961-63; instr. Am. govt. William Woods Coll., Fulton, 1963-64; exec. asst. to Rep. James Roosevelt, 1964; dir. rsch. and publs. Dem. Nat. Com., 1965-66; Congressional liaison aide HUD, 1967-69; chief info. liaison Ctr.for Family Planning Program Devel., Planned Parenthood-World Population, 1969-71; dir. policy coordination Commn. on Population and Am. Future, 1971-72; exec. dir. Citizens Com. on Population and Am. Future, 1972-73, Paul Douglas Consumer Rsch. Ctr., 1973-77, Consumer Fedn. Am., 1973-77; asst. sec. food and consumer svcs. Dept. Agr., Washington, 1977-81; pres. Foreman & Co., 1981-86, ptnr. Foreman & Heidepriem, 1986-94; pres. Foreman & Heidepriem, Inc., 1994—; coord. Safe Food Coalition, 1987—; bd. dirs. Adams Nat. Bank. Editor: Regulating for the Future, 1991. Exec. dir. Ctr. for Women Policy Studies, 1983-84; mem. Interdeptl. Task Force on Women; mem. D.C. Commn. on Status Women, 1973-74; bd. dirs. Consumer's Union, 1982-83, chmn., 1993—; bd. dirs. Food Rsch. and Action Ctr., 1983—, Christianity and Crisis, 1990—; vice-chmn. Ctr. Nat. Policy, 1982-84, bd. dirs., 1981—; trustee Washington U., St. Louis, 1987-95. Recipient Disting. Alumni award Washington U., 1979. Mem. Women's Equity Action League (past pres. local chpt.), Nat. Planning Assn. (dir. 1985—), Pi Beta Phi. Presbyterian. Home: 5408 Trent St Chevy Chase MD 20815-5514 Office: Foreman & Heidepriem Inc 1100 New York Ave NW Ste 1030 Washington DC 20005-3934

FOREMAN, ELEANOR TERESA (TERRY FOREMAN), artist; b. Balt., Sept. 6, 1958; d. Douglas Joseph and Dorothy Ann (Eichelberger) F.; m. John Jennings Crowther, June 16, 1979; 1 child, Brenna Ann. BA, William Paterson Coll., Wayne, N.J., 1980. Graphic designer AT&T Bell Labs., Short Hills, N.J., 1980-84; graphic designer Design in Mind, Middletown, N.Y., Caldwell, N.J., 1984-89, Newark, Del., 1990-96; jewelry designer Design in Mind, Newark, 1992-96; art tchr. Ctr. for Creative Arts, Yorklyn, Del., 1992-96; show organizer Newark Studio Tour, 1992-96; founding mem. Kaleidescope Gallery, Newark, 1993-94; staff person Newark Arts Alliance, 1995—; shirt designer Sleigh Bell Run, Newark Ctr. for Creative Learning, 1994-95; crafts coord. Newark Arts Alliance, 1993-96; chair artisans com. Harvest Moon Festival De Nature Soc., Ashland, Del., 1995. Artist, designer commemorative pin Del. Women's Conf., 1994, exhibited in art show, 1996. Mem. Am. Craft Coun., Newark Arts Alliance (bd. mem. 1993-94). Home and Office: 307 Mason Dr Newark DE 19711

FOREMAN, LAURA, dancer, choreographer, conceptual artist, writer, educator; b. L.A.; d. Michael and Gladys (Charnas) F.; m. John Everett Watts. Dir. dance, physical fitness and recreation depts. and movement specialist cert. program, Foreman Dance Theatre artist-in-residence. New Sch. Social Rsch., N.Y.C., 1971—; founder, dir. Choreographers Theatre, N.Y.C.; artist-in-residence Channel 13 TV Lab., 1978, Holographic Film Found., N.Y.C., 1983; dance dir., bd. dirs. Composers and Choreographers Theatre, Inc.; mem. dance panel N.Y. State Coun. on Arts; cons. Nat. Endowment Humanities; mem. Artists Talk on Art, The Performance Project, N.Y. Theater Bridge, Writers Rm., N.Y.C.; visual arts panel Ill. Arts Coun., Seattle Arts Commn.; documentary and arts panel Nat. TV Emmy Awards; bd. dirs. Ear Inc., N.Y.C.; tchr. master classes New Sch., Parsons Sch. of Design, Art Student League, Met. Mus. Art, Chapin Sch. Choreography and performanc art includes Memorials, Study, A Time, Perimeters, Epicycles, SkyDance for skywriters and helicopters, Margins, Signals, Laura's Dance, Spaces (Collage I-IV), Locrian, Performance, a deux, Postludes, Monopoly, Program, Heirlooms, Entries, others.; video includes TimeCoded Woman I, II, III (2 silver, 1 gold award Houston Internat. Film Festival 1979, 80, 81, Bronze medal Internat. Film and TV Festival of N.Y., 1981); conceptual work (with John Watts) includes WallWork, crowd-created art work, 1981, Coney Island Cray-Pas, 1981, Concourse Cray-Pas, The Philadelphia Story, 1981; installations include Roomwork, 1981, WindoWork, 1982, 91; one-woman shows Portico Gallery, Phila., Limbo, N.Y.C., Souyun Yi Gallery, N.Y.C., Kleinert Arts Ctr., Woodstock, N.Y.; two-person shows Souyun Yi Gallery, Webb & Parsons Gallery, Vt.; over 50 group shows including Bronx, N.Y., Wustum., Wis., Hudson Highlands, N.Y., Chgo. Peace, Ill., and Pasadena, Calif., museums; permanent collections include Antwerp Mus.; off-Broadway shows City Junket, 1980; published in The Act, Downtown, Letters, Pinehurst Jour., Confrontation, ACM, Santa Clara Review, Up Front Muse Internat., Lamia, Ink mags., (short story collection) Pig Iron Anthology. Grantee CAPS, 1970, 73, N.Y. State Coun. Arts, 1970-74, Nat. Endowment Arts, 1971, 73, 77, 78, Vogelstein Found., 1985, Pub. Arts Commn., JBR Found., 1989; fellow Blue Mountain, 1985, 90, Dorset Colony, 1985, 88, MacDowell Colony, 1986, Djerassi Found., 1987, Vt. Studio Sch. and Colony, 1988, Act II Colony, 1988, Ragdale Found., 1990, Watershed Ctr. for Ceramic Arts, Edward Albee Found., Byrdcliffe Arts Colony, 1991, Cummington Cmty. for the Arts, 1992, Lookout Sculpture Park, 1994, Pallenville Found., 1994, Mary Anderson Ctr., 1994, Hambidge Ctr., Ga., 1995, Pouch Cove Studio Cst. John's NK, 1996, Contemporary Artists Ctr., Mass., 1996. Mem. Artists and Scis. in Collaboration (founder), Artists Talk on Art. Home: 94 Chambers St New York NY 10007-1800

FOREST, CHARLENE LYNN, cell biologist, educator; b. N.Y.C., Feb. 27, 1947; d. Harold Matthew and Sadie (Biller) Friedman; m. Richard Mark Forest, June 29, 1969. BS, Cornell U., 1968; MS, Adelphi U., 1972; PhD, Ind. U., 1976. Postdoctoral fellow Harvard U., Cambridge, Mass., 1976-79; asst. prof. Bklyn. Coll., CUNY, 1979-83, 84-86, assoc. prof., 1986—; prin. investigator, grant assoc. Rsch. Found. CUNY, Bklyn., 1983-84. Contbr. articles to profl. publs. Grantee NIH, 1980-83, NSF, 1983-85, 85-88; recipient Career Advancement award NSF, 1989-90. Mem. AAAS, Am. Soc. Cell Biology, Genetics Soc. Am., Soc. Protozoologists, Assn. Women in Sci., Am. Soc. Plant Physiologists, N.Y. Soc. Electron Microscopists, N.Y. Acad. Scis., Sigma Xi.

FOREST, EVA BROWN, nurse, supervisor and paralegal; b. Ontario, Va., July 7, 1941; d. William Butler and Ruth Pauline (Simpson) Brown; m. Willie J. Forest Jr., Sept. 16, 1961; children: Geraid, Darryl, Angela. AA, Bismarck (N.D.) State Coll., 1981; BSN, U. Mary, Bismarck, 1984. RN, Colo. Charge nurse St. Alexius Med. Ctr., Bismarck, 1984-85, Cedars Health Care Ctr., Lakewood, Colo., 1989-90; staff devel. coord. Park Avenue Bapt. Home, Denver, 1990-91; supr., charge nurse Cedars Health Care Ctr., Lakewood, Colo., 1991—; charge nurse Villa Manor Health Ctr., Lakewood, Colo., 1991-93; supr., charge nurse Stovall Care Ctr., Denver, 1995-96. Vol. for cultural exch. lang., culture and fashions YWCA, Kano, Nigeria; vocalist gospel music workshop, N.D.; pianist adult and children's choir, N.D.; mem. MADD, Habitat for Humanity Internat., HALT, Vols. of Am. Mem. Nat. Multiple Sclerosis Soc., Internat. Platform Assn., DAV Commdrs. Club.

FORESTER, ERICA SIMMS, decorative arts historian, consultant, educator; b. N.Y.C., Feb. 13, 1942; d. Leon Marcus and Selma (Rosen) Simms; m. Bruce Michael Forester, Dec. 21, 1962; children: Brent Peter, Robin Ann, Russell Charles. BA, Cornell U., 1963; MA, Columbia U., 1964; cert., N.Y. Sch. Interior Design, 1973; AAS in Interior Design, Parsons Sch. Design, 1982. Owner Erica Forester, Interiors, Bronxville, N.Y., 1973—; mem faculty Parsons Sch. Design, N.Y.C., 1982—; lectr. Hudson River Mus., 1984, Eastchester Hist. Soc., 1989, Bartow Pell Mansion, 1990, Scarsdale Adult Sch., 1991, The Decorative and Fine Arts Soc. of N.J., 1995, N.Y. U., 1995; guest curator Scarsdale Hist. Soc., 1987. Author: (with others) At Home in Westchester: Style and Design, 1836-1886, The Evolution of Elegant Dining. Mem. adv. bd. Am. Field Svc. Rye Country Day Sch., 1984-88; mus. adv. bd. Scarsdale Hist. Soc. Mem. Allied Bd. Trade, Decorative Arts Trust, Assn. Ind. Historians of Art. Home and Office: 55 Northway Bronxville NY 10708-2325

FORESTER, JEAN MARTHA BROUILLETTE, innkeeper, retired librarian, educator; b. Port Barre, La., Sept. 7, 1934; d. Joseph Walter and Thelma (Brown) Brouillette; m. James Lawrence Forester, June 2, 1957; children: Jean Martha, James Lawrence. BS, La. State U., 1955; MA (Carnegie fellow 1955-56), George Peabody Coll. Tchrs., 1956. Libr. Howell Elem. Sch., Springhill, La., 1956-58; asst. post libr. Fort Chaffee, Ark., 1958; command libr. Orleans Area Command, U.S. Army, Orleans, France, 1958-59; acquisitions libr. Northwestern State U., Natchitoches, La., 1960; serials libr. La. State U., New Orleans, 1960-66; mem. faculty La. State U., Eunice, 1966-85, asst. libr., 1972-85, assoc. libr., 1985-87, acting libr., 1987-88, dir. libr., 1988-89, libr. emeritus, 1989—; asst. prof., 1972-85, faculty senator, 1978-80, 85-86, 87-89; innkeeper Crown'n'Anchor Inn, Saco, Maine, 1989—. Co-author: Robertson's Bill of Fare; contbr. articles to profl. jour. Active Eunice Assn. Retarded Children. Mem. La. Libr. Assn. (sect. sec. 1971-72, coord. serials interest group 1984-85), UDC, Delta Kappa Gamma (chpt. parliamentarian 1972-74, rec. sec. 1984-86), Alpha Beta Alpha, Phi Gamma Mu, Phi Mu, Order Eastern Star. Democrat. Baptist.

FORINA, MARIA ELENA, gifted education educator; b. Santiago, Cuba, Apr. 10, 1942; came to U.S., 1972; d. Jorge Fernando and Maria Elena (De Gongora) Chaves; m. Antonio Forina, May 28, 1961; children: Maria Elena, Amalia, Jose, Jorge Antonio. AA, Somerset County Coll., 1975; BS, U. Tex. Pan Am., Edinburg, 1982, M in Gifted Edn., 1995. Cert. elem. tchr., bilingual tchr., gifted edn. tchr., Tex.; SOI cert. trainer. 1st grade tchr. Pharr-San Juan-Alamo (Tex.) Ind. Sch. Dist., 1981-83, gifted edn. resource tchr., 1983-88, 6th grade gifted edn. tchr., 1988—, AMS writing trainer, 1991—. Eucharistic minister Resurrection Cath. Ch., Alamo, 1982—, CCD tchr., 1986—, mem. blue ribbon com., 1988—, mem. pastoral coun., 1993—. Mem. ASCD, Nat. Coun. Tchrs. Math., Nat. Coun. Tchrs. English, Tex. Assn. for Gifted and Talented, Phi Kappa Phi, Delta Kappa Gamma. Republican. Home: 842 Fannin Box 3901 Alamo TX 78516 Office: Alamo Mid Sch 1819 W US Highway 83 Alamo TX 78516-2102

FORKAN, PATRICIA ANN, association executive; b. N.Y.C., June 13, 1944; d. Robert James and Elaine May (Van Horn) F.; BA in Polit. Sci., Pa. State U., 1966; postgrad. Am. U., 1968-69. Manpower analyst Dept. Labor, Washington, 1967-69; nat. coordinator Fund for Animals, N.Y.C., 1970-76; v.p. program and communications Humane Soc. of U.S., Washington, 1976-86, sr. v.p. 1987-91, exec. v.p., 1992—; bd. dirs. Solar Elec. Light Fund;

mem. U.S. del. Internat. Whaling Commn., 1978, 93, 94 Re-negotiation of Conv. for Regulation of Whaling, 1978, U.S. del. North Pacific Fur Seal Commn., 1985; mem. U.S. Public Adv. Com. to Law of the Sea, 1978-83; bd. dirs. Coun. for Ocean Law; advisor, contbr. weekly TV show Living with Animals, 1985-91; advisor Animal Polit. Action Com.; sr. v.p. Humane Soc. Internat., 1991—; coun. woman Friendship Heights (Md.) Village, 1993—; pres. Nat. Assn. Humane and Environ. Edn., 1994—. Contbr. articles to environ. and animal welfare publs.; co-host weekly radio show, 1986-87. Office: Humane Soc of US 2100 L St NW Washington DC 20037-1525

FORMAN, BETH ROSALYNE, entertainment industry professional; b. N.Y.C., Oct. 15, 1949; d. Philip and Dorothy Lea (Vilensky) F. BA in English with honors, NYU, 1971; MA with honors, Columbia U., 1972; MBA in Fin., Rutgers U., 1980. Asst. to contr. Colin Hochstin Co., N.Y.C., 1971-78; instr. Columbia U., N.Y.C., 1974-76; adj. faculty Bergen Community Coll., Paramus, N.J., 1985-87; communications cons. B.R. Forman & Co., Paramus, 1981-87; proposal mgr. Ogden Svcs.Corp., N.Y.C., 1988-89; dir. tech. svcs. Ogden Entertainment Svcs., Rosemont, Ill., 1990-92; dir. mktg. comms. Ogden Entertainment Svcs., N.Y.C., 1993—. Bd. dirs. new leadership div. United Jewish Community Bergen County, River Edge, N.J., 1981-87, chmn. fundraiser, 1983, chmn. edn. com., 1983-86, treas., 1984-86; mem. steering com. Viewpoints div. Am. Jewish Com., 1991-93. Pres.'s fellow Columbia U., 1973; recipient Masters award Ogden Svcs. Corp., 1994. Mem. NAFE, Internat. Platform Assn., Women in Comm. (v.p. spl. programs 1992-93 Chgo. chpt., mem. career devel. com. 1994-95, mem. pub. rels. com. and Matrix awards fundraising com. 1995-96), Columbia U. Club of N.Y., Mensa. Democrat. Home: 9060 Palisade Ave North Bergen NJ 07047 Office: Ogden Entertainment 2 Pennsylvania Plz New York NY 10121

FORMAN, BRENDA JOYCE, administrative assistant; b. Detroit, Oct. 18, 1957; d. Frank Sr. and Queen Esther (Evans) F. Student, Wayne State U., 1975-77; Assoc. degree, Detroit Coll. Bus., 1979. Exec. sec. University City A Citizens Dist. Coun., Detroit, 1978-85; adminstrv. asst. Travelers Aid Soc., Detroit, 1985—. Office: Travelers Aid Soc Detroit 3d Fl 211 W Congress Detroit MI 48226

FORMAN, JEANNE LEACH, piano and voice educator; b. L.A., Mar. 3, 1916; d. Rowland E. and Charlotte F. (Van Wickle) Leach; student U. Redlands, 1934-36, UCLA, 1937; m. Edward S. Forman, July 28, 1945; children: Bonnie Jeanne Forman Ottinger, Karen Lynn Forman Maginnis, Wendy K. Forman Bolduc. Pvt. tchr. piano, Pasadena, Calif., 1945-52, Tucson, 1952-58, Sunnyvale, Calif., 1958-75, Santa Barbara, Calif., 1976—; owner, dir. Jeanne Forman Studios, Sunnyvale; owner/dir. Jeanne Forman Enterprises (Music to Write By), 1982—; owner J. Forman Advt. Agy.; propr. Jeanne Forman Advt. and Enterprises; founder Classic Acts of Santa Barbara, 1991—; writer L.A. Times, 1978-80; columnist The Galeria Santa Barbara News Press, 1978; publicity writer Music Tchrs. Assn.; tchr. of blind Santa Clara County Assistance League; lectr. on blind techniques, vocal techniques, rapport in communications; free lance writer; gen. edn. staff Brooks Inst. Photography; voice specialist, 1990-91; Santa Barbara guest appearances There is a Way, Sta. KHJ-TV, L.A.; author, presenter seminars; voice specialist with speech difficulties or tonal problems, and with attention disorder deficiency. Author: Security, 1984, Secret of the Pig, 1984; composer: I Love to Hear the Bells, 1986, Christmas Is Here; compositions performed by U. Calif., Santa Barbara, 1971. Coach Civic Light Opera. Mem. Calif. Assn. Profl. Music Tchrs., Music Tchrs. Nat. Assn. Home: 1119 Alameda Padre Serra Santa Barbara CA 93103-2004

FORMIGONI, MAURI, artist, educator, gallery director; b. Louisville, Nov. 6, 1941; d. Maurice Vernon and Dorothy Marie (Neeld) Monihon; m. Ugo Carlo Formigoni, Sept. 15, 1965 (div. 1988); children: Gregg, Marco, Tania; m. Danijel Žuré, Jan. 27, 1992. BA, Kalamazoo Coll., 1963; postgrad., Sch. of Art Inst., Chgo., 1966-68; MA, Sangamon State U., 1972. Rsch. asst. U. Chgo., 1963-66; courtroom artist ABC-TV, Chgo., 1973; assoc. prof. visual arts U. Ill., Springfield, 1985—, gallery dir., 1985—; part-time instr. Lincoln Land C.C., Springfield, 1972-83. Mural commd. by Ill. Dept. Rev. Commn., 1988; exhibited in solo shows at Daut Pasha Hamman Mus., Skopje, Macedonia, 1991, Artemesia Gallery, Chgo., 1994, more than 40 group exhibits. Project Completion grantee Ill. Arts Coun., 1982, Chmn.'s grantee Ill. Arts Coun., 1994, Artist's grantee Springfield Area Arts Coun., 1988; Fulbright fellow, 1990-91. Mem. Coll. Art Assn., Chgo. Artists' Coalition, Fulcrum Gallery Soho. Home: 549 W Fulton Chicago IL 60661 Office: U Ill at Springfield Shepard Rd Springfield IL 62794

FORNELL, MARTHA STEINMETZ, art educator, artist; b. Galveston, Tex., Dec. 19, 1920; d. Joseph Duncan and Martha Lillian (McRee) Steinmetz; m. Earl Wesley Fornell, Sept. 20, 1947 (dec. Mar. 1969). B.Mus. cum laude, U. Tex., 1943; postgrad. U. Houston, 1953-56, Lamar U., 1957-60. Music cons., fgn. program editor Voice of America, USIA, N.Y.C., 1944-46; advt. cons. fed. agys., San Antonio, 1946-47; tchr. music secondary schs., Houston, 1953-56; tchr. art Beaumont (Tex.) Ind. Sch. Dist., 1956-79; collages exhibited Galerie Paula Insel, N.Y.C., 1974-84, Ponce, P.R., 1976-79, 82, 84, 87; group show participant Ann. Am. Nat. Miniature Show, Laramie, Wyo., Beaumont Art Mus. Annual, 1960, Houston Art League Easter Annual, 1960, Austin Women's Club, 1961. Recipient Circuit awards Tex. Fine Arts Assn., 1962-64, Invitational awards, 1964-65. Mem. Tex. Fine Arts Assn., Mu Phi Epsilon. Contbr. articles to Am.-German Rev. Address: 2303 Evalon St Beaumont TX 77702-1309

FORNERIS, JEANNE M., lawyer; b. Duluth, Minn., May 23, 1953; d. John Domenic and Elva Lorraine (McDonald) F.; m. Michael Scott Margulies, Feb. 6, 1982. AB, Macalester Coll., 1975; JD, U. Minn., 1978. Bar: Minn. 1978. Assoc. Halverson, Watters, Bye, Downs & Maki, Ltd., Duluth, Minn., 1978-81, Briggs & Morgan, P.A., Mpls. and St. Paul, 1981-83; ptnr. Hart & Bruner, P.A., Mpls., 1983-86; assoc. gen. counsel M.A. Mortenson Co., 1986-90, v.p., gen. coun., 1990—; instr. women's studies dept. U. Minn., Mpls., 1977-79. Author profl. edn. seminars; author, editor articles. Bd. dirs. Good Will Industries Vocat. Enterprises, Inc., 1979-81; chmn. bd. trustees Duluth Bar Library, 1981; mem. United Way Family and Individual Services Task Force, Duluth, 1981. Nat. Merit Assn. scholar, 1971. Fellow Am. Coll. Construction Lawyers; mem. ABA, Am. Arbitration Assn. (mem. large complex case panel), Minn. State Bar Assn., Hennepin County Bar Assn., Minn. Women Lawyers (bd. dirs.). Democrat. Roman Catholic. Office: MA Mortenson Co 700 Meadow Ln N Minneapolis MN 55422-4817

FORNEY, VIRGINIA SUE, educational counselor; b. Little Rock, Sept. 15, 1925; d. Robert Millard and Susan Amanda (Ward) Tate; m. J.D. Mullen, Jr., Oct. 13, 1945 (div. 1966); children: Michael Dunn, Patricia Sue; m. Bill E. Forney, Apr. 29, 1967. Student Tex. State Coll. for Women, 1943-46; BFA, U. Okla., 1948; postgrad. Benedictine Heights Coll., Tulsa, 1957-58; M.Teaching Arts, Tulsa U., 1969; postgrad. Okla. State U., intermittently, 1969—. Cert. secondary tchr., sch. counselor, vis. sch. counselor, Okla. With Sta. WNAD, U. Okla., 1947-49; tchr. lang. arts Tulsa Bd. Edn., 1959-73; women's counselor Tulsa YWCA, 1980; vis. sch. counselor Tulsa County Supt. of Schs. Office, 1980-86; dir. spl. project Tulsa County Supt. Schs. Office, 1986-91; owner, dir. Svc. to Families in Bus. and Industry, 1991—. Mem. budget com. United Way Greater Tulsa, 1980-86, edn. com. Planned Parenthood Greater Tulsa, 1980-86; mem. Tulsa County adv. coun. Okla. State U., 1983-85; chairperson Tulsa Coalition for Parenting Edn., 1983-84; chairperson problems of youth study Tulsa Met. C. of C., 1984-85; mem. gen. bd. March of Dimes Greater Tulsa, 1985; pres. evening alliance All Souls Unitarian Ch., 1993-94. Mem. Am. Assn. for Counseling and Devel., Internat. Assn. Pupil Personnel Workers (state bd. dirs. 1982-86), Okla. Assn. Family Resource Programs (regional v.p. 1982-86, state pres. 1986-87), Program Internat. Ednl. Exchange (community coordinator for Tulsa 1986-90), LWV Okla. (chairperson juvenile justice study 1976-77), LWV Met. Tulsa (mem. exec. bd. 1993-95), Tulsa Parents As Tchrs. Inc. (founding pres. 1991-92, exec. bd. 1992—). Democrat. Unitarian. Avocation: piano.

FORNI, PATRICIA ROSE, nursing educator, university dean; b. St. Louis, Feb. 14, 1932; d. Harold and Glenda M. (Keay) Brown. B.S.N., Washington U., St. Louis, 1955, M.S. (USPHS trainee), 1957; Ph.D. (USPHS fellow), St. Louis U., 1965; postgrad. (USPHS scholar), U. Minn., summers 1968, 70. Staff nurse McMillan EENT Hosp., St. Louis, summer 1955, Renard Psychiat. Hosp., St. Louis, part-time 1955-57; rsch. asst. Washington U. Sch. Nursing, St. Louis, 1957-59, rsch. assoc., 1959-61, asst. prof., 1964-66, assoc. dean in charge grad. edn., assoc. prof. gen. nursing sci., 1966-68; assoc. prof. pub. health nursing Wayne State U., Detroit, 1968-69, asst. dir. for manpower and edn. Ill. Regional Med. Program, Chgo., 1969-71; project dir. Midwest Continuing Profl. Edn. for Nurses, St. Louis U., 1971-75; dean, prof. nursing So. Ill. U., Edwardsville, 1975-88; dean, prof. Coll. Nursing U. Okla., Oklahoma City, 1988—; grant proposal reviewer Divsn. Nursing, USPHS, 1972-79, 88, 91, NSF, 1978, U.S. Dept. Edn., 1980; active Ill. Implementation Commn. on Nursing, 1975-77, Okla. State Health Plan Adv. Com., 1994—. Mem. peer rev. panel Nursing Outlook, 1987-91; mem. editl. bd. Health Care for Women Internat., 1984—, Jour. Profl. Nursing, 1988-90. Chairwoman articulation of nursing programs task force Okla. State Regents for Higher Edn., 1990-91; bd. dirs. Greater St. Louis Health Sys. Agy., 1976-81, Adult Edn. Coun. Greater St. Louis, 1973-76, Edwardsville unit Am. Cancer Soc., 1981-88; mem. adv. com. Okla. Health State Plan, 1994—. Fellow WHO, Sweden, Finland, 1985. Mem. Nat. League for Nursing (accreditation site visitor 1979—, nominating com. Coun. Baccalaureate and Higher Degree Programs 1979-82, pub. policy and legis. com. 1981-85, bd. dirs. 1991-93, treas. 1991-93, mem. fin. com. 1991-95), Nat. League for Health Care (trustee 1991-93), Am. Nurses Assn. (chmn. continuing edn. publs. com. 1975-76), Mo. Nurses Assn. (chmn. edn. com. 1973-77), Greater St. Louis Soc. Health Manpower Edn. and Tng. (chmn. legis. com. 1974-75), Midwest Alliance in Nursing (1st governing bd. 1979-80, 93—, chmn. nominations com. 1980, 81, mem. fin. com. 1993-94, chair fin. com. 1994—, treas. 1994—), Am. Assn. Colls. Nursing (program com. 1978-82, mem.-at-large, bd. dirs. 1990-92, chair rsch. com. 1990-92), Ill. Coun. Deans/Dirs. Baccalaureate and Higher Degree Programs in Nursing (chmn. 1979-81), Am. Acad. Nursing (treas., chairwoman fin. com., mem. gov. coun. 1989-93, editor Newsletter 1982-87), Ill. Nurses Assn. (commn. on adminstrn. 1983-87, commn. on edn. 1987-89), Okla. Nurses Found. (pres. bd. trustees 1990-93), Sigma Theta Tau Internat. (charter mem. Epsilon Eta chpt. 1980). Office: U Okla Coll Nursing PO Box 26901 Oklahoma City OK 73126

FORONDA, ELENA ISABEL, secondary school educator; b. N.Y.C., Jan. 15, 1947; d. Severino Deliso and LaVerne (Ibanez) F. BS in Music, Hunter Coll., CUNY, 1969, MA in Music Edn., 1971. Tchr. vocal music N.Y.C. Pub. Sch. System, 1970—; asst. dir. tchr. placement Hunter Coll., City U. N.Y., summers 1971-72; examination asst. N.Y.C. Pub. Sch. System Bd. Examiners, 1987-89. Sponsor children in World Vision Internat.; del. Asian Am. Women's Caucus, 1977; mem. Hunter Coll. choirs, 1968-69, 71; pianist, minister of music Ch. of The Holy Spirit, Bklyn., 1988-90; lay reader, lay eucharistic minister L.I. Diocese Episcopal Ch., 1993. Dist. winner Nat. Piano Playing Auditions, 1965; recipient N.Y. State permanent cert. Dept. Edn., 1971. Mem. Music Educators Nat. Conf., Music Educators Assn. N.Y.C., N.Y. State Sch. Music Assn., Amateur Chamber Music Players (N.Y.C.). Democrat.

FORREST, IRIS, publisher; b. N.Y.C., Dec. 4, 1925; d. Elliot Albert and Sade (Roth) Daitz; children: Richard Lee, Douglas Edward. BA, Finch Coll., 1944. Editor/publisher: Computer Tales of Fact and Fantasy, 1993, Computer Legends, Lies and Lore, 1994. Mem. Actors Equity Assn., Publishers Mktg. Assn., Fla. Publishers Assn. Office: Ageless Press PO Box 5915 Sarasota FL 34277-5915

FORREST, KATHERINE VIRGINIA, writer; b. Windsor, Ont., Can., Apr. 20, 1939; d. Leland Wilson and Mary Elizabeth (Gulhuly) McKinlay. Student, Wayne State U., UCLA. With GM Corp., Detroit, Mich., 1957-62; adminstr., mgr. Technicolor, Inc., L.A., 1962-72, Reynolds Metals Co., L.A., 1972-78; sr. editor The Naiad Press, Tallahassee, Fla., 1983-95. Author: Curious Wine, 1983, Daughters of a Coral Dawn, 1984, Amateur City, 1984, An Emergence of Green, 1986, Murder at the Nightwood Bar, 1987, Dreams and Swords, 1987, The Beverly Malibu, 1987, Murder by Tradition, 1989, Flashpoint, 1991, Liberty Square, 1996, Apparition Alley, 1997; editor numerous books. Mem. PEN Internat.

FORREST, TRUDY GREEN, school psychologist, counselor, special educator; b. Glens Falls, N.Y., Nov. 24, 1943; d. Floyd Wilson and Patricia May (Hess) Green; m. Alan Wayne Forrest, Sept. 11, 1965 (div. Apr. 23, 1973). BS in Elem. Edn., State U. N.Y., 1965; MA, St. Bonaventure (N.Y.) U., 1969; Edn. Spec., U. Con., 1973; M Tchr. of Rajah Yoga, Inst Simplified Kundalini Yoga, 1976. Cert. sch. psychology, sch. guidance counselor, spl. educator, elem. educator. Elem. tchr. Olean (N.Y.) Pub. Schs., 1965-68; spl. edn. tchr. East Hartford (Con.) Schs., 1968-71; learning disability cons. Bloomfield (Con.) Pub. Schs., 1971-74; diagnostic prescriptive tchr. Children's Svcs. Region II Mental Health Ctr., Oxford, Miss., 1974-81; instr. ednl. psychology Univ. Miss., 1974-80; intern counseling psychology Region II Mental Health Ctr., Oxford, 1978-79; sch. psychologist, tchr. Oxford Pub. Schs., 1981-82, spl. edn. tchr., autistic, 1982-92; spl. edn. tchr., cross categorial Harnett County Schs., Lillington, N.C., 1992—; v.p. Coun. for Exceptional Children, Oxford, 1974-75; v.p., state rep. Assn. Retarded Citizens, Oxford, 1989-90; bd. mem. Domestic Violence Project, Oxford, 1980-90; sch. psychologist testing, counseling Moore County Schs., 1993, Randolph County Schs., 1994; sch. psychologist Northampton County, 1995—; mem. N.C. Sch. Psychology Forum, 1994—; writer behavior programs; presenter in field. Bd. mem. Cmty. Goodfood Coop., Oxford, 1980-92; mem. Sierra Club, Oxford, 1980-82, Dem. Women, Oxford, 1981-92, Nat. Orgn. Women, Oxford, 1976-80; apptd. mem. State Dept. Edn. Inst. Learning Disabilities, 1970. Recipient Tchr. Inst. for Excellence award State Dept. Edn., Albany, N.Y., 1966. Mem. Nat. Assn. Sch. Psychologists, N.C. Assn. Sch. Psychologists, Internat. Reading Assn., Orton Dislexia Soc., Phi Delta Kappa. Democrat. Jewish. Home: 1321 Carolina Dr Sanford NC 27330

FORSELIUS, VANESSA LENARD, economist; b. McAllister, Okla., Nov. 5, 1954; d. Jack Harvey and Barbara Jean (Escue) Lenard; m. Arth Robert Forselius, Apr. 6, 1985; stepchildren: Jessica, Robert, Christina. BS in Agrl. Econ., Okla. State, 1977, MS in Agrl. Econ., 1979. Specialist devel. economist Okla. Coop. Extension Svc., Stillwater, 1979-85; program prin., economist Indsl. Siting Divsn. Wyo. Dept. Environ. Quality, Cheyenne, 1988—. Mem. Cheyenne Kennel Club (Jack Buttrick Meml. award 1996), Australian Shepherd Club Am. Democrat.

FORSETH, LYNN MARIE, college administrator; b. Milw., Oct. 7, 1956; d. Jack Paul and Elizabeth Ann (Van Zeeland) Spridco; m. Michael Vernon Forseth, June 27, 1981; children: Nicole Anne, Rachel Marie. BS in Elem. Edn., U. Wis., 1978, MS in Continuing and Vocat. Edn., 1985; MS in Ednl. Psychology, U. Wis., Milw., 1992. Elem. tchr. New Berlin (Wis.) Pub. Schs., 1978, Mukwonago (Wis.) Pub. Schs., 1978; registration clk. Milw. Area Tech. Coll., 1978-79, student svcs. specialist, 1979-86, basic edn. instr., 1986, project coord., 1987-88, student svcs. adminstr., 1987—; Wis. Leadership Identification Program participant Wis. State Bd. Vocat., Tech. and Adult Edn., Madison, 1984-85. mem. ACA, Am. Vocat. Assn., Am. Assn. Women in C.C.s, Am. Coll. Counseling Assn., Nat. Assn. for Career Devel., Wis. Vocat. Assn. (state com. 1987-88), Milw. Vocat. Assn. (pres. 1987-88, bd. dirs. 1985-86, award of merit 1987), Sigma Epsilon Sigma, Pi Lambda Theta. Home: 2760 S 149th St New Berlin WI 53151-3702 Office: Milw Area Tech Coll 1200 S 71st St Milwaukee WI 53214-3110

FORSNESS, KITTY ALETHA, lead and asbestos abatement administrator; b. Wolf Point, Mont., June 4, 1963; d. Dewey Charles and JoAnn (Russell) F. BA in Journalism, U. N.D., Williston, 1988. Cert. asbestos, hazmat and lead supr. Supr. TLH, Seattle, 1991-94, CAA, Auburn, Wash., 1994, Coralco, Honolulu, 1994, Crown Delta, Seattle, 1994, Thermatech, Bellevue, Wash., 1995; owner, operator Kit's Korner, Puyallup, Wash., 1995-96; lead and asbestos abatement supr. Coralco, Honolulu, 1996—. Address: HC 33 Box 5035 Wolf Point MT 59201 also: # 159-B 854-688 Ala Mahiku Dr Waianae HI 96792

FORSTEN, DEBORAH I., marketing professional; b. Dayton, Tenn., Apr. 9, 1955; d. William Richard and Helen Pearl (Janhauser) F. BS in Phys. Edn., U. Tenn., Knoxville, 1976, MS in Edn., 1979. Asst. to dir. communication U.S. Gymnastics Fedn., Indpls., 1981-84; coord. spl. projects U. Ill, Urbana-Champaign, 1986-91; program developer Zenith Mgmt. and Desktop Design, Dayton, Tenn., 1991-93; dir. communication St. Louis Sports Commn., 1993-95; dir. mktg., ops. Palm Beach (Fla.) County Sports Commn., 1995—; coach Illini Twisters Gymnastics Club, Champaign, Martinettes Gymnastics Sch. and Athletic World, Longmont, Colo. Author: YMCA Progressive Gymnastics Program, 1987, SPlash, 1985, Tear in Saint Louis Sports, 1994, (with M. Murphy) On the Guard, 1986; contbr. articles to profl. jours., mags. and newspapers. Mem. Nat. Assn. Women in Communications, U.S. Gumnastics Fedn., Nat. Assn. Gymnastics Judges. Office: PBC Sports Commn Ste 202 1555 Palm Beach Lakes Blvd West Palm Beach FL 33401

FORSTER, SUSAN BOGART, computer educator; b. Hackensack, N.J., June 6, 1944; d. Charles William and Lillian (Vito) Bogart; m. John D. Forster, June 17, 1967; children: Gregory, Brian. BA, Mt. Holyoke Coll., 1966; MEd, George Mason U., 1985. Tchr. adult edn. Fairfax (Va.) County Pub. Schs., 1983-84; programmer Fairfax County Pub. Schs., Annandale, Va., 1984-85; computer dir. Potomac Sch., McLean, Va., 1985-93; computer trainer, tchr. The Langley Sch., McLean, Va., 1994—; dir. computer Summer Inst., Washington, 1993—; program developer Adult Computer Literacy Program, McLean, 1991-92; adj. prof. edn. Marymount U., 1993—, George Mason U., Fairfax, Va., 1993—. Mem. Computer Assn. Ind. Schs. (program chair 1990-91). Home: 1900 Wintergreen Ct Reston VA 22091-5114

FORSYTH, PRISCILLA ELIZABETH, lawyer; b. Estherville, Iowa, July 12, 1961; d. Gordon Jameson and Martha Joan Forsyth. Student, U. Kans., 1979-81; BA in Econs., U. Iowa, 1983, JD, 1986. Bar: Ariz. 1986, Iowa 1992, U.S. Dist. Ct. (no. dist.) Iowa 1993. Law clk., bailiff Judge Frederick J. Martone, Phoenix, 1986; dep. Maricopa County Pub. Defender, Phoenix and Mesa, Ariz., 1987-92; asst. atty. Dickinson County, Spirit Lake, Iowa, 1992; pvt. practice Milford, Iowa, 1993—. Mem. Iowa State Bar Assn. (coun. mem. criminal sect. 1994—, chmn. criminal law sect., 1996-97), Nat. Assn. Criminal Def. Lawyers, Assn. Trial Lawyers of Am., Dickinson County Bar Assn. (pres. 1992-93), Spirit Lake Kiwanis Club, PEO, Iowa Great Lake Area C. of C. (bd. dirs. 1993—), Ariz. State Bar Assn. Office: PO Box 295 910 10th St Milford IA 51351

FORSYTH, TRUDY LOUISE, mechanical engineer; b. Denver, May 18, 1958; d. Royce Delmer and Betty Louise (Selby) F.; m. Frank Hamblin, June 22, 1991 (div. Dec. 1995). BS in Mech. Engr., U. Colo., 1983, MS in Mech. Engr., 1989. Grad. tchr. asst. U. Colo., Denver, 1980-83, exec. sec. staff coun., 1996—; sr. engr. Martin Marietta, Denver, 1984-93; staff project coord. Nat. Renewable Energy Lab., Golden, Colo., 1994—; summer engr. Pub. Svc. Co., Denver, 1982; instr. part-time Red Rocks C.C., Lakewood, Colo., 1981-85. Pres. Kids in Need of Dentistry, Denver, 1995-96; mem. Mile-Hi coun. bd. Girl Scouts Am., Denver, 1993-94; fin. chair State Bd. Edn., Denver, 1992; bass clarinetist/clarinetist in cmty. orchestras. Home: 2396 S Columbine St Denver CO 80210 Office: NREL/NWTC 1617 Cole Blvd Golden CO 80401

FORSYTHE, PATRICIA HAYS, development professional; b. Curtis, Ark.; d. John Chambers and Flora Jane (Eby) Hays; m. Kurt G. Pahl, Dec. 15, 1962 (div. Dec. 1980); children: Thomas Walter, Susan Clara; m. Robert E. Forsythe, June 20, 1981; 1 child, Nathaniel Ryan. BA, Calif. State U., Los Angeles, 1974; MSLS, U. So. Calif., 1976. Asst. to dir. devel. office The Assocs., Calif. Inst. Tech., Pasadena, 1978-81; exec. dir. Iowa City Pub. Library Found., 1982-89; dir. devel. Hoover Presdl. Libr. Assn., West Branch, Iowa, 1989-94, exec. dir., 1994—. Contbr. articles to profl. jours. Recipient Outstanding Fund Raising Exec. award Ea. Iowa, 1990, honorary Paul Harris fellow, 1994. Mem. ALA, LWV (editor 1985-87), Nat. Soc. Fund Raising Execs. (bd. dirs. 1987-89, chmn. Ea. Iowa Philanthropy Day 1990-91, bd. dirs. Ea. Iowa chpt. 1986—), Iowa City C. of C., West Branch C. of C. (bd. dirs.), Iowa Life Shares Assn. (bd. dirs., pres. 1995-96), Libr. Adminstrn. and Mgmt. Assn., Women in Mgmt., Hancher Guild (audience devel. 1981-85, pres. 1985-86), Univ. Athletic Club, Rotary (program chair 1992-96). Congregationalist. Home: 1806 E Court St Iowa City IA 52245-4643 Office: Hoover Presdl Libr Assn PO Box 696 West Branch IA 52358-0696

FORT, BRENDA LOUISE, critical care nurse; b. Detroit, Aug. 19, 1955; d. William Talmadge and Hattie Belle (Walton) Walker; m. John Allen Fort, Jan. 29, 1983; children: Christopher Jeremy, Daniel Nicholas, Bethany Lynne. BA, U. Mich., 1977; BSN, Ga. State U., 1987. RN. Staff nurse VA Med. Ctr., Decatur, Ga., 1987-95, critical care nurse, 1995—. Disaster health nurse ARC, Atlanta, 1994—, health fair coord., 1994, CPR instr., 1993—. Mem. ANA, AACN (cert.), Sigma Theta Tau, Phi Kappa Phi. Home: 3453 Wren Rd Decatur GA 30032 Office: VA Med Ctr 1670 Clairmont Rd Decatur GA 30033

FORTI, CORINNE ANN, corporate communications executive; b. N.Y.C., July 26, 1941; d. Wilbur Walter and Sylvia Joan (Charap) Bastian; B.A., CUNY, 1963; m. Joseph Donald Forti, Aug. 18, 1962 (dec.); 1 child, Raina. Adminstrv. asst. Ednl. Broadcasting Corp., 1963-65; adminstrv. asst. W.R. Grace & Co., N.Y.C., 1965-67, pub. relations rep., 1967-70, mgr. info. services, 1970-79, dir. info. services, 1980-86, dir. info. and advt., 1986-87; pres. Bastian-Forti Communications, 1988-89, Forti Communications Inc., 1989—; lectr. photography and graphics Am. Mgmt. Assn. Bd. dirs. YM/YWCA Day Care, Inc. Named to Acad. Women Achievers, YWCA, 1979; recipient citation award in communications Nat. Council of Women, 1979. Mem. Am. Women in Radio and TV, Chem. Mfrs. Assn., Am. Mgmt. Assn., Women Execs. in Pub. Relations. Republican. Roman Catholic. Home and Office: 1246 Calle Yucca Thousand Oaks CA 91360-2239

FORTI, LENORE STEIMLE, business consultant; b. Houghton, Mich., Sept. 9, 1924; d. Russell Nicholas and Agnes (McCloskey) Steimle; m. Frank Forti, May 29, 1950 (dec.). BBA summa cum laude, Northwood U., 1973, Dr.Laws, 1969. Asst. corp. sec., purchasing agt. Fed. Life & Casualty Co., Detroit, 1942-53; supr. sectl. J.L. Hudson Co., Detroit, 1953-57, adminstrv. asst. to exec. v.p., 1957-86; instr. Wayne State U. and U. Mich. Adult Edn., Detroit, 1958-71; creator, dir. Seminars for Profl. People, 1971—. Co-author: The Professional Secretary; contbr. articles to profl. jours. Asst. br. dir. planning City of Detroit for Civil Def.; chmn. bd. trustees PSI Rsch. and Ednl. Found.; trustee PSI Retirement Home Complex, Albuquerque; elected dir. Property Owners and Residents Assn., Sun City West Mcpl. Govt., 1994; past pres. Women's Bd. Northwood U., Midland, Mich.; pres. parish coun. Our Lady of Lourdes Ch., Sun City West, Ariz., 1988, pres. ladies guild, 1990, pres. singles club, 1995; 1st v.p. Vol. Bur. of Sun Cities, 1989. Elected One of Detroit's Top Ten Working Women, 1969; elected to Exec. and Profl. Hall of Fame. Mem. Profl. Sec. Internat. (internat. pres. 1967-69), Future Secs. Assn. (nat. coord.), Lioness Club (pres. 1991-92), Sun City West Singles Club (pres. 1988, pres. Singles Club Ch. 1995). Republican. Roman Catho . Home and Office: 12613 W Seneca Dr Sun City West AZ 85375-4635

FORTIER, DANA SUZANNE, psychotherapist; b. Fresno, Calif., Jan. 15, 1952; d. Dan and Louise (Metkovich) Ninkovich; m. Timothy Fortier, Jan. 29, 1994. BA in Journalism summa cum laude, Calif. State U., Fresno, 1974; BSN, Calif. State U., 1979, MSW with distinction, 1986. Registered nurse, Calif; lic. social worker, Calif. Staff nurse Valley Med. Ctr., Fresno, 1980-81; pub. health nurse Fresno County Health Dept., 1981-83; therapist II Sierra Community Hosp., Fresno, 1986-87; women's svcs. coord. Turning Point Youth Svcs., Visalia, Calif., 1987-89; psychotherapist and cons. in pvt. practice Visalia, 1989—; instr. San Joaquin Valley Coll., 1994—; clins. cons. in field. Contbr. articles to profl. jours. Mem. Task Force on Pregnant Mothers, 1990—. Mem. Calif. Women's Commn. on Drugs and Alcohol, Calif. Advocacy for Pregnent Women, Soc. for Clin. Social Wk., Nat. Assn. Social Workers, Visalia Bus. and Profl. Women's Clubs. Republican. Office: 304 S Johnson St Visalia CA 93291-6136

FORTNEY, DIANE ELINE OSBORN, accountant, financial analyst; b. Rockford, Ill., May 1, 1958; d. Lloyd William and Lila Jean Belle (Lidke) Osborn; m. Gary Michael Fortney, May 17, 1980; children: Jessica, Douglas. BS in Acctg., Mankato (Minn.) State U., 1980. CPA, Minn.; cert. tax profl. Intern gen. acctg. PEP Svcs., Bloomington, Minn., 1979; asst. tax preparer J. Meyer Acctg., Roseville, Minn., 1979-80; staff acct. Samuel Held & Assocs., St. Louis Park, Minn., 1980-82; head acct. Republic Telcom, Bloomington, 1982-84; consolidation acct. CTS Fabri-Tek, Inc., Eden Prairie, Minn., 1984-86; fin. analyst Micro Component Tech., Inc., Shoreview, Minn., 1986-90; pvt. practice acctg., Inver Grove Heights, Minn., 1983—. Tutor Mankato State U., 1978-79; treas. Salem Cmty. Child Care Ctr., Inver Grove Heights, 1986-93; treas. Mt. Bethel United Meth. Ch.,

1991—, chair adminstrv. bd., 1996—; bd. dirs. BEST Found.; Minn. del. White House Conf. on Small Bus., 1995, vice chair regional implementation team, 1995—. Mem. AICPA, Minn. Soc. CPAs, SSP/IGH C. of C. (bd. dirs. 1995—), Minn. C. of C. (small bus. com.), Am. Bus. Women's Assn. (pres. Key Wakota charter chpt. 1988-89, Woman of Yr. 1987), Micro Component Tech. Inc. Employees Club (pres. 1987-90), Nat. Soc. Tax Profls. Methodist. Office: Fortney Place 6775 Cahill Ave Inver Grove Heights MN 55076

FORTSON-RIVERS, TINA E. (THOMASENA ELIZABETH FORTSON-RIVERS), computer and social studies educator; b. Anderson, S.C.; d. Thomas Henry and Mary (Oliver) Fortson; m. Michael M. Rivers, Sept. 12, 1962 (div. 1973); children: Michael II, George Thomas, Kashiya Elaine. BA, Spelman Coll., 1962; MEd, Bowie State U., 1979; MS, Johns Hopkin U., 1982. Cert. adminstrn., supervision, Md. Tchr. Tulip Grove Elem. Sch., Bowie, Md., 1973-79, Kenmoor Elem. Sch., Landover, Md., 1979-82; computer coord. Benjamin Stoddert Mid. Sch., Temple Hills, Md., 1982-86; computer tng. specialist Prince Georges County Pub. Schs., Upper Marlboro, Md., 1986—; ednl. cons. Wicat, Provo, Utah, 1985-91; design cons. Computer Lady, Capitol Heights, Md., 1990-92; del. U.S.-Russia Conf. on Edn., 1994; del. Initiative for Edn., Sci. and Tech. to Republic of South Africa, 1995. Author: Education Software Correlation to PGCPS Social Studies Curriculum, 1992. Mem. Com. of 100, Prince Georges County Schs., Upper Marlboro, 1985. Mem. Mid. States Coun. for Social Studies (bd. dirs. 1979—, conf. program chair 1989, regional conf. coord. 1992-93, pres. 1994-96), Md. Coun. for Social Studies (treas. 1982-83), Prince Georges County Coun. for Social Studies (pres. 1981-82), Nat. Coun. for Social Studies (membership com. chmn. 1994), Alpha Delta Kappa (sec. Eta 1992-94, membership chair 1994-96, pres.-elect 1996—, Md. dist. chair 1994-96, corr. sec. 1996—). Methodist. Office: Prince Georges County Pub Schs 8437 Landover Rd Landover MD 20785-3502

FORTUNATO, JOANNE ALBA, athletic director; b. Phila.; d. Frank and MaryAnn (Vasquez) Torcaso. BS, Temple U., 1957, MS, 1959; PhD, U. So. Calif., L.A., 1973, Northwestern U., Chgo., 1986. Tchr. Phila. Pub. Sch. System, 1957-64; asst. prof. Trenton (N.J.) Coll., 1964-68, Cen. Conn. State Coll., New Britain, 1968-69; teaching asst. U. So. Calif., L.A., 1970-71; asst. prof. CUNY, Bklyn., 1971-75; assoc. athletic dir. and prof. Northwestern U., Chgo., 1975-80; athletic dir. Keene (N.H.) State Coll., 1981-93; commr. athletics New Eng. Collegiate Conf., 1990-93, Calif. C.C.'s, 1995—; commr. New Eng. Collegiate Conf., 1990-93; chair infraction com. Ea. Collegiate Athletic Conf., Centerville, Mass., 1984-89; regional chair W soccer Nat. Collegiate Athletic Assn., 1987-90; commr. Div. I champ, AIAW, Washington, 1983-86. Recipient Instl. Svc. award Italian Olympic Com., Rome, 1965, Ann. Leadership award Internat. Orgn. Women Execs., 1978, Citation of Recognition USVBA, 1972. Mem. AAHPERD, Nat. Assn. Coll. Women Athletic Adminstrs., Nat. Assn. Coll. Dirs. of Athletics. Home: 3090 Sierra Blvd Sacramento CA 95064 Office: CCLC/COA 2017 O St Sacramento CA 95864

FORTUNE, LAURA CATHERINE DAWSON, elementary school educator; b. Louisville, Feb. 2, 1931; d. Lewis Harper and Zelma Ruth (Hocutt) Dawson; m. James Ralph Fortune, Jan. 10, 1950; children: Elaine, Jean, Tom, Joe. BS, R.I. Coll., 1969, MEd, 1972; postgrad., Longwood Coll., Farmville, Va., 1980-88, U. Va., 1977-90. Cert. math. tchr., elem. edn. tchr., mid. sch. tchr. Elem. sch. tchr. North Kingston (R.I.) Schs., 1969-74; 6th grade tchr. Campbell County Schs., Altavista, Va., 1974-92, sch. divsn. grantwriter, 1992-96, instructional coord., 1987-91. Mem. unit com. Rep. Party, Campbell County; tchr. adv. coun. Rep. Party, Va., past chmn.; mem. Va. Gov.'s Commn. on Champion Schs., 1994-96; leader Girl Scouts U.S.A., mem. parent com., 1961-69; treas. Narrow River Preservation Assn., 1970-74; mem. Edn. Commn. of States. Mem. NEA (Rep. Educators Caucus past chair), ASCD, Va. Edn. Assn. (Rep. Educators Caucus), Campbell County Edn. Assn., Phi Delta Kappa. Baptist. Address: RR 2 Box 324 Evington VA 24550-9717

FORWARD, DOROTHY ELIZABETH, legal assistant; b. Medford, Mass., Oct. 12, 1919; d. Roy Clifford and Julia (Lane) Hurd; student UCLA, 1964; m. Winston W. Forward, Sept. 29, 1942. Sec. nat. dir. fund raising ARC, Washington, 1943-46; legal sec. William W. Waters, Esq., Los Angeles, 1953-56; office mgr. Winston W. Forward, Ins. Adjuster, Arcadia, Calif., 1956-64; legal asst. John M. Podlech, Esq., Pasadena, 1964-79; dir. Calif. Probate Insts., Arcadia, 1970—; ind. probate legal asst., 1979—; condr. workshops in probate procedures, 1967-92. Recipient ARC Meritorious Service award, 1945. Mem. Nat. Assn. Legal Secs., Legal Secs. Inc., Calif. Assn. Legal Secs. (parliamentarian 1982-84), Pasadena Legal Secs. Assn. (Sec. of Yr. 1974, 75, 77, Freedom Through Edn. award 1975, pres. 1976-78), Los Angeles County Forum of Legal Secs. (chmn. 1978-80), Nat. Assn. Legal Assts. (charter), Arcadia Travelers Club (recording sec. 1993, 94). Contbg. author: Calif. Legal Secretary's Handbook, 1984, 85. Office: PO Box 660311 Arcadia CA 91066-0311

FORYST, CAROLE, mortgage broker; b. Chgo., Apr. 8; d. James M. and Marie V. Foryst; m. Anthony H. Cordesman, Feb. 14, 1976; children: Justin G., Alexander Scott. Student, Rosary Coll., 1958-61, Cite Universite de Grenoble, France, 1961, Hunter Coll., 1964-67, Roosevelt U., 1970-71. Fin. reporter Chgo. Sun-Times, 1969-72; fin. reporter Los Angeles Times, 1972; staff asst. to sec. U.S. Dept. Treasury, Washington, 1973-76; dep. dir. pub. affairs U.S. Dept. Interior, Washington, 1976; asst. v.p. Assn. Am. Railroads, Washington, 1977-78; v.p. AMTRAK, Washington, 1979-81; assoc. adminstr. budget and policy Urban Mass Transp. Adminstrn., Washington, 1981-84; comml. real estate broker Barnes, Morris & Pardoe, Washington, 1984-88, Larry Hogan & Assocs., Inc., Landover, Md., 1988-93; mortgage broker Mortgage Investment Corp., Vienna, Va., 1993-94, Windsor Mortgage Co, McLean, Va., 1994—; mem. fin. svc. com. Treas. Dept., Fed. Credit Union, 1991-93, Pub. Internat. Bus. Insights, 1991-93, Glbal Techs. Co., 1993—, Hotels and Comm. Real Estate Co., 1993—. Republican. Home: 960 Carya Ct Great Falls VA 22066-1929

FOSCARINIS, MARIA, lawyer; b. N.Y.C., Aug. 8, 1956; d. Nicolas and Rosa F. BA, Barnard Coll., 1977; MA, Columbia U., 1978, JD, 1981. Bar: N.Y. 1982, U.S. Dist. Ct. (so. and ea. dists.) N.Y. 1983, D.C. 1986, U.S. Dist. Ct. D.C., U.S. Ct. Appeals (D.C. cir.). Law clk. to judge U.S. Ct. Appeals (2d cir.), N.Y.C., 1981-82; assoc. Sullivan & Cromwell, N.Y.C., 1982-85; counsel Nat. Coalition for Homeless, Washington, 1985-89; founder and dir. Nat. Law Ctr. on Homelessness and Poverty, Washington, 1989—. Notes editor Columbia U. Law Rev., 1980-81. Harlan Fiske Stone scholar, 1978-79; John Dewey fellow. Mem. ABA (commr. Homelessness and Poverty, 1989-95). Home: 1444 Rhode Island Ave NW Washington DC 20005-5455 Office: Nat Law Ctr Homelessness & Poverty 918 F St NW Ste 412 Washington DC 20004-1406

FOSCARINIS, ROSA, pediatrician, allergist; b. Burlington, Vt., Apr. 7, 1916; d. Gerassimos and Maria (Focarinis) Moshopoulos; m. Nicolas Foscarinis, July 22, 1946; 1 child, Maria. MD, Nat. U. Athens, 1940. Diplomate Am. Bd. Pediat. Rotating intern Fordham Hosp., N.Y.C., 1948-49; pediat. resident Gouverneur Hosp., N.Y.C., 1949-50, attending pediat. allergy, 1977—; pediat. resident Postgrad. Hosp., N.Y.C., 1950-51; allergy tng. Mount Sinai Hosp., N.Y.C., 1955-72; pvt. practice N.Y.C., 1951-86; attending pediat. Med. Ctr. NYU, N.Y.C., 1951-93, clin. assoc. prof., 1971—; attending pediat. Bellevue Hosp. Ctr., N.Y.C., 1963-91; cons. pediatrician Manhattan State Hosp., N.Y.C., 1965-75; attending pediatrician Astoria Gen. Hosp., N.Y.C., 1973-87; cons. allergy T. Cardinal Cooke, N.Y.C., 1982—. Recipient award City of N.Y. Dept. Hosps., 1964, citation Med. Soc. State N.Y., 1990. Fellow Am. Acad. Pediat.; mem. Am. Coll. Allergy and Immunology (com. food allergy 1984-86), N.Y. State Med. Soc., N.Y. County Med. Soc., N.Y. Allergy Soc. Home: 64 E 94th St New York NY 10128

FOSGATE HEGGLI, JULIE DENISE, producer; b. El Paso, Tex., Feb. 17, 1954; d. Orville Edward and Patricia (Ward) Fosgate; m. Bjarne Heggli, June 20, 1980; children: Elise Mai, Kristin April. BA in Broadcasting, U. So. Calif., 1976, MA in Journalism, 1978. On-board editor Royal Viking Line, San Francisco, 1978-80; editor Stentor, Trondheim, Norway, 1981; staff Grunion Gazette, Long Beach, Calif., 1981; news editor Nine Network Australia, Los Angeles, 1981-82; editor South Coast Metro News, Costa Mesa, Calif., 1981-82; v.p. The Newport Group, Newport Beach, Calif., 1982-85; exec. editor Orange County This Month, Newport Beach, 1985; exec. dir. mktg. Gen. Group Cos., Harbor City, Calif., 1985-87; sr. v.p. mktg. Automax Corp., L.A., 1987-88, Gen. Group Internat., Harbor City, Calif., 1988-90; assoc. producer Zoo Life Tv Spls., L.A., 1991; asoc. producer NBC News, Burbank, Calif., 1992-94; v.p. mktg. Western Nat., Scottsdale, Ariz., 1994—. Mem. Phi Beta Kappa. Home: 9640 E Davenport Scottsdale AZ 85260-6154 Office: Western Nat 7272 E Indian School Rd Scottsdale AZ 85251-3921

FOSHAY, MAXINE VALENTINE SHOTTLAND, civic worker, public relations executive; b. N.Y.C., Feb. 14, 1921; d. Maximillian Stanford and Violet Gertrude (Turner) Shottland; m. Robert Lethbridge Foshay, Mar. 16, 1956. B.A., Royal Acad. Dramatic Arts (London), 1943. Field rep. Am. Cancer Soc., N.Y.C., 1967-68; dir. fund raising and pub. rels. Preventive Medicine Inst., Strang Clinic 1969-71; dir. fund raising and pub. rels. Fedn. Handicapped, N.Y.C., 1971-72; exec. dir. Irvington House, 1972-73; chmn. group affiliates Meml. Sloan Kettering, 1960-66; v.p. Meml. Sloan Kettering Soc., 1966-67; vol. Meml. Sloan Kettering Cancer Soc., 1956-77; prin. Maxine V. Foshay and Assocs., 1977—; v.p. Victoria Home for Retired Men and Women, Ossining, N.Y., 1988—; bd. dirs. Elder Craftsman, N.Y.C.; dir. devel. Children's Asthmatic Found. N.Y. Mem. Daus. Brit. Empire State N.Y. (1st v.p. 1980-84, statewide pres. 1984-88, Medal Brit. Empire Her Majesty's Honours List 1987).

FOSHER, MARY JANE, humanities educator; b. Shakopee, Minn., Dec. 19, 1946; d. William Harold and Mary Agnes (MacEachern) Block; children: Cassandra, Jonathan. BA, Notre Dame Coll., 1969; MS, U. N.H., 1987. English tchr. Raymond (N.H.) High Sch., 1980—; dir. English curriculum Raymond Sch. Dist., 1987—. Bd. dirs. A Safe Place, Portsmouth, N.H., 1993—. Mem. Nat. Coun. Tchrs. English, New Hampshire Feminist Connection (founding, bd. dirs.), NOW (v.p., sec. Seacoast chpt. 1994—), N.H. Assn. Tchrs. English (bd. dirs. 1995—). Democrat. Office: Raymond High Sch 45 Harriman Hill Rd Raymond NH 03077

FOSNAUGH, DARLA JOY, accountant; b. Decatur, Ind., Dec. 8, 1971; d. Roger Lee and Marilyn Jane (Sprunger) Fox. BS in Acctg., Ind. Inst. Tech., 1994. Libr. asst. Ind. Inst. Tech., Ft. Wayne, 1990-91, lab. technician, 1991, teaching asst., 1991-92, tutor, 1992-94, asst. to accounts payable mgr., 1992-93; internal acct. Graber Ins. Inc., Berne, Ind., 1990—; cons. acct. A/Z Tech, Inc., Ft. Wayne, 1993-94. Ind. Inst. Tech. Alumni scholar, 1993, Realizing A Dream scholar, 1992; named All-Am. scholar. Mem. Inst. Mgmt. Accts., Alpha Chi, Phi Beta Lambda (sec., pres. 1992-94). Mennonite Ch. Home: 895 W 500 S Berne IN 46711

FOSS, LYNNE ARLENE, pediatric nurse practitioner; b. Oslo, May 26, 1961; d. Gerald Peter and Bernyce Anne (Arrajj) F.; m. Brian Andrew Brown, Jan. 15, 1990. BSN, U. Del., 1984; cert. PNP, USAF, 1989; MSN, U. Wash., 1995. Nat. cert. PNP. Commd. 2d lt. USAF, 1984, advanced through grades to maj., 1994; staff nurse USAF, Las Vegas, 1984-86, Lakenheath, Eng., 1986-88; PNP USAF, Rapid City, S.D., 1989-93, Great Falls, Mont., 1995—; spkr. Iowa Nurse Practitioner Conf., 1991, Uniformed Nurse Practitioner Conf., 1992, Soc. Rsch. on Child Devel. Symposium, 1995. Fellow Nat. Assn. PNPs, Uniformed Nurse Practitioner Assn.

FOSSLAND, JOEANN JONES, professional speaker, marketing consultant; b. Balt., Mar. 21, 1948; d. Milton Francis and Clementine (Bowen) Jones; m. Richard E. Yellott III, 1966 (div. 1970); children: Richard E. IV, Dawn Joeann; m. Robert Gerard Fossland Jr., Nov. 25, 1982. Student, Johns Hopkins U., 1966-67; cert. in real estate, Hogan's Sch. Real Estate, 1982. Owner Kobble Shop, Indiatlantic, Fla., 1968-70, Downstairs, Atlanta, 1971; seamstress Aspen (Colo.) Leather, 1972-75; owner Backporch Feather & Leather, Aspen and Tucson, 1975-81; area mgr. Welcome Wagon, Tucson, 1982; realtor assoc. Tucson Realty & Trust, 1983-85; mgr. Home Illustrated mag., Tucson, 1985-87; asst. pub., gen. mgr. Phoenix, Scottsdale, Albuquerque, Tricities Tucson Homes Illustrated, 1990-93; pres. Advantage Solutions Group, Cortaro, Ariz., 1993—; power leader Darryl Davis Seminars Power Program, 1995—. Designer leather goods (Tucson Mus. Art award 1978, Crested Butte Art Fair Best of Show award 1980). Voter registrar Recorder's Office City of Tucson, 1985-91; bd. dirs. Hearth Found., Tucson, 1987—, pres., 1994; bd. dirs. Ariz. Integrated Residential & Ednl. Svcs., Inc., 1989-95, pres. 1994-95). Mem. NAFE, Women's Coun. Realtors (leadership tng. grad. designation, pres. Tucson chpt. 1995, Ariz. state pres. 1996, Tucson Affiliate of Yr. award 1991), Tucson Assn. Realtors (Affiliate of Yr. award 1988). Democrat. Presbyterian. Office: ADvantage Solutions Group PO Box 133 Cortaro AZ 85652-0133

FOSTER, (MARY) CHRISTINE, literary agent; b. L.A., Mar. 19, 1943. BA, Immaculate Heart Coll., 1967; M in Journalism, UCLA, 1968. Tchr., 1962-65, Pacific U., Tokyo, 1968; dir. R & D Metromedia Prodns. Corp., L.A., 1968-71; dir. devel. and prodn. svcs. Wolper Orgn., L.A., 1971-76; mgr. film programs NBC-TV, L.A., 1976-77; v.p. movies for TV and mini-series Columbia Pictures TV, L.A., 1977-81; v.p. series programs Columbia TV, L.A., 1981; v.p. program devel. Group W Prodns., L.A., 1981-87; ptnr. The Agy., L.A., 1988-90; agent Shapiro-Lichtman Talent Agy., L.A., 1990—; tchr. UCLA Ext., 1987—; lectr., spkr. in U.S. and internat. Mem. exec. com. Humanitas Awards, 1986—, Caths. in Media, 1993—; mem. activities com. Acad. TV Arts & Scis., 1989-91; mem. L.A. Roman Cath. Archiodean Comm. Com., 1986-89; bd. dirs. Women in Film, 1977-78. Office: Shapiro-Lichtman Talent Agy 8827 Beverly Blvd Los Angeles CA 90048*

FOSTER, FAITH WILHELMINA, school counselor, educational consultant; d. William and Estelle (Taylor) Smith; m. Esau Foster Sr., Aug. 21, 1971 (div. 1988); children: Esau II, Shani Lynn. BS, Ctrl. State U., 1965; MEd, Kent State U., 1970. Lic. profl. counselor; cert. tchr., prin. Tchr. Cleve. Pub. Schs., 1965-69, 70-71; counselor University City (Mo.) Pub. Schs., 1972-75; probation officer criminal courts Allegheny County, Pitts., 1977-80; counselor Cleveland Heights/University Heights Bd. Edn., 1983—; career edn. counselor Upward Bd., 1983—. Author: Career Education in Middle School Education, 1974. Mem. citizens adv. coun. City of Cleveland Heights, 1991—; chairperson civil rights AFT, Cleveland Heights/University Heights, 1993—; chairperson Sch. Am. Delta Sigma Theta, Cleve., 1993—. Mem. ASCD, Phi Delta Kappa. Home: 1080 Rushleigh Rd Cleveland OH 44121-1444

FOSTER, FRANCES, actress; b. Yonkers, N.Y., June 11, 1924; d. George Henry and Helen Elizabeth (Lloyd) Brown Davenport; m. Morton Goldsen, Sept. 11, 1982; m. Robert Standfield Foster, Mar. 29, 1941 (dec.); 1 son, Terrell Robert. Student, Am. Theatre Wing, N.Y.C., 1949-52. Artist in residence CCNY, N.Y.C., 1973-77; actress Negro Ensemble Co., N.Y.C., 1967-86. Appeared in plays throughout the world including, Munich Olympics, 1972; World Theatre Festival, London, 1969, Australia, 1977. Recipient Obie award, 1985. Mem. SAG, AFTRA, Actors Equity Assn. (councillor 1953-67). Democrat.

FOSTER, GERALDINE U., pharmaceutical company executive. Sr. v.p. investor rels. Schering-Plough Corp., Madison, N.J., 1995—. Office: Schering-Plough Corp 1 Giralda Farms Madison NJ 07940-1027*

FOSTER, JOAN S., retired elementary educator; b. Bridgeport, Conn., Aug. 14, 1931; d. Edward and Ella (Murphy) Smith; children: Frederick M., Michael S., Ellen Mary, Charlotte. BA in Speech, Coll. of New Rochelle, 1952; postgrad., WCSU, 1965, Sacred Heart U. Cert. elem. educator, Conn. Elem. educator St. Francis Ch. Sch., New Milford, Conn., St. Xavier Ch. Sch., New Milford, Conn., Pettibone Sch., New Milford, Conn.; catechist, 1976-96; office of the dean WCSU, Danbury, Conn., 1993, supr., 1993-94; pre-GED tchr. Foothills Educators, 1994-95. Contbr. articles and poems to newspapers. Catechist St. Francis Ch.; libr. trustee New Milford, 1988-93; adv. bd. Teach the Children New Daycare, New Milford; adv. bd. Danbury (Conn.) News Time, 1987-92. Nat. Endowment grantee in poetry and poets, 1985. Mem. Conn. Edn. Assn., WEA, Delta Kappa Gamma Internat., Lay Missionary of Charity. Republican. Roman Catholic. Home: Box 973 New Milford CT 06776

FOSTER, JODIE (ALICIA CHRISTIAN FOSTER), actress; b. L.A., Nov. 19, 1962; d. Lucius and Evelyn (Almond) F. BA in Lit. cum laude, Yale U., 1985. Acting debut in TV show Mayberry, R.F.D, 1969; numerous other TV appearances including My Three Sons, The Courtship of Eddie's Father, Gunsmoke, Bonanza, Paper Moon, 1974-75; TV spl. The Secret Life of T.K. Dearing, 1975; TV movies Rookie of the Year, Smile, Jenny, You're Dead; motion picture appearances Napoleon and Samantha, 1972, Menace on the Mountain, One Little Indian, 1973, Tom Sawyer, 1973, Kansas City Bomber, 1972, Bob & Carol & Ted & Alice, 1973, Alice Doesn't Live Here Anymore, 1974, Taxi Driver, 1976 (Acad. award nominee for Best Supporting Actress), Echoes of a Summer, 1976, Bugsy Malone, 1976, Freaky Friday, 1976, Moi, Fleur Bleue, 1977, Casotto, 1977, The Little Girl Who Lives Down the Lane, 1977, Candleshoe, 1977, Foxes, 1980, Carny, 1980, O'Hara's Wife, 1982, Svengali, 1983, Hotel New Hampshire, 1984, The Blood of Others, 1984, Mesmerized, 1986, Siesta, 1986, Five Corners, 1986, Siesta, 1987, Stealing Home, 1988, Five Corners, 1988, The Accused, 1988 (Acad. award for Best Actress, 1989), Backtrack, 1989, The Silence of the Lambs, 1991 (Golden Globe award for Best Actress in Drama, 1992, Acad. award for Best Actress, 1992), Shadows and Fog, 1992, Sommersby, 1993, Maverick, 1994; dir., actress: Little Man Tate, 1991; prodr., actress: Nell, 1994 (Acad. award nominee for Best Actress 1995); dir., prodr. Home For the Holidays, 1995; prodr. Assassins, 1996. Recipient Golden Globe award, 1989. Office: EGG Pictures Production Co 7920 Sunset Blvd Ste 200 Los Angeles CA 90046*

FOSTER, JOY VIA, library media specialist; b. Besoco, W.Va., Aug. 11, 1935; d. George Edward and Burgia Stafford (Earls) Via; m. Paul Harris Foster, Jr., Dec. 8, 1956 (dec. Dec. 20, 1962); children: Elizabeth Lee, Michael Paul. BS, Radford Coll., 1971; MS, Radford U., 1979. Cert. pub. sch. libr., Va. Clk. Va. Tech. and State U., Blacksburg, 1955-57; clk. Christiansburg (Va.) Primary Sch., 1971-72, libr., 1972-85; libr. Auburn Mid. and High Sch., Riner, Va., 1985—. Meml. chmn. Am. Cancer Soc., Christiansburg, 1965-66; area chmn. Am. Heart Fund, Christiansburg, 1990-93, block worker, 1985-91. Mem. NEA, ALA, Am. Assn. Sch. Librs., Montgomery County Edn. Assn. (v.p. 1988-89, sec. 1989-91, bldg. rep. 1991, sec. 1995-96), Va. Ednl. Media Assn., Va. Ednl. Assn., Women of the Moose. Presbyterian. Office: Auburn Mid and H S 4163 Riner Rd Riner VA 24149-2513

FOSTER, KATHRYN WARNER, newspaper editor; b. Charleston, S.C., Sept. 16, 1950; d. Jack Huntington Warner and Theodora (Heinsohn) Miller; m. William Chapman Foster, Sept. 11, 1971; children: William Huntington, Jonathan Chapman. BA in English, Newberry Coll., 1972. Obituary writer, TV editor Greenville (S.C.) News-Piedmont, 1971-72, asst. lifestyle editor, 1972-73, feature editor, 1973-78; Living Today copy editor Miami (Fla.) Herald, 1978-83, asst. weekend editor, 1984-86, asst. travel editor, 1986-91, 96—, editor in home and design dept., 1992-93, editor Getaways midweek travel page, 1993-94, assoc. editor Health Beat, 1995-96; editor Miami Herald Dining Guide, 1988-91, asst. editor Destinations mag., 1990-91; speaker S.W. Fla. Writer's Conf., Ft. Myers, 1992. Contbr. articles to newspapers. Sec. Palmetto Elem. PTA, Miami, 1990-91. Recipient Penney-Mo. 1st pl. award for feature sects. U. Mo. Sch. Journalism, Columbia, 1978. Lutheran. Office: Miami Herald Travel Dept 1 Herald Plz Miami FL 33132-1609

FOSTER, KIM, art dealer, gallery owner; b. Washington, Nov. 22, 1956; d. James R. and Clair Lynn (Block) Foster; m. Antonio Petracca, Oct. 30, 1994. BA, Sarah Lawrence Coll.; MA, Johns Hopkins U. Lic. stockbroker, N.Y. Asst. treas. Bankers Trust Co., N.Y.C., 1980-83; asst. v.p. Marine Midland, N.Y.C., 1984-85; commodities credit mgr. Shearson Lehman, N.Y.C., 1985-86; v.p. Bayerische Vereinsbank, N.Y.C., 1988-94; pres. Kim Foster Gallery, N.Y.C., 1993—; dir. Foster Industries, Inc., Pitts.; v.p. Fostin Securities, Inc., Wilmington, Del., 1995—. Adv. bd. Ben Gurion U., N.Y. chpt., N.Y.C., 1993-94; bd. dirs. Shotgun Prodns., N.Y.C., 1994—; speech writer Gov. James R. Thompson, Chgo., 1985. Mem. Mus. Modern Art. Republican. Jewish. Office: Kim Foster Gallery 62 Crosby St New York NY 10012

FOSTER, MARCIA WILLIAMS, national account manager; b. Mobile, Ala., Sept. 28, 1950; d. D.V. and Erma Ganelle (Deese) Williams; m. Ronald Stewart Foster, Aug. 21, 1971 (div. Nov. 1987), remarried Sept. 1, 1990; children: Michael Stewart, Susan Genelle. Student, Spring Hill Coll., 1968-71; cert. gen. ins., Ins. Inst. Am., 1983. Cert. ins. profl., ins. counselor. Ins. sec., receptionist Millette & Assocs. Inc., Pascagoula, Miss., 1973-74; personal lines rep. Ross-King-Walker, Inc., Pascagoula, 1974-76; personal lines customer svc. Kennedy Ins. Agy., Inc., San Jose, Calif., 1978-79; personal lines customer svc. Baumhauer-Croom Ins., Inc., Mobile, 1976-78, underwriting sec., asst. to pres., 1980-82; adminstrv. asst. to pres. Lyon Fry Cadden Ins. Agy., Inc., Mobile, 1982-94; account mgr., nat. accounts Willis Corroon Corp. of Mobile, Mobile, Ala., 1994—. Vol. Cystic Fibrosis Found., Mobile, 1985-90, Matthews City Park, Ranger Babe Ruth, Mobile, 1989—. Named Ala. State Ins. Woman of Yr., Ala. Ind. Ins. Agts., 1985. Mem. Ins. Women of Mobile (ednl. course instr. 1987—, pres. 1986-87, Presdl. Svc. award 1984, Mobile Ins. Woman of Yr. 1985, Anna S. Loding Meml. award 1990), Nat. Assn. Ins. Women Internat. (chmn. Ala. state conf. 1992, asst. region III dir. 1986-87, mem. Ala. coun.), Soc. Cert. Ins. Counselors (cert.). Episcopalian. Home: 3584 Pepper Ridge Dr Mobile AL 36693-2555 Office: Willis Corroon Corp of Mobile PO Box 2407 Mobile AL 36652-2407

FOSTER, MARTHA TYAHLA, educational administrator; b. Coaldale, Pa., Apr. 22, 1955; d. Stephen and Frances (Solomon) Tyahla; m. David Marion Foster, Jan. 3, 1981. BA with distinction, U. Va., 1977, MEd, 1981, EdS, 1981. Legis. asst. U.S. Ho. of Reps., Washington, 1977-79; asst. dean summer session U. Va., Charlottesville, 1981; program cons. campus activities U. Houston, 1981; coordinator student affairs Capitol Inst. Tech., Kensington, Md., 1982-83, asst. dean students, Laurel, Md., 1983-84, assoc. dean students, 1984-86, dean students, 1986-87; bd. dirs. Curry Sch. Edn. Found. U. Va., 1987-90. Mem. Arlington County Commn. on Status of Women, 1985-88; chmn. Christian edn. Christ Meth. Ch., 1994—; coun. mem.- at-large Arlington United Way, 1995—. Named Woman of Yr. Bus. and Profl. Women's Club, Vienna, Va., 1986. Methodist. Lodge: Order of Eastern Star (worthy matron 1988-89, trustee 1993-96).

FOSTER, MARY KATHERINE, teacher; b. N.J., Aug. 15, 1954; d. Rocco John DeFelippis and Mary Margaret Reilly; m. Edwin Richard Foster, Feb. 26, 1984; children: Rider Rocco, Ford Reilly. BSE, Bloomsburg (Pa.) State Coll., 1975. Cert. English tchr., N.J. Tchr. Lancaster (Pa.) Cath. H.S., 1978-80; part time tchr. CETA program Boonton (N.J.) H.S., 1980-81; tchr. Our Lady of Mt. Carmel Sch., Boonton, N.J., 1983-95, The Wilson Sch., Mountain Lakes, N.J., 1995—; tchr. adult edn. program, Montville, N.J., 1987. Nat. Coun. Tchrs. of English. Roman Catholic. Home: 321 William St Boonton NJ 07005 Office: The Wilson Sch 271 Boulevard Mountain Lakes NJ 07046

FOSTER, NANCY HASTON, columnist, author; b. Austin, Tex., June 7; d. Arch B. and Verlea (Jones) Haston; m. Joe D. Foster Jr. (div.). BJ, U. Tex., BA in Sociology. Writer, pub. rels. dept. Trinity U., San Antonio, Tex.; social worker pub. welfare dept. State of La., Lafayette; instr. sociology U. Tex., Austin; columnist San Antonio Light, 1982-83, San Antonio Express-News, 1989-90; freelance writer, 1977—. Co-author: San Antonio, A Texas Monthly Guidebook, 1983, rev. edit., 1989, 94; author: The Alamo and Other Texas Missions to Remember, 1984, Texas Missions, A Texas Monthly Guidebook, 1995; contbg. editor, writer: Texas, Fodor's Travel Guides, 1985, rev. edit., 1991, Fodor's American Cities, 1986, rev. edit., 1988, Texas, A Texas Monthly Guidebook, 1993; contbr. articles to popular mags. Mem. Women in Communications, Phi Beta Kappa. Home and Office: 412 Cloverleaf Ave # 3 San Antonio TX 78209-4115

FOSTER, R. PAM, interior designer; b. Fleet, Hants, Eng., June 17, 1946; came to U.S., 1991; d. William Henry and Mabel (Selby) Melville; m. Ernest William Bracken, Feb. 4, 1991; children from a previous marriage: Paul Melville, Nina Kathleen. Student in Bus., Clark's Coll., Guildford, Surrey, Eng., 1964. From sec. to dir. sales Brit. Caledonian Airways, Gatwick, Eng., 1969-71, sr. mktg. exec., 1985-89; v.p. Transcontinental Svcs., London, 1973-81; owner, pres. Claremont Travel Ltd., Hurstpierpoint, Eng., 1981-85; mgr. interior design Brit. Airways, London, 1989-91; pres., owner House of

Melville, Inc., Leesburg, Va., 1993—. designer interior for Airbus A320 Launch Aircraft for Brit. Airways. Local organizer Cystic Fibrosis Rsch. Trust, Sussex, Eng, 1974-84. Office: House of Melville RR 1 Box 361 Leesburg VA 22175-8811

FOSTER, RUTH MARY, dental association administrator; b. Little Rock, Jan. 11, 1927; d. William Crosby and Frances Louise (Doering) Shaw; m. Luther A. Foster, Sept. 8, 1946 (dec. Dec. 1980); children: William Lee, Robert Lynn. Grad. high sch., Long Beach, Calif. Sr. hostess Mon's Food Host of Coast, Long Beach, 1945-46; dental asst., office mgr. Dr. Wilfred H. Allen, Opportunity, Wash., 1946-47; dental asst., bus. asst. Dr. H. Erdahl, Long Beach, 1948-50; office mgr. Dr. B.B. Blough, Spokane, Wash., 1950-52; bus. mgr. Henry G. Kolsrud, D.D.S., P.S., Spokane, 1958—, Garland Dental Bldg., Spokane, 1958—. Sustaining mem. Spokane Symphony Orch. Mem. Nat. Assn. Dental Assts., DAV Aux., DAV Comdrs. Club, Wash. State Fedn. Bus. and Profl. Women (dir. dist. 6), Spokane's Lilac City Bus. and Profl. Women (past pres.), Nat. Alliance Mentally Ill, Wash. Alliance Mentally Ill, Internat. Platform Assn., Spokane Club, Credit Women's Breakfast Club, Dir.'s Club, Inland N.W. Zool. Soc., Pioneer Circle of Women Helping Women. Democrat. Mem. First Christian Ch. Office: Henry G Kolsrud DDS PS 3718 N Monroe St Spokane WA 99205-2850

FOSTER, SANDRA KAY, sales official; b. Dallas, June 6, 1948; d. Joseph Daniel and Harriet Jean (Ledbetter) Stephens; children: Joseph B., James Anthony. Student, Northlake Coll., Dallas, 1993-94, So. Oreg. State Coll., 1995. Lic. profl. sales counsellor, Oreg. With Merc. Bank and Southwestern Bell Tel., Dallas, 1966-70; co-owner, operator Jiffy Mart and Triple A Dairy Farm, Brookhaven, Miss., 1970-83; adminstrv. asst. Stahl-Urban Co., Brookhaven, 1971-78; convenience store mgr. Craddock Oil Co., McComb, Miss., 1984-85; ind. contractor Home Interiors, Dallas, 1985-87; with temp. agys., Waxahachie and Ennis, Tex., 1985-87; fin. aid officer, receptionist United Travel Schs. and MTA Sch./Careercom, Dallas, 1987-88; asst. in-store mktg. mgr. Amre, Inc., Dallas, 1989-90; broker trainee Sunset Securities/Reach Exploration/Impala Exploration, Dallas, 1989-90; with Telemktg. Svcs., Dallas, 1989-92; aviation clk., safety asst. FAA, Dallas, 1992-94; sales counsellor Hillcrest/Memory Gardens/Conger Morris, Medford, Oreg., 1994—. Mem. NAFE, AAUW, Nat. Mus. for Women in Arts. Democrat. Methodist. Home: 402 Piccadilly Ct Medford OR 97504

FOSTER, SCARLETT LEE, public relations executive; b. Charleston, W.Va., Dec. 14, 1956; d. William Christoph Foster, Jr. and Anne (Howes) Conway. B in Comm., Bethany Coll., 1979. Dir. pub. rels. Allergy Rehab. Found., Charleston, 1979-80; dir. pubs. Contractors Assn. W.Va., Charleston, 1980-82; comm. rep. Monsanto Co., Nitro, W.Va., 1982-84, 1984-87; mgr. environ. and community rels. Monsanto Co., St. Louis, 1987-89, mgr. pub. rels., 1989-91, mgr. fin. pub. rels., 1991-93, dir. pub. rels., 1993-94, dir. pub. affairs, 1994—. Bd. dirs. Sta. KWMU Pub. Radio, St. Louis, 1992—; trustee Bethany (W.Va.) Coll., 1994—. Named Outstanding Alumni of Achievement Bethany Coll., 1990. Mem. Internat. Assn. Bus. Communicators (2 Gold Quill awards of Merit). Episcopalian. Office: Monsanto Co A2SP 800 N Lindbergh Blvd Saint Louis MO 63167

FOSTER, SUSAN CHANDLER, educator; b. Montgomery, Ala., Sept. 21, 1949; d. Horace Leonard and Mary Charles (Howell) Chandler; m. Tony Shirley (div. Jan. 1979); 1 child, Scott; m. Donald Glenn Wilson, Aug. 27, 1994. AS, Enterprise State Jr. Coll., 1976; BS, Troy State U., 1981; MS, U. So. Calif., 1984. Staff asst. Sec. of the Army, Pentagon, Washington, 1985-86; program mgr. Dept. Chief of Staff Logistics, Pentagon, Washington, 1986; dept. mgr. CACI, Inc., Arlington, Va., 1986-89; program mgr. SONEX, Inc., Fairfax, Va., 1990; fin. team leader TRESP, Inc., Alexandria, Va., 1991-93; mem. faculty Army Mgmt. Staff Coll., Fort Belvoir, Va., 1993—, dept. chair. Befriend vol. Dept. of Human Svcs., Alexandria, 1994-95. Mem. Assn. of U.S. Army. Office: Army Mgmt Staff Coll 5500 21st St Ste 3702-3 Fort Belvoir VA 22060

FOSTER, VIRGINIA, retired botany educator; b. Joseph, Oreg., Feb. 4, 1914; d. Perry Alexander and Genevieve (Shain) F. BS, U. Wash., 1949, MS, 1950; PhD, Ohio State U., 1954. Prof. Judson Coll., Marion, Ala., 1956-58; prof. Miss. State Coll. for Women, Columbus, 1958-59, LaVerne (Calif.) Coll., 1959-60, Calif. Western U., San Diego, 1960-61, Pensacola (Fla.) Jr. Coll., 1962-84. Author: (lab. manual) The Botany Laboratory, 1976, rev. edit., 1985, 3d edit., 1991. Home: 9270 Scenic Hwy Pensacola FL 32514-8054

FOSTER VARGAS, KATHLEEN DIANE, legal administrator; b. Boston, Feb. 22, 1951; d. Joseph Ernest and Barbara Shirley (Dundas) Emge; children: Christian Andrew Fabian, Michelle Diane; m. Howard Vargas, 1995. BA in Anthropology/Archaeology, Pacific Luth. U., 1984, MA in Anthropology/Archaeology, 1984; JD, Am. Coll. of Law, 1989. Tchr. English Castillo Escuela, Guadalajara, Mexico, 1972-74; rsch. asst. U. Calif., Irvine, 1978-80; rsch. assoc. Hoko River Archaeol. Project, Pullman, Wash., 1981-84; law clk., investigator Law Offices of Leonard Moen, Tacoma, 1984-86; law clk. Law Offices of Thomas Moga, Upland, Calif., 1986-90; hearing rep. Law Offices of Grant Lynd, Westminster, Calif., 1990—; disc jockey, music dir. Sta. KUCI Radio, Calif., 1978-80, Sta. KPLU Radio, 1981-82. Asst. (film) Battered Women/Convicted Killers, 1981. Asst. leader Brownies/Girl Scouts, Puyallup, Wash., 1981-85. Recipient Am. Jurisprudence award for appellate advocacy Lawyers Coop/Bancroft Whitney Pub., 1988, Am. Jurisprudence award for uniform comm. code, 1988. Mem. Bus. and Profl. Women's Assn., Nat. Notary Assn. Democrat. Office: Law Offices of Grant A Lynd 14340 Bolsa Chica Rd Ste B Westminster CA 92683-4868

FOTHERGILL, KATE ESTHER, public health service officer; b. Washington, Apr. 16, 1964; d. William R. and Priscilla Kate (Royce) F. BA in Polit. Sci., Tufts U., 1986; MPH, U. N.C., 1992. Dir. pubs. Nat. Ctr. Edn. Maternal & Child Health, Washington, 1987-89; program asst. Calif. Med. Assn., San Francisco, 1989-90; rsch. asst. Sch. Pub. Health U. N.C., Chapel Hill, 1991-92; dept. dir. Sch. Health Policy Initiative, N.Y.C., 1992-95; dir. support ctr. Advocates Youth, Washington, 1995—; mem. adv. coun. Com. Sch. Health AMA, Chgo., 1994—; program evaluator Durham Substance Abuse Svcs., 1990-91; exec. coun. Nat. Assembly Sch.-Based Health Care, Washington, 1995—. Contbr. articles to profl. jours. Tutor Martha's Table, Washington, 1995—; vol. Luther Pl. Shelter, Washington, 1986-88. Mem. APHA, ACLU, Nat. Assembly Sch. Based Healthcare. Democrat. Office: Advocates for Youth 1025 Vermont Ave #200 Washington DC 20005

FOTI, MARGARET ANN, association executive, editor; b. Phila., Dec. 15, 1944; d. Samuel A. and Margaret M. (DiBiase) F. B.A., Temple U., 1975, M.A. in Communications, 1985, PhD in Comm., 1995. Tech. editor U. Pa., Phila., 1962-64, asst. to bus adminstr., 1964-65; sr. editorial asst. Cancer Rsch. Jour., Phila., 1965-69, mng. editor, 1969—; exec. dir. Am. Assn. Cancer Rsch., Phila., 1982—, dir. publs., 1990—; adminstrn., pub. edn., devel., editorial and pub. cons., lectr. in field. Contbr. articles to profl. jours. Pres. Nat. Coalition for Cancer Rsch., 1994-96. Recipient Cert. of Appreciation Am. Assn. Cancer Rsch., 1975, 85, 90. Mem. AAAS, Am. Soc. Assn. Execs., Am. Assn. Cancer Rsch., European Assn. for Cancer rsch., European Assn. Sci. Editors, Internat. Fedn. Sci. Editors, Soc. Sch. Publs., Soc. for Scholarly Publs. (pres. 1996—), Coun. Biology Editors (pres. 1980-81), Coun. Engrs. and Sci. Soc. Execs. Democrat. Roman Catholic. Home: 220 Locust St Apt 24A Philadelphia PA 19106 Office: Am Assn Cancer Rsch 150 S Independence Mall W Philadelphia PA 19106-3483

FOUCART VINCENTI, VALERIE, art educator; b. Williamsport, Pa., Nov. 16, 1953; m. Stephen C. Vincenti. BS in Art Edn., Mansfield (Pa.) State U., 1975; MFA in Weaving, Marywood Coll., Scranton, Pa., 1993. Art tchr. Lycoming Valley Mid. and Roosevelt Mid. Schs. Williamsport Area Sch. Dist., 1975—; tchr. gifted arts program Pa. State U., Wilkes-Barre, Lehman Campus, 1990. Editor The Lion newsletter St. Mark's Luth. Ch., Williamsport, 1985-88. Playground arts instr. Williamsport Recreation Commn., summers 1980's; vol. ARC, Williamsport, 1980's. Recipient 3rd pl. award painting and photography Bald Eagle Art League and Williamsport Recreation Commn., 1975-76, Nat. Program Stds. award Nat. Art Edn. Assn., 1994. Mem. NEA, Nat. Art Edn. Assn., Pa. Art Edn. Assn., Pa. State Edn. Assn., Williamsport Edn. Assn. (faculty rep.), Nat. Mus. of the Am. Indian, Susquehanna Valley Spinners and Weavers Guild, Bald Eagle Art League, Handweavers Guild Am., Williamsport-Lycoming Arts Coun., Lycoming County Hist. Soc., Kappa Pi (Zeta Omicron chpt.). Democrat. Lutheran. Office: Williamsport Area Sch Dist 201 W 3rd St Williamsport PA 17701-6409

FOUCHA, LAURA THERESA, computer graphics designer, film maker, writer; b. New Orleans, Mar. 24, 1947; d. Frederick Lake and Lucille Mary (Normand) F. BA, U. New Orleans, 1973. Reg. radiologic technologist. Radiologic technologist Uptown Physicians Group, New Orleans, 1969-73; dept. mgr. D.H. Holmes, New Orleans, 1969-73; asst. mgr. Gen. Cinema Theatres, New Orleans, 1973-75; computer graphics designer New Orleans, 1975—; videographer Lens To Creation, New Orleans, 1993—; camerawoman New Orleans Women in Video, 1982-89. Film maker: Gunchase to Nowhere, 1970 (1st prize 1970); author: (book) Tribunal of Anarchy, 1995. Vol. City of New Orleans, 1962-64; campaign worker Candidates Campaigns, 1964-74; activist NOW, New Orleans, 1979—. Recipient Certificate of Recognition award City of New Orleans, 1962, Key to the City, 1965, Cert. of Appreciation Vet's. Adminstrn., 1963, Best Actress award New Orleans Cmty. Theater, 1979. Mem. NOW (New Orleans chpt. pres. 1986-88), Agenda For Children, Timberwolf Preservation Soc., Soc. for Creative Anachronism, Ravenswood Archery Assn. (pres. 1995—). Home: PO Box 72125 New Orleans LA 70172

FOUCHÉ, HELEN STROTHER, editorial design executive; b. Washington, Apr. 19, 1939; d. James Herschel and Elizabeth Ellen (Wright) Strother; m. Robert Michael Fouché, Oct. 20, 1962; children: James Michael, David Carroll, Stephen Charles. BA cum laude, Auburn U., 1960; student, Belles Artes, Managua, Nicaragua, 1964-65; student Intensive Lang. Tng., Fgn. Svc. Inst., 1961, 73; grad., Am. Transp. Inst., 1983. Asst. producer-dir. Internat. TV Svcs., U.S. Info. Agy., Washington, 1960-62; diplomatic svcs. with fgn. svc. husband U.S. Dept. of State, Europe, Africa, Cen./So. Am., 1963-81; art instr. for internat. children's classes La Paz, Bolivia, 1979; community liaison officer U.S. Embassy, La Paz, 1979-81; internat. group coord. Group Travel Unlimited, Alexandria, Va., 1983-84, mktg. creative/tech. writer, 1985-86; mng. editor Am. Leisure Industries, Lanham, Md., 1986-87; editor, cons. Washington Editorial Svcs., DC and Met. area, 1987-88; pres. Washington Editorial Svcs. Inc., Washington, Arlington, Va., 1988—; founding bd. dirs. Fgn. Svc. Youth Found., Washington, 1989-91; cons. Overseas Briefing Ctr., Fgn. Svc. Inst., U.S. Dept. of State, Arlington, 1981-93; travel cons., tour mgr. Acad. Travel Abroad, Inc., 1990—, Travelcorp Inc., 1991—; in mktg. sales Va. Divsn. of Tourism, 1994—; media cons. designed slide shows, wrote scripts for non-profit causes. Contbg. editor, columnist: Diplomatic Digest, others; editor FS EYE for U.S. Dept. of State, 1991-94; mem. editorial bd. Fgn. Svc. Jour., 1989-92; executed murals, Crippled Children's Ward Managua (Nicaragua) Gen. Hosp., 1964, Montessori Sch., La. Paz, 1980; contbr. articles to profl. publs. Pres. Episcopal Ch. Women of St. Michael's, 1989-90, mem. vestry, 1990-94; mem. Altar Guild, 1982—, lector, 1984—. Recipient Vol. of Yr. award, Tampa, Fla., 1970; named one of Outstanding Young Women of Am., 1973. Mem. AAUW, DAR, Assn. of Am. Fgn. Svc. Women (bd. mem., editorial com., newsletter editor), Nat. Press Club, Internat. Women's Media Found., Jamestown Soc., Order of Charlemagne, Alpha Gamma Delta Alumnae Assn. Democrat. Episcopalian. Home and Office: Washington Editorial Svcs PO Box 5884 Arlington VA 22205

FOUNTAIN, KAREN SCHUELER, physician; b. Aberdeen, S.D., Oct. 14, 1947. BA, No. State Coll., Aberdeen, S.D., 1968; MD, U. Md., Balt., 1972. Diplomate Nat. Bd. Med. Examiners, Am. Bd. Radiology in Therapeutic Radiology. Intern Md. Gen. Hosp., Balt., 1972-73, resident in radiation oncology, 1973-74; fellow in radiation oncology Mayo Clinic, Rochester, Minn., 1974-76, cons. in oncology, 1976-81; clin. asst. prof. Columbia U., N.Y.C., 1981-83, residency program dir. dept. radiation oncology, 1981-93, clin. assoc. prof., 1983—; mem. med. bd. Presbyn. Hosp., N.Y.C., 1983-86; faculty coun. mem. Columbia U., 1982-89; del. N.Y. State Radiological Soc., N.Y.C., 1987—. Fellow Am. Coll. Radiology, N.Y. Acad. Medicine; mem. Am. Soc. Therapeutic Radiology and Oncology, Radiol. Soc. N.Am., Am. Radium Soc., Am. Soc. Clin. Oncology, Am. Assn. for Women Radiologists (bd. dirs. 1995—), N.Y. Roentgen Soc. (sect. chmn. 1989-90). Office: Columbia-Presbyn Med Ctr Rad Onc 622 W 168th St New York NY 10032-3702

FOUNTAIN, LINDA KATHLEEN, health science association executive; b. Fowler, Kans., Apr. 30, 1954; d. Ralph Edward and Ruth Evelyn (Cornelson) Young; m. Andre Fountain. BS in Nursing, Cen. State U., Edmond, Okla., 1976. RN, Okla. Staff nurse med./surg. and coronary care unit Presbyn. Hosp., Oklahoma City, 1976-79; mgr. nursing Hillcrest Osteo. Hosp., Oklahoma City, 1979-80; staff nurse, mgr. Oklahoma U. Teaching Hosp., Oklahoma City, 1981-82; pres. New Life Programs, Oklahoma City, 1981-88, Nursing Entrepreneurs, Ltd., Oklahoma City, 1988—; mgr. Internat. Health Supply, Oklahoma City, 1988—; coord. lactation cons. program State of Okla., 1981—, new life car seat rental program at various hosps., 1983-92, also speaker Success Co., Oklahoma City, 1984—; owner Rainbows Overhead Graphic Media, Oklahoma City, 1984-91; speaker in field. Founder Praxis Coll., Oklahoma City, 1988. Named Mentor of Yr., Okla. Metroplex Childbirth Network, Oklahoma City, 1984. Mem. Am. Nurses Assn., Internat. Lactation Cons. Assn., Internat. Platform Assn., Bodyworkers and Wellness Therapies Assn. Office: Nursing Entrepreneurs Ltd PO Box 75393 Oklahoma City OK 73147-0393

FOURCARD, INEZ GAREY, foundation executive, artist; b. Bklyn.; d. George W. and Frances E. (MacDonald) Garey; student Pratt Inst., 1946-48; BFA, McNeese State U., 1963; diploma Maestro di Pitturia Arti Modernea e Contemporaneo, Salsomaggiore, Italy, 1982. Waldren Arthur Fourcard, Aug. 7, 1948; children—Chrystal Frances, Sharon Lynn, Waldren Arthur, Andrea Renee, David Marquard, Anita Lynn. Exhibited in numerous one man shows throughout U.S., also in Eng., France and Spain; 3 paintings on loan to Gov. La., 1974-77; mem. gifted and talented sect. of Spl. Edn. State of La., 1971-73; mem. adv. council Child Centered/Parent Tutored Kindergarden Program, 1974—; mem. La. Task Force for Community Edn., 1974-75; v.p. La. Assn. for Sickle Cell Anemia, 1974—; named best statewide vol.; mem. Calcasieu Parish Bicentennial Com., 1974—; exec. dir., founder Southwestern Sickle Cell Anemia Found., Lake Charles, La., 1973—, producer, dir. 7 Sickle Cell Telethons, Sta. KPLC-TV, 1980-87; bd. dirs., exec. dir., found. World Sickle Cell Anemia/Thalassemia Found.; del. to Dem. Nat. Convs., 1980, 84. Named Hon. Citizen of Fort Worth, 1977; recipient Award of Merit, Human Relations Council of Lake Charles Deanery, award for services to sickle cell disease Sigma Gamma Rho, award for community service Phi Beta Sigma, Gold medal first prize Accademia Italia della Arti e del Sarvo, Italy, 1980, Statua della Vittoria Centro Studie Richerche Delle Nazioni, Italy, 1985. Democrat. Roman Catholic. Important works include The Widow in pvt. collection Bertrand Russell Peace Found., London. Home: 1414 Saint John St Lake Charles LA 70601-2470 Office: 730 Enterprise Blvd Lake Charles LA 70601-4516

FOURNIER, MAUREEN MARY, physical education educator; b. Chgo., Feb. 27, 1952; d. George Joseph and Lauretta Marie (Tangney) Lewis; m. Thomas Joseph Fournier, Sept. 21, 1979; children: Jennifer Lynn, Michele Marie. BS in Edn., No. Ill. U., 1973; MS in Edn., Chgo. State U., 1983. Recreation leader Alsip (Ill.) Park Dist., 1973-75; tchr. phys. edn. Sch. Dist. 126, Alsip, 1974—; pres. Alsip Coun. Local 943 IFT, Alsip, 1976-80, 85-87, 92—, chairperson tchrs. negotiation team, 1993, 96, chmn. phys. edn. curriculum com., 1992-94, mem. curriculum steering com., 1992—, chmn. fine arts curriculum com., mem. sch. improvement plan com.; mgr. Oak Lawn (Ill.) Girls Softball, 1990-91, 94, 95, 96. Mem. AAHPERD, Ill. Assn. of Health, Phys. Edn., Recreation and Dance. Office: Sch Dist 126 Lane Sch 4600 W 123rd St Alsip IL 60658-2522

FOURNIER, REBECCA EILEEN FINES, fundraising executive; b. Alton, Ill., Oct. 10, 1960; d. Galen Wayne and Betty Jean (Phleger) Fines; m. Dennis Francis Fournier, Apr. 10, 1988; 1 stepchild, Leah Denise Fournier Fulton. BA in Mass. Comm., Journalism, So. Ill. U., Edwardsville, 1981; MS in Orgnl. Comm., Leadership Dynamics, So. Ill. U., Carbondale, 1991. Cert. fundraising exec. Dir. comm. Olney (Ill.) Ctrl. Coll., 1981-82; asst. to pres. Muskingum Area Tech. Coll., Zanesville, Ohio, 1982-83; asst. dir. Sch. Engring. Washington U., St. Louis, 1983-87; asst. dean Coll. Bus. So. Ill. U., Carbondale, 1987-92; exec. dir. Pana (Ill.) Cmty. Hosp. Found., 1992-94; dir. devel. BBF Family Svcs., Chgo., 1994—; sr. ptnr. CommuniCreations, Inc., Naperville, Ill., 1995—. Bd. dirs. Am. Cancer Soc., Pana, 1992-94. Named to Women in Leadership, Coro Found., 1990, Faculty Advisor of the Yr. COBA Coun., So. Ill. U., 1991. Mem. NAFE, Nat. Soc. Fundraising Execs. (program, mentoring, cert. and diversity coms. Chgo. chpt. 1994—, program com. chair Springfield chpt. 1992-94), So. Ill. U. Edwardsville Alumni Assn. (life, v.p. 1985-87), So. Ill. U. Carbondale Alumni Assn. (life). Democrat. Presbyterian. Office: BBF Family Svcs 3333 W Arthington Ste 139 Chicago IL 60624

FOUSER, BETH LOUISE, art historian; b. Ann Arbor, Mich., July 5, 1966; d. Robert and Wilma Jean (Quick) F. BA, U. Mich., 1988; MA, U. Victoria, 1993. Intern Guggenheim Mus., N.Y.C., 1986; tchg. asst. U. Victoria, B.C., 1989-93, rsch. asst., 1990-91, art rschr., 1992; supr. Kinko's Copy Ctr., Ann Arbor, 1994-95; adminstrv. asst. U. Mich., Ann Arbor, 1995-96, project mgr. color slide project Am. Com. South Asian Art, 1995—; guest lectr. Art Gallery Greater Victoria, B.C., 1992; presenter S.E. Asian Studies Asian Studies Conf., Seattle, 1992. Author: The Lord of the Golden Tower, 1996. Fgn. Lang. Area Study fellow U. Wash., Seattle, 1993. Mem. Am. Assn. Mus., Am. Com. for South Asian Art. Home: 1402 Culver Rd Ann Arbor MI 48103

FOUTS, ELIZABETH BROWNE, psychologist, metals company executive; b. New Orleans, July 5, 1927; d. Donovan Clarence and Mathilde Elizabeth (Hanna) B.; m. James Fremont Fouts, June 19, 1948; children: Elizabeth, Donovan, Alan, James. BA, Tulane U., 1948; MS, N.E. La. U., 1973, postgrad., 1984. Cert. sch. psychologist, La.; cert. reality therapist, La. Instr. spl. ed., psychol. cons. N.E. La. U., Monroe, 1971-73; sch. psychologist Ouachita Parish Schs., Monroe, 1973-87; sec.-treas Fremont Corp., Monroe, 1967—, Auric Metals Corp., Salt Lake City, 1975—; dir. La Fonda Hotel, Santa Fe, N.Mex., 1993—; pres. Family Resource Ctr. N.E. La. U., 1993-94; pres. Sunbelt Reality Therapist, 1989-90; Mem. exec. bd. Episc. Diocese Western La., 1986-87, commn. ministry, 1987-94; pres. family resource ctr. N.E. La. U., 1993-94; bd. dirs. Assn. for Retarded Citizens, Monroe, 1982-88, treas., 1984, pres., 1987. Named Outstanding Sch. Psychologist State of La., 1987. Mem. Nat. Assn. Sch. Psychologists, La. Sch. Psychologists Assn. (pres. 1978-79, Outstanding Woman Sch. Psychologist 1984, newsletter editor 1988-93). Avocations: biking, skiing, swimming. Home: PO Box 7070 Monroe LA 71211-7070 Office: 4002 Bon Aire Dr Monroe LA 71203-3015

FOWLER, ANN L., hotel executive; b. Gainesville, Fla., Jan. 19, 1949; d. Claude W. and Eldreth (Hart) Lovett; m. Bernie A. Fowler, Apr. 25, 1966; children: Laura Fowler Marden, David A. AA, Columbia (Mo.) Coll.; postgrad., Santa Fe C.C., Gainesville, Fla., Fla. Real Estate Inst., Gainesville. Office mgr. Leonard Constrn./Monsanto, Lakeland, Fla., 1973-76; mgr. F&A Cleaning Svc., Baumholder, West Germany, 1976-78; office mgr. Hart Bldg. & Constrn., Gainesville, Fla., 1978-80; dir. U.S. Army Rec Ctr.-Tours & Travel, Karlsruhe, West Germany, 1980-87; coord. Gator Boosters, Inc., Gainesville, 1989-91; asst. gen. mgr. Residence Inn, Marriott, Gainesville, 1991-94; dir. catering Holiday Inn-West, Gainesville, 1994-95, sr. sales mgr., 1995—; bridal/catering cons. Affairs by Faye, Gainesville, 1989—. Vol. Pick-An-Angel, Alachua County, Fla., 1988—, Hospice House, Alachua County, 1994—, Alzheimer's Assn., Alachua County, 1994—; bd. dirs. Gainesville Sports Organizing Com., 1994-96; mem. adv. bd. Santa Fe C.C., 1996—. Mem. Pilot Club Greater Gainesville (pres.- elect 1996), Soc. Govt. Meeting Planners, Fla. Soc. Assn. Execs., Rotary Club Gainesville, Beta Sigma Phi (Woman of Yr. Alpha Beta chtp. 1991, Gainesville City Coun. 1992, Gainesville Area 1993). Republican. Baptist. Home: 4151 NW 39th Way Gainesville FL 32606 Office: Holiday Inn-West 7417 NW 8th Ave Gainesville FL 32606

FOWLER, ARDEN STEPHANIE, music educator; b. N.Y.C., May 24, 1930; d. Arthur Simon and Lenore Irene (Strouse) Bender; m. Milton Fowler, Aug. 6, 1951; children: Stacey Alison, Crispin Laird. Student, Traphagen Sch., 1947-49; BA, Marymount Coll., Tarrytown, N.Y., 1976; MusM, U. So. Fla., 1978. Designer Rubeson's Sportswear, N.Y.C., 1949-51; free-lance designer Dobb's Ferry, N.Y., 1952-72; organist/choir dir. Children's Village, Dobb's Ferry, N.Y., 1972-74; music specialist Highland Nursery Sch., Chappaqua, N.Y., 1972-76; pvt. voice tchr., vocal coach, 1972—; music therapist Cedar Manor Nursing Home, Ossining, N.Y., 1974-76; founder, pres. Gloria Musicae Chamber Chorus, Sarasota, Fla., 1979-85, mng. dir., 1985-89; soloist various chs. and choruses, N.Y., Fla., 1953—; mem. faculty vocal music dept. St. Boniface Conservatory, Sarasota, 1979-81; music critic Sarasota Herald Tribune, 1986-91; lectr. music history Edn. Ctr., Longboat Key, Fla.; vol. music for early childhood Head Start. Freelance travel writer, 1985—. Mem. Chorus Am., Assn. Profl. Vocal Ensembles, Friends of the Arts (hon.), Sigma Alpha Iota, Phi Kappa Phi. Democrat. Episcopal. Home: 4244 Marina Ct Cortez FL 34215-2518

FOWLER, BARBARA HUGHES, classics educator; b. Lake Forest, Ill., Aug. 23, 1926; d. Fay Orville and Clara (Reber) Hughes; m. Alexander Murray Fowler, July 14, 1956; children: Jane Alexandra, Emily Hughes. BA, U. Wis., 1949; MA, Bryn Mawr Coll., 1950, PhD, 1955. Instr. classics Middlebury (Vt.) Coll., 1954-56; asst. prof. Latin Edgewood Coll., Madison, Wis., 1961-63; mem. faculty U. Wis., Madison, 1963—; prof. classics U. Wis., 1976—, John Bascom prof., 1980—, prof. emeritus, 1991—. Author: The Hellenistic Aesthetic, 1989, The Seeds Inside a Green Pepper, 1989, Hellenistic Poetry, 1990, Archaic Greek Poetry, 1992, Love Lyrics of Ancient Egypt, 1994, Songs of a Friend, 1996; also articles. Fulbright scholar Greece, 1951-52; Fanny Bullock Workman travelling fellow, 1951-52. Mem. Am. Philol. Assn., Archaeol. Inst. Am., Classical Assn. Middle West and South. Home: 1102 Sherman Ave Madison WI 53703-1620 Office: U Wis 910 Van Hise Hall Madison WI 53706

FOWLER, BETTY JANMAE, dance company director, editor; b. Chgo., May 23, 1925; d. Harry and Mary (Jacques) Markin; student Art Inst., Chgo., 1937-39, Stratton Bus. Coll., Chgo., 1942-43, Columbia U., 1945-47; B.A., Eastern Wash. U., 1984; 1 dau., Sherry Mareth Connors. Mem. public relations dept. Girl Scouts U.S.A., N.Y.C., 1961-63; adminstrv. asst. to editor-in-chief Scholastic Mags., N.Y.C., 1963-68; adminstrv. dir. Leonard Fowler Dancers, Fowler Sch. Classical Ballet, Inc., N.Y.C., 1959-78, tchr. ballet, 1959-61; pvt. practice Ecol. Lifestyle Advisor, 1980—; editor Bulletin, Kiwanis weekly publ., Spokane, Wash., 1978-82, adminstrv. sec. Kiwanis Club; instr. Spokane Falls Community Coll., 1978. Founder Safe Water Coalition Wash. State, 1988. Cert. metabolic technician Internat. Health Inst. Avocations: travel, reading. Office: Safe Water Coalition Washington State W 5615 Lyons Ct Spokane WA 99208

FOWLER, CECILE ANN, nurse, professional soloist; b. Paterson, N.J., Feb. 14, 1920; m. Chester A. Fowler, Mar. 9, 1942. Grad., Passaic (N.J.) Gen. Hosp. Nursing Program, 1941. Nurse Beth Israel Hosp., Newark, 1941-42, Orange (N.J.) Meml. Hosp., 1942-50; asst. receptionist Dr. Stokes, Urologist, East Orange, N.J., 1943-44; nurse Mountainside Hosp., Montclair, N.J., 1960-69, head nurse, premature and newborns, 1966-67; profl. soloist, 1952-69; part-time nurse Upper Three Hosps., 1950-60; co-founder The Oratorio Soc. of N.J., Montclair, 1952; mem. quartet First Baptist Ch., Montclair. Active various coms. PTA, 1951-62; co-founder CD, Little Falls, N.J., 1967; sponsor Met. Opera Guild N.Y., 1977—; child sponsor World Vision, 1983—; mem. Rep. Presdl. Task Force, 1987; founder Challenger Ctr. for Math., Space and Sci. Edn., 1990—, Ptnrs. in Hope: St. Jude's Rsch. Ctr., 1991—; mem. Friends of Richard Tucker Music Found., 1987—. Recipient Vocal Accomplishment award Griffith Music Found., 1944, 45, medal of Merit, Pres. Reagan, 1988, Pres. Bush, 1990, Rep. Presdl. Legion of Merit, 1992. Mem. Lincoln Ctr. for the Performing Arts, Friends of Carnegie Hall, Friends of Richard Tucker Music Found., Am. Biog. Inst. Am. (rsch. bd. advs. 1989—, dep. gov., life mem., fellowship, Commemorative Medal of Honor 1991), Heritage Found. (U.S. English mem. 1986—), U.S. Senatorial (preferred mem.), Little Falls Woman's Club (edn. chmn. 1979-81), Montclair Operatta (various chairmanships 1943—, gov. 1990-92). Republican. Roman Catholic. Home: 9 Lotz Hill Rd Clifton NJ 07013-2312

FOWLER, CHARLOTTE ANN, occupational health nurse; b. Shreveport, La., June 10, 1954; d. William James Jr. and Erin Kathleen (Taylor) F. Student, N.E. La. U., 1973-74, La. State U., Shreveport, 1977-78; ADN, Northwestern State U., Shreveport, 1982. RN, La. RN in oper. rm.

Schumpert Med. Ctr., Shreveport, 1982-85; RN in oper. rm. La. State U. Med. Ctr., Shreveport, 1985-86, RN in recovery rm. and surg. ICU, 1986-87, RN in psychiatry, 1987-88, RN in recovery rm., 1988-89, RN in surg. ICU, 1989-90, RN clin. coord. dept. of surgery divsn. oral maxifacial surgery, 1990-93, nursing adminstrn. RN, house mgr., 1993—. Author: (with others) American Poetry Anthology, 1989. Dist. coord. La. Nurses' Network for Impaired Profls., 1987-90; bd. dirs., lay rep. Met. Cmty. Ch., Shreveport. Mem. ANA, Am. Assn. Occupl. Health Nurses, Critical Care Soc., La. State Nurses Assn., Shreveport Dist. Nurses Assn. Home: 625 Wilkinson Shreveport LA 71104 Office: La State U Med Ctr Occupl Health Clinic 1501 Kings Hwy PO Box 33932 Shreveport LA 71130-3932

FOWLER, CYNTHIA ANN BROWN, secondary school educator; b. Roanoke, Ala., Jan. 25, 1947; d. Grover E. and Velma I. Brown; m. Christopher R. Fowler, Dec. 19, 1965 (div. Oct., 1995); children: Mike, David, Kara. BA magna cum laude, La Grange (Ga.) Coll., 1986; MEd, West Ga. Coll., 1991; EdS, Troy State U., Phenix City, Ala., 1994. Cert. English educator, Ga. Owner ABC Nursery Sch., La Grange, Ga., 1972-86; job tng. instr. Ga. Dept. Labor, La Grange, 1985-86; tchr. Troup County Bd. Edn., La Grange, 1986—; instr. West Ga. Tech., La Grange, 1993-95; advisor Future Tchr. Club, Troup H.S., La Grange, 1989-96, Debate Team, 1994-95; chair Student Support Team Com., Troup H.S., 1995, 96, prin.'s leadership team; story teller Nat. Storytelling, 1990-96. Contbr. articles to profl. publs., poetry and essays to newspapers and mags. Treas., coord. Dem. Women, La Grange, Ga., 1993-96; vol. Alumnae Club, La GrangeColl., 1995-96. Named Tchr. of Yr. Troup H.S., 1991. Mem. AAUW, NEA, Nat. Coun. Tchrs. of English, N.Am. Storytellers, Phi Delta Kappa, (sec. orgn. team 1991-93). Democrat. Home: 49 N Barnard Ave Lagrange GA 30240 Office: Troup HS 1920 Hamilton Rd Lagrange GA 30240

FOWLER, ELIZABETH MILTON, real estate executive; b. Watertown, Fla., Jan. 11, 1919; d. Arthur Wellington and Mattie Jean (Hodges) Milton; m. Albert L. Fowler, Jr., Aug. 6, 1948; children: Patricia Dawn Cecilia, Richard Gordon Sean. Student Bowling Green Bus. U., 1938-39; Cultural HHD (hon.), World U. Roundtable, 1988. Sec. to dir. Workmen's Compensation Div., Fla. Indsl. Commn., Tallahassee, 1940-41; sec. to supt. div. Gibbs Ship Yard Repair, 1942-44; sec. to elec. engrs. Reynolds, Smith & Hills, Architects and Engrs., 1946-49; sec. to pres. Aichel Steel Corp., Jacksonville, Fla., 1949-50; adminstr. office mgr. for prin., vice-prin. Am. Dependent Sch., Moron Air Base, Spain, 1961-63; owner, mgr. Elizabeth Properties, Jacksonville, 1956—. Chmn. ways and means com. Chattanooga High Sch. PTA, 1956-57; asst. den mother Cub Scout Troop, 1970; block worker Gov. Reagan's Presdl. Campaign. Recipient Spl. Appreciation award Eglin AFB, Fla., 1969. Mem. Nat. Assn. Female Execs., Am. Security Council (nat. adv. bd.), Dade County Crimewatch Orgn. Republican. Avocations: art and interior design, horseback riding, collecting fine porcelain, reading, politics and world affairs. Died Sept. 3, 1996. Home and Office: 20101 SW 92nd Ave Miami FL 33189-1808

FOWLER, ELIZABETH SUSAN, systems analyst, artist; b. Petersburg, Va., Sept. 27, 1957; d. William A. and Norma J. (Mocabee) F. BA in Anthropology, U. Okla., 1978, MA in Comm., 1993; postgrad., U. Toronto, Ont., Can., 1979-80; publs. specialist cert., George Washington U., 1982. Graphic coord. Georgetown U., Washington, 1981-83; mgr. quality assurance Raytheon, Arlington, Va., 1983-90; prin. sys. analyst Logicon Syscon, Arlington, 1991—. Mem. Vienna Art Soc., Penthouse Investment Club (pres. 1994—). Democrat. Methodist. Home: 116 Rinker Gate Fort Valley VA 22652

FOWLER, LINDA MCKEEVER, hospital administrator, management educator; b. Greensburg, Pa., Aug. 7, 1948; d. Clay and Florence Elizabeth (Smith) McK.; m. Timothy L. Fowler, Sept. 13, 1969 (div. July 1985). Nursing diploma, Presbyn. U. Hosp., Pitts., 1969; BSN, U. Pitts., 1976, M in Nursing Adminstrn., 1980; D in Pub Adminstrn., Nova U., 1985. Supr., head nurse Presbyn. Univ. Hosp., Pitts., 1969-76; mem. faculty Western Pa. Hosp. Sch. Nursing, Pitts., 1976-79; acute care coord. Mercy Hosp., Miami, 1980-81; asst. adminstr. nursing North Shore Med. Ctr., Miami, 1981-84, v.p. patient care, 1984-88, Golden Glades Regional Med. Ctr., Miami, 1988-89, Humana Hosp.-South Broward, Hollywood, Fla., 1989-91, assoc. exec. dir. nursing; v.p./CNO Columbia Regional Med. Ctr. at Bayonet Point, 1991-96; COO/CNO Greenbrier Valley Med. Ctr., 1996—; mem. adj. faculty Barry U., Miami, 1984—, Broward C.C., Ft. Lauderdale, 1984—, Nova U., 1986—; cons. Strategic Health Devel. Inc., Miami Shores, Fla., 1986—, So. Coll., Cleveland, Tenn., 1995-96. Bd. dirs. Pasco County Am. Cancer Soc., 1992-95. Dept. HEW trainee, 1976, 79-80. Recipient Pres.'s award Columbia Healthcare Corp., 1995. Mem. Am. Orgn. Nurse Execs. (legis. com. 1988-90), Fla. Orgn. Nurse Execs. (bd. dirs. 1986-88), South Fla. Nurse Adminstrs. Assn. (sec. 1983-84, bd. dirs. 1984-86), U. Pitts. Alumni Assn., Presbyn. U. Alumni Assn., Portuguese Water Dog Club Am. (bd. dirs. 1988-89), Ft. Lauderdale Dog Club (bd. dirs. 1981-82, 83-85, v.p. 1982-83), Am. Kennel Club (dog judge), Sigma Theta Tau. Lutheran. Home: 27 Potomac Crossway Lewisburg WV 24901-8917 Office: Columbia Greenbrier Valley Med Ctr PO Box 497 202 Maplewood Ave Ronceverte WV 24970

FOWLER, MARTI, secondary education educator; b. St. Louis, Mar. 25, 1952; d. Chester Felix and Emily (Kohout) Czarcinski; m. Robert Lee Fowler, Mar. 26, 1988. BA, So. Ill. U., 1973, MA, 1981. Cert. tchr. English, speech and theatre, Mo. Tchr. asst. Hazelwood Sch. Dist., St. Louis, 1974-76; instr. Jefferson Coll., 1991-92, St. Louis C.C. at Meramec, St. Louis, 1990—; tchr. Hazelwood E. High Sch., St. Louis, 1976—. Co-playwright/lyricist: (musical theatre) Difficult Choices, 1988; dir. and choreographer numerous prodns., 1973—. Mem. Am. Alliance for Theatre in Edn. (Mo. state chmn. 1993—), Theatre Edn. Assn. (Mo. State chmn. 1993—, coord. Md. State Thespian Conf. 1996), Speech Theatre Assn. of Mo., Speech Comm. Assn., Internat. Thespian Soc., Zeta Phi Eta (pres. 1972-73). Home: 15685 Silver Lake Ct Chesterfield MO 63017 Office: Hazelwood E High Sch 11300 Dunn Rd Saint Louis MO 63138-1047

FOWLER, MARY EMILY, federal agency administrator; b. Pasadena, Calif., May 17, 1942; d. William A. and Ardiane Fowler; m. Lawrence S. Salowin, July 31, 1990. BA in Polit. Sci., Stanford U., 1965; M in Internat. Affairs, Columbia U., 1969. From mgmt. intern to chief population program review staff Agy. Internat. Devel., Washington, 1967-75; chief energy outreach br. Office of Conservation, Energy Rsch. & Devel. Adminstrn., Washington, 1976-77; chief state coord. br. Energy Ext. Svc., Washington, 1977-79; acting dir. Office of Energy Mgmt. & Ext. Office of Conservation and Solar Energy, Washington, 1980-81; energy conservation specialist State and Local Assistance Programs, Washington, 1981-83; dir. bldg. svcs. div. Office of Bldgs. & Community Systems, Washington, 1984-85; dir. resdl. & comml. conservation program Office Tech. and Fin. Assistance, Washington, 1985-88, dir. weatherization programs div., 1988-91, assoc. dep. asst. sec., 1991-94, acting dep. asst. sec., 1995-96, assoc. dep. asst. sec. for bldg. tech. state and cmty. programs, 1996—; bd. dirs. Pub. Mgr., 1988-95. Recipient Meritorious Honor award U.S. AID, 1972. Mem. Am. Soc. Pub. Adminstrn. (bd. dirs. nat. capitol area chpt. 1984-87, chpt. svc. award 1986), Sr. Execs. Assn., Federal Exec. Inst. Alumni Assn. (treas. 1987-89), Phi Beta Kappa. Office: Dept Energy Energy Efficiency & Renew Energy EE-40 1000 Independence Ave SW Washington DC 20585

FOWLER, SUSAN MICHELE, real estate broker, entrepreneur; b. East Liverpool, Ohio, Jan. 6, 1952; d. George Robert and Mary Helen (Gilliland) F.; m. Paul Joseph Cusumano, Nov. 5, 1988. BA, West Liberty Coll., 1973; MEd, Kent State U., 1995. Lic. real estate broker, Ohio. Sales rep. Tropic-Cal, L.A., 1974-76; project mgr. R&B Enterprises, L.A., 1977-80; regional leasing mgr. First Union Mgmt., Inc., Cleve., 1981-82; comml. real estate broker Adler, Galvin, Rogers, Inc., Cleve., 1983-86, Coldwell Banker Comml. Real Estate, Cleve., 1986-90; pres. Comml. Real Estate Co., Cleve., 1990—; owner Susan M. Fowler Comml. Real Estate Co., Chagrin Falls, Ohio, 1990—, Empower Yourself Seminars, Chagrin Falls, 1992—; v.p., dir. offices First Union Real Estate Investment Trust, Cleve.; pres. Christopher Real Estate Investment, Cleve., 1989—, Christopher Mgmt. Co., Cleve., 1989—; founder, speaker Empower Yourself Seminars, 1992. Trustee, pres. West Side Community Mental Health Ctr., Cleve., 1985—; trsutee, v.p. Child Conservation Coun., Cleve., 1988—; trustee Big Bros. and Big Sisters Greater Cleve., 1989, Visions for Youth, 1991; mem. Cleve. Mus. Art, Geauga County Humane Soc., Fairmount Arts Centre. Mem. Comml. Real Estate Women, Cleve. Area Bd. Realtors (speakers bur.), Nat. Assn. Realtors, Ohio Assn. Realtors, Cleve. Mus. Art, Pine Lake Trout Club. Home: 810 Sun Ridge Ln Chagrin Falls OH 44022 Office: Empower Yourself Seminars PO Box 23255 Chagrin Falls OH 44023-0255

FOWLER, TERRI (MARIE THERESE FOWLER), artist; b. Decatur, Ga., Sept. 26, 1949; d. John Francis and Marjorie (Benson) Herndon; m. John Charles Fowler, July 29, 1972; children: Courtney Marie, Douglas Edwin. Studied with Carolyn Wyeth, Wyeth Sch. Art, 1972. speaker to arts groups, schools. One-man shows include Hampden Sydney Coll., 1973, Longwood, Coll., 1976, C&S Bank, Camden, S.C., 1979, Benfield Gallery, 1985-93; exhibited in cen. chpt. Va. Mus., 1972 (recipient award 1973), Colonial Williamsburg, 1974-77, Md. St. House, Md. St. Senate, 1983-85; works selected by Am. Heart Assn. for Holiday Card Series, 1986-87, commnd. Prince Edward County Bicentennial Com., 1976; represented in many nat. and internat. pvt. collections. Active Girl Scouts Am. cen. Md.; sec. citizens adv. com. Annapolis Mid. Sch. Mem. Balt. Watercolor Soc., Md. Fedn. Art. Annapolis Watercolor Club., San Diego Watercolor Soc., U.S. Naval Acad. Womens Club and Garden Club. Home: 123 Groh Ln Annapolis MD 21403-4008

FOWLER, TILLIE KIDD, congresswoman; b. Milledgeville, Ga., Dec. 23, 1942; d. Culver and Katherine Kidd; m. L. Buck Fowler, 1968; children: Tillie, Elizabeth. BA in Polit. Sci., Emory U., 1964, JD, 1967. Legis. asst. Rep. Robert G. Stephens, 1967-70; counsel White House Office of Consumer Affairs, 1970-71; mem. 103d-104th Congresses from 4th Fla. dist., 1993—. Pres. Jr. League Jacksonville, Fla., 1982-83; chmn. Fla. Humanities Coun., 1989-91; pres. Jacksonville City Coun., 1989-90, mem., 1985-91; mem. bd. visitors U.S. Naval Acad., 1995-96. Republican. Office: US Ho of Reps 413 Cannon House Office Bldg Washington DC 20515

FOWLER, VIVIAN DELORES, insurance company executive; b. Knoxville, Tenn., Sept. 26, 1946; d. Rance James Pierce and Margaret Willadene (Crowe) Compton; m. James Hubert Fowler, May 12, 1979. Student, U. Tenn., Knoxville. CPCU. Clk. The Travelers Ins. Co., Knoxville, 1967-84, adminstv. staff, 1984, comml. mktg. asst., 1984-86; comml. account analyst The Travelers Ins. Co., Nashville, 1986-89, sr. account analyst, 1989-90, account mgr., 1990-93; regional asst. mgr. small bus. unit coml. lines The Travelers Ins. Co., Atlanta, 1993—; regional underwriting mgr. select accounts mktg. Travelers/Aetna Ins. Co., Atlanta, 1996. Lay witness speaker, United Meth. Ch., Knoxville 1979-82; charter mem. St. Thomas Hosp. Found. Soc., 1990; mem. Arthritis Found., 1991. Mem. NAFE, Soc. CPCU, Soc. Cert. Ins. Counselors (cert. 1987), Nat. Assn. of Ins. Women (cert. Profl. Ins. Woman 1975), Internat. Platform Assn. Republican. United Methodist. Home: 604 Ashley Forest Dr Alpharetta GA 30202-6133 Office: Travelers Aetna Ins Co 3500 Piedmont Rd NE Ste 400 Atlanta GA 30305

FOWLES, CHARLOTTE MARIE, English language educator; b. Little Rock, May 24, 1956; d. Lee Roy Fowles and Vera Martha (Mullins) Jones. BA, U. Wyo., 1980; postgrad., U. Nat. Automoma de Mexico, San Antonio, 1984-85. Tchr. English Carbon County Sch. Dist. 2, Hanna, Wyo., 1981-83, South San Antonio Ind. Sch. Dist., 1983-87; asst. English tchr. Japan Exch. of Teaching Ministry of Edn., Miyazaki City, Japan, 1987-89; tchr. ESL San Antonio Coll., 1989-90, Pass Lang. Square, Osaka, Japan, 1991-92; instr. English and history Seian Girls' Pvt. H.S., Kyoto, Japan, 1992-96; instr. Osaka Kokusai Coll. Fgn. Lang., Osaka, 1996—; cons. Minaminaka Bd. Edn., Nichinan City, Japan, 1987-88. Richardson Trust scholar, 1974. Mem. Am. Fedn. Tchrs., Nat. English Tchrs., Tex. Tchrs. of English, Japanese Assn. Lang. Tchrs., Alumni of the Japan Exch. and Teaching Program, Phi Sigma Iota. Democrat. Episcopalian. Home: 3620 N College Dr Cheyenne WY 82001-1974 Office: Osaka Kokusai Coll Fgn Lang, 8-21 Minami-Kawahori-cho, Tennoji-ku Tennoji-ku Osaka 543, Japan

FOWLKES, NANCY LANETTA PINKARD, social worker; b. Athens, Ga.; d. Amos Malone and Nettie (Barnett) Pinkard; m. Vester Guy Fowlkes, June 4, 1955 (dec. 1965); 1 child, Wendy Denise. BA, Bennett Coll., 1946; MA, Syracuse U., 1952; MSW, Smith Coll., 1963; MPA, Pace U., 1982. Dir. publicity Bennett Coll., Greensboro, N.C., 1946-47, 49-50; asst. editor Va. Edn. Bull. ofcl. organ Va. State Tchrs. Assn., Richmond, 1950-52; asst. office mgr. Cmty. Svc. Soc., N.Y.C., 1952-55; social caseworker, asst. supr. Dept. Social Svcs., Westchester County, White Plains, N.Y., 1959-67, supr. adoption services, 1967-77, supr. adoption and foster care, 1977-89; mem. adv. bd. White Plains Adult Edn. Sch. First v.p. Eastview Jr. High Sch., 1970-71; area chmn. White Plains Community Chest, 1964; sec. Mt. Vernon Concert Group, 1952-54; fund raising co-chmn. Urban League Guild of Westchester, 1967; pres. White Plains Interfaith Council, 1972-74; pres. northeastern jurisdiction United Meth. Ch., 1988-92; chmn. adminstrv. bd. Meth. Ch., 1970-72, 82-83, vice chmn., 1978-80, vice chmn. trustees, 1973-77, treas., 1978-83; lay speaker, v.p. Met. dist. United Meth. Women, 1977-79, exec. bd. N.Y. conf., N.Y. conf. rep. Upper Atlantic Regional Sch., 1981-83, mem. nominating com., 1982-83, trustee N.Y. conf., 1982-88, pres. N.Y. conf., 1983-87, conf. United Meth. Women, bd. dirs. Global Ministries United Meth. Ch., 1988—, women's divsn., 1988—, v.p., chair sect. finance women's divsn., 1992—, chair program divsn. N.Y. Conf., 1989-93; bd. dirs. Family Service of Westchester, Bethel Meth. Home, Ossining, N.Y.; bd dirs. White Plains YWCA, 1985—, Scarritt Bennett Ctr., Nashville, Tenn., 1990—, Gum Moon Women's Residence, San Francisco, 1992—, White Plains-Greenburg NAACP, 1993—. Mem. Nat. Assn. Social Workers, Acad. Cert. Social Workers, Jack and Jill of Am. Inc. (chpt. pres. 1954-56, regional sec.-treas 1967-71), Nat. Bus. and Profl. Women's Club (chpt. sec. 1954-56), Internat. Platform Assn., Theta Sigma Phi (Sec.-Treas.), Zeta Nu Omega, Alpha Kappa Alpha (pres. 1960-64, treas. 1975-78). Club: Regency Bridge (pres. 1963-65). Home: 107 Valley Rd White Plains NY 10604-2316

FOX, BETTY, insurance agent, consultant; b. Chgo., July 30, 1935; d. Abraham and Lucille (Manesewitz) Axelrod; m. Ira Rosenberg; children: Deborah Kravitz, Esther Fox Ham, Adam. Student, U. Ill., Chgo., 1953; CLU, The Am. Coll., 1989, ChFC, 1990. Art tchr. Suburban Fine Arts Ctr., Highland Park, Ill., 1963-75; commodities broker Rosenthal et al, Chgo., 1975-78; registered rep. The Equitable, Northbrook, Ill., 1978—; Painter represented in nat. collection (blue ribbon award 1971). Bd. dirs. Suburban Fine Arts Ctr., Highland Park, Ill., 1962—; vol Jewish Vocat. Svc., Chgo.; active Alliance for Mental Illness. Recipient Purchase prize Kemper Ins. Co., Nat. Wine Art Competition. Mem. Nat. Assn. Life Underwriters, Million Dollar Round Table, Chgo. Women Ins. Assn. (treas. 1989), Nat. Assn. Women Life Underwriters, Lake County Life Underwriters, 500 Club (pres. 1990, agy. CLU advisor 1989-92, chmn. Agts. Forum 1992-94). Office: Equitable Life Assurance Co 500 Skokie Blvd Ste 300 Northbrook IL 60062-2864

FOX, CONNIE MARIE, artist; b. Fowler, Colo., Mar. 6, 1925; d. Hurley Wellington and Eva Katherine (Marty) F.; m. Blair Morton Boyd, April 14, 1954 (Oct. 1969); children: Megan Boyd, Brian Boyd. BFA, U. Colo., Boulder, 1947; MA, U. N.Mex., Albuquerque, 1954. Head art depts. Boulder H.S., U. Hill Jr. H.S., Boulder, 1947-48; tchr. U. N.Mex., Albuquerque, 1955-58, Albuquerque Modern Mus., 1956-58; tchr. Carnegie-Mellon U., Pitts., 1969-71, chmn. freshman curriculum com., 1970-71; tchr. New Experimental Coll., Thy, Denmark, 1971-72, Sweetwater Art Ctr., Sewickly, Pa., 1973-79, Southampton Coll., L.I. U., 1980-82; faculty mem. master workshop Southampton Coll., 1983-84; tchr. Art Barge, Napeague, N.Y., 1985-92; mem. painting faculty Vt. Studio Ctr., Johnson, 1990; mem. bd. dirs., v.p. Pitts. Broadcasting Corp., 1974-76, Sweetwater Art Ctr., Sewickley, 1976-79, Anne Mackesey Dance Co., Sag Harbor, N.Y., 1986; mem. first com. Art in Public Places, East Hampton, 1987; curator (with Allan Frumkin) The New Frontier: Art From Western Queens, Queens Coun. on the Arts, 1987; master workshop Southampton Coll., L.I. U., 1988; lectr. Victor D'Amico Inst. Art, East Hampton, 1988, Mus. of Fine Art, U. N.Mex., Albuquerque, 1989, Weir Farm Heritage Trust, Wilton, Conn., 1992, Parrish Art Mus., 1993. Public collections include Albright-Knox Art Gallery, Buffalo, N.Y., Albuquerque Mus., Bklyn. Mus., Fayez-Sarofim, Inc., Houston, Greater Lafayette (Ind.) Mus. of Art, Greenville (N.C.) Mus. of Art, Guild Hall Mus., East Hampton, N.Y., Herbert F. Johnson Mus. of Art, Cornell U., Ithaca, N.Y., IND-COM, Pitts., Nat. Women's Mus., Washington D.C., New Sch. for Social Rsch., N.Y.C., Pacific Enterprises, First Interstate World Ctr., L.A., Parrish Mus., Southampton, N.Y., Roswell (N.Mex.) Mus. and Art Ctr., Santa Barbara (Calif.) Mus. of Art, Simpson, Thatcher and Bartlett, N.Y.C., U. N.Mex., Albuquerque, Weatherspoon Art Gallery, U. N.C., Greensboro, Xerox Corp., Stamford, Conn.; solo exhbns. include Elaine Benson Gallery, Bridgehampton, N.Y., 1981, Southampton Coll. Fine Arts Gallery, 1983, Peter S. Loonam Gallery, Bridgehampton, 1983, Il Punto Blu, Southampton, 1984, Ingber Gallery, N.Y.C., 1985, 86, 88, Vered Gallery, East Hampton, N.Y., 1985, 86, 88, 89, 90, East Hampton Ctr. for Contemporary Art, 1987, U. Mass., Amherst, 1989, Peconic Gallery, Suffolk Cmty. Coll., Riverhead, N.Y., 1991, Benton Gallery, Southampton, 1992, 93, Parrish Art Mus., Southampton, 1994, Weatherspoon Gallery, U. N.C. at Greensboro, 1994, Arlene Bujese Gallery, East Hampton, 1994, Ashawagh Hall, East Hampton, 1996, numerous others; Lorraine Kessler Gallery, Poughkeepsie, N.Y., 1992, Renee Fotouhi Fine Art, East Hampton, 1992, U. Art Gallery, Staller Ctr. for the Arts, SUNY, Stony Brook, 1994, Brenda Taylor Gallery, N.Y.C., 1996, Arlene Bujese Gallery, East Hampton, 1996, numerous others; contbr. numerous articles to profl. jours.; director, prodr. video interviews of artists, dealers and their galleries, 1982—. Recipient First award Southwest Biennial Mus. of N.Mex., Santa Fe, 1957, Purchase award Highlands U., 1959, First Purchase award Tri-State Exhibit, Amarillo, Tex., 1960, Circle Invitational Roswell Mus. of Art, 1960, Beatrice J. Ryan award San Francisco Mus. of Art, 1965, Joan Mitchell Found. award, 1995.

FOX, DONNA BRINK, music educator; b. Pipestone, Minn., June 7, 1950; d. Carroll Marion and Nellie (De Groot) Brink; m. George Bernard Fox, Aug. 30, 1975; 1 child, Elizabeth Ann. BA, Calvin Coll., 1972; MMus, Ohio U., 1975; PhD, Ohio State U., 1982; postgrad. Mgmt. Devel. Program, Harvard U., 1996. Music tchr. Calvin Christian Schs., Grand Rapids, Mich., 1972-74; vis. instr. Ohio U., Athens, 1975-76; asst. prof. Ill. State U., Normal, 1980-84; from asst. prof. to assoc. prof. Eastman Sch. Music, Rochester, N.Y., 1984—; bd. dirs. Aesthetic Edn. Inst., Rochester, 1994—; cons. in field. Grantee Young Audiences of Rochester, 1994, 95; recipient Eisenhart award for Disting. Tchg., Eastman Sch. of Music, 1996, Outstanding Alumni award Ohio U., 1994. Mem. ASCD, Am. Edn. Rsch. Assn., Nat. Assn. Edn. Young Children, Music Educators Nat. Conf. (spl. interest group 1986-90), Am. Orff-Schulwerk Assn. (rsch. adv. review panelist 1992—), N.Y. State Sch. Music Assn. (chair early childhood group 1991-95). Office: Eastman Sch Music 26 Gibbs St Rochester NY 14604

FOX, ELLEN, academic administrator; b. N.Y.C., Apr. 5, 1946; d. Edward and Faith-Hope (Green) Kahn; divorced; 1 child, Jenny Fox. BA in English magna cum laude, L.I. Univ., 1967, MA in English, 1969. With student affairs office grad. sch. arts and scis. Harvard U., Cambridge, Mass., 1980—, dir. student svcs., 1994—. Author: (poem in anthology) A Break in the Clouds, 1993. Co-founder, pres. Nat. Lymphatic and Venous Found Inc., Cambridge, 1978-81. Mem. Nat. Assn. Student Personnel Adminstrs., Assn. Coll. and Univ. Housing Officers Internat. Address: PO Box 748 Cambridge MA 02140-0007

FOX, FRANCES JUANICE, retired librarian, educator; b. Vicksburg, Miss., Aug. 17, 1916; d. Willie Amercy Thaxton and Fannye Lou (Spell) Hepfer; m. Leonard John Fox, Feb. 25, 1937; children: Frances Juanice, L. John Jr., Kenneth L., Robert T., William E., Elizabeth Jean. AA, Phoenix Coll., 1959; BS in Edn., Ariz. State U., 1963, MS in Edn., Libr., 1972. Cert. kindergarten, primary, and elem. tchr., cert. libr., cert. religious edn. Diocese of Phoenix. Substitute tchr. Eseambia County Sch. Dist., Pensacola, Fla., 1936-38; kindergarten tchr. Lollipop Ln. Sch., Phoenix, 1960-61, 1st United Meth. Day Sch., Phoenix, 1961-62; tchr. grade 3 Wilson Elem. Sch., Phoenix, 1962-63; summer libr. R.E. Simpson Elem. Sch., Phoenix, 1964, 65; preschool tchr. Jewish Community Ctr., Phoenix, 1967-68; libr. Audio Visual Ctr. Sts. Simon and Judge Elem. Sch., Phoenix, 1969-82; cataloger First Untied Meth. Ch. Libr., Phoenix, 1963, Baker Ctr. Ariz. State Univ. Meth. and Hillel Students Libr., Tempe, 1969; tchr. ch. sch., 1942-69, ret., 1969. Contbr. poetry to varius publs., including Nat. Libr. Poetry, 1995, Poetic Voices of Am., 1990, 95, World Book of Poetry. 1990; co-compiler: (libr. manual) Diocese of Phoenix, 1980-81. Organizer, leader Girl Scouts USA, Birmingham, Ala., 1951, 52, Phoenix, 1976-83; leader cub scouts Boy Scouts Am., Birmingham, 1950-52, Phoenix, 1952 55; swim instr. ARC, Fla., Ariz., 1933, 34, 53, 54; dance instr. Circle Game and Beginning Dance, Wesley Cmty. Ctr., Phoenix, 1966, 67; sch. tchr. Meth. Ch., 1939-69. Scholar Phoenix Coll., Ariz. State Coll., 1959; recipient Gold Poet award World Book of Poetry, 1990, Honorable Mention Poetic Voices of Am., 1990, Internat. Twentieth Century Achievement award Cambridge Edn., 1994. Mem. ALA, Ariz. State Libr. Assn. (com. on continuing edn. 1979-81), Gold Star Wives of Am. Inc. (pres. 1993-94, nat. parlementarian 1990-91), DAV Aux. (life), Ariz. PTA (life mem., organizer, v.p.), Phi Theta Kappa, Iota Sigma Alpha Honor Soc. Methodist. Home: 2225 W Montebello Ave Phoenix AZ 85015-2327

FOX, GRETCHEN HOVEMEYER, staff assistant, freelance editor, genealogical consultant; b. Erie, Pa., Jan. 2, 1940; d. Ernst Henry and Marjory Etta (Hollister) Hovemeyer; m. Kenneth Roland Fox, Apr. 23, 1989. AB, Radcliffe Coll., 1961. Manuscript sec. Internat. Tax Program Harvard U. Law Sch., Cambridge, Mass., 1961-63; copy editor Internat. Tax Program Harvard U. Law Sch., Cambridge, 1963-65, editorial asst., 1965-66, publs. asst., 1966-76, editorial and pub. dir., 1976-89; freelance editor, cons. pub. and genealogy Cambridge, 1989—; database/rsch. asst. innovations program John F. Kennedy Sch. of Govt., Harvard U., Cambridge, Mass., 1991-93, staff asst. innovations program, 1993—. Co-compiler: Bibliography on Taxation of Foreign Operations and Foreigners: 1968-75, 1976, Bibliography on Taxation of Foreign Operations and Foreigners: 1976-82, 1983; contbr. articles on geneal. to prof. jours.; designer computer software. Mem. New Eng. Hist. Geneal. Soc., Orange County Geneal. Soc. (pub. cons. 1983-91), Sullivan County (N.Y.) Hist. Soc., DAR (chpt. registrar, chpt. historian 1978-83). Office: Harvard U John F Kennedy Sch Govt 79 JFK St Cambridge MA 02138-5801

FOX, JANE ELIZABETH BOYER, secondary education educator; b. York, Pa.; d. Paul A. and Virginia M. (Allison) Boyer; m. Terry G. Fox; children: Randall B., Ryan A. BS in Edn., Shippensburg U., 1965, MEd, 1968. Cert. tchr. Tchr. Gettysburg (Pa.) Area Sch. Dist., 1965-70, Upper Adams Sch. Dist., Biglerville, Pa., 1979—. Home: 724 Sunset Ave Gettysburg PA 17325-2727 Office: Upper Adams Sch Dist N Main St Biglerville PA 17307

FOX, JANICE ANNETTE, dietitian; b. Fredericksburg, Tex., Sept. 23, 1953; d. James Ross and Yvonne (Wegenhoft) Leonard; m. Chad Wayne Fox, July 28, 1973 (div. Jan. 1985); children: Vanessa Grace, James Chad. BS in Food & Nutrition cum laude, Tex. A&I U., 1975. Registered dietitian. Dietetic asst. Valley Bapt. Med. Ctr., Harlingen, Tex., 1975-76, dietetic trainee, 1976-77, dietician, 1977-78; food svc. dir. Beeville (Tex.) Ind. Sch. Dist., 1978-83; dietitian self-employed The Fountain Family Bus., Universal City, Tex., 1983-85; food svc. dir. Edgewood Ind. Sch. Dist., San Antonio, 1985-94, Victoria Ind. Sch. Dist., 1994-95; asst. food svc. dir. San Antonio Ind. Sch. Dist., 1996—; nursing home cons. Huber Manor, Beeville, 1979-83; instr. Bee County Coll., Beeville, 1979-83, Palo Alto Coll., San Antonio, 1987—. Recipient Sunkist Grower's award, 1977. Mem. San Antonio Dietetic Assn., Tex. Dietetic Assn., Am. Dietetic Assn., Tex. Sch. Food Svc. Assn. Methodist. Home: PO Box 1236 Johnson City TX 78686 Office: San Antonio Ind Sch Dist 806 N Salado San Antonio TX 78207

FOX, JUDITH CAROL, sculptor, conservator; b. Elizabeth, N.J., Feb. 14, 1957; d. Sheldon and Anitta (Boyko) F. Student, R.I. Sch. of Design, Providence, 1974, Sch. Painting and Sculpture, Skowhegan, Maine, 1986; BA, Yale U., 1978; postgrad., Ecole Superior des Beaux Arts, Paris, 1979; MA, Inst. Fine Arts. NYU, 1983. Excavator archeology Haifa U., Israel, 1981; fellow in objects conservation Mus. Cultural Hist. U. Calif.,, L.A., 1982-83, Ctr. for Conservation and Tech. Studies, Harvard U., Cambridge, Mass., 1983-84; conservator of cast collection N.Y. Acad. Art, N.Y.C., 1984-87; contract conservator Bklyn. Mus., 1987, 89; contract conservator modern and contemporary Solomon R. Guggenheim Mus., N.Y.C., 1988-94; vis. artist Middlebury (Vt.) Coll., 1989, Empire State Program, N.Y.C., 1989, Tyler Sch. of Art, Phila., 1992, adj. instr. 1992; adj. instr. Yale U., 1992-90, Sch. of Visual Arts, N.Y.C., 1994; vis lectr. Akad. de Bildenden Kunst, Vienna, 1994; presenter Amherst Coll. Artist's Studio, 1994; conservator, pvt. galleries and collections, 1979—. Solo-exhibits include Yale U. Art and Architecture Gallery, New Haven, 1977, Bruno Fachetti Gallery, N.Y.C.,

1987, The Virgin Mary, Saint Theresa and Cinderella, P.P.O.W., N.Y.C., 1993, Sphinx Chapel, 1996, Christine König Galerie, Vienna, 1994, Rena Bransten Gallery, San Francisco, 1996; selected group exhibitions: Limbo Gallery, N.Y.C., 1985, The Palladium, 1985, Jack Tilton Gallery, 1989, 91, Washburn Gallery, N.Y.C., 1990, Morris Mus., Morristown, N.J., 1990, Fla. Internat. U. Art Mus., Miami, 1991, Lorence Monk Gallery, N.Y.C., 1991, White Columns, N.Y.C., 1992, Blum Helman Warehouse, N.Y.C., 1992, The First World, N.Y.C., 1992, 95, Haggerty Mus. of Art, Milw., 1993, Phyllis Kind Gallery, N.Y.C., 1993, Ronald Feldman Gallery, N.Y.C., 1993, Salzburger Kuntzverein, Austria, 1994, Proctor Arts Ctr., Annandale on Hudson, N.Y., 1994, The Jewish Mus., Washington, 1994, Nohra Haine Gallery, N.Y.C., 1994, Galerie RÛdiger Schöttle, Munich, 1994, Revolution, Ferndale, Md., 1995, Herter Art Gallery U. Mass., Amherst, 1995, Kunst-Werke, Berlin, 1995, Venice Bienniale, Venice, 1995, Calif. Ctr. for the Arts, 1995, 96. Contbr. work to benefit auction various charities, N.Y.C., 1994—. Recipient Jonathan Edwards award Yale U., 1978 commission Townsend Harris Hall Acquisition Com., CCNY, 1993; grantee NEA, 1988, 94. Other: Penny Pilkington W Olsoff 532 Broadway New York NY 10012 Office: Amann Conservation Assocs 211 W 61st St New York NY 10023

FOX, JUDITH ELLEN, personnel executive; b. N.Y.C., Aug. 2, 1941; d. Murray A. and Harriette Schneider; student Pa. State U., 1959-60; m. Jerry Fox, Aug. 16, 1964; children: Brian Spencer, Jennifer Leslie. Asst. pers. dir. Miles Shoe Co., N.Y.C., 1961-63; freelance writer, photographer Coronet, The Progressive, U.S. Catholic, numerous local and nat. periodicals, 1962-77; asst. pers. dir. Wallachs, Inc., N.Y.C., 1963-64; co-owner, photographer J. Fox Photographers, Stony Brook, N.Y., 1968-72; mgr. Forbes Temporaries, Richmond, Va., 1975-78; pres., chief exec. officer Judith Fox Cos., Inc., Richmond & Charlottesville, 1978— (One of Inc. mag. 500, 1987), Rosemary Scott Temps., N.Y.C., 1983—, Judith Fox Tech. & Profl. Richmond and Charlottesville, 1991—, Judith Fox Tng. for Growth, 1994—; adv. bd., chmn. Women in Bus. com. Women's Bank, 1981-83; chmn. customer adv. bd. Va. Power, 1981-84, chmn. task force 12th Street Hydroelectric Plant Project, 1983-84; mem. communications cons. group, 1985-87; cons. to pvt. industry, govt., 1980—. Charter mem. Bus. Who Care; mem. exec. adv. coun. E. Claiborne Robins Sch. Bus., 1993—; mem. Met. Regional Water Rev. Panel, 1993—; mem. gov.'s joint sub-com. to study Bus., Profl. and Occupl. Lic. Tax, 1993-94; mem. adv. bd. Massey Cancer Ctr., 1993-95; mem. Richmond met. bd. capital region Crestar Bank, 1994—; bd. dirs. Multiple Sclerosis Soc., Ctrl. Va. chpt., 1979-80, Richmond Met. Coun. Am. Heart Assn., 1992-93, U. Va. Sch. Nursing, 1996—, Keswick Estate Owners Assn., 1995—, Ctrl. Va. Ednl. Telecomms. Corp., 1994—, Va. Festival of Am. Filro, 1994—; bd. govs. Keswick Club, 1995—; mem. pers. com. Am. Heart Assn.; Pres.' Roundtable James Madison U., 1987-89; Local Corp. Gifts Com. The Campaign for Va. Commonwealth U., 1987-89; mem. exec. com. Gov's Adv. Com. Small Bus., 1982-86; steering com. women's health adv. coun. Va. Commonwealth U./Med. Coll. Va., 1988, v.p. 1989-90, mem. bus. coun., 1991—, mem. strat. planning com., 1993—, mem. mktg. com., 1993—; mem. corp. patrons com. Va. Mus. of Fine Arts, 1988-89; chair Industrialist of Yr. Awards Com. Sci. Mus. of Va., 1986—, bd. dirs., 1985—; organizer and dir. Regency Bank, 1987-93; bd. dirs. Met. Richmond YMCA, 1982-86, Pvt. Industry Coun., 1983-86, Jr. Achievement Richmond, Inc., 1988-94; vice-chmn. Richmond area U.S. Olympic Com., 1983-86; co-founder, exec. bd. mem. Richmond Assn. Bus. Owners, 1982-84, acting pres., 1982; mem. The Com. of 200, 1994—. Named Richmond Small Businesswoman of Yr., 1987, one of Richmond's 100 Most Influential People, 1986, Outstanding Businesswoman of Yr. YWCA, 1988; Judith Fox Cos. named one of Inc. mag. 500, 1987. Mem. Nat. Assn. Temporary and Staffing Svcs., Nat. Tech. Svcs. Assn., N.Y. Assn. Temporary Svcs., Va. C. of C. (small bus. com. 1983-85), Metro Richmond C. of C. (chmn. small bus. coun. 1982-84, bd. dirs. 1983-86, exec. com. 1984-86, mem. legis. affairs com. 1981-88), Va. Assn. Temp. Svcs. (v.p. 1981-88). Office: 7301 Forest Ave Richmond VA 23226-3792 also: 3042-C Berkmar Dr Charlottesville VA also: 1790 Broadway Ste 702 New York NY 10019-1412

FOX, KELLY DIANE, financial advisor; b. Brockton, Mass., Sept. 9, 1959; d. James H. and Betty Jane (Calloway) F.; m. Alan David Goldberg, July 6, 1985; 1 child, Andrew Jason. BA, Allegheny Coll., 1980; postgrad. in Bus. Adminstrn., Suffolk U., 1983-84; student Temple U., London, 1978, Syracuse U., London, 1979. Asst. mgr. Casual Male, Braintree, Mass., 1980, Hit or Miss, Braintree, 1981-82; merchandiser Foxmoor, West Bridgewater, Mass., 1982; distbr. Hill's Dept. Stores, Canton, Mass., 1982-85; asst. buyer BJ's Wholesale Club, Natick, Mass., 1985-92; fin. advisor, Am. Express Fin. Advisors, 1993—. Cheerleading coach Avon High Sch., Mass., 1982-83; co-chair enrichment program Falls Elem. Sch.; active John Woodcock Sch. Coun., 1993-94; treas., Attleboro Area Coun. for Children; bd. dir. Atteboro Area Parents Anonymous. Methodist. Avocations: dance, exercise, cooking, art galleries.

FOX, LORRAINE SUSAN, marketing professional; b. L.A., Feb. 8, 1956; d. Robert Lazar and Valerie Joan (Barker) Fox; m. Clark Byron Siegel, July 19, 1981 (div. Nov. 1989). AB with distinction, Stanford U., 1979; MBA, U. Chgo., 1983. Sr. fin. analyst MacIntosh div., Apple Computer, Cupertino, Calif., 1983-84, Sun Microsystems Inc., Mountain View, Calif., 1984-85; mgr. fin. planning and analysis Sun Microsystems Inc., Mountain View, 1985-86, project mgr., 1986-88, mgr. project mgmt., 1988-90, sr. product mktg. mgr., 1990-93, mgr. mktg. strategy, 1993-95; dir. multimedia product mktg. new media divsn. Oracle Corp., Redwood Shores, Calif., 1995, sr. dir. product mktg. Sun Products divsn., 1995-96; v.p. mktg. Centerview Software, Inc., San Francisco, 1996—. Vol. fundraiser Stanford (Calif.) U., 1983-88; vol. Sun Microsystems Cmty. Vols., Mountain View, 1989—; alumni rep. undergrad. commn. on edn. Stanford U. Mem. Commonwealth Club, Stanford Profl. Women's Club, Churchill Club. Home: 707 Bryant St Palo Alto CA 94301-2554 Office: Centerview Software Inc 185 Berry St San Francisco CA 94107

FOX, LYNN SMITH, federal government official; b. Spartanburg, S.C., Apr. 19, 1955; d. James Leonard and Dorothy Harriet (Wilson) Smith; m. William Lloyd Fox, Aug. 1, 1981; 1 child, Harriet Buffington. Student, Wofford Coll., 1974; BA cum laude, Smith Coll., 1977; MBA, George Washington U., 1982. Legis. asst. Rep. John J. LaFalce, Washington, 1982-83; profl. staff mem. Subcom. on Econ. Stabilization, Ho. Banking Com., Washington, 1983-85; congl. liaison asst. Fed. Res. Bd., Washington, 1986-88, spl. asst. to bd., 1992-94, dep. congl. liaison, 1994—; dir. corporate rels. Harvey Mudd Coll., Claremont, Calif., 1990-92. Vice chair Inland Hospice, Claremont, 1992; class officer Smith Coll. Alumnae, Northampton, Mass., 1993—. Univ. fellow George Washington U., 1981-82. Mem. Women in Housing and Fin. (vice chair 1986), Washington Literacy Coun. (bd. dirs. 1996—). Home: 3526 Woodbine St Chevy Chase MD 20815-4039 Office: Fed Res Bd 20th & Constitution Ave NW Washington DC 20551

FOX, MARCIA THERESA, accountant; b. Brunswick, Maine, Sept. 25, 1967; d. Douglas M. and Melinda A. (Curless) F. BBA in Acctg., Western Conn. State U., 1994. Credit mgr. Barrett Roofing and Supply, Inc., Danbury, Conn., 1987-91; acctg. asst. Howard D. Burtis, CPA, Danbury, 1991-94; acct. Allen & Tyransky, CPAs, Danbury, 1994—. Councilwoman City of Danbury, 1995-97; treas. com. to elect Lew Wallace, State Rep., Danbury, 1996. Scholar AAUW, 1993, Western Conn. State U. Alumnae, 1993. Mem. Inst. Mgmt. Accts. (dir. newsletter 1995-96, scholar 1992), Danbury Dems. (v.p. 1996-97), Danbury Ski Club. Home: 95 Park Ave # 4 Danbury CT 06810 Office: Allen & Tyransky CPAs 158 Deer Hill Ave Danbury CT 06810

FOX, MARGERY Q., anthropology educator; b. N.Y.C., Mar. 30, 1928; d. Otto Henry Court Quitzau and Marguerite Elisabeth Ernst; m. Frederick B. Fox, Nov. 25, 1954 (dec. Sept. 1991); children: Peter Q., Hugh Charles. BA, Smith Coll., 1949; MA, NYU, 1967, PhD, 1973. Asst. designer Max Liebman Prodns. (NBC-TV), N.Y.C., 1951-56, various Broadway prodns., N.Y.C., 1953-60; prof. anthropology/sociology Fairleigh Dickinson U., Teaneck, N.J., 1967-87; adj. prof. Hawaii Pacific U., Honolulu, 1973-74; founder women's studies program Fairleigh Dickinson U., Teaneck, 1977; lectr. R.S.V.P., Paramus/Teaneck, 1992—; project dir. NEH Grant, 1983. Author: (with others) Women as Healers, 1989; contbr. articles to profl. jours. Co-dir. Women's Outreach Ctr., Teaneck, 1978-80; adv. bd. dirs. Palisades Chamber Orch., Englewood, N.J., 1973—. Pre-doctoral Rsch. grantee NSF, 1971; Rsch. grantee Fairleigh Dickinson U., 1976, 87. Home: 200 Winston Dr Apt 804 Cliffside Park NJ 07010

FOX, MARY ANN WILLIAMS, librarian; b. Savannah, Ga., Jan. 16, 1939; d. Alton F. and Arthur (Colquitt) Williams; m. William Francis Fox, Dec. 26, 1960 (div. 1984); children: Katherine Frances, William Francis Jr. BA, U. Ga., 1960; MLS, Rutgers U., 1984. Libr. Metuchen (N.J.) Pub. Libr., 1983-85, Mable Smith Douglas Libr. Rutgers U., New Brunswick, N.J., 1984, Firestone Libr. Princeton (N.J.) U., 1985, The Hun Sch. of Princeton, 1985—; bd. dirs. Region 5 Libr. Coop., N.J., 1985-92. Trustee East Brunswick (N.J.) Pub. Library, 1979-92; bd. dirs., Cen. Jersey YWCA, New Brunswick, 1985-88, Cen. Atlantic Conf. United Ch. of Christ, 1985-88. Mem. ALA, N.J. Libr. Assn., N.J. Ind. Sch. Assn. (chair libr. sect. 1988—), Edn. Media Assn. N.J. (bd. dirs. 1987—), Librs. of Middlesex (pres.). Democrat. Mem. United Ch. of Christ. Home: 10 Redcoat Dr East Brunswick NJ 08816-2759 Office: Hun Sch Princeton Edgerstone Rd Princeton NJ 08540

FOX, MARY LOU, paralegal; b. Conneaut, Ohio, Feb. 19, 1932; d. John R. and Mildred D. (Williams) Waltz; m. Kenneth E. Fox, Aug. 4, 1956; children: Kevin S., Gregory S., Susan L. Fox Markowitz. BS in Edn., Westminster Coll., New Wilmington, Pa., 1953; MS in Edn., U. Pitts., 1956. Tchr. Mt. Lebanon Sch. Dist., Pitts., 1953-56; tchr. Ellwood City (Pa.) Sch. Dist., 1956-57, substitute tchr., 1957-66; paralegal Fox & Fox, P.C., Ellwood City, 1966—. Bd. dirs. Almira Home, New Castle, Pa., 1976-95, chmn., 1984-86; chmn. Heritage Bd., Ellwood City, 1985-90; vice chmn. Ellwood Area Devel. Com., 1985-93; precinct committeewoman Beaver County Rep. Com., 1994-96. Mem. AAUW, Town and Country Garden Club (past pres.), Ellwood City Coll. Club (past pres.). Methodist. Office: 323 6th St Ellwood City PA 16117

FOX, MARYE ANNE, chemistry educator; b. Canton, Ohio, Dec. 9, 1947. BS, Notre Dame Coll. of Ohio, 1969; MS, Cleve. State U., 1970; PhD, Dartmouth Coll., 1974; postgrad., U. Md., 1974-76. Prof. chemistry U. Tex., Austin, 1976-91, Rowland Pettit Centennial prof., 1986-92, M. June and J. Virgil Waggoner regents chair chemistry, 1992—, v.p. rsch., 1994—; mem. Nat. Sci. Bd., 1991-96, vice-chair, 1994-96. Assoc. editor Jour. Am. Chem. Soc., 1986-94; mem. adv. bd. Jour. Organic Chemistry, Chem. Engring. News, Chem. Review; contbr. numerous articles to profl. jours. Recipient Agnes Faye Morgan Rsch. award Iota Sigma Pi, 1984, Arthur C. Cope scholar award Am. Chem. Soc., 1988; Garvan medal Am. Chem. Soc., 1988, Havinga medal Leiden U., 1991, Monie A. Ferst award, 1996; named to Hall of Excellence, Ohio Found. Ind. Colls., 1987, The Best of the New Generation, Esquire Mag., 1984; Alfred P. Sloan Rsch. fellow, 1980-82, Camille and Henry Dreyfus tchr. scholar, 1981-85. Fellow AAAS; mem. NAS, Am. Acad. Arts and Sci., Am. Philos. Soc. Home: 5203 Valburn Cir Austin TX 78731-1142 Office: Univ Tex Dept Chemistry Austin TX 78712

FOX, MIRIAM ANNETTE, state legislative fiscal analyst; b. Cuba, N.Y., May 27, 1959; m. Frederick S. Fox, Jan., 1991. BA in Polit. Sci., Idaho State U., 1984; MS in Pub. Mgmt. & Policy, Carnegie-Mellon, 1986. Semiconductor line technician Gould/AMI, Pocatello, Idaho, 1978-84; legal rsch. analyst Manning, Holmes And Winmill Law Firm, Pocatello, 1983-84; market rsch. intern Internat. Trade Adminstrn., Pitts., 1985; rsch. intern Health & Welfare Planning Assn., Pitts., 1985-86; acctg. clk. Carnegie Mellon U., Pitts., 1986; tax revenue analyst Pa. House Appropriations Com., Harrisburg, 1987-91, sr. tax revenue analyst, 1991-93, sr. fiscal analyst, 1993—; designee to Pa. Sch. Employees Retirement Sys. Bd., 1993—. Mem. Capitol Hill Dem. Women's Club, Phi Kappa Phi. Office: Pa House Reps Appropriations Com 512 E9 Main Capitol Bldg Harrisburg PA 17108-0054

FOX, MURIEL, public relations executive; b. Newark, Feb. 3, 1928; d. M. Morris and Anne L. (Rubenstein) F.; m. Shepard G. Aronson, July 1, 1955; children: Eric R., Lisa S. Student, Rollins Coll., 1944-46; B.A. summa cum laude, Barnard Coll., 1948. Art critic, bridal editor Miami (Fla.) News, 1946; reporter U.P.I., 1946-48; polit. speechwriter, publicist, 1949-50; with Carl Byoir & Assos., N.Y.C., 1950-86; TV-radio writer Carl Byoir & Assos., 1950-52, dir. TV-radio dept., 1952-57, v.p., 1956-74, group v.p., 1974-76, exec. v.p., 1977-85; pres. subs. MediaCom Communications Tng., 1975-85, By/Media Inc., 1981-85; sr. cons. Hill & Knowlton, Inc., 1986-90; dir. Harleysville Ins. Co., Rorer Group Inc.; Co-chmn. Vice Presdl. Task Force on Women, 1968; mem. steering com. Women's Forum, 1974-79, pres., 1976-78; mem. Women's Econ. Adv. Com., N.Y.C., 1974-78; mem. nat. adv. com. Nat. Women's Polit. Caucus; mem. nat. adv. bd. Women Today, Ethnic Woman. Bd. dirs. N.Y. Diabetes Assn., 1956-66; bd. dirs. Holy Land Conservation Fund, United Way of Tri-State, Internat. Rescue Com., 1977-84; v.p. Rockland Ctr. for the Arts, 1985—. Named one of 100 Top Corp. Women Bus. Week mag., 1976; recipient Matrix award Women in Communications, 1977, Bus. Leader of Year award ADA, 1979; Disting. Alumna award Barnard Coll., 1985; Eleanor Roosevelt Leadership award, 1985. Mem. NOW (founder, v.p. 1967-70, chmn. bd. 1971-73, chmn. nat. adv. com. 1973-74, bd. dirs. legal defense and edn. fund 1974—, v.p. fund 1977-78, pres. 1978-81, chmn. bd. 1981—, Muriel Fox Communications Leadership award 1991, Our Hero award 1995), Am. Women in Radio and TV (bd. dirs. 1950-51, chmn. nat. publicity com. 1955-57, chmn. nat. pub. rels. com. 1957-59, Achievement award 1983), Am. Arbitration Assn. (bd. dirs. 1983-87). Home and Office: 66 Hickory Hill Rd Tappan NY 10983-1804

FOX, PATRICIA SAIN, academic administrator; b. Indpls., Jan. 8, 1954; d. Thomas Troy and Faye Melba (Martinez) Sain; m. Donald Lee Fox, Aug. 26, 1978; children: Ashley Marie, Aimee Elizabeth. BS in Acctg., Ind. U., 1980; MBA, Butler U., 1985. Adminstrv. asst. Sch. Engring. and Tech. Ind. U.-Purdue U., Indpls., 1980-83, asst. to the dean Sch. Engring. and Tech., 1983-86, asst. dean Sch. Engring. and Tech., 1986—; cons. Gene Glick Mgmt. Co., Indpls., 1986-87. Eucharistic minister St. Christopher Ch., Speedway, Ind., 1987—. Mem. Am. So. for Engring. Edn. Roman Catholic. Office: Ind U-Purdue U Sch Engring & Tech 799 W Michigan St Indianapolis IN 46202-5195

FOX, PAULA (MRS. MARTIN GREENBERG), author; b. N.Y.C., Apr. 22, 1923; d. Paul Hervey and Elsie (de Sola) F.; m. Richard Sigerson (div. 1954); children: Adam, Linda, Gabriel; m. Martin Greenberg, June 9, 1962. Student, Columbia U. Condr. writing Seminars U. Pa. Author: 22 children's books and 6 novels, including How Many Miles to Babylon, 1966, Portrait of Ivan, 1968, Blowfish Live in the Sea, 1970; (novels) Poor George, 1967, Desperate Characters, 1970, The Western Coast, 1972, The Slave Dancer, 1974 (John Newbery medal), The Widow's Children, 1976, The Little Swineherd and Other Tales, 1978, A Place Apart, 1983 (Am. Book award), A Servant's Tale, 1984, One-Eyed Cat, 1985 (Newbery honor book 1985), Maurice's Room, 1985, The Moonlight Man, 1986, The Stone-Faced Boy, 1987, The Village by the Sea, 1988, Lily and the Lost Boy, 1989, The God of Nightmares, 1990, Monkey Island, 1991, Amzat and His Brothers, 1993, Western Wind, 1993, The Eagle Kite, 1995. Recipient Arts and Letters award Nat. Inst. Arts and Letters, 1972, Hans Christian Andersen medal, 1978, fiction citation Brandeis U., 1984, Empire State award for children's lit., 1994; Guggenheim fellow, 1972. Mem. P.E.N., Authors League. Address: care Robert Lescher 67 Irving Pl New York NY 10003-2202

FOX, RENÉE CLAIRE, sociology educator; b. N.Y.C., Feb. 15, 1928; d. Paul Fred and Henrietta (Gold) F. A.B. summa cum laude, Smith Coll., 1949, L.H.D., 1975; Ph.D., Harvard U., 1954; M.A. (hon.), U. Pa., 1971; Sc.D. (hon.), Med. Coll. Pa., 1974, St. Joseph's Coll., Phila., 1978; D. honoris causa, Katholieke U., Belgium, 1978; LHD (hon.), La Salle U., Phila., 1988; DSc (hon.), Hahnemann U., 1991. Rsch. asst. Bur. Applied Social Rsch., Columbia U., 1953-55, rsch. assoc., 1955-58; lectr. dept. sociology Barnard Coll., 1955-58, asst. prof., 1958-64, assoc. prof., 1964-66; lectr. sociology Harvard U., 1967-69; rsch. fellow Center Internat. Affairs, 1967-68, research assoc. program tech. and soc., 1968-71; prof. sociology, psychiatry and medicine U. Pa., Phila., 1969—, Annenberg prof. social scis., 1978—, chmn. dept. sociology, 1972-78; sci. adviser Centre de Recherches Sociologiques, Kinshasa, Zaïre, 1963-67; vis. prof. sociology U. Officielle du Congo, Lubumbashi, 1965; vis. prof. Sir George Williams U., Montreal, Que., Can., summer 1968; Phi Beta Kappa vis. scholar, 1973-75; dir. humanities seminar med. practitioners NEH, 1975-76; maitre de cours U. Liège, Belgium, 1976-77; vis. prof. Katholieke U., Leuven, Belgium, 1976-77; Wm. Allen Neilson prof. Smith Coll., Mass., 1980; dir. d'Etudes Associè, Ecole des Hautes Etudes en Sciences Sociales, Paris, summer 1989; George Eastman vis. prof. Oxford U., 1996—; mem. bd. clin. scholars program Robert Wood Johnson Found., 1974-80; mem. Pres.'s Commn. on Study of Ethical Problems in Medicine, Biomed. and Behavioral Rsch., 1979-81; dir. human qualities of medicine program James Picker Found., 1980-83; Fae Golden Kass lectr. Harvard U. Sch. Medicine and Radcliffe Coll., 1983, Kate Hurd Mead lectr. Med. Coll. Pa./Coll. Physicians Phila., 1990, Lori Ann Roscetti Meml. lectr. Rush-Presbyn.-St. Luke's Med. Ctr., Chgo., 1990; vis. scholar Women's Ctr., U. Mo., Kansas City, 1990, vis. scholar Case Western Reserve Sch. of Med., 1992; opening address 13th Internat. Conf. on Social Scis. and Medicine, Hungary, 1994, vis. prof. U. Calif., San Francisco Sch. of Med., 1994; lectr. founds. of medicine Faculty of Medicine McGill U., Montreal, Can., 1995. Author: Experiment Perilous, 1959, (with Willy DeCraemer) The Emerging Physician, 1968, (with Judith P. Swazey) The Courage to Fall, 1974, rev. edit. 1978, Essays in Medical Sociology, 1979, 2d edit., 1988, L'Incertitude Medicale, 1988, The Sociology of Medicine: A Participant Observer's View, 1989, (with Judith P. Swazey) Spare Parts: Organ Replacement in American Society, 1992, In the Belgian Château: The Spirit and Culture of European Society in an Age of Change, 1994; assoc. editor: Am. Sociol. Rev, 1963-66, Social Sci. and Medicine; mem. editorial com.: Ann. Rev. Sociology, 1975-79; assoc. editor Jour. Health and Social Behavior, 1985-87; mem. editorial adv. bd. Tech. in Soc., Sci., 1982-83; mem. editorial bd. Bibliography of Bioethics, 1979—, Culture, Medicine and Psychiatry, 1980-86, Jour. of AMA, 1981-94, Am. Scholar, 1994—, Current Revs. in Publs., 1994—; vice chair adv. bd. Am. Jour. Ethics and Medicine; contbr. articles to profl. jours. Bd. dirs. Medicine in Pub. Interest, 1979-94; mem. tech. bd. Milbank Meml. Fund, 1979-85; mem. overseers com. to visit univ. health svcs. Harvard Coll., 1979-86; trustee Russell Sage Found., 1981-87; vice chmn. bd. dirs. Acadia Inst., 1990—. Recipient E. Harris Harbison Gifted Teaching award Danforth Found., 1970, Radcliffe Grad. Soc. medal, 1977, Lindback Found. award for teaching U. Pa., 1989, Centennial medal Grad. Sch. Arts and Scis. Harvard U., 1993; Wilson Ctr., Smithsonian Instn. fellow, 1987-88, Guggenheim fellow, 1962; Fulbright Short-Term Sr. scholar to Australia, 1994. Fellow African Studies Assn., AAAS (dir. 1977-80, chmn. sect. K 1986-87), Am. Sociol. Assn. (council 1970-73, 79-81, v.p. 1980-81), Am. Acad. Arts and Scis. (co-chair Class III section I membership com., 1994—), Inst. Medicine (Nat. Acad. Scis., council 1979-82), Inst. Soc., Ethics and Life Scis. (founder, gov.); mem. AAUP, AAUW, Assn. Am. Med. Colls., Social Sci. Research Council (v.p., dir.), Eastern Sociol. Soc. (pres. 1976-77, Merit award 1993), N.Y. Acad. Scis., Soc. Sci. Study Religion, Inst. Intercultural Studies, 1969-93, (asst. sec. 1969-78, sec. 1978-81, 89-92, v.p. 1987-89), Am. Bd. Med. Specialists, Coll. of Physicians of Phila. (council, 1993—), Phi Beta Kappa (senate 1982-87). Home: 135 S 19th St Philadelphia PA 19103-4912

FOX, SALLY GOERS, movement theatre artist, educator; b. Angaston, Australia, Nov. 23, 1952; arrived in U.S., 1979; d. Herald Melville and Doris Mary (Roach) Goers; m. Lay Christopher Fox, Apr. 7, 1982. BA with honors, Flinders U., South Australia, Australia, 1973; MAH, SUNY, Buffalo, 1996. Performer Theatre Magenia, Paris, 1974-76; founding mem. Neue Gruppe Kulturarbeit, Bremen, West Germany, 1976-79; artistic dir. The Mime Workshop, Rochester, N.Y., 1979-82; staff mem. Rochester Zen Ctr., 1982-83; asst. adminstr. Genesee Valley Zen Ctr., Rochester, 1984-85; acting coach Patch Theatre Co., Australia, 1989; stilts dancer Australia and N.Y., 1989—; tchg. artist Aesthetic Edn. Inst., Rochester, 1991—; performing and tchg. artist Young Audiences, Rochester, 1992—; advisor arts in edn. Genesee Valley Coun. on Arts, Mt. Morris, N.Y., 1995, 96; artist-in-residence N.Y. Found. for Arts, 1996; tchg. artist N.Y. State Coun. for Arts, 1993-96. Resource artist Monroe County Libr. Sys., Rochester, 1994-96. Travel grantee Australia Coun., 1974, 75. Mem. Nat. Movement Theatre Assn., Theatre Comms. Group. Zen. Office: Theatre Askew Box 200 Springwater NY 14560

FOX, SANDRA GAIL, insurance marketing executive; b. N.Y.C., Aug. 12, 1960; d. Joseph A. and Rhoda (Levine) Fried; m. David A. Fox, Sept. 21, 1986; children: Alexander, Peter. BA, Ind. U., 1982. Examiner nat. compliance Dean Witter, N.Y.C., 1983-84, sales supr. active assets account, 1984-85, mktg. assoc., 1985-86; ind. mktg. cons. Hackensack, N.J., 1986-87; dir. alt. distbn. mktg. Mut. of N.Y., Teaneck, N.J., 1987-89, dir. spl. markets and annuities, 1989-94; asst. v.p. annuities mktg., 1994—; mem. work life force com. Mut. N.Y., Teaneck, 1991—. Vol. presch. activities YW-YMHA, Wayne, N.J., 1993-94; fundraiser United Jewish Fedn., Bergen and Passaic, N.J., 1982—, Nat. Kidney Found., 1984. Griswald acad. scholar Ind. U., 1980, 81. Mem. Nat. Assn. Variable Annuities (edn. com., publ. chair 19936), Phi Beta Kappa. Office: Mutual of NY 500 Frank W Burr Blv Teaneck NJ 07666

FOX, SARAH, lawyer; b. Buffalo, Dec. 12, 1951; d. Austin McCracken and Jean McLean (Coatsworth) F. BA, Yale U., 1973; JD, Harvard U., 1982. Bar: N.Y. 1982, D.C. 1983. Reporter Buffalo Courier-Express, 1973-79; staff counsel Internat. Union of Bricklayers & Allied Craftsmen, Washington, 1982-90; chief labor counsel Senate Labor and Human Resources Com., Washington, 1990-94, minority chief labor counsel, 1995-96; bd. dirs. NLRB, Washington, 1996—. Office: NLRB 1099 14th St NW Ste 11300 Washington DC 20570

FOX, SELENA MARIE (SUZANNE BISSET CARPENTER), minister, priestess, psychotherapist, counselor; b. Arlington, Va., Oct. 20, 1949; d. Thomas Richard and Anne Elise (Fox) Bisset; m. Dennis Darrel Carpenter, June 7, 1986. BS in Psychology with honors, Coll. William and Mary, 1971; postgrad., Rutgers U., 1972, Madison Area Tech. Coll., Wis., 1973-75; MS in Counseling, U. Wis., 1995. Min. Circle Sanctuary, Mt. Horeb, Wis., 1974—; psychotherapist Wellspring Clinic, Madison, Wis., 1996—; guest min. Unitarian Universalists, Wis., others, 1980—; speaker chs. and spiritual communities, U.S. and Can., 1975—; speaker, organizer regional, nat., internat. ecospiritual/pagan festivals, 1977—; del., speaker World Coun. Chs. Conf., Toronto, 1988, Parliament of World's Religions, Chgo.,1993, Nature Religion Today conf., Eng., 1996, others; guest speaker tchr. at univs., 1980—; founder, exec. dir. Circle Sanctuary Nature Preserve, 1983—; founder Sch. for Priestesses, 1986, Lady Liberty League, 1991; Wiccan civil rights leader; founder, convener Nature Religions Scholars Network within Am. Acad. Religion, 1996. Author: Goddess Communion Rituals, 1988, When Goddess is God: Pagans, Recovery, and Alcoholics Anonymous, 1995; cons. (Time-Life book series) Mysteries of the Unknown, 1990; founding editor Circle Guide to Pagan Groups, 1979, Circle Network News quar., 1980, Circle Guide to Pagan Arts, 1992; recordings include Magical Journeys, 1981, Ritualist: Sacred Cave Ritual, 1996; founder Circle's Network, Worldwide Nature Spirituality Assn., 1978, Wiccan Shamanism, 1979, Pagan Academic Network, 1992; contbr. articles and rituals to books and jours., 1975—; nat./internat. Nature Spirituality spokesperson on TV, and radio, for films, mags., newspapers, others, 1979—. Mem. adv. bd. Madison Area Interfaith Network. Recipient Feature Writing Excellence award PROCOM/WABC, Madison, 1978. Mem. APA, ACA, Assn. for Transpersonal Psychology, Am. Acad. Religion, Nat. Geneal. Soc., Inst. Noetic Scis. Mem. Circle Sanctuary/Nature Spiritualist. Office: Circle Sanctuary PO Box 219 Mount Horeb WI 53572-0219

FOX, SUSAN E., legal assistant; b. Uniontown, Pa., June 17, 1955; d. James Ira Sr. and Elizabeth Ann (Kirk) F. BS in Journ., W.Va. U., 1977; Cert. Completion, Nat. Ctr. for Paralegal Tng., Atlanta, 1977. Legal asst. Jackson, Kelly, Holt & O'Farrell, Charleston, W.Va., 1978-79, Dennis, Corry, Webb & Carlock, Atlanta, 1979-84, Dennis, Corry, Porter & Thornton, Atlanta, 1984-89, Ga.-Pacific Corp., Atlanta, 1989—. Bd. dirs. Met. Atlanta Coun. on Alcohol and Drugs, 1991-92, treas., 1992-93, pres., 1993-94; bd. dirs. DeKalb Rape Crisis Ctr., 1994-96; bd. dirs. Ga.-Pacific Svc. Force, 1995-96; chmn., mem. devel. Jr. League of DeKalb County, Decatur, Ga., 1989-90, cmty. rsch. chmn., 1990-91, corr. sec., 1991-92, pres.-elect, 1994-95, pres., 1995-96; mem. Leadership DeKalb, 1995; Olympic vol., Equestrian Venue Comm. Ctr., 1996. Mem. Ga. Assn. Legal Assts. (newsletter asst. 1980-81, mem. chmn. 1981-82), Embroiderers Guild of Am., Atlanta Needlepoint Guild (sec. 1992-93, chmn. cmty. projects), High Mus. of Art. Republican. Presbyterian. Home: 2207 Harbor Pointe Pkwy Dunwoody GA 30350-3158 Office: Georgia-Pacific Corp 133 Peachtree St Atlanta GA 30303

FOXWELL, BETSY MEERSCHAUT, gifted education educator; b. Chgo., July 29, 1938; d. Robert Lee and Margaret (Howells) Meerschaut; m. Warren Roger Foxwell, June 10, 1961. BA, U. Wis., 1960. Tchr. of gifted Chgo. Bd. Edn., 1961—; mem. edn. com. Ill. Hist. Preservation Agy., 1990—; mem. adv. bd. Chgo. Metro History Fair, 1987—; asst. state dir. Future Problem Solving Program, 1994—. Bd. dirs. Park Ridge (Ill.) Youth Campus, 1986—; fundraising chmn. Maine Mental Health, 1985, 86. Recipient Kate Maremont award Ill. PTA, 1984, Ill. Nat. History Day Tchr. award Nat. HIstory Day, 1993, Honored Tchr. award Ill. Math. and Sci. Acad., Aurora, 1990, 92, 94. Mem. Nat. Coun. Tchg. Social Studies, Nat. Coun. Tchrs. English, Orgn. Am. Historians, Ill. Assn. Tchrs. English. Home: 522 N Home Ave Park Ridge IL 60068-3036

FOX-WOLFGRAMM, SUSAN JO, business management educator; b. Denver, Mar. 14, 1961; d. Al and Angela Marlene (Allen) Fox; m. Dietrich George Wolfgramm, May 21, 1993. BS, U. Colo., 1983; MPA, Tex. Tech. U., 1984, PhD, 1991. Pers. asst. intern Tex. Dept. Human Resources, Lubbock, 1984; lectr. Tex. Tech. U., Lubbock, 1985-91; prof. San Francisco (Calif.) State U., 1991—; senator Acad. Senate, San Francisco (Calif.) State U., 1993—. Sch. Bus. grantee San Francisco (Calif.) State U., 1992, 93; Samuel Moore Walton Free Enterprise fellow Students in Free Enterprise, Inc., 1992—; Price-Babson Coll. fellow Ctr. for Enterpreneurial Studies, Babson Coll., Mass., 1994. Mem. San Francisco State Univ. Women's Assn. (pres.), Commonwealth Club Calif., Beta Gamma Sigma. Office: San Francisco State Univ 1600 Holloway Ave San Francisco CA 94132

FOY, SISTER MARY SHEILA, school system administrator; b. Phila., Aug. 7, 1939; d. Edward Daniel and Dorothy Mary (Murphy) F. AB, Immaculate Coll., 1970; MEd, West Chester (Pa.) U., 1978; postgrad., St. Joseph's U., 1993-94. Cert. secondary edn. tchr., Pa. Svc. rep. spl. projects Bell Tel., Pa., 1957-58; tchr. grades 5-8 Archdiocese of Phila., Phila., 1961-80; tchr. French grades 9-12 Diocese of Harrisburg, Shemokin, Pa., 1980-84; tchr. French grades 10-12 Diocese of Scranton, Hazelton, Pa., 1984-86; adminstr. Archdiocese of Phila., Drexel Hill, Pa., 1986-93, Phila., 1993—; mem. adv. bd. Sister's Coun. of Phila., Phila., 1970-80, Sister's Coun. of Harrisburg (Pa.), 1982-84, secondary edn. Sister's of Immaculate Heart of Mary, Immaculata, Pa., 1985—. Francophone scholar Am. Assn. of Tchrs. of French, 1981. Mem. Nat. Cath. Edn. Assn. (mem. region 3 regional bd.). Office: St Maria Goretti HS 1736 S 10th St Philadelphia PA 19148-1644

FRACKMAN, NOEL, art critic; b. N.Y.C., May 27, 1930; d. Walter David and Celeste (Barman) Stern; m. Richard Benoit Frackman, July 2, 1950; 1 child, Noel Dru Pyne. Student Mt. Holyoke Coll., 1948-50; BA, Sarah Lawrence Coll., 1952, MA, 1953; postgrad. Columbia U., 1964-67; MA, Inst. Fine Arts, NYU, 1976, PhD, 1987. Art critic Scarsdale Inquirer (N.Y.), 1962-67, Patent Trader, Mt. Kisco, N.Y., 1962-71; assoc. Arts Mag., N.Y.C., 1968-92; lectr. Aldrich Mus. Contemporary Art, Ridgefield, Conn., 1967-75, Gallery Passport Ltd., N.Y.C., 1968—; contractual lectr. Met. Mus. Art, N.Y.C., 1994-95; curator of edn. Storm King Art Ctr., Mountainville, N.Y., 1973-75; instr. continuing edn. div. SUNY, Purchase, 1988—; bd. dirs. Friends of the Neuberger Mus. Art, Purchase (N.Y.) Coll., Shah U. N.Y., 1994—. Author (catalogue) John Storrs, Whitney Mus. of Am. Art, 1986; contbr. articles and/or revs. to various mags. including: Arts Mag., Harper's Bazaar, Feminist Art Jour., Art Voices. Sarah Williston scholar, 1948-50; recipient 1st prize, coll. publs. contest Mademoiselle mag., 1961. Mem. Internat. Assn. Art Critics, Art Table Inc., Coll. Art Assn. Home: 3 Hadden Rd Scarsdale NY 10583-3327

FRAHM, SHEILA, senator, lieutenant governor, former state legislator; b. Colby, Kans., Mar. 22, 1945; m. Kenneth Frahm; children: Amy, Pam, Chrissie. BS, Ft. Hays State U., 1967. Mem. bd. edn. State of Kans., 1985-88; mem. Kans. Senate, Topeka, 1988-94, senate majority leader, 1993-94; lt. gov. State of Kans., 1995-96; U.S. senator from Kans., 1996—. Mem. AAUW (Outstanding Br. Mem. 1985), Thomas County Day Care Assn., Shakespeare Fedn. Women's Clubs, Farm Bur., Kans. Corn Growers, Kans. Livestock Assn., Rotary (Paul Harris fellow 1988). Republican. Address: 6005 SW 39th St Topeka KS 66610-1369 Office: US Senate 141 Hart Senate Office Bldg Washington DC 20410

FRAIMAN, SUSAN DIANA, English language and literature educator; b. N.Y.C., Jan. 4, 1957; d. Arnold Guy and Genevieve (Lam) F.; m. Eric William Lott, Aug. 20, 1988; 1 child, Cory Michael Fraiman-Lott. BA summa cum laude, Princeton U., 1978; PhD, Columbia U., 1988. Asst. prof. dept. English U. Va., Charlottesville, 1987-93, assoc. prof., 1993—; dir. undergrad. studies dept. English, U. Va., 1994-96. Author: Unbecoming Women: British Women Writers and the Novel of Development, 1993; contbg. editor: Columbia Dictionary of Modern Literary and Cultural Criticism, 1995; contbr. articles to profl. jours. Mem. Women's Studies Exec. Bd., 1987—, Women's Ctr. Coord. Coun., 1989-92. Sesquicentennial assoc. U. Va. Ctr. for Advanced Studies, 1996-97, Fulbright fellow, France, 1978-79. Mem. MLA, U. Va. Women Faculty and Profl. Assn., Phi Beta Kappa. Home: 409 Altamont St Charlottesville VA 22902 Office: Dept English Bryan Hall Univ Va Charlottesville VA 22903

FRAKES, MARY H., journalist, publisher; b. Memphis, Nov. 28, 1950; d. John Biddle and Margaret (Walker) Hamsher. BA, Vanderbilt U., 1972. Asst. city editor Palm Beach (Fla.) Post, 1979-82; city editor Transcript-Telegram, Holyoke, Mass., 1982-83; mng. editor The Robb Report, Acton, Mass., 1983-86; editor-in-chief High Tech. Bus., Boston, 1987-88; owner N.E. Writers Syndicate, Cambridge, Mass., 1988-91; asst. v.p. Fidelity Investments, Boston, 1991-96; v.p. internet svcs. Reality Online, Norristown, Pa., 1996—. Contbg. editor Boston Phoenix mag., 1988-91. Recipient Editl. Excellence award Folio mag., 1995, Gold Quill Award of Excellence, Internat. Assn. Bus. Communicators, 1994. Mem. Women in New Media. Office: Reality Online 1000 Madison Ave Norristown PA 19403

FRAME, ANNE PARSONS, civic worker; b. Berkeley, Calif., Jan. 3, 1904; d. Reginald Hascall and Maude (Bemis) Parsons; A.B., Mills Coll., 1924; postgrad. Columbia, 1924-25; m. Frederic D. Tootell, Apr. 3, 1926 (div. July 1935); children: Geoffrey H., Natalie (Mrs. Oliver); m. Jasper Ewing Brady, Jr., July 31, 1935; (dec. Dec. 1944); 1 son, Hugh Parsons; m. Howard Andres Frame, Mar. 29, 1948 (dec. Dec. 1986). Dir. Parsons, Hart & Co., Seattle, Hillcrest Orchard Co., Seattle. Mem. bd. mgmt. Palo Alto br. A.R.C., 1955-61; trustee Children's Hosp. & Med. Ctr., Seattle, 1942-48; bd. dirs. Children's Health Coun., Palo Alto, Calif., 1953-63, 64-76, pres., 1954-58, assoc. mem., Seattle, 1986—; sponsor Nat. Recreation Assn., 1942-66, trustee, 1948-66; sponsor Nat. Recreation and Park Assn., 1966—, trustee, 1966-73; trustee Nat. Recreation Found., 1964—; 1st v.p. Children's Hosp. at Stanford Sr. Aux., 1965-67, bd. dirs. Hosp., 1967-85; former mem. adv. com. Holbrook-Palmer Park; trustee Mills Coll., 1952-62; bd. dirs. Holbrook-Palmer Recreation Park Found., 1968-86; bd. govs. San Francisco Symphony Assn., 1949-79; mem. Atherton (Calif.) Park and Recreation Commn., 1968-81. Mem. LWV, Bowne House Hist. Soc., San Mateo County, Seattle, Chgo., Calif. hist. socs., Calif. Heritage Council, San Francisco Mus. Art, Seattle Art Mus., Museum Soc., Nat. Trust for Historic Preservation, Nat. Soc. Colonial Dames Am. Episcopalian. Clubs: Sunset, Tennis (Seattle), Woodside-Atherton Garden (bd. dirs. 1966-68), Francisca (San Francisco), Menlo Country (Calif.), Seattle Garden Club.

FRAME, NANCY DAVIS, lawyer; b. Brookings, S.D., Dec. 13, 1944; m. J. Davidson Frame, Mar. 28, 1970 (d. Oct. 1994); 1 child, Katherine Adele. BS, S.D. State U., 1966; MA, Georgetown U., 1968, JD, 1976. Bar: D.C. 1976. Atty., advisor AID, Washington, 1976-81, asst. gen. counsel, 1981-86; dep. dir. Trade and Devel. Agy., Washington, 1986—. Recipient Superior Honor award AID, 1984, Presdl. Rank award, 1993; Fulbright fellow , 1966, NDEA fellow, 1967. Mem. ABA, Fed. Bar Assn. Home: 5819 Magic Mountain Dr Rockville MD 20852-3231 Office: Trade and Devel Agy SA 16 Washington DC 20523

FRANCA, CELIA, ballet director, choreographer, dancer, narrator; b. London, Eng., June 25, 1921; m. James Morton, Dec. 7, 1960. Student, Guildhall Sch. Music, Royal Acad. Dancing; LLD (hon.), Assumption U. of Windsor, 1959, Mt. Allison U., 1966, U. Toronto, 1974, Dalhousie U., 1976, York U., 1976, Trent U., Peterborough, Ont., Can., 1977, McGill U., 1986; DCL (hon.), Bishop's U., 1967; DLitt (hon.), Guelph U., 1976; DFA, Carleton U., Ottawa, 1995. Founder, artistic dir. Nat. Ballet Can., Toronto, 1951-74; co-founder Nat. Ballet Sch., Toronto, 1959; Mem. jury 5th Internat. Ballet Competition, Varna, Bulgaria, 1970, 2d Internat. Ballet Competition, Moscow, 1973. Debut: corps de ballet Mars, The Planets (Tudor), Mercury Theatre, London, 1936; soloist, Ballet Rambert, London, 1936-38, leading dramatic dancer, Ballet Rambert, 1938-39, guest artist, Ballet Rambert, 1950, dancer, Ballet des Trois Arts, London, 1939, Arts Theatre Ballet, London, 1940, Internat. Ballet, London, 1941, leading dramatic dancer, Sadler's Wells Ballet, 1941-46, guest artist, choreographer, Sadler's Wells Theatre Ballet, London, 1946-47, dancer, tchr., Ballets Jooss, Eng., 1947, ballet mistress, leading dancer, Met. Ballet, London, 1947-49, dancer, Ballet Workshop, London, 1949-51, prin. dancer, Nat. Ballet Can., 1951-59; prin. roles include Black Queen in Swan Lake; title roles in Lady from the Sea; choreographer: ballets, including Midas, London, 1939, Cancion, London, 1942, Khadra, London, 1946, Dance of Salome, BBC-TV, 1949, The Eve of St. Agnes, BBC-TV, 1950, Afternoon of a Faun, Toronto, 1952, Le Pommier, Toronto, 1952, Casse-Noisette, 1955, Princess Aurora, 1960, The Nutcracker, 1964, Cinderella, 1968, numerous others for CBC, Can. Opera Co.; author: The National Ballet of Canada: A Celebration, 1978. Hon. patron Osteoporosis Soc. Can. Decorated Order of Can.; recipient Key to City of Washington, 1955, Woman of Yr. award B'nai B'rith, 1958, award for outstanding contbn. to arts Toronto Telegram, 1965, Centennial medal, 1967, Hadassah award of merit, 1967, Molson award, 1974, award Internat. Soc. Performing Arts Adminstrs., 1979, Can. Dance award, 1984, Gold Card IATSE local 58, 1984, diplôme d'honneur Can. Conf. Arts, 1986, Woman Yr. award St. George's Soc. Toronto, 1987, Order of Ont., 1987, Gov. Gen. award, 1994, Children's Charity award Variety Club of Ont., 1995; twice visited China at invitation of Chinese govt. to teach; in Beijing mounted full-length Coppelia, 1980; honored as one of founders of Can.'s maj. ballet cos. at Alta. Ballet Co.'s 15th anniversary, 1981. Office: 203 350 Queen Elizabeth Dr, Ottawa, ON Canada K1S 3N1 also: 157 King St E, Toronto, ON Canada M5C 1G9

FRANCAVILLA, BARBARA JEAN, human services administrator; b. Montclair, N.J., Nov. 18, 1955; d. John Joseph and Angela (Rapa) F. MA, Montclair State U., 1995. Mental health counselor Cmty. Substance Abuse Saint Clares Hosp., Boonton, N.J., 1992—; prevention specialist Inst. for Prevention Saint Barnabas Behavioral Health Network, Union, N.J., 1995—; dir. Livingston (N.J.) Youth and Cmty. Svcs. St. Barnabas Hosp., 1995—. Mem. bd. Livingston (N.J.) Municipal Alliance, 1995—. Mem. Am. Counseling Assn., N.J. Counseling Assn., Phi Kappa Phi, Alpha Kappa Delta. Office: Livingston Youth/Cmty Svcs St Barnabas Hosp Monmouth Ct Comty Ctr Livingston NJ 07039

FRANCE-DEAL, JUDITH JEAN, parochial school educator; b. Falls City, Nebr., June 27, 1941; d. Paris and Georgia Elizabeth (Reiger) France; m. Gary Arthur Deal, Dec. 30, 1960; children: Kevin, Timothy. Student, Bapt. Inst. Christian Workers, Bryn Mawr, Pa., 1959; grad., Liberty Bible Inst., 1994. Vol. worker with many orgns., 1957—; receptionist Central Ins. Co., Omaha, Nebr., 1960-62; vol. PTA, Cub Scouts, etc., Wis., 1966-76; tchr. spl. edn. First Bapt. Ch., Dallas, 1985-88, vol. tutor ESL, 1985—; inspirational spkr.; tchr. English and Bible studies 1st Bapt. Ch., Richardson, Tex., 1989—; pres., founder God's Internat. ABCs, Inc.; model for numerous advts. and commls. Author: Center of Our Lives, 1994. Chaplain-min. to cancer patients Tulsa Cancer Treatment Ctr. Recipient numerous writing awards. Mem. Internat. Platform Assn. Republican. Office: Gods Internat ABC Inc 1000 14th St Ste 122 Plano TX 75074-6249

FRANCE-LITCHFIELD, RUTH A., reading and literacy specialist; b. Cleve., Mar. 17, 1945; d. Edward Agnew and Elizabeth Ann (Way) France; children: Katherine Ann, Charles Robert. AA, Christian Coll., Columbus, Mo., 1965; BS in Elem. Edn. and French, U. Mo., 1969; MEd in Reading, U. Hawaii, 1974; cert. advanced grad. study, Boston U., 1995. Cert. advanced grad. study, consulting tchr. of reading, French K-9, Mass. Elem. tchr. Claude O. Markoe Sch., Fredericsted, St. Croix, V.I., 1969-70; tchr. Ecole Active Bilingue, Paris, 1970-71; elem. tchr. Punahou Sch., Honolulu, 1971-74; nat. cons., asst. editor, editor, asst. to mng. editor The Economy Co.-McGraw Hill Divsn., Oklahoma City, 1974-81; pvt. cons., tutor U.S. Army, West Germany, 1981-84; tchr., substitute Community Nursery Sch., Lexington, Mass., 1985-89; substitute tchr. Lexington (Mass.) Pub. Schs., 1989-91; instrnl. aide Bridge Elem. Sch., Lexington, 1991-92, reading recovery trainee, 1992-93; reading recovery tchr. Davis Elem. Sch., Bedford, Mass., 1994, Bridge Elem. Sch., Lexington, 1992—; rsch. asst. Harvard U. Sch. Edn., 1993; pvt. tutor, 1995—; workshop presenter in field. Contbr. articles to profl. publs. Mem. ASCD, Internat. Reading Assn. (bd. dirs. Greater Boston coun., v.p. elect), Nat. Reading Assn., Mass. Reading Assn., Ohio Reading Assn., New Eng. Reading Assn., Mass. Assn. Bilingual Edn., Reading Recovery Coun. of N.Am., Phi Delta Kappa, Thi Lambda Theta, Pi Lambda Theta. Republican. Home: 6 Conestoga Rd Lexington MA 02173-6427 Office: 55 Middleby Rd Lexington MA 02173-6920

FRANCESCHI, BETTI, artist; b. Cleve.; children: Chris, Antonia. Student, Ind. U., Carnegie Inst. Tech., Pitts.; BS, Hunter Coll., N.Y.C., 1977. Author, artist: The Still Point, 1987 (6 nominations to Nat. Trust show 1987, London and Frankfurt Book Fair Exhbns.); one-woman shows include Nat. Mus. Dance, 1991, N.Y. State Theater, N.Y.C. Ballet, 1992, Philharmonic Ctr. for the Arts, Naples, Fla., 1993. Home and Studio: 2680 Broadway # 5A New York NY 10025-4411

FRANCH, NORA, re-engineering specialist; b. Kansas City, Kans., Aug. 16, 1955; d. Ernest Sr. and Frances (McQuaid) Voiles; m. Gary L. Franch; 1 stepchild, Kathleen Blair. BS in Bus. Adminstrn., Nat. Coll., Denver, 1983; MSS in Applied Communications, U. Denver, 1992. Office mgr. U.S. Army, Anchorage, 1976-79; lease adminstrn. K-N Energy Co., Lakewood, Colo., 1980-83; paralegal Welborn, Dufford, Brown Law Firm, Denver, 1982-84; sec. Colo. N.G., Englewood, 1984-85, staffing specialist, 1985-86, EEO mgr., 1986-88, human resources mgr., 1988-93; reengring. specialist Def. Fin. and Acctg. Svcs., 1993—; instr. grad. sch. Webster U., 1996—; instr. Nat. Coll., 1992, Wester U. Grad. Sch., 1996. Home: 2096 Sandhurst Dr Castle Rock CO 80104-2392

FRANCHINI, ROXANNE, banker; b. N.Y.C., Mar. 20, 1951; d. Tullio and Jean (Brady) F. Student, Emerson Coll., Ricker Coll., New Sch. Social Rsch. With Princess Marcella Borghese div. Revlon, N.Y.C., 1972-73; stewardess TWA Airlines, 1973-74; asst. to pres. N.Y. Shipping Assn., N.Y.C., 1974-79; benefits mgr. Kidde, Inc., N.Y.C., 1979-83; 2d v.p. pension trust fin. svcs. Chase Manhattan Bank, N.A., N.Y.C., 1983-85, v.p. mgr. global securities, 1985-89; v.p., sales dir. global custody worldwide securities svcs. Citibank, N.Y.C., 1989-91; v.p. Mellon Bank, Pitts., 1991—. Chair fin. local fund raising campaigns. Mem. AAUW, Internat. Ops. Assn., Nat. Investment Co. Svc. Assn., Nat. Assn. Colls. and Univ. Bus. Offices.

FRANCIOSI, BARBARA LEE, designer, fiber artist; b. Batavia, N.Y., Oct. 25, 1931; d. Henry Curtis and Ferne Marie (Jewitt) Parcells; m. Raymond Louis Cates, June 23, 1950 (div. 1960); children: Gwynne Cates Chandler, Edward Paul Cates; m. Pat Franciosi, Feb. 1, 1964. Grad., Ctrl. City Bus. Coll., Syracuse, N.Y., 1949. Med. sec., asst. Harold Courtney, MD, Syracuse, N.Y., 1949-51; dir., owner Barbara Schs. of Dance, Preble, N.Y., and Groton, Conn., 1951-63; legal asst. Melvin Scott, Atty., New London, Conn., 1961-75; designer, owner Fiber Artistry by Barbara Lee, Groton, 1978—. Sec. Dem. City Com., Groton, Conn., 1972-76; candidate dist. judge of probate State of Conn., 1974; vice chmn. Dem. Town Com., Groton, 1976-80; elected Groton Town Coun., 1971, Rep. Town Meeting, Groton, 1969-71, 77-79; mem. Lyman Allyn Art Mus. Mem. Am. Craft Coun., Coun. Am. Embroiderers, Mystic Art Assn., Soc. Conn. Crafts. (bd. dirs., corr. sec. 1983-86). Office: Fiber Artistry by Barbara Lee 30 W Elderkin Ave Groton CT 06340-4933

FRANCIS, ANNETTE, author; b. Waco, Tex.; d. Abraham Samuel and Selma (Saul) Levy; m. Bry Benjamin, June 27, 1955 (div. Feb. 1975); 1 child, Alan Dean. Student, Sophie Newcomb Coll., 1945-47; BFA, Coll. of Music of Cin., 1949. Copy supr. RKO Teleradio Pictures, N.Y.C., 1955-56; promotion mgr. drugs and toiletries McCall's mag., N.Y.C., 1957-59; v.p. Reminder Binders, Inc., N.Y.C., 1974-84; pub. rels. dir. Palm Beach (Fla.) Opera, 1986-87; spl. projects dir. Nat. Found. for Advancement in Arts, Miami, Fla., 1988-89; pres. Bravo! Books, Inc., Palm Beach, Fla., 1988-92, Boston, 1992—; freelance editl. cons., Boston, 1992—. Co-author: (with Bry Benjamin) In Case of Emergency-What to Do Until the Doctor Arrives, 1965, New Facts of Life for Women, 1969, (with Paula Hober) The Mozart Diet, 1988, Cooking with Shakespeare, 1989; author: Smart English: The Easy-to-Use, Instant-Access Guide to Proper Written and Spoken English, 1995; contbr. monthly med. column to Am. Home mag., 1966-69. Mem. ASCAP, Harvard Musical Assn. Home and Office: 1 Longfellow Pl Apt 519 Boston MA 02114-2404

FRANCIS, BETTY BUGHER, elementary education educator; b. St. Petersburg, Fla., July 30, 1950; d. Henry James and Mary June (Ayers) Bugher; m. Marvin Tilmon Francis, Oct. 10, 1981; children: Michael Shane, Abbi Linn. BS in Edn., U. Fla., 1972; M in Early Childhood Edn., Ga. State U., Atlanta, 1980. Tchr. Yankeetown (Fla.) Elem. Sch., 1972-73, Flat Shoals Elem. Sch., Conyers, Ga., 1973-79, Barksdale Elem. Sch., Conyers, 1979-88, Honey Creek Elem. Sch., Conyers, 1988—; mento Rockdale Schs., Conyers, 1990—; tchr. support specialist Rockdale County Schs., Conyers, 1992—. Mem. Honey Creek Homeowners, Conyers, 1989—; habitat chair Honey Creek PTA, 1993—; mem. local sch. adv. coun. Edwards Mid. Sch., Conyers, 1994; mem. leadership acad. Rockdale Sch. Bd., Conyers, 1993—. Named Outstanding Young Woman of Rockdale County, Rockdale Jaycees, 1979, HOney Creek Tchr. of Yr., 1990. Mem. Rockdale Profl. Assn. of Ga. Educators (sec. 1990—), Profl. Assn. Ga. Educators (bldg. rep.), Rockdale Internat. Reading Assn. (sec. 1993-94), Ga. Internat. Reading Assn., Ga. Wildlife Fedn., Alpha Delta Kappa. Republican. Methodist. Office: Honey Creek Elem Sch 700 Honey Creek Rd SE Conyers GA 30208-3516

FRANCIS, CAROLYN RAE, music educator, musician, author, publisher; b. Seattle, July 25, 1940; d. James Douglas and Bessie Caroline (Smith) F; m. Barclay Underwood Stuart, July 5, 1971. BA in Edn., U. Wash., 1962. Cert. tchr., Wash. Tchr. Highline Pub. Schs., Seattle, 1962-64; musician Olympic Hotel, Seattle, 1962-72; 1st violin Cascade Symphony Orch., 1965-78; tchr. Bellevue (Wash.) Pub. Schs., 1965-92; founder/pres. Innovative Learning Designs, Mercer Island, Wash., 1984—; profl. violinist for TV, recs., mus. shows, 1962-85; violist Eastside Chamber Orch., 1984-86; pvt. tchr. string instruments, 1959—; spkr. in-svc. workshops, convs., music educators numerous cities, 1984—, adjudicator music festivals; instr. MIDI applications for educators, 1992—. Author-pub. Music Reading and Theory Skills (curriculum series), Levels 1, 2, 1986, Level 3, 1984; contbr. articles to profl. jours., 1984—. Mem. Snohomish Indian Tribe. Bellevue Schs. Found. grantee, 1985-86, 86-87, 89-90. Mem. NEA, Am. String Tchrs. Assn. (regional mem. chmn. 1992-94), Music Educators Nat. Conf., Music Industry Coun. Office: Innovative Learning Designs 7811 SE 27th St Ste 104 Mercer Island WA 98040-2961

FRANCIS, JANICE RUTH, realtor; b. Denver, Apr. 2, 1943; d. Donald Allen and Pearle Mary (Colby) Morgan; m. Homer Lee Francis; children: John A., Jennifer A., Kara J. Student, U. Colo., Colorado Springs, 1966. Realtor Francis/Boehnke Ltd., Colorado Springs, 1980—. Mem. Nat. Assn. Realtors, Colo. Assn. Realtors, Pike's Peak Assn. Realtors, Tuesday Arts. Roman Catholic. Home: 1826 E San Miguel Colorado Springs CO 80909 Office: Francis/Boehnke 2910 Beacon Colorado Springs CO 80907

FRANCIS-FELSEN, LORETTA (LOREE FRANCIS-FELSEN), nursing educator; b. Youngstown, Ohio, May 26, 1947; d. Frank Anthony and Ann (Beraduce) Capuzello; 1 child, Julie Frances Felsen. AAS, Youngstown State U., 1972, BS, 1976; MSN, Cath. U. Am., 1981; PhD, Columbia Pacific U., San Rafael, Calif., 1991. Lic. nurse, Fla., D.C., Md., Ohio. Employee health nurse lamp plant GE, Youngstown, 1972-76; charge nurse intermediate and med./surg. clients St. Elizabeth Med. Ctr., Youngstown, 1976-78; head nurse SICU/CCU Sibley Meml. Hosp., Washington, 1978-79; instr. dept. nursing Anne Arundel C.C., Annapolis, Md., 1979-81; instr. Marymount Coll., Arlington, Va., 1981; dir. ICU/CCU So. Md. Hosp. Ctr., Clinton, Md., 1981-82; clin. nurse specialist Office of Dr. Edwin Westura, Camp Springs, Md., 1982-84; instr. ADN program Charles County C.C., LaPlata, Md., 1984-85; asst. prof., coord. undergrad. program dept. nursing Bowie (Md.) State U., 1987-91; on-call asst. DON Greater Laurel-Beltsville Hosp., Laurel, Md., 1989-91; asst. prof. Coll. Nursing U. Fla., Gainesville, 1991—; mem. minority mentor program, mem. adminstrv. coun. U. Fla., 1994—; mem. nursing adv. coun. Bowie State U., 1989-91; mem. profl. practice com. Alachua Gen. Hosp., Gainesville, 1992—; vice chair, chair dist. HHS Bd., 1994; presenter in field. Mem. editl. adv. bd. Nursing Health S.C.O.P.E., Jacksonville, Fla., 1991-93; contbr. or co-contbr. articles to profl. publs. Vol. nurse Westwood Mid. Sch., Gainesville, 1993-94; vol. Kids Am. Day, Glen Springs Elem. Sch., Gainesville, 1992, treas. safety patrols, 1991-92; vol. Career Day, Fairland Elem. Sch., Silver Spring, 1991. Recipient nurse traineeship Cath. U. Am., 1988. Mem. ANA (cert. in gerontol. nursing), NLN, Nat. Rural Health Assn., Fla. Rural Health Assn., Sigma Theta Tau (pres.-elect Alpha Theta chpt. 1994-95, chpt. vice-chairperson, chpt. program chairperson 1993-94, pres. 1995—, faculty advisor, co-chairperson induction 1992-93, chpt. eligibility chairperson 1992-93). Home: 4127 NW 34th Pl Gainesville FL 32606-6151

FRANCK, ARDATH AMOND, psychologist; b. Wehrum, Pa., May 5, 1925; d. Arthur and Helen Lucille (Sharp) Amond; m. Frederick M. Franck, Mar. 18, 1945; children—Sheldon, Candace. B.S. in Edn., Kent State U., 1946, M.A., 1947; Ph.D., Western Res. U., 1956. Cert. high sch. tchr., elem. supr., sch. psychologist, speech and hearing therapist. Instr., Western Res. U., Cleve., summer 1953, U. Akron, 1947-50; sch. psychologist Summit County Schs., Ohio, 1950-60; cons. psychologist Wadsworth Pub. Schs., Ohio, 1946-86; dir. Akron Speech & Reading Ctr., Ohio, 1950—; pres. Twirling Unlimited; cons., dir. Hobbitts Pre-Sch., 1973-88. Author: Your Child Learns, 1976. Pres. Twirling Unltd., 1982—. Mem. Am. Speech and Hearing Assn., Internat. Reading Assn., Ohio Psychol. Assn., Mensa, Soroptimist (Akron). Home: 631 Ghent Rd Akron OH 44333-2629 Office: Akron Speech & Reading Ctr 700 Ghent Rd Akron OH 44333-2632

FRANCKE, GLORIA NIEMEYER, pharmacist, editor, publisher; b. Dillsboro, Ind., Apr. 28, 1922; d. Albert B. and Fannie K. (Libbert) Niemeyer; m. Donald Eugene Francke, Apr. 15, 1956. BS in Pharmacy, Purdue U., 1942; PharmD, U. Cin., 1971; postgrad. U. Mich., 1945; PharmD (hon.) Purdue U., 1988—. Pharmacist, Dillsboro Drug Store, 1943-44; instr. Sch. Pharmacy, Purdue U., Lafayette, Ind., 1943; asst. to chief pharmacist U. Mich. Hosp., Ann Arbor, 1944-46; assoc. editor Am. Jour. Hosp. Pharmacy, Washington, 1944-64; asst. dir. Div. Hosp. Pharmacy of Am. Pharm. Assn., Washington, 1946-56; exec. sec. Am. Soc. Hosp. Pharmacists, Ann Arbor, 1949-60; acting dir. dept. comms., Washington, 1963-64; drug lit. specialist Nat. Library Medicine, Bethesda, Md., 1965-67; clin. pharmacy teaching coord. VA Hosp., Cin., 1967-71; asst. clin. prof. clin. pharmacy Coll. Pharmacy, U. Cin., 1967-71; chief program evaluation br. Alcohol and Drug Dependence Svc., VA, Ctrl. Office, Washington, 1971-75; dir. Pharmacy Intelligence Ctr., Am. Pharm. Assn., Washington, 1975-85; mem. Roche Hosp. Pharmacy Adv. Bd., 1971-74; judge for ann. Lunsford Richardson Pharmacy awards, 1963, 64; mem. com. standards for drug abuse treatment and rehab. programs Joint Commn. Accreditation of Hosps., 1974-75. Author: (with D. E. Francke, C. J. Latiolais and N.F. H. Ho) Mirror to Hospital Pharmacy, 1964. Contbr. articles on hosp. pharmacy and clin. pharmacy to profl. jours. Recipient Harvey A.K. Whitney award Mich. Soc. Hosp. Pharmacists, 1953, Disting. Alumnus award Purdue U. Sch. of Pharmacy, 1985, Remington Honor medal, 1987, Career Achievement award Profl. Frat. Assn., 1991, Fedn. Internat. Pharm. Lifetime Achievement in the Practice of Pharmacy award, 1996; also various commendations. Mem. Internat. Pharm. Fedn., Am. Inst. History of Pharmacy (exec. sec. 1968-78), Tex. Soc. Hosp. Pharmacists (hon.), Am. Pharm. Assn. (hon. chmn. 1986, named the Gloria Niemeyer Francke Leadership Mentor award in her honor 1995), Am. Soc. Hosp. Pharmacists (Donald E. Francke medal 1995), Drug Info. Assn., Kappa Epsilon, Rho Chi. Presbyterian. Home and Office: 3900 Cathedral Ave NW # 208A Washington DC 20016-5201

FRANCKE, LINDA BIRD, journalist; b. N.Y.C., Mar. 14, 1939; d. Samuel Curtis and Janet (King) Bird; m. G.D. Mackenzie, Jan. 12, 1961; 1 son, Andrew Mackenzie; m. Albert Francke III, Oct. 7, 1967; 2 daughters: Caitlin, Tapp. Student, Bradford Jr. Coll., 1958. Copywriter Young & Rubicam, Inc., N.Y.C., 1960-63, Ogilvy & Mather, Inc., N.Y.C., 1965-67; contbg. editor N.Y. Mag., N.Y.C., 1968-72, 80—; gen. editor Newsweek Mag., N.Y.C., 1972-77; columnist N.Y. Times, 1977—; TV news commentator Spl. Edit., 1978-79; dir. New Directions; juror Am. Book Awards,

1981; Co-chmn. Writer's Resource Center, Southampton, N.Y. Works in numerous anthologies, including, The New York Spy, 1967, The Power Game, 1970, Running Against the Machine, 1969, Women: A Book for Men, 1979, Hers: Through Women's Eyes, 1985, America Firsthand, Vol. II: From Reconstruction to the Present, 1994; author: The Ambivalence of Abortion, 1978, Growing Up Divorced, 1983; collaborator: First Lady from Plains, 1984, Ferraro: My Story, 1985, Q Woman of Egypt, 1987, Daughter of Destiny, 1989. Mem. Women's Commn. for Refugee Women and Children, Internat. Rescue Com. Inc.; chmn. East End Choice; candidate N.Y. State Assembly, 2d Dist., 1990; del. to Dem. Nat. Conv., 1992; bd. dirs. Bridgehampton Child Care & Recreational Ctr., Inc., The Retreat. Recipient award Cannes Film Festival, 1969, Nat. Clarion award, 1994. Mem. Authors Guild, Women's Media Group N.Y.C. Home: PO Box 55 Sagaponack NY 11962

FRANCO, ANNEMARIE WOLETZ, editor; b. Somerville, N.J., Sept. 18, 1933; d. Frederick Franz and Bertha (Laugginger) Woletz; m. Frederick Nicholas Franco, June 11, 1977. Student, Wood Coll. of Bus. Editorial asst. Internat. Musician, then assoc. editor, 1965-88, ret., 1988. Republican. Presbyterian. Home: 166 Wellstone Dr Palm Coast FL 32164-4111

FRANEY, BILLIE NOLAN, political activist; b. Eveleth, Minn., Sept. 17, 1930; d. Mark and Ann Murray Nolan; m. Neil Joseph Franey; children: Kathleen, Timothy, Nora, Colin, Patrick. Student, Carleton Coll., 1948-49, U. Minn., 1949-50; BA, Coll. St. Scholastica, 1952. Social worker Cath. Welfare, Mpls., 1952-53; Contbr. articles to profl. jours. Chair Indian Affairs, Minn. Mrs. Jaycees, 1962; mem. Charter Commn., White Bear Lake, Minn., 1962-65; pres. White Bear Lake LWV, 1965-67; lobbyist Common Cause of Minn., 1979, Minn. LWV, 1980, AAUW, 1987-89; mem. met. futures task force Met. Coun., 1988-89; co-chair Women Come to The Capitol, Minn. Women's Consortium. Named Outstanding Young Women of Am., 1966; revipient Sister Ann Edward Scholar award The Coll. of St. Scholostica, 1992. Mem. AAUW (pres. 1992-94, St. Paul program v.p. 1990-92, legis. pub. policy chair 1987-89, Minn. chpt. legis. pub. policy v.p. 1987-89, scholarship named for as a gift from St. Paul AAUW 1989, Women as Agts. of Change award 1991), Coun. Met. Area LWV (chair 1981-83, program and study chair 1979-81, bd. mem. 1978-79). Home: 1323 Hedman Way White Bear Lake MN 55110-3360

FRANK, ANN-MARIE, sales administration executive; b. Omaha, July 27, 1957; d. Joseph Anthony and Louise Virginia (DiMauro) Malingagio; m. Jon Lindsay Frank, July 13, 1985; 1 child, Jon L. BA in Fine and Communication Arts, Loyola Marymount U., L.A., 1980, MBA, 1988. Region adminstrv. mgr. Data Gen. Corp., Manhattan Beach, Calif., 1986-90; adminstrv. customer svc. mgr. Candle Corp., L.A., 1991-92, mgr. fin. svcs. western area, 1992-93; mgr. sales adminstr. nat. ops. Candle Corp., Santa Monica, 1993-96; dir. royalty and records adminstrn. Herbalife Internat., Inglewood, Calif., 1996—. Dir., editor: (creative drama) Patchwork, 1982 (Rochester, N.Y. trophy). Republican. Roman Catholic. Home: 3311 Raintree Ave Torrance CA 90505-6618 Office: Herbalife Internat 9800 La Cienega Blvd Inglewood CA 90301

FRANK, BETTY POPE, editor; b. Detroit, Dec. 9, 1914; d. Melville S. and Belle O. (Oberfelder) Welt; m. Vernon K. Pope, Dec. 18, 1938 (div. 1961); children: John, Anne, Barbara; m. Morton Frank, Dec. 31, 1963. BA, Vassar Coll., 1936. Staff editor Look Mag., Des Moines, 1936-40; staff writer The Open Road, N.Y., 1940-41; freelance writer N.Y.C., 1941-59; articles editor Good Housekeeping, N.Y.C., 1960-77, contract writer, 1977-80; editor, cons. Family Circle, N.Y.C., 1980-87; ret., 1987—; bd. dirs. U. Bridgeport, 1978—. Mem. adv. com. Vassar Quar., 1960s and 70s. Bd. dirs. Planned Parenthood, Westchester County, 1951-60. Recipient Best Article published award Mag. Writers & U. Mo., 1979. Mem. Cosmopolitan Club (bulletin com. 1988-91). Democrat. Home and Office: 19-10 Meadow Lakes Hightstown NJ 18520

FRANK, ELIZABETH, English literature educator, author; b. L.A., Sept. 14, 1945. d. Melvin G. and Anne R. Frank; 1 child, Anne Louise Buchwald. Student Bennington Coll.; BA, MA, PhD, U. Calif.-Berkeley. Joseph E Harry prof. modern langs. and lit. Bard Coll., Annandale-on-Hudson, N.Y., 1982—. Author: Jackson Pollock, 1983, Louise Bogan: A Portrait (Pulitzer prize for biography 1986), Esteban Vicente, 1995. Office: The Lantz-Harris Agy 156 Fifth Ave # 617 New York NY 10011 also: Bard Coll Dept Lang & Lit Annandale On Hudson NY 12504

FRANK, ELIZABETH AHLS, art educator; b. Cin., Sept. 27, 1942; d. Edward Henry and Constance Patricia (Barnett) Ahls; m. James Russell Frank, Aug. 10, 1963; children: Richard Scott, Robert Edward. BA, U. Denver, 1964; MA, U. South Fla., 1988. Cert. profl. educator, Fla. Remedial reading tchr. Willoughby (Ohio)-Eastlake Schs., 1971-72; third grade tchr., grade level chairperson Lee County Pub. Schs., Fort Myers, Fla., 1972-79, art tchr., 1979—; long range planning curriculum com. Lee County Pub. Schs., 1992-94, model sch. planning com., 1995-96. Contbg. author Davis Art Edn. Publs., Worcester, Mass. Vol. Mann Performing Arts Hall, Fort Myers, 1986-96, Harborside Convention Ctr., 1991-95; sec. Colonial Acres Homeowners Assn., North Fort Myers, Fla., 1994-96. Mem. Fla. Art Edn. Assn. (workshop presenter 1989, 91, 92), Southwest Fla. Audubon Soc., Southwest Fla. Rose Soc., Calusa Nature Ctr., Lee Art Edn. Assn. (founder, pres. 1991-92, Art Educator of Yr. 1991-92), Nat. Edn. Assn., Fla. Tchg. Profession, Tchrs.'s Assn. Lee County (bldg. rep., exec. bd. 1972-96, M.M. Bethune Humanities award 1992), Phi Kappa Phi, Phi Delta Kappa, Delta Kappa Gamma (scholar 1988, pres. 1988-90). Democrat. Home: 8236 W Jamestown Cir North Fort Myers FL 33917 Office: Suncoast Elem 1858 Suncoast Ln North Fort Myers FL 33917

FRANK, GLORIA T., lawyer; b. N.Y.C.. BA magna cum laude, Hunter Coll., 1980; JD, Fordham U., 1983. Ptnr. Anderson Kill Olick & Oshinsky, P.C., N.Y.C. Mem. ABA, N.Y. State Bar Assn., Bar of City of N.Y. Office: Anderson Kill Olick & Oshinsky PC 1251 Ave of the Americas New York NY 10020-1182*

FRANK, JOAN GALE, audio/video producer; b. Santa Monica, Calif., July 22, 1956; d. Sherman and Mary Frank; m. Jon Allen Bell, Oct. 16, 1992. BA, UCLA, 1979, MPH, 1981; MEd, San Francisco State U., 1984. Video prodr. Lockheed, Santa Clara, Calif., 1984-85, Hitachi Data Sys., Santa Clara, 1985-91; pres., owner Big Mouth Pubs., San Francisco, 1991—; instr. audio prodn. Learning Annex of San Francisco, 1995; cons. Internet projects, San Francisco, 1995—. Author: Instant Guts!, 1993; writer/prodr.: (documentary) Prototype for Managed Care, 1995. Tchr. illiterate adults San Francisco adult Learning Ctr., 1996—; active No. Calif. Wildlife Express, Marin, 1995; vol. Urban Forest, San Francisco, 1995; video prodr. Silon Valley Charity Ball, Santa Clara, 1991. Recipient Award of Excellence San Jose Film Commn., 1991, Internat. TV Assn., 1992, Award of Creative Excellence U.S. Indsl. Film Festival, 1990. Mem. Marin Small Pubs. Assn. (bd. dirs. 1993—, program chmn. 1994—), Pub. Mktg. Assn., Toastmasters Internat. (Toastmaster of Yr. 1994, Best Internat. Speaker 1993, v.p. edn. 1992-95). Office: 95 Red Rock Way #M108 San Francisco CA 94131

FRANK, JUDITH ANN (JANN FRANK), entrepreneur, small business owner; b. Fresno, Calif., Feb. 10, 1938; d. Walter R. Frank and Ethel Joan (Klomburg) Brinkerhoff; m. David Rogers, Oct. 1956 (div. June 1973). BA, Calif. State U., Fullerton, 1989, postgrad., 1990-91; postgrad., Chapman U., 1991-93. Vault teller, new accounts, comml. Bank of Am., Fresno, 1956-64; new accounts and note teller Security First Nat. Bank, Fresno, 1965-68; br. bookkeeper, supr. Wells Fargo Bank, Santa Clara and San Jose, Calif., 1968-78; student asst. Fullerton Coll. Career Planning and Placement Ctr., 1982-83; owner, operator Distant Drums, 1994—, Jann Frank Enterprises, Placentia, Calif., 1996—. Phys. and occupational intern transitional tng. program for brain injured adults and impaired sr. citizens Rehab. Inst. So. Calif., Orange, 1978-80, 92-93, vol. 1993; vol. Sr. Citizens Transp., Lunch and Counseling Program, Fullerton, 1981-82, City Wide Disaster Drill, Whittier, Calif., 1987; vol. grad. Evoluton of Psychotherapy Conf., Anaheim, Calif., 1990; bd. dirs. Native Am. Inst.; amb. Placentia (Calif.) C. of C.; mem. Women's Referral Svc. Recipient Commendation for Vol. Svc. Orange County Coun. Women in C. of C., 1980, Disting. Svc. award Rehab. Inst. So. Calif., Orange, 1993; tuition scholarship grantee Chapman U., Orange, 1991. Fellow Am. Biog. Inst., Internat. Biog. Assn.; mem. Smithsonian Inst., Order Internat. Fellowship, Mus. Am. Indian, Assn. Humanistic Psychology, Calif. Indian Art Assn., Order of Internat. Fellowship, Golden Key, Alpha Gamma Sigma. Office: Distant Drums & Jann Frank Enterprises 601 W Santa Fe Ave # N85 Placentia CA 92870

FRANK, MARY LOU, retired elementary education educator; b. Cleve., May 18, 1915; d. William Henry and Martha Ann (Brown) Parsons; m. Russell Edward Frank, May 18, 1935; children: Richard Edward, James Russell. BS in Edn., Cleve. State U., 1960; MS in Edn., U. Akron, Ohio, 1967, Miami U., Oxford, Ohio, 1934-35; student, Baldwin-Wallace Coll., 1933-34. Cert. tchr., Ohio. Substitute tchr. Cleve. Pub. Schs., 1963; tchr. elem. Brecksville (Ohio) City Sch. Dist., 1953-71; tchr. elem. Lee County Bd. of Edn., Ft. Myers, Fla., 1971-74, ret., 1974; mem. ambassadors to China from Fla., Children's Palaces Homes Hosps., 1980. Martha Holden Jennings Found. scholar, 1963-64, grantee, 1965. Mem. U.S. Power Squadron Aux. (pilot), Collier Reading Coun., Delta Kappa Gamma. Home: 61 Impala Ct # 23 Fort Myers FL 33912-6338

FRANK, MARY LOU BRYANT, psychologist, educator; b. Denver, Nov. 27, 1952; d. W.D. and Blanche (Dean) Bryant; m. Kenneth Kerry Frank, Sept. 9, 1973; children: Kari Lou, Kendra Leah. BA, Colo. State U., 1974, MEd, 1983, MS, 1986, PhD, 1989. Tchr. Cherry Creek Schs., Littleton, Colo., 1974-80; from grad. asst. to dir. career devel. Colo. State U., Ft. Collins, 1980-86; intern U. Del., Newark, 1987-88; psychologist Ariz. State U., Tempe, 1988-93; assoc., lead prof. psychology Clinch Valley Coll. U. Va., Wise, 1992-96, asst. acad. dean, 1993-95; head psychology dept., prof. North Ga. Coll., 1996—; instr. Colo. State U., Ft. Collins, 1981-82, counselor, 1984-85, 86-87; psychologist Ariz. State U., Tempe, 1989-92; assoc. prof. psychology Clinch Valley Coll. U. Va., 1992-96. Author: (program manual) Career Development, 1986; contbr. book chpts. on eating disorders and existential psychotherapy. Mem. APA, AACD, Phi Kappa Phi, Phi Beta Kappa, Pi Kappa Delta, Psi Chi. Office: North Ga Coll Psychology Dept 207 Dunlap Hall Dahlonega GA 30533

FRANK, MYRA LINDEN, consultant; b. Richmond, Va., Oct. 26, 1950; d. J. C. and Myra Teresa (Lanzarone) Frank; m. Timothy Franklin Long (div. Jan. 1981); m. Robert Andrew Hudson (div. 1994). BA, Erskine Coll., 1972; student, Inst. Fin. Edn., 1982-88. Chief activities therapist S.C. Dept. Corrections, Columbia, 1973-75, acting prin., 1975-77, coll. coord., 1977-78; owner, operator Carolina Coast Seafood, Aiken and Beaufort, S.C., 1978-80; from teller to savs. counselor Security Fed. Savs. & Loan, Aiken, 1981-83; customer svc. rep. Bankers 1st Savs. & Loans, Augusta, Ga., 1983-84, mgr. br. adminstrn., 1984-85; coord. automated teller machines, banking officer 1st Fed. Savs. Bank, Brunswick, Ga., 1985-88; ptnr., cons. electronic banking/software devel. RAH Systems, Brunswick, 1988-93; ptnr. specific application computer programming, software tng. Details & More, Greenville, S.C., 1989-90, ptnr. event planning, various mfg. positions and mktg./sales, 1989-91; cons. office and computer svcs. Mauldin, S.C., 1992-93; lectr. S.C. Edn. Tchrs. Assn., Columbia, 1974, S.C. Assn. Social Workers, Columbia, 1975, Bus. and Profl. Women's Club, Columbia, 1978; small bus. owner, distbr. Nuskin product line, 1987-90; ind. mktg. rep. Network 2000/U.S. Spring, 1988-92; computer specialist Top Food Svcs. Carolina, Inc., Duncan, S.C., 1989-9o; adminstrv./sales mgr. Custom Catering, Duncan, 1990; cons. Contract Office/Computer Svcs., Greenville, 1992—. Book rev. writer A Class Act, Greenville, 1996—; appeared with Aiken Cmty. Theatre, 1981. Bd. dirs. Quest Soc., Greenville, 1992-95; mem. hospice com. Am. Cancer Soc., Augusta, 1981; lectr. St. John's United Meth. Ch., 1981-82; registrar, treas. Sugar Creek Soccer Club, Greenville, 1996—. Mem. A Creative Gathering Writers Group. Democrat. Home and Office: PO Box 333 Mauldin SC 29662-0333

FRANK, NANCE SUE, yacht captain; b. Key West, Fla., Mar. 3, 1949; d. Bernard and Rose S. (Steieman) Frank. BA, U. Fla., 1970. Dir. USVI Marine Industries, St. Thomas, 1985-86; founder, dir. Caribbean Women's Championship, St. Thomas, 1985-86; capt., pres. U.S. Women's Challenge, Key West, Fla., 1988—; co-founder, capt. U.S./Soviet Sailing Summit, 1989-92; dir. 1st Women's Regatta, Phila., 1990; skipper 1st Team of Women, Annapolis, Md., Newport, R.I., 1991, 92, Bermuda, 1992, N.Y.C., Southampton, Eng., 1993; pub. Women's Offshore Racing jour., 1989-93; nat. spokesperson Safety-At-Sea Inst., Newport, 1991-93. Chairperson Monroe County Arts Coun., Key West, 1995-96. Recipient Liberty Bell award Mayor Goode, Phila., 1990. Mem. USSailing, Royal Ocean Racing Club. Home: 1717 George St Key West FL 33040

FRANK, NANCY BALLARD, editor, artist; b. Ann Arbor, Mich., June 28, 1919; d. Harold Lyman and Aline Morley (Smith) Ballard; m. Albert Eugene Frank, May 25, 1942; children: Chana, Robert Worth, Nancy Frank Brewster, Morley Frank Panyko. Student, Smith Coll., 1937-40, Vogue/Ray Sch. Interior Decorating, 1940-41, Princeton U., 1976-77. Editor: Arlington Along the Battenkill: Its Pictured Past, 1993 (Am. Assn. State & Local History Commendation cert., Vt. Hist. Soc. Merit award 1994); exhibited in group shows at So. Vt. Art Ctr., 1987—. Docent Nat. Portrait Gallery, Washington, 1972-74; exhibit chmn. Hist. Soc. Princeton, N.J., 1976-80; duplicating, monitoring Recording for Blind, Princeton, 1975-91; curator photo archives Russell Vermontiana Collection, Arlington, Vt., 1987—. Mem. Arts & Crafts Assn. of Rossmoor (bd. dirs., corr. sec. 1995—). Democrat. Episcopalian. Home: 345 C Old Nassau Rd Jamesburg NJ 08831-1840

FRANK, PAULA FELDMAN, business executive; b. Tulsa; d. Maurice M. and Sarah (Bergman) Feldman; m. Gordon D. Frank, Dec. 15, 1955; children: Cynthia Jan, Margaret Jill. B.S., Northwestern U., 1954. Directed, wrote and appeared in TV films for Nat. Safety Coun., Chgo., 1954-55; appeared in TV commls., 1955-56; asst. prodn. mgr. Kling Films, Chgo., 1956; pres. Gaston Ave. Optical Inc., ret. 1992; Dallas. Social chmn. Baylor Hosp. Vol. Corp., Dallas, 1962—; asst. dir. Des Plaines (Ill.) Theater Guild, 1956-57, Pearl Chappell Playhouse, Dallas, 1962-63, Dallas Theater Center, 1964. Mem. Hockaday Alumni Assn., Tau Gamma Epsilon, Phi Beta, Sigma Delta Tau. Home: 7123 Currin Dr Dallas TX 75230-3645

FRANK, RUBY MERINDA, employment agency executive; b. McClusky, N.D., June 28, 1920; d. John J. and Olise (Stromme) Hanson; m. Robert G. Frank, Jan. 14, 1944 (dec. 1973); children: Gary Frank, Craig. student Coll. Mankato, Minn., Aurora (Ill.) U. Exec. sec., office mgr. Nat. Container Corp., Chgo., 1943-50; owner, pres. Frank's Employment, Inc., St. Charles, Ill., 1957—; corp. sec. Sta. WFXW-FM, Geneva, 1988—; chmn. Baker Hotel, 1989-91; sec. bd. trustees Delnor Hosp., St. Charles, 1959-78, chmn. bd., 1985-87; vocat. adviser Waubonsee Coll.; bd. dirs. Aurora U., corporate sec. 1994. Contbr. weekly broadcast Sta. WGSB, 1970-80, weekly interview program Sta. WFXW. Active mem. Women's aux.; vice chmn. Kane County (Ill.) Rep. Com., 1968-77; pres. Women's Rep. Club, 1969-77; local bd. Am. Cancer Soc.; adv. council Dellora A. Norris Cultural Arts Ctr.; bd. govs. Luth. Social Svc. Baker Hotel, sec. 1987, vice chmn. 1988, chmn. Baker Hotel, 1989-90; bd. dirs. St. Charles Hist. Soc., 1989, Ill. Chamber Symphony, Dorchester Assn.; co-vice chmn. Delnor Community Health System; bd. dirs., exec. bd. Aurora Found., 1989—, v.p., 1990-92, pres. 1993—. Recipient Exec. of Yr. award Fox Valley PSI; Charlemagne award for community service, 1982; Mentor of Bus. Women award, 1991. Mem. St. Charles C. of C. (pres., bd. dirs. 1976-82, amb.), Kane-DuPage Pers. Assn. (v.p. 1971—), Nat., Ill. employment assns., Ill. Assn. Pers. Cons. (dir.), Women in Mgmt., St. Charles Country Club, St. Charles Ambs. Club (pres.), The Club of Pelican Bay (Naples, Fla.). Lutheran. Home: 1104 Adare Ct Saint Charles IL 60174 Office: Arcada Theater Bldg 12 S 1st Ave Saint Charles IL 60174-1947

FRANKEL, ALICE KROSS, physician, director; b. N.Y.C., Feb. 3, 1929; d. Isidor and Anna (Moscowitz) Kross; m. Julian B. Schorr, May 14, 1951 (div. 1963); children: David, Ellen; m. Marvin E. Frankel, Aug. 22, 1965; 1 stepchild, Eleanor Frankel Perlman; 1 child, Mara. BA, Oberlin (Ohio) Coll., 1949; MD, Columbia U., 1953. Pvt. practice N.Y.C., 1956-66, 85—, Larchmont, N.Y., 1966-85; assoc. clin. prof. psychiatry Med. Coll. Cornell U., N.Y.C., 1970-90; dir. Child Devel. Ctr. Jewish Bd. Family & Children's Svcs., N.Y.C., 1984—; supervising and tng. psychoanalyst Psychoanalytic Ctr. Tng. & Rsch. Columbia U., N.Y.C., 1984—. Mem. Am. Psychiat. Assn., Am. Psychoanalytic Assn., Am. Acad. Child and Adolescent Psychiatry, Assn. for Child and Adolescent Analysis, N.Y. County Med. Soc., N.Y. State Med. Soc. Democrat. Jewish. Office: Jewish Bd Family Childrens Svcs Child Devel Ctr 120 W 57th St New York NY 10019-3320*

FRANKEL, BARBARA BROWN, cultural anthropologist; b. Phila., Dec. 24, 1928; d. Paul and Sarah (Magil) Brown; m. Herbert L. Frankel, Feb. 27, 1949 (dec. Sept. 1976); children: Claire R. Sholes, Joan L. Frankel, David S. Frankel; m. Donald T. Campbell, Mar. 19, 1983 (dec. May 1996). PhB, U. Chgo., 1947; BA, Goddard Coll., 1966; MA in Anthropology, Temple U., 1970; PhD, Princeton (N.J.) U., 1974. Asst. prof. Lehigh U., Bethlehem, Pa., 1973-77, assoc. prof., 1977-85, assoc. dean arts and sci., 1981-83, prof. anthropology, 1985-93, prof. emerita, 1994—; rsch. assoc. prof. Boston U., 1980-81. Author: Childbirth in the Ghetto, 1977, Transforming Identities, 1989; contbr. articles to profl. jours. Bd. dirs. Pinebrook Svcs. for Children and Youth, Whitehall, Pa., 1987-93. Grad. fellowship for Women Danforth Found., Princeton U., 1969-73; predoctoral fellowship AAUW, 1971-72; rsch. grant Mellon Faculty Devel. Grant, Boston U., 1980-81, Provost's Rsch. award Lehigh U., 1987. Fellow Am. Anthropol. Assn. (mem. ethics commn. 1994-95), Soc. for Applied Anthropology (chair ethics com. 1986-88); mem. AAAS, Phila. Anthropol. Soc. (pres. 1988), LWV (study com. chair 1994-96), Phi Beta Kappa (pres. Beta chpt. 1989-90). Democrat. Agnostic Jewish. Home: 637 N New St Bethlehem PA 18018-3936 Office: Lehigh U Sociology & Anthropology 681 Taylor St Bethlehem PA 18015-3169

FRANKEL, DIANE, museum institute administrator; b. N.Y.C., Nov. 13, 1942; d. Harry and Frances Bejosa; m. Charles Louis Frankel, July 10, 1966; children: Alexander, Matthew. BA in Psychology, U. Calif., Berkeley, 1964; MA in Museum Edn., George Washington U., 1976. Cert. in Mus. Mgmt. Outreach educator U. Botswana, Lesotho and Swaziland, 1974-75; assoc. dir. edn. San Francisco Mus. Modern Art, 1976-80; dir. Ctr. for Mus. Studies John F. Kennedy U., Orinda, Calif., 1980-85, assoc. dean Sch. Liberal and Profl. Arts., 1980-85, dean Sch. Liberal and Profl. Arts, 1985-86; exec. dir. Bay Area Discovery Mus., Sausalito, Calif., 1986-93; dir. Inst. Mus. Svcs., Washington, 1993—; chair Career Day, ArtTable, San Francisco, 1989, 92, chair Washington chpt., 1995-96. Co-founder Wise-Up support group for women candidates, San Francisco. Mem. Assn. Youth Museums (coun. 1991—), Am. Assn. Museums (chair Women Dirs. Breakfast 1992, 93). Office: Inst of Museum Svcs 1100 Pennsylvania Ave NW Washington DC 20004-2501

FRANKEL, JUDITH JENNIFER MARIASHA, clinical psychologist, consultant; b. Bklyn., May 25, 1947; m. Anthony R. D'Augelli, Sept. 1, 1968 (div. 1985); children: Jennifer Hadley Frankel, Rebekah Lindsay Frankel. BA, New Coll. at Hofstra U., 1968; MA, U. Conn., 1971, PhD, 1972. Lic. psychologist, Pa. Rsch. psychologist Family Consultation Ctr., Roslyn, N.Y., 1968, Conn. State Dept. Mental Health, Hartford, 1969-71; staff intern VA Hosp., West Haven, Conn., 1971-72; asst./assoc. prof., dir. program devel. and evaluation Pa. State U., State College, 1972-81; pvt. practice psychology State College, 1976—; psychol. cons. PYRAMID Orgn., Walnut Creek, Calif., 1975-78, N.Y. Dept. Mental Health, 1976, Nat. Inst. Alcohol Abuse Prevention, Nat. Inst. Drug Abuse Prevention, Nat. Youth Alternatives Program, 1975-79, Meadows Psychiatric Ctr. Women's Program, 1993-95; v.p. Mental Health Profls., State College, 1978-80, pres., 1980-82; exec. bd. Ctrl. Pa. Psychol. Assn., 1989-90. Author: Decisions Are Possible, 1975, Communication and Parenting Skills, 1976, Helping Others, 1980; contbr. articles to profl. jours. Campaigner Stein for Rep., 1982, Wachob for Congress, 1984; chair cmty. action Congregation Brit Shalom, State College, 1985-87, coord. ednl. liaison, 1985-87; v.p. Jewish Cmty. Coun. Women, 1988-90, pres., 1990-93, bd. dirs. Congregation Brit. Shalom, 1985-87, 90-93; v.p. Hadassah, 1995—. USPHS fellow, U. Conn., 1969-71. Mem. APA (clin. psychology, psychology of women, ind. practice, & health psychology divsns.), Pa. Psychol. Assn., Ea. Psychol. Assn., Ctrl. Pa. Psychol. Assn. (exec. bd. 1989-90), Jewish Cmty. Coun. women (bd. dirs. 1990-94), Hadassah (v.p. programming 1995—), Phi Beta Kappa, Phi Kappa Phi. Democrat. Jewish.

FRANKENTHALER, HELEN, artist; b. N.Y.C., Dec. 12, 1928; d. Alfred and Martha (Lowenstein) F.; m. Robert Motherwell, Apr. 5, 1958 (div.); m. Stephen DuBrul, Jr., July 1994. BA, Bennington Coll., 1949; LHD (hon.), Skidmore Coll., 1969, Hofstra U., 1991; DFA (hon.), Smith Coll., 1973, Moore Coll. Art, 1974, Bard Coll., 1976, NYU, 1979; DFA, Phila. Coll. Art, 1980, Williams Coll., 1980; DFA (hon.), Marymount Manhattan Coll., 1989, Adelphi U., 1989, Washington U., St. Louis, 1989; D.Art, Radcliffe Coll., 1978, Amherst Coll., 1979; D.Art (hon.), Harvard U., 1980; DFA (hon.), Yale U., 1981, Brandeis U., 1982, U. Hartford, 1983, Syracuse U., 1985, Dartmouth Coll., 1994. tchr., lectr. Yale U., 1966, 67, 70, Hunter Coll., 1970, Princeton U., 1971, Cooper Union, N.Y.C., 1972, Washington U. Sch. Fine Arts, 1972, Skidmore Coll., 1973, Swathmore Coll., 1974, Drew U., 1975, Harvard, 1976, Radcliffe Coll., 1976, Bard Coll., 1977, Detroit Inst. Arts, 1977, NYU, U. Pa., Sch. Visual Arts, Goucher Coll., Wash. U., Yale Grad. Sch., U. Ariz., 1978, Graphic Arts Council N.Y., 1979, Harvard U., 1980, Phila. Coll., 1980, Williams Coll., 1980, Yale U., 1981, Brandeis U., 1982, U. of Hartford, 1983, Syracuse U., 1985, Sante Fe Inst. Fine Arts, 1986, 90, 91; U.S. rep. Venice Biennale, 1966. One-woman shows include, Tibor de Nagy Gallery, N.Y.C., 1951-58, Andre Emmerich Gallery, N.Y.C., 1959-73, 75, 77, 78, 79, 81, 82, 83, 84, 86, 87, 89, 90, 91, 92, 93, Jewish Mus., N.Y., 1960, Everett Ellin Gallery, Los Angeles, 1961, Galerie Lawrence, Paris, 1961, 63, Bennington Coll., 1962, 78, Galleria dell'Ariete, Milan, 1962, Kasmin Gallery, London, 1964, David Mirvish Gallery, Toronto, 1965, 71, 73, 75, Gertrude Kasle Gallery, Detroit, 1967, Nicholas Wilder Gallery, Los Angeles, 1967, Andre Emmerich Gallery, Zurich, 1974, 80, Swarthmore (Pa.) Coll., 1974, Solomon R. Guggenheim Mus., N.Y.C., 1975, Corcoran Gallery Art, Washington, 1975, Seattle Art Mus., 1975, Mus. Fine Arts, Houston, 1975, 85, 86, Ace Gallery, Vancouver, B.C., Can., 1975, Rosa Esman Gallery, N.Y.C., 1975, 83, 89, 3d Internat. Contemporary Art Fair, Paris, 1976, 81, retrospective Whitney Mus. Am. Art, 1969, Whitechapel Gallery, London, Eng., 1969, Kongress-Halle, Berlin, Kunstverein, Hannover, 1969, Heath Gallery, Atlanta, 1971, Galerie Godard Lefort, Montreal, 1971, Fendrick Gallery, Washington, 1972, 79, John Berggruen Gallery, San Francisco, 1972, 79, 82, Portland (Oreg.) Art Mus., 1972, Waddington Galleries II, London, 1973, 74, Janie C. Lee Gallery, Dallas, 1973, Houston, 1975, 76, 78, 80, 82, Met. Mus. Art, N.Y.C., 1973, Gallery Diane Gilson, Seattle, 1976, Greenberg Gallery, St. Louis, 1977, Galerie Wentzel, Hamburg, Germany, 1977, Jacksonville (Fla.) Art Mus., 1977-78, Knoedler Gallery, London, 1978, 81, 83, USIA exhbn., 1978-79, Atkins Mus. Fine Art, William Rockhill Nelson Gallery Art, Kansas City, Mo., 1978, 80, Saginaw Art Mus., Mich., 1980, Gimpel and Hanover and Andre Emerich Galleries, Zurich, 1980, Gallery Ulysses, Vienna, 1980, Knoedler Gallery, London, 1981, 83, Buschlen/Mowalt Fine Arts, Vancouver, 1989, Mus. Modern Art, N.Y.C., 1989, Douglas Drake Gallery, N.Y.C., 1989, Mizografia Gallery, L.A., 1989, Gerald Peters Gallery, Santa Fe, 1990, Kukje Gallery, Seoul, Korea, 1991, Assn. Am. Artists, N.Y.C., 1992, Knoedler & Co., N.Y.C., 1992, 94, Nat. Gallery Art, Washington, 1993, San Diego Mus. Art, 1993, Mus. Fine Arts, Boston, 1994, Contemporary Arts Ctr., Cin., 1994, numerous others; exhibited in group shows including, Whitney Mus., 1958, 71, 75-79, 82, 89, Carnegie Internat., Pitts., 1955, 58, 61, 64, Columbus Gallery Fine Arts, 1960, Guggenheim Mus., 1961, 76, 80, 82, Seattle World's Fair, 1962, Art Inst. Chgo., 1963, 69, 72, 76, 77, 82, 83, San Francisco Mus. Art, 1963, 68, Krannert Mus., U. Ill., 1959, 63, 65, 67, 80, Washington Gallery Modern Art, 1963, Pa. Acad. Fine Arts, 1963, 68, 76, N.Y. World's Fair, 1964, Am. Fedn. Arts Circulating Exhbn., 1964, U. Austin Art Mus., 1964, Rose Art Mus. Circulating Exhbn., 1964, Detroit Inst. Arts, 1965, 67, 73, 77, U. Mich. Mus. Art, 1965, Md. Inst., 1966, Norfolk Mus. Arts and Scis., 1966, Venice Biennale, 1966, Smithsonian Instn., 1966, Expo '67, Montreal, 1967, Washington Gallery Modern Art, 1967, Ga. Mus. Art, Athens, 1967, U. Okla. Mus. Art, Norman, 1968, Philbrook Art Center, Tulsa, 1968, Cin. Mus., 1968, U. Calif. at San Diego, 1968, Mus. Modern Art, N.Y.C., 1969, 75, 76, 80, 82, Met. Mus., N.Y.C., 1969-70, 76, 79, 81, Va. Mus., Richmond, 1970, 74, 87, Balt. Mus. Art, 1970, 76, 89, Boston U., 1970, Boston Mus. Fine Arts, 1972, 82, 90, Des Moines Art Center, 1973, Mus. Fine Arts, Houston, 1974, 82, Smith Coll. Mus. Art, Northampton, Mass., 1974, El Instituto de Cultura Puertorriquena, San Juan, 1974, Basil (Switzerland) Art Fair, 1974, 76, Finch Coll. Mus. Art, N.Y.C., 1974, S.I. Mus., 1975, Denver Art Mus., 1975, Visual Arts Mus., N.Y.C., 1975, 76, Mus. Modern Art, Belgrade Yugoslavia, 1976, Chrysler Mus., Norfolk, Va., 1976, Everson Mus., Syaracuse, N.Y., Galleria d'Arts Moderna, Rome, 1976, Grey Art Gallery, N.Y.C., 1976-78, 81, Bklyn

Mus., 1976-77, 82, Edmonton Art Gallery, Alta., Can., 1977, 78, Albright-Knox Mus., Buffalo, 1978, Fogg Art Mus., Harvard U., 1978, 83, Art Gallery Ont., 1979, Hirshorn Mus. and Sculpture Garden, Washington, 1980, Phoenix Art Mus., 1980, Nat. Gallery Art, Washington, 1981, Tate Gallery, London, 1981, Walker Art Ctr., Mpls., 1981, Milw. Art Mus., 1982, Mus. Fine Arts, Boston, 1982, Whitney Mus. Am. Art , N.Y., 1982, St. Louis Art Mus., 1982, High Mus. Art, Atlanta, 1989, Nelson-Atkins Mus. Art, Kansas City, Nat. Gallery Can., 1990, Williams Coll. Mus. Art, Williamstown, Mass., 1991, Aldrich Mus. Contemporary Art, Ridgefield, Conn., 1992, Mus. Modern Art, Mexico City, 1992, Yokohama Mus. Art, Japan, 1992, Marugame Inokuma-Genichiro Mus. Contemp. Art, 1992, Mus. Modern Art, Wakayama, 1992, Tokushima Modern Art Mus., Japan, 1992, Hokkaido Obihiro Mus. Art, 1993, Whitney Mus. Am. Art, Stamford, Conn., 1993, Gallery One, Toronto, Can., 1994; represented in permanent collections, Bklyn. Mus., Met. Mus. Art N.Y., , Solomon R. Guggenheim Mus., NYU, Mus. Modern Art, Albright-Knox Art Gallery, Buffalo, Whitney Mus., N.Y.C., U. Mich., High Mus., Atlanta, Milw. Art Inst., Wadsworth Atheneum, Hartford, Newark Mus., Yale U. Art Gallery, U. Nebr. Art Gallery, Carnegie Inst., Pitts., Detroit Inst. Art, Balt. Mus. Art, Univ. Mus., Berkeley, Calif., Bennington (Vt.) Coll., Art Inst. Chgo., Cin. Art Mus., Cleve. Mus. Art, Columbus Gallery Fine Arts, Honolulu Acad. Arts, Contemporary Arts Assn., Houston, Pasadena Art Mus., William Rockhill Nelson Gallery Art, Kans. City, Kans., Kans. City Art Inst., Atkins Mus. Fine Arts, Kans. City, Kans., City Art Mus., St. Louis, Mus. Art, R.I. Sch. Design, Providence, San Francisco Mus. Art, Everson Mus., Syracuse, N.Y., Smithsonian Instn., Walker Art Inst., Mpls., Washington Gallery Modern Art, Wichita Art Mus., Brown Gallery Art, Nat. Gallery Victoria, Melbourne, Australia, Australian Nat. Gallery, Canberra, Victoria and Albert Mus., London, Eng., Tokyo Mus., Ulster Mus., Belfast, No. Ireland, Elvehjem Art Center, U. Wis., Israel Mus.-Instituto Nacional de Bellas Artes, Phila. Mus. Art, Phoenix Art Mus., Corcoran Gallery Art, Boston Mus. Fine Arts, Springfield (Mass.) Mus. Fine Arts, White Mus., San Antonio, Abbott Hall Art Gallery, Kendal, Eng., Mus. Contemporary Art, Nagaoka, Japan, Guggenheim Mus., N.Y.C., 1984, others; was subject of film Frankenthaler: Toward a New Climate, 1978. Trustee Bennington Coll., 1967—. Fellow Calhoun Coll., Yale U., 1968—; recipient 1st prize for painting Paris Biennale, 1959, Gold medal Pa. Acad. Fine Arts, 1968, Great Ladies award Fordham U., Thomas Moore Coll., 1969, Spirit of Achievement award Albert Einstein Coll. Medicine, 1970, Gold medal Commune of Catania, III Biennale della Grafica d'Arte, Florence, Italy, 1972, Garrett award 70th Am. Exhbn., Art Inst. Chgo., 1972, Creative Arts award Nat. Women's div. Am. Jewish Congress, 1974, Art and Humanities award Yale Women's Forum, 1976, Extraordinary Woman of Achievement award NCCJ, 1978, Alumni award Bennington Coll., 1979, N.Y.C. Mayor's award , 1986, Lifetiem Achievement award Coll. Art Assn., 1994. Mem. NEA, Am. Acad. (vice-chancelor 1991), Am. Acad. Arts and Scis., Nat. Coun. Arts, Nat. Inst. Arts and Letters. Office: M Knoedler & Co Inc 19 E 70th St New York NY 10021-4907

FRANK-FITZNER, FONTAINE LYNNE, geriatrics, medical and surgical nurse; b. Detroit; m. George H. Fitzner. AA with honors, Jackson Community Coll., Mich., 1984; BSN with honors, Ea. Mich. U., 1988; Assoc. in Geriatric Nursing Care, Ea. Mich. U.-Mich. State U., 1990. RN, Mich., Fla. Staff nurse Suncoast Hosp., Largo, Fla., 1988-89; charge nurse VA Hosp., Ann Arbor, Mich., 1989; infection control practitioner Med. Ctr. Hosp., Punta Gorda, Fla., 1992-93; health svcs. coord. Cigna Health Plan of Fla. Inc., Tampa, 1993-96; clin. rev. specialist Liberty Mut. Ins. Co., Tampa, 1996—. Mem. ANA, Fla. Nurses Assn., Nat. League of Nursing, Sigma Theta Tau.

FRANKIE, SUZANNE OPENLANDER, librarian; b. Toledo, June 20, 1935; d. Gerald P. and Catherine (Phillips) Openlander; m. Richard J. Frankie, June 30, 1962. BA, Bowling Green State U., 1957; MLS, U. Mich., 1959; D Pub. Adminstrn., George Washington U., 1980. Reference libr. undergrad. lib. U. Mich., Ann Arbor, 1959-62; reference libr. Wayne State U., Detroit, 1962-66; head libr. Ctr. for Vocat. Edn. Ohio State U., Columbus, 1966-70; asst. dir. ERIC Clearinghouse on Libr. and Info. Scis. ASIS, Washington, 1970-73; assoc. exec. dir. Assn. Rsch. Librs., Washington, 1973-79; dir. pub. svcs. library NYU, N.Y.C., 1980-82; dean of the libr. Oakland U., Rochester, Minn., 1983—; part-time faculty Wayne State U., 1991-92; mem. com. on accreditation, ALA, Chgo., 1986-92. Mem. U. Mich. Sch. Info. Alumni Assn. (pres. 1994-95), Detroit Area Libr. Network (pres. 1994), Mich. Libr. Consortium (pres. 1987-88, bd. dirs. 1983-88). Office: Oakland University Library Rochester MI 48309

FRANKIEWICZ, MARCIA JEAN, telemarketing executive; b. East Chicago, Ind., July 9, 1947; d. Edward Stanley and Bernice Jean (Pikula) F.; m. Richard Joseph Palchak, Apr. 22, 1989; children: Sarah Frankiewicz-Palchak, Jason Frankiewicz-Palchak. BS in Edn., Western Mich. U., 1969; MS in Spl. Edn., U. Wis., Whitewater, 1981. Tchr., unit leader Wilson Elem. Sch., Janesville, Wis., 1969-79; spl. edn. tchr. Brown Deer (Wis.) High Sch., 1979-84, trainer, 1983-84; spl. svcs. mgr. Braeger Chevrolet, Inc., Milw., 1984-85; telemktg. mgr. Gander Mountain, Inc., Wilmot, Wis., 1985-86; pres., owner MJ Dimensions, Milw., 1986—; guest WISN Radio, Milw., 1988; speaker and seminar leader in field. Advisor mktg. edn. adv. com. Milw. Pub. Schs., 1987—. Mem. Wis. Telemktg. Mgrs. Assn. (pres. 1987-89), Sales and Mktg. Execs. Milw. (v.p. programs 1989-90, bd. dirs. 1991-94), Internat. Assn. Pers. Women (bd. dirs. 1984-87), Pers. Indsl. Rels. Assn. Milw. (various coms.), Wis. Women Entrepreneurs, Alpha Omicron Pi, Kappa Delta Pi. Roman Catholic. Office: MJ Dimensions 2670 N Lake Dr Milwaukee WI 53211-3837

FRANKING, HOLLY MAE, software publisher; b. Washington, D.C., May 13, 1944; d. Nelson W. and Dorothy Elizabeth (O'Connor) F.; m. John Robert Slegman, Aug. 16, 1986. BA in English, Mt. St. Mary's Coll., 1967; MA in English, Loyola U., L.A., 1970; MA in Philosophy, U. Kans., 1986, PhD in English, 1988. Cert. preschool, kindergarten, grades 1-12, adult tchr., Calif., jr. coll. tchr., Calif. Grade 3 tchr. Valley Sch., L.A., 1968-69; grade 4 tchr. St. Elizabeth Sch., Van Nuys, Calif., 1970-72, grades 5,6 tchr., vice prin., 1972-77; grades 7, 8 tchr. St. Mel Sch., Woodhills, Calif., 1977-78, Woodland Hills, Calif., 1978-79; grades 7, 8 tchr. St. Elizabeth Sch., Van Nuys, Calif., 1978-82; grades 10-12 tchr. Taft High Sch., L.A., 1982-83; pres., co-founder, software pub., author Diskotech, Inc., Prairie Village, Kans., 1987—; faculty rep. for sch. bd. St. Elizabeth Sch., Van Nuys, 1973-78. Author: (computerized video novel) Negative Space, 1990, CD-ROM version, 1995, Dr. Franking's Language Lessons, 1990; editor: Mae Franking's "My Chinese Marriage," 1991; pub.: How to Be Happily Employed in the 1990s, 93, Martensville Nightmare CD-ROM, 1996; author, pub. software; pub. PCcards (1st multimedia greeting cards 1992); book reviewer Kansas City Star newspaper, 1994. Democrat. Home: 6240 Rosewood Shawnee Mission KS 66205 Office: Diskotech Inc 7930 State Line Rd Ste 210 Prairie Village KS 66208-3704

FRANKL, RAZELLE, management educator. BA in English, Temple U., 1955; MA in Polit. Sci., Bryn Mawr Coll., 1966; MBA in Organizational Devel., Drexel U., 1973; PhD, Bryn Mawr Coll., 1984. Chair codes and ordinance com. Exec Com. Neighborhood Improvement Program, Lower Merion Twp., 1967-68; pres. LWV Lower Merion Twp., 1967-68; v.p. for organizational affairs LWV, Springfield, Mass., 1968-70; chair environ. quality com. LWV Radnor Twp., 1970-71; instr. applied behavioral sci. Drexel U. Sch. Bus., 1972-73; planner office of mental health/mental retardation Dept. Pub. Health, City of Phila., 1971-73, planner office of health planning, 1971-73; coord. for health programs Phila. '76 Inc. (Official Bicentennial Corp.), 1972-74; adj. faculty dept. mgmt. adminstrv. studies div. Sch. Bus. Rowan Coll. N.J. (formerly Glassboro State Coll.), 1974-77, 81-82; asst. prof. Glassboro (N.J.) State Coll., 1982-88, assoc. prof. dept. mgmt., 1988-95, prof., 1995—. Author: Televangelism: The Marketing of Popular Religion, 1987, Popular Religion and the Imperatives of Television: A Study of the Electric Church, 1984; author: (with others) Religious Television: Controversies and Conclusions, 1990, Teleministries as Family Businesses, 1990;, New Christian Politics, 1984; contbr. articles to profl. jours. Dir. Nat. Bd. Med. Coll. Pa., chair spring program; chair, bd. dirs. Anti-Violence Partnership of Phila. Rsch. grantee Rowan Coll. N.J. (formerly Glassboro State Coll.), 1986-87, 90, 91, 93-94, 94-95, All-Coll. Rsch. grantee, 1987-88. Mem. Am. Acad. Mgmt. (chair membership com. div. mgmt. edn. and devel., chair media rels. com., div. women in mgmt.), Soc. for Human Resource Mgmt., Am. Sociol. Assn., Ea. Sociol. Soc., Assn. for Sociology Religion, Religious Rsch. Assn., Soc. for Sci. Study Religion (chair womens caucus), Internat. Sociol. Assn., Assn. for Rsch. on Non-profit Orgns. and Vol. Action. Home: 536 Moreno Rd Wynnewood PA 19096-1121

FRANKLIN, ARETHA, singer; b. Memphis, 1942; d. Clarence L. and Barbara (Siggers) F.; m. Ted White (div.); m. Glynn Turman, Apr. 11, 1978. First record at age 12; rec. artist with Columbia Records, N.Y.C., 1961, then with Atlantic records, now with Arista Records; albums include Aretha, 1961, Electrifying, 1962, Tender Moving and Swinging, 1962, Laughing on the Outside, 1963, Unforgettable, 1964, Songs of Faith, 1964, Running Out of Fools, 1964, Yeah, 1965, Soul Sister, 1966, Queen of Soul, Take it Like You Give It, 1967, Lee Cross, Greatest Hits, 1967, I Never Loved a Man, 1967, Once in a Lifetime, Aretha Arrives, 1967, Lady Soul, 1968, Greatest Hits, Vol. 2, 1968, Best of Aretha Franklin, Live at Paris Olympia, 1968, Aretha Now, 1968, Soul 69, 1969, Today I Sing the Blues, 1969, Soft and Beautiful, Aretha Gold's, 1969, Satisfaction, I Say a Little Prayer, 1969, This Girl's in Love With You, 1970, Spirit in the Dark, 1970, Don't Play that Song, 1970, Live at the Fillmore West, 1971, Young Gifted and Black, 1971, Aretha's Greatest Hits, 1971, Amazing Grace, 1972, Hey Hey Now, 1973, Star Collection, 1978, First 12 Sides, 1973, Let Me Into Your Life, 1974, With Every Thing I Feel in Me, 1975, You, 1975, Sparkle, 1976, Ten Years of Gold, 1976, Sweet Passion, 1977, Almighty Fire, 1978, La Diva, 1979, Aretha, 1980, Who's Zoomin' Who, 1985, One Lord, One Faith, One Baptism, 1987, Aretha Sings the Blues, 1965, 85, Lady Soul, 1988, Through the Storm, 1989, What You See Is What You Sweat, 1991, Jazz to Soul, 1992, Aretha After Hours; appeared in film: Blues Brothers, 1980; performer: (Showtime prodn.) Aretha, 1986; concert tours in U.S. and Europe. Named Top Female Vocalist, 1967; named Number One Female Singer 16th Internat. Jazz Critics Poll, 1968; recipient Grammy award for best female rhythm and blues vocal, 1967-74, 81, 85, 87, 88 for best rhythm and blues rec., 1967, for best soul gospel performance, 1972, for best rhythm and blues duo vocal (with George Michael, 1987); Am. Music award, 1984; Kennedy Center Honor, 1994. Address: 8450 Linwood St Detroit MI 48206-2379 Office: care Wm Morris Agency 151 S El Camino Dr Beverly Hills CA 90212-2704*

FRANKLIN, BARBARA HACKMAN, former government official; b. Lancaster, Pa., Mar. 19, 1940; d. Arthur A. and Mayme M. (Haller) Hackman; m. Wallace Barnes, Nov. 29, 1986. BA with distinction, Pa. State U., 1962; MBA, Harvard U., 1964; D of Bus. Adminstrn. (hon.), Bryant Coll., 1973; D of Commerce (hon.), Drexel U., 1990; D of Comml. Sci. (hon.), U. Hartford, 1994; JD (hon.) Briarwood Coll., 1996. Mgr. environ. analysis Singer Co., N.Y.C., 1965-68; asst. v.p. Citibank, N.Y.C., 1969-71; asst. on White House staff for recruiting of women to positions in govt., Washington, 1971-73; commr., vice chmn. U.S. Consumer Product Safety Commn., Washington, 1973-79; sr. fellow, dir. govt. and bus. program Wharton Sch., U. Pa., Phila., 1979-88; pres., CEO Franklin Assocs., Washington, 1984-92; alt. rep. pub. del. 44th session UN Gen. Assembly, 1989-90; sec. commerce Dept. Commerce, Washington, 1992-93; pres. and CEO Barbara Franklin Enterprises, Washington, 1995—; adviser to comptroller gen. U.S., 1984-92, 94—; bd. dirs., chair audit com. Aetna Life and Casualty Co., 1979—, Dow Chem. Co., 1980—, AMP, Inc., 1993—, J.A. Jones, Inc., 1995—, MedImmune, Inc., 1995—, NASDAQ Stock Market, 1996—, Guest Svc., Inc., 1995—; Automatic Data Processing, Inc., 1984-92, Armstrong World Ind., 1989-92, Black & Decker Corp., 1985-92, Westinghouse Electric Corp., 1980-92, Nordstrom, 1988-92; pub. mem. Auditing Standards Bd. Planning Com., 1989; pub. mem., bd. dirs., chair audit com. Am. Inst. CPA's, 1979-86. Apptd. by Pres. Reagan then Bush to Pres.'s Adv. Com. Trade Policy and Negotiations, 1982-86, 89-92, chair task force on tax reform, 1985-86; co-chmn. Nat. Fin. Com. George Bush for Pres., 1985-88; Conn. reps. fin. chair, 1993-94; bd. visitors Def. Systems Mgmt. Coll., Dept. Def., 1986-89; svcs. policy adv. Com. of U.S. Trade Representatives; apptd. by Gov. Thornburgh to State Bd. Edn., Commonwealth Pa., 1980-81; bd. regents U. Hartford, 1986-88. Trustee Pa. State U., 1976-82. Recipient Disting. Alumni award Pa. State U., 1972, Disting. Woman award Northwood Inst., 1972, Mother Gerard Phelan medal Marymount Coll., 1972, Catalyst award for Corp. Leadership, 1981, Excellence in Mgmt. award Simmons Coll., 1981, Am. Assn. Poison Control Ctrs. award, 1979, cert. appreciation, Am. Acad. Pediatrics, 1979, Dirs. Choice award Nat. Women's Econ. Alliance, 1987, Corp. Social Responsibility award CUNY, 1988, John J. McCloy Auditing award, 1992, Womens Nat. Rep. Club award, 1993; Kappa Alpha Theta Graduate fellow, 1962, Edith Gratia Stedman, Harvard U., fellow, 1962; named one of 50 Most Influential Corp. Dirs. Am. Mgmt. Assn., 1990. Fellow Nat. Assn. Corp. Dirs.; mem. NACD (Blue Ribbon commn. bd. and CEO evaluation 1994), Women's Forum Washington, Nat. Women's Econ. Alliance Found. (bd. govs. 1984-92, 94—, Dir.'s Choice award 1987), Nat. Com. U.S.-China Rels. (Atlantic coun. dir.), Internat. Women's Forum (founding mem.), Asia Soc., Coun. Fgn. Rels. (U.S.-China Bus. Coun.), Exec. Women in Govt. (founding mem., vice chmn. 1973), Heritage Found. (chair internat. trade adv. coun.), Bretton Woods Com., Washington Forum, Alumni Coun. Pa. State U., 1925 F Street Club, Washington (bd. govs.), Women's Nat. Rep. Club (bd. govs. 1969-71), Econ. Club N.Y., Econ. Club D.C. Congregational. Avocations: exercise, skiing, hiking, reading. Office: 2600 Virginia Ave NW Ste 506 Washington DC 20037-1905 also: 1875 Perkins St Bristol CT 06010-8910

FRANKLIN, BARBARA KIPP, financial advisor; b. Jackson, Mich., Jan. 7, 1943; d. Robert Charles and Barbara Jean (Boardman) F.; m. Peter G. Stone. BBA, U. Mich., Ann Arbor, 1967. Chartered fin. analyst; cert. fin. planner. Freelance journalist various Mich. and Ohio newspapers, 1968-71; pub. relations rep. Bayerische Motoren Werke, Munich, Germany, 1969-71; acct. exec. Dean Witter Reynolds, Los Angeles, 1975-77; trust rep. First Interstate Bank, 1978-79; trust adminstr. Union Bank, Los Angeles, 1980-81; trust portfolio mgr. Fidelity Bank, Phila., 1981-84; trust portfolio mgr., v.p. Provident Nat. Bank, Phila., 1984-91; pvt. practice Del. and Pa., 1992—; corp. sec. Flavour of Britain Tea Shop, 1996—; treas. Flavor of Britain Catalog Co. Ltd., 1996—. Mem. Hist. Soc. Chester County; bd. dirs., exec. com., treas. Children's Country Week Assn., Chester County, 1988—. Mem. DAR, Assn. Investment Mgmt. and Rsch., Inst. Chartered Fin. Analysts, Inst. CFP, Nat. Assn. Life Underwriters, Delaware Valley Soc. CFP (bd. dirs. 1991-93, sec. 1993-96), Chester County Chamber of Bus. and Industry, Estate Planning Coun. Phila., Estate Planning Coun. Chester County, Phila. Securities Assn., Fin. Analysts Phila.

FRANKLIN, BONNIE SELINSKY, federal agency administrator; b. Oakland, Calif., Mar. 17, 1944; d. Harold Joseph and Madge (Warden) Selinsky; m. Alfred Carl Franklin, Jan. 24, 1981; 1 child, Amy Beth. AB in Am. Studies, George Washington U., 1966, MBA in Acctg., 1977. Tax auditor IRS, Baileys Crossroads, Va., 1966-71; from program analyst to tax law specialist IRS, Washington, 1971-77, from program analyst appeals to chief procedures sect., 1979-82, tech. asst. to nat. dir. appeals, 1985—; regional analyst conf. IRS, Atlanta, 1977-79. Chair Arlingtonians for a Better County, Arlington, Va., 1994—; active Friends of the Libr., Arlington, 1996—. Mem. LWV, Womens Nat. Dem. Club. Democrat. Lutheran.

FRANKLIN, LYNNE, business communications consultant, writer; b. St. Paul, Minn., Aug. 24, 1957; d. Lyle John Franklin and Lois Ann (Cain) Kindseth; m. Lawrence Anton Pecorella, Sept. 2, 1989; 1 stepchild, Lauren. BA in Psychology and English, Coll. St. Catherine, 1979; MA, Hamline U., 1989. Residential treatment counselor St. Joseph's Home, Mpls., 1979-80; staff writer Comml. West Mag., Mpls., 1980-81; acct. exec. Edwin Neuger & Assocs., Mpls., 1981-83, Hill and Knowlton, Mpls., 1983-84; mgr. pub. rels. Gelco Corp., Eden Prarie, Minn., 1984-86; dir. financial rels. Dunstan & Assocs., Mpls., 1986; cons. MC Assocs., Chgo., 1986-87; v.p. Fin. Rels. Bd., Chgo., 1987—; principal Wordsmith, Glenview, Ill., 1993—; judge achievement awards Internat. Assn. of Bus. Communicators, Mpls., 1986, presenter fin. rels., 1990; judge achievement awards Publicity Club of Chgo., 1992-94; presenter annual report seminar Nat. Investor Rels. Inst., Chgo., 1992. Author: (novel) Second Sight, 1989. tchr. Great Books Program, St. Paul, 1976-79, Minn. Literacy Coun., 1985-87. Recipient Ann. Report Excellence award Fin. World Mag., 1991-96, MerComm-ARC Competition, 1992-96. Office: Wordsmith 2019 Glenview Rd Glenview IL 60025-2849

FRANKLIN, MARGARET LAVONA BARNUM (MRS. C. BENJAMIN FRANKLIN), civic leader; b. Caldwell, Kans., June 19, 1905; d. LeGrand Husted and Elva (Biddinger) Barnum; m. C. Benjamin Franklin, Jan. 20, 1940 (dec. 1983); children: Margaret Lee (Mrs. Michael J. Felso), Benjamin Barnum. B.A., Washburn U., 1952; student, Iowa State Tchrs. Coll., 1923-25, U. Iowa, 1937-38. Tchr. pub. schs. Union, Iowa, 1925-27, pub. schs., Kearney, Nebr., 1927-28, Marshalltown, Iowa, 1928-40; advance rep. Redpath-Vawter-Chautauquas, 1926, Associated Chautauquas, 1927-30. Mem. Citizens Adv. Com., 1965-69; mem. Stormont-Vail Regional Ctr. Hosp. Aux.; bd. dirs. Marshalltown Civic Theatre, 1938-40, pres. 1938-40; bd. dirs. Topeka Pub. Libr. Found., 1984-92; mem. Park Ave. Christian Ch., N.Y.C.; 1st sec. beautification com. City of Topeka, 1951. Recipient Waldo B. Heywood award Topeka Civic Theatre, 1967, Vol. Svc. award Topeka Pub. Libr., 1991. Mem. DAR (state chmn. Museum 1968-71), AAUW (50+ Yr. mem.), Gemini Group of Topeka, Topeka Geneal. Soc., Topeka Civic Symphony Soc. (dir. 1952-57, Svc. Honor citation 1960), Doll Collectors Am., Shawnee County Hist. Soc. (dir. 1963-75, sec. 1964-66), Stevengraph Collectors Assn., Friends of Topeka Public Libr. (dir. 1970-79, Disting. Svc. award 1980), PEO Sisterhood, Philanthropic and Ednl. Orgn. (pres. chpt. 1956-57, coop. bd. pres. 1964-65, chpt. honoree 1969), Native Sons and Daus. Kans. (life), Nonoso, Topeka Stamp Club, Western Sorosis Club (pres. 1960-61), Minerva Club (2d v.p. 1984-85), Woman's Club (1st v.p. 1952-54), Knife and Fork Club, Alpha Beta Gamma. Republican.

FRANKLIN, MARY ANN WHEELER, retired administrator, educator, higher education and management consultant; b. Boston; d. Arthur Edward Wheeler and Madeline Ophelia (Hall) Wheeler-Brooks; m. Carl Matthew Franklin; 1 child, Evangeline Rachel Hall Franklin-Nash. BS, U. N.H., 1942; MEd, U. Buffalo, 1948; EdD, U. Md., 1982. Cert. tchr., N.Y., Ga. Instr. edn. W.Va. State Coll., Institute, 1947; tchr. gen. sci. John Marshall Jr. High Sch., Bklyn., 1952; assoc. prof. sci. Elizabeth City (N.C.) State Coll., 1960; asst. dean coll. Morgan State U., Balt., 1967-77, asst. dean Coll. Arts and Scis., 1977-78, asst. v.p. acad. affairs, 1978-82; asst. prof. bus. Catonsville (Md.) Community Coll., 1982; asst. to dean evening and weekend coll. So. U. New Orleans, 1983-92; cons. numerous locations Herford County Tchrs., Murfreesboro, N.C., 1961, St. Catherine's Sch., Elizabeth City, 1962-64, Archbishop Keough H.S., Balt., 1970-80, Hampton Inst. Va. St. Paul Coll., 1972; bd. dirs. Archbishop Keough H.S.; presenter confs., seminars and workshops; spkr. in field. Editor Academic Affairs Newsletter, 1980-82, Morgan State Coll. Catalog, 1969-82; author: The How and Why of Testing at Elizabeth City State College, 1962, Report on Princeton University Program for Physics Teachers in HBCU's, 1964, Learning Summer Camp Code, National Library of Poetry, 1992, 93, 94, 95, Interrogations of a Metropolis, 1993, Who Are We/Who We ARe, 1994. Mem. com. higher edn. Citizens League, Balt., 1979-81; assoc. dir. youth camp NCCJ, 1974-75, bd. dirs., 1969-80; dir., originator Vestibule Program and Parents Workshop for New Citizens and Residents, SUNO Summer Learning Camp, 1984-95; pres. Lake Willow Homeowners Assn., 1994-96. Fellow NSF, Harvard U., 1958-59, Carnegie-Ford-NSF, Princeton U., 1964; recipient Education award Am. Assn. of Coll. Tchrs. Edn., 1966. Mem. AAUW, Am. Mgmt. Assn., Nat. Coun. Negro Women (bd. dirs. 1984), Am. Assn. Higher Edn., Am. Assn. Continuing Higher Edn., Nat. Assn. Trainers and Educators for Alcohol and Substance Abuse Counselors (pres. accreditation coun.'s alcohol and drug counseling program in higher edn.), La. Assn. Continuing Higher Edn., Md. Assn. Higher Edn., Urban League, Delta Sigma Theta, Phi Sigma, Pi Lambda Theta.

FRANKLIN, MELISSA, physicist; b. Edmonton. BS, Univ. of Toronto; PhD, Stanford Univ., Calif. Asst. prof. Univ. of Ill., Champaign-Urbana; jr. fellow Harvard Univ., Cambridge, Mass., prof. physics, 1992—. Office: Harvard Univ Dept of Physics Jefferson Lab Cambridge MA 02138-6502

FRANKLIN, PHYLLIS, professional association administrator; b. N.Y.C., Apr. 21, 1932; d. Matthew Pine and Helen Lutsky; m. Irwin Franklin, Apr. 21, 1958 (div. 1971); children: James, Jody. AB, Vassar Coll., 1954; MA, U. Miami, 1965, PhD, 1969; LHD (hon.), George Washington U., 1986. From asst. to assoc. prof. U. Miami, Coral Gables, 1969-80; spl. asst. to dean Coll. Arts & Scis. Duke U., Durham, N.C., 1980-81; dir. English programs MLA, N.Y.C., 1981-85, exec. dir., 1985—; adj. prof. English programs NYU, 1987-88. Editor ADE Bull., 1981-85, Profession, 1985—. Fellowship, Danforth Found., 1966-68, Am. Council on Edn., 1980-81; stipend NEH, 1971. Mem. USSR Acad. Scis., Am. Coun. Learned Socs. (bd. dirs. 1987-89, commn. on humanities and social scis. 1987-88, chair conf. secs. 1987-90), Nat. Humanities Alliance (bd. dirs. 1986-88, v.p. 1990-91, pres. 1991), Nat. Fedn. Abstracting and Info. Svcs. (bd. dirs. 1994—). Democrat. Jewish. Office: Modern Language Assn 10 Astor Pl New York NY 10003-6935

FRANKLIN, RACHEL ALLEN, nursing educator; b. Hartsville, S.C., June 26, 1957; d. David Lewis and Anna Divver (Vaughan) Allen; m. Lonnie William Franklin, Apr. 16, 1989. BSN, Clemson U., 1979; MN, U. S.C., 1983, postgrad., 1994. RN, S.C.; cert. specialist med.-surg. nursing, adult nurse practitioner. Nurse intern McLeod Regional Med. Ctr., Florence, S.C., 1979-80, staff nurse, charge nurse coronary care unit, 1980-82; staff nurse, charge nurse MCCU Providence Hosp., Columbia, S.C., 1982-84, cardiac rehab. specialist, 1984-88; assoc. degree nursing instr. Midlands Tech. Coll., Columbia, S.C., 1984; clin. specialist cardiology Richland Meml. Hosp., Columbia, S.C., 1988-90, coord. nurse extern program, 1990; clin. instr. Coll. Nursing U. S.C., Columbia, 1990-96, clin. asst. prof., 1996—; instr. RN refresher course SCAHEC, Columbia, 1993-96; BLS instr. Am. Heart Assn., Columbia, 1988—; content expert, item writer ANCC, Washington, 1994-95; lectr. Romanian Critical Care Course Providence Hosp., Columbia, 1993. Contbr. articles to profl. jours. Mem. Lake Murray Power Squadron, Columbia, 1990. Mem. ANA (Ctrl. Midlands chpt.), Sigma Theta Tau. Methodist. Home: 711 Woodcreek Ct Columbia SC 29212 Office: U SC Coll Nursing Pickens & Green St Columbia SC 29208

FRANKLIN, SHARON JANINE, educational writer, designer; b. July 27, 1945. BA in English, UCLA, 1967; MLS, U. Oreg., 1975. Exec. dir. Visions for Learning Inc., Eugene, 1989—; developer ednl. multimedia materials Franklin & Cron/Devel. Group, Eugene, 1994—. Author: Explore Science series, 1995; editor: The Writing Notebook, 1986—. Home: 2676 Emerald St Eugene OR 97403-1634 Office: Franklin & Cron Devel Grp 2676 Emerald St Eugene OR 97403

FRANKLIN, SHIRLEY MARIE, marketing consultant; b. Kansas City, Mo., Apr. 13, 1930; d. Eric E. and Marie M. (Kilpatrick) Snodgrass; div. 1967; 1 child, Scot Wesley. BA, State U. Iowa, 1952; MS, Simmons Coll., 1954; MA, Kans. U., 1974. Cert. tchr., Kans., Mass., N.J., Ariz., Calif. Tchr., adminstr. various schs., 1952-76; gifted student program designer Leavenworth County (Kans.) Pub. Schs., 1976-77; sales cons., mgr. Sealight Co., Inc., Kansas City, Mo., 1978-82; dir. chain sales Haagen Dazs Ice Cream Co., Teaneck, N.J., 1982-87; program dir. case space mgmt. Ice Cream Industry, 1986-88; prin. Shirley Franklin Consulting, Basehor, Kans., 1987—; apptd. U.S. brands dir. Mövenpick Co., Zurich, Switzerland, 1990—; mktg. cons. Franklin & Assocs., 1994—; speaker at dairy industry meetings, seminars. Contbr. articles to profl. jours. and mags. Foster parent World Vision, Pasadena, Calif., 1986—; mem. nat. com. steering com. U.S. Congress Arts Caucus, Washington, 1988, 89; vol. ct. appointed spl. advocate for children in trouble, Kans., 1994; apptd. City Planning Commn., 1996—. Recipient Excellence in Sales Promotions award Dairy and Food Industries Supply Assn. Mem. Internat. Ice Cream Assn. (mktg. coun. 1979—), Delta Delta Delta. Republican. Episcopalian. Home and Office: 3741 N 155th St PO Box 233 Basehor KS 66007-9205

FRANKS, CECELIA ANITA, secondary school educator; b. Athens, Ala., June 30, 1938; d. Vanal B. and Elsie Mae (Tillery) Broadway; m. Charles W. Franks, Aug. 16, 1959; children: Charles Timothy, Randy Alan. BS, Athens State Coll., 1970. Sec. Anderson Ford Co., Huntsville, Ala., 1960-61, Ford Motor Co, McRae, Ga., 1964, Park Chrysler Plymouth, Macon, Ga., 1965-68; tchr. W. Laurens Jr-Sr H.S., Dublin, Ga., 1969—; Sponsor Jr. H.S. Co-Ed Y Club, West Laurens Jr. H.S., Dublin, Jr. H.S. Beta Club, Future Bus. Leaders of Am., 1984—; mem., chmn. adv. com. for Vocat. Edn., official in competitive events at both local and state levels; chmn. student support com., child study team. Chmn. Am. Cancer Soc. 1983-93; vol. Lions Club, 1983—, active in many charitable and comty. projects especially those involving youth. Mem. Ga. Assn. Educators. Home: 1112 Edgewood Dr Dublin GA 31021-5522 Office: West Laurens HS RR 5 Box 138 Dublin GA 31021-8897

FRANKS, LUCINDA LAURA, journalist; b. Chgo., July 16, 1946; d. Thomas Edward and Lorraine Lois (Leavitt) F.; m. Robert M. Morgenthau, Nov. 1977; children: Joshua Franks Morgenthau, Amy Elinor Morgenthau. B.A., Vassar Coll., 1968. Journalist specializing youth affairs, civil strife in No. Ireland UPI, London, 1968-73, N.Y. Times, N.Y.C., 1974-77; freelance writer N.Y. Times Mag., N.Y. Times Book Rev., The Atlantic, The New Yorker, N.Y. mag., The Nation; Vis. prof. Vassar Coll., 1977-82; Ferris prof. journalism Princeton U., 1983. Author: Waiting Out A War: The Exile of Private John Picciano, 1974, Wild Apples, 1991. Recipient Pulitizer prize for nat. reporting, 1971, N.Y. Newspaper Writers Assn. award, 1971; Nat. Headliners award, Soc. Silurians journalism award, 1976. Mem. Am. PEN Club (membership bd.), Author's League, Coun. on Fgn. Rels., Writers Rm. Inc. (past pres.). Address: 1085 Park Ave New York NY 10128-1168

FRANKSON-KENDRICK, SARAH JANE, publisher; b. Bradford, Pa., Sept. 24, 1949; d. Sophronus Ahimus and Elizabeth Jane (Sears) McCutcheon; m. James Michael Kendrick, Jr., May 22, 1982. Customer service rep. Laros Printing/Osceola Graphics, Bethlehem, Pa., 1972-73; assoc. editor Babcox Publs., Akron, Ohio, 1973-74; assoc. editor Bill Communications, Akron, 1974-75, sr. editor, 1975-77, editor-in chief, 1977-81; assoc. pub. Chilton Co./ABC Pub., Chgo., 1981-83, pub., 1983-89, group pub., Radnor, Pa., 1989-93; group v.p. Chilton Co., Radnor, Pa., 1993—; exec. MBA prof. Northwood U., mem. adv. coun. Recipient Automotive Replacement Edn. award Northwood Inst., 1983, award for young leadership and excellence Automotive Hall of Fame, 1984; mem. bd. dirs. Automotive Hall of Fame. Mem. Automotive Found. for Aftermarket (trustee), Automotive Parts and Accessories Assn. (bd. dirs., exec. com., sec. treas., strategic planning com., edn. com., Disting. Svc. award 1993), Automotive Svc. Industry Assn. (bd. dirs. automotive divsn. com.), Automotive Svc. Assn. Mgmt. Inst. (bd. trustee). Republican. Club: Knollwood Country (Lake Forest, Ill.). Office: Chilton Co/ABC Pub 201 Chilton Way Radnor PA 19089

FRANK WAKE, ANN MARIE, English language and literature educator; b. Sterling, Ill., Dec. 9, 1959; d. William G. and Karen S. (Baker) Frank; m. Andrew K. Wake, July 5, 1991. BA cum laude, Ill. Wesleyan U., 1982; PhD, U. Mich., 1989. Asst. prof. English Elmhurst (Ill.) Coll., 1989—; divsn. chair humanities Elmhurst Coll., 1994—. Rotary fellow, 1986-87. Mem. MLA, NOW, N.Am. Soc. Studies of Romanticism, Midwest Modern Lang. Assn., Ill. Staff and Curriculum Developers Assn., Phi Kappa Phi. Democrat. Office: Elmhurst Coll 190 Prospect Ave Elmhurst IL 60126

FRANSE, JEAN LUCILLE, secondary school educator; b. Comanche, Okla., Jan. 24, 1932; d. Robert Sydney and Mary Lee (Hooper) McDonald; children: Steven E. Franse, John K. Franse, James M. Franse. BS, Eastern N.Mex. U., 1969, MA, 1976; postgrad., Tex. Tech. U. Cert. ESL, mid-mgmt. Telephone operator Mountain States Telephone, Clovis, N.Mex., 1950-51; mktg. rschr. Opinions Unltd., Amarillo, Tex., 1985-88; sch. tchr. Farwell (Tex.) Ind. Schs., 1969—; bookkeeper, pres. Franse Irrigation, Inc., Farwell, 1985—. Author: (poetry) World of Poetry Anthology, 1991 (Golden Poet award 1991), Our World's Favorite Poems (Outstanding award 1993), Outstanding Poets of 1994, 1994 (Merit award 1994). Mem. Christian Coalition, Dallas, 1994, Ctr. for Am. Values, Washington, 1993-94, Liberty Alliance, Forest, Va., 1994. Mem. ASCD. Home: PO Box 580 Farwell TX 79325-0580 Office: Farwell Ind Sch Dist Box F Farwell TX 79325

FRANSE, KAREN BALCH, editor; b. Menomonee Falls, Wis., Sept. 14, 1964; d. William Perry and Kitty (Parker) B.; m. Ulrich Bonn (div. Jan. 1990); m. John E. Franse, July 6, 1996. BA in Comms., Broadcast Journalism, Pepperdine U., Malibu, Calif., 1985; MA in Counseling Psychology, Nat. U., Irvine, Calif., 1995. Cert. mediator. Mktg. coord. Schmidt-Cannon, Inc., City of Industry, Calif., 1986-88; copywriter The Practice Builder Advtg. Agy., Irvine, Calif., 1988; proprietor The Write Stuff, El Toro, Calif., 1989-91; mng. editor Macartist Mag., Santa Ana, Calif., 1989-91; asst. publs. editor Ingram Micro Inc., Santa Ana, Calif., 1988-91; sr. editor CMP Publs. Inc., Irvine, Calif., 1991—; psychotherapist trainee College Hosp., Costa Mesa, Calif., 1994-95. Past mem. bd. dirs., mem.-at-large, v.p. Cedar Glen Homeowners Assn. Mem. Psi Chi Honor Soc. Office: CMP Media 19200 Von Karman # 360 Irvine CA 92715

FRANTZ, CAROLE TERRI, lawyer; b. Greenville, S.C., Feb. 24, 1949; d. Frank and Joyce B. (Fayard) Bailey; m. Thomas R. Frantz, Aug. 22, 1972 (div. June 1985); 1 child, Ricky; m. Robert H. McKenzie, Jr., Nov. 30, 1991. BA, Westhampton Coll., 1971; JD, Coll. William and Mary, 1974. cert. Bar: Va. 1974, U.S. Ct. Appeals (4th cir.) 1976. Assoc. Day and Summs, Norfolk, Va., 1974-76; asst. commonwealth atty. Norfolk Commonwealth's Atty.'s Office, 1976-81; dep. commonwealth's atty. Virginia Beach (Va.) Commonwealth's Atty.'s Office, 1982-89; pvt. practice Virginia Beach, 1990—. Active North End Civil League, Virginia Beach, 1985-90; dir. Women's Health Forum, Washington, 1985-86; com. mem. Virginia Beach Dem. Com., 1987-95. Mem. Nat. Coll. Criminal Def. Attsy., Va. Trial Lawyers Assn., Virginia Beach Bar Assn. (com. chair 1982-95, chmn. juvenile and domestic rels. ct. com. 1984), Women's Forum (com. chair 1978-95, membership chairperson 1979). Office: 1711 Mediterranean Ave Virginia Beach VA 23451

FRANTZ, CECILIA ARANDA, psychologist; b. Nogales, Ariz., Aug. 6, 1941; d. Tomas Nāvarro and Maria Guadalupe (Covarrubias) A.; m. Roger Allen Frantz, May 27, 1972; 1 child, Kimberly Marie Whelan. BA, U. Ariz., 1966; MA, Ariz. State U., 1972, PhD, 1975. Lic. clin. psychologist, Ariz., sch. psychologist, Va. Tchr. Wilson Sch. Dist., Phoenix, 1966-70; psychologist Child Evaluation Ctr., Phoenix, 1973-75; sch. psychologist Wilson Sch. Dist., Phoenix, 1975-78, spl. edn. dir., 1977-78, schs. supt., 1978-81; acting dir. Nat. Inst. Handicap Rsch. U.S. Dept. Edn., Washington, 1981-82, dep. asst. sec. dept. elm. and secondary edn., 1982-87; asst. dir. Bush's Nat. Steering Com. Campaign Hdqrs., Washington, 1987-88; pvt. practice Washington, 1988—; sch. psychologist Cath. Diocese of Arlington, Va., 1990-92; Arlington County Schs., Arlington, Va., 1992—; cons. U.S. Dept. Edn., Washington, 1987—. Mem. APA, Am. Assn Sch. Adminstrs., Ariz. State Psychol. Assn., Ariz. State Sch. Psychologists Assn., Maricopa Soc. Clin. Psychologists (sec. 1976-77). Republican. Roman Catholic. Home: 4501 Arlington Blvd Apt 609 Arlington VA 22203-2740

FRANTZ, GILDA GLORIA, Jungian analyst; b. Bklyn., Dec. 29, 1926; d. Jack Feldrais and Ruth (Gersten) Striplin; m. Kieffer Evans Frantz, Apr. 21, 1950 (dec. May 1975); children: Carl Gilbert (dec.), Marlene Maris. MA, Antioch U., L.A., 1978. Founding editor Psychol. Perspectives C.G. Jung Inst. of L.A., 1969-76, interviewer, adv. com. Matter of Heart, 1975-81, pres., 1980-83, chmn., 1980-83, tng. analyst, 1977—; adv. coun. Paul Brunton Philos. Found.; lectr. and workshop presenter in field. Editorial bd. Jour. of Contemporary Jungian Psychology; editorial adv. bd. Chiron, A Rev. of Jungian Analysis; contbr. articles to profl. jours. Co-facilitator support group for significant others of people with AIDS, Sherman Oaks (Calif.) Hosp.; keynote speaker Nat. Conf. Jungian Analysts, Lake Tahoe, 1994. Mem. Soc. of Jungian Analysts of So. Calif., Internat. Assn. Analytical Psychology (spkr. 13th congress 1995, Internat. Symposium on Grief and Bereavement (adv. bd. 1983—), Nat. Archive for Rsch. in Archetypal Symbolism (exec. bd., sec. 1984-89).

FRANTZVE, JERRI LYN, psychologist, educator, consultant; b. Huntington Beach, Calif., Sept. 9, 1942; d. Rolland and Marjorie (Ferrin) Weiland. Student, Purdue U., 1964-68; BA in Psychology and History, Marian Coll., 1969; MS in Organizational Psychology, George Williams Coll., 1976; PhD in Indsl. and Organizational Psychology, U. Ga., 1979. Case worker Marion County Welfare Dept., Indpls., 1970-71; sr. mktg. rsch. analyst Quaker Oats Co., Barrington, Ill., 1971-75; mgmt. cons. J.L. Frantzve & Assocs., Bklyn., 1978—; asst. prof. sch. of mgmt. SUNY, Binghamton, 1979-83; pers. rsch. and acad. affairs coord. Conoco/DuPont, Ponca City, 1983-86, dir. employee rels., 1986-88; cons. psychologist Mass., 1988-89; assoc. prof. psychology Radford (Va.) U., 1989-94; cons. Brooklyn, N.Y., 1994—; instrn. cons. USAF, Rome, N.Y., 1979-83; dir. Israel Overseas Rsch. Program, Ginozar, Israel, 1982, Japanese Overseas Rsch. Program, Tokyo, 1983; coord. rsch. Ctr. for Gender Studies, Radford U., 1989-94. Author: Behaving in Organizations: Tales from the Trenches, 1983, Guide to Behavior in Organizations, 1983; contbr. articles to profl. jours. Bd. dirs. Broome County Alcoholism Clinic, Binghamton, N.Y., 1980-83, bd. dirs. Broome County Mental Health Clinic, Binghamton, 1981-83; del. Dem. Caucus, Okla., 1985. Mem. APA (com. on women in psychology 1986-88), AAUW, Acad. Mgmt. (placement dir. Ea. chpt. 1982), Internat. Pers. Mgmt. Assn., Assn. for Women in Psychology, Delta Sigma Pi. Home and Office: 1804 Glenwood Rd Brooklyn NY 11230-1816

FRANZ, HOLLY JO, lawyer, partner; b. Mpls., July 2, 1957; d. Gerald A. and Delores E. (Dahle) F. BS, Mont. State U., 1983; JD, U. Mont., 1986. Bar: Mont., 1986, U.S. Dist. Ct., 1986. Ptnr. Gough, Shanahan, Johnson and Waterman, Helena, Mont., 1986—; exec. bd. Mont. Water Resources Assn., Helena, 1993—. Author: Montana Law Journal, 1986. Legis. Com. Women's Law Caucus, Missoula, Mont., pres. or bd. mem. The State Bar of Mont. (Women's Law Sect.), 1986—, treas. Mont. Women's Lobby, Helena, 1990-95. Recipient Award of Merit Mont. Legal Svcs., 1984, Belle Winestine award Mont. Women's Lobby, 1993. Mem. ABA, First Jud. Bar Assn. Office: Gough Shanahan Johsnson & Waterman 33 S Last Chance Gulch Helena MT 59601

FRANZ, WANDA, association administrator. BA in Anthropology, U. Washington, 1965; MS in Family Resources, W. Va. U., 1970, PhD in Developmental Psychology, 1974. Pres. Nat. Right to Life Comm., D.C.; prof. divsn. of family resources W.Va. U., Morgantown, 1974—. Office: Nat Right to Life Com 419 7th St NW Ste 500 Washington DC 20004-2205

FRANZEN, JANICE MARGUERITE GOSNELL, magazine editor; b. LaCrosse, Wis., Sept. 24, 1921; d. Wray Towson and Anna Heldena (Renstrom) Gosnell; m. Ralph Oscar Franzen, Feb. 15, 1964. BS cum laude, Wis. State U., LaCrosse, 1943; MRE, No. Bapt. Theol. Sem., 1947. Tchr. history and social sci. Galesville (Wis.) High Sch., 1943-45; registrar Christian Writers Inst., Chgo., 1947-49; dir. Christian Writers Inst., 1950-63, dir. studies, 1964-86; fiction editor Christian Life Mag., Wheaton, Ill., 1950-63, woman's editor, 1964-72, exec. editor, 1972-86; mem. editorial bd. Creation House, Wheaton, 1972-86; with Christian Life Missions, Lake Mary, Fla., 1971-95; speaker writers confs. Author: Christian Writers Handbook, 1960, 61, The Adventure of Interviewing, 1989; editor: Christian Author, 1949-54, Christian Writer and Editor, 1955-63; compiler, contbr.: The Successful Writers and Editors Guidebook, 1977; contbr. articles to various mags. Sec. Christian Life Missions, 1971-95. Home: 3N455 Mulberry Dr West Chicago IL 60185-1185

FRANZETTI, LILLIAN ANGELINA, former automobile dealership owner; b. N.Y.C., Nov. 24, 1925; d. Anthony and Jenny (De Santis) Spilotro; m. Louis Mario Franzetti, Apr. 27, 1946 (dec. Oct. 1986); 1 child, Paul. Student, Bergen C.C. Clk. typist U.S. Guarantee Ins. Co., N.Y.C., 1943-44, payroll asst. mgr., 1944-46; clk. typist N.J. Div. of Motor Vehicles, Westwood, 1950-54; office mgr. Lakeview Motors, Inc., Woodcliff Lake, N.J., 1954-58; mgr., owner Lakeview Motors, Inc., Westwood, 1958-93; sec. Tri-State Jeep, Eagle Adv. Assn., Tappan, N.Y., 1978-93. Recipient Bus. Mgmt. award, Am. Motors Corp., 1978. Republican. Roman Catholic.

FRASCA, JOANNE MARIE, secondary education educator; b. Rome, N.Y., July 13, 1955; d. Joseph E. and Susanna (Puglia) F. BS in English, State Univ. Coll. at Brockport, 1977. Cert. tchr. English 7-12, N.Y. English tchr. Staley Jr. H.S., Rome, N.Y., 1979—, English dept. coord., 1986-90, mem. lang. arts curriculum com., 1992-93. Mem. Rome Tchrs. Assn. (bldg. rep. 1984—, pub. rels. com. 1986—). Home: 605 Healy Ave Rome NY 13440-5415

FRASER, ARVONNE SKELTON, former United Nations ambassador; b. Lamberton, Minn., Sept. 1, 1925; d. Orland D. and Phyllis (Du Frene) Skelton; m. Donald M. Fraser, June 30, 1950; children: Thomas Skelton, Mary MacKay, John Du Frene, Lois MacKay (dec.), Anne Tallman (dec.), Jean Skelton Fraser. BA, U. Minn., 1948; LLD (hon.), Macalester Coll., 1979. Staff asst. Office Congressman Donald M. Fraser, 1963-70, adminstrv. asst., campaign mgr., 1970-76; regional coord. Carter-Mondale Com., 1976; counsellor office presdl. pers. The White House, 1977; coord. office women in devel. U.S. Agy. Internat. Devel., Washington, 1977-81; dir. Minn. and Chgo. coms. peace petition dr. Albert Einstein Peace Prize Found., Chgo., 1981-82; co-dir. ctr. on women and pub. policy Hubert H. Humphrey Inst. Pub. Affairs, U. Minn., Mpls., 1982-94; head U.S. del. Commn. On The Status of Women, UN, 1993-94, U.S. rep., amb., 1994; bd. dirs. Nat. Dem. Inst. Internat. Affairs, Women's Econ. Devel. Corp., Nat. Women's Law Ctr., Washington Women's Network, Women's Campaign Fund, Nat. Women's Edn. Fund, Minn. DFL Edn. Found.; mem. U.S. del. UN Decade for Women World Conf., Copenhagen, 1980, Internat. Women's Yr. Conf., Mexico City, 1975, UN Commn. on Status of Women, 1974, 78, Internat. Bur. Edn. Conf., Geneva, 1977; cons. Kenya Women's Leadership Conf., 1984; organiser, chairperson Orgn. Econ. Coop. and Develp./Devel. Assistance com./Women in Devel. experts group for aid-donor nations, 1978-80; dir. Ford. Found. Women's Equity Action League Fund Intern Project and World Plan Project, treas. 1974-77, bd. dirs. 1970-77, 81-83, nat. pres. 1972-74, past legis. chairperson Washington office;. Author: U.N. Decade for Women: Documents and Dialogue, 1987; (with others) Women in Washington: Advocates for Public Policy, 1983. Trustee Macalester Coll., St. Paul, 1982-84; candidate Lt. Gov. Minn., 1986. Recipient Disting. Svc. award Women's Equity Action League, 1977, Superior Honor award U.S. Agy. Internat. Devel., 1981, Elizabeth Boyer award Women's Equity League, 1984, Leader of Leaders Outstanding Achievement award Mpls. YWCA, 1979, Resourceful Woman award Tides Found., 1992; sr. fellow Humphrey Inst. Pub. Affairs U. Minn., 1981-94, emeritus 1995; Prominent Women in Internat. Law award Am. Soc. of Internat. Law, 1995, Mpls. Internat. Citizen award, 1995. Mem. Minn. Bar Assn. (maintenance guidelines com. 1991-93). Home: 821 7th St SE Minneapolis MN 55414-1331 Office: 821 7th St SE Minneapolis MN 55414

FRASER, ELEANOR RUTH, radiologist, administrator; b. Woodlake, Calif., May 31, 1927; d. Morton William and Dorothy Jean (Harding) F. BA magna cum laude, Pomona Coll., 1949; MD, Stanford U., 1954. Diplomate Am. Bd. Radiology. Resident in radiology Los Angeles County Hosp., L.A., 1957; radiologist St. Joseph Hosp., Orange, Calif., 1957-61; pvt. practice Anaheim, Calif., 1961-78; radiologist Radiology Nuclear Med. Group, Bakersfield, Calif., 1978-85; dir. radiology Kern Valley Hosp., Lake Isabella, Calif., 1985—, chief of staff, 1992—. Mem. AMA, Calif. Med. Assn., Kern County Med. Assn., Soc. Nuclear Medicine, Kern Valley Exchange Club (sec. 1992-94), Phi Beta Kappa. Methodist. Home & Office: PO Box 1657 Lake Isabella CA 93240-1657

FRASER, JOAN CATHERINE, lawyer; b. Lawrence, Mass., Jan. 11, 1950; d. John Arthur and Catherine Louise (Swartz) Raymond; m. Robert Francis Fraser, May 26, 1978 (div. 1982); 1 child, Sarah Catherine; m. Jay Michael Rosengarden, June 4, 1994. AA, Essex C.C., 1982; BA, U. Balt., 1984, JD, 1988. Bar: Md. 1990, U.S. Dist. Ct. Md. 1996, U.S. Ct. Appeals (4th cir.) 1996. Asst. prof. Essex C.C., Balt., 1984-88; felony law clk. Office of Pub. Defender, Balt., 1984-88; jud. law clk. Office of Judge Richard Rombro, Balt., 1988-90; assoc. Rosenberg & Brown, Balt., 1990-91, Law Office of Susan Green, Balt., 1991-92; pvt. practice Balt., 1992—. With U.S. Army, 1976-79. Mem. NOW, Nat. Criminal Def. Atty.'s Assn., Md. Criminal Def. Atty.'s Assn., Balt. City Bar. (Libr. Co.). Office: 359 N Calvert St Baltimore MD 21202

FRASER, PRUDENCE, television producer. Exec. prodr. TriStar TV, Culver City, Calif. Exec. prodr. (TV series) The Nanny. Office: TriStar TV 9336 W Washington Blvd Culver City CA 90323 also: care CBS Television City 7800 Beverly Blvd Los Angeles CA 90036*

FRATT, DOROTHY, artist; b. Washington, Aug. 10, 1923; d. Hugh and Martha (Holt) Miller; m. Nicholas Diller Fratt, Sept. 4, 1943 (div. 1965); children: Nicholas, Hugh, Gregory, Peter; m. Curtis Calvin Cooper, Nov. 3, 1972. Studied with Nicolai Cikovsky, 1940; student, Mt. Vernon Coll., 1940-42, Am. U., 1942-43, Phillips Collection Art Sch., 1942-43; studied with Karl Knaths, 1943. mem. commissioning panel for NEA grant, Scottsdale, Ariz., 1971; mem. adv. bd. U. Art Mus. Ariz. State U., Tempe, 1989-95. Exhibited at UN Club Gallery, 1948, Desert Art Gallery, Scottsdale, Ariz., 1959, Tucson Art Ctr., 1964, Phoenix Art Mus., 1964, 75, Riva Yares Gallery, Scottsdale, 1965, 82, 89, 94, 95, Calif. Legion Honor, San Francisco, 1965, Mickelson Gallery, Washington, 1967, State-Wide Touring Exhibit, 1974, Scottsdale Ctr. for Arts, 1980, Carson-Sapiro Gallery, Denver, 1981, Thomas Beabor Gallery, La Jolla, Calif., 1985, U. Ariz. Gallery, Tucson, 1986; represented in pub. collections at Phoenix Art Mus., Tucson Mus., Ariz. State Mus., Tempe; represented in various corp. collections. Mem. Fine Arts Commn., Phoenix, 1965-71; mem. Sotheby Symposium Quality in Art, N.Y.C., 1990.

FRATTINI, SALLI, broadcast executive; m. Robert Hess; 2 children. BS in Mass Comm., Northeastern U., 1982. Prodn. mgr. Sullivan Assocs., Boston, 1982-86, Entertainment Tonight, 1986; supervising prodr. Zink Comm., N.Y.C., 1986-88; broadcast mgr. NBC-Olympics, Seoul, Korea, 1988, Barcelona, Spain, 1992; freelancr line prodr. MTV Networks, N.Y.C., 1988-92, v.p. and exec. in charge of prodn., 1992—. Office: MTV Networks 1515 Broadway New York NY 10036*

FRAUENS, MARIE, editor, researcher; b. Kansas City, Mo., July 10, 1902; d. Frank Henry and Margaret (Stansch) F. AA, Kansas City (Mo.) Jr. Coll., 1921; BJ, U. Mo., 1924; MA, Columbia U., 1947; postgrad., Naval Res. Officers Sch., Washington, 1955-64, Indsl. Coll. Armed Forces, 1964. Instr. swimming, Kansas City, 1919-21; rschr. Mo. State Hist. Soc., 1922-24; teaching prin., dir. extra curricular newspaper and dramatics club Wardell (Mo.) High Sch., 1924-27; math. editor Row Peterson and Co., Evanston, Ill., 1927-35; chief editor high sch. program McGraw-Hill Book Co., N.Y.C., 1935-43; commd. lt. (j.g.) USNR, 1943, advanced through grades to permanent commn. as lt. comdr., 1949, liaison officer U.S. Navy-U.S. Armed Forces Inst., 1943-44, tng. officer Bur. Ordnance, 1944-47; tech. writer Naval Res. Tng. Publs. Project, 1947-49; ret. from Res., 1965; tng. dir. John I. Thompson and Co., Washington, 1949-57; tech. writer Dept. Navy, Washington, 1957; adminstrv. officer Office of Sec. Def., Washington, 1958-69; freelance editor, rschr., Washington, 1969-86, Kansas City, Mo., 1986—, messages of Gov. Ky. to gen. assembly for Ky. Hist. Soc., 1974-76; editor The Machine Gun, Vol. II, Part VII for Lt. Col. George Chinn, USMC, 1952; editor reports for, also exec. sec. Spl. Com. Adequacy of Range Facilities, Dept. Def., 1958; completed authentic restoration of 1882 town house on Capitol Hill, 1980. Active first aid, health courses ARC, 1917-18; girls' advisor YWCA, Kansas City, 1921; counselor Chgo. settlement house, 1930-35; active Red Cross Fund, D.C., 1949; mem. bd. dirs. Naval Gun Factory Welfare and Recreation Assn., 1947-49; mem. work group to develop Interagy. Sci. and Engring. Exhibit The Vision of Man, Office Sec. Def., 1963-65. Decorated mil. medals. Mem. Naval Res. Assn., Ret. Officers Assn., Res. Officers Assn., Naval Order U.S., Am. Def. Preparedness Assn., Union Cemetery Hist. Soc., Nat. Trust Hist. Preservation, Pi Gamma Mu. Contbr. to Commn. Implications of Armed Services Ednl. Programs. Author manuals, pamphlets in field of naval ops. Avocation: genealogical and historical rsch. Home and Office: 435 W 10th St Kansas City MO 64105-2221

FRAVEL, ELIZABETH WHITMORE, accountant; b. Hagerstown, Md., Oct. 17, 1951; d. John W. and Dorothy E. (McCullough) Whitmore; children: Christine E., John W. BBA, Bridgewater Coll., 1973. CPA. Jr. staff acct. Rockingham Meml. Hosp., Harrisonburg, Va., 1973-75; mgr. customer service Pentamation Enterprises Inc., Sparks, Md., 1975-83; sr. acct. Good Samaritan Hosp., Balt., 1983-84; pvt. practice acctg. Balt., 1984-86, Annapolis, Md., 1986—; staff acct. Hammond & Heim Chartered Accts., Annapolis, Md., 1987-89; contr. Smith Bros., Inc., Galesville, Md., 1989-94; dir. office mgmt. and fin. Md. Spl. Olympics, Columbia, Md., 1995—. Treas. Belmont Condominium Assn., Balt., 1983-85. Mem. AICPAs, Md. Assn. CPAs, Md. Soc. Accts.

FRAWLEY, SISTER CLAIRE, educator; b. Elmira, N.Y., Nov. 7, 1929; d. James Edward and Alice (Keating) Frawley. BS, Nazareth Coll., 1957, BA, 1966; postgrad., Siena Coll., 1967, U. Dayton, 1967-68, Cath. U., 1969-73; MRE, Divine Word, 1972. Sch. administr., tchr. Parish Schs., Rochester, Ithaca, Elmira, N.Y., 1950-80; founder, exec. dir. St. Claires Homes, Escondido Calif., homes for homeless women and children, youth minister, Escondido, established and administered program for youth and young adults. Recipient Women Helping Women award Soroptimists, Womens Internat. Living Legacy award; scholar Nat. U. Mem. NAFE, Assn. of Christian Therapists, Calif. Mental Health Assn., Womens Internat., Coalition of Human Svc. Agencies, Child Abuse Coalition, Inland Dirs. Coalition. Home: # 321 243 S Escondido Blvd Escondido CA 92025-4116

FRAWLEY, MELISSA J., banker; b. Ft. Lauderdale, Fla., Mar. 19, 1969; d. William James and Jean Marie Frawley. BSBA, U. Fla., 1991; MBA, U. Ga., 1996. Credit analyst Port St. Lucie (Fla.) Nat. Bank, 1991-93; sr. credit analyst Barnett Bank, Port St. Lucie, 1993-95; comml. real estate mgr. Wachovia Bank, Atlanta, 1996—. Merit-based grad. assistantship U. Ga., 1995-96; Wachovia Bank scholar U. Ga., 1996. Home: # 7 247 E Cloverhurst Ave Athens GA 30605

FRAZER, DIANNE KAY, daycare administrator, consultant; b. La Junta, Colo., Sept. 4, 1952; d. Richard Orville and Shirley Ann (Hurrelbrink) Bullard; m. Frederick Harold Frazer, Oct. 2, 1976; 1 child, Amy Tahirih. BA in Edn., Augustana Coll., 1974. Presch. tchr. Wee Wisdom Presch., Bettendorf, Iowa, 1978; adult basic edn. specialist Skills, Inc., Moline, Ill., 1979-81; day care ctr. mgr. Creative World Sch., Davenport, Iowa, 1981-82; substitute tchr. Davenport (Iowa) Cmty. Sch. Dist., 1979, 83; edn. coord. Project N.O.W. Head Start, Silvis, Ill., 1983-87; head start dir. Project N.O.W. Head Start, Silvis, 1987-91, head start, day care dir., 1991—; adv. bd. mem. Black Hawk Coll. Child Devel. Dept., Moline, 1990—, Black Hawk Coll. Literacy Program, Moline, 1993—; cons. head start reviewer Devel. Assocs., Inc., Arlington, Va., 1990—; cons. grant reviewer Ellsworth Assocs., Inc., Vienna, Va., 1994. Head start del. Citizen Amb. Program, People to People Internat., Russia and Poland, 1992. Ill. State scholar State of Ill., 1970-74. Mem. NAFE, Nat. Head Start Assn., Assn. for Childhood Edn. Internat., Quad Cities Chpt. Nat. Assn. for the Edn. Young Children (bd. mem. 1984-85), Ill. ASCD, People to People Internat. Office: Project NOW Head Start 85 9th St Silvis IL 61282-1048

FRAZIER, DIANE COURTRIGHT, special education educator; b. Rochester, N.Y., June 3, 1954; d. Charles Earl and Eleanor (Palumbo) Courtright; m. Terry Lee Frazier, Sept. 20, 1975 (separated); 1 child, Charles Stephen. BS in Elem. Edn. and Spl. Edn., Keene State Coll., 1977, M in Counseling and Consultation, 1984; postgrad., U. Vt. Cert. spl. edn. tchr., reading specialist, Vt., elem. edn., spl. edn. and counseling and guidance profl., N.H. Resource tchr. Marlborough (N.H.) Schs., 1980-81, Westmoreland (N.H.) Schs., 1981-84; reading specialist Brattleboro (Vt.) Union H.S., 1984-94, faculty coun. chair, 1991-93, N.E. area sch. evaluator, 1991-92; spl. svcs. coord. Adminstrv. Unit 29, Keene, N.H., 1994—; instr. Franklin Pierce Coll., Rindge, N.H., 1990-91; mem. sch.-to-work initiative program So. Vt. Career Edn. Ctr., Brattleboro, 1993-94. Mem. ASCD (ednl. leadership com. 1994-95), Coalition of Essentials Schs. (preschool grant initiative, inclusion facilitator). Home: 154 Washington St Keene NH 03431 Office: 34 West St Keene NH 03431-3371

FRAZIER, KAREN (CARRIE FRAZIER), casting director; b. L.A., Mar. 29, 1957; d. Richard Gregory and Marcia Fay (Cummins) F.; m. Judge Reinhold, Nov. 1, 1985 (div. Apr. 1993). BA, Sarah Lawrence Coll., Bronxville, N.Y., 1979. Asst. to dir. Amy Heckerling, 1980-85; asst. to editor Union 776, 1980-85; casting dir., 1985—. Home: 1282 1/2 Devon Ave Los Angeles CA 90024 Office: CSA 6565 Sunset Blvd #306 Los Angeles CA 90028

FRAZIER, WILMA RUTH, emergency nurse, clinical educator; b. Dimmitt, Okla., Dec. 16, 1949; d. Charles William and Agnes May (Behrends) Pennington; m. Robert Lee Frazier, Aug. 25, 1967; children: Troy Linn, Matthew A., Robbie G., Brandy R., Nathan L. AAS, No. Okla. Coll., 1992; postgrad., Okla. U. Health Sci., 1994—. RN. Tchr. Perry Head Start, 1988-90; purchasing clk. Perry (Okla.) Meml. Hosp., 1984-88, nursing asst., 1990-92, med./surg. nurse, 1992-94, inpatient supr., 1994, emergency rm. nurse, 1992—, preceptor nurse externs, 1993—, dietary quality assurance team, 1994, clin. educator, 1996—; Sunday sch. tchr. First Christian Ch., Perry, 1988—, mem. Christian Women's Fellowship, 1968—; mem. Perry Band Boosters Perry Sch. Bands, 1987—; active PTA, Perry Pub. Schs., 1975—. Mem. Student Nurse Assn., Phi Theta Kappa. Republican. Home:

RR 2 Box 59 Perry OK 73077-9802 Office: Perry Meml Hosp 501 N 14th St Perry OK 73077-5021

FREAD, PHYLLIS JEAN, counselor, educator; b. Pahala, Hawaii, May 21, 1927; d. Logan Allen and Joyce (Barnes) Pruitt; m. John W. Fread (dec.); children: James R., John A. BA, Cornell Coll., 1948; MEd, U. Oreg., 1956. Cert. tchr., counselor, Oreg. Tchr. Seattle Pub. Schs., 1948-50, West Valley H.S., Millwood, Wash., 1950-52; tchr. Roseburg (Oreg.) Dist. 4, 1954-65, dean students, 1965-80; French instr. Umpqua C.C., Roseburg, Oreg., 1984-93; diagnostic counselor AFS, Portland, Oreg., 1988—; hosting dir. AFS, Portland, 1990—. Named Vol. of Month, Roseburg C. of C. Mem. AAUW (treas. 1958-63), Zonta Club of Roseburg (pres. 1976-78, 83-84, gov. dist. 8 1996—). Republican. Methodist. Home: 1336 NW Whipple Roseburg OR 97470

FREASIER, AILEEN W., special education educator; b. Edcouch, Tex., Nov. 12, 1924; d. James Ross and Ethel Inez (Riley) Wade; m. Ben F. Freasier, Mar. 9, 1945 (dec.); children: Ben. C., Doretha J. Christoph, Barbara F. McNally, Raymond E., John F. BS HE, Tex. A and I Coll., 1945; MEd, La. Tech. U., 1966; postgrad. 90 hours, La. Tech. U. Tchr. Margaret Roane Day Care Ctr., Ruston, La., 1965-71; tchr. spl. edn. Lincoln Parish Schs., Ruston, 1971-81; individualized edn. program facilitator La. Tng. Inst. Monroe Spl. Sch. Dist. # 1, 1981-89; ednl. diagnostician LTI Monroe (La.) SSD # 1, 1985-95; R.S.V.P. vol. tutor, Lincoln Parish Detention Ctr., 1995—; citizen amb. People Conf. on Edn., Beijing, 1992, South Africa, 1995; presenter in field. Mem. editl. bd. Jour. Correctional Edn., 1983—, learning tech. sect. editor, 1991-95. Treas. Ruston Mayor's Commn. on Women. Named Spl. Sch. Dist. #1 Tchr. of Yr., 1988; recipient J.E. Wallace Wallin Educator of Handicapped award La. Fedn. CEC, 1994, Meritorious Svc. award La. Dept. Pub. Safety and Corrections, 1995. Mem. AAUW (pres. Ruston br. 1995-96, state co-chair diversity task force 1993—, La. Named Gift honoree AAUW Edn. Found. 1994), CEC-TAM (treas. La. divsn. 1993-96), Am. Assn. Mental Retardation, Internat. Correctional Edn. Assn. (spl. edn. spl. interest group, newsletter editor 1991-94, chmn. 1994-96), Lincoln Parish Ret. Tchrs. Assn. (newsletter editor 1996-97), Phi Delta Kappa (past pres., newsletter editor), Kappa Kappa Iota (state past pres., nat. scholarship com. 1995-97, Eta State Loretta Doerr award 1995). Home: PO Box 1595 Ruston LA 71273-1595

FREDERICH, KATHY W., social worker; b. Ashland, Ky., Apr. 19, 1953; d. James Greeley and Jo Ann (Sparks) Walker; divorced; m. Harry Donald Frederich, Sept. 5, 1987; stepchild, David Scott. BA with distinction, U. Ky., 1978; MS with honors, Ea. Ky. U., 1994. Tng. supr. Blue Grass Assn. for Retarded Citizens, Lexington, Ky., 1971-75, Bur. Vocational Rehab., Lexington, 1976-77; social worker Ky. Dept. for Social Svcs., Lexington, 1978-79, field office supr., 1979-85; social work/domestic violence prog. specialist, conf. coord. Ky. Dept. for Social Svcs., Frankfort, 1985—, tng. instr., 1987—; instr. Ky. Sheriff's Acad., 1986-92, domestic violence Ky. State Police, 1995—; cert. instr. Levington Fayette div. police, 1981-87, 90-91; cons., trainer for field staff and related profls. statewide, Ky., 1983—; mem. adv. bd. Assn. for Older Kentuckians, 1989-93; mem. Ky. Law Enforcement Tng. Project, 1989-91; mem. Atty. Gen.'s Task Force on Domestic Violence Crime, 1991-93, Legis. Task Force on Domestic Violence, 1994-95; coord. 1st Nat. Teleconf. on Domestic Violence and Family Preservation Svcs., 1994; mem. Gov.'s Coun. Domestic Violence, 1996—; staff facilitator Nat. Coll. Dist. Attys. domestic violence conf., 1995; mem. Domestic Violence Jud. Edn. Planning Com., 1995-96. Contbr. to profl. publs. including Ky. Prosecutor's Manual on Domestic Violence, Ky. Hosp. Mag. on Abuse, Ky. Adult Abuse Med. Protocol, Custody and Visitation Manual, and others. Mem. ad hoc grant com. Violence Against Women Act, 1995. Recipient Outstanding Svc. award Lexington Fayette div. of Police, 1984, Ky. Sheriff's Acad. Hon. Grad., 1989, tributes, 1986, 87, 88, Outstanding Kentuckian award Gov. Martha Layne Collins, 1987, Outstanding Young Am. Women award, 1987, Outstanding Victim Adv. award Lexington Urban County Govt., 1990, Outstanding Victim Advocacy award Ky. Victims' Coalition, 1993, Outstanding Svcs. Recognition Senate Ky. Gen. Assembly, 1995, Ky. Commn. Women, 1996; named Ky. Col., 1985. Mem. Ky. Domestic Violence Assn. (homicide-suicide task force 1990-94). Democrat.

FREDERICK, BERNICE BARKER, realtor, broker; b. Hudson, N.C., Oct. 13, 1917; d. James Albert and Princa E. (Miller) Barker; m. Cecil Banks Mullis, Mar. 19, 1936 (div. Feb. 1969); children: Brent B., Kary B., Robert, David; m. Francis D. Frederick, Feb. 14, 1970 (dec. June 1980). Student, Columbia Bus. Coll., Midlands Tech. Coll., U. S.C. Realtor Bonieu Real Estate, Columbia, S.C., 1959-63, Columbia Real Estate, 1963-66; sales mgr. Edens Real Estate, Columbia, 1966-70; realtor Edens & Avant Comml. Realtors, Columbia, 1971—. Scout leader, tchr. Sunday sch., music leader 1st Bapt. Ch. Columbia, 1952-59; vol. Bapt. Hosp., 1965-75; v.p. Richland County Assn. Parents & Tchrs., Columbia, 1950s. Mem. Nat. Realtors Assn., S.C. Realtors Assn. Democrat. Home: 4665 Crystal Dr Columbia SC 29206 Office: Edens & Avant Realtors 1901 Main St Columbia SC 29202

FREDERICK, MYRNA SUE LABRY, sales executive, beauty consultant; b. Abbeville, La., Nov. 22, 1950; d. Noah and Jeanne (Vincent) LaBry; m. Conley J. Frederick, Jan. 22, 1972; children: Dawn M. Frederick Vincent, Shauri F. Richard, Ryan C., Brett J. Student, U. Southwestern La., Lafayette, 1968-69. Ins. office mgr. and cashier Kaplan, La., 1969-73; owner Baton Studio, Kaplan, 1973-79; mgr., fashion buyer, bookkeeper, cashier Kaplan, 1973-91, landscape artist, 1973—; ind. profl. sales dir. Mary Kay Cosmetics, 1992—; ind. profl. beauty cons., 1989—. Mem. Vermilion Arts Coun. Mem. Am. Bus. Women (sec., treas., v.p., pres. 1985-90, Outstanding Woman of Yr. 1990), Krew Chic Alapie (v.p., sec., treas., reporter), Kaplan Jaycee Jaynes (sec., treas., pres. 1974-79, Oustanding Woman of Yr. 1977, Dist. Woman of Yr. 1977-78). Democrat. Roman Catholic. Home: 115 Pelican St Kaplan LA 70548-5652

FREDERICK, PATRICIA LYNN, art educator; b. Milw., Aug. 4, 1949; d. Edwin Aloysius and Lois (Nelson) Sieren; m. Gregory R. Frederick; children: Kelly C., Christopher G. BA, St. Norbert Coll., 1971; MFA, Md. Inst. Coll. of Arts, 1994. Chair art dept. Pius XI H.S., Milw., 1977—; advisor Pius XI chpt. Nat. Art Honor Soc., Milw., 1987—; com. mem. Wis. Regional Scholastic Com., Milw., 1988—. Exhibited in group shows Walkers Point Gallery Exhibit, 1993, Milw. Area Tchrs. of Art, 1984—. Named Tchr. of Yr., Milw. Archdiocese, 1990, Herb Kohl Tchr. of Yr., Kohl Found., 1991, Art Tchr. of Yr., Francis Hook Scholarship Fund, 1993, Disting. Tchr., Presdl. Scholars Program, 1995; recipient tchr.-mentor, scholastic art awards Scholastic, Inc., 1994. Mem. Nat. Art Educators Assn., Wis. Art Educators Assn., Milw. Area Tchrs. of Art (past pres., bd. dirs. 1989—). Home: 4723 W Woodlawn Ct Milwaukee WI 53208-3656 Office: Pius XI H S 135 N 76th St Milwaukee WI 53213-3560

FREDERICK, PAULA F., health facility administrator; b. Portland, Oreg., Apr. 14, 1954; d. Robert Paul and Gertrude Agnes (Krein) F.; m. Stephen Wilson DeBruhl, Aug. 25, 1978 (div. 1992); children: Brandon Frederick DeBruhl, Colin Frederick DeBruhl. BA with honors, Portland State U., 1976, MS, MEd with honors, 1977. Cert. in mental health psycho-therapy Wash.; nat. cert. in addictions specialty (psycho-therapy). Rschr. F.U.D., Fairbanks, Alaska, 1977-80; tchr. Women's Ctr., Knoxville, Tenn., 1980-82; sr. psychotherapist Child and Family Svcs., Family Crisis Ctr., Knoxville, 1980-82; asst. adminstr. Comprehensive Care Corp. Care Unit Hosp., Kirkland, Wash., 1983-88; adminstr. Rader Inst., Auburn, Wash., 1988-93, Seattle, 1993—; rsch. asst. Portland (Oreg.) State U., 1976-77; cons. Vancouver (Wash.) Women's Ctr., 1978-80, Knoxville Women's Ctr., 1980-82; sec., treas., bd. dirs. Tenn. Victims of Abuse & Violence Coalition, Knoxville, 1981-82. Author, co-author publs. in field. Mem. ACA, State of Wash. Mental Health Counselors Assn. Office: Rader Inst of Wash Plz 451 SW 10th St Ste 100 Renton WA 98055

FREDERICK, SUSAN LOUISE, preschool educator; b. Somers Point, N.J., May 2, 1964; d. Ingeborg Louise (Böhmer) Kimbark; m. R. Scott Frederick, Oct. 6, 1984. BS in Edn. with honors, Millersville (Pa.) U., 1993. Cert. elem. and early childhood tchr. Graphic artist Datcon Instrument Co., East Petersburg, Pa., 1984-86; day care provider Small Steps Early Learning Ctr., Lancaster, Pa., 1986-89; substitute elem. tchr. Lancaster County Sch. Dists., 1993-94; elem. co-op tchr. Manheim Twp. Parent's Co-op, Lancaster, 1993, 95; day care provider Small Frey's Children's Ctr., Manheim, Pa., 1991-96; pre-kindergarten, presch. tchr. St. Peter's Presch., Lancaster, 1993—. Bd. of Christian edn. St. Paul's United Ch. of Christ, Manheim, Pa., 1985-87, co-dir. vacation bible sch., 1987; mem. Manheim Area Jaycees, 1988-89. Mem. ASCD, Phi Kappa Phi. Home: 125 E Ferdinand St Manheim PA 17545

FREDERICK, VIRGINIA FIESTER, state legislator; b. Rock Island, Ill., Dec. 24, 1916; d. John Henry and Myrtle (Montgomery) Heise; B.A., U. Iowa, 1938; postgrad. Lake Forest Coll., 1942-43, LLD, 1994; m. C. Donnan Fiester (dec. 1975); children—Sheryl Fiester Ross, Alan R., James D.; m. Kenneth Jacob Frederick, 1978. Free-lance fashion designer, Lake Forest, Ill., 1952-78; pres. Mid Am. China Exchange, Kenilworth, Ill., 1978-81; mem. Ill. Ho. of Reps., Springfield, 1979-95, asst minority leader, 1990-95. Alderman, first ward Lake Forest, 1974-78; del. World Food Conf., Rome, 1974; mem. Ill. Commn. on Status of Women subcom. pensions and employment, 1976-79; co-chmn. Conf. Women Legislators, 1982-85; bd. trustees Lake Forest Coll., 1995; city supr. City of Lake Forest, Ill., 1995-96. Named Chgo. Area Woman of Achievement, Internat. Orgn. Women Execs., 1978. Recipient Lottie Holman O'Neal award, 1980, Jane Addams award, 1982, Outstanding Legislator award Ill. Hosp. Assn., 1986, VFW Svc. award, 1988, Joyce Fitzgerald Meml. award, 1988, Susan B. Anthony Legislator of the Yr. award, 1989, award Delta Kappa Gamma, 1991, Outstanding Legislator award, 1995, Svcs. for Srs. award, Ill. Dept. Aging, 1991, Ethics in Pols. award, Rep. Women's Club, 1992, Woman of Achievement award YWCA North Eastern Ill., 1994, Ill. Women in Govt. award, 1994. Mem. LWV (local pres. 1958-60, state dir. 1969-75, mem. nat. com. 1975-76), AAUW (local pres. 1968-70, state pres. 1975-77, state dir. 1963-69, mem. nat. com. 1967-69, Legislator of Yr. award 1993), UN Assn. (dir.), Chgo. Assn. Commerce and Industry (dir.). Methodist. Home: 1290 N Western Ave Lake Forest IL 60045-1317

FREDERICKS, JOAN DELANOY, retired health science administrator; b. Dobbs Ferry, N.Y., Feb. 27, 1928; d. Robert Bert and Amelia (DeLanoy) F.; m. Stanley Whetstone, Mar. 20, 1993. BA, Skidmore Coll., Saratoga Springs, N.Y., 1949; MA, Syracuse U., 1954. Rsch. asst. C.F. Kettering Found., Yellow Springs, Ohio, 1949-50; rsch. tech. Syracuse (N.Y.) U. Med. Sch., 1950-54, Duke U. Med. Sch., Durham, N.C., 1954-58, NIH, Bethesda, Md., 1958-88; ret., 1988; chemist Nat. Inst. Arthritis and Metabolic Diseases, NIH, Bethesda, 1958-63, scientific grant asst. Nat. Inst. Heart, Lung and Blood Diseases, Bethesda, 1963-70, asst., program dir. Nat. Inst. Arthritis Metabolism and Digestive Diseases, 1970-81, exec. sec. div. Rsch. Grants, 1981-88; cons. in field. Vol. Sibley Meml. Hosp., Washington. Mem. Sumner Sq. Condominium Assn. (sec., v.p. 1988-92).

FREDERICKS, PATRICIA ANN, real estate executive; b. Durand, Mich., June 5, 1941; d. Willis Edward and Dorothy (Plowman) Sexton; m. Ward Arthur Fredericks, June 12, 1960; children: Corrine Ellen, Lorraine Lee, Ward Arthur II. BA, Mich. State U., 1962. Cert. Grad. Real Estate Inst., residential broker, residential salesperson; cert. real estate broker. Assoc. Stand Brough, Des Moines, 1976-80; broker Denton, Tuscon, 1980-83; broker-trainer Coldwell Banker, Westlake Village, Calif., 1984-90; broker, br. mgr. Brown, Newbury Park, Calif., 1990-94; dir. tng. Brown Real Estate, Westlake Village, Calif., 1994—; gen. mgr., dir. mktg. Coldwell Banker Town & Country Real Estate, Newbury Park, Calif., 1994—; dir. mktg. Coldwell Banker Town and Country, 1995—; bd. sec. Mixtec Corp., Thousand Oaks, 1984—. Contbr. articles to profl. jours. Pres. Inner Wheel, Thousand Oaks, 1991, 96-97; bd. dirs. Community Leaders Club, Thousand Oaks, 1991, Conejo Future Found., Thousand Oaks, 1989-92, Wellness Community Ventura Valley, 1994—. Mem. Calif. Assn. Realtors (dir. 1988-95 regional chairperson 1995, vice chairperson expn. 1997), Conejo Valley Assn. Realtors (sec., v.p., pres.-elect 1989-92, pres. 1993, Realtor of Yr. 1991), Pres.'s Club Mich. State U., Com. 100, Cmty. Concerts Assn., Alliance for the Arts, Conejo Valley Symphony Guild, Wellness Cmty., Indian Wells Country Club, North Ranch Country Club. Home: 171 E Thousand Oaks Blvd Thousand Oaks CA 91360 Office: Town and Country Coldwell Banker 2277 Michael Dr Newbury Park CA 91320-3340

FREDERICKS, SHARON KAY, nurses aide; b. Grand Rapids, Mich., July 12, 1942; d. Leroy and Edith Luella (Crawford) F. Cert. in Interior Decorating, LaSalle U., 1975; AAS, Community Svc. Asst., Kalamazoo Valley Coll., 1982; assoc. paralegal studies, Internat. Corr. Schs., Scranton, Pa., 1991; AAS in Bus. Mgmt., Davenport Coll., 1994. Cashier Goodwill Industries, Battle Creek, Mich., 1963; dishwasher Woolworths, Kalamazoo, 1963; nurses aide Mary L. Bocher, Kalamazoo, 1964-69, Sisters St. Joseph, Nazareth, Mich., 1976—; kitchen aide Saga Foods, Kalamazoo Valley C.C., 1981-82, Saga Foods, Nazareth Coll., 1983-84. Vol. Portage Ctrl. Jr. and Sr. High Sch., 1961-62, Bronson Meth. Hosp., Kalamazoo, 1961-62; vol. nurse aide ARC, 1964-69, Bloodmobiles, 1970-75, Borgess Med. Ctr., 1977; sec.-treas. 3d Order St. Francis Secular, 1976-79, pres., dir. pres. pub. rels. and bulls., 1979-81; participant neighborhood watch Vine Neighborhood, Kalamazoo, 1985-88; vol. Cath. Family Svcs., 1991—; vol., adminstrv. aide, Kalamazoo, 1991—; vol. monitor Kalamazoo Women's Festival, 1991, 92. Thomas F. Reed Jr. scholar Davenport Coll.; recipient John Edgar Hoover gold medal, 1991; named vol. of month, Kalamazoo Regional Psychiat. Hosp., July 1976; named vol. of week Catholic Family Svcs., Sept. 13, 1993, Oct. 1995. Mem. Nat. Spl. Child Advocates. Roman Catholic. Home: 2310 Inverness Ln Apt 204 Kalamazoo MI 49001-1459

FREDERIKSEN, MARILYNN ELIZABETH CONNERS, physician; b. Chgo., Sept. 12, 1949; d. Paul H. and Susanne (Ostergren) Conners; m. James W. Frederiksen, July 11, 1971; children: John Karl, Paul S., Britt L. BA, Cornell Coll., 1970; MD, Boston U., 1974. Diplomate Am. Bd. Ob-Gyn., Am. Bd. Maternal-Fetal Medicine, Am. Bd. Clin. Pharmacology. Pediat. intern U. Md. Hosp., 1974-75, resident in pediat., 1975-76; resident in ob-gyn. Boston Hosp. for women, 1976-79; fellow in maternal fetal medicine Northwestern U., 1979-81, fellow clin. pharmacology, 1981-83; instr. ob-gyn. Northwestern U., Chgo., 1981-83, asst. prof. ob-gyn., assoc. clin. pharmacology, 1983-91, assoc. prof. ob-gyn., assoc. in clin. pharmacology, 1991—, sect. chief gen. ob-gyn., 1993—; mem. gen. faculty com. Northwestern U., Chgo., 1994—, mem. ob-gyn. adv. panel, 1985—, U.S. Pharm. Com. Revision, Rockville, Md., 1986—; del. U.S. Pharm. conv. Northwestern U. Med. Sch., 1990, 95; bd. dirs. Northwestern Med. Faculty Found., 1995—; mem. gen. clinic rsch. ctr. com. NIH, 1989-93, chairperson, 1992-93; mem. Task Force Working Group on Asthma in Pregnancy Nat. Heart, Lung and Blood Inst., 1991-92. Mem. editorial bd. Clin. Pharmacology & Therapeutics, 1993; contbr. numerous articles to profl. jours. Bd. dirs. Cornell Coll. Alumni Assn., Mt. Vernon, Iowa, 1986-90, Northwestern Med. Faculty Found., 1995—. Recipient Pharm. Mfrs. Assn. Found. Faculty Devel. award, 1984-86, Civil Liberties award ACLU, 1991. Fellow Am. Coll. Ob-Gyn.; mem. Soc. Perinatal Obstetricians, Ctrl. Assn. Obstetricians and Gynecologists, Am. Med. Womens Assn., Am. Soc. Clin. Pharmacology and Therapeutics (chmn. sect. pediat. and perinatal pharmacology 1993-96, bd. dirs. 1994—), Chgo. Gynecologic Soc. (treas. 1994—), Phi Beta Kappa. Republican. Episcopalian. Home: 2002 Devon Ave Park Ridge IL 60068-4306 Office: Northwestern U 680 N Lake Shore Dr Ste 1000 Chicago IL 60611-4402

FREDERKING, KATHY HAHN, elementary school educator; b. Dodge City, Kans., Mar. 24, 1954; d. Donald and V. June (West) Hahn; m. Hal Frederking, Aug. 20, 1978; children: Jerrod, Joel, Emileigh. BS, Ft. Hays State U., 1975; MLS, Emporia State U., 1994. Cert. elem. edn. tchr., Kans. Tchr. Unified Sch. Dist. 328, Wilson, Kans., 1976-79, Unified Sch. Dist. 443, Dodge City, 1979—; bldg. rep. NEA, Dodge City, 1987-94; mem. tech. com. Unified Sch. Dist. 443, Dodge City, 1992-95. Co-dir. youth fellowship Holy Cross Luth. Ch., Dodge City, 1991—. Mem. Kans. Reading Assn. (co-chair state conf. April 1994, zone 5 coord. 1991—), Delta Kappa Gamma, Phi Delta Kappa. Republican. Lutheran.

FREDIANI, DIANE MARIE, graphic designer, interior designer; b. Bklyn., June 20, 1963; d. Albert Michael and Mary (Piantino) F. BFA in Graphic Design, Centenary Coll., 1985, teaching cert., 1991. Cert. graphic designer. Cashier, dept. supr. Reynolds, Hackettstown, N.J., 1982-85; window displays and promotions staff Reynolds, Hackettstown, 1985-86; clerical asst. AT&T, Basking Ridge, N.J., 1986-87; typesetter, bd. artist AT&T, Parsippany, N.J., 1988-89; project coord. interior design AT&T, Basking Ridge, 1989—; graphic designer St. Mary's Sch., Hackettstown, 1985—; nominee for White House Fellowship Com., 1994. Mem. Centenary Alumni Assn. (forensic judge oral speaking competitions 1993—). Roman Catholic. Home: 109 Pleasant View Rd Hackettstown NJ 07840-1017 Office: AT&T 295 N Maple Ave Basking Ridge NJ 07920-1002

FREDRICK, SUSAN WALKER, tax company manager; b. Painesville, Ohio, Nov. 17, 1948; d. Floyd Clayton and Margaret (Merkel) Walker; m. Stephan Douglas Fredrick, Oct. 20, 1973. BS, Mt. Union Coll., Alliance, Ohio, 1970; MS, U. Conn., 1973. Research asst. Boyce Thompson Inst., Yonkers, N.Y., 1971-74; dir. quality control Lawley, Matusky, Skelly, Tappan, N.Y., 1974-75; field supr. Ecological Analysts, Middletown, N.Y., 1975-76; scientist Pandullo Quirk Assocs., Wayne, N.J., 1976-78; editor Biosis. Info. Service, Phila., 1978-80; tax preparer H&R Block, Inc., King of Prussia, Pa., 1978-80; dist. mgr. H&R Block, Inc., Malvern, Pa., 1980—; guest lectr. Temple U., 1981-86. Mem. Nat. Assn. Enrolled Agts., Pa. Soc. Enrolled Agts., Nat. Assn. Underwater Instrs. (active instr.), Keystone Divers Club (West Chester, Pa.). Office: H&R Block Inc Great Valley Shopping Ctr # 18 Rtes 401 & 30 Malvern PA 19355

FREDRICKSON, LOLA JEAN, communications company executive; b. Mpls., Feb. 8, 1945; d. Clifford James Byron and Ardythe (Ellen) F. BS in Applied Art and Design, U. Minn., 1969, MS in Plant Scis. and Chemistry, 1969; MMI, Carlson Sch. of Mgmt., 1990. Editorial asst. dept. econs. U. Minn., Mpls., 1965-70; mem. faculty, rsch. asst., student advisor U. Minn., 1973-80; mgr. documentation control EG&G Idaho, Inc. at Idaho Nat. Engring. Lab., Idaho Falls, 1980-81; mgr. tech. publs. and indsl. security EG&G Washington Analytical Svcs. Ctr., Inc., Newport, R.I., 1981-84; tech. communications con. Mpls. and St. Paul, 1984-85; owner, pres. Fredrickson Communications, Inc., Mpls., 1985—; speaker in field. Contbr. numerous articles to profl. publs. Founder, pres., bd. dirs. Advantage Communications, Inc., 1986-91. Mem. Soc. for Tech. Communications, Mpls. Women's Rotary (bd. dirs. 1993—), Mpls. Women's Club, Gamma Sigma Delta. Office: Fredrickson Communications 119 N 4th St Ste 513 Minneapolis MN 55401-1792

FREDRIK, BURRY, theatrical producer, director; b. N.Y.C., Aug. 9, 1925; d. Fredric Kreuger and Erna Anita (Burry) Gerber; m. Gerard E. Meunier, Dec. 27, 1945 (div. 1949). Grad., Sarah Lawrence Coll., 1947. Ind. theatrical dir., producer U.S. and abroad, 1955—; lit. mgr., dir. Boston Post Road Stage Co., 1988-92; artistic dir. Fairfield County Stage Co. (formerly Boston Post Road Stage), 1992-93. Producer: (Broadway plays) Too Good To Be True, 1964-65 (nominated Tony award 1965), Travesties, 1975-76 (Tony award 1976), An Almost Perfect Person, 1977, The Night of the Tribades, 1978, To Grandmother's House We Go, 1981, The Royal Family, 1975-76, (off-Broadway plays) Thieves Carnival, 1955 (Spl. Tony award 1955), Exiles, 1956 (OBIE award 1956), Buried Child (Pulitzer prize 1980); dir.: (nat. tours) Misalliance, 1953, Milk and Honey, 1963, Dark at the Top of the Stairs, 1958, Dear Love, 1971, To Grandmother's House We Go, 1982, (off-Broadway prodns.) The Decameron, 1961, Catholic School Girls, 1981, (Broadway prodn.) Wild and Wonderful, 1972. Home: 51 Hillside Rd N Weston CT 06883-1513

FREE, ANN COTTRELL, writer; b. Richmond, Va.; d. Emmett Drewry and Emily (Blake) Cottrell; m. James Stillman Free, Feb. 24, 1950; 1 child, Elissa. Grad. Collegiate Sch. for Girls, Richmond, 1934; student Richmond div. Coll. William and Mary, 1934-36; AB, Barnard Coll. Columbia U., 1938. Reporter Richmond Times Dispatch, 1938-40; Washington corr., Newsweek, 1940-41, Chgo. Sun, 1941-43, N.Y. Herald Tribune, 1943-46; pub. info. dir. UNRRA China Mission, Shanghai, 1946-47; corr. Middle and Nr. East and Europe, 1947-48; writer-photographer Marshall Plan, Washington and Western Europe, 1949-50; Washington corr. N.Am. Newspaper Alliance, 1955-80; contbg. editor Between the Species; contbr. newspapers and mags., including Washington Star and Washington Post; Washington editor EnviroSouth Quar., 1977-82; pres. Flying Fox Press. Mem. Friends of the Rachel Carson Nat. Wildlife Refuge (hon. founding mem.); chmn. Mrs. Roosevelt's Press Conf. Assn., 1943; cons. expert Rachel Carson Coun.; v.p. Vieques (P.R.) Humane Soc.; coord. Albert Schweitzer Summer Fellows Program; bd. dirs. Albert Schweitzer Fellowship; pres. Albert Schweitzer Coun. on Animals and Environment. Recipient Dodd Mead-Boys' Life Writing award, 1963, Albert Schweitzer medal, Animal Welfare Inst., 1963, Jr. Book award certificate Boys Clubs of Am., 1964; Humanitarian of Yr. awards Washington Animal Rescue League, 1971, Montgomery County Humane Soc., 1971, Washington Humane Soc., 1983, News Writing award Dog Writers Assn. Am., 1975, 78, Rachel Carson Legacy award, 1987, Disting. Alumni award The Collegiate Schs., 1992, Cert. Appreciation Dept. of Interior Fish and Wildlife Svc. and Rachel Carson Nat. Wildlife Refuge, 1995; recognition Dept. Interior, 1970; inducted Va. Comms. Hall of Fame, 1996. Mem. Soc. Woman Geographers, Nat. Press Club, Am. News Women's Club. Author: Forever the Wild Mare, 1963, Animals, Nature and Albert Schweitzer, 1982, No Room, Save in the Heart, 1987, Since Silent Spring: Our Debt to Albert Schweitzer and Rachel Carson, 1992. Home: 4700 Jamestown Rd Bethesda MD 20816-2923 also: Lantz Mill Edinburg VA 22824

FREE, HELEN MAE, chemist, consultant; b. Pitts., Feb. 20, 1923; d. James Summerville and Daisy (Piper) Murray; m. Alfred H. Free, Oct. 18, 1947; children: Eric, Penny, Kurt, Jake, Bonnie, Nina. BA in Chemistry, Coll. of Wooster, Ohio, 1944, DSc (hon.), 1992; MA in Clin. Lab. Mgmt., Ctrl. Mich. U., 1978, DSc (hon.), 1993. Cert. clin. chemist Nat. Registry Clin. Chemistry. Chemist Miles Labs., Elkhart, Ind., 1944-78, dir. mktg. svcs. rsch. products div., 1978-82, chemist, mgr., cons. diagnostics divsn. Bayer Corp., 1982—; mem. adj. faculty Ind. U., South Bend, 1975—. Author: (with others) Urodynamics and Urinalysis in Clinical Laboratory Practice, 1972, 76. Contbr. articles to profl. jours. Patentee in field. Women's chmn. Centennial of Elkhart, 1958. Recipient Disting. Alumni award Coll. of Wooster, 1980, award Medi Econ. Press, 1986, Lab. Pub. Svc. Nat. Leadership award, 1994; named to Hall of Excellence, Ohio Found. Ind. Colls., 1992; named Woman of Yr. YWCA, 1993; Killy Found. laureate, 1996. Fellow AAAS, Am. Inst. Chemists (co-recipient Chicago award 1967), Royal Soc. Chemistry; mem. Am. Chem. Soc. (pres. 1993, bd. dirs., chmn. Chemistry Week task force, bd. com. pub. affairs and pub. rels., chmn. women chemists com. internat. activities com., grants and awards com., profl. and member relations com., nominating com., council policy pub. affairs and budget, Service award local chpt. 1981, councilor; Garvan medal 1980, co-recipient Mosher award, 1983, (first recipient) Helen M. Free Pub. Outreach award, 1995, Helen M. Free award named in honor 1995), Am. Assn. for Clin. Chemistry (council, bd. dirs., nominating com. and pub. relations com., nat. membership chmn., profl. affairs coordinator, pres.), Assn. Clin. Scientists (diploma of honor 1992), Am. Soc. Clin. Lab. Sci. (chmn. assembly, Achievement award 1976), Nat. Com. Clin. Lab. Standards (bd. dirs.), Soc. Chem. Industry (hon.), Iota Sigma Pi (hon.), Sigma Delta Epsilon (hon.). Presbyterian. Lodge: Altrusa (pres. 1982-83, bd. dirs.). Home: 3752 E Jackson Blvd Elkhart IN 46516-5205 Office: Bayer Corp Diagnostics Divsn 1884 Miles Ave Elkhart IN 46514

FREE, MARY MOORE, anthropologist; b. Paris, Tex., Mar. 6, 1933; d. Dudley Crawford and Margie Lou (Moore) Hubbard; m. Dwight Allen Free Jr., June 26, 1954 (dec.); children: Hardy (dec.), Dudley (dec.), Margery, Caroline. BS, So. Meth. U., 1954, MLA, 1981, MA, 1987, PhD, 1989. Instr. So. Meth. U., Dallas, 1982-89, prof. continuing edn., 1989-90, prof. Dedman Coll., 1990—, adj. asst. prof. dept. anthropology, 1990—; prof. Richland C.C., Dallas, 1986; house anthropologist Baylor U. Med. Ctr., Dallas, 1990—; adv. bd. geriatrics Vis. Nurse Assn., Dallas, 1984-91; presenter in field anthropology, medicine; bd. Dedman Coll. SMU Excellence in Sci. Lecture Series. Author: The Private World of the Hermitage: Lifestyles of the Rich and Old in an Elite Retirement Home, 1995; contbr. chpts. in sci. books, ednl. TV, and articles to Anthropology Newsletter, Am. Anthropologist, Am. Jour. Cardiology, Cahiers de Sociologie Economique et Culturelle-Ethnopsycholie, Jour. Heart Failure, Jour. Internat. Soc. Dermatology, other profl. jours.; mem. editl. bd. Baylor U. Med. Ctr. Procs. Bd. dirs. New Hearts & Lungs, Baylor Med. Ctr., 1994; active various svc. and social orgns. Named one of Notable Women of Tex., 1984. Fellow Am. Anthrop. Assn., Inst. for Study of Earth and Man; mem. AAAS, Internat. Soc. Heart Failure (sci. adv. bd.), Dallas Women's Club, Dallas Petroleum Club, Brook Hollow Golf Club, Pi Beta Phi. Methodist. Home: 4356 Edmondson Ave Dallas TX 75205-2602 Office: Baylor U Med Ctr 3500 Gaston Ave Dallas TX 75246-2045

FREECE, DEBBIE ANN, trade association executive; b. Dayton, Ohio; d. Lloyd M. and Dorothy E. (Deblin) Cannon; m. Eric W. Freece; children: Ian C., Katclyn A. BSN, Ohio State U., 1974, MS, 1979. Cert. gerontol. nurse ANCC. DON Arlington Ct. Nursing Home, Columbus, Ohio, 1974-78; project dir. Ohio Dept. Health, Columbus, 1979-82; pvt. practice geriatric nurse cons. Columbus, 1983-91; exec. dir. Mid-Ohio Dist. Nurses Assn., Columbus, 1991—; cons. Ohio Tchg. Network, Columbus, 1987-90, Ohio Health Care Bd., Columbus, 1993-95, Legis. Study Com., Columbus, 1993-95. Pres. Evangelical Luth. Ch. Women Ascension Luth. Ch., Columbus, 1985-88, pres. presch. bd., 1990-93. Mem. Ohio Nurses Assn. (del. 1995—, Dorothy A. Cornelius Leadership fellow 1995), Alpha Tau Delta Epsilon Pi (sec. 1990-95), Sigma Theta Tau. Republican. Office: Mid-Ohio Dist Nurses Assn 1460 W Lane Ave Columbus OH 43221

FREED, RITA EVELYN, curator, Egyptologist, educator; b. Newark, June 29, 1952; d. Samuel David and Gertrude (Houseman) F. BA in Classical and Nr. Ea. Archaeology, Bibl. Studies, Wellesley Coll.; cert. in museology, NYU, MA, PhD. Exhbn. asst. Egypt's minor arts Mus. Fine Arts, Boston, 1978-82, curator dept. Ancient Egyptian, Nubian and Near Ea. Art, 1989—; curator Egyptian exhbn. univ. gallery Memphis State U., 1983, curator Egyptian antiquities, founding dir., 1984-89, assoc. prof. dept. art, 1983-89; adj. prof. Wellesley Coll., 1991—; part-time rsch. asst. dept. Egyptian and classical art Bklyn. Mus., 1976-78; rschr. Egyptian dept. Met. Mus. Art, 1977-78, lectr. dept. pub. edn., 1978; lectr. art Adelphi U., 1978-79; mem. archaeol. survey team Idalion Excavations, Dhali, Cyprus, 1973; site supr. excavation of Philistine temple, Tel Qasile, Tel Aviv, 1973; field archaeologist expdn. photographer Mendes Excavations, Ea. Delta, Egypt, 1977; small finds registrar Memphis Excavations, Mitrahineh, Egypt, 1988; epigrapher Giza Mastabas Project, Egypt, 1989; co-project dir. Boston-Penn Expdn., Bersheh, Egypt, 1990, Saqqara, Egypt, 1992—. Contbr. articles and revs. to profl. jours. and books; author exhbn. catalogues. Ford Found. fellow, Slater Fgn. Study fellow; Trustee fellow and Durant scholar of Wellesley Coll.; NSF rsch. grantee. Mem. Am. Rsch. Ctr. in Egypt (bd. govs.), Soc. for Study Egyptian Antiquities, Egypt Exploration Soc., Egyptological Seminar, Internat. Assn. Egyptologists (N.Am. rep.), Internat. Coun. Mus. (Am. rep.), Am. Assn. Mus., Phi Beta Kappa. Jewish. Office: Mus Fine Arts 465 Huntington Ave Boston MA 02115-5523

FREED, RUTH S., anthropologist; Prof. anthropology Seton Hall U., South Orange, N.J., 1971-81, research assoc. Am. Mus. Natural History, N.Y.C., 1975—. Co-author (with Stanley A. Freed): Man From the Beginning, 1967, Shanti Nagar: The Effects of Urbanization in a Village in North India, vol. I, Social Organization, 1976, vol. II, Aspects of Economy, Technology and Ecology, 1978, vol. III, Sickness and Health, 1979; Rites of Passage in Shanti Nagar, 1980, Enculturation and Education in Shanti Nagar, 1981, The Psychomedical Case History of a Low Caste Woman of North India, 1985, Fertility, Sterilization, and Population Growth in Shanti Nagar, India: A Longitudinal Ethnographic Approach, 1985, Uncertain Revolution: Panchayati Raj and Democratic Elections in a North Indian Village, 1987, Ghosts: Life and Death in North India, 1993. Office: Am Mus Natural History Dept Anthropology Central Park West at 79th St New York NY 10026

FREEDGOOD, ANNE GOODMAN, editor; b. Mount Vernon, N.Y., Mar. 24, 1917; d. Jules Eckert and Mai Farr (Pfouts) Goodman; widowed; 1 child, Julia. B.A., Bryn Mawr Coll., 1938. Writer Office War Info., London, Paris, Munich, 1944-46; book editor N.Y. Star, N.Y.C., 1949-50; editor Harpers Mag., N.Y.C., 1950-58, Doubleday, N.Y.C., 1958-71, Random House, N.Y.C., 1971-87; cons. editor Summit Books, N.Y.C., 1988-91; sr. editor Harcourt Brace, N.Y.C., 1991-93; editor-at-large William Morrow & Co., N.Y.C., 1994—. Author short stories; contbr. articles to various publs. Home: 425 Riverside Dr New York NY 10025-7775

FREEDLENDER, SUSAN See HOMESTEAD, SUSAN E.

FREEDMAN, ANNE BELLER, public speaking and marketing consultant; b. Gardner, Mass., June 22, 1949; d. Gabriel Philip Freedman and Natalie Engler (Beller) Lyons; m. Edward A. Fischer, May 20, 1979; 1 child, Lynne Heather. BSJ U. Fla., 1971. Staff writer Coral Gables Times, Miami, 1972-73; reporter Miami News, 1973-74; assoc. editor Miami Phoenix, 1974-75; freelance writer, Miami, 1975-80; corr. Advt. Age, Miami, 1977-81; pres. Exec. S.O.S., Inc., Miami, 1980-90; pres. Speak Out, Inc., Coral Gables, 1990—; ptnr. Speak Out/Lewison-Singer, Inc., Coral Gables, 1991-94; instr. Fla. Internat. U. Producer cable TV show Not For Women Only, 1992, pub. rels., 1990-92; author: Unforgettable Speeches and Presentations in 8 Easy Steps, 1991, rev. edit. 1996; mem. edit. bd. Enterprising Woman Mag., 1996—. Bd. dirs. Miami/Bogota-Calé Sister Cities Program, 1983-85; host Focus South Cable TV Show, 1990-91; mem. steerin com. Fla. Internat. U. Coun. of 100. Mem. South Miami/Kendall C. of C. (editor monthly newsletter 1980-83, dir., 1982-85, chmn. bus. com. 1985-89, editor ann. directory and buyer's guide 1986-87, 89—, Presdl. award 1983, 89), Nat. Assn. Women Bus. Owners (chair public relations 1981, dir. tng. and devel. 1987—, chmn. corp. ptnrs., v.p. 1989-91, co-chmn. Recognition awards, 1992, pub. rels. chair 1990-93, dir. tng. and devel. 1993-94, exec. chair 1994—, established bus. chair 1995-96, bd. dirs.), Coral Gables C. of C. (chmn., dir. 1993—, mem. edit. bd. 1995-96), Greater Miami C. of C. Clubs: Toastmasters (pres. 1984). Home: 6721 SW 113th Pl Miami FL 33173-1954 Office: 1541 Sunset Dr Ste 201 Coral Gables FL 33143

FREEDMAN, AUDREY WILLOCK, economist; b. Cleve., Nov. 25, 1929; d. Sylvester Rhodes and Hilda Louise (Reiber) Willock; m. Monroe H. Freedman, Sept. 24, 1950; children: Alice, Sarah, Caleb, Judah. BA in Econs., Wellesley Coll., 1951. Staff economist Communication Workers Am., AFL-CIO, Washington, 1958-60; staff economist Bur. Labor Stats., U.S. Dept. Labor, Washington, 1961-67, staff economist Manpower Adminstrn., 1968-71; mem. policy staff Cost of Living Coun., liaison U.S. Pay Bd., Washington, 1971-72; sr. cons. Orgn. Resources Counselors, N.Y.C., 1973-75; sr. rsch. assoc. Conf. Bd., N.Y.C., 1976-92; pres. Audrey Freedman & Assocs., N.Y.C., 1992—; chmn. bus. rsch. adv. coun., U.S. Bur. Labor Stats., 1992-94; bd. dirs. Manpower, Inc., mem. compensation com., 1991—; frequent TV commentator, spkr. in field. Author: Security Bargains Reconsidered, 1978, Managing Labor Relations, 1979, Industry Response to Health Risk, 1981, The Changing Human Resource Function, 1991, Contingent Work and the Role of Labor Market Intermediaries, 1996; author (annual) The Human Resources Forecast, 1996, (monthly newsletter) Unconventional Wisdom, 1996. Recipient Disting. Svc. award U.S. Dept. Labor, 1967, Presdl. citation, 1972. Mem. Am. Fedn. Govt. Employees (v.p. local chpt. 1965-68, chmn. civil rights com. 1964-69), Am. Econ. Assn., Indsl. Rels. Rsch. Assn. Jewish. Home: 30-49 79th St Flushing NY 11370-1509 Office: 111 Broadway Fl 5 New York NY 10006-1901

FREEDMAN, GAIL, financial analyst; b. Oyster Bay, N.Y., Dec. 26, 1963; d. Noble Aubrey and Dorothy Ann Langille; m. Jonathan Eric Freedman, Oct. 23, 1993. BA in Polit. Sci., Bethany (W.Va.) Coll., 1986; MBA in Mktg. and Fin., U. So. Calif., 1992; student, UCLA, 1996—. Cert. in healthcare mgmt. Legis. intern legis. affairs Dept. Treasury, Washington, 1985, adminstrv. asst. adminstrn., 1986, rsch. asst. legis. affairs, 1986-88; spl. asst. Congressman Thomas McMillen, Washington, 1988; sr. legal asst. Pepper, Hamilton & Scheetz, Washington, 1988-90; cons. L.A. County Dept. Transp., 1990-91; licensing intern Applause Co., Woodland Hills, Calif., 1991; mgr. rsch. unit Tobacco Control Program, L.A., 1992-93; fin. analyst L.A. County Dept. Health Svcs., PHP Fin. Mgmt., 1993-95, PacifiCare of Calif, Cypress, 1995—; mentor to students U. So. Calif. Grad. Sch. Bus., L.A., 1991—. Author: (poetry) Fortnight, 1981, The Harbinger, 1985; author commentary newspaper The Tower, 1985-86. Founder, singer Sunday Sound, L.A., 1993—. Mem. U. So. Calif. Commerce Assn., Healthcare Fin. Mgmt. Assn., Kappa Delta Konnection. Home: 512 S Ogden Dr Los Angeles CA 90036-3231 Office: PacifiCare of Calif 5701 Katella Ave Cypress CA 90630

FREEDMAN, JUDITH GREENBERG, state senator, importer; b. Bridgeport, Conn., Mar. 11, 1939; d. Samuel Howard and Dorothy (Hoffman) G.; m. Samuel Sumner, Dec. 24, 1964; 1 child, Martha Ann. Student, Boston U., 1957-58, U. Mich., 1958-59; BS, So. Conn. State U., 1961, MS, 1972. Tchr. Hollywood (Fla.) Pub. Schs., 1961-62, White Plains (N.Y.) Pub. Schs., 1962-64, Wilton (Conn.) Pub. Schs., 1964-66; tchr. Weston (Conn.) Pub. Schs., 1966-72, tutor, 1977-80, tchr., 1982-84; owner Judith's Fancy, Westport, Conn., 1984—; mem. Conn. Senate, 1987-88; ranking mem. human svcs. com., 1987-88, ins. com., 1987-88, ranking mem. appropriations com., 1989-94, chmn. program rev. and investigation, 1992-94, chmn. commn. on innovation and productivity, 1994—; dep. pres. pro tem Conn. State Senate, 1995—, chmn. edn. com., 1995—. Pres., v.p. 4th Congl. Rep. Women's Assn., 1976-80; pres. Rep. Women of Westport, 1976-79; mem. Bd. Edn., Westport, 1983-87, 89—; treas. Conn. Order Women Legislators. Mem. Order of Women Legislators (treas.). Jewish. Home: 17 Crawford Rd Westport CT 06880-1823

FREEDMAN, KERRY JO, art educator; b. Chgo., July 21, 1954; d. Arthur Jacob and Sally Ann F.; m. Arthur Lawrence Norberg. BFA, U. Ill., 1977, MA, 1980; PhD, U. Wis., 1985. Art tchr. Blue Island (Ill.) Pub. Schs., 1977-79; instr. Fedn. Art Sch., Champaign, Ill., 1980, U. Ill. Art Sch. for Gifted High Sch. Students, 1981; grad. asst. U. Wis., Madison, 1981-85; asst. prof. U. Minn., Mpls., 1985-92, assoc. prof., 1992—; adv. bd. Walker Art Ctr., Mpls., 1985-94, Jour. of Art and Design Edn., U.K., 1994-98. Co-author: Postmodern Art Education: An Approach to Curriculum, 1996, Transforming Computer Technology: Information Processing for the Pentagon, 1996; contbr. articles to profl. jours. Named to Outstanding Young Women of Am., 1982; fellow Ohio State U., 1989-90, Charles Babbage Inst., 1989-90. Mem. Am. Ednl. Rsch. Assn. (officer arts and learning 1989-92), Nat. Art Edn. Assn. (editorial bd. studies in art edn., 1993-97), Internat. Soc. for Edn. Through Art, U.S. Soc. for Edn. Through Art, ASCD. Office: Univ Minn 159 Pillsbury Dr SE Minneapolis MN 55455-0208

FREEDMAN, MARYANN SACCOMANDO, lawyer; b. Buffalo, Sept. 12, 1934; d. James Vincent and Rosaria (Rizzo) Saccomando; m. Robert Paul Freedman, Apr. 9, 1961; children: Brenda Marie, Donald Vincent. JD, U. Buffalo, 1958. Bar: N.Y. 1959, U.S. Dist. Ct. (we. dist.) N.Y. 1959, U.S. Supreme Ct. 1963. Law clk. Saperston McNaughton & Saperston, Buffalo, 1957-59, assoc., 1959-61; ptnr. Freedman & Freedman, Buffalo, 1961-75; confidential legal rsch. asst. Buffalo City Ct., 1972-75; asst. atty. gen. N.Y. State Dept. Law, Buffalo, 1975-77; confidential law clk., matrimonial referee N.Y. State Supreme Ct., Buffalo, 1977-90; spl. counsel Lavin & Kleiman, 1991-95; of counsel Cohen & Lombardo, P.C., Buffalo, 1995—; asst. prof. Erie Community Coll., Buffalo, 1975-76; lectr. Erie County Emergency Med. Technician Program, Buffalo, 1975-83, Buffalo and Erie County Police Acad., 1975-86. Bd. editors N.Y. State Bar Jour. Trustee, YWCA, Buffalo, 1982-85; chmn. United Way Task Force on Legal Svcs., Buffalo, 1983; chair Buffalo Philharm. Orch. Stabilization Com., 1991-94; mem. dean's adv. coun. sch. law State U. Buffalo, 1991-93; bd. dirs. Downtown Nursing Home, Buffalo, 1982-91, Better Bus. Bur., Buffalo, 1983-92. Recipient Buffalo Bison award City of Buffalo, 1976, Legal Svcs. for Elderly and Handicapped Award, 1986, SUNY Buffalo Disting. Alumni award, 1986, Hilbert Coll. Pres.'s medal, 1987, Wise Woman award Nat. Orgn. Italian-Am. Women, 1987, Barrister award Nat. Columbus Day Com., 1987, Westchester Legal Svcs. award, 1987; named Outstanding Woman in Law, U. Buffalo Community Adv. Council, 1984, Outstanding Citizen Buffalo News, 1986, Disting. Alumnus, U. Buffalo Law Alumni, 1988, Woman of Yr., Buffalo Philharm. Orch., 1993. Mem. ABA (ho. dels. 1986—), N.Y. State Bar Assn. (pres. elect, chair ho. of dels. 1986-87, pres. 1987-88, Ruth G. Schapiro award 1994), Erie County Bar Assn. (pres. 1981-82, Spl. Svc. award 1984, Lawyer of Yr. 1987), Cattaraugus County Bar Assn. (Law Day award 1986), Aid to Indigent Prisoners Soc. (pres. 1981-82), Women Lawyers Assn. Western N.Y. (pres. 1962-64), N.Y. State Bar Found. (bd. dirs., v.p. 1994—). Clubs: Zonta (pres. 1978-79, area dir. dist. IV, 1982-83, 79-80). Office: 343 Elmwood Ave Buffalo NY 14222

FREEDMAN, SANDRA WARSHAW, former mayor; b. Newark, Sept. 21, 1943; m. Michael J. Freedman; 3 children. BA in Govt., U. Miami, 1965. Mem. Tampa (Fla.) City Coun., 1974—, chmn., 1983-86; mayor City of Tampa, 1986-95. Bd. dirs. Jewish Community Ctr., 1974-75, Boys and Girls Clubs Greater Tampa, Hillsborough Coalition for Health, Tampa Community Concert Assn.; mem. sports adv. bd. Hillsborough Community Coll., 1975-76; sec. Downtown Devel. Authority, 1977-78; bd. dirs., v.p. Fla. Gulf Coast Symphony, 1979-80; vice chmn. Met. Planning Orgn., 1981-82; corp. mem. Neighborhood Housing Service; bd. fellows U. Tampa; mem. steering com. Hillsborough County Council of Govt.'s Constituency for Children; mem. exec. bd. Tampa/Hillsborough Young Adult Forum; chmn. bd. trustees Berkeley Prep. Sch.; trustee Tampa Bay Performing Arts Ctr., Inc., Tampa Mus.; mem. ethics com. Meml. Hosp.; mem. Tampa Preservation, Inc., Tampa/Hillsborough County Youth Council, Davis Islands Civic Assn., Tampa Hist. Soc., Met. Ministries Adv. Bd., Rodeph Sholom Synagogue, Sword of Hope Guild of Am. Cancer Soc., Friends of the Arts. Recipient Spessar L. Holland Meml. award Tampa Bay Com. for Good Govt., 1975-76, Human Rights award City of Tampa, 1980, award Soroptimist Internat. Tampa, 1981, Status of Women award Zonta of Tampa II, 1986, Woman of Achievement award Bus. & Profl. Women, Jewish Nat. Fund Tree of Life award, Disting. Citizen award U. South Fla., 1995, Nat. Conf. of Christian and Jews Humanitarian award, 1995; named to Fla. Home Builders Hall of Fame. Mem. Hillsborough County Bar Aux., Greater Tampa C. of C., C. of C. Com. of 100 (exec. com.), Fla. League of Cities (bd. dirs.), Tampa Urban League, Nat. Council Jewish Women, U. Miami Alumni Assn., Athena Soc., Hadassah. Office: 3435 Bayshore Blvd #700 Tampa FL 33629

FREEDMAN, SARAH WARSHAUER, education educator; b. Wilmington, N.C., Feb. 23, 1946; d. Samuel Edward and Miriam (Miller) Warshauer; m. S. Robert Freedman, Aug. 20, 1967; 1 child, Rachel Karen. BA in English, U. Pa., 1967; MA in English, U. Chgo., 1970; MA in Linguistics, Stanford U., 1976, PhD in Edn., 1977. Tchr. English Phila. Sch. Dist., 1967-68, Lower Merion High Sch., 1968-69; instr. English U. N.C., Wilmington, 1970-71; instr. English and Linguistics Stanford Univ., 1972-76; asst. and assoc. prof. English San Francisco State Univ., 1977-81; asst. prof. Edn. Univ. Calif., Berkeley, 1981-83, assoc. prof. Edn., 1983-89; dir. Nat. Ctr. for the Study of Writing and Literacy, 1985—; prof. Edn. Univ. Calif., 1989—; cons. Nat. Bd. of Profl. Teaching Standards, 1993; mem. nat. adv. bd. Children's TV Workshop program Ghostwriter, Nat. Standards in English Lang. Arts, 1993-94. Author: Exchanging Writing, Exchanging Cultures, Lessons in School Reform from the United States and Great Britain, 1994, Response to Student Writing, 1987; editor: The Acquisition of Written Language: Response and Revision, 1985; contbr. chpts. to books and articles to profl. jours. Recipient Richard Meade award for Pub. Rsch. in Tchr. Edn. Nat. Coun. Tchrs. English, 1989, 94; fellow Nat. Conf. on Rsch. in English, 1986; Rockefeller Found. grantee Bryn Mawr Coll., 1992, Nat. Ctr. for Study of Writing and Literacy grantee Office Ednl. Rsch. and Improvement, 1985-95, Minority Undergrad. Rsch. Program grantee U. Calif., 1988, 89, 92, 93, numerous other grants. Mem. Nat. Coun. Tchrs. English (mem. standing com. on rsch. 1981-87, ex-officio 1987—, chair bd. trustees rsch. found. 1990-93), Am. Ednl. Rsch. Assn. (chair spl. interest group on rsch. in writing 1983-85, numerous other coms.), Linguistic Soc. Am., Am. Assn. Applied Linguistics, Internat. Reading Assn. Office: U Calif Dept Edn Berkeley CA 94720

FREEMAN, ANNE FRANCES, artist; b. Milw., Sept. 13, 1936; d. Edward Joseph and Agatha Gertrude (Mihm) Huether; m. John Henry Freeman, June 27, 1964; children: John Edward, Robert William. BA, Elmira Coll., 1964. Rsch. assoc. The Corning (N.Y.) Mus. Glass, 1957-59, coord. ednl. svcs., 1959-61, curator edn., 1962-63; freelance graphic artist, writer Corning Glass Works, 1963-64; asst. to dir. communications & employee rels. Crouse Hinds Corp., Syracuse, N.Y., 1964-65; freelance artist Southborough, Mass., 1977—; tchr., jr. curator The Corning Mus. Glass, 1961-63, editor jr. curator's newsletter, 1961-63. Author: Glass and Man, 1962. Chair Southborough Sch. Bd., 1976-77, Algonquin Regional High Sch. Com. Bd., Northborough, Mass., 1978-79; treas. Southborough Cultural Arts Coun., 1983-85, chmn., 1986. Mem. Friends of Southborough Arts Ctr., ARTS Worcester. Roman Catholic.

FREEMAN, CORINNE, financial services, former mayor; b. N.Y.C., Nov. 9, 1926; d. Bernard J. Hirschfeld and Sidonie (Daxe) Lichtenstein; m. Michael S. Freeman, Mar. 14, 1948; children: Michael L., Stephan J. Adelphi Coll. Sch. Nursing, 1944-47. RN, N.Y., Mass. Nurse numerous hosps. in N.Y. and Mass., 1948-64; mayor St. Petersburg, Fla., 1977-85; mem. Pinellas County Sch. Bd., St. Petersburg, Fla., 1989—; fin. advisor Prudential Securities; bd. dirs. Creativity in Child Care. Chmn. Social Svc. Allocations Com., St. Petersburg, 1972-76, City Budget Rev. Com., 1973-76, Youth Svc. System, Pinellas County, 1975-76, West Coast Regional Water Supply Authority; past mem. community redevel. com. U.S. Conf. of Mayors; past pres. Fla. League Cities; past mem. Pinellas County Mayors Coun.; past mem. Nat. League of Cities Revenue and Fin. Task Force; pres. LWV, St. Petersburg, 1970-72, 75-76; trustee Fire Pension Bd., St. Petersburg, 1989-92, Bayfront Med. Ctr.; adv. com. Jr. League St. Petersburg, 1990-92. Recipient Disting. Alumni award Adelphi U. Mem. Fla. Nursing Assn. Republican. Home: 2101 Pelham Rd N Saint Petersburg FL 33710-3659 Office: 5858 Central Ave Saint Petersburg FL 33707-1728

FREEMAN, ELAINE LAVALLE, sculptor; b. Boston, May 22, 1929; d. John and Ellen (Tufts) Lavalle; m. Felix Joachim Freeman, Jr., June 16, 1951 (div. 1974); children: John Lavalle, William Baker, Ellen Candler. Student, NAD, 1973, Art Students League, N.Y.C., 1947-49, 70-73; BA, Fordham U., 1986. Profl. sculptor N.Y.C. and Southampton, N.Y., 1973—; instr. sculpture Sculpture Ctr. Sch., N.Y.C., 1977-81; vol. gallery asst. Sculpture Ctr., N.Y.C., 1979—; exec. com., sec., bd. trustees Sculpture Ctr., N.Y.C., 1985—; mem. Catherine Lorillard Wolfe Art Club, N.Y.C., Southampton (N.Y.) Artists. One woman shows include Wheeler Gallery, Providence, 1979, Sculpture Ctr., N.Y.C., 1977, Southampton Gallery, N.Y.C., 1975; exhibited in group shows including Nat. Acad., Audubon Artists, Allied Artists, Parrish Mus., Nat. Arts Club, Am. Standard Corp. Gallery, Sculpture Ctr. Gallery, Huntington Twp. Art League, East Edn Arts Coun., 1973—. Bd. dirs. Southampton Fresh Air Home for Crippled Children, 1980-86, sec., 1981-83, treas. 1980. Recipient Judges award Parrish Art Mus., Southampton, 1974, Am. Carving Sch. award Allied Arts, N.Y.C., 1977, Anna Huntington Hyatt award Catherine Lorillard Wolfe Art Club, N.Y.C., 1983, 1st prize sculpture Catherine Lorillard Wolfe Art Club, 1994. Mem. Southampton Bathing Corp., Colony Club, Meadow Club. Democrat. Episcopalian. Home: 119 W 77th St New York NY 10024-6927

FREEMAN, JANET L., librarian; b. Winston-Salem, N.C., Nov. 5, 1946; d. Vernon Charles and Lula M. (McHan) F. BA, U. N.C., Greensboro, 1969; MLS, George Peabody Coll. Tchrs., 1971. Ref. libr. Ga. Southwestern Coll., Americus, 1971-73; tech. svcs. libr. Furman U., Greenville, S.C., 1973-75; dir. libr. svcs. Wingate (N.C.) Coll., 1975-84; coll. libr. Meredith Coll., Raleigh, N.C., 1984—. Mem. ALA, N.C. Libr. Assn. (bd. dirs. 1987-89, pres.-elect. 1989-91, pres. 1991-93), Southeastern Libr. Assn. Home: 2774 Rue Sans Famille Raleigh NC 27607-3051 Office: Meredith Coll 3800 Hillsborough St Raleigh NC 27607-5237

FREEMAN, LAURETTA BRANDES, early childhood education educator, consultant; b. Bklyn., Dec. 24, 1922; d. Sol and Lena (Einhorn) Brandes; m. Lawrence Collier Freeman, June 25, 1946; children: James Robert, Scott Nathaniel. BA, Hunter Coll., 1943; MA, Columbia U., 1947. Cert. nursery-3d grade tchr., N.Y. Tchr. N.Y.C. Pub. Sch., 1944-48, N.J. Pub. Sch., 1948-49, 50-51; dir. Montclair (N.J.) Coop. Sch. Inc., 1964-86; instr. Montclair State U., 1979—, Kean Coll., Union, N.J., 1995—; cons. Ctr. for Ednl. Svc., Glen Ridge, N.J., 1989—, Partnership Group Inc., Pa., 1989—, Performance Evaluation Project, N.J. State Dept., 1970-76; mentor Nat. Acad. Early Childhood Programs, 1990—; nat. rep. coun. Early Childhood Recognition, 1986—. Co-author: Daisy, 1995. Mem. Women's Internat. League for Peace and Freedom, N.J., 1948—, former pres.; mem. Peace Action, N.J., 1958—; bd. dirs./evaluator Encomium Arts Coun., N.J., 1988—; mem. AARP Vote Program, N.J., 1995. Recipient Women Who Have Made a Difference award YWCA, N.J., 1983, grant Schumann Found., 1985-86, 89. 90, Woman of Yr. award Women's Internat. League for Peace and Freedom, 1996. Mem. Assn. for Edn. of Young Children (Essex Hudson treas. 1987—), Coalition Infant Toddler Educators, N.J. Assn. for Edn. for Young Children (Month of Young Child chair 1987-91). Office: Ctr Ednl Svcs 18 Hillside Ave Glen Ridge NJ 07028

FREEMAN, LINDA MARIE, college educator; b. Kansas City, Mo., Aug. 28, 1949; d. Harry William and Hulda Marie (Perala) Peterson; m. Roger Donald Freeman, June 19, 1971; children: Christopher, Angela. BA, MacAlester Coll., 1971. Exec. sec. Gen. Mills, Mpls., 1971-72; ind. cons. Mary Kay Cosmetics, St. Paul, Duluth, Minn., 1975-80; owner, founder Iron Range Computer Svcs., Hibbing, Minn., 1980-94; systems analyst Jasper Engring., Hibbing, 1982-83; instr. computer sci. Hibbing Tech. Coll., 1988-89; owner, founder M.P. Resources, Hibbing, 1994—; chmn. Hibbing Park Bd., 1980-82, adv. bd. Hibbing Tech. Coll., 1989-91; cons. on computer system, City of Hibbing, 1993-94. Author: poetry, 1989-94; editor, writer (newsletters) Seasoned Saints Newsletter, 1994—, Towards More Productivity, 1994. Del. to regional and state convs. Rep. Orgn., Minn., 1980—; bd. dirs., treas. Victory C. Acad., Hibbing, Minn., 1988-92. Recipient Pres. award Hibbing C. of C, 1984, Speech Contest award, Toastmasters Hibbing, 1986. Mem. Salolampi Found. (bd. dirs., publicity and computer coms. 1996—), Swan Lake Country Club. Home and Office: MP Resources 834 W 47th St Hibbing MN 55746

FREEMAN, MARJORIE KLER, interior designer; b. Phila., June 30, 1929; d. Joseph H. and Elizabeth VanHoesen (Vaughan) Kler; m. John Martin Hale, Dec. 26, 1953 (div. 1974); children: John Marshall, David Maclain; m. Bruce George Freeman, Dec. 17, 1983. Cert. in interior design, Pratt Inst., 1951, BFA, 1952, MA, U. Mich., 1954. Dir. design studio Handicraft Furniture Co., Ann Arbor, Mich., 1953-63; design cons. dorms U. Mich., Ann Arbor, 1955-62; design cons. U. Del., Newark, 1963-67; bldg. and maint. designer and studio mgr. Vallery Miller Interiors, Woodland Hills, Calif., 1969-74; office mgr. Joseph H. Kler, MD, New Brunswick, N.J., 1974-83; pres. Marjorie Kler Interiors Inc., Princeton, N.J., 1980—; design cons. East Jersey Olde Towne, Inc., Piscataway, 1974. Author/editor cookbooks: Educated Palate, 1969, Grand Slam, 1990, Indian Queen Tavern, 1991. Pres. Bucceleuch Mansion Found., New Brunswick, 1983—; past pres., v.p. East Jersey Olde Towne, Inc., 1983-90, 91—. Mem. DAR (Jersey Blue chpt.), Nat. Huguenot Soc., Huguenot Soc. N.Y., Princeton C. of C., Penn Hall Alumnae Assn. (pres., bd. dirs. 1989—), Trowel Club New Brunswick (pres. 1993), Daus. of Cin., Soc. Daus. of Holland Dames. Republican. Presbyterian. Home and Office: 6 Mimosa Ct Princeton NJ 08540-9423

FREEMAN, MARJORIE SCHAEFER, mathematics educator; b. Chevy Chase, Md., Sept. 23, 1924; d. Herbert Stanley and Helen (Hummer) Schaefer; m. John C. Freeman, June 14, 1947; children: John C. III, Walter H., Jill F. Hasling, Cathryn F. Disch, Helen Freeman, Paul D. AB, Randolph-Macon Womans Coll., 1946; MS, Brown U, 1949; postgrad., U. Houston, 1973-75. Computer asst. Inst. for Advanced Study, Princeton, N.J., 1949-50; rsch. asst. Tex. A&M Rsch. Found., College Station, 1954-55; instr. Tex. A&M U., College Station, 1955; cons. Gulf Cons., Houston, 1955-56; instr. South Tex. Jr. Coll., Houston, 1961-74; asst. prof. U. Houston-Downtown, 1974-90, asst. prof. emeritus, 1990—; systems analyst, programmer TERA, Inc., Houston, 1985; cons. Inst. for Storm Rsch., Houston, 1979-86; adv. bd. Weather Rsch. Ctr., Houston, 1987—. Mem. Math. Assn. Am., South Tex. Obedience Club, S.W. Tracking Assn., Am. Chesapeake Club. Home: 4404 Mount Vernon St Houston TX 77006-5814

FREEMAN, MARY ANNA, librarian; b. Sentinal, Okla., July 24, 1943; d. Wylie Lee and Thelma Anna (Elam) Johnson; m. Charles Edward Freeman, Jr., Aug. 26, 1963; children: Charles Edward III, Juliana Elizabeth, Mark Adrian, Lee Agustin. BS, Abilene Christian U., 1963; M.L.S., Tex. Woman's U., 1981. Tchr. 4th grade Las Cruces Pub. Sch. (N.Mex.), 1963-64; tchr. 2d grade, 1964-67; head audiovisual dept. El Paso (Tex.) Pub. Library, 1972; head librarian Guillen Jr. H.S., El Paso, 1974-95; asst. librarian Andress H.S., El Paso, 1995-96, head libr., 1996—. Treas., Guillen PTA, El Paso, 1983-85, 86-89; mem. partnership in edn. liaison, 1986-90. Mem. ALA, Tex. Library Assn. Office: Andress HS 5400 Sun Valley El Paso TX 79924

FREEMAN, MARY LOUISE, state senator; b. Willmar, Minn., Oct. 21, 1941; d. James Martin and Luella Anna (Backlund) Hawkinson; m. Dennis Lester Freeman, June 10, 1962; children: Mark D., Sara L., Cary D., Maret S. BA, Gustavus Adolphus Coll., 1963. Substitute tchr. Arrowhead Edn. Assn., Storm Lake, Iowa, 1982-93; tchr., cons. Midwest Power, Des Moines, 1991-94; mem. Iowa Senate, Des Moines, 1994—; mem. early childhood intervention com., 1994—, mem. disaster prevention svcs. com., 1994—. Del. alt. Rep. Nat. Conv., Kansas City, 1976; active Midwest-Can. Relations

Co., 1994—. Mem. Am. Legis. Exch. Coun., Nat. Coun. State Govt. Lutheran. Home: 311 E Lakeshore Dr Storm Lake IA 50588-2539 Office: Iowa State Senate State Capitol Des Moines IA 50319*

FREEMAN, MYRNA FAYE, county schools official; b. Danville, Ill., Oct. 30, 1939; d. Thomas Gene and Dorothy Olive (Chodera) F.; m. Lonnie Lee Choate, Aug. 16, 1959 (div. 1987); children: Leslie Rene, Gregory Lonn. BA in Pub. Adminstrn., San Diego State U., 1977, MA in Edn. Adminstrn., 1987. Employee benefits mgr. City of San Diego, 1974-84; asst. risk mgr. San Diego County Office Edn., San Diego, 1984—; instr. Sch. Bus. Mgrs. Acad., Assn. Calif. Sch. Adminstrs., 1985—, Ins. Edn. Assn., Cert. Employee Benefits Specialist courses, 1991—. Author: Book, Adm. Impact of Implement Leg. 1987; Author: Article Risk Mgmt.- Emp. Benefits 1985, Risk Mgmt. - Workers' Comp. 1986, Risk Mgmt. - Loss Control 1986. Mem. Kaiser Consumer Coun., 1977-84, pres., 1979-80; bd. dirs. S.D. County Affirmative Action Adv. Bd., 1985; mem. adv. com. Vista Health Plan Pub. Policy, 1994—; mem. adv. coun. Kaiser On-the-Job, 1994—. Recipient Award of Appreciation COMBO-Cultural Arts of San Diego 1977. Mem. Risk Ins. Mgmt. Soc. (pres. San Diego chpt. 1988), Calif. Assn. Sch. Bus. Ofcls. (chmn. risk mgmt. R&D comm. 1987-88), San Diego Group Ins. Claims Coun. (pres. 1987), S.D. Employers Health Cost Coalition (vice-chmn. 1987), Calif. Women in Govt. (bd. dirs. 1983-84), Calif. Assn. of Joint Powers Authority, Pub. Agys. Risk Mgmt. Assn., Pub. Risk Ins. Mgmt. Assn., Internat. Found. Employee Benefits Plans, San Diego Workers' Compensation Forum, Sigma Kappa, Phi Kappa Phi, Internat. Platform Assn. Republican. Methodist. Home: 4345 Cartulina Rd San Diego CA 92124-2102 Office: San Diego County Office Edn 6401 Linda Vista Rd # 405 San Diego CA 92111-7319

FREEMAN, NATASHA MATRINA LEONIDOW, nursing administrator; b. Nyack, N.Y., June 12, 1958; d. Paul and Matrina (Butich) L.; m. Douglas Edward Freeman, Oct. 20, 1990; children: Alexandra, Mary. AAS, Rockland C.C., 1979; BS in Nursing cum laude, SUNY Coll. Technology, Utica, 1982; MS in Nursing magna cum laude, Syracuse U., 1985. RN, N.Y.; cert. nurse adminstr. Staff nurse Englewood Hosp., N.J., 1979-80; charge nurse Mary Imogene Bassett Hosp., Cooperstown, N.Y., 1980-82, nursing svc. coord., 1983-86, asst. dir. sys. devel., 1986-87; assoc. nursing practice coord. Strong Meml. Hosp.-U. Rochester, N.Y., 1987-88, asst. dir. nursing Bayfront Med. Ctr., St. Petersburg, Fla., 1988—. Translator: Excellence in Russian Language, 1976 (Otrada award). Served as 1st lt. USAFR, 1990-91, Persian Gulf War, Saudi Arabia. Mem. Fla. Orgn. Nurse Execs., Tampa Bay Orgn. Nurse Execs., Sigma Theta Tau. Office: Bayfront Med Ctr 701 6th St S Saint Petersburg FL 33701-4814

FREEMAN, PATRICIA ELIZABETH, library and education specialist; b. El Dorado, Ark., Nov. 30, 1924; d. Herbert A. and M. Elizabeth (Pryor) Harper; m. Jack Freeman, June 15, 1949; 3 children. BA, Centenary Coll., 1943; postgrad., Fine Arts Ctr., 1942-46, Art Students League, 1944-45; BSLS, La. State U., 1946; postgrad., Calif. State U., 1959-61, U. N.Mex., 1964-74; EdS, Peabody Coll., Vanderbilt U., 1975. Libr. U. Calif., Berkeley, 1946-47; libr. Albuquerque Pub. Schs., 1964-67, ind. sch. libr. media ctr. cons., 1967—. Painter lithographer; one-person show La. State Exhibit Bldg., 1948; author: Pathfinder: An Operational Guide for the School Librarian, 1975, Southeast Heights Neighborhoods of Albuquerque, 1993; compiler, editor: Elizabeth Pryor Harper's Twenty-One Southern Families, 1985; editor: SEHNA Gazette, 1988-93. Mem. task force Goals for Dallas-Environ., 1977-82; pres. Friends of Sch. Librs., Dallas, 1979-83; v.p., editor Southeast Heights Neighborhood Assn., 1988-93. With USAF, 1948-49. Honoree AAUW Ednl. Found., 1979; vol. award for outstanding service Dallas Ind. Sch. Dist., 1978; AAUW Pub. Service grantee 1980. Mem. ALA, AAUW (dir. Dallas 1976-82, Albuquerque 1983-85), LWV (sec. Dallas 1982-83, editor Albuquerque 1984-88), Nat. Trust Historic Preservation, Friends of Albuquerque Pub. Libr., N.Mex. Symphony Guild, Alpha Xi Delta. Home: 3016 Santa Clara Ave SE Albuquerque NM 87106-2350

FREEMAN, PEGGY RENEA, accountant; b. Gadsden, Ala., Oct. 8, 1966; d. Russell Leon and LaVada Inez (Weaver) Lemons; m. Robert Stanley Freeman, Mar. 15, 1986; children: Teri Inez, Robert Kyle. AS, Gadsden State C.C., 1986; BS, Jacksonville (Ala.) State U., 1993. Office clk. R.L. Polk & Co., Gadsden, 1984-85; sec. Shamrock Rentals, Gadsden, 1986; bookkeeper Ala. Contrs. Equipment, Gadsden, 1986-87, City of Hokes Bluff, Ala., 1988; tutor Gadsden State C.C., 1991-92; editor H & R Block, Gadsden, 1991-93; tax preparer Student Acctg. Assn., Jacksonville, 1992-93, Ret. Sr. Volunteer, Gadsden, 1994, Steed Acctg. Svcs., Attalla, Ala., 1995-96; acct. Manpower (Delphi Packard Electric Systems), Gadsden, Ala., 1995—. Mem. Student Acctg. Assn., Inst. Mgmt. Accts. Assn. Home: 5032 Louise St Gadsden AL 35903

FREEMAN, SUSAN TAX, anthropologist, educator; b. Chgo., May 24, 1938; d. Sol and Gertrude Tax.; m. Leslie G. Freeman, Jr., Mar. 20, 1964; 1 dau., Sarah Elisabeth. B.A., U. Chgo., 1958; M.A., Harvard U., 1959, Ph.D., 1965. Asst. prof. anthropology U. Ill., Chgo., 1965-70; assoc. prof. U. Ill., 1970-78, prof., 1978—, chmn., 1979-82; panelist NEH, Council for Internat. Exchange of Scholars; mem. anthropology screening com. Fulbright-Hays Research Awards, 1975-78; mem. ad hoc com. on research in Spain Spain-U.S.A. Friendship Agreement, various yrs., 1977-84; field researcher Mex., 1959, Spain, 1962—, Japan, 1983. Author: Neighbors: The Social Contract in a Castilian Hamlet, 1970, The Pasiegos-Spaniards in No Man's Land, 1979; asso. editor: Am. Anthropologist, 1971-73, Am. Ethnologist, 1974-76. Named to Inst. for the Humanities, U. Ill. Chgo., 1987-88; Wenner-Gren Found. for Anthrop. Research grantee, 1966, 83; NIMH grantee, 1967, 68-71; Nat. Endowment Humanities fellowships , 1978-79, 89-90. Fellow Am. Anthrop. Assn. (nominating com. 1981-82), Royal Anthrop. Inst. Gt. Britain and Ireland; mem. Soc. for Anthropology of Europe (exec. com. 1987-88), Soc. Spanish and Portuguese Hist. Studies (exec. com. 1990-92), Coun. European Studies (steering com. 1990-92), Internat. Inst. Spain (corporator, bd. dirs. 1982-87), Centro Estudios Sorianos (hon.), Assn. Anthropologia Castilla y Leon (hon.). Home: 5537 S Woodlawn Ave Chicago IL 60637-1620 Office: U Ill Dept Anthro M/C 027 1007 W Harrison St Chicago IL 60607-7135

FREEMAN-GIBB, LAURIE ANNE, nursing educator; b. Sudbury, Ont., Can., Feb. 4, 1963; d. Robert Maurice Freeman and Valerie Joan (Vaillancourt) Chaloux; m. David Garnet Gibb; children: Jeana Celine, Evan Robert. BS, U. Windsor, Ont., 1983, BSN, 1987. RN, Mich., Ont.; ACLS, BLS instr. trainee. RN surg. svcs. Harper Hosp., Detroit, 1987-88, RN MRI dept., 1988-89, RN med. ICU, 1989-93, cardiology coord., 1993-94, nurse educator, 1994—; patient focused care edn. & tng. task force Harper Hosp., Detroit, 1995-96, edn. & rsch. coun., 1994-96, image nursing com., 1995-96. Mem. spkrs. bur. AIDS Com. Windsor, 1987—; mem. parents coun. David E. Maxwell pub. Sch., Windsor, 1996. Recipient DMC Strategic Initiative award, 1995. Mem. AACN (Ednl. Advancement scholarship 1996), Nat. Nursing Staff Devel. Orgn. Office: Harper Hosp Edn Dept 3990 John R Detroit MI 48201

FREEMAN-ZUNIGA, ROCHELLE ELLEN, electrologist, medical technologist; b. Chgo., June 25, 1943; d. Bernard M. and Harriet (Itzkowitz) Laskov; m. Leonard Irwin Freeman, Mar. 1, 1964 (div. Dec. 1969); m. Jorge Clemente Zuniga, Jan. 4, 1992; children: Irma Squires, Jorge Jr. Cert. Med. Technologist, Cook Cty. Grad. Sch. Med. Tech, Chgo., 1962; BA in Bus. & Biology, North Park Coll., 1978; Assoc. of Selective Studies, Mesa Coll., San Diego, 1980; Assoc., Coll. Electrology, San Diego, 1985. Registered electrologist, Bd. Barbering and Cosmetology, Calif. Owner, operator New Image Ctr. AKA New Image Electrolysis Ctr., San Diego, 1985—. Precinct asst. Dem. Orgn., Chgo., 1970. Mem. Internat. Soc. Clin. Lab. Tech. (cert.), Electrologist Assn. Calif., Am. Electrology Assn., Internat. Guild of Profl. Electrologist, Clin. Lab. Scientists. Home: 7807 Nightingale Way San Diego CA 92123-2726 Office: New Image Ctr AKA New Image Electolysis Ctr 7677 Ronson Rd Ste 200 San Diego CA 92111

FREESE, KATHERINE, physicist, educator; b. Freiburg, Germany, Feb. 8, 1957; came to U.S., 1957; d. Ernst and Elisabeth Gertrude Maria (Bautz) F.; m. Fred Chester Adams, June 27, 1987; 1 child, Douglas Quincy Adams. BA, Princeton U., 1977; MA, Columbia U., 1981; PhD, U. Chgo., 1984. Postdoctoral fellow Harvard/Smithsonian Ctr. for Astrophysics, Cambridge, Mass., 1984-85, Inst. for Theoretical Physics, Santa Barbara, Calif., 1985-87, U. Calif., Berkeley, 1987-88; asst. prof. physics MIT, Cambridge, 1988-91; assoc. prof. physics U. Mich., Ann Arbor, 1991—; gen. mem. Aspen Ctr. for Physics, 1991—. Contbr. articles to profl. jours. William Rainey Harper fellow U. Chgo, 1982; Sloan Found. fellow, 1989; Presdl. Young Investigator NSF, 1990, rsch. grantee, 1991, 94; Presdl. fellow U. Calif., 1987. Mem. Am. Phys. Soc., Assn. for Women in Sci. Democrat. Office: U Mich Dept Physics Ann Arbor MI 48109

FREESE, MELANIE LOUISE, librarian, professor; b. Mineola, N.Y., May 12, 1945; d. Walter Christian and Agnes Elizabeth (Jensen) F. BS in Elem. Edn., Hofstra U., 1967, MA in Elem. Edn., 1969; MLS, L.I. U., 1977. Cert. tchr., N.Y. Bibliographic searcher acquisitions dept. Adelphi U. Swirbul Libr., Garden City, N.Y., 1973-79, res. desk libr., 1979-83; catalog libr., assoc. prof. Hofstra U. Axinn Libr., Hempstead, N.Y., 1984—; ch. librarian St. Peters Evang. Luth. Ch., Baldwin, N.Y., 1977—. Founder libr. Salvation Army Wayside Home and Sch. for Girls, Valley Stream, N.Y., 1993. Mem. ALA, Nassau County Libr. Assn. (corr. sec. acad. and spl. librs. divsn. 1986-88, v.p., pres.-elect 1989-90, pres. 1991), Bus. and Profl. Women's Club (pres. Nassau County chpt. 1990-92, Woman of Yr. 1994). Republican. Office: Hofstra U Axinn Library 1000 Fulton Ave Hempstead NY 11550-1030

FREEZE, KARLA E., accountant; b. Nashville, Nov. 12, 1957; d. Garth Fort and Jacque Sue (Irwin) F. AA, Bauder Coll., 1979; AS, Lakeland Coll., 1993; BS, Eastern Ill. U., 1994. Decorating cons. Sherwin Williams Co., Mattoon, Ill., 1979, asst. mgr., 1982-83; asst. mgr. Sherwin Williams Co., Dallas, 1984, store mgr., 1984-85, credit specialist, 1985-87; dir. acctg. Design Trend Internat. Interiors, Dallas, 1987-91, contr., 1995—; self employed designer, Mattoon, 1979-82. Mem. Inst. Mgmt. Accts., Inst. Internal Auditors. Office: Design Trend Internat Interiors 3030 LBJ Fwy Ste 230 LB4 Dallas TX 75234

FREHSE, BECKY ANN, artist, art educator; b. Harvard, Ill., Jan. 23, 1955; d. Gerald Donald and Sally Mareta (Stock) F.; m. Gregory Livingston Youtz, Nov. 28, 1987; children: Katherine Violet Youtz, Clara Jade Youtz. BFA, Ariz. State U., 1980; MFA, Ctrl. Wash. U., 1984. Artist in residence Wash. State Arts Commn., Olympia, Wash., 1984-85; lectr. and artist in residence Pacific Luth. U., Tacoma, Wash., 1986-94; dir. The Women's Ctr. Pacific Luth. U., Tacoma, 1992-95; art instr. Charles Wright Acad., Tacoma, 1995—. Artist; exhibits nationally. Vol. Peace Corps, Tunis, Tunisia, 1985-86. Grants Artists Program grantee Artist Trust, Seattle, 1995. Mem. AAUW, NOW, Womens Caucus for Art (del. and panelist at 4th U.N. Non-Govt. Orgn. Forum, Huairou, People's Rep. China, 1995). Home: 10016 S Patterson Tacoma WA 98444

FREI, CATHERINE HELEN, elementary education educator; b. N.Y.C., Oct. 26, 1944; d. Fredrick and Rose T. (Kozell) Meyer; m. Robert W. Frei, Nov. 25, 1967; children: Robert, Randall, Ryan. BS, East Stroudsburg State Coll., 1966, M in Phys. Edn., 1991. Cert. health and phys. edn. tchr., N.J. Tchr. phys. edn. Ridgefield Park (N.J.) H.S., 1966-68, Andover (N.J.) Regional Schs., 1977—; boys basketball coach Andover Regional Schs., 1978-91, girls softball coach, 1978-86; dir. coaches Andover Soccer Club, 1980-81; instr. gymnastics Andover PTA Program, 1992-94. Karate instr. Sussex County Karate Sch., 1986-94. Recipient Gov.'s Recognition award State of N.J., 1990. Mem. AAHPERD, Andover Regional Edn. Assn. (treas. 1988-91, pres. 1992-94), Harley Owners Group. Home: 8 Park Ln Newton NJ 07860-2741

FREIBERGER, JANA LYNN, paper company executive; b. Carlsbad, N.Mex., Nov. 17, 1957; d. Dale L. and Billie Ree (Grantham) F.; m. Dennis Ray Morgan, Jan. 14, 1984; 1 child, Erin Freiberger Morgan. BSChemE, Montana State U., 1979. Process engr. Procter & Gamble, Green Bay, Wis., 1979-80, pulp mill team mgr., 1980-81, digester area mgr., 1981-84, total quality dept. mgr., 1984-85, Puffs design team leader, 1986, Puffs Plus dept. mgr., 1987-89; orgn. devel. mgr. Procter & Gamble, Grande Prairie, Alta., Can., 1990-92; environ. dept. mgr. Weyerhaeuser, Grande Prairie, Alta., Can., 1992-93; orgn. devel. mgr. North Pacific Paper Corp., Longview, Wash., 1994—. Vol. support group facilitator Oddysey House, Grande Prairie, 1991-92. Home: 2347 Cascade Way Longview WA 98632 Office: North Pacific Paper Corp 3401 Industrial Way Longview WA 98632

FREIBERT, LUCY MARIE, humanities educator; b. Louisville, Oct. 19, 1922; d. Joseph Anthony and Amelia Josephine (Stich) F. BA in English, Nazareth Coll., 1957; MA in English, St. Louis U., 1962; PhD in English, U. Wis., 1970. Joined Sisters of Charity of Nazareth. Elem. tchr. St. Cecilia Sch., Louisville, 1947-51, Holy Name Sch., Louisville, 1951-57; secondary tchr. Presentation Acad., Louisville, 1957-60; prof. English Spalding Coll., Louisville, 1960-71; prof. English U. Louisville, 1971-93, prof. emerita of English, 1993—. Co-editor: Hidden Hands, An Anthology of American Women Writers, 1790-1870, 1985; contbr. articles to profl. jours. Named Woman of Distinction, Ctr. for Women and Families, 1993. Mem. MLA (life), NOW, Nat. Women's Studies Assn., Melville soc. Roman Catholic. Home: 1507 Hepburn # 2 Louisville KY 40204 Office: U Louisville Dept English Louisville KY 40292

FREIDEL, JUDY ANN, artist, illustrator; b. Madison, Wis., June 11, 1955; d. Robert Leo and Agnes Theresa (Langer) F. BA in Art, U. Ctrl. Ark., 1977. Owner, artist Red Hen Studio, Hot Springs, Ark., 1991—; freelance comml. artist and illustrator, 1977—; represented by Birchstone Gallery. Artwork included in American Artist of the Bookplate, 1993, Best of Colored Pencil II, 1994, Creative Colored Pencil, 1995; represented in pvt. collection St. Joseph Regional Health Ctr. Mem. Colored Pencil Soc. Am. Roman Catholic.

FREIFELD, MURIEL ILSA, early childhood consultant; b. N.Y.C., Aug. 2, 1923; d. Eli Israel and Anna Becker; m. Milton Freifeld, Nov. 18, 1943; children: Martin, Nina Freifeld Giles, Alison Freifeld Cowan. BA in Psychology, Hunter Coll., 1945; MA in Teaching, Trinity Coll., 1985. Tchr. Atlantic Highlands (N.J.) Pub. Schs., 1946-47, Dayton (Ohio) Pub. Schs., 1947-48; dir. presch. Jewish Cmty. Ctr., Springfield, Mass., 1954-57, Cin., 1958-60; dir. nursery sch. Jewish Cmty. Ctr., Easton, Pa., 1962-67; tchr. kindergarten Rockaway Twp. (N.J.) Pub. Schs., 1967-75; dir., tchr. Head Start Easton (Pa.) Pub. Schs., 1965; tchr., specialist Head Start Montgomery County Schs., Rockville, Md., 1975-85; pres., founder New Visions for Child Care, Potomac, Md., 1991—; founder, CEO New Visions for Caregivers, 1996—; chair adv. bd. New Visions for Child Care, 1993-94; cons. Head Start Peer Review, Phila., 1993—; researcher in field. Artist paintings, pen and ink drawings. Vol. Children's Inn, Bethesda, Md., 1991—, Hebrew Home, Rockville, 1993—, NIH-Pediatric Oncology, Bethesda, 1993-94; hospice worker Jewish Social Svcs., Rockville, 1994—. Project Head Start grantee, 1965. Mem. AAUW, Am. Counseling Assn., Nat. Assn. for Edn. of Young Children (validator 1990—), Assn. Childhood Edn. Internat., Hunter Coll. Alumni Assn. (program chair 1991-93, bd. dirs.). Home and Office: 10737 Deborah Dr Potomac MD 20854-2714

FREILICH, JOAN SHERMAN, utilities executive; b. Albany, N.Y., Nov. 3, 1941; d. Julius and Bess (Bergner) Sherman; m. Sanford J. Freilich, Jan. 24, 1965. AB in French magna cum laude, Barnard Coll., 1963; MA in French, Columbia U., 1964, PhD in French, 1971, MBA in Fin., 1980. Instr. CCNY, Columbia U., N.Y.C., 1965-75; tchr. Walden Sch., N.Y.C., 1970-74; asst. to the dean Coll. New Rochelle, N.Y., 1974-75, dir. admissions, 1975-78; sr. acct. Consol. Edison Co. N.Y., N.Y.C., 1978-81, mgr. acctg. rsch., 1981-82; contr. power generation Consolidated Edison Co. N.Y., N.Y.C., 1982-86, gen. mgr. power generation, 1986-89, exec. asst. to pres., 1989, asst. v.p. corp. planning, 1989-90, v.p. corp. planning, 1990-92, v.p., contr., chief acctg. officer, 1992-96; sr. v.p., CFO, 1996—. Author: Paul Claudel's "Le Soulier de satin": A Stylistic, Structuralist and Psychoanalytic Interpretation, 1973; assoc. editor Claudel Studies, 1973-78; contbr. articles to profl. jours. Publ. grantee Humanities Rsch. Coun. Can., 1972; Pres.'s fellow Columbia U., 1964, Henry Todd fellow, 1967; recipient scholarship N.Y. State Bd. Regents, 1959, Nat. Merit Found., 1959, Columbia U., 1965. Mem. Fin. Execs. Inst., YWCA Acad. of Women Achievers, Phi Beta Kappa, Beta Gamma Sigma. Office: Consolidated Edison Co NY 4 Irving Pl New York NY 10003-3502

FREILICHER, JANE, artist; b. N.Y.C., Nov. 29, 1924; d. Martin and Bertha (Niederhoffer); m. Joseph Hazan, Feb. 17, 1957; 1 dau., Elizabeth. A.B., Bklyn. Coll., 1947; postgrad., Hans Hoffman Sch. Fine Arts, 1947; M.A., Columbia U., 1948. vis. lectr., critic art schs., colls. One-woman shows include Tibor de Nagy, 1952-68, John Bernard Myers Gallery, 1971, Fischbach Gallery, 1975, 77, 79-80, 83, 85, 88, 90, 92, 95, Utah Mus. Fine Arts, 1979, Lafayette Coll., 1981, Kansas City Art Inst., 1983, David Heath Gallery, Atlanta, 1990; group exhbns. include Met. Mus. Art, 1979-80, Denver Art Mus., 1979, Pa. Acad., 1981, Am. Acad. and Inst. of Arts and Letters, 1981, 84-85, Bklyn. Mus. 1984, Yale U., 1986, Tibor de Nagy Gallery, 1992, Whitney Mus., 1995; represented in permanent collections Met. Mus. Art, Hirschorn Mus., Bklyn. Mus., N.Y. U., Rose Art Mus., Whitney Mus., others; travelling retrospective in Currier Gallery Art, Parrish Mus., Contemporary Arts Mus., McNay Mus., 1986-87; illustrator Turandot and Other Poems, 1953, Paris Review, 1965. Recipient Eloise Spaeth award Guild Hall Mus., East Hampton, N.Y., 1991; AAUW fellow, 1974; Nat. Endowment Arts grantee, 1976. Mem. NAD (academician) (Saltus Gold medal 1987, Benjamin Altman landscape prize 1995), Am. Acad. Arts and Letters.

FREIMAN, LELA KAY, secondary school educator; b. Canton, Miss., Oct. 2, 1939; d. Lyle K. and Mae Susan (Billman) Linch; m. James F. Freiman, Sept. 5, 1965 (div. Feb. 1975); 1 child, Jennifer Leigh. Student, Northwestern State Coll., Natchitoches, La., 1957-59; BA, U. Iowa, 1962; MEd, U. Ariz., 1977. Tchr. speech, English and drama Sturgeon Bay (Wis.) H.S., 1962-65; spl. edn. tchr. Naylor Jr. H.S., Tucson, 1975-83; tchr. drama Sahuaro H.S., Tucson, 1983—; summer camp dir. Sahuaro coun. Girl Scouts U.S.A., Tucson, 1977-87; mem. adv. coun. drama dept. U. Ariz., Tucson; participant Nat. faculty for Humanities, Santa Fe, Tucson, 1988-89. Former leader, trainer, camp dir. Girl Scouts U.S.A., Sturgeon Bay, Wis. Rapids, Waukesha, Wis., Ariz., rep. Nat. Leadership Conf., Washington, 1983, bd. dirs. Sahuaro coun., 1992-95; first aid com., instr. AFA, CPR ARC, Tucson; instr. CPR Am. Heart Assn.; Sunday sch. tchr., supt., mem. coun. Luth. Chs., Wis. Rapids, Waukesha, now Tucson; v.p. bd. dirs. S.W. Actors Studio, Tucson, 1987-92; adult mem. Ariz. State Thespian Bd. Recipient Thanks Badge, Sahuaro coun. Girl Scouts U.S.A., 1976, 88, Cross and Crown award Luth. Scouters So. Ariz., 1983, Mainstream Tchr. of Yr. award Assn. for Retarded Citizens So. Ariz., 1989. Mem. NEA, Am. Alliance for Theatre and Edn., Internat. Thespian Soc. of Ednl. Theatre Assn., Ariz. Theatre Educators Assn. (state sec. 1989-90, state treas. 1990-91, com. to draft curriculum guidelines for Ariz. Ho. of Reps., Theatre Educator of Yr. 1994-95), Ariz. Edn. Assn., Tucson Edn. Assn. Home: 7517 E Beach Dr Tucson AZ 85715-3649 Office: Sahuaro HS 545 N Camino Seco Tucson AZ 85710-3067

FREISER, ELEANOR HELENE, school system administrator, educator, educational analyst; b. Bklyn., Nov. 18, 1946; d. Alexander and Ruth (Herrick) Freiser; children: Jonathan Zak, Michael Hisler. BS in Edn., L.I. U., 1968; MS in Edn., Queens Coll., Flushing, N.Y., 1973, Profl. Diploma in Supervision/Adminstrn., 1995. With N.Y.C. Bd. Edn., Bklyn., 1968—, tchr. PS 25, PS 309 Dist. 16, with Office of Ednl. Rsch., adminstr. test adminstrn. unit, ednl. analyst h.s. evaluation and early childhood units, adv. coun. for occupl. edn.; program dir. College Point (N.Y.) Rd. Runners Track Club, 1972-78. Mem. Kappa Delta Pi.

FREITAG, LINDA JOAN, human resource manager; b. New Rochelle, N.Y., Sept. 1, 1961; d. John M. and Doris F. (Press) F.; m. Henry R. Ilian, Oct. 1, 1988; 1 child, Julia Simone Freitag Ilian. BA in Psychology with distinction, U. Va., 1983; MS in Social Work, Columbia U., 1985; MS in Indsl. and Labor Rels., Cornell U. and Baruch Coll., 1995. CSW, N.Y. Employment mgr. Met. Opera Assn., N.Y.C., 1985—. Bd. dirs., sec. Beth Am, The People's Temple, N.Y.C., 1989-91; bd. dirs. Reform Temple of Forest Hills, N.Y., 1995—. Mem. Soc. for Human Resource Mgmt., Psi Chi, Beta Gamma Sigma. Democrat. Jewish.

FREITAG, NANCY THEODORA, medical device complaint investigator; b. Mineola, N.Y., Dec. 8, 1953; d. Howard E. Freitag and Edna T. (Schmarl) Freitag Fain; m. Frank J. Louden, June 15, 1983 (div. Aug. 1987); 1 child, Kristina. Student, Nassau C.C., Garden City, N.Y., 1991-94, St. Joseph's Coll., Patchogue, N.Y., 1996—. Cert. emergency med. technician, N.Y. Head cashier, supr. Terrace Inn, Milledgeville, Ga., 1985; fraud investigator Chase Manhattan Bank, Garden City, 1985-87; med. asst. Ob/Gyn. Contemporary Care Ctr. Winthrop U. Hosp., Mineola, 1987-90; investigator Olympus Am. Inc., Melville, N.Y., 1994—. Treas. Mineola Vol. Ambulance Corps, 1980. Mem. Assn. for Surg. Tech., Assn. for Advancement of Med. Instrumentation. Lutheran.

FREITAS, ELIZABETH FRANCES, lawyer; b. N.Y.C., Aug. 19, 1963; d. Joao A. and Alva Marie (Alvarez) F. BA cum laude, Cath. U. Am., 1985; BBA cum laude, CUNY-Baruch Coll., 1994; JD, Bklyn. Law Sch., 1993. Bar: N.J. 1993, N.Y. 1994, D.C. 1995. Intern U.S. Internat. Trade Com., Washington, 1985-86; archivist asst. Nat. Leadership Coun./GOPAC, Washington, 1985; telephone mgr. Citizen Action, Washington, 1986-87; telemarketer Decision Ctr., N.Y.C., 1988; intern Lawyers Com. for Human Rights, N.Y.C., 1992-93; pvt. practice Advocacy Inc., N.Y.C., 1994—; part-time atty. Americana Agy., N.Y.C., 1995; chair film com. L.I. U., 1981-82. Editor: (lit. mag.) New Leaf, 1980. Mem. Get Out the Vote com. Citizen Action, Washington, 1986-87. Recipient Bausch and Lomb Sci. award, 1981; Phillips fellow L.I. U., 1981-82. Mem. ABA, ACLU, N.Y. Bar Assn., Amnesty Internat., Pi Gamma Mu, Beta Gamma Sigma, Golden Key Nat. Honor Soc. Democrat. Catholic. Home and Office: # 3A 561 W 169th St New York NY 10032

FRENCH, DEBORAH FERN, banking executive; b. Chattanooga, Apr. 22, 1953; d. Fern Sinclair and Nina Evelyn (Andes) F. Student, U. Tenn., 1971-75. Cert. trust and fin. advisor; cert. trust compliance profl. Trust sec. Sun Trust Bank, Chattanooga, 1983-84, adminstrv. asst., 1984-88, asst. trust officer, 1988-90, trust officer, 1990-92, sr. trust officer, 1992-94, asst. v.p., 1994—. Treas. Make A Wish Found.-Ea. Tenn. chpt., Chattanooga, 1992—; mem. Scenic City chpt.-Optimist Internat., Chattanooga, 1995. Mem. Nat. Assn. Trust Auditors and Compliance Profls., Inst. Cert. Bankers, Estate Planning Coun. Chattanooga, Chattanooga Tax Practitioners, Greater Chattanooga Area Planned Giving Coun. (charter). Presbyterian. Office: Sun Trust Bank Chattanooga 736 Market St Mail Ctr 0312 Chattanooga TN 37411

FRENCH, ELIZABETH IRENE, biology educator, violinist; b. Knoxville, Tenn., Sept. 20, 1938; d. Junius Butler and Irene Rankin (Johnston) F. MusB, U. Tenn., 1959, MS, 1962; PhD, U. Miss., 1973. Tchr. music Kingsport (Tenn.) Sympony Assn., 1962-64, Birmingham (Ala.) Schs., 1964-66; NASA trainee in biology U. Miss., Oxford, 1969-73; asst. prof. Mobile (Ala.) Coll. (name now U. Mobile), 1973-83, assoc. prof., 1983-94, prof., 1994—; orch. contractor Am. Fedn. Musicians, 1983—; 1st violin Kingsport Symphony Orch., 1962-64, Birmingham Symphony Orch., 1964-66, Knoxville Symphony Orch., 1965-68, Memphis Symphony Orch., 1970-73, Mobile Opera-Port City Symphony, 1974—. Violin recitalist Ala. Artists Series, 1978-81. Named Career Woman of Yr., Gayfer's, Inc., 1985. Mem. Assn. Southeastern Biologists, Human Anatomy and Physiology Soc. (nat. com. to construct standardized test on anatomy and physiology), Wilderness Soc., Ala. Acad. Scis. (presenter 1996), Ala. Ornithol. Soc., Mobile Bay Audubon Soc., Am. Fedn. Musicians, Ala. Fedn. Music Clubs (chmn. composition contest 1986—, historian 1991-95), Schumann Music Club (pres. 1977-79, 85-87, 94—). Republican. Episcopalian. Home: 36 Ridgeview Dr Chickasaw AL 36611-1317 Office: U Mobile PO Box 13220 Mobile AL 36663-0220

FRENCH, LINDA JEAN, lawyer; b. Newark, N.Y., Nov. 12, 1947; d. Allyn B. and Willa E. (Cronk) Wrench; m. William J. French, Aug. 27, 1966; children: Mark W., David A. BA summa cum laude, William Jewell Coll., 1969; JD with distinction, U. Mo., 1978. Bar: Mo. 1978, U.S. Dist. Ct. (we. and ea. dists.) Mo. 1978, U.S. Ct. Appeals (8th and 10th cirs.) 1978, U.S. Ct. Appeals (D.C. cir.) 1979. Assoc. Blackwell Sanders Matheny Weary & Lombardi, Kansas City, Mo., 1978-82, ptnr., 1983-84; gen. counsel, sec. Payless Cashways Inc., Kansas City, 1984-86, v.p., gen. counsel, sec., 1986-91, sr. v.p., gen. counsel, sec., 1991—; lectr. U. Mo. Bus. Sch., Kansas City, 1991. Pres. Town and Country Homes Assn., Shawnee Mission, Kans.,

1987, v.p., 1985-86; chmn. commn. adult and student recruitment William Jewell Coll., Liberty, Mo., 1984, chmn. commn. on comms., 1991, 92-93, mem. alumni bd. govs., 1987-93, v.p., 1991-93, exec. com., 1987-88, 91-93; bd. dirs. Legal Aid Western Mo., 1989-94, treas., 1991-93, exec. com., fin. com., audit com., 1992-93; bd. dirs. Greater Kansas City Jr. Achievement, 1985-86, Kansas City Tomorrow Leadership Program, 1988-89, alumni bd., 1991-92, alumni assn.; bd. dirs. ARC-Greater Kansas City chpt., 1992—, fin. com., 1992—, exec. com. 1993—, vice chair, 1994-95, chair, 1996—; bd. dirs. Diastole, 1993—, Trinity Luth. Hosp. Found., 1994—, U. Mo. Kansas City Gallery of Art, 1994—. Named one of Outstanding Young Women in Am., 1974, one of Top 100 Women in Corp. Am. Bus. Month, 1989, one of Top Women Execs. in Kansas City, 1992; recipient Citation of Achievement award William Jewell Coll., 1988. Mem. ABA (mem. com. on labor and employment law, mem. com. on bus. law), Mo. Bar Assn., Kansas City Met. Bar Assn. (vice chmn., then chmn. corp. house counsel com. 1986-88, lectr. CLE program), Kansas City Assn. Women Lawyers, Am. Corp. Counsel Assn. (v.p. 1992-93), Am. Soc. Corp. Secs., Lawyers Assn. Kansas City (bd. dirs. 1990—, sec. 1991—, chairperson pub. rels. com. 1990-91, chairperson program com. 1991-92, chairperson long-range planning com. 1992-93, pres.-elect 1993-94, pres. 1994-95, bd. dirs. found. 1993—, pres. 1995—), U. Mo. Kansas City Alumni Assn., William Jewell Alumni Assn., Kansas City Club. Presbyterian. Office: Payless Cashways Inc PO Box 419466 2300 Main St Kansas City MO 64108-2415

FRENCH, MARGARET DIANA, operating room nurse; b. Birmingham, Eng., Dec. 9, 1956; came to U.S., 1994; d. Almira Clarissa French; 1 child, Dwane. Diploma, Kingston Sch. Nursing, Jamaica, 1979; student, Pace U., 1995. RN, cert. nurse oper. rm., N.Y. Nurse Kingston Pub. Hosp., 1979-83, Jewish Meml. Hosp., Boston, 1984; nurse Brookdale Hosp., Bklyn., 1985—, preceptor oper. room, 1990—; nurse Maimonides Hosp., Bklyn., 1993—. Appeared on cover Spectrum Mag., 1993. Mem. Assn. Oper. Rm. Nurses (local edn. com. 1992-93), N.Y. State Nurses Assn. Home: 7 Hegeman Ave Apt 10G Brooklyn NY 11212 Office: Brookdale Hosp Med Ctr 1 Brookdale Plz Brooklyn NY 11212

FRENCH, MARILYN, author, critic; b. N.Y.C., Nov. 21, 1929; d. E. Charles and Isabel (Hazz) Edwards; m. Robert M. French, Jr., June 4, 1950 (div. 1967); children: Jamie, Robert. BA, Hofstra Coll., 1951, MA, 1964; PhD, Harvard U., 1972. Secretarial, clerical worker, 1946-53; lectr. Hofstra Coll., 1964-68; asst. prof. Holy Cross Coll., Worcester, Mass., 1972-76; Mellon fellow Harvard U., 1976-77; writer, lectr., 1967—. Author: (criticism) The Book as World: James Joyce's Ulysses, 1976, Shakespeare's Division of Experience, 1981; (novels) The Women's Room, 1977, The Bleeding Heart, 1980, Her Mother's Daughter, 1987, Our Father: A Novel, 1994, My Summer With George, 1996; (non-fiction) Beyond Power: On Women, Men and Morals, 1986, The War Against Women, 1992; introductions to Edith Wharton's Summer and The House of Mirth, 1981, My Summer with George, 1995. Mem. MLA, James Joyce Soc., Virginia Woolf Soc. *

FRENCH, STEPHANIE TAYLOR, arts administrator; b. Newark; d. William Taylor and Connie V. French; B.A., Wellesley Coll., 1972; M.B.A., Harvard U., 1978; m. Amory Houghton, III, Sept. 8, 1979; children: Christina French Houghton, Amory Taylor Houghton. Traffic mgr. Radio Sta. KFRC, 1973-74; free-lance on-air performer, producer San Francisco and Oakland cable TV stas., 1973-76; dir. European Gallery, San Francisco, 1974-75; acct. exec. Young & Rubican, N.Y.C., 1978-79; acct. supr. Rives Smith Baldwin & Carlberg, Houston, 1980-81; mgr. cultural affairs and spl. programs Philip Morris Cos. Inc., N.Y.C., 1981-86, dir. cultural and contbns. programs, 1986-90, v.p. corp. contbn. ans cultural affairs bds., 1990—. Bd. dirs. The Joffrey Ballet, Am. Fedn. of Arts, Am. Council on Arts, Parsons Dance Co., Nat. AIDS Fund, the Thomas S. Kenan Inst. for the Arts, Harkness Ctr. for Dance, Dance Com. of the Met. Mus. Art, The Contbns. Coun. of the Conf. Bd. Adv. Com. of Bill T. Jones/Arnie Zane Co., Dance Theatre Workshop. Apptd. mem. Gov. of N.Y. to Empire State Arts Commn., Mayor of N.Y.C. to the exec. com. N.Y.C. Econ. Devel. Corp. Clubs: Harvard Bus. Sch. Network of Women Alums, Harvard Bus. Sch., Wellesley. Home: 320 E 72d St Apt 6C New York NY 10021 Office: Philip Morris Cos Inc 120 Park Ave New York NY 10017-5523

FRESCH, MARIE BETH, court reporting company executive; b. Norwalk, Ohio, Jan. 16, 1957; d. Ralph Roy and Vonda Mae (Brunkhorst) Spiegel; m. James R. Fresch, Aug. 5, 1978; 1 child, Alexandra Jane. AS in Bus., Tiffin U., 1977; cert. in ct. reporting, Acad. Ct. Reporting, 1979. Registered profl. reporter, Ohio. Ofcl. reporter Seneca County Common Pleas Ct., Tiffin, Ohio, 1979-80; owner, operator Marie B. Fresch & Assocs., Norwalk, 1980—. Recipient Cert. of Merit, Nat. Ct. Reporters Assn., 1990. Mem. Nat. Ct. Reporters Assn., Ohio Ct. Reporters Assn. (student promotions and pub. rels. coms. 1986—), NOW (sec. Port Clinton chpt. 1984-86, treas. 1986-87, 91), Am. Legion Aux., Kappa Delta Kappa. Democrat. Methodist. Lodge: Order of Eastern Star (esther 1979-81). Home and Office: 47 Warren Dr Norwalk OH 44857-2447

FRESQUEZ, BEATRICE C., counselor; b. Quantico, Va., Aug. 18, 1969; d. Luis Ramon and Cecilia Irene (Castro) F.; m. Raul Eduardo Pedroso, Feb. 19, 1994. B in Rehabilitative Svcs., U. Fla., 1990, MEd in Sch. Counseling, 1993, EdS in Sch. Counseling, 1993. Nat. cert. counselor; cert. sch. counselor, Fla. Enrollment counselor Stanley Kaplan Edn. Ctr., Gainesville, Fla., 1989-92; employment counselor HRS-Project Independence, Palatka, Fla., 1991; practica in counseling Hawthorne H.S., Gainesville, 1992, Westwood Middle Sch., Gainesville, 1993; job tng. counselor Metro Dade County, Miami, Fla., 1993; counselor intern G. Holmes Braddock Sr. H.S., Miami, Fla., 1993, counselor, 1994—. Presenter in field. Mem. ACA, Am. Sch. Counseling Assn., Fla. Counseling Assn., Fla. School Counseling Assn. Democrat. Roman Catholic. Office: G Holmes Braddock Sr H S 3601 SW 147 Ave Miami FL 33165

FRESTEDT, JOY LOUISE, cytogeneticist and molecular biologist; b. Oak Park, Ill., Jan. 31, 1959; d. James Albert Machnicki and Wanda Louise (McConnaughhay) Katzman; m. Robert LeVance Frestedt, Aug. 8, 1987; 1 child, Megan Marie. BA, Knox Coll., 1980; PhD, U. Minn., 1996. Cytogeneticist Ill. Masonic Med. Ctr., Chgo., 1980-81; med. tech., asst. scientist, rsch. asst. U. Minn., Mpls., 1981-89, 91-96; cancer rsch. scientist III Roswell Park Cancer Inst., Buffalo, 1989-90; grad. fellow Sci. Mus. Minn., St. Paul, 1993-95; rsch. scientist St. Jude Med. Inc., St. Paul, 1996—; grants reviewer U. Minn., 1994; mem. exec. bd. Grad. Women in Sci., 1994-2003, pres., 1996—; exec. bd. Minn. Acad. Sci., St. Paul, 1994-96. Adv. bd. Operation Smart, YWCA, St. Paul, 1994-96. Mem. AAAS, Coalition of Women Grad. Students, Preparing Future Faculty, Am. Assn. Cancer Rsch., Assn. Molecular Pathology, Am. Soc. Investigative Pathology, Am. Soc. Leukocyte Biology. Home: 5727 W 42d St Saint Louis Park MN 55416-3101

FRETER, LISA, non-profit association administrator; b. Washington, Aug. 25, 1951; d. Theodore Henry and Elizabeth Crawford (Stout) Freter; m. David O'Shea Dawkins, Dec. 10, 1975 (div. May 1995); 1 child, Meghan Elizabeth. Student, Towson State Coll., 1969-70, U. de las Americas, Cholula, Puebla, Mex., 1972-73; BSBA, U. Phoenix, 1992. Owner B&B Liquors, Denver, 1979-81; dir. pubs. Gt. Western Assn. Mgmt., Denver, 1985-88; adminstrv. asst., conf. coord. Employment and Tng. divsn. Arapahoe County, Aurora, Colo., 1988-93; dir. confs. 3AI Affiliated Advt. Agys. Internat. Inc., Aurora, Colo., 1994-95; office mgr. Cin. Works, 1996—. Author: (poems) The San Miguel Writer, 1970, Xalli, 1971; exec. producer Law Enforcement Torch Run for Spl. Olympics Video, 1986, videotaped pub. svc. announcements, 1987; producer, dir. (video) Private Industry Council, 1989; contbr. articles to mags.; editor various newsletters. Exec. dir. Colleagues Police for Edn., Support, Denver, 1983-85; liaison Colo. Assn. Chiefs of Police, 1983-85; coord. Law Enforcement Torch Run for Spl. Olympics, 1986-88. Mem. Freedoms Found. Valley Forge (v.p. pub. rels. 1988-92, 93-94, pres. 1992-93), Colo. Gang Investigators Assn. (exec. dir. 1989-90, v.p. membership 1993-94, newsletter editor 1994-95), Colo. Soc. Assn. Execs., Profl. Conv. Mgmt. Assn., Cin. Soc. Assn. Execs. Home: 5784 Eaglesridge Ln Cincinnati OH 45230-1386

FRETZ, DEBORAH M., oil industry executive; m. Philip Fretz; two children. BS in Biology and Chemistry, Butler U., 1970; MBA, Temple U. Virologist Merck, Sharp & Dohme; fin. analyst Sun Co., Inc., 1977—, mgr. fin. analysis group, 1985-88, dir. wholesale fuels mktg., 1988-89, gen. mgr. fuels, 1989, pres. Sun Pipe Line Co. and Marine Terminals, sr. v.p. Sunoco Logistics, 1994—. Office: Sun Co Inc Ten Penn Ctr 1801 Market St Philadelphia PA 19103-1699

FREUND, CYNTHIA M., dean, nursing educator. BSN, Marquette U., 1963; MSN, U. N.C., 1973, FNP, 1974; PhD in Bus. and Health Adminstrn., U. Ala., 1981. Staff nurse McHenry (Ill.) Hosp., 1963, 64-65, VA Hosp., Wood, Wis., 1963-64; instr. Milw. County Instns., Wauwatosa, Wis., 1965-68, supr. Milw. County Rehab. and Chronic Disease Hosp., 1968-70; instr. Sch. Nursing U. Wis., Milw., 1972-73; dir. FNP program Area L Health Edn. Ctr., Tarboro, N.C., 1973-74; asst. prof., assoc. dir. FNP program U. N.C., Chapel Hill, 1974-78, assoc. prof., chair social and adminstrv. sys. dept., 1984-92, dean, prof. nursing, 1992—; asst. prof. U. Pa., Phila., 1981-84, sr. rsch. assoc. Leonard Davis Inst. Health Econs., 1981-84, dir. MSN nursing adminstrn. program, PhD in nursing/MBA joint degree, 1981-84; mem. Gov. Advocacy Com. for Children and Youth State of Wis., 1973; mem. N.C. Med. Data Base Commn., N.C. Gen. Assembly, 1985-89; mem. nursing adv. panel P.E.W. Health Professions Commn., 1991-92; mem. nat. adv. com. for project future requirements for nurse practitioners and nurse midwives Dept. Health and Human Svcs., 1993-94, mem. joint adv. com. to project future requirements for primary care physicians, and others, Bur. Health Professions, 1994-95; cons., presenter in field. Author: (with D. del Bueno) Power and Politics in Nursing Administration, 1986 (Am. Jour Nursing Book of Yr. 1986), Nursing: A Kaleidoscopic View, 1991 (Am. Jour. Nursing Book of Yr. 1991); author chpts. to books; mem. editl. bd. Nursing Econs., 1982-84, manuscript reviewer, 1982—; manuscript reviewer Jour. Profl. Nursing, 1984—, Health Svc. Rsch., 1984—, Planning for Higher Edn., 1986; contbr. articles to profl. jours. Pub. Health Svc. Doctoral fellow Nat. Ctr. for Health Svcs. Rsch., 1980-81, Rsch. fellow Nat. Health Care Mgmt. Ctr., 1980-81; recipient Profl. Svc. Alumni award Marquette U., 1992. Fellow Am. Acad. Nursing; mem. ANA (vice-chair coun. FNP and clinicians 1977-78, cert. adult nurse practitioner 1977, Jessie M. Scott award 1990), Nat. League Nursing, Acad. Mgmt., Am. Orgn. Nurse Execs., Am. Hosp. Assn. Office: U NC Sch Nursing CB # 7460 Carrington Hall Chapel Hill NC 27599-7460

FREUND, DEBORAH MIRIAM, transportation engineer; b. Bklyn., Apr. 9, 1957; d. Harry and Bertha (Fried) F.; m. Garey Douglas White, Feb. 22, 1981. BSCE, Washington U., 1979, MSc, 1982. Registered profl. engr., Tex. Grad. rsch. asst. Washington U., St. Louis, 1979-81; transp. planning engr. Mid-Am. Regional Coun., Kansas City, Mo., 1981-83; civil engr. Fed. Hwy. Adminstrn., Washington, 1983-85, rsch. hwy. engr., 1985-90, transp. specialist, 1990-92, sr. transp. specialist, 1992—; mem. Com. Operator and Vehicle Performance and Simulation Transp. Rsch. Bd., Washington, 1993—; presenter in field. Fellow Coun. Excellence in Govt., Washington, 1995-96. Mem. ASCE (sec. hwy. divsn. rsch. com. 1988-90), Soc. Automative Engrs. (co-chair total vehicle com. 1995—), Inst. Transp. Engrs., Sigma Xi (assoc.). Office: Fed Hwy Adminstrn 400 7th St SW Rm 3107 Washington DC 20590

FREUND, EMMA FRANCES, medical technologist; b. Washington; d. Walter R. and Mabel W. (Loveland) Ervin; m. Frederic Reinert Freund, Mar. 4, 1953; children: Frances, Daphne, Fern, Frederic. BS, Wilson Tchrs. Coll., Washington, 1944; MS in Biology, Catholic U., Washington, 1953; MEd in Adult Edn., Va. Commonwealth U., 1988; cert. in mgmt. devel. Va. Commonwealth U., 1975, supr. devel.; student SUNY, New Paltz, 1977, J. Sargeant Reynolds C.C., 1978. Cert. Nat. Cert. Agy. for Clin. Lab. Pers, supervisory devel., Va. Tchr. math. and sci. D.C. Sch. System, Washington, 1944-45; technician in parasitology lab., zool. div., U.S. Dept. Agr., Beltsville, Md., 1945-48; histologic technician dept. pathology Georgetown U. Med. Sch., Washington, 1948-49; clin. lab. technician Kent and Queen Anne's County Gen. Hosp., Chestertown, Md., 1949-51; histotechnologist surg. pathology dept. Med. Coll. Va. Hosp., Richmond, 1951—, supr. histology lab., 1970-88, mgr., supr. 1988—; cons. profl. meetings and workshops histotechnology, head infosvcs. Histo-Help; mem. exam. coun. Nat. Cert. Agy. Med. Lab. Pers. Asst. cub scout den leader Robert E. Lee coun. Boy Scouts Am., 1967-68, den leader, 1968-70. Co-author: (mini-course) Instrumentation in Cytology and Histology, 1985; editor Histo-Scope Newsletter. Mem. AAAS, NAFE, AAUW, Am. Soc. CLin. Lab. Sci. (rep. to sci. assembly histology sect. 1977-78, chmn. histology sect. 1983-85, 89-96), Va. Soc. Med. Technology, Richmond Soc. Med. Technologists (corr. sec. 1977-78, dir. 1981-82, pres. 1984-85), Va. State Soc. Histotechnology (pres. 1994—), Nat. Certification Agy. (clin. lab. specialist in histotech., clin. lab. supr., clin. lab. dir.), N.Y. Acad. Scis., Am. Assn. Clin. Chemistry (assoc.), Am. Soc. Clin. Pathologists (cert. histology technician), Nat. Geog. Soc., Va. Govtl. Employees Assn., Nat. Soc. Histotech. (by-laws com. 1981—; C.E.U. com. 1981—, program com. regional meeting 1984, 85, chmn. regional meeting 1987, program chmn. regional mtg. 1992), Am. Mus. Natural History, Smithsonian Instn., Am. Mgmt. Assn., Clin. Lab. Mgmt. Assn., Nat. Soc. Historic Preservation, Sigma Xi, Phi Beta Rho, Kappa Delta Pi, Phi Lambda Theta, Omicron Sigma. Home: 1315 Asbury Rd Richmond VA 23229-5305

FREY, KATIE MANCIET, educational administrator; b. Tucson, Ariz., Dec. 31, 1952; d. Hector Encinas and Lilian Eloisa (Hanna) Manciet; m. Richard Patrick Frey, Jul. 20, 1974; 1 child, Stacy Ann. BS, U. Ariz., 1974, MEd, 1982, PhD, 1987. Tchr. physical edn. Amphitheater Pub. Schs., Tucson, 1974-81, rsch. specialist, 1982-85, dir. rsch. & devel., 1985-88, asst. supt., 1988-89, assoc. supr., 1989—; gymnastics coach Amphitheater Pub. Schs., Tuscon, 1974-81, rsch chair supr. Ad Hoc Adv. Coun. on Sch. Dropouts, Ariz., 1987, mem. Gov. Edn. Conf., Ariz., 1989, mem. State Supr. Task Force on Sch. Violence, Ariz., 1993-94, Mayor's Sch. Dist. Action Task Force, Tucson. 1993—. Mem. APEX, Tucson, 1987—, Traveler's Aid Soc. of Tucson, 1993—, Citizen's Adv. Coun. U. Ariz., 1994—; mem. tech. adv. bd. Town of Oro Valley, 1995—; mem. exec. steering com. K-16 Edn. Coun. So. Ariz. Recipient APEX Apple award U. Ariz., 1994. Mem. Am. Assn. for Superivision and Curriculum Devel., Nat. Organ. for Women, Am. Assn. of U. Women, U. Ariz. Hispanic Alumni Assn., Coll. Assn. for the Devel. and Renewal of Edn., Ariz. Hispanic Sch. Adminstrn.

FREY, MARGARET KATHRYN, artist; b. San Diego, Nov. 20, 1961; d. Leonard Hamilton and Kathryn (Thurston) F. BFA, R.I. Sch. Design, 1988. Owner Moovy Co. Computer & Animation Co., N.Y.C., 1992—. Acad. award nom. for animation art direction The Chicken from Outer Space, 1995. Mem. ASIFA (bd. dirs. 1990—, editor jour. 1994—). Home: 951 Amsterdam Ave # 2C New York NY 10025

FREY, MARGO WALTHER, career counselor, columnist; b. Watertown, Wis., July 1, 1941; d. Lester John and Anabel Marie (Bergin) Walther; m. James Severin Frey, June 29, 1963; children: Michelle Marie Frey Loberg, David James. BA in French, Cardinal Stritch Coll., 1963; MS in Counseling and Guidance, U. Wis., Milw., 1971; EdD in Adult Edn., Nova U., 1985. Nat. bd. cert. career counselor. Acad. counselor biology dept. Ind. U., Bloomington, 1975-76; dir. career planning and placement Cardinal Stritch Coll., Milw., 1977-89; pres. Career Devel. Svcs., Inc., Milw., 1989—; weekly columnist Milw. Sentinel, 1994-95. Mem. Bloomington (Ind.) women's commn. com. on employment assessment Displaced Homemakers Task Force, 1975. Named to Practitioner's Hall of Fame, Nova U., 1985. Mem. ASTD (bd. dirs. 1992), Wis. Career Planning and Placement Assn. (bd. dirs. 1987), Wis. Assn. Adult and Continuing Edn. (bd. dirs. 1983-85), Milw. Coun. Adult Learning, Human Resource Mgmt. Assn., Tempo (bd. dirs. 1995—).

FREYD, JENNIFER JOY, psychology educator; b. Providence, Oct. 16, 1957; d. Peter John and Pamela (Parker) F.; m. John Q. Johnson, June 9, 1984; children: Theodore, Philip, Alexandra. BA in Anthropology magna cum laude, U. Pa., 1979; PhD in Psychology, Stanford U., 1983. Asst. prof. psychology Cornell U., 1983-87, mem. faculty coun. of reps., 1986-87; assoc. prof. psychology U. Oreg., Eugene, 1987-92, prof., 1992—; mem. dean's adv. com. U. Oreg., 1990-91, 92-93, mem. exec. com. Ctr. for the Study of Women in Soc., 1991-93, mem. child care com., 1987-89, 90-91; fellow Ctr. for Advanced Study in the Behavioral Scis., 1989-90; elected mem. faculty coun. of reps. Cornell U., 1986-87; mem. dean's adv. com. U. Oreg., 1990—, exec. com. Ctr. for Rsch. Study of Women in Soc., 1991-92, Inst. of Cognitive and Decision Scis., 1991—. Author: Betrayal Trauma: The Logic of Forgetting Childhood Abuse, 1996; editl. bd. Jour. Exptl. Psychology: Learning, Memory, and Cognition, 1989-91; guest reviewer Am. Jour. Psychology, Am. Psychologist, others; contbr. articles to profl. jours. Recipient Graduate fellowship NSF, 1979-82, Univ. fellowship Stanford U., 1982-83, Presdl. Young Investigator award NSF, 1985-90, IBM Faculty Devel. award, 1985-87, fellowship Ctr. for Advanced Study in the Behavioral Scis., 1989-90, John Simon Meml. fellowship Guggenheim Found., 1989-90, Rsch. Scientist Devel. award NIMH, 1989-94; other rsch. funding. Fellow AAAS, APA, Am. Psychol. Soc.; mem. Psychonomic Soc., Sigma Xi. Office: U Oreg 1227 Dept Psychology Eugene OR 97403-1227

FREYER, DANA HARTMAN, lawyer; b. Pitts., Apr. 17, 1944; m. Bruce M. Freyer, Dec. 21, 1969. Student, L' Institut De Hautes Etudes Internationales, Geneva, 1963-64; BA, Conn. Coll., 1965; postgrad., Columbia U., 1968, JD, 1971. Bar: N.Y. 1972, Ill. 1974, U.S. Dist. Ct. (no. dist.) Ill. 1974, U.S. Ct. Appeals (7th cir.) 1976, U.S. Supreme Ct. 1977, U.S. Dist. Ct. (so. dist.) N.Y. 1978, U.S. Dist. Ct. (ea. dist.) N.Y. 1981, U.S. Ct. Appeals (2d cir.) 1982. Staff atty. Legal Aid Soc. Westchester County, Mt. Vernon, N.Y., 1971-72; assoc. Friedman & Koven, Chgo., 1973-77; assoc. Skadden, Arps, Slate, Meagher & Flom, N.Y.C., 1977-88, spl. counsel, 1988-93, ptnr., 1993—; pres. Westchester Legal Services, Inc., White Plains, N.Y., 1985-87, bd. dirs. Mem. ABA, Bar Assn. of City of N.Y. Office: Skadden Arps Slate Meagher & Flom 919 3rd Ave New York NY 10022*

FREYER, VICTORIA C., fashion and interior design executive; b. Asbury Park, N.J.; d. Spiros Steven and Hope (Pappas) Pappaylion; m. Cyril Steven Arvanitis, Dec. 26, 1950 (div. 1975); children: Samuel James, Hope Alexandra. BA, Georgian Court Coll., 1950; student, N.Y. Sch. Interior Design, 1971-72. Mgr. Homestead Restaurant, Ocean Grove, N.J., 1946-58; art supr. Lakewood (N.J.) Pub. Schs., 1950-51; interior designer London, 1975-76, F. Korasic Assocs., Oakhurst, N.J., 1977-78; owner, operator Virginia Interiors, McLean, Va., 1974-90; interior designer Anita Perlut Interiors, McLean, 1986; owner, operator Victoria Freyer Interiors, McLean, 1986—; fashion cons. Nordstrom Splty. Store, McLean, 1988-92; fashion seminar coord. Nordstrom Splty. Store, Tysons Corner, Va., 1992—; lectr. Girl Scouts U.S., Rep. Women of Capitol Hill, Washington Hosp. Ctr., Women's Am. ORT, Nat. Assn. Cath. Women, Bethesda Naval Hosp., NIH, others. Pres. Monmouth County Med. Aux., 1964; originator 1st lecture series Monmouth Coll., Long Branch, N.J., 1965; guest moderator Alexandria (Va.) Hosp. Series, 1988; mem. Women's Symphony Com., Washington, 1988—; guest speaker Girl Scouts U.S. Coun. Nation's Capitol, 1988-90, Nuclear Energy Coun., 1989, pers. dept. CIA, 1989-90, Internat. Women's Group Washington, 1989-90. Recipient Recognition awards Girl Scout Coun. Nation's Capitol, 1991, No. Region Beta Pi, 1991, Beta Sigma Pi, 1991. Mem. AAUW (program chmn. 1968, guest speaker many orgns.). Greek Orthodox. Home and Office: 7630 Provincial Dr Mc Lean VA 22102-7631

FREYMUELLER, CYNTHIA LOUISE, educational consultant; b. Chgo., July 29, 1940; d. Eugene Willard and Dorothy Harriet (Rutstrom) Larson; m. John Craig Freymueller; children: Jeffrey T., Brian J., Sarah S. BA, San Diego State U., 1962; GATE cert., U. Calif., Riverside, 1982. Cert. elem. tchr., K-8, Calif. Tchr. LaMesa Spring Valley Sch. Dist., 1962-64, Ctrl. Sch. Dist., Rancho Cuca, Calif., 1976-81; mentor, tchr. Snowline J.U. Sch. Dist., Phelan, Calif., 1981—. Recipient Hon. Svc. award PTA Ctrl. Sch., 1978, Foothill Coun. PTA, 1979. Mem. AAUW (women's issues com.), Mountain Desert Reading Assn., Calif. Reading Assn., Delta Kappa Gamma. Home: 18524 Kamana Rd Apple Valley CA 92307-1454

FREYTAG, ADDIE LOU, nurse; b. Crestview, Fla., May 16, 1941; d. William Harold and Nellie (Davis) McCullough; m. Charles Lee Freytag, Oct. 14, 1961 (dec. 1992); children: Cassandra Duncan, Camilla Gay, C. Preston. RN, Orange Meml. Hosp., 1961; grad., Tex. Woman's U., 1973; BS in Edn., U. Tenn., 1988, MSN, 1991. RN, Tenn., Fla.; cert. pediat. nurse practitioner, family nurse practitioner. Staff nurse Hariman (Tenn.) Hosp., 1961-66, Oak Ridge (Tenn.) Hosp., 1966-70; office nurse Dr. Lewis Preston, Oak Ridge, 1970-74; family nurse practitioner Mountain Peoples Health Coun., 1974-76; with Child Health & Devel., Wartburg, Tenn., 1977-80, Community Health Ctr., Deer Lodge, Tenn., Highland Health Ctr., Elgin, Tenn.; staff nurse Parkwest Hosp. Knoxville Superior Home Health, Wartburg, 1989; family nurse practitioner Oak Grove Primary Care Clinic, Oneida, Tenn., 1992—; mem. med. staff Scott County Hosp., Oneida, 1992. Past county commr. Morgan County. Recipient honorable mention Felder Photo Contest, 1988, 95; George B. Boland Nurse's scholar. Mem. ANA (cert. family nurse practitioner 1982), Tenn. Nurses Assn., Nat. Assn. Pediat. Nurse Assocs. and Practitioners (cert. pediat. nurse practitioner 1977), Nurse Practitioners Assn. for Continuing Edn., Tenn. Pac, Nurses in Advanced Practice. Home: 226 Letorey Rd Wartburg TN 37887-3135

FREYTAG, SHARON NELSON, lawyer; b. Larned, Kans., May 11, 1943; d. John Seldon and Ruth Marie (Herbel) Nelson; children: Kurt David, Hillary Lee. BS with highest distinction, U. Kans., Lawrence, 1965; MA, U. Mich., 1966; JD cum laude, So. Meth. U., 1981. Bar: Tex. 1981, U.S. Dist. Ct. (no. dist.) Tex. 1981, U.S. Ct. Appeals (5th cir.) 1982, U.S. Supreme Ct. 1993; cert. civil appellate law. Tchr. English, Gaithersburg (Md.) H.S., 1966-70; instr. English, Eastfield Coll., 1974-78; law clk. U.S. Dist. Ct. for No. Dist. Tex., 1981-82, U.S. Ct. Appeals 5th Cir., 1982; ptnr. litigation and appellate sect. Haynes and Boone, Dallas, 1983—, vis. prof. law Southern Meth. U., 1985-86; faculty Appellate Adv. program NITA. Editor-in-chief Southwestern Law Jour., 1980-81; contbr. articles to law jours. Woodrow Wilson fellow. Recipient John Marshall Constl. Law award, Baird Cmty. Spirit award, 1995. Mem. ABA (mem. litigation sect., chair subcom. on local rules), Fed. Bar Assn. (co-chmn. appellate practice and advocacy sect. 1990-91), Tex. Bar Assn. (mem. appellate coun.), Dallas Bar Assn. (mem. appellate coun.), Higginbotham Inn of Ct., Barristers, Order of Coif, Phi Delta Phi, Phi Beta Kappa. Lutheran. Office: Haynes & Boone 3100 NationsBank Plz Dallas TX 75202

FRIAUF, KATHERINE ELIZABETH, metal company executive; b. Balt., Oct. 13, 1956; d. John Beecher Friauf and Elizabeth Withers (Wilson) Struever. Student, Columbia Coll., Chgo., 1979-81. Cert. sound engr. Owner, operator Midwest Emery Freight System, Chgo., 1978-80; driver BCB Dispatch, Inc., Rochester, N.Y., 1980-88; dispatcher, systems analyst BCB Dispatch, Inc., LeRoy, N.Y., 1988-89; corp. controller Rochester Plating Works, Inc., 1988—; pres., co-owner Rochester Vibratory Inc., 1991—; dir. Rochester Plating Works, Inc., 1988—. Mem. NAFE, Rochester Women's Network (patron mem.). Presbyterian. Office: Rochester Vibratory Inc 4 Cairn St Rochester NY 14611-2416

FRIDAY, KATHERINE ORWOLL, artist; b. Granite Falls, Minn., Dec. 3, 1917; d. Melvin Sylvester and Anna Elizabeth (Hustvedt) Orwoll; m. Erling Bjarne Struxness, May 8, 1943 (div. 1961); children: John Eric Struxness, Mimi Ann McNicholas, Martha Jane Begin; m. George Edward Friday, Apr. 12, 1969. Student, U. Minn., 1935-36, 40-41, Frederick Mizen Sch. of Art, Chgo., 1941. Designer, illustrator Josten's, Owatonna, Minn., 1936-49, 42-43; layout artist Tempo Inc., Chgo., 1941-42, Vogue-wright Studios, Chgo., 1943-44; layout illustration Allan D Parson Agy., Chgo., 1945, Ad-Art, Wichita, 1952-54, 63; indsl. designer Harold W. Darr Assoc., Mpls., 1959-61; layout illustration Lydiard Assoc., Mpls., 1961-63, 64, Skyline Studio, Mpls., 1964-66, Comm. Cons., Wilmington, Del., 1971; freelance illustration Chgo., 1945-48, Hutchinson, 1948-58; art dir. SPF Adv. Intermedia, Mpls., 1966-69, Arne Westerman Adv., Portland, 1970-71, Battle Advt., Wyncote, Pa., 1971-72; creative dir. A'La Carte Art, Bellevue, Wash., 1973-77; graphic illustration Courseware, Moffat Field, Quantic, and Los Altos, Calif., 1978-81; ret., 1981. Mem. Miniature Artists of Am., Fla. Miniature Art Soc. (1st pl. 1989, 91, 2d pl. 1990, 94), Ga. Miniature Artists (1st pl. 1991, 94, 2d pl. 1990), Miniature Printers, Sculptors, Gravers Soc., Oreg. Soc. of Artists, Main St. Artists, Cider Painters.

FRIDLEY, SAUNDRA LYNN, internal audit executive; b. Columbus, Ohio, June 14, 1948; d. Jerry Dean and Esther Eliza (Bluhm) F. BS, Franklin U., 1976; MBA, Golden Gate U., 1980. Accounts receivable supr. Internat. Harvester, Columbus, Ohio, San Leandro, Calif., 1972-80; sr. internal auditor Western Union, San Francisco, 1980; internal auditor II, County of Santa Clara, San Jose, Calif., 1980-82; sr. internal auditor Tymshare, Inc., Cupertino, Calif., 1982-84, div. contr., 1984; internal audit mgr. VWR Scientific, Brisbane, Calif., 1984-88, audit dir., 1988-89; internal audit mgr. Pacific IBM Employees Fed. Credit Union, San Jose, 1989-90, Western Staff Svcs., Inc.,

Walnut Creek, Calif., 1990—; internal audit mgr., 1990-92; dir. quality assurance, 1992—; owner Dress Fore the 9's, Brentwood, Calif., 1994—; pres., founder Bay Area chpt. Cert. Fraud Examiners, 1990. Mem. NAFE, Friends of the Vineyards, Internal Auditors Speakers Bur., Assn. Cert. Fraud Examiners (founder, pres. Bay area chpt., we. regional gov. 1996—), Inst. Internal Auditors (pres., founder Tri-Valley chpt.), Internal Auditor's Internat. Seminar Com., Internal Auditor's Internat. Conf. Com. vocations: woodworking, gardening, golfing. Home: 19 Windmill Ct Brentwood CA 94513-2502 Office: Western Staff Svcs 301 Lennon Ln Walnut Creek CA 94598-2418 also: Dress Fore The 9's 613 1st St Ste 19 Brentwood CA 94513-1322

FRIED, ELEANOR REINGOLD, psychologist, educator; b. Quantico, Va., Jan. 4, 1943; d. Morris and Eleanor (Wilson) R.; divorced, 1984; children: Joshua Mark, Noah Seth, Adam Lawrence. BS cum laude, Boston U., 1964; MS in Clin. Sch. Psychology, CUNY, 1971; postgrad. Fordham U., 1971-73; MA in Clin. Psychology, The Fielding Inst., 1980, PhD in Clin. Psychology, 1981. Lic. psychologist, N.J.; diplomate Am. Bd. Forensic Examiners. Psychology intern Roosevelt Hosp., N.Y.C., 1971-73; cons. Inwood House, N.Y.C., 1971-83; staff therapist Univ. Consultation Center Mental Hygiene, Bronx, N.Y., 1974-79, clin. instr., 1976-80; sr. clin. psychologist moderate security unit North Princeton Developmental Ctr., 1983—; cons. Early Childhood Learning Center, Paramus, N.J., 1978-80, Found. for Religion and Mental Health, Briarcliff Manor, N.Y., 1979-82, Inwood House, N.Y.C., 1981-83, prin. clin. psychologist Ewing Residential Ctr., Trenton, N.J., 1987-88, Ind. Child Study Teams, East Orange, N.J; pvt. practice, Princeton, N.J.; expert witness in criminal cts. Mem. APA (assoc.), N.J. Psychol. Assn., Nat. Assn. Treatment Sex Offenders, Kappa Tau Alpha. Office: 601 Ewing St # C-20 Princeton NJ 08540-2757

FRIED, RONNEE, marketing research company executive; b. N.Y.C., Dec. 16, 1947; d. Phillip Frank Fried and Gloria Edith (Pfeffer) Sandow. B.A., George Washington U., 1969. Field dir. AHF Mktg. Research, N.Y.C., 1969-73; project dir. Decisions Ctr. Inc., N.Y.C., 1973-76, Ogilvy & Mather Advt., N.Y.C., 1977; assoc. group mgr. Data Devel. Corp., N.Y.C., 1977-81; ptnr., exec. v.p. Brown Koff & Fried Inc., N.Y.C., 1981—. bd. dirs. Chain Lightning Theatre Inc. Mem. speakers bur. Greater N.Y. Conf. Soviet Jewry, 1979—. Mem. Am. Mktg. Assn. (Effie Awards Judging co-chmn. 1982, membership com. 1981, Recognition award 1982, career counselor), Advt. Women N.Y. Jewish. Avocation: competitive ballroom dancing. Home: 454 Broome St New York NY 10013-2602 Office: Brown Koff & Fried Inc 112 Madison Ave New York NY 10016-7416

FRIEDAN, BETTY NAOMI, author, feminist leader; b. Peoria, Ill., Feb. 4, 1921; d. Harry and Miriam (Horwitz) Goldstein; m. Carl Friedan, June 1947 (div. May 1969); children: Daniel, Jonathan, Emily. AB summa cum laude, Smith Coll., 1942, LHD (hon.), 1975; LHD (hon.), SUNY, Stony Brook, 1985, Cooper Union, 1987; Doctorate (hon.), Columbia U., 1994. Rsch. fellow U. Calif., Berkeley, 1943; lectr. feminism univs., women's groups, bus. and profl. groups in U.S. and Europe; founder NOW, 1st pres., 1966-70, chairwoman adv. com., 1970-72, mem. bd. dirs. legal def. and edn. fund; organizer Nat. Women's Polit. Caucas, 1971, Internat. Feminist Congress, 1973, First Women's Bank, 1973, Econ. Think Tank for Women, 1974; v.p. Nat. Assn. Repeal Abortion Laws, 1970-73; Disting. vis. prof. sch. journalism and studies of women and men in soc., U. So. Calif., 1987; vis. prof. sociology Temple U., 1972, Queens Coll., 1975; vis. lectr. Calhoun Coll., fellow Yale U., 1974; lectr. New Sch. Social Research, N.Y.C., 1971; sr. research assoc. Ctr. Social Scis., Columbia U., N.Y.C., 1979-81; bd. dirs. NOW Legal Defense and Education fund; co-chmn. Nat. Comms. Women's Equality; del. White Ho. Conf. on Family, 1980; del. UN Decade for Women Confs. in Mexico City, Copenhagen, Nairobi; mem. LORAN Commn. Harvard Community Health Plan; vis. scholar U. S. Fla., Sarasota, 1985; Disting. vis. prof. Sch. Journalism and Social Work Sch. U. So. Calif. Author: The Feminine Mystique, 1963, It Changed My Life: Writings on the Women's Movement, 1976, The Second Stage, 1981, The Fountain of Age, 1993; mem. editl. bd. Present Tense mag.; contbg. editor McCall's mag., 1971-74; contbr. Atlantic Monthly; contbr. articles to New York Times, Cosmopolitan, Saturday Rev., Family Circle, Good Housekeeping, McCall's, Newsweek, American Behavioral Scientist, Social Policy, and others; papers being collected by Schlesinger Libr. Harvard U. Mem. exec. com. Am. Jewish Congress, co-chair nat. commn. women's equality, 1984-85; mem. nat. bd. Girl Scouts USA, 1976-82; mem. N.Y. County Democratic Com. Recipient Humanist of Yr. award, 1974, Eleanor Roosevelt Leadership award, 1989; Inst. Politics fellow Kennedy Sch. Govt., Harvard U., 1982, rsch. fellow Ctr. Population Studies, Harvard U., 1982-83, Chubb fellow Yale U., 1985, Andrus Ctr. Gerontology fellow U. So. Calif., 1986, guest scholar Woodrow Wilson Ctr. for Internat. Scholars, 1995-96, disting. vis. prof. George Mason U., 1995, Mt. Vernon Coll., 1996. Mem. AFTRA, PEN, Author's Guild, Women's Ink, Women's Forum, Mag. Writers, Am. Soc. Journalists and Authors (1st recipient Mort Weisinger award for outstanding mag. journalism 1979, Author of Yr. 1982), Assn. Humanistic Psychology, Am. Sociology Assn., Gerontol. Soc. Am., Cosmos Club, Nat. Press Club, Phi Beta Kappa. Address: 420 7th St NW Apt 1010 Washington DC 20004-2215

FRIEDBERG, MARLYN S., real estate company executive; b. Phila., May 13, 1938; d. Milton and Sylvia Leah (Silver) Soss; m. Eugene Alexander Friedberg; children: Ahron, Alanna, Jared. BS, Temple U., 1959. Lic. real estate salesperson, N.J., real estate broker, N.J.; cert. real estate broker, N.J. Elem. sch. tchr. Emerson Elem. Sch., Teaneck, N.J., 1960-63; real estate salesperson Saydah Realtors, Tenafly, N.J., 1973-82; real estate broker Dick O'Connor Real Estate, Tenafly, N.J., 1982-83; owner, pres. Lenk-Friedberg Properties, Cresskill, N.J., 1983-94, Friedberg Properties & Assoc., Cresskill, Englewood Cliffs, Tenafly, N.J., 1994—; dir. bd. realtors Eastern Bergen County Bd. Realtors, Palisades Park, N.J., 1989—. Pres. Ladies Auxilliary Columbia Presbyn. Hosp., N.Y.C.; com. mem. PTA Horace Mann Sch., Riverdale, N.Y. Fellow Rotary Found. of Rotary Internat. (com. mem. 1990-91, Paul Harris Fellow 1992); mem. Nat. Assn. Realtors, Knickbocker Heights Assn. (pres.), Alpine Swim & Tennis Club (pres. 1986-92). Home: PO Box 838 Alpine NJ 07620 Office: Friedberg Properties & Assocs 18 Union Ave Cresskill NJ 07628

FRIEDE, HEATHER ELLEN, computer consultant; b. Martinsville, Va., Nov. 24, 1968; d. Richard E. Friede and Victoria E. (Niemann) Friel. BS in Bus. Adminstrn., U. Kans., 1991, BS in Computer Sci., 1991. Computer cons., programmer, analyst Am. Mgmt. Sys., Lakewood, Colo., 1991-92; computer cons., sr. programmer, analyst Am. Mgmt. Sys., Lisbon, Portugal, 1992-95; computer cons., prin. Am. Mgmt. Sys., Madrid, 1995—. Mem. NOW, NAFE, As Quintas Profl. Women of Lisbon, Upsilon Pi Epsilon. Office: Am Mgmt Sys 14033 Denver West Pky Golden CO 80401

FRIEDEL, HELEN BRANGENBERG, counselor, therapist; b. Kampsville, Ill., May 16, 1938; d. Carl Morris and Martha Marie (Zipprich) Brangenberg; m. John Laverne Friedel; children: Vincent Joseph, John Francis. BS, So. Ill. U., 1969, MS, 1973. Lic. profl. counselor, Mo. Educator Archdiocese of St. Louis, 1956-87; counselor Diocese of Belleville, Waterloo, Ill., 1988-89, Christian Bros. H.S., St. Louis, 1989—; pvt. practice Florissant, Mo., 1987—. Mem. parents adv. bd. St. Louis Prep. Sem., Florissant, 1973-79; youth moderator Sacred Heart Parish, Florissant, 1967-71, lector and eucharistic min. Mem. ACA, Mo. Counseling Assn. (bd. dirs. 1986-88, 90-93, sec. 1990, pres. 1992, legis. chair 1992-93, Kitty Cole Human Rights award 1993), St. Louis Counseling Assn., Mo. Multicultural Counselors, Mid Rivers Counseling Assn. (pres. 1986), Am. Sch. Counselors Assn., Mo. Sch. Counselors Assn., St. Louis Learning Disabilities Assn. (bd. dirs. 1994), Kappa Delta Pi. Roman Catholic. Home: 425 Saint Marie St Florissant MO 63031-5830 Office: Christian Bros Prep HS 6501 Clayton Rd Saint Louis MO 63117-1705

FRIEDEN, JANE HELLER, art educator; b. Norfolk, Va., Aug. 25, 1926; d. Samuel Ries and Saida (Seligman) Heller; m. Joseph Lee Frieden, Dec. 23, 1950 (dec. 1990); children: Nancy Frieden Crowe, Robert M., Andrew M. AA, Coll. of William and Mary, Norfolk, Va., 1945; BA, Coll. of William and Mary, Williamsburg, Va., 1947; MA, Columbia U., 1950. Lic. pvt. pilot. Tchr. art City of Norfolk Pub. Schs., 1947-48, Hudson Day Sch., New Rochelle, N.Y., 1948-49, Mt. Vernon (N.Y.) Pub. Schs., 1949-50, City of Norfolk Pub. Schs., 1950-51; prof. art Coll. William and Mary Extension, Williamsburg, 1957-72, U. Va. Extension, Norfolk, 1972-78, Community Colls. State of Va., Chesapeake and Hampton, 1978-82, St. Leo Coll., Norfolk, 1982-95; travel agt., 1977-89. Author: (dictionary) A is For Art, 1978-82; artist water color paintings and ink drawings at several shows. Asst. Gen. Douglas MacArthur Meml. Archives, Norfolk, 1945-95; vol. Chrysler Mus. Art, Norfolk, 1991—, Va. Symphony Aux., 1992—, Norfolk Little Theatre Box Office, 1991—, Meals on Wheels, 1962-66, Make-A-Wish Found., 1996, ARC, 1953-95, greylady project, 1956-62, bloodmobile project, 1966-80; tchr. drawing Ghent Venture, 1993; reader for the visually handicapped Intouch Network WHRO-TV, 1991—; mem. archives com. Ohef Sholom Temple; bd. dirs. Norfolk Little Theatre, 1996. Mem. Internat. Orgn. Women Pilots (treas. 1978-85), Tidewater Artists Assn. (bd. dirs. 1975-80, 91—, treas. membership coun.), Tidewater Orchid Soc., Am. Orchid Soc., Norfolk Soc. Arts, United Daus. Confederacy, Hermitage Soc., Norfolk Ex Libris Soc. Coll. William & Mary (mem. steering com. 1993—), Va. Belles (reunion com. 1993—). Republican. Jewish. Home: 221 Oxford St Norfolk VA 23505-4354

FRIEDHEIM, JAN V., education administrator; b. Corpus Christi, Tex., Oct. 20, 1935; d. Roy Lee Conyers and Bertha Victoria (Ostrom) Hamm; m. John R. Eisenhour, Nov. 22, 1962 (div. 1983); m. Stephen B. Friedheim, Sept. 1, 1984; children: Neenah, Stephen II, Robert. BS, U. Tex., 1957; hon. doctorate, Constantinian U., Malta, 1994. Chmn. bd. Exec. Secretarial Sch., Dallas, 1960—; vice chmn. Tex. Vocat.Adv. Bd., Austin, 1979-86; mem. adv. com. Dept. Edn., Washington, 1980-84; commr. So. Assn. Colls. and Schs. Commn. on Occupl. Edn. Instns., 1994—; mem. adv. com. State Postsecondary Rev. Entity, 1994; bd. dirs. Tex. Assn. Pvt. Schs., Career Coll. and Schs. of Tex., 1994—; commr. Coun. on Occupl. Edn., 1995—. Bd. dirs. Career Colls. and Schs. of Tex., 1995—. Mem. Assn. Ind. Colls. and Schs. (chmn. bd. dirs. 1980-81, commn. 1978-79, commr. 1974-79, Disting. Mem. 1974, 81, Mem. of Yr. 1979), Southwestern Assn. Pvt. Schs. (pres. 1982), Metroplex Assn. Pvt. Schs. (pres. 1989-90, 92-93), So. Assn. Colls. and Schs. (trustee 1981-85, commn. on occupational edn. instns. 1994—), Tex. Assn. Pvt. Schs. (bd. dirs. 1992—), Career Colls. and Schs. Tex. (bd. dirs. 1995—). Home: 6450 Patrick Dr Dallas TX 75214-2444

FRIEDLAND, BILLIE LOUISE, former human services administrator; b. Los Alamos, New Mex., Jan. 6, 1944; d. William Jerald and Harriet Virginia (Short) Van Buskirk; m. David Friedland. BS in Edn., Calif. U. of Pa., 1972, MS in Psychology, 1986; postgrad., W.Va. U., 1992—. Sales mgr., buyer Friedland's Ladies Ready-To-Wear, Monessen, Pa., 1969-72; tchr. Belle Vernon (Pa.) Area Schs., 1973-74; head social scs. dept. Yeshiva Achei Tmimim, Pitts., 1974-75; caseworker, outreach to children and their families project Fayette County Mental Health and Mental Retardation Clinic, Uniontown, Pa., 1975, ctr. supr. outreach to children and their families project, 1976; case mgr., family support svcs. coord. Diversified Human Svcs. Inc., Monessen, 1978-89, supr. cmty. living arrangements, 1989-92; grad. asst. Affiliated Ctr. for Deve. Disabilities W.Va. U., Morgantown, 1992-93, grad. asst. dept. spl. edn., 1993—; founder 1st Infant/Toddler Day Care Project, Fayette County, 1976-78. Mem. NAACP, Am. Assn. Mental Retardation, Coun. for Exceptional Children, W.Va. Fedn. Coun. for Exceptional Children (chairperson divsn. mental retardation/developmental disabilities), Nat. Assn. Dual Diagnoses, Conf. on Black Basic Edn. Office: WVa U Sch Human Resources Dept Spl Edn 507 E Allen Hall Morgantown WV 26506-6122

FRIEDLANDER, PATRICIA ANN, marketing executive; b. Chgo., May 9, 1944; d. James Farrell and Therese Mary (Pfeiler) Crotty; m. Daniel B. Friedlander, July 3, 1971 (div. Apr. 1978); children: Michael Derek, David Colin; m. Denis R. Johnson, Feb. 24, 1994. BA, Cardinal Stritch Coll., 1966; MA, U. Wis., Milw., 1968; postgrad., U. Chgo., 1968-69, U. London, 1968—. Instr. U. Wis., Milw., 1966-68, Chgo. State U., 1968-71, Argo Community High Sch., Summit, Ill., 1971-73, Park Dist., Park Forest South, Ill., 1973-77; counselor Will County Mental Health Clinic, Park Forest South, 1977-78; sales rep. Prentice-Hall, Inc., Englewood Cliffs, N.J., 1978-84; nat. sales mgr. Dow Jones Irwin, Homewood, Ill., 1984-87; dir. mktg. Nat. Textbook Co., Lincolnwood, Ill., 1987-88; mgr. mktg. Scott Foresman & Co., Glenview, Ill., 1988-90; corp. advt. dir. Giltspur, Inc., Itasca, Ill., 1990-96; dir. Mktg. Comms. Exhibitgroup/Gitspur, Roselle, Ill., 1996—; dir. Printer's Row Bookfair, Chgo., 1985; pub. cons.; spkr. and author in trade show and pub. field; mem. Ctr. for Exposition Rsch. Den mother Cub Scouts Am., Park Forest South, 1981-84. Mem. Bus. Mktg. Assn., Am. Book Travelers, Midwest Book Travelers (pres. 1983-87), Am. Mgmt. Assn., Am. Mktg. Assn., Health Care Conv. & Exhibitors Assn., Internat. Exhibitors Assn. (del.), Exhibit Designers and Prodrs. Assn. (del.), Computer Exhibit Mgrs. Assn. Home: 2320 W Farwell Ave Chicago IL 60645-4735 Office: Exhibitgroup/Giltspur 200 N Gary Ave Roselle IL 60172

FRIEDMAN, ALICE DIANE, internist, gastroenterologist, educator; b. Houston, Aug. 21, 1957; d. Ben and Susanna Rose (Stern) F. BS in Medicine, Tex. A&M U., 1979, MD, 1981; MS in Aerospace Medicine, Wright State U., 1994. Lic. physician, Tex., Va., Md., Ohio, Ark. Resident in internal medicine U. of Va. Affiliated Hosp., Roanoke-Salem, Va., 1981-84; fellow in gastroenterology U. Md. Hosp., Balt., 1984-86; pvt. practice Mahorner Clinic, New Orleans, 1986-87, Lubbock, Tex., 1988-92; resident in aerospace medcine Wright State U., Dayton, Ohio, 1992-94; rsch. asst. Logicon Inc., Dayton, 1993-94; asst. prof. in internal medicine U. Ark. for Med. Scis., Little Rock, 1994—; instr. U. Md., Balt., 1984-86; clin. asst. prof. Tex. Tech. U., Lubbock, 1989-91; cons. Dayton-Vets. Hosp., 1993-94. Contbr. case reports, abstracts, studies to profl. publs. Bd. dirs. S.W. Lubbock Kiwanis, 1989-92. Rsch. grantee Schering Inc., 1995. Fellow ACP, Am. Coll. Gastroenterology; mem. AMA, Am. Gastroenterol. Assn., Am. Soc. Internal Medicine, Am. Soc. Parenteral and Enteral Nutrition. Office: U Ark for Med Scis Slot 567 4301 W Markham St Little Rock AR 72205

FRIEDMAN, ANN GAIL, writer, educator; b. Highland Park, Ill., Apr. 6, 1954; d. Tom Richard and Maxine Ruth (Murstein) F.; m. Thomas Alix Johnston, Sept., 1980. BA in Studio Art, Western Wash. U., 1979; MA in Art History, U. Wash., 1987. Lectr. art history Western Wash. U., Bellingham, 1989, 95—, visual resources mgr., 1993—; art critic Bellingham (Wash.) Herald, 1995—; pre-screener Birmingham (Ala.) Internat. Ednl. Film Festival, 1991-92, edn. cons. art edn. coun. Birmingham Mus. of Art, 1992. Curator, author: Counterpoint and Color: Prints by S.W. Hayter, 1991, The Art of Helen Loggie, 1993. Commr. Bellingham Mcpl. Arts Commn., Bellingham, 1993—. Office: Dept Art Western Wash U Bellingham WA 98225-9068

FRIEDMAN, BARBARA, artist, educator; b. N.Y.C., Mar. 15, 1955; d. William Robert and Erica Gertrude (Urech) F.; m. Brian Templin Seitz, May 16, 1985 (div. May 1992); 1 child, Sabina Rebecca; m. Nickolas Pappas, Dec. 4, 1993; 1 child, Sophia Stavrula. BA, Beloit Coll., 1976; BFA, RISD, 1979; MFA, U. Calif., Berkeley, 1983. Assoc. prof. art Pace U., Pleasantville, N.Y., 1983—; mem. rev. bd. Art in General, N.Y.C., 1994-95; mem. panel Artists Talk on Art, N.Y.C., 1995. One-woman shows at Dana Reich Gallery, San Francisco, 1983, Art Awareness, Lexington, N.Y., 1984, White Columns, N.Y., 1984, Queens Mus., N.Y., 1985, Real Art Ways, Hartford, Conn., 1985, Phillip Dash Gallery, N.Y., 1986, 87, Windows on White, N.Y., 1988, Hollins Coll. Art Gallery, Roanoke, Va., 1990, 55 Mercer, N.Y., 1991, Roanoke Mus. of Fine Arts, 1992, Hewlett Gallery, Pitts., 1992, The Bellport, N.Y., 1995; group exhibitions include Artists Space, N.Y., 1983, Terry Dintenfass Gallery, N.Y., 1984, The Drawing Ctr., N.Y., 1984, SoHo Ctr. for Visual Arts, N.Y., 1984, Grey Art Gallery, NYU, 1985, Aldrich Mus. Contemporary Art, Conn., 1985, White Columns, 1985, Marianne Deson Gallery, Chgo., 1985, Artspace, San Francisco, 1987, Queens Mus., 1988, Carlo Lamagna Gallery, N.Y., 1989, The Gallery, N.Y., 1991, P.S. 1 Mus., N.Y., 1992-93, Tweed Gallery, N.Y., 1993, Richard Anderson Gallery, N.Y., 1993, Art in Gen., N.Y., 1993, Exit Art, n.Y., 1993, N.Y. Law Sch., 1994, Sullivan County Mus., 1995. Regents fellow for art U. Calif., Berkeley, 1982, Va. Ctr. for Creative Arts fellow, 1985; award residency Yaddo, Saratoga Springs, N.Y., 1993; recipient Best in Show award Roanoke City Art Show, 1991, award for Arts in Transit, Met. Transp. Authority, 1994. Home: 138 W Broadway New York NY 10013

FRIEDMAN, CYNTHIA, film company executive. Sr. v.p., CFO Orion Pictures Corp., L.A. Office: Orion Pictures Corp 1888 Century Park E Los Angeles CA 90067*

FRIEDMAN, DIAN DEBRA, elementary education educator; b. Balt., June 12, 1943; d. Bernard Maurice and Sondra Seletta (Dolgoff) Jacobs; m. Irving Joel Friedman, June 24, 1965; children: Benjamin Aaron, Joshua Jason. AA, Miami (Fla.)-Dade Jr. Coll., 1963; BS in Elem. Edn., Fla. State U., 1965. With contracts and grants Fla. State U., Tallahassee, 1965-66; substitute tchr. Chicopee (Mass.) Sch. Systems, 1965-66; elem. tchr. City of Springfield, Mass., 1966-76; real estate salesperson Gene Kelly Real Estate, Suffield, Conn., 1985-87; ednl. tutor Suffield (Conn.) Sch. Sys., 1987—, mem. curriculum coun., 1986-90; tchr. Computer Tots; substitute tchr., tchr. asst. Agawam (Mass.) Pub. Schs. Bd. dirs. The Village for Families and Children, Inc., Hartford, Conn., 1986—, pub. issues com., 1994—; bd. dirs. Child and Family Charities, Inc., Hartford; chairperson Suffield Aux. The Village for Families and Children, Inc., 1978-80, mem. 1973—; mem. Citizens for Suffield, 1990—, Friends of Suffield Libr., 1973—, Springfield Mass. Cyclonauts. Mem. Fla. State Alumni Club, Suffield Woman's Club. Democrat. Jewish. Home: 119 Marbern Dr Suffield CT 06078-1542

FRIEDMAN, ELAINE FLORENCE, lawyer; b. N.Y.C., Aug. 22, 1924; d. Henry J. and Charlotte Leah (Youdelman) F.; m. Louis Schwartz, Apr. 10, 1949; 1 child, James Evan. BA, Hunter Coll., 1944; JD, Columbia U., 1946. Bar: N.Y. 1947, U.S. Dist. Ct. (so. and ea. dists.) N.Y., U.S. Ct. Appeals (2d cir.), U.S. Supreme Ct. 1954. Assoc. Oseas, Pepper & Siegel, N.Y.C., 1947-48, Bernstein & Benton, N.Y.C., 1948-51, Copeland & Elkins, N.Y.C., 1951—; sole practice N.Y.C., 1953—; bd. dirs. Health Ins. Plan of Greater N.Y. Mem Fedn. Internat. des Femmes Juristes (v.p. U.S. chpt. 1993-95), N.Y. Bar Assn., Women's City Club, Hunter Coll. Alumni Assn., Columbia Law School Assn. Jewish. Home: 2 Agnes Cir Ardsley NY 10502-1709 Office: 60 E 42nd St New York NY 10165

FRIEDMAN, FRANCES, public relations executive; b. N.Y.C., Apr. 8, 1928; d. Aaron and Bertha (Itzkowitz) Fallick; m. Clifford Jerome Friedman, June 17, 1950; children—Kenneth Lee, Jeffrey Bennett. B.B.A., CCNY, 1948. Dir. pub. relations Melia Internat., Madrid, N.Y.C., 1971-73; sr. v.p. Lobsenz-Stevens, N.Y.C., 1973-75; exec. v.p. Howard Rubenstein Assocs., N.Y.C., 1975-83; pres., prin. Frances Friedman Assocs., N.Y.C., 1983-84; pres., chmn. bd. dirs. GCI Group Inc., N.Y.C., 1984-91, pub. rels. and editorial cons., 1991-93; mng. dir. L.V. Power & Assoc., Inc., 1993—. Bd. dirs. ACRMD-Retarded Children, N.Y.C., 1983-85, City Coll. Fund, N.Y.C., 1970-79; mem. adv. bd. League for Parent Edn., N.Y.C., 1961-65; editor South Shore Democratic Newsletter, North Bellmore, N.Y., 1958-61, press sec. N.Y. State Assembly candidate, 1965, N.Y. State Congl. candidate, 1968; officer Manhasset Dem. Club, N.Y., 1965-69; mem. adv. com. N.Y.C. Council candidate, 1985. U. New Haven Bartels fellow, 1993. Mem. Pub. Relations Soc. Am., Women in Communications (Matrix award for pub. relations 1989), The Counselors Acad., Pride and Alarm, City Club N.Y. Democrat. Jewish. Home: 860 Fifth Ave New York NY 10021-5856

FRIEDMAN, FREDRICA SCHWAB, editor, publisher; b. N.Y.C., Aug. 29, 1939; d. Joseph H. and Ruth (Landis) Schwab; m. Stephen J. Friedman, June 25, 1961; children: Vanessa V., Alexander S. BA, Vassar Coll., 1961; MA, Columbia U., 1963. Assoc. articles editor Holiday Mag., N.Y.C., 1966-68; contbg. editor Travel & Leisure Mag., N.Y.C., 1969-70; editorial cons. Saturday Rev. Mag., N.Y.C., 1971-74; sr. editor Reader's Digest Press, N.Y.C., 1974-77; sr. staff editor Reader's Digest Condensed Books, N.Y.C., 1977-84; sr. editor Little, Brown & Co., N.Y.C., 1985-88, exec. editor, assoc. pub., v.p., 1988—, editl. dir., assoc. pub., v.p., 1996; chair Matrix Awards, 1996. Recipient Matrix award Women in Comm., 1992. Mem. Women's Forum, Women's Media Group, The Peer Group, Leadership Circle of Woman's Campaign Fund. Home: 1185 Park Ave New York NY 10128-1308 Office: Little Brown & Co 1271 Avenue Of The Americas New York NY 10020

FRIEDMAN, LINDA ANNE, lawyer; b. Cleve., Oct. 6, 1952; d. Thomas John and Elaine (Urban) Bunsey; m. Doug Friedman, Aug. 6, 1978; children: Jessica, Rachel. Student, Sorbonne U., Paris, 1971-72; AB, Kenyon Coll., 1973; JD, Vanderbilt U., 1976. Bar: Ala. 1976. Law clk. U.S. Dist. Ct. (no. dist.) Ala., Birmingham, 1976-77; ptnr. Bradley, Arant, Rose & White, Birmingham, 1977—; legal editor Channel 6 TV, Birmingham, 1993-94. Co-author: Protecting Intellectual Property, 1988, Unfair Competition in Alabama, 1989; editor: (chpts. in books) State Trademark and Unfair Competition, 1986—, State Antitrust Practice and Statutes, 1991. Fundraiser March of Dimes, Birmingham, 1990; co-chmn. bus. leaders divsn. Birmingham Jewish Fedn., Birmingham, 1992, 93; VIP Starathon, United Cerebral Palsy, Birmingham, 1993—. Named one of Top 40 under 40, Birmingham Bus. Jour., 1992. Mem. Ala. Bar Assn. (chmn. antitrust 1986-90, bd. bar examiners 1988-89, other offices, Continuing Legal Edn. award 1990), Am. Law Inst., Bus. and Profl. Women (steering com. 1992-93), Kiwanis. Office: Bradley Arant Rose & White 1400 Park Place Tower 2001 Park Pl Birmingham AL 35203-2735

FRIEDMAN, MARIA ANDRE, public relations executive; b. Jackson, Mich., June 12, 1950; d. Robert Andre and Mary MacLean (Thompson) Hoving; m. Stanley N. Friedman, July 22, 1973; children: Alexandra, Adam. BA cum laude, U. Md., 1972, MA, 1979; DBA, Nova U., 1993. Writer, U.S. Bur. Mines, Washington, 1973-78; head writer Nat. Ctr. for Health Svc. Rsch. and Health Care Tech. Assessment, DHHS, Rockville, Md., 1978-85, chief publs. and info. br. Agy for Health Care Policy and Rsch., 1986-89; dir. office pub. affairs Health Care Financing Adminstrn., Washington, 1990—, acting assoc. adminstr. for comm., 1992-93, sr. rsch. advisor, Balt., 1994-95, dir. disemination staff ORB, 1995-96. Mem. Assn. Health Svcs. Rsch., Acad. of Mgmt. Home: 713 Brandon Green Dr Silver Spring MD 20904 Office: Health Care Fin Adminstrn 7500 Security Blvd Baltimore MD 21244

FRIEDMAN, MILDRED, designer, educator, curator; b. L.A., July 25, 1929; d. Nathaniel and Hortense (Weinsveig) Shenberg; m. Martin Friedman; children: Lise, Ceil, Zoe. BA, UCLA, 1951, MA, 1952; DFA (hon.), Mpls. Coll. Art, 1984; DFA, Hamlin U., 1987. Instr. design L.A. City Coll., 1952-54; archtl. designer Cerny Assocs., Mpls., 1957-69; design curator Walker Art Ctr., Mpls., 1970-90; freelance cons. N.Y.C., 1990—; architecture and design panel Nat. Endowment Arts, 1975-78, policy panel design arts, 1979-82, presdl. design awards jury, 1991; vis. com. sch. architecture and planning MIT, 1985-88, grad. sch. design Harvard U., 1994—; bd. dirs. Internat. Design Conf., Aspen, 1989-91, Chgo. Inst. Architecture and Urbanism, 1990-93, Nat. Inst. Archtl. Edn., 1993—; design jury Am. Acad. Rome, 1991; guest instr. UCLA, 1992; jury to select architect for Whitehall Ferry Terminal, N.Y.C., 1992; vis. instr. Harvard U., 1993; cons. Battery Park City Authority, N.Y.C.; guest curator Bklyn. Mus., Can. Ctr. Architecture. Editor Design Quar., 1970-91, numerous catalogues. Recipient Outstanding Achievement award YWCA, 1984, Outstanding Svc. award U. Minn., 1991; fellow Intellectual Interchange program Japan Soc., 1982; grantee Nat. Endowment Arts, 1992-93. Mem. AIA (hon., nat. awards jury 1981, 87, bd. dirs. Minn. chpt. 1984-86, Inst. Honors 1994).

FRIEDMAN, PAMELA RUTH LESSING, art consultant, financial consultant; b. N.Y.C., Jan. 15, 1950; d. Fred William and Helen D. (Kahn) Lessing; m. Neil David Friedman, May 28, 1972; children: Elizabeth Lessing, Paul Lessing. BA, U. Rochester, 1972; MSLS, U. N.C., Chapel Hill, 1974. Dep. libr. Am. Soc. Internat. Law, Washington, 1974-76; with edn. dept. Nat. Air and Space Mus., Smithsonian Inst., Washington, 1976-84; ind. cons. fin. and art Boulder, Colo., 1984—; pub. C.S.B. Co., Boulder, 1989—; lectr. in fields, 1989—; cons. Denver Art Mus., 1989-91, Asian Art Coordinating Coun., Denver, 1990—; pres. Kylin Resources, Boulder, Colo., 1995—. Author: (reference book) Chinese Snuff Bottles, 1990; editor: (reference book) Flight Service Directory, 1975. Rep. S.E.V.A.B., Smithsonian Instn., 1979-81, mem. exec. bd. docent coun. Nat. Air and Space Mus., 1977-81; mem. trustee coun. U. Rochester, N.Y., 1992, mem. vis. com. coll. of arts and scis. U. Rochester, 1994—; bd. dirs., mem. exec. com., bd., treas. Colo. Music Festival, Boulder, 1983-89; mem. exec. bd. Women's Incentive Fund Colo. U., Boulder, 1988—; rep. Leadership Boulder, 1986-87; v.p. bd. dirs. Lessing Found., N.Y., 1988—; mem. exec. bd. Interfaith Coun., Boulder, 1987-90; life mem. RAF Mus., 1977—. Recipient Internat. Gold Test Pin award Swiss Skiing Fedn., St. Moritz, 1975. Mem. Internat. Chinese Snuff Bottle Soc., Army and Navy Club (Washington), Beach Point Club (Mamaroneck, N.Y.), Game Creek Club (Vail, Colo.). Home and Office: 503 Kalmia Ave Boulder CO 80304-1733

FRIEDMAN, PAULINE POPLIN, civic worker, consultant; b. Scranton, Pa., Apr. 2, 1930; d. Harry and Lillian (Kushner) Poplin; m. Sidney Friedman, Aug. 3, 1952; children: Anne Friedman Glauber, Robert. BS, Pa. State U., 1952. Cons. AID, Washington, 1993—. Trustee Temple Israel, 1985-87, Jewish Cmty. Ctr., 1992—; mem. coun. King's Coll., 1992—; pres. Home Health Svcs.-vis. Nurse Assn., Kingston, Pa., 1987-88, Coun. Family Agys., Harrisburg, Pa., 1987-88, Family Svc. Wyoming Valley, Wilkes-Barre, 1988-90; mentor Leadership Wilkes-Barre; mem. pres.' coun. Wilkes U., 1991—, King's Coll.; v.p. United Way, Interfaith Coun. Wyoming Valley; bd. dirs. Ethics Inst. N.E. Pa., Dallas, 1994—, St. Vincent De Paul Soup Kitchen; bd. alumni coun. Pa. State U.; mem. Jewish Cmty. Bd. Whoming Valley. Recipient Humanitarian award Interfaith Coun. Wyoming Valley, 1989, Phillip Mitchell Cmty. Svc. award Pa. State U., 1990, Woman of Yr. award Family Svc. Wyoming Valley, 1993, Pathfinders award Luzerne County Women's Conf., 1995, Disting. Svc. award B'nai Brith, 1996. Home: 796 Milford Dr Kingston PA 18704-5308

FRIEDMAN, POLLY, public relations executive, marketing professional; b. Orange, N.J., Nov. 9, 1932; d. Sidney and Doris (Simons) Adler; m. Eugene M. Friedman, Jan. 14, 1954; children: Robert A. Friedman, Nancy Friedman Meagher. Student, Beaver Coll., 1951-53, NYU, 1953-54. Dir. pub. rels. Albert Einstein Med. Ctr., Phila., 1975-77, Pa. Coll. Optometry, Phila., 1977-79; mgr. media project devel. Sun Oil Co., Phila., 1979-86; dep. dir. Greater Phila. Econ. Coalition, Phila., 1986-88; exec. dir. The Nat. Constitution Ctr., Phila., 1992-94; pres. Polly Friedman & Assoc., Phila., 1988—; dir. mktg. Grant Thornton, Phila., 1995—; com. mem. White House Conf. on Small Bus., Pa.; hon. bd. mem. Nat. Archives Week, Phila., 1993; conf. spkr. Nat. Park Svc., Washington, 1993, Nat. Parks and Conservation Assn., 1993, 94, Nat. Newspaper Assn., 1993; mem. adv. com. Ambler Music Festival at Temple U., Phila., 1992-94; mem. pub. rels. coun. Phila. Coalition on Domestic Violence, 1986, 87; cons. Fed. Res. Bank, Phila., 1994—. Recipient Silver Anvil Best Pub. Rels. Event award Pub. Rels. Soc. of Am., 1979, Pepperpot award (Phila. chpt.), 1979, Best Pub. Affairs Radio Series Pa. Assn. Broadcasters, 1993. Office: PO Box 46 Spring House PA 19477-0046

FRIEDMAN, SUE TYLER, technical publications executive; b. Nürnberg, Germany, Feb. 28, 1925; came to U.S., 1938; d. William and Ann (Federlein) Tyler (Theilheimer); m. Gerald Manfred Friedman, June 27, 1948; children: Judith Fay Friedman Rosen, Sharon Mira Friedman Azaria, Devora Paula Friedman Zweibach, Eva Jane Friedman Scholle, Wendy Tamar Friedman Spanier. Student, Beth Israel Sch. Nursing, 1941-43. Exec. dir. Ventures and Publs. Gerald M. Friedman, 1964—; owner Tyler Publs., Watervliet and Troy, N.Y., 1978-86; treas., dir. Northeastern Sci. Found., Inc., Troy, 1979—; treas. Gerry Exploration, Inc., Troy, 1982-88; office mgr. Rensselaer Ctr. Applied Geology, Troy, 1983—. Pres. Pioneer Women/Na'amat, Tulsa, 1961-64, treas., Jerusalem, Israel, 1964, pres., Albany, N.Y., 1968-70; bd. dirs. Temple Beth-El, 1965—, dir. Hebrew Sch., 1965-80; mem. social program com. Internat. Sedimentological. Congress, 1979. Named Hon. Alumna, Dept. Geology, Bklyn. Coll. at CUNY, 1989; Sue Tyler Friedman medal for distinction in history of geology created in her honor Geol. Soc. London, 1988; recipient Disting. Svc. award Temple Beth-El, 1991, Scroll of Honor, State of Israel Bonds, 1981. Mem. Geology Alumni Assn. (hon.). Jewish. Home: 32 24th St Troy NY 12180-1915 Office: Northeastern Sci Found Inc/Bklyn Coll CUNY Rensselaer Ctr Applied Geology 15 3d St PO Box 746 Troy NY 12181-0746

FRIEDMAN, SUSAN LYNN BELL, job training and community relations specialist; b. Lafayette, Ind., May 23, 1953; d. Virgil Atwood and Jean Loree (Wiggins) B.; m. Frank H. Friedman, July 31, 1976; 1 child, Alex Charles. B.A., Purdue U., 1975; M.S., Ind. State U., 1981. Asst. dir. pub. relations Vincennes U. Jr. Coll., Ind., 1977-83; dir. Knox County C. of C., Vincennes, 1983-84; asst. to pres. Am. Assn. Community and Jr. Colls., Washington, 1985-87; owner/pres. SBF Promotions, 1987—; mgr., program developer Family Resources, Inc., 1988-89; partnership coord. Beaufort (S.C.) County Sch. Dist., 1989-90; job tng. coord. Heart of Ga. Tech. Inst., 1990-92, econ. devel. v.p., 1992-96; exec. dir. Tex. Assn. Ptnrs. in Edn., 1996—. Bd. dirs. Women in Need of God's Shelter, Inc., 1991-96, Ga. Common Cause, 1992-96, pres., 1993-95; mem. Dublin-Laurens Leadership Class, 1994-95; Hoosier scholar, 1971, 72; pres. Annandale BPW, Vincennes, Ind. and Beaufort, S.C., 1995-96; pres. BPW Dublin. Mem. NAFE, Am. Assn. Women in Community and Jr. Colls. (nat. liaison 1985-87), LWV (chpt. v.p. 1982-84), ACLU, BPW Austin, TSAE, TSPRA, NAPE, TAPE, NOW, Austin Kiwanis. Home: 8612 Bobcat Dr Round Rock TX 78681-3700 Office: 400 W 15th St Ste 910 Austin TX 78701-1647

FRIEDMANN, ROSELI OCAMPO, microbiologist, educator; b. Manila, Nov. 23, 1937; came to U.S., 1968; d. Eliseo Amio and Generosa (Campana) Ocampo; m. Emerich Imre Friedmann ; children: Maria Roseli, Rodolfo. BSc in Botany, U. Philippines, 1958; MSc in Biology, Hebrew U. of Jerusalem, 1966; PhD in Biology, Fla. State U., 1973. Rsch. assoc. Inst. Sci. and Tech., Manila, 1958-67; rsch. asst. Queen's U., Kingston, Ont., Can., 1967-68; teaching asst. Fla. State U., Tallahassee, 1968-73, rsch. assoc., 1973—; asst. prof. dept. biology Fla. A&M U., Tallahassee, 1975-84, assoc. prof., 1984-87, prof., 1987—. Contbr. articles to sci. jours. Recipient Resolution of Commendation, State of Fla., Tallahassee, 1978, Antarctic Svc. medal U.S. Congress, Tallahassee, 1981. Mem. Soc. Phycologique France, Phycological Soc. Am., Planetary Soc., AAAS, U.S. Fedn. Culture Collections, Am. Soc. Microbiology, Assn. Women in Sci., Sigma Xi. Office: Fla A&M U Martin Luther King Blvd Tallahassee FL 32307

FRIEDMAN PHILLIPS, PAULINE See VAN BUREN, ABIGAIL

FRIEDRICH, KATHERINE ROSE, educational researcher; b. Ft. Benning, Ga., Mar. 16, 1964; d. Robert Louis and Judith Ann (Dupont) F. BS in Math. and Psychology, S.W. Tex. State U., 1987; MS in Ednl. Psychology, Tex. A&M U., 1990, postgrad. Grad. rsch. asst. dept. sociology Tex. A&M U., College Station, 1989, grad. rsch. asst. dept. ednl. psychology, 1989-91, grad. teaching asst., 1991-92; program evaluator Ctr. for Alternative Programs Bryan (Tex.) Ind. Sch. Dist., 1991; rsch. specialist dept. rsch. and evaluation Houston Ind. Sch. Dist., 1993—; rsch. cons. U. Oreg., Eugene, 1987-88, Tex. A&M U., 1991-92. Vol. Doing Something, Washington, 1992-93. Am. Ednl. Rsch. Assn. rsch. fellow with NSF, 1992-93; scholar for acad. excellence Tex. A&M U., 1990-91. Mem. Advanced Studies of Nat. Databases (sec. 1994-95), Am. Ednl. Rsch. Assn., So. Ednl. Rsch. Assn. Roman Catholic. Office: Houston Ind Sch Dist Dept Rsch Evaluation 3830 Richmond Ave Houston TX 77027

FRIEDRICH, MARGRET COHEN, guidance and student assistance counselor; b. Balt., June 4, 1947; d. Joseph Cohen and Judith (Kline) Cohen Roisman; m. Jay Joseph Friedrich, May 16, 1971; children: David Benjamin, Marc Adam, Samantha Lauren. BEd, U. Miami, Fla., 1969, MEd, 1970. Cert. alcoholism and addiction counselor, alcoholism and drug counselor. Grad. asst. U. Miami, Coral Gables, Fla., 1969-70; tchr. Balt. Bd. Edn., 1970; guidance counselor Ridgewood Bd. Edn., N.J., 1970—; student asst. coord., 1986—, chmn. student assistance com., 1986—; alcoholism counselor Bergen County Dept. Health, Paramus, N.J., 1981-82; in-service tchr. Ridgewood Bd. Edn., 1983, supr., coordinator peer counseling program h.s. 1973-93; with Assn. Mental Health and Counseling of No. N.J., 1985-89; pres. BFH, 1987—, Maggie Assoc.; exec. officer BFPR; cons. N.J. Student Assistance Program, student asst. cons. N.J. Dept. Edn., chmn. student asst. com.; presenter Coll. Bd. Conf., 1992, CEEB Conf., Phila, 1992. Author tech. papers. Exec. bd. Hadassah, Ridgewood-Glen Rock, N.J., 1971-80; youth leadership com. United Jewish Appeal, Bergen County, 1974-75; sec. Bergen County Youth Com. Substance Abuse, Paramus, 1980-90, conf. coord. com., 1983; treas. Ridgewood Coalition Substance Use and Abuse, 1983-84, Ridgewood Substance Abuse Prevention Commn., 1989-91; participant Pres.'s Drug-Free Am.; facilitator Gov.'s N.J. Drug-Free TeleConf.; co-chmn. fundraiser, treas. United Parents/Safe Homes, Ridgewood, 1984; mem. core com. Ridgewood Against Drugs; lectr./educator Passaic County Juvenile Conf. Com., Paterson, N.J., 1984. Reisman scholar, 1969; U. Miami teaching asst., 1970, recipient Recognition award, 1968, disting. Leadership award N.J. Assn. St. Asst. Profls. Mem. N.J. Assn. Alcoholism and Drug Counselors, Nat. Assn. Suicidology, N.J. Edn. Assn., Ridgewood Edn. Assn., Bergen County Edn. Assn., N.J. Task Force on Women and Alcohol, Nat. Assn. Coll. Adminstr. Counselors, N.J. Personnel and Guidance Assn., Women of Accomplishment, Sigma Delta Tau. (exec. bd. 1965-69). Democrat. Jewish. Office: Ridgewood High Sch Ridgewood NJ 07451

FRIEND, ELAINE BYRD, retired savings and loan executive; b. Smith County, Miss., Aug. 14, 1930; d. Clive Llewellyn and Annie Ruth (Husband) Byrd; m. Perry F. Friend, Jr., Mar. 28, 1953 (div. Apr. 1980); children: Melanie A. Taylor, Perry L., Susan V. Levens, Leah E. Gillespie. Cert., Fin. Inst. Edn., Chgo., 1971, 75-77, 80, Coun. on Mgmt., 1990. Lic. life ins. agt. Credit investigator Credit Bur. Laurel, Miss., 1948-52; credit mgr. Sherwin-Williams Paint Co., 1952-54; bookkeeper, teller Laurel Fed. Savs. and Loan Assn., 1954-58, mgr. savs. dept., 1959-61, with tax and ins. dept., 1968-74, sec. to the pres., 1974-79, asst. corp. sec., 1979-85, corp. sec., 1985-95. Bd. dirs., mem. fin. com. United Way Pine Belt, Laurel, 1989—, chair metro campaign, 1992; sponsor Laurel Little Theater, 1965—; block chair Am. Heart Assn., 1992. Recipient Best 1st local campaign award Cystic Fibrosis Found., Little Rock, 1979. Mem. Fin. Women Internat. (Magnolia Group chair, sec., v.p. 1987-90, pres. 1990-91), Nat. Assn. Bank Women (Miss. coun. Group Membership award 1989), Nat. Assn. Ins. Women (chair state conf. 1990), Ins. Women (chair state conf. 1990), Ins. Women Laurel (bd. dirs., numerous offices including pres. 1975—, chair long range planning com. 1992—, Ins. Woman of Yr. 1980, chmn. state conf. 1981), Laurel YWCA. Baptist. Home: 105 Shore Dr Long Beach MS 39560-3121

FRIEND, MELINDA KAY, archivist; b. Keyser, W.Va., Oct. 5, 1961; d. Clarence William and Rita Mae (Shipe) F. AA, Potomac State Coll., 1981; BA, W.Va. U., 1983, MA, 1988. Asst. manuscripts libr. Md. Hist. Soc., Balt., 1988-91; asst. editor/advt. mgr. Md. Hist. Mag., Balt., 1988-89, mng. editor, 1990-91; archivist Libr. of Congress, Washington, 1991—; archivist, cons. U. Md. Balt. Campus, 1989-92. Democrat. Roman Catholic. Home: 3264-G Normandy Woods Dr Ellicott City MD 21043 Office: Libr of Congress Manuscript Divsn 101 Independence Ave SE Washington DC 20540

FRIEND, MIRIAM RUTH, personnel company executive; b. Scranton, Pa., May 19, 1925; d. Benjamin and Etta (Weiss) Loewy; m. Sidney Friend, Aug. 27, 1950. BA, Syracuse U., 1947; cert., Inst. Pub. Welfare Tng. Cornell U., 1950. Social worker Child Placement div. N.Y. State Dept. Welfare, Binghamton and Ithaca, 1948-52; v.p. Office Help Temps., Yonkers, N.Y., 1954-83; pres. Friend & Friend Personnel Agy., Yonkers, N.Y., 1985—. Mem. Eliz Seton Coll. Adv. Council; pres. Pvt. Industry Council, Yonkers, 1981-82, Yonkers Gen. Hosp. Aux., 1983-84, Big Bros./Big Sisters, Yonkers, 1978-80; bd. dirs. Salvation Army, Yonkers, 1977—; publicity chmn. Sen. John E. Flynn Salute, 1986; chmn. breakfast com. Yonkers C. of C., 1978; chmn. Work Opportunities Referral for Kids, Wednesdays Together, 1993—; bd. dirs. Community Planning Council; trustee Yonkers Gen. Hosp., 1978—. Recipient Disting. Service award United Way, 1983, Community Service award Yonkers Council of Chs., 1984, Woman in Bus. award YWCA, 1986; named Pioneer of Industry Ind. Office Services, Hilton Head, S.C., 1984. Mem. Assn. Bus. Profl. Women, Psi Chi, Racquet Club, Amackassin Club (Yonkers), Soroptimists (pres. 1970-72), Rotary. Home and Office: 11 Abbey Pl Yonkers NY 10701-1715

FRIES, HELEN SERGEANT HAYNES, civic leader; b. Atlanta; d. Harwood Syme and Alice (Hobson) Haynes; student Coll. William and Mary, 1935-38; m. Stuart G. Fries, May 5, 1938. Bd. mem. Community Ballet Assn., Huntsville, Ala., 1968—; mem. nat. nurses aid com. ARC, 1958-59; dir. ARC Aero Club, Eng., 1943-44; supr. ARC Clubmobile, Europe, 1944-46; mem. women's com. Nat. Symphony Orch., Washington, 1959—, chmn. residential fund drive for apts., 1959; bd. dirs. Madison County Republican Club, 1969-70; mem. nat. council Women's Nat. Rep. Club N.Y., 1963—, chmn. hospitality com., 1963-65; bd. dirs. League Rep. Women, 1952-61; patron mem., vol. docent Huntsville Mus. Art, Huntsville Lit. Assn.; vol. docent Weeden House, Twickenham Hist. Preservation Dist. Assn., Inc., Huntsville; mem. The Garden Guild, Huntsville, The Collectors Guild Constn. Hall Village, Huntsville, Historic Huntsville Found., Hunstville Mus Art. Recipient cert. of merit 84th Div., U.S. Army, 1945. Mem. Nat. Soc. Colonial Dames Am., Daus. Am. Colonists, DAR, Nat. Trust Hist. Preservation, Va., Nat., Valley Forge (Pa.), Eastern Shore Va., Huntsville-Madison County hist. socs., Assn. Preservation Va. Antiquities, Greensboro Soc. Preservation, Tenn. Valley Geneal. Soc., Friends of Ala. Archives, Nat. Soc. Lit. and Arts, Va. Hist. Soc., English Speaking Union, Turkish-Am. Assn., Army-Navy Club, Washington Club, Capitol Hill Club, Army-Navy Country Club, Garden Club, Redstone Yacht Club, Huntsville Country Club, Heritage Club, Botanical Garden Club. Home: 409 Zandale Dr SW Huntsville AL 35801-3462

FRIES, LITA LINDA, school system administrator; b. Merced, Calif., Feb. 16, 1942; d. Alfred Earl and Juanita Lora (Brown) Griffey; m. George Richard Fries, Feb. 3, 1962; 1 child, Damon Brant. BA, U. Calif., Berkeley, 1966; MS, Calif. State U., 1976. Cert. elem. tchr., secondary tchr., ednl. adminstrator, reading specialist. Tchr. Peace Corps, Mwanza, Tanzania, 1963-65; tchr. Oakland (Calif.) Unified Sch. Dist., 1966-74, tchr. spl. assignment, 1974-84, principal, Burckhalter, 1984-85, program mgr., 1985-90, administr., 1990-92, coord. state and fed. programs, 1992—. Mem. East Bay Reading Assn. (editor 1982-83), Pi Lamda Theta (membership chairperson 1986-88), Delta Kappa Gamma, Phi Delta Kappa. Democrat. Office: Oakland Unified Sch Dist 1025 2nd Ave Oakland CA 94606-2212

FRIES, MATTIE DEVERS, media specialist; b. Winchester, Va., Jan. 3, 1950; d. Henry Lee and Helen (Estep) Devers; m. John Wayne Fries, July 17, 1976; 1 child, Megan Renee. AA, Shenandoah Coll., Winchester, 1970; BS, Madison Coll., Harrisonburg, Va., 1972; MEd, Shenandoah U., Winchester, 1993. 3rd grade tchr. Shenandoah County Pub. Schs., Strasburg, Va., 1972-73; libr., media specialist Clarke County Pub. Schs., Berryville, Va., 1973—, gifted edn. tchr., 1990—; computer coord. Berryville Primary Sch./Clarke County Pub. Schs., 1987—. Potomac Edison Co. hardware grantee, 1988. Mem. NEA, Va. Ednl. Media Assn., Va. Ednl. Assn., Clarke County Edn. Assn., Phi Delta Kappa, Alpha Delta Kappa (treas. 1994—). Baptist. Home: RR 1 Box 173-b Boyce VA 22620-9801 Office: Berryville Primary Sch 317 W Main St Berryville VA 22611-1230

FRIES, MAUREEN HOLMBERG, English literature educator; b. Buffalo, July 14, 1931; d. Howard Henry and Margaret Teresa (Wiley) Holmberg; children: Jeb Stuart, Howard Gordon, John Pelham, Sheila Maureen. AB magna cum laude, D'Youville Coll., 1952; MA, Cornell U., 1953; PhD, SUNY-Buffalo, 1969. Advt. copywriter Eastman Advt. Co., Ithaca, N.Y., 1953-54, Coe Advt. Co., Syracuse, N.Y., 1954; free-lance journalist, Buffalo, 1964-69; teaching fellow SUNY-Buffalo, 1965-69; asst. prof. N.Y. State U. Coll. at Fredonia, 1969-73, assoc. prof., 1973-77, prof. medieval Brit. lit., 1977-90, disting. teaching prof., 1990—; Moss chair of excellence in English, U. Memphis, 1995; lectr. and cons. in field; participant, chmn. numerous confs. Editor: (with Jeanie Watson) The Figure of Merlin in the 19th and 20th Centuries, 1990, Approaches to Teaching the Arthurian Tradition, 1992; compiler A Biography By and About British Women Writers, 1971; contbr. articles to profl. jours., chpts. to books; mem. editorial bd. Quondam et Futurus: A Jour. of Arthurian Interpretations, 1984—. Reader various publs. Recipient Chancellor's award for Excellence in Teaching, 1977, Callista Jones award, 1982, D'Youville Coll. Alumni Svc. award, 1991; Kasling Meml. lectureship State U. of N.Y. Coll. at Fredonia, 1985; NEH fellow, 1975-76; SUNY Faculty Rsch. awards, 72, 73, 79, 80, Am. Philos. Soc., summer 1978, Am. Coun. Learned Socs. travel grant, summer 1978, NEH, 1979; Fulbright Rsch. and Lecturing award, sr. professorship Universitat Regensburg, Fed. Republic Germany, Apr.-July 1984, other awards, grants, fellowships. Mem. Am. Classical League, Internat. Assn. Univ. Profs. of English, Internat. Courtly Lit. Soc., Medieval Acad. of Am., MLA (chairperson Arthurian Discussion Group, mem. exec. com. 1978-82, organizer, chairperson other ann. meetings northeastern and southeastern chpts.), Société Internationale Arthurienne. Democrat. Roman Catholic. Office: SUNY Coll 241 Fenton Hall Fredonia NY 14063

FRIESEN, JANIS M., public relations executive; b. Wichita, Kans., Mar. 20, 1958; d. Gilbert G. and Ethel M. (Farha) F.; m. Butch Lowe. BA in Journalism, Wichita State U., 1980, MA in Comm., 1986. Pub. rels. coord. Mycro-Tek, Wichita, 1981-85; asst. v.p. advt. and comm. Bank IV, Wichita, 1985-91; pub. rels. dir. Sullivan Higdon & Sink, Wichita, 1991-93; pres. Friesen & Assocs., Wichita, 1993-94; ptnr. Allison-Friesen Advt. & Pub. Rels., Wichita, 1994—. Trustee Botanica, The Wichita Gardens, 1987-96. Mem. Pub. Rels. Soc. Am. (past pres. 1991, Pub. Rels. Profl. Yr. 1991), Am. Fedn. Wichita. Office: Allison-Friesen PO Box 47691 Wichita KS 67201-7691

FRIESTEDT, AMÉDÉE CHABRISSON, systems analyst; b. Washington, Aug. 9, 1949; d. Wallace Eugene Danforth and Dorothy Anne (Ball) F. BA in Psychology, George Washington U., 1973; postgrad., Howard U., 1974-79; MS in Physiology and Biophysics, Georgetown U., 1988; postgrad., Walden U., 1993—. Fin. records rep. George Washington U. Hosp., Washington, 1977-84; tech. writer, programmer Computer Scis. Corp., Fairfax, Va., 1984-87; sr. sys. analyst Network Mgmt., Inc., Fairfax, 1987-90; project sys. requirements analyst Unisys Corp., McLean, Va., 1990-92; lead sys. analyst Martin Marietta Tech. Svcs., Lockheed Martin, Inc., Bethesda, Md., 1992—; dir. computer ops. dept. physiology and biophysics Georgetown U., Washington, 1986-89; presenter in field. Editor: The Nurture of the Small, 1993, For Every Child, (newsletter) Every Child By Two. Mem. U.S.-China Capital Cities Friendship Coun., Inc., 1995; v.p. D.C. Head Injury Found., 1988-89. Recipient cert. of appreciation and letter of commendation Office of Personnel Mgmt., EPA, 1987, letter of commendation Gen. Svcs. Adminstrn., 1988, Office Rsch. and Devel., EPA, 1995. Mem. AAAS, NAFE, AAUW, Nat. Fedn. Bus. and Profl. Women (rec. sec. 1984-89), Women's Caucus for Art (pub. rels., newsletter editor, membership com.). Office: Lockheed Martin 401 M St SW WIC Washington DC 20460

FRINDELL, ELIZABETH ANN, English educator; b. Portsmouth, Va., July 27, 1946; d. Bernard Ralph and Florence Elizabeth (Arnold) Sherman; m. Guy Harlan Frindell, June 22, 1968 (div. July 1988); children: Karen Lynne, Alan Hugh. BA, U. Md., 1968; MA, Johns Hopkins U., 1975, U. Wash., 1985. Tchg. cert. Calif. English, drama tchr. Montgomery County Schs., Rockville, Md., 1968-75; adj. faculty speech, English Olympic Coll., Bremerton, Wash., 1977-91; English, debate tchr. South H.S., Bakersfield, Calif., 1991—; English tchr. Olympic H.S., Silverdale, Wash., 1980-81, Shelton (Wash.) H.S., 1987-88; cons. in field, 1985-90. Mem. AAUW, NEA. Unitarian-Universalist. Home: 505 Sun Rose Ave Bakersfield CA 93308

FRISCH, PATRICIA F., pastoral psychotherapist; b. Huntington, N.Y., Oct. 17, 1948; d. Joseph Robert and Ann (McCamphill) Fitzgerald; m. Richard Francis Frisch, Aug. 29, 1970; children: Richard Francis, Mark Thomas. BS in Edn., U. Dayton, Ohio, 1970; MTS in Theology, Spring Hill Coll., Mobile, Ala., 1987; MA in Pastoral Counseling, La Salle U., Phila., 1992; postgrad, Loyola Coll., Balt., 1994—. Lic. profl. counselor. Dir. religious edn. St. Ann's Parish, Phoenixville, Pa., 1987-88, Holy Rosary Parish, Claymont, Del., 1988-89; acad. advisor La Salle U., Phila., 1991-93; counselor Help Counseling, Inc., West Chester, Pa., 1993-94; pastoral counselor Our Risen Savior Parish, Spartanburg, S.C., 1994—. Mem. ACA. Roman Catholic. Office: The Anchoring Place 347E Blackstock Rd Spartanburg SC 29301

FRISCH, ROSE EPSTEIN, population sciences researcher; b. N.Y.C., July 7, 1918; m. David H. Frisch; children: Henry J., Ruth Frisch Dealy. BA, Smith Coll., 1939; MA, Columbia U., 1940; PhD, U. Wis., 1943. Assoc. prof. population scis. Harvard U., Cambridge, Mass., 1984-92, assoc. prof. emerita, 1992—. Contbr. articles to profl. jours. John Simon Guggenheim Meml. fellow, 1975-76. Mem. AAAS, Endocine Soc. Am., Population Soc. Am., Sigma Xi (nat. lectr. 1989-90). Office: Harvard U Ctr Population Studies 9 Bow St Cambridge MA 02138-5103

FRITH, ANNA BARBARA, artist; b. Fort Collins, Colo., Jan. 3, 1925; d. Adam Christian and Rose Virginia (Ayers) Tepfer; m. Donald Eugene Frith, May 7, 1949; children: Eugenia, Martin, Johanna, Juliet. AA in Painting, Colo. Women's Coll., Denver, 1944; Cert. in Illustration, Cleve. Sch. of Art, 1946; BFA in Painting (Hon.), Cleve. Western Reserve U., 1947; MA in Painting, Denver U., 1950; attended, U. Ill., Champaign, 1975-89. Tchr. figure drawing Denver Art Mus., Chappell House, Denver, 1942, 43, 44, 45; tchr. ceramic sculpture San Bernardino (Calif.) Jr. Coll., 1950, 51, 52; tchr. art H.S. San Bernardino, 1953; part-time tchr. women's classes U. Ill., Champaign, 1955-80; tchr. Sat. and pvt. classes; conductor workshops in field. Exhbns. include Gilman/Gruen Gallery, Chgo., The Peoria (Ill.) Art Guild, Prairie House Gallery, Springfield, Ill., Modern Mus. Art, N.Y.C., 1950; one-woman shows include Julian McPhee Univ. Gallery, San Luis Obispo, Calif., Calif. Poly. U., 1996. Recipient Mary Agnes Page award Cleve. Inst. of Art, 1946, 5th Yr. Scholarship award, 1946. Republican. Presbyterian. Home: 310 Poppinga Way Santa Maria CA 93455

FRITH, JANET LAVON MINER, community health nurse, educator; b. Denver, Sept. 2, 1940; d. Stanley Eugene and Florence Catherine (Nelson) Miner; m. William B. Frith, Oct. 14, 1967; children: Michelle, Christine, Theresa, Katherine, Elizabeth, Jennifer, Patricia. Diploma, Carroll Coll., Helena, Mont., 1961; BSN, U. Wyo., Laramie, 1985. RN, cert. sch. nurse, substitute tchr. Staff nurse Sheridan Meml. Hosp., 1961-62, 65-67, 69-74, 88—, VA Hosp., Ft. McKenzie, 1962-63, 67-69; office nurse P. M. Schunk M.D., Sheridan, 1973-82, Dr. L.G. Booth, 1974; clin. instr. Sheridan Coll., 1985-95; sch. nurse Sch. Dist. 1, Big Horn, Wyo., 1990—; office nurse oncology clinic Whedon Found., Sheridan, 1984—; hospice instr., vol. nurse Sheridan County Hospice, 1983-96; substitute RN, tchr. Sch. Dist. #2 Sheridan County, 1984—; substitute office nurse Women's Clinic, N.E. Wyo., 1984—. Mem. Wyo. State Bd. Nursing, 1989-95; bd. dirs. Sheridan County Hospice. Mem. ANA, NEA, Nat. League Nursing, Nat. Assn. Sch. Nurses, Wyo. Hospice Orgn. (charter 1984-96, treas. 1984-94), Wyo. Sch. Nurses Assn., Wyo. Nurses Assn., Wyo. League Nursing, Wyo. Edn. Assn., Sheridan County Edn. Assn., Sigma Theta Tau.

FRITTS, LILLIAN ELIZABETH, retired nurse; b. N.Y.C., July 19, 1923; d. William Franklin and Elzora Jane (Hodge) Bowen; A.D.N., R.N., Central Peidmont Community Coll., 1969; m. Thurman Luther Fritts, Aug. 5, 1944; children—William Luther, Franklin Lee, George Allen. Emergency room nurse Lexington (N.C.) Meml. Hosp., 1953-58; office nurse James T. Welborn, M.D., Lexington, 1958-60; staff nurse Haven Nursing Ctr., Lexington, 1960-61; pvt. duty nurse, 1961-63; owner, ptnr. Buena Vista Nursing Ctr., Lexington, 1964-91, ret., 1991; adult extension tchr. Davidson County Community Coll., 1978, adv. bd. nursing program, 1969-79; pres. Piedmont dist. Long Term Nursing Dirs., 1986-88, Long Term Care Piedmont Nurses Assn., 1987-89. Mem. Am. Nurses Assn., N.C. Nurses Assn., Lic. Practical Nurse Orgn. (state sec. 1958-60), N.C. Lic. Practical Nurse Assn., Dist. 9 Nurse Assn. N.C., N.C. Health Care Facilities Services Assn., Gideons Internat. Baptist. Home: 797 Hill Everhart Rd Lexington NC 27295-7102

FRITZ, ETHEL MAE HENDRICKSON, writer; b. Gibbon, Nebr., Feb. 4, 1925; d. Walter Earl and Alice Hazel (Mickish) Hendrickson; BS, Iowa State U., 1949; m. C. Wayne Fritz, Feb. 25, 1950; children: Linda Sue, Krista Jane. Dist. home economist Internat. Harvester Co., Des Moines, 1949-50; writer Wallace's Farmer mag., Des Moines, 1960-64; free-lance writer, 1960—. Chmn. Ariz. Council Flower Show Judges, 1983-85; media rels. Presdl. Inaugural Com., 1988. Accredited master flower show judge. Mem. Women in Communications (pres. Phoenix profl. chpt.; nat. task force com. 1980—), Am. Soc. Profl. and Exec. Women, Am. Home Econs. Assn., SW Writers' Conf., Ariz. Authors Assn., Phi Upsilon Omicron, Kappa Delta. Republican. Methodist. Club: PEO. Author: The Story of an Amana Winemaker, 1984, Prairie Kitchen Sampler, 1988, The Family of Hy-Vee, 1989.

FRITZ, MARY G., state legislator; b. Cambridge, Mass., May 8, 1938; d. Patrick John and Kathleen Sherry; m. William W. Fritz, Aug. 24, 1963; children: William Jr., Kathleen, Michael, Heather, Matthew, David. BA, Emmanuel Coll., Boston, 1959. Cert. tchr., Conn. Tchr. Wallingford (Conn.) Bd. Edn., 1979-83; dir., owner nursery sch., Yalesville, Conn., 1969-78; mgr. furniture store, Yalesville, 1977-81; legislator 90th dist. State of Conn., 1983-84, 87—. Bd. dirs. Wallingford Day Care, 1985—; adv. bd. Substance Abuse Coalition, Cheshire, Conn., 1985—; adv. coun. August Early Intervention Ctr., Cheshire, 1985—. Mem. Grange Club. Democrat. Roman Catholic. Home: 43 Grove St Wallingford CT 06492-1606

FRIZZELL, LINDA DIANE BANE, exercise physiologist; b. Council Bluffs, Iowa, May 6, 1950; d. Howard Austin and Dorothy (Eyberg) Bane; m. Richard J. Frizzell, Sept. 5, 1971; children: William, Michelle, Audra,

Austin. Cert. athletic trainer, John F. Kennedy Coll., 1970; BA, Parsons Coll., 1972; postgrad., U. Iowa, 1973; MS, Bemidji State U., 1988; PhD, U. N.D., 1991. Lic. phys. edn. tchr., coach, adaptive phys. edn. tchr., Minn.; cert. auto mech., nursing asst.; trained medication aide; water safety instr.; life guard tng. instr.; cert. leisure profl.; qualified mental retardation profl.; cert. personal trainer, CPR, first aid instr. Mgr. swimming pool, dir. swimming lessons Town of Oakland (Iowa), 1971; head cross country, men and women's track and field, asst. coach women's basketball, dir. women's instramurals, phys. edn. instr. Parsons Coll., Fairfield, Iowa, 1972-73; mgr. parts and svc. head mech. Winebrenner Ford, Walker, Minn., 1974-76; tchr., coach Laporte (Minn.) Sch., 1976-81; coach Cass Lake (Minn.) Sch., 1981-85; grad. asst. coach men and women track and field Bemidji (Minn.) State U., 1987; community edn. instr., mem. adv. bd. Walker (Minn.)-Hackensack Schs., 1987-90; mgr. warrany parts and svc. Walker Electric & Hardware, 1987-90; recreation dir. Town of Walker, 1991; therapeutic recreation specialist Ah-Gwah-Ching (Minn.) SNF, 1987-91; grad. rsch. asst. Bureau Ednl. Svcs., U. N.D., Grand Forks, 1989-91; exec. dir. tng. facility developmentaly disable adults Deer River Hired Hands, 1991-92; cons. Bush Grant Study, U. N.D.; presenter at AAHPERD nat. conv. (conf. scholarship 1990, 91, 95); adj. prof. Bemidji State U., 1993—; ind. cons. excercise physiology, rehabilitative therapy, leisure edn., health edn., 1991—; tribal health planner. Leech Lake Reservation, 1993—; speaker for various nat. orgns. on adult aging, devel. and exercise, and innovations in health care and education for rural areas. Designed and copyrighted a wellness circuit for older adults; contbr. articles in field. Minn. rep. to Coun. on Aging and Adult Devel.; active mem. Nat. Minority Involvement Com.; mem. Gov.'s Task Force on Health Promotion and Phys. Fitness for Srs. Grantee Indian Health Svc.-Tribal Mgmt., 1994, State Minn. Cmty. Health Ctr., 1994, Bur. Primary Healthcare/Maternal & Child Health Sch. Based Health Clinic & Wellness Program, 1994. Mem. Am. Assn. Leisure and Recreation (mem. com. on aging), Am. Coll. Sports Medicine (profl., govt. affairs com., Minn. rep.), Nat. Assembly Sch. Based Health Ctrs. (co-chair health edn. sect., sect. rep. to exec. com.), Am. Assn. Health Edn. (govs. task force on health promotion and phys. fitness for srs.).

FRIZZELL, LUCILLE BRIDGERS, retired librarian; b. Yazoo City, Miss., Dec. 17, 1925; d. Thomas Alfred Bridgers and Maie Hollingsworth; m. Byron Waters Frizzell, July 24, 1952; children: Peter Graham, David Edward, Mark Dillard. BS, East Tenn. State U., 1977, MS, 1980. Lic. lay eucharistic min. Sec. U.S. Steel Corp., 1946-53; libr. Steel Coll., Johnson City, Tenn., 1980-82, Bristol Coll., Johnson City, 1982-84, Draughons Jr. Coll., Johnson City, 1984-90. Mem. AAUW, DAR (treas. Johnson City chpt. 1959-60), Nat. Soc. So. Dames (v.p. East Tenn. chpt. 1986-88, v.p. Tenn. state chpt. 1990-92), Watauga Assn. Genealogists (charter), Washington County Hist. Soc. (charter), Monday Club, Delta Kappa Gamma. Republican. Episcopalian. Home: 3320 Bondwood Cir Johnson City TN 37604-8907

FROELICH, BEVERLY LORRAINE, foundation director; b. Vancouver, B.C., Can., Oct. 23, 1948; came to U.S., 1968; d. Kenneth Martin and Ethel (Seale) Pulham; m. Eugene Leonard Froelich, Dec. 26, 1971; children: Craig, Grant. Cert. in fundraising, U. So. Calif., 1986; profl. designation in pub. rels., UCLA, 1987. Cert. fund raising exec. Contract analyst Universal Studios, Calif., 1968-71; exec. dir. Olive View, UCLA Med. Ctr. Found., Sylmar, Calif., 1987—; pres. Beverly Froelich Pub. Rels., Sherman Oaks, Calif., 1988-90; prin. Tracy Susman & Co., Sherman Oaks, 1986-88. Co-author: (program) Overcoming Chronic Arthritis Pain, 1989; contbg. writer hosp. earthquake preparedness guidelines Hosp. Coun. So. Calif., 1991. Founder San Fernando Valley br. Arthritis Found., Encino, 1983, pres., 1983-87, mktg. com.; exec. com. Jeopardy "Balancing the Odds" Found.; bd. dirs. health care com. VICA, Futures IV com., United Way; devel. com. Crespi H.S. Recipient Nat. Vol. Svc. award Arthritis Found., 1986, Jane Wyman Humanitarian award Arthritis Found., 1991, Disting. Svc. award Arthritis Found., 1990. Mem. Nat. Soc. Fund Raisers (exec. com. San Fernando Valley chpt.), Valley Industry and Commerce Assn., UCLA Alumni Assn., Publicity Club of L.A. Home: 14152 Valley Vista Blvd Sherman Oaks CA 91423 Office: Olive View Med Ctr Found Doctors Bldg 14445 Olive View Dr Sylmar CA 91423

FROGGE, BEVERLY ANN, nurse, consultant; b. Wichita, Kans., Jan. 1, 1943; d. Owen Elba Frogge and Maudie Frances (Gillette) Surber; m. Jake C. Saubers (sept. 5, 1967 (div. May 1989); 1 child, Jeff Lee. Attended, So. Meth. U., 1960-61, St.Mary of Plains Coll., 1961-62; diploma, Wichita-St. Joseph Sch. Nursin, 1964; attended, UCLA, 1965. Registered profl. nurse, Kans.; cert. health facility surveyor. Instr. LPN Program Neosho C.C., 1970-73; pub. health nurse Woodson Co., Yates Ctr., Kans., 1973-75; health facility surveyor Kans. Dept. Health & Environ., Topeka, 1975-77; nursing dir. Neosho Meml. Hosp., Chanute, Kans., 1977-84, Regency Health Care Ctr., Yates Ctr., 1985-89; psychiatric nurse VA Med. Ctr., Topeka, 1989—; dir. Neosho Meml. Hosp. Home Health Agy., Chanute, 1977-84; instr. Disaster Preparedness, Yates Ctr., 1973-75; cons. in field, 1975-77. Author: (textbook) Anatomy & Physiology Medical Treatment, 1965-67; contbg. author: (poetry) National Anthology of College Poetry, 1961; radio presenter weekly broadcast, 1978-84. Founder, dir., instr. Dresser Sch. U.S. Peace Corps, Makele, Ethiopia, 1965-67, spkr., 1967; adv. com. mem. Vocat. Edn. State Kans., Neosho C.C., Chanute, 1980-81. Home: 910 SW High Topeka KS 66606-1827

FROGGE, HELENE MARGARETE, educator, administrator, consultant; b. Bakersfield, Calif., June 26, 1965; d. Herbert George and Hella Helene Frogge. BA in Polit. Sci., U. Calif., San Diego, 1987; postgrad., UCLA, 1987-89; cert. in tchg., Chapman U., 1989-90; MA in Ednl. Adminstrn., Calif. State U., Bakersfield, 1995. Cert. tchr., Calif. Educator Antelope Valley H.S. Dist., Lancaster, Calif., 1990-91; educator, adminstr. Eastside Union Sch. Dist., Lancaster, Calif., 1991-95, Acton-(Calif.) Aqua Dulce Unified Sch. Dist., 1995—; cons. sch. safety, Lancaster, 1993-95. Mem. ASCD, AAUW, NOW. Home: 44714 Fenhold St Lancaster CA 93535-3417 Office: Acton Agua-Dulce Unified 3620 Antelope Woods Rd Acton CA 93510

FROLICK, PATRICIA MARY, retired elementary education educator; b. Portland, Oreg., May 17, 1923; d. Fred Anthony and Clara Cecelia (Riverman) F. BS in Edn., Marylhurst Coll., 1960; MS in Edn., Portland State U., 1970; student, U. Oreg., 1975; MA in Theology, St. Mary's Coll., Moraga, Calif., 1977. Joined Roman Cath. Order Sisters of Holy Names of Jesus and Mary, 1943. Left order in 1974. Elem. sch. tchr. Catholic Sch. System, Oreg., 1943-69; tchr., libr. Hood River Pub. Schs., 1970-74, Bend-La Pine (Oreg.) Pub. Schs., 1981-93; ret., 1993; part-time tchr's. asst., Portland, 1993—. Mem. NEA, Oreg. Edn. Assn., Met. Mus. Art (assoc.), Nat. Mus. Women in Arts (charter). Democrat. Roman Catholic. Home: 3465 SE 153rd Ave Portland OR 97236-2265

FROMKIN, AVA LYNDA, management consultant, healthcare risk management services; b. Toronto, Ont., Can., May 3, 1946; d. Joseph and Sara Ann (Hurovitz) F.; came to U.S., 1948, naturalized, 1953; BSN, U. Miami, 1969, cert. adminstrv. scis., 1975, MBA, cert. health adminstrn., 1983. Diplomate Am. Bd. Risk Mgmt. of Healthcare; lic. risk mgr. Nurse, Mt. Sinai Med. Ctr., Miami Beach, Fla., 1970-71, 73-76; dir. surg. svcs. Cedars of Lebanon Health Care Ctr., Miami, 1976-82; adj. prof. intraoperative nursing program Miami (Fla.)-Dade C.C., 1982-83; prin. A. Lynda Fromkin, Inc., Miami, Fla., 1982-94. Mem. ANA, Fla. Nurses Assn., Am. Soc. Post Anesthesia Nurses, Assn. Oper. Rm. Nurses (dir. Miami chpt. 1979-80), F.H.A. Soc. Healthcare Risk Mgmt., Alzheimer's Care Com. Notables, U. Miami Pres. Circle. Home: 555 NE 34th St Apt 2306 Miami FL 33137-4059

FROSCH, BETH STACEY, chiropractor; b. Bethpage, N.Y., Mar. 16, 1965; d. Herbert and Lillian (Botknecht) F. BS, SUNY, Oneonta, 1987; D in Chiropractic Medicine, N.Y. Chiropractic Coll., 1991. Recipient Disting. Svc. award N.Y. Chiropractic, 1993; named Outstanding Young Woman, 1991. Mem. Fla. Chiropractic Soc., N.Y. Chiropractic Soc., Palm Beach Chiropractic Soc., C. of C. Delray Beach (chamber amb., chamber com. mem.), Rotary Club Delray. Home: 9794 Nickels Blvd #806 Boynton Beach FL 33436 Office: 112 S Federal Hwy #2 Boynton Beach FL 33435

FROST, CAROL D., geology educator; b. Salem, Oreg., May 23, 1957; d. O.W. and Mary D. (Bills) F.; m. Eric W. Nye, Dec. 21, 1980; children: Charles W., Ellen M. AB, Dartmouth Coll., 1979; PhD, U. Cambridge, 1984. From asst. prof. to prof. U. Wyoming, Laramie, 1983—; NSF panelist, 1992-96. Mem. Mineralogical Soc. Am., Geochem. Soc., Geol. Soc. Am. (edtl. bd. 1990-96). Office: Dept Geology/Geophysics U Wyo Laramie WY 82071-3006

FROST, CLAUDIA W., lawyer; b. Houston, Feb. 17, 1954. BA, U. Tex., 1975; MA, U. Houston, 1978, JD magna cum laude, 1982. Bar: Tex. 1982. Teaching asst. legal comm., oral advocacy U. Houston, 1981-82; pvt. practice Baker & Botts, LLP, Houston. Editor-in-chief Houston Law Rev., 1981-82. ABA, State Bar of Tex. (cert. civil trial law and civil appellate law), Tex. Bd. Legal Specialization, Houston Bar Assn., Order of the Barons, Phi Delta Phi. Office: Baker & Botts 1 Shell Plz 910 Louisiana St Houston TX 77002*

FROST, DEBBIE JEAN, nurse; b. Norman Okla., Sept. 24, 1971; d. Gary Gene and Karen Eleanora (Thomas) F. BS in Nursing, U. Okla., 1994. RN, Okla. Phys. therapy aide Bone & Joint Hosp., Okla. City, 1989-93, nurse's aide, 1993; mental health worker Willow View Mental Health, Spence, Okla., 1993-94; charge nurse Willow View Mental Health, Spence, 1994—. Vol. Med. Mission to Nicaragua, 1st Presbyn. Ch., Galveston, Tex. Recipient Outstanding Youth award Epsilon Sigma Alpha, 1986. Mem. NOW, Okla. Nurses Assn., Alpha Gamma Delta. Democrat. Baptist. Office: Willow V Mental Health Sys 2601 N Spence Rd Spence OK 73084

FROST, DEIRDRE JANE, marketing executive; b. Tarrytown, N.Y., Oct. 8, 1953; d. Gerard Charles and Margaret Catherine (Bennings) Frost; m. Barry Frederick Davidoff, June 1, 1991. BA in Polit. Sci. and English, Manhattanville Coll., 1975; MA in Internat. Rels., Georgetown U., 1979; MBA, Sacred Heart U., Fairfield, Conn., 1993. Rsch. assoc. SRI Internat., Croydon, Eng., 1979-82; mktg. analyst Booz-Allen & Hamilton, N.Y.C., 1982-84; strategic planning Barclays Bank, Scarsdale, N.Y., 1984-86; software mktg. mgr. Ashton-Tate, Westport, Conn., 1986-89; mktg. comms. mgr. Army Aviation Assn., Westport, 1989-94; internat. exhbns. mgr. Am. Aerospace and Def. Industries, Inc., Harrison, N.Y., 1995—. Mem. Royal Inst. Internat. Affairs (London), Georgetown Club (bd. dirs., v.p. 1989-92, officer 1993—).

FROST, DIANA, lawyer; b. San Jose, Calif., Apr. 20, 1954; d. Richard George Frost and Frances Edna (Atkins) Harkess; m. Douglas Edward Friedman, Sept. 14, 1980; children: Maxwell Douglas, Kyle Edward. BA, Bard Coll., 1976; JD, Fordham U., 1985. Bar: N.Y., U.S. Dist. Ct. (so., ea. dists) N.Y. Contracts mgr. St. Martin's Press, N.Y., 1980-82; litigation assoc. Coudert Bros., N.Y., 1986-91; sr. counsel Random House, Inc., N.Y., 1991—. Contbr. article to profl. jour. Office: Random House Inc 201 E 50th St New York NY 10022-7703

FROST, ELIZABETH ANN MCARTHUR, physician; b. Glasgow, Scotland, Oct. 29, 1938; came to U.S., 1963; d. Robert Thomas and Annie M. (Ross) F.; m. Wallace Capobianco, Sept. 4, 1965 (dec. May 1988); children: Garrett, Ross, Christopher, Neil. MBChB, U. Glasgow, 1961. Diplomate Am. Bd. Anesthesiology, Royal Coll. Ob-Gyn., London. Intern in surgery Royal Infirmary, Glasgow, 1961-62; intern in medicine Victoria Infirmary, Glasgow, 1962; intern in obstetrics Royal Maternity Hosp., Glasgow, 1962-63; resident in internal medicine Englewood (N.J.) Hosp., 1963-64; resident in anesthesiology N.Y. Hosp., N.Y.C., 1964-66; instr. in anesthesiology Albert Einstein Coll. Medicine, Bronx, N.Y., 1966-68, asst. prof. to assoc. prof., 1968-81, prof. anesthesiology, 1981-91, mem. dept. history of medicine, 1973-91; prof., chmn. dept. anesthesiology N.Y. Med. Coll., Valhalla, N.Y., 1992—; dir. div. neuroanesthesia Albert Einstein Coll. Medicine and Affiliated Hosps. Book reviewer New Eng. Jour. of Medicine, 1983—; editor Preanesthetic Assessment, Anesthesiology News, 1984—, Gen. Surgery News, 1991; author/contbr. books; contbr. articles to profl. jours. Mem. N.Y. State Soc. Anesthesiologists, Am. Soc. of Anesthesiologists, Assn. of Univ. Anesthesiologists, Soc. of Neurosurg. Anesthesia and Neurologic Supportive Care, Am. Assn. of Neurol. Surgeons, Anesthesia History Assn., Internat. Trauma Anesthesia and Critical Care Soc. Office: NY Medical Coll Valhalla NY 10595

FROST, ELLEN ELIZABETH, psychologist, b. N.Y.C., July 16, 1947; d. John Joseph and Josephine Mary (Cornell) F.; m. Jerry Melnick, Jan 8, 1982; children: Mariel Frost, Matt James. B.A. magna cum laude, St. John's U., 1969; M.A. (N.Y. State regents fellow, 1969, USPHS fellow, 1969-72), Fordham U., 1981, Ph.D., 1982; candidate N.Y.U. Postdoctoral Program for Psychotherapy and Psychoanalysis, 1982-84. Clin. psychology intern Columbia-Presbyn. Psychiat. Inst., N.Y.C., 1972-73; asst. team leader, staff psychologist Bensonhurst inpatient unit, South Beach Psychiat. Center, Bklyn., 1973-75, sr. psychologist, Bensonhurst outpatient dept., 1975-81, assoc. psychologist, supr., 1982-89; clin. supr. New Hope Guild, Bklyn., 1983—; faculty L.I. Inst. Mental Health, 1990—, supr., 1993—. Mem. Am. Psychol. Assn., Sigma Xi. Office: 200 E 33rd St # 25J New York NY 10016-4874

FROST, ELLEN LOUISE, political economist; b. Boston, Apr. 26, 1945; d. Horace Wier and Mildred (Kip) F., m. William F. Pedersen, Feb. 2, 1974; 1 son by previous marriage, Jai Kumar Ojha; children: Mark Francis Pedersen, Claire Ellen Pedersen. B.A. magna cum laude, Radcliffe Coll., 1966; M.A., Fletcher Sch. Law and Diplomacy, 1967; Ph.D., Harvard U., 1972. Teaching fellow, instr. Harvard U., Wellesley Coll., 1969-71; legis. asst. Office of Senator Alan Cranston, Washington, 1972-74; fgn. affairs officer Dept. Treasury, Washington, 1974-77; dep. dir. Office of Internat. Trade Policy and Negotiations, 1977; dep. asst. sec. of def. for internat. econ. and tech. affairs Dept. Def., Washington, 1977-81; dir. govt. programs Westinghouse Electric Corp., Washington, 1981-88; corp. dir., internat. affairs United Techs. Corp., Washington, 1988-91; sr. fellow Inst. for Internat. Econs., Washington, 1992-93; counselor to U.S. Trade Rep., Washington, 1993-95; sr. fellow Inst. for Internat. Econs., Washington, 1995—. Author: For Richer, For Poorer: The New U.S.-Japan Relationship, 1987. Trustee Aspen Inst. Berlin, 1990-92. NSF trainee, 1967-69. Mem. Internat. Inst. Strategic Studies, Coun. Fgn. Rels., Phi Beta Kappa. Office: Inst Internat Econs 11 Dupont Cir NW Washington DC 20036-1207

FROST, LYNN LAPLANTE, physical education educator; b. Saranac Lake, N.Y., July 21, 1960; d. Robert Carlton and Eileen Gen (Madden) LaPlante; m. Peter Scott Frost, Dec. 19, 1981; children: Tim, Jayme, Krista. BS in Phys. Edn., Springfield Coll., 1982. Itinerant tchr. adapted phys. edn. Howard County Pub. Sch. Sys., Columbia, Md., 1984—. Contbr. articles to profl. jours. Washington Post grantee, 1988. Mem. Md. Adapted Phys. Edn. Consortium, 1993—. Roman Catholic. Home: 639 Saint Georges Station Rd Reisterstown MD 21136-1721 Office: Howard County Pub Sch Sys 5451 Beaverkill Rd Columbia MD 21044-1946

FROST, MARY BETH, manufacturing company executive; b. Mesa, Ariz., June 3, 1955; d. David Richmond and Lea Charlotte (Caldwell) F.; 1 child, Marian Lea. BS, U. Utah, 1979; MBA, Harvard U., 1988. Foreman Magma Copper, San Manuel, Ariz., 1979-82; engr., asst. gen. foreman Amax Lead Co., Boss, Mo., 1982-86; cons. Arthur D. Little, Cambridge, Mass., 1987; ops. mgr. Rachem. Corp., Menlo Park, Calif., 1988-94; gen. mgr. Nashua (N.H.) Corp., 1994—. Mem. Soc. Mining Engrs., Soc. Women Engrs. (co-founder), Menlo Park C. of C. (pres.-elect 1993-94). Home: 14 Colonial Way Exeter NH 03833 Office: Nashua Corp 44 Franklin St Nashua NH 03060

FROST, ROSE, library sciences executive; b. Saginaw, Mich., Jan. 20, 1950; d. Philip Raymond and Angeline Alice (Brink) Grybowski. AA, Delta Coll., 1969; BA, Mich. State U., 1971; MA, U. S. Fla., 1977. Cert. permanent profl. librarian, Mich. Library aide, librarian Orlando Pub. Library, Fla., 1973-78; sales rep. Baker & Taylor, Momence, Ill., 1978-81; pub. relations officer Saginaw Pub. Library, 1981-83; librarian Delta Coll., University Center, Mich., 1983-85; supr. user services Grace Dow Library, Midland, Mich., 1985-88; exec. dir. Presque Isle Dist. Library, Rogers City, Mich., 1988-93; dir. Ransom Dist. Libr., Plainwell, Mich., 1993-94; exec. dir. libr. svcs., Mt. Pleasant Vets. Meml. Libr., Mt. Pleasant, Mich., 1995—; chmn. Video Cassettes in Pub. Libraries Conf., 1986; chmn. adv. coun. Northland Library Coop., 1989-90; v.p. Tots Aboard Presch., 1992-93. Chmn. networking YWCA, Bay City, Mich., 1985; trustee Carrollton (Mich.) Pub. Schs., 1985-88. Mem. ALA, Mich. Libr. Assn. (pub. rels. com. 1981-84, chmn. intellectual freedom com. 1985-87, presenter Best of Show awards 1984, panel mem. conf. 1984, awards com. 1991-93), AAUW (newsletter editor 1983-84), Mich. Libr. Assn. (task force alternative funding 1990-94), Mich. Libr. Assn. Leadership Acad. Avocations: classical music, theater, travel, swimming, reading.

FROSTIC, GWEN, paper company executive; b. Sandusky, Mich., Apr. 26, 1906; d. Fred Watson and Sara (Alexander) F. A in Teaching, Eastern Mich. U., 1965; BA, Western Mich. U., 1971; LLD (hon.), Ea. Mich. U., 1965; HHD (hon.), Western Mich. U., 1971; DFA (hon.), Mich. State U., 1973; DLitt (hon.), Alma Coll., 1977. Art tchr. Deabron (Mich.) Pub. Schs., 1927-39; tool designer Ford Motor Co., Dearborn, 1940-90; pres. Presscraft Papers, Benzonia, Mich., 1991—; mem. state bd. Bus. and Profl. Women, Wyandotte, 1930-60. Author: My Michigan, 1957, A Walk With Me, 1958, These Things are Ours, 1960, A Place of Earth, 1962, To Those Who See, 1965, Wingborne, 1967, Wisps of Mist, 1969, Beyond Time, 1971, Contemplate, 1973, The Enduring Cosmos, 1976, The Infinite Destiny, 1978, The Evolving Omnity, 1981, The Caprice Immensity, 1983, Multiversality, 1985, Heuristic, 1987, Chaotic Harmony, 1989, Abysmal Acuman, 1991, Aggrandize, 1993, Synthesis, 1995. Recipient Southwest Mich. Mensa award, 1981, Franfort C. of C. award, 1981, Ohio Gov.'s Youth Art Exhbn. award, 1981, Huron Valley Mich. Botanical Club award, 1982, Crooked Tree Girl Scout Coun. award, 1982, Mich. Outdoor Edn. Assn. award, 1983, Internat. Assn. Printing House Craftsmen award, 1984, Mich. Capitol Girl Scout Coun. award, 1985, Women's Nat. Farm and Garden Club award, 1986; named to Mich. Womens Hall of Fame, 1986, Jr. Achievment Bus. Hall of Fame, 1991. Mem. Nat. Fedn. Garden Club, PEO, Order Ea. Star, Alpha Delta Kappa, Delta Kappa Gamma, Omicron Nu, Alpha Sigma Tau. Republican. Home and Office: 5140 River Rd Benzonia MI 49616

FROST-KNAPPMAN, (LINDA) ELIZABETH (ELIZABETH FROST KNAPPMAN), publishing company executive; b. Washington, Oct. 1, 1943; d. Edward Laurie and Lorena (Ameter) Frost; m. Edward William Knappman, Nov. 6, 1965; 1 child, Amanda. BA, George Washington U., 1965; postgrad., U. Wis., 1966, NYU, 1966. Editor Natural History Press, N.Y.C., 1967-69, William Collins and Sons, London, 1970-71; sr. nonfiction editor Doubleday and Co., N.Y.C., 1972-80, William Morrow and Co., Inc., N.Y.C., 1980-82; founder, pres. New Eng. Pub. Assocs. Inc., Chester, Con., 1982—; lectr. New Eng. colls. and univs. Author: The World Almanac of Presidential Quotations, 1993, The ABC-CLIO Companion to Women's Progress in America, 1994 (Outstanding Acad. Book-Reference of Yr. award ALA); co-author: (under name Elizabeth Frost with David Shrager) The Quotable Lawyer, 1986, (with Kathryn Collen-DuPont) Women Suffrage in America: An Eyewitness History, 1992; gen. editor: (CD-ROM) Am. Jour.: Women in Am., 1994. Mem. Assn. Authors Reps., Authors Guild, Am. Soc. Journalists and Authors, Haddam Hist. Soc., Conn. Gilbert and Sullivan Soc., Conn. Network of Entrepreneurial Women. Home: PO Box 805 Higganum CT 06441 Office: New Eng Pub Assocs Inc PO Box 5 Chester CT 06412*

FRUCHTER, ROSALIE KLAUSNER, elementary school educator; b. Bklyn., May 1, 1940; d. Marcus and Sarah (Twersky) Klausner; m. Marvin Fruchter, Aug. 15, 1970; children: Marcus, Alexander. BA, Bklyn. Coll., 1960; MA, Nat. Louis U., Evanston, Ill., 1988; postgrad., U. Chgo., 1962-65. Tchr. William H. Ray Sch./Chgo. Bd. Edn., 1961—; cons. math project U. Chgo., 1985-87; presenter in field. Contbr. to math book: One Minute Math, 1990. Bd. dirs. Jewish Community Ctr. of Hyde Park, Chgo., 1978-84, Congregation KAM Isaiah Israel, Chgo., 1984-91, 93—; co-founder Nurit chpt. Hadassah, Hyde Park, 1980; mem. Hyde Park Neighborhood Club, Chgo., 1975—; mem. adv. bd. Humana Michael Reese Hyde Park HMO. Recipient Kate Maremont award Chgo. PTA, 1980, award Chgo. Found. for Edn., 1994; Chgo. Found. for Edn. grantee, 1990, 92, 93, 94, Oppenheimer grantee, 1991. Mem. ASCD, Nat. Coun. Tchrs. Math., Nat. Coun. Tchrs. English, Acad. Econ. Edn., Ill. Sci. Tchrs. Found., Chgo. Tchrs. Union, Internat. Reading Assn., Ill. Resource Coun., Pi Lambda Theta. Democrat. Home: 5434 S Hyde Park Blvd Chicago IL 60615-5802

FRUDAKIS, ROSALIE, small business owner; b. Bloomsburg, Pa., May 29, 1952; d. Jacob Louis and Mary (Kalish) Gluchov; m. Zenos Antonios Frudakis, Jan. 9, 1976. BA in Social Work, Elizabethtown Coll., 1973; postgrad., Temple U., 1974. Art therapist Inst. of Pa. Hosp., Phila., 1974-75; dir. art therapy Bacharach Rehab. Ctr., Pomona, N.J., 1975-76; co-founder, officer of found. Frudakis Acad. Fine Arts, Phila., 1976-85; founding ptnr., pres. Frudakis Gallery, Phila., 1976-85; founding ptnr. The Support System, Inc., Phila., 1984-87; ptnr. Frudakis Studio, Glenside, Pa., 1985—; devel. cons. Mus. at Drexel U., Phila., 1988-91. Patentee for game and method for encouraging self-improvement. V.p. fin. and adminstrn. Bach Festival, Phila., 1992-93; mng. dir. Convergence Dancers and Musicians, 1993—; mgr. Pa. Pro Musica, 1995—. Mem. Nat. Sculpture Soc. (allied profl. mem., devel. cons. 1985—, exhbn. project mgr. 1987). Home: 2355 Mount Carmel Ave Glenside PA 19038-4103

FRUEHAUF, VICKIE, photographer, educator; b. Harvey, Ill., June 13, 1968; d. Robert and Patricia C. (Tanzillo) F. BA in Comm., Am. U., 1990; MFA in Photography, George Washington U., 1994. Assoc. prof. art George Washington U., Washington, 1995—; lectr. art Am. U., Washington, 1996—; lectr. photography Mount Vernon Coll., Washington, 1995; instr. photography Fairfax (Va.) County Office of Adult and Cmty. Edn., 1994—. Exhibited in solo show at Am. U., 1996; group shows include Washington Women Photographers, Beijing, China, 1994, 2d Ann. Regional Juried Art Competition, Savage Mill, Md., 1995, 96, Photo 95, Arlington, Va., 1995, China Impressions, Fairfax, Va., 1995, 1st Ann. Fine Arts Show, San Marcos, Tex., 1996, 3rd place award Mattawoman Juried All-Media Exhbn., 1996.

FRUEHWALD, KRISTIN G., lawyer; b. Sidney, Nebr., May 15, 1946; d. Chris U. and Mary E. (Boles) Bitner; m. Michael R. Fruehwald, Feb. 23, 1980; children: Laurel Elizabeth, Amy Marie. BS with highest distinction in History, U. Nebr., 1968; JD summa cum laude, Ind. U., 1975. Bar: Ind. 1975, U.S. Dist. Ct. (so. dist.) Ind. 1975. Assoc. Barnes & Thornburg, Indpls., 1975-81, ptnr., 1982—; speaker in field. Contbr. articles to profl. jours. Bd. dirs. Indpls. Parks Found., 1995—, Arts Ind., 1994—, Ind. Continuing Legal Edn. Forum, 1993—, treas.; bd. dirs. James Whitcomb Riley Meml. Assn., 1995—, Planned Giving Group Ind.; bd. dirs., treas. Ind. Fed. Cmty. Defenders, Inc., 1993—; bd. dirs. Indpls. Bar Found., 1992—, vice chmn., 1995—; bd. dirs. Ind. affiliate Am. Heart Assn., 1977-81, vice chmn. Marion County chpt., 1981; trustee The Orchard Sch., 1993—, vice chmn., 1995. Fellow ABA (chmn. distributable net income subcom. 1985-91, sect. taxation, mem. com. adminstrn. decendant's estates, mem. com. significant current legislation, real property, probate and trust sect.), Am. Coll. Trust and Estate Counsel (chmn. Ind. state laws com. 1992-95), Ind. Bar Found., Ind. State Bar Assn. (bd. mgrs. 1989-90, chmn. probate, trust and real property sects. 1987-88, mem. sect. taxation, mem. ho. of dels. 1987—); mem. Indpls. Bar Assn. (pres. 1993, chmn. estate planning and adminstrn. sect. 1982-83, chmn. long range fin. planning com. 1988-89), Indpls. Estate Planning Coun., Internat. Assn. Fin. Planners, Ind. Probate Code Study Commn. Office: Barnes & Thornburg 11 S Meridian St Ste 1313 Indianapolis IN 46204-3506

FRUND, H. KATHRYN, painter, graphic designer; b. Hartford, Conn., Oct. 12, 1955; d. Walter Charles and Anne may (Zupka) Frund; m. Steven Haynes Whinfield, Oct. 10, 1993. BFA, Cleve. Inst. Art, 1979; student, Sch. Visual Arts, N.Y.C., 1981-82. Designer Merchandising Workshop, N.Y.C., 1981-86; sr. art dir., designer The Guild Group, Pleasantville, N.Y., 1987-94; artist/paintings and assemblages Newtown, Conn., 1980—. Exhibited in shows at LeverHouse, N.Y.C., 1993, 94, John Slade Ely House, New Haven, 1993, Butler Inst. Am. Art, 1995, Kohn, Pederson, Fox Gallery, N.Y.C., 1995, others. Recipient awards Mattatuck Mus., Waterbury, Conn., 1992, Conn. Acad. Fine Arts, 1992, Stamford Mus. and Nature Ctr., 1995, others. Mem. Silvermine Artist Guild, N.Y. Soc. Women Artists. Democrat. Episcopalian. Home: 4 Glover Ave Newtown CT 06470

FRUTH, BERYL ROSE, physician; b. Carey, Ohio, Mar. 27, 1952; d. Oscar W. and Alice (Arnett) Fruth. BA in Chemistry magna cum laude, Asbury Coll., 1973; MD, Ohio State U., 1977. Diplomate Am. Acad. Family Practice. Intern Grant Hosp., Columbus, Ohio, 1977-78, resident, 1978-79, chief resident, 1979-80; pvt. practice, Columbus, 1980-93; family physician Columbus Community Physicians, Inc., Grove City, Ohio, 1993—; asst. dir. family practice residency Grant Hosp., 1980-81; med. dir. Columbus Dispatch, 1983-93, St. Anthony Breast Evaluation Ctr., 1986—; lectr. Columbus Cancer Clinic, 1984; mentor family practice dept. Ohio State U., physician preceptor Sch. Medicine. Contbr. Ohio State U. Med. Sch. Learning Module in Alcoholism, 1983-84. Named Alumna of Yr., Vanlue Sch., Ohio. Fellow Am. Acad. Family Physicians; mem. AMA, Am. Med. Women's Assn., Acad. Family Practice. Office: 2041 Stringtown Rd Grove City OH 43123-2930

FRY, ANNE EVANS, zoology educator; b. Phila., Sept. 11, 1939; d. Kenneth Evans and Nora Irene (Smith) F. AB, Mount Holyoke Coll., 1961; MS, U. Iowa, 1963; PhD, U. Mass., 1969. Instr. Carleton Coll., Northfield, Minn., 1963-65; asst. prof. Ohio Wesleyan U., Delaware, 1969-74, assoc. prof., 1974-80, prof., 1980—. Contbr. articles to profl. jours. Recipient Welch Teaching award Ohio Wesleyan U., 1976. Mem. AAAS, Am. Inst. Biol. Scis., Am. Soc. Zoologists, Ohio Acad. Sci., Soc. Devel. Biology, Sigma Xi. Office: Ohio Wesleyan U Delaware OH 43015

FRY, DORIS HENDRICKS, museum curator; b. Bristol, Pa., Jan. 20, 1918; d. John Reading and Mary Cordelia (Mariner) Hendricks; m. Wayne Franklin Fry, Aug. 30, 1944; children: Christine Mariner Bode, David Whiteley, Janet Margaret. Student, Temple U. Sch. Music, 1936-40. Cert. tchr. Hist. Soc. Early Am. Decoration, Inc. Art tchr. home studio Delmar, N.Y., 1957—; art tchr. The Arts Ctr., Albany, N.Y., 1972-76, Albany Inst. History and Art, 1972-76; tchr. Mus. Hist. Soc. Early Am. Decoration, Albany, 1982-90, dir., curator, 1981-88; trustee Hist. Soc. Early Am. Decoration, Albany, 1976-86; dir. Sch. Mus. Hist. Soc. Early Am. Decoration, Albany, 1979-81, chmn. tchr. cert. com., 1979-80; class coordinator Albany Inst. History and Art, 1972-76; lectr. Hitchcock Mus., Conn., Conn. Valley Mus., Mass., 1981-82, N.Y. State Mus. Contbr. articles to profl. jours. and popular mags. Recipient awards Hist. Soc. Early Am. Decoration, including Disting. Service award, 1986, Pres.'s award, 1989. Mem. PEO.

FRY, MARION GOLDA, retired university administrator; b. Halifax, N.S., Can., Apr. 16, 1932; d. George W. and Marion I. (Publicover) F. Grad., U. King's Coll., 1953, DCL, 1985; MA, Dalhousie U., 1955; BLitt, Oxford U., 1958; DLitt, Trent U., 1989. Asst. prof. philosophy, asst. dean of women Bishop's U., 1958-64; prin. Catharine Parr Traill Coll., Trent U., 1964-69, assoc. prof. philosophy, 1964-86, v.p., 1975-79; pres. U. of King's Coll., Halifax, 1987-93. Home: 652 Walkerfield Ave, Peterborough, ON Canada K9J 4W2

FRY, MILDRED COVEY, assistant regional library director; b. Canton, Ohio, Mar. 31, 1940; d. Homer D. and Freda A. (Heldman) Covey; m. James W. Fry, July 26, 1957 (div. 1985); 1 child, Christine Lee Fry Clarke. BA, Capital U., Columbus, Ohio, 1982; MLS, Kent (Ohio) State U., 1986. Libr. asst. Stark County Dist. Libr., Canton, 1958-61; asst. dir. Mayne Williams Pub. Libr., Johnson City, Tenn., 1965-66; circulation desk supr. Ohio State U. Libr., Edn. and Psychology, 1966-82; training coord. Online Computer Libr. Ct., Columbus, 1982-84; asst. dir. Cleve. Area Met. Libr. System, 1986—; owner Polaris Leadership Ctr., Cleve., 1996—. Developer Libr. Leadership 2000 Inst., Ohio, 1993—. Recipient Leadership award for LL 2000, ASCLA, 1996. Mem. ASTD, ALA, Continuing Libr. Edn. Network and Exch. Round Table (exec. bd., sec. 1990-92, mem. PLA leadership devel. com. 1994-95), Libr. Adminstrn. and Mgmt. Assn., Am. Soc. Assn. Execs., Ohio Libr. Assn. (bd. dirs. 1990-93), First Families of Ohio. Democrat. Home: 6511 Marsol Rd Ste 307 Cleveland OH 44124 Office: Cleve Area Metro Libr 20600 Chagrin Blvd Ste 500 Cleveland OH 44122-5334

FRY, RITA ALIESE, lawyer; b. Memphis, May 28, 1946; d. McKinley and Lucile (Hoskins) High; m. Adelbert Fry; 1 child, Vincent J. BA, Loyola U., 1973; JD, Northwestern U., 1979. Bar: Ill. 1980, U.S. Dist. Ct. (no. dist.) Ill. 1980, U.S. Ct. Appeals (7th cir.) 1993, U.S. Supreme Ct. 1993. Asst. pub. defender Office of Cook County Pub. Defender, Chgo., 1980-86; sr. supervising atty. City of Chgo. Dept. Law, Ill., 1986-88; 1st asst. pub. defender Office of Cook County Pub. Defender, Chgo., 1988-92; pub. defender of cook county Office of Cook County Pub. Defender, 1992—; mem. adv. bd. BNA Criminal Practice Manual, 1993, MacArthur Justice Ctr., 1993; mem. adv. com. Northwestern U. Sch. Law of Short Courses, 1993—; bd. dirs. Pub. Interest Law Initiative; bd. visitors No. Ill. U. Law Sch., 1992-94; exec. com. Cook County Criminal Justice Coordinating Coun.; mem. Cir. Ct. Liaison Com., 1993; mem. Ill. Supreme Ct. Subcom. on the Selection and Adminstrn. of Juries, 1993—, U.S. Senate Jud. Nominations Commn. for the State of Ill., 1993; many others. Recipient Ida Platt award Cook County Bar Assn., 1992, Kizzy award Kizzy Scholarship Fund Revlon, Inc., 1992, Sixth Amendment award Bill of Rights Bicentennial Celebration Indp. Voters of Ill., 1992. Mem. ABA (coun. mem. sect. of criminal justice), Am. Mgmt. Assn., Black Women Lawyers Assn., Chgo. Bar Assn. (bd. mgrs. 1992-94), Chgo. Conf. Black Lawyers, Chgo. Coun. Lawyers, Cook County Bar Assn., Ill. Pub. Defenders Assn. (bd. dirs.), Ill. State Bar Assn., Nat. Assn. for Criminal Def. Lawyers, Nat. Bar Assn., Nat. Lawyers Guild, Nat. Legal Aid and Defenders Assn., The Fellows of Am. Bar Found. Office: Cook County Pub Defender 200 W Adams St Chicago IL 60606-5208

FRYAR, CAROLYN R., personnel recruiting firm executive. Sr. v.p., gen. mgr. Kelly Svcs., Inc., Troy, Mich., 1991—. Office: Kelly Svcs Inc 999 W Big Beaver Rd Troy MI 48084-4716*

FRYBERGER, ELIZABETH ANN, financial consultant; b. Oakland, Calif., Sept. 7, 1947; d. Marion Raymond Holden and Della Elois Nunley; m. Richard Fryberger, Aug. 19, 1972; 1 child, Laura. BA cum laude, U. Minn., 1987. Registered rep.; accredited investment mgmt. cons.; cert. qualified plans consultant. Investment exec. PaineWebber, Duluth, Minn., 1987-91; trust and investment officer North Shore Bank of Commerce, Duluth, 1991-93; fin. cons. Merrill Lynch, Duluth, 1993—. Co-chair Follow Your Dreams Festival, Duluth, 1990; sect. chair United Way, Duluth, 1994; treas. Cmty. Investment Fund, Duluth, 1993-95; v.p. Ind. Sch. Dist. 709 Endowment Fund, Duluth, 1994—; pres. Project SOAR, Duluth, 1991; mem. Jr. League, Duluth, Leadership Duluth, 1990. Mem. NAFE, Second Tuesday Networking Group (founder), Nat. Ctr. for Women and Retirement Rsch., Profl. Women's Network, Arrowhead Estate Planning Counsel, Superior Syndicate, Women's Network-Merrill Lynch, Greysolon Toastmasters (past pres.). Office: Merrill Lynch 130 W Superior St Duluth MN 55802

FRYE, DEIRDRE LYNN, elementary educator; b. Riverside, Calif., Feb. 24, 1962; d. Victor Carr and Arlene June (De Heer) Timmons; m. Gary Harlan Frye, Jan. 27, 1990. BS in Biology, Seattle U., 1984. Cert. tchr., Calif. Vet. asst. Fred Hutchinson Cancer Rsch. Ctr., Seattle, 1984-85; from lab. asst. I to sr. rsch. asst. U. Calif., Riverside, 1986-90; sr. lab. technician Loma Linda (Calif.) U. Med. Sch., 1990-92; 8th grade integrated sci. tchr. Colton (Calif.) Jr. H.S., 1993—; lead tchr. Calif. Earth Sci. Acad., San Bernardino, summer, 1995; family life adv. com., sci. curriculum devel. com. Colton Joint Unified Sch. Bd., 1993—; salish participant Calif. State U., San Bernardino, 1993—. Campaigner, canvasser Colton Educators Assn., 1993; active altar guild St. Francis Ch. Lead Tchr. grant Calif. Earth Sci. Acad., 1994-95. Mem. NSTA, Calif. Sci. Tchrs. Assn., Calif. Tchrs. Assn. Democrat. Episcopalian. Home: 2271 W College Ave San Bernardino CA 92407 Office: Colton Jr HS 670 W Laurel Colton CA 92324

FRYE, HELEN JACKSON, federal judge; b. Klamath Falls, Oreg., Dec. 10, 1930; d. Earl and Elizabeth (Kirkpatrick) Jackson; m. William Frye, Sept. 7, 1952; children: Eric, Karen, Heidi; 1 adopted child, Hedy; m. Perry Holloman, July 10, 1980 (dec. Sept. 1991). BA in English with honors, U. Oreg., 1953, MA, 1960, JD, 1966. Bar: Oreg. 1966. Public sch. tchr. Oreg., 1956-63; with Riddlesberger, Pederson, Brownhill & Young, 1966-67, Husband & Johnson, Eugene, 1968-71; trial judge State of Oreg., 1971-80; U.S. dist judge Dist. Oreg. Portland, 1980—. Office: US Dist Ct 119 US Courthouse 620 SW Main St Portland OR 97205-3037*

FRYE, HOLLY LASHELLE, accountant; b. Portsmouth, Va., Feb. 16, 1963; d. James Milford and Virginia Gwen (Sunds) F. BA, Doane Coll., 1985. CPA, Minn. Sr. auditor Deloitte & Touche, St. Paul, 1985-90; asst. corp. underwriter Krelitz Industries, Inc., Mpls., 1990-93; mgr. fin. acctg. Merrill Corp., St. Paul, 1993-96; dir. fin. sales ops. TRO Learning Inc., Edina, Minn., 1996—; asst. corp. contr. Micro-Component Technologies, Inc., St. Paul, 1993. Active St. Paul Jaycees, St. Paul, 1987-90. Mem. Minn. Soc. of CPA (pub. rels. com. 1990—). Office: TRO Learning Inc 4660 W 77th St Edina MN 55435

FRYE, JUDITH ELEEN MINOR, editor; b. Seattle; d. George Edward and Eleen G. (Hartelius) Minor; student UCLA, 1947-48, U. So. Calif., 1948-53; m. Vernon Lester Frye, Apr. 1, 1954. Acct., office mgr. Colony Wholesale Liquor, Culver City, Calif., 1947-48; credit mgr. Western Distbg. Co., Culver City, 1948-53; ptnr. in restaurants, Palm Springs, L.A., 1948, ptnr. in date ranch, La Quinta, Calif., 1949-53; ptnr., owner Imperial Printing, Huntington Beach, Calif., 1955—; editor, pub. New Era Laundry and Cleaning Lines, Huntington Beach, 1962—; registered lobbyist, Calif., 1975-84. Mem. Textile Care Allied Trade Assn., Laundry & Dry Cleaning Suppliers Assn., Calif. Coin-op Assn. (exec. dir. 1975-84, Cooperation award 1971, Dedicated Svc.award 1976), Nat. Automatic Laundry & Cleaning Coun. (Leadership award 1972), Women Laundry & Drycleaning (past pres., Outstanding Svc. award 1977), Printing Industries Assn., Master Printers Am., Nat. Assn. Printers & Lithographers. Office: 22031 Bushard St Huntington Beach CA 92646-8409

FRYER, JUDITH DOROTHY, lawyer; b. N.Y.C., Feb. 14, 1950; d. Jerome M. and Gloria (Abrams) F.; m. Daniel P. Biggs, June 4, 1972; chidren: Jeremy Fryer-Biggs, Zachary Fryer-Biggs. BA, Washington U., 1972; JD, Hofstra U., 1975. Bar: N.Y. 1976. Assoc. Carro, Spanbock, Fass & Geller, N.Y.C., 1978-82, ptnr., 1982-86; ptnr. Finley & Kumble, N.Y.C., 1987; counsel Kaye, Scholer, Fierman, Hays & Handler, N.Y.C., 1988-89, ptnr., 1989-95; shareholder Greenberg Traurig, N.Y.C., 1995—; Bd. advisers Capital Sources for Real Estate newsletter, 1994—. Author: Roll-up Transactions-The Current Picture, 1992, Taking a REIT Public, 1994, Surprises in Recent REIT and Rollup Offerings, 1994, Integration Issues in Real Estate Securities Offerings, 1995; editor current devels.: Real Estate Securities & Capital Markets newsletter, 1989-90, editor, 1990-92. Fellow Am. Bar Found.; mem. ABA (chair subcom. equipment leasing programs 1988-91, chair subcom. on partnerships & REIT products 1991-96, chair subcom. on partnerships, trusts and unincorporated assns. 1994—, chair women rainmakers interest group 1996—), Assn. of Bar of City of N.Y., Nat. Assn. Real Estate Investment Trusts (exec. com. 1994-95, bd. govs. 1994—), Investment Program Assn. (securities law and regulatory affairs com.), Real Estate Investment Assn. (founding mem). Office: Greenberg Traurig 153 East 53rd St New York NY 10022-3506

FRY-WENDT, SHERRI DIANE, psychologist; b. Clinton, Mo., Mar. 30, 1958; d. Charles Pierce and Norma Geraldine (Croft) Fry; m. Joseph Otto Wendt, May 24, 1980; children: Benjamin, Ethan, Nathaniel. BSE, Cen. Mo. State U., 1979, MS, 1981; PhD, U. Mo., 1989. Lic. psychologist, Mo. Mental health therapist Wyandot Mental Health Ctr., Kansas City, Kans., 1981-88; EAP contract psychologist Menninger Found., Topeka, 1988-89; contract psychologist Tri-County Mental Health Ctr., Kansas City, 1988-89; pvt. practice Kansas City, 1988—; tng. provider local and state level, 1985—; expert witness State of Kans., 1985—. Youth group sponsor Hillside Christian Ch., Kansas City, 1982-86, children's choir dir., 1983-87, deaconess, 1983-93, dir. vacation bible sch., 1992, 93; deaconess Fairview Christian Ch., co-chair Christian edn.; mem. ethics com. Kansas City region Christian Ch. (Disciples of Christ). Mem. APA, Internat. Soc. Study of Multiple Personality and Dissociation, Greater Kansas City Psychol. Assn., Phi Kappa Phi, Psi Chi. Office: 4901 Main St Ste 408 Kansas City MO 64112-2635

FRYXELL, GRETA ALBRECHT, marine botany educator, oceanographer; b. Princeton, Ill., Nov. 21, 1926; d. Arthur Joseph and Esther (Andreen) Albrecht; m. Paul A. Fryxell, Aug. 23, 1947; children: Karl Joseph, Joan Esther, Glen Edward. BA, Augustana Coll., 1948; MEd, Tex. A&M U., 1969, PhD, 1975. Tchr. math and sci. jr. high schs. Iowa, 1948-52; research asst. Tex. A&M U., College Station, 1968-71, research scientist, 1971-80, asst. prof. oceanography, 1980-83, assoc. prof., 1983-86, prof., 1986-94, prof. emeritus, 1994—; adj. prof. botany U. Tex., Austin, 1993—; vis. scientist U. Oslo, 1971; chmn. adv. commn. Provasoli-Guillard Ctr. for Culture Marine Phytoplankton, Bigelow Lab, Maine, 1985-87; hon. curator N.Y. Bot. Gardens, 1992—; courtesy prof. U. Oreg., 1994—. Editor: Survival Strategies of the Algae, 1983; contbr. articles to profl. jours. Recipient Outstanding Woman award Brazos County, College Station, 1979, Outstanding Achievement award Augustana Coll., Rock Island, Ill., 1980; Faculty Disting. Achievement award in rsch. Tex. A&M U., 1991, Geoscis. and Earth Resources Adv. Coun. medal, 1993; grantee NSF. Mem. AAAS, AAUW, ACLU, Phycol. Soc. Am. (editoral bd. 1976-79, 82-85, chairperson Prescott award com. 1991, Award of Excellence in Phycology 1996), Brit. Phycol. Soc., Internat. Phycol. Soc., Am. Soc. Limnology and Oceanography, Am. Soc. Plant Taxonomists, Internat. Diatom Soc. (coun. 1986—), Tex. Assn. Coll. Tchrs. Democrat. Unitarian-Universalist. Office: U Tex Botany Dept Austin TX 78713-7640

FUCHS, ANNA-RIITTA, medical educator, scientist; b. Helsinki, Finland, Feb. 8, 1926; came to U.S., 1964; d. Martti Adolf and Rut Ester (Sario) Olsson; m. Fritz Fuchs, May 19, 1948; children: Anneli, Martin, Peter Erik, Lars Frederik. MS in Chemistry with honors, U. Helsinki, 1950; DSc, U. Copenhagen, 1978. Research assoc. Inst. Hygiene Med. Physiology, U. Copenhagen, 1952-62; adj. in reproductive physiology Inst. Med. Physiology, U. Copenhagen, 1962-65; research assoc. bio.-med. div. The Population Council, Rockefeller U., N.Y.C., 1965-71, staff scientist bio.-med. div., 1971-77; faculty mem. pharmacology Cornell U. Med. Sch., N.Y.C., 1973-80, assoc. prof. reproductive biology dept. ob-gyn and dept. physiol. biophysics, 1977-86, prof. reproductive biology dept. ob-gyn and dept. physiology and biophysics, 1986—; vis. scientist dept. ob-gyn. Fed. U. Bahia, Salvador, Bahia, Brazil, 1966; vis. prof. reproductive biology Dept. ob-gyn. Chulalongkorn U., Bangkok, 1972-73, 85; cons. dept. ob-gyn. Dept. Health U.S. Virgin Islands, St. Thomas, 1986; Fogarty sr. internat. fellow Inst. Hormone and Fertility Rsch. U. Hamburg, Germany, 1994-95. Mem. editl. bd. Am. Jour. Physiology: Endocrinology and Metabolism, 1982-85, Clinica e Investigacion en Ginecologica y Obstetrica, Barcelona, Spain, 1977—; guest editor: Directions in Obstetric Perinatology, spl. issue Am. Jour. Perinatology, 1989; editor: (with F. Fuchs and P. Stubblefield) Preterm Birth, 1993; contbr. chpts. to books, more than 200 sci. articles to prof. jours. Elected friend N.Y.C. Commn. on the Status of Women, 1985. Served with Lotta Svard Finnish women's aux., 1939-44. Decorated Medal of Freedom of Finland, 1944. Fellow N.Y. Acad. Sci. (vice chmn., 1988, program chmn. com. for women in sci. 1982-88); mem. AAAS, Soc. for Gynecologic Investigation, Endocrine Soc., Soc. for the Study Reproduction, Soc. for the Study Fertility, Assn. for Women in Sci. (treas. 1978-80), Gynecol. Assn. Finland (hon.). Lutheran. Club: Larchmont (N.Y.) Yacht. Office: Cornell U Med Coll 1300 York Ave Rm S412 New York NY 10021-4805

FUCHS, ANNE SUTHERLAND, magazine publisher; b. Volta Redonda, Brazil, Apr. 19, 1947; d. Paul Warner and Evelyn Coffman; m. James E. Fuchs, Feb. 6, 1982. Student, U. Paris at Sorbonne, 1967-68, Western Coll. for Women, 1966-67; BA, NYU, 1969. V.p., pub. Woman's Day Spl. Interest Mags.-CBS Mags., N.Y.C., 1980-82, Cuisine Mag., CBS Mags., N.Y.C., 1982-84; v.p., pub. Woman's Day mag. DCI Comm., Inc., N.Y.C., 1985-88; sr. v.p., pub. ELLE mag., N.Y.C., 1988-90, Vogue, N.Y.C., 1990-94; group pub. Harper's Bazaar, N.Y.C., 1994—; chmn. mag. and print com. U.S. Info. Agy., 1989—. Chmn. women's bd. Madison Sq. Boys and Girls Club, N.Y.C.; mem. Com. 200, USIA; bd. dirs. N.Y.C. Partnership, N.Y.C. Partnership Found. Mem. Fin. Women's Assn. N.Y., N.Y. Jr. League, Advt. Women of N.Y., Women in Communications, Women's Forum, Com. of 200, Fin. Women's Assn. N.Y. Club: Economic (N.Y.C.). Office: Harper's Bazaar Hearst Mags 1700 Broadway Fl 37 New York NY 10019-5905*

FUCHS, BETH ANN, research technician; b. Moberly, Mo., July 22, 1963; d. Larry Dale and Marilyn Sue (Summers) Williams; m. Fred Albano Fuchs Jr., Sept. 30, 1989. AA, Cottey Coll., 1983; BS in Engring., U. N.Mex., 1987. Bookkeeper, chemistry technician U. N.Mex., Albuquerque, 1984-88; rsch. engr. Sandia Nat. Labs., Albuquerque, 1988—. Contbr. articles to profl. jours. Mem. Am. Vacuum Soc. Republican. Home: 336 Espejo St NE Albuquerque NM 87123-1111 Office: Sandia Nat Labs Mail Stop 0603 Divsn 1314-1 PO Box 5800 Albuquerque NM 87185-0603

FUCHS, ELAINE V., molecular biologist, educator; b. Hinsdale, Ill., May 5, 1950; d. Louis H. and Viola L. (Lueck) F.; m. David T. Hansen, Sept. 10, 1988. BS in Chemistry with honors, U. Ill., Urbana, 1972; PhD in Biochemistry, Princeton U., 1977. Postdoctoral fellow dept. biology MIT, 1977-80; asst. prof. U. Chgo., 1980-85, assoc. prof., 1985-88, prof. dept. molecular genetics and cell biology, 1989—, Amgen prof. basic scis., 1993—, investigator, Howard Hughes Med. Inst., 1988—. Assoc. editor Jour. Cell Biology, 1993—; contr. numerous articles to profl. jours. Recipient R.R. Benesely award Am. Assn. Anatomists, 1988, Searle Scholar award Chgo. Cmty. Trust, 1981-84, Presdl. Young Investigator award NSF, 1984-89, NIH Merit award, 1993, Wm. Montagna award Soc. Investigative Dermatology, 1995. Fellow Am. Acad. Arts and Scis.; mem. NAS (elected mem.), Inst. Medicine of NAS, Am. Assn. Cell Biology (Keith Porter award 1996), Am. Assn. Biol. Chemists, Phi Beta Kappa. Office: U Chgo Howard Hughes Med Inst Dept Molecular Genetics 5841 S Maryland Ave Rm 314N Chicago IL 60637-1463

FUDGE, ANN MARIE, marketing executive; b. Washington, Apr. 23, 1951; d. Malcolm R. and Bettye (Lewis) Brown; m. Richard E. Fudge, Feb. 27, 1971; children: Richard Jr., Kevin. BA, Simmons Coll., 1973; MBA, Harvard U., 1977; DHL (hon.), Adelphi U., 1995. Manpower specialist GE, Bridgeport, Conn., 1973-75; mktg. asst. Gen. Mills, Mpls., 1977-78, asst. product mgr., 1978-80, product mgr., 1980-83, mktg. dir., 1983-86; assoc. dir., strategic planning Gen. Foods, White Plains, N.Y., 1986-87, mktg. dir., 1987-89, v.p. mktg. and devel., 1989-91, exec. v.p., gen. mgr., 1991-94; exec. v.p. Kraft Foods, 1994—; pres. Maxwell House Coffee Co., White Plains, N.Y., 1994—; bd. dirs. Simmons Coll., Boston, Liz Claiborne, Inc., Allied Signal, Inc.; trustee Thunderbird, The Am. Grad. Sch. of Internat. Mgmt. Bd. mem. Women's Economic Devel. Corp., St. Paul, 1984-86; chairperson Allocations Panel-United Way, Mpls., 1983-86; vol. Big Sisters/Big Bros., Fairfield County, Conn., 1988-90. Recipient Leadership award YWCA, Mpls., 1980, Black Achievers award Harlem YMCA, 1988, Candace award Nat. Coalition of 100 Black Women, 1991, 92, Corp. Women's Network award, 1994, She Knows Where She's Going award Girls, Inc., 1994. Mem. Exec. Leadership Coun. (pres. 1994—), Com. of 200, N.Y. Women's Forum. Office: Kraft Foods 250 North St White Plains NY 10625-0001

FUENNING, ESTHER RENATE, adult education educator; b. Florence, Mo.; d. Albert Theodore and Elizabeth (Muenzinger) F. BS, U. Nebr.; MA, Columbia U., 1952; doctoral program in recreation, U. Ill., Champaign, 1955-61. Dean of women Carthage (Ill.) Coll., 1949-50; asst. social dir. Ill. Union U., 1955-61; dean of women So. State Tchrs. Coll., Springfield, S.D., 1961-63; asst. dir. student activities Ill. Tchrs. Coll., South Chicago, 1963-64; prof. Wilbur Wright Coll., Chgo., 1964-77; sub. tchr. Chgo. Pub. Schs., 1977-82; tchr. dept. aging and disability Sr. Citizens Ctrs., Chgo., 1980—; dir. pub. relations Wright City Coll., 1964-77; del. Internat. Leisure and Recreation Congress, Krefeld, Germany, World Leisure and Recreation Assn, USSR. Author pamphlets in field; author: Upbeat With Esther, series of materials for sr. citizens, 1993—. Tour guide adults abroad Wright City Coll., 1986—; del. for sr. citizens conf. Wilbur Wright Coll., 1984, organized art fair, 1968—; ofcl. White House Conf. on Aging, Washington, 1955, Ill. White House Conf. on Aging, Springfield, 1990. Recipient Gov. Thompson Sr. Leadership award, Outstanding Svc. award Wright Coll. Alumni, Dedicated and Outstanding Leadership award Wright Coll., 1975, Cert. of Recognition adult edn. activities Wright City Coll., 1988, scholarship Gov.'s Conf. for Aging Network, 1991, Cert. of Life-Time Achievement Women's History Month, 1994, 96; inducted Chgo. Sr. Citizen Hall Fame. Republican.

FUENTES, DAISY, televison personality; b. Havana, Cuba, Nov. 17, 1966; d. Maria and Amado F.; m. Timothy Adams, Aug. 5, 1991. Bergen Comm. Coll., 1984-86. News reproter/weather anchor WXTV, New York, 1986-87; weather anchor WNJU-TV, New York, 1987-90; VJ MTV Networks, New York, 1988—. recipient: Outstanding Women in Media award, Latin Coalition for Fair Media, 1992. Office: MTV Networks 1515 Broadway New York NY 10036*

FUENTES MUNOZ, GUADALUPE, price monitor; b. Mexico City, Feb. 6, 1959; d. Hilario and Ana Maria (Muñoz) F. AA, L.A. Trade Technical Coll., 1985; BS, Calif. State U., L.A., 1996. Acctg. clk. Young's Mktg. Co., L.A., 1986-88; bookkeeper Petrolane Inc., Long Beach, Calif., 1988-89, Gol-Sol-Arco, L.A., 1989-90; price integrity specialist Ralph's Grocery, L.A., 1990—. Roman Catholic. Home: 11744 Adenmoor Ave #B Downey CA 90241 Office: Ralphs Grocery Co 1100 W Artesia Compton CA 90025

FUFUKA, NATIKA NJERI YAA, retail executive; b. Cleve., Feb. 21, 1952; d. Russell and Mindoro Reed. AA, AAB, Cuyahoga Community Coll., Cleve., 1973; BA, Mich. State U., 1975; postgrad., Cleve. State U. Asst. pers. dir. May Co., Cleve., 1975-78; merchandiser J.C. Penney, Cleve., 1978-80; sports mgr. Joseph Hornes, Cleve., 1980-81; fashion buyer Higbee, Cleve., 1981-86; merchandise exec. Fashion Bug, Euclid, Ohio, 1986-92; pres., CEO Mindy's Return to Fashion, Cleve., 1993—. Bd. dirs. Ohio Youth Adv. Coun.; vice chair Joint Com. on Medicad Provider Impact for State of Ohio, 1992; mem. Mayor's Census Task Force, Cuyahoga County Women Bus. Enterprise Adv. Coun., Cleve. Female Bus. Enterprise Adv. Coun., Displaced/Single Parent Homemakers Adv. Coun., Cuyahoga Community Coun., Cuyhoga Hills Boys Adv. Coun.; chair Centralized Resource Referral Svc. Panel United Way, 1993, mem. Gen. Assembly, 1993—; vice chair federated allocation panel United Way of Greater Cleve; bd. dirs. Women Community Found., 1993—, Career Beginning Program Bd., 1993—. Ford Found. scholar, 1975; recipient Jesse Jackson Voter Registration award, 1984, Leadership award United Way, 1991, Vol. Leadership recognition City of Cleve., 1991. Mem. NAFE, Assn. MBA Execs., Black Profl. Assn., Nat. Assn. Negro Bus./Profl. Women, Am. Profl. Exec. Women, Am. Women Bus. Assn., Nat. Assn. Black Female Entrepreneurs, Severance Merchant Mall Orgn., Op. Big Vote, Nat. Coun. Negro Women, Nat. Polit. Congress Black Women (nat. founder mem., founder mem. Ohio state chpt.), Nat. Hook-Up, 100 Black Women Coalition, Black Congl. Caucus Braintrust, Small Minority Bus. Braintrust, Corp. Braintrust, Black Women Agenda, Black Women Roundtable, Black Focus (pres. bd. trustees), 21st Congl. Dist. Caucus (exec. bd. mem., chair bus. women com., certs. of appreciation for outstanding svc. 1985, 86), Urban League Greater Cleve., Op. Push of Greater Cleve. (bd. dirs.), Project Vote (asst. dir., Voter Registration award 1984), Midwest Vote Project, Women Vote Project, Women-Space, United Black Fund, Greater East Cleve. Dem. Club, Minority Women Polit. Action Com., LWV, Cuyahoga Women Polit. Caucus, Ohio Pub. Interest Campaign, Ohio Rainbow Coalition, Ohio Dem. Women Com., Network Together, Black Elected Dem. Ofcls. Ohio, Cleve. City Club, 16th Dist. Club, Project M.O.V.E, Kinsman Youth Devel. Proclam and Scholarship Cmty. Liasion. Democrat. Pentecostal. Home: 12001 Martin Luther King Jr Dr Cleveland OH 44105-4581

FUGATE, JUDITH, ballet dancer; b. Hamilton, Ohio, Nov. 23, 1956. Student, Sch. Am. Ballet. Dancer N.Y.C. Ballet, 1973—, soloist, 1979-86, prin. dancer, 1986—. Dancer numerous ballets including The Nutcracker, Don Quixote, A Midsummer Night's Dream, Concerto Barocco, Gounod Symphony, Valse-Fantaisie, Divertimento # 15, Fancy Free, Liebeslieder Walzer, Dances at a Gathering, The Fours, Seven by Five, A Fool for You, I'm Old Fashioned, Seven by Five, Ivesiana, Ma Mere l'Oye, N.Y.C. Ballet's Balanchine Celebration, 1993, Apollo, Coppélia, Jewels, Union Jack. Office: NYC Ballet Inc NY State Theater Lincoln Ctr Plz New York NY 10023 Office: 1501 Strawberry Rd Mohegan Lake NY 10547-1046*

FUGELBERG, NANCY JEAN, secondary education educator; b. Tarentum, Pa., Mar. 6, 1947; d. Stanley and Mary (Struhar) Homer; m. Darrell Marvin Fugelberg, Aug. 27, 1977. Cert. master piano classes and music lit. Mozarteum, Salzburg, Austria, 1968; B in Music Edn., Mount Union Coll., 1969; postgrad. Kent State U., 1973-76; EdM in Curriculum and Instrn., Ashland U., 1989. Music tchr. Alliance Sch. Dist., Ohio, 1969-

70, Minerva Sch. Dist., Ohio, 1970—; ch. organist First Imamnuel United Ch. of Christ, Alliance, Ohio, 1969-85. Pianist for musicals Carnation Players, Alliance, 1969-72; asst. organist, accompanist various chs. Recipient award for working with handicapped children Minerva Sch. Dist., 1981; Alumni Service award Mu Phi Epsilon, 1983, 84; named One of Outstanding Young Women Am., 1981. Mem. NEA, Minerva Tchrs. Assn., Ohio Edn. Assn., Mu Phi Epsilon (chpt. v.p. 1980-82, pres. 1982-84, historian and music therapy chmn. 1984—). Republican. United Ch. of Christ. Avocations: plants, traveling, playing keyboards shows. Address: 345 S Rockhill Ave Alliance OH 44601-2257

FUGGI, GRETCHEN MILLER, education educator; b. Westerly, R.I., Aug. 26, 1938; d. John Louis and Harriet (Schied) M.; m. William Joseph Fuggi, Aug. 15, 1960; children: Gretchen, Juliann, John, Kristen. BS, So. Conn. State U., 1960, MS, 1969, 6th yr. diploma, 1991, 6th yr. Ednl. Leadership diploma, 1994. Reading cons. Washington Magnet Sch., West Haven, Conn., 1974—; adj. prof. So. Conn. State U., New Haven, 1988—. Pres. Cath. Charity League of Greater New Haven, 1989-90; bd. dirs. New Haven Symphony Aux., 1992—. Mem. AAUP, Internat. Reading Assn., Conn. Reading Assn., Stonington Hist. Soc. of Conn., Delta Kappa Gamma Soc. Internat. Roman Catholic. Home: 19 Westview Rd North Haven CT 06473-2013

FUJITSUBO, LANI CHARLENE, psychology educator; b. L.A., June 21, 1954; d. WIlliam Sadao and Sylvia Toshiko (Shigihara) F. BA, SCC, Costa Mesa, Calif., 1980; MA, U.S. Internat. Univ., San Diego, 1988, PhD, 1991. Lic. psychologist, Oreg., Alaska. Psychology intern Children's Hosp., Orange, Calif., 1990-91; prof., psychologist U. Alaska, Fairbanks, 1991-93; prof. So. Oreg. State Coll., Ashland, 1993—, dir. testing, 1994—; pvt. practice, Ashland, 1993—; cons., 1991—. Bd. dirs. Girl Scout Coun., Winema, Oreg. Mem. Am. Psychol. Assn., Western Psychol. Assn., Oreg. Psychol. Assn., Assn. Women in Psychology. Democrat. Office: So Oreg State Coll 1250 Siskiyou Blvd Ashland OR 97520

FUJIWARA, ELIZABETH JUBIN, lawyer; b. New Orleans, Dec. 20, 1945; d. Otha Ernest and Yvette Marie (Jubin) Barron ; children: Jean Paul Jubin Toshiro, Maria Sachiko Yonahara, Cathleen Sumiko Yonahara. Student, U. Dallas, Irving, 1963-64; BA in Sociology, Loyola U., New Orleans, 1967; MSW, U. Hawaii, 1971, JD, 1983. Exec. dir. ACLU of Hawaii, Honolulu, 1975-77; specialist in equal edn. opportunity Hawaii Dept. Edn., Honolulu, 1977-78; asst. dir. Inst. Productive Behavior, Honolulu, 1978-80; faculty rsch. asst. William S. Richardson Sch. Law, U. Hawaii, Honolulu, 1981; law clk. to presiding justice Intermediate Ct. Appeals Hawaii, Honolulu, 1984-86; pvt. practice law Honolulu, 1986—. Editor: Women's Legal Rights in Hawaii, 1990, 2d edit., 1991, Our Rights, Our Lives, 1990. Active Hawaii Women's Polit. Action Caucus, 1983-85, 89—, Ad Hoc Com. Abortion Rights, 1977-79; organizer Coalition Against Capital Punishment, 1976-78; Peacer Corps trainee in P.R. and Guatemala, 1968. Named one of Outstanding Young Women of Yr. State Commn. on Status of Women, 1976, Outstanding Hawaii Woman Lawyer of Yr., 1988. Mem. Hawaii Bar Assn. (employment sect. officer 1993-94), Nat. Employment Lawyers Assn. (founder and pres. Hawaii chpt. 1993-94), Assn. Trial Lawyers Am., Hawaii Women Lawyers (co-chair pay equity com. 1985-87, spouse abuse and women prisoners legal penal project 1985-88, mem. legis. com. 1985-87, bd. dirs.), Kappa Beta Gamma. Democrat. Buddhist. Office: 737 Bishop St Ste 1655 Honolulu HI 96813-4623

FUJIWARA, MITSUKO, chemist, researcher; b. Okayama, Japan, Dec. 7, 1966; came to U.S., 1979; d. Akira and Masako (Kitao) F. BA summa cum laude, Cornell U., 1988; PhD, Calif. Inst. Tech., 1993. Lab. technician Cornell Med. Coll., N.Y.C., summer 1986, 87, Bayer, A.G., Leuerkusen, Germany, summer 1988; undergrad. rsch. asst. Cornell U., Ithaca, N.Y., 1986-88; grad. rsch. asst. Calif. Inst. Tech., Pasadena, 1989-93, grad. tchg. asst., 1989-91, grad. lab. asst., 1992-93; prin. rsch. chemist Unilever Rsch., Edgewater, N.J., 1993-95; rsch. scientist, 1995—; cons. Cryopharm Corp., Pasadena, 1990-92. Author abstracts in field; contbr. article to profl. jour.; patentee in field. Mem. Am. Chem. Soc., Biophys. Soc., Phi Beta Kappa, Phi Kappa Phi. Office: Unilever Rsch 45 River Rd Edgewater NJ 07020

FUKUSHIMA, CATHERINE, museum program director; b. Phila., Mar. 29, 1961; d. Toshiyuki and Marion Anne (MacDaid) F.; m. Robert Perris, May 31, 1992. BA in Art History, Conn. Coll., New London, 1983. Gallery dir. Mus. Am. Folk Art, N.Y.C., 1989-93; mgr. sch., youth and family programs The Bklyn. Mus., 1994—. Mem. com. N.Y.C. Mus. Educators Roundtable, 1993—, chair conf., 1995.

FULBRIGHT, HARRIET MAYOR, foundation administrator; b. N.Y.C., Dec. 13, 1933; d. Brantz and Evelyn (Griswold) M.; m. William Watts, Aug. 4, 1954 (div. 1975); children: Evelyn G. Ward, Shelby S. Watts, Heidi H. Mayor; m. J. William Fulbright, Mar. 10, 1990. BA, Radcliffe Coll., Cambridge, Mass., 1955; MFA, George Wash. U., 1975. Chair art dept. Maret Sch., Washington, 1975-80; asst. dir. Congl. Arts Caucus, Washington, 1980-82, Alliance of Ind. Coll. Art, Washington, 1982-84; exec. sec. Internat. Congress Art History, Washington, 1984-87; exec. dir. Fulbright Assn., Washington, 1987-91; pres. The Ctr. for Arts in the Basic Curriculum, Washington, 1991—; bd. dirs. Coun. for Basic Edn., 1991-95, World Learning, INc., 1993—, Nat. Coun. for Internat. Visitors, 1993-95; vice chair Reves Internat. Ctr.; mem. J.W. Fulbright Fgn. Scholarship Bd., 1992—, Acad. for Ednl. Devel., 1995—. Author: How To Get Your Own Pre-School Play Group; editor: Fulbrighters Newsletter. Pres. Maret Sch. Bd. Honoree, Young Audiences, 1994. Mem. Nat. Coun. Stds. in the Arts. Office: Ctr Arts Basic Curriculum PO Box 379 East Hampton NY 11937

FULCHER, (MARIAN) PEGGY KOTOWSKI, reading recovery educator; b. Wyandotte, Mich., Oct. 9, 1948; d. Michael Florian and Minnie Elrus (Ford) K.; m. Morris Wayne Fulcher, Aug. 7, 1982. BA in Home Econs. Edn., Marygrove Coll., 1970; M in Guidance and Counseling, Wayne State U., 1975; M in Reading, Eastern Mich. U., 1990, adminstrv. cert. student, 1994. Home econs. and social studies tchr. Warren Consolidated Schs., Sterling Heights, Mich., 1970-74, tchr., counselor, 1975-76; sub. tchr. Livingston County Schs., Hartland, Howell, Mich., 1977-78; home econs. and social studies tchr. Hartland Consolidated Schs., 1978-82, tchr., site mgr. alternative edn., 1982-93, chpt. 1 tchr., 1993-94, chpt. 1/reading recovery tchr., 1994—. Active Fenton (Mich.) Village Players, 1977—, Flint (Mich.) Cmty. Players, 1988-91, Hartland Players, 1980, 86-88, Livingston County Players, Brighton, Mich., 1993-94. Mem. ASCD, AAUW, Reading Recovery Coun. Mich., Internat. Reading Assn., Mich. Reading Assn., Livingston County Reading Assn. Office: Hartland Consolidated Schs PO Box 900 Hartland MI 48353-0900

FULD, ALICE K., journalist; b. N.Y.C., June 29, 1939; d. Morris H. and Kay (Zimmerman) Kinzler; m. Gilbert L. Fuld; children: Rachel, Sarah. BA, Radcliffe, 1961. Staff writer Book of Knowledge, N.Y.C., 1962-64, Scholastic Magazines, N.Y.C., 1964-71; arts critic Keene (N.H.) Sentinel, 1973-88, arts and entertainment editor, 1988—. Dir. Keene (N.H.) Housing Auth., 1974-79, Keene Family YMCA, 1978-84, Hospice of Cheshire County, N.H., 1985-89. Democrat. Office: Keene Sentinel 60 West St Keene NH 03431

FULLER, ANNE ELIZABETH HAVENS, English language and literature educator, consultant; b. Pomona, Calif., Jan. 20, 1932; d. Paul Swain and Lorraine Elizabeth (Hamilton) Havens; m. Martin Emil Fuller, II, June 17, 1961; children: Katharine Hamilton, Peter David Takashi. A.B., Mount Holyoke Coll., 1953; B.A. (Fulbright scholar), Somerville Coll., Oxford U., 1955, M.A., 1959; Ph.D. (Univ. fellow), Yale U., 1958. Instr. English Mount Holyoke Coll., 1957-59; instr. Pomona Coll., 1959-61; asst. prof. U. Fla., Gainesville, 1961-63; lectr. U. Denver, 1964-68, 71-73; assoc. prof., chmn. center for lang. and lit. Prescott (Ariz.) Coll., 1968-70; tchr. Colo. Rocky Mountain Sch., 1970-71; dean of faculty Scripps Coll., Claremont, Calif., 1973-80; prof. English Scripps Coll., 1973-80; spl. asst. to pres., sec. to corp. Claremont U. Center, 1981-83; v.p. for acad. affairs Austin Coll., Sherman, Tex., 1982-84, faculty mem., 1984-96; mem. SW dist. Rhodes Scholar Selection Com., 1975-83. Bd. dirs. Am. Council on Edn., 1979-81. Mem. Assn. Am. Colls. (dir. 1977-81, chmn. 1980-81), Am. Conf. Acad. Deans (dir. 1976-79), Commn. on Women in Higher Edn., Am. Assn. Higher Edn., Modern Lang. Assn. Am. Democrat. Episcopalian. Home: 6407 Christy Ave NE Albuquerque NM 87109

FULLER, CASSANDRA MILLER, programmer analyst; b. Norwalk, Conn., Dec. 10, 1965; d. George Louis and Bernice (Simmons) Miller; m. David Norman Fuller, Dec. 24, 1988. BS, S.C. State Coll., 1987; MBA, U. Bridgeport, 1995. Interior decorator's apprentice Marty Rae Interiors, Orangeburg, S.C., 1984-85; asst. mgr. Dairy Queen, Orangeburg, S.C., 1986-87; day mgr. The Bedford, Stamford, Conn., 1987-88; dept. mgr. Burlington Coat Factory Warehouse, Danbury, Conn.; asst. mgr. Kidstuff, Inc., Orange, Conn., 1989-92; Postage By Phone customer assistance specialist Pitney Bowes, Stamford, Conn., 1992-96, assoc. programmer analyst, 1996—; cons. Orangeburg Metro Transit 1987. Mem. Nat. Assn. Negro Bus. and Profl. Women's Clubs Inc., Nat. Black MBA Assn., NAFE, Kappa Omicron Phi. Democrat. Baptist. Office: Pitney Bowes Inc MSC 30-16 1 Elmcroft Rd Stamford CT 06902

FULLER, CHERRY LYN, librarian; b. San Angelo, Tex., Sept. 28, 1946; d. Jack Ivan Harmon and Mary Helen (Lindsey) Kapavik; m. Edward Eugene Prose, Dec. 16, 1967 (div. Feb. 1980); children: Jennifer Lyn, Lauren Nicole; m. David Lee Fuller, July 16, 1982. BA, U. Tex., 1967; MS, U. North Tex., 1985. Cert. tchr., Tex. Tchr. Poultney (Vt.) Elem. Sch., 1967-70, Bradford Elem. Sch., San Angelo, Tex., 1970-71, Fannin Elem. Sch., San Angelo, Tex., 1971-76, 77-80; dir. grant program in econs. San Angelo (Tex.) Ind. Sch. Dist., 1976-77; tchr. Roanoke (Tex.) Elem. Sch., 1980-84; libr. N.W. Mid. Sch., Justin, Tex., 1984-96; dir. Libr. Media Svcs. Edn. Svc. Ctr., Region XI, Ft. Worth, 1996—; cons. lib. automation Nichols Advanced Technologies, Edmunton, Alta., Can., 1993—. Author: Bringing MOLLI to Life, 1993; co-author: Bring Athena to Life, 1995. Mem. ALA, ASCD, Am. Assn. Sch. Librs., Tex. Libr. Assn., Tex. State Tchrs. Assn., Tex. Computer Educator Assn., Tex. Mid. Sch. Assn., Kappa Kappa Iota. Republican. Presbyterian. Home: 1000 Gibbons Rd S Argyle TX 76226-6336 Office: NW Mid Sch 18700 Texan Dr Justin TX 76247-8702

FULLER, CHERYL A., women's health nurse; b. Barre, Vt., Sept. 7, 1943; d. O. Fay and Julia Harriet (Gale) Allen; m. Richard A. Fuller, June 26, 1965; children: Richard, Lori Ann. BS, U. Vt., 1965; MS, SUNY, Binghamton, 1980; cert., NYU, 1985, postgrad. RN, Pa., N.Y. Asst. prof. nursing Wilkes Coll., Wilkes Barre, Pa.; rsch. asst. in fertility antibody diagnostics N.Y.C.; nurse practitioner Wyoming Valley Gyn-Ob Assocs., Kingston, Pa.; nurse practitioner Maternal and Family Health Svcs., Wilkes Barre, dir. nursing and med. svcs.; asst. prof. nursing U. Scranton, Pa. Mem. Assn. Women's Health, Obstetrics, and Neonatal Nurses, Northeast Pa., Nurse Practitioner's Assn., Am. Fertility Soc., Sigma Theta Tau (Outstanding Nurse Practitioner). Home: 64 Elmcrest Dr Dallas PA 18612-9168

FULLER, CHRISTINE ANN, medical technology company professional; b. Ottawa, Ont., Can., Feb. 3, 1960; d. Gerald Brendon and Catherine Ellen (Schneider) F. AA in Comm., Cmty. Coll. of the Air Force, 1988; BA in History and Polit. Sci., Incarnate Word Coll., 1992; MA in Am. History, S.W. Tex. State U., 1993. Enlisted USAF, 1979, advanced through grades to staff sgt.; morse systems operator USAF, Iraklion AS, Crete, Greece, 1979-81, Wheeler AFB, Hawaii, 1981-83, Osan AB, Korea, 1983-84; morse and printer systems supr. USAF, RAF Chicksands, Eng., 1984-86; unit tng. and evaluations mgr. USAF, Kelly AFB San Antonio, Tex., 1986-90; ret. USAF, 1990; peer tutor Jim Saunders for Senator, San Antonio, 1994; lead coord. med. device reporting HK Med. Technologies Inc., San Antonio, 1995—; cert. med. device reporter Shotwell & Carr, Houston, 1995—; cert. risk mgmt. Medmarc, San Francisco, 1995—. Vol. Rep. Party campaign, San Antonio, 1992; del. Rep. Senatorial Conv., San Antonio, 1992; campaign coord. Dem. Party campaign, San Antonio, 1994. With USAFR, 1990-94.

FULLER, GAYLE BARNES, psychotherapist; b. Houston, June 30, 1950; d. Gaylord Perry Barnes and Nannell (Julian) Siver; m. Michael Fuller, June 19, 1970 (div. 1980); children: Jon Michael (dec.), Jeremy Anthony; m. Thomas J. Herter Jr., Sept. 4, 1987 (div. Aug. 1996). BA, Sam Houston State U., 1976; MEd, U. Houston, 1996. Lic. profl. counselor, Tex. Elem. sch. tchr. Alta Loma Inc. Sch. Dist., Houston, 1975-77, Spring Ind. Sch. Dist., Houston, 1977-80, Conroe Ind. Sch. Dist., Houston, 1980-81; paralegal Thomas J. Herter and Assocs., Houston, 1982-85; case mgr. Liddell, Sapp, Zivley, Hill and LaBoon, Houston, 1986-91; rsch. asst. for children of battered women project Psychology Dept., U. Houston, 1994; family therapy Juvenile Cts., CASA, Houston. Ct. vol. Child Advocates, Inc., Houston. Baptist.

FULLER, KATHRYN SCOTT, environmental association executive, lawyer; b. N.Y.C., July 8, 1946; d. Delbert Orison and Carol Scott (Gilbert) F.; m. Stephen Paul Doyle, May 29, 1977; children: Sarah Elizabeth Taylor, Michael Stephen Doyle, Matthew Scott Doyle. BA English, Am. Lit., Brown U., 1968, LHD (hon.), 1992; JD with honors, U. Tex., 1976; postgrad., U. Md., 1980-82; DSci. (hon.), Wheaton Coll., 1990; LLD (hon.), Knox Coll., 1992. Bar: Tex. 1977, D.C. 1979. Rsch. asst. Yale U., New Haven, Conn., 1968-69, Am. Chem. Soc., 1970-71, Harvard U. Mus. Comparative Zoology, Cambridge, Mass., 1971-73; law clerk Dewey, Ballantine, Bushby, Palmer & Wood and Vinson & Elkins, N.Y.C., Houston, 1974-76, U.S. Dist. Ct. (so. dist.), Tex., 1976-77; atty., advisor Office Legal Counsel Dept. Justice, Washington, 1977-79, atty. Wildlife and Marine Resources sect., 1979-80, chief Wildlife and Marine Resources sect., 1981-82; exec. v.p., dir. Traffic USA, pub. policy, gen. counsel World Wildlife Fund, Washington, 1982-89, pres., CEO, 1989—. Contbr. articles to profl. jours. Adv. com. Trade Policy and Negotiations; Pres'. Commn. Environ. Quality; bd. dirs. Brown U.; trustee The Ford Found.; mem. World Bank Adv. Com. on Sustainable Devel. Recipient William Rogers Outstanding Grad. award Brown U., 1990, UN Environment Programme Global 500 award, 1990; outstanding woman law student Tex. scholar, 1975. Mem. State Tex. Bar, D.C. Bar (coun. fgn. rels., internat. coun. environ. law, overseas devel. coun.), Zonta Internat. (hon.). Office: World Wildlife Fund 1250 24th St NW Washington DC 20037-1124*

FULLER, SUE, artist; b. Pitts.; d. Samuel Leslie and Carrie (Cassedy) F. B.A., Carnegie Inst. Tech., 1936; M.A., Columbia U., 1939. Producer: movies String Composition, 1970, 74; one-woman shows include Bertha Schaefer Gallery, McNay Art Inst., San Antonio, Norfolk Mus. Currier Gallery, Corcoran Gallery, Smithsonian Instn., others; exhibited in group shows including Aldrich Mus., Corcoran Gallery, Phila. Mus., Mus. Modern Art, Whitney Mus., Bklyn. Mus., Brit. Mus., London, others; represented in permanent collections Addison Gallery Am. Art, Larry Aldrich Mus., Chgo. Art Inst., Des Moines Art Ctr., Ford Found., Met. Mus., Guggenheim Mus., Whitney Mus. Am. Art, Tate Gallery London, Brit. Mus. London, Library of Congress, others; commd. works include Unitarian Ch. All Souls, N.Y.C., 1980, Tobin Library, McNay Art Mus., San Antonio, 1984. Recipient Alumni Merit award Carnegie Mellon U., 1974, CAA/WCA Nat. Honor award, 1986; Louis Comfort Tiffany fellow, 1948; Guggenheim fellow, 1949; Nat. Inst. Arts and Letters grantee, 1950; Eliot Pratt Found. fellow, 1966-68; Mark Rothko Found. grantee, 1973; U. Cin. Nat. Sculpture Conf.: Works by Women honoree, 1987. Home: PO Box 1580 Southampton NY 11969-1580

FULLER, WRENDA SUE, music and secondary school educator; b. Aberdeen, S.D., Oct. 21, 1947; d. LeRoy William and Annette Karlene (Robinette) Herther; m. Larry Fray Fuller, Aug. 22, 1970; 1 child, Heather Sue. BA in Music, History, Dakota Wesleyan U., 1969; MA in Govt., U. Va., 1970. Sr. state human resources planner Commonwealth of Va., Richmond, 1970-73; cons. Social Security Adminstrn., S.W. Va., 1973-74; educator Russell County Sch. Bd., Lebanon, Va., 1974—. Author: (directory) Listing and Evaluation of Available Human Services in Russell County, 1975; also articles. Mem. Health Svcs. Adv. Bd., S.W. Va., 1982-84; pres. Lebanon Women's Club, 1982-84; minister of music, Lebanon Meml. United Meth. Ch., 1982—; sponsor Boy Scouts Bloomington, Ind. (nat. winner mock trial), 1994, Nat. Hist. Day, College Park, Md., 1994. Named Outstanding Young Educator Jaycees, 1980, Econs. fellow U. Va., Charlottesville, 1988. Mem. NEA, Music Educators Nat. Conf. (chmn. dist. VII, Va., 1989-91, 95—), Am. Choral Dirs. Assn. Home: RR 4 Box 81 Lebanon VA 24266-9734

FULLER-MCCHESNEY, MARY ELLEN, sculptor, writer; b. Wichita, Kans., Oct. 20, 1922; d. Edward Emory and Karen Mabel (Rasmussen) Fuller; m. Robert Pearson, Dec. 17, 1949. AA, U. Calif., Berkeley, 1943. Staff writer Currant. Author: (art book) Period of Exploration, Oakland Museum, 1973, also 3 mystery novels, short stories, poems and articles on art; exhibited sculpture at Syracuse (N.Y.) Mus., San Francisco Mus., Oakland (Calif.) Mus., Calif. State U., Sonoma, Santa Rea Civic Ctr., U. Calif., Davis, San Jose (Calif.) State U., U. Oaxaca, San Francisco art festivals and many galleries; prin. works include Dos Leones, San Francisco, 1974, Children's Sculpture Park, Salinas, Calif., Falcon, San Jose, Calif., Yuba Totem, Yuba City, Calif., Playground, San Francisco, Olympic Lions, Squaw Valley, Calif., Petaluma (Calif.) Libr. Sculptures, West Side Pump Sta., San Francisco, 4 garden sculptures L.A. State Office Bldg., Broadway Totem, Walnut Creek, Calif. Ford Found. fellow, 1965-66; Nat. Endowment Arts grantee, 1975. Home and Studio: 2955 Sonoma Mt Rd Petaluma CA 94954

FULLERTON, GAIL JACKSON, university president emeritus; b. Lincoln, Nebr., Apr. 29, 1927; d. Earl Warren and Gladys Bernice (Marshall) Jackson; m. Stanley James Fullerton, Mar. 27, 1967; children by previous marriage—Gregory Snell Putney, Cynde Putney Mitchell. B.A., U. Nebr., 1949, M.A., 1950; Ph.D., U. Oreg., 1954. Lectr. sociology Drake U., Des Moines, 1955-57; asst. prof. sociology Fla. State U., Tallahassee, 1957-60; asst. prof. sociology San Jose (Calif.) State U., 1963-67, asso. prof., 1968-71, prof., 1972-91, dean grad. studies and research, 1972-76, exec. v.p. univ., 1976-78, pres., 1978-91; ret., 1991; bd. dirs. Assoc. Western Univs., Inc., 1980-91; mem. sr. accrediting commn. Western Assn. Schs. and Colls., 1982-88, chmn., 1985-86; mem. Pres.'s Commn. Nat. Collegiate Athletic Assn., 1986-91; bd. dirs. Am. Coll. Assn., 1991. Author: Survival in Marriage, 2d edit, 1977, (with Snell Putney) Normal Neurosis: The Adjusted American, 2d edit, 1966. Carnegie fellow, 1950-51, 52-53; Doherty Found. fellow, 1951-52. Mem. Phi Beta Kappa, Phi Kappa Phi, Chi Omega. Home: 1643 Tompkins Hill Rd Fortuna CA 95540-9728

FULLERTON, NANCY LEE, elementary school and music educator; b. Wheeling, W. Va., June 28, 1951; d. Harley Richard and Dannie Lou (Burkett) Lilley; m. Thomas Michael Fullerton, May 15, 1977; children: April Dawn, Shawn Michael, Jennifer Lynn. BA in Music Edn., Fairmont State Coll., 1973; postgrad. studies in Edn. Adminstrn., W. Va. U., 1993—. Travelling music tchr. Upshur County Schs., Buchannon, W. Va., 1973-76; substitute tchr. Marshall County Schs., Moundsville, W. Va., 1976-90; elem. music specialist Marshall County Schs., Cameron, W. Va., 1990—; dir. chancel choir First Christian Ch., Cameron, 1977—, program chmn., 1986-88, Sunday sch. supt., 1992—; advisor Camerette Theta Rho Girls' Club, 1979—. Election worker Marshall County, Cameron, 1990-91. Mem. NEA, W.Va. Edn. Assn., Music Educators Nat. Conf., W.Va. Music Educators Assn., Sunmbeam Rebekah Lodge, Sigma Alpha Iota (pres.). Republican. Mem. Disciples of Christ Ch. Office: Cameron Elem Sch 12 Church St Cameron WV 26033-1217

FULLWOOD, ALTBURG MARIE, women's health nurse; b. Scharbeutz, West Germany, May 6, 1933; d. Hans F. and Cacilie A. (Bliesmer) Burmann; m. Marvin Fullwood, Sept. 6, 1963; children: Randal O., Renée M. Diploma, St. Georg Hosp., Hamburg, West Germany, 1953, Kleemann Sch., Kiel, West Germany, 1954; ADN, U. N.C., Wilmington, 1984. RN, N.C.; cert. psychiat./mental health nurse. Nurse German Social Security System, Hamburg; exec. sec. to dir. Fla. State U., Eglin AFB; civil service pers. Dept. of Army, Southport, N.C.; psychiat. nurse New Hanover Regional Med. Ctr., Wilmington.

FULRATH, IRENE, corporate marketing executive; b. N.Y.C., Nov. 15, 1945; d. Logan and Grace (Sheehy) F. B.A., Wheaton Coll., Ill., 1967. Media exec. Doyle Dane Bernbach, N.Y.C., 1967-72; account exec., retail sales mgr. Sta. WABC, N.Y.C., 1972-84; account exec. Sta. WABC-TV, N.Y.C., 1984-86; regional sales mgr., Am. Express Co., 1987—. Mem. Fin. Advt. and Mktg. Assn. (bd. dirs. 1981-84, sec. 1984-85, v.p. 1985-86, pres 1986-87). Republican. Presbyterian. Avocation: travel. Home: 150 E 56th St New York NY 10022-3631

FULTON, CARLA RAE, human resources manager; b. Clarion, Iowa, July 18, 1953; d. Don C. and Marietta (Walker) Greenfield; m. Kenneth W. Townsley, May 24, 1975 (div. 1987); m. James P. Fulton, July 17, 1994. BA, U. North Tex., 1975, MBA, 1982. Human resources specialist Mobil Oil Corp., Dallas, 1976-82; human resources mgr. S & A Restaurant Corp., Dallas, 1982-85; sr. compensation analyst Frito-Lay, Dallas, 1985-86; asst. dir. human resources Fed. Home Loan Bank, Dallas, 1986-89; sr. mgr. human resources DSC Communications Corp., Plano, Tex., 1989-92, Pier I Imports, Fort Worth, 1993—. Mem. Dallas Forty, 1990; mem. adv. coun. Seay Behavioral Ctr. Mem. Soc. Human Resource Profls., Dallas Human Resource Mgmt. (v.p. 1986-90), Nat. Human Resource Systems Profls. (sec. 1986), Dallas Human Resource Systems Profls. (founding mem., pres. 1985-86). Republican. Methodist. Home: 7111 Mimosa Ln Dallas TX 75230-5441

FULTON, CHERYL LYNN, customer service administrator; b. Chgo., Feb. 21, 1947; d. Theodore Edward and Elsie Amelia Whiffen; m. Richard Lawrence Gniadek, Nov. 15, 1969 (dec. Feb. 1979); m. Richard John Fulton, Sept. 2, 1995. BSBA, Ill. State U., 1969. Prodn. sec. Universal Tng. Systems, Lincolnwood, Ill., 1969-71; exec. sec. Alliance Am. Insurers, Chgo., 1971-78; temp. sec. Kelly Svcs., Grand Rapids, Mich., 1978-79; sec. Honeywell, Inc., Grand Rapids, Mich., 1979-80, sales corr., 1980-81; adminstr. customer quality Honeywell, Inc., Ft. Washington, Pa., 1981-84; rep. customer service Honeywell, Inc., Valley Forge, Pa., 1984-88; fin. acct. Honeywell, Inc., Ft. Washington, 1987-91; br. support supr. Honeywell, Inc., Valley Forge, 1991-92; supr. Regional Customer Svc. Ctr. Honeywell, Inc., Ft. Washington, Pa., 1992-95; field svcs. mgr. Honeywell, Inc., Valley Forge, Pa., 1995—. Mem. NAFE, Am. Bus. Women's Assn. (New Directions Charter chpt., pres. 1986, Woman of Yr. 1985), Instrument Soc. Am. (treas., edn. com. Phila. sect., sec., treas., 3d v.p., 2d v.p., 1st v.p., pres. 1994-95). Democrat. Roman Catholic. Home: 857 Thoreau Ct Warminster PA 18974-2057 Office: Honeywell Inc PO Box 916 Valley Forge PA 19403

FULTON, DIANN MARIE, consultant; b. York, Pa., Nov. 24, 1966; d. Gene Reese and Louise Arlene (Louey) F. BS in Acctg., York Coll. Pa., 1988; MBA, Loyola Coll., Md., 1992. CPA, Md., 1988; CMA, 1996. Cons. Price Waterhouse Gateway Group, Arlington, Va., 1992—; mem. govt. fin. mgmt. tech. interest group Price Waterhouse, 1994—. Mem. Md. Assn. CPAs, Inst. Mgmt. Accts., Assn. Govt. Accts. Home: 1950 North Point Blvd # 210 Tallahassee FL 32308 Office: Price Waterhouse Gateway Group 1616 N Ft Myer Dr Arlington VA 22209

FULTON, SHERRI LEAH, elementary education educator; b. Tipton, Mo., Jan. 24, 1968; d. Robert Lee and Sharon Regina (Schreck) F. BS in Edn., Ctrl. Mo. State U., 1990; MS in Edn., Troy State U., 1996. 6-8th grade tchr. Moniteau R-V, Latham, Mo., 1990-92; 6th grade tchr. N.W. Middle Sch., Clarksville, Tenn., 1992-93; 1st grade tchr. Norman Smith Elem., 1993-94; early childhood ctr. tchr. Dawning Point, Enterprise, Ala., 1994-96. Mem. Gamma Sigma Sigma (pres., 1st v.p., sec., Outstanding mem. 1990), Kappa Delta Pi. Home: 3165 Harbor Ln Apt 2-202 Plymouth MN 55447

FULTON-MARTINEZ, KATHLEEN, insurance company official; b. Kansas City, Kans., Sept. 20, 1960; d. Clarence Davy Crockett and Shirley Frances Fulton; m. Daryl Gerard Martinez, May 14, 1994. BA in Bus., Baker U., 1994. Ins. processor Mut. Benefit Life Ins. Co., Kansas City, Mo., 1978-81; lab. technician II, U. Kans. Med. Ctr., Kansas City, 1981-87; office rep. Mid-Am. Cardiology, Kansas City, Mo., 1987-88; ins. claims rep. Blue Cross Blue Shield Kansas City, 1988-93, electronic media claims ins. field rep., 1993—; cons., Kansas City, 1992—. Com. asst. League Dem. Women Voters, Kansas City, 1982, 84, 90. Mem. NAFE, Am. Bus. Women's Assn., Phi Theta Kappa. Methodist. Office: Blue Cross Blue Shield Kansas City 2301 Main St Kansas City MO 64108-2423

FULTZ, LISA ANN, counselor; b. Demopolis, Ala., Oct. 11, 1964; d. Leroy and Carol (Williams) Fultz; m. Lee McGilberry, June 26, 1983 (div. Feb. 1993). BA in Lang. Arts, Livingston (Ala.) U., 1989; MEd in Counseling and Guidance, U. Montevallo, Ala., 1994. Tchr. English and Spanish Sumter Acad., York, Ala., 1989-92; child devel. tchr. Crosscreek Bapt. Ch. Child Devel. Ctr., Pelham, Ala., 1993-94; mental health worker I Chilton-

Shelby Mental Health, Clanton, Ala., 1994-95; residential counselor Shelby Youth Svcs., Alabaster, Ala., 1994-95, Family Connection, Inc., Alabaster, 1995—; counselor, tchr. Glenwood Health, Birmingham, Ala., 1995—. Mem. ACA, Chi Sigma Iota, Kappa Delta Pi. Democrat. Baptist. Home: 4741 Hwy 22 Montevallo AL 35115 Office: Family Connection Inc Walker Run #2 Alabaster AL 35007

FULWEILER, PATRICIA PLATT, civic worker; b. N.Y.C., Mar. 19, 1923; d. Haviland Hull and Marie-Louise (Fearey) Platt; m. Spencer Biddle Fulweiler, Oct. 5, 1946; children: Marie-Louise Fulweiler Allen, Pamela Spencer, Hull Platt, Spencer Biddle. AB cum laude, Bryn Mawr Coll., 1945; MBA, Columbia U., 1950. Jr. copywriter, asst. account exec. Dorland Internat. Pettingell & Fenton, N.Y.C., 1945-46; statistician, fin. staff treas.'s office GM, N.Y.C., 1950-52; asst. account mgr. investment dept. Fiduciary Trust Co., N.Y.C., 1953-61; bd. dirs. Chapin Brearley Exchange, Inc., 1964-74, treas., 1966-71, pres., 1971-73. Bd. dirs. Knickerbocker Greys, 1965—, treas., 1970-75; bd. dirs., treas. City Gardens Club, N.Y.C., 1974-79, chmn. ways and means com., 1974-81; bd. dirs. Nat. Soc. Colonial Dames State N.Y., 1973-82, asst. treas., 1973-82; mem. fin. com. Alumnae Assn. Bryn Mawr Coll., 1970-76; bd. dirs. Daus. of Cin., 1974-81, scholarship adminstr., 1976-81; pres. Ladies Christian Union, 1982-87, chmn. fin. com., 1987-94; rec. sec. Women's Assn. St. James Ch., N.Y.C., 1972-75, co-chmn. Spring Festival, 1974-75, chmn., 1975-76, treas., 1976-81, mem. Altar Guild, 1975—; treas. Churchwomen's League for Patriotic Svc., 1982-86; mem. scholarship com. Youth Found., 1981—, pres., 1990—; membership chmn. Huguenot Soc. Am., registrar, 1986—. Mem. Soc. Sponsors of USN, Alumnae Coun. Spence Sch., Colonial Dames Am. (bd. dirs. 1987-93), Nat. Soc. Colonial Dames, Colony Club, Thursday Evening Club, Wilson Point Beach Assn. Club. Republican. Home: 3 Hilltop Rd Norwalk CT 06854-5001 Address: 158 East 83rd St New York NY 10028

FUNG, AMY SHU-FONG, accountant; b. Hong Kong, Sept. 23, 1949; came to U.S., 1970; d. Wing-Chee and Fung-Siu (Tsang) Leung; m. Gee-You Fung, Mar. 17, 1970; children: Alice, Deborah. BS in Acctg., CUNY, 1982. Acct. Cath. Charities Diocese of Bklyn. Inc., N.Y.C., 1982-83; sr. acct. Beth Israel Med. Ctr., N.Y.C., 1983-85, St. John Episcopal Home for Aged and Blind, N.Y.C., 1986-87, Internat. Ctr. for Disabled, N.Y.C., 1988-91, United Jewish Appeal-Fedn. Jewish Philanthropies N.Y., N.Y.C., 1992-94. Home: 359 Colon Ave Staten Island NY 10308-1415

FUNICELLI, BETTY LYNN, accountant; b. Altoona, Pa., Mar. 20, 1963; d. Ray Joseph and Donna Jean (DeLancey) F. BS in Acctg., Pa. State U., 1985. CPA, Pa. Sr. mgmt. acct. Guy J. Landolfi, CPA, Altoona, 1985-90; pres. Betty Lynn Funicelli, PC, Altoona, 1990—. Mem. worship com., adminstrv. coun., choir dir., ch. pianist Greenwood United Meth. Ch., Altoona, 1985—, jr. youth asst. leader, 1989—, chmn. ch. pastor-parish rels. com.; mem. Cen. Pa. Youth Ministries, Duncansville, 1989—; bd. dirs. treas., chmn. fin. com. Tri-County unit Epilepsy Found. Western Pa., Altoona, 1991-93. Scholar Altoona Area Sch. Dist., 1981, Espy scholar Pa. State U., 1982-83. Mem. AICPA, Pa. Inst. CPA's, Am. Bus. Women's Assn. (treas. Horseshoe Curve chpt. 1991-92, chmn. hospitality com. 1990-91, Woman of Yr. award 1991), Altoona C. of C., Quota Club, Internat. Order Rainbow (life), Alpha Lambda Delta. Home: 1618 Princeton Rd Altoona PA 16602-7437 Office: The Pines Plaza Unit II 1637 E Pleasant Valley Blvd Altoona PA 16602-7337

FUNK, DOROTHEA, public health nurse; b. St. Louis, Oct. 26, 1916; d. John Arthur and Pearl M. (Dial) Johnson; m. Frank E. Funk, Jan. 3, 1941 (dec. Jan. 1996). Diploma, Leo N. Levi Meml. Hosp., Hot Springs Nat. Park, Ark. RN, Ark. Asst. dir. nursing svc. Helena (Ark.) Hosp.; nurse-investigator Little Rock Health Dept.; pub. health nurse Clark County Health Dept., Arkedelphia, Ark.; nurse coord. for health manpower recruitment Ark. State Nurses Assn.; patient-coord. and liaison nurse Medi-Ctr. of Am., Inc.; health manpower coord. Ark. Nursing Assn., Little Rock, 1970-73; trustee Ark. Nurses Found., Little Rock, 1996. Vol., field rep. Women's Meml.-Meml. Found. Ind., Arlington, Va.; mem. Ark. Gov.'s Commn. on Status of Women; mem. Spl. Task Force on Delivery of Health Care; active ARC, Ark. Red Cross. Lt. Nurse Corps, U.S. Army, World War II. Recipient Health Planning award in Ark., 1979, Jerome S. Levy award Ctr. Ark. Health Systems Agy., 1983, Lifetime Achievement award Ark. Nurses Coalition, 1994. Mem. ANA, Ark. State Nurses Assn. (pres. dist. 10 1971-73, state pres., state treas., chmn. pub. health nursing, trustee 1996-97), Ark. Pub. Health Assn. (life mem.), Bus. and Profl. Women's Club (co-dir. S.W. Ark. Fedn., club pres.), Altrusa Internat. (club treas. 1969-71), Am. Bus. Women's Assn., North Little Rock Women's City Club. Home: Lakewood House 701 4801 North Hills Blvd North Little Rock AR 72116-7601

FUNK, ELLA FRANCES, genealogist, author; b. Domino, Ky., Apr. 7, 1921; d. Roy William and Edna Rene (Cummins) Roach; m. Eugene Boyd Funk, June 20, 1942; children: Susan Teresa, Eugene Boyd. B of Liberal Studies, Mary Washington Coll., 1982. Exec. sec. Lang. Labs., Inc., Bethesda, Md., 1969-70; office mgr. legal firm Donovan Leisure Newton & Irvine, Washington, 1970-76; genealogist, hist. researcher, writer, 1976—; class lectr., bd. dirs. Mary Washington ElderStudy Program; vol. Assn. Preservation Va. Antiquities; mem. Presbyn. Ch., Fredericksburg, Va. Named Exec. of Week, Sta. WGMS, Washington, June 1975; recipient Blue Ribbon winner for poem Va. Fedn. Women's Clubs, 1994. Life mem. Nat. Geneal. Soc.; mem. Hist. Fredericksburg Found., DAR, Alpha Phi Sigma, Sigma Phi Gamma. Club: Woman's (Fredericksburg, Va.). Lodge: Order Eastern Star. Author: Cummins Ancient, Cummins New, vol. 1, 1978, vol. 2, 1980, Joseph Funk, a biography, 1984, Benjamin's Way, 1988, (short stories) Christmas In The Abbey, 1988 (ribbon winner 1989), Dangerous Mission (Va. Fedn. Women's Clubs ribbon 1991), The Phobia (Va. Fedn. Women's Clubs ribbon 1994), My Son and the Westwind (Women's Club blue ribbon 1996). Recipient ribbon for poem "The Good Ship", 1990. Home: 4405 Turnberry Dr Fredericksburg VA 22408-9548

FUNKE, FRANCINE, artist; b. Bklyn., July 4, 1945; d. Abraham and Mollie (Wilensky) Feldman; m. Michael Jeffrey Funke, Dec. 2, 1968; children: Randall Joel, Elliot Gordon. BFA, Cornell U., 1967; MFA, Hunter Coll., 1972. juror Conn. Commn. on Arts Art in Pub. Spaces Program, Hartford, 1993. Exhibited paintings and sculpture in numerous one-woman shows including Barbara Braathen Gallery, N.Y.C., Tiffany & Co., N.Y.C., 1986, Russell Senate Rotunda, Washington, 1995, Scottsdale (Ariz.) Ctr. for Arts, 1995, Walter Wickiser Gallery, N.Y.C., 1995, Mus. Art, Ft. Lauderdale, Fla., 1994; group exhbns. include Cambridge (Mass.) Multicultural Arts Coun., 1993, Aldrich Mus. of Contemporary Art, Conn., 1993, Parrish Art Mus., Southampton, N.Y., 1996, Dowling Coll., N.Y., 1996; represented in permanent collections including Mus. of Art, Ft. Lauderdale, Aldrich Mus. Contemporary Art; author, designer: (book) On Fire, Poem and Paintings, 1995. Recipient Stone Meml. award Cornell U., 1967. Jewish. Home and Studio: 33 Barncroft Rd Stamford CT 06902

FURBER, SYLVIA ABEL, psychotherapist, educator; b. Boston, Oct. 3, 1915; d. Harry and May (Albert) Abel; m. Allan Furber (dec.), Jan. 31, 1942; children Joan Furber Kalafatas, Richard Mark. BS, U. Mass., 1936; MA, Boston U., 1962. Cert., lic. social worker, Mass. Tchr. Boston Pub. Schs., 1936-40; libr. edn. reference Newark, 1940-41; tchr. Brockton (Mass.) Pub. Schs., 1950-60; dept. chmn. Fisher Jr. Coll., Boston, 1961-65; pvt. practice as psychotherapist, cons., lectr. Sharon, 1965-80, Delray Beach, Fla., 1980—; lectr. Mae Volen Sr. Ctr., Boca Raton, Fla., 1993-94, Kings Pt. Sr. Ctr., Delray Beach, Fla., 1979—; adj. prof. Massasoit Coll., Brockton, Mass., 1960-61, Stonehill Coll., N. Easton, Mass., 1961-62, Emerson Coll., Boston, 1961-65; lectr., cons., presenter in field. Reviewer: (books)(Deepak Chopra) Ageless Body, Timeless Mind, 1993, (Betty Friedan) The Fountain of Age, 1993, (Bill Moyers) Healing and the Mind, 1993, (M. Czikszentimihalyi) The Evolving Self, 1993, (Antonio Damasio) Descartes' Error, 1994, (Barry Panter) Creativity and Madness, 1995. Pres. Parents Fedn., Boston, 1945-47; founder 1st chpt. NOW, 1960—; mem. Delray Citizens for Social Responsibility, Delray Beach, Fla., 1980—. Mem. Am. Group Psychotherapy Assn., Am. Personnel and Guidance Assn., S.E. Fla. Assn. Psychoanalytic Psychology, Humanist Soc. S. Fla. Home: 109 Prudence Ln Cotuit MA 02635

FURCI, JOAN GELORMINO, early childhood education educator; b. Torrington, Conn., Jan. 3, 1939; BS, Western Conn. State Coll., Danbury, 1960; MS, U. Hartford, 1966; Ed.D., Nova U., Ft. Lauderdale, Fla., 1975. Tchr., Conn., 1960-68, dir. Early Childhood Program Univ. Sch., Nova U., 1971-90; asst. prof. Nova Coll., 1990-94, early childhood tchr., N.C. Tng. and Tech. Assistance Ctr., Morganton, 1995—; cons. Early Childhood Program, N.Y., N.C., 1968—; bd. dirs. United Way Child Care Centers, Broward County. Pres. Kids in Distress, 1987-88. Mem. Nat. Assn. for Edn. Young Children, Assn. for Childhood Edn. Internat. Home: 281 Cold Creek Rd Canton NC 28716-9612

FUREN, SHIRLEY ANN, marketing professional; b. Pomona, Calif., Sept. 12, 1936; d. Orville Emmett and Mary Evelyn (Carmack) Strickland; m. Ralph R. Rickel, Sept. 3, 1954 (div.); children: Lynda Diane, Lorrie Anne, Stanley Rupert; m. Walter E. Furen, Sept. 25, 1976. B Univ. Studies with distinction, U. N.Mex., 1975; Massage Therapist, Healing Arts Inst., Roseville, Calif., 1994. Cert. massage therapist, Calif. Adminstrv. asst. Psychiat. Inst. Am., Washington, 1977; exec. sec. Am. Assn. Schs. Podiatric Medicine, Washington, 1978-79; profl. model Julie Nation Acad., Santa Rosa, Calif., 1980-88; owner Spheres, Roseville, 1991—. Vol. Andrea Lambert, M.F.C.C., Gold River, Calif., 1992-95; vol. hostess Ted Gaines for City Coun., Roseville, 1993; vol. fundraiser Matrix Gallery, Sacramento, Crocker Art Mus., Sacramento; staffer Matrix Gallery Aux., 1994—; wedding coord. Culinary Guild, Trinity Cathedral, 1989—. Mem. ASCE (chmn. 1992, 93), Sacramento Capital Club, Mercedes Benz Assn. Episcopalian. Home and Office: Spheres No 7 Oak Forest Lane Santa Rosa CA 95409

FUREY, ANNEMARIE PATRICIA, apparel designer; b. Kingston, N.Y., Oct. 11, 1966; d. Peter Joseph II and Anne Barbara (Cioffi) F.; m. Todd Douglas Sheinfeld, Sept. 10, 1994. BFA, RISD, 1988. Product mgr. Mast Industries, Andover, Mass., 1988-91; head sweater designer Boston Traders, Lynn, Mass., 1991-92; product mgr. Burton Snowboards, Burlington, Vt., 1992-95; head design and sourcing Brystie, Morrisville, Vt., 1995—. Vol. Mad River Valley Winter Carnival, Waitsfield, Vt., 1992—. Home: PO Box 534 Waitsfield VT 05673 Office: Brystie 1 Lamolle Industrial Pkwy Morrisville VT 05661

FURGIUELE, MARGERY WOOD, educator; b. Munden, Va., Sept. 28, 1919; d. Thomas Jarvis and Helen Godfrey (Ward) Wood; BS, Mary Washington Coll., 1941; postgrad. U. Ala., 1967-68, Catholic U. Am., 1974-76, 80; m. Albert William Furgiuele, June 19, 1943; children—Martha Jane Furgiuele MacDonald, Harriet Randolph. Advt. and reservations sec. Hilton's Vacation Hide-A Way, Moodus, Conn., 1940; sec. TVA, Knoxville, 1941-43; adminstrv. asst., ct. reporter Moody AFB, Valdosta, Ga., 1943-44; tchr. bus. Edenton (N.C.) H.S., 1944-45; tchr. bus., coord. Culpeper (Va.) County High Sch., 1958-82; ret., 1982; tchr. Piedmont Tech. Edn. Ctr., 1970—. Co-leader Future Bus. Leaders Am., Culpeper, mem. state bd., 1979-82; state advisor 1978-79, Va. Bus. Edn. Assn. Com. chmn., 1978-79. Certified geneal. record Searcher; author of two books, contbr. articles to profl. jours. Mem. Am. Orchid Soc., African Violet Soc., Country Club (Culpeper). Home: 1630 Stoneybrook Ln Culpeper VA 22701-3336

FURMAN, SUE, owner public relations agency; b. Phila., Aug. 3, 1945; d. Seymour and Ruth (Pripstein) Costilo; m. Richard A. Furman, Aug. 20, 1966; children: Michael Brett (dec.), Deborah Elizabeth. BA in comm., Temple U., Phila., 1982. Prodn. asst., prodr., dir. Sta. WPHL-TV 17, Phila., 1981-84; spl. events coord. Sta. KYW-TV 3, Phila., 1984-88; dir. mktg. Oxford Valley Mall, Langhorne, Penn., 1989-90; v.p. The Hayes Group, Dresher, Penn., 1992-95; pres. Furman Comm., Blue Bell, Penn., 1995—; cons. Internat. Franchise Assn., Washington, 1995—. Mem. Greater Phila. C. of C. (bd. dirs.). Home: 105 Muirfield Dr Blue Bell PA 19422 Office: Furman Comm 105 Muirfield Dr Blue Bell PA 19422

FURNEY, LINDA JEANNE, state legislator; b. Toledo, Sept. 11, 1947; d. Robert Ross and Jeanne Scott (Hogan) F. BS in Edn., Bowling Green State U., 1969; postgrad., U. Toledo. Tchr. Washington Local Schs., Toledo, 1969-72, Escola Americano do Rio de Janiero, 1972-74; asst. mgr. banquets Holiday Inn, Perrysburg, Ohio, 1976-77; tchr. Springfield Schs., Holland, Ohio, 1977-83; council mem. City of Toledo, 1983-86; mem. Ohio State Senate, Columbus, 1987—, mem. edn. com., rules com., reference & oversight com., fin. com., minotiry whip. Dem. precinct committeewoman Toledo, 1980-90; mem. Toledo Bd. Edn., 1982-83; mem. adv. bd. Toledo Chem. Abuse Reduced through Edn. & Svcs. Recipient Citizen award Ohio Assn. Edn. Young Children, Stanley K. Levinson award Planned Parenthood Northwest Ohio, Educator of Yr. award Phi Delta Kappa. Mem. NOW, AAUW, NAACP, ACLU (Found. award), Toledo Mus. Art, Toledo Zoo. Congregationalist. Home: 2626 Latonia Blvd Toledo OH 43606-3620 Office: State House Senate Columbus OH 43215

FURNISH, DOROTHY JEAN, retired religious studies educator; b. Plano, Ill., Aug. 25, 1921; d. Reuben McKinley and Mildred (Feller) F. BA, Cornell Coll., Mt. Vernon, Iowa, 1943; MA, Northwestern U., 1945, PhD, 1968. Cert. dir. Christian edn. United Meth. Ch. Dir. Christian edn. Trinity Meth. Ch., Hutchinson, Kans., 1945-52, 1st United Meth. Ch., Lincoln, Nebr., 1952-65; prof. Christian edn. Garrett-Evang. Theol. Sem., Evanston, Ill., 1968-88, adj. dir. M Christian Edn. in Ministry degree, 1988-90; ret., 1990—, freelance writer, lectr., 1990—. Author: Exploring the Bible with Children, 1975, DCE/MCE: History of a Profession, 1976, Living the Bible with Children, 1979, Experiencing the Bible with Children, 1990, Adventures with the Bible: A Sourcebook for Teachers of Children, 1995; also articles. Bd. dirs., treas. Kinheart Women's Ctr., Evanston, 1984-92. Mem. Assn. Profs. and Researchers in Religious Edn., United Meth. Assn. Scholars Christian Edn. Home and Office: PO Box 2374 Boulder CO 80306-2374

FURSE, ELIZABETH, congresswoman, small business owner; b. Nairobi, Kenya, 1936; came to U.S., 1958, naturalized, 1972; m. John Platt; 2 children (from previous marriage). BA, Evergreen State Coll., 1974; postgrad., U. Wash., Northwestern U., Lewis & Clark Coll. Dir. Western Wash. Indian program Am. Friends Svc. Com, 1975-77; coord. Restoration program for Native Am. Tribes Oreg. Legal Svc., 1980-86; co-owner Helvetia Vineyards, Hillsboro, Oreg.; mem. 103rd-104th Congresses from 1st Oreg. dist., 1993—, mem. oversight and investigations com. commerce, trade and hazardous materials, mem. telecomm. and finance com. Co-founder Oreg. Peace Inst., 1985. Office: 316 Cannon HOB Washington DC 20515*

FURSTMAN, SHIRLEY ELSIE DADDOW, advertising executive; b. Butler, N.J., Jan. 26, 1930; d. Richard and Eva M. (Kitchell) Daddow; grad. high sch.; m. Russell A. Bailey, Oct. 1, 1950 (div. Oct. 1967); m. William B. Furstman, Dec. 24, 1977. Asst. corporate sec. Hydrospace Tech., West Caldwell, N.J., 1960-62; sec. to pres. R.J. Dick Co., Totowa, N.J., 1962-63, Microlab, Livingston, N.J., 1963; asst. corporate sec. Astrosystems Internat., West Caldwell, N.J., 1963-65; corporate sec. Internat. Controls Corp., Fairfield, N.J., 1965-73; sec. to pres. Global Financial Co., Nassau, Bahamas, 1974-75; office mgr. Internat. Barter, Nassau, 1975-76; sec. to pres., corp. sec. Haas Chem. Co., Taylor, Pa., 1976-77; asst. to pres., pub. Am. Home mag., N.Y.C., 1977-78; v.p., office mgr. Gilbert, Whitney & Johns, Inc., Whippany, N.J., 1979-95; ret., 1996. Home: 4 Oceans West Blvd # 606D Daytona Beach FL 32118

FURTH, YVONNE, advertising executive. Pres. Kobs and Draft Advt., Chgo. Office: Kobs & Draft Advt Inc 142 E Ontario St Chicago IL 60611-2818*

FURUKAWA, JUDITH KAREN, lawyer; b. Sunnyside, Wash., May 20, 1954; d. Hiroshi and Marion Kimiko (Mizuki) Furukawa; m. Richard Gordon King, Aug. 11, 1990; 1 child, Sarah Kimiko. BA in Spanish lang. and lit., Lewis and Clark Coll., Portland, Oreg., 1976, MA in Tchg. Spanish, 1978; JD, Am. U., Washington, 1989. Bar: Pa. 1989, D.C. 1994. Tchr., counselor McMinnville (Oreg.) Pub. Schs., 1978-86; assoc. Regan Assocs., Chdt., Washington, 1992-94, Law Office of Martha Jennings, Washington, 1990-92, 95—. Recipient Cmty. Svc. award Oreg. Human Devel. Corp., Tigard, 1982, named outstanding bd. mem., 1986. Mem. Am. Immigration Lawyers Assn., Nat. Lawyers Guild. Office: Law Office Martha Jennings 1325 18th St NW # 203 Washington DC 20036

FUSELER, ELIZABETH ANNE, librarian; b. Phila., June 15, 1947; d. Demitry John and Adah (Mench) Pollock. AB, Coll. William and Mary, 1968; MS, Drexel U., 1972, cert. advanced study, 1993. Head biology libr. U. Pa., Phila., 1969-73; head cataloger Marine Biol. Lab., Woods Hole, Mass., 1973-74; libr. Nat. Marine Fisheries, Woods Hole, 1974-75; libr. dir. Tex. A & M U., Galveston, 1975-81, U.S. Merchant Marine Acad., Kings Point, N.Y., 1981-83; rsch. mgr. ISI, Phila., 1986-89; head scis. and tech. Colo. State U. Librs., Ft. Collins, 1989-95; dir. Lamar U. Libr., Beaumont, Tex., 1995—. Recipient Blackwell award ALA, 1994. Mem. Internat. Assn. Aquatic and Marine Sci. Librs. and Info. Ctrs. (pres. 1979-80, pres./pres.-elect 1991-94, editor proceedings, 1990-92.

FUSON, KAREN LEE, sculptor; b. Deming, N.Mex., May 31, 1944; d. Benno Arnold and Catherine Fay (Wegter) Krause; m. Phillip Lawrence Fuson, Aug. 20, 1965; 1 child, Michelle Lee. BA, Western N.Mex. U., 1966; MA, Calif. State U., Fullerton, 1983. Represented by Patricia Correia Gallery, Bergamont Station Art Ctr., Santa Monica, Calif.; founding dir. Gallery 318, L.A., 1983-84; instr. art Calif. State U., Fullerton, 1983-84. One-woman shows include Gallery 318, L.A., 1984, 86, Orange County Ctr. Contemporary Art, Santa Ana, Calif., 1985, Westmont Coll. Art Ctr., Santa Barbara, Calif., 1988, Williams Lamb Gallery, Long Beach, Calif., 1989, Clack Art Ctr., Alma, Mich., 1993, Chemeketa Coll. Art Gallery, Salem, Oreg., 1994, Reed Whipple Cultural Ctr. Gallery, Las Vegas, 1995. MSU Northwest Art Ctr., Minot, N.D., 1996,others; group shows include Gallery 318, 1983, Simard Gallery, L.A., 1984, Orange County Ctr. Contemporary art, 1985, Santa Barbara Contemporary Arts Forum, 1996, The Art Museum of Santa Cruz, 1996, Santa Monica Coll. Art Gallery, 1987, Security Pacific Gallery at the Plaza, L.A., 1988, Williams Lamb Gallery, 1990, Rhodes Gallery, San Pablo, Calif., 1991, Claudia Chapline Gallery, Stinson Beach, Calif., 1992, N. Mex. State U. Art Gallery, Las Cruces, 1993, Laguna Art Mus., Laguna Beach, Calif., 1994, Patricia Correia Gallery, Santa Monica, 1995, Pacific Design Ctr., L.A., 1995, Laguna Art Museum, 1995, 96, Riverside (Calif.) Art Mus., 1996, others; included in numerous private collections and in the permanent collection of the Laguna Art Museums. Office: 2944 Randolph Ave Ste 7 Costa Mesa CA 92626

FUTRAL, NANCY WRIGHT, retired educator; b. Hattiesburg, Miss., Sept. 30, 1936; d. James Edward and Maggie (Taylor) Wright; m. Guy Clemmons Futral; children: Rebecca, Cynthia, Valerie, Elizabeth. BA, Miss. Coll., 1957; MEd, Southeastern La. U., 1972. English tchr. Mandeville (La.) H.S., 1968-73, Covington (La.) H.S., 1974-88; corp. tchr. PNC Bank, Louisville, 1988-92. Bd. dirs. KET, Lexington, Ky., 1984-92; bd. dirs. Seven Counties Svc., Louisville, 1988—. Mem. AAUW, Ky. Home Extension. Democrat. Baptist.

FUTRELL, MARY ALICE HATWOOD, dean, education association administrator; b. Alta Vista, Va., May 24, 1940; d. Josephine Austin; m. Donald Lee Futrell. BA, Va. State U., 1962; MA, George Washington U., 1968, EdD, 1992; postgrad., U. Md., U. Va., Va. Poly Inst. and State U.; DHL (hon.), Va. State U., George Washington U., 1984, Spellman Coll., 1986, Cen. State U., 1987; DEd, Eastern Mich. U., 1987; hon. doctorates, U. Lowell, Adrian Coll.; EdD, George Washington U., 1992. Bus. edn. tchr. Parker-Gray High Sch., Alexandria, Va., 1963-65; bus. edn. tchr., dept. chmn. George Washington High Sch., 1965-80; pres. NEA, Washington, 1983-89, Edn. Internat., Washington, 1993—; sr. fellow, assoc. dir. George Washington U. Ctr. for the Study of Edn. and Nat. Devel., 1989-92; dir. Inst. for Curriculum Stds. and Tech., Washington, 1992—; dean Grad. Sch. of Edn. and Human Devel. George Washington U., 1995—; mem. adv. com. on tchr. cert. State of Va., 1977-82, adv. com. to U.S. Commn. on Civil Rights, 1978; mem. Gov.'s Com. on Edn. of Handicapped, 1977; state rep. to Edn. Commn. of States, 1982; mem. Carnegie Found.'s Nat. Panel on Study of Am. High Sch., Carnegie Forum on Edn. and Economy, task force on teaching as profession; mem. edn. adv. council Met. Life Ins. Co.; trustee Joint Council on Econ. Edn.; mem. study commn. on Global Perspectives in Edn.; mem. Va.-Israel Commn., Nat. Select Com. on Edn. Black Youth; mem. Nat. Bd. for Profl. Teaching Standards; chairperson edn. com. Nat. Council for Accreditation Tchr. Edn.; mem. task force on educationally disadvantaged Com. for Econ. Devel. Mem. editorial bd. ProEdn. mag.; bd. advisers Esquire Register, 1985. Mem. women's council Democratic Nat. Com., Dem. Labor Council; former pres. ERAmerica, nat. chairperson; mem. U.S. Nat. Commn. to UNESCO; mem. adv. council Internat. Labor Rights Edn. and Research Fund; mem. Nat. Dem. Inst. for Internat. Affairs, Nat. Labor Com. for Democracy and Human Rights; bd. advisers Project VOTE; mem. Martin Luther King Jr. Fed. Holiday Commn.; trustee Nat. History Day; bd. dirs. U.S. Com. for UNICEF, Nat. Found. for Improvement Edn., Citizen-Labor Energy Coalition. Recipient Human Rights award NCCJ, 1976, cert. of appreciation UN Assn., 1980, Disting. Service medal, Columbia Univ., 1987, Schull award Ams. for Dem. Action, Pres.'s award NAACP, numerous others; named Outstanding Black Bus. and Profl. Person, Ebony mag., 1984, One of 100 Top Women in Am., Ladies Home Jour. mag., 1984, One of 12 Women of Yr., Ms. mag., 1985, One of Top 100 Blacks in Am., Ebony mag., 1985-89; Ford Found. and Nat. Com. on U.S.-China Relations grantee, 1981. Mem. NEA (bd. dirs. 1978-80, task force on sch. vols. 1977-78, head human relations com. to 1980, sec.-treas. 1980-83) (Creative Leadership in Women's Rights award 1982), Edn. Assn. Alexandria (pres. 1973-75), Va. Edn. Assn. (pres. 1976-78) (Fitz Turner Human Rights award 1976), Edn. Internat. (pres. 1993—), World Confedn. Orgns. of Teaching Profession (pres. 1990-93, exec. com., v.p. 1988—, chmn. women's caucus, 1984—, women's concerns com., chmn. fin. commn., 1986-89, pres. 1990), Am. Assn. Colls. Tchr. Edn., Am. Assn. State Colls. and Univs. Office: George Washington U 2134 G St NW Washington DC 20037-2797

FUTTER, ELLEN VICTORIA, museum administrator; b. N.Y.C., Sept. 21, 1949; d. Victor and Joan Babette (Feinberg) F.; m. John A. Shutkin, Aug. 25, 1974; children—Anne Victoria, Elizabeth Jane. Student, U. Wis., 1967-69; AB magna cum laude, Barnard Coll., 1971; JD, Columbia U., 1974, LLD (hon.); LLD (hon.), Hamilton Coll., N.Y. Law Sch.; DHL (hon.), Amherst Coll., Hofstra U. Bar: N.Y. 1975. Assoc. Milbank, Tweed, Hadley & McCloy, N.Y.C., 1974-80; acting pres. Barnard Coll., N.Y.C., 1980-81, pres., 1981-93; president American Museum of Natural History, New York, NY, 1993—; bd. dirs. Bristol Myers Squibb, CBS, Inc., Consol. Edison of N.Y.; trustee Am. Mus. Natural History, Coun. on Econ. Devel. Ptnr. N.Y.C. Partnership; bd. dirs. The Am. Assembly. Recipient Spirit of Achievement award Albert Einstein Coll. Medicine/Yeshiva U., Abram L. Sachar award Brandeis U., Elizabeth Cutter Morrow award YWCA, Distinction medal Barnard Coll., Excellence medal Columbia U. Mem. ABA, Am. Acad. Arts and Scis., N.Y. State Bar Assn., Assn. Bar City N.Y., Nat. Inst. Social Scis., Coun. Fgn. Rels., Cosmopolitan Club, Century Club, Phi Beta Kappa. Office: Am Mus Natural History Central Park West at 79th New York NY 10024*

FUXA, PATRICIA FRANCES, elementary education educator; b. Nacogdoches, Tex., Sept. 29, 1948; d. John Edward and Patricia Alice (Wood) Stone; m. Robert Jacob Fuxa, Dec. 27, 1965 (div. 1990); children: Jane Marie Fuxa-Johnson, Bryan D., Bradley S., Barry L. BS in Elem. Edn., Phillips U., 1986, MEd, 1995; postgrad., U. Va., 1995. Cert. elem. edn., jr. high social studies, Okla. Tchr. Coolidge Elem. Sch., Enid, Okla., 1986-87, Monroe Elem. Sch., Enid, 1987—; writer, advisor sci. curriculum com. Enid Pub. Schs., 1990—, social studies curriculum com., 1994—; tchr. Project Wild Okla. Wildlife Commn., 1986—; mem. edn. and design coms. Leonardo's Discovery Warehouse and Adventure Quest, 1994—. Author: (poetry) Images, 1986. Chairperson Jr. Svc. League, Pampa, Tex., 1972-74; leader Great Salt Plains coun. Boy Scouts Am., Enid, 1976-78, 84, Cherokee Strip coun. Girl Scouts U.S.A., Enid, 1977; booster Big Blue Band, Enid, 1982-94; religious educator St. Gregory Cath. Ch., Enid, 1975-88. Grantee Enid Pub. Sch. Found., 1991, 90. Mem. NEA, Okla. Edn. Assn., Okla. Reading Coun., Cherokee Strip Reading Coun., Enid Edn. assn., Okla. Alliance for Geog. Edn., Delta Kappa Gamma. Republican. Roman Catholic. Office: Monroe Elem Sch 400 W Cottonwood Ave Enid OK 73701-2113

FUZEK, BETTYE LYNN, secondary education educator; b. Knoxville, Tenn., Oct. 24, 1924; d. Wallace Paul and Bess (Wallace) Bean; m. John F. Fuzek, May 31, 1943; children: Mary Ann, Mark Lynn, Martha Elizabeth. Student, U. Tenn., 1944-45, East Tenn. State U., 1959-64; BS, Milligan Coll., 1966; postgrad. summers, various schs., 1966—. Sci. tchr.

Dobyns-Bennett High Sch., Kingsport, Tenn., 1969-72; subs. tchr. Sullivan County High Schs., Kingsport, 1973-86; violin tchr. Symphony Assn. of Kingsport Talent Edn. Prog., 1973-80, Kingsport Suzuki Assn., 1980-90; pvt. tchr. violin, 1990—; violinist Kingsport Symphony Orch., 1980-85. Tchr. Literacy Coun. Kingsport, Inc., 1990—. Mem DAR. Presbyterian. Home: 4603 Mitchell Rd Kingsport TN 37664-2125

FYDA-MAR, MARY CATHERINE, systems engineer, consultant; b. Oil City, Pa., Aug. 4, 1952; d. John Joseph and Lela Marie (Thompson) Fyda; m. Thomas Webb Mar, June 17, 1978; 1 child, Christina Ann. BS, Mich. State U., 1973, MA, 1975. Exec. dir. H.E.R.E. Rape Crisis Clinic, Placentia, Calif., 1977-78; lectr. Calif. State U., Fullerton, 1978; software engr., project engr. Rockwell Internat., Anaheim, Calif., 1978-91, systems engr., 1996—; computer tchr. Fairmont Pvt. Sch., Anaheim Hills, Calif., 1992-94. NSF fellow, 1974; Nat. Merit scholar, 1970. Mem. IEEE, Computer Soc. IEEE, Nat. Mgmt. Assn., Phi Kappa Phi, Phi Beta Kappa. Democrat. Episcopalian. Office: Rockwell Internat 3370 Miraloma Ave Anaheim CA 92803

GAAR, MARILYN AUDREY WIEGRAFFE, political science educator; b. St. Louis, Sept. 22, 1946; d. Arthur and Marjorie Estelle (Miller) W.; m. Norman E. Gaar, Apr. 12, 1986. AB, Ind. U., 1968, MA, 1970, MS, 1973. Mem. faculty Stephens Coll., Columbia, Mo., 1971-73, Johnson County C.C., Overland Park, Kans., 1973—; interviewer Fulbright Hayes Tchr. Exch. fellowship candidates, Kansas City, Mo., 1982-92; mem. state selection com. Congress Bundestag Youth Exch. Program, Kans., 1985; pres. faculty del. Kans. Assn. C.C.s, 1984-85; gov.'s appointee, admissions interviewer, mem. selection palen Sch. Medicine U. Kans., 1991-95, mem. admissions criteria and admissions process rev. com., 1992. Author: Profile of Kansas Government, 1990; contbg. editor to instr.'s manual Am. Democracy (by Thomas Patterson). Pres. LWV Johnson County, 1987-89, prodr. 1990 Candidates Forum, mem. governing bd., 1993-95; mem. Johnson County Elder Net Coalition, 1988; mem. governing bd. Johnson County Mental Health Ctr., 1981-86, chmn., 1985-86; vol., translator Russian Refugee Resettlement Program of Jewish Family and Children Svcs., Kansas City, 1979-81; alt. mem. Rep. Party State Com., Kans., 1984-86; chmn. Rep. Party City Com., Shawnee, Kans., 1982-86; bd. dirs. Substance Abuse Ctr., Johnson County, 1983-85; treas. Heart of Am., Japan Am. Soc., 1979; program chmn. Kans. Fedn. Rep. Women, 1984-87; hon. dir. Rockhurst Coll., Kansas City; bd. dirs. Huntington Farms Homes Assn., Leawood, Kans., 1993-95. Grantee Europaische Akademie, West Berlin, 1984, 92, Fulbright Hayes, The Netherlands, 1982, Japan, 1975; univ. fellow NEH, 1990. Mem. C.C. Humanities Assn., Kans. Polit. Sci. Assn., Internat. Rels. Coun., People to People, Soc. Fellows, Nelson-Atkins Mus. Arts, Dobro Slovo Nat. Slavic Honor Soc., Phi Beta Kappa, Phi Sigma Alpha. Episcopalian. Office: Johnson County C C 12345 College Blvd Shawnee Mission KS 66210-1283

GAB, HELEN PAULIN, lawyer; b. Evansville, Ind., Dec. 27, 1957; d. Eugene Jr. and Jeanette Helen (Kuzma) Paulin; m. Derald Lee Gab, Aug. 13, 1983; children: Allison Elizabeth, Audrey Louise, Jared Michael, Adrienne Millicent. BA in Social Work, Ind. State U., 1981; MA in Social Work, Washington U., St. Louis, 1984, JD, 1984. Bar: U.S. Ct. Appeals (9th cir.), U.S. Claims Ct., U.S. Dist. Ct. (ea. dist.) Mo., Mo., Ill. Legis. rsch. asst. Consolidated Neighborhood Svcs., 1981; legal intern Forst and Levy, 1981; summer legal intern Bryan, Cave, McPheeters & McRoberts, St. Louis, 1983, assoc., 1984-93; ptnr. Bryan, Cave, LLP, St. Louis, 1993—; mem. Women in the Profession Com., St. Louis, 1990, Securities Com. of the Bus. Law Sect., St. Louis, 1990, Task Force on Family Issues Affecting Lawyers, St. Louis, 1990, Adult Abuse Com., St. Louis, 1989. Co-chairperson Amos Place Welcoming Com., University City, Mo., 1990. Named one of Outstanding Young Women of Am., 1983; honor scholar Washington U., 1982, 83, 84, Fisse scholar Washington U., Breckinridge scholar 2d prize Washington U., Erna Ardnt scholar, Robert Adamson scholar Ind. State U., Betty Blumberg scholar Chi Omega; dean's fellow social work Washington U. Mem. ABA, Mo. Bar Assn., Ill. Bar Assn., Bar Assn. Met. St. Louis, Women's Lawyers Assn. Met. St. Louis, Assn. Trial Lawyers Am., Order of Coif, Chi Omega. Democrat. Roman Catholic. Office: Bryan Cave LLP 211 N Broadway Ste 3600 Saint Louis MO 63102-2750

GABALDON, DIANA, writer; b. 1950; d. Jacqueline (Sykes) Gabaldon; m. Doug Watkins; children: Laura Juliet, Samuel Gordon, Jennifer Rose. MS in Marine Biology, PhD in Ecology. Asst. prof. rsch. environ. studies, freelance writer. Author: Outlander, 1991 (Best First Novel award B. Dalton bookstores 1991, Best Book Yr. award Romance Writer's Am. 1991), Dragonfly in Amber, 1992, Voyager, 1994; software reviewer Byte mag.; contbr. articles to profl. jours.; author comic strips Disney. Office: Bantam Doubleday/Del 1540 Broadway New York NY 10036*

GABAY, ELIZABETH LEE, infectious diseases physician; b. Milw., Oct. 20, 1951; d. George Gerald and Margaret Louise (Tracy) G.; m. Stephen K. Liu, June 29, 1974; children: Katherine Liu, Margaret Liu. BS, U. Wis., Milw., 1973; MD, U. Wis., 1976. Diplomate Am. Bd. Internal Medicine, Am. Bd. Infectious Diseases, Am. Bd. Geriatrics. Internal medicine physician FHP, Long Beach, Calif., 1981-90, chmn. infectious disease dept., 1990—. Contbr. articles to profl. jours. Fellow ACP; mem. Am. Soc. Microbiology. Roman Catholic. Office: PO Box 2607 Bellingham WA 98227

GABBERT, J(OSEPHINE) ANN, nurse, administrator; b. Ft. Worth, Feb. 19, 1956; d. Weldon Saye Darnell and Mary E. (Richards) Darnell Strasheim; children: Amanda, Maryann; m. Adam Gabbert. BS in Nursing, Mary Hardin Baylor Oll., Belton, Tex., 1978; postgrad., U Tex., Arlington, Dallas Bapt. U. Clinician II Surg. ICU/Recovery Rm. M.D. Anderson Hosp. and Tumor Inst., Houston, 1977-84; staff nurse emergency rm. DFW Med. Ctr., Grand Prairie, Tex., 1984-87; agcy. nurse Spl. Care Nurses, Dallas, 1988-89; nurse mgr. emergency rm. Charlton Meth. Hosp., Dallas, 1988-89; claims rep. AMNA Corp., Dallas, 1990; staff nurse emergency svcs. dept. Parkland Meml. Hosp., Dallas, 1990-92; PRN, staff nurse emergency rm., relief supr. Midway Park Med. Ctr., Lancaster, Tex., 1989-91, dir. home health, 1993-94; CEO, owner Elite Care II Home Health Agy., Midlothian, Tex. Mem. ANA, Tex. Nurses Assn. Home: 1033 Glen Oak Dr Burleson TX 76028-6267

GABEL, CONNIE, chemistry educator; b. Green Bank, W.Va.; d. William Ashby and Marie (Galford) Lowry; m. Richard Gabel; children: Greg, Keith, Debbie. BS in Chemistry magna cum laude, James Madison U.; MA in Ednl. Adminstrn., U. Colo., 1984. Teaching asst. U. Wis., Madison, 1969-70, specialist endocrinology, 1970-71; tchr. Dept. Defense Schs., Tokyo, 1972-74, Poudre R-1 Schs., Ft. Collins, Colo., 1975-78; tchr. Boulder (Colo.) Valley Schs., 1985-87, interim asst. prin., 1984-85; interim supt. Jefferson County Schs., Golden, Colo., 1992; tchr. Mapleton Pub. Schs., Thornton, Colo., 1992-95; internat. studies Egyptian program Regis U., Denver, 1994; instr. Colo. Sch. Mines, 1995-96; dean of students Horizon H. S., Thornton, Colo., 1995-96; rechr. AMC Cancer Rsch. Ctr., Denver, 1993, rsch. cons. Colo. U. Med. Ctr., Denver, 1994; cons. sch. fin. Colo. Dept. Edn., Denver, 1984; display tech Boulder-chemistry rsch., 1995. Charter mem., pres. Friends Louisville (Colo.) Libr., 1985—; charter mem., pres., v.p. Coal Creek Rep. Women, Louisville, 1987—; precinct chair, mem. Boulder County Reps., 1988—; mem. Nat. Rep. Women, Washington, 1987—. Mem. AAAS, AAUW, Nat. Assn. Sci. Tchrs., Am. Chem. Soc. (edn. divsn.), Colo. Assn. Sci. Tchrs., ASCD, MESA (dir., advisor 1992—, mem. state level adv. bd. 1993—), Phi Delta Kappa. Office: Horizon H S 5321 E 136th Ave Brighton CO 80601

GABEL, KATHERINE, academic administrator; b. Rochester, N.Y., Apr. 9, 1938; d. M. Wren and Esther (Conger) G.; m. Seth Devore Strickland, June 24, 1961 (div. 1965). AB, Smith Coll., Northampton, Mass., 1959; MSW, Simmons Coll., 1961; PhD, Syracuse U., 1967; JD, Union U., 1970; bus. program, Stanford U., 1984. Psychol. social worker Cen. Island Mental Health Ctr., Uniondale, N.Y., 1961-62; psychol. social worker, supt. Ga. State Tng. Sch. for Girls, Atlanta, 1962-64; cons. N.Y. State Crime Control Coun., Albany, 1968-70; faculty Ariz. State U., Tempe, 1972-76; supt. Ariz. Dept. of Corrections, Phoenix, 1970-76; dean, prof. Smith Coll., 1976-85; pres. Pacific Oaks Coll. and Children's Sch., Pasadena, Calif., 1985—; advisor, del. UN, Geneva, 1977; mem. So. Calif. Youth Authority, 1986—. Editor: Master Teacher and Supervisor in Clinical Social Work, 1982; author report Legal Issues of Female Inmates, 1981, model for rsch. Diversion program Female Inmates, 1984. Vice chair United Way, Northampton, 1982-83; chair Mayor's Task Force, Northampton, 1981. Mem. Nat. Assn. Social Work, Acad. Cert. Social Workers, Nat. Assn. Edn. Young Children, Western Assn. Schs. and Colls., Pasadena C. of C., Athenaeum, Pasadena Rotary Club. Democrat. Presbyterian. Office: Pacific Oaks Coll 5 Westmoreland Pl Pasadena CA 91103-3565

GABELER-BROOKS, JO, artist; b. Baton Rouge, Feb. 14, 1931; d. Gustav Adolph Jr. and Ruth Adelaide Stein; m. Charles Pierce Gabeler Jr., Feb. 17, 1951 (div. Feb. 1973); children: Ann Speed, Charles Pierce III, T. Dolph, Caroline Hart; m. Ralph Brooks, Aug. 8, 1990. BA, Stephens Coll., 1950; studied with Edward Betts, Judi Betts, Al Brouillette, Jeanne Dobie, Ray Ellis, Dong Kingman, Fred Messersmith, John Pike, Tony Van Hasselt, Millard W, ells. illustrator (book) The Golf Courses at the Landings on Skidaway Island, 1993. Currently showing at John Tucker Fine Arts, Savannah, Ga.; one-woman shows include Elliott Mus., Stuart, Fla., 1986, Scarborough House, Savannah, 1988; exhbns. include Fla. Watercolor Soc., Mus. Arts and Scis., Daytona, Fla., 1978, Brevard Art Ctr. and Mus., Melbourne, 1981, State Capitol, Tallahassee, 1982, Boca Raton Mus. Art, 1984, 86, Houston Pub. Libr., 1981, Galveston (Tex.) Art League, 1983; represented in permanent collections The Moody Found., Elliott Mus., The Rosenberg Libr., Transco Energy Co. Houston, Allied Bank of Seabrook, Tex. Mem. Fla. Watercolor Soc. (Pres.'s award 1981, 82, Purchase award 1986, signature life mem.), Salmagundi Club, Galveston Art League (pres. 1981-82, Purchase award 1982), Profl. Artist Guild, Landings Art Assn. (pres. 1990). Home: 11 Mainsail Crossing Savannah GA 31411-2723

GABERT, NORI LAUREN, lawyer; b. Houston, Aug. 15, 1953; d. Lenard Morris and Dahlia (Edelstein) G. BA, U. Houston, 1975, JD, 1979. Bar: Tex. 1980, U.S. Dist. Ct. (so. and ea. dists.) Tex. 1980. Staff atty. securities bd. State of Tex., Houston, 1980-81; v.p., assoc. gen. counsel, sec. Am. Capital Asset Mmgt. Inc., Houston, 1981—. Mem. ABA, Houston Bar Assn. Office: Am Capital Asset Mgmt Inc 46th Fl 2800 Post Oak Blvd Fl 46 Houston TX 77056-6106*

GABLER, ELIZABETH, film company executive. Exec. v.p. 20th Century Fox, Beverly Hills, Calif. Office: 20th Century Fox PO Box 900 Beverly Hills CA 90213-0900*

GABLIK, SUZI, art educator, writer; b. N.Y.C., Sept. 26, 1934; d. Anthony Julius and Geraldine (Schwartz) G. BA, Hunter Coll., 1955. Vis. prof. art Sydney Coll. Arts, 1980, U. of the South, Sewanee, Tenn., 1982, 84, U. Calif., Santa Barbara, 1985, 86, 88, Va. Commonwealth U., Richmond, 1987, Va. Tech., Blacksburg, 1990, U. Colo., Boulder, 1990; endowed lectr. U. Victoria, B.C., 1983, Colo. Coll., 1983, U. Santa Barbara, 1985, Va. Tech., 1989. Author: Magritte, 1979, Has Modernism Failed?, 1984, The Reenchantment of Art, 1991, Conversations Before the End of Time, 1995. Home: 3271 Deer Run Rd Blacksburg VA 24060

GACNIK, BONITA L., computer science, mathematics educator; b. Pueblo, Colo., Feb. 3, 1948; d. Stanley J. Sr. and Viola M. (Wolf) G. BS in Math, U. So. Colo., 1970; MA in Math, U. S.D., 1988, MA in Computer Sci., 1989. Software engr. Nat. Ctr. for Atmospheric Rsch., Boulder, Colo., 1970-84; asst. prof. Mount Marty Coll., Yankton, 1989—, dir. acad. computing, 1991—. Cantor, choir Sacred Heart Monastery, Yankton, 1985—; vol. Kiwanis, Yankton, 1989—. Mem. Pi Mu Epsilon, Upsilon Pi Epsilon. Democrat. Roman Catholic.

GAEDE, JANE TAYLOR, pathologist; b. Washington, July 8, 1941; d. Raleigh Colston and Margaret (Lamb) Taylor; m. William Hanks Gaede, Feb. 12, 1966; children: Geoffrey Terence, Bruce Lucas. BA, U. Miss., 1962; MD, Duke U., 1966. Diplomate Am. Bd. Pathology. Intern in surgery N.C. Bapt. Hosp., Winston-Salem, N.C., 1966-67; resident in pathology Duke Med. Ctr., Durham, N.C., 1967-71, asst. prof. pathology, 1974—; asst. prof. pathology Med. Univ. S.C., Charleston, 1971-74; staff pathologist VA Med Ctr., Durham, 1974—. Author: Clinical Pathology for the House Officer, 1982. Fellow Am. Soc. Clin. Pathologists; mem. DAR (1st vice regent local chpt. 1992-94, regent 1996—), N.C. Soc. Pathologists. Presbyterian. Office: Duke Univ Med Ctr Dept Pathology PO Box 3712 Durham NC 27710

GAETA-HARPER, THERESA, psychotherapist; b. Altoona, Pa., July 6, 1955; d. Joseph D. and Anna M. (Malfara) Gaeta; m. Kevin W. Harper, Oct. 16, 1982. BA in Psychology, St. Francis Coll., 1977; grad. cert., Roosevelt U., 1986, MA in Clin. Psychology, 1989. Clinically cert. substance abuse counselor. Clin. therapist Family Guidance Ctr., Chgo., 1985-86, counseling coord., 1986-87, dir., clin. therapist, 1987-89; pvt. practice psychotherapy Chgo., 1989-91; mgr. vol. dept., clin. therapist Howard Brown Health Ctr., Chgo., 1989-96; cons., psychotherapist Rush Presbyn.-St. Luke's Med. Ctr., 1995—; seminar and workshop trainer, educator Howard Brown Health Ctr., Chgo., 1989-96, nat. trainer and educator, 1991-94. Producer video Active Duty, 1992. Vol. Guild for the Blind, Chgo., 1990-94, Cris Radio, Chgo., 1987-88; bd. dirs. Lakeview Mental Health Ctr., Chgo., 1989-91. Recipient Friend for Life award Howard Brown Health Ctr., 1992, Hon. Recognition PWA Support award, 1991; finalist Internat. Health and Med. Film Festival, 1994. Mem. ACA, Am. Mental Health Counselors, Midwestern Psychol. Assn., Coalition Ill. Counselors. Democrat. Roman Catholic.

GAFFEY, VIRGINIA ANNE, anesthetist; b. Boston, Sept. 6, 1933; d. James Hugh and Virginia (Glennon) G. BS in Edn., Fitchburg State Coll., Mass., 1955; cert. nurse anesthetist, Carney Hosp. Sch. Anesthesia, Boston, 1957. Cert. registered nurse anesthetist. Dir. Sch. Anesthesia Carney Hosp., Boston, 1957-86; staff anesthetist S.E. Anesthesia Assocs., Boston, 1986—. Elected mem. Milton Bd. Health, 1970—. Recipient Helen Lamb Educators award, 1982. Mem. Am. Assn. Nurse Anesthetists (past pres. 1969-70), Mass. Assn. Nurse Anesthetists, New Eng. Assembly Nurse Anesthetists, Milton Vis. Nurses Assn. (mem. and chmn. profl. adv. com.). Home: 230 Edge Hill Rd Milton MA 02186-5324

GAFFIN, JOAN VALERIE, secondary school educator; b. N.Y.C., Nov. 25, 1947; d. William John and Louise Eleanor (Liebig) Philibert; m. Ira Martin Gaffin, May 7, 1981. BS in Bus. Edn., Rider U., 1971; MA in Student Personnel Svcs., Montclair State U., 1978. Cert. coop. bus. edn. coord., bus. edn. adminstr. and coord. Bus. edn. instr., coord. Econ. Manpower Corp., N.Y.C., 1971-72; bus. edn. coord., educator Northern Valley Regional H.S., Old Tappan, N.J., 1972—; gymnastics instr. Twp. of Teaneck, N.J., 1985—; adj. grad. prof. Montclair State U., Upper Montclair, N.J., 1994—. Recipient N.J. Gov.'s Outstanding Tchr. of Yr. award, 1986. Mem. NEA, Nat. Bus. Edn. Assn., N.J. Bus. Edn. Assn. (legis. com. mem. 1990-92, bd. dirs. 1991—, chmn. critical issues task force 1991-95, N.J. bus. tchr. of yr. 1993), N.J. Edn. Assn., Eastern Bus. Edn. Assn. (educator of yr. 1993), N.J. Cooperative Bus. Edn. Coord.'s Assn. (Bergen sector sec. and pres., coord. of yr. 1993), Northeast Bergen Ind. Assn. (treas., bd. dirs. 1978—), Northern Valley Edn. Assn. (sec. 1978-80, 85-86, 91-92, tchr. recognition award 1990-91). Home: 852 W Crescent Ave Allendale NJ 07401 Office: Northern Valley Regional HS Central Ave Old Tappan NJ 07675

GAFFNEY, BERYL, Canadian legislator; d. Heath and Mary Clark; m. J. Cuthbert Gaffney, June 14, 1952; children: Michael, Kenneth, Patti, Gail, Alyson. Regional councillor City of Nepean, Regional Municipality of Ottawa-Carleton, Ont., Can., 1978-88; M.P. Ho. Commons, 1988. Liberal. Office: House of Commons, Offices of House Members, Ottawa, ON Canada K1A OA6

GAFFNEY, MARIE WINIFRED, English language educator; b. Hartford, Conn., Dec. 12, 1965; d. Steve and Catherine T. (Dockery) Kulcsar; Cyril F. Gaffney, July 25, 1992. BA, Fairfield U., 1987; MS, Ctrl. Conn. State U., 1991. Cert. Tchr. Enlish tchr. S. Catholic H.S., Hartford, Conn., 1987-88, Sage Park Middle Sch., Windsor, Conn., 1989—; cmty. mgr. Am. Heart Assoc., Hartford, Conn., 1988-89; bd. dirs. Internat. Consulting and Trade, Inc. Joseph Korzenik fellow in Holocaust Tchg., U. Hartford Maurice Greenberg Ctr. for Judaic Studies, 1995; recipient Celebration of Excellence award for edn., State of Conn. Mem. Nat. Council of Tchrs. of English, Nat. Edn. Assn., Assn. of Supr. and Curriculum Devel. Office: Sage Park Middle Sch 25 Sage Park Rd Windsor CT 06095

GAFFNEY, SUSAN, federal official. BA, Wilson Coll., 1965; MA in Advanced Internat. Studies, John Hopkins. Staff analyst to dep. commr. Dept. Housing Preservation and Devel., City of N.Y., 1970-79; dir. policy, plans and programs Office of Inspector Gen., Agy. for Internat. Devel., 1979-82; asst. inspector gen. Gen. Svcs. Adminstrn., 1982-87, dept. inspector gen., 1987-91; chief mgmt. integrity br. Office of Mgmt. and Budget, 1991-93; inspector gen. Dept. Housing and Urban Devel., 1993—. Recipient Presdl. Meritorious Rank award, Disting. Honor award, Disting. Leadership award Joint Fin. Mgmt. Improvement Program. Office: HUD Office of the Inspector General 451 7th St SW Rm 8256 Washington DC 20410-0001

GAGEL, BARBARA JEAN, health insurance administrator; b. Celina, Ohio, Nov. 19, 1943; d. Vincent James and Theresa Barbara (Goettemoeller) G. BA, Miami U., 1965; MBA, U. Chgo., 1977. Asst. dir. for internat. trade State of Ill., Chgo., Brussels, Hongkong and Sao Paulo, Brazil, 1973-76; dir. office of mgmt. and planning Office Human Devel. Svcs., Chgo., 1976-79; dep. regional adminstr. Health Care Financing Adminstrn., Chgo., 1979-82, regional adminstr., 1982-87; dir. bur. of prog. ops. Health Care Financing Adminstrn., Balt., 1987-92; dir. health stds. and quality bur. Health Care Fin. Adminstrn., Balt., 1992-96; pres., CEO AdminaStar, Inc., Indpls., 1996—. Recipient Presdl. Disting. Rank award 1988, 94, Presdl. Meritorious Rank award 1987, 92; named Fed. Exec. of Yr., 1987. Home: 10461 Spring Highlands Dr Indianapolis IN 46290 Office: AdminaStar Inc 6801 Hillsdale Ct Indianapolis IN 46250

GAGNON, EDITH MORRISON, ballerina, singer, actress; b. Chgo., Apr. 8; grad. Chalif Sch. Dancing, N.Y.C.; student Northwestern U.; voice student Forest Lamont of Chgo. Opera Co.; grad., trained with Ivan Tarasoff Chalif Sch. of N.Y.; m. Alfred Gagnon, Feb. 3, 1977; children by previous marriage—Joyce, Morton. Premiere ballerina Pavley and Oukrainsky Russian Ballet of Chgo., performer with Chgo., Met., Ravinia Opera Cos.; appeared Birthday of Infanta, Greenwich Follies, The Five O'Clock Girl; founder, dir., instr. Sch. of Dance, St. Louis; singer in concert, Carnegie Hall; commentator radio programs Women on the Home Front, Sta. KSD, St. Louis, and CD program Sta. WEW, St. Louis U.; voice coach, producer, performer benefit performances, St. Louis, San Francisco area. Pres. Pets Unlimited, San Francisco; bd. dirs. Artists Embassy. Mem. Pacific Musical Soc. (v.p. San Francisco), Equity Guild. Clubs: Burlingame Country; International Embassy, Francisca

GAHAN, KATHLEEN MASON, small business owner, retired educational counselor, artist; b. Long Beach, Calif., May 23, 1940; d. Robert Elwyn and Jean Mason (Campbell) Fisher; m. Keith Victor Gahan, Apr. 21, 1961; children: Carrie Jean, Christie Sue. BA, Calif. State U., Long Beach, 1962, MA, 1967; student, Studio Arts Ctrs. Internat., Florence, Italy, 1992. Cert. gen. secondary educator, adminstr., Calif. Tchr. Long Beach Unified Sch. Dist., 1963-70; tchr. Porterville (Calif.) Union High Sch. Dist., 1970-76, counselor, 1976-95, ret., 1995; coord. gifted and talented edn. Porterville High Sch., 1976-83, coach acad. decathlon team, 1977-82, 85; adminstr. Counseling for Collegeable Hispanic Jrs., Porterville, 1988-90, Counseling for Ptnrship. Acad. in Bus., 1990-95; tchr. faculty and staff computer workshop Porterville High Sch., 1992-94; proprietor El Mirador Ranch, Strathmore, Calif., 1978-96; salesman real estate, Porterville, 1981-82; income tax return preparer, Lindsay, Calif., 1983-84; organizer SAT preparation workshop, 1981-83. Editor: (cookbook) Mexican Cooking in America, 1974; editor (craft patterns) Glory Bee, 1979-84; group exhibits photography Porterville Coll., 1989, oil paintings, Coll. of Sequoias, 1992; one woman show Porterville Coll., 1995, Cort Gallery, Three Rivers, Calif., 1995. Leader 4-H, Lindsay, 1971-79; mem. exec. com. Math. Sci. Conf. for Girls, Tulare County, 1982-85; adminstr. Advanced Placement Program, Porterville, 1979-95; mem. bible study Ch. of Nazarene; charter mem. Tulare County Herb Soc., 1983-85. Recipient 1st pl. Mus. Art, Long Beach, 1961, Orange Blossom Festival Art Show, Lindsay, 1988, 2d pl. Coll. of Sequoias Art Show, Visalia, 1988, Hon. mention Orange Blossom Festival Art Show, Lindsay, 1992, commendation Gov. Bd. and Dist. Adminstrn., Portersville, Calif., 1975, 82, 95; named Coach of Champion Acad. Decathlon Team, Tulare County, 1982, 85. Mem. AAUW, Am. Assn. Individual Investors, Women in the Senate and House, San Joaquin Herb Soc. Republican. Home: PO Box 431 Lindsay CA 93247-1626

GAILEY, JOAN DALE, business management educator; b. Beaver Falls, Pa., May 10, 1940; d. Irvin D. and Elizabeth Jane (Hollander) Anderson; m. Ronald L. Gailey, Aug. 15, 1957; 1 child, Ronald. BSBA, Geneva Coll., 1975; MBA, Youngstown State U., 1980; PhD, U. Pitts., 1987. Libr. tech. Community Coll. Beaver County, Monaca, Pa., 1969-74; customer liaison, floor supr. LTV Steel, Aliquippa, Pa., 1975-79; instr. Youngstown (Ohio) State U., 1980-83; asst. prof. bus. mgmt. Kent State U., East Liverpool, Ohio, 1984-91, assoc. prof. bus. mgmt., 1992—; cons. in bus. mgmt., 1988—; dir. Kent State East Liverpool Bus. Resource Ctr. Abstract editor: Interface, 1994, 95; contbr. articles to profl. jours. Mem. Rochester (Pa.) Area Planning Commn., 1989, Rochester Area Mktg. Com., 1990; tutor Adult Lit. Coun., Monaca, 1984-91; mem. adv. bd. Ret. Sr. Vol. Program, Lisbon, Ohio, 1990, vice chair, 1993—, facilitator Columbiana County Mini-Loan Fund, 1994—. Recipient Kent State Teaching Devel. award, 1990, Kent State Profl. Devel. award, 1992. Mem. Am. Ednl. Rsch. Assn. (editor newsletter 1993-94, program chair 1992), Midwest MLA, Ohio Bus. Tchrs. Assn., Humanities and Tech. Assn., Assn. for Bus. Communication, Alpha Mu (Outstanding Mktg. Tchr. 1983). Office: Kent State U 400 E 4th St East Liverpool OH 43920-3402

GAILLARD, MARY KATHARINE, physics educator; b. New Brunswick, N.J., Apr. 1, 1939; d. Philip Lee and Marion Catharine (Wiedemayer) Ralph; children: Alain, Dominique, Bruno. BA, Hollins (Va.) Coll., 1960; MA, Columbia U., 1961; Dr du Troiseme Cycle, U. Paris, Orsay, France, 1964, Dr-es-Sciences d'Etat, 1968. With Centre National de Recherche Scientifique, Orsay and Annecy-le-Vieux, France, 1964-84; maitre de recherches Centre National de Recherche Scientifique, Orsay, 1973-80; maitre de recherches Centre National de Recherche Scientifique, Annecy-le-Vieux, 1979-80, dir. research, 1980-84; prof. physics, sr. faculty staff Lawrence Berkeley lab. U. Calif., Berkeley, 1981—; Morris Loeb lectr. Harvard U., Cambridge, Mass., 1980; Chancellor's Disting. lectr., U. Calif., Berkeley, 1981; Warner-Lambert lectr. U. Mich., Ann Arbor, 1984; vis. scientist Fermi Nat. Accelerator Lab., Batavia, Ill., 1973-74, Inst. for Advanced Studies, Santa Barbara, Calif., 1984, U. Calif., Santa Barbara, 1985; group leader L.A.P.P., Theory Group, France, 1979-81, Theory Physics div. LBL, Berkeley, 1985-87; sci. dir. Les Houches (France) Summer Sch., 1981; cons., mem. adv. panels U.S. Dept. Energy, Washington, and various nat. labs. C0-editor: Weak Interactions, 1977, Gauge Theories in High Energy Physics, 1983; author or co-author 140 articles, papers to profl. jours., books, conf. proceedings. Recipient Thibaux prize U. Lyons (France) Acad. Art & Sci., 1977, E.O. Lawrence award, 1988, J.J. Sakurai prize for theoretical particle physics, APS, 1993; Guggenheim fellow, 1989-90. Fellow Am. Acad. Arts and Scis., Am. Physics Soc. (mem. various coms., chairperson com. on women, J.J. Saburai prize 1993); mem. AAAS, NAS. Office: U Calif Dept Physics Berkeley CA 94720

GAINER, BARBARA JEANNE, radiology educator; b. Omaha, Dec. 9, 1938; d. Merrill Lester and Ressie (Kirby) Steele; m. Glenn Thomas Gainer, Oct. 26, 1968; 1 child, Kelly Jeanne Gainer. BA, Austin Coll., 1960; MD, U. Tex. Southwestern, 1966. Diplomate Am. Bd. Radiology. Rotating intern Meth. Hosp. Dallas, 1966-67, resident in diagnostic radiology, 1967-70; chief radiology RE Thomason Gen. Hosp., El Paso, Tex., 1971-77; pvt. practice Radiology Cons., El Paso, 1977-78; from asst. to assoc. prof. radiology Tex. Tech. Health Scis. Ctr., El Paso, 1978-90, prof., 1990—; med. advisor radiologic tech. program El Paso C.C., 1979—; chief med. staff Thomason Gen. Hosp., 1989-90. Bd. dirs. Planned Parenthood, El Paso, 1983-86. Mem. AMA, Am. Coll. Radiology (councilor), Radiol. Soc. N.Am., Tex. Radiol. Soc., Tex. Med. Assn., Assn. Univ. Radiologists. Republican. Presbyterian. Home: 8727 Marble Dr El Paso TX 79904-1709 Office: Tex Tech Health Scis Ctr at El Paso 4800 Alberta Ave El Paso TX 79905-2709

GAINES, SARAH FORE, retired foreign language educator; b. Roxobel, N.C., Aug. 21, 1920; d. Stonewall Jackson Fore and Ethel Gattis; m. Clyde Ritchie Bell (div. 1974); m. John Coffman Gaines. AB, U. N.C., 1941, MA, 1944, PhD, 1968, MLS, 1982. Instr. U. N.C., Greensboro, 1967-69, asst. prof., 1970-75, assoc. prof., 1976-85, assoc. prof. emeritus, 1985—. Author: Charles Nodier, 1971; also articles, book revs. Home: 3017 Robin Hood Dr Greensboro NC 27408-2618

GAINFORT, LOUISE KATHERINE ANN, nutritionist; b. Highland Park, N.J., May 13, 1930; d. Thomas and Sally (DeFranco) De Candia; m. George Kenneth Gainfort, Sept. 16, 1950; children: John Hopkins, Amy Elizabeth Gainfort Katz, Sally Katherine Gainfort Lackey. Student, U. Pa. Nutritionist cholesterol screenings Health Screening Assn., Marlton, N.J., 1987-95; mgr. Gainfort Assocs., Marlton, 1989-95; nutritionist TLC Health Care, Marlton, 1994-96; bd. dirs. Juvenile Diabetes Assn., South Jersey, Chanticleer Condo Assn., Cherry Hill; organizer AARP, Maple Shade, N.J., 1985-89; spkr. and lectr. in field. Author: Gourmet Cooking for Health, 1980, Easy Ways to Control Cholesterol, 1994, Children's Cholesterol, 1996; contbr.: Rodales Natural Foods Cookbook, 1984.

GAIPA, NANCY CHRISTINE, pharmacist; b. Benton Harbor, Mich., Oct. 11, 1949; d. Frank Thomas and Anne Marie (Scardina) G. BS, Marygrove Coll., Detroit, 1971; BS in Pharmacy, Wayne State U., 1992; postgrad. in Cons. Pharmacy, Ferris State U., 1996. Registered pharmacist, Mich.; cert. secondary educator, Mich. Educator Regina High Sch., Harper Woods, Mich., 1971-88; staff pharmacist Perry Drugs, Northville, Mich., 1993, Meijers, Inc., Westland, Mich., 1993—. Vol. Detroit Welfare Reform Coalition, 1989-91, Maral, Southfield, Mich., 1991. State of Mich. scholar, 1967-71. Mem. NOW, Detroit Area Women's Network, Am. Pharm. Assn., Mich. Pharmacists Assn., Golden Key Nat. Honor Soc., Iota Gamma Alpha, Rho Chi. Office: Meijers Inc Westland MI 48185

GAISSER, JULIA HAIG, classics educator; b. Cripple Creek, Colo., Jan. 12, 1941; d. Henry Wolseley and Gertrude Alice (Lent) Haig; m. Thomas Korff Gaisser, Dec. 29, 1964; 1 son, Thomas Wolseley. A.B., Brown U., 1962; A.M., Harvard U., 1966; Ph.D., U. Edinburgh (Scotland), 1966. Asst. prof. Newton Coll. (Mass.), 1966-69, Swarthmore Coll. (Pa.), 1970-72, Bklyn. Coll., 1973-75; assoc. prof. dept. Latin Bryn Mawr Coll. (Pa.), 1975-84, prof., 1984—, editor Bryn Mawr Latin Commentaries, 1983—. Mem. Mid-East selection com. Marshall Scholarships, Washington, 1975-89, chmn., 1984-89; mem. mng. com. Intercollegiate Ctr. for Classical Studies in Rome, Stanford, Calif., 1984-92, chmn. 1988-92. Author: Catullus and His Renaissance Readers, 1993. Decorated MBE. Marshall scholar, U. Edinburgh, 1962-64; NEH summer stipend, 1977; research grantee Am. Philosophical Soc., 1980, 93; ACLS Travel grant, 1985, fellow 1989-90; NEH sr. fellow, 1985-86, 93-94; resident Rockefeller Study and Conf. Ctr., Bellagio, Italy, 1994; Phi Beta Kappa Vis. scholar, 1996—. Mem. Am. Philological Assn. (dir. 1985-88), Renaissance Soc. Am., Internat. Neo-Latin Soc. Office: Bryn Mawr Coll Dept Latin Bryn Mawr PA 19010

GAJL-PECZALSKA, KAZIMIERA J., surgical pathologist, pathology educator; b. Warsaw, Poland, Nov. 15, 1925; came to U.S., 1970; d. Kazimierz Emil and Anna Janina (Gervais) Gajl; widowed; children: Kazimierz Peczalski, Andrew Peczalski. Student, Jagiellonian Univ., Cracov, Poland, 1945-47; MD, Warsaw U., Poland, 1951, PhD in Immunopathology, 1964. Diplomate Polish Bd. Pediatrics, Polish Bd. Anatomic Pathology, Am. Bd. Pathology. Attending pediatrician Children's Hosp. for Infectious Diseases, Warsaw, Poland, 1953-58, head, pathology lab., 1958-65; adj. prof. Postgrad. Med. Sch., Warsaw, Poland, 1965-70; fellow U. Minn., Mpls., 1970-72, asst. prof. dept. pathology, 1972-75, assoc. prof. dept. pathology, 1975-79, prof. dept. pathology, 1979—, dir. immunophenotyping and flow lab., 1974—, dir. cytology dept. pathology, 1976-95. Author chpts. to book; contbr. of numerous papers to profl. jours. Fellow WHO, Paris, 1959, London, 1962, Paris, 1967, U.S. Pub. Health Svcs. fellow, 1968-69; recipient Scientific Com. award Polish Ministry of Health and Social Welfare, 1964. Mem. Am. Soc. Experimental Pathology, Am. Soc. Cytology, Internat. Acad. Pathology, British Soc. Pediatric Pathology, Polish Soc. Pathology, Polish Soc Pediatricians. Roman Catholic. Office: U Minn Dept Pathology U Health Ctr PO Box 609 Minneapolis MN 55455

GALANOPOULOS, KELLY, biomedical engineer; b. Athens, Greece, Jan. 4, 1952; came to U.S. 1970, naturalized, 1976; d. Panayotis and Catherine (Calas) G.; m. Dale S. Kruchten, Sept. 4, 1982; children: Catherine Roberta Kruchten, Stephanie Diane Kruchten. BA, CUNY, 1974; MS, Poly. Inst. N.Y., 1978, postgrad., 1982—; postgrad. L.I. U., 1982—. Dir. bio-med. engring. Wyckoff Heights Hosp., Bklyn., 1980-83, Bronx Lebanon Hosp., N.Y.C., 1983-89; dir. clin. engring. Mt. Sinai Med. Ctr., N.Y.C., 1991—; cons. Environ. Co., N.Y.C., 1980-85, Joint Purchasing, N.Y.C., 1980—; premier health alliance of N.Y. biomed. engring. adminstrs., 1991—; lectr. in field. Mem. Am. Soc. for Hosp. Engring. of Am. Hosp. Assn., Am. Coll. Clin. Engrs., Assn. Advancement Med. Instrumentation, IEEE, Soc. Women Engrs., N.Y. Acad. Scis. Office: Mt Sinai Med Ctr 1 Gustave L Levy Pl New York NY 10029-6504

GALANTE, VALERIE, psychologist; b. West Point, N.Y., May 7, 1962; d. Gaetan Charles Galante; m. James Bryant Hittner, Nov. 26, 1994. BA in Psychology, Rutgers U., 1984; MA in Clin. Psychology, Fairleigh Dickinson U., 1986; PhD in Clin. Psychology, Hofstra U., 1990; postgrad. in Buddhist studies, Naropa Inst. Lic. clin. psychologist, R.I., S.C. Postdoctoral fellow in health psychology Mich. State U./St. Joseph Hosp., Flint, 1991-92; clin. psychologist in pvt. practice Charleston, S.C., 1991—; faculty dept. psychology Citadel, Charleston, S.C., 1996—. Featured columnist The Health Psychologist, 1994-95. Vol. cons. mayor's commn. for children, youth and families, 1995—. Mem. APA (divsns. of clin. psychology and health psychology), AABT, AAAPP, Psi Chi.

GALATI, VERONICA ANTOINETTE, artist; b. Bayridge Bklyn., Feb. 24, 1935; d. Vito and Assunta (Destito) G. BS, NYU, N.Y.C., 1957; MA, Hunter Coll., N.Y.C., 1977. Cert. tchr. music/art, N.Y. Artist, tchr. H.S. of Art and Design, N.Y.C., 1970-86; tchr. anatomy N.Y. Acad. Art, N.Y.C., 1984; art instr. anatomy, sculpture Sculpture Ctr., N.Y.C., 1987-88; artist-tchr. anatomy, life drawing, painting and sculpture. Artist sculpture Decision's Frown Warwick Art League, 1993 (2nd prize); exhibited in group shows at Cannes Film Festival, N.Y.C., 1960's, Monaco Internat. Art Exposition, 1965, Am. Painters in Paris, 1975, Gloria Cortella Gallery, N.Y.C., 1977, Queens Mus., N.Y., 1981, Sculpture Ctr. Gallery, N.Y.C., 1986-87, Marcoleo Ltd., N.Y.C., 1986—, Warwick Art League, 1993—, Arts Coun. of Orange County Middletown Arts Ctr., 1993—, Maxwell Davidson Gallery, N.Y.C., 1992, Mickey Mantel Restaurant and Sports Bar, N.Y.C., 1992, Gallery 53 Artworks, Cooperstown, N.Y., 1992—. Recipient Concours Drawing prize Students League, 1963, John Myers painting scholarships New Sch., 1965-66, Anatomy scholarship N.Y. Acad. Art, N.Y.C., 1984, Sculpture fellowship Sculpture Ctr., N.Y.C., 1986, Excellence in Painting/Internat. Juried Art Competition, Met. Mus. Art and L.A. County Mus. curators, 1988, Sculputre award Warwick Art League, N.Y., 1993; named Outstanding Tchr. of Art, N.Y.C. Art Tchrs. Assn., 1986. Mem. Orange County Coun. Arts. Democrat.

GALATY, CAROL POPPER, health policy administrator; b. Buffalo, Mar. 31, 1943; d. David Henry and Florence Popper; m. David Holt Galaty, June 21, 1965 (div. Apr. 1975); children: Mara Elise; m. James Hill, June 25, 1978; children: Andy, Bruce. BA in Zoology, Pomona Coll., 1964. Vol. Peace Corps, Ghana, West Africa, 1964-66; various positions HEW, 1966-68; founder, mem., bd. dirs. Planned Parenthood of Green Bay, Wis., 1969-74; assoc. dir. Com. for Nat. Health Ins., Washington, 1975-76; Office ofChild Health in Office of Asst. Sec. for Health, HEW, Washington, 1976-78; exec. dir. Fed. Internat. Yr. of the Child, Dept. HHS, Washington, 1978-80; dir. CHAMPUS Liaison Office, Washington and Aurora, Colo., 1981-83; dir. health benefits Office Asst. Sec. Def., DOD, Washington, 1983-90; dep. dir. ops. spl. projects Def. Med. Systems Support DOD, Falls Church, Va., 1990-91; dir. office of program devel., maternal/child health bur. Dept. HHS, Rockville, Md., 1991—; cons. Chilean Health Systems, Santiago, 1976-77; mem. HRSA managed care and infrastructure bldg. work groups Dept. HHS, 1994—; mem. health care reform team White House, 1993. Bd. dirs. Returned Peace Corps Vols., 1989-91; mem. adv. group Nat. Women's Polit. Caucus, Washington, 1975-78; mem. Office Sec. Def. Sr. Exec. Women, Washington, 1981-91. Mem. Northeastern Wis. Health Planning Coun. (econ. task force 1973-75), Milw. Planned Parenthood (bd. dirs. 1970-73), Wis. Family Planning Coordinating Coun. (bd. dirs. 1970-72). Democrat. Jewish. Office: Parklawn Bldg 5600 Fishers Ln Rockville MD 20857-0001

GALATZAN, TAMAR GINNA, lawyer, arbitrator; b. L.A., Oct. 20, 1969; d. Ted Tuvia and Sharon Lee (Adler) G. BA in Polit. Sci. magna cum laude, UCLA, 1991; JD, U. Calif., San Francisco, 1994. Bar: Calif. 1994. Dir. opposition rsch. Assemblyman Terry Friedman Campaign, Encino, Calif., 1992; law clk. L.A. City Atty., 1993; regional adminstr. Calif. Dem. Party, L.A., 1994; field rep. Assemblywoman Barbara Friedman, Sherman Oaks, Calif., 1995-96; western states asst. counsel Anti-Defamation League, L.A., 1996—; arbitrator Arbitration and Mediation, Internat., Sacramento, 1995—. Mem. NOW (pres. UCLA chpt. 1990-91), UCLA Alumni Assn., Phi Beta Kappa. Democrat. Office: Anti-Defamation League 10495 Santa Monica Blvd Los Angeles CA 90025

GALAVITZ, MARIE L., counselor educator; b. Simpson, Pa., Jan. 12, 1928; d. Julius Joseph and Cecilia Stella (Pinkshaw) G.; m. Leonard W. Rosenbloom, Oct. 16, 1958 (div. Aug. 26, 1991); children: David Elia Rosenbloom, Daniel Paul Rosenbloom. BS, Mansfield State Tchrs. Coll., 1949. Cert. secondary educator. Tchr. Vincentown (N.J.) Schs., 1949-53; elem. edn. Middletown (N.J.) Schs., 1953-60; reading specialist Washington Sch., Levittown Twp., Pa., 1969-72; remedial reading tchr. Somerset County (N.J.) H.S., 1973; addictions counselor Carrier Psychiat. Clinic, Belle Meade, N.J., 1976-79; reading and learning disabilities specialist Runney (N.J.) Prep. Sch., 1980-82; addictions counselor West Pines Hosp., Colo., 1989-90; counselor educator, pres., mgr. High Hopes Ltd., Park City, Utah, 1985—. Mem. NOW, ACLU, AARP, Nat. Assn. Alcohol & Drug Abuse, Nat. Victim Ctr., Utah Assn. Alcohol Drug Addictions. Home and Office: High Hopes Ltd PO Box 1212 Park City UT 84060

GALBRAITH, DIANA, elementary education educator. BA, Mills Coll., 1969; multiple subject K-12 credential, Calif. State U., Chico, 1987. Elem. tchr. pub. schs., Chico, 1986-87; mid. sch. tchr. Sanborn Sch., Salinas, Calif., 1987-88, elem. tchr., 1988—; tchr. Greenfield (Calif.) Elem. Sch., summer 1987; presenter in field. Mem. Ctrl. Calif. Tchrs. English (bd. dirs. 1995-96). Home: 380 Belden St Monterey CA 93940

GALBRAITH, NANETTE ELAINE GERKS, forensic and management sciences company executive; b. Chgo., June 15, 1928; d. Harold William and Maybelle Ellen (Little) Gerks; m. Oliver Galbraith III, Dec. 18, 1948; children: Craig Scott, Diane Frances Galbraith Ketcham. BS with high honors with distinction, San Diego State U., 1978. Diplomate Am. Bd. Forensic Document Examiners. Examiner of questioned documents San Diego County Sheriff's Dept. Crime Lab., San Diego, 1975-80; sole prop. Nanette G. Galbraith, Examiner of Questioned Documents, San Diego, 1980-82; pres., examiner of questioned documents Galbraith Forensic & Mgmt. Scis., Ltd., San Diego, 1982—; one of keynote speakers Internat. Assn Forensic Scis., Adelaide, South Australia, 1990. Contbr. articles to profl. jours. Fellow Am. Acad. Forensic Scis. (questioned documents section, del. to Peoples Rep. of China 1986, USSR, 1988); mem. Am. Soc. Questioned Document Examiners, Southwestern Assn. Forensic Document Examiners (charter), U. Club Atop Symphony Towers, Phi Kappa Phi. Republican. Episcopalian. Office: Galbraith Forensic & Mgmt Scis Ltd 4370 La Jolla Village Dr Ste 400 San Diego CA 92122-1249

GALE, CONNIE R(UTH), lawyer; b. Cleve., July 15, 1946; m. Curtis S. Gale, Dec. 20, 1967. Student, Miami U., Oxford, Ohio, 1964-66; BA with distinction, U. Mich., 1967, JD, 1971; MBA, Mich. State U., 1981. Bar: mich. 1971. Law clk. to presiding justice Mich. Supreme Ct., Lansing, 1971-72; asst. atty. gen. State of Mich., Lansing, 1973; corp. counsel Chrysler Corp., Highland Park, Mich., 1973-81; assoc. gen. counsel Fed.-Mogul Corp., Southfield, Mich., 1981-86; v.p., gen. counsel, sec. Allnet Communication Svcs., Inc. (subs. ALC), Bingham Farms, Mich., 1987-95, ALC Communications Corp., Bingham Farms, 1987-95; of counsel Raymond & Prokop PC, Southfield, 1995—. Mem. ABA (meetings com. bus. law sect.), Mich. Bar Assn. (chmn. in-house counsel com. 1984-93, chair bus. law sect. 1991, alt. dispute resolution com. 1986-89), Am. Corp. Counsel Assn. (chmn. securities law com. Detroit chpt. 1990, chmn. membership 1991, treas. 1992, sec. 1993, v.p. 1994, pres. 1995), Phi Kappa Phi. Office: Raymond & Prokop PC 2000 Town Ctr Ste 2400 Southfield MI 48075

GALE, DIANE M., medical software company administrator; b. Webster, Mass., June 23, 1966; d. Anthony J. and Jeannette L. (Hebert) Napierata; m. Robert Gale, Feb. 14, 1993. BS, U. Bridgeport. Cert. med. technologist. Med. technologist U. Mass. Med. Ctr., Worcester; software installer Meditech, Canton, Mass.; salesperson Meditech, Canton, mgr. Home: 60 Janes Way Bridgewater MA 02324

GALE, MARTHA JAYNE, lawyer; b. Fort Wayne, Ind., Aug. 20, 1945; d. Francis LaMoyne and Maxine Ann (Taylor) G. BS, Cornell U., 1967; JD, Temple U., 1975; diploma, Phila. Sch. Psychoanalysis, 1996. Probation officer N.Y. City Cts., Bronx, 1967-70; law clk. Hon. Matthew Bullock, Phila., 1975-78; asst. atty. gen. Pa. Dept. Justice, Phila., 1978-81; chief asst. city solicitor City of Phila. Law Dept., 1981-86; adminstr. Legal Rsch., Inc., Phila., 1986-92; assoc. Law Offices Barry Ginsberg, Phila., 1992—. Mem. Pa. Trial Lawyers Assn., Phila. Bar Assn., Phila. Trial Lawyers Assn. Home: 1420 Locust St # 14F Philadelphia PA 19102

GALE, SYLVIA ELIZABETH, child protection specialist; b. Nanuet, N.Y., Sept. 6, 1949; d. Maynard Elton and Marguerite F. (Goldsmith) G.; 1 child, Elizabeth R. BA, U. N.H., 1971; postgrad., Antioch Grad. Sch., 1982-83. Coord., dir. Rape and Assault Svcs., Nashua, N.H., 1976-80; investigation specialist dept. health and human svcs. N.H. Divsn. for Children, Youth & Families, Concord, 1980—; advisor, mem. steering com. Sexual Assault and Recovery Through Awareness and Hope (SARAH, Inc.), Derry, N.H., 1988—; facilitator N.H. Child Fatality Rev. Com., N.H., 1991—; advisor Baby Steps to Recovery, Nashua, 1992-95. Pres., bd. dirs. Gateway Family Health Ctr., Nashua; bd. dirs. Neighbor to Neighbor Clinic, Nashua, 1991—; vol. sponsor, bd. dirs. N.H. Parents Anonymous, 1985-88; mem. N.H. Task Force to Prevent Child Abuse, 1989-92, 96—, N.H. Atty. Gen.'s Task Force on Child Abuse & Neglect, 1995—. Recipient Roger Fossum award N.H. Atty. Gen.'s Task Force on Child Abuse. Mem. Am. Profl. Soc. on Abuse Children (Pres.'s honor roll 1994), No. New Eng. Profl. Soc. on Abused Children (covening bd. dirs. 1990—), Nat. Abortion Rights Action League, N.H. Women's Lobby. Home: 4 Clergy Cir Nashua NH 03063

GALEN, ELAINE, painter; b. Bklyn., July 12, 1928. BA, U. Pa., 1951; MA, NYU, 1963. Instr. NYU, 1970-73, Prairie State Coll., Ill., 1974-79, Lake Forest (Ill.) Coll., 1979-80; assoc. prof. SUNY, Purchase, 1981—; instr. Manhattanville Coll., Purchase, 1981-89, Columbia U., N.Y.C., 1984-89. Exhbns. include Whitney Mus. Am. Art, N.Y.C., 1961, Bklyn. Mus. Internat., 1963, 78, Pa. Acad. Fine Arts, Peale House., 1972, State Mus. Ill., 1974, Art Inst. Chgo., 1978, The Jewish Mus., 1988, Soho 20, N.Y.C., 1988, 90, 92, 94, Neuberger Mus., Purchase, N.Y., 1992-94, Tampa Mus. Art, 1994, Gallery 1756, Chgo., 1996, numerous others; collections include U.S. Info. Agy., Cyprus, 1996—. Recipient Florsheim grant, 1991.

GALEY, SUSAN ELIZABETH, artist; b. Duncan, Okla., July 1, 1968; d. Joseph Herbert and W. Louise (Freeman) G.; m. Malcolm Paul Christhilf, June 1, 1993. BFA, Cameron U., 1990; postgrad., U. Tex., San Antonio, 91-92. Instr. drawing U. Tex., 1992; resident fellow Blue Mountain Ctr., Adirondacks, N.Y., 1993; asst. to dir. Jansen-Perez Galleries, Inc., San Antonio, 1992; juror Spring Exhbn. Edinboro (Penn.) U., 1994. Exhibited in group shows at Women's Caucus for Art, Penn., 1994, The Parthenon, Nashville, 1994, Moravian Provincial Mus., Czechoslavakia, 1993, Leslie Powell Gallery, Lawton, Okla., 1993. McMahon Fine Arts scholar, Cameron U., 1988, 89, 90, Fine Arts scholar, U. Tex., 1992. Mem. Women Artists' Visual Expressions. Home: 502 Erie St Edinboro PA 16412

GALIGARCIA, CARMEN MARIA, artist, educator; b. Havana, Cuba, Mar. 31, 1936; came to U.S., 1967, naturalized, 1972; d. Estefano Gregorio and Lilia (Del Castillo) G.; m. Juan Manuel Velasco, Nov. 28, 1934 (div. Oct. 1980); 1 child, Nelson Ignacio; m. John Sidney Michael Albert, Feb. 21, 1988. BS, Sch. Commerce Havana, 1957, Sch. Plastic Art San Alejandro, Havana, 1960; BFA in Art, BS in Art Edn., Fla. Internat. U., 1995. Cert. tchr., Fla. Analyst for wide body aircraft Ea. Airlines, Miami, Fla., 1972-91; tchr. fine arts Sunset Sr. H.S., Miami, 1995—; ofcl. poster artist South Fla. Orchid Soc. One woman shows include Galeria Teodora Braga, Belem, Brazil, 1980, Big Five Club, Miami, 1982-83, 86, Equus Art Gallery, Miami Beach, 1992, Galeria Vanidades, Miami Springs, 1996, others; group shows include Embassy Gallery, Miami, 1987, Centre Art Gallery, Indpls., 1988, Palais de Luxembourg, Paris, 1988, IX Internat. Biennial, Valparaiso, Chile, 1989, Inst. Cultural Domecq, Mexico City, 1990, First Salon L.Am. Religious Paintings, 1992, Mus. Sci., 1985-94, others. Bd. dirs. Fla.-Israel Cultural Soc., Miami, 1987—. Recipient 1st prize for watercolors South Fla. Orchid Soc., 1985, 86, 87, 1st hon. mention for watercolors Nat. Capital Orchid Soc., 1991. Mem. Nat. Mus. Women in Arts, Nat. Trust for Hist. Preservation. Republican. Roman Catholic. Home and Studio: 14001 SW 92d Ave Miami FL 33176

GALITELLO-WOLFE, JANE MARYANN, artist, writer; b. Torrington, Conn., Aug. 27, 1942; d. Morris D. and Rose A. (Abate) Galitello; children: Henry Berg III, Jason Sterling, Marissa Tracy. Student, Ward Sch. Elec., 1961, Porter-Chester Coll., 1982. Nurse aide Palm Bay, Fla., 1989; decorator, designer Waterbury, Conn.; electronic engr. Torrington, Conn.; sales rep. Thomaston, Conn.; dance tchr. San Jose, Calif.; freelance artist, writer Torrington. Author: Your Gift of Life, 1991 (award 1993), Snow Bird Melt, 1991, Tody, Heart Desire; published 3 songs including Shadow of Love. Faith healer; active Govt. for Abuse Through Nation and Unity of Nation; advocate for the homeless; active Untied We Stand in Love; min. Your Gift of Life, WBCC-CoCo Radio. Home: PO Box 61851 Palm Bay FL 32906-1851

GALITZ, LAURA MARIA, secondary education educator; b. Chgo., Apr. 16, 1951; d. John Anthony and Barbara Jean (Bunche) Lauzon; m. Richard Allen Galitz, June 17, 1973; children: Melissa Jean, Kimberly Anne. BS in Biology, DePaul U., 1973. Cert. tchr., Ill. Tchr. St. Viator H.S., Arlington Heights, Ill., 1973-76; sales rep. E.R. Squibb & Sons, Princeton, N.J., 1976-77; fin. analyst Motorola, Inc., Schaumburg, Ill., 1978-81; substitute tchr. Palatine, 1990; substance abuse prevention coord. Lake Zurich (Ill.) Schs., 1991-94; tchr. earth sci. and chemistry Grant Cmty. H.S., Fox Lake, Ill., 1994—. Bd. dirs. Lake Zurich Mid. Sch.-North PTO, 1991—, sec., 1994-95, pres., 1995—; music parent coord. Seth Paine Sch. PTO, 1993-94, vol. coord., 1992-93; vol. coord. Thomas Jefferson Sch. PTA, 1985-90; vol. tchr. Palatine and Lake Zurich Schs., 1989—; project co-dir. Ela Area Cmty. Partnership, Lake Zurich, 1991; referendum co-chmn. Citizens for New Schs., 1990-91, head spkrs. com., 1991; dep. registrar Lake County, Ill. Co-recipient Partnership award Lake County Fighting Back Project, 1991. Office: Grant Cmty HS 285 E Grand Ave Fox Lake IL 60020-1634

GALIZZI, MONICA, economics researcher; b. Piacenza, Italy, Nov. 12, 1961; came to U.S., 1987; d. Giovanni and Giuliana (Vecchiotti) G.; m. Enrico Cagliero, June 25, 1994; 1 child, Diana Anna. BS, U. Cattolica, Milan, Italy, 1986; M in Polit. Economy, Boston U., 1990, PhD in Econs., 1994; D in Polit. Economy, U. Milan, Italy, 1990. Rsch. asst. dept. econs. Cath. U., Milan, Italy, 1986-87; instr. micro- and macro-economics, dept. econs. Boston U., 1989-92; postdoctorate rsch. fellow in econs. of labor markets U. Limburg, Maastricht, The Netherlands, 1993-94; economist Workers Compensation Rsch. Inst., Cambridge, Mass., 1994—. Mem. Am. Econ. Assn., European Econ. Assn., Ea. Econ. Assn. Home: 31 Pickman Dr Bedford MA 01730-1009 Office: Workers Compensation Rsch Inst 101 Main St Cambridge MA 02142-1519

GALL, BETTY BLUEBAUM, office services executive; b. Williamson, W.Va., June 11, 1944; d. Thomas Jefferson Bluebaum and Ollie Mae (Moore) Bluebaum Walker; Charles B. Walker (stepfather); 1 child, Thomas Ethan. Ptnr., dir. Chicagoland Register, dating service, Chgo., 1974-84; cooking instr. Elizabeth Benson Internat. Cooking Lessons, 1978-84; owner Ethnic Party People Catering, 1981-92, Phone-A-Friend Dating Service, Chgo., 1984-90, Betty Gall Office Svcs., Chgo., 1991—. Mem. comm. dept. Little City Found., 1989-91. Home: 6314 N Troy St Chicago IL 60659-1414

GALLAGHER, ANNE PORTER, business executive; b. Coral Gables, Fla., Mar. 16, 1950; d. William Moring and Anne (Jewett) Porter; m. Matthew Philip Gallagher, Jr., July 31, 1976; children: Jacqueline Anne, Kevin Sharkey. BA in Edn., Stetson U., 1972. Tchr. elem. schs., Atlanta, 1972-74; sales rep. Xerox Corp., Atlanta, 1974-76, Fed. Systems, Rosslyn, Va., 1976-81; sales rep. No. Telecom Inc. Fed. Systems, Vienna, Va., 1981-84, account exec., 1984-85, sales dir., 1985-94, mktg. dir., 1995-96; bus. devel. dir. Informix Federal, Vienna, Va., 1996—; v.p. Fed. Pub. Sector Timeplex Fed. Systems, Inc., Fairfax, Va. Exec. com. N. Va. United Way. Mem. NAFE, Info. Tech. Assn. of Am. (exec. com.), Armed Forces Comm. and Electronics Assn., Pi Beta Phi. Episcopalian. Avocations: skiing, aerobics. Home: 4052 Seminary Rd Alexandria VA 22304-1646 Office: Informix Fed 8605 Leesburg Pike Ste 700 Vienna VA 22182

GALLAGHER, DIANE SHUGRUE, human resources professional; b. N.Y.C., Dec. 31, 1936; d. Dwyer William and Leona (MacDonald) Shugrue; children: Maura, William, Katherine, Claire. AA, Colby Sawyer Coll., 1957; BS in Orgnl. Behavior, Lesley Coll., 1988. Newspaper columnist South of Boston Mirror, Scituate, Mass., 1973-76; TV talk show host WBZ TV, Boston, 1975-77; placement dir. Katharine Gibbs Sch., Boston, 1981-83; human resources rep. Wang Labs., Lowell, Mass., 1983-85, Fidelity Investments, Boston, 1985-88; human resources cons. Analog, Houghton-Mifflin, Boston, 1989-90; vol. Peace Corps, Cape Verden, West Africa, 1990-92; staff rep. Peace Corps, Boston, 1993—; mem. Boston Coun. Internat. Visitors, 1970-80; career counselor Roxbury (Mass.) H.S., 1981-90; bd. mem. Greater Boston Rehab. Svcs., Cambridge. Commr. Gov. Commn. on Status of Women, Boston, 1971-76, Internat. Women Year Commn., Boston, 1976; bd. mem., advisor to pres. Colby-Sawyer Coll., 1970-76, Mass. Coll. Art, 1972-78, Marion Ct. Coll., 1982-88; chairwoman Child Care Task Force, Boston, 1974; bd. mem. Harvard Ponds Condo Assn., Brookline, Mass., 1993—; active Harvard Host Fmaily Program, 1970—. Mem. Returned Peace Corps Assn. Home: 83 Harvard Ave Brookline MA 02146 Office: Peace Corps 10 Causeway St Boston MA 02222

GALLAGHER, ELIZABETH WORRELL, fund raising consultant; b. Phila., June 9, 1936; d. Granville II and Marguerite (Boyle) Worrell; m. William J. Gallagher, Mar. 21, 1981; children: Liza Powell, Lynne Samson, Sara Noon, Lawrence Coughlin. BA, Sweet Briar Coll., 1958. Assoc. Marsteller, McCade, Inc., Washington, 1971-74; dir. devel. Nat. Cathedral Sch., Washington, 1974-88; assoc. Russell Reynolds, Inc., Washington, 1988-90; exec. dir. devel. Georgetown U., Washington, 1990-94; sr. cons. Marts & Lundy, Inc., Lyndhurst, N.J., 1994—. Office: Marts & Lundy Inc 1280 Wall St W Lyndhurst NJ 07071

GALLAGHER, LINDY ALLYN, banker, financial consultant; b. Kalamazoo, Sept. 27, 1954; d. Karl P. Joslow and Audrey S. Phillips; m. Thomas J. Gallagher, Nov. 29, 1975; children: James Allyn Buckley, Phillip Graham, Charles Bedloe. BS, U. Pa., 1975; MBA, Columbia U., 1982. Faculty, researcher U. Pa., Phila., 1976-80; corp. banking officer Bank of Montreal, N.Y.C., 1982-84; v.p. Citibank NA, N.Y.C., 1984-89; v.p. manager Chase Manhattan Bank, N.Y.C., 1989-90; pres. The Allyn Co., New Canaan, Conn., 1990—; treas., dir. 957 Lexington Corp., 1981-87. Editor Columbia Jour. World Bus., 1980-82. Mem. Women's Nat. Rep. Club, 1986—; commr. Town of New Canaan, 1991—; treas., sec. Young Women's League New Canaan, Inc., 1992-94. Mem. Stanwich Club, The Penn Club (N.Y.C.). Republican. Episcopalian.

GALLAGHER, LORI MEGHAN, lawyer; b. Raton, N.Mex., 1958. BA, U. N.Mex., 1980, JD, 1984. Bar: Tex. 1984. Ptnr. Andrews & Kurth, LLP, Houston. Editor-in-chief: N.Mex. Law Rev., 1983-84. Mem. ABA, Houston Bar Assn., State Bar Tex. Office: Andrews & Kurth LLP 600 Travis Ste 4200 Houston TX 77002*

GALLAGHER, NANCY ANNE, college official; b. Henniker, N.H., July 15, 1952; d. Bernard Leon and Theresa Marie (Damour) Young; m. Joseph John Gallagher, Oct. 2, 1971; children: Jennifer Joan, James Joseph. Student, St.

Anselm Coll., 1986—. Clk. bus. office New Eng. Telephone, Manchester, N.H., 1970-74; operator switchbd. St. Anselm Coll., Manchester, 1978-87, dir. telecommunications, 1987—. Tchr. St. Raphael Ch., Manchester, 1986-90; vol. libr. St. Raphael Sch., Manchester, 1974-76. Mem. NAFE, Assn. Coll. and Univ. Telecom. Adminstr. (state coord.), N.H. Telecom. Assn. (program v.p. 1992-95, pres. 95—), N.H. Women in Higher Edn. Assn. Roman Catholic. Office: St Anselm Coll 100 Saint Anselms Dr Manchester NH 03102-1323

GALLAGHER, PAULA MARIE, real estate appraiser; b. Omaha, Nov. 10, 1959; d. Kenneth Leroy and Phyllis Virginia (Stopak) G. Diploma, Nebr. Coll. Bus., 1978-79; student, Met. Tech. Community Coll., Omaha, 1979-81, U. Nebr., Omaha, 1981-85, 91, Coll. St. Mary, Omaha, 1986-90; BS, Bellevue U., 1993. Lic. real estate appraiser and broker, Nebr. Legal sec. McCormick Cooney Mooney & Hillman P.C., Omaha, 1979; word processor Firstier Bank, Omaha, 1979-83, staff asst., 1983-84; appraiser trainee Morrissey Appraisal Svcs., Omaha, 1985-88, real estate appraiser, 1988—; residential mem. Am. Inst. Real Estate Appraisers. Mem. Appraisal Inst. (sr. residential appraiser), Am. Bus. Women's Assn. (rec. sec. 1984-85, treas. 1988-89, Women of Yr. award 1989), Omaha Women's C. of C. (pres.-elect 1996—, mem. edn. com. 1990-92, mem. fin. com. 1991, dir. cmty. recognition 1992, dir. edn. 1993, chmn. fin. style show 1995). Roman Catholic. Home: 10321 N 186th Ave Bennington NE 68007-6165 Office: Morrissey Appraisal Svcs 11314 Davenport St Omaha NE 68154-2630

GALLAGHER, RUTH RYALL, retired social worker; b. Sparta, Wis., Oct. 11, 1925; d. Ernest Van Rensselaer and Henrietta Lorraine (Achtenberg) Ryall; m. Frederick Walter Gleeson, Aug. 6, 1953 (dec. Feb. 1962); m. Thomas Patrick Gallagher, June 12, 1965. BA in Journalism, U. Wis., 1948; MA in Sociology, Case Western Res. U., 1965; MSW, U. Utah, 1974. Lic. clin. social worker, Utah. Reporter, freelance writer, sociology instr. Utah, 1974-90; Worked as reporter, free-lance writer and sociology instr, 1948-74, social worker State of Utah, 1974-90. Author: Words Most Often Misspelled and Mispronounced, 1963. Mem. Welfare Reform Coalition, Salt Lake City, 1994—. Mem. LWV. Democrat. Home: 1571 Glen Arbor Salt Lake City UT 84105

GALLAGHER, SIOBHAN EILEEN, public relations executive, consultant, researcher; b. Torrington, Conn., Dec. 10, 1960; d. Leonard Wesley and Mary Page (Burns) G.; m. Raymond Russell Hyatt, Nov. 19, 1994. BA cum laude, McGill U., Montreal, 1983; MBA, Simmons Coll., 1989. Adminstrv. asst. Advest, Inc., Boston, 1984-86; rsch. assoc., asst. v.p. Moseley Securities Corp./The Flagship Group, Boston, 1986-88; sr. rsch. analyst for socially responsible investing U.S. Trust Co., Boston, 1989-93; mgr. pub. rels. DSP Devel. Corp., Cambridge, Mass., 1989—; cons. on socially responsible investing and mktg. and comm., Mass., 1993—; mem. adv. coun. Applebrook Farms, Vt., Mass., 1992. Vol. Medford (Mass.) Recycling Com., 1993-94, also various women's orgns., Mass., 1989—. Mem. NOW, Nat. Women's Health Network, Nat. Mus. Women in Arts, Feminist Majority Found., Boston Women Communicators, Simmons Coll. Alumni Orgn. Office: DSP Devel Co 1 Kendall Sq Cambridge MA 02139-1562

GALLAGHER-KOSMATKA, PATRICIA ANNE, secondary school mathematics educator, dean; b. La Crosse, Wis., Oct. 4, 1961; d. Donald J.and Erna M. (Kelzer) Gallagher; m. Gregory L. Kosmatka, Nov. 7, 1992. BS in Math., U. Wis., La Crosse, 1983, M in Edn. and Profl. Devel., 1989. Cert. tchr. secondary math., Wis. Math. tchr. Amery Middle Sch., Amery, Wis., 1983-84, Assumption H.S., Wis. Rapids, Wis., 1984-94; dean of acads. Assumption H.S., Wis. Rapids, 1994—. Mem. teen citizen com. C. of C., Wis. Rapids, 1992—. Roman Catholic. Office: Assumption HS 445 Chestnut St Wisconsin Rapids WI 54494

GALLAHER, CAROLYN COMBS, secondary education educator; b. Lakewood, Ohio, June 27, 1939; d. Andrew Grafton and Wilhelmina D. (Jackson) Combs; m. Thomas F. Gallaher, Apr. 2, 1966; children: Andrew Brooks, Sloan T.F., Sarah Jane Bloodworth. BA, Duke U., 1961; MA, Columbia U., 1965; postgrad., Manhattanville Coll. Cert. history and Spanish tchr., N.Y. Tchr. Am. High Sch., San Salvador, El Salvador, 1961-62; Peace Corps vol. Ednl. TV, Colombia, South America, 1965-67; tchr. Tarrytown (N.Y.) High Sch., 1969-70, The Masters Sch., Dobbs Ferry, N.Y., 1979-93; dept. head, Lightner endowed history chair The Masters Sch., Dobbs Ferry, 1988-93; grad. asst. ESL inst. Manhattanville Coll., Purchase, N.Y., 1994-95; adj. prof. ESL Equal Opportunity Ctr. Westchester C.C., 1994—; originator ann. Conf. Advanced Placement Students; curriculum cons.; presenter Western Europe Inst. Workshop Columbia U.; NIS-US Tchr. Exchange Program. Mem. various bds. Life Ctr.-Environ. Organ, Larchmont, N.Y., 1976—; vestry St. John's Episcopal Ch., Larchmont, 1986-89. Recipient Fulbright grant U.S. Govt., Yugoslavia, 1989, NEH grant U.S. Govt., Dept. Edn. grant U.S. Govt. Mem. Nat. Coun. Social Studies, Westchester Coun. Social Studies, Phi Delta Kappa. Home: 2 Lyons Pl Larchmont NY 10538-3810

GALLANT, JENNIFER RUTH, family practice physician; b. Cambridge, Mass., Aug. 13, 1957; d. William Franklin and Martha Jeanne (Brawley) Dorrill; m. Thomas Paul Gallant, Aug. 6, 1978; children: Michael William, Patrick Hunter. MusB with high distinction, Ind. U., 1979; MD cum laude, Ohio State U., 1989. Diplomate Am. Bd. Family Practice. Concert pianist, 1979-86; resident in family practice Hunterdon Med. Ctr., Flemington, N.J., 1989-92, chief resident, 1990-91; mem. faculty, attending physician Mid-Hudson Family Practice Residency Program, Poughkeepsie, N.Y., 1992-93; pvt. practice, Poughkeepsie, 1993—; adj. prof. Tulane U., New Orleans, 1980-84; artistic dir. First Monday Contemporary Chamber Ensemble, New Orleans, 1983-84; vis. asst. prof. music Ohio U., Athens, 1984-86. Appeared with New Orleans Philharm., Chautauqua Symphony, Jefferson Chamber Orch. performances in N.Y.C., Washington, Pitts., Geneva. Vol. Lend-a-Hand Ctr., 1970-74, Columbus Free Clinic, 1986-87; counselor YMCA Camp for Mentally Retarded Children, 1975-78. Mem. AMA, Am. Acad. Family Practice, Am. Med. Women's Assn., Alpha Omega Alpha. Office: Dutchess Family Medicine 1123 Rte 52 Ste 48 Fishkill NY 12524

GALLANT, MAVIS, author; b. Montreal, Que., Can., Aug. 11, 1922. Hon. doctoral degree, U. St. Anne, N.S., Can., 1984, York U., Toronto, 1984, U. Western Ont., 1990; hon. doctoral degree, Queen's U., 1992, U. Montreal, 1995, Bishop's U., 1995. Writer-in-residence U. Toronto, 1983-84. Author: Green Water, Green Sky, 1959, 60, A Fairly Good Time, 1970; short stories The Other Paris, My Heart Is Broken: 8 Stories and a Short Novel (Brit. title An Unmarried Man's Summer), 1964, The Affair of Gabrielle Russier; introductory essay, 1971; The Pegnitz Junction, a Novella and Five Short Stories, 1973, The End of the World and Other Stories, 1974; short stories From the Fifteenth District, 1979, Home Truths, 1981, Overhead in a Balloon, 1985; play What Is To Be Done? (produced Toronto 1982), 1984, Paris Notebooks: Essays and Reviews, 1986, (short stories) In Transit, 1989, (short stories) Across the Bridge, 1993; The Moslem Wife and other stories, 1994; contbr. to New Yorker, 1951—. Decorated Order of Can.; recipient Gov.-Gen.'s Lit. award, 1982. Fellow Royal Soc. Lit.; fgn. hon. mem. Am. Acad. and Inst. Arts and Letters. Home: 14 rue Jean Ferrandi, Paris VI, France

GALLARDO, HENRIETTA CASTELLANOS, writer; b. San Antonio, July 16, 1934; d. Francisco Garcia and Elisa Duarte (Moreno) Castellanos; m. Albert Joseph Gallardo, Aug. 19, 1965; children: Frank Cantu, Roger Cantu, Gloria Michelle. Cert., Draughn's Bus. Coll., San Antonio, 1952. Sec. Kelly Air Force Base, San Antonio, 1952-53; exec. sec. U. Tex., Dallas, 1974-82; interior decorator Plano, Tex., 1983-85, writer. Author: Tangled Web of Destiny, 1992, Marsh & Co., 1993. Mem. Internat. Platform Assn. Democrat. Catholic. Home: 2212 Parkhaven Dr Plano TX 75075-2013

GALLATIN, NANCY MAE, elementary education educator; b. Downing, Mo., Oct. 5, 1934; d. Russell W. and Louise I. (Farland) Morgan; m. Harlie Kay Gallatin, Aug. 5, 1954; children: Kaylene Cox, Rhonda Proffitt, Morgan. A in Edn., Hannibal-LaGrange Coll., 1954; BA, SW Baptist Coll., 1970. 2d grade tchr. Englewood Elem. Sch., Kansas City North, Mo., 1954-57; libr. sec. U. Ill., Urbana, 1965-69; 1st, 2d grade tchr. Fair Play (Mo.) Elem. Sch., 1970-77; kindergarten tchr. Bolivar (Mo.) R-I Sch., 1977-85, reading tchr. grades 1-3, 1985-95; reading tchr. grades 4-5 Bolivar Intermediate Sch., 1995—. Active PTA, Bolivar, 1969—; Sunday sch. tchr. 1st Bapt. Ch., Bolivar, 1962—. Mem. Internat. Reading Assn., Classroom Tchrs. Assn., Mo. State Tchr.'s Assn., Lakes Country Coun. Reading, Kappa Kappa Iota (pres. local chpt. 1992-95, pres. S.W. area coun. 1995—). Office: Bolivar Intermediate Sch 1300 N Hartford Bolivar MO 65613

GALLAWAY, MARTHINE S., artist; b. Oakland, Calif., June 15, 1913; d. Hector Lorillard and Alma Amelia (Steffensen) Solares; m. Howard Murray Gallaway, June 14, 1936; children: Heather, Bruce, Brian, Kent, Kirk. BA, U. Nev., 1934. Muralist on ceramic tiles. Developer high-fired ceramic glazes allowing refined detail in tile commns.; artist numerous tile commns. churches, restaurants, pvt. homes.; tile commns. published in numerous mags. Past pres. Arundel (Calif.) PTA, Carlmont High Sch. PTA, San Carlos, Calif.; libr. bldg. com. San Carlos, 1965, city hall bldg. com. 1960; vol. Woodside (Calif.) Store County Mus. Mem. Am. Soc. Interior Designers, Hist. Preservation Com. Designers, AAUW (charter mem., pres. 1955), Nat. Mus. of Women in the Arts (charter), Cap & Scroll, Zeta Tau Alpha. Home: 1400 Native Sons Rd Woodside CA 94062-4731

GALLEGLY, GENNA G. SHELTON, instructional systems specialist, educator; b. Poplar Bluff, Mo., Oct. 4, 1950; d. John c. and Sue A. (Johnston) Shelton; 1 child, Jason C. BS of Edn., Ark. State U., 1974, MS of Edn., 1983, EdS, 1984; postgrad./ABD, U. Ark. Tchr. elem. edn. North Little Rock (Ark.) Schs., 1975, McGehee (Ark.) Pub. Sch., 1975-78, Naylor (Mo.) Pub. Sch., 1980-82; grad. asst. Ark. State U., Jonesboro, 1982-84, tutorial coord., instr. pass program, 1984-87; instrnl. sys. specialist Edn./Tng. Ctr. Engr. Constrn. Mgmt. Dept. Vets. Affairs, North Little Rock, 1987—; mgr. fed. women's program Little Rock VA Med. Ctr., 1992-94; presenter distance learning confs. Mem. AAUW, Internat. Assn. Continuing Edn./Tng. Office: ETCECM (138E) 2200 Fort Roots Dr North Little Rock AR 72116

GALLETTI, KAREN JEAN, publishing company executive; b. Modesto, Calif., Aug. 5, 1957; d. Frank Galletti and Zella Ilene (Ladd) Weed; m. Jeffrey Neil Sokol, Sept. 21, 1981 (div. 1983). Student, West Valley Coll., Saratoga, Calif., 1984-88, Stanford U., 1987; BA, Long Island (N.Y.) U., 1993. Asst. mgr. Blossom Hill Tennis Shop, Los Gatos, Calif., 1973-75; supr. Hewlett-Packard Corp., Palo Alto, Claif., 1976-79; recieving inspector Gen. Electric Corp., San Jose, Calif., 1979-81; planner Gen. Electric Corp., 1981-82, engring. analyst, 1982-83, engring. specialist, 1983-85; engr. Internat. Telephone & Telegraph, Clifton, N.J., 1985-86; project mgr. Internat. Telephone & Telegraph, Nutley, N.J., 1986—; owner Small Bus. of Am., Los Gatos, Calif., 1988—, dir. rsch. and devel., Peregrine McCoy Ltd., 1991—. Vol., Peace Corps, Pa., 1988. Mem. Writers Guild Am., U.S. Songwriters Assn., ASME, Nat. Autobon Soc., The Bullet, Anistaisias, Blossom Hill Tennis Club, Almaden Valley Athletic Club, Marina Athletic Club.

GALLIAN, VIRGINIA ANNE, educator; b. St. Louis, Dec. 29, 1933; d. Martin Charles and Flora Olinda (Rocklage) Schake; children: John Charles, Paige Renee. BS, U. Mo., 1955, MS, 1966; student, U. San Jose, Calif., 1961, U. North Tex., Denton, 1971. Tchr. Hazelwood (Mo.) Pub. Schs., 1955, Ft. Dix Post Sch., Trenton, N.J., 1956, Ft. Bragg Post Sch., Fayetteville, N.C., 1956-58, Fergusen-Florrisant (Mo.) Pub. Schs., 1958-59; music supr. Jefferson City (Mo.) Pub. Schs., 1959-60; tchr. Union Sch. Dist., San Jose, 1960-63, 67, 68, Bridgeport (Calif.) Pub. Schs., 1963-65, Columbia (Mo.) Pub. Schs., 1965-67; music tchr. Denton Ind. Sch. Dist., 1970-95; adj. Tex. Woman's U., 1996—; instr. U. North Tex., 1995. Mem. AAUW, Tex. State Tchrs. Assn. (lobbyist 1985—, bd. dirs. 1988-93), Denton Edn. Assn. (chmn. 1985-95), Sigma Alpha Iota (chaplain 1972-74), Phi Delta Kappa. Republican. Methodist.

GALLIHER, CLARICE A. ANDREWS, secondary education educator; b. Laporte, Minn., June 28, 1922; d. Clarence Ray and Luella Anna (Leitch) Andrews; m. Ralph Galliher, June 5, 1943 (dec. Oct. 1985); children: William, Rosemary, Rosanne, Andrew. BS in Secondary Edn., St. Cloud State Coll., 1942; MS, Bemidji State U., 1967. Tchr. math. Ind. Sch. Dist. 111, Baudette, Minn., 1942-43, tchr. math. and sci. Ind. Sch. Dist. 306, Laporte, Minn., 1943-47; tchr. math. Ind. Sch. Dist. 564, Thief River Falls, Minn., 1965-79; clk. Ind. Sch. Dist. 303 Bd. Edn., Guthrie, Minn., 1948-65; mem. sch. survey com. Hubbard county, Minn., 1961-65. Author of poems; contbr. travel articles to pubs. Mem. United Way, Thief River Falls, 1975-77, pres., 1977; mem. Bus. and Profl. Women's Club, Thief River Falls, 1973-89, pres., 1977-78, chair Pennington County Ind. Reps., 1974; life mem. N.W. Med. Ctr. Aux., 1980—, sec., 1989-92, v.p., 1992-93, pres., 1993-94; v.p. United Meth. Women, 1987-90, pres., 1994—; adminstrv. coun. sec. Thief River Falls United Meth. Ch., 1984-91. Mem. AARP, AAUW, NEA (life), Nat. Coun. Tchrs. Math. (life), Minn. Edn. Assn. (life), N.W. Minn. Ret. Educators (v.p. 1993-94), Ret. Educators Assn. Minn. (life), Am. Legion Aux. (life), Mensa (life), Delta Kappa Gamma Soc. Internat. (editor Minn. newsletter 1981-85).

GALLINARI, KAREN LUCILLE ILLUZZI, lawyer; b. S.I., N.Y., Apr. 25, 1960. BA, NYU, 1982; JD cum laude, N.Y. Law Sch., 1988. Bar: N.Y. 1988, Conn. 1988, U.S. Dist. Ct. (so. and ea. dists.) N.Y. 1988. Ptnr. Anderson, Kill, Olick & Oshinsky, P.C., N.Y.C., to 1996; gen. counsel S.I. Univ. Hosp., 1996—. Mem. Human Rights Jour., 1985-86, rsch. editor, 1987; contbr. articles to profl. jours. Mem. ABA, Am. Soc. Law and Medicine. Office: Anderson Kill Olick & Oshinsky PC 1251 Avenue of Americas New York NY 10020-1182*

GALLINGER, LOIS MAE, medical technologist; b. Hibbing, Minn., Sept. 5, 1922; d. Clarence Adolph and Dorothy Mae (Stoller) Belanger; m. Ben Elton Gallinger, Sept. 1, 1956; children: Carol Elda, Gregory John. BS, U. Minn., 1946; Med. Tech. Intern, Coll. St. Scholastica, 1948-49. Cert. med. technologist. X-ray technologist Leigh Clinic, Grand Forks, N.D., 1946-47, Nicollet Clinic, Mpls., 1947-48; med. technologist Little Traverse Hosp., Petoskey, Mich., 1949-52; med. and x-ray technologist Lakeside Med. Ctr., Duluth, Minn., 1952-60; med. technologist St. Mary's Med. Ctr., Duluth, 1961-87; retired, 1987. Treas. Benedictine Health Ctr. Aux., Duluth, 1984—, Women's Assocs. Duluth Symphony, 1986—; cookie chmn. No. Pine Girl Scouts USA, Duluth, 1969; bd. dirs. St. Paul's Episc. Women's Club, Duluth, 1970s, greeter's chmn., 1970s, corr. sec., 1990-94, publicity chmn., 1994; vol. Am. Cancer Soc., 1993—, Am. Lung Assn., 1993. Mem. AAUW, Am. Soc. Med. Tech., Minn. Soc. Med. Tech. (regional historian 1969), Duluth Women's Club. Home: 364 Leicester Ave Duluth MN 55803-2203

GALLINOT, RUTH MAXINE, educational consultant; b. Carlinville, Ill., Feb. 16, 1925; d. Martin Mike and Augusta (Kumpus) G. BS, Roosevelt U., Chgo., 1971, MA with honors, 1974; PhD, The Union Inst., Cin., 1978. Adminstrv. asst., exec. sec. Karoll's Inc., Chgo., 1952-66; asst. dean Cen. YMCA Community Coll., Chgo., 1966-81, dir. life planning inst., 1979-80; pres. Gallinot & Assocs., Chgo., St. Louis and Bethalto, Ill., 1980—; mem. task force Office Sr. Citizens and Handicapped, City of Chgo., 1971-79; mem. criteria and guidelines com. Internat. Assn. for Continuing Edn. and Tng., 1983-86, survey and rsch. com., 1984-88; team chair accreditation evaluation team Accrediting Commn. Ind. Colls. and Schs., Washington, 1983-88; instr. Grad. Sch., USDA, 1984—, Coun. Rehab. Affiliates, Chgo., 1985—. Developer leisure time adult edn. series for elderly Uptown model cities area dept. human resources City of Chgo., 1970; editor: Certified Professional Secs. Rev., 1983; reporter Greater Alton Pub. Co., 1987-89; contbr. articles to profl. jours. Chmn. Commn. Status of Women in State of Ill., 1963-68; del. White House Conf. on Equal Pay, 1963, White House Conf. on Civil Rights, 1965, City of Chgo. White House Conf. on Info. and Library, 1976, State of Ill. White House Conf. Info. Services and Library Services, 1977; life mem. Mus. Lithuanian Culture, Chgo., 1973—; pub. mem. Fgn. Service Selection Bd. U.S. Dept. State, 1984; bd. dirs. Luths. for Chgo., 1978-83, also founding member; member adv. edn. com. Chgo. Commn. Human Relations, 1968-75 fundraising chmn. Bethalto (Ill.) Sr Citizens new bldg. furnishings, 1990-91, pres. 1995—. Recipient Leadership in Civic, Cultural and Econ. Life of the City award YWCA, Chgo., 1972, Achievement in Field Edn. award Operation P.U.S.H., Chgo., 1975. Mem. Profl. Secs. Internat. (past pres., ednl. cons. 1980-84), Edn. Network Older Adults (v.p., sec. 1979-86), Nat. Assn. Parliamentarians (Ill. and Chgo. chpts.), Literacy Coun. Chgo. (bd. dirs. 1979-86), Zonta of Alton (treas. Chgo. club 1965-66). Lutheran. Home and Office: Gallinot & Assocs 210 James St Bethalto IL 62010-1318

GALLO, PIA, art historian; b. N.Y.C., May 10, 1956; d. Thomas Joseph and Maria Dolores (Daniele) Gallo; m. Peter Van Wagner, Sept. 2, 1989; 1 child, Annalisa Van Wagner. Student, John Cabot Coll., Rome, 1974-76; BA in English, Hiram (Ohio) Coll., 1978; postgrad., U. Chgo. Pvt. art dealer specializing in old master and modern prints Chgo., 1981—, N.Y.C., 1995—. Author catalogues: Pietro Testa, 1989, Recent Acquisitions, 1986, Herman Armour Webster, 1983, American Prints, 1981. Mem. Internat. Fine Print Dealers Assn., Arts Club of Chgo. Office: PO Box 389 New York NY 10021-0006

GALLOWAY, EILENE MARIE, space and astronautics consultant; b. Kansas City, Mo., May 4, 1906; d. Joseph Locke and Lottie Rose (Harris) Slack; student Washington U., St. Louis, 1923-25; AB, Swarthmore Coll., 1928; postgrad. Am. U., 1937-38, 43; LLD (hon.), Lake Forest Coll., 1990, Swarthmore Coll., 1992; m. George Barnes Galloway, Dec. 23, 1924; children: David Barnes, Jonathan Fuller. Tchr. polit. sci. Swarthmore Coll., 1928-30; editor Student Svc., Washington, 1931; staff mem., edn. div. Fed. Emergency Relief Adminstrn., 1934-35; asst. chief info. sect., div. spl. info. Library of Congress, 1941-43, editor abstracts Legis. Reference Svc., 1943-51, nat. def. analyst, 1951-57; specialist in nat. def., 1957-66; sr. specialist internat. rels. (nat. security) Congl. Rsch. Svc., 1966-75; cons. internat. space activities, 1975—. staff mem. Senate Fgn. Rels. Com., 1947; profl. staff mem. U.S. group Interparliamentary Union, 1958-66; cons. Senate Armed Svcs. Com., 1953-74, Ford Found., 1958; spl. cons. spl. Senate Com. on Space and Astronautics, 1958; spl. cons. to Senate Com. on Aero. and Space Sci., 1958-77; cons. to Senate Com. on Commerce, Sci. and Transp., 1977-82; chmn. com. edn. and recreation Washington, 1937-38; forum leader 1976-79; guest Soviet Acad. Sci., 1982, adult edn. U.S. Office Edn., 1938; mem. Internat. Inst. Space Law of Internat. Astronautical Fedn., 1958—, U.S. mem. bd. dirs., v.p., 1967-79, hon. dir., 1979—, Fedn. ofcl. observer at sessions UN Com. on Peaceful Uses Outer Space and legal sub-com., 1970-94, mem. com. for rels. with internat. orgns., 1979—; mem. Am. Rocket Soc.'s Space Law and Sociology Com., 1959-62; mem. adv. panel Office Gen. Counsel, NASA, 1971; adviser outer space del. U.S. Mission to UN Working Group on Direct Broadcast Satellites, 1973-75; observer UN Conf. Exploration and Peaceful Uses of Outer Space, Vienna, 1982; lectr. NAS, 1973, U.S. CSC, Exec. Seminar Center, Oak Ridge, 1973, 74, 75, 76, 78; ednl. counselor Purdue U., 1974; lectr. Inst. Air and Space Law McGill U., 1975, Inter Am. Def. Coll., 1977, 78, U. Akron, 1984, 91; mem. panel on solar power for satellites and U.S. space policy Office Tech. Assessment, 1979-80, 82-86, cons., 1982; cons. COMSAT, 1983, FCC Commn. on U.S. Telecomm. Policy, 1983-87; spkr. internat. space law UN, N.Y.C., 1995; mem. NASA Nat. Adv. Com. on Internat. Space Sta., 1996—; active European Space Agy. Internat. Lunar Workshop, 1994. Pres., Theodore Von Karman Meml. Found., 1973-84; mem. alumni council Swarthmore Coll., 1976-79; mem. organizing com., author symposium on Conditions Essential For Maintaining Outer Space for Peaceful Uses, Peace Palace, Netherlands, 1984; bd. advisers Students for Exploration and Devel. of Space, 1984—. Rockefeller Found. scholar-in-residence, Bellagio, Italy, 1976; elected to Coun. of Advanced Internat. Studies, Argentina, 1985, Uruguayan Centro de Investigacion y Difusion Aeronautica-Expacial, 1985. Recipient Andrew G. Haley gold medal Internat. Inst. Space Law, 1968; dist. svc. award Libr. Congress, 1975; NASA Gold Medal for Pub. Svc., 1984, USAF Space Command plaque, 1984; Internat. Acad. Astronautics' Theodore Von Karman award, 1986, Women in Aerospace Lifetime Achievement award, 1987, Lifetime Achievement award Internat. Inst. Space Law, 1989; Wilton Park fellow, Eng., 1968. Fellow AIAA (tech. com. on legal aspects of aeros. and astronautics 1980-84, internat. activities com. 1985—, European space agy. internat. lunar workshop, 1994), Am. Astronautical Soc.; mem. LWV (chmn. study groups housing, welfare in D.C., 1937-38, mem. tech. com. on law and sociology task force on legal aspects 1979—), World Peace Through Law Ctr., Am. Soc. Internat. Law, Am. Astronautical Soc., Lamar Soc. Internat. Law, Internat. Acad. Astronautics (trustee, chmn. sect. on social scis. 1982-93, Mars exploration sub-com., 1991—, trustee emeritus 1995—), Internat. Law Assn., Phi Beta Kappa, Delta Sigma Rho, Kappa Alpha Theta. Episcopalian. Author: Atomic Power: Issues Before Congress, 1946; (with Bernard Brodie) The Atomic Bomb and the Armed Services, 1947; History of United States Military Policy on Reserve Forces, 1775-1957, 1957; Guided Missiles in Foreign Countries, 1957; The Community of Law and Science, 1958; United Nations Ad hoc Committee on Peaceful Uses of Outer Space, 1959; Satellites: A Force for World Peace, World (Security and the Peaceful Uses of Outer Space), 1960; International Cooperation and Organization for Outer Space, 1965; Space Treaty Proposals by the United States and U.S.S.R., 1966; Treaty on Principles Governing the Activities of States in the Exploration and Use of Outer Space, Including the Moon and Other Celestial Bodies: Analysis and Background Data, 1967; Remote Sensing of the Earth by Satellites: Legal Problems and Issues, 1973, 75; The Future of Space Law, 1976; Consensus as a Basis for International Space Cooperation, 1977; The Role of the United Nations in Earth Resources Satellites, 1972; Consensus Decisionmaking by the UN Committee on the Peaceful Uses of Outer Space, 1979; Settlement of Space Law Disputes, 1980; Agreement Governing the Activities of States on the Moon and Other Celestial Bodies, 1980, Perspectives of Space Law, 1981; Conditions for Success of International Space Institutions, 1982; Space Manufacturing, 1981; U.S. Space Policy and Programs, 1982; Space Station, 1986; U.S. National Space Legislation and Peaceful Uses Of Outer Space, 1987; Expanding Article IV of 1967 Space Treaty, 1982; History and Development of Space Law, 1982, Definition of Space Law, 1989, Law, Science and Technology for the Moon/Mars Missions, 1990, Legal and Regulatory Framework for Solar Power Satellites, 1992, The Space Agy. Forum and Internat. Coop., 1993; editor: Space Law Symposium, 1958; The Legal Problems of Space Exploration, 1961; United States International Space Programs, 1965; International Cooperation in Outer Space: A Symposium, 1972, Use of the Geostationary Orbit, 1988; assoc. editor Advances in Earth Oriented Applications of Space Tech., 1978-82, Acta Astronautica Jour., Space Technology: Industrial and Commercial Applications; mem. editorial adv. bd. Jour. Space Law, U. Miss. Law Sch., Space Communication and Broadcasting, 1984-89. Home: 4612 29th Pl NW Washington DC 20008-2105

GALLOWAY, KAREN, nursing educator; b. Canton, Ohio, Feb. 25, 1950; d. Per Lee Guy and Edythe Viola (Arter) Hornbeck; m. Edward Doyle Galloway, June 22, 1985; children: Ryan Edward, Meghan Michelle. Diploma in Nursing, Akron (Ohio) Gen. Hosp., 1968-71; BS in Edn., U. Tenn., Knoxville, 1975, MS in Edn., 1982; BSN, U. N.C., Charlotte, 1992; PhD in Edn., LaSalle U., 1996. Cert. operating rm. nurse; cert. laser nurse. Operating rm. nurse Ft. Sanders Presbyn. Hosp., Knoxville, 1971-76; instr./coord. surg. technologists program Knoxville City Schs., 1976-85; instr./coord. nursing asst. program Adult Evening Sch., Knoxville, 1978-84; eye neuro operating rm. nurse Good Samaritan Hosp., San Jose, 1985-87; operating rm./laser nurse South Valley Hosp., Gilroy, Calif., 1987-89; instr./coord. Louise Harkey Sch. Nursing, Concord, N.C., 1989—; adv. com. Knoxville Health Occupations Program, 1976-85; CPR instr. day care ctrs. Am. Heart Assn., 1986—. Coach cheerleading YMCA, Kannapolis, N.C., 1992—. Mem. Assn. Operating Rm. Nurses (bd. dirs. 1975, del. to nat. conv. 1990), Nat. League Nursing (mem. computer tech. group), Sigma Theta Tau, Pi Lambda Theta. Republican. Methodist. Office: Louise Harkey Sch Nursing Cabarrus Meml Hosp 431 Copperfield Blvd Concord NC 28025-2927

GALLOWAY, LILLIAN CARROLL, modeling agency executive, consultant; b. Hazard, Ky., Sept. 23, 1934; d. William Zion and Clemma (Lewis) Carroll; m. Thomas Roddy Galloway, Dec. 21, 1957; children: David Junkin, Scott Thomas, Donald Lewis. Student, Cumberland Coll., 1955, Ea. U., Richmond, Ky., 1956, U. Cin., 1958, John Robert Powers Sch., Cin., 1958. Tchr. Vandalia (Ohio) Elem. Sch., 1954-56, Kenwood Elem. Sch., Louisville, 1956-57, Cin. Pub. Schs., 1957-64; founder, pres. Fairfax Model Agy., Washington, 1964-67, Cin. Model Agy. Internat., 1967—, Lillian Galloway Modeling Acad., Cin., 1971—, Children Model Agy. Internat., Cin., 1985—; cons., co-owner John Robert Powers Modeling Sch., Cin., 1957-64; pres. Student Model Bds., Cin., 1984—; dir. Career Day, Cin., 1967—. Mem. Cin. Better Bus. Bur., 1967—; trustee Knox Presbyn. Ch., Cin. Named Cin.'s Outstanding Bus. Woman, Sta. WCPO-TV, 1985, Outstanding Alumni, Cumberland Coll., 1988. Mem. DAR, Modeling Assn. Am. (chmn. convs. 1975-77), Am. Modeling Assn. Internat. (pres. 1976-77), Cin. Advertisers Club (membership and program coms., Outstanding Bus. Women award 1985), Exec. Women Internat. (program com., chmn. bd. dirs. 1986, Woman of Achievement award 1986), Cin. C. of C., Cumberland Coll. Alumni Assn.

(pres. 1982), English Speaking Union, Order Ky. Cols., Cin. Woman's Club (bd. dirs. 1992—, lecture/entertainment chmn. 1992—), Town Club (bd. dirs. 1988—), Order Ea. Star (organist 1953—). Republican. Home: 6027 Stirrup Rd Cincinnati OH 45244-3917 Office: 6047 Montgomery Rd Cincinnati OH 45213-1611

GALLOWAY, SISTER MARY BLAISE, mathematics educator; b. Mendota, Ill., June 30, 1933; d. Otto William and Rita Irene (Cannon) G. BS in Math., St. Joseph's Coll., 1965; MS in Math. Edn., U. Ill., 1970; MS in Adminstrn., U. Notre Dame, 1985. Tchr. elem. edn. St. Augustine Sch., Richmond, Mich., 1952-58, Holy Rosary Sch., Duluth, Minn., 1958-65; asst. prin. Sacred Heart Acad., Springfield, Ill., 1983-85, co-prin., 1985-87; instr. math. Marian Cath. H.S., Chicago Heights, Ill., 1965-75, 90—, instr. math., chair math. dept., 1975-83, asst. prin., 1987-90; mem. curriculum com., adv. bd., registrar Marian Cath. H.S., Chicago Heights, 1987-90, faculty coun., 1994—. Grantee Ill. State U., 1992, 95, Ohio State U., 1992, U. Ill., 1990. Mem. Nat. Coun. Tchrs. Math., Ill. Coun. Tchrs. Math., Math. Tchrs. Assn. Chgo. (Master Tchr. 1994, pres. 1996—). Roman Catholic. Home and Office: 700 Ashland Ave Chicago Heights IL 60411

GALLUP, JANET LOUISE, business official; b. Rochester, N.Y., Aug. 11, 1951; d. John Joseph and Mildred Monica (O'Keefe) VerHulst; 1 son, Jason Hicks. BA, Hofstra U., 1973; MA (grad. asst.), Calif. State U., Long Beach., 1979. Asst. trader E.F. Hutton, N.Y.C., 1973-75, Los Angeles, 1975, instr. Calif. State U., Long Beach, 1978-79; fin. analyst Rockwell Internat., Seal Beach, Calif., 1979-85, coordinator mgmt. and exec. devel. and succession planning, 1985-91; mgr. orgn. and employee devel. activities, Hughes Aircraft, 1991-95; mgr. tng. ops. Smart & Final Co., L.A., 1995—. Vol. Cedar House Ctr.-Child Abuse, Long Beach, 1976. Democrat. Roman Catholic. Office: Smart & Final Co 4719 S Boyle Ave Los Angeles CA 90058

GALLUPS, VIVIAN LYLAY BESS, federal contracting officer; b. Vicksburg, Miss., Jan. 14, 1954; d. Vann Foster and Lylay Vivian (Stanley) Bess; m. Ordice Alton Gallups, Jr., July 12, 1975. BA, Birmingham So. Coll., 1975, MA in Mgmt., 1985; MA in Edn., U. Ala., Birmingham, 1975. Cert. purchasing mgr. Nat. Assn. Purchasing Mgmt. Counselor Columbia (S.C.) Coll., 1975-76; case mgr. S.C. Dept. Social Services, Lexington, 1976; benefit authorizer, payment determination specialist then recovery reviewer Social Security Adminstrn., Birmingham, 1977-85; adminstrv. contracting officer U.S. Dept. Def., Birmingham, Ala., 1992-94; supr. contract adminstr. Def. Logistics Agy. U.S. Dept. Def., Ft. Belvoir, Va., 1994-95; contract adminstr., now supervisory contract adminstr. Def. Logistics Agy., Ft. Belvoir, Va., 1995—. Hospice vol. Bapt. Med. Ctr.-Montclair, Birmingham, 1982; trustee, treas. Resurrection House, Birmingham, 1984-85; vol. counselor Cathedral Ch. of Advent, Birmingham, 1987. Mem. Nat. Contract Mgmt. Assn. (cert. profl. contracts mgr., chpt. sec. 1987, pres. 1990-93, nat. dir. 1993-94), Assn. of Luth. Ch. Musicians. Lutheran. Home: 14144 Reverend Rainsford Ct Upper Marlboro MD 20772 Office: US Def Dept Def Logistics Agy 2875 John J Kingman Rd Rm 4422 Fort Belvoir VA 22060

GALOTTI, DONNA, publishing executive; b. Mountainside, N.J., Feb. 8, 1955; d. Jack and Analid Kalajian; m. Ron Galotti, Oct. 14, 1981. BS, Penn State U., 1975. Internat. credit analyst Irving Trust Co., N.Y.C., 1976-77; ad sales rep. BMT Pub., N.Y.C., 1977-79; ad sales rep. Woman's Day Mag., N.Y.C., 1979-81, cosmetics mgr., 1981-83, ea. mgr., 1984-87; v.p., advt. dir. Ladies' Home Jour., N.Y.C., 1987-89, v.p., pub., 1989—; pub. Cosmopolitan Mag. Home: 100 Park Ave New York NY 10017-5516 Office: Cosmopolitan Hearst Magazines 224 West 57th St New York NY 10019*

GALVAN, MARY THERESA, economics and business educator; b. Rockford, Ill., Dec. 19, 1957; d. Dino F. and Ida M. Dal Fratello; m. John D. Galvan, June 27, 1987; children: Marie K., John M., Kathleen T. BA, Rockford Coll., 1979; MA, No. Ill. U., 1981, PhD, 1988. Instr. No. Ill. U., DeKalb, 1979-81; asst. prof. Rockford Coll., 1981-87; assoc. prof. bus. and econs. St. Xavier Coll., Chgo., 1987-92; assoc. prof. mktg. North Ctrl. Coll., Naperville, Ill., 1992—, dir. Ctr. for Rsch., 1994—; chmn. grad. studies com. North Ctrl. Coll., 1996—; cons. Fed. Res. Bank Chgo., 1988—. Lector, St. Elizabeth Seton Parish, Naperville, 1987—, pres. Women's Network. Earhart Found. fellow, 1988; Hegelar Carus scholar, 1987.. Mem. AAUW, Am. Econs. Assn., Am. Mktg. Assn., Am. Statis. Assn. (v.p. 1994—), Western Econs. Assn. Internat., Midwest Bus. Adminstrn. Assn., Midwest Econs. Assn., Phi Delta Kappa, Omicron Delta Epsilon. Office: North Ctrl Coll 30 N Brainard St Naperville IL 60540-4607

GÁLVEZ, ELIZABETH, counselor; b. Santiago, Chile, Feb. 2, 1953; came to the U.S., 1972; d. Miguel Alejandro Aceituno and Sylvia Alejandrina (Morales) Gálvez; children: Paul Anthony, Sara Elizabeth. AA in Liberal Arts, West Hills Coll., 1988; B in Multiculturalism, Humboldt State U., 1991, MEd, 1992. Regional dir. Young Edn. Sys., San Diego, 1983-85; instrnl. asst. Lemoore (Calif.) Sch. Dist., 1986-87; health educator Rural Human Svcs., Crescent City, Calif., 1989-90; coll. instr. Coll. of the Redwoods, Crescent City, 1991-95; counselor Humboldt State U., Arcata, Calif., 1992-96; human resource specialist Del Norte Career Ctr., Crescent City, 1994—; instr. Health Sport, 1991-95; art/adv. com. mem. Del Norte Assn. Cultural Awareness, Crescent City, 1992-95; advisor, cons. Del Norte H.S., Crescent City, 1992-95. Home: 120 Cherrywood Ct Crescent City CA 95531

GALVIN, NOREEN ANN, nurse, educator; b. New Haven, Dec. 9, 1943; d. John Joseph and Helen Jane (Doherty) G.; divorced; children: Eileen M., Paula T., Beth A. Diploma in Nursing, Hosp. St. Raphael Sch. Nursing, 1964; BSN, Cath. U. Am., 1967, MSN, 1979. Staff nurse Greater S.E. Community Hosp., Washington, 1970-72, asst. head nurse, 1972-75; nurse assoc. Guy W. Gargour, M.D., Bethesda, Md., 1975-76; lectr. Prince George's Community Coll., Largo, Md., 1975-78; asst. dir. nursing So. Md. Hosp. Ctr., Clinton, 1977-82, dir. planning, 1982-85; nursing adminstr. Parkwood Hosp., Clinton, 1985-86; staff nurse Phsycians Meml. Hosp., La Plata, Md., 1986-88; prof. Charles County C.C., La Plata, 1988—; nurse cons. Nancy C. Taber, Ft. Washington, Md., 1983-85. Pres. Brandywine (Md.) Dem. Club, 1979, 88, Brandywine Heights Citizens Assn., 1980—; vice chmn. So. Md. Health Systems Agy., Clinton, 1985-90. St. Raphaels Hosp. scholar, 1964. Mem. ANA, Acad. of Med.-Surg. Nursing, Orgn. for the Advancement Assoc. Degree Nursing, Md. Nurses Assn. (bd. dirs. 1989—, dist. 9 sec. 1995—), Lioness (3d v.p. Brandywine chpt. 1985-86, pres. 1994—), Sigma Theta Tau. Roman Catholic. Office: Charles County Coll PO Box 910 La Plata MD 20646-0910

GAMBARDELLA, ROSEMARY, federal judge. BA, JD, Rutgers U. Admitted to bar, 1980. Judge U.S. Bankruptcy Ct. for Dist. N.J., Newark. Office: US Bankruptcy Ct M L King Jr Fed Bldg 50 Walnut St Newark NJ 07102-3506*

GAMBILL, JANE, communications systems developer; b. Oak Ridge, Tenn., July 14, 1958; d. Everett Floyd and Sarah (Martin) G. BA in Math. and Computer Sci., U. Tenn., 1980; MS in Computer Sci., U. N.C., 1982. Mem. tech. staff Bell Labs., Denver, 1982-95; disting. mem. tech. staff AT&T Bell Labs., Denver, 1995-96, Lucent Techs., Bell Labs., Denver, 1996—; mentor Young Scholars Program Colo. Sch. Mines, Golden, 1988—. Co-inventor plug-and-play calling features. Mem. Phi Beta Kappa. Methodist. Office: Lucent Techs 11900 N Pecos St Denver CO 80234

GAMBLE, ANN FYHR, music educator; b. Bklyn., Jan. 22, 1949; d. Ellef Hansen and Ana Alarcón (Riollano) Fyhr; m. Richard Lawson Gamble, Aug. 28, 1971; 1 child, Matthew Hansen. BMus Edn., Westminster Choir Coll., 1970. Cert. music K-12; cert. tchr. N.J. Elem. music tchr. East Windsor Pub. Schs., Hightstown, N.J., 1970-71; middle sch. music tchr. Middletown (R.I.) Pub. Schs., 1971-76; dorm parent/music tchr. Fay Sch., Southborough, Mass., 1976-84; music tchr. Fay Sch., Southborough, 1984—, chairperson music dept., 1984—. Mem. Am. Choral Dirs. Assn., Music Educators Nat. Conf., Am. Guild of English Handbell Ringers (com. for handbells in music edn. 1992—, clinician 1992—, guest condr. area I MA Youth Ring, 1994-96). Episcopalian. Office: Fay Sch 48 Main St Southborough MA 01772-1509

GAMBRELL, LUCK FLANDERS, corporate executive; b. Augusta, Ga., Jan. 17, 1930; d. William Henry and Mattie Moring (Mitchell) Flanders; m. David Henry Gambrell, Oct. 16, 1953; children: Luck G. Davidson, David Henry, Alice Kathleen, Mary G. Rolinson. AB, Duke U., 1950; diplome d'etudes françaises, L'Institut de Touraine, Tours, France, 1951. Chmn. bd. LFG Co., 1960—. Mem. State Bd. Pub. Safety, 1981-90; bd. dirs. Atlanta Symphony Orch., 1982-85; mem. Chpt. Nat. Cathedral, Washington, 1981-85; mem. World Service Council YWCA, 1965—, council Presbytery Greater Atlanta, 1988; elder First Presbyn. Ch., Atlanta; chmn. bd. dirs. Student Aid Found., Atlanta, 1992—; mem. Bd. Councilors The Carter Ctr., Emory U. Mem. Atlanta Jr. League, Alpha Delta Pi.

GAMBRELL, SARAH BELK, retail executive; b. Charlotte, N.C., Apr. 12, 1918; d. William Henry and Mary (Irwin) Belk; B.A., Sweet Briar Coll., 1939; D. Humanities (hon.), Erskine Coll., 1970, U. N.C.-Asheville, 1986; m. Charles Glenn Gambrell (dec.); 1 child, Sarah Belk Gambrell. Officer, dir. Belk Stores, various locations, 1947—. Hon. trustee emeritus Princeton (N.J.) Theol. Sem.; trustee Johnson C. Smith U., Charlotte, N.C., Warren Wilson Coll., Swannanoa, N.C., Florence Crittenton Svcs., Charlotte, Hezekiah Alexander Found., Charlotte, Found. for Good Bus., Raleigh, (hon.) Cancer Rsch. Inst.; trustee nat. bd. YWCA; bd. dirs. Parkinson's Disease Found., N.Y.C., N.C. Cmty. Found., Raleigh, Charlotte Philharmonic Orch., (hon.) bd. dirs. YWCA, N.Y.C. Mem. Fashion Group, Inc., Jr. League N.Y.C., Nat. Soc. Colonial Dames, DAR. Home: 300 Cherokee Rd Charlotte NC 28207-1908 Office: 6100 Fairview Rd Ste 640 Charlotte NC 28210-3277

GAMER, FRANCES, elementary educator; b. Boston, Feb. 12, 1946; d. Morris and Rose Gamer. BS in Edn., Boston State Coll., 1967, MEd, 1969; EdD, U. Mass., 1991. Cert. elem. tchr., reading tchr., supr., prin., Mass. Tchr. Boston Pub. Schs., Dorchester, Mass., 1967-80, Roxbury, Mass., 1980—; mem. adv. bd. Horace Mann Ednl. Found., Boston, 1992—; cons. Renaissance Charter Sch., Boston, 1994—. Contbr. articles to profl. jours. Friend John F. Kennedy Libr., Boston; active Wang Ctr. for Performing Arts, Boston. Mem. ASCD, Coun. Exceptional Children, Learning Disabilities Network, Coun. Tchrs. English, Whole Lang. Assn. Mass., Boston Reading Coun., Phi Delta Kappa. Office: Mendell Elem Sch 164 School St Roxbury MA 02119

GAMMELL, GLORIA RUFFNER, professional association administrator; b. St. Louis, June 19, 1948; d. Robert Nelson and Antonia Ruffner; m. Doyle M. Gammell, Dec. 11, 1973. AA in Art, Harbor Coll., Harbor City, Calif., 1969; BA in Sociology, Calif. State U., Long Beach, 1971. Cert. fin. planner. Bus. analyst Dun & Bradstreet, Los Angeles, 1971-81; sales rep. Dun & Bradstreet, Orange, Calif., 1971-93; rep. sales Van Nuys, Calif., 1981-90; pres. sec. Gammell Industries, Paramount, Calif., 1993-95, also bd. dirs.; regional dir. Am. Mgmt. Assn., 1995—. Mem. Anne Banning Assistance League, Hollywood, Calif., 1981-82; counselor YWCA, San Pedro, Calif., 1983-84; fundraiser YMCA, San Pedro, 1984-85; mem. womens adv. com. Calif. State Assembly, 1984-89. Recipient Best in the West Presdl. Citation, 1981-86, 89, 90. Home: 991 W Channel St San Pedro CA 90731-1415

GAMPEL, ELAINE SUSAN, investment management analyst and consultant; b. New Haven, Apr. 12, 1950; d. Stanley Irwin and Marion (Levine) G.; m. Alan Joseph Tedeschi, Sept. 9, 1984; children: Zachary Joseph Tedeschi Matthew Samuel Gampel Tedeschi. BS in Spl. Edn., Boston U., 1972; MS in Counseling, So. Conn. State U., New Haven, 1975. Cert. investment mgmt. analyst Wharton Sch. Bus., Investment Mgmt. Cons. Assn. Spl. edn. tchr. Ansonia (Conn.) Pub. Schs., 1972-77; v.p., investment mgmt. cons. Paine Webber Inc., Denver, 1977-89; 1st v.p. investments, sr. cons. Dean Witter Reynolds, Denver, 1993—; bd. dirs. the Denver Nuggets. Bd. dirs. United Cerebral Palsy of Denver, 1984-93; mem. outside editorial bd. Denver Post, 1991—; mem. investment com. Women's Found. of Colo., Denver, 1992—. Mem. Investment Mgmt. Cons. Assn. (cert. com. 1990—). Office: Dean Witter Reynolds 370 17th St Ste 5100 Denver CO 80202-5651

GANAWAY, NORMA JEAN, vocational counselor; b. South Bend, Ind., Apr. 9, 1927; d. Welvin Sr. and Alphia (Bond) G. Grad., Thomas Comml. Sch., 1947; cert. in bus., Ind. U., 1980, cert. in supervisory devel., 1980. Sec. to contr. Robertson's Dept. Store, South Bend, 1947-62, sec. to divsnl. mgr. mdse., 1962-68; dir. Urban Tech. Asst. Project, South Bend, 1971; asst. dir. Neighborhood Assn. Model Cities, South Bend, 1971-74; client svc. specialist CETA Program, South Bend, 1974-83; vocat. counselor Workforce Devel. Svcs. No. Ind., South Bend, 1983-94. Sec. Sunday Sch. Pilgrim Bapt. Ch., 1942-43, 50, pres. fellowship club, 1968-69, active red circle; bd. dirs. St. Joseph County YWCA, 1968-71, chmn. Y teenage com 1969-70; bd. dirs., pub. rels. com. Campfire Girls, 1969, 2d v.p., 1972; sec. bd. dirs. Hansel Ctr. Neighborhood Svcs., 1972-73; nat. bd. dirs. YWCA of U.S.A, N.Y.C., 1973-76; apptd. by mayor Commn. Status of Women, 1975, 76; housing commr. City of South Bend Pub. Housing, 1991—; active, past bd. dirs. South Bend Urban League; Rep. committeewoman, South Bend; dir. dist. # 2 St. Joseph County Rep. Women, 1994—. Recipient Woman of Yr. award South Bend-Mishawaka C. of C., 1970, Counselor award Ind. Vocat. Tech. Coll., 1990, Woman of Yr. award Ind. State Women in the NAACP, 1995, NAACP Midwest Region III, 1995, Svc. award East Chgo. br. NAACP, 1995, Appreciation award Order Ea. Star, 1993-95; Ganaway scholarship named in her honor, Workforce Devel. Svcs., 1993. Mem. NAACP (nat. life; state chair 1969—, Ind. conf., Achievement award 1990) Sorelle Entre Nous Club (pres., organizer 1951—, chair Ebony Fashion Show 1992), Order Ea. Star (grant chpt. Ind., dist. dep. grand matron 1968, Dist. Yr. award 1988-91, exec. dir. pub. rels. 1993-94, appreciation placque grand chpt. 1993-95), Imperial Ct. Daus. Isis (illustrious commandress 1962, imperial NAACP coord. 1967-89, Community Leader Am. award 1971). Home: 214 Birdsell St South Bend IN 46628-2107

GANGELL, BERNADETTE ANNE, librarian, writer, biologist; b. Hartford, Conn., Aug. 14, 1959; d. Lawrence Justus and Madeline Elizabeth (Clark) G. BA, St. Joseph Coll., 1983, postgrad., 1985-90; MA, Nat. U., Dublin, Ireland, 1992. Teaching asst. Mary Walsh Sch. Dance, Bloomfield, Conn., 1975-77; clerical asst. Ct. Jud. Dept., Hartford, 1978-83; asst. to law libr. Robinson & Cole, Esqs., Hartford, 1985-87; tech. asst. Prosser Pub. Libr., Bloomfield, Conn., 1983-91; med. toxicologist Keverly Labs., Inc., Bloomfield, 1990-91; researcher, writer Dublin, 1991-93; libr. Newington (Conn.) Libr., 1994—, Bristol (Conn.) Pub. Libr., 1994—; writer, craft designer Bloomfield, 1994—. Scholar, State of Conn., 1978. Mem. Irish No. Aid, Conn. Guild Craftsmen. Republican. Roman Catholic. Home: 32 Wintonbury Ave Bloomfield CT 06002-2416

GANN, JO RITA, social services administrator, association executive; b. Talihina, Okla., June 2, 1940; d. Herbert and Juanita Rita (Fields) G. BS, Okla. Bapt. U., 1962; M Theatre Arts, Portland State U., 1970. Tchr. Oklahoma City Pub. Schs., 1962-64; teen dir., dir. health edn. YWCA, Oklahoma City, 1964-67; camp dir., teen dir. YWCA, Portland, Oreg., 1967-72; asst. dir., program coordinator YWCA, Flint, Mich., 1972-75; exec. dir. YWCA, Salem, Oreg., 1975—; chair N.W. regional staff YWCA, 1983, mem. constn. commn. YWCA, 1981-84, nat. com. to study purpose, 1988-91, del. to World Coun., Norway, 1991; CEO bus. panel Oregonian's Pub. Co. Co-author: A New Look at Supervision, 1980. Del. UN Conf. for Non-Govtl. Orgns.; internat. study del. on world econ. interdependence to Ghana; spkr. Global Concerns, Salem and Portland, 1981—; mem. president's coun. Salem Summerfest, 1985, 86; mem. strategic planning com. Nat. YWCA. Mem. Nat. Assn. YWCA Exec. Dirs. (bd. dirs.), United Way Agy. Execs. (chair 1987, 88). Democrat. Office: YWCA 768 State St Salem OR 97301-3849

GANNAWAY, CAROLYN MARIE, middle school educator; b. Kenosha, Wis., Sept. 30, 1949; d. Nicholas and Rose Lucy (Manna) Bordo; m. Paul Joseph Gannaway, May 2, 1970; children: Steven, Michael, Jason, Gregory. BA in English, U. Wis.-Parkside, Kenosha, 1971; MA in Classroom Guidance and Counseling, Carthage Coll., 1989. Cert. tchr., Wis. Tchr., team leader Racine (Wis.) Unified Sch. Dist., 1972—. Named Tchr. of Yr., Wis. PTA, 1995. Office: Gilmore Mid Sch 2330 Northwestern Ave Racine WI 53404

GANNON, SISTER ANN IDA, retired philosophy educator, former college administrator; b. Chgo., 1915; d. George and Hanna (Murphy) G. A.B., Clarke Coll., 1941; A.M., Loyola U., Chgo., 1948, LL.D., 1970; Ph.D., St. Louis U., 1952; Litt.D., DePaul U., 1972; L.H.D., Lincoln Coll., 1965, Columbia Coll., 1969, Luther Coll., 1969, Marycrest Coll., 1972, Ursuline Coll., 1972, Spertus Coll. Judaica, 1974, Holy Cross Coll., 1974, Rosary Coll., 1975, St. Ambrose Coll., 1975, St. Leo Coll., 1976, Mt. St. Joseph Coll., 1976, Stritch Coll., 1976, Stonehill Coll., 1976, Elmhurst Coll., 1977, Manchester Coll., 1977, Marymount Coll., 1977, Governor's State U., 1979, Seattle U., 1981, St. Michael's Coll., 1984, Nazareth Coll., 1985, Holy Family Coll., 1986, Keller Grad. Sch. Mgmt., Our Lady of Holy Cross Coll., New Orleans, 1988. Mem. Sisters of Charity, B.V.M.; tchr. English St. Mary's High Sch., Chgo., 1941-47; residence, study abroad, 1951; chmn. philosophy dept. Mundelein Coll., 1951-57, pres., 1957-75, prof. philosophy, 1975-85, emeritus faculty, 1987—, archivist, 1986—. Contbr. articles philos. jours. Mem. adv. bd. Sec. Navy, 1975-80, Chgo. Police Bd., 1979-89; bd. dirs. Am. Coun. on Edn., 1971-75, chmn., 1973-74; nat. bd. dirs. Girl Scouts USA, 1966-74, nat. adv., 1976-85; trustee St. Louis U., 1974-87, Ursuline Coll., 1978-92, Cath. Theol. Union, 1983-89, DeVry, Inc., 1987—, Duquesne U., 1989-91, Montay Coll., 1993-95; bd. dirs. Newberry Libr., 1976—, WTTW Pub. TV, 1976—, Parkside Human Svcs. Corp., 1983-89. Recipient Laetare medal, 1975, LaSallian award, 1975, Aquinas award, 1976, Chgo. Assn. Commerce and Industry award, 1976, Hesburgh award, 1982, Woman of Distinction award Nat. Conf. Women Student Leaders, 1985, Outstanding Svc. award Coun. Ind. Colls., 1989, Woman of History award for edn. AAUW, 1989; named One of 100 Oustanding Chgo. Women, Culture in Action, 1994. Mem. Am. Cath. Philos. Assn. (exec. coun. 1953-56), Assn. Am. Colls. (bd. dirs. 1965-70, chmn. 1969-70), Religious Edn. Assn. Am. (pres. 1973, chmn. bd. 1975-78), North Cen. Assn. (commn. on colls. and univs. 1971-78, chmn. exec. bd. 1975-77, bd. dirs.), Assn. Governing Bds. Colls. and Univs. (bd. dirs. 1979-88, hon. bd. dirs. 1989-92). Office: Loyola U Office Archives Sullivan Ctr 6525 W Sheridan Rd Chicago IL 60626 Home: Loyola U Coffey Hall 6525 N Sheridan Rd Chicago IL 60626-5311

GANNON, SARA MCFADDEN, training manager; b. Whiteford, Md., Apr. 28, 1928; d. Ernest Keese and Helen Marie (Hardesty) McFadden; m. Charles Benton Gannon, Aug. 30, 1948; children: Michael Benton, Katharine Marie. BS in Edn., Towson U., 1948; MEd, Worcester State Coll., 1975. Elem. sch. tchr. Balt. City Sch. Dept., 1948-55; dir. pvt. nursing sch. Penn Hills (Pa.) Presbyn. Ch., 1964-66; kindergarten team leader Westboro (Mass.) Sch. Dept., 1966-84; tng. mgr. Yankee Engring. Co., Bolton, Mass., 1987—; adj. prof. Worcester State Coll. Profl. storyteller. Libr. trustee Westboro Pub. Libr., 1988-91; pres. women's fellowship Congl. Ch., Westboro, 1967-69, bd. deacons, 1971-74, clk. of ch., 1984-87. Mem. Nat. Assn. Preservation and Perpetuation of Storytelling in Am., Phi Delta Kappa. Home: 21 Wheeler Rd Westborough MA 01581

GANS, ERNA IRENE, printing company executive; b. Bielsko, Poland; d. Adolf and Rosa (Pelzman) Reicher; came to U.S., 1948, naturalized, 1953; BA, Roosevelt U., 1971; MA, Loyola U., Chgo., 1974; m. Henry Gans, Apr. 16, 1947 (dec. Oct. 1987); children: Alan, Howard. Asst. prof. dept. sociology Loyola U., Chgo., 1976; pres. Internat. Label & Printing Co., Bensenville, Ill., 1972-93. Chmn., Skokie (Ill.) Youth Commn., 1968-88; bd. govs. Israel Bond Orgn.; founder, chmn. Holocaust Meml. Found. Ill.; mem. U.S. Holocaust Meml. Council. Recipient Edward S. Sparling award Roosevelt U., 1987, 3d Ann. Humanitarian award Holocaust Meml. Found. Ill., 1988. Mem. Am. Sociol. Assn., Nat. Fedn. Ind. Bus., Am. Acad. Polit. and Social Sci. Republican. Jewish. Clubs: B'nai B'rith (pres. 1976-81). Home: 2812 Woodland Dr Northbrook IL 60062-6930 Office: 537 N Edgewood Ave Wood Dale IL 60191-2600

GANSLER, HELEN JONES, elementary and secondary education educator; b. St. Louis, Nov. 28, 1941; d. Glenn B. Jones and Lucille Mary Overschmidt; m. William H. Gansler, Aug. 13, 1966; children: Dania, Angelina, Harold, Mary, Michael, Stephen. BA, Webster (Mo.) Coll., 1963; MA, U. Mo., Kansas City, 1972; degree in gifted edn., U. Mo., St. Louis, 1992. 2d grade tchr. Westridge Elem. Sch., Bullwin, Mo., 1963-67; Spanish tchr. Lafayette H.S., Ellisville, Mo., 1967-68; 2d grade tchr. Bowles Elem. Sch., Fenton, Mo., 1968-69, John Diemer Sch., Overland Park, Kans., 1969-72; reading specialist Valley Park (Mo.) Sch., 1972—. Prodr. (videos) Dear Dad, 1995; author: Reflections of a Proud Community, 1988. Chair Sacred Heart Pro Life, Eureka, Mo., 1992-94. Mem. Gifted Assn. Mo., St. Louis Assn. for Gifted Edn., Tri County Birthright Assn.

GANTZ, SUZI GRAHN, special education educator; b. Chgo., May 17, 1954; d. Robert Donald and Barbara Edna (Ascher) Grahn; m. Louis Estes Gantz, July 11, 1976; children: Christopher, Joshua. BS in Edn. of Deaf and Hard of Hearing, U. Ill., 1976. Tchr. A.G. Bell Sch., Chgo., 1976-80, 88—; sales asst. Bob Grahn & Assocs., Chgo., 1982-84; with sales dept. Isis/My Sisters Circus, Chgo., 1984-86; interpreter Glenbrook North High Sch., Northbrook, Ill., 1986-87; interpreter, aide Lake Forest (Ill.) Dist. 67, 1987-88. Mem. Northbrook Citizens for Drug and Alcohol Alliance, 1988—; cubmaster Boy Scouts Am., Northbrook, 1990-93. Mem. Ill. Tchrs. of the Hearing Impaired, A.G. Bell Soc., Coun. on Exceptional Children. Home: 485 Laburnum Dr Northbrook IL 60062-2259 Office: AG Bell Sch 3730 N Oakley Ave Chicago IL 60618-4813

GANZ, PATRICIA ANNE, medical educator, physician; b. L.A., Mar. 23, 1948; d. Raymond W. and Ida (Shrier) Conn; m. Tomas Ganz, Aug. 16, 1970; children: David, Rebecca. BA magna cum laude, Harvard-Radcliffe, 1969; MD, UCLA, 1973. Diplomate Am. Bd. Internal Medicine, Am. Bd. Med. Oncology. Chief resident in medicine med. ctr. UCLA, 1977-78; from asst. to assoc. prof. medicine San Fernando Valley program UCLA, Sepulueda, 1978-90, prof., 1990-92; prof. schs. medicine and pub. health UCLA, 1990—; dir. divsn. cancer prevention and contorl rsch. Jonsson Comprehensive Cancer Ctr., L.A., 1993—. Office: UCLA Divsn Cancer Prevention & Control Rsch 1100 Glendon Ave Ste 711 Los Angeles CA 90024-3511*

GANZEL, LINDA SUE, secondary school educator in art and English; b. Nebraska City, Nebr., Aug. 13, 1965; d. Robert and Ruby Ann Wrigg G. BA in Edn., Peru (Nebr.) State Coll., 1987. Student tchr. Techumseh (Nebr.) Pub. Sch., 1987; English and art tchr. Macy (Nebr.) Pub. Schs., 1987-95; tchr. English, journalism Walthill (Nebr.) Pub. Sch., 1995-96; art and journalism instr. Mead Pub. Sch., 1996—; GED instr. Nebr. Indian C.C., Winnebago, Nebr., 1991-92; coord. Young Nebr. Animation project, Macy, Nebr., U. Nebr. at Kearny and Nebr. Arts Coun., 1992-94. Sponsor Fellowship of Christian Athletes, Macy, Nebr., 1991-95; counselor, tchr. I Can Camps, Macy, 1991-95. Recipient Dorothea A. Kropp Art scholarship, Campbell Kropp Found., Nebr. City, 1983-87. Mem. NEA, Nat. Coun. Tchrs. of English, Nebr. Art Education Assn., Sigma Tau Delta, Kappa Delta Pi. Republican. Office: Mead Public Sch Walthill Pub Sch Mead NE 69069

GAONA, GALE F., motivation professional; b. Passaic, N.J., Nov. 10, 1961; d. Walter and Lois Marlene (Freeman) Siwiec; m. Bernabe Gaona III, Dec. 21, 1984; children: Christina, Jessica. BS, Ctrl. Mo. State U., 1983; postgrad., Brooks Inst., 1984. CEO West Coast Photographics, Santa Barbara, Calif., 1985-89; cons. Coldwell Banker, Ojai, Calif., 1989-90; CEO Timeless Network, Oak View, Calif., 1989—; creator parenting course Lighting the Fire, 1993; dir. mus. exhibit The Champion Within, 1995. Office: Timeless Network 105 S Oak # 218 Ventura CA 93022

GAPE, SERAFINA VETRANO, decorative artist and designer; b. Villa Franco, Sicily, Italy, Oct. 4, 1945; came to U.S., 1947; d. Augustino and Maria (Tramuta) Vetrano; m. William Evan Gape, Jan. 27, 1965; children: William Edward, Andrea Marie. BA cum laude, SUNY, Utica, 1982. Apprentice/journeyman/master Augustino Vetrano, New Hartford, N.Y., 1955-70; artist N.Y., 1970—; owner, designer Decorative Painting/Lit. Restoration Co., N.Y., 1980—; art tchr. Mohawk Valley C.C., Utica, N.Y., 1988; decorative arts guide Fountain Elms/Hist. HouseMus., Utica, 1985—; cons., lectr. various chs., businesses, art orgns. Exhibited in group and one-woman shows including Italian Cultural Ctr., Utica, 1987, Ctrl. N.Y. Cmty. Arts Coun., N.Y.C., 1985 (awarded in a variety of mediums including oil, watercolor, acrylic and pastels); represented in pvt. collections in U.S., Can., Eng.; works include restoration and redesign of interiors of numerous chs. throughout Ctrl. N.Y. State, includes Our Lady of Lourdes, Utica, N.Y., 1994, Sts. Peter & Paul, Passaic, N.J., 1993, St. Mary's of Mt. Carmel, Utica, 1996, Holy Trinity, Utica, 1996, St. Joseph's, Boonville, N.Y., 1995, others. Recipient 2d pl. mixed media award Rural Show, SUNY, 1995, 2d pl. oil award Rome (N.Y.) Comty. Art, 1994, Best in Show pastel award Utica Pub. Libr., 1994, Painting of the Month award Utica Art Assn., 1995. Mem. Munson-Williams-Proctor Inst., Kirkland Art Ctr., Utica Art Assn. (pres. 1984-87), Italian Cultural Ctr., Leatherstocking County Stencillers (v.p. 1990-91, pres. 1993-94), Stencil Artisans League. Home: 652 Daytona St Utica NY 13502-1110

GARABEDIAN, BETTY MARIE, elementary education educator, retired; b. Worcester, Mass., June 24, 1928; d. Henry L. and Marie A. (Holquist) Olson; m. Peter Garabedian, Aug. 20, 1960. BA, Bob Jones U., 1950; MEd, Boston U., 1961. Elem. tchr. Town of Shrewsbury, Mass., 1950-54, remedial reading tchr., 1950-57; elem. supr. Auburn, Mass., 1957-67; elem. tchr. Douglas, Mass., 1967-87. Pres. Shrewsbury Tchrs. Club Assn., 1954-56, Auburn Tchrs. Assn., 1960-61. Recipient Horace Mann Outstanding Tchr. award, State of Mass., 1985-86. Mem. Boston U. Alumni, AAUW, Christian Appalachian Project; Delta Kappa Gamma (pres. 1961-62). Mem. Armenian Evangelical-United Ch. of Christ.

GARAND, BRENDA JOY, sculptor, educator; b. Peterborough, N.H., Nov. 1, 1959; d. Albert Leo and Louise Mary (Kelley) G. BFA, U. N.H., 1981; MFA, Queens Coll./CUNY, 1983. Asst. prof. studio art Queens Coll./CUNY, Flushing, 1983-95, Dartmouth Coll., Hanover, N.H., 1995—. Fulbright grantee, France, 1987-88. Mem. Fulbright Assn., Coll. Art Assn. Office: Dartmouth Coll Hanover NH 03755

GARATE, REBECCA, elementary school bilingual educator; b. Denver City, Tex., Aug. 27, 1956; d. Joe and Amparo (Manzano) Nevarez; m. Jesse Garate, June 30, 1975; 1 child, Rebecca Diane. AA, N.Mex. Jr. Coll., 1983; BS, Coll. of S.W., 1986; bilingual endorsement, Tex. Tech U., 1988. Spl. edn. aide Denver City Jr. H.S., 1977-87; 3d grade tchr. Kelley Elem. Sch., Denver City, 1987-89, 2d grade bilingual tchr., 1989—; mem. textbook proclamation adv. com. Tex. Edn. Agy., Austin, 1990. Mem. Assn. Tex. Profl. Educators. Home: PO Box 1464 Denver City TX 79323-1464

GARAVAGLIA, SUSAN BERGER, decision systems designer; b. N.Y.C., May 10, 1948; d. Joseph and Traudy (Huss) Berger; m. Jack Anthony Perricone, Dec. 31, 1971 (div. 1983); m. Paul Louis Garavaglia, May 31, 1986. B Mus, The Juilliard Sch., 1971; MBA, Baruch Coll., 1981; PhD, CUNY, 1993. Project mgr. Abraham & Straus, Bklyn., 1977; mgr. Adela Investment Co., N.Y.C., 1977-78; v.p. N.Y. Ops. Cosmac Mgmt. Sys., N.Y.C., 1978-80; pres., owner The Sys. Advantage Ltd., N.Y.C., 1980-86; v.p. Chase Manhattan (N.Y.) Bank, 1986-92; asst. v.p. Dun & Bradstreet, Murray Hill, N.J., 1992—; adj. asst. prof. N.Y.U., 1981-88, instr. The New Sch., N.Y.C., 1983-84, adv. bd. Smart-F$, N.Y.C., 1992—, treas. N.Y. Women Economists, N.Y.C., 1994—. Author: Prolog: Programming Techniques and Applications, 1987; contbr. articles to profl. jours. Mem. N.Y. Women Economists. Office: Dun & Bradstreet Info Svcs 1 Diamond Hill Rd Murray Hill NJ 07974

GARAY, ERICA BLYTHE, lawyer; b. N.Y.C., Mar. 8, 1953; d. Harold and Gladys M. (Messing) G.; m. Gary S. Schachter, Dec. 22, 1973 (dec. Aug. 1980); m. Michael B. Siehs, June 10, 1984; children: Rachel Claire, Kaitlin Anne. BA, SUNY, Binghamton, 1973; JD, St. John's U., Jamaica, N.Y., 1978. Bar: N.Y. 1979, U.S. Dist. Ct. (so. and ea. dists.) N.Y. 1979, U.S. Dist. Ct. (no. dist.) Calif. 1986, Calif. 1987, U.S. Dist. Ct. (cen. dist.) Calif. 1987, U.S. Ct. Appeals (fed. cir.) 1987. Asst. corp. counsel N.Y.C. Law Dept., 1978-82; assoc. Willkie Farr & Gallagher, N.Y.C., 1982-83, Rivkin, Radler & Kremer, Uniondale, N.Y., 1983-85; ptnr. Rivkin, Radler & Kremer, Uniondale, 1986—. Editor ABA newsletter Equal Access, 1995-96. Bd. dirs. L.I. Ctr. for Bus. and Profl. Women; bd. dirs. Ctr. for Family Resources; pres., bd. dirs. Women Econ. Developers of L.I. St. Thomas More scholar St. John's U., 1976-78; recipient St. Thomas More award St. John's U., 1978. Mem. ABA (chair consumer and personal rights litigation com. 1996—). Democrat. Office: Rivkin Radler & Kremer EAB Plaza Uniondale NY 11556

GARBACZ, PATRICIA FRANCES, school social worker, therapist; b. Hamtramck, Mich., Nov. 26, 1941; d. Stanley and Frances (Harubin) G. BS, Siena Heights Coll., 1969; M. Pastoral Counseling, St. Paul U., Ottawa, Can., 1972; ThM, St. John Provincial Sem., 1983; MSW, Wayne State U., 1989. Cert. social worker Acad. Cert. Social Workers; cert. sch. social worker; lic. marriage and family therapists. Assoc. dir. vocations Archdiocese of Detroit, 1975-77; co-dir. of inst. for women Archdiocese of Lusaka (Zambia), 1977-78; pastoral minister Archdiocese of Detroit, 1979-80, assoc. dir. preformation, 1980-84; tchr., ministry coord. Bishop Borgess High Sch., Redford, Mich., 1984-86; tchr., dept. chair Aquinas High Sch., Southgate, Mich., 1986-88; therapist Community Coun. on Drug Abuse/Livonia (Mich.) Counseling, 1988-89; substance abuse therapist Oxford Inst., St. Clair Shores, Mich., 1989-91; sch. social worker Lakeshore Pub. Schs., St. Clair Shores, 1990—; therapist Macomb Child Guidance, 1989—. Mem. NASW, Am. Assn. Marriage and Family Therapists, Mich. Assn. Sch. Social Workers.

GARBER, DOROTHY HELEN, rancher, artist; b. Fredricktown, Mo., Oct. 7, 1917; d. Chester Payton and Bessie Belle (Sykes) Brewington; m. H. Derwood Garber, 1933 (dec.); children: Patricia Kay, Marici Lea; m. Samuel T. Ramey, Sept. 1959 (div. Dec. 1971). Rancher Patty K. Ranch, Hotchkiss, Colo., 1945—; bookkeeper, owner Garber Clo, Hotchkiss, 1954-56, co-owner, mgr., 1966-80; owner, mgr., buyer Dorothy's, Hotchkiss, 1956-66. Artist, judge, exhibitor, lectr. and demonstrator. One-woman shows include Western Colo. Ctr. for Arts, Grand Junction, Hotel Colorado Art Gallery, Glenwood Springs, Colo., Aristracrat, Paonia, Colo., Finishing Touch Gallery, Hotchkiss, Pavilion, Montrose, Colo., etc.; exhibited in group shows at Montrose Pavilion, Mitchell Mus., Trinidad, Colo., Old Pass Gallery, Raton, N.Mex., Doherty Gallery, Delta, Colo., Castano Gallery, Denver, Rocky Mountain Nat. Watercolor Exhibition, Golden, Colo., San Diego Internat. Watercolor Soc. Exhibition, State Fair Fine Arts Gallery, Albuquerque, The Tubac Mus., Tubac, Ariz., Albuquerque Mus. Fine Arts, Western Colo. Ctr. for Arts, Grand Junction, etc. Mem. Am. Watercolor Soc., Nat. Watercolor Soc., Western Fedn. Watercolor (signature mem.), N.Mex. Watercolor Soc. (founder), Western Colo. Watercolor Soc. (past pres., adv. bd.), Hotchkiss Fine Arts (pres., charter mem.), Delta Fine Art, Allied Artist. Democrat. Baptist. Home and Office: 697 3950 Rd Hotchkiss CO 81419

GARBER, SHARON N., medical/surgical nurse; b. Lynn, Mass., Sept. 20, 1963; d. Paul S. and Lynne (Sosna) Cohen; m. Kenneth A. Garber, Apr. 6, 1986; children: Andrew Charles, James Lee, Peter Edward. BSN, Adelphi U., 1985; MS in Nursing, Columbia U., 1990; postgrad., U. R.I., 1995. Staff nurse, orthopedics Atlanticare Med. Ctr., Lynn; staff nurse, operating room/endoscopy St. Mary's Hosp., Orange, N.J.; adult nurse practitioner Providence Ambulatory Health Assn. Mem. Sigma Theta Tau.

GARBUTT, SUSAN JOHNSON, nursing administrator; b. Astoria, N.Y., Nov. 7, 1954; d. Vilho S. K. and Helen W. (Suomela) Johnson; m. George John Garbutt, June 20, 1976; children: Sarah Beth, Timothy. BS in Nursing, Hartwick Coll., 1976; MSN, Med. Coll. of Ga., 1981. RN, N.Y., Fla.; cert. BLS instr. Staff nurse, shift supr. U. Hosp. ECF, Augusta, Ga., 1979-81; admissions nurse St. Joseph Hosp., Augusta, 1982-84, nurse discharge coord., 1984-85; asst. DON Abbey Nursing Ctr., St. Petersburg, Fla., 1987-89, Ctrl. Park Lodge, Pinellas Park, Fla., 1989-90; admitting mgr. HCA Med. Ctr. Hosp., Largo, Fla., 1990-91; care plan coord., nursing supv. Jacaranda Manor, St. Petersburg, 1992-93; resident care plan coord. Sabal Palms Health Care Ctr., Largo, 1993, asst. DON, 1993—. Troop leader Girl Scouts of the U.S., Largo, 1990-92, svc. team mem. Sandpiper neighborhood, 1991-92; sec. Tutterow Stars, Largo, 1994-96. Mem. ANA, Fla. Nurses Assn. (coun. on rsch.), Assn. Practitioners in Infection Control, Pinellas Area Nurse Educators (pres. 1995—). Republican. Lutheran. Home: 3159 138th Pl Largo FL 34641-3828 Office: Sabal Palms-Health Care Ctr 499 Alternate Keene Rd Largo FL 34641-1652

GARCHIK, LEAH LIEBERMAN, journalist; b. Bklyn., May 2, 1945; d. Arthur Louis and Mildred (Steinberg) Lieberman; m. Jerome Marcus Garchik, Aug. 11, 1968; children—Samuel, Jacob. B.A., Bklyn. Coll., 1966. Editorial asst. San Francisco Chronicle, 1972-79, writer, editor, 1979-83, editor This World,, 1983-84, columnist, 1984—; also author numerous book and movie reviews, features and profiles; Author: San Francisco; the City's Sights and Secrets, 1995; panelist (radio quiz show) Mind Over Matter; contbr. articles to mags. Vice pres. Golden Gate Kindergarten Assn., San Francisco, 1978; pres. Performing Arts Workshop, San Francisco, 1977-79; bd. dirs. Home Away From Homelessness, 1995—. Recipient 1st prize Nat. Soc. Newspaper Columnists, 1992. Mem. Deutsche Music Verein, Media Alliance, Newspaper Guild, ACLU (bd. dirs. San Francisco chpt. 1977-79). Democrat. Jewish. Home: 156 Baker St San Francisco CA 94117-2111 Office: San Francisco Chronicle 901 Mission St San Francisco CA 94103-2905

GARCÍA, BETH BAXTER, sculptor, writer; b. Oakland, Calif., Jan. 4, 1918; d. Howard Edward and Rena (Scott) Baxter; m. John Locke García, 1942 (div. 1974); children: Baxter Juan, Holland Gene. BA in Creative Art, Mills Coll., 1939, MA in Creative Art, 1941. One person shows include Carmel (Calif.) Art Assn., 1978; two person shows include Villa Montalvo, Saratoga, Calif., 1964, New Monterey Ctr., Monterey, Calif., 1967; exhibited in group shows Dallas Mus. Fine Art, 1959, Oakland (Calif.) Mus. Art, 1959, Calif. State Fair, Sacramento, 1965, Monterey County Fair, 1956-65, Ch. of the Wayfarer, Carmel, 1967, Carmel Art Assn., 1956—. Recipient Popular award Ch. of the Wayfarer, 1967, 1st prize ribbons Monterey County Fair Fine Arts, 1956, 57, 58, 63, 64, 65, 1st Ann. Chamber Arts award Portland (Oreg.) Chamber, 1980. Mem. Carmel Art Assn. (bd. dirs. 1958-59, 77-79, 85-86). Home: 25673 Flanders Dr Carmel CA 93923

GARCIA, EDNA I., secondary education educator; b. Humacao, P.R., Feb. 16, 1951; d. Agustin and Benigna Garcia; children: Clemente, Myrna. BA, Internat. Inst. of Ams., Hato Rey, P.R., 1983; postgrad., U. Bridgeport, 1985, Housatonic Coll., Bridgeport, Conn., 1989, Fairfield U., 1995; student paralegal studies, Profl. Career Devel. Inst., Atlanta, 1990—. Notary pub.; cert. Spanish tchr. Coord. social sci., outreach worker Spanish Am. Devel. Agy., Bridgeport, 1973-79; tchr. English Dept. Pub. Edn., Carolina, P.R., 1979-83; ESL tchr. Bassic High Sch., Bridgeport, Conn., 1985-95. Mem. citizens adv. com. on contract compliance Mayor's Office; state rep. 128th Dist. Conn., 1993—; mem. Dem. Town Com., 1994—; bd. dirs. The Kennedy Ctr., Inc., 1994—. Recipient Humanitarian award Conn. Edn. Assn., 1988, Jefferson award Sta. WTNH-TV Channel 8, 1991, Outstanding Achievement award The Hispanic Soc., Inc., 1991. Mem. NAFE, NOW, ASPIRA (founding mem.), ATENO (founding mem.), Nat. Hispanic Caucus of State Legislators, Latinos for Progress, Nat. Assn. Latino Elected Ofcls. Democrat. Home: 1465 E Main St Apt 2B Bridgeport CT 06608-1120

GARCIA, FRANCES, accountant; b. Wichita Falls, Tex., July 21, 1941; d. Genaro Garcia and Rosalia Nunez. BBA, Midwestern State U., 1968. Audit mgr. Arthur Andersen and Co., Austin and Dallas, Tex., 1968-77; commr. U.S. Copyright Royalty Tribunal, Washington, 1977-82; auditing ptnr. Quezada Navarro and Co., L.A., 1982-86; dir. of recruiting U.S. Gen. Acctg. Office, Washington, 1986—, dir. internal evaluation, 1994—. Mem. Am. Assn. Hispanic CPAs (pres. 1987-90), Spanish Edn. Devel. Ctr. (treas. 1992—). Home: 2510 Virginia Ave NW Washington DC 20037

GARCIA, GAIL G., photojournalist, editor; b. Jeanerette, La., Nov. 5, 1957; d. John J. and Myrtle (Landry) Grisiaffi; m. Donovan L. Garcia, Sept. 10, 1977; children: Raymond L., Virginia C. Grad., Teche Tech. Inst., 1976. Owner, mgr. Bayou Sounds & Security, Jeanerette, 1977-89; mgr. Sears Catalog Agy., Jeanerette, 1984-85; sec. Jeanerette Enterprise, 1983, editor, 1983-84; photojournalist, corr. Daily Advertiser, Lafayette, La., 1985-91; lifestyle editor Franklin (La.) Banner-Tribune, 1993—. V.p. Jeanerette Bus. & Profl. Women, 1984, pres.-elect, 1985, pres., 1986. Recipient Young Careerist award Bus. & Profl. Women, 1986, Outstanding Woman Yr. award, 1988. Mem. La. Press Assn. Office: St Mary & Franklin Banner Tribune 115 Wilson St Franklin LA 70538

GARCIA, ISA, accountant; b. Havana, Cuba, Sept. 4, 1953; came to U.S., 1962; d. Jose Antonio and Ketty (Exposito) Caraballo; m. Federico Garcia, June 11, 1977; children: Michael F., Christina L. B.Acctg., U. Miami, Coral Gables, Fla., 1975. CPA, Fla. Auditor Deloitte Haskins & Sells, Miami, 1975-77; ptnr. Garcia & Garcia, CPAs, P.A., Miami, 1985—; fin. dir. U. Miami, Coral Gables, 1977—. Fin. com. mem. St. Brendan's Cath. Ch., Miami, 1995—; pres. sch. adv. bd. St. Brendan's Elem. Sch., Miami, 1987-91. Mem. AICPAs, Fla. Inst. CPAs, Cuban Am. CPAs, Beta Alpha Psi (sec. 1974-76), Phi Kappa Phi. Office: Garcia and Garcia CPAs PA 8221 Coral Way Miami FL 33155

GARCIA, JOY P., counselor coordinator, educator; b. Manila, The Philippines, Mar. 3, 1965; came to U.S., 1986; d. Armando Lazaro Garcia and Miriam (Garcia) Rorabaugh. BS in Math., Philippine Normal U., Manila, 1985; MEd in Math., Millersville U., 1989, MEd in Guidance and Counseling, 1991. Cert. in secondary sch. counseling Pa. Instr. Bethel High Sch., Manila, 1985-86; grad. admissions asst. Millersville (Pa.) U., 1987-91, instr., tutorial coord. Upward Bound Program, 1991—, counselor coord., 1991—; assoc. supr. Ednl. Testing Svc./Praxis Test Series, 1991—. Recipient Eugene K. Robb scholarship, 1991, James C. Atty scholarship, 1991, Nat. Sci. and Tech. Assn. scholarship, 1981-85. Mem. ACA, ASCD, NAFE, Assn. for Multicultural Counseling and Devel., Am. Coll. Pers. Assn., Am. Sch. Counselors Assn., Assn. Religious and Value Issues in Counseling, Lancaster County Counselors Assn., Assn. Pa. State Coll. and Univs. Faculties. Office: Millersville U Upward Bound Program Millersville PA 17551

GARCIA, JUNE MARIE, library director; b. Bryn Mawr, Pa., Sept. 12, 1947; d. Roland Ernest and Marion Brill (Hummel) Traynor; m. Teodosio Garcia, July 17, 1928; children: Gretchen, Adrian. BA, Douglass Coll., 1969; MLS, Rutgers U., 1970. Reference libr. New Brunswick (N.J.) Pub. Libr., 1970-72, Plainfield (N.J.) Pub. Libr., 1972-75; br. mgr. Phoenix Pub. Libr., 1975-80, extension svcs. adminstr., 1980-93; dir. San Antonio Pub. Libr., 1993—. Recipient Productivity Innovator award City of Phoenix, 1981. Mem. ALA (life, coun. 1986-90, 93—, pres. Pub. Libr. Assn. 1991-92, new stds. task force 1983-87, goals, guidelines and stds. com. 1986-90, chairperson 1987-90, Libr. Adminstrn. and Mgmt. Assn., Assn. Libr. Svc. Children, Young Adult Svcs. Divsn.), REFORMA, Tex. Libr. Assn., Freedom Read Found. (bd. dirs.), Ariz. State Libr. Assn. (pres. 1984-85, Libr. of Yr. award 1986, Pres.'s award 1990), Beta Phi Mu. Home: 3731 Twisted Oaks Dr San Antonio TX 78217-3422 Office: San Antonio Pub Library 203 S Saint Mary's St San Antonio TX 78205-2786

GARCIA, KATHERINE LEE, comptroller, accountant; b. Portland, Oreg., Nov. 4, 1950; d. Gerald Eugene and Delores Lois (Erickson) Moe; m. Buddy Jesus Garcia; Nov. 19, 1977; children: Kevin, Brett, Rodd. BS cum laude, U. Nev., 1976. CPA, Idaho, Nev. Retail clk. Raleys, Food King, Reno, 1968-76; sr. acct. Pieretti, Wilson and McNulty, Reno, 1976-78, Deloitte Haskins and Sells, Boise, Idaho, 1979-81; sr. acct. Washoe County, Reno, 1981-83, chief dep. comptr., 1983-94, comptroller, 1994—. Treas., bd. dirs. Friends of 4 (pub. TV), Boise, 1979-81; tutor RAD program, 1995—. Recipient Cert. of Excellence in Fin. Reporting, Govt. Fin. Officer's Assn., 1982—. Mem. AICPA, Nev. Soc. CPAs (chmn. state and local govt. com. 1992-93), Govt. Fin. Officers Assn. (mem. spl. rev. com. 1989—, state rep.), Nev. Govt. Fin. Officers Assn. (treas. 1989-91, reader for blind 1992—). Republican. Home: 655 Joy Lake Rd Reno NV 89511-5766 Office: Washoe County PO Box 11130 Reno NV 89520-0027

GARCÍA, MARY ELIZABETH, Spanish and English as second language educator; b. Winter Haven, Fla., Mar. 3, 1931; d. Walter Roberts and Mary Elmira (Williams) Rozier; m. Guillermo García, Sept. 21, 1957; children: Mary Leonor, Guillermo Clyde. BA, U. Fla., 1956; MA, Maryville Coll., 1983. Cert. tchr. Spanish, ESL, bilingual lang. edn., Fla. Tchr. Spanish and civics Palatka (Fla.) Sr. H.S., 1956-58; tchr. ESL Centro Colombo-Americano, Bogotá, Colombia, 1959, Medellín, Colombia, 1960-65, Cali, Colombia, 1965-66; tchr. English and history The Internat. Sch., Maracay, Venezuela, 1969-71; area head in lit. U. Venezuela, Maracay, 1975-85; dir. bilingual program Price Mid. Sch., Interlachen, Fla., 1985-88; chair fgn. lang. Crescent City (Fla.) H.S., 1988-95; tchr. ESOL courses for tchrs. Putnam County, Palatka, 1991-96; adj. prof. Spanish Stetson U., Deland, Fla., 1995—; Venezuelan del. 1st Caribbean Conf., Santo Domingo, Dominican Republic, 1995; spkr. 2d ann. TESOL Conf., Carabalelda, Venezuela, 1994, TESOL Conf., U. Met. Caracas, Venezuela, 1985. Mem. TESOL, Hon. Spanish Soc. (sponsor 1988-95), Am. Assn. Tchrs. of Spanish and Portuguese, Venezuelan TESOL (founding mem., state rep. 1988-85), Phi Beta Kappa, Phi Kappa Phi. Democrat. Baptist. Home: PO Box 639 120 Parkin Rd Pomona Park FL 32181 Office: Stetson U Campus Box 8423 Deland FL 32720

GARCIA, MARY JANE MADRID, state legislator; b. Dona Ana, N.Mex., Dec. 24, 1936; d. Isaac C. and Victoria M. Garcia. A.A., San Francisco City Coll., 1956; B.S., N.Mex. State U., 1982, B.A. in Anthropology, 1983, M.A. in Anthropology, 1985. Interpretor, translator to USAF Capt., Hotel Balboa, Madrid, Spain, 1962-63; exec. sec. to city mgr. City of Las Cruces, N.Mex., 1964-65; adminstrv. asst. RMK-BRJ, Saigon, Socialist Republic Vietnam, 1966-72; owner Billy the Kid Gift Shop, Mesilla, N.Mex., 1972-81; pres., owner Victoria's Night Club, Las Cruces, 1981—; state senator Dist. 38, N.Mex.; with archaeol. excavations N.Mex. State U. Anthropology Dept., summer 1982, spring 1983. Bd. dirs., sec-treas. Dona Anna Mutual Domestic Water Assn.; mem. Subarea Council Health Systems Agy., 1979; bd. dirs. Sun Country Savings Bank, Las Cruses, 1985; treas. Toney Anaya for U.S. Senate, 1978; active Toney Anaya for N.Mex. Gov., 1979-82. Mem. N.Mex. Retail Liquor Assn. Democrat. Roman Catholic. Home: Isaac Garcia St PO Box 22 Dona Ana NM 88032-0022 Office: Senate of N Mex State Capital Santa Fe NM 87503*

GARCIA, WILMA THACKSTON, English language and literature educator; b. Detroit, Jan. 11, 1933; d. James Bruce Thackston and Gertrude (Epps) Thackston Molinar; div.; children: Lorraine Garcia-McGlynn, Sally, Catherine Garcia-Lindstrom, John, Martha Garcia-Carr, Joseph, Rachel Garcia-Bieszak, William. A in Liberal Arts, Oakland C.C., Bloomfield Hills, Mich., 1971; BA in English, Oakland U., 1973, MA in English, 1975; PhD in English and Folklore, Wayne State U., 1983. Cert. secondary tchr., Mich. From spl. instr. to assoc. prof. Oakland U., Rochester, Mich., 1976—; speaker in field. Author: Mothers and Others, 1985; contbr. articles to profl. jours. Recipient Meritorious Alumni award Oakland C.C., 1986, Headliner award Women of Wayne State U., 1987; honoree Wonder Woman award Pontiac Women's Survival Ctr., 1989. Mem. NOW, ACLU, Mich. Coll. English Assn. (past. pres., bd. dirs., Disting. Svc. award 1992), Coll. English Assn. (bd. dirs. 1991-94), Nat. Coun. Tchrs. English. Home: 656 W Hazelhurst Ferndale MI 48220 Office: Oakland U 510 Wilson Hall Rochester MI 48309-4401

GARCIA, YOLANDA VASQUEZ, educational services manager, educator; b. San Antonio, Nov. 27, 1948; d. Eleodoro and Antonia (Hernandez) Vasquez; (div. 1985); children: Yvette Flores, Marisa Flores, Julie Garcia. BA, Our Lady of the Lake, 1971; MA, U. Tex., San Antonio, 1977. Cert. counseling and guidance. Elem. sch. tchr. San Antonio (Tex.) Ind. Sch. Dist., 1972-76; elem. sch. tchr. Northside Ind. Sch. Dist., San Antonio, 1977-81, itenerant ESL tchr., 1981-87, sch. counselor, 1988-93, adminstr.; student tchr. supr. U. Tex., Austin, 1993—. Scholar Our Lady of the Lake, San Antonio, 1968, U. Tex., San Antonio, 1976, Inst. de Cooperacion, Madrid, Spain, 1985; fellow U. Tex., Austin, 1993. Mem. TESPA, Am. Edn. Rsch., Coun. for Exceptional Children, Tex. Assn. Bilingual Edn., Kappa Delta Pi. Democrat. Roman Catholic. Home: 6834 Brookvale San Antonio TX 78238 Office: Northside Pre-K Ctr 11937 I H 10 W San Antonio TX 78230

GARCIA C., ELISA DOLORES, lawyer; b. Bklyn., Nov. 8, 1957; d. Vincent Garcia, Jr. and Dolores Elizabeth (Canedo) Marmo; m. John Jay Hasluck, Feb. 28, 1987; 1 child, Brooke Elisabeth. BA, MS, SUNY, Stony Brook, 1980; JD, St. John's U., 1985. Bar: N.Y. 1986. Cons. Energy Devel. Internat., Pt. Jefferson, N.Y., 1980-83; assoc. Willkie Farr & Gallagher, N.Y.C., 1985-89; sr. counsel GAF Corp./Internat. Specialty Products, Wayne, N.J., 1989-94; asst. regional counsel for L.Am., Philip Morris Internat., Rye Brook, N.Y., 1994—. Mem. Glen Rock (N.J.) Planning Bd., 1992-95, chmn., 1994-95. Mem. ABA, N.Y. State Bar Assn. Roman Catholic. Office: Philip Morris Internat 800 W Chester Ave Rye Brook NY 10573

GARCIA-HILL, LENY JUDITH, human resources specialist; b. Puerto Cortes, Honduras, Ctrl. America, Mar. 23, 1959; came to U.S., 1966; d. Amado Lopez and Petrona (Ruiz) Garcia; m. Tommy C. Hill, May 20, 1995; 1 child, Matias Lambert Jr. A.Bus. Studies, Delgado C.C., New Orleans, 1988; BS in BA, So. U., New Orleans, 1992. Pers. sec. Bunny Bread, Inc., New Orleans, 1980-89, asst. pers. mgr., 1989-92; dir. human resources Huval Bakery, Inc., Lafayette, La., 1992-93; human resources specialist Flowers Industries, Inc., Thomasville, Ga., 1993—. Mem. Coun. for Cath. Women, Thomasville, 1993, NAACP. Mem. NAFE, Soc. for Human Resource Mgmt. (South Ga. chpt. edn. advocate 1995—). Home: PO Box 1338 Thomasville GA 31799 Office: Flowers Industries Inc US Hwy 19 S Thomasville GA 31792

GARCIA-PRICHARD, DIANA, research scientist, chemical physicist; b. San Francisco, Oct. 27, 1949; d. Juan and Matilde (Robleto) Garcia; m. Jimmie Andrew Steely, Sept. 21, 1969 (div. Aug. 1979); children: Erik Jimmie Steely, Andrea Yvette Steely; m. Mark Stephen Prichard, Oct. 2, 1982. BS in Chemistry and Physics cum laude, Calif. State U., Hayward, 1983; MS in Phys. Chemistry, U. Rochester, 1985, PhD in Chem. Physics, 1988. Post doctoral fellow U. Rochester, N.Y., 1989; rsch. scientist PhotoSci. Rsch. divsn. Eastman Kodak, Rochester, N.Y., 1989-92, project mgr. color paper mfg., 1992-94, sr. rsch. scientist, 1994—; presenter in field. Bd. trustees Monroe C.C., Rochester, 1994—; mem. planning & adv. bd. Math., Sci. & Engring. Hispanics, Rochester, 1993—; mem. adv. bd. EPA Minotiry Acad. Instns. Traineeship Program, College Park, Md., 1996—; mem. adv. coun. 7th Judicial Adv. Coun., 1995—; mem. Clinton/Gore transition team Cluster Sci., Space & Tech., 1992; mem. adv. com. NSF Edn. & Human Resource Directorate, 1993—. Mem. Am. Chem. Soc. (adv. bd. Chem. & Engring. News mag. 1994—), Hisp. Orgn. Leadership & Advancement Kodak Employees (pres., founder), Latinas Unidas (pres., founder), Sigma Xi, Sigma Phi Sigma. Democrat. Office: Eastman Kodak Co Rsch Divsn 1669 Lake Ave Rochester NY 14650-1731

GARCIA Y CARRILLO, MARTHA XOCHITL, pharmacist; b. Austin, Tex., Dec. 7, 1919; d. Alberto Gonzalo and Guadalupe Eva (Carrillo) Garcia; m. Jerjes Jose Rodriguez, Oct. 9, 1943 (dec. 1987); children: Marie Eugenia, Jerjes Alberto, Nicanor Francisco. BS in Pharmacy, U. Tex., 1944. RPh, Tex. Retail pharmacist Ward Drug Store, Austin, Tex., 1952-57, Sommer's Drug Store, San Antonio, 1957-62, Skillern's Drug Store, Dallas, 1962-66; hosp. pharmacist Brackenridge Hosp., Austin, 1968-75; retail pharmacist Thorp Lane Pharmacy, San Marcos, Tex., 1975-77, The Pharmacy, San Marcos, 1975-79, MHMR Pharmacy, Austin, 1975-78, Ace Drug Co., Austin, 1979-82; ret. Recipient Citation of Achievement Tex. State Bd. Pharmacy, 1996. Mem. Am. Pharm. Assn., Tex. Pharmacy Assn., Capitol Area Pharmacy Assn., Tex. State Hist. Assn., Ex-Students Assn. U. Tex. (life, Golden Anniversary cert. 1994). Republican. Home: 21107 Ridgeview Rd Lago Vista TX 78645-4617

GARD, BEVERLY J., state legislator; b. N.C., Mar. 8, 1940; m. Donald Gard; children: David, Doug. BS, U. Tenn. Biochemist Eli Lilly & Co.; councilwoman City of Greenfield, Ind., 1976-88; mem. Ind. State Senate from 28th dist., 1988—. Mem. Hancock Assn Retarded Citizens, Ind. Assn. Cities and Towns. Republican. Methodist. Office: State Senate State Capital Indianapolis IN 46204*

GARD, JUDY RICHARDSON, artist, educator; b. Woodward, Okla., Mar. 11, 1938; d. Russell Eugene and Bertie Easter (Bailey) Richardson; m. Robert Lee Gard, Aug. 31, 1958; children: Michael Cameron, Matthew Davis. Attended, U. Okla., 1956, 57, Volkshochschule, Wiesbaden, Germany, 1963, Am. U., 1967. Tchr. Watercolor Art Soc., Houston, 1983-90, Arrowmont Sch. Arts and Crafts, Gatlinberg, Tenn., 1992, Okla. Art Workshops, Tulsa, 1992-96; demonstrator Elrod Elem. Sch., Houston, 1975, 78-79, U. Houston, 1986; juror Soc. Layerists in Multimedia, Albuquerque, 1992, San Antonio Art League, 1992, EXPO Photog. Soc., Tulsa, 1994; critic, demonstrator Okla. Art Workshops, 1994-95; lectr. Charles Page H.S., Sand Springs, Okla., 1994. Featured artist in book, The New Spirit of Watercolor, 1989. Named Best of Show, Western Fedn. Watercolorists Tucson, 1975, Art League Houston, 1979, Tex. Watercolor Soc., 1977, 80; recipient Honor award Watercolor USA Honor Soc., 1993. Mem. Am.

Watercolor Soc. (Washington Sch. of Art award 1976, High Winds medal 1987), Tulsa Artists Guild, Tex. Watercolor Soc.

GARDE, SUSAN REUTERSHAN, accountant; b. Southampton, N.Y., Sept. 5, 1953; d. Robert Gordon and Ann Patricia (Cronin) Reutershan; m. John Franklin Garde III, May 20, 1989; children: John Franklin IV, Sean Robert. BS, Skidmore Coll., 1975; MBA, Fla. Inst. Tech., 1983, MS in Mgmt., 1991. Budget analyst Grumman Aerospace Corp., Bethpage, N.Y., 1975-76, program planner, 1976-79; sr. budget planner Grumman Aerospace Corp., Stuart, Fla., 1979-81, program planner, 1981-82; adminstr. rsch. ctr. United Technologies, West Palm Beach, Fla., 1982-86; sr. adminstr. United Technologies Inc., West Palm Beach, 1986-87, United Technologies Optical Systems Inc., West Palm Beach, 1988-94; cost acct. Harbor Br. Oceanog. Inst., Inc., Fr. Pierce, Fla., 1994-96, sr. cost acct., 1996—. Mem. Am. Bus. Women's Assn. (pres. Orchid chpt. 1986-87, Sailfish chpt. 1985), Skidmore Alumni Assn., Skidmore Club S.E. Fla. Republican. Roman Catholic. Home: 5100 9th St Vero Beach FL 32966-2841 Office: Harbor Br Oceanog Inst 5600 US Hwy 1 N Fort Pierce FL 34946-7320

GARDEBRING, SANDRA S., judge. Grad., Duke U. and Harvard U.; JD, U. Minn. Dir. EPA; commr. Minn. Pollution Control Agy., Minn. Dept. Human Svcs.; judge Minn. Ct. Appeals; assoc. justice Minn. Supreme Ct., 1991—; chmn. bd. regional planning agy. Met. Coun. Mem. Ctr. Victims of Torture; mem. lawyers com. Internat. Human Rights, LWV; past bd. dirs. St. Paul United Way, Camp DuNord, Project Environment Found., Clean Sits. Office: Minn Supreme Ct Minn Jud Ctr Ste 421 25 Constitution Ave Saint Paul MN 55155-1500*

GARDENIER, EDNA FRANCES, nursing educator; b. Teaneck, N.J., June 30, 1935; d. Andrew Cairns and Edna Frances (Manney) O'Neil; diploma Newark Beth Israel Sch. Nursing, 1955; BS in Nursing, Seton Hall U., S. Orange, N.J., 1965; MEd, Tchrs. Coll. Columbia U., 1970; EdD SUNY, Albany, 1990; m. Harvey James Gardenier, Aug. 25, 1961; children: Andrew, William. Staff nurse N.J. hosps., 1955-65; pub. health nurse, 1965-70; mem. nursing faculty Dutchess C.C., Poughkeepsie, N.Y., 1970—, program chmn. nursing, 1971-83, acting head dept. health technologies, 1983-92, head nursing dept., 1983—; mem. overall nursing faculty N.Y. State Regents Coll., 1981-92; mem. nurse edn. com. SUNY; mem. Dutchess County chpt. Am. Heart Assn., 1974-90; nutrition adv. coun. Dutchess County Coop. Edn., 1970-79. USPHS trainess, 1968-70. Mem. Am. Assn. Women in Jr. and C.C.s, N.Y. Asso. Degree Nurse Coun., N.Y. State Nurses Assn., N.Y. State Two Year Coll. Assn., Sigma Theta Tau. Home: Rd 1 Box 85 Holsapple Rd Dover Plains NY 12522 Office: Dutchess C C Pendell Rd Poughkeepsie NY 12601

GARDINER, JUDITH KEGAN, English language and women's studies educator; b. Chgo., Dec. 17, 1941; d. Albert and Esther (Oswianza) Kegan; divorced; children: Viveca, Carita. BA, Radcliffe Coll., 1962; MA, Columbia U., 1964, PhD, 1968. Prof. English and women's studies U. Ill., Chgo., 1969—, acting dir. women's studies, 1989, 91. Author: Rhys Stead Lessing, 1989; editor: Provoking Agents, 1995; editor Feminist Studies, 1989—; also articles. Organizer Newberry Libr. Feminist Lit. Criticism Group, Chgo., 1985-95. Fellow NEH, 1988. Office: U Ill Dept English M/C 162 601 S Morgan Chicago IL 60607-7120

GARDINER, STEPHANIE JOANN, staff office nurse, endoscopy nurse; b. Columbus, Ohio, Feb. 6, 1956; d. Elton Clarence and Frieda Louise (Baas) Renner; m. Jay Vernon Gardiner, Dec. 23, 1978; children: Nickalas, Tiffany, Timothy. Diploma, Springfield Hosp. Sch. Nursing, 1978. RN, Ohio. Staff nurse Meml. Hosp., Marysville, Ohio, 1978-80, Newport (R.I.) Hosp., 1980; charge nurse Long Lake Manor, Port Orchard, Wash., 1984; float nurse to staff nurse Palomar Meml. Hosp., Escondido, Calif., 1986-87; staff nurse, drs. endoscopy call nurse Gastroenterology Ltd., Virginia Beach, Va., 1991-95; endoscopy staff nurse Virginia Beach Gen. Hosp., 1991-95, endoscopy call nurse, 1993-95. Mem. Ea. Stars, Soc. of Gastroenterology Nurses and Assocs., Inc., Providence Presbyn. Handbells, Providence Presbyn. Youth Handbells. Republican. Home: 1586 Barlow Rd Hudson OH 44236

GARDINER, SUSAN NIVEN, purchasing executive; b. N.Y.C., Aug. 28, 1956; d. Robert MacPherson Gardiner and Janet (Eaton) Gardiner Glover; m. René Raul Trespalacios, Oct. 12, 1991. BA in French Lang. and Lit., Smith Coll., 1978. Prodn. mgr. Wunderman, Ricotta & Kline, N.Y.C., 1978-79; prodn. supr. Random House Enterprises, N.Y.C., 1979-81; print svcs. mgr. Esquire Mag., N.Y.C., 1981-82; purchasing agt. Playtex, inc., Stamford, Conn., 1982-84; purchasing buyer Gen. Foods Corp., White Plains, N.Y., 1984-86; asst. v.p. promotional purchasing Lancome, Inc., N.Y.C., 1986—. Mem. Assn. Graphic Arts (judge 1991—). Home: 8 Brandywine Ter Morristown NJ 07960-3503 Office: Lancome Inc 575 Fith Ave New York NY 10017

GARDINIER, CAROLYN ANN SHADDIX, reading educator; b. Daytona Beach, Fla., Oct. 24, 1956; d. James Edward and Carolyn Virginia (Galbreath) Shaddix; m. James Edward Gardinier, Mar. 24, 1976; children: William Thomas Andrew, Carolyn Jane-Elizabeth. AS in Art, Recreation, Daytona Beach C.C., 1977; BS in Edn., U. Ctrl. Fla., Orlando, 1989. Mcpl. recreation leader Volusia County Recreation Div., Deland, Fla., 1974-83; tchrs. aide Hillcrest Sch., Daytona Beach, Fla., 1985-86; adminstrv. aide Seabreeze H.S., Daytona Beach, Fla., 1986-87; tchr. Volusia County Schs., Deland, Fla., 1989-94, Reading Recovery tchr., 1994-96. Mem. Hurst Elem. Sch. PTA. Recipient Future's grant Future's Inc., Daytona Beach, Fla., PTA grant Hurst PTA. Mem. Volusia County Reading Assn., Fla. Reading Assn., Internat. Reading Assn., Delta Kappa Gamma, Phi Delta Kappa. Home: 3021 Rollins Ave Daytona Beach FL 32118-3132 Office: Hurst Elementary School 1340 Wright St Holly Hill FL 32117-1850

GARDNER, ANN JEANNETTE, family and child therapist; b. Leominster, Mass.; d. Fernand Arthur and Florence Mildred (Frodyma) Rouleau; m. Allan Donald Gardner; 1 child, Matthew Allan. B of Social Work, R.I. Coll., 1991; MA in Counseling Psychology, R.I. Coll., Providence, 1994. Residential treatment worker No. R.I. Cmty. Mental Health Ctr., Woonsocket, R.I., 1986-91; crisis intervention case mgr. NRICMCH, Woonsocket, R.I., 1991-92, house mgr., 1992-94; family and child therapist Mental Health Svcs., Johnston, R.I., 1994—. Mission bd. Greenville (R.I.) Bapt. Ch., 1993-96, lay minister, 1994—, deacon, 1996—. Recipient Merit award Woonsocket (R.I.) Police Dept., 1988. Mem. ACA, Am. Mental Health Counselors Assn. Baptist. Office: Mental Health Svcs 311 Doric Ave Cranston RI 02920

GARDNER, ANN L., social anthropologist, researcher; b. Dayton, Ohio, Sept. 21, 1961; d. Owen Ben and Gladys Elizabeth (Brown) G. BA, Friends World Coll., 1982; non-degree work in Arabic lang., Am. U., Cairo, Arab Republic of Egypt, 1983-85; MA in Anthropology, U. Tex., 1987, PhD, 1994. Rsch. grantee Nat. Geog. Soc., 1990, NSF, 1989-91, Wenner-Gren, 1990, U.S. Info. Agy. adminstered by Am. Rsch. Ctr. in Egypt, 1989-90; Arabic lang. fellowship U. Tex., summer 1988, Am. U. Cairo, 1984-85. Home: 3026 Clay St San Francisco CA 94115-1624

GARDNER, ANNE LANCASTER, lawyer; b. Corpus Christi, Tex., Aug. 19, 1942; d. Jack Quinn and DeWitte (Benton) Lancaster; 1 child, Travis Gregory. BA, U. Tex., 1964, LLB, 1966.Bar: Tex., 1966; asst. dir. continuing legal edn. State Bar Tex., 1966-67; law clk. to U.S. Dist. Ct. judge, 1967-71; ptnr. Simon, Peebles, Haskell, Gardner & Betty, Ft. Worth, 1971-85, McLean, Sanders, Price, Head & Ellis, P.C., Ft. Worth, 1985-88, Shannon, Gracey, Ratliff & Miller, Ft. Worth, 1988—, chair appeals sect. Mem. adv. commn. State Bd. Legal Specialization Appellate Civil Law, chair, 1993-94; mem. adv. com. Supreme Ct. Tex., 1993-96; chair merit selection Panel for U.S. Magistrate Judges, no. dist. Tex., 1995. Fellow Tex. Bar Found. (life); mem. ABA, Tarrant County Bar Assn. (dir., v.p., pres. elect 1993, pres. 1994), Tex. Assn. Def. Counsel (bd. dirs.), Tex. Assn. Def. Counsel (bd. dirs.). Editor legal jours.

GARDNER, ELLA HAINES, artist; b. Montfort, Wis.; d. Robert Daniel and Gena Helena (Helgeson) Haines; m. Russell Robert Gardner, June 1, 1937; children: Russell R., Wayne, Keith. One-woman shows include Bank of granton, Wis., 1977-96, Marshfield (Wis.) Living Ctr., 1985-96, First Nat. Bank, Neillsville, Wis., 1982-84, Dept. Industry, Labor and Human Rels., Madison, Wis., 1987, Marshfield Libr., 1990, 91, The Mabel Tainter Meml. Mus., Menomonie, Wis., 1996; two-woman shows include Jail Mus., Neillsville, 1985; exhibited in group shows at Rahr West Mus., Manitowoc, Wis., 1982, gov.'s Office, Madison, 1983, 88-89, King (Wis.) Treatment Ctr., 1983, Tuffs Mus., Neillsville, 1983, Gray Owl Exhibit, Athens, Wis., 1988, Silverman Gallery, Spring Green, Wis., 1989, New Visions Gallery, Marshfield, 1989, 90, Art for Faith, Janesville, 1990; represented in numerous pvt. collections. Charter mem. Nat. Mus. Women in the Arts. Recipient K & M Kuemmerlin award, 1986, Grumbacher Bronze award, 1987, Northwood Art Assn. award, 1987, Traveling Show award, 1987, Obermiller Edn. award, 1993, Ctrl. Wis. State Fair award, 1973-96. Mem. Wis. Regional Artists Assn. (Meml. award 1988, Contour award 1978, 81, 84, 85, 86, 87, 88, 91, 93), Wis. Women in the Arts. Home: 10598 Hwy H Marshfield WI 54449

GARDNER, KATHLEEN D., gas company executive, lawyer; b. Fayetteville, Ark., July 14, 1947; d. Harold Andrew and Bess (Gunn) Dulan; m. Robert Gardner, June 7, 1969 (dec. Sept. 1974); 1 child, Christina Ann. BS, U. Ark., 1969, JD, 1978; MA, U. Ala., 1972. Atty., corp. officer SW Energy Co., Fayetteville, 1978-85; asst. gen. counsel, asst. v.p. Ark. La. Gas Co., Little Rock, 1985-86, gen. counsel, v.p., 1986—; chmn. Regional Tng. Program, Birmingham, Ala., 1972-75. Bd. dirs. the New Sch. Fayetteville, 1978-79, Robert K. Gardner Meml. Fund, Fayetteville; past bd. dirs. Keep Ark. Beautiful Commn., Ballet Ark., Ark. Mus. Sci. and History, Vis. Nurse Corp. Named Outstanding Young woman Fayetteville Jaycettes, Ark. Jaycettes, recipient Woman of Achievement in Energy award, 1990; named to Top 100 Women in Ark., Ark. Bus. Newspaper, 1995, 96. Mem. ABA, Ark. Bar Assn. (sec. natural resources sect. 1981), Pulaski County Bar Assn., Am. Gas Assn., DAR, Ark. Assn. Def. Counsel, Am. Arbitration Assn. (Ark. adv. coun.), Alpha Delta Pi. Episcopal. Office: Ark La Gas Co 400 E Capitol Ave Little Rock AR 72202-2418

GARDNER, LEE ROBBINS, psychiatrist; b. Balt., June 6, 1934; d. Bernard S. and Lee (Fraidin) Robbins; m. Robert Williams, Oct., 1990; children: Andrew, Nancy, Julie. BA, Barnard, 1955; MD, Columbia U., 1959, cert. adult psychoanalysis, 1979, cert. child psychoanalysis, 1981. Intern St. Luke Hosp., 1959-60; resident N.Y. State Psychiat. Inst., N.Y.C., 1962-66; attending psychiatrist N.Y. State Psychiat. Inst., 1966—; asst. clin. prof. psychiatry Columbia Coll. Physicians and Surgeons, N.Y.C., 1982—; collaborating faculty Columbia Psychoanalytic Ctr., Columbia U., 1980—; bi-annual lectr. N.J. Coll. Medicine & Dentistry. Jewish.

GARDNER, LISA ANN, risk management and insurance educator, consultant; b. Ottumwa, Iowa, June 8, 1962; d. Ronald Eugene and Mary Ann (Bloss) G. AA, Indian Hills C.C., Ottumwa, 1981; BS, U. Wyo., 1984; MBA, Drake U., 1988; PhD, Ga. State U., 1992. Residence hall dir. Indian Hills C.C., Ottumwa, 1985-87; acad. advisor Buena Vista Coll., Ottumwa, 1985-87; grad. rsch. asst. Drake U., Des Moines, 1987-88; grad. rsch. asst. Ga. State U., Atlanta, 1988-90, grad. teaching asst., 1990-92; asst. prof. Old Dominion U., Norfolk, Va., 1992-93, U. Nev., Las Vegas, 1993-95; Gerald D. Stephens chair in risk mgmt. and ins. Bradley U., Peoria, Ill., 1995—. Contbr. articles to profl. jours. Recipient Program Devel. grant AEtna Life and Casualty Found., 1987, Doctoral Dissertation Rsch. award State Farm Cos., 1991, Program Devel. grant Va. Chpt. Risk and Ins. Mgmt. Soc., 1993, Rsch. grant Old Dominion U., 1993; named Bell South scholar Ga. State U., 1988-92, Helen C. Leith fellow Ga. State U., 1988-92, Spencer Ednl. Found. scholar Atlanta Chpt. Risk and Ins. Mgmt. Soc., 1990. Mem. Am. Risk and Ins. Assn., So. Risk and Ins. Assn., Inst. for Ins. and Risk Mgmt., Beta Gamma Sigma (Delta chpt. of Ga.). Office: Bradley U Foster Coll Bus Dept Fin/Quantitative Meth 1501 W Bradley Ave Peoria IL 61625

GARDNER, LIZ See WEDDINGTON, ELIZABETH GARDNER

GARDNER, SANDRA BEYER, sales manager; b. Shawano, Wis., June 2, 1960; d. David O. and Ernestine Alice (Hodel) Beyer; m. Stuart Charles Gardner, Dec. 12, 1992. BS in Agr. and Food Sci., U. Wis., 1982. Quality assurance technologist The Larsen Co., Green Bay, Wis., 1982-84; tech. coord. Schepps Inc., Dallas, 1984-85; tech. sales rep. Crest Foods Co., Ashton, Ill., 1985-88; regional sales mgr. Nat. Sea Products, Portsmouth, N.H., 1988-89; dist. sales mgr. J.M. Smucker Co., Orrville, Ohio, 1989-91, nat. accounts mgr. west, 1991—. Presbyterian. Office: 2131 N Collins St Ste 433 Arlington TX 76011-2811

GARDNER, SHERYL PAIGE, gynecologist; b. Bremerton, Wash., Jan. 24, 1945; d. Edwin Gerald and Dorothy Elizabeth (Herman) G.; m. James Alva Beat, June 20, 1986. BA in Biology, U. Oreg., 1967, MD cum laude, 1971. Diplomate Am. Bd. Ob-Gyn. Intern L.A. County Harbor Gen. Hosp., Torrance, Calif., 1971-72, resident in ob-gyn., 1972-75; physician Group Health Assn., Washington, 1975-87; pvt. practice Mililani, Hawaii, 1987—; med. staff sec. Wahiawa (Hawaii) Gen. Hosp., 1994-95. Mem. Am. Coll. Ob-Gyn., Am. Soc. Colposcopy and Cervical Pathology, Hawaii Med. Assn., Sigma Kappa, Alpha Omega Alpha. Democrat. Office: 95-1249 Meheula Pkwy #B10A Mililani HI 96789-1720

GARFIELD, JOAN BARBARA, statistics educator; b. Milw., May 4, 1950; d. Sol. L. and Amy L. (Nusbaum) G.; m. Michael G. Luxenberg, Aug. 17, 1980; children: Harlan Ross and Rebecca Ellen (twins). Student, U. Chgo., 1968; BS, U. Wis., 1972; MA, U. Minn., 1978, PhD, 1981. Assoc. prof. ednl. psychology Coll. Edn., U. Minn., Mpls., 1981—, coord. rsch. and evaluation The Gen. Coll., 1984-87. Mem. Am. Ednl. Rsch. Assn., Math. Assn. Am., Nat. Coun. Tchrs. of Math., Internat. Assn. for Statis. Edn., Am. Statis. Assn., Internat. Study Group on Learning Probability and Stats. (sec. 1987-95). Jewish. Office: U Minn Dept Edn Psychology 332 Burton Hall Minneapolis MN 55455

GARFIELD, PHYLLIS H., international program administrator, educational consultant; b. Columbus, Nebr., Aug. 21, 1950; d. Carl and Wilma (Phillips) Rafferty; m. Alan J. Garfield, Sept. 2, 1979; children: Eliot, Margaret, Carolan. AA, Platt C.C., Columbus, Nebr., 1972; BA, Midland Luth. Coll., Fremont, Nebr., 1974; student, Phillips U., Marburg, Germany, 1973-74; postgrad., Creighton U., 1975-79. Asst. to dean of students Marycrest Coll., Davenport, Iowa, 1980-83; cons. and v.p. Digigraphic Systems, Inc., Davenport, 1985—; internat. travel advisor Digigraphic Systems, Inc., Meenaleck, Ireland, 1992—; internat. study advisor Teikyo Marycrest U., Davenport, 1981—. Pres. Temple Emanuel Sisterhood, Davenport, 1993—. Fulbright fellow, Marburg, 1973-74. Home: 34 Oak Ln Davenport IA 52803-3124 Address: Meenaleck Letterkenny, County Donegal Ireland

GARFINKEL, BARBARA ANN, pianist, educator, musicologist; b. Elizabeth, N.J., Dec. 19, 1931; d. Irving and Lillian (Treister) Slavin; m. Burton Garfinkel, June 28, 1952; children: Steven, Joan Struss. BS in Edn., Boston U., 1953. Cert. vocal music instr., piano instr. Pvt. piano tchr. Millburn, N.J., 1949-52, Livingston, N.J., 1968-90; elem. sch. tchr. Nahant (Mass.) Pub. Schs., 1953-54, Maplewood (N.J.) Pub. Schs., 1954-56; profl. pianist, vocalist, 1984—; music tchr. Downs Syndrome Children, Livingston, 1982-85; choir dir. Daughers of Miriam, Clifton, N.J., 1986, Cranford (N.J.) Home Continuing Care, 1990. Composer liturgical and show music; performer one woman shows vocal and piano. Vol. pianist Grotta Nursing Home, West Orange, N.J., 1988-93; judge teen piano finalists Garden State Art Ctr., Holmdel, N.J., 1985-95; local leader Dem. Party, Livingston, 1990—; v.p. Christ Hosp. Auxiliary, Jersey City, 1980-85; instrs. Russian, Israeli, Chinese immigrants, 1980-93; diplomat World Jewish Congress, 1995—. Mem. N.J. Music Tchrs. Assn., Schumann Music Study Club (program chair 1994-95), Pro Musica Hon. Music Club, Pi Lambda Theta. Home: 2 Tiffany Ct Montville NJ 07045

GARFINKEL, FRAN SYLVIA, professional business coach, financial planner; b. Bronx, Jan. 21, 1959; d. Sol and Louise Marion (Goldberg) G. BS in Recreation, Calif. State U., 1981. Adminstr. Recreation and Parks Dept., 1981-84; fin. planner IDS/Am. Express, Glendale, Calif., 1986-91; So. Calif. regional mgr./retirement planning specialist IRM Corp., 1991-93; dir. fin. planning/ednl. instns. Gateway Investment Svcs., Glendale, Calif., 1993-96; pvt. practice profl. bus. coach, 1996—. Bd. dirs. Calif. State U. Northridge Student Union, 1983-85; mem. Calif. State U. Alumni Council, Long Beach, Calif., 1984-86. Named one of Outstanding Young Women in Am., 1981, 84, recipient Outstanding Contbds., Calif. State U. Northridge Student Union, 1985. Mem. NAFE (network dir. 1987—), Bus. and Profl. Women (chmn. ways and means com. Verdugo Hills chpt. 1987, chmn. Young Careerist 1988—), Calif. State U. Northridge Assoc. Students (hon. life), Pasadena Jaycees (bd. dirs. 1991-94, v.p. individual devel. 1991-92, v.p. adminstrn. 1992-93, exec. v.p. 1993-94, Tripod bd. dirs. 1990-91), Calif. Jaycees (Presdl. Medallion of Honor 1992-93, outstanding v.p. 1992-93), Toastmasters Internat. (ednl. v.p., pres. 1990). Republican.

GARFINKEL, RUTH, non-profit executive director; b. Altoona, Pa., Aug. 11, 1941; d. Sam and Mathilda (Lych) Rider; m. Alan A. Garfinkel, June 9, 1963; children: Marc Rider, J. Asher. BS in BA, Robert Morris Coll., Pitts., 1978. Tchr. bus. Allegheny Intermediate Unit, Pitts., 1979-80, Fox Chapel H.S. Adult Edn., Pitts., 1979-80; sch. dir. Zoar Home, Pitts., 1980-87; dir. adult svcs. Jewish Cmty. Ctr., Pitts., 1987-88; adminstrv./vol. dir. Nat. Coun. Jewish Women, Pitts., 1988-91, exec. dir., 1991—. Mem. Leadership Pitts. XI, 1994-95; bd. dirs. Riverview Towers Sr. Adult Housing, Pitts., 1995-96; mem. steering com. Family Health Coun., Pitts., 1994-96, Pitts. Bd. Pub. Edn.-Evenstart, 1994-96. Mem. Nat. Soc. Fundraising Execs., Pa. Assn. Voluntarism, Robert Morris Coll. Alumni Assn. (Heritage award 1994), Exec. Women's Coun. Democrat. Home: 2 Shadyside Ln Pittsburgh PA 15232

GARGAN, ANNAMARIE, accountant; b. Huntington, N.Y., July 5, 1962; d. Frank Patrick and Loretta Jean (Mele) G. BS in Acctg., St. John's U., Jamaica, N.Y., 1984; MBA in Fin., L.I. U., 1988. Accounts receivable clk. Cantor Bros., Farmingdale, N.Y., 1984-85; asst. to treas. Orthodox Ch. in Am., Oyster Bay Cove, N.Y., 1985-88; asst. contr., sr. acct. Assn. for Advancement of Blind and Retarded, Jamaica, 1988-89; staff acct. Career Employment Svcs. (name now CHI Fin. Svcs.), Westbury, N.Y., 1989-90, sr. acct., 1990-94, mgr. acctg. sys., 1994—. Mem. Inst. Mgmt. Accts., St. John's U. Alumni Assn. Office: Career Horizons Fin Svcs 177 Crossways Park Dr Woodbury NY 11797

GARIBALDI, MARIE LOUISE, state supreme court justice; b. Jersey City, Nov. 26, 1934; d. Louis J. and Marie (Serventi) G. BA, Conn. Coll., 1956; LLB, Columbia U., 1959; LLM in Tax. Law, NYU, 1963. Atty. Office of Regional Counsel, IRS, N.Y.C., 1960-66; assoc. McCarter & English, Newark, 1966-69; ptnr. Riker, Danzig, Scherer & Hyland, Newark, 1969-82; assoc. justice N.J. Supreme Court, Newark, 1982—. Contbr. articles to profl. jours. Trustee St. Peter's Coll.; co-chmn. Thomas Kean's campaign for Gov. of N.J., 1981, mem. transition team, 1981; mem. Gov. Byrne's Commn. on Dept. of Commerce, 1981. Recipient Disting. Alumni award NYU Law Alumni of N.J., 1982; recipient Disting. Alumni award Columbia U., 1982. Fellow Am. Bar Found.; mem. N.J. Bar Assn. (pres. 1982), Columbia U. Sch. Law Alumni Assn. (bd. dirs.). Roman Catholic. Home: 34 Kingswood Rd Weehawken NJ 07087-6930*

GARIL, MARSHA SATER, secondary education educator; b. Wilmington, N.C., Aug. 9, 1945; d. Stanley L. and Celia Bernice (Levine) Sater; m. Stanley Garil, Jan. 3, 1982. AB, Coll. William and Mary, 1968; MST, Rutgers U., 1974. Cert. tchr. math., physics, gifted edn., Va. Tchr. math. Fairfax County Pub. Schs., Fairfax, Va., 1968—; chmn. dept. math. West Potomac H.S., Alexandria, Va., 1987-95; tchr. Thomas Jefferson H.S. for Sci. and Tech., Alexandria, 1995—; in curriculum devel. Fairfax County Pub. Schs., 1989, 91, tchr. staff devel. courses, 1986—; trainer A Process Approach to Algebra 1, U. Hawaii, 1993—. Mem. NEA, Va. Edn. Assn., Fairfax Edn. Assn., Nat. Coun. Tchrs. Math., Va. Coun. Tchrs. Math., No. Va. Coun. Tchrs. Math. Office: Thomas Jefferson HS Sch/Tec 6560 Braddock Rd Alexandria VA 22312

GARISON, LYNN LASSITER, real estate executive; b. El Dorado, Ark., Dec. 19, 1954; d. Robert Weaver and Iris Amy (Horton) Lassiter; m. James Wallace Garison, Jr., Dec. 11, 1982. Student, Randolph-Macon Woman's Coll., 1973-76; BS, Tex. A&M U., 1978. Lic. real estate broker, Tex. From broker assoc. to regional mgr. J. B. Goodwin, Realtors, Residential, Inc., Austin, Tex., 1979-82; comml. broker assoc. Christon Co., Realtors, Inc., Dallas, 1983-87; v.p. Dallas Mkt. Ctr., Dallas, 1987-89; regional v.p. Tenenbaum and Assocs., Inc., Dallas, 1989-92; pres. Artemis Co., Dallas, 1992—; bd. dirs. Consumer Credit Counseling Svc. Bd. dirs. Dallas Coun. World Affairs; mem. Mayor's Task Force on Child Abuse, Highland Pk. Presbyn. Ch. Mem. DAR, Daus. of the Republic of Tex., Nat. Assn. Corp. Real Estate, Cert. Comml. Investment Mem., Urban Land Inst., Rotary Internat. (bd. dirs. Park Cities club, v.p.). Home: 4317 Greenbrier Dr Dallas TX 75225-6640

GARLAND, BEVERLY LYN, computer graphic artist; b. Havelock, N.C., Dec. 13, 1964; d. John Douglas and Harriet Ann (Whitworth) G. BS, U. Tex., 1988. Secnery painter Strong Prodns., Austin, Tex., 1987-91; computer artist, art dir. Origin Sys., Inc., Austin, 1991-95; computer artist, art dir., co-founder Titanic Entertainment, Austin, 1995—. Graphic web site, 1996; archtl. designer residence in Austin. Constrn. crew leader Hands on Housing, Austin, 1994. Mem. Amnesty Internat., Common Cause, 3D Studio Users' Group, Sierra Club of Austin, Webgrrls of Austin. Office: Titanic Entertainment 507 Powell St Austin TX 78703

GARLAND, DANNA LORANE, elementary school educator; b. Sapulpa, Okla., June 23, 1961; d. Ray Thomas and Frances Lorane (Newland) Graham; m. Gordon Ray Garland, Aug. 4, 1984; children: Kylie Lorane, Keaton Nicole. BS, Northeastern State U., 1983, MS in Adminstrn., 1990; cert. in elem. edn., U. Ctr. at Tulsa, 1986. Cert. tchr., Okla. Elem. phys. edn. tchr. Glenpool (Okla.) Pub. Sch., 1984-87, 2d grade tchr., 1987-89, 5th grade tchr., 1989-95, mem. textbook com., 1989—, mem. staff devel., chmn., 1990-92, grade chmn., 1991-94, asst. prin., 1995—. Mem. Glenpool PTA, 1990-94. Grantee Tulsa Edn. Fund, 1994, grantee Glenpool Found., 1995. Mem. ASCD. Office: Glenpool Elem Sch PO Box 1149 Glenpool OK 74033-1149

GARLAND, KATHLEEN, school librarian, media educator, consultant; b. Cleve., Oct. 8, 1942; d. David Brown and Eileen Eva (Bon) G.; m. Galen Edwin Rike, June 30, 1984. BS in Edn., Ohio U., 1964; MSLS, Case Western Reserve U., 1968, PhD, 1980. cert. in school library media, elem. edn., N.Y. 5th grade tchr. E. Cleve. (Ohio) Schs., 1964-66; librarian Dist. No. 2 West Orangeburg cen. Sch., Piermont, N.Y., 1968-70; school media specialist Forest Hills Sch. Dist., Cin., 1970-76; asst. prof. Rutgers U., New Brunswick, N.J., 1980-83; asst. prof., asst. chair Ball State U., Muncie, Ind., 1983-86; coord. sch. media program., asst. prof. SUNY at Buffalo, N.Y., 1987-90, U. Mich., Ann Arbor, 1990-95; coord. media svcs. Kelloggsville Sch. Dist., Grand Rapids, Mich., 1995—; mem. cont. edn. com. Western N.Y. Library Resources Coun., Buffalo, N.Y., 1988-91; mem. sch. library system adv. coun. Erie Bd. Coop. Svcs., Buffalo, N.Y., 1988-90; cons. Holt (Mich.) High Sch., 1992—. Contbr. chpt. to book, articles to profl. jours. Mem. Mich. Electronic Libr. Adv. Coun., Libr. of Mich., 1996—. Recipient rsch. grantee Assn. Libr. and Info. Scis. Edn., 1985, U.S. Dept. Edn., 1989, 93. Mem. ALA, ASCD, Am. Assn. Sch. Librarians. (Highsmith Rsch. grant, 1994), Am. Soc. Info. Sci., Assn. Library and Info. Sci. Edn., Assn. Library Svc. to Children, Freedom to Read Found.

GARLAND, MEG, advertising executive; b. Ft. Worth, Sept. 19, 1946; d. Robert Neal and Mary Jewell (Saul) G.; children: Blayn Elizabeth Garland Barnard, Mary Blayr Garland Barnard. B.Advt.Art and Design, Tex. Tech U., 1969. Teaching asst. Tex. Tech U., Lubbock, 1968; graphic designer Storm Printing Corp., Dallas, 1969; art dir. Ratcliff Advt., Dallas, 1969-71; owner, prin. Triad Assocs., Waco, Tex., 1972—. Scholarship grantor Tex. Tech. U., 1988; bd. dirs. Am. Cancer Soc., Waco and McLennan County, 1989-91, Freeman Ctr., 1994—, v.p. 1995-96; mem. Woodway Beautiful Commn., 1995-98, Dist. 2x3 Lions Cabinet, 1995-96. Recipient Spl. award Waco Assn. Retarded Citizens, 1976, Tex. Assn. Retarded Citizens, 1977, Pathfinders, YWCA, 1988, varous design awards, 1966—. Mem. Hewitt C. of C., Waco Founder Lions Club (pres. 1994). Methodist. Office: PO Box 8688 Waco TX 76714-8688

GARLAND, SYLVIA DILLOF, lawyer; b. N.Y.C., June 4, 1919; d. Morris and Frieda (Gassner) Dillof; m. Albert Garland, May 4, 1942; children:

Margaret Garland Clunie, Paul B. BA, Bklyn. Coll., 1939; JD cum laude, N.Y. Law Sch., 1960. Bar: N.Y., 1960, U.S. Ct. Appeals (2d cir.), 1965, U.S. Ct. Claims, 1965, U.S. Supreme Ct., 1967, U.S. Customs Ct., 1972, U.S. Ct. Appeals (5th cir.), 1979. Assoc. firm Borden, Skidell, Fleck and Steindler, Jamaica, N.Y., 1960-61, Fields, Zimmerman, Skodnick & Segall, Jamaica, 1961-65, Marshall, Brater, Greene, Allison & Tucker, N.Y.C., 1965-68; law sec. to N.Y. Supreme Ct. justice, Suffolk County, 1968-70; ptnr. firm Hofheimer, Gartlir & Gross, N.Y.C., 1970—; asst. adj. prof. N.Y. Law Sch., 1974-79; mem. com. on character and fitness N.Y. State Supreme Ct., 1st Jud. Dept., 1985—, vice chmn., 1991—. Author: Workman's Compensation, 1957; Labor Law, 1959; Wills, 1962; contbg. author: Guardians and Custodians, 1970; editor-in-chief Law Rev. Jour., N.Y. Law Forum, 1959-60 (service award 1960); contbr. article to mag. Trustee N.Y. Law Sch., 1979-90, trustee emeritus, 1991—; pres. Oakland chpt. B'nai Brith, Bayside, N.Y., 1955-57. Recipient Disting. Alumnus award, N.Y. Law Sch., 1978. Mem. ABA (litigation sect.), N.Y. State Bar Assn., Queen's County Bar Assn. (sec. civil practice 1960-79), N.Y. Law Sch. Alumni Assn. (pres. 1976-77), N.Y. Law Forum Alumni Assn. (pres. 1963-65). Jewish. Home: 425 E 58th St New York NY 10022-2300

GARLETTS, TWILA UMBEL, advocate; b. Uniontown, Pa., Dec. 17, 1955; d. Wade and Margaret Theresa (Rocheck) U.; m. Gary Paul Garletts; 1 child, Nathan Umbel. BA summa cum laude, U. Pitts., 1987. Sales rep., receptionist Uniontown (Pa.) Newspapers, Inc., 1973-88; sec., ins. coord. Dr. Ronald R. Sepic, D.D.S., Uniontown, 1989-93; keyboarder Tapsco, Inc., Akron, Pa., 1994—. Active numerous movements involving children rights and healthcare issues; co-founder Treasures of Human Expression Arts Coun. Mem. animal rights orgns. Republican. Presbyn. Home: 3080 Todd Ln Lancaster PA 17601

GARMAN, NORMA JEAN, home care agency administrator; b. Camp Taylor, Ky., Feb. 23, 1939; d. William Edward and Emma Pauline (Wade) Eppihimer; divorced; stepchildren: Lewis, Rubin, Gayna, Brenton; m. Melvin LeRoy Garman, June 11, 1987; children: Constance, James, Timothy, William R., Sharon, Barbara. AA, Sierra Coll., 1986. C.N.A., Calif., Oreg.; H.H.A., Calif. Sec., bookkeeper Landino Constrn. & Well Drilling, Santa Cruz, Calif., 1972-74; H.H.A. Carepoint Home Health, Auburn, Calif., 1986-88, Kimberly Quality Care, Eugene, Oreg., 1989-90, 92-93, Lebanon (Oreg.) Hosp.-Home Health, 1991-92; owner Valley Homecare & Referral, Inc., Sweet Home, Oreg., 1993—. Office: Valley Homecare & Referral Inc PO Box 603 1150 S Main Lebanon OR 97355

GARMAN, TERESA AGNES, state legislator; b. Ft. Dodge, Iowa, Aug. 29, 1937; d. John Clement and Barbara Marie (Korsa) Lennon; m. Merle A. Garman, Aug. 5, 1961; children: Laura Ann Garman Hansen, Rachel Irene Garman Coder, Robert Sylvester, Sarah Teresa Garman Powers. Grad. high sch., Ft. Dodge. With employee relations dept. 3M Co., Ames, Iowa, 1974-86; mem. Iowa Ho. of Reps., Des Moines, 1986—. Asst. majority leader, mem. platform com., del. Rep. Nat. Conv., 1988, del., mem. platform com., 1992; mem. Iowa Rep. Ctrl. Com. Mem. Rep. Farm Policy Coun., Story County Rep. Women, Story County Pork Prodrs., Farm Bur., Story City C. of C., Nev. C. of C. Roman Catholic. Home: RR 2 Ames IA 50010-9802 Office: State Capitol Des Moines IA 50319

GARMEL, MARION BESS SIMON, journalist; b. El Paso, Tex., Oct. 15, 1936; d. Marcus and Frieda (Alfman) Simon; m. Raymond Louis Garmel, Nov. 28, 1965 (dec. Feb. 1986); 1 child, Cynthia Rogers. Student, U. Tex., El Paso, 1954-55; BJ, U. Tex., 1958. Exec. sec. Nat. Student Assn., Phila., 1958-59, pub. rels. dir., 1960-61; sec. World Assembly Youth, Paris, Brussels, 1959-60; dictationist Wall Street Jour., Washington, 1961; libr., staff writer Nat. Observer, Silver Spring, Md., 1961-70; art critic Indpls. News, 1971-91, editor Free Time sect., 1975-91, critic radio and TV, 1991-95; theater critic Indpls. Star and News, 1995—; television critic Indpls. News, 1995—. Mem. Nat. Fedn. Press Women (1st Place Critics award 1974), Hadassah Women's Zionist Orgn. Am. (life), Women's Press Club Ind. (1st Place Critics award 1995). Jewish. Home: 226 E 45th St Indianapolis IN 46205-1712 Office: Indpls Star and News 307 N Pennsylvania St Indianapolis IN 46204-1811

GARMIRE, ELSA MEINTS, electrical engineering educator, consultant; b. Buffalo, Nov. 9, 1939; d. Ralph E. and Nelle (Gubser) Meints; m. Gordon P. Garmire, June 11, 1961 (div. 1975); children: Lisa, Marla; m. Robert Heathcote Russell, Feb. 4, 1979. AB in Physics, Harvard U., 1961; PhD in Physics, MIT, 1965. Rsch. scientist NASA Electronics Rsch. Ctr., Cambridge, Mass., 1965-66; rsch. fellow Calif. Inst. Tech., Pasadena, 1966-73; sr. rsch. scientist U. So. Calif. Ctr. for Laser Studies, L.A., 1974-78, prof. elec. engring. and physics, 1981-92, assoc. dir. Ctr. for Laser Studies, 1978-83, dir., 1984—, William Hogue prof. of engring., 1992—; vis. fellow Standard Telecommunication Labs., Eng., 1973-74; cons. Aerospace Corp., L.A., 1975-91, sci. adv. bd. Air Force, Washington, 1985-89, TRW, L.A., 1988-89, McDonnell Douglas, St. Louis, 1990-93. Contbr. over 200 sci. papers and articles to profl. publs.; patentee in field. Recipient Soroptimist Achievement award Soroptimist Club L.A., 1970, K.C. Black Award N.E. Electronics Rsch. and Engring. Meeting, 1972, Soc. Women Engrs. Achievement award 1994, U. So. Calif. Rschr. award, 1994; named Mademoiselle Women of Yr. Mademoiselle Mag., 1970. Fellow IEEE (bd. dirs. 1985-89), Optical Soc. Am. (bd. dirs. 1983-86, pres. 1992, pres. 1993), Am. Phys. Soc. (bd. dirs. 1994—); mem. NAE (life), Soc. Women Engrs. (sr., life), Harvard Radcliffe Club (v.p. 1984-86). Democrat. Office: Univ So Cal Ctr Laser Studies Denney Rsch Bldg / Univ Park Los Angeles CA 90089

GARNER, CARLENE ANN, fundraising consultant; b. Dec. 17, 1945; d. Carl A. and Ruth E. (Mathison) Timblin; m. Adelbert L. Garner, Feb. 17, 1964; children: Bruce A., Brent A. BA, U. Puget Sound, 1983. Adminstrv. dir. Balletacoma, 1984-87; exec. dir. Tacoma Symphony, 1987-95; prin. New Horizon Cons., Tacoma, 1995—; cons. Wash. PAVE, Tacoma, 1983-84. Treas. Coalition for the Devel. of the Arts, 1992-94; pres. Wilson High Sch. PTA, Tacoma, 1983-85; chmn. Tacoma Sch. Vol. Adv. Bd., 1985-87; pres. Emmanuel Luth. Ch., Tacoma, 1984-86, chmn. future steering com., 1987-93; sec.-treas. Tacoma-Narrows Conf., 1987—; vice chmn. Tacoma Luth. Home. Mem. N.W. Devel. Officers Assn. (chair Tacoma/Pierce County com.), Am. Symphony Orch. League, Jr. Women's Club Tacoma (pres. 1975-76, pres. Peninsula dist. 1984-86), Wash. CFWC (pres. 1988-90, 3d v.p. 1990-92, 2d v.p. 1992-94, 1st v.p. 1994-95, pres.-elect 1996—, Clubwoman of Yr. 1977, Outstanding FREE chmn. Gen. Fedn. 1995), Commencement Bay Woman's Club (pres. 1990-92, trustee, chair nat. conv.). Lutheran. Home: 1115 N Cheyenne St Tacoma WA 98406-3624 Office: New Horizon Cons 1115 N Cheyenne Tacoma WA 98406-3625

GARNER, CECELIA VANESSA, bank consultant; b. Richmond, Va., Aug. 23, 1968; d. Pearl L. Garner. BSW, Va. Commonwealth U., 1991; AAS/Paralegal, U. Richmond, 1994; postgrad. in adminstrv. of justice, J. Sargeant Reynolds Sch., Richmond, 1996. Telemktg. mgr. Olan mills Portrait Studios, Richmond, 1986-88; delinquent accounts collector Va. Edn. Loan Authority, Richmond, 1988-90; atty./agy. liaison Crestar Bank Card/Legal Recovery, Richmond, 1990—. Mem. Daily Planet Vols., Richmond, 1987—, Mother's Against Drunk Drivers, Richmond, 1994—. Mem. ABWA, Richmond Assn. of Legal Assts., NAFE, Phi Theta Kappa. Democrat. Baptist.

GARNER, DORIS TRAGANZA, education educator; b. Phila., Oct. 13, 1934; d. Charles Thomas and Elizabeth Marie (Blatteau) Traganza; m. Joseph Anthony DeMatteo, Apr. 12, 1958 (dec. Aug. 1968); children: Maria Louise, Carol Ann, Nicholas Joseph, Elizabeth Joan, Charles Traganza, Ann Seton; m. Doyle Daniel Garner, July 11, 1970 (div. Feb. 1989); 1 child: Jean Estelle. BA in Psychology cum laude, U. Pa., 1955; postgrad., Temple U., 1955-59; MS in Ednl. Adminstrn., SUNY, Albany, 1978, EdD in Ednl. Adminstrn. and Higher Edn., 1983. Cert. tchr., N.Y. Elem. tchr. Phila. Sch. Dist., 1955-59; asst. to asst. dean grad. studies SUNY, Albany, 1977-78, asst. to asst. v.p. acad. affairs, 1979; curriculum rsch. assoc. John Jay Coll., CUNY, N.Y.C., 1979; asst. in higher edn. doctoral office N.Y. State Edn. Dept., Albany, 1979-84, coord. program rev. master's programs, 1985-87, assoc. in higher edn. coll./univ. evaluation, 1987-89, asst. to dep. commr. higher edn. and professions, 1989-95, divsn. dir. coll./univ. evaluation, 1995—; mem. staff N.Y. State Regents Task Force on Tchg. N.Y. State Edn. Dept., 1996—; chair session on state policy Am. Assn. Colls. for Tchr. Edn., New Orleans, 1988; presenter at confs. in field. Mem. Shaker H.S. Theater Support, Latham, N.Y., 1988, 90; pianist at charity functions, Albany, N.Y., 1992-94; cmty. theater actor Stagecrafters, Phila., 1951. Home: 27 Henkes Ln Latham NY 12110-5013

GARNER, JO ANN STARKEY, educator; b. Ft. Hamilton, N.Y., Dec. 25, 1934; d. Joseph Wheeler and Irene Dorothy (Vogt) Starkey; m. James Gayle Garner, Mar. 2, 1957; children: Mary Vivian Pine, Margaret Susan Gillis, Kathryn Lynn. BA in History, Govt., Law, U. Tex., Austin, 1956; postgrad., Trinity U., 1973. Cert. deaf edn. and elem. tchr., Tex. Kindergarten tchr. Platenstrasse Internat. Sch., Frankfurt, Fed. Republic Germany, 1964-66; tchr. of deaf Sunshine Cottage Sch. for Deaf, San Antonio, 1966—; speech cons. Trinity U., 1978, cooperating tchr., 1978-87. Mem. San Antonio Fiesta Commn. Mem. Tex. Alexander Graham Bell Assn. (charter), Tex. State Geneal. and Hist. Soc., San Antonio Geneal. and Hist. Soc., The Bright Shawl, Rep. Nat. Com., German-Texan Heritage Soc., Ind. Hist. Soc., Pioneers of Ind., Mecklenburg (N.C.) Geneal. Soc., Pioneers of Ill., Ill. Geneal. Soc., Tex. Pioneers, Alpha Delta Pi. Republican. Mem. Catholic Episcopal Ch. Home: 2027 Edgehill Dr San Antonio TX 78209-2023 Office: Sunshine Cottage Sch for Deaf 103 Tuleta Dr San Antonio TX 78212-3176

GARNER, JOYCE CRAIG, artist; b. Covington, Ky., Dec. 4, 1947; d. William Fayette and Mildred Ollie (Hodge) Craig; m. Gordon Reed Garner, Aug. 19, 1967; children: Angie Reed, Craig Charles, Scott William, Will Michael. BS, U. Ky., 1968. One-woman shows include Ctrl. Bank Gallery, Lexington, 1988, 91, Yvonne Rapp Gallery, Louisville, 1989, 91, 93, 94, Bluegrass Airport Gallery, Lexington, 1991, Headley-Whitney Mus., Lexington, 1992, Malton Gallery, Cin., 1994, Jewish Cmty. Ctr., Louisville, 1995, Hot House Gallery, Indpls., 1996; group exhibits include Three Rivers Arts Festival, Pitts., 1995, Turman Gallery Ind. State U., Terre Haute, 1995, 96, Louisville Visual Art Assn., 1995, 96, Indiana (Pa.) U., 1995, 96, Indpls. Art Ctr., 1995, 96, Carnegie Art Ctr., Covington, Ky., 1995, 96, Midwest Mus. Am. Art, Elkhart, Ind., 1995, 96, many others; represented in permanent collections Grand Ctrl. Office Bldg., St. Louis, U. Hosp., Cin., St. Luke's Hosp., Newport, Ky., Assn. Met. Sewage Agys., Washington, C.P.I. Corp., St. Louis, KAISER, Atlanta, Ctrl. Bank, Lexington, Balke Properties, St. Louis, Brown & Williamson, Louisville, others; art in embassies program U.S. Mission to European Cmtys., Brussels. Resident fellow Hambidge Ctr., 1994. Unitarian-Universalist. Home: 7300 Happy Hollow Ln Prospect KY 40059

GARNER, JULIE LOWREY, occupational therapist; b. Paris, Tex., Aug. 6, 1953; d. John Robert and Rachel (Garner) Lowrey; m. Kenneth Wayne Garner, Jan. 29, 1983. BS, U. Tex., Galveston, 1975; MS, Tex. Woman's U., 1982. Cert. occupational therapist, Tex.; cert. to administer and interpret So. Calif. Sensory Integration Tests Sensory Integration Internat., neurodevel. treatment approach to cerebral palsy. Occupational therapist Presbyn. Hosp. Dallas, 1976-77; occupational therapist region X Ednl. Svc. Ctr., Richardson, Tex., 1977; occupational therapist Duncanville (Tex.) Ind. Sch. Dist., 1977-81, 89-90, Grand Prairie (Tex.) Ind. Sch. Dist., 1978-81, U. Tex., Dallas, 1981-83, Lewisville (Tex.) Ind. Sch. Dist., 1983-85, Collin County Coop. Spl. Svcs., Wylie, Tex., 1983-89, Commerce (Tex.) Ind. Sch. Dist., 1990—. Bd. dirs. United Cerebral Palsy Assn. Dallas, 1980-84. Recipient Hurdle Cert. of Honor Soroptimist Internat., Dallas, 1976. Mem. Am. Occupational Therapy Assn., Sensory Integration Internat. Methodist. Home: 1313 Flameleaf Dr Allen TX 75002-4424

GARNER, MILDRED MAXINE, retired religious studies educator; b. nr. Liberty, N.C., Mar. 15, 1919; d. Robert Monroe and Maize (Kimrey) G. B.A., U. N.C., Greensboro, 1939; M.A., Union Theol. Sem., N.Y.C., 1946; Ph.D., U. Aberdeen, Scotland, 1952. Tchr. English, history, journalism Roanoke Rapids, N.C., 1939, 41-42; asst. editor Bibl. Recorder, Raleigh, N.C., 1940; dir. religious activities Woman's Coll., U. N.C. at Greensboro, 1942-50; assoc. prof. religion Meredith Coll., Raleigh, 1952-58; prof. religion Sweet Briar (Va.) Coll., 1958—, Wallace Eugene Rollins prof. religion, 1969-84, prof. emeritus, 1984—, chmn. dept., 1961-62, 63-72, 74-78, 81-84; fellow summer seminar history and culture India U. Va., 1964, summer seminar history and culture China, 1965; summer seminar South Asia Duke U., 1966, summer seminar Banaras Hindu U., Varanasi, India, 1977; Fulbright scholar U. Aberdeen, 1950-51, 51-52; program advanced religious studies fellow Union Theol. Sem., 1955-56; Am. Inst. Indian Studies fellow, Poona, India, 1962-63, Inst. Judaism, Vanderbilt Div. Sch., Nashville, 1979; deacon Pullen Meml. Bapt. Ch., Raleigh, 1952-58. Author: First Baptist Church, Liberty, North Carolina, 1886-1986, 1986. Trustee 1st Bapt. Ch., Liberty, 1991-96, Chatham Hosp., Siler City, N.C., 1992-94, Liberty Pub. Libr., 1996-99; chmn. adv. com. Liberty Sr. Adults Assn., 1993—; grand marshal Holiday Parade, Liberty, 1991. Mem. Fulbright Alumni Assn., Phi Beta Kappa. Republican. Baptist. Lodge: Rotary (hon. Liberty chpt.). Home: PO Box 427 Liberty NC 27298-0427

GARNER, SHARON RENE, management professional; b. Mpls., Mar. 28, 1959; d. Floyd Brewer and Florence Gertrude (Colver) Mims; m. Tommy Ray Garner, Mar. 9, 1979; children: Tommy Ray II, Katie Marie. AS in Data Processing, John C. Calhoun Jr. Coll., 1979; BBA in Acctg., Athens State Coll., 1996. Mgr. Dairy Queen, Russellville, Ala., 1980-83; asst. mgr. Dairy Queen, Athens, Ala., 1983-95; ins. clk. Emm Dee Drug Co., Athens, 1995; acctg. clk. Valley Mgmt., Inc., Decatur, Ala., 1995-96; project mgr. asst. Valley Mgmt., Inc., Decatur, 1996—. Leader, asst. cub master Boy Scouts Am., Cotaco, Ala., 1991-94; treas. Youth Alliance Bowling Assn., Decatur, 1988-95; mem. Cotaco (Ala.) Comty. League, 1988—. Mem. Inst. Mgmt. Accts. (spl. events coord. 1995-96). Methodist. Office: Valley Mgmt Inc Rt 2 Box 33 Hwy 67 Decatur AL 35603

GARNER, WILLA YOST, pesticide toxicologist; b. Washington, Aug. 14, 1936; d. Willard Henry and Myrtle Estelle (Yost) G.; children: K. Gregory, Carla Renee O'Gwin. AA, Montgomery Coll., Rockville, Md., 1968; BS, U. Md., 1970, MS, 1972, PhD, 1979. Clk. CIA, Washington, 1956-58; grants mgmt. officer NIH, Bethesda, Md., 1958-68; chemist, product mgr., sect. chief U.S. EPA, Washington, 1974-82, br. chief health effects br., 1982-84, sr. chemist, 1984-89; pres. GARNDAL Assocs., Inc., Monument, Colo., 1990—; cons. Garndal Assocs., Inc., Monument, Colo., 1989—. Author, co-editor: Good Laboratory Practices, 1988, Good Laboratory Practice Standards, 1992. Fellow Am. Chem. Soc. (treas. divsn. agrochem. 1984-88, vice chmn. 1988, chmn.-elect 1989, chmn. 1990, councilor 1995—), Soc. Quality Assurance, Soc. Environ. Toxicology and Chemistry, Sigma Xi, Phi Kappa Phi. Democrat.

GARNETT, LINDA KOPEC, nurse, researcher; b. Springfield, Mass.; d. Frank J. and Anna (Paul) Kopec; m. Thomas R. Garnett, Oct. 6, 1990. BS in Nursing cum laude, Fitchburg (Mass.) State Coll., 1983; MS in Health Svcs. Adminstrn., Ctrl. Mich. U., 1996. RN. Nurse intern Med. Coll. Va. Hosps., Richmond, nurse clinician in neurosci. ICU; terr. mgr., patient care specialist Kinetic Concepts Therapeutic Svcs., Richmond; rsch. coord. dept. neurology Med. Coll. Va./Va. Commonwealth U., Richmond. Mem. Sigma Theta Tau.

GARNICK, DIANE M., accountant; b. Bellmore, N.Y., Jan. 19, 1967; d. Donald and Gwen (Cotter) Burbach; m. Joe Garnick, Aug. 26, 1989; children: Michelle, Amanda. BBA, Hofstra U., 1996; AS, Suffolk C.C., 1994. With comml. lending dept. Anchor Savs., Hewlett, N.Y., 1987-92; intern UN, N.Y.C., 1994; with tax compliance dept. Ernst & Young, LLP, N.Y.C., 1994-95; with global securities dept. J.P. Morgan, N.Y.C., 1995-96; with Deloitte and Touche LLP, N.Y.C., 1996—. Author: Socioeconomic Impact of Lending into Russia, 1996. Vol. Com. to Elect Frank Petrone, Huntington, N.Y., 1993; active Rep. Club Hofstra U., 1994-96; mem. bd. scholarship com. SUNY, N.Y.C., 1992—. John Astor Meml. scholar, 1992; recognized for outstanding performance Fin. Women Internat., 1995, Acad. Achievement USA Today, 1993. Mem. Inst. Mgmt. Accts. (pres. 1994—), Fin. Mgmt. Assn., Beta Gamma Sigma, Phi Theta Kappa. Home: 25 North Ln Huntington NY 11743 Office: Deloitte and Touche LLP 2 World Fin Ctr New York NY 10281

GAROFALO, JANEANE, actress, comedienne; b. 1965. BA in History and Am. Studies, Providence Coll. TV appearances include The Ben Stiller Show, 1992-93, The Larry Sanders Show, 1992—, Saturday Night Live, 1994-95, Comedy Product, 1995, emcee, prodr., (movies) Late for Dinner, 1991, Armistead Maupin's Tales of the City, 1993, Reality Bites, 1994, Bye Bye Love, 1995, Cold Blooded, 1995, The Truth about Cats and Dogs, 1996. Office: care Messina Baker Entertainment 955 S Carillo Ste 100 Los Angeles CA 90048*

GARONZIK, SARA ELLEN, stage director; b. Phila., Jan. 12, 1951; d. Milton and Bernice (Kohn) G. BA in Spanish cum laude, Temple U., 1972. Producing artistic dir. The Phila. Theatre Co., 1982—. Bd. dirs. Greater Phila. Cultural Alliance, Artreach, Citizens for the Arts in Pa. and Artspace. Recipient prize Sigma Delta Pi, 1972. Office: Phila Theatre Co The Belgravia-Ste 300 1811 Chestnut St Philadelphia PA 19103

GARR, CHERYL DENISE, research chemist; b. Idaho Falls, Idaho, May 2, 1960; d. Jerry Lee and Jane Ellen (Wise) Gross; m. Westley Dean Garr, June 27, 1987; children: Taylor Kristen, Jamie Lynn. BS in Chemistry, Evergreen State Coll., Olympia, Wash., 1986; PhD in Chemistry, U. Oreg., 1992. Postdoctoral fellow Panlabs Inc., Bothell, Wash., 1992, scientist, 1992—, group leader, 1995-96, project mgr. synthetic and combinatorial chemistry, 1996—. Contbr. articles to Jour. Am. Chem. Soc., Jour. Inorganic Chemistry, Bio-organic Med. Chemistry, Jour. Biomolecular Screening. Mem. Am. Chem. Soc., Soc. for Biomolecular Screening, SIM. Home: 22717 NE 195th St Woodinville WA 98072-7538 Office: Panlabs Inc 11804 N Creek Pky S Bothell WA 98011-8805

GARR, TERI (ANN), actress; b. Lakewood, Ohio, 1952; m. John O'Neil, Nov. 1993; 1 adopted child, Molly. Began career as dancer performing with San Francisco Ballet at age 13; in original road show co. of West Side Story; stage appearences include One Crack Out, 1978, Broadway, 1978, Ladyhouse Blues, 1979, Night of 100 Stars II, 1985; appeared in films including Viva Las Vegas, Head, 1968, Maryjane, 1968, Moonshine War, 1970, The Conversation, 1974, Young Frankenstein, 1974, Won Ton Ton, The Dog Who Saved Hollywood, 1976, Oh God!, 1977, Close Encounters of the Third Kind, 1977, Mr. Mike's Mondo Video, 1979, The Black Stallion, 1979, Honky Tonk Freeway, 1981, The Escape Artist, 1982, Tootsie, 1982, One From the Heart, 1982, The Sting II, 1983, The Black Stallion Returns, 1983, Mr. Mom, 1983, Firstborn, 1984, After Hours, 1985, Miracles, 1987, Out Cold, 1988, Let It Ride, 1989, Short Time, 1990, Waiting for the Light, 1990, Mom and Dad Save the World, 1992, Dumb and Dumber, 1995; TV movies include Doctor Franken, 1980, Prime Suspect, 1982, The Winter of Our Discontent, 1983, To Catch a King, 1984, Intimate Strangers, 1986, Fresno, 1986, Pack of Lies, 1987, Teri Garr in FlapJack Floozie, 1988, Drive, She Said (Trying Times), 1987, Mother Goose Rock n Rhyme, Stranger in the Family, 1991, Deliver Them From Evil: The Taking of Alta View, 1992, Fugitive Nights: Danger in the Desert, 1993; regular on TV series The Sonny and Cher Comedy Review, 1974, Good and Evil, 1991, Good Advice, 1994, Duckman, 1994, The Women of the House, 1995; other TV appearances include Law and Order, 1976, Fresno, Late Night with David Letterman, The Frog Prince, Tales from the Crypt. Office: care Brillstein/Grey 9150 Wilshire Blvd Ste 350 Beverly Hills CA 90212-3430*

GARRARD, MIMI, choreograper, director dance company; b. Gastonia, N.C., Mar. 16, 1936; d. James Moseley Garrard and Ethel Castor (Keesler) Garrard Duncan; m. James Lemuel Seawright, June 22, 1960; 1 child, Andrew. BA, Sweet Briar Coll., 1958; cert. in tchg., choreography-performance, Henry Street Playhouse, N.Y.C., 1963. Performer Murray Louis Dance Co., N.Y.C., 1962-64, Alwin Nikolais Dance Co., N.Y.C., 1961-65; performer Mimi Garrard Dance Co., Inc., N.Y.C., 1965-91, dir., 1965—; instr. Henry Street Playhouse, 1962-69, Columbia U. Tchrs. Coll., 1978-85, Radford U., 1987, 88, Dalcroze Sch. Music, 1981-93; condr. periodic workshops Mimi Garrard Dance Studio, 1969—; tchr. master classes throughout u.S. Mimi Garrard Dance Theatre, 1971—. Contbr. articles to profl. jours.; choreographer numerous dances, 1962—, latest being Walking on Gravel, Moving Toward Two, Reflection, 1990, Sincopes, Pedacito de Tiempo, 1991, Otello, 1991, 1991, Metrick One, Metrick Two, 1992, Oasis, On A Time, 1993, The Other Side of a Coin, 1994, Renderings, Potpourri, 1995, Tripartita, Agua and Fuego, Hoodoo Zephyr, Romanze, 1996; designer costumes, sets and lighting for her choreography; prodr. (with James Seawright) Medium Is the Medium, Sta. WGBH, nat. ednl. TV, Boston, 1968, Boston Symphony Experiment, 1972, Enigma of Scriabin, CBS Camera Three, 1970;. Mem. DTW. Home and Studio: 155 Wooster St New York NY 10012

GARREN, CHRISTINE ELIZABETH, author, educator; b. Phila., Dec. 15, 1957; d. William MacElreath and Marjorie Faye (Sanders) Branham; m. Samuel Baity Garren, May 24, 1980. BA, U. N.C., Greensboro, 1987, MFA, 1990. Vis. writer in residence Guilford Coll., Greensboro, N.C., 1995. Author: Afterworld, 1993. Democrat. Mem. Soc. of Friends. Home: 1608 N College Park Dr Greensboro NC 27403

GARRETT, GLORIA SUSAN, social services professional; b. Tampa, Fla., Nov. 30, 1951; d. Howard Leon and Marie Leonora (Garcia) G.; m. Michael Thomas McClain, May 16, 1973; children: Molly Kathleen Garrett McClain, Andrew Michael Garrett McClain. Student, Agnes Scott Coll., 1969-71, U. South Fla., 1971-72; BA, Ga. State U., 1977, MEd, 1979. Sr. caseworker DeKalb County Dept. Family and Children Services, Decatur, Ga., 1979-80, 82-84, prin. caseworker, 1980-82, 84-85, casework supr., 1985-86, sr. casework supr., 1986-91; disability adjudicator Ga. Disability Adjudication Sect., Decatur, 1991-93, sr. disability adjudicator, 1993-94, case cons., 1994-96, disability adjudication casework supr., 1996—. Mem. Nat. Assn. Disability Examiners, Ga. Assn. Disability Examiners. Office: Disability Adjudication PO Box 1187 Decatur GA 30031-1187

GARRETT, JILL HOPE, broadcast journalist; b. N.Y.C., Aug. 7, 1954; d. Carlton Ray and Mary Hope (Jackson) G. Grad. high sch., Wilkes-Barre, Pa., 1972. Clk.-stenographer EEOC, Washington, 1973; ministry, 1974-76; sec. prodn. asst. Sta. WBAX Radio, Edwardsville, Pa., 1976-77; photographer, reporter Sta. KJAC-TV, Port Arthur, Tex., 1977-79; news producer Sta. WVIA-TV, Pittston, Pa., 1979-80; reporter Sta. WNYT-TV, Albany, N.Y., 1980-83; morning anchor/reporter Sta. WCPO-TV, Cin., 1983-90; anchor, producer Sta. WNEP-TV, Scranton, Pa., 1990—. Former vol. Cin. Zoo. Home: 438 S River St Wilkes Barre PA 18702-3725 Office: Sta WNEP TV 16 Montage Mountain Rd Scranton PA 18507-1753

GARRETT, KAREN A., auditor, financial analyst; b. Little Rock, Ark., May 25; d. Eugene C. Gideon; m. Wesley L. Garrett, June 5. BBA, U. Ctrl. Ark., 1990. CPA, Ark.; CMA. Staff acct. Thomas and Thomas CPA's, Little Rock, 1990-93; sr. auditor Engstrom, Grayson and Green CPA's, North Little Rock, 1993-96, St. Vincent Infirmary Med. Ctr., Little Rock, 1996—. Assoc. adviser AIA Explorer Post, Little Rock, 1996; tchr. Liberty Missionary Bapt. Ch., Little Rock, 1993—. Mem. Am. Soc. Women Accts. (Ctrl. Ark. chpt. pres. 1994-96, treas. 1993-94), AICPA, Inst. Mgmt. Accts. (treas. 1996-97), Ark. Soc. CPAs. Office: St Vincent Infirmary Med Ctr #2 St Vincent Circle Little Rock AR 72205

GARRETT, KATHRYN ANN (KITTY GARRETT), legislative clerk; b. Antlers, Okla., July 10, 1930; d. Stansell Harper and Vena Clifford (Crawford) Byers; m. William Donald Garrett, Jan. 13, 1955 (dec. June 1992); children: William Mark, Amy Kathryn, Ann Elizabeth Garrett Jenni. Student, Okla. A&M U., 1948-50. Sec. Garform Industries, Wagoner, Okla., 1951-52; sec. to exec. sec. Okla. Edn. Assn., Oklahoma City, 1952-55; sec. revenue and taxation com. Ho. Reps., State of Okla., Oklahoma City, 1969-76, bill clk./ins. clk., 1976-84, asst. chief clk./jour. clk., 1985-93; ret., 1994. Mem. Am. Soc. Legis. Clks. and Secs. (assoc.), Okla. Heritage Assn., Sooner Book Club. Democrat. Home: 1429 Wilburn Dr Oklahoma City OK 73127-3253

GARRETT, LAURIE, science correspondent; b. L.A., Sept. 8, 1951; d. Banning and Lou Ann (Pierose) G. Grad. with honors, U. Calif., 1975, postgrad. With KPFA, Berkeley, Calif., Calif. Dept. Food and Agr.; freelance journalist So. Europe, E. Africa, 1979; freelance reporter, 1980-88; sci. corr. Newsday, N.Y.C., 1988—; vis. fellow Harvard Sch. Pub. Health, 1992-93. Author: The Coming Plague: Newly Emerging Diseases in a World Out of Balance, 1994; contbr. articles to periodicals including Omni, Washington Post, L.A. Times, Foreign Affairs, others; TV appearances include Dateline, McNeil/Lehrer Newshour, Nightline, others; contbr. reports including

Science Story (George Foster Peabody Broadcasting award 1977), Hard Rain: Pests, Pesticides, and People (Edwin Howard Armstrong Broadcast award 1978), The VDT Controversy (Nat. Press Club award Best Consumer Journalism 1982), Why Children Die in Africa (Media Alliance Meritorious Achievement award in Radio 1983, World Hunger Media award First Prize 1987), AIDS in Africa (J.C. Penney/Mo. Journalism Cert. Merit, award of Excellence Nat. Assn. Black Journalists Second Place, 1989), Breast Cancer (Best Beat Reporter Deadline Club N.Y. 1993, First Place N.Y. State AP Writing Contest Press Club L.I., Soc. Silurians 1994), AIDS in India (Bob Considine award Overseas Press Club Am. 1995), Ebola Virus Outbreak in Zaire (Pulitzer prize in Explanatory Journalism, 1996). Office: Newsday 235 Pinelawn Rd Melville NY 11747 also: care Charlotte Sheedy 65 Bleecker St New York NY 10012*

GARRETT, LINDA SILVERSTEIN, financial planner; b. Pitts., May 14, 1949; d. Maurice J. and Mary H. (Reagan) Silverstein; m. Mark B. Garrett, Apr. 1, 1978 (div. Aug. 1987). BS in Social Work, W.Va. U., 1972. CFP, Fla.; registered rep. N.Y. Stock Exch., Nat. Assn. Securities Dealers. Group worker, dir. Miami Jewish Home & Hosp. for the Aged, 1976-80, registered rep., 1980-84; rsch. asst. Prescott, Ball & Turben, North Miami, Fla., 1980-84; acct. exec. Prudential Securities, Ft. Lauderdale, Fla., 1984-88; v.p. Morgan Keegan, Ft. Lauderdale, 1988-89; fin. cons. Merrill Lynch, Ft. Lauderdale, 1989-94; v.p. Dean Witter, Plantation, Fla., 1994—. Instr., lectr. Assn. Women CPA, Ft. Lauderdale, 1985; cons. Jr. Achievement, Broward County, Fla., 1993; counselor Switchboard Miami, 1976-80; active Archdiocese Miami Planned Giving Coun. 1988-90, lectr. 1988-89; mem. exec. com. profl. adv. coun. Found. Jewish Philanthropies, 1995—, Gwen Cherry chpt. Women's Political Caucus, 1995—. Mem. Internat. Assn. Fin. Planners, Nat. Coun. Aging. Democrat. Jewish. Home: 544 NE 17th Way Fort Lauderdale FL 33301-1352 Office: Dean Witter Reynolds Cornerstone 1 1200 S Pine Island Rd # Rp Plantation FL 33324-4413

GARRETT, NANCY ELIZABETH ROBERTS, editor; b. Terre Haute, Ind., Dec. 5, 1954; d. Jack Richford and Anne Marie (Dennison) Roberts; m. William H. Garrett Jr., Jan. 2, 1978 (div. Sept. 1986). BS in Journalism cum laude, Ind. State U., 1977. Sports reporter Terre Haute Tribune-Star, 1975-76; sports reporter Paris (Ill.) Daily Beacon-News, 1977-80, reporter, photographer, 1981-85, mng. editor, 1985—; editor Marshall (Ill.) Independent, 1980-81; corr. Sta. WTWO-TV, Terre Haute, 1978-89; media adviser State Sen. Harry Woodyard, Chrisman, Ill., 1983-89; advt. cons. Rep. William Black, Danville, Ill., 1986-88. Author, editor Series Clark County Park Dist., 1980-81 (2d pl. award Ill. Press Assn.). Deacon Paris Presbyn. Ch., 1982, elder, 1985-92; commr. to 202d gen. assy. United Presbyn. Ch., 1990; co-chmn. Bicentennial Fund, Presbyn. of Southeastern Ill., 1990—; mgr. Paris Youth Ctr., 1981-86; pres. Edgar County Young Rep., Paris, 1987-89; dir. Cmty. Concert Assn.; cheer coord. Mayo Mid. Sch., 1987-88; drama dir. Paris High Sch., 1987—, cheerleading coord., 1989-92; Rep. precinct committeeman, 1990-92; founding dir. Paris Summer Theater Co., 1992; dir. Edgar County Fair Queen Pageant, 1992-94, asst. dir. May Fete, 1993—; mem editl. bd. Ins. State U.; host "Stage Door" Sta. WPRS, WACF. Mem. Assn. Soc. Profl. Journalists, Ind. State U. Nat. Alumni Coun., Ill. Pageant Dirs. Assn., Sigma Delta Chi. Presbyterian. Home: 406 S Central Ave Paris IL 61944-2107 Office: Paris Daily Beacon-News North Main St North Main St Paris IL 61944

GARRETT, NANCY LEE, government agency administrator; b. Indpls., Jan. 4, 1945; d. Floyd and Myrtle Marie (Leffew) Feasel; m. Henry James Brucker, Jr., Mar. 26, 1966 (div. Apr. 1988); children: Ryan Todd, Kristen Kathleen; m. Raymond Anthony Garrett, Oct. 19, 1991; 1 child, Kevin Anthony. AS, U. Wis., Stevens Point, 1982; BS, Univ. State of N.Y., Albany, 1991; postgrad., Ball State U., 1993—. Owner, v.p. Best Way Maintenance Corp., Highland, Ind., 1976-78; owner, operator Seven Oaks Farm, Plover, Wis., 1981-84; marketer Sentry Ins. Hdqtrs., Stevens Point, 1984-86; journalist Oneida County News - Review/Three Lakes News, Eagle River, Wis., 1987; educator/asst. educator Wayne Twp. Schs., Inpls., 1990; phys. security specialist U.S. Fed. Protective Svc., Indpls. and Chgo., 1991-96; dep. dist. dir. U.S. Fed. Protective Svc., Indpls., 1996—. Editor/writer: (news periodical) FPS Vigil, 1991-94. Mem. NAFE, Fed. Exec. Assn. (Indpls.), Am. Soc. Indsl. Security. Roman Catholic. Office: US Federal Protective Svc 693 Minton-Capehart Fed Bdg 575 N Pennsylvania St Indianapolis IN 46204

GARRETT, SANDY LANGLEY, school system administrator; b. Muskogee, Okla., Feb. 8, 1943; 1 child, Charles Langley (Chuck). BS in Elem. Edn., Northeastern U., Tahlequah, Okla., 1968, MS in Counseling, 1980; grad. John F. Kennedy Sch. Govt., Harvard U., 1989. Lic. tchr., adminstr., supt. std., Okla. Tchr. Hillsdale Schs., Muskogee, Okla., 1968-80, coord. gifted program, 1980-82; coord. gifted and talented State Dept. Edn., Oklahoma City, 1982-85, dir. rural edn., 1985-87, exec. dir. ednl. svcs., 1987-88, state supt., 1991—; sec. edn. Gov.'s Office, Oklahoma City, 1988—; chair State Bd. Edn., Oklahoma City, 1991—, State Vo-Tech. Edn., Oklahoma City, 1991—; bd. dirs. So. Regional Edn. Bd.; regent Okla. Colls., 1991—; mem. Nat. Coll. Bd. Equality Project; chair. Okla. Lit. Initiatives Commn.; mem. So. Regional Edn. Bd. Co-author: (curriculum guide) Gifted Galaxy; mem. editorial bd. Rural and Small Schs.; contbr. articles to profl. jours. Co-chair Dem. Party, Muskogee, 1978; del. Dem. Nat. Conv., N.Y.C., 1980, 82; mem. Leadership Okla., 1990. Recipient Cecil Yarbrough award, 1989, Claude Dyer Legis. award, 1989. Mem. Muskogee County Ednl. Assn., Delta Kappa Gamma, Phi Delta Kappa, Delta Kappa Gamma. Methodist. Home: Apt 2410 11300 N Pennsylvania Ave Oklahoma City OK 73120-7776 Office: State Dept Edn 2500 N Lincoln Blvd Oklahoma City OK 73105-4503*

GARRETT, SHIRLEY GENE, nuclear medicine technologist; b. Evanston, Ill., Apr. 19, 1944; d. Nathan and Emma Louise (Uecker) G. AA, Oakton C.C., 1977; AS in Nuc. Medicine, Triton Coll., 1980; BA, Northea. Ill. U., 1983; MA, Govs. State U., University Park, Ill., 1985. Cert. nuclear medicine technologist. Nuc. medicine technologist Chgo. Osteo. Hosp., 1980-88, Little Co. of Mary Hosp., Evergreen Park, Ill., 1989; nuclear medicine technologist Lutheran Gen. Hosp., Lincoln Park, Ill., 1989; nuc. medicine technologist Mt. Sinai Hosp., Chgo., 1990-92; technologist nuc. medicine Swedish Covenant Hosp., Chgo., 1992-93; pres. Providence Hosp. of Cook County, Chgo., 1994—. Contbr. articles to profl. jours. Vol. Ravenswood Hosp., Chgo., 1986—, Mt. Sinai Hosp., 1990-92, Congl. Health Ministry, Ch. of St. Lukes. Mem. Soc. Nuc. Medicine (mem. bylaws com. technologist sect. Ctrl. chpt. 1982-83, 85-86, 92—, mem. continuing edn. com. 1986-87, chmn. nominating com. 1987-88, 92-93, mem. edn. com. 1988-89, pres.-elect 1989-90, mem. bd. govs. 1990-92, pres. 1991-92, chmn. bylaws com. 1992-93), Assoc. and Tech. Affiliates Chgo. Area (coord. edn. 1981-84, mem. adv. bd. 1983-84, 87-88, pres. 1985-87, chmn. nominating com. 1987-89). Lutheran.

GARRETT, VIKKI RAE, transportation planner; b. Pensacola, Fla., Jan. 17, 1967; d. Edgar Ray and Patricia Ann (Lodge) G. AA, Pensacola Jr. Coll., 1987; BS, U. West Fla., 1990, postgrad., 1996—. Field acct. Contractor, Pensacola, 1991-92; transp. planner Fla. Dept. of Transp., Pensacola, 1992—; mem. Women's Transportation Seminar, Boston, 1995—. Home: 1411 E Lee St Pensacola FL 32503

GARRISON, ALTHEA, government official; b. Hahira, Ga., Oct. 7, 1940; d. Charles and Lenora Mae (Davis) G. AS, Newbury Jr. Coll., 1978; BS, Suffolk U., 1982; cert. in social studies, Harvard U., 1986; MS, Lesley Coll., 1984. Counselor, supr. Charlotte House Dorchester (Mass.), 1977-77; with EDP dept., sr. assessor Mass. Dept. Revenue, Boston, 1979-81; sr. examiner Office State Compt., Boston, 1982-90; human resource mgr. Office of State Comptr. Commonwealth of Mass., 1991—; state rep. gen. ct. 5th suffolk Rep. Dist., Mass., 1992-95; bd. dirs. Uphams Corner Health Ctr., Dorchester, 1983—, v.p., 1987—, Disting. Svc. award, 1991. Charter mem. adv. bd. Christian Record Braille, Lincoln, Neb., 1983; alumna coun. Lesley Coll. Grad. Sch., Cambridge, Mass., 1986-88; active Nat. Rep. Congl. Com., 1988—, Rep. Presdl. Task Force, 1989—, Met. Area Planning Coun., 1994; charter founder Ronald Reagan Rep. Ctr., Washington, 1989; nominee City Coun. Dorchester, 1989, State Rep. Rep. Primary, 1990; town com. woman Ward 13, Boston, 1992, commn. vice-chair, treas. city com., 1994—. Recipient Senator's citation Commonwealth Mass., 1982, Merit medal Rep. Task Force, 1989, Appreciation cert. Mass. Rep. Party, Outstanding Vol. award Suffolk U., 1991, Achievement cert. Conf. New Legislators, 1993, Rep. Leadership award, 1993-94, Book award Dearborn Middle Sch., 1994, Excellent Svc. award Holborn, Gannett, Gaston, Otisfield Betterment Assn., 1995; hon. fellow John F. Kennedy Libr., 1987-90; named One of 100 Women Making History North Shore Women's Coalition, Rep. Presdl. Legion of Merit Honor Roll, 1993. Mem. Am. Mgmt. Assn., Nat. Assn. Govt. Employees (negotiator, organizer 1979-81), Suffolk U. Gen. Alumni Assn. (bd. dirs. 1986-89), Heritage Found., Nat. Found. Cancer Rsch. (hon., citation 1991), DAV Comdrs. Roman Catholic. Home: 18 Jerome St Apt 2 Dorchester MA 02125-2021

GARRISON, BETTY BERNHARDT, retired mathematics educator; b. Danbury, Ohio, July 1, 1932; d. Philip Arthur and Reva Esther (Meter) Bernhardt; m. Robert Edward Kvarda, Sept. 28, 1957 (div. 1964); m. John Dresser Garrison, Jan. 17, 1968; 1 child, John Christopher. BA, BS, Bowling Green State U., 1954; MA, Ohio State U., 1956; PhD, Oreg. State U., 1962. Teaching asst. Ohio State U., Columbus, 1954-56; instr. Ohio U., Athens, 1956-57, San Diego State Coll., 1957-59; teaching asst. Oreg. State U., Corvallis, 1959-62; asst. prof. San Diego State U., 1962-66, assoc. prof., 1966-69, prof., 1969-96. Reviewer of articles and books, 1966—; contbr. articles to profl. jours. NSF fellow, 1960-61, 61-62. Mem. Am. Math. Soc., Math. Assn. Am. Home: 5607 Yerba Anita Dr San Diego CA 92115-1027

GARRISON, F. ELAINE, copy editor; b. Trenton, Mo., Jan. 16, 1957; d. Eugene and Arlene (Elliott) G. AA, Trenton Jr. Coll., 1976; B in Mass Comm., Ctrl. Mo. State U., 1978. Features editor Daily Dunkin Democrat, Kennett, Mo., 1981-89; agriculture editor Daily Am. Republic, Poplar Bluff, Mo., 1989-90; news editor News Guardian, Cape Girardeau, Mo., 1990; state editor Mo. Agri-News, Columbia, 1990-91; news editor, features editor, copy desk chief Sedalia (Mo.) Democrat, 1991—. Bd. dirs. Mo. Bootheel Humane Soc., Kennett, 1980-86, pres., 1987. Mem. Tiger's Lair Feline Fanciers (bd. dirs. 1994-95, 95-96). Methodist. Office: Sedalia Democrat 700 S Massachu Sedalia MO 65301

GARRISON, TRACY MICHELLE, educational organization official; b. Tuskegee, Ala., Dec. 27, 1966; d. James Lemuel Jr. and Nancy Regina (Hooten) G. BS in Secondary Edn., U. Tex., 1988, MA in U.S. History, 1990. Cert. tchr., Tex. Tchr. world geography Johnston H.S., Austin (Tex.) Ind. Sch. Dist., 1990-93, tchr. advanced placement U.S. history, 1993-95; program assoc. Facing History and Ourselves, Inc., Brookline, Mass., 1995—; instr. U.S. history Austin C.V., 1992-95; cons. AP U.S. history S.W. region Coll. Bd., Austin, 1994-95. Music coord. Univ. Cath. Ctr., Austin, 1988-95. Mem. Phi Delta Kappa. Democrat. Home: 3 Englewood Ave Brookline MA 02146 Office: Facing History and Ourselves Nat Found 16 Hurd Rd Brookline MA 02146

GARRISON, WANDA BROWN, environmental consultant; b. Madison County, N.C., Sept. 16, 1936; d. Roy Lee Brown and Zella Arizona (Miller) Brown Hannah; m. Charles Mitchell Garrison, July 9, 1955; children—Roy Lee, Marsha Joan; 1 step-son, Charles Mitchell, Jr. Student air-line hostess Weaver Airlines, St. Louis, 1954-55; student Haywood Tech. Coll., Clyde, N.C., 1967-68; student IBM, Asheville, N.C., 1977; student in data processing Agy. Record Control, Atlanta, 1978. Operator Day Co., Waynesville, N.C., 1954-57; driver Haywood County Schs., Waynesville, 1970-71; operator Am. Enka, N.C., 1972-75; bookkeeper L. N. Davis Ins. Co., Waynesville, 1975-80; stock preparation Champion Internat., Canton, N.C., 1980-89; cons. Garrison and Assocs. Environ. Solutions, Pensacola, Fla. Sec./treas. James Chapel Baptist Ch., Haywood County, N.C., 1965-77; pres. Fire Dept. Aux., Crabtree, N.C., 1973—; pres. Women Mission Union, Crabtree Bapt. Ch., Haywood County, 1977-80; v.p. Gideon Aux., Haywood County, 1982-84, pres., 1984-87; state aux. follow-up rep., 1984-87, state zone leader, 1987-88. Recipient Life Saving plaque Lion's Club, Waynesville, 1972. Mem. AFL-CIO. Republican. Home: 513 S 2nd St Pensacola FL 32507-3313

GARRISON-FINDERUP, IVADELLE DALTON, writer; b. San Pedro, Calif., Oct. 4, 1915; d. William Douglas and Olive May (Covington) Dalton; m. Fred Marion Garrison, Aug. 8, 1932 (dec. Nov. 1984); children: Douglas Lee, Vernon Russell, Nancy Jane; m. Elmer Pedersen Finderup, Apr. 8, 1994. BA, Calif. State U., Fresno, 1964; postgrad., U. Oreg., 1965, U. San Francisco, 1968. Cert. secondary tchr., Calif. Tchr. Tranquillity (Calif.) High Sch., 1964-78, West Hills Coll., Coalinga, Calif., 1970-74; lectr. in field. Author: Roots and Branches of Our Garrison Family Tree, 1988, Roots and Branches of Our Dalton Family Tree, 1989, The History of James' Fresno Ranch, 1990, 3d edit., 1993, There is a Peacock on the Roof, 1993, (with Vernon R.) William Douglas Dalton, a Biography, 1995. Mem. DAR (sec.), Archaeology Inst. Am., Frazier Clan N.Am., Fresno City and County Hist. Soc. (life), Fresno Archaeology Soc. (sec.), Children of the Am. Revolution (sr. pres.), Westerners Internat., Fresno Gem and Mineral Soc., Thora # 11 Dannebrog, Friends of the Libr. Republican. Lutheran. Office: Garrison Libr 3427 Circle Ct E Fresno CA 93703-2403

GARRITY, CHERYL LYNNE, lawyer, political activist; b. Pittsfield, Mass., Dec. 9, 1965; d. Charles Andrews and Mary Patricia (O'Brien) G. BS in Polit. Sci., U. Mass., 1988; JD, Northeastern U., 1991. Bar: Mass. 1991. Legal intern Arthur & Jaworski, Reading, Mass., 1989, Bd. Bar Overseers, Boston, 1989, Ronan Segal & Harrington, Salem, Mass., 1990, Greater Boston Legal Svcs., 1990; atty. Ronan, Segal & Harrington, Boston, 1992-93; ind. contractor Mass., 1993-94; pvt. practice Boston, 1994—; lobbyist NOW, Boston, 1992-95. Bd. dirs. Women's Statewide Legis. Network, Boston, 1993-95; mem. Domestic Violence Coun., Boston, 1992—, Malden (Mass.) Charter Commn., 1994-95, Coalition Ind. Madlen Schs., 1995. Named Woman Achiever New Eng. Sch. Law-Woman's Caucus, 1996. Mem. NOW (pres. 1994—), Nat. Lawyer's Guild, Malden Asian Pacific Am. Coalition. Office: NOW 971 Commonwealth Ave Boston MA 02215

GARRITY, CHERYL RUMLEY, counselor; b. Reidsville, N.C., Feb. 2, 1947; d. Abe Jones and Mary Miles (Snead) Rumley; m. William Joseph Garrity; children: Marnie Lynn, Angela Michelle, Michael Joseph. BA, U.N.C., 1969, MEd, 1981. Nat. cert. counselor; lic. profl. counselor, N.C.; cert. reality therapist. Migrant edn. counselor Madison-Mayodan City Schs., Madison, N.C., 1981-84, Western Rockingham City Schs., Madison, 1984-87; counselor Scott Elem. Sch., Madison, 1987-89, Dillard Primary Sch., Madison, 1989—. Vol. Hanging Rock State Park, Danbury, N.C., 1994-96; mem. Rockingham County Naturalists Club, Reidsville, N.C., 1995-96; mem. Sierra Club, Boulder, Colo. Mem. Am. Counseling Assn., N.C. Counseling Assn., Am. Sch. Counselor's Assn., N.C. Sch. Counselor's Assn. Office: Dillard Primary Sch 810 Cure Dr Madison NC 27025

GARROTT, FRANCES CAROLYN, architectural technician; b. Bowling Green, Ky., Mar. 10, 1932; d. Irby Reid and Carrie Mae (Stahl) Cameron; m. Leslie Othello Garrott, Oct. 12, 1951 (dec. Feb. 1978); children: Dennis Leslie, Alan Reid; adopted children: Carolyn Maria, Karen Roxana; m. Raymond William Scerbo, May 31, 1978 (div. Oct. 1990). Student Fla. State U., 1951, St. Petersburg Jr. Coll., 1962-74; grad. Pinellas Vocat. Tech. Inst., 1975. With Sears, Roebuck and Co., Rapid City, S.D., 1951-52, St. Petersburg, Fla., 1961-62; bookkeeper Ohio Nat. Bank, Columbus, 1953-54, Sunbeam Bakery, Lakeland, Fla., 1955-56; with Christies Toy Sales, Pennsauken, N.J., 1958-60; exec. sec. Gulf Coast Automotive Warehouse, Inc., Tampa, Fla., 1970-73, office mgr., 1975-78; sec., treas., chief pilot, co-owner Tech. Devel. Corp., St. Petersburg, Fla., 1970-78; freelance archtl. draftsman and designer, archtl. cons., constrn. materials estimator, 1975—, Fla. state judge Vocat. Indsl. Clubs of Am. Skills Olympics, 1986. Nat. Assn. Women in Constrn. scholar, 1974. Mem. Nat. Assn. Women in Constrn., Alpha Chi Omega. Democrat. Home and Office: 8156 Timberidge Loop W Lakeland FL 33809

GARROW, JANICE FAYE, music educator; b. St. Charles, Mo., Jan. 13, 1967; d. Charles Nicholas and Dorothy Frances (Burkemper) Vomund; m. Marshall Jay Garrow, Aug. 18, 1990; 1 child, Carly Rae. B of Music Edn., U. Mo., 1989; MA in Edn., Maryville U., 1994. Cert. vocal music educator, Mo. Instr. piano, organ Eberhardt Music, St. Charles, Mo., 1982-89; elem. music instr. Washington (Mo.) Sch. Dist., 1989—; organist Immaculate Heart of Mary Ch., New Melle, Mo., 1994—. Choir mem. Washington (Mo.) Civic Chorus, 1990-92. Mem. NEA, Mo. Nat. Edn. Assn., Mo. Music Educators Assn., Music Educators Nat. Conf. Office: South Point Elem Sch 2300 Southbend Dr Washington MO 63090-3719

GARSIDE, MARLENE ELIZABETH, advertising executive; b. Newark, Dec. 1, 1933; d. Abraham and Shirley (Janow) Carnow; BS in Commerce and Fin., Bucknell U., 1955; m. Stanley Kramer, Aug. 7, 1955 (dec. 1967); children: Deborah Frances, Elizabeth Anne; m. Martin Lutman, Aug. 27, 1969 (dec. 1981); m. Michael J. Weinstein, Apr. 9, 1983 (dec. 1984); m. Normand Garside, Apr. 5, 1986. Asst. rsch. dir. Modern Materials Handling Co., Boston, 1955-57; econ. analyst, project adminstr. United Rsch. Co., Cambridge, Mass., 1957-58; free lance tech. writer, econ. analyst, 1958-66; asst. mgr. survey planning and market rsch. IBM, White Plains, N.Y., 1967-69; mgr. rsch. svcs. McKinsey & Co., Cleve., 1969-72; former v.p., dir. Am. Custom Homes, former dir. Liberty Builders, Inc., Cleve.; owner, v.p., dir. Am. Custom Builders Inc., Cape Coral, Fla., 1978—; ptnr., dir. Star Realty Inc., Cape Coral, 1980—; account exec. Media Graphics, Inc., Naples, Fla., 1984; advt. mgr. Fox Electronics, Ft. Myers, Fla., 1984-86; v.p. Langdon Advt., Ft. Myers, 1987-88; asst. mgr. facility svcs. State of Fla. Dept. Health and Rehabilitative Svcs., Ft. Myers, 1988-90, facility svcs. mgr., 1990-92, gen. svcs. mgr., 1992—. Mem. Econ. and Indsl. Devel. Task Force, City of Cape Coral, 1979. Mem. Nat. Assn. Homebuilders, Bldg. Industry Assn., Constrn. Industry Assn., Nat. Bd. Realtors. Home: 1482 Sautern Dr Fort Myers FL 33919-2744 Office: State of Fla Dept Health Rehab Svcs 2295 Victoria Ave Fort Myers FL 33901-3884

GARVEY, ELLEN BRIDGET, airline pilot; b. Flushing, N.Y., July 6, 1956; d. Michael J. and Gisela H. (Hess) G.; (div.); children: Brandon Staples, Stephanie Staples. BA, SUNY, Albany, 1978. Cert. comml. pilot, instrument rating, flight engr., private pilot. Supr. ILT CBPO Hanscom AFB, Mass., 1980-81, supr. ILT Edn. Office, 1981-82; pilot N.H. Air Nat. Guard, Portsmouth, 1984-92; pilot Am. Airlines, N.Y.C., 1987-88, Boston, 1988—. Mentor York (Maine) Jr. H.S., 1994; vol. fundraiser Ronald McDonald House, Portland, Maine, 1994. Major USAF and Air Nat. Guard, 1979-92.

GARVEY, EVELYN JEWEL, retired mental health nurse; b. Carrizozo, N.Mex., Aug. 23, 1931; d. Everett E. and Jewel A. (Bullard) Bragg; m. Robert J. Garvey, July 10, 1949; children: Nancy, Annie, Catherine, Robert, Michael, Betty. AD, Ea. N.Mex. Coll., 1972. RN, N.Mex.; cert. EMT., N.Mex. Staff nurse N.Mex. Rehab. Ctr., Roswell, 1972; staff nurse Villa Solano State Sch., Roswell, 1972-79, DON, 1979-81; staff nurse Ft. Stanton (N.Mex.) Hosp., 1981-95, Sunset Villa Nursing Home, Roswell, N.Mex., 1995-96; ret., 1996.

GARVEY, JEANNE WOLTER, state legislator, realtor; b. Bridgeport, Conn., Jan. 13, 1939; d. Henry Adolph and Bertha Helen (Morazes) Wolter; m. Henry Hulton Garvey, Jr., Apr. 28, 1962; children: Henry Hulton, III, Kendra Garvey Owen, Colleen Elizabeth. Student, Western Conn. State U., Mattatuck C.C. Grad. Real Estate Inst. Rsch. lab. asst. Nestle Co., New Milford, Conn., 1957-63; realtor, apprisor DeVoe Realty Co., New Milford, 1976-93, Settlers and Traders Realtors, New Milford, 1993—; state rep. Conn. Legislature, Hartford, 1993—; mem. various coms. New Milford Bd. Realtors, 1976—, Conn. Bd. Realtors, Hartford, 1976—. mem., past. dir. New Milford Hist. Soc., 1971—; mem. New Milford Rep. Town Com., 1993—. Mem. Nat. Order Women Legislators, Nat. Assn. Realtors (various coms. 1976—). Roman Catholic. Office: Conn Legis Office Bldg Capital Ave Hartford CT 06106*

GARVEY, JOANNE MARIE, lawyer; b. Oakland, Calif., Apr. 23, 1935; d. James M. and Marian A. (Dean) G. A.B. with honors, U. Calif., Berkeley, 1956, M.A., 1957, J.D., 1961. Bar: Calif. bar 1962. Assoc. firm Cavaletto, Webster, Mullen & McCaughey, Santa Barbara, Calif., 1961-63, Jordan, Keeler & Seligman, San Francisco, 1963-67; ptnr. Jordan, Keeler & Seligman, 1968-88, Heller, Ehrman, White & McAuliffe, 1988—; bd. dirs. Mexican-Am. Legal Def. and Ednl. Fund; chmn. Law in a Free Soc., Continuing Edn. of Bar; mem. bd. councillors U. So. Calif. Law Center. Recipient Paul Veazy award YMCA, 1973, Internat. Women's Yr. award Queen's Bench, 1975, honors Advs. for Women, 1978, CRLA award. Fellow Am. Bar Found.; mem. ABA (state del., chmn. SCLAID, chmn. delivery of legal svcs.), Calif. State Bar (v.p., gov., tax sect., del., Jud Klein award, Joanne Garvey award), San Francisco Bar Assn. (pres., pres. Barristers), Am. Law Inst., Calif. Women Lawyers (founder), Order of Coif, Phi Beta Kappa. Democrat. Roman Catholic. Home: 16 Kensington Ct Kensington CA 94707-1010 Office: 333 Bush St San Francisco CA 94104-2806

GARVEY, KATHERINE HESTON, gerontology nurse; b. Galesburg, Ill., Dec. 28, 1944; d. Ernest Edwin and Eunice Corinne (Hollister) Heston; m. Edward Anthony Garvey, Nov. 25, 1967; children: Travler Franklin, Edward Anthony II, Anne Elizabeth, Michael Joseph, Thomas Heston. BS, U. Md., 1981; MA, John F. Kennedy U., 1993. RN, Calif. Staff nurse ICU Children's Meml. Hosp., Chgo., 1967-68; staff nurse pediatrics St. Joseph's Hosp., Chgo., 1968-70; staff nurse neonatal ICU Prentice Woman's Hosp., Chgo., 1970-73; staff nurse newborn nursery Anne Arundel Gen. Hosp., Annapolis, Md., 1974-82; advisor/counselor Group Health, Washington, 1982-83; patient/home care educator John Muir Med. Ctr., Walnut Creek, Calif., 1984-92; minimun data set coord. Jewish Home for Aged, San Francisco, 1992—. Youth educator St. John Vlanney Ch., Walnut Creek, 1985; vol. St. Anne's Crisis Nursery, Concord, Calif., 1993. Recipient Contbg. scholarship Contra Costa Alternative Sch., Orinda, Calif., 1988-93. Mem. AAUW (sec. 1985, 86, membership v.p. 1987, 88, program v.p. 1989, 90, ednl. found. v.p. 1995-96). Roman Catholic.

GARVIN, ANN BAKER, religious organization administrator, consultant; b. Topeka; 2 children. BA in Math. and Chemistry, Ky. State U.; MA in Math., Fisk U. Former tchr. math. high sch., 23 yrs; owner, dir. Midwest Bus. Cons., Topeka; nat. pres. Ch. Women United, N.Y.C., 1992-96. Bd. regents Washburn U., Topeka, 1981-92; bd. dirs. YWCA, YMCA, officer United Way; mem. bd. daycare ctr.; mem. N.E. Kans. Health Sys. Planning Agy.; steward St. John AME Ch., Topeka, regional and nat. leader Women's Missionary Soc.; Kans. bd. dirs. Ch. Women United, 1979-86, mem. nat. nominating com., 1986-92; pres. Women in Cmty. Svc., 1989-91, bd. dirs. Office: Ch Women in USA 475 Riverside Dr Rm 812 New York NY 10115-0050

GARVIN, GERALDINE MCKINLEY, retired psychology educator; b. Boyne City, Mich., Jan. 3, 1922; d. Donald A. and Isabel M. (Phillips) McKinley; m. James Hinkley Garvin; children: James H., Jr., Nancy Garvin Shor. BA with honors, Wellesley Coll., Wellesley, 1943; MEd, U. Del., Newark, 1962. Cert. tchr., Del. Historian war records project U.S. Govt., Washington, 1943-44; adminstr. U.S. Govt. Bermuda Base Command, Bermuda, 1945-46, Del. Preschool Assn., Wilmington, 1949-77; prof. psychology Widener U., Del., 1966-84. Editor: Delaware Women Remembered, 1977, S Legacy from Delaware Women, 1982. Jr. bd. Med Ctr. of Del., 1965—; mem. Foster Care Rev. Bd., apptd. by Gov. duPont, Del., 1977; bd. dirs. United Way, 1985-89; moderator Women of Westminster, 1990-92; deacon, 1993—, Westminster Presbyn. Ch.; pres. Mental Health Assn. Del., 1985-89. Mem. Lincoln Club, Del. World Affairs Coun., English-speaking Union (nat. bd. mem., chair Region III). Presbyterian. Home: 2302 Delaware Ave Wilmington DE 19806

GARVIN, JANE MARIE, marketing professional; b. Mankato, Minn., May 25, 1950; d. Neil T. and Yvonne G. (Foley) G. BS in Internat. Bus. Mgmt., S.W. State U., Marshall, Minn., 1990; Cert. in Internat. Trade Law and European Cmty. Law, Am. U., Paris, 1992. Mktg. cons. John Ryan & Co., Madrid, Spain, 1991-92; mktg. dir. The Rust Cons. Group, Mpls., 1992-95; v.p., gen. mgr. Datapower Internat., Inc., Mpls., 1995—. Mem. AAUW, Am. Mktg. Assn., Pi Gamma Mu. Office: Datapower Internat Inc 1450 Energy Park Dr Ste LLII Saint Paul MN 55108

GARWOOD, JULIE, author; b. 1946. Author: (historical romance novels) Gentle Warrior, 1985, Rebellious Desire, 1986, Honor's Splendor, 1987, The Lion's Lady, 1988, The Bride, 1989, Guardian Angel, 1990, The Gift, 1990, The Prize, 1991, The Secret, 1992, (novels for young adults), A Girl Named Summer, 1985 (Scholastic award), (as Emily Chase) What's A Girl to Do, 1985 (Scholastic award), Castles, 1993, Saving Grace, 1993, Prince Charming, 1994, For the Roses, 1995. Office: PO Box 7574 Leawood KS 66211*

GARWOOD-DAGGETT, CARLEEN MCCUISTION, animal breeder; b. Ft. Worth, Oct. 14, 1908; d. Noah and Elizabeth (Jordan) McCuistion; m. Floyd Ray Garwood, May 14, 1924 (dec.); 1 child, Robert Jordan; m. Walter M. Daggett, Apr. 15, 1965. BS, Tex. A&M U., 1981. Cert. med. record libr. Mem. Descs. of the Plantagenet Kings of Eng., Descs. of Charlemagne, Am. Royal Descent. Republican. Baptist.

GARY, HAZEL WILLAINE, oncological nurse; b. Pitts., June 13, 1949; d. Wilbert Dalton and Hazel Marion (Adams) T.; m. Luther Darnell Gary, May 17, 1975; children: Terri Lynn, Cassandra Marie, Ermus Age. LPN, Great Plain Votech., 1972; ASN, Allegheny C.C., 1979. RN, Ky. Nurse Meml. Hosp., Lawton, Okla., 1972-73; 3-11 charge nurse Montefiore Hosp., Pitts., 1979-80; 11-7 asst. nurse mgr. Southwest Jefferson Hosp., Louisville, Ky., 1983-84; RN IV therapy Hardin Meml. Hosp., Elizabethtown, Ky., 1986-92; staff nurse Lakeview Rehab. Hosp., Elizabethtown, Ky., 1987-89; head office nurse Elizabethtown Hematology-Oncology PC, Ky., 1992—. sec. Radcliff Softball Assn., 1983, Gold Vault Senate, 1993—. Mem. Oncology Nursing Soc. Jehovah Witness. Home: 2494 Lake Rd Radcliff KY 40160-9711

GARY, JULIA THOMAS, minister; b. Henderson, N.C., May 31, 1929; d. Richard Collins and Julia Branch (Thomas) G. BA, Randolph-Macon Woman's Coll., 1951; MA, Mt. Holyoke Coll., 1953; PhD in Chemistry, Emory U., 1958; MDiv cum laude, Candler Sch. Theology, 1986. Ordained to Meth. Ch. as deacon, 1986, as elder 1989. Instr. Mt. Holyoke Coll., South Hadley, Mass., 1953-54, Randolph-Macon Woman's Coll., Lynchburg, Va., 1954-55; from asst. prof. to prof. chemistry Agnes Scott Coll., Decatur, Ga., 1957-84, dean, 1969-84; pastor-in-charge St. Matthew United Meth. Ch., East Point, Ga., 1987-92; bd. dirs. Global Health Action, Inc., Atlanta, treas., 1991—; chair coord. coun. Decatur Area Emergency Assistance Ministry, 1995—. Contbr. articles to profl. jours. Recipient Alumnae Achievement award Randolph-Macon Woman's Coll., 1990. Mem. Zonta of Atlanta (pres. 1979-81, Zonta of the Yr. 1988), Phi Beta Kappa, Sigma Xi. Home: 117 Bruton St Decatur GA 30030-3767

GARY, NANCY ELIZABETH, nephrologist, academic administrator; b. N.Y.C., Mar. 4, 1937; d. Walter Joseph and Charlotte Elizabeth (Sayer) G. BS, Springfield (Mass.) Coll., 1958; MD, Med. Coll. Pa., 1962. Diplomate Am. Bd. Internal Medicine, Am. Bd. Nephrology. Resident Nassau County Med. Ctr., East Meadow, N.Y., 1962-64; resident St. Vincent's Hosp. and Med. Ctr., N.Y.C., 1964-65, chief renal sect., 1967-74; fellow in nephrology Georgetown U. Med. Ctr., Washington, 1965-67; instr. medicine NYU Sch. Medicine, N.Y.C., 1968-74; asst. prof. U. Medicine and Dentistry of N.J.-Rutgers Med. Sch., Piscataway, 1974-76, assoc. prof., 1976-81, prof., 1981-88, assoc. dean, 1981-87, exec. assoc. dean, 1987-88; dean Albany (N.Y.) Med. Coll., 1988-90; sr. med. adv. to adminstr. health care financing HHS, Washington, 1990-92; clin. prof. medicine George Washington U. Sch. Medicine, 1991—; prof. medicine Uniformed Svcs. U. Health Scis., Bethesda, Md., 1992—; exec. v.p., dean Sch. Medicine Uniformed Svcs. U. Health Scis., 1992-95; clin. prof. Howard U. Coll. Medicine, Washington, 1992—; pres., CEO Ednl. Commn. Fgn. Med. Grads., Phila., 1995—. Contbr. chpts. to books, articles to profl. jours. Robert Wood Johnson Health Policy fellow NAS Inst. Medicine, 1987-88; recipient Joseph F. Boyle, M.D. award for Disting. Pub. Svc., Am. Soc. Internal Medicine, 1992. Mem. ACP (Master), AMA, Nat. Kidney Found., Alpha Omega Alpha. Office: Ednl Commn Fgn Med Graduates 3624 Market St Philadelphia PA 19104

GARY, TONI BERRYHILL, school counselor, psychotherapist; b. Belzoni, Miss., Mar. 2, 1951; d. Thomas Richard and Alyene Cornealia (Ellis) Berryhill; m. Clarence Addison Hall III, Feb. 3, 1972 (div. Mar. 1976); 1 child, Clarence Addison IV; m. Mark Loftin Gary, Dec. 23, 1977 (div. Apr. 1990); children: Kristina Lynn, James Thomas. BS, Miss. State U. for Women, Columbus, 1972; MEd, Delta State U., Cleve., 1991. Lic. profl. counselor; nat. cert. counselor, nat. cert. sch. counselor. Social worker Humphreys County Welfare Dept., Belzomi, Miss., 1974-76; bookkeeper Gary Flying Svc., Inverness, Miss., 1978-90; counselor The Indianola (Miss.) Acad., 1991—. Editor. The Share-Cropper, 1977. Cons., counselor Teen Pregnancy Prevention Project, Sunflower County Make a Difference Day, 1995; pres. PTO, Ctrl. Delta Acad., 1975-78. Recipient Pres. award Miss. Women's Agrl. Aviation Assn., 1985; named Woman of Yr. Miss. Agrl.Aviation Assn., 1986. Mem. ACA, Miss. Women's Agrl. Aviation Assn. (pres. 1987),. Baptist. Home: 702 3d St Inverness MS 38753 Office: The Indianola Acad Dorsett Dr Indianola MS 38751

GARZA, ALICIA ANN, elementary educator; b. Detroit, Oct. 18, 1942; d. Lewis Vernon and Catherine Augusta (Ackermann) Weidemann; m. Fred Garza, Apr. 7, 1967; children: Max Darrin, Stephanie Dianne. BS in Edn., Wayne State U., 1965; MA in Reading, Oakland U., 1979. Cert. early reading tchr., Mich. Tchr. Detroit Pub. Schs., 1965-68; tchr. Fraser (Mich.) Pub Schs., 1968-89, title I facilitator, 1989—. Citizen amb. People to People, Spokane, Wash., 1995; literacy advocate Macomb Reading Coun., Macomb County, Mich., 1995. Mem. NEA, Internat. Reading Assn., Nat. Tchrs. English, Mich. Reading Assn., Fraser Edn. Assn., Mich. Edn. Assn., Childrens Book Coun. Lutheran. Home: 1232 Bradbury Dr Troy MI 48098

GARZA, ELIZABETH YVONNE, secondary education educator; b. Galveston, Tex., Aug. 6, 1969; d. Enrique and Maria Josephine (Partridge) Garza. BA in Math., U. Tex., 1991. Cert. secondary tchr. Tchr. Newman Smith H.S., Carrollton, Tex., 1991—; faculty sponsor Key Club, Carrollton, 1992—.

GARZA, MELITA MARIE, journalist; b. Madrid, Oct. 19, 1959; came to U.S., 1961; d. Carlos Mario and Linda Rose (Caballero) G. BA, Harvard U., 1983; postgrad., Poynter Inst. Reporter, writer L.A. Times, 1984-85, Milw. Jour., 1986-89, Chgo. Tribune, 1989—; discussion leader Am. Press Inst., Reston, Va., 1995; spkr., instr. Wilmington (Del.) Writers Workshop, 1995. Bd. dirs. SciTech mus., Aurora, Ill., 1991—; mem. com. on fgn. rels. Chgo. Coun. on Fgn. Rels., 1991—. Named one of top 20 young people in U.S. newspaper industry Newspaper Assn. Am., 1993, one of 100 Women Making a Difference Today's Chgo. Women, 1996; recipient Excellence in Journalism award Ill. Coalition for Immigrant and Refugee Protection, 1995, Cardinal's Comm. award for Profl. Excellence Archdiocese of Chgo., 1996. Mem. Nat. Assn. Hispanic Journalists (v.p. bd. dirs. 1989-94, Pres.' award 1994), Internat. Women's Media Found., Harvard Club of Chgo. (v.p. 1993-94), Radcliffe Club of Chgo. (pres. 1993-94). Roman Catholic. Office: Chgo Tribune 435 N Michigan Ave Chicago IL 60611

GARZILLI, ENRICA, religious studies educator; b. Citta di Castello, Italy, Aug. 13, 1957; came to U.S., 1992; d. Elpidio and Guiseppina (Celani) G.; m. Fabrizio Fiore, Apr. 1, 1981; 1 child, Andrea Rachele Fiore. PhD, U. Rome La Sapienza, 1985, postgrad., 1987; postgrad., U. for Foreigners, Perugia, Italy, 1989. Sr. fellow Ctr. for Study of World Religions Harvard U., Cambridge, Mass., 1992-95, mng. editor, editor-in-chief orient. series, 1993-95, lectr. in Sanskrit, 1993-95, vis. rschr. Law Sch., 1994—. Author: The Bhāvopahāra of Carrapanl Nātha, 1993, Translating, Translations, Translators, 1996; editor-in-chief Internat. Jour. Tantric Studies, 1995—, Jour. South Asia Women Studies, 1995—. Fellow U. ROme La Sapienza, 1986-87, sr. fellow CSWR, Harvard U., 1992-94; rsch. affiliate fellow Indian Ministry of Edn., Delhi U., 1987-89. Mem. Società Dante Alighieri (life), Internat. Sanskrit Studies, Assn. Italy-India (award 1987), Am. Acad. Religions, Assn. Asian Studies, Amnesty Internat. Home: Apt 511 1306 Massachusetts Ave Cambridge MA 02138 Office: U Perugia, Piazza Morlacchi 1, 06100 Perugia Italy

GASAWAY, LAURA NELL, law librarian, legal educator; b. Searcy, Ark., Feb. 24, 1945; d. Merel Roger and Carnell (Miller) G. BA, Tex. Woman's U., 1967, MLS, 1968; JD, U. Houston, 1973. Bar: Tex. 1974. Catalog libr. U. Houston, 1968-70, catalog-circulation libr., 1970-72, asst. law libr., 1972-73, law libr., asst. prof. law, 1973-75; dir. law libr., prof. law U. Okla., Norman, 1975-85; dir. law libr., prof. law U. N.C., 1985—; copyright cons. Recipient Calvert prize U. Okla., 1978, 81, Compton award Ark. Librs. Assn., 1986. Fellow Spl. Librs. Assn. (H.W. Wilson award 1983, John Cotton Dana award 1987, Fannie Simon award, 1992); mem. ABA, State Bar Tex., N.C. Bar Assn.,, Am. Assn. Law Librs. (pres. 1986-87). Democrat. Author: (with Maureen Murphy) Legal Protection for Computer Programs, 1980; (with James Hoover and Dorothy Warden) American Indian Legal Materials, A Union List, 1981, (with Bruce S. Johnson and James M. Murray) Law Library Management during Fiscal Austerity, 1992, (with Sarah K. Wiant) Libraries and Copyright: A Guide to Copyright in the 1990s, 1994. Office: U NC Law Libr CB #3385 Chapel Hill NC 27599-3385

GASIOR, DAWN MARIE, elementery education educator; b. Chgo., Nov. 30, 1957; d. Joseph Anthony and LaVerne Theresa (Ptacin) Slowinski; m. Thomas Joseph Gasior, Aug. 22, 1986; children: Daniel Thomas, Aimee Elizabeth, Sara Marie, Nathan Joseph. BA in Elem. Edn., Northeastern Ill. U., 1979. 1st grade tchr. Our Lady of Guadalupe Sch., Chgo., 1979-80; kindergarten and 2nd grade tchr. St. Symphorosa Sch., Chgo., 1980—. Mem. Assn. Childhood Edn. Internat. Roman Catholic. Office: St Symphorosa Sch 6125 S Austin Ave Chicago IL 60652

GASPAR, ANNA LOUISE, retired elementary school teacher, consultant; b. Chgo., May 12, 1935; d. Miklos and Klotild (Weiss) G. BS in Edn., Northwestern U., 1957. Cert. elem. tchr., Calif. Tchr. 6th grade Pacific Palisades Elem. Sch., L.A., 1957-58; tchr. 1st grade Eastman Street Elem. Sch., L.A., 1959, Glassell Park, L.A., 1959-62, Stoner Ave. Elem. Sch., L.A., 1962-67; 2nd-4th grade tchr. Brentwood Elem. Sch., L.A., 1967-78; tchr. 4th and 5th grades Brockton Avenue Elem. Sch., L.A., 1978-90; vol., established Swakopmund Tchrs. Resource Ctr., Peace Corps, Namibia, 1991-93; tchr. English, Atlantic Sr. Primary Sch., Swakopmund, Namibia, 1992; career info. cons. Peace Corps., 1991—; substitute tchr. various schs., Las Vegas, 1994—. Mem. Hadassah, Bet Knesset Bamidbar. Mem. Internat. Platform Assn., Friends of Edn. Assn., Calif. Ret. Tchrs. Assn., Northwestern U. Alumni Assn. Democrat. Jewish. Home: 2700 Hope Forest Dr Las Vegas NV 89134-7322

GASPARRINI, CLAUDIA, publishing company executive, scientist, writer; b. Genova, Italy, Apr. 25, 1941; came to U.S., 1984; d. Corrado and Tina (Pizzuti) G. D in Earth Scis., U. Rome, 1965; cert. in English, U. Cambridge, Eng., 1965, Pitman Inst., London, 1965. Sr. tech. U. Toronto, Can., 1966-67; rsch. asst. U. Toronto, 1967-70, rsch. assoc., 1970-72; phys. scientist II Geol. Survey Can., Ottawa, 1973; rsch. scientist Nat. Inst. for Metallurgy (now Mintek), Johannesburg, South Africa, 1974-75; ind. cons. Toronto, 1976; pres., owner Minmet Sci. Limited, Toronto, 1977—, Jacksonville, Fla., 1982-86, Tucson, 1986—; pres., owner The Space Eagle Pub. Co., Inc., Toronto, Tucson, 1986—, 88—; advisor Chinese chpt. Internat. Precious Metals Inst., 1996—; presenter in field. Author: Gold and Other Precious Metals-The Lure and the Trap, 1989, How to Get the Most Out of the Legal System Without Spending a Fortune, 1990, Gold and Other Precious Metals-From Ore to Market, 1993, Murder of the Mind-The Practice of Subtle Discrimination, 1993, When You Make the Two One, 1994, (as Gloria J. Duv) How to Run a Successful Mail Order Business by Defrauding the Public, 1995; mem. bd. editors Chinese mag. Gold Sci. and Tech., 1996—; contbr. articles to profl. jours. and books. Scientist Sci. by Mail Program, Boston Mus. Sci., 1991-92; mem. rsch. bd. advisors Am. Biog. Inst., Raleigh, N.C., 1990—; hon. mem. Internat. Biog. Ctr. Adv. Coun., Cambridge, Eng., 1992—. Recipient Cert. Appreciation Outstanding Svc. Internat. Precious Metals Inst., 1994; named hon. mem. organizing com. Internat. Conf. on Precious Metals, Kosice, Slovakia, Oct. 25-27, 1995. Mem. Can. Inst. Mining and Metallurgy, Internat. Precious Metals Inst., Soc. for Geology Applied to Mineral Deposits (councillor 1996—), Assn. Women in Sci., Ariz. Geol. Soc. Home: 6651 N Campbell Ave Apt 102 Tucson AZ 85718-1360 Office: Minmet Sci Limited PO Box 41687 Tucson AZ 85717-1687 also: 2 Lansing Sq Ste 703, Willowdale, ON Canada M2J 4P8 also: Via Ugo de Carolis 62, Rome 00136, Italy

GASPARRO, MADELINE, banker; b. Jersey City, Oct. 5, 1928; d. Donato and Anna (D'Urso) D'Achille; m. Dominick J. Gasparro, Apr. 30, 1949; children: Dorothy, Joseph, Donato, Frank. Grad. high sch., Jersey City. Salesperson credit dept. and employee sales J.C. Penney, Parlin, N.J.; head teller Amboy Madison Nat. Bank, Old Bridge, N.J., bank mgr.; br. mgr., 1983—. Chpt. chmn. South Amboy Hosp., mem. fin. com.; eucharist minister St. Bernadette Ch. of Parlin. Mem. NAFE, Nat. Assn. Bank Women (past hostess), Fin. Women Internat. (chmn. membership Raritan Bay group 1990-91, v.p. 1991-92, pres. 1992-93), Altar Rosary Soc. (past pres.). Address: 17 Parkway Pl Parlin NJ 08859-1905

GASPERINI, ELIZABETH CARMELA (LISA GASPERINI), advertising professional, graphic designer; b. Newark, Sept. 26, 1961; d. Enrico Caesar and Wanda Claudia (Stanziale) G. BFA, Caldwell (N.J.) Coll., 1983. Advt. specialist J.C. Penney Corp., Wayne, N.J., 1982-83; asst. prodn. mgr. Internat. Postal Mktg. Corp., Montville, N.J., 1983-84; art dir. Healy, Dixcy & Forbes, W. Caldwell, N.J., 1984-86; sr. mktg. specialist Am. Varityper Corp., E. Hanover, N.J., 1986-88; product promotion mgr. Brother Internat. Corp., Somerset, N.J., 1988-90; mktg. specialist Ishida USA Inc., Lincoln Park, N.J., 1990-92; mktg. promotions mgr. Nat. Electronic Info. Corp., Secaucus, N.J., 1992-95; self-employed mktg. cons. Towaco, N.J., 1995—; telemktg. specialist Sears, Roebuck & Co., Fairfield, N.J., 1984-96; owner, cons. Gasperini Graphics, Towaco, N.J., 1984—; art cons. Italico Pubs., Livingston, N.J., 1982—. Mem. N.J. Art Assn., N.J. Italian-Am. Assn. (cons. 1982—). Republican. Roman Catholic. Home: 10 Willard Ln Towaco NJ 07082-1517

GASPERONI, ELLEN JEAN LIAS, interior designer; b. Rural Valley, Pa.; d. Dale S. and Ruth (Harris) Lias; student Youngstown U., 1952-54, John Carrol U., 1953-54, Westminster Coll., 1951-52; grad. Am. Inst. Banking; m. Emil Gasperoni, May 28, 1955; children: Sam, Emil, Jean Ellen. Mem. Coeurde Coeur Heart Assn., Orlando Opera Guild, Orlando Symphony Guild. Mem. Jr. Bus. Women's Club (dir. 1962-64), Sweetwater Country Club (Longwood, Fla.); Lake Toxaway Golf and Country Club (N.C.). Presbyterian. Home: 1126 Brownshire Ct Longwood FL 32779-2209

GASQUE, DIANE PHILLIPS, funding analyst; b. Madison, Wis., Mar. 31, 1954; d. Codie Odel and Ruth Elaine (Oimoen) Phillips.; m. Wyndham Henry Burriss, Feb. 5, 1977 (div. 1979); m. Allard Harrison Gasque, Nov. 14, 1992; 1 child, Folline Elaine Gasque. BA, Midlands Tech., Columbia, S.C. Cert. Notary S.C. With inventory control Oxford Industries, Columbia, S.C.; processing agent NCR, Columbia, S.C.; comml. loan officer S.C. Nat., Columbia, S.C.; personnel dir. Witten Sales, Columbia, S.C.; funding agt. Resource Bankshares Mortgage Group, 1995—. Mem. The Order of the Confederate Rose. Republican. Presbyterian. Home: 3728 Linbrook Dr Columbia SC 29204

GASS, GERTRUDE ZEMON, psychologist, researcher; b. Detroit; d. David Solomon and Mary (Goldman) Zemon; m. H. Harvey Gass, June 19, 1938; children: Susan, Roger. BA, U. Mich., 1937, MSW, 1943, PhD, 1957. Lic. clin. psychologist, Mich. Mem. faculty Merrill-Palmer Inst., Detroit, 1958-69, lectr., 1967; mem. faculty Advanced Behavioral Sci. Ctr., Grosse Pointe, Mich., 1969-72; pvt. practice clin. psychology Birmingham, Mich., 1972—; adj. prof. psychology U. Detroit, 1969-75; cons. Continuum Ctr. Oakland U., Rochester, Mich., 1961-77, Traveler's Aid, Detroit, 1959-75; pres. Shapero Sch. Nursing, Detroit, 1967-72, cons. 1958-78; psychol. cons. Physician's Ins. Co. of Mich., 1988—, mgt. Mich. Bell Telephone, 1979-82. Mem. Adv. Com Sch. Needs, 1954-56; trustee Sinai Hosp. Detroit, 1972—; bd. dirs. Tribute Fund United Community Services, 1955-67. Fellow Am. Assn. Marriage-Family, Am. Orthopsychiatric Assn. (v.p. 1975-76), Mich. Psychol. Assn.; mem. Am. Psychol. Assn., Psychologists Task Force (v.p. 1977-84), Mich. Inter-Profl. Assn. (pres. 1976-78), Mich. Assn. Marriage Counselors (1979-80, pres. 1979-80), Mental Health Adv. Svc., Blue Cross and Blue Shield of Mich., Phi Kappa Phi, Pi Lambda Theta. Office: 30200 Telegraph Rd Bingham Farms MI 48025-4502

GASSER-SANZ, EVA CLAUDIA, lawyer, consultant; b. Caracas, Venezuela, Nov. 11, 1967; d. Jorge Hernan Gasser-Sanz and Franziska M. Gasser; m. Alfred L. Brophy, June 5, 1993. BA, Columbia U., 1989; JD, Georgetown U., 1993. Bar: Okla., U.S. Dist. Ct. (we. dist.) Okla. Intern Legal Action Ctr. for Homeless, N.Y.C., summer 1987, Sanctuary for Families, N.Y.C., summer 1988; paralegal MFY Legal Svcs., N.Y.C., 1989-90; legal intern Ayuda/Clinica Legal Latina, Washington, 1992, Greater Boston Legal Svcs., 1993-94; assistive tech. specialist Okla. Disability Law Ctr., Oklahoma City, 1994-95; coord. early settlement Oklahoma City U. Sch. Law, 1995—. Contbr.: Transitions: Exeter Remembered, 1961-87, 1990. Mem. Planned Parenthood Fedn. Am., 1995. Pub. interest law scholar Georgetown U. Law Ctr., 1991-93. Mem. ABA, NOW, Okla. Bar Assn., Okla. Hispanic Profl. Assn. Unitarian.

GAST, LINDA KAY, accountant, financial executive; b. San Antonio, Apr. 15, 1949; d. Jerry Joseph and Dolores Mae (McCurry) Rasmussen; m. Steven Alan Schwartzberg, Apr. 19, 1970; m. Johnny R. Gast, Jan. 8, 1994; 1 child, Laurie Rachelle; stepchildren: Laura Lee, Stacy Jo, Josh Daniel. BS, Lindenwood Coll., 1987. CPA, Mo. Office mgr. Coopers & Lybrand, St. Louis, 1982-84; controller The Type House, Inc., St. Louis, 1984-86; cons. Arthur Young & Co., St. Louis, 1986-87; v.p. fin. Amedco Health Care, Inc., Wright City, Mo., 1987-90; CFO RAPCO Internat., Inc., Jackson, Mo., 1990-94, exec. v.p., CFO, 1995—, CEO, 1996—; bd. dirs. RAPCO Holding Co. Pres. bd. trustees Congregation B'nai Torah, St. Charles, Mo., 1987-90; bd. dirs. Hidden Valley, Burfordville, Mo. Mem. Wright City C. of C., Beta Sigma Phi (v.p. St. Peters, Mo. chpt. 1988-89, Woman of Yr. 1988-89). Home: 241 Clay Ln Whitewater MO 63785-6051

GAST, MARY SUSAN, minister, religious organization administrator; b. Benton Harbor, Mich., Oct. 27, 1945; d. Charles Adolph and Mary Ann (Pihulic) G.; m. Roger Dean Straw, Mar. 20, 1971; 1 child, Susannah Martin Straw-Gast. BA cum laude, Mich. State U., 1970; D of Ministry, Chgo. Theol. Sem., 1975, DD (hon.), 1994. Ordained to ministry, United Ch. Christ, 1975. Campus min. Iowa State U., Ames, 1975-78; pastor 1st Congl. United Ch. Christ, Union City, Mich., 1978-81, Smith Meml. United Ch. Christ, Grand Rapids, Mich., 1981-86; dir. S.W. Mich. Riverside Project in Nuclear Disarmament, Grand Rapids, 1981-84; assoc. conf. min. Ind.-Ky. Conf. United Ch. Christ, Indpls., 1986-91; exec. dir. coorinating ctr. for women in ch. and soc. United Ch. Christ, Cleve., 1991—; denominational rep. Religious Coalition for Reproductive Choice, 1991—; pers. and organizational life and conflict cons., 1991—. Active Project Oversea, Union City, 1979-81; comty. organizer Smith Ctr., Grand Rapids, 1982-86; peace monitor S. African elections Black Sash, 1994; participant UN Forum on Women, China, 1995. Mem. Phi Beta Kappa. Office: United Church of Christ 700 Prospect n Ave Ste 304 Cleveland OH 44115

GASTAÑAGA, CLAIRE GUTHRIE, consultant; b. London, May 8, 1949; d. John Reiley and Rebecca Jane (Jeffers) Guthrie; m. Javier Enriqué Gastañaga del Manzano, Dec. 21, 1991. BA, Mich. State U., 1971; JD, U. Va., 1974. Bar: Va. 1974, N.J. 1977, D.C. 1983. Staff atty. U.S. Dept. HEW, Office for Civil Rights, Washington, 1974-76; asst. sec., univ. counsel Princeton (N.J.) U., 1976-79; asst. gen. counsel Am. Coun. Edn., Washington, 1979-82; pvt. practice Hogan and Hartson, Washington, 1982-86; interim pres. Chatham Coll., Pitts., 1982-83; dep. atty. gen. Commonwealth of Va., Richmond, Va., 1986-93, chief dep. atty. gen., 1993-94; cons. The Gastañaga Group, Richmond, 1994—. Contbr. articles to profl. jours. Mem. bd. trustees Chatham Coll., Pitts., 1981-87; mem. commn. to reengineer city govt. City of Richmond, 1996—; participant Leadership Metro Richmond, 1995-96; mem., bd. dirs., founder Make Women Count, Richmond, 1993—. Named Outstanding Women in Law, YWCA, 1994, Outstanding Woman Atty., Va. Women Attys. Assn., 1986. Fellow Nat. Assn. Coll. and Univ. Attys. (bd. dirs. 1984-87); mem. Met. Richmond Women's Bar. Office: CG2 Cons Divsn Gastañaga Group 2123 Park Ave Richmond VA 23220

GASTEYER, CARLIN EVANS, museum administrator, museum studies educator; b. Jackson, Mich., Mar. 30, 1917; d. Frank Howard and Marian (Spencer) Evans; student Barnard Coll., 1934-35; B.A., CUNY, 1983; m. Harry A. Gasteyer, Jan. 8, 1944; 1 dau., Nancy Catherine. Clk., First Nat. City Bank, 1939-42; statistician Bell Telephone Labs., 1942-45; dir. asst. S.I. Mus., 1956-61; bus. mgr. Mus. of the City of N.Y., 1961-63; mus. adminstr., 1963-66; asst. dir. Monmouth (N.J.) Mus., 1966-67, Mus. of City of N.Y., 1967-70; vice dir. adminstrn. Bklyn. Mus., 1970-74; dir. planning Snug Harbor Cultural Center, S.I., N.Y., 1975-79; cable TV Cons., 1980—; adj. lectr. mus. studies Coll. S.I. CUNY, 1985—. Active Girl Scouts. Co-founder, pres. Jr. Mus. Guild, S.I. Mus., 1956-58. Mem. N.Y.C. Local Sch. Bd. 54, 1960-61. Mem. Am. Assn. Mus., Mus. Council of N.Y.C. Home: 50 Fort Pl Staten Island NY 10301-2415

GASTON, BONNIE FAYE JAMES, elementary education educator; b. Littlefield, Tex., Apr. 17, 1931; d. John William and Kittie (Drake) James; m. Milburn Fenton Gaston, May 26, 1954; children: Terry Lynn, Dale Weldon, Randy Lee. BS in Edn., Tex. Tech U., 1952, postgrad. Tchr. Plainview, Tex., 1952-54, 55-58, San Angelo, Tex., 1954-55, Hale Ctr., Tex., 1968-72, 73-76, Olton, Tex., 1977-92; condr. tchrs. workshops; mem. sch. evaluating vis. team. Author, pub.: Gaston Enrichment Skills, 1979. Dist. sec. PTA. Recipient Outstanding Young Homemaker award State Senator Andy Rogers, Notable Women of Tex. award, 1984-85. Mem. Tex. Assn. for Improvement Reading (cons. West Tex. U.), Assn. Tex. Profl. Educators (local pres., sec. dist. 17), AAUW, Smithsonian Assocs., Nat. Mus. Women in Arts, Delta Kappa Gamma. Baptist. Home: 1119 Holliday Dr Plainview TX 79072

GATELEY, EDWINA, public speaker, women's advocate; b. Lancaster, Lancashire, Eng., May 20, 1943; came to U.S., 1979; d. John Christopher and Catherine Adelaine (Pye) G.; 1 adopted child, Niall Kizito. BEd, Sedgley Park Coll., Manchester, Eng., 1964; M in Theol. Studies, Cath. Theol. Union, Chgo., 1981. Cert. tchr., Eng.; HIV counsellor, Ill. Tchr. Diocese of Masaka, Uganda, E. Africa, 1964-67, St. William's Sch., Liverpool, Eng., 1967-68; founder, dir. The Vol. Missionary Movement, London, 1969-79, Genesis House, Chgo., 1983-88; writer, speaker, minister, activist pvt. practice, Grand Rapids, Mich., 1988—; pres. Vol. Missionary Movement, London, 1969-85, Chgo., 1987-90, Genesis House, Chgo., 1989-96; bd. dirs. Marys Pence, Chgo., 1989-92. Author: (books) Psalms of a Laywoman, 1981, I Hear a Seed Growing, 1990, A Warm, Moist, Salty God, 1993, God Goes on Vacation, 1994, There Was No Path So I Trod One, 1995. Named Cath. Woman of Yr., Eng. and Wales, 1979; recipient Spirit of St. Francis award (outstanding Cath. laywoman in Ill.), 1984, Assn. Chgo. Priests award, 1986, Cook County State Atty. Recognition award, 1986, U.S. Cath. Mission Assn. award, 1986, Chgo. Commn. of Human Rels. award, 1987, Pope John XXIII award Viterbo Coll., La Crosse, Wis., 1988, Clare award, Clinton, Iowa, 1993, Loretto award, St. Louis, 1995; named in her honor: Gately Hall residence opened in Southampton, Eng., 1995, Edwina Homes, Chgo., 1995. Mem. NOW, Vol Missionary Movement (cons.), Marys Pence (advisor, Wise Woman Counsel), Call to Action. Home: 248 Carroll SE Grand Rapids MI 49506 Office: Genesis House 911 W Addison Chicago IL 60613

GATES, BARBARA LYNN, school administrator, educator; b. Billings, Mont., May 13, 1954; d. Joseph Isacc and Ima Evelyn (Daugherty) G. B.S. in Elementary Edn., Eastern Mont. Coll., 1976. Cert. tchr., Mont. Tchr., Union Sch., Lindsay, Mont., 1976-79, Greycliff Sch., Mont., 1979-80; supr. Alliance Christian Sch., Lewistown, Mont., 1981-83, prin., supr., 1983-86; prin., supr. Paradise Christian Acad., Lewistown, Mont., 1986-91.

GATES, DEBORAH WOLIN, petroleum company executive, lawyer; b. Jan. 20, 1955; m. Stephen A. Gates. BA, Coll. William & Mary, 1976; JD, U. Va., 1979; LLM, U. Wash., 1986. Bar: Va. 1979, Wash. 1982, Ky. 1990. Atty. EPA, Seattle, 1979-89; sr. atty. Ashland Petroleum Co. (divsn. Ashland, Inc.), Russell, Ky., 1989-90; sr. group counsel Ashland Petroleum Co. (divsn. Ashland Oil Co.), Russell, Ky., 1990-92, v.p. environ, health and safety dept., 1992—; adj. prof. U. Puget Sound Law Sch., Tacoma, 1986-89; active API Subcom. on Environ. and Health Law, Washington, 1990—. Bd. dirs. The Nature Conservancy of Ky., Lexington, 1992—, v.p., bd. dirs. 1995—; active Comty. Hospice. Recipient Tristate Women in Industry award YWCA, 1994. Mem. ABA (vice chmn. native Am. resources sect. 1985-89), Ky. Bar Assn. (dir., corp. counsel sect.). Home: PO Box 472 Russell KY 41169-0472 Office: Ashland Petroleum Co Env Health and Safety Dept 2000 Ashland Dr Russell KY 41169

GATES, DONNA MARIE, special education educator; b. Milton, Fla., Dec. 14, 1961; d. Lawrence C. and Theresa M. (Bechard) Bonneau; m. David J. Gates, June 25, 1994. BS in Edn., Fitchburg State Coll., 1983. Head counselor, counselor WAARC-Camp Joy, Worcester, Mass., 1977-81; house staff Cape Cod Summer Vacation Program, Hyannis, Mass., 1982; case mgr. NCM Friends of Retarded Coop. Apt. Program, Fitchburg, Mass., 1983; head tchr. May Inst., Chatham, Mass., 1983-85; tchr. Asabet Valley Collaborative Elem. Spl. Needs Program, Marlborough, Mass., 1985-88; primary resource tchr. Town of Auburn (Mass.), 1988—; tchr. Project Challenge Assabet Valley Collaborative, 1993. Mem. Mass. Tchrs. Assn., Coun. Exceptional Children, Alpha Delta Kappa.

GATES, DOROTHY LOUISE, retired sociology educator; b. National City, Calif., Feb. 21, 1926; d. Harold Roger and Bertha Marjorie (Lippold) Gates. BA, U. Calif., Santa Barbara, 1949; MA, U. Hawaii, 1963, PhD, 1975; postdoctoral student U. Uppsala (Sweden), 1976, Bedford Coll., London, 1978, Cuban Ministry of Justice, 1979, Cambridge U., Eng., 1986. Dept. probation officer, Riverside County, Calif., 1950-54, 55-61; dir. La Morada, probation facility, Santa Barbara County, 1963-65; prof. sociology San Bernardino Valley Coll. (Calif.), 1965-87, prof. emeritus, 1987—; part-time tchr. criminology U. Redlands, Calif.; chmn. Riverside County Juvenile Justice and Delinquency Prevention Commn., 1971-88. Pres. Women's Equity Action League, Hawaii, 1972; mem. adv. group Riverside County Justice System, 1982. bd. dirs. San Bernardino County Mental Health Assn., Symphony Guild, Cooper Burkhart House, Riverside, Alzheimer Assn., Riverside & San Bernardino counties; mem. adv. council Ret. Sr. Vol. Program, San Bernardino; acad. pres. San Bernardino Valley Coll., 1986; pres., trustee Riverside Community Coll., 1989—. Recipient Cert. of Recognition, Riverside YWCA; named Citizen of Achievement, San Bernardino LWV, 1985; NEH fellow U. Va., 1977; named Outstanding Prof. San Bernardino Valley Coll., 1987. Mem. AAUW, LWV, Western Gerontology Assn., Am. Soc. Criminology, State of Hawaii Sociol. Soc., Calif. Probation, Parole and Correctional Assn. (award 1969), Calif. Women's Assn. Edn. and Rsch., Urban League, Kiwanis (past pres.). Address: 4665 Braemar Pl # 212 Riverside CA 92501-3017

GATES, JODIE, dancer; b. Sacramento. The Joffrey Ballet Sch., 1981. Prin. dancer The Joffrey Ballet, N.Y.C., 1983—. Appeared in TV series Dance in America, The Tonight Show; guest appearances with cos. throughout Am. and abroad. Active mem. Dancers Responding to AIDS. Office: The Joffrey Ballet 130 W 56th St New York NY 10019-3818 Home: 924 Pine St # 2R Philadelphia PA 19107-6128*

GATES, LISA, small business owner, chef, caterer; b. Washington, July 11, 1955; d. Chester Robert and Peggy Jean (Dalton) Gates; m. Sergio Vivoli, Nov. 3, 1978 (div. Nov. 1984); m. Mitchell Cohen, Sept. 21, 1987 (div. Febr. 1995). AA, Fleming Coll., Florence, Italy, 1974. Dir. The Am. Sch. in Switzerland, Lugano, 1974-80; counter person Bar Gelateria Vivoli, Florence, 1978-80; costumer, choreographer, scene designer English Theatre of Florence, 1978; tchr. Dance Sch. Theatre, Florence, 1978-81; sec., treas. Vivoli Da Firenze, Inc., L.A., 1981-82; event coord. Calif. Catering Co., Beverly Hills, Calif., 1983; chef, sales rep. St. Germain To Go, West Hollywood, Calif., 1984; chef, cons. Posh Affair Catering Co., L.A., 1984-87; owner, chef, party planner Lisa Gates-Vivoli Catering, L.A., 1985—; catering mgr. Maple Drive Restaurant, Beverly Hills, 1990-91; pvt. chef, 1991—. Mem. Mus. Contemporary Art, L.A., L.A. County Mus. Art, L.A. Theatre Ctr., NOW, L.A., Music Ctr. Unified Fund. Recipient Outstanding Achievement in Art award Bank of Am., Miraleste, Calif., 1972. Mem. Am. Inst. Wine and Food, Roundtable for Women in Foodsvc., Internat. Soc Women Chefs and Restaurateurs. Democrat. Home and Office: 1227 N Orange Grove Ave West Hollywood CA 90046-5311

GATES, LORI ANN, history educator; b. Eugene, Oreg., Feb. 3, 1965; d. Bruce M. Gates and Naomi M. Gates Taylor. AA, Lane C.C., Eugene, 1982; BA in History with honors, U. Oreg., 1984, MA in History, 1986; PhD in History, U. Toronto, Ont., 1991. Instr. Lane C.C., Eugene, 1989-90; vis. asst. prof. U. Oreg., Eugene, 1990-91; asst. prof. history Mo. Valley Coll., Marshall, 1991—, dean social scis., 1993—. Regional liaison History Day in Mo., Saline County, 1994—; pres. Saline County Hist. Soc., Marshall, 1993-95. Mem. Am. Hist. Assn., Medieval Acad. of Am., World History Assn. Office: Missouri Valley College 500 E College St Marshall MO 65340-3109

GATES, MARTINA MARIE, food products company executive; b. Mpls., Mar. 19, 1957; d. John Thomas and Colette Clara (Luetmer) G. BSBA in Mktg. Mgmt. cum laude, Coll. St. Thomas, 1984, MBA in Mktg., 1987. Tchrs. asst. Mpls. Area Vocat. Tech. Inst., Mpls., 1978-79; sec., regional sales mgr. Internat. Multifoods, Mpls., 1979, sec. bakery mix, mktg. mgr., 1979-80, sec., v.p. sales and new bus. devel., 1980, customer svc. rep. regional accounts, 1980-81, customer svc. rep. nat. accounts, 1981-82, credit coordinator indsl. foods div., 1982-85, asst. credit mgr. consumer foods div., 1985, advt./sales promotion mgr. indsl. foods div., 1985-86, asst. credit mgr. fast food and restaurant div., 1986-87, dir. devel. USA and Can. franchise area, 1987-89; dir. franchise devel. FIRSTAFF, Inc., Mpls., 1989-90; dir. adminstrn. Robert Half Internat., Inc., Mpls., 1990-94; dir. client svcs. The NPD Group, Inc., Chgo., 1994—. Vol. seamstress Guthrie Theater Costume Shop, Mpls., 1975—; alumni mem. New Coll. Student Adv. Council St. Thomas, St. Paul, 1984—; vol. Mpls. Aquatennial, 1987. Mem. Omicron Delta Epsilon.

GATES, PHYLLIS GAIL, speechwriter, public relations consultant; b. Omaha, Feb. 3, 1941; d. Ferdinand Joseph and Mary Catherine (Wienehe) Knipping; m. Thomas F. Crawler, Feb. 3, 1967 (div. Jan. 1979); m. Gary Paul Gates, May 31, 1989; 1 stepchild, Christopher. BS in English and Speech, U. Nebr., 1964, postgrad., 1965. English and speech tchr. Norris H.S., Hickman, Nebr., 1964-66; speech and debate instr. U. Nebr., Lincoln, 1967; dir. advt. and publicity Pegasus divsn. Western Publ., N.Y.C., 1967-69; v.p. corp. comms. Esquire mag. Esquire Inc., N.Y.C., 1969-79; v.p. comms. CBS Mags., N.Y.C., 1979-91; dir. editl. svcs. Paramont Comms. (now Viacom), N.Y.C., 1991; freelance speechwriter, pub. rels. cons. N.Y.C., 1991—; condr. courses, workshops, lectr. in field. Author career guide: Magazine Career Directory, 1986, 4th edit., 1989; contbr. articles to profl. publs. Mem. devel. com. YWCA, 1990—. Named to Acad. of Women Achievers, YWCA, 1983. Mem. Women in Comms. (matrix chair 1983), Mag. Pubs. Am. (chair pub. rels. com.), N.Y. Found. for Arts (trustee 1986—, sec. 1990-93), Nat. Assn. for Visually Handicapped (bd. dirs. 1982-89), Nebr. Soc. of N.Y. (bd. dirs. 1985—), Advt. Club of N.Y. (bd. dirs. 1982-83). Home and Office: 2 East End Ave New York NY 10021

GATES, ROBERTA PECORARO, nursing educator; b. Elmira, N.Y., May 22, 1948; d. Patrick George and Verle Elizabeth (Warriner) Pecoraro; m. William Franklin Gates III, May 20, 1972; 1 child, William Franklin IV. BSN, U. Ariz., 1970; MSN in Family Nursing, U. Ala., Huntsville, 1981. Cert. clin. specialist in med.-surg. nursing. Charge nurse St. Mary's Hosp. and Mental Health Ctr., Tucson, 1970-72; asst. head nurse Torrance (Calif.) Meml. Hosp., 1973-74; dist. nurse Sierra Sands Sch. Dist., Ridgecrest, Calif., 1974-76; instr. Albany (Ga.) Jr. Coll., 1978-80, John C. Calhoun Coll., Decatur, Ala., 1981-83; learning resources coord. Albany State Coll., 1984-85; asst. prof. Sinclair C.C., Dayton, Ohio, 1990-91, Darton Coll., Albany, 1986-89, 92—; cons. Cmty. Health Inst., Albany, 1993, Early County Bd. Edn., Blakely, Ga., 1994. Author: A Model for Adolescent Health Promotion in the Dougherty County Community, 1993. Mem. Ga. Coun. Prevention of Child Abuse, Albany, 1988, 93; mem. Albany Mus. Art, 1993—; mem. Cmty. Ptnrs. Health Care Initiative, Dayton, 1990-91; bd. dirs. March of Dimes, Albany, 1986-89; mem. Albany-Dougherty 2000, DOCO Alternative Adv.Bd., State Consortium Early Intervention, Babies Can't Wait, 1995. Named to Outstanding Young Women of Am., 1983. Mem. Sigma Theta Tau, Phi Kappa Phi. Office: Darton Coll 2400 Gillionville Rd Albany GA 31707-3023

GATES, SHERRIE MOTT, chemotherapy nurse; b. Selma, Ala., Aug. 3, 1943; d. Walter Glover and Elvin (McKinney) Mott; m. Frederick Kilbourne Gates Jr., May 29, 1964; children: Dannial Kilbourne, William Shawn. Diploma, Carraway Meth. Sch. Nursing, Birmingham, Ala., 1964. Cert. med.-surg. nurse, ANCC. Staff med.-surg. nurse Good Samaritan Hosp., West Palm Beach, Fla., 1964-67; relief evening supr., emergency nurse, staff nurse Belle Glade (Fla.) Gen. Hosp., 1970-74; emergency rm. nurse Prattville (Ala.) Gen. Hosp., 1976-92; head nurse emergency rm. Autauga Med. Ctr., Prattville, 1986-90, 3-11 shift supr., 1990-92; ambulatory care staff/relief supr. VA Hosp., Montgomery, Ala., 1992-93; chemotherapy nurse VA Med. Ctr., Montgomery, Ala., 1993—. Office: VA Medical Center 215 Perry Hill Rd Montgomery AL 36109-3725

GATEWOOD, JULIA ELLEN SHIRLEY, educator, rancher; b. Ottawa County, Kans., July 18, 1927; d. Thomas James and Mary May (Matthews) Shirley; m. Moody J. Gatewood, May 4, 1946; children: Teresa Ann, James Thomas. BA in Edn., San Jose (Calif.) State U., 1964; MA in Edn., Reading Specialist, U. Santa Clara, Calif., 1973. Tchr. aide Mt. Pleasant Sch. Dist., San Jose, 1953; tchr. elem., jr. H.S. Milpitas (Calif.) Sch. Dist., 1964-78; substitute tchr. Dora (Mo.) Sch. Dist., 1984-90, West Plains (Mo.) Sch. Dist., 1990-95; beef cattle rancher Ozark County (Mo.) Farm, 1980—; mem. curriculum com. K-12 Reading Devel., Milpitas, 1971-75; bd. dirs. St. Francis Farm for Law Violotors, West Plains, Mo., 1981-86; historian, bd. dirs. Mo. Coun. on Arts, West Plains, 1985—. Author poetry, short stories. Sec.-treas. Oak Mount Cemetery, Ozark County, 1981—; organizer petition to include rural telephone into West Plains, Mo., 1983-85; committeeman to establish West Plains Farmer's Market, 1991-92; organizer, campaigner Mo. Ho. Reps., Ozark County, 1993. Fellow AAUW, Artists Guild West Plains (v.p. 1981-82). Office: Rt 17 Box 360 West Plains MO 65775

GATEWOOD, TELA LYNNE, lawyer; b. Cedar Rapids, Iowa, Mar. 23; d. Chester Russell and Cecilia Mae (McFarland) Weber. BA with distinction, Cornell Coll., Mt. Vernon, Iowa, 1970; JD with distinction, U. Iowa, 1972. Bar: Iowa 1973, Calif. 1974, U.S. Supreme Ct. 1984. Instr. LaVerne Coll., Pt. Mugu, Calif., 1973; asst. city atty. City of Des Moines, 1973-78; sr. trial atty. and supervisory atty. EEOC, Dallas, Phila., 1978-91, acting regional atty. Dallas Dist., 1987-89; adminstrv. judge EEOC, Dallas, 1991-94; adminstrv. law judge Social Security Adminstrn., Oklahoma City, 1994—. Bd. dirs. Day Care Inc., Des Moines, 1975-78, sec., 1977, pres., 1978. Mem. ABA (labor law, litigation, govt. svc., judiciary sects.), AAUW, NAFE, Nat. Assn. Female Judges, Fed. Bar Assn., U.S. Supreme Ct. Bar Assn., Calif. Bar Assn. Office: Social Security Adminstrn Office of Hearings and Appeals 420 W Main St Ste 400 Oklahoma City OK 73102

GATI, TOBY T., federal official; b. Bklyn., July 27, 1946; m. Charles Gati; 2 children; 3 stepchildren. BA, Pa. State U., 1967; MA in Russian Lit., Columbia U., 1970, M in Internat. Affairs, 1972. Rsch. asst, project dir., dep. v.p., v.p., sr. v.p. UN Assn. of the U.S.A., 1972-93; spl. asst. to the pres. for nat. security affairs Nat. Security Coun., sr. dir. for Russia, Ukraine and Eurasian States, 1993; asst. sec. for intelligence and rsch. Dept. State, Washington, 1993—; cons. ABC World Tonight, 1986, Ford Found., 1987-89, BDM Internat., 1989; mem. Coun. on Fgn Rels., Internat. Inst. for Strategic Studies. Office: Intelligence & Rsch Bureau 2201 C St NW Washington DC 20520-0001

GATIPON, BETTY BECKER, medical educator, consultant; b. New Orleans, Sept. 8, 1931; d. Elmore Paul and Theresa Caroline (Sendker) Becker; m. William B. Gatipon, Nov. 22, 1952 (dec. 1986); children: Suzanne, Ann Gatipon Sved, Lynn Gatipon Pashley. BS magna cum laude, Ursuline Coll., New Orleans, 1952; MEd, La. State U., 1975, PhD, 1983. Tchr. Diocese of Baton Rouge, 1960-74, edn. cons. to sch. bd., 1974-78; dir. Right to Read program Capital Area Consortium/Washington Parish Sch. Bd., Franklington, La., 1978-80; dir. basic skills edn. Capital Area Consortium/Ascension Parish Sch. Bd., Donaldsonville, La., 1980-82; instr. Coll. Edn. La. State U., Baton Rouge, 1982-84; evaluation cons. La. Dept. Edn., Baton Rouge, 1984-85; dir. basic skills edn. Capital Area Basic Skills/East Feliciana Parish Sch. Bd., Clinton, La., 1985-86; program coord. La. Bd. Elem. and Secondary Edn., New Orleans, 1987-89; dir. divsn. of med. edn., dept. family medicine Sch. Medicine La. State U. Med. Ctr., New Orleans, 1989—; evaluator East Feliciana Parish Schs., 1982-86; presenter math. methods workshops Ascension Parish Schs., 1980-84. Author curriculum materials, conf. papers; contbr. articles to edn. jours. Curatorial asst. La. State Mus., New Orleans, 1987—; soprano St. Louis Cathedral Concert Choir, New Orleans, 1988—; chmn. Symphony Store, New Orleans Symphony, 1990—; lector St. Angela Merici Ch. Mem. Am. Ednl. Rsch. Assn., Assn. Am. Med. Colls., Midsouth Ednl. Rsch. Assn., La. Ednl. Rsch. Assn., Soc. Tchrs. Family Medicine, New Orleans Film and Video Buffs, Phi Kappa Phi, Phi Delta Kappa. Roman Catholic. Home: 105 10th St New Orleans LA 70124-1258 Office: LA State U Med Ctr Sch Medicine 1542 Tulane Ave New Orleans LA 70112-2825

GATLIN, NOVELLA ANNA MARIA, collection specialist, business consultant; b. St. Louis, Nov. 23, 1942; d. George Wilbur Thompson and Flossie Lavetta Carter; m. Alton Lee Gatlin, Mar. 3, 1962; children: Kimberly Ann, Michael David. AA in Liberal Arts, Forest Park C.C., St. Louis, 1973; postgrad., LaSalle Extension U., Chgo., 1973-80. Clk. for various depts. City of University City, Mo., 1971-82, dep. collector fin. dept., 1982-88, collection specialist fin. dept., 1988—; bus. cons. Jr. Achievement of Miss. Valley, University City, 1991—. Writer Credit Profls. Internat. Connection quar. newsletter, 1995, 96, St. Louis Credit Profls. Internat. quar. newsletter, 1996. With U.S. WAC, 1961-62. Recipient 5 Yr. Svc. award Jr. Achievement Miss. Valley, 1996. Mem. Internat. Credit Assn. Mo. (chmn., writer quar. newsletter 1995-96, 2d v.p. 1995-96), Mo. Credit Assn. (bd. dirs. 1992-94), St. Louis Credit Profls. Internat. (treas. 1990-91, v.p. 1991-92, pres. 1992-93, 94-95, 95—, past. pres. 1993-94, credit profl. of yr. award 1992-93, credit profl. of yr. award dist. VII 1995-96, individual excellence in edn. dist. VII 1996, dist. VII treas. 1994-95, dist. VII 2d v.p. 1995-96, dist. VII 1st v.p. 1996—). Office: City of University City 6801 Delmar Blvd University City MO 63130

GATRELL, JOSELLE BERNSTEIN, government official; b. Long Branch, N.J., Sept. 7, 1942; d. Benjamin and Theresa Bernstein; m. Jacob W. Gatrell (div. Nov. 1982). BS, U. Md., 1964; cert. in stats. of health scis., Yale U., 1966; MS, Am. U., Washington, 1974. Statistician, programmer Nat. Ctr. for Health Stats., Rockville, Md., 1967-73; sect. chief Nat. Inst. Drug Abuse, Rockville, 1975-78, chief info. resources mgmt. br., 1978-82, asst. dir. Info. Resources Mgmt., 1982-83; chief data mng. br. Office Toxic Substances EPA, Washington, 1983-85, info. mgmt. specialist Info Resources Mgmt., 1985-86; statistician Nat. Inst. Mental Health, Rockville, 1965-67, chief info. mgmt. and analysis br., 1986-88; statistician FDA, Rockville, 1973-75, dir. div. regulatory info. systems, 1988—. Mem. Phi Kappa Phi. Home: 5400 Rapidan Ct Lothian MD 20711 Office: FDA 5600 Fishers Ln Rockville MD 20857-0001

GATTI, ROSA MARIE, television network executive; b. Phila., June 27, 1950; d. William Jules and Ruth Marie (Hahn) G. BA in French, Villanova U., 1972. Sports info. dir. Villanova (Pa.) U., 1974-76, Brown U., Providence, 1976-80; dir. communications ESPN, Bristol, Conn., 1980-81, v.p. communications, 1981—, now sr. v.p. comm. & human resources. Mem. Women in Cable, Internat. Radio and TV Soc., Football Writers, Cable TV Advt. and Mktg., Cable TV Pub. Affairs Assn. Office: ESPN ESPN Plaza Bristol CT 06010*

GATTING, CARLENE J., lawyer; b. Hartford, Conn., Apr. 12, 1955; d. Charles W. and Jean A. (Murkowicz) G. BS, U. Conn., 1977; JD, Rutgers U., 1983. Counsel Skadden, Arps, Slate, Meagher & Flom, N.Y.C., 1987—. Mem. ABA. Office: Skadden Arps Slate Meagher & Flom 919 3rd Ave New York NY 10022

GATTO, LYNN, elementary education educator; b. Bridgeport, Conn., Mar. 26, 1952; d. Murray and Ann (Bookholtz) Astarita; m. Richard Gatto. BS in Elem. Edn., Monmouth Coll., 1973; MA in Spl. Edn., Nazareth Coll., 1978. Cert. elem., spl. edn. tchr., N.Y. Tchr. spl. edn./primary self-contained Rochester (N.Y.) City Schs., 1973-77, tchr. spl. edn./resource room, 1978-86, 1st grade tchr., 1988, 4th grade tchr., 1989—; 1st grade tchr. Palm Beach Schs., Boca Raton, Fla., 1987; lead tchr. elem. sci. Rochester City Schs., 1992-94, tchr. trainer, 1990—. Author: Reading, Riting and Rithmetic Through Science, 1993; contbr. articles to profl. jours. Recipient Spirit of Ms. Frizzle award Instructor Mag., 1995, Excellence in Sci. Teaching award, 1993. Mem. Nat. Sci. Tchrs. Assn., Sci. Tchrs. Assn. N.Y. State, Delta Kappa Gamma (chpt. pres. 1992-94). Office: No 39 Sch 145 Midland Ave Rochester NY 14621-4051

GATULIS, NANCY A., elementary education educator; b. Boston, May 10, 1950; d. Albert J. and Philomena (Colella) DiCesare; m. Paul P. Gatulis, Mar. 22, 1985; 1 child, Eric M. Harris. BS, Bridgewater State Coll., 1972; MEd, Curry Coll., 1988. Cert. elem. tchr. 4th grade tchr. Dexter Sch., Dedham, Mass., 1973-82; 5th grade tchr. Avery Sch., Dedham, Mass., 1982—. Exhibited photography at Milton Art Mus., 1994, South Shore Art Ctr., Cohasset, 1995. Mem. PTO, Dedham, 1973—; sec. Milton Camera Club, 1986—, past pres., editor monthly newsletter, 1992—; pres., bd. dirs. Cebra Tennis Club, Hyde Park, Mass., 1980—. Mem. ASCD, NEA, Mass. Tchrs. Assn., Dedham Edn. Assn., Whole Lang. Tchrs. Assn., Milton Art Assn. Republican. Roman Catholic. Home: 176 Reedsdale Rd Milton MA 02186-3920 Office: Avery Sch 123 High St Dedham MA 02026-2829

GAUB, KIMBERLY KAY, elementary school educator; b. Billings, Mont., Sept. 9, 1960; d. Theodore and Selma Wilma (Krueger) G. BS, Coll. Great Falls, 1984; MEd, Mont. State U., 1995. Cert. tchr., Mont. Clk.-typist Great Falls (Mont.) Schs., 1977-86, libr. aide, 1984-85, substitute tchr., 1985-86, chpt. I math. tutor, 1986-89, reading resource tchr., 1989-92, chpt. I reading resource tchr., 1992—. Recipient award Heisey Found., 1976. Mem. NEA, Internat. Reading Assn. (del. 1992, 94), Great Falls Reading Coun. (membership dir. 1990-91, treas. 1991-92, v.p. 1992-93, pres. 1993-94, 94-95, cert. 1994, membership dir. 1995-96), Mont. State Reading Coun. (grad. scholarship 1993), Great Falls Edn. Assn., Mont. Edn. Assn., Phi Delta Kappa, Delta Kappa Gamma. Democrat. Lutheran. Home: 1111 33rd St S Great Falls MT 59405-5408 Office: Great Falls Pub Schs Mountain View Elem Sch 3420 15th Ave S Great Falls MT 59405-5514

GAUDET, JEAN ANN, librarian, educator; b. Oakland, Calif., Dec. 28, 1949; d. Edwin Joseph and Teresa Maureen (McDonnell) G. BS, Madison Coll., Harrisonburg, Va., 1971; MLS, George Peabody Coll. for Tchrs, Nashville, 1973. Libr., gifted edn. tchr. Prince William County Schs., Manassas, Va., 1971—. Chmn. Site-Based Mgmt. Com., Dumfries, Va., 1989-92; chmn. Cmty. Choir, Woodbridge, Va., 1983-85; citizen ambassador People to People, Russia and Poland, 1992, China, 1993, Australia, 1994. Mem. ALA, Va. Edn. Media Assn., Va. Assn. for Edn. of Gifted, Delta Kappa Gamma (sec. 1994—), Beta Phi Mu, Alpha Beta Alpha. Home: 16820 Francis West Ln Dumfries VA 22026-2110 Office: Potomac Sr High Sch 16706 Jefferson Davis Hwy Dumfries VA 22026-2130

GAUDIERI, MILLICENT HALL, association executive; b. East Liverpool, Ohio, Jan. 26, 1941; d. John Thompson and Sara (Pollock) Hall; m. Alexander V.J. Gaudiere, June 10, 1967; 1 son, Alexandre Barclay Everson. A.A., Centenary Coll., Hackettstown, N.J., 1961; postgrad., U. Pitts., 1962. Polit. researcher U.S. embassy, Paris, 1964-65; asst. to pres. RTV Internat., Inc., N.Y.C., 1966-71; exec. dir. Assn. Art Mus. Dirs., Montreal, Que., Can., 1973—. Bd. dirs. Ga. Pub. Radio, Savannah, 1978-79. Mem. N.Y. Jr. League (dir. 1973-75 Vol. of Yr. award), Am. Assn. Mus. Republican. Presbyterian. Office: Assn of Art Mus Dirs 41 E 65th St New York NY 10021-6508

GAUDREAU, GAYLE GLANERT, computer resource educator; b. Hartford, Conn., June 10, 1944; d. Edward Eugene and Evelyn Ruth (Manning) Glanert; m. George C. Gaudreau, Nov. 15, 1974; children: Christopher, Matthew, Nathan. BS in Bus. Edn., Ctrl. Conn. State U., New Britain, 1969, MS in Edn., 1974; postgrad., U. Conn. Cert. tchr. bus. edn., coord. coop. work experience, Conn. Group leader Pratt & Whitney Aircraft, East Hartford, Conn., 1964-67; coord. bus. edn. Wethersfield H.S., 1969-92; computer resource tchr. Wethersfield (Conn.) Bd. Edn., 1992—; part-time instr. Manchester (Conn.) C.C., 1973-74; mem. adv. bd. State of Conn. Bus. Edn., 1992; mem. adv. bd. bus. edn. Ctrl. Conn. State U., 1993—; cooperating tchr. State of Conn.; mem. Wethersfield Technology Com., 1993—. Named Disting. Educator, Wethersfield Bd. Edn.; recipient edn. alumni award Ctrl. Conn. State U. Sch. Bus., 1996. Mem. NEA, Wethersfield Edn. Assn., Conn. Educators Computer Assn., Conn. Bus. Educators' Assn., Phi Delta Kappa, Pi Lambda Theta, Delta Pi Epsilon. Home: 1 Falcon Ln Glastonbury CT 06033-2731 Office: Wethersfield HS 411 Wolcott Hill Rd Wethersfield CT 06109-2934

GAUDREAU, TINA MARIE, chemical engineer; b. Norwich, Conn., Feb. 25, 1963; d. Albert Ernest and Margaret (Rude) G. BSChemE, Tufts U., 1985. Engr. N.E. Utilities, Hartford, Conn., 1985-93, Babcock & Wilcox Nuclear Tech., Lynchburg, Va., 1993-95; prin. cons. Gebco Engring., Sebastopol, Calif., 1995—. Mem. Am. Nuclear Soc., Nat. Assn. Corrosion Engrs. Home: 4607 Rishell Ct Concord CA 94521

GAUER, SANDRA LEE, public health nurse; b. Lampasas, Tex., Sept. 24, 1946; d. Kenneth Lee and Vada Alta (Van Liew) Morris; m. Jerry James Gauer, Feb. 26, 1966; children: Rick, Russell. ADN, McLennan C.C., Waco, Tex., 1992. RN, Tex. Nursing asst. Westview Manor Nursing Home, McGregor, Tex., 1975-76, LVN charge nurse, 1977-78; LVN staff nurse Hillcrest Bapt. Hosp., Waco, 1978-82, Tex. Dept. Corrections, Gatesville, Tex., 1983-91; RN Tex. Dept. Corrections, Gatesville, 1993—; RN relief charge nurse Hillcrest Med. Ctr., Waco, 1992-93; RN coord. infectious dis. Hilltop Unit Tex. Dept. Corrections, Gatesville, 1994—. Mem. ANA, Tex. Nurses Assn., N-STAT. Baptist. Home: 3051 Canaan Church Rd Crawford TX 76638-3335 Office: Tex Dept Criminal Justice 1500 State Sch Rd Gatesville TX 76528

GAUGER, MICHELE ROBERTA, photographer, studio administrator, corporate executive; b. Elkhorn, Wis., Feb. 28, 1949; d. Robert F. and Christiane J. (Guiffaut) Marszalek; m. Richard C. Gauger, May 3, 1969 (div.). Student U. Wis., Superior, 1967-69, U. Wis., Whitewater, 1978-80, Winona Sch. Profl. Photography-Chgo., 1984-91; Degree in Photographic Craftsmenship, Profl. Photographers of Am., 1990, MA in Photography, 1994. Wedding photographer Fossum Studio, Elkhorn, 1973-78; owner Photography by Michele, Whitewater, 1978-81; pres., photographer, mgr., Michele Inc. of Wis., Whitewater, 1981—, Foxes Reg., 1987; speaker Wedding Photographers Internat. Conv., Las Vegas, Nev., 1987, 89, Nashville, 1988, 93, Tenn. Profl. Photographers Assn., Nashville, 1987, Twin Cities Profl. Photographers, Mpls., 1987; lectr. Supra Color Seminar, Mpls., 1987, 89, San Francisco Profl. Photographers Assn., 1988, Monterey Profl. Photographers Assn., Nev. Profl. Photographers Assn., 1989, Mich. Profl. Photographers Assn., 1989, 94, Wis. Profl. Photographers Assn., 1993, 94, N.J. Profl. Photographers, Assn., 1995. Contbr. articles to profl. jours.; works exhibited Chinese Nat. Gallery, Beijing, 1987, 88, 89, 91, 94, 95. Mem. Nat. Arbor Found, Nebr., 1984—. Recipient 1st place Wedding Photography award Internat. Wedding Photography, 1983, 84, 87, 88 (two awards), 89, 91, 96, 2nd place award, 1985, 96, Grand award, 1988; named to Wis. Ct. Honor, 1991, 96. Mem. Profl. Photographers Am. (Natl. Loan Collectional 1984), Exhibited Chinese Nat. Gallery, Beijing, China (2d place award 1988, Bronze medal 1989), Wis. Profl. Photographer Assn., Wedding Photographer Internat., Winona Sch. Profl. Photography Alumni Assn., Whitewater C. of C. Republican. Roman Catholic. Avocations: world travel, big game hunting, horseback riding, cooking. Home and Office: Michele Inc N7240 Sand Pyramid Whitewater WI 53190-9802

GAUL, MALINDA ANN, lawyer; b. Greenville, S.C., Jan. 20, 1958; d. Alexander and W. Ann (Watson) Gozur; m. Grant Andrew Gaul, Jan. 28, 1984. BA, Baylor U., 1979, JD, 1982. Bar: Tex. 1982, U.S. Dist. Ct. (we. dist.) Tex. 1985, U.S. Dist. Ct. (so., no. and ea. dists.) Tex. 1990, U.S. Ct. Appeals (5th cir.) 1990, U.S. Ct. Appeals (fed. cir.) 1994, U.S. Supreme Ct. 1990. Assoc. Kosub, Langlois & Van Cleave, San Antonio, 1982-84; asst. Law Offices Julia Navelli, Rome, N.Y., 1984-86; ptnr. Kosub & Gaul, San Antonio, 1986-94, Gaul and Dumont, San Antonio, 1995—. Mem. ABA, Tex. Bar Assn., Bexar County Women's Bar Assn., Kappa Kappa Gamma, Zeta Phi Eta. Democrat. Baptist. Office: Gaul and Dumont 105 S St Mary's Ste 950 San Antonio TX 78205

GAULIN, LYNN, experiential education educator; b. Chgo., Nov. 26, 1937. BA, U. R.I., 1979, MA in Adult Edn., 1991; MSW, Boston Coll., Newton, Mass., 1981. Lic. social worker, Mass. Planner King Philip Elder Svcs., Foxboro, Mass., 1981-84; field coord. U. R.I., Kingston, 1984—, acting dir., 1995-96, instr. human sci. and svcs., 1988—, acting dir. Office Internship and Field Experience, 1995-96. Chmn. North Attleboro (Mass.) Dem. Town Treas. Com., 1990-96; mem., chmn. sch. com. North Attleboro Pub. Schs., 1981-91; mem. North Attleboro Bd. Selectmen, 1991-94; mem. edn. com., chmn. leadership com. Commn. on Women, Providence, 1989—. Mem. Acad. Cert. Social Workers, Assn. Profl. and Acad. Women, New Eng. Orgn. Human Svc. Edn. (bd. dirs., membership chairwoman 1994—), Nat. Soc. Exptl. Edn., Phi Beta Kappa, Phi Kappa Phi (pres. U. R.I. chpt. 1994-95). Democrat. Home: PO Box 664 605 Broadway North Attleboro MA 02760-1167 Office: U RI Taft Hall Kingston RI 02881

GAULT, TERESSA ELAINE, special education educator; b. South Williamson, Ky., Feb. 25, 1959; d. Donald Lee and Glenna Faye (Kirk) Varney; m. Marc Allen Widener, Sept. 1, 1979 (div. Aug. 1994); 1 child, Dawn Elise Widener; m. Robert William Gault III, July 29, 1995. EdB, Ohio U., 1980, MEd, 1992. Cert. tchr. grades 1-8, Ohio; cert. tchr. multiple, severely, profoundly retarded grades K-12, Ohio. Substitute tchr. Lancaster City (Ohio) Schs., 1980-81, tchr. multihandicapped, 1990—; tchr. St. Mary Elem. Sch., Lancaster, Ohio, 1981-88; habilitation specialist II Licking County Bd. Mental Retardation/Developmental Disabilities, Heath, Ohio, 1988-89; presch. instr. MH Perry County Cmty. Schs., New Lexington, Ohio, 1989-90; instr. computer Fairfield Career Ctr., Carroll, Ohio, 1988, Southeastern Bus. Coll., Lancaster, Ohio, 1988-89. Recipient Letter of Commendation The Ohio House of Reps., 1993. Mem. Nat. Edn. Assn., Ohio Edn. Assn., Lancaster Edn. Assn. Democrat. Methodist. Home: 2656 Heidelberg Dr Lancaster OH 43130 Office: West Elem Sch Lancaster City Schs 625 Garfield Ave Lancaster OH 43130

GAUNCH, PAMELA JEWEL, bank executive; b. Charleston, W.Va., May 9, 1951; d. Donald Wayne and Phyllis Jean (Peters) Turley; m. James Michael Gaunch, Mar. 13, 1971; 1 child, Michael Wayne. Student, W.Va. Inst. Tech., 1967-69, W.Va. State Coll., 1969-71, 88-89; AS, U. Charleston, 1990. Svc. cons. Rodger House Pontiac-Buick-GMC, Nitro, W.Va., 1994-95; tchr. Boone County Bd. Edn., Madison, W.Va., 1969-71; customer svc. mgr., computer sys. mgr., teller Bank One-W.Va., Charleston, 1971-74, 88-91, 1995—; office mgr. Connie Whiteside State Farm Agy., Charleston, 1991-92; sales rep., svc. cons. Stephens Auto, Danville, W.Va., 1992-93; sales rep. C&O Motors, St. Albans, 1993, Big Sandy Furniture, Dunbar, W.Va., 1993-94. Republican. Baptist. Home: HC 64 Box 928 Ashford WV 25009 Office: Bank One 707 Virginia St E Charleston WV 25312

GAUTHIER, MARY ELIZABETH, librarian, researcher, secondary education educator; b. Tudor, Alta., Can., May 17, 1917; d. Harold Bertram and Mary Evelyn (Foley) Bliss; m. Louis Lyons Gauthier, May 31, 1947 (dec. 1976). PhB, Northwestern U., 1970; MA in Edn., Lewis U., 1976; EdD, Pacific States U., London, 1979. Clk. LaGrange (Ill.) Pub. Libr., 1956-57; package libr. AMA, Chgo., 1958-60; staff libr. Duff, Anderson & Clark, Chgo., 1960-63; libr./tchr. Fremont Sch. Dist. 79, Mundelein, Ill., 1970-75; substitute tchr. Valleyview Sch. Dist. 365-U, Romeoville, Ill., 1978-89; dormitory dir./tchr. Project Upward Bound, Romeoville, Ill., 1984-94, enrichment studies, 1991-94; ind. researcher South Bend, Ind., 1990-94; instr. Joliet (Ill.) Jr. Coll., 1986-89; cons. Wash. High Sch.; bd. of advisors Ivy Tech. Coll., Southbend, 1993. Contbr. monograph and articles to profl. jours.; author: Some Basic Principles of New Scientific Attitudes in Education, 1980. Active Manor Pk. Community Assn., Ottawa, Can., 1953. With RCAF, 1943-45. Recipient Gold medal Internat. Symposium on the Mgmt. of Stress, Monte Carlo, 1979; grantee Ill. State Bd. Edn., 1985, Ind. U. South Bend, 1992. Mem. AAAS, N.Y. Acad. Scis.

GAUTIER, ELIZABETH JOLENE, accountant, consultant; b. Claremore, Okla., Apr. 15, 1958; d. Jack Milton and Beverly Jo (Duke) Miller; m. Roger Allen Gautier, June 19, 1980; 1 child, Heather Dawn. AD in Bus., Tulsa Jr. Coll., 1988; B in Bus., Langston U., 1989. Acct. Am. Airlines Inc., Tulsa, Okla., 1979-81; computer operator JR Norton Co., Phoenix, 1981-83; full charge bookkeeper REC Specialties, Inc., Camarillo, Calif., 1983-84; acct. Sandstone, Inc., Tulsa, 1984-89; acctg. and DP mgr. Colorgraphics Corp., Tulsa, 1989-90; mgr. cost acctg. Springtime Growers, San Diego, 1991-93; adminstr. cost acctg. GTE Interactive Media, Carlsbad, Calif., 1993-96; acctg. mgr. Airline Interiors, Simula Co., San Diego, 1996—; tax cons. Elizabeth Gautier's Tax Svc., San Diego, 1992—. Auditor Carl Sandburg PTA, San Diego, 1994-95, treas., 1995-96, pres., 1996—; leader Girl Scouts of U.S., Troop 8103, San Diego, 1993-95. Fellow mem. Int. Mgmt. Accts. (cert.). Republican. Office: Airline Interiors 9940 Mesa Rim Rd San Diego CA 92121

GAVARINI, JEHANNE-MARIE, artist, educator; b. Saint Jean de Maurienne, Savoie, France, Nov. 10, 1953; Came to the U.S., 1978; d. André-Louis-Victor and Mireille-Carmen (Bonfils) G. BA, U. Calif., Berkeley, 1991; MFA, U. Calif., Davis, 1994. Asst. prof. in sculpture Lafayette Coll., Easton, Pa., 1995; founder of theater co. Le Cirque Des Femmes, Toulouse, France, 1979-81, Charivari, San Francisco, 1978-79. Solo exhbns. include Loaded Subject, 1994, Passé Simple, 1995, No Opening, 1995, Notre pain de chaque jour, 1996, Exil, 1997. Mem. and founder Disarming Women, San Francisco, 1981-86; mem. Non Nuclear Family, San Francisco, 1981-83. Recipient 1st prize San Jose Art League, 1991, Merit award San Francisco Women Artists Gallery, 1992, 1st prize Matrix Gallery, Sacramento, 1993. Mem. Nat. Mus. Women in the Arts, Coll. Art Assn., Pi Delta Phi. Office: Williams Ctr for the Arts Lafayette Coll Easton PA 18042

GAVIN, JOAN ELAINE, special education educator; b. Onalaska, Wis., July 26, 1950; d. Vernon and Helen Ruth Weinberg; m. A.M. Gavin, June 13, 1986; stepchildren: John Edward, Daniel James, Mark Ambrose, Scott Michael. BS in Elem. Edn., U. Wis., La Crosse, 1973, MS in Spl. Edn., ED/LD, 1975. Cert. 1-8 elem. tchr., tchr. emotionally disturbed and learning disabled, Wis.; cert. crisis prevention intervention; cert. CPR. Tchr. emotionally disturbed and learning disabilities De Soto (Wis.) Area Schs., 1975-79; tchr. elem. emotionally disturbed coop. program Elroy Kendall-Wilton Schs., Elroy, Wis., 1979-84, Wilton, Wis., 1984-86, Kendall, Wis., 1986-93; elem. tchr. Elroy-Kendall-Wilton Schs., Elroy, 1993—; mem. dist.-wide in-svc. com. Elroy-Kendall-Wilton Schs., 1986—, facilitator AODA program, mem. CORE com. AODA, 1994—. Developer, bd. dirs., treas. Kinship of Elroy, Inc., 1980-89; pres., coord. county-wide program Kinship, Inc., 1984—; active Kids for Kids. Honor scholar, 1968; grantee NSF Sci. Enhancement Project, U. Wis., 1985, 86, 88, 89, 90. Mem. Coun. for Exceptional Children, Am. Legion Aux., U. Wis.-LaCrosse Alumni Assn. Office: 1100 Academy St Elroy WI 53929

GAVIN, MARY JANE, medical, surgical nurse; b. Prairie Du Chien, Wis., Sept. 1, 1941; d. Frank Grant and Mary Elizabeth Wolf; m. Alfred William Gavin, Nov. 9, 1963; children: Catherine Heidi Elizabeth, Carl Alfred Eric. Student, North Cen. Coll., Naperville, Ill., 1959-61; BS, RN, U. Wis., 1964; postgrad., Deepmuscle Tng. Ltd., 1980; postgrad. in deep muscle therapy. RN, Wis. Staff nurse U. Wis. Hosps., Madison; RN home response VA, Milw. Unit chair Badger Girls State, 1991—; mem. Wis. Am. Legion Aux.; mem. task force for handicapped Eastside Wis. Evang. Luth. Ch., Madison, 1993. U. Wis. scholar. Mem. Monona Grove Am. Legion Aux. (pres. Unit 429). Home: 702 Fairmont Ave Madison WI 53714-1424

GAVIN, PAULA LANCE, professional society administrator; b. Nassau, N.Y., July 25, 1945; d. Paul P. and Gisela M. (Saume) Lance; m. John J. Gavin, July 23, 1983; children: Jennifer, Jason. BA, U. Del., 1967. With AT&T, N.J., 1967-90; pres. YMCA of Greater N.Y., N.Y.C., 1990—; mem., chair N.Y. Stock Exch. Adv. Com., N.Y.C., 1993—; bd. dirs. Health Ins. Plan, N.Y.C., 1995—. Bd. dirs. N.Y.C. Partnership and C. of C. Office: YMCA 333 7th Ave New York NY 10001

GAWEHN-FRISBY, DOROTHY JEANNE, freelance technical writer; b. Omaha, Jan. 20, 1931; d. Robert Floyd and Margaret Marie (Sitzman) Sealock; m. Kenneth Emil Gawehn, Apr. 17, 1951 (div. Jan. 1985); children: Marilyn Gawehn Jeffries, Kenneth M., Eric M., Celeste Gawehn-Yates; m. Charles Frisby, Mar. 17, 1990. Grad. high sch., Omaha. Systems technician Nat. Welding Co., Richmond, Calif., 1962-63; lead data entry operator United Grocers Co., Fresno, Calif., 1964-68, data processing mgr., 1968-72, computer operator shift supr., Oakland, Calif., 1972-76, documentation specialist, 1976-82; mgr. adminstrv. systems Baddour, Inc., Memphis, 1983-89; with Fed. Express Corp., 1989-91; sr. tech. writer Autozone, Memphis, 1991-95; freelance writer; contract tech. writer with Ctrl. Technical Svcs. Reader for the blind Sta. WTTL, Memphis, 1983-89; vol. worker Crisis and Suicide Intervention, Memphis, 1985-89, Docent for Ramesses exhibit, 1987. Recipient Key to Memphis. Mem. Internat. Tng. Communication (club pres. 1989-90, 96—, Communicator of Yr. award, Dixie region 1988-89, coun. 4 exec. bd. 1992-93), Data Processing Mgmt. Assn (Performance award 1973, Yosemite chpt.), Mensa (chmn. 1989-90, 96). Republican. Roman Catholic. Avocations: backpacking, reading, writing, travel, hiking. Home and Office: 6644 Elkgate Memphis TN 38141-1205

GAWEL, MAUREEN SALTZER, newspaper executive; b. Winchester, Mass., Mar. 21, 1959; d. William Charles Saltzer and Janet Ann (Quigley) Child; m. O. Lee Brotherton, June 27, 1981 (div. 1984); m. Robert Chester Gawel, Oct. 14, 1996; 1 child, Lauren Roberta. BS in Journalism summa cum laude, Boston U., 1981; postgrad., Northeastern U., Boston, 1984, U. Calif., Riverside, 1994. Freelance corr. Concord (N.H.) Monitor, 1981-82; advt. sales rep. N.H. Times, Concord, 1981-82, circulation mgr., 1982-83; circulation and promotion mgr. Century Publs. Inc., Winchester, Mass., 1983-84, asst. gen. mgr., 1984-85; ad dir., ops. mgr. Provincetown (Mass.) Adv., 1985-86; gen. mgr. Healdsburg (Calif.) Tribune, Lesher Communications, 1986-87, Valley Times, Lesher Communications, Pleasanton, Calif., 1987-90; corp. oper. bd. dirs. Lesher Communications Inc., Walnut Creek, Calif.; pub., v.p. Victor Valley Daily Press and Barstow Desert Dispatch divsn. div. Freedom Newspapers, Victorville, Calif., 1990—. Bd. dirs. Desert Cmtys. United Way, campaign chmn., 1992, v.p., 1993, pres., 1994; bd. dirs. Victor Valley Cmty. Svcs. Coun., pres., 1993; hotline listener First Call for Help; treas. High Desert Regional Econ. Devel. Authority, pres. 1995-96; bd. dirs. Victor Valley Coll. Found. Recipient Woman of Achievement award Bus. and Profl. Women, San Orco, 1991, Golden Nike award, 1991, 94, Hall of Fame-Bus. award for State of Calif., 1992, Humanitarian award Desert Comtys., United Way, 1991, Outstanding Exec. Achievement award U. Calif. Riverside, 1994-95; named Citizen of Yr., Boy Scouts Am. Serrano Dist., 1994. Mem. Am. Newspaper Pubs. Assn., Calif. Newspaper Pubs. Assn. (1st v.p. so. unit 1993, pres. 1994, state bd. dirs. 1994—, 2d pl. excellence award 1989), Internat. Newspaper Mktg. Assn., Internat. Newspaper Advt. and Mktg. Execs. Assn. (best TV comml. award 1992), Apple Valley C. of C., Victorville C. of C. (leadership com., fundraising com.), Rotary. Democrat. Home: 20672 Sholic Rd Apple Valley CA 92308-6367 Office: Victor Valley Daily Press PO Box 1389 Victorville CA 92393-1389

GAWTHROP, DAPHNE WOOD, performing company executive. Exec. dir. Sacramento Ballet. Office: 1631 K St Sacramento CA 95814-4019*

GAWTHROP, LINDA ANNE, circulation assistant; b. Washington, Nov. 26, 1950; d. Louis August and Viola Pearl (Holland) Miller; m. Richard Carr Gawthrop, Sept. 9, 1978; children: Richard C. II, Kevin C. BA with distinction, U. R.I., 1972; M of Planning, U. Va., 1979. Rsch. asst. Dept. Agr., Beltsville, Md., 1972-74; asst. dir. The Nature Conservancy, Arlington, Va., 1974-78; asst. land use planner Wapora, Inc., Chgo., 1978-80; environ. protection specialist EPA, Chgo., 1980-81; mem. nat. heritage task force U.S. Dept. Interior, Washington, 1978; workshop leader women's studies program U. Ill., Chgo., 1981; presenter application earth sci. info. to planning process seminar U.S. Geol. Survey, Reston, Va., 1977. Contbg. author: (report and recommendation) The Preservation of Natural Diversity, 1975, Lowest Common Denominator File--An Information Management System, 1976. Bd. officers Mosby Woods PTA, Fairfax, Va., 1994, Edgelea Woods Comty. Assn., Vienna, Va., 1995, Young Woman's Christian Home, Washington, 1996, Christian Womens Club, Fairfax, 1996. Recipient Gold Oak Leaf award The Nature Conservancy, 1977. Mem. Am. Planning Assn., Toastmasters Internat., Phi Sigma. Democrat. Methodist.

GAY, CATHERINE, corporate communications consultant. BA, U. So. Calif.; postgrad., Hebrew U. Reporter Caracas Daily Jour., 1963; writer, 1965-67; asst. to dir. fgn. pub. rels. Israel Mus., Jerusalem; nat. coord. of programs AZYF; dir. spkrs. bur. ZOA; broadcaster WEVD Radio Sta., N.Y.C., 1976-78; assoc. prodr. Howard Enders Prods., 1978-79; cons., 1978-81; exec. dir. Ctr. for Comm., Inc., 1981-90; v.p. pub. affairs Maxwell/Macmillan Group, 1990; pub., strategic comms. cons. Internat. Adv. Coun., N.Y.C., 1990—. Recipient Gold award Internat. Teleconferencing Assn., 1987. Mem. Coun. on Fgn. Rels., Soc. of Profl. Journalists, Advt. Women of N.Y. Address: 6 Prince St New York NY 10012

GAY-BRYANT, CLAUDINE MOSS, retired physician; b. Alma, Ga., Nov. 30, 1915; d. Fred and Rosa (Mercer) Moss; B.S., Coll. William and Mary, 1935; M.D., U. Va., 1939; m. Lendall C. Gay, June 29, 1940 (dec. 1969); children: Gordon B., Spencer B.; m. J. Marion Bryant, 1974 (dec. 1986). Intern, Gallinger Mcpl. Hosp., Washington; practice medicine specializing in family practice, Washington, 1940-91 ; mem. staff, exec. bd. Sibley Meml. and Capitol Hill Hosp., Washington; ret. 1990; mem. Pres.'s Council on Malpractice, 1965; mem. health adv. commn. HEW, 1971-78; U.S. del. Med. Women's Internat. Congress, 5 times; del. Pres.'s Workshop on Non-Govtl. Orgn. Trustee Moss Charity Trust Fund, 1966—; adv. bd. Med. Coll. Pa., 1977; mem. president's council Coll. William and Mary. Recipient Capitol Hill Community Achievement award, 1986; Claudine Moss Radiological Ampatheatre donated to U. Va. Med. Sch., 1991. Fellow Am. Acad. Family Practice (del. 1971-81; alt. del. to ho. dels. 1964-71); mem. Assn. Med. Women Internat. (del. 1966-72, councillor 1978-84), Royal Acad. Medicine, Pan Am. Med. Soc., D.C. Acad. Gen. Practice (pres.), Am. Med. Women's Assn. (councilor orgn. and mgmt. 1972-73, v.p. 1974, nat. pres. 1977, Blackwell medal 1988), D.C. Med. Women's Assn. (pres.), AMA, D.C. Med. Soc. (dir., exec. bd., past v.p., mem. nominating com. 1970, 81, relative value study com. 1970-72, constn. and constn. bylaws com., sec. family practice sect. 1966, 69, 78), DAR Regent. Clubs: Women's Roundtable for Health Issues, Washington Forum (pres. 1987-88), Zonta (dir.). Home: 5030 Loughboro Rd NW Washington DC 20016-2613

GAYLOR, ANNE NICOL, editor, foundation executive; b. Tomah, Wis., Nov. 25, 1926; d. Jason Theodore and Lucie Edna (Sowle) Nicol; m. Paul Joseph Gaylor, Jr., Dec. 29, 1949; children: Andrew, Ian Stuart, Annie Laurie, Jamie Lachlan. BA, U. Wis., 1949. Founder Freedom from Religion Found., Madison, Wis., 1976, pres., 1978—; editor Freethought Today. Author: Abortion is a Blessing, 1975, Lead Us Not into Penn Station, 1983. Founder, adminstr. Women's Med. Fund, Inc., Madison, 1972, Zero Population Growth Referral Service, Madison, 1970; founder, pres. Protect Abortion Rights, Inc., Madison, 1978. Recipient Achievement award Zero Population Growth, 1983, Humanist Heroine award Am. Humanist Assn., 1985. Home: 726 Miami Pass Madison WI 53711-2933

GAYLOR, ANNIE LAURIE, editor; b. Madison, Wis., Nov. 2, 1955; d. Paul Joseph and (Lucie) Anne (Nicol) G.; m. Daniel Edwin Barker, May 30, 1987; 1 child, Sabrina Delata. BA in Journalism, U. Wis., 1980. Founder, editor, pub. Feminist Connection newspaper, Madison, 1980-84; editor Freethought Today Freedom From Religion Foundation, Inc., Madison, 1985—; coord. Feminist Caucus of Am. Humanist Assn., Madison, 1991—. Author: Woe to the Woman: The Bible Tells Me So, 1981, Betrayal of Trust: Clergy Abuse of Children, 1988; editl. page editor: Daily Cardinal newspaper, U. Wis., Madison, 1978. Bd. dirs. Women's Med. Fund, Madison, 1989—; maj. activist recall of Judge Archie Simonson, Madison, 1977; maj. activist campaign to save Ms. Forward statue, Madison, 1995. 9th pl. student scholar Hearst Found., 1978, student scholar Ken Purdy Scholarship, U. Wis., 1980. Democrat. Office: Freedom From Religion Found PO Box 750 Madison WI 53701

GAYNOR, LEAH, radio personality, commentator, broadcaster; b. Irvington, N.J.; d. Jack and Sophia Kamish; AA, Miami Dade C.C., 1970; BA, Fla. Internat. U., 1975, postgrad., 1975—; m. Robert Merrill, Mar. 27, 1954 (dec.); children: Michael David (dec.), Lisa Heidi (dec.), Tracy Lynn (dec.). Owner, operator Lee Gaynor Assos., pub. relations, Miami, Fla., 1970-72; exec. dir. Ft. Lauderdale (Fla.) Jaycees, 1970-71; host interview program Sta. WGMA, Hollywood, Fla., 1971-73, stas. WWOK and WIGL-FM, Fla., 1973-79; occupational specialist Lindsey Hopkins Edn. Ctr. Dade County Pub. Schs., publicity-pub. rels., Miami, 1971-91; ednl. specialist Office Vocat., Adult, Career and Community Edn. Dade County Pub. Schs. 1991-94; broadcaster talk show sta. WEDR-FM, 1983-93; host, producer weekly half-hour pub. service talk program, The Leah Gaynor Show, 1985-94. Mem. Citizens Adv. Com. Career and Vocat. Edn., 1973; mem. adv. com. North Miami Beach High Sch., 1977-79; mem. publicity Com. Ctr. Fine Arts, Mus. Sci.; mem. Coalition Community Edn.; bd. dirs. Alternative Programs, Inc. Mem. Women in Comm., Am. Women in Radio and TV (dir. publicity Goldcoast chpt. 1974-76), Alliance Career Edn. (publicity chmn.). Democrat. Home: 1255 NE 171st Ter Miami FL 33162-2755

GAYNOR, MARGARET CRYOR, program director; b. Oak Park, Ill.; children: Andrew Thorp, Mary Leland. Student, Wellesley Coll., U. Ariz.; BA in Am. Studies, George Washington U., 1974; postgrad., Fed. Exec. Inst. Caseworker, spl. asst. U.S. Senate, Washington, 1962-65, 69-70; assoc. dir. for congl. rels. U. S. OEO, Washington, 1970-73; dir. Office of Govt. Rels. Smithsonian Instn., Washington, 1973-92, dir. Office of Policy and Program Devel., 1992-94, asst. dir. Office Planning Mgmt. and Budget, 1995—. Past treas. LEADER Fund of Women in Govt. Rels., bd. dirs.; former mem. Alexandria Archaeology Commn. Home: 220 N Alfred St Alexandria VA 22314-2408

GAZDAG, GAIL ELIZABETH, psychology associate; b. Rockville Center, N.Y., Mar. 4, 1950; d. Russell Carl and Claire Elizabeth (Robinson) G.; m. Jerry Michael Plummer, Apr. 14, 1990. BA in Psychology, L.I. U., 1972, MPS, 1979; PhD in Psychology, Vanderbilt U., 1994. Psychology asst. Manhattan Devel. Ctr., N.Y.C., 1972-78, Suffolk Devel. Ctr., Melville, 1978-82; psychology assoc. Rosewood Ctr., Balt., 1994—. Contbr. articles to profl. jours. Comml. Travelers scholar, 1979. Mem. NOW, Am. Assn. Mental Retardation, Assn. Behavior Analysts. Home: 7F Tentmill Ln Baltimore MD 21208 Office: Rosewood Ctr Psychology Dept Rosewood Ln Owings Mills MD 21117

GEALT, ADELHEID MARIA, museum director; b. Munich, May 29, 1946; came to U.S., 1950; d. Gustav Konrad and Ella Sophie (Daeschlein) Medicus; m. Barry Allen Gealt, Mar. 15, 1969. BA, Ohio State U., 1968; MA, Ind. U., 1973, PhD, 1979. Registrar Ind. U. Art Mus., Bloomington, 1972-76, curator Western art, 1976—, acting/interim dir., 1987-89, dir., 1989—; adj. assoc. prof. H.R. Hope Sch. Fine Arts, Ind. U., Bloomington, 1985-89, assoc. scholar, 1986, assoc. prof., 1989—; mem. nat. adv. coun. Valparaiso U. Art Mus. Author: Looking at Art, 1983, Domenico Tiepolo The Punchinello Drawings, 1986; co-author: Art of the Western World, 1989, Painting of the Golden Age: A Biographical Dictionary of Seventeenth-Century European Painters, 1993. Grantee Nat. Endowment for Arts, 1982, 83, Am. Philos. Soc., 1985, NEH, 1985. Mem. Assn. Art Mus. Dirs. Office: Ind U Art Mus 7th St Bloomington IN 47405-3024

GEANDOMENICO, ANNE-MARIE, elementary school educator; b. Bklyn., Dec. 13, 1967; d. William Joseph and Jean Ann (Fortunato) G. BS in Elem. Edn., C.W. Post/L.I. U., 1989, MS in Early Childhood Elem. Edn., 1992; postgrad., Setric-Salisbury Ctr., 1993. Cert. elem. tchr., N.Y. Kindergarten tchr. Lee Ave/Woodland Ave. Sch., Hicksville, N.Y., 1989-90; kindergarten tchr. Lee Ave. Sch., Hicksville, 1989-90, third grade tchr., 1990-92, kindergarten tchr., 1992-94, fourth grade tchr., 1994—; site based mgmt. mem. Lee Ave. Sch., Hicksville, 1993—; mem. Dist. Curriculum Coun., 1995—. Vol. catechist St. Kilian's Ch., Farmingdale, N.Y., 1983-93, Outreach vol., 1985—. Recipient Pope Pious X Catechist award 1993. Mem. C.W. Post Alumni Assn., Nassau Reading Coun., Hicksville Congress of Tchrs. (bowling team capt. 1990—). Home: 127 Motor Ave Farmingdale NY 11735-4032 Office: Lee Ave Elem Sch 7th St Hicksville NY 11801

GEANURACOS, ELSIE DA SILVA, foreign language educator; b. Bklyn., Dec. 29, 1922; d. John and Maria (Nascimento) Da Silva; m. George J. Geanuracos, Jan. 28, 1945; children: Constance, Patricia, James, Joan, John. BA, Hunter Coll., 1944; student Columbia U., 1944-47. 1st tchr. Portuguese lang. N.Y.C. Sch. System, 1945-50, Spanish tchr., 1945-50; prof. Spanish U. Bridgeport, Conn., 1969, 72, 73, Housatonic Community Coll., Bridgeport, 1970; founder, adviser Portuguese Scholarship Program, U. Bridgeport, 1973—, sec. Halsey Internat. Scholarship Program, 1974, mem. bd. assocs., instr. Spanish, Womens' Inst. U. Bridgeport; tutor Tutoring Ctr. Bridgeport. Com. mem. Womens' Aux. to Fairfield County Med. Assn., Am. Cancer Soc. Bridgeport chpt.; Chmn. dissemination com. Fairfield chpt. Autism Soc. Conn. translator Bridgeport Hosp. Aux.; mem. bd. assoc. U. Bridgeport; mem. Bklyn. Hist. Soc., Bklyn.; mem. Greater Bridgeport Symphony Guild. Recipient citation for community service Am. Cancer Soc. Bridgeport chpt.; citation as an internationalist UN Assn., 1975; 10-yr. service plaque Portuguese Scholar Ship Program of HISP, 1983. Mem. AAUW (treas. Fairfield chpt.), UN Assn., Judeo-Christian Women's Assn. (mistress of ceremonies first awards luncheon 1974), Alpha Delta Pi. Avocations: swimming, reading, drapery making, knitting, traveling. Home: 102 Lu Manor Dr Fairfield CT 06432-1434

GEARHART, MARGUERITE THERESA, school nurse, health educator, nurse, counselor; b. Camden, N.J., Mar. 21, 1936; d. Arthur Thomas AThey and Marguerite Theresa (Phelps) Hurry; m. Gene Ray Reget, June 21, 1958 (div. July 1990); children: Cynthia Goldberg, Pamela Zambelli, Jeannine Serra, Marguerite Reget; m. Michael Roy Gearhart, Aug. 19, 1990. RN, St. Mary Hosp. Sch. Nursing, Phila., 1956; BA magna cum laude, Jersey City State Coll., 1976; MA, Montclair State U., 1982. RN, N.J.; cert. health educator, N.J. Post partum obstet. head nurse Atlantic City (N.J.) Hosp., 1956-57; pediatric psychiat. nurse Ea. Pa. Psychiat. Hosp., Phila., 1957; communicable disease hosp. nurse L.A. County Hosp., 1958; pediatrics head nurse Clarksville (Tenn.) Meml. Hosp., 1959; staff nurse Cape Fear Valley hosp., Fayetteville, N.C., 1963-64; neonatal special care nurse St. John's Hosp., Santa Monica, Calif., 1965-67; staff nurse Valley Community Hosp., Santa Maria, Calif., 1968-72; pediatric health educator Wm. J. Tibbs MD, Santa Maria, 1970-71; community health nurse Community Nursing Svc., E. Orange, N.J., 1976-79; sch. nurse, health educator, chairperson Morristown (N.J.)-Beard Sch., 1979-96, chem. abuse counselor/educator, 1986-94; psychiat.-chem. dependency staff RN Fair Oaks Hosp./Charter Behavioral Health Sys., Summit, N.J., 19990-95. Author, presenter: (booklet) (with Carol Sauer) How to Begin a Drug Prevention Program, 1986. Pres. Profl. Nurses Orgn. Mil. Wives, Munechweller, Germany, 1960, co-leader Campfire Girls, Santa Maria, 1968-69; mem. Nat. LWV, Santa Maria, 1969-72; vol. Santa Maria Assn. Retarded Children, 1969-72. Grantee Drug Free Schs., N.J., 1989-95. Mem. Am. Nurses Assn., Am. Sch. Health Assn., N.J. Sch. Nurses Assn., St. Mary Hosp. Alumni Assn., People to People Internat. (nursing del. to Rep. of China 1984). Home: 1832 Enfield Ave Port St Lucie FL 34952 Office: Morristown-Beard Sch PO Box 1999 Morristown NJ 07962-1999

GEARHART, MARILYN KAYE, mathematics and biology educator; b. Tucson, Apr. 11, 1950; d. Raymond Fred and Joan Gazelle (White) Hagerty; m. Lon David Gearhart, Mar. 22, 1975; children: Amanda Kaye, Shannon Leigh. BA in Elem. Edn. with dis, Manchester Coll., 1972; MS in Elem Edn. summa cum, Ind. U., 1976; BS in Math. with high hon, Tri-State U., 1985; postgrad., Ind. U., 1983-89. Substitute tchr. South Bend (Ind.) Community Sch. Corp., 1971-72; tchr. DeKalb County Ea. Community Sch. Dist., Butler, Ind., 1972-77; founder, tchr. Pleasant View Christian Early Learning Ctr., Angola, Ind., 1981-85; also bd. dirs. Pleasant View Christian Early Learning Ctr., Angola; micro computer tchr. Purdue U., Ft. Wayne, Ind., 1984; substitute tchr. Met. Sch. Dist. Steuben County, Angola, 1985; tchr. math. and biology DeKalb County Cen. United Sch. Dist., Auburn, Ind., 1985--. Author: (textbook) The Impossibility of Achieving and Maintaining an Utopia, 1971. Sponsor freshman class DeKalb H.S., 1987-89, sophomore class, 1989-96, Students Against Drunk Driving, Auburn, 1985-90, Butler Elem. Little Hoosiers, 1973-77; mem. attendance and gifted and talented coms. DeKalb H.S., 1989-90; coach Acad. Decathlon and Hoosier Acad. Super Bowl, 1989—, Hoosier Spell Bowl, 1993—; leader Girl Scouts U.S., 1986-91, mem., coord. product sales Svc. Unit, 1989-90; del. Rep. State Conv., 1996. Dir's. award Jr. Hist. Soc., 1981-85; maths. and sci. scholars Tri-State, 1985; grantee Tchrs. Retng. Fund. Ind.-State, 1983-85. Mem. NEA, AAUW (treas. 1987-89), Dekalb High Sch. Band and Show Choir Parents, Beta Beta Beta. Mem. Christian Ch. Home: 910 Duesenberg Rd Auburn IN 46706-3223 Office: DeKalb High Sch County Rd 427 Waterloo IN 46793

GEARHART, SHIRLEE MORTON, art educator; b. Jacksonville, N.C., Feb. 3, 1935; d. Clyde and Adell (Gurganus) M.; m. James Lee Gearhart, July 3, 1959; children: Jamy Lee, Ann-Marie; m. John Curtiss Welles, Apr. 28, 1982. BS in Edn., East Carolina U., 1957, MA in Art Edn., 1961. Art tchr. New Hanover County Schs., Wilmington, N.C., 1959—. Mem. N.C. Art Edn. Assn. (Secondary Art Tchr. of Yr. 1993-94), Delta Kappa Gamma. Democrat. Presbyterian. Home: 4 Bahama Dr Wrightsville Beach NC 28480-5002

GEARIN, LOUVAN ANITA, retired school librarian; b. St. Louis, July 5, 1917; d. William Sherman and Ira Mae (Haskell) Brabham. BA, Fisk U., 1937; BSLS, Atlanta U., 1949; MSLS, U. Mich., 1955. Cert. tchr., Mo. Libr. Lincoln Inst., Ky., 1950-53; reference libr. Tuskegee (Ala.) Inst., summers 1951-54; jr. high and sr. high libr. Webster Groves (Mo.) Schs.,

1954-82; ret., 1982; cons. selection of titles M. W. Wilson Libr. Catalog, N.Y.C., 1974-82; cons. book bait, reference and subscription books, rev. com. for young adults ALA, Chgo., 1980-82. Vol. Eldercare Ctr., U. Mo., St. Louis, 1985—, County Older Resident Program, St. Louis County, 1987—, Meals on Wheels, Creve Couer, Mo., 1982—. Recipient award Mo. Assn. Sch. Librs., 1984, Vol. award U. Mo., St. Louis, 1985. Mem. AAUW (sec. 1970-82). Home: 11999 Villa Dorado Dr Saint Louis MO 63146

GEARY, LINDA, artist, educator; b. Santa Rosa, Calif., Feb. 14, 1960; d. William and Therese (Hassler) G. BA in Fine Art, U. San Diego, 1982, BA in English, 1982; MFA in Painting and Drawing, U. Del., 1986. Printer Crown Point Press, San Francisco, 1990-91; artist, painter Oakland, Calif., 1986—; art instr. Contra Costa Coll., San Pablo, Calif., 1994—; budget and proposals intern Southern Exposure, San Francisco, 1994. One-woman shows include Branson Sch., Ross, Calif., 1987, Claudia Chapline Gallery, 1991, 93, Okeanos Press, 1994, Ohlone Coll., Fremont, Calif., 1995, Triangle Gallery, San Francisco, 1996; exhibited in group shows at Del. Ctr. Contemporary Art, Wilmington, 1985-86, L.A. County Mus. Art, 1986, U. Wis., Oshkosh, 1986, San Jacinto Coll., 1986, Columbia Coll., 1989-90, Berkeley Art Ctr., 1991, Terrain Gallery, Newport, R.I., 1992, 94, U. Del., 1994, U. Pacific, Stockton, 1994, San Jose (Calif.) Inst. Contemporary Art, 1995; represented in permanent collections at Quadus Corp., Mpls., Banke Nat. Paris, San Francisco, numerous pvt. collections. Recipient Emerging Artists award Del. State Arts Coun., 1987, Gold award Art of Calif. mag., 1993; grantee Pollock-Krasner Found., 1995. Democrat.

GEARY, MARIE JOSEPHINE, art association administrator; b. Boston, Dec. 1, 1933; d. Vincent and Maryanne (DeAngelo) Bianco; m. John Francis Geary, Oct. 11, 1959; 1 child, John Francis Jr. Diploma, Medford High Sch., 1951. Registrar grad./postgrad. div. Tufts U. Sch. Dental Medicine, Boston, 1951-60; reporter, arts editor Chelmsford (Mass.) Newsweekly, 1970-82; owner, mgr. Village Sq. Art Gallery, Chelmsford, 1976-80; founder, owner A Way With Words, Chelmsford, 1980—; founder, dir. Eastcoast Quilters Alliance, Westford, Mass., 1988—; mktg. cons. Westford Regency Inn, 1991. Contbr. articles to profl. mags. Pub. rels. dir. New Eng. Quilt Mus., Lowell, 1986-88; founder, pres. Chelmsford Art Soc., 1970-75; founder, bd. dirs. Chelmsford Cultural Coun., 1980-84; founder, dir. pub. rels. Chelmsford Crafters, Inc., 1976-80; publicity dir. Chelmsford Town 4th of July Celebration, 1971-74; founder Women in Bus. Conf., 1994; adv. bd. Clear Lake Furniture. Mem. Am. Quilting Soc., Chelmsford Quilters (pres. 1985-89), New Eng. Quilters Guild (Compass editor 1985-88), Chelmsford Book Discussion Soc., Quilters Connection (Quiltations editor 1992-93, v.p. 1994-95, pres. 1995-96), Middlesex Women's Network, Women in Bus. (formed 1993, coord. 1st conf. 1994), Enterprising Women. Republican. Roman Catholic. Home: 38 Amble Rd Chelmsford MA 01824-1968 Office: Eastcoast Quilters Alliance PO Box 711 Westford MA 01886-0021

GEARY, NANCY THOMPSON, elementary school educator; b. New Kensington, Pa., Jan. 14, 1955; d. James Harold Jr. and Mary Jane (Shope) Thompson; m. Joseph L. Geary, July 12, 1980; 1 child, Matthew Joseph. BS in Edn., Indiana U. Pa., 1976, MS in Reading, 1981. Cert. reading specialist Pa. Dept. Edn. Elem. tchr. Indiana Area Sch. Dist., 1976—; mem. bur. tchr. prep. evaluation team Pa. Dept. Edn., Harrisburg, 1991—; mem. tchr. edn. adv. com. Indiana U. Pa., 1983-86. Mem. citizen's adv. coun. Indiana Area Sch. Dist., 1991—; mem. exec. bd. Ben Franklin Elem. Sch. PTA, Indiana, 1993—; Cub den leader Boy Scouts Am., Indiana, 1992-94; vol. children's libr. Indiana Free Libr., 1992-93. Pa. Tech. Initiative grantee Pa. Dept. Edn., 1983. Mem. AAUW, Nat. Assn. Educators of Young Children, Internat. Reading Assn., Ind. Reading Coun. (mem. membership and publicity coms.), Ind. Area Edn. Assn. (treas.), Pa. State Edn. Assn., Keystone State Reading Assn. (presenter ann. conf. 1993-94), Phi Delta Kappa. Office: Ben Franklin Elem Sch Indiana Area Sch Dist 95 Ben Franklin Rd Indiana PA 15701

GEBBIE, KATHARINE BLODGETT, astrophysicist; b. Cambridge, Mass., July 4, 1932. BA, Bryn Mayr Coll., 1957; BSc, U. London, 1960, PhD, 1965. Rsch. assoc. astrophysics Joint Inst. Lab. Astrophysics, U. Colo., 1967-68, lectr. physics and astrophysics, 1974-77; astrophysicist Nat. Bur. Standards, 1968-85, supervisory physicist, 1985-89; dir. physics lab. Nat. Inst. Standards and Tech., 1990—; adj. prof. astrophys., planetary and atmospheric scis. U. Colo., 1977-89. Fellow Joint Inst. Lab. Astrophysics, Am. Phys. Soc.; mem. AAAS, Internat. Astron. Union, Internat. Com. Weights and Measures, Royal Astron. Soc., Sigma Xi. Office: Nat Inst Standards & Tech Physics Lab Bldg 221 Rte 270 Gaithersburg MD 20899

GEBBIE, KRISTINE MOORE, health science educator, health official; b. Sioux City, Iowa, June 26, 1943; d. Thomas Carson and Gladys Irene (Stewart) Moore; m. Lester N. Wright; children: Anna, Sharon, Eric. BSN, St. Olaf Coll., 1965; MSN, UCLA, 1968; DPH U. Mich., 1995. Project dir. USPHS tng. grant, St. Louis, 1972-77; coord. nursing St. Louis U., 1974-76, asst. dir. nursing, 1976-78, clin. prof., 1977-78; adminstr. Oreg. Health Div., Portland, 1978-89; sec. Wash. State Dept. Health, Olympia, 1989-93; coord. Nat. AIDS Policy, Washington, 1993-94; asst. prof. Sch. Nursing Columbia U., 1994—; assoc. prof. Oreg. Health Scis. U. Portland, 1980—; chair, U.S. dept. energy secretarial panel on Evaluation of Epidemiologic Rsch. Activities, 1989-90; mem. Presdl. Commn. on Human Immunodeficiency Virus Epidemic, 1987-88. Author: (with Deloughery and Neuman) Consultation and Community Orgn., 1971, (with Deloughery) Political Dynamics: Impact on Nurses, 1975; (with Scheer) Creative Teaching in Clinical Nursing, 1976. Bd. dirs. Luth. Family Svcs. Oreg. and S.W. Wash., 1979-84; bd. dirs. Oreg. Psychoanalytic Found., 1983-87. Recipient Disting. Alumna award St. Olaf Coll., 1979; Disting. scholar Am. Nurses Found., 1989. Fellow Am. Acad. Nursing; mem. Assn. State & Territorial Health Ofcls., 1988 (pres. 1984-85, exec. com. 1980-87, McCormick award 1988), Am. Pub. Health Assn. (exec. bd.), Inst. Medicine, N.Am. Nursing Diagnosis Assn. (treas. 1983-87), Am. Soc. Pub. Adminstrn. (adminstrn. award II 1983). Office: Columbia U Sch Nursing 630 W 168th St New York NY 10032-3702

GEBHARD, DIANE KAY, county administrator, political advisor; b. Indpls., Aug. 9, 1947; d. John Allen and Ruth Ethel (Bolin) Wortman; children: Christine Cummings, David McNeely II; m. Gary O. Gebhard, Sept. 16, 1994. Grad. h.s., Indpls. Dep. clk. Johnson County Clk.'s Office, Franklin, Ind., 1976-84; adminstrv. asst. Ind. State Senate, Indpls., 1984-88, Ind. Ho. of Reps., Indpls., 1988-95; Perry County adminstr. County Commrs., Tell City, Ind., 1995—. Campaign cons. State Rep. Dennis Heeke, Jasper, Ind., 1994, State Rep. Larry Lutz, Evansville, Ind., 1996. Named Ky. Col., Gov. Ky., 1992. Mem. Am. Legion Aux., Indpls. Press Club, Women of the Moose. Democrat. Office: Perry County Commrs 2219 Payne Tell City IN 47586

GEBHARD, LAVERNE ELIZABETH, retired accounting educator; b. Milw., Aug. 30, 1936; d. Frank and Helen Gebhard. BS, Marquette U., 1958, MBA, 1964. CPA, cert. internal auditor, cert. cost analyst. Internal auditor Fed. Res. Bank Chgo., 1958-60; gen. acct. City Products, 1960-61; tchr. bus. Milw. Pub. Schs., 1961-65; from instr. to lectr. to sr. lectr. U. Wis., Milw., 1966-93; cons. New Berlin, Wis., 1993—; CMA exam. adminstr. ICMA-Milw. site, Montvale, N.J., 1984—. Contbr. articles to profl. jours. Vol. advisor Milw. Hist. Soc., La Farge Learning Ctr., others. Recipient Citizen Ambassador award People to People, Inc., 1991—. Mem. Inst. Internal Auditors, Wis. Inst. CPAs (ch. bd. dirs. 1984—, mem. numerous coms., cons. 1984-86), Inst. Mgmt. Accts., Beta Gamma Sigma, Delta Pi Epsilon, Beta Alpha Psi (faculty advisor, founder). Home: 12685 Bobwood Rd New Berlin WI 53151

GECEL, CLAUDINE, investment analyst; b. Brookline, Mass., July 31, 1957; d. Joseph and Sally Gecel. BS cum laude, SUNY, Albany, 1979; postgrad., Boston U., 1981, NYU, 1981-83. CFA. Investment analyst Dreyfus Corp., N.Y.C., 1981-85, Quadrex Group, London and N.Y.C., 1986; fin. analyst Disclosure, Inc., N.Y.C., 1987-91; sales analyst Harcourt General, N.Y.C., 1992-94; investment analyst Smith Barney Equity Rsch., N.Y.C., 1995—. Friend White Columns Alt. ARt Space, N.Y.C., 1986—, New Mus. Contemporary Art, N.Y.C. 1987—; fundraiser Met. Opera Assn., 1991—. Mem. N.Y. Soc. Securities Analysts, Assn. Investment Mgmt. Rsch., Fgn. Policy Assn., French Alliance, N.Y. Road Runners Club. Home: 227 E 59th St New York NY 10022-1424 Office: Smith Barney 388 Greenwich St 30th Fl New York NY 10013

GEDEON-MARTIN, DIANE MARIE, small business owner, consultant; b. Detroit, Oct. 4, 1957; d. Howard M. and Susan D. (Lalian) Gedeon; m. Roger J. Martin, Aug. 22, 1980. B.A., Oakland U., Rochester, Mich., 1979. Announcer WLAV-AM/FM, Grand Rapids, Mich., 1979-80, weathercaster WTOL-TV, Toledo, Ohio, 1980; announcer, prodn. dir. WMHE-FM, Toledo, 1980-82; mktg. dir. Food Service Enterprises, Inc., Port Clinton, Ohio, 1982-83; account exec. McCann-Erickson, Troy, Mich., 1983-84; advt./promotion mgr. WPBN/WTOM-TV, Traverse City, Mich., 1985-86; mktg. supr. Little Caesar Enterprises, Detroit, 1986-88; mktg. mgr. Wendy's Internat., Inc., 1988-91; devel. dir. Mich. Humane Soc., 1991-92; owner, cons. The Write Source, Bloomfield Hills, Mich., 1993—; mem. faculty Wayne State U. Coll. Lifelong Learning. Mem. Nat. Soc. Fund Raising Execs., Women in Comms. Avocations: stained glass windows, equestrian sports, dog obedience training. Office: 4671 Burnley Bloomfield Hills MI 48304-3720

GEDRIS, IRENE JADVYGA, elementary school educator; b. Kaunas, Lithuania, July 19, 1932; came to U.S., 1961; d. Jonas and Edith (Weise) Ulickas; m. Algis E. Gedris, Apr. 2, 1961; children: Ingrid N., Audrey E. BS in Elem. Edn., Cleve. State U., 1973; MEd in Learning Disabilities, John Carroll U., 1985. Cert. elem. and learning disabilities tchr., Ohio. Chpt. 1 reading tchr. Willoughby (Ohio)-Eastlake Schs., 1993-95, 2d, 4th, 5th and 6th grade tchr., 1994—, grade level chmn., 1994—; bd. dirs. Am. Profl. Partnership for Lithuanian Edn., West Hartford, Conn., elem. curriculum coord., 1991—. Editor coloring book Colorful Scouting, 1993, 94. Martha Holden Jennings Found. grantee, 1992. Mem. ASCD, Internat. Alliance for Invitational Edn. Home: 355 Royal Oak Blvd Richmond Hts OH 44143-1709 Office: Royalview Elem Sch 31500 Royalview Dr Willowick OH 44095-4256

GEE, IRENE, food products executive, school administrator; b. N.Y.C., Aug. 17, 1950; d. Jimmy Set and Lin Fung (Ng) G.; m. Oct. 17, 1981. B.A., Hunter Coll., 1971; M.S. in Family and Consumer Studies, Lehman Coll., 1974, M.S. in Guidance and Counseling, 1978, M.S. in Adminstrn. and Supervision Coll. New Rochelle. Cert. secondary prin. Tchr., Olinville Jr. H.S., Bronx, N.Y., 1971-75, Lehman Coll., Bronx, 1975-77, Harry Eiseman Jr. H.S., Bklyn., 1978-80; asst. prin. adminstrn. A. Philip Randolph Campus H.S., 1994—; food stylist, recipe developer Ladies Home Jour., 1977-78; food stylist, recipe developer Woman's Day Mag., 1979—, home economist, 1980—; owner, operator Irene's Catering, 1984—; food coordinator Evander Childs High Sch.; food cons. Corn Products Corp., 1978—; food stylist Nabisco, 1978, also Perdue Co.; reciper writer, judger natural food contsts Scholastic Mag.; judge nat. contests Choices mag.; developer recipe booklets various cos. including Progresso and Fla. Mushrooms; cons. food cos. and publs.; comml. model Mauna Loa Macadamia Nuts, Lewis & Neale; recipe developer Lipton Co. Food exhibitor Avant Grade Foods; contbr. articles to Forecast and Choices mags. Mem. ACA, Nat. Assn. Secondary Suprs. and Prins., Nat. Assn. Secondary Sch. Prins (Asst. Prin. of Yr. 1996), Am. Home Econs. Assn., Home Economists in Bus., N.Y.C. Adminstrv. Women in Edn., Omicron Nu. Contbr. articles Woman's World mag.

GEE-MCAULEY, KAREN SUZANNE, public relations executive; b. L.A., Apr. 30, 1962; d. Melvin and Ellen (Tom) G.; m. Skeet McAuley, June 25, 1994. BA in Journalism and Internat. Rels., U. So. Calif. Pub. rels. asst. J.W. Robinson's, L.A., 1982-85; jr. acct. exec. Madeline Zuckerman Pub. Rels., Tustin, Calif., 1985-86; from acct. exec. to v.p. Ruder Finn, L.A., 1986-90; from v.p. to exec. v.p. The Blaze Co., Venice, Calif., 1990-96, pres., 1996—. Mem. Town Hall. Mem. Pub. Rels. Soc. Am., Am. Inst. Wine and Food (bd. dirs.). Home: 3516 Madera Ave Los Angeles CA 90039-1930 Office: Blaze Co 228 Main St Ste 4 Venice CA 90291-5202

GEER, JERRI DIANE, retired career officer, photographer; b. Kilgore, Tex., Oct. 28, 1946; d. James Hallead and Lois Pearl (Bryant) G. BS, U. Southwestern La., 1969; AA, N. Seattle C.C., 1986; BFA, U. Washington, 1989. Phys. edn. tchr. Orleans Parish Schs., New Orleans, 1969-71, L.A. Unified Sch. Dist., 1971-72; ensign USCG, 1973, advanced through grades to lt., 1979, aide to the admiral, 1975-76, legal counselor, 1978-82, human rels./civil rights officer, 1978-82, sr. watch officer, marine safety officer, 1979-82, ret., 1982. Photographer: (for book) Photographer's Forum, Best of College Photography Annual, 1989; exhibited in group shows U. Washington, No Boundaries N.W. Travel Art Exhibit, 1993-94, 95-96 (Juror's Special Recognition 1993), Arts Commn., City of Sea-Tac, Washington, 1995. Decorated Meritorious Unit Commendation with silver letter and gold star. Mem. Nat. Mus. Women in Arts (charter mem.), Women in Mil. Svc. Meml. (charter mem.), Photographic Coun. Seattle, Seattle Art Mus., Disabled Am. Vets., USCG Officer's Assn. Democrat. Methodist. Home: 513 NE 79th St Seattle WA 98115

GEERTZ, HILDRED STOREY, anthropology educator; b. N.Y.C., Feb. 12, 1927; d. Walter Rendell and Helen (Anderson) Storey; m. Clifford Geertz, 1948 (div. 1979); children: Erika, Benjamin. BA, Antioch Coll., Yellow Springs, Ohio, 1948; PhD, Radcliffe Coll., 1956. Lectr. U. Chgo., 1963-68; from assoc. prof. to prof. anthropology Princeton (N.J.) U., 1970—; chmn. dept. anthropology Princeton U., 1972-77, 86, 88-89. Author: The Javanese Family, 1961, Kinship in Bali, 1974, Images of Power: Balinese Paintings Made for Gregory Bateson and Margaret Mead, 1994, (with Lawrence Rosen) Meaning and Order in Moroccan Society, 1979; editor: State and Society in Bali, 1992. Office: Princeton Univ Dept Anthropology Princeton NJ 08544

GEFFEN, BETTY ADA, theatrical personal manager; b. Lachine, Que., Can., May 12, 1911; came to U.S., 1942, naturalized, 1945; d. Joseph and Minnie (Illievitz) Gottheil; student public schs., Montreal, Que.; m. Jacob N. Geffen, Dec. 23, 1944; 1 child, JoAnn Merle. Sec., Saul Cohen/Trustee in Bankruptcy, Montreal, 1926-28, Maxwell Cummings Real Estate, 1928-30, Monroe Abbey, Atty., 1930-31; with Tic-Toc, Stanley Grill and Chez Maurice, Montreal, 1931-41; sec. H.L. Green, N.Y.C., 1941-44; pvt. theatrical personal mgr., casting cons., N.Y.C., 1950—; v.p., sec. Mor-Lite Corp., 1994—; cons. Consab Assocs. Corp., N.Y.C., 1977-95. Trustee Israel Cancer Rsch. Fund., 1977-95; vol. Floating Hosp. Mem. NATAS, Women of the Motion Picture Industry, Motion Picture Pioneers (life), Internat. Platform Assn., The Nat. Mus. Women in the Arts (charter). Democrat. Clubs: Variety Women N.Y. (v.p. 1977-81, pres. 1982-86, chmn. bd. 1986-88), Brandeis U. Home and Office: 17 W 71st St Apt 7A New York NY 10023-4142

GEFFNER, DONNA SUE, speech pathologist, audiologist, educator; b. N.Y.C.; d. Louis and Sally (Weiner) G. BA magna cum laude, Bklyn. Coll., 1967; MA, NYU, 1968, PhD (NDEA fellow), 1970, postgrad., Advanced Inst. Analytic Psychotherapy, 1973-75. Asst. prof. Lehman Coll., 1971-76; assoc. prof. dept. speech St. John's U., 1976-81, prof., 1982—, dir. Speech and Hearing Ctr., 1976—, chmn. dept. speech comm. scis. and theater, 1983-92, developer M.A. program in speech pathology and audiology; pvt. practice, 1980—; cons. to corp. execs.; TV producer and hostess NBC, 1977-78, CBS, 1978-79. Contbr. articles to profl. jours. and textbooks; issue editor Jour. Topics in Lang. Disorders, 1980; editor ASHA monograph, 1987. Active N.Y. State Licensure Bd., 1993—. Emmy nominee for Outstanding Instrnl. Program, 1978; recipient award Pres.'s Com. on Employment of Handicapped, Pres.'s medal for Outstanding Faculty Achievement St. Johns U., 1987, Dist. Achievement award NYC Speech Lang.-Hearing Assn., 1994; N.Y. State Edn. Dept. grantee, 1976-78, CUNY Rsch. Found. grantee, 1972. Fellow Am. Speech, Lang. and Hearing Assn. (legis. councillor 1978-87, 90-94, Ednl. Standards Bd., v.p. acad. affairs 1995—); mem. N.Y. State Speech and Hearing Assn. (pres. 1978-80), Audiology Study Group N.Y. Office: St John's U Speech and Hearing Ctr 8000 Utopia Pky Jamaica NY 11432-1335

GEHLKE, CAROL JEAN, entrepreneur, realty outsourcing company executive; b. Pasadena, Calif., Apr. 27, 1953; d. Ellsworth Clarence and Dorothy Adelia (Douglas) G. BA, U. Calif., Irvine, 1975. Lic. realtor, Calif. Tng. asst. Host-Internat. Industries, Van Nuys, Calif., 1973-78; waitress Rusty Pelican, Newport Beach, Calif., 1975-78; flight attendant TWA, St. Louis, 1979-80; realtor assoc. Walker & Lee Real Estate, Newport Beach, 1980-84; realtor assoc., mgr. sales and mktg. divsn. Great Western Real Estate, Santa Ana, 1984-86; CEO REO Nationwide, Newport Beach, 1986—. Mem. Nat. Assn. Realtors, Calif. Assn. Realtors, Orange Coast Assn. Realtors. Republican. Home: 210 Lille Ln # 317 Newport Beach CA 92663 Office: REO Nationwide 23 Corporate Plz Dr Ste 180 Newport Beach CA 92660

GEHM, DENISE CHARLENE, ballerina, arts administrator; b. Miami, Fla., Dec. 14, 1951; d. Charles William and Verna Mae (Wiley) Gehm; m. Gary Edward MacDougal, June 15, 1992. BA cum laude, NYU, 1994; studied ballet with, George Milenoff, Thomas Armour. Soloist ballerina Harkness Ballet Co., N.Y.C., 1970-71, Nat. Ballet Washington, 1971-73; prin. ballerina Chgo. Ballet, 1974, Ballet de Caracas, Venezuela, 1975; featured ballerina Joffrey Ballet, N.Y.C., 1976-91. Appeared in Broadway plays West Side Story, 1979, Phantom of the Opera, 1988; with Rudolf Nureyev in Nijinsky's L'Apres-Midi d'Un Faune, 1979; prin. dancer Homage to Diaghilev, Broadway and State Theatre N.Y., 1979; featured roles include Joffrey's Nutcracker, Arpino's Suite St.-Saens, Cranko's Taming of the Shrew, Ashton's Midsummer Night's Dream, Robbin's N.Y. Export Opus Jazz; performed in numerous maj. cities, theatres and festivals including Champs Elysees in Paris, Herod Atticus Odeon, Athens, An der Vien, Vienna, and Spoleto (Italy)/U.S.A. festivals; featured in numerous TV commls. and print. Recipient Founders Day award NYU, 1994; Harkness House for Ballet and Arts scholar, 1969.

GEHRET, GEORGIANA UNDERHILL, illustrator; b. Elmira, N.Y., July 21, 1948; d. Alpheus Finch and Claribel (Rockwell) Underhill; m. Reginald Richard Gehret; children: Austin U., McCray R. AA, Stephens Coll., 1968; BA, U. Ala., 1970; MS, Elmira Coll., 1974. Prodn. asst. Elmira (N.Y.) City Schs., 1970-71; writer, reporter WENY-TV, Horseheads, N.Y., 1972-73; coord. media svcs. S.A. Boces, Bath, N.Y., 1973-78; illustrator Georgiana Illustrations, Bath, N.Y., 1976—. Illustrator: (children's book) Rocky, The Reindog, 1987; writer: (manual for law enforcement agys.) Sexual Abuse, 1984; designer line of 72 greeting cards marketed as Georgiana Illustrated. Pres. Bath (N.Y.) Ctrl. Sch. Bd. Edn., 1987-94, ARC Steuben chpt., 1990-92, Steuben Area Sch. Bds. Assn., Hornell, N.Y., 1992-93; bd. dirs. N.Y. State Rural Schs., 1988-92, Heart Assn., Bath, 1993—, Ctrl. Steuben United Way, Corning, N.Y., 1995; treas. Dem. Orgn., Bath, 1994—. Mem. AAUW (pres. Bath, N.Y. 1982-86, bd. dirs. N.Y. divsn. 1984-88), Greater Bath C. of C. (pres. 1994-96, Mem. of Yr. 1988, Bus. Woman of Yr. 1994). Home: 125 E Washington St Bath NY 14810

GEHRING, CLAUDIA MARY, instructional assistant; b. Cottonwood, Idaho, Oct. 2, 1937; m. David Joseph Gehring, Jan. 21, 1958; children; Shannon, Bruce, Tami, Brenda, Shane. Student, Coll. St Gertrude, 1956, 71. Cashier, bank teller Idaho 1st Nat. Bank, Cottonwood, 1956-60; store clerk Cash and Carry Grocery, Cottonwood, 1981-84; instructional asst. Jt. Sch. Dist. # 242, Cottonwood, 1984—. Religious educator St. Mary Parish, Cottonwood, 1971-81, sec. St. Mary Religious Education Bd., 1973-78; bd. mem. St. Mary's Parish Bd., 1971-73; judge Local Election Bd., 1968-80; girl scout leader Girl Scout Council, Cottonwood, 1968-74. Named Outstanding Young Woman of Yr. Cottonwood Jaycees, 1971. Roman Catholic. Home: 1005 East Box 372 Cottonwood ID 83522

GEHRING, ELIZABETH T.F., mechanical engineer; b. Washington, Apr. 5, 1962; d. Charles C.Y. and Helen M. Feng; m. John L. Gehring, May 25, 1991; children: Kasinee Jean Wenjing Gehring, Nola Renon Inez Gehring. B of Archtl. Engring., Pa. State U., 1985; MSc, U. Colo., 1990. Registered profl. engr., Colo. Mech. engr. SME Engrs., Inc., Rockville, Md., 1985-86, Albert Kahn Assoc., Inc., Detroit, 1986-88, U.S. Bur. of Reclamation, Denver, 1990-93, ME Engrs. Inc., Denver, 1993-96; prin. Gehring & Assocs., 1996—. Pres. Kings Ridge Home Owners Assn., Boulder, 1993—. Recipient Am. Western U. fellowship Dept. of Energy, 1990. Mem. ASHRAE. Home and Office: 4842 Franklin Dr Boulder CO 80301

GEHRKE, JEANNETTE ELAINE, nurse; b. Iowa Falls, Iowa, Oct. 3, 1959; d. Russell Windell and Eleanor Mae (Hoversten) Anders; m. John Lee Gehrke, June 7, 1986; children: Bethany Marie, Brandon Daniel. ADN, North Iowa Area C.C., Mason City, 1980. RN; cert. BLS, ACLS, PALS, TNCC, Advanced Trauma Mgmt. Med.-surg. staff nurse Ellsworth Hosp., Iowa Falls, Iowa, 1980-87, 11-7 supr., emergency rm. supr., emergency rm. and oper. rm. supr., 1987-88; dir. nursing Valley View Hosp., Eldora, Iowa; emergency rm. staff, charge nurse Mercy Hosp., Cedar Rapids, Iowa, 1989-94; emergency rm. and house supr. St. Anthony's Hosp., Carroll, Iowa, 1994-95; staff nurse Audubon County Meml. Hosp., Audubon, Iowa, 1995—. Leader Girls Scouts Am. Mem. Emergency Nurses Assn., Audubon Womens Assn., Presbyn. Womens Circle. Presbyterian. Home: 1006 Grandview Dr Audubon IA 50025-1432

GEHRKE, KAREN MARIE, accountant; b. Gaylord, Minn., Apr. 12, 1940; d. Stanley Henry and Frieda Marie (Hammel) Ostermann; m. Orville Raymond Gehrke, Oct. 21, 1961 (div. Aug. 1994); children: Kimberly, Karla, Kent. Grad. high sch., Gaylord, 1958. Inspector Fingerhut Mfg., Gaylord, 1959-60; rewinder 3M, Hutchinson, Minn., 1960-61; packer 3M, Hutchinson, 1971-72; sec. Boehmke Ins. Agy., Gaylord, 1961-63, Law Office of H.A. Knobel, Gaylord, 1964-68; teller First State Fed. Savs. and Loan, Hutchinson, 1969; sec. Wally's Tire Shop, Hutchinson, 1970, Lyle R. Jensen, CPA, Hutchinson, 1974-84; owner Karen M. Gehrke L.P.A., Hutchinson, 1984—. Mem. Nat. Assn. Female Execs., Nat. Soc. Pub. Accts., Minn. Assn. Pub. Accts., Hutchinson Area C. of C.

GEIBEL, SISTER GRACE ANN, college president; b. Sept. 17, 1937. BA in Piano and Music Edn., Carlow Coll., 1961; MA in Music Edn., U. Rochester, 1967, PhD in Music, 1975. Tchr. elem. and high schs., 1959-67, ch. musician, 1972-80; assoc. prof. and co-chmn. music dept. Carlow Coll., Pitts., 1981-82, acting acad. dean, 1982-83, dean, 1983-88, v.p. acad. affairs, 1984-88, pres., 1988—; mem. pres.'s coun. Pitts. Coun. on Higher Edn., numerous other ednl. orgns. Bd. dirs. Program for Female Offenders, Pitts. Rsch. Inst., United Way of Allegheny County, Oakland Cath. H.S.; mem. adv. bd. Mom's Ho., Pitts. Symphony Soc., Pitts. Opera, Pitts. Pub. Theater. Mem. Pitts. Athletic Assn., Duquesne Club, Zonta Club (mem. internat. bd.). Office: Carlow Coll Office of the President 3333 5th Ave Pittsburgh PA 15213-3165

GEIER, CLAIRE, advertising executive. Ptnr. Earle Palmer Brown, Bethesda, Md. Office: Earle Palmer Brown/Bethesda 6935 Arlington Rd Bethesda MD 20814-5212*

GEIER, SHARON LEE, special education educator; b. Dayton, Ohio, Nov. 21, 1943; d. Robert Stanley Murphy and Mary Frances (Ross) Briggs; m. Arthur M. Geier, Jan 23, 1965; children: Arthur William, Bradford Robert. BA, Wilmington (Ohio) Coll., 1965; cert. spl. edn., Wright State U., 1976; MS in Edn., U. Dayton, 1995. Cert. elem. tchr., Ohio, edn. handicapped. Tchr. 1st grade Fairborn (Ohio) City Schs., 1965-66, Kettering (Ohio) City Schs., 1967-71; tchr. 1st grade Xenia (Ohio) City Schs., 1975-81, tchr. 3d grade, 1981-82, tchr. learning disabled, 1982—; tchr. specifically learning disabled Camp Progress Centerville (Ohio) Schs., summers, 1977, 78. Founder, pres. Twig 6 Children's Med. Ctr. Aux., Dayton, 1971-73, chmn. Jr. Aux., 1972-74. Recipient Doer award Miami Valley Regional Ctr. and Dayton Area Citizens for Spl. Edn., 1988; Martha Holden Jennings scholar, 1980-81; Named Spl. Educator of Yr., 1993. Mem. AAUW, ASCD, Coun. Exceptional Children (Outstanding Chpt. Pres. Ohio Fedn. 1989, pres. Greene County chpt. 1987-89, treas. Ohio divsn. learning disabilities 1989-91, pres. 1991-93), Ohio Fedn. Coun. for Exceptional Children (liaison S.W. region 1989-94, liaison chmn. 1992-93, 93-94, sec. 1994—), Green Key Honor Soc. Republican. Home: 160 Honey Jane Dr Beavercreek OH 45434-5711

GEIGER, ANN MARIE, epidemiologist; b. Athens, W.Va., Oct. 9, 1965; d. Dale E. and Mary Lu (De Right) G. AB, Harvard-Radcliffe U., 1987; MPH, U. Mich., 1992, PhD, 1995. Rsch. asst. Brigham and Women's U., Boston, 1987-90; rsch. asst. U. Mich., Ann Arbor, 1990-94, tchg. asst., 1992-93; sr. investigator Kaiser Permanente Rsch., Pasadena, Calif., 1995—. Contbr. articles to profl. jours. Grantee Mich. Health Care Edn. and Rsch. Found., 1993, U. Calif. Breast Cancer Rsch. Program, 1996; predoctoral fellow U. Mich., 1994-95. Mem. APHA, Soc. for Epidemiologic Rsch. Office: Kaiser Permanente Rsch 393 E Walnut St Pasadena CA 91188

GEIGER, LINDA SCHAEFER, accountant; b. Oshkosh, Wis., June 30, 1952; d. Ronald John Schaefer and Kathleen Mae (Mentzel) Zabel; m. David Carl Geiger, July 27, 1974; children: Nancy Lin, Jill Kathleen. BS in Med. Tech., U. Wis., Oshkosh, 1976, MBA, 1986. Cert. mgmt. acct. Med. technologist Cons. Lab./St. Agnes Hosp., Fond du Lac, Wis., 1976-86; bus. mgr. Cons. Lab. of Wis., Fond du Lac, 1986-89; acct. Willow Foods, Beaver Dam, Wis., 1990-91; accounts receivable/credit mgr. Miles Kimball, Oshkosh, 1991-95, fin. acctg. mgr., 1995—. Mem. Inst. Mgmt. Accts. (cert., dir. membership 1991-94, v.p. membership 1994-96). Mem. United Ch. of Christ. Office: Miles Kimball 41 W 8th Ave Oshkosh WI 54901

GEISELHARDT-HEAD, BARBARA THERESA, nursing administrator; b. Denver, Sept. 6, 1961; d. Alfred and Helene Marie (Birkofer) Geiselhardt; m. Mark Dean Head, Aug. 29, 1992. BSN, Creighton U., 1984; MSN, U. Colo., Denver, 1992. Cert. ABLS, BLS. Charge nurse med. oncology Univ. Hosp., Denver, 1985-87, staff nurse med. ICU, 1987-88, sr. staff nurse med. ICU, 1988-89, nurse mgr. med. ICU, 1989-90, nurse mgr. bone marrow transplant unit, 1990—, bone morrow transpalnt program, 1990—, dir. oncology svcs., 1996—; clin. faculty U. Colo. Sch. Nursing, Denver, 1992—; clin. teaching assoc. Univ. Hosp., 1985-87. Mem. AACCN, Oncology Nursing Soc., Spl. Interest Group-Bone Marrow Transplantation, Spl. Interest Group-Mgmt. Adminstrn., S.W. Oncology Group (nurse oncologist com. 1991—), Sigma Theta Tau. Roman Catholic. Office: Univ Hosp 4 West BMTU 4200 E 9th Ave Denver CO 80220-3706

GEISELHART, LORENE ANNETTA, English language educator; b. Rake, Iowa, June 28, 1929; d. Charles Tobias and Altha May (Mills) Knutson; m. James Willis Geiselhart, June 1, 1947 (div. 1971); children: Nancy Joyce, Larry Paul, Richard Ray, Kathleen Ann. Cert., Luther Coll., 1949; BA, U. No. Iowa, 1965, MA, 1989; postgrad., U. Iowa, 1990—. Pub. sch. tchr. Postville, Iowa, 1947-48; adminstrv. asst. to county supt. schs. Decorah, Iowa, 1948-49; pub. sch. tchr. Galesville and Trempealeau, Wis., 1949-51, Iowa Braille and Sight-Saving Sch., Vinton, 1959-70, South Winneshiek Community Sch., Ossian, Iowa, 1970-94; instr. English to univ. students Nanchong Inst. Edn., Sichuan, China, 1995-96; student tchr. supr. Luth. Coll., Decorah, 1971-94; instr. English to univ. students Inst. Edn., Nanchong, Sichuan Province, China, 1995-96. Sec. Calmar (Iowa) Improvement Assn., 1987-92; active Calmar Luth. Ch. Coun., 1975-80, 89-91, mem. choir, 1975-80, pres. Ch. Circle, 1975-77, 88-92. Mem. AAUW (pres. 1969-70, sec. 1990-92), NEA, Iowa Reading Coun., Iowa State Edn. Assn., NE Iowa Rosemaling Assn. (sec. 1991-94), Delta Kappa Gamma (pres. Beta Eta chpt. 1978-81, state fellowship com. 1982-84, grantee 1988). Democrat.

GEISELMAN, LUCYANN, college president; m. Robert L. Harrington; 1 child, Gabriella. BA in Religion, Tex. Christian U., MA in Theology; PhD in Edn., U. Chgo. Former v.p. Eisenhower Med. Ctr., Rancho Mirage, Calif.; v.p. for planning and Advancement Calif. Inst. of Arts, 1989-91; pres. Mt. Vernon Coll., Washington, 1991—. Office: Mt Vernon Coll Office of Pres 2100 Foxhall Rd NW Washington DC 20007-1199

GEISELMAN, PAULA JEANNE, psychologist, educator; b. Ohio, June 30, 1944; d. Paul and Rosemary (Dawson) Parsley. AB in Psychology with honors, Ohio U., 1971, MS in Exptl. Psychology, 1976; PhD in Physiol. Psychology, UCLA, 1983. Adj. asst. prof. UCLA, 1986-91; dir. psychophysiol. rsch. UCLA Sch. Medicine, 1986-91; assoc. prof. dept. psychology La. State U., Baton Rouge, 1991—; adj. assoc. prof. Pennington Biomed. Rsch. Ctr. La State U., Baton Rouge, 1991—; lectr. in field. Reviewer for Sci. Jour., Am. Jour. Physiology, Physiology and Behavior, Brain Research Bulletin, Appetite: Determinants and Consequences of Eating and Drinking; contbr. numerous articles to profl. jours. Mem. Soc. Neurosci., AAAS, N.Am. Assn. Study of Obesity, Women in Neurosci., Assn. Acad. Women, Am. Psychol. Assn., Am. Psychol. Assn., Eastern Psychol. Assn., Western Psychol. Assn. (head of physiol. psychol., chair. Animal Feeding and Behavior paper session 1981), Assn. Advancement Psychology, Internat. Brain Research Orgn., World Fedn. Neuroscientists, Brit. Brain Research Assn. (hon.), European Brain and Behavior Soc. (hon.), N.Y. Acad. Scis., Sigma Xi, Psi Chi. Office: La State U Psychology Dept Pennington Biomed Rsch Ctr 6400 Perkins Rd Baton Rouge LA 70808-4124

GEISENDORFER, ESTHER LILLIAN, retired nursing educator; b. Ferryville, Wis., May 18, 1927; d. Peter C. and Christie G. (Quamme) Walker; m. James V. Geisendorfer, Sept. 23, 1949; children: Jane Stokke, Karen Geisendorfer-Lindgren, Lois Buchnis. Student, U. Wis.-LaCrosse, 1944-45; RN, Fairview Hosp. Sch. Nursing, Mpls., 1948. Staff nurse Worthington (Minn.) Clinic, 1948-50; pvt. duty nurse, Sioux Falls, S.D., 1950-51; obstet. nurse Fairview Hosp., Mpls., 1951-53; staff nurse St. Anthony Hosp., Rock Island, Ill., 1953-54; obstet. nurse Fairview Hosp., Mpls., 1954-58, post anesthesia recovery nurse, 1958-62, emergency room nurse, 1962-66, obstet. nurse, 1966-68, head nurse obstetrics, 1968-76; staff devel. instr., clinician, Bellin Meml. Hosp., Green Bay, Wis., 1976-92, ret.; instr. in prenatal and Lamaze classes Ob-Gyn Assocs. of Green Bay Ltd.; editorial cons. Krames Communications. Mem. Wis. Assn. Perinatal Care, Nordfjord Laget in Am., Wis. Nurses Assn. (Disting. Svc. award 1981), Nurses Assn. Am. Coll. Obstetrics and Gynecology (cert., founder Northeast Wis. chpt.), Wis. Acad. Scis., Arts and Letters, Nat. Perinatal Assn. Lutheran. Home: 1001 Shawano Ave Green Bay WI 54303-3020

GEISER, ELIZABETH ABLE, publishing company executive; b. Phillipsburg, N.J., Apr. 28, 1925; d. George W. and Margaret I. (Ross) G. A.B. magna cum laude, Hood Coll., 1947. Promotion mgr. coll. dept. Macmillan Co., N.Y.C., 1947-54; promotion mgr. R.R. Bowker, N.Y.C., 1954-60; sales mgr. R.R. Bowker, 1960-67, dir. mktg., 1967-70, v.p., 1970-73, sr. v.p., 1973-75, sr. v.p., pub. book divsn.; adj. prof., dir. U. Denver Pub. Inst., 1976—; sr. v.p. Gale Rsch. Co., 1976-91, cons., 1991—; cons. Excerpta Medica, Elsevier, 1976-82; lectr. pub. procedures Radcliffe Coll., 1966-75; lectr. schs. libr. sci. U. Wash., U. So. Calif.; panel mem. TV series Living Library, 1970. Editor: The Business of Book Publishing, 1985. Contbr. Manual of Bookselling, 1969. Mem. bd. trustees Hood Coll., 1993—. Inducted into Publishing Hall of Fame, 1988. Mem. Assn. Am. Pubs. (exec. coun. prof. and scholarly pub. div. 1989-91, adv. coun. Frankfurt book fair 1971, sch. and libr. promotion and mktg. com. 1972-76, bd. dirs. 1982-85), ALA (pres. exhibits roundtable 1968-70, bd. dirs. exhibits roundtable 1968). Presbyterian. Home: 24 Forest Dr Springfield NJ 07081-1124 Office: 335 E 51st St Apt 5E New York NY 10022-6765

GEISER, JANIE MARIE, theater director, filmmaker, designer; b. Baton Rouge, July 24, 1951; d. Frederick James and Anne Genevieve (Thompson) G.; m. Lewis D. Klahr. BFA, U. Ga., 1973. Curator Nexus Contemporary Art Ctr., Atlanta, 1977-80, Ctr. for Puppetry Arts Mus., Atlanta, 1980-82; artist, freelance illustrator, 1982—; panel mem. NEA Commissioning Program, Washington, 1995, Ga. Coun. on Arts, Atlanta, 1983. Dir., designer, conception: (film) The Red Book, 1994 (New Dirs. New Films award Mus. Modern Art 1996), (theatrical work) Evidence of Floods, 1994 (N.Y. Dance and Performance award 1995); dir., designer: (theatrical work) Stories From Here, 1989 (Obie award 1989); dir., designer, writer: (theatrical work) Blue Night, 1984. Guggenheim fellow John Simon Guggenheim Found., 1992, theater fellow NEA, 1990, 94, design fellow N.Y. State Coun. on Arts, 1991, 95; Alive TV commn. Twin Cities Pub. TV, 1994. Mem. Union Internat. de la Marionette (Performance awards 1981, 86, 89), Millenium Film Workshop. Home: # 7 340 E 9th St New York NY 10003

GEISINGER, JANICE ALLAIN, accountant; b. Iroquois County, Ill., June 21, 1927; d. Carl Oliver and Constance Kathryn (Risser) Irps Allain; m. Robert Bond Geisinger, Oct. 17, 1947 (div. 1976); children: Jacque K., Holly D., Terry Joe. AA, Blackburn U., Carlinville, Ill., 1947. Lab. technician Mich. Health Lab., East Lansing, 1947-48; with Southwestern Bell Telephone, Tulsa, 1948-49; bookkeeper Geisinger Ent., Dallas, 1951-69; salesman Earl Page Real Estate, Irving, Tex., 1969-71; food purchaser Town & Country vending, Dallas, 1971-75; bookkeeper/sec. Belco C & I Wiring Inc., Irving, 1976-85; leasing bookkeeper Copiers Etc., Inc., Dallas, 1985-89; bookkeeper Kennedy Elec. Inc., Mesquite, Tex., 1989; ret., 1990; cons. Ross Mech., Irving, 1989-95; asst. bookkeeper Metroplex Dental Group, 1990—. Crew leader Census Bur., Dallas, 1990. Mem. Am. Contract Bridge Assn. Home: 1216 E Grauwyler Rd Irving TX 75061-5031

GEISLER, ROSEMARY P., computer dealer, marketing executive; b. Chgo., Apr. 5, 1947; d. James Vincent and Raffaella Mary (DeSeno) Pastorello; student Triton Coll., 1970-72; B.A., DePaul U., 1981; m. Ervin R. Geisler, Aug. 17, 1968. Asst. market analyst Evans Products Co., Rolling Meadows, Ill., 1970-76; office svcs. mgr., asst. market analyst Comdisco, Inc., Rosemont, Ill., 1976-78, asst. mktg. product mgr., 1978-80, dir. dealer rels., 1980-81, mktg. product mgr., market maker, 1981-83, asst. v.p., 1983-85, v.p., 1985, sr. v.p. mktg. div., 1985-89, exec. v.p. mktg. div., 1989-95, pres. dis. sys. divsn., 1995—. Mem. Des Plaines (Ill.) Youth Commn. Mem. LifeSpan Orgn. (bd. dirs.), DePaul U. Alumni Assn. Home: 85 Brinker Rd Barrington IL 60010-5132 Office: Comdisco Inc 6111 N River Rd Des Plaines IL 60018-5158*

GEISLER, SHERRY LYNN, justice of the peace, city magistrate; b. Durango, Colo., Aug. 18, 1956; d. George Walter and Evelyn Ruth (MacLean) Geisler; m. Harvey Lee Slade, June 6, 1981 (div. Aug. 11, 1993); 1 child, Sherry (Rachel) Orona. Grad. H.S., Springerville, Ariz., 1974; student, Northland Pioneer Coll., Springerville, Ariz. Clk. Round Valley Justice Ct., Springerville, 1981-84; chief clk. Round Valley Justice Ct., 1984-88, office mgr., judge pro tem, 1988-93, justice of the peace, 1993—; city magistrate City of Springerville and Eagar, Ariz., 1993—; mentor judge Ariz. Supreme Ct., 1994—; edn. chair Ariz. Justice Ct. Assn, 1995-96. Mem. Nat. Judges Assn., Am. Judges Assn., Ariz. Cts. Assn., State of Ariz. Justice of the Peace Assn. (pres.). Ariz. Magistrates Assn. Democrat. Home: PO Box 1202 Springerville AZ 85938 Office: Round Valley Justice Ct PO Box 1356 Springerville AZ 85938-1356

GEIST, JILL MARIE, medical writer; b. Oak Park, Ill., Nov. 11, 1959; d. Raymond Joseph and Julia Thersa Weiner; children: Samantha Rae, Jacob Lee. Student, Coll. of Lake County, Grayslake, Ill., 1982-86. Line worker Zenith Microcircuits, Elk Grove, Ill., 1978, inspector, 1978, prodn. screen specialist, 1978-79, group leader screen print, 1979-80, process control inspector, 1980-81, engring. technician, 1981-83; engring. specialist Abbott Labs., Abbott Park, Ill, 1983-89, process devel. engr., 1989-93; new product coord. Abbott Labs., Abbott Park, Ill., 1993-95, med. writer, 1995—. Patentee in field. Pres., co-founder Abbott Parent Network, Abbott Park, Ill., 1989-91, pres. emeritus, 1992. Office: Abbott Labs D-7B4AP6A-2 100 Abbott Park Rd Abbott Park IL 60064-3501

GEIST, KARIN RUTH TAMMEUS MCPHAIL, secondary education educator, realtor, musician; b. Urbana, Ill., Nov. 23, 1938; d. Wilber Harold and Bertha Amanda Sofia (Helander) Tammeus; m. David Pendleton McPhail, Sept. 7, 1958 (div. 1972); children: Julia Elizabeth, Mark Andrew; m. John Charles Geist, June 4, 1989 (div. 1995). BS, Juilliard Sch. Music, 1962; postgrad., Stanford U., 1983-84, L'Academia, Florence and Pistoia, Italy, 1984-85, Calif. State U., 1986-87, U. Calif., Berkeley, 1991, 92. Cert. tchr., Calif.; lic. real estate agt., Calif. Tchr. Woodstock Sch., Musoorie, India, 1957, Canadian, Tex., 1962-66; tchr. Head Royce Sch., Oakland, Calif., 1975-79, 87—, Sleepy Hollow Sch., Orinda, Calif., 1985—; realtor Freeholders, Berkeley, Calif., 1971-85, Northbrae, Berkeley, Calif., 1985-92, Templeton Co., Berkeley, 1992—; organist Kellogg Meml., Musoorie, 1956-57, Mills Coll. Chapel, Oakland, 1972—; cashier Trinity U., San Antonio, 1957-58; cen. records sec. Riverside Ch., N.Y.C., 1958-60; sec. Dr. Rollo May, N.Y.C., 1959-62, United Presbyn. Nat. Missions, N.Y.C., 1960, United Presbyn. Ecumenical Mission, N.Y.C., 1961, Nat. Coun. Chs., N.Y.C., 1962; choral dir. First Presbyn. Ch., Canadian, Tex., 1962-66; assoc. in music Montclair Presbyn. Ch., Oakland, 1972-88; site coord., artist, collaborator Calif. Arts Coun. Artist; cons. music edn. videos and CD Roms Clearvue EAV, Chgo., 1993—. Artist: produced and performed major choral and orchestral works, 1972-88; prodr. Paradiso, Kronos Quartet, 1985, Magdalena, 1991, 92, Children's Quest, 1993—. Grantee Orinda Union Sch. Dist., 1988. Mem. Berkeley Bd. Realtors, East Bay Regional Multiple Listing Svc., Calif. Tchrs. Assn., Commonwealth Club (San Francisco). Democrat. Home: 7360 Claremont Ave Berkeley CA 94705-1429 Office: Templeton Co 3070 Claremont Ave Berkeley CA 94705-2630

GEITHMAN, JUDITH ANN MORTENSON, secondary education educator; b. Mpls., Oct. 11, 1946; d. Chester Oliver and Ellen Dorthea (Aadland) Mortenson; m. Theodore Wayne Geithman, Dec. 23, 1967; children: Amanda Michelle, Jennifer Renata. BS in English, Fla. State U., 1967; MS in English, U. So. Miss., 1985; MA in Humanities, U. West Fla., 1991. Cert. tchr., Fla. English tchr. Melbourne (Fla.) H.S., 1968-69, Merritt Island (Fla.) H.S., 1969-70, Riviera Jr. H.S., St. Petersburg, Fla., 1970-72, Lemon Bay H.S., Englewood, Fla., 1978—. Braille typist Epsilon Sigma Alpha, Merritt Island, 1969-70, reader for books on tape Libr. Congress, 1970; pres. Young Women's Philanthropic Orgn., Englewood, 1977-78. Home: 2290 Buckskin Dr Englewood FL 34223 Office: Lemon Bay HS 2201 Placida Rd Englewood FL 34224

GELB, JUDITH ANNE, lawyer; b. N.Y.C., Apr. 5, 1935; d. Joseph and Sarah (Stein) G.; m. Howard S. Vogel, June 30, 1962; 1 child, Michael S. B.A., Bklyn. Coll., 1955; J.D., Columbia U., 1958. Bar: N.Y. 1959, U.S. Dist. Ct. (so. dist. and ea. dist.) N.Y. 1960, U.S. Ct. Appeals (2d cir.) 1960, U.S. Ct. Mil. Appeals 1962. Asst. to editor N.Y. Law Jour., N.Y.C., 1958-59; confidential asst. to U.S. atty. ea. dist. N.Y., Bklyn., 1959-61; assoc. Whitman & Ransom, N.Y.C., 1961-70, ptnr., 1971-93; ptnr. Whitman Breed Abbott & Morgan, N.Y.C., 1993—. Mem. ABA (individual rights sect., real property & trust law sect.), Fed. Bar Counsel, N.Y. State Bar Assn. (trusts and estates com.), N.Y. State Dist. Attys. Assn., Assn. of Bar of City of N.Y., Columbia Law Sch. Alumni Assn. (bd. dirs.), Girls, Inc. (resources com.), Princeton Club. Home: 169 E 69th St New York NY 10021-5163 Office: Whitman Breed Abbott & Morgan 200 Park Ave New York NY 10166-0005

GELDER, DONNA RAE, elementary school educator; b. Canton, N.Y., Jan. 14, 1943; d. William Raymond and Elizabeth Helen (Winship) G. BA, SUNY, Potsdam, 1965, MS in Reading, 1972, reading specialist cert., 1974. Cert. elem. tchr., reading tchr., N.Y. 1st grade tchr. Queensbury (N.Y.) Sch., 1965-67, 73-81, developmental 1st grade tchr., 1967-72, summer Headstart tchr., 1986-88, supervising tchr., 1968-81, reading tchr., 1981—, summer sch. reading tchr., 1984, 87, 88,94; leader, chair classroom clinic N.Y. State Reading Conf., Kiamesha Lake, N.Y., 1976. Author: Reading Is Magic, 1974, Spotlight on Fifty Years - A History of the Glens Falls Operetta Club, 1986; complier: Fifty Years of Directors, Casts, and Crews, Glens Falls Operetta Club Programs, 1985. Mem. com. Mohican coun. Boy Scouts Am., Glens Falls, 1983—, mem. exec. bd., 1987—; mem. com. Adirondack coun. Girl Scouts U.S., Queensbury, 1965—; mem. com., bd. dirs., historian Glens Falls Operetta Club/Glens Falls Cmty. Theater, 1965—. Recipient Appreciation award Adirondach coun. Girl Scouts U.S., 1984, Silver Beaver award Mohican coun. Boy Scouts Am., 1991, 3d Pl. Hon. Mention award N.Y. State Assn. Compensatory Educators, 1994. Mem. AAUW, DAR, Internat. Reading Assn., Kappa Delta Pi. Republican. Methodist. Office: Queensbury Elem Sch 431 Aviation Rd Queensbury NY 12804-2914

GELLAS, BONNIE, employee benefits communications executive; b. Trenton, N.J., July 21, 1949; d. George G. and Dorothy (Skokos) G. BA in History, Wilkes U., 1971; MA in Curriculum Devel., Columbia U., 1975. Tchr. secondary sch. social studies Newburgh (N.Y.) Free Acad., 1971-73, The Baldwin Sch., N.Y., 1974-75; curriculum developer Life Office Mgmt. Assoc., N.Y., 1975-78; comm. cons. Martin E. Segal Co., N.Y., 1978-82, Johnson & Higgins, N.Y., 1982-85; sr. comm. cons. Marjorie Gross & Co., N.Y., 1985-90; v.p., dir. comm. The Segal Co., N.Y., 1990-95, sr. v.p., 1995—. mem. bd. dirs. Greater N.Y. Bridge Assn., 1991—. Mem. WEB, Internat. Found. Employee Benefit Plans, 1990—. Office: The Segal Co One Park Ave New York NY 10016-5895

GELLER, BUNNY Z., poet, writer, publisher, sculptor, artist; b. N.Y.C., May 21, 1926; d. Herman and Shirley (Shonfeld) Juster; m. Lester Roy Geller; children: Judy Lynn, Robert Douglas, Sheryl Sue, Wayne Mitchell. Student, UCLA, 1944-46, Fla. Internat. U., 1989-96. invited artist Pegasus Internat. Corp., N.J., 1981-85, Internat. Art Expo., N.Y., 1982-83; invited guest artist Broward County Main Lib., Ft. Lauderdale, Fla., 1988. Author: (poems) Bunny Geller Original Poetry, 1995, Choices, 1996, (nonfiction) Bunny Geller Original Sculpture, 1985; one woman shows include Bowery Savings Bank, N.Y.C., 1978, Lynn Kottler Galleries, N.Y.C, 1978, Hollywood (Fla.) Art Mus., 1978-79; group exhibns. include All Broward Exhibit 78, Ft. Lauderdale, Fla., 1978, Old Westbury Hebrew Congregation, Westbury, N.Y., 1978, De Ligny Galleries, Ft. Lauderdale, Fla., 1979, 1983-84, Internat. Treas. Fine Art, Plainview, N.Y., 1978, 79, 80, 81, Artists Equity Assn. Hollywood (Fla.) Art Mus., 1979, Limited Edition Galleries, Bal Harbour, Fla., 1979, Temple Beth-El, Boca Raton, Fla., 1979, Expo 79, Pompano, Fla., 1979, Hilda Rindom Galleries, Hallendale, Fla, 1980, Jockey Club Art Gallery, Miami, 1980, 81, 83, 84, Gallery SO-HO 7 , Ltd., Great Neck, N.Y., 1979-80, Gallery at Turnberry, Turnberry Isle, Fla., 1980-81, Galleria Martin, Palm Beach, Fla., 1981, Contextual Fine Arts, Ft. Lauderdale, Fla., 1980-81, Art and Culture Ctr. of Hollywood (Fla.), 1981, Miami Convention Ctr., 1981, Anita Gordon Gallery, Inc., North Miami Beach, 1981, Collier Art Internat., Ltd., Westbury, N.Y., 1981, Tavistock Country Club, Haddonfield, N.J., 1982, Internat. Art Expo, N.Y.C., 1982, 83, Ohio All Arabian Show and Buckeye Sweepstakes, Columbus, 1982, West Elec. Co., Hopewell, N.J., 1982, Devon (Pa.) Arabian Horse Show, 1982, Bondstreet Art Gallery, Pitts., 1982, Blumka II Gallery, N.Y.C., 1982, Kerby Gallery, Cedar Grove, N.J., 1982, Washington Internat. Horse Show, Gaithersburg, Md., 1982, Pegasus Internat. Corp., Pennington, N.J., 1982, Patricia Judith Art Gallery, Boca Raton, Fla., 1983-84, Panache Gallery, Ft. Lauderdale, Fla., 1983, The Nelson Rockefeller Collection, Inc., N.Y.C., 1983, Shorr Goodwin Gallery, N.Y.C., 1983, Carrier Found. Auxiliary, Belle Meade, N.J., 1983, First Annual Internat. Wildlife Exposition, Atlantic City, N.J., 1983, Palm Beach, Fla., 1984-85, Robert's One-of-a-Kind, Bal Harbour, Fla., 1984, Hallandale (Fla.) Pub. Lib., 1984-85, Galleria Camhi, Bar Harbor Is., Fla., 1984-85, Tatem Galleries, Ft. Lauderdale, Fla., 1984-85, Westbury (N.Y.) Meml. Lib., 1984, Trenton Country Club, 1984, Designers' Showcase 1985 Cashelmara, Glen Cove, N.Y., 1985, UN Conf., Nairobi, 1985; featured in (book) Artists/USA, 1979-80, The Am. Album, Nat. Mus. Women Arts permanent collection, Washington, 1985, Art Expo N.Y. catalogue, 1983, 92, Limited Collectors Edition, 1982, Town and Country mag., 1982, Gold Coast Life mag., 1983, Art in America mag., 1983-84, Sunstorm Arts Mag., 1984; represented in permanent collection Kushi Found. Pres. Sisterhood Westbury Hebrew Congregation, Westbury, N.Y., 1967-69; judge Fine Art and Craft Show, Ft. Lauderdale, Fla., 1979-81; art adv. coun. Westbury Meml. Libr., 1990-94. Recipient 1st prize Carrier Found. Aux. 2d Ann. Arts Festival, 1983. Mem. Nat. Mus. Women in the Arts (assoc.), Nat. Libr. Poetry (Editor's Choice award 1995), Internat. Soc. Poets (disting. mem. 1995, Poet of Merit 1995, semi-finalist symposium 1995). Home: 400 Diplomat Pkwy #711 Hallandale FL 33009

GELLER, DIANE JOYCE, lawyer; b. Glen Cove, N.Y., Aug. 6, 1953; d. Isadore and Rose (Herskovitz) Goldstein; m. Joseph H. Geller, July 4, 1973; 2 children. BA, C.W. Post Coll., 1975; JD, Hofstra U., 1978. Bar: N.Y. 1978, U.S. Dist. Ct. (ea. and so. dists.) N.Y. 1978, U.S. Supreme Ct. 1990, Tenn. 1991. V.p. adminstrn. Counsel Synergy Group, Farmingdale, N.Y., 1978-83; gen. counsel, assoc. risk mgr. LRF Risk Mgmt., Great Neck, N.Y., 1984-85; gen. counsel Alpha Surg. Enterprises, Inc., White Plains, N.Y., 1985-86; v.p., gen. counsel Am. Med. Ins. Co., Hicksville, N.Y., 1986-89; counsel, corp. sec. Uniforce Temp. Pers., Inc., New Hyde Park, N.Y., 1989—; bd. advisors lawyers assistance program Adelphi U. Bd. Advisors, Garden city, N.Y.. Mem. ABA, Nassau County Bar Assn. Home: 32 Broadfield Pl Glen Cove NY 11542-2004 Office: Uniforce 1335 Jericho Tpke New Hyde Park NY 11040-4613*

GELLER, JANICE GRACE, nurse; b. Auburn, Ga., Feb. 25, 1938; d. Erby Ralph and Jewell Grace (Maughon) Clack; m. Joseph Jerome Geller, Dec. 23, 1973; 1 child, Elizabeth Joanne. Student, LaGrange Coll., 1955-57; BS in Nursing, Emory U., 1960; MS, Rutgers U., 1962. Nat. cert. group psychotherapist; cert. clin. nurse specialist. Psychiat. staff nurse dept. psychiatry Emory U., Atlanta, 1960; nurse educator Ill. State Psychiat. Inst., Chgo., 1961; clin. specialist in mental retardation nursing Northville, Mich., 1962; faculty Coll. Nursing Rutgers U., Newark, 1962-63, faculty Advanced Program in Psychiat. Nursing, 1964-66; faculty Coll. Nursing U. Mich., Ann Arbor, 1963-64; faculty, Teheran (Iran) Coll. for Women, 1967-69; clin. specialist psychiat. nursing Roosevelt Hosp., N.Y.C., 1969-70; faculty, guest lectr. Columbia U., N.Y.C., 1969-70; supr. Dept. Psychiat. Nursing Mt. Sinai Hosp., N.Y.C., 1970-72; pvt. practice psychotherapy N.Y.C., 1972-77, Ridgewood, N.J., 1977-96; faculty, curriculum coord. in psychiat. nursing William Alanson White Inst. Psychiatry, Psychoanalysis and Psychology, N.Y.C., 1974-84; mem. U.S. del. of Community and Mental Health Nurses to People's Republic of China, 1983. Contbr. articles to profl. jours.; editorial bd. Perspectives in Psychiat. Care, 1971-74, 78-84; author: (with Anita Marie Werner) Instruments for Study of Nurse-Patient Interaction, 1964. Mem. Bergen County Rep. Com., 1989. Recipient 10th Anniversary award Outstanding Clin. Specialist in psychiat.-mental health nursing in N.J., Soc. Cert. Clin. Specialists, 1982; Fed. Govt. grantee as career tchr. in psychiat. nursing, Rutgers U., 1962-63; cert. psychiat. nurse and clin. specialist, N.J., N.Y. Mem. AAAS, ANA (various certs.), N.C. Nurses Assn., Soc. Cert. Clin. Specialists in Psychiat. Nursing (chmn.), Coun. Specialists in Psychiat./Mental Health Nursing, Am. Group Psychotherapy Assn. (cert. group psychotherapist), Am. Assn. Mental Deficiency, World Fedn. Mental Health, Sigma Theta Tau. Address: 307 Chatterson Dr Raleigh NC 27615-3137

GELLER, NANCY, broadcast executive. V.p. original programming HBO Time Warner Entertainment, N.Y.C. Office: HBO Time Warner Entertainment 1100 Ave of the Americas New York NY 10036*

GELLERT, GEORGIA MARRS, public relations executive; b. Denver, Oct. 8, 1917; d. William Middelton and Blanche (Boak) Marrs; student U. Denver, 1936-37; m. Winfield Turrell Barber, Jan. 18, 1941 (dec. May 1948); m. 2d, Nathan Henry Gellert, Mar. 12, 1954 (dec. Nov. 1959); m. 3d, James Kedzie Penfield, May 19, 1978. Soc. editor Denver Post, 1937-41; tech. writer, editor Consol. Vultee Aircraft, USN Radio and Sound Lab., San Diego, 1944-46; mgr. box office Central City Opera House Assn., Denver, 1948; soc. editor Denver Post, 1949-51; publicity dir. N.A.M., San Francisco, 1951-54; asst. exhibits dir. Seattle Worlds Fair, 1960-62; pub. relations dir. Seattle Center, 1962-64; free lance pub. relations, Seattle, 1964—; dir. Pacific Search Press, 1977-87. Trustee Seattle Symphony Orch., 1960-88, sec. bd., 1964-65, v.p., mem. exec. com., 1973-76, 79-83; dir. Allied Arts of Seattle, 1960-90; dir. Pottery N.W., Seattle, 1966-68; trustee Seattle Childrens Home, 1954-61, pres., 1959-61; trustee Gov's. Mansion Found., 1972-88, mem. exec. com., 1975-80, trustee emeritus, 1992—; trustee Seattle Ctr. Found., 1984-94. Mem. Women in Communications, Pi Beta Phi. Episcopalian. Clubs: Denver Womans Press, Seattle Tennis, Washington Athletic. Home and Office: 1232 38th Ave E Seattle WA 98112-4448

GELLMAN, GLORIA GAE SEEBURGER SCHICK, marketing professional; b. La Grange, Ill., Oct. 5, 1947; d. Robert Fred and Gloria Virginia (McQuiston) Seeburger; m. Peter Slate Schick, Sept. 25, 1978 (dec. 1980); 2 children; m. Irwin Frederick, Gellman, Sept. 9, 1989; 3 children. BA magna cum laude, Purdue U., 1969; student, Lee Strasberg Actors Studio; postgrad., UCLA, U. Calif.-Irvine. Mem. mktg. staff Seemac, Inc. (formerly R.F. Seeburger Co.); v.p. V.I.P. Properties, Inc., Newport Beach, Calif. Profl. actress, singer, artist, writer; television and radio talk show hostess, Indpls., late 1960s; performer radio and television commls., 1960s—. Mem. Orange County Philharm. Soc., bd. dirs. women's com.; mem. Orange County Master Chorale, Orange County Performing Arts Ctr., v.p., treas. Crescendo chpt. OCPAC Ctr. Stars, 1st v.p. membership; bd. dirs. Newport Harbor (Calif.) Art Mus., v.p. membership, mem. acquisition coun.; bd. dirs., mem. founders soc. Opera Pacific, mem. exec. com. bd. dirs.; patron Big Bros./Big Sisters Starlight Found.; mem. Visionaries Newport Harbor Mus., Designing Women of Art Inst. Soc. Calif.; pres. Opera Pacific Guild Alliance; immediate past pres. Spyglass Hill Philharm. Com.; v.p. Pacific Symphony Orch. League; mem. Calif. State Libr. Found. Bd., U. Calif. Irvine Found. Bd., mem. devel. com., pub. affairs and advocacy com.; chmn. numerous small and large fundraisers. Recipient Lauds and Laurels award U. Calif., Irvine, 1994, Gellman Courtyard Sculpture honoring contbn. to Sch. of Humanities, U. Calif., Irvine. Mem. AAUW, AFTRA, SAG, Internat. Platform Assn., Actors Equity, U. Calif.-Irvine Chancellor's Club, U. Calif.-Irvine Humanities Assocs. (founder, pres., bd. dirs.), Mensa, Orange County Mental Health Assn., Balboa Bay Club, U. Club, Club 39, Islanders, Covergirls, Alpha Lambda Delta, Delta Rho Kappa. Republican. Home: PO Box 1993 Newport Beach CA 92659-0993

GELMAN, ELAINE EDITH, nurse; b. Bklyn., Feb. 16, 1927; d. Michael Levi and Shirley (Drezner) Rodkinson; m. David Graham Gelman, Apr. 6, 1952; children: Eric, Andrew, Amy. BS, CUNY, Queens, 1946; RN, NYU, 1948. Cert. PNP. Mem. oper. rm. staff, supr. Queens Gen. Hosp., Bellevue, Beth-El Hosp., N.Y.C., 1948-61; mem. labor and delivery rm. staff, supr. Georgetown Hosp., Washington, 1962-66; pub. health nurse N.Y.C. Dept. Pub. Health, 1966-72; PNP Roosevelt Hosp., N.Y.C., 1972-82; pvt. practice N.Y.C., 1982-95. Mem. Dem. County Com., N.Y.C., 1984—; apptd. mem. N.Y. State Bd. Nursing, 1990—, exec. dir. N.Y. State Coalition Nurse Practitioners, Inc., 1996—. Named Nurse of Distinction N.Y. State Legis., 1991; recipient Spl. Presdl. award N.Y. State Coalition of Nurse Practitioners, 1991. Fellow Nat. Assn. PNPs (legis. chmn. 1986-88, cert. of recognition 1986, 87), Coalition of Nurse Practitioners, Inc. (pres. 1984-85, 87-88). Jewish. Home: 229 W 78th St New York NY 10024-6604

GELPI, BARBARA CHARLESWORTH, English literature and women's studies educator; b. El Centro, Colombia, Dec. 17, 1933; came to U.S., 1951; d. Lionel Victor and Frances Ardelle (Heins) Charlesworth; m. Albert Joseph Gelpi, June 14, 1965; children—Christopher, Adrienne. A.B., U. Miami, Fla., 1955, M.A., 1957; Ph.D., Radcliffe Coll., Cambridge, Mass., 1962. Asst. prof. U. Calif.-Santa Barbara, 1962-64; asst. prof. Brandeis U., Waltham, Mass., 1964-67; lectr. Stanford U., Calif., 1967-81, assoc. prof., 1981-92, prof., 1992—. Author: Dark Passages, 1965, Shelley's Goddess: Maternity, Language, Subjectivity, 1992; editor: Adrienne Rich's Poetry, 1975, Adrienne Rich's Poetry and Prose, 1993, Feminist Theory, 1982, Signs: Jour. of Women in Culture & Society, 1980-85; The Lesbian Issue, 1985; Women's Poverty, 1986; assoc. editor: Victorian Women, 1981. Mem. MLA (program com. 1981-84), Nat. Women's Studies Assn., Philol. Assn. Pacific Coast. Democrat. Roman Catholic. Home: 870 Tolman Dr Stanford CA 94305-1026 Office: Stanford U Dept English Stanford CA 94305

GELTNER SCHWARTZ, SHARON, communications executive; b. Lakeland, Fla., Dec. 10, 1958; d. Bernard Benjamin and Gail (Bergad) G.; m. Eric Michael Schwartz, Dec. 30, 1995. AA, Wm. Rainey Harper Coll., 1978; BJ, U. Ill., 1980. Editor White House Weekly Feistritzer Publs., Washington, 1980, Instl. Investor, Washington, 1981-83; freelance writer Alexandria, Va., 1984-90; feature writer, investigative reporter, fgn. corr. Knight Ridder Newspapers, Boca Raton, Fla., 1990-92; book editor Weiss Rsch., Palm Beach Gardens, Fla., 1994-95; comm. mgr. Achievers Unltd., West Palm Beach, Fla., 1995—; writer, rschr. The Naisbitt Group, Washington, 1985-86; legal rschr. David James Ltd., Bethesda, Md., 1986-87; invited panelist The Poynter Inst. Media Studies, 1992. Author: (with others) Weekends Away from Washington, D.C., 1989, Fodor's Wall Street Journal Guide to Business Travel, 1991; contbr. articles to Quill, Washington Journalism Rev., Media Bus. Quar., Am. Writer. Participant Women's March on Washington, 1986; fundraiser United Jewish Appeal, Washington, 1986-88.; rep. D.C. writers in Bangkok Royal Thai Embassy, Washington, 1986, Palm Beach County, Fla., Yellow Feathers gridiron, 1990-91. Recipient Nat. Headliner award for outstanding news reporting Press Club of Atlantic City, 1993. Mem. NOW, Washington Ind. Writers (Michael Halberstam award 1983), House and Senate Periodical Corrs., Amnesty Internat., Fla. Press Assn., Nat. Writers Union (del. nat. conv. 1994), Regional Reporters Assn., Nat. Women's Art Mus. (charter), U. Ill. Alumni Assn. Investigative Reporters and Editors. Home: Apt 500 I 1441 Brandywine Rd West Palm Beach FL 33409-2049

GELTZER, SHEILA SIMON, public relations executive; b. N.Y.C.; d. Sidney E. and Bertie (Rome) Simon; m. Howard E. Geltzer, Sept. 10, 1967; children: Jeremy Niles, Gabriel Lewis. BA, Queens Coll., 1961. With Philip Lesly Co., N.Y.C., 1962-63, Benjamin Co., N.Y.C., 1963-68; ptnr. Simon and Geltzer, Inc., N.Y.C., 1968-74, Ries and Geltzer, N.Y.C., 1974-79; prin. Geltzer and Co., Inc., N.Y.C., 1979—. Mem. Pub. Relations Soc. Am. (counselors acad.), Women in Communications, Women in Pub. Relations, Nat. Council of Women. Office: Geltzer & Co Inc 1301 Ave of the Americas New York NY 10019

GEMMELL-AKALIS, BONNI JEAN, psychotherapist; b. Lansing, Mich., Mar. 11, 1950; d. James Stewart Gemmell and Alpha Alice (Hackenberg) Vanden Bosch; m. Thomas Joe Akalis, Dec. 14, 1974 (div. Sept. 94); children: Scott Aaron, Ty Alexander, Zachary Alan. BS, Ctrl. Mich. U., 1972, MA, 1974. Ltd. lic. psychologist, Mich.; cert. social worker, Mich. Clin. psychologist, sr. mental health therapist Lincoln Ctr. for Emotionally Disturbed Children & Youth, Lansing, 1974-77; outpatient psychologist Grand Rapids (Mich.) Child Guidance Clinic, 1978-81; pvt. practice Grand Rapids Psychiat. Svcs., 1981-88; pvt. practice Associated Therapists, Inc., Grand Rapids, 1988—, pres., 1989-90. Grad. fellow Ctrl. Mich. U., 1972-73. Mem. Mich. Psychoanalytic Coun., Mich. Women Psychologists, Mich. Assn. Profl. Psychologists, Am. Group Psychotherapy Assn. (founder nat. registry 1996), Grand Rapids Area Psychology Assn., Psi Chi. Home: 632 Duxbury Ct SE Grand Rapids MI 49546-9605 Office: 1025 Spaulding Ste B Grand Rapids MI 49546

GEMMILL, ELIZABETH H., corporate executive; b. Phila., Dec. 7, 1945; d. Kenneth W. and Helen H. G.; m. Douglas B. Richardson, July 15, 1977; children—Katherine Preston Richardson, Hollis Bentley Richardson. A.B., Bryn Mawr Coll., 1967; J.D., Boston U., 1970. Bar: Mass. 1970, Pa. 1973. Assoc. firm vom Baur, Coburn, Simmons & Turtle, Boston, 1970-71; staff atty. Cape Cod Legal Services, Inc., Hyannis, Mass., 1971-73; asst. dist. atty. City of Phila., 1973-74; atty., asst. sec. Girard Bank, Phila., 1974-75; sec., treas., counsel Girard Bank, 1975-76, v.p. cust. svcs., 1976-78, v.p., gen. auditor, 1979-81, sr. v.p. pers. dept., 1981-83, sr. v.p., regional banking group head, 1983-85; v.p. Drexel U., Phila., 1986-87; v.p., sec. Tasty Baking Co., Phila., 1988—; bd. dirs. Am. Water Works, Inc., Pvt. Industry Coun. Bd. dirs. Met. YMCA Phila. and Vacinity, 1979-88, 90—, Presbyn.-U. Pa. Med. Ctr., 1982—, WHYY Inc., 1981-94, Phila. Coll. Textiles and Sci., Salvation Army, Forum Exec. Women. Mem. ABA, Pa. Bar Assn., Phila. Bar Assn., Am. Soc. Corp. Secs. (pres. Mid. Atlantic group), Nat. Investors Rels. Inst., Pa. Chamber Bus. and Industry. Office: Tasty Baking Co 2801 W Hunting Park Ave Philadelphia PA 19129-1306

GENDRON, CAROL J., neonatal nurse; b. Big Rapids, Mich., Dec. 23, 1952; d. Lewis H. and Helen E. (Wooster) Maynard; m. Thomas D. Gendron, Sept. 15, 1979; children: Erin, Megan. Assoc. Degree in Nursing, Kalamazoo Valley C.C., Mich., 1979; BS in Nursing, U. Mich.,, 1995. RN, Mich.; cert. in neonatal nursing NACOG, cert. grief counseling Resolve Through Sharing. Staff nurse neonatal intensive care unit Bronson Meth. Hosp., Kalamazoo, 1979-81, 82-90; care coord. for neonatal intensive care unit Bronson Meml. Hosp., Kalamazoo, 1990-95; case mgr., quality mgr. Bronson Meth. Hosp., Kalamazoo, 1995—; pub. health nurse Allegan County Health Nurse, Allegan, Mich., 1981. Recipient Bronson Nursing scholarship Bronson Meth. Hosp., 1994-95. Mem. SWMPA, Parent Care, Inc. Office: Bronson Meth Hosp 252 E Lovell Kalamazoo MI 49007

GENDRON, MICHÈLE MARGUERITE MADELEINE, librarian; b. Paris, Mar. 15, 1947; came to U.S., 1950; d. Gerard Joachim and Denise Marie Louise (Le Morvan) G. BA, Orlinda Pierce Coll. for Women, Athens, Greece, 1969; MS, U. Ill., 1971. Libr. Free Libr. Phila., 1971-75, head, Kingsessing Br., 1975-76, head, Ramonita G. de Rodriguez Br., 1976-91, curator spl. collections ctrl. children's dept., 1991-92, head, lit. dept., 1992—; cons. devel. Hist. Children's Lit. Collection Montgomery County-Norristown (Pa.) Pub. Libr., 1993-94; organizing mem. Pa. Libr. Assn.'s 1st Conf. Svcs. to Youth, Harrisburg, Pa., 1987-89, Women's Network's 1st Conf. on P.R. Woman in Phila., 1981. Author: (bibliographies) Booklist, 1983; contbr. bibliographies Destination World, 1979, Stories to Share, 1985. Trustee Legal Svcs. Fund Dist. Coun. 47 of Am. Fedn. State, County and Mcpl. Employees, 1985-95, mem. exec. bd. Local 2186, 1996—. Recipient Charles Scribner award Scribner Pub., 1976, Nat. Security Forum award Air War Coll., 1985. Mem. ALA (Assn. Libr. Svcs. Children, Mildred Batchelder award selection com. 1979-81, 85-87, internat. rels. com. 1981-85, chair 1984-85, libr. instrn. round table 1991-93), Pub. Libr. Assn. (mktg. to pub. librs. 1991—, svcs. to multicultural populations 1991, sec. exec. com. mktg. pub. libr. svcs. sect. 1995-96), Alliance Francaise de Phila., Beta Phi Mu. Roman Catholic. Office: Free Libr of Phila Lit Dept 1901 Vine St Philadelphia PA 19103-1116

GENDZWILL, JOYCE ANNETTE, retired health officer; b. Milw., Aug. 8, 1927; d. Felix Vincent and Antoinette Marie (Borske) G.; m. Lauren E. Trombley, June 13, 1952 (div. Jan. 1960); children: Regan Eve Trombley Kovacich, Eugene Vincent, Paul Quentin. BS, U. Mich., 1949, MD, 1952, MPH, 1961. Cert. pub. mgr., Ala. Internship USPHS, Detroit, Cleve., 1952-53; dir. extern edn. Beyer Meml. Hosp., Ypsilanti, Mich., 1953-54; resident in radiology St. Luke's Hosp., Denver, 1954-55; health officer Dickinson-Iron Dist. Health Dept., Stambaugh, Mich., 1959-76; dir. bur. local health svc. Ala. Dept. Pub. Health, Montgomery, Ala., 1976-81; asst. state health officer Ala. Dept. Pub. Health, Montgomery, 1981-91; ret., 1991. Mem. AMA, So. Med. Assn., Mensa, Phi Beta Kappa, Delta Omega, Phi Kappa Phi. Home: 6580 Thorman Rd Port Charlotte FL 33981-5579

GENÉT, BARBARA ANN, accountant, travel counselor; b. N.Y.C., Oct. 14, 1935; d. Arthur Samuel and Louise Margaret (Schneider) G. Profl. cert. in acctg., U. Calif., La Jolla, 1995, student, 1996—. Asst. to chmn. bd., asst. v.p. pub. rels. Brink's Inc., Chgo., 1976-78; co-owner, pres. Ask Mr. Foster, Chgo., 1982-90; with Profl. Cmty. Mgmt., Laguna Hills, Calif., 1990-92; travel counselor E.J. Brown & Assocs., San Diego, 1992-94; tchr.'s asst. U. Calif-San Diego, La Jolla, 1996—; rep. Becker CPA-CMA Rev., San Diego, 1995—. Becker scholar, 1995, scholr Marks CPA Rev., 1996. Mem. Am. Soc. Woman Accts., Inst. Mgmt. Accts., Inst. Cert. Travel Agts., Rancho Santa Fe Bus. and Profl. Women's Club, Order Ea. Star, Ladies of Shrine N.Am. Office: U Calif Dept Bus and Mgmt 9500 Gilman Dr La Jolla CA 92093-0176

GENGENBACH, SYLVIA ANN, English language and literature educator; b. Shell Lake, Wis., May 1, 1949; d. Leonard Walter and Geraldine Frances (Clark) Voight; m. Edward Carl Gengenbach, oct. 13, 1973; 1 child, Grant Edward. BA in Secondary Edn., U. Wis., Eau Claire, 1971, MA in English, 1976; MEd in Second Langs and Cultures, U. Minn., 1987. Tchr. English Phillips (Wis.) High Sch., 1971-75; instr. Chippewa Valley Tech. Coll., Eau Clair, Wis., 1976-81; sr. lectr. English U. Wis.-Stout, Menomonie, 1981—, dir. English Lang. Inst., 1987—. Mem. Nat. Assn. Fgn. Student Affairs, Minn. Tchrs. ESL, Wis. Tchrs. ESL, Wis. Assn. Fgn. Student Affairs. Office: U Wis-Stout Dept English Meomonie WI 54751

GENOVICH-RICHARDS, JOANN, health care services consultant, educator; b. Detroit, July 23, 1954; d. Steven Edward and Catherine Ann (Malaspina) Genovich; m. David Edward Richards, Aug. 15, 1975. BSN, U. Mich., 1976; MSN, Wayne State U., 1978; MBA, Oakland U., 1985; PhD, U. Mich., 1993. Mental health coord. Midland (Mich.) Hosp. Ctr., 1978-79; outpatient nursing supr. Henry Ford Hosp., Detroit, 1979-82; adminstrv. dir. nursing St. John Hosp. Macomb Ctr., Mt. Clemens, Mich., 1986; dir. quality svcs., cons., dir. nursing Mercy Health Svcs., Farmington Hills, Mich., 1983-89; instr. nursing Oakland U., Rochester, Mich., 1985-92, interim dean Nursing Sch., 1992; asst. prof. Sch. Nursing and Pub. Health, U. N.C., Chapel Hill, 1993; asst. v.p. planning and devel. Nat. Com. Quality Assurance, 1993-95; expert appointment Ctr. Quality Measurement & Improvement Agy. for Health Care Policy & Rsch.; bd. dirs. Sisters of St. Joseph Health System, Ann Arbor; clin. faculty Joint Commn. on Accreditation of Healthcare Orgns., Chgo., 1986-90. Contbr. chpt. to book and articles to profl. jours. Recipient Project grant, Inst. of Medicine, 1989. Mem. ANA, Mich. Nurses Assn., Nat. Assn. Quality Assurance Profls., Am. Soc. for Quality Control, Aircraft Owners and Pilots Assn. Roman Catholic. Home: 12322 Prairie Dr Sterling Heights MI 48312-5230

GENRICH, JUDITH ANN, real estate executive; b. Milw., Mar. 10, 1949; d. Einar and Eleanor Svea (Russell) Barnes; m. Nathan Mark Genrich, Oct. 23, 1971; children: Krista Svea, Erik Leif. BA, Gustavus Adolphus Coll., 1970; grad., Wis. Sch. Real Estate, Milw., 1979; postgrad., Carroll Coll., 1980, U. Wis., 1978-80, 92. Tchr. Oak Grove Middle Sch., Bloomington, Minn., 1970-71, Mukwonago (Wis.) High Sch., 1971-72; sales mgr. Lincoln Park Homes, West Allis, Wis., 1972-73, v.p., 1973-74, pres., 1974—; chmn. Mfrd. Housing Subdivision Sec., Madison, 1978-80; sec. Southeastern Wis. Housing, Milw., 1981-82, treas., 1982-84. Bd. dirs. Waukesha YMCA, 1985-87, v.p. 1987-89; bd. dirs. YMCA Heritage Found., 1994—; bd. dirs. Waukesha County United Way, 1984-87; mem. alumni bd. Gustavus Adulphus Coll., St. Peter, Minn., 1974-80; trustee The Cooper Inst., Naples, Fla., 1987-93, mem. adv. bd., 1993—. Recipient Dedicated Svc. award Wis. Mfrd. Housing, 1975-84, 88. Mem. West Allis C. of C., Wis. Mfrd. Housing Assn. (bd. dirs. 1975-80), Ind. Bus. Assn. Wis. (trustee University Lake 1991—), Merrill Hills Country Club (chair golf 1991), Milw. Women's Dist. Golf Assn. (bd. dirs. 1993, v.p. 1994, pres. 1995-96), Vasa Lodge, Eagle Creek Country Club, Chenequa Country Club. Republican. Lutheran. Home: 5219 State Road 83 Hartland WI 53029-9306

GENTILCORE, EILEEN MARIE BELSITO, elementary school principal; b. Glen Cove, N.Y.; d. Samuel Francis and Nellie Theresa (McKenna) Belsito; m. James Matthew Gentilcore, Aug. 4, 1951; children: Kevin, John, Scott. BS in Edn., SUNY, Potsdam; MS in Edn., Hofstra U., 1968, profl. diploma, 1976, EdD, 1979. Tchr., first grade Sea Cliff (N.Y.) Schs., 1951-52; tchr., pre-K Germany Officers Sch., Munich, 1952-53; tchr., first grade Peekskill (N.Y.) Schs., 1953-54; tchr., second grade Syosset (N.Y.) Ctrl. Sch. Dist., 1954-55, reading cons., 1970-84, head tchr., 1974-84, principal, 1985-96; ret., 1996; bicentennial adv. bd. Syosset Community, 1976; adv. bd. mem. Telicare, Uniondale, N.Y., 1978-80. Author: Developmental Learning, 1979. Mem. Nassau County Graffiti Task Force, 1994—. N.Y. State PTA fellow, 1971, 72, 73, Hofstra fellow, 1971; recipient Jenkins award, 1968, Hon. Life, 1976, Pius X award Rockville Ctr. Diocese, 1985, Paul Harris Rotary award, 1992, Disting. Svc. award, N.Y. State PTA Dist. Coun., 1996. Mem. Syosset Prins. (pres. 1992), Syosset-Woodbury Rotary (pres. 1993-95), Gift of Life Rotary (pres. 1996—, dist. gov. 7250 aide 1995, med. mission to Russia 1995, vocat. dir. 1996—), Kappa Delta Pi, Alpha Sigma Omicron, Phi Beta Kappa. Roman Catholic.

GENTILE, MARY O'CONNOR, curriculum supervisor; b. Worcester, Mass.; d. John D. and Evelyn A. O'Connor; m. Francis V. Gentile, July 8, 1972; children: Richard, Mary, Christopher, Evelyn. BA, Chestnut Hill Coll., 1966; MA, Boston Coll., 1968; MEd in Reading, Northeastern U., 1972; MEd, Villanova U., 1977. Cert. educator, Pa., Mass. Reading specialist Dedham (Mass.) Sch. Dist., 1967-70, Franklin (Mass.) Sch. Dist., 1970-72; supr. curriculum and instrn. Bensalem (Pa.) Sch. Dist., 1972—. Mem. AAUW (bd. mem. 1973-79), OSIA (Montemuro Lodge); mem. Internat. Reading Assn. (bd. mem. Bucks County coun. 1991—), Bucks County Fed. Program Coords. (chair 1992—). Office: Bensalem Sch Dist 3000 Donallen Dr Bensalem PA 18966

GENTILE, MELANIE MARIE, record producer, marketing and public relations consultant, writer; b. N.Y.C., Apr. 27, 1944; d. Frank Joseph and Jean Ferreri; m. R.P. Gentile, Apr. 4, 1964 (div. 1982); children: Robert, Jessica. Student, Calif. State U., 1967-70. Pres. U.S. venture Yasu Corp. of Tokyo, 1971-86; cons. in mktg., 1986-89; exec. prodr. and pres. Schrimshaw Prodn. Co. and Record Co., Nashville, 1975—; owner Triad Music, 1996—; account exec., creative cons. Erwin Wasey Advt. Corp.; freelance creative cons. Jacques Yves Cousteau, 1968—. Author: Look Back But Don't Stare. Mem. ASCAP (CMA award Acad. of Country Music, Billboard mag.). Home and Office: PO Box 588 Beakes Rd Cornwall NY 12518

GENTRY, ALBERTA ELIZABETH, elementary education educator; b. Richter, Kans., Feb. 18, 1925; d. John Charles and Dessie Lorena (Duvall) Briles; m. Kenneth Neil Gentry, June 1, 1947; children: Michal Neil, Alan Dale, Elisa Ann. BE, Emporia (Kans.) Tchrs. Coll., 1975. Cert. tchr., Kans. Tchr. Chippewa Rural Sch., Ottawa, Kans., 1943-44; prin., tchr. Pomona (Kans.) Grade Sch., 1944-47, tchr., 1960-61; tchr. Silverlake Rural Sch., Pomona, 1947-48, Hawkins Rural Sch., Ottawa, 1948-49, Davy Rural Sch., Ottawa, 1950-53, Eugene Field Sch., Ottawa, 1953-54, Centropolis Grade Sch., Ottawa, 1964; tchr. Appanoose Elem. Sch., Pomona, 1964-90, ret., 1990; trainer student tchr., 1985-86. Author: Proven Ideas for Classroom Teachers, 1988. Project leader, supporter 4-H, Franklin County, Kans., 1963-67; den mother Boy Scouts Am., Ottawa, 1955-66; dir. Bible sch., tchr. Trinity Meth. Ch., Ottawa, 1955-70, supt., 1955-66, mem. choir, 1947—. Named to Kans. Tchrs. Hall of Fame, 1991. Mem. NEA, Kans. Tchrs. Assn., Kans. Edn. Assn., Alpha Delta Kappa (sec. 1988-90). Republican. Methodist. Home: PO Box 2 Pomona KS 66076-0002

GENTRY, BARBARA BEATRICE, educational consultant; b. Utica, N.Y., Oct. 21, 1948; d. James Russell and Beatrice Hazel (Vanderhoop) G. BS in Social Work, Utah State U., 1974; MA in Guidance and Counselor Edn., U. Wyo., 1975. Head counselor U. Wyo. Divsn. Student Ednl. Opportunity, Laramie, 1976-78; assoc. dir. U. Wyo. Divsn. Student Ednl. Opportunity, Laromie, 1985-86; edn. unit dir. N.Am. Indian Ctr. of Boston, 1978-83; ptnr. Indian and Mexican Crafts, Oak Bluffs, Mass., 1986-93; multicultural coord. Ea. Mich. U., Ypsilanti, 1990-92; Wampanoag tribal edn. dir. Wampanoag Tribe of Gay Head, Gay Head, Mass., 1992-93; sr. assoc. ORBIS Assocs., Washington, 1993—; cons. Indian Vocat. Edn. U.S. Dept. Edn., Washington, 1990, Springfield (Mass.) Mus., 1992, Nat. Indian Adult Edn. Conf., 1994, 95, Mich. Indian Critical Issues Conf., 1994, 95, N.Y. State Indian Edn. Conf., 1996, U.S. Dept. of Edn., Office of Indian Edn., 1981. Mem. election com. Boston Indian Coun., 1980-81. Mem. Nat. Indian Edn. Assn., Nat. Indian Adult Edn. Assn., Mich. Assn. Programs, Ea. Mich. U. Woman's Assn., Wampanoog Tribe of Gay Head. Office: Orbis Assocs 1411 K St NW Ste 700 Washington DC 20008

GENTRY, JEANNE LOUISE, lecturer, writer; b. Portland, Oreg., Sept. 12, 1946; d. Louis Darell and Mary Louise (Lane) G.; m. Gini Mario Martini, June 13, 1965 (div. 1968); children: Deborah Corinna Martina, Darell James Martini. Student, Northwestern Coll. Bus., Portland, 1968, Mt. Hood Community Coll., Gresham, Oreg., 1986. Receptionist, sec. to pres. Met. Printing Co., Portland, 1969-73; adminstrv. asst. Lifespring, Inc., Portland, 1974-77; cons. Jeanne Mort Co., Boring, Oreg., 1978-80; office mgr. Beef Palace Provisioners, Gresham, 1980-82; bus. cons. Boring, 1983-90; owner Good As New Doll Hosp., Boring, 1990-92; adminstrv. projects mgr. Profl. Svc. Industries, Portland, 1992—. Co-compiler: Lebanon Pioneer Cemetery, 1991, rev. edit. 1995. Apptd. to Oreg. Pioneer Cemetery Commn., 1995. Mem. Geneal. Coun. Orgn. (sec. 1991-94), Nat. Geneal. Soc., Fellowship of Brethren Genealogists, Geneal. Forum of Oreg. (Newsletter staff), Ind. Geneal. Soc. (charter), East Tenn. Hist. Soc., Oreg. Hist. Cemeteries Assn. (pres. 1992-96, exec. dir. 1996—), Pellissippi Geneal. and Hist. Soc., Lebanon Geneal. Soc. Home: 16385 SE 232nd Dr Boring OR 97009-9124

GENTRY, SANDRINA JANE, healthcare administrator; b. Sandusky, Ohio, Apr. 7, 1951; d. Charles William and Alice Sandra (Magi) G.; m. Richard Thomas Brittain, Sept. 6, 1985. RN, Providence Hosp. Sch. Nursing, 1972; BE, U. Toledo, 1978, MEd, 1980. Psychiat. staff nurse St. Charles Hosp., Toledo, 1972-73; pub. health nurse Toledo Health Dept., 1973-78; insvc. educator Toledo Hosp., 1978-79, dir. insvc. edn., 1978-81, dir. output alcoholism program, 1981-83; wellness instr. Blue Cross-N.W. Ohio, Toledo, 1984-85; dir. personnel health svcs. Monroe (Mich.) County Health Dept., 1985-90; dir. nursing Charter Hosp., Toledo, 1990-91; corp. dir. quality Franciscan Svcs. Corp., Sylvania, Ohio, 1993—. Author Worksite Based Health Promotion Programs, 1984. Mem. Sr. Citizens Adv. Bd., Monroe, 1985-90; disaster svc. cons. ARC, Monroe, 1985-90; bd. dirs. Am. Heart Assn., Monroe, 1985-90. Recipient Prenatal Care Program award Mich. Dept. Pub. Health, 1989. Mem. APHA, Am. Orgn. Nursing Execs., Mich. Home Health Assembly, Nat. Assn. for Home Care. Democrat. Office: Franciscan Svcs Corp 6832 Convent Blvd Sylvania OH 43560-2853

GENTRY, TINA J. M., executive secretary, legal assistant; b. Kampala, Uganda, July 19, 1963; d. Doyle E. and Mikiko (Takeuchi) G. BA, Tex. Christian U., 1985; postgrad studies Legal Asst., George Washington U., 1995—. Profl. asst. Price Waterhouse, Washington, 1987-88; rsch. asst. WIRES, Ltd., Washington, 1988-89; exec. sec. The Riggs Nat. Bank, Washington, 1989-94, ITT Defense and Electronics, McLean, Va., 1994—. Office: ITT Defense & Electronics 1650 Tysons Blvd Ste 1700 Mc Lean VA 22102

GENTRY, VICKI PAULETTE, museum director; b. Bessemer, Ala., June 2, 1952; d. Gerald Vance and Marjorie Jean (Bush) George; children: Alissa Hubbard, Rebecca Hubbard. Office worker Mining Corp. of the South, Vance, Ala., 1978-79; artist, sign painter Bob's Sign Shop, Midfield, Ala., 1979-80; dir. Iron & Steel Mus. of Ala., McCalla, 1980—; program completion Office of Mus Programs, Smithsonian, Washington, 1987. Artist (book) Tannehill Crafts, 1982. Events Planner Ala. Reunion State of Ala., Montgomery, 1989. Recipient Top 20 Events in the South East award SE Tourism Soc., Atlanta, 1986-87, 88, 91, Head Start Vol. award, 1994. Mem. Ala. Preservation Alliance, Soc. Indsl. Archaeology, Nat. Trust for Hist. Preservation, Birmingham Area Mus. Assn., Am. Assn. State and Local History (program completion 1980), Am. Assn. Mus., Ala. Mus. Assn. (sec.-treas. 1983-85, Meritorious Svc. award 1983), Ala. State Employees Assn. (pres. Tannehill chpt. 1993-95). Democrat. Baptist. Home: 16920 Brooke Dr Mc Calla AL 35111-8504 Office: Tannehill Historical State Park 12632 Confederate Pky Mc Calla AL 35111-9508

GENUNG, SHARON ROSE, pediatrician; b. Williamsport, Pa., Oct. 6, 1951; d. Joseph Patrick and Jeanette (Mossendew) Lynch; m. Norman Bernard Genung, June 9, 1973; children: Jeffrey, Sarah. BS in Microbiology cum laude, Mich. State U., 1973; MS in Clin. Microbiology, U. Ark., 1979, MD, 1984. Lic. physician, Wash., Ark. Clin. resident in pediatrics Wright State U./Children's Med. Ctr., Dayton, Ohio, 1987; dir. pediatrics USAF Hosp. Fairchild, Spokane, Wash., 1987-88, dir. med. svcs., 1988-91; pvt. practice in pediats. Kapstaffer, Maixner & Genung, Spokane, 1991—; instr. in pediatric advanced life support, neonatal resuscitation. Contbr. articles to profl. jours. Maj. USAF M.C., 1980-91. Fellow Am. Acad. Pediatrics; mem. So. Med. Assn., Wash. State Soc. Pediatrics, Spokane Med. Soc., Spokane Pediatric Soc., Spokane Women's Assn. Physicians, Alpha Omega Alpha. Office: Kapstaffer Maixner & Genung 105 W 8th Ave Ste 318 Spokane WA 99204-2318

GEOGHEGAN, PATRICIA, lawyer; b. Bayonne, N.J., Sept. 9, 1947; d. Frank and Rita (Mihok) G. BA, Mich. State U., 1969; MA, Yale U., 1972, JD, 1974; LLM, NYU, 1982. Bar: N.Y. 1975. Assoc. Cravath, Swaine & Moore, N.Y.C., 1974-82, ptnr., 1982—. Mem. ABA, N.Y. State Bar Assn., Assn. of Bar of City of N.Y. Office: Cravath Swaine & Moore 825 8th Ave New York NY 10019-7416

GEO-KARIS, ADELINE JAY, state legislator; b. Tegeas, Greece, Mar. 29, 1918; student Northwestern U., Mt. Holyoke Coll.; LLB, DePaul U. Bar: Ill. Founder Adeline J. Geo-Karis and Assocs., Zion, Ill.; former mcpl., legis. atty. Mundelein, Ill., Vernon Hills, Ill., Libertyville (Ill.) Twp., Long Grove (Ill.) Sch. Dist.; justice of peace; former asst. state's atty.; mem. Ill. Ho. of Reps., 1973-79; mem. Ill. Senate, 1979—, asst. majority leader, 1992—; mayor, City of Zion, Ill. Served to lt. comdr. USNR., Res. ret. Recipient Americanism medal DAR; named Woman of Yr. Daughters of Penelope, Outstanding Legislator Ill. Fedn. Ind. Colls. and Univs., 1975-78, Legis. award Ill. Assn. Park Dists., 1976. Sponsor Guilty but Mentally Ill Law. Greek Orthodox. Office: Ill State Senate State Capitol Springfield IL 62706

GEORGE, CAROLE SCHROEDER, computer company executive; b. Bloomington, Ind., Mar. 20, 1943; d. Melburne Evert and Neva Mae (Bechtel) Gibson; m. Richard D. White, Aug. 31, 1962 (div. 1972); 1 child, Kenneth Donald; m. Charles R. Schroeder, Apr. 7, 1973 (div. 1983); m. Thomas H. George III, May 4, 1991. BS in Pharmacy, Wayne State U., 1972; postgrad., Va. Commonwealth U., 1980-83. Registered pharmacist, Mich. Va. Staff pharmacist St. Joseph Hosp., Pontiac, Mich., 1972-73; dir. pharmacy St. Mary Hosp., Livonia, Mich., 1974-76; resident Detroit Receiving Hosp., 1977-78; clin. faculty pharmacy Med. Coll. of Va., Richmond, 1978-83; dir. pharmacy ops. Med. Coll. Va. Hosps., Richmond, 1978-83; mktg. mgr. TDS Healthcare Systems Corp., Atlanta, 1983-86; sr. cons. Gerber Alley, Norcross, Ga., 1986; dir. product mgmt. Baxter Healthcare Systems, Reston, Va., 1986-89; sr. v.p. Integrated Systems Tech. Inc., Reston, 1989-96; prin. Intelligent Bus. Consulting, Reston, 1996—. Mem. Am. Soc. of Hosp. Pharmacists, Am. Pharm. Assn., Nat. Assn. for Healthcare Quality, Rho Chi.

GEORGE, DIANE ELIZABETH, librarian, educational technology and computer education educator; b. L.I., N.Y., July 12, 1952; d. Arnold J. and Jeanette A. (Hester) G. BS, So. Conn. State U., 1974, MS in Libr. Sci., 1976, MS in Ednl. Tech., 1977. Cert. intermediate adminstr., libr. media specialist K-12, elem. edn. 1-8, driver's edn. Libr. media specialist New Canaan (Conn.) Pub. Schs., 1976-77, North Haven (Conn.) Pub. Schs., 1977-80, Branford (Conn.) Pub. Schs., 1980—; ednl. cons. to SEED Project, New Haven; Conn. del. N.E. Regional Ednl. Leadership Conf., 1983; participant forum Linking Children with Nature, Roger Tory Peterson Inst., 1988. Mem. libr. power adv. com. New Haven Pub. Edn., 1995—. Recipient Faculty Excellence award Branford Intermediate Sch., 1985-86. Mem. Assn. for Supervision and Curriculum Devel., Conn. Educators Computer Assn. (bd. dirs. 1989—), Conn. Ednl. Media Assn. (bd. dirs. 1984-85, cert. of appreciation 1984). Office: Branford Intermediate Sch 185 Damascus Rd Branford CT 06405-6107

GEORGE, ELIZABETH, author; b. 1949. English tchr. Mater Dei H.S., Santa Ana, Calif., 1974-75, El Toro (Calif.) H.S., 1975-87; creative writing tchr. Coastline Coll., Costa Mesa, Calif., 1988—, Irvine (Calif.) Coll., 1989, U. Calif., Irvine, 1990. Author: A Great Deliverance, 1989, Payment in Blood, 1989, Well Schooled in Murder, 1990, A Suitable Vengeance, 1991, For the Sake of Elena, 1992, Missing Joseph, 1993, Playing for the Ashes, 1994. Recipient Anthony award, 1989, Le Grand Prix de Litterature Policiere, 1990. Office: Bantam-Doubleday-Dell 1540 Broadway New York NY 10036*

GEORGE, JEAN CRAIGHEAD, author, illustrator; b. Washington, July 2, 1919; d. Frank Cooper and Carolyn (Johnson) Craighead; m. John L. George, Jan. 28, 1944 (div. Jan. 1964); children: Twig Craighead Pittenger, John Craighead, Thomas Lothar. B.A., Pa. State U., 1941. Reporter Washington Post, 1943-44; artist Pageant mag., 1945; reporter United Features, 1945-46; roving editor Reader's Digest, 1973-80; continuing edn. tchr. Chappaqua, N.Y., 1960-68. Author, illustrator: My Side of the Mountain, 1959, Summer of the Falcon, 1962, Gull Number 737, 1964, The Thirteen Moons, 1967-69, Coyote in Manhattan, 1968, River Rats, Inc., 1968, Who Really Killed Cock Robin, 1971, Julie of the Wolves, 1972, American Walk Book, 1978, Cry of the Crow, 1980, Journey Inward, 1982, The Talking Earth, 1983, One Day in the Alpine Tundra, 1984, How to Talk to Your Animals, 1985, One Day in the Prairie, 1986, Water Sky, 1987, (mus.) One Day in the Woods, 1988, The Shark Beneath the Reef, 1989, On the Far Side of the Mountain, 1990, One Day in the Tropical Rain Forest, 1990, The Missing 'Gator of Gumbo Limbo, 1992, The Fire Bug Connection, 1993, The First Thanksgiving, 1993, Dear Rebecca, Winter Is Here, 1993, Animals Who Have Won Our Hearts, 1994, Julie, 1994, To Climb a Waterfall, 1995, Acorn Pancakes & Dandelion Salad, 1995, There's an Owl in the Shower, 1995, Everglades, 1995, The Case of the Missing Cutthroat Trout, 1996, The Tarantula in My Purse, 1996, Survival Filmstrips, 1984, (film) My Side of the Mountain, 1995, Nature Filmstrips, 1978-80, One Day in the Woods Musical for Children, 1996. Recipient Aurrainne award, 1957; Newbery Honor Book award, 1961; medal, 1973; Hans Christian Andersen Honor List award, 1964; Pa. State Woman of Yr. award, 1968; World Book award, 1971; Kerlan award, 1982; U. So. Miss. award, 1986, Washington Irving award, 1991, 92, Knickerbocker award, 1991. Address: 20 William St Chappaqua NY 10514-3114

GEORGE, JOYCE JACKSON, judge emeritus, lawyer; b. Akron, Ohio, May 4, 1936; d. Ray and Verna (Popadich) Jackson; children: Michael Eliot, Michelle René. BA, U. Akron, 1962, JD, 1966; postgrad. Nat. Jud. Coll., Reno, 1976, NYU Sch. Law, 1983; LLM, U. Va., 1986. Bar: Ohio 1966, U.S. Dist. Ct. (no. dist.) Ohio 1966, U.S. Ct. Appeals (6th cir.) 1968, U.S. Supreme Ct. 1968. Tchr. Akron Bd. Edn., 1962-66; asst. dir. law city of Akron, 1966-69, pub. utilities advisor, 1969-70, asst. dir. law, 1970-73; sole practice, Akron, 1973-76; referee Akron Mcpl. Ct., 1975, judge, 1976-83; judge 9th Dist. Ct. Appeals, Akron, 1983-89; judge, Peninsula, Ohio, 1989; U.S. atty. No. Dist. Ohio, 1989-93; v.p. adminstrn. Telxon Corp., Akron, Ohio, 1993—; tchr., lectr. Ohio Jud. Coll., Nat. Jud. Coll.; cons. in field. Author: Judicial Opinion Writing Handbook, 1981, 2d edit. 1986, 3d edit., 1993, Referee's Report Writing Handbook, 1992; contbr. articles to profl. publs. Recipient Outstanding Woman of Yr. award Akron Bus. and Profl. Women's Club, 1982; Alumni Honor award U. Akron, 1983, Alumni award U. Akron Sch. Law, 1991; Dept. Treasury award, 1992; named Woman of Yr. in politics and govt. Summit County, Ohio, 1983. Mem. ABA, Ohio Bar Assn.

GEORGE, KATIE, lawyer; b. Chillicothe, Ohio, Sept. 4, 1953; d. Harry Paul and Tina Lillian George; m. Nov. 25, 1972 (div. Nov. 1983); 1 child, Alison; m. Timothy John Nusser, June 30, 1985. BBA, U. Toledo, 1983, JD, 1986, MBA, 1989. Bar: Ohio 1987, U.S. Dist. Ct. (no. dist.) Ohio 1993, Fla. 1994. Law clk. Allotta, Singer & Farley, Co., LPA, Toledo, 1985-86; mgmt. specialist Dept. Pub. Utilities City of Toledo, 1987-91, acting commr. Dept. Health, 1992-93, acting mgr. Dept. Pub. Safety, 1991-94; pvt. practice Toledo, 1987-96, Pensacola, Fla., 1996—; asst. dist. legal counsel State of Fla., 1996—; part-time instr. U. Toledo, 1987-88. Bd. dirs. City of Toledo BlockWatch, 1993. Mem. Fla. Bar Assn. Home and Office: 160 Gaermental Ctr Ste 601 Pensacola FL 32501

GEORGE, MARY SHANNON, state senator; b. Seattle, May 27, 1916; d. William Day and Agnes (Lovejoy) Shannon; B.A. cum laude, U. Wash., 1937; postgrad. U. Mich., 1937, Columbia U., 1938; m. Flave Joseph George; children—Flave Joseph, Karen Liebermann, Christy, Shannon Lowrey. Prodn. asst., asst. news editor Pathe News, N.Y.C., 1938-42; mem. fgn. editions staff Readers Digest, Pleasantville, N.Y., 1942-46; columnist Caracas (Venezuela) Daily Jour., 1953-60; councilwoman City and County of Honolulu, 1969-74; senator State of Hawaii, 1974-94, asst. minority leader, 1978-80, minority policy leader, 1983-84, minority floor leader, 1987, minority leader, 1987-94, chmn. housing com., 1993, transp. com., 1981-82; mem. Nat. Air Quality Adv. Bd., 1974-75, Intergovtl. Policy Adv. Com. Trade, 1988-93, White House Conf. Drug Free Am., 1988. Vice chmn. 1st Hawaii Ethics Commn., 1968; co-founder Citizens Com. on Constl. Conv., 1968; vice-chmn. platform com. Republican Nat. Conv., 1976, co-chmn., 1980; bd. dirs. State Legis. Leaders Found., 1993-94, Hawaii Planned Parenthood, 1970-72, 79-86, Hawaii Med. Services Assn., 1972-86; mem. adv. bd. Hawaii chpt. Mothers Against Drunk Driving, 1984—. Recipient Jewish Men's Club Brotherhood award, 1974, Disting. Svc. award Hawaii Women Lawyers, 1991, Mahalo award Friends of Libr. Hawaii, 1991; Outstanding Legislator of Yr. award Nat. Rep. Legislators Assn., 1985; named Woman of Yr., Honolulu Press Club, 1969, Hawaii Fedn. Bus. and Profl. Women, 1970; Citizen of Yr., Hawaii Fed. Exec. Bd., 1973, 76. Mem. LWV (pres. Honolulu 1966-68), Mensa, Phi Beta Kappa. Author: A Is for Abrazo, 1961. Home: 782G N Kalaheo Ave Kailua HI 96734-1910

GEORGE, MILDRED M., sentencing advocate; b. Erie, Pa., Apr. 6, 1925; d. John Alexander and Hannah Clare (Mowrey) McKinnon; m. Edward Michael George, Apr. 24, 1949 (dec. Feb. 1993); children: Edward M. Jr., David, Sarah, John (dec.), Hannah. AS, Palm Beach Jr. Coll., 1974; BA, Fla. Atlantic U., 1985. Cert. in mental health tech. Aide Fla. Parole Commn., Delray Beach, 1974-76, Dept. Offender Rehab., Delray Beach, 1976-78; probation supr. Dept. Corrections, Delray Beach, 1978-85; program dir. divsn. comprehensive alternatives Office of Pub. Defender, West Palm Beach, Fla., 1985—; cons. Sentencing project, Washington, 1993; advisor Legal Case Mgmt. project, Tallahassee, 1994—; pres., bd. dirs. PRIDE, Inc., West Palm Beach, 1995—. Bd. dirs. Urban League, West Palm Beach, 1985-95 (Appreciation award, 1990, Svc. award, 1996); active Am. Civil Liberties Union, 1986— (Freedom award, 1995), Freedom of Choice, Inc., Palm Beach County, 1987—, Fla. Women's Consortium, 1990—; mem. adv. bd. United Way Vol. Bur., Palm Beach County, 1990-93; mem. Dist. 9-A Alcohol, Drug Abuse and Mental Health planning coun., West Palm Beach, 1991-93; gov's appointment Dist. 9 Health and Human Svcs. bd., West Palm Beach, 1993—. With USN, 1945-47. Recipient Davis Productivity award Fla. TaxWatch, 1991, Svc. to Indigents award PRIDE, 1992, Women in Leadership award Public Svc. Sector Exec. Women of the Palm Beaches, 1993, Appreciation award Comprehensive Alcohol Rehab. program, 1994, Pioneer award, 1995, Butterfly award Wayside House, 1994, Cert. of Appreciation The Sentencing Project, 1996. Mem. NOW (Susan B. Anthony award, 1996), Mental Health Assn., Nat. Assn. Sentencing Advocates, Human Svcs. Coalition of Palm Beach County, Partnership for Drug Free Cmty., Palm Beach Assn. Criminal Defense Lawyers (certificate of Recognition, 1996). Home: 86 MacFarlane Dr Delray Beach FL 33483 Office: Office of Pub Defender 421 Third St West Palm Beach FL 33401

GEORGE, NANCY MARIE, nurse practitioner; b. Royal Oak, Mich., Oct. 16, 1959; d. Robert Thomas George Sr. and Agnes Julia (Davidson) Younge. Diploma in Nursing, Bronson Sch. Nursing, Kalamazoo, 1989; BS, Mich. Technol. U., 1990; MS, U. Mich., 1993. Cert. nurse practitioner, RN, Mich. Tchr. U.S. Peace Corps, Kenya, Africa, 1982-85; clin. nurse Mott Childrens Hosp., Ann Arbor, Mich., 1989-93; adult nurse practitioner Primary Care Nursing, Detroit, 1993-94; adolescent nurse practitioner Oakwood Teen Ctr., Romulus, Mich., 1994—; mem. Clinical Adv. Bd. Nurse Practitioner Assn. Continuing Edn., Chgo., 1995—, mktg. com. Advance Practice Council, Mich. Nurses Assn., symposium planning com., Advance Practice Coun.-Mich. Nurses Assn., Okemos, Mich., 1995—; child family rep., Mich. Nurses. Assn., 1995—; presenter in field. Fellow Am. Acad. Nurse Practitioners, mem. Mich. Nurses Assn., Sigma Theta Tau. Office: Oakwood Teen Health Ctr 9650 S Wayne Rd Romulus MI 48174

GEORGE-LEPKOWSKI, SUE ANN, echocardiographic technologist; b. Altoona, Pa., Sept. 17, 1948; d. Charles Frederick and E. Anita (Haller) G.; m. Walter Lepkowski. AS, BS in Agronomy, Pa. State U., 1968, 70, MEd in Agronomy, Biol. Scis., Edn., 1972; PhD, Columbia & Columbia Pacific U., 1980; DS, Columbia Pacific U., 1981. Internship echocardiology West Pa. Hosp., Pitts., 1979-80; echocardiology tech. Bronson Meth. Hosp., Kalamazoo, 1981-82; echocardiographic technologist Nalle Clinic, Charlotte, 1983-85; tech. dir. Carolina Cardiology, Asheville, N.C., 1985-86; chief echocardiographic technologist Candler Gen. Hosp., Savannah, Ga., 1986-88; echocardiography, clin. specialist, technical spl. edn. specialist, chief technologist Self Meml. Hosp., Greenwood, S.C., 1988—; cons., rschr., lectr. in field. Contbr. articles to profl. jours.; co-author: Clinical 2-D Echocardiography. Mem. choir Carolina Mountain Brass, Gospell Quartet; percussionist Images; edn. chmn. Greenwood Lupus Group, pres.; edn. chmn. S.C. Lupus Found. Recipient ACP award, Berkeley-Whittinger award for rsch. and acad. excellence. Mem. Am. Soc. Ultrasonic Tech. Specialists, Am. Inst. Ultrasonic Medicine, Soc. Diagnostic Med. Sonographers, Am. Registry Diagnostic Med. Sonographers (registered diagnostic med. sonographer, registered diagnostic cardiac sonographer), Altoona/Pa. State U. Alumni Assn., Columbia Pacific U. Alumni Assn., Altoone High Alumni Assn., IPTAY, S.C. Ultrasound Soc., N.C. Ultrasound Soc., Am. Soc. Echocardiography, Pa. State Carolina Club, USGA, PGA, LPGA, Rollings Platform Assn., Phi Epsilon Phi. Mem. Dutch Reformed Ch. Home: 531 Willson St Apt 3 Greenwood SC 29649-1560 Office: Self Meml Hosp 1325 Spring St Greenwood SC 29646-3860

GEORGES, LINDA SWINSON, anesthesiologist, pediatrician; b. Orangeburg, S.C., Feb. 26, 1948; d. Rodney Southerland and Marian (Edwards) Swinson; m. Gregory Lee Georges, Aug. 21, 1982; children: Lauren Elizabeth, Graham Leigh. BS, Emory U., 1970; MD, Med. Coll. Ga., 1976. Surgery intern Med. Coll. Ga., Augusta, 1977, anesthesiology resident, 1979; anesthesiology fellow U. Utah, Salt Lake City, 1980, instr. dept. anesthesiology, 1980-81, asst. prof., 1981-88; pediat. anesthesia and critical care fellow Children's Hosp. Phila., 1983; asst. prof. anesthesiology U. N.C., Chapel Hill, 1991—. Office: 914 Kings Mill Rd Chapel Hill NC 27514-4923

GEORGINO, SUSAN MARTHA, city redevelopment services administrator; b. Phila., Apr. 1, 1950; d. Joseph Francis and Eleanor (Kelley) Boyle; m. Richard Romano (div.); 1 child, Sean; m. Victor Georgino. BA, Calif. State U., L.A., 1975, MPA, 1983. Adminstrv. officer Maravilla Found., Montebello, Calif., 1978-81; adminstrv. analyst City of Burbank (Calif.), 1982-84, project mgr., 1984-87, asst. dir. community devel., redevel. adminstr., 1987-89; dir. redevel. svcs. City of Brea (Calif.), 1989—; bd. dirs. Calif. Redevel. Assn. Bd. officer Soroptomist Internat., Brea, 1991; active La Providencia Guild, Burbank, 1990, Parks and Recreation Commn., Burbank, 1991, 93; vice chair City of Burbank's Performing Arts Grant Awards Program, 1994. Mem. Nat. Assn. Redevel. and Housing Ofcls. (bd. dirs. 1986-87), Calif. Assn. Econ. Devel. Ofcls., Orange County Consortium (bd. dirs.), Bus. Coun. Econ. Devel., Lambda Alpha Internat. (bd. dirs. Orange County chpt., v.p. 1996—). Roman Catholic. Office: City of Brea One Civic Ctr Circle Brea CA 92621

GEORGOPOULOS, MARIA, architect; b. Moussata, Cefalonia, Greece, Apr. 2, 1949; came to U.S., 1973; d. Vassilios and Joulia Georgopoulos; m. 1972 (div. 1974); 1 child, Demetrios. BArch, Nat. Poly. Sch. Greece, Athens, 1972; MS, Columbia U., 1976. Registered architect, N.Y., Greece. Project mgr. Architects Design Group, N.Y.C., 1976-79, Griswold, Heckel & Kelly, N.Y.C., 1979-80; project dir. Lehman Bros., Kuhn Loeb Inc., N.Y.C., 1980-85; v.p. L.F. Rothschild Inc., N.Y.C., 1985-89, sr. project mgr., 1989-90; dir. of facilities mgmt. Dreyfus Corp., N.Y.C., 1990—. Mem. AIA, Am. Women Entrepreneurs, Greek Inst. Architects. Greek Orthodox. Club: Douglaston (N.Y.). Home: 14 Melrose Ln Douglaston NY 11363-1221 Office: The Dreyfus Corp 200 Park Ave New York NY 10166-0005

GERAGHTY, ANDREA, lawyer; b. Pitts., July 9, 1952; d. Charles and Wilma Marie (Rizzardi) Ocepek; m. Guy E. Geraghty, June 21, 1986; children: Ryan Charles, Claire Kathryn. BA, Indiana U. Pa., 1974; JD cum laude, Duquesne U., 1983. Bar: Pa. 1983, U.S. Dist. Ct. (we. dist.) 1983, U.S. Ct. Appeals (3rd cir.) 1987. Sr. staff mediator Westmoreland County Bur. of Consumer Affairs, Greensburg, Pa., 1975-77; consumer svcs. rep. Pa. Pub. Utility Commn., Pitts., 1977-81; law clk. Mansmann, Cindrich & Huber, Pitts., 1981-83; legal writing and rsch. instr. Duquesne U. Sch. Law, Pitts., 1982-83; lawyer Hollinshead, Mendelson, Bresnahan & Nixon, Pitts., 1983-96; sole practitioner Pitts., 1996—. Editor: (newsletter) Real News, 1991—. Bd. dirs. Duquesne U. Sch. of Law Alumni Assn., Pitts., 1991-93. Mem. Allegheny County Bar Assn. (sec. real property sect. 1995-96, coun. on professionalism 1992—), Pa. Bar Assn. (liaison real property probate trust sect. 1995—), Women's Bar Assn. (exec. bd. 1994—). Home: 6930 Rosewood St Pittsburgh PA 15208 Office: 1310 Allegheny Bldg Pittsburgh PA 15219

GERAGHTY, MARGARET KARL, financial consultant, portfolio manager; b. Bklyn., May 31, 1947; d. Edward H. and Margaret Honora (Miller) Karl; m. John Matthew Geraghty, Sept. 9, 1972; 1 child, Elizabeth. BA, Marymount Coll., Tarrytown, N.Y., 1969; MA, Hunter Coll., 1974; advanced profl. cert., Stern Grad. Bus. Sch. NYU, 1978. Fin. analyst GM, N.Y.C., 1969-73; dir. fin. analysis Equitable, N.Y.C., 1973-77; asst. v.p. Equitable Life Holding Corp., N.Y.C., 1977-79, Equitable Life Assurance Soc., N.Y.C., 1979-84; v.p. Equitable Capital Mgmt. Corp., N.Y.C., 1984-91; fin. and investment cons. in pvt. practice, 1991—; bd. dirs. Equico Securities. Trustee Marymount Coll., 1984—, chmn. fin. com., 1988—; trustee Mt. St. Dominic Acad., Caldwell, N.J., 1987-90; treas. Cath. Big Bros., N.Y.C., 1987-91; co-chmn. Centennial Scholarship Fund, 1986-89; mem. Friends of Ridgewood Libr., Family Counseling Aux. Recipient Gloria Gaines award Marymount Coll., 1979, Golden Dome award, 1994. Mem. Fin. Women's Assn., Coll. Club Ridgewood, Rep. Club. Home and Office: 250 Palmer Ct Ridgewood NJ 07450-2316 also: 400 East Ave Bay Head NJ 08742-4706

GERARD, SUSAN JANE, secondary education educator; b. Spokane, Wash., Feb. 8, 1962; d. Michael Arthur and Jane Carol (Sheppard) Hussey; m. Thomas Roy Gerard, Dec. 20, 1986; children: Andrew Thomas, Stephen Michael, Kymberley Sue. BA in History and Edn. with honors, Gonzaga U., 1984, MA in Tchg. and History, 1987, postgrad., 1990; postgrad., Ea. Wash. U., 1990. Cert. tchr., adminstrn., Wash. Tchr. social studies Lewis and Clark H.S., Spokane, 1984—, freshman track coach, 1984-88, debate coach, 1986-88, mem. sch. care team, 1985—; adj. prof. edn. Whitworth Coll., 1995—; advanced placement European history essay exam grader, 1996—. Contbr. articles to profl. publs. Voter registrar Spokane County Election Bd., 1983—. Cataldo acad. scholar Gonzaga U., 1984-87. Mem. ASCD, NEA, Wash. Edn. Assn., Spokane Edn. Assn. (bldg. rep. 1985-87), Phi Alpha Theta, Kappa Delta Pi, Alpha Sigma Nu. Roman Catholic. Home: 14025 E 23rd Ave Veradale WA 99037 Office: Lewis and Clark HS 521 W 4th Ave Spokane WA 99204-2603

GERARD-SHARP, MONICA FLEUR, communications executive; b. London, Oct. 4, 1951; came to U.S., 1975; d. John Hugh Gerard-Sharp and Doreen May (Kearney) Dewhurst; m. Ali Edward Wambold, Nov. 21, 1981; children: Marina, Daniela, Dominica. BA in Philosophy and Lit. with honors, U. Warwick, Eng., 1973; MBA in Fin., Mktg. and Internat. Bus., Columbia U., 1980. Editor Inst. Chem. Engrs., London, 1973-74; sub-editor TV Times Ltd., London, 1974-75; press officer, editor UN, N.Y.C., 1975-78; bus. mgr. Time-Life Video, N.Y.C., 1980-81; mgr. fin. analysis Time-Life Films, N.Y.C., 1981; v.p. T.V.I.S., N.Y.C., 1982-83; dir. strategy and devel. video group Time Inc. Info. Svcs., N.Y.C., 1984-85; asst. treas., officer Time Inc., N.Y.C., 1985-87; pub. Travel Todays mags. Fairchild Pubs. subs. Capital Cities/ABC, N.Y.C., 1987-88; dir. video programming Fairchild Pubs., Capital Cities/ABC, N.Y.C., 1988-89; pub. Entrée and Home Fashions Mag., N.Y.C., 1988-90; pres. Monali Inc., N.Y.C., 1991—; cons. UN Bus. Council, N.Y.C., 1979; bd. rep. U.S.A. Network, N.Y.C., 1983-85; bd. dirs. Maga-Link, Communications Bridge; trustee The Richmond Theater, London. Editor: Everyone's United Nations, 1977; contbg. editor Asia Pacific Forum, 1976-77; contbr. articles to profl. jours. and mags., 1973-78. Treas. Help the Aged, Eng. Bronfman fellow, 1979-80. Mem. Nat. Acad. Cable Programming, Am. Film Inst., Beta Gamma Sigma. Roman Catholic. Home: Deer Park Sunset Hill Rd Pleasant Valley NY 12569 Office: Monali Inc 26 E 80th St New York NY 10021

GERBERG, JUDITH LEVINE, human resource company executive; b. N.Y.C., Mar. 21, 1940; d. Murray Joseph and Pearl (Berens) Levine; m. Mort Gerberg, Feb. 1, 1969; 1 child, Lilia Anya Berens. BA in Comparative Lit., Columbia U., 1963, postgrad. in organizational devel., 1989; MA in Psychology and Art, NYU. Registered art therapist; cert. clin. mental health counselor; nat. cert. counselor. Program dir. Women's Selling Game, N.Y.C., 1979-84; mem. faculty Parsons Sch. Design, N.Y.C., 1979-85; pres. Judith Gerberg Assocs., N.Y.C., 1984—; orgnl. devel. mgmt. valuing diversity, team bldg., comm. skills, stress mgmt.; founder Powerhouse, 1st outplacement for creative profls. Co-author: The New York Women's Directory, 1973; contbr. articles and book revs. to various publs. Chmn. pub. rels. Profl. Women's Caucus, 1972; facilitator N.Y.C. Contr.'s Women's Econ. Task Force, 1994-95. N.Y. State scholar. Mem. Am. Art Therapy Assn. (life, bd. dirs. 1980-84), N.Y. Art Therapy Assn. (founding v.p. 1975), The Forum at Stephen Wise (co-chmn. 1986-87), Fin. Women's Assn., Women's Venture Fund. Home: 35 W 82nd St New York NY 10024-5607 Office: 250 W 57th St Ste 1019 New York NY 10107-1019

GEREAU, MARY CONDON, corporate executive; b. Winterset, Iowa, Oct. 10, 1916; d. David Joseph and Sarah Rose (Stack) Condon. Student, Mt. Mercy Jr. Coll., 1935-37; BA, U. Iowa, 1939, MA, 1941; m. Gerald Robert Gereau, Jan. 14, 1961. Program dir. ARC, India, 1943-45; dean of students Eastern Mont. Coll., 1946-48; supt. pub. instrn. state of Mont., 1948-56; sr. legis. cons. NEA, 1957-73; dir. legis. Nat. Treasury Employees Union, 1973-76; legis. asst. to Senator Melcher, Mont., 1976-86; pres. Woman's Party Corp., 1991—. Contbr. articles on state govt. and edn. to profl. jours. Co-chmn. Truman Commerative Com., 1994—. Mem. Coun. Chief State Sch. Officers (bd. dir. 1953-56, pres. 1956), Rural Edn. Assn. (exec. bd. 1953-56), Nat. Women's Party (v.p. 1984-91), Equal Rights Ratification Coun. (nat. chmn.), NEA. Named Conservationist of Yr. Mont. Conservation Coun., 1952, Roll Call Cong. Staffer of Yr., 1985; recipient Disting. Svc. award VFW, 1951, Disting. Svc. award, Chief State Sch. Officers, 1956. Mem. U.S. Congress Burro Club (pres. 1983-84).

GERHARD, NANCY LUCILE DEGE, school counselor, educator; b. St. Paul, July 23, 1939; d. Carl H. and Mildred L. (Toenjes) Dege; m. Rick A. Gerhard, June 25, 1960; children: Geoffrey Austin, Mark Alan. BS in Elem. Edn. magna cum laude, Gustavus Adolphus Coll., 1960; MA in Sch. and Guidance Counseling, Chapman U., 1978. Cert. English tchr., guidance counselor, elem. tchr., adminstr., Calif. Tchr. English Orange (Calif.) Unified Sch. Dist., 1987-93, mentor tchr., 1990-93, coach Middle Sch. Demonstration Program, 1990-93, h.s. counselor, 1993—; mem. Calif. Lang. Arts Instructional Materials Evaluation Panel, 1988; cons. UCI Writing Project, Calif. Lit. Project. Mem. ASCD, NEA, Coun. for Basic Edn., Calif. Tchrs. Assn., Orange Unified Edn. Assn. Office: Orange High Sch 525 N Shaffer St Orange CA 92667-6824

GERHARDT, LILLIAN NOREEN, magazine editor; b. New Haven, Sept. 28, 1932; d. Victor Herbert and Lillian Angela (Beecher) G. BS, So. Conn. State U., 1954; MLS, U. Chgo., 1962. Children's libr. New Haven Pub. Libr., 1954-55; 1st asst. reference dept. Meriden (Conn.) Pub. Libr., 1955-58, head reference dept., 1958-61; assoc. editor Kirkus Svc., Inc., N.Y.C., 1962-66; exec. editor Sch. Libr. Jour. Book Rev., R.R. Bowker Co., Juvenile Projects, N.Y.C., 1966-71; editor in chief Sch. Libr. Jour., 1971—; v.p. Cahners Mags., N.Y.C., 1992—; lectr. Columbia U. Sch. Library Service, 1969-72. Sr. editor: Best Books for Children, 1967-70; sr. editor, project coordinator: SLJ Book Review Cumulative, 1969, Children's Books in Print, 1969, Subject Guide to Children's Books in Print, 1970; editor-in-chief Sch. Libr. Jour., v.p. Cahners magazines, 1992. Recipient Disting. Alumnus award So. Conn. State U. div. libr. sci., 1978, Cahners medal of excellence, 1993, 94, Jesse H. Neal award Am. Bus. Press, 1994. Mem. ALA (mem.-at-large coun. 1976-80, Mildred Batchelder award com. 1970, Newbery-Caldecott award com. 1970, Grolier Found. award 195), Conn. Liby Assn. (hon.), Woman's Nat. Book Assn., Assn. Libr. Svcs. to Children (pres. 1978-79). Office: Cahners Mags SLJ 249 W 17th St New York NY 10011-5300

GERHART, DOROTHY EVELYN, insurance executive, real estate professional; b. Monett, Mo., Apr. 20, 1932; d. Manford Thomas and Norma Grace (Barrett) Ethridge; m. Robert H. Gerhart, Apr. 11, 1952 (div. Dec. 1969); children: Sandra Gerhart Kreamer, Richard A., Diane Gerhart Lacey. Grad. high sch., Tucson; student, U. Ariz., 1950-53. Lic. real estate broker. Owner, pres. Gerhart Ins., Inc., Tucson, 1967-70, 89—; agt. Mahoney-O'Donnell Agy., Tucson, 1970-73, Gerhart & Mendelsoh Ins., Tucson, 1973-78; agt., mgr. personal lines dept. Tucson Realty and Trust, 1978-83; ins. agt. San Xavier Ins. Agy., Tucson, 1985-89; pres. Gerhart Ins., Inc., Tucson, 1989-93, Koty-Leavitt Ins., Inc. (formerly Gerhart Ins., Inc.), Tucson, 1993—, Gerhart Realty, Inc., Tuscon, 1993—. Vol. Palo Verde Psychiat. Hosp. Mem. Nat. Fedn. Ind. Bus., Ind. Ins. Agts. Tucson (bd. dirs. 1973, 74, v.p. 1975, pres. 1976, First Woman Pres.), Fed. Home Life Ins. Co. (Pres.'s Club award 1986), Nat. Fedn. Small Bus., Altrusa Club of Tucson (bd. dirs. 1984, membership chmn. 1985, fund raising chmn. 1986). Republican. Address: PO Box 13421 Tucson AZ 85732-3421 Office: Gerhart Realty Inc # 200 6339 E Speedway Tucson AZ 85710

GERHART, GLENNA LEE, pharmacist; b. Houston, June 11, 1954; d. Henry Edwin and Gloria Mae (Mrnustik) G. BS in Pharmacy, U. Houston, 1977. Registered pharmacist, Tex. Staff pharmacist Meml. City Med. Ctr., Houston, 1977-84, asst. dir. pharmacy, 1984—. Mem. Am. Pharm. Assn., Am. Soc. Hosp. Pharmacists, Tex. Pharm. Assn., Tex. Soc. Health-System Pharmacists, Harris County Pharm. Assn., Plumeria Soc. Am., U. Houston Alumni Orgn. (life), Houston Cat Club, Nat. Cougar Club, Slavonic Benevolent Order of Tex., Greentrails Ladies Club, Kappa Epsilon. Republican. Methodist. Home: 19811 Cardiff Park Ln Houston TX 77094-3031 Office: Meml City Med Ctr 920 Frostwood Dr Houston TX 77024-2312

GERIKE, ANN ELIZABETH, psychologist; b. Casper, Wyo., Aug. 24, 1933; d. Marcus Gustav and Lillie Helene (Grobengieser) G.; m. John W. Robinson, Oct. 20, 1959 (div. Mar. 1978); children: David Gerike, Margaret Ann, Catherine Elizabeth. BA, U. Nebr., 1955, MA, 1956, PhD, 1983; postgrad., Glasgow U., 1957-60. Editor U. Nebr. Press, Lincoln, 1962-80; clin. psychologist Mental Health and Mental Retardation Authority Harris County, Houston, 1984-87; pvt. practice Mpls., 1988—; clin. psychologist Pyramid Counseling Ctr., Mpls., 1988—; aging specialist Employee Adv. Resource, Control Data Corp., Mpls., 1988-89. Pres. Older Women's League, Houston, 1986; bd. dirs. Twin Cities Gray Panthers, Mpls., 1988—; nat. chair Gray Panthers Ageism Task Force, 1995—. Mem. APA, Minn. Psychol. Assn., Minn. Gerontol. Soc., Minn. Women Psychologists, Nat. Women's Studies Assn. (convenor Aging and Ageism Caucus 1986-95). Democrat. Unitarian. Office: Midlife Counseling 5841 Cedar Lake Rd S Ste 201 Saint Louis Park MN 55416-5657

GERING, SANDRA EILEEN, art dealer, curator; b. Washington, Oct. 5, 1942; d. Jack and Marian (Brill) Marks; m. Norman Charles Gering, May 30, 1964 (div. Nov. 1987); children: Brett Michael, Craig Stephen. AS, U. Bridgeport, 1962. Owner, pres. Sandra Gering Gallery, N.Y.C., 1985—; adv. bd. Genart, N.Y.C., 1993—; bd. mem. N.Y. Kunsthale, N.Y.C., 1993. Pub. (catalogues) Anastasi, Bradshaw, Cage, Marioni, Rauschenberg, Tobey, 1990, William Anastasi, 1991, Dove Bradshaw: Works, 1969-93, 1993. Mem. Art Table. Home: 14 W 11th St New York NY 10011

GERMAN, JUNE RESNICK, lawyer; b. N.Y.C., Feb. 24, 1946; d. Irving and Stella (Weintraub) Resnick; m. Harold Jacob German, May 31, 1974; children: Beth Melissa, Heather Alice, Bret. BA, U. Pa., 1965; JD, NYU, 1968. Bar: N.Y. 1968, U.S. Dist. Ct. (ea. and so. dists.) N.Y. 1974, U.S. Ct. Appeals (2d cir.) 1973, U.S. Supreme Ct. 1973. Atty., sr. atty., supervising atty, Mental Health Info. Svc., N.Y.C., 1968-77; atty./advisor Course in Human Behavior Mems. of N.Y. State Judiciary, Nassau and Suffolk County, 1980; pvt. practice Huntington, N.Y., 1985—. Contbg. author: Bioethics and Human Rights, 1978, Mental Illness, Due Process and the Acquitted Defendant, 1979; contbr. chpts. to books, articles to profl. jours. Chmn. Citizen's Ad Hoc Com. on the Construction of the Dix Hills Water Adminstrn. Bldg., Huntington, N.Y., 1985-90; mem. Citizens Adv. Com. for Dix Hills Water Dist., Huntington, 1992—; dir. House Beautiful Assn. at Dix Hills, 1986—; dir. Citizens for a Livable Environment and Recycling, Huntington, 1989-93; committeeperson Dem. Party, Suffolk County, N.Y., 1986—. Mem. Suffolk County Bar Assn. Jewish. Office: 150 Main St Huntington NY 11743

GERMER, LAURA VAUGHAN, social services administrator; b. Syracuse, N.Y., Feb. 18, 1938; d. Luther Wesley and Harriet (Vaughan) Smith; m. Harold Dickinson Germer Jr., June 13, 1959; children: Paul Harold, John Luther, Elizabeth Vaughan Germer Hottel. BA, Kalamazoo Coll., 1959; MS, Emporia State U., 1977. Classroom asst. Tempe Union Sch. Dist., Guadalupe, Ariz., 1978-79; adminstrv. asst., intake counselor Clin. Psychology Ctr., Ariz. State U., Tempe, 1979-81; adminstrv. asst. Am. Bapt. Chs. of Pa. and Del., Valley Forge, Pa., 1981-84, adminstrv. asst. pub. rels. divsn. Bd. Internat. Ministries, 1984-90; info. and referral specialist East Ctrl. Kans. Area Agy. on Aging, Ottawa, 1990—. Bd. dirs. Am. Bapt. Women's Ministries Ctrl. Region, 1995—, Ch. Women United, Kans., 1995—. Mem. AAUW (bd. dirs. Ottawa br. 1992—), PEO Sisterhood (chpt. corr. sec. 1972-74, pres. 1974-76, guard 1991-92), Ottawa Univ. Women (pres. 1995-96), Older Kansans Info. and Referral Specialists Assn., Franklin County Women's Club. Democrat. Home: PO Box 21 Ottawa KS 66067-0021 Office: Ea Ctrl Kans Area Agy Aging 132 S Main St Ottawa KS 66067

GERONCA, CARMELINA ESCOSIA, real estate appraiser, consultant; b. Canlaon City, N. Occid., The Phillipines, May 19, 1944; came to U.S., 1970; d. Pedro Patino and Carmen (Escosia) G. BS in Commerce, Bus. Adminstrn., U. Negros Occidental Recoletos, Bacolod City, The Philippines, 1967. Cert. real estate appraiser Internat. Soc. Real Estate Appraisers, Chgo.; registered real estate appraiser, Calif. Sr. real estate appraiser Comty. Redevel. Agy., L.A., 1970-90; pres. Carmelina-Michael Appraisal Co., Inc., L.A., 1990—; profl. advisor, Sci. Mus. Sch., L.A. Unified Sch. Dist.; project mgr. Manual Arts Elem. Sch., L.A., 1992. Author: (book) Demonstration Appraisal Report for Commercial Buildings, 1990. Mem. Kahirup Internat., LA, Builder Lions Club L.A., Nergenses of Am., L.A., United Ilonggo, L.A. Mem. NAFE, Assn. Real Estate Execs/. Democrat. Roman Catholic. Home and Office: Carmelina-Michael Appraisal Co Inc 2658 Glendower Ave Los Angeles CA 90027

GERONEMUS, DIANN FOX, social work consultant; b. Chgo., July 4, 1947; d. Herbert J. and Edith (Robbins) Fox; BA with high honors, Mich. State U., 1969; MSW, U. Ill., 1971; 1 dau., Heather Eileen. Diplomate Am. Bd. Clin. Social Work; lic. clin. social worker, marriage and family therapist, Fla.; cert. case mgr.; bd. cert. diplomate clin. social work. Social worker neurology, neurosurgery and medicine Hosp. of Albert Einstein Coll. Medicine, 1971-74; prin. social worker ob-gyn and newborn infant service Rush-Presbyn.-St. Luke's Med. Center, Chgo., 1974-75; social worker neurology, adminstr. Multiple Sclerosis Treatment Center, St. Barnabas Hosp., Bronx, N.Y., 1975-77, socio-med. researcher (Nat. Multiple Sclerosis Soc. grantee), dept. neurology and psychiatry, 1977-79, dir. social service, 1979-80; field work instr. Fordham U. Grad. Sch. Social Service, 1979-80; preceptor, social work program Fla. Atlantic U., Fla. Internat. U.; mem. edn. com., med. adv. bd., program cons. Nat. Multiple Sclerosis Soc., 1980-83, area service cons., 1983-86 ; pvt. practice psychotherapy; social work cons.; cons. in gerontology, rehab. and supervision, 1980—. Mem. Ombudsman Coun., 1992-94, vice chmn. 1993-94. Mem. NASW, Acad. Cert. Social Workers, Registry Clin. Social Workers, Am. Orthopsychiat. Assn. Jewish. Contbr. articles to profl. jours. Home: 833 NW 81st Way Fort Lauderdale FL 33324-1216

GERRINGER, ELIZABETH (THE MARCHIONESS DE ROE DEVON), writer, lawyer; b. Edmund, Wis., Jan. 7, 1934; d. Clyde Elroy and Matilda Evangeline Knapp; m. Roe (Don Davis) Devon Gerringer-Busenbark, Sept. 30, 1968 (dec. Dec. 1972); student Madison Bus. Coll., 1952, San Francisco State Coll., 1953-54, Vivian Rich Sch. Fashion Design, 1955, Dale Carnegie Sch., 1956, Arthur Murray Dance Studio, 1956, Biscayne Acad. Music, 1957, L.A. City Coll., 1960-62, Santa Monica (Calif.) Jr. Coll., 1963; JD U. Calif., San Francisco, 1973; postgrad. Wharton Sch., U. Pa., 1977, London Art Coll., 1979; Ph.D., 1979; attended Goethe Inst., 1985. Bar: Calif., 1965. Actress, Actors Workshop San Francisco, 1959, 65, Theatre of Arts Beverly Hills (Calif.), 1963, also radio; cons. and systems analyst for banks and pub. accounting agys.; artist, poet, singer, songwriter, playwright, dress designer. Pres., tchr. Environ Improvement, Originals by Elizabeth; atty. Dometrik's, JIT-MAP, San Francisco, 1973—; steering com. explorations in worship, ordained min. 1978. Author: The Cardinal, 1947, Explorations in Worship, 1965, The Magic of Scents, 1967, New Highways, 1967, The Grace of Romance, 1968, Happening - Impact-Mald, 1971, Seven Day Rainbow, 1972, Zachary's Adversaries, 1974, Fifteen from Iowa, 1977, Bart's White Elephant, 1978, Skid Row Minister, 1978, Points in Time, 1979, Special Appointment-A Clown in Town, 1979, Happenings, 1980, Candles, 1980, Votes from the Closet, 1984, Wait for Me, 1984, The Stairway, 1984, The River is a Rock, 1985, Happenings Revisited, 1986, Comparative Religion in the United States, 1986, Lumber in the Skies, 1986, The Fifth Season, 1987, Summer Thoughts, 1987, Crimes of the Heart, 1987, Toast Thoughts, 1988, The Contrast of Russian Literature Through the Eyes of Russian Authors, 1988, A Thousand Points of Light, 1989, The Face in the Mirror, 1989, Sea Gulls, 1990, Voices on the Hill, 1991, It's Tough to Get a Matched Set, 1991, Equality, 1991, Miss Geranium Speaks, 1991, Forest Voices, 1991, Golden Threads, 1991, Castles in the Air, 1991, The Cave, 1991, Angels, 1991, Real, 1991, An Appeal to Reason, 1992, We Knew, 1992, Like It Is, 1992, Politicians Anonymous, 1993, Wheels Within Wheels, 1994, A Tree for All Seasons, 1995, The Visitor, 1995, There are no Ghettoes, 1996, Time Frames, 1996. Mem. Assn. of Trial Lawyers of Am. Address: 1008 10th St # 275 Sacramento CA 95814-3502

GERRISH, CATHERINE RUGGLES, food company executive; b. Winona, Minn., July 10, 1911; d. Clyde O. and Frances (Holmes) Ruggles; m. Hollis G. Gerrish, Sept. 10, 1946. AB, Radcliffe Coll., 1932, AM, 1934; PhD, Harvard U., 1937. Rsch. asst. Harvard U., 1937-39; instr., asst. prof. econs. U. Ill., 1939-42, assoc. prof., 1946; economist Bur. Budget, Exec. Office President, 1943-45; asst. editor Quar. Jour. Econs., 1951-69; treas., v.p. Squirrel Brand Co., Cambridge, Mass., 1966—. Corporater The Cambridge Homes, pres., 1990-91. Mem. Am. Econ. Assn., Nat. Tax Assn., Coll. Club of Boston (pres. 1948-51), Radcliffe Alumnae Assn. (pres. 1953-55). Home: 207 Grove St Cambridge MA 02138-1013 Office: 17 Boardman St Cambridge MA 02139-1927

GERRITSEN, MARY ELLEN, vascular and cell biologist; b. Calgary, Alta., Can., Sept. 20, 1953; came to U.S., 1978; d. Thomas Clayton and Alice Irene (Minton) Cooper; m. Paul William Gerritsen, May 24, 1975 (div. 1977); m. Thomas Patrick Parks, Oct. 11, 1980; children: Kristen, Madelene. BSc summa cum laude, U. Calgary, 1975, PhD, 1978. Postdoctoral fellow U. Calif., San Diego, 1978-80; asst. prof. N.Y. Med. Coll., Valhalla, 1981-86, assoc. prof., 1986-90; sr. staff scientist Pharm. divsn. Bayer Corp., West Haven, Conn., 1990-93, head inflammation exploratory rsch., 1990—, prin. staff scientist, 1993—; vis. scientist Harvard U., 1996; cons. Insite Vision, Alameda, Calif., 1987-89, Boehringer Ingelheim Pharms., Ridgefield, Conn., 1985-88; adj. assoc. prof. N.Y. Med. Coll., 1990—. Mem. editorial bd. Microvascular Rsch., 1988-96, Am. Jour. Physiology, 1993—, Am. Jour. Cardiovascular Pathology, 1996—; editor-in-chief Microcirculation, 1993—; editor N.Am. Vascular Biology Orgn. Newsletter; contbr. articles to profl. jours. I. W. Killam Found. fellow, 1976, Med. Rsch. Coun. Can. fellow, 1978. Mem. Am. Soc. for Pharmacology and Exptl. Therapeutics, Am. Physiol. Soc., Assn. Rsch. on Vision and Ophthalmology, Am. Soc. Investigational Pathology, Soc. Leukocyte Biology, Am. Soc. Cell Biology, Microcirculatory Soc. (mem. coun. 1989-92, chairperson publs. com. 1991-93, Mary Weideman award 1985, Young Investigator award 1984), N.Am. Vascular Biology Orgn. (mem. steering com. 1993, mem. coun. 1994—, editor-in-chief newsletter 1994—). Office: Bayer Corp Pharm Divsn Inst Bone/Jt Disease/Cancer 400 Morgan Ln West Haven CT 06516-4140

GERRY, DEBRA PRUE, psychotherapist; b. Oct. 9, 1951; d. C.O. and Sarah E. Rawl; m. Norman Bernard Gerry, Apr. 10, 1981; 1 child, Gisele Psyche Victoria. BS, Ga. So. U., 1972; MEd, Armstrong State U., 1974; PhD, U. Ga., 1989. Cert. Ariz. Bd. Behavioral Health Examiners. Spl. edn. tchr. Chatham County Bd. Edn., Savannah, Ga., 1972-74; edn. and learning disabilities resource educator Duval County Bd. Edn., Jacksonville, Fla., 1974-77; ednl. resource counselor spl. programs adminstr. Broward County Bd. Edn., Ft. Lauderdale, Fla., 1977-81; pvt. practice Scottsdale, Ariz., 1990—. Contbr. author coll. textbooks; contbr. articles to profl. jours. Vol., fundraiser, psychol. cons., group leader Valley AIDS Orgns., Phoenix, 1990-96; fundraiser Hosp. Health Edn. Programs, Scottsdale, 1992-93; mem. com. for women's issues Plz. Club, Phoenix, 1992-93; pres. Laissez Les Bon Temps Rouler, Wrigley Club, Phoenix, 1993-96; bd. dirs. Sojourner's Ctr., Phoenix; appointee Ariz. Supreme Ct., Foster Care Rev. Bd., Phoenix, 1996-99. Recipient Rudy award Shanti Orgn., 1991. Mem. APA, NOW, ACA, Internat. Soc. Poets (disting. mentor, Poet of Merit award 1996), Nat. Assn. Women Bus. Owners, Assn. for Multicultural Coun., Assn. for Specialists in Group Work, Mensa, Phi Delta Kappa, Kappa Delta Epsilon, Sigma Omega Phi, Kappa Delta Pi.

GERSH, IRIS GAIL, writer, English educator; b. Kerhonkson, N.Y., Oct. 17, 1950; d. Nathan Gersh and Lillian (Kaminsky) Fredericks. BA in Sociology cum laude, Boston U., 1972; MFA in Creative Writing, Fla. Internat. U., 1995. Creative writing instr. Broward County Sch. Bd., Ft. Lauderdale, Fla., 1991-95; adj. instr. English, creative writing, tutor Writing Ctr. Nova Southeastern U., Ft. Lauderdale, 1994—. Author: (poetry): Sunscripts 94-anthology, 1994, (fiction) Thema, 1990, The Alembic, 1996. Recipient South Fla. Poetry Inst. 1st prize for poem, 1990. Mem. Assoc. Writing Programs, People for Ethical Treatment Animals, Amnesty Internat., Sierra Club.

GERSHON, NINA, federal judge; b. Chgo., Oct. 16, 1940; d. David and Marie Gershon; m. Bernard J. Fried, May 15, 1983. BA, Cornell U., 1962; LLB, Yale U., 1965; postgrad., London Sch. Econs., 1965-66. Former magistrate judge U.S. Dist. Ct. (so. dist.) N.Y., N.Y.C.; U.S. dist. judge Eastern Dist. N.Y., Bklyn., 1996—. Fulbright scholar. Office: US Courthouse 225 Cadman Plz Brooklyn NY 11201*

GERSKE, JANET FAY, lawyer; b. Chgo., Nov. 14, 1950; d. Bernard G. Gerske and L. Fay (Knight) Capron; m. James P. Chapman, Dec. 5, 1982. BS, Northwestern U., 1971; JD, U. Mich., 1978. Bar: Ill. 1978, U.S. Dist. Ct. (no. dist.) Ill. 1978. Pvt. practice, Chgo., 1978-80, 84—; assoc. Jerome H. Torshen Ltd., Chgo., 1980-84. Chpt. chmn. Ind. Voters Ill./Ind. Precinct Orgn., Chgo., 1982-84; co-chmn. Ill. Women's Agenda Com., 1985-88, fin. officer, 1987-88; dir. Chgo. Abused Women Coalition, 1986-90, sec., treas., 1988-90. Mem. Women's Bar Assn. Ill. (co-chmn. rights of women com. 1985-86, dir. 1988-90), Chgo. Bar Assn. (co-chmn. legal status of women com. young lawyers sect.), Nat. Orgn. Social Security Claimants' Rep. Democrat. Home: 850 W Oakdale Ave Chicago IL 60657-5122 Office: 203 N LaSalle St Chicago IL 60601

GERSONI-EDELMAN, DIANE CLAIRE, author, editor; b. Bklyn., Apr. 16, 1947; d. James Arthur and Edna Bernice (Krinski) Gersoni; B.A. cum laude, Vassar Coll., 1967; m. James Neil Edelman, Oct. 5, 1975; children—Michael Lawrence, Sara Anne. Asst. editor, then asso. editor Sch. Library Jour. Book Rev., 1968-72; free lance writer, 1972-74, 77—; writer, editor Scholastic Mags., Inc., N.Y.C., 1974-77; author: Sexism and Youth, 1974; Work-Wise: Learning About the World of Work from Books, 1980; cons., speaker in field. Club: Vassar (N.Y.C.). Contbr. articles, book revs. to anthologies, newspapers, mags. Home: care Edelman 301 E 78th St New York NY 10021-1322

GERSTEIN, ESTHER, sculptor; b. N.Y.C., May 20, 1924; d. Leon and Lillian (Peretz) Grizer; m. Leonard B. Gerstein, Mar. 31, 1946; children: Lee Steven, Laurie Susan. Student, Pratt Inst., 1941-42, NYU, 1942-43; pvt. study, various sculptors; student, Cooper Union, 1946-48. Asst. tchr. Art Students League, N.Y.C., 1944-46; painting tchr. pvt. sch. Great Neck, N.Y., 1961-63; founder, instr. sculpture and painting Studio 33, Westbury, N.Y., 1964-72; sculptor and painter pvt. studios, Boca Raton, Fla.; lectr. Norton Mus., Palm Beach, Fla., 1985. Exhibited in group shows at Hecksher Mus., Huntington, N.Y., Norton Mus., Palm Beach, Fla., Kellenberg Gallery, C.W. Post Coll., L.I., Firehouse Gallery, Nassau Cmty. Coll., L.I., Lever House, N.Y.C., Grace Bldg., N.Y.C., Hofstra U., Lighthouse Gallery, Tequesta, Fla., Montoya Art Gallery, Palm Beach, Del-Aire Country Club, Boca Raton, Fla., Bocaire Country Club, Boca Raton, Polo Country Club, Boca Raton, Nathan Rosen Gallery, Boca Raton, Lynn U., Boca Raton, Naza Gallery, Boca Raton; one man show includes TV spl.; represented in numerous pvt. and corp. collections throughout U.S. Art Students League scholar, 1944, Cooper Union scholar, 1946. Mem. Artists Guild Norton Mus., Nat. League Am. Pen Women.

GERSTEIN, REVA, university chancellor; d. David and Diana (Kraus) Appleby; m. Bertrand Gerstein, 1939 (div. 1971); children: Irving Russell, Ira Michael; m. David Raitblat, 1979. BA, U. Toronto, 1938, MA, 1939, PhD, 1945, LLD (hon.), 1996; LLD, U. Western Ont., Can., 1972; DLitt (hon.), Lakehead U., 1974; LLD (hon.), U. Guelph, 1975, Queen's U., Can., 1981, York U., 1994, U. Toronto, 1996. Registered psychologist, Ont., Can. Lectr. dept. psychology U. Toronto, 1939-49, York U., 1965-73; dir. McGraw-Hill Ryerson Ltd., 1974-87; founder, chmn. bd. dirs. Gerstein Crisis Ctr., 1988—; chancellor U. Western Ont., Toronto, 1992—; fellow Founders Coll., York U.; mem. Niagara Inst., Inst. Rsch. and Pub. Policy, 1978, Cardinal Emmett Carter's Panel on Economy, 1983, Mental Health Care Commn. Dist. Health Coun., 1983-87; chmn. Mayor's Task Force on Discharged Psychiat. Patients, 1983; mem. Premier's Health Strategy Coun., 1988-91; bd. dirs., chmn. Can. Inst. Advanced Rsch., 1989—; bd. dirs. Avon Products Ltd. Nat. pres. Can. Coun. Children and Youth, 1957-65, Nat. Coun. Jewish Women, 1955-59, internat. v.p., 1955-59; chmn., coord. Social Plan Coun. Youth Project, 1969-71; chmn. adv. coun. on policy to Leader of Opposition, Ottawa, 1977; vice chmn., chmn. capital campaign Hosp. for Sick Children, mem. found., trustee, 1975—; bd. dirs. Stratford Shakespearean Festival Inc., 1977, hon. sec., 1979, senator, 1980; chmn. hosp. coun. Met. Toronto, 1984-87; bd. dirs., exec. mem. Nat. Arts Ctr., 1988-91; bd. dirs. Royal Conservatory of Music, 1990—; mem. Can. Opera Co., Art Gallery of Ont., Royal Ont. Mus., Can. Coun. Christians and Jews, Ont. Police Commn., 1982-88; founder Toronto Friends of Stratford, Nat. Coun. Human Rights Found. Decorated officer Order of Can., Order of Ont.; recipient Albert Einstein Coll. of Medicine award, 1956, Centennial medal, 1967, C.M. Hincks Nat. award for mental health, 1987; named B'nai Brith Women of Yr., 1961. Fellow Can. Psychol. Assn. (hon., life); mem. APA, Can. Mental Health Assn. (nat. dir.), Ont. Psychiat. Found. (pres. 1987—), Nat. Assn. Children's Hosps. and Related Instns., Ont. Psychiat. Assn. (hon. life), Ont. Psychol. Assn., Ont. Chiefs of Police Assn. (hon.). Office: 625 Avenue Rd Apt 703, Toronto, ON Canada M4V 2K7

GERSTEL, JUDITH ROSS, film critic; b. Winnipeg, Man., Can., Dec. 19, 1944; d. Marvyn and Rachel (Kesten) Ross; m. Alan N. Gerstel, Nov. 6, 1963; children: Jennifer, Sasha (dec.). Student, U. Man., 1960-63; BA, U. Buffalo, 1964. Music and dance critic Buffalo Courier-Express, 1965; producer WGBH-FM, Cambridge, Mass., 1966-67; writer, critic Mpls. Star, 1968-71; writer, broadcaster CBC-TV, Windsor & Toronto, Can., 1974-77; TV producer CBC-TV, Can., 1977-81; asst. editor, feature writer Detroit Free Press, KRTN, 1988-91, film critic, 1991—. Recipient award for TV, Can. Music Coun., 1977; nominated for best documentary writer Assn. Can. TV and Radio Artists, 1979; Nat. Arts Journalism fellow U. So. Calif., 1994—. Mem. Nat. Soc. Film Critics. *

GERSTEL, LINDA, lawyer; b. Forest Hills, N.Y., June 5, 1962. BA magna cum laude, Columbia U., 1983; JD, Temple U., 1986. Bar: Conn. 1986, N.Y. 1987, D.C. 1987, U.S. Dist. Ct. (so. and ea. dists.) N.Y. 1987. Ptnr. Anderson Kill Olick & Oshinsky, P.C., N.Y.C. Note and comment editor Temple Internat. and Comparative Law Jour. Mem. Conn. Bar Assn., N.Y. Bar Assn., D.C. Bar. Office: Anderson Kill Olick & Oshinsky 1251 Ave of the Americas New York NY 10020-1182*

GERSTENBERGER, DONNA LORINE, humanities educator; b. Wichita Falls, Tex., Dec. 26, 1929; d. Donald Fayette and Mabel G. AB, Whitman Coll., 1951; MA, U. Okla., 1952, PhD, 1958. Asst. prof. English U. Colo., Boulder, 1958-60; prof. U. Wash., 1960-96, prof. emeritus, 1996—, chmn. undergrad. studies, 1971-74, assoc. dean Coll. Arts and Scis., dir. Coll. Honors and Office Undergrad. Studies, 1974-76, chmn. dept. English, 1976-83, vice chmn. faculty senate, 1984-85, chmn. faculty senate, 1985-86; cons. in field; bd. dirs. Am. Lit. Classics; mem. grants-in-aid com. Am. Coun. Learned Socs.; chmn. region VII, Mellon Fellowships in Humanities, 1982-92; mem. adv. com. Grad. Record Exams, 1990-93, Coun. Internat. Exch. of Scholars, 1992-95. Author: J.M. Synge, 1964, 2d edition, 1988, The American Novel: A Checklist of Twentieth Century Criticism, vols. I and II, 1970, Directory of Periodicals, 1974, The Complex Configuration: Modern Verse Drama, 1973, Iris Murdoch, 1974, Richard Hugo, 1983; editor: Microcosm, 1969, Swallow Series in Bibliography, 1974—; assoc. editor: Abstracts of English Studies, 1958-68; founder, editor jour. Seattle Review, 1983—. Bd. dirs. N.W. Chamber Orch., Seattle, 1975-78, Wash. Friends Humanities, 1991—; trustee Wash. Commn. Humanities, 1985-91, pres., 1988-90; mem. vis. com. Lehigh U., 1987-92; pres. Am. Commn. for Irish Studies/West, 1989-91. Am. Council Learned Socs. grantee, 1962, 88; Am. Philos. Soc. grantee, 1963. Mem. MLA, Am. Com. Irish Studies. Office: U Wash GN-30 Dept English Seattle WA 98195

GERSTING, JUDITH LEE, computer science educator, researcher; b. Springfield, Vt., Aug. 20, 1940; d. Harold H. and Dorothy V. (Kinney) MacKenzie; m. John M. Gersting, Jr., Aug. 17, 1962; children: Adam, Jason. BS, Stetson U., 1962; MA, Ariz. State U., 1964, PhD, 1969. Assoc. prof. computer sci. U. Ctrl. Fla., Orlando, 1980-81; asst. prof. computer sci. Ind. U.-Purdue U., Indpls., 1970-73, assoc. prof., 1974-79, prof., 1981-93; prof. computer sci. U. Hawaii, Hilo, 1994—; staff scientist Indpls. Ctr. for Advanced Rsch., 1982-84. Author: The Programming Process/Pascal, 1989, Mathematical Structures for Computer Science, 1993, Visual Basic Programming, 1996; contbr. articles to computer sci. jours. Mem. Assn. for Computing Machinery, IEEE Computer Soc. Office: U Hawaii 200 W Kawili St Hilo HI 96720-4075

GERTNER, NANCY, federal judge, legal educator; b. May 22, 1946; d. Morris and Sadie Gertner; m. John C. Reinstein, Apr. 27, 1985; 3 children. BA cum laude with honors, Columbia U., 1967; MA, JD, Yale U., 1971; degree (hon.), New England Sch. Law, 1979. Bar: Mass., U.S. Dist. Ct., U.S. Ct. Appeals (1st and 3rd cirs.), U.S. Supreme Ct. Law clerk to Hon. Luther M. Swygert U.S. Ct. Appeals (7th cir.), Chgo., 1971-72; ptnr. Silverglate, Gertner, Fine & Good, 1973-90, Dwyer, Collora & Gertner, 1990-94; judge U.S. Dist. Ct. Mass., Boston, 1994—; instr. Sch. Law Boston U., 1972-86, 87-90; vis. prof. Law Sch. Harvard U., 1985-86; mem. civic justice adv. com. to U.S. Dist. Ct., 1991; mem. adv. com. U.S. Ct. Appeals (1st cir.), 1991-92. Contbr. articles to legal jours. Bd. dirs. Women's Rights Com. Recipient Mass. Choice award, 1987, Black Educator's Alliance award Profl. Svc. to Edn., 1983, New England Hadassah award, 1992, Abigail Adams award Mass. Women's Polit. Caucus Edn. Fund., 1994. Mem. Assn. Trial Lawyers Am. (basic trial advocacy course com., vice chair 1985-86), Mass. Acad. Trial Lawyers, Mass. Half-Way Houses, Inc. (house com.), Mass. Civil Liberties Union (bd. dirs., Abraham T. Alper award for Excellence in Civil Liberties, 1980), Boston Bar Assn. (lawyers com. for civil rights under law, steering com. 1979—). Office: John W McCormack Courthouse 90 Devonshire St Rm 707 Boston MA 02109-4501

GERTRUDE, KATY See WILHELM, KATE

GERWIN, LESLIE ELLEN, public affairs and community relations executive, lawyer; b. L.A., May 18, 1950; d. Nathan and Beverly Adele (Wilson) G.; m. Bruce Robert Leslie, July 3, 1978; 1 child, Jonathan Gerwin Leslie. BA, Prescott Coll., 1972; JD, Antioch Sch. Law, 1975; MPH, Tulane U., 1988. Bar: D.C. 1975, N.Y. 1981, U.S. Dist. Ct. D.C. 1977, U.S. Dist. Ct. (so. dist.) N.Y. 1980. Staff asst. U.S. Congress, Washington, 1970-72; cons. Congl. Subcom., Washington, 1972-73; instr. U. Miami Law Sch., Coral Gables, Fla., 1975-76; assoc. prof. law Yeshiva U., N.Y.C., 1976-86; vis. assoc. prof. law Tulane Law Sch., New Orleans, 1983-84; pub. policy cons. New Orleans, 1987—; with Ariadne Cons., New Orleans, 1994—; dir. devel. and community rels. Planned Parenthood La., Inc., New Orleans, 1989-90; legal advisor La. Coalition for Reproductive Freedom, 1990-92; exec. v.p. Met. Area Com., New Orleans, 1992-94; exec. dir. Met. Area Com. Edn. Fund, New Orleans, 1992-94; bd. dirs. Inst. for Phys. Fitness Rsch., N.Y.C., 1982-86, Challenge/Discovery, Crested Butte, Colo., 1977-80; cons. FDA, Washington, 1977-78, U. Judaism, L.A., 1974-75; mem. Met. Area Com. Leadership Forum, New Orleans, 1988. Contbr. articles to profl. jours. Mem. Ind. Dem. Jud. Screening Panel, N.Y.C., 1980; bd. dirs. New Orleans Food Bank for Emergencies, 1987-89; profl. adv. com. MAZON-A Jewish Response to Hunger, L.A., 1986-89; bd. dirs. Second Harvesters Food Bank Greater New Orleans, 1989-94, La. State LWV, 1990-91, Anti-Defamation League, New Orleans, 1989-95, Jewish Endowment Found., 1987-93; trustee Jewish Fedn. Greater New Orleans, 1989-95, Fed. Emergency Mgmt. Agy. Bd., Emergency Food and Shelter Program, S.E. La., 1988—; v.p. Tulane U. B'nai B'rith Hillel Found., 1987-90; steering com. Citizens for Pers. Freedom, 1989-91; steering com. Metro 2000, 1989-90; sec. New Orleans sect. Nat. Coun. Jewish Women, 1990-91, state pub. affairs chmn., 1992-96; bd. Contemporary Arts Ctr., 1993—; chair, bd. advocates Planned Parenthood La., 1995—; v.p. Edn. Tikvat Shalom Conservative Congregation, 1995—, chair New Orleans Israel Bonds, 1996—; me. Cmty. Rels. Com., 1986—, vice chair, 1995—. Fellow Inst. of Politics, 1990-91; scholar Xerox Found., 1972-75; Decorated Order of Barristers; named One of Ten Outstanding Young Women of Am., 1987; recipient Herbert J. Garon Young Leadership award Jewish Fedn. Greater New Orleans, 1990; named YWCA Role Model, 1992. Mem. ABA, N.Y. Bar Assn., N.Y. Acad. Scis., Am. Pub. Health Assn., D.C. Bar Assn., Nat. Moot Ct. Honor Soc., Pub. Health Honor Soc., Calif. State Dem. Club (Key Svc. award 1988), Delta Omega.

GERWIN, MARY BERRY, legislative staff member, federal and state government lawyer; m. Edward F. Gerwin Jr.; children: Kathleen, Kristen. BA summa cum laude, U. Maine, 1977; JD cum laude, Georgetown U., 1980. Bar: D.C. Legis. aide to Senator William S. Cohen, Washington, 1981—; counsel sub-com. on oversight of govt. mgmt. Senate Com. on Govt. Affairs, Washington, 1981-86, minority staff dir. and chief counsel sub-com. on oversight of govt. mgmt., 1986-91; minority staff dir. and chief counsel Senate Special Com. on Aging, Washington, 1991—. Assoc. editor: Tax Lawyer Law Review. Pres. bd. dir. Senate Employee's Child Care Ctr. Mem. Alpha Kappa Delta, Phi Kappa Phi. Office: Special Com on Aging SD-31 Dirksen Office Bldg Washington DC 20510-6400*

GESELL, GERALDINE CORNELIA, classical archaeology educator; b. Evanston, Ill., July 23, 1932; d. Walter Bertram and Lillian Marie (Robinson) G. BA, Vassar Coll., 1953; MA, U. Okla., 1955; PhD, U. N.C., 1972. Latin tchr. John Marshall High Sch., Oklahoma City, 1955-67; asst. prof. U. Tenn., Knoxville, 1972-79, assoc. prof., 1979-85, prof., 1985—, Lindsay Young prof., 1988—; exec. dir. Kavousi (Greece) Excavations, 1984—. Author: Town, Palace, and House Cult in Minoan Crete, 1985; contbr. articles to Am. Jour. Archaeology Hesperia. Mem. Archaeological Inst. Am., Classical Assn. of Mid. West and South, Vergilian Soc., Torch Club. Office: U Tenn Dept Classics 710 McClung Tower Knoxville TN 37996-0471

GESKE, ANNA DIERS, university official; b. Hampton, Iowa, June 12, 1931; d. Hermann A. and Viola J. (Ager) Diers; m. David H. Geske, Aug. 20, 1953 (dec. Dec. 1967); children: Elise Ann, Matthew David; m. Lee A. Teichthesen, June 8, 1974. BA, Wartburg Coll., 1953; MA, U. Iowa, 1957. Cert. tchr., Iowa, Mass. Tchr. English and theater Nichols H.S., West Br. H.S., Iowa, 1953-56; instr. English, Northeastern U., Boston, 1958-59; lectr. English Cornell U., Ithaca, N.Y., 1968-75, adminstr. Mellon postdoctoral fellowships, 1975-89, adminstr. Cornell Coun. for Arts, 1975—; mem. adv. bd. Olive Press, 1991-93; panel mem. fundraising for arts and econ. impact on arts. Mem. adv. coun. Sage Chapel, Ithaca, 1986-90; mem. adv. bd. Firehouse Theatre, Ithaca, 1996—; grant panelist Tompkins County Arts Coun., Ithaca; bd. dirs. Mental Health Assn. Tompkins County. Mem. Assn. Performing Arts Presenters, Nat. Mus. Women in Arts, Mus. Modern Art, Met. Mus. Art. Democrat. Lutheran. Office: Cornell U Cornell Coun for Arts 341 Caldwell Hall Ithaca NY 14853

GESKE, JANINE PATRICIA, judge; b. Port Washington, Wis., May 12, 1949; d. Richard Braem and Georgette (Paulissen) Geske; m. Michael Julian

Hogan, Jan. 2, 1982; children: Mia Geske Berman, Sarah Geske Hogan, Kevin Geske Hogan. Student, U. Grenoble, U. Rennes; BA, MA in Teaching, Beloit Coll., 1971; JD, Marquette U., 1975. Bar: Wis. 1975, U.S. Dist. Ct. (ea. & we. dists.) Wis. 1975, U.S. Supreme Ct. 1978. Tchr. elem. sch. Lake Zurich, Ill., 1970-72; staff atty., chief staff atty. Legal Aid Soc., Milw., 1975-78; asst. prof. law, clin. dir. Law Sch. Marquette U., Milw., 1978-81; hearing examiner Milw. County CETA, Milw., 1980-81; judge Milw. County Circuit Ct., Milw., 1981-93; justice Supreme Ct. Wis., 1993—; dean Wis. Jud. Coll.; mem. faculty Nat. Jud. Coll.; instr. various jud. tng. programs, continuing legal edn. Fellow ABA, mem. Am. Law Inst., Wis. Bar Assn., Milw. Bar Assn., Dane County Bar Assn., Nat. Women Judges Assn., 7th Cir. Bar Assn., Alpha Sigma Nu. Roman Catholic. Office: Wis Supreme Ct PO Box 1688 Madison WI 53701-1688

GESSNER, BARBARA ANN, continuing education educator; b. Sheboygan, Wis.; d. Hugo R. and Edna (Heinecke) G. BS, U. Wis., 1964; MS, Wayne State U., 1968; PhD, U. Wis., 1979. Staff nurse U. Hosp., Madison, 1959-63; instr. U. Wis. Extension, Madison, 1964-67; rsch. asst. Yale U. Sch. Nursing, New Haven, Con., 1969-71; nursing specialist U. Wis. Extension, Madison, 1971-77, asst. prof., 1977-80, assoc. prof., 1980-83, prof., chmn., 1983-85; prof. U. Wis., Madison, 1985—; mem. adv. commn. nurse longterm care Am. Nurses Found., Kansas City, Mo., 1982-84; chairperson cont. edn. Am. Nurses Assn., Kansas City, 1985-89, cabinet mem. on nursing edn., 1988-90; site vis. accreditation Am. Nurses Creditialing Ctr., Washington. Author: (with others) The Head Nurse: Her Leadership Role, 1975, The Practice of Continuing Education in Nursing, 1983; contbr. articles to profl. jours. Mem. Am. Heart Assn., Wis., named Outstanding Nurse, 1984. Project dir. grantee Wis. Bd. Nursing, 1978; project dir. Cont. Edn. Leadership grantee Divsn. Nursing, 1984-85. Mem. Am. Assn. for Adult and Cont. Edn., Wis. Nurses Assn. (fin. com. 1989-94), Wis. League for Nursing (nominating com. 1993), Midwest Nursing Rsch. Soc. Office: U Wis Madison Sch of Nursing 600 Highland Ave Madison WI 53792-2455

GEST, KATHRYN WATERS, press secretary; b. Boston, Mar. 20, 1947; d. Mendal and Anna Waters; m. Theodore O. Gest, May 28, 1972; 1 child, David Mendal. B.S., Northwestern U., 1969; M.S., Columbia U., 1970. Reporter The Patriot-Ledger, Quincy, Mass., 1968; writer Europe desk Voice of Am., Washington, 1969; reporter St. Louis Globe-Democrat, 1970-77; reporter Congl. Quar., Washington, 1977-78, news editor, 1978-80, asst. mng. editor, 1980-83, mng. editor, 1983-87; St. Louis corr. Time Mag., 1975-77, The Christian Sci. Monitor, 1976-77; press sec. to Sen. William S. Cohen, Washington, 1987—; chmn., U.S. del. Internat. Labor Orgn. Tripartite Meeting on Conditions of Employment and Work of Journalists, Geneva, 1990. Recipient award for investigative reporting Inland Daily Press Assn., 1975. Mem. Soc. Profl. Journalists. Club: Nat. Press. Office: Office of Sen William S Cohen 322 Hart Senate Office Bldg Washington DC 20015

GETCHELL, SYLVIA FITTS, librarian; b. Dover, N.H., July 3, 1925; d. Perley Irving and Marguerite Elizabeth (Marden) F.; m. L. Forbes Getchell, July 17, 1948; children: Ann Marden, Faith Perley, Edward Fitts, William Forbes. BA in History magna cum laude, U. N.H., 1947; BS in Libr. Sci., Simmons Coll., 1948. Profl. cataloger Libr. Columbia U., N.Y.C., 1948-51, U. N.H., Durham, 1951-52; sch. libr. Newmarket (N.H.) Pub. Schs., 1970-85; curator Stone Sch. Mus., Newmarket, 1966—. Author: Marden Family Genealogy, 1974, Tide Turns on the Lamprey: History of Newmarket, N.H., 1984, Fitts Families: A Genealogy, 1989. Bd. govs. Am. Ind. Mus., Exeter, N.H., 1992—; bd. dirs., past pres. Newmarket Hist. Soc., 1966—, Piscataqua Pioneers, Portsmouth, N.H., 1969—; 18th Century reenactor First Newmarket Militia, 1973—; troop leader Girl Scouts USA, Newmarket; mem. budget com. Town of Newmarket; chair ann. fund drive local chpt. ARC; collector, Sun. sch. tchr. Newmarket Community Ch.; state treas. Aux. of N.H. Dental Soc.; mem. N.H. Hist. Soc. Mem. DAR (mem. and sec. attic commn. N.H. chpt. 1994—), New Eng. Hist. Geneal. Soc., Newmarket Women's Club (past treas.), Huguenot Soc. N.H. Republican. Home: 51 N Main St Newmarket NH 03857-1216

GETTELMAN, ROBIN CLAIRE, media specialist; b. Milw., Jan. 6, 1952; d. Robert Otto and Virginia Mae (Proffit) G.; m. Ted Bayard Johnson, Sept. 25, 1976 (div. Jan. 1985). BS in Secondary Edn., U. Wis., 1974; MA in Librarianship, U. Denver, 1975. Dir. instructional material ctr. Cripple Creek (Colo.)-Victor Sch. Dist., 1975-81; dir. Franklin Ferguson Meml. Libr., Cripple Creek, 1975-81; dir. instructional materials ctr. D.C. Everest Jr. High Sch., Schofield, Wis., 1981—; dist. media coord. D.C. Everest Area Schs., Schofield, 1988—; reviewer Sch. Evaluation Consortium, Madison, Wis., 1986, Marshfield, Wis., 1987, reviewer, coord., Ashland, Wis., 1989; chair media com. D.C. Everest Area Schs., Schofield, 1988—. Recipient Svc. award of the Yr., Franklin Ferguson Meml. Libr., 1981. Mem. Wis. Sch. Libr. Media Assn. (chair profl. devel. com. 1983, chair 1984, 85 confs. exec. bd. 1985), Wis. Ednl. Media Assn., Wausau Area Jaycees (community dir. 1986-87, chair cancer ski-a-thon 1987, chair 4th of July concessions 1989, Project Chmn. of the Month 1987). Methodist. Home: 2405 Petunia Rd Wausau WI 54401-9351 Office: DC Everest Jr High Sch 1000 Machmueller St Schofield WI 54476-3811

GETTIG, RHONDA GAIL, elementary education educator; b. Bowie, Tex., Jan. 23, 1955; d. Ray Nored and Lillie Pearl (Roberts) Duncan; m. Robert Gerald Head, Jan. 18, 1974 (div. Sept. 1978); m. David Richard Gettig, July 18, 1981; 1 child, William Lyndall Jeremy. BS in Bus. Adminstrn., Cameron U., Lawton, Okla., 1984, postgrad, 1989-90, 95—. cons. Ava Maria Montessori Sch., Lawton, 1982-84. Mem. 1st Baptist East, Lawton, 1982—. Sgt. U.S. Army, 1976-79. Mem. NAFE, Cameron U. Alumni Assn. Democrat. Baptist.

GETTY, CAROL PAVILACK, government official; b. Wilmington, Del., Apr. 9, 1938; d. Frank Clifton and Maxine (Remaly) McGrew; m. Lawrence Lee Pavilack, Aug. 18, 1960 (div. 1980); children: Douglas Brooks, Joann Clements; m. James John Getty, May 8, 1985. BA, Wellesley Coll., 1960; MS in Criminal Justice, Ariz. State U., 1978; postgrad. U. S.C., U. Mo. Engring. aide Air Rsch., Phoenix, 1960-63; computer analyst Motorola, Phoenix, 1963; tchr. math. Phoenix County Day Sch., 1964-69; mem. Ariz. Bd. Pardons and Paroles, Phoenix, 1978-83; commr. U.S. Parole Commn., Kansas City, Mo., 1983-90, chmn., 1991-92, commr. 1992—; tech. adviser Maricopa County Alts. to Incarceration Commn., 1980-83. Treas., asst. treas., sec., impact community action, admissions and fin. Jr. League, 1970—; docent, treas. Phoenix Art Mus. League, 1968-79; vice chmn. Criminal Justice Adv. Com., Phoenix, 1973-78. Mem. Exec. Women in Govt., Am. Soc. Pub. Adminstrs., Assn. Patroling Authorities (regional v.p.), Ctrl. Exchange, Jr. League, Soroptimists (chancellor's adv. com. to the women's ctr. UMKC), Wellesley Club (fed. exec. bd.). Unitarian. Home: 7709 NW Westside Dr Kansas City MO 64152-1539 Office: US Parole Commn 5550 Friendshp Blvd Ste 420 Chevy Chase MD 20815

GETTY, ESTELLE, actress; b. N.Y.C., July 25, 1923; m. Arthur Gettleman, Dec. 21, 1947; children: Barry, Carl. Student, New Sch. for Social Rsch., Herbert Berghof Studios; studied with Gerald Russak. Appeared in numerous stage prodns. on and off Broadway including Death of a Salesman, The Glass Menagerie, All My Sons, 6 Rms Rv Vu, Blithe Spirit, Arsenic and Old Lace, I Don't Know Why I'm Screaming, Widows and Children, Torch Song Trilogy, 1981-83; film appearances include The Chosen, 1982, Tootsie, 1983, Mask, 1984, Protocol, 1984, Mannequin, 1987, Stop or My Mom Will Shoot, 1991; TV appearances include (series) The Golden Girls, 1987-92, (Emmy award as outstanding supporting actress in a comedy series 1988, Golden Globe award for best actress in a comedy, Am. Comedy award for best supporting actress in a series 1990), Golden Palace, 1992-93; (TV movies) No Man's Land, 1984, Victims for Victims: The Teresa Saldana Story, 1984, Copacabana, 1985; author: If I Knew Then What I Know Now...So What?, 1988. Office: Innovative Artists Talent and Literary Agency 1999 Ave of Stars Ste 2850 Los Angeles CA 90067 Office: Green/Siegel & Associates 8730 W Sunset Blvd Ste 470 Los Angeles CA 90069-2210*

GETZ, CHERYL ANN, basketball coach; b. Cleve., Mar. 3, 1960; d. Leroy Conrad and Violet Wilma (Saunders) G. BS in Phys. Edn., U. Cin., 1979-82; MA in Athletic Adminstrn., Cen. Mich. U., 1984; postgrad., U. San Diego. Grad. asst. coach Cen. Mich. U., Mt. Pleasant, 1982-84; asst. basketball coach U. Dayton, Ohio, 1984-86, George Washington U., Washington, 1986-87; head basketball coach Ea. Mich. U., Ypsilanti, 1987-92; asst. basketball coach U. San Diego, 1992—. Mem. NOW, AAUW, Am. Ednl. Rsch. Assn., Women's Basketball Coaches Assn. Democrat. Office: U San Diego 5998 Alcala Park San Diego CA 92110

GETZ, CHRISTINA L., critical care nurse, educator, business owner; b. Massillon, Ohio, Feb. 6, 1964; d. Charles Gordon and Pamela Lynn (Silvis) Vogt; m. Dennis S. Getz, June 30, 1985; children: Joseph Daniel, Brandon Michael. Diploma in nursing, Massillon Community Hosp. Sch., 1986. Cert. CCRN, ACLS instr., PALS. Staff nurse critical care and emergency dept. Dr.'s Hosp., Massillon; policy and procedure com. Doctor's Hosp., Massillon, 1989-91, chairperson, 1991, clin. ladder devel. com., 1990-91; co-developer Intra-Aortic Balloon Pump Edn. program, 1991; instr., 1991-93; guest spkr. WTIG Radio, 1992; co-owner Critical Care Connection, Bolivar, Ohio. Mem. AACN.

GETZENDANNER, SUSAN, lawyer, former federal judge; b. Chgo., July 24, 1939; d. William B. and Carole S. (Muehling) O'Meara; children—Alexandra, Paul. B.B.A., Loyola U., 1966, J.D., 1966. Bar: Ill. bar 1966. Law clk. U.S. Dist. Ct., Chgo., 1966-68; assoc. Mayer, Brown & Platt, Chgo., 1968-74, ptnr., 1974-80; judge U.S. Dist. Ct., Chgo., 1980-87; ptnr. Skadden, Arps, Slate, Meagher & Flom, Chgo., 1987—. Recipient medal of excellence Loyola U. Law Alumni Assn., 1981. Mem. ABA, Chgo. Council Lawyers. Office: Skadden Arps Slate Meagher Flom 333 W Wacker Dr Chicago IL 60606-1218

GEVANTMAN, JUDITH, financial analyst, consultant; b. Pitts., May 25, 1949; d. Chaim and Charlotte Selma (Max) G. AB cum laude, Goucher Coll., Towson, Md., 1971; postgrad., NYU, 1971-74; MPA, Harvard U., 1977. Dep.dir. N.Y.C. Addiction Svcs. Agy., 1971-74; asst. v.p., supr. Moody's Investors Svc., N.Y.C., 1978-85; v.p., dir. mcpl. rsch. Wertheim, Schroder & Co., N.Y.C., 1986-87; v.p., mgr. fixed income rsch. Mabon, Nugent & Co., N.Y.C., 1988; ptnr. Rsch. Assocs., Bklyn., 1989—; chmn. bd. dirs. GemStone Investors Assurance Corp., 1990—; cons. Downstate Med. Sch., Bklyn.,1975, Harvard U. Med. Sch., Boston, 1976, Boston Mus. Sci., 1977. Bd. dirs. Bruekelen Owners Corp., Bklyn., 1982-83; alumni rep. Goucher Coll., 1985—; trustee Congregation Bnai Avraham, Brooklyn Heights, N.Y., 1988—. UN fellow U. Kans., 1970, Univ. fellow NYU, 1971-73; Senatorial scholar Md. Legisature, 1967-71; Urban Corp. grantee, 1970. Mem. Mcpl. Forum N.Y., Mcpl. Analyst Group N.Y., Harvard Club (N.Y.C.).

GEWIRTZ, GERRY, editor; b. N.Y.C., Dec. 22, 1920; d. Max and Minnie (Weiss) G.; m. Eugene W. Friedman, Nov. 11, 1945; children: John Henry, Robert James. BA, Vassar Coll., 1941. Editor Package Store Mgmt., 1942-44, Jewelry Mag., 1945-53; freelance editor promotion dept. McCall's Mag., Esquire, 1953-56; free-lance fashion and gifts editor Jewelers Circular Keystone, N.Y.C., 1955-71; editor, pub. The Fashionables, 1971-74, The Forecast, 1974—, Nat. Jeweler, Ann. Fashion Guide, 1976-80; editor, assoc. pub. Exec. Jeweler, 1980-83; editor The Fashion Source (formerly Internat. Fashion Index), N.Y.C., 1984—; freelance editor and mktg. specialist, 1995—; ptnr. Gary Gewirtz-Editl. and Mktg. Corr. Internat. Mktg. News. Mem. exec. com. Inner City Council of Cardinal Cooke, N.Y.; chairperson women's task force United Jewish Appeal Fedn.; former bd. govs. Israel Bonds; former trustee Israel Cancer Research Fund, Central Synagogue; bd. dirs. Double Image Theater; former pres. women's aux. Brandeis U. Honored guest Am. Jewish Com., 1978; Israel Cancer Research Fund, 1978-81; recipient Disting. Community Service award Brandeis U., 1987; named to Jewellry Hall Fame, 1988. Mem. N.Y. Fashion Group, Nat. Home Fashions League (former pres.), Women's Jewelry Assn. (pres. 1983-87, named editor who has contbd. most to jewelry industry 1984). Home: 45 Sutton Pl S New York NY 10022-2444

GEWIRTZ, MINDY L., organizational and human relations consultant; b. N.Y.C., Mar. 19, 1951; d. Martin and Miriam (Altman) Lebovicz; m. Gershon C. Gewirtz, Sept. 7, 1971; children: Yussy, Henoch, Sora Leah, Adina, Doniel. MPS, N.Y. Inst. Tech., 1977; MSW, SUNY, Albany, 1981; PhD in Orgnl. Sociology, Boston U., 1995. Lic. ind. clin. social worker; diplomate Am. Bd. Clin. Social Workers. Project coord. Ringel Inst. Gerontology SUNY-Albany, 1980-82; coord. sr. adult dept. Jewish Family Svcs., Albany, 1983-84; dir. eldercare connection long distance caregiving svc. Jewish Family and Children's Svc., Boston, 1984-93; pres. Strategic Bus. Solutions, Boston, 1988—; postgrad. fellow orgnl. devel. & human resources cons. Boston Inst. Psychotherapy, 1990; adj. asst. prof. Boston U. Sch. Social Work; cons. Ibis Cons. Group, Cambridge, 1990—; orgn. and mgmt. cons. Boston Digital Equipment Corp., Boston, 1988-92; orgnl. cons. Malden Mills, Lawrence, Mass., 1992—. Author: (with E. and N. Newman) Elderly Criminals, 1984; assoc. author: Human Dilemmas in Work Organizations, 1994; contbr. articles to profl. jours. and publs. Mem. Boston Work and Family Forum, New England Human Resources Assn., Greater Boston Orgnl. Devel. Network. Recipient Max Siporin Social Work fellow. Mem. NASW, ACSW (bd. cert. diplomate), Am. Assn. Bus. Women (career advancement fellow), Phi Beta Kappa. Home: 23 Browne St Brookline MA 02146-3804

GEYER, CAROLYN KAY SMITH, English language and journalism educator; b. Denton, Tex., Apr. 9, 1936; d. Elbert Geron and Hazel Beatrice (Lynn) Smith; m. Charles William Geyer, Aug. 23, 1959; children: Mark William, Thomas Hugh. BA in English, Augustana Coll., 1958; MA in English, Auburn U., 1965; PhD in Edn., U. Nebr., 1985. Intermediate tchr. Tex. Sch. for Deaf, Austin, 1958-59; lang. tchr. S.D. Sch. for Deaf, Sioux Falls, 1960-62; instr. English Auburn (Ala.) U., 1965-67, Augustana Coll., Sioux Falls, 1971-76; coll. rep. Harcourt Brace Jovanovich, Inc., 1976-77; tchr. English O'Gorman High Sch., Sioux Falls, 1977-80; asst. prof. English Augustana Coll., Sioux Falls, 1980-86, asst. acad. dean and assoc. prof., 1986-87, assoc. acad. dean, dir. adult learning, 1987-92, chair English and Journalism dept., 1992—, faculty rep. to bd. regents, 1992-94, chair faculty Personnel Coun., 1995, prof. English, 1995—; regional mgr. Coun. of Adult and Exptl. Learning, N.D., S.D., Mont., 1985-90; S.D. state liaison for U.S. West's Pathways to the Future, 1990-91; vis. scholar dept. adult edn. Syracuse U., 1991; state corp. rep. Am. Coll. Testing, S.D., 1986-88; instl. rep. Coll. Bd., Augustana Coll., 1987-91. Contbr. articles to profl. jours. Mem. Tech. Info. Project on Environ. Issues in S.D., 1988—; bd. dirs. S.D. chpt. ARC, Sioux Falls, 1980-83. Recipient Faculty Growth award Am. Luth. Ch., 1983, Leadership grantee, 1986; U. Nebr. Regents fellow, 1984; Kellogg Found. project LEARN grantee, 1986-88, Devel. grantee Bush Faculty, S.D. Humanities Coun. grantee; recipient Granskou Award for Rsch., Augustana Coll. Alumni, 1990. Mem. NOW, AAUP, Luth. Women's Caucus (program com.), Feminists for Diversity in Luth. Colls. and Sems., Greenpeace, Nature Conservancy. Democrat. Lutheran. Office: Augustana Coll 2001 S Summit Ave Sioux Falls SD 57197-0001

GEYER, KAREN LEA, reporter, editor; b. Pampa, Tex., June 6, 1952; d. William Dudley and Mardell (Mask) McKendree; m. David Wesley Geyer, Aug. 11, 1972; children: Nathan David, Neil John William, Kendra Lea. Student, U. Tex. State U., 1970-71, Cen. Area Vo-Tech., Drumright, Okla., 1987. Various positions Drumright News Jour., 1985-86; reporter Drumright Gusher, 1987-88; reporter, Lifestyles editor, tour condr., spkr. Cushing (Okla.) Daily Citizen, 1992—. Editor: (mag.) Young at Heart. Mem. curriculum com. Olive H.S., 1995—, mem. gifted/talented adv. com., 1995—; active PTO, band, All Sports Boosters, basketball, softball, 1977—. Mem. Okla. Press Assn. (participant news clinics), Cushing C. of C. (mem. environ. com. 1996—). Republican. Baptist. Home: Rt 1 Box 411 Drumright OK 74030 Office: Cushing Daily Citizen 115 S Cleveland Cushing OK 74023

GFELLER, DONNA KVINGE, clinical psychologist; b. Chgo., Jan. 15, 1959; d. Milton Melvin and Doris Ann (Chapman) Kvinge; m. Jeffrey Donald Gfeller, Aug. 2, 1986. BS in Biol. Scis., Ill. State U., 1980, MS in Clin. Psychology, 1984; PhD in Clin. Psychology, Ohio U., 1987. Lic. psychologist. Staff psychologist Cardinal Glennon Children's Hosp., St. Louis, 1986-87, sr. psychologist, 1988-89, dir. dept. psychology, 1990—. Mem. APA (divsn. clin. psychology, sect. on clin. child psychology), Soc. Pediatric Psychology, World Wildlife Fund. Office: Cardinal Glennon Children's Hosp 1465 S Grand Blvd Saint Louis MO 63104-1003

GHALY, EVONE, SHEHATA, pharmaceutics and industrial pharmacy educator; b. Cairo; d. Shehata Ghaly Shenouda and Amalia Elias Tadros; m. Nagdy Roshdy Mehany; children: Maichel Nagdy Roshdy, Mary Nagdy Roshdy. B in Pharm. Scis., Assiut U., Egypt, 1970; M in Pharm. Sci., Cairo U., 1979, PhD of Pharmaceutics, 1984; postdoctoral fellow, Phila. Coll. Pharm., 1986-88. Specialist and pharmacist in R&D Arab Drug Co., Cairo, 1970-75, sr. pharmacist in R&D, mgr. rsch. devel., 1975-86; assoc. rschr. Phila. Coll. Pharm., 1988-89; vis. prof., asst. prof. Sch. Pharmacy U. P.R., San Juan, 1989-92, assoc. prof., 1992—; cons. Smith Kline & Beecham, Inc., P.R., 1990—, Eli Lilly found., P.R., 1993—, Merck Sharp and Dohme Inc., P.R., 1994; instr., lectr. FDA, 1991, Warmer Lambert Inc., P.R., 1993-94, Ciba Geigy Inc., P.R., 1995. Contbr. articles to profl. jours. Grantee Colorcon Pharm. Inc., 1993-94, Baker Norton Pharm. Inc., 1993, INDUNIV Rsch. Ctr., 1990-92, 92-93, IBM, NIH-BRSG, 1991-92, Knoll AG Co., 1983, others. Mem. AAAS, Fed. Internat. Pharmaceutics, Am. Assn. Pharm. Scientists, Am. Pharm. Assn., Am. Assn. Coll. Pharmacy, Controlled Release and Bioactive Material, Sigma Xi, Rho Chi. Home: Condominio Puerta Sol 2000 San Juan PR 00926 Office: Univ PR Sch Pharmacy GPO Box 5067 San Juan PR 00936

GHARIB, SUSIE, television newscaster; b. N.Y.C., Nov. 27, 1950; d. Ali and Homa (Razzaghmanesh) G.; m. Fereydoun Nazem, Jan. 20, 1973; children: Alexander, Taraneh. BA magna cum laude, Case Western Res. U., 1972; M in Internat. Affairs, Columbia U., 1974. Reporter Cleve. Plain Dealer, 1972-73; assoc. editor Fortune Mag., N.Y.C., 1974-83; anchor, reporter Bus. Times/ESPN, N.Y.C., 1983-85; bus. reporter ABC News, N.Y.C., 1986-87; anchor Fin. News Network, N.Y.C., 1989-90, CNBC Network, Ft. Lee, N.J., 1993—; moderator/host Xerox Corp., Stanford, Conn., 1989-95, KPMG Peat Marwick, N.Y.C., 1992-95; cons. Adam Smith's Money World/PBS, N.Y.C., 1987. Bd. dirs. First Fortis, Inc., 1991—, Ice Theatre of N.Y., 1988-90. Mem. Overseas Press Club, Phi Beta Kappa, Sigma Delta Chi. Democrat. Home: 44 E 73rd St New York NY 10021-4173 Office: CNBC 2200 Fletcher Ave Fort Lee NJ 07024-5005

GHEN, EDYTHE SOLBERG, artist; b. Wakefield, Mass., May 1, 1922; d. Frederick Carl and Ethel (Keander) Solberg; m. William Russell Ghen; children: Karen, William Jr. Student, Mass. Coll. Art, 1940-41, Salem State Coll., 1974-78, Montserrat Sch. Art, 1984-86, 88-90. Sec., art editor War Dept., Boston, 1942-43; comml. artist Loudon Advt., Boston, 1943-44; sec. to pres. Benjamin Franklin U., Washington, 1944-45; art tchr. Beverly (Mass.) Adult Edn., 1958-60; art tchr. psychiat. divsn. J.B. Thomas Hosp., Peabody, Mass., 1970-72; pvt. practice Beverly, 1964—; lectr. various orgns., 1960—. Author two manuals on stained glass; author, illustrator children's picture books; work featured in book Best of Watercolor, 1995. Vol. Am. Lung Assn., pres., founder Essex County Fresh Air for Non-Smokers, 1964—. Recipient Beverly Arts Coun. awards, 1987, 88, Collidge awards Topsfield Fair, 1984, 87, vol. award Am. Lung Assn., 1976, Lifetime Achievement award Mass. Coll. Art, 1993, Painting in "Best of Watercolors: internat. book, 1995, numerous others. Mem. Copley Soc. Boston (sagendorf award 1992, Juror's Choice award 1994), Rockport Art Assn. (Moore award 1988, Wengenroth award 1991, Goldberg award 1996), North Shore Arts Assn. (Sketchgroup award 1988, Callow award 1988, Anderson award 1993), Acad. Artists Springfield (Guild Boston Artists award 1988), Guild Beverly Artists (Best of Show awards 1984, 90, 91, Best of Watercolor award 1995), New England Watercolor Soc. Methodist. Home: 42 E Corning St Beverly MA 01915-4735

GHEZ, ANDREA MIA, astronomy and physics educator; b. N.Y.C., June 16, 1965; d. Gilbert and Susanne (Gayton) G.; m. Tom La Tourette, May 1, 1993. BS, MIT, 1987; MS, Calif. Inst. Tech., 1989, PhD, 1993. Hubble postdoctoral fellow U. Ariz., Tucson, 1992-93; vis. rsch. scholar Inst. Astronomy, Cambridge, England, 1994; asst. prof. physics and astronomy UCLA, 1994—. Recipient Young Investigator award NSF, 1994, Fullam Dudley award, 1995; fellow Pacific Telesis, 1991, Sloan fellow, 1996. Mem. Am. Astron. Soc., AAUW (Anne Jump Cannon award 1994), Phi Beta Kappa. Home: 8641 Kirkwood Dr Los Angeles CA 90046 Office: UCLA Dept Astronomy 405 Hilgard Ave Los Angeles CA 90095

GHRAMM, JANE HARRIS, transport economist; b. Southampton, N.Y., Sept. 8, 1950; d. Frank E. and Eleanor A. (Hedberg) Harris; m. John William Ghramm, Nov. 11, 1978; children: Shannon Morgan, Lindsay Havens. BS in Fgn. Svc./Internat. Rels., Georgetown U., 1972; MSc in Econs., London Sch. Econs., 1973. Assoc. planner Port of Portland, Oreg., 1974-75; sr. planner for marine terminals and econ. devel. Port of Portland, 1975-77; ind. cons. The World Bank and UN Devel. Program, Washington, 1978-84; founding ptnr. Preinvest, Inc., Bethesda, Md., 1984—; vice-chmn. Clarke County Planning Commn., Berryville, Va., 1990—; mem. Clarke County Hist. Preservation Commn., Berryville, 1992—, Clarke County Sanitary Authority, Berryville, 1994-95. Vol. Winchester (Va.) Med. Ctr., 1978-84; event chmn. Handley Libr., Winchester, 1982-84; vol. coord. Va. Dept. Transp. Rd. Pick-Ups Crews, 1991—; dir. Friends of the State Arboretum of Va., 1990—; pres., trustee Belle Grove, Inc.-Nat. Trust for Historic Preservation Property, 1995—. Mem. Am. Planning Assn., Internat. Assn. Maritime Economists. Episcopalian.

GIACCHI, JUDITH ADAIR, elementary education educator; b. Rochester, N.Y., Dec. 8, 1947; d. William Robert Peters and L. Virginia (Coulter) Peters Sweet; m. Alphonse Robert Giacchi, Aug. 8, 1970; children: Christina Marie, Anthony Robert. BS, SUNY, Buffalo, 1969. Permanent cert. tchr., N.Y. Data processing control clk. Neisner Bros., Inc., Rochester, 1969-70; tchr. Syracuse (N.Y.) City Sch. Dist., 1970—; tchr. insvcs. and workshops Syracuse sch. dists., 1972—; master tchr. Syracuse U., 1983—, chmn. bldg. level team, 1988—, collaborative Field Team Rep., mem, 1988—; rep. N.Y. State Tchrs. Retirement Sys. convs. and N.Y. State United Tchrs. convs., 1987-89. Contbr. articles to profl. publs. Corr. sec., rec. sec., legis. chmn. Nate Perry Sch. PTA, Liverpool, N.Y., 1983-95; troop aide Girl Scouts U.S.A., Liverpool, 1982-86; rep., mem. strategy com. Syracuse Labor Coun., 1995—. Recipient award N.Y. State Legislature, 1994, various minigrants. Mem. N.Y. State United Tchrs. Fedn. (rep. convss. 1990-92), Onondaga County Tchrs. Assn. (award 1989), Syracuse Tchrs. Assn. (various coms., chief bldg rep. 1984-90). Office: Webster Elem Sch 500 Wadsworth St Syracuse NY 13208

GIACOMINI, BARBARA JAN, archaeologist; b. Cleve., Mar. 14, 1954; d. Stephen and Barbara Sylvia (Vidusic) Szemenyei; m. Roddy Lyman Giacomini, Oct. 27, 1973 (div. Dec. 1995); children: Skye, Bianca, Roddy Jr. BA in Anthropology, Calif. State U., Fullerton, 1991, MA in Anthropology, 1993. Crew archaeologist RMW Paleo Assocs., Mission Viejo, Calif., 1990-93; assoc. archaeologist Brian F. Mooney & Assocs., San Diego, 1993-95, ASM Affiliates, Encinitas, Calif., 1995—. Pres. PTO, Del Obispo Elementary Sch., 1985-87; drug prevention chmn. County Jr. Women's Club, Orange County, Calif., 1985-87; bd. mem. youth task force Nat. Coun. on Alcoholism, Orange County, 1979-87; leader Girl Scouts U.S., San Juan Capistrano, Calif., 1982-87; soccer, San Juan Capistrano, 1982-87. Named Woman of Yr. AAUW, 1987; rsch. grantee Dept. Assoc. Coun., Calif. State U., Fullerton, 1993. Mem. Soc. Profl. Archaeologists (cert.), Archaeol. Inst. Am. (bd. dirs. 1993—), Am. Schs. Oriengal Rsch., Orange County Soc. Democrat. Methodist. Home: 25632 Dana Mesa San Juan Capistrano CA 92675

GIACONE, ANNA MARIE, social studies educator; b. Benton, Ill., Oct. 24, 1946; d. Joe John and Katie (Garauaglia) Mayeski; m. Ronald J. Giacone, June 26, 1968; children: Gina, Jim, Jennifer. BA, So. Ill. U., 1968. Tchr. Lakeview Sch., Hoffman Estates, Ill., 1968-69, Webster Jr. H.S., Benton, 1969-70, Benton H.S., 1988—. Trustee Benton Pub. Libr. Mem. NEA, Nat. Coun. for Social Studies, Ill. Coun. for Social Studies, Ill. Edn. Assn., Benton Edn. Assn. Republican. Roman Catholic. Office: Benton HS 511 E Main St Benton IL 62812-2522

GIANAKOS, PATRICIA ANN, social worker; b. Warren, Ohio, Oct. 14, 1948; d. Jimmie Lambros and Julie (Mougianis) G. BA in Pre-Profl. Social Work, Kent State U., 1970. Lic. social worker. Aid for aged workers Trumbull County Human Svcs. Dept., Warren, 1970-71, social svc. worker, 1971-88, adult svcs. worker, 1988—, mem. excellence com., 1991, 93, contbg. editor County Line newsletter, 1991—, mem. awards com., 1991-93, chmn. awards com., 1993—; mem. Trumbull County Task Force on Wellness in

Later Yrs., Warren, 1991-92. Vol. St. Demetrios Festival, Warren, 1979—; mem. Dem. Nat. Com., Warren, 1992—, Ladies Philoptochos Soc., Warren, 1979—; co-founder, adviser Sr. Citizens Orgn. St. Demetrios Ch., Warren, 1979—. Mem. ACA, NASW, Am. Bus. Women's Assn., Assn. for Adult Devel. and Aging, Nat. Com. for Prevention of Elder Abuse. Greek Orthodox. Home: 1786 Dodge Dr NW Warren OH 44485-1823 Office: Trumbull Cou Human Svcs 150 S Park Ave Warren OH 44481-1018

GIANCOLA, MARY ANN, school nurse; b. Locust Dale, Pa., Jan. 10, 1942; d. Frederick and Mary Ellen (Enders) Regitz; m. Philip Robert House, May 18, 1962 (div. Aug. 1982); children: Shawn House, Andre House, Fritz House; m. Dennis Allen Giancola, July 9, 1983. Diploma in nursing, Ashland State Gen. Hosp., 1962; BS in Pub. Sch. Nursing, West Chester State Coll., 1966; MEd in Counseling/guidance, West Chester U., 1981; postgrad., Ind. U. of Pa., 1987, Pa. State U., 1990-92, St. Joseph's U., 1990-92, West Chester U., 1985, 87, 91-92, Okla. State U., 1990, U. Alaska, 1991, Millersville U., 1991, Phila. Coll. Textiles & Scis., 1992. RN, Pa. Staff nurse Pa. Hosp., Phila., 1962-63, Coatesville (Pa.) Hosp., 1963, Embreeville (Pa.) State Hosp., 1963-66; sch. nurse North Brandywine Mid. Sch. Coatesville Area Sch. Dist., Coatesville, 1977—, counselor, 1983-84; chair blood drive Coatesville Area Sch. Dist., 1991—, nurse coord., 1987-89, mem. bldg. induction/dist. coun., 1988—, mem. profl. devel. coun., 1988—. Cmty. Safety and First aid instr. ARC, West Chester, Pa., 1982—; co-chair North Brandywine Mid. Sch. Daffodil Days, Am. Cancer Assn., 1993—. Mem. Nat. Assn. Sch. Nurses, Chester County Sch. Nurses (v.p. 1992-94, pres. 1994-95, 95-96), NEA, Pa. State Edn. Assn., Coatesville Area Tchrs. Assn. (bldg. rep. 1983-85), Delta Kappa Gamma Internat. Soc. (1st v.p. 1996—). Methodist. Home: 1341 Robin Rd Coatesville PA 19320-4509 Office: North Brandywine Mid Sch 200 Reeceville Rd Coatesville PA 19320-1520

GIARDI, DIANE M., ceramics educator, sculptor, art school administrator; b. West Hartford, Conn., June 11, 1957. Student comparative arts program, Florence, 1978; BS in Art Edn., U. Vt., 1979; Cert. in Graphic Design, Mass. Coll. Art, 1985; MFA in Ceramics, Syracuse U., 1994. Milieu counselor Kennedy Meml. Hosp. Children, Brighton, Mass., 1979-81, activities coord., 1981-83; art tchr. Creative Ednl. Assocs., Boston, 1981-83; graphic artist, supr. Extraversion, Waltham, Mass., 1983-84; art dir. Info. Gatekeepers, Inc., Boston, 1984-86; art tchr. New Eng. Home for Little Wanderers, Boston, 1986-87; creative dir. Wilde Advtsg. Assocs., Inc., Portland, Me., 1987-89; freelance designer Giardi Designs, Cape Porpoise, Me., 1987-90; asst. instr. Syracuse (N.Y.) U., 1992, 93, instr., 1992, 93, 94; ceramics instr., administr. Heartwood Sch. Art, 1995—; ceramics prof. U. So. Maine, 1996—; represented by The Sheridan Gallery, Belmont, Mass., 1984, Fire Opal Gallery, Jamaica Plains, Mass., 1985, Bazaar Gallery, Brookline, Mass., 1986, Gallery 33, Portsmouth, N.H., 1987-89, The Roberta Wood Gallery, Fayetteville, N.Y., 1993—, Eureka Craft Gallery, Syracuse, N.Y., 1994—, Ogunquit (Maine) Art Assn. Gallery, 1995—. One woman exhbns. include Phoebes Gallery, Syracuse, N.y., 1994, Eureka Craft Gallery, 1994, Ogunquit Art Assn. Gallery, 1996; group exhbns. include Danforth St. Gallery, Portland, 1989, 90, White Cube Gallery Syracuse (N.Y.) U., 1991, Mission Landing Gallery, Syracuse, N.Y., 1992, Lowe Gallery, Syracuse, 1992, U. La., 1993, U. Tenn., 1993, 12 Rms. 4 Gallery, Syracuse, 1993, Octagon Ctr. for the Arts, Ames, Iowa, 1993, The Upper Gallery, 1993, The Everson Mus. Art, 1993, HUB Galleries and Pa. State U., University Park, 1993, Ea. Wash. U. Gallery Art, Cheney, 1993, West Chester, Pa., 1993, Galleria Mesa, 1994, Lafayette (La.) Art Gallery, 1994, The Newark Mus., 1994, Carnegie Mus. Art, Pitts., 1994, The Potters Gallery, West Chester, Pa., 1994, Hoyt Gallery, New Castle, Pa., 1995, Maine Coast Gallery, Rockport, Maine, 1996, The Ogunquit Art Assn. Gallery, 1996. Bd. dirs. Danforth St. Gallery, Portland, 1988-90, Ogunquit Art Assn., 1996—; active Hospice York, Maine; creator, developer Arts in Hospice, York. Grantee Me. Coun. Arts, 1989, 90. Mem. Am. Craft Coun., Coll. Art Assn., Maine Alliance Art Edn., Nat. Coun. Edn. for the Ceramic Arts, Ogunquit Art Assn. (bd. dirs. 1996—). Home: 1140 Tatnic Rd Wells ME 04090

GIARRETTO, ANNA EINFELD, marriage, family and child counselor; b. San Francisco, Mar. 8, 1932; d. William Edward and Anna (Irvine) Buck; m. Richard B. Einfeld, July 7, 1950 (div. Aug. 1957); children: Lise, Christopher and Rebecca Einfeld; m. Henry Giarretto, Aug. 1973. BA in Edn., San Francisco State U., MA in Counseling Psychology; postgrad., Calif. Inst. Integral Studies. Lic. religious sci. practitioner United Ch. of Religious Sci.; lic. marriage, family and child counselor, Calif. Group facilitator San Francisco Venture, 1965-70; therapist Ctr. for Human Comms., Los Gatos, Calif., 1970-75; co-founder, clin. dir., trainer The Giarretto Inst.: Child Sexual Abuse Treatment Program, Santa Clara County, Calif., 1975-85, co-dir., 1985-91; religious sci. practitioner United Ch. of Religious Sci., 1992—; pvt. practice as marriage, family and child counselor San Rafael, Calif., 1991—. Developed child sexual abuse treatment concepts illustrated in TV film Something About Amelia; appeared on talk shows included Oprah, Sally Jessie Raphael, Phil Donahue. Recipient Women of Achievement in Cmty. Svc. award Santa Clara Women's Fund, 1989, numerous otehr awards; State of Calif. grantee. Mem. Calif. Assn. Marriage, Family and Child Counselors.

GIBA, JULIA UNITAS, sales manager; b. Pitts., Apr. 18, 1963; d. William Vincent Unitas and Gertrude Elizabeth McCrory; m. Raymond Anthony Yeckley, Jan. 9, 1988 (div. June 1989); 1 child, Alexis Rae; m. Paul Robert Giba, Nov. 20, 1993; 1 child, Gillian Elizabeth. BS, Indiana U. of Pa., 1987. Dir. sales Hampton Inn., Pitts., 1990-92; sales mgr. Embassy Suites, Coraopolis, Pa., 1992-94, sr. sales mgr., 1995—. Voice over artist Gold's Gym, 1991, Oriental Rug Gallery, 1991. Mem. Alpha Gamma Delta. Home: 217 Seegar Rd Upper Saint Clair PA 15241 Office: Embassy Suites Hotel 550 Cherrington Pky Coraopolis PA 15108

GIBB, ROBERTA LOUISE, lawyer, artist; b. Cambridge, Mass., Nov. 2, 1942; d. Thomas Robinson Pieri and Jean Knox Gibb. Student, Boston Mus. Fine Arts, 1962-65; BS, U. Calif., La Jolla, 1969; JD, N.E. Sch. Law, 1978. Bar: Mass. 1978. Rsch. asst. in opistemology MIT, Cambridge, 1972—; legis. aid Mass. State Legislature, 1973-75; pvt. practice law, 1980—; cert. title examiner Mass. Land Ct., Boston, 1987—; assoc. Cohen & Burg Attys., Boston, 1988-89; founder, pres. Inst. for the Study of Natural Sys., 1978—. Author: The Art of Inflation, 1978, To Boston With Love, 1980; sculptor and painter. Named to Road Runner's Hall of Fame, Alexandria, Va., Acad. of Women Achievers YWCA, Spl. Recognition, 1996. Mem. U.S. Assn. Club Rome, Boston Athletic Assn., Rockport Art Assn., Alumni Assn. Univ. Calif.

GIBBARD, JUDITH R., library director; b. N.Y.C., Jan. 27, 1945; d. Charles J. and Esther (Polonsky) Popovits; m. Bruce Gregory Gibbard, June 19, 1966. AB in Edn., U. Mich., 1966, AM in English, 1968; MLS, Syracuse U., 1978. Cert. pub. libr., cert. secondary English/French tchr. Slide cataloger history of art dept. U. Mich., Ann Arbor, 1969-70; tchr. Assn. des Habitants de la Ville de Meyrin, Switzerland, 1970-71; cataloger Cornell U. Olin Libr., Ithaca, N.Y., 1972-78; head cataloging sect. Suffolk Coop. Libr. System, Bellport, N.Y., 1979-81; cataloging svcs. div. chief Suffolk Coop. Libr. System, Bellport, 1981-82; head tech. svc./automation Patchogue (N.Y.)-Medford Libr., 1983-89, asst. dir., 1989-90, dir., 1991—. Coord. Community Youth Com., Patchogue, 1992. Mem. Pub. Libr. Assn. (chair cataloging needs com. 1989-90), N.Y. Libr. Assn., Suffolk County Libr. Assn. (mem.-at-large 1988-89). Office: Patchogue-Medford Libr 54-60 E Main St Patchogue NY 11772

GIBBONS, JULIA SMITH, federal judge; b. Pulaski, Tenn., Dec. 23, 1950; d. John Floyd and Julia Jackson (Abernathy) Smith; m. William Lockhart Gibbons, Aug. 11, 1973; children: Rebecca Carey, William Lockhart Jr. B.A., Vanderbilt U., 1972; J.D., U. Va., 1975. Bar: Tenn. 1975. Law clk. to judge U.S. Ct. Appeals, 1975-76; assoc. Farris, Hancock, Gilman, Branan, Lanier & Hellen, Memphis, 1976-79; legal advisor Gov. Lamar Alexander, Nashville, 1979-81; judge 15th Jud. Cir., Memphis, 1981-83, U.S. Dist. Ct. (we. dist.) Tenn., Memphis, 1983—. Fellow Am. Bar Found., Tenn. Bar Found.; mem. ABA, Tenn. Bar Assn., Memphis Bar Assn., Order of Coif, Phi Beta Kappa. Presbyterian. Office: US Dist Ct 1157 Federal Bldg 167 N Main St Memphis TN 38103-1816

GIBBONS, MARTHA BLECHAR, psychotherapist, educator, consultant; b. Santa Fe, Aug. 9, 1950; d. Theodore Joseph and Margaret Estelle (Harvey) Blechar; m. Myles David Gibbons, June 18, 1977; 1 child, Adam David. BSN, San Jose (Calif.) State U., 1973; MS in Maternal-Child Nursing, Med. Coll. of Va., 1977, PNP, 1978; PhD in Human Devel., U. Md., 1990. PNP Pa. Hosp., Phila.; clin. nurse specialist pediatric urology dept. Children's Hosp. of Phila.; cmty. health nurse Frankfurt (Germany) Mil. Cmty.; psychiat. liaison nurse Tex. Children's Hosp., Houston; pediatric oncology nurse practitioner M. D. Anderson Hosp. and Tumor Inst., Houston; clin. nurse specialist pediatric oncology dept. NIH, Bethesda, Md.; pvt. practice psychotherapy and cons. Chevy Chase, Md.; pediat. psychiat. liaison NIH; dir. pediat. nurse practitioner program sch. nursing U. Md.; assoc. dir. children's program St. Francis Ctr., Washington. Editor (newsletter) Children's Hospice Internat. Fellow Nat. Assn. Pediatric Nurse Assocs. and Practitioners (bd. dirs. Chesapeake chpt., pres.); mem. ANA, Assn. Death Edn. & Counseling, Md. Nurses Assn., D.C. Nurses Assn., Assn. Pediatric Oncology Nurses, Assn. for Care Children's Health, Sigma Theta Tau. Home: 6669 Barnaby St NW Washington DC 20015-2331 Office: 5135 MacArthur Blvd NW Washington DC 20016 also: 4500 N Park Ave Ste 801N Chevy Chase MD 20815

GIBBONS, MARY PEYSER, civic volunteer; b. N.Y.C., Dec. 15, 1936; d. Frederick Maurice and Catherine Mary (McKelvey) Peyser; m. John Martin Gibbons, Dec. 26, 1955; children: Catherine Way, Mary Sloan, John, Fredericka Kerr, Myles. Trustee Wadsworth Atheneum, 1978-80, 81-90, 91—, Hartford Art Sch., 1985-95; regent U. Hartford, 1988-94, 95—; bd. dirs. Hartford Ballet, 1981-95, Conn. Valley Girl Scouts, 1994-95, U.S. Found. World Fedn., Friends of Museums, 1990—; vol. Com. Art Mus., U.S. and Can., 1982-91; corporator St. Francis Hosp., 1990—, Hartford Ballet, 1995—. Mem. Am. Assn. Mus. Vols. (pres. 1986-89, adv. bd. 1991—), Hartford Golf Club, Town and Country Club. Office: Sefton & Sheil Ltd 1130 Prospect Ave Hartford CT 06105-1124

GIBBONS, TERRY EL, elementary education educator; b. Joliet, Ill., Sept. 12, 1953; d. Herbert Charles and Janice Ruth Strautz; m. Murray Francis Gibbons III, Aug. 15, 1981; children: Allison Gibbons, Brian Gibbons. BE, U. Mo., 1975. Cert. spl. edn., art edn., elem. tchr., Tex., edn. all levels, Mo. Spl. edn. tchr. Galveston (Tex.) Ind. Sch. Dist., 1975-77; spl. edn. tchr. Temple (Tex.) Ind. Sch. Dist., 1977-85, art tchr., 1985—. Named Educator of Month Temple Rotary, 1992-93. Mem. Tex. Classroom Tchrs. Assn., Tex. Art Edn. Assn., Nat. Art Edn. Assn. Home: 82 Great West Loop Belton TX 76513-9243 Office: Lamar Mid Sch Temple Ind Sch Dist 2120 N 3rd St Temple TX 76501-1361

GIBBS, HOPE KATZ, journalist; b. Phila., July 8, 1964; d. Joel S. and Bobbi A. (Brownstien) K.; m. Michael Gibbs, 1995; 1 child, Anna Paige. Studied abroad, Tel Aviv U., 1983-84; BA in Communications, U. Pa., 1986; postgrad., George Washington U., 1988-89, 91—. Cert. massage therapist. Staff writer Dominion Post, Morgantown, W.Va., 1986-87; asst. editor Miami (Fla.) Herald, 1987-88; editor Adler Pub. Co., Washington, 1988-89; assoc. editor New Miami mag., 1989-91; publs. specialist George Washington U., Washington, 1991—; freelance writer Washington, 1993—. Journalist; author short stories, poetry. Founder The Writing's on the Wall. Mem. NOW, Save the Whales. Democrat. Jewish. Home: 7 W Braddock Rd Alexandria VA 22301-2143

GIBBS, JUNE NESBITT, state senator; b. Newton, Mass., June 13, 1922; d. Samuel Frederick and Lulu (Glazier) Nesbitt; m. Donald T. Gibbs, Dec. 8, 1945; 1 child, Elizabeth. BA in Math., Wellesley Coll., 1943; MA in Math., Boston U., 1947; postgrad. computer sci., U. R.I., 1981-84. Mem. Republican Nat. Com. from, R.I., 1969-80; sec. Republican Nat. Com., 1977-80; mem. R.I. State Senate, 1985—; mem. def. adv. com. Women in Services, 1970-72, vice chmn., 1972. Mem. Middletown Town Council, 1974-80, 82-84, pres., 1978-80. Served to lt. (J.G.) USNR, 1943-46. Home: 163 Riverview Ave Middletown RI 02842-5324 Office: RI State Senate State Capitol Providence RI 02903

GIBBS, MARGARET CATHERINE, retired public administration educator; b. Hot Springs, Ark., Apr. 7, 1914; d. Leonard Everett and Kate (Ludwig) King; m. George Gibbs IV, June 27, 1942; children: George V., Thomas Ashley, Katherine Wellington Gibbs Gengoux, Sarah Randolph Gibbs Beetem. BA cum laude, U. So. Calif., 1936, MPA, 1941; PhD in Govt., Claremont Grad. Sch., 1973. Exec. sec. Univ. Religious Conf., L.A., 1937-38; mng. editor Palos Verdes Estates (Calif.) Bull., 1941-42; tchr. English to Latin Am. diplomats Washington, 1942; tchr. L.A. City High Schs., 1945-49; corr. L.A. Times, Claremont, Calif., 1950-62; lectr. pub. adminstrn. U. So. Calif., L.A., 1973-81; emeritus prof., chmn. dept. pub. adminstrn. Calif. State U., San Bernardino, 1975-80; cons. undergrounding com. League Calif. Cities, 1969; del. 2d U.S.-Japan Computer Conf., Tokyo, 1975, Inst. Adminstrv. Svcis., Mex., 1974, Abidjan, 1977. Contbr. articles to profl. jours. Bd. dirs. League Calif. Cities, 1962-70; mem. L.a. County Com. for Coord. Delinquency, 1964-66; trustee Citrus C.C., Glendora, Calif., 1974-81; mem. Claremont City Coun., 1962-70; mem. program adv. com. Calif. State U., San Bernardino, 1977-92; bd. councillors Sch. Edn., U. So. Calif., L.A., 1985-91; docent Rancho Santa Ana Bot. Garden, 1983-93. Recipient Beautiful Activist award Broadway Dept. Store and Germaine Monteil, 1972, merit award U. So. Calif., 1987; grantee Western Electric Fund, 1979. Mem. AAUW, LWV, Am. Soc. Pub. Adminstrn. (nat. coun. 1979-82, Outstanding Achievement award Inland chpt. 1982), Trojan League, Internat. Congress Adminstrv. Sci., L.A. Philharmonic Assocs., Saturday Afternoon Club Ukiah, Alpha Kappa Psi. Democrat. Episcopalian. Home: 1199 S Dora St Apt B26 Ukiah CA 95482-8313

GIBBS, MARY BRAMLETT, banker; b. Corona, Calif., Sept. 18, 1953; d. Kenneth Frank and Kathy Lee (Hill) Harris; m. Charles Merrill Gibbs, 1987; 1 child, Meryl Elisabeth. Student U. Md., 1974-77, Southwestern Grad. Sch. Banking. Br. mgr. Peoples Nat. Bank of Md., Suitland, 1972-77; with Post Oak Bank, Houston, 1977-82, asst. v.p. ops. mgmt., 1980-82; v.p. loan ops. First City Nat. Bank Houston, 1982-89; sr. v.p. First Interstate Bank Tex., 1989-96; mgr. market devel. & pub. rels. Bank One, Houston, 1996—. Bd. dirs., life mem. Big Sisters-Big Bros. of Houston; mediator Neighborhood Justice Ctr., 1981; mem. Christ Ch. Cath.; bd. dirs. Tex. So. U. Found., Houston Met. Ministries, Houston Area Urban League, Houston Fire Mus. Named Outstanding Young Houstonian, 1985, Woman on the Move, 1987; recipient Disting. Leadership award Nat. Assn. Community Leadership, 1990. Mem. Nat. Assn. Bank Women, NOW, Houston C. of C. (chair leadership Houston policy coun., chair Houston CRA officers coun. 1994—, bd. dirs. Project Print 1992—). Contbr. articles to profl. jours. Office: Bank One 910 Travis 4 Houston TX 77002

GIBBY, DIANE LOUISE, physician, plastic surgeon; b. Miami, Feb. 5, 1957; d. John and Mabel (Kunce) G.; m. Rodney J. Rohrich. BS, Duke U., Durham, N.C., 1975; MD, U. Miami, 1980. Diplomate Am. Bd. Gen. Surgery, Bd. Plastic and Reconstructive Surgery. Clin. asst. prof. U. Tex. Southwestern, Dallas, 1987—; pvt. practice plastic surgery Med. City Dallas, 1987—; founder Women's Ctr. for Plastic and Reconstructive Surgery, 1992. Fellow Am. Coll. Surgeons; mem. Am. Soc. Plastic and Reconstructive Surgeons, Am. Med. Soc., Tex. Soc. Plastic Surgeons, Dallas Soc. Plastic Surgeons, Aesthetic Soc. Office: 7777 Forest Ln C820 Dallas TX 75230

GIBBY, MABEL ENID KUNCE, psychologist; b. St. Louis, Mar. 30, 1926; d. Ralph Waldo and Mabel Enid (Warren) Kunce; student Washington U., St. Louis, 1943-44, postgrad., 1955-56; B.A., Park Coll., 1945; M.A., McCormick Theol. Sem., 1947; postgrad. Columbia U., 1948, U. Kansas City, 1949, George Washington U., 1953; M.Ed., U. Mo., 1951, Ed.D., 1952; m. John Francis Gibby, Aug. 27, 1948; children—Janet Marie (Mrs. Kim Williams), Harold Steven, Helen Elizabeth, Diane Louise (Mrs. Roderick Rohrich), John Andrew, Keith Sherridan, Daniel Jay. Dir. religious edn. Westport Presbyn. Ch. Kansas City, Mo., 1947-49; tchr. elementary schs., Kansas City, 1949-50; high sch. counselor Arlington (Va.) Pub. Schs., 1952-54; counselor adult counseling services Washington U., 1955-56; counseling psychologist Coral Gables (Fla.) VA Hosp., 1956—; counseling psychologist Miami (Fla.) VA Hosp., 1956—, chief counseling psychology sect., 1982-86; sr. psychologist Office Disability Determination Fla. Hdqrs., 1987-94. Sec. bd. dirs. Fla. Vocat. Rehab. Found. Recipient Meritorious Service citation Fla. C. of C., 1965, President's Com. on Employment of Handicapped, 1965; commendation for meritorious service Com. on Employment of Physically Handicapped Dade County, 1965, named Outstanding Rehab. Profl., 1966, 81; named Profl. Fed. Employee of Year, Greater Miami Fed. Exec. Council, 1966; Outstanding Fed. Service award Greater Miami Fed. Exec. Council, 1966; Fed. Woman's award U.S. Civil Service Commn., 1968, Community Headliner award Theta Sigma Phi, 1968, Outstanding Alumni award Park Coll., 1968, Freedom award The Chosen Few, Korean War Vets. Assn., 1986; certificate of appreciation Bur. Customs, U.S. Treasury Dept., 1969, Fla. Dept. Health and Rehab. Services, 1970. Mem. Am., Dade County (past sec.) psychol. assns., Nat., Fla. (past dir. Dade County chpt.) rehab. assns., Nat. Rehab. Counseling Assn. (past sec.). Patentee in field. Home: 7107 Aberdeen Ave Dallas TX 75230-5406

GIBBY-SMITH, BARBARA, psychologist, nurse; b. Woodburn, Oreg., Dec. 13, 1938; d. Chester Clifton and Marvel Elizabeth (Hill) Gibby; m. Roy Milton Smith, June 2, 1957 (div. June 1990); children: Thomas Clifton, Jeffery Shawn, Mark Anderson. ADN, Chemeketa C.C., Salem, Oreg., 1972; BS, SUNY, Albany, 1980; MS, Western Oreg. State Coll., 1982; D of Psychology, Pacific U., Forest Grove, Oreg., 1993. Diplomate Am. Bd. Profl. Disability Cons.; cert. disability specialist. Adminstr. Birch St. Manor, Dallas, Oreg., 1973-81; disability determination specialist State of Oreg. Workers' Compensation Dept., Salem, 1983-85; counselor Women's Crisis Ctr., Salem, 1986-88; rehab. counselor Employer Rehab. Svcs., Portland, Oreg., 1985-87; therapist, counselor Pacific U., Hillsboro, Oreg., 1988-89, Forest Grove, 1989-91; intern in psychology Portland State U., 1991-92, Kaiser-Permanente, Salem, 1991-92; resident in psychology Tillamook (Oreg.) Counseling Ctr., 1993-95; hosp. privileges Tuality Healthcare, 1996—; group therapy counselor Women's Crisis Ctr., Dallas, 1982-83; eating disorders group therapy facilitator, Salem, 1986-88. Active Women's Coalition Orgn., Salem, 1988—. Mem. APA (clin. neuropsychology divsn. 40), Am. Coll. Forensic Examiners (diplomate), Oreg. Psychol. Assn., Prescribing Psychologist Assn. Democrat. Office: Mountain View Counseling Ctr Ste 500 1911 Mountain View Ln Forest Grove OR 97116 also: Mountain View Med Ctr Ste 200 1909 Mt View Ln Ste 200 Forest Grove OR 97116

GIBLIN, MARY ELLEN, mental health professional; b. Warsaw, N.Y., July 31, 1943; d. William Marcy and Mary Agnes (Conroy) Hurlburt; m. Robert Paul Giblin, Aug. 27, 1966; 1 child, Darlene Mary. BA in Psychology, SUNY Empire State Coll., Albany, 1975; MS in Pub. Adminstrn., Russell Sage Coll., 1978; PhD in Urban and Environ. Studies, Rensselaer Poly. Inst., 1991. Residential supr., tng. and edn. coord., transp. coord Eleanor Roosevelt Devel. Svcs., O.D. Heck Devel. Ctr., Schoharie, N.Y., 1974-81; policy analyst bur. program design Office of Mental Retardation and Devel. Disabilities, Albany, N.Y., 1981-83, statewide community residence coord. bur. residential svcs., 1983-84, asst. dir. bur. operational design, program evaluation, 1984-87, supr. design and evaluation unit bur. program design, 1987-90, asst. dir. bur. consumer and family supports, 1990—; instr. pub. policy grad. program SUNY Empire State Coll., 1992—. Contbr. articles to profl. jours. Mem. adv. coun. Schenectady (N.Y.) County Office for the Aging, 1994-96. Mem. ASPA (coun. rep. 1992-94, co-chair Ann. Inst. 1990-91, 93-94, treas. 1995-96), Empire State Coll. Bd. Govs. (sec. 1993-96, pres. 1996—), Empire State Coll. Alumni-Student Assn. (chair phonothon 1992, 95, 96, Alumni of Yr. 1993), Am. Assn. on Mental Retardation. Office: Office Mental Retardation & Devel Disabilities 44 Holland Ave Albany NY 12229

GIBSON, ALTHEA, retired professional tennis player, golfer, state official; b. Silver, S.C., Aug. 25, 1927; d. Daniel and Annie B. (Washington) G.; m. William A. Darben, Oct. 17, 1965; m. Sydney Llewellyn, Apr. 11, 1983. B.S., Fla. A&M Coll., 1953; D. Pub. Service (hon.), Monmouth Coll., 1980; LittD (hon.), U. N.C., Wilmington, 1987; LHD (hon.), Upsala Coll., 1989. Amateur tennis player U.S., Europe, and S.Am., 1941-58; asst. instr. dept. health and phys. edn. Lincoln U., Jefferson City, Mo., 1953-55; made profl. tennis tour with Harlem Globetrotters, 1959; community rels. rep. Ward Baking Co., 1959; joined Ladies Profl. Golf Assn. as profl. golfer, 1963; apptd. to N.Y. State Recreation Council, 1964; staff mem. Essex County Park Commn., Newark, 1970; recreation supr. Essex County Park Commn., 1970-71; dir. tennis programs, profl. Valley View Racquet Club, Northvale, N.J., 1972; tennis pro Morven, 1973—; athletic commr. State of N.J., Trenton, 1975—; recreation mgr. City of East Orange, N.J., 1980; mem. N.J. State Athletic Control Bd., 1986; spl. cons. Gov.'s Coun. Phys. Fitness and Sports, N.J., 1988—; winner world profl. tennis championship, 1960, Wimbledon Women's Singles Championship, 1957, 58, Wimbledon Women's Doubles Championship, 1956-58, U.S. Women's Singles Championship, 1957, 58. Appeared in the movie The Horse Soldiers, 1958; author: I Always Wanted to Be Somebody, 1958. Named Woman Athlete of Yr., AP Poll, 1957-58; named to Lawn Tennis Hall of Fame and Tennis Mus., 1971, Black Athletes Hall of Fame, 1974, S.C. Hall of Fame, 1983, Fla. Sports Hall of Fame, 1984, Sports Hall of Fame of N.J., 1994. Mem. Alpha Kappa Alpha. Home: PO Box 768 East Orange NJ 07019-0768*

GIBSON, BARBARA ARLENE, nurse, writer; b. Port Jefferson, N.Y., July 6, 1942; d. David M. and Marion G. (Nyman) Ramos; m. Robert R. Gibson, Feb. 10, 1979; children: Joan M. Gunther, Karen L. Mullins. AAS, Suffolk County C.C., 1976. RN, Fla. Team leader Tarpon Springs (Fla.) Gen. Hosp., 1977-80; office mgr. Bob's Concrete Pumping Svc., Clearwater, Fla., 1980-89; nurse team leader St. Anthony's Hosp., St. Petersburg, Fla., 1981-89; founder Fibromyalgia Network Greater Tampa Bay, Fla., 1989-90; lectr. on fibromyalgia syndrome, 1989—; freelance writer. Author, pub.: The Fibromyalgia Handbook, 1990, 2d edit., 1995, Fibromyalgia: Exploring the Possibilities, Vol. I, Sumatriptan, 1994; freelance writer; former med. columnist Suncoast CFIOS Support Group Newsletter. Home: 1443 Mission Dr W Clearwater FL 34619-2744 Office: Gemini Press PO Box 4546 Clearwater FL 34618-4546

GIBSON, BEATRICE ANN, retired systems analyst, artist; b. Canton, Ohio, Feb. 4, 1926; d. Paul Cummins Gibson and Luella Mae (Clements) Gibson Ward. Student, Cleve. Sch. Art, 1941-44, Carnegie Mellon U., 1945-47; BA, U. Chgo., 1951; postgrad., Northwestern U., 1955-57, Oxbow Summer Sch., 1957-59, Sch. Art Inst. Chgo., 1956-60; ind. study, Italy, Greece, Spain, France, England, 1960-61, France, Netherlands, England, 1987; postgrad., EBA Sch. Art, San Francisco, 1988. Procedure analyst U.S. Steel Corp., Chgo., 1955-61; methods analyst Continental Ins. Cos., San Francisco, 1962-64; forms, methods analyst Ins. & Securities Inc., San Francisco, 1964-74; sr. systems analyst Calif. State Automobile Assn., San Francisco, 1974-91; ret., 1991; mem., editor, officer San Francisco Ins. Women's Assn., 1962-68. One-woman exhibits include Diablo Valley Coll., Pleasant Hill, Calif., 1983, EBA Sch. Art, San Francisco, 1991; group exhbns. include Old Town Art Fair, Chgo., 1955, Navy Pier Exhbn., 1956, Laguna Beach (Calif.) Gallery, 1963, San Francisco Civic Ctr. Exhbn., 1964, Hayward (Calif.) Art Show, 1983, EBA Sch. Art, 1988-93. Recipient Recognition award Calif. State Automobile Assn., 1991. Mem. Assn. Systems Mgmt. (emeritus, editor, sec. 1968—, v.p. 1973-74, pres. San Francisco chpt. 1975-76, Disting. Svc. Merit award 1978, Achievement award 1985).

GIBSON, DENICE YVONNE, telecommunications, networking and computer executive; b. Grants Pass, Oreg., Apr. 6, 1955; d. Harry Charles Gibson and Bettye Yvonne Bentley Stein. BS in Psychology, U. San Francisco, 1980; MS in Systems Mgmt., U. So. Calif., 1982; postgrad., Stanford U., 1983; PhD in Instl. Mgmt., Pepperdine U., 1990. Documentation coord./systems analyst Argonaut Ins., Menlo Park, Calif., 1977-78; tech. ops. mgr. Amdahl Corp., Sunnyvale, Calif., 1978-85; sr. dir. worldwide mktg. Candle Corp., L.A., 1985-89; v.p. mktg. Panoramic Inc., San Jose, 1989-90; v.p. devel. Tandem Computers, Plano, Tex., 1990-92, v.p. devel. and support, 1992-93; v.p. devel. and support Tandem Corp., Cupertino, Calif., 1993—, v.p. Quality Initiative Ctr.; adj. prof. U. Calif., Santa Cruz, 1993-95; v.p. quality Tandem Computers, Cupertino, 1995-96; gen. mgr. Novell Computers, Provo, Utah, 1996—; adj. prof. info. sys. mgmt. U. San Francisco, 1984-86; adj. faculty mem. U. Phoenix, 1995—; guest lectr. Stanford U., U. Calif., Berkeley, U. Calif., Santa Clara; adj. faculty U. Calif., Santa Cruz, 1994, U. San Francisco, 1994; cons. Nat. Sch. Safety Ctr., 1987, Fed. Law Enforcement Tng. Ctr., 1987, Nat. Soc. Secs., 1986, Pacific Bell, 1985, Elxsi Computers, 1983, Trilogy, 1983. Contbr. articles to profl. jours. Mem. IEEE, Engring. Soc., Am. Soc. Tng. and Devel., Am. Mgmt. Assn., Internat. Platform Assn.

GIBSON, ELEANOR JACK (MRS. JAMES J. GIBSON), retired psychology educator; b. Peoria, Ill., Dec. 7, 1910; d. William A. and Isabel

(Grier) Jack; m. James J. Gibson, Sept. 17, 1932; children: James J., Jean Grier. BA, Smith Coll., 1931, MA, 1933, DSc (hon.), 1972; PhD, Yale U., 1938, DSc (hon.), 1996; DSc (hon.), Rutgers U., 1973, Trinity Coll., 1982, Bates Coll., 1985, U. S.C., 1987, Emory U., 1990, Middlebury Coll., 1993; LHD (hon.), SUNY, Albany, 1984, Miami U., 1989. Asst., instr., asst. prof. Smith Coll., 1931-49; research assoc. psychology Cornell U., Ithaca, N.Y., 1949-66; prof. Cornell U., 1972—, Susan Linn Sage prof. psychology, 1972—; fellow Inst. for Advanced Study, Princeton, 1959-60, Inst. for Advanced Study in Behavioral Scis., Stanford, Calif., 1963-64, Inst. for Advanced Study, Ind. U., fall 1990; vis. prof. Mass. Inst. Tech., 1973, Inst. Child Devel., U. Minn., 1980; Disting. vis. prof. U. Calif., Davis, 1978; vis. scientist Salk Inst., La Jolla, Calif., 1979; vis. prof. U. Pa., 1984; Montgomery fellow Dartmouth Coll., 1986; Woodruff vis. prof. psychology Emory U., 1988-90. Author: Principles of Perceptual Learning and Development, 1967 (Century award), (with H. Levin) The Psychology of Reading, 1975, Odyssey in Learning and Perception, 1991. Recipient Wilbur Cross medal Yale U., 1973, Howard Crosby Warren medal, 1977, medal for disting. svc. Tchrs. Coll. Columbia U., 1983, Nat. Medal Sci., 1992, Lifetime Achievement award Internat. Soc. for Ecol. Psychology; Guggenheim fellow, 1972-73, William James fellow Am. Psychol. Soc., 1989. Fellow AAAS (div. chairperson 1983), Am. Psychol. Assn. (Disting. Scientist award 1968, G. Stanley Hall award 1970, pres. div. 3 1977, Gold medal award 1986); mem. NAS, Eastern Psychol. Assn. (pres. 1968), Soc. Exptl. Psychologists, Nat. Acad. Edn., Psychonomic Soc., Soc. Rsch. in Child Devel. (Disting. Sci. Contbn. award 1981), Am. Acad. Arts and Scis., Brit. Psychol. Soc. (hon.), N.Y. Acad. Scis. (hon.), Italian Soc. Rsch. in Child Devel. (hon.), Phi Beta Kappa, Sigma Xi. Home: RR 1 Box 265A Middlebury VT 05753-9705

GIBSON, ELISABETH JANE, principal; b. Salina, Kans., Apr. 28, 1937; d. Cloyce Wesley and Margaret Mae (Yost) Kasson; m. William Douglas Miles, Jr., Aug. 20, 1959 (div.); m. Harry Benton Gibson Jr., July 1, 1970. AB, Colo. State Coll., 1954-57; MA, San Francisco State Coll., 1967-68; EdD, U. No. Colo., 1978; postgrad. U. Denver, 1982. Cert. tchr., prin., Colo. Tchr. elem. schs., Santa Paula, Calif., 1957-58, Salina, Kans., 1958-63, Goose Bay, Labrador, 1963-64, Jefferson County, Colo., 1965-66, Topeka, 1966-67; diagnostic tchr. Ctrl. Kans. Diagnostic Remedial Edn. Ctr., Salina, 1968-70; instr. Loretto Heights Coll., Denver, 1970-72; co-owner Ednl. Cons. Enterprises, Inc., Greeley, Colo., 1974-77; resource coord. Region VIII Resource Access Project Head Start Mile High Consortium, Denver, 1976-77; exec. dir. Colo. Fedn. Coun. Exceptional Children, Denver, 1976-77; asst. prof. Met. State Coll., Denver, 1979; dir. spl. edn. N.E. Colo. Bd. Coop. Edn. Svcs., Haxtun, Colo., 1979-82; prin. elem. jr. h.s., Elizabeth, Colo., 1982-84; prin., spl. projects coord. Summit County Schs., Frisco, Colo., 1985-92; prin. Frisco Elem. Sch., 1985-91; cons. Montana Dept. Edn., 1978-79, Love Pub. Co., 1976-78, Colo. Dept. Inst., 1974-75; cons. Colo. Dept. Edn., 1984-85, mem. proposal reading com., 1987—; pres. Found. Exceptional Children, 1980-81; pres. bd. dirs. N.E. Colo. Svcs. Handicapped, 1981-82; bd. dirs. Dept. Ednl. Specialists, Colo. Assn. Sch. Execs., 1982-84; mem. Colo. Title IV Adv. Coun., 1980-82; mem. Mellon Found. grant steering com. Colo. Dept. Edn., 1984-85; mem. Colo. Dept. Edn. Data Acquisition Reporting and Utilization Com., 1983, Denver City County Commn. for Disabled, 1978-81; chmn. regional edn. com. 1970 White House Conf. Children and Youth; bd. dirs. Advocates for Victims of Assault, 1986-91; mem. adv. bd. Alpine Counseling Ctr., 1986-92; mem. placement alternatives commn. Dept. Social Svcs., 1986—; mem. adv. com. Colo. North Ctrl. Assn., 1988-91; sec. Child Care Resource and Referral Agy., 1992—; mem. Child Care Task Force Summit County, 1989-92; mem. tchr. cert. task force Colo. State Bd. Edn., 1990-91; chair Summit County Interagy. Coord. Coun., 1989-93. Recipient Vol. award Colo. Child Care Assn., 1992, Ann. Svc. award Colo. Fedn. Coun. Exceptional Children, 1981; San Francisco State Coll. fellow, 1967-68. Mem. Colo. Assn. Retarded Citizens, Assn. Supervision Curriculum Devel., Nat. Assn. Elem. Sch. Prins., North Cen. Assn. (state adv. com. 1988-91), Order Eastern Star, Kappa Delta Pi, Pi Lambda Theta, Phi Delta Kappa. Republican. Methodist. Author: (with H. Padzensky) Goal Guide: A minicourse in writing goals and behavioral objectives for special education, 1975; (with H. Padzensky and S. Sporn) Assaying Student Behavior: A minicourse in student assessment techniques, 1974; contbr. articles to profl. jours. Home: 14354 E Caley Ave Aurora CO 80016 Office: Sylvan Learning Ctr 8200 S Quebec Englewood CO 80112

GIBSON, FLORENCE ANDERSON, talking book company executive, narrator; b. San Francisco, Feb. 7, 1924; m. V.H. Carlos Gibson, Aug. 30, 1947; children: Nancy Derwent, Christopher Carlos, Katherine Wayne Bolland, Diana Corona. Student, Finch Jr. Coll., N.Y.C., 1941-42; BA in Dramatic Lit., U. Calif., Berkeley, 1944; student, Neighborhood Playhouse, N.Y.C., 1944-45. Radio actress San Francisco, 1944, 46, 47; chmn. Washington com. Am. Field Svc., 1958-60, 62-65; founder, chmn. Peruvian Com. Am. Field Svc., Lima, 1960-62; treas., distbn. mgr. Living Garden and Concern 1975 calendars, 1971-75; sec. exec. com Fgn. Student Svc. Coun., 1973-76; narrator Talking Books Libr. of Congress div. for Blind and Physically Handicapped, 1975-96; narrator Recorded Books, Inc., 1979; founder, pres. Audio Book Contractors, Inc., 1982—; narrator more than 733 unabridged books on cassettes. Actress, appearing in Blithe Spirit, 1945, Ah, Wilderness, 1946, Traffic Ct. TV series, others. Bd. dirs. Fgn. Student Svc. Coun., Concern, Inc., Rec. for the Blind, Children's Theater of Washington; vol. in occupational therapy Children's Hosp., Washington, 1949-50; vol. lobbyist student exch. program Am. Field Svc. Recipient 3 Parents' Choice awards, 1983, 84, 86; named Best Female Narrator, Book World; selected as A Notable Children's Recording, ALA, 1987, 88, 89. Home: 4626 Garfield St NW Washington DC 20007-1025 Office: Audio Book Contractors Inc PO Box 40115 Washington DC 20016-0115

GIBSON, JANIS ELAINE, elementary school educator; b. Houston, Aug. 1, 1945; d. Herbert Paul and Olga Marie (Manz) Haschke; m. Joe Henry Gibson, May 29, 1944; children: Buck C., Jesse J. BS in Edn., Tex. Tech U., 1969; MEd with splty. in reading, Ark. Tech. U., 1991. Cert. tchr. grades 1-6, cert. reading specialist K-12, Ark. Tchr. Omaha (Ark.) Schs., 1970-72, Bergman (Ark.) Schs., 1976—; K-4 Crusade trainer. Mem. NEA, ASCD, Ark. Edn. Assn., Internat. Reading Assn., Ark. State Reading Coun. (rsch. grantee 1992-93, State Edn. Literacy award 1996), Ozark Reading Coun. (membership chair 1995, 96—). Home: RR 1 Box 322 4135 E Persimmon Pt Lead Hill AR 72644-9637 Office: Hwy 7 N Bergman AR 72615

GIBSON, JUDITH M., federal agency administrator; b. Detroit, Aug. 4, 1947; d. Teophiel A. and Helen K. (Laethem) DeM. BA, Wayne State U., 1969. Specialist manpower devel. Dept. Labor, Washington, 1970-74; various analyst positions Fed. Energy Adminstrn., Washington, 1974-78; dir. scheduling, staffing, adminstrn. econ. registration adminstrn. Dept. Energy, Washington, 1978-79, dir. divsn. resource mgmt., 1979-82, acting dir. resource mgmt. office inspector gen., 1982-83, chief mgmt. and budget, 1983-87, dir. adminstrn. budget and disclosure, 1987-88, exec. dir., 1988-92, asst. inspector gen. policy, planning and mgmt., 1992—. Mem. Assn. Govt. Accts., Exec. Women in Govt. Office: Dept Energy Office Inspector Gen 1000 Indpendence Ave SW Washington DC 20585

GIBSON, LUANNE EILEEN, visual artist, educator; b. Toledo, Jan. 14, 1955; d. Omar Frank and Roseann Mae (Nickerson) Smith; m. William Patrick Gibson, May 1, 1982; 1 child, Shayna Nicole. Student, U. Toledo, 1977-1979; BA, Mont. State U., 1993. Ind. visual artist Bozeman, Mont., 1993—; art instr. Inst. Lifetime Learning, 1996. Artist (neck piece) The World Diploma of Design & Crafts, 1994. Vol. art tchr. elem. sch., Bozeman, 1994-95. Mem. Nat. Mus. Women in the Arts, Phi Kappa Phi.

GIBSON, PATRICIA ANN, health care administrator; b. Joplin, Mo., Nov. 14, 1942; d. Arrell Morgan and Dorothy (Deitz) G. BA in English, U. Okla., 1963, MLS, 1966, PhD in Edn., 1977. English tchr. Norman (Okla.) Pub. Schs., 1963-65; pub. svcs. librarian U. Okla. Health Scis. Ctr., Oklahoma City, 1966-68, serials librarian, 1971-72, dir. media prodn., 1972-77; coord. library svcs. Okla. Regional Med. Program, 1968-70; head reference dept. Wichita State U., 1978-80; mgr. library devel. DataPhase Systems, Inc., Kansas City, Mo., 1980-82; v.p. program adminstrn., libr. dir. Am. Acad. Family Physicians Found., Kansas City, 1982—; cons. Am. Coll. Cardiology Library, 1986-87. Contbr. articles to profl. jours. Chmn. regional screening com. Am. Field Svc., Kansas City, 1987-89; bd. dirs. Midwest Ear Inst., 1993—. Kellogg Found. grantee, 1987-88. Mem. Med. Libr. Assn. (disting. mem. Acad. Health Sci. Librs., chmn. med. libr. edn. sect. 1989-90, med. soc. librs. sect. 1991-92), Kansas City Met. Libr. Network (pres. 1986, sec. 1987-89), Health Scis. Libr., Group Greater Kans. City (pres. 1992—), Nat. Network Med. Librs. (regional adv. com. midcontinental region 1991—, regional adv. com. 1994—). Democrat. Presbyterian. Office: Am Acad Family Physicians Found 8880 Ward Pkwy PO Box 8418 Kansas City MO 64114-0418

GIBSON, PAULA LAUREN, lawyer, screenwriter; b. Denver, 1956. BA, UCLA, 1978; JD, Southwestern U., 1981. Bar: Calif. 1981. Assoc. Potter, Bradish and Ellinghouse, Encino, Calif., 1981-82; sr. corps. counsel Calif. Dept. of Corps., Los Angeles, 1982-84; dep. atty. gen. State of Calif., Los Angeles, 1984—; gen. counsel Twilight Films div. Nefertiti Entertainment Group, Beverly Hills, Calif., 1985-93. Author: (film treatment) Never to be Abducted from my Heart, 1987, Seven Times Over, 1994; screenwriter Due and Payable, 1987. Recipient Outstanding Achievement in civil litigation award Atty. Gen., 1994. Mem. L.A. County Bar Assn.

GIBSON, SARAH ANN SCOTT, art librarian; b. Harrisburg, Pa., Mar. 2, 1932; d. John Young Scott and Alice Virginia (Cooper) Rowe; m. Walter Samuel Gibson, Dec. 16, 1972. AB in History, Smith Coll., 1953; postgrad., Université de Strasbourg, France, 1953-54, École du Louvre, Paris, 1965-66; MLS, Case Western Reserve U., 1968, MA in Art History, 1972, PhD in Libr. and Info. Sci., 1975. Asst. cataloger Denison U., Granville, Ohio, 1958-69; asst. prof. U. Mich., 1972-73; asst. prof. Case Western Reserve U., 1975-82, asst. dean Sch. Libr. Sci., 1979-82, assoc. prof., 1982-86; exec. officer Matthew A. Baxter Sch. Info. and Libr. Sci., 1984-86; libr. Sterling & Francine Clark Art Inst., Williamstown, Mass., 1987—; vis. prof. Sch. Info. Studies Syracuse U., 1986. Author: (with Lois Swan Jones) Art Libraries and Information Services: Development, Organization and Management, 1986, (with others) Book Illustration From Six Centuries in the Library of the Sterling & Francine Clark Art Institute Library, 1990; assoc. editor RILA Internat. Repertory of Lit. of Art, 1986-87; contbr. articles to profl. jours. Fulbright fellow, 1953-54. Mem. Art Librs. Soc. N.Am., Jr. League Cleve., Princeton Club N.Y.C., Historians Netherlands Art. Home: RR 2 461H Mason Hill Rd Pownal VT 05261 Office: Sterling & Francine Clark Art Inst 222 South St # 8 Williamstown MA 01267-2822

GIBSON, VIRGINIA LEE, lawyer; b. Independence, Mo., Mar. 5, 1946. BA, U. Calif., Berkeley, 1972; JD, U. Calif., San Francisco, 1977. Bar: Calif. 1981. Assoc. Pillsbury, Madison & Sutro, San Francisco, 1980-83; ptnr. Chickering & Gregory, San Francisco, 1983-85, Baker & McKenzie, San Francisco, 1985—. Mem. ABA (employee benefits subcom. tax sect.), Internat. Found. Employee Benefit Plans, Am. Compensation Assn. (internat. compensation and benefits com.), Calif. Bar Assn. (exec. com. tax sect. 1985-88), San Francisco Bar Assn. (internat. and comparative law taxation sects.), Western Pension and Benefits Conf. (pres. San Francisco chpt. 1989-91, program com. 1984-88). Office: Baker & McKenzie 2 Embarcadero Ctr Ste 2400 San Francisco CA 94111-3909

GICALETTO, SABRINA MARIA, accountant; b. McAlester, Okla., Aug. 18, 1967; d. James A. and Barbara Elaine (Dobson) G. BS in Bus. Adminstrn. cum laude, U. Tulsa, 1989, M Taxation magna cum laude, 1996. CPA, Okla. Sr. auditor Arthur Anderson & Co., Tulsa, 1989-92; contr. Flint Industries, Inc., Tulsa, 1992—. Script writer Your Day in Court, 1996. Treas. Crop Walk Hunger, Tulsa, 1991. Fellow Okla. Soc. CPAs; mem. Beta Gamma Sigma. Democrat. Episcopalian. Office: Flint Industries Inc 1624 W 21st St Tulsa OK 74107

GIDEON-HAWKE, PAMELA LAWRENCE, fine arts small business owner; b. N.Y.C., Aug. 23, 1945; d. Lawrence Ian Verry and Lily S. (Stein) Gordon; m. Jarrett Redstone, June 27, 1964; 1 child, Justin Craig Hawke. Grad. high sch., Manhattan. Owner Gideon Gallery Ltd., L.A. and Las Vegas, 1975—; prin. Pamela L. Gideon-Hawke Pub. Rels., L.A., 1984—. Pres. San Fernando Valley West Point Parents Club, 1990—. Named Friend of Design Industry Designers West Mag., 1987. Mem. Am. Soc. Interior Designers (publicist), Internat. Soc. Interior Designers (trade liaison 1986-88), Network Exec. Women in Hosp. (pres. Las Vegas chpt., pres. Las Vegas program, L.A. chair), Internat. Furnishings and Design Assn. (pres.). Office: Gideon Gallery Ltd 8121 Lake Hills Dr Las Vegas NV 89128 also: 8748 Melrose Ave Los Angeles CA 90069-5015

GIEBEL, MIRIAM CATHERINE, librarian, genealogist; b. Williamsburg, Iowa, Oct. 10, 1934; d. John Timothy and Helen Gertrude (Wright) Donahoe; m. William Herbert Giebel, Sept. 30, 1967; 1 child, Sara Ann Giebel Ward. BS, Marquette U., Milw., 1956; MS in Library Science, Rosary Coll., River Forest, Ill., 1960; Cert. Paralegal, Roosevelt U., Chgo., 1992; Cert. in Family History Rsch., Brigham Young U., Provo, Utah, 1992. Asst. acquisitions dept. Marquette U., Milw., 1956-58; tech. svcs. librarian Chicago Heights (Ill.) Pub. Libr., 1959-63; librarian Little Company of Mary Nursing, Evergreen Park, Ill., 1963-64; asst. librarian hdqrs. ALA, Chgo., 1964-67; extension, reference librarian Chicago Heights (Ill.) Pub. Libr., 1974—. Mem. Ill. Fedn. Bus. Profl. Women (state library chair 1994-96), U.S. Daughters of 1812 (Ill. state registrar 1994—, chpt. pres. 1991—), DAR (chpt. registrar 1994—), Soc. Ind. Pioneers (life). Roman Catholic.

GIENAPP, HELEN FISCHER, jewelry company owner; b. Saginaw, Mich., Oct. 9, 1921; d. John Frederick and Dorothea (Schleicher) Fischer; m. Walter Lawrence Gienapp, Oct. 10, 1942; children: Karen Lynne, Roger Alan, David Paul, Marcia Lou, Richard Kevin. Grad. h.s., Saginaw. Adminstrv. asst. Muskegon (Mich.) Devel. Corp., 1961-66; exec. asst. to pres. Greater Detroit C. of C., 1966-80; owner Internat. Jewelry, Ferndale, Mich., 1990—. Pres. Internat. Luth. Women's Missionary League, St. Louis, 1979-83; dir. Hist. Trinity, Inc., Detroit, 1990—, English dist. Luth. Ch.-Mo. Synod, Farmington, 1988—, Mission Opportunities Short Term Ministries, Ann Arbor, Mich., 1995. Named Luth. Woman of Yr., Mich. Dist. of Luth. Ch.-Mo. Synod, 1983. Mem. Valparaiso U. Guild, Women's Econ. Club Detroit. Home: 371 Channing Ferndale MI 48220-2555

GIER, AUDRA MAY CALHOON, environmental chemist; b. Bella Vista, Peru, Aug. 21, 1940; came to U.S., 1944; d. Nathan Moore and Olivia Cleo (Hite) Calhoon; m. Delta Warren Gier, Apr. 4, 1968. BA, Austin Coll., 1962; MS in Chemistry, Kans. State Coll., 1964; MA in History of Sci., U. Wis., 1974; postgrad., York U., Toronto, Can., 1974-79. Food technologist Midwest Rsch. Inst., Kansas City, Mo., 1963-64; chemist Mobay (formerly Chemagro), Kansas City, 1964-67; instr. chemistry St. Andrews Presbyn. Coll., Laurinburg, N.C., 1967-68; chemist Cardinal Chem. Co., Columbia, S.C., 1968; asst. prof. chemistry Lea Coll., Albert Lea, Minn., 1969-72; psychology intern emergency unit Thistletown Regional Centre for Children & Adolescents, Toronto, Ont., Can., 1975-77; assoc. prof. chemistry Cleveland Chiropractic Coll., Kansas City, 1979-84; adj. faculty Pk. Coll., Parkville, Mo., 1982-92; environ. chemist, quality assurance specialist Ecology & Environ., Inc., Overland Park, Kans., 1987-95; pres. Delta and Assocs., Inc., Kansas City, 1988-92; co-founder, v.p. Midwest Sci. Found., Kansas City, 1990—; mem. adj. faculty Donnelly Coll., 1992-94, dean adminstrn. health scis. program, 1992—; mentor tng. program Option Inst. and Fellowship, Sheffield, Mass., 1994—. Author: Highlights of Organic Chemistry, 1985; co-editor: (with D.W. Gier) History and Directory of Chemical Education, 1974, (with D.W. Gier) Peace is Something Speshl; co-inventor, co-patentee acetylenic ketones as herbicides. Mem. adv. bd. Kansas City Interfaith Peace Alliance, 1980-95, bd. dirs., 1982-85, pres., 1985-86; bd. dirs. Prairie Star Dist./Unitarian-Universalist Midwest (Upper), 1985-91; co-chair Bragg Symposium on Humanism, Kansas City, 1980-90; chair Social Responsibility Com., Prairie Star Dist. UUA, 1986-91; mem. N.Am. Com. for Humanism and Fellowship of Religious Humanists. Recipient Social Justice award Social Justice Com. Prairie Star Dist, 1985; named Woman of Yr., 1982, Humanist of Yr., 1987, All Souls Unitarian Ch., Kansas City. Mem. NAFE, AAUW, ACLU, DAR, NARAL, Am. Chem. Soc., Am. Soc. for Quality Control (cert.), Inst. for Soc. Ethics and Life Scis., Midwest Bioethics Ctr., Planned Parenthood, Assn. for Quality and Participation, Habitat for Humanity. Democrat. Home: 421 W 99th St Kansas City MO 64114-3908

GIER, KARAN HANCOCK, counseling psychologist; b. Sedalia, Mo., Dec. 7, 1947; d. Ioda Clyde and Lorna (Campbell) Hancock; m. Thomas Robert Gier, Sept. 28, 1968. BA in Edn., U. Mo., Kansas City, 1971; MA Teaching in Math/Sci. Edn., Webster U., 1974; MA in Counseling Psychology, Western Colo. U., 1981; MEd Guidance and Counseling, U. Alaska, 1981; PhD in Edn., Pacific Western U., 1989. Nat. cert. counselor. Instr. grades 5-8 Kansas City-St. Joseph Archdiocese, 1969-73; ednl. cons. Pan-Ednl. Inst., Kansas City, 1973-75; instr., counselor Bethel (Alaska) Regional High Sch., 1975-80; ednl. program coord. Western Regional Resource Ctr., Anchorage, 1980-81; counselor U. Alaska, Anchorage, 1982-83; coll. prep. instr. Alaska Native Found., Anchorage, 1982; counselor USAF, Anchorage, 1985-86; prof. U. Alaska, Anchorage, 1982—; dir. Omni Counseling Svcs., Anchorage, 1984—; prof. Chapman Coll., Anchorage, 1988—; workshop facilitator over 100 workshops on the topics of counseling techs., value clarification, non-traditional teaching approaches, peer-tutor tng. Co-author: Coping with College, 1984, Helping Others Learn, 1985; editor, co-author: A Student's Guide, 1983; contbg. author developmental Yup'ik lang. program, 1981; contbr. photographs to Wolves and Related Canids, 1990, 91; contbr. articles to profl. jours. Mem. Am. Bus. Women's Assn., Blue Springs, Mo., 1972-75, Ctr. for Environ. Edn., World Wildlife Fund, Beta Sigma Phi, Bethel, Alaska, 1976-81. Recipient 3d place color photo award Yukon-Kuskokwim State Fair, Bethel, 1978, Notable Achievement award USAF, 1986, Meritorious Svc. award Anchorage Community Coll., 1984-88. Mem. Coll. Reading and Learning Assn. (editor, peer tutor sig leader 1988—, Cert. of Appreciation 1986-93, bd. dirs. Alaska state, coord. internat. tutor program, Spl. Recognition award 1994-95), AACD, Alaska Assn. Counseling and Devel. (pres. 1989-90), Alaska Career Devel. Assn. (pres.-elect 1989-90), Nat. Rehab. Assn., Nat. Rehab. Counselors, Greenpeace, Human Soc. of U.S. Wolf Haven Am., Wolf Song of Alaska. Home and Office: Omni Counseling Svcs 8102 Harvest Cir Anchorage AK 99502-4682

GIER, PATRICIA CHAPMAN, elementary education educator; b. Butte, Mont., June 27, 1949; d. Kenneth D. and Peggy (Hansen) White and John R. Chapman Jr.; m. Ronald E. Gier, Dec. 23, 1982; children: Thomas Duane, Kristi Nicole, Alexandra Novichkova; stepchidren: Ronald E. Jr., Randall E., Richard E. BA in Elem. Edn., U. Mo., 1985; MA in Teaching, Webster U., 1993. Cert. tchr., Mo., Kans. Tchr., sci., math. Kans. City (Mo.) Sch. Dist., 1986-87; tchr. Christa McAuliffe Elem. Sch., Shawnee Mission, Kans., 1987-90, Belinder Elem. Sch., 1990—; facilitator Project Learning Tree Am. Wilderness Leadership Tng. Sch., 1990. Lifetime mem. PTA; mem. Jr. League, also various youth comty. svc. orgns., child abuse and neglect orgns. Mem. NEA, Internat. Reading Assn., Nat. Assn. Math. Tchrs., Nat. Assn. Sci. Tchrs., Kans. Assn. Conservation, Jr. League (Mo. chpt.).

GIERLASINSKI, KATHY LYNN, accountant; b. Chewelah, Wash., May 21, 1951; d. John Edward and Margaret Irene (Seefeldt) Rail; m. Norman Joseph Gierlasinski, May 23, 1987. BBA, Gonzaga U., 1984. CPA, Wash. Legal sec. Redbook Pub. Co., N.Y.C., 1974-75, Howard Michaelson, Esquire, Spokane, Wash., 1975-76; sec. Burns Internat. Security Svcs., Spokane, 1977-79; sec. to contr. Gonzaga U., Spokane, 1979-81, acctg. asst., 1981-82; staff acct. Martin, Holland & Petersen, CPA's, Yakima, Wash., 1984-87; acct., supr. Strader Hallet & Co., P.S., Bellevue, Wash., 1988-91; acct. Miller & Co., P.S., Woodinville, Wash., 1991-93; pres. Gierlasinski & Assocs., P.S., Bothell, Wash., 1993—; treas. White Pass Ski Patrol, Nat. Ski Patrol Systems, Wash., 1987-90; editor, chmn. audit com. Mt. Spokane Ski Patrol, 1983-84. Mem. AICPA, Am. Soc. Women Accts. (charter, editor 1987), Wash. Soc. CPA (sec. Sammamish Valley chpt. 1990-92, pres. 1992-93, 93-94), Washington Soc. of Cert. Pub. Accts. (chair adv. coun. 1995-96, tax com., govt. affairs com., dir. 1996—), Bus. and Profl. Women of Woodinville (treas. 1994-95), Northshore C. of C. Republican. Lutheran. Home: 28623 NE 47th Pl Redmond WA 98053

GIFFEN, LOIS KEY, artist, psychosynthesis counselor; b. Hollis, Okla., Dec. 18, 1932; d. Andrew Finley and Audra Agnes (Griffith) Key; m. Robert Edward Giffen, June 26, 1954; children: John Andrew, Mark Alexander. BA, U. Chgo., 1951, attended, 1951-54; diploma, Inst. Psychosynthesis, London, 1988. Artist, 1945—; social group worker Neighbourhood Clubs, Oklahoma City, Okla., 1956-59; tchr. Unity of the Keys, Key West, Fla., 1994—; workshop facilitator Fla. Coalition for Peace and Justice, 1990; organizer for tchg. student mediators in elem. schs. Peace Edn. and Awareness Ctr., Santa Barbara, 1992-93. Editor The London Bridge Mag., 1981-84, The CCL Cookbook, 1986; one-woman shows include Gippsland Regional Art Ctr., Sale, Victoria, Australia, 1973, Anjuian Angkatan Pelakis Semalaysia, Kuala Lumpur, 1976, Am. Consulate-USIS, Benghazi, Libya, 1962. V.p., mem. bd. dirs. Internat. Women's Club, Benghazi, Libya, 1960-65; mem. bd. dirs. Gippsland Regional Art Ctr., Sale, Victoria, Australia, 1971-73; com. chmn., mem. bd. dirs. Am. Women's Club, London, 1981-88; mem. bd. dirs. Commonwealth Countries League, London, 1982-88, Welcome to London Internat. Club, London, 1983-88; mem. Univ. Women's Club, London, 1985-88. Mem. Assn. for Transpersonal Psychology, Assn. for the Advancement of Psychosynthesis, Bus. & Profl. Women's Club, Marathon Art League, Marathon Sailing Club. Democrat. Mem. Unity Ch. Home: 1600 79th St Ocean Marathon FL 33050

GIFFIN, BARBARA HAINES, education coordinator; b. Mt. Holly, N.J., July 2, 1944; d. Harvey and Loris (Mantell) H.; m. Donald William Giffin, Mar. 25, 1967; children: Sherri Christine, Darrell Wesley. BS, Ind. U. of Pa., 1966; MEd, U. South Fla., 1982. Cert. tchr. Fla., N.J., Pa. Instr. No. Burlington (N.J.) County High Sch., 1966-68, Sterling High Sch., Sommerville, N.J., 1968-71, U. Tampa, Fla., 1975-77; instr., coord. Pinellas Tech. Edn. Ctr., St. Petersburg, Fla., 1977—, Fire Chief's Assn., 1994—; Mem. adv. bd. Operation Par, Inc., St. Petersburg, 1992-93; mem. exec. bd. Pinellas Adult Vocat. Edn., St. Petersburg, 1991-92; treas., membership chair PAVE, 1994-95; v.p. Bus. Edn. Assn. Pinellas, 1988. Mem. All Children's Guild, 1995—; corr. sec. Dillard's Career Club, 1994—. Recipient Nat. Recognition award for Exemplary Vocat. Edn. Programs, 1991. Mem. Am. Vocat. Assn., Shriners Aux. Democrat. Episcopalian. Home: 12338 Capri Cir N Treasure Is FL 33706-4974 Office: Pinellas Tech Edn Ctr 901 34th St S Saint Petersburg FL 33711-2209

GIFFIN, MARGARET ETHEL (PEGGY GIFFIN), management consultant; b. Cleve., Aug. 27, 1949; d. Arch Kenneth and Jeanne (Eggleton) G.; m. Robert Alan Wyman, Aug. 20, 1988; 1 child, Samantha Jean. BA in Psychology, U. Pacific, Stockton, Calif., 1971; MA in Psychology, Calif. State U., Long Beach, 1973; PhD in Quantitative Psychology, U. So. Calif., 1984. Psychometrist Auto Club So. Calif., L.A., 1973-74; cons. Psychol. Svcs., Inc., Glendale, Calif., 1975-76, mgr., 1977-78, dir., 1979-94; rschr. Social Sci. Rsch. Inst., U. So. Calif., L.A., 1981; dir. Giffin Consulting Svcs., L.A., 1994—; instr. Calif. State U., Long Beach, 1989-90; mem. tech. adv. com. on testing Calif. Fair Employment and Housing Commn., 1974-80, mem. steering com., 1978-80. Mem. Am. Ednl. Rsch. Assn., Soc. Indsl. Organizational Psychology, Am. Psychol. Assn., Personnel Testing Coun. So. Calif. (pres. 1980, exec. dir. 1982, 88, bd. dirs. 1980-92). Home and Office: 260 S Highland Ave Los Angeles CA 90036-3027

GIFFIN, MARY ELIZABETH, psychiatrist, educator; b. Rochester, Minn., Mar. 30, 1919; d. Herbert Ziegler and Mary Elizabeth (Nace) G. BA, Smith Coll., Northampton, Mass., 1939; MD, Johns Hopkins, 1943; MS, U. Minn., 1948. Diplomate Am. Bd. Psychiatry and Neurology. Cons. in neurology and psychiatry Mayo Clinic, Rochester, 1949-58; med. dir. Josselyn Clinic, Northfield, Ill., 1958-89; pvt. practice psychiatry Northfield, 1989—; mem. faculty Inst. for Psychoanalysis, Chgo., 1963-89. Contbr. numerous articles to profl. jour. Mem. Ill. Psychiat. Soc., Am. Acad. Child Psychiatry. Republican. Mem. Am. Bapt. Ch. Home: 1190 Hamptondale Ave Winnetka IL 60093-1812 Office: 1 Northfield Plz Ste 300 Northfield IL 60093-1214

GIFFORD, KATHIE LEE, television personality, singer; b. Paris, Aug. 16, 1953; d. Aaron Leon and Joan Epstein; m. Paul Johnson (div.); m. Frank Gifford, Oct. 18, 1986; children: Cody Newton, Cassidy Erin. Student, Oral Roberts U., Tulsa. Gospel singer; singer $100,000 Name That Tune Quiz Show; co-host Morning Show, 1985-88, LIVE with Regis and Kathie Lee, 1988—; author: The Quiet Riot, 1976, I Can't Believe I Said That, 1992; (with Regis Philbin) Cooking With Regis and Kathie Lee, 1993, Entertaining With Regis and Kathie Lee, 1994; marketer clothing collection Kathie Lee for Plaza South; album: Sentimental, 1993, It's Christmas Time, 1993; sang Nat. Anthem, Super Bowl, 1995; host, co-writer, co-producer, CBS television special, Kathie Lee...Looking for Christmas, 1994. Office: Live With Regis & Kathie Lee WABC-TV Seven Lincoln Square New York NY 10023*

GIFFUNI, CATHE, researcher, writer; b. N.Y.C., July 18, 1949; d. Joseph V. and Flora (Baldini) G. BA, Hollins Coll., 1970; postgrad., Columbia U., 1971-72. Author: Bessie Head: A Bibliography, 1986, A Bibliography of Louise Arner Boyd, 1986, James Courage: A Checklist of Published Primary and Secondary Sources, 1987, Joseph O'Neill: A Bibliography, 1987, Annie Smith Peck: A Bibliography, 1987, A Bibliography of the Film Scores of Ralph Vaughan Williams, 1988, Clarice Lispector: A Complete English Bibliography, 1988, Laura Z. Hobson: A Bibliography, 1988, Lajos Zilahy: A Bibliography, 1988, A Bibliography of Margaret Leech, 1988, A Bibliography of the Mystery Writings of Leonardo Sciascia, 1989, Maurice Gee: A Bibliography, 1990, Witi Ihimaera: A Bibliography, 1990, Zofia Kossak: An English Bibliography, 1990, Iris Origo: A Bibliography, 1990, A Bibliography of the Mystery Writings of Elspeth Huxley, 1991, Joseph Roth: An English Bibliography, 1991, Leo Perutz: An English Bibliography, 1991, An English Bibliography of Alejo Carpentier, 1992, The Prose of David Malouf: A Bibliography, 1992, An English Bibliography of the Writings of Primo Levi, 1992, A Bibliography of the Writings of Natalia Ginzburg, 1993, Catherine Drinker Bowen: A Bibliography, 1993, A Bibliography of Vera Caspary, 1995. Address: 240 E 27th St New York NY 10016-9277

GIGLIOTTI, FRANCES MARIE, primary education educator; b. Phila., Nov. 15, 1969; d. Richard John and Frances Marie (Chiriaco) G. BA, Glassboro State/Rowan Coll., 1992. Beginners tchr. East Greenwich Bd. Edn., Mickleton, N.J., 1992—; mem. sci. curriculum com. East Greenwich Schs., 1992—, mem. sch. planning com., 1993—; tutor math and reading, Turnersville, N.J., 1993-94. Recipient Disting. Tchr. Candidate award Commr. Edn., N.J., 1992. Mem. Kappa Delta Pi. Office: Jeffrey Clark Sch 7 Quaker Rd Mickleton NJ 08056-1306

GIL, JOAN ELLEN, secondary education educator, consultant; b. N.Y.C., Mar. 17, 1944; d. Sam S. and Helen (Riff) Harkavy; m. J. Eduardo Gil, Dec. 30, 1967; children: Carolyn, Sandra, Diana. AA, Centenary Coll. for Women, Hackettstown, N.J., 1963; BA, Pa. State U., 1965; postgrad., U. Las Americas, Mexico City, 1966-67, Mich. State U., Mexico City, 1968-74. Cert. primary and secondary tchr., Tex.; cert. in internat. rels. and fgn. svc. Elem. tchr. Am. Found. Sch., Mexico City, 1966-76; tchr. social studies Loretto Acad., El Paso, 1978-88; migrant tchr. Anthony (Tex.) Ind. Sch., 1988-89; tchr. computers Canutillo (Tex.) Ind. Sch. Dist., 1989—; pvt. cons., El Paso area, 1993—. Pres. UN Assn., El Paso, 1988—. Recipient Writing Contest award NATO, 1986; West Tex. Writing Project fellow, 1993. Mem. AFT. Home: 5400 Orantes Pl El Paso TX 79932-3027 Office: Canutillo Ind Sch Dist PO Box 100 Canutillo TX 79835-0100

GILB, CORINNE LATHROP, history educator; b. Lethbridge, Alta., Can., Feb. 19, 1925; d. Glen Hutchison and Vera (Passey) Lathrop; m. Tyrell Thompson Gilb, Aug. 19, 1945; children: Lesley Gilb Taplin, Tyra. BA, U. Wash., 1946; MA, U. Calif., Berkeley, 1951, law student, 1950-53; PhD, Harvard U., 1957. History lectr. Mills Coll., Oakland, 1957-61; prof. humanities San Francisco State U., 1964-68; rsch. assoc. U. Calif., Berkeley, 1953-68; prof. history Wayne State U., Detroit, 1968-94, co-dir. Liberal Arts Urban Studies program, 1976-86; dir. planning City of Detroit, 1979-85; spl. cons. Calif. Legislature, 1963, 64; vis. scholar Hoover Instn., Stanford U., fall 1993; UN Nongovtl. Orgn. rep. Internat. Orgn. for Unification of Terminological Neologisms, 1995—. Author: Conformity of State to Federal Income Tax, 1964, Hidden Hierarchies, 1966, numerous chpts. in books; contbr. articles to profl. jours. Vol. writer Silicon Valley Global Trading Ctr., 1995-96. Guggenheim fellow, 1957; grantee Social Sci. Rsch. Coun. Mem. Internat. Soc. Comparative Study of Civilizations (five terms exec. coun., 1st v.p. 1995—), No. Calif. World Affairs Coun., various acad. assns. Presbyterian.

GILBERT, EDES POWELL, headmistress; b. Bklyn., Mar. 25, 1932; d. Talcott Williams Powell and Helen Ann (Ranney) Anderson; m. Rexford Wilson, Aug. 18, 1954 (div. 1976); children—Timothy Rexford, Christopher Lawrence, Sarah Edes; m. Peter Gilbert, July 2, 1980 (dec. Mar. 1989). A.B., Vassar Coll., 1953; M.Ed., Lesley Coll., 1970. Cert. tchr., N.Y., Mass. Tchr. Tenacre Country Day Sch., Wellesley, Mass., 1966-70; dir. admissions, dir. studies Dexter Sch., Brookline, Mass., 1970-75; headmistress Mary Inst., St. Louis, 1976-83, Spence Sch., N.Y.C., 1983—. Trustee St. Louis Repertory Theatre, 1980-83; bd. dirs. Ensemble Studio Theatre, N.Y.C., 1985, St. David's Sch., N.Y.C., 1984-88, Profl. Children's Sch., 1990-95, TIAA-CREF. Mem. Nat. Assn. Prin. Schs. for Girls, Headmasters Assn. (pres. 1992), Headmistresses of East, Nat. Assn. Ind. Schs. (v.p. 1983-90), Country Day Sch. Headmasters (pres. 1993). Democrat. Episcopalian. Avocations: travel; reading; walking; theatre. Office: Spence Sch 22 E 91st St New York NY 10128-0657

GILBERT, JO, psychologist; b. L.A., July 25, 1949; d. Joseph Raymond and Rochelle Rose (Burdman) G.; divorced; 1 child, Branden Christopher Smale. BA in Psychology cum laude, UCLA, 1972; postgrad., U. Houston, 1971-72, William Marsh Rice U., 1972-77; PhD in Clin. Psychology, Calif. Sch. Profl. Psychology, 1980. Lic. psychologist, Calif.; qualified med. evaluator. Psychol. intern, researcher, then counselor Olive St. Bridge, Fresno, Calif., 1978-80; registered psychologist FCEOC Project Pride, Fresno, 1980-82; psychologist Fox, Pick and Assocs., Napa, Calif., 1982-85; pvt. practice Napa, 1985—; ptnr. Napa-Solano Psychotherapy Svcs., 1993—; adj. faculty in forensic psychology Calif. Sch. Profl. Psychology, Berkeley, 1987; faculty U. San Francisco, 1987-88; presenter at profl. confs.; mem. Sacramento County panel ct.-appointed psychologists, Yolo County panel ct.-appointed psychologists, Solano County panel ct.-appointed psychologists. Contbr. articles to profl. publs. Mem. APA, Calif. Psychol. Assn. (assoc. sec. 1994-95), Napa Valley Psychol. Assn. (past pres.), Soc. Personality Assessment. Democrat. Jewish.

GILBERT, JOAN STULMAN, petroleum company executive; b. N.Y.C., May 10, 1934; student Conn. Coll. for Women, 1951-53; m. Phil E. Gilbert, Jr., Oct. 6, 1968; children: Linda Cooper, Dana, Patricia. Br. coord. Vol. Service Bur., Westchester, N.Y., 1970-72; Westchester Lighthouse (pub. relations dir. 1972-76); exec. dir. Westchester Heart Assn., 1976-77; mgr. community rels. Texaco Inc., White Plains, N.Y., 1977—. Bd. dirs. Am. Heart Assn., Coll. Careers, Phoenix Theatre, v.p.; bd. dirs. ARC, Pvt. Industry Coun., Westchester Philharmonic; former bd. Choate Rosemary Hall, United Way of Westchester; chmn. bd. The Street Theater; former trustee Westchester Coun. for the Arts, former bd. dirs.; trustee Teatown Lake Reservation, former bd. dirs. Recipient awards Girl Scouts, Am. Heart Assn., Am. Diabetes Assn., Westchester Putnam Affirmative Aciton Program, Arthritis Found., ARC, Urban League Westchester. Mem. Pub. Rels. Soc. Am. (chpt. pres. 1977), Advt. Club (dir.), Women in Comms., Public Issues Coun. of The Conference Bd., Sales and Mktg. Execs. Westchester (former dir.), Advertising Club of Westchester, Westchester County Assn. Home: The Croft 1595 Spring Valley Rd Ossining NY 10562-2002 Office: Texaco Inc 2000 Westchester Ave White Plains NY 10650-0001

GILBERT, LIANE MARIE, research scientist executive; b. Long Branch, N.J., June 20, 1949; d. Charles Wilson and Edith Doris (Johnson) Case; m. Roger William Gilbert, July 17, 1971; children: David Aaron, Charles Paul. BA in Psychology, Monmouth U., West Long Branch, N.J., 1972; MA in Teaching, Trenton State Coll., 1979. Cert. tchr. of handicapped, N.J. Tchr. spl. edn., dir. afternoon program S.E.A.R.C.H., Ocean, N.J., 1972-74; tchr. spl. edn. Jackson (N.J.) Twp. Sch. System, 1974-79; exec. dir. Otologic Edn., Inc., Shrewsbury, N.J., 1980-88; dir. clin. rsch. Nat. Patent Analytical Systems, Inc., Roslyn Heights, N.Y., 1983-86, v.p. rsch., 1986-88; pres. Westerman Rsch. Assocs., Inc., Shrewsbury, N.J., 1988—; participant numerous convs., profl. organs. and spl. interest groups, U.S.A., Israel and The Netherlands, 1974—; software devel. expert to knowledge engr. for Visual Perceptual System, 1984—; v.p. Otologic Edn., Inc., Shrewsbury, 1988—. Co-contbr. articles and chpts. to profl. publs.; U.S. and Can. patentee computer-aided drug-abuse detection. Fundraiser Am. Heart Assn., 1991; active MADD; activist Nat. Audubon Soc. Mem. Internat. Regulatory Affairs Profls. Soc., Nat. Graphic Soc., Assn. Clin. Pharmacologists, Regulatory Affairs Profls. Soc., Monmouth County Assn. Children with Learning Disabilities, Psi Chi, Sigma Xi. Office: Westerman Rsch Assocs Inc 499 Broad St Shrewsbury NJ 07702-4003

GILBERT, LISA JANE, psychiatrist; b. Cleve., July 4, 1959; d. Jack Flint and Sophie Jean (Kulway) G. BS, Kent State U., 1981; MD, Case Western Res. U., 1986. High sch. tchr. Cleveland Heights Univ. Heights Bd. of Edn., 1981-86; resident physician Cleve. Clinic Found., 1990-94; cmty. psychiatrist Westside Cmty. Mental Health, Cleve., 1994—; pvt. practice Dunkle and Assoc., Cleveland Heights, 1994—. Mem. Am. Psychiat. Assn., Physicians Com. for Responsible Medicine, Assn. of Gay and Lesbian Psychiatrists, Gay and Lesbian Med. Assn. Home: 850 S Green Rd Apt 7 South Euclid OH 44121-3460 Office: Dunkle & Assocs 12417 Cedar Rd Ste 21 Cleveland Heights OH 44106

GILBERT, MELISSA, actress; b. Los Angeles, May 8, 1964; d. Paul and Barbara (Crane) G.; m. Bo Brinkman (div.); 1 son, Dakota; m. Bruce Boxleitner, Jan. 1, 1995; stepchildren: Lee, Sam. Student, U. So. Calif. Actress: (TV movies) Little House on the Prairie, 1974, Christmas Miracle in Caulfield, U.S.A., 1977, The Miracle Worker, 1979, The Diary of Anne Frank, 1980, Splendor in the Grass, 1981, Little House: Look Back to Yesterday, 1983, Choices of the Heart, 1983, Little House: Bless All the Dear Children, 1984, Family Secrets, 1984, Little House: The Last Farewell, 1984, Choices, 1986, Penalty Phase, 1986, Family Secrets, Killer Instincts, Without Her Consent, Forbidden Nights, 1990, Blood Vows: The Story of a Mafia Wife, Joshua's Heart, 1990, Donor, The Lookalike, 1990, Conspiracy of Silence: The Shari Karney Story, 1992, With Hostile Intent, 1993, Shattered Trust, 1993, House of Secrets, 1993, Dying to Remember, 1993, Cries From the Heart, 1994, Against Her Will: The Carrie Buck Story, 1994, The Babymaker: The Dr. Cecil Jacobson Story, 1994; (TV series) Little House on the Prairie, 1974-82, Little House: A New Beginning, 1983, Stand By Your Man, 1992, Sweet Justice, 1994-95 (TV spls.) Battle of the Network Stars, 1978, 79, 81, 82, Celebrity Challenge of the Sexes, 1980, Circus Lions, Tigers and Melissa, Too, 1977, Dean Martin Celebrity Roast, 1984, (stage prodns.) Night of 100 Stars, 1982, The Glass Menagerie, 1985, A Shayna Maidel, 1987 (Outer Critics Circle Award), (feature films) Nutcracker Fantasy, 1979, Sylvester, 1985, Ice House, 1989. Office: William Morris Agy 151 S El Camino Dr Beverly Hills CA 90212-2704*

GILBERT, NANCY LOUISE, librarian; b. Norfolk, Va., Nov. 3, 1938; d. Oscar Linwood Jr. and Mary Margaret (Nicholls) Gilbert. BA, Greensboro Coll., 1961; MLS, U. North Carolina, 1968. Libr. Va. Beach (Va.) Pub. Libr., 1968, U.S. Army, Worms, Crailsheim and Mannheim, Fed. Republic Germany, 1968-74, Pentagon Libr., Washington, 1974-80, U.S. Army Mil. History Inst., Carlisle Barracks, Pa., 1980—. Mem. ALA, Spl. Librs. Assn., Mid-Atlantic Region Archives Conf.

GILBERT, SARA, actress; b. 1975; d. Harold Abeles and Barbara Gilbert. Appeared as Darlene Connor in TV series Rosanne, 1988—, (TV movies) Sudie & Simpton, 1990, Calamity Jane, (TV spls.) ABC Weekend Spl., 1988, Valvolene Nat. Driving Test, 1989, 4th Ann. Am. Comedy Awards, 1990, Tom Arnold: The Naked Truth, 1991, In a New Light, 1992, 43 Ann. Foley's Thanksgiving Day Parade, 1992, CBS Schoolbreak Spls., 1992, (syndicated game show) Fun House, 1989, (talk show) At Rona's, 1989, (film) Poison Ivy, 1992. Office: care ABC 2040 Ave of the Stars Los Angeles CA 90067*

GILBERT, SUZANNE HARRIS, advertising executive; b. Chgo., Mar. 8, 1948; d. Lawrence W. and Dorothea (Wilde) Harris; children: Kerry, Elizabeth, Gregory. B.S., Marquette U., 1965; MBA, U. Chgo., 1985. Fin. analyst Leo Burnett Co., Chgo.; sr. v.p. fin. adminstrn., sec.-treas. Clinton E. Frank Inc., Chgo., 1975-85; with Campbell-Ewald Co., Detroit, 1985—; formerly group sr. v.p., Campbell-Ewald, Warren, Mich., exec. v.p., chief fin. and adminstrv. officer, 1990—; mem. bd. dirs. Boys Hope Detroit; mem. bd. advs. U. Detroit Mercy Coll. of Bus. Mem. Am. Assn. Advertising Agys. (fiscal control com.), Econ. Club Detroit, Fin. Execs. Inst., Better Bus. Bur. (mem. bd. dirs.). Office: Campbell-Ewald 30400 Van Dyke Ave Warren MI 48093-2316

GILBERTI, JUDITH ANNE, secondary school educator; b. Jersey City, Jan. 6, 1957; d. Charles Joseph and Rose Elizabeth (Mastropasqua) G. BS in Home Econs., Saint Mary-of-the-Woods Coll., 1979; MS in Edn., Monmouth Coll., 1994. Tchr., coach Essex Catholic Girls H.S., Irvington, N.J., 1979-86, Middletown (N.J.) Twp. Bd. Edn., 1986—; cheer coach, judge Met. Cheerleading Judges Assn., 1995; class sec., alumnae assn. Saint Mary-of-the-Woods Coll., 1990—; adv. bd. mem. alumnae assn. Mother Seton Regional H.S., Clark, N.J., 1994—. Vol., supporter Muscular Dystrophy Assn., ALS divsn. N.J./N.Y., 1990—. Recipient Cheer Coach of Yr. award Nat. Cheerleaders Assn., 1982-83, Gov. Tchrs. Recognition award N.J. State Dept. Edn., 1989. Mem. Am. Counseling Assn., Am. Assn. Family and Consumer Scis., N.J. Assn. Mid. Level Educators, Nat. Fedn. Interscholastic Spirit Assn., Alpha Delta Kappa (historian, treas., pres.- elect 1990—), Kappa Delta Pi. Roman Catholic. Home: 401 Aldene Rd Roselle NJ 07203 Office: Middletown Twp Bd Edn 59 Tindall Rd Middletown NJ 07748

GILBRECH, ELIZABETH MARIE, cable television company executive; b. Paterson, N.J., Nov. 6, 1960; d. William Martin and Mary Ellen (Conry) Hannigan; m. Arthur Stanton Gilbrech, Oct. 8, 1988; children: Katherine Marie, Michael George. BSBA, Montclair State Cll., 1985; M Profl. Studies in Interactive Telecom., NYU*, 1988. Mktg. support asst. IBM, Parsippany, N.J., 1983-84; mktg. support rep. Xerox Corp., Morris Plains, N.J., 1984-85; telecom. cons. Goldman Sachs & Co., N.Y.C., 1985-87; staff cons. Arthur Andersen & Co., Stamford, Conn., 1987-88; sr. network engr. Salomon Inc., Rutherford, N.J., 1988-94; mgr. compression sys. HBO, Hauppauge, N.Y., 1994-95; v.p. multimedia ops. Popcorn Channel, N.Y.C., 1995—. Com. mem. N.Y. Women's Agenda, N.Y.C., 1993-94; mem. disaster action team ARC, Bergen County, N.J., 1994-96. Scholar Internat. Comm. Assn., 1985-86. Mem. Internat. Interactive Comm. Assn. (chmn. subcom. 1993-94), Fin. Women's Assn. N.Y. (profl. devel. com. 1995-96), N.Y. New Media Assn., Wall Street Telecom. Assn. (co-chmn. emerging techs. com. 1993-94), N.Y. PC Assn. (adv. bd. multimedia interest gruop 1993-94). Democrat. Home: 95 Crescent Pl Allendale NJ 07401 Office: Popcorn Channel 1120 Ave of Americas 6th Fl New York NY 10036

GILCHREST, BARBARA A. D., dermatologist; b. Port Chester, N.Y., 1945. MD, Harvard U., 1971. Cert. dermatology, internal medicine. Intern Boston City Hosp., 1971-72, resident internal medicine, 1972-73, resident dermatology, 1973-76; fellow photobiology Harvard U., Boston, 1974-75; chief dermatology U. Hosp., Boston, Boston City Hosp.; prof., chmn. dermatology Boston U. Sch. Medicine, 1985—. Mem. AAAS, Am. Acad. Dermatology, Assn. Am. Physicians, Am. Soc. for Clin. Investigation, Soc. for Investigative Dermatology. Office: Boston U Sch Medicine Dermatology 80 E Concord St Boston MA 02118-2394

GILCHRIST, ELLEN LOUISE, writer; b. Vicksburg, Miss., Feb. 20, 1935; d. William Garth and Aurora (Alford) G.; children: Marshall Peteet Walker, Jr., Garth Gilchrist Walker, Pierre Gautier Walker. BA in Philosophy, Millsaps Coll., 1967; postgrad., U. Ark., 1976; LittD (hon.), Millsaps Coll., 1987; LHD (hon.), U. So. Ill., 1991. Freelance writer, journalist; commentator, morning edit. of news Nat. Pub. Radio, Washington, 1984, 85. Author: The Land Surveyor's Daughter, 1979, In The Land of Dreamy Dreams, 1981, The Annunciation (Book of Month Club alternate in U.S. and Sweden), 1983, Victory Over Japan (Am. Book award 1984), 1984, Drunk With Love, 1986, Falling Through Space, 1987, The Anna Papers, 1988, Light Can Be Both Wave and Particle, 1989, I Cannot Get You Close Enough, 1990 (Miss. Inst. Arts and Letters award 1990, fiction award Miss. Libr. Assn. 1990), Net of Jewels, 1992, Starcarbon, 1994, Anabasis, A Journey to the Interior, 1994, The Age of Miracles, 1995, Rhoda, A Life in Stories, 1995, The Courts of Love, 1996; (poems) Riding Out the Tropical Depression; contbr. short stories poems to literary publs. Recipient Poetry award U. Ark., 1976, Craft in Poetry award N.Y. Quar., 1978, Fiction award The Prairie Schooner, 1981, Poetry award Miss. Arts Festival, 1968, Saxifrage award, 1983, Fiction award Miss. Acad. Arts and Sci., 1982, 85, Am. Book award Victory Over Japan, 1984, J. William Fulbright prize U. Ark., 1985, Lit. award Miss. Inst. Arts and Letters, 1985, 90, 91; 2 Pushcart prizes, O. Henry Short Story award, 1995; grantee NEA, 1979. Mem. Author's Guild.

GILDEN, ROBIN ELISSA, elementary education educator; b. Albany, N.Y., Aug. 1, 1950; d. Avrom Irwin and Virginia (D'Arcangelo) G. BS, Pa. State U., 1972, cert. in teaching, 1977. Cert. elem. tchr., Pa. Tchr. West Allegheny Sch. Dist., Imperial, Pa., 1972—. Fundraiser Mary Rensel Meml. Fund, Pitts., 1992—. Recipient NASA Tchr. in Space Program, 1986. Mem. Pa. Edn. Assn. (bldg. rep. 1984-86, 91-93), Pa. Framework, PTA, Pa. State Alumni Assn., ASCD. Home: 1256 Pennsbury Blvd Pittsburgh PA 15205-1638 Office: McKee Sch 1501 Oakdale Rd Oakdale PA 15071-3638

GILE, MARY STUART, educational executive; b. Montreal, Que., Can., Mar. 24, 1936; d. William Gillies and Hazel Irene (Stuart) Sinclair; m. Robert Hall Gile, Mar. 29, 1974; children—D. Christopher, Julia Mary, John, Robertson Sinclair. BS, McGill U., 1957; MEd, U. N.H., 1971; EdD, Vanderbilt U., 1982. Specialist phys. edn. Protestant Sch. Bd. Greater Montreal, 1957-64, kindergarten tchr. White Mountains Sch. Bd., Littleton, N.H., 1965-67; dir. Open Door Kindergarten, Salem, N.H., 1967-69; coord. State Follow Through, State of N.H., 1969-80, N.H. Right to Read, 1973-74, U.S. Sec.'s Initiative in Excellence chpt. 1 Edn. Consol. and Improvement Act, 1983-84; sr. cons. edn. N.H. State Dept. Edn., Concord, 1969-85; v.p. edn. and devel. Acad. Applied Sci., Concord, 1985-90; prof., dept. head early childhood edn. N.H. Tech. Inst., Concord, 1990—; state dept. staff assoc. to U. N.H., Durham, 1970-74; mem. Gov.'s Task Force on Sexual Harassment, Concord, 1981-83; chair N.H. Trust Fund for Prevention of Child Abuse and Neglect, 1986-94, Commr.'s Com. on Alt. Work Schedules, Concord, 1982-84, gov. appt. state child abuse neglect prevention leadership team; commr.'s rep. State Day Care Adv. Com., Concord, 1984-85; commn. rep. N.H. State Child Care Adv. Com., 1994—; pres., faculty NNTI, 1995—. Contbr. articles to profl. jours. Pres. Concord Parents and Children, 1977-82; chmn. Citizens Adv. Bd. to Community Devel., 1978-82; chair Edn. Leadership Concord, 1993-94, chair selection com., 1994—; bd. govs. Merrimack County United Way, 1983-88; pres. N.H. Assn. for Mental Health, 1984-86. Recipient Appreciation cert. Maine Dept. Edn., 1984, cert. outstanding achievement N.H. State Bd. Edn., 1985, Imperial Oil Ltd. scholar, 1953; U. N.H. early childhood fellow, 1969; recipient Leo J. Rubin award United Way Merrimack County, 1993. Mem. N.H. Assn. for Edn. Young Children, Phi Delta Kappa. Congregationalist. Avocations: skiing, music, theater, hiking.

GILES, ANNE DIENER, flutist; b. Rochester, N.Y., Oct. 13, 1948; d. Frederick William and Alma Mary (Bastian) Diener; m. Allen Giles, Sept. 26, 1970; 1 child, Katherine Anne. BMus, Juilliard Sch., 1970, MS, 1971. Prin. flutist L.A. Philharm. Orch., 1971—; instr. flute U. So. Calif., L.A., 1990—; vis. prof. flute Rice U., Houston; instr. master classes, L.A., Santa Barbara, Wyo., Fla., Tojo Sch., Tokyo. Solo performances with orch. include (West Coast premiere) Bernstein "Halil," 1983, (world premiere) Stucky Concerto for 2 flutes and orch., 1995, Bach Brandenburg Concertos with P. Zukerman, Mozart Complete Works for Flute and Orch.; featured soloist L.A. Philharm. recs.: Debussy "Afternoon of a Faun," Leinsdorf, Ravel "Daphnis & Chloe." Recipient Bronze medal Competition Internat., Geneva, Switzerland, 1973. Mem. Nat. Flute Assn., Music Tchrs. Nat. Assn. Office: LA Philharm Orch 135 N Grand Ave Los Angeles CA 90012-3013*

GILES, JEAN HALL, retired corporate executive; b. Dallas, Mar. 30, 1908; d. C. D. and Ida (McIntyre) Overton; m. Alonzo Russell Hall, II, Jan. 23, 1923 (dec.); children: Marjorie Hodges, Alonzo Russell III; m. Harry E. Giles, Apr. 24, 1928 (div. 1937); 1 child, Janice Ruth; 1 adopted child, Marjean Giles. Grad. Hamilton State U., PhD (hon.), 1973. comdg. officer S.W. Los Angeles Women's Ambulance and Def. Corps., 1941-43; maj., nat. exec. officer Women's Ambulance and Def. Corps, 1944-45; capt., dir. field ops. Communications Corps of the U.S. Nat. Staff, 1951-52; dir. Recipe of the Month Club. Active Children's Hosp. Benefit, 1946; coord. War Chest Motor Corps, 1943-44; dir. Los Angeles Area War Chest Vol. Corps and Motor Corps, 1945-46; realtor Los Angeles Real Estate Exchange, 1948—, now ret.; also partner Tech. Contractors, Los Angeles. Bd. dirs. Tchr. Remembrance Day Found. Inc. Mem. Am. Biol. Inst., Internat. Biol. Assn. Eng. (hon., adv.), L.A. C. of C. (women's div.), A.I.M., Los Angeles Art Assn., Hist. Soc. So. Calif., Opera Guild So. Calif., Assistance League So. Calif., Needlework Guild Am. (sect. pres. L.A.), First Century Families Calif., Internat. Platform Assn. Clubs: Athletic; Town Hall, The Garden (L.A.); Pacific Coast. Home: 616 Magnolia Ave Long Beach CA 90802-1243

GILES, MARY LOU ANDERSON, retired educator, small business owner; b. Jamestown, N.Y., July 29, 1930; d. Warren Charles Anderson and Vivian Ione Mills Anderson-Larson; m. William S. Giles, July 16, 1955 (dec. Jan. 1983); children: Andrew Giles, Grace Johnson, Elaine Sardi. BS in Elem. Edn., SUNY, Fredonia, 1952. Cert. elem. tchr., N.Y. Tchr. Jamestown (N.Y.) Schs., 1952-54, Cassadaga (N.Y.) Schs., 1954-56, Riverside (Calif.) Schs., 1957-60, 64-66, Bemus Point (N.Y.) Schs., 1966-90; co-owner Giles Vending, Jamestown, 1994—; treas. Bemus Point Tchrs. Union, 1975-76. Trustee United Meth. Ch., Falconer, N.Y., 1990-95, founder, Contemporary Choir, 1995; mem. Pre-sch. bd., Falconer, 1994-95. Republican. Home: 15 E Elmwood Ave Falconer NY 14733 Office: Giles Vending 133 Stowe St Jamestown NY 14701

GILES, PATRICIA CECELIA PARKER, retired art educator, graphic designer; b. Chgo., Mar. 8, 1925; d. Frederick Louis and Bernice Clara (Kennedy) Parker; m. Lewis Wentworth Giles, June 20, 1946 (div. 1960); children: Alan Julian, Kay Celeste. BS in Fine Arts, U. Ill., Urbana, 1946; postgrad., Howard U., Washington D.C., 1947, U. Mass., Amherst, 1974-75, Washington Sch. Psychology, 1962. Reg. sec. tchr. art Ill., 1972. Sec. tchr. art Randall Jr. High, Washington, D.C., 1947-48; art cons. Elem. Sch., Washington, 1952-53; tchr., chmn. art dept. Theodore Roosevelt H.S., Washington, 1959-60, Boys Sr. H.S., Washington, 1961-63, Carter G. Woodson Jr. H.S., Washington, 1963-72, Howard D. Woodson Sr. H.S., Washington, 1973-85; v.p. D.C. Art Assn., 1964-65; cons. art-math. with humanities Upward Bounders U. Md., College Park, 1966-67; potential supervisor of student tchg. in art therapy Planning Program Staff George Washington U., Washington, 1972; visual arts coord. D.C. Congress P.T.A. Cultural Arts, Washington, 1972; artist-in-residence Washington Seniors Wellness Ctr., 1987-88. Painter: (oil painting) Mud and Roots, 1971 (award 1971), Mural: Infinite Joy, 1991 (Golden Dolphins Commendation award 1991), Kenkin, oils, 1992 (award 1992); author: (book of poetry) Mud and Roots, 1976. Taught art workshop in cmty. Fort DuPont Civic Assn., Washington, 1960, defining creative art Channel 14 WOOK-TV, Washington, 1963, comparing and interacting with cultures and govts. Am. Forum for Internat. Study, Senegal, Ghana, Ethiopia, Kenya, Tanzania, 1970; peer leader in tennis and yoga Washington Seniors Wellness Ctr., Washington, 1995. Recipient Commendation award Ft. DuPont Civic Assn., Washington, 1960, 1st prize for watercolor Architect's Wives Assn., 1962, Gold medals D.C. Senior Olympics in Tennis & Swimming, 1993. Mem. Nat. Conf. of Artists, D.C. Nat. Tennis Assn. (sr., 2d Place Trophy 1990), Golden Dolphins (Outstanding Swimming Trophy 1993). Democrat. Seventh Day Adventist. Home: 3942 Blaine St NE Washington DC 20019

GILES, VIRGINIA DENISE, artist; b. Mena, Ark., Feb. 8, 1959; d. Charles Thomas Adkins and Sylvia Ann (Mitchell) Ventris; m. Mark Joel Giles, Sept. 1, 1979; children: Max Ausborn, Ian Stewart, Lee Elizabeth. AAS in Human Svcs., Westark C.C., 1979; BA in Fine Arts, Ark. Tech. U., 1992. Artist Palmer Gallery 800, Hot Springs, Ark., 1993—, Art Form Gallery, Van Buren, Ark., 1994—; coord. local artist gallery Ark. River Valley Arts Ctr., Russellville, 1993, liaison between visual arts com., 1993. One-woman shows include Ark. River Valley Arts Ctr., 1993; exhibited in group shows at Ark. River Valley Arts Ctr., 1991, 92, Ft. Smith, Ark., 1995, Art in the Park, Russellville, Ark., 1995. Vol. Cir. of Friends, Russellville, 1994—. Recipient Best of Show and 2 Hon. Mention awards Ark. River Valley Arts Ctr., 1992, Best of Show award, 1995. Mem. Nat. Mus. for Women in Arts (slides in registry), Ark. Artist Registry/Arts Coun. (slides in registry). Studio: 1705 S Boston Pl Russellville AR 72801

GILFOYLE, NATHALIE FLOYD PRESTON, lawyer; b. Lynchburg, Va., May 4, 1949; d. Robert Edmund and Dorothea Henry (Ward) Gilfoyle; m. Christopher Y.W. Ma, Sept. 9, 1978; children: Olivia Otey, Rohan James. B.A., Hollins Coll., Roanoke, Va., 1971; J.D., U. Va., Charlottesville, 1974. Bar: Mass. 1974, D.C. 1977. Staff counsel Rate Setting Commn., Boston, 1974-76; ptnr. Peabody, Lambert & Meyers, Washington, 1976-84; ptnr. McDermott, Will and Emery, 1984-96; dep. gen. counsel APA, 1996—; bd. dirs. Washington Lawyers Com. Civil Rights Under Law, Washington, 1982—; participating counsel Vol. Lawyers for Arts, Boston, 1974-76,

Washington, 1978—. Bd. dirs. ACLU Nat. Capital Area, Washington, 1980-83, Filmore Early Learning Ctr., 1977-81, St. Columba's Nursery Sch., 1992—, D.C. Bar Atty. Client Arbitration Bd., chmn. Mem. ABA, D.C. Bar Assn., Mass. Bar Assn., Women's Bar Assn. Episcopalian. Office: McDermott Will & Emery 1850 K St NW Washington DC 20006-2213

GILIEN, NANCY CAMPBELL, nursing consultant; b. Russellville, Ark., Jan. 4, 1926; d. Robert Arthur and Celeste Dabney (Campbell) Ragsdale; m. Sasha B. Gilien, Nov. 29, 1964 (dec. Nov. 1971); 1 child, Thea. BSN, Vanderbilt U., 1947; MPH, U. Calif., Berkeley, 1960; MA in Anthropology, UCLA, 1970. RN, Calif. Staff nurse comty. hosps., Little Rock, 1947-50; pub. health nurse City Health Dept., Little Rock, 1951-52, Fgn. Svc., U.S. Dept. of State, Rangoon and Tokyo, 1953-57; nursing cons. Childrens Hosp., L.A., 1960-64, North Bay Regional Ctr., Napa, Calif., 1973-89, Napa, 1989—. Contbr. chpts. to nursing textbooks; contbr. articles to profl. jours. Chair pub. health com. Calif. Assn. for Retarded, statewide, 1963. Mem. APHA, Calif. Nurses Assn. (bd. officers area 9 1975-79). Home: 3477 Valle Verde Dr Napa CA 94558

GILL, CAROL SUSAN, educational consultant; b. Chelsea, Mass., Mar. 7, 1939; d. Maurice S. and Frances (Disken) Deitch; m. Arthur Gill, Dec. 28, 1979; children: Deborah, Marjorie. BA, Radcliffe Coll., 1962; MAT, Manhattanville Coll., 1971. Cert. tchr., N.Y. Chair social sci. dept. Masters Sch., Dobbs Ferry, N.Y., 1971-79, dir. coll. guidance, 1977-81; assoc. dir. admissions Barnard Coll., N.Y.C., 1981-85; pres., ednl. cons. Carol Gill Assoc., Dobbs Ferry, 1985—; lectr. in field. Contbr. articles to profl. jours. Mem. NOW, Coalition Legal Abortion, Am. Counseling Assn., Nat. Assn. Coll. Admission Counseling, Ind. Ednl. Cons. Assn. Office: Carol Gill Assocs 369 Ashford Ave Dobbs Ferry NY 10522

GILL, DIANE LOUISE, psychology educator, university official; b. Watertown, N.Y., Nov. 7, 1948; d. George R. and Betty J. (Reynolds) G. BS in Edn., SUNY, Cortland, N.Y., 1970; MS, U. Ill., 1974, PhD, 1976. Tchr. Greece Athena High Sch., Rochester, N.Y., 1970-72; asst. prof. U. Waterloo, Ont., Can., 1976-78; asst. prof. U. Iowa, Iowa City, 1979-81, assoc. prof., 1981-86; assoc. prof. sport & exercise psychology U. N.C., Greensboro, 1987-89; prof. U. N.C., Greenboro, 1989—; assoc. dean U. N.C., Greensboro, 1992—. Author: (book) Psychological Dynamics of Sports, 1986; editor Jour. of Sport and Exercise Psychology, 1985-90; editorial bd. Jour. of Applied Sport Psychology, 1988—; contbr. articles to profl. jours. Fellow AAHPERD (rsch. consortium pres. 1987-89), APA, Am. Psychol. Soc., Assn. for Advancement of Applied Sport Psychology, Am. Acad. Kinesiology and Phys. Edn.; mem. N.Am. Soc. for Psychology of Sport and Phys. Activity (pres. 1988-91). Democrat. Office: U NC Dept Exercise and Sport Sci Greensboro NC 27412

GILL, E. ANN, lawyer; b. Elyria, Ohio, Aug. 31, 1951; d. Richard Henry and Laura (Beeler) G.; m. Robert William Hempel, Aug. 4, 1973; children: Richard, Peter, Mary. AB, Barnard Coll., 1972; JD, Columbia U., 1976. Bar: N.Y. 1977, U.S. Supreme Ct. 1982. Assoc. Mudge, Rose, Guthrie & Alexander, N.Y.C., 1976-77; assoc. Dewey Ballantine, N.Y.C., 1977-84, ptnr., 1985—. Mem. ABA, N.Y. State Bar Assn., Nat. Assn. Bond Lawyers. Home: 255 W 90th St New York NY 10024-1109 Office: Dewey Ballantine 1301 Ave Of The Americas New York NY 10019-6022

GILL, EVALYN PIERPOINT, editor, publisher; b. Boulder, Colo.; d. Walter Lawrence and Lou Octavia Pierpoint; student Lindenwood Coll., BA, U. Colo.; postgrad. U. Nebr., U. Alaska, MA, Cen. Mich. U., 1968; m. John Glanville Gill; children: Susan Pierpoint, Mary Louise Glanville. Lectr. humanities Saginaw Valley State Coll., University Center, Mich., 1968-72; mem. English faculty U. N.C., Greensboro, 1973-74; editor Internat. Poetry Rev., Greensboro, 1975-92; pres. TransVerse Press, Greensboro, 1981—. Bd. dirs. Eastern Music Festival, Greensboro, 1981—, Greensboro Symphony, 1982—, Greensboro Opera Co., 1982—, Weatherspoon Assn.; chmn. O. Henry Festival, 1985, 95. Mem. Am. Lit. Translators Assn., MLA, N.C. Poetry Soc., Phi Beta Kappa. Author: Poetry By French Women 1930-1980, 1980, Dialogue, 1985, Southeast of Here: Northwest of Now, 1986, Entrances, 1996; editor: O. Henry Festival Stories, 1985, 87, Women of the Piedmont Triad: Poetry and Prose, 1989, Edge of Our World, 1990; contbr. poetry to numerous mags. Home: 2900 Turner Grove Dr N Greensboro NC 27455-1977

GILL, JO ANNE MARTHA, middle school educator; b. L.A., July 8, 1940; d. James Hurse Wilson and Martha Grace (Hanson) Wilson Horn; m. Richard Martin Gill, Apr. 18, 1959; 1 child, Richard James. BA in Interdisciplinary Studies, Nat. U., San Diego, 1989; MA in Ednl. Adminstrn., Calif. State U., San Bernardino, 1992. Cert. tchr. pre-sch. through adult edn., social sci., adminstrn. Tchr. grades 6 and 7 Palm Springs (Calif.) Unified Sch. Dist., 1989-94, tchr. 8th grade U.S. history, gifted/regular, 1994—; prof. edn. Calif. State U., San Bernardino; cons. Desert Schs. Consortium, Palm Springs, 1993-95, Inland Empire History/Social Studies, Riverside, Calif., 1991-95; adv. bd. Inland Empire Lit. Project, 1994—; mem. leadership team Inland Area History/Social Sci. Summer Inst., U. Calif., Riverside, 1994—. Contbr. articles to profl. jours. Mem. Calif. State History Standards and Course Models Commn.; coach mid. sch. demonstration program. Inland Area History/Social Sci. Adv. Acad. fellow, 1991, NEH fellow, 1993, Calif. History/Social Sci. Project/UCLA fellow, 1994; recipient 1st pl. award/tchr. multimedia group presentation Nat. History Day, 1996. Mem. AAUW (home tour guide 1993), Calif. Coun. for the Social Studies (presenter conf. workshop 1993, 95, 96), Calif. Assn. for Gifted (presenter ann. conf. workshop 1994, 96), Inland Empire Coun. for the Social Studies (pres. 1994-96), Delta Kappa Gamma (scholarship fundraising com. 1993-94). Democrat. Roman Catholic. Office: Palm Springs Unified Schs 333 S Farrell Dr Palm Springs CA 92262-7905

GILL, KATHY, nursing educator; b. Paris, June 13, 1954; d. William E. and Lorene (Bell) Burns; children: Arthur, Patrick, Colin. BS, Lindenwood Coll., 1976; BSN, St. Louis U., 1980; MSN, Wichita State U., 1994. RNC; cert. childbirth educator; advanced RN practitioner. Surg. ICU staff nurse HCA Wesley Med. Ctr., Wichita, Kans., 1980-87, maternal-child educator cons., 1987-90; lectr. sch. medicine U. Kans., Wichita, 1990-92; adjunct faculty ASPO/Lamaze Childbirth Educator Cert. Program, 1991—; asst. prof. divsn. nursing Kans. Newman Coll., Wichita, 1992—; lectr. in field. Contbg. author: Maternal Newborn Nursing: Theory and Practice; contbr. articles to profl. jours. Elizabeth Bing scholar, 1992. Fellow Am. Coll. Childbirth Educators; Assn. Women's Health, Obstetrical and Neonatal Nurses, Am. Soc. Psychoprophylaxis in Obstetrics, Nat. Assn. Multicultural Edn., Sigma Theta Tau (past newsletter editor).

GILL, LINDA A., advertising executive. Sr. v.p., mgmt. supr. Girgenti, Hughes, Butler & McDowell, N.Y.C. Office: Girgenti Hughes Butler & McDowell 100 Ave of the Americas New York NY 10013*

GILL, LINDA TRACY, accountant; b. Cin., Oct. 20, 1951; d. George William and Helen Mary (Lauber) Tracy; m. Robert D. Gill, June 29, 1979; children: Dennis, Brian. BS summa cum laude in acctg., U. Cin., 1976; MBA in Taxation, Xavier U., 1982. CPA, Ohio. Media clk. Procter & Gamble, Cin., 1970-74, media staff asst., 1974-76; staff auditor Arthur Young & Co., Cin., 1976-78, mem. tax staff, 1978-81, tax mgr., 1981-84; mgr. tax dept. Aronowitz, Chaiken & Hardesty, Cin., 1984-87, ptnr., 1988-92; founder, CEO Giffin/Gill, 1995—; founder Women Entrepreneurs, Inc., 1984. Recipient Women in Bus. Advocate award SBA, 1987, Individual Progress award Greater Cin. C. of C., 1989; named YWCA Career Woman of Achievement, 1992. Mem. Am. Inst. CPAs, Ohio Soc. CPAs (Pres.'s award 1994), Cin. Women CPAs, Bus. and Profl. Women's Club. Office: Giffin/Gill 4701 Creek Rd Ste 240 Cincinnati OH 45242-8330

GILL, MARY C., lawyer; b. Indpls., May 21, 1955; d. Ben Dailey and Alice M. (Harrison) G.; m. Dennis R. Kruszewski, Sept. 24, 1983; 1 child, Cory Oliver Raub. BA, Ind. U., 1979; JD, Emory U., 1983. Bar: Ga. 1983. Ptnr. Alston & Bird, Atlanta, 1983—; adj. prof. Emory U. Sch. Law, Atlanta, 1990-93. Mem. Ga. Bar Assn., Atlanta Bar Assn., Atlanta Younger Lawyers Assn. (bd. dirs. 1989-91). Office: Alston & Bird One Atlantic Ctr 1201 W Peachtree St NW Atlanta GA 30309-3400*

GILL, PATRICIA JANE, human resources executive; b. Mt. Vernon, N.Y., Jan. 20, 1950; d. J. Morgan and Magdalina (Manganiello) G. BA in History, St. Mary's Coll., 1971; MA in Counseling, NYU, 1973; MBA in Mktg., Fordham U., 1979; postgrad., Columbia U. Tchr., counselor Mt. Vernon Bd. Edn., 1970-74; tng. mgr. St. Luke's Hosp., N.Y.C, 1974-78; dir. personnel Bernard Hodes Advt., N.Y.C., 1978-80; mgr. mgmt. programs group Devel. Dimensions Internat., Pitts., 1980-82; v.p. Swan Cons., N.Y.C., 1982-83; nat. sales mgr. Reader's Digest, Pleasantville, N.Y., 1983-84; pres. Alexis-Gill, Inc., White Plains, N.Y., 1985; cons. in field. Author: Roleplaying, 1979. Worker Project Hope, New Rochelle, N.Y., 1986—. Mem. Am. Soc. Tng. and Devel. (pres. 1988), Nat. Speakers Assn. Episcopalian. Office: Alexis-Gill Inc 222 Mamaroneck Ave Ste 207 White Plains NY 10605-1316

GILL, RONNIE JOY, newspaper editor; b. Bklyn., Dec. 13, 1949; d. Robert and Frances (Noble) Ginsberg; m. Martin Harvey Gill, Nov. 24, 1971 (div. Nov. 1984). BA, Queens Coll., 1971. Adminstrv. asst. Technicolor, Inc., N.Y.C., 1971-72; daily TV listing editor Newsday, Inc., Melville, N.Y., 1972-74, TV book listing editor, 1974-79, editor, editing supr., 1979-87, editor, editing mgr., 1987-90, TV Plus editor, 1990-92; TV Plus/Entertainment Guides editor, 1992—, nationally syndicated travel columnist, 1995—. Contbr. numerous articles to publs., 1973—. Jewish. Office: Newsday 235 Pinelawn Rd Melville NY 11747-4226

GILLAM, LINDA DAWN, physician, researcher; b. Corner Brook, Nfld., Can., Sept. 23, 1952; d. Donald Samuel and Vera (Pieroway) G.; m. Vincent Charles DiCola, Aug. 30, 1985 (div. 1995); children: John William DiCola, Laura Ann DiCola. BS, McGill U., Montreal, Que., Can., 1972; MD, Queen's U., Kingston, Ont., Can., 1976. Diplomate Am. Bd. Internal Medicine, Am. Bd. Cardiovascular Disease. Intern U. Toronto, 1976; resident in medicine St. Michaels Hosp., Toronto, 1977-79; fellow in cardiology U. Toronto, 1979-81, Mass. Gen. Hosp., Boston, 1981-83; instr. in medicine Harvard U. Med. Sch., Boston, 1983-86; clin. asst. prof. medicine U. Conn., Farmington, 1986-95, clin. assoc. prof., 1995—; dir. echocardiography U. Conn. Health Ctr., Farmington, 1986-90, Hartford (Conn.) Hosp., 1990—; mem. adv. bd. Mallucrodt Med., St. Louis, 1994—; spkr. in field. Contbr. articles to profl. jours. Coord. children's program North Edgehill Assn., New Haven, 1993—; active St. Thomas's Episcopal Ch., New Haven, 1993—. Rsch. grantee Can. Heart Assn. Fellow Am. Coll. Cardiology (chair chpt. reimbursement com. 1994—, gov. 1996—); mem. AMA, Conn. State Med. Soc., Am. Soc. Echocardiography (legis. com., regulatory affaris com. 1993—, bd. dirs. 1995—), Am. Heart Assn. (task force on guidelines for echocardiography). Office: Hartford Hosp 80 Seymour St Hartford CT 06102-5037

GILLAM, PAULA SAMPLE, artist, educator; b. Cleve., Mar. 1, 1939; d. Howard Donaldson and Elizabeth Minerva (Slater) Sample; d. Virginia W. (stepmother) Sample. m. Jerry Michael Gillam, Sept. 14, 1962 (div. May 1974); children: Thea Elizabeth, Chad Michael; m. James W. Butler, Aug. 1, 1981 (div. May 1996). BFA, Cleve. Inst. Art, 1975; postgrad., Kent State U., 1979-81, U. Akron, 1979-81. Instr. Cleve. Mus. Art, 1965-68, 72-78, Cooper Sch. Art, Cleve., 1974-78, Cuyahoga C.C., Cleve., 1977, U. Akron, Ohio, 1978-81, Art Inst. Fort Lauderdale, Fla., 1981—; artist-in-residence traveling summer program Akron Mus. Art, 1978. One person shows include Coral Springs (Fla.) Libr., 1983, Gilles Patrick Studio/Gallery, Fort Lauderdale, 1984, Art Inst. Fort Lauderdale, 1985, 87, Margate Libr., 1985; exhibited in group shows at Cleve. Mus. Art, 1961, 62, 63, 64, 65, 68, Chautauqua (N.Y.) Inst., 1963-67, 69, 74, Canton (Ohio) Inst. Art, 1974, Cooper Sch. Art, Cleve., 1975-79, Women's Caucus Art, Akron, 1978, Summit County Libr., Akron, 1978, Massillon (Ohio) Mus., 1979, U. Akron, 1979, 80, Kent (Ohio) State U., 1980, Boca Raton (Fla.) Mus. Art, 1982-85, 91, 93, Art Inst. Fort Lauderdale, 1982—, Moosart Gallery, Miami, Fla., 1984, Mus. Art, Fort Lauderdale, 1984, 87, 91, 95, Gilles Patrick Studio/Gallery, 1985, 86, Barbara Gillman Gallery, Miami, 1986, Main Libr., Miami, 1986, Palm Beach C.C., Lake Worth, Fla., 1993, Soc. Four Arts, Palm Beach, Fla., 1993, Broward C.C., Davie, Fla., 1996. Substitute tchr. sch. and workshops Cuyahoga County Bd. Mental Retardation, Cleve.; active swim program for spl. edn. students, West Shore YMCA, 1971-74; coord. vols. for George McGovern, Fairview Park, 1972; v.p. 23rd Dist. Caucus, Cleve., 1973; campaign chairperson Robert Weller for Ohio Senate, Cleve., 1973-74; bd. mem. Women's Polit. Caucus, Cleve., 1973-75; den mother Cub Scouts, 1979, asst. to den mother, 1980. Mem. Met. Mus. Art, Mus. Art Fort Lauderdale, Mus. Art Boca Raton. Democrat. Unitarian. Home: 325 NW 5th Ave Boca Raton FL 33432 Office: Art Inst Ft Lauderdale 1799 SE 17th St Fort Lauderdale FL 33316

GILLASPIE, LYNN CLARA, education educator, director clinical experience; b. Winchester, Ky., Oct. 23, 1953; d. Bramblette Francis and Annette (Faulconer) G. BS in Elem. Edn., U. Tenn., 1976, MS in Elem. Edn./Reading, 1979; EdD in Curriculum and Supervision, Vanderbilt U., 1993. Cert. elem. educator, reading, gifted educator, Ky., Tenn. Tchr. lang. arts Morristown (Tenn.) City Schs., 1976-78; tutor, grad. asst. U. Tenn., Knoxville, 1978-79; reading tchr., migrant math. tchr., adult basic educator Clark County Schs., Winchester, Ky., 1979-90; vis. instr., supr. student interns Eastern Ky. U., Richmond, 1990-91; teaching asst. Vanderbilt U., Nashville, 1991-93; assoc. prof., dir. clin. experiences U. North Ala., Florence, 1993—; cost ctr. head U. North Ala., Florence, 1993—, tchr. edn. coun. mem., 1993—, chair first yr. tchr. survey task force, 1993—. Co-author: University of North Alabama Teacher Education Handbook, 1994, Facilitating Reform: One Laboratory School's Collaborative Enterprise, 1994; author: University of North Alabama Student Internship Handbook, 1994; contbr. articles to profl. jours. Recipient Eliza Claybrooke Meml. scholarship Vanderbilt U., 1993. Mem. ASCD, Internat. Reading Assn., Am. Ednl. Rsch. Assn., Assn. Tchr. Educators, Am. Assn. Colls. for Tchr. Edn., Ala. Assn. Tchr. Educators (sec.-treas. 1995-96), Kiwanis, Phi Delta Kappa (v.p. U. North Ala. chpt. 1994-95), Alpha Upsilon Alpha, Kappa Delta Pi, Alpha Delta Kappa. Disciples of Christ. Office: U North Ala Box 5125 U North Alabama Florence AL 35632-0001

GILLEM, ELISE MARIE (ELISE MARIE MICHAELS), radio and television personality; b. Kalamazoo, Dec. 24, 1958; d. Kenneth James and Mary Louise (Lemon) Fleckenstein; m. Mark Thomas Gillem; children: Charles Cortez, Gracie Lee. Grad. high sch., Kalamazoo. Radio personality Sta. KTIL, Tillamook, Oreg., 1983-84; personality, news dir. Sta. KXIQ/KGRL, Bend, Oreg., 1984-88, Sta. KLRR/KBND, Bend, Oreg., 1988-94; promotion and pub. affairs dir. Sta. KTVZ-TV, Bend, Oreg., 1994—. Prodr. Living with Renal Failure, 1986 (hon. mention Oreg. AP); writer, host weekly TV show Your Next Home; creator, host, prodr. TV show The Earth Friendly Home; prodr., host Ctrl. Oreg. Today. Bend coord. Oreg. Donor Program Miracle Mile Walk. Home: 19115 Pumice Butte Rd Bend OR 97702-8948 Office: Sta KTVZ 62990 O B Riley Rd Bend OR 97701-9001

GILLEO, SANDRA V., elementary education educator; b. Somerville, N.J., May 8, 1944; d. Sam B. and Frances (Green) Hammer; m. Robert James Gilleo (div. Dec. 1981); children: Robert T.I., Felise V. BA, Trenton (N.J.) State Coll., 1967; MA, Newark State Coll., 1971. Cert. tchr., N.J., Pa. Tchr. elem. Franklin Twp. Sch. Dist., Quakertown, N.J., 1966-67, Bricktown (N.J.) Twp. Sch. Dist., 1967-69; reading specialist Lawrence Twp. Sch. Dist., Lawrenceville, N.J., 1969-72; elem. tchr. New Hope-Solebury (Pa.) Sch. Dist., 1972—. Libr. Village Libr. of Wrightstown, Pa., 1972—; vol. John B. Anderson presdl. campaing, Bucks County, Pa., 1980; mem. Second Monday adv. com. for women, Doylestown, Pa., 1982-894; tchr. Temple Judea of Bucks County, 1991; active James Michener Art Mus., Churchville Nature Ctr. With USNR, 1965-71. Mem. Franklin Twp. Edn. Assn., Brick Edn. Assn., Lawrenceville Edn. Assn., New Hope-Solebury Edn. Assn., Churchville Nature Ctr., Michener Art Mus. Jewish. Home: 2650 Windy Bush Rd Newtown PA 18940-3601 Office: New Hope-Solebury Elem Sch N Sugan Rd Solebury PA 18963-9998

GILLES, DOROTHY KATHLEEN, special education educator, arts/play therapist; b. Chgo., Nov. 12, 1936; d. John William and Margaret Kathleen (Schueller) Cordes; m. Peter Edmund Gilles, Oct. 6, 1956 (div. Aug. 1985); children: Peter Alan, John Harry, Mark David. BME, Northwestern U., 1971; MEd, Nat. Coll. Edn., 1972; PhD, St. Louis U., 1978. Diplomate Nat. Inst. Expressive Therapy; cert. reality therapist Inst. Reality Therapy; cert. expressive therapist. Spl. edn. educator Met. Sch., St. Louis, 1974-75; music tchr. Granite City (Ill.) Sch. Dist., 1976-77; univ. instr., asst. prof. So. Ill. U., Edwardsville, 1979-82; ednl. diagnostician, music tchr. Spl. Sch. Dist., St. Louis, 1983-85; spl. edn. tchr. L.A. Unified Sch. Dist., 1985-86; instr. Nat. U., San Diego, 1986-88; spl. edn. tchr. South Bay Union Sch. Dist., Imperial Beach, Calif., 1988, Francis Howell Sch. Dist., St. Charles, Mo., 1989—; arts therapist Opening Doors, Edwardsville, St. Charles, St. Louis, 1990—; program co-chair Very Spl. Arts Festival, So. Ill. U., Edwardsville, 1979, insvc. workshop leader, 1979-82, coord. acad. credit, chair evaluation com., 1982; invited spkr. 2d Internat. Symposium Music Edn. for Handicapped, 1981. Contbr. articles on music edn. for spl. children to profl. jours. including Outlook, Music Therapy Perspectives, Edn. for the Handicapped. Den mother Boy Scouts Am., Evanston, Ill., 1962; program chair PTO, Evanston, 1965; youth choir dir. Presbyn. ch., Edwardsville, 1973. Recipient Alumni Achievement award Nat. Coll. Edn., 1979. Mem. Nat. Expressive Therapy Assn., Nat. Guild Hypnotists (cert. hypnotherapist), St. Louis Psychol. Assn., Mental Health Assn. Greater St. Louis, Midwest Reality Therapy Assn., Profl. Women's Alliance, Sigma Alpha Iota (pres. 1962-64, Sword of Honor), Kappa Delta, Pi Kappa Lambda. Democrat. Religious Science. Home: 101 Surrey Ln Edwardsville IL 62025 Office: Met Counseling Ctr Ste 224 443 N New Ballas Rd Saint Louis MO 63141

GILLESPIE, DONNA FAY, novelist; b. Gainesville, Fla., July 21, 1948; d. Joe Gill and Orlene Fay (Cox) G. BA in Fine Art, U. Fla., 1970. Author: The Light Bearer, 1994.

GILLESPIE, HELEN DAVYS, marketing/industry consultant, writer; b. San Jose, Calif., Nov. 23, 1954; d. Robert Bruce and Helen Davys (Street) G.; m. Nigel George Haden, May 1, 1982 (div. June 1986). BA in English with honors, Calif. State U., Chico, 1976; postgrad. in English, U. Sheffield, Eng., 1976-77, Calif. State U., Chico, 1977-78. Cert. bus. communicator. Bus. analyst Dun & Bradstreet, San Jose, 1978-80; personal asst. Times Computer Svcs., London, 1980; adminstr. Exec. Aviation, Palo Alto, Calif., 1981; sr. writer/editor Tymnet/McDonnell Douglas, San Jose, 1982-86; mgr. sales support Pactel Spectrum Svcs., Walnut Creek, Calif., 1987; mgr. product communications Varian Assocs., Inc., Sunnyvale, Calif., 1987-90; mgr. mktg. communications Allergan Humphrey, San Leandro, Calif., 1990-91; owner Write Away Comm., San Jose, Calif., 1987—, Isographics Internat., 1994—; editor, pub. LIMS/Letter, 1995—, LIMSource web site, 1996—. Mem. Mus. Modern Art, San Jose. Mem. Bus. Mktg. Assn., Airline Owners and Pilots Assn., Writers Connection, Art Inst. Chgo., Mus. Soc. San Francisco, Commonwealth Club, Am. Soc. Quality Control.

GILLESPIE, JACQUELYN RANDALL, psychologist; b. Paris, France, Oct. 10, 1927; came to U.S., 1932; d. John Roberts and Hazel Maurine (Hammel) Hunter; m. Thomas Gilbert Gillespie, Apr. 27, 1947 (dec. May 1995); children: Thomas Randall, Catherine Claire Gillespie Laroche. AB, Calif. State U., Long Beach, 1959; MS, Calif. State U., Fullerton, 1965; PhD, Calif. Grad. Inst., L.A., 1977. Lic. psychologist, psychoanalytic psychotherapist, Calif. Guidance cons. Lowell Sch. Dist., Whittier, Calif., 1963-69; psychologist Fullerton (Calif.) High Sch., 1969-82; pvt. practice Orange, Calif., 1976-90; assoc. prof. Calif. Grad. Inst., L.A., 1978-90. Author: Projective Use of Mother-and-Child Drawings, 1994; co-author: (reading text) Diagnostic Analysis of Reading Errors, 1981; contbr. articles to profl. jours. Grantee State of Calif., 1979; rsch. award Calif. Assn. Sch. Psychologists, 1972. Mem. APA (assoc.), Calif. Assn. Lic. Ednl. Psychologists (pres. 1983). Episcopalian. Home: 421 Meadowlark Ln # A Naples FL 34105-2459

GILLESPIE, KAREN GLENA, trucking company dispatcher; b. Chgo., Feb. 2, 1946; d. Carl Marnius and Glena Belle (Garmon) Christiansen; m. Richard F. Gillespie, Mar. 11, 1967 (div. Dec. 1969). Scalemaster Howard Thomas Gravel Co., Paxton, Ill., 1967-70; constrn. truck driver various rd. bldg. cos., Champaign and DeKalb, Ill., 1970-74, Stahl Constrn. Co., DeKalb, 1974-88; scalemaster Elmer Larson, Inc., DeKalb, 1988-95, dispatcher, 1995—. Mem. various local bands, DeKalb, 1969-92. With USN, 1966. Home: 1642 Pershing Ave Rockford IL 61109

GILLESPIE, MARY KREMPA, psychologist, consultant; b. New Haven, Oct. 31, 1941; d. Albert Charles and Marye (Bemis) Krempa; m. J. Joseph Gillespie, Sept. 1, 1962 (div. 1979); children: Carolyn Gillespie Kottmeyer, James Joseph III (dec.). AA in Classical Music cum laude, Mount Aloysius Coll., 1961; BA in Psychology cum laude, Immaculata (Pa.) Coll., 1973; MA in Clin. Psychology, West Chester (Pa.) U., 1974; postgrad., Temple U., 1976-80; PhD in Social Psychology, Walden U., 1988. Lic. psychologist Pa. Dir. tng. Rape Crisis Coun., West Chester, Pa., 1974-77; exec. dir. Open Door Counseling Ctr., West Chester, 1975-77; therapist Temple U. Community Counseling Clin., Phila., 1977-78; doctoral intern Coatesville (Pa.) Vets. Hosp., 1978-79; sr. psychologist Delaware Valley Pscyhol. Svcs., Phila., 1979-81; dir. Substance Abuse Programs Resource Spectrum, Phila., 1980-81; psychologist 1810 Counseling Ctr., Phoenixville, Pa., 1983-85, Ambler (Pa.) Psychol. Svcs., 1980-83; clin. supr., profl. mentor Eaglesmere Psychology Assocs., Malvern, Pa., 1980—, dir., 1983—; mem. staff Eugenia Hosp., Lafayette Hills, Pa., 1988—; dir. tng. Rape Crisis Coun., West Chester, Pa., 1974-77; vocat. counselor Haverford (Pa.) State Hosp., 1975; rsch. cons. Mind's Eye Ednl. Sys., Wayne, Pa., 1989-92; corp. cons. in field, 1975—; clin. cons. Chester County Hosp., Occupational Health Ctr., 1988—, Children's Hosp. U. Pa., 1990—, The Reed Group, Rensselaer, N.Y., 1994—, Bus. Devel. and Tng. Ctr., Great Valley Ctr., Malvern, 1994—; occupational health psychologist Sterling-Winthrop Drugs, Collegeville, Pa., 1992—; expert witness in field; spkr. in field. Author: Outcome Study of an Innovative Paradoxical Treatment for Panic Attacks, 1988. Bd. dirs. Chester County Rape Crisis Coun., 1976-78; adminstr. U.S. Healthcare Managed Mental Health Care Capitation, 1979-90. Recipient Univ. fellowship Temple Univ., Phila., 1976-77. Fellow Pa. Psychol. Assn. (mem. legis. network 1980—), Phila. Coll. of Physicians; mem. APA (mem. legis. network 1980—), Am. Assn. Applied Psychophysiology and Biofeedback (cert. practitioner), Pa. Soc. Behavioral Medicine and Biofeedback, Am. Psychosomatic Soc., Prescribing Psychologists Register, Sierra Club (mem legis. network 1985—), Audubon Club (mem. legis. network 1985—), Phi Theta Kappa, Psi Chi. Home: RR 3 Box 2350 Malvern PA 19355-9803 Office: Eaglesmere Psychology Assoc 2350 Pheasant Hill Ln Malvern PA 19355-9712

GILLESPIE, PENNY HANNIG, business owner; b. Schenectady, N.Y., June 4, 1954; d. William Armand and Freda (Penney) H.; m. Kenneth Scofield Keyes, Jr., Sept. 2, 1984 (div. Aug. 1992). Student, U. Ariz., 1972-74. Cert. EMT, Ariz., N.Y.; completion in skills tng. for profls. in Hakomi psychotherapy, Oreg. Co-founder Ken Keyes Coll., Coos Bay, Ore., 1982-91; pvt. practice counseling Eugene, Ore., 1991-95; founder, pres. The Wellness Network, Eugene, Oreg., 1994—. Co-author: Gathering Power Through Insight and Love, 1986, Handbook to Higher Consciousness: The Workbook, 1989; editor: How to Enjoy Your Life in Spite of It All, 1980, The Hundredth Monkey, 1982, Your Heart's Desire, 1983, Your Life Is a Gift, 1987, Discovering the Secrets of Happiness, 1988, PlanetHood, 1988, The Power of Unconditional Love, 1990. Bd. dirs. Living Love Ch., 1980-91, sec., v.p.; founding bd. dirs., sec., sec.-treas., v.p. The Vision Foundation, Inc., 1982-91; founding bd. dirs., sec., sec.-treas. Cornucopia, The Living Love Ch. of Ky., 1982-91; vol. Victim Advocate Lane County Dist. Attys. Victim/Witness Svcs. Program, Oreg., 1993. Recipient peace award Coalition for Justice and Peace, Ariz. State U. and the Inst. Peace Edn., 1989; award as site mgr. for Anne Frank exhibit Jewish Fedn. Lane County, Ore., 1993. Home: PO Box 21942 Eugene OR 97402-0413

GILLESPIE, SUSAN JOAN, nurse, educator; b. Teaneck, N.J., June 4, 1958; d. Daniel J. and Edna J. (Stevenson) G. AAS, Bergen C.C., 1979; BSN, Dominican Coll., 1981; MPA, L.I. U., 1995. RN, N.J. Staff nurse emergency rm., pediatrics, nursery, maternity Barnert Meml. Hosp., Paterson, N.J., 1979-85; staff nurse hemodialysis Holy Name Hosp., Teaneck, 1985-86, insvc. edn. coord., 1986-90; coord. insvc. edn. Palisades Med. Ctr., North Bergen, N.J., 1990—, relief adminstrv. supr., 1992—. Mem. Sigma Phi Omega, Phi Alpha Alpha. Home: 380 Knickerbocker Rd 1C Dumont NJ 07628

GILLETT, MARY CAPERTON, military historian; b. Richmond, Va., Apr. 28, 1929; d. Lewis Hopkins and Mary Caperton (Horsley) Renshaw; m. Richard Clark Gillett, June 7, 1949; children: Richard Clark Jr., Glenn Douglas, Mary Caperton, Priscilla Elizabeth, Blakeney Diana. Student,

Wellesley Coll., 1946-49; BA, Am. U., 1966, MA, 1971, PhD, 1978. Historian U.S. Navy Dept., Washington, 1966-69, U.S. Dept. Army, Washington, 1972—. Author: The Army Medical Department, 1775-1818, 1981, The Army Medical Department, 1818-1865, 1988, The Army Medical Department, 1865-1917, 1995; contbr. articles to profl. jours. Mem. Am. Assn. for History of Medicine, Am. Hist. Assn., Western Hist. Assn., The Westerners.

GILLETTE, ETHEL MORROW, columnist; b. Oelwein, Iowa, Nov. 27, 1921; d. Charles Henry and Myrne Sarah (Law) Morrow; student Coe Coll., 1939-41; BA, Upper Iowa U., 1959; MA, Western State Coll., 1969; m. Roman A. Gillette, May 6, 1944 (dec. 1992); children: Melody Ann, Richard Allan, William Robert (dec. 1993). Stenographer, Penick & Ford, Cedar Rapids, Iowa, 1941-43, FBI, Washington, 1943-44; tchr. Fayette (Iowa) High Sch., 1959-60, Jordan Jr. High Sch., Mpls., 1960-64, Montrose (Colo.) High Sch., 1964-68; family living, religion editor The News-Record, Gillette, Wyo., 1977-79, columnist Distaff Side, 1979-84. Mem. Western Writers Am., WestWind Writers/NMA (pres. 1994), Nat. Writers Club. Contbr. articles to various mags. Home: 1804 Locust Rd Montrose CO 81401-5825

GILLETTE, MARCIA DRUCKER, marketing executive; b. San Mateo, Calif., July 11, 1954; d. Arnold Plaine and Regina Jeanette (Segall) Drucker; m. David Allan Gillette, Aug. 1, 1976. BA in Comms., Wash. State U., 1975; MS in Info. Sys. Tech., George Washington U., 1989. Broadcast traffic coord. KCBS Newsradio, San Francisco, 1975-77; advt. traffic coord. The Gap Stores, Inc., San Bruno, Calif., 1977-79; video dir. Indsl. Tng. Corp., Herndon, Va., 1980-81; software program coord. GE, Arlington, Va., 1981-84; v.p., analyst Sigma Sys., Inc., Falls Church, Va., 1984-91; dir. tech. comms. TV Answer, Inc., Reston, Va., 1991-93; ind. writer MDG Comms., Alexandria, Va., 1994; mgr. affiliates programs Versatility, Inc. (formerly NPRI, Inc.), Fairfax, Va., 1995—; freelance video prodr. WETA-TV, Arlington, 1982-88. Editor newsletter The Spark, 1990-94; contbr. articles to mags. and profl. publs. Mem. Assn. Women in Comms. (futures task force 1995—, pres. Washington chpt. 1995-96, chair N.E. regional conf. 1994-95), Am. Women in Radio and TV, Soc. Tech. Comms., MG Car Club (bd. dirs. Washington chpt. 1981-94). Office: Versatility Inc Ste 600 11781 Lee Jackson Meml Hwy Fairfax VA 22033

GILLETTE-BAUMANN, MURIEL DELPHINE, nurse; b. Pasadena, Calif., Nov. 10, 1945; d. Edwin and Jean Helen (Fremont) Gillette; m. Larry Houston Potter, Dec. 31, 1971 (dec. 1979); children: Melissa Darlene Genevieve Potter Stephens, Bryan Scott; m. Robert George Baumann Jr., Aug. 18, 1980; 1 child, Robert George III. Student, Western Coll. for Women, Oxford, Ohio, 1963-65; BSN, UCLA, 1968; M of Nursing, Oreg. Health Scis. U., 1991. Sch. nurse, health tchr. Hawthorne (Calif.) Intermediate Sch., 1969-70; nurse St. John's Hosp., Santa Monica, Calif., 1969-71; camp nurse L.A. Girl Scout Coun., 1969-71; nurse UCLA Med. Ctr., 1967-70; ICU/CCU/pediatrics nurse Mercy Med. Ctr., Roseburg, Oreg., 1971-79; nurse Umpqua Valley Community Hosp., Myrtle Creek, Oreg., 1981-91; health edn. dir. City of Myrtle Creek, 1986-91; nurse practitioner Umpgua Nat. Forest, Roseburg and Glide, Oreg., 1991-93; camp nurse, health coord. Oreg. Trail Boy Scout Coun., Roseburg, 1991—, Western Rivers Girl Scout Coun., Roseburg, 1984-90. Musician quartet, orch., soloist; artist in oils; poet. Bd. dirs. River 'N Dell Day Care Ctr., Myrtle Creek, 1983-85; trustee Augusta Bixler Farms, Inc., Stockton, Calif., 1976—; mem. Douglas County Cancer Screening Com. Capt. USAF, 1970-89. Umpqua Valley Hosp. Aux. scholar, 1989; L.A. Watercolor Soc. traveling art collection award, 1963. Mem. UCLA Alumni Assn., Umpqua Valley Hosp. Aux., Oreg. Health Sci. U. Alumni Assn., OES, Delta Zeta. Republican. Presbyterian. Home: PO Box 668 Myrtle Creek OR 97457-0104

GILLEY, ELIZABETH A., lawyer; b. Boston, Aug. 23, 1960. BA, George Washington U., 1983, JD with honors, 1986. Bar: Ga. 1986, U.S. Dist. Ct. (no. dist.) Ga. 1986, U.S. Ct. Appeals (11th cir.) 1986. Ptnr. Alston & Bird, Atlanta. With U.S. Army, 1978-81. Mem. State Bar Ga. (environmental law sect.), Atlanta Bar Assn. (chmn. continuing legal edn. com. 1991-92, environmental law sect.). Office: Alston & Bird 1 Atlantic Ctr 1201 W Peachtree St Atlanta GA 30309-3424*

GILLIAM, MARY, travel executive; b. Pampa, Tex., Apr. 18, 1928; d. Roy and Hylda O. (Bertrand) Brown; divorced; 1 child, Terry K. AA, Amarillo (Tex.) Bus. Coll., 1949. Flight attendant Braniff Internat. Airways, Dallas, 1950-53; from reservation agt. to mgr. passenger sales Trans-World Airlines, various locations, 1953-81; exec. v.p. Lakewood (Colo.) Travel, 1981; mgmt. cons. Bank One Travel, Columbus, Ohio, 1981-82; pres. Icaria Travel, Inc., Tucson, Ariz., 1986—, Intensive Trainers Inst., Tucson, 1983-92. Mem. Ariz. Rep. Com., 1978—. Recipient Award of Excellence Trans-World Airlines, N.Y.C., 1972, Pres.' Hall of Fame award, 1973. Mem. Am. Soc. Travel Agts. (Industry Svc. award 1980), Inst. Cert. Travel Agts., Ariz. Travel Agts. Assn. Republican. Methodist. Office: Icaria Travel Inc 616 Rio San Pedro Green Valley AZ 85614

GILLIAM, PAULA HUTTER, transportation company executive; b. N.Y.C.; d. Irving and Edna Phyllis (Manes) Hutter; m. Stanley Spencer Rolnick (div.); children: Jeffry Hutter Gilliam, Pamela Sara Bielory; m. Peter Gilliam, 1981. AA, Centenary Coll., 1961. Pres. Paula Rolnick Sales, N.Y.C., 1970-74; mdse. mgr. Kirby Block Internat., N.Y.C., 1974-78; pres. P.M.G. Internat. Ltd, N.Y.C., 1981—; v.p. Rical Air Express, Inc., N.Y.C., Rical Ocean Forwarding, N.Y.C.; ptnr. The Golden Unicorn Restaurant; mem. adv. bd. for internat. bus. Fashion Inst. Tech., 1991—. Producer (Broadway show) Stardust, 1987; exec. producer (plays) Long Days Journey Into the Night, 1988, Ah Wilderness. V.p. Murray Hill Com., N.Y.C., 1982—, chmn. block party, 1983-92, bd. dirs and sec. house owners com.; bd. advisors 132 E 35th St., N.Y.C., 1984-86; vol. aide June Eisland Coun. Women, Riverdale, N.Y., 1979—; bd. dirs. Theater Off Park, 1983-88, Black Goat Entertainment and Enlightenment, 1994. Mem. Women in Internat. Trade (bd. dirs. 1991-96), Women's Traffic Club, Met. Traffic Club. Democrat. Home and Office: 132 E 35th St New York NY 10016-3892

GILLIARD, JUDY ANN, speaker, writer, broadcasting station executive; b. Ventura, Calif., Aug. 21, 1946; d. Sam Albert and Betty (Hardacre) G. A in Hotel and Restaurant Mgmt., Santa Barbara (Calif.) Community Coll., 1974. Calif. teaching credential. Supr. dining room Santa Barbara Biltmore, 1972-73; supr. food service, instr. dining room ops. Santa Barbara Community Coll., 1972-73; cons. J. Gilliard & Co., Santa Barbara, 1973-74; exec. mgr. Head of the Wolf Restaurant, Palm Springs, Calif., 1974-76; salesperson Indio (Calif.) Daily News, 1976-77; sales cons. Jurgensons Restaurant, Palm Springs, 1977-79; account exec. Sta. KPSI-FM, Palm Springs, 1978-84, gen. sales mgr., 1984-88, v.p., gen. mgr., 1988-92; owner, pres. JAG & Co., 1992—. Co-author: The Guiltless Gourmet, 1983, The Guiltless Gourmet Goes Ethnic, 1990, European Cuisine from the Guiltless Gourmet, 1991, Beyond Alfalfa Sprouts and Cheese, 1993; author: The Flavor Secret, 1994. Mem. Am. Heart Assn. (bd. dirs.), Nat. Spkrs. Assn., Palm Spring C. of C. (bd. dirs.), Desert Advt. Club (bd. dirs.), Am. Inst. Food and Wine, Internat. Food, Travel and Writers Assn., Internat. Assn. Cooking Profls. Home: 876 Calle de Mimosa Palm Springs CA 92262-6112

GILLICE, SONDRA JUPIN (MRS. GARDNER RUSSELL BROWN), sales and marketing executive; b. Urbana, Ill.; d. Earl Cranston and Laura Lorraine (Rose) Jupin; m. Gardner Russell Brown, Jan. 12, 1980; 1 child, Thomas Alan Gillice. BS, Lindenwood Coll.; MBA, Loyola Coll. Pers. officer N.Y. Citibank, 1968-70, 1st Nat. Bank of Chgo., 1970-72; mgr. human resources Potomac Electric Power Co., Washington, 1973-81; dir. pers. U.S. Synthetic Fuels Corp., Washington, 1981-86, v.p. human resources, Guest Svcs., Inc., 1987-90; v.p. sales and mktg., 1990-93; pres. Rus Son, Inc., 1994—; sr. v.p. govt. rels. Drake Beam Morin, Inc., 1994—. Mem. bd. govs. Loyola Coll., Nat. Coal Coun., mem. exec. com.; mem. nat. bd. Med. Coll. Pa.; bd. dirs. Restaurant Assn. Met. Washington, 1991-94, Nat. Women's Econ. Alliance. Mem. AAUW (pres. Falls Church br. 1976-78), Edison Electric Inst. (chmn. tng. and mgmt. devel. com.), Am. Soc. Pers. Adminstrs., Greater Met. Washington Bd. Trade, Soroptimists (pres. Washington chpt. 1979-80), DAR, Army Navy Country Club, Soc. Magna Charta Dames, Edgartown Yacht Club, Georgetown Club. Republican.

GILLICK, BETSY BRINKLEY, financial analyst; b. Richmond, Va., May 11, 1959; d. Martha Lou (Caplinger) B. BBA, James Madison U., 1981, MBA, 1983. Procurement analyst Calculon Corp., Germantown, Md., 1983-85; agt. purchasing, subcontracts ORI/Calculon Corp., Rockville, Md., 1986-87; adminstr. contracts ORI/Calculon Corp., Rockville, 1987-89; sr. contracts adminstr. ARC Profl. Svcs. Group subs. ORI/Calculon Corp, Rockville, 1989-90, sr. fin. analyst, 1990-93; sr. fin. and contracts analyst Otsuka Am. Pharm. Inc., Rockville 1993-94, fin. and contracts mgr., 1994-96; R & D bus. mgr., 1996—. Mem. Nat. Contract Mgmt. Assn. Democrat. Presbyterian. Home: 18420 Cape Jasmine Way Gaithersburg MD 20879-4644 Office: Otsuka Am Pharm Inc 2440 Research Blvd Rockville MD 20850-3238

GILLIE, MICHELLE FRANCOISE, industrial hygienist; b. Phila., Oct. 24, 1956; d. Marino and Marcelle Jeannine (Boyer) Lazarich; m. Alan Deane Gillie, May 22, 1982; children: Patrick Alan, Caroline Elizabeth. BS, Pa. State U., 1977; MS, Drexel U., 1981. Diplomate Am. Bd. Indsl. Hygiene. Clin. chemist Pa. Hosp., Phila., 1976-80; indsl. hygienist Stewart-Todd Assocs., Wayne, Pa., 1981-82, S.W. Occupational Health Svcs., Houston, 1982-84; clin. toxicologist Smith-Kline-Beckman Labs., Houston, 1984-85; sr. indsl. hygienist Am. Analytical Labs., Akron, Ohio, 1985-88; indsl. hygiene cons. AMP Technical Svcs., Cleve., 1988-91; sr. indsl. hygienist Environ. Mgmt., Inc., Anchorage, 1991-92; indsl. hygiene cons. AMP Tech. Svcs., Bakersfield, Calif., 1992-94; health and safety mgr. Brown & Root Environ., Wayne, Pa., 1994—. Mem. Am. Indsl. Hygiene Assn. (pub. rels. com. chair Midnight Sun chpt. 1991-92). Home: 711 E Boot Rd West Chester PA 19380-1229

GILLIGAN, SANDRA KAYE, private school director; b. Ft. Lewis, Wash., Mar. 22, 1946; d. Jack G. and O. Ruth (Mitchell) Wagoner; m. James J. Gilligan, June 3, 1972; 1 child, J. Shawn Gilligan. BS in Edn., Emporia State U., 1968, MS in Psychology, 1971; postgrad., Drake U., 1976, U. Mo., St. Louis, 1977-79. Tchr. Parklane Elem. Sch., Aurora, Colo., 1968-69, Bonner Springs (Kans.) Elem., 1970; stewardess Frontier Airlines, Denver, 1969; grad. teaching asst. Emporia (Kans.) State U., 1970-71; lead tchr. Western Valley Youth Ranch, Buckeye, Ariz., 1971-74; staff mem. program devel., lead tchr. The New Found., Phoenix, Ariz., 1974; ednl. therapist Orchard Pl., Des Moines, 1974-76; ednl. cons. Spl. Sch. Dist. of St. Louis County, 1976-79; founding dir. The Churchill Sch., St. Louis, 1979—; instr. Webster Coll., Webster Groves, Mo., 1978-80; adj. prof. Maryville Coll., St. Louis, summer 1985; mem. profl. adv. bd. Learning Disabilities Assn., St. Louis Learning Disabilities Assn.; keynote speaker Miss. Learning Disabilities Assn. Conv., 1991; site visitor blue ribbon schs. program U.S. Dept. Edn., 1992; cert. trainer Human Potential Seminars; presenter in field; bd. dirs. St. Louis Confederation Ind. Schs. Active St. Louis Jr. League. Mem. Learning Disabilities Assn., Orton Dyslexia Soc. Home: 14721 Greenleaf Valley Dr Chesterfield MO 63017-5514 Office: The Churchill Sch 1035 Price School Ln Saint Louis MO 63124-1533

GILLILAND, M. SHANNON, museum director; b. Chgo., Jan. 11, 1948; d. Robert Franklin and Clarisse L. (Weeks) O'Keefe; m. Greg Allan Gilliland, Feb. 9, 1969; children: Deborah Jean Gilliland Schmidt, Mary Catherine. AS in Biology and Chemistry, Amarillo Coll., 1968; postgrad., Wet Tex. State U., 1968, U. Houston, 1968-69, U. San Diego, 1973-75. Dir. Longview (Tex.) Art Mus., 1993—. Trustee Lucille P. Weeks, 1980—, Megaan M. Poindexter Trust, 1990—; cub den leader Boy Scouts Am., 1968-69; libr. vol. St. Marys Sch., Longview; bulletin writer, editor, reception coord., CCD tchr. St. Marys Ch., Longview; chair, edn. coord., preparator, curator, sec., bd. dirs. Longview Art Mus.; bd. trustees, sec., 1st v.p., pres. Southside DayCare Ctr.; active Girl Scouts Am.; pres. St. Marys and St. Anthony Parishes Ladys Guild. Mem. Greenbriar Garden Club (pres., 1st v.p., 2d v.p., sec.-treas.). Roman Catholic. Home: 616 Cynthia Dr Longview TX 75601 Office: Longview Art Mus 102 W College Longview TX 75601

GILLILAND, MARCIA ANN, nurse clinician, infection control specialist; b. Kansas City, Mo., Sept. 15, 1949; d. Robert Joseph and Mary Agnes (Paup) Caton; m. John Lee Gilliland, Mar. 28, 1974 (dec. Oct. 1983); children: Marcella Lyn, John Patrick, Devon Marie. ADN, Kansas City C.C., 1979; BSN, Webster U., 1990. RN, Kans. Staff nurse U. Kans. Med. Ctr., Kansas City, 1979-84, infection control coord., 1984—, facilitator HIV/AIDS wellness group, 1991—; community health nurse Cath. Charities, Kansas City, 1980-82; pres., owner Kansas City Total Image, Overland Park, Kans., 1981-83. Active Rep. Committeewoman, Overland Park, Kans., 1994; Rep. candidate Overland Park City Coun., Kans., 1995. Mem. Nat. Speakers Assn., Assn. Profls. in Infection Control and Epidemiology (pres. Kansas City chpt., 1993-94), Assn. Nurses in AIDS Care. Republican. Home: 9430 Riggs St Overland Park KS 66212-1443 Office: U Kans Med Ctr 3901 Rainbow Blvd Kansas City KS 66160-0001

GILLILAND, MARION CHARLOTTE S., volunteer; b. Duluth, Minn., Dec. 29, 1918; d. John Oscar and Jenny Olympia (Wangberg) Spjut; m. Charles Herbert Gilliland, Mar. 6, 1942; children: Charles Herbert Jr., Marion Charlotte Jr., Patricia Ann, Norman Paul, Cynthia Eileen. BA in Anthropology with honors, U. Fla., 1963, MA in Anthropology, 1965. Author: The Material Culture of Key Marco, Florida, 1976, Key Marco's Buried Treasure, 1989, Dearest Daught and Popsy Wells; Two Artists named Sawyer, 1995, The Calusa Indians of Florida, 1995; contbr. articles to newspapers and profl. jours. Pres. Alachua County (Fla.) Childrens Com., 1959-61, Alachua County Scholarship and Loan Fund, 1960-62, Gainesville (Fla.) Womens Forum 1993-94; v.p. govtl. rels. div. Gainesville C. of C., 1977-79; health com. Human Svcs. Planning Coun., Gainesville, 1980-84; bd. dirs. Fla. Arts Celebration, Gainesville, 1984-91; sec. Friends of Music U. Fla., 1994—, pres., 1990-92; pres. Gainesville Women's Forum, 1993-94. Recipient Peggy Wilcox Svc. award State of Fla., 1985, Woman of Distinction award Santa Fe C.C., 1993, Women Who Make a Difference award Girl Scouts U.S., 1996. Mem. Fla. Med. Assn. Aux. (pres. 1969-70, bd. dirs. 1970-73), AMA Aux. (sec. 1975-76, v.p. so. regional 1976-78, historian 1978-79), Alachua County Med. Aux. (pres. 1960-61), So. Anthorpol. Soc., Fla. Anthropol. Soc., Archael. Inst. Am., Nat. Assn. Underwater Investigators, Fla. Mus. Assocs., Fla. Women's Alliance (charter mem.), Mortar Bd. (hon.), Phi Kappa Phi. Home: 3031 SW 70th Ln Gainesville FL 32608-5216

GILLILAND, MARY MARGARETT, healthcare consultant; b. Leland, Miss., Dec. 23, 1942; d. Lindon Edward and Allie Earlene (Saulters) Palmore; m. Carl Ralph Gilliland, Jan. 12, 1963; children: Carl Ralph, Gini Lynn. Diploma in Nursing, Greenwood Leflore, 1963; B of Healthcare Adminstrn., East Tex. State U., 1976; M of Human Rels. and Mgmt., Abilene Christian U., 1978; BS, Tex. Woman's U., 1991, MS, 1993. RN, Tex. Staff nurse Sunflower County Health Dept., Indianola, Miss., 1965-66; asst. dir. nursing Presbyn. Hosp. Dallas, 1966-80, assoc. dir. nursing, 1980-87, assoc. exec. dir., 1987-91; healthcare cons. G&S Healthcare Cons., Allen, Tex., 1991—; adj. faculty Tex. Woman's U., Denton. Contbr. articles to profl. jours. Mem. ANA, Am. Orgn. Nurse Execs., Tex. Orgn. Nurse Execs., Tex. Nurses Assn. (continuing edn. com, Great 100 Nurses 1991), Nurses Alumni Assn. (sec.) Sigma Theta Tau, Phi Kappa Phi. Home: 2101 Rigsbee Dr Plano TX 75074-4913 Office: G&S Healthcare Cons Raceway Profl Bldg I 200 Boyd Pl Allen TX 75002-2560

GILLILAND, TERRI KIRBY, accountant; b. Tuscaloosa, Ala., Oct. 4, 1954; d. William Park and Bobbie (Fitts) Kirby; m. Glenn Scott Gilliland, Aug. 31, 1991; 1 child, Joshua Scott. BS in Commerce and Bus. Adminstrn., U. Ala., Tuscaloosa, 1977. CPA, Ala. Staff acct. Yeager & Christian CPAs, Tuscaloosa, 1979-84; chief acct. HealthSouth Rehab. Corporation, Birmingham, Ala., 1984-86; sr. acct. DeWitt & DeWitt CPAs, Tuscaloosa, 1986-93; acct. II-tax Hunt Refining Co., Tuscaloosa, 1993—; mem. regional adv. com. U.S. Small Bus. Adminstrn., Birmingham, 1991-93. Participant Leadership Tuscaloosa, 1988-89. Mem. AICPA, Am. Soc. Women Accts. (treas. West Ala. chpt. 1991-92, sec. 1992-93), Ala. Soc. CPAs, Inst. Mgmt. Accts. (acquisition dir.). Baptist. Home: 3015 1st Ct Tuscaloosa AL 35405-2201 Office: Hunt Refining Co PO Box 038995 Tuscaloosa AL 35403-8995

GILLIOM, JUDITH CARR, government official; b. Indpls., May 19, 1943; d. Elbert Raymond and Marjorie Lucille (Carr) G. B.A., Northwestern U., 1964; M.A., U. Pa., 1966. Feature writer, asst. women's editor Indpls. News, summers 1961-63; research asst. cultural anthropology Northwestern U., 1963-64, asst. instr. freshman English, 1964; editorial asst. to dir. div. cardiology Phila. Gen. Hosp., 1965-67; asst. to ophthalmologist-in-chief Wills Eye Hosp., Phila., 1967-69; editor, writer Nat. Assn. Hearing and Speech Agencies, Washington, 1969-70; free-lance speech writer White House Conf. Children and Youth, 1969-70; free-lance editor, writer, abstractor, 1971-78; free-lance speechwriter President's Com. Mental Retardation, 1971-78; dir. publs. Nat. Assn. Hearing and Speech Action, Silver Spring, Md., 1972-74; dir. communications Nat. Assn. Hearing and Speech Action, 1975-77; editor Hearing & Speech Action mag., 1969-70, 72-77; program mgr. Interagy. Com. on Handicapped Employees, 1978, dep. exec. sec., 1979-83; mgr. disability program Dept. Def., 1983—; cons. U.S. Archtl. and Transp. Barriers Compliance Bd., 1976-77, Office Ind. Living for Disabled, HUD, 1977-78, Office for Handicapped Individuals, HEW, 1978, Women's com. Pres.'s Com. Employment Handicapped, 1985-86. Mem. Nat. Spinal Cord Injury Assn., 1970-90, editor, pub. conv. jour., 1974-82, bd. dirs. D.C. chpt., 1975-81, 89-90, nat. trustee, 1975-81, nat. bd. dirs., 1978-79; bd. dirs. Nat. Ctr. for a Barrier-Free Environment, 1979-84, v.p., 1980-81, pres., 1981-82; nat. bd. dirs., treas. League Disabled Voters, 1980-85; local bd. dirs. Easter Seal Soc. Disabled Children and Adults, 1985-90; active Montgomery County Commn. on Poeple with Disabilities, 1989-95; mem. Taxicab Svcs. Adv. Com., 1995—. Woodrow Wilson fellow, 1965. Mem. Phi Beta Kappa, Delta Delta Delta. Home: 901 Arcola Ave Silver Spring MD 20902-3401 Office: Dept Def The Pentagon Rm 3A272 Washington DC 20301-4000

GILLISPIE-FRIEDMAN, VIRGINIA C., poet, writer, nurse; b. Chgo., Mar. 28, 1966; d. Judith Irene Friedman. Student, Smith Coll., Northampton, Mass., 1984-86; BA, U. Calif., Santa Cruz, 1990; postgrad. Sch. Nursing, U. Colo., 1994. Poet, writer short fiction Denver, 1980—. Contbr. poetry and fiction to various publs. Active PBS, Colo. Women's Lobby, Sta. KUVO, Denver. Recipient Editor's Choice award Nat. Libr. Poetry, Owing Mills, Md., 1995, 96, 3rd pl. award, 1996, 1st pl. award Lavender Life Mag., N.Y., 1996. Mem. Nat. Gerontol. Nurses Assn., Smith Coll. Alumnae Assn., U. Calif. Alumnae Assn. Democrat. Jewish.

GILLMAN, GRETA JOANNE, physician; b. Montreal, Quebec, Can., Aug. 18, 1945; d. Hyman and Fanny (Izenberg) G.; m. Vic Bhoopat, Oct. 17, 1970; children: Lisa, Mitchell. MD, U. Calif., Irvine, 1969. Physician specialist L.A. County Hosp., 1973—; asst. clin. prof. UCLA, 1976—. Home: 13492 Grinnell Cir Westminster CA 92683-1734 Office: LA County Hosp 10005 Flower St Bellflower CA 90706-5412

GILLMOR, HELEN W., federal judge; b. 1942. BA, Queen's Coll. of CUNY, 1965; LLB magna cum laude, Boston Univ. Sch. of Law, 1968. With Ropes & Gray, Boston, 1968-69, Law Offices of Alexander R. Gillmor, Camden, Maine, 1970, Torkildson, Katz, Jossem, Fonseca, Jaffe, Moore & Hetherington, Honolulu, 1971-72; law clk. to Chief Justice William S. Richardson Hawaii State Supreme Ct., 1972; dep. pub. defender Honolulu, 1972-74; district court judge Family Ct., 1st circuit, State of Hawaii, 1977-83, Dist. Ct., 1st circuit, 1983-85; with Gillmor & Gillmor, Honolulu, 1985-94; district judge U.S. Dist. Ct. Hawaii, 9th circuit, 1994—; counsel El Paso Real Estate Investment Trust, El Paso, 1969; lectr. U.S. Agy. for Internat. Devel., Seoul, South Korea, 1969-70, Univ. of Hawaii, 1975. Office: Prince J K Kuhio Fed Bldg Box 50128 300 Ala Moana Blvd Rm C-414 Honolulu HI 96850

GILLMOR, KAREN LAKO, state legislator, strategic planner; b. Cleve., Jan. 29, 1948; d. William M. and Charlotte (Sheldon) Lako; m. Paul E. Gillmor, Dec. 10, 1983; children: Linda D., Julie E., Paul M. BA cum laude, Mich. State U., 1969; MA, Ohio State U., 1970, PhD, 1981. Asst. to v.p. Ohio State U., Columbus, 1972-77, spl. asst. dean law, 1979-81; asst. to pres. Ind. Cen. U., Indpls., 1977-78; rsch. asst. Burke Mktg. Rsch., Indpls., 1978-79; v.p. pub. affairs Huntington Nat. Bank, Columbus, 1981-82; fin. cons. Ohio Rep. Fin. Com., Columbus, 1982-83; chief mgmt. planning and rsch. Indsl. Commn. Ohio, Columbus, 1983-86; mgr. physician rels. Univ. Hosps., Columbus, 1987-91; cons. U.S. Sec. Labor, Washington, 1990-91; mem. Regional Bd. Rev., Industrial Commn., Ohio, 1991-92; assoc. dir. Ctr. Healthcare Policy and Rsch. Ohio State U., 1991-92; mem. Ohio General Assembly, 1993—; legis. liaison Huntington Bancshares, Ohio, Ohio State U., Columbus. Grantee Andrew W. Mellon Found. 1978, Carnegie Corp. 1978; named Outstanding Freshman Ohio Legislator, Ohio, 1994, Bulldog of the Treasury; recipient Pres. award Ohio State Chiropractic Assn., 1994, Pub. Svc. award Am. Heart Assn., 1995, Nat. Freshman Legislator of Yr., 1995. Mem. Women in Mainstream, Women's Roundtable, Ohio Fedn. Rep. Women, Am. Assn. Higher Edn., Coun. Advancement and Support Edn., DAR, Phi Delta Kappa. Methodist. Clubs: University (Columbus). Office: The Statehouse Columbus OH 43215-4276

GILLMOR, ROGENE GODDING, medical technologist; b. El Dorado, Kans., Jan. 25, 1939; d. Marc Antone and Verda May (Bogue) Godding; m. Charles Stewart Gillmor Jr., Nov. 28, 1964; children: Charles Stewart III, Alison Bogue. AA in Liberal Arts, Cottey Coll., 1958; BA in Biology, Stanford U., 1960; postgrad., Wesleyan U., U. Hartford, Foothills Coll. Rsch. asst. genetics Joshua Lederberg lab. Stanford U., 1960-62; assoc. scientist space biology/medicine Lockheed Missiles & Space Co., Palo Alto, Calif., 1962-64; rsch. asst. biology Princeton (N.J.) U., 1965-66, Wesleyan U., Middletown, Conn., 1967-69; lab. technician immunochemistry Hartford (Conn.) Hosp., 1978-84, instr. immunology clin. lab. edn. program, 1985-89, lab. supr. proteins/immunology dept. pathology and lab. medicine, 1986—; rschr. various labs, France and Switzerland, 1984-85. Contbr. articles to profl. jours. Leader Girl Scouts U.S., 1977-85; trustee, deacon Higganum (Conn.) Congl. Ch., 1980—. Recipient Achievement award Girl Scouts U.S., 1985. Mem. Am. Assn. Clin. Chemistry, Am. Soc. Clin. Pathologists (cert. immunology specialist), Am. Soc. Clin. Lab. Sci., Wesleyan Potters (pres. 1982-84), Haddam, Conn. Hist. Soc. (sec. 1970-72), PEO Sisterhood. Home: 29 Spencer Rd Higganum CT 06441-4034 Office: Hartford Hosp Dept Pathology & Lab Medicine 80 Seymour St Hartford CT 06102

GILLOOLY, EDNA RAE See **BURSTYN, ELLEN**

GILMAN, KAREN FRENZEL, legal assistant; b. Syracuse, N.Y., Jan. 11, 1947; d. Charles Henry and Cora Adell (Haith) Frenzel; m. Lawrence Sanford Gilman, June 5, 1970 (div. Feb. 9, 1977). AAS in Horticulture, SUNY, Morrisville, 1967; BS, Cornell U., 1969, MS in Floriculture and Ornamental Hort., 1971; attended, Syracuse Univ. Coll., 1983. Cert. legal asst. Floral designer Fortino of Fayetteville (N.Y.), 1965-69, 76-79, 81-84, Fallon's Florist, Raleigh, N.C., 1973-74; salesperson Finley Fine Jewelry, N.Y.C., 1979-80; legal asst. Agway, Inc., Dewitt, N.Y., 1984; legal asst. gen. legal Carrier Corp., Syracuse, N.Y., 1984-91, legal asst. intellectual property, 1992—; mem. adv. bd. legal asst. program Syracuse U. Coll., 1986-90. Contbr. articles to profl. jours. Henry Strong Denison fellow, 1969. Mem. Pi Alpha Xi, Phi Theta Kappa. Office: Carrier Corp PO Box 4800 Carrier Pkwy Syracuse NY 13221

GILMER, N. JENNIFER, management consultant; b. Atlanta; d. William Swift Jr. and Nancy Elizabeth (Williams) G. BBA, U. Ga., 1989, MBA, 1991. Cert. mgmt. cons. Computer support Coll. Bus. U. Ga., Athens, 1986-88; mktg. support IBM, Atlanta, 1988-90; sr. mgr. Deloitte & Touche Consulting Group, Atlanta, 1991—. Mem. Inst. Mgmt. Cons. (treas. Atlanta chpt. 1995—). Office: Deloitte & Touche Consulting Group Ste 2000 285 Peachtree Ctr Ave Atlanta GA 30303

GILMORE, CATHERINE RYE, arts administrator; b. Birmingham, Ala., Mar. 7, 1947; d. Thomas Aloyisius and Eva Catherine (Hydinger) Crawford; m. James William Rye, May 25, 1968 (div.); children: James William III, Susan Crawford Rye; m. Victor Alan Gilmore, May 23, 1986. BA in Theatre, Birmingham So. U., 1968; postgrad., U. Ala., Birmingham. Actress profl. cabaret theatre Atlanta and Birmingham, 1970-80; talk show host WBMG-TV, Birmingham, 1980-82; exec. dir. Met. Arts Coun., Birmingham, 1996—; instr. U. Ala., Birmingham, 1979-80. Stage appearances include Peter Pan, 1974, Sweet Charity, 1975, Wit's Other End Cabaret Theatre, 1976-80. Mem. The Women's Network, Birmingham; leadership class Birmingham C. of C., 1989. Recipient Silver Bowl award Festival of Arts, Birmingham, 1989, Obelisk award Arts Cmty., Birmingham, 1978; named one of Top 10 Corporate Women in Birmingham, 1996. Episcopalian. Office: Metropolitan Arts Council 2001 Park Place North Birmingham AL 35203

GILMORE, JUNE ELLEN, psychologist; b. Middletown, Ohio, Oct. 22, 1927; d. Linley Lawrence and Elizabeth Kathleen (Barker) Wetzel; m. John Lester Gilmore, July 6, 1945; children: John Lester Jr., Michael Edward. BS, Miami U., Oxford, 1961; MS, Miami U., 1964. Lic. psychologist, Ohio. Intern in psychology Hamilton (Ohio) City Schs., 1963-64; psychologist Talawanda, Shiloh, Trenton Schs., Butler County, Ohio, 1964-66, Franklin (Ohio) City Schs., 1966-72, Wapakoneta (Ohio) City Schs., 1972-76, Cin. City Schs., 1978-86; pvt. practice psychology, 1975—; planner, evaluator Warren/Clinton Counties Mental Health Bd., Ohio, 1986-88; adj. instr. Wright State U., Dayton, Ohio, 1989-90. Co-author: Summer Children-Ready or not for School, 1986, The Rape of Childhood--No Time to be a Kid, 1990. Sec. Tri County Drug Coun., Lima, Ohio, 1975; chmn. Auglaize County Social Svcs., Wapakoneta, 1973-75; bd. dirs. Butler County Alcohol and Drug Addiction Svcs. Bd., 1990—, sec., 1992-94. Mem. Ohio Sch. Psychologists Assn. (exec. bd. 1982-86), Southwestern Ohio Sch. Psychologist Assn. (pres.), Southwest Council Exceptional Children (Pres.), Nat. Assn. Sch. Psychologists, Ohio Psychol. Assn., Butler County 648 Mental Health Bd. (bd. dirs. 1978-86, pres. 1983-84). Republican. United Methodist. Home and Office: 6120 Michael Rd Middletown OH 45042-9402

GILMORE, LINDA LOUISE TRAYWICK, nursing educator; b. Alexander City, Ala., Dec. 4, 1962; d. James Winston and Vena Louise (Curlee) Traywick; m. Gerald Bates Gilmore, Aug. 24, 1985; 1 child, Ethan Bates Gilmore. AS, Alexander City State Jr. Coll., 1984; RN, Sylacauga Hosp. Sch. Nursing, 1985; BSN, U. Ala., Birmingham, 1988; MSN, Troy State U., 1992. RN, Ala.; cert. med.-surg. nurse, chemotherapy, and oncology clin. nurse, BLS instr., oncology nurse. Staff nurse U. Ala. Hosps., Birmingham, 1985-89, S.E. Ala. Med. Ctr., Dothan, 1989-94; ADN instr. Wallace Coll., Dothan, 1991-95; asst. prof. BSN program Troy (Ala.) State U., 1996—; quality assurance rep. perinatal divsn. Univ. Hosp., Birmingham, 1986-88; discharge planning rep. S.E. Ala. Med. Ctr., Dothan, 1989-91; faculty advisor Wallace Assn. Nursing Students, Dothan, 1993-95; mem. courtesy com. Wallace Coll., 1994-95; mem. drug computation com. Wallace ADN, 1994-95. Choir mem., soloist Bay Springs Bapt. Ch., Dothan, 1990—, guest speaker Hospice care Sr. Citizen Group, 1992, guest speaker nursing Bible Sch. Class, 1993, discipleship tng. tchr., 1993—, dir. children's choir grades 1-3, 1995—; vol. firefighter Bay Springs Vol. Fire Dept., Dothan, 1993—. Mem. ANA, Oncology Nursing Soc., Ala. State Nurses Assn. (v.p. dist. 7 1993-95). Baptist. Office: Troy State U Collegeview Bldg Troy AL 36082

GILMORE, LOUISA RUTH, retired nurse, retired firefighter; b. Pitts., Oct. 31, 1930; d. Albert Leonard and Bertha Christina (Birch) Huber; m. William Norman Kemp, May 27, 1950 (div. 1975); children: Janyce Louise Kemp Lipson, Barbra Lea Kemp Bilharz, Robert William, Paul Lee, Charles Albert; m. Robert James Gilmore, Sept. 1, 1989. Diploma in nursing, San Bernardino C.C., Needles, Calif., 1983. Office nurse Santa Fe Clinic, Needles, 1953-57; spl. duty nurse Needles Cmtys. Hosp., 1957-62; nurse supr. Santa Fe Clinic, 1962-79; staff nurse in surgery Needles Desert Cmtys. Hosp., 1979-90; Cell Tech ind. distbr. Reliv Products, Temple, Tex., 1991—; instr. CPR Needles Desert Cmtys. Hosp., 1987-90; med. officer San Bernardino County Fire Dept., Needles, 1980-83, pub. info. officer, 1983-85, vol. fire fighter, 1983-90; ind. distbr. Reliv Products, 1991-95, Cell Tech., 1996—. Mem. Calif. State Fireman Assn., Needles Firefighters Assn. (treas. 1987, 88), Beta Sigma Phi-Zeta Gamma (treas. 1966, sec. 1967, v.p. 1968, pres. 1969, named Sweetheart Queen 1969), Order of Rose (life).

GILMORE, MARJORIE HAVENS, civic worker, lawyer; b. N.Y.C., Aug. 16, 1918; d. William Westerfield and Elsie (Medl) Havens; AB, Hunter Coll., 1938; JD, Columbia, 1941; m. Hugh Redland Gilmore, May 8, 1942; children: Douglas Hugh, Anne Charlotte Gilmore Decker, Joan Louise. Admitted to N.Y. State bar, 1941, Va. bar, 1968; rsch. asst. N.Y. Law Revision Commn., 1941-42; assoc. firm Spence, Windels, Walser, Hotchkiss & Angell, N.Y.C., 1942, Chadbourne, Wallace, Parke & Whiteside, N.Y.C., 1942-43; atty. U.S. Army, Washington, 1948-53. Sec., Thomas Jefferson Jr. High Sch. PTA, 1956-58; chmn. by-laws rev. com., Long Point Corp., Ferrisburg, Vt., 1981-93; parliamentarian Wakefield High Sch. PTA, 1959-60, chmn. citizenship com., 1960-61; publicity chmn. Patrick Henry Sch. PTA, sec., 1964-65; parliamentarian Nottingham PTA, 1966-69; mem. extra-curricular activities com. Arlington County Sch. Bd.; area chmn. fund drive Cancer Soc., 1955-56; active Girl Scouts U.S.A., 1963-70; mem. '41 com. Columbia Law Sch. Fund. Recipient Constl. Law award Hunter Coll., 1938. Mem. Arlington Fedn. Women's Clubs (rec. sec. 1979-80), No. Dist. Va. Fedn. Women's Clubs (chmn. legis. com. 1986-88, chmn. pub. affairs No. dist. 1988-90), Columbia Law Sch. Alumni Assn., Alpha Sigma Rho. Presbyn. Club: Williamsburg Woman's of Arlington (corr. sec. 1970-72, 1st v.p. 1972-74, pres. 1974-76, chmn. communications 1981-82, chmn. legis. com. 1982-86, 90—). Home: 3020 N Nottingham St Arlington VA 22207-1268

GILMORE, NANCY JEAN, journalist; b. Omaha, Sept. 18, 1936; d. Robert H. and Sophye D. (Bruckner) McKinney; m. William Y. Gilmore III (div. 1976); children: William IV, Robert, Steven. AB, U. Ill., Urbana, 1958. Asst. feature editor Chgo. Daily News, 1960-65; mgr. advt. and promotion Bundy-Morgan Realtors, Medinah, Ill., 1977-81; editor Ill. Quar. U. Ill. Alumni Assn., Urbana, 1990-96; chmn. pub. rels. Fashion Group, Chgo., 1962-65. Author: The Magic of Medicare, 7, 8 or 9, 1994; editor jour. Ill. Alumni News, 1981-90. Recipinet 1st pl. award for instnl. advt. Nat. Assn. Realtors, 1979, Case award, 1984, 86, 87. Mem. Exec. Women's Club.

GILMORE, ROBIN HARRIS, emergency department nurse; b. Wilmington, N.C., Apr. 23, 1964; d. John Sidney and Emily (Newton) Harris; m. Christopher Alan Gilmore, Feb. 20, 1993. AAN, Southeastern C.C., 1987. RN, ACLS, BTLS, MICN. From staff nurse to asst. nurse mgr. ER Columbus County Hosp., Whiteville, N.C., 1993-95; critical care nurse mgr., current CCU, ICU, ED Columbus County Hosp., Whiteville, 1995—. Mem. Emergency Nurses Assn. Republican. Baptist. Home: PO Box 1835 Rd#1546 Whiteville NC 28472 Office: Columbus County Hosp 500 Jefferson St Whiteville NC 28472

GILMORE, ROBIN LEE, neurologist, educator; b. Dayton, OHio, July 8, 1950; d. Charles Bronson and Dorris Nell Lake) Gilmore; m. Dennis Ira Nedelman, Dec. 23, 1974 (div. Oct. 1981); 1 child, Cassandra Beatrice; m. Peter Nash Colonnese, Oct. 14, 1989. BS summa cum laude, U. Cin., 1972; MD with honors in surgery, Ohio State U., 1975. Intern in medicine U. Fla., Gainesville, 1975-76, resident, 1976-78, chief resident, 1978-79, fellow dept. neurology, 1979-80, asso. prof. neurology, 1990-95, prof., 1995—; asst. prof. medicine East Tenn. State U., Johnson City, 1980-82; asst./assoc. prof. neurology U. Ky., Lexington, 1982-90; vis. scientist Cleve. Clinic Found., 1990. Contbr. articles to profl. jours. Bd. dirs. Epilepsy Found. of Fla., Gainesville, 1990-91; mem. Ky. Multiple Sclerosis Soc., Lexington, 1985-90. Recipient Clin. Investigator Devel. award NIH, 1985-90. Fellow Am. Acad. Neurology, Am. Clin. Neurophysiology Soc. (sec. 1995—), Am. Epilepsy Soc., So. EEG Soc. (pres. 1988, sec. 1984-87, Caton award 1980), Am. Bd. Clin. Neurophysiology (bd. dirs.), Alpha Omega Alpha. Office: Univ of Florida College of Medicine PO Box 100236 Gainesville FL 32610-0236

GILMORE, VANESSA D., federal judge; b. St. Albans, N.Y., Oct. 26, 1956. BS, Hampton U., 1977; JD, U. Houston, 1981. Bar: Tex. 1982, U.S. Ct. Appeals (5th cir.), U.S. Dist. Ct. (so. dist.) Tex. Fashion buyer Foley's Dept. Store, 1977-79; atty. Vickery, Kilbride, Gilmore & Vickery, Houston, 1981-85, 86-94, Sue Schecter & Assocs., Houston, 1985-86; judge U.S. Dist. Ct. (So. dist.) Tex., Houston, 1994—; spkr. ATLA, San Diego, 1990, ABA, Atlanta, 1991, N.Y.C., 1993, Leadership Tex., Austin, 1992, Hampton U. Alumni Assn., Dallas, 1992, Laredo Bus. and Profl. Women's Assn., 1993, XI Ann. Border Gov.'s Conf., Monterrey, Mex., 1993, Gov.'s Bus. Devel. Coun., Ausitn, 1993, Tex. A&M U., 1993, State Bar of Tex., Austin, 1993, Houston Bus. Coun., 1993, Minority Enterprise Devel. Week, Houston, 1993, Holman St. Bapt. Ch., 1994, Greater Houston Women's Found., 1994, The Kinkaid Sch., 1995, So. Meth. U., Dallas, 1996, South Tex. Coll. of Law, 1996, among others. Contbr. articles to profl. jours. Bd. dirs. Post Oak Park Townhomes, Houston Ballet, Tex. So. Univ. Found., Neighborhood Recovery Community Redevel. Corp., 1992-95; chair African Am. Art Adv. Assn., Mus. Fine Arts; mem. scv. acad. nominations bd. Rep. Jack Fields, Tex., 1993, 94; active Texans for NAFTA; mem. Tex. Dept. Commerce, 1991-94, chairperson, 1992-94; mem. adv. bd. St. Joseph's Hosp.; mem. Leadership Tex. Named One of Houston's Black Achievers, Human Enrichment of Life Program, 1989; recipient Citizen of the Month award Houston Defender, 1990, YWCA award, 1991, Austin Met. Resource Bus. Ctr. award, 1991, Houston Bus. and Profl. Men's Club award, 1992, Disting. Svc. award Nat. Black MBA Assn., 1994, Cmty. Svc. award Holman St. Bapt. Ch., 1994. Mem. ABA, ATLA, NAACP (chair chs. and orgns. com. Freedom Fund banquets 1989-93), Am. Leadership Forum, Tex. Trial Lawyers Assn., Tex. Lyceum Assn., Houston Bar Assn., Houston Lawyers Assn., U. Houston Law Alumni (bd. dirs. 1993—), W.J. Durham Legal Soc., Links, Inc. (Mo. chpt., chair LEAD substance abuse and teen pregnancy prevention program 1990-91). Office: Fed Bldg 515 Rusk St Ste 10026 Houston TX 77002-2605

GILOLEY, NANCY JEAN, private school educator; b. Phila., Feb. 10, 1952; d. Edward F. and Bernadette M. (Obert) Campbell; m. John Peter Giloley, Nov. 7, 1970. AAS in Early Childhood, Del. County C.C., Media, Pa., 1985; BS in Elem. Edn., Cabrini Coll., Radnor, Pa., 1987; MEd, Widener U., 1988. Cert. elem. tchr., Pa. Adminstrv. asst. Shevlin Fin. Group, Broomall, Pa., 1976-90; educator St. Matthias Sch., Bala Cynwyd, Pa., 1987-89, St. Andrew Sch., Drexel Hill, Pa., 1990-95, Radnor (Pa.) Sch. Dist., 1995—; trustee Del. County C.C., Media, 1987-92. Bruckmann scholar, 1986. Mem. Delta Epsilon Sigma. Democrat. Roman Catholic. Home: 240 Kathmere Rd Havertown PA 19083

GILPIN, HEIDI L., dance educator, consultant; b. Dec. 20, 1962. BA summa cum laude, Amherst Coll., 1984; MA, Harvard U., 1987, PhD, 1993. Tchg. asst. Harvard U., Cambridge, Mass., 1986-91; dramaturg Frankfurt (Germany) Ballet, 1989—; prof. U. Calif., Riverside, 1991—; presenter in field. Boston corr. Sphinx, 1988-89; consulting editor comparative lit. Harvard Rev., 1985-89; mng. editor Copyright, 1986-88, founding co-editor, 1986-93; founding co-editor Parallax, 1989—, current editor.; contbr. articles to profl. jours.; conceptual author/dramaturg Frankfurt Ballet, 1990, 91, 92, 95; cons., advisor (video documentary) Chance Favours the Prepared Mind, Belgian TV, 1990, I Think the Body Likes to Move, 1990; dramaturg Alonzo King and LINES Contemporary Ballet, San Francisco, 1994, N.Y., 1994; contbr. articles to profl. jours. Dir. Internat. Inst. for New Dramaturgy, Amsterdam, The Netherlands, 1990—. Recipient scholarship Harvard U., 1985-93, Bryn Mawr Coll. fellowship, 1985, Bernhard Blume prize for excellence, 1987, Women's Studies fellowship, 1987, Rsch. fellowship Radcliffe Coll. Pres., 1987, Travelling scholarship Harvard U., 1991-92, 92-93, Rufus B. Kellogg Meml. fellowship Amherst Coll., 1986, 88-89, 89-90, Amherst Meml. fellowship Amherst Coll., 1989-90, numerous other grants. Mem. MLA, Am. Assn. Tchrs. German, Am. Assn. Tchrs. French, Am. Comparative Lit. Assn., Am. Soc. for theatre Rsch., Assn. Theater in Higher Edn., Dramaturgische Gesellschaft, Internat. Fedn. Theatre Rsch., Lit. Mgrs. and Dramaturgs of Ams., Soc. Dance History Scholars, Women in Theater, Women in German, Women in French, Phi Beta Kappa. Office: Univ Calif Dept Dance Riverside CA 92521-0328

GILPIN, PERI, actress. Appeared in (TV series) Frasier. Office: care NBC 3000 W Alameda Blvd Burbank CA 91523*

GILROY, JANET NOLL, academic administrator; b. Elizabeth, N.J., June 12, 1959; d. Richard Francis and Mildred Frances (Rotolo) Noll; m. William Gerard Gilroy, Apr. 23, 1983; 1 child, Meaghan Frances. BS in Polit. Sci., U. Scranton, 1981, MS in Counselor Edn., 1988. Claims adjuster The Ohio Casualty Group, Union, N.J., 1981-83; admissions counselor Dexter Hanley Coll. U. Scranton, Pa., 1983-88, coord. admissions, 1988-95, dir. admissions, 1995—; presenter Pa. Vocat. Ednl. Conf., 1990, Nat. Conf. on Student Retention, 1990. Named to Outstanding Young Women of Am., 1985; Perkins grantee, U. Scranton, 1989-90, 90-91. Mem. Northeast Pa. Counseling Assn. (v.p. 1990-92), Am. Counseling Assn., Am. Counsel Higher Edn., ASCD, Pa. Counseling Assn., Mid. States Assn. Collegiate, Registrar's ad Officers of Admissions. Roman Catholic. Home: 1617 N Webster Ave Dunmore PA 18509 Office: Dexter Hanley Coll U Scranton Scranton PA 18510-4582

GILROY, SUE ANNE, state official. Sec. of state State of Ind., 1995—. Office: Office of the Sec of State State House Rm 201 Indianapolis IN 46204-2728*

GILSON, BARBARA FRANCES, editor; b. Bklyn., May 6, 1946; d. Osmar Frank and Marie Elizabeth (Micka) G.; m. Robert Sawicki, June 29, 1962 (div. Sept. 1972); 1 child, Blake. BA in English, Smith Coll., 1976. Editor Literary Guild, Military Book Club Doubleday & Co., Inc., N.Y.C., 1968-78; sr. sponsoring editor McGraw-Hill Latinoamericana, Bogota, Colombia, 1978-83; sr. editor Barrons Edn. Series, Woodbury, N.Y., 1983-84; exec. editor Monarch Press Simon & Schuster, N.Y.C., 1984-96, sr. editor Arco Pub., 1984-96; editl. dir. Schaum McGraw-Hill, N.Y.C., 1996—. Contbr. poems, articles, short story to profl. publs.

GILSTRAP, LEAH ANN, media specialist; b. Seneca, S.C., Sept. 12, 1950; d. Raymond Chester and Eunice Hazel (Long) G. BA in History, Furman U., 1976, MEd, 1982; MLS, U. S.C., 1991. Cert. tchr., media specialist, S.C. Tchr., spl. edn. Greenville (S.C.) County Sch. Dist., 1978-79, tchr., 1978-92, media specialist, 1992—. Mem. NEA (del. 1991-95), ALA, S.C. Assn. Sch. Librs., S.C. Edn. Assn. (bd. dirs. 1994—), Greenville County Edn. Assn. (bd. dirs. 1988—, governance chair 1988—, v.p. 1996—), Greenville County Coun. Media Specialists (bd. dirs. 1993-94). Democrat. Baptist. Home: 130 Howell Cir Apt 184 Greenville SC 29615-4915 Office: Bryson Mid Sch 3657 S Industrial Dr Simpsonville SC 29681-3238

GILSTRAP, MYRNA LOY, business educator; b. Greenville, Tex., May 25; d. LeRoy Pratt and Esther Lee (Gamble) Minter; m. Noble Gilstrap; children: Noble Denard, Gerald Lenn. BBA, Prairie View A&M U., 1957, MA, 1962; MS, E. Tex. State U., 1969; PhD, Tex. Woman's U., 1994. Cert. tchr., Tex. Tchr. Ladonia (Tex.) Pub. Schs., 1957-58, Greenville (Tex.) Pub. Schs., 1958-71; instr. to assoc. prof. E. Tex. State U., Commerce, 1971—; dir. Hunt County Head Start Program, Greenville, 1980-86. Editl. mem. Collegiate Press, 1992-96; contbr. articles to profl. jours. Adv. bd. mem. Salvation Army, Greenville, 1987-90, North Tex. Transp., Irving, 1984-88; dir. regional competition Regional U. Interscholastic League, Commerce, 1994-95; mem. city coun. Greenville City Coun., 1973-79, mayor-pro-tem, 1983-89; election judge, Greenville Sch. Bd.; del. Nat. Dem. Conv., Atlanta, 1988. Recipient State Woman in Govt. award Tex. State Bus. and Profl. Women, Houston, 1992, Yellow Rose of Tex. award Gov. George Bush, Jr., Austin, 1996; named Woman of the Yr., Bus. and Profl. Women's Club, Greenville, 1995. Mem. Tex. Bus. Edn. Assn. (Dist. 10 pres. 1985-86 (tchg. award 1980, 84), Tex. Assn. of Coll. Tchrs., Hunt County Bus. and Profl. Women's Club (1st v.p. 1994), Delta Kappa Gamma (2d v.p. 1995—). Democrat. Baptist.

GINGERICH, NAOMI R., emergency room nurse; b. Linwood, Mich., Sept. 18, 1945; d. Leroy and Mary Alice (Driver) G. Diploma in Nursing, Kansas City (Mo.) Gen. Hosp., 1967. RN, Pa., Md., Fla.; cert. advanced trauma life support. Charge nurse emergency rm. Kansas City (Mo.) Gen. Hosp. and Med. Ctr., 1967-70, oper. rm. nurse, 1971-74; charge nurse emergency rm. Univ. Med. Ctr., Kansas City, Kans., 1970-73; oper. room charge nurse Lancaster (Pa.) Gen. Hosp., 1974-79, charge nurse emergency rm., 1979-88; staff nurse emergency room Preferred Nursing Pool, Balt., 1988-90; with home health care, emergency room Norrell Health Care, Sarasota, Fla., 1990-91; office nurse Landisville Family Practice, 1991-92; on-call night nurse Hospice of Lancaster County, 1992—. Home: 13 Hilltop Rd Lititz PA 17543-8625 Office: Hospice Lancaster County PO Box 4125 685 Good Dr Lancaster PA 17604-4125

GINGRICH, LISA COX, advertising and marketing executive, consultant; b. Phila., Oct. 17, 1956; d. George Carl and Helen Elizabeth (Cox) G.; m. Peter Michael Thompson, Aug. 24, 1991. BA, U. Pa., 1978. Lic. real estate agt. Account exec. SSC&B:LINTAS, N.Y.C., 1981-83, Weightman Advt., Phila., 1983-85, Henderson Advt., Greenville, S.C., 1985-87; account supr. Lintas:N.Y., N.Y.C., 1987-89; advt. dir. Impact & Echo/BBDO, Kuwait City, Kuwait, 1991; prin. cons. Communicate!ink, Fairfield, Conn., 1989—; corp. cons. Internat. Al Ghanim Corp., Kuwait City, 1991. Vol. Rep. orgns., Fairfield and Westport, Conn., 1987—; tutor Literacy Vols., Norwalk, 1990—; interviewer, assessor secondary sch. com. U. Pa., Fairfield, 1990—. Decorated Dame Sovereign Mil. Order of Temple of Jerusalem; recipient cert. of recognition Dept. State, Abu Dhabi, United Arab Emirates, 1992. Mem. Fairfield County Beagles, Cedar Point Yacht Club, Club-Abu Dhabi. Home and Office: 320 Jennings Rd Fairfield CT 06432

GINN, CONNIE MARDEAN, nurse; b. Nevada, Mo., July 22, 1951; d. Walter Jess and Marjorie Dean (Bowman) Andrews; 1 child, Justin Andrew Hutchinson; m. Robert Bob Ginn, Feb. 18, 1978; 1 child, Heather Diane. LPN, Okla., Pa.; cert. gastrointestinal nurse clinician. Med./surgical nurse Jane Phillips Mem. Med. Ctr., Bartlesville, Okla., 1971-72, Baptist Med. Ctr., Oklahoma City, 1972-73; emergency rm. nurse Baptist Med. Ctr., 1973-75, with, 1975-77; with South Community Hosp., Oklahoma City, 1977-79; digestive disease nurse James L. Stammer, M.D. and area hosps., Oklahoma City, 1979-86; clin. coord. Regional Gastroenterology Assocs., Ben G. Lazarus, D.O., Lancaster, Pa., 1986-88; nurse Springer Clinic, Paul W. Hathaway, M.D., Tulsa, 1988-90; gastrointestinal clinician Hillcrest Med. Ctr., 1990-94; nurse coord. Family Med. Care of Tulsa, 1994—; dir. Okla. Ednl. Seminars, 1983-85, course coord., 1983-85. Presented articles on diseases and patient care to various confs. Pro rescuer and vol. ARC, vol. health and safety, vol. first aid and safety, first responder, instr. Mem. Soc. Gastroenterology Nurses and Assocs. (regional del. to nat. seminars 1982-85, dir. at large 1984-86, co-divsn. chmn. regional socs. 1984, mem. program com. 1985, mem. scholarship com. 1987-88), Regional Soc. Gastrointestinal Assts. (pres.-elect Okla. and Ark. 1981-82, pres. Okla. 1980-85, founder and first pres. Okla. 1982), Northeastern Okla. Soc. Gastrointestinal Nurses and Assocs. (founder, bd. advisors 1991—), Pa. Soc. Gastrointestinal Assts., Nat. Soc. Gastrointestinal Nurses and Assocs., Nat. Assn. LPNs, LPN Assn. Pa., Nat. Soc. Physicians Nurses, Nat. Coun. Nurses, Am. Assn. Christian Counselors. Republican. Home: 11386 S Date St Jenks OK 74037-3240 Office: Family Med Care of Tulsa 7600 S Lewis Ave Tulsa OK 74136-6836

GINN, VERA WALKER, educational administrator; b. Jacksonville, Fla., Dec. 22, 1949; d. Grady (dec.) and Pearl Walker; m. Perry L. Ginn, Mar. 16, 1969; children: Perry Jr., Spencer. BA in Edn., Fla. Atlantic U., 1972; MS, Nova U., 1985; specialist in edn., Barry U., 1991. Cert. ednl. leadership, reading, elem. edn., ESOL. Tchr. grades 3 and 4 Plantation (Fla.) Park Elem., 1973-82, Griffin Elem., Cooper City, Fla., 1982-85; tchr. grades 6-8 Seminole Middle, Plantation, 1985-90; lead tchr. Chpt. 1 Adminstrv. Office, Ft. Lauderdale, 1990-92, tchr. on spl. assignment, 1992-93, specialist chpt. 1 secondary, 1993—; adj. prof. Fla. Atlantic U., Ft. Lauderdale, 1995; advisor Fla. Future Educators Am., Plantation, 1990-91. Mem. ASCD, Internat. Reading Assn., Fla. Reading Assn., Fla. Assn. Sch. Adminstr., Secondary Reading Coun. Fla., Broward County Reading Coun., Phi Delta Kappa. Democrat. Baptist. Home: 6700 SW 20th St Plantation FL 33317-5107 Office: Chpt 1 Adminstrv Office 701 NW 31st Ave Fort Lauderdale FL 33311-6627

GINOP, ANITA LEUOLLA, elementary education educator; b. Cheboygan, Mich., Mar. 8, 1966; d. Gerald Allen Brown and Patricia D. Hershey Thornton; m. Kenneth Edward Ginop, Aug. 6, 1988; children: Zachary Emil, Kelsey Catherine. BS, Ctrl. Mich. U., Mt. Pleasant, 1988. Tchr. sixth grade math. and sci. Littlefield Schs., Alanson, Mich., 1990—. Office: Littlefield Schs 7400 North St Alanson MI 49706

GINOSAR, D. ELAINE, elementary education educator; b. Red Lodge, Mont., June 14, 1937; d. Alvin Henry and Dorothy Mary (Roberson) Wedemeyer; children: Nathan B., Daniel M., David M. BA, Calif. State U., Northridge, 1964, MA, 1977. Cert. elem. tchr., reading and learning disabilities. Tchr. Sacramento City Unified Sch. Dist., 1977—; math. leader, 1992-95; owner, operator rental properties. Pres. Davis (Calif.) Flower Arrangers, 1993-96. Host family for U. Calif. Davis to 15 fgn. students from Japan, Thailand, Mexico, South Korea, 1990-95. Named Woman of Yr. Am. Biog. Soc., 1996. Mem. AAUW (edn. equity chair 1993-95, edn. chair 1965-93, readers theater, women's history week 1990, 91, treas. 1995—), Calif. Tchrs. Assn. Republican. Presbyterian. Home: 3726 Chiles Rd Davis CA 95616-4346

GINSBERG, ANN S., lawyer; b. N.Y.C., Aug. 23, 1966. BA, Johns Hopkins U., 1988; JD, Columbia U., 1991. Bar: N.J. 1991, U.S. Dist. Ct. N.J. 1991, N.Y. 1992, D.C. 1993, U.S. Dist. Ct. (so. and ea. dists.) N.Y. 1993. Law clk. to presiding judge Appellate Divsn., Hackensack, N.J., 1991-92; ptnr. Anderson Kill Olick & Oshinsky, P.C., N.Y.C.; dir. Moot Ct. exec. com. Columbia U., 1991. Mem. ABA, Bergen County Bar Assn., N.Y. County Bar Assn., N.J. Bar Assn., N.Y. Bar Assn., Phi Beta Kappa. Office: Anderson Kill Olick & Oshinsky PC 1251 Ave of the Americas New York NY 10020-1182*

GINSBERG-FELLNER, FREDDA, pediatric endocrinologist, researcher; b. N.Y.C., Apr. 21, 1937; d. Nathaniel and Bertha (Jagendorf) Ginsberg; m. Michael J. Fellner, Aug. 27, 1961; children: Jonathan R., Melinda F. Bramwit. AB, Cornell U., 1957; MD, NYU, 1961. Diplomate Am. Bd. Pediatrics, Am. Bd. Pediatric Endocrinology. Intern Albert Einstein Coll. Medicine, N.Y.C., 1961-62, fellow in pediatrics, 1962-63, 64-65, 66-67, resident in pediatrics, 1963-64, 65-66, clin. instr. pediatrics, 1967; assoc. in pediatrics Mt. Sinai Sch. Medicine, N.Y.C., 1967-69, asst. prof., 1969-75, assoc. prof., 1975-81, dir. div. pediatric endocrinology, 1977—, prof. pediatrics, 1981—. Mem. med. scis. rev. com. Juvenile Diabetes Found., 1985-88, mem. scis. adv. bd., 1991-95; mem. N.Y. State Coun. on Diabetes, Albany, 1988-89; chmn. Camp NYDA for Diabetic Children, Burlingham, 1977-89. Recipient Humanitarian award, Juvenile Diabetes Found., 1994; grantee NIH, 1977—, Am. Diabetes Assn., 1978, March of Dimes, 1983-87, Juvenile Diabetes Found., 1982-88, 93-95, Wm. T. Grant Found., 1985-89. Fellow Am. Acad. Pediatrics; mem. Am. Diabetes Assn. (chmn. 1992-94, Outstanding Contbns. award 1991, Svc. award 1994), Soc. Pediatric Rsch., Am. Pediatric Soc., Endocrine Soc., Lawson Wilkins Pediatric Endocrine Soc., N.Y. Diabetes Assn. (pres.-elect 1985-87, pres. 1987-89, Svc. award Camp NYDA 1989, Max Ellenberg Profl. Svc. award 1993). Office: Sinai Med Ctr Dept Pediats Box 1659 1176 Fifth Ave New York NY 10029-6504

GINSBURG, FAYE DIANA, anthropology educator; b. Chgo., Oct. 28, 1952; d. Benson Earl and Pearl (Miner) G.; m. Fred Ralph Myers, Feb. 14, 1988; 1 child, Samantha Ginsburg Myers. BA in Ancient Studies cum laude, Barnard Coll., 1974; PhD in Anthropology, CUNY, 1986. Part-time faculty Lang Coll., New Sch. for Social Rsch., N.Y.C., 1984-87; vis. asst. prof. anthropology New Sch. for Social Rsch., 1985-86; asst. prof. anthropology NYU, N.Y.C., 1986-91, assoc. prof. anthropology, 1991-95, prof. anthropology, 1995; dir. Certificate Program in Culture and Media, Dept. Anthropology, NYU, 1986—, dir. Ctr. for Media, Culture and History and Rockefeller Humanities Fellowship Program, NYU, 1993—. Author: Contested Lives: The Abortion Debate in American Community, 1989 (Hans Rosenhaupt Meml. Book award 1989, Village Voice Outstanding Books of 1989, Eileen Basker Meml. award for rsch. on gender and health, Soc. Med. Anthropology, 1990, Sociology of Culture Book award, Am. Sociol. Assn., 1992), 2d edit. 1996, Uncertain Terms: Negotiating Gender in American Culture, 1990; co-editor (with Rayna Rapp): Conceiving the New World Order: The Global Politics of Reproduction, 1995. Advisor Margaret Mead Film Festival, Am. Mus. of Natural History, N.Y.C., 1986—. Recipient Meml. Found. for Jewish Culture rsch. grant, 1978, NEH Youthgrant, 1978-79, Ford Found. Travel and Rsch. grant (Thailand), 1981, Sigma Xi rsch. award, 1983, Wenner-Gren Found. Conf. grant, 1990-91, N.Y. Coun. for the Humanities major grant, 1992-93; recipient Global Village Documentary award, 1980, visitorship, Humanities Rsch. Ctr. Australian Nat. U., Canberra, 1989, Disting. Alumni award CUNY, 1994; Keynote Spkr. Australian Anthropology Assn. meetings, Sydney, 1994; AAAS Mass Media fellow, 1981, Charlotte Newcombe fellow in ethics and values, 1982-83, AAUW fellow 1983-84, Presdl. fellow NYU, 1991-92, Guggenheim fellow 1991-92, MacArthur fellow 1994—. Home: 3 Washington Sq Village 14M New York NY 10012 Office: NYU Dept Anthropology 25 Waverly Pl New York NY 10003

GINSBURG, IONA HOROWITZ, psychiatrist; b. N.Y.C., Dec. 2, 1931; d. A. Eugene and Gertrude (Seidman) Horowitz; m. Selig M. Ginsburg, Aug. 15, 1954 (div. 1984); children: Elizabeth, Jessica. AB, Vassar Coll., 1953; MD, Columbia U., 1957. Diplomate Am. Bd. Psychiatry and Neurology. Pvt. practice N.Y.C., 1961—; instr. psychiatry Columbia U., N.Y.C., 1961-81, asst. clin. prof. psychiatry, 1981-95, assoc. clin. prof. psychiatry, 1995—; psychiatrist student health svc. NYU, N.Y.C., 1978—; cons.-liaison psychiatrist Columbia Presbyn. Med. Ctr., N.Y.C., 1982—. Contbr. articles to profl. jours. Med. adv. bd. Nat. Psoriasis Found. Recipient Josie Bradbury Travel award Psoriasis Assn. Gt. Britain. Mem. Am. Soc. Adolescent Psychiatry, N.Y. Soc. Adolescent Psychiatry (pres. 1986, cert. of appreciation 1986), Am. Psychiat. Assn., Am. Psychosomatic Soc., Met. Coll. Mental Health Assn. (pres. 1980), Assn. Psychocutaneous Medicine N.Am. (sec.-treas. 1994-95, v.p. 1995—).

GINSBURG, RUTH BADER, United States supreme court justice; b. Bklyn., Mar. 15, 1933; d. Nathan and Celia (Amster) Bader; m. Martin David Ginsburg, June 23, 1954; children: Jane Carol, James Steven. AB, Cornell U., 1954; postgrad., Harvard Law Sch., 1956-58; LLB Kent scholar, Columbia Law Sch., 1959; LLD (hon.), Lund (Sweden) U., 1969, Am. U., 1981, Vt. Law Sch., 1984, Georgetown U., 1985, DePaul U., 1985, Bklyn. Law Sch., 1987, Amherst Coll., 1991, Rutgers U., 1991, Lewis and Clark Coll., 1992, Radcliffe Coll., 1994, NYU, 1994, Columbia U., 1994, Smith Coll., 1994, L.I. U., 1994, U. Ill., 1995, Brandeis U., 1996; DHL (hon.), Hebrew Union Coll., 1988. Bar: N.Y. 1959, D.C. 1975, U.S. Supreme Ct. 1967. Law sec. to judge U.S. Dist. Ct. (so. dist.) N.Y., 1959-61; rsch. assoc. Columbia Law Sch., N.Y.C., 1961-62, assoc. dir. project internat. procedure, 1962-63; asst. prof. Rutgers U. Sch. Law, Newark, 1963-66, assoc. prof., 1966-69, prof., 1969-72; prof. Columbia U. Sch. Law, N.Y.C., 1972-80; U.S. Cir. judge U.S. Ct. Appeals, D.C. Cir., Washington, 1980-93; assoc. justice U.S. Supreme Ct., Washington, 1993—; Phi Beta Kappa vis. scholar, 1973-74; fellow Ctr. for Advanced Study in Behavioral Scis., Stanford, Calif., 1977-78; lectr. Aspen (Colo.) Inst., 1990, Salzburg Seminar, Austria, 1984; gen. counsel ACLU, 1973-80, bd. dirs., 1974-80. Author: (with Anders Bruzelius) Civil Procedure in Sweden, 1965; Swedish Code ofJudicial Procedure, 1968; (with others) Sex-Based Discrimination, 1974, supplement, 1978; contbr. numerous articles to books and jours. Fellow Am. Bar Found.; mem. AAAS, Am. Law Inst. (coun. mem. 1978-93), Coun. Fgn. Rels. Office: US Supreme Ct 1 1st Ave SW Washington DC 20024-5105

GINSBURGH, BROOK, association administrator; b. Phila., Oct. 4, 1942; d. Harrison Stanford and Florence Virginia (Campbell) G. Diploma in nursing, Chestnut Hill Hosp., 1963. RN, Pa. Pediatric nurse Chestnut Hill Hosp., Phila., 1963-66; pediatric charge nurse Ea. Pa. Psychiatric Inst., Phila., 1967-69, Nazareth Hosp., Phila., 1970-76; adminstrv. asst. Subcontractors Assn. Del. Valley, Ardmore, Pa., 1977-79; exec. dir. Am. Subcontractors Assn. Del. Valley, Ardmore, Pa., 1979—; editor monthly newsletter, pub. ann. directory, 1980—. V.p. Condominium Bd. Dirs., 1991-96. Mem. NAFE, Am. Soc. Assn. Execs., Pa. C. of C. Office: Am Contractors Assn Del Vly PO Box 586 63 W Lancaster Ave Ardmore PA 19003

GINSBURGH, JUDY CAPLAN, music specialist, consultant; b. Alexandria, La., July 14, 1956; d. Edwin Joseph and Jacqueline Sonia (Segall) Caplan; m. Robert Howard Ginsburgh, Dec. 30, 1979; children: Rachel, Aaron, Jonathan. BM in Vocal Performance, Ind. U., 1978. Mgr., buyer Foley's, Houston, 1978-79; pers. adminstr. Lord and Taylor, Chgo., 1979-81; exec. sec. Beth El Hebrew Congress, Alexandria, Va., 1982-85; profl. singer, 1982—, music cons., 1985—; founder, dir. Freelance Musicians Assn., Alexandria, La., 1990—; dir. Jewish Entertainment Resource Directory, Alexandria, La., 1994; cons., spkr. early childhood orgns., 1985—. Author, performer Shalom Yeladim/Hello Children (Parent's Choice award), 1994, Chanukah Favorites (Parent's Choice award), 1992. Pres. Rapides Arts & Humanities Coun., Alexandria, 1991-92; coord. Cmty. Concert, Alexandria, 1992—. Recipient Mazel Tov award, 1989, Spl. Music award Religious Heritage Am., 1990, La. Artists Roster La. Divsn. Arts, 1989—; Arts Edn. grantee States La., Tex., 1991—. Mem. Nat. Assn. Recording Arts & Scis., Coalition Advancement Jewish Edn. (bd. dirs. 1994—), Matinee Music Club, Nat. Assn. Edn. Young Children, So. Assn. Children Under Six, Assn. Childhood Edn. Internat., Guild Temple Musicians, Women's Cantors Network. Office: Ginsburgh Enterprises PO Box 12692 Alexandria LA 71315

GINTER, DOLORES DENA (DEDE GINTER), public relations consultant; b. Chgo., Aug. 22, 1929; d. Benjamin and Dorothy Vera (Doroshow) Henner; m. Edward M. Ginter, Nov. 22, 1950; children—Susan Allyn, Barbara Ann. Student Northwestern U., 1948-49. Dir. pub. relations and programming Muckenthaler Cultural Ctr., Fullerton, Calif., 1970-73; dir. pub. relations Rubin Advt. Inc., Fullerton, 1975-78; pres. Ginter Assocs., Fullerton, 1978—. Author chpts. in book. Contbr. articles to jours. in field. Active Nat. Women's Polit. Caucus, Orange County, Calif., 1975—; campaign dir. local, county, city, state candidates, jud. candidates, 1960-80; chmn. Fullerton Bicentennial Commn., 1974-76; trustee Girls' Clubs of Orange County, 1981-85; trustee Mus. North Orange County, 1978-82; 83, 84; council on extended edn. Calif. State U.-Fullerton, 1982—, profl. adviser pub. relations sequence, 1984—. Recipient Outstanding Citizen award City of Fullerton, 1976. Mem. Pub. Relations Soc. Am. (accredited, fellow counselor's acad., Protos award 1980, 81, 82, 83, 84, 86, Disting. Service award, 1986, numerous awards of excellence, bd. dirs. 1980—, v.p. Orange County chpt. 1982-83, bd. dirs. 1984—), Publicity Club of Los Angeles. Democrat. Jewish. Club: Press of Orange County (Most Valuable Mem. award 1982). Office: Ginter Assocs 1816 Yermo Pl Fullerton CA 92833*

GIOIA, MARTHA ELLEN, secondary educator; b. Boston, Sept. 12, 1947; d. John B. and Rebecca B. (Hancock) G.; m. John T. Burke, Sept. 7, 1965 (div. Jan. 1992); children: Deborah A., James P.; m. Harold N. Allen, July 10, 1993. BA in English, Trenton (N.J.) State Coll., 1979; MA in Counselor Edn., San Jose (Calif.) State U., 1992. Cert. tchr. N.J. Tchr. Monroe Twp. H.S., Jamestown, N.J., 1980; rschr. for devel. Santa Catalina Sch., Monterey, Calif., 1983-85; tchr. San Benito H.S., Hollister, Calif., 1985—; English dept. chairperson San Benito H.S., Hollister, 1995—; bd. dirs. Ctrl. Calif. Coun. of Tchrs. of English, 1995—. Vol. Santa Cruz Art Mus., 1994—. Office: San Benito HS 1220 Monterey St Hollister CA 95003

GIOIELLA, EVELYN, dean, nursing educator. BS in Nursing with distinction, Cornell U., 1959; MA in Pub. Health Nursing, NYU, 1963, PhD in Nursing, 1977. Cmty. health instr. Sch. Nursing Lenox Hill Hosp., 1963-73; asst. prof., curriculum coord. Sch. Nursing CCNY, 1976-78, assoc. prof., dir. curriculum & curriculum rsch. Sch. Nursing, 1978-89, acting dean, assoc. prof., 1979-80, dean, prof. nursing, 1980-83; dean, prof. nursing Hunter-Bellevue Sch. Nursing, N.Y.C., 1983—; cons. Russell Sage Coll., N.Y.C., U. P.R., St. Anselm Coll., N.H., U. Fla., St. Louis U., U. Wis., Madison, Dept. Health, Taiwan, Taipei City Nurses Assn. Homecare Unit, Taipei Coll. Nursing, Kaochsiong U., Tien Med. Ctr.; vis. prof. Shanghai Med. U., 1991-94; presenter in field. Editor: The History of the Lenox Hospital School of Nursing, 1973, Nursing Care of the Aging Client, 1985 (AJN Book of Yr. award 1985), Gerontology in the Professional Nursing Curriculum, 1986; contbr. chpts. to books and articles to profl. jours. Recipient Disting. Alumnus award Cornell U.-N.Y. Hosp. Sch. Nursing Alumni Assn.; named one of YWCA Acad. Women Achievers; grantee Diamond Found., 1989-95, Helene Fuld Health Trust, 1989-90, Astor Found., 1994. Fellow Am. Acad. Nursing (panel on aging 1991—); mem. ANA (coun. nurse rschrs. nurse rep. 1984—, coun. gerontol. nursing), N.Y. State Nurses Assn. (bd. com. strategic planning 1991-93, geriatric nurse practice group, coun. edn. 1985-88), Assn. Am. Colls. Nursing (sec. 1986-90, mem. edn. stds. task force 1987-91), Nat. League for Nursing, Sigma Theta Tau (v.p. Upsilon chpt. 1983-87, mem. Alpha Phi chpt. 1986—, charter mem. Cornell chpt., disting. educator award 1978). Office: Hunter Bellevue Sch Nursing 421 East 25th St New York NY 10010*

GIORDANO, ANN CHRISTINE, photographer; b. Westwood, N.J., July 24, 1961; d. Mario and Olga (Palmer) Giordano. BFA in Photography, Parsons Sch. of Design, N.Y.C., 1983. Asst. photographer Calif. Acad. Scis., San Francisco, 1986-88; archival photographic coord. Richard Avedon Studio, N.Y.C., 1985—, asst. curator, 1990-91; studio mgr., technical photo asst. Victor Schrager, N.Y.C., 1992-94; curator, exhbn. coord. Patrick Demarchelier Studio, N.Y.C., 1995—. Photographer: (book) City Dogs, 1994, Animal Attractions, 1995; artist: (book) Time Capsule, 1995. Recipient Workshop Excellence medal Fachochschule Dortmund Fachbereich Design, 1983, Workshop Scholarship award Friends of Photography, 1987. Mem. Camera Club of N.Y. (bd. trustees, mem. dir. 1991-94).

GIORDANO, JOAN AUGUSTA, artist; b. N.Y.C., Sept. 8, 1942; d. Vincent James and Antoinette (Narducci) Baldassano; children: Jeffrey, Glenn. BA, Wagner Coll., 1962; MFA, Pratt Inst., 1978. Co-founder, adminstr. Art Lab. Snug Harbor Cultural Ctr., 1975-80; founder, adminstr. Visual Exch., S.I., N.Y., 1980-83; curator The Sarah Inst., N.Y.C., 1980-85; asst. dir. Rockland Ctr. for Arts, Nyack, N.Y., 1985-87; curator Rockland Ctr. for Arts; dir. continuing edn. fine arts program Coll. of S.I., 1977-81, instr. painting, 1976-78; artist, instr. Studio in a Sch., N.Y.C., 1988-91; instr. LaGuardia C.C., CUNY, 1978-80, Union Coll., N.J., 1978-80; vis. artist workshops U. South Fla., Tampa, Awa Awagami Hall Japanese Handmade Paper Mem.'s Cir., Hall of Awa, Tokushima, Japan, 1996; vis. artist Ringling Sch. Art, Sarasota, Fla.; exhbn. Mauro Graphics Gallery, S.I.; curator Rockland Ctr. for Arts. One-woman shows include Gallery DuBost, Paris, 1981, Sutton Gallery, N.Y.C., 1982, 84, Nuance Gallery, Tampa, Fla., 1987, Walter Wickiser Gallery, N.Y.C., 1993-97, Queens Coll. Art Ctr., CUNY; mus. exhbn. tour Southeast, Lamar Dodd Art Ctr. and Mus., Ga., 1995, Art Inst. for the Permian Basin, Tex., 1995, Longview Art Mus., Tex., 1996, Danville Mus. Fine Arts, Va., 1996; exhibited in group shows at Met. Mus., N.Y.C., 1975, S.I. Mus., 1976, Sutton Gallery, N.Y.C., 1981, U. Wis., Superior, 1983, Clayton Gallery, Tampa, 1990, A.J. Lederman Fine Arts, 1992, Alan Stone Gallery, N.Y.C., 1986-87, Feminine Dialogue UNESCO, Paris, 1982, Gallery Brocken, Tokyo, Hashimoto Gallery, Tokyo, 1996; represented in permanent collections N.Y. Pub. Libr., Best Collection, Sidney Louis and Longview Mus. Collection and pvt. collections. Founder Urban Artists for Earth, N.Y.C., 1993. Recipient Julian Weissglass award for painting S.I. Mus., 1978; named grad. fellow Hunter Coll., CUNY, 1973, Va. Ctr. Creative Arts, 1979, Yaddo Artists, 1980. Mem. N.Y. Artists Equity (bd. dirs.), Ironclad Artists (bd. dirs., sec. 1990-96). Home and Studio: 136 Grand St New York NY 10013-3127

GIORDANO, LAURA ANN, quality management professional; b. Bronx, N.Y.; d. Joseph P. and Viola N. (Seymour) Morrissey; m. Joseph P. Giordano. BS in Nursing, Molloy Coll., Rockville Centre, N.Y., 1978; MBA, Adelphi U., Garden City, N.Y., 1985. RN, N.Y., Ariz.; cert. profl. in health care quality. Staff nurse Winthrop U. Hosp., Mineola, N.Y., 1978-79; staff nurse nursing supr. alcohol treatment ctr. Creedmoor Psychiat. Ctr., Queens, N.Y., 1979-80, asst. adminstr., cen. systems coord. acute admissions div., 1980-84, asst. dir. edn. and tng., 1984-85; community program rep. Office Community Behavioral Health Ariz. Dept. Health Svcs., Phoenix, 1985-87; clin. quality assurance coord. Ariz. State Hosp., Ariz. Dept. Health Svcs., Phoenix, 1987-90; dir. quality mgmt. svcs. div. behavioral health svcs. Ariz. Dept. Health Svcs., 1990-93; health outcomes project mgr., coop. projects specialist Health Svcs. Adv. Group Inc., Phoenix, 1994—. Mem. Am. Coll. Med. Quality, Ariz. Assn. for Healthcare Quality, Nat. Assn. for Healthcare Quality, Sigma Theta Tau, Delta Mu Delta.

GIORGI, ELSIE AGNES, physician; b. N.Y.C., Mar. 8, 1911; d. Anacleto and Maria (Maserati) G. BA, Hunter Coll., 1931; MD, Columbia U., 1949. Diplomate Am. Bd. Internal Medicine. Intern Cornell 2d med. div. Bellevue Hosp., N.Y.C., 1949-50, asst. resident in medicine Cornell 2d med. div., 1950-52, chief resident in medicine Cornell 2d med. div., 1952-53, chief gen. med. clinics Cornell 2d med. div., 1953-59, assoc. attending physician Cornell 2d med. div., 1953-62, physician, specialist in internal medicine, 1953-61; physician, specialist in internal medicine L.A., 1962—; psychiat. trainee Cedars of Lebanon Hosp., Los Angeles, 1961-62, assoc. attending physician, 1962—; dir. div. home care and extended care, Cedars-Sinai Med. Ctr., Los Angeles, 1962-66; chief adolescent clinic, med. dir. clinics Mt. Sinai Hosp., Los Angeles, 1962-66, assoc. attending physician dept. medicine, 1962-69, attending physician, 1970—; med. dir., coordinator U. So. Calif. Family Neighborhood Health Services Ctr. for Watts, 1966-67; attending physician Los Angeles County Hosp., U. So. Calif. Med. Ctr., 1966-71; assoc. mem. dept. internal medicine Orange County Med. Ctr., Calif., 1969—, dir. ambulatory care services, 1969-72; staff St. John's Hosp., Santa Monica, Calif., 1970—; asst. prof. clin. medicine, attending sr. physician internal medicine Cornell U. Med. Coll., 1957-62; asst. prof. clin. medicine UCLA, 1962-66, guest lectr. Sch. Social Welfare, 1964—, assoc. clin. prof. medicine and community medicine Sch. Medicine, 1972—, PRIMEX, 1972-73; asst. prof. medicine Sch. Medicine, U. So. Calif., 1966-69, adj. prof. medicine, community medicine, family medicine Coll. Medicine, U. Calif., Irvine, 1969-72; cons. Martin E. Segal Co., 1969—, VA Hosp., Long Beach, Calif., 1972—, Washington, 1972—; cons. health care sect. Social Security Adminstrn., Balt., Los Angeles County Health Dept., Calif. Council for Health Plan Alternatives, Burlingame, Regional Med. Care Program, 1971-73, Tb and Health Assn. of Los Angeles; mem. nat. adv. bd. Nat. Council Sr. Citizens, Washington; mem. adv. com. USPHS, Calif. Dept. Pub. Health; mem. med. adv. com. Vis. Nurse Assn., Los Angeles, 1976; mem. adv. bd. Life Extension Inst., N.Y.C.; mem. edn. com. Am. Cancer Soc., San Francisco; cons. ednl. films. Author sect. in textbook; contbr. articles to profl. publs. Active Town Hall, Los Angeles; vol., bd. dirs. South Central Child Care Ctrs. for South Central Los Angeles; mem. nat. adv. bd. for legal research and services for elderly Nat. Council Sr. Citizens; mem. UCI-21 project com. U. Calif. Recipient Achievement award AAUW, 1968, Better Life award Am. Nursing Home Assn., 1974, lifetime commitment award Watts Health Found., 1987; named to Hall of Fame, Hunter Coll. Alumni Assn., 1976; feature This Is Your Life progam TV Sta. KNBC, 1984. Mem. AMA, New York County Med. Assn., Calif. Med. Assn., Los Angeles County Med. Assn., Los Angeles County Soc. Internists, Am. Pub. Health Assn. (med. care sect.), Gerontol. Soc., Western Gerontology Assn., Comprehensive Health Planning Assn., Nat. Acad. Scis., Inst. Medicine. Home: 153 S Lasky Dr Ste 3 Beverly Hills CA 90212-1721

GIOSEFFI, (DOROTHY) DANIELA, poet, author, educator; b. Orange, N.J., Feb. 12, 1941; d. Daniel Donato and Josephine (Buzevska) G.; m. Richard J. Kearney, Sept. 7, 1965 (div.); 1 child, Thea D.; m. Lionel B. Luttinger, June 6, 1986. BA, Montclair State Coll., 1963; MFA, Cath. U. of Am., 1966. Cons., poet Poets-in-the-Schs., Inc., N.Y.C., 1972-85; freelance writer, lectr. at numerous univs. throughout U.S. and Europe; appeared on Nat. Pub. Radio, CBC, BBC; spkr. on world peace and disarmament, 1979—; keynote spkr. Am. Forum for Global Edn. Nat. Conf., Miami, Fla., 1994, State Coun. of Tchrs. of English Conf., Orlando, Fla., 1995. Author: (novel) The Great American Belly, 1977, 4th edit., 1979, (collection of poems) Eggs in the Lake, 1979, Word Wounds and Water Flowers, 1995 (non-fiction) Earth Dancing: Mother Nature's Oldest Rite, 1981, Women on War and Survival: International Voices for the Nuclear Age, 1988 (am. Book award 1990), On Prejudice: A Global Perpective, 1993—, Dust Disappears: Translations of Carilda Oliver Labra of Latin America, 1995, In Bed With the Exotic Enemy, 1996, The Psychic Touch, 1996, (plays) The Golden Daffodil Dwarf, Care of the Body, The Sea Hag in the Cave of Sleep, 1988; mem. editl. bd. Voices in Italian Americana, Purdue U., 1990—; short stories include Daffodil Dollars (PEN Short Fiction award 1990); contbr. poetry and fiction to numerous periodicals and anthologies: performer stage presentations of work throughout U.S. and Europe. Pres. Bklyn. Citizens for Sane Nuclear Policy, 1987-89; participant IV Feminist Internat. Bookfair, Barcelona, Spain, 1989, Miami Internat. Bookfair, 1990; mem. exec. bd., chmn. media watch com. Writers and Pubs. Alliance for Nuclear Disarmament, 1978-91. Recipient poetry and fiction award Creative Artists' Pub. Svc. Program, N.Y. State Coun. on Arts, 1971; grantee N.Y. State Coun. on Arts, 1972, 77, World Peace award Ploughshares Fund, 1989, Womens' Leadership Devel. Mem. PEN Am. Ctr., Acad. Am. Poets, Actors Equity Assn., Nat. Book Critics Cir., Poets' House, Skylands Writers and Artists Assn. (pres.). Address: PO Box 15 Andover NJ 07821-0015

GIOVAN, TRIA, photographer; b. Chgo., Mar. 6, 1961; d. Anthony Constantine and Mary Niles (Arnold) G. BA in Photography, Hampshire Coll., 1983. Solo shows include Henry St. Settlement, N.Y.C., 1988, Union Sq. Gallery, N.Y.C., 1989, Art for Transit, Grand Ctrl. Terminal, N.Y.C., 1991, Condesso Lawler Gallery, N.Y.C., 1994; group shows include Hebrew Union Coll., N.Y.C., 1990, Barret House Gallery, Poughkeepsie, N.Y., 1990, Phillips Hill Gallery, Solebury, Pa., 1993, Bonnie Benrubi Gallery, N.Y.C., 1994; permanent collections include Bklyn. Mus., Mus. Modern Art, N.Y.C., N.Y. Pub. Libr., Jewish Mus., N.Y.C.; author: The Elusive Island-Photographs of Cuba, 1996; photographs also included in Aperture-Cuban Photography, 1995, Am. Photography ann., Photographers Forum, Graphis-Fine Art Photography. Active NOW, NARAL, Emily's List. Home: 60 East 12th St #9B New York NY 10003

GIOVANAZZI, DIANE MARY, social worker; b. Pitts., Apr. 30, 1954; d. Albert George and Dorothy Catherine (Connors) G. BA in Social Work, U. Pitts., 1981, MA in Social Work, 1986. Lic. social worker. Child care worker Allegheny Valley Jr. Sch., Pitts., 1975-78; coord. Big Brothers/Big Sisters YMCA, Pitts., 1979-80; child therapist Holy Family Inst., Pitts., 1979-86, supr. partial hosp. program, 1986-87, supr. helping families in crisis, 1987—; mem. western area consortia Health Start, Inc., Pitts., 1992—; coord. Sto-Rox Youth Svcs. Network, McKees Rocks, Pa., 1990—. Recipient Disting. Svc. cert. Allegheny County Children and Youth Svcs. and Juvenile Ct., 1994. Office: Holy Family Inst 324 Munson Ave Mc Kees Rocks PA 15136

GIOVANNI, KATHARINE CROMWELL, meeting planning company executive; b. N.Y.C., May 20, 1961; d. Roger J.K. and Joan (Van Pelt) C.; m. Ronald M. Giovanni, Aug. 29, 1992; children: Matthew J., Jeremy J. BA, Lake Forest Coll., 1984. Pres., founder Meeting Planning Plus, Inc., Cary, N.C., 1994—. Mem. Nat. Assn. Women Bus. Owners, Mtg. Profls. Internat. Episcopalian. Office: Meeting Planning Plus Inc 2221 Appledown Dr Cary NC 27513

GIRA, CATHERINE RUSSELL, university president; b. Fayette City, Pa., Oct. 30, 1932; d. John Anthony and Mary (Stephen) Russell; m. Joseph Andrew Gira, July 17, 1954; children—Cheryl Ann, Thomas Russell. B.S., Calif. State U., 1953; M.Ed., Johns Hopkins U., 1957, M.L.A., 1972; Ph.D., Am. U., 1975. Tchr. Balt. County, Balt., 1953-60, head dept., 1958-60; writing cons. Md. State Dept. Edn., 1960-68; instr. Johns Hopkins U., Balt., 1964-65; from asst. prof. to prof. U. Balt., 1965-81, acting dean, 1981-82, provost, 1982-91; pres. Frostburg (Md.) State U., 1991—. Contbr. articles to profl. jours. Am. U. scholar, 1973-75. Mem. Am. Assn. Univ. Adminstrs. (bd. dirs. 1984-87, pres.-elect 1987, pres. 1988-90), Fedn. State Humanities Couns. (bd. dirs. 1990-94, vice-chair 1993-94), Md. Humanities Coun. (chmn. 1989-90), Md. Assn. Higher Edn. (bd. dirs. 1983-85, pres. 1986-87), Shakespeare Assn. Am., Edgar Allan Poe Soc. (bd. dirs. 1982—). Methodist. Home: 324 Braddock Rd Frostburg MD 21532-2300 Office: Frostburg State U Office of Pres Frostburg MD 21532-2302*

GIRARD, ANDREA EATON, communication executive, consultant; b. N.Y.C., Oct. 16, 1946; d. Samuel Robert and Mimi (Eaton) G. Student, Syracuse U., 1964-66; BA cum laude, Finch Coll., 1968; MA, Columbia U., 1971. Talent coord./prodn. asst. Guber-Ford-Gross Prodns., N.Y., 1968-70; v.p. Charing Cross Press, N.Y.C., 1970-72; assoc. producer, talent dir.TV shows "To Tell the Truth" and "Snap Judment" Goodson Todman Prodns., N.Y.C., 1972-80; programming exec. David Letterman-NBC, N.Y.C., 1980; dir. of talent, producer Daytime/Arts and Entertainment Networks (Hearst/ABC Video Enterprises), N.Y.C., 1981-84; dir. current programming acquisition, sr. producer Lifetime Network (Hearst/ABC/Viacom Entertainment Svcs.), N.Y.C., 1984-86; pres. Girard Communications, N.Y.C., 1986—, dir. med. communications advantage internat., 1990-91; v.p. PRNY, N.Y.C., 1990-92; CEO Panache Communications Inc., N.Y.C., 1992—; judge Emmy awards Internat. Film and TV Festival; speaker pub. rels. coun. sch. of continuing edn. NYU; media cons. to med. industry, 1987—. Producer, writer (documentaries) Cave Dwellers of Crete, 1974, Sponge Divers of Kalymnos, 1979, Gypsies of the Camargue, 1983. Active fund raising bd. Jersey Wildlife Preservation Trust, N.Y.; active hospitality com. United Nations, N.Y., Big Apple Com. for the Benefit of the Image of N.Y. Mem. NATAS, NAFE, Women in Comm., Nat. Assn. Women Bus. Owners, Internat. Assn. Cooking Profls. Office: Panache Comms 201 E 77th St Ste 7F New York NY 10021-2082

GIRARD, JUDY, broadcast executive. BS in Radio-TV-Film, Ithaca Coll. With WPVI-TV, Phila., 1968; program mgr. WBNG-TV, Binghamton, N.Y.; sta. mgr. WOWK-TV, Huntington, W.Va.; dir. programming ops. and promotion WBAL-TV, Balt., WTAE-TV, Pitts.; dir. ops. and programming WTVJ-TV, Miami, 1987-89; dir. broadcasting WNBC-TV, 1989-91, v.p. broadcasting, 1991-93; sr. v.p. programming and prodn. Lifetime Television, N.Y.C., 1993—. Developer new movie franchise: Lifetime Original Movie. Named Alumna of the Yr., Ithaca Coll., 1992. Office: Lifetime Tel 16th and 17th Fls 309 W 49th St New York NY 10019-7316

GIRARD, NETTABELL, lawyer; b. Pocatello, Idaho, Feb. 24, 1938; d. George and Arranetta (Bell) Girard. Student, Idaho State U., 1957-58; BS, U. Wyo., 1959, JD, 1961. Bar: Wyo. 1961, D.C. 1969, U.S. Supreme Ct. 1969. Practiced in Riverton, 1963-69; atty.-adviser on gen. counsel's staff HUD; assigned Office Interstate Land Sales Registration, Washington, 1969-70; sect. chief interstate land sales Office Gen. Counsel, 1970-73; ptnr. Larson & Larson, Riverton, 1973-85; pvt. practice Riverton, 1985—; guest lectr. at high schs.; condr. seminar on law for layman Riverton br. A.A.U.W., 1965; condr. course on women and law; lectr. equal rights, job discrimination, land use planning. Editor Wyoming Clubwoman, 1966-68; bd. editors Wyo. Law Jour., 1959-61; writer Obiter Dictum column Women Lawyers Jour., Dear Legal Advisor column Solutions for Seniors, 1988-94; featured in Riverton Ranger, 1994; also articles in legal jours. Chmn. fund dr. Wind River chpt. ARC, 1965; chmn. Citizens Com. for Better Hosp. Improvement, 1965; chmn. subcom. on polit. legal rights and responsibilities Gov.'s Commn. on Status Women, 1965-69, mem. adv. com., 1973-93; rep. Nat. Conf. G ovs. Commn., Washington, 1966; local chmn. Law Day, 1966, 67, country chmn. Law Day, 1994, 95, 96; mem. state bd. Wyo. Girl Scouts USA, sec. 1974-89, mem. nat. bd., 1978-81; state vol. adv. Nat. Found., March of Dimes, 1967-69; legal counsel Wyo. Women's Conf., 1977; gov. apptd. State Wyo. Indsl. Siting Coun., 1995—. Recipient Spl. Achievement award HUD, 1972, Disting. Leadership award Girl Scouts U.S.A., 1973, Franklin D. Roosevelt award Wyo. chpt. March of Dimes, 1985, Thanks Badge award Girl Scout Coun., 1987, Women Helping Women award in recognition of effective advancement status of women Riverton Club of Soroptimist Internat., 1990, Spl. award plaque in appreciation and recognition of 27 yrs. of svc. to State of Wyo., Wyo. Commn. for Women, 1964-92, Appreciation award Wyo. Sr. Citizens and Solutions for Srs., 1994. Mem. AAUW (br. pres.), Wyo. Bar Assn., Fremont County Bar Assn., D.C. Bar Assn., Women's Bar Assn. D.C., Internat. Fedn. Women Lawyers, Am. Judicature Soc., Assn. Trial Lawyers Am., Wyo. Trial Lawyers Assn., Nat. Assn. Women Lawyers (del. Wyo., nat. sec. 1969-70, v.p. 1970-71, pres. 1972-73), Wyo. Fedn. Women's Clubs (state editor, pres.-elect 1968-69, treas. 1974-76), Prog. Women's Club (pres.-elect. 1994-95), Riverton Chautaqua Club (pres. 1965-67), Riverton Civic League (pres. 1987-89), Kappa Delta, Delta Kappa Gamma (state chpt. hon.). Home: 224 Sunset Dr PO Box 687 Riverton WY 82501 Office: 513 E Main St Riverton WY 82501-4440

GIRE, SHARON LEE, state legislator; b. Jan. 13, 1944; m. Dana A. Gire. BS in Edn., Ohio State U., 1965, postgrad. in counseling psychology, 1966; MSW, Wayne State U., 1975. Program dir. YWCA, Macomb, Mich., 1969-71, cons. ctrl. region teen program, 1971-73; commr. Macomb County, 1984-86; chairperson budget com., pers. com., data processing subcom., bldg. and grounds subcom.; state rep. Mich. Ho. of Reps., 1987—, co-chair human svcs., children com. and youth, mem. pub. health, housing and urban affairs com., mem. consumers econ. devel. and energy com.; mem. Mich. Assn. Counties Legis. Conf., Mich. Assn. Counties Ann. Conf., Mich. Assn. Counties Seminar County Govt., Mich. Mcpl. League State Legis. Confs., Mich. Mcpl. League Annual Confs., Mich. Mcpl. League Regional Meetings, Mich. Mcpl. League Workshops. Mem. Mt. Clemens Bd. Zoning Appeals, 1977-84; mem. Mich. Women in Mcpl. Govt., 1978-84; mem. comml. and indsl. devel. com., 1978-84; city liaison for student govt. day, 1979-84; mayor pro-tem City of Mt. Clemens, 1979-84; vice chairwoman Mich. Mcpl. League Region 5, 1982; dir. N.E. Interfaith Ctr., 1977-84. Home: 37567 Radde St Clinton Township MI 48036-2936*

GIRGA, LAURA, accountant; b. Sheboygan, Wis., May 16, 1945; d. John and Mildred (Sager) Felsinger; m. Lawrence Girga, Sept. 3, 1983; children: Elizabeth, Cheryl. AS in Acctg. with honors, Lakeshore Tech. Coll., 1988; BA with honors, Lakeland Coll., 1994. Office clk. Zimmermann Printing Co., Sheboygan; cost acct. Nemschoff Chairs Inc., Sheboygan, asst. credit mgr.; fin. analyst Brunen Corp., Milw.; acctg. TCG/TrumpCo., Waukesha. Mem. Inst. Mgmt. Accts. (pres. Waukesha area chpt. 1996—). Home: 2107 Inverness Dr Waukesha WI 53186

GIRLING, BETTIE JOYCE MOORE, home health executive; b. Midlothian, Tex., Feb. 10, 1930; d. Robert and Florence Irene (Shaw) Moore; BS in Edn., Daniel Baker Coll., 1952; MSSW, U. Tex., Austin, 1956; m. Robert George William Girling, III, Sept. 2, 1960; children: Robert George William IV, Maria Julia Anastasia, Samuel Marcus Shaw, Katherine Susan Jane. Tchr., Clairemont (Tex.) Ind. Sch. Dist., 1952-53; caseworker

Tex. Dept. Public Welfare, 1953-57, licensing supr., Dallas, 1960; caseworker Austin State Sch. for Mentally Retarded, 1957-60; with adoption intake Edna Gladney Home, Ft. Worth, 1961-65; rschr. Child Welfare League Am., N.Y.C., 1966; organizer, exec. dir. Girling Home Care, Austin, 1967-69; asst. dir. agy. programs Girling Health Care, Inc., ex-v.p., COO multi-state, Tex., La., N.Y., Okla., Tenn., comprehensive health care agy., 1967—; owner, operator child care facility, 1973-75; mem. long range planning com. Grad. Sch. Social Work, Bd. U. Tex.-Austin Sch. Nursing; mem. home health services adv. council Tex. Dept. Health; organizer, coord. profl. workshops; mem. adv. bd. U. Tex. Sch. Social Work, Austin, 1996. Mem. NASW, Tex. Hosp. Assn., Tex. Home Health Agys., Nat. Assn. Home Health Agys., Women's Symphony League of Austin, Austin Symphony Orchestra Soc. (bd. dirs.), Austin Womens Club, Austin Country Club (co-chair Austin Lyric Austin Ball 1988, 89), Daniel Baker Ex-Students Assn. Tex. Recipient Ida Mae Hebert award Tex. Assn. for Home Care, 1994, Disting. Alumni award Daniel Baker Coll. Ex-Students Assn., 1988. Democrat. Baptist. Office: Girling Health Care Inc PO Box 4294 Austin TX 78765-4294

GIROLAMI, LISA S., film producer; b. Modesto, Calif., Sept. 13, 1960; d. Guido and Kristine (White) G. BA, Calif. State U., Long Beach, 1983. Assoc. prodn. exec. Walt Disney Pictures/Touchtone, Burbank, Calif., 1985-87; prodn. exec. Buena Vista Pictures, Burbank, Calif., 1987-89; producer Theme Park Prodns. div. Walt Disney, Burbank, Calif., 1989-90; show designer Walt Disney Imagineering, Glendale, Calif., 1990-92; line prodr. Disney's Virtual Reality Attraction, 1992-94; mgr. prodn. Disney Interactive Software, Burbank, 1995-96; show producer Universal's Islands of Adventure, Universal City, Calif., 1996—. Prodn. exec. films including Honey I Shrunk The Kids, Heartbreak Hotel, DOA, Disorganized Crime, Ernest Saves Christmas, Where the Heart Is, 1989; producer theme park films including the Lottery, Monster Sound Show; prodn. coord. films including Critters, 1985; set mgr. films Reanimator, 1985, Terminator, 1984; asst. dir. films including Summers End, Calling Home; sr. asst. to v.p. prodn. films including Ruthless People, Outrageous Fortune, Color of Money, Adventures in Babysitting, Who Framed Roger Rabbit?, Good Morning Vietnam, Tough Guys, Down and Out in Beverly Hills; prodn. mgr. numerous commls. Roman Catholic. Office: MCA Recreation Svcs Bldg 488/7 100 Universal City Plz Universal City CA 91608

GIROUARD, GAIL PATRICIA, family practice physician; b. Acushnet, Mass., Mar. 26, 1956; d. Ernest and Doris Elizabeth (Whalley) G. BS in Earth Sci. with honors, Bridgewater State Coll., 1978; MS in Molecular Biology with honors, Creighton U., 1989, MD, 1994. Cert. tchr., Mass., EMT, Mass. Sci. tchr. Keith Jr. H.S., New Bedford, Mass., 1978-89; resident Creighton Family Practice, St. Joseph's Hosp., Omaha, 1994—; sci. tchr. Sea Lab, New Bedford, summer 1989; summer sch. tchr., New Bedford, 1980-89; personal fitness trainer, New Bedford, 1985-89; tchr., trainer weight training for women program Bright Nights, 1989; EMT, New Bedford, Mass. Physician at homeless clinics, Omaha, 1995. Mem. AMA, Am. Assn. Family Practice, Am. Med. Women's Assn. Roman Catholic. Office: Creighton Family Practice 3047 S 72d St Omaha NE 68124

GIROUARD, SHIRLEY ANN, nurse, policy analyst; b. New London, Conn., Jan. 16, 1947; d. Maxime Albert Girouard and Irene Barbara (Arnold) Reid. BA in Sociology, Ea. Conn. State Coll., 1972; MA in Sociology, U. Conn., 1974; MSN, Yale U., 1977; PhD in Policy Analysis, Brandeis U., 1988. Nurse Woodstock (Conn.) Pub. Health Assn., 1968-70; staff nurse Clinton (Conn.) Convalescent Ctr., 1970-72; ins. edn. coord. Middlesex Meml. Hosp., Middletown, Conn., 1973-75; clin. nurse specialist Dartmouth Hitchcock Med. Ctr., Hanover, N.H., 1977-83; staff nurse Dartmouth Hitchcock Med. Ctr., Hanover, 1983-84; legis. cons., lobbyist N.H. Nurses Assn., Concord, 1985-87; program officer Robert Wood Johnson Found., Princeton, N.J., 1987-92; exec. dir. N.C. Ctr. Nursing, 1992-93, Am. Nurse's Assn., 1993-94; health policy and nursing cons. pvt. and pub. sector orgns., Washington, 1994-95; dir. child health planning & Evaluation Nat. Assn. Children's Hosps. and Related Instns., Alexandria, Va., 1995—; pvt. practice cons., 1983-87; profl. devel. cons., Lebanon, N.H., 1983-87; health policy and nursing cons. Author: (chpt.) Health Policy and Nurse Services, 1989; mem. editorial bd. Clin. Nurses Specialist Jour., 1986—; contbr. articles to profl. jours. State rep. N.H. Legislature, Concord, 1982-84; counselor City of Lebanon Coun., 1984-87. Fellow Am. Acad. Nursing; mem. ANA (project dir. 1986), N.C. State Nurses Assn., Sigma Theta Tau. Democrat. Office: Nat Assn Childrens Hosps & Related Instns 401 Wythe St Alexandria VA 22314

GISH, ANNABETH, actress; b. Albuquerque, Mar. 13, 1971. Student, Duke U., 1993. Appeared in (film) Desert Bloom, Hiding Out, Mystic Pizza, Shag, Coupe de Ville, Wyatt Earp, The Red Coat, Nixon, The Last Supper, Beautiful Girls; (TV) (series) Courthouse (Movies) Hero in the Family, When He's Not a Stranger, The Last To Go, Lady Against the Odds, Silent Cries, (mini-series) Scarlett. Office: care Internat Creative Mgmt 8942 Wilshire Blvd Beverly Hills CA 90211*

GIST, MARILYN ELAINE, organizational behavior and human resource management educator; b. Tuskegee, Ala., May 9, 1950; d. Lewis A. and Grace (Perry) G. BA in Edn., Howard U., 1972; MBA, U. Md., 1982, PhD in Bus. Aminstrn. Organizational Behavior, 1985. Tchr. Montgomery County Pub. Schs., Rockville, Md., 1972-76; mgmt. intern NASA Goddard Space Flight Ctr., Greenbelt, Md., 1976-79; procurement mgr. NASA Goddard Space Flight Ctr., Greenbelt, 1980-81, staff asst. to dir. mgmt. ops., 1983-85; dir. contracts OAO Corp., Greenbelt, 1981-83; prof. organizational behavior U. N.C., Chapel Hill, N.C., 1985-87; prof. organized behavior and human resources U. Wash., Seattle, 1987—; staff cons. U. Md., Coll. Park, 1979-84, CIA, Langley, Va., 1984-85; adj. prof. human resources Cornell U., 1995-96. Contbr. articles to profl. jours. Recipient Outstanding Student award Alumni Assn. Internat. U. Md., 1985, Alan Nash Outstanding Doctoral Student award U. Md., 1985, Chancellor's Disting. lectr. award U. Calif., Irvine, 1993; U. Md. Academic Research grantee, 1982-85. Mem. Acad Mgmt. (Outstanding Paper award 1987), Am. Psychological Assn., So. Mgmt. Assn. Democrat. Roman Catholic. Office: U Wash Sch Bus Adminstrn MacKenzie Hall DJ 10 Seattle WA 98195

GITNER, DEANNE, writer; b. Lyons, N.Y., Jan. 8, 1944; d. Myron and Mary (Kurland) Gebell; m. Gerald L. Gitner, June 24, 1968; children: Daniel Mark, Seth Michael. AB, Cornell U., 1966. Cert. English tchr. Tchr. English Gates (N.Y.) Chili Cen. Sch., 1966-68, Wantagh (N.Y.) Jr. and Sr. High Sch., 1968-70, F. Weiner Sch., Houston, 1980-81; writer Bellaire Texan, Houston, 1980; rep. sales McDougal Littel & Co., Chgo., 1981-83; writer Millburn Short Hills Ind., New Providence, N.J., 1987-93; comm. coord. Millburn Twp. (N.J.) Pub. Schs., Milburn, N.J., 1993—. Contbr. articles to profl. publs. Bd. mem. TU-36, Summit, N.J. Mem. Nat. Coun. Jewish Women (v.p. Houston sect. 1976-79, pres. 1980-81, v.p. Essex County N.J. sect. 1983-88, pub. rels. com. 1981-90, chmn. nat. bull. subcom. 1990-93, Vol. award), Soc. Profl. Journalists, Nat. Fedn. Press Women, N.J. Press Women (2d prize comm. contest 1992, hon. mention 1990, 1st prize 1993, 94, 3d prize nat. contest 1994, newsletter editor 1992), N.J. Sch. Pub. Rels. Assn., Cornell Club No. N.J. (v.p. 1992, 93, pres. 1994, 95). Office: Millburn Twp Pub Schs 434 Millburn Ave Millburn NJ 07041-1210

GITTLER, WENDY, artist, art educator, writer; b. Manhattan, N.Y.; d. Lewis Frederic and Esther (Becker) G. Studied with George Grosz, Art Students League, N.Y., 1958-59; studied with Camillio Egas, N.Y.C., 1960; BS in Art History, Columbia U., 1963; MA in Art History, Hunter Coll., 1967; postgrad., NYU, 1968; MFA, Bklyn. Coll., 1973; postgrad., U. Paris, 1977-78. Lectr. art NYU, N.Y.C., 1966-68; lectr. art history Farleigh Dickson, Teaneck, N.J., 1966-68; lectr., art history Hunter Coll., N.Y.C., 1968-80; lectr. art history Sch. Visual Arts, N.Y.C., 1979-86; lectr. Met. Mus., N.Y.C., 1988-89; lectr. art history Parsons Sch. of Design, N.Y.C., 1989—; lectr. N.Y. Studio Sch., N.Y.C., 1991—; instr. studio U. Haifa, Israel, 1971; curator First Street Gallery, N.Y.C., 1992; lectr. Brown U., R.I., 1993, South Fla. Art Ctr., 1990, Lowe Art Mus., U. Miami, Fla., 1984; moderator artists panels Artists Equity, N.Y.C., 1995-96. One-woman shows include First St. Gallery, N.Y.C., 1995, 88, 82, 76; exhibited in group shows at Blue Mountain Gallery, N.Y.C., 1995, Ashawag Hall, East Hampton, N.Y., 1995, LeHigh U., Bethlehem, Pa., 1984, Gallery of Fine Arts, N.Y.C., 1976, N.Y. City C.C., 1975; contbg. author art jours., exhibit catalogues. Mem. Coll. Art Assn., Fedn. Modern Painters and Sculptors, Channel 13. Home: 780 W End Ave New York NY 10025

GITTMAN, ELIZABETH, education educator; b. N.Y.C., Mar. 15, 1945; d. Kallman and Rebecca (Santcroos) G.; m. Aug. 5, 1965 (div. 1977); children: Stephen Loeb, Leslie Loeb, Sherry Loeb; m. Victor Arnel, Mar. 5, 1981. BS, NYU, 1966; MS, CUNY Queens Coll., 1969; PhD, Hofstra U., 1979, Cert. Advanced Study, 1987. Cert. ednl. adminstr., N.Y. Tchr. N.Y.C. Bd. Edn., Kew Gardens, 1966-68; instr. New Sch. for Social Rsch., N.Y.C., 1980-81; ind. cons., 1981-84; coord. instl. rsch. and evaluation Bd. Coop. Ednl. Svcs. of Nassau County, Westbury, N.Y., 1984-94; assoc. prof. N.Y. Inst. Tech., Old Westbury, 1994—; adj. prof. L.I. U., Brookville, N.Y., 1987-93. Mem. high risk youth rev. com. Ctr. Substance Abuse Prevention, U.S. Dept. HHS, 1990-95; developer numerous ednl. programs. Hofstra U. Doctoral fellow, 1976. Mem. APA, Am. Ednl. Rsch. Assn., Am. Evaluation Assn., Nat. Coun. Measurement in Edn., Northeastern Ednl. Rsch. Assn. (editor 1993-95, treas. 1996—, membership com. 1989-90, nominating com. 1991, program co-chair 1993, program com. 1989-92, bd. dirs. 1993—), L.I. ASCD, Kappa Delta Pi, Phi Delta Kappa (rsch. rep. 1990-91, sec. 1991-93, conf. co-chair 1992, v.p. 1993-94, pres.-elect 1994-95, pres. 1994-96, exec. bd. 1990—). Republican. Jewish. Office: Sch Edn NY Inst Tech Old Westbury NY 11568

GIUFFRIA, TINA B., accountant; b. Kenner, La., Feb. 9, 1972; d. Larry Herman Holder and Linda Jean Le Grande Briant; m. Robert M. Giuffria Jr. BS in Acctg., U. New Orleans, 1994; MBA, Loyola U., 1996. Asst. mgr. Mothers Work/Maternité, New Orleans, 1989-91; asst. acct. FNBC, New Orleans, 1991-94; lead tax auditor The Gary W. Lambert Co., Gretna, La., 1994—. Mem. partnership in edn. com. Young Leadership Coun., New Orleans, 1993-94; shadow program dir. Sigma Iota Epsilon, New Orleans, 1993-94. Recipient Scholarship and Svc. award Sigma Iota Epsilon, 1994. Republican. Roman Catholic. Home: 2001 Cypress Creek Rd Apt D322 New Orleans LA 70123

GIULIANTI, MARA SELENA, mayor, civic worker; b. N.Y.C., June 3, 1944; d. Leon and Bertha (Jablonky) Berman; m. Donald Giulianti, May 29, 1966; children: Stacey Alexander, Michael Alan. BA, Tulane U., 1966. Social worker L.A. County Social Svcs., 1966-68; adminstrv. asst. neurosurg. cons. D. Giulianti, MD, Hollywood, Fla., 1980-83; campaign mgr. City Commr. Suzanne Gunzburger, Hollywood, 1982; mayor City of Hollywood, 1986-90, 92—; vice chmn. Broward Employment and Tng. Adminstrn., 1987-89, 92—, chmn., 1989-90, 92—; mem. exec. bd. Fla. League Cities, Tallahassee, 1986-90, 92-94, bd. dirs., 1990-91, 94—; mem. econ. devel. task force Nat. League Cities, Washington, 1987-90, human devel. policy com., 1992-94, fin., adminstrn. and intergovtl. rels. steering com., 1994—; mem. Broward County Met. Planning Orgn., 1986-90. Contbr. articles to local newspapers. Pres. Women in Distress, Broward County, 1982-83, bd. dirs., 1983-90, trustee, 1994—; v.p. CHARLEE Family Care Homes, Broward County, 1986-88, bd. dirs., 1988-92; mem. Broward County Commn. on Status Women, 1984-86, Fla. Commn. on Drug and Alcohol Concerns, Tallahassee, 1984-85, Broward County Dem. Exec. Com., 1984-88; pres. Hills Dem. Club, 1991-94; bd. trustees Graves Mus. of Archeol. and Nat. History, Dania, Fla., 1993—; bd. dirs. Hollywood Econ. Growth Corp., 1994-95. Recipient Hannah G. Solomon award, 1983, Giraffe Stick Your Neck Out award Women's Advocacy - the Majority/Minority, 1986, Leadership award Leadership Hollywood Alumni, 1987, City of Peace award Israel Bonds, Broward County, 1987, Broward County Woman of Yr., Am. Jewish Congress, 1988, Menorah award Histadrut, 1990; named Woman of Yr. Women in Comms., Inc., 1990; inducted Broward County Women's Hall of Fame, 1996. Mem. Nat. Coun. Jewish Women (nat. bd. dirs. 1985-89), Jewish Fedn. So. Broward (chair community rels. com. 1981-82, bd. dirs. 1982-90), Broward County Med. Aux. (br. pres. 1977-78), Nat. Jewish Community Rels. Adv. Coun. (exec. bd. 1985-87), Rotary. Democrat. Office: PO Box 229045 Hollywood FL 33022

GIVENS, DEBORAH TAYLOR, newspaper publisher; b. Gary, Ind., June 19, 1953; d. Harvey Cecil and Dolores Dean (Moore) Taylor; m. Roger Grady Givens, Dec. 3, 1977; children: Chris, Cynthia, Craig, Carla, Elizabeth. BS, Ball State U., 1974. Editor Green River Rep., Morgantown, Ky., 1974-78; health environmentalist Ky. State Dept. Health, Morgantown, 1979-80; editor, pub., founder Butler County Banner, Morgantown, 1982—. Chairperson 50th Anniversary Salute/Banquet for WWII Vets., Butler County, 1995, Green River Catfish Festival, 1988; troop leader Girl Scouts U.S., 1975-77, 86-89. Recipient Journalism Alumnus award Ball State U., Muncie, Ind., 1978. Mem. Ky. Press Assn. (Freedom of Info. award 1978, numerous writing, photography and design awards). Democrat. Methodist. Office: Butler County Banner Green River Republican 119 N Main St Morgantown KY 42261

GIVENS, JANET EATON, writer; b. N.Y.C., July 5, 1932; d. Irving Daniel and Matilda (Schmelzle) E.; m. Richard Ayres Givens, Aug. 24, 1957; children—Susan Ruth, Jane Lucile. B.A., Queens Coll., 1953; M.A., Columbia U., 1955. Lic. tchr., N.Y. Tchr. pub. elem. schs., Silver Spring, Md., 1953-55, Mamaroneck, N.Y., 1955-59; supr. prospective tchrs., part-time lectr. Queens Coll., N.Y.C., 1959-68. Author: The Migrating Birds, 1964; Something Wonderful Happened, 1982; Just Two Wings, 1984; contbg. author: Tensions Our Children Live With, 1959. V.p. PTA, Pub. Sch. 219, Queens, N.Y., 1972-73, del. to United Parents Assn., 1971-72, editor PS 219 News, 1971-73. Home: 14711 68th Rd Flushing NY 11367-1332

GIZA, MARIE THERESA, elementary school educator, secondary school educator; b. Balt., May 1, 1931; d. Joseph Frank and Frances Theresa (Staniec) G.; B.A., Coll. of Notre Dame of Md., 1953; M.A., Cath. U. Am., 1960; Cert. Advanced Studies in Edn., Johns Hopkins U., 1972, M.S., 1982; postgrad. (scholar) U. Oslo, 1973. Elem. tchr. St. Jerome's Sch., Balt., 1953-56; social studies tchr. Cath. High Sch. of Balt., 1956-62, guidance counselor, 1962; Polish language instr. evening coll. Essex Community Coll., 1975-77; primary and intermediate tchr. Balt. Highlands Elem. Sch., 1962-92, ret., 1992; instr. in-service creative writing course for tchrs., Balt. County, 1978-80; cons. on social studies and econs. Carroll County Schs., 1983. Sec. Polish Nat. Alliance, Group 692, 1975-78; treas. PTA, 1974-76; mem. ethnic adv. com. for Balt. City Sch. Tchrs., 1979-83; pres. St. Stanislaus Parish Council, 1978-80, former pres. Southeast Area Council, Balt. Archdiocese; instr. Polish Nat. Alliance Language Sch. Father Koble Soc. Language Sch. St. Casimir's Parish, 1978-82; seminar lectr. to Lithuanian tchrs., Vilnius, Lithuania 1995; tchr. of English Lujiang U., Xiamen, China, 1992; 1st sec. Archdiocesan Pastoral Council, Balt. Recipient Elinor Pancoast award for excellence in teaching econs., 1978; cert. of merit Joint Council on Econ. Edn. and Internat. Paper Co. Found., 1982; Balt. Polish Community award, 1980; NDEA fellow in lang. arts to Kutztown State Tchrs. Coll., 1956; Russian scholar, Georgetown U., 1963-64, Fulbright scholar, India, 1990; recipient scholarships Jagiellonian U., Cracow, Poland, 1974. Cath. U. Lublin, Poland, 1976, Mikotaj Kopernik U., Torun, Poland, 1978, tchr. of yr. award in social studies Md. Coun. for Social Studies, 1992. Mem. NEA, Nat. Coun. Tchrs. English, Nat. Coun. for the Social Studies, Nat. Coun. Geographic Edn., Nat. Assn. for Ethnic Studies, Md. Geographic Alliance, Md. Tchrs. Assn., Tchrs. Assn. Baltimore County (One of Outstanding Tchrs. award 1983), Md. Coun. Tchrs. English Language Arts (disting. svc. award 1993, tchr. of yr. elementary 1985), Md. Council Tchrs. of English (tchr. of yr. award 1988), Women Educators of Balt. County (pres. 1992-93), Smithsonian Assn., Eta Sigma Phi, Delta Epsilon Sigma, Phi Delta Gamma, Pi Lambda Theta (cert. award for outstanding presentation on China 1994). Democrat. Roman Catholic. Contbr. articles to Creative Teacher; contbr. articles to profl. jours.; speaker in field. Home: 4000 N Charles St Apt 701 Baltimore MD 21218-1735

GLACEL, BARBARA PATE, management consultant; b. Balt., Sept. 15, 1948; d. Jason Thomas Pate and Sarah Virginia (Forwood) Wetter; m. Robert Allan Glacel, Dec. 21, 1969; children: Jennifer Warren, Sarah Allane, Ashley Virginia. AB, Coll. William and Mary, 1970; MA, U. Okla., 1973, PhD, 1978. Tchr. Harford County (Md.) Schs., 1970-71; tchr. Dept. Def. Schs., W.Ger., 1971-73; ednl. counselor U.S. Army, Germany, 1973-74; mgmt. cons. Barbara Glacel & Assocs., Anchorage, 1980-86, Washington, 1986-88; ptnr. Pracel Prints, Williamsburg, Va., 1981-85; sr. mgmt. tng. specialist Arco Alaska, Inc., 1984-85; gen. mgr. mgmt. programs Hay Systems, Inc., Washington, 1986-88; CEO VIMA Internat., Burke, Va., 1988—; 2d v.p., bd. dirs. Chesapeake Broadcasting Corp. Md.; adj. prof. U. Md., 1973-74, Suffolk U., Boston, 1974-77, C.W. Post Ctr., L.I. U., John Jay Coll. Criminal Justice, N.Y.C., 1979-80, St. Thomas Aquinas Coll., N.Y.C., 1981, St. Mary's Coll., Leavenworth, Kans., 1981, Anchorage C.C., 1982; acad. adviser Ctrl. Mich. U., 1981-82; asst. prof. U. Alaska, Anchorage, 1983-85; mem. adj. faculty Ctr. for Creative Leadership, 1986—; guest lectr. U.S. Mil. Acad.; mem. U.S. Army Sci. Bd., 1986-90; mem. U.S. Dept. Def. Sci. Bd. Quality of Life Panel, 1994-95. Author: Regional Transit Authorities, 1983; (with others) 1000 Army Families, 1983, The Army Community and Their Families, 1989, Light Bulbs for Leaders, 1994. Chmn. 172d Inf. Brigade Family Coun. Recipient Comdr.'s award for pub. svc. U.S. Dept. Army, 1984, U.S. Army Patriotic Civilian Svc. award 1991, U.S. Army Forscom Svc. award 1993; AAUW grantee, 1977-78. Mem. ASTD (bd. dirs. Anchorage chpt.), Am. Psychol. Assn., Soc. for Indsl. and Organizational Psychology, Instrnl. Systems Assn. (v.p. 1993-96), Soc. of Alumni Coll. of William and Mary (bd. dirs. 1992—). Home: 5290 Lyngate Ct Burke VA 22015-1688 Office: VIMA Internat 5290 Lyngate Ct Burke VA 22015-1688

GLACKIN, JUDITH M., secondary school counselor, educator; b. Pitts., Sept. 11, 1951; d. Paul Bernard and Mary Elizabeth (Baum) G. BS in Edn., Slippery Rock (Pa.) U., 1973, MS in Edn., 1992. Cert. tchr. and secondary sch. guidance counselor. Tchr. Karns City (Pa.) H.S., 1972-92, guidance counselor, 1992—. Mem. Am. Counseling Assn., Am. Sch. Counselors Assn., Butler County Counselors (v.p. 1995—). Office: Karns City HS 1446 Kittanning Pike Karns City PA 16041

GLAD, SUZANNE LOCKLEY, retired museum director; b. Rochester, N.Y., Oct. 2, 1929; d. Alfred Allen and Lucille A. (Watson) Lockley; m. Edward Newman Glad, Nov. 7, 1953; children: Amy, Lisanne Glad Lantz, William E. BA, Sweet Briar Coll., 1951; MA, Columbia U., 1952. Exec. dir. New York State Young Reps., N.Y.C., 1951-57; mem. pub. rels. staff Dolphin Group, L.A., 1974-83; scheduling sec. Gov.'s Office, Sacramento, 1983-87; dep. dir. Calif. Mus. Sci. and Industry, L.A., 1987-94; ret. Mem. Calif. Rep. League, Pasadena, 1969—; mem. Assistance League of Flintridge, 1970—, Flintridge Guild Children's Hosp., 1969-89. Mem. Sweet Briar Alumnae of So. Calif. (pres. 1972), Phi Beta Kappa, Tau Phi. Episcopalian.

GLADKI, HANNA ZOFIA, civil engineer, hydraulic mixer specialist; b. Krakow, Poland, Dec. 30, 1933; came to U.S., 1984; d. Stanislaw Wojtanowski and Maria (Ekiert) Wojtanowska; m. Jozef Gladki, July 2, 1955 (dec. 1982); 1 child, Ania. ScD, Tech. U., Warsaw, Poland, 1966; postgrad. degree, Agrl. U., Wroclaw, Poland, 1977. Asst. prof. Agrl. Acad. Krakow, 1966-70, assoc. prof., 1970-81, chair dept., 1973-83, dean of faculty, 1977-81, prof., 1981-85; hydraulic mixer specialist ITT Flygt Corp., Norwalk, Conn., 1985—; presenter at profl. confs. Contbr. articles to profl. publs. Mem. AIChE, N.Am. Mixing Forum, Internat. Assn. Hydraulic Rsch. Roman Catholic. Home: 79 Melville St Stratford CT 06497-5723 Office: ITT Flygt Corp PO Box 1004 Trumbull CT 06611-0943

GLADSTONE, CAROL LYNN, assistant principal; b. N.Y.C., Aug. 14, 1944; d. Albert Ludwig and Jeanne (Eisner) Adler; m. Edward Gladstone, Nov. 20, 1973. BA, Hunter Coll., 1965; MA, CCNY, N.Y.C., 1967; PhD, Columbia Pacific U., 1988, postgrad., 1993-94. Cert. tchr. English, French, sch. dist. adminstr., Ariz., Conn., N.J., N.Y. English/reading tchr. Jr. High Sch. #120, N.Y.C., 1965-66; reading coord. Dewitt Clinton High Sch., Bronx, 1966-74; asst. chair John F. Kennedy High Sch., Bronx, 1974-85; asst. prin. James Monroe High Sch., Bronx, 1985—; prin. PM/Saturday Sch. James Monroe H.S., 1993-94; trainer of adminstrv. staff Bronx. Supt.'s Office, 1992—, Manhattan Supt.'s Office, 1989-90; adj. prof. Coll. of New Rochelle, N.Y., 1988-89, Lehman Coll., Bronx, 1987-88. Contbr. articles to profl. jours.; author: Competence in Cloze, 1989; author series of books: Gladstone Comprehensive Writing Program, 1986-88. Sec. Westchester (N.Y.) Alzheimer's Disease Assn., 1980-87; reporter Pub. Access Cable TV, Westchester, 1982-83. Named Supr. of Yr. Bronx Supt.'s Office, 1990-91, 94-95, Educator of Yr. Assn. Tchrs. N.Y., 1987-88, 90-91, Educator as Writer Mayor of City of N.Y., 1986; N.Y. Inst. for Humanities fellow, 1994. Mem. ASCD (assoc.), N.Y. State English Coun. (Educator of Excellence 1992-93, 95-96, regional dir. 1994—), N.Y. State Reading Assn., Bronx Assn. Prins. of English (standing com. on English 1995), Nat. Bd. for Profl. Teaching Standards, Nat. Coun. Tchrs. English.

GLAESSMANN, DORIS ANN, former county official, consultant; b. Northampton, Pa., Feb. 18, 1940; d. Frank G. and Theresa (Fischl) Zwikl; m. Edward Glaessmann, Sept. 1, 1962; children: Edward Jr., Robert F. Grad. high sch., Northampton, 1958. Sec., bookkkeeper John F. Moore Agy., Inc., Allentown, Pa., 1958-64; ct. clk. Criminal div. Clk. of Cts. Office, Allentown, 1968-69, asst. dep. clk., 1969-76, chief dep. clk., 1976-82; clk. of cts., criminal and civil divsns. Lehigh County, Allentown, 1982-95; cons., 1995—. Den mother, sec. Cub Scout Pack 140, Allentown, Pa., 1973-78; mem., past bd. dirs., 1st v.p. Quota Club Allentown, 1983—; mem. coun. St. Peter's Evang. Luth. Ch., Allentown, 1984-89. Mem. Pa. Prothonotaries and Clks. Assn. (past pres., treas. 1993—), Pa. Elected Women's Assn. (past sec.-treas. and pres. Lehigh Valley chpt.). Democrat. Home: 945 E Lynnwood St Allentown PA 18103-5250

GLANCY, DOROTHY JEAN, lawyer, educator; b. Glendale, Calif., Sept. 24, 1944; d. Walter Perry and Elva T. (Douglass) G.; m. Jon Tobias Anderson, June 8, 1979. BA, Wellesley Coll., 1967; JD, Harvard Law Sch., 1970. Bar: D.C. 1971, Calif. 1976, U.S. Dist. Ct. D.C. 1971, U.S. Ct. Appeals (D.C. cir.) 1972. Assoc. Hogan & Hartson, Wash., 1971-73; counsel U.S. Senate Judiciary Subcomm. on Constitutional Rights, Wash., 1973-74; fellow in Law & Humanities Harvard U., Cambridge, Mass., 1974-75; asst. to assoc. prof. law Santa Clara U., Calif., 1975-82, prof. law, 1984—; vis. prof. law U. Arizona, Tucson, 1979; asst. gen. counsel U.S. Dept. of Agr., 1982-83; cons. Commn. Fed. Paperwork, Wash., 1976; dir. summer Law Study Program in Hong Kong, 1985-90; advisor Restatement, Third Property: Servitudes, 1986—. Dir. legal rsch. project regarding privacy and intelligent trnsp. systems Fed. Hwy. Adminstrn., 1993-95; mem. coun. Harvard Law Sch. Assn., 1991—; v.p. Presidio Hts. Assn. Neighbors, 1990—. Fellow Wellesley Coll., Harvard U. Mem. ABA (chair ethics com. of sect. on natural resources, energy and environ. law, 1993—, coun. mem. 1995—), State Bar Calif. (mem. environ. law sect., exec. com. 1993—), Am. Assn. Law Schs. (chair environ. law sect. 1992-93, chair property sect. 1996—), Am. Law Inst., Calif. Women Lawers, Soc. Am. Law Tchrs., Phi Beta Kappa. Democrat. Office: Santa Clara U Sch Law Santa Clara CA 95053

GLANTZ, GINA, consultant; b. N.Y.C., Apr. 3, 1943; d. Nathan L. and Lillian (Rosenbaum) Stritzler; m. Ronald A. Glantz, Oct. 17, 1968; children—Amy Samantha, Peter Samuel. B.A., U. Calif.-Berkeley, 1965. Chief of staff County Exec. Peter Shapiro, County of Essex, N.J., 1978-82; owner, mgr. Gina Glantz Cons., Springfield, N.J., 1982-83; sr. cons. Mondale for Pres., Washington, 1984; nat. field dir. Mondale/Ferraro, Inc., Washington, 1984; ptnr. Martin & Glantz, Mill Valley, Calif. and Rosslyn, Va., 1985—. Home: 96 Avenue Del Norte San Anselmo CA 94960-2510 Office: Martin & Glantz 100 Shoreline Hwy Mill Valley CA 94941-3645

GLASBERG, PAULA DRILLMAN, advertising executive; b. Dusseldorf, Germany, Nov. 22, 1939; came to U.S., 1940, naturalized, 1942; d. Solomon and Regina (Rubin) Drillman; m. H. Mark Glasberg, June 19, 1960; children: Scot Bradley, Hilary Jennifer. BA, Bklyn. Coll., 1957; MA, New Sch. Social Research, 1959, PhD, 1962. Rsch. asst. McCann-Erickson, N.Y.C., 1962-64; v.p. Marplan, Inc., N.Y.C., 1964-70, Tinker/Pritchard Wood, Inc., N.Y.C., 1970-72; exec. v.p., chmn. exec. com. Rosenfeld, Sirowitz & Lawson, Inc., N.Y.C., 1972-78; exec. v.p., chmn. exec. com., dir. Marschalk Co. div. Interpublic Group of Cos., N.Y.C., 1978-1982; exec. v.p., dir., dir. strategic planning McCann-Erickson World Wide, Inc., 1983—, world wide exec. v.p., dir. strategic planning, 1990—; assoc. prof. Columbia U. Sch. Bus. Adminstrn., 1991—; bd. dirs. Stern Coll. for Women, 1987—; sponsor mem. Yeshiva U. Women's Orgn., 1985—. Fellow APA, NAS, Nat. Rsch. Coun., Nat. Assn. Psychologists; mem. AAAS, Am. Assn. Advt. Agys., Am. Mktg. Assn., Advt. Rsch. Found., Internat. Platform Assn. Office: McCann-Erickson World Wide Inc 750 3rd Ave New York NY 10017-2703

GLASER, ANN KARRICK, marketing professional. Cert. fin. mgmt., IBM Advanced Bus. Inst., 1989; BA cum laude, Hollins Coll., 1985. From statis.

programmer to client rep. IBM Corp., 1984-93; internat. acct. cons. AT&T Comm., 1993-94; freelance mktg. profl. Bradford series divsn. Sargent Mfg., 1995-96; pub. rels. and mktg. comm. cons. Kerr Kelly Thompson, Greenwich, Conn., 1996, pub. rels. and mktg. cons., 1996—; sports mktg. partnership & properties divsn. Advantage Internat. Mktg.; event planner Atre Internat. Cons., Inc., 1986-87. V.p. promotion and publicity Conn. Speedskating Assn.; co-dir. Fairfield (Conn.) Network Exec. Women, 1995-96; chair pub. rels. com. Jr. League Stamford-Norwalk (Conn.); reunion program co-chair, career assistance network rep., local area chair S.E. Fla., Hollins Coll.; organizer USO; prodr. tennis tournament fund raiser Sunrise Presbybn. Ch.; cons. Jr. Achievement; tutor Learn to Read/Project Literacy. Home: 65 Marsh Rd Easton CT 06612-1296

GLASER, VERA ROMANS, journalist; b. St. Louis; d. Aaron L. and Mollie (Romans); m. Herbert R. Glaser, Apr. 16, 1939; 1 dau., Carol Jane Barriger. Student, Washington U., St. Louis, George Washington U., Am. U., 1937-40. Reporter-writer Nat. Aero. mag., 1943-44; reporter Washington Times Herald, 1944-46; pub. relations specialist Great Lakes-St. Lawrence Assn., 1950-51; promotion specialist, writer Congl. Quar. News Features, 1951-54; writer-commentator radio sta. WGMS, Washington, 1954-55; mem. Washington bur. N.Y. Herald Tribune, 1955-56; press officer U.S. Senator Charles E. Potter, 1956-59; dir. pub. relations, women's div. Rep. Nat. Com., 1959-62; press officer U.S. Senator Kenneth B. Keating, 1962-63; Washington corr. N.Am. Newspaper Alliance, 1963-69, bur. chief, 1965-69; columnist, nat. corr. Knight-Ridder Newspapers, Inc., 1969-81; assoc. editor Washingtonian Mag., 1981-88, contbg. editor, 1988—; columnist Maturity News Svc., 1988-94; mem. Pres.'s Commn. on White House Fellows, 1969, Pres.'s Task Force on Women's Rights and Responsibilities, 1970; judge 1981 Robert Kennedy Journalism Awards. Free-lance writer nat. publs.; radio and TV appearances on Stas. WTOP-TV, ABC, PBS, C-SPAN. Mem. nat. bd. Med. Coll. Pa., 1977-88; bd. dirs. Washington Press Club Found., 1986-88; bd. dirs. Internat. Women's Media Found., 1990—. Mem. White House Corrs. Assn., Nat. Press Club (bd. govs. 1988, 89), Washington Press Club (pres. 1971-72), Cosmos Club. Unitarian. Home and Office: 5000 Cathedral Ave NW Washington DC 20016

GLASGOW, AGNES JACKIE, social welfare administrator, therapist; b. El Paso, Tex., July 23, 1941; d. Carl Lecota Pace and Henrietta Ford (Cozart) Robertson; m. Morgan Walton, Sept. 20, 1958 (div. 1979); children: Scotty Gene, Carley Earlene Walton DeVore; m. Phillip Sidney Glasgow, Aug. 9, 1986. Lic., Trinidad State Jr. Coll., Colo., 1968; AAS, Met. State Coll., Denver, 1979, BS, 1980; MPA, U. Colo., Denver, 1987. Cert. substance abuse counselor, Colo., Tenn. Pvt. practice Life Counseling Ctr., Denver, Memphis, 1980—; coord. masters program for substance abuse Met. State Coll., Denver, 1980-81; exec. dir. Concord Commons Counseling Ctr., Decatur, Ill., 1981-82; child care specialist Adams Community Mental Health Ctr., Commerce City, Colo., 1982-84; adolescent family counselor Parkside Lodge Colo., Thorhton, Colo., 1984-86; family therapist Charter Lakeside Hosp., Memphis, 1986-87; counselor, coord. Shelby State Community Coll., Memphis, 1987-88; supr. adolescent and young adult program Meth. Outreach, Memphis, 1988-90; sr. mental health specialist dual diagnosis unit Meth. Hosp. Cen., 1990—, relapse prevention specialist, 1994—; cons., part-time instr. Shelby State C.C., Memphis. Contbr. articles to profl. jours. Com. mem. Youth Suicide Task Force, Memphis, 1988—. Recipient Vol. of Yr. award United Way, Decatur, Ill., 1982, Cmty. Svc. award scholarship Mental Health Soc., 1983, Outstanding Svc. award, 1989, Disting. Svc. award Sheriff Dept., Memphis, 1988; nominated Diamond award Memphis Mental Health Assn., 1994. Mem. Nat. Orgn. Human Svc. Workers, Nat. Orgn. Substance Abuse Counselors, Surrender Al Anon (group rep.), Am. Assn. Counseling & Devel., Psi Chi (treas. 1979-80). Republican. Methodist. Office: 10 Thomas 1265 Union Ave Memphis TN 38104-3415 also: 1835 Union Ave Ste 203 Memphis TN 38104-3900

GLASGOW, KAREN, special education educator; b. N.Y.C., May 20, 1954; d. Douglas G. Glasgow. BS in Edn., U. Wis., 1976; MS in Spl. Edn., U. So. Calif., 1979. Spl. edn. tchr. Lanterman Sch., L.A. Chairperson commn. gender equity L.A. Unified Sch. Dist. Mem. Assoc. Adminstrs. L.A., Women in Ednl. Leadership, Coun. Black Adminstrs.

GLASS, AMY BORRESS, lawyer; b. Bklyn., Apr. 13, 1964. AB, Smith Coll., 1986; JD, Yeshiva U., 1989. Bar: N.Y. 1989, U.S. Dist. Ct. (so. and ea. dists.) N.Y. 1990. Ptnr. Anderson Kill Olick & Oshinsky, N.Y.C. Notes and comments editor Cardozo Arts and Entertainment Law Jour., 1988-89. Mem. Assn. of Bar of City of N.Y., N.Y. State Bar Assn., ABA. Office: Anderson Kill Olick & Oshinsky 1251 Ave of the Americas New York NY 10020*

GLASS, CAROL PAULA, rabbi; b. Hartford, Conn., Dec. 14, 1953; d. Bernard Lewis and Faye Ruth (Lipman) G.; m. Michael Bruce Swartz, Dec. 27, 1987; children: Nadav, Barak. BA in Religion, Barnard Coll., 1975; M Jewish Edn., Jewish Theol. Sem., 1977; M Hebrew Letters, Hebrew Union Coll., 1982; cert. in pastoral counseling, Postgrad. Ctr. Mental Health, 1984. Ordained rabbi, 1984. Rabbi North Shore Havurah, Great Neck, N.Y., 1984-85; exec. dir. Hillel Found. at Am. U., Washington, 1985-90; counselor, staff trainer Jewish Family and Children's Svc., Canton, Mass., 1990-91; rabbi, univ. chaplain Boston U./Hillel Found., 1991—. Contbr. articles to profl. publs. Co-founder Jewish Women's Resource Ctr., N.Y.C., 1976—; mem. adv. bd. urban concerns task force JCRC, Boston, 1993—; mem. governing bd. Danielsen Inst., Boston, 1995—. Mem. Ctrl. Conf. Am. Rabbis, Women's Rabbinic Network (regional rep. 1993-95), Mass. Bd. Rabbis, Religious Coalition for Reproductive Rights. Home: 15 Nardone Rd Newton MA 02159 Office: Hillel Found Boston U 233 Bay State Rd Boston MA 02215

GLASS, DOROTHEA DANIELS, physiatrist, educator; b. N.Y.C.; d. Maurice B. and Anna S. (Kleegman) Daniels; m. Robert E. Glass, June 23, 1940; children: Anne Glass Roth, Deborah, Catherine Glass Barrett, Eugene. BA, Cornell U., 1940; MD, Woman's Med. Coll. Pa., 1954; post-grad., U. Pa., 1960-61; DMS (hon.), Med. Coll. Pa., 1987. Diplomate: Am. Bd. Phys. Medicine and Rehab. (guest bd. examiner 1978, 89). Intern Albert Einstein Med. Center, Phila., 1954-55, clin. asst. dept. medicine, 1956-59, attending phys. medicine and rehab., 1968-70, chmn. dept. phys. medicine and rehab., sr. attending, 1971-85; chief rehab. medicine VA Med. Ctr., Miami, Fla., 1985-95; clin. prof. dept. orthopaedics and rehab. U. Miami Sch. Medicine, 1985—; Lois Mattox Miller fellow preventive medicine Woman's Med. Coll. Pa., 1955-56, instr. preventive medicine, 1956-59, instr. medicine, 1960-62; resident phys. medicine and rehab. VA Hosp., Phila., 1959-62, chief phys. medicine and rehab., 1966-68, cons., 1968-82; asst. clin. dir. Jefferson Med. Coll. Hosp., Phila., 1963-66, Camden County Stroke Program, Cooper Hosp., Camden, N.J., 1963-66; gen. practice medicine, Phila., 1956-59; asst. med. dir., chief rehab. medicine and rehab. Moss Rehab. Hosp., Phila., 1968-70, med. dir., 1971-82, sr. cons., 1982—; mem. active staff Temple U., Phila., 1968—, asso. prof. rehab. medicine, 1968-73, prof., 1973—, dir. residency tng. rehab. medicine, 1968-82; program dir. Rehab. Research and Tng. Center, 1977-80, chmn. dept. rehab. medicine, 1977-82; staff physician Hosp. Med. Coll. Pa., Phila., 1955-59, vis. asso. prof. neurology, 1973-79, clin. prof., 1977-82, vis. prof., 1982-96; mem. cons. staff Frankford Hosp., Phila., 1968-82, Phila. Geriatric Center, 1975-82; mem. active staff Willowcrest-Bamberger Hosp., Phila., 1980-82; asso. phys. medicine and rehab. U. Pa. Sch. Medicine, Phila., 1962-66; asst. prof. clin. phys. medicine and rehab., 1966-68; asst. clin. dir. dept. phys. medicine and rehab. Jefferson Med. Coll., Phila., 1963-66. Contbr. articles to profl. jours. Mem. profl. adv. com. Easter Seal Soc. Crippled Children and Adults Pa., 1975-82; active Goodwill Industries Phila., 1973-82, Cmty. Home Health Svcs. Phila., 1974-82, Ea. Pa. chpt. Arthritis Found., 1968-82. Recipient humanitarian svc. cert. Gov.'s Com. on Employment Handicapped, 1974, Outstanding Alumnae award Commonwealth of Pa. Bd., Hosp. Med. Coll. Pa., 1975, humanitarian award Pa. Easter Seal Soc., 1981, John Eiselie Davis award Am. Kinesiotherapy Assn., 1988, Carl Haven Young svc. award, 1994. Mem. AMA, Am. Acad. Med. Dirs., Am. Acad. Phys. Medicine and Rehab. (disting. clinician award 1995), Am. Assn. Electromyography and Electrodiagnosis (assoc.), Am. Assn. Sex Educators, Counselors and Therapists, Am. Burn Assn., Am. Coll. Antiology, Am. Coll. Utilization Rev., Am. Congress Rehab. Medicine (bd. govs., pres. 1986-87, gold Key award 1989), Am. Heart Assn. (coun. on cerebrovascular disease), Am. Lung Assn. Phila. and Montgomery County (bd. dirs. 1977-79), Am. Med. Women's Assn., Assn. Acad. Physicatrists, Assn. Med. Rehab. Dirs. and Coordinators, Coll. Physicians Phila., Emergency Care Rsch. Inst., Gerongol. Soc., Internat. Assn. Rehab. Facilities, Internat. Rehab. Medicine Assn., Pan Am. Med. Assn., Fla. Med. Assn., Fla. Soc. Phys. Medicine and Rehab. (pres. 1975-77), Pa. Med. Soc. (phys. medicine and rehab. adv. com. 1975-82), Pa. Thoracic Soc., Martin County Med. Soc., Delaware Valley Hosp. Coun. Forum, Phila. Med. Soc., Phila. PSRO (bd. dirs. 1975-82), Phila. Soc. Phys. Medicine and Rehab. (pres. 1968-69), Laennec Soc. Phila., Martin County Med. Assn., Royal Soc. Health, Alpha Omega Alpha.

GLASS, GLENDA JUNE, clinical microbiologist; b. Boise, Idaho, Oct. 8, 1950; d. James Myron and Elleen Grace (Heales) Glass; m. Tariq Khalidi, 1972. BS in Med. Tech., U. Nev., Reno, 1973. Cert. clin. lab. technologist, Calif.; cert. med. technologist. Clin. microbiologist Biomed. Resources, Concord, Calif., 1976-78, M.D. Anderson Hosp., Houston, 1978-80; supr. microbiology Fong Diagnostic Lab., Sacramento, 1981-91, quality assurance technologist, 1991-92; clin. microbiologist St. Joseph's Regional Health System, Stockton, Calif., 1992—. Supporter Women Escaping a Violent Environment, Sacramento; mem. Planned Parenthood; sponsor Childreach, Warwick, R.I. Fleischman scholar, 1969; Doctor's Wives scholar, 1972. Mem. NOW, Am. Soc. Clin. Pathologists, Am. Soc. for Microbiology.

GLASS, JANICE LYNN, nurse; b. Norristown, Pa., Mar. 30, 1957; d. G. David and Eleanor (Lepre) Pascale; m. Marc Glass, Oct. 7, 1984; 1 child, Matthew David. AAS, Montgomery County C.C., 1984. RN, Pa. Psychiatric technician Norristown (Pa.) State Hosp., 1978-83; med.-surg. nurse Montgomery Hosp., Norristown, 1984-85, peritoneal dialysis nurse, 1985, oncology nurse, 1986-89, recovery rm. nurse, 1989—; drug and alcohol nurse Valey Forge Med. Ctr., Norristown, 1993—; sch. nurse NAHS, Norristown, 1995—; legal nurse cons. Med.-Legal Cons. Inst., Houston. Contbr. editorials to newspapers, chpt. to book. Active Dem. Nat. Com., Nat. Abortion Rights Action League, Ams. United for Separation of Ch. and State, People for the Am. Way. Mem. NOW.

GLASS, JEAN ANN, special education services professional; b. Phoenix, Ariz., Mar. 15, 1934; d. James Leslie Giffin and Helen Lucille Griffith; m. Dwaine Charles Glass, Nov. 26, 1952; children: Michael James, Stephen Charles, Daphne Ann, Diona Lynn, Helen Louise, Geoffrey Giffin. Student, U. Nev., 1950-52; AA in Psychology, Mt. San Antonio Coll., 1973, AS in Mental Health, 1974; BA in Behavioral Sci., Calif. Polytechnic U., 1975; MA in Spl. Edn., Calif. State U., L.A., 1979, MA in Psychology, 1983; MS in Devel. Disabilities Programming, U La Verne, 1981, postgrad., 1981-85; postgrad., Azusa Pacific U., 1989. Instr. devel. disabled Chaffey C.C., Alta Loma, Calif., 1975-79; tchr., program dir. sch.- age parenting and infant devel. El Monte (Calif.) Union High Sch. Dist., 1981—; family life educator Nat. Coun. Family Rels., Mpls., 1988—; therapeutic recreation specialist Nat. Coun. Therapeutic Recreation, Thiells, N.Y., 1975—; rschr., psychiat. technician Frank D. Lanterman State Hosp. & Devel. Ctr., Pomona, Calif., 1981-94. Recipient cert. commendation State of Calif., 1985, City of El Monte, 1993. Mem. DAR, AAUW, Coun. Exceptional Children, Archaeol. Survey Assn. So. Calif., Inc., Bibl. Archaeology Soc., San Gabriel/Pomona Valley Alumnae Panhellenic Assn., Calif. Fedn. Chaparral Poets, Gamma Phi Beta. Republican. Mem. LDS Ch. Office: El Monte Union High Sch Dist 3537 Johnson Ave El Monte CA 91731

GLASS, LAUREL ELLEN, gerontologist, developmental biologist, physician, retired educator; b. Selma, Calif., Oct. 1, 1923; d. Sydney L. and Marie (Damron) G. B.A., U. Calif.-Berkeley, 1951; Ph.D., Duke U., 1958; M.D., U. Calif., San Francisco, 1974. Teaching asst. zoology Duke U., 1953-56; rsch. assoc. Pathology Rsch. Lab. Med. Rsch. divsn. VA Hosp., Durham, N.C., 1957-58; part-time instr. anatomy Duke U. Med. Sch., 1958; instr. dept. anatomy U. Calif. Med. Sch., San Francisco, 1958-61, asst. prof., 1961-66, assoc. prof., 1968-72, prof., 1972-89, prof. emeritus, 1989—, prof. psychiatry, 1984-89, prof. emeritus, 1989—, dir. Ctr. on Deafness, 1984-89, adj. prof. family and community medicine, 1983-89; dir. project on adaptation to adult onset hearing loss Langley Porter Psychiat. Inst., U. Calif. Med. Sch., San Francisco, 1989-92; mem. San Francisco adv. com. Child Health and Disability Prevention Program, 1974-79; mem. exec. com., bd. dirs. Mission Neighborhood Health Ctr., 1974-77; mem. med. adv. com. Coalition for Med. Rights of Women, 1974-87; mem. adv. bd. P.R. Orgn. Women Health Edn. Project, 1976-78; v.p. Developmental Disabilities Programs, Inc., 1976-87. Mem. edn. commn. NAACP, Ocean View-Merced Heights Community Stblzn. and Improvement Project, exec. com. Ocean View-Ingleside Dist. Council, Bay Area Social Planning Council, 1969-73, adv. council Nat. Ctr. for Vision and Aging, 1986-94; bd. dirs. Service Com. on Pub. Edn., 1963-66, Constl. Rights Found., 1965-73, Deaf Counseling, Adv. and Referral Agency (DCARA), 1985-86, Hearing Soc. for the Bay Area, Inc., 1984-86, 93—; trustee Self-Help for Hard of Hearing People, Inc., 1986-89, Glide Found., 1966-75, Gallaudet U., Washington, 1986—; bd. govs. Pub. Advs. Inc., 1975-79; mem. San Francisco Bd. Edn., 1967-71, pres., 1969; regent Lone Mountain Coll., 1973-76; pres. United Meth. Congress of the Deaf, 1993—. Mem. Am. Assn. Anatomists, Gerontol. Soc. Am., Am. Soc. on Aging, Self Help for Hard-of-Hearing People, Inc., Assn. Late Deafened Adults, Am. Deafness and Rehab. Assn., NOW, Phi Beta Kappa, Sigma Xi. Democrat. Methodist. Home: 1300 NE 16th Ave Apt 1408 Portland OR 97232-1467

GLASSBURN, TRACY ANN, geochemist, researcher; b. St. Petersburg, Fla., Oct. 7, 1962; d. Paul Douglass and Sharon Lou (DeVore) Glassburn; m. Stefan Ryszard Witek, Nov. 26, 1986 (div. Apr. 1991); m. Paul Slusarewicz, May 7, 1995. BSc, Coll. William and Mary, 1984; MS, Lehigh U., Bethlehem, Pa., 1987; PhD, U. London, 1993; DIC, Imperial Coll. Sci., Tech., London, 1993. Grad. rsch. asst. Lehigh U., Bethlehem, 1984-85, grad. teaching asst. geology, 1985-86, rsch. asst. dept. materials sci., 1987; rsch. scientist Cookson Rsch. Group, plc, London, 1988; teaching asst. geology Imperial Coll. Sci., Tech. and Medicine, London, 1989-92, rsch. asst. geology, 1990-91, rsch. assoc. geology, 1993-94; geochem. cons. Enfield, N.H., 1995—. Author abstracts in profl. jours. Mem. Brit. Geol. Soc., Paleontological Soc., Sigma Xi, Phi Eta Sigma, Alpha Lambda Delta, Sigma Gamma Epsilon. Home: 1725 Robinhood Ln Clearwater FL 34624-6449 Office: Shaker Farm 431-T RR2 Enfield NH 03748

GLASSCOCK, PAMELA, artist; b. New Haven, Aug. 26, 1950; d. Thomas Tilden and Ludmila (Majkut) G.; m. Tony King, Jan. 15, 1982; children: George King, John King. BA, Stanford U., 1972. Exhibited in shows at Susan Cummins Gallery, Anne Reed Gallery, N.Y. Acad. Scis., Fresno (Calif.) Mus. Fine Art, Bank of Am. Hdqrs. Vol. art tchr. pub. schs., 1992-96. Home: 480 Bohemian Hwy Freestone CA 95472

GLASSER, LYNN SCHREIBER, publisher; b. Chgo., Sept. 19, 1943; d. Alexander Paul and Beatrice (Bollard) Schreiber; m. Stephen A. Glasser, Dec. 30, 1965; children: Susan, Laura, Jeffrey, Jennifer. BA, Chatham Coll., 1965. Publs. editor Inst. CLE U. Mich. Law Sch., Ann Arbor, 1966-68; asst. to dir. Practising Law Inst., N.Y.C., 1968-71; v.p., COO Law Jour. Press and Law Jour. Seminars, N.Y.C., 1971-78; exec. v.p., pub. Law & Bus./Harcourt Jovanovich, Inc., N.Y.C., 1978-86; co-pres. Prentice Hall Law & Bus., Englewood Cliffs, N.J., 1986-94; cons. Simon and Schuster, N.Y.C., 1994-95; pres. Glasser Publ. Inc., Little Falls, N.J., 1995—; organizer, originator over 1000 CLE seminars, 1986—; organizer Woman Advt. Conf., N.Y.C., Chgo. and San Francisco, 1993-94; chmn. Woman Bus. Lawyer Conf., N.Y.C. and San Francisco, 1994. Trustee N.J. Chamber Music Soc., Montclair, 1989—; Cmty. Found. of N.J., Morristown, 1995—; co-donor Lynn & Stephen Glasser Scholarship Fund, Colgate U., 1988—, Bloomfield Coll., 1993—. Mem. Rockefeller Ctr. Club (N.Y.C.). Office: 150 Clove Rd Little Falls NJ 07424

GLASSER, SUSAN BETH, journalist; b. Montclair, N.J., Jan. 14, 1969; d. Stephen A. and Lynn (Schreiber) G. AB, Harvard U., 1990. From staff writer to editor Roll Call Newspaper, Washington, 1990—. Office: Roll Call Newspaper 900 2d St NE Washington DC 20002

GLASSMAN, CAROLINE DUBY, state supreme court justice; b. Baker, Oreg., Sept. 13, 1922; d. Charles Ferdinand and Caroline Marie (Colton) Duby; m. Harry Paul Glassman, May 21, 1953; 1 son, Max Avon. LLB summa cum laude, Williamette U., 1944. Bar: Oreg. 1944, Calif. 1952, Maine 1969. Atty. Title Ins. & Trust Co., Salem, Oreg., 1944-46; assoc. Belli, Ashe, Pinney & Melvin Belli, San Francisco, 1952-58; ptnr. Glassman & Potter, Portland, Maine, 1973-78, Glassman, Beagle & Ridge, Portland, 1978-83; justice Maine Supreme Judicial Ct., Portland, 1983—; lectr. Sch. Law, U. Maine, 1967-68, 80. Author: Legal Status of Homemakers in State of Maine, 1977. Mem. Am. Law Inst., Oreg. Bar Assn., Calif. Bar Assn., Maine Bar Assn., Maine Trial Law Assn. Roman Catholic. Home: 56 Thomas St Portland ME 04102-3639 Office: ME Supreme Jud Ct 142 Federal St Portland ME 04101-4151

GLASSMAN, JUDITH DALE, chocolate company owner, realtor; b. Newark, N.J., July 21, 1945; d. William Margo and Sonya (Janoff) Gale; m. Barnett Glassman, Nov. 24, 1967 (dec. Aug. 1976); children: Heather, Tara, Jolie. Student, U. Miami, 1967. Lic. realtor, Fla. Realtor Hollywood, Fla., 1970—; owner chocolatier Tender Loving Chocolates, Hollywood, 1980—. Bd. dirs. Miami Chamber Symphony, 1991—. Democrat. Jewish.

GLATMAN-STEIN, MARCIA, executive search company executive; b. N.Y.C., Feb. 28, 1944; d. Martin and Jean (Bykowsky) Eisenberg; m. Allan Glatman, June 27, 1965 (div. 1979); children: Jill, Kim; m. Seymour Stein, Nov. 22, 1983. BA, Hunter Coll., 1965, MA, 1969. Cert. tchr., N.Y. Tchr. N.Y.C. Bd. Edn., 1965-70; counselor Rockland Community Coll., Suffern, N.Y., 1976-77; acct. mgr. Alexander Ross Assoc., N.Y.C., 1978-80; sr. acct. mgr. Stevenson Group, N.Y.C., 1981-83; v.p. Richards Cons., N.Y.C., 1983-84, E.G. Todd Assocs., N.Y.C., 1984-88; pres. HRD Cons., Inc., Clark, N.J., 1989—. Pub. (newsletter) Trends in Human Resources. Mem. ASTD, Internat. Assn. of Corp. and Profl. Recruiters, Am. Compensation Assn., Human Resource Planning Assn., Soc. for Human Resource Mgmt. Office: HRD Cons Inc 60 Walnut Ave Clark NJ 07066-1606

GLAZ, BETTY GEHLHAUSEN, public information specialist, writer, poet; b. Evansville, Ind., Feb. 5, 1944; d. Ambrose A. and Ruby I. (Lauderdale) Gehlhausen; m. Thomas Carl Glaz, May 1, 1965; children: Nancy Glaz Watkins, John-Mark. BA in English magna cum laude, U. S.C., 1993. Mem. svcs. spl. Soc. Automotive Engrs., Warrendale, Pa., 1977-79; adminstrv. asst. Mony Fin. Svcs., Columbia, S.C., 1982-85; legal sec. Finkel Law Firm, Columbia, 1985-87; exec. support specialist State Bd. Tech. Edn., Columbia, 1987-92; editor/pub. Kaleidoscope of Carolina, Columbia, 1993—; free-lance writer Columbia, 1993—; pub. info. specialist Gov.'s Office Commn. on Women, Columbia, 1993—. Author essays, poems. Bd. mem. Women's Cmty. Residence, West Columbia, S.C., 1993—. Mem. AAUW (chair pub. info. com. 1995-97), Soc. Profl. Journalists, S.C. Writers Workshop, Phi Beta Kappa. Roman Catholic. Home: 1004 Cold Branch Dr Columbia SC 29223-5540

GLAZE, LYNN FERGUSON, development consultant; b. Oakland, Calif., May 24, 1933; d. Kenneth Loveland and Constance May (Pedder) Ferguson; m. Harry Smith Glaze, Jr., July 3, 1957; children: Catherine, Charles Richard. B.A., Stanford U., 1955, M.A., 1966. Devel. dir. Greenwich Acad., Conn., 1982-84; devel. cons. Del. Learning Ctr., Brandywine Mus., Opera Del., Ctr. for Creative Arts St. Michael's Day Nursery, 1984—. Pres. Darien-Norwalk YWCA, Conn., 1973-76; sec. Darien Republican Town com., Darien, 1974-79; dist. chmn. Darien Rep. Meeting, 1974-76, mem. Rep. Nat. Conv. Platform Com., 1988; vestry St. Luke's Ch., Darien, 1979-82; justice of the peace, Darien, 1981-84; bd. dirs. Ingleside Homes, Inc., 1986-92; mem. Gov.'s Small Bus. Council, 1987, EEOC, New Castle County, 1991-94. Fellow Coro Found., 1981.

GLAZER, JANE ANN, tax specialist; b. Cin., Oct. 13, 1962; d. James Ralph Beimesche and Carol Ann Stenger; m. Ronald Paul Glazer, Dec. 12, 1981 (div. Feb. 1986); children: Jeffrey Paul, Jason Edward. BS in Acctg., U. Cin., 1989, MS in Taxation, 1994. CPA, Ohio. Tax clk. Winegardner & Hammons Inc., Cin., 1985-88; asst. tax mgr. Cin. Bell Inc., 1988-89, tax mgr., 1989-90, tax specialist, 1991—. Asst. leader Boys Scouts Am., Cin., 1993-94. Mem. AICPA, Ohio Soc. CPAs (tax comm.), Inst. of Mgmt. Accts. (sec. 1988-90, bd. mem. 1989-91), Tel. Pioneers of Am. Republican. Roman Catholic. Office: Cincinnati Bell Inc Rm 102-815 201 E Fourth St Cincinnati OH 45039

GLAZER, KATE THOMPSON, artist; b. St. Louis, July 15, 1959; d. Morton Shane Glazer and Kate Edmonstone (Borders) Moore. MFA, Art Inst. Chgo. Sch., 1987; ind. study program, Whitney Mus. Am. Art, 1992-93. Contbr: (catalogue) Mapping a Response to Moma, 1995; contbr. articles to jours. Tracing Cultures, 1994, Politiques, 1994, Whitewalls, Fall/Winter, 1994; exhibited work in group shows at Name Gallery, Chgo., 1991, Viafarini, Milan, Italy, 1991, Dart Gallery, Chgo., 1992, Creast Hardware Show, N.Y.C., 1994, Living Room Show, N.Y.C., 1995, Am. Fine Arts Show, N.Y.C., 1995, Disney Land After Dark, Berlin, 1996; collaborator Atoptic Site, Tokyo Bay, 1996. Helena Rubenstein fellow, 1993-94, K.S. Goodman and Graff Merit Scholarship, 1986.

GLAZER, REA HELENE See KIRK, REA HELENE

GLAZER, ROSE MARIE EVANS, lawyer; b. Ogden, Utah, Oct. 27, 1966; d. Eldon Eugene and Maria Emma (Carerras) Evans; m. William Frank Glazer, Aug. 11, 1990; children: Carl Joseph, Samantha Lee. BBA, So. Meth. U., Dallas, 1987, BS, 1987, JD, 1990. Bar: Tex. 1990, U.S. Dist. Ct. (no. dist.) Tex. 1991, U.S. Ct. Appeals (5th cir.) 1991. Assoc. Jones, Day, Reavis & Pogue, Dallas, 1990-96; atty. Am. Airlines, Dallas/Ft. Worth Airport, 1996—. Mem. ABA, Dallas Bar Assn. Home: 6923 LaMangadr Dallas TX 75248 Office: MD 5675 PO Box 619616 Dallas TX 75261-9616

GLAZOV, SHEILA NEWMAN, professional speaker, creativity consultant; b. Chgo., Feb. 2, 1945; d. Alexander Isadore and Sylvia Elizabeth (Feldman) Newman; m. Jordan Edward Glazov, Apr. 9, 1967; children: Joshua, Noah. BS, Ohio State U., 1966. Cert. profl. spkr., Ill. Tchr. Ill. Sch. Dist. 64, Park Ridge, 1967-70; owner Sheila Glazov Enterprises, Mammoth Lakes, Calif., 1980-85; pres. Visual Impact Planning, Barrington, Ill., 1985—; adj. faculty William Rainey Harper Coll., Palatine, Ill., 1993—, dir. sml. bus. adv. bd., 1995—, dir. Career Transition Ctr., Prospect Heights, Ill., 1994—. Co-founder Eastern Sierra Jewish Cmty. Synagogue, Mammoth Lakes, 1985; dir. Congregation Kneseth Israel, Elgin, Ill., 1985—. Named One of One-Hundred Women Making a Difference, Today's Chgo. Woman newspaper, 1995. Mem. Nat. Spkrs. Assn., Profl. Spkrs. of Ill. (Award of Merit 1995), Northwest Suburban Assn. of Commerce and Industry (Mem. of Distinctin 1993, 94, 95, foundercons. and trainers forum 1993-94), Toastmasters (chpt. historian 1994-95). Jewish.

GLEASON, CYNTHIA S., public relations executive, educator; b. Portage, Wis., Mar. 2, 1949; d. Walter E. and Arleen (Slette) G.; m. William J. Kostka, Jr., Apr. 6, 1974; children—Jennifer Kostka, William Kostka III. B.A. in Journalism, U. Wis., 1972. Intern, U. Wis.-Madison Med. Ctr. Office of Pub. Info., 1970, State of Wis. Dept. Natural Resources, Madison, 1971; writer-researcher, jr. account exec. William Kostka & Assocs., Denver, 1972—, sr. account exec., 1974-77, v.p., 1977-79, sr. v.p., 1979-81, exec. v.p., 1981—; instr. dept. journalism U. Colo. Bd. dirs. Juvenile Offenders In Need, Inc., Denver; active Guardians Ad Litem. Recipient Pub. Relations Person of Year award Southland Corp., 1976. Mem. Pub. Relations Soc. Am. (accredited; counselors acad.), Denver Press Club. Home: 13955 E Hamilton Dr Aurora CO 80014-3942 Office: William Kostka & Assocs 1409 Larimer Sq Denver CO 80202-1723*

GLEASON, JOANNA, actress; b. Toronto, Ont., Can., June 2, 1950; d. Monty and Marilyn (Plotell) Hall. Grad., UCLA. Broadway debut I Love My Wife, Ethel Barrymore Theatre, 1977; Broadway appearances include Hey! Look Me Over, 1981, The Real Thing, 1984, A Hell of a Town, 1984, A Day in the Death of Joe Egg, 1985, It's Only a Play, 1985, Social Security, 1986, Into the Woods, Old Globe Theatre, San Diego and Martin Beck Theatre, N.Y.C., 1987 (Antoinette Perry award for leading actress in a mus., N.Y. Outer Critics Circle award, Drama Desk award), Nick and Nora, 1991; appeared in films Heartburn, 1986, Hannah and Her Sisters, 1986, Crimes and Misdemeanors, 1989, FX2: The Deadly Art of Illusion, 1991; TV appearances include Why Us?, 1981, Great Day, 1983, Still the Beaver, 1983, Life Under Water, 1989, The Boys, 1991, For Richer, For Poorer, 1992, Born Too Soon, 1993, For The Love of Aaron, 1994, series Hello, Larry,

1979-80, Chain Reaction, 1980, Love and War, 1992. Mem. Actors' Equity Assn. Office: UTA 9560 Wilshire Blvd 5th Floor Beverly Hills CA 90212*

GLEASON, MARY MARGARET, church administrator; b. Chgo., Mar. 2, 1952; d. William Francis and Mary Lorraine (Leonard) Cloonan; m. William M. Gleason, Sept. 23, 1972; children: Michael William, David Martin, Bethany Lorraine. BA in Comm., U. Ill., Springfield, 1996. Activity dir. Octavia Manor, Colfax, Ill., 1972-74; tchr. aide Broadwell (Ill.) Sch., 1988-91; bank teller Elkhart (Ill.) Bank, 1991-94; receptionist, sec. St. Patrick's Ch., Elkhart, 1993—, coord. religious edn., 1988—; advisor Religious Edn. Commn., Elkhart, 1988-96; office mgr., coord. St. John's Evang. Lutheran Ch., 1996. Mem. Women in Comm. Home: 492 1100th St Middletown IL 62666

GLEASON, MARY NORA, social worker; b. Passaic, N.J., July 20, 1965; d. John M. and Theresa (Montagnino) G.; m. David See Palmer, Dec. 10, 1994. BA summa cum laude, Drew U., 1987; MA, U. Chgo., 1989. Lic. clin. social worker, N.J.; cert. sch. social worker, N.J. Bilingual child and family therapist Dover (N.J.) H.S.-Sch.-Based Youth Svcs. Program, 1989-93; sch. social worker, svc. broker Jersey City Pub. Schs., 1993—; mem. Interagy. Task Force-Jersey City Pub. Schs., 1994—. Tutor Horizon Teen Ctr., Jersey City, 1994-95. Mem. NASW, Phi Beta Kappa.

GLEATON, HARRIET E., retired anesthesiologist; b. Altoona, Pa., Aug. 25, 1937; d. Munsey Sinclair and Anna Morgan (Scofield) G. BA, Franklin & Marshall Coll., 1959; MD, Temple U., 1962. Diplomate Am. Bd. Anesthesiology. Intern Mt. Sinai Hosp., N.Y.C., 1962-63; resident in anesthesiology Hosp. U. Pa., 1963-65; fellow Hosp. U. Pa., Phila., 1965-66, instr. anesthesiology, 1966-69; clin. anesthesiologist Michael Reese Hosp., Chgo., 1969-71; assoc. prof. U. Okla., Oklahoma City, 1971-81; clin. anesthesiologist Jane Phillips Episcopal Meml. Med. Ctr., Bartlesville, Okla., 1981-92; pvt. practice, 1992. Mem. AMA, Am. Soc. Anesthesiologists, Nature Conservancy, World Wildlife Fedn., Environ Def. Fund, Sierra Club.

GLEEMAN, MARSHA, film company executive. Pres. MGM/UA Music Metro-Goldwyn-Mayer, Inc., Santa Monica, Calif. Office: Metro-Goldwyn-Mayer 2500 Broadway St Santa Monica CA 90404*

GLEICH, CAROL S., health professions education executive; b. Kewanee, Ill., Jan. 18, 1935; d. Carl and Edna (Krause) Gleich BA, U. Iowa, 1958, MS, 1967, PhD in Health Sci. Edn., 1972. From instr. to asst. prof. pathology U. Iowa, 1971-77; program dir. med. tech. program, asst. prof. dept. pathology U. Iowa, Iowa City, 1972-77; edn. specialist divsn. allied health, 1977-88; chief resource devel. sec., 1988-90; health manpower edn. officer, physician manpower and credentialing, chief spl. projects and data analysis br. divsn. medicine, exec. sec. coun. on grad. med. edn., 1991-95; chief, area health edn. ctr. nat. program, 1996; Bur. Health Professions, Health Resources and Services Adminstrn., HHS, Rockville, Md., from 1977, allied health cons. to Egypt; chief Area Health Edn. Ctrs.; gov. consult in internat. health profl. edn., 1996; dir. Geriatric Edn. Ctrs. of PHS; adj. assoc. prof. U. Md. Sch. Medicine; mem. Iowa Health Manpower Com., 1976—; cons. U. Wis. System Acad. Affairs, 1976; panelist and participant workshops; presenter and del. to internat. congress. Cert. clin. chemistry technologist, Nat. Registry Clin. Chemistry. Mem. Am. Soc. Allied Health Professions, Nat. Coun. for Internat. Health, Am. Soc. Clin. Pathologists (assoc.; cert. med. technologist; sec. ASCP Bd. Registry, 1975-77), Am. Soc. Clin. Lab. Sci., D.C. Soc. Med. Tech. (Outstanding Med. Technologist of Yr. 1975), Beta Beta Beta (Pub. Health Svc. award 1995), Alpha Mu Tau. Assoc. editor Am. Jour. Med. Tech., 1974-83, Jour. Allied Health, 1982-85; contbr. articles to profl. pubs., papers to confs. Home: 14800 Rocking Spring Dr Rockville MD 20853-3635 Office: Parklawn Bldg Room 9A-27 5600 Fishers Ln Rockville MD 20857-0001

GLEICHMANN, FRANCES EVANGELINE, retired elementary educator; b. Marion, N.C., Sept. 24, 1920; d. Alexander Rudolph and Margaret Katherine (McNeely) McCulloch; m. August O. Gleichmann, Dec. 1, 1945. AA, Pfeiffer Coll., 1940; BS in Edn., Asheville Coll., 1942; postgrad., Mount St. Agnes Coll., Johns Hopkins U., U. Md., U. R.I. Elem. tchr. Balt. City Pub. Schs., 1942-85; cooperating tchr. for student tchrs. from Towson State U. Balt. City Pub. Schs., 1957-59. Recipient Econ. Edn. Tchr. award Devel. Econ. Edn. Program Com., 1985, Disting. Alumni award Pfeiffer Coll., 1973, Tate award Balt. C. of C. and Tate Industries, 1975, Salute 13 award Sta. WJZ TV, 1980, Golden Poet award World of Poetry, 1985-88. Mem. NEA, Md. State Ret. Tchrs. Assn., Balt. City Ret. Tchrs. Assn., Alpha Delta Kappa (Md. state publicity chmn. 1988-90, Alpha Delta Kappa week chmn. 1986-88), Shenandoah Valley Writers Guild. Home: 10 Dungarrie Rd Baltimore MD 21228-3401

GLEIM, MICHELLE LINN, secondary education music educator; b. Dayton, June 12, 1966; d. Joe Paul and Thelma Jean (Blockburn) Brittain; m. Gary Lee Gleim, May 14, 1994. B of Music Edn., Ohio State U., 1988, MA, 1996. Band dir. Minford (Ohio) High Sch., 1982—. Mem. Ohio Music Edn. Assn. Republican. Methodist. Home: 4523 Blue Run Rd Lucasville OH 45648-8776 Office: Minford High Sch 135 Falcon Rd Minford OH 45653-8670

GLENN, ANDREA POUTASSE, editor; b. Cleve., Sept. 13, 1951; d. Eugene Francis Poutasse and Helen (Kingston) Ingram; m. Grant Matthew Glenn, Aug. 4, 1973; children: Alexander, Charles, Margaret. BS, Kans. State U., 1973. Advt. copywriter Emerson/Franzke Advt., Topeka, 1973-78; editor Kansas! mag. Kans. Dept. Commerce, Topeka, 1978—. Author, editor: Kansas In Color, 1981. Mem. Auburn-Washburn Bd. Edn., 1991—; active Jr. League Topeka, 1981-92; bd. dirs. Mulvane Art Ctr., Topeka, 1987-92, Hist. Topeka, Inc., 1985-88. Mem. Regional Pubs. Assn. Episcopalian. Home: 7828 SW 37th St Topeka KS 66614-4939 Office: Kans Dept Commerce 700 SW Harrison St Ste 1300 Topeka KS 66603-3755

GLENN, CONSTANCE WHITE, art museum director, educator, consultant; b. Topeka, Oct. 4, 1933; d. Henry A. and Madeline (Stewart) White; m. Jack W. Glenn, June 19, 1955; children: Laurie Glenn Buckle, Caroline Glenn Galey, John Christopher. BFA, U. Kans., 1955; postgrad., U. Mo., 1964-69; MA, Calif. State U., 1974. Dir. Univ. Art Mus. & Mus. Studies program, from lectr. to prof. Calif. State U., Long Beach, 1973—; art cons. Archtl. Digest, L.A., 1980-89. Author: Jim Dine Drawings, 1984, Roy Lichtenstein: Landscape Sketches, 1986, Wayne Thiebaud: Private Drawings, 1988, Robert Motherwell: The Dedalus Sketches, 1988, James Rosenquist: Time Dust: The Complete Graphics 1962-92, 1993; contbg. editor: Antiques and Fine Arts, 1991-92. Vice-chair Adv. Com. for Pub. Art, Long Beach, 1990-95; chair So. Calif. adv. bd. Archives Am. Art, L.A., 1980-90; mem. adv. bd. ART/LA, 1986-94, chair, 1992; mem. adv. bd. Decorative Arts Study Ctr., San Juan Capistrano, Calif., 1990-95. Recipient Outstanding Contbn. to Profession award Calif. Mus. Photography, 1986. Mem. Am. Assn. Mus., Assn. Art Mus. Dirs., Coll. Art Assn., Art Table, Long Beach Pub. Corp. for the Arts (arts adminstr. of yr. 1989), Kappa Alpha Theta. Office: Univ Art Mus 1250 Bellflower Blvd Long Beach CA 90840-0004

GLENN, DEBORAH PORTER, graphics educator, artist, photographer, painter; b. Quantico, Va., Feb. 11, 1960; d. Frank Brinley IV and Linda (Ames) Porter; m. Cooper Glenn, Oct. 28, 1995. BA in English, Skidmore Coll., 1982; Cert., NYU, 1983, Pratt Inst., 1985; MS in Mixed Media, Pratt Inst., 1988. Ad dept. asst. Crown Pub. Inc., N.Y.C., 1983-84; asst. to editor/pub. ADS Mag. Internat., N.Y.C., 1984; asst. dir. meeting planning Bus. Week Mag., N.Y.C., 1984-85; freelance graphic artist, 1986—; tchg. asst. Maine Photo Workshops, Rockport, 1988-89; asst. prof. Sch. of Arts Stephens Coll., Columbia, Mo., 1989-93; prof. graphic design dept. Savannah (Ga.) Coll. Art and Design, 1993-95; vis. artist U. So. Colo., 1991. Shows include Bucks Rock Art Camp, New Milford, Conn., 1986, 87, Open Loft Space, Williamsburg-Bklyn., 1986, Mus. of Photo, La., 1986, 87, Pratt Inst., 1987, Maine Photo Workshops, Rockport, 1988, Worcester Artist Group, Mass., 1988, Ctr. for Photography, Woodstock, N.Y., 1989, Stephens Coll. Gallery, Columbia, 1989, 90, 91, 92, 93, 1st Ann. Invite Rocheport (Mo.) Art Festival, 1990, 91, 92, Columbia Art League, 1990, Randall Gallery, St. Louis, 1990, The Todd Gallery, 1990, Mary In, St. Louis, 1990, St. Louis Artist Guild, Webster, Mo., 1991, Field Mus., Chgo., 1991, Ctr. Conf. Art, St. Louis, 1991, Arts Rsch. Cncl., Mo., 1991, Spiva Art Ctr., Joplin, Mo., 1991, Ft. Smith Art Ctr., Ark., 1991, St. Louis Nat. Bank, 1991, Williams Woods Coll., Fulton, Mo., 1992, Suffolk C.C. Gallery, Riverhead, N.Y., 1992, Huntingdon Coll., Montgomery, Ala., 1992, Heifer Prof. Conf., Little Rock, 1992, Days Inn, Columbia, 1992, InterAction Agy., Arlington, Va., 1992, Ctr. Contemporary Art, St. Louis, 1992, 93, Elliot Smith Contemporaty Art, St. Louis, 1992, Brady Cmty. Gallery, Columbia, 1993, Blue Note Club, Columbia, 1993, Martin Schweig Gallery, St. Louis, 1993, Savannah Coll. Art and Design, Savannah, 1993, Orange County Ctr. for Contemporary Art, Santa Ana, Calif., 1993, Nat. Vague Art Exhibit, Phoenix, 1993, U. West Fla., Pensacola, 1994, Rear Window Gallery, Winchester, Va., 1994, Oasis Gallery, Savannah, 1994, Savannah County Court House Gallery, 1994, Park Lane Hotel, Boston, 1994, 1st City Club, Savannah, 1995, Sidewalk Arts Festival, Savannah, 1995, Arts on the River, Savannah, 1995. Instr., photo area head Bucks Rock Art Camp, New Milford, Conn., 1986, 87; instr. 92d St YM-YWCA, N.Y.C., 1987-88; vol. Cath. Relief Svcs., Amman, Jordan, 1989, Light Connection, Columbia, Mo., 1990, Heifer Project Internat., Dominican Republic, 1991, Group Home # 14, Columbia, Mo., 1992, Ga. Hist. Soc., Quito, Equador, 1993, Diabetes Assn., Savannah, 1994, Bethesda House, Savannah, 1994, Save A Cow, Uganda, Africa, 1994, United Way, Savannah, 1995—, City Savannah, 1995—, JEA:Morning Star, Savannah, 1995—, Alliance for Cultural Democracy, N.Y.C., 1995—. Recipient Firestone Baars Grant, 1991, 92, Summer Study grant Coll. Tchg., Stony Lake, Mich., 1992. Mem. AAUW, Alliance Cultural Democracy, Coll. Arts Assn., Environ. Def. Fund, Savannah MAC Users Group-Computers, Women's Mus. Home: 121 E 54th St Savannah GA 31405

GLESMANN, SYLVIA-MARIA, artist; b. Spardorf/Erlangen, Germany, June 8, 1923; arrived in the U.S., 1925; d. Rolf-Joseph and Auguste (Schultheiss) Hoffmann; m. John Brainerd Glesmann, Apr. 30, 1948; children: Glenn M., Eric B., Jonathan M. Degree, Acad. Fine Arts, Nurnberg, Germany, 1940, Acad. Fine Arts, Munich, 1944. instr. Somerville Adult Edn. Classes. Paintings exhibited in group shows including Carrier Clinic, 1993, Bergen Mus., 1993, Morris Mus., 1993, Nabisco Brands, 1993, Tribute to Spring Cultural and Heritage Gallery, Somerville, N.J., 1993, 94, 95, Salmagundi Juried Mems. Show, 1994, Garden State Water Color Assn., Princeton, N.J., 1994, Barrons Art Ctr., 1993, Art on the Ave. Group Show of Flowers, 1991, Nat. Assn. Women Artists Show, N.Y.C., 1991, The "Big Picture" NAWA, N.Y., 1994, "105 Exhibition" SoHo, 1994, Bridgewater N.J. County Libr. Show, 1996; others; exhibited painting in more than 22 one woman shows including Childrens Specialized Hosp., Mountainside, N.J., N.U.I. Corp., Bridgewater, N.J., 1987, Salmagundi Club Juried Show, N.Y.C., 1995, Am. Artists Profl. League Juried Show, 1995, Somerset County Libr., Bridgewater, N.J., 1996, others. Recipient over 50 awards in water color. Mem. Am. Artists Profl. League (pres. N.J. chpt. 1988-91), Nat. Assn. Women Artists, Raritan Valley Arts Assn. (pres. 1976-78), Somerset Art Assn. (chairwoman 10th outdoor art show), Nat. Assn. Women Artists, Salmagundi Club, Nat. Mus. for Women in Arts (charter mem.). Lutheran. Home and Office: 36 Twin Oaks Rd Bridgewater NJ 08807-2343

GLESS, SHARON, actress; b. L.A.; m. Barney Rosenzweig. Student, Gonzaga U. Appeared in TV series Faraday and Company, 1973-74, Marcus Welby, M.D., 1974-75, Switch!, 1975-78, Turnabout, 1979, House Calls, 1981-82; star TV series Cagney and Lacey, 1982-88 (6 Emmy nominations 1982-88, Emmy award 1986, 87, Golden Globe award 1985), The Trials of Rosie O'Neill, 1990-92 (Golden Globe award 1990, Emmy nomination 1991, 92); appeared in TV miniseries The Immigrants, 1978, Centennial, 1978, The Last Convertible, 1979; numerous other guest appearances in TV series; TV movies include All My Darling Daughters, 1972, My Darling Daughters' Anniversary, 1973, Clinic on 18th Street, 1974, Richie Brockelman: The Missing 24 Hours, 1976, The Islander, 1978, Crash, 1978, Kids Who Knew Too Much, 1979, Moviola: The Scarlett O'Hara War, 1980, Revenge of the Stepford Wives, 1980, Hardhat and Legs, 1980, The Miracle of Kathy Miller, 1981, Palms Precinct, 1982, Hobson's Choice, 1983, The Sky's No Limit, 1984, Letting Go, 1985, The Outside Woman, 1989, Honor Thy Mother, 1992, Separated by Murder, 1994, Cagney and Lacey: The Return, 1994; motion pictures include The Star Chamber, 1983; theatrical debut in Watch on the Rhine, 1989; theater: Misery (London), 1992-93; films include Airport 1975, 1974, The Star Chamber, 1983. Recipient Genii award Hollywood Women in Radio and TV, Best Actress award Viewers for Quality TV, Milestone award, 1988, SI award, 1991, Crystal Airwaves Media award Coalition for Clean Air, 1987, Gideon Media award, 1992, Disting. Artist award, 1992; named Woman of Yr., Ms mag., NCA Woman of Year, 1987, Entertainer of Yr., 1987. Office: William Morris Agy c/o Carly Berman 151 S El Camino Dr Beverly Hills CA 90212-2704*

GLICK, ANNA H., lawyer; b. Salzburg, Austria, Apr. 25, 1947. BA, CUNY, Bklyn., 1967; MA, Temple U., 1969; JD, NYU, 1982. Bar: N.Y. 1983. Ptnr. Cadwalader, Wickersham & Taft, N.Y.C. ABA (mem. bus. law sect.), Order of Coif. Office: Cadwalader Wickersham & Taft 100 Maiden Ln New York NY 10006*

GLICK, CYNTHIA SUSAN, lawyer; b. Sturgis, Mich., Aug. 6, 1950; d. Elmer Joseph and Ruth Edna (McCally) G. AB, Ind. U., 1972; JD, Ind. U.-Indpls., 1978. Bar: Ind. 1978, U.S. Dist. Ct. (so. dist.) Ind. 1978, U.S. Dist. Ct. (no. dist.) Ind. 1981. Adminstrv. asst. Gov. Otis R. Bowen, Ind., 1973-76; dep. pros. atty. 35th Jud. Cir., LaGrange County, Ind., 1980-82, pros. atty., 1983-90; pvt. practice, LaGrange, Ind., 1989—. Campaign aide Ind. Rep. State Cen. Com., Indpls., 1972-73. Named Hon. Speaker Ind. Ho. of Reps., 1972, Sagamore of the Wabash, Gov. Ind., 1974. Fellow Ind. Bar Found.; mem. ABA, Ind. State Bar Assn., LaGrange County Bar Assn. (pres. 1983-86), DAR, Bus. and Profl. Women's Club, Order of Ea. Star, Phi Delta Phi, Delta Zeta. Republican. Methodist. Home and Office: 113 W Spring St Lagrange IN 46761-1843

GLICK, JANE MILLS, biochemistry educator; b. Memphis, Nov. 26, 1943; d. Albert Axtell Jr. and Mary Louise (Baynes) Mills; m. John Harrison Glick, May 25, 1968; children: Katherine Anne, Sarah Stewart. AB, Randolph-Macon Woman's Coll., 1965; PhD, Columbia U., 1971. Postdoctoral trainee NIH, Bethesda, Md., 1971-73; postdoctoral fellow Sch. of Medicine Stanford (Calif.) U., 1973-74; rsch. asst. prof. biochemistry Sch. Dental Medicine U. Pa., Phila., 1974-77; asst. prof. biochemistry Med. Coll. Pa., Phila., 1977-82, assoc. prof. biochemistry, 1982-90, prof. biochemistry, 1990-94; sr. rsch. investigator Inst. Human Gene Therapy, U. Pa. Sch. Medicine, 1994—; mem. metabolism study sect. NIH, 1993—. Assoc. editor: Jour. Lipid Rsch., 1985-86, mem. editorial bd., 1987—; contbr. articles to profl. jours. Trustee Episcopal Acad., Merion, Pa., 1989—. Recipient Rsch. Svc. award NIH, 1975-77, Young Investigator award, 1980-83, Teaching award Lindback Found., 1985. Mem. AAAS, AAUP (sec. 1990-92), Arteriosclerosis Coun. Am. Heart Assn. (program com. 1990-93), Am. Soc. for Biochemistry and Molecular Biology, Am. Soc. for Human Genetics, Phi Beta Kappa, Sigma Xi. Presbyterian. Office: U Pa Med Coll Inst Human Gene Therapy 3400 Spruce St # 601 Philadelphia PA 19104

GLICK, KAREN LYNNE, college administrator; b. Bucyrus, Ohio, Sept. 2; d. Phillip Dole and Bernice Grace Glick; BSJ, Bowling Green State U., 1967, MA, 1979; children: M. Todd, K. Christine. Editor, Bowling Green (Ohio) State U., 1972-74; account exec. Howard E. Mitchell, Jr., Advt., Findlay, Ohio, 1974-77; asst. to dir. Student Devel. Program, Bowling Green State U., 1977-79; dir. pub. info. Bluffton (Ohio) Coll., 1980-83; asst. to v.p. for instl. advancement Findlay (Ohio) Coll., 1983-85; assoc. dir. devel. Bluffton Coll., 1985-90; assoc. dir. divisional support Miami U., Oxford, Ohio, 1990-93; sr. regional dir. devel. U. Ill. Found., Urbana, 1993—. Anglican. Mem. Bowling Green U. Press Club (charter 1983). Office: U Ill Found Harker Hall MC-386 1305 W Green St Urbana IL 61801-2919

GLICK, NANCY LYNN, public relations executive; b. N.Y.C., Aug. 23, 1948; d. Robert Lehman Burnstine and Lynn Phillips Manulis; m. Louis Gerstley Hecht, June 21, 1977; m. Michael Raymond Leaveck, Nov. 27, 1987. BS in Journalism, Boston U., 1970. Pub. rels. specialist Nat. Paint & Coatings Assn., Washington, 1971-72; dep. press sec. U.S. Office Consumer Affairs, Washington, 1972-76; press officer FDA, Washington, 1976-79; account exec., dir., v.p., sr. v.p. Hill & Knowlton, Washington, 1979-89; SVP/practice dir., 1991—; SVP Porter/Novelli, Inc., Washington, 1989-91; mem. adv. com. Nat. Rehab. Hosp., Washington, 1993—. Named Pub. Rels. All Star, Pub. Rels. Jour., 1992; recipient award of excellence Pub. Rels. Soc. Am., 1995. Office: Hill & Knowlton 600 New Hampshire Ave NW Washington DC 20037

GLICKENHAUS, SARAH BRODY, speech therapist; b. Mpls., Mar. 8, 1919; d. Morris and Ethel (Silin) Brody; BS, U. Minn., 1940, MS, 1945; m. Seth Morton Glickenhaus, Oct. 23, 1944; children: James Morris, Nancy Pier. Speech therapist Davison Sch. Speech Correction, Atlanta, 1940-42; speech pathologist U. Minn., Mpls., 1945-46; speech therapist Queens Coll., N.Y.C., 1946-48; speech therapist VA, N.Y.C., 1949-50; pvt. practice, New Rochelle, N.Y., 1950-71; speech therapist Abbott Sch. United Free Sch. Dist. 13, Irvington, N.Y., 1971-79; pvt. practice, Scarsdale, N.Y., 1979—; tutor learning disabled children New Rochelle Public Schs., 1968-71. Mem. AAAS, Am. Speech Hearing & Lang. Assn., N.Y. State Speech &Hearing Assn., Westchester Speech & Hearing Assn. Club: Harvard (N.Y.C.). Jewish. Home and Office: 100 Dorchester Rd Scarsdale NY 10583-6051

GLICKMAN, ELAINE JEANNE, artist; b. Des Moines, Jan. 21, 1922; d. Isaac Davidson and Rae (Miller) Ginsberg; m. Eugene David Glickman, Mar. 15, 1942; children: Richard Lorin, James Allan. Student, Northwestern U., 1939-41, Am. Acad. Art Chgo. Columnist, illustrator Register Tribune, Des Moines, 1942-44; art tchr. Solo shows include Bernard Heights Country Club, 1994-95, Remington, 1996; group shows include La Jolla Art Assn., Poway Ctr. Performing Arts, 1994-95, San Diego Med. Soc., 1995. Bd. dirs., past pres. Davenport Mus. of Art; vol. nurse's aide Camp Dodge Iowa, Des Moines, Cook County Hosp., Chgo., Broadlawn County Hosp., Des Moines, 1943-44. Mem. LWV. Democrat. Home: 12876 Circulo Dardo San Diego CA 92128

GLICKMAN, MARLENE, non-profit organization administrator; b. Evansville, Ind., May 13, 1936; d. Morris Jack and Sarah (Krawll) Foreman; m. Marshall Levi Glickman, Jan. 9, 1956; children: Cynthia Anne, Joseph Leonard. Student, Ohio State U., 1954-56. Area dir. The Am. Jewish Com., Buffalo, 1982—. Pres. Human Rights Adv. Coun., Western N.Y., 1988—; bd. dirs. YWCA, Buffalo and Erie County, 1990—, Buffalo Fedn. Neighborhood Ctrs. Inc., 1994—, Sheehan Meml. Hosp., Inc., 1994—, sec.; co-pres., bd. dirs. Western N.Y. Martin Luther King Jr. Commn., 1991—; mem. United Way Agy. Allocations Com.; chairwoman Towns and Villages divsn. United Way, 1981; pres. N.E. Lakes coun. Union Am. Hebrew Congregations, 1982-86, Meals on Wheels of Buffalo and Erie County, 1981-83, Coun. Congl. Pres. Erie County, 1979-81, Temple Beth Am, 1978-80, Sisterhood Temple Beth Am, 1969-71, 76-77; vice chair gen. campaign United Jewish Appeal, 1980, chair woman's divsn., 1979; active western N.Y. Vision for Tomorrow 2000 C. of C./Buffalo Partnership. Recipient Abraham Pugash Cmty. Rels. award for establishing Kosher Meals on Wheels, Jewish Family Svc., Buffalo and Erie County, N.Y., 1975; Am.-Pol Eagle Citizen of Yr., 1995. Mem. Union Am. Hebrew Congregations (bd. dirs. 1982—, exec. com.), Commn. on Synagogue Music Facilitators, Joint Cantorial Placement Commn., Hadassah (life), Assn. Reform Zionists Am. (del. to Israel 1987), Brandeis Women's Com., Nat. Coun. Jewish Women (life, Hannah G. Solomon award 1985), Assn. Jewish Comty. Rels. Workers, Jewish Communal Svc. Assn. Office: The Am Jewish Com 3407 Delaware Ave Buffalo NY 14217-1421

GLIDDEN, NELLIE EVELYN DILL, federal agency administrator; b. Gardiner, Maine, Feb. 16, 1927; d. Benjamin Corin and Leona Mary (Michaud) Dill; m. Vernard Glidden, May 15, 1949 (dec. Apr. 1978); children: Scott Prentiss, Shelley Lynn Glidden Rowley. Grad. high sch., Gardiner, Maine. Clk. typist VA, Washington, 1945, Dallas, 1946-47, Togus, Maine, 1947-52; sec. Maine Army Nat. guard, Augusta, 1952-66; clk. typist Social Security Adminstrn., Augusta, 1966-72; data review tech. Social Security Adminstrn., Waterville & Augusta, Maine, 1972-76; svc. rep. Social Security Adminstrn., Augusta, 1976-84; personnel clk. Maine Army Nat. Guard, 1984-85; retired, 1985. Pres. Pray St. PTA, Gardiner, 1961, 62, 63; mem. cable TV franchaise com. City of Gardiner, 1995-96, apptd. to charter com., 1996; tchr. Sunday sch. grades 7 & 8 Winter St. Bapt. Ch., Gardiner, 1961-71, tchr. adult class, 1986—, mem. prison ministry Kennebec County Correctional Ctr., Augusta, 1985—, nursing ministry, 1991—. Mem. Nat. Assn. Retired Fed. Employees (pres. 1990-91, Meritorious Svc. award 1991). Republican. Home: RR 5 Box 1540 Brunswick Rd Gardiner ME 04345

GLIER, INGEBORG JOHANNA, German language and literature educator; b. Dresden, Germany, June 22, 1934; came to U.S., 1972; d. Erich Oskar and Gertrud Johanne (Niese) G. Student, Mt. Holyoke Coll., 1955-56; Dr. phil. (Studienstiftung des deutschen Volkes), U. Munich, Germany, 1958; Dr. phil., Habilitation, 1969; M.A. (hon.), Yale U., 1973. Asst., lectr. U. Munich, 1958-69, universitätsdozentin, 1969-72; vis. prof. Yale U., 1972-73, prof. German, 1973—, chmn. dept., 1979-82; chmn. Medieval Studies Yale U., New Haven, 1986-93, chmn. Women's Studies, 1995-96; sr. faculty fellow Yale U., 1974-75; vis. prof. U. Cologne, Germany, 1970-71, U. Colo., Boulder, spring 1983, U. Tubingen, summer 1984. Author: Struktur und Gestaltungsprinzipien in den Dramen John Websters, 1958, Deutsche Metrik, 1961, Artes amandi, Untersuchung zu Geschichte, Überlieferung und Typologie der deutschen Minnereden, 1971; contbr. articles, book reviews to profl. jours. Mem. Internationaler Germanisten-Verband, Modern Lang. Assn., Mediaeval Acad. Am., Am. Assn. Tchrs. German, Internat. Courtly Lit. Soc., Wolfram von Eschenbach Gesellschaft. Home: 111 Park St Apt 12T New Haven CT 06511-5421 Office: Yale Univ Dept Germanic Langs PO Box 208210 New Haven CT 06520-8210

GLINSKI, HELEN ELIZABETH, operating room nurse; b. Gouverneur, N.Y., Apr. 9, 1944; d. Arthur Andrew and Lillian May (MacKenzie) Turnbull; m. David Lee Joseph Glinski, May 13, 1967; children: David Lee Joseph II, Christopher John. Diploma of Nursing, House of Good Samaritan, Watertown, N.Y., 1965; registered nurse 1st asst., Del. County C.C., 1992. RN, N.Y.; Cert. Nurse Operating Room. Staff nurse operating rm. House of Good Samaritan, Watertown, N.Y., 1965-66; staff nurse operating rm. Cmty. Gen. Hosp., Syracuse, N.Y., 1966-68, acting headnurse operating rm., 1968-69, 70, acting asst. head nurse, inservice instr., 1969-70, 70-71; staff nurse operating rm. E.J. Noble Hosp., Gouverneur, N.Y., 1971-72; head nurse, supr. operating rm. Edward John Noble Hosp., Gouverneur, N.Y., 1972-77; sr. staff nurse operating rm. Mercy Hosp., Watertown, N.Y., 1978-79; staff nurse operating rm. Roswell Pk. Meml. Inst., Buffalo, 1979-85, Buffalo VA Med. Ctr., 1985-95; nurse 1st asst. oper. rm. VA Med. Ctr., West Palm Beach, Fla., 1995—; mem. RN First Asst. Spl. Assembly, 1992—. Collector Am. Cancer Assn., Buffalo, 1991, 92, 93. Recipient Performance award Dept. Vet. Affairs, Buffalo, 1988, 91, 93. Mem. Assn. Oper. Rm. Nurses (bd. dirs. 1992-93, 96—, corr. sec. 1986-91, pres.-elect 1993-94, pres. 1994-95, officer western N.Y. chpt.). Episcopalian. Home: 737 Mill Valley Pl West Palm Beach FL 33409-7613

GLOBIG, SABINE A., biology educator; b. Stuttgart, Germany, Nov. 13, 1949; came to U.S., 1953; d. Herbert and Ursula Ruth (Vesely) G. BA in Internat. Studies, Am. U., 1972; MS in Horticulture, Rutgers U., 1988. Cert. tchr. h.s., N.J. Adj. instr. biology Union County Coll., Cranford, N.J., 1980-91; teaching asst./adj. Rutgers U., New Brunswick, N.J., 1984-87; tchr. biology Millburn (N.J.) H.S., 1987-89; rsch. asst. Ctr. for Agrl. Molecular Biology Rutgers U., 1990; teaching lab. mgr. William Paterson Coll., Wayne, N.J., 1991-92; asst. prof. Hazard (Ky.) C.C., 1992—. Author poster presentation Internat. Horticultural Congress, 1996. Mem. Perry County Humane Soc., Hazard, 1993—; mem. exec. bd., co-founder Adopt-A-Pet Program, Hazard, 1993-95. Mem. Ky. Acad. Scis., Mensa. Office: Hazard C C Divsn Natural Sci Hwy 15 N Hazard KY 41701

GLOSUP, LORENE See DEAN, DEAREST

GLOTZER, LIZ, film company executive. BA, Bennington Coll., 1983; MFA, U. So. Calif., 1985. Dir. devel. Samuel Goldwyn Co.; staff mem. Castle Rock Pictures, Beverly Hills, Calif., 1987-94, pres. of prodn., 1994—. Prodr. (film) Sibling Rivalry, 1990; exec. prodr. (film) The Shawshank Redemption, 1994. Office: Castle Rock Pictures 335 N Maple Dr Ste 135 Beverly Hills CA 90210

GLOVER, GERALDINE JOANN, counselor; b. Kalispell, Mont., May 29, 1958; d. Gene Lindy and Lucille Annette (Danielson) G. BA in Liberal

Arts, St. John's Coll., Santa Fe, 1980; BS in Edn., U. N.Mex., 1987; MA in Counseling, Appalachian State U., Boone, N.C., 1990; PhD, U. North Tex., 1996. Assoc. Thornburg Mgmt. Co., Santa Fe, 1985-86; tchr. Santa Fe Pub. Schs., 1986-89; resident dir. Appalachian State U., 1989-90; coord. Mountain Valley Therapeutic Nursery, Mountain City, Tenn., 1990-93; rsch. asst., tchg. fellow Ctr. for Play Therapy U. North Tex., Denton, Tex., 1993-96; supr. play therapists Ctr. for Play Therapy, Denton, Tex., 1994-95; presenter in field. Mem. Johnson County Foster Care Rev. Bd., Mountain City, 1991-93; cmty. mem. Kellogg Grant Program, Johnson County, 1992-93. Scholar U. North Tex., 1994-95, rsch. grantee, 1995-96. Mem. ACA, AAUW (scholar 1994-95), Assn. for Play Therapy (registration chmn. San Antonio conf. 1994-95). Democrat. Home: PO Box 22933 Santa Fe NM 87502

GLOVER, JANET BRIGGS, artist; b. Allahabad, India, June 22, 1919; came to U.S., 1924; d. George Weston and Mary Ames (Hart) Briggs; m. Alan Marsh Gover, Feb. 5, 1949; children: Keith Terrot, John Carroll, Beth Marsh Glover Wittig. BA, Bennington Coll., 1943; postgrad., New Sch. Social Rsch., 1969-70. Artist, draftsman Chartmakers, Inc., N.Y.C., 1943-45; apprentice to Oscar Ogg Book of Month Club, N.Y.C., 1946; 2d grade tchr. Hartridge Sch., Plainfield, N.J., 1947-48, Country Day Sch., Lancaster, Pa., 1948-49; chmn. art dept. Women's Club Chatham, N.J., 1964-65, lectr. art, 1981-86; publicity chmn. N.J. Ctr. Visual Arts, Summit, 1980-81. One-man shows include Present Day Club, Princeton, N.J., 1967, Gallery 9 Upstairs, Chatham, 1978; group shows include Key Gallery, N.Y.C., 1980; contbg. editor N.J. Music and Arts Mag., 1970-71; art critic Madison Eagle, 1975-78. Recipient 1st prize Morris County Art Assn., 1966, Princeton Art Assn., 1969, Cmty. Art Assn., 1980. Mem. Chatham Twp. Art League (co-founder, 1st pres. 1988-90, editor Artist's Album 1993-95), Drew U. Art Assn. (membership chmn. 1990-94). Democrat. Unitarian. Home and Studio: 30 Oak Hill Rd Chatham NJ 07928-1552

GLOVER, KAREN E., lawyer; b. Nampa, Idaho, Apr. 14, 1950; d. Gordon Ellsworth and Cora (Frazier) G.; m. Thaddas L. Alston, Aug. 17, 1979; children: Samantha Glover Alston, Evan Glover Alston. AB magna cum laude, Whitman Coll., 1972; JD cum laude, Harvard U., 1975. Bar: Wash. 1975, U.S. Dist. Ct. (we. dist.) Wash. 1975. Assoc. Preston, Thorgrimson Ellis & Holman, Seattle, 1975-80; ptnr. Preston Gates & Ellis, Seattle, 1981—. Chmn. bd. dirs. United Way King County, Seattle, 1993-94; chair bd. overseers Whitman Coll., Walla Walla, Wash., 1995—; mem. bd. trustees King County Libr. Sys., Seattle, 1992—. Mem. Wash. State Bar Assn. (corp. and tax sects.), Seattle Pension Roundtable, Columbia Tower Club, Sand Point Country Club, Rainier Club. Episcopalian. Office: Preston Gates & Ellis 50th Flr 701 5th Ave Seattle WA 98104-7016

GLOVER, LISA MARIE, transportation company executive; b. Detroit, Oct. 14, 1963; d. Ronald and Denise (Wellons) G. BS, Tuskegee U., 1986; MS, Morgan State U., 1988. Lic. real estate agt. Summer intern IBM, Charlotte, N.C., 1982, GM, Pontiac, Mich., 1983, 84, 85, Turner Constrn., Detroit, 1986; grad. intern State of Md., Dept. Transp., Balt., 1987-88; planner Dept. Transp., Detroit, 1988-90, asst. to dir., 1990-91, mgr. Office of Contract Compliance, 1991-93; transp. engr., cons. M2 Internat., Detroit, 1993-94; owner Trans. Svcs., Inc., 1994—; rep. Detroit Dept. Transp. SEMCOG, Transp. Adv. Coun., Detroit, 1988-93, Labor Mobility Project Steering Com., Detroit, 1991. Mem. Civic Ctr.-Optimist Club, 1992—, mem. 14th Congl. Dist. Young Dems., spl. projects com., 1992, young adults com. NAACP, 1989-91; math. tutor Ednl. Guidance and Tutoring Ctrs., Inc., 1996—. Mem. NAFE, Assn. Gen. Contractors Am. (pres. 1985-86), Conf. Minority Transp. Ofcls., Tuskegee Nat. Alumni Assn., Morgan State Student Transp. Assn. (sec. 1986-87), Trade Union Leadership Coun. Young Adults, Alpha Kappa Alpha (sponsor teen group 1989—). Democrat. Mem. African Meth. Episcopal Ch.

GLOVER, MAGGIE WALLACE, state legislator; b. Florence, S.C., Aug. 29, 1948; d. Fulton and Ethel (Greene) Wallace. 1 child, Marisa. BA, Fayetteville St. U., 1970; MEd, Marion Coll., 1982. Former mem. S.C. Ho. of Reps., dist. 62; mem. S.C. Senate. Active sch. bd. trustees, Florevce Sch. Dist., 1983-86, 86-89. With AUS 1974-77. Mem. NAACP. Democrat. Home: PO Box 8000F Florence SC 29501 Office: Senate House State House Columbia SC 29211*

GLOVER, POLLY STONE, English language educator; b. Camden, Tenn., Sept. 7, 1940; d. Alton Brooks and Zula Mai (Kee) Stone; m. William Polk Glover, Aug. 13, 1961; children: Elizabeth Brooke Glover Emery, Dale Beaird, Joshua Stone. EdD, Vanderbilt U., 1987, MA in Tchg., 1962; BA, Union U., 1961. Tchr. English Obion County Cen. H.S., Troy, Tenn., 1962-63; instr. dept. English U. Tenn., Martin, 1963-66, asst. prof., 1966-80, assoc. prof., 1980-89, prof., 1989—, coord. Student Learning Ctr., 1978—; bd. dirs. Tenn. Humanities Coun., Nashville, Tenn. Writers Alliance, Nashville; advisor Alpha Phi Omega, Martin. Author: Marks on the Land: The Story of Obion, 1975, So...You're Going to College: Assignments for Success, 1996; contbr. articles to profl. jours. including Tenn. English Jour., Tenn. Ednl. Leadership, Off to Coll. Bd. dirs., chair Obion County Pub. Libr. Bd., Union City, Tenn., 1960s, 70s, Reelfoot Regional Libr. Bd., Martin; bd. dirs. Tenn. Adv. Coun. on Librs., Nashville, 1977-80, Obion County Bd. Edn., Union City, 1982-84; pres. trustees sect. Tenn. Libr. Assn., Nashville, 1970s. Mem. Nat. Assn. for Devel. Edn., Nat. Coun. Tchrs. English, Tenn. Assn. for Devel. Edn. (Outstanding Devel. Educator 1989), Phi Kappa Phi, Sigma Tau Delta.

GLÜCK, LOUISE ELISABETH, poet; b. N.Y.C., Apr. 22, 1943; d. Daniel and Beatrice (Grosby) G.; m. Charles Hertz (div.); 1 child, Noah Benjamin; m. John Dranow, 1977 (separated). Student, Sarah Lawrence Coll., 1962, Columbia U., 1963-65; LLD, Williams Coll., 1993, Skidmore Coll., 1995, Middlebury, 1996. Vis. poet Goddard Coll., U. N.C., U. Va., U. Iowa; Elliston prof. U. Cin., 1978; vis. faculty Columbia U., 1979; faculty M.F.A. program Goddard Coll., also Warren Wilson Coll., Swannanoa, N.C.; Holloway lectr. U. Calif., Berkeley, 1982; vis. prof. U. Calif.-Davis, 1983; Scott prof. poetry Williams Coll., 1983, faculty, 1984—; Regents prof. poetry UCLA, 1985-88; vis. prof. Harvard U., 1995; Hurst prof. poetry Brandeis U., 1996; delivered Phi Beta Kappa poem harvard U. commencement, 1990; baccalaureate spkr. Williams Coll. Author: Firstborn, 1968, The House on Marshland, 1975, Descending Figure, 1980, The Triumph of Achilles, 1985, Ararat, 1990, The Wild Iris, 1992 (Pulitzer Prize for poetry 1993), Proofs and Theories (collected essays), 1994, Meadowlands, 1996. Grantee Rockefeller Found., Nat. Endowment for Arts, 1969-70, 79-80, 88-89, Guggenheim Found., 1975-76, 87-88, NEA, 1988-89; recipient lit. award Am. Acad. and Inst. Arts and Letters, 1981, award in poetry Nat. Book Critics Cir., 1985, Melville Cane award Poetry Soc. Am., 1986, Sara Teasdale Meml. prize Wellesley Coll., 1986, Bobbitt Natil prize Libr. Congress, 1992, Pulitzer prize, 1996, William Carlos Williams award, 1993, PEN/Martha Albrand award Non-Fiction, 1995; named Poet Laureate of Vt., 1994. Fellow Am. Acad. Arts and Scis.; mem. Am. Acad. Arts & Letters, Phi Beta Kappa (hon.).

GLUECK, MARY A., psychiatric and mental health nurse, administrator; b. Bridgetown, Barbados; came to U.S., 1952; d. Hubert and Christina Cumming; m. Stephen G. Glueck (dec.). Grad. sch. nursing, St. Joseph's Mercy Hosp., Georgetown, Guyana. RN, Calif. Clin. svcs. mgr. med.-surg., geropsychiat. rehab. Crystal Springs Rehab. div. San Mateo County Gen. Hosp., San Mateo, Calif. Mem. Mid. Mgrs. Assn., Am. Psychiat. Nurses Assn. Home: 4505 Sandra Ct Union City CA 94587-4853

GLUECK, SYLVIA BLUMENFELD, writer; b. Tulsa, Dec. 23, 1925; d. Maurice and Sina (Turk) Blumenfeld; m. Norton Shushan Glueck, June 15, 1947; children: Nancy Eisen, Milton Glueck. BJ, U. Mo., Columbia, 1949. Publicity dir. Sta. WDSU, New Orleans, 1946-47; advt. copywriter Swiftway Direct Mail, New Orleans, 1961; freelance writer and author New Orleans and San Antonio, 1965—. Author book, 1990; contbr. fiction articles to mags. and newspaper features, 1984-85, 90 (Golden Pro award 1986). Mem. AAUW, Women in Communication, Alamo Writers, San Antonio Profl. Writers Group, Mensa. Home and Office: 309 W Magnolia Ave Apt 1 San Antonio TX 78212-3216

GLYNN, MARY ANN THERESA, management educator; b. N.Y.C., Mar. 25, 1951; d. Francis P. and Nora T. (Broderick) G.; married, Jan. 8, 1972 (div. 1979); 1 child, Kathryn Elizabeth. BA, Fordham U., 1972; MA, Rider Coll., 1978; MBA, L.I. Univ., 1982; PhD, Columbia U., 1988. Dir. grad. admissions L.I. Univ., Westchester, N.Y., 1978-83; prof. mgmt. devel. program Smith Coll., Northampton, Mass., 1991—; asst. prof. Sch. of Orgn. and Mgmt. Yale U., New Haven, 1987-93; assoc. prof. Emory Bus. Sch. Emory U., Atlanta, 1993—. Cons. editor Jour. Applied Behavioral Sci., 1991—, Jour. Mgmt.; contbr. articles to profl. jours. Fellow Columbia U., 1983-88. Mem. Acad. Mgmt., Strategic Mgmt. Soc., Beta Gamma Sigma, Delta Mu Delta. Office: Emory U Bus Sch 1602 Mizell Dr Atlanta GA 30322

GMUR, JUDY ANNE, licensing and merchandising executive, educator; b. Long Beach, Calif., July 12, 1952; d. Buckner New and Janet Blanchard (Kluger) Harris; m. James Edward Gmur, Nov. 1975 (div. 1979). BA, Calif. State U., Long Beach, 1975. Buyer May Co. So. Calif., L.A., 1975-78, Macy's Calif., San Francisco, 1978-83; divisional merchandise mgr. Miller's Outpost, Ont., Can., 1983-89; v.p. gen. merchandise Jay Jacobs, Seattle, 1990; pres. Club Monaco, U.S., Santa Monica, Calif., 1991-92; v.p. licensing Chauvin, Internat., Rancho Dominguez, Calif., 1993-94; dir. trademarks & licensing UCLA, 1996—; instr. Fashion Inst. Design & Merchandising, L.A., 1995—. Mem. NOW, Planned Parenthood Fedn. Am., Surfrider Found., Fashion Group Internat.

GO, BETTY SY, family practice physician; b. Cebu, The Philippines, Nov. 8, 1956; came to U.S., 1988; d. Bonifacio and Zoila (Po) Sy; m. Benjamin Ang Go, Dec. 7, 1985; 1 child, Michelle Lynn,. BS in Med. Tech., Velez Coll., Cebu City, Philippines, 1978, MD, 1983. Diplomate Am. Bd. Family Physicians. Asst. instr. L.A. Coll. Chiropractic, Whittier, Calif., 1991; resident family practice St. Mary of Nazareth Hosp. Ctr., Chgo., 1991-94; family practitioner Meml. Hosp., Carthage, Ill., 1994-96; pvt. practice, Metamora, Ill., 1996—. Mem. AMA, Am. Acad. Family Physicians. Office: Midwest Health Renewal Ctr 205 S Engelwood Dr Metamora IL 61548

GOBLE, ELISE JOAN H., pediatric ophthalmologist; b. Winnipeg, Man., Can., Jan. 23, 1932; d. Michael Samuel and Sarah (Corbin) Hollenberg; m. John Lewis Goble, Oct. 4, 1956; children: John Robert, Michael William. Assoc. in Music, U. Man., 1949, MD, 1956. Resident Columbia Presbyn. Eye Inst., N.Y.C., 1956-59; pvt. practice pediatric ophthalmology San Mateo, Calif., 1959—. Mem. San Mateo Sch. Health Com.; mem. Coordinating Coun. Developmental Disabilities, San Mateo; founder San Mateo chpt. Nat. Assn. Autistic Citizens. Fellow ACS, Am. Bd. Ophthalmology, Am. Bd. Pediatrics; mem. Am. Assn. Pediatric Ophthalmology & Strabismus (charter mem.), San Mateo County Med. Soc., Calif. Med. Assn. Home: 2007 New Brunswick Dr San Mateo CA 94402-4012 Office: 100 S Ellsworth Ave Ste 507 San Mateo CA 94401-3929

GOCHNAUER, ELISA ANNE, marketing executive; b. Bellefonte, Pa., Sept. 4, 1960; d. Theodore Frank and Doris Lee (Smith) Schneider; m. Dean Joe Gochnauer, Apr. 23, 1994. Student, Shippensburg U., 1978-80; BA, Millersville U., 1982. Cert. nursing asst. Sales svc. coord. Fleur de Lait Foods, Ltd., New Holland, Pa., 1982-87; sales adminstr. Northfield Specialty Foods, Lancaster, Pa., 1987-88; mktg. asst. Charles Chips Corp., Lancaster, 1988-89, dir. mktg. svcs., 1989-93; with inside sales R/W Connection, Lancaster, 1994; mktg. asst. Red Rose Transit Authority, Lancaster, 1995-96, mgr. mktg., 1996—. Republican. Lutheran. Home: 748 Lawrence Blvd Lancaster PA 17601-1418 Office: Red Rose Transit Authority 45 Erick Rd Lancaster PA 17601-3111

GOCKLEY, BARBARA JEAN, corporate professional; b. Pitts., July 26, 1951; d. William Ervin and Dorothy Marie (Wolf) Cain; m. William Lee Gockley, Mar. 29, 1975 (div. Aug. 1989); children: Ervin Cain, Marianne Cain, William Cain, Malinda Cain. Student, Indiana U. Pa., 1969-71, Thomas Edison State Coll., 1986-88; BA in Bus. Mgmt. and Mktg. Mgmt., Alvernia Coll., 1993. Cert. in purchasing mgmt. Asst. materials mgr. Redman Mobile Homes, Ephrata, Pa., 1972-75; mgr. inventory control Gym-Kin, Inc., Reading, Pa., 1975-77; supr. prodn./inventory control Wyomissing Converting, Reading, 1979-82; mgr. prodn./inventory control Dorma Door Controls, Inc., Reamstown, Pa., 1982-85, project mgr., 1985-86; materials mgr. Powder Coatings Group-Morton Internat., Reading, 1986-94; dir. purchasing Dexter Corp., Waukegan, Ill., 1994—; dir. programs Congress for Progress Inc., 1984-88, vice chmn., 1988-89, chmn., 1989-90; dir. programs Pansophic/ASD User Group Internat. Conf., 1991, 92; instr. Berks Campus, Pa. State U., Reading, 1985-86. Dir. Reinholds (Pa.) PTA, 1978-81; bd. dirs. Cocalico Sch. Bd., Denver, Pa., 1985-89. Mem. Am. Prodn. and Inventory Control Soc. (cert. prodn. and inventory mgmt., treas. Schuylkill Valley chpt. 1981-82, pres. 1982-84, dir. membership region IX 1985-86, asst. v.p. 1987, v.p. 1988-89, Internat. Vol. Svc. award 1986), Nat. Assn. Purchasing Mgrs., Assn. Mfg. Excellence, NAFE, Am. Bus. Women's Assn., Soc. Mfg. Engrs., Mothers of Twins Club (nominating chmn. Lancaster, Pa. 1977-78). Republican. Presbyterian. Office: Dexter Corp East Water St Waukegan IL 60085

GODBEY, HELEN KAY, city official; b. Ft. Worth, Jan. 18, 1946; d. Paschal Lee and Ester Katherine (Williams) Godbey; children: Tammy Denise Thompson, Shelly Rae Thompson. AAS, Tarrant County Jr. Coll., 1985; B in Career Arts Dallas Bapt. U., 1987; MPA, U. Tex., Arlington, 1991. Cert. mcpl. clk., Tex. peace officer. Ct. clk. City of Ft. Worth, 1966-68; transcriber for ct. reporters, Dallas and Tarrant Counties, 1970-75; sec. City of Euless Police Dept., Tex., 1975-81; city sec. Euless, 1981-89; asst. city mgr., 1989-93; city mgr., Burleson, Tex., 1993—; speaker, instr. law enforcement and mgmt. topics Tex. A&M U., Tarrant County Jr. Coll. Police Acad., 1979-81; speaker IBM, various computer groups, Tex., Calif., 1983—, North Tex. State U. Ctr. for Community Svcs., Denton, 1984, 87—. Recipient Disting. Svc. awards Euless Police Dept., 1976, 79, Linda Keithley award for women in pub. mgmt., 1996. Mem. Internat. Inst. Mcpl. Clks. Advanced Acad. (co-chair 1989-90, com. on technol. devel. 1984-89, constl. revisions), Tex. Mcpl. Clks. Assn. Inc. (trustee officer 1987-88, treas. com. 1989, v.p. 1990), Internat. City Mgmt. Assn., North Tex. City Mgmt. Assn., Tex. City Mgmt. Assn. (pub. rels. & membership com., profl. devel. com.), Internat. City Mgmt. Assn. (academe affairs com. 1992—), Kiwanis (v.p. Mid-Cities chpt. 1989-90). Baptist. Avocations: golf, hiking, skating. Home: 1101 Glen Oak Dr Burleson TX 76028-6269 Office: 141 W Renfro St Burleson TX 76028-4261

GODDARD, CAROL ANN, newspaper editor; b. Chgo., Mar. 26, 1941; d. Robert Charles and Cecilia Margaret (Vonesh) Bosh; m. Joseph S. Goddard Jr., Feb. 9, 1966 (div. Mar. 1981); children: Laura Anne, Leslie Elizabeth. BA, DePauw U., 1963; postgrad., Northwestern U., 1964, U. Ill., 1979, No. Ill. U., 1980-81. Adminstrv. asst. A.G. Becker, Chgo., 1963-67; owner P&C Mktg., Hinsdale, Ill., 1975-79; reporter Doings newspaper, Hinsdale, 1979-82, assoc. editor, 1982-84, mng. editor, 1984-86; mng. editor Pioneer Press, Oak Park, Ill., 1986-90; exec. editor Pioneer Press, Park Ridge, Ill., 1990-91; bur. chief Lake County Pioneer Press, Bannockburn, Ill., 1992—. Chmn. Hinsdale Concert Com., 1989, Hinsdale Plan Commn., 1989-91; trustee Village of Hinsdale, 1991-95; bd. dirs. Sarah's Inn (abused women's shelter), Oak Park, 1989-91. Mem. Suburban Press Club Chgo. (bd. dirs. 1980-93, treas. 1980-81, pres. 1986-87, editl. award), Zonta. Roman Catholic. Home: 1300 Central St # 301 Evanston IL 60201 Office: Pioneer Press 2201 Waukegan Rd Deerfield IL 60015-1577

GODDARD, KAREN M., retail shop owner; b. Boston, Apr. 12, 1961; d. David E. and Elizabeth A. (Kennedy) G.; children: Keara Sexton, Lee Sexton. BS, Notre Dame Coll., Manchester, N.H., 1983. Legal asst., office mgr. Smith, Connor & Wilder, PA, Nashua, N.H., 1984-87; owner, retailer Mother & Child, Amherst and Nashua, N.H., 1990—. Editor newsletter Mother & Child, 1992—. Mem. planning com. Earth Day, Nashua, 1995—, Teddy Bear Picnic Fund Raiser, 1994—; mem. event planning Nature Conservancy, Concord, N.H., 1995-96; active NOW, 1994—, Downtown Revitalization Com., 1995—,. Mem. Women Owners Network, Coop Am. Bus. Network. Home: 29 McKean St Nashua NH 03060 Office: Mother & Child 111 W Pearl St Nashua NH 03060

GODDARD, KATHERINE SMITH (KITTY GODDARD), education and technology consultant; b. Dallas, Nov. 19, 1947; d. Robert Cowley and Ruth (Townsend) Smith; m. Richard A. Goddard, Oct. 2, 1970; 1 child, Pamela Chistine. BA, So. Meth. U., 1969. Classroom tchr. Richardson (Tex.) Ind. Sch. Dist., 1969-73, adminstrv. asst. dept. instrn., 1985-89; creative cons. ednl. software divsn. Jostens Learning Corp., Dallas, 1989-91; adminstrv. asst. to prin. St. Thomas Aquinas Cath. Sch., Dallas, 1992-94; cons. Richardson, 1991—; info. provider on Am. Online Nat. Staff Devel. Coun., Dallas, 1993-95; dir. devel. and pub. rels. Am. Inst. Musical Studies, Dallas, 1993—; edn. and tech. cons., owner CallKitty, Richardson, 1992—; Design/editor (catalog) Richardson Ind. Sch. Dist. Staff Devel. Catalog, 1987-89, design team America 2000, 1992; (dir.) St. Thomas Aquinas Cath. Sch. Dir., 1993; developer, editor Tech. Model-Hamilton Park Pacesetter Magnet Sch., Richardson Ind. Sch. Dist., 1996. Editor (newsletter) RISDiskourse. Exec. bd. Richardson Woman's Club, 1983-89, PTA, Richardson, 1978-86; exec. bd., v.p. Friends of the So. Meth U. Librs.-Colophon, Dallas, 1992—; adminstrv. bd. Spring Valley United Meth. Ch., Dallas, 1991-92. Recipient Key to the City, City of Port Arthur, 1965. Mem. Tex. State PTA (hon. life, Membership award 1977, Scrapbook award 1978), Nat. Staff Devel. Coun., So. Meth. U. Alumni Assn. (evaluator), Highland Park H.S. Alumni Assn. Reunion (alumni dir. 1990-95). United Methodist. Home and Office: 1411 Seminole Dr Richardson TX 75080

GODDARD, SANDRA KAY, elementary education educator; b. Steubenville, Ohio, Oct. 31, 1947; d. Albert Leonard and Mildred Irene (Hill) G. BS in Edn., Miami U., Oxford, Ohio, 1969; MEd, Miami U., 1973. Tchr. elem. grades Gregg Elem.-Edison Local Schs. Dist., Hammondsville, Ohio, 1969—; mem. curriculum and textbook com. Jefferson County Schs., Steubenville, 1994-95; active Spl. Olympics, 1992, 93; presenter in field. Publicity chmn., rec. sec., box office chmn. Steubenville Players, 1981-83; mem. Edison Local Adv. Coun. on Drug Edn., 1987—; mem. Edison Local Curriculum Instrn. Com., 1993—; state judge Ashland Oil Tchr. Achievement awards, 1988-90; regional and state judge Odyssey of the Mind, 1992—, bd. dirs. region XI, 1993-94, regional dir. Region XI, 1994—, state bd. dirs. Ohio Odyssey of the Mind, 1994—; exec. com. Gregg Elem. PTO, 1990-92; instr. 1st aid and cmty. CPR, ARC, 1990—, instr.-trainer 1993—, county disaster team. Martha Holden Jennings scholar, 1972-73; minigrantee Jefferson County Schs., 1991, 94. Mem. NEA (del. to rep. assembly 1979, 85, 86, 87, 88), Ohio Edn. Assn. (exec. com. 1983-89, pres.'s cabinet 1985-87, appeals bd. 1994—), Ea. Ohio Edn. Assn. (pres. 1978-79, exec. com. 1983-89), Edison Local Edn. Assn. (pres. 1974-75, v.p. 1986-88, 89-91, exec. com. 1991-94, mem. negotiation's team 1987, 90, 93), Ohio Valley UNISERV Coun. (treas. 1986-92), Delta Kappa Gamma (legis. chair 1990-92). Democrat. Methodist. Home: 200 Fernwood Rd Apt 11 Steubenville OH 43952-9200 Office: Gregg Elem Sch RR 1 Bergholz OH 43908-9801

GODDARD, THELMA TAYLOR, critical care nurse, nursing educator; d. James Oscar and Goldie Pearl (Hawkins) Taylor; m. Kenneth L. Goddard; children: Catherine, Sharon, K. John. ADN, W.Va. No. Community Coll., Weirton, 1980; BSN, West Liberty State Coll., 1986; MSN, W.Va. U. Staff critical care nurse Weirton (W.Va.) Med. Ctr., Pitts., West Pa., Pitts.; instr. nursing W.Va. No. C.C., W.Va. U., Morgantown; staff critical care nurse Cen. Med. Ctr., Pitts.; nursing instr. Waynesburg (Pa.) Coll., 1991-92, Carlow Coll., Pitts., 1992-94; instr. nursing Allegheny County C.C., Pitts., 1993-94; asst. prof. Wheeling (W.Va.) Jesuit Coll., 1994—; critical care nurse Ctrl. Med. Ctr., Pitts., 1990-94. Mem. ANA, AACCN, Sigma Theta Tau, Phi Theta Kappa. Office: Wheeling Jesuit Coll 342 Donahue Hall Wheeling WV 26003

GODDEN, JEAN W., columnist; b. Stamford, Conn., Oct. 1, 1933; d. Maurice Albert and Bernice Elizabeth (Warvel) Hecht; m. Robert W. Godden, Nov. 7, 1952 (dec. Dec. 1985); children: Glenn Scott, Jeffrey Wayne. BA, U. Wash., 1974. News editor Univ. Dist. Herald, Seattle, 1951-53; bookkeeper Omniarts Inc., Seattle, 1963-71; writer editorial page Seattle Post-Intelligencer, Seattle, 1974-80, editorial page editor, 1980-81, bus. editor, 1981-83, city columnist, 1983-91; city columnist Seattle Times, 1991—. Author: The Will to Win, 1980, Hasty Put Ins, 1981. Communicator of the Yr. U. Wash. Sch. of Comm., 1995. Mem. LWV (dir. 1969-71), Wash. Press Assn. (Superior Performance award 1979), Soc. Profl. Journalists, Mortarboard, City Club, Phi Beta Kappa. Office: The Seattle Times PO Box 70 Seattle WA 98111-0070

GODDESS, LYNN BARBARA, commercial real estate broker; b. N.Y.C., Mar. 3, 1942; d. Eugene Daniel and Hazel Cecile (Kinzler) G.; divorced. BS, Columbia U., 1963, postgrad., 1964-66. Coord. John M. Burns Assembly Campaign, N.Y.C., 1963; dir. spl. events, projects Kenneth B. Keating Senatorial Campaign, N.Y.C., 1964; dist. dir. fund raising Muscular Dystrophy Assn. Am. Inc., N.Y.C., 1965-66; exec. acct. fund raising, pub. relations Victor Weingarten Co., N.Y.C., 1966-67, Oram Group (formerly Harold L. Oram Inc.), N.Y.C., 1967-70; dir. devel. City Ctr. Music Drama Inc., N.Y.C., 1970; sales person Whitbread-Nolan, N.Y.C., 1971-73; from asst. v.p. to sr. v.p. Cross and Brown Co., N.Y.C., 1973-1985; sr. dir. Cushman & Wakefield, Inc., N.Y.C., 1985—. Trustee Young Adult Inst. Mem. Nat. Soc. Fund Raisers, Assn. Fund Dirs., Real Estate Bd. N.Y. (named Most Ingenious Broker Yr. 1975), Women's Forum (bd. dirs.). Office: Cushman & Wakefield Inc 51 W 52nd St New York NY 10019-6119

GODFREY, ALINE LUCILLE, music specialist, church organist; b. Providence, R.I., Dec. 4, 1943; d. Bernard Almasse and Rita Linda (Laramee) Brindamour; m. George Ruben Godfrey, Aug. 22, 1981; 1 child, Murray Aaron. BA, Rivier Coll., 1970; cert. of attendance, Am. Conservatory of Music, Fontainebleau, France, 1972; M of Music, U. Notre Dame, 1975. Cert. tchr. profl. all level music, provisional elem.-gen., Tex. Choir dir. Scituate (R.I.) High Sch., 1970-74; tchr. grade 4 McDowell Intermediate Sch., Hondo, Tex., 1974-75; tchr. grade 5 Wilson Elem. Sch., Harlingen, Tex., 1975-76; organist St. Albans Episcopal Ch., Harlingen, 1977-80; music specialist St. Mary's Sch. and Immaculate Conception Sch., Brownsville, Tex., 1977-79; choral accompanist Harlingen H.S., 1979-80; tchr. grade 6 Sam Houston Sch., Harlingen, 1980-81; music dir. St. Alban's Episcopal Sch., Harlingen, 1987-90; choral accompanist Marine Military Acad., Harlingen, 1988-90; tchr. Stuart Place Elem. Sch., Harlingen, 1990-91; msic specialist Harlingen Ind. Sch. Dist., 1991—; organist St. James Ch., Manville, R.I., 1972-74, First United Meth. Ch., Mercedes, Tex., 1987-93; pianist, accompanist Cardinal Chorale, Harlingen, 1980-81. Composer: Songs for Tots, 1983; playwright: (musical) Why the Bells Rang, 1988, American Tribute, 1995; arranger, dir. (musicals) Across the U.S.A., 1988, Around the World at Wilson School, 1992; dir. Under the Big Top, 1989, United We Stand, 1991; music dir.: Together, 1995, Christmas in the West, 1995, Every Day is Earth Day, 1996. Vol. Hosts Program, Harlingen, 1981, Riofest, 1983, Dishman Spring Festival, Combes, Tex., 1993, 94, Wilson Spring Fest, 1996; dir. Crockett Sch. dedication, 1993. Mem. Tex. State Tchrs. Assn., Tex. Music Educators Assn., Smithsonian Instn., PEO Sisterhood (historian), Am. Assn. Ret. Persons. Home: PO Box 875 Combes TX 78535-0875 Office: Wilson Elem Sch Primera Rd Harlingen TX 78552

GODFREY, EUTHA MAREK, elementary school educator, consultant; b. Balt., Mar. 25, 1937; d. Louis Joseph and Estelle Virginia (Stickels) Marek; m. Stanley I. Lewis (div. June 1970); children: Mark W. Lewis, Ronald A. Lewis, Kari S. Howard; m. Carl Godrey Sr., Nov. 20, 1983 (dec. July 1993). BM in Music Edn., Peabody Conservatory John's Hopkins U., 1959; postgrad., N.C. A & T State U., 1972-75, U. N.C., 1974-76. Cert. early childhood edn. Tchr. Murray County Schs., Chatsworth, Ga., 1959-60, Fulton County Schs., Roswell, Ga., 1960-62; music tchr. Balt. County Schs., Baltimore, Md., 1962-63; band, chorus tchr. Guilford County Schs., Greensboro, N.C., 1963-67, kindergarten tchr., 1967-73; cons., early childhood State Dept. Pub. Instruction, Raleigh, N.C., 1972-76; early childhood tchr. Peeler and Erwin Magnet Schs., Greensboro City Schs., N.C., 1973-91; cons. Divsn. of Reading, State Dept. Pub. Instruction, Raleigh, N.C., 1976-82; dir. music Palm Coast United Methodist Ch., Palm Coast, Fla., 1993—; cons., presenter, Individually Guided Edn., St. Louis, 1977; workshop presenter, Greensboro City Assn. for Edn. of Young Children, 1980-90; accreditation team, Southern Assn. of Schs. and Colls. State of N.C., 1977-91. Bd. dirs. Family Life Ctr., Palm Coast, 1992-95; mem. exec. com. Dem. Party, Greensboro, N.C., 1975; vol. Flagler County Pub. Libr., Palm Coast. Greensboro Pub. Sch. Fund grantee, 1987-88; Full Competative scholar Peabody Conservatory, 1955. Mem. AAUW, N.C. Ret. State Employees, Nat. Edn. Assn. Retired, N.C. Assn. Ret. Educators, Fellowship of United Meth. Musicians in Worship, Royal Sch. Ch. Music, Am. Choral Dir.'s Assn., Music & Other Arts, Am. Guild English Handbell Ringers, Choristers Guild, Mu Phi Epsilon. Home: 39 Westmore Ln Palm Coast FL 32164-4031

GODFREY, JOYZELLE EFFIE, economic development and small business consultant; b. Ft. Thompson, S.D., Jan. 18, 1942; d. Lawrence Michael and Nina Mae (Menzie) Gingway; m. Gene Rilling, Sept. 1963 (div. May 1970); children: Rodney, Mike, Neil, Nicolle, Yvette; m. Jerry Dean Godfrey, Sept. 1985 (div. Nov. 1993). BS, Black Hill State U., 1973; MPA, U. S.D., 1985. Mgr. Lakota Devel. Coun. St. Joseph's Indian Sch., Chamberlain, S.D., 1989—; small bus. cons. to Native Am. entrepreneurs. Author of poetry and short stories. Humanities scholar. Mem. Lambda Iota Tau Soc. Home: PO Box 257 Fort Thompson SD 57339-0257 Office: PO Box 440 Fort Thompson SD 57339

GODING, JUDITH GERMAINE, residential facility administrator, musician; b. Lynchburg, Va., Mar. 8, 1947; d. John Lewellyn and Louise Irene (McCormick) G. BA in Music, Lynchburg Coll., 1969, MEd in Spl. Edn., 1975; EdD in Sch. Adminstrn., Vanderbilt U., 1984. Cert. tchr., Va. Tchr. Cen. Va. Tng. Ctr., Lynchburg, 1969-79, program coord., 1979-82, ctr. dir., 1982—; tchr. Cen. Va. Cmty. Coll., Lynchburg, 1978, 86; organist, choirmaster Peakland United Meth. Ch., Lynchburg, 1970-79, 84-87; interim organist, choir dir. Madison Hts. (Va.) Bapt. Ch., 1990-91; interim organist First Christian Ch., Lynchburg, 1989-90, Euclid Christian Ch., Lynchburg, 1991—; pianist Piedmont Club, Lynchburg, 1975-93; presenter workshops. Contbr. articles to profl. jours. Mem. Cmty. Concerts Assn.; bd. dirs. Lynchburg Symphony. Recipient Edith Carrington award Lynchburg Fine Arts Ctr., 1988, Outstanding Achievement of Accomplishment in Human Svcs. Mgmt., Devel. Disabilities Svcs. Mgrs., Inc., 1989, Disting. Alumni award Lynchburg Coll., 1993, T. Gibson Hobbs award, 1995 and others. Mem. Ctrl. Va. Alumni Club (pres. 1990-94), Lynchburg Coll. Alumni Assn. (pres. 1994—). Home: 1911 Mimosa Dr Lynchburg VA 24503-2329 Office: Cen Va Tng Ctr PO Box 1098 Lynchburg VA 24505-1098

GODWIN, GAIL KATHLEEN, author; b. Birmingham, Ala., June 18, 1937; d. Mose Winston and Kathleen (Krahenbuhl) G.; m. Douglas Kennedy, 1960 (div. 1961), m. Ian Marshall, 1965 (div. 1966). Student, Peace Jr. Coll., Raleigh, N.C., 1955-57; B.A. in Journalism, U. N.C., 1959; M.A. in English, U. Iowa, 1968, Ph.D., 1971. News reporter Miami Herald, 1959-60; rep., cons. U.S. Travel Service, London, 1961-65; editorial asst. Saturday Evening Post, 1966; instr. Univ. Iowa, Iowa City, 1967-71; lectr. Iowa Writer's Workshop, 1972-73, Vassar Coll., 1977, Columbia U. Writing Program, 1978, 81. Author: (novels) The Perfectionists, 1970, Glass People, 1972, The Odd Woman, 1974 (Nat. Book award nomination 1974), Violet Clay, 1978 (Am. Book award nomination 1980), A Mother and Two Daughters, 1982 (Am. Book award nomination 1982), The Finishing School, 1985, A Southern Family, 1987, Father Melancholy's Daughter, 1991, The Good Husband, 1994; (short stories) Dream Children, 1976, Mr. Bedford and The Muses, 1983;editor: (with Shannon Ravenel) The Best American Short Stories 1985, 1985; librettist: (with Robert Starer) The Last Lover, 1975, Journals of a Songmaker, 1976, Apollonia, 1979, Anna Margarita's Will, 1981, Remembering Felix, 1987. Recipient Thomas Wolfe Meml. award Lipinsky Endowment of Western N.C. Hist. Assn., 1988, Janet Kafka award U. Rochester, 1988; fellow Center for Advanced Study, U. Ill., Urbana, 1971-72; Am. specialist USIS, 1976; Nat. Endowment Arts grantee, 1974-75; Guggenheim fellow, 1975-76; recipient award in lit. Am. Acad. and Inst. of Arts and Letters, 1981. Mem. PEN, ASCAP, Authors Guild, Authors League. Home: PO Box 946 Woodstock NY 12498-0946

GODWIN, JOYCE ANN, governance and business services consultant; b. Washington, July 25, 1943; m. Earl R. Godwin. BA in Govt., Fla. State U., 1965; MA in Polit. Sci. and Pub. Adminstrn., George Washington U., 1967. Dir. inquiry service Nat. League Cities, Washington, 1965-68; mem. polit. sci. faculty Calif. State Coll., San Jose, 1968-71; mgr. govtl. and pub. affairs San Jose (Calif.) C. of C., 1968-69, gen. mgr., 1969-70, acting exec. v.p., 1970-71, dir. staff devel. Meml. Med. Ctr., Corpus Christi, Tex., 1971-73; dir. edn. Southwest Community Health Svcs., Albuquerque, 1973-74, dir. pers., 1974-79, v.p. mgmt. svcs., 1979-85, v.p. diversification, 1985-86, sec. corp., bd. dirs., 1982-93, v.p. bus. devel. and external rels., 1989-93; pres. Southwest Bus. Ventures Inc., 1986-93, Vanguard Properties Inc., 1986-93; chmn. Hosp. Home Health, Inc., 1988-90, Home Care Enterprises, 1985 88, N.Mex. Self Insurers Guarantee Fund Commn., 1993, Quality N.Mex., 1994—; bd. dirs. Pub. Svc. Co., N.Mex., 1989—; chmn. spl. litigation com., 1989-91, chmn. compensation com., 1990-92, chmn. corp. and pub. responsibility com., 1990—, chmn. nom. com. 1991—; v.p. Southwest Health Found., 1981-93; vice chmn. Mission Aviation Fellowship, 1989—; chmn. Air Svc. Internat., 1993—; vice chmn. Internat. Students, Inc., 1995-96, chmn., 1996—; bd. dirs. ECFA, 1996—. Contbr. articles to profl. publs. Chmn. orch. rels. com. N.Mex. Symphony Orch., 1985-87, exec. com., 1985-87, bd. dirs., 1983-89; assoc. gen. chmn. United Way, 1987, campaign chmn., 1988, bd. dirs., 1987-89. Named one of Outstanding N.Mex. Women, Gov. of N.Mex., 1988; recipient Leadership award Leadership Albuquerque Alumni Assn., 1990. Mem. Greater Albuquerque C. of C. (chmn. roadrunners, bd. dirs., exec. com. 1984, chmn. statewide econ. devel. task force 1985, officer 1985-91, v.p. econ. affairs div. 1985, v.p. ednl. affairs div. 1986, v.p. membership 1987, chmn.-elect 1988-89, chmn. 1989-90).

GODWIN, MARY JO, editor, librarian consultant; b. Tarboro, N.C., Jan. 31, 1949; d. Herman Esthol and Mamie Winifred (Felton) Pittman; m. Charles Benjamin Godwin, May 2, 1970. BA, N.C. Wesleyan Coll., 1971; MLS, East Carolina U., 1973. Cert. libr., N.C. From libr. asst. to asst. dir. Edgecombe County Meml. Library, Tarboro, 1970-76, dir., 1977-85; asst. editor Wilson Library Bull., Bronx, N.Y., 1985-89, editor, 1989-92; dir. govt. sales The Oryx Press, Phoenix, 1993-95; dir. mktg. svc. The Oryx Press, Phoeniz, 1995—; mem. White House Conf. on Librs. and Info. Svcs. Task Force; bd. dirs. Libr. Pub. Rels. Coun., 1992-95. Bd. dirs. Friends of Calvert County Pub. Libr., 1994, Osborn Sch. Dist. Found.; mem. Ariz. Ctr. for the Book. Recipient Robert Downs award for intellectual freedom U. Ill. Grad. Sch. of Libr. Sci., 1992. Mem. ALA (3M/Jr. Mem. Roundtable Profl. Devel. award 1981), N.C. Libr. Assn. (sec. 1981-83), Info. Futures Inst., Ind. Librs. Exchange Roundtable (v.p., pres. elect 1994, pres. 1995—). Democrat. Episcopalian. Office: The Oryx Press 4041 N Central #700 Phoenix AZ 85012

GODWIN, SARA, writer; b. St. Louis, Feb. 18, 1944; d. Robert Franklin II and Annabelle (Palkes) G.; children: Jane, Josh; m. Charles D. James, May 1, 1990. BA, Calif. State U., 1967; postgrad., UCLA, 1968-70, U. Calif., Berkeley, 1970-71, W.I. Inst. Fairleigh Dickinson U., St. Croix, V.I., 1971-72; MA, Dominican Coll., 1974. Writer, editor Ortho Books Standard Oil of Calif., San Francisco, 1975-77; writer, editor Gannett Corp., San Rafael, Calif., 1977-79; sr. writer Shaklee Corp., San Francisco, 1979-88; freelance writer Marin County, Calif., 1988—; featured speaker Ask the Gardener, Sta. KSFO, San Francisco, 1980-81. Author: Seals, 1990, Gorillas, 1990, Scott's See and Do: Lawns and Groundcovers, 1995; contbr. to The Sea, 1993, Last Puff, 1990 (Lit. Guild selection), The Angler's Companion, 1991, Hummingbirds, 1991, The Gardener's Companion, 1992 (N.Y. Times Rev., Garden Book Club selection), Landscaping Decks and Patios, 1994; scriptwriter documentary Discover Canada, Discovering the USA; manuscript editor all About Perennials, 1992; prin. lexicographer Nat. Gardening Assn. Dictionary of Horticulture, 1994; author: Smith and Hawken Book of Basic Gardening, 1996, Microsoft Complete Gardening CD-ROM, 1996, Frommer's Boston CD-ROM, 1996; contbr. cover stories and feature articles to numerous U.S. and fgn. mags. Recipient 1st prize Calif. Press Women, for travel writing, 1982, corp. communications, 1983, personal column, 1984. Mem. Pacific Asia Travel Assn., Authors Guild, Am. Soc. Journalists and Authors, Garden Writers Assn. Am. Home: PO Box 1503 Ross CA 94957-1503

GOEBEL, CAROL LOUISE, sculptor; b. Dayton, Ohio, June 19, 1946; d. Robert Scott Goebel and Virginia Louise (Dolohan) Goebel Fisher; m. Christopher Cherney; 1 child, Timothy Robert Goebel Cherney. BFA, Miami U., Oxford, Ohio, 1968; MFA, Pratt Inst., Bklyn., 1970. Pres. Dutch Girl Painters, Inc., N.Y.C., 1973—; pres. CERES, N.Y.C., 1988-92, bd. dirs., 1988—, mem. steering com. 1988-96; co-coord. Women and Health exhbns. at A.I.R., Denise Bibro Fine Art, Ceres, Soho 20, 1993, Voices for Choice exhbns. A.I.R., Ceres, Soho 20, 1991; panelist A.I.R. Gallery, N.Y.C., 1984, Soho Photo Gallery, N.Y., 1992; panel co-chair Nat. Conv. Women's Caucus for Art, Chgo., 1992. Illustrator: Aromatherapy, Personal Journey Through Your Senses, 1994; one-person shows include Pratt Inst., Bklyn., 1970, Open Studio, N.Y.C., 1975, Chuck Levitan Gallery, N.Y.C., 1979 Ceres Gallery, N.Y.C., 1987, 90, 92, 95, Broadway Windows, N.Y.C., 1989, Queens Mus. of Art at Bulova Ctr., 1992, Denise Bibro Fine Art, 1996; exhibited in group shows at Chuck Levitan Gallery, N.Y.C., 1976, U.S. Mil. Acad., West Point, N.Y., 1977, Arsenal Gallery, N.Y.C., 1979, Project Union Square, N.Y.C., 1981, Fairleigh Dickinson U., Teaneck, N.J., 1981, AIR Gallery Invitation Exhbn., N.Y.C., 1981-85, Thorpe Intermedia Gallery, Sparkill, N.Y., 1984, AIR Gallery, N.Y., 1984, Douglass Coll., Rutgers U., New Brunswick, N.J., 1985, Erector Square Gallery, New Haven, 1986, Miami Art Mus., Miami U., Oxford, Ohio, 1986, Ceres Gallery, N.Y.C., 1986, 87, 91, Soho 20 Gallery, N.Y.C., 1986, 91, Arregui Hsai Fine Art, Coral Gables, Fla., 1989, 90, Jewish Mus., N.Y.C., 1989, Manhattan C.C., N.Y.C., 1989, Grand Ctrl. Terminal, N.Y.C., 1989, Aljira Gallery, Newark, 1990, Wunsch Arts Ctr., Glen Cove, N.Y., 1990, Gallery 128, N.Y.C., 1991, Krasdale Gallery, Bronx, 1991, 94, Grand Army Plaza, Bklyn., 1991, Snug Harbor Cultural Ctr., S.I., N.Y., 1992, 95, Prince St. Gallery, N.Y.C., 1992, Raritan Valley C.C. Gallery, N.J., 1992, One Main Sculpture Space, Bklyn., 1993, Nabisco Gallery, East Hanover, N.J., 1995, The Writer's Pl, Kansas City, Mo., 1995, St. Mark's Ch.-in-the-Bowery, N.Y.C., 1996, others. Mem. Women's Caucus for Art (bd. mem. N.Y. chpt. 1989-96, treas. 1988-90, v.p. 1990-95). Home: 48 Grand St New York NY 10013 Office: 76 Franklin St New York NY 10013

GOEDICKE, PATRICIA, poet, educator; b. Boston, June 21, 1931; d. John Bernard and Helen Victoria (Mulvey) McKenna; m. Leonard Wallace Robinson, June 3, 1971. BA, Middlebury Coll., 1953; MA, Ohio U., 1965. Lectr. Ohio U., Athens, 1963-68, Hunter Coll., N.Y.C., 1969-71; assoc. prof. U. Guanajuato, Mex., 1972-79; assoc. prof. U. Mont., Missoula, 1988-90, prof., 1991—; vis. writer Kalamazoo (Mich.) Coll., 1977; guest poet Sarah Lawrence Coll., Bronxville, N.Y., 1980-81; vis. poet U. Mont., 1981-83; mem. adv. bd. Calapooya Collage, Salem, Oreg., 1987—, Hellgate Writers, Missoula, 1989—; judge Oreg. Literary awards, Portland, 1995; artist's residency Rockefeller Found., 1993. Author: (poetry) Between Oceans, 1968, For the Four Corners, 1976, The Trail That Turns on Itself, 1978, The Dog That Was Barking Yesterday, 1980, Crossing the Same River, 1980, The King of Childhood, 1984, The Wind of Our Going, 1985, Listen, Love, 1986, The Tongues We Speak, 1989, Paul Bunyan's Bearskin, 1992, Invisible Horses, 1996; contbr. poems to numerous anthologies & mags. and articles to profl. jours.; consulting editor Eastern Wash. State U. Press, Cheney, 1995. Recipient award NEA, 1969, Duncan Frazier prize, 1976, Coordinating Coun. Lit. Mags. prize, 1976, William Carlos Williams prize New Letters, 1977, Pushcart Prize, 1977-78, Carolyn Kizer Poetry prize Monmouth Inst., 1987, Strousse award Prairie Schooner, 1987, Spl. commendtion Arvon Internat. Poetry Competition, 1987, Edward Stanley award, 1992, Walter Hall award Hubbub, 1995; rsch. grantee U. Mont., 1989; NEA creative writing fellow, 1976-77. Fellow MacDowell Colony; mem. Poetry Soc. Am., Assoc. Writing Programs, Acad. Am. Poets (assoc.), Poets Editors Novelists USA, Poets Editors Novelists West. Democrat. Office: U Mont Dept English Missoula MT 59812

GOEGLEIN, GLORIA J., state legislator; b. Ft. Wayne, Ind., Jan. 13, 1931; d. Alton F. and Nellie I. (Black) Woods; m. Leonard O. Goeglein, Oct. 17, 1954; children: Julia, Chris, Mark. Auditor Allen County, Ind., 1979-86; purchasing dir. City of Ft. Wayne, 1988-90; mem. Ind. Ho. of Reps., Indpls., 1990—; mem. Ways and Means Com., 1993-95, Govtl. Affairs Com., 1991-94, Cities and Town Com., 1991-92, Autism Commn., 1991-94, Local Govt. Fin. Study Commn., 1991-94, Mental Health Commn., 1994—, chair, 1996; mem. Interim Study Com. on State Govt. Mgmt. Issues, 1994, Local Govt. Com., 1995—, chair, 1996; mem. Ind. Adv. Commn. on Intergovernmental Rels., 1995—, Interim Study Com. on State Mgmt. Issues, 1995, Families, Children and Human Affairs Com., 1996, Mental Health Practices Study Com., chair, 1996; mem. Interim Study Com. on Procurement Law, 1996. Mem. Allen County Coun., 1974-78, v.p., 1975-78. Home: 9339 Maysville Rd Fort Wayne IN 46815-5820

GOEHNER, DONNA MARIE, university dean; b. Chgo., Mar. 9, 1941; d. Robert and Elizabeth (Cseke) Barra; m. George Louis Goehner, Dec. 16, 1961; 1 child, Michelle Renee. BS in English, So. Ill. U., 1963; MSLS, U. Ill., 1966, CAS in L.S., 1974; PhD in Edn., So. Ill. U., 1983. Rsch. assoc. U. Ill., Urbana, 1966-67; high sch. librarian St. Joseph-Ogden Sch. System, St. Joseph, Ill., 1967-68; curriculum lab librarian Western Ill. U., Macomb, 1968-73, periodicals librarian, 1974-76, coordinator for tech. svcs., 1977-78, acquisitions and collection devel. librarian, 1979-86, acting dir. library, 1986, dean library svcs., 1988—; assoc. Univ. librarian for tech. and adminstrv. svcs. Ill. State U., Normal, 1986-88. Contbr. articles to profl. jours. Mem. ALA, Assn. Coll. and Rsch. Libraries (chmn. univ. libraries sect. 1988-89), Ill. Assn. Coll. and Rsch. Libraries (pres. 1985-86), Ill. Library Assn. (Acad.Librarian of Yr. 1989). Home: 1001 Wigwam Hollow Rd Macomb IL 61455-1035 Office: Univ Library Western Ill U Macomb IL 61455

GOEHRING, MAUDE COPE, retired business educator; b. Persia, Tenn., Jan. 5, 1915; d. James Lawrence and Bobbie C. (Ross) Cope; m. Harvey John Goehring Jr., Aug. 12, 1950 (dec. Mar. 1992). BS in Edn., Ind. U. of Pa., 1948; MEd, U. Pitts., 1950; student, Lebanon Valley Coll., 1944-45. Tchr. Penn Hills Sr. High Sch., Pitts., 1948-68; tchr. U. Pitts., 1959-60, ret., 1968; vol. chmn. ICU, operating rm. info. desk Margaret R. Pardee Meml. Hosp., Hendersonville, N.C., 1989-95; vol. Carolina Village Health Ctr., 1994—; coord. Henderson County Ct. House Vols., Hendersonville, 1983-89; cons., counselor tax aid program Am. Assn. Ret. Persons, Hendersonville, 1981-96. Neighborhood chmn. Girl Scouts U.S., Butler County Pa., 1976-79; bd. dirs. ARC, Hendersonville, 1986-91; sec.-treas., bd. dirs. Crime Stoppers of Henderson County, 1991-96; nat. bd. dirs. Second Wind Hall of Fame, 1991-95. Mem. AAUW (officer 1975-76), Gideon Internat. Aux. (pres., sec. 1969-70), Delta Pi Epsilon (life, Gamma chpt., pres., sec. 1956-59, nat. del. 1957). Republican. Lutheran. Home: 21 Kestrel Ct Hendersonville NC 28792-2838

GOELDEN-BOWEN, MICHELLE MARIE, occupational therapist; b. Dallas, Oct. 28, 1966; d. David Louis and Barbara Marie (Michiels) Goelden; m. Richard George Bowen, Feb. 6, 1988. BS in Occupational Therapy, Tex. Woman's U., 1993. Lic. Exec. Coun. Phys. Therapy Occupational Therapy Examiners. Occupational therapist Plano (Tex.) Rehab. Hosp., 1993-94, Comty. Rehab. Ctrs., Dallas, 1993, Sundance Rehab. Corp., Dallas, 1994-96; home health occupational therapist Arcadia Healthcare, Lewisville, Tex., 1994—; occupational therapist Therapists Unltd., Dallas, 1994-96, Premier Health Staff, Inc., Bedford, Tex., 1996—; reviewer new product ideas or therapy materials The Psychol. Corp. Therapy Skill Builders, San Antonio, 1996. Mem. NAFE, World Fedn. Occupational Therapy, Am. Occupational Therapy Assn., Tex. Occupational Therapy Assn., Golden Key Nat. Honor Soc. Home: 4254 Malone Ave The Colony TX 75056-3066 Office: 1905 Central Dr Ste 200 Bedford TX 76021

GOERES, MINDY SUSAN, contracting specialist; b. Pensacola, Fla., Oct. 2, 1959; d. John S. and Edna Ruth (Garrett) Connolly; m. Ross P. Goeres, July 2, 1988. BA in Bus., Capital U., 1990; postgrad., Troy State U. Phys. sci. technician U.S. Army, Landstuhl, Germany, 1994-95; cooper cap intern USAF, Holloman AFB, N.Mex., 1995-96. Mem. Nat. Contracts Mgmt. Assn. (cert. assoc. contracts mgr.), Am. Homebrewers Assn. (cert. judge 1991-96), Am. Home Wine and Beer Trade Assn., Delta Sigma Pi (life). Unitarian Universalist.

GOERNER, SALLY J., system study center administrator, consultant; b. St. Louis, Sept. 30, 1952; d. Edwin Bayard and Marie M. (Schmidt) G.; m. Theodore G. Lindeman, Jan., 1975 (div. June 1978); m. John Stewart Petty, July 10, 1980; 1 child, Diana. BA magna cum laude, Colo. Coll., 1974; MS, SUNY, 1977; MEd, U. N.C., 1982; PhD with distinction, Saybrook Inst., 1989. Systems programmer NCR Corp., Ithaca, N.Y., 1975-79; co-founder Asyst Design Svcs., 1976, bus. sys. cons., 1976-79; sr. software engr. Adaptronics, McLean, Va., 1979-81; pvt. practice psychotherapy, 1982-85; mem. sci. staff Bell No. Rsch. Labs., Research Triangle Park, N.C., 1983-85; sr. tech. comms. specialist Data Gen. Corp., 1986-92; dir., cons. Triangle Ctr. Study of Complex Syss., Chapel Hill, N.C., 1992—. Author: Chaos and the Evolving Ecological Universe, 1994, Life After The Clockwork Universe, 1996, Complexity and the Web World, 1996; contbr. chpts. to books, articles, reviews to profl. jours. Recipient Excellence award Soc. Technical Communicators, Women of Achievement Award Orange County Women's Assn. Mem. APA, Am. Psychol. Soc., Am. Soc. Syss. and Cybernetics, Internat. Soc. Syss. Scis. (Sir Geoffrey Vickers award for Excellence), Internat. Soc. Ecol. Psychology, European Acad. Evolutionary Mgmt., Soc. Chaos Theory in Psychology and the Life Scis. (pres.), Gen. Evolution Rsch. Group, Phi Beta Kappa. Mem. Unitarian-Universalist Ch. Office: Triangle Ctr Study Complex 374 Wesley Ct Chapel Hill NC 27516*

GOERSS, BETTY LOU, education educator; b. Carthage, Mo., Dec. 2, 1942; d. John W. and Pauline (Holland) Wickstrom; m. Danny Allen Phillips, Sept. 4, 1960 (dec. Feb. 1981); children: Tom W., Timothy A., Ted L.; m. Arthur Wilson Goerss, Apr. 21, 1984. BS in Elem. Edn., Radford Coll., 1974; MEd, U. Pitts., 1981, EdD, 1993. Cert. elem. tchr., reading specialist, reading supr., Pa. 6th grade tchr. Roanoke (Va.) City Schs., 1974-76; tchr. Duquesne (Pa.) Pub. Schs., 1976-80; reading specialist Allegheny Intermediate Unit, Pitts., 1980-93; asst. prof. Coll. Mt. St. Joseph, Cin., 1993—; cons. Performance Resources Cons., Inc., Fairfield, Ohio, 1987-94, U. Pitts., 1990-91, City of Pitts. Schs., 1990-91; chair athletics com., mem. grad. com. Coll. Mt. St. Joseph. Tchr. Fairfield (Ohio) Ch. of Christ, 1994—. Named Outstanding Tchr., Allegheny Intermediate Unit, Pitts., 1992. Mem. Internat. Reading Assn., Tchrs. Whole Lang., Assn. Ednl. Rsch., Ohio Coun. Intern. Reading Assn. (mem. rsch. and studies com.), Coll. Reading Assn. Republican. Home: 120 Blair House Pl Fairfield OH 45014

GOETTEL, DEBORAH R., environmental engineer; b. Kansas City, Mo., Sept. 29, 1958; d. Charles Howard and Ernestine (Orr) Elms; m. Mitchell Dean Hanley, Sept. 24, 1977 (div. 1979); children: Joshua, Mitchell; m. Daniel Edward Goettel, Jan. 24, 1982 (dec.). BSCE, U. Minn., 1994, postgrad. Lab. tech., field svc. staff Weyerhauser Co., Elgin, Ill., 1980-83; lab. tech. Container Corp. Am., Carol Stream, Ill., 1983-84; tchr. St. Augustin Sch., Austin, Minn., 1984-87; environ./safety coord. Mid-Continent Engr., Mpls., 1993-94; cons. environ. engr. Montgomery Watson, Wayzate, Minn., 1995—. Editor Montgomery Watson Newsletter; contbr. articles to profl. jours. Vol., cons. Senator Wellstone's Office, Mpls., St. Paul, 1995—. Mem. NOW, Women's Forum, Am. Electroplaters and Surface Finishers, Indsl. Consortium Environ. Mgmt. Roman Catholic. Home: 6525 James Ave South Richfield MN 55423

GOETZ, CECELIA HELEN, lawyer, retired judge; b. N.Y.C.; d. Isador and Sylvia (Cohen) G.; children: Matthew I. Spiegel, Robert Spiegel. BA cum laude, NYU, 1940, LLB, 1940, LLM in Taxation, 1957. Bar: N.Y. 1940, U.S. Dist. Ct. (so. and ea. dists.) N.Y. 1951, Fla. 1954, U.S. Ct. Appeals (2d cir.) 1958, U.S. Ct. Appeals (1st cir.) 1952, U.S. Ct. Appeals (9th cir.) 1967. Atty. claims div. (now civil div.) Dept. Justice, Washington, 1943-46; assoc. counsel Office Chief of Counsel for War Crimes, Nuremberg, Ger., 1946-48; ptnr. Goetz & Goetz, N.Y.C., 1949-51; asst. chief counsel Office Price Stblzn., Washington, 1951-52; spl. asst. to atty. gen., tax div., Dept. Justice, Washington, 1952-53; assoc. Weisman, Celler, Allan, Spett & Sheinberg, N.Y.C., 1953-58, Kaye, Scholer, Fierman, Hays & Handler, N.Y.C., 1958-64; ptnr. Herzfeld & Rubin, P.C., N.Y.C., 1964-78; judge U.S. Bankruptcy Ct., Eastern Dist. N.Y., Bklyn., 1978-93; of counsel Herzfeld & Rubin, P.C., N.Y.C., 1994-95. Mem. Assn. Bar City N.Y., N.Y. State Bar Assn., ABA, N.Y. County Lawyers Assn., NYU Law Rev. Alumni Assn., N.Y. Women's Bar Assn., Women's Bar Assn. State N.Y. Nat. Conf. Bankruptcy Judges, Nat. Assn. Women Judges, Assn. Women Judges State N.Y., Women's City Club N.Y. Office: 3400 North Ocean Dr Singer Island FL 33404-3201

GOETZ, SALLY LOANN, social services administrator; b. Sylvania, Ohio, Mar. 9, 1935; d. Gustav Peter and Edna Louise (Groth) Fischer; m. Ronald William Raymond, June 22, 1955 (dec. June 1988); children: David Keith, Mark Allan, Neil Stephen; m. LaVern Carl Goetz, Aug. 21, 1994. Student, U. Toledo, 1984. Sec. Gen. Mills, Inc., Toledo, 1959-69; sec., mgr. human resources Hudson's Dept. Store, Toledo, 1972-87; office adminstr. Lee Eye Inst., Monroe, Mich., 1987-89; sec., exec. dir. Sylvania Cmty. Svcs. Ctr., Inc., 1990—; co-owner Moments In Time, Sylvania, 1990-93. Mem. Nat. Assn. Fund Raising Execs. Republican. Lutheran. Home: 6708 Gettysburg Dr Sylvania OH 43560 Office: Sylvania Cmty Svcs Ctr Inc 6850 Monroe St Sylvania OH 43560-1922

GOFF, LILA JOHNSON, historical society administrator; b. Redwood Falls, Minn., Jan. 10, 1944; d. Byron Willard and Camilla (Henry) Johnson; m. Robert Eugene Goff, Apr. 24, 1974; children: Emily Lee, Matthew Byron. BA in History, U. Minn., 1965, MA in History, 1995. Chief Oral History Office Minn. Hist. Soc., St. Paul, 1967-69, head Audio Visual Library, 1969-76, asst. dir. for library and mus. collections, 1976-85, asst. dir. for library and archives, 1985—. Dep. coord. Minn. State Hist. Records Adv. Bd. Mem. Oral History Assn. (pres. 1989-90), Oral History Assn. Minn. (pres. 1985-87), Orgn. Am. Historians, Nat. Assn. Govt. Archivists and Records Adminstrs. (bd. dirs. 1992-94), Coun. State Hist. Records Coords. (chair 1994-95), Rsch. Librs. Group (bd. dirs. 1996—). Home: 1151 Orange Ave E Saint Paul MN 55106-2076 Office: Minn Hist Soc Libr and Archives Div 345 Kellogg Blvd W Saint Paul MN 55102-1903

GOFORTH, MARY ELAINE DAVEY, secondary education educator; b. Barnesville, Ohio, Sept. 9, 1922; d. Frederick Richard and Lola (Knox) Davey; m. Richard Eugene Goforth, Sept. 9, 1944; 1 child, Diane Lynell Goforth-Ohning. B.M.Ed., Oberlin Coll., 1944; MA in Edn., Coll. of Mt. St. Joseph, 1987. Cert. edn. Music tchr. Leipsig, Ohio, 1944-45, Perry Local, 1945-47; English tchr. Ohio No. Univ., 1946; English and music tchr. Perry Sch., Lima, Ohio, 1945-47; English tchr. Stone Creek, Ohio, 1947-51, Barnesville, Ohio, 1952-53, Tuscarawas, Ohio, 1957-59; English tchr. Conotton Valley Sch., Bowerston, Ohio, 1960-62; English tchr. New Philadelphia, Ohio, 1964-68, Indian Valley, Midvale, Ohio, 1973-88, Indian Valley, Gnadenhetten, Ohio, 1988-93. Author poems. Pres. New Philadelphia (Ohio) Tchrs.' Assn., 1967. Named Indian Valley Tchr. of Yr., 1985, Candidate for Ohio Tchr. of the Yr., 1985; Martha Holden Jennings scholar, 1985. Home: 2123 E High Ave New Philadelphia OH 44663-3323

GOGAN, CATHERINE MARY, dental educator; b. Buffalo, Feb. 9, 1959; d. John Francis and Mary Louise (Solomon) G. BA, SUNY, Buffalo, 1981, DDS, 1985, MS, 1995. Resident Erie County Med. Ctr., Buffalo, 1985-86, attending dentist, 1986—, dental residency coord., 1987—, dental dir. skilled nursing facility, 1989—; pvt. practice Buffalo, 1986—; clin. instr. SUNY, Buffalo, 1987-88, asst. prof., 1988—. Editor mag. UB Dental Report, 1989-94 (Golden Scroll award); contbr. articles to profl. jours. Fellow Am. Assn. Hosp. Dentists; mem. ADA, Am. Assn. Dental Schs., Orgn. Tchrs. Oral Diagnosis, Acad. Dentistry for Persons with Disabilities, Am. Soc. Geriatric Dentistry, U. Buffalo Dental Alumni Assn. (sec. 1988-89, v.p. 1989-90, pres. 1990-91), Mt. Mercy Acad. Alumni Assn. (bd. dirs. 1990-91), Omicron Kappa Upsilo n (v.p., pres.-elect chpt., pres. chpt. 1996-97). Roman Catholic. Office: SUNY at Buffalo Dept Oral Diagnostic Scis 355 Squire Hall Buffalo NY 14214

GOGGANS, CATHY DIANE, nurse; b. Abilene, Tex., Dec. 17, 1957; d. James Lawrence and Shirley Ann (Mangum) G. Diploma RN, Meth. Hosp. Sch. Nursing, 1983; AA, Cisco (Tex.) Jr. Coll., 1983; BSN, Angelo State U., 1988. RN, Tex.; cert. pediatric nurse, cert. neonatal nurse. Staff nurse in nursery Hendrick Med. Ctr., Abilene, 1983-88, staff nurse in pediatrics, 1988-95; clin. coord. Abilene Internal Medicine, 1989-90; pediatric home health staff nurse Kimberly Quality Care, 1990; staff nurse Hendrick House Calls, Abilene, 1995—. Vol. March of Dimes, 1995—. Baptist. Home: 1817 Peach St Abilene TX 79602-4748 Office: Hendrick Hosue Calls 1393 Ambler Abilene TX 79601-2316

GOGGIN, JOAN MARIE, school system specialist; b. Boston, Nov. 15, 1956; d. Richard and Florence Muriel (Stone) G. BS in Edn., Westfield State Coll., 1978; MS in Edn., Lesley Coll., 1981. Spl. needs tchr. Supervisory Union # 53, Pembroke, N.H., 1978-79; grad. intern, head tchr. Ednl. Collaborative Greater Boston, Brookline, Mass., 1979-80; vocat. counselor Charles River Assn. for Retarded Citizens, Needham, Mass., 1981-83; dir. vocat. svcs. Community Assistance Corp., New Orleans, 1983-84; tchr. of pre-sch. children with severe spl. needs St. Charles Parish Pub. Schs., Luling, La., 1985-88; career placement and tng. specialist Plymouth (Mass.) Carver Regional Sch. Dist., 1988-92; inclusion facilitator Plymouth Pub. Schs., 1992—; ednl. cons. Ednl. Performance Sys., 1994—; cons. on self advocacy Mass. Assn. for Retarded Citizens, 1980-83; ednl. cons. Human Devel. Ctr., La. State U., New Orleans, 1984-85, D.K. Hollingsworth &

Assocs., Metairie, La., 1984-88, vocat. cons. United Cerebral Palsy, Harahann, La., 1984-85; program coord. JTPA Project, Plymouth Sch. Dist., 1989-91, program. adminstr., 1991-93, exec. prodr. Bridging the Gap, We All Belong Together, 1991-93. Exec. prodr.: Bridging the Gap: Transition to Independence, We All Belong Together; author tng. program for paraprofls. Active Mass. Dept. Edn. Task Force on Criteria for Spl. Edn. Svcs., 1992-93, mem. com. Individual Edn. Plan, 1990-93. Recipient Hon. Mention Tchr. of Yr. award Mass. Coun. Exceptional Children; grantee Mass. Dept. Edn., 1988—. Mem. NEA, Assn. for Severely Handicapped. Democrat. Office: Mt Pleasant Sch Pupil Pers Svcs 253 S Meadow Rd Plymouth MA 02360

GOGOLIN, MARILYN TOMPKINS, educational administrator, language pathologist; b. Pomona, Calif., Feb. 25, 1946; d. Roy Merle and Dorothy (Davidson) Tompkins; m. Robert Elton Gogolin, Mar. 29, 1969. BA, U. LaVerne, Calif., 1967; MA, U. Redlands, Calif., 1968; postgrad., U. Washington, 1968-69; MS, Calif. State U., Fullerton, 1976. Cert. clin. speech pathologist; cert. teaching and sch. adminstrn. Speech and lang. pathologist Rehab. Hosp., Pomona, 1969-71; diagnostic tchr. L.A. County Office of Edn., Downey, Calif., 1971-72, program specialist, 1972-74, cons. lang., 1975-76, cons. orgns. and mgmt., 1976-79, dir. administrv. affairs, asst. to supt., 1979-95; dep. supt., 1995—; cons. lang. sch. dists., Calif., 1975-79; cons. orgn. and mgmt. and profl. assns., Calif., 1976—; exec. dir. L.A. County Sch. Trustees Assn., 1979—. Founding patron Desert chpt. Kidney Found., Palm Desert, Calif., 1985. Doctoral fellow U. Washington, 1968; named One of Outstanding Young Women Am., 1977. Mem. Am. Mgmt. Assn., Am. Speech/Hearing Assn., Calif. Speech/Hearing Assn., Am. Edn. Research Assn. Baptist. Office: LA County Office Edn 9300 Imperial Hwy Downey CA 90242-2813

GOHEEN, JANET MOORE, counselor, sales professional; b. Everett, Mass., Sept. 29, 1945; d. Franklin Pierce and Virginia Louise (Murphy) Moore; m. Peter Arthur Goheen, Apr. 2, 1967; children: Kevin Murphy Moore Goheen, Andrew Hudson Moore Goheen. BA, Ohio Wesleyan U., 1967; MS, U. Bridgeport, 1979. Cert. profl. guidance counselor, Ohio. Tchr. English Nordinia Hills High Sch., Macedonia, Ohio, 1967-69, White Plains (N.Y.) High Sch., 1969-71, Hudson (Ohio) High Sch., 1982-83; tchr. emotionally disturbed Palisades Learning Ctr., Paramus, N.J., 1986-87; sales cons. The Longaberger Co., Dresden, Ohio, 1983-84, br. advisor, 1984-90, regional advisor, 1990—; middle sch. counselor Hudson Middle Sch., 1988—; tchr. ESL Hitchcock Presbyn. Ch., Scarsdale, N.Y., 1976-79, Aurora (Ohio) City Schs., 1979-81, Hudson Local Schs., 1980-82. Mem. Jr. League of Scarsdale, 1976-79, Jr. League of Akron, 1979-82, Jr. League No. N.J., Ridgewood, 1983-85; mem. alumni bd. dirs. Ohio Wesleyan U., Delaware, Ohio, 1990-93. Mem. Am. Sch. Counselors Assn., Ohio Sch. Counselors Assn., Kappa Kappa Gamma, Kappa Delta Pi. Home: 97 Manor Dr Hudson OH 44236-3406 Office: Hudson Middle Sch 77 N Oviatt St Hudson OH 44236-3043

GOINS, FRANCES FLORIANO, lawyer; b. Buffalo, Jan. 30, 1950; d. William and Anita (Graziano) Floriano; m. Gary Mitchell Goins; children: Matthew W., Mark W. MusB, Cleve. Inst. Music, 1971; MusM, Case Western Res. U., 1973, JD, 1977. Bar: Ohio 1977, U.S. Dist. Ct. Ohio 1978, U.S. Ct. Appeals (6th cir.) 1979, N.Y. 1984, U.S. Ct. Appeals (2d cir.) 1991. Law clk to Hon. Frank J. Battisti U.S. Dist. Ct. (no. dist.) Ohio, Cleve., 1977-78; ptnr. Squire, Sanders & Dempsey, Cleve., 1986—; mem. vis. com. bd. overseers Case Western Res. U., Cleve., 1984—; faculty Nat. Inst. Trial Advocacy, Cleve., 1991-92, 96; faculty, lectr. trial advocacy seminar Cleve. State U. Sch. Law, 1989-90. Editor-in-chief law rev. Case Western Res. Sch. Law, 1976-77. Trustee, chairperson devel. com. Lyric Opera Cleve., 1985-92; trustee Shoreby Club Cleve., 1989-91; v.p. bd. trustees Bay Village Montessori Sch., 1994-96. Mem. ABA (bus. law sect., bus. lit. com., subcom. on corporate governance 1995—, fed. regulation of securities com., subcom. on civil litigation and SEC enforcement matters 1992—), Ohio State Bar Assn. (ad hoc com. on bus. cts. 1994—), Cleve. Bar Assn. (com. on women and the law 1987—, ethics com. 1988-90, securities law inst. 1991, 92, 93, jud. selection com. 1996—). Democrat. Roman Catholic. Office: Squire Sanders & Dempsey 4900 KeyCorp Ct 127 Public Sq Cleveland OH 44114-1216

GOLASHESKY, CHRYSA ZOFIA, telecommunications company executive; b. Bayonne, N.J., Feb. 16, 1957; d. John Stanley and Margaret Walterine (Stanko) G. BS, Pa. State U., 1978; MBA, Rutgers U., 1980. Cert. Christian Founds. for Ministry. Mktg. analyst ITT - Domestic Transmission Systems, Inc., N.Y.C., 1980-81; market rsch. analyst ITT - U.S. Transmission Systems, Inc., N.Y.C., 1981-82; project mgr., market researcher ITT - U.S. Transmission Systems, Inc., Secaucus, N.J., 1982-85, mktg. mgr., 1985-86; product mgr. Metromedia Long Distance, Inc., Secaucus, 1986-87, dir. product mgmt., 1987-88, dir. mktg., 1988-89; dir. product mktg. Metromedia/ITT Long Distance, Inc., Secaucus, 1989-91; v.p. product mktg. Metromedia Communications Corp., East Rutherford, N.J., 1991-95; v.p. account rels. World Com, 1995—. Mem. edon. com. OLA Parish, Bayonne, N.J., 1986—; mem. Christian Founds. for Ministry, Irvington, N.J., 1988-91; v.p. account rels. LDDS World Com., N.E. Region East Rutherford, 1995. Roman Catholic. Home: 101 W 24th St Bayonne NJ 07002-2701 Office: World Com 1 Meadowlands Plz East Rutherford NJ 07073-2137

GOLBERT, SANDRA, artist; b. San Juan, P.R., Nov. 9, 1937; d. Leonard and Hortensia (Portilla) G.; div.; children: Michelle, Jeanette, Pedro. Student, Haystack Sch. Workshops, Parsons Sch. of Design. One-woman shows include Curacao (Netherlands, Antilles) Mus., 1974, La Fortaleza Gov.'s Mansion, San Juan, 1984, Origenes-Origins, San Juan, 1990, John Harms Ctr., Englewood, N.J., 1994, Art for Body and Wall, St. Thomas, V.I., 1994; group exhibitions include Centro de Amistad, Guadalajara, Mex., 1972, Art Ventures Gallery, Princeton, N.J., 1985, Citibank Gallery and Ponce Mus., 1989, Ateneo Puertorriqueno, San Juan, 1989, Women's Art Works II, Rochester, N.Y., 1992, Convergence '92, Washington, 1992, The Farrell Collection, Washington, 1992, Paramount Ctr. for Arts, Peekskill, N.Y., 1992, Lever House, N.Y.C., 1992, America House, Piermont, N.Y., 1992, Coleen Greco Gallery, Suffern, N.Y., 1992, Barbara Gibson Gallery, Nyack, N.Y., 1993, Nat. Arts Club, N.Y.C., 1993, Marymount Coll., Tarrytown, N.Y., 1993, Jacob K. Javits Fed. Bld., N.Y.C., 1994, West Broadway Gallery, Soho, N.Y., 1994, Watchung Ctr., N.J., 1995, Johnson & Johnson HQ, New Brunswick, N.J., 1995, Old Ch. Cultural Ctr., Demerest, N.J., 1995, NAWA, Athens, 1996, Art for Body and Wall 11, Curacao, 1996; represented in permanent collection at Jane Voorhees Zimmerli Mus., Rutgers Univ., New Brunswick. Recipient grant NEA, 1991, grant Pollock-Krasner Found., 1991, residency Millay Colony for Arts, 1993; fashion designs published in Vogue Mag., 1959. Mem. Salute to Women in Arts, Nat. Assn. Women Artists (bd. dirs.), Arts Coun. Rockland, Assn. Puerto Rican Women Artists. Home and Office: PO Box 193 Piermont NY 10968

GOLD, ALISON LESLIE, writer; b. N.Y.C.; d. William I. and Shirley E. Greenwald; 1 child, Thor. BA, New Sch., N.Y.C., 1968. Author: (with Miep Gies) Anne Frank Remembered, 1987; author: Clairvoyant, 1991. Recipient Merit of Ednl. Distinction award Anti-Defamation League, N.Y.C., 1987, Christopher award Christian Brothers, N.Y.C., 1988; named Best of Best Am. Libr. Assn., 1994.

GOLD, ARLINE, educational administrator. EdD, Columbia U., 1987. Prin. George W. Miller Elem. Sch., Nanuet, N.Y. Recipient elem. sch. recognition award U.S. Dept. Edn., 1989-90, Internat. Invitational Sch. award, 1990-91, champions of edn. award, 1995-96. Office: George W Miller Elem Sch 50 Blauvelt Rd Nanuet NY 10954-3445

GOLD, CATHERINE ANNE DOWER, music history educator; b. South Hadley, Mass., May 19, 1924; d. Lawrence Frederick Dower and Marie (Barbieri) Barber; m. Arthur Gold, Mar. 24, 1994; children: Carolyn D. Gold, Judith G. Enteen. AB, Hamline U., 1945; MA, Smith Coll., 1948; PhD, The Cath. U. Am., 1968. New Eng. rep. Gregorian Inst. Am., Toledo, 1948-49; tchr. music, organist St. Rose Sch., Meriden, Conn., 1949-53; supr. music Holyoke (Mass.) Pub. Schs., 1953-55; instr. music U. Mass., Amherst, 1955-56; prof. music Westfield (Mass.) State Coll., 1956-90; columnist and freelance writer Holyoke Transcript Telegram, 1991-93; organist St. Theresa's Ch., South Hadley, 1937-41, St. Michael's Ch., N.Y., 1945-46; concert series presenter Westfield State Coll., 1987-91, rschr. tchr.; vis. scholar U. So. Calif., 1969; vis. assoc. prof. music Herbert Lehman Coll. CUNY, 1970-71. Author: Puerto Rican Music Following the Spanish American War, 1898-1910, 1983; (monograph) Yella Pessl, 1986, Alfred Einstein on Music, 1991, Yella Pessl: First Lady of the Harpsichord, 1993; presenter Irish Concert Springfield Symphony Orch., 1981 (plaque 1982). Pres. Coun. for Human Understanding Holyoke, 1981-83, Friends of Holyoke Pub. Libr., 1990-91; bd. dirs., chmn. nominating com. Holyoke Pub. Libr., 1987-89; bd. dirs. Holyoke Pub. Libr. Corp., 1991-94, Women's Symphony League, The Symphony Orch., 1992-94; bd. dirs., sec. Life Long Learning Soc. of Fla. Atlantic U., 1994—; presiding officer inauguration Dr. Irving Buchman pres. of Westfield State Coll.; mem. ethics com. Holyoke Hosp., 1988-94; sec. Haiti Mission, 1982-94; bd. overseers Mullen U., 1993; hon. mem. bd. Coun. Human Understanding, 1994; hon. mem. WSC Found., 1994; co-chair United Jewish Appeal/Jewish Fedn. Boca Lago Women's Divsn., 1996-97. Recipient citation Academia InterAmericana de P.R., 1978, Holyoke Pub. Libr., 1983, plaque Mass. Tchrs. Assn., Boston, 1984, medal Equestrian Order Holy Sepulchre of Jerusalem, Papal Knighthood Soc., Boston, 1984, Performance award Gov. Dukakis, Mass., 1988, award for Puerto Rican Jour. Al. Margens, 1992, Human Rels. award Coun. for Human Understanding, Holyoke, 1994, award Trustee's Cir. Westfield State U., 1994; named Lady Comdr., 1987, with star, 1990, Career Woman of Yr., 1988; fellow Internat. Biographical Assn., 1991; Westfield State U. concert series named Catherine A. Dower Performing Arts Series in her honor, 1991; recipient 1st prize in Raddock Eminent Scholar Chair Essay Contest of Fla. Atlantic U., 1996. Mem. Am. Musicol. Soc., The Coll. Mus. Soc., Ch. Music Assn. Am. (journalist), Acad. Arts and Scis. of P.R. (medal 1977), Internat. Platform Assn., Friends of the Holyoke Pub. Libr. (pres. 1990-91), Irish Am. Cultural Inst. (chmn. bd. 1981-89), Holyoke Quota (v.p. 1976-79, pres. 1979-81, 90-92, chmn. speech and hearing com. 1987-94), B'nai B'rith of Boca Lago (sec. bd. dirs. 1994—), Lifelong Learning Soc. Fla. Atlantic U. (sec. 1994—). Democrat. Home: 8559 Casa Del Lago Boca Raton FL 33433-2107

GOLD, CHRISTINA A., cosmetics company executive. Grad., Carleton U., Ottawa; degree (hon.), U. Montreal, 1991. With human resources, sales, mktg., fin. and mgmt. depts. Avon Can., 1970-89, pres., CEO, 1989-93, head oper. bus. unit, 1993; sr. v.p., pres. Avon North Am., N.Y.C., 1993—. Mem. adv. coun. Carleton U. Mem. Conf. Bd. (bd. dirs.), Direct selling Assn. (bd. dirs.). Office: Avon Products Inc 9 W 57th St New York NY 10019

GOLD, DONNA LAUREN, writer; b. White Plains, N.Y., Apr. 24, 1953; d. Irving and Judy (Fleminger) G.; m. Bill Carpenter; 1 child, Daniel Carpenter-Gold. Student, Bennington Coll., 1971-72; BA, UCLA, 1975; MA, New Sch. for Social Rsch., N.Y.C., 1980. V.p. Friendly Publs. Internat., N.Y.C., 1977-80, Zurich, 1978-79; writer/producer Barry Howard Assocs., Larchmont, N.Y., 1983-84; art editor Kennebec Jour., Augusta, Maine, 1990-91; writer, journalist, 1981—; Stockton Springs, Maine, 1990—. Editor: Maine Progressive, 1987-89; author: Country Roads of Maine, 1995; sculptor: Sacred Spaces, 1993; author poetry. Organizer, facilitator Peace and Justice in Cen. Am., Augusta, 1985-88; organizer June 12 Com./Photoshow, N.Y.C., 1982. Recipient 1st pla. arts criticism, Maine Press Assn., 1990. Mem. Maine Writers and Pubs. Alliance, Phi Beta Kappa. Democrat. Jewish. Home: Rte 1 Box 1297 Stockton Springs ME 04981

GOLD, JANET NOWAKOWSKI, Spanish language educator; b. Torrington, Conn., Oct. 24, 1948; d. Peter S. and Virginia (Eseppi) Nowakowski; m. Hector Zamora, Dec. 1974 (div. Spet. 1978); m. Stephen Gold, June 28m 1981. BA, Albertus Magnus Coll., 1971; MEd, Worcester State Coll., 1981; PhD, U. Mass., 1990. Elem. sch. tchr. Tegucigalpa, Honduras, 1971-72; instr. English Centro Internat. de Idiomas, Cuernavaca, Mexico, instr. ESL, 1973; tchr. Spanish-English bilingual program Worcester (Mass.) Elem. Sch., 1974-82; tchg. asst. U. Mass., Amherst, 1984-88; instr. Spanish lang. and lit. Bates Coll., Lewiston, Mass., 1989-91; asst. prof. Spanish La. State U., Baton Rouge, 1991-95, U. N.H., Durham, 1995—. Author: Clementina Suarez: Her Life and Poetry, 1995; contbr. books Reinterpreting the Spanish American Essay: Studies in Nineteenth and Twentieth Century Women's Essays, 1994, A Dream of Light and Shadow: Portraits of Latin American Women Writers, 1995; contbr. articles and revs. to Hispanic studies jours. Fulbright grantee, Honduras, 1988-89. Mem. MLA, Am. Assn. Tchrs. Spanish and Portuguese,Latin Am. Studies Assn., Millay Soc., Asociacion de Literatura Femenina Hispanica, Maine Writers and Publ. Alliance. Home: PO Box 959 Camden ME 04843 Office: U NH Dept Spanish Murkland 209 Durham NH 03824*

GOLD, LISA DAWN, artist; b. Phila., June 26, 1959; d. David Irwin and Rosalie (Steelman) G. BFA, Pratt Inst., 1980, MFA, 1987; postgrad., Byram Shaw Sch. Art, London, 1980. Various editl. positions Conde Nast Publs., N.Y.C., 1980-84; prin. Born of Brush Studios, N.Y.C., 1981—, color cons., 1987—. One-woman shows include Stux Gallery, N.Y.C., 1993, Mangel Gallery, Phila., 1995; groups shows include Katona (N.Y.) Mus. Art, 1992, Renee Fotouhi Fine Arts, East Hampton, N.Y., 1995, Kagon Martos Gallery, N.Y.C., 1996; represented in permanent collections Ara Art Coll., Phila., pvt. collectors. Grantee Ford Found., Pratt Inst., 1980, Nat. Endowment for Arts, Drawing Ctr., 1988. Office: BOBSI 195 Chrystie St New York NY 10002 also: PO Box 1956 Telluride CO 81435

GOLD, LOIS MEYER, artist; b. N.Y.C., June 2, 1945; d. Seymour Roy and Carol (Rubin) Meyer; m. Leonard Marshall Gold, Oct. 14, 1971; 1 child, Eric Marshall. BA, Boston U., 1967; MA, Columbia U., 1970. Tchr. Lenox Sch., N.Y.C., 1972-84, Columbia Grammar Sch., N.Y.C., 1975-76; artist, free-lance N.Y.C., 1976—; represented by Lizan-Tops Gallery, N.Y.C., Summa Gallery, N.Y.C. Prin. works appear in permanent mus. collections including Herbert F. Johnson Mus. Art, Ithaca, N.Y., corp. collections, including Bklyn. Union Gas Co., Bristol Myers Squibb, Imperial Oil, others; featured artist The Artists Mag., 1993 (Landscape award 1993); pub. in: Pastel School, Reader's Digest, The Pastel Painter's Solution Book, Painting Shapes & Edges, Fresh Flower Painting, North Light Books. Recipient Artists Mag. Landscape award, 1991, 93, Pastel Soc. Am. Juried Scholarship award, 1994-95. Mem. Pastel Soc. Am., Nat. Assn. of Women Artists (Pauline Law award 1988, Works on Paper award 1988), Cassatt Pastel Soc., Studio Ctr. Artist's Assn. Home: 45 E End Ave New York NY 10028-7953

GOLD, MARLYN H., art educator; b. N.Y.C., Mar. 10, 1952; d. John Joseph and Irene (Turney) Hommel; m. Daniel Wayne Gold, Mar. 6, 1976; children: Jacob, Olivia. BA in Teaching Art., Sam Houston State U., 1976. Art tchr. Conroe (Tex.) Ind. Sch. Dist., 1977-85, Kerrville (Tex.) Ind. Sch. Dist., 1988—; ednl. adv. bd. Cowboy Artist of Am., Kerrville, 1992-94; presenter in field. Mem. Nat. Art Educators Assn., Tex. Art Educators Assn. (presenter convs. 1994). Roman Catholic. Office: Peterson Mid Sch K ISD 605 Tivy St Kerrville TX 78028-4600

GOLD, PHRADIE KLING See KLING, PHRADIE

GOLD, RUTH FORMAN, education educator; b. Bklyn., Oct. 10, 1932; d. Louis and Bertha (Wolkowitz) Forman; m. Bernard Gold, Nov. 23, 1952 (dec. May 1994); children: Alan Mark, Anyta Joan Costales. BA, Bklyn. coll., 1953, MA, 1955; EdD, Columbia U., 1973. Tchr. N.Y.C. Pub. Schs., Bklyn., 1953-58, East Meadow (N.Y.) Schs., 1958-60; lectr. Hofstra U., Hempstead, N.Y., 1961-72; from asst. prof. to prof. Adelphi U., Garden City, N.Y., 1972-86; prof. spl. edn. Hofstra U., 1986—, chair dept. counseling, rsch., spl. edn. and rehab., 1993-96, coord. gerontology, 1996—; mem. adv. bd. C.W. Post Tchr. Tng. Grant, Greenvale, N.Y., 1992-95; cons. Ctr. for Devel. Disabilities, Woodbury, N.Y., 1991-94. Co-author: Education the Learning Disabled, 1982; contbr. chpts. to books. Named Person of the Yr. Long Is. Assn. Spl. Edn. Adminstrs. Mem. Assn. for Children with Learning Disabilities (mem. adv. bd. 1972-84, bd. dirs. 1984-90, bd. trustees 1990—), Coun. for Exceptional Children (v.p. N.Y. State chpt. 1987-88, pres. N.Y. state divsn. for early childhood 1984-85). Office: Hofstra U Hempstead Tpke Hempstead NY 11553-1200

GOLD, RUTH HELEN BABS, retired elementary education educator, volunteer; b. Bklyn., Feb. 2, 1928; d. Meyer and Augusta (Yachelson) Bernstein; m. Isadore Roy Gold, Dec. 28, 1949 (dec.); children: Matthew David, Jennifer Ellen Gold Levy, Daniel Marshall. BA, Smith Coll., 1949; MA, Columbia U., 1950. Cert. brailist Libr. of Congress; cert. elem. tchr., N.Y. Tchr. early childhood N.Y.C. Pub. Schs., 1950's-70's, ret., 1970's; office mgr. Physicians Office, N.Y.C., 1980's, caregiver, 1990's. Literary braillist Helen Keller Inst., Libr. of Congress, 1970—. Mem. Nat. Coun. Jewish Women (Bklyn. sect. bd. dirs., 1950's—, past Bklyn. sect. v.p., nat. standimg com. bylaws, 1982-90, nat. spl. com. quota 1985-86, northeast dist. chair by laws 1984-86, action line vol. 1993—, Outstanding Dedication and Commitment award 1991), Nat. Braille Assn., Alumnae Assn. Smith Coll.

GOLDBERG, ANNE CAROL, physician, educator; b. Balt., June 12, 1951; d. Stanley Barry and Selma Ray (Freiman) G.; m. Ronald M. Levin, July 29, 1989. AB, Harvard U., 1973; MD, U. Md., 1977. Diplomate Am. Bd. Internal Medicine, Am. Bd. Endocrinlolgy and Metabolism. Intern in medicine Michael Reese Hosp., Chgo., 1977-78; resident in medicine Michael Reese Hosp., 1978-80; fellow in endocrinology Washington U., St. Louis, 1980-83, instr. medicine, 1983-85, asst. prof. medicine, 1985-94, assoc. prof. medicine, 1994—, clin. dir. lipid reseach clinic, 1987—. Mem. steering com. Cholesterol Coalition, St. Louis, 1988-93. Fellow ACP; mem. AMA, Am. Diabetes Assn., Am. Heart Assn., Am. Fedn. Clin. Rsch., Am. Med. Women's Assn., Alpha Omega Alpha. Democrat. Jewish. Office: Washington U Med Sch PO Box 8046 660 S Euclid Saint Louis MO 63110

GOLDBERG, BARBARA M., consultant; b. Providence, Apr. 16, 1950; d. Bernard and Bertha Goldberg. BEd, Ithaca Coll., 1972; M Adult Edn., U. R.I., 1976, MBA, 1996. Cert. tchr., N.Y., R.I. Instr. Adult Correctional Instns., Cranston, R.I., 1972-73; dir. Providence Adult Edn., 1973-75; pres. Edn. Resource Assocs., Pawtucket, R.I., 1975-85; cons., mng. ptnr. Equine Resource Assocs., Cranston, 1981-90, Entelechy Resource Assocs., Cranston, 1990—; bd. dirs. N.E. Ctr. for Orgnl. Efficiency, Boston, 1992-96. Named Adult Educator of Yr., Nat. Assn. Adult Educators, 1981, R.I. Adult Edn. Assn., 1981. Mem. Cranston C. of C. (v.p. 1995-96), Exec. Round Table, Am. Horse Shows Assn., Cranston-Warwick Hadassah, Little Rhody Model A Ford Club. Jewish. Office: Entelechy Resource Assocs 6 Buttercup Rd Cranston RI 02920

GOLDBERG, BETH SHEBA, artist, educator, art therapist; b. N.Y.C.; d. Max and Hannah Segal; m. Benjamin Goldberg; children: Murray, Ilene, Gerald, Jeffrey. BA cum laude, Bklyn. Coll., 1955, MS in Guidance Sch. Counseling with honors, 1957; MA with distinction, Hofstra U., 1995. Tchr. Ohel Moshe Day Sch., Bklyn., 1954-55, N.Y. Bd. Edn., Bklyn., 1955-57, Amherst Sch. System, Snyder, N.Y., 1957-58, Farmingdale (N.Y.) Sch., 1959-60, Hebrew Acad. of Nassau Bd. Edn., 1977-92; art therapy intern South Oaks, Amityville, 1994, South Nassau Hosp., Oceanside, 1995. Exhibed in various one-woman shows and group exhibits including Salmaguni, Firehouse Gallery, Island Artists Gallery, Chelsea; represented in pvt. collections including Dupont Corp. Hon. trustee Farmingdale Jewish Ctr., 1992—; v.p. Ea. L.I. Women's League, 1982-86; pres. Lionesses, Farmingdale, 1973-74; pres. Sisterhood Farmingdale Jewish Ctr., 1969-70. Mem. Art Circle 2100, Contemporary Art Soc., Pequa Art Assn. (pres.), Nat. League Am. Pen Women (v.p.), Am. Art Therapy Assn., Clin. Art Therapy, Creative Art Therapist, Huntington Twp. Art League, Visual Art Alliance League, Psi Chi (v.p.), Kappa Delta Pi (v.p.), Chi Sigma Iowa. Home: 23 Tanwood Dr Massapequa NY 11758-8548

GOLDBERG, BETTY (WEINGARTEN), accountant; b. Oakland, Calif., June 8, 1961; d. Leo and Sarah Weingarten; m. Ephraim Z. Goldberg, Dec. 26, 1983; children: Talia, Yoel, Moriel, Penina. Tchg. cert., New Sch. for Women, 1981; BS in Math. and Computer Sci., Touro Coll. for Women, 1983; cert. for tax preparation, Yeshiva U., 1986. Cert. client rep. IRS. Judaic studies tchr. Valley Torah Ctr. H.S., North Hollywood, Calif., 1981-82; sys. analyst Bell Comms. Rsch., Livingston, N.J., 1983-86; tax preparer Better Tax Svc., N.Y.C., 1988; tax acct. McCurry & Co., CPAs, Boca Raton, Fla., 1989—; tax svc. cons., Boca Raton, 1993—. Sunday sch. tchr., tutor, Boca Raton, 1989—. Mem. Nat. Soc. Tax Profls., Fla. Soc. Enrolled Agents.

GOLDBERG, BONITA WILLIAMS, artist, consultant; b. Cin., June 30, 1947; d. Clifford James and Mary Margaret (Rolfsen) Williams; m. Michael Frederick, Nov. 16, 1968; children: Tracey, Scott, Jason. AA, Thomas More Coll., Crestview Hills, Ky., 1987, BES, 1988. Sr. sales rep. Cin. Bell, 1967-69; decorator sales Designs & Blinds, Fairfield, Ohio, 1980-84; art cons. Works of Art, West Chester, Ohio, 1987-90, Village Frame Schop, Cin., 1990-92; sales McAlpin, Cin., 1992-94; art cons. AB Closson Art Gallery, Cin., 1994—; gallery docent Contemporary Art Ctr., Cin., 1988-90; sec.-treas. Base Art Gallery, Cin., 1990—. Exhbns. include Middletown Fine Arts Ctr., 1988, 90, 91, 92 (1st place drawing award), Works of Art Gallery, 1989, Art Acad. of Cin., 1992, Mason Art Show, 1992 (hon. mention), Pendelton Art Ctr., 1993, Base Gallery, 1993-95, Women's Art Club, 1994, 95, others. Art instr. YMCA, Florence, Ky., 1986. Mem. Fitton Art Ctr., Contemporary Art Ctr., Base Art (treas.-sec. 1993-95). Roman Catholic. Home: 5458 Yosemite Dr Fairfield OH 45014

GOLDBERG, JANE G., psychoanalyst; b. New Orleans, May 31, 1946; d. Meyer and Madeleine Malvina (Levy) Goldberg; children: Molly Malvina. BA, Washington U., 1968; postgrad., Pratt Inst., 1969-72; MA, New Sch. for Social Rsch., 1971; PhD, CUNY, 1978. Lic. psychologist, N.Y.; cert. psychoanalyst N.Y., psychoanalytic psychotherapist, N.Y. Pvt. practice psychotherapy and psychoanalysis N.Y., N.J., 1973—, pvt. practice supervision psychotherapy and psychoanalysis, 1980—; staff psychotherapist art therapy program Hillside Hosp., Queens, N.Y., 1970-72, Advanced Ctr. for Psychotherapy, Jamaica, N.Y., 1974-81; rsch. assoc. dept. psychology New Sch. for Social Rsch. Grad. Faculty, N.Y.C., 1971-72, dept. med. oncology Kingsbrook Jewish Med. Ctr., Bklyn., 1979-80; faculty psychology dept. CUNY, N.Y.C., 1972-76; faculty Fifth Ave. Ctr. for Counseling and Psychotherapy, N.Y.C., 1982-84, Ctr. for Modern Psychoanalytic Studies, N.Y.C., 1984—; mem. faculty Treatment and Referral Svc. N.Y.C., 1984—, Psychoanalytic ctr. N.J., Morristown, 1986—, Boston Ctr. Modern Psychoanalytic Studies, 1986—; lectr. in field. Author: Psychotherapeutic Treatment of Cancer Patients, 1982, Deceits of the Mind (and their effects on the body), 1991, The Dark Side of Love: the positive role of our negative emotions, 1993; mng. editor: Modern Psychoanalysis; column writer: "News and Notes" in Modern Psychoanalysis; TV talk show co-host: "Schmoozing, " N.Y.C.; numerous mag. and newspapers interviews; numerous TV and radio appearances; contbr. articles to profl. jours. Asst. to exec. dir. Found. for the Advancement of Cancer Therapies; dir. La Casa de Vida Natural, Rio Grande, P.R., 1987—, La Casa Day Spa, N.Y.C., 1993—. Home: 41 E 20th St New York NY 10003-1324

GOLDBERG, LEE WINICKI, furniture company executive; b. Laredo, Tex., Nov. 20, 1932; d. Frank and Goldie (Ostrowiak) Winicki; student San Diego State U., 1951-52; m. Frank M. Goldberg, Aug. 17, 1952; children: Susan Arlene, Edward Lewis, Anne Carri. With United Furniture Co., Inc., San Diego, 1953-83, corp. sec., dir., 1963-83, dir. environ. interiors, 1970-83; founder Drexel-Heritage store Edwards Interiors, subs. United Furniture, 1975; founding ptnr., v.p. FLJB Corp., 1976-86, founding ptnr., sec. treas., Sea Fin., Inc., 1980, founding ptnr., First Nat. Bank San Diego, 1982. Den mother Boy Scouts Am., San Diego, 1965; vol. Am. Cancer Soc., San Diego, 1964-69; chmn. jr. matrons United Jewish Fedn., San Diego, 1958; del. So. Pacific Coast region Hadassah Conv., 1960, pres. Galilee group San Diego chpt., 1960-61; supporter Marc Chagall Nat. Mus., Nice, France, U. Calif. at San Diego Cancer Ctr. Found., Smithsonian Instn., L.A. County Mus., San Diego Mus. Contemporary Art, San Diego Mus. Art; pres. San Diego Opera, 1992-94. Recipient Hadassah Service award San Diego chpt., 1958-59; named Woman of Dedication by Salvation Army Women's Aux., 1992, Patron of Arts by Rancho Sante Fe Country Friends, 1993. Democrat. Jewish.

GOLDBERG, LESLIE ROBERTA, management development, employee relations and training executive; b. N.Y.C.; d. William and Margaret (Waterman) G. BA, Hunter Coll., 1969; MS, Lehman Coll., 1974. Cert. in human rels., human resources, tng. Instructional design specialist Yonkers (N.Y.) Bd. Edn., 1969-87; sales and tng. specialist Commerce Clearing House Inc., N.Y.C., 1987-89; human resources devel. cons. Sussman-Automatic Corp., N.Y.C., 1987—; tng. and devel. mgr. Kirk Paper Co., L.A., 1989-91; mgmt. edn. program mgr. Employers Group (formerly Mchts. & Mfrs. Assn.), L.A., 1992-95; human resources mgr. AIDS Project, L.A., 1995—; cons. job search skills for profls. Employment and Devel. Dept., State of

Calif., 1992; counselor, cons. Worknet, L.A., 1992—; featured in Fortune Mag., TV-KHSC. Mem. ASTD, Profls. in Human Resources Assn. (program chairperson 1994).

GOLDBERG, LUELLA GROSS, diversified financial services company executive; b. Mpls., Feb. 26, 1937; d. Louis and Beatrice (Rosenthal) Gross; m. Stanley M. Goldberg, June 23, 1958; children: Ellen Goldberg Luger, Fredric, Martha Goldberg Aronson. BA, Wellesley Coll., 1958; postgrad. in philosophy, U. Minn., 1958-59. Dir. Reliastar Fin. Corp., 1995—; bd. dirs. Northwestern Nat. Life Ins. Co., Mpls., 1976-95, TCF Bank, Mpls., TCF Fin. Corp., Mpls., Piper Funds, Mpls., Hormel Foods Corp., Austin, Minn. Pres. Minn. Orch. Women's Assn., Mpls., 1972-74; bd. dirs. Minn. Orch. Assn., 1972—, chmn., 1980-83, Mpls. chpt. United Way, 1978-88, Ind. Sector, Washington, 1984-90; regent St. John's U., Collegeville, Minn., 1974-83; trustee U. Minn. Found., Mpls., 1978—; mem. bd. overseers Sch. Mgmt., U. Minn., Mpls., 1980—; chmn. bd. trustees Wellesley (Mass.) Coll., 1985-93, acting pres., 1993; trustee Northwest Area Found., 1994—. Recipient Disting. Svc. award Minn. Orch. Assn., 1983, Community Svc. Leadership award Mpls. YWCA, 1986, Disting. Svc. to Higher Edn. award Minn. Pvt. Coll. Coun., 1992, Humanitarian award NCCJ, 1992. Mem. Nat. Women's Econ. Alliance, Minn. Women's Econ. Round Table, Phi Beta Kappa. Club: Cosmopolitan (N.Y.C.). Home: 7019 Tupa Dr Minneapolis MN 55439-1643

GOLDBERG, NORMA LORRAINE, retired public welfare administrator; b. South Bend, Ind., May 6, 1929; d. James Albert and Minnie Sylvia (Kaplan) Seamon; m. Albert Goldberg, Apr. 19, 1959 (dec. Dec. 1976); children: Lisa Ann, Paul Ephraim. B.S., Ind. U.-Bloomington, 1950; postgrad. Sch. Social Work, Ind. U.-Indpls., 1950-52. Sch. social worker Indpls. Pub. Schs., 1951-53; with Marion County Dept. Pub. Welfare, Indpls., 1953-66, 71-73, asst. dir., 1961-64, dir., 1964-66, intake supr., 1971-73; asst. dir. Ind. Dept. Pub. Welfare, Indpls., 1973-79, dir., 1979-87, regional adminstr., rep. Family Support Adminstrn., Dallas, 1987-91; spl. project officer Adminstrn. Children and Families, 1991-94, asst. regional administr., 1994-95; mem. steering com. Whitehouse Conf. on Children and Youth, Indpls., 1982-83; mem. program com. Gov.'s Conf. on Children and Youth, Indpls., 1982-83. Founder Welfare Service League, Indpls., 1968, pres., 1968-71, mem., 1968—. Mem. steering com. Indpls. sect. Nat. Council Jewish Women, 1982-87; mem. steering com. Guardian ad Litem Project; mem. Republican Round Table, Indpls., 1983-87 ; city chmn. adult bd. B'nai B'rith Youth Orgn., 1985-86. Recipient Gov.'s Voluntary Action Program Community Service award Gov. of Ind., 1980. Mem. Assn. Women Execs., Dallas Council World Affairs, Dallas Women's Found., Ind. Conf. on Social Concerns (state coordinator 1963-64), Network of Women in Bus., Indpls. Council of Women (program chmn. 1968-71). Club: The 500, Inc. Lodge: Order Eastern Star.

GOLDBERG, PAMELA WINER, strategic consultant; b. Boston, Oct. 14, 1955; d. Arthur Leonard and Marilyn (Miller) Winer; m. Marc Evan Goldberg, June 11, 1983; children: Frederick Warren, Alyssa Rachel, Meredith Hayley. BA, Tufts U., 1977; MBA, Stanford U., 1981. Day care dir. Community Action Inc., Haverhill, Mass., 1977-79; lending assoc. Bankers Trust Co., N.Y.C., 1980-81; mgr., bank officer, corp. fin. dept. Citicorp, N.Y.C., 1981-82; assoc. dir., mergers and acquisitions group State Street Bank, Boston, 1983-85; ind. strategic cons. Wellesley, Mass., 1986—. Mem. exec. bd. Friends Beth Israel Hosp., Boston, 1987—; mem. exec. bd. trustees Temple Beth Elohim, Wellesley, 1992—; trustee Recuperative Ctr., Boston, 1988-95; bd. dirs. Wellesley League Women Voters, 1995—; mem. Hunnewell Sch. PTO Bd., 1991—. Home and Office: 31 Lathrop Rd Wellesley MA 02181-7011

GOLDBERG, RITA MARIA, foreign language educator; b. N.Y.C., Oct. 1, 1933; d. Abraham Morris and Hilda (Weinman) G. B.A. (N.Y. State Regents scholar), Queens Coll., 1954; M.A., Middlebury Coll., 1955; Ph.D., Brown U., 1968. Mem. faculty Queens Coll., N.Y.C., 1956, Oberlin (Ohio) Coll., 1957; mem. faculty St. Lawrence U., Canton, N.Y., 1957—; Dana prof. modern langs. St. Lawrence U., 1975—, chmn. dept., 1972-75, 83-91; chmn. Regional Conf. Am. Programs in Spain, 1979-81; mem. Nat. Fulbright Selection Com., 1990-92; mem. advanced placement test devel. com. for Spanish, Ednl. Testing Svc., 1993—, chair, 1996—. chmn. Regional Conf. Am. Programs in Spain, 1979-81; mem. Nat. Fulbright Selection Com., 1990-92; mem. advanced placement test devel. com. for Spanish, Ednl. Testing Svc., 1993—, chair, 1996—. Spanish Ministry of Fgn. Affairs scholar, 1954-56; Danforth grantee, 1960-62, 63-64; Brown U. scholar, 1960-62. Mem. Am. Assn. Tchrs. Spanish and Portuguese, AAUP, MLA, Am. Council Teaching of Fgn. Langs., N.E. Modern Lang. Assn., N.Y. State Assn. Fgn. Lang. Tchrs., Phi Beta Kappa, Sigma Delta Pi. Roman Catholic. Home: 45 Judson St Canton NY 13617-1146 Office: St Lawrence U Dept Modern Langs Lits Canton NY 13617

GOLDBERG, WHOOPI (CARYN JOHNSON), actress; b. N.Y.C., Nov. 13, 1955; d. Robert and Emma (Harris) Johnson; m. David Claessen (div.); m. Lyle Trachtenberg, Oct. 1, 1994 (div. Oct. 1995); 1 child, Alexandrea Martin. Mem. San Diego Repertory Theatre, 1975-80, Blake St. Hawkeyes, Berkeley, Calif., 1980-84. Author: Alice; appeared in one-person show Whoopi Goldberg on Broadway, 1984-85, Living on the Edge of Chaos, 1988 (Calif. theatre award outstanding achievement); films include The Color Purple, 1985, Jumpin' Jack Flash, 1986, Burglar, 1986, Telephone, 1987, Fatal Beauty, 1987, Clara's Heart, 1988, Beverly Hills Brats, 1989 (cameo), Homer and Eddie, 1989, The Long Walk Home, 1990, Ghost, 1990 (Acad. award best supporting actress, 1991), Soapdish, 1991, House Party 2 (cameo), The Player, 1992, Sister Act, 1992, Wisecracks, 1992, Sarafina!, 1992, Made in America, 1993, National Lampoon's Loaded Weapon 1, 1993, Sister Act 2: Back in the Habit, 1993, The Lion King, 1994 (voice), The Little Rascals, 1994, Naked in New York (cameo), 1994, Corrina, Corrina, 1994, Star Trek: Generations, 1994, The Pagemaster, 1994 (voice), Boys on the Side, 1995, Bogus, 1996, The Ghost of Mississippi, 1996, Eddie, 1996, Tales from the Crypt Presents: Bordello of Blood, 1996, The Associate, 1996; TV film: Kiss Shot, 1989, My Past Is My Own; TV series: Star Trek: The Next Generation, 1988-94, Bagdad Cafe, CBS, 1990; TV specials include: Tales from the Whoop: Hot Rod Brown, Class Clown, 1990; host TV talk show The Whoopi Goldberg Show, 1992-93. Named NAACP Entertainer of the Yr., 1990, Humanitarian of Yr. Starlight Found., 1989; recipient, Hans Christian Andersen Award for outstanding achievement by a dyslexic, 1987, grammy award for album of Broadway show, 1985; nominated for Emmy, 1996. *

GOLDBERGER, BLANCHE RUBIN, sculptor, jeweler; b. N.Y.C., Feb. 2, 1914; d. David and Sarah (Israel) Rubin; m. Emanuel Goldberger, June 28, 1942 (dec. 1994); children—Richard N., Ary Louis. B.A., Hunter Coll., N.Y.C., 1934; M.A., Columbia U., 1936; Certificat d'Etudes, Sorbonne, Paris, 1936; postgrad. Westchester Arts Workshop Sculpture and Jewelry, White Plains, 1961-70, Silvermine Coll. Arts, 1962, Nat. Acad. Arts, N.Y.C., 1968. Tchr. French and Hebrew, N.Y.C. High Sch. System, Scarsdale Jr. and Sr. High Schs. One-woman shows include: Bloomingdale's, Eastchester, N.Y., 1975, Scarsdale Pub. Library, N.Y., 1976, Temple Israel, White Plains, N.Y., 1975, Greenwich Art Barn, Conn., 1972 Westlake Gallery, White Plains, N.Y., 1981; exhibited in group shows at Hudson River Mus., Yonkers, N.Y., 1978, Silvermine-New Eng. Ann., Silvermine, Conn., 1979; represented in permanent collection at Scarsdale High Sch. Library, N.Y.; sculpture commn. Jewish Community Ctr. White Plains, N.Y., 1988; commn. Manchester, Vt.; also pvt. collections. Recipient award Beaux Arts of Westchester, White Plains, N.Y., 1967, First Prize, White Plains Art Show, Holocaust Meml. Bronze Plaque for Synagogue Congregation Israel; various commns. for calli collis calligraphic collages. Mem. Nat. Assn. Women Artists, Nat. Assn. Tchrs. French, Scarsdale Art Assn. (bd. dirs.; first prizes for sculpture). Jewish. Avocations: lecturing on sculpture, reading contemporary lit. in Hebrew, the violin, classical music concerts, callicollies.

GOLDBLATT, EILEEN WITZMAN, arts administrator, executive director; b. N.Y.C.; d. Ben and Sylvia Witzman; m. Myron Everett Goldblatt Jr.; children: Tracy Ellen, David Laurence. BS, Russell Sage Coll., 1967; MS, Bank Street Coll, 1980. Tchr., tchr. trainer N.Y.C. Bd. Edn., 1967-73, dir. mus. and cultural programs, 1984-89; ednl. cons. Cooper-Hewitt Mus., N.Y.C., 1979-80; dir. mus., collaborative sch./cultural voucher programs Mus. Collaborative, Inc., N.Y.C., 1981-84; exec. dir. Young Audiences/N.Y., 1990—; creator N.Y.C. Arts and Cultural Edn. Network and Arts and Cultural Edn. Network Menu, 1986-90, Cultural Instn. Network Menu, 1984-85; creator N.Y.C. Cultural Instn. Network. Author: (workbook) Electroworks, 1980), (exhbn. guide) Smithsonian: A Treasure Hunt, 1979, (curriculum) The Ancient Egyptians, 1980. Trustee N.Y.C. Sch. Art League; mem. cultural del. People to People Internat., People's Republic China, 1988, 96; mem. Class of 1990 Leadership Am. Mem. Am. Assn. Mus., Internat. Coun. Mus. (com.), Am. Women in Enterprise, Women's City Club N.Y., City Club N.Y. Home: 500 E 83rd St New York NY 10028-7201 Office: Young Audiences NY 1 E 53rd St New York NY 10022-4201

GOLDEN, ELLEN FRANCES, economic development practitioner; b. Washington, Oct. 8, 1946; d. Gerald and Rose (Cohen) G.; m. Duane Alan Paluska, June 18, 1983. BA in Art History, Barnard Coll., 1968; MA in Pub. Policy and Mgmt., U. So. Maine, 1994. With Coastal Enterprises, Inc., Wiscasset, Maine, 1978—, comm. coord., ops. mgr., project developer, sr. program officer. Bd. dirs., co-founder Women's Devel. Inst., Augusta, Maine, 1991-93, Women's Bus. Devel. Corp., Bangor, Maine, 1986-88; commr. Maine Commn. for Women, Augusta, 1988-92; bd. dirs. Maine Women's Lobby, Augusta, 1987-93; mem. Commn. on Women's Voices in the Economy Ctr. for Policy Alternatives, Washington, 1995—; bd. trustees Maine Initiatives, Augusta, 1994—, pres.; bd. dirs. Assn. for Enterprise Opportunity, Chgo., 1992-96. Named Women Bus. Advocate of Maine U.S. SBA, 1987, Minority Bus. Advocate for Maine, 1994. Mem. Phi Kappa Phi. Office: Coastal Enterprises Inc PO Box 268 Water St Wiscasset ME 04578

GOLDEN, ELOISE ELIZABETH, community health nurse; b. Hope, Ind., Nov. 20, 1938; d. John M. and Hazel E. (Gosch) Holder; m. Don Golden, Aug. 2, 1959; children: David, Susanne. Diploma, Ball State U., 1959. RN. Office nurse Columbus, Ind.; staff nurse Pub. Health Dept. Bartholomew County, Columbus; parish nurse, clinicare staff nurse, housecall coord. Bartholomew County Hosp., Columbus, intake coord. Hospice, 1991—. Lutheran. Home: 11635 E 600 N Hope IN 47246

GOLDEN, JENNIE DILLY, secondary education educator; b. Parsons, W.Va., July 17, 1940; d. Frank A. and Virginia C. (Schumaker) Dilly; m. Robert W. Golden, July 25, 1964. BS, Youngstown State U., 1972, MS, 1974. Bus. edn. tchr. Boardman (Ohio) H.S., 1972-78, Barbour Bd. Edn., Philippi, W.Va., 1980—. Mem. NEA, W.Va. Ednl. Assn., Barbour County Ednl. Assn. Office: Philip Barbour Complex Rte 2 Box 168 Philippi WV 26416

GOLDEN, KIMBERLY KAY, critical care, flight nurse; b. Munich, July 31, 1961; came to U.S., 1961; d. Henry Davis and Mary Walker G. AA, Hinds Jr. Coll., Raymond, Miss., 1980, ASN, 1984; BSN, U. Miss., Jackson, 1987, AS in EMT-Paramedic, 1990. Cert. ACLS instr., PALS provider and instr.; emergency nurse, crit. care RN; cert. paramedic, Miss., Tenn. Staff nurse neuro ICU U. Miss. Med. Ctr., 1984-85, staff nurse surg. ICU, 1985-87; staff nurse emergency rm. Rankin Gen. Hosp., Brandon, Miss., 1987-88; flight nurse Lifestar Helicopter Flight Svc., 1988-91; staff nurse emergency rm., ICU Nightingale Nursing, Jackson, 1988-91, Riveroaks Hosp., Jackson, 1990-91; staff RN emergency rm., Aerovesta flight Midland Meml. Hosp., Tex., 1991-93; flight nurse Hosp. Wing BTLS, Memphis, Tenn., 1993—; examiner Nat. Registry EMT-P; advanced trauma life support station instr.; affiliate faculty paramedic program U. Miss. Faculty scholar Hinds Jr. Coll., 1983. Mem. AACN, Nat. Flight Assn., Emergency Nurses Assn. Baptist. Office: PO Box 140466 Austin TX 78714-0466

GOLDEN, LESLIE BLACK, real estate agent; b. Dallas, Aug. 21, 1955; d. Aubrey C. Jr. and Martha (Cartwright) Black; m. G. Hawkins Golden II, Sept. 21, 1985; children: G. Hawkins III, John Houston. BBA, U. Tex., 1977. Advt. prodn. asst. Neiman Marcus, Dallas, 1977-78; group account exec. Registry Hotel, Dallas, 1978-80, sales mgr., 1982-83; sales mgr. Doubletree Inn., Dallas, 1980-82, Sheraton Park Cen., Dallas, 1983-85; real estate agt. Golden-King Properties, Dallas, 1985-94, Golden Homes, Dallas, 1994—. Mem. Jr. League Dallas, 1988—; bd. dirs. Innovators of Dallas Symphony Orch., 1986-89, chmn. arrangements 1988, chmn. coloring book fundraiser, 1989, hon. trustee Dallas Symphony Orch., 1988-89; chair phone com., auditor chmn. jr. group Dallas Garden Club, 1983—, bd. dirs. 1987-89; bd. dirs. Yellow Rose Gala com. Multiple Schlerosis, Dallas, 1985-89; chmn. Easter Egg Hunt Dallas So. Meml. 1987-96. bd. dirs. 1987-89; docent Dallas Zoo, 1989-93; vol. Freedom Ride Found., 1987; Highland Park Presbyn. Day Sch. Parents Coun., 1990-96, auction solicitations com.; Dallas Children's Theatre Guild, 1992—; vol. Equest., 1993—; co-chair Ridefest, 1994, 95, chair ann. awards banquet, 1996—, Equest. aux., 1991—, bd. dirs. 1995-96, Showcase com. 1980, 96. Mem. The Science Pl., Dallas Mus. Art, Dallas Zoo, Channel 13, Dallas Childrens Theater Guild, Dallas Country Club, Park Cities Club, Kappa Alpha Theta Alumni. Office: Golden King Properties 8533 Ferndale Rd Ste 202 Dallas TX 75238-4401

GOLDEN, SOMA, newspaper editor; b. Washington, Aug. 27, 1939; m. William Behr; 2 children. BA, Radcliffe Coll.; MA, Columbia U. Mem. econs. staff Bus. Week Mag., Washington, 1962-73; with The New York Times, 1973—, mem. editorial bd., 1977-82, editor Sunday bus. sect., 1982-87, nat. news editor, 1987-93, asst. mng. editor, 1993—; adj. prof. Columbia U., N.Y.C., 1961-76. Office: The New York Times Co 229 W 43rd St New York NY 10036-3913

GOLDENBERG, LISA ROBIN, marketing professional; b. Phila., Feb. 6, 1964; d. Jerald Jacob and Lynne (Finkelstein) Brownstein; m. Michael P. Goldenberg, May 28, 1989; children: Lauren, Jaclyn. Student, Phila. Coll. Textiles & Sci., 1987—. Sales, purchasing Delaware Steel Co., Blue Bell, Pa. Fundraiser Jewish Fedn. Greater Phila., 1985—; campaign chairwoman Young Leadership Coun., Phila., 1995—. Mem. Assn. Steel Distbrs., Am. Women in the Metals Industry. Democrat. Jewish. Home: 75 Ridings Way Ambler PA 19002

GOLDENBERG, MYRNA GALLANT, English language and literature educator; b. Bklyn., Mar. 8, 1937; d. Harry and Fay (Solomon) Gallant; m. Neal Goldenberg, Jan. 27, 1957; children: Elizabeth, David Brian, Eve Lisa. BS cum laude, CCNY, 1957; MA, U. Ark., 1961; PhD, U. Md., 1987. Faculty, dept. English Montgomery Coll., Rockville, Md., 1971—, chmn. dept., 1979-81, coord. gen. edn., 1981-90, coord. women's studies program, 1990-94; adj. faculty humanities dept. Johns Hopkins U., judaic studies, women's studies, honors coll. English U. Md.; English grad. dept. adj. faculty, U. Va.; dir. project to integrate scholarship on women and minorities into the curriculum Ford Found., 1993-94; co-dir. project integrating scholarship of women in curricula of selected Md. C.C.s, FIPSE, 1988-90; chmn. Montgomery County Commn. on Humanities, 1984-91; chmn. Title IX adv. com. Montgomery County Pub. Schs., 1985-89; lectr. in field. Contbr. author/author: Common and Uncommon Concerns: The Complex Role of Community College Department Chairpersons/Enhancing Department Leadership, 1990, Different Horrors/Sane Hell: Women Remembering the Holocaust, Thinking the Unthinkable: Human Meanings of the Holocaust, 1990, Writing Everybody In: Two-Year College English: Essays for a New Century, 1994; contbg. editor: Belles Lettres, 1989—; editor: C.C. Humanities Rev.; editor: Community College Guide to Curriculum Change, 1990; contbr. articles to profl. jours. Recipient Disting. Humanities Educator award C.C. Humanities Assn., 1989, Outstanding Faculty Mem. award Montgomery Coll., 1990, Teaching award Md. Assn. for Higher Edn., 1991; acad. adminstrn. fellow Am. Coun. on Edn., 1981-82; Lowenstein Wiener fellow U. Md., 1983. Mem. MLA (sec.), Nat. Women's Studies Assn. (sec.), Assn. Jewish Studies, Nat. Coun. Tchrs. English, Phi Kappa Phi. Home: 9328 Garden Ct Rockville MD 20854-3962

GOLDENRING, JANE, film production company executive. BA, Wesleyan U. Legis. asst. U.S. Senator Christopher Dodd, 1977-82; account rep. MNA Inc., 1983-86; chief exec., v.p., sr. v.p. Touchstone Pictures/Walt Disney Studios, Burbank, Calif., 1986-96; proes. Goldenring Prodns., Burbank. Supr. films White Fang, Cocktail, Gross Anatomy, My Father the Hero, The Ref, Jefferson in Paris, Last Dance, Phenomenon. Mem. Women in Film (bd. dirs.). Office: Walt Disney Studios 500 S Buena Vista St Burbank CA 91521*

GOLDICH, SANDRA MCGINTY, secondary school educator, consultant; b. Alexandria, La., Aug. 3, 1945; d. Herschel McGinty and Patricia (Hammonds) Corley; m. Ward Christopher Hooter II, Nov. 29, 1960 (div. Sept. 1977); children: Ward Christopher III, Patricia Lynlee Hooter Touchet; m. Mark S. Goldich, July 1, 1978. BA in Edn., La. State U., New Orleans, 1966. Cert. tchr., La. Tchr. Andrew Jackson H.S., Arabi, La., 1966-69, Alexandria (La.) Country Day Sch., 1978-84, Peabody Sixth Grade Ctr., Alexandria, 1984—; geography tchr., cons. La. Geography Edn. Alliance, Baton Rouge, 1992—, Nat. Geog. Soc. Summer Geography Inst., 1992; presenter in field; reviewer Nat. Geography Standards Goals 2000, 1992-93, Nat. Geog. Standards Workshop, 1995. Contbr. articles to profl. jours. Life mem., pres. St. Frances Cabrini Hosp. Aux., Alexandria, 1976-78; ptnr. in literacy Alexandria Daily Town Talk, 1991—. Recipient award Nat. Geog. Soc., Expect the Best award, 1989-92, Competetive Grant award La. Quality Edn. Support Fund, 1995—; grantee Jr. League of Alexandria, 1993-94, Rand McNally, 1990. Mem. AAUW (pres. 1976-78), Nat. Coun. Geog. Edn., La. Mid. Sch. Assn. (presenter 1993, 96, award of excellence 1995-96), La. Coun. for Social Studies (presenter 1993—), La. Geography Edn. Alliance (sec./treas. 1995—, Faculty Inst. award 1992—), Assn. Profl. Educators La., Rapides Assn. Educators (sec. 1992-94), Delta Kappa Gamma (pres. Beta Xi 1994—, quad. pres. Ctrl. La. 1994-95). Republican. Roman Catholic. Home: 1703 Shirley Park Pl Alexandria LA 71301-4040 Office: Peabody Sixth Grade Ctr PO Box 1747 Alexandria LA 71309-1747

GOLDIN, CHERYL BONNIE, airline official; b. Milw., Sept. 25, 1959; d. Frederick and Dione (Rakita) G. Student, Hochschule Musik-DarstellendeKunst, Vienna, Austria, 1976-79. Fares agt. TWA, N.Y.C., 1979-83; travel agt. Travel Specialists, N.Y.C., 1983-85; fares agt., instr. Brit. Airways, Jackson Heights, N.Y., 1985—, shop steward, 1986-88. Democrat. Jewish. Home: 115 Old Short Hills Rd West Orange NJ 07052

GOLDIN, CLAUDIA DALE, economics educator; b. N.Y.C., May 14, 1946; d. Leon and Lucille (Rosansky) G. BA magna cum laude with distinction, Cornell U., 1967; MA, U. Chgo., 1969, PhD, 1972; MA (hon.), U. Pa., 1985, Harvard U., 1990; DHL (hon.), U. Nebr., Lincoln, 1994. Asst. prof. econs. U. Wis., Madison, 1971-73; asst. prof. Princeton (N.J.) U., 1973-79, vis. fellow indsl. relations sec., 1987-88; vis. lectr. Harvard U., Cambridge, Mass., 1975-76, prof., 1990—; assoc. prof. U. Pa., Phila., 1979-85, prof., 1985-90; vis. fellow The Brookings Instn., 1993-94; mem. Inst. Advanced Study, Princeton, 1982-83; rsch. assoc., project dir. Nat. Bur. Econ. Rsch., Cambridge, 1979—. Author: Urban Slavery in the American South, 1976, Understanding the Gender Gap, 1990; editor: Strategic Factors in 19th Century American Economic History, 1992, The Regulated Economy, 1994, Jour. Econ. History, NBER Series on Long-Term Factors in Econ. Devel.; edtl. bd. Am. Econ. Rev., 1985-91, Quar. Jour. Econs., 1992—, Rev. Econs. & Statistics; contbr. articles to profl. publs. Recipient NSF award, 1975-77, 79-81, 81-82, 84-86, 87-89, 92-93, 96-99, Spencer Found. rsch. award, 1996-99; Guggenheim fellow, 1987-88. Fellow Econometric Soc.; mem. Am. Acad. Arts and Scis., Am. Econ. Assn. (v.p. 1990-91), Econ. History Assn. (trustee 1984—, v.p. 1988-89). Office: Harvard U Dept Econs Cambridge MA 02138

GOLDIN, MARION FREEDMAN, television news producer, reporter; b. N.Y.C., Sept. 5, 1940; d. Milton I. and Alice S. Freedman; m. Norman W. Goldin, Mar. 19, 1967 (dec. Sept. 1992). BA, Barnard Coll.; MA, Harvard U. Sec./researcher Eric Sevareid, 1963-69; researcher/assoc. producer CBS Morning News, 1969-72; producer "60 Minutes" CBS News, 1972-82; sr. producer, asst. to exec. producer "20/20" ABC News, 1982-84; sr. producer "Expose" NBC News, 1990-91; pres. Marigold Unltd., 1988-90, 92—.

GOLDING, CAROLYN MAY, government administrator; b. Essex County, N.J., July 1, 1941; d. Wesley Irwin and Florence Grace (Smith) G.; m. Gary Anthony Derosa, Oct. 18, 1975 (div. Sept. 1982). B.A., Duke U., 1963, postgrad., 1965-66. Tchr. English, Parkersburg High Sch. (W.Va.), 1963; asst. to registrar Duke U., Durham, N.C., 1963-65; mgmt. intern Dept. Labor, Washington, 1966-67, in various other positions, 1967-72, dep. assoc. regional adminstr. Employment and Tng. Adminstrn., San Francisco, 1972-77, comptroller, Washington, 1977-78, regional adminstr., San Francisco, 1979-82, dir. Unemployment Ins. Svc., Dept. Labor, Washington, 1982-87, adminstr. employment security, Dept. Labor, 1987-88, dep. asst. sec. employment and tng., 1988-96. Recipient Disting. Career Service award Dept. Labor, 1979, Fed. women's Career award Sec. Labor, 1983, Presdl. Meritorious rank, 1987, 95, Philip Arnow award, U.S. Dept. Labor, 1988. Mem. Internat. Women's Forum, Women's Forum of Washington, Am. Civil Liberties Union, The Writer's Ctr., Pi Sigma Alpha. Episcopalian.

GOLDING, KAREN LESLEY, show horse manager, equestrian; b. Wolverhampton, Eng., Aug. 25, 1950; came to U.S., 1970; d. Leslie Frank and Olive (Johnstone) G. Student, Eastleigh Tech. Coll., Eastley, Eng., 1969. With Customer Svc. Office, Nat. Gas Bd., Portsmouth, Eng., 1967-70; groom Bloodstock Farm, New Hope, Pa., 1970-73, Winter Place Farm, Salisbury, Md., 1973-75; mgr. F.E. Dixon Sr., Phila., 1975-85, Vintage Farm, Collegeville, Pa., 1985—; stage mgr. World Cup, Geneva, 1996; mem. U.S. Equestrian Team, groom Montreal Olympics, 1976, team mgr. Pan Am. Games, P.R., 1979, Caracas, Venezuela, 1983, Olympic Games, Barcelona, Spain, 1993, coach for virgin lands, Barcelona, 1992. Mem. Am. Horse Show Assn. Home: 837 Bridge Rd Collegeville PA 19426 Office: Vintage Farm 426 Hildeboital Rd Collegeville PA 19426

GOLDING, SUSAN, mayor; b. Muskogee, Okla., Aug. 18, 1945; d. Brage and Hinda Fay (Wolf) G.; children: Samuel, Vanessa. Cert. Pratique de Langue Francaise, U. Paris, 1965; BA in Govt. and Internat. Rels., Carleton Coll., 1966; MA in Romance Philology, Columbia U., 1974. Asssoc. editor Columbia U. Jour. of Internat. Affairs, N.Y.C., 1968-69; teaching fellow Emory U., Atlanta, 1973-74; instr. San Diego Community Coll. Dist., 1978; assoc. pub., gen. mgr. The News Press Group, San Diego, 1978-80; city council mem. City of San Diego, 1981-83; dep. sec. bus., transp., housing State of Calif., Sacramento, 1983-84; county supr. dist. 3 County of San Diego, 1984—; mayor City of San Diego, 1992—; founder Internat. Trade Commn., San Diego, 1985; chmn. San Diego Drug Strike Force, 1987-88, Calif. Housing Fin. Agy., Calif. Coastal Commn.; mem. San Diego County Commn. on the Status of Women; bd. dirs. San Diego County Water Authority; trustee So. Calif. Water Com., Inc.; founder Mid City Comml. Revitalization Task Force, Strategic Trade Alliance, 1993, Calif. Big 10 City Mayors, 1993; chair Pub. Svcs. and Safety Com. San Diego City Coun., Select Com. on Affordable Rental Housing, Gov. Calif. Mil. Base Reuse Task Force, 1994; co-chair City County Reinvestment Task Force; vice-chair Transp. and Land Use Com. of City Coun.; edtablished San Diego World Trade Ctr., 1993, San Diego City/State/County Regional Permit Assistance Ctr., 1994; mem. adv. bd. U.S. Conf. of Mayors, 1994. Bd. dirs. Child Abuse Prevention Found., San Diego Conv. and Vis. Bur., Crime Victims Fund, United Cerebral Palsy, San Diego Air Quality Bd., San Diego March of Dimes, Rep. Assocs.; adv. bd. Girl Scouts U.S.; trustee So. Calif. Water Comm.; mem. Rep. State Cen. Com.; co-chair com. Presidency George Bush Media Fund, Calif.; chair San Diego County Regional Criminal Justice Coun., race rels. com. Citizens Adv. Com. on Racial Intergration, San Diego Unified Sch. Dist.; hon. chair Am. Cancer Soc's. Residential Crusade, 1988. Recipient Alice Paul award Nat. Women's Polit. Caucus, 1987, Calif. Women in Govt. Achievement award, 1988, Willie Velasquez Polit. award Mex. Am. Bus. and Profl. Assn., 1988, Catalyst of Chance award Greater San Diego C. of C., 1994, Woman Who Means Bus. award San Diego Bus. Jour., 1994, Internat. Citizen award World Affairs Coun., 1994; named One of San Diego's Ten Outstanding Young Citizens, 1981, One of Ten Outstanding Rep. County Ofcls. in U.S.A., Rep. Nat. Com., 1987, San Diego Woman of Achievement Soroptimists Internat., 1988. Mem. Nat. Assn. of Counties (chair Op. Fair Share, mem. taxation and fin. com.), Nat. Women's Forum. Jewish. Office: Office of the Mayor City Administration Bldg 11th Fl 202 C St San Diego CA 92101-4806*

GOLDMAN, ARLENE LESLIE, distribution company executive; b. Paterson, N.J., July 7, 1956; d. Jacob and Bertha (Deck) G.; student Am. U., 1974. Asst. store mgr., asst. buyer Latt's Country Squire, Washington, 1976-77; ops. mgr. Complement, Washington, 1977-78; with Bidermann Industries, 1978-83, prodn. mgr. Jean-Paul Germain div., N.Y.C., 1979-80, dir. ops., 1980-81, v.p., 1981-83; nat. sales mgr. Ralph Lauren div., 1984-86; ind. cons., 1986; v.p. adminstrn. N.E. region BT Office Products Internat. Inc., N.Y.C., 1986—; bd. dirs. Yeshiva U. Mem. Friend Whitney Mus., Met. Mus. Art (sustaining mem.), ORT. Home: 23 E 10th St Apt 608 New York NY

10003-6136 Office: BT Office Products Internat 303 W 10th St New York NY 10014-2521

GOLDMAN, BARBARA DEREN, film and theatrical producer; b. Bridgeport, Conn., Dec. 22, 1949; m. James Goldman, Oct. 25, 1975. Pres. Barbara Deren Assocs., N.Y.C., 1975—, Raoulfilm Inc., N.Y.C., 1979—; co-pres. Magellan Entertainment, 1994—; v.p. Trans-Internat. Revisions, 1980—. Co-author: Where to Eat in America, 1987; contbr. to book Feast of Wine and Food, 1987; producer Tolstoy, London, 1996.

GOLDMAN, ELISABETH PARIS, sole practice lawyer; b. Pittsburgh, Pa., Jan. 11, 1939; d. Harold H. and Silvia F. (Koenigsberg) Paris; m. Alvin Lee Goldman, Nov. 23, 1956; children: Polly, Douglas. BA, Queens Coll., 1964; JD, U. Ky., 1975. Bar: Ky. 1975, Calif. 1977. Chief law clk. Supreme Ct. Ky., Frankfort, 1975-76; pvt. practice Elisabeth Goldman PSC, Lexington, Ky., 1977—. Mem. ACLU Louisville, Ky., 1987-90, Hadassah, Chamber Music Soc., Fayette County Health Care Bd.; pres. Ctrl. Ky. Jewish Fedn., 1993-95, Ctrl. Ky. Civil Liberties Union, 1988-90, James Lane Allen PTA, Lexington, Ky., 1971-72. Recipient Pro-Bono Svc. award Ky. Bar Assn., Frankfort, 1994, 95. Mem. Am. Acad. Adoption Attys., Phi Beta Kappa. Democrat. Office: Elisabeth Goldman PSC 118 Lafayette Ave Lexington KY 40502-1704

GOLDMAN, JANICE GOLDIN, psychologist, educator; b. Phila., Feb. 15, 1938; d. Samuel and Dorothea (Berenson) Goldin; m. Arthur S. Goldman, Aug. 31, 1958; children: Jill Ann Goldman-Callahan, Joshua N., Jennifer S. BA, U. Pa., 1960, MA, 1962; MS, Hahnemann Med. Coll., 1972, D in Psychology, 1975. Lic. psychologist, Pa. Chief psychologist Charles Peberdy Child Psychiatry Ctr. Hahnemann U., Phila., 1975-87, from clin. asst. to assoc. prof., 1985-87; pvt. practice Jenkintown, Pa., 1977—; cons. Haverford (Pa.) State Hosp., 1982, Assn. for Mental Health Affiliates with Israel, 1984, 86; mem. profl. adv. bd. Pub. Radio Sta WHYY, Phila., 1984-86; workshop leader Women's Ctr. of Montgomery County, Jenkintown, 1982—. Contbr. articles to profl. jours. Board dirs. Assn. for Mental Health Affiliate with Israel, nationwide, 1984-88, Or Hadash Synogogue, Wyncote, Pa., 1989. Mem. APA, Am. Family Therapy Acad., Nat. Register Health Svc. Providers, Phila. Soc. Clin. Psychology (sec. 1977-79), Am. Amnesty Internat., Internat. Soc. for Study Dissociation, Greater Phila. Soc. Clin. Hypnosis, Am. Soc. Clin. Hypnosis, Phi Beta Kappa. Democrat. Office: The Plaza at Foxcroft 1250 Greenwood Ave Jenkintown PA 19046-2901

GOLDMAN, LISA EACHUS, health facility administrator; b. Waltham, Mass., June 24, 1955; d. George Bloomfield and Genivive (Foti) Gallub; m. Edward Elliot Goldman, July 1, 1984; children: Melissa Ann, Audrey Carol. BS, Barry U., 1983, MBA, MPA, 1994. Tchr. Dade County and Miami (Fla.) Tech. Inst., 1982-84; v.p. Point Adult Communities, North Miami Beach, Fla., 1984-92; CEO, owner Fla. Behavioral Network, Miami, 1993—; pres. Statewide Mgmt. & Fin. Svcs. Corp., Miami, 1993—; exec. v.p. Assocs. in Geriatric Psychology, Inc., Pembroke Pines, 1992—; ptnr. Goldsel Inc., Fort Lauderdale, Fla., 1990-92; real estate investor, Miami, 1976-88; instr. acctg. Barry U., 1993. Co-author: Bi-Lingual Resource Jour., 1990, 91. Active Miami Shores Performing Theater; mem. bd. overseers U. Miami. Mem. Alzheimer's Assn. (v.p. 1993), Fla. State Coun. on Alzheimer's Disease, Nat. Long Term Care Com. (bd. dirs. Dade County chpt. 1991), Nat. Coun. Jewish Women (v.p. 1989-91), S.O.A.R.I.N.G. (chpt. pres.), Infants in Need Inc. Home: 7120 W Cypresshead Dr Parkland FL 33067 Office: Fla Behavioral Network 1001 Ives Dairy Rd Ste 206 Miami FL 33179

GOLDMAN, PATRICIA GROLLMAN, foundation administrator; b. Easton, Pa., June 24, 1939; d. Herman and Elaine Millicent (Knobel) Grollman; m. Richard Harris Goldman, June 21, 1959; children: Elaine Merrill, Stephen Louis. BA, Wellesley Coll., 1960; MPA, Suffolk U., 1979. Contbg. editor/reporter Newton (Mass.) Times, 1972-76; editor Golden Times, Newton, 1976-80; freelance pub. rels. exec. Newton, Boston, 1976-80; rsch. assoc., editor Vasquez-Nuttall Assocs., Newton, 1981-84; exec. dir. Asthma & Allergy Found. of Am., Chestnut Hill, Mass., 1989—. Agy. rep. Combined Health Appeal, 1994-96; mem. planning com. United Against the Asthma Epidemic, Boston, 1995-96; commr. Human Rights Commn., Newton, 1981-92; pres. Friends of Beth Israel Hosp., Boston, 1986-88; v.p., chair com. LWV, Newton, 1967-71; bd. dirs. Friends of Dana-Farber Cancer Inst., Boston, 1980-82; chmn. bd. Culture sharing, Inc., Newton, 1984-86; pres. Beethoven Sch. PTA, Newton, 1970-71. Grantee Asthma Partnership for Cleaner Air, 1996, Mass. Tobacco Control Project, 1994-96. Mem. Nat. Soc. Fundraising Execs., Mass. Health Coun., Belmont Country Club. Office: Asthma & Allergy found Am New Eng Chpt 220 Boylston St Chestnut Hill MA 02167

GOLDMAN, PHYLLIS, writer, ballet educator; b. Cleve., Feb. 20, 1932; d. Henry Hoenig and Molly (Friedman) G.; m. William Lloyd Goldman, Aug. 3, 1956; children: Meredith, Suzanne, Nina. BS in Edn., Ohio State U. Dance tchr. 92nd Street YMHA, N.Y.C., 1970-75, Am. Dance Machine, N.Y.C., 1977-82; writer Back Stage BPI Comms., N.Y.C., 1986—. Contbg. articles to profl. jours.; screenwriter. Home: 1225 Park Ave New York NY 10128

GOLDMAN, SHERRY ROBIN, public relations executive; b. Queens, N.Y., Mar. 2, 1958; d. Daniel and Alice (Epstein) G. BA, Hofstra U., 1980. Assoc. editor Gralla Publs., N.Y.C., 1980-84; account supr. G.S. Schwartz & Co. Publs., N.Y.C., 1984-87; v.p. Ruder-Finn, Inc., N.Y.C., 1987-95, sr. v.p., 1992-95; cons., 1995—; sr. v.p. The Rowland Co., 1995-96; pres. Goldman Comms., 1996—. Mem. Pub. Rels. Soc. Am. (bd. dirs. N.Y. chpt. 1993—, Silver Anvil award 1991), Nat. Assn. Profl. Environ. Communicators.

GOLDMAN, SUSAN JOSEPH, public relations executive; b. Newark, N.J., Oct. 4, 1957; d. Joseph and Deborah (Shapiro) Firkser; m. Richard G. Goldman, March 22, 1992. BS in Journalism, Northwestern U., 1979. Asst. editor Chicagoland Monthly, Chgo., 1979; feature editor Chgo. Daily Law Bulletin, 1980; acct. exec. Leigh Communications, Chgo., 1981; dep. press sec. Stevenson for Gov., Chgo., 1982; acct. exec. Carl Byoir & Assocs., Chgo., 1983-85; sr. acct. exec., acct. group supr., v.p. Golin/Harris Communications, Chgo., 1985-93, sr. v.p., 1993—. Researcher (book) Women's Networks, 1979. Recipient Silver Anvil award Pub. Rels. Soc. Am., 1986, 2 awards of excellence Pub. Rels. Soc. Am., 1995, Silver Trumpet award Publicity Club of Chgo., 1986, 87, 90, 92, 95. Office: Golin Harris Comms 500 N Michigan Ave # 200 Chicago IL 60611-3704

GOLDRING, NANCY DEBORAH, artist, educator; b. Oak Ridge, Jan. 25, 1945; d. David and Evelyn (Lasky) G.; m. N. Ubaldo Arregui, May 16, 1981. BA, Smith Coll., 1967; MFA, NYU, 1969-70. Instr. English lit. U. Pisa, Italy, 1967-68; lectr. sculpture Sch. Visual Arts, N.Y.C., 1970-71; lectr. art history Fashion Inst. Tech., N.Y.C., 1971; vis. lectr./critic RISD, Providence, 1974-75; artist-in-residence Haverford Coll., Pa., 1978; prof. dept. art Montclair (N.J.) State U., 1972—; lectr., cons. in field. Solo exhbns. include Carlsson Meml. Gallery, Bridgeport, Conn., 1979, Gladstone-Villani Gallery, N.Y.C., 1979, Monique Knowlton Gallery, N.Y.C., 1979, Nassau County Mus., 1980, 81, Inst. for Architecture and Urban Studies, N.Y.C., 1980-81, Am. Cultural Ctrs. Jerusalem and Tel Aviv and Gallery of Haifa U., 1982, Miss. Mus. Art, The Open Gallery, Jackson, Miss., 1983, Herzliya Mus., Ithaca Coll., 1984, A&M Artworks, N.Y.C., 1984-85, Michael Bennett Gallery, N.Y.C., 1986, Galleria S.Fedele, Milan, Italy, 1986, Inst. d'Arte, Dossa Dossi, Ferrara, Italy, 1986, Drury Coll., Mo., 1988, Jayne H. Baum, N.Y.C., 1988, 90, 93, Meridian Gallery, San Francisco, 1991, Istituto d'Arte Dosso Dossi, Ferrara, Italy, 1991, Eliot Smith Gallery, St. Louis, 1992, Grand Cen. Sta., N.Y.C., 1992, Jayne H. Baum Gallery, N.Y.C., 1993, Hampshire Coll. Amherst Coll., 1993, Elliot Smith Gallery, St. Louis, 1994, Duane Reed Gallery, 1996, ACTA Internat., Rome, 1996; exhibited in group shows at Muse Gallery, Phila., 1980, Rabinovitch Gallery, 1981, Ohio State Galleries, Columbus, 1982, Gallery North, Setauket, N.Y., 1982, Mus. Modern Art, 1983, Galleria D'Arte E Architettura Moderna, Rome, 1983, 84, A.I.R. Gallery, N.Y.C., 1984, 86, Allen/Wincor Gallery, N.Y.C., 1985, Jayne H. Baum Gallery U. Calif., Berkeley, 1987, 88, 89, 90, SSC&B, Lintas Internat., N.Y.C., 1987, Alternative Mus. N.Y.C., 1987, 88, Copley Soc., Boston, 1987, R.H. Love Gallery, Chgo., 1988, Haggerty Mus., Milw., 1988, White Columns, 1989, Squibb Corp., Princeton, 1989, Bard Coll., 1989, Nat. Mus. Am. Art, 1989, Nat. Mus. Am. Art, Washington, 1989, Jayne H. Baum Gallery, N.Y., 1989, Burden Gallery, N.Y., 1990, Photographic Resource Ctr. with Boston Archtl. Ctr., 1990, The West Collection Traveling exhbn., 1990-91, Andrea Ruggieri Gallery, Washington, 1990, Ellis Island, N.Y., 1990-92, Polaroid at Fotokine, Cologne, Germany, 1990, Art Mus. at Fla. Internat. U., 1991, Montclair State U., 1991, Pacific Security, L.A., 1992, Campion Corp., 1992, Palazzo Cini, Ferrera, Italy, 1993, Elliot Smith Gallery, St. Louis, 1993, Caldwell Coll., N.J., 1994, Southeast Mus., Daytona, Fla., 1995, NYU, 1995, Duane Reed Gallery, St. Louis, 1995, Ctr. Photography, Tokyo, 1996, others; represented in permanent collections at Bibliotheque Nationale, Paris, Herzliya Mus., Israel, Eastman Kodak Mus., I.T.T. of N.J., Padiglione d'Arte Contemporanea, Milan, IBM, Polaroid Corp., Citybank, NYNEX Corp., others; contbr. articles to profl. jours. Grantee Montclair State U. Art Dept., 1982-87, N.Y. State Coun. Arts, 1978-79, 77-78, 86—; NDEA fellow, 1967; Fulbright fellow, 1967-68; NYU grad. teaching fellow, 1969-70, Fulbright fellow, 1995-96, others. Mem. Interarts. Address: 463 West St Apt A1112 New York NY 10014-2040 Office: Montclair State Coll Art Dept Calcia Hall Upper Montclair NJ 07043

GOLDSMITH, CAROLINE L., arts executive; b. N.Y.C., Nov. 25, 1925; d. Reuben and Gladys (Garf) Steinholz; m. Mortimer M. Lerner, Dec. 1, 1948 (div. Nov., 1968); children: Lawrence, David; m. John F. Goldsmith. BA, Cornell U., 1946. Pres. dir. Gallery Passport Ltd., N.Y.C., 1960-66; sr. v.p. Ruder Finn Arts and Comm. Counselors, N.Y.C., 1966—; exec. dir. Arttable, Inc., N.Y.C., 1980-94. Mem. Community Bd., N.Y.C., 1987-94. Mem. Am. Assn. Mus., Am. Fedn. Arts, Internat. Coun. Mus. Coll. Art Assn., Smithsonian Inst., Century Assn., Internat. Women's Forum (bd. dirs.). Democrat. Jewish. Home: 375 W End Ave New York NY 10024-6568 Office: Ruder Finn Arts & Comm Counselors 301 E 57th St New York NY 10022-2900

GOLDSMITH, CATHY ELLEN, special education educator; b. N.Y.C., Feb. 18, 1947; d. Eli D. and Gertrude A. G. BS, NYU, 1968, MA in Elem. Edn., 1971, MA in Ednl. Psychology, 1974. Cert. phys. handicapped, K-6 elem. edn. tchr., N.Y. 2d grade tchr. N.Y.C. Bd. Edn., 1968-69, tchr. learning disabled students (spl. edn.), 1969-86, tchr. emat. disturbed learning disabled students, 1986-87, tchr. learning disabled students, 1987-88, tchr. trainable retarded students, 1988—. Represented in permanent collections Bobst Libr. NYU. Recipient Charles Oscar Maas Essay award in Am. History, 1968, Disting. Alumni Svc. award NYU, 1987. Mem. Nat. Profl. Assn. in Edn., Coun. for Exceptional Children, Coun. for Learning Disabilities, Found. for Exceptional Children, Orton Dyslexia Soc., N.Y. State-N.Y.C. Assn. Tchrs. Handicapped, NYU Alumni Leadership Coun. (rec. sec., v.p.), Pi Lambda Theta (past pres., past historian). Home: 3 Washington Sq Village New York NY 10012-1836

GOLDSMITH, DARA J., lawyer; b. L.A., Sept. 26, 1966; d. Donald Robert and Barbara Bence Gelbman; m. Michael Goldsmith. BA, Calif. State U., Northridge, 1987; JD, Pepperdine U., 1990; LLM, U. Miami, 1994. Atty. Haney & Assocs., Las Vegas, Nev., 1991-96, Goldsmith & Guymon, Las Vegas, 1996—; chairperson Trial By Peers, Las Vegas, 1994-96. Mem. Latin Am. Bar Assn. (sec. 1995-96), Clark County Bar (bd. dirs. 1991-96, Outstanding Vol. 1994). Office: Goldsmith & Guymon Ste 1404 300 S 4th St Las Vegas NV 89101

GOLDSMITH, ETHEL FRANK, medical social worker; b. Chgo., May 31, 1919; d. Theodore and Rose (Falk) Frank; m. Julian Royce Goldsmith, Sept. 4, 1940; children: Richard, Susan, John. BA, U. Chgo., 1940. Lic. social worker, Ill. Liaison worker psychiat. consultation service U. Chgo. Hosp., 1964-68; med. social worker Wyler Children's Hosp., Chgo., 1968—. Treas. U. Chgo. Service League, 1958-62, chmn. camp Brueckner Farr Aux., 1966-72; pres. Bobs Roberts Hosp. Service Commn., 1962; bd. dirs. Richardson Wildlife Sanctary, 1988—; mem. Field Mus. Women's Bd., 1966—; bd. dirs. Hyde Park Art Ctr., 1964-82, Chgo. Commons Assn., 1967-77, Alumni Assn. Sch. Social Service Adminstrn., 1976-80, Self Help Home for Aged, 1985—. Recipient Alumni Citation Pub. Service, U. Chgo., 1972. Mem. Phi Beta Kappa. Home: 5631 S Blackstone Ave Chicago IL 60637-1827 Office: Wyler Hosp Dept Social Svc 5841 S Maryland Ave Chicago IL 60637-1463

GOLDSMITH, KATHLEEN MAWHINNEY, accountant; b. Bklyn., July 16, 1957; d. James R. and Carmela (Ditria) Mawhinney; m. Marc Bruce Goldsmith, Oct. 7, 1979; children: James Ryan, Jaclyn Samantha. BS, Alfred U., 1979; MBA, U. Conn., 1986. CPA, Conn. Acct., Price Waterhouse, Stamford, Conn., 1979-83; contr. OCE Bus. Systems Inc., Stamford, 1983-89; dir. planning and control Gestetner, Greenwich, Conn., 1989-90, dir. adminstrn., 1990-91, dir. ops., 1991-92; dir. Gestetner Svcs., 1992-93, dir ops. and corp. contr., 1993-94, CFO, 1994—. Adv., Jr. Achievement, 1980-81. Named one of Outstanding Young Women of Am. Mem. Am. Inst. CPAs, Conn. Soc. CPAs, Phi Kappa Phi, Delta Mu Delta. Home: 24 Lamppost Dr West Redding CT 06896-1120 Office: Gestener Corp 599 W Putnam Ave Greenwich CT 06830-6005

GOLDSMITH, NANCY CARROL, business and health services management educator; b. Conemaugh, Pa., May 11, 1940; d. John and Mary (Appley) Stinich; m. Sidney Goldsmith, Apr. 2, 1966. RN, Temple U., 1961; Assoc. summa cum laude, C.C. Phila., 1984; BS in Health Care Mgmt. summa cum laude, Phila. Coll. Textiles and Sci., 1986; MA in Health Care Adminstrn. summa cum laude, Antioch U., Yellow Springs, Ohio, 1988; PhD in Health Svcs. and Hosp. Adminstrn. summa cum laude, Southwest U., New Orleans, 1990. Nurse, head nurse to med. surg. supr. Temple U. Hosp., Phila., 1961-67; nursing rsch. assoc. Smith Klein & French, Inc. and Ames Med. Co., Phila. and Elkhart, Ind., 1967-69; sr. nursing rsch. assoc. NIH, Washington, 1969-75; adminstrv. supr. nursing svcs. Rolling Hill Hosp. and Diagnostic Ctr., Elkins Park, Pa., 1975-87, lectr. legal aspects nursing, 1980-90, dir. cost containment strategies, 1987-89, lectr. in health svcs. mgmt., 1989—, asst. dir. nursing svcs., 1988-89, nursing svcs. dir., 1989-90; prof. health svcs. adminstrn. and svcs. Phila. Coll. Textiles and Scis., 1991—, prof. bus. mgmt., 1992—; mem. adv. bd. health and wellness programs Phila. Coll. Textiles and Sci., 1993—; prof. managed care in health svcs. adminstrn. Ea. Coll., St. Davids, Pa., 1996—; lectr. Sr. Edn. League, 1992—; lectr. healthcare fin. and health svcs. adminstrn. Pa. State U., 1994; lectr. health svcs. reform C.C. Phila., 1993—, Free Libr. Phila., 1994—; instr. med./surg. nursing Sch. Nursing, Temple U., 1964-67, chmn. ann. fundraising, 1978-86. Author 2 books. Inventor use of dextrostix in hypoglycemic range, 1972 (Rsch. award 1974); co-patentee multipurpose biopsy needle, 1972; mem. editorial bd. Coll. Textiles Newletter, 1993—. Recipient Mayor's Liberty Bell award City of Phila., 1978, Legion of Honor award Chapel of Four Chaplains, 1981, Capitol award Nat. Leadership Coun., 1991, Excellence in Teaching Highest award Pa. Coll. Textiles and Sci., 1993; named to Hall of Fame, Internat. Profl. and Bus. Women's Assn., 1994. Mem. Am. Hosp. Assn., Am. Mgmt. Assn., Temple U. Nurse's Alumni Assn. (bd. dirs., v.p. 1991-92, pres. 1993-94, dir. continuing edn. com. 1986—), Temple U. Gen. Alumni Assn. (bd. dirs. 1980-88, 93—, Disting. Svc. award 1984), Downtown Club Temple U., Phi Beta Kappa, Phi Theta Kappa (pres. Delta of Pa. chpt. 1991-94, Honors Hall of Fame 1991). Jewish. Office: Phila Coll Textiles & Sci School House Ln Henry Ave Philadelphia PA 19144

GOLDSTEIN, AMY JAEL, editor; b. Princeton, N.J., May 24, 1961; d. Mymon Goldstein and A. Rice Lyons; m. Owen O'Donnell, July 22, 1995. AB, Vassar Coll., Poughkeepsie, N.Y., 1982. With Peterson's Guides, Princeton, N.J., 1983-91, mng. editor, 1989-91; with Games Mag., N.Y.C., 1992-96, mng. editor, 1995-96. Mem. Princeton Folk Dance Group (pres. 1984-92), Phi Beta Kappa.

GOLDSTEIN, CONSTANCE SUE, magazine editor; b. Pitts., Jan. 18, 1931; d. Sol and Lena (Levenson) Bornstein; m. Richard N. Goldstein, Aug. 5, 1952 (div. 1973); children: Judy Goldstein Richardson, Glen, Nancy. BA with honors in Journalism, U. Pa., 1951. Editor The Counselor mag., Langhorne, Pa., 1972-74; exec. editor Successful Meetings mag., Phila., 1974-81; v.p., account exec. United Travel, Jenkintown, Pa., 1981-82; editor Corp. Meetings and Incentives mag. Adams/Laux Pub., N.Y.C., 1982—; discussion leader Gt. Books Found., Phila., 1970—. Contbr. articles to mags. Pres. PTA, Willow Grove, Pa., 1968; v.p. LWV, Jenkintown, 1970. Mem. Soc. Incentive Travel Execs. (program chmn. ann. meeting, 1990, bd. dirs. 1990-96), Meeting Planners Internat. (v.p. 1978-79), Soc. Am. Travel Writers, Class of 1952 (U. Pa. sec. 1993). Democrat. Jewish. Office: Corp Meetings & Incentives Mags 1180 Ave Americas 11th Fl New York NY 10036

GOLDSTEIN, CORINNE A., lawyer; b. Birmingham, Ala., Mar. 2, 1951. BA with honors, Wellesley Coll., 1973; JD magna cum laude, U. Mich., 1976. Bar: D.C. 1976. Adj. prof. George Washington U. Nat. Law Ctr., Washington, 1981-84; ptnr. Covington & Burling, Washington. Contbr. chpts. to handbooks. Mem. ABA (vice-chair water quality com.). Office: Covington & Burling PO Box 7566 1201 Pennsylvania Ave NW Washington DC 20044-7566*

GOLDSTEIN, DEBRA HOLLY, judge; b. Newark, Mar. 11, 1953; d. Aaron and Erica (Schreier) Green; m. Joel Ray Goldstein, Aug. 14, 1983; children: Stephen Michael, Jennifer Ann. BA, U. Mich., 1973; JD, Emory U., 1977. Bar: Ga. 1977, Mich. 1978, D.C. 1978, Ala. 1984. Tax analyst atty. Gen. Motors Corp., Detroit, 1977-78; trial atty. U.S. Dept. Labor, Birmingham, Ala., 1978-90; U.S. adminstrv. law judge office hearing and appeals Social Security Adminstrn., Birmingham, 1990—; new judge faculty U.S. adminstrv. law judges Social Security Adminstrn., 1991, 93—. Mem. editorial bd. The Ala. Lawyer, 1994—, The Addendum, 1995—. Chairperson Women's Coordinating Bur., Birmingham, 1983-85; active United Way, Birmingham, 1983, 87, 90, active adult edn. Temple Beth-El, bd. dirs., 1993-94, co-chair workshop initiative group, 1993-94; program chmn. Sisterhood, 1987-88, adminstrv. v.p., 1989-90, 90-92; scholarship chairperson Nat. Coun. Jewish Women, 1986; mem. steering com. Birmingham Bus. and Profl. Women Fedn., 1987-88, 95—; leader Brownie Troop, 1992—, bd. dirs. Cohaba Girl Scout Coun., 1996—; mem. enrichment com. Cherokee Bend Sch., 1992-93, 94-95, chmn. enrichment com., 1995-96; mem. edn. com. Temple Emanu-El, 1995—; active Leadership for Diversity Initiative, 1995-96. Mem. ABA, Ga. Bar Assn., D.C. Bar Assn., Mich. Bar Assn., Birmingham Bar Assn. (mem. law day com., scholarship com. 1994—), Ala. Bar Assn., Zonta (v.p. 1983-84, bd. dirs. 1988-89, 90-92, intercity chmn. 1995, co-pres. 1996—), B'nai B'rith Women (chair S.E. region 1984-86, counselor 1986-88, Women's Humanitarian award 1981), Hadassah (local bd. dirs. 1979-83, adminstrv. v.p. 1989-90, 90-92). Jewish. Office: Social Security Adminstrn Office of Hearings and Appeals 117 Gemini Cir Birmingham AL 35209-5840

GOLDSTEIN, DONNA MERYL, anthropologist educator; b. Bklyn., Sept. 3, 1960; d. Alex Sam and Reneé (Zimmerman) G. BS, Cornell U., 1982; MEd, Harvard U., 1985; PhD, U. Calif., Berkeley, 1994. Asst. prof. U. Colo., Boulder, 1994—. Recipient Fulbright scholarship, 1990. Office: U Colo Dept Anthropology CB233 Boulder CO 80309

GOLDSTEIN, JUDITH SHELLEY, reading and learning specialist; b. Bklyn., Mar. 5, 1935; d. Maurice and Mary (Goldstein) G. BA, Adelphi U., 1956; MA, Columbia U., 1957; EdD, Hofstra U., 1984. Cert. permanent tchr. in reading, spl. and elem. edn., N.Y. Early childhood tchr. N.Y.C. Sch. System, Bklyn., 1957-80; reading specialist Southampton (N.Y.) Unified Sch. Dist., 1981-87; spl. edn. tchr. Amagansett (N.Y.) Sch., 1987-88; mem. adj. faculty C.W. Post Campus, L.I. U., Brookville, N.Y., 1984-88; supr. clin. practice Southampton Campus L.I. U., 1988-95; exec. dir. nursery sch. Jewish Ctr. of Hamptons, East Hampton, N.Y., 1988-89; bd. dirs. Alternatives East End Counseling Project, Southampton, 1989—; adj. assoc. prof. Southampton Campus L.I. U., 1989-94, Dowling Coll., 1990-92; adj. asst. prof. Suffolk County C.C., 1989-95, adj. assoc. prof. 1995—. Mem. Guild Hall, East Hampton, 1980—; v.p. edn. Hadassah, East Hampton, 1989-92; chair Am. Affairs, 1993—; tchr. religious ch. Jewish Ctr. of the Hamptons, 1990—. Mem. ASCD, AAUW (v.p. programming 1987-89, sec. 1993—), Internat. Reading Assn. Democrat. Home: 138 Windward Rd East Hampton NY 11937-3189

GOLDSTEIN, MARCIA LANDWEBER, lawyer; b. Bklyn., Aug. 7, 1952; d. Jacob and Sarah Ann (Danovitz) Landweber; m. Mark Lewis Goldstein, June 3, 1973. AB, Cornell U., 1973, JD, 1975. Bar: N.Y. 1976, U.S. Dist. Ct. (so. and ea. dists.) N.Y., U.S. Ct. Appeals (2d, 7th and 9th cirs.). Assoc. Weil, Gotshal & Manges, N.Y.C., 1975-83, ptnr., 1983—; adv. bd. Colliers on Bankruptcy, 15th edit. Mem. ABA (com. on creditors' rights, corp. counse. com.), Assn. of Bar of City of N.Y. (bankruptcy and reorgn. com.), Practicing Law Inst. (ALI-ABA panels, NYU bankruptcy workshop panel), Nat. Bankruptcy Conf. Office: Weil Gotshal & Manges 767 5th Ave New York NY 10153

GOLDSTEIN, MARSHA FEDER, tour company executive; b. Chgo., July 7, 1945; d. Charles S. and Geraldine (Shulman) Feder; m. Michael Warren Goldstein, Dec. 26, 1966; 1 child, Paul Goldstein. B.A., Roosevelt U., Chgo., 1967. Tchr. art Chgo. Pub. Schs., 1967-68; free-lance artist, Chgo., 1968-71; tchr. architecture Brandeis U., Northfield, Ill., 1974-80; tour guide My Kind of Town Tours, Highland Park, Ill., 1975-79, owner, 1979—; owner, Tours at the Mart, 1992—; art cons. Randall Pub. Co., Inc., 1984—. Editor: Highland Park by Foot or Frame, 1980. Contbr. to book in field. Chmn., commr. Highland Park Hist. Preservation Commn.; bd. dirs. Roosevelt U., Chgo.; charter mem. Nat. Mus. Women in the Arts. Recipient Cert. of Completion, Chgo. Arch. Found., 1975. Mem. Nat. Assn. Women Bus. Owners (bd. dirs. Chgo. chpt., pres.), Women's Exec. Network, Chgo. Assn. Commerce & Industry, Chgo. Conv. and Tourism Bd. (mem. devel. com.), Chgo. Soc. Assn. Execs., Milw. Conv. and Tourism Bd., The Auditorium Bldg. Soc. (founder, chmn. 1994). Republican. Jewish. Club: Brandeis U. Nat. Women (bd. dirs., v.p. 1977—). Home: 1585 Tara Ln Lake Forest IL 60045-1221 Office: My Kind of Town Tours PO Box 924 Highland Park IL 60035-0924

GOLDSTEIN, MARY KANE, physician; b. N.Y.C., Oct. 24, 1950; d. Edwin Patrick and Mary Kane; m. Yonkel Noah Goldstein, June 24, 1979; children: Keira, Gavi. Philosophy degree, Columbia U., 1973, MD, 1977; MS in Health Svcs. Rsch., Stanford U., 1994. Resident Duke U. Med. Ctr., Durham, N.C., 1977-80; asst. prof. medicine U. Calif., San Francisco, 1980-84; staff physician Cowell Student Health Ctr. U. Calif., Santa Cruz, 1984-85, clin. instr. dept. family and cmty. preventive medicine, 1984-85; staff physician Mid-Peninsula Health Svc., Palo Alto, Calif., 1986-88; dir. grad. med. edn. divsn. gerontol. Stanford (Calif.) U., 1986-93, Agy. for Health Care Policy Rsch. fellow Sch. Medicine, 1991-94; sect. chief for gen. internal medicine Palo Alto (Calif) VA Med. Ctr., 1994-96; editor Computer Ctr. Pubs., N.Y.C., 1971-72; computer programmer Columbia U., N.Y.C., 1972-73; faculty assoc. Stanford Sch. Medicine, 1992; chair ethic com. U. Calif./Natividad Med. Com., San Francisco, 1984. Author chpt. to book; contbr. articles to profl. jours. Recipient Rsch. award Far West HSR & D, 1990, Expanding Rsch. award Charles H. Dana Found., 1990, Cost Implications award Hartford Found. Geriatric Ctr., 1991, Preference Assessment in Geriatrics award Palo Alto Inst. for Rsch. and Edn., 1992. Fellow Am. Geriatrics Soc. (bd. dirs. 1996—); mem. Am. Bd. Family Practice (bd. dirs. 1993—), Am. Fedn. Clin. Rsch., Geriatric Test Com. Office: Palo Alto VA Med Ctr 182B MPD 3801 Miranda Ave Palo Alto CA 94304-1207

GOLDSTEIN, PEGGY R., sculptor; b. N.Y.C., Jan. 16, 1921; d. Francis Mortimer and Ruth (Schram) Rosenfeld; m. E. Ernest Goldstein, June 22, 1941; children: Susan Lipschitz, Daniel Frank. AB, Smith Coll., 1941; student, Art Inst. Chgo., 1941-42, Corcoran Sch. Art, 1951-52, Acad. de la Grand Chaumière, Paris, 1952-53, Atelier 17, Paris, 1953, 66-67, Acad. de Peinture Orientale, Paris, 1973-75. tchr. Anacostia Neighborhood Mus., Smithsonian Instn., Washington, 1967-68, Am. Coll., Paris, 1976-77. One woman shows include Creative Gallery, N.Y.C., 1951, 53, Springfield Mus. Fine Arts, Mass., 1956, SW Tex. State Coll., San Marcos, 1960, Laguna Gloria, Austin, 1956, 61, Maison du Décor, Washington, 1968, Gottesman and Ptnrs., London, 1976, Galerie Lambert, Paris, 1970, 73, 77, 78, Galerie de la Cathédrale, Fribourg, 1981, Galerie Cimaise, Lausanne, 1983, Galerie Cardas, Lausanne, 1983, Galerie Valentine, Bex, 1984, Galerie Farel, Aigle, 1982, 85, Le Vieux Bourg, Denges, 1987, Galerie Motte, Geneva, 1989, Animalart, Austin Tex., 1995; exhibited in group shows at Salon de la Jeune Sculpture, 1961, 71-76, Salon de Mai, 1970, 72, 73, 77, Galerie Horizon, 1978—, Galerie Picpus, Montreux, 1981, Biennale of Fedn. Internat. de la Médaille, 1983, 85, 87, Création 85, Montreux, 1986, France-Chine, Marseille, 1987, Gravure, Paris, 1987, Galerie Siret, Paris, 1987—, U. Fribourg, 1988, La Fondation Taylor, Paris, 1990, Galerie Les Hirondelles, Coppet,

1990, Bibliothèque Nationale, Paris, 1992; U.S. Info. Agy. exhbns. Latin Am.; represented in permanent collections Bibliothèque Nationale, Paris, Nat. Archives, Washington, Musée Jenisch, Vevey, Bibliothèque Nationale, Berne; also pvt. collections; executed bronze outdoor sculpture, Nat. Hdqrs. Am. Camping Assn., Ind., 1987, 2 bronze mural sculptures, Austin, 1988; designer 20 medals Adminstrn. des Monnaies et Médailles, Ministère de Fin., Paris, 1973-86; illustrator: At Home After 1840, 1965; author, calligrapher: Lóng is a Dragon: Chinese Writing for Children, 1990 (Gold award Parents Choice 1991); author, calligrapher, illustrator: Ma Ma Hu Hu, An Introduction to Chinese Writing, 1995; contbr. articles to jours. Recipient Sculpture prize Soc. Washington D.C. Artists, 1954, Small Sculpture award Ball State Tchrs. Coll., 1961, Prize UPFS Concours de Masque, 1977; Prèfecture de Paris grantee, 1971; nominated Outstanding Ptnr., Ptnrs. in Edn., Austin Adopt-a-Sch., 1995-96. Fellow Creation 85, Le Bois Grave, Headliners Club (Austin, Tex.). Home: 1619 Northumberland Rd Austin TX 78703-3143

GOLDSTEIN, PHYLLIS ANN, art historian, educator; b. Chgo., Apr. 27, 1926; d. Frederick and Belle Florence (Hirsch) Jacoby; m. Seymour Goldstein, Nov. 19, 1947 (dec. 1980); children: Arthur Bruce, Kathy Susan Goldstein Maultasch. BA, Hunter Coll., 1948; MA, Hofstra U., 1985. Tchr. home econs. Cin. Pub. Schs., 1948-50; nutrition instr. Brandeis U. Nat. Women's Com., Westbury, N.Y., 1975-78, instr. art history, 1984-91; lectr. art history Brandeis U., Westbury, N.Y., 1992—; instr. art history Herricks Adult Community Edn. Program, 1990-91. Camp counselor, troop leader Girl Scouts U.S., N.Y.C., Cin., 1942-51; cub leader Boy Scouts Am., Westbury, 1963-64; active Sisterhood of Temple Beth Avodah, Westbury, 1958-70, pres. 1964-65; active Sisterhood of Temple of Beth Am., Merrick, N.Y., 1980-91; life mem. Brandeis U. Nat. Women's Com., lectr. art history, 1992—; vol. Fairchild Tropical Gardens, 1994—. Mem. Modern Mus. Art, Ft. Lauderdale (Fla.) Mus. Art, Jewish Mus. N.Y., Met. Mus. Art, Williamsburg Mus., Mus. Modern Art, Mus. Art Ft. Lauderdale. Democrat.

GOLDSTEIN, SANDRA C., lawyer; b. Bklyn., May 12, 1964. BA, Barnard Coll., 1984; JD, NYU, 1987. Bar: N.Y. 1988. Ptnr. Cravath, Swaine & Moore, N.Y.C. Office: Cravath Swaine & Moore Worldwide Plz 825 Eighth Ave New York NY 10019*

GOLDSTEIN, SUZANNE, retail buyer; b. Queens, N.Y., Nov. 20, 1960; d. Alan Goldstein and Sandra (Zucker) Kaczetow. Student, Adelphi U., 1978-80, Long Beach (Calif.) State U., 1980-82. Buyer, mgr. Nordstrom, Oakbrook, Ill. Home: Apt 1004 3660 N Lakeshore Dr Chicago IL 60613

GOLDSTEIN, VALERIE PAT, community education administrator; b. Bklyn., Jan. 4, 1943; d. Joseph and Blanche (Pivar) Gotthelf; m. Allen Rene Morganstein, July 6, 1963 (div. 1974); 1 child, Jennifer Leigh Morganstein; m. Joseph Goldstein, June 25, 1988. BA, Bklyn. Coll., 1964, MS in Edn., 1967. Cert. elem. sch. tchr., N.Y. Tchr. gifted children Pub. Sch. Dist. 335, Bklyn., 1964-71; cmty. health edn. specialist West County Health Dept., White Plains, N.Y., 1981-86, ednl. media program specialist, 1986-93, adminstr. cmty. edn. program, 1993—. Mem., spkr. to N.Y. State Assembly, Westchester Women's Adv. Group, 1989—; mem. com. on tng. revisions for wastewater treatment plant operators N.Y. State Dept. Environ. Conservation; asst. to chmn. govt. campaign com. United Way Westchester, 1983, asst. to chmn. health campaign com., 1984; selected Westchester County Mid. Mgmt. Program, 1987—. Recipient commendation N.Y. State Pub. Health Assn. and Pub. Health Assn. N.Y.C., 1989. Mem. N.Y. State Pub. Health Assn. (bd. dirs. 1989—, pres. Lower Hudson Valley region 1993—), Women's Healthcare Network (bd. dirs. 1994—). Home: 1001 Scarsdale Rd Scarsdale NY 10583 Office: Westchester County Dept Health Edn and Info 19 Bradhurst Ave Hawthorne NY 10532-2140

GOLDSTON, BARBARA M. HARRAL, editor; b. Lubbock, Tex., Jan. 26, 1937; d. Leonard Paul and Olivette (Stuart) Harral; m. John Rowell Toman (div. 1963); 1 child, Stuart Rowell; m. Olan Glen Goldston, 1989. BE, Tex. Christian U., 1959; MLS, U. Hawaii, 1968; postgrad., Golden Gate U., 1980-82. Tchr. pub. elem. schs., various cities, Tex. and Hawaii, 1959-66; contracts abstractor, indexer Champlin Oil Co., Ft. Worth, 1963-64; adminstrv. asst. engring. Litton Industries, Lubbock, Tex., 1964-65; mgr. rsch. library Hawaii Employers' Coun., Honolulu, 1968-72; rsch. cons. Thailand Hotel Study, Touche-Ross Assocs., Honolulu, 1974; dir. med. library U. S.D.-Sacred Heart Hosp., Yankton, 1977-79; editor, adminstrv. coord. book div. ABC-Clio, Inc., Santa Barbara, Calif., 1981-88; free-lance rsch./editorial cons. Albuquerque, 1988-89; instr. Santa Fe Community Coll., 1989—; owner Sandbar Prodns., Albuquerque, 1993—; ptnr. Broome-Harral, Inc., Albuquerque, 1989—. Author, editor with others Hist. Periodical Dir., 5 vols., World Defense Forces compendium. Contbr. Boy's Ranch, Amarillo, Tex., 1987—; mem. Lobero Theater Group, Santa Barbara, 1975-76; mem., treas. Yankton Med. Aux., 1977-79. Mem. ALA, Spl. Libraries Assn., Med. Libraries Assn., Am. Soc. Info. Sci., Albuquerque C. of C., Albuquerque Conv. and Visitors Bur., Better Bus. Bur. Albuquerque, Tex. Christian U. Alumni Assn., Delta Delta Delta. Republican. Episcopalian. Home: 11137 Academy Ridge Rd NE Albuquerque NM 87111 Office: PO Box 3824 Albuquerque NM 87190-3824

GOLIAN, LINDA MARIE, librarian; b. Woodbridge, N.J., Mar. 27, 1962; d. Joseph John Golian and Mary Grace (Juba) Rodriguez; m. Gary S. Lui, Oct. 6, 1988. BA, U. Miami, 1986; MLIS, Fla. State, 1988; EdS, Fla. Atlantic U., 1995, postgrad., 1996—. Libr. tech. asst. U. Miami, 1981-86; serials control libr. U. Miami Law Sch., 1986-89; serials dept. head Fla. Atlantic U., Boca Raton, 1990—; adj. instr. Fla. Atlantic U. Coll. Continuing & Distance Edn., 1993—, U. So. Fla. Coll. Libr. Sci., 1995—; program specialist Marriott Statford Ctr. Sr. Living Comty., Boca Raton, 1994-96. Vol. story teller Aid to Victims of Domestic Assault, Delray Beach, Fla., 1994—. Mem. NOW, AAUW, NAFE, NLA, SLA, NASIG, ASCD, SELA, ALISE, ALA (mem. ACRL, ALCTS, LAMA and RASD divsns., mem. CLENE, IFRT, LIRT, NMRT and SORT Round Tables, women's studies sect. comm. com. 1994—, serials com. nomination com., Miami local arrangements com. 1994, chair libr. sch. outreach 1994—, 3M profl. devel. grantee 1995), Laubach Literary Vols. of Am., Am. Assn. Adult and Continuing Edn., Fla. Libr. Assn. (serials libr. of yr. 1994, grantee 1987). Republican. Roman Catholic. Office: Fla Atlantic U Wimberly Libr PO Box 3092 Boca Raton FL 33431

GOLIN, JOYCE ARLENE, public information officer; b. Beverly, Mass., Aug. 29, 1964; d. John J. and Constance A. (McNeil) McMahon; m. Robert M. Golin, Sept. 16, 1989. BS in Speech cum laude, Emerson Coll., 1986. Pub. rels. asst. S.D. Warren Co., Boston, 1986-88; conf. coord. New Medico Assn., Lynn, Mass., 1988-89; mktg. specialist Caravan for Commuters, Boston, 1989-90; exec. dir. Peabody (Mass.) Downtown Partnership, 1990-94; pub. info. officer Mass. Divsn. Energy Resources, Boston, 1995—. Bd. dirs. Spar & Spindle Girl Scout Coun., North Andover, Mass., 1993—; city councillor City of Beverly, Mass., 1994—; coun. rep. Econ. Devel. Coun., Beverly, 1994—; chmn. Com. on Fin. and Property, Beverly, 1996—. Mem. LWV. Home: 36 Sonning Rd Beverly MA 01915

GOLLIN, SUSANNE MERLE, cytogeneticist, cell biologist; b. Chgo., Sept. 22, 1953; d. Harvey A. and Pearl (Reiffel) G.; m. Lazar M. Palnick; 1 child, Jacob Hillel Palnick, Oct., 1991. BA in Biology, Northwestern U., 1974, MS, 1975, PhD, 1980. Diplomate Am. Bd. Med. Genetics, Clin. Cytogenetics. Postdoctoral fellow U. Rochester Med. Ctr. (N.Y.), 1979-81; rsch. assoc. in cell biology Baylor Coll. of Medicine, Houston, 1981-83, rsch. assoc. in genetics, 1983-84; asst. prof. dept. pathology and pediatrics U. Ark. Med. Scis., 1984-87; dir. cytogenetics lab. Ark. Children's Hosp., 1984-87; assoc. mem. Pitts. Cancer Inst., 1987-95, mem., 1995—; asst. prof. human genetics U. Pitts., 1987-95, dir. clin. cytogenetics lab., 1988—, assoc. prof. human genetics, 1995—; mem. pediatric oncology group., mem. exec. com. Ark. Genetics Program, 1984-87; mem. organizing com. Am. Cytogenetics Conf., 1990—; mem. Allegheny County Bd. Health, 1992—, clin. lab. improvement adv. com. Ctrs. Disease Control and Prevention, HHS, 1994—; vis. sci. Deutsches Krebsforschungszentrum, Heidelberg, Germany, 1995. Contbr. articles to profl. jours. Mem. deans' adv. com. Pa. Sch. Excellence for Healthcare Profls., 1991-95; mem. faculty senate exec. com. U. Pitts. Grad Sch. Pub. Health, 1992—, pub. health affirmative action com., 1992-94, v.p. faculty senate, 1994-95; vol. Lighthouse for the Blind, Houston, 1983; chmn. med. ethics and civil liberties com. ACLU, Pitts., 1989-91; alt. del. Dem. Nat. Conv., 1992. Fellow Am. Coll. Med. Genetics (founder); mem. AAAS, Am. Assn. Cancer Rsch., Women in Cancer Rsch., Am. Soc. Human Genetics, Am. Soc. Cell Biology, Soc. Analytical Cytology, Pitts. Cancer Inst., Southwest Oncology Group (core com. cytogenetics), Pitts. Cytogenetics Club (founder, coord. 1989-95), Sigma Xi. Avocations: gardening, photography, pulled thread embroidery. Office: U Pitts Dept Human Genetics 130 Desoto St Pittsburgh PA 15213-2535

GOLLIS, ELAINE SANDRA, nurse, administrator; b. Fall River, Mass., Mar. 30, 1938; d. Harold and Esther (Packer) G.; m. Pasquale Margiotta, May 16, 1968 (div. Oct. 1986); children: Ellen, Mark. Nurse, Worcester City Hosp., 1959; BS, Post Coll., 1989; MS, Hartford Grad. Ctr., 1992. RN, Conn.; cert. nurse adminstr. Dir. nursing Hebrew Home and Hosp., Hartford, Conn., 1963-68, Jewish Home for Aged, San Francisco, 1968; clin. supr. Hebrew Home and Hosp., Hartford, 1971-81, coord. patient care, 1981-82, clinic coord. ambulatory care, 1982-84, ombudsman, 1984, acting dir. nursing, 1984-85, asst. dir. nursing, 1985-95, assoc. dir. nursing svcs., 1995—; clin. assoc. dept. behavioral sci. Sch. Dental Med. U. Conn., Farmington, 1986—. Mem. ANA (cert. nurse adminstr.), Conn. League for Nursing, Conn. Hosp. Assn., Conn. Assn. Not-For-Profit Providers For the Aging (dir. nurses coun.). Jewish. Office: Hebrew Home and Hosp 1 Abrahms Blvd West Hartford CT 06117-1508

GOLONKA, ANNE M., women's rights activist; b. Buffalo, Feb. 14, 1936; d. William James and Violet Lilian (Hunt) Young; divorced; children: Elizabeth, Gregory, Mary Grace, Christopher, Stephen, Catherine, Jean, Andrew, John. Transportation supervisor Grand Island (N.Y.) Sch. Dist., 1973-82; correction officer City of Las Vegas, 1982-91, corrections sgt., 1991-92. Pres. NOW, Las Vegas, 1995-96. Mem. AARP, AAUW, LWV, Nev. Sr. Coalition., Ret. Pub. Employees Nev., Police Protection Assn., Women's Polit. Caucus. Home: 5157 D Garden Ln Las Vegas NV 89119

GOLUB, SHARON BRAMSON, psychologist, educator; b. N.Y.C., Mar. 25, 1937; m. Leon M. Golub, June 1, 1958; children: Lawrence E., David B. Diploma, Mt. Sinai Hosp. Sch. Nursing, 1957; BS, Columbia U., 1959, MA, 1966; PhD, Fordham U., 1974. Head nurse Mt. Sinai Hosp., N.Y.C., 1957-59; contbg. editor RN Mag., Oradell, N.J., 1967-74; asst. prof. psychology Coll. New Rochelle, N.Y., 1974-79, assoc. prof., 1979-86, prof., 1986—, dir. women's studies, 1978-79, chmn. dept. psychology, 1979-82; pvt. practice individual and group psychotherapy Harrison, N.Y., 1976—; adj. prof. psychiatry N.Y. Med. Coll., Valhalla, 1980-94. Editor: Menarche, 1983 (Assn. Women in Psychology Disting. Pub. award 1984, Book of Yr. award Am. Jour. Nursing 1984), Lifting the Curse of Menstruation, 1983, Health Care of the Female Adolescent, 1984, Health Needs of Women as They Age, 1984, PERIODS from Menarche to Menopause, 1992; (with Rita Jackaway Freedman) Psychology of Women: Resources for a Core Curriculum, 1987; editor Women and Health, 1982-86, mem. editorial bd., 1986—; mem. editorial bd. Psychology of Women Quar., 1989—. Grantee Nat. Libr. Medicine, 1983-84; NIH rsch. fellow, 1971-74. Fellow Am. Psychol. Assn. (chmn. task force on teaching psychology of women 1980-83), Am. Psychol. Soc., Am. Assn. Applied and Preventive Psychology; mem. Soc. for Menstrual Cycle Rsch. (pres. 1981-83, bd. dirs. 1981-93), Assn. Women in Psychology, Phi Beta Kappa, Sigma Xi, Psi Chi. Office: Coll New Rochelle Dept Psychology New Rochelle NY 10805

GOLUBSKI, LISA LEANN, secondary school educator; b. Council Grove, Kans., Feb. 16, 1971; d. Larry Leon and Karen Kay (Borkert) Landgren; m. Rick Edward Golubski, June 25, 1994. BSE in English and Journalism, Emporia State Univ., 1993. Cert. tchr. English, Journalism, 7-12. English tchr. United Sch. Dist. #313, Buhler (Kans.) H.S., 1993—. Mem. NEA, ESU Ambassadors (newsletter editor 1991-93), Emporia State U. Alumni Assn., Kappa Delta Pi (sec.), Nux Zeta of Chi Omega (chpt. correspondent, house mgr.). Home: 737 Westhaven Dr Newton KS 67114 Office: Buhler HS 611 N Main St Buhler KS 67522

GOMBAR, CHRISTINA MARIE CATHERINE, writer, marketing professional; b. Fort Campbell, Ky., Nov. 21, 1959; d. Gordon and Barbara Rose (Evanstock) G.; m. Peter Harold Leviten, May 15, 1988. BA in Journalism and English, U. R.I., Kingston, 1982; MA in Creative Writing and English, CUNY, N.Y.C., 1993. Editl. asst. Matthew Bender Pub., N.Y.C., 1982-83; asst. editor mag. Jewelers-Circular Keystone/AJM, N.Y.C., 1983-86; corp. comms. writer Am. Internat. Group, N.Y.C., 1986-87; pub. rels. mgr. Standard & Poors, N.Y.C., 1988-92, freelance writer various publs., 1993-95; mktg. specialist TIAA-CREF, N.Y.C., 1995—; assoc. editor Global City Review, N.Y.C., 1994—. Author: (book) Great American Women Authors, 1996; contbr. articles to mags. and jours. Adv. bd. EFAP, Marymount Coll.; driver, distributor Coalition for the Homeless, N.Y.C., 1992-94. Recipient Creative Writing fellowship N.Y. Found. for the Arts, 1995, Goodman Fund grant, 1993, Geraldine Griffin Moore award CCNY, 1993. Mem. PEN (assoc.), Internat. Assn. Bus. Communicators. Democrat. Roman Catholic. Home: 32 Round Hill Rd Dobbs Ferry NY 10522

GOMEZ, SYLVIA, pediatric critical care nurse; b. L.A., July 27, 1960; d. Antonio and Belia (Rubalcava) G. AA, East L.A. Coll., 1980; BSN, Calif. State U., L.A., 1985. Cert. pediatric nurse, CCRN. RN staff relief Personal Care Home Health Care, San Gabriel, Calif., 1984-86; RN staff nurse LAC/USC Pediatric Pavilion, L.A., 1983-86; RN relief nurse Care Visions Corp., Encino, Calif., 1990-93; RN staff nurse/PICU Huntington Meml. Hosp., Pasadena, Calif., 1986—; RN staff nurse/CTICU Children's Hosp. L.A., 1994—. Mem. Calif. Nurses Assn., ANA, AACN, Soc. Pediatric Nurses, Alpha Tau Delta Phi Pi (chpt. historian 1994—). Democrat. Roman Catholic. Home: 273 East Markland Dr Monterey Park CA 91755

GONCE, PAMELA KAY, accountant; b. Amarillo, Tex., Aug. 2, 1956; d. Nick Joe Nelson and Ann (Sain) Mulanax; m. Michael Dean Gonce, June 14, 1974; 1 child, Christopher Shane. AS in Bus. Adminstrn., Amarillo Coll., 1989; BBA in Acctg., West Tex. State U., 1992. Sr. acct. fin. analysis dept. Mason & Hanger, Silas Mason Co., Inc., Amarillo, Tex., 1993—. Mem. Inst. Mgmt. Accts. Home: 1905 Beech St Amarillo TX 79106-4505 Office: Mason & Hanger Silas Mason Co, Inc P O Box 30020 Amarillo TX 79177

GONDA, SUSAN, history educator; b. Detroit, Apr. 4, 1956; d. Frank Andrew and Eleanor Gonda. BA, San Diego State U., 1990; MA, UCLA, 1993, postgrad. Legal sec./paralegal various firms, Detroit, 1974-81; adminstrv. asst. U. Calif. San Diego Med. Sch., 1981-90; teaching asst. in history UCLA, 1992-94, teaching fellow, 1994—; co-coord. Women's Resource Ctr. San Diego Stae U., 1987-90; presenter in field. Author articles and essays. Recipient awards and fellowships. Mem. Am. Hist. Assn., Law and Society Assn., Orgn. Am. Historians, Coording Com. on Women in the Hist. Profession, So. Calif. Women's Studies Assn., Western Assn. Women Historians, Phi Alpha Theta.

GONG, CAROLYN LEI CHU, real estate agent; b. Visalia, Calif., July 10, 1949; d. Robert C. and Lynn P. (Low) G. BA in Health Sci., Calif. State U., Long Beach, 1973; MA in Sociology, Calif. State U., L.A., 1980. Cert. jr. coll. tchr., Calif. Social worker County of L.A., El Monte, Calif., 1974-76, children treatment counselor, 1976-81; children svcs. worker County of L.A., Norwalk, 1981-89; real estate agt. Coldwell Banker, Diamond Bar, Calif., 1989-90, First Team Real Estate, Dana Point, Calif., 1991-92, Grubb & Ellis Real Estate, Dana Point, Calif., 1994—, 1994-95, San Clemente, Calif., 1995—. Active March of Dimes Walk-a-Thon, Toys for Tots, Sugar Plum Tree, Am. Cancer Soc., Am. Heart Assn., Disabled Vet., Easter Seal. Mem. NAFE, Nat. Assn. Realtors (Mult-million Prodn. award 1989—, Relocation award 1995), Calif. Assn. Realtors, Asian Bus. League, Tennis Connection. Republican. Home: 33144 Ocean Rdg Dana Point CA 92629-6010 Office: Grubb & Ellis Real Estate 635 Camino de los MaresSte 100 San Clemente CA 92673

GONGLEWSKI, GRACE, actor; b. Johnstown, Pa., Oct. 31, 1963; d. Zygmund Anthony John and Sylvia Blanche (MacFadyen) G. BFA, N.C. Sch. Arts, 1987. outreach mem. The Walnut St. Theatre, Phila., 1987-88, The Drama Guild, Phila., 1993-94; tchr. teen acting Arden Theatre Co., Phila., 1990—; tchr. adult improvisation Wilma Theatre, Phila., 1995-96. Appeared in performances at Arden Theatre Co., Phila. Alliance for Performance Alternatives, Walnut St. Studio Theatre, Cheltenham Arts Ctr., The Wilma Theatre, others. Recipinet Barrymore award for outstanding supporting actress in a musical Performing Arts League Phila., 1995, F. Otto Haas award Performing Arts League Phila., 1995. Mem. NOW, AFRTA, Actors Equity Assn. Democrat. Brethren. Home: 2825 Poplar St Philadelphia PA 19130

GONGOS, SUSAN CLARE, financial advisor; b. Chgo., Jan. 22, 1945; d. Clarance Oliver and Diane Mercedes (Southern) Sathre; m. Deno Gongos, May 1966 (div. July 1978); children: Lexie Gongos Senior, Demi Diana. BSBA in Biology, French, U. Tex., Arlington, 1968; postgrad. in Elec. Engring., U. Tex., Austin, 1974. Tchr. biology Irving (Tex.) H.S., 1968-74; instr. anatomy and physiology Arapahoe C.C., Littleton, Colo., 1975; substitute tchr. sci. Littleton, Cherry Creek (Colo.) Pub. Schs., 1976-78; dir. Randell Moore Sch., Denver, 1978-82; fin. advisor Cigna Fin. Svcs., Englewood, Colo., 1982—. Mem. Leadership Denver, Denver C. of C., 1983, Leadership Denver alumni, 1985-86; mem. 50 for Colo., Colo. Assn. Commerce and Industry, Denver, 1985, exec. bd. bus. leaders network, 1994-96. Mem. Alpha Phi. Office: Cigna Fin Advisors 6300 S Syracuse W # 500 Englewood CO 80111

GONNELLA, NINA CELESTE, biophysical chemist; b. Phila., Dec. 22, 1953; d. Anthony and Antoinette E. Gonnella. BA, Temple U., 1975; PhD, U. Pa., 1979; postdoctoral, Calif. Inst. Tech., 1979-81, Columbia U., 1981-83; research assoc., Yale U., 1984. Sr. rsch. scientist CIBA Geigy Pharm. Co., Summit, N.J., 1983-88, staff scientist II, 1989-93, rsch. fellow I, 1993-94, mgr., 1994—; vis. rsch. fellow Yale U., 1984; invited lectr. CCNY, CIBA Geigy, Basel, Temple U., Varian Assocs., Internat. Soc. Magnetic Resonance Conf. Contbr. articles to profl. jours. NSF fellow, 1976-79. Mem. AAAS, ACS, Phi Lambda Upsilon. Office: Ciba Geigy 556 Morris Ave Summit NJ 07901-1330

GONNERMAN, CHARNEY LOUISE, association administrator; b. Luverne, Minn., Nov. 25, 1945; d. George William and Margaret Lucile (Arnold) Ziegahn; m. William Wallace Wilmot, June 7, 1967 (div. May 1976); children: Jason Lamar, Carina Louise; m. David Allen Gonnerman, Sept. 27, 1980; stepchildren: Melissa Diane, Paula Marie. BA, Augustana Coll., Sioux Falls, S.D., 1967. Dist. dir. Totem coun. Girl Scouts U.S.A., Seattle, 1967-70; presch. tchr. 1st Congl. Ch., Missoula, Mont., 1974-76, YWCA, Missoula, 1973-74; asst. state dir. S.D. Green Thumb, Sioux Falls, 1978-80; dir. Aging Svcs. Ctr., Sioux Falls, 1980; exec. dir. Vol. and Info. Ctr., Sioux Falls, 1980-83, YWCA, Sioux Falls, 1983-91; bus. owner Primerica Fin. Svcs., 1991-92; exec. dir. YWCA, Billings, Mont.; co-owner, mgr. Small World, Missoula, 1975; dir. vols. ARC, 1991, Luth. Social Svcs., Sioux Falls, 1991-94. Bd. dirs. YWCA, Missoula, 1971-73, Mont. Women's Lobby, 1995—, Pub. Utilities Commn., Billings, 1995—, Child Care Coalition, Billings, 1995—; organizer, dir. Isabella County Recycling, Mt. Pleasant, Mich., 1970-73; trainer, leader Girl Scouts U.S.A., Mt. Pleasant, 1970-73, leader, Brandon, S.D., 1982; bd. dirs. Interagy. Steering Com., Sioux Falls, 1981-83, Child Protection Coun., 1981-83, Valley Drive Recreation Ctr., 1984, Aging Svcs. Ctr., 1979, Family Violence Coalition, 1985, S.D. Office Volunteerism, 1984; mem. Nat. Abortion Rights Action League, 1990-96, numerous others. Recipient Women Serving S.D. award S.D. Advocacy Network for Women, 1990. Mem. Nat. Assn. YWCA Execs., Nat. Assn. Fund Raising Execs., AAUW, NOW, Nat. Women's Polit. Caucus, Mont. Assn. Female Execs., Sioux Falls Pers. Assn., Nat. Parks and Conservation Assn., Badger Wilderness Assn., Rotary. Democrat. Methodist. Home: 1102 Pepper Lane Billings MT 59102

GONNERMAN, KAREN ELIZABETH, occupational health nurse; b. Dixon, Ill., Apr. 16, 1943; d. Harold Edward and Ruth Marie (Kling) Spencer; m. Marcus Paul Gonnerman, Sept. 20, 1964; children: Gregory Spencer, Debra Marie Gonnerman Schuler. Diploma in Nursing, Swedish Am. Hosp. Sch. Nursing, Rockford, Ill., 1964. RN, Ill.; cert. occupational health nurse-specialist; cert. CPR. Staff nurse gen. surgery Streator (Ill.) Mcpl. Hosp., 1964-65; asst. head nurse orthopedics Luth. Gen. Hosp., Park Ridge, Ill., 1965-66; staff nurse obstetrics Sycamore (Ill.) Mcpl. Hosp., 1967-69; office nurse dermatology Dr. William Slinger, Rockford, 1969-70; office nurse allery Allergy Assocs., Rockford, 1970-78; office nurse Freeport (Ill.) Clinic, S.C., 1978-79; occupl. health nurse Thermos Co., 1980-85; occupl. health nurse/pers. mgr. Zedco Inc., 1985-87; indsl./cmty. rels. mgr., cons. case mgmt./job analysis Freeport Clinic, S.C., 1988-95; med. mgmt. cons. Disability Mgmt. Network, Ltd., 1995—; program coord. New Horizons Health Svcs., Freeport, 1992-95; educator/speaker Freeport Clinic, 1988-95; bd. dirs. Sojourn House, Inc., Freeport, 1992-94. Classified sect. leader United Way, No. Ill., 1985-95; state rep. campaign fin. chmn. Rep. Party, Ill. Dist. 74, 1988, 90; adult advisor/chmn. Internat. Drug Free Uouth, Stephenson County, Ill., 1991-95; mem. Miss Freeport scholarship adv. com. Miss Am. Pageant Sys., 1988-93. Mem. Am. Assn. Occupational Helath Nurses, No. Ill. Assn. Occupational Health Nurses (bd. dirs. 1991-92, rec. sec. 1993-94), Freeport C. of C. (wellness task force 1990-95). Office: Freeport Clinic SC 1036 W Stephenson St Freeport IL 61032-4865

GONSOULIN GHATTAS, WENDY ANN, choreographer, dancer; b. New Iberia, La., Jan. 14, 1965; d. Claude Cleaveland and Margaret Ann Gonsoulin; m. Rony Joseph Ghattas, June 26, 1987. BFA, U. Southwestern La., 1988, postgrad. in speech-language pathology. Sales assoc. Zales Jewelers, LaFayette, La., 1986-92; choreographer The Performing Art Cons., Ltd., New Iberia, 1989—; instr. creative dance Cathy's Daycare Ctr., New Iberia, 1990—. Prin. dancer (musical) Cajun Odyssey, 1990, (concert with symphony) An Evening with the Acadiana and State of La Danse, 1991. Dance instr. for deaf students Daspit Elem. Sch., New Iberia, 1990—; bd. dirs. New Iberia Community Concert, 1991—; mem. svc. commn. Our Lady of Wisdom Cath. Ch., LaFayette, 1991—; founder PAC Reperatory Ensemble Modern Dance Co. Mem. Am. Bus. Women Assn. (nominee Outstanding Young Woman award 1991), Profl. Dance Tchr. Assn., Nat. Student Speech-Lang.-Hearing Assn., New Iberia Downtown Merchants Assn., Iberia Gen. Hosp Adv. bd., 1996, Cofounder Dance Teachers Alliance, 1996, Grant recipient for inner sch. Art Program, Dance Educators Am., Delta Delta Delta (libr. 1983-84, marshall 1984-85), mem. Gama Beta Phi. Democrat. Home: PO Box 43031 Lafayette LA 70504-3031 Office: The Performing Arts Cons Lt 101 Julia St PO Box 9125 New Iberia LA 70562

GONZALES, ANGELA ANN, sociology educator; b. San Bernardino, Calif., June 3, 1964; d. Jesse Mary and Erlene (Onsae) G. BA, U. Calif., Riverside, 1990; AM, Harvard U., 1993, MA, 1994, postgrad., 1995—. Social analyst Congl. Rsch. Svc., Washington, 1991; rsch. asst. Harvard U., Cambridge, Mass., 1991-93, teaching fellow, 1992-94; dir. edn. Hopi Tribe, Kykotsmovi, Ariz., 1994-95; lectr. U. Calif., Berkeley, Calif., 1995—; lectr. San Francisco State U., 1996. Chair Coun. Native Am. Students Harvard U., 1993-95. Recipient Alumni award U. Calif., Riverside, 1990; Harvard U. fellow, 1990-96, Ford fellow Nat. Rsch. Coun., 1992-95. Mem. Am. Sociology Assn., Nat. Indian Educators Assn., Am. Acad. Religion. Home: 1227 Talbot Ave Berkeley CA 94706

GONZALES, LISAMARIE, elementary and secondary education educator; b. Sept. 23, 1967. BS in Bus., BA in TV, San Jose State U., 1990, MA in Edn. Adminstrn., 1994. Multiple subject tchg. credential, Calif. Tchr. lang. arts C.W. Fair Mid. Sch., San Jose, 1992-93; tchr. Carlton Elem. Sch., San Jose, 1993; tchr. sci. and math. T.R. Pollitita Mid. Sch., Daly City, Calif., 1993—; presenter workshops. Contbr. articles to profl. jours. Vol. Youth Focus, 1986-94, Miss America Scholarship Program, San Jose, 1988-94. Grantee Peninsula Cmty. Found., 1993, 94, Coca-Cola Found., 1993—, Hewlett Packard, 1993—. Mem. AAUW, Nat. Sci. Tchrs. Assn., Nat. Coun. Tchrs. Math., Earthwatch. Office: TR Pollicita Mid Sch 550 E Market St Daly City CA 94014-2103

GONZALES, SHARON L., nursing administrator, educator; b. Abilene, Kans., Apr. 13, 1945; d. Raymond E. and Pauline G. (Long) Engle; m. Richard L. Gonzales, Dec. 28, 1968; children: Brian, Jill, Joy. Diploma, Stormont-Vail Sch. Nursing, Topeka, 1966; BSN with honors, Pittsburg (Kans.) State U., 1974; MSN, U. Kans., Lawrence, 1989. Instr., clin. staff nurse Colmery O'Neil VA Med. Ctr., Topeka; instr. Stormont-Vail Sch. Nursing, Topeka; divsn. dir. inpatient nursing svcs. St. Francis Hosp. and Med. Ctr., Topeka. Mem. ANA, Kans. State Nurses Assn. (bd. dirs. Dist. 1), Am. Orgn. Nurse Execs., Kans. Orgn. Nurse Execs., Sigma Theta Tau (v.p. Eta Kappa chpt., now pres.).

GONZALES, STEPHANIE, state official; b. Santa Fe, Aug. 12, 1950; 1 child, Adan Gonzales. Degree, Loretto Acad. for Girls. Office mgr. Jerry Wood & Assocs., 1973-86; dep. sec. of state Santa Fe, 1987-90, sec. of state, 1991; bd. dirs. N.Mex. Pub. Employees Retirement, N.Mex. State Convassing Bd., N.Mex. Commn. Pub. Records. Mem. exec. bd. N.Mex. AIDS Svc.; mem. Commn. White House Fellowships. Mem. Nat. Assn. Secs. State, United League United Latin Am. Citizens (women's coun.). Office: Office of the Sec of State State Capitol Rm 420 Santa Fe NM 87503*

GONZALES, YOLANDA G., rehabilitation services professional; b. El Paso, Tex., July 12, 1953; d. Margarito Jacquez and Concha (Blanco) Garcia; m. Ernesto H. Gonzales, Jr., Feb. 14, 1986; children: Brian Garcia, Kyle L. Gonzales. Sec. Ft. Stockton (Tex.) C. of C., 1970; ins. head Meml. Hosp., Ft. Stockton, 1973-79; dental asst. Paul Pearce, DDS, Ft. Stockton, 1981; rehab. svc. technician Tex. Rehab. Comm., Odessa, 1979-93. State dir. Jaycees, Ft. Stockton, 1980-83, treas. Jaycee Women; den leader Boy Scouts Am., Ft. Stockton, 1984; active Crisis Intervention/MHMR, Ft. Stockton; counselor asst. St. Joseph Cath. Ch., Ft. Stockton; chair human rights com. Comanche Flats ICF-MR Facility. Named Woman of Yr. Jaycees, 1983-84. Mem. Permain Basin Comm. Svc. Orgn. (v.p.), mem. Legion of Mary (aux. mem. St. Mary's Cath. Ch.). Office: ABLE Ctr for Ind Living 208 W 23rd Odessa TX 79764

GONZALEZ, CARMEN GRACIA, lawyer; b. Havana, Cuba, Jan. 6, 1962; d. Francisco and Carmen (Bonachea) G. BA, Yale U., New Haven, Conn., 1985; JD, Harvard Law Sch., Cambridge, Mass., 1988. Bar: Calif. 1988, D.C. 1989. Law clerk to Judge Thelton E. Henderson U.S. Dist. Ct. (no. dist.) Calif., San Francisco, 1988-89; atty. Pillsbury, Madison & Sutro, San Francisco, 1989-91, Pacific Gas & Electric Co., San Francisco, 1991-94; asst. regional counsel U.S. EPA, San Francisco, 1994—; with ABA Ctrl. and East European Law Initiative, Ukraine, 1996—; adj. prof. law Sch. Law Golden Gate U., San Francisco, 1996—. Mem. ABA, Hispanic Nat. Bar Assn., La Raza Lawyer's Assn. Office: US EPA Office of Regional Counsel 75 Hawthorne St San Francisco CA 94105

GONZALEZ, IRMA ELSA, federal judge; b. 1948. BA, Stanford U., 1970; JD, U. Ariz., 1973. Law clk. to Hon. William C. Frey U.S. Dist. Ct. (Ariz. dist.), 1973-75; asst. U.S. atty. U.S. Attys. Office Ariz., 1975-79, U.S. Attys. Office (ctrl. dist.) Calif., 1979-81; trial atty. antitrust divsn. U.S. Dept. Justice, 1979; assoc. Seltzer Caplan Wilkins & McMahon, San Diego, 1981-84; judge U.S. Magistrate Ct. (so. dist.) Calif., 1984-91; ct. judge San Diego County Superior Ct., 1991-92; dist. judge U.S. Dist. Ct. (so. dist.) Calif., San Diego, 1992—; adj. prof. U. San Diego, 1992. Mem. Girl Scout Women's Adv. Cabinet. Mem. Calif. Bar Assn., Ariz. Bar Assn., Nat. Assn. Women Judges, Lawyers' Club San Diego, Calif. Judges Assn., Thomas More Soc., La Raza Lawyers, Inns of Ct. Office: Edward J Schwartz US Courthouse 940 Front St Ste 5135 San Diego CA 92101-8911*

GONZÁLEZ, LUCIE CLETA, artist, retired dressmaker, writer; b. Mexico City, Apr. 26, 1911; d. Francisco F. and Clotilde Cesaria (Segura) G. Ed., Ethel Traphagan Sch. Fashion, N.Y.C., 1934-37, Xavier Barile Sch. Fine Art, N.Y.C., 1950-52. Mem. office staff Nat. Mailorder, N.Y.C., 1930; instr. sewing Singer Sewing Ctr., Mexico City, 1945; mem. adminstrv. staff front office Hotel Taft, N.Y.C., 1945-56; dressmaker various shops, N.Y.C., 1956-86; ind. tchr. Spanish lang. N.Y.C., 1986; artist, writer Rockland, Maine, 1995—. Author: Dress and Pattern Making, 1982; contbr. articles to various publs., 1980-82; contbr. column to Rockland Free Press publ., 1995; artist one woman show Twelfth St. Gallery, N.Y.C., 1961; three woman show Piano Gallery, Jackson Heights, N.Y., 1987; prize winner's show Whitney Mus. of Art, N.Y.C., 1954; group shows: Lynn Cotler Gallery, N.Y.C., 1978, Jackson Heights Art Club, 1981-94. Active YWCA, N.Y.C., 1930-75. Recipient 1st prize in watercolor Village Art Ctr., N.Y.C., 1945, hon. awards, 1940-50, hon. mention awards, various orgns., 1950-94. Mem. Women in Arts (Washington), Maine Media Women. Republican. Roman Catholic. Home: 9 Water St Rockland ME 04841-3540

GONZÁLEZ, MARIA CRISTINA, university official; b. Ft. Stockton, Tex., Mar. 15, 1957; d. Alejandro Ramón and Senaida (Ureta) G. BS, North Tex. State U., 1978; MA, SUNY, Buffalo, 1982; PhD, U. Tex., 1986. Project dir. Office of Gov., State of Tex., Austin, 1984-86; lectr. U. Ill., Chgo., 1986; asst. prof. Rutgers U., New Brunswick, N.J., 1986-88, U. North Tex., Denton, 1988-90; asst. prof. Ariz. State U., Tempe, 1990-94, dir. campus cmtys. program, 1994—; trainer Indian Health Svc., Phoenix, 1992-94, Hispanic Leadership Inst., Phoenix, 1994—; mem. faculty L.Am. program John F. Kennedy Spl. Warfare Ctr., Ft. Bragg, N.C., 1993-94; intern Nat. Assn. for Native Am. Children of Alcoholics, Seattle, 1995—. Contbg. author: The Leaning Ivory Tower, 1995; author, performer Painting the White Face Red, 1994, Unveiling of a Human Spirit, 1995. Bd. dirs. N.J. chpt. Nat. Com. for Prevention Child Abuse, 1986-87, Tonatierra Cmty. Devel. Orgn., Phoenix, 1994; lector St. Theresa's Ch., Phoenix, 1995. Recipient award for outstanding contbns. in child abuse prevention Tex. Migrant Coun., 1985; Fulbright fellow, Mex., 1988-89. Mem. Speech Comm. Assn., Internat. Comm. Assn., Western States Comm. Assn. (chmn. 1995-96). Democrat. Home: PO Box 60484 Phoenix AZ 85082-0484 Office: Ariz State U Campus Cmtys Program Box 870212 Tempe AZ 85287-0212

GONZALEZ, MARIA DEL CARMEN, translator; b. Havana, Cuba, Aug. 22, 1956; came to U.S., 1967; d. Raul and Esther (Almeida) G.; children: Katerina Seligmann, Kyle Anthony Engstrom. BA cum laude, U. Miami, 1977; postgrad., Fla. Internat. U., 1980-81. Lic. real estate agt., Fla.; cert. securities series 7 and 63; lic. group I and variable ins. agt. Staff writer Buenhogar Editorial Am., Miami, 1977-78; adminstrv. asst. to Commr. Armando La Casa Miami, 1978-79; interpreter, translator Assoc. Interpreters, Miami, 1980-85; real estate agt. Internat. Mktg. Realty, Miami, 1981-82; mgr., owner Angelini Imported Children's Wear, Miami, 1982-85; fin. rep. United Resources, Dallas, 1985-87; acct. exec. Dean Witter, Dallas, 1987-88; fin. cons. Merrill Lynch, San Antonio, 1988-90; pres. Translating Concepts, Inc., Internat. Networking Concepts, San Antonio, 1990—; v.p. R-U-Fit Fitness and Nutrition Ctr., San Antonio; judge UTSA Fgn. Lang. Contest, San Antonio, 1990-93. Vol. interpreter City of San Antonio, 1990-91. Mem. Phi Kappa Phi, Pi Delta Phi, Sigma Delta Pi. Roman Catholic. Home and Office: Translating Concepts 2333 NW 1st St Miami FL 33125-5203

GONZALEZ, ROSITA CHRISTINE, photographer; b. Seoul, Korea, Nov. 15, 1967; d. Enrique F. and Frances D. (Taylor) G.; m. Jonathan Mark Sleeman. BA, Austin Peay State U., Clarksville, Tenn., 1990; MS, U. Tenn., Knoxville, 1992. Tchr. photography Arnstein Jewish Cmty. Ctr., Knoxville, 1991; instr. photography U. Tenn., Knoxville, 1993, editor, graphic designer, 1992-95; freelance photographer Kigali, Rwanda, 1995—. Exhibitor photographs When May I Come?, 1990, When May I Come and Not Now, 1991, Restless Sleep, 1991, At Home in London, 1994. Vol., designer Planned Parenthood of East Tenn., 1994-95. Mem. Soc. Newspaper Design (prs. 1991-92), Phi Kappa Phi, Omicron Delta Kappa, Kappa Tau Alpha. Democrat. Home: 340 Unaka St Newport TN 37821 Office: BP 1321, Kigali Rwanda

GOOCH, CAROL ANN, psychotherapist consultant; b. Meridian, Miss., Apr. 17, 1950; d. James Tackett and Chris M. Page; (div.); 1 child, Aaron Patrick Gooch. BS, Fla. State U., 1972, DS, 1975; MS, Troy State U., 1974. Lic. profl. counselor, Tex.; lic. chem. dependency counselor, Tex.; lic. marriage and family therapist, Tex.; cert. chem. dependency specialist, Tex.; cert. compulsive gambling counselor, Tex. Tchr. Okaloosa Sch. Dist., Fort Walton, Fla., 1972-77; counselor USAF, Osan AFB, Korea, 1977-79; sch. counselor Tomball (Tex.) Sch. Dist., 1983-90; cons. Montgomery (Tex.) Sch. Dist., 1992—; psychotherapist pvt. practice, Houston, 1990—; cons. school systems, Houston, 1990—; coord. sr. program Forest Springs Hosp., Houston, 1993—, Cypress Creek Hosp., 1994—. Vol. cons. PTO, Woodlands, Tex., 1990. Recipient fellowship Fla. State U., Tallahassee, 1973, Nat. Disting. Svc. award Ex Coun. U.S. Pubs., N.J., 1989; named Outstanding High Sch. Counselor, Tomball Ind. Sch. Dist., 1989. Mem. AAUW, ACA, ASCD, Tex. Sch. Counselors Assn., Am. Mental Health Counselors Assn., Tex. Mental Health Counselors Assn., Am. Bus. Women's Assn., Fla. State U. Alumni Assn., Kappa Delta Pi. Home and Office: Carol A Gooch MS LPC PO Box 1308 Montgomery TX 77356

GOOCH, CAROLYN FRANCES, school nutrition services company executive; b. Louisiana, Mo., July 4, 1951; d. Kenneth Porter and Frances Carolyn (Geujen) Morris; m. William Ronald Gooch, Jan. 29, 1977; children: Angela Marie, Christina Carolyn. BS in Home Econs., U. Mo., 1973. Home economist Amana (Iowa) Refrigeration, 1973-75; youth specialist Mo. Coop. Extension, Higginsville, 1975-77; sec., tchr.'s aide Poplar Bluff (Mo.) High Sch., 1978-79; area home economist Mo. Coop. Extension, Buffalo, 1980-82; mktg. specialist Mo. Dept. Agr., Jefferson City, 1983-87; supr. sch. food svc. Mo. Dept. Elem. and Secondary Edn., Jefferson City, 1987-90; dir. ops. Opaa Food Mgmt., Chesterfield, Mo., 1990-94; dir. tech. sales Sch. Nutrition Svcs., Zartic, Inc., Rome, Ga., 1994—; owner The Care Basket, Vandalia, Mo., 1988-95; cons. Mo. Soybean Merchandising Coun., Jefferson City, 1988-90; recipe developer Nat. Pork Prodrs. Assn., Des Moines, 1991; presenter workshops in field. Mem. NAFE, Am. Sch. Food Svc. Assn. (Mktg. award 1990), Mo. Sch. Food Svc. Assn. (local arrangement co-chair 1988-89, newsletter editor 1990), Am. Home Econs. Assn., Mo. Home Econs. Assn. (sec. 1989-91), Home Economists in Bus., Beta Sigma Phi (pres. 1988-89, Girl of Yr. 1988-89). Home: 36 Ridgeview Dr Silver Creek GA 30173 Office: Zartic Inc 438 Lavender Dr Rome GA 30165-2262

GOOD, CHERYL DENISE, veterinarian; b. Ann Arbor, Mich., June 3, 1961; d. Leslie Morton and Phyllis Irene (Isaacson) Werbel; m. Mark Alan Good, Apr. 1, 1989; children: Miranda Leigh, Ian Matthew, Alan David. BS in Biology, Mich. State U., 1983, DVM, 1988. Veterinarian Westborn Animal Hosp., Dearborn, Mich., 1988-95; veterinarian, owner Burns Animal Hosp., Dearborn, 1995—; vet. cons. Dearborn Animal Shelter, 1993—. Bd. dirs. Friends for Dearborn Animal Shelter, 1993—. Mem. AVMA, Mich. Vet. Med. Assn., U.S. C. of C., Dearborn C. of C. Jewish. Office: Burns Animal Hosp 24604 Michigan Dearborn MI 48124

GOOD, DORINE KAY, accountant; b. Waco, Tex., May 15, 1947; d. Donald Frank and Anna Jane (Koontz) Venosdel; m. William Charles Good, July 7, 1967; children: Daryl William, Ruth Ann. BS in Acctg. magna cum laude, DeVry Inst. Tech., 1994. Acctg. clk. JD Bennetts Restaurant, Redding, Calif., 1986-88; libr. & order clk. Shasta County Libr., Redding, Calif., 1986-88; crew sponsor McDonalds Restaurant, Redding, Calif., 1988-89; office mgr., bookkeeper Mi Ranchito Mex. Food, Phoenix, 1989-91; placement asst. DeVry Inst., Phoenix, 1992-94; acct. Valley Pipe & Supply Inc., Fresno, Calif., 1995—. Project leader 4-H Clubs, Redding, 1980-84; tchr. Ch. Groups, Fresno, 1995; womens missionary dir. Shasta Bapt. Assn., Redding, 1987-89; choir mem. varius chs., Redding and Phoenix. Mem. Inst. Mgmt. Accts. Republican. Baptist. Home: 790 W Bastow #146 Clovis CA 93612 Office: Valley Pipe & Supply 1810 Santa Clara Fresno CA 93721

GOOD, JOAN DUFFEY, artist; b. Irvington, N.J., Apr. 8, 1939; d. Joseph Edmund and Mary Kathleen Duffey; m. Robert Whitney Meyers, Feb. 19, 1960; children: Robert Whitney Jr., Mary Kathleen; step-children: Alison H., Forrester H.; m. Allen Hovey Good, June 12, 1976. Student, Rosemont Coll., 1958-59, Summit Art Ctr., 1973-78; BA in Psychology and Studio Art, Drew U., 1987. Represented by Jain Marunouchi Gallery Soho, N.Y.C., 1991-92, Abney Gallery Soho, N.Y.C., 1992; interior designer Maytime Festival of Homes, 1985; freelance interior design cons., 1987-89; bd. dirs. Atlantic Nat. Acquisition and Mergers, Inc., Short Hills, N.J.; bd. dirs. N.J. Ctr. for Visual Arts, Summit, curatorial assoc. gallery com., 1989-90, cocurator exhbns., 1990-94, asst. gallery curator, 1991-92, gallery curator, 1992-94, pres. 1994-95, exec. dir., 1995—; archivist Oak Knoll Sch., 1988-95. One-woman show World Trade Ctr., N.Y.C., 1988; exhibited in group shows Madison (N.J.) Pub. Libr., 1986, Chatham (N.J.) Pub. Libr., 1987, Korn Gallery, Drew U., 1986, 87, 89, 90, N.J. Ctr. for Visual Arts, 1987, 88, 89, 90, Oak Knoll Sch. Alumnae Art Exhibit, 1989, 90; represented in numerous private collections, Mass., Fla., Tex., N.J., N.Y., Calif. V.p., pres., membership chmn. PTO, 1966-69; homecoming com. mem. Oak Knoll Sch. Alumnae Bd., Summit, 1989, 90, historian, 1988-94, archivist, 1988-95. Mem. N.J. Ctr. for Visual Arts, The Drew Art Assn., Chatham Fish & Game Assn., Mantoloking Yacht Club, Summit Tennis Club. Republican. Roman Catholic. Home: 15 Hobart Ave Short Hills NJ 07078-2026

GOOD, LAURIE ANN, elementary education educator; b. Mpls., Nov. 16, 1954; d. James Walter and Donna Roberta (Closson) Farrier; m. Paul Martin Good, July 30, 1977; children: Andrea, Amanda, James, Katherine. BS in Edn. summa cum laude, Bemidji State U., 1977; MA in Curriculum, U. St. Thomas, 1986-88; PhD in Lit. Edn., U. Minn., 1996. Tchr. 3d grade Albany (Minn.) Area Schs., 1977-78; tchr. 5th grade Anoka (Minn.) - Henn Sch. Dist., 1978-79, tchr. 1st grade, 1979-89, tchr. 2d grade, 1989-96, multiage 1st-3d grade tchr., 1996; grad. asst. U. Minn., Mpls., 1993; instr. U. Minn., 1996; sprk. in field. Campaign Vol. State Rep. Charlie Weaver, Anoka, 1991—; collection vol. March of Dimes, Anoka, 1990—. U. Minn. scholar, Mpls., 1993. Mem. Nat. Coun. Tchrs. English, Internat. Reading Assn., Minn. Reading Assn., Phi Kappa Phi. Office: Eisenhower Elem Sch 151 Northdale Blvd NW Coon Rapids MN 55448-3359

GOOD, LINDA LEE, music educator, musician; b. Seattle, Jan. 24, 1940; d. Roy S. Grannis and Florence Virginia (Sprague Grannis) Shropshire; m. Leonard J. Good, Apr. 22, 1962; children: Nancye. BA, U. Wash., 1964; MA, U. Hawaii, 1970. Tchr. Pacific Prep. Acad., Honolulu, 1965; tchr., cofounder Island Strings, Langley, Wash., 1974—; tchr. Evergreen Sch., Seattle, 1976-78, Skagit Valley Coll., Langley, 1981-85. Performer (string band) Indigo, 1986—, (tape) Gather 'Round, 1992, (CD) Clara's Fiddle, 1996. Pres. Island Arts Coun., Whidbey Island, Wash., 1986-88, bd. dirs., 1980-93; bd. dirs. Cmty. Concerts Assn., Whidbey Island, 1984-87; music dir. Unitarian Universalist Congregation, Whidbey Island, 1994—. Recipient grant Hawaii Found., 1966. Mem. Suzuki Assn. of Americas, Internat. Suzuki Assn., Wash. State Suzuki Assn., Nat. Music Tchrs. Assn., Citizens for Sensible Devel., Whidbey Environ. Action Network. Home and Office: PO Box 131 Langley WA 98260

GOOD, LINDA LOU, elementary education educator; b. Zanesville, Ohio, May 30, 1941; d. John Robert and Alice Laura (Fulkerson) Moore; B.S. in Elem. Edn., Ohio U., 1964; m. Larry Alvin Good, Jan. 11, 1964; children—Jason (dec.), Alicia and Tricia (twins), Amy Jo. Tchr., West Muskingum Sch. Dist., 1962-64; 1st grade tchr., Bellevue, Ohio, 1964-68, 2d grade tchr., Zanesville Sch. System, 1970—; head tchr. Munson Sch., Zanesville. Co-chmn. Zane Trace Commemoration; pres. Munson-Garfield Schs. PTA; mem. Trinity Presbyn. Ch. Mem. NEA, Ohio Edn. Assn., Zanesville Edn. Assn., Eastern Ohio Tchrs. Assn. Presbyterian.

GOOD, MARY LOWE (MRS. BILLY JEWEL GOOD), government official; b. Grapevine, Tex., June 20, 1931; d. John W. and Winnie (Mercer) Lowe; m. Billy Jewel Good, May 17, 1952; children: Billy, James. BS, Ark. State Tchrs. Coll., 1950; MS, U. Ark., 1953, PhD, 1955, LLD (hon.), 1979; DSc (hon.), U. Ill., Chgo., 1983, Clarkson U., 1984, Ea. Mich. U., 1986, Duke U., 1987; hon. degree, St. Mary's Coll., 1987, Kenyon Coll., 1988, Stevens Inst. Tech., 1989, Lehigh U., 1989, Northeastern Ill. U., 1989, U. S.C., 1989, N.J. Inst. Tech., 1989; hon. law degree, Newcomb Coll. of Tulane U., 1991; DSc (hon.), Manhattan Coll., 1992, Ind. U., 1992; LLD (hon.), Coll. of William and Mary, 1992; DSc (hon.), SUNY, Binghamton, 1994, Rensselaer Polytechnic Inst., 1994; DSC, Monmouth U., 1995, La. State U., 1995. Instr. Ark. State Tchrs. Coll., Conway, summer 1949; instr. La. State U., Baton Rouge, 1954-56; asst. prof. La. State U., 1956-58; asso. prof. La. State U., New Orleans, 1958-63; prof. La. State U., 1963-80; Boyd prof. materials sci., div. engrng. research La. State U., Baton Rouge, 1979-80; v.p., dir. research UOP, Inc., Des Plaines, Ill., 1980-84; pres. Signal Research Ctr. Inc., 1985-87; pres. engineered materials research div. Allied-Signal Inc., Des Plaines, Ill., 1986-88; sr. v.p.-tech., Allied-Signal Inc., Morristown, N.J., 1988-93; under sec. of commerce for technology Dept. of Commerce, Washington, DC, 1993—; chmn. Pres.'s Com. for Nat. Medal Sci., 1979-82; mem. Nat. Sci. Bd., 1980-91 (chmn. 1988-91), chmn., 1988-90; mem. adv. bd. NSF Chemistry Sect., 1972-76; mem. com. medicinal chemistry NIH, 1972-76, Office of USAF Rsch., 1974-78, chemist div. Brookhaven and Oak Ridge Nat. Labs., 1973-83, chem. tech. div. Oak Ridge Nat. Lab., catalysis program Lawrence-Berkeley Lab.; catalysis program coll. engrng. La. State U.; vice chmn. Nat. Sci. Bd., 1984, chmn., 1988-90; bd. dirs. Cin. Milacron Inc., bd. dirs. Ameritech. Contbr. articles to profl. jours. Mem. Nat. Sci. Bd., 1980-91; mem. Pres.' Coun. Advisors for Sci. and Tech., 1991-93, chmn., 1988-91. Recipient Agnes Faye Morgan rsch. award, 1969, Disting. Alumni citation U. Ark., 1973, Scientist of Yr. award Indsl. R&D mag., 1993, Delmer S. Fahrney medal Franklin Inst., 1988, N.J. Women of Achievement award Douglass Coll., Rutgers U., 1990, Indsl. Rsch. Inst. medal, 1991, Disting. Svc. award NSF, 1992, Roe award ASME, 1993, Gold medal SME, 1995, Earle K. Barnes award ACS, 1995, 96; AEC tng. grantee, 1967, NSF Internat. travel grantee, 1968, NSF rsch. grantee, 1969-80, Albert Fox Demers award, 1992; hon. fellow Royal soc. of Chemistry, 1995. Fellow AAAS, Am. Inst. Chemistry (Gold medal 1983), Chem. Soc. London; mem. NAE, Swedish Acad. Engrng., Am. Chem. Soc. (1st woman dir. 1971-74, regional dir. 1972-80, chmn. bd. 1978, 80, pres. 1987, Garvan medal 1973, Herty medal 1975, award Fla. sect. 1979, Charles Lathrop Parsons award 1991), Internat. Union Pure and Applied Chmistry (pres. inorganic div. 1980-85), Zonta (past pres. New Orleans club, chmn. dist. status of women com. and nominating com., chmn. internat. Amelia Earhart schoolarship com. 1978-88, pres. internat. Found. 1988-93, mem. internat. bd. 1988-90), Phi Beta Kappa, Sigma Xi, Iota Sigma Pi (regional dir. 1967-93, hon. mem. 1983). Home: 3321 O St NW Washington DC 20007-2814 Office: Dept of Commerce Office Tech Admn 14th and Constitution Ave NW Washington DC 20230

GOOD, REBECCA MAE WERTMAN, learning and behavior disorder counselor, grief and loss counselor, hospice nurse; b. Barberton, Ohio, May 13, 1943; d. Frederick Daniel Wertman and Freda Beam Wertman Lombardi; m. William Robert Good Jr., Aug. 15, 1964; children: William Robert III, John Joseph, Matthew Stephan. RN diploma, Akron Gen. Med. Ctr., Ohio, 1964; BS in Psychology, Ramapo Coll., Mahwah, N.J., 1986; MA in Counseling, NYU, 1990. RN, N.Y.; nat. cert. counselor. Staff nurse Green Cross Gen. Hosp., Cuyahoga Falls, Ohio, 1965-68; staff nurse, relief supr., psychiat. nurse F.D.R. VA Hosp., Montrose, N.Y., 1971-72; geriatric staff and charge nurse Westledge Extended Care Facility, Peekskill, N.Y., 1972-77; infirmary and ICF nurse St. Dominics Home, Orangeburg, N.Y., 1981-83; allergy and immunology nurse Dr. Andre Codispoti, Suffern, N.Y., 1979-89; rsch. asst. counselor NYU, N.Y.C., 1989-90; Rockland advocate Student Advocacy Inc., White Plains, N.Y., 1989-90; exec. dir. Rockland County Assn. for Learning Disabled, Orangeburg, 1990-91; life skills counselor Bd. Coop. Edn., West Nyack, N.Y., 1991-93; learning and behavior disorders counselor, Suffern, 1991-93, Salt Lake City, 1994—; hospice nurse United Hospice Rockland, 1991-93; assessment and referral counselor/case mgr. CPC Olympus View Hosp., Salt Lake City, 1994—; practitioner, tchr. Therapeutic Touch, 1990—. Co-chmn. Rockland County Coordinating Coun. for Devel. Disabled Offenders, New City, N.Y., 1990-93; bd. visitors Rockland Children's Psychiat. Ctr., Orangeburg, 1991-93, sec., 1992; mem. U.S. Congressman Benjamin Gilman's Handicapped Adv. Com., Rockland County, 1985-94; pres. Ramapo Ctrl. Sch. Dist. Spl. Edn. PTA, 1982-86. Ramapo Coll. of N.J. Pres.'s scholar, 1986. Mem. ACA, Utah Counselors Assn., Children and Adults with Attention Deficit Disorders (coord. Rockland chpt. 1992-93), Hospice Nurses Assn., Nurse Healers Profl. Assn., Utah Networker Nurse Healers Profl. Assn. Episcopalian. Office: 7730 S Quicksilver Dr Salt Lake City UT 84121-5500

GOOD, VIRGINIA JOHNSON, real estate executive; b. Onancock, Va., Mar. 1, 1919; d. Obed Wilbur and Sallie Mildred (Deyerle) Johnson; m. William Dennis Good, Jan. 14, 1941 (dec. Apr. 1970). Bus. cert., Elon College, N.C., 1937; real estate cert., U. Miami, 1973; student, Montgomery County Jr. Coll., 1974. Acct. Carolina Biol. Supply Co., Elon College, N.C., 1935-39, Sears Roebuck, Richmond, Va., 1939-40, Ritchie Electric, Charlottesville, Va., 1940-41; mgmt. investor Dr. & Mrs. William D. Good Real Estate, Washington and Gaithersburg, Md., 1941-70, Good Properties, Washington and Miami Beach, Fla., 1970-94, Dennis Apts., Miami Beach, Fla., 1972-94; owner Good Properties, Orlando, Fla., 1994—; Mem. D.C. Apt. Owners/Mgmt. Assn., Washington, 1970-84, Miami Beach Apt. Owners Assn., 1970-86, North Shore Apt. Owners Assn., Miami Beach, 1986-88. Exec. com. Anti Rock Quarry, Dawsonville, Md., 1959, Save Our Coast, Miami Beach, 1982-86; mem. Montgomery County Hist. and Geneal. Soc., Rockville, Md., 1977—, Nat. Geneal. Soc., 1980—, Greater Miami Geneal. Soc., Miami, 1982—, Va. Hist./Geneal. Soc., Richmond, 1988—, Bradley Blvd. Civic Assn., Bethesda, Md., 1989. Mem. La Gorce Country Club, Miami Beach, Columbia Country Club (Chevy Chase, Md.), DAR, Nat. Soc. So. Dames, United Daus. of Confederacy, Nat. Soc. Colonial Dames of XVII Century, Nat. Huguenot Soc. Mem. United Church of Christ. Home & Office: 3607 Lake Sarah Dr Orlando FL 32804

GOODAKER, DIANNE MCCRYSTAL, language educator; b. Harrodsburg, Ky., Jan. 2, 1948; d. Garnett A. and Lois M. (Gibson) McCrystal; m. Gary R. Goodaker, June 14, 1969; children: Thomas A., Ann M. BA, McNeese State U., 1983, MEd, 1988. Cert. tchr. English. Tchr. English Washington-Marion H.S., Lake Charles, La., 1984-89, A.M. Barbe H.S., Lake Charles, 1989—; humanities tchr. Gov.'s Program for Gifted Children, Lake Charles, 1991—; cons. McNeese Writing Project, Lake Charles, 1990—. Mem. NEA, Nat. Assn. Secondary Sch. Prins., Nat. Coun. Tchrs. English, Calcasieu Assn. Educators. Democrat. Roman Catholic. Home: 516 Central Pky Lake Charles LA 70605-6236 Office: A M Barbe H S 2200 W Mcneese St Lake Charles LA 70605-4114

GOODALE, SUSAN DANA, family therapist, consultant; b. Peoria, Ill., Dec. 23, 1944; d. Charles Angus and Peggy Mona (Cook) McLee; m. Del Eugene Goodale, July 27, 1968; 1 child, Mark. BA in English/Journalism/Edn. cum laude, Ill. State U.; MA in Counseling, Bradley U., 1971, MA i Edn. Adminstrn., 1984. Cert. 7-12 tchr., counselor edn. adminstrn.; lic. clin. profl. counselor. Tchr. Ill. Valley Ctrl. H.S., Chillicothe, 1967-87, asst. prin., 1987-90; prin. Rome (Ill.) Sch., 1990-93; family therapist Counseling & Family Svc., Peoria, 1993-94, Behavioral Health Advantages, Peoria, 1994—; prep dir. Ill. Ctrl. Coll., East Peoria, 1994-95; grad. instr. Ill. State U., Normal; cons. in field; spkr. in field. Freelance feature writer Peoria Jour. Star, 1987—. Recipient Sch.-Bus. Partnership award ISBE, Friend Youth award outstanding contbns. to edn. Optimists Club, Chillicothe, 1992, Innovative Programs in IntegratedAcad. and Vocat. Edn. award Ill. State Bd. Edn., 1992, Ednl. Leadership and Human Devel. Exemplary Alumni award Bradley U., 1992, Friends Spl. Edn. award Spl. Edn. Assn. Peoria County Exceptional Svc. to Students with Spl. Needs, 1991, Outstanding Educator award U. Chgo., 1989, IVC Band Pride and Performance award, 1988. Mem. ASCD, Am. Counseling Assn., Am. Mental Health Counselors Assn., Nat. Assn. Secondary Sch. Prins., Internat. Assn. Marriage and Family Counselors, Ill. Prin.'s Assn., Ill. Sch. Pub. Rels. Assn., Pub. Rels. Assn. Ctrl. Ill., Women in Mgmt. (Peoria chpt.), Ill. Vocation Assn., Phi Delta Kappa. Home: 212 E Lakeview East Peoria IL 61611 Office: Behavioral Health Advantage 410 Fayette Peoria IL 61602

GOODALL, FRANCES LOUISE, nurse, production company assistant; b. Gove, Kans., Apr. 30, 1915; d. Francis Mitchell and Ella Aurelia (Brown) Sutcliffe; m. Richard Fred Goodall, Feb. 22, 1946; children: Roy Richard, Gary Frederick. Student, U. Kans., 1932-33, Ft. Hays State Coll., 1933-34; BS in Nursing, U. Wash., 1939. RN, Wash. Nurse King County Hosp. System, Seattle, 1939-41; office nurse Dr. Cassius Hofrictor, Seattle, 1941-42; founder Goodall Prodns., Seattle, 1971—. Pres. Hawthorne Elem. Sch. PTA, Seattle, 1960-61, Caspar Sharples Jr. High Sch. PTA, Seattle, 1967-68; historian Seattle Coun. PTAs, 1964-65, 68-69; den mother Boy Scouts Am., Seattle, 1963-67; active United Good Neighbors, Seattle, 1964-68; treas. Women's Overseas Svc. League, Seattle, 1970-74, treas., 1987-91. 1st lt. Nurses Corps, AUS, 1942-46, PTO. Recipient vol. award King County Hosp. System, 1964, Acorn award Franklin High Sch. PTA, 1965, Woman Achievement cert. award Past Pres. Assembly, 1992. Mem. U. Wash. Alumni Assn. (v.p. 1966-70), U. Wash. Nursing Alumni Assn., Seattle Mus. Art Soc. (assoc., social com., bd. dirs.), Pres's. Forum, Seattle Fedn. Women's Clubs (chmn. community improvement program 1990—), Seattle Geneal. Soc., Lake City Emblem Club, Order Eastern Star, Seattle Sorosis (pres. 1990—), Sigma Sigma Sigma, Kappa Delta (pres. Seattle alumni 1954-55, sec. alumnae coop. bd. 1963-82), Nat. Assn. Parliamentarians (pres. parliamentary law unit 1989-93, treas. 1960-61, 64-66, 75-89, 93-94), Am. Legion (life mem. Fred Hancock post #19 Renton, Wash.). Republican. Presbyterian. Home: 4111 51st Ave S Seattle WA 98118-1265

GOODART, NAN L., lawyer, educator; b. San Francisco, Apr. 4, 1938. BA, San Jose State U., 1959, MA, 1965; JD, U. of the Pacific, 1980. Bar: Calif. 1980, U.S. Dist. Ct. (ea. dist.) Calif. 1981. Tchr. Eastside Union High Sch., San Jose, Calif., 1960-65; counselor San Jose City Coll., 1965-75;

atty. Sacramento, 1981—; speaker numerous seminars throughout no. Calif. and other western states, 1988—. Author: Who Will It Hurt When I Die? A Primer on the Living Trust, 1992 (Nat. Mature Media award 1993), The Truth About Living Trusts, 1995. Judge pro tem Sacramento County Small Claims Ct., 1988-96; instr. continuing edn. of bar Am.'s Legal Ctr., Sacramento, 1992—. Mem. Nat. Acad. Elder Law Attys., Calif. State Bar Assn., Sacramento County Bar Assn. Office: Law Offices Nan L Goodart 7230 S Land Park Dr Ste 121 Sacramento CA 95831-3658

GOODBERRY, DIANE JEAN (OBERKIRCHER), mathematics educator, tax accountant; b. Buffalo, June 24, 1950; d. Ralph Arthur and Muriel Carol (Glaeser) O.; m. Lawrence D. Goodberry, Sr. BS in Math. Edn., State Univ. Coll., Brockport, N.Y., 1972, MS in Ednl. Adminstrn., 1974. Cert. in secondary math. edn., N.Y. Uni-Pay clk. Marine Midland Bank, Buffalo, 1968-72; asst. registrar State Univ. Coll., Brockport, 1972-74; home instrn. tutor Clarence (N.Y.) Ctrl. Sr. H.S., 1974-75; part-time inst. Erie C.C., Buffalo, 1975-86; instr. math. Ednl. Testing Methods, Buffalo, 1984-90, Buffalo Pub. Sch. System, 1974—; mem. curriculum devel. com. Buffalo Pub. Schs., 1988, 92—; cooperating tchr. BRIET-U. Buffalo, 1990—; part-time tax acct. Vol., World Univ. Games, Buffalo, 1993. Mem. AAUW, Women Tchrs. Assn. (bd. dirs., v.p. 1993-94, pres. 1994—), Assn. Math. Tchrs. N.Y. State, Theodore Roosevelt Rough Riders, Nat. Coun. Math. Republican. Methodist. Home: 10644 Crump Rd Holland NY 14080 Office: South Park HS 150 Southside Pky Buffalo NY 14220-1552

GOODE, CLARA ANN, accountant, budget analyst; b. Marschall County, Ala., July 26, 1946; d. John T. and Jannie B. (Higgins) Harris; m. George M. Goode, Aug. 1, 1980; children: D. Neal, Jeffrey S. BSBA, U. Ala., Huntsville, 1991, MS in Mgmt., 1994. Cert. govt. fin. mgr. Safety and security technician Monsanto, Guntersville, Ala., 1972-78, team leader, 1978-80; program coord. U. Ala., Huntsville, 1990-92, sr. rsch. program coord., 1992—. Recipient scholarship U. Ala., 1990. Mem. Assn. Govt. Accts. Office: Univ Ala RI M-17 Huntsville AL 35899

GOODE, ERICA TUCKER, internist; b. Berkeley, Calif., Mar. 25, 1940; d. Howard Edwin and Mary Louise (Tucker) Sweeting; m. Bruce Tucker (div. 1971); m. Barry Paul Goode, Sept. 1, 1974; children: Adam Nathaniel, Aaron Benjamin. BS summa cum laude, U. Calif., Berkeley, 1962, MPH, 1967; MD, U. Calif., San Francisco, 1977. Diplomate Am. Bd. Internal Medicine. Chief dietitian Washington Hosp. Ctr., Washington, 1968; pub. health nutritionist Dept. Human Resources, Washington, 1969-73; intern Children's Hosp. (now Calif. Pacific Med. Ctr.), San Francisco, 1977-78, resident, 1978-80, chief med. resident internal medicine, 1979-80; pvt. practice internal medicine San Francisco, 1980—; expert witness med.-legal issues, Calif., 1990—; lectr., tchr. med. house staff Children's Hosp., 1982—; assoc. prof. medicine U. Calif., San Francisco, 1984—. Contbr. articles to profl. publs. Co-chair Physicians for Clinton, No. Calif., 1992. Mem. AMA, ACP, Calif. Med. Assn., Calif. Soc. Internal Medicine, San Francisco Med. Soc., U. Calif. Alumni Assn. (del.), Alpha Omega Alpha. Office: Goode Brayer Dobrow Watanabe & Liberman 3801 Sacramento St # 100 San Francisco CA 94118-1625

GOODE, JANET WEISS, elementary school educator; b. Chattanooga, Tenn., Sept. 3, 1935; d. Albert H. and Dorothy E. (Crandall) Weiss; m. Gene G. Goode, June 11, 1961; children: Jennifer E., Amy V. BS in Biology, Carson-Newman Coll., 1957; MA in Botany, Vanderbilt U., 1959; MEd, Lynchburg Coll., 1980. Cert. postgrad. profl. tchr., Va. Instr. gen. biology, botany, zoology, animal ecology Carson-Newman Coll., Tenn., 1959-61; tchr. biology, chemistry Salem Acad., Winston-Salem, N.C., 1961-64; tchr. chemistry Wade Hampton High Sch., Greenville, S.C., 1964-65; tchr. sci. Va. Treatment Ctr. for Children, Richmond, 1966; tchr. biology Quantico (Va.) H.S., 1969-70; pvt. tutor Madison Heights, Va., 1980-85, James River Day Sch. and Seven Hills Sch., Lynchburg, Va., 1980-85; reading specialist Title I reading program Monellson Mid. Sch., Madison Heights, 1985-93; reading specialist Amherst County Adult Basic Edn. Program, 1992-94, 95—; reading specialist Title I reading and Reading Recovery Pleasant View Elem. Sch., Monroe, Va., 1993—; vis. instr. U. Chattanooga, summer 1960; mem. learning disabilities del. to Russia and Lithuania, Citizen Amb. Program, 1993. Editor: (newsletter) Topics for Title I; author: Can You Read a Baseball Card?; co-author: Transitional Intervention Program. Sponsor sch. lit. mag. Monellson Mid. Sch., Pleasant View Elem. Sch.; organist, newsletter editor for Ptnr. Ch. com. First Unitarian Ch.; mem. Friends of Libr., Madison Heights Br. Libr., helper ann. book sale. Recipient Reading Tchr. of the Year Piedmont Va. Area Reading Coun., 1993-94. Mem. NEA, Va. Edn. Assn., Amherst Edn. Assn., Orton Dyslexia Soc., Piedmont Area Reading Coun. (past newsletter editor, past treas.), Va. State Reading Assn., Internat. Reading Assn., Reading Recovery Coun. of N.Am., Lynchburg Stamp Club, Kappa Delta Pi, Phi Delta Kappa (past sec.).

GOODE, MARGARET NIGHAN, nurse; b. Norristown, Pa., Dec. 5, 1949; d. Raymond Andrew and Dorothy Mae (O'Neill) Nighan; m. Michael Geoffrey Goode, Dec. 26, 1970; children: Penelope Anne, Geoffrey Raymond. ADN, Chestnut Hill Hosp., Phila., 1967-70; BSN, George Mason U., 1988, postgrad. in nursing, 1996—. RN: Md., Va., Pa.; cert. HIV/AIDS Red Cross instr.; cert. addiction RN; CPR cert. Staff nurse Dominion Hosp., Falls Church, Va., 1988-91, CATS-Addiction Program, Fairfax, Va., 1989-91, Veterans Hosp., Washington, 1991-93; charge nurse Another Way, Inc., Wheaton, Md., 1993—. Pres. Jermantown Elem. Sch. PTA, Fairfax, 1983-85; Fairfax City Coun. rep. adv. coun. Fairfax County Schs.; mem. Fairfax City Alcohol Policy Com.; mem. 20/20 Commn., Fairfax. Mem. AAUW, Drug and Alcohol Nurses Assn., Sigma Theta Tau, Phi Theta Kappa. Roman Catholic. Home: 3851 Chain Bridge Rd Fairfax VA 22030 Office: Another Way, Inc. 11308 Grandview Ave Wheaton MD 20902

GOODE, STACY J., real estate broker; b. Charlottesville, Va., Feb. 25, 1942; d. Henry Wirt Jackson and Mary Stacy (Dodge) Boyle; children: Sarah Catherine, Henry Thomas II. BS in Sec. Edn., Longwood Coll., Farmville, Va., 1964; postgrad., Butler U., Indpls., 1966-67. Lic. real estate broker, Va.; CRS, GRI. Tchr. Indpls. Ind. Pub. Sch., 1966-69, Richmond (Va.) Pub. Sch., 1963-64, 69-70, Charlottesville (Va.) Pub. Schs., 1964-66; assoc. broker Nancy Chandler Assocs., 1980—. Mem. Ghent Square Archtl. Review Bd., 1987—; mem. parents adv. bd. Norfolk Pub. Schs. (vice-chmn. 1996—). Mem. AAUW, Nat. Historic Trust, Nat. Assn. Realtors, Va. Assn. Realtors, Tidewater Assn. Realtors (residential sales coun., Gold award 1986, 89, 92, 93, 94, 95, 96, Silver award 1983, 86, 88, 91, Bronze award 1982, 84, 85, 87, Platinum award 1991, Diamond award 1996, mem. Circle of Excellence 1981—), The Chrysler Mus., The Norfolk Yacht & Country Club. Democrat. Office: Nancy Chandler Assocs 701 W 21st St Norfolk VA 23517

GOODFELLOW, ROBIN, musician, educator; b. Portland, Oreg., Jan. 25, 1940; d. Ted and Lois Goodfellow; m. Victor Wong, 1970 (div. 1977); m. Charles Hixon, Mar. 17, 1991. AA with honors, Merritt Coll.; student, U. Calif., Berkeley, 1960—. 1st flute and piccolo Santa Rosa (Calif.) Symphony, 1958-60; dir. Queen's Ha' Penny Consort, Berkeley, Calif., 1960-80; dir., tchr. Mandala Fluteworks, Oakland, Calif., 1970—; mem. adv. bd., illustrator Exptl. Music Inst. Mag., Nicasio, Calif.; performer, instr. and cons. in field. Author, illustrator in field.

GOODFELLOW, ROBIN IRENE, surgeon; b. Xenia, Ohio, Apr. 14, 1945; d. Willis Douglas and Irene Linna (Kirkland) G. B.A. summa cum laude, Western Res. U., Cleve., 1967; M.D. cum laude, Harvard U., 1971. Diplomate Am. Bd. Surgery. Intern, resident Peter Bent Brigham Hosp., Boston, 1971-76; staff surgeon Boston U., 1976-80, asst. prof. surgery, 1977-80; pvt. practice medicine specializing in surgery Jonesboro, La., 1980-81; practice medicine specializing in surgery Albion, Mich., 1984-87, Coldwater, Mich., 1987—. Bd. Overseers Case Western Res. U., 1977-82. AAUW fellow, 1970. Fellow ACS; mem. AMA, Phi Beta Kappa. Republican. Methodist.

GOODHART, KAREN STEPHAN, sales executive; b. Bklyn., Jan. 14, 1947; d. Frank Herman and Bernadette (Brady) S.; m. James Stanley Goodhart, June 7, 1969 (div. Jan. 1983); children: Kristen Stephanie, Erika Lee. BA, Alvernia Coll., 1969. Elem. tchr. Schuylkill Valley Sch., Leesport, Pa., 1969-78; mgr. sales Radio Shack, Reading, Pa., 1978-84, The Computer Source, Reading, 1984; buyer Boscov's, Reading, 1985-86; with sales dept. Info. Mgmt., Blue Bell, Pa., 1986; mgr. sales Bio-Med Pa., Inc., Allentown, 1986-87, v.p. sales, 1987-88; v.p. sales Med. Disposal Services, Inc., Reading, 1988-89; v.p. nat. mktg. Nat. Med. Waste Inc, 1989-92; pres., CEO Enviro Med, Balt., 1992-94; environ. cons. K K and R Assocs., Wyomissing, Pa., 1994—; bd. dirs. Nat. Solid Waste Mgmt. Assn. Mem. Am. Soc. Health Care, Nat. Exec. Housekeeping, Assn. Practitioners Infection Control. Democrat. Roman Catholic. Office: K K and R Assocs PO Box 7002 Wyomissing PA 19610-6002

GOODHUE, MARY BRIER, lawyer, former state senator; b. London, 1921; naturalized, 1942; d. Ernest and Marion H. (Hawks) Brier; m. Francis A. Goodhue, Jr., May 15, 1948 (dec. Sept. 1990); 1 child, Francis A. III. BA, Vassar Coll., 1942; LLB, U. Mich., 1944. Bar: N.Y. 1945. Assoc. Root, Clark, Buckner & Ballantine, N.Y.C., 1945-48; asst. counsel N.Y. State Crime Commn., N.Y.C., 1951-53, Moreland Commn., N.Y.C., 1953-54; mem. firm Goodhue, Arons & Neary and predecessors, Mt. Kisco, 1955—; mem. N.Y. State Assembly from 93d Dist., 1975-78, N.Y. State Senate, 1979-92. Trustee Katonah Mus. Art, Vis. Nurse Assn., Hudson Valley, John Jay Homestead; N.Y. del. Nat. Women's Conf., Houston, 1977. Mem. ABA, West Bar Assn., No. Westchester Bar Assn. Office: 126 Barker St Mount Kisco NY 10549-1502 also: Rock Gate Farm Rd Mount Kisco NY 10549

GOODIN, JULIA C., medical investigator, state official, educator; b. Columbia, Ky., Mar. 10, 1957; d. Vitus Jack and Geneva (Burton) G. BS, Western Ky. U., 1979; MD, U. Ky., 1983. Diplomate Am. Bd. Clin. and Anatomic Pathology, Am. Bd. Forensic Pathology. Intern Vanderbilt U. Med. Ctr., Nashville, 1983, resident in anatomic and clin. pathology, 1984-87; fellow in forensic pathology Med. Examiner's Office, Balt., 1987-88; asst. med. examiner Office of Chief Med. Examiner, Balt., 1988-90; dep. chief med. examiner State of Tenn., 1990-94; asst. med. examiner Nashville, 1990-93, chief med. examiner, 1993-94; asst. med. investigator State of N.Mex., Albuquerque, 1994-96; asst. prof. U. N.Mex., Albuquerque, 1994-96; clin. assoc. prof. U. of South Ala. Sch. Medicine, 1996—; asst. med. examiner State of Ala., 1996—; state med. examiner Ala. Dept. Forensic Scis., Mobile, 1996—; clin. prof. U. Md. Med. Sch., Balt., 1988-90, Vanderbilt U. Med. Ctr., 1990-94. Comdr. USNR, 1985—. Mem. Am. Acad. Forensic Sci., Assn. Mil. Surgeons of U.S., AMA. Home: 352 McDonald Ave Mobile AL 36604 Office: Mobile Med Examiner 2451 Fillingim St Mobile AL 36617

GOODIN, KATE, communications consultant; b. Detroit, July 23, 1956. BA, U. Mich., 1978. Assoc. producer WJBK-TV, Southfield, Mich., 1978-79; reporter WILX-TV, Lansing, Mich., 1979-80, WZZM-TV, Grand Rapids, Mich., 1980-84; freelance producer Southfield, 1984-86; producer MVP Comms., Troy, Mich., 1986-90; pres. Detroit Producers Assn., 1992-93; ptnr. KG Comms., Royal Oaks, Mich., 1990—. Vol. Mich. Humane Soc., Auburn Hills, 1988-94. Mem. Detroit Producers Assn. (bd. dirs. 1990-92, pres. 1992-93), Internat. TV Assn. Office: KG Comms PO Box 1728 Royal Oak MI 48068

GOODING, GRETCHEN ANN WAGNER, physician, educator; b. Columbus, Ohio, July 2, 1935; d. Edward Frederick and Margaret (List) Wagner; m. Charles A. Gooding, June 19, 1961; children: Gunnar Blaise, Justin Mathias, Britta Meghan. BA magna cum laude, St. Mary of the Springs Coll., Columbus, 1957; MD cum laude, Ohio State U., 1961. Diplomate Am. Bd. Diagnostic Radiology. Intern Univ. Hosps., Columbus, 1961-62; rsch. fellow Boston City Hosp., 1962-63, Boston U., 1963-65; with dept. radiology U. Calif., San Francisco, 1975—, assoc. prof. in radiology, 1981-85, prof., vice chmn., 1986—; asst. chief radiology VA Med. Ctr., San Francisco, 1978-87, chief radiology, 1987—, chief ultrasonography, 1975—; chair com. acad. pers. U. Calif., San Francisco, 1993-94; speaker in field. Co-editor Radiologic Clinics of N.Am., 1993—; mem. editorial bd. San Francisco Medicine, 1986-95, Applied Radiology, 1987-89, Current Opinion in Radiology, 1992-93, The Radiologist, 1993—, Emergency Radiology, 1993—; contbr. articles to profl. jours. Fellow Am. Coll. Radiology (mem. commn. on ultrasound 1984-96), Am. Inst. Ultrasound in Medicine (bd. govs. 1981-84, chair convention program 1986-88, Presdl. Recognition award 1984); mem. AMA, San Francisco Med. Soc. (chmn. membership com. 1992-94, bd. dirs. 1996—), RSNA (course com. 1984-88, tech. exhibit com. 1992-96), Bay Area Ultrasound Soc. (pres. 1979-80), Soc. Radiologists Ultrasound (chair membership com. 1991-93), ARRS, AUR, CRS, Calif. Med. Assn., Am. Assn. Women Radiologists (pres. 1984-85, trustee 1991-94), VA Chiefs of Radiology Assn. (pres.-elect, pres. 1994-95), San Francisco Radiological Soc. (pres. 1990-91), Hungarian Radiological Soc. (hon.), Pakistan Radiological Soc. (hon.). Office: VA Med Ctr Radiology Svc 4150 Clement St San Francisco CA 94121-1545

GOODKIN, DEBORAH GAY, internal management consultant; b. Oceanside, N.Y., Dec. 8, 1951; d. Harold and Rose (Mostkoff) G.; m. Glenn Richard; children: Samuel Goodkin Richard, Sarah Goodkin Richard. BA, Syracuse U., 1972; M. Urban Planning, NYU, 1977. Planner, Nassau-Suffolk Planning, Hauppauge, N.Y., 1972; asst. to treas. Nat. Assn. Savs. Banks, N.Y.C., 1973; planning aide Dept. City Planning, N.Y.C., 1973-79; planner, real property mgr. N.Y.C. Bd. Edn., 1979-81, dir. Capital Budget Bur., 1981-85; supervising mgmt. engr. Port Authority N.Y. & N.J., 1985-90, mgr. fin. sys., 1989-96; sr. cons. Tchrs. Ins. Annuity Assn., 1996—; cons. C Corp., L.A., 1983—. Security cons. Dem. Nat. Com., N.Y.C., 1980; founder, pres. Allendale Opportunity and Enrichment Program. Recipient C.F.O. Award of Excellence, 1987, 92. Mem. Women in Govt. (guest lectr. 1983), Syracuse U. Alumni Assn., NYU Alumni Assn. Author: (zoning law) Bay Ridge Zoning Dist., 1978. Artist: Show of Selected Works, Sireuil, France, 1983. Office: Tchrs Ins Annuity Assn 730 3rd Ave New York NY 10017

GOODMAN, BONNIE MICHELLE, marketing executive; b. Phila., June 20, 1959; d. Albert Carl and Evelyn Ruth (Ross) Powell; m. Howard Bruce Goodman, Oct. 27, 1990; 1 child, Jillian Tawna. BA, UCLA, 1981. Rsch. asst. Hill and Knowlton, L.A., 1982, asst. acct. exec., 1982-83, acct. exec., 1983-84, sr. acct. exec., 1984-86, acct. supr., 1986-88, group supr., 1988-90, v.p., 1990-91, sr. v.p., 1991—. Recipient Adweek Spl. Events Mktg. award Adweek, 1989. Mem. Pub. Rels. Soc. Am. (Prism award 1993), Ad Club L.A., Hispanic Pub. Rels. Assn.

GOODMAN, CAROLYN, advertising executive; b. Chatham, Kent, U.K., Dec. 10, 1956; came to U.S., 1983; d. Dudley Cyril Harry and Barbara June (Le Lievre) Francis; m. Peter Earl Goodman, Apr. 15, 1989; 1 child, Robert Francis. BA, Carleton U., Ottawa, Ont., Can., 1977; Diploma of Creative Advertising, Algonquin Coll., Ottawa, 1980. Typesetter, paste-up artist The Ottawa Jour., 1979; copywriter, prodr. Sta. CFCN-TV, Lethbridge, Alta., 1980; account exec. Cockfield Brown, Inc., Calgary, Alta., 1980-83, Chiat/Day Inc., San Francisco, 1983-84; sr. account exec. DDB Needham Inc., San Francisco, 1984-88; v.p., mktg. mgr. 1st Nationwide Bank, San Francisco, 1988-90; v.p., group product mgr. Bank of Am., San Francisco, 1990; v.p., mgmt. supr. Ogilvy & Mather Direct, San Francisco, 1990-92; v.p., acct. dir. Cohn & Wells, San Francisco, 1992-93; sr. v.p., gen. mgr. Cohn & Wells, Toronto, 1994-95; owner, pres. Goodman Direct, San Anselmo, Calif., 1995-96; v.p., gen. mgr. 360 Group, San Rafael, Calif.; cons. b-to-b Bell Can., BC TEL, Cohn & Wells, McCann-Erickson. Office: 360 Group 700 5th Ave San Francisco CA 94109*

GOODMAN, CATHY LEIGH, film producer; b. Suffern, N.Y., Sept. 21, 1959; d. Stanley Goodman and Francine (Moskowitz) Luscher. AAS, SUNY, Suffern, 1979; BS, Pace U., 1980. Asst. prodn. mgr. Rockland Arena, Suffern, N.Y., 1977-80; gen. mgr. HEI Prodns., N.Y.C., 1981-84, Miller Mgmt., L.A., 1984-85; mktg. mgr. Landmark Edn., San Francisco, 1985-89, Ray Tusken & Assocs., Hollywood, Calif., 1989-90; personal exec. asst. Gene Simmons (rock band Kiss), Beverly Hills, 1991-93; dir. ops. The Ministry of Film, L.A., 1993—. Assoc. prodr. (TV series) Erotic Confessions, 1995—, (feature film) Digging to China, 1996; music cons. (cable feature film) The Legend of Gator Face, 1996. Mem. Assn. Celebrity Personal Assts. (bd. dirs. 1993—), Women in Film, Women in Music Bus. Assn. Office: The Ministry of Film 9220 Sunset Blvd #224 Los Angeles CA 90069

GOODMAN, DARLENE EARNHARDT, nursing educator; b. Concord, N.C., Dec. 22, 1953; d. Hugh J. and Juanita J. (Paxton) Earnhardt; div.; 1 child, Aaron Locke. BSN, U. N.C., Charlotte, 1977, postgrad., 1991—. Staff nurse Cabarrus Meml. Hosp., Concord, N.C., 1977-81; nursing instr. sch. of nursing Cabarrus Meml. Hosp., Concord, 1981-84, cert. neonatal resuscitation instr., 1991—; nurse mgr. birthing ste. Lake Norman Regional Hosp., Moorsville, N.C., 1990-91; nursing instr. maternity Louise Harkey Sch. of Nursing, Concord, N.C., 1991—; patient edn. nurse childbirth Lake Norman Regional Hosp., Mooresville, 1990-91; diabetes educator Cabarrus Meml. Hosp., Concord, 1994; advisor Assn. Nursing Students, Cabarrus Meml. Hosp., 1990—. Chmn. United Way Lake Norman Regional Hosp., Mooresville, N.C., 1990, Cabarrus Meml. Hosp., Concord, N.C., 1994. Mem. ANA, N.C. Nurses Assn., Assn. Women's Health, Obstet. and Neonatal Nurses, Sigma Theta Tau (charter Gamma Iota chpt.). Democrat. Presbyterian. Office: Louise Harkey Sch Nursing 431 Copperfield Blvd Concord NC 28025

GOODMAN, ELIZABETH ANN, lawyer; b. Marquette, Mich., Aug. 11, 1950; d. Paul William and Pearl Marie Goodman; m. Herbert Charles Gardner, Sept. 24, 1977. Student, U. Munich, 1970-71; BA cum laude, Alma (Mich.) Coll., 1972; JD cum laude, U. Mich., 1977. Bar: Minn. 1978, Mich. 1978, U.S. Dist. Ct. Minn. 1979. Cert. real property law specialist, real property sect. Minn. Bar Assn. High sch. tchr. Onaway (Mich.) High Sch., 1973-74; assoc. Dorsey and Whitney LLP, Mpls., 1978-82; ptnr. Dorsey and Whitney, Mpls., 1983—. Mem. ABA (natural resource, energy and environ. law sect., real property, probate and trust law sect., vice chair environ. aspects of real estate transactions), Minn. Bar Assn., Hennepin County Bar Assn. Office: Dorsey & Whitney LLP 220 S 6th St Minneapolis MN 55402-4502

GOODMAN, ELLEN, elementary education educator; b. Starkville, Miss., Dec. 27, 1958; d. Arthur Louis Jr. and Grace W. (Henry) G. BS, Miss. State U., 1981, MEd, 1982, 93. Cert. nursery, kindergarten, K-3 elem. tchr., elem. adminstr., Miss. Tchr. kindergarten and remedial reading Magnolia Heights Sch., Senatobia, Miss., 1982-83; tchr. Aiken Village Presch., Mississippi State, Miss., 1983-84, dir., 1984-86; tchr. kindergarten Starkville Sch. Dist., 1986—. Recipient Excellence in Tchg. award Miss. Power Found., 1990, Tchr. of Month award Starkville Exch. Club, 1993, Tchr. of Yr. award Starkville Sch. Dist., 1993. Mem. NAESP, Miss. Early Childhood Assn. (local pres. 1991-92), Pilot Club (pres. 1989-90), Phi Delta Kappa (sec. 1992-94, Outstanding Pub. Sch. Tchr. award 1989), Delta Kappa Gamma (sec. 1994-95). Presbyterian. Home: 2103 Douglas MacArthur Dr Starkville MS 39759 Office: Sudduth Elem Sch 101 Greenfield St Starkville MS 39759-2222

GOODMAN, ELLEN HOLTZ, journalist; b. Newton, Mass., Apr. 11, 1941; d. Jackson Jacob and Edith (Weinstein) Holtz; m. Robert Levey; 1 dau., Katherine Anne. B.A. cum laude, Radcliffe Coll., 1963; hon. degrees, Mt. Holyoke Coll., Amherst Coll., U. Pa., U. N.H. Researcher, reporter Newsweek Mag., 1963-65; feature writer Detroit Free Press, 1965-67; feature writer columnist Boston Globe, 1967-74, assoc. editor, 1986—; syndicated columnist Washington Post Writers Group, 1976—; radio commentator Spectrum, CBS, 1978-80, NBC, 1979-80; commentator NBC Today Show, 1979-81. Author: Close to Home, 1979, Turning Points, 1979, At Large, 1981, Keeping in Touch, 1985, Making Sense, 1989, Value Judgments, 1993. Trustee Radcliffe Coll. Nieman fellow Harvard U., 1974; named New Eng. Newspaper Woman of Year New Eng. Press Assn., 1968; recipient Catherine O'Brien award Stanley Home Products, 1971, Media award Mass. Commn. Status Women, 1974, Columnist of Year award New Eng. Women's Press Assn., 1975, Pulitzer Prize for Commentary, 1980, prize for column writing Am. Soc. Newspaper Editors, 1980, Hubert H. Humphrey Civil Rights award, 1988, William Allen White award 1995. Office: Globe Newspapers Co 135 Morrissey Blvd Dorchester MA 02125-3310

GOODMAN, ERIKA, dancer, actress; b. Phila.; d. A. Allan and Laura (Baylin) G. Student, Sch. of Am. Ballet, 1961-63; BA in Theatre and Dance, Empire State Coll., 1993; master classes, Princeton Ballet, 1994, Hartford Ballet Co., 1995. Mem. faculty Actors and Dirs. Lab., N.Y.C., 1979—; founding mem. ensemble theater co. The Barrow Group, N.Y.C., 1986—; mem. dance faculty CCNY, 1990; mem. dance faculty CCNY, 1990; guest tchr. ballet Balettakademeln, Stockholm, 1986, 89; instr. master classes Rutgers U., East Carolina U., 1989, Hofstra U., U. Kans., 1990, Harvard U., summer 1993, Cornell U., Skidmore Coll., Vassar Coll., 1992—, Conn. Coll.; vis. prof. ballet, head ballet dept. CCNY, 1992—, lectr. world arts, 1993—. Dancer N.Y.C. Ballet Co., 1964-65, prin. dancer Joffrey Ballet, N.Y.C., 1966-75; performer (with Barrow Group) Seymour in the Heart of Winter, Perry St. Theatre, N.Y.C., 1986, When You Comin' Back Red Rider, 1987, Feather Hat, Three Sisters, 1989; casting dir. (films) Hazing in Hell, Neon Red; dir. ballet rehearsal Ballet Hispanico. Richard Porter Leach fellow, 1992-93.

GOODMAN, GAIL SUSAN, psychology educator; b. L.A., Feb. 27, 1949; d. Haskell Gus and Ruth (Marks) G. BA, UCLA, 1970, MA, 1971, PhD, 1977. NICHD postdoctoral fellow U. Denver, 1977-80, postdoctoral rschr., 1981-82, asst. prof., 1982-87, assoc. prof., 1987-88; assoc. prof. SUNY, Buffalo, 1988-91, prof., 1991-92; prof. U. Calif., Davis, 1992—; cons. in field. Editor: Child Victims, Child Witnesses, 1993; contbr. chpts. to books and articles to profl. jours. Grantee in field. Fellow APA (pres. divsn. child, youth and family 1991-92, pres. divsn. psychology and law 1996-97, divsn. Soc. for the Psychol. Study of Social Issues, Robert Chow award), Am. Psychol. Soc.; mem. Am. Profl. Soc. of the Abuse of Children (founding mem., adv. bd., Career Scientist award 1991), Soc. for Rsch. on Child Devel. (chair ethics com. 1995—). Office: Dept Psychology Univ Calif Davis CA 95616

GOODMAN, GERTRUDE AMELIA, civic worker; b. El Paso, Tex., Oct. 24, 1924; d. Karl Perry and Helen Sylvia (Pinkiert) G. BA, Mills Coll., 1945. Pres. El Paso chpt. Tex. Social Welfare Assn., 1963-65, bd. dirs. 1965-70, state bd. dirs., 1965-70; state bd. dirs. Pan-Am. Round Table, El Paso, 1966—, bd. dirs. 1970-71, sec., 1973-74, life mem.; founder, 1st chmn. El Paso Mus. Art Mem. Guild, 1962-68; bd. dirs. Mus. Art Assn., 1962-69, also v.p.; chmn. dir. El Paso C. of C. women's Dept., 1976-77; bd. dirs. Rio Grande Food Bank, 1988-94; bd. dirs. El Paso Pub. Libr., 1972-80, pres. bd. dirs., 1978-80; pres. El Paso County Hist. Soc., 1981-82, bd. dirs., 1986-92; mem. planning com. El Paso United Way, 1953—; mem. El Paso Mus. Art Bd. Coun. Recipient Hall of Honor award El Paso County Hist. Soc., Nat. Human Rels. award NCCJ, 1981, numerous awards for civic vol. work. Home: 905 Cincinnati Ave El Paso TX 79902-2435

GOODMAN, JOAN FRANCES, avionics manufacturing executive; b. N.Y.C., Oct. 25, 1941; d. Jack and Evelyn (Fine) G.; m. Stephen Gordon Glatzer, Oct. 2, 1982 (dec. Dec. 1987). BS, Alfred U., 1963; MA, NYU, 1967. RN, N.Y. Psychiatric liaison nurse Hosp. Albert Einstein Coll. Medicine, N.Y.C., 1968-73; nursing care coord. United Hosp., Port Chester, N.Y., 1974-80; asst. to pres. Glatzer Industries, New Rochelle, N.Y., 1980-87; pres., chief exec. officer Glatzer Industries Corp., New Rochelle, 1987—, Emergency Beacon Corp., New Rochelle, 1987—, ELTS Ltd., Inc., New Rochelle, 1987—. Mem. ANA, Nat. League Nursing, Chief Exec. Network (Westchester and Rockland County chpts.), Westchester Assn. Women Bus. Owners, Am. Women's Econ. Corp., Nat. Coun. Women in Aviation, Women in Aviation Internat. Office: Glatzer Industries Corp 15 River St New Rochelle NY 10801-4351

GOODMAN, KAREN LACERTE, financial services executive; b. Mesa, Ariz., Nov. 9, 1946; d. Howard Lee and Margaret (Duncan) G.; m. Grant A. Lacerte, Feb. 1, 1964; children: Arthur Grant Jr., Arcel Leon Rene. Student, George Washington U., 1974-76. Prodn. mgr. Data Corp. of Am., Reston, Va., 1967-73; pres. Transco Leasing Co., Washington, 1974-78; sec., treas. to v.p. Certa Data Corp., Orlando, Fla., 1989—; pres. Fin. Rsch. Assocs., Inc., Orlando, 1979—; cons. in field, 1979—; dir. statis. seminars in field. Editor, pub.: Financial Studies of the Small Business (annual publ.), 1976—. Mem. Am. Heart Assn., Winter Haven, Fla., MADD, 1985—. Mem. Greater Orlando C. of C. Republican. Home: 6759 Winterset Gardens Rd Winter Haven FL 33884-3154 Office: Financial Rsch Assocs 510 Avenue J SE Winter Haven FL 33880-3781

GOODMAN, MARGARET GERTRUDE, government administrator; b. East Troy, Wis., Aug. 29, 1947; d. Andrew J. and Florence M. (Zinn) G.; 1 child, Mary Zinn. BA, Beloit Coll., 1969; MA, Johns Hopkins U., 1971. Legis. asst. to Rep. Clement J. Zablocki Ho. of Reps., Washington, 1971-73, staff cons. Com. Fgn. Affairs, 1977-93; fgn. policy analyst Congl. Rsch. Svc., Libr. Congress, Washington, 1973-77; regional dir. for Asia and Pacific Peace Corps, Washington, 1993—. Mem. Soc. Internat. Devel. (pres. Washington chpt. 1982-84, internat. v.p. 1988-91), Women in Fgn. Policy Assn., Asia Soc. Democrat. Office: Peace Corps 1990 K St NW Rm 7616 Washington DC 20526-0001

GOODMAN, MYRNA MARCIA, school nurse; b. Bklyn., Mar. 5, 1936; d. Louis and Anna R. (Bernowitz) Sheinberg; m. Stanley M. Goodman, June 30, 1957; children: Farrell Jay, Blayne Barrie, Devin Josh, Danica Janine. Diploma, L.I. Coll. Hosp., Bklyn., 1956; B in Elected Studies, Thomas More Coll., 1980; postgrad., Xavier U., 1984-86. Cert. sch. nurse, Ohio. Sch. nurse, supr. health and wellness svcs. L.I. Coll. Hosp., 1956-58; nurse, office mgr. Pediatric Assocs. of Fairfield (Ohio), Inc., 1962-72; nurse Fairfield City Sch. Dist., 1972-89, dir. health svcs., 1989-92, supr. health and wellness svcs., 1992—, sch. nurse Kindergarten Ctr., 1995; sch. nurse Kindergarten Ctr.; sec. Fairfield City Safety Coun., 1987-90; mem. Intervention Team for At-Risk Students, 1987-90, 95-96, Del. to Study Sch. Health, Australia, 1989; keynote spkr. Ohio Comprehensive Sch. Health Conf., 1991; conf. spkr. Ohio Assn. Health, Phys. Edn., Recreation and Dance, 1990, Nat. Sch. Bds. Assn., 1993. Mem. adv. coun. on drug free schs. and cmty. Butler County Mental Health Assn., 1988; chmn. sch. site com. Am. Heart Assn., 1981, coord. heart-at-work program; chmn. employee wellness com., spkr. del. assembly Ohio affiliate, 1992, pres., 1995, co-pres. Hamilton-Fairfield div., 1995, mem. adv. com. for county practical nurse program, 1994-95; pres. Fairfield Tempo Club, 1976; com. mem. Fairfield Sister City Program; mem. Modern Music Masters, 1976; mem. adv. coun. Daytime Ctr. for Girls; bd. dirs. Greater Hamilton Safety Coun., 1988; mem. adv. com. Fairfield Pub. Presch.; chmn. adv. com. Fairfield Schs. Food Svc. Recipient Outstanding Svc. award Fairfield Cen. Sch., 1974, 77, 78, 89, Letters of Recognition for Outstanding Svc. to Fairfield Sch. Dist. Supt., 1980, 86, 89, 90, March of Dimes, Am. Lung Assn., 1980, Am. Heart Assn., 1988, 89, 90, Hall of Fame award Am. Heart Assn., 1992, co-recipient Cert. of Appreciation, Am. Heart Assn. Sch. Site Task Force, 1992. Mem. NEA, ASCD, Ohio Edn. Assn., Ohio Assn. Sch. Nurses (conf. speaker 1993), S.W. Ohio Sch. Nurses Assn. (sec. 1987-90), Am. Sch. Health Assn., Nat. Assn. Sch. Nurses, Parents and Tchrs. for Children, Ohio Assn. Secondary Sch. Adminstrs., Nat. Assn. Secondary Sch. Adminstrs. Home: 5180 Suwannee Dr Fairfield OH 45014-2482 Office: Fairfield City Sch Dist 211 Donald Dr Fairfield OH 45014-3006

GOODMAN, NANCY JANE, small business owner; b. Monett, Mo., May 9, 1946; d. William F. and Audie L. (Stolle; m. Douglas L. Goodman, May 9, 1969; children: Kelly, Gregory, Kristi, Anthony, Richard. Student, Drury Coll., Springfield, Mo., 1969-70, Crowder Coll., Neosho, Mo., 1991-93. Lic. real estate salesperson, Mo., notary public. Supr. Family Svcs., Aurora, Mo., 1972-87; exec. sec. Little Tikes Toy Co., Aurora, 1987-90, buyer, 1990—; pres., owner DJ's Catering, Aurora, 1991—. Author: South American Travel, 1985. Area rep. Am. Intercultural Students, Aurora, 1989—. Named to Outstanding Young Women of Am., 1984. Mem. NAFE, Am. Purchasing Soc., Optimist Club (charter pres., lt. gov. Western Mo. dist. 1996—), Phi Theta Kappa. Home: 519 W College St Aurora MO 65605-2833

GOODMAN, PEGGY JOYCE, early childhood educator, author; b. Lawton, Okla., Oct. 28, 1939; d. Orvell Hoyett and Myrtle Marie (Graham) Currey; m. Lanny Joe Goodman, June 18, 1966; children: Kelley Goodman Peacock, Kevin Bryan, Kyle Currey. BME, Abilene Christian U., 1961; MEd, Tex. Woman's U., 1977, EdD, 1990. Cert. in all level music edn., elem. edn., mid-mgmt. adminstrn. Elem. music eductor Lawton Pubs. Schs., 1961-63; early childhood music specialist Dallas Pub. Schs., 1963-67, 70-71, 75—, curriculum writer, 1985-86, chpt. I music supr., 1992; elem. music educator Irving (Tex.) Pubs. Schs., 1967-70; adj. prof. Tex. Woman's U., Denton, 1990, 94. Contbg. author: Young Children: An Introduction to Early Childhood, 1986. Recipient Golden Oak award Oak Cliff Jaycees, 1981, Jack Lowe award, 1980. Republican. Mem. Ch. of Christ. Office: Dallas Pub Schs Phyllis Wheatley Campus 2908 Metropolitan Ave Dallas TX 75215

GOODMAN, PHYLLIS L., public relations executive; b. N.Y.C., Sept. 7, 1946; d. Bernard Jacob and Claire (Rosenberg) Goodman. BS, Cornell U., 1967. Ext. home economist Nassau County Ext. Svc., Mineola, N.Y., 1967-68; editl. asst. Funk & Wagnalls, N.Y.C., 1968-69; sr. v.p. Glick & Lorwin, Inc., N.Y.C., 1969-80, Sci. and Medicine, N.Y.C., 1980-82; v.p. Hill and Knowlton, Inc., N.Y.C., 1982-85; assoc. v.p. comm. and pub. affairs St. Luke's-Roosevelt Hosp. Ctr., N.Y.C., 1985-92; owner Goodman Berry Pub. Rels., Albuquerque, 1993-95; v.p. corp. comm. Sun Healthcare Group, Inc., Albuquerque, 1995—; mem. com. pub. affairs Greater N.Y. Hosp. Assn., 1988-92. Mem. Am. Soc. Health Care Mktg. and Pub. Rels. (treas. N.Mex. chpt. 1993-94), Pub. Rels. Soc. Am. (accredited, pres. N.Mex. chpt. 1996), Healthcare Pub. Rels. and Mktg. Soc. Greater N.Y. (pres. 1990-91), Westside C. of C. N.Y.C. (bd. dirs. 1986-92), Pi Lambda Theta. Office: Sun Healthcare Group Inc 101 Sun Ln NE Albuquerque NM 87109-4367

GOODMAN, VALERIE DAWSON, psychiatric social worker; b. Bluefield, W.Va., Feb. 2, 1948; d. Francis Carl and Lesly (Collett) Dawson; m. David William Goodman, June 9, 1985; 1 child, Amanda Lynn. BS, W.Va. U., 1970, MS, 1972; MSW, U. Md., 1980. Lic. clin. social worker, Md. Social worker Md. Children's Aide Family Svcs. Soc., Balt., 1972-78; social worker III Montgomery County Dept. Social Svcs., Rockville, Md., 1980-81; clin. social worker Johns Hopkins Hosp., Balt., 1981-83; pvt. practice Suburban Psychiat. Assoc. Hopkins at Greenspring Station, Balt., 1986—; supr. Johns Hopkins Hosp., 1983-86, chair Brogden com., 1984-85, spl. events com. depression and related affective disorders dept. psychiatry, 1994; spkr. in field. Parent vol. Park Sch. Mem. Kappa Delta. Home: 54 Bellchase Ct Pikesville MD 21208-1300 Office: Suburban Psychiat Svc Md Adult Ctr ADD Johns Hopkins at Greenspring Sta Falls Concourse Falls Rd Ste 306 Lutherville MD 21093

GOODMAN, YETTA M., secondary education educator; b. Cleve., Mar. 10, 1931; d. William and Dora (Shapiro) Trachtman; B.A. in History, Los Angeles State Coll., 1952, M.A. in Elem. Edn., 1956; Ed.D. in Curriculum Devel., Wayne State U., 1967; m. Kenneth S. Goodman, 1952; children: Debra, Karen, Wendy. Elem. and secondary tchr., public schs., Los Angeles, 1952-63; supr. pre-service teaching experiences Wayne State U., 1963-67; asst. to prof. U. Mich., Dearborn, 1967-75; prof. edn., co-dir. program in lang. and literacy U. Ariz., 1975—; regents prof., U. Ariz., 1990—; speaker, cons. lang. and lit. devel. Active in orgns. concerned with censorship and children's rights. Recipient Faculty Recognition award Tucson Trade Bur., 1978, Outstanding Tchr. Educator of Reading award Internat. Reading Assn., 1983. Mem. Nat. Council Tchrs. English (bd. dirs. 1976—, pres. 1978-79, Disting. Svc. award 1994), Center Expansion of Lang. and Thinking (bd. dirs. 1972—, pres. 1976-79), Internat. Reading Assn. (chairperson and active mem. various coms. 1962—, bd. dirs. 1994—, elected into Reading Hall Fame 1994), Internat. Assn. Supervision and Curriculum Devel., Am. Ednl. Rsch. Assn., Assn. Childhood Edn. Internat. (bd. dirs. internat. centre for study literacy processes 1988—). Jewish. Author: How Children Construct Literacy: Piagetian Perspectives, 1990; (with C. Burke and B. Sherman) Reading Strategies: Focus on Comprehension, 1981; (with D. Watson and C. Burke) Reading Miscue Inventory: Alternate Procedures, 1986, (with K. Goodman and Wendy Hood) The Whole Language Evaluation, 1989, Organizing for Whole Language, 1991; (with K. Goodman and L. Bird) The Whole Language Catalogue, 1991; (with S. Wilde) Literacy Events in a Community of Young Writers, 1992, (with K. Goodman and L. Bird) The Whole Language Catalogue: Supplement on Authentic Assessment, 1992, The Language Catalogue: Forms for Authentic Assessment, 1994 (with Ann M. Marek) Retrospective Miscue Analysis Revaluing Readers and Reading, 1996; contbr. numerous articles, chpts. to profl. publs.; also audio tapes scripts video, films. Home: 5649 E 10th St Tucson AZ 85711-3268 Office: U Ariz Coll Edn Program in Lang and Literacy Tucson AZ 85721

GOODSON, CAROL FAYE, librarian; b. Detroit, Mar. 28, 1947; d. Norman Elwood and Wilma Mary (Harmon) G.; m. Lawrence J. Price, May 10, 1974 (div. 1977). BA, SUNY, Buffalo, 1970, MLS, 1972; MA, West Ga. Coll., 1996. Libr. SUNY, Buffalo, 1970-72, St. Louis Pub. Libr., 1973-77; community sch. dir. St. Louis Bd. Edn., 1977-80; reference libr. Ga. Dept. Edn., Atlanta, 1981-84; head pub. svcs. Atlanta campus Mercer U., Chamblee, Ga., 1985; mem. Dominican Sisters of Nashville, 1985-90; asst. dir. Clayton County Libr. System, Jonesboro, Ga., 1990-91; coord. off-campus libr. svcs. West Ga. Coll., Carrollton, 1991—; state coord. Ga. Summer Reading Club, 1991; owner and moderator, ALA-PLAN listserv., FISC-L listserv and WOODY-L listserv. Editor GA Conf., AAUP Summary. Pres. Tower/Literacy Vols. Am., Clayton County, 1991; active Leadership, 1990-91. Mem. AAUP (exec. com. 1994—, editor Ga. newsletter 1996—), ALA, Ga. Libr. Assn., Southeastern Libr. Assn., Libr. Info. Tech. Assn., (program planning com. 1992—, sec. 1993—), Assn. Coll. Rsch. Librs. (clip notes com. 1992—, extended campus libr. svcs. sect., comm. com. 1994—), Beta Phi Mu, Phi Kappa Phi, Omicron Delta Kappa, Sigma Tau Delta. Home: 210 Oak Ave Carrollton GA 30117-3726 Office: West Ga Coll Ingram Libr Carrollton GA 30118

GOODSON, SHANNON LORAYN, behavioral scientist, author; b. Beaumont, Tex., May 26, 1952; d. James Ernest and Lorayn (Miller) G. BS in Psychology, Lamar U., 1974, MS in Organizational Psychology, 1977. Co-founder, pres., CEO Behavioral Scis. Rsch. Press, Inc., Dallas, 1979-92, pres., 1992—; presenter in field; guest on various radio talk shows. Co-author: (with G.W. Dudley) Earning What You're Worth?, 1992, Psychology of Call Reluctance, 1986; contbr. articles to profl. jours. and periodicals. Mem. SE Psychol. Assn. Office: Behavioral Scis Rsch Press 12803 Demetra Dr Ste 100 Dallas TX 75234-6101

GOODSON, STEPHANIE LEE, medical illustrator; b. Kansas City, Mo., Aug. 15, 1969; d. Richard Lee and Rita (Corona) G. BFA, Columbus Coll., 1992; MS, Med. Coll. Ga., 1996. Tchr. Columbus (Ohio) Coll. Art and Design, 1991-94; intern Eisenhower Army Med. Ctr., Augusta, Ga., 1995—. Artistic contbr.: Kansas City, Kansas Architecture: A Gift to the Future, 1989, Society of Illustrators, Illustrators 32, 1990, (calenders) Sumner Academy of Arts and Science, 1986, 87. Rsch. grantee Vesalius Trust, 1996; scholar to Columbus Coll. Art and Design, Nat. Scholastics Competition, Kansas City, 1987, Retail Advt. scholar Columbus Coll. Art and Design, 1988, Illutration scholar Columbus Coll. Art and Design, 1989, Arthur and Sarah J. Kobacker scholar Columbus Coll. Art and Design, 1991. Mem. Assn. Med. Illustrators.

GOODSPEED, BARBARA, artist; b. Gardner, Mass., Sept. 1, 1919; d. George Daniel and Bernice (Lucas) G. Diploma Stoneleigh Coll., 1939, Famous Artist Schs., Westport, Conn., 1955. Free-lance photographer, N.Y.C., 1941-52, Christmas card designer, Sherman, Conn., 1952-69, oil and watercolor, fine arts artist, Sherman, 1969—. Illustrator: Forever Flowers, 1979. Recipient Merit award Sheffield Art League, 1979, 81, 83, others; named Artist of Yr., Art League of Harlem Valley, 1981. Fellow Am. Artists Profl. League (John Dole Meml. award, Parsons award 1991); mem. Salmagundi Club(Jane Peterson Meml. award), Hudson Valley Art Assn., Acad. Artists, Nat League Am. Pen Women, Kent Art Assn., Inc. (pres. 1970-72, 80-83, 85-88, 91-93, medal of Merit 1979, Grumbacher Gold medal 1989, 91, K.A.A. award, 1995), Housatonic Art League (v.p., bd. dirs. 1977-83), Catharine Lorillard Wolfe Art Club (bd. dirs. 1990-93, travel show 1996, Corp. award). Avocations: camping, crafts. Home and Studio: 11 Holiday Point Rd Sherman CT 06784-1624

GOODSTADT, SUZANNE LOUISE, artist; b. Boston, Nov. 28, 1950. Degree in fine arts, Accademia DiBelle Arti, Florence, Italy; degree in fashion design, Garland Jr. Coll., Boston; student, Mus. Fine Arts, Boston, Mass. Coll. Art, Boston, Sch. Visual Arts, N.Y.C., Art Students League, N.Y.C. Owner gallery Suzanne's Gallery, N.Y.C.; instr. Fairleigh Dickinson U., Guggenheim Mus., 1985; fine art cons. Dyansen Gallery, N.Y., 1985, Boston Mus. of Sci., 1988, Brodney Gallery of Fine Arts, Boston, 1988-90; promotion cons. Manhattan Theater Club, 1985; art dealer European artists; art cons. TV, Channel D, 1980, Lee Ansel, 1980. Exhibited in group shows at Palazzo Strozzi Il Centro D'Incontro Per Stranieri, Florence, 1971, Mus. of Fine Arts, Boston, Mass. Coll. of Art, Boston.

GOODSTEIN, LAURIE BETH, journalist; b. N.Y.C., June 25, 1960; d. Daniel Victor and Joan G. (Waxgiser) G.; m. Peter Grand, June 19, 1993; 1 child, Gabriel. BA, U. Calif. Berkeley, 1984; MFA, Columbia U., 1989. Editl. asst. The Washington Post, 1989-93, staff writer, 1993—; judge Leslie Sander Social Justice Awards, N.Y.C., 1989—. Named John Templeton Religion Reporter of Yr. Religion Newswriters Assn., 1995, Supple Religion Newswriter of Yr., 1995. Jewish. Office: The Washington Post 1150 15th St NW Washington DC 20071

GOODSTEIN-SHAPIRO, FLORENCE (FLORENCE GOODSTEIN WALTON), artist, art historian; b. N.Y.C., July 22, 1931; d. Philip and Cecelia (Pletchnow) Goodstein; m. Ivan Shapiro, June 24, 1951 (div. Jan. 1957); 1 child, Lisa Jean Shapiro; m. John A. Walton, Sept. 30, 1968. BS, CCNY, 1952; student, Cooper Union Inst., N.Y.C., 1950-52, Hans Hofmann Sch. Fine Arts, N.Y.C., 1956-58, U. Calif., Long Beach, 1970-71; MA in Art History, U. Minn., 1973. Asst. prof. art history Lakewood Coll., White Bear Lake, Minn., 1971-72; lectr. art history Mpls. Inst. Art, 1973-74; bd. dirs. Banfill-Locke Cmty. Art Ctr., Fridley, Minn., 1981. Exhibited in shows at Roko Gallery, N.Y.C., 1962, Smithsonian Inst., Washington, 1963, Aspects Gallery, N.Y.C., 1964, Loeb Gallery/NYU, 1966, Los Angeles County Art Mus., 1969, Bonython Gallery, Sudney, Australia, 1969, Peter M. David Gallery, Mpls., 1985, 91, Artbanque, Mpls., 1986, Coll. St. Catherine, St. Paul, 1988, McGallery, Mpls., 1994; represented in collections at 3M Co., St. Paul, U. Minn. Mus., Martin Luther King Jr. Mus., Atlanta, Fairview Southdale Hosp., Mpls., Ctrl. Lakes C.C., Brainerd, Minn., others. Mem. Cooper Union Alumni Assn. Democrat. Jewish. Office: Goodstein-Shapiro Studio 8066 Ruth St NE Fridley MN 55432

GOODWIN, BARBARA A., retired nurse, military officer; b. Phila., Dec. 23, 1938. Diploma, Boston City Hosp. Sch. Nursing, 1959; BS, U. Pa., 1968; MS, U. Colo., 1972; grad., Sq. Officer Sch., 1973, Air Command & Staff Coll., 1974, Air War Coll., 1977. Commd. officer USAF, advanced through ranks to brig. gen., 1988, nurse, 1962—; staff nurse USAF, Otis AFB, Mass.; clinic nurse USAF Clinic, Naha Air Base, Okinawa, Japan, 1963-65; clinic staff nurse USAF Hosp., Minot AFB, N.D., from 1965; flight nurse Aeromed. Evacuation Squadron, Rhein-Mein AFB, Frankfurt, Fed. Republic Germany, 1968-71; charge nurse med. unit USAF Med. Ctr., Scott AFB, Ill., 1972-73; clin. nurse specialist Malcolm Grow USAF Med. Ctr., Andrews AFB, Md., 1973-74, surg. nursing practice coord., from 1974; asst. chief nurse USAF Regional Hosp., Lakenheath, Eng., 1974-76; adminstrv. staff officer Office of Chief Air Force Nurse Corps, Bolling AFB, D.C., 1979-83; chmn. dept. nursing David Grant USAF Med. Ctr., Travis AFB, Calif., 1983-84; asst. for nursing svcs. Hdqrs. Mil. Airlift Command, USAF Med. Ctr., Scott AFB, Ill., 1984-88; chief USAF Nurse Corps, Office Surgeon Gen., USAF Hdqrs., Washington, 1988-91; ret., 1991. Decorated D.S.M., Legion of Merit with one oak leaf cluster. Mem. ANA, Aerospace Med. Assn., Assn. Mil. Surgeons of USAF Assn., Bus. and Profl. Women., Sigma Theta Tau.

GOODWIN, DORIS HELEN KEARNS, history educator, writer; b. Rockville Centre, N.Y., Jan. 4, 1943; d. Michael Aloisius and Helen Witt (Miller) Kearns; m. Richard Goodwin, 1975; three sons. BA magna cum laude, Colby Coll., 1964; PhD, Harvard U., 1968. Intern Dept. State, D.C., 1963, Ho. of Reps., D.C., 1965; rsch. assoc. U.S. Dept. Health, Edn., and Welfare, D.C., 1966; spl. asst. to Willard Wirtz U.S. Dept. Labor, D.C., 1967; spl. asst. to President Lyndon B. Johnson, 1968; asst. prof. Harvard U., Cambridge, 1969-71, assoc. prof. govt., 1972; spl. cons. to President Johnson, 1969-73; asst. dir. Inst. Politics, 1971—; hostess "What's the Big Idea", WGBH-TV, Boston, 1972; polit. analyst news desk, WBZ-TV, Boston, 1972; mem. Women's Polit. Caucus, Mass., 1972, Faculty Coun. Harvard U., 1971, Dem. Party Platform Com., 1972; trustee Wesleyan U., Colby Coll., Robert F. Kennedy Found. Author: Lyndon Johnson and the American Dream, 1976, The Fitzgeralds and the Kennedys: An American Saga, 1987, No Ordinary Time: Franklin and Eleanor Roosevelt-The Homefront in World War II, 1994 (Pulitzer Prize for history 1995); contbr.: Telling Lives: The Biographer's Art, 1979; forward: Mortal Friends: A Novel, 1992. Named Fulbright fellow, 1966, White House fellow, 1967. Mem. Am. Polit. Sci. Assn., Coun. Fgn. Relations, Women Involved, Group for Applied Psychoanalysis, Signet Soc., Phi Beta Kappa (outstanding young women of yr. award 1966), Phi Sigma Iota. Roman Catholic. Office: c/o Dori Lawson 307 Main St Concord MA 01742*

GOODWIN, JEAN MCCLUNG, psychiatrist; b. Pueblo, Colo., Mar. 28, 1946; d. Paul Stanley and Geraldine (Smart) McClung; m. James Simeon Goodwin, Aug. 8, 1970; children: Laura (dec.), Amanda Harding Goodwin, Robert Caleb, Paul Joshua, Elizabeth Cronin Goodwin. BA in Anthropology summa cum laude, Radcliffe Coll., 1967; MD, Harvard U., 1971; MPH, UCLA, 1972. Diplomate Am. Bd. Psychiatry and Neurology, Am. Bd. Forensic Psychiatry. Resident in psychiatry Georgetown U. Hosp., Washington, 1972-74; resident in psychiatry U. N.Mex. Sch. Medicine, 1974-76, asst. dir., dir. psychiat. residents tng., 1979-85; prof. Med. Coll. Wis., 1985-92, U. Tex. Med. Br., Galveston, 1992—; from inst. to assoc. prof. dept. psychiatry U. N.Mex. Sch. Medicine, 1976-85; cons. protective services Dept. Human Services, N.Mex., 1976-84; lectr. profl. groups. Author: Effects of High Altitude on Human Birth, 1969, Sexual Abuse: Incest Victims and Their Families, 1982, 2d edit., 1989, Redisovering Childhood Trauma: Historical Casebook and Clinical Applications, 1993, Mischief and Mercy, 1993; mem. editl. bd. Jour. Traumatic Stress, 1985-93, Dissociation, 1988—; contbr. numerous articles on child abuse to profl. jours. Chmn. work group on child sexual abuse Surgeon Gen.'s Conference on Violence and Pub. Health, Leesburg, Va., 1985; mem. adv. bd. Nat. Resource Ctr. on Child Sexual Abuse, 1989-96. Recipient Saville Prize in Family Planning, UCLA Sch. Pub. Health, 1972, Esther Haar award Am. Acad. Psychoanalysis, 1990, Cornelia Wilbur award Internat. Soc. for Study of Dissociation, 1994; Nat. Cen. Child Abuse and Neglect grantee, 1979-82, Nat. Inst. Aging grantee, 1980-85. Fellow Internat. Soc. Study Dissociation (exec. com. 1991-96), Am. Psychiat. Assn. (dist. br. treas., sec. N.Mex. br. 1980-82, exhibits and programs subcoms. 1985-91); mem. Am. Profl. Soc. on Sexual Abuse in Children (bd. dirs. 1986-90), Am. Med. Women's Assn. (state dir. N.Mex. 1978-80). Democrat. Roman Catholic. Office: U Tex Med Br Dept Psychiatry and Behavioral Sci Galveston TX 77555

GOODWIN, MARY CHRISTINE, art history educator; m. Scott George Lemley, Dec. 16, 1989; children: Sean, Sierra. BA, U. Calif., Santa Cruz, 1975; MA, Boston U., 1977, PhD, 1990. Instr. U. Alaska, Anchorage and Fairbanks, 1985-90; asst. prof. art history Calif. State U., San Bernardino, 1991—. Home: PO Box 2558 Wrightwood CA 92397-2558 Office: Calif State U Art Dept 5500 University Pky San Bernardino CA 92407

GOODWIN, MARYELLEN, state legislator; b. Providence, Sept. 27, 1964. Student, R.I. Coll. mem. 12th Ward Dem. Com., R.I. Young Dems. Mem. state senate State of R.I., 1986—. Roman Catholic. Home: 325 Smith St Providence RI 02908-3759 Office: RI State Senate State House Rm 318 Providence RI 02903*

GOODWIN, NANCY LEE, corporate executive; b. Peoria, Ill., Aug. 11, 1940; d. Raymond Darrell and Mildred Louise (Brown) G. B.A. (Nat. Meth. scholar, Nat. Merit scholar), MacMurray Coll., 1961; M.A., U. Colo., 1963; Ph.D., U. Ill., 1971. Tchr. Roosevelt Jr. High Sch., Peoria, 1961-62; counselor U. Ill., Urbana, 1963-66; staff assoc., asst. prof. edn. measurement U. Ill., Chgo., 1967-71; asst. v.p., assoc. prof. stats. Fla. Internat. U., Miami, 1971-78; pres. Greenfield (Mass.) Community Coll., 1978-82, Arapahoe Community Coll., Colo., from 1982; corp. owner MTF Enterprises; prof. Nat. U.; owner C.A.T.S. Inc., 1987—; corp. mgr. DRM Enterprises; dir. Cons. Mid-Am. Computer Corp., First Chance Network U.S. Office Edn., 1972-78. Mem. Com. on Ill. Govt., Higher Edn. Task Force; mem. Vol. Action Center, Miami, 1972-78; active Girl Scouts U.S.A.; mem. Franklin/Hampshire Area Service Planning Team, 1978; incorporator Franklin County (Mass.) United Way, Farren Meml. Hosp.; adv. Franklin County Public Hosp.; bd. dirs. Women's Inst. Fla., Franklin County Arts Council, Franklin County Devel. Corp., Western Welcome Week, Inc.; bd. dirs., mem. fin. monitoring com. New Eng. Soy Dairy, 1980. Recipient Merit award Chgo. Tchrs. Assn., 1969; citation Girl Scouts U.S.A., 1973. Mem. NEA, Am. Assn. Higher Edn., Am. Ednl. Research Assn., Assn. Instl. Research, Centennial C. of C. (dir. 1983). Home: 5228 Del Rey Ave Las Vegas NV 89102-1414

GOODWIN, SHARON ANN, academic administrator; b. Little Rock, May 19, 1949; d. Jimmy Lee and Eddie DeLois (Cluck) G.; m. Mitchell Shayne Mick, May 4, 1968 (div. Mar. 1973); 1 child, Heather Michelle; m. Raymond Eugene Vaclavik, June 24, 1974 (div. Aug. 1982); 1 child, Tasha Rae Vaclavik. BA in Psychology, U. Houston-Clear Lake, 1980; MEd in Higher Edn. Adminstrn., U. Houston, 1990. Various clerical positions Gen. Telephone Co., Dickinson, Tex., 1969-80; state dir. Challenge, Inc., Oklahoma City, 1980-82; gen. mgr. Mr. Fix It, Houston, 1982-85; assoc. dir. admissions U. Houston, Tex., 1985-92; adminstr. Inst. for the Med. Humanities U. Tex. Med. Br., Galveston, 1992—. Mem. legis. com. Comm. Workers, Dickinson and Austin, 1975; mem. centennial choir U. Tex. Med. Br., Galveston, 1992, 95; vol. Dickens on the Strand, Galveston, 1993—. Recipient Honorable Mention, World of Poetry, 1986, Golden Poet award World of Poetry, 1987. Mem. AAUW, Assn. of Am. Med. Colls.-Group on Institutional Planning. Home: PO Box 517 League City TX 77574-0517 Office: Univ Tex Med Br Inst for the Med Humanities 301 University Blvd Galveston TX 77555-1311

GOODWIN, S(HEILA) DIANE, drug information scientist; b. Durham, N.C., Jan. 19, 1958; d. Leon Jackson and Mattie (Wilson) G. BS in Pharmacy, U. N.C., 1981; PharmD, Med. Coll. Va., 1986. Registered pharmacist, N.C., Va., Colo. Staff pharmacist Durham (N.C.) County Gen. Hosp., 1981-84; asst. prof. U. Fla. Coll. Pharmacy, Gainesville, 1988-89; clin. rsch. pharmacist Duke U. Med. Ctr., Ctr. AIDS Rsch., Durham, 1990-91; asst. prof. U. Colo., Sch. Pharmacy, Denver, 1991-94; drug info. sci. Burroughs Wellcome Co., Research Triangle Park, N.C., 1994-95; mgr. HIV/herpes program devel. Care Mgmt. divsn. Glaxo Wellcome, Inc., Research Triangle Park, 1995—; cons., reviewer, researcher, lectr. in field. Contbr. articles to profl. and sci. jours. Clin. pharmacy fellow Duke U. Med. Ctr., 1986-87, Millard Fillmore Hosp., 1987-88. Mem. Am. Coll. Clin. Pharmacy (chmn. pub. and profl. rels. com. 1991-92, Schering rsch. grantee 1990, chmn. pubs. com. 1996), Am. Soc. Health Sys. Pharmacists, Am. Soc. Microbiology, Soc. Infectious Diseases Pharmacists, Am. Pharm. Assn., Am. Soc. Clin. Pharmacology and Therapeutics, Kappa Epsilon, Rho Chi. Democrat. Baptist. Office: Glaxo Wellcome Inc 5 Moore Dr Research Triangle Park NC 27709

GOODYEAR, JULIE ANN, marketing and fundraising specialist; b. Lafayette, Ind., Dec. 10, 1956; d. Charles Robert and Leona Mae (Widmer) Stroop; m. Michael Clark Goodyear, May 31, 1986; children: Elizabeth, Katharine, (twins) Charles and David. BA, Purdue U., 1983; MA, U. N.D., 1985. Asst. mktg. dir. Mo. Repertory Theater, Kansas City, 1985-88; dir. mkg. and pub. rels. Northlight Theater, Chgo., 1988-91; membership mgr. Chgo. Bot. Gardens, Glencoe, Ill., 1991-92; mgr. rel. mktg. Evanston (Ill.) Hosp. Corp., 1992-93, sr. devel. officer, 1993—. Active Dawes Elem. Sch. PTA, Evanston, 1992—; pres. Ctrl. Evanston ChildCare Parents Bd., 1993-94. Design winner for poster Saks 5th Ave., 1986. Mem. Nat. Soc. Fundraising Execs., Assn. Healthcare Philanthropy, Jr. League of Evanston-North Shore. Home: 1804 Cleveland St Evanston IL 60202

GOOGINS, LOUISE PAULSON, financial planner; b. Iola, Wis., June 14, 1941; d. Walter August and Helen Veronica (Waldoch) Paulson; m. James R. Googins, June 19, 1965 (div. 1978); children: Michael James, Shane Paul. BS, Stevens Point State U., 1963; MA, U. Wis., 1976, Coll. Fin. Planning, Denver, 1984. Recreational therapist Cen. Wis. Colony, Madison, Wis., 1966-69; tchr. mentally retarded Madison Schs., Madison, 1969-71; supr. student tchrs. U. Wis., Madison, 1972-76; tchr. learning disabled Monona, Wis., 1976-78; rep. FPC Secs. & Charter Securities, Madison, 1978-83; prin., pres. Googins & Co. Inc., Madison, 1983—. Bd. dirs. REBOS House, Madison, 1982-95, pres. 1987-90. Mem. Inst. CFPs, Madison South Rotary (bd. dirs. 1993—, sgt. at arms 1990-91, pres.-elect 1995-96). Office: Googins & Co Inc 437 S Yellowstone Dr Madison WI 53719-1096

GOOGINS, SONYA FORBES, state legislator, retired banker; b. New Haven, Nov. 9, 1936; d. Edward and Madeline Forbes; m. Robert Reville Googins, June 21, 1958; children: Shawn W. and Glen. R. BE, U. Conn., 1958; postgrad., Dartmouth Inst., 1978. Tchr. Manchester (Conn.) High Sch., 1958-61; pres. Colonial Printing Co., Glastonbury, 1971-76; br. mgr., bank officer Conn. Nat. Bank, Hartford, 1982-89; mem. Conn. Ho. of Reps., 1994—. Mayor, Town of Glastonbury, 1983-85, 87-91, 93-95; mem. Town Coun., 1979-94; mem. Rep. Town Com.; mem. Capitol Region Coun. Govts., 1983-91, chmn., 1989-94; chmn. govt. divsn. Great Hartford United Way, 1992; bd. dirs. Conn. Capitol Region Growth Coun., 1992—; active Adv. Commn. Intergovtl. Rels., 1992—. Recipient Outstanding Svc. award Friends of Glastonbury Youth, 1990, Disting. Svc. award Capitol Region Coun., 1994; named Glastonbury Rep. of Yr., 1992. Mem. Greater Hartford Automobile Assn. Am. (bd. dirs.), Glastonbury Bus. and Profl. Women (past pres. and founder, Woman of Yr. 1988), Glastonbury C. of C., Glastonbury Jr. Woman's Club (past pres.). Roman Catholic. Home: 74 Forest Ln Glastonbury CT 06033-3918

GOOLKASIAN, PAULA A., psychologist, educator; b. Methuen, Mass., Aug. 9, 1948; d. Paul K. and Sadie T. (Touma) G.; m. Francis C. Martin, July 29, 1978; 1 child, Christopher. BA, Emmanuel Coll., 1970; MS, Iowa State U., 1972, PhD, 1974. Asst. prof. U. N.C., Charlotte, 1974-79, assoc. prof., 1979-85, prof. psychology, 1985—, pres. faculty, 1989—; cons. in field. Contbr. articles to profl. jours. Nat. Def. Ednl. Act. fellow, 1971-74; grantee NSF, NIH, and numerous others. Mem. AAAS, APA, Psychonomics Soc., Ea. Psychol. Assn., Internat. Soc. Psychophysics, Soc. for Computers in Psychology (sec.-treas. 1989-91, pres. 1994), Sigma Xi, Phi Kappa Phi. Home: 7107 Preston Ct Charlotte NC 28215-3625 Office: U NC Dept Psychology Charlotte NC 28223

GOOREY, NANCY JANE, dentist; b. Davenport, Iowa, May 8, 1922; d. Edgar Ray and Glenna Mae (Williams) Miller; m. Douglas B. Miller, Sept. 12, 1939 (div. 1951); children: Victoria Lee, Nickola Ellen, Douglas George, Melahna Marie; m. Louis Joseph Roseberry Goorey, Feb. 22, 1980. Student, Wooster (Ohio) Coll., 1939-40; DDS, Ohio State U., 1955. Cert. in gen. anesthesiology. Mem. faculty coll. dentistry Ohio State U., Columbus, 1955-86, dir., chmn. div. dental hygiene coll. dentistry, 1969-86, asst. dean coll. dentistry, 1975-86, mem. grad. faculty colls. dentistry and medicine, 1980—, asst. dean, prof. emeritus colls. dentistry and medicine, 1986—; moderator, prodn. chmn. Lifesavers 40 Prodns., 1981—. Producer, video program Giving Your Mouth a Sporting Chance, 1990, video Operation TACTIC. Chmn. State Planning Com. for Health Edn. in Ohio, Columbus, 1976-77, 87-88, 95—; founder, chmn. Coun. on Health Info., Columbus, 1981-85, pres., 1985-86; trustee Caring Dentists Found., Mayor's Drug Edn. and Prevention Program, Columbus, 1980—; mem. edn. com. Franklin County Rep. com., exec. com., 1993—; mem. human svcs. com. The Columbus Found. Recipient Vol. of Yr. award Columbus Health Dept., 1988-89, Dental Hygiene Nancy J. Goorey award Ohio State U., 1988. Fellow Am. Coll. Dentists (pres.-elect 1989-90), Am. Soc. Dental Anesthesiology, Internat. Coll. Dentists; mem. ADA (nat. consumer advisor 1975-78), Am. Assn. Dental Schs. (v.p., pres. 1972-77), Ohio Dental Assn. (cons. 1979—, mem. subcoun. on dentists concerned for dentists 1994—, chmn. subcoun. chem. dependency, Ohio Disting. Dentist 1983), Columbus Dental Soc. (pres. bd. dirs. 1986-87, 89-91, chmn. coun. on constn. and bilaws on jud. affairs 1989—), Ohio State U. Starling Womens Club (pres. 1982-83), Ohio State U. Faculty and Profl. Womens Club (pres. 1971-72), The Found. of the Acad. of Medicine (v.p. 1993-94), Ohio State Med. Assn. Alliance (chmn. state com. legis. affairs 1993-94, chmn. state health promotions com. 1994-95, v.p. 1995—), Acad. of Medicine Aux. (pres. 1992-93), Omicron Kappa Upsilon (chmn. Sports Dentistry com. 1995-96), The Columbus Found. (human svcs. com.), Caring Dentists Found. (trustee). Republican. Episcopalian. Office: Ohio State U Coll Dentistry 305 W 12th Ave Columbus OH 43210-1249

GOOSTREE, DIANE SCHEMMEL, pharmaceutical executive; b. Highland Park, Ill., Feb. 23, 1956; d. Louis and Rosa (Gresham) Schemmel; m. Robert Lynn Goostree, Sept. 18, 1982; 1 child, Jonathan. BSChemE, U. Kans., 1979; MBA, U. Mo., 1985. Engr. DuPont, Houston, 1979-80, Bayer, Kansas City, Mo., 1980-83; mgr. global comml. devel. Hoechst Marion Roussel, Kansas City, 1984-95; dir. bus. devel. Dura Pharmaceuticals, San Diego, 1995—. Mem. Soc. Licensing Execs. Office: Dura Pharmaceuticals 5880 Pacific Center Blvd San Diego CA 92121

GOOTMAN, PHYLLIS MYRNA, physiology, biophysics, educator; b. N.Y.C., June 8, 1938; d. Albert and Ida (Krieger) Adler; m. Norman Gootman, June 1, 1958; children: Sharon Hillary, Craig Seth. BA cum laude, Barnard Coll., 1959; PhD, Yeshiva U., 1967. Rsch. assoc. dept. physiology and biophysics U. Wash., Seattle, 1963; instr. dept. physiology Albert Einstein Coll. Medicine, Bronx, N.Y., 1966-70, asst. prof., 1970-73; asst. prof. SUNY, Bklyn., 1973-75, assoc. prof., 1975-81, prof., 1981—; vis. asst. prof. dept. physiology Albert Einstein Coll. Medicine, Bronx, 1973-76, vis. prof. dept. Physiology and Biophysics, 1984-92; mem. clin. campus, 1989—. Contbr. articles to profl. jours.; mem. editl. bd. Jour. of Development Physiology, 1986-95. Recipient Hendel Family award Brandeis U., 1957; John Miles Davidson fellow in physiology Albert Einstein Coll. Medicine, 1973; recipient numerous grants. Fellow Royal Soc. Medicine; mem. AAAS, Soc. for Neurosci., Biophys. Soc., Am. PHysiol. Soc., Am. Heart Assn., Am. Inst. Biol. Scis., Am. Autonomic Soc. (exec. bd.), Microcirculatory Soc., Soc. for Exptl. Biology and Medicine, Am. Assn. Lab Animal Sci., Internat. Soc. for Devel. of Neurosci. Office: SUNY Health Sci Ctr Bklyn Dept Physiology Box 31 450 Clarkson Ave Brooklyn NY 11203-2098

GOPLEN, DONNELLE, mental health services administrator; b. Loco, Okla., Nov. 5, 1936; d. Allen R. and Dorothy R. (Carmichael) Bean; BA with honors, U. N.Mex., 1974, MA, 1977; postgrad. Family Therapy Inst., 1981-82; m. Bruce C. Goplen, Sept. 26, 1969; children: Stephen Harvey, Donald Harvey. State welfare worker State Welfare Agy., N.Mex., 1975-77; counseling intern Presbyn. Hosp., Albuquerque, 1977; social worker State of N.Mex., 1977-78; vol. mental health aide Prince William County (Va.) Cmty. Mental Health Center, 1978-79, coordinator Social Activity Center; program coordinator mental health family services program Cmty. Svcs. Bd. of Prince William County, Prince William Women For... (founding mem. 1992—). Mem. Nat. Cert. Counselors. Home: 18414 Cedar Dr Triangle VA 22172-1416 Office: Prince William Cmty Svcs Bd 7969 Ashton Ave Manassas VA 22110-2885

GORDIMER, NADINE, author; b. Republic of South Africa, Nov. 20, 1923; d.Isidore and Nan (Myers) Gordimer; m. Reinhold Cassirer, Jan. 29, 1954; children: Oriane, Hugo. Ed., Convent Sch., Springs, Republic of South Africa. Author: (story collections) Face to Face, 1949, The Soft Voice of the Serpent, 1952, Six Feet of the Country, 1956, Friday's Footprint, 1960 (W.H. Smith and Son Literary award 1961), Not for Publication, 1965, Livingstone's Companions, 1971, Selected Stories, 1975, Some Monday for Sure, 1976, A Soldier's Embrace, 1980, Town and Country Lovers, 1980, Something Out There, 1984, Crimes of Conscience, 1991, Jump, 1991, Why Haven't You Written?, 1992; (polit. and lit. essays) The Essential Gesture, 1988, Three in a Bed, 1991; (literary criticism) The Black Interpreters, 1973, Writing & Being: Charles Eliot Norton Lectures, 1995; (novels) The Lying Days, 1953, A World of Strangers, 1958, Occasion for Loving, 1963, The Late Bourgeois World, 1966, A Guest of Honour, 1970 (James Tait Black Meml. prize 1973), The Conservationist, 1974 (Booker prize for fiction Nat. Book League 1974), Burger's Daughter, 1979, July's People, 1981, A Sport of Nature, 1987, My Son's Story, 1991, None to Accompany Me, 1994; (other) On the Mines, 1973, Lifetimes Under Apartheid, 1986; editor: (with Lionel Abrahams) Southern African Writing Today, 1967. Decorated comdr. de l'Ordre des Arts et des Lettres (France), 1986; recipient Thomas Pringle award English Acad. South Africa, 1969, CNA award, 1974, 79, 81, 91, Grand Aigle d'Or, 1975, Disting. Svc. in Lit. Commonwealth award, 1981, MLA award, 1982, Nelly Sachs prize (Germany), 1985, Malaparte award (Italy), 1986, Bennett award, 1986, Benson medal, 1990, Nobel Prize for Literature, 1991; Neil Gunn fellowship Scottish Arts Coun., 1981. Fellow Royal Soc. Lit.; mem. AAAS, Com. European Authors, Am. Acad. (hon.), Inst. Arts and Letters (hon.), PEN (v.p.). Home: Parktown West, 7 Frere Road, Johannesburg 2193, South Africa

GORDLY, AVEL LOUISE, state legislator, community activist; b. Portland, Oreg., Feb. 13, 1947; d. Fay Lee and Beatrice Bernice (Coleman) G.; 1 child, Tyrone Wayne Waters. BS in Adminstrn. of Justice, Portland State U., 1974; Grad. John F. Kennedy Sch. Govt., Harvard U., 1995. Phone co. clk. Pacific West Bell, Portland, 1966-70, mgmt. trainee, 1969-70; work release counselor Oreg. Corrections Divsn., Portland, 1974-78, parole and probation officer, 1974-78; dir. youth svcs. Urban League of Portland, 1979-83; dir. So. Africa program Am. Friends Svc. Com., Portland, 1983-89, assoc. exec. sec., dir. Pacific N.W. region, 1987-90; freelance writer Portland Observer, Portland, 1988-90; program dir. Portland House of Umoja, 1991; mem. Oreg. Ho. of Reps., Portland, 1991—, mem. joint ways and means com., adv. mem. appropriations com., rules and reorgn. com., low income housing com., energy policy rev. com., others; mem. joint ways and means com. on edn., mem. gov. drug and violent crime policy bd., mem. Oreg. liquor control commn. task force, mem. sexual harrassement task force, mem. Hanford waste bd., mem. Gov.'s Commn. for Women, Gov.'s Drug and Violent Crime Policy Bd.; originator, producer, host Black Women's Forum, 1983-88; co-producer, rotating host N.E. Spectrum, 1983-88. Mem. corrections adv. com. Multnomah Cmty.; mem. adv. com. Oregonians Against Gun Violence; mem. Black Leadership Conf.; treas., bd. dirs. Black United Fund; co-founder, facilitator Unity Breakfast Com.; co-founder Sisterhood Luncheon; past project adv. bd. dirs. Nat. Orgn. Victims Assistance; past citizen chmn. Portland Police Bur.; past mem. coordinating com. Portland Future Focus Policy Com.; past coord. Cmty. Rescue Plan; past vice chmn. internat. affairs Black United Front; past sec. Urban League Portland, past vice chmn. and exec. com.; past adv. com. Black Ednl. Ctr.; past vice chmn. Desegregation Monitoring; also past adv. com., past chmn. curriculum com., founder African Am. Leg. Issues Roundtable; founder Black Women Gathering; other past orgn. coms. Recipient Outstanding Cmty. Svc. award NAACP, 1986, Outstanding Women in Govt. award YWCA, 1991, Girl Scout-Cmty. Svc. award, 1991, N.W. Conf. of Black Studies-Outstanding Progressive Leadership in the African-Am. Cmty. award, 1986, Cmty. Svc. award Delta Sigma Theta, 1981, Joint Action in Cmty. Svc.-Vol. and Cmty. Svc. award, 1981, Quality of Life Photography award Pacific Power & Light Co., 1986, Am. Leadership Forum Sr. fellow, 1988, Equal Opportunity award, Urban League, 1996, Outstanding Alumni, 1996, PSU. Mem. NAACP.

GORDON, ALICE JEANNETTE IRWIN, secondary and elementary education educator; b. Detroit, Mar. 18, 1934; d. Manley Elwood and Jeannette (Coffron) Irwin; m. Edgar George Gordon, Feb. 4, 1967; children: David Alexander, John Scott. BA in Elem. Edn., Mich. State U., 1956; MA in Child Devel., U. Mich., 1959, EdS in Ednl. Psychology, 1967, MA in Reading, 1990. Cert. K-12 tchr., Mich. Elem. tchr. Detroit Pub. Schs., 1956-67, reading tchr., 1967-68; secondary tchr. English and reading Parchment Pub. Schs., 1989-94; secondary reading specialist Kalamazoo Pub. Schs., 1994-96; jr. high reading specialist South Middle Sch., Kalamazoo, 1996—; reading therapist Western Mich. U., Kalamazoo, 1992-96. Mem. alumni bd. Mich. State U. Coll. Edn., 1990—; chmn. Century Ball, Nazareth Coll., Kalamazoo, 1987; co-chmn. Evening of Nte, Kalamazoo Symphony, 1989; precinct del. Kalamazoo Rep. Com., 1989, 92, 96; mem. Mich. Adult Edn. Practitioner Inquiry Project, 1994, 95, 96. Fellow U. Mich., 1963, 66; coop. learning grantee Mich. Dept. Edn., 1990. Mem. Internat. Reading Assn., Mich. Reading Assn., Homer Carter Reading Assn., P.E.O., Jr. League, Lawyers Wives Auxillery, Kappa Delta Pi, Phi Delta Kappa (v.p.), Alpha Omega Pi. Presbyterian. Home: 4339 Lakeside Dr Kalamazoo MI 49008-2802 Office: South Middle Sch Kalamazoo MI 49008-3610

GORDON, ANNE KATHLEEN, editor; m. Phillip L. Berman. BA, U. Denver, 1979; postgrad., Columbia Grad. Sch. Journalism, 1983. Fin. writer Rocky Mountain Bus. Jour., Denver, 1981; fin. writer Sun-Tattler, Hollywood, Fla., 1982-83, fin. editor, 1983; asst. bus. editor Ft. Lauderdale (Fla.) News, 1983-85; bus. editor The Denver Post, 1985-88, asst. mng. editor, 1988; news cons. Sta. KCNC-TV, Denver, 1988-89, assignment mgr., 1989-90; editor Jackson Hole News, 1990-92; editor Sunday Mag. The Plain Dealer, Cleve., 1993—. Author: A Book of Saints, 1994. Recipient Best of Show award Colo. Press Assn., 1981, 86, Woman of Yr. award Broward County Bus. and Profl. Women's Assn., 1983, 1st Pl. Spot News award Colo. Associated Press, 1986, 1st Pl. Breaking News award Colo. Press Assn., 1986, Gen. Excellence award Wyo. Press Assn., 1991, Gen. Excellence award Nat. Newspaper Assn., 1992. Home: 1060 Erie Cliff Dr Lakewood OH 44107-1214 Office: The Plain Dealer 1801 Superior Ave Cleveland OH 44104

GORDON, AUDREY KRAMEN, university administrator; b. Chgo., Nov. 18, 1935; d. Edward J. and Anne (Levin) K.; children: Bradley, Dale, Holly. BS with highest distinction, Northwestern U., 1965, MA, 1967, postgrad., 1971; MA, U. Chgo., 1970; PhD, U. Ill., Chgo., 1991. Cert. in clin. pastoral edn. Lectr. Northwestern U., Evanston, Ill., 1966-74; vis. asst. prof. Beloit (Wis.) Coll., 1974-75; research specialist U. Ill., Chgo., 1983-86, dir. continuing edn. Sch. Pub. Health, 1986-91, lectr. community health scis., 1988-91, dir. coll. advancement Sch. Pub. Health, 1991-92; coord./counselor Jewish Hospice, Chgo., 1984-89; asst. prof. community health scis. Sch. Pub. Health U. Ill., Chgo., 1992—; sr. rsch. specialist Ctr. for Pub. Health Practice, Sch. Pub. Health, U. Ill., 1992—; lectr. Loyola U. Stritch Sch. Medicine, Maywood, Ill., 1982—; pres. Rainbow Hospice Orgn., 1984-88, mem. profl. adv. bd., 1988—. Co-author: They Need To Know: How To Teach Children About Death, 1979; co-editor: Hospice and Cultural Diversity, 1995. Recipient Northwestern Univ. Alumni Merit award, 1993. Mem. APHA, Ill. Pub. Health Assn., Ill. Hospice Orgn. (pres. 1989-90), Nat. Hospice Orgn. (coun. of profls.), Alpha Sigma Lambbda, Alpha Kappa Lambda, Delta Omega.

GORDON, BETH, advertising executive. Exec. v.p., mng. dir. Media Edge N.W. Ayer & Ptnrs., N.Y.C. Office: N W Ayer Inc Wordwide Plz 825 8th Ave New York NY 10019-7498*

GORDON, BONNIE HEATHER, writer, editor; b. Phila., Oct. 18, 1952; d. Herman E. and Jean (Twersky) G.; m. Ed Kaplan, Apr. 2, 1978; 1 child, Philip Gordon Kaplan. BA in English, Temple U., 1975. Pub.'s rep. Columbia U. Press, N.Y.C., 1975-76; asst. editor mag. div. Dun-Donnelly Corp., N.Y.C., 1976-78; asst. editor High Times mag. Tixeon Inc., N.Y.C., 1978-79; staff editor Nat. League for Nursing, N.Y.C., 1981-82; freelance writer and editor N.Y.C., Cin., Phila., N.J., 1982-91; editor Law Sch. Admission Coun., Newtown, Pa., 1991—. Author: Thus May Be Figured in Numberless Ways, 1985; editor, pub. Sapiens, 1983; writer, prodr. documentary video Which Is Why Poetry Is Weightlifting, 1991. Mem. bus. and profl. br. Nat. Coun. Jewish Women, 1989-90. Winner Blue Chip Cable Access award, 1992. Mem. Editl. Freelancers Assn., Women in Comm., Ednl. Press Assn. Am., Phila. Ind. Film Video Assn., Phi Beta Kappa.

GORDON, DEBRA GWEN, music educator; b. Clinton, Iowa, Apr. 5, 1951; d. Otto Edward and Edna Firm (Griffin) Bruhn; m. Roger L. Gordon, July 30, 1983. BA in Music Edn., U. Iowa, 1973; MA in Music Edn., U. No. Iowa, 1985. Cert. music tchr. Elem. music tchr. Lincoln Community Schs., Mechanicsville, Iowa, 1973-76; elem. music tchr., German tchr. Hudson (Iowa) Community Schs., 1976-93; instr. music edn. U. No. Iowa, 1993—; mem. North Ctrl. Accredidation Team, 1980—; clinician, presenter at various convs., 1977—; mem. musician's del. to China and Kazakhstan, 1992. Author: Capsule Units for Music Teachers, 1983, Teaching Examples: Ideas for Music Educators, 1994, Strategies for Teaching K-4 General Music, 1996; contbr. numerous articles to mags. Grantee Iowa Dept. Edn., 1985, 87. Mem. Iowa Music Educators (bd. dirs., exec. sec. 1984—), Am. Choral Dirs. Assn., Nurse Educators Nat. Conf., Phi Delta Kappa, Pi Kappa Lambda. Democrat. Lutheran. Office: U No Iowa 121 Russell Hall Cedar Falls IA 50614-0246

GORDON, ELLEN RUBIN, candy company executive; d. William B. and Cele H. (Travis) Rubin; m. Melvin J. Gordon, June 25, 1950; children: Virginia, Karen, Wendy, Lisa. Student, Vassar Coll., 1948-50; B.A., Brandeis U., 1965; postgrad., Harvard U., 1968. With Tootsie Roll Industries, Inc., Chgo., 1968—, corp. sec., 1970-74, v.p. product devel., 1974-76, sr. v.p., 1976-78, pres., COO, 1978—, also dir.; v.p., dir. HDI Investment Corp.; bd. dirs. CPC Internat., Inc.; mem. coun. on divsn. biol. scis. and Pritzker Sch. Medicine U. Chgo. Mem. adv. coun. J.L. Kellogg Grad. Sch. Mgmt. at Northwestern U., Stanford U. Grad. Sch. Bus.; mem. bd fellows Harvard U. Med. Sch.; mem. univ. resources and overseers com. Harvard U.; trustee, mem. Com. for Econ. Devel., Northwestern U. Assocs.; active Pres. Export Coun. Recipient Kettle award, 1985. Mem. Nat. Confectioners Assn. (bd. dirs.). Office: Tootsie Roll Industries Inc 7401 S Cicero Ave Chicago IL 60629-5818

GORDON, GERD STRAY, retired historian, educator, writer; b. Stavanger, Norway, Nov. 15, 1912; came to U.S., 1948; d. Johannes and Ella (Stray) Johansen; m. Johan Vogt (div.); children: Mette Wernøe, Gerd Ada Vogt, Christina Isaksen; m. Raymond Gordon; 1 child, Karen Allyn. Student, Oslo U., 1937-41; BA, Fla. State U., 1960; MA, U. Pitts., PhD, 1978. Cert. tchr., Fla., Pa. Accredited corr. Aftenposten-Norsk Dameblad, Oslo, 1948-55; tchr. Panama C.Z. Schs., Panama Episc. Sch., 1960-61, Am. Coop. Sch., Tunis, Tunisia, 1962-64; tchr. Am. Internat. Sch., Bangkok, 1965-68, Djakarta, Indonesia, 1968-69; tchr. Am. Sch., New Delhi, 1969-70, Pitts. Pub. Sch. Sys., 1970-83; freelance lectr., 1983—; lectr. Slippery Rock (Pa.) U., U. Kans., Lawrence, Vanderbilt U., Nashville; presenter Symposium of Scandinavian Historians. Author: Kvinnen Idag (Woman Today), 1952; contbr. articles to numerous publs including Dictionary of Scandinavian History, 1986. Dem. ofcl., Denver, 1952-57, election judge, 1954-58; bd. dirs., rep., Planned Parenthood, Denver and Pitts., 1952-89; participant Citizen Day Com. signed S.P. Kinney II Denver Woman's Press Club, 1965, Senate of Pa., 1985. Resistance worker during German occupation of Norway, World War II. Recipient Outstanding Citizen award Norwegian Resistance; Ella Lyman Cabot Trust grantee U. Pitts. Mem. Denver Women's Press Club (bd. dirs. 1952—), Pitts. U. Historian Alumnae Orgn., Fla. State U. Alumnae Assn., AAUW (bd. dirs. Pitts. chpt. 1984—), LWV (past bd. dirs. Denver and Pitts. chpts.), Countryside Garden Club (bd. dirs. 1970—). Home: 224 Rockingham Rd Pittsburgh PA 15238-3014

GORDON, IRENE MARLOW, radiology educator; b. White County, Tenn., May 21, 1943; d. Paul Terah and Mary Eva (Holloway) Marlow; m. Shigern Chino, July 14, 1969 (div.); children: Hatsuyo Mary Chino, Kazumi Elaine Chino, Junzo Paul Chino, Hazuki Carol Chino, Fumiko Catherine Chino; m. James Robert Gordon, Sept. 6, 1979. BS, U. Dayton, 1966; MD, Ohio State U., 1970, MS, 1974. Intern in medicine and pediat. St. Lukes Hosp., San Francisco, 1970-71; resident in gen. radiology Ohio State U. Hosp., 1971-74; fellow in radiation and oncology U. Calif., Irvine; clin. instr. dept. radiology Ohio State U., Columbus, 1971-74; asst. clin. prof. divsn. radiation therapy U. Calif., Irvine, 1976-78, acting chief divsn. radiation therapy, 1976-77; asst. clin. prof. divsn. radiation therapy Harbor-UCLA Med. Ctr., L.A., 1981-82; clin. asst. prof. radiology, radiation oncology Ind. U. Med. Ctr., Indpls., 1992—; bd. dirs. Health Talents Internat., Sentinel Med. Rev. Orgn., sec., 1985-89, Hoosier Oncology Group, mem. exec. com., 1993—; mem. staff St. Joseph & Children's Hosp., Orange, Calif., 1974-82, Long Beach Meml. Med. Ctr., 1979-82; dir. radiation oncology St. Elizabeth Hosp. and Med. Ctr. Regional Treatment Ctr., Lafayette, Ind., 1982—. Translator for deaf Ouabache Ch. of Christ, Lafayette, 1993—; bd. dirs. Tippecanoe County chpt. ARC, 1992—. Mem. AMA, Am. Coll. Radiology (cert.), Am. Soc. Therapeutic Radiology and Oncology, Radiology Soc. N.Am., Am. Endocurie Soc., Am. Coll. Radiation Oncology, Am. Soc. Clin. Oncology, Tippecanoe County Med. Assn. (pres. 1994—), Ind. 9th Dist. Med. Assn. (pres. 1994). Office: Regional Treatment Ctr 1116 N 16th St Lafayette IN 47904-2119

GORDON, JANINE M., advertising agency executive; b. N.Y.C., Oct. 2, 1946; d. Moses Fortune and Emma (Leo) Mager. BA, U. Pa., 1968. Asst. buyer Bloomingdale's, N.Y.C., 1968-69; fashion credits editor Harper's Bazaar, N.Y.C., 1969-72; assoc. dir. pub. relations Cotton, Inc., N.Y.C., 1972-73; press officer Harrods Ltd., London, 1973-74; project mgr. J.C. Penney Co., Inc., N.Y.C., 1974-75; dir. pub. relations Bozell, Inc., N.Y.C., 1975-77; exec. v.p. corp. comm., mem. oper. com. Saatchi & Saatchi Advt., 1977-94; pres. Saatchi & Saatchi Pub. Rels., 1987-94, Janine Gordon & Assocs., N.Y.C., 1994-95, Waring LaRosa GordonPub. Rels., N.Y.C., 1995-96, Emmerling Post Gordon Pub. Rels. Inc., 1996—. Mem. Pub. Rels. Soc. Am., Advt. Women N.Y., Cosmopolitan Club.

GORDON, JUNE ANN, educator; b. Long Beach, Calif., Nov. 16, 1950; d. James Gordon and Muriel (Carr) Parker; m. Dale Wilson (div.); m. William Henry Heid, June 19, 1988. BA, Stanford (Calif.) U., 1972; MA, Western Washington U., 1989; PhD, U. Wash., 1991. English tchr. YMCA, Toyama, Japan, 1983; source lang. coord. Computer Curriculum Corp., Palo Alto, 1982-85; program coord. Stanford (Calif.) U., 1985-86; rsch. assoc. U. Wash., Seattle, 1990-92; lectr. Antioch U., Seattle, 1992-93; lectr., adminstr. Western Wash. U., Bellingham, 1986-93; prof. U. Wash., Seattle, 1992-94, U. Calif., 1996—; cons. in field. Contbg. editor China: Inside the People's Republic, 1971; contbr. articles to profl. jours. Mem. Am. Anthropology Assn., Japan Am. Soc., Am. Assn. of Higher Edn., Nat. Assn. for Women in Edn. Assn. of Tchr. Edn. Home: 1906 20th St C-11 Bellingham WA 98225 Office: U Calif Crown Coll 230 Santa Cruz CA 95064

GORDON, KATHERINE ANSON, accountant; b. L.A., Dec. 7, 1953; d. John Hahn and Martha Mildred (Moyer) Anson; m. Richard Duke Nunn, June 26, 1976 (div. May 1991); children: Krista Holly, John Duke; m. John Stephen Gordon, Apr. 25, 1992. AA, Pasadena City Coll., 1974; BA, Calif. State U., L.A., 1976. CPA, Oreg. Acctg. supr., asst. v.p. Am. Fed. Savs. and Loan, Salem, Oreg., 1976-90; tax supr. Aldrich, Kilbride and Tatone LLP, Salem, 1991—. Vol. parent Boy Scouts Am., Salem, 1988—; asst. leader Girl Scouts U.S., Salem, 1987-92. Honoree YWCA Tribute to Outstanding Women, Salem, 1996. Mem. AICPAs, Oreg. Soc. CPAs, Beta Sigma Phi (city coun. pres. 1990—, treas. 1996—, Woman of the Yr. 1992). Republican. Episcopalian. Home: 1786 Snowbird Dr NW Salem OR 97304 Office: Aldrich Kilbride & Tatone LLP 1011 Commercial St NE #120 Salem OR 97301

GORDON, KIM, singer; b. 1953; m. Thurston Moore. Recs. include Sonic Youth, Experimental Jet Set, Trash and No Star, 1994, (with Lydia Lunch) Screaming Fields of Sonic Love, 1995, Washing Machine, 1995. Office: DGC Records 9150 Sunset Blvd Los Angeles CA 90068*

GORDON, MARY CATHERINE, author; b. L.I., N.Y., Dec. 8, 1949; d. David and Anna (Gagliano) G.; m. James Brain, 1974 (div.); m. Arthur Cash, 1979; children: Anna Gordon, David Dess Gordon. BA, Barnard Coll., 1971; MA, Syracuse U., 1973. Tchr. English Dutchess Community Coll., Poughkeepsie, N.Y., 1974-78, Amherst (Mass.) Coll., 1979-80, Barnard Coll., 1988—. Author: (novels) Final Payments, 1978, The Company of Women, 1981, Men and Angels,1985, The Other Side, 1989, The Rest of Life, 1993, (short stories) Temporary Shelter, 1987, Good Boys and Dead Girls and Other Essays, 1991, The Rest of Life: Three Novellas, 1993. Recipient Kafka prize for Fiction, 1979, 82. Roman Catholic. Office: Viking Penguin Publicity Dept 375 Hudson St New York NY 10014-3658 also: Barnard Coll Dept of English 606 West 120th St New York NY 10027-5706*

GORDON, NANCY M., congressional administrator; b. Thunder Bay, Ont., Can., Nov. 10, 1943; came to U.S., 1959; d. Walter Ernest and Hilda May Gordon. BA in Econs., U. Calif., Berkeley, 1964; PhD in Econs., Stanford U., 1970. Asst. prof. Carnegie Mellon U., Pitts., 1969-74; econ. policy fellow Brookings Instn., Washington, 1975-76; sr. rsch. assoc. The Urban Inst., Washington, 1976-79; exec. dir. task force on women The White House, Washington, 1979, sr. advisor to asst. to pres., 1979-80; asst. dir. health and human resources Congl. Budget Office, Washington, 1980—. Author: (with others) The Subtle Revolution, 1979; contbr. chpts. to profl. jours. Pres., bd. dirs. Worldwide Assurance Employees Pub. Agys., 1987-90. Woodrow Wilson Found. fellow, 1964, IBM fellow, 1965, Stanford-Wilson Dissertation fellow Stanford U., 1967. Mem. Am. Statis. Assn. (chair com. on status of women in econ. profession, vice chair com. on women in sci.), Am. Econ. Assn. Home: 5500 Friendship Blvd Bethesda MD 20815-7219 Office: Congl Budget Office US Congress Second and D Sts SW Washington DC 20515

GORDON, PEGGY SUE, administrative assistant; b. Seattle, Dec. 1, 1962; d. Gary Edward and Brenda Kay (Rineholt) Watson; m. Neal David Gordon, Apr. 29, 1989 (dec. Sept. 1992); 1 child, Elizabeth Michelle. Sec. M.J. Meats, Lynnwood, Wash., 1987-89, Quantum Wood Windows, Everett, Wash., 1990-93; office mgr. Amundson & Squires, Inc., Lynnwood, 1993—. Deacon Ch. of the Good Shepherd, 1996—. Office: Amundson & Squires Inc 3400 188th St SW #629 Lynnwood WA 98037

GORDON, PENELOPE EVERALL, computer consultant; b. San Francisco, Sept. 8, 1965; d. Marshall Hewitt and Eleanor Helen (Everall) G.; m. Kristian Arthur Baakkonen, June 28, 1987 (div. Oct. 1994). BS in Engring., Harvey Mudd Coll., 1987; BA in Engring. Mgmt., Claremont McKenna

Coll., 1987; MBA in Mktg., St. Mary's Coll., Moraga, Calif., 1991. Engr.-in-tng., Md. Mktg. rep. Impel Computer Sys., Berkeley, Calif., 1987-89; sys. engr. IBM, Oakland, Calif., 1989-93; project mktg. engr. IBM, Austin, Tex., 1994; availability svcs. specialist IBM, Balt., 1995—. Mem. Soc. Women Engrs., Harvey Mudd Coll. Alumni Assn. (bd. dirs. 1993—). Christian Scientist. Office: IBM 100 E Pratt St Baltimore MD 21202

GORDON, RENA JOYCE, health services researcher, educator; b. Detroit, Mar. 4, 1936; d. Joseph Lazar and Edna Dorothy (Rosenfeld) Feigelman; m. Leonard Gordon, Dec. 25, 1955; children: Susan Melinda, Matthew Seth, Melissa Gail. BS with honors, Wayne State U., 1957; MA, Ariz. State U., 1971, Ariz. State U., 1978; PhD, Ariz. State U., 1983. Resource tchr. Detroit Pub. Schs., 1966-67; faculty assoc. Ariz. State U., 1971-76; rsch. stat. analyst Ariz. Dept. Health Svcs., Phoenix, 1981-82; rsch. asst. prof. dir. Phoenix Rural Health Office Coll. Medicine U. Ariz., 1983-89; exec. dir. Ariz. Coun. for Mothers and Children, 1992-94; pres. Gordon Rsch. Assocs., Scottsdale, 1994—; rsch. cons. Clin. Gerontology Unit, St. Luke's Hosp., Phoenix, 1982-83; adj. prof. dept. geography Ariz. State U., 1988—; vis. prof. Am. Grad. Sch. Internat. Mgmt., Glendale, Ariz., 1989; rsch. lectr. dept. family and cmty. medicine, U. Ariz. Coll. Medicine, Tucson, 1989—. Author: Arizona Rural Health Provider Atlas, 1984, 87; contbr. chpts. to books and articles to profl. jours. Mem. Camelback Hosps. Coun. Ctr., adv. com. 1982-88, chmn. 1983-84, St. Luke's Behavioral Health Ctr., 1988-92, bd. trustees, Phoenix. Recipient various awards U. Mich., Ariz. State U., challenge grant The Flinn Found. Mem. AAUW (bd. dirs. 1987-88), APHA., Ariz. Pub. Health Assn. (bd. dirs. 1986-88), Assn. Am. Geographers (med. geography sect.).

GORDON, SHARON J., special education educator; b. Calif., 1972; m. Ted H. Gordon, July 2, 1972; 1 child, Matthew. BA, San Jose State U., 1969, MA, 1973. Cert. tchr., Calif. Speech lang. pathologist Walnut Creek (Calif.) Elem. Sch. Dist., 1969, San Ramon Unified Sch. Dist., Danville, Calif., 1969-75; speech lang. pathologist Cotati-Rohnert Park (Calif.) Sch. Dist., 1975-80, spl. edn. educator lang. handicapped students, 1980-92, spl. edn. educator, 1992—; mem. leadership team Waldo Rohnert Sch., 1993—. Pres. Congregation Rodef Sholom, San Rafael, Calif., 1989-91; social action chair no. Calif. Union Am. Hebrew Congregations, San Francisco, 1985-88; chair Jewish Cmty. Rels. Coun., San Rafael, 1992-94. Named Woman of Yr. ORT, 1991. Mem. Am. Speech Lang. Hearing Assn., Calif. Speech Lang. Hearing Assn., Calif. Tchrs. Assn. Office: Waldo Rohnert Sch 550 Bonnie Ave Rohnert Park CA 94928-3897

GORDON, SUSAN JOAN, physician, educator; b. Atlantic City, Aug. 14, 1942. Student Goucher Coll., 1959-62; M.D., Jefferson Med. Coll., 1966. Diplomate Am. Bd. Internal Medicine, Am. Bd. Gastroenterology. Intern in medicine Hahnemann Med. Coll. and Hosp., Phila., 1966-67; resident in medicine Jefferson Med. Coll. Hosp., 1967-69; instr. Thomas Jefferson U. Phila., 1971-73, asst. prof., 1973-78, assoc. prof., 1978-87, clin. prof. medicine, 1987—; jr. coordinator medicine Jefferson Med. Coll., Phila., 1971-82. Contbr. articles to profl. jours. Mem. Am. Gastroenterol. Assn. (mem. biliary sect., abstract reviewer, chairperson clin. biliary sect.), Am. Assn. Study Liver Disease, Pa. Med. Soc., Phila. Gastrointestinal Rsch. Forum, Sigma Xi. Office: Jefferson Med Coll 480 Main Bldg 132 S 10th St Philadelphia PA 19107-5244

GORDON, TINA, sculptor, art therapist; b. N.Y.C.; d. Abraham and Rose (Scoff) Schapiro; m. Norman B. Gordon (div.); children: Jane, Judith, Marc. BA in Fine Arts, Goddard Coll., 1972; postgrad., NYU, 1978-80; student, Nat. Acad. Art, N.Y.C., 1981-83, Parsons Sch. Design, N.Y.C., 1983-88. Art tchr. East River Montessori Sch., N.Y.C., 1969-72; instr. Nassau Cmty. Coll., 1973-76; art therapist Manhattan Psychiat. Ctr., N.Y.C., 1977-87; curator ann. juried non-member exhbn. sculpture and photography; jury of awards for Wash. Square outdoor art club, 1995, 96. Exhibited in shows at Nat. Acad. Art, 1977, 78, 80, Nat. Art Club, N.Y.C., 1978, 79, 80, 83, 88, Thompson Gallery, N.Y.C., Salamagundi Art Club, N.Y.C., 1979-90, Pen and Brush, N.Y.C., 1984-89, L.I. Artists Guild, 1970, 71, 72, numerous others; commns. for Manhattan Psy. Ctr. Jury mem. Allied Artists Am., 1995-96, Pen and Brush Artists, 1995-96, Washington Sq. Outlook Artists, 1995-96, Salmagundi Art Club, 1996—. Recipient Philip Isenberg 1st prize in Sculpture, Salmagundi Art Soc., 1994. Mem. Salmagundi Art Soc. (curator, chmn. ann. open juries exhbn. 1994, jury of awards 1996—), Elliot Liskin award in sculpture 1984, 86, First Prize Sculpture award), Nat. Assn. Women Artists, Pen and Brush (bd. dirs., 1994, 96—, Merit award 1985, 87, 88, 89, jury of acceptance 1995, 96), Am. Soc. Contemporary Artists, Burr Artists, Allied Artists of Am. (elected as jury of acceptance 1995, 96), Knickerbocker Artists (Roman Bronze award 1981, 83), Nat. Sculpture Soc. (assoc.). Home: 24 5th Ave New York NY 10011-8858

GORDON-MOUNTIAN, LESLEY DARA, office manager, dancer; b. New Haven, Conn., Mar. 21, 1954; d. David Cole and Pearl Doris (Greenberg) G.; m. Vassilii Vladimirovich Mountian, Mar. 3, 1991. BA with distinction and deptl. honors, Northwestern U., 1976. Sr. asst. buyer I. Magnin, San Francisco, 1978-81; dancer Khadra Internat. Folk Ballet, San Francisco, 1986-91; dir., v.p., mem. exec. com. Khandra Internat. Folk Ballet, San Francisco, 1989-91; office mgr. Banque Paribas, San Francisco, 1981—, assoc., 1994—; Choreographer Duquesne U. Tamburitzans. Bd. dirs. Calif. Artists Series, San Francisco, 1989-90; coord. Hartley House Food Dr., N.Y.C., 1972, Soviet Jewish Emigre Svcs., San Francisco, 1991; solicitor Casa de las Madres, San Francisco, 1991—, Americares, New Canaan, Conn., 1993—. Recipient Richter Internat. scholarship Northwestern U., Paris, 1975, Regents scholarship SUNY, 1971, scholastic award Alpha Lambda Delta. Jewish. Office: Banque Paribas 101 California St Ste 3150 San Francisco CA 94111

GORE, TIPPER (MARY ELIZABETH GORE), wife of vice president of the United States; b. Washington, Aug. 19, 1948; m. Albert Gore Jr., May 19, 1970; children: Karenna, Kristin, Sarah, Albert III. BA in psychology, Boston U., 1970; MA in psychology, George Peabody Coll. Freelance photographer; chmn. Congl. Wives Task Force, 1978-79. Author: Raising PG Kids in an X-Rated Society, 1987. Co-founder Parents Music Resource Ctr., Arlington, Va., 1985. Office: Old Exec Office Bldg Rm 200 Washington DC 20501*

GOREAU, ANGELINE, writer; b. Sept. 12, 1951; d. Theodore Nelson and Eloise (Keaton) G.; m. Stephen Jones McGruder, Mar. 19, 1983; 1 child, Keaton Angeline. BA, Barnard Coll., 1973. Hodder fellow Princeton (N.J.) U., 1982-83; lectr. Vassar Coll., Poughkeepsie, N.Y., 1980's; judge for various prizes. Author: Reconstructing Aphra, 1980, The Whole Duty of a Woman, 1984; contbr. articles to mags., newspapers, essays to books. Fellow NEH, 1976, Nat. Endowment for Arts, 1981, Belgian Ministry of Culture, Hodda fellow, 1982-83. Mem. PEN, Book Critics' Cir., Authors' Guild.

GORELICK, ELLEN CATHERINE, museum director, curator, artist, educator, civic volunteer; b. Chgo., Jan. 2, 1946; d. Martin Francis and Doris Harriet (Adams) Heckmann; m. Walter Lee Gorelick, Dec. 19, 1970. AA cum laude, Coll. of Sequoias, 1976; BA cum laude, Calif. State U., Fresno, 1979, MA in Art, 1982. Book divsn. corr. Time, Inc., Chgo., 1964-68; accounts receivable supr. Tab Products Co., San Francisco, 1968-69; exec. sec. Foremost-McKesson, Inc., San Francisco, 1969-71, McCarthy Land Co., Visalia, Calif., 1972-74; adminstrv. dir. Creative Ctr. for Handicapped, Visalia, 1979-80; curator Tulare (Calif.) Hist. Mus., 1984-87, dir., curator, 1994—; mem. adj. faculty Coll. of Sequoias, Visalia, 1985—. Bd. dirs. Tulare-Kings Regional Arts Coun., pres., 1989-90; bd. dirs. Tulare County Art League, pres., 1977-78; bd. dirs. Leadership Tulare, founding CORE com., 1991-93, alumni chair, 1992-93; bd. dirs. Tulare County U. Calif. Campus Expansion task force, Visalia, 1988-91, Tulare City Sch. Dist. Classrooms for Kids Campaign, co-chair, 1989; mem. Tulare City Hist. Soc. long range planning com., 1995; mem. Tulare County Symphony Assn., 1992-95, sec., 1993—. Named Artist of Yr., Tulare-Kings County Arts Coun., 1988; recipient cert. of appreciation City of Tulare, 1989, Tulare County Bd. Suprs., 1991, Woman of Distinction award Soroptimists, Tulare, 1994. Mem. Tulare Palette Club (pres. 1984-85, Artist of Yr. award 1985). Democrat. Roman Catholic. Office: Tulare Hist Mus 444 W Tulare Ave Tulare CA 93274

GORELICK, JAMIE SHONA, lawyer; b. N.Y.C., May 6, 1950; d. Leonard and Shirley (Fishman) G.; m. Richard E. Waldhorn, Sept. 28, 1975; children: Daniel H., Dana E. BA, Radcliffe Coll., 1972; JD, Harvard U., 1975. Bar: D.C. 1975, U.S. Dist. Ct. D.C. 1976, U.S. Tax Ct. 1976, U.S. Ct. Claims 1976, U.S. Ct. Appeals (D.C. cir.) 1976, U.S. Ct. Appeals (5th cir.) 1977, U.S. Supreme Ct. 1979, U.S. Ct. Appeals (Fed. cir.) 1982, U.S. Ct. Internat. Trade 1984, U.S. Dist. Ct. Md. 1985, U.S. Ct. Appeals (4th cir.) 1986, U.S. Ct. Appeals (3d cir.) 1988. Assoc. Miller, Cassidy, Larroca & Lewin, Washington, 1975-79, 80, ptnr., 1981-93; asst. to sec., counselor to dep. sec. U.S. Dept. Energy, Washington, 1979-80; gen. counsel Dept. Def., Washington, 1993-94; dep. atty. gen. Dept. Justice, Washington, 1994—; mem. Nat. Commn. Support Law Enforcement, Washington, 1995—; chmn.'s adv. coun. U.S. Senate Jud. Com., 1988-93; teaching mem. trial advocacy workshop Harvard Law Sch., Cambridge, Mass., 1982, 84; mem. overseers com. to visit Harvard Coll, 1989-93; vice chmn. task force evaluation of audit investigative inspection components Dept. Def., Washington, 1979-80; mem. sec.'s transition team Dept. Energy, Washington, 1979; bd. dirs. Found. for Change, Nat. Women's Law Ctr., Mental Health Law Project. Bd. editors Corp. Criminal Liability Reporter, 1986-93, Rico Litigation Reporter, 1986-93; adv. bd. RICO Law Reporter, Corp. Criminal Liability Reporter; co-author: Destruction of Evidence, 1989; contbr. articles to profl. jours. Fellow Am. Bar Found.; mem. ABA (chmn. complex crimes litigation com. litigation sect. 1984-87, vice chmn. complex crimes litigation com. 1983-84, Nat. Commn. to Support Law Enforcement, 1995—, sec. litigation sect. 1988-90, coun. mem. 1990-93, com. on profl. discipline, house of delegates 1991-93), D.C. Bar (pres. 1992-93, bd. govs. 1982-88, sec. bd. govs. 1981-82, bar found. advisors 1985-93, legal ethics com.), Womens Bar Assn., Am. Law Inst. Office: Dep Atty Gen US Dept Justice Rm 4111 Main 10th & Constitution Ave NW Washington DC 20530-0001

GORELICK, MOLLY CHERNOW, psychologist, educator; b. N.Y.C., Sept. 17, 1920; d. Morris and Jean Chernow; m. Leon Gorelick, Apr. 12, 1941; children: Walter, Peter. AB, UCLA, 1948, MA, 1955, EdD, 1962. Tchr., counselor Los Angeles City Bd. Edn., 1948-61; instr., chief guidance svcs. Exceptional Children's Found., Los Angeles, 1963-70; prof. Calif. State U., Northridge, 1970-91, prof. emeritus, 1991—; research project dir. Vocat. Rehab. Adminstrn. HEW, Los Angeles, 1964-66, project dir., 1971-75; owner, dir. Hi-Ho Day Camp, 1950-57; cons. Riverside County Schs., 1962-70, Kennedy Child Study Ctr., 1975-79; rschr. Preschool Integration of Children with Handicaps, 1971-75; invited lectr. on mental retardation, Eng., Uruguay, Mex., Argentina, China, Poland and Brazil. Co-author: Rescue series, 5 vols., 1967-68; contbr. articles to profl. jours. Former mem. adv. bd. Calif. State Regional Diagnostic Ctr. Children's Hosp., Mirman Sch. Gifted Children, Calif. Ednl. Ctr., Friendship Day Camp; adv. bd. UCLA Sch. Social Welfare. Mem. APA, Western Psychol. Assn., NEA, Coun. Exceptional Children, Am. Assn. Mental Retardation, Phi Beta Kappa, Pi Lambda Theta, Pi Gamma Mu, Phi Kappa Phi. Office: Calif State U Northridge CA 91330

GOREN, NANCE, artist, art educator; b. N.Y.C., July 23, 1948; d. Shelley and Beulah (Schweitzer) G. BFA, Washington U., St. Louis, 1970; MA, L.I. Univ., 1975; MFA, SUNY, Albany, 1986. Instr. Ann Arundel C.C., Arnold, Md., 1977-78, Prince Georges C.C., Largo, Md., 1977-78; prof. art The Sage Colls., Albany, N.Y., 1980—; dir. Rathbone Gallery, The Sage Colls., 1980-82, chair fine arts divsn. 1983-87, acad. advisor 1980—. Exhbns. include Albany Inst. History & Art, 1978, 81, Western Washington U., 1984 (Purchase award 1984), Hist. Soc. Saratoga Springs, N.Y., 1996, The Museums of Stony Brook, N.Y., 1996. Recipient grad. assistantship C.W. Post Coll., Greenvale, N.Y., 1973-75, faculty rsch. grants The Sage Colls., 1982, 85, 96, Cert. of Merit Nat. Acad. Advising Assn., 1991. Mem. Nat. Mus. Women in the Arts, Women's Caucus for Art, Inter-Soc. Color Coun., Chautauqua Art Assn. Office: The Sage Colleges 140 New Scotland Ave Albany NY 12208

GORENCE, PATRICIA JOSETTA, judge; b. Sheboygan, Wis., Mar. 6, 1943; d. Joseph and Antonia (Marinsheck) G.; m. John Michael Bach, July 11, 1969; children: Amy Jane, Mara Jo, J. Christopher Bach. BA, Marquette U., 1965, JD, 1977; MA, U. Wis., 1969. Bar: Wis. 1977, U.S. Dist. Ct. (ea. and we. dists.) Wis. 1977, U.S. Ct. Appeals (7th cir.) 1979, U.S. Supreme Ct. 1980. Asst. U.S. atty. U.S. Atty.'s Office, Milw., 1979-84, 1st asst. U.S. Atty., 1984-87, 89-91, U.S. Atty., 1987-88; dep. atty. gen. State of Wis. Dept. Justice, Madison, 1991-93; assoc. Ginbel, Reilly, Guerin & Brown, Milw., 1993-94; U.S. magistrate judge U.S. Dist. Ct. Wis., Milw., 1994—. Bd. dirs. U. Wis.-Milw. Slovenian Arts Coun., 1988—, Milw. Dance Theatre, 1993—. Recipient Spl. Commendation, U.S. Dept. Justice, 1986, IRS, 1988. Mem. ABA, Nat. Assn. Women Judges, Fed. Magistrate Judges Assn., Milw. Bar Assn. (Prosecutor of Yr. 1990), State Bar Wis. (chair professionalism com. 1988—, vice chair legal edn. commn. 1994—, Pres. award 1995), 7th Cir. Bar Assn. (chair rules and practices com. 1991-95), Assocs. for Women Lawyers.

GORMAN, JANE MARILYN, retired elementary school educator; b. Southampton, N.Y., Oct. 20, 1934; d. Joseph Alexander and Anna Clarabel (Maslin) Shott; m. Ronald Keith Gorman, Sept. 15, 1957; 1 child, Keith Owen. BS in Music Edn., SUNY, Potsdam, 1956. Music tchr. Liverpool (N.Y.) Ctrl. Schs., 1956-58; tchr. GED jr. high level U.S. Army, Saumar, France, 1959; substitute tchr. music Rochester (N.Y.) City Schs., 1959-60; elem. tchr. Simi Valley (Calif.) Unified Sch. Dist., 1963-91; ret. Mem. AAWU, Calif. Ret. Tchrs. Assn., Sweet Adelines (pres. 1968-70), Order Ea. Star. Republican.

GORMAN, KAREN MACHMER, optometric physician; b. Poughkeepsie, N.Y., June 4, 1955; d. James Andrew and Joan (Benton) Machmer; m. D.L. McCartney III, Aug. 16, 1976 (div. June 1982); m. N. David Gorman, Oct. 16, 1985; 1 stepchild, Danette Y. Gorman. BS in Optometry, U. Houston, 1976, OD, 1978; therapeutic pharm. lic., U. Mo., St. Louis, 1993. Diplomate Nat. Bd. Examiners Optometry; lic. optometrist, Colo., Mo., Tex. Pvt. practice Dallas, 1978-83, 1984-85, Hurst, Tex., 1984-85, St. Joseph, Mo., 1986—; charter mem. optometric adv. panel Pearle, Inc., 1991-93; lectr. on eyecare to community groups; free-lance journalist St. Joseph News-Press, Benson (N.C.) Rev. Contbr. poetry to lit. jours. including Nat. Libr. of Poetry and Typo mag., articles to profl. jours. including St. Joseph News Press and Benson (N.C.) Review; lead actress (play) None Come Back Innocent, Robidoux Resident Theatre, St. Joseph, 1990, Hay Fever, 1991, The Best Man, 1992, Wedded But No Wife, 1993, Mousetrap, 1993, Diary of Anne Frank, 1994, Death and the Maiden, 1995, Veronica's Room, 1996. Vol. Dallas Humane Soc., 1981, YWCA Women's Abuse Shelter; patron Robidoux Resident Theatre, St. Joseph, 1988-92, Ice House Theatre, St. Joseph, Kemper Albrecht Art Mus., St. Joseph, St. Joseph Animal Shelter; sponsor, coach, cheerleader and drill team Mo. Western State Coll., St. Joseph, 1985-86; legis. corr. Humane Soc. U.S., 1990-92; mem. Nat. Soc. Newspaper Columnists. Recipient Optometric Recognition awards Pearle, Inc., 1986-90; U. Houston scholar, 1972-76. Mem. U. Houston Alumni Assn., CWENS, Nat. Assn. Newspaper Columnists, St. Joseph Lit. Guild, Tau Sigma.

GORMAN, LILLIAN R., human resources executive; b. N.Y.C., July 4, 1953; d. Helmuth H. and Ida A. (Malitsch) Degen; BA in Psychology, Lehman Coll., CUNY, 1975; MA in Indsl. Psychology, Case Western Res. U., 1978, PhD in Indsl. Psychology, 1979; MBA in Corp. Fin., U. So. Calif., 1986; m. Mark R. Gorman, Oct. 23, 1976. Econ. benefits asst. Girl Scouts U.S.A., N.Y.C., 1971-75; psychologist Personnel Rsch. Svcs., Personnel Rsch. & Devel. Corp., Cleve., 1975-79, consulting psychologist, 1977-78; mgr. personnel rsch. 1st Interstate Bank, L.A., 1979-82, v.p., mgr. human resource planning and devel., 1982-85; v.p., mgr. human resource planning and exec. devel. 1st Interstate Bancorp, L.A., 1985-86; sr. v.p., human resources dir. 1st Interstate Bank of Calif., 1986-90; exec. v.p. human resources divsn. 1st Interstate Bancorp, L.A., 1990-96; v.p. human resources divsn. Edison Internat., Rosemead, Calif., 1996—; cons. psychology Bd. dirs. INROADS/L.A., 1986—. Mem. APA, Soc. for Psychologists in Mgmt. (bd. dirs. 1993-97). Orgn. for Women Execs., Soc. for Human Resources Mgmt. Home: 1332 Allenford Ave Los Angeles CA 90049-3612

GORMAN, MAUREEN J., lawyer; b. Rockford, Ill., Dec. 17, 1955; d. John William and Joanne Mary (Ollman) G.; m. Alan O. Sykes, 1980. BA, Coll. William and Mary, 1978; JD, Yale U., 1981. Bar: D.C. 1983, Ill. 1987. Law clk. to Hon. Warren W. Eginton U.S. Dist. Ct. Conn., 1981-82; assoc. Caplin & Drysdale, Washington, 1982-85; legis. atty. joint com. on taxation U.S. Congress, Washington, 1985-86; assoc. Mayer, Brown & Platt, Chgo., 1986-88, ptnr., 1988—. Mem. ABA (chairperson subcom. tech. corrections, employee benefits com., tax sect. 1987-91). Home: 343 E 1st St Hinsdale IL 60521-4241 Office: Mayer Brown & Platt 190 S La Salle St Chicago IL 60603-3410

GORMAN-GORDLEY, MARCIE SOTHERN, personal care industry franchise executive; b. N.Y.C., Feb. 25, 1949; d. Jerry R. and Carole Edith (Frendel) Sothern; m. N. Scott Gorman, June 14, 1969 (div.); children: Michael Stephen, Mark Jason; m. Mark A. Gordley, June 26, 1994. AA, U. Fla., 1968; BS, Memphis State U., 1970. Tchr., Memphis City Sch. System, 1970-73; tng. dir. Weight Watchers of Palm Beach County and Weight Watchers So. Ala., Inc., West Palm Beach, Fla., 1973—, area dir., then pres., 1977—; pres. Markel Ads, Inc. Cubmaster Troop 130. Hon. lt. col. a.d.c. Ala. Militia. Mem. Women' Am. ORT (program chmn. 1975), Optometric Soc. (sec. 1973), Weight Watchers Franchise Assn. (chair mktg. com., mem. advt./mktg. coun., chairperson region IV bd. dirs., treas., 2d v.p. 1991, 1st v.p.), Nat. Orgn. Women, Exec. Women of the Palm Beaches, Am. Bus. Women's Assn., Nat. Assn. Female Execs., Zonta. Home: 429 N Country Club Dr Lake Worth FL 33462-1003 Office: 2459 S Congress Ave West Palm Beach FL 33406-7616

GORNEY, PAULA JEAN WARDIN, gas company specialist; b. Saginaw, Mich., Apr. 5, 1955; d. Carl Leon and Bonnie Jean (Tilden) Wardin; m. Paul Girard Gorney, Apr. 15, 1978. Secretarial degree, Cen. Mich. U., 1975; BA in Honors summa cum laude, Saginaw Valley State U., 1992. Divsn. sec. Alcoholism Svcs. Saginaw County Health Dept., Saginaw, 1976-79; computer sys. coord. Mulholland Equipment, Saginaw, 1979; exec. sec. Valley Oxygen co., Bay City, Mich., 1980-85; splty. gas specialist Mich. Airgas, Bay City, 1985-96, market mgr. specialty and med. gases, 1996—; presenter in field of women's studies. Bd. dirs. alumni bd. Saginaw Valley State U., University Center, Mich., 1992—; supporting mem. Ctr. for Women and Religion, U. Calif., Berkeley, 1992—; mem. Womens Internat. League for Peace and Freedom, 1993—. Mem. AAUW, NOW, Mich. Women Studies Assn., Alpha Chi (Delta chpt. pres. 1992-95), Nat. Honor Scholarship Soc.

GORR, ELAINE GRAY, therapist, elementary education educator; b. Pitts., Oct. 3, 1949; d. Elmer and Elizabeth Gray; m. Joseph Charles Bonasorte, June 20, 1969 (div. 1972); 1 child, Leah Christine Bonasorte; m. Arthur Richard Gorr, Aug. 12, 1983; children: Arthur Richard, Stephen, Ellen Jane, Bruce, Matthew. BS in Psychology, U. Pitts., 1972; MA in Counseling/Psychology, Norwich U., 1993; postgrad., Walden U., 1992-96. Cert. elem. sch. counselor, Pa., elem. tchr., Pa. Tchr. Pitts. Pub. Schs., 1973-89; pvt. practice counselor, therapist Pitts., 1992—. Mem. APA, ACA, Am. Sch. Counseling Assn.

GORSKE, MARGOT ELIZABETH, nurse administrator; b. Wilmington, Del., Oct. 7, 1955; d. Ronald Leander and Sandra Jean (Harstly) Smith; m. Wilton Scot Gorske, June 14, 1986; children: Wilton Benjamin, Alyson Elizabeth. BA, Beloit Coll., 1979; BSN, U. Tex., Austin, 1988; MS in Nursing, Troy State U., 1994. Clin. staff nurse Eisenhower Med. Ctr., Ft. Godon, Ga., 1988-89; asst. head nurse Winn Army Hosp., Ft. Stewart, Ga., 1989-92, murse mgr., 1992-93; clin. staff nurse Martin Army Hosp., Ft. Benning, Ga., 1994-95; clin. instr. Columbus (Ga.) Coll. Sch. Nursing, 1994-95, LaGrante (Ga.) Coll. Sch. Nursing, 1995; divsn. coord. Psychiat. Nursing Svcs. Care South, Columbus, 1995—; presenter in field. With U.S. Army Nurse Corps, 1988-93, res., 1993-96. U. Tex. scholar, 1985-88, Beloit Coll. scholar, 1974-79. Mem. Am. Psychiat. Nurses Assn., Sigma Theta Tau. Democrat. Mem. LDS Ch. Office: Care South St Francis Hosp 1900 Hamilta Rd Columbus GA 31964

GORSKI, HEDWIG IRENE, journalist, poet; b. Trenton, N.J., July 18, 1949; d. Joseph and Irene (Bus) G.; m. Alfred Wishart Jr., Nov. 1, 1973 (div. 1979); m. D'Jalma Garnier III, Dec. 26, 1979. AA, Mercer County C.C., 1969; BFA, Nova Scotia Coll. Art Design, 1976; MA, U. Southwestern La., 1997. Program coord. Tex. Circuit Writers Svc. Orgn., Austin, 1981-83; exec. dir. Perfection Prodns., Lafayette, La., 1985—. Performance poet East of Eden Band, audio tape, 1985, Charted Can. Radio; author: Snatches of the Visible Unreal, 1990, others. Grantee Nat. Endowment for the Arts, 1996. Mem. Soc. Profl. Journalists. Democrat. Roman Catholic. Home: 327 Clinton St Lafayette LA 70501

GORTNER, SUSAN REICHERT, nursing educator; b. San Francisco, Dec. 23, 1932; d. Frederick Leet and Erida Louise (Leuschner) R.; m. Willis Alway Gortner, Aug. 25, 1960 (dec. Sept. 1993); children: Catherine Willis, Frederick Aiken. AB, Stanford U., 1953; M Nursing, Western Res. U., 1957; PhD, U. Calif., Berkeley, 1964; postgrad., Stanford U., 1983. Staff nurse, instr., supr. Johns Hopkins Hosp. Sch. Nursing, Balt., 1957-58; instr. to asst. prof. Sch. Nursing U. Hawaii, Honolulu, 1958-64; staff scientist, rsch. adminstr. div. nursing USPHS, Bethesda, Md., 1966-78; assoc. dean rsch. Sch. Nursing U. Calif., San Francisco, 1978-86, acting chmn. dept. family health, 1982, prof. dept. family health care nursing, 1978-94; prof. emerita, 1994—; fellow, assoc. mem. faculty Inst. Health Policy U. Calif., San Francisco, 1979-94, mem. affiliated faculty Inst. for Aging and Health, 1981-94, adj. prof. internal medicine dept. gen. medicine, 1989-94, dir. cardiac recovery lab. Sch. Nursing, 1987-95, spl. asst. to dean, 1993-94; Fulbright lectr., rsch. scholar Norwegian Fulbright Commn., Oslo, 1988. Contbr. articles, papers to profl. publs., chpts. to books. Health advisor N. Fork Assn., Soda Springs, Calif., 1981—. Disting. scholar Nat. Ctr. Nursing Rsch., 1990; named Disting. Alumna Frances Payne Bolton Sch. Nursing, 1983. Fellow Am. Acad. Nursing; mem. ANA (chair exec. com., coun. nurse rsch. com. 1976-80, cabinet on nursing rsch. 1984-86), Am. Heart Assn. (coun. cardiovascular nursing exec. com. 1987-91, coun. epidemiology 1989—, Katharine A. Lembright award 1991, fellow in cardiovascular nursing coun. 1992), Sigma Theta Tau (Alpha Eta chpt., Margretta M. Styles award 1990). Home: PO Box 1056 Soda Springs CA 95728-1056 Office: U Calif 4th And Parnassus # N411Y San Francisco CA 94143

GORUM, VICTORIA, computer engineer; b. Tucson, Ariz., Dec. 30, 1951; d. Alvin E. and Virginia L. (Don Carlos) G. BS in Zoology, U. Mass., 1974; MS in Math., Elec. Engring., U. Nev., 1982. Rsch. asst. Worcester Found. for Exptl. Biology, Shrewsbury, Mass., 1974-76, Stanford Rsch. Inst., Menlo Park, Calif., 1976-77; sr. rsch. asst. Lawrence Berkeley (Calif.) Labs., 1977-79; tech. writer Lynch Communications, Reno, 1981-82; cons. CPL Inc., Sunnyvale, Calif., 1982-83; mgr. software support Zilog, Inc., Campbell, Calif., 1983-85; mgr. network support Sun Microsystems, Mountain View, Calif., 1986-90; mgr. net. info. systems Next Computer, Inc., Fremont, Calif., 1990-93; mgr. network ops. Adobe Systems, Mountain View, Calif., 1993-94; v.p. ops. Break Away Tech. Svcs., 1994-96; pres. Network Tech. Exp. Inc., 1996—. Mem. Assn. for Computing Machinery, IEEE, Am. Needlepoint Guild, Embroidery Guild Am. Home: 14737 Clayton Rd San Jose CA 95127-5213

GORVETT, GAYLE SHAWN, legal assistant; b. Denver, Dec. 16, 1968; d. Robert Lindley and Lou June (Luske) G. BA in Internat. Bus., DePauw U., 91; postgrad., Northwestern U., 1996—. Cert. proficient in bus. French, French C. of C., Paris. Japanese Exch. and Tchg. asst. English tchr. Japanese Ministry of Edn., Shime, 91-92; investment analyst Prudential Capital Group, Chgo., 1993-94; legal asst. antitrust group Sidley & Austin, Chgo., 1994—. Young Profl. Chgo. Coun. on Fgn. Rels., 1993—; active Chgo. Cares Vol. Orgn., Chgo. Vol. Legal Svcs. Mem. Japanese Exch. and Tchg. Alumni Assn., Delta Gamma. Republican. Home: 30 E Huron St Chicago IL 60611

GORYN, SARA, textiles executive, real estate developer, psychologist; b. Lima, Peru, Dec. 28, 1944; came to U.S., 1988; d. Ricardo and Lola (Braiman) Grunfeld; m. Jorge Goryn, June 18, 1966 (dec. Sept. 1985); children: Karen, Monica, Lea. B in Psychology, Cath. U., Lima, 1978, M in Psychology, 1985; BA in Bus., Queens Coll., 1989-91. Sec. Inst. Internat. Edn., Lima, 1963-66; head dept. clin. psychology Coll. Leon Pinelo, Lima, 1978-85; pvt. practice Lima, 1978-85; founder Nido Picaflores, Lima, 1980; gen. mgr. Fabritex Peruana, Lima, 1985-88, Michelle Textiles, Charlotte, N.C., 1989—; v.p. Monica Investment, Charlotte, 1990-93, pres., 1993—; bd. dirs. Fabritex Peruana, Lima, MLK Internat., Charlotte, SOFAS y MAS,

Lima. Author learning disabilities curriculum, 1980. Mem. Soc. Israelita Peru, Lima, 1966—, Hebraica, Lima, 1966—. Mem. Peru Psychol. Soc. Democrat. Home: 3600 Castellaine Dr Charlotte NC 28226-6386

GORZKA, MARGARET ROSE, elementary education educator; b. Akron, Ohio, Sept. 2, 1945; d. Alfonso Sebastian and Hannah Jean (Morris) Brown; m. Joseph Frank Gorzka Sr., Nov. 24, 1966; children: Joseph Frank Jr., Julie-Anne. BS in Elem. Edn., Akron U., 1968; MS in Elem. Edn., Nazareth Coll., 1986. Permanent cert. N-6. Tchr. 1st grade # 3 Sch. Rochester (N.Y.) City Schs., 1967-68, St. John the Evangelist, Rochester, 1968-70, Mother of Sorrows, Rochester, 1971-72; tchr. kindergarten St. John's Sch., Spencerport, N.Y., spring 1978; tchr. 1st, 2d, 3d grades St. Rita's, West Webster, N.Y., 1978-79; tchr. 1st grade St. Anne's, Rochester, 1979-81, St. Jerome's, East Rochester, N.Y., 1981-86; tchr. kindergarten, 1st grade East Rochester Union Free Schs., East Rochester, 1986-91; tchr. 1st grade Fairport (N.Y.) Cen. Schs., 1991—; geselle trainer East Rochester Union Free Schs., 1987—, essential elements of effective instrn. trainer, 1987-91, clin. supervision trainer, 1987-91; cons. and presenter in field. Mem. fundraising com. Advent House, Fairport, 1993—; PTA chair for Parent Edn., 1995-96; mem. staff devel. Fairport Cen. Sch. Dist., 1996-97. Grantee Sci. Wizards at Work, 1994; recipient Disting. Svc. award East Rochester PTA, 1986, Crystal Apple award, 1995, PASE award, 1995, Team Performance Recognition award for Fairport Cen. Sch. dist., 1993-94, Phoebe Apperson Hearst Outstanding Edn. Excellence award 1996. Mem. N.Y. State United Tchrs., Fairport Edn. Assn., Phi Mu Alumnae (v.p. 1970s). Republican. Roman Catholic. Home: 1 Cobblestone Dr Fairport NY 14450-3152

GORZYCKI, DIANE ELAINE, middle school educator; b. Austin, Tex., Nov. 9, 1953; d. George C. and Patricia (Crowson) G.; m. Jack G. Harbour, Dec. 17, 1983 (div. 1988); 1 child, Scott A. Harbour. BMus, U. Tex., 1975. Band dir. Saegert Mid. Sch., Seguin, Tex., 1976-77, Porter Jr. H.S., Austin, Tex., 1977-93, Bailey Mid. Sch., Austin, 1993—; adjudicator Univ. Interscholastic League, Tex., 1988—. Cub scout leader Boy Scouts Am., Austin, 1995—. Mem. Nat. Bandmasters Assn., Music Educators Nat. Conf., Tex. Bandmasters Assn., Tex. Music Adjudicators Assn, U. Tex. Longhorn Alumni Band (pres. 1992-93, bd. dirs. 1995—), Tex. Music Educators Assn. (clinician 1988—, pres. region 18 1994—), U. Tex. Ex-Students Assn. (life), Tau Beta Sigma, Sigma Alpha Iota, Phi Beta Mu, Phi Delta Kappa. Home: 7424 Whistlestop Dr Austin TX 78749 Office: Bailey Mid Sch Band 4020 Lost Oasis Hollow Austin TX 78739

GOSE, CELESTE MARLENE, writer; b. Laramie, Wyo., Jan. 2, 1959; d. Richard Vern Gose and Agnes Jean (Allen) McGregger. BS, U. Wyo., 1984; student, U. UNA, Belo Horizonte, Brazil, 1982. Freelance writer Scottsdale, Ariz., 1990—; writer Today's Ariz. Woman. N.Mex. prodn. coord. (feature movies) Twins, 1988, Young Guns, 1988, (cable) The Tracker, 1987; asst. prodn. coord. (feature movies) Outrageous Fortune, The Sunday Disney Movie; asst. unit publicist The Milagro Beanfield War, 1986; casting asst. (TV) Lonesome Dove, 1988, Sparks, 1989, The Fantasticks, 1995; author: Your Daggar or Mine?, 1991, (song lyrics) Awake Inside a Dream, 1990, Caught in Eternity, 1990, Drum Sticks on the Moon, 1990, Of A Different Spirit, 1994, Stardust and Loneflower, 1994, Coyotes Don't Bark, 1995, The Reluctant Actress, Have No Regrets (screenplay) Junkyard Palace. Mem. Ariz. 602-Film Prodr's. Warehouse, Women in Comm., Internat. Arabian Horse Assn., Brazilian Inst. Ariz., Ariz. Club. Republican. Home and Office: 31206 N 65th St Cave Creek AZ 85331-6126

GOSE, KAREN KAMARA, state arts administrator; b. Seattle, July 4, 1955; d. Alvin Frederick Jr. and Donna Muriel (Malde) Kamara; m. Michael Gordon Gose, Mar. 20, 1978; children: John Michael, Elisabeth Jane. BA, The Evergreen State Coll., 1982. Adminstrv. asst. to v.p. and provost The Evergreen State Coll., Olympia, Wash., 1983-86; arts program mgr. II Wash. State Arts Commn., Olympia, 1986-88, 1988-90, asst. dir., 1990-93, acting exec. dir., 1993-94, exec. dir., 1994—; bd. dirs. Western States Arts Fedn., Santa Fe. Editor: Peoples of Washington, 1989. Office: Wash State Arts Commn 234 E 8th Ave Olympia WA 98504-2675

GOSE GALLOWAY, GRACE SMITH, wholesale lumber company executive; b. Burke's Garden, Va., Oct. 14, 1909; d. Tilden Hendricks and Margaret (Wynn) Short; m. Lionel Charles Smith, Oct. 30, 1927 (dec. Sept. 1956); children: Lionel Elizabeth and Hilah Mae (twins); m. John Paul Gose, Mar. 28, 1959 (dec. May 1981); m. G.H. Galloway, Dec. 28, 1985 (dec. Dec. 1994). B.S. in Biology, Concord Coll., Athens, W.Va., 1954, B.S. in Vocat. Home Econs., 1956; postgrad.; lifetime cert. W.Va. U., 1976. Cert. tchr., W.Va. Elem. tchr., pub. schs., Sommers County, W.Va., 1954-61; supt. women's prison, Penoe Spring, W.Va., 1961-65; high sch. tchr., pub. schs., Raleigh County, W.Va., 1965-68, 70-79; owner, operator L. C. Smith Mine Timbers, Jumping Branch, W.Va., 1979—; active in real estate, Jumping Branch, 1945—. Commr. Pub. Svc. Dist. Water of Summers County,, Nimitz and Jumping Branch. Mem. Internat. Assn. Chiefs of Police (life), Nat. Ret. Tchrs. Assn. Democrat. Methodist. Lodge: Order Eastern Star. Avocations: selling real estate, travel in U.S. and Canada. Home and Office: Box 81 HC 85 Jumping Branch WV 25969-0081

GOSS, GEORGIA BULMAN, translator; b. N.Y.C., Dec. 1, 1939; d. James Cornelius and Marian Bright (McLaughlin) Bulman; m. Douglas Keith Goss, Dec. 21, 1957; children: Kristin Anne, David. BA, U. Mich., 1961. Libr., High Altitude Obs., Boulder, Colo., 1963-64, U.S. Bur. Standards, Boulder, 1964-65; cons. editor Spanish lang. pilots' tng. manual, 1981-82; freelance translator, Englewood, Colo., 1982—. Mem. U. Mich. Alumni Assn., Phi Sigma Iota. Republican. Episcopalian. Home and Office: D-1 # 105 7755 E Quincy Ave Denver CO 80237-2312

GOSS, MONIQUE ZENAIDA, artist, educator; b. Toulouse, France, Apr. 29, 1941; came to U.S., 1947; d. Julian and Margaret (Pick) Epstein; m. Robert Goss; children: Julie Anne, Jamie Lisa. BS, NYU, 1968; MA, Towson State U., 1981; postgrad., Hunter Coll., Johns Hopkins U., Md. Inst. Coll. Art. Program coord. Mayor's Com. on Art and Culture, Balt., 1976-78; artist in residence Dept. of Health, Arundal County, 1994, Frederick (Md.) Arts Coun., 1995, Md. Arts Coun., 30 locations, 1995—; tchr. Md. Artist-in Edn. Program Murals, Dundalk C.C.; adj. prof. watercolor painting Towson Coll.; tchr. continuing edn. geriatric programs Essex C.C.; tchr. Artscape-Recreation Ctrs., Balt. City; art tchr. Pimlico Jr. H.S., Robert Poole Jr. H.S.; tchr. enrichment programs Balt. City Pub. Schs., Belair H.S., Cross Country Elem. Sch., Balt. City Recreation Ctr., Oasis Geriatric Ceramics Program, Balt., 10 yrs. of pvt. instrn.; curator Art Gallery 247, Balt., mural exhibit Balt. Mus. Art. Represented in permanent collections at N.Y.U., Towson State Coll., John F. Kennedy Inst., Johns Hopkins Hosp., Mayor's Adv. Com. on Art and Culture, Balt.; bldg. murals include John F. Kennedy Inst., Balt., 1978, Native Am. Indian Ctr., Balt., 1979, Timonium State Fairgrounds, Balt., 1979, Pikesville Shopping Ctr., Balt., 1979, Luskin Dept. Store, Eastpoint, Md., 1979, Carroll County (Md.) Agr. Ctr., 1979, Nicki Paul Agy., World Trade Ctr., Balt., 1980, Geriatric Thesis Mural, Balt., 1980, Hamilton Recreation Ctr., Balt., 1980, New Era Ctr., Balt., 1980, The Chocolate Factory, Balt., 1980, Spanish Maison Restaurant, Balt., 1980, Youth Benefit Elem., Fallston, Md., 1981, Waverly Recreation Ctr., Balt., 1982, Booker T. Washington Jr. High, Balt., 1983, Edison H.S., Montgomery County, Md., 1988, Lewistown Elem., Frederick County, Md., 1989, Easton Elem., Dorcester County, Md., 1990, Ocean City Elem., Worcester County, Md., 1990, Thomas Pullen Magnet Sch., Prince George's County, Md., 1991, John Carroll H.S., Harford County, 1991, Belair Sr. Ctr., Harford County, 1992, Belair Mid. Sch., Harford County, 1992, New Windsor Mid. Sch., Carroll County, 1992, Stephen Decatur Mid. Sch., Berlin, Md., 1993, Allen Apts.-Parole Md., Anne Arundel County, Md., 1993, Panorama Elem. Sch., Prince George's County, Md., 1994, Echodale Elem. Sch., Balt. County, 1994, Emmittsburg Elem. Sch., Frederick, Md., 1994, South Frederick Elem. Sch., 1994, Youth Ctr. Frederick Recreation Ctr., 1995, Parkway Elem. Sch., Frederick County, Md., 1995, White Flint Mall, Montgomery County, Md., Rockledge Elem. Sch., Prince George's County, 1995, Free State Mall, Bowie, Md., Rodger's Forje Elem., 1996, others. Mem. steering com. Bill Clinton; vol. Del. Maggie McIntosh, Md. House, 1994. Recipient yearly artist in edn. grants Md. State Arts Coun., 1980—, awards Frederick Arts Coun., Timonium Jaycees Art Show, WCBM, Lake Show Honor Sect., Towsontown Ct. Arts Festival award. Democrat. Jewish. Home: 2505 Pinebrush Rd Baltimore MD 21209

GOSS, PATRICIA ELIZABETH, secondary education educator; b. Cheyenne, Wyo., June 6, 1958; d. Alan Robert and Donna Jean (Hirst) G.; m. Michael Holland Argall, Nov. 6, 1993. BA, Colo. Women's Coll., 1979; MA, U. Denver, 1980; postgrad., U. Colo., 1986. Cert. secondary tchr., Colo. Exec. dir. Denver Dem. Com., 1980-82; coord. 3d Congl. dist. Mondale for Pres. Campaign, Colo., 1984; tchr. mid. sch. gifted and talented Denver Pub. Schs., 1988-90, tchr. history, 1991—; supr. student tchrs. Regis Coll., Denver, 1996. Contbr. articles to profl. jours. Chmn. precinct com. Denver Dem. Com., 1980—, mem. exec. com., 1980-86. Mem. NEA (congl. contact team 1993—, rep. assembly del. 1993, 96), Colo. Edn. Assn. (legis. action team 1991—, bd. dirs. 1992—), Denver Classroom Tchrs. Assn. (dir. govtl. rels. 1991—), DAR, Order Ea. Star, Alpha Delta Kappa. Presbyterian. Home: 1378 Locust Denver CO 80220 Office: George Washington HS 655 S Monaco Pky Denver CO 80224

GOSSELL, TERRY RAE, advertising agency executive, small business owner; b. Rockford, Ill., Jan. 24, 1947; d. Virgil Houston and Wilma Beatrice (Cox) Pierce; m. Ronald Richard Gossell, Mar. 3, 1979 (div. Apr., 1983); children: Cameo Ann Elliott, Ronica Rae. Grad. high sch., Loves Park, Ill.; arts cert., U. Kans., 1962. Artist Rockford (Ill.F) Silk Screen Process, 1967-72, Grocery Co-op Advt., Ocala, Fla., 1973-74; art dir. Carlson & Co. Advt., Rockford, Ill., 1975; co-owner R.S.S.P. Graphics & Typesetting, Rockford, 1975-76; owner Graphic Comm., Inc., Rockford, 1976-79, T.R. Gossell Advt., Rockford, 1979-82; owner The Gossell Agy., Phoenix, 1982-88, Rockford, 1988—. Author, artist: (comic book) The Gang from Carl Hayden High Sch., 1986-87. Advisor No. Ill. Advt. Coun. Explorer Post #423, Rockford, 1990-92. Recipient Merit and 1st Place awards Rockford Advt. Club, 1978, 79, 1st Place award of Excellence, Nat. Assn. Pers. Cons., San Diego, 1985, Cert. of Merit, BMA Tower awards, 1994. Mem. Am. Advt. Fedn., No. Ill. Advt. Coun. (pres. 1992-94, merit, 1st and 2nd pl. awards 1980, 81, 91, 93, 94, 95), bd. dir., Greater Rockford Adv. Club,1996—. Democrat. Lutheran. Office: The Gossell Agy 5002 Sherwood Forest Rd Rockford IL 61109-2735

GOSSEN, RENEE HEBERT, retail executive; b. Lafayette, LA, Sept. 1, 1951; d. Joel L. and Elsie L. (Lasseigne) Hebert; m. Jeffrey Marc Gossen; children: Rahlyn Renee, Jenee Michelle. BS, U. Southwestern LA, 1973. Owner, mgr. Mondays Child, Lafayette, 1982—. Home: 111 Monteigne Dr Lafayette LA 70506-5422 Office: Mondays Child 4111 Johnston St Lafayette LA 70503

GOSSETT, SUSAN DIANNE, counselor educator; b. Atlanta, July 1, 1953; d. Herman R. and Edna (Hart) G. BS in Bus., Judson Coll., 1974; cert. elem. tchr., Berry Coll., 1975; MS in Guidance and Counseling, Jacksonville State U., 1979; EdD in Counselor Edn., U. Ala., 1992. Nat. cert. counselor, nat. cert. sch. counselor, cert. AA sch. counselor K-12, Ala., cert. tchr. class B K-8, Ala., sch. psychometrist, Ala.; lic. profl. counselor, Ala. Tchr. elem. edn. Spring Garden (Ala.) High Sch., 1976-79; guidance counselor Cherokee County Schs., Centre, Ala., 1979-90; grad. asst. instr., doctoral intern U. Ala., Tuscaloosa, 1990-91, asst. prof., 1991, rsch. asst., 1992; sch. counselor Centre Mid. Sch., 1992-93; asst. prof., coord. sch. counseling program Troy State U., Phenix City, 1993—; head start tchr. Spring Garden High Sch., summer 1976; freshmen counselor, summer 1987, 88, 89; freshmen counseling supr., summer 1990; adj. faculty U. Ala., Tuscaloosa, 1992; presenter Am. Sch. Counselor Nat. Conf., Little Rock, 1989, Nat. Mid. Sch. Assn. Regional Conf., Birmingham, Ala., 1989. Thelma J. M. Smith scholar, 1990-91. Mem. ACA, Am. Sch. Counseling Assn., Am. Assn. Specialists in Group Work, Am. Assn. Counselor Edn. and Supervision, So. Assn. Counselor Edn. and Supervision (presenter conf. 1991), Ala. Counseling Assn. (grad. student com. 1991-92), Ala. Sch. Counselors Assn., Ala. Assn. for Specialists in Group Work (sec. 1989-90), Chpt. III Ala. Assn. for Counseling and Devel. (presenter confs. 1987, 91, 92), Kappa Delta Pi, Chi Sigma Iota, Phi Kappa Phi. Democrat. United Methodist. Office: Troy State U One University Pl Phenix City AL 36869

GOTLIEB, JAQUELIN SMITH, pediatrician; b. Washington, Oct. 20, 1946; d. Turner Taliaferro and Lois Barbara (Fisk) Smith; m. Edward Marvin Gotlieb, June 25,1970; children: Sarah Ruth, Aaron Franklin, David Jacob. BS in Zoology, Duke U., 1968; MD, Med. Coll. Va., 1972. Diplomate Am. Bd. Pediat. Rotating intern Med. Coll. Va. Hosps.-Va. Commonwealth U., Richmond, 1972-73, resident in pediat., 1973-74; pvt. practice Richmond, 1974-75, Stone Mountain, Ga., 1976-86, 87—; resident in pediat. U. Colo., Denver, 1975-76; med. dir., cons. CIGNA Healthplan Ga., Atlanta, 1986-87; sch. physician Richmond City Schs., 1974-75. Bd. dirs. Ga. Health Found., Atlanta, 1985-95, vice chmn., 1995—. Fellow Am. Acad. Pediat. (Ga. chpt. bd. dirs. 1996—); mem. Med. Assn. Ga., Ga. Perinatal Assn. (bd. dirs. 1994—), DeKalb Med. Soc. (chmn. com. 1976). Office: Pediatric Ctr 5405 Memorial Dr Ste D Stone Mountain GA 30083-3258

GOTO, MIDORI See MIDORI

GOTSCH, AUDREY ROSE, environmental health sciences educator, researcher; b. Milw., May 30, 1939; d. Carlos Louis and Florence Olga (Clausing) Grandy; m. Thomas Gotsch, June 20, 1959; children: Christine Anne Robinson, Allison Lorraine. BS, Ind. U., 1963; MPH, U. Mich., 1966; DrPH, CHES, Columbia U., 1976. Pvt. practice as dental hygienist Lafayette, Ind., 1962-63, Springfield, Ill., 1963-65; health educator Ill. Dept. Health, Springfield, 1966-67, N.J. State Dept. Health, Trenton, 1968; assoc. prof., chief dept. environ. and cmty. medicine U. Medicine and Dentistry N.J. Robert Wood Johnson Med. Sch., Piscataway, 1978-93, prof., chief dept. environ. and cmty. medicine, 1993—, acting chair dept. environ. and cmty. medicine, 1994-95; dir. pub. edn. and risk com. divsn. Environ. and Occupational Health Scis. Inst., 1983—; cons. Nat. Hospice Demonstration Programs, 1980, Hospice of Ctrl. N.Y., Syracuse, 1980, Nat. Cancer Inst., 1981—, Fox Chase Cancer Ctr., Phila., 1983, Medcom, Inc., Calif., 1985, NIH, Heart, Lung and Blood Inst., Bethesda, Md., 1985—, and others; assoc. mem. grad. faculty, Rutgers U., New Brunswick, N.J., 1984—; mem. Outreach Task Force, The Cancer Inst. N.J., 1991—; assoc. mem. Inst. for Health, Health Care Policy and Aging Rsch., Rutgers, 1992; councilor, Coun. on Edn. for Pub. Health, 1990-96, pres. 1993-96; mem. Coun. Edn. for Pub. Health, 1990-96, sec., 1991-93, pres., 1993-96; chair ednl. programs com. Environ. Health Found., 1995—; mem. steering com. Cmty. Environ. Health Assessment, NACCHO and Nat. Ctr. Environ. Health, CDC, 1995—. Author: (with others) Communication of Risk, 1992, Education for Health: Strategies for Change, 1978, The Environment and the Community: Environmental Health Lesons for Grades 10-12, 1990, Occupational Health Awareness: Lessons for Vocational Students in Secondary Schools, 1990, Healthy Environment--Healthy Me for Kindergarten-Sixth Grade, 1991, 92, Environmental Decision Making, 1994, and others; mem. editl. bd. Health Edn. Quar., 1986-89; editor-in-chief INFOletter: Environmental and Occupational Health Briefs, 1988-95; contbr. reports, articles and abstracts to profl. jours. and newspapers; videos Alexandria's Clean-Up Fix-Up Parade, 1988, Alu-man the Can, 1987 (Sci. Commendation Cath. Audio Visual Educators 1991), Safety Sense, 1989, Sam's Safety Star Award, 1988, Down the Drain, 1989, Keeping the Lid on Air Pollution, 1989 (Cable award Programming Excellence CTN N.J. 1990), Inside Story on Air Pollution, 1990, What To Do With All Our Garbage?, 1990, Talkin' Trash, 1992; contbr. numerous articles to profl. jours. Mem. N.J. Pub. Health Coun., Trenton, 1987—, sec., 1992-94, vice chair, 1994-96; task force Gov.'s Conf. on Aging, 1980-81. USPHS fellow, 1965-66, 72-74; grantee Nat. Inst. Environ. Health Scis., 1987—, NSF, 1991-95, N.J. Bus. Roundtable, 1989-92, N.J. Dept. Edn., 1991-92, U.S. EPA, 1991-95, N.J. Dept. Environ. Protection and Energy, 1991-92, numerous others; C.V. Mosby scholar, 1962; recipient Sec.'s award U.S. Dept. Health and Human Svcs., 1988, 94, Statewide Faculty Recognition award N.J. Bd. Higher Edn., 1989. Mem. Am. Pub. Health Assn. (Pub. Health Edn. and Health Promotion sect., Occupational Safety and Health sect.), Assn. for the Social Scis. in Health, Assn. Tchrs. of Preventive Medicine, Soc. for Pub. Health Edn. (Greater N.Y., N.J. chpts.), Internat. Union for Health Edn., Soc. Toxicology (Mid-Atlantic chpt.), Nat. Ctr. for Health Edn., Nat. Hospice Orgn., N.J. Hospice Orgn. (bd. trustees 1980-82), N.J. Pub. Health Assn., Soc. for Pub. Health Edn., Soc. for Risk Analysis, Sigma Phi Alpha, Sigma Xi. Lutheran. Office: U Medicine & Dentistry NJ Robert Wood Johnson Med Sch EOHSI 681 Frelinghuysen Rd Piscataway NJ 08855-1179

GOTSCH, GWEN RHODA, editor, writer; b. Detroit, July 28, 1954; d. Herbert Maurice and Marilyn Helen (Masch) G.; m. Lon Arthur Grahnke; Aug. 14, 1982; children: Kristoffer, Eliza, Kurt. BA, Augustana Coll., Rock Island, 1975. Reference libr. LaLeche League Internat., Franklin Park, Ill., 1979-84; sr. editor LaLeche League Internat., Schaumburg, Ill., 1984—. Author: Breastfeeding Pure and Simple, 1993; contbr. articles to profl. jours. Lutheran.

GOTT, MARJORIE EDA CROSBY, conservationist, former educator; b. Louisville; d. Alva Baird and Nellie (Jones) Crosby; m. John Richard Gott, Jr., Mar. 12, 1946 (dec. Sept. 1993); 1 child, J. Richard III. AB in Math., U. Louisville, 1934; postgrad., U. Ky., 1938-42. Nationally accredited flower show judge, landscape design critic and judge. Underwriter Commonwealth Life Ins. Co., Louisville, 1934-37; tchr. English Hikes Sch., Buechel, Ky., 1937-43; civilian chief statis. control unit Materiel Command, Army Air Force, Dayton, Ohio, 1943-46; tchr. psychology Bapt. Hosp. and Gen. Hosp., Louisville, 1950-52; dedicated Ky.'s Floral Clock to All Kentuckians Who Take Pride in the Beauty of Their State Commonwealth of Ky.,1961. Author: (booklet) How a Garden Club Beautifies a City, 1967. Pres. Young Women's Rep. Club of Louisville and Jefferson County, 1938-40; pres. Beautification League Louisville and Jefferson County, 1963-64; co-chair Keep Ky. Cleaner-Greener, 1963-68; bd. dirs. Scenic Ky., Inc., 1989—, Nat. Coun. State Garden Clubs, 1961-83. Recipient Conservation award of merit Commonwealth of Ky., 1963, Landscape Design Critics award Nat. Coun. State Garden Clubs, 1979. Mem. Woman's Club of Louisville (pres. 1973-75, hon. 1991—), Garden Club of Ky. (pres. 1961-63), Nat. Assn. Parliamentarians (founder, pres. Louisville unit 1961-63), Louisville Astron. Soc. (hon.). Presbyterian. Home: 136 Indian Hills Trl Louisville KY 40207-1541

GOTTOVI, KAREN ELIZABETH, former state legislator, political consultant, researcher; b. Rochester, N.Y., Feb. 2, 1941; d. Richard Allan Eckberg and Vivian Emma (Chall) Eckberg; m. Daniel Gottovi, June 23, 1962; children: Daniel Richard, Peter Andrew, Nancy Christine. BA, Wells Coll., 1962; MS in LS, U. N.C., 1972. Tchr. English, Pittsford (N.Y.) Cen. High Sch., 1962-65, 66; reference libr. Wilmington (N.C.) Pub. Libr., 1972-75; commr. New Hanover County, Wilmington, 1976-84; polit. cons. Ind. Opinion Rsch. & Communications, Inc., Wilmington, 1985-91; mem. N.C. Ho. of Reps., Raleigh, 1990-94; mem. N.C. Coastal Resources Commn., Raleigh, 1980-88; bd. dirs. N.C. Ctr. for Pub. Policy Rsch., Raleigh, 1978-90. Bd. dirs. Lower Cape Fear United Way, Wilmington, 1976-84; mem. New Hanover Bd. Social Svcs., Wilmington, 1977-84, Pub. Libr. Adv. Bd., Wilmington, 1989-94, Women's Forum N.C., Raleigh, 1977—; committeewoman Dem. Nat. Com., Washington, 1980-88; mem. N.C. Commn. for Nat. and Community Svcs., 1994—. Recipient Susan B. Anthony award New Hanover NOW, 1985; named Legislator of Yr. N.C. Wildlife Fedn., 1994. Mem. Nat. Conf. State Legislatures (communications com. 1991—), Am. Assn. Polit. Cons., LWV (pres. New Hanover 1973-75), Phi Beta Kappa. Unitarian. Home: 116 Martingale Ln Wilmington NC 28409-2020*

GOTTSCHALL, JOAN B., judge; b. Oak Ridge, Tenn., Apr. 23, 1947; d. Herbert A. and Elaine (Reichbaum) G. BA cum laude, Smith Coll., Mass., 1969; JD, Stanford Univ., Calif., 1973. Bar: Ill. 1973. Assoc. Jenner & Block, 1973-76, 78-81, ptnr., 1981-82; staff atty. Fed. Defender Program, 1976-78, Univ. of Chgo., Office of Legal Counsel, 1983-84; magistrate judge U.S. Dist. Ct. (no. dist.) Ill., Chgo., 1984—; mem. vis. com. Divinity Sch., Univ. of Chgo.; mem. vis. com. on coll. and student activities Univ. of Chgo., co-vice-chmn. Chgo. Bar Assn. Alliance for Women; bd. dirs. Just the Beginning Found.; mem. com. Seventh Cir. Judicial Conf. Mem. Am. Bar Assn., Chgo. Bar Assn., Law Club of the City of Chgo., Am. Inns of Ct., Am. Law Inst. Office: Everett McKinley Dirksen Bldg 219 S Dearborn St Ste 2490 Chicago IL 60604-1802*

GOUGÉ, SUSAN CORNELIA JONES, microbiologist; b. Chgo., Apr. 18, 1924; d. Harry LeRoy and Gladys (Moon) Jones; student Am. U., Washington, 1942-43, La. Coll., 1944-45; BS, George Washington U., 1948; postgrad. Georgetown U., 1956-58, 66-69, Vt. Coll. of Norwich U., M.A. in Pub. Health, 1984; m. John Oscar Gougé, Aug. 7, 1943; children: John Ronald, Richard Michael (dec.), Claudia Renée Gougé Carr. Med. technician Children's Hosp. Research Lab., Washington, 1948-49; bacteriologist George Washington U. Research Lab., D.C. Gen. Hosp., 1950-53; med. microbiologist Walter Reed Army Inst. Research, Washington, 1953-61; research asst. Dental Research, Walter Reed Army Med. Ctr., 1961-62; microbiologist antibiotics div. FDA, 1962-63; supr. quality control John D. Copanos Co., Pharms., Balt., 1963-64; research tng. asst. infectious diseases and tropical medicine Howard U. Med. Sch., 1964-65; research assoc. Georgetown U. Lab. Infectious Diseases, D.C. Gen. Hosp., 1966-69; mycologist Georgetown U. Hosp. Lab., 1969-70; microbiologist Research Found. of Washington Hosp. Ctr., 1971-73; dir. quality control Bio-Medium Corp., Silver Spring, Md., 1973-76; microbiologist Alcolac, Inc., Balt., 1976-77; microbiologist div. labs., dept. human resources Community Health and Hosps. Adminstrn., Washington, 1978-79; microbiologist div. ophthalmic devices, Office Device Evaluation Ctr. for Devices and Radiol. Health, FDA, Rockville, Md., 1979—. Sec. to exec. bd. Bethesda Project Awareness, 1970-71; vol. lead poisoning detection testing project, D.C. Office Vols. Internat. Tech. Assistance, 1970-71; vol. Zacchaeus Free Clinic, Washington, 1979-84, Winchester Med. Ctr., 1994—. Mem. Nat. Capital Harp Ensemble, 1941-65; mem. parish social concerns com. Roman Cath. Ch., 1972-84; mem. Winchester Med. Ctr. Aux., 1994—. Recipient medal community service; registered microbiologist Nat. Registry Microbiologists; specialist microbiologist Am. Acad. Microbiology. Mem. AAAS, VITA, Am. Soc. for Microbiology, Am. Inst. Biol. Scis., Am. Chem. Soc., Internat. Union Pure and Applied Chemistry, N.Y. Acad. Scis., Am. Pub. Heath Assn., Bus. and Profl. Women (Capital Club, rec. sec. 1973-74, 1st v.p. 1974-75, pres. 1975-76), Winchester Bus. and Profl. Women, World Affairs Council of Washington D.C., Winchester-Frederick County Hist. Soc., Toastmasters Internat. (charter sec. BMD Club #3941 1979-80), Pi Kappa Delta, Sigma Xi. Methodist. Office: FDA Div Ophthalmic Devices Office Device Evaluation 9200 Corporate Blvd Rockville MD 20850-3229

GOUGH, CAROLYN HARLEY, library director; b. Paterson, N.J., Sept. 23, 1922; d. Frank Ellsworth and Mabel (Harrison) Harley; m. George Harrison Gough, Sept. 21, 1944; children: Deborah Ann Gough Bornholdt, Douglas Alan. B.A., Coll. William and Mary, 1943; M.L.S., Drexel U., 1966. Research asst. Young and Rubicam, Inc., N.Y.C., 1943-44; library dir., asst. prof. Cabrini Coll., Radnor, Pa., 1966-81; chmn. Palm Beach County Library Bd., 1984-86. Mem. resources study com. Tredyffrin Twp. Library, 1964-65; docent Henry Morrison Flagler Mus., 1982—. Mem. Tri-State Coll. Library Coop. (v.p. 1973-74, pres. 1974-75), Assn. Coll. and Research Libraries (dir. 1978-81), AAUP, DAR (Palm Beach chpt.), Beta Phi Mu, Kappa Delta. Republican. Episcopalian. Clubs: Questers, Inc. (1st nat. v.p. 1964-66), Atlantis Golf, Atlantis Women's (co-pres. 1982-83), Sir Robert Boyle Soc. Home: 458 S Country Club Dr Atlantis FL 33462-1238

GOUGH, JESSIE POST (MRS. HERBERT FREDERICK GOUGH), retired education educator; b. Nakon Sri Tamaraj, Thailand, Jan. 26, 1907 (parents Am. citizens); d. Richard Walter and Mame (Stebbins) Post; B.A., Maryville Coll., 1927; M.A. in English, U. Chgo., 1928; Ed.D., U. Ga., 1965; m. Herbert Frederick Gough, June 30, 1934; children: Joan Acland (Mrs. Alexander Reed), Herbert Frederick. Tchr. English, Linden Hall, Lititz, Pa., 1930-32; tchr. Fairyland Sch., Lookout Mountain, Tenn., 1955-64; rsch. asst. English curriculum studies ctr. U. Ga., 1964-65; asso. prof. elem. edn. LaGrange (Ga.) Coll., 1965-73, prof., 1973-75; prof. N.W. Ga. area tchr. edn. svcs., 1969-71. Mem. Walker County (Ga.) Curriculum Coun., 1959-61, Walker County Ednl. Planning Bd., 1958-60. Mem. Am. Ednl. Rsch. Assn., Internat. Reading Assn., Nat., Ga. edn. assns., Delta Kappa Gamma. Home: 1005 Mountain Creek Rd Chattanooga TN 37405-1638

GOUGH, PAULINE BJERKE, magazine editor; b. Wadena, Minn., Jan. 7, 1935; d. Luther C. and Zita Pauline (Halbmaier) Bjerke; BA, U. Minn., Mpls., 1957; BS, Moorhead (Minn.) State Coll., 1970; MS, Ind. U., Bloomington, 1972, EdD, 1977; children: Mary Pauline, Sarah Elizabeth, Philip Clayton. Reporter women's page San Jose (Calif.) Mercury-News, 1957-58; with rsch. dept. Campbell-Mithun Advt., Mpls., 1958-60; tchr. Univ. Elem. Sch., Bloomington, 1970-79; freelance writer Agy. Instructional TV, Bloomington, 1974-80; mem. adj. faculty Ind. U.-Purdue U., Indpls., summers 1976, 77; asst. editor Phi Delta Kappan, Bloomington, 1980-81, mng. editor,

1981-88; editor, 1988—; mem. profl. staff Phi Delta Kappa, 1981—, also leader insts. on writing for publ. Recipient Disting. Alumna award Moorhead State U., 1982. Mem. Phi Beta Kappa, Phi Delta Kappa. Author articles in field. Home: 3570 S Oakridge Dr Bloomington IN 47401-8926 Office: Phi Delta Kappa PO Box 789 408 N Union Bloomington IN 47402

GOULD, BETTY CHAIKIN, elementary school educator; b. Bklyn., Apr. 19, 1928; d. Julius and Jeannette (Lipkin) C.; m. Joseph Gould, Dec. 9, 1951; children: Nancy Marla, Jodie Ellen. BA, L.I. U., 1950; MA, Columbia U., 1954. Lic. guidance counselor. Tchr. Yorktown Cen. Sch. Dist., Yorktown Heights, N.Y. Recipient Edgar Lilien Meml. award. Mem. N.Y. LWV. Home: 1471 Old Logging Rd Yorktown Heights NY 10598-6242

GOULD, DEB LEE, grief counselor; b. Chicago Heights, Ill., Nov. 16, 1955; d. Robert Henry Lee and Geraldyn Lee (Conlan) Hogan; m. Daniel Roy Gould, July 7, 1979; children: Kristen (dec.), Kevin, Brian. BPE, U. Ill., 1977, MS, 1978; Surg. Tech. Cert. of Achievement, Lansing (Mich.) C.C., 1982; MEd in Counseling, U. N.C., Greensboro, 1993. Cert. elem. tchr., Ill.; nat. cert. counselor. K-4 phys. edn. tchr. Allen Elem. Sch., Lansing, 1978-82; surg. technologist intern Ingham Med. Ctr., Lansing, 1982; heart monitor technician St. Mary Hosp., Manhattan, Kans., 1982-83; pvt. practice grief counseling Greensboro, N.C., 1993—; grief counselor Hospice of Greensboro, Inc., 1993-94; presenter, cons. Compassionate Friends Support Group, Greensboro, 1994—. Author/editor MCAD Comm. Network newsletter, 1991—; contbr. articles to profl. jours. Vol. Hospice of Greensboro, Inc., 1990-94; grief support vol. The Transition Ctr., Greensboro, 1991-93; active various cmty. philanthropic activities Alpha Omicron Pi Alumni Group, Champaign, Ill., 1984-87. Mem. ACA, N.C. Assn. Death Edn. & Counseling (ethics com. chair 1991—), Assn. for Death Edn. and Counseling, Internat. Assn. of Marriage and Family Counseling. Roman Catholic. Home and Office: 805 Montrose Dr Greensboro NC 27410

GOULD, KATHERINE TURNER, author, special education consultant; b. Kearny, N.J., Apr. 15, 1925; d. William Richard Turner and Helen Theresa Burns; m. Joseph P. McAvoy; children: Patricia Kelly, Maureen Amaya, William McAvoy, Daniel McAvoy; m. Timothy Gould. BA in Edn., William Paterson Coll., 1964, MA in Reading, 1969. Cert. L.D. tchr. cons. Tchr. Main St. Sch., Denville, N.J., 1964-69, tchr. cons., 1969-81. Author: Stories & Activities for Articulation Reinforcement, 1989, The Price of Rage, Grace of Healing, 1994. Recipient Disting. Alumni of Yr. award William Paterson Coll., 1991. Mem. AAUW (Outstanding Creative Writer award 1995). Home: 1604 S Oceanshore Blvd Flagler Beach FL 32136

GOULD, LINDA FLEWELLEN, lawyer; b. Ft. Lauderdale, Fla., June 21, 1958; d. William B. Jr. and Martha Eleanor (Crenshaw) F.; m. Robert William Gould Jr., June 19, 1982. BS in Chemistry summa cum laude, Furman U., 1979; JD with high honors, U. Fla., 1982. Bar: Colo. 1982, U.S. Dist. Ct. Colo. 1983, Fla. 1983, Ga. 1990. Ptnr. Berniger, Berg, Rioth & Diver, P.C., Colorado Springs, Colo., 1982-93, Gould & Whitley, Colorado Springs, Colo., 1993—. Mem. El Paso County Bar Assn.

GOULD, MARTHA BERNICE, retired librarian; b. Claremont, N.H., Oct. 8, 1931; d. Sigmund and Gertrude Heller; m. Arthur Gould, July 29, 1960; children: Leslie, Stephen. BA in Edn., U. Mich., 1953; MS in Library Sci., Simmons Coll., 1956; cert., U. Denver Library Sch. Community Analysis Research Inst., 1978. Childrens librarian N.Y. Pub. Libr., 1956-58; adminstr. library services act demonstration regional library project Pawhuska, Okla., 1958-59; cons. N.Mex. State Libr., 1959-60; childrens librarian then sr. childrens librarian Los Angeles Pub. Libr., 1960-72; acctg. dir. pub. srvices, reference librarian Nev. State Libr., 1972-74; pub. services librarian Washoe County (Nev.) Libr., 1974-79, asst. county librarian, 1979-84, county librarian, 1984-94; ret., 1994. Contbr. articles to jours. Exec. dir. Kids Voting/USA, Nev., 1996; treas. United Jewish Appeals, 1981; bd. dirs. Temple Sinai, Planned Parenthood of Nev., Planned Parenthood No. Nev., 1996—, Tucker Meadows Habitat for Humanity, 1995—; trustee RSVP, North Nevadans, for ERA; No. Nev. chmn. Gov.'s Conf. on Libr., 1990; mem. bd. Campaign for Choice, No. Nev. Food Bank, Nev. Women's Fund (Hall of Fame award 1989); mem. No. Nev. NCCJ, Washoe County Quality Life Task Force, 1992—; chair Sierra (Nev.) Comty. Access TV; presdl. appointee Nat. Commn. on Librs. and Info. Sci., 1993-96; mem. adv. bd. Partnership Librs. Washoe County; apptd. by Pres. Clinton vice chair Nat. Commn. on Librs. and Info. Svcs., 1994—. Recipient Nev. State Libr. Letter of Commendation, 1973, Washoe County Bd. Commrs. Resolution of Appreciation, 1978, ACLU of Nev. Civil Libertarian of Yr. 1988, Freedom's Sake award AAUW, 1989, Leadership in Literacy award Sierra chpt. Internat. Reading Assn., 1992, Woman of Distinction award 1992, Nev. Libr. Assn. Libr. of Yr., 1993. Mem. ALA (bd. dirs., intellectual freedom roundtable 1977-79, intellectual freedom com. 1979-83, coun. 1983-86), ACLU (bd. dirs. Civil Libertarian of Yr. Nev. chpt. 1988, chair gov.'s conf. for women 1989), Nev. Libr. Assn. (chmn. pub. info. com. 1972-73, intellectual freedom com. 1975-78, govt. rels. com. 1978-79, v.p., pres.-elect 1980, pres. 1981, Spl. Citation 1978, 87, LIbr. of Yr. 1993).

GOULD, ROBERTA, poet; b. Bklyn., July 16; d. Michael and Leah (Edelson) G. BA, Bklyn. Coll.; MA, U. Calif., Berkeley, 1962. Author: (poetry) Dream Yourself Flying, 1979, Writing Air, Written Water, 1980, Only Rock, 1985, Esta Naranja, 1990, Not By Blood Alone, 1990, Live Show, 1994; contbr. poetry to N.Y. Times, Village Voice, Green Mountain Rev., Mid Am. Rev., Pacific Coast, Downtown, Cath. Worker, Milkweed, Manhattan Poetry, Chapultepec Rev., numerous others; editor Light, a Poetry Rev., 1979-87. N.Y. State scholar; Mexican Exch. scholar, 1960. Mem. AAUW.

GOULDER, CAROLJEAN HEMPSTEAD, psychologist; b. Houston, Minn., Apr. 9, 1933; d. Orson George and Jean Helen (Lischer) Hempstead; m. L. Lynton Goulder, Jr., May 26, 1956 (div. 1978); children: Jean Virginia, David Thomas, Ann Rachel; m. John T. Blake, Apr. 12, 1986. BS, Hamline U., 1956; CAGS, R.I. Coll., 1975, MA in Sch. Psychology, 1972; postgrad., Nova U., 1977-78. Cert. sch. psychologist, R.I., cert. nat. sch. psychologist Nat. Assn. Sch. Psychologists. Dept. head, instr. Highsmith Hosp., Fayetteville, N.C., 1956-57; instr. nursing New Eng. Deaconess Hosp., Boston, 1957-58; dir. psychol. svcs. Burrillville Sch. Dept., Harrisville, R.I., 1972-79, sch. psychologist, 1972—; coord. presch. handicapped, 1985-86; lectr. pediatric problems Sturdy Meml. Hosp., Attleboro, Mass., 1970-72; cons. Wheeler Sch., Providence, 1970-73. Chmn. 2d Congl. Ch. Sch., Attleboro, Mass., 1962-65, mem. religious edn. com., kindergarten com. and choir, 1965; active 1st Unitarian Ch., Providence, 1982—. Mem. R.I. Sch. Psychologists Assn., Nat. Assn. Sch. Psychology, Am. Psychol. Assn. (assoc.), Mass. Psychol. Assn. (assoc.), Delta Kappa Gamma. Office: AT Levy Sch Spl Svcs Office Harrisville RI 02830

GOULDING, NORA See CLARK, SUSAN

GOULD-LISCO, DEBRA ANN, accountant; b. Melrose, Mass., Jan. 2, 1956; d. Frederick H. Jr. and Claire M. (Lewis) Gould; m. Allen S. Lisco; children: Elizabeth A. Worsdell, Christina M. Worsdell. AS in Acctg., Johnson & Wales U., 1981; postgrad., Tampa Coll. Acct., mktg. specialist Radiology Assocs., New Port Richey, Fla., 1991—; co-owner Bacé Specialties, New Port Richey, 1995—, Consumers Outlet, New Port Richey, 1996. Bd. dirs. Am. Cancer Soc., New Port Richey: vol. Girl Scouts Am., Holiday, Fla. Mem. Epsilon Phi Delta.

GOULET, LORRIE, sculptor; b. Riverdale, N.Y., Aug. 17, 1925. Student, Inwood Potteries Studios, N.Y.C., 1932-36, Black Mountain Coll., N.C., 1943-44. One-woman shows Clay Club Sculpture Ctr., N.Y.C., 1948, 55, Cheney Libr., Hoosick Falls, N.Y., 1951, Contemporaries Gallery, N.Y.C., 1959, 62, 66, 68, Rye Art Ctr., N.Y., 1966, New Sch. Assocs., N.Y.C., 1968, Temple Emeth, Teaneck, N.J., 1969, Kennedy Galleries, N.Y.C., 1971, 73, 75, 78, 80, 82, 86, Carolyn Hill Gallery, N.Y.C., 1988, 91, Caldwell (N.J.) Coll., 1989; group shows include Mus. Natural History, 1936, Whitney Mus. Am. Art, N.Y.C., 1948, 49, 50, 53, 55, Met. Mus. Art, N.Y.C., 1951, Detroit Inst. Arts, 1960, Pa. Acad., 1950, 51, 52, 54, 59, 64, NAD, N.Y.C., 1966, 75, 77, Corcoran Gallery, Washington, 1966, Hofstra Mus., N.Y.C., 1990, The McNey Mus., 1990, The Copley Soc., Boston, 1991, The Spanish Inst., 1992, Lehigh U. Art Gallery, 1992, Iowa State U. Brunne Gallery, 1992, Paine Art Ctr., Oshkosh, Wis., 1992, Mitchell Art Gallery St. John's Coll., Annapolis Md., 1992, Revealed Form, Erie Art Mus., Erie, Pa., 1995; represented in permanent collections Hunter Mus., Chattanooga, Tenn., N.J. State Mus., Wichita Mus. Art, Hirschhorn Sculpture Mus., Washington, also pvt. collections. Tchr. Mus. Modern Art, 1957, 64, Scarsdale Studio Workshop, 1959, 61, New Sch., 1961-75, Art Students League, 1981—. Recipient numerous art awards, various commns. Fellow Nat. Sculpture Soc. (coun.); mem. Artists Equity, Audubon Artists, Sculptors Guild, Visual Artists and Galleries Assocs., Nat. Acad. Design (academician 1989, mem. coun. 1994), Fedn. Arts (del. 1992-93, bd. dirs.).

GOURLEY, ELAINE AUDREY, school system administrator, consultant; b. Norwalk, Conn., Oct. 3, 1937; d. William and Lydia (Szilagyi) Pinces. BS, UCLA, 1959; MS, U. So. Calif., 1964, EdD, 1980. Cert. adminstrn., tchr. elem. and secondary, life. Tchr. L.A. Unified Sch. Dist., 1959-66, asst. prin., prin. elem., 1966-91; supt. Hermosa Beach (Calif.) Sch. Dist., 1991-92; cons. L.A. Unified Sch. Dist., 1993—; cons. Aga Khan Found., Washington, 1994-95; supr. Calif. State U., Dominquez Hills, 1994-95. Author: Classroom Captions-Bilingual, 1981; contbg. author: Child Wants to Learn, 1977; lectr., spkr. in field. Mem. Riviera Homeowners Assn., Torrance, Calif., 1966—. Mem. Brentwood Bel Air Womens Club, Rep. Women Federated (Dist. chair 1993-95), Delta Kappa Gamma (pres. 1972-74), Kappa Delta Pi (pres. 1984-87). Home: 4233 Paseo de las Tortugas Torrance CA 90505

GOURLEY, HELEN ELIZABETH, physicist; b. Rochester, N.Y., Apr. 22, 1931; d. Karl Friedrich and Emma Christine (Kramer) Vogele; m. Edward Henry Gustafson, June 9, 1959 (div. Oct. 1968); 1 child, Rebecca Christine Gustafson-O'Hare; m. Darrell Lavonne Gourley, Apr. 18, 1973; children: Brandon Wayne, Lisa Amber. BS in Physics with hons., U. Rochester, 1953. Calif. state tchr.'s credential for electro-optics and electronics, gen. contractor's lic. Rsch. physicist U. Calif. Med. Ctr., San Francisco, 1953-55; project engr. Beckman Instruments, Richmond, Calif., 1955-60; sr. scientist Nuclear Rsch. Instruments, Berkeley, Calif., 1960-65; program mgr. Quantic Industries, San Carlos, Calif., 1965-70; owner, chief optical scientist System Scis. Group, San Francisco, 1971—; dir., mem. Nat. Adv. Group for Nat. Tech. Inst. for the Deaf, Rochester Inst. Tech., Rochester, 1979-83; mem. nat. spkr.'s bur. Am. Phys. Soc., Washington, 1990—; lectr., seminar leader for various U. Calif. Physics Depts. Contbr. seminars and symposiums to various profl. meetings. Spkr. Lion's Club, "Women and Small Business", San Francisco, 1984, 86; presenter laser workshops for h.s. girls, San Francisco, 1983—; organizer, chmn. Tech-Net Consultant Group, San Francisco, 1992—. Recipient Bausch & Lomb Science award and scholarship Bausch & Lomb Optical Co., 1949, N.Y. State scholarship, 1949-53, Pres.'s award Internat. Soc. for Optical Engring., 1964. Mem. Optical Soc. No. Calif. (pres. 1990-91), Optical Soc. of Am. (Nat. Edn. Coun. 1984-88), The Internat. Soc. for Optical Engring. (spkr. 1964—). Office: System Scis Group 389 Benito Way San Francisco CA 94127

GOURLEY, MARY E., education educator; b. Yonkers, N.Y., Apr. 20, 1934; d. Rivers W. and Elizabeth (Johnston) Best; m. Robert N. Gourley, July 25, 1970; children: Janice, Christine, Gail, Lynn, Brooke, James. BA in Elem. Edn., Davis and Elkins (W.Va.) Coll., 1957; MS in Supervision, Portland State U., 1970; postgrad., U. So. Calif.; EdD, U. Sarasota, 1994. Cert. prin., adminstr., Oreg. Asst. prof. Portland (Oreg.) State U.; staff specialist NW Regional Edn. Lab., Portland; program dir. spl. edn. N.H. Dept. Edn., Concord; cons., evaluator Western Mich. U., Kalamazoo; ednl. cons., chief exec. officer Gourley Assoc., Inc., 1991-94; assoc. prof. U. Sarasota, Fla., 1994—. Author: Inservice Education, 1977, Staff Evaluation Training Manual, 1978, Evaluation Criteria for the Assessment of Vocational and Technical Education, 1989, Kellogg Youth Initiatives Program Final Report, 1994. Spl. fellow IDEA, 1984. Mem. ASCD, Am. Assn. Sch. Adminstrs., Phi Delta Kappa. Home: 109 5th St S Bradenton Beach FL 34217-2531 Office: U Sarasota 5250 17th St Sarasota FL 34235

GOURLEY, PAULA MARIE, art educator, artist, designer bookbinder; b. Carmel, Calif., Apr. 29, 1948; d. Raymond Serge Voronkoff and Frances Eliseyvna (Kovtynovich) G.; m. David Clark Willard, Feb. 10, 1972 (div. Oct. 1973). AA, Monterey (Calif.) Peninsula Coll., 1971; BA, Goddard Coll., 1978; MFA, U. Ala., 1987; pvt. bookbinding study with, Donald Glaister, Roger Arnoult, Paule Ameline, Michelene de Bellefroid, Francoise Bausart, Sun Evrard, James Brockman. Radiologic technologist Cen. Med. Clinic, Pacific Grove, Calif., 1970-71, Community Hosp. of Monterey, 1972-75, Duke U. Med. Ctr., Durham, N.C., 1975-77; dept. head, ultrasound technologist Middlesex Meml. Hosp., Middletown, Conn., 1977-79; asst. prof. U. Ala., Tuscaloosa, 1985-93, assoc. prof., 1993—; asst. dir. Inst. for the Book Arts, U. Ala., 1985-88, coord., 1988-94, co-dir. M.F.A. program in the book arts, 1994—; U.S. rep. Les Amis de la Reliure d'Art, Toulouse, France, 1989—; founding dir. Southeastern chpt. Guild of BookWorkers, 1995—; coord. journalist for U.S. to Art et Metiers du Livre, Revue Internat., Paris; established Pelegaya Press and Paperworks, 1978. Editor First Impressions (newsletter), 1988—; contbr. articles to profl. jours.; numerous nat. and internat. bookbinding exhbns., 1978-95. Vol. PLUS Literacy Program, Tuscaloosa, 1991—. U. Ala. grantee, 1988, 89, 90, 92; recipient Diplome of honneur Atelier d'Arts Appliques, France, 1986, Craft fellowship Ala. State Coun. on Arts, 1993-94. Mem. Am. Registry Radiologic Technologists, Am. Registry Diagnostic Med. Sonographers, Guild of Bookworkers (founder and bd. dirs. Southeastern regional chpt., editor, pub. newsletter True Grits), Hand Bookbinders Calif., Bookbinders Internat. (v.p. U.S. 1989—), Pacific Ctr. for the Book Arts, Am. Craft Coun., Ala. Craft Coun., Can. Bookbinders and Book Artists Guild, Nat. Mus. Women in Arts, Am. Craft Coun. Nat. Trust for Historic Preservation, Phi Beta Kappa Internat. Scholars. Home: 2811 6th St Tuscaloosa AL 35401-1759 Office: U Ala Main Libr # 517 Tuscaloosa AL 35487

GOVAN, GLADYS VERNITA MOSLEY, retired critical care and medical/surgical nurse; b. Tyler, Tex., July 24, 1918; d. Stacy Thomas and Lucy Victoria (Whitmill) Mosley; m. Osby David Govan, July 20, 1938; children Orbrenett K. (Govan) Carter, Diana Lynn (Govan) Mosley. Student, East Los Angeles Coll., Montebello, Calif., 1951; lic. vocat. nurse, Calif. Hosp. Med. Ctr., L.A., 1953; cert., Western States IV Assn., L.A., 1978. Lic. vocat. nurse, Calif.; cert. in EKG. Intravenous therapist Calif. Hosp. Med. Ctr., cardiac monitor. nurse; ret. Past pres. PTA, also hon. mem., 1963—; charter mem. Nat. Rep. Presdl. Task Force.

GOVIER, MARY ATHERTON, internist; b. Bellefonte, Pa., Apr. 27, 1948; d. John Peabody and Virginia Rae (Kaufmann) G.; m. John Michael Cashman, June 24, 1978; children: Katherine Govier, John Atherton, Matthew Haynes. BA in Chemistry, Grinnell Coll., 1970; MA in Edn., Stanford U., 1972; MD, U. Mo., 1977. Diplomate Am. Bd. Internal Medicine. Resident in internal medicine U. Iowa, Iowa City, 1977-80; pvt. practice, Manitowoc, Wis., 1980—; med. dir. Shady Lane Nursing Home, Manitowoc, 1984—, bd. dirs., 1985-87; med. advisor Holy Family Meml. Home Care, Manitowoc, 1987-96, Lakeshore Family Svcs., Manitowoc, 1996—; chief staff Holy Family Meml. Med. Ctr., Manitowoc, 1992-94. Former mem. bd. dirs. Cmty. Concerts, Manitowoc; mem. auction com. Roncalli H.S., Manitowoc, 1993—. Mem. ACP, Am. Med. Women's Assn., Am. Soc. Parenteral and Enteral Nutrition, Med. Soc. Wis., Wis. Assn. Med. Dirs., Manitowoc County Med. Soc., Phi Beta Kappa, Alpha Omega Alpha. Democrat. Roman Catholic. Home: 818 Winnetka Ct Manitowoc WI 54220 Office: Internal Medicine Assocs 1900 Woodland Dr Manitowoc WI 54221-1630

GOWDEY, DOROTHY E., artist; b. Everett, Wash., Mar. 12, 1918; d. Albert N. and Gladys I. (Mallory) Smith; m. Dwight M. Gowdey, Dec. 4, 1945; children: Kathleen A. Hesseltine, Christine E., Sharon L. Art student, Cornish Sch., 1938-39, P. Camfferman, E. Zeigler,, and others, 1941-46, Factory of Visual Arts, 1970-74, Janet Laurel, 1981-85; student nursing, Seattle Pacific Coll.; RN, Swedish Hosp. RN, Wash. One-woman art shows include: Providence Hosp., 1985, Internat. Snow Leopard Trust Show, 1985, Nat. League of Am. Pen Women Biennial St. Exhbn., 1985-93, Churchill Club/Okayama, Japan, 1986, Eastside Assn. of Fine Arts, 1986, 89, 91, Mercer Island Visual Arts League, 1986, 87, 89, 90, Puget Sound Sumi Artists, Wash. Biennial, 1987-89, Tacoma Show, 1991-94, Moss Bay Gallery, 1993-94, Olympic Arts, Avoir Gallery, Kirkland, Wash., 1991, Museo Piccolo Gallery, Langley, Wash., 1993-94, Anacortes Arts and Crafts Festival, 1993, Moss Bay Gallery, 1995; numerous group exhibits. Organizer, mem. Nellie Goodhue Group Homes for the Retarded, Seattle, 1970—; mem. ARC, Tex., 1963—, Down Syndrome Congress, Atlanta, 1971—. Recipient 1st prize Churchill Club, Okayama, Japan, 1986, Watercolor prize Western Wash. State Fair, 1990, numerous other art awards. Mem. Nat. League of Am. Pen Women (award of excellence 1987), Women Painters of Wash. (pres. 1984-86), Women in the Arts (charter), Seattle Art Mus., Puget Sound Sumi Artists, Olympic Arts (pres. 1992-93). Democrat. Presbyterian. Home: 11536 6th Ave NW Seattle WA 98177

GOWDY, MIRIAM BETTS, nutritionist; b. Nelsonville, Ohio, Jan. 9, 1928; d. Charles Donald and Lillian Mary (Linscott) B.; m. Robert Averill Gowdy, Oct. 12, 1950 (div. 1977); children: Carol Jo, Robert Jr., Bruce. BA in Home Econs., Ohio Wesleyan U., 1949; student, Duke U., 1949-50, Calif. State U., L.A., 1975-76. Registered dietitian. Dietitian L.A., 1977-91; cons. Nat.-in-Home Health, Van Nuys, Calif., 1984-87; clin. dietitian Lake Mead Hosp., 1991-94; pvt. practice cons. nutritionist Las Vegas, Nev., 1994—; contracting dietitian Pulse Health Svcs., Las Vegas, 1995—; contract dietitian Pulse Health Svcs., 1995—. Mem. Am. Diabetes Assn. (con. San Fernando Valley unit 1976-80, bd. dirs. N.W. chpt. 1977-82), Nev. Dietetic Assn. (nominating com. 1995—), So. Nev. Dietetic Assn. (mem. chmn. 1991-92, pres. 1993-94), Cons. Nutritionists (chmn.-elect So. Calif. chpt. 1979-81), Calif. Dietetic Assn. (chmn. diabetes care practice 1979-81), Am. Heart Assn. (mem. governing bd. N.W. chpt. 1988-89), Sierra Club, Nat. Audubon Soc. Republican. Methodist. Home and Office: 9713 White Cloud Dr Las Vegas NV 89134-7840 Office: 9713 White Cloud Dr Las Vegas NV 89134-7840

GOWDY, NANNENE, minister; b. Cin., Mar. 3, 1941; d. Victor John Gowdy and Jeanette Elizabeth (Bryant) Sessions; m. Alphonse Wright, Oct. 19, 1968 (div. 1983); children: Alphonse Victor Wright, Alyce Elizabeth Gowdy-Wright. BS, Boston U., 1963, MEd, 1975; MDiv, Andover Newton Theol., 1982. Ordained to ministry, 1982. Tchr. Billerica (Mass.) H.S., 1963-66, Belmont (Mass.) H.S., 1966-69; min. 1st Congl. Soc., Jamaica Plain, Mass., 1982-83, South Nassau Unitarian, Freeport, N.Y., 1983-88, First Ch. Unitarian, Littleton, N.Y., 1988—; bd. trustees, mem. Unitarian Universalist Assn., Boston, 1993—; pres. Urban Ch. Coalition, Boston, 1986-93; cons. Conversations with the Bible, 1994, Special Times, 1995. Co-author (curriculum) Timeless Themes from the Bible, 1988. Pres. Interfatih Clergy Assn., Freeport, 1985-88, Liberty Pk. Housing Devel., Freeport, 1986-88; treas. Interfaith Nat. Network, Freeport, 1985-88. Named Hon. Supporter Women on Job, 1985. Unitarian Universalist. Office: First Ch Unitarian 19 Foster St Littleton MA 01460

GOWENS, VERNEETA VIOLA, journalist; b. South Holland, Ill., Mar. 19, 1913; d. William and Mary Cawthorne (Fowler) Gibson; m. Albert Gowens, July 17, 1936; children: Victoria Ann Gowens Utke, Mary Ann Gowens Buer. Educated public schs., Bryant and Stratton Bus. Coll. Clk., pub. rels. worker Chgo. and Riverdale Lumber Co., Chgo., 1934-45; feature writer, women's editor Tribune Publs., Harvey, Ill., 1960-62; feature writer, women's editor Star-Tribune, Williams Press, Chicago Heights, Ill., 1963-78; freelance writer; script writer variety shows Ship Ahoy, 1963, Fair 'n' Square, 1964; contbr. to Internat. Altrusan, 1974, Ch. Herald, 1977. Sunday sch. tchr., youth leader 1st Ref. Ch., South Holland; mem. editl. coun. Ch. Herald, Ref. Ch. in Am., 1976-82; pres. Dist. 150 PTA, 1965-66; adv. com. program in ltd. occupation tng. Thornton H.S., 1963-69; mem. South Holland Indsl. Commn., 1965-68; bd. dirs. Family Svc. and Mental Health Ctr. of South Cook County, Ill., 1974-77; mem. South Holland unit Salvation Army, 1958—; judge Internat. Teen Pageant, 1969; mem. South Holland Cmty. Chest, 1978-87; adv. bd. Thornton C.C. nursing program, 1976-83; mem. spl. events and publicity coms. South Holland Centennial, 1994; active South Holland Diamond Jubilee, 1969, South Holland Cable Commn., 1984—, South Holland Centennial Com., 1994. Recipient award South Holland C. of C., 1970, Genoa coun. K.C., 1974, Village of South Holland, 1969, 1st pl. in contest No. Ill. U., 1974, 75, award Suburban Press Found., 1969, 1st pl. award Ill. Press Assn., 1973, 50 other awards in writing. Mem. Ill. Women's Press Assn. (Woman of Yr. 1974, award 1978), Nat. Fedn. Press Women (1st pl. Sweepstakes award 1976). Home: 16830 S Park Ave South Holland IL 60473

GOYAK, ELIZABETH FAIRBAIRN, public relations executive; b. Chgo., Oct. 7, 1922; d. Lewis Howard and Berenice Marie (Bowers) Fairbairn; m. Edward Anthony Goyak, May 20, 1951. BEd, So. Ill. U., 1943; MA, No. Ill. U., 1979. Reporter Internat. News Svc., Chgo., 1945-49, Chgo. Tribune, 1949-52; writer Gardner & Jones, Chgo., 1954-59, Aaron Cushman & Assocs., Chgo., 1959-60; v.p. Daniel J. Edelman, Chgo., 1960-76; mgr. pub. rels. Stone Container Corp., Chgo., 1976-82; pres. pub. rels. Firm Chgo. Connection, Matteson, Ill., 1982—. Dir. pub. rels. Dem. Women for Adlai Stevenson, 1952; founder, pres. bd. dirs. Matteson Pub. Libr., 1958-87; chmn. Matteson Bicentennial Commn., 1973-76. Mem. Pub. Rels. Soc. Am. (accredited, Silver anvil award 1975), Publicity Club Chgo. (sec., bd. dirs. 1964-76, Golden Trumpet award 1965, 66, 75), Chgo. Press Vets. Mem. United Ch. Christ. Home and Office: 21310 Butterfield Pky Matteson IL 60443-2460

GOYER, VIRGINIA L., accountant; b. Troy, N.Y., July 19, 1942; d. Clarence Archie and Edna Alice (Toussaint) G.; m. James Cobb Stewart, May 17, 1986. BS, Rochester Inst. Tech., 1975, MBA, 1976. Tax mgr. Deloitte Haskins & Sells, Rochester, N.Y., 1976-82; pres. Lamanna & Goyer, PC, CPAs, Rochester, 1982-89; owner Goyer & Assocs., CPAs, Rochester, 1989-93; pres. Virginia L. Goyer, CPA, P.C., Rochester, 1993—. Mem. adv. bd. Salvation Army, Rochester, 1985-88, Rochester Inst. Tech. Deferred Giving, 1988-89; mem. bd. Nat. Women's Hall of Fame. Mem. AICPA (nat. coun. 1995—), Fla. Inst. CPA's, N.Y. State Inst. CPA's (bd. dirs. 1990-93, v.p. 1994-95, 1st woman pres. Rochester chpt. 1988-89), Rochester Women's Network, Nat. Assn. Women Bus. Owners (bd. dirs. 1992-93), Estate Planning Coun. (bd. dirs. 1987-89), NOW. Office: 354 Westminster Rd Rochester NY 14607-3233

GOZEMBA, PATRICA ANDREA, women's studies and English language educator, writer; b. Medford, Mass., Nov. 30, 1940; d. John Charles and Mary Margaret (Sampey) Curran; m. Gary M. Gozemba, Sept. 4, 1967 (div. Feb. 1975). BA, Emmanuel Coll., Boston, 1962; MA, U. Iowa, 1963; EdD, Boston U., 1975. Tchr. Waltham (Mass.) High Sch., 1963-64; prof. Salem (Mass.) State Coll., 1964—; vis. fellow East-West Ctr., 1995. Editor: New England Women's Studies, 1977-87; mem. editorial bd. Thought and Action, 1990-93; contbr. articles to profl. jours. Mem. NEA (standing com. 1982-93), NOW, NAACP, Nat. Women's Studies Assn. (gov. bd. 1977-89), Nat. Coun. Tchrs. English, Nat. Gay and Lesbian Task Force, Mass. State Coll. Assn. (editor 1982-90, 92—), Herb Soc. Am. Democrat. Home: 17 Sutton Ave Salem MA 01970-5728 Office: Salem State Coll Women Studies Dept Salem MA 01970

GRABAREK, DONNA L., bank accountant; b. Wilkes-Barre, Pa., Jan. 30, 1971; d. Edward P. and Helen G. BS in Acctg. and Econs., King's Coll., Wilkes-Barre, Pa., 1993. Audit assoc. Coopers & Lybrand, Parsippany, N.J., 1993-95; asst. mgr. global fin. dept. Citibank-N.Am., Long Island City, N.Y., 1995—. Recipient award for acctg. excellence, Pa. Inst. of CPA's, 1993. Mem. AICPAs, Inst. Mgmt. Accts. (dir. student affairs and student manuscript competition 1993). Office: Citibank N Am 1 Court Sq Long Island City NY 11101

GRABAUSKAS, PATRICIA ANNE, nurse midwife; b. Woonsocket, R.I., Feb. 15, 1941; d. Francis John and Lillian Claire (Gardner) Sheehan; m. D. Anthony Grabauskas, Oct. 27, 1962 (div. 1988); children: Daniel, Lisa, David, Karen. BSN cum laude, Worcester State Coll., 1981, BS in Sociology, 1981; MSN in Midwifery, Georgetown U., 1988. Cert. nurse midwife, Am. Coll. Nurse Midwives. Staff, head nurse St. Vincent Hosp., Worcester, Mass., 1962-86; staff nurse midwife Prince George's Hosp., Cheverly, Md., 1988-89; asst. dir. midwifery Columbia Hosp. for Women, Washington, 1989-93; dir. midwifery svcs. Fallon Clinic, Inc., Worcester, 1993-96; dir. nurse midwifery Mass. Gen. Hosp., Boston, 1996—. Mem. Am. Coll. Nurse Midwives, Georgetown U. Alumnae Assn., Sigma Theta Tau, Iota Phi. Republican. Roman Catholic. Office: Mass Gen Hosp Dir Nurse Midwifery Boston MA 02114

GRABER, SUSAN P., judge; b. Oklahoma City, July 5, 1949; d. Julius A. and Bertha (Fenyves) G.; m. William June, May 3, 1981; 1 child, Rachel June-Graber. BA, Wellesley Coll., 1969; JD, Yale U., 1972. Bar: N.Mex. 1972, Ohio 1977, Oreg. 1978. Asst. atty. gen. Bur. of Revenue, Santa Fe, 1972-74; assoc. Jones Gallegos Snead & Wertheim, Santa Fe, 1974-75, Taft Stettinius & Hollister, Cin., 1975-78; assoc., then ptnr. Stoel Rives Boley Jones & Grey, Portland, Oreg., 1978-88; judge, then presiding judge Oreg. Ct. Appeals, Salem, 1988-90; assoc. justice Oreg. Supreme Ct., Salem, 1990—. Mem. Gov.'s Adv. Coun. on Legal Svcs., 1979-88; bd. dirs. U.S. Dist. Ct. of Oreg. Hist. Soc., 1985—, Oreg. Law Found., 1990-91; mem. bd. visitors Sch. Law, U. Oreg., 1986-93. Mem. Oreg. State Bar (jud. adminstrn. com. 1985-87, pro bono com. 1988-90), Ninth Cir. Jud. Conf. (chair exec. com. 1987-88), Oreg. Jud. Conf. (edn. com. 1988-91, program chair 1990), Oreg. Appellate Judges Assn. (sec.-treas. 1990-91, vice chair 1991-92, chair 1992-93), Am. Inns of Ct. (master), Phi Beta Kappa. Office: Oreg Supreme Ct 1163 State St Salem OR 97310-1331

GRABINSKI, C. JOANNE, gerontologist, educator; b. Bend, Oreg., Dec. 8, 1941; d. Jack George and Helen Margaret (Thomsen) Huffman; m. Roger Neil Grabinski, Aug. 13, 1966; 1 child, Lawrence Neil. BS, MS in Home Econ. Edn., Oreg. State U., 1963, 68; MA in Ednl. Adminstrn./Cmty. Leadership, Ctrl. Mich. U., 1976, MA in Family Rels., 1980; postgrad., Mich. State U., 1982-87. Dept. chair, tchr. home econs. Oakridge (Oreg.) Jr./Sr. High Sch., 1963-67, Briggs Jr. High Sch., Springfield, Oreg., 1967-68; prof. home econs. Lane C.C., Eugene, Oreg., 1968-69; residence hall dir., assoc. dir. Western Mich. U., Kalamazoo, 1970-72; dir., spl. interest coord. Mt. Pleasant (Mich.) Pub. Schs., 1976-77; money mgmt. counselor Coop. Ext. Svc./DSS, Mt. Pleasant, 1977-78; asst. prof. ednl. adminstrn./community leadership Ctrl. Mich. U., Mt. Pleasant, 1976, 77, asst. prof. home econs., 1980-86, dir./asst. prof. interdisciplinary gerontology program, 1984-91; pres., cons. cjgGERONTOLOGY, Mt. Pleasant, 1991—; project dir. Region 7 Alzheimer's Disease and Related Conditions Caregiver Edn. Project, Mich. Dept. Mental Health, Ctrl. Mich. U., 1986-91; adj. prof. gerontology, lectr. Western Mich. U., Kalamazoo, 1992-94; continuing edn. rep., lectr. gerontology Ea. Mich. U., 1992-96, continuing edn. coord.-gerontology Ea. Mich. U., 1996—; Ea. Mich. U. Elderwise liaison, 1995-96; ctr. coord. Ea. Mich. U. at NMC U., 1996—. Mem. editl. bd. AGHE Exch., 1988-91, asst. editor, 1988-91; contbr. articles to profl. jours. Bd. dirs. Hospice of Cen. Mich., Mt. Pleasant, 1986-89, Cen. Mich. U. Dames, 1974-78, pres., 1976-77; bd. dirs. Mt. Pleasant Welcome Wagon Newcomers Club, 1972-76, pres., 1974-75; team mem. Bldg. Ties, Isabella County, Mich., 1983-84. Marie Dye Grad. fellow Mich. Home Econ. Assn., 1983; named Outstanding Faculty Mem., Ctrl. Mich. U. Mortar Bd. Mem. Am. Soc. on Aging, Gerontol. Soc. Am., Nat. Coun. on Aging, Mich. Coun. on Family Rels. (bd. dirs. 1984-87), Nat. Coun. Family Rels., Assn. Gerontology Higher Edn. (instnl. rep.), Kappa Omicron Nu, Omicron Nu, Kappa Omicron Phi, Phi Delta Kappa. Democrat. Lutheran. Home: 310 Apricot Ln Mount Pleasant MI 48858-6156 Office: Gerontology PO Box 868 Mount Pleasant MI 48804-0868

GRABNER, CAREN SUE, food service manager; b. Longview, Tex., Feb. 11, 1955; d. Keith C. and Patricia (Kuhn) Shaffer; m. Michael A. Grabner, Oct. 7, 1978 (div. Nov. 1989). Grad. high sch., Ft. Wayne, Ind. Exec. mgr. Ponderosa, Ft. Wayne, 1972-79; gen. mgr. Sizzler Steak House, Ft. Wayne, 1980-83; mgr. Pizza Hut, Ft. Wayne, 1984-86; sr. mgr. Burger King, Ft. Wayne, 1986-87; mgr. Ponderosa, Ft. Wayne, 1987-88; gen. bus. mgr. Taco Bell, Inc., Grand Rapids, Mich., 1988—.

GRABNER, CAROLINE L., health services administrator; b. Hamilton, Mont., July 4, 1944; d. Edwin Ole and Margaret Mary (Jones) Bringen; married, Oct. 16, 1966; children: Charles Edwin, Arline Lucretia. Student, Montgomery Coll., 1986—. Travel clk. USN, Washington, 1963-64, secret control clk. USN Spl. Projects, Washington, 1964-66; grants tech. asst. NIH, Bethesda, Md., 1985-90; temp. lead GTA trainer NIH, Bethesda, 1990-91, lead GTA trainer, 1991-93, com. mgmt. asst., 1993-95, chief sci. rev. and evaluations award office, 1995—, chief travel office, 1995—. Mem. Concord club, Inc. Home: 5518 Lincoln St Bethesda MD 20817-3724

GRACE, BETTE FRANCES, accounting executive; b. Hanford, Calif., Apr. 16, 1957; d. Boyd Lowell Sharp and Janet Praria Judd; m. Clyde Jon Nold, May 4, 1974 (div. 1987); children: Mandolin P., Christopher J.; m. James Frank Cangiamilla, Aug. 27, 1988 (div.); m. Michael E. Grace, Feb. 14, 1996. AA in Bus., Gavilan Coll., Gilroy, Calif., 1992; BS in Bus./Acctg., San Jose State U., 1994, postgrad., 1994—. Fin. controller Hollister (Calif.) Disposal, Inc., 1984-92; owner, operator Hollister Bookkeeping and Tax Svc., 1985—; acct. mgr. Ridgemark Golf & Country Club, Hollister, 1992—; staff acct. Michael E. Grace, CPA, Hollister; fin. controller John Smith Landfill, Inc., Hollister, 1986-92, Ajax Portable Svc., Hollister, 1987-92. Supporter Monterey County (Calif.) Symphony Guild, 1991—; parent mem. Calif. High Sch. Rodeo Assn., Hollister, 1991—; dir. 33rd Dist. Agrl. Assn., San Benito County Fair Bd., 1992-94; asst. fin. chmn. AT&T Pebble Beach Nat. Pro-Am. Mem. Internat. Assn. Hospitality Accts., El Gabilan Young Ladies Inst., NAFE. Republican. Roman Catholic. Office: Michael E Grace CPA PO Box 1352 Hollister CA 95024-1352

GRACE, HELEN KENNEDY, foundation administrator; b. Beresford, S.D., Mar. 30, 1935; d. Walter James and Ethel Elvira (Soderstrom) Kennedy; B.S. in Nursing, Loyola U., Chgo., 1963; M.S. in Nursing, U. Ill., Chgo., 1965; Ph.D. in Sociology, Northwestern U., 1969, LLD Valparaiso U., 1992; DSc (hon.) S.D. State U., LHD (honoris causa) Loyola U., 1993; m. Elliott A. Grace, Nov. 20, 1961; 1 dau., Elizabeth Ann. Nursing adminstr. Ill. Dept. Mental Health, 1963-67; faculty Coll. of Nursing, U. Ill., Chgo., 1967-82, instr., 1967-69, asst. prof., 1969-71, assoc. prof., 1971-73, prof., assoc. dean for grad. study, 1973-77, dean coll. of Nursing 1977-82; program dir. W.K. Kellog Found., Battle Creek, Mich., 1982-86, coord. health programs, 1986-91, v.p. program, 1991-95; spl. asst. to pres./CEO, 1995—. Recipient Disting. Alumnus award Loyola U., Coll. of Nursing U. Ill., Centennial Alumni award Am. State and Land Grant Univs. Mem. Am. Nurses Assn., Nat. League for Nursing (governing bd. 1978-86), Am. Acad. of Nursing (governing council 1976-80), Am. Sociol. Assn. Author: Mental Health Nursing: A Psychosocial Approach, 1977, 2d edit., 1981; Families Across the Life Cycle: Family Studies for Nursing, 1977; The Development of a Child Psychiatric Treatment Program, 1971; Current Issues in Nursing, 1981, 4th edit. 1993. Office: 1 Michigan Ave E Battle Creek MI 49017-4005

GRACE, JULIANNE ALICE, investor relations firm executive; b. Riverdale, N.Y., Oct. 29, 1937; d. Arthur Edward and Julia May (McCarthy) Thompson; m. Daniel Vincent Grace, July 2, 1960; children: Daniel Vincent III, Deirdre Elizabeth. BA, Marymount Manhattan Coll., 1959; MA, Fordham U., 1960. Dir. admissions Marymount Manhattan Coll., N.Y.C., 1966-72; mgr. human resources The Perkin-Elmer Corp., Norwalk, Conn., 1972-78, dir. human resources, 1978-81, asst. sr. v.p. semiconductor equipment, 1981-83, asst. pres., 1983-85, v.p., asst. to chief exec. officer, 1985-86; v.p. adminstrn. The Perkin-Elmer Corp., Norwalk, 1986-90, v.p. corp. rels., 1990-95; pres. The Jagcom Group, New Canaan, Conn., 1995—. Bd. dirs. Norwalk and Wilton chpts. ARC, 1975-85, Metropool, 1991—, Waveny (Conn.) Care Ctr.; trustee Norwalk YMCA, 1986-94; active Norwalk C.C. Found., 1986-90, Fairfield 2000; mem. corp. cabinet U. Conn. Downstate Initiative, 1995—. Woodrow Wilson Nat. Found. fellow, 1959-60. Mem. Econ. Soc. Conn., Nat. Investor Rels. Inst. (sr. exec. roundtable), Fairfield Pub. Rels. Assn., Women in Comm., Regional Plan Assn. (com.), Sports Car Club Am., Roton Point Club (Rowayton, Conn.), Wolfpit Running Club. Home and Office: 54 Louises Ln New Canaan CT 06840-2120

GRACE, MARCIA BELL, advertising executive; b. Pitts., July 29, 1937; d. Daniel Henry and Gertrude Margaret (Loew) Bell; m. Roy Grace, May 16, 1966; children: Jessica Bell, Nicholas Bell. AB, Harvard U., 1959. V.p., assoc. creative dir. Doyle Dane Bernbach, N.Y.C., 1964-77; sr. v.p., creative dir. Wells, Rich, Greene, Inc., N.Y.C., 1977-85, exec. v.p., creative dir., 1986-90; cons. Marcia Grace & Co., N.Y.C., 1990—. Recipient 1st Pl. ANDY award Advt. Club N.Y., 1968, 70, 72, 75, 1st Pl. Gold award The One Show, 1973, 78, Hall of Fame award The Clio Show, N.Y.C., 1982, 86.

GRACE, PRISCILLA ANNE, labor union executive; b. Ft. Worth, Mar. 20, 1943; d. John Paul and Pauline (Greer) G.; children: Kenneth C. Caldwell Jr., George E. Caldwell, Kristina Caldwell Henry. Grad. pvt. sch., Our Lady of Victory Sch., Ft. Worth. Telephone operator Southwestern Bell Telephone, Ft. Worth and Houston, 1968-70; letter carrier U.S. Postal Svc., Humble, Tex., 1973-85; officer local 283, Nat. Assn. Letter Carriers, Houston, 1984—; chmn. bd. dirs. Houston Postal Credit Union, 1990—; mem. exec. bd. Harris County AFL-CIO, Houston, 1988—. Editor Houston Letter Carrier Newsletter, 1978-84. Mem. Nat. Assn. Letter Carriers (chmn. nat. election com. 1990, 94, Mem. of Yr. award local 283, 1978). Lutheran. Office: Nat Assn Letter Carriers 2414 Broadway St Houston TX 77012-3812

GRACE, SUE, state legislator; b. Milw.; m. Vincent Grace. Mem. Ariz. Ho. of Reps.; mktg. specialist. Named Legis. of Yr., Mental Health Assn., 1991. Republican. Office: Ariz House of Reps Capitol Complex 1700 W Washington Phoenix AZ 85007-2890*

GRACEY, JANET ENGLISH, church administrator; b. Wolcott, Ind., Aug. 11, 1937; d. Victor Floyd and Mae Avanelle (Norwood) English. Student, U. Mich., 1955-56, New Sch. for Social Rsch., 1960-62. Cons. Nat. Endowment for Arts, Washington, 1969; exec. asst. spl. studies project Rockefeller Bros. Fund, N.Y.C., 1963-70; dir. rsch. Associated Couns. of Arts, N.Y.C., 1970-73; dir. spl. projects Theatre Devel. Fund, N.Y.C., 1973-77, dir. program planning and rsch., 1978-83, dir. ops., 1983-90; dir. adminstrn. Ch. of the Holy Apostles/Holy Apostles Soup Kitchen, N.Y.C., 1991—; panel mem. N.Y. State Coun. on Arts, 1985-86. Office: Ch of the Holy Apostles 296 Ninth Ave New York NY 10001

GRACY, CAROLYN DIANE, elementary education educator; b. Springfield, Ohio, Oct. 20, 1953; d. Donald Grant and Carol Louise (Rader) Gross; m. Dail William Gracy, July 12, 1975; children: Janelle, Bridget, Valerie, Hillary. Bof Music Edn., Wittenberg U., 1975; MS in Elem. Edn., U. Dayton, 1994. Instr. piano, music purchaser, studio dir. Kincaid's Is Music, Springfield, Ohio, 1971-75; tchr. music West Liberty Salem (Ohio) Local Sch., 1975-79; co-owner Gracy's Gardens, New Carlisle, Ohio, 1983-91; substitute tchr. 6 Sch. Dists., Springfield/Dayton/Urbana, Ohio, 1989-90; tchr. music Ridgewood Pvt. Sch., Springfield, 1990-91; tchr. music Springfield City Schs., 1991-94, tchr. 2d grade, 1994—; instr. music for elem. tchrs. workshop Springfield City Schs., 1994. Organist New Carlisle Meth. Ch. Mem. NEA, Ohio Edn. Assn., Springfield Edn. Assn., Music Educators Assn. Republican. Mem. Brethren Ch. Home: 8066 Stott Rd New Carlisle OH 45344-9517 Office: Springfield City Schs Emerson Elem Sch 601 Selma Rd Springfield OH 45505-2034

GRADER, PATRICIA ALISON LANDE, editor; b. L.A., Mar. 23, 1960; d. Frederick and Irma Rose (Davidson) L.; m. Scott P. Grader, Feb. 11, 1995. Student, Washington U., St. Louis, 1977-79; BA with high distinction, U. Calif., San Diego, 1982. Editl. asst. Crown Pubs., N.Y.C., 1982-83; asst. editor St. Martin's Press, N.Y.C., 1983-84; editor Atheneum Pubs., N.Y.C., 1984-87; v.p., sr. editor Simon & Schuster, Inc., N.Y.C., 1987-91; v.p., dir. IMG-The Julian Bach Literary Agy., N.Y.C., 1992-95; exec. editor Avon Books, N.Y.C., 1995—; mentor internship program Simon & Schuster, 1991; mem. adminstrv. com. IMG, 1992-95; speaker in field. Mem. Women in Pub., Pi Beta Phi. Office: Avon Books 1350 Ave of the Americas New York NY 10019

GRADIE, CHARLOTTE MAY, history educator; b. Putnam, Conn., Nov. 7, 1949; d. Robert Richmond and Avis Leonia (Gregg) Gradie; m. Frank Palmer Hendrick, Dec. 30, 1978; children: Rachel May Hendrick, Emily Rose Hendrick, Adam Palmer Hendrick. BA, U. Conn., 1973, MA, 1975, PhD, 1990. Assoc. prof. history Sacred Heart U., Fairfield, Conn., 1990—; cons. Conn. Humanities Coun., Middletown, 1993—; cons. scholar So. Conn. Libr. coun., Hamden, 1992—. Contbr. articles to profl. jours. Bd. dirs. Haddam (Conn.) Hist. Soc. Andrew W. Mellon grantee, 1994; Sacred Heart U. rsch. grantee, 1993-94. Mem. Phi Alpha Theta. Methodist.

GRADO-WOLYNIES, EVELYN (EVELYN WOLYNIES), clinical nurse specialist, educator; b. N.Y.C., Apr. 2, 1944; d. Joseph Frederick and Evelyn Marie (Ronning) Grado; m. Jon Gordon Wolynies, July 12, 1964; children: Jon Andrew, Kristine Elisabeth. AAS, Burlington County Coll., 1990; AS, Camden C.C., 1990; BSN cum laude, Thomas Jefferson U., 1991, MSN summa cum laude, 1992; PhD in Nursing Studies, Johns Hopkins U., 1993. RN, N.J., Pa., cert. clin. nurse specialist. Charge nurse Hampton Hosp., Westampton, N.J., 1990-92; adjunct clin. instr. psychiat. nursing Burlington County Coll., Pemberton, N.J., 1992-93; project leader Alzheimer's disease clin. drug study Olsten Health Care, Cherry Hill, N.J., 1992-95, psychiat. case mgr., 1992-94; CNS neuropsych in Huntingtons Disease Dr. Allen Rubin, Camden, N.J., 1992; psychiat. case mgr. Moorestown (N.J.) Vis. Nurses Assn., 1992; charge nurse, group therapist, rschr. Friends Hosp., Phila., 1994—; pvt. practice hypnotherapy/psychotherapy; cons. psychiat. care, Alzheimer's Disease, RN/home health aide instr. Olsten-Kimberly Home Care. Contbr. articles to nursing jours. Mem. Burlington County Coll. Alumni Bd.; founder, dir. Support Group for Adult Children with Aging Parents; Developed music therapy/exercise program for Geriatric Psych patients. Recipient Juanita Wilson award, 1991, Farber fellowship, 1991-92.; Nurse in Washington intern, 1992; named to Burlington County Coll. Hall of Fame, 1994. Mem. Am. Assn. of Neuroscience Nurses, Am. Psychiat. Nurses Assn., N.J. State Nurses Assn., Sigma Theta Tau (Delta Rho chpt.), Phi Theta Kappa. Home: PO Box 3604 Cherry Hill NJ 08034-0550

GRADY, CHERYL R., telecommunications executive; b. Texas City, Tex., Nov. 19, 1958; d. William J. III and Marjorie L. (McAleer) G.; m. John M. Kelly, Dec. 19, 1981 (div. Jan. 1987). BS in Engring. Tech., Tex. A&M U., 1981. Engr. Pacific Bell, San Ramon, Calif., 1982-93; dir. mktg. Pacific Bell, San Ramon, 1993—. Roman Catholic. Office: Pacific Bell Network Integration 6379 Clark Ave Dublin CA 94568

GRAESSER, AMY LYNN, elementary education educator; b. Sterling, Ill., Aug. 23, 1971; d. Kenneth L. and Shirley A. (Weires) G. BEd, Augustana Coll., 1993. 4th grade tchr. Antioch (Ill.) Dist. 34 Schs., 1993-94, 5th grade tchr., 1994—. Mem., vol. Antioch Jr. Women's Club, 1993—, chairperson edn., 1994—; pres. Antioch Cmty. Band, 1994—. Office: WC Petty Sch 850 Highview Dr Antioch IL 60002

GRAF, DOROTHY ANN, business executive; b. Nashville, Mar. 21, 1935; d. Henry George and Martha Dunlap (Hill) Meek; student Montgomery Coll., 1979—; m. Peter Louis Graf, Oct. 28, 1971; children—Sidney E. Pollard, Deborah Lynn Pollard, Robert George Pollard, Michelle Joy Graf. Office mgr. Pa. Life Ins. Co., Miami and Dallas, 1957-72; exec. sec. to med. dir. Pitts. Children's Hosp., 1974; sec. G.E./TEMPO, Washington, 1974-76; adminstrv. asst. to sr. v.p. Logistics Mgmt. Inst., Washington, 1976-81, dir. adminstrv. svcs., 1981—, dir. recruiting and tng., 1995—; dir. KHI Svcs., Inc. Mem. Washington Tech. Personnel Forum. Democrat. Baptist. Home: 20404 Remsbury Pl Gaithersburg MD 20879-4369 Office: 2000 Corporate Rdg Mc Lean VA 22102-7805

GRAF, NANCY ELLEN, school librarian, consultant; b. Twin Falls, Idaho, June 8, 1946; d. Verne J. and Mary Ellen (Fry) Eisinger; m. Richard Stanley Graf, Aug. 3, 1968. BS, U. Idaho, 1968; MEd, Ctrl. Wash. U., 1972. Tchr. Stevens Jr. High, Pasco, Wash., 1968-72; libr. Chief Joseph Jr. High, Richland, Wash., 1972-82; libr., media spl., dir. Libr. Media Ctr. Hanford Secondary, Richland, 1982—; presenter state and nat. confs. ASCD, Am. Assn. Sch. Librs., Assn. Edn., Comm. and Tech., Nat. Coun. Computers in Edn. Contbr. articles to profl. jours. Bd. dirs. Sch. Employees Credit Union, Richland, 1980—. Mem. Assoc. For Edn. Comm. and Tech., Wash. Libr. Media Assoc., Phi Delta Kappa, Delta Kappa Gamma. Office: Hanford Secondary Sch 450 Hanford St Richland WA 99352

GRAF, STEFFI, professional tennis player; b. 1969; d. Peter and Heidi Graf. Winner numerous profl. women's tennis tournaments including Italian Open, 1987, French Open, 1987, The Golden Grand Slam (Australian Open, French Open, Wimbledon, U.S. Open, Olympics), 1988, Berlin Open, 1988, Wimbledon, 1989, 91, 93, 95, German Open, 1989, 91, 94, U.S. Open, 1989, 91, 92, 93, 95, U.S. Hardcourt Championship, 1989, 91, Australian Open, 1990, 94, Players Challenge, 1990, French Open, 1993, 95-96, Paris Open, 1995, Lipton Open, 1995; WTA Tour Champ, 1995; ranked no. 1 in world for more consecutive weeks than any other player in tennis history. *

GRAFF, LOIS MARIE, retired accounting educator; b. Cleve., Feb. 25, 1926; d. Ferdinand E. and Marie Dorothy (Seegert) Boehmer; m. Richard Allison Graff, June 26, 1948; children: Richard N., Alison M., Douglas E. BS in Bus. cum laude, Miami U., Oxford, Ohio, 1947; MBA, Baldwin-Wallace Cll., 1980; PhD in Accountancy, Massey U., Palmerston North, New Zealand, 1989. CPA, Ohio. Acct. City of Parma Heights, Ohio, 1963-86; pvt. practice acctg. Parma Heights, 1963-86; instr. Cuyahoga C.C., Parma, Ohio, 1976-79; asst. prof. Baldwin-Wallace Coll., Berea, Ohio, 1980-83, Cleve. State U., 1983; treas. Parma Sch. Dist., 1984-86; vis. tchg. fellow Massey U., 1987-89; instr. in acctg. U. So. Ala., Mobile, 1989; assoc. prof. acctg. Coastal Carolina U., Conway, S.C., 1990-94; cons., advisor Law Firm of Graff and Assocs., Columbus, Ohio, 1995—; cons. Open Poly. of New Zealand, Wellington, summer 1991. Contbr. articles to profl. publs. Pres. Parma Bd. Edn., 1972-84, Snowview PTA and others, 1955-71; leader Girl Scouts U.S., Parma, 1962-66; Sunday sch. tchr. Denison Ave. Congl. Ch., Cleve., 1948-53, Parma-South Presbyn. Ch., Parma Heights, 1955-65; vol. tutor Horry County Lit. Coun., 1995—. Named to All Ohio Sch. Bd., Ohio Sch. Bd. Assn., 1982, Alumnae of Yr., The Andrews Sch., 1983, Sons of Liberty Bowl, Cassidy Team, 1986. Mem. AAUW, Ohio Soc. CPAs (legis. com. 1970's), S.C. Tax Coun., Acctg. Assn. of Australia and New Zealand, Phi Beta Kappa, Beta Gamma Sigma. Republican. Home: 171 Quail Run Conway SC 29526

GRAFF, MARNETTE KATHLEEN, writer, nurse; b. Oct. 8, 1951; d. Giovanni Laurance and Kathleen Marnette (Loschmidt) Travia; m. John J. Burk, July 28, 1973 (div. Mar. 1983); 1 child, Sean Christian Burk; m. Arthur Leonard Graff, May 4, 1991. AAS, Nassau C.C., 1971; student, NYU, 1987-90; BS, St. Joseph's Coll., 1996. RN, N.Y. Med.-surg. RN Mercy Hosp., Rockville Centre, N.Y., 1971-75; utilization rev. coord. Grandell SNF-HRF, Long Beach, N.Y., 1975-76; insvc. dir. to dir. nursing svcs. Port Jefferson (N.Y.) Nursing Home, 1977-79; utilization rev. coord. Island Peer Rev. Orgn., Hauppauge, N.Y., 1979; dir. utilization rev. J.T. Mather Meml. Hosp., Port Jefferson, 1979-88, utilization rev. cons., 1988—; v.p. Gallery of Two Sisters, Blithe Spirit, Ltd., Miller Place, N.Y., 1988-90; med. dir. Cinema World Movie Studios, Greenpoint, N.Y., 1990-96; writer Nursing Spectrum, Hempstead, N.Y., 1989-96; instr. Beaufort County C.C., Washington, N.C., 1996; med. cons. ABC, N.Y.C., 1990—. Author: (screenplay) Building Blocks, 1989, Comin' Around Again, 1993; editor/author: (anthology) Feminine Intuition, 1991; script cons.; also short stories and essays; columnist Beaufort Hyde News, Belhaven, N.C. Episcopalian. Home and Office: Gull Cottage PO Box 26 Scranton NC 27875

GRAFF, NANCY KERR, public relations professional; b. Springfield, Mo., Apr. 17, 1942; d. Roger H. and Genevieve Emily (Vinyard) Taylor; m. Richard H. Kerr, July 24, 1962 (dec. Feb. 1979); children: N. Allison Kerr, Richard T. Kerr; m. W. Curtis Graff, Feb. 21, 1981; stepchildren: Stephen Curtis, Elisabeth Kay. BS in Edn., U. Mo., 1964. Cert. in prins. of fund devel. Fund Raising Sch. San Francisco. Tchr. English Springfield (Mo.) Pub. Schs., 1964-67; tchr. speech and drama Columbia (Mo.) Pub. Schs., 1967-68; dir. pub. rels. Burrell Comty. Mental Health, Springfield, 1977-81; pub. info. speciaist City Utilities Springfield, 1981; v.p. mktg. and adminstrn. Ozark InfoView Videotex, Springfield, 1984-85; pres. Graff and Assocs. Pub. Rels., Springfield, 1985-89; coord. comty. rels. Springfield Pub. Schs., 1989—; dir. devel. Springfield Pub. Schs. Found. 1990—; commr. Springfield Planning Zoning Commn., 1981; bd. dirs. S.W. Regional Adv. Coun. for Drug and Alcohol Abusers, 1978-80. Sustaining mem., bd. dirs. Jr. League Springfield, 1966—, dir. pub. rels., 1975-77, bd. dirs., vice-chmn. jr. league thrift shop, 1972-75. Mem. Nat. Soc. Fund Raising Execs. (nat. and local mem.), Nat. Assn. Ptnrs. in Edn. (nat. presenter 1995), Women in Comms. (nat. and local mem.), Network (founding and charter mem.), Rotary Internat. (com. chair S.E. chpt. 1990—), Springfield Ad Club. Republican. Episcopalian. Office: Springfield Pub Schs 940 N Jefferson Springfield MO 65802

GRAFF, RANDY, actress; b. Bklyn., May 23, 1955. Grad., Wagner Coll. Profl. theater debut in Gypsy, Village Dinner Theater, Raleigh, N.C.; appeared in Godspell, Raleigh; other appearances include Pins and Needles, Roundabout Theatre, N.Y.C., 1978, Something Wonderful, Westchester Regional Theatre, Harrison, N.Y., 1979, Sarava, Mark Hellinger Theatre, N.Y.C., 1979, Coming Attractions, Playwrights Horizons, Mainstage Theatre, N.Y.C., 1980, Keystone, McCarter Theatre, Princeton, N.J., 1981, A...My Name is Alice, Village Gate Theatre, N.Y.C., 1984, Amateurs, Playhouse in the Park, Cin., 1985, Fiorello!, Goodspell Opera House, East Haddam, Conn., 1985, Absurd Person Singular, Phila. Drama Guild, Phila., 1986, Les Miserables, Broadway Theatre, N.Y.C., 1987, City of Angels, Va. Theatre, N.Y.C., 1989 (Drama Desk award Featured Actress in Musical 1989, Tony award Supporting of Featured Actress in Musical 1990), Falsettos, 1993, Laughter on the 23rd Floor, 1993, Moon Over Buffalo, Martin Beck Theatre, 1995-96; (TV shows) include Mad About You, Law & Order, Love & War, Pros & Cons; (films) Key's to Tulsa, 1995. Recipient Drama Desk award, 1990, Antoinette Perry award for best featured actress in musical, 1990. Office: 210 W 70th St New York NY 10023

GRAFFEO, MARY THÉRÈSE, music educator, performer; b. Mineola, N.Y., Jan. 20, 1949; d. Michael Joseph and Florence Marie (Lonette) G. BA in Music Edn., Adelphi U., 1972; MusM in Vocal Performance, Kent State U., 1982. Cert. music tchr. N.Y. Tchr. music, therapist Nassau County Bd. Coop. Ednl. Svcs., Westbury, N.Y., 1972-85; tchr. music, developer curricula Great Neck (N.Y.) Pub. Schs., 1985-87; tchr. music Syosset (N.Y.) Pub. Schs., 1987-88, 89-90, Jericho (N.Y.) Pub. Schs., 1988-89; tchr. music, developer creative programs Lawrence (N.Y.) Pub. Schs., 1990-92; tchr. music Herricks Pub. Schs., New Hyde Park, N.Y., 1992-93, Hempstead (N.Y.) Pub. Schs., 1993—; music dir. summer programs Friends Acad., Locust Valley, N.Y., 1989-94. Author: (curriculum) Music for the Trainable Mentally Retarded, 1973, (book) Creative Enrichment Programs/America: The First 200 Years in Song, 1990; co-author: The Remediation of Learning Discrepancies Through Music, 1980; composer: (mus. play) Red Riding Hood's Day, 1993, The Bell of Atri, 1994, The Children's Song, 1995. Cultural adv. bd. Lawrence Pub. Schs., 1990-92, Hempstead Pub. Schs., 1993—; founding mem. United We Stand Am., Dallas, 1992—. Scholar Adelphi U., 1968-72, Blossom Festival Sch., Kent, Ohio, 1978-79. Mem. NEA, Music Educators Nat. Conf., N.Y. State United Tchrs., N.Y. State Sch. Music Assn., Nassau Music Educators Assn. Democrat. Roman Catholic. Home: 300 Edwards St Roslyn Heights NY 11577-1140 Office: Early Childhood Ctr 436 Front St Hempstead NY 11550-4212

GRAFT, JULIE ANN, secondary physical educator educator; b. Chgo., June 7, 1965; d. Anthonius Walterius and Margaret Elizabeth (Martell) G. BS, U. Wis., LaCrosse, 1988; MA, U. Minn., 1993. Cert. lifeguard ARC. Athletic trainer Profl. Phys. Therapy, Shakopee, Minn., 1988-89, No. Phys. Therapy, Fridley, Minn., 1989-90; lifeguard N.W. YMCA, Shoreview, Minn., 1989-90, South St. Paul YMCA, 1990-93; tchr. phys. edn. Edina (Minn.) Kindergarten Ctr., 1991; grad. asst. U. Minn., Mpls., 1991-93; tchr. phys. edn. Evanston Twp. H.S., Evanston, Ill., 1993-94; pool dir. Northmoor Country Club, Highland Park, Ill., 1994; tchr. phys. edn. New Trier H.S., Winnetka, Ill., 1994—. AAHPERD, Nat. Athletic Trainers Assn. (cert.). Home: 1220 Central St Apt 3W Evanston IL 60201-1652 Office: New Trier Twp HS 385 Winnetka Ave Winnetka IL 60093-4238

GRAFTON, SUE, novelist; b. Louisville, Apr. 24, 1940; d. Cornelius Warren and Vivian Boisseau (Harnsberger) G.; children: Leslie, Jay, Jamie; m. Steven Humphrey, Oct. 1, 1978. BA, U. Louisville, 1961. lectr. L.A. City Coll., Long Beach (Calif.) City Coll., U. Dayton (Ohio) Writers Conf., Midwest Writers Conf., Canton, Ohio, Calif. Luth. Coll., Thousand Oaks, Santa Barbara (Calif.) Writers Conf., L.A. Valley Coll., Antioch Writers Conf., Yellow Springs, Ohio, S.W. Writers Conf., Albuquerque, Smithsonian Campus on the Mall, Washington, and others. Author: (novels) Keziah Dane, 1967, The Lolly-Madona War, 1969, "A" is for Alibi, 1982 (Mysterious Stranger award 1982-83), "B" is for Burglar, 1985 (Shamus award 1986, Anthony award 1987), "D" is for Deadbeat, 1987, "E" is for Evidence, 1988 (Doubleday Mystery Guild award 1989), "F" is for Fugitive, 1989 (Doubleday Mystery Guild award 1990, The Falcon award 1990), "G" is for Gumshoe, 1990 (Doubleday Mystery Guild award 1991, Anthony award

1991, Shamus award 1991), "H" is for Homicide, 1991 (Doubleday Mystery Guild award 1992), "I" is for Innocent, 1992 (Doubleday Mystery Guild award 1992, Mystery Scene Am. Mystery award 1993), Kinsey and Me, 1992, "J" is for Judgement, 1994, "K" is for Killer, 1994 (Shamus award 1994); editor: Writing Mysteries, 1992; author short fiction, short stories, screenplay, teleplay TV episodes. Mem. Writers Gild Am. West, Mystery Writers Am. Inc. (pres. 1994), Private Eye Writers Assn. (pres. 1989-90), Crime Writers Assn.

GRAFTON, SUSAN FRANCES, economic developer; b. New Orleans, Aug. 2, 1957; d. Walter Weldon and Lottie Frances (Vance) G.; m. John Dale Cody Jr., Nov. 26, 1988; 1 child, Paul Austin Grafton Cody. BA in Bus. Adminstrn. and Polit. Sci., Ouachita Bapt. U., 1979; M of Urban and Regional Planning, U. Miss., Oxford, 1981. Cert. econ. developer Am. Econ. Devel. Coun. Asst. planning dir. Calcasieu Parish, Lake Charles, La., 1981-87; dir. planning and econ. devel. Carbon County, Rawlins, Wyo., 1987-91; mgr. econ. devel. City of Westminster, Colo., 1991—; bd. sec. Colo. Lending Source, Denver, 1995—; bd. dirs. Adams County Econ. Devel. Corp., Denver; ex-officio bd. mem. Jefferson Econ. Coun., Golden, Colo.; exec. bd. mem. Metro Denver Network. Chmn. Carbon County United Way, Rawlins, 1989-90; mem. Soroptomist Internat., Rawlins, 1987-91. Named Outstanding Young Woman, 1986. Mem. La. Flood Plain Mgrs. Assn. (hon. lifetime mem. 1991), Rotary Internat. Democrat. Baptist. Office: City of Westminster 4800 W 92d Ave Westminster CO 80030

GRAGG, ANNA MABEL, financial analyst; b. Klamath Falls, Oreg., Aug. 27, 1964; d. Lawrence Frederick and Carlene Elaine (Cornish) Halousek; m. Tay Winfield Gragg, June 19, 1994; 1 child, Cheryl Hannah. BS, Calif. State U., 1990. Sr. acct. Contadina Foods, Woodland, Calif., 1991-92; project officer Cal-Mortgage, Sacramento, Calif., 1993—. Mem. Am. Soc. Pub. Adminstrn., Sacramento Vegetarian Soc. Republican. Seventh Day Adventist. Office: Cal-Mortgage Rm 210 818 K St Sacramento CA 95814

GRAHAM, ANITA LOUISE, correctional and community health nurse; b. Casa Grande, Ariz., Sept. 17, 1959; d. Therman Louis and Annie Clessie (Dornan) Nichols; m. Richard Arthur Christy, Aug. 27, 1990; children: Amanda Sue Foster, Kristi Lynn Foster. AS in Practical Nursing, Ctrl. Ariz. Coll., 1982; AAS, Gateway C.C., Phoenix, 1985, Degree in Health Svc. Mgmt., 1992. RN, Ariz., Okla.; cert. BLS, ACLS, Chemotherapy. Cert. nursing asst. Hoemako Hosp., Casa Grande, 1977-82; lic. practical nurse Mesa (Ariz.) Luth. Hosp., 1982-85; RN Mesa Gen. Hosp., 1985-86, East Mesa Care Ctr., 1986-88; RN, case mgr. Interim Healthcare, Phoenix, 1988-93; RN, nurse clinician PDR Carum Care, Phoenix, 1991-95; correctional RN Ariz. Dept. Corrections, Florence, 1993-95; IV nurse clinician Signature Home Care, 1994-96; mem. RN adv. bd. Interim Healthcare, 1990-93; RN, nurse clinician PDR Caravan, Phoenix, 1991—. Mem. Ariz. Nurses Assn. Republican. Home: 1646 N Pennington Dr Chandler AZ 85224-5115

GRAHAM, ANNE MARIE CYNTHIA, electrical engineer; b. Detroit, Nov. 6, 1961; d. Kenneth Patrick Graham and Patricia Lukasik Pondell; 1 child, Martin Rodriguez. BS, Boston U., 1990. Short-term mcpl. bond trader Scudder, Stevens & Clark, Boston, 1985-88; engring. aide Fed. Dept. Transp., Cambridge, Mass., 1988-90; electronics engr. FAA, Boston, 1990-93, Detroit, 1993-94; process leader Ford Motor Co., Dearborn, Mich., 1994, electronics engr., 1994—. Vol. citizen case reviewer Mass. Dept. Social Svcs., Lowell, Mass., 1992-93; aviation educator women in aviation FAA 99's, 1990-93. Mem. LWV (moderate polit. candidate forums/interviews), Soc. Women Engrs.

GRAHAM, ARLENE R., artist; b. Bethlehem, Pa., Nov. 13, 1945; d. Arnold Jefferson Rosenkranz and Mimi Caroline (Rosenberg) Wolnstein; m. David Charles Graham, May 8, 1971; children: Mark David, Jonathan Stephen. BA, Ripon Coll., 1967; MA, Tufts U., 1971. Ceo Fiberworks, Beavercreek, Ohio, 1982—; artist-in-residence Metro. Arts Coun., Dayton, Ohio, 1993. Treas. Supportive Advocates for Gifted Edn., Beavercreek, 1987-93. Mem. Weavers Guild Miami Valley (pres. 1995—), Handweavers Guild Am., Ohio Designer Craftsmen, Midwest Weavers Assn., Beavercreek Women's League, Hadassah. Jewish. Home and Office: Fiberworks 3102 Maginn Dr Beavercreek OH 45434

GRAHAM, BARBARA S., electric power industry executive. Sr. v.p., treas., CFO Delmarva Power & Light Co., Wilmington, Del. Office: Delmarva Power & Light 800 King St Wilmington DE 19899*

GRAHAM, CYNTHIA ARMSTRONG, banker; b. Charlotte, N.C., Jan. 3, 1950; d. Beverly Weller and Katherine (Anderson) Armstrong; m. Walter Raleigh Graham Jr., May 23, 1970. AB in Chemistry, Bryn Mawr Coll., 1971; MBA in Fin. with distinction, U. Pa., 1976. Computer programmer Philco-Ford, Ft. Washington, Pa., 1973-74; asst. dir. admissions Wharton Sch., U. Pa., Phila., 1974-76; asst. v.p. N.C. Nat. Bank, Charlotte, 1976-80; v.p. Barclays Am. Corp., Charlotte, 1980-86; sr. v.p. Barclays Bank Del., N.A., Wilmington, 1986-87, Barnett Banks, Inc., Jacksonville, Fla., 1987—; chmn., pres. Barnett Mcht. Svcs., Inc., Jacksonville, 1987-89, TeleCheck Southcoast, 1987-89, Barnett Card Svcs. Corp., Jacksonville, 1989—; bd. advisors Nat. DAta Corp., Atlanta, 1987-88; delivery sys. advisor VISA U.S.A., Inc., San Mateo, Calif., 1987-91; mcht. svcs. advisor MasterCard, Internat., N.Y.C., 1989-92; mem. U.S. regional bus. com. MasterCard, 1992—; card products advisor VISA U.S.A., Inc., San Mateo, 1991-94, VISA Internat., 1994, mem. mktg. com., 1994—; bd. dirs. Interlink Network, Inc., U$A Value Exchg., 1995—. Mem. Jacksonville Women's Network, 1988-92, bd. dirs., 1991-92, treas., 1992; mem. bd. suprs. Spaceport Fla., 1990-92. Mem. Am. Bankers Assn. (exec. com. card divsn. 1991-94, vice chmn. 1993, chmn. 1994), Jacksonville C. of C. Office: Barnett Card Svcs Corp Bldg 400 9000 Southside Blvd Jacksonville FL 32256-8418

GRAHAM, DIANNE DOUGLAS, advertising agency executive; b. Cherrypoint, N.C., Oct. 11, 1953; d. Gordon and Barbara Allyn (Wolfe) G.; m. Suresh Kumar Kandiah, Oct. 16, 1989. BA, Smith Coll., 1975. Creative supr. Grey Advt., N.Y.C., 1980-84; assoc. and creative dir. Saatchi & Saatchi, N.Y.C., 1984-90; creative dir. Rubin-Ehrenthal, N.Y.C., 1992-95, DDG Advt., N.Y.C., 1995—. Mem. coun. African Wildlife Found., Washington, 1989-92, planning com. Asia Cir., N.Y., 1995—. Recipient Lion-African Wildlife Found. award Cannes Festival, Clio gold pub. svc. award, N.Y. Addy gold-UKLA award. Mem. Asia Soc., Smith Club. Office: DDG Advt 158 E 61st St New York NY 10021

GRAHAM, FRANCES KEESLER (MRS. DAVID TREDWAY GRAHAM), psychologist, educator; b. Canastota, N.Y., Aug. 1, 1918; d. Clyde C. and Norma (Van Surdam) Keesler; m. David Tredway Graham, June 14, 1941; children: Norma, Andrew, Mary. BA, Pa. State U., 1938; PhD, Yale U., 1942; DSc (hon.), U. Wis., 1996. Acting dir. St. Louis Psychiat. Clinic, 1942-44; instr. Barnard Coll., 1948-51; research assoc. Sch. Medicine, Washington U., St. Louis, 1942-48, 53-57, U. Wis., Madison, 1957-64; asso. prof. pediatrics and psychology U. Wis., 1964-68, prof., 1968-86, Hilldale research prof., 1980-86; prof. U. Del., Newark, 1986-89, prof. emerita, 1989—; Disting. faculty lectr., U. Del., Newark, 1989; cons. Nat. Inst. Neurol. Diseases and Blindness perinatal research br.; mem. exptl. psychology research review com. NIMH, 1970-74, NRC, 1971-74; mem. bd. sci. counselors NIMH, 1977-81, chmn., 1979-81; mem. Pres.'s Commn. for Study of Ethical Problems in Medicine and Biomed. and Behavioral Research, 1980-82. Mem. editorial bd. Jour. Exptl. Child Psychology, 1964-67, Child Devel., 1966-68, Jour. Exptl. Psychology, 1968-73, Psychophysiology, 1968-73; contbr. articles to profl. jours. Recipient Rsch. Scientist award NIMH, 1964-89, Disting. Alumna award Pa. State U., 1983, Wilbur L. Cross medal Yale U., 1992, Gold medal Am. Psychol. Found., 1995. Fellow AAAS (chmn. sect. psychology 1979, mem. nominations com. 1992-95), APA (coun. 1975-77, pres. div. physiol. and comparative psychology 1978-79, G. Stanley Hall award 1982, Disting. Scientist award 1990); mem. NAS, Am. Psychol. Soc. (William James fellow 1990), Soc. Rsch. Child Devel. (council 1965-71, pres. 1975-77, Disting. Sci. Contbns. award 1991), Soc. Psychophysiol. Rsch. (dir. 1968-71, 72-75, pres. 1973-74, Disting. Contbns. award 1981), Soc. Exptl. Psychologists, Soc. Neurosci., Fedn. Behavioral Psychol. and Cognitive Scis. (exec. com. 1991-94), Psychonomic Soc., Acoustical Soc. Am., Internat. Soc. Devel. Psychobiology, Phi Beta Kappa, Sigma Xi. Home: 311 Dove Dr Newark DE 19713-1211

GRAHAM, JAN, state attorney general; b. Salt Lake City. BS in Psychology, Clark U., Worcester, Mass., 1973; MS in Psychology, U. Utah, 1977, JD, 1980. Bar: Utah. Ptnr. Jones, Waldo, Holbrook & McDonough, Salt Lake City, 1979-89; soliciter gen. Utah Atty. Gen.'s Office, Salt Lake City, 1989-93; atty. gen. State of Utah, 1993—; adj. prof. law U. Utah Law Sch.; bar commr. Utah State Bar, 1991; master of bench Utah Inns Ct. VII; mem. Utah Commn. on Justice in 21st Century; bd. dirs. Jones, Waldo, Holbrook & McDonough; bd. trustees Coll. Law U. Utah (pres.). Fin. devel. chair YWCA; chair Ctrl. Bus. Improvement Dist.; mem. Salt Lake City Olympic Bid Com. 1988 Games. Named Woman Lawyer Yr. Utah, 1987. Mem. Am. Arbitration Assn. (nat. panel arbitrators), Women Lawyers Utah (co-founder, mem. exec. com.). Office: Office of Attorney General 236 State Capitol Bldg Salt Lake City UT 84114-1202*

GRAHAM, JESSICA ALICE, performing company executive; b. Honolulu, June 9, 1969; d. Edward Lloyd and Alice Chloe (Bennett) G. AA, Alvin (Tex.) C.C., 1989; BA in Comm., Stephen F. Austin State Univ., 1992. Pub. rels. asst. Houston Ballet, 1992-93, adminstrv. asst., 1993-95, adminstrv. coord., edn. coord., 1995—. Sunday sch. tchr., Clear Lake, Tex., 1994-95; nat. poetry judge Literacy Advance Houston, 1994-96. Recipient Golden Poet award Library of Poetry, 1985, 87, Silver Poet award, 1986, 90. Mem. Women in Comm., Inc. (hospitality chair 1993-94, publicity chair, regional conf. co-chair 1995-96, sec., 1996—, Who's Who in Poetry award 1992, Pres.'s award 1996), Internat. Assn. Bus. Communicators.

GRAHAM, JEWEL FREEMAN, social worker, lawyer, educator; b. Springfield, Ohio, May 3, 1925; d. Robert Lee and Lula Belle Freeman; m. Paul N. Graham, Aug. 8, 1953; children: Robert, Nathan. BA, Fisk U., 1946; student, Howard U., 1946-47; MS in Social Svc. Adminstrn., Case Western Res. U., 1953; JD, U. Dayton, 1979; LHD (hon.), Meadville-Lombard Theol. Sch., 1991. Bar: Ohio; cert. social worker. Assoc. dir. teenage program dept. YWCA, Grand Rapids, Mich., 1947-50; coord. met. teenage program YWCA, Detroit, 1953-56; dir. program for interracial edn. Antioch Coll., Yellow Springs, Ohio, 1964-69, from asst. prof. to prof., 1969-92, prof. emeritus, 1992—; mem. Ohio Commn. on Dispute Resolution and Conflict Mgmt., 1990-92. Mem. exec. com. World YMCA, Geneva, 1975-83, 87—, pres., 1983; bd. dirs. YWCA of the U.S.A., 1970-89, pres., 1979-85; bd. dirs. Antioch U., 1994—. Named to Greene County Women's Hall of Fame, 1982, Ohio Women's Hall of Fame, 1988; named 1 of 10 Outstanding Women of Miami Valley, 1987; recipient Ambassador award YWCA of the U.S.A., 1993. Mem. ABA, Nat. Assn. of Social Workers (charter), Nat. Coun. of Negro Women (life), Alpha Kappa Alpha. Democrat. Unitarian Universalist. Office: Antioch Coll Livermore 51 Yellow Springs OH 45387

GRAHAM, JORIE, author; b. N.Y.C., May 9, 1951; d. Curtis Bell and Beverly (Stoll) Pepper; m. James Galvin. BFA, NYU, 1973; MFA, U. Iowa, 1978. Asst. prof. Murray (Ky.) State U., 1978-79, Humboldt State U., Arcata, Calif., 1979-81; instr. Columbia U., N.Y.C., 1981-83; mem. staff U. Iowa, Iowa City, 1983—; poetry editor Crazy Horse, 1978-81. Author: Hybrids of Plants and of Ghosts, 1980 (Great Lakes Colls. Assn. award 1981), Erosion, 1983, The End of Beauty, 1987, Region of Unlikeness, 1991, Materialism, 1993; editor: (with David Lehman) The Best American Poetry 1990, 1990. Recipient Am. Acad. Poets award, 1977, Young Poet prize Poetry Northwest, 1980, Pushcart prize, 1980, 82, American Poetry Review prize, 1982; Bunting fellow Radcliff Inst., 1982, Guggenheim fellow, 1983, John D. and Catherine T. MacArthur Found. fellow, 1990; grantee Ingram-Merrill Found., 1981. Office: U Iowa Dept Creative Writing Iowa City IA 52242*

GRAHAM, KATHARINE, newspaper executive; b. N.Y.C., June 16, 1917; d. Eugene and Agnes (Ernst) Meyer; m. Philip L. Graham, June 5, 1940 (dec. 1963); children: Elizabeth Morris Graham Weymouth, Donald Edward, William Welsh, Stephen Meyer. Student, Vassar Coll., 1934-36; AB, U. Chgo., 1938. Reporter San Francisco News, 1938-39; mem. editorial staff Washington Post, 1939-45, mem. Sunday circulation and editorial depts., pub., 1969-79; pres. Washington Post Co., 1963-73, 77, chmn. bd., 1973-93, CEO, 1973-91, chmn. exec. com., 1993—; co-chmn. Internat. Herald Tribune; ind. trustee Reuters Founders Share Co. Ltd.; vice chmn. bd. dirs. Urban Inst.; mem. Coun. on Fgn. Rels., Overseas Devel. Coun.; past chmn. N.Y. Pubs. Assn. Life trustee U. Chgo.; hon. trustee George Washington U.; mem. collectors com. The Nat. Gallery of Art, Washington; active D.C. Com. Pub. Edn. Fellow Am. Acad. Arts and Scis.; mem. Am. Soc. Newspaper Editors, Nat. Press Club, Coun. Fgn. Rels., Overseas Devel. Coun., Met. Club, Cosmopolitan Club, 1925 F Street Club. Home: 2920 R St NW Washington DC 20007-2920 Office: Washington Post Co 1150 15th St NW Washington DC 20071-0001*

GRAHAM, KIRSTEN R., computer science educator; b. Inglewood, Calif., July 20, 1946; d. Ray Selmer and Ella Louise (Carter) Newbury; m. Frank Sellers Graham, July 31, 1981. BS, U. Wis., Oshkosh, 1971; MS, U. Colo., 1980; postgrad., Army War Coll., 1987. Cert. Flight instr. Chief info. svc. Mont. State Dept. Labor and Industry, Helena, Mont.; dir., personal property and bus. lic. div. County of Fairfax, Va.; analyst officer U.S. Army Pentagon, Washington; battalion commdr. U.S. Army, Frankfurt, West Germany; assoc. prof. U.S. Army, West Point, N.Y.; tchr. computer tech. Helena Coll. Tech., U. Mont.; del. People-to-People Women Computer Sci. Profls. program., China. Del. to People's Republic of China Citizen's Amb. Program, 1993. LTC U.S. Army, 1964-88. Mem. Assn. for Computing Machinery, Am. Fedn. Tchrs.

GRAHAM, LAURIE, editor; b. Evanston, Ill., Nov. 22, 1941; d. Thomas Harlin and Mary Elisabeth (Stoner) Graham; m. George McKay Schieffelin, Dec. 12, 1980 (dec. Jan. 1988); m. Robert Dale Shearer, Apr. 6, 1994. Student, Mt. Holyoke Coll., 1959-61; BA, U. Colo., 1963. Editor Charles Scribner's Sons, N.Y.C., 1969-87. Author: Rebuilding the House, 1990; mem. editl. bd. Creative Nonfiction, 1994—, (press series) Emerging Writers in Creative Nonfiction, Duquesne U., 1994—. Mem. PEN, N.Y. Jr. League, Colony Club. Home: 1000 Grandview Ave Pittsburgh PA 15211-1362

GRAHAM, LOIS CHARLOTTE, retired educator; b. Denver, Mar. 20, 1917; d. James Washington Brewster and Martha Wilhemina (Raukohl) Plunkett; m. Milton Clinton Graham, June 30, 1940 (dec.); children: Charlotte, Milton, Charlene, James. Student, Okla. City U., 1935-36; AB, Ouachita Bapt. U., 1939; postgrad., U. Nev., Reno, 1953, 63, 68, Ark. State U., 1954, 59. Cert. tchr., Colo., Nev., Ark. Tchr. Fairmount Sch., Golden, Colo., 1939-40, Melbourne (Ark.) Sch., 1940-41, Blytheville (Ark.) Jr. H.S., 1944-45, Hawthorne (Nev.) Elem. Sch., 1952-81; substitute tchr. Mineral County Sch. Dist., Hawthorne, 1988-94; sr. resource cons. dept. geriatrics U. Nev.-Reno Med. Sch., 1988-90, del. to Rural Health Conf., Hawthorne, 1990; officer Mineral County Tchrs. Assn., 1955-65; ad hoc com. Nev. State Tchrs., 1965. Mem. Mineral County Emergency Planning Com., 1991—; asst. to pres. High Sch. PTA, Hawthorne, 1958, Elem. PTA, Hawthorne, 1961; pianist, choir dir., tchr. various chs., 1927—; active Older Am. Friends of Libr. Recipient Disting. Svc. award. Mem. AAUW (membership v.p. 1988-91, pres. 1991-92, 94-95, 96—), AARP (pres. 1995—), Ret. Pub. Employees of Nev. (membership v.p. 1994-96, pres. 1996—), Older Ams., Friends Libr., Delta Kappa Gamma (v.p. 1991-92). Republican. Baptist. Home: PO Box 1543 Hawthorne NV 89415-1543

GRAHAM, MARY ANNE, electrical engineer; b. Salt Lake City, Feb. 19, 1967; d. Richard Lee and Mary Elizabeth (Ayrton) G. BS in Engring., Colo. Sch. Mines, 1990. Elec. engr. Tenneco Energy, Houston, 1995—. Capt. U.S. Army, 1990-95. Decorated Army Achievement medal. Mem. NOW, Women's Sports Found. Home: 12411 Rincon Houston TX 77077 Office: Tenneco Energy PO Box 2511 Houston TX 77252-2511

GRAHAM, PATRICIA ALBJERG, education educator, foundation executive; b. Lafayette, Ind., Feb. 9, 1935; d. Victor L. and Marguerite (Hall) Albjerg; m. Loren R. Graham, Sept. 6, 1955; 1 child, Marguerite Elizabeth. BS, Purdue U., 1955, MS, 1957, DLett (hon.), 1980; PhD, Columbia U., 1964; MA (hon.), Harvard U., 1974; DHL (hon.), Manhattanville Coll., 1976; LLD (hon.), Beloit Coll., 1977, Clark U., 1978; DPA (hon.), Suffolk U., 1978, Ind. U., 1980; DLitt (hon.), St. Norbert Coll., 1980; DH (hon.), Emmanuel Coll., 1983; DHL (hon.), No. Mich. U., 1987, York Coll. of Pa., 1989, Kenyon Coll., 1991, Bank St. Coll. Edn., 1993; LLD (hon.), Radcliffe Coll., 1994. Tchr. high sch. Norfolk, Va., 1955-56, 57-58, N.Y.C., 1958-60; lectr., asst. prof. Ind. U., 1964-66; asst. prof. history of edn. Barnard Coll. and Columbia Tchrs. Coll., N.Y.C., 1965-68; assoc. prof. Barnard Coll. and Columbia Tchrs. Coll., 1968-72, prof., 1972-74; dean Radcliffe Inst., 1974-77; also v.p. Radcliffe Coll., Cambridge, Mass., 1976-77; prof. Harvard U., Cambridge, Mass., 1974-79, Warren prof., 1979—; dean Grad. Sch. Edn., 1982-91; pres. Spencer Found., Chgo., 1991—; dir. Nat. Inst. Edn., Washington, 1977-79, trustee Northwestern Mut. Life., 1980—. Author: Progressive Education: From Arcady to Academe, 1967, Community and Class in American Education: 1865-1918, 1974, S.O.S. Sustain Our Schools, 1992. Bd. dirs. Dalton Sch., 1973-76, Josiah Macy, Jr. Found., 1976-77, 79—; trustee Beloit Coll., 1976-77, 79-82, Found. for Teaching Econs., 1980-87; dir. Spencer Found., 1983—, Johnson Found., 1983—, Hitachi Found., 1985—, Carnegie Found. for Advancement of Teaching, 1984-92. Am. Council on Edn. fellow Princeton U., 1969-70. Mem. AAAS (coun. 1993—), Sci. Rsch. Assocs. (dir. 1980-89), Nat. Acad. Edn. (pres. 1985-89), Am. Hist. Assn. (v.p. 1985-89), Phi Beta Kappa. Episcopalian. Office: The Spencer Found 900 N Michigan Ave Ste 2800 Chicago IL 60611-1542 also: Harvard U Grad Sch Edn Cambridge MA 02138

GRAHAM, SHEILA MARION, publisher, editor; b. Bristow, Okla., June 8, 1936; d. Clifford Frederick and Thelma Ernestine (Putz) Van Orsdol; m. Wesley Duane Dennis, Nov. 1955 (div. Oct. 1961); children: Shara Guss, David Dennis (dec.), Tina Dennis, Steven Dennis, Eileen Dennis; m. Eddie Gene Graham, Dec. 21, 1977. AA in Liberal Arts, Antelope Valley Coll., Lancaster, Calif., 1993; BA in Bus. Mgmt., U. Phoenix, 1995; postgrad., Azusa Pacific U., 1995—. Assoc. editor The Worldwide News, Big Sandy, Tex., 1976-77; assoc. editor The Worldwide News, Pasadena, Calif., 1977-80, sr. editor, 1980-96; assoc. editor The Plain Truth mag., Pasadena, 1980-90, mng. editor, 1990-96; pub. Christian Women InTouch, Arcadia, Calif., 1996—; mem. adv. bd. Pasadena Women's Ministry, 1996—; nat. coord. of women's ministry Worldwide Ch. of God, Pasadena, 1996—. Editor newsletter Christian Women In Touch, 1996. Mem. Women in Comm., L.A. Press Club. Office: Christian Women InTouch PO Box 2028 Arcadia CA 91077

GRAHAM, SYLVIA ANGELENIA, wholesale distributor, retail buyer; b. Charlotte, N.C., Mar. 27, 1950; d. John Wesley and Willie Myrl (Ray) White; m. James Peter Cleveland Fisher, Apr. 23, 1967 (div. Sept. 1972); 1 child, Wesley James Fisher; m. Harold Walker Graham, Sept. 14, 1972 (dec. June 1994); 1 child, Angelique Jane Graham. Cert., Naval Reserve Force Detachment Mgmt. Sch., 1985; air cargo specialist cert., Air U., 1987. Store owner Naval Air Terminal/Naval Transp. Support Unit, Norfolk, Va., 1985—; fleet liaison technician Naval Material Transp. Orgn., Norfolk, 1988-93; passenger svc. rep. Naval Material Transport Orgn., Norfolk, Va.; distbr. Blair Divsn. of Merchants, Lynchburg, Va., 1988—, Mason Shoe Co., Chippewa Falls, Wis., 1988—; driver Greater Charlotte Transp. Co., 1988—, Watkins Products, Winona, Minn., 1992—, Citizens Def. Products, St. Joseph, Mo., 1993—; dealer Creative Card Co., Chgo., 1995—; jewelry dealer Merlite Industries, N.Y.C., 1994; dealer Creative Cards, Chgo., 1995—; mem. Nat. Safety Coun., Charlotte, 1988—, "C" team Watkins Products, Lincoln, Nebr., 1992—; sec. Popular Club Plan, Dayton, N.J., 1990—; pub. Citizens Def. Products, 1993—; sponsor The Paralyzed Vets. Am., Wilton, N.H., 1994—. Crusader Cancer Ctr. for Detection and Preventin Drive, Seattle, 1991—; blcok chmn. Easter Seal Soc., 1988—. With USN, 1991, Persian Gulf; USNR, 1992, Somolian Relief Effort; USN, 1993-94. Named Top Dealer, Home Showcase Products, Lynchburg, Va. Mem. NAFE, Nat. Enlisted Res. Assn., Naval Enlisted Res. Assn., Nat. Pk. and Conservation Assn., Nat. Trust Hist. Preservation, Direct Selling Assn., Navy League of the U.S., Libr. of Congress Assocs., Nature Conservancy. Democrat. Pentecostal. Home: PO Box 16066 Charlotte NC 28297-6066

GRAHAM, SYLVIA SWORDS, educator; b. Atlanta, Nov. 15, 1935; d. Metz Jona and Christine (Gurley) Swords; m. Thomas A. Graham, Nov. 29, 1958 (div. 1970). BA, Mary Washington Coll., Fredericksburg, Va., 1957; MEd, W. Ga. Coll., Carrollton, 1980; SEd, W. Ga. Coll., 1981; postgrad., Coll. William and Mary, 1964-67. Tchr. Atlanta pub. schs., 1957-58, Newark County pub. schs., Newark, Calif., 1960-61; tchr. history Virginia Beach (Va.) pub. schs., 1964-75, Paulding County pub. schs., Dallas, Ga., 1976—; tour dir. Paulding High Sch. trips, Far East, 1985, USSR, 1989, Australia, 1988-89. County chmn. Rep. Party, 1987-89, county chmn. for re-election of Newt Gingrich, 1982; mem. Gingrich edn. com., 1983, 88; 1st vice chmn. 6th Congl. Dist., 1989-90, chmn. 1989-90; chmn. 7th Congl. Dist., 1992-95; del. Nat. Rep. Conv., 1992. Named Star Tchr., Paulding County C. of C., Dallas, Ga., 1989. Mem. Dallas Woman's Club (pres. 1982-84, 1st v.p. 1986-88, pub. affairs chmn. 1986—, treas. for Civic Ctr. fund 1984—), Phi Kappa Phi. Republican. Baptist. Home: 204 Hart Cir Dallas GA 30132-1115

GRAHN, BARBARA ASCHER, publisher; b. Chgo., Mar. 26, 1929; d. Harry L. and Eleanor (Simon) Ascher; m. Robert D. Grahn, Dec. 23, 1952; children: Susan Grahn Gantz, Nancy Lee, Wendy. BA, Miami U., Oxford, Ohio, 1950. Promotion dir. George Williams Coll., Chgo., 1950-52; sales mgr. Chatham Mfg., Chgo., 1952-54; research asst. Standard Rate and Data Service, Skokie, Ill., 1968-70, adminstr. editorial services, 1970-75, asst. editor, 1975-77; editor Wilmette, Ill., 1977-87; assoc. pub. Std. Rate and Data Svc., Wilmette, Ill., 1987-95, quality assurance mgr., 1995-96. Precinct capt. Ill. Reps., 1956-58; pres. Cmty. Club of Jewish Women, Skokie, 1958-60; bd. dirs., treas. North Shore Towers Condo Assn., Skokie, 1986-90, 93—. Mem. NAFE, Chgo. Ad Club, Alpha Epsilon Phi. Office: SRDS 1700 Higgins Rd Des Plaines IL 60018-5621

GRAINGER, NESSA, artist; b. Atlantic City, N.J., Sept. 15; d. Barnet and Pauline (Gittelman) Posner; m. Murray Grainger; children: Richard Greenbaum, Margie Friedman. BFA, Phila. Mus. Sch., 1950; postgrad., Tyler Sch. Art, Phila., 1954-55, Pa. Acad. Art, Phila., 1962-64. One-woman shows include Douglas Coll., N.J., 1990, The Interchurch Ctr., N.Y.C., 1992, Elliott Mus., Stuart, Fla., 1993, Ocean County Artists Guild, 1994, Warner-Lambert Corp. Hdqrs., Morris Plains, N.J., 1996, NAD; exhibited in group shows at Am. Watercolor Soc. Ann. Exhbn., 1995, NAD, 1992, 96; represented in permanent collections, including Nat. Gallery of Art Libr., Washington, Mus. Modern Art Libr., N.Y.C., Newark Mus., Bergen Mus. Arts and Scis., N.J., Elliott Mus., Zhejiang Provincial Mus., Hangzhow, China. Recipient Best Landscape award, 1986, Nicholas Reale medal, 1993, 1st prize Essex Watercolor Soc., award of merit Perkins Art Ctr., 1987, 1st prize for abstract watercolor Miniature Art Soc. N.J., 1988, Catherine Wolfe Gold Medal of Honor award, 1994, Calendar award Pa. Watercolor Soc., 1995, Merit award Balt. Watercolor Soc., 1996, Merit award La. Watercolor Soc., 1996. Mem. Nat. Assn. Women Artists (pres. 1989-91, medal of honor 1973, Molly M. Canaday award, Kopet award), N.J. Watercolor Soc. (pres. 1982-84, silver medal of honor 1985, Forbes award 1985, ODS award 1987, Mitzuki Kovacs award 1988, Henry Gasser award 1996), N.J. Watercolor Soc. (Orthodiagnostics award 1992), Phila. Watercolor Club (Village Art award 1995), Knickerbocker Artists (silver medal of honor 1992), Allied Artists Am. (Henry Grasser Meml. award 1993), Audubon Artists (v.p. watermedia 1988, Koffler award 1987, Silver medal 1989, Elsie Ject Key award 1993, Liquitex award 1995, Dale Meyers Honor medal 1996), Am. Soc. Contemporary Artists (Doris Kreindler award), Soc. Exptl. Artists. Home: 212 Old Turnpike Rd Califon NJ 07830-3306

GRALA, JANE MARIE, securities firm executive; b. Phila.; d. Stanley Frank and Anna Stephanie (Yurkiewicz) G. BS, Rutgers U., Camden, 1976; MBA, Winthrop U., 1979; postgrad., Am. Mgmt. Assn., N.Y.C., 1980-82, Am. Inst. Real Estate Appraisers, Chgo., 1985. Mgr. acctg. dept. NDI Engring. Co., Pennsauken, N.J., 1968-72, project mgr., 1972-76; rep. sales Am. Cyanamid, Wayne, N.J., 1976-80; dist. mgr. Am. Appraisal Assocs., Phila., 1980-86; assoc. v.p. investments Prudential Securities Incorporated, Clearwater, Fla., 1986—; adj. prof. fin. area Tampa (Fla.) Coll., 1995—. Mem. Nat. Assn. Accts. (dir. advt. So. Jersey chpt. 1983-86), Assn. MBA Execs., Bus and Profl. Women's Assn., Nat. Assn. for Female Execs., Chi Delta, Phi Chi Theta. Republican. Office: Prudential Securities Inc 28100 Us Highway 19 N Ste 100 Clearwater FL 34621-2656

GRALAPP, MARCELEE GAYL, librarian; b. Winfield, Kans., Nov. 2, 1931; d. Benjamin Harry and Lelia Iris G. BA, Kansas State Teacher's Coll.,

1952; MA, U. Denver, 1963. Children's libr. Hutchinson Pub. Libr., Kans., 1952-57, Lawrence Pub. Libr., Kans., 1957-59; assoc. libr. Boulder Pub. Libr., Colo., 1959-66, libr. dir., 1966—; vis. faculty U. Denver, 1965-66, 67, Kans. State Teacher's Coll., Emporia, 1965. Chmn. state plan for libr. devel. Libraries-Colo., 1974; city staff liaison Boulder Arts Commn., 1979—; bd. dirs. Boulder Ctr. for Visual Arts, 1975-79; treas. Irving Libr. Network, Inc. Recipient Governor's award Colo. Council on Arts and Humanities, 1981. Mem. ALA, Mountain Plains Libr. Assn., Colo. Libr. Assn. (legis. com. 1970-78, Lifetime Achievement award 1992), Boulder Hist. Soc., Boulder Philharm. Soc., Chautauqua Assn., Denver Art Mus., Delta Kappa Gamma. Democrat. Home: 3080 15th St Boulder CO 80304-2614 Office: Boulder Pub Libr PO Drawer H 1000 Canyon Blvd Boulder CO 80306

GRAMBS, JENNIFER IANNACONE, writer; b. Newark, Apr. 5, 1945; d. Anthony T. Iannacone and Mary E. (Butler) Koser; m. Jeffrey Wood Grambs, Sept. 28, 1970; 1 child, Alison Rebecca. BA in English Lit., Hunter Coll., 1980, MA in English Lit., 1986. City editor The East Orange (N.J.) Record, 1965-67; asst. to fashion columnist Eugenia Sheppard, N.Y. Post Women's Wear Daily, 1967-73; bus. owner The Jennifer Grambs Collection, N.Y.C., 1985—. Author: Alaska, 1990, Texas, 1990, Florida, 1990; contbr. articles to profl. publs.; also film and video work. Hotline vol. Self-Help for Women with Breast Cancer (S.H.A.R.E.), 1994—.

GRAMES, JUDITH ELLEN, building engineering inspector, artist, educator; b. Inglewood, Calif., Feb. 7, 1938; d. Glover Victor and Dorothy Margaret (Burton-Bellingham) Hendrickson; divorced; children: Nansea Ellen Ryan, Amber Jeanne Shelley-Harris, Carolyn Angel Longmire, Susan Elaine Gomez, Robert Derek Shallenberger. Cert in journalism, Newspaper Inst. Am., N.Y.C., 1960; AA, Santa Barbara City Coll., 1971; BA, U. Calif., Santa Barbara, 1978, cert. in teaching, 1979. Cert. bldg. inspector, plumbing inspector, Calif. Editor, reporter, photographer Goleta Valley Sun Newspaper, Santa Barbara, 1968-71; editor, team asst. Bur. of Ednl. Rsch. Devel., Santa Barbara, 1971; bus. writer, graphics cons. Santa Barbara, 1971-77; art and prodn. dir. Bedell Advt. Selling Improvement Corp., Santa Barbara, 1979-81; secondary sch. tchr. Coalinga (Calif.) Unified Sch. Dist., 1981-83; bldg. inspector aide Santa Barbara County, Lompoc, 1983-88, from bldg. engring. inspector I to III, 1988—. Exhibited in group shows at Foley's Frameworks and Interiors, 1984, Grossman Gallery, 1984, Lompoc Valley Art Assn., 1984— (numerous awards including Best of Show 1985, 1st place 1984, 94, 2d place 1984, 86, 88, 96, 3d place 1987, 89, Hon. Mention 1986, 90, 91); featured artist Harvest Arts Festival, 1989, Cypress Gallery, 1994; contbr. poetry to anthologies. Mem. disaster response team Calif. Bldg. Ofcls., 1992—; exec. bd. dirs. Lompoc Mural Soc., 1991—. Delta Kappa Gamma scholar. Mem. NOW, Nat. Abortion Rights Action League, Nat. Mus. of Women in the Arts, Internat. Conf. Bldg. Ofcls., Engrs. and Technicians Assn., Lompoc Valley Art Assn., Toastmasters Internat. (Outstanding Speaker awards 1991-93). Office: Santa Barbara County 624 W Foster Rd Santa Maria CA 93455-3623

GRAN, JANICE ELIZABETH, home healthcare nursing administrator; b. Cambridge, Mass., Aug. 14, 1947; d. Kenneth Ralph and Grace Minnie (Taylor) Medor; children from previous marriage: James W. Rutledge, Robert A. Rutledge, Lori A. Rutledge; m. David Carl Gran, Dec. 27, 1992. ADN, No. Essex C.C., Haverhill, Mass., 1981; BSN, U. Lowell, 1989. RN, Mass., N.H.; cert. BLS. Staff nurse St. Joseph's Hosp., Lowell, Mass., 1981-86, GI specialty nurse, 1986-93; primary nurse Nursing Svcs. Homecare, Salem, N.H., 1994-95; adminstr. Ocean Med. Svcs., Marlboro, N.H., 1995; exec. dir., adminstr. Greenbriar Home Health Svcs., Maren, Mass., 1996—. Vol. Pop Warner Football, Dracut, Mass., 1979-81, Middlesex St. Shelter, Lowell, 1985-89, Nat. Multiple Sclerosis Soc., 1988—; campaign mgr. Local Sch. Com. Candidate, Lowell, 1986. Mem. ANA, Sigma Theta Tau. Office: Greenbriar Home Health Services Cross Point Tower I 8th Fl 900 Chelmsford St Lowell MA 01851

GRANATA, DONNA ASSUNTA, photographer, educator; b. Encino, Calif., July 15, 1963; d. Charles Anthony Granata and Jo Ann (Thomas) Clark; m. Rick H. Berger, Sept. 16, 1995. AA, AS, Ventura (Calif.) C.C., 1990; BA, Brooks Inst. of Photography, Santa Barbara, Calif., 1993. Cultural arts instr. Comty. Svcs. Office of Cultural Affairs City of Ventura, Calif., 1988—; spl. programs asst. Office of Cultural Affairs City of Ventura, 1994—; owner, photographer Donna Granata Photography, Casitas Springs, Calif., 1989—; art studio intern Chiat Day Advt., Inc., Venice, Calif., 1990; docent, arts workshop instr. Carnegie Art Mus., Oxnard, Calif., 1990-93; guest lectr., seminar and workshop presenter, statewide, 1988—. Photographer: solo shows include The Creative Imagery of Donna Granata, Ventura City Hall, 1992, Brewhouse Grill, Santa Barbara, Calif., 1992, Images of Artists Agulars, Ventura, 1993, Transitions, A Fusing of Photography and Paint, Art City II, Ventura, 1993, The World of Art City (Audio visual slide documentary Ventura City Hall, 1995), The Beauty of Greece, Early World Restaurant, Brentwood, Calif., 1992—; selected group shows: Brooks Inst. of Photography, Santa Barbara, 1990, 93, Art City II, 1992, 93, 95, Ventura County Fair, 1991, 92, 94-96, Carnegie Art Mus., 1995, Buenaventura Art Assn., Ventura, 1995, Calif. Luth. U., Thousand Oaks, 1996, Charles E. Probst Ctr. Performing Arts, 1996; writer, dir. prodr. 17 minute slide show: The World of Art City, 1995; founder, writer, photographer, Focus on the Masters, 1995. Founding bd. dirs., mem. Kim Loucks Meml. Arts Edn. Scholarship Com., Ventura, Calif., 1995—; guest docent The J. Paul Getty Mus., Malibu, Calif., 1988-93; vol. Dia De Los Muertos Outreach Program, 1994. Recipient Betty Brooks Holt scholarship Brooks Inst. of Photography, 1992, Best of Coll. Photography Annual pub. finalist, 1987, 88, 90, 91, 92, 93, Best of Photography Annual pub. finalist, 1988, 89, 90, 91, 92, 93; 1994 Ventura County Fair 1st pl. Children, 1st pl. Creative; Best of Photography Annual 4th pl. color, Photographers' Forum, 1993, 2d pl. black and white (coll.), 1993; grantee City of Ventura, Office of Cultural Affairs, 1994-95, Ojai Studio Artists, 1996. Mem. Advt. Photographers Am. (L.A. chpt.). Office: PO Box 2619 Ventura CA 93002

GRANDA, NANCY MAGGIACOMO, history educator, guidance counselor; b. Sharon, Conn., July 10, 1951; d. Edward Louis and Ann (Wascziko) Maggiacomo; m. Rudolph Granda, Nov. 18, 1995; stepchildren: Christopher, Joseph. BA, Marist Coll., 1973; MA, U. South Fla., 1977. Cert. tchr., Fla. Tchr. Tampa (Fla.) Cath. H.S., 1973-77; guidance counselor Hillsborough County Sch. Bd., Tampa, 1978—; guidance counselor Dept. of Def. Dependant Schs., Subic Naval Sta., The Philippines, 1989-92. Pres. LWV, Hillsborough County, Tampa, 1982-84; bd. dirs. LWV Fla., Tallahassee, 1984-86, pres., 1993-95. Mem. Phi Delta Kappa. Democrat. Roman Catholic. Home: 4619 Longfellow Ave Tampa FL 33629 Office: TR Robinson HS 6311 S Lois Ave Tampa FL 33616

GRANDIN, TEMPLE, livestock equipment designer, educator; b. Boston, Aug. 29, 1947; d. Richard McCurdy and Eustacia (Cutler) G. BA in Psychology, Franklin Pierce Coll., 1970; MS in Animal Sci., Arizona State U., 1975; PhD in Animal Sci., U. Ill., Urbana, 1989. Livestock editor Ariz. Farmer Ranchman, Phoenix, 1973-78; equipment designer Corral Industries, Phoenix, 1974-75; ind. cons. Grandin Livestock Systems, Urbana, 1975-90, Fort Collins, Colo., 1990—; lectr., asst. prof. animal sci. dept. Colo. State U., Fort Collins, 1990—; chmn. handing com. Livestock Conservation Inst., Madison, Wis., 1976—. Author: Emergence Labelled Autistic, 1986, Recommended Animal Handling Guidelines for Meat Packers, 1991, Livestock Handling and Transport, 1993, Thinking in Pictures, 1995; contbg. editor Meat and Poultry mag., 1987—; contbr. articles to profl. jours. Recipient Meritorious Svcs. award Livestock Conservation, Madison, Wis., 1986, Disting. Alumni award Franklin Pierce Coll., 1989, Industry Innovators award Meat Mktg. and Tech. Mag., 1994, Brownlee award for internat. leadership in sci. publ. promoting respect for animals Animal Welfare Found. of Canada, 1995, Harry Roswell award Scientists Ctr. for Animal Welfare, 1995; named One of Processing Stars of 1990 Nat. Provisioner, 1990. Mem. Autism Soc. Am. (bd. dirs. 1988—, Trammel Crow award 1989), Am. Soc. Animal Sci. (Animal Mgmt. award 1995), Am. Soc. Agrl. Cons. (bd. dirs. 1981-83), Am. Soc. Agrl. Engrs., Am. Meat Inst. (supplier mem., Industry Advancement award 1995), Am. Registry of Profl. Animal Scis. Republican. Episcopalian. Home: Grandin Livestock Systems 2918 Silver Plume Dr C-3 Fort Collins CO 80526 Office: Colo State U Animal Sci Dept Fort Collins CO 80523

GRANDY, JERILEE, research scientist; b. Pitts., Oct. 22, 1942; d. George W. and Ada A. (Minnotte) Taylor. BA in Philosophy, U. Pitts., 1964. Rsch. asst. Bur. Rsch. in Neurology and Psychiatry, Princeton, N.J., 1965-66; programmer, numerical analyst Princeton U., 1966-70; programmer Mathematica Inc., Princeton, 1970-72; sr. statis. asst. Ednl. Testing Svc., Princeton, 1972-73, rsch. assoc., 1973-80, sr. rsch. assoc., 1980-83, assoc. rsch. scientist, 1983-87, rsch. scientist, 1987—; mem. proposal rev. coms. NSF, Washington, 1990—, U.S. Dept. Edn., Washington, 1993—; keynote speaker Math. Conf., Allentown, Pa., 1993. Contbr. numerous articles to profl. jours. Vol. instr., EMT; state coun. del. Pennington (N.J.) First Aid Squad, 1989-94, ARC, Flagstaff, Ariz., 1994—; mem. N.J. First Aid Coun., Mercer County, 1993, del., historian, 1991-94. Rsch. grantee NEH, 1983, 94, NSF, 1988-90, 93, U.S. Dept. Edn., 1987. Mem. AAAS (proposal reviewer, conf. organizer 1994-95), Am. Ednl. Rsch. Assoc. Home and Office: 4540 E Flintwood Ln Flagstaff AZ 86004

GRANGER, KAY, mayor; b. Greenville, Tex., 1943; children: Jonh Dean, Chelsea, Brandon. Tex. Wesleyan U., 1964, U. Tex., Arlington, 1976. Mem. zoning com. City of Ft. Worth, 1980-88; mem. pvt. industry coun., 1988-89; councilwoman City of Ft. Worth, 1989-91, mayor, 1991-95; owner Kay Granger & Assocs. Recipient Leadership award state of Tex., 1986, Woman of Yr. award, 1987, Bus. and Profl. Woman award, 1987. Mem. Am. Planning Assn., Internat. Sister Cities Assn., Women's Policy Forum (bd. dirs.), East Ft. Worth Bus. and Profl. Assn. (bd. dirs.), Ft. Worth Bus. and Estate Planning Coun., Meadowbrook Bus. and Profl. Womens Assn., East Ft. Worth C. of C. (vice chmn.). Methodist. Address: 308 Williams Rd Fort Worth TX 76120-1616*

GRANOVSKY, MELISSA S. GOLDSTEIN, lawyer, psychologist; b. San Mateo, Calif., Oct. 26, 1968; d. Stewart Goldstein and Jo Cooper; m. David S. Granovsky, Nov. 5, 1994. BA in Justice, The Am. U., 1990; MA in Clin. Psychology, Widener U., 1995, JD, PsyD, 1997. Asst. to adminstr. econ. reg. adminstrn. U.S. Dept. Energy, Washington, 1988-90; rsch. asst. psychology dept. Temple U., Phila., 1990-91; child life counselor Phila. Child Guidance Ctr. Phila., 1990-91; psychotherapist Childrens Crisis Treatment Ctr., Phila., 1991-92; clk. to Hon. Sheldon Jelin Ct. Common Pleas, Phila., 1993; family therapist Robin's Nest, Glassboro, N.J., 1993-94; intern psychologist Phila. Mental Health Ctr., 1995—; clk. Blank, Rome, Comisky and McCauley, Phila., 1992—; lectr. Ea. Psychol. Assn., Phila., 1996. Asst. to dep. gen. counsel Bush Quayle 1988 Presdl. Campaign, 1988; vol., donor, mem. Fedn. for United Jewish Appeal, Phila.; active Girl Scouts U.S. Recipient Am. Jurisprudence award West Pub. Co., 1993, Pyramid award Phi Sigma Sigma, 1990. Mem. ABA, APA (presenter 1993), NAFE, AAUW, Pa. Bar Assn., Phila. Bar Assn. (legal/psychol. svcs. provider Vols. for Indigent program), Women in Comms., Nat. Mus. Women in the Arts. Jewish. Home: 1732 Rodman St Philadelphia PA 19146 Office: Blank Rome Comisky & McCauley 1100 Four Penn Center Plz Philadelphia PA 19103

GRANT, AMY, singer, songwriter; b. Augusta, Ga., 1961; d. Burton Grant; m. Gary Chapman; 3 children: Matthew Garrison Chapman, Millie Chapman, Sarah Cannon Chapman. Student, Furman U., Vanderbilt U. Albums include Amy Grant, 1976, My Father's Eyes, 1977, Never Alone, 1978, Amy Grant in Concert, 1979, Amy Grant in Concert II, 1980, Age to Age (Grammy award), 1983, A Christmas Album, 1983, Straight Ahead, 1984, Unguarded (Grammy award), 1985, Lead Me On, 1988, Heart in Motion, 1991; (with Vince Gill) House of Love, 1994. Recipient 3 Dove awards Gospel Music Assn., Grammy award for contemporary gospel performance NARAS, 1982, for female gospel performance, 1983, 84, for female gospel vocal, 1985. Office: Blanton Harrell Entertainment 2910 Poston Ave Nashville TN 37203*

GRANT, SISTER BARBARA LEE, nun, religions community leader; b. Jackson, Miss., Aug. 13, 1946; d. Robert Emmett and Patricia (Horan) G. BSN, Marillac Coll., 1970; M of Health Adminstrn., Washington U., St. Louis, 1980. Joined Sisters of Mercy, St. Louis, 1964. Staff nurse St. John's Mercy Med. Ctr., St. Louis, 1970-74; adminstrv. asst. St. Edward Mercy Med. Ctr., Ft. Smith, Ark., 1974-78; resident Mercy Health Svcs., Farmington Hills, Mich., 1980-81; asst. adminstr. Mercy Hosp., New Orleans, 1981-85, COO, 1985-87, CEO, 1987-94; exec. v.p. Mercy & Bapt. Med. Ctr., New Orleans, 1993-95; sabbatical, 1995-96; leadership team Sisters of Mercy, St. Louis, 1996—. Trustee Mercy Regional Med. Ctr., Laredo, Tex., 1984-90, Mercy Med. Group S.W. Mo., Rolla, 1992-94; bd. dirs. St. Thomas Health Svcs., New Orleans, 1989-92; chairperson Met. Hosp. Coun., New Orleans, 1991; mem. exec. com. Met. Area Com., 1991-95; trustee St. John's Regional Health System, 1994-95. Mem. La. Cath. Health Assn. (pres. 1989-90). Home and Office: 2039 N Geyer Rd Saint Louis MO 63131

GRANT, CYNTHIA D., writer; b. Brockton, Mass., Nov. 23, 1950; d. Robert Cheyne and Jacqueline Ann (Ford) G.; m. Daniel Heatley; 1 child: Morgan; m. Erik Neel; 1 child, Forest. Author: Joshua Fortune, 1980 (Woodward Park Sch. annual book award 1981), Summer Home, 1981, Big Time, 1982, Hard Love, 1983, Kumquat May, I'll Always Love You, 1986, Phoenix Rising, 1989 (Mich. Libr. Assn. Young Adult Caucus best book of yr. 1990, PEN/Norma Klein award 1991, Detroit Pub. Libr. Author Day award 1992), Keep Laughing, 1991, Shadow Man, 1992, Uncle Vampire, 1993 (ALA best books for young adults list 1994), Mary Wolf, 1995. Recipient Book of Distinction award Hungry Mind Review, 1993, 94. Mem. PEN (Norma Klein award 1991), Soc. Children's Book Writers and Illustrators. Home: PO Box 95 Cloverdale CA 95425-0095 Office: care Atheneum Children's Books 1230 Avenue of the Americas New York NY 10020

GRANT, FRANCES BETHEA, technical editor, writer; b. Sumter, S.C., Jan. 25, 1932; d. Edward Samuel and Mildred (Ladson) Bethea; m. Victor Rastafari Grant, July 2, 1960 (div.); children: Christine Sharon, Pamela Ellen. BA, SUNY, Albany, 1954; postgrad., Temple U., summers 1955-59; MS, Coll. St. Rose, Albany, 1984. Cert. tchr., S.C., biology, social studies, English, gen. sci., social studies tchr., guidance counselor, Pa., social studies tchr., N.Y. Tchr. history Wilson Jr. H.S., Florence, S.C., 1954-57; tchr. sci. Bartlett Jr. H.S., Phila., 1957-60, head sci. dept., 1959-60; tchr. Schenectady Pub. Schs., 1960-61, 75; music resource tchr. Refreshing Spring Day Care Ctr., Schenectady, 1976; tech. editor GE Knolls Atomic Power Lab., Schenectady, 1976-89; tech. editor, writer Westinghouse Machinery Apparatus Operation, Schenectady, 1989-96; vis. lectr. Schenectady County C.C., 1981-83, Hudson Valley C.C., Troy, N.Y., 1974, 75, 92, 93, 95; pvt. instr. guitar and autoharp Skidmore Coll., Saratoga Springs, N.Y., 1976; tchr., poet Rensslaerville (N.Y.) Inst., 1987, 88, 89; vis. writing tchr. Schenectady Sch. Sys., 1979-81; entrepreneur Fran G's Candies; mem. task force GE Program to Increase Minority engring. grads., Schenectady, 1977-86; 1st black effective listening instr. GE Knolls Atomic Power Lab., Schenectady, 1988-89, Westinghouse Machinery Apparatus Operation, Schenectady, 1992; effective listening trainer Grant Enterprises, Albany, N.Y., 1988. Author, editor: Something to Believe In, 1973; author: There's More to Tell, 1976; poet, ventriloquist, spkr. Martin Luther King Program, 1995; puppeteer, ventriloquist Puppet People, 1978-95; editor newsletter Jaycee, 1967-68, Families for the Future, 1969-71; book reviewer Schenectady Pub. Libr., 1976. Founder, dir. Minority Women's Breast Cancer Network, Albany, 1992—; mem. bd. Families for the Future, Schenectady, 1967-69, Refreshing Spring Day Care Ctr., Schenectady, 1973-76; v.p. Empire State Black Arts and Cultural Festival Com., Albany, 1984-86; chairperson youth com. Black Family Conf., State Mus., Albany, 1985; mem. planning com. Critical Black Issues, N.Y. State Mus., Albany, 1988; cmty. rep. AAUW Martin Luther King Day, Schenectady, 1985-87; bd. mem. Hamilton Hill Art Ctr., Schenectady, 1985-86, YWCA of Albany, 1986-92, YWCA of Schenectady, 1992-95; vol. YWCA of Phila., 1958-60; mem. YWCA Women and Teens in Violence, Schenectady, 1993-95; founder, 1st chairperson Diversity in Schenectady, AAUW Study Group, 1993-95; mem. nat. nominating com. YWCA/USA, Eastern states region, 1994-96; com. mem. Troy Conf. Ethnic Minority Scholarship Com., Latham, N.Y., 1990-96; vol. Vanguard Albany Symphony Orch., 1980-86, 91-92. Recipient Centennial award GE Knolls Atomic Power Lab., Schenectady, 1978, Scholar award First Reformed Ch., Albany, 1980, award of excellence Westinghouse Machinery Apparatus Operation Facility, Schenectady, 1994. Mem. AAUW (life, publicity chair 1973-74, chairperson internat. rels. 1973-74, scholar award 1981, 83, cmty. action grant 1992, Edn. Found. grant honoree 1995), Nat. Orgn. Black Chemists and Chem. Engrs. (copy editor newsletter 1995—), Nat. Assn. Black Storytellers, Internat. Listening Assn. (life.), Nat. Coun. Negro Women (life), Bus. and Profl. Women, Nat. Story Telling Assn., N.Am. Assn. Ventriloquists, Puppeteers of Am., Fellowship of Christian Puppeteers.

GRANT, JACQUELYN, minister, religion educator; b. Georgetown, S.C., Dec. 19, 1948; d. Joseph James and Lillie Mae (Ward) G. BA, Bennett Coll., 1970; MDiv, I.T.C., 1973; MPhil, Union Theol. Sem., 1980, PhD, 1985. Assoc. in rsch. Harvard Divinity Sch., Cambridge, 1977-79; grad. fellow Harvard U., Cambridge, 1979-80; prof. Interdenominational Theol. Ctr., Atlanta, 1980-88, 94—, assoc. prof., 1989-94; prof. Interdenominational Theol. Ctr., 1994—; area chairperson Interdenominational Theol. Ctr., Atlanta, 1990—; vis. lectr. and prof. in field. Author: White Women's Christ and Black Women's Jesus, 1989; contbr. articles to profl. jours. Recipient Fellowship Am. Assn. Theol. Schs., 1987-88, Doctoral fellowship Rockefeller Found., 1973-75, Scholarship Interdenominational Theol. Ctr., 1970-73. Mem. Soc. for Study Black Religion, Black Theology Project, Ecumenical Assn. 3rd World Theologians, Am. Acad. Religion, World Coun. Churches (commn. mem.). African Methodist Episcopal.

GRANT, JANETT ULRICA, medical/surgical nurse; b. Mavis Bank, St. Andrew, Jamaica, Jan. 15, 1956; came to U.S., 1990; d. John Edgerton and Daisy Ann (Sterling) Welsh; m. Aurnandy Alfanso Grant, Nov. 25, 1978; children: Avril, Adrian, Christophe. Grad., Kingston (Jamaica) Sch. Nursing, 1978, diploma in midwifery, 1988. RN, N.J.; cert. med.-surg. nurse. Mem. staff med. surg. nursing Isaac Barrant Hosp., St. Thomas, Jamaica, 1978-79; mem. staff med. surg. nursing Kingston Pub. Hosp., 1979-87, acting sister supr., 1988-90; mem. staff med. surg. nursing Newark Beth Israel Med. Ctr., 1990—, team leader Med.-Surg. Unit, 1995—; alt. unit rep. Coun. Nursing Practice, Newark Beth Israel Med. Ctr., 1994. Mem. planning com. Salvation Army Basic Sch., Kingston, 1988-90. Mem. N.J. State Nurses Assn., Jamaica Nurses Assn. (N.J. chpt.). Methodist.

GRANT, JUDITH IVERSEN, family health nurse, nursing administrator; b. Sioux City, Iowa, Mar. 30, 1952; d. Harry Andrew and Gertrude Roberta Iversen; m. George Alexander Grant, June 21, 1979 (dec. Feb. 1989); 1 child, Tyler Ross. BSN, Marquette U., 1974; postgrad., U. San Francisco, 1990-93. Cert. pub. health nurse, Calif.; lic. residential care facility for elderly, Calif.; adminstr. cert. RCFE and pub. health. Staff RN, relief supr. Midwest Med. Placement Agy., Milw., 1974-75; nursing supr. Marion Heights, Inc., Milw., 1975-76; patient care coord. Milw. Psychiat. Hosp./Dewey Ctr., Wauwatosa, Wis., 1976-77; RN, staff relief Med. Pers. Pool, Profl. Nurses Bur., Stat Nursing Svcs., San Francisco, 1977-89; asst., acting nurse mgr. Pacific Med. Ctr., San Francisco, 1979-84; staff devel. instr., clin. cons. San Francisco (Calif.) Gen. Hosp. Med. Ctr., 1984-85, adminstrv. nursing supr., 1985-89; RN neonatal ICU Children's Hosp./Pediatric Trauma Ctr., Oakland, Calif., 1986-87; nursing supr. Children's Hosp./Pediatric Trauma Ctr., Oakland, 1987-88; RN per diem U. Calif. San Francisco, 1984-88; pvt. practice North Sioux City, S.D., 1988—; cons., ind. nurse Marin County, Calif., 1979-84; co-coord. for group formation Bay Area Adminstrv. Nursing Suprs., 1986-87; postgrad. rsch. asst. pediat. pain study U. Calif.-San Francisco, Sch. Nursing, 1987; pvt. practice nurse cons., San Francisco, 1990-94; coord. cmty. edn., dir. Silver Advantage/Older Adult Svcs., Marian Health Ctr., Sioux City, Iowa, 1994—; nursing instr., cons. Morningside Coll., Sioux City, 1994—. Author (with others) Siouxland: An Anthology, 1995, Capturing Our Heritage, Vol. 1, 1996. Vol. Jerry Brown for Pres./We the People, San Francisco, 1991—; mem. Nat. Wildlife Fedn., Washington, 1991—; dir. Senior Writer Project, 1996; parish dir. Cath. of the Epiphany, Sioux City, Iowa; founder, exec. dir. Caring 4-U, 1996—, Crossroad, Inc. Grantee Iowa Humanities Bd. Mem. Nat. Wellness Assn., Nat. League for Nursing (coun. for nursing ctrs., coun. for nursing practice, coun. for the study for rsch. in nursing edn., coun. for nursing informatics, coun. cmty. health svcs.), Nat. Assn. Neonatal Nurses, Neonatal Nurses No. Calif., Iowa Nurses Assn., Neonatal Nurses of Iowa, Calif. Nurses Assn. (named expert nurse 1991), World Affairs Coun. No. Calif., The Smithsonian Assocs., Jr. League, Nat. Trust for Hist. Preservation, Siouxland Writer's Project. Roman Catholic. Home: 4303 W 19th St Sioux City IA 51103 Office: PO Box 1458 North Sioux City SD 57049-1458

GRANT, MAGGIE RUTH, school principal; b. Roanoke Rapids, N.C., Feb. 4, 1934; d. John and Pearl (Pair) Harrison; m. James Grant, Sept. 1, 1956; children: Christopher Mark, Kevin Stacy, Karen Charise. BA Early Childhood Edn. magna cum laude, Queens Coll., CUNY, 1972; MA in Elem. Edn., Adelphi U., 1974. Cert. K-6 tchr. Nurse Jewish Hosp., Bklyn., 1955-60; elem. tchr. Martin L. King Sch., Wyandanch, N.Y., 1972-83, prin., 1983-87; prin. Mary G. Clarkson Sch., Bay Shore, N.Y., 1987-96. Mem., rec. sec. Sherwood Civic Assn., Westbury, N.Y., 1985-88. Named Disting. Prin., NAACP, 1994. Mem. ASCD, Nat. Assn. Elem. Sch. Prins., Nat. Alliance Black Sch. Educators, Assn. Childhood Edn. Internat. Democrat. Christian. Home: 826 Pepperidge Rd Westbury NY 11590-1423

GRANT, MARGARET M. DOYLE, lawyer; b. Columbus, Ohio, Apr. 13, 1957; d. Frederick Joseph and Mary Olga (Blaskovich) Doyle; m. Jeffrey D. Grant, May 19, 1990. BA, Coll. William & Mary, 1979; JD, U. Va., 1983. Bar: N.Y., D.C. Assoc. White & Case, N.Y.C., 1983-85, Washington, 1985-88; v.p., assoc. gen. counsel Riggs Nat. Bank, Washington, 1988-94; sr. comml. counsel Overseas Pvt. Investment Corp., Washington, 1994—. ESL tutor Sacred Heart Adult Edn., Washington, 1991—. Mem. Am. Soc. Internat. Law, N.Y. Bar Assn., D.C. Bar Assn. (vice chair in-house counsel com., sect. on corps., fin. and securities law 1994—). Roman Catholic. Office: Overseas Pvt Investment Corp 1100 New York Ave Washington DC 20524*

GRANT, MIRIAM ROSENBLOUM, educator, journalist; b. Collinsville, Ala.; d. Harry M. and Rae (Rosenberg) Rosenbloum; m. Morton A. Grant, Nov. 17, 1952 (dec. 1967). AB, U. Ala., 1935; postgrad., U. Miami, 1968-69, Fla. Internat. U. Cert. tchr., Fla. Reporter Chattanooga Free Press., 1936-41, Birmingham (Ala.) Post, 1942; reporter, movie editor, drama critic Chattanooga News-Free Press, 1943-49; thcr., head journalism dept., newspaper and yearbook adviser North Miami (Fla.) Sr. High Sch., 1969-89. Recipient Disting. Svc. award Chattanooga Little Theater, 1949, Golden Medallion Fla. Scholastic Press Assn., 1987, named life member, 1990, service award Coll. Fraternity Editors Assn., 1989. Mem. AAUW, U. Ala. Nat. Alumni Assn. (coun. mem.-at-large 1960-61), Ceramic League Miami (Corr. sec. 1963-64), Women's Panhellenic Assn. Miami (Sec. 1992-93), nat. Panhellenic Editors Conf. (vice chmn. 1986-87, chmn. 1987-89), Sigma Delta Tau (nat. pres. 1950-54, editor The Torch mag. 1968—, honor key 1988, scholarship named in her honor as 1st mem. to serve 50 yrs. on sorority nat. coun. 1991, archivist 1992—, devel. com. 1996—, CFEA recognition award as editor 1993), Theta Sigma Phi, Phi Lambda Pi, Rho Lambda, Sigma Delta Chi.

GRANT, NANCY MARIE, marketing professional, journalist; b. Tilden, Nebr., Jan. 2, 1941; d. William Gerald and Evelyn Marie (Baughman) Whitford; m. Marvin Ostberg, 1961 (div. 1969); children: Jill Marie Ostberg Bennett, Carrie Ostberg Chun; m. Richard Grant, 1973 (div. 1975). BA in Journalism, U. Nebr., 1963; postgrad., U. Oreg., 1968, Portland State U., 1978, U. Wash., 1979-83; diploma, Bailie Sch. Broadcasting, Seattle, 1984; postgrad., Seattle Cen. C.C., 1992, Computer & Bus. Tng. Inst., Bellevue, Wash., 1993. Internship gen. assignment reporter Lincoln (Nebr.) Jour., 1962-63; asst. state editor Lexington (Ky.) Leader, 1963; freelance writer Shreveport Times, AP, Natchatoches, La., 1964; info. rep. 1 & 2 Univ. Oreg. News Bur., Old Oreg. Alumni Mag., Faculty Staff Newsletter, Eugene, 1965-70; dir. pub. rels. U. Portland, Oreg., 1971; info. rep. 3 Oreg. Hwy. Div. and Motor Vehicles, 1972-77; founder, bus. mgr. Grant Mktg., Seattle, Wash., 1979; exec. dir., founder Wash. Neurol. Alliance, Seattle, 1985—. Editor U. Oreg. Faculty-Staff Newsletter, 1969; editor, writer U. Portland Alumni Mag., 1970, Hwy Newsletter and film, 1971-77. Lobbiest Wash. Neurol. Alliance; mem. Gov.'s Com. on Disability Issues and Employment, 1983-86; bd. dirs. Wash. Assembly, 1983-86, Highland Community Ctr., Bellevue, Wash., 1984-86. Recipient Hearst award, 1963, No. 1 in country for hwy. pub. affairs event, 1973. Mem. NAFE, LWV, Am. Assn. Women Bus. Owners, Internat. Platform Assn. Democrat. Unitarian. Home and Office: Nassau Arms Apts 285 Franklin Ave Princeton NJ 08540-2716

GRANT, PEGGY (MARGARET MARY GRANT), art gallery administrator, artist, consultant; b. Balt., Sept. 19, 1929; d. Edward J. and Estelle T. (Smith) Brennan; m. Adam M. Grochowski Grant (dec. June 1992); children: Thomas Gregory, Adam Mark. BFA, Md. Inst. Coll. Art, 1952. Designer Palmer Paint, Detroit, 1953-55, Craftmaster Corp., Toledo, 1956-80; art curator Owens-Ill. Corp., Toledo and N.Y.C., 1981-84; art cons., Toledo, 1985—; dir. 20 North Gallery, T, 1995—. Writer art exhibit catalogs, 1981-89. Bd. dirs. Arts Commn. Greater Toledo, 1991—, Blair Mus. Lithophanes, Toledo, 1993—; mem. Poznan (Poland)-Toledo Sister City Alliance, 1994—; mem. com. for cultural diversity Toledo Mus., 1991—; mem. docent bd. Toledo Mus. Art, 1988—. Recipient Disting. Svc. in Art Edn. award Ohio Art Edn. Assn., 1984. Mem. Glass Art Soc., Athena Art Soc. (bd. dirs., chmn. jury), Glass Collectors Club Toledo (bd. dirs. 1985—, pres. 1992-93). Roman Catholic. Home: 2821 Latonia Blvd Toledo OH 43606 Office: 20 North Gallery 20 N St Clair St Toledo OH 43604

GRANT, PENNY, pediatrics educator; b. N.Y.C., Dec. 19, 1959; d. Stanley Charles and Hilda (Kleinerman) G.; m. Lee Mark Cohen, Feb. 28, 1987. BA, Columbia U., 1980; MD, N.Y. Med. Coll., 1984. Diplomate Nat. Bd. Med. Examiners, Am. Bd. Pediatrics. Intern N.Y. Hosp. Cornell Med. Ctr., N.Y.C., 1984-86; resident Jackson Meml. Hosp., U. Miami, Fla., 1986-88, dir. pediatric care network, 1989-90; pediatrician Pediatric Assocs., P.A., Hollywood, Fla., 1988-89; clin. asst. prof. dept. pediatrics U. Miami, 1989—; dir. Univ. Pediat. Assocs., Miami, 1993-95; pediatrician Bay Harbor (Fla.) Pediatrics, 1995—; med. dir. Broward County Child Protection Team, Ft. Lauderdale, Fla., 1996—. Mem. Am. Acad. Pediatrics. Office: Bay Harbor Pediatrics Ste 402 1160 Kane Concourse Bay Harbor FL 33154

GRANT, SALLY K., nursing home administrator; b. Massillon, Ohio, Dec. 29, 1949; d. Henry Kiehl and Mary Helen (Rosché) Krier; m. Russell J. Grim, Dec. 22, 1967 (div. Oct. 1980); m. Harold J. Grant, Jan. 4, 1992 (dec. Feb. 1992). BS, Kent State U., 1978; MBus., Ohio State U., 1987. Lic. nursing home adminstr., Ohio. Dir. Western Stark County Comty. Action, Canton, Ohio, 1979-84; sr. adminstr. Medi Mgmt., Inc., Hudson, Ohio, 1984—; adminstr. Maple Wood Care Ctr., Streetsboro, Ohio, 1989—; mem. adv. bd. Are Nursing Home Tng. Ctr., Mansfield, Ohio, 1993-94, AIDS Outreach Program, Akron, Ohio, 1993-94. Pres. Stark County (Ohio) Rep. Women, 1973-78; mem. Arthritis Found., Portage County, Ohio, 1987-88; bd. dirs. Interfaith Campus Ministry, Kent State U., 1990-91; mem. Hudson Common Trustees, pres., 1994-96. Mem. Streetsboro C. of C. (pres. 1994-95). Presbyterian. Home: 37 Hudson Common Hudson OH 44236 Office: Maple Wood Care Ctr 1645 Maple Wood Dr Streetsboro OH 44241

GRANT, SHIRLEY MAE, retired business affairs director; b. Barberton, Ohio, Feb. 4, 1936; d. Chester Claude and Virginia Hutchison (Crispin) Culp; m. Stewart K. Grant, June 19, 1960 (dec. 1975); children: Michelle C. Grant Fontes, Sabrina K. Fox, Michael S. AA in Liberal Arts, Graceland Coll., 1956; BS in Edn. magna cum laude, Calif. State Ul., Long Beach, 1965, MS in Counseling/Student Affairs, 1974; AA in Real Estate, Fullerton Coll., 1979. Lic. real estate broker; life cert. community coll. instr. Asst. registrar Graceland Coll., Lamoni, Iowa, 1956-58; adminstrv. asst., dean of students Calif. State U., Long Beach, 1958-61; tchr. Vista Unified/Rossmoor, Los Alamitos, Calif., 1965-70; asst. dean admissions and records Calif. State U., Long Beach, 1970-74; dir. sch. and coll. rels. Calif. State U., Fullerton, 1974-77; dir. sch. and coll. res. Calif. State U., Dominguez Hills, Carson, Calif., 1978-80; coord. tour and travel Knotts Berry Farm, Buena Park, Calif., 1980-85; chief info. officer Pro Value, Cerritos, Calif., 1985-89, Gen./Vascular Surg. Assocs., Long Beach, 1989-93; dir. bus. affairs Unyeway, Ramona, Calif., 1993-95; ret., 1995. Steering com. Calif. Women in Higher Edn., Sacramento, 1977. Danforth scholar, 1954, Univ. scholar, 1974. Mem. Nat. Honor Soc. (pres. 1954).

GRANT, VIRGINIA ANNETTE, newspaper editor, journalist; b. Abilene, Tex., Jan. 21, 1941; d. Thomas Spenser and Dorris Barnett (Turner) G.; m. Steele Commager, Mar. 8, 1983 (dec. Apr. 1984). B.A., Brown U., 1963. Writer, editor Mademoiselle Mag., N.Y.C., 1965-68; reporter, feature writer Newsweek Mag., N.Y.C., 1968-69; asst. editor articles and fiction Seventeen Mag., N.Y.C., 1970-77; editor Living sect. N.Y. Times, N.Y.C., 1977-81, dep. style editor, 1981-82, editor Weekend sect., 1982-90, editor cultural affairs N.Y. Times Sunday Mag., 1990-94; art editor, arts & leisure sec., Sunday edit. N.Y. Times, 1994—. Democrat. Office: NY Times 229 W 43rd St New York NY 10036-3913*

GRANT, VIRGINIA LEE KING, nutritionist, consultant; b. Pineville, Mo., Oct. 10, 1918; d. Arthur Judson and Blanche Bell (Boyd) King; m. Weston G. Lawson, June 14, 1942 (div. Aug. 1959); children: Victoria, Robert, Weston G. Jr., Melissa; m. H. Scott Grant, Dec. 31, 1983. BS, Kans. State U., 1939; MS, U. Tenn., 1972. Registered dietitian; lic. nutritionist and dietitian. Instr. nutrition St. Joseph Hosp. Sch. Nursing, Memphis, 1957-61; instr. nutrition U. Tenn. Coll. Nursing, Memphis, 1957-61, clin. dietitian dept. medicine Diabetic Clinic, 1961-63, clin. dietitian Clin. Rsch. Ctr., 1961-65, head rsch. dietitian, 1965-73, chief rsch. dietitian, 1973-85, asst. prof. medicine, 1973-85; nutrition cons., Memphis, 1985—; nutrition cons. Rosewood Convalescent Ctr., Memphis, 1961-65. Food and nutrition columnist Comml. Appeal, Memphis, 1961-65; contbr. articles to profl. jours. Block chmn. Memphis Neighborhood Watch Program, Memphis Police Dept., 1984—. Travel grantee AMA, 1968. Mem. Am. Dietetic Assn. (career guidance com. 1967-68, Lydia J. Roberts fellow 1972-73), Tenn. Dietetic Assn. (pres. 1963, past chmn. numerous coms.), Memphis Dist. Dietetic Assn. (pres. 1961, past chmn. numerous coms., Dietitian of Yr. award 1981), Memphis Area Nutrition Coun. (pres. 1979-80). Republican. Roman Catholic. Home: 5151 Tarrytown Dr Memphis TN 38117-2125

GRANTHAM, PATRICIA ANN, social worker; b. Kansas City, Mo., Aug. 14, 1959; d. Fred G. and Rose Mary (Hall) G. BA, St. Mary Leavenworth Coll., 1981; MS, U. Ill., 1986; postgrad., Ctrl. Mich. U., 1988-90. Lic. clin. social worker, Mo. Mgr. client svcs. Cath. Charities, Rome, N.Y., 1982-85, Child Saving Inst., Omaha, 1986-91; rsch. asst. U. Ill., Champaign, 1985-86; psychiat. social worker St. Luke's Northland Hosp., Smithville, Mo., 1992-95, Northwoods Psychiat. Svcs., Gladstone, Mo., 1995—. Bd. dirs. St. Mary Coll., Kansas City, 1994—. Roman Catholic. Home: 1113 W Cedar Olathe KS 66061 Office: Northwoods Psychiat Svcs 5700 N Broadway Gladstone MO 64118

GRANTMAN, CAROL LEIGH, federal agency administrator; b. Red Wing, Minn., Jan. 12, 1956; d. Dale Julian and Virginia Mae (Klein) G.; m. (div. Aug. 1992); 1 child, John Joseph Whelan. BA, Coe Coll., 1978. Spl. agt. IRS Criminal Investigation, Des Moines, 1978—. Deacon Westminster United Presbyn. Ch., Des Moines, 1992-95. Mem. Alpha Omicron Pi. Republican. Presbyterian. Office: IRS Criminal Investigation 210 Walnut St Rm 347 Des Moines IA 50309

GRANTUSKAS, PATRICIA MARY, elementary education educator; b. Irvington, N.J., Jan. 17, 1952; d. Albert L. and Mary D. (Gradeckis) G. BA summa cum laude, Kean Coll., Union, N.J., 1973, MA, 1977 and 1993, supr.'s cert., 1980. Cert. prin. supr., tchr., reading specialist, elem. tchr. Reading clinician Reading Inst., Kean Coll., 1977-80; instr. reading Newark Acad., Livingston, N.J., 1983—; reading specialist, test and basic skills coord. Garwood (N.J.) Bd. Edn., 1977-89; reading instr. Summer Clinic Pingry Sch., N.J., 1977-82; reading specialist, coord. basic skills Harrington Park (N.J.) Bd. Edn., 1989—; remedial reading tchr. Garwood (N.J.) Pub. Schs., 1973-77; pvt. tutor. Mem. YMCA. chairperson award of Excellence. Mem. ASCD, N.J. ASCD, Nat. Coun. Tchrs. English, Internat. Reading Assn. (hon. coun., Pres.'s Club), N.J. Edn. Assn., N.J. Reading Assn. (bd. dirs. 1991-94, sec. bd. dirs. 1989-90), Garwood Tchrs. Assn., Harrington Park Edn. Assn., Suburban Reading Coun. (past pres., bd. dirs.), Delta Kappa Gamma, Kappa Delta Pi, Phi Kappa Phi. Office: Harrington Park Sch 191 Harriot Ave Harrington Park NJ 07640-1401

GRAPIN, JACQUELINE G., journalist; b. Paris, Dec. 15, 1942; came to U.S., 1985; d. Jean and Raymonde (Ledru) G.; m. Michel Le Goc, June 4, 1971; children: Claire, Julien. Degree, Institut d'Etudes Politiques, Paris, 1966; Degree in Law, U. Paris, 1967; Auditeur, Inst. des Hautes Etudes de Def. Nat., Paris, 1980. Staff writer LeMonde, Paris, 1967-81; dir.-gen. Interavia Pub. Group, Geneva, 1982-86; pres. The European Inst., Washington, 1989—; econ. corr. Le Figaro, Washington, 1987—; prof. Inst. d'Etudes Politiques, Paris, 1974-77. Author: Guerre Civile Mondiale, 1977, Radioscopie des Etats-Unis, 1980, Fortress America, 1984, Pacific America, 1987; assoc. editor World Paper, Boston, 1980-93; contbr. articles to profl. jours. Trustee Aspen Inst. for Humanistic Studies, N.Y.C., 1981-96; bd. dirs. Internat. Women's Media Found., Internat. Action Against Hunger. Recipient Prix Vauban Inst. des Hautes-Etudes, Paris, 1977, Ordre de la Legion d'Honneur, 1993. Mem. Internat. Inst. Strategic Studies Longon, Swiss Soc. of the French Legion of Honor, Pen Club, Nat. Press Club, Kenwood Golf Club (Washington), Polo Club (Paris). Home: 4745 Massachusetts Ave NW, 1231 Washington Switzerland Office: The European Inst Ste 223 4910 Massachusetts Ave NW Washington DC 20016-2345

GRASER, BERNICE ERCKERT, elementary school principal; b. Buffalo, May 5, 1933; d. George Snead Sr. and Ada Louise (Sheasley) Erckert; m. Stanley Richard Graser, May 8, 1953; children: Deberah Dawn Walvoord Rogers. BA magna cum laude, Coll. Gordon & Barrington, 1963; MA, R.I. Coll., 1965; postgrad., Boston U., 1969-71. Cert. elem., pre-sch.-high sch. handicapped tchr.; cert. spl. edn. adminstr.; cert. sch. psychologist. Spl. edn. instr. United Coll. Gordon (Mass.) & Barrington; prin. Pleasant View Sch. for Handicapped Children, Providence; spl. edn. supr. Meeting Street Sch., East Providence; prin. Wm. D'Abate Meml. Elem. Sch., Providence; established State Model Child Opportunity Zone at Wm. D'Abate Sch.; cons. on ednl. reform; speaker on critical ednl. issues; presenter workshops and confs. Producer TV broadcast Internat. Celebrations of Cultures; contbr. articles to profl. jours. Named Sch. Adminstr. of Yr., State of R.I., 1993; grantee: U.S. Govt. Dept. Edn.1971—, 1991-93; Very Spl. Arts, State of R.I., 1985-87. Home: 45 Clarke Rd Barrington RI 02806-4037

GRASMICK, NANCY S., superintendent of schools; b. Balt.; m. Louis J. Grasmick. BS in Elem. Edn., Towson State U., 1961; MS in Deaf Edn., Gallaudet U., 1965; PhD in Communicative Scis. with distinction, Johns Hopkins U., 1979; LHD (hon.), Towson State U., 1992, Goucher Coll., 1992, U. Balt., 1996. Tchr. deaf William S. Baer Sch., Balt., 1961-64; tchr. hearing and lang. impaired children Woodvale Sch., Balt., 1964-68; supr. Office Spl. Edn. Balt. County Pub. Schs., 1968-74; prin. Chatsworth Sch., Balt., 1974-78; asst. supt. Balt. County Pub. Schs., 1978-85, assoc. supt., 1985-89; sec. juvenile svcs. Dept. Juvenile Svc., Balt., 1991; spl. sec. children, youth and families Gov.'s Exec. Office, Balt., 1989-95; supt. schs. Md. Dept. Edn., Balt., 1991—; mem., chmn. interagy. com. on sch. constrn. Gov.'s Subcabinet for Children, Youth and Families; mem. interagy. coord. coun. Gov.'s Adv. Bd. Juvenile Justice, Gov.'s Workforce Investment Bd.; mem. profl. stds. and tchr. edn. bd. Md. Assocs. for Dyslexic Adults and Youth; mem. State Bd. Edn. profl. adv. bd. Met. Balt. Assn. Learning Disabled Children. Trustee Md. Retirement and Pension Sys.; bd. dirs. Coll. Bound Found., Balt. Symphony Orch.; pres. Child Care Found.; mem. Md. Pub. Broadcasting Commn., Gov.'s Coun. Adolescent Pregnancy, Gov.'s Drug and Alcohol Abuse Commn.; mem. adv. coun. Scholastic, Inc. Recipient Medallion award Jimmy Swartz Found., 1989, Louise B. Makofsky Meml. award Md. Conf. Social Concern, 1990, Child Advocacy award Am. Acad. Pediats., 1990, Humanitarian award March of Dimes, 1990, Disting. Citizen's award Md. Assn. Non-pub. Spl. Edn. Facilities, 1991, Women of Excellence award Nat. Assn. Women Bus. Owners, 1991, Andrew White medal Loyola Coll., 1991, Nat. Edn. Adminstr. of Yr. award Nat. Assn. Ednl. Office Profls., 1992, Nat. award computing to asst. persons with disabilities Johns Hopkins U., 1992, Vernon E. Anderson Disting. Lecture award for outstanding leadership in edn. Coll. Edn., U. Md., 1992, DuBois Circle Award of Honor, 1992, Disting. Alumna of Yr. award Johns Hopkins U., 1992, Pub. Affairs award Md. C. of C., 1994, Educator of the Yr. award Am. Coun. on Rural Spl. Edn., Profl. Legal Excellence award Md. Bar Found., Inc.; named Communicator of Yr. by Speech and Hearing Agy., 1990, Marylander of Yr. by Advt. and Profl. Club of Balt., 1990, Most Disting. Woman Girl Scouts Ctrl. Md., 1994; selected as one of Md.'s Top 100 Women, Warfields, 1996. Mem. Phi Delta Kappa (Excellence in Edn. award), Pi Lambda Theta. Office: Md Dept Edn 200 W Baltimore St Baltimore MD 21201-2500

GRASSI, KATHERINE D., sales manager; b. N.Y.C., Apr. 22, 1954; d. Walter Robert and Marie Dolores (Mulligan) Popp; m. Joseph John Grassi, Jan. 19, 1975; children: Alex Joseph, Alene Katherine. BA cum laude, Sonoma State U., 1993. Sales rep. D.C. Heath Pubs., Lexington, Mass., 1982-84, telemarketing supr., 1984-93, dist. sales mgr., 1993-95; regional sales mgr. Houghton Mifflin Pub. Co., Boston, 1995—. Mem. AAUW. Democrat. Roman Catholic. Home: PO Box 21 Novato CA 94948 Office: Houghton Mifflin Co 222 Berkeley St Boston MA 02116

GRASSIE, YVONNE GAIL, lawyer; b. Chgo., July 29, 1960; d. Joseph Roberts and Josette Yafa (Krespi) G. BA with honors, U. Chgo., 1982; JD, Washington U., St. Louis, 1987. Bar: Fla. 1987. Tchr. Berlitz, Madrid, 1982-83; internat. dept. asst. Banco Zaragozano, Madrid, 1982-83; internat. credit mgr. Sherwood Med., St. Louis, 1983-84; legal intern House Banking Com., Washington, 1987; assoc. Paul Landy Bailey & Harper P.A., Miami, Fla., 1987-89, Stearns, Weaver, Miller et al., Miami, 1989-90, Matzner, Ziskind et al., Miami, 1990-92; owner Salo Design by Yvonne, Miami, 1993—; pvt. practice Miami, 1993—. Editor Washington U. Law Quarterly, 1985-87; contbr. articles to law rev. Pres. bd. dirs. Miami Coalition for Homeless, 1994—; bd. dirs. Dade County Homeless Trust, Miami, 1994— Urban League, 1996—; bd. mem. Dade County Performance Commn., Miami, 1995—; intake atty. Legal Svcs. Pro Bono Homeless Project, Miami, 1990-94. Scholar McGeorge U., 1985. Mem. So. Poverty Law Ctr., Nat. Women's Polit. Caucus, NOW.

GRASSO, KATHLEEN ALICE, English language educator; b. Binghamton, N.Y.; d. Daniel Anthony and Alice Eleanor (Sturek) G. BS in Elem. Edn., SUNY, Cortland, N.Y., 1975; BA in Bus. Adminstrn., U. Md., 1992; MEd, Trenton State Coll., 1992. 2d grade tchr. St. John's Sch., Binghamton, 1975-76; Am. history tchr. Union Endicott (N.Y.) H.S., 1976-77; 3rd and 4th grade tchr. Charlotte Kenyon Sch., Chenango Forks, N.Y., 1978-79; 6th-8th grade reading and English tchr. St. Columbia Sch., Oxon Hill, Md., 1981-82; 7th-9th grade tchr. Friendly H.S., Ft. Washington, Md., 1984-88; 9th-12th grade ESL tchr. Okinawa, Japan, 1988-90; ESL tchr. Johnson City (N.Y.) H.S., 1990—; ESL dir. Tokyo-Frostvalley YMCA, N.Y., 1992; English as fgn. lang. instr. Prague Castle, Czech Rep., 1994. Youth leader D.C. Air N.G., 1982. Recipient USAR Phys. Tng. award U.S. Army, 1991, Innovative Teaching award WSKG-TV, 1994. Mem. TESOL. Home: 8 Delmar St Binghamton NY 13903

GRASSO, MARY ANN, theatre association administrator; b. Rome, N.Y., Nov. 3, 1952; d. Vincent and Rose Mary (Pupa) Grasso. BA in Art History, U. Calif., Riverside, 1973; MLS, U. Oreg., 1974. Dir. Warner Rsch. Collection, Burbank, Calif., 1975-84; mgr. CBS TV/Docudrama, Hollywood, Calif., 1984-88; exec. dir. Nat. Assn. Theatre Owners, North Hollywood, Calif., 1988—; instr. theatre arts UCLA, 1980-85, Am. Film Inst., L.A., 1985-88. Screen credits: The Scarlet O'Hara Wars, This Year's Blonde, The Silent Lovers, A Bunnies Tale, Embassy. Mem. Nat. Assn. Theatre Owners (exec. dir.), Bus. and Profl. Women's Assn. (Woman of Achievement award 1983), RP Internat. (The Vision award), Acad. Motion Picture Arts and Scis., Friends of the Motion Picture Pioneers, Earth Comm., Phi Beta Kappa. Democrat. Office: Nat Assn Theatre Owners 4605 Lankershim Blvd # 340 North Hollywood CA 91602-1818

GRATZ, CINDY CARPENTER, dance educator, choreographer; b. Corpus Christi, Tex., Nov. 20, 1958; d. Regan and Sara (Medellin) Carpenter; m. Robert David Gratz, Dec. 30, 1995. BA, UCLA, 1980, MA, 1982; PhD, NYU, 1990. Adj. instr. dance NYU, N.Y.C., 1987-90, adj. asst. prof., 1990-91; asst. prof. dance Sam Houston State U., Huntsville, Tex., 1991—; artist-in-residence Dan-Ching Acad., Taiwan City, Taiwan, 1986, Brenau Coll., Gainesville, Ga., 1988, U. Nebr., Lincoln, 1989; dir. Washington Square Repertory Dance Co., N.Y.C., 1990-91; founder, dir. Janus Dance Projects, N.Y.C., 1986-91, Prime Time: Srs. in Motion Dance Co., Huntsville, 1992—, The Cindy Carpenter Dance Co., Huntsville, 1995—. Choreographer, performer Afterimages, 1992; choreographer, dir. Post Post Dances: Another Artist Slips Away, 1995; dir., choreographer, performer (play) Stepping Out, 1995; choreographer Cheval, 1995. Mem. exec. bd. Huntsville Cmty. Theatre, 1994—. Grantee Chi Tau Epsilon, 1994, Huntsville Arts Commn., 1994—. Mem. AAUP (pres. local chpt. 1994—), AAUW (v.p. local chpt. 1994—), Sam Houston State U. Women (officer 1991—). Home: 2223 Mustang Ln San Marcos TX 78666 Office: Sam Houston State U Dance Program Box 2269 Huntsville TX 77341-2269

GRAU, MARCY BEINISH, former precious metal trader, banker, consultant; b. Bklyn., Aug. 7, 1950; d. Joseph Beinish and Gloria (Rosenbaum) Bennett; m. Bennett Grau, Nov. 19, 1978; 3 children. AB with high honors, U. Mich., 1971; postgrad., Columbia U., 1972, N.Y. Inst. Fin., 1973. Asst. to chmn. Bancroft Convertible Fund, N.Y.C., 1973-75; precious metals trader J. Aron & Co., N.Y.C., 1975-81, mgr. metals mktg., 1981-83; v.p. Goldman, Sachs & Co/J. Aron, N.Y.C., 1983-88; investment banking cons., N.Y.C., 1988-90. Editor Precious Metals Rev. and Outlook, 1980—; contbr. article to profl. jours. Vol. worker pediatrics dept. Lenox Hill Hosp., N.Y.C., 1978-79; asst. The Holiday Project, The Hunger Project, N.Y.C., 1978-83; vol. Yorkville Common Pantry, N.Y.C., 1984; tutor Yorkville Neighborhodd Assn., N.Y.C., 1984; assoc. Child Devel. Ctr., N.Y.C.; trustee Congregation B'Nai Jeshurun, 1989—, pres., 1991-94, chair, 1994—; trustee Ethical Fieldston Fund, 1994—. Mem. Phi Beta Kappa. Democrat. Jewish. Home and Office: 300 W End Ave New York NY 10023-8156

GRAU, SHIRLEY ANN (MRS. JAMES KERN FEIBLEMAN), writer; b. New Orleans, July 8, 1929; d. Adolph and Katherine (Onion) G.; m. James Kern Feibleman, Aug. 4, 1955; children: Ian, James, Nora Miranda, William, Katherine. BA, Tulane U., 1950. Author: (short stories) The Black Prince and Other Stories, 1955, The Hard Blue Sky, 1958, The House on Coliseum Street, 1961, The Keepers of the House, 1964 (Pulitzer prize for fiction 1965), The Condor Passes, 1971, The Wind Shifting West and Other Stories, 1973, Evidence of Love, 1977, Nine Women, 1986, Roadwalkers, 1994; writer publs. including Holiday, New Yorker, New World Writing, Mademoiselle, Saturday Evening Post, Atlantic, The Reporter, 1954—. Mem. Phi Beta Kappa. Office: 210 Baronne St Ste 1120 New Orleans LA 70112-1713

GRAUER, EVA MARIE, sculptor, artist; b. Memphis, Jan. 13, 1925; d. Otto Franklin and Mary Eva (Nichols) Lyons. Student, Southwestern Coll., Memphis, Memphis Acad. Arts. Ind. sulptor, artist, archtl. restorer, art instr. Memphis, 1955—. Sculptures represented in permanent collections including: Overbrook Acad., Nashville, St. Jude Hosp., Memphis, St. Mary's Cathedral, Memphis, numerous pvt. collections; contbr. articles to numerous pubs.; contbr. art, WKNO-TV, Memphis, Memphis Brooks Mus. Showcase. Mem. Brooks Art League. Episcopalian. Home and Studio: 1261 W Perkins Rd Memphis TN 38117-6120

GRAUER, SANDRA LEE, biology educator, nurse; b. Charleston, S.C., Jan. 30, 1950; d. William Jacob and Bella (Goldman) G. BS, U. S.C., 1972; BSN, Med. Coll. Ga., 1976; postgrad., Clemson U., 1983-86, Med. U. S.C., Charleston, 1987-90; MEd in Biology, The Citadel Evening Coll., Charleston, 1991. RN, N.C. Charge nurse Eugene Talmadge Meml. Hosp., Augusta, Ga., 1977, Anderson (S.C.) Meml. Hosp., 1978-80; agrl. sci. asst. Clemson (S.C.) U., 1980-83, sci. rschr., 1983-86, tchg. asst. biology, 1985-86; sci. rschr. Med. U. S.C., Charleston, 1987-89; instr. biology Trident Tech. Coll., Charleston, 1988-95, Limestone Coll., Gaffney, S.C., 1996—. Elks state and local scholar Elks Lodge, 1968-71, Saul Alexander scholar, 1968-72; instnl. grantee Med. U. S.C., 1988. Mem. AAUW (membership chair 1995-96, participant women's polit. forum 1996), Am. Soc. for Cell Biology, Nature Conservancy, S.C. Coastal Conservation League, Sigma Xi, Gamma Sigma Delta. Jewish. Home: 870 Colony Dr Apt 13 Charleston SC 29407

GRAUMLICH, BETTY SINCLAIRE WOMMACK, lawyer; b. Suffolk, Va., Aug. 6, 1957; d. Forrest Sinclaire and Jane (Burchett) Wommack; m. August Kiger Graumlich III, Apr. 29, 1995. BA, U. Va., 1979; JD, U. Va. Sch. Law, 1983. Bar: D.C. 1983, Va. 1989, U.S. Ct. Appeals (4th cir., 5th cir.). Clk. U.S. Dist. Ct. (no. dist.) Tex., Dallas, 1983-84; assoc. Kirkland & Ellis, Washington, 1984-89, McSweeney Burtch & Crump, Richmond, Va., 1989-92; prin. McSweeney Burtch & Crump, 1992—. Sec., bd. dirs. Ships Watch Homeowners Assn., Duck, N.C., 1995-96; adv. bd. Emergency Shelter, Inc., Richmond, 1995—. Mem. ABA, Va. Bar Assn. (coun., sect. labor and employment law 1995—), Order of Coif, Westwood Club (sec., bd. dirs. 1995-96). Methodist. Office: McSweeney Burtch & Crump 11 S 12th St Richmond VA 23219

GRAUPNER, SHERYLL ANN, elementary education educator; b. Independence, Mo., Sept. 19, 1947; d. Horace Alvin and Estelle (LeJeune) G. BS in Edn., Ctrl. Mo. State U., 1969; MEd, U. Mo., Kansas City, 1972. Tchr. Independence Pub. Schs., 1969—; chairperson Procter Sch. North Ctrl., Independence, 1982, co-chairperson, 1989; math connection tchr. Mo. State Ednl. Incentive Grant, Independence, 1987, 94. Mem. NEA, Internat. Reading Assn., Nat. Congress Parents and Tchrs.

GRAVELIN, JANESY SWARTZ, elementary education educator; b. Cleve., Mar. 28, 1952; d. Jesse Franklin and Adele Myra (Pesek) Swartz; m. Christopher James Hof, June 15, 1974 (div. May 1988); 1 child, Zachary Christopher Hof; m. David Paul Gravelin, June 6, 1991. BS in Edn., Bowling Green State U., 1974; MEd, U. South Fla., Ft. Myers, 1985. Cert. elem., spl. edn. tchr., adminstr., supr., Fla., Ohio. Infant stimulation tchr. Wood Lane Sch., Bowling Green, 1974-76, developmentally delayed tchr., 1976-77; 1st grade tchr. Peace River Elem. Sch., Charlotte Harbor, Fla., 1978-85; 3rd grade tchr. Peace River Elem. Sch., Charlotte Harbor, 1985-90, computer edn. tchr., 1990—; yearbook advisor Peace River Elem. Sch., 1991—; com. mem. So. Assn. Colls. and Schs., 1989. Recipient Fla. Merit Tchr. award State of Fla., 1984. Mem. Phi Delta Kappa (v.p. 1994-96). Home: 21043 Cascade Ave Port Charlotte FL 33952 Office: Peace River Elem Sch 22400 Hancock Ave Port Charlotte FL 33980

GRAVELY, JANE CANDACE, computer company executive; b. Rocky Mount, N.C., Dec. 1, 1952; d. Edmund Keen and Janice Eleanor (Beavon) G.; m. Barney Ben Linthicum, July 13, 1985 (div. 1991). BS, N.C. Wesleyan Coll., 1974, MEd, Coll. William and Mary, 1980. Circulation and promotion mgr. Va. Gazette, Williamsburg, 1975-80; computer analyst, chief exec. officer Affordable Computer Systems, Rocky Mount, 1982-85, Goldsboro, N.C., 1985-95; sr. sys. analyst Nat. Tech. Group, Goldsboro, N.C., 1996—; instr. bus., math., computers Nash Tech. Coll., Rocky Mount, 1980-83; instr. math., computers N.C. Wesleyan Coll., Rocky Mount, 1983-85, instr. computers, 1985-89. Mem. NAFE, United Meth. Womens Circle (pres. 1990-91), Goldsboro C. of C. (Chamber Amb. Com. of 100, sec. 1994), Kiwanis, Goldsboro Club (2d v.p. 1994—), Omicron Delta Kappa. Republican.

GRAVER, MARY KATHRYN, medical, surgical nurse; b. Rehrersburg, Pa., Nov. 8, 1934; d. Levi B. and Emma A. (Sensenig) Gibbel; m. C. W. Graver, June 27, 1959; children: Elizabeth Ann, Craig Warren, Timothy John, Kathryn Renate. RN, Coatesville (Pa.) Sch. Nursing, 1956; BA, Eastern Coll., St. Davids, Pa., 1994. Staff nurse pediatrics unit Phila. Gen. Hosp., 1956; staff nurse med./surg. unit Coatesville Hosp., 1957; staff nurse maternal and med./surg. units Ephrata (Pa.) Hosp., 1958-59; staff nurse Bryn Mawr (Pa.) Hosp., 1976-93.

GRAVES, DANA LOUISE, elementary school educator; b. Takoma Park, Md., Mar. 15, 1948; d. John William and Patricia Eloise (langdon) Perkins; m. George William Graves, Nov. 7, 1977; 1 child, Jennifer; 1 stepchild, Michael. BA, Elon Coll., N.C., 1970. Cert. tchr. elem. edn., Va. Tchr. 5th grade Hope Valley Sch., Durham, N.C., 1971, tchr. 2d grade, 1971-72; tchr. 4th grade Alanton Elem. Sch., Virginia Beach, Va., 1972-73, tchr. 2d grade, 1973-77; tchr. 3d grade North Springfield Elem. Sch., 1978; tchr. 2d grade Hunt Valley Sch., Fairfax, Va., 1985-86, 1987—. Parent mem./helper Girl Scouts U.S., Fairfax, 1987—. Tchr. of Yr. at Alanton Elem. Sch., Virginia Beach Pub. Schs., 1976-77, Cert. of Appreciation for outstanding contbn., dedication and commitment Children and Adults with Attention Deficit Disorders of No. Va., 1994. Mem. NEA, Va. Edn. Assn., Fairfax Edn. Assn., Virginia Beach Edn. Assn., Nat. Coun. Tchrs. English, Nat. Sci. Tchrs. Assn., Greater Washington Reading Coun., Internat. Reading Assn., Va. State Reading Assn. Roman Catholic. Home: 5023 Dequincy Dr Fairfax VA 22032-2432

GRAVES, DIANE JOHNSTON, academic librarian; b. Pitts., June 12, 1957; d. Allan Howard and M. Elaine (Graham) Johnston; m. Paul A. Cimbala, June 23, 1979 (div. 1989); m. William C. Graves, Feb. 17, 1990; 1 child, Elena Marie. BA in English, Emory U., 1979, M of Librarianship,

1981. Editl. asst. Emory U. Publs., Atlanta, 1979-80; social scis. libr. Miami U., Oxford, Ohio, 1981-83; rsch. asst. Fla. Senate, Tallahassee, 1983-84; asst. libr. for support svcs. Augusta (Ga.) Coll., 1984-87; sr. regional rep. Faxon Co., Westwood, Mass., 1987-89; head of serials Ill. Inst. Tech., Chgo., 1989-90; acquisitions libr. U. Ill., Chgo., 1990-91; asst. univ. libr. Loyola U., Chgo., 1991-94; assoc. dean librs. U. Miss., University, 1994-96; libr. dir. Hollins Coll., Roanoke, Va., 1996—. Editor: (periodical) Libr. Adminstrn. and Mgmt., 1993-94, assoc. editor, 1991-92; co-editor: (monographic series) Advances in Library Resource Sharing, 1991-92; mem. editl. bd. College and Research Libraries, 1996—; contbr. articles to profl. jours. Mem. Am. Libr. Assn., Assn. Coll. and Rsch. Librs., Libr. Adminstrn. and Mgmt. Assn. (Cert. Appreciation 1996), Assn. Libr. Collections and Tech. Svcs., Adoptive Families of Am. Episcopalian. Home: 2310 Wembley Ct Daleville VA 24083 Office: Hollins Coll Fishburn Libr Roanoke VA 24020

GRAVES, KATHRYN LOUISE, dermatologist; b. Kansas City, Kans., Mar. 9, 1949; d. Jack Clair and Ruth Marjory (Prentice) Schroll; m. Jeffery Jackson Graves, Mar. 31, 1973; children: Jeffery Justin, Jonathon Tyler, Kathryn Camille. BA, U. Kans., 1971; MD, U. Kans., Kansas City, 1974. Diplomate Am. Bd. Dermatology. Intern St. Lukes Hosp., Kansas City, 1975-76, resident in internal medicine, 1976; resident dermatology Sch. Medicine U. Kans., Kansas City, 1976-79; dermatologist Hutchinson (Kans.) Clinic P.A., 1979—; mem. med. staff Hutchinson Hosp., 1979—. Fellow Am. Acad. Dermatology; mem. AMA, Kans. Dermatology Soc., Kans. Med. Assn., Reno County Med. Assn., Hutchinson C. of C., Gamma Phi Beta (standards chair 1973—). Republican. Methodist. Home: 211 Countryside Dr Hutchinson KS 67502-4457 Office: Hutchinson Clinic 2101 N Waldron St Hutchinson KS 67502-1131

GRAVES, LORRAINE ELIZABETH, dancer, educator, coach; b. Norfolk, Va., Oct. 5, 1957; d. Thomas Edward and Mildred Fayette (Odom) G. BS, Ind. U., 1978. Dancer, Regisseuse Dance Theatre of Harlem, N.Y.C., 1978—, ballet mistress, 1980—, prin. dancer, 1982—; guest tchr. N.C. Sch. of Arts, Winston-Salem, 1987, 93, Gov.'s Sch. for Arts, U. Richmond, 1990-95, Carlton Johnson Acad. of Dance, 1991-95, Okla. Summer Arts Inst., 1993-94, The Flint Sch. Performing Arts, Dance Theatre of Harlem, Kennedy Ctr. Residency Program, 1993-94; resident guest tchr. Gov.'s Magnet Sch. for Arts, Norfolk, Va., 1988-91, S.C. Gov. Sch. for Arts, 1995. Appeared with Dance Theatre of Harlem as Princess of Unreal Beauty in live TV prodn. of Firebird, 1982, as Myrta, Queen of the Willis in NBC prodn. of Creole Giselle, 1987; performed at White House, 1981, also at the closing ceremonies of the 1984 Olympics, 1984, toured with Dance Theatre of Harlem, USSR, 1988, South Africa, 1992; guest artist Young People's Concert series, N.Y. Philharm., 1988, Detroit Symphony, 1989, River City Ballet, Memphis, 1991, 92, N.W. Fla. Ballet, 1994; regisseuse Dance Theater of Harlem, 1989. Fellow Am. Guild Mus. Artists. Episcopalian.

GRAVES, MARGERY A., elementary education educator; b. Champaign, Ill., Dec. 16, 1931; d. Herbert L. and Margery E. (Fish) White; m. John E. Graves, June 23, 1956; children: Beth Graves Lenz, Cheryl Graves Mehta. BA, Drury Coll., 1953; MS Edn., Drake U., 1991. Tchr. Des Moines Pub. Schs., 1953-56, Ames (Iowa) Pub. Schs., 1956-59, Newton (Iowa) Comm. Schs., 1967-95; mem. coms. lang., social studies, whole lang., early childhood, report card, Newton Schs., 1977-94; founder pub. ctr. for student books, Emerson Hough Sch., Newton, 1988. Pres. LWV, Newton, Willowbrook Adult Day Care Bd., Newton. Mem. Delta Kappa Gamma. Democrat. Unitarian. Home: 7006 S 28th Ave E Newton IA 50208

GRAVES, MARIE MAXINE, public relations executive, OSHA consultant; b. Cullman, Ala., Feb. 15, 1957; d. Hugh Max and Nellie Marie (Elliott) G. AS in Psychology, Wallace State Coll., Hanceville, Ala., 1977; student, OSHA courses, 1993—. Sales clk. Rexall Drugs, Hanceville, 1973-78; office mgr., pub. rels. Hanceville Tire Co., 1978-83, Warren Supply Co., Hanceville, 1983-86; office mgr., pub. rels., rsch., OSHA cons. Hanceville Dental Clinic, 1986-92; office mgr., pub. rels. Conn Surveyors, Cullman, Ala., 1992—; part time OSHA cons. Hanceville Dental Clinic, 1992-95. Beat committeman Dem. Exec. Com., Hanceville, 1980—; exec bd. pub. rels., fin., Cullman County Dems., 1980—; mem. Cullman County Dem. Women, pres. 1993-94; founder, sponsor Cullman County Young Dems.; steering com. Dem. Nat. Com., Washington, 1990—. Mem. NOW (pres. Greater Birmingham chpt., sec. Ala.). Baptist. Home: 414 Blountsville St NE Hanceville AL 35077 Office: 202 1st Ave SE Ste M Cullman AL 35055

GRAVES, MAUREEN ANN, counselor; b. Sioux City, Iowa, July 10, 1946; d. Jack Milford and Elizabeth Mildred (St. George) Dryden; m. Thomas Darrel Graves, Oct. 9, 1965; children: Michael James, Lorrie Michelle. G-rad., Gestalt Inst. Iowa, 1980. Cert. drug and alcohol counselor, Nebr.; cert. profl. asst., U. S.D.; cert. hypnotherapist. Counselor Siouxland Coun. on Alcoholism and Drug Abuse, Sioux City, 1979-81; counselor, co-founder New Hope Alcohol and Addiction Ctr., South Sioux City, Nebr., 1981—; cons. St. Luke Hosp. Addiction Ctr., Sioux City, 1987—; trainer Va. Satir-Internat. Tng. Inst., Crested Butte, Colo., 1988-89. Vol. co-facilitator Siouxland Coun. on Alcoholism and Drug Abuse, Sioux City, 1976-79; mem. exec. team couple World Wide Marriage Encounter, N.E. Nebr., 1979-82; trainer Va. Satir-Internat. Tng. Inst., Crested Butte, Colo., 1992; co-leader Satir Family Camp, San Jose, 1992, 93, 94, 95, 96; mem. Avanta Governing Coun., 1994-96. Mem. Avanta Network, Am. Mental Health Counselors Assn., Moscow Inst. for Profl. Devel. of Psychologists and Social Workers (founding), AACD. Roman Catholic. Home: 424 W 16th St South Sioux City NE 68776-2233 Office: New Hope Alcoholism & Addiction Ctr Inc PO Box 35 South Sioux City NE 68776

GRAVES, REBECCA O., public health nurse, consultant; b. Nashville, Jan. 25, 1941; d. Earl T. and Anna (Davis) Odom; m. Edward L. Graves, Dec. 22, 1964; children: Angela R., Alison R. BSN, Tuskegee U., 1965. RN, Tenn.; cert. intravenous therapy critical care nurse. Staff med.-surg. nurse L. Richardson Meml. Hosp., Greensboro, N.C.; coord. health svcs. Shaw U., Raleigh, N.C.; staff nurse, coord. health svcs. State of N.C., Raleigh; intravenous therapy nurse, clin. coord. IV therapy Hubbard Hosp., Nashville; pub. health nurse cons. State of Tenn., Nashville. Mem. Intravenous Nurses Soc., Tenn. Nurses Assn., Tenn. Pub. Health Assn. Home: 4111 Dalemere Ct Nashville TN 37207-1211

GRAY, ANN MAYNARD, broadcasting company executive; b. Boston, Aug. 22, 1945; d. Paul Maynard and Pauline Elizabeth MacFadyen; children: Richard R. Gray III, Dana Maynard Gray. BA, U. Mich., 1967; MBA, NYU, 1971. With Chase Manhattan Bank, N.Y.C., 1967-68, Chem. Bank, N.Y.C., 1968-73; asst. sec. Chem. Bank, 1971-73; asst. to treas., then asst. treas. ABC, Inc., 1974-76, treas., 1976-81, v.p. planning, 1979-86; v.p. Capital Cities/ABC, Inc. (merged 1986), 1986—; sr. v.p. fin. ABC TV Network Group, 1988-91; pres. Diversified Pub. Group Capital Cities/ABC, Inc., 1991—; bd. dirs. Cyprus AMAX Minerals Co., PanEnergy Corp. Trustee Martha Graham Ctr. of Contemporary Dance, N.Y.C., 1989-92, Cancer Care, Inc., 1991—. Office: Capital Cities ABC Inc 77 W 66th St New York NY 10023-6201

GRAY, BARBARA BRONSON, nurse, writer; b. Van Nuys, Calif., June 3, 1955; d. Gerald M. and Jane Marie (Strauss) Bronson; m. Thomas Stephen Gray, Aug. 27, 1977; children: Jonathan Thomas, Katherine Marie. BS, UCLA, 1977, M in Nursing, 1981. RN, Calif. Staff nurse Valley Presbyn. Hosp., Van Nuys, Calif., 1977-80; asst. adminstr. Calif. Med. Ctr., L.A., Calif., 1981-84; freelance writer Agoura, 1984—; exec. dir. Nurseweek, 1995—; cons. St. John's Hosp. and Health Ctr., Santa Monica, Calif., 1986-90, Los Robles Regional Med. Ctr., Thousand Oaks, Calif., 1993—; lectr. UCLA Sch. Nursing, 1991—. Author: 120 Years of Medicine in Los Angeles County, 1991; contbr. articles to jours., mags. and newspapers; syndicated by L.A. Times Syndicate. Recipient Outstanding Achievement award Perinatal Network, Santa Clara County, Calif., 1994; named Writer of Yr., Nurseweek, 1991; Kellogg fellow, 1979-81. Mem. Nat. Assn. Sci. Writers, Sigma Theta Tau (Cert. of Appreciation 1994, Internat. Media award 1995). Republican. Episcopalian. Home: 4909 Cardinal Way Agoura CA 91301-4762

GRAY, CAROL LIPPERT, public relations executive; b. N.Y.C., Mar. 31, 1950; d. Michael and Lenore (Bortstein) Lippert; m. Lewis William Gray, Sept. 5, 1970 (dec. 1992); children: Holly, Meredith. BA in History, Douglass Coll., 1970; MS in Broadcast Journalism, Boston U., 1976. Reporter, copywriter Sta. WCTC Radio, New Brunswick, N.J., 1967-70; benefit authorizer Social Security Adminstrn., Phila., 1970-73; writer, prodr., host talk show Don Christ Studios, Collingswood, N.J., 1976; freelance writer, 1976—; mng. editor Carstens Pubs., Newton, N.J., 1981-83, All Am. Crafts, Sparta, N.J., 1984-88; ptnr. Gray/Blanchard Enterprises, Newton, 1988-90; editor Creative Pub. Group, Newton, 1988-90; mgr. pub. rels. The Seeing Eye, Morristown, N.J., 1990—. Author: Weight Watchers 365-Day Menu Cookbook; mem. editl. adv. bd. Morris County C. of C., 1995—; contbr. articles to profl. jours. Pres., sec. Sussex County Arts Coun., Newton, 1982-92; v.p. Hilltop Country Day Sch., Sparta, 1987-92. Mem. Nat. Fedn. Press Women, N.J. Press Women, Internat. Assn. Bus. Commumicators, Pub. Rels. Soc. Am., N.J. Ad Club. Office: The Seeing Eye Washington Valley Rd Morristown NJ 07963-0375

GRAY, DAHLI, accounting educator and administrator; b. Grand Junction, Colo., Dec. 28, 1948; d. Forrest Walter and Mary (Crockett) G.; 1 child, Kimberly. BS, Ea. Oreg. State U., 1971; MBA, Portland (Oreg.) State U., 1976; D of Bus. Adminstrn., George Washington U., 1984. Instr. acctg. Portland State U., 1976-79, George Mason U., Fairfax, Va., 1980, George Washington U., Washington, 1981-82; asst. prof. Oreg. State U., Corvallis, 1983-86; research fellow U. Notre Dame, South Bend, Ind., 1986-88; assoc. prof. Am. U., Washington, 1988-90; chairperson, Walpert, Smullian & Blumenthal prof. Towson (Md.) State U., 1990-92; chairperson Morgan State U., Balt., 1992—. Contbr. articles to profl. jours. Named Tchr. of Yr., Alpha Lambda Delta, 1986; Peat Marwick Mitchell & Co. fellow, 1986-88. Mem. Internat. Assn. Acctg. Research and Edn., Am. Inst. CPA's, Nat. Assn. Accts. (Andrew Barr award 1982, 84, Cert. Merit 1982), Am. Acctg. Assn., Inst. Cert. Mgmt. Accts. Democrat. Home: T-3 202 Duke of Kent Ln Cockeysville MD 21030 Office: Morgan State U Sch Bus and Mgmt Acctg and Fin Dept Baltimore MD 21239

GRAY, DAWN PLAMBECK, public relations/newletter publishing executive; b. Chgo., Aug. 23, 1957; d. Raymond August and Eunice Eve (Fox) Plambeck; m. Richard Scott Gray, Apr. 13, 1985; children: Zachary, Rae. BS, Northwestern U., 1979. Desk asst. Sta. WCFL, Chgo., 1979-80; writer UPI Internat., Chgo., 1980; asignment editor Cable News Network, Chgo., 1980-81; account exec. Aaron Cushman and Assoc., Chgo., 1981-83; account exec. Ruder Finn & Rotman, Chgo., 1983-84, account supr., 1984-86, dir. consumer group, 1986-87; dir. pub. rels. Tassani Communications, Chgo., 1987-90; v.p. Marcy Monyek & Assoc., Chgo., 1990; pres. Moments Inc., Chgo., 1991—. Mem. Network Women Entrepreneurs. Office: Moments Inc 6 N Michigan Ave Ste 1514 Chicago IL 60602-4809

GRAY, DEBORAH DOLIA, business writing consultant; b. Elmo, Mo., Jan. 25, 1952; d. Gerald Lee and Rosalie (Thompson) G. BS in Music and Journalism cum laude, U. Nebr., 1976; MFA, Columbia U., 1988. Reporter The Lincoln (Nebr.) Star, 1975-78; spl. writer, feature projects The Fort Lauderdale (Fla.) News, 1978-79; reporter Miami (Fla.) News, 1979-80; curriculum specialist John Jay Coll. Criminal Justice, N.Y.C., 1980-84; tng. specialist Mgmt. Devel. Systems Inc., N.Y.C., 1985—; writing cons. various non-profit agys. and corps. Contbr. articles to profl. jours. Hollingsworth fellow Columbia U., 1985. Home: 200 W 93rd St Apt 3-I New York NY 10025-7402

GRAY, DEBORAH MARY, wine importer b. Sydney, N.S.W., Australia, Feb. 4, 1952; came to U.S., 1973; d. Anthony Eric and Mary Patricia (O'Mullane) Gray; m. Theodore Ralph Culbertson, July 31, 1971 (div. 1979); m. Scott Cameron Struthers, Jan. 31, 1981 (div. 1988). Student St. Petersburg Jr. Coll., 1978-85, Eckerd Coll., 1988-90. Fin. counselor Wuesthoff Meml. Hosp., Rockledge, Fla., 1973-75; adminstrv. dir. Dresden & Ticktin, MDs, P.A., St. Petersburg, Fla., 1976-80; exec. dir., v.p. Am. Med. Mgmt., Inc., Clearwater, Fla., 1980-90; pres., dir. All Women's Health Ctr., Inc., St. Petersburg, 1980-90, All Women's Health Ctr. North Tampa, Inc., Fla., 1980-90, All Women's Health Ctr. Tampa, Inc., 1980-90, Women's Ob-Gyn. Ctr. Countryside, Inc., 1984-90, All Women's Health Ctr. Sarasota, Fla., 1980-90, All Women's Health Ctr. Ocala, Fla., 1980 90, All Women's Health Ctr. Gainesville, Fla., 1981-90, Lakeland Women's Health Ctr., Fla., 1980-90, Ft. Myers Womens Health Ctr., Fla., 1980-90, All Women's Health Ctr. Jacksonville, Fla., 1980-90, Nat. Women's Health Svcs., Inc., Clearwater, Fla., 1983-90, D.M.S. of Ft. Myers, Inc., 1985-90, Alternative Human Svc., 1979, treas., v.p., dir. Birthing Mgmt. Inc., 1985-90; healthcare cons., 1990-92; N.Am. mgr. Cowra Wines, Australia, 1991-95; owner, sole proprietor The Australian Wine Connection, Breckenridge, Colo., 1992—; dir. Perinatal Ct. Ga. Bapt. Med. Ctr., 1990-92. Mem. bd. agy. that facilitates hard to place children adoptions One Ch. One Child, 1990-94.

GRAY, DIANE, dancer, choreographer; b. Painesville, Ohio, May 29, 1941; d. Gordon Dallas and Bettie (Kerr) G.; m. James William Viera, May 15, 1971; 1 child, James William II. BS, Juilliard Sch., 1963; MS in Edn., Hunter Coll., 1987. Chorus dancer Martha Graham Dance Co., N.Y.C., 1963-69, soloist, 1969-71, prin. dancer, 1972-79, assoc. artistic dir., 1993—; artist-in-residence various Univs., worldwide, 1965—; tchr. Martha Graham Sch., N.Y.C., 1963—; also dir. Martha Graham Sch., 1983—; dir. Dances by Diane Gray, N.Y.C., 1979-83. Mem. Kappa Delta Pi. Office: Martha Graham Sch 316 E 63rd St New York NY 10021-7702

GRAY, DOROTHY N., policy analyst; b. Tallahassee, July 8, 1946; d. Walter Floyd and Marjorie Clarice (Sanders) G.; m. Walter P. Godfrey, Dec. 17, 1966 (div. July 1976); 1 child, Staphanie Lee; m. Paul E. Lincolnhol, June 9, 1984. AA, Chipola Jr. Coll., 1966; BS in Vocat. Home Econs., Fla. State U., 1973, MPA, 1985. Drafter, sec. Franklin Co., Prinston, W.Va., 1970-71; legal sec. Red Lobster Inns, Orlando, Fla., 1972-73, Abrams, Anton, Robbins, Resnick & Sneider, Hollywood, Fla., 1974-75, Holland & Knight, Tallahassee, 1976-77, Pub. Defenders Office, Tallahassee, 1978, Mcpl. Ode Corp., Tallahassee, 1979; workers' compensation examiner Dept. Labor & Employment Security, Tallahassee, 1980-85; senate analyst Senate Appropations Com., Tallahassee, 1985-86; policy analyst Office Policy Analysis, Govt. Accountability, Tallahassee, 1986—. Mem. Dem. exec. Com., 1980-81. Mem. NOW, Nat. Leadership Program Evaluation Assn., Nat. Conf. Senate Legislators, Southeast Educators Assn. Home: 1608 Chinnapakin None Tallahassee FL 32301

GRAY, ELIZABETH DODSON, theologian, writer, speaker; b. Balt., July 13, 1929; d. Fitzhugh J. and Lillian (Northam) Dodson; m. David Dodson Gray, July 2, 1987; children: Lisa, Hunter. BA, Smith Coll., 1951; BD, Yale U., 1954. Rsch. assoc. MIT Sloan Sch. Mgmt., Cambridge, 1974-76; vis. prof. Williams Coll., Williamstown, Mass., 1977; Theol. opportunities program coord. Harvard Divinity Sch., Cambridge, 1978—; adj. faculty Boston Coll., Chestnut Hill, 1981-90, Antioch N.E. Grad. Sch., Keene, N.H., 1990-91. Author: Green Paradise Lost, 1979, Patriarchy as a Conceptual Trap, 1982, Sacred Dimensions of Women's Experience, 1988, Sunday School Manifesto, 1994; co-author: Growth and Its Implications for the Future, 1974, Children of Joy, 1976. Film for TV, Adam's World, about her work and thoughts, Nat. Film Bd. Can., 1988. Mem. U.S. Assn. Club of Rome (co-vice chmn. 1979-82). Home: 4 Linden Sq Wellesley MA 02181 Office: Harvard Divinity Sch 45 Francis Ave Cambridge MA 02181

GRAY, FRANCINE DU PLESSIX, author; b. Warsaw, Poland; came to U.S., 1941, naturalized, 1952; d. Bertrand Jochaud and Tatiana (Iacovleff) du Plessix; m. Cleve Gray, Apr. 23, 1957; children: Thaddeus Ives, Luke Alexander. B.A., Barnard Coll., 1952; Litt.D. (hon.), CUNY, Oberlin Coll., U. Santa Clara, St. Mary's Coll., U. Hartford. disting. vis. prof. CCNY, 1975; vis. lectr. Yale U., New Haven, 1981-82; Ferris prof. Princeton U., 1986. Author: Divine Disobedience: Profiles in Catholic Radicalism, 1970 (Nat. Cath. Book award), Hawaii: The Sugar-Coated Fortress, 1972 , Lovers and Tyrants, 1976, World Without End, 1981, October Blood, 1985, Adam & Eve and the City, 1987, Soviet Women: Walking the Tightrope, 1989, Rage and Fire: A Life of Louise Colet, 1994. Guggenheim Found. fellow, 1991-92. Mem. Am. P.E.N., Am. Acad. Arts and Letters. Democrat. Roman Catholic.

GRAY, GWEN CASH, real estate broker; b. Cowpens, S.C., Oct. 24, 1943; d. Woodrow C. and Marie (Hamrick) Cash; m. Charles H. Gray, Oct. 24, 1987 ; children: Dianne Marie Young, Teena Michele Bulman. BS, Limestone Coll., Gaffney, S.C., 1984. Real estate sales rep. and mgr. ERA Miller & Gray Real Estate, Spartanburg, S.C., 1983-89, real estate sales rep., co-owner, broker-in-charge, 1989—; bd. dirs. Nations Bank Gaffney; lectr. in field. Contbr. articles to profl. jours. Advisor S.C. Peach Festival, Gaffney, 1977—, Clemson U. Extension Svc., 1987—. Named Woman of Yr. Bus. and Profl. Women, 1979, Woman of Yr. S.C. Rural Electric Coop., 1984. Mem. Am. Farm Bur., Nat. Bd. Realtors, S.C. Farm Bur., S.C. Bd. Realtors, Spartanburg Bd. Realtors (officer), S.C. Hort. Soc. (bd. dirs.), S.C. Assn. Agr. Agts. (Friend of Extension award 1986), Spartanburg Multiple Listing Svc. (bd. dirs.). Baptist. Democrat.

GRAY, HANNA HOLBORN, history educator; b. Heidelberg, Germany, Oct. 25, 1930; d. Hajo and Annemarie (Bettmann) Holborn; m. Charles Montgomery Gray, June 19, 1954. AB, Bryn Mawr Coll., 1950; PhD, Harvard U., 1957; MA, Yale U., 1971, LLD, 1978; LittD (hon.), St. Lawrence U., 1974, Oxford (Eng.) U., 1979; LLD (hon.), Dickinson Coll., 1979, U. Notre Dame, 1980, Marquette U., 1984; LittD (hon.), Washington U., 1985; HHD (hon.), St. Mary's Coll., 1974; LHD (hon.), Grinnell (Iowa) Coll., 1974, Lawrence U., 1974, Denison U., 1974, Wheaton Coll., 1976, Marlboro Coll., 1979, Rikkyo (Japan) U., 1979, Roosevelt U., 1980, Knox Coll., 1980, Coe Coll., 1981, Thomas Jefferson U., 1981, Duke U., 1982, New Sch. for Social Research, 1982, Clark U., 1982, Brandeis U., 1983, Colgate U., 1983, Wayne State U., 1984, Miami U., Oxford, Ohio, 1984, So. Meth. U., 1984, CUNY, 1985, U. Denver, 1985, Am. Coll. Greece, 1986, Muskingum Coll., 1987, Rush Presbyn. St. Lukes Med. Ctr., 1987, NYU, 1988, Rosemont Coll., 1988, Claremont U. Ctr. Grad Sch., 1989, Moravian Coll., 1991, Rensselaer Poly. Inst., 1991, Coll. William and Mary, 1991, Centre Coll., 1991, Macalester Coll., 1993, McGill U., 1993, Ind. U., 1994, Med. U. of S.C., 1994; LLD (hon.), Union Coll., 1975, Regis Coll., 1976, Dartmouth Coll., 1978, Trinity Coll., 1978, U. Bridgeport, 1978, Dickinson Coll., 1979, Brown U., 1979, Wittenburg U., 1979, Dickinson Coll., 1979, U. Rochester, 1980, U. Notre Dame, 1980, U. So. Calif., 1980, U. Mich., 1981, Princeton U., 1982, Georgetown U., 1983, Marquette U., 1984, W.Va. Wesleyan U., 1985, Hamilton Coll., 1985, Smith Coll., 1986, U. Miami, 1986, Columbia U., 1987, NYU, 1988, Rosemont Coll., 1988, U. Toronto, Can., 1991; LDH, U. Del., 1994, Haverford Coll., 1995, Tulane U., 1995; LLD, Harvard U., 1995; LHD, McGill U., 1993, Macalester Coll., 1993, Ind. U., 1994, Med. U. S.C., 1994, Haverford Coll., 1995, Tulane U., 1995; LLD, Harvard U., 1995. Instr. Bryn Mawr Coll., 1953-54; teaching fellow Harvard, 1955-57, instr., 1957-59, asst. prof., 1959-60, vis. lectr., 1963-64; asst. prof. U. Chgo., 1961-64, asso. prof., 1964-72; dean, prof. Northwestern U., Evanston, Ill., 1972-74; provost, prof. history Yale U., 1974-78, acting pres., 1977-78; pres. U. Chgo., Ill., 1978-93; prof. dept. history U. Chgo., 1978—, Harry Pratt Judson disting. svc. prof. history, 1994—; bd. dirs. Cummins Engine Co., J.P. Morgan & Co., Morgan Guaranty Trust Co., Atlantic Richfield Co., Ameritech; fellow Center for Advanced Study in Behavioral Scis., 1966-67, vis. scholar, 1970-71; vis. prof. U. Calif., Berkeley, 1970-71. Editor: (with Charles Gray) Jour. Modern History, 1965-70; contbr. articles to profl. jours. Mem. Nat. Coun. on Humanities, 1972-78; trustee Yale Corp., 1971-74, Com. on Econ. Devel., Bryn Mawr Coll., Howard Hughes Med. Inst., Marlboro Sch. Music; bd. dirs. Andrew W. Mellon Found.; mem. bd. regents The Smithsonian Instn. Decorated Grosse Verdienstkreuz (Germany); fellow Newberry Libr., 1960-61, hon. fellow St. Anne's Coll., Oxford (Eng.) U., 1978—; Fulbright scholar, 1950-51; recipient Grad. medal Radcliffe Coll., 1976, Yale medal, 1978, Medal of Liberty award, 1986, Medal of Freedom, 1991, Frontrunner award Sara Lee, 1991, Laureate Lincoln Acad. Ill., 1988, Charles Frankel prize, 1993, Centennial medal Harvard U., 1994; Disting. Svc. award in edn. Inst. Internat. Edn., 1994. Fellow Am. Acad. Arts and Scis.; mem. Renaissance Soc. Am., Am. Philos. Soc. (Jefferson medal 1993), Nat. Acad. Edn., Coun. Fgn. Rels. Chgo., Coun. on Fgn. Rels. N.Y. (bd. dirs.), Phi Beta Kappa (vis. scholar 1971-72). Office: U Chgo Dept History 1126 E 59th St Chicago IL 60637-1580

GRAY, JENNIFER FRANCINE, photographer, illustrator; b. Kansas City, Oct. 20, 1956; d. James Franklin and Mary Jane (Stevenson) G.; m. Harold Whitehurst Jr., Dec. 26, 1981 (div. 1983); 1 child, Jesse James. BA in Liberal Arts, The Evergreen State Coll., 1989. Portrait studio mgr. JC Penney Co., Seattle, 1989-91; owner, operator Cove Gallery, Shelton, Wash., 1991-93; photographer, illustrator GrayWorks, Lilliwaup, Wash., 1993—. Chmn. Shelton (Wash.) Arts Commn., 1991-94. Mem. Peninsula Art Assn. (mem. bd. 1991-95). Home: P O Box 1150 Hoodsport WA 98548

GRAY, KARLA MARIE, state supreme court justice. BA, Western Mich. U., MA in African History; JD, U. Calif., San Francisco, 1976. Bar: Mont. 1976, Calif. 1977. Law clk. to Hon. W. D. Murray U.S. Dist. Ct., 1976-77; staff atty. Atlantic Richfield Co., 1977-81; pvt. practice law Butte, Mont., 1981-84; staff atty., legis. lobbyist Mont. Power Co., Butte, 1984-91; justice Supreme Ct. Mont., Helena, 1991—. Mem. Mont. Supreme Ct. Gender Fairness Task Force. Fellow Am. Bar Found., Am. Judicature Soc., Internat. Women's Forum; mem. State Bar Mont., Silver Bow County Bar Assn. (past pres.), Nat. Assn. Women Judges. Office: Supreme Ct Mont Justice Bldg Rm 323 215 N Sanders St Helena MT 59601-4522

GRAY, KATHERINE, marriage and family counselor and support therapist; b. Los Angeles, July 6, 1941; d. Edward David and Marjorie Ross; m. Daniel C. Gray, Feb. 5, 1965; children: Michael, Lisa. BA, Calif. State U., Sacramento, 1983, MS in Edn. Cons. and Counseling, 1987, MS in Sch. Counseling. Instr. Shasta Coll., Redding, Calif., 1965-69; owner Water Ojai Valley Chapel, Ojai, Calif., 1971-77, Lipp & Sullivan, Marysville, Calif., 1977—; instr. Yuba Coll., 1988—; pres. Interagy. Council, 1988—; cons. and organizer various community outreach programs in edn. Contbr. articles to profl. jours. and newspapers. County coordinator, bd. dirs. Am. Cancer Soc., Marysville, 1980—; mem. exec. com., bd. dirs., com. chairperson Gateway Projects, Yuba City, Calif., 1980—; bd. dirs. Mercy Guild, Yuba City, 1980—, Easter Seals; past bd. dirs., com. chairperson Campfire Inc., Yuba City and Morro Bay, Calif., 1979-80; past pres. Ojai Valley-Oxnard Symphony Orch. Assn., Ventura County, Calif., 1975; Sacramento focus program coordinator 4-H, Yuba and Sutter Counties, 1985—; exec. officer, bd. dirs. Gateway Projects, 1985-87; pres. Interagy. Council of Yuba & Sutter Counties, 1988—. Mem. Calif. Funeral Dirs. Assn. (mem. legis. bd. com., edn., ethics and mem. bd. com.), Calif. Assn. for Counseling and Devel., Sacramento Area Gifted Assn., Children's Home Soc. (chpt. bd. sec.). Lodges: Soroptimists (past bd. dirs.), Rainbow for Girls (pres., bd. dirs. 1985-87). Avocations: music, art, travel, historical studies. Home: PO Box 611 Yuba City CA 95992-0611 Office: PO Box 148 629 D St Marysville CA 95901-5527

GRAY, KATHERINE HARRIS, commercial banker; b. Durham, N.C., May 18, 1962; d. A. Brooks and Margaret Marie (Rees) Harris; m. James William Gray, June 16, 1984; children: Allison Rees Gray. BA, U. Pa., 1984, MA, 1984. Credit analyst, jr. lender Wilmington (Del.) Trust Co., 1987-89; br. mgr., lender Madison Bank of Md., Silver Spring, 1989-90; HUD multi-br. mgr. First Am. Bank, Silver Spring, 1990-93; comml. lender Citizens Bank of Md., Laurel, 1993—; rep. Montgomery County Bankers Small Bus. Loan Fund, Bethesda, Md., 1994—; rep. Prince Georges Econ. Revitalization Loan Fund, Landover, Md., 1993—; tchr. Mid-Atlantic chpt. Am. Inst. Banking, 1990—. Pres. The Dwelling Place, Gaithersburg, Md., 1990—. Mem. Greater Gaithersburg C. of C., Rotary Club (treas.). Quaker. Office: Citizens Bank of Md 6410 Rockledge Dr Bethesda MD 20814

GRAY, KATHERINE WILSON, newspaper editor; b. Sumter, S.C., Aug. 23, 1940; d. Thomas III and Suzanne Barden (Winstead) Wilson; m. Kermit S. King (div. 1980); children: Suzanne E., John D.; m. Robert Faulkner Gray II, July 14, 1990. AB in Journalism cum laude, U. N.C., 1961. Reporter Charlotte (N.C.) Observer, 1961-62; advt. and news copywriter Sta. WWOK-FM, Charlotte, 1962-63; advt. copywriter Belk, Charlotte, 1963-64; asst. dir. pub. rels. Winthrop Coll., Rock Hill, S.C., 1964-67; exec. women's editor The State and Columbia (S.C.) Record, 1968-69, reporter, 1979-84; assoc. editl. page editor Columbia Record, 1984-87, editl. page editor, 1987-88; assoc. editl. page editor The State, Columbia, 1988—. Bd. dirs. Greater Columbia Fighting Back Task Force against Alcohol and Drug Abuse, 1990—, Columbia Commn. Children and Youth, 1992-95. Recipient Blue Cross-Blue Shield award, 1981, Media Person of Yr. award Animal Protection League, 1989; Tribute to Women in Industry honoree YWCA Midlands, 1991. Mem. Nat. Fedn. Press Women (award 1992), Nat. Conf. Editl. Writers, Media Women S.C. (award, Media Woman of Yr. 1987), S.C. Press

Assn. (10 awards 1980-94), Columbia Media Club, Summit Club, Phi Beta Kappa, Kappa Tau Alpha. Home: 124 Sims Ave Columbia SC 29205 Office: The State Record Co Inc PO Box 1333 Columbia SC 29202-1333

GRAY, LOIS SPIER, labor relations educator, consultant; b. St. Louis, Oct. 17, 1923; d. Charles and Mae (Imboden) Spier; m. Edward Franklin Gray (dec. July 1995). BA, Park Coll., 1943; MA, U. Buffalo, 1955; PhD, Columbia U., 1965; LLD (hon.), Park Coll., 1991. Economic analyst U.S. Mil Intelligence, Washington, 1944-45; field examiner Nat. Labor Rels. Bd., Buffalo, 1945-46; dir. we. dist. N.Y. State Sch. Indsl. and Labor Rels. Cornell U., 1947-56, dir. met. N.Y. State Sch. Indsl. and Labor Rels., 1956-76, prof. N.Y. State Sch. Indsl. and Labor Rels., 1974—, assoc. dean N.Y. State Sch. Indsl. and Labor Rels., 1976-88; cons. ednl. instns. in U.S. and abroad on curriculum design and evaluation; chair N.Y. State Apprenticeship and Tng. Coun., 1975-96. Author: Socio-Economic Profiles of Puerto Rican New Yorkers, 1976; author, editor: Under the Stars: Labor Relations in Arts and Entertainment, 1996; contbr. articles to profl. jours. Recipient Labor Edn. award N.Y. State AFL-CIO, 1995, Hispanic Labor Com., 1993. Mem. Indsl. Rels. Rsch. Assn. (nat. exec. bd. 1980-84), Labor History Assn. (Labor Edn. award 1985, OSHA award 1988), Univ. and Coll. Labor Edn. Assn. (nat. pres. 1965-67), N.Y. Occupl. Safety and Health Assn., Ams. for Dem. Action (Social Justice award 1979), Wagner Archives (bd. dirs.). Home: 3 Washington Square Village New York NY 10012 Office: Cornell Univ 16 E 34th St New York NY 10016

GRAY, MARGARET ANN, management educator, consultant; b. Junction City, Kans., Sept. 19, 1950; d. Carl Ray and Mayme Louise (Kopmeyer) G.; m. Dennis Wayne Stokes, June 9, 1973 (div. July 1981); m. Robert Frederick Carlson Jr., Nov. 21, 1987. BEd, Pittsburg State U., Kans., 1972; MBA, Wichita State U., 1981. Tchr., Sch. Dist. 1, Kansas City, Mo., 1972-73; tchr. Haysville Sch. Dist., Kans., 1974-81, dist. coord., 1979-81; instr. mgmt. Wichita State U., 1981-85; mgmt. devel. rep. Beech Aircraft Corp. a Raytheon Co., Wichita, 1985-87, mgr. mgmt. devel. and tng., 1988-91; tng. and devel. coord. MIT, Cambridge, 1991—; cons. Dartnell Inst., Chgo., 1983—; assoc. dir. Ctr. for Entrepreneurship, Wichita State U., 1984-85. Bd. dirs. Kans. Found. for partnerships in Edn., 1986—; mem. speaker's bur. United Way, 1986—, vol. tng. dir., 1987—, tng. com., 1987—, top leadership cabinet, 1989; bd. dirs. Kans. Literacy Group, 1989, Sedgwick County div. Am. Heart Assn., 1990; active Leadership 2000. Named Outstanding Young Alumnus Pitts. State U., 1991. Mem. ASTD (bd. dirs. Sunflower chpt.), Wichita C. of C. (bus. edn. success team 1988—), Rotary, Beta Gamma Sigma. Democrat. Roman Catholic. Club: Turnip (Wichita). Avocations: ballet, cross country skiing, classical music, hot air ballooning.

GRAY, NANCY ANN OLIVER, college administrator; b. Dallas, Apr. 23, 1951; d. Howard Ross and Joan (Dawkins) Oliver; m. Doyle P. Gray, Nov. 24, 1973 (div. Jan. 1985); children: Paul, Jeff, Scott; m. David Nelson Maxson, Oct. 5, 1985. BA, Vanderbilt U., 1973; MEd, North Tex. State U., 1975; postgrad., Vanderbilt U., 1976-79. Cert. fund raising exec. Tchr. Highland Park High Sch., Dallas, 1973-75; chmn. drama dept. Harpeth Hall Sch., Nashville, 1975-77; assoc. dir. devel. Vanderbilt U., Nashville, 1977-78, assist. dean students, 1978-80; dir. spl. gifts U. Louisville, 1982-86; dir. major gifts Oberlin (Ohio) Coll., 1986-90; dir. capital programs The Lawrenceville (N.J.) Sch., 1990-91; v.p. devel. and univ. rels. Rider U., Lawrenceville, 1991—; bd. dirs. Jr. Achievement Ctrl. N.J.; cons. United Way, Cleve., 1988-90, Oberlin Coll., 1990, Princeton Project '55, 1992-93; guest lectr. Vanderbilt U., Nashville, 1987-88. Trustee Oberlin Libr., 1989, Oberlin Sch. Endowment Bd., 1988-90, Oberlin Early Childhood Ctr., 1986-88, Vanderbilt U., Nashville, 1973-77; bd. dirs. Vanderbilt U. Alumni Assn., Nashville, 1984-85, George Washington coun. Boy Scouts Am., 1996—; mem. Jr. League, 1984-89, various coms. Named Outstanding Young Woman of Am., 1982, Outstanding Woman Achievement, Lorain County (Ohio) YWCA, 1988. Mem. Nat. Soc. Fund-Raising Execs. (pres. Louisville chpt. 1985-86), Coun. for Advancement Support to Edn. (conf. presenter). Home: 32 Laurel Wood Dr Trenton NJ 08648-1000 Office: Rider U Trenton NJ 08648-0125

GRAY, PHYLLIS ANNE, librarian; b. Boston, Jan. 2, 1926; d. George Joseph and Eleanor (Morrison) G. Ph.B., Barry Coll., 1947, M.B.A., 1979; MS in Libr. Sci., Cath. U. Am., 1950. Librarian U.S. Air Force Base, Miami, Fla., 1952-53; asst. librarian Brockway Meml. Library, Miami Shores, Fla., 1953-55; head librarian North Miami Pub. Library, 1955-59; supervising librarian Santa Clara County Library, San Jose, Calif., 1959-61; library dir. City of Commerce (Calif.) Pub. Library, 1961-68; adminstrv. librarian Miami Dade Pub. Library, 1969-76; library dir. Miami Beach (Fla.) Pub. Library, 1978-86; dir. Surf-Bal Bay Pub. Library, Surfside, Fla., 1987-91; Democrat. Roman Catholic. Councilwoman Bal Harbour Village, 1979-83; treas. Women in Govt. Service, 1981-86, pres., 1988-89. Mem. ALA, Am. Soc. Pub. Adminstrn., Fla. Library Assn., Barry U. Alumni Assn., Fla. Pub. Library Assn. Democrat. Roman Catholic. Club: Pilot (rec. sec. 1981-82, pres. 1982-83). Home: 54 Park Dr Apt 6 Bal Harbour FL 33154-1344

GRAY, SANDRA RAE, retired secondary school educator; b. East Palestine, Ohio, Nov. 8, 1932; d. Kenneth Ray Morris and Nina Olivia (Jamsen) Rex; m. Donald Noel Gray Jr., Nov. 9, 1951; children: Pamela, Donald, Douglas. BA in speech communications, Calif. State U., 1967, MA in speech communications, 1974. Tchr. Tustin (Calif.) Unif. Sch. Dist., 1971-95, ret., 1995; tchr. Riverside (Calif.) Sch. Dist., 1968-71; teaching asst. U. Souther Calif., L.A., 1974-77; tchr. Saddleback Coll., Mission Viejo, Calif., 1982-84, Calif. State U., L.A., 1976. Pres. adv. coun. annual fund Calif. State U., 1992-95; pres. Calif. State Speech Coun., 1976-78; chmn. Nat. Forensic League (Big Orange Chpt.), Ripon, Wis., 1992-93. Recipient Calif. State Speech Coun. Hall of Fame Calif. H.S. Speech Assn., 1982. Mem. AAUW. Republican. Protestant. Home: 13671 Falmouth Dr Tustin CA 92680

GRAY, SHEILA HAFTER, psychiatrist, psychoanalyst; b. N.Y.C., Oct. 19, 1930; m. Oscar Shalom Gray, Apr. 8, 1967. MD, Harvard U., 1958. cert. Washington Psychoanalytic Inst., 1969. Intern St. Elizabeths Hosp., Washington, 1958-59; resident McLean Hosp., Belmont, Mass., 1959-61; clin. and rsch. fellow Mass. Gen. Hosp., Boston, Mass., 1961-62; staff psychiatrist Chestnut Lodge, Inc., Rockville, Md., 1962-64; practice medicine, specializing in psychiatry and psychoanalysis Washington, 1964—; clin. asst. prof. psychiatry U. Md. Sch. Medicine, Balt., 1968-75, clin. assoc. prof., 1975-83, clin. prof., 1983—; instr. Washington Psychoanalytic Inst., 1971-75, tchg. analyst, 1975-96; tchg. analyst Balt.-Washington Inst. for Psychoanalysis, 1996—; mem. staff U. Md. Hosp., Balt.; physician mem. Commn. on Mental Health, Superior Ct. of D.C., 1972—; bd. govs. Nat. Capital Reciprocal Ins. Co., 1981—; treas. NCRIC Physicians Orgn., 1994—; cons. Walter Reed Army Med. Ctr., Washington, 1983—. Mem. Mayor's Adv. Com. on Mental Health Svcs. Reorgn., Washington, 1984; mem. adv. panel for Mayor's Environ. Design Awards Program, 1988-89; mem. exec. com. D.C. Fedn. Civic Assns., 1984—, asst. rec. sec., 1985, rec. sec., 1986-88, 2d v.p., 1989-90, pres., 1991-92, del.-at-large, 1993—; v.p. programs Women's Equity Action League Met. D.C., 1986; commr. D.C. Adv. Neighborhood Commn., 1986-88; mem. Met. Washington Coun. of Govt.'s Partnership for Regional Excellence, 1992—. Fellow Am. Psychiat. Assn. (chair com. quality assurance and improvement, Coun. on Econ. Affairs, 1996—); mem. Am. Psychoanalytic Assn. (diplomate Bd. Profl. Stds.), Am. Acad. Psychoanalysis (trustee 1996—), Washington Psychiatric Soc. (councillor 1981-83), Med. Soc. D.C. (exec. bd. 1982, ho. dels. 1992—), Washington Psychoanalytic Soc. (chmn. bd. dirs. psychoanalytic clinic and councillor ex officio 1987-90), Palisades Citizens Assn. (bd. dirs. 1980—, treas. 1983-84, pres. 1984-86). Office: PO Box 40612 Palisades Sta Washington DC 20016

GRAY, VIRGINIA HICKMAN, political science educator; b. Camden, Ark., June 10, 1945; d. George Leonard and Ethel Massengale (Bell) Hickman; m. Charles Melvin Gray, Oct. 16, 1944; 1 child, Brian Charles. BA with honors, Hendrix Coll., 1967; MA, Washington U., St. Louis, 1969, PhD, 1972. Asst. prof. polit. sci. U. Ky., Lexington, 1971-73; from asst. prof. to assoc. prof. U. Minn., Mpls., 1973-83, prof., 1983—, chairperson dept. polit. sci., 1985-88; guest scholar Brookings Inst., Washington, 1977-78; vis. prof. U. Oslo, 1985, U. B.C., 1992, U. N.C., 1993-94; NSF vis. prof. for women, 1993-94. Co-author: The Organizational Politics of Criminal Justice, 1980, Feminism and the New Right, 1983, Politics in the American States, 1983, 6th edit., 1996, American States and Cities, 1991, The Population Ecology of Interest Representation, 1996. Bd. dirs. Group Health Inc., 1992-98. Fellow Woodrow Wilson Found., 1970, NDEA, 1969-70; grantee Swedish Bicentennial Found., 1985; recipient rsch. assistantship NSF, 1968-69. Mem. Am. Polit. Sci. Assn. (coun. 1991-92), Midwest Polit. Sci. Assn. (coun. 1984-86), Policy Studies Orgn. (coun. 1977-79). Democrat. Unitarian. Home: 1776 Pinehurst Ave Saint Paul MN 55116-2117 Office: U Minn Dept Polit Sci 1414 Soc Sci Bldg Minneapolis MN 55455

GRAY, YVETTE LYNN, human resources executive; b. Tokyo, July 29, 1967; 1 child, Markus Kendall Allen; m. Jeffery L. Gray. BS, Bowie State U., 1991. Cert. profl. in human resources. Employee rels. supr. Computer Scis. Corp., Calverton, Md., 1991—. Mem. Nat. Mgmt. Assn., Soc. for Human Resources Mgmt., Washington Tech. Pers. Forum. Democrat. Baptist. Home: 6247 Figtree Ct Beltsville MD 20705 Office: Computer Sciences Corp 4061 Powder Mill Rd Calverton MD 20705

GRAY-BUSSARD, DOLLY H., energy company executive; b. Wilmington, Del., July 29, 1943; d. Henry Odell and Dorothy (Knotts) Gray; m. Robert William Bussard, Mar. 17, 1981; stepchildren: Elise Bright, William Bussard, Robert L. Bussard, Virginia B. Barausky. BA in History and English Lit., U. Calif., San Diego, 1984; MA in History, Georgetown U., 1990. Coord. Orgn. Human Devel., San Diego, 1977-78; owner, prin. Hello Dolly, La Jolla, Calif., 1978-80; ptnr. Linda Chester Lit. Agy., La Jolla, 1978-80; owner, pres. Unicorn Literary Agy., La Jolla, 1980-85; pres., chmn. bd. Energy/Matter Conversion Corp., Manassas Park, Va., 1988—; vis. lectr. writers' confs. U. Calif., San Diego, 1979-81. Co-author: The Best of San Diego, 1981. Mem. NAFE, Am. Hist. Assn., Cosmos Club, Phi Alpha Theta. Episcopalian. Office: EMC2 8505 Euclid Ave #3 Manassas Park VA 20111

GRAY-LITTLE, BERNADETTE, psychologist; b. Washington, N.C., Oct. 21, 1944; d. James and Rosalie (Lanier) Gray; m. Shade Keys Little, Nov. 21, 1971; children—Maura, Mark. Asst. prof. psychology, U. N.C.-Chapel Hill, 1971-76, assoc. prof., 1976-82, prof., 1982—, chair dept., 1993—. NIMH fellow, 1967-68; Fulbright fellow, 1970-71; NRC fellow, 1982-83. Fellow Am. Psychol. Assn.; mem. Phi Beta Kappa. Office: U NC Psychology Dept Cb # 3270 Chapel Hill NC 27599

GRAY-NIX, ELIZABETH WHITWELL, occupational therapist; b. Milton, Mass., Apr. 9, 1956; d. Roland and Susan (Brooks) Gray; m. Ronald Harding Nix; 1 child, Roger Harrison Nix. BS, Utica Coll. of Syracuse U., N.Y., 1978. Reg. occupational therapist. Staff occupational therapist Walter E. Fernald State Sch., Waltham, Mass., 1978-82; head occupational therapist Walter E. Fernald State Sch., 1982-84, clin. supr., 1984—. Trustee Mass. Jaycees Charitable Trust, Mansfield, 1983-91; dir.-at-large South End Hist. Soc., Boston, 1983-85, fundraising dir., 1985-87; alumni rep. Beaver country Day Sch., Brookline, 1974—, alumni sec., 1988-94. 0ecipient Baystater award #060, Mass. Jaycees, 1984, Armbruster Keyman award, 1981, Award of Merit, Maddak, Inc., 1991, 96, Jaycee Internat. Senatorship award, 1992. Mem. Mass. Occupational Therapists Assn., State Employed Occupational Therapists Assn. (union rep.), Am. Occupational Therapists Assn., World Fedn. Occupational Therapists, Jaycees Internat. (Mass. sec., pres. Riverside chpt. 1983, mem. coun. Newton chpt. 1979-82, state sec. 1994-95), Boston Ctr. for Arts (mem. coun. 1979-84). Home: 90 Pelham Island Rd Sudbury MA 01776-3132 Office: Walter E Fernald Devel Ctr 200 Trapelo Rd Waltham MA 02154-6332

GRAYSON, GRACE RIETHMULLER, teacher, consultant; b. Johannesburg, Transvaal, South Africa, Apr. 21, 1917; came to U.S., 1946; d. Frederick Edward Christian and Martha Johanna (Broodrijk) Riethmuller; m. Lincoln Blaisdell Grayson, Nov. 10, 1946; children: David Arthur, Guy. Student, Tchrs. Coll., 1934; cert. tchr., U. Calif., Berkeley, 1969; student, Diablo Valley Coll., Berkeley, 1978-83. Master judge emeritus flower shows and landscape design. Supr. revenue posting dept. NSW Tramways, Sydney, Australia, 1939-46; freelance writer Australia and U.S.A., 1945-57; columnist Cooma (Australia)-Monaro Express, 1953-57; corr. Australian Broadcasting Commn., Sydney, 1954-57; pvt. practice crafts instr. Pleasant Hill, Calif., 1962-64; class instr. floral design Woolworths, Walnut Creek, Calif., 1966-69; tchr. arts and crafts Mt. Diablo (Calif.) Unified Sch. Dist., 1965-73; ret., 1973; curator accessories Mus. Fashion, Lafayette, Calif., 1987—; cons. in field. Contbr. articles to profl. jours. Benefactor Heather Farms Garden Ctr., Walnut Creek; supporting mem. Berkeley Repertory Theatre, 1975—; fundraiser Alexander Lindsay Mus. Natural History, Walnut Creek, 1981—. Mem. Fan Assn. N.Am. (pres. 1986-88, chmn. rsch. com. 1988—), Fan Circle Internat. (corr.), Assn. Culturale "Il Ventaglio," Bologna (Italy) (hon. mem.), East Bay Fan Guild, Walnut Creek Civic Arts Assn., Diablo Women's Garden Club, Calif. Garden Clubs Inc. (life). Democrat. Episcopalian. Home: 2133 Pine Knoll Dr Apt 16 Walnut Creek CA 94595-2187

GRAYSON, PAULA S., biofeedback clinician, mental health nurse; b. Louisville, Ky., Nov. 20, 1953; d. Paul and Joan Lee (Schoenbachler) Dickerson; m. W. Paul Grayson, July 29, 1978; children: Alaina Brock, Benton Paul,. Nursing ad., Jefferson C.C., U. Ky., Louisville, 1973; BA in Psychology, U. Mo., Kansas City, 1988, MA in Psychology, 1991. Cert. Biofeedback Clinician, Biofeedback Certification Inst. Am.; RN, Ky. Nurse med., surg., ICU St. Joseph's Infirmary, Louisville, Ky., 1973-75; recovery room nurse Louisville Gen. Hosp., 1975-77; ICU supr. Charity Hosp., New Orleans, 1977-79; mgr. surg. ward City of Memphis Hosp., 1979-81; prn. float, supr. Trinity Luth. Hosp., Kansas City, Mo., 1981-89; mental health nurse Trinity Luth. N., Kansas City, 1992-94; clinician Biofeedback North, Kansas City, Mo., 1994; biofeedback clinician, 1994—. Mem. Assn. Applied Psychophysiology and Biofeedback, Psi Chi. Episcopalian. Office: Biofeedback North Ste H 3805 N Oak Kansas City MO 64116

GRAYSON, TELMA M., lawyer; b. Cuba, Sept. 10, 1965. BA, NYU, 1987; JD, Boston Coll., 1990. Bar: N.Y. 1991, U.S. Dist. Ct. (so. and ea. dists.) N.Y. 1994. Ptnr. Anderson Kill Olick & Oshinsky, P.C., N.Y.C. Mem. ABA, N.Y. State Bar Assn. Office: Anderson Kill Olick & Oshinsky PC 1251 Ave of the Americas New York NY 10020-1182*

GRAZIANI, LINDA ANN, secondary education educator; b. Erie, Pa., Aug. 16, 1951; d. Edward and Christine (Karsznia) Grzelak; m. Richard Martin Graziani, Aug. 4, 1973; 1 child, Kristen Lynn. BS, Pa. State U., 1973; MBA, Gannon U., 1978. Asst. twsp. sec. Lawrence Park Twsp., Erie, Pa., 1968-73; bus. edn. tchr. Millcreek Sch. Dist., Erie, 1973-74, Fairview (Pa.) Sch. Dist., 1974-76, 83—, Girard (Pa.) Sch. Dist., 1976; adult edn. instr. Erie (Pa.) County Tech. Sch., 1978-85; active Bus. Adv. Coun., Millcreek, Pa., 1994—. Bd. dirs. Lake Erie Jr. Women's Club, Erie, 1977-83, St. Stephen's Preschool, Fairview, 1982-83; eucharistic min. Holy Cross Ch., Fairview, 1982—. Mem. Nat. Bus. Edn. Assn., Pa. State Edn. Assn., Pa. Bus. Edn. Assn., Erie County Bus. Edn. Assn., Inst. Mgmt. Accts., Phi Chi Theta. Democrat. Roman Catholic. Home: 680 Hawthorne Trce Fairview PA 16415-1723 Office: Fairview HS 7460 Mccray Rd Fairview PA 16415-2401

GRAZIANO, CATHERINE ELIZABETH, nursing educator; b. Providence, Dec. 2, 1931; d. William J. and Catherine E. (Keegan) Hawkins; m. Louis W. Graziano, Oct. 9, 1954; children—Mary Lou, William F., Catherine E., Paul, Carol. B.S., Salve Regina Coll., Newport, R.I., 1949-53, M.S., Salve Regina Coll., 1984; M.S., Boston Coll., 1965; PhD, Pacific Western U., 1988. Instr. nursing Salve Regina U., 1953-66, asst. prof., 1966-74, assoc. prof., 1974-82, prof., 1982—, chair dept. nursing, 1974-93; staff-charge nurse St. Joseph's Hosp., Providence, 1953-93, part-time faculty, 1960, 65; mem. R.I. Bd. Nurse Registration and Edn., 1970-79, pres., 1977-79; charter mem., sec. R.I. Health, Sci. and Edn. Council, 1972-78; adj. asst. prof. Coll. Nursing U. R.I., 1986—; mem. R.I. State Senate, 1992—. Active local and nat. senatorial campaigns. Mem. R.I. Nurses Assn. (pres. 1969-71, 73-75), Am. Nurses Assn., Women Educators (charter), Nursing Leadership Council R.I. (charter; chair 1981-82, sec. 1982—), Nat. League Nursing (accreditation site visitor 1990—), Sigma Theta Tau (R.I. State senator 1992—). Roman Catholic. Home: 42 Rowley St Providence RI 02909-5521 Office: Salve Regina U Ochre Point Ave Newport RI 02840

GREASER, CONSTANCE UDEAN, automotive industry executive; b. San Diego, Jan. 18, 1938; d. Lloyd Edward and Udean Greaser. BA, San Diego State Coll., 1959; postgrad. U. Copenhagen Grad. Sch. Fgn. Students, 1963, Georgetown U. Sch. Fgn. Service, 1967; MA, U. So. Calif., 1968; Exec. MBA, UCLA, 1981. Advt., publicity mgr. Crofton Co., San Diego, 1959-62; supr. Mercury Publs., Fullerton, Calif., 1962-64; supr. engring. support services div. Arcata Data Mgmt., Hawthorne, Calif., 1964-67; mgr. computerized typesetting dept. Continental Graphics, Los Angeles, 1967-70; v.p., editorial dir. Sage Publs., Inc., Beverly Hills, Calif., 1970-74; head publs. RAND Corp., Santa Monica, Calif., 1974-90; mgr. communications Am. Honda Motors Co., Torrance, Calif., 1990—. Mem. nat. com. Million Minutes of Peace Appeal, 1986, Nat. Info. Standards Orgn., 1987-93, nat. com. Global Cooperation for Better World, 1988. Recipient Berber award Graphic Arts Tech. Found., 1989. Mem. Women in Bus. (pres. 1977-78), Graphic Comm. Assn. (bd. dirs. 1994—), N.Am. Environ. Task Group, Soc. for Scholarly Pubs. (nat. bd. dirs.), Women in Communication, Soc. Tech. Communication, Brahma Kumaris World Spiritual Orgn. Co-author: Quick Writer-Build Your Own Word Processing Users Guide, 1983; Quick Writer-Word Processing Center Operations Manual, 1984; editor: Urban Research News, 1970-74; mng. editor Comparative Polit. Studies, 1971-74; contbr. articles to various jours. Office: Am Honda Motor Co 1919 Torrance Blvd Torrance CA 90501-2722

GREATHOUSE, FRANCES MARY WAGNER, elementary education educator; b. Shippenville, Pa., May 13, 1944; d. Arthur Martin and Frances Mary (Kurtzhals) Wagner; m. E. John Greathouse, June 14, 1969; children: Trisha Ann, Todd Jacob, Jason Michael. BS in Elem. Edn./Speech Correction, Clarion U., 1968; cert. in religion studies, Mercyhurst Coll., 1994. Cert. elem. edn. and speech correction, Pa. Speech therapist Venango County Intermediate Unit VI, Franklin, Pa., 1968-72; substitute tchr. Valley Grove Schs., Crawford Ctrl. Schs., Meadville, Pa., 1973-90; homebound instrn. Crawford Ctrl. Schs., Meadville, 1990, first grade tchr., 1991-92, substitute tchr., 1992-93, 93, 94, permanent substitute tchr. grade 2, 1994, 95—; cons. Erie (Pa.) Cath. Diocese, 1984—. V.p. pastoral coun., guild mem. Our Lady of Lourdes Ch., Cochranton, Pa., 1994. Named Catechist of Yr., Erie (Pa.) Cath. Diocese, 1982. Mem. NEA, Pa. State Edn. Assn. Democrat. Home: 25511 Oak Dr Cochranton PA 16314-9029

GREATHOUSE, PATRICIA DODD, retired psychometrist, counselor; b. Columbus, Ga., Apr. 26, 1935; d. John Allen and Patricia Ottis (Murphy) Dodd; m. Robert Otis Greathouse; children: Mark Andrew, Perry Allen. BS in Edn., Auburn (Ala.) U., 1959, M in Edn., 1966, AA in Counselor Edn., 1975. Cert. secondary tchr., Ala., Ga. Tchr. Columbus High Sch., 1959-61, Phenix City Bd. Edn., 1957-58; tchr. pub. schs. Russell County (Ala.) Bd. Edn., Phenix City and Seale, 1961-69, 71-80, 82-83, counselor pub. schs., 1969-82, 83-93; psychometrist Russell County (Ala.) Bd. Edn., Seale, 1980-82; county psychometrist Russell County (Ala.) Bd. Edn., Phenix City, 1983-93. Editor: (ann.) Tiger Tales, 1973 (award 1980). Treas. Ladonia PTA, Phenix City, 1966-68, parliamentarian, 1987-88; leader Ladonia chpt. 4-H Club, Phenix City, 1961-80; active March of Dimes, Am. Heart Assn.; rep. Mardi Gras; tchr. Sunday Sch., Vacation Bible Sch. N. Phenix Bapt. Ch.; vol. Reach to Recovery Am. Cancer Soc., 1980—. Named Mardi Gras Queen Phenix City Moose Club, 1987, hon. life mem. Ladonia PTA, 1967, Outstanding Tchr. of Yr., 1972; recipient Silver Clover award 4-H Club, 1966, Outstanding PTA Performance award 1986-87; nominated to Tchr. Hall of Fame, 1980-81, 81-82, 82-83. Mem. NEA, AARP, Russell County Edn. Assn. (pres.-elect 1973), Ala. Edn. Assn., Ala. Pers. and Guidance Assn., Ala. Assn. Counseling and Devel., Coun. Exceptional Children, Am. Bus. Women's Assn. (pres. Phenix City charter chpt. 1986-87, Woman of Yr. 1987, Perfect Attendance award, treas. 1990-95, sec. 1995—, tri-county coun.), Daus. of Nile (pres. Phenix City club 1980-81, 83-84, Outstanding Svc. award, sec. 1994—), Ret. Tchrs. Assn. (ctrl. sr. activities ctr. 1993, sr. citizens' sec. 1993), Muscogee County Geneal. Soc., Jetettes (v.p. Phenix City club 1976, 80), Jaycettes, Order of Eastern Star (worthy matron 1981-82), Riverview Sr. Citizens, Delta Kappa Gamma (sec. 1979-80, pres. 1990-94), Kappa Iota. Democrat. Baptist. Home: 1502 Nottingham Dr Phenix City AL 36867-1941

GREAUX, CHERYL PREJEAN, federal agency administrator; b. Houston, July 30, 1949; m. Robert Bruce Greaux. BA, Tex. So. U., 1967; MA, U. Tex., 1973. Mgr. compliance programs Dept. Labor, N.Y.C., 1973-80; corp. human resources mgr. Allied Signal Inc., Morristown, N.J., 1980-85; account exec., sourcing specialist Dean Witter Reynolds, N.Y.C., 1986-88; dir. civil rights staff USDA Rural Devel., Washington, 1994—; cons. Gen. Foods, White Plains, N.Y., 1985, Seagrams, N.Y.C., 1984. Author: Struggling Within or Success from Within? 1973. Lectr. Nat. Urban League, 1980—; cons. Nat. Urban Affairs Coun., N.Y., 1981-86; bd. dirs. Ednl. Opportunity Fund, N.J., 1985-87. Mem. Edges Group, Delta Sigma Theta. Baptist. Home: 6323 Summer Day Ct Burke VA 22015 Office: Dept Agr 14th and Independence SW Washington DC 20250

GREAVER, JOANNE HUTCHINS, mathematics educator, author; b. Louisville, Aug. 9, 1939; d. Alphonso Victor and Mary Louise (Sage) Hutchins; 1 child, Mary Elizabeth. BS in Chemistry, U. Louisville, 1961, MEd, 1971; MAT in Math., Purdue U., 1973. Cert. tchr. secondary edn. Specialist math Jefferson County (Ky.) Pub. Schs., 1962—; part-time faculty Bellarmine Coll., Louisville, 1982—, U. Louisville, 1985—; project reviewer NSF, 1983—; advisor Council on Higher Edn., Frankfort, Ky., 1983-86; active regional and nat. summit on assessment in math., 1991, state task force on math., assessment adv. com., Nat. Assessment Ednl. Progress standards com.; lectr. in field. Author: (workbook) Down Algebra Alley, 1984; co-author curriculum guides. Charter mem. Commonwealth Tchrs. Inst., 1984—; mem. Nat. Forum for Excellence in Edn., Indpls., 1983; metric edn. leader Fed. Metric Project, Louisville, 1979-82; mem. Ky. Ednl. Reform Task Force, Assessment Com., Math. Framework, Nat. Nat. Assessment Ednl. Progress Rev. Com. Recipient Presdl. award for excellence in math. teaching, 1983; named Outstanding Citizen, SAR, 1984, mem. Hon. Order Ky. Cols.; grantee NSF, 1983, Louisville Community Found., 1984-86. Mem. Greater Louisville Council Tchrs. of Math. (pres. 1977-78, 94—, Outstanding Educator award 1987), Nat. Council Tchrs. of Math. (reviewer 1981—), Ky. Coun. Tchrs. of Math. (pres. 1990-91, Jeff County Tchr. of Yr. award 1985), Math. Assn. Am., Kappa Delta Pi, Delta Kappa Gamma, Zeta Tau Alpha. Republican. Presbyterian. Avocations: tropical fish; gardening; handicrafts; travel; tennis. Home: 11513 Tazwell Dr Louisville KY 40241 Office: Gheens Acad 4425 Preston Hwy Louisville KY 40213-2033

GREBEY, NANCY V., bank executive. Sr. v.p. mktg. Crestar Fin. Corp., Richmond, Va., 1994—. Office: Crestar Fin Corp 919 E Main St Richmond VA 23261-6665*

GRECCO, CHERYL ANN, computer educator; b. Hoboken, N.J., July 15, 1966; d. Michael John and Kathleen Rita (Ryan) G. BA in Sociology, Rutgers U., 1988. Cert. elem. tchr., N.J. Jr. H.S. computer tchr. Anna L. Klein Elem. Sch., Guttenberg, N.J., 1988—; girls basketball coach Anna L. Klein Elem. Sch., Guttenberg, N.J., 1991—. Recipient Congl. Tchr.'s scholarship State of N.J., 1986, 87, 88. Mem. NEA, N.J. Edn. Assn., Guttenberg Edn. Assn. (sec. 1994-95, 88—), Hudson-Bergen Athletic League (co-pres.). Office: Anna L Klein Elem Sch 301 69th St Guttenberg NJ 07093

GRECO, ROSEMARIE B., bank executive; b. 1946. Grad. magna cum laude, St. Joseph's U.; LLD (hon.), Temple U. From br. sec.to pres., CEO Fidelity Bank, 1968-91; former chief retail svcs. officer CoreStates Fin. Corp.; former CEO CoreStates 1st Pa. Bank; currently pres., CEO CoreStates Bank, Phila. Office: CoreStates Bank N.A. 1500 Market St Philadelphia PA 19101

GREELEY, GALE ELIZABETH, psychiatrist; b. Portland, Oreg., Sept. 20, 1944; d. Charles Allison and Frances Elizabeth (MacBain) MacArthur; m. Robert Greeley, Jan. 24, 1967 (div. Feb. 1969); m. Burt J. Kempner, June 22, 1980; 1 child, Nathan Daniel. BA, Temple U., 1966; MD, Med. Coll. Pa., 1976. Diplomate Am. Bd. Psychiatry and Neurology. Instr. psychiatry Med. Coll. Pa., Phila., 1979-80; staff psychiatrist St. Elizabeths Hosp., Washington, 1981-85; asst. prof. U. South Fla., Tampa, 1985-88; pvt. practice Tampa, 1987—; staff psychiatrist Mental Health Care, Inc., Tampa, 1992—; asst. prof. George Washington U., Washington, 1983-85; mem. clin. faculty U. So. Fla., Tampa, 1987-94. Mem. Am. Psychiat. Assn., Am. Med. Women's Assn. Democrat.

GREEN, ALLISON ANNE, retired secondary education educator; b. Flint, Mich., Oct. 5, 1936; d. Edwin Stanley and Ruth Allison (Simmons) James; m. Richard Gerring Green, Dec. 23, 1961 (div. Oct. 1969). BA, Albion Coll., 1959; MA, U. Mich., 1978. Cert. tchr., Mich. Tchr. phys. edn. Southwestern High Sch., Flint, 1959-62; tchr. math. Harry Hunt Jr. High Sch., Portsmouth, Va., 1962-63; receptionist Tempcon, Inc., Mpls., 1963-64; tchr. phys. edn. and math. Longfellow Jr. High Sch., Flint, 1964-81, tchr. math., 1981-92, tchr. lang. arts and social studies, 1986-87. Mem. Fair Winds council Girl Scouts U.S., 1943—, leader Lone Troop, Albion, Mich., 1957, sr. tchr. aide adviser, 1964-67; mem. Big Sisters Genesee and Lapeer Counties, 1964-68; mem. adminstrv. bd. Court St. United Meth. Ch., vice chmn. 1995, chmn. 1996—, treas. edn. work area, mission commn., sec. council on ministries, mem. worship com. United Meth. Women Soc. Christian Service, also chmn. meml. com. Mem. NEA, Mich. Edn. Assn., Mich. Assn. Mid. Sch. Educators, United Tchrs. Flint (bldg. rep.), Delta Kappa Gamma (treas. 1982-88, profl. affairs chmn. 1978-80, legis. chmn. 1980-82, pres. 1988-90), Alpha Xi Delta (pres. Flint, alumnae, v.p., treas., corp. pres. Albion Coll., alumnae dir. province 1972-77, Outstanding Sr. Albion Coll. 1959), Embroiderers Guild Am. (sec. 1977-80, maps rep. 1980-82), Phi Delta Kappa (historian 1985-91, treas. 1991-92). Home: 1002 Copeman Blvd Flint MI 48504-7326

GREEN, ANGELA LOUISE, neonatal nurse practitioner; b. Mobile, Ala., Mar. 31, 1963; d. Fred Lawrence and Carlene Floyce (Plemons) Penry; m. Jerril Wayne Green, June 5, 1993; 1 child, Zackary Rayn Eubanks. BS, Auburn U., 1986; MS, U. South Ala., 1993. Cert. RN practioner, Ala., Pa. Staff nurse East Ala. Med. Ctr., Opelika, 1986-87, Mobile Infirmary, 1987-88, U. South Ala. Med. Ctr., Mobile, 1988-89; pediat. cardiology clin. nurse specialist U. South Ala., Mobile, 1989-93, neonatal nurse practioner, 1993-94; neonatal nurse practioner Children's Hosp. Pitts., 1994—. Mem. Nat. Assn. Neonatal Nurses, Three Rivers Assn. Neonatal Nurses, Sigma Theta Tau. Home: 3152 Shady Ave Pittsburgh PA 15217 Office: Childrens Hosp Pitts 3705 Fifth Ave Pittsburgh PA 15213

GREEN, BARBARA STRAWN, psychotherapist; b. Cleve., May 31, 1938; d. Charles Everard and Dorothy Haring (Strawn) G. BA, Pa. State U., 1960; MS, Columbia U., 1962; postgrad. in psychotherapy and psychoanalysis, Postgrad. Ctr. for Mental Health, N.Y.C., 1975. Cert. social worker, N.Y.; lic. social worker, Pa.; cert. Rutgers Summer Sch. Alcoholism Studies, 1982. Social worker VA, N.Y.C., 1962-66; sr. psychiat. social worker in child psychiat. Downstate Med. Ctr., Bklyn., 1966-71; staff therapist Inst. for Contemporary Psychotherapy, N.Y.C., 1971-73; social worker Lower East Side Service Ctr., N.Y.C., 1975-77; intake coordinator alcoholism program Postgrad. Ctr. for Mental Health, N.Y.C., 1981-82; program coordinator Bowery Residents Com., N.Y.C., 1984-86; pvt. practice psychotherapy N.Y.C., 1973—, Dingmans Ferry, Pa., 1994—; sec. alcoholism com. N.Y.C. chpt. NASW, 1987-89. Author: Jogging the Mind, 1995. Participant N.Y.C. Marathon, 1991, 92. Mem. Social Workers Helping Social Workers (chmn. 1982-84).

GREEN, BARBARA-MARIE, publisher, journalist, poet; b. N.Y.C., Mar. 21, 1928; d. James Matthew and Mae (McCarter) G. BA, CCNY, 1951, MA, 1955; ABD, NYU, 1978. Adminstr., tchr. English, 1952-82; tchr. English Newtown High Sch., Elmhurst, Queens, N.Y., 1961; asst. prin. Jr. High Sch. 142, Queens, N.Y., 1963; founder, pub. The "Creative" Record, Virginia Beach, Va., 1988-92; keynote speaker; pres. Bar 'JaMae Comm. Inc. Founder, publisher The Good News, East Elmhurst, N.Y., 1985-88; author: (book of poetry) Dreams and Memories, 1996; contbr. poetry to publs. Ch. and cmty. reporter N.Y. Voice; mem. libr. action com. Corona (N.Y.)-East Elmhurst, Inc.; mem. Langston Hughes Cmty. Libr. and Cultural Ctr., Corona, Harpers Ferry Hist. Assn., Va. Symphony League; mem. Crispus Attucks Theater Restoration Com., Norfolk. Recipient Profl. award Nat. Assn. Negro Bus. and Profl. Women's Club Inc., 1964, Trophy "Career Woman of Yr.", County Line Guild of Career Women, 1967, Cert. of Appreciation Women's Equality Action League, 1978, Antioch Bapt. Ch., 1982, Cert. of merit City of N.Y., 1982, Community Svc. award Arlene of N.Y., 1990, N.Y. State Resolution commemorating the "Good" News, 1985, Participation award Coalition of 100 Black Women, Valuable Service citation Phi Delta Kappa; named Star Among Stars, 1991; named to African-Am. Biographies Hall of Fame, Atlanta, 1994. Mem. Nat. Assn. Negro Musicians (life; bd. dirs. Chgo. 1984-91, ea. region dir. 1990-91), Harpers Ferry Hist. Assn., Poetry Soc. Va., Nat. Assn. Black Journalists, Zonta Internat., Va. Fedn. Bus. and Profl. Women's Clubs (corr. sec. 1992, 1st v.p. 1993, pres. 1993, chair coastal region pub. rels. com. staet level 1994—), N.Y.C. Ret. Suprs. Assn., Chesapeake C. of C., Phi Delta Kappa, Alpha Kappa Alpha. Baptist. Office: Bar JaMae Comm Inc PO Box 64412 Virginia Beach VA 23467-4412

GREEN, BETH INGBER, intuitive practitioner, counselor, musician, composer; b. N.Y.C., Feb. 28, 1945; d. Frank and Lillian Ingber; m. John Ingber Green, 1995. BA, Bklyn. Coll., 1970; MA, UCLA, 1978. Cert. in intuitive consulting, counseling, tchg. and learning, body and kinetic intervention. Spiritual dir. and founder The Stream, L.A., 1980-86; ptnr., co-founder The Healing Partnership, L.A. and Ramona, 1986-90; spiritual dir. and founder The Triple Eye Found., Escondido, Calif., 1990-93; intuitive practitioner, counselor, cons. and tchr. Ramona, 1980—; owner Let's Talk, Ramona, Calif.; spiritual activist, co-founder Rising Mountains Setting Suns, Ramona, 1993-95; co-founder Spiritual Activist Movement, L.A. and Ramona, 1993-95; owner Treehouse Music. Author: The Autobiography of Mary Magdalene, 1988; spoken tapes include: The Healing of God, The Alienation of Love, Spirituality: The Last Block to Freedom, Beyond the Mystery, Sasa in the Clouds; videotapes include Breaking the "I" Barrier, 19. West Coast coord. Wages for Housework Campaign, L.A., 1974-78; co-founder The Looseleaf Directory: Linking Bodies, Minds and Spirits in the Healing Arts, 1994-95.

GREEN, BETTY NIELSEN, education educator, consultant; b. Copenhagen, Apr. 30, 1937; came to U.S., 1979; d. Alfred Christian Josef and Lilly Nielsen; m. Philip Irving Green, Apr. 16, 1962; children: Ruth, Erin, Nils. AA in Fgn. Lang., Daytona Beach C.C., 1981; BA in Liberal Arts, U. Ctrl. Fla., 1986; MS in TESOL, Nova Southeastern U., 1988; EdD in Curriculum and Instrn., U. Ctrl. Fla., 1994. Cert. tchr., Fla.; cert. TESOL trainer, Fla. Tchr. TESOL, program mgr. English Lang. Inst. Daytona Beach C.C., Fla., 1986-91; tchr. TESOL, fgn. lang. specialist Volusia County Schs., Daytona Beach, 1991—; tchr. trainer, facilitator Nova Southeastern U., Ft. Lauderdale, Fla., 1991—; cons. TESOL, Ormond Beach, Fla., 1991. Author, editor Teaching Assistant Manual, 1987; editor Unitarian Universalist Soc. newsletter, 1987—. Pres. Unitarian Universalists, Ormond Beach, 1982-84, N.E. Cluster Unitarian Universalists, Volusia, 1982-86; pres., v.p. S.E. Unitarian Universalists Sem. Inst., Blacksburg, Va., 1985-89. Mem. TESOL, ASCD, Nat. Coun. Tchrs. of English, Fla. Fgn. Lang. Assn., Fla. Assn. Bilingual Edn. Suprs. (sec. 1995), Phi Kappa Phi, Kappa Delta Pi. Democrat. Home: 771 W River Oak Dr Ormond Beach FL 32174-4641 Office: Volusia County Schs 729 Loomis Ave Daytona Beach FL 32114

GREEN, BONNIE JEAN, early childhood administrator; b. Crookston, Minn., Oct. 23, 1950; d. Francis Romain and Dorothy Marion (Boatman) Bagne; m. Steven Douglas Wedger, July 21, 1973 (div. Feb. 1985); m. Charles Edward Green Jr., June 15, 1985; stepchildren: Andrew Green, Russell Green. BS in Edn. magna cum laude, U. N.D., 1972; cert. human rels., Minn. State U., 1973; postgrad., U. Minn., 1975-83. Cert. elem./early childhood edn. adminstr. Math/reading tutor bilingual students U. N.D., Grand Forks, 1969-71; 1st grade tchr. Park Rapids (Minn.) Ind. Sch. Dist., 1972-73; asst. dir./curriculum writer, tchr. Child Devel. and Learning Ctr., Burnsville, Minn., 1973-75, dir., 1975-87; caring ministry outreach Luth. Ch. of Incarnation, Davis, Calif., 1990—; facilitator-parent edn. program Dakato County Vo-Tech, 1973-78; advisor, cons. Dakota County Childcare Coun., 1977-83; advisor, tchr. cert. program Augsburg Coll., Mpls., 1977-78; supr. student tchrs. Coll. of St. Catherine, Augsburg, St. Paul, 1977-87; cons. Minn. Edn. for Young Children, 1978, State of Minn., 1979-81, Am. Luth. Ch., Mpls., 1981-83; cons., kindergarten curriculum Burnsville Sch. Dist., 1983; liaison coord. Head Start Program, Burnsville, 1985-87. Vol. Prince of Peace Luth. Ch., Burnsville, 1975-87 facilitator parents of divorce, 1984-87; vol. Yolo Wayfare Ctr., Woodland, Calif., 1992; bd. dirs. Riverwoods Homeowners Assn. Arch. Control, 1978-85; mem., vol. Holy Cross Luth., Wheaton, Ill., 1987-89, Luth. Ch. of Incarnation, Davis, 1989—, curriculum planner, 1989; publicity chair, bd. dirs. U. Calif. Farm Circle, Davis, 1989—; fundraiser Wheaton (Ill.) Newcomers, 1987-89. Mem. Nat. Assn. for Edn. Young Children, PEO (guard, treas.), Pi Lambda Theta. Home and Office: 39648 Lupine Ct Davis CA 95616-9756

GREEN, BRENDA ANN PECK, museum director; b. Midwest City, Okla., Sept. 4, 1966; d. Esten E. and Neoma N. (Passmore) Peck; m. Louis M. Green, Feb. 26, 1995. BS in Edn., Okla. State U., 1988; MA in Mus. Studies, U. Ctrl. Okla., 1991. Cert. secondary social sci. tchr. Intern Guggenheim Mus., N.Y.C., 1990; project historian U. Okla., Norman, 1991-92; promotions mgr., vol. coord. Harn Homestead Mus., Oklahoma City, 1992-94; mus. dir. Edmond (Okla.) Hist. Soc., 1994—; curator exhibit Anne Frank in the World: 1929-45. Mem. Leadership Edmond, Up with Edmond, Preservation Okla., Oklahoma City, Edmond Arts and Humanities Coun.; com. chair Jewish Fedn. Oklahoma City. Mem. Am. Assn. Mus., Okla. Mus. Assn., Okla. Hist. Soc., Kappa Alpha Theta, Phi Alpha Theta. Democrat. Jewish. Home: 4013 NW 18th St Oklahoma City OK 73107

GREEN, CAROL H., lawyer, educator, journalist; b. Seattle, Feb. 18, 1944; B.A. summa cum laude in History and Journalism, La. Tech. U., 1965; MSL, Yale U., 1977; JD, U. Denver, 1979. Reporter, Shreveport (La.) Times, 1965-66; reporter Guam Daily News, 1966-67; city editor Pacific Jour., Agana, Guam, 1967-68; reporter, editorial writer, 1968-76, legal affairs reporter, 1977-79, asst. editor editorial page, Denver Post, 1979-81, house counsel, 1980-83, labor rels. mgr., 1981-83; assoc. Holme Roberts & Owen, 1983-85; v.p. human resources and legal affairs Denver Post, 1985-87; mgr. circulation, 1988-90, gen. mgr. Distribution Systems Am., Inc., 1990-92; dir. labor rels., Newsday, 1992-95, dir. comm. and labor rels., 1996—; mem. corrections task force Colo. Criminal Justice Standards and Goals, 1985 speaker for USIA, India, Egypt; mem. Mailers Tech. Adv. Com. to Postmaster Gen., 1991-92. Bd. dirs. YWCA, Mile Hi Red Cross, Trans. Coun., Denver C. of C. Recipient McWilliams award for juvenile justice, Denver, 1971; award for interpretive reporting Denver Newspaper Guild, 1979. Mem. ABA (forum on communications law), Colo. Bar Assn. (bd. govs. 1985-87, chairperson BAR-press com. 1980), Newspaper Assn. Am. (mem. human resources and labor rels. com.), Denver Bar Assn. (co-chairperson jud. selection and benefits com. 1982-85, 1st v.p. 1986), Colo. and Internat. Women's Forum, Leadership Denver. Clubs: Huntington Camera. Episcopalian. Office: Newsday 235 Pinelawn Rd Melville NY 11747-4226

GREEN, CAROLE L., lawyer; b. Queens, N.Y., Mar. 17, 1959; d. Gerald Harry and Mary (Clark) G. AB cum laude with distinction, Dartmouth Coll., 1980; JD, Harvard Law Sch., 1983. Bar: N.Y. Congl. aide to rep. John Conyers U.S. House of Reps., Washington, 1980; assoc. real estate Kaye, Scholer, Fierman, Hays & Handler, N.Y., 1983-85, Richards & O'Neil, N.Y., 1985-87; gen. counsel Petrie Stores Corp., Secaucus, N.J., 1987-88; assoc. counsel Mfrs. Hanover Trust Co., N.Y., 1988-91; v.p., asst. gen. counsel Chemical Bank, N.Y., 1991—. Mem. ABA (mem. minority in-house counsel group 1994—), N.Y. State Bar Assn., Practicing Attys. for Law Students, Inc. (founding mem. 1986—), Black Alumni of Dartmouth Assn. Office: Chemical Bank 270 Park Ave Fl 40 New York NY 10017-2014

GREEN, CATHERINE L., special education educator; b. Alexandria, Va., Apr. 13, 1959; d. Russell James and Betty Joyce (Sellers) G. AA, Gulf Coast C.C., Panama City, Fla., 1980; BS in Social Sci., Fla. State U., 1991. Cert. tchr. spl. edn., emotionally handicapped. Tchr. emotionally handicapped Carabelle (Fla.) H.S., 1992; tchr. emotionally handicapped Merritt Brown Middle Sch., Panama City, Fla., 1992—, head emotionally handicapped dept., 1993—, coach girl's volleyball, 1992—, coach girl's basketball, 1993, mem. leadership team Onward Toward Excellence team, 1994—; site supr. JTPA Work Enclave, Panama City, 1993—. Youth dir. Springfield Meth. Ch., Panama City, Fla., 1985-90. Mem. ASCD, Coun. for Exceptional Children. Democrat. Home: 7337 Copenhagen Ln Panama City FL 32404-5327 Office: Merritt Brown Middle Sch 5044 Merritt Brown Way Panama City FL 32404-2090

GREEN, EDITH JUDITH, registered nurse; b. Camden, N.J., Jan. 28, 1937; d. Arthur William Fields and Emily Gladys (Heal) Glover; m. Edward Russell Green, Apr. 1958 (dec. Mar. 1975); children: Rachel, Edward, Thomas, Ellen, David, Russell. RN, Thomas Jefferson U., 1958; BS, Syracuse U., 1985; MPS, SUNY, New Paltz, 1991. RN. Staff nurse Vis. Nurse Assn., Utica, N.Y., 1982-84; psychiat. nurse St. Elizabeth Hosp., Utica, 1980-84; insvc. trainer Greystone Inc., Wappingers Falls, N.Y., 1988-89; counselor, educator Teen Parents Program YWCA, Poughkeepsie, N.Y., 1987-88; educator HIV and Sexuality Planned Parenthood, Poughkeepsie, 1990-93; staff nurse Prison Health Svcs., Poughkeepsie, 1989—; adj. prof. Dutchess C.C., Poughkeepsie, 1993—. Author: Ellery Queen Mystery Magazine, 1984. Active many local polit. groups. Mem. NOW (pres. 1987-90), Am. Assn. Sex Educator, Counselors and Therapists, Mystery Writer's Am., Family Planning Advocates, Internat. Women's Writers Group. Episcopalian. Office: Prison Health Svcs 150 N Hamilton St Poughkeepsie NY 12601-2011

GREEN, ELEANOR MYERS, veterinarian, educator; b. Phila., Feb. 10, 1948; d. Wade Cooper and Eleanor Ruth (McWherter) Myers; m. George Ashby Green, Dec. 19, 1970; children: George Ashby Jr., Stacy Elizabeth, William Wade. Student, U. South Fla., 1965-67, U. Fla., 1967-69; DVM, Auburn U., 1973. Diplomate Am. Coll. Vet. Internal Medicine, Am. Bd. Vet. Practitioners (pres. 1993-95, past pres. 1995-96). Ptnrship, owner Guntown (Miss.) Vet. Clinic, 1973-76; asst. prof. Miss. State U., Starkville, 1976-84; assoc. prof. U. Mo., Columbia, 1984-91; prof. U. Tenn., Knoxville, 1991-96; prof., chair dept. U. Fla., Gainesville, 1996—. Mem. Am. Assn. Equine Practitioners, Tenn. Vet. Med. Assn., Am. Vet. Med. Assn., Internat. Soc. Vet. Perinatology, Tenn. Horse Coun., Am. Assn. Vet. Clinicians (pres.-elect 1994-95, pres. 1995-96), Rotary Internat. Presbyterian. Office: U Fla Dept Large Animal Clin Scis Gainesville FL 32610-0136

GREEN, GAYLA MAXINE, elementary school educator; b. Gastonia, N.C., Sept. 1, 1951; d. Woodrow and Mildred Louise (Cagle) G. BS, Mars Hill Coll., 1973; cert. in intermediate edn., Sacred Heart Coll., 1974; MA in Edn., Western Carolina U., 1977, EdS, 1985. Cert. tchr., N.C. Elem. phys. edn. tchr. Gaston County Schs., Gastonia, N.C., 1974—; line assoc. rides Paramount's Carowinds, Charlotte, N.C., 1992-94; adj. instr. Belmont (N.C.) Abbey Coll., 1985-87, Gaston Coll., Dallas, N.C., 1986-87, Sacred Heart Coll., Belmont, 1980-84; games cons. Gaston Coll. Day Camp, Dallas, 1993—; counselor, group leader Civitan Youth Camp, Bolling Springs, N.C., 1979-81. Contbr. articles to profl. jours. Coach Spl. Olympics, Gaston County, N.C., 1986—; ch. music asst. First Bapt. Ch., Gastonia, N.C., 1983-88, Covenant Bapt. Ch., Gastonia, 1988—. Named one of Outstanding Young Women of Am., 1982, 84. Mem. AAHPERD, ASCD, N.C. Alliance for Health, Phys. Edn., Recreation and Dance, U.S. Phys. Edn. Assn., Phi Kappa Phi, Kappa Delta Pi. Democrat. Home: 202 Dallas Bessemer City Dallas NC 28034

GREEN, JEAN HESS, psychotherapist; b. Flushing, Mich., Aug. 10, 1930; d. Ozro Kline and Thelma Lucille (Cook) Hess; m. Warren Dale Sarley, Mar. 21, 1952 (div. 1971); children: Gaie Lee, Patton Garret, Erin Jessie; m. Peter B. Green, Jan. 4, 1972. BA, Mich. State U., 1955; MS, Columbia Pacific U., San Rafael, Calif., 1988, PhD, 1994. Cert. Rubenfeld synergist. Tchr. secondary English, Norwich (N.Y.) Pub. Schs., 1960-61; claims rep. Social Security Adminstrn., Rochester, N.Y., 1961-63; mgr. Maplewood Apts., Syracuse, N.Y., 1972-76; dir. overseas scholarships Episcopal Ch., USA, N.Y.C., 1979-81; dir. audio books N.Y. Pub. Libr., N.Y.C., 1987-89; pvt. practice psychotherapy, N.Y.C. and Mt. Vernon, N.Y., 1985—; workshop presenter Mariandale Ctr., Ossining, NY., 1986—. Mem. Assn. for Humanistic Psychology, C.G. Jung Found., Analytical Psychology Club N.Y. (rec. sec. 1988-94, pres. 1994-96). Democrat. Roman Catholic. Home and Office: 472 Gramatan Ave Apt 4W Mount Vernon NY 10552 Office: 222 E 5th St New York NY 10003

GREEN, JOANTA HERMION, electrical engineer; b. Cleve., Nov. 14, 1960; d. Joseph Ezkiel and Clarece Hermion (Marshall) G. BS in Chemistry and Biology, U. Md., 1983; MS in Econ. Devel., N.H. Coll., 1987; postgrad., U. Malaya, Kuala Lumpur, Malaysia, 1990; PhD in Energy Systems, U. Edinburgh, Scotland, 1992. Lab. tech. USDA, 1980-83; dep. headmistress, tchr. Chepareria (West Pokot, Kenya) Girl's Secondary Sch., 1983-86; project engr. renewable energy R & D div. Bechtel Group Inc., San Francisco, 1992-95; owner J.H. Green Enterprises, Sausalito, Calif., 1995—; ind. expert spl. energy program Deutsche Gesellschaft für Technische Zusammenarbeit GmbH, Eschborn, Germany, 1990-92; vis. fellow energy program Asian and Pacific Devel. Ctr., Kuala Lumpur, 1990-91; rsch. assoc. environmentally compatible energy strategies project Internat. Inst. Applied Systems Analysis Laxenburg, Austria, 1991-92; presenter in field. Contbr. articles to profl. publs. Mem. AAAS, Assn. Energy Engrs., Inst. Energy (U.K.), NAFE. Office: J H Green Enterprises 338 Sausalito Blvd Sausalito CA 94965

GREEN, JOYCE HENS, federal judge; b. N.Y.C., Nov. 13, 1928; d. James S. and Hedy (Bucher) Hens; m. Samuel Green, Sept. 25, 1965 (dec.); children: Michael Timothy, June Heather, James Harry. BA, U. Md., 1949; JD, George Washington U., 1951, LLD, 1994. Practice law Washington, 1951-68, Arlington, Va., 1956-68; ptnr. Green & Green, 1966-68; assoc. judge Superior Ct., D.C., 1968-79; judge U.S. Dist. Ct. for D.C., 1979—; judge presiding U.S. Fgn. Intelligence Surveillance Ct., 1988-95; bd. advisors George Washington U. Law Sch. Co-author: Dissolution of Marriage, 1986, supplements, 1987-89; contbr. supplements Marriage and Family Law Agreements, 1985-89. Chair Task Force on Gender, Race and Ethnic Bias for the D.C. Cir. Recipient Alumni Achievement award George Washington U., 1975, Profl. Achievement award, 1978, Outstanding Contbn. to Equal Rights award Women's Legal Def. Fund, 1976, hon. doctor of Laws George Washington U., 1994, U.S. Dept. Justice Edmund J. Randolph award 1995. Fellow Am. Bar Found.; ABA (jud. adminstrn. divsn., chair elect nat. conf. fed. trial judges), Fed. Judges Assn., Nat. Assn. Women Judges, Va. Bar Assn., Bar Assn. D.C. (jud. honoree of Yr. 1994), D.C. Bar, D.C. Women's Bar Assn., (pres. 1960-62, women lawyer of yr. 1979), Exec. Women in Govt. (chmn. 1977), Lawyers Club of Washington, Woman's Forum of Washington D.C. Office: US Dist Ct US Courthouse 333 Constitution Ave NW Washington DC 20001-2802

GREEN, JULIA LYNNE, financial services professional; b. Mpls., Nov. 17, 1959; d. Kenneth and Roberta (Pinsky) G. BA, Mt. Holyoke Coll., 1980; cert. in Adminstrn. and Mgmt., Harvard U., 1994; postgrad., Boston U., 1994—. Staff asst. Harvard Coll., Cambridge, Mass., 1980-81; promotion asst. MIT Press, Cambridge, 1981-82; freelance proofreader O'Reilly Assocs., Newton, Mass., 1987; sr. sec. dept. computer sci. Boston U., 1986-87; sr. sec. mut. series fund State St. Bank, Boston, 1987-89; trans. processor mut. series fund Boston Fin. Data Svcs., Quincy, Mass., 1990-92; account specialist Zweig, Boston Fin. Data Svcs., Quincy, 1990-92, Romac & Assocs., 1992-93, Fidelity Investments, 1993—. Mem. WGBH, Boston Computer Soc., Mt. Holyoke Club Boston, Quill and Scroll. Home: 107 Spring St Apt A-3 Watertown MA 02172-3471

GREEN, JUNE LAZENBY, federal judge; b. Arnold, Md., Jan. 23, 1914; d. Eugene H. and Jessie T. (Briggs) Lazenby; m. John Cawley Green, Sept. 5, 1936. JD, Am. U., 1941. Bar: Md. 1943, D.C. 1945. Claims adjuster Lumbermans Mut. Casualty Co., Washington, 1942-43, claims atty., 1943-47; pvt. practice Washington, 1947-68, Annapolis, Md., 1950-68; judge U.S. Dist. Ct. D.C., 1968—; mem. spl. ct. Regional Reorganization Railroad Act, 1987—; examiner bar, Washington, 1963-68. Named Woman Lawyer of Yr., 1965; recipient Lifetime Achievement award Alumni Assn. of Am. U., 1986. Mem. ABA, Md. Bar Assn., Bar Assn. D.C. (bd. dirs. 1966-68, award 1984), Women's Bar Assn. D.C. (pres. 1955-57), Federal Judges Assn., Am. Jud. Soc. Home: 464 W Joyce Ln Arnold MD 21012-2207 also: 550 N St SW Washington DC 20024-4643 Office: US Dist Ct US Courthouse 333 Constitution Ave NW Washington DC 20001-2802

GREEN, KAREN DANIELLE, psychotherapist; b. Springfield, Ohio, May 3, 1953; d. Daniel and Loretta Louise (Parsons) G.; 1 child, Hadley Louise Green. BA, Hiram (Ohio) Coll., 1975; MA, W. Ga. Coll., 1981; MDir, Starr King Sch. Ministry, 1987; attended, Calif. Inst. Integral Studies, 1992-93. Cert. individual, marriage and family therapist, clinical hypnotherapist; diplomate logotherapy; ordained Unitarian Universalist minister, 1989. Child care worker Clark County Children's Home, Springfield, 1975-76; juvenile probation and parole counselor Health and Rehab. Svcs., Sarasota, Fla., 1977-78; exec. dir. Safe Place and Rape Crisis Ctr., Sarasota, Fla., 1978-79; psychotherapist New Coll., Sarasota, Fla., 1980-81, Stanford Rsch. Inst., Menlo Park, Calif., 1985-86; pvt. practice Berkeley, Calif., 1985-93, Sarasota, Fla., 1980-83, 94—; cons. Safe Place and Rape Crisis Ctr., Sarasota, 1980-81, St. Vincent de Paul, San Francisco, 1991; bd. dirs. Sarasota Help and Referral Svc., 1981-83, Mental Health Assn., Sarasota, 1981-83. Playwright: Conversations With Mama, 1984. Vol. therapist Children of War, San Francisco, 1985; bd. dirs. NOW, Sarasota, 1981-89, pres., NOW, Berkeley, 1989-91; ministerial vol. Pastors for Peace, Mpls., 1990. Mem. Unitarian Universalist Ministerial Assn. (bd. dirs. Pacific Ctrl. Dist., Berkeley, 1991-92), Am. Assn. Marriage and Family Therapy.

GREEN, LINDA GAIL, international healthcare and management consultant; b. Kalamazoo, Nov. 29, 1951; d. Jesse Floyd and Mattie Dean (Fulcher) G. BS in Nursing, Fla. State U., Tallahassee, 1974; postgrad., Nova U., Ft. Lauderdale, Fla. Staff nurse med./surg. unit St. Mary's Hosp., West Palm Beach, Fla., 1974, staff nurse coronary care, 1974-75, relief charge nurse ICU, 1975-76, asst. nursing care coord. post anesthesia recovery rm., 1976-78, insvc. instr., 1978-81, asst. dir. staff devel. and edn., 1981-83; dir. insvc. H.H. Raulerson Hosp., Okeechobee, Fla., 1983-84; adminstr. Med. Personnel Pool, Palm Beach, Fla., 1984-90; regional exec. healthcare divsn. Interim Svcs., Inc. (formerly Pers. Pool of Am.), Ft. Lauderdale, 1990-93; pres. L.G.I. Consulting/Cmty. Health Educator, West Palm Beach, 1993—; Spkr. in field. Author: Sexual Harassment in Home Healthcare, 1993; pub. Everything the Doctor Ordered. Past bd. dirs. Vinceremos Therapeutic Riding Ctr., Inc. for Physically and Mentally Challenged, 1990-95. Mem. ANA, AHA (heart walk industry leader 1994, 95), Fla. Nurses Assn., Palm Beach County Health Educators (past sec.), Palm Beach County Patient Educators (pres. 1989, Leadership and Spirit awards 1989), Royal Palm Beach Bus. Assn., Palms West C. of C. (v.p. 1987-88, Dedicated and Outstanding Svc. award 1989, Cert. of Appreciation 1986, 87), Zonta Internat. (pres. 1994-95, past v.p. Palms West chpt., del. to internat. conf., Hong Kong, 1992), Exec. Women of Palm Beaches. Office: PO Box 15301 West Palm Beach FL 33416-5301

GREEN, LINDA LOU, systems analyst; b. Cape Girardeau, Mo., Sept. 12, 1946; d. Barney Oldfield and Opal (Jeffries) G. BA, East Carolina U., 1967, MA, 1969; postgrad., U. Utah, 1969-70; grad., Naval War Coll., Newport, R.I., 1985, Command and Staff Coll., Ft. Leavenworth, Kans., 1990. Cert. in collegiate teaching. Asst. prof. history Jackson (Miss.) State U., 1970-72, Va. State U., Petersburg, 1972-74; commd. 1st lt. U.S. Army, 1974, advanced through grades to lt. col., 1991, ret., 1996; logistics engr. land systems div. Gen. Dynamics Corp., Warren, Mich., 1983-84; systems analyst Raytheon Svc. Co., Huntsville, Ala., 1984-86; pres. Green & Assocs. Inc., Huntsville, 1985-86; logistics engr., cost analyst, br. mgr. Applied Rsch. Inc., Huntsville, 1986-90; sr. ILS analyst Native Am. Svcs. Inc., Huntsville, Ala., 1990; sr. systems analyst BDM Internat. Inc., 1990; pres. Green and Assocs., Inc., Huntsville, 1990-91; sr. logistics analyst Sigmatech Inc., 1991-95; pvt. cons., 1995—; instr. U. Md., Fed. Republic Germany, 1975-77, Calhoun Community Coll., Huntsville, 1990-91; lectr. in field. Author: Study Guides for American History, 1969, The Family Tree, 1989, Logistics Engineering, 1991, The Town Crier: Descendents of Timothy and Elizabeth Trigg/Reagan, 1995, Town Crier: The Descendents of Archibald McCarver, 1996, Town Crier: The Ancestors of the Missouri Shrums, 1996. Mem. Rep. Nat. Com., Washington, 1986-91. Mem. LWV, Soc. Logistics Engrs. (bd. dirs. TVC chpt. 1992-93, chpt. Logistician of Yr. 1993, recipient Nat. Field award in Integrated Logistics Support 1994), Assn. U.S. Army (bd. dirs. Redstone, Huntsville chpt. 1988-91), Res. Officers Assn., Ret. Officers Assn., DAR, United Daus. of the Confederacy, Daus. of Union Vets. of the Civil War. Baptist. Office: Green and Assocs Inc 708 Lily Flagg Rd SE Huntsville AL 35802-3435

GREEN, MARJORIE, automotive distribution, import and manufacturing company executive; b. N.Y.C., Sept. 27, 1943; d. Benjamin Maxon and Harriet (Weslock) Gruzen; m. Thomas Henry Green, May 31, 1964. Student Antioch Coll., 1961-63, CCNY, 1964-65. Adminstrv. asst. edni. research U. Calif.-Berkeley, 1965-76; v.p., co-owner Automotion, Santa Clara, Calif.,

1973—. Adv. bd. Import Car mag. Mem. Am. Fedn. State, County and Mcpl. Employees (pres. U. Calif. chpt. 1967), Porsche Club Am (v.p. Golden Gate region 1974, treas. region 1975). Home: 10666 W Loyola Dr Los Altos CA 94024-6513 Office: Automotion 193 Commercial St Sunnyvale CA 94086-5202

GREEN, MARJORIE JOAN, elementary education educator; b. Sacramento, Apr. 8, 1938; d. Albert Robertson and Mabel Elizabeth (Wallington) Oughton; m. Norman Everett Green, Mar. 22, 1959; children: Scott Allan, Victoria Elizabeth Green-Spicer. BA, Calif. State U., Sacramento, 1959, MA, 1981. Cert. gen. edn. tchr., lang. devel. specialist, reading specialist, adminstr., Calif. Classroom tchr., reading recovery/title I tchr. San Juan Unified Sch. Dist., Carmichael, Calif., 1967-71, 91-95, reading specialist, 1971-91. Author: (curriculum guide) On the Write Track with Spelling, 1992, Teacher to Teacher: A Professional's Handbook, 1993. Bd. dirs. Fair Oaks (Calif.) Theater Festival, 1984-89, Concert Dance Found., Carmichael, 1976-79, Capital Cadets, Sacramento, 1974-76. Mem. Internat. Reading Assn., Calif. Reading Assn., Sacramento Area Reading Assn. (rec. sec. 1986-87, bd. dirs. 1980-82). Lutheran. Office: Carmichael Sch 6141 Sutter Ave Carmichael CA 95608-2738

GREEN, MARY HESTER, evangelist; b. Oxford, N.C., May 6, 1941; d. Melvin and Martha Elizabeth (Bridges) Hester; m. Joe Lewis G., Dec. 24, 1962; children: Reginald, Renee G. Johnson, Terri Lynatta. AA in Applied Sci., SUNY, 1979; diploma in Christian Edn., Am. Bible Coll., 1984; BA in Christian Edn., City U., L.A., 1989, postgrad., 1989—; postgrad. in Christian Edn., N.C. Cen. U., 1985-86; BTh, Trinity Theol. Sem., 1993; postgrad., Shaw Div. Sch., Raleigh, N.C., 1993—; Grad. of Theology, Trinity Theol. Sem., 1994; B of Religios Edn., Christian Bible Coll., Rocky Mount, N.C., 1995; BRE, Christian Bible Coll., 1995. Charge nurse Newark City Hosp., 1967-69, Lincoln Hosp., Durham, N.C., 1974-79; team leader Duke Med. Ctr., Durham, 1969-90; part-time nurse Vets. Hosp., 1990; TV program producer Inspirational Moments, 1996—, producer TV program; instr. ARC, 1991—. Deaconess Pine Grove Ch., Creedmoor, N.C., 1971—, Sunday sch. tchr., 1972-80, mem. choir. 1970—; mem. staff Bapt. Tng. Union, 1974—, mem. scholarship com.; leader Girl Scouts U.S., 1976-79; active St. Joseph Found. Heritage Ctr., Contact Durham Inc., Nat. Coun. Women, Today's Women Orgn. Recipient Cert. Recognition YWCA, Durham, 1985, Disting. Svc. award Lincoln Hosp., 1976, Honor award Zeta Phi Beta, 1995. Mem. NAFE, Am. Soc. Notaries, Internat. Platform Assn., Century Club Winston Salem U., Masons, Order Ea. Star. Democrat. Home: 5301 Whippoorwill St Durham NC 27704-1250

GREEN, MARY LOUISE, elementary school educator; b. Greenville, S.C., June 28, 1952; d. Guerry Wofford, Sr. and Anna Stovall (Zimmerman) G. BA, Winthrop Coll., 1973, MA, 1974. Cert. tchr., S.C. Tchr. social studies Hughes Acad., Greenville, S.C., 1974—. Mem. First Bapt. Ch., Greenville, S.C. Grantee State Dept. of Edn., 1989-92. Mem. ASCD, AAUW, Palmetto State Tchrs. Assn., Alpha Delta Kappa (past state pres. 1994-96), others. Office: Hughes Acad Sci and Tech 122 De Oyby Ave Greenville SC 29605

GREEN, MIRIAM BLAU, psychologist; b. New Castle, Pa., Sept. 21, 1932; d. Jacob Mont and Anne (Levine) Blau; m. Alvin Green, June 13, 1954; children: Andrew, Marie, Jennifer. BA with high honors, U. Mich., 1954; EdM, Harvard U., 1955; EdD, Columbia U., 1960. Lic. psychologist, N.Y.; diplomate Am. Bd. Profl. Psychology. Tchr. history Maimonides Sch., Boston, 1955-57; sch. psychologist Bur. Child Guidance, N.Y.C., 1960-67, Great Neck (N.Y.) Pub. Schs., 1967-81; instr. State U. Coll. Old Wesbury, Westbury, N.Y., 1982-85; fellow child psychoanalysis Postgrad. Ctr. Mental Health, N.Y.C., 1983-86, fellow family therapy, 1982-84, asst. coord. family program, 1985-89, dir. family and couples tng. program, 1989-91; mem. faculty, supr. Inst. for Child, Adolescent and Family Studies, 1991—; pvt. practice Great Neck and N.Y.C., 1983—; NIMH trainee Columbia U., 1958-60; lectr., instr. Queens Coll., CUNY, 1962-63; cons. Jewish Family Svc. of Bergen County, N.J., 1991-92; faculty supr. Postgrad. Ctr. Mental Health, 1991—. Mem. Am. Psychol. Assn. (div. sec. 1989—), N.Y. State Psychol. Assn., Nassau County Psychol. Assn., Psychol. Practioners L.I. (bd. dirs. 1987-89), Phi Beta Kappa. Jewish. Home: 22 Arleigh Rd Great Neck NY 11021-1338 Office: 145 E 48th St New York NY 10017-1254

GREEN, NANCY H., insurance company executive; b. La Grange, Mo.. BA in Philosophy, Wooster (Ohio) Coll., 1966; grad. advanced mgmt. program, Harvard U., 1985. CLU, ChFC. Credit and media rsch. analyst Prentice Hall, Inc., Englewood Cliffs, N.J., 1966-68; pub. rels. officer United Jersey Bank, Hackensack, N.J., 1968-72; mem. pub. rels. staff Equitable Cos., Inc., N.Y.C., 1972-82, v.p. pub. rels., 1982-85, head corp. comm., 1985-87, sr. v.p., head corp. rels. dept., 1987-88; pres., CEO Equitable Found., N.Y.C., 1988-92; sr. v.p., head corp. rels., human resources policy and svc. Equitable Life Assurance Soc. U.S., N.Y.C., 1994—. Coord. summer jobs program N.Y.C., Nat. Alliance Bus., 1974; exec. in residence Ala. State U., 1980, Mount Holyoke Coll., 1984. Mem. Pub. Rels. Soc. N.Y. (past pres.), Wisemen, Pub. Rels. Seminar. Office: Equitable Life Assurance Soc 787 7th Ave New York NY 10019-6018

GREEN, NANCY LOUGHRIDGE, higher education executive; b. Lexington, Ky.; d. William S. and Nancy O. (Green) Loughridge; BA in Journalism, U. Ky., 1964; MA in Journalism, Ball State U., 1971; postgrad. U. Ky., 1968, U. Minn., 1968. Tchr. English and publs. adv. Clark County High Sch., Winchester, Ky., 1965-66, Pleasure Ridge Park High Sch., Louisville, 1966-67, Clarksville (Ind.) High Sch., 1967-68, Charleston (W.Va.) High Sch., 1968-69; asst. publs. and pub. info. specialist W.Va. Dept. Edn., Charleston, 1969-70; tchr. journalism and publs. dir. Elmhurst High Sch., Ft. Wayne, Ind., 1970-71; adviser student publs. U. Ky., Lexington, 1971-82; gen. mgr. student publs. U. Tex., Austin, 1982-85; pres., pub. Palladium-Item, Richmond, Ind., 1985-89, News-Leader, Springfield, Mo., 1989-92; asst. to the pres., Newspaper Divsn. Gannett Co., Inc., Washington, 1992-94; exec. dir. coll. advancement Clayton State Coll., Morrow, Ga., 1994—; dir. Harte-Hanks urban journalism program, 1984; pres. Media Cons., Inc., Lexington, 1980; dir. urban journalism workshop program Louisville and Lexington newspaper pubs., 1976-82; sec. Kernel Press, Inc., 1971-82. Contbr. articles to profl. jours. Bd. dirs. Jr. League, Lexington, 1980-82, Manchester Ctr., 1978-82, pres., 1979-82; chmn. Greater Richmond Progress Com., 1986-87, bd. dirs. 1986-89; pres. Leadership Wayne County, 1986-87, bd. dirs., 1985-89; bd. dirs. Richmond Community Devel. Corp., 1987-89, United Way of the Ozarks, 1990-92, ARC, 1990-92, Springfield Arts Coun., 1990-91, Bus. Devel. Corp., 1991-92, Bus. Education Alliance, 1991-92, Caring Found., 1991-92, Cox Hosp. Bd., 1990-92, Springfield Schs. Found., 1991-92; mem. adv. bd. Ind. U. East, 1985-89, Richmond C. of C., 1987-89, Ind. Humanities Coun., 1988-89, Youth Communications Bd., 1988-92, Opera Theatre No. Va., 1992-94, Atlanta chpt. AIWF, 1995—. Recipient Coll. Media Advisers First Amendment award, 1987, Carl Towley award Journalism Edn. Assn., 1988, Disting. Svc. award Assn. Edn. Journalism and Mass Comm., 1989; named to Ball State Journalism Hall of Fame, 1988, Coll. Media Advisers Hall of Fame, 1994. Mem. Student Press Law Ctr. (bd. dirs. 1975—, pres. 1985-87, 94—, v.p. 1992-94), Assoc. Collegiate Press, Journalism Edn. Assn., Nat. Council Coll. Publs. Advs. (pres. 1979-83), Disting. Newspaper Adv. 1976, Disting. Bus. Adviser, 1984). Columbia Scholastic Press Assn. (Gold Key 1980), So. Interscholastic Press Assn. (Disting. Service award 1983), Nat. Scholastic Press Assn. (Pioneer award 1982), Soc. Profl. Journalists, Clayton County C. of C. (internat. com. chmn. 1996—).

GREEN, PATRICIA PATAKY, school system administrator, consultant; b. N.Y.C., June 18, 1949; d. William J. and Theresa M. (DiGianni) P.; m. Stephen I. Green, Dec. 7, 1975. BS, U. Md., 1971, MEd, 1977, PhD, 1994. Tchr. Prince George's County (Md.) Pub. Schs., 1971-83; elem. instrnl. adminstrv. specialist Thomas Stone Sch., Mt. Ranier, Md., 1984-85, Glenridge Sch., Lanham, Md., 1984, Greenbelt (Md.) Ctr. Sch., 1983-84, Prince George's County Pub. Schs., 1985-91; prin. Columbia Park Sch., Landover, Md., 1985-91; asst. supt. Prince George's County Pub. Schs., 1991-95, chief divsnl. adminstr. pupil svcs., 1995—; cons. nationwide sch. systems, 1987—; seminar/workshop presenter in field. Editor, writer (newsletter) Tooth or Consequences, 1980—; featured in numerous mags. and on TV shows; contbr. articles to profl. jours. Recipient Nat. Sch. Recognition award U.S. Dept. Edn., 1988, Outstanding Adminstr. award Prince George's County C. of C., 1990, Outstanding Rsch. award Md. Assn. Supervision and Curriculum Devel., 1995, Outstanding Educator award Prince George's County, 1983. Mem. NAESP (Excellence of Achievement award 1988), ASCD, NEA, Nat. Sch. Bds. Assn., Nat. Assn. Secondary Sch. Prins., Am. Ednl. Rsch. Assn., Phi Kappa Phi. Kappa Delta Pi.

GREEN, PHYLLIS, artist, educator; b. Mpls., June 10, 1950; d. Max and Clarice (Pink) Wasserman; m. Gerald Marvin Green, June 21, 1970 (div. 1985); m. Ave EarlPildas, Sept. 17, 1995. BA, U. Man., Can., 1972; attended, Calif. State U., Fullerton, 1977-78; MFA, UCLA, 1981. Asst. prof. Emily Carr Coll. Art and Design, Vancouver, Can., 1982-83; studio asst. Laddie John Dill, Venice, Calif., 1979-86; bus. mgr. Gallery at the Doolittle, Hollywood, Calif., 1986; instr. Jr. Arts Ctr., L.A., 1987-91, Barnsdall Arts Ctr., L.A., 1987-91, Westside Arts Ctr., Santa Monica, Calif., 1987-91, Glendale (Calif.) Coll., 1992, Loyola Marymount U., L.A., 1989—; lectr. UCLA, 1996—; guest lectr. U. Alta., Can., Vancouver C.C., Langara, Alta. Coll. Art, Calgary, Banff Ctr. Arts, Alta., USC, L.A., others; mem. sculpture symposium Claremont (Calif.) Grad. Sch., 1987-89, vis. artist, 1990; mem. artist adv. bd. L.A. Mcpl. Art Gallery, 1992-94; cons. Old Pasadena (Calif.) Streetscapes and Alley Walkways Improvement Plan, 1994. Solo exhibitions include Artspace, L.A., 1982, Turnbull, Lutjeans, Kogan Gallery, Costa Mesa, Calif., 1983, Charles Scott Gallery, Emily Carr Coll. Art and Design, 1983, Natalie Bush Gallery, San Diego, 1986, Mendenhall Gallery, Whittier (Calif.) Coll., 1987, Fine Arts Gallery, Long Beach (Calif.) City Coll., 1988, Jan Baum Gallery, L.A., 1988, 90, 93, 94, Stephen Rosenberg Gallery, N.Y.C., 1989, Art Gallery at Pierce Coll., Woodland Hills, Calif., 1991, Todd Madigan Gallery, Calif. State U., Bakersfield, 1994, Art Gallery at Rio Hondo Coll., Whittier, 1995; group exhibitions at Jan Baum Gallery, 1992, 93, 95, (catalogue) Laband Art Gallery, Loyola Marymount U., 1992, 95, Todd Madigan Gallery, 1994, Space Gallery, L.A., 1994, 1994, TRI Gallery, L.A., 1994, Channing Peake Gallery, Santa Barbara, Calif., 1995, Laguna Mus. Art, 1995, Contemporary Artists Collective, Las Vegas, Nev., 1995, Armand Hammer Mus. and Cultural Ctr., L.A., 1995, José Drudis-Biada Gallery, Mt. St. Mary's Coll., L.A., 1995, Mus. de Arte y Diseno Contemporaneo, San Jose, Costa Rica, 1995, Victoria Room and Push Gallery, San Francisco, 1995, The Lotus Motel, L.A., 1995, Feldman Gallery, Pacific Design Ctr., L.A., 1996, (catalogue) Armory Ctr. Arts, Pasadena, 1996, numerous others; public art includes Hope St. Promenade Intersection Design Competition, Hollywood Fences Project, MTA A-R-T program, 1994, Montebello / Commerce Metrolink Sta., 1994. Recipient Spl. Juror's award Laguna (Calif.) Mus. Art, 1986; fellow Calif. Arts Coun., 1990, Nat. Endowment Arts, Washington, 1986; grantee Can. Coun., Ottawa, 1981, Cultural Affairs Dept. City L.A., 1996. Studio: 3902 Grand View Blvd Los Angeles CA 90066

GREEN, ROBIN, film company executive. Sr. v.p. TV prodn. Castle Rock Entertainment, Beverly Hills, Calif. Office: Castle Rock Entertainment 335 N Maple Dr Ste 135 Beverly Hills CA 90210*

GREEN, ROSE BASILE (MRS. RAYMOND S. GREEN), poet, author, educator; b. New Rochelle, N.Y., Dec. 19, 1914; d. Salvatore and Caroline (Galgano) Basile; m. Raymond S. Green, June 20, 1942; children: Carol-Rae Green Sadano, Raymond Ferguson St. John. BA, Coll. New Rochelle, 1935; MA, Columbia U., 1941; PhD, U. Pa., 1962; LHD (hon.), Gwynedd-Mercy Coll., 1979, Cabrini Coll., 1982. Tchr. Torrington H.S., Conn., 1936-42; writer, researcher Fed. Writers Project, 1935-36; freelance script writer Cavalcade of Am., NBC, 1940-42; assoc. prof. English, univ. registrar Tampa U., Tampa, 1942-43; spl. instr. English, Temple U., Phila., 1953-57; prof. dept. English, Cabrini Coll., Radnor, Pa., 1957-70, chmn. dept., 1957-70. Author: Cabrinian Philosophy of Education, 1967, (criticism) The Italian-American Novel, 1972, (poetry books) To Reason Why, 1971, Primo Vino, 1972, 76 for Philadelphia, 1975, Woman, The Second Coming, 1977, Lauding the American Dream, 1980, Century Four, 1981, Songs of Ourselves, 1982, (transl.) The Life of Mother Frances Cabrini, 1984, The Pennsylvania People, 1984, Challenger Countdown, 1988, Five Hundred Years of America, 1492-1992, 1992, The Distaff Side: Great Women of Am. History, 1995; editor faculty jour. A-Zimuth, 1963-70. Exec. dir. Am. Inst. Italian Studies; dir. lit. com. Phila. Art Alliance; bd. dirs., trustee Free Libr. of Phila.; v.p., dir. Nat. Italian-Am. Found.; chair Nat. Adv. Coun. Ethnic Heritage Studies; adv. bd. Women for Greater Phila.; dir. Balch Inst. Phila. Decorated cavalier Republic of Italy; named Woman of Yr. Pa. Sons of Italy, 1975, Disting. Dau. of Pa., 1978; recipient Nat. Amita award for lit., 1976, Nat. Bicentennial award for poetry DAR, 1976, other awards for contbns. to lit. and edn. Fellow Royal Soc. Arts (London); mem. AAUW (dir.-at-large), Am. Acad. Polit. and Social Sci., Acad. Am. Poets, Acad. Polit. Sci., Am. Studies Assn., Ethnic Studies Assn., Nat. Council Tchrs. English, Am.-Italy Soc. (dir. 1952—), Eastern Pa. Coll. New Rochelle Alumnae (pres. 1951-54), Cosmopolitan Club, Franklin Inn Club (Phila.), Kappa Gamma Phi. Home: 308 Manor Rd Lafayette Hill PA 19444-1741

GREEN, RUTH SUDDATH, retired archivist; b. Kingstree, S.C., Aug. 10, 1924; d. George William and Pauline Beulah (Suddath) Green. BS, Columbia Coll., 1945, BA, 1949; MA, U. N.C., 1951. From indexer to head inventory and arrangement divsn. S.C. Dept. Archives and History, Columbia, 1955-95. Asst. editor: Jour. of the (S.C.) Commons House of Assembly, Sept. 10, 1746-June 13, 1747, Jan. 19, 1748-June 29, 1748, Mar. 28, 1749-Mar. 19, 1750 (3 vols.). Mem. South Caroliniana Soc. Methodist. Home: 830 Poinsettia St Columbia SC 29205-2040

GREEN, RUTHANN, marketing and management consultant; b. Streator, Ill., July 14, 1935; d. John Joseph and Edna Marie (Peters) G. BS in Edn., U. Ill., 1957. Elem. tchr. Jefferson Sch., Davenport, Iowa, 1957-59; tchr. Hinsdale (Ill.) Jr. High Sch., 1959-62; ednl. cons. Harcourt Brace & World, Chgo., 1962-63; exec. sec. Everpure, Inc., Oakbrook, Ill., 1963-68; ednl. cons. Houghton Mifflin Co., Europe, 1968-69, Palo Alto, Calif., 1969-77; sr. mktg. mgr. Houghton Mifflin Co., Boston, 1977-87; v.p., nat. sales mgr. Riverside Pub. Co., Chgo., 1987-89; v.p., dir. mktg. McDougal, Littell & Co., Evanston, Ill., 1990-92; v.p., gen. mgr. Open Court Pub. Co., Chgo., 1992-94; pres. Peters & Green, Inc., Chgo., 1994—. Author: WSIL: Why Should I Listen, 1987, 93, A Garfield Memoir, 1995. Mem. Chicagoland Radio Info. Svc., Inc. Recipient Svc. award Am. Arbitration Assn., 1987, Golden Reel of Excellence Internat. TV Assn., 1983. Mem. Am. Mktg. Assn., Nat. Assn. Women Bus. Owners, Internat. Reading Assn., U.S. Bd. on Books for Young People, People for Am. Way, Common Cause, Am. Arbitration Assn. Home and Office: 1310 N Ritchie Ct Apt 21A Chicago IL 60610-2178

GREEN, SHARON JORDAN, interior decorator; b. Mansfield, Ohio, Dec. 14, 1948; d. Garnet and L. Wynell (Baxley) Fraley; m. Trice Leroy Jordan Jr., Mar. 30, 1968 (dec. 1973); children: Trice Leroy III, Caerin Danielle, Christopher Robin; m. Joe Leonard Green, Mar. 13, 1978. Student, Ohio State U., 1966-67, 75-76. Typist FBI, Washington, 1968; ward clk. Means Hall, Ohio State U. Hosp., Columbus, 1970; x-ray clk. Riverside Hosp., Columbus, 1971; contr., owner T&D Mold & Die, Houston, 1988—; interior decorator, franchise owner Decorating Den, Houston, 1989-91; owner T&D Interior Decorator, Houston, 1992—. Tchr. aide Bedford Sch., Mansfield, Ohio, 1976-77, Yeager Sch., 1981-82; pres. N.W. Welcome Wagon, Houston, 1980-81, Welcome Club, El Paso, 1986-87; active North Houston Symphony, 1992—, North Houston Performing Arts, 1993—, Mus. Fine Arts, Houston, 1993—, Edn. and Design Resource Network, 1993—, The Wellington Soc. for Arts, 1994, Jr. Forum, 1995, Rep. Nat. Com., 1995—; vol. Harris County Juvenile Probation Dept., 1996. Home: 16247 Morningbrook Dr Spring TX 77379-7158

GREEN, SHELLEY Z., lawyer, university counsel; b. N.Y.C.. AB, Vassar Coll.; JD, Harvard U. Bar: N.Y. 1975, D.C. 1976, Pa. 1981, U.S. Supreme Ct. 1981. Assoc. Sutherland Asbill & Brennan, Washington; atty. advisor HEW, Washington; asst. gen. counsel U. Pa., Phila., assoc. gen. counsel, gen. counsel, 1982—. Office: U Pa 221 College Hall Philadelphia PA 19104

GREEN, SHIA TOBY RINER, therapist; b. N.Y.C.; d. Murray A. and Frances Riner; student CCNY; BA, Antioch Coll., MA, 1976; m. Gary S. Green, Sept. 4, 1957; children: Margot Laura, Vanessa Daryl, Garson Todd. Press. and legis. sec. U.S. Ho. of Reps., Washington, 1960-71; cons. Rehab. Services Adminstrn., Social and Rehab. Services, HEW, 1972-73; asst. dir. State of Md. Foster Care Impact Demonstration Project, 1977-78; therapist Alexandria (Va.) Narcotics Treatment Program, 1979-84, Assocs. Psychotherapy Ctrs., Gaithersburg, Md., 1984—; mem. treatment com. Alexandria Case Mgmt. and Treatment of Child Sexual Abuse. Mem. exec. bd. Children's Adoption Resource Exchange, Washington; vol. worker Girl Scouts U.S.A., also Boy Scouts Am., 1970-74. Mem. APA, Md. Psychol. Assn., Am. Assn. Marriage and Family Therapy. Co-author: Permanent Planning in Maryland—A Manual for the Foster Care Worker. Home: One Lake Potomac Ct Potomac MD 20854 Office: 8915 Shady Grove Ct Gaithersburg MD 20877-1308

GREEN, SUSAN ELIZABETH, systems designer; b. Orlando, Fla., Dec. 30, 1960; d. Semion Barto and Vivian Lunsford (Posey) Hendrix; m. Donald Keith Green, July 13, 1991. BSBA, Miss. Coll., 1982. Asst. office mgr. Stein Mart, Jackson, Miss., 1982-83; customer svc. rep. Executone of Miss., Jackson, 1983-84, admnstrv. asst., 1984-85; advt. cons. L.M. Berry Co., Jackson, 1985-86; customer svc. rep. TelPlus Comm., Jackson, 1986-87; customer support rep. South Ctrl. Bell, Montgomery, Ala., 1987-91; systems designer I Bell South Bus. Systems South Ctrl. Bell, Montgomery, Mobile, 1991-95; systems designer II Bell South Bus. Systems South Ctrl. Bell, Montgomery, 1995—. Sunday sch. tchr. youth First Bapt. Ch. Montgomery, 1988-91; counselor Hugh O'Bryan Youth Found. Weekend, Montgomery, 1990; policies and procedures team Vaughn Forest Bapt. Ch., Montgomery, 1995-96, third and fourth grade girls mission group, 1995-96. Republican. Baptist. Home: 3858 Llyde Ln Montgomery AL 36106 Office: Bell South Bus Systems 4001 Carmichael Rd Ste 450 Montgomery AL 36106

GREENAWALT, PEGGY FREED TOMARKIN, advertising executive; b. Cleve., Apr. 27, 1942; d. Bernard H. and Gyta Elinor (Arsham) Freed; m. Gary Tomarkin, Aug. 7, 1966 (div. 1981); children: Craig William, Eric Lawrence; m. William Sloan Greenawalt, Oct. 31, 1987. BS, Simmons Coll., 1964. Asst. account exec. Howard Marks/Norman, Craig & Kummel, Inc., N.Y.C., 1964-66; account exec. Shaw Bros. Advt. Co., N.Y.C., 1966-67; copywriter Claire Advt. Co., N.Y.C., 1967; ptnr. Copywriters Coop., Hartsdale, N.Y., 1970-73; copy chief Howard Marks Advt., N.Y.C., 1973-80; sr. copywriter Wunderman, Ricotta & Kline, N.Y.C., 1980-82; v.p., assoc. creative dir. Ayer-Direct (N.W. Ayer), N.Y.C., 1982-84; sr. v.p., creative dir. D'Arcy Direct (D'Arcy, MacManus & Masius), N.Y.C., 1984-86; creative and mktg. cons., 1986—; pres. Tomarkin/Greenawalt, Inc., 1986—; judge Echo Awards, Caples Awards. Author: Kiss, The Real Story, 1980. Dem. dist. Leader. Mem. Direct Mktg. Assn., Women in Communications, Direct Mktg. Club N.Y., Westchester Assn. Women Bus. Owners (past pres.). Home: 24 Lewis Ave Hartsdale NY 10530 Office: 45 E 30th St New York NY 10016-7323

GREENBERG, AMY BETH, counselor; b. Bklyn., Nov. 26, 1964; d. Nathan and Rosalind (Bloom) Silver; m. Derek Greenberg, Jan. 15, 1995. BA in Psychology, SUNY, Buffalo, 1986; M Counseling, San Francisco State U., 1996. Clinic dir. SUNY, Buffalo, 1985-86; social worker Hamlin Terrace, Buffalo, 1986; office mgr. Choice Med. Group, Redwood City, Calif., 1987; asst. supr. RCH, Inc., San Francisco, 1987-91; rehab. mgr. The Arc San Francisco, 1991-95; counselor Women's Recovery Assn., Burlingame, Calif., 1995-96; vocat. rehab. specialist Miramonte Mental Health, 1996—. Pledge operator Pub. TV-Buffalo, 1986; helpline vol. Nat. Coun. on Alcoholism, San Francisco, 1995. Mem. ACA, Counseling Students Assn., Calif. Assn. Marriage and Family Therapists. Office: Miramonte Mental Health 206 California Ave Palo Alto CA 94306

GREENBERG, ARLINE FRANCINE, artist, photographer; b. N.Y.C.; m. Sidney Greenberg. BA, Hunter Coll.; postgrad., NYU; AS, Parson Sch. Design, Pratt Inst. Ind. practice cons. firm in jewelry and design; v.p. Reliable Textile Co., N.Y.C.; fashion dir. Burlington Klopman Fabrics, N.Y.C., 1988-92; guest lectr. AWED and F.I.T. Contbr. fashion articles to newspapers. Recipient Medal in Fine Arts; scholar NYU. Mem. AATT, AWARE, Fashion Group, Fashion News Workship, The Info. Exch.. Home: 555 Kappock St Apt 15D Riverdale NY 10463-6458

GREENBERG, BLU, author; b. Seattle, Jan. 21, 1936; d. Sam and Sylvia (Genser) Genauer; m. Irving Greenberg; children: Jeremy, David, Deborah, Jonathan, Judith. BA, Bklyn. Coll., 1957; BA in Religious Edn., Yeshiva U., 1958; MA in Clin. Psychol., City U., N.Y.C., 1967; MS in Jewish History, Yeshiva U., 1977. Instr. Dept. Religious Studies Coll. Mt. St. Vincent, N.Y.C., 1970-77; lectr. Pardes Inst., Jerusalem, 1974-75; guest lectr. Harvard U., Princeton U., Dartmouth U., U. Ind., and various other colls. Author: How to Run a Traditional Jewish Household, 1983, On Women and Judaism: A View from Tradition, 1982; (poetry) Black Bread: Poems, After the Holocaust, 1994, mem. exec. bd. Project Kesher, 1996—; mem. adv. bd. Lilith mag.; mem. editl. bd. Hadassah mag., 1986—. Mem. exec. bd. Coalition for Soviet Jews, 1987—; trustee Jewish Found. for Christian Rescuer's 1990—; mem. steering com. Women of Faith in 80's, 1980-92, The Dialogue Project, 1989—; pres. JWB Jewish Book Coun., 1983-86, mem. exec. bd.; mem. exec. bd. Fedn. Commn. on Synagogue Rels., 1976, chair, 1982-86, chair women's task force, 1976-80; co-founder, mem. exec. bd. U.S.-Israel Women to Women, 1978-93; chairperson Jewish Women Leaders Cons., 1988-91; mem. commn. to equality of women Am. Jewish Congress, 1981—, task force on bioethics, 1989—; mem. profl. adv. bd. William Petschek Nat. Jewish Family Ctr., 1990—, Jewish Women's Resrouce Ctr., 1982—, chair 1993—; bd. dirs. Covenant Found., 1991-94. Named Woman Valor Riverdale Jewish Ctr., 1971, Woman of Yr. United Jewish Appeal-Bronx Div., 1971, Bronx Woman of Yr., 1990; recipient Myrtle Wreath Lit. award Camden County Hadassah 1976, Nassau County, 1991, Lit. award B'nai B'rith women 1981, Women of Achievement Memoirist Am. Jewish Com., 1990, Riverdale Jewish Cmty. Coun. Svc. award, 1988, B'nai B'rith Disting. Humanitatian award, Riverdale, 1993. Mem. Sh'ma (mem.editorial bd. 1979-93), Jewish Publ. Soc. (mem. editorial bd. 1985—), Jewish Women's Resource Ctr. (mem. adv. bd. 1982—), Jewish Book Council Am. (pres. 1983-86), Fedn. Commn. Synagogue Rels. (chmn. exec. bd. 1982-86), U.S.-Israel Women to Women (co-founder, mem. exec. bd. 1978-94), Women Faith Eighties (mem. steering com. 1980-92), B'nai B'rith Commn. Adult Edn. (mem. exec. bd. 1989-92). Home and Office: 600 W 246th St Bronx NY 10471-3611

GREENBERG, CAROLYN PHYLLIS, anesthesiologist, educator; b. San Francisco, July 7, 1941. AB, Stanford U., 1962; MD, U. Calif., San Francisco, 1966. Diplomate Am. Bd. Anesthesiology. Rotating intern L.A. County Hosp., 1966-67; resident in anesthesiology Presbyn. Hosp., N.Y.C., 1967-69, vis. fellow in anesthesiology, 1969-70, asst. attending anesthesiologist, 1971-90, assoc. attending anesthesiologist, 1990—, med. dir. ambulatory surgery, 1986—; asst. attending anesthesiologist N.Y. Hosp., 1970-71; instr. anesthesiology Cornell Med. Sch., 1970-71; assoc. anesthesiology Columbia U., N.Y.C., 1971-74, asst. prof. clin. anesthesiology, 1974-90, assoc. prof. clin. anesthesiology, 1990—. Contbr. book chpts., articles to profl. jours. Mem. Am. Soc. Anesthesiologists, N.Y. State Soc. Anesthesiologists (Media award 1992), Med. Soc. N.Y., Soc. Ambulatory Anesthesia (treas. 1994—, Ambulatory Anesthesia Rsch. Found. award 1992), Malignant Hyperthermia Assn. of U.S. (hotline cons. 1983—). Jewish. Office: Presbyn Hosp Dept Anesthesiology 622 W 168th St New York NY 10032-3702

GREENBERG, ELINOR MILLER, college administrator, consultant; b. Bklyn., Nov. 13, 1932; d. Ray and Susan (Weiss) Miller; m. Manuel Greenberg, Dec. 26, 1955; children: Andrea, Julie, Michael. BA, Mt. Holyoke Coll., 1953; MA, U. Wis.-Madison, 1954; EdD, U. No. Colo., 1981; LittD (hon.), St. Mary-of-the-Woods, Ind., 1983; LHD (hon.), Profl. Sch. Psychology, Calif., 1987. Exec. dir. Arapahao Inst. for Community Devel., Littleton, Colo., 1969-71; founding dir. Univ. without Walls, Loretto Heights Coll., Denver, 1971-79, asst. acad. dean, 1982-84, asst. to pres., 1984-85; regional exec. officer Coun. for Adult and Experiential Learning, Chgo., 1979-91; founding exec. dir. US West Comm. CWA, Pathways to the Future, 1986-91; rsch. assoc. Inst. for Rsch. on Adults in Higher Edn., U. Md., U. College., 1991, exec. dir. project Leadership, 1986—; pres., chief exec. officer EMG and Assocs.; sr. cons. US West Found., No. Telecom, Rose Found., Cogeoinfo., 1992—; regional coord. Mountain and Plains Partnership Health Scis. Ctr. U. Colo., 1996—; cons. in field. Co-editor, contbr.: Educating Learners of All Ages, 1980; co-author: Designing Undergraduate Education, 1981, Widening Ripples, 1986, Leading Effectively, 1987, In Our Fifties: Voices of Men and Women Reinventing Their Lives, 1993; editor, contbr.: New Partnerships: Higher Education and the Nonprofit Sector, 1982, Enhancing Leadership, 1989, Weaving: The Fabric of a Woman's Life, 1991,

Liberal Education Journal, 1992; guest editor Liberal Edn., 1992; feature writer Colo. Woman News, 1993—, Women's Bus. News, 1995—; contbr. Sculpting The Learning Organization, 1993; contbr. articles to profl. jours. Bd. dirs., exec. com. Anti Defamation League of B'nai B'rith, Denver, 1981—, chair women's leadership com., 1991-93, bd. dirs., 1985—; mem. Colo. State Bd. for Community Colls. and Occupational Edn., 1981-86, vice chair, 1984-85; bd. dirs. Internat. Women's Forum, 1986-88, Internat. Women's Forum Leadership Found., 1991-95, Griffith Ctr., Golden, Colo., 1982-86, Colo. Bd. Continuing Legal and Jud. Edn., 1984—; pres. Women's Forum of Colo., 1986; v.p. Women's Forum Colo. Found., 1987; mem. adv. bd. Anchor Ctr. Blind Child, Colo. Coalition Prevention Nuclear War, Mile Hi Girl Scouts, Nat. Conf. on Edn. for Women's Devel., Community Adv. Bd. Colo. Woman News, adv. com. Colo. Pvt. Occupational Sch., 1990—; co-chair Gov.'s Women's Econ. Devel. Taskforce, Women's Econ. Devel. Coun., 1988—; mem. bd. visitors U. Hosp., U. Colo., 1990-91, gov. apptd. Colo. Math., Sci. and Tech. Commn., chair, 1991-93, co-telecom. adv. commn. TAC 14, chair, 1993-95; founding steering com. Colo. Women's Leadership Coalition, 1988—. Named Citizen of Yr., Omega Psi Phi, Denver, 1966, Woman of Decade Littleton Ind. Newspapers, 1970; grantee W. K. Kellogg Found., 1982, Weyerhaeuser Found., 1986, Fund for Improvement of Post Secondary Edn., 1977, 80; recipient Sesquicentennial award Mt. Holyoke Coll. Alumni Assn., 1987, Minoru Yasui Community Vol. award, 1991, Women of Excellence award Cmty. Women's Leadership Coalition, 1995. Mem. Am. Assn. for Higher Edn., Assn. for Experiential Edn. (editorial bd. 1978-80), Nat. conf. Women's Devel. Edn., Kappa Delta Pi. Democrat. Jewish. Home: 6725 S Adams Way Littleton CO 80122-1801

GREENBERG, EVA MUELLER, librarian; b. Vienna, Austria, July 19, 1929; came to U.S., 1939; d. Paul and Greta (Scheuer) Mueller; m. Nathan Abraham Greenberg, June 22, 1952; children: David Stephen, Judith Helen, Lisa Pauline. AB, Harvard/Radcliffe Coll., 1951; MLS, Kent State U., 1975. Head reference McIntire Libr., Zanesville, Ohio, 1978; with Lorain (Ohio) Pub. Libr., 1978-81; head reference Elyria (Ohio) Pub. Libr., 1981-82; reference libr. adult svcs. Cuyahoga County Pub. Libr., Strongsville, Ohio, 1983-89; head adult svcs. Oberlin (Ohio) Pub. Libr., 1989—. Contbr. articles to profl. jours. Grantee Ohio Humanities Coun. for Pub. Programs. Mem. ALA, Ohio Libr. Assn. (coord. community info. task force). Home: 34 S Cedar St Oberlin OH 44074-1520 Office: Oberlin Pub Libr 65 S Main St Oberlin OH 44074-1603

GREENBERG, HINDA FEIGE, library director; b. Bayreuth, Germany, Feb. 26, 1947; came to U.S., 1951; d. Samuel Leon and Sima (Schampagnere) F.; m. Joseph Lawrence, July 6, 1968; children: David Micah, Jacob Alexander. BA, Temple U., 1969; MLS, Rutgers U., 1981; doctoral candidate, Drexel U., 1991—. Assoc. librarian Ednl. Testing Svc., Princeton, N.J., 1981-86; dir. info. ctr. Carnegie Found., Princeton, 1986—. Assoc. editor Jour. Reading, Writing and Learning Disabilities, 1984-86. Mem. Princeton/Trenton Spl. Librs. Assn. (pres. 1985-86). Office: Carnegie Found 5 Ivy Ln Princeton NJ 08540-7218

GREENBERG, INA FLORENCE, retired elementary education educator; b. N.Y.C., May 1, 1933; d. David Samuel and Nettie (Schapiro) Grossman; m. Ira Greenberg, Dec. 24, 1966 (dec. Dec. 1991); 1 child, Charles Joseph. BS in Edn., CCNY, 1955, MS in Edn., 1958. Cert. elem. tchr., N.Y. Tchr. elem. Pub. Sch. 2 Bronx, N.Y.C., 1955-69; tchr. writing Pub. Sch. 46 Bronx, N.Y.C., 1983-95; retired, 1995. Mem. Hadassh (Bay Club chpt., pres. Orah group Yonkers chpt. 1992-93), B'nai B'rith (Bay Club unit, pres. Lincoln Pk. chpt. 1977-79), Sigma Tau Delta.

GREENBERG, LENORE, public relations professional; b. Flushing, N.Y.; d. Jack and Frances Orenstein. BA, Hofstra U.; MS, SUNY. Dir .pub. rels. Bloomingdale's, Short Hills, N.J., 1977-78; dir. comms. N.J. Sch. Bds. Assn., Trenton, 1978-82; dir pub. info. N.J. State Dept. Edn., Trenton, 1982-90; assoc. exec. dir. Nat. Sch. Pub. Rels. Assn., Arlington, Va., 1990-91; pres. Lenore Greenberg & Assocs., Inc., 1991—; adj. prof. pub. rels. Rutgers U. Freelance feature writer N.Y. Times. Mem. bd. assocs. McCarter Theatre, Princeton, N.J.; mem. Franklin Twp. Zoning Bd. Adjustment; mem. Franklin Twp. Human Rels. Commn.; chair Somerset County LWV; instr. Bus. Vols. for the Arts. Recipient award Am. Soc. Assn. Execs., award Women in Comms., award Internat. Assn. Bus. Communicators; Gold Medallion awrd Nat. Sch. Pub. Rels. Assn. Mem. Pub. Rels. Soc. Am. (accredited; pres. N.J. State chpt., nat. nominating and accreditation coms., Silver Anvil award), Nat. Health/Edn. Consortium. Home and Office: 15 Tunnell Rd Somerset NJ 08873-2916

GREENBERG, SHOSHANA (GREENBERG SHIRLEY E.), artist; b. N.Y.C., Feb. 28, 1926; d. Alexander and Bessie (Fleischman) Singer; m. Arnold E. Greenberg, Aug. 2, 1952; children: Noah J., Seth M. BFA with Distinction, Calif. Coll. of Arts/Crafts, Oakland, 1972, MFA with highest distinction, 1979. Exhbns. include: A Mosaic of Jewish Experience, 1991, Jewish Community Mus., San Francisco, 1989, 1991, Jewish Comm. Libr., San Francisco, 1990, Judah L. Magnes Mus., Berkeley, 1986-87, Skirball Mus., L.A., 1985, Judah Magnes Mus., Berkeley, Calif., 1983, 1993 (Max and Sophie Adler award), Nat. Jewish Mus., Washington, 1996, numerous others; contbr. to art catalogs, including Forms for Faith, 1986-87, Location/Dislocation, 1980; contbr. profl. jours. and publs. Mem. Jewish Arts Community of the Bay (founding mem., pres. 1989-93). Home: 1816 Virginia St Berkeley CA 94703

GREENBERG, SUSAN ANN, lawyer; b. Bklyn., Mar. 15, 1957; d. Irving Arthur and Betty (Mayo) G. BA in Econs., Boston U., 1978; JD, Bklyn. Law Sch., 1981; LLM in Labor Law, NYU, 1986. Bar: N.Y. 1982, U.S. Dist. Ct. (ea. and so. dists.) N.Y. 1982. Assoc. Law Offices of Bert W. Subin P.C., N.Y.C., 1981-82; atty. N.Y. Life Ins. Co., N.Y.C., 1982-83, asst. counsel, 1982, assoc. counsel, v.p., 1982—; sec., bd.dirs. N.Y. State Adv. Council Employment Law, N.Y.C., 1985—, mem. Equal Employment Adv. Council, 1983—. Bus. editor Bklyn. Jour. Internat. Law, 1980-81. Mem. ABA. *

GREENBERGER, ELLEN, psychologist, educator; b. N.Y.C., Nov. 19, 1935; d. Edward Michael and Vera (Brisk) Silver; m. Michael Burton, Aug. 26, 1979; children by previous marriage—Kari Edwards, David Silver. B.A., Vassar Coll., 1956; M.A., Harvard U., 1959, Ph.D., 1961. Instr. Wellesley (Mass.) Coll., 1961-63, asst. prof., 1963-67; sr. research scientist Johns Hopkins U., Balt., 1967-76; prof. psychology and social behavior U. Calif., Irvine, 1976—. Author: (with others) When Teenagers Work, 1986; contbr. articles to profl. jours. USPHS fellow, 1956-59; Margaret Floy Washburn fellow, 1956-58; Ford Found. grantee, 1979-81; Spencer Found. grantee, 1979-81, 87, 88-91. Fellow APA, Am. Psychol. Soc.; mem. Soc. Rsch. in Child Devel., Soc. Rsch. on Adolescent Devel. Office: Univ Calif Sch Of Social Ecology II Irvine CA 92717

GREENBERGER, MARSHA MOSES, sales executive; b. Lakewood, N.J., Mar. 15, 1943; d. Bernard David and Ethel (Gordon) Moses; m. Paul Edward Greenberger (div. 1969); 1 child, Nathan Scott. Student, Kent (Ohio) State U., 1961-62. Mgr. gen. sales Ellison Products, Fairfield, N.J., 1972-79; gen. mgr. Indsl. Maintenance Corp., Cherry Hill, N.J., 1979-83; co-owner corp. sect. Ven-Mar Sales, Inc., Blairstown, N.J., 1983-89; pres. MGM Sales, 1989—. Office: MGM Sales 29 High Ridge Rd Randolph NJ 07869-4567

GREENBLATT, MIRIAM, author, editor, educator; b. Berlin; d. Gregory and Shifra (Zemach) Baraks; B.A. magna cum laude, Hunter Coll.; postgrad. U. Chgo., Spertus Coll.; m. Herbert Halbrecht (div. 1960); m. Howard Greenblatt, 1962 (div. 1978). Tchr., New Trier (Ill.) High Sch., 1978-81; editor Am. People's Ency., Chgo., 1957-58; editor Scott, Foresman & Co., Chgo., 1958-62; pres. Creative Textbooks, Evanston, Ill., 1972—. V.p. Chgo. Chpt. Am. Jewish Com., 1977-79, mem. nat. exec. council, 1980-84; treas. Glencoe Youth Services, 1981-83. Mem. Nat. Council Social Studies, Ill. Council Social Studies, Am. Hist. Assn., Nat. Coun. History Edn. Author: (with Chu) The Story of China, 1968, (with Cuban) Japan, 1971, The History of Itasca, 1976, (with others) The American People, 1986, James Knox Polk, 1988, Franklin Delano Roosevelt, 1989, John Quincy Adams, 1990, (with Jordan and Bowes) The Americans, 1996, (with Welty) The Human Expression, 1992, The War of 1812, 1994, (with Lemmo) Human Heritage, 1995, Cambodia, 1995; edit. cons. Peoples and Cultures Series, 1976-78; subject area cons. World Geography and Cultures, 1994; contbg. editor A World History, 1979. Jewish. Address: 2754 Roslyn Ln Highland Park IL 60035

GREENE, ADELE S., management consultant; b. Newark; d. Adolph and Sara (Schubert) Shuminer; m. Alan Greene (div.); 1 child, Joshua. Student, Juilliard Sch. Music, 1942-44, NYU, 1942-44, New Sch. Social Research, 1944-47; diploma in mgmt., Harvard Bus. Sch., 1978. Account exec. Ruder and Finn Inc., N.Y.C., 1964-66, sr. assoc., 1966-68, v.p., 1968-72, sr. v.p., 1972-76; v.p. pub. affairs Corp. Pub. Broadcasting, Washington, 1976-78; pres., CEO TV Program Group, Washington, 1978-80; pres. Greene and Assocs., N.Y.C., 1981—; exec. dir. Am. Friends of Brit. Mus., 1994—; instr. pub. relations and community affairs, NYU 1974-76; bd. dirs. Sci. Program Group, Washington 1976-81; treas., bd. dirs. Coliseum Park Apts. Co-author: Teen-Age Leadership, 1971. Advisor The Acting Co., Understudies, N.Y.C., 1987—; pres., COO Am. Craft Coun., 1980-81, trustee, 1976-81; bd. dirs. Union Settlement, N.Y.C., 1987-90; trustee Duke Ellington Sch. Arts, Washington, 1977-81. Mem. Pub. Relations Soc. Am. (silver anvil award 1971), Nat. Assn. Edn. Broadcasters, Am. Women Radio and TV. Home and Office: 30 W 60th St New York NY 10023-7902

GREENE, BARBARA ANN MARY, English educator; b. Pembroke, Ont., Can., Sept. 1, 1945; d. Aldred and Mary (Hutchinson) G.; 1 child, Caroline. BA in English, U. Toronto, Ont., 1966, postgrad., 1966-67, 86-87; MPA, Harvard U., 1981. Secondary tchr. English, media studies, dramatic arts North York (Ont.) Bd. Edn., Willowdale, Ont., 1967-72, 81-82, 1986-88; M.P. from Don Valley North Can. Ho. Commons, 1988-93; secondary tchr. English, media studies North York (Ont.) Bd. Edn., 1993—. Elected contr. City of North York, 1972-80, 82-85; mem. Met. Toronto Coun., 1972-80, 82-85, exec. mem., budget subcom. mem., 1974-80, 82-85; dep. mayor North York, 1974-80; mem. Parliament Ottawa, Ont., 1988-93. Roman Catholic.

GREENE, BARBARA NANCY, art consultant; b. Boston, May 7, 1943; d. Bernard M. and Gertrude (Kramer) Millman; children: Robert Kaufman, Peter Kaufman. AA, U. Fla., 1962; BA, Goucher Coll., 1964; student, Johns Hopkins U., 1963. Cert. art educator, Fla.; cert. secondary English edn., Fla. Co-dir. Gloria Luria Gallery, Miami, Fla., 1978-82, asst. to dir., 1982-83; owner, dir. Greene Gallery, Inc., Miami, Fla., 1983-96; art cons. Greene Gallery, Inc., Pompano Beach, Fla., 1991—; v.p. in charge programming U. Miami, 1994-96. Creator of art exhibit: Latin American Art, Lowe Art Mus., 1995. Fundraiser Channel 2 Pub. TV, Lowe Art Mus.; docent, chair Lowe Art Mus.; past cons. Temple Bath Am., South Dade Jewish Cmty. Ctr.; active Friends of Art, Lowe Art Mus., South Dade Cmty. Ctr., Friends of Chamber Music Soc., Bach Soc., Friend Arts Fla. Internat. U. Art Mus., Jewish Home for Aged; bd. dirs. South Fla. Art Ctr., curator selected exhibits. Jewish. Home and Office: 1012 N Ocean Blvd #1105 Pompano Beach FL 33062

GREENE, CHERYL, advertising executive. Exec. v.p. acctg., planning dir. Deutsch Inc., N.Y.C. Office: Deutsch Dworin 215 Park Ave S New York NY 10003-1603*

GREENE, DONNA S., newspaper editor; b. Middlesboro, Ky., Mar. 28, 1955; d. Charles Rufus and Alene Juanita (Meyers) G. Student, Cumberland Coll., 1975, Southeast C.C., 1977. Libr. clk. Middlesboro Pub. Libr., 1971-76; home svc. aide Dept. Social Svcs. Commonwealth Ky., Pineville, 1976-85; lifestyles editor Middlesboro Daily News, 1985—. Vol. Ky. Young Democrats, Frankfort, 1975-80, Young Dems. Am., Washington, 1975-80; bd. dirs. Cumberland Trails United Way, publ. chmn., 1996—; treas. Yellow Creek Concerned Citizens, 1981-85; exec. bd. dirs. Cumberland Gap Area Arts Coun.; Ky. del. Nat. Dem. Conv., 1996; sec./treas. Bell County Dem. Woman's Club; deacon 1st Christian Ch. Named Outstanding Young Dem., 1981. Mem. Ky. Press Assn. (first place lifestyles 1992, 93, 94, best spl. sect. 1992). Mem. Disciples of Christ Ch.

GREENE, ELIZABETH IVORY, real estate company official; b. N.Y.C., Jan. 17, 1929; d. Percy Van Eman Ivory and Elizabeth (Schofield) Post Price; m. James Benno Greene Jr. (dec.); children: Elizabeth Tylawsky, James Benno III, Edgar Charles Ivory. BA, Bennington Coll., 1952. Sculptor Hansen Lamps, N.Y.C., 1952-57; real estate agent Ely-Cruikshank Co., N.Y.C., 1968-70; prin. Greene Realty Ltd., N.Y.C., 1970—, Apocalyptic Holdings Ltd., N.Y.C., 1972—. Bd. dirs. Bus. Improvement Dist. Greenwich Village, N.Y.C.; trustee City & County Sch., N.Y.C.; mem. Rep. Nat. Com., 1996. Recipient scholarship Bennington (Vt.) Coll., 1949-52. Mem. Small Property Owners Action Network (founder, pres. 1983—), Nat. Ctr. Neighborhood Enterprise, Village Visiting Neighbors (bd. dirs. 1987-89), DAR (John Jay chpt.), Greenwich Village C. of C. (bd. dirs.), Assn. Village Homeowners, N.Y. Mycological Soc. Home and Office: Small Property Owners Action Network SPAN 279 W 12th St New York NY 10014-1911

GREENE, ENID, congresswoman; b. San Rafael, Calif., Oct. 5, 1958. BS in Pol. Sci., U. Utah, 1980; JD, Brigham Young U., 1983. Caseworker, rsch. asst. U.S. Rep. Dan Marriott, R., 1982; atty. Ray, Quinney & Nebeker, 1983-90; dep. chief of staff Gov. Norman H. Bangerter, 1990-92; corp. counsel Novell, Inc., 1993-94; mem. 104th Congress from 2nd Utah dist., Washington, 1995—. Office: US House Reps 515 Cannon House Office Bldg Washington DC 20515-4402

GREENE, KATHRYN ELIZABETH, educational administrator; b. Dallas, Oreg., July 22, 1937; d. Fredrick Ernest Holtz and Esther Jane (Ross) Patton; m. Anthony Angel Cardenas, Nov. 25, 1962 (div. July 1976); children: Charles Anthony, David Edward; m. Ire Theophilus Greene, Apr. 13, 1981. BA, Linfield Coll., 1960; MS, U. Oreg., 1985. Purchasing agt. Martinez (Calif.) Unified Sch. Dist., 1978-80, Eugene (Oreg.) 4J Sch. Dist., 1980-83, City of Lompoc, Calif., 1985-90; dir. purchasing Washoe County Sch. Dist., Reno, 1990—. Vol. Ct. Apptd. Spl. Adv. (CASA),Reno, 1992—. Mem. Nat. Assn. Purchasing Mfrs. (cert., pres. No. Nev. chpt. 1994-96), Nat. Purchasing Inst. (bd. dirs. 1991-94), Calif. Assn. Pub. Purchasing Ofcls. (bd. dirs. 1988-89). Methodist. Office: Washoe County Sch Dist 425 E 9th St Reno NV 89520

GREENE, KAY C., psychologist, author; b. Yankton, S.D., July 10, 1939; d. Fred Orin and Evelyn Irene (Sundy) Green. B.Mus. in Edn., U. Nebr., 1962; MA in Psychology, New Sch. Social Rsch., 1980, PhD in Clin. Psychology, 1983. Lic. psychologist, Md., N.Y., D.C. With Gulf States Utilities, Beaumont, Tex., 1963-64, Tatham, Laird & Kudner, N.Y.C., 1965-66; mgmt. cons. John Wiersma Cons., Washington, 1966; advt. coord. Sullivan Stauffer Colwell & Bayles, N.Y.C., 1966-67; acting supr., ticket agt., svc. rep. Am. Airlines, N.Y.C., 1967; exec. sec. to v.p./chief engr. WPIX-TV, N.Y.C., 1967-72, adminstrv. asst. to news chief, 1967-72; office mgr. Lawrence Letter Svc., N.Y.C., 1973-78; clin. psychologist in pvt. practice N.Y.C., 1985—; regional trainer APA Hope (HIV) Project, 1992—; tchr. music, English, spl. edn. MacArthur Jr. H.S., Beaumont, 1964-65; student music tchr. U. Nebr. Exptl. H.S., Lincoln, 1961-62; lectr. in field; condr. seminars in field; appeared on Donahue, Good Morning, Kelly and Co., Survival into the 21st Century, Turning Inward; radio shows include The Alan Colmes Show, WABC, N.Y., Alan Colmes, WPIX, N.Y., Open Session, Ben Reese, WNYE, N.Y., From Head to Heart, WXLO, N.Y., Foundation Focus, WNEW, N.Y., Wellness Workshop, WNWK FM, N.Y., others; pres. Bridge of Change; sr. rep. UN Hdqrs. for World Fedn. Mental Health, organizer various confs., keynote spkr. various internat. confs. past staff therapist/sr. staff psychologist Fifth Ave. Ctr. for Counseling and Psychotherapy, N.Y.C. Contbr. articles to profl. jours. Named Internat. Woman of the Yr. in recognition of svcs. to mental health Internat. Biog. Centre, 1993-94; recipient Disting. Leadership award Internat. Directory of Disting. Leadership. Mem. APA (Nat. AIDS task force 1988—), Am. Fedn. TV and Radio Artists, Authors Guild, Authors League, Internat. Coun. of Psychologists, Internat. Platform Assn., C.G. Jung Found. for Analytical Psychology, N.Y. Acad. Sci., N.Y. State Psychol. Assn., Screen Actors Guild, Soc. for Psychol. Study of Social Issues, World Assn. for Psychosocial Rehab., World Fedn. Mental Health. Home and Office: 30 Waterside Plz #13E New York NY 10010-2630

GREENE, LYNNE JEANNETTE, fashion designer; b. Albany, N.Y., Aug. 27, 1938; d. Zebulon Stevens and Helen Matilde (Maier) Robbins; m. Stanley E. Greene, Jan. 31, 1962 (dec. June 27, 1987); 1 child, Stuart Nathaniel; m. Michael Alan Karlan, Sept. 29, 1991. Student, Goucher Coll., 1956-57; BA with honors, Parsons Sch. Design, 1960. Asst. designer Haymaker Sportswear (David Crystal), N.Y.C., 1959-61; designer Craig Craely Sportswear and Dresses, N.Y.C., 1961-63, Flair Lingerie, N.Y.C., 1964-66; designer, owner Kaleidoscope Lingerie, N.Y.C., 1966-67; head designer Contessa/Monique/Fisher Lingerie, N.Y.C., 1967-71; creative dir. Eye of the Peacock Sportswear, N.J., 1968-72; head designer, owner Lynne Greene Designs Retail, Montclair, N.J., 1972-74; designer, pres. Little Greene Apples Inc., Montville, N.J., 1971—; designer, dir. mktg. Lady Lynne Lingerie, Guy Laroche Lingerie, N.Y.C., 1973-93, Val Mode by Lynne Greene, N.Y.C., 1993—; lingerie critic Pratt Inst., 1984—. Patentee in field; illustrator books, pamphlets in fashion and packaging fields; commn. artist and illustrator. Active participant Montville Soccer Assn, 1972-88, fund drives for Am. Heart Assn., Cancer Inc. Mem. The Fashion Group. Republican. Unitarian Universalist.

GREENE, NATALIE CONSTANCE, protective services official; b. Ft. Benning, Ga., Nov. 26, 1960; d. Wilbur Murray and Vernel Jeanette (Smalls) G. BS in Phys. Edn., East Stroudsburg U., 1983; AAS in Gen. Bus., Mercer County C.C., 1989, postgrad., 1991—; postgrad., Coll. of Air Force, 1991—. Mil. pay clk. Dept. Def.-U.S. Army, Trenton, N.J., 1984-85, Dept. Def.-USAF, McGuire AFB, N.J., 1985-86; spl. police officer Willingboro (N.J.) Police Dept., 1986-90; budget asst. Dept. Def., West Trenton, N.J., 1986-88; edn. planner, budget officer Dept. Edn., Edison, N.J., 1988-89; mcht. svcs. clk. Chem. Bank, Cherry Hill, N.J., 1989-90; transit police officer Southea. Pa. Transp. Authority, Phila., 1990—. Master sgt. USAFR, 1980—. Recipient Desert Shield/Storm award, 1992, Cert. of Appreciation, CAP, 1991, Willingboro Twp., 1991, Morton Elem. Sch., 1991, Outstanding Young Women of N.J., 1989. Mem. NAFE, VFW, Air Force Sgts. Assn., Air Force Assn., Fraternal Order Police, Fraternal Order Transit Police, Noncommd. Officers Acad. Grad. Assn., Nat. Orgn. Black Law Enforcement. Baptist. Home: 132 Crestview Dr Willingboro NJ 08046-3538

GREENE, REBECCA RACHEL, lawyer; b. Berlin, Germany, Nov. 14, 1947; parents U.S. citizens; m. Peter Alan Greene, June 22, 1969; children: Abraham, Ethan. BA, Barnard Coll., 1968; MA, Washington U., 1970; PhD, Columbia U., 1977; JD, Rutgers U., Newark, 1984. Bar: N.J. 1985, D.C. 1991, N.Y. 1992. Rsch. asst. Internat. Bank for Reconstrn. and Devel., Washington, 1970-71; rsch. fellow Cornell Med. Ctr., N.Y.C., 1974-76; vis. asst. prof. Colgate U., Hamilton, N.Y., 1979-80; staff atty. Union County Legal Svcs., Elizabeth, N.J., 1986-88; examiner N.J. Divsn. for Consumer Affairs, Newark, 1988—, regulatory officer, 1990—. Contbr. articles to profl. jours. Regents Coll. Tchg. fellow, 1968-69; Danforth fellow in history, 1968-69; Josiah Macy fellow, 1974-76; fellow in history of medicine NIH, 1978-80. Home: 246 Lenox Ave South Orange NJ 07079-1408

GREENE, SHARON WILLIAMS, school librarian; b. Norfolk, Va., Oct. 17, 1953; d. Richard Parker and Evelyn Mae (Burrows) Williams; m. Randy Lee Greene, Mar. 18, 1977; children: Marilyn Denise, Angela Michelle. BS in Counseling Psychology, Presbyn. Coll., 1974. Cert. assoc. guidance, S.C. Guidance counselor Riverside Middle Sch., Saluda, S.C., 1974-77; office mgr. Franklin Springs (Ga.) Ch., 1986-89; tchr. W. Wyman King Acad., Batesburg, S.C., 1991-94, libr., 1994—; mem. S.C. children's book award com., 1996—; part-time counselor Saluda County Alcohol and Drug Abuse Commn., 1991-94; mem Com. to Prepare Middle Sch. Guidance Objectives, Columbia, S.C., 1976. Leader Girl Scouts U.S.A., Franklin Springs, 1986-91. Recipient Newcomer award Girl Scouts U.S.A., 1987. Mem. Am. Contract Bridge League, Highland Ave. Pentecostal Holiness Women's Ministry (pres. 1994—). Office: W Wyman King Acad RR 1 Box 287 Batesburg SC 29006-9526

GREENE, STEPHANIE HARRISON, marketing executive; b. Lake Forest, Ill., June 20, 1950; d. Howard Harrison and Gloria Juliet (Christensen) Greene. BA in Journalism and Advt., Syracuse U., 1972; MBA in Mktg., Cornell U., 1975. With Weeden & Co., Boston, 1972-73; product rep. Allis Chalmers, Matteson, Ill., 1975-76; asst. product mgr. Midwest Am./Am. Hosp. Supply, Des Plaines, Ill., 1976-77; product mgr. Borden, Inc., Columbus, Ohio, 1977-80; product line mgr. John Sexton & Co./Beatrice, Chgo., 1980-82; product mgr. non-foods PYA/Monarch/Sara Lee, Greenville, S.C., 1982-84; mktg. mgr. Fuller Brush/Sara Lee, Winston-Salem, 1984-89; pres. Corbett Harrison Greene, Mundelein, Ill., 1984—; mktg. mgr. The Greehill Corp., Libertyville, Ill., 1989—; bd. dirs. Career Pub., Mundelein, v.p., 1993—. Editor: The Quotation Dictionary, 1968. Active Wilmette (Ill.) Chorus, 1993-95, Village Follies, 1994, Winnetka (Ill.) Theatre, 1992—, bd. govs., 1994-96, v.p., 1995-96, pres., 1996—; mem. Chancel Choir, Libertyville, Ill., 1995—. Mem. Print Prodn. Club, Cornell U. Alumnae Assn. (pres. Class of 1975), Johnson Club (amb. 1990, 91, pres. 1992-94), Holly Tree Garden Club (treas. 1983-84), Serendipity Garden Club (treas. 1978-79), Pi Beta Phi. Republican. Episcopalian. Home: 408 Hampton Ter Libertyville IL 60048-3334 Office: The Greehill Corp 15521 W Rockland Rd Libertyville IL 60048-9674

GREENE, VANESSA ANDREA, television producer; b. London, Sept. 15, 1954; d. William John and Alice May (Stratford) Linsell; m. David Brian Greene, Jan. 22, 1975 (div. Apr. 1981); 1 child, Linsel Adam. Exec. prodr., prodr./writer Rape and Marriage: The Rideout Case, CBS, 1980, Wait Till Your Mother Gets Home, NBC, 1982, Hobsons Choice, CBS, 1984, Under the Influence, CBS, 1986, Secret Witness, CBS, 1987, Money..Power..Murder, CBS, 1989-90, Deadly Desire, 1991, Writers Block, 1929, With Hostile Intent, CBS, 1993, Search for Grace, CBS, 1994, Nothing Lasts Forever, CBS, 1995, Stolen Women, CBS, 1996; writer: (with Alan Adler) Star Trek, The Next Generation, The Loss episode, 1991, The Body, 1995. Recipient Scott Newman award for best TV film of 1987 dealing with drug and alcohol abuse Newman Found., L.A., 1987. Office: CBS 7800 Beverly Blvd Los Angeles CA 90046

GREENE, WENDY SEGAL, special education educator; b. New Rochelle, N.Y., Jan. 9, 1929; d. Louis Peter and Anne Henrietta (Kahan) Segal; m. Charles Edward Smith (div. 1952); m. Richard M. Greene Jr. (div. 1967); children: Christopher S., Kerry William, Karen Beth Greene Olson; m. Richard M. Greene Sr., Aug. 29, 1985 (dec. 1986). Student, Olivet Coll., 1946-48, Santa Monica Coll., 1967-70; BA in Child Devel., Calif. State U., Los Angeles, 1973, MA in Elem. Edn., 1975. Cert. tchr., Calif. Counselor Camp Watitoh, Becket, Mass., 1946-49; asst. tchr. Outdoor Play Group, New Rochelle, 1946-58; edn. sec. pediatrics Syracuse (N.Y.) Meml. Hosp., 1952-53; with St. John's Hosp., Santa Monica, Calif., 1962-63; head tchr. Head Start, L.A., 1966-77; tchr. spl. edn. L.A. Unified Sch. Dist., 1977—, Salvin Spl. Edn. Ctr., L.A., 1977-85, Perez Spl. Edn. Ctr., L.A., 1986-; instr. mktg. rsch. for motivational rsch. Anderson-McConnell Agy., 1966; mentor tchr. L.A. Unified Sch. Dist., 1992—. Contbr. to house organ of St. John's Hosp.; co-editor of newspaper for Salvin Sch., L.A. and The Eagle, Perez Sch., L.A., 1988—; contbg. reporter El Aguiler (The Eagle), Perez. Bd. dirs. Richland Ave. Youth House, L.A., 1960-63, Emotional Health Assn., L.A., 1961-66, Richland Ave. Sch. PTA, 1959-63; vol. Hospice of St. Joseph Hosp., Orange, Calif., 1985—; mem. cmty. adv. com. spl. edn. Tustin Unified Sch. Dist., 1994—. Mem. AAUW, So. Calif. Assn. Young Children, Olivet Coll. Alumni Assn., United Tchrs. L.A., Westside Singers (L.A.), Kappa Delta Pi. Jewish. Home: 14291 Prospect Ave Tustin CA 92680-2316

GREENE LLOYD, NANCY ELLEN, infosystems specialist, physicist; b. Worcester, Mass., Nov. 4, 1947; d. William Arthur II and Dorothy Goddard (Fuller) Green; children: Ellen Dorothy, Gwyneth Tegan; m. Stephen C. Lloyd, July 25, 1992. BS in Physics, Ohio State U., 1969, MS in Physics, 1971. Instr. physics U. Colo., Colorado Springs, 1971-73; physics programmer U. N.Mex., Albuquerque, 1973-76; data analyst Los Alamos (N.Mex.) Nat. Lab., 1975-77, programmer, 1977-78, mem. tech. staff controlled thermonuclear reaction divsn., 1978-81, mem. tech. staff Accelerator Tech. div., 1981-84, mem. tech. staff adminstrv. data processing divsn., 1984-85, mem. tech. staff dynamic experimentation divsn., 1985-94, staff mem. supr., 1989-90, acting sect. leader, 1990-91, acting dep. divsn. leader, 1992, chief ops. explosives tech. and applications divsn., 1992-94, mem. tech. staff environ., safety, and health divsn. Instl. Affairs Office, 1994—; speaker in field. Vol. Los Alamos Schs., 1980-88, Fountain Valley Sch., Colo., 1990-91. Nat. Merit scholar, Mich. State U., 1965, Nat. Defense Edn. Act Title IV fellow, Ohio State U., 1969. Mem. NAFE, IEEE, N.Mex. Digital Equipment Computer Users Soc. (exec. com. 1984-87, 88-90, registration chair computer conf. 1984-87, vice-chair 1988-89, publicity 1989-90), VAX Computer Local Users Group (chmn. 1981-82, sec. 1989-92), N.Mex. Square and Round Dance Assn. (dist. co-chair 1996—), Toastmasters. Office: Los Alamos Nat Lab PO Box 1663 K491 Los Alamos NM 87545-0600

GREENEY, LAURA ANNE, editor, English educator; b. Bklyn., July 18, 1961; d. John H. and Florence E. (Taylor) G. BA in English, Fordham U., 1982; MA in English, NYU, 1985. Copy and prodn. editor Garland Pub., Inc., N.Y.C., 1983-86; devel. editor Paragon House Pubs., N.Y.C., 1986-88; sr. editor Brunner/Mazel Pubs., N.Y.C., 1989; adj. instr. English Fordham U., N.Y.C., 1988—, assoc. dir. Coll. Writing Ctr., 1990-95; assoc. editor River Reporter literary supplement, Barryville, N.Y., 1990-95; sr. editor Panel Pubs., N.Y.C., 1995—; freelance editorial cons., 1989—; freelance writer Ednl. Testing Svcs., Princeton, N.J., 1993—. Contbr. articles to newspapers. Mem. Women's Nat. Book Assn., NAFE. Home: 294 11th St Brooklyn NY 11215-3911 Office: Panel Pubs 36 W 44th St Rm 1316 New York NY 10036

GREENFIELD, LINDA SUE, nursing educator; b. Dover, Del., Aug. 5, 1950; d. Norman Raymond and Eleanor Henrietta (Harmon) Connell; m. Douglas Herman Greenfield, Dec. 27, 1976; children: Leah, Paige. BSN, Cath. U., 1972; MSN cum laude, Boston U., 1977; postgrad., Coll. New Rochelle, 1986-88, Adelphi U., 1994—. RN; cert. registered nurse anethetist. Staff nurse emergency rm. & ICU Washington Hosp. Ctr., 1974-75; operating rm. nurse Mass Eye & Ear, Boston, 1975; ICU nurse Peter Bent Brigham Hosp., Boston, 1975-76; surg. nurse practitioner Kingsbrook Jewish Hosp., Bklyn., 1976-79; surgical nurse Met. Hosp. Sch. Nurse Anesthetists, 1979-81; RN anethetist Brookdale Hosp., Bklyn., 1981-82, Winthrop U. Hosp., Mineola, N.Y., 1991-95; adj. prof. Adelphi U., Garden City, N.Y., 1995—. Bd. officer Manhasset Newcomers, N.Y., 1988-90; bd. dirs. Friends of Manhasset Libr., N.Y., 1990-94; mem. Make a Wish Found., Port Washington, N.Y., 1990—. Lt. U.S. Army, 1970-74. Mem. NOW, Am. Assn. Nurse Anesthetists, 1 in 9, Sch. Cmty. Assn., Noetic Soc., Nat. Assn. Homeopathy, Nat. Assn. for Holistic Nurses, Sigma Theta Tau. Home: 34 Aldershot Ln Manhasset NY 11030

GREENFIELD, MEG, journalist; b. Seattle, Dec. 27, 1930; d. Lewis James and Lorraine (Nathan) G. BA summa cum laude, Smith Coll., 1952; Fulbright scholar, Newnham Coll., Cambridge (Eng.) U., 1952-53; DHL (hon.), Smith Coll., 1978, Georgetown U., 1979, Wesleyan U., 1982, Williams Coll., 1987, Princeton U., 1990. With Reporter mag., 1957-68, Washington editor, 1965-68; editorial writer Washington Post, 1968-70, dep. editorial page editor, 1970-79, editorial page editor, 1979—; columnist Newsweek, 1974—. Recipient Pulitzer prize for editorial writing 1978. Mem. Am. Soc. Newspaper Editors, Phi Beta Kappa. Home: 3318 R St NW Washington DC 20007-2309 Office: Washington Post Co 1150 15th St NW Washington DC 20005-2780

GREENHOUSE, LINDA JOYCE, journalist; b. N.Y.C., Jan. 9, 1947; d. Herman Robert and Dorothy Eleanor (Greenlick) G.; m. Eugene R. Fidell, Jan. 1, 1981; 1 child, Hannah Margalit Fidell. BA, Radcliffe Coll., 1968; M of Studies in Law, Yale U., 1978; D.H.L. (hon.), Brown U., 1991; JD (hon.), Colgate U., 1993. Asst. to James Reston The N.Y. Times, N.Y.C., 1968-69, met. reporter, 1970-74, state polit. reporter, 1974-77; supreme ct. corr. The N.Y. Times, Washington, 1978-85, 88—, congl. corr., 1986-88. Bd. dirs. Yale Law Sch. Fund, New Haven, 1984-91; adv. com. Schlesinger Lib. on the History of Women in Am. Radcliffe Coll., 1995—. Fellow Am. Acad. Arts and Scis.; mem. Yale Law Assn. (exec. com. 1993—), Harvard Club Washington (bd. dirs. 1989-92). Office: The NY Times 1627 I St NW Washington DC 20006-4007

GREEN-NIGRO, CAROLYN JEAN, nursing educator; b. Detroit, May 15, 1943; d. Wade Enlo and Mildred Mary Ellen (Robbins) G.; m. John Bruce Maloney, May 23, 1964 (div. May, 1970); children: Kathryn Michelle, Deborah Lynn; m. Charles Carl Nigro, II, Nov. 16, 1990. Nursing diploman, Independence Sanitarium & Hosp, Mo., 1964; AA, Johnson County C.C., Overland Park, Kans., 1977; BS in Nursing, U. Kans., Kansas City, 1981, MS in Nursing, 1985; PhD in Nursing, U. Kans., 1995. Staff nurse Independence (Mo.) Sanitarium & Hosp., 1964-70; head nurs. Med. Ctr. of Independence, 1970-73; dir. nursing Olathe (Kans.) Comty. Hosp., 1974-77; quality assurance coord. Suburban Med. Ctr., Overland Park, Kans., 1979-82; nursing faculty Johnson County C.C., Overland Park, 1983—; adv. bd. staff devel. Overland Park Regional Med. Ctr., Overland Park, 1990—, rsch. com. 1992; profl. adv. coun. Am. Nursing Svcs., Overland Park, 1995. Author: (books) Study Guide to Accompany Phipps: Medical Surgical Nursing, 1994, Instructor's Manual for same, 1994 (Publisher's award, 1995), Instructor's Manual for Leukonett's Gerontological Nursing, 1994; (computer software) Multiple Sclerosis: Cases, 1995. Vol Good Samaritan Project, 1986-88; bd. dirs. Am. Heart Assn., Overland Park, Kans., 1988-92. Recipient Burlington No. Faculty Achievement award, Overland Park, Kans., 1993. Mem. ANA, AACN, Kansas City Hosp. Assn. (Employee of Yr 1972), Kans. Nurses Assn. (pres. dist. 2 1995—), Am. Assn. Operating Rm. Nurses, Navy Nurse Corps Assn., Phi Delta Kappa. Office: Johnson County CC 12345 College at Quivira Overland Park KS 66210

GREENSPAN, GLADYS, textile designer; b. N.Y.C., Sept. 14, 1923; d. Irving and Celia Appelbaum; m. Alex Greenspan, July 30, 1944; 1 child, Jeffrey. Doctor, Bklyn. Mus. Art Student, League, Queen's Coll. Textile designer Textile-Virgil Studio, N.Y.C., 1941-61, Ameritex, N.Y.C., Steintex, N.Y.C., Jane Albert Studios, N.Y.C.; active drawing with pastels, YMCA-YMHA, Queens, N.Y., 1976-78. Exhbns. include Roslyn Mus. Fine Arts, Long Beach Mus., Nat. Art League, Emil Leonard Gallery, Smithtown Twp. Art Coun., St. James, n.Y., Gaddard Ctr. for Visual Arts, Ardmore, Okla., Mus. of Southwest U. Mus., Midland, Tex., U. of the South, Tenn., Richmond (Ind.) Art Mus., Owtanna Arts Ctr., Minn., others; permanent collection in Jane-Voorhees-Zimmerli Mus. of Rutgers U. Awards include Best-in-Show Bayside Art League, Meml. award Jacob Javits Fed. Bldg., Paul Mellon Art Ctr., others. Mem. Pastel Soc. Am., Nat. Assn. Women Artists, Profl. Artist Guild Boco Mus./Fla., Artist Guild of Norton Mus./Fla., Artist Network of Great Neck/L.I., N.Y. Home: 6080 Huntwick Terr Apt 307 Delray Beach FL 33484

GREENSPAN-MARGOLIS, JUNE E., psychiatrist; b. N.Y.C., June 28, 1934; d. Benjamin Robert and Theresa (Cooperstein) Edelman; divorced; 1 child, Alisa Greenspan; m. Gerald J. Margolis. AB, Bryn Mawr Coll., 1955; MD, Med. Coll. Pa., 1959; grad., Inst Phila Assn Psychoanalysis, Bala Cynwyd, 1975. Intern Albert Einstein Med. Ctr., Phila., 1959-60; pvt. practice medicine specializing in pediatrics Cinnaminson, N.J., 1961-67; psychiat. resident Hahnemann Med. Coll., Phila., 1967-71; practice medicine specializing in adult and child psychiatry, psychoanalysis Jenkintown, Pa., 1971—; instr. U. Pa. Sch. Medicine, Phila., 1975-77, clin. assoc. 1977-81, clin. asst. prof. 1981-85, clin. assoc. prof. 1986—; tng. and supervisory analyst Inst. of the Phila. Assn. Psychoanalysis, Bala Cynwyd, Pa., 1986—. Fellow Am. Coll. Psychoanalysts; mem. AMA, Am. Psychiat. Assn., Am. Psychoanalytic Assn. (cert. adult and child psychoanalysis), Am. Acad. Child Psychiatry, Ctr. for Advanced Psychoanalytic Studies (Princeton). Office: Benson East Suite 223-C 100 Old York Rd Jenkintown PA 19046

GREENSTEIN, SHARON DIANE, hospital administrator, nurse, educator; b. Boston, May 18, 1962; d. George David and Barbara Evelyn (Bloom) G.; m. Robert Dean Sellers, Oct. 6, 1991; 1 child, Bryan Jacob. BSN, U. Pa., 1984; MBA, U. Chgo., 1989. RN, Pa., Ill. Nurse Grad. Hosp., Phila., 1984-87, U. Chgo. Hosps., 1987-88; provider rels. cons. Pru Care Ill., Des Plaines, 1988; cons. Price Waterhouse, Chgo., 1989; dir. fin. svcs. Rush-Presbyn.-St. Luke's Med. Ctr., Chgo., 1990—; instr. Rush U., Chgo., 1990—. Mem. Chgo. Health Execs. Forum. Jewish. Home: 636 N Ridgeland Ave Oak Park IL 60302 Office: Rush-Presbyn-St Luke's Med Ctr 1653 W Congress Pky Chicago IL 60612

GREENWALD, LYNDA J., small business owner; b. Phila., Apr. 8, 1968; d. Mark John and Carol (Rockower) Goldstein; m. Thomas Zoltan Greenwald. BS, So. Conn. State U., 1990, MS, 1991. Resource devel. asst. ACORD, Wallingford, Conn., 1990-91; daycare owner/provider The Carousel Home Child Care, Inc., Dresher, Pa., 1991—. Home: 3855 Blair Mill Rd 231Q Horsham PA 19044-2848

GREENWALT, MARY SUSAN, counselor; b. St. Louis, Dec. 26, 1946; d. LeGrand West and Susan Frances (Frier) Wheeler; m. Allen Duane Greenwalt, Apr. 11, 1992; stepchildren: Scott Harrison, Emily Megan. BS, So. Ill. U., 1968, MS, 1972; MBA, St. Louis U., 1982. Tchr. Lindbergh Sch. Dist., St. Louis, 1968-79, counselor, 1979—. Stage mgr. V-P Fair, St. Louis, 1984-93; vol. St. Louis Nursery Found. Book Fair, 1985-93. Recipient Tuition grant for women MBA students IBM, 1977. Mem. NEA, Mo. Edn. Assn., Lindbergh Edn. Assn. (pres. 1982-83), Am. Counseling Assn., Mo. Sch. Counselors Assn., St. Louis Suburban Sch. Counselors Assn. (Elem. Counselor of Yr. 1993), Jr. League St. Louis, Alpha Gamma Delta (St. Louis Alumnae Club). Republican. Methodist. Home: 14 Girard Dr Saint Louis MO 63119-4802 Office: Crestwood Elem Sch 1020 S Sappington Rd Saint Louis MO 63126-1005

GREENWOOD, HARRIET LOIS, environmental banker, researcher; b. Detroit, Oct. 4, 1950; d. Samuel H. and Elizabeth Ann (Bode) G.; m. Michael E. Carlson, Aug. 23, 1981 (div. Sept. 1986); m. Eric J. Halbeisen, Sept. 5, 1987; 1 child, Robin Faith. BA in Biology, Antioch Coll., 1972; MS in Teaching, Antioch Coll. of New Eng., 1975; postgrad. U. Mich., 1985-87. Dir. environ. studies Swanson Environ., Southfield, Mich., 1978-80; project mgr. ESEI, Ecol. Scis., Detroit, 1981-82; pres. Greenwood & Assocs., Detroit, 1982-83; mgr. environ. studies Environ. Rsch. Group, Ann Arbor, Mich., 1983-85; environ. policy specialist Clayton Environ., Southfield, 1985-91; pres. Environ. Tng. Svcs., Detroit, 1991-93; personal trust officer Comerica Bank, 1993—; part-time instr. Wayne State U., 1992—; rec. clk. Detroit Friends Meeting, 1985-88; bd. dirs. Friends Sch. Detroit, 1987-89. U. Mich. fellow, 1985-86. Mem. East Mich. Environ. Acton. Coun., Mich. Assn. Environ. Profls., Mich. Bankers Assn. (environ. com.), Nat. Assn. Environ. Profls. (ASTM com. E-50 on environ. assessment S.W. Detroit environ. vision project); Mich. Air and Waste Mgmt. Assn., Environ. Bankers Assn. Quaker. Avocations: English country dancing, rapper sword dancing, cross country skiing. Office: Comerica Bank Trust Real Estate-3228 PO Box 75000 Detroit MI 48275-0001

GREENWOOD, JANET KAE DALY, psychologist, educational administrator; b. Goldsboro, N.C., Dec. 9, 1943; d. Fulton Benton and Kelminy Ethel Esther (Ball) Daly; 1 child, Gerald Thompson. AA, Peace Coll., 1963; BS in English and Psychology, East Carolina U., 1965, MEd in Counseling, 1967; postgrad., N.C. State U., 1967-69, U. London, 1969; PhD in Counseling and Higher Ednl. Adminstrn., Fla. State U., 1972. Tchr. English Kinston (N.C.) City Schs., 1965-66, Goldsboro City Schs., 1966-67; counselor and psychometrist primary and secondary schs. County of Wake, N.C., 1967-69; coord. Am. Inst. for Fgn. Study, 1969; supr. student tours in Eng., France, Switzerland, Italy, and Capri, 1969; counselor Fla. State U., Tallahassee, 1969-72; asst. dir. counseling Rutgers U., New Brunswick, N.J., 1972-73; cons. to v.p. for student svcs. Rutgers U., New Brunswick, 1973-74, lectr. in counseling psychology, 1972-74; coord. and assoc. prof. counselor edn. U. Cin., 1974-77, adviser to grad. students, 1974-77, vice provost student affairs, 1977-81; cons. guidance South Plainfield Pub. Schs., 1973-76; adviser Parents Without Ptnrs., 1976; pres. Longwood Coll., Farmville, Va., 1981-87, U. Bridgeport, Conn., 1987-92; cons., ptnr. Heidrick & Struggles, Washington D.C., 1992—, bd. dirs. The Hydraulic Co., Gov.'s Partnership to Prevent Substance Abuse in the Workforce, audit com. and cmty., govt. rels. com. Contbr. articles to profl. jours. Mem. Gov.'s Ad Hoc Edn. Com. on Tchr. Edn. and Counselor Edn., State of Ohio, 1975; mem. state planning commn. Nat. Identification of Women Project; chair Twin Rivers Tenants Rights Assn., 1972-74; bd. dirs. Bridgeport Hosp., Bridgeport Bus. Coun.; mem. adv. com. Bridgeport Pub. Edn. Fund; bd. dirs. Conn. Ballet Theatre, chair South End streeting com; mem. mgmt. adv. com. City of Bridgeport; mem. adv. com. United Way Tri-State; chair South End Partnership Com; mem. The Schiavone Steering Com./Downtown Bridgeport Project, YWCA Bd., Champion/United Way, United Way Community Human Svcs. Planning Coun., Bridgeport Symphony Bd., Bridgeport Opera Bd., Bridgeport Area Coll./Univ. Consortium, Conn. Conf. Ind. Colls., The Newcomen Soc. of U.S., The United Way Ea. Fairfield County; mem. adv. bd. Sacred Heart/St. Anthony Sch., Roosevelt Sch; mem. ct. com. Regional Plan Assn. Fairfield 2000; bd. dirs. Conn. Ballet Theatre; chair The Bridgeport Regional Bus. Coun. Brass Ring Task Force on Leadership; bd. govs. Fairfield County Study; mem. hon. bd. dirs. Conn. Earth Day 20, Inc.; chair L.I. Sound Western Regional Coun.; mem. L.I. Sound Assembly; mem. membership com., campus partnership subcom. Drugs Don't Work program, 1989—. Recipient Spl. award Black Arts Festival, Meritorious Svc. award Am. Assn. State Colls. and Univs. Mem. AAUP, Am. Coll. Pers. Assn. (editor and chair media bd. 1975—), Am. Pers. and Guidance Assn., Cin. Pers. and Guidance Assn., Ohio Psychol. Assn., Cin. Psychol. Assn., Organizational Behavior Assn., Am. Sch. Counselors Assn., Ohio Sch. Counselors Assn., Assn. for Women Faculty, Ohio Counselor Edn. and Supervision Assn., Kappa Delta Pi.

GREENWOOD, JANET KINGHAM, sanitarian, county official; b. Houston, Sept. 29, 1939; d. Harold Lloyd and Angelina (Mann) Kingham; m. James Richard Greenwood, June 13, 1959; children: Cynthia Anne, Patricia Greenwood Hardcastle. BA in Sociology cum laude, U. Houston, 1975. Registered sanitarian, Tex. Sanitarian-in-tng. Galveston County Health Dist., LaMarque, Tex., 1975-76, sanitarian II, 1976-79, sanitarian III, 1979-81, sr. sanitarian, 1981-88, sanitarian supr., 1988-90, chief sanitarian, 1990-93, dir. environ. and consumer health, 1993—; mem. Sanitarian's adv. Com., Austin, Tex., 1984, vice chmn., 1985. Vol. St. Joseph's Hosp., Houston, 1951-53; mem. recycling com. City of Galveston, 1990-96. Fellow Tex. Pub. Health Assn. (governing council, 1980-81, legis. com. 1981-83, scholarship com. 1988-90, exhibit procurement com. 1992-93, chair exhibit procurement com. 1993-96, benefits com. 1991-95, sect. chmn. 1980-81, President's award 1985, 90, 94, 95, 96, edn. and tng. grantee 1978, fund raising com. 1992-96, 2d vice pres. 1994, 1st v.p. 1995, pres. elect, 1996, pub. health mus. com. 1992-96); mem. Nat. Environ. Health Assn. (governing coun. 1988-89, merit award 1988), Internat. Milk, Food and Environ. Sanitarians, Tex. Environ. Health Assn. (pres. 1987-89), Gulf Coast Tex. Environ. Health Assn. (pres. 1981, President's award 1986), Tex. Assn. Mcpl. Health Ofcls. (charter), La Marque Rotary. Democrat. Roman Catholic. Office: Galveston County Health Dis 1205 Oak St La Marque TX 77568-5925

GREENWOOD, JOEN ELIZABETH, economist, consultant; b. Mineral Point, Wis., Aug. 29, 1934; d. John Edward and Lillian Laile (Rohr) G. BS, MA, U. Wis., 1956, 57; postgrad., Newnham Coll. Cambridge U., Eng., 1961-62; diploma in advanced mgmt. program, Harvard Bus. Sch., 1983. Instr. econs. Wellesley (Mass.) Coll., 1962-68; sr. assoc. Charles River Assocs., Boston, 1968-79, v.p., 1979—; mem. bd. editors Energy Jour., 1979-83. Co-author: Folded, Spindled and Mutilated: Economic Analysis and U.S. v. IBM, 1983; contbr. to profl. publs. Mem. Commonwealth of Mass. Pub. Health Coun., Boston, 1973-79. Earhart fellow U. Calif.-Berkeley, 1960-61; Fulbright scholar U.K., 1961-62. Mem. Internat. Assn. Energy Economists (v.p. 1978-84, exec. v.p. 1981-84), Nat. Coal Coun., U. Wis. Alumni Assn. (bd. dirs. 1987-93), Wis. Alumni Assn. Greater Boston (pres. 1987-89), Boston Club, Harvard Club, Phi Beta Kappa. Home: 108 Chestnut St Cambridge MA 02139-4704 Office: Charles River Assocs 200 Clarendon St Boston MA 02116-5021

GREENWOOD, MARYSCOTT, lobbyist; b. Camp Le June, N.C., Dec. 16, 1965; d. Eugene Brady and Margery (Owen) Fallon; m. James Henry Greenwood, June 9, 1990; 1 child, Margery Grace. BA, U. Vt., 1988. Fin. dir. Dem. Party of Ga., Atlanta, 1990-92, exec. dir., 1992-94; dir. intergovtl. affairs, chief state/fed. lobbyist Office of the Mayor of Atlanta, Ga., 1994—; bd. dirs. The Margaret Mitchell House, Atlanta; adv. bd. mem. The Urban Study Inst., Atlanta, 1994—. Participant Program for State and Local Execs., John F. Kennedy Sch. Govt., Harvard U., Cambridge, Mass., 1995. Mem. Ga. C. of C. (govt. affairs coun. 1994—), Ga. Mcpl. Assn. (fin. policy com. 1994—). Roman Catholic. Office: Office of the Mayor 55 Trinity Ave SW Atlanta GA 30335

GREER, CYNTHIA FAYE, university administrator, legal educator, mediator; b. Madison, Tenn., Oct. 22, 1954; d. Leo Curtis Sr. and Vera Evelyn (Dickens) G. BA, David Lipscomb U., Nashville, 1976; MEd, Ga. State U., 1978; EdD, Pepperdine U., 1988. Cert. in dispute resolution; cert. counselor and mediator. Secondary English tchr. Greater Atlanta Christian Sch., 1977-80; dir. career svcs. David Lipscomb U., Nashville, 1980-81; dir. career svcs. and alumni rels. Pepperdine Sch. Law, Malibu, Calif., 1981-82, asst. dean, 1982-92, assoc. dean instnl. advancement, 1992—. Editor Pepperdine Law Quar., 1981—. Mem. Malibu Vol. Patrol, 1994—. Mem. ABA, Calif. State Bar (com. on continuing legal edn. 1990-93), Am. Assn. Law Schs. (sec. sects. on student svcs. 1995, exec. com. 1995). Office: Pepperdine Sch Law 24255 Pacific Coast Hwy Malibu CA 90263

GREER, DOROTHY ELIZABETH SLAUGHTER, construction and engineering firm executive; b. Knoxville, Tenn., July 4, 1946; d. Elmer and Dorothy Elizabeth (Covington) Slaughter; children: William Curtis, Andrew Joseph, Nathan Alton. BS, U. Tenn., 1969; postgrad., Sonoma State U., 1980, So. Ill. U., 1989-90, Kennedy-Western U., 1991. Vice pres. Greco, Inc., Victorville, Calif., 1975-80; substitute tchr. Fundacion Educativa, Barranquilla, Colombia, 1983-87; owner, mgr. Greer and Assocs., Houston, 1981-83, Carlinville, Ill., 1987-90; prin. Greer and Assocs., Charlotte, N.C., 1990-93; owner MMI Enterprises, Knoxville, Tenn., 1993—; vol. project mgr. design and constrn. of ch. bldg. 9th Ch. Christ Scientist, Houston, 1983. Roundtable commr., mem. tng. staff Houston area Boy Scouts Am., 1982-83, Springfield, Ill. area, 1987-90; mem. tng. staff Scouts de Colombia, 1984-87. Recipient Cub Scout Woodbadge, Boy Scouts Am., 1983, named Master Commr. Sci., 1989. Mem. Am. Inst. Constructors, Constrn. Specifications Inst. (sec. 1992-94), Profl. Constrn. Estimators Assn. Am. (historian 1991), Nat. Assn. Women in Constrn. Office: MMI Enterprises 3010 Cox Ln Knoxville TN 37914-9508

GREEVER, JANET GROFF, history educator; b. Philadelphia, Sept. 12, 1921; m. William St. Clair Greever, Aug. 24, 1951; 1 child. BA, Bryn Mawr Coll., 1942, MA, 1945; MA, Harvard U., 1951, PhD, 1954. Resident head grad. houses Radcliffe Coll., Cambridge, Mass., 1947-48; resident head undergrad. hall Bryn Mawr (Pa.) Coll., 1949-51, instr. history, 1949-50; asst. prof. history Wash. State U., Pullman, 1962-63, U. Idaho, Moscow, 1965-66; ind. rschr., lectr. history Moscow, Idaho, 1954—; interim lectr. history Whitman Coll., Walla Walla, Wash., 1978; Idaho regional admissions cons. and interviewer Bryn Mawr COll., 1955-81. Author: Jose Ballivian y El Oriente Boliviano, 1987. bd. dirs. U. Idaho Libr. Assocs., Moscow, 1979-81, pres. 1980-81. Pa. State scholar, 1938-42, History fellow Bryn Mawr (Pa.) Coll., 1944-45, Margaret M. Justin fellow AAUW, Washington, 1948-49; grantee Lucius N. Littauer Found., N.Y.C., 1948-49. Mem. Am. Hist. Assn. (life), Conf. on Latin. Am. History (life), Latin Am. Studies Assn., Soc. for Am. Archaeology (life), Archaeol. Inst. Am. (life), Phi Alpha Theta. Home: 315 S Hayes St Moscow ID 83843-3419

GREEVER, MARGARET QUARLES, mathematics educator; b. Wilkensburg, Pa., Feb. 7, 1931; d. Lawrence Reginald and Ella Mae (LeSueur) Quarles; m. John Greever, Aug. 29, 1953; children: Catherine Patricia, Richard George, Cynthia Diane. Cert. costume design, Richmond Profl. Inst., 1952; student, U. Va., 1953-56; BA in Math., Calif. State U., Los Angeles, 1963; MA in Math., Claremont Grad. Sch., 1968. Cert. tchr. specializing in Jr. Coll. math., Calif. Tchr. math. Chaffey Unified High Sch. Dist., Alta Loma, Calif., 1963-64, Los Angeles Unified Sch. Dist., 1964-65, Chino (Calif.) Unified Sch. Dist., 1965-81; from asst. prof. to prof. Chaffey Coll., Rancho Cucamonga, 1981—; phys. sci. divsn. chmn. Chaffey Coll., Alta Loma, 1985-92; dean, phys., life, health sci., 1992—. Mem. LWV, Nat. Coun. Tchrs. Math., Am. Math. Assn. Two-Yr. Colls., Calif. Math. Coun., Assn. Calif. C.C. Adminstrs., Assn. Instr. Adminstrs., Women in Higher Edn., Pi Lambda Theta. Office: Chaffey Coll 5885 Haven Ave Rancho Cucamonga CA 91737-3002

GREEY, KATHLEEN MARGARET, librarian; b. Princeton, N.J., May 8, 1937; d. Edward Alexander and Grace Catherine (Gapen) G. BA, Oreg. State Coll., 1959; MA, U. Denver, 1960. Reference libr. Wethersfield (Conn.) Pub. Libr., 1960-63, San Francisco Pub. Libr., 1963-67; edn. libr., assoc. prof. Portland (Oreg.) State U., 1968—. Mem. Spl. Librs. Assn., Oreg. Libr. Assn., Oreg. Ednl. Media Assn., Phi Kappa Phi (chpt. sec. 1980-83, 84-86, 87—), Kappa Delta Pi (chpt. treas. 1986—), Oreg.-Fujian Book Exch. Com. (co-chair 1992—). Democrat. Unitarian. Office: Portland State U Libr PO Box 1151 Portland OR 97207

GREFE, JEAN BUTLER, secondary education art educator; b. Denver, May 28, 1942; d. Paul Porter Butler and Nelle Montana (Stewart) Clark; divorced; children: Christopher, Frederick. BS, East Carolina U., 1963. Cert. secondary art tchr., Va. Ptnr. Grefe & Grefe, Great Falls, Va., 1971-89; art tchr., chair dept. Fairfax (Va.) County Pub. Schs., 1981—, curriculum writer, 1993, 94; cons. Countryside Day Sch., Sterling, Va., 1984; life model study leader Smithsonian Instn., Washington, 1994—; sponsor, cons. reenactment video Project Enlightenment: Corcoran Mus., 1994; mem. Disciplined Based Art Edn. seminar Getty Found., U. Cin., 1994, Advanced DBAE Getty Seminar, Cranbrook, 1995, Freer Gallery of Art Tchr. Inst., 1995. Exhibited photographs at group shows, 1993, 94, 95, 96. Named Cafritz Found. artist Nat. Endowment for Arts, 1987-90. Mem. Nat. Art Edn. Assn., Va. Art Edn. Assn. (Tchr. of Yr. 1986, 87), Am. Scandinavian Cultural Union, Washington Ctr. for Photography, Wasa Drott Lodge, Delta Phi Delta. Lutheran. Home: 1514 Farsta Ct Reston VA 22090-4910

GREGERSON, LINDA, English educator; b. Elgin, Ill., Aug. 5, 1960; d. Olaf Thorbjorn and Karen Mildred Gregerson; m. Steven Mullaney, 1980; children: Emma, Megan. BA, Oberlin Coll., 1971; MA, Northwestern U., 1972; MFA, U. Iowa, 1977; PhD, Stanford U., 1987. Actress Kraken, 1972-75; staff editor Atlantic Monthly, Boston, 1982-87; asst. prof. U. Mich., Ann Arbor, 1987-94, assoc. prof. English, 1994—; vis. assoc. prof. Boston U., 1985-86; instr. MIT, 1985-87; mem. usage panel Am. Heritage Dict. Author: (poetry) Fire in the Conservatory, 1982, The Reformation of the Subject: Spenser, Milton, and the English Protestant Epic, 1995; work represented in The Pushcart Prize XIX: Best of the Small Presses, 1994, Nautre's Ban: Women's Literature about Incest from the Twelfth Century to the Present; contbr. to books contemporary Literary Criticism; contbr. poems to lit. mags. Recipient Levinson Prize award Poetry, 1991, Consuelo Ford award Poetry Soc. Am., 1992; Mellon fellow Nat. Humanities Ctr., 1991-92, Fellow Nat. Endowment Arts, 1992; Arts Found. grantee, Mich., 1994. Mem. MLA (mem. exec. com., Divsn. Lit. of Renaissance), Shakespeare Assn. Am., Renaissance Soc. Am., Spenser Soc. Am. (Isabel MacCaffrey award 1992), Milton Soc. Office: U Mich Dept English Lang and Lit 7611 Haven Hall Ann Arbor MI 48109-1045 Address: 4881 Hidden Brook Ln Ann Arbor MI 48105-9663*

GREGG, ANDREA MARIE, nursing administrator, educator, researcher; b. Savannah, Ga., Nov. 2, 1946; d. Walter Michael and Dorothy Marie (Coleman) Crawford; m. John Jasper Schuman Jr., July 2, 1967 (div. Aug. 1981); children: Alicia, John, Robert; m. John Franklin Gregg, Mar. 12, 1982; children: Nancy, Jay. Diploma in nursing, St. Joseph's Sch. Nursing, Savannah, 1967; BSN, Armstrong State Coll., 1976; MSN, Med. Coll. Ga., 1978; DSN in Nursing Adminstrn., U. Ala., Birmingham, 1993. RN, Ga., Fla., Ala. Staff nurse, asst. head nurse, head nurse, v.p. nursing Meml. Med. Ctr., Savannah, 1967-82; dir. nursing St. Jude's Nursing Ctr., Jacksonville, Fla., 1982-83; assoc. adminstr. patient care Nemours Children's Hosp., Jacksonville, Fla., 1983-86; asst. prof. nursing U. Fla., Jacksonville, 1986—; dir. Jacksonville urban campus Coll. Nursing, U. Fla., Jacksonville, 1995—; NIH trainee, 1988-93; cons. Nemours Children's Clinic, Jacksonville, 1991, Meml. Home Health Svcs., Savannah, 1992; statistician cons. Fla. Allergy and Immunology Soc., Jacksonville, 1993. Contbr. articles to profl. jours. Bd. dirs. Child Guidance Ctr., Inc., Jacksonville, 1994-95, chmn. bd. dirs., 1995—; bd. dirs. S.E. Ga. Health Sys. Agy., 1980-82; mem. Am. Heart Assn., Jacksonville, 1994. Mem. Nat. League for Nursing, Fla. League for Nursing (treas., bd. dirs. 1994-96), Ala. Acad. Sci., Sigma Theta Tau. Office: U Fla Coll Nursing Bldg 1 2d Fl 653 W 8th St Jacksonville FL 32209-6561

GREGG, LAUREN, women's soccer coach; b. Rochester, Minn., July 20, 1960. BS in Psychology, U. N.C.; MS in Counseling and Consulting Psychology, Harvard U. Asst. soccer coach U. N.C., 1983; asst. coach Harvard U., Cambridge, Mass.; head coach U. Va., 1987-95; asst. coach U.S. Women's Nat. Soccer Team. Named Coach of Yr. Nat. Soccer Coaches Assn. Am., 1990; recipient Gold medal Atlanta Olympics, 1996; Marie Jane postgrad. scholar. Office: US Soccer Fedn US Soccer House 1801-1811 S Prairie Ave Chicago IL 60616*

GREGG, MARIE BYRD, retired farmer; b. Mount Olive, N.C., Jan. 12, 1930; d. Arnold Wesley and Martha (Reaves) Byrd; m. Robert Allen Gregg,

July 11, 1953; children: Martha Susan, Kathryn Elizabeth, Kenneth Allen. BA in Elem. Edn., Furman U., 1951. Tchr. 3rd grade Greenville (S.C.) City Schs., 1951-53; med. social worker Ctrl. Carolina Rehab. Hosp., Greensboro, N.C., 1959-61; window display designer Kerr Rexall Drugs, Durham, N.C., 1960's; shop owner Something Else Antiques, Lima, Ohio, 1979-81; farm owner Mt. Olive, 1978-92. Democrat. Methodist. Home and Office: 212 Baucom Park Dr Greer SC 29650-2972

GREGGS, ELIZABETH MAY BUSHNELL (MRS. RAYMOND JOHN GREGGS), retired librarian; b. Delta, Colo., Nov. 7, 1925; d. Joseph Perkins and Ruby May (Stanford) Bushnell; m. Raymond John Greggs, Aug. 16, 1952; children: David M., Geoffrey B., Timothy C., Daniel R. BA, U. Denver, 1948. Children's librarian Grand Junction (Colo.) Pub. Library, 1944-46, Chelan County Library, 1948, Wenatchee (Wash.) Pub. Library, 1948-52, Seattle Pub. Library, 1952-53; children's librarian Renton (Wash.) Pub. Library, 1957-61, dir., 1962, br. supr. and children's services supr., 1963-67; area children's supr. King County Library, Seattle, 1968-78, asst. coordinator children's services, 1978-86; head librarian Valley View Library of King County Library System, Seattle, 1986-90; cons., organizer Tutor Ctr. Library, Seattle South Community Coll., 1969-72; mem. Puget Sound (Wash.) Council for Reviewing Children's Media, 1974—, chmn., 1974-76; cons. to children's TV programs; participant Children's Lit. People to People Tour of South Africa, 1996. Editor: Cayas Newsletter, 1971-74; cons. to Children's Catalog, Children's Index to Poetry. Chmn. dist. advancement com. Kloshee dist. Boy Scouts Am., 1975-78; mem. Bond Issue Citizens Group to build new Renton Libr., 1958, 59; mem. exec. bd. Family Edn. and Counseling Ctr. on Deafness, 1991-94. Recipient Hon. Service to Youth award Cedar River dist. Boy Scouts Am., 1971, Award of Merit Kloshee dist., 1977, winner King County Block Grant, 1990. Mem. ALA (Newbery-Caldecott medal com. 1978-79, com. chmn. 1983-84; membership com. 1978-80, Boy Scouts com. children's svcs. div. 1973-78, chmn. 1976-78, exec. bd. dirs. Assn. for Libr. Svc. to Children 1979-81, mem. coun. 1985-92, chmn. nominating com. 1986-87, councillor 1989-92, exec. bd. 1989-92, exec. com. 1989-92, coun. orientation com. 1987-89), Wash. Libr. Assn. (exec. bd. children's and young adult svcs. div. 1970-78, chmn. membership com. 1983-90, publs. com. 1988-92, emeritus 1991, mem. elections com.), King County Right to Read Coun. (co-chmn. 1973-77), Pierce-King County Reading Coun., Wash. State Literacy Coun. (exec. bd. 1971-77), Wash. Libr. Media Assn. (jr. high levels com. 1980-84), Pacific N.W. Libr. Assn. (young readers' choice com. 1981-83, chmn. div. 1983-85, exec. bd. 1983-85). Methodist. Home: 11448 Rainier Ave S Seattle WA 98178

GREGO, LAUREN HARRIS, reading specialist; b. Kingston, Pa., Feb. 8, 1950; d. Lazarus C. and Doris (Searfoss) Harris; m. Michael F. Grego, Aug. 5, 1978; children: Paul Michael, David Harris; 1 child from previous marraige: Kimberly O'Hara Kauffman. BA in English, Wilkes Coll., Wilkes-Barre, Pa., 1974; MS in Reading Edn., Marywood Coll., Scranton, Pa., 1978. Libr. West Pittston (Pa.) Pub. Libr., 1975-77; reading tchr. Scranton Sch. Dist., 1977-78; reading specialist Mifflin County Sch. Dist., Lewistown, Pa., 1978—; newspaper in edn. coord. Stone Arch Reading Count.-The Sentinel, 1991—; rschr., cons. Performance Learning Sys., Nevada City, Calif., 1981—; co-chmn. goal team 1 Mifflin County 2000, dir. organizer county-wide jump into reading program. Bd. dirs. Mifflin County 2000, Lewistown, 1994—, Juanita Mifflin Literacy Coalition, Lewistown, 1990; den leader Cub Scout Troop 7. Mem. ASCD, Keystone State Reading Assn., Stone Arch Reading Coun. (v.p. 1993-95, pres. 1995—), Internat. Reading Assn., Phi Delta Kappa. Methodist. Home: 265 Cornfield Cir Lewistown PA 17044-9750

GREGOIRE, CHRISTINE O., state attorney general; b. Auburn, Wash.; m. Michael Gregoire; 2 children. BA, U. Wash.; JD cum laude, Gonzaga U., 1977. Clerk, typist Wash. State Adult Probation/ Parole Office, Seattle, 1969; caseworker Wash. Dept. Social and Health Scis., Everett, 1974; asst. atty. gen. City of Spokane, Wash., 1977-81, sr. asst. atty. gen., 1981-82; dep. atty. gen. City of Olympia, Wash., 1982-88, atty. gen., 1993—; dir. Wash. State Dept. Ecology, 1988-92. chair Puget Sound Water Quality Authority, 1990-92, Nat. Com. State Environ. Dirs., 1991-92, States/B.C. Oil Spill Task Force, 1989-92. Mem. Nat. Assn. Attys. Gen. (consumer protection and environment com., energy com., children and the law subcom.). *

GREGOIRE, SISTER THERESE GERMAINE, secondary education educator; b. Lowell, Mass., June 12, 1942; d. Lionel G. and Gertrude C. (Houle) G. BS in Edn., U. Mass., Lowell, 1971; postgrad., Nicholls State U., 1983-87. Cert. elem. edn., secondary math. and computers, La., elem. edn., Mass., nat. cert. Nat. Bd. Profl. Teaching Standards. 1st grade tchr. St. Joseph Sch., Haverhill, Mass., 1962-64, tchr. grades 5, 6, 1971-73; 1st and 3d grade tchr. Maltrait Meml. Sch., Kaplan, La., 1964-66, jr. high math. and sci. tchr., libr., 1973-79; tchr. grades 5, 6, libr. Notre Dame Sch., Ogdensburg, N.Y., 1966-68; tchr. grades 7-12 math. and computers Mt. Carmel Sch., New Iberia, La., 1979-88; tchr. grades 9-12 math. and computers Vermilion Cath. High Sch., Abbeville, La., 1988—. Vol. tchr. Plantation Edn. Program, New Iberia, 1981; provider workshops in computer use and stamp collecting Boy Scouts of Am., Ogdensburg, 1966-68, Boy Scouts Am., New Iberia, Abbeville, 1979-90. Mem. Nat. Coun. Tchrs. Math., La. Assn. Tchrs. Math., Nat. Cath. Edn. Assn., La. Assn. Computer Using Educators. Democrat. Roman Catholic. Office: Vermilion Cath High Sch 425 Park Ave Abbeville LA 70510-3500

GREGOR, DOROTHY DEBORAH, librarian; b. Dobbs Ferry, N.Y., Aug. 15, 1939; d. Richard Garrett Heckman and Marion Allen (Richmond) Stewart; m. A. James Gregor, June 22, 1963 (div. 1974). BA, Occidental Coll., 1961; MA, U. Hawaii, 1963; MLS, U. Tex., 1968; cert. in Library Mgmt., U. Calif., Berkeley, 1976. Reference libr. U. Calif., San Francisco, 1968-69; dept. libr. Pub. Health Libr. U. Calif., Berkeley, 1969-71, tech. services libr., 1973-76; reference libr. Hamilton Libr., Honolulu, 1971-72; head serials dept. U. Calif., Berkeley, 1976-80, assoc. univ. libr. tech. svcs. dept., 1980-84, univ. libr., 1992-94; ret., 1994; chief Shared Cataloging div. Libr. of Congress, Washington, 1984-85; univ. libr. U. Calif.-San Diego, La Jolla, 1985-92, OCLC asst. to pres. for acad. and rsch. libr. rels., 1995—; instr. sch. libr. and info. studies U. Calif., Berkeley, 1975, 76, 83; cons. Nat. Libr. of Medicine, Bethesda, Md., 1985, Ohio Bd. Regents, Columbus, 1987; trustee Online Computer Libr. Ctr., asst. to pres. for acad. and rsch. libr. rels., 1995—; dir. Nat. Coordinating Com. on Japanese Libr. Resources, 1995—. Mem. ALA, Libr. Info. Tech. Assn., Program Com. Ctr. for Rsch. Libr. (bd. chair 1992-93, Hugh Atkinson award 1994).

GREGOR, MARLENE PIERCE, primary education educator, elementary science consultant; b. Oak Park, Ill., Apr. 22, 1932; d. Kenneth Bryant and Dorothy (Bloeser) Pierce; m. G. Ray Timmons, Aug. 1, 1953 (div. 1972); children: Gregg R., Todd P., Wendy S. Timmons McGuire; m. Norman Rittenhouse, 1972 (div. 1976); m. Harold Laurence Gregor, May 30, 1987. BS in Elem. Edn., U. Ill., 1953; MS in Elem. Edn., Ill. State U., 1974, postgrad., 1975-91. Tchr. 2d grade Wethersfield Community Unit Schs., Kewanee, Ill., 1953-54; primary tchr. Fairbury (Ill.) Cropsey Schs., 1965-84, Prairie-Cen. Community Unit #8 Schs., Fairbury, 1984-91; ret. Prairie-Ctr. Community Unit # 8 Schs., Fairbury, 1991; item writer Stanford Achievement Test Psychol. Corp., San Antonio, 1989, sci. assessment Ill. State Bd. Edn., Springfield, 1987-88; grant reader Ctr. Sci. Literacy, Springfield, 1991-93; textbook reviewer The Wheetley Co., Wilmette, Ill., 1994-95. Author: (with others) Horizons Plus Science Stories-Grade 2, 1992, Toys That Teach Science, 1993, Celebrating Science, 1990, Award Winning Nutrition Education Lessons and Units, 1994; mem. sci. tchrs. writing team Ill. State U., 1992; contbr. articles and stories to various pubs. Bd. dirs. Friends of the Arts Ill. State U., Normal, 1980-86, 92—, v.p., 1994-96; mem. Bloomington Mayoral Downtown Commn., 1993—, sec., 1994-96, chair pro tem, 1996—; mem. adv. bd. Kid's Crossing Mus., 1993-95; mem. steering com. Downtown Heritage Festival, Bloomington, 1995, 96, Ill. State U. Fell Arboretum, 1994—, co-chair edn. subcom., 1995—; mem. Leadership McLean County Class of 1996; bd. trustees Ill. Symphony Orch., 1996—. Named Outstanding Tchr. Sci. NSF-Ill. State U., 1985, Honors Sci. Tchr. Ill. State U., 1985, 86, 87; Chpt. II Mini grantee Edn. Svc. Ctr. #13, 1985-90; recipient Creative Nutrition award Nutrition and Edn. Tng. Ctr., 1989. Mem. ASCD, NEA, Nat. Sci. Tchrs. Assn. (presenter conv. 1985, 87), Coun. for Elem. Sci. Internat., Ill. Edn. Assn. (Tchr. Excellence award 1989), Ill. Ctr. Sci. Literacy (adv. mem. 1991-93), Ill. Sci. Tchrs. Assn. (sec. 1989-93, Presdl. Excellence Sci. Tchg. award 1991, State Finalist), Delta Kappa Gamma (v.p. chpt. 1990-92). Presbyterian. Home: 107 W Market St Bloomington IL 61701-3917

GREGORICH, PENNY DENISE, production procurement analyst; b. Newark, Ohio, May 27, 1968; d. William Raymond and Ethel Faye (Wineman) G. AS in Office Adminstrn., Ctrl. Ohio Tech. Coll., 1989, AS in Bus. Mgmt., 1991; student, Otterbein Coll., 1991—. Sec./clk. Rockwell Internat., Newark, 1985-86, accounts receiveable coll. co-op., 1987-89, inventory control specialist, 1989-90, purchasing buyer/analyst, 1990-92, material procurement analyst, 1992—; bookkeeper's asst. Spenley Newspapers/Fostoria Times Rev., Newark, 1986-87. Licking County Joint Vocat.-Tech. Sch./Coop. Office Edn. historian, 1985-86; driver participant Miss Ohio Parade, Mansfield, 1990. Mem. NAFE, Assoc. Humane Soc., Capital Area Humane Soc., Licking County Humane Soc., Ctrl. Ohio Tech. Coll. Alumni Assn., Phi Theta Kappa. Office: Rockwell Internat Rt 79 Heath OH 43056-1440

GREGORY, ANN YOUNG, editor, publisher; b. Lexington, Ky., Apr. 28, 1935; d. David Marion and Pauline (Adams) Young; m. Allen Gregory, Jan. 29, 1957; children: David Young, Mary Peyton. BA with high distinction, U. Ky., 1956. Sec. Ky. edit. TV Guide, Louisville, summer 1956; traffic mgr. Sta. WVLK, Lexington, 1956-61; part time tchr. adult basic edn. Wise County (Va.) Sch. Bd., St. Paul, 1966-72; adminstrv. asst. Appalachian Field Svcs., Children's TV Workshop, St. Paul, 1971-74; editor, co-pub. Clinch Valley Times, 1974—; pres. Clinch Valley Pub. Co., Inc., St. Paul, 1974—; mem. mktg. com. Mountain Empire TechPrep Consortium, 1993—. Editor, text writer: The Flood of '77 in the St. Paul Area, 1977; weekly newspaper columnist Of Shoes...and Ships...and Sealing Wax, 1974—. V.p. St. Paul PTA, 1970-73; trustee Lonesome Pine Regional Libr. Bd., 1972-80, chmn., 1978-80; chmn. com. to establish br. libr. in St. Paul, opened 1975; mem. adv. bd. Pro-Art, Wise County chpt. Va. Mus. Fine Arts, 1979-86; co-leader Brownie troop Girl Scouts U.S.A., 1971-76, bd. dirs. Appalachian Coun., 1983-1995, 1st v.p., 1985-91; mem. adv. bd. Wise County YMCA, 1977-80; mem. Wise County Bd. Edn., 1975—, vice chmn., 1981-95; pres. So. Region Sch. Bds. Assn., 1987-88; mem. Va. Edn. Block Grants Adv. Com., 1981-86, Region I State Literacy Coun., 1989-91; mem. Local Vocat. Adv. Coun., 1980—, chmn., 1981—; mem. statewide planning coun. Va. Dept. Edn.; mem. Va. Coun. on Vocat. Edn., 1987-95, chmn., 1989-91; mem. exec. com. Va. H.S. League, 1984-88; past pres. Wise County Humane Soc., Inc.; bd. dirs. Va. Sch. Bds. Assn., 1979-89, pres., 1985-86; bd. dirs. Va. Literacy Found., 1987-89; bd. dir., Appalachia Ednl. Lab., 1995—; sec., treas. S.W. Va. Pub. Edn. Found. Bd., 1993—; mem. Mountain Empire C.C. Found. Bd., 1994—; mem. adv. com. Va. State Supt. Pub. Instrn., 1993-96; mem. devel. and cmty. rels. com., mem. music adv. com. Clinch Valley Coll.; mem. adv. bd. Wise Appalachian Regional Hosp. Named Outstanding Clubwoman of Yr., St. Paul Jr. Women's Club, 1964, 66, Outstanding Citizen, S.W. Va. dist. Va. Fedn. Women's Clubs, 1968, Woman of Yr. Wise County/ Norton Dem. Women's Club, 1986; recipient Rufus Beamer award Va. Poly. Inst., 1989, William P Kanto Meml. award for contbns. to edn. Clinch Valley Coll., Mountain Empire C.C. and Wise County and Norton Pub. Schs., 1990; Ky. Broadcasters Assn. scholar, 1956; named Citizen of Yr. Wise County C. of C., 1990. Mem. Va. Press Assn. (1st place award for editorial writing 1976), Nat. Press Women, Va. Press Women, Nat. Newspaper Assn., Women in Communications, Nat. Sch. Bds. Assn. (pub. rels. com., nominating com. 1987), Mortar Bd., Delta Kappa Gamma (hon. mem. Alpha Psi chpt.), Phi Beta Kappa, Alpha Delta Pi, Chi Delta Phi, Alpha Epsilon Rho, Alpha Lambda Delta, Theta Sigma Phi. Democrat. Methodist. Home: PO Box 303 Saint Paul VA 24283-0303 Office: PO Box 817 Saint Paul VA 24283-0817

GREGORY, BETTINA LOUISE, journalist; b. N.Y.C., June 4, 1946; d. George Alexander and V. Elizabeth Friedman; m. John P. Flannery, II, 1981; 1 child, Diana Elizabeth. Student, Smith Coll., 1964-65; diploma in acting, Webber-Douglas Sch. Dramatic Art, London, 1968; BA in Psychology, Pierce Coll., Athens, Greece, 1972; LittD (hon.), Susquehanna U., 1988, St. Thomas Aquinas U., 1992; LLD (hon.), Wilmington Coll., 1989; D in Journalism (hon.), U. Findlay, 1990. Reporter Sta. WVBR-FM, Ithaca, N.Y., 1972-73, Sta. WCIC-TV, Ithaca, 1972; reporter, anchorwoman Sta. WGBB, Freeport, N.Y., 1973, Sta. WCBS, N.Y.; freelance reporter, writer AP, N.Y.C., 1973-74; freelance reporter N.Y. Times, 1973-74; with ABC News, 1974—; corr. ABC News, Washington, 1977-79; White House corr. ABC News, 1979—, sr. gen. assignment corr., 1980—; elected rep. for corr.'s ABC News Women's Adv. Bd. Reporter TV spl. Flaws in the Shield, 1989 (1st pl. Headliner award), A&E's Biography of Hillary Rodham Clinton, 1994 (Best Documentary ACE award 1994). Recipient 1st Place award Nat. Feature News, Odyssey Inst., N.Y., 1978, Clarion award Women in Communications, Inc., 1979, hon. mention Nat. Commn. on Working Women, 1979, Media award for Am. Agenda segment on homeless World Hunger Found., 1990, Cable Ace Best Documentary award, 1995, Edward R. Murrow award for coverage of O.J. Simpson Murder trial, 1996; named one of top 10 investigative reporters, TV Guide, 1983. Mem. Radio TV Corrs. Assn., White House Corrs. Assn. Clubs: Newswomen's N.Y. (recipient Front Page award 1976); Nat. Press; Washington Press. Office: ABC News Washington Bur 1717 Desales St NW Washington DC 20036-4401

GREGORY, CAROLYN HOLMES, poet, editor, journalist; b. Rochester, N.Y., Jan. 27, 1950; d. Harry P. and Anna Gertrude (Holmes) Miller; m. Peter T. Bates. BA, U. Mich., Ann Arbor, 1972, MA, 1980. Author: (books) The Wait, 1982, For Lovers and Other Losses, 1982, Tour of Light, 1996, Playing By Ear, 1996. Fellow Mass. Coun. for the Arts; mem. NOW, New England Poetry Club, Poetry Soc. of Am. Home: 50 Green St # 106 Brookline MA 02146

GREGORY, CONNIE LEE, small business owner; b. Mt. Pleasant, Ia., Mar. 27, 1954; d. Arved Clinton Gregory and Edith Belle (Blythe) Stearns. Lic. Nurse, Hawkeye Inst., Waterloo, Iowa, 1983; AA, Southeastern Community, Burlington, Iowa, 1989; BA in Journalism, Western Ill. U., Macomb, 1991. Pre-press technician Alaniz & Sons Inc., Mt. Pleasant, Iowa, 1991-95, chmn. newsletter, 1991-94; owner QECETH Enterprises, 1994—; correctional officer Dept. Correction, Ft. Madison, Iowa, 1995—. Foster parent Dept. Human Svcs., Burlington, Iowa, 1991—; publicity chmn. non-profit orgn., 1985. With U.S. Army, 1977-80. Mem. NAFE, Am Entrepreneurs Assn., Internat. Women's Writing Guild, Sigma Tau Delta (prodn. editor 1990). Home: 215 W Front Wayland IA 52654-0244 Office: PO Box 244 Wayland IA 52654

GREGORY, ELEANOR ANNE, artist, educator; b. Seattle, Jan. 20, 1939; d. John Noel and Eleanor Blanche G.; BA, Reed Coll., 1963; MFA, U. Wash., 1966; MEd, Columbia U., 1978, EdD., 1978. Art tchr. Seattle Pub. Schs., 1970-75; instr. N.Y.C. C.C., 1977, Manhattan C.C., N.Y.C., 1978; asst. prof. N.Mex. State U., Las Crucas, 1978-79; asst. prof. art Purdue U., West Lafayette, Ind., 1979-82, West Tex. State U., Canyon, 1982-84; mgr. Watson's Crick Gallery, West Lafayette, 1982-83; lectr. Calif. State U., Long Beach, 1985-87, L.A. Unified Sch. Dist., 1988—. One woman shows: Columbia U. Tchrs. Coll., 1976, Watson's Crick Gallery, West Lafayette, 1980, 81, Gallery I, Purdue U., 1980, W. Tex. State U., 1983, Amarillo Art Ctr., 1984, Sch. Visual Concepts, Seattle, 1985; group shows include: El Paso (Tex.) Art Mus., 1979, Ind. State Mus., Indpls., 1980, Lafayette (Ind.) Art Mus., 1982, T. Billman Gallery, Long Beach, 1987; represented in permanent collection: Portland (Oreg.) Art Mus. Mem. Nat. Art Edn. Assn. (pres. women's caucus chpt. 1988-90, v.p.-elect Pacific region 1994-96, v.p. pacific region, 1996—), N.Y. Soc. Scribes, L.A. Soc. Calligraphy, Internat. Soc. Edn. Through Art, Art Educators of L.A. (pres. 1993-95). Episcopalian.

GREGORY, HOLLY WANDA JANUSZKIEWICZ, lawyer; b. Rutland, Vt., May 14, 1956; d. Tadeusz and Marjorie Beatty (Martinson) Januszkiewicz; m. Robert Stephen Gregory, Aug. 23, 1987; 1 child, Thaddeus Robert. BA with honors, SUNY, Purchase, 1978; JD summa cum laude, N.Y. Law Sch., 1986. Bar: N.Y. 1987. Law clk. U.S. Ct. Appeals (2d cir.), Albany, N.Y. and N.Y.C., 1986-87; assoc. Trade Practices & Regulatory Law Dept. Weil, Gotshal & Manges, N.Y.C., 1987—; counsel WestFest, Inc., N.Y.C., 1988-91. Editor: Journal of Proprietary Rights, 1989-91; exec. editor: N.Y. Law Sch. Law Rev., 1985-86. Frederick C. Scholem scholar N.Y. Law Sch., 1983-86. Mem. ABA (antitrust sect.). Soc. of Friends. Office: Weil Gotshal & Manges 767 5th Ave New York NY 10153

GREGORY, JEAN WINFREY, ecologist, educator; b. Richmond, Va., Feb. 13, 1947; d. Thomas Edloe and Kathryn (McFarlane) Winfrey; m. Ronald Alfred Gregory, Dec. 13, 1973. BS in Biology, Mary Washington Coll., 1969; MS in Biology, Va. Commonwealth U., 1975, postgrad. in pub. adminstrn., 1982-90; MA in Environ. Sci., U. Va., 1983. Cert. fisheries sci. Lab. specialist A Cardiovascular Div. Med. Coll. Va., Richmond, 1969-70; pollution specialist State Water Control Bd. (now Dept. Environ. Quality), Richmond, 1970-77, pollution control specialist B, 1977-81, ecologist, 1981-85, ecology programs supr., 1985-88, environ. program mgr., 1988—; adj. faculty Va. Commonwealth U., Richmond, 1978-93. Contbr. articles to profl. jours., 1972-88. Named One of Outstanding Young Women of Am., 1974; EPA fellow, Va., 1974-76. Mem. Am. Soc. Limnology and Oceanography, N.Am. Lake Mgmt. Soc., N.Am. Benthological Soc., Ecol. Soc. Am., Romance Writers Am., Sisters in Crime. Democrat. Methodist. Office: Office Water Environ Rsch Stds PO Box 10009 Richmond VA 23240

GREGORY, LESLIE FINLAYSON, tax accountant, financial consultant, realtor; b. Halifax, N.S., Can., Nov. 18, 1956; d. F. Douglas and Beverley Jeanne (Adams) Finlayson; m. Michael R. Gregory, May 15, 1981 (div. 1982); children from previous marriage: Jarrell (Geno) Hurley II, Jason Douglas Hurley. AA magna cum laude, Diablo Valley Coll., Pleasant Hill, Calif.; BS in Fin., Mktg. and Bus. Adminstrn. Mgmt., Calif. State U., Hayward, 1990. Lic. tax acct.; lic. real estate agt. Investment analyst Camilto Mgmt. Co., Lafayette, Calif., 1980-82; office mgr. Gilbert Constrn., Martinez, Calif., 1982-84; acctg. mgr. Richmond (Calif.) Drydock, 1981-82; A/P mgr. Sassoon-Sherman, Oakland, Calif.; tax acct. Beneficial Tax, Pleasant Hill, 1985-88; realtor Mason-McDuffie Real Estate, Clayton, Calif., 1990—; fin. cons., tax acct. Gregory & Assocs., Sonora, Calif., 1983—; tax/audit. rep., Concord, Calif.; mng. representative Excel Comms., 1994—. Mem. NAFE, Nat. Soc. of Pub. Accts., Nat. Assn. Realtors, Calif. Assn. Realtors, Contra Costa Bd. Realtors (participant canned food dr. Walnut Creek, Calif. 1990—), Moose, BAM, R.E. Fin. Planners. Republican. Office: Mason McDuffie Real Estate 5400 B 1 Ignacio Valley Rd Concord CA 94520

GREGORY, MYRA MAY, religious organization administrator, educator; b. N.Y.C., Sept. 21, 1912; d. Thomas and Anna (Collins) G. Diploma, Maxwell Tchrs. Tng. Sch., Bklyn., 1933; BS in Edn., Bklyn. Coll., 1940, MA in History, 1952. Cert. music tchr. Tchr. N.Y.C. Bd. Edn., Bklyn., 1943-75; social worker Berean Bapt. Ch., Bklyn., 1932-48, supr., 1932-94, fin. sec. Sunday sch., 1935-94; bd. dirs. Berean-Vacation Bible Sch., Bklyn., 1935-86; tchr. Protestant Coun., N.Y.C., 1940-81; bd. dirs. Recreation Bedford-Stuyvesant Area Project, Bklyn.; dir. seminar Christian Teaching, Bklyn., 1974-86, 1990—. Bd. mgrs. Bklyn. Sun. Sch. Union, 1974—; bd. dirs. Bklyn. Divsn. Coun. of Chs.; 1984—; pres. Bklyn. divsn. Coun. of Ch. N.Y.C., 1984-86. Named Tchr. of Yr. Cmty. Sch. Bd. Dist. 14, Bklyn., 1973, Outstanding Tchr., Stuyvesand divsn., Bklyn. Sunday Sch. Union, 1977, Educator/Leader Berean Bapt. Ch., 1977; recipient Ecumenism citation Borough Pres.'s Office, Bklyn., 1985, Religious Educator citation Bklyn. Ch. Women United, Inc., 1993, Cmty. Svc. awrd Mayors Office, N.Y.C., 1993, Ecumenical Svc./Educator Honors Office the Coun. City of N.Y., 1994, Lifetime Achievement award Bklyn. Coll., 1995, Outstanding Svc. award Coun. Chs. the City of N.Y., 1995. Mem. ASCD, Am. String Tchrs. Assn., Am. Viola Soc., Assn. Childhood Edn. Internat., Orgn. Am. Historians, Ctr. Study of Presidency, Assn. Bible Tchrs. Democrat.

GREGORY, SANDRA K., accountant, consultant; b. Gallatin, Tenn., Mar. 10, 1957; d. Harry L. and Mary F. (Stone) Neil; m. Lanny L. Gregory. AAS in Gen. Bus. magna cum laude, Vol. State Cmty. Coll., Gallatin, 1993. Gen. acct. supr. Globe Bus. Furniture, Hendersonville, Tenn., 1986-89; acct. Keller Furniture, Goodlettsville, Tenn., 1989-90, Corroon & Black, Nashville, 1990, K.O. Lester Co., Inc., Lebanon, Tenn., 1993—; cons. in field. Mem. Inst. Mgmt. Accts. Home: PO Box 534 Hendersonville TN 37077

GREGORY, SHEILA THERESE, education educator; b. Washington, Oct. 17, 1963; d. Karl Dwight and Tenicia Ann (Banks) G.; m. Anthony Kelly Jones, Aug. 15, 1992. BA in Comm. and Journalism, Oakland U., Rochester, Mich., 1984; MPA in Health Care Adminstrn., Wayne State U., 1989; PhD in Higher Edn. Adminstrn., U. Pa., 1994. Sys. analyst/project leader Mich. Bell Tel. Co., Oak Park, 1986-89; exec. asst. to pres. St. Joseph Mercy Hosp., Pontiac, Mich., 1989-91; coord. higher edn. U. Pa., Phila., 1992-94; asst. prof. higher edn., student devel. adminstr. Kingsboro C.C.-CUNY, Bklyn., 1994—; cons. Idaho State U., Pocatello, 1994—; mem. adv. bd. Jour. Cultural Diversity and Health, 1994—, Assn. Black Nursing Faculty Jour., 1994—. Author: Black Women in the Academy, 1995; contbr. articles and rev. to profl. publs. Mem. Acad. for Humanities and Scis., CUNY, 1994. Mem. Nat. Congress Black Faculty (co-chairperson bd. dirs. 1993, co-chairperson R & D 1993—, editor newsletter 1994—), Am. Ednl. Rsch. Assn., Assn. for Study of Higher Edn., Am. Assn. Higher Edn., Assn. Black Women in Higher Edn. Office: Kingsborough C C-CUNY 2001 Oriental Blvd Rm L-514 Brooklyn NY 11235-2336

GREGORY, SUSAN B., lawyer; b. Terre Haute, Ind., Apr. 30, 1965; d. Robert Leroy and Patricia Mary (French) Eddleman; m. Kevin L. Gregory, Aug. 13, 1988. BS, BA, Purdue U., 1987; JD, U. Ill., 1991. Bar: Ind. 1991, U.S. Dist. Ct. (so. dist.) Ind. 1991. Assoc. Baker & Daniels, Indpls., 1991-93; corp. atty. USA Group, Inc., Fishers, Ind., 1993—. Charter mem. Beacon Soc. in Support of Meth. Hosp., Indpls., 1993—. Mem. Purdue U. Sch. Consumer and Family Scis. Alumni Assn. (pres. 1995), Indpls. Zoo Guild, Order of Coif, Order of Barristers, Phi Beta Kappa, Phi Kappa Phi, Omicron Delta Kappa, Omicron Nu. Home: 123 Morningside Dr Brownsburg IN 46112-1073

GREGORY, VALISKA, writer; b. Chgo., Nov. 3, 1940; d. Andrej and Stephania (Lascik) Valiska; m. Marshall W. Gregory, Aug. 18, 1962; children: Melissa, Holly. BA cum laude, Ind. Ctrl. Coll., 1962; MA, Univ. Chgo., 1966; postgrad., Vassar Inst. Pub. Writing, 1984, Simmons Coll., 1986. Music and drama tchr. White Oak Elem. Sch., Whiting, Ind., 1962-64; tchr. Oak Lawn (Ill.) Meml. H.S., 1965-68; lectr. English U. Wis., Milw., 1968-74; adj. prof. English U. Indpls., 1974-83; adj. prof. English Butler U., Indpls., 1983-85, writer-in-residence, 1993—; fellow Butler Writer's Studio, 1989-92; founding dir. Butler U. Midwinter Children's Litf. Conf., 1989-92; spkr., workshop leader schs., libr., confs., 1993—. Author: Sunny Side Up, 1986 (Chickadee Mag. Book of Month award 1986), Terribly Wonderful, 1986 (Grandparent's Mag. Best Book award 1986), The Oatmeal Cookie, 1987 (Best of Best Book list Chgo. Sun-Times), Riddle Soup, 1987 (Best of Best Book list Chgo. Sun-Times), Through the Mickle Woods (named Pick of List Am. Booksellers Assn. 1992, State Ind. Read Aloud-List 1993), Happy Burpday, Maggie McDougal!, 1992 (State Ind. Read-aloud List 1993), Babysitting for Benjamin (Parent's Choice Honor award 1993). Recipient Ill. Wesleyan U. Poetry award, 1982, hon. mention Billee Murray Denny Nat. Poetry Award Bilee Murray Denny Poetry Found., 1982, Hudelson award Children's Fiction Work-In-Progress, 1982, Artistic Excellence and Achievement award State Art Treasure Arts Ind., 1989; Individual Artist Master fellow Ind. Arts Commn. and Nat. Endowment for Arts, 1986. Mem. AAUW (Creative Writer's pres. 1984-86), Author's Guild, Authors League Am., Soc. Children's Book Writers and Illustrators, Nat. Book Critic's Circle, Children's Reading Round Table, Soc. Midland Authors. Democrat. Office: Butler U 4600 Sunset Ave Indianapolis IN 46208*

GREGUS, LINDA ANNA, government official; b. Hartford, Conn., Mar. 24, 1956; d. Steven and Sylvia Christine (Ramunno) G. AB, Bowdoin Coll., 1978; MA in Law and Diplomacy, Tufts U., 1985. Vol. VISTA, Phoenix, 1978-79; research asst. Econ. Research Assocs., Boston, 1979; ops adminstr. CRT Inc., Hartford, Conn., 1980-82; program officer U.S. Dept. of State, Washington, 1986-90; intelligence officer CIA, Washington, 1990—. Recipient Milo Peck Scholarship Town of Windsor, Conn., 1984. Republican. Home: 1904 Wilson Ln Mc Lean VA 22102-1958

GREIDER, CAROL WIDNEY, molecular biologist; b. San Diego, Apr. 15, 1961. Student, George-August Univ., Göttingen, Fed. Republic Germany, 1981-82; BA in Biology, U. Calif., Santa Barbara, 1983; PhD in Molecular

Biology, U. Calif., Berkeley, 1987. Fellow Cold Spring Harbor (N.Y.) Lab., 1988-90, staff investigator, 1990-92, sr. staff investigator, 1992-94, sr. staff scientist, 1994—. Contbr. numerous articles, revs., book chpts. George-August Univ. Auslandsamt scholar, 1981, Regents scholar U. Calif., 1981, Pew Biomed. Scis. scholar; recipient Allied Signal Outstanding Project award, 1992, Gertrude Elion Cancer Rsch. award Am. Assn. Cancer Rsch., 1994, Rhodes award, 1996, Glenn Found. award Am. Assn. Cell Biology, 1995. Mem. Phi Beta Kappa. Office: Cold Spring Harbor Lab PO Box 100 1 Bungtown Rd Cold Spring Harbor NY 11724

GREIF, SANDRA NICOLE, social worker; b. Camden, N.J., Sept. 13, 1971; d. Nicholas Frank and Barbara Fee (Pawlowski) G. BSW, Georgian Ct. Coll., 1993; MSW, U. Pa., 1995. Lic. social worker, N.J. Residential counselor intern Family Svc. of Burlington County, Mt. Holly, N.J., 1993; domestic violence counselor Providence House, Toms River, N.J., 1993; sch. social worker Burlington County Sch. of Spl. Svcs., Mt. Holly, 1993-94; clin. therapist intern St. Francis Counseling Ctr., Brant Beach, N.J., 1994-95; clin. social worker Providence House, Willingboro, N.J., 1995—. Designer pamphlet Feeling Good About Saying No to Sexual Abuse, 1994. Vol. children's groupworker Family Svcs. of Burlington County, 1991; sexual assault vol. St. Francis Counseling Ctr., Brant Beach, 1995; employee campaign chairperson United Way, Willingboro, 1995; cert. cmty. CPR and first aid vol. ARC, N.J., 1996. Recipient Outstanding Campaign award United Way of Burlington, 1996. Mem. NASW, AAUW, NOW, Nat. Coalition for Homeless, Women's Health Network, Delta Tau Kappa, Kappa Gamma Pi.

GREIMAN, APRIL, graphic designer; b. Rockville, N.Y., Mar. 22, 1948. BFA, Kansas City (Mo.) Art Inst., 1970; studied design with Armin Hoffmann and Wolfgang Weingart, Allgemeine Kunstgewerbeschule, Basel, Switzerland, 1970-71. Free-lance designer N.Y.C., 1971-75; asst. prof. Phila. Coll. Art, 1971-75; cons. MOMA, N.Y.C., 1975-76; founder April Greiman Inc., L.A., 1976; dir. design program Calif. Inst. Arts., L.A., 1982-84. One woman shows include Arc en Reve, Ctr. d'Architecture, Bordeaux, France, 1994; exhibited in group shows at Albright Knox Gallery, Buffalo, 1979, Cooper Hewitt Mus., Walker Art Ctr., Mpls., Mus. Modern Art, Smithsonian. Nat. Endowment for Arts grantee, 1987; winner The Modern Poster MOMA, 1989. Mem. Am. Inst. Graphic Arts (past nat. bd. dirs., past pres. L.A. chpt.), Alliance Graphique Internat. (mem. exec. com. 1991-93). Office: April Greiman Inc 620 Moulton Ave Apt 211 Los Angeles CA 90031-3288*

GREITZER, CAROL, councilwoman; b. N.Y.C., Jan. 3, 1925; d. Harry H. and Rae (Balinson) Hutter; m. Herman S. Greitzer, 1949 (div. 1965); 1 child, Elizabeth; m. Joshua S. Vogel, 1990; stepchildren: Laura, David, Robert. BA, Hunter Coll., 1945; MA, NYU, 1950. Editor Topic Publ., N.Y.C., 1945-49; copy chief Murdock Advt., Washington, 1950-54; copywriter J. Walter Thompson, N.Y.C., 1957-60, L.W. Frohlich Advt., N.Y.C., 1965-69; coun. mem. N.Y.C. Coun., 1969-91, ret., 1991. Contbr. articles to various mags. and jours. Dem. Dist. Leader, Manhattan, 1961-69; pres. Village Ind. Dems., N.Y.C., 1960; founding pres. Nat. Abortion Rights Action League, 1969-72, chair exec. com. 1972-74; founder, bd. dirs. Parks Coun., N.Y.C., 1962-88; founder Com. for Artists Housing, 1963-70, Transit Riders Action Com., SAFE TA, others; mem. Commn. on Status of Women, 1975-89; chair transit and consumer affairs coms.; co-founder, original bd. dirs. First Women's Bd., N.Y.C., 1975. Home: 59 W 12 St New York NY 10011

GRENFELL, GLORIA ROSS, freelance journalist; b. Redwood City, Calif., Nov. 14, 1926; d. Edward William and Blanch (Ross) G.; m. June 19, 1948 (div. Nov. 15, 1983); children: Jane, Barbara, Robert, Mary. BS, U. Oreg., 1948, postgrad., 1983-85. Coll. bd., retail sales Meier & Frank Co., Portland, Oreg., 1945; book sales retailer J.K. Gill & Co., Portland, Oreg., 1948-50; advisor Mt. Hood Meadows Women's Ski Program, Oreg., 1968-78; corp. v.p. OK Delivery System, Inc., Oreg., 1977-82; ski instr. Willamette Pass, Oreg., 1983-85, Mt. Shasta, 1986; Campfire girls leader Portland, 1958-72; freelance journalist Marina, Calif., 1986—. Mem. Assn. Jr. League Internat., 1957-87; mem. Monterey County Mental Health Adv. Commn., 1994—, So. Poverty Law Ctr., 1994—, No. Mariposa County History Ctr., Calif. Recipient Golden Poles award Mt. Hood Meadows, 1975. Mem. Soc. Profl. Journalists, Profl. Ski Instrs. Am., U.S. Ski Coaches Assn., Calif. State Sheriffs' Assn. (assoc.), Monterey History and Art Assn., Yosemite Assn., Monterey Sports Ctr., Friends of Sea Otter, Mariposa County C. of C., Monterrey Bay Area Nat. Alumnae Panhellenic, Order Ea. Star, DAR (Commodore Sloat chpt.), Citizens for Law and Order, Mortar Board, Kappa Alpha Theta. Democrat. Episcopalian. Home and Office: 3128 Crescent Ave Lot 9 Marina CA 93933-3131

GRESHAM, ANN ELIZABETH, retailer, horticulturist executive, consultant; b. Richmond, Va., Oct. 11, 1933; d. Allwin Stagg and Ruby Scott (Faber) Gresham. Student, Peace Coll., Raleigh, N.C., 1950-52, East Carolina U., 1952-53, Penland Sch., N.C., 1953-54, Va. Commonwealth U., 1960-64. Owner, prin. Ann Gresham's Gift Shop, Richmond, 1953-56; pres., treas. Gresham's Garden Ctr., Inc., Richmond, 1955-79; v.p. Gresham's Nursery, Inc., Richmond, 1959-73, pres., treas., 1973-84; pres., treas. Gresham's Country Store, Richmond, 1964—; tchr., 1982—. Bd. dirs. Bainbridge Community Ministry, 1979, Handworkshop, 1984-89; class agt. Peace Coll., Raleigh, 1987-88, mem. alumnae council, 1987, 88—, bd. visitors, 1987-93; focus group mem. Hand Workshop, Richmond, 1983, bd. dirs., 1984-87. Mem. Midlothian Antique Dealers (treas. 1975-79), Richmond Quilt Guild (chpt. v.p. 1983-84), Nat. Needlework Assn., Quilt Inst., Am. Hort. Soc. Episcopalian. Clubs: Chesmond Women's (v.p. 1979-80), James River Woman's (Richmond) (tres. 1990-92). Home and Office: Gresham's Inc 2324 Logan St Richmond VA 23235-3462

GRESHAM, DOROTHY ANN, operating room nurse, educator; b. Washington, Ga., Oct. 5, 1954; d. Daniel Webster Sr. and Mary Lee (Smith) Dunn; m. Roy Lee Gresham, July 5, 1975; children: Isaac Patrick, Jillian Jeanine, Phillip Michael. Diploma in Nursing, Ga. Bapt. Sch. Nursing, Atlanta, 1975; BSN, Creighton U., 1987. RN, Nebr., Ga., Ala., Mo.; cert. nurse operating rm., HIV/AIDS instr., ARC nurse, BLS, ACLS. Staff nurse recovery rm., eye, ears and throat nurse Ga. Bapt. Hosp., Atlanta, 1975-76; gen. duty nurse Wills Meml. Hosp., Washington, Ga., 1976; staff nurse recovery rm. and emergency rm. Southeastern Bapt. Hosp., San Antonio, 1977-78; staff nurse med.-surgery, oper. and recovery rm. Johnson County Hosp., Warrensburg, Mo., 1979-81; mem. operating rm. staff, asst. supr. Whiteham AFB (Mo.) Hosp., 1982-83; med.-surg. and oper. rm. staff nurse Barksdale AFB (La.) Hosp., 1983-85; staff nurse operating rm. Erlingh Bergquist Regional Hosp., Offutt AFB, Nebr., 1986-88; staff nurse telemetry unit, crital care and on-call nurse St. Joseph Hosp., Omaha, 1987-88; staff nurse, charge nurse ICU West Ala. Gen. Hosp., Northport, Ala., 1988-90; mem. oper. rm. staff Air Univ. Hosp., Maxwell AFB, Ala., 1989-90; staff nurse operating rm. Langley AFB (Va.) Hosp., 1990-91, 502d Med. Group, Maxwell AFB, 1991-94; HIV/AIDS instr. ARC, Ramstein and Landstuhl, Germany, 1994—; cmty. health nurse, early interventionist Incirlik AFB, 1996—; part-time clin. instr. Capstone Coll. Nursing, Tuscaloosa, Ala., 1989-90; substitute tchr., nurse Dept. Def. Dependent Schs., Kaiserslautern Mil. Cmty., Germany, 1994-95; instr. Emet Ctrl. Tex. Coll. Europe Campus, 1994—; oper. rm. staff nurse Landstuhl 2d Gen. Hosp., 1995-96. Maj. USAF, 1991-94. Decorated Nat. Def. Svc. medal; recipient Recognition for Outstanding Svc. cert. 1st Med. Group Langley AFB, 1991, Appreciation cert. USAF, 1991, numerous others. Mem. AACN, ANA, Nat. League for Nursing, Assn. Operating Rm. Nurses, Sigma Theta Tau. Baptist. Home: PSC 94 Box 467 APO AE 09824

GRESS, DONNA MARY, health facility administrator; b. Nebraska City, Nebr., May 30, 1958; d. Henry Joseph and Verna Louise (Damme) G. Student, Rsch. Med. Ctr., Avila Coll., 1976-77, U. Nebr., 1981-83. Accredited record technician on patient care unit U. Kans. Med. Ctr., Kansas City, 1977-79; cancer registrar Archbishop Bergan Mercy Hosp., Omaha, 1979-84; cancer registry coord. Presbyn. Intercmty. Hosp., Whittier, Calif., 1984-90; supr. cancer registry St. Mary Med. Ctr., Long Beach, Calif., 1990—; mem. software beta testing divsn. C/Net, Sacramento, 1988—, mem. adv. bd., 1990-93; mem. spkrs. bur. commn. cancer ACS, Chgo., 1994—; lectr. in field. Author, asst. editor: (with others) Cancer Registry Management, 1996; contbr. articles to profl. jours. Mem. Am. Health Info. Mgmt. Assn., Nat. Cancer Registrars Assn. (alt. liaison commn. cancer ACS 1995—, chmn. edn. com. 1996-97, chmn. edn. subcom. bldg. blocks data base mgmt. workshop 1995-96, mem. formal edn. subcom. 1995-96), Calif. Cancer Registrars Assn. (bd. dirs. del. 1989, v.p. 1992, pres. 1994-96, chmn. various coms.), So. Calif. Cancer Registrars Assn. (v.p. 1988, pres. 1989, chmn. various coms.). Roman Catholic. Office: St Mary Med Ctr 1050 Linden Ave Long Beach CA 90813

GRESSETT, LISA, advertis ng professional; b. Birmingham, Mar. 14, 1960; d. Linzy and Ileen (Woodard) G.; 1 child, Jennifer Louise Hatin. BA in Mktg., U. South Ala., 1983; postgrad. in bank mktg., U. Colo., 1993. Mktg. profl. Placer Savs., Auburn, Calif., 1985; asst. mktg. dir. McClellan Fed. Credit Union, North Highlands, Calif., 1989; mktg. dir. Continental Pacific Bank, Vacaville, Calif., 1989-94; owner Market Edge, Vacaville, 1994—; judge Internat. Assn. of Bus. Communicators, Sacramento, 1995. Bd. dirs. Children's Network, Solano County, 1995—, Local Devel. Corp., Vacaville, 1994—. Mem. Art Dirs. and Artists Club, Printing Industries of No. Calif., Rotary (fellowship chmn. 1994-96, bd. dirs. 1996—). Republican. Office: Market Edge Ste F 312 Cernon St Vacaville CA 95688

GREY, DEBORAH CLELAND, Canadian government official; b. Vancouver, B.C., Can., July 1, 1952; d. Mansell Caverhill Grey and Lilian Joyce (Russell) Levy; m. Lewis Larson, Aug. 7, 1993. BA, U. Alta., Edmonton, Can., 1978, B of Edn., 1979. Tchr. Frog Lake (Alta.) Indian Res., 1979-80, Dewberry (Alta.) Sch., 1980-89; M.P. Ho. of Commons, Ottawa, Ont., Can., 1989—. Caucus chmn. Reform Party, 1993—, apptd. dep. parliamentary leader, 1995—. Recipient Can. 125 medal, 1993, Alumni award of distinction Trinity Western U., 1996. Home: Box 69, Heinsburg, AB Canada T0A 1X0 Office: Ho of Commons, Parliament Bldgs, Ottawa, AB Canada K1A 0A6

GREY, JENNIFER, actress; b. N.Y., Mar. 26, 1960; d. Joel and Jo (Wilder) G. appearances include: (stage) Album, 1980, The Twilight of the Golds, 1993, (film) Reckless, 1984, Red Dawn, 1984, The Cotton Club, 1984, Reckless, 1984, American Flyers, 1985, Ferris Beuller's Day Off, 1986, Dirty Dancing, 1987 (Golden Globe award nom. for best actress 1988), (voice) Light Years, 1988, Bloodhounds of Broadway, 1989, Stroke of Midnight, 1991, Wind, 1992, (T.V. movies) Murder in Mississippi, 1990, Criminal Justice, 1990, Eyes of a Witness, 1991, A Case for Murder, 1993; other TV appearances include Friends, 1995. Office: c/o Creative Artists Agy Inc 9830 Wilshire Blvd Beverly Hills CA 90212-1804*

GREY, RUTHANN E., pharmaceutical company executive; b. Buffalo, N.Y., May 13, 1945; d. Wilson Campbell and Rosalie (Briggs) Evege; m. Daine A. Grey, Aug. 25, 1990; children: Daine, Jr., Keenan, Nichole. BS, SUNY, Buffalo, 1966, MS, 1970, PhD, 1980; postgrad., Harvard U., 1988. Tchr. Bennett High Sch., Buffalo, 1966-69; prof. Erie C.C., Buffalo, 1970-73; adminstr. No. Va. Community Coll., Annandale, 1975-76, Wayne State U., Detroit, 1978-80; dir. pub. affairs Burroughs Corp., Detroit, 1981-86; exec. asst. to chmn. bd. dirs. The Equitable, N.Y.C., 1986-89; mgr. pub. affairs N.Y. Times, N.Y.C., 1989-90; mgr. divsn. corp. rels. Pub. Svc. Corp. Colo., Denver, 1990-93; v.p. comm. and pub. affairs Hoechst Celanese, Bridgewater, N.J., 1993—; v.p. global media and external rels. Hoechst Marion Roussel, Bridgewater; cons. A+ For Kids, Newark, 1989-90, Rockefeller Found., N.Y.C., 1989-90. Bd. dirs. Citizens Scholarship Found., Minn., 1990-94. Mem. Pub. Rels. Seminar, Arthur Page Soc., The Wisemen, Pub. Rels. Rsch. Found. Home: 28 Stonegate Dr Watchung NJ 07060-5471 Office: Hoechst Celanese Box 6800 Bridgewater NJ 08807-0800

GREYTAK, SHARON ANN, film director, writer, producer; b. Bridgeport, Conn., May 13, 1958; d. Joseph and Anna Dorothy (Niznik) G. BFA magna cum laude, U. Hartford, 1980; MFA, Calif. Inst. Arts, 1982. Film maker, N.Y.C., 1982—. Writer, prodr., dir. (documentary) Weirded Out and Blown Away, 1986, (dramatic feature films) Hearing Voices, 1990, The Love Lesson, 1994; films shown at Margaret Mead Film Festival, 1986, Joseph Papp's Pub. Theatre, 1986, Sta. WNET-13, 1986, 90, (all N.Y.C.), , 1987 Am. Film Inst.'s Directing Workshop for Women, 1987 and 93 N.Y. Found. for the Arts Fellow in Film, Florence (Italy) Film Festival, 1989, Houston Internat. Film Festival, 1990, 1994 Am. Film Inst.'s Ind. Filmmaker fellowship, L.A. Internat. Film Festival, 1990, 96, Films de Femmes Internat. Fest Women Dirs., Creteil, France, 1990; represented in permanent collections Mus. Modern Art, N.Y.C.; one woman shows at Mus. Modern Art 1983, 86, 90, 96, Mus. Fine Arts, Boston, 1990, Wadsworth Atheneum, Hartford, 1995. Mem. exec. bd. Leo Dratfield Endowment, v.p., 1988-90; v.p. MacDowell Colony Fellows Exec. Com., 1993-98. Democrat. Address: 85 8th Ave Apt 2K New York NY 10011-5122

GRIEB, ELIZABETH, lawyer; b. Chestertown, Md., Nov. 14, 1950; d. Henry Norman and Lillian (Ballard) Grieb; m. George Stewart Webb, Aug. 18, 1979 (div. 1990); children: Timothy Stewart, Margaret Elizabeth. BA English, Wells Coll., 1972; JD cum laude, U. Balt., 1977. Bar: Md. 1977. Assoc. Piper & Marbury, Balt., 1977-84, ptnr., 1984—. Adv. bd. U. Md. Sys. Downtown Ctr., Balt., 1990-92; bd. dirs., sec. Choice Jobs, Inc., Balt., 1991-93; pres. U. Balt. Alumni Assn., 1994-95; bd. dirs. Balt. Zoo, 1995—. Mem. Md. State Bar Assn. (chair securities laws com. 1990-92), Ho. of Ruth (bd. dirs. 1994—), Ctr. Club. Episcopal. Office: Piper & Marbury 36 S Charles St Baltimore MD 21201-3020*

GRIEBEL, PAMELA SUE, elementary school educator; b. Lakewood, Ohio, Oct. 18, 1957; d. Theodore Ralph Olm and Faith Joy (Sherman) Heckenberg; m. Brian R. Griebel, July 25, 1980; children: Mallory, Brian. BEd, U. Dayton, 1980; MEd, Baldwin Wallace Coll., 1987. Cert. elem. tchr., reading specialist, Ohio. 6th grade tchr. St. Peter & Paul Sch., Garfield Heights, Ohio, 1980-81; 3d grade tchr. St. Raphael Sch., Bay Village, Ohio, 1981-84; 2d and 4th grade tchr. Lakewood (Ohio) City Schs., 1984—; mem. supt.'s adv. coun. Lakewood City Schs., 1993-95; mem. Math. Pilot/Textbook Selection Team, 1993; team leader, writer Venture Capital Grant Team. Hospitality chmn. St. Raphael Home & Sch., 1994-95; presch. religion tchr. St. Raphael Ch., 1994-96, uniform resale co-chair, 1995—; supr. student coun. Roosevelt Sch., 1987—. Martha Holden Jennings grantee, 1989. Mem. Internat. Reading Assn., Lakewood Tchrs. Assn., Delta Gamma Kappa. Roman Catholic. Home: 27006 E Oviatt Rd Bay Village OH 44140-2335 Office: Lakewood City Schs 1470 Warren Rd Lakewood OH 44107-3918

GRIEDER, KAREN SUZANNE, insurance company administrator; b. Paterson, N.J., Apr. 26, 1957; d. John Robert and Suzanne Jeanne (Ferrand) G. AA with honors, Golden West Coll., Huntington Beach, Calif., 1982; student in Spl. Arts Studies, Richmond Coll., London, 1983; BA with distinction, Calif. State U., Long Beach, 1984; grad., Ins. Inst. Am.; student, Coll. For Appraisers. News and pub. affairs Sta. KBIG, L.A., 1984; in mktg. and fundraising Sta. KLON, Long Beach, Calif., 1984-87; program producer Sta. KABC and ABC Talkradio Network, L.A., 1987-90; claims adjuster, legal negotiator Farmers Ins., 1990—. Mem. Nat. Assn. Broadcast Employees and Technicians. Office: PO Box 1447 Orange CA 92668-0447

GRIER, BARBARA G. (GENE DAMON), editor, lecturer, writer; b. Cin., Nov. 4, 1933; d. Phillip Strang and Dorothy Vernon (Black) Grier; life ptnr. Donna J. McBride, 1972—; grad. high sch. Author: The Lesbian in Literature, 1967, (with others) 2d edit., 1975, 3d edit., 1981, 4th edit.; The Least of These (in Sisterhood is Powerful), 1970; The Index, 1974; Lesbiana, 1976; The Lesbian Home Jour., 1976; The Lavender Herring, 1976; Lesbian Lives, 1976, The Mysterious Naiad, 1994, The First Time Ever, 1995, Dancing in the Dark, 1996; editor: (with Katherine V. Forrest) The Erotic Naiad, 1992, The Romantic Naiad, 1993; pub. The Ladder mag., 1970-72, fiction and poetry editor, 1966-67, editor, 1968-72; dir. promotion Naiad Press, Reno, Nev., 1973—, treas., 1976—, v.p., gen. mgr., Tallahassee, Fla., 1980—, CEO, 1987—, pres., 1995—. Democrat. Home: RR 1 Box 3319 Havana FL 32333-9759 Office: Naiad Press Inc PO Box 10543 Tallahassee FL 32302-2543

GRIFFEY, KAREN ROSE, special education educator; b. Phila., May 15, 1955; d. Arnold and Jacqueline (Wasserman) Salaman; m. Kenneth Paul Griffey, June 18, 1988; 1 child, Jessica; stepchildren: Kristina, Joseph. BS in Elem. Edn., W. Chester U., Pa., 1977; cert. Paralegal Studies, Nat. Ctr. Paralegal Tng., Atlanta, 1986; MS in Interrelated, U. Ga., 1994. Adult habilitation program Jewish Vocat. Svc., Phila., 1977-79; instr. Phila. Sch. Sys., 1979-81; tchr. 3rd grade Fla. Sch. Sys., Fort Myers, 1981-86; paralegal Atlanta, 1986-89; tchr. Interrelated Sharp Middle Sch., Covington, Ga., 1989-91; tchr. Spl. Kindergarten Rorterdale and Fairview Elem., Covington, Ga., 1991—; tchr., liaison, bd. mem., PAC rep., bldg. rep. Tchrs. Assn. Lee County, Fort Myers, Fla., 1981-86. Tchr. liaison Senators and Reps. in Fla. Legis., Tallahassee, 1981-86; PAC bd., 1981-86; exec. bd. mem. Leadership Team. of Tchrs. Assn. Lee County, Ft. Myers, Fla., 1981-86; Bargaining Team mdm. Tchrs. Assn. Lee County, Ft. Myers, Fla., 1981-86. Recipient Svc. award for working with handicapped, Phila. Sch. Sys., 1973; Phila scholarship Phils Sch. Sys., Mayor's Sch., Phila., 1973; NEA Svc. award in Edn., NEA, Ft. Myers, Fla., 1980. Mem. Coun. for Exceptional Children, Nat. Mus. of Women in the Arts, B'Nai B'rith, Spl. Olympics, Nat. Multiple Sclerosis Soc., Kappa Delta Pi. Democrat. Jewish. Home: 65 Stone Creek Dr Covington GA 30209-9053

GRIFFEY, LINDA BOYD, lawyer; b. Keokuk, Iowa, Aug. 6, 1949; d. Marshall Coulter and Geraldine Vivian (White) Boyd; m. John Jay Griffey, June 24, 1972. BS in Pharmacy, U. Iowa, 1972; JD, Duke U., 1980. Bar: Calif. 1980; lic. pharmacist, Iowa, N.C. Pharmacist Davenport (Iowa) Osteo. Hosp., 1972-75, Wagner Pharmacy, Clinton, Iowa, 1975-77, Durham (N.C.) County Gen. Hosp., 1977-80; assoc. O'Melveny & Myers, L.A., 1980-88, ptnr., 1988—; speaker, writer in field. Active L.A. Philharm. Bus. & Profl. Assn. Mem. ABA (employee benefits com. tax sect.), Am. Law Inst., L.A. County Bar Assn. (chair employee benefits com. 1994-95), L.A. Duke Bar Assn. (pres. 1987-90, 91-92), Rotary (bd. dirs. 1995—). Office: O'Melveny & Myers 400 S Hope St Los Angeles CA 90071-2801

GRIFFIN, DIANE EDMUND, research physician, virologist, educator; b. Iowa City, Ia., May 12, 1940; d. Rudolph William and Doris Irene (Swanson) Edmund; m. John Wesley Griffin, June 13, 1965; children: Christopher Todd, Erik Edmund. BA, Augustana Coll., Rock Island, Ill., 1962; MD, Stanford U., 1968, PhD, 1970. Diplomate Am. Bd. Internal Medicine, Am. Bd. Infectious Diseases. Resident in medicine Stanford (Calif.) U. Hosp., 1968-70; fellow Johns Hopkins U. Sch. Medicine, Balt., 1970-73, asst. prof., 1973-79, assoc. prof., 1979-86, prof., 1986—; prof., chair molecular microbiol. immunology Johns Hopkins U. Sch. Pub. Health, 1994—; investigator Howard Hughes Med. Inst., Balt., 1973-79; mem. virology study sect. NIH, 1982-86; mem. adv. com. Nat. Multiple Sclerosis Soc., 1986-92; mem. microbiology and infectious diseases rsch. adv. com. NIH, 1989-92, chair, 1992-94. Author films and tapes; contbr. chpts. to books, articles to profl. jours. Grantee NIH, 1983—, Nat. Multiple Sclerosis Soc., 1986—, WHO, 1993—, Muscular Dystrophy Assn., 1996—. Fellow Infectious Diseases Soc. Am.; mem. Am. Soc. for Clin. Investigation, Am. Soc. for Virology (council 1987-89), Interurban Clin. Club. Democrat. Lutheran. Office: Johns Hopkins Sch Pub Health 615 N Wolfe St Baltimore MD 21205

GRIFFIN, ELEANOR, magazine editor. Exec. editor Southern Living, Birmingham. Office: Southern Living 2100 Lakeshore Dr Birmingham AL 35209*

GRIFFIN, GLADYS BOGUES, critical care nurse, educator; b. Elizabeth City, N.C., July 18, 1937; d. Matthew Boques and Lucy Griffin Boques Eason; m. Oct. 21, 1957 (div.); children: Terry, Lucy, Misty, Derrick. AAS, Nassau (N.Y.) Community Coll., 1972. RN, N.C.; cert. ACLS. Nurse Long Beach (N.Y.) Meml. Hosp., 1968-70, staff nurse team leader, 1972-75, head nurse, 1975-76; staff nurse Critical Care Unit Albemarle Hosp., Elizabeth City, 1976-78, staff nurse Surg. Intensive Care Unit then coord., 1978—; BLS instr., head nurse surg. intensive care —, 1981-87; pub. speaker health related topics, Long Beach and Elizabeth City. Featurered Life Styles of Elizabeth City. Named one of Disting. Women N.C., 1989. Mem. Am. Assn. Critical Care Nurses, ARC Nurses, Soc. Notary Pub., NAFE, N.Y. Nurses Assn. Democrat. Home: 616 Crooked Run Rd Elizabeth City NC 27909-7538

GRIFFIN, GLORIA JEAN, elementary school educator; b. Emmett, Idaho, Sept. 10, 1946; d. Archie and Marguerite (Johnson) G. AA, Boise (Idaho) Jr. Coll., 1966; BA, Boise Coll., 1968; MA in Elem. Curriculum, Boise State U., 1975. Cert. advanced elem. tchr., Idaho. Tchr. music, tutor, Boise; sec. Edward A. Johnson, atty., Boise; tchr. Head Start, Boise; elem. tchr. Meridian (Idaho) Sch. Dist., 1968—; developer multi-modality individualized spelling program; co-developer program for adapting curriculum to student's individual differences. Author: The Culture and Customs of the Argentine People As Applied to a Sixth Grade Social Studies Unit. Sec. PTA. Named Tchr. of Yr., Meridian Sch. Dist., 1981. Mem. NEA, Internat. Reading Assn., Idaho Edn. Assn., Meridian Edn. Assn. (bldg. rep.), Idaho Reading Coun., Horizons Reading Coun., Alpha Delta Kappa (rec. sec.). Office: Silver Sage Elem Sch 7700 Snohomish St Boise ID 83709-5975

GRIFFIN, (ALVA) JEAN, entertainer; b. Detroit, June 1, 1931; d. Henry Bethel White and Ruth Madelyn (Gowen) Durham; m. Francis Jay Griffin, July 8, 1958 (dec.); stepchildren: Patra, Rodney; 1 adopted child, Donald; children: Rhonda Jean, Sherree Lee. Student, Anderson Coll., 1952-53; DD (hon.), Ministry of Salvation, Chula Vista, Calif., 1990, Ministry of Salvation, 1990. Ordained minister, 1990. Supr. Woolworth's, Detroit, 1945-46; operator, supr. Atlantic Bell Telephone Co., Detroit, 1947-51, Anderson, Ind., 1952-56; sec. to div. mgr. Food Basket-Lucky Stores, San Diego, 1957-58; owner, mgr. Jay's Country Boy Markets, Riverside, Calif., 1962-87; entertainer, producer, dir., singer Mae West & Co., 1980—; owner The Final Touch, Colorado Springs; tchr. art Grant Sch., Riverside, 1964-65; tchr., adviser Mental Retarded Sch., Riverside, 1976-77; instr. Touch for Health Found., Pasadena, Calif., 1975-79; cons., hypnotist, nutritionist, Riversaide, 1976-79; mem., tchr. Psi field parapsychology. Mem. Rep. Presdl. Task Force, 1983. Recipient svc. award Rep. Presdl. Task Force, 1986. Mem. Parapsychology Assn. Riverside (pres. 1981-82). Mem. Ch. of Religious Science New Thought. Home: 201 W Chapel Rd Sedona AZ 86336-7031

GRIFFIN, KARIN M.B., graphic artist, training developer; b. Chattanooga, Tenn., Apr. 9, 1950; d. Charles Cleveland and Mary Evelyn (McCurdy) Brewer; m. Philip Wayne Griffin; children: Jessica Leigh Griffin, Joshua Brewer Griffin. AA, St. Johns River Coll., Palatka, Fla., 1970; BFA, Middle Tenn. State U., Murfreesboro, 1979. Graphic arts specialist Saturn, Spring Hill, Tenn., 1989—. Home: 1210 General McArthur Dr Brentwood TN 37027

GRIFFIN, KELLY ANN, public relations executive, consultant; b. Buffalo, May 20, 1964; d. Michael Gerald and Patricia Frances (Lippert) G.; m. Thomas Richard Kleinberger, Oct. 11, 1992. B in Polit. Sci., SUNY, Geneseo, 1986; postgrad., CUNY, Bklyn., 1994—. Legis. asst. to N.Y. State Assembly Spkrs. Stanley Fink and Mel Miller Buffalo, 1986-87; acct. exec. Griffin Media Group, N.Y.C., 1987-88, acct. supr., v.p., 1988-90, pres., CEO, 1990-94; pub. rels. cons. N.Y.C., 1994—; assoc. dir. N.Y. State Funeral Dirs. Assn., N.Y.C., 1992-94, Met. Funeral Dirs. Assn., N.Y.C., 1992-94, Nat. Coun. Elected County Execs., N.Y.C., 1993—; instr. remedial reading Cornell U. Sch. Industry/Lab. Rels., Buffalo, 1987. Editor N.Y. State AFL-CIO Unity, 1988-90, Nat. Coun. Elected County Execs. News, 1993—, N.Y. State Funeral Dirs. Assn./Met. Funeral Dirs. Assn. News, 1992-94, Amalgamated Transit Union News, 1988-90. cons. Interfaith Assembly on Homelessness, N.Y.C., 1994—, Voter Assistance Commn., N.Y.C., 1990-92; participant, cons. Erie County Dem. Party, Buffalo, 1985-87; mem. assocs. steering com. Children's Health Fund, N.Y.C., 1991—. Recipient Acad. award DAR, 1978. Mem. Pub. Rels. Soc. N.Y.C. Roman Catholic. Home: 640 W 231st St Apt 7B Riverdale NY 10463 Office: Griffin Media Group PO Box 203 New York NY 10009-0203

GRIFFIN, LAURA M., retired educator; b. Woodland, Calif., Aug. 14, 1925; d. George Everette Ramsey and Bertha (Storz) Ramsey Lowe; m. Roy J. Griffin, Nov. 19, 1944; children: Robert Eugene, Dennis Charles, Kathleen Ann. AA in Social Sci., Sacramento City Coll., 1969; BA in Geography, Calif. State U., Sacramento, 1972. Cert. elem. and secondary tchr., Calif.; Master Gardener. Sec. Alameda Naval Air, Alameda, Calif., 1944-45, Cal-Western Life Ins., Sacramento, 1945-47, Pacific Sch. Dist., Sacramento, 1956-57; substitute tchr. Sacramento Unified Sch. Dist., 1974-75; tchr. Mt. Diablo Unified Sch. Dist., Concord, Calif., 1976-91; ret., 1991; dir. Heather Farm Garden Ctr., Walnut Creek, Calif., 1985-86, edn. chmn., 1986-87, pres., 1987-88, fin. sec., 1993-94; sec. investment group AAUW, Walnut Creek, 1978-79. Guardian Jobs Daus.-Bethel 325, Walnut Creek, 1978-79; leader Girl Scouts Am., Sacramento, 1971-72; den mother Boy Scouts Am.,

Sacramento, 1957-60; publicity chmn. membership Northgate Music Boosters, Walnut Creek, 1976-77. Recipient Heather Farm Garden Ctr. Outstanding Svc. award, 1994-95, Bert A. Bertolero Gardening award, 1996. Mem. Heather Farm Garden Club (pres. 1987-88, Outstanding Svc. award 1994-95), Walnut Creek Garden Club (pres. 1983-84, civic project chmn. 1994-95, 95-96), Order of Eastern Star. Republican.

GRIFFIN, LINDA L., English language and speech educator; b. Yale, Mich., Dec. 23, 1942; d. Benjamin and Ruth (Steenbergh) Hinton; m. James Griffin, Nov. 23, 1980. BA, U. Mich., 1965, MA, 1967; postgrad., Bowling Green (Ohio) State U., 1975, U. N.C., 1985; PhD, U. South Fla., 1996. Tchr. English and speech Sandusky (Mich.) H.S.; instr. Jackson (Mich.) C.C., Terra Tech. Coll., Fremont, Ohio, Edison C.C., Naples, Fla.; frequent speaker and presenter, including harp lecture programs; mem. NEH Shakespeare Seminar, 1985; keynote speaker Collier County Tchrs. Assn. Conf., 1987. Recipient Edison C.C. Excellence in Teaching award. Mem. MLA, South Atlantic MLA, S.E. Medieval Assn., Medieval Inst., S.C. Renaissance Assn., Nat. Coun. Tchrs. English, Flger Shakespeare Libr., So. State Comm. Assn., Fla. Comm. Assn. (pres. 1989-90), Phi Kappa Phi. Home: 9781 Bobwhite Ln Bonita Springs FL 33923-4416 Office: 7007 Lely Cultural Pky Naples FL 33962-8976

GRIFFIN, MARY FRANCES, retired library media consultant; b. Cross Hill, Laurens County, S.C., Aug. 24, 1925; d. James and Rosa Lee (Carter) G. BA, Benedict Coll., 1947; postgrad., S.C. State Coll., 1948-51, Atlanta U., 1953, Va. State Coll., 1961; MLS, Ind. U., 1957. Tchr.-librarian Johnston (S.C.) Tng. Sch., Edgefield County Sch. Dist., 1947-51; librarian Lee County Sch. Dist., Dennis High, Bishopville, S.C., 1951-52, Greenville County (S.C.) Sch. Dist., 1952-66; library cons. S.C. Dept. Edn., Columbia, 1966-87; vis. tchr. U. S.C., 1977; bd. dirs. Greater Columbia Lit. Coun.; mem. Richland County unit Assault on Illiteracy. Recipient Cert. of Living the Legacy award Nat. Council Negro Women, 1980. Mem. ALA, Assn. Ednl. Communications and Tech. S.C., Assn. Curriculum Devel., AAUW (pres. Columbia br. 1978-80), Southeastern Library Assn. (sec. 1978-80), S.C. Library Assn. (sec. 1979), S.C. Assn. Sch. Librarians, Nat. Assn. State Ednl. and Media Personnel. Baptist. Home: PO Box 1652 Columbia SC 29202-1652 also: 1100 Skyland Dr Columbia SC 29210-8127

GRIFFIN, NANCY RENAY, legal secretary; b. Phila., Feb. 27, 1962; d. Dominick Patrick and Anna Marie (Bunting) Griffin. AA, Peicre Jr. Coll., Phila., 1982; student, New Hampshire Coll., Brunswick, Maine, 1983-84, LaSalle U., 1992-93, Holy Family Coll., 1994. notary public. Legal sec. Matty & Ferroni, Phila., 1981, Hepburn, Willcox, Hamilton, Phila., 1982; radioman U.S. Navy, Naples, Italy, 1982-86, USNR, Phila., 1986-90; supr. legal sec. Toolan & Yanni, Phila., 1987-94; legal sec. Sheller, Ludwig & Badey, Phila., 1994—. Recipient good conduct medal U.S. Navy, 1986, meritorious svc. medal, 1990. Mem. NAFE, Phila. Legal Secs. Assn. (corr. sec. 1991-92), Phi Theta Kappa. Office: Sheller Ludwig & Badey 3d Fl 1528 Walnut St Fl 3 Philadelphia PA 19102-3604

GRIFFIN, SHEILA MB, electronics marketing executive; b. Chgo., June 17, 1951; d. George Michael and Frances Josephine (Sheehan) Spielman; m. Woodson Jack Griffin, Dec. 30, 1972; children: Woodson Jack, II, Kelly Sheehan. BS, U. Ill., 1975, MBA, 1979. Personal banking rep. Am. Express Banking, Boeblingen, Fed. Republic Germany, 1973-74; market rsch.analyst Market Facts, Chgo., 1975-77; mgr. strategic rsch. Motorola, Inc., Schaumburg, Ill., 1977-83, mgr. mktg. resource, 1985-88, mgr. spl. projects Corp. Strategy Office, 1988-89, dir. corp. advt. worldwide, 1989-93, dir. bus. assessment corp. strategy office, 1993-94, dir Global Applied Market rsch. consumer business office, 1994-96, dir. multimedia strategy office; gen. mgr. mktg. rsch. and info. Ameritech Mobile Communications, Inc., Schaumburg, 1983-85. Trustee (founding), Ill. Math. and Sci. Acad., 1985—. Mem. U. Ill. Chgo. MBA Alumni Assn. (founder, pres. 1984-86), U. Ill. Alumni Assn. (bd. dirs. 1984-86, Disting. Alumni 1985, Constituent Leadership award 1989). Home: 3017 Glen Eagles Ct Saint Charles IL 60174-8832 Office: Motorola Inc 1303 E Algonquin Rd Schaumburg IL 60196-4041

GRIFFIN, SYLVIA GAIL, reading specialist; b. Portland, Oreg., Dec. 13, 1935; d. Archie and Marguerite (Johnson) G. AA, Boise Jr. Coll., 1955; BS, Brigham Young U., 1957, MEd, 1967. Cert. advanced teaching, Idaho. Classroom tchr. Boise (Idaho) Pub. Schs., 1957-59, 61-66, 67-69, reading specialist, 1969-90, 91-95, inclusion specialist, 1995—, early childhood specialist, 1990-91, inclusion specialist, 1995—; tchr. evening Spanish classes for adults, 1987-88; lectr. in field; mem. cons. pool U.S. Office Juvenile Justice and Delinquency Prevention, 1991—. Author: Procedures Used by First Grade Teachers for Teaching Experience Readiness for Reading Comprehension, The Short Story of Vowels, A Note Worthy Way to Teach Reading. Advisor in developing a program for dyslexics Scottish Rite Masons of Idaho, Boise. Mem. NEA, AAUW, Internat. Reading Assn., Orton Dyslexia Soc., Horizon Internat. Reading Assn., Idaho Edn. Assn. (pub. rels. dir. 1970-72), Boise Edn. Assn. (pub. rels. dir. 1969-72, bd. dirs. ednl. polit. involvement com. 1983-89), Alpha Delta Kappa. Office: 5007 Franklin Rd Boise ID 83705-1106

GRIFFIN-THOMPSON, MELANIE, accounting firm executive; b. Corpus Christi, Tex., Oct. 25, 1949; d. Roy Albert and Ola Emma (Hunt) G.; m. Robert Thompson; children: Maurice Dale, Donald Dwight, Merideth Thompson, Laura Thompson. BBA summa cum laude, Corpus Christi State U., 1977; MBA, Tex. A&M U., 1994. CPA, Tex.; cert. fin. planner. Sec.-treas. Roy Hunt, Inc., Corpus Christi, 1970-78, dir., 1970-82; v.p. White, Sluyter & Co., Corpus Christi, 1978-80; pres. Whittington & Griffin, Corpus Christi, 1980-82, also dir.; sec.-treas., dir. Sand Express, Inc., Corpus Christi, 1975-82; prin. Melanie Hunt Griffin & Assocs., CPAs, Corpus Christi, 1982-84; v.p. Fields, Nemec & Co., P.C., Corpus Christi, 1984—; mem. edn. and tng. task force White Ho. Conf. Small Bus., 1993; adj. prof. Tex. A&M, Corpus Christi. Contbr. articles to profl. jours. Devel. chair Am. Heart Assn., chmn. bd. 1989-90, Leadership Corpus Christi Alumni, 1982—; mem. adv. coun. Tex. A&M U., Corpus Christi. Recipient Women in Careers award YWCA, 1989, Outstanding Svc. award Corpus Christi chpt. CPA's, 1990-93. Mem. AICPA (personal fin. planning dir. small bus. taxation com. 1990-93), Tex. Soc. CPAs (bd. dirs. 1987—, v.p. 1988-89, 93-94, treas. 1995-96, pres. elect 1996-97, pres. Corpus Christi chpt. 1987-88, chmn. devel. new legis. leaders 1990-93, vice chair CPAs Helping Schs. 1994-95, Outstanding Svc. award 1990-91, Presdl. citation, pres. elect, 1996-97), Corpus Christi State U. Alumni Assn. (bd. dirs. 1987-90), Tex. State CPAs Ednl. Found. (trustee 1990-93), Exec. Women Internat. (chmn. philanthropy com. 1986-87), Corpus Christi Rotary (bd. dirs. 1996—). Home: 10817 Stonewall Blvd Corpus Christi TX 78410-2429 Office: Fields Nemec & Co PC 501 S Tancahua PO Box 23067 Corpus Christi TX 78403

GRIFFITH, LINDA MARIE, county government official; b. Helena, Mont., Sept. 22, 1949; d. Lawrence Eugene and Mary Ceona (Price) Smith; m. Dennis J. Willis Sr., July 6, 1968 (div. 1972); children: Dennis John Willis Jr., Andrew Bonnell Christian; m. Eugene Donald Griffith, Sept. 20, 1995. Cert. Paralegal, Kennesaw Coll., Marietta, Ga., 1986-88; Cert. Pub. Mgmt., U. Ga., 1991. Ga. state lobbyist. Reservations mgr. Guest Travel, Mpls., 1968-74; sales staff North Cen. Airlines, Mpls., 1974-76; dir. conv. and groupsales Summit Travel, Mpls., 1976-81; mktg. and sales mgr. Internat. Travel, Tampa, Fla., 1981-82; asst. dir. ops. and maintenance Cobb Community Transit, Marietta, Ga., 1989-95; legis. liaison office of fed. and state rels. Met. Atlanta Rapid Transit Authority, 1995-96, mgr. paratransit svcs., 1996—. Author (poetry): Battle of the Clouds, 1991 (Golden Poet award 1991). Civic leader East Cobb Civic Assn./Alpine Lakes Homeowners, Marietta, 1983-89; campaign mgr. Com. to Elect Thea Powell County Commr., Marietta, 1985-86; planning commr. Cobb County, Marietta, 1986-89; legis. liaison Cobb County Rep. Party, 1988-89; exec. com. Cobb County Rep. Party, 1988-89; legis. liaison Ga. Transit Assocs., 1991—; active mgmt.-edn. EXCEL-Cobb County. Recipient Award for Service as Planning Commr. Cobb County Bd. Commrs., 1989. Mem. Ga. Transit Assn., Women's Transp. Seminar, Am. Planning Assn., Assn. County Commrs. (policy com. 1986-88), Am. Pub. Transp. Assn. Republican. Office: Met Atlanta Rapid Transit Paratransit Svcs 2424 Piedmont Rd NE Atlanta GA 30324

GRIFFITH, MARY H., corporate communications executive. BA in English, Centre Coll., Danville, Ky. Sr. v.p., dir. pub. rels. 1st Nat. Bank Louisville, until 1990; with Nat. City Corp., Cleve., 1990—, sr. v.p. mktg. comm., 1992—. Bd. dirs. Centre Coll.; active numerous city and state civic orgns. Recipient Disting. Alumni award Centre Coll., 1991. Office: Nat City Corp Nat City Ctr 1900 E 9th St Cleveland OH 44101

GRIFFITH, MARY L. KILPATRICK (MRS. EMLYN I. GRIFFITH), civic leader; b. Gadsden, Ala., Mar. 22, 1926; d. Lewis A. and Willie (Reid) Kilpatrick; m. Emlyn I. Griffith, Aug. 13, 1946; children: William L., James R. AB, Huntingdon Coll., 1947. Pres. Evergreen Twig, Rome, N.Y., 1966-67, Rome Home, 1973-75, Rome Coll. Found., 1990-93, Ctrl. Assn. Blind and Visually Impaired, 1992-96; mem. Bd. Edn. Rome City Sch. Dist., 1967-77; del. U.S.-China Joint Session on Trade and Law, Beijing, 1987, Soviet-Am. Conf. on Comparative Edn., Moscow, 1988, Gov.'s Conf. on Librs., 1990. Bd. dirs. Kirkland Coll. Coun., 1967-75, Rome chpt. Am. Field Svc., 1969-77, Utica Coll. Found., 1974-80, George Jr. Republic, 1974-88, Pub. Broadcasting Coun. Ctrl. N.Y., 1977-83, Rome Art and Cmty. Ctr., 1978-84, 1st Presbyn. Ch., Rome, 1979-85, Ctrl. N.Y. Libr. Resources Coun., 1992—, Utica Symphony Orch., 1989-94, Cmty. Found., 1992—, Oneida Cmty. Mansion House Mus., 1994—. Recipient Rose for Living award Rotary Club, 1973, Civic award for conspicuous pub. service Colgate U., 1978. Mem. AAUW, PEO (pres. 1965-66), Wednesday Morning Club (pres. 1968-70). Home: Golf Course Rd Rome NY 13440

GRIFFITH, MELANIE, actress; b. N.Y.C., Aug. 9, 1957; d. Tippi Hedren; m. Steven Bauer (div.); 1 child, Alexander; m. Don Johnson, 1989 (div.); 1 child, Dakota; m. Antonio Banderas, 1996. Student, Hollywood Profl. Sch., 1981; studied acting with, Stella Adler. Acting debut in Night Moves, 1975, other films include The Drowning Pool, 1975, Smile, 1975, One on One, 1977, Roar, Joyride, 1977, Underground Aces, Body Double, 1984, Fear City, Something Wild, 1986, Cherry 2000, 1988, The Milagro Beanfield War, 1988, Stormy Monday, 1987, Working Girl, 1988 (Acad. Award nomination), In the Spirit, The Grifters, Pacific Heights, 1990, Bonfire of the Vanities, Shining Through, Paradise, 1991, A Stranger Among Us, 1992, Born Yesterday, 1993, Milk Money, 1994, Nobody's Fool, 1994, Two Much, 1996, Mulholland Falls, 1996, Lolita, 1996; TV appearances include (series) Carter Country, (mini-series) Once an Eagle, Buffalo Girls, 1995, (movies) Daddy, I Don't Like This, Steel Cowboy, The Star Marker, (pilots) She's in the Army Now, Golden Gate; guest in Alfred Hitcock Presents. Recipient Golden Globe award, 1989. *

GRIFFITH, NANCI, singer, songwriter; b. Austin, Tex., 1954; d. Griff and Ruelene G. BA Edn., U. of Tex., Austin. Former kindergarten & 1st grade teacher Austin SD; recording artist, 1978—. albums include: There's a Light Beyond These Woods, 1978, Poet in My Window, 1982, Once in a Very Blue Moon, 1985, Last of the True Believers, 1986, Lone Star State of Mind, 1987, Little Love Affairs, 1988, One Fair Summer Evening, 1988, Storms, 1989, Late Night Grande Hotel, 1991, The MCA Years - A Retrospective, 1993, Other Voices, Other Rooms, 1993 (Grammy award Best Folk album), The Best of Nanci Griffith, 1993, Flyer, 1994; appeared in Nanci Griffith on Broadway, 1994. Office: care Gold Mountain Entertainment 1111 16th Ave S Ste 302 Nashville TN 37212*

GRIFFITH, PATRICIA KING, journalist; b. San Francisco, Jan. 20, 1934; d. Earl Beardsley and Frankie Mae (Kelly) King; m. Winthrop Gold Griffith, Oct. 4, 1958 (div. Jan. 1986); children: Kevin Winthrop, Christina Suzanne. BA, Stanford U., 1955. Copy asst., reporter Washington Post, 1956-57, 60-64; reporter San Francisco Examiner, 1957-59; Washington bureau chief Monterey Herald and Toledo Blade, Washington, 1979-81; investigative reporter Monterey (Calif.) Peninsula Herald, 1973-79, city editor, 1981-83, mng. editor, 1983-88; Washington bureau chief, White House corr. Toledo Blade and Pitts. Post-Gazette, Washington, 1988—. Bd. dirs. Lyceum of Monterey Peninsula, 1977-79, All Sts. Episcopal Day Sch., Carmel, Calif., 1977-79, Monterey Coll. Law, 1978-79; sr. warden St. Dunstan's Episcopal Ch., Carmel Valley, Calif., 1983-84. Recipient Silver Gavel award ABA, 1978. Mem. Stanford Alumni Assn., Nat. Press Club, Gridiron Club, Stanford Club Washington, Stanford Cap and Gown Soc. Home: 3001 Veazey Ter NW Washington DC 20008-5454 Office: Blade Comm 955 National Press Building Washington DC 20045-1901

GRIFFITH, SHEILA MERCEDES, underwriter; b. Phila., Oct. 6, 1957; d. Oscar Arlington and Jane Vernetta (Jervis) Blenman; m. Sherlock Herbert Griffith, Aug. 1, 1992. BA, U. Del., 1979; MS, Drexel U., 1983. Acct. Childhood Ctr. Drexel U., Phila., 1982-83; jr. cons. Garafolo & Sons., Ardmore, Pa., 1984; underwriter, sr. underwriter Gen. Accident Ins., Phila., 1985-92, personal lines underwriting supr., 1992-93, staff specialist underwriter, 1993—. Usher St. Mary's Episcopal Ch., Ardmore, 1991—, altar guild, 1993—. Named Outstanding Young Woman Am., 1979. Mem. NAFE, Delta Sigma Theta. Democrat. Home: 121 Europa Blvd Cherry Hill NJ 08003 Office: Gen Accident Ins Co 436 Walnut St Philadelphia PA 19106

GRIFFITH, SIMA LYNN, investment banking executive, consultant; b. N.Y.C., Sept. 7, 1960; d. Morris Benjamin and Mary (Buberoglü) Nahum; m. Clark Calvin Griffith, Sept. 13, 1987. BA in English, Amherst Coll., 1982. Account exec. D.F. King & Co., Inc., N.Y.C., 1982-84; asst. v.p. D.F. King & Co., Inc., 1984-86, v.p., 1986-88; v.p. Wells & Miller, Mpls., 1988; with Griffith, Levi Capital, Inc, Mpls., 1988—; co-chmn. seminars, 1987; bd. advisors Pacer, Inc. Mem. Internat. Assn. Bus. Communicators (bd. govs. 1987-88), Pub. Relations Soc. Am. (bd. govs. investor relations sec. 1987—), Nat. Investor Relations Inst. Office: Griffith Levi Capital Inc 4830 IDS Ctr 80 S 8th St Minneapolis MN 55402-2100*

GRIFFITH FRIES, MARTHA, controller; b. Brockton, Mass., Sept. 9, 1945; d. Ishmael Hayes and Jettie L. (Dudley) Davis; m. Jack C. Griffith, May 29, 1965 (dec. June 1984); Michael S., David M.; m. Dan H. Fries, Nov. 5, 1994. Student, U. Ark., 1962-64; BA, Ball State U., 1967. Prin. Griffith Acctg. Co., Indpls., 1968-70; probate adminstr. Johnson & Weaver, Indpls., 1970-74; personnel adminstr. Hercules Inc., Houston, 1974-76; adminstr. Lapin Totz & Mayer, Houston, 1976-80; bus. mgr. Pasadena (Tex.) Citizen, 1980-84; contr. Houston Community Newspapers, 1984-88, DCI Pub., Alexandria, Va., 1989-90, Telescan Inc., Houston, 1990-93, Advolink, Inc., 1993—. Commr. Houston council Boy Scouts Am., 1983. Recipient Dist. Merit awards Boy Scouts Am., Houston, 1983. Mem. Internat. Newspaper Fin. Execs. (com. mem. 1986-89), Collier Jackson Users Group (moderator 1986-89), Nat. Assn. Female Execs. Democrat. Baptist. Address: 17218 Telegraph Creek Dr Spring TX 77379-4840

GRIFFITH JOYNER, FLORENCE DELOREZ, track and field athlete; b. L.A., Dec. 21, 1959; d. Robert and Florence Griffith; m. Al Joyner; 1 child: Mary Ruth Joyner. Student, Calif. State U., Northridge, UCLA; PhD (hon.), Am. U., Washington, 1994. Co-owner NUCO Nails, Camarillo, Calif., 1994—; Designed line of sportswear, and uniforms for NBA Ind. Pacers. Actress (prin. role film) The Chaser, (recurring role TV drama) Santa Barbara, guest 227 TV situation comedies; host, commentator various sports events; guest numerous talk shows. Co-chairperson Pres. Coun. on Phys. Fitness & Sports, 1993—, founder The Florence Griffith Joyner Youth Found. Winner Silver medal Summer Olympics, L.A., 1984, 3 Gold medals, 1 Silver medal Summer Olympics, Seoul, Republic of Korea, 1988; U.S. Olympic Com. Sports Woman of the Year 1988, TAC Jesse Owens outstanding track and field athlete, 1988, Internat. Jesse Owens award Most Outstanding amateur athlete, 1988, Tass News Agy. Sports Personality of Yr., 1988, Internat. Fedn. Bodybuilders Most Outstanding Physique 1980s, 1988, UPI and AP Sportswoman of the year, 1988; named Athlete of Yr. Track and Field, 1988, recipient of the Harvard Found. award for outstanding contribution to the field of athletics, 1989, Essence Mag's. Sports award Extraordinary Accomplishments in Athletics, 1989, Golden Camera award from German Advt. Industry, 1989, James E. Sullivan Meml. award as most outstanding athlete in Am., 1989. Address: NUCO Nails Inc PO Box 67853 Via Alondra Camarillo CA 93012*

GRIFFITHS, BARBARA GAYLE, physician, artist; b. Valley Forge, pa., Dec. 30, 1955; d. Cadvan Owen and Barbara Frances (Williams) G. Student, U. Paris, 1977; BA, Mills Coll., 1978; MPH, U. Calif., Berkeley, 1979; MD, U. Ctrl. del Este, Dominican Republic, 1982. Intern Hosp. St. Raphael/Yale-New Haven Hosp., 1983-84; fellow in med. edn. U. Calif., San Francisco, 1984-86, resident in diagnostic radiology, 1986-89; surg. asst. pvt. practice plastic and reconstructive surgery L.A., 1979-83; urgent care dept. physician Med. Clinic of Sacramento, 1989-92; urgent care physician Kaiser Permanente Med. Group, South Sacramento, Calif., 1989-95; lead physician Folsom Clinic, 1992-94; med. dir. Readicare Indsl. Med. Clinics, Sacramento, 1993-94; site dir. Am. Health Med. Group, Sacramento, 1995; med. dir. Rocklin (Calif.) Clinic, Sutter Occupl. Health Svcs., 1995—; presenter in field. Contbr. articles to profl. publs., illustrations to med. jours.; art exhibited in shows at Nat. Soc. Plastic and Reconstructive Surgery, 1977, Mills Coll. Art Gallery, 1978, Med. Clin. of Sacramento, 1990, Sacramento Fine ARts Ctr., 1991. Bd. dirs. Rsch. Found. for Plastic Surgery, Del., 1985—; pres., bd. dirs. Internat. Found. Med.-Surg. Self Help Clinics, 1992—. Acad. senate grantee in trauma rsch. U. Calif., San Francisco, 1985-86; recipient Achievement award Lawrence Berkeley Labs., 1978; Mills Coll. scholar, 1974-78. Mem. AMA, NAFE, Am. Bd. Occupl. & Preventive Medicine, Calif. Med. Assn., Am. Coll. Occupl. and Environ. Medicine, Western Occupl. Med. Assn., Profl. Women in Health Care Network (founder Placer-Sacramento chpt.), Roseville C. of C., Rocklin C. of C. Home: 3937 Maudray Way Carmichael CA 95608 Office: Sutter Health 6000 Fairway Dr Ste 1 Rocklin CA 95677

GRIFFITH-THOMPSON, SARA LYNN, resource reading educator; b. Kansas City, Mo., July 27, 1965; d. Hugh Wallace and Mary Elizabeth (Mullinix) Griffith; m. Joey Lee Thompson, May 30, 1992. BS in Edn., Ctrl. Mo. State U., 1986, MS in Edn., 1992. Tchr. grade 4 East Lynne (Mo.) Sch. Dist., 1987-88, Pleasant Lea Elem., Lee's Summit, Mo., 1988-93; tchr. grade 4 resource reading K-6 Trailridge Elem., Lee's Summit, 1993—; asst. After Sch. Group, Lee's Summit, 1993-94; mem. Tchr. Expectation Student Achievement, Lee's Summit, 1992, sponsor Student Coun., Lee's Summit, 1994-96, supr. Student Tchrs., Lee's Summit, spring 1992. Recipient Excellence in Tchg. award Lee's Summit C. of C., 1992. Mem. Internat. Reading Assn. (bldg. rep. 1994—, presenter Plains regional 1995, state conf. 1996), Mo. State Tchr. Assn., PEO, Grand Cross, Optimist Club (super friends), Phi Delta Kappa. Office: Trailridge Elem 3651 SW Windemere Dr Lees Summit MO 64082-4412

GRIGGS, BOBBIE JUNE, civic worker; b. Oklahoma City, Feb. 14, 1938; d. Robert Jefferson and Nora May (Green) Fish; m. Peter Harvey Griggs, Apr. 16, 1955; children: Diana (dec.), Terry, James. Grad. high sch., Salina, Kans. Commissary rep. Family Mag., Charleston AFB, S.C., 1976—; rep. Avon Corp., Charleston, S.C., 1976—; freelance demonstrator to USAF and USN orgns. Charleston, 1976—; rep. Salute Mag., Charleston AFB, 1986—; consumer edn. counselor Air Force-Navy exchs. Oster Kitchen Appliances, Charleston, 1987-90. Contbr. World's Largest Poem for Peace, 1991, Selected Works of our Best Poets, 1992, In A Different Light, 1992. Youth advisor, Charleston AFB, 1966-78; vol. doll distbn. program Salvation Army; clinic vol. ARC, Charleston AFB, 1967-75, chmn. family svcs. publicity and spl. projects, 1989; clinic vol. Clara Barton award, 1972; vol. Spoleto Festival, 1989—, Twin Oaks Retirement Ctr., 1992—, Chapel SUMMOM program, 1991—; asst. coord., publicity chmn. Family Svcs., 1967-83, named vol. of quarter, 1970, 72, 74, 76, named vol. of yr., 1970; active various scouting orgns., 1967—; asst. kindergarten Sunday sch. supt. Chapel I, 1966-68; active North Charleston (S.C.) Christian Women's Club, 1988—, hosp. chmn., mem. Charleston AFB Protestant Women's Club., 1965—; tchr. Bible sch., 1984-89; vol. tutor Lambs Elem., 1992, Trident Literacy Assn. (Laubach Literacy Action cert. 1992); coun. rep. Charleston AFB parish coun., 1988—; mem. Rocketeers Actors Group, Goals 2000 com. 1993—, Barnabas Outreach program, 1991—, Clown Ministry Charleston AFB, 1993—; chairperson Helping Hands Charleston AFB, 1991—, Voyagers Sunday Sch. Class Project, Summerville Homeless Shelter Charleston AFB, 1993—, Publicity Protestant Women, 1993—; vol. Lambs Elem., 1992—, Twin Oaks Retirement Ctr., 1992—, Barnabas Outreach Com., 1991—, Military Retirees, 1994—, counselor Jr. Achievement Program, 1994; mem. Charleston Raptor Ctr., 1996, S.C. Homeless Shelter Planning com., 1995-96, Am. Indian Heritage Coun., 1996. Recipient 1,000 Hours award Air Force Times, 1971, 1st Pl. award Designer Craftsman show, 1967-71, Dedicated Svc. award Charleston AFB, 1981, Hurricane Hugo Hero award, 1989, 1st Pl. award Bake-Off Contest YMCA, 1981, Hist. Charleston Trail Hike award Cub Scouts, 1988, Family Svcs. Vol. of Quar. award, 1990, Family Svcs. 6,000 Hour award, 1990, Golden Poet award, 1991, 1992, In a Different Light award Libr. Congress, 1991; named Enlisted Wife of Yr., Charleston AFB, 1974, Family Svcs. Vol. of Quarter Charleston AFB, 1990, Family Svcs. 6000 Hour award, 1991, Outstanding Vol. Svc. award Operation Desert Shield/Storm, 1991, Family Svcs. Spl. Recognition award, 1991, Appreciation acknowledgement Pres. of U.S., 1991, First Lady Barbara Bush, 1992, Pres. of U.S., 1994, First Lady Hillary Clinton, 1994, Disting. Vol. award Charleston County Sch. Dist., 1995, Retiree Volunteer of the Quarter Charleston AFB, 1995, Vol. of Month Lambs Elem. Sch., 1995, Voting Slogan award Sec. Def., 1995. Mem. Nat. Trust Hist. Preservation, Smithsonian Inst., Charleston AFB Non-Commd. Officers' Wives Club (pres. 1971-73, publicity chmn. 1969-70, wife of month 1967, wife of quarter 1973), Rocketeers Actors Group, Friends of Dock St.-Ushers.

GRIGGS, EMMA, management executive; b. Cleveland, Ark., Feb. 8, 1928; d. James and Frazier (Byers) Wallace; m. Augusta Griggs, Mar. 20, 1954 (dec.); children: Judy A., Terri V. Grad. h.s., Chgo. Pres., CEO Burlington No. Inc., Inglewood, Calif., 1986—. Republican. Home: 2601 W 81st St Inglewood CA 90305-1418

GRIGGS, RUTH MARIE, retired journalism educator, writer, publications consultant; b. Linton, Ind., Aug. 11, 1911; d. Roy Evans Price and Mary Blanche (Hays) P.; m. Paul Philip Griggs, Aug. 4, 1940. BS, Butler U., 1933; postgrad. U. So. Calif., 1938, Northwestern U., 1939; MA, U. Wyo., 1944. Cert. tchr. journalism, English, speech, bus. edn. Travel writer Indpls. Star, 1927-37; summer reporter Worthington Times, Ind., 1928-33; journalism, speech tchr. Warren Cen. High Sch., Indpls., 1937-37; tchr. bus. edn., journalism Greene Twp. High Sch., South Bend, Ind., 1937-38; tchr. journalism, English, bus. edn. Howe High Sch., Indpls., 1938-46; tchr. journalism Butler U., Indpls., 1946-48, evenings 1972-76; dir. publs. Broad Ripple High Sch., Indpls., 1948-77; summer journalism workshop instr. numerous univs. 1949-80. Author: History of Broad Ripple, 1968; co-author: Handbook for High School Journalism, 1951; Teacher's Guide to High School Journalism, 1965, Marquette Memoirs, 1996. Dow Jones Newspaper Fund fellow U. Minn., 1967; named Nat. Journalism Tchr. of Yr. Wall Street Jour., 1968, Woman of Achievement Woman's Press Club of Ind., 1984; recipient Rabb award Women's Press Club of Ind., 1988, Disting. Alumni award Butler U. Alumni Bd., 1989. Mem. AAUW, DAR, Journalism Edn. Assn. (v.p., pres. 1963-69, Towley award 1965), Women in Communications (pres. Indpls. 1969-70, Wright award 1969, Kleinhenz award 1978), Nat. Fed. Press Women (youth projects bd. 1979-87, Recognition award 1991), Columbia Scholastic Press Assn. (Gold Key award 1964, Golden Crown 1975, life mem. 1977), Ind. High Sch. Advisers Assn. (pres. 1972, Sengenberger award 1965), Delta Zeta (Ind. Woman of Yr. 1984). Republican. Presbyterian.

GRIGSBY, MARGARET ELIZABETH, physician; b. Prairie View, Tex., Jan. 16, 1923; d. John Richard and Lee (Hankins) G. BS, Prairie View State Coll., 1943; MD, U. Mich., 1948. Diplomate: Nat. Bd. Med. Examiners, Am. Bd. Internal Medicine. Intern Homer G. Phillips Hosp., St. Louis, 1948-49, asst. resident medicine, 1949-50; asst. resident Freedmen's Hosp., Washington, 1950-51, asst. physician, 1952-56, attending physician, 1956; practice medicine specializing in internal medicine Washington, 1953-54; instr. medicine Howard U., Washington, 1952-57, asst. prof., 1957-60, assoc. prof., 1960-66, prof., 1966-93, prof. emerita, 1993—, chief of infectious diseases, 1952-71, lectr. sch. social work, 1955-59, adminstrv. asst. dept. medicine sch. social work, 1961-63; epidemiologist USPHS, Ibadan, Nigeria, 1966-68; hon. vis. prof. preventive and social medicine U. Ibadan, 1967-68; cons. AID, Dept. State, 1970-71; mem. adv. com. anti-infective agents FDA, 1970-72. Contbr. articles to med. jours. Rockefeller Found. fellow Harvard U., 1951-52; research fellow Thorndike Meml. Lab., Boston City Hosp., 1951-52; China Med. Bd. fellow tropical medicine U. P.R., 1956; Commonwealth Fund Fellow U. London, 1962-63. Fellow ACP; mem. Nat. Med. Assn., Med. Soc. D.C., Royal Soc. Tropical Medicine and Hygiene, Am. Soc. Tropical Medicine and Hygiene, Medico-Chirug. Soc. D.C., Assn. Former Interns and Residents Freedman's Hosp., U. Mich. Alumni Assn., Prairie View Alumni Assn., Sigma Xi, Alpha Epsilon Iota, Alpha Kappa Alpha, Alpha Omega Alpha. Office: Howard U Dept Medicine 2041 Georgia Ave NW Washington DC 20060-0001

GRIGSBY-STEPHENS, KLARON, corporate executive; b. East Prairie, Mo., Feb. 15, 1952; d. Claron Grigsby and Sylvia Mae (Grigery) Oliver; m. Richard Earl Stephens, Aug. 13, 1986. Exec. asst. Quasar Petroleum Corp., Ft. Worth, 1974-80; sales mgr. ITT Life Ins. Corp., Ft. Worth, 1980-83; media buyer Boca Blue Star, Boca Raton, Fla., 1983-84; video editor Video Workshop, Pompano Beach, Fla., 1984-85; pres. Stephens Alfa Corp., Pompano Beach, 1985—. Contbr. articles to profl. jours., also numerous poems. Sgt. USAF, 1970-74. Mem. Alfa Romeo Owners Club, Challenger Ctr. (Washington, hon.). Office: 1321 S Dixie Hwy W Pompano Beach FL 33060-8520

GRILLO, JOANN DANIELLE, mezzo-soprano; b. Bklyn., May 14, 1939; d. John Daniel and Lucille Ann (De Pierre) G.; m. Richard Kniess, July 23, 1967; 1 child, John Richard. BS in Music, Hunter Coll., 1976; studied voice with Marinka Gurewich, Daniel Ferro, Lorenzo Anselmi, Joan Dornemann, Loretta Corelli, Franco Iglesias.; also courses, Met. Opera. Founder, mng. dir. Ambassadors of Opera and Concert World Wide, 1981—. Appeared in Aida, Madame Butterfly, N.Y. City Opera, 1962, with Paris Opera, Teatro San Carlo, Naples, Italy, Zurich (Switzerland) Stadttheatre, Opera of Marseille, France, 1964, Frankfurt (Fed. Republic of Germany) Opera as Carmen, Amneris and Jocasta, 1967-68, Amneris in Aida at Teatro Municipal, Rio di Janeiro, 1989; European debut in Werther at Gran Teatro Liceo, Barcelona, Spain, 1963, 78; debut with Met. Opera, N.Y.C., 1963, resident artist, 1963—; debut with Vienna Staatsoper as Carmen, 1978, English debut in Verdi Requiem at Buxton Festival, 1991; performed Carmen with Paris Opera, 1981; appearances include Met. Opera, Vienna Staatsoper, Paris Opera, Paris Opera Comique, Amsterdam Opera, Hamburg Staatsoper, Deutsche Oper am Rhein, Opera of Madrid, Internat. Festival Split, Bellas Artes Mexico City, Israel Nat. Opera, Dallas Civic Opera, Washington Opera Soc., N.Y.C. Opera, Opera Nice, Washington Opera Soc., Phila. Opera, Cin. Opera, others; roles include in Don Carlos, Il Trovatore, Carmen, Samson et Dalila, Damnation de Faust, Die Walkure, Das Rheingold, Götterdammerung, Tannhauser, others; toured U.S. for Civic Concert Orgn., 1959, 1961; performed concert for UN World AIDS Day, N.Y.C., 1996; presented concerts with Ambassadors of Opera in Europe, Latin Am. and Far East, including Istanbul, Cairo, Nairobi, Dubai, Abu Dhabi, Bahrain, Muscat, Karachi, Lahore, Hong Kong, Seoul, Kyongju, Manila and Bangkok, 1996. Kathryn Long scholar Met. Opera. Roman Catholic. Office: Ambs of Opera 240 Central Park S Ste 16M New York NY 10019-1413

GRIM, ELLEN TOWNSEND, artist, retired art educator; b. Boone County, Ind., Nov. 1, 1921; d. Horace Wright and Sibyl Conklin (Lindley) Townsend; m. Robert Little Grim, Apr. 5, 1952; children: Nancy Ellen Grim Davis, Howard Robert. BA in Art, U. Wash., 1946; MA in Art, UCLA, 1950; postgrad., Otis Art Inst., L.A., 1970-71. Cert. secondary tchr., Calif. Art tchr., chairperson secondary Calif. and L.A. Unified Sch. Dist., 1947-82; retired, 1982; artist L.A., 1975—; guest speaker on art TV and cable, L.A., 1993. One-woman shows include Ventura County Mus. Art, 1982, Riverside Mcpl. Mus., 1984, Craft and Folk Art Mus., L.A., 1986, S.W. Mus., L.A., 1987, Calif. Heritage Mus., 1991, others; exhibited in more than 100 group shows. 1st lt. USMC, 1943-45. Recipient Purchase prize Gardena Fine Arts Collection, 1982, Watercolor West award San Diego Watercolor Soc. Internat., 1983, N.Mex. Watercolor Soc. award, 1989, 1st pl. award Fine Arts Fedn., 1987, 1st pl. award Art Educators L.A., 1988, 89, others. Mem. Nat. Watercolor Soc. (historian 1989-90, Painting award 1989), Women Painters West (membership chair, mem.-at-large 1983-89, Painting award 1985, 86, 89, 92, 93, 95), L.A. Art Assn. (bd. dirs. 1993-95), Pasadena Soc. Artists (Painting award 1986, 88, 90, 92, 93), Collage Artists Am. (1st pl. award 1995), Women Marines Assn. and Alliance of Women Vets., Alpha Phi, Pi Lambda Theta.

GRIMBALL, CAROLINE GORDON, sales professional; b. Columbia, S.C., Dec. 21, 1946; d. John and Caroline Grimball. B.A. in Polit. Sci., Converse Coll., 1968; postgrad., S.C. Law Sch., 1968-69. Asst. buyer, buyer Rich's, Inc., Atlanta, 1971-78, spl. events fashion coordinator, Columbia, S.C., 1978-83; gen. mdse. mgr. Rackes, Inc., Columbia, 1983-84, Parasol Boutique, Columbia, 1984-86; retail cons. Retail Mdsg. Service Automation, Columbia, 1986-88; sales rep. Palmetto Promotions, 1989-93; retail mdse. supr. Riverbanks Zoo & Garden, 1993—. Pres. Columbia Action Coun., 1990-92; bd. dirs. Palmetto Leadership Coun., 1991-92, Palmetto State Orch. Assn., Columbia, 1979-89, Women's Symphony Assn., Columbia, 1985; com. chmn. Columbia Action Coun., 1984-85, exec. com., 1989—. Named one of Outstanding Young Women Am., 1979, 80; recipient Community Service award Rich's, Inc., 1981. Mem. Nat. So. Colonial Dames Am., Columbia Jr. League. Democrat. Episcopalian. Club: Columbia Drama. Avocations: bridge, reading, needlepoint, tennis. Home: 4000 Bloomwood Rd Columbia SC 29205-2847

GRIMES, DAPHNE BUCHANAN, priest, artist; b. Tulsa, Apr. 12, 1929; d. George Sidney and Dorothy Elnora (Dodds) Buchanan; m. Thomas Edward Grimes, Nov. 6, 1964 (dec. Oct., 1986). BFA, U. Houston, 1952; MA, Columbia U., 1954; MA in Religion, Episcopal Seminary of the Southwest, 1985. Ordained deacon Episcopalian Ch., 1982, priest, 1986. Tchr. history Rockland County Day Sch., Nyack, N.Y., 1959-61; dir. Am. Sch., Tunis, Tunisia, 1962-64; priest vicar St. Andrew's Ch., Meeteetse, Wyo., 1987-90; dir. Thomas the Apostle Ctr., Cody, Wyo., 1990—; stewardship chmn. Diocese Wyo., 1979-85, mem. bd. diocesan coun., 1987-90, chmn. social svcs., 1987-91. Author of poems. Chaplain West Park County Hosp., Cody, Wyo., 1981-84, West Park County Long Term Care Ctr., Cody, 1982—; bd. dirs. Park County Arts Coun., 1995—. Mem. Cody Country Arts League, Cmty. of Celebration (spiritual adv. 1990—), Order of Julian of Norwich (assoc.), St. Andrew's Cmty. (assoc.). Home and Office: Thomas the Apostle Ctr 45 Road 3CX-S Cody WY 82414

GRIMES, EVANGELINE, secondary school educator; b. Washington, Apr. 24, 1945; d. Luther Sylvester and Queen Mildred (Williams) Johnson; m. Leavie Ander Grimes, June 28, 1964 (div. Oct. 1989); children: Gwendolen, Tameka, Veronika, Patricia Kennedy, Joseph Kennedy. BS in Elem. Edn., Ind. State U., 1982. Lic. tchr., Ind. Sec. drug abuse sect. outpatient clinic N.J. Neuro-Psychiat. Inst., Newark, 1969-72; sec., supr. Potomac Electric Power Co., Washington, 1972-78; sec. Afro-Am. Studies dept. Ind. State U., Terre Haute, 1979-80, pub. rels. coord. Black Student Union, 1979-80; substitute tchr. Vigo County Sch. Corp., Terre Haute, 1982-86; tchr. 7-9th grades Greater Victory Temple Acad., Terre Haute, 1993—. Ecclesiastes affairs chair Greater Victory Temple, Terre Haute, 1991-92, writing minister, 1990—; mem. PTA, Woodrow Wilson Jr. H.S., 1992-93; choir mem. Voices of Wisdom, 1994—; missionary Apostolic Bible Student Assn. of Pentecostal Assemblies of the World, Inc., 1993-94. Democrat. Apostolic Ch. Democrat. Apostolic Ch. Home: PO Box 8455 2927 Jefferson St Terre Haute IN 47802-8544 Office: Greater Victory Temple Acad 1100 S 17th St Terre Haute IN 47807

GRIMES, HEILAN YVETTE, publishing executive; b. Hamilton, Ohio, Sept. 16, 1949; d. J and Claudette (Hinkle) G. Grad., New Eng. Sch. Photography, 1987. Founder, pres. Dot & Line Graphics, 1975—, Color Computer Weekly, 1982—, Hollow Earth Pub., 1983—. Author: Norse Mythology, 1984, Legend of Niebelungenlied, 1984, Using QuarkXPress 3.3, The Laxdaela Saga, Beginning Internet, Beginning QuarkXPress, The Newton Source Book, Page Mill/Site Mill, Hot Metal Pro; founder (mag.) Byte, 1974, Macpower, 1993. Recipient various photographic awards and grants. Democrat. Office: PO Box 1355 Boston MA 02205-1355

GRIMES, MARGARET WHITEHURST, medievalist, educator; b. New Bern, N.C., Oct. 12, 1917; d. Robert Emmet and Margaret Edna (Ervin) Whitehurst; m. Alan Pendleton Grimes, May 16, 1942; children: Margaret, Alan P. Jr., Katherine E., Peter E. BA, U. N.C., 1938; MA, Mich. State U., 1967, PhD, 1969. Instr. Mich. State U., E. Lansing, 1969-71; asst. prof. humanities asst. prof. humanities, E. Lansing, 1971-75; assoc. prof. Mich. State U., E. Lansing, 1975-80, prof., 1980-86, prof. emeritus, 1986—; chmn., organizer Medieval Studies Consortium, Mich. State U., E. Lansing, 1991—. Contbr. articles to profl. jours.; presenter to medieval studies groups. Mem. Medieval Assn. Midwest, Dante Soc. Am., Medieval Acad. Am., Mich. State U. Dante Soc. (chmn., founder 1985). Democrat. Home: 728 Lantern Hill Dr East Lansing MI 48823-2828 Office: Mich State U Ctr Integrative Studies Linton Hall East Lansing MI 48824

GRIMES, MARTHA, author; b. Pittsburgh, Pa.; d. D.W. and June (Dunnington) G.; div.; 1 s.: Kent Van Holland. BA, MA, U. Md. Formerly instr. English U. Iowa, Iowa City; asst. prof. Frostburg State Coll., Frostburg, Md.; prof. Montgomery Coll., Takoma Park, Md., 1970—. Author: mystery novels The Man With a Load of Mischief, 1981, The Old Fox Deceiv'd, 1982, The Anodyne Necklace, 1983 (Nero Wolfe Award for best mystery of yr.1983), The Dirty Duck, 1984, The Jerusalem Inn, 1984, Help the Poor Struggler, 1985, The Deer Leap, 1985, I Am the Only Running Footman, 1986, The Five Bells and Bladebone, 1987, The Old Silent, 1989, Send Bygraves, 1989, The Old Contemptibles, 1991, End of the Pier, 1992, The Horse You Came In On, 1993, Rainbow's End, 1994, Hotel Paradise, 1994. Address: care Random House 201 E 50th St New York NY 10022-7703*

GRIMES, MARY ANNE, nurse; b. Kansas City, Kans., June 19, 1936; d. John Andy and Bertha Helen (Ball) G. RN, St. Joseph's Hosp. Cert. sch. nurse. Staff nurse St. Joseph's Hosp., Phoenix, 1957-61; office nurse Family Med. Clinic, Phoenix, 1961-62; pvt. duty nurse Central Registery, Phoenix, 1962-65; office nurse, mgr. Phoenix Urologic Clinic, 1965-79; sch. nurse Wilson Sch. Dist. 7, Phoenix, 1980-84, Balsz Sch. Dist. # 31, 1984-94; health svc. coord. Cath. Coalition for Urban Schs., Diocese of Phoenix, 1995-96, S.W. Elem. Sch., 1996—. Primary fund raiser Classical Chorus Bach and Madrigal Soc., also sec., bd. dirs.; campaign worker Republican gubernatorial election, Phoenix, 1968, 70; sec.-treas. Cen. Phoenix Coun. for Child Abuse Prevention, 1991-95; patron Spreckels Organ Soc., San Diego, Cantemus Classical Chorus, Phoenix, 1990. Mem. Am. Bus. Women's Assn. (pres. 1974-75, Woman of Yr. Met. chpt. 1995, chpt. pres. 1995—), Nat. Assn. Sch. Nurses Inc., Ariz. Sch. Nurse Assn. Republican. Roman Catholic. Home: 1805 N 21st Pl Phoenix AZ 85006-2415 Office: SW Sch 1111 W Dobbins Rd Phoenix AZ 85041

GRIMES, PAMELA RAE, elementary school educator; b. Cumberland, Md., Dec. 30, 1943; d. Robert Elmer and Mary Evelyn (Hill) McFarland; m. George Edward Grimes, Feb. 9, 1962; children: George Edward Jr., Robert Eric, Jonathon William, David James, Richard Allen. AA, Am. River Coll., 1965; BA, Calif. State U., Sacramento, 1975, MA, 1975; cert. in computer literacy, Sacramento Unified Sch. Dist., 1981. Cert. elem. tchr., Calif. Tchr. aide O.W. Erlewine Elem. Sch., Sacramento, 1965-67, elem. gate tchr., 1969-71; tchr. aide Cohen Elem. Sch., Sacramento, 1967-69; libr., tchr. 1st through 6th grades Golden Empire Elem. Sch., Sacramento, 1979-89; tchr. Hubert Bancroft Elem. Sch., Sacramento, 1989-95; staff trainer Literacy Curriculum & Instrn. Dept., 1995—; mentor tchr. Sacramento City Unified Sch. Dist., 1985-95; fellow, mem. Calif. History/Social Sci. course of study, 1991; mem. libr./lit. course of study, 1975, CORE lit. com., 1979, lang. arts assessment com., 1990—, CLAS adv. com., 1993-94, Literacy Task Force, 1995, adv. com. assessment testing, 1995; co-chair 20-1 Class Size Reduction Tng. SCUSD, Young Authors program, curriculum alignment project; literacy leader, facilitator CSIN, 1996—; No. Calif. coord. Ottawa U., 1991—. Ednl. cons. Children's Mus. Com., 1985—, Sacramento History Ctr., 1985. Fellow Calif. Lit. Project, 1989, Area III Writing Project, 1988, Calif. Social Studies Inst., 1990. Fellow Calif. Geog. Inst., East Asian Humanities Inst.; mem. NEA, ASCD, SARA, CRA, IRA, Nat. Coun. Tchrs. English, Geography Inst. (social studies project.stds. com. 1991), Calif. Alliance Elem. Edn., Calif. English Tchrs. Assn., Calif. Tchrs. Assn. Democrat. Methodist. Home: 9005 Harvest Way Sacramento CA 95826-2203

GRIMES, RUTH ELAINE, city planner; b. Palo Alto, Calif., Mar. 4, 1949; d. Herbert George and Irene (Williams) Baker; m. Charles A. Grimes, July 19, 1969 (div. 1981); 1 child, Michael; m. Roger L. Sharpe, Mar. 20, 1984; 1 child, Teresa. AB summa cum laude, U. Calif., Berkeley, 1970, M in City Planning, 1972. Rsch. and evaluation coord. Ctr. Ind. Living, Berkeley, 1972-74; planner City of Berkeley, 1974-76, sr. planner, 1983—, analyst, 1976-83; bd. dirs. Vets. Asssistance Ctr., Berkeley, pres., 1978-93; bd. dirs. Berkeley Design Advisors, treas., 1987-94. Author: Berkeley Downtown Plan, 1988; contbr. numerous articles to profl. jours. and other publs. Bd. dirs. Berkeley-Sakai Sister City Assn., 1994—, pres., 1995—, Ctr. Ind. Living. Honored by Calif. State Assembly Resolution, 1988; Edwin Frank Kraft scholar, 1966. Mem. ASPA, Am. Inst. Cert. Planners, Am. Planning Assn., Mensa, Lake Merrit Joggers and Striders (sec. 1986-89, pres. 1991-93), Lions Internat. (bd. dirs. Berkeley club 1992-94), U. Calif. Coll. Environ. Design Alumni Assn. (bd. dirs., treas. 1994-96). Home: 1330 Bonita Ave Berkeley CA 94709-1925 Office: City of Berkeley 2121 Mckinley Ave Berkeley CA 94703-1519

GRIMES, TRESMAINE JUDITH RUBAIN, psychology educator; b. N.Y.C., Aug. 3, 1959; d. Judith May (McIntosh) Rubain; m. Clarence Grimes, Jr., Dec. 22, 1984; children: Elena Joanna, Elijah Jeremy. BA, Yale U., 1980; MA, New Sch. for Social Rsch., 1982; MPhil, PhD, Columbia U., 1990. Advanced tchg. fellow Jewish Bd. Family and Childrens Svcs., N.Y.C., 1980-82; tchg./rsch. asst. Tchrs. Coll., Columbia U., N.Y.C., 1983-84; rschr., historian Youth Action Program, N.Y.C., 1984-86; psychologist Hale House for Infants, N.Y.C., 1986-89; asst. rschr. Bank St. Coll., N.Y.C., 1988; addiction program adminstr. Harlem Hosp. Ctr., N.Y.C., 1989-91; assoc. prof. and chair dept. psychology S.C. State U., Orangeburg, 1991—; adj. prof. psychology Tchrs. Coll., Columbia U., N.Y.C., 1990-91. Named Outstanding Young Women of Am., 1981. Mem. APA, Southeastern Psychol. Assn., Delta Sigma Theta, Kappa Delta Pi, Psi Chi. Democrat. Office: SC State Univ Box 7003 300 College St NE Orangeburg SC 29117-0001

GRIMES-FREDERICK, DOROTHEA D., communications executive; b. New Orleans; d. Morris and Rosemary (Birch) Grimes; m. John H. Frederick. BS in Physics, So. U., Baton Rouge, 1974; EDD, Rutgers U., 1980. Tchr. physics Piscataway (N.J.) Sch. System, 1975-78; tech. asst. AT&T Bell Labs., Murray Hill, N.J., 1978-80; mem. tech. staff. AT&T Bell Labs., Piscataway, 1980-85; tech. supr. small system devel. lab. AT&T Bell Labs., Middletown, N.J., 1985-88; tech. supr. quality system devel. AT&T Bell Labs., Parsippany, N.J., 1988-89; dept. head communications systems devel. lab. AT&T Bell Labs, Middletown, 1989-94; sr. coach, technology planning AT&T Bell Labs, Basking Ridge, N.J., 1994-95; sr. dir. Lucent Techs. (an AT&T Co.), Basking Ridge, N.J., 1995—. Contbr. articles to profl. jours. Mem. YWCA Mgmt. Forum, Summit, N.J., 1988, bd. dirs., 1989-93. Mem. AAAS, IEEE, Assn. Computing Machinery, Am. Ednl. Rsch. Assn., Coalition of 100 Black Women. Office: Lucent Techs (an AT&T Co) 211 Mount Airy Rd Rm 2e110 Basking Ridge NJ 07920-2311

GRIMLEY, CYNTHIA PATRIZI, rehabilitation consultant, special education educator; b. Sharon, Pa., Mar. 29, 1958; d. James Donald Sr. and Delores Virginia (Maykowski) Patrizi; m. Kevin Neil Grimley, Apr. 11, 1987; children: Ronald James, Jennifer Rose. BS, Youngstown (Ohio) State U., 1981; MS, Calif. State U., 1986. Lic. multiple subject tchr., spl. edn. and elem. tchr., severly handicapped edn. tchr.; specialist credential, Calif.; cert. rehab. counselor, case mgr., human resources generalist. Residential program worker, supr., classroom tchr. Mercer County Assn. for the Retarded, Hermitage, Pa., 1980-82; tchr. spl. edn. Hermitage Sch. Dist., 1982-83; cons. property mgmt. Lorden Mgmt. Co., Covina, Calif., 1983-84; tchr. spl. edn. Fullerton (Calif.) Elem. Sch. Dist., 1984-87; vocat. rehab. cons. Profl. Rehab. Cons., Santa Ana, Calif., 1986-89, Pvt. Sector Rehab., Fullerton, 1989—i. Contbr. curriculum, articles in field. Coach Spl. Olympics, Fullerton, 1982-87; sec. So. Calif. Rehab. Exch., 1989, mem.-at-large, 1990, treas., 1991. Polish Art Club scholar, 1977. Fellow Am. Bd. Vocat. Experts, Am. Acad. Pain Mgmt., Am. Bd. Disability Analysts; mem. NEA, Nat. Assn. Rehab. Profls. in the Pvt. Sector, Calif. Assn. Rehab. Profls., Assn. Retarded Citizens, Soc. for Human Resource Mgmt. Democrat. Roman Catholic. Office: Pvt Sector Rehab 2555 E Chapman Ave Ste 300 Fullerton CA 92831-3618

GRIMLEY, JANET ELIZABETH, newspaper editor; b. Oelwein, Iowa, Dec. 3, 1946; d. Harold E. and Ida Mae (Anderson) Teague; m. Terry L. Grimley, June 15, 1968; 1 child, Brynn Sara Mae Grimley. BA, U. Iowa, Iowa City, 1969; attended, U. Wash., Seattle, 1979-82. Asst. mng. editor Seattle Post-Intelligencer; publs. dir. Marycrest Coll., Davenport, Iowa, 1969-70; reporter Quad-Cities Times, Davenport, Iowa, 1970-74; reporter Seattle Post-Intelligence, Seattle, 1974-76, feature editor, 1976-95, asst. mng. editor, 1995—; v.p. Am. Assn. Sunday and Feature Editors; mem. Newspaper Features Coun. Mem. Shoreline Strategic Planning Com., Seattle, 1993; co-chair Shoreline Capitol/Bond Com., Seattle, 1994, Einstein Site Coun., Seattle, 1994-95. Mem. Junior League of Seattle (bd. dirs. 1989-90, exec. bd. 1991-92), City Club Seattle. Office: Seattle Post Intelligencer 101 Elliott Ave W Seattle WA 98119

GRIMLEY, JUDITH LEE, speech and language pathologist; b. Bklyn., Dec. 15, 1939; d. Harold H. and Pauline (Flecker) Rosenblum; m. Philip M. Grimley, June 24, 1962; children: Daniel, David, Ben. Student, Pa. State U., 1957-59; BS, Boston U., 1961; MA, U. Md., 1983. Tchr. Wantagh (N.Y.) Pub. Sch., 1961-62, San Mateo (Calif.) Pub. Sch., 1962-63; speech-lang. pathologist Montgomery County Pub. Schs., Rockville, Md., 1982—; presenter Am. Speech Hearing Assn., 1985, 91, 93. Pres. Kehila Chadasha Congregation, Rockville, 1990-92, program chairperson, 1988-90, edn. co-chair, 1984-86; mem. supporting screens test for Tay Sachs disease com. Nat. Capital Tay Sachs Found., 1972-78. Recipient scholarship N.Y. State, 1957. Mem. Am. Speech-Hearing Assn. (cert.), Montgomery County Edn. Assn. (co-chair speech lang. liaison com. 1992-94), Md. Speech Lang. Hearing Assn., Md. State Tchrs. Assn., Speech and Hearing Discussion Group, Pi Lambda Theta. Home: Five Lakenheath Ct Potomac MD 20854

GRIMM, ESTHER R., artist, educator; b. Covington, Ky., June 10, 1942; d. Henry R. Kuhn and Eleanor Marie (Reichel) Wolfe; m. Ralph Edward Grimm, Oct. 10, 1964; children: Edward Mathias, David Charles. Student, Wright State U. art instr. Shaw Elem. Sch., Beavercreek, Ohio, 1980-81; self-employed art tchr., Beavercreek, 1980-94; speaker in field. Co-author/illustrator: Disease Control Unit, 1980 (1st pla. in Hosp. Comm. award 1980). Vol. art instr. various children's groups, 1980-82; active children's church, Hawker United Ch. of Christ, Beavercreek, 1980-84. Various awards in field. Mem. Ohio Arts and Crafts Guild, Mich. Guild of Artists, Ohio Designer/Craftsmen Guild. Home: 2441 Glenboro Dr Beavercreek OH 45431

GRIMM, PAULA, advertising executive, strategic planner; b. Troy, N.Y., Nov. 10, 1950; d. Frederick Henry and Helen Marie (Johnson) G.; m. David K. Mickle. BA in Am. Studies, Manhattanville Coll., Purchase, N.Y., 1974. Rsch. assoc. Scali McCabe, Sloves, N.Y.C., 1974-79, assoc. rsch. dir., 1981-86; rsch. group head Dancer, Fitzgerald, Sample, N.Y., 1979-81; exec. v.p., dir. strategic planning and rsch. Saatchi & Saatchi DFS/Pacific, Torrance, Calif., 1986—. Mem. Townhall of L.A., 1989-90. Recipient Outstanding Woman of Yr. in Automotive Industry award McCalls, Wards Automotive and Internat. Auto Show. Mem. Am. Mktg. Assn., Western States Advt. Agys., AEF Advt. Ednl. Found., ECO/Advt. Adv. Alliance. Home: 601 N Gardner St Los Angeles CA 90036-5712 Office: Saatchi & Saatchi 3501 Sepulveda Blvd Torrance CA 90505-2538

GRIMMER, BEVERLEY SUE, consumer products executive; b. Olathe, Kans., June 9, 1950; d. Edward Mathines Rice and Jessie LaVaun (Cade) Waymire; m. Danny Joe San Romani, June 4, 1977 (div. May 1991); 1 child, Justin (dec.); m. Gary G. Grimmer, June 21, 1992. Student, Kans. State Tchrs. Coll., 1968-71, U. Kans., 1975-77. Employee trainer, dept. mgr. T.G.&Y. Stores, Emporia, Kans., 1968-70; office mgr. Office of Staff Judge Adv. 3d Armored Div., Frankfurt, Fed. Republic of Germany, 1971-75, Don W. Lill, Atty. at Law, Emporia, 1976-77; instr., sub. tchr. Kodiak (Ala.) C.C. and Kodiak Pub. Sch. System, 1979-81; legal sec. Kaito & Ishida, Honolulu, 1983-84; adminstr. Alcantara & Frame, Honolulu, 1984-86; ind. contractor Hughes Hubbard & Reed, N.Y., Honolulu, 1986-88; paralegal Carlsmith, Ball, Wichman, Murray, Case, Mukai & Ichiki, Honolulu, 1988-91; spl. agt. Vanuatu (Hawaii) Maritime Agy., 1989—; ch. adminstr. Ctrl. Union Ch., Honolulu, 1991-94; owner Gentle Memories, Kailua, Hawaii, 1995—; Gubernatorial coun. appointee Juvenile Justice State Adv. Coun., 1993-94; mem. women's health week com. State of Hawaii, Commn. on Status of Women, 1994. 1st v.p. Christmas in April Oahu, 1995, bd. dirs., 1995—; auction pub. chair Acad. Arts Guild, 1993; mem. Contemporary Arts Mus.; cmty. rels. and arrangements chairs for Tuxes 'n Tails Black and White Ball, Hawaiian Humane Soc., 1993, 94; mem. Hawaii Lupus Found.; bd. dirs. Armed Forces YMCA, 1995—; mem. vestry St. Christopher's Ch., 1995—. Recipient Order of Golden Swivel Shot award Comdt. USCG, 1981, 89, 1st Runner-up Maritime Week Maritime Employee award Propeller Club U.S., 1986, Letter of Appreciation, Dept. Navy, 1983, Cert. of Commendation, U.S. Army, 1975. Mem. Am. Heart Assn. (chair Celebrity Celebration 1994, silent auction co-chair 1996 Heart Ball), Coast Guard Officers' Spouses Club (nominating chair 1989, pres. 1982, 87, 88), Awa Lau Wahine (Coast Guard rep. 1988, 87, corr. sec. 1983, Boutiki chair 1982), Rotary (vice chair Friends of Foster Kids Picnic 1994, chair 1995), Jr. League (cmty. v.p. 1993, rec. sec. 1990), Navy League, Propeller Club Port of Honolulu (bd. govs. alt. 1990), Hawaii Legal Aux. (v.p. 1994, pub./publs. chair 1994). Republican. Episcopalian. Home and Office: 159 Kakahiaka St Kailua HI 96734-3474

GRIMMER, MADONNA MARIE, government resource specialist; b. Buffalo, May 1, 1929; d. Edward Henry and Marie Margaret (Schaff) Bauer; m. Donald Irving Grimmer, Nov. 11, 1950; children: Mary Ellen, Donald James, Diane Marie, John Michael, Gary Thomas, Patricia Ann. AA, Montgomery Coll., Rockville, Md., 1979. Cert. in Handicapped Assistance Curriculum, 1981. Freelance photographer Rockville, 1957-74; resource specialist Montgomery County Govt., Rockville, 1974-94; cons.; mem. Alcoholism Adv. Bd., Montgomery County Govt., 1974-76, mem. Spouse Abuse Adv. Bd., 1976-77, mem. Abused Persons Adv. Bd., 1978-81, mem. Fin. Counseling Adv. Bd., 1983-92, info. and referral cons., 1987-92. Editor: Directory of Community Resources, 1977-90, Directory of Licenses and Inspections, 1990, 92, Quick Guide to Community Resources, 1977-1992. Active in fin. counseling svc. Coop. Extension, Rockville, 1974-85. Recipient Outstanding Svc. award Montgomery County Govt., 1992; named Toastmaster of Yr., 1992. Roman Catholic. Home: 404 Broadwood Dr Rockville MD 20851

GRIMMER, MARGOT, dancer, choreographer, director; b. Chgo., Apr. 5, 1944; d. Vernon and Ann (Radville) G.; m. Weymouth Kirkland; 1 child, Ashley Samantha Grimmer Kirkland; student Lake Forest; 1963, Northwestern U., 1964-68. Dancer, N.Y.C. Ballet prodn. of Nutcracker Chgo., 1956-57, Kansas City Starlight Theatre, 1958, St. Louis Mcpl. Theatre, 1959, Chgo. TentHouse-Music Theater, 1960-61, Lyric Opera Ballet, Chgo., 1961, 63-66, 68, Ballet Russe de Monte Carlo, N.Y.C., 1962, Ruth Page Internat. Ballet, Chgo., 1965-70; dancer-choreographer Am. Dance Co., Chgo., 1972—, artistic dir., 1972—; dancer, choreographer Bob Hope Show, Milw., 1975, Washington Bicentennial Performance, Kennedy Ctr., 1976, Woody Guthrie Benefit Concerts, 1976-77, Assyrian Cultural Found., Chgo., 1977-78, Iranian Consulate Performance, Chgo., 1978, Israeli Consulate Concert, Chgo., 1980, Chgo. Coun. Fine Arts Programs, 1978-87, U.S. Boating Indsl. Show, 1981—; dir.-tchr. Am. Dance Sch., 1971—; tchr. master classes U. Ill, 1975, 83, Anderson Hall, Occidental and Sebastopol Cmty. Ctr., Calif., 1988-90, Park Point Club, Santa Rosa, Calif., 1988-89, Oakland (Calif.) Dance Collective, 1989—; soloist Showcase to Benefit Sebastopol Ctr. For Arts, Calif., 1990, benefit performances Chgo. Area Settlement Houses, Lake Forest, Ill., 1991-94, Milw. Charities, 1992; appeared in TV commls. and indsl. films for Libbys Foods, Sears, GM, others, 1963—, also in feature film Risky Business, 1982; soloist in ballet Repertory Workshop, CBS-TV, 1964, dance film Statics (Internat. Film award), 1967; soloist in concert Ravinia, 1973; important works include ballets In-A-Gadda-Da-Vida, 1972, The Waste Land, 1973, Rachmaninoff: Theme and Variations, 1973, Le Baiser de la Fee and Sonata, 1974, Four Quartets, 1974, Am. Export, 1975, Earth, Wind and Fire, 1976, Blood, Sand and Empire, 1977, Disco Fever, 1978, Pax Romana, Xanadu, 1979, Ishmael, 1980, Vertigo, 1982, Eye in the Sky, 1984, Frankie Goes to Hollywood, 1986, Power House Africano, 1987, Cole Porter Tribute, 1994, In the Mood, 1995, others; dance critic Mail-Advertiser Publs., 1980-82; host cable TV show Spotlight, 1984-85, View-points, 1987. Ill. Arts Coun. Grantee, 1972-75, 78; Nat. Endowment Arts grantee, 1973-74. Mem. Actors Equity Assn., Screen Actors Guild, Am. Guild Mus. Artists. Home: 970 Vernon Ave Glencoe IL 60022-1266 Office: 442 Central Ave Highland Park IL 60035-2651

GRIMSHAW, MARGARET LOUISA, historian; b. Port Arthur, Tex., June 27, 1955; d. Charles Wendell and Roberta Jean (Simpson) McClelland; m. (div.); children: Charles, Adam, Matthew, Margaret. AB, U. Wis., 1978; MA, San Diego State U., 1989; PhD, UCLA, 1996. Grad. student rep. Am. Hist. Assn., Washington, 1991-94; exec. dir. County Alliance for a Responsible Edn. System, San Diego, 1994—; grad. student rep. Eleanore Roosevelt Centennial Conf., San Diego, 1984. pres. North Coastal coun. PTA, San

Diego, 1995—. Recipient Hon. Svc. award Earl Warren Jr. High PTA, Solana Beach, 1995. Mem. Am. Hist. Assn., Orgn. Am. Historians, Am. Assn. for the History Medicine, Western Assn. Women Historians. Methodist. Home: 13005 Walking Path Pl San Diego CA 92130

GRIMSLEY, BESSIE BELLE GATES, special education educator; b. Iola, Kans., Feb. 22, 1938; d. Dwight Leonard and Ruth Bebee (Colwell) Gates; m. Dale Dee Grimsley, Feb. 14, 1959; 1 child, Lendi Lea Grimsley Bland. BS in Edn., Emporia State U., 1962, MS in Edn., 1970. Music tchr. Hamilton, Kans., 1957-58; music tchr. Belle Plaine, Kans., 1958-59; 3rd grade tchr. Johnson, Kans., 1959-61; mid. sch. tchr. Kendall, Kans., 1961-63-68; kindergarten tchr. Alma, Kans., 1968-69; music, reading, phys. edn., math. tchr. Council Grove, Kans., 1969-94; chpt. I reading, math. tchr. Council Grove, 1994—; polit. chmn. USD #417 Tchr.'s Orgn., Council Grove, 1992-94, pres., 1987-89, uniserve rep., 1987-93. Vice chmn. Lyon County Dem. com., 1988-94; mem. planning bd. Americus, Kans. zoning commn., 1985—; mem. Americus Fall Festival com. (parade chmn. 1992-94). Mem. Americus C. of C. (pres. 1993-95), Emporia Antique Auto Club (sec.-treas. 1993-94), 4-H Alumni, VFW Aux., Am. Legion Aux., Woman's Kans. Day Club (2d v.p. 1994). Presbyterian. Home: Box 147 555 Locust Americus KS 66835 Office: Alta Vista Elem Sch RR 2 Box 2A Alta Vista KS 66834-9300

GRINDAL, MARY ANN, sales professional; b. Michigan City, Ind., Sept. 9, 1942; d. James Paxton and Helen Evelyn (Koivisto) Gleason; m. Bruce Theodore Grindal, June 12, 1965 (div. Sept. 1974); 1 child, Matthew Bruce. BSBA, Ind. U., 1965. Sec. African studies program Ind. U., Bloomington, 1965-66; rsch. aide Ghana, West Africa, 1966-68; exec. sec. divsn. biol. scis. Ind. U., Bloomington, 1968-69; office asst. Dean of Students office Middlebury (Vt.) Coll., 1969-70; exec. sec. Remo, Inc., North Hollywood, Calif., 1974-76; sec., asst. to product mgrs. in cosmetic and skin care Redken Labs., Canoga Park, Calif., 1976-79; various sec. and exec. sec. positions L.A., 1979-81, 85-89; exec. sec. Sargent Industries, Burbank, Calif., 1981-85; sales asst. Chyron Graphics, Burbank, Calif., 1989—. Author of poems and essays. Mem. U.S. Navy Meml. Found. Mem. DAR (chpt. registrar 1988-91, chpt. regent 1991-94, chpt. chmn. pub. rels. and pub. 1994—, chpt. chaplain 1996—, mem. spkrs. staff 1995—, state chmn. Am. Heritage 1994-96, state chmn. Calif. DAR scholarship com. 1996—), Nat. Soc. Colonial Dames (rec. sec. 1989-90), Daus. of Union Vets. of Civil War, 1961-65, Inc., Nat. Soc. Daus. of Am. Colonists, Ladies of Grand Army of the Republic, Inc., Nat. Soc. Dames of the Ct. of Honor. Episcopalian.

GRINNELL, HELEN DUNN, musicologist and arts administrator; b. N.Y.C., Nov. 22, 1936; d. Kempton and Susan Barret (Gill) D.; children: Taylor, James Bodman; m. Alexander Grinnell, July 6, 1991. New Eng. Conservatory, 1957-60; BMus, San Francisco Conservatory of Music, 1968; MA in Musicology, Am. U., 1982. Dir. Opera and Symphony Previews, San Francisco, 1966-67; instr. piano, music theory, San Francisco, 1969-71, Wilmington, Del., 1973-76; dir. constituent rels. Office of Congressman William Mailliard, Washington, 1973; arts coord. Del. State Arts Coun., 1977-78; music libr. Am. U., Washington, 1981-84; pres. Arts Info. Specialists (name changed to Arts Info. Specialists), 1984—, dir. Discovering Music, 1984—; dir. Rsch. Ctr. for Chinese Mus. Iconography, 1984—; cons. Boys Clubs of Am. Young Artists Program, Met. Mus. Art Dept. Musical Intruments. Author: Chinese Musical Iconography: A History of Musical Instruments Depicted in Chinese Art, 1987, Chinese Musical Iconography: A Catalogue, 1988, National Symphony Orchestra Discography, 1988, Yayue Depicted on Ancient Chinese Bronzes, 1994; program annotator Dumbarton Concert Series, Smithsonian Institution, Kennedy Ctr. Stagebill, Handel Festival Orch., Nat. Chamber Orch.; editor: American Women Composers' Forum; steering com. Friends of Music Smithsonian Instn. Bd. dirs. Spring Opera of San Francisco, 1967-71, Wilmington Music Sch., 1973-78, Washington Performing Arts Soc., 1980-90, Nat. Symphony Orch., Washington, 1979-82, Bargemusic Ltd., 1992—, Nat. Orchestral Assn., 1993—, Shelter Island Hist. Soc., 1993—, New Eng. Conservatory Alumni Assn., 1995—; chmn. acad. policy com., trustee San Francisco Conservatory of Music, 1967-71; bd. overseers New Eng. Conservatory, 1985-90; chmn. archl. rev. bd. Village of Dering Harbor, N.Y., 1991—. Mem. Am. Musical Instruments Soc., Am. Musicol. Soc., Amateur Ski Club N.Y., Shelter Island Yacht Club, Cosmopolitan Club. Office: 25 E 86th St Ste 2E New York NY 10028

GRISE, CHERYL, electric power industry executive. Sr. v.p., chief adminstrv. officer Northeast Utilities, Berlin, Conn., 1995—. Office: Northeast Utilities 107 Selden St Berlin CT 06037*

GRISH, MARILYN KAY, speech educator; b. Detroit, Jan. 20, 1951; d. George and Olga (Yanowsky) G.; 1 child, Christina Kay. BS, Ea. Mich. U., 1973, MA, 1974; EdD, Nova U., 1985. Speech pathologist Sch. Bd. Broward County, Ft. Lauderdale, Fla., 1974-90; adminstr. Sch. Bd. Broward County, Ft. Lauderdale, 1990—; instr. Nova Southeastern U., Ft. Lauderdale, 1990—, grant writer, 1992—; adv. bd. mem. Family and Sch. Ctr., Ft. Lauderdale, 1992-94. Supporter Broward Edn. Found., Ft. Lauderdale, 1994—, United Way, Ft. Lauderdale, 1990—, Orthodox Ch. Am., 1974—, Nova Southeastern U. Sch. & Parents Assn., 1994—. Grantee Title II Math. Sci. Project, 1992-93. Mem. Am. Speech and Hearing Assn. (hospitality com. nat. conv. 1994), Fla. ASCD (tech. jour. editor 1992—), Fla. Speech, Lang. and Hearing Assn. (publicity chairperson state conv. 1986). Democrat. Office: Nova Southeastern U 3301 College Ave Fort Lauderdale FL 33314-7721

GRISHAM, JEANNIE, artist; b. Opportunity, Wash., June 26, 1942; d. Lyle Gordon and Lela Georgia (Miller) Jacklin; m. John Paul Grisham, July 4, 1965; children: Jill Jacklin Grisham Ross, Jennifer Jean Grisham Marks, John Paul Jr. Attended, Wash. State U., 1960-62; grad., Burnley Sch. Profl. Art (now Seattle Art Inst.), 1962-64; postgrad., Lyme (Conn.) Acad. Fine Art, 1981-82; studied with, Gerald Brommer, Jerry Caron, Brent Heighton, Katherine Chang Liu, Marilyn Hughy Phillis, Barbara Nechis, Carol Orr, Lou Taylor, Alex Powers, Irving Shapiro, Frank Webb. Exhibits include U.S. Naval Acad., Annapolis, Md., 1974, San Diego Watercolor Soc., 1982-83, San Diego Art Inst., 1982-83, Western Fedn. Watercolor Soc., 1982-83, Deerpath Art Festival, Lake Forest, Ill., 1985-88, Deerpath Art Gallery, Lake Forest, 1985-88, David Adler Show, Libertyville, Ill., 1987-88, Curtis Gallery, Libertyville, 1987-88, Eastside Assn. Fine Art, Kirkland, Wash., 1989, 90, Ea. Wash. Watercolor Soc., Richland, 1989, Mercer Island (Mich.) Art Festival, 1989, Frye Art Mus., Wash., 1990, 91, 93, Bainbridge Arts and Crafts Solo Show, 1989, 91, 93, 94, Northwest Watercolor Soc., 1991, 92, 94, 95, 96, Women Painters of Wash., 1993, 94, 95, 96, Midwest Watercolor Soc., 1992, 93, NWWS Waterworks, 1992, 94, 95, , 96, Nat. Watercolor Soc., 1996, many others; works included in various publs. Mem. Am. Watercolor Soc. (assoc.), Midwest Watercolor Soc. (assoc.), Nat. Watercolor Soc. (signature mem.), Northwest Watercolor Soc. (pres. emeritus, signature mem.), Women Painters of Wash. Home: 10044 Edgecombe Pl NE Bainbridge Island WA 98110

GRISSOM, JOANN (TERRY), physical education educator; b. Indpls., Aug. 4, 1938; d. Joseph Andrew and Vannia Dee (Stone) Terry; m. Leo Warner Grissom Jr., Nov. 23, 1963; children: Vernice Ann, LaWayne Lee. BS, Tenn. State U., 1960, MS, 1968; postgrad., Ball State U., 1966-76. Tchr. phys. edn. Shortridge H.S., Indpls., 1960-72, acting dean of girls, asst. dean of girls, 1972-73; guidance counselor Shortridge Jr. H.S., Indpls., 1968-72; tchr. phys. edn. Arlington H.S., Indpls., 1986—; offical Olympics, 1984, Pan Am. Games, 1987. Mem. 80 meter hurdle Olympic team, 1960, long jump Olympic team, 1964; mem. Pan. Am. team, 1959, 63; recipient gold medal for 80 meter hurdles Pan Am. Games, 1963. Lutheran. Home: 4223 Norrose Dr Indianapolis IN 46226

GRISSOM, PATSY COLEEN, college administrator, English educator; b. Mt. Pleasant, Tex., Jan. 9, 1934; d. Thomas A. and Cleo (Jones) G. BA, East Tex. State U., 1955; MA, Syracuse U., 1957; PhD, U. Tex., 1966. Student dean, head resident Syracuse (N.Y.) U., 1955-57; head resident, instr. English Hanover (Ind.) Coll., 1957-58, Trinity U., San Antonio, 1958-61; teaching asst., assoc. dean of students U. Tex., Austin, 1961-64; assoc. dean of students, asst. prof. English Trinity U., San Antonio, 1964-72, v.p. student affairs, prof. English, 1972—. Named Outstanding Prof., Trinity U. chpt. Mortar Bd., 1976. Mem. AAUW, Nat. Assn. Student Personnel Adminstrs., Nat. Assn. Women Deans and Counselors. Democrat. Presbyterian. Office: Trinity Univ Box 99 715 Stadium Dr San Antonio TX 78212

GRISWOLD, JOAN BAIRD, artist; b. Oberlin, Ohio, Mar. 1, 1954; d. Thomas Franklin and Marian Baird (Diehl) G.; m. Donald Benson Jurney. BA, Beloit Coll., 1977. tchr. painting and drawing, Great Barrington, Mass., 1989—. One-woman shows include South Gallery, Beloit, 1977, Broadway Frames and Gallery, N.Y.C., 1981, 83, David Wright Gallery, Wellfleet, Mass., 1986, 87, David Gavin Gallery, Millerton, N.Y., 1987, Five Points Gallery, East Chatham, N.Y., 1988, 89, 90, 91, 92, 93, 94, Forecast Gallery, Garrison, N.Y., 1988, Conn. Gallery, Marlborough, 1989, Garrison Art Ctr., 1989, Jacob Fanning Gallery, Wellfleet, 1989, 90, 92, Helio Galleries, N.Y.C., 1991, Hoorn-Ashby Gallery, N.Y.C., 1993, 94, 95, Kent (Conn.) Gallery, 1995; group exhbns. include Five Points Gallery, 1987, 88, 89, 91, 92, Berkshire Open Studios, Great Barrington, 1987, Bayless Gallery, Norfolk, Conn., 1987, Gallery at Mill River, Mass., 1988, Jacob Fanning Gallery, 1988, 91, 92, 93, Westenhook Small Works, Sheffield, 1988, 89, 90, Greene Gallery, Guilford, Conn., 1988, Conn. Gallery, 1988, Riversbend Art Gallery, West Stockbridge, Mass., 1989, Store Hill Gallery, South Egremont, Mass., 1989, Scarborough Gallery, Chappaqua, N.Y., 1989, Naumkeag Carriage House Art Show, Stockbridge, 1989, John Pence Gallery, San Francisco, 1989, 90, Hoorn-Ashby Gallery, Nantucket, Mass., 1990, 91, 92, 93, 94, Clapp & Tuttle Gallery, Woodbury, Conn., 1991, Art of 100 Pearl, Hartford, Conn., 1992, Millbrook (N.Y.) Gallery, 1992, Pioneer Gallery, Cooperstown, N.Y., 1992, Berkshire Artisans, Pittsfield, Mass., 1992, Geoffrey Young Gallery, 1992, 93, Underhill Inn, Hillsdale, N.Y., 1994, Salisbury (Conn.) Land Trust, 1994, Randall Tuttle Fine Arts, Woodbury, Conn., 1994, Barney's Benefit, N.Y.C., 1994; represented in pvt. collections. Bd. dirs. Sheffield (Mass.) Land Trust, 1994—; mem. Sheffield Arts Coun., 1991-93. Recipient Portraiture prize Ridgefield Guild of Artists, 1986, Frame award Sheffield Art League, 1986, Excellence award Sheffield Art League, 1987, Purchase award Sheffield Art League, 1990, 3d prize Bridgeport Nat. Juried Expn., 1991. Home: 778 Hewins St PO Box 813 Sheffield MA 01257 Studio: 292 Main St Rm 35 Great Barrington MA 01230

GRIVNA, DORIS M., elementary education educator; b. Rochester, Pa., Feb. 22, 1947; d. Lloyd F. and D. Emily (Agnew) Miller; m. Drew Grivna, Apr. 20, 1974; children: Marc A., Aaron J. BE, Clarion U., 1969. Tchr. elem. Potter Schs., Monaca, Pa., 1969-72, Ctr. Area Sch., Monaca, 1972—; residential camp dir. ARC Beaver County, Monaca, 1991—. Mem. Marion Guild, Beaver, Pa., 1984—, Assn. for Retarded Citizens, Beaver County, 1974—. Mem. NEA, Internat. Reading Assn., Nat. Coun. Tchrs. English, Pa. Edn. Assn., Keystone State Reading Coun., Ctr. Area Ednl. Assn., Leotta C. Hawthorne Coun. Roman Catholic. Home: 109 Hill Dr Beaver PA 15009-1205 Office: Center Grange Elem Sch 225 Center Grange Rd Aliquippa PA 15001-1420

GRMEK, DOROTHY ANTONIA, accountant; b. Cleve., July 7, 1930; d. Louis and Antonia (Korosec) Lipanye; m. M. Charles Stelmach, June 13, 1953 (div. May 1977); children: Monica Doran Meade, Dwayne Alan Stelmach, Dale Richard Stelmach; m. William Edward Grmek, Aug. 18, 1978. BBA in Acctg., Fenn Coll., 1953. Chief acct. Pyromatics, Inc., Willoughby, Ohio, 1975-87; acct., exec. sec. Auctor Assocs., Inc., Cleveland Heights, 1972-96; ptnr., tax cons. Diversified Bus. Svc., Rocky River, Ohio, 1980—; contr., human rels. specialist Telefast Industries, Inc., Berea, Ohio, 1988-94; treas., buyer River Toy Box, Inc., Rocky River, 1990—. Mem. Slovene Nat. Benefit Soc. (ins. agt. 1982—, charter mem., fin. sec. lodge 781 1982—, Cleve. Fedn. Lodges rec. sec. 1968-72, fin. sec. 1972-82). Home: 3645 Kings Post Pky Rocky River OH 44116-3816 also: River Toy Box Inc 20130 Center Ridge Rd Rocky River OH 44116-3500

GROAH, LINDA KAY, nursing administrator and educator; b. Cedar Rapids, Iowa, Oct. 5, 1942; d. Joseph David and Irma Josephine (Zitek) Rozek; diploma St. Luke's Sch. Nursing, Cedar Rapids, 1963; student San Francisco City Coll., 1976-77; BA, St. Mary's Coll., Moraga, Calif., 1978; BS in Nursing, Calif. State U.; MS in Nursing, U. Calif.; m. Patrick Andrew Groah, Mar. 20, 1975; 1 child, Kimberly; stepchildren: Nadine, Maureen, Patrick, Marcus. Staff nurse to head nurse U. Iowa, 1963-67; clin. supr., dir. oper. and recovery room Michael Reese Hosp., Chgo., 1967-73; dir. oper. rooms Med. Ctr. Cen. Ga., Macon, 1973-74; dir. oper. and recovery rooms U. Calif. Hosps. and Clinics, San Francisco, 1974-90, asst. dir. hosps. and clinics, 1982-86; svc. dir. Kaiser Found. Hosp., San Francisco, 1990—; asst. clin. prof. U. Calif. Sch. Nursing, San Francisco, 1975—; cons. to oper. room suprs., to div. ednl. resources and programs Assn. Am. Med. Colls., 1976—; condr. seminars. Mem. Nat. League for Nurses, Am. Nurses Assn. (vice chmn. operating room conf. group 1974-76), Assn. Oper. Room Nurses (com. on nominations 1979-84, treas. 1985-87, 93-95, bd. dirs. 1991-93, pres.-elect 1995-96, pres. 1996—, bd. trustees 1995—, pres. found., 1992-95, Excellence award in Preoperative Nursing 1989), Ctr. for Study Dem. Instns. Author: Perioperative Nursing Practice, 1983, 3d edit., 1996; contbr. articles on operating room techniques to profl. jours. and textbooks; author, producer audio-visual presentations; author computer software. Home: 5 Mateo Dr Belvedere Tiburon CA 94920-1071 Office: 3020 Bridgeway Ste 399 Sausalito CA 94965-2839

GROAT, KATHLEEN DELORES, social services administrator; b. Stoughton, Wis., Mar. 25, 1941; d. Kennerd Arnold and Eleanor Marie (Utermark) Loftus; m. Charles Edwin Groat, Mar. 25, 1966; 1 child, Christopher Charles. BS, U. Wis., 1963, MPA, 1990. Cert. social worker, Wis. Social worker Dane County Dept. Human Svcs., Madison, Wis., 1963-66; social worker supr. Waukesha (Wis.) County Human Svcs., 1966-68, outagamie County Human Svcs., Appleton, Wis., 1968-72; youth work counselor Columbia Project, Appleton, 1980-85; family svcs. dir. Trettin-Lederer Funeral Chapel, Appleton, 1987-90; exec. dir. Fair Housing Coun., Appleton, 1990-95; agy. adminstr. Adoption Svcs., Inc., Appleton, Wis., 1989—; adv. bd. community action program, Appleton. Bd. dirs. SOUL, Ltd., Appleton, 1979-84; chair 8th Congrl. Dist. Dem. Party, N.E. Wis., 1992—, vice chair Wis. Women's Network, 1995-96, chair Outagamie Co. Dem. Party, 1990-92, treas., 1985-90; elected alderman 14th dist. Appleton Common Coun., 1996—. Democrat. Lutheran. Office: Valley Guardians Inc PO Box 9050 Appleton WI 54911

GRODSKY, DAWN LYNN, editor; b. St. Louis, Mar. 3, 1967; d. Harry Richard and Gloria Rosalyn (Kornblatt) G. BA in Media Comms., Webster U., 1989. Editor, reporter Island Reporter, Sanibel, Fla., 1991-92; copy editor Island Packet, Hilton Head, S.C., 1993; city editor Daily Breeze Newspaper, Cape Coral, Fla., 1994; editor Observer Newspapers and Gulf Coast Woman, Ft. Myers, Fla., 1994—; on-air host Sta. WSFP-FM, 1995—. Mem. Fla. Press Assn.

GRODSKY, JAMIE ANNE, lawyer; b. San Francisco; d. Gerold Morton and Kayla Deane (Wolfe) G. BA in Human Biology/Natural Scis. and History with distinction, Stanford U., 1977; MA in Econ. Geography, U. Calif., Berkeley, 1985; JD, Stanford Law Sch., 1992. Ednl. dir. Oceanic Soc., San Francisco, 1979-81; rsch. asst. Woods Hole (Mass.) Oceanog. Inst., 1983; analyst Office Tech. Assessment U.S. Congress, Washington, 1984-89; counsel Com. Natural Resources, U.S. Ho. of Reps., Washington, 1993-94; counsel to Senator Dianne Feinstein, com. judiciary U.S. Senate, Washington, 1995—. Articles editor Stanford Law Rev.; contbr. articles to profl. jours.

GROER, CONNIE JEAN, accounting educator; b. Annapolis, Md., Jan. 8, 1957; d. Donald Duncan Daugherty and Doris Irene Bolles Long; m. John L. Groer, Aug. 17, 1984. BS in Acctg., Frostburg (Md.) State U., 1980, MBA, 1982. CPA, Md. Staff acct. Faw, Casson & Co., CPAs, Annapolis, Md., 1982-84; supr. Hammond & Heim, Chartered, Annapolis, 1984-87; vis. lectr. Frostburg State U., 1987-90; asst. prof., chair Frostburg State U., 1990-94, assoc. prof. acctg., 1994—. VITA Site 212 coord. IRS, Balt., 1988-95. Mem. AICPA, Md. Assn. CPAs (Outstanding Md. Acctg. Tchg. award 1993), Am. Acctg. Assn. Republican. Office: Frostburg State U 340 Frampton Hall Frostburg MD 21532

GROFF, SUSAN CAROLE, elementary education educator; b. Marshalltown, Iowa, Feb. 16, 1954; d. Ernest Jerome and Alice Marjorie (Harmon) G.; m. Wayne A. Van Arendonk, Aug. 14, 1994. BS, Iowa State U., 1976; MS in Edn., U. Kans., 1981; edn. specialist, U. Iowa, 1984. Resource rm. aide Pinckney Elem., Lawrence, Kans., 1976-77; tchr. spl. edn. Booth Elem., Wichita, Kans., 1977-78; tchr. resource rm. Clinton (Iowa) Community Schs., 1978-80; tchr. spl. edn. Henry Sabin Elem., Clinton, 1980-83; cons. No. Trails Area Edn. Agy., Clear Lake, Iowa, 1984-86; tchr. resource rm. Tomiyasu Yr.-Round Sch., Las Vegas, Nev., 1986-88, 90-92; tchr. elem. edn. Tomiyasu Yr.-Round Sch., Las Vegas, 1988-90, 92-94; cons. Heartland Area Edn. Agy., Johnston, Iowa, 1994-96; tchr. spl. edn. Haysville (Kans.) Middle Schs., 1996—; student tchr. supr. U. Iowa, Iowa City, 1983, grad. asst., 1984. Treas. U.S. Rep., Iowa, 1974-75. Recipient Excellence in Edn. award Clark County Sch. Dist., Las Vegas, 1992. Mem. Iowa State Edn. Assn., Iowa State Cons. Assn., Coun. for Exceptional Children, U. Iowa Alumni Assn. (life), Iowa State U. Alumni Assn. (life), U. Kans. Alumni Assn. Democrat. Jewish. Home: 2359 N Parkridge Ct Wichita KS 67212

GROFT, KATHERINE IRENE, secondary education educator, artist; b. Lancaster, Pa., Feb. 27, 1960; d. Homer Charles and Laura Virginia (de la Sierra) Schelling; m. Jere Michael Groft, July 31, 1987. BS in Art Edn. magna cum laude, Millersville U. Pa., 1993. Cert. K-12 art tchr., Pa. Beverage mgr. Plaza at Angel Fire, N.Mex., 1984-86; gallery, printing libr. and lab. asst. Millersville U. Pa., 1988-93, young artist-in-residence, 1993; tchr. art McCaskey H.S., Sch. Dist. Lancaster, 1993—; tchr. art youth program Pa. Sch. Art and Design, Lancaster, 1993—. One-woman shows include Artemis, Lancaster, 1996, 1994; group shows include Border's Book Store, Lancaster, 1994, Bube's Brewery, Mt. Joy, Pa., 1994, Doshi Ctr. for Contemporary Art, Harrisburg, Pa., 1996, Elizabethtown (Pa.) Coll., 1995; created bronze sculpture Quetzalcoati and Tenochtitlan, 1994. Vol. New Art Voices, Lancaster, 1993—. Presdl. scholar Millersville U. Pa., 1991, scholar Greater Beneficial Union Found., 1991-93. Mem. Nat. Art Edn. Assn., Pa. Edn. Assn., Lancaster Edn. Assn., Mus. Women in Arts, Phi Kappa Phi. Democrat. Office: McCaskey HS 445 N Reservoir St Lancaster PA 17602

GROGAN, BETTE LOWERY, steel fastener distribution executive; b. Seminole, Okla., Nov. 18, 1931; d. C.J. and Martha C. (Eakin) Lowery; m. Morris Rowell, Feb. 8, 1947 (div. Oct. 1960); children: Ronald Michael, Kathy D. Rowell Ray; m. John Kenneth Grogan, Oct. 28, 1967. Student Del Mar Coll., 1949-51, So. Meth. U., 1963-65. Sec., office mgr. Carrigan Realty, Orlando, Fla., 1958-61; dist. sec. Tektronics, Inc., Orlando, 1961-63; legal sec. Jenkens, Anson, Spradley & Gilchrist, Dallas, 1963-67; real estate broker, Dallas, 1967-77; v.p. Grogan & Co., Dallas, 1972-77; pres. Fla. Threaded Products Inc., Orlando, 1977—; dir. Women's Bus. Ednl. Council (pres. 1986, chmn. bd. 1987), Inc., Orlando, pres., 1986. Mem. Planning and Zoning Commn., Carrollton, Tex., 1972-74; bd. dirs. Jr. Achievement, Orlando, 1981-83, Healthcare Cost Containment Bd., Fla. Def. Conversion and Transition Commn., 1993—; del. Gov.'s Conf. on Small Bus., 1987, 89, 91, White House Conf. on Small Bus., Fla., 1986; sec.-treas. Cmty. Health Purchasing Alliance, State of Fla., 1993—. Named Cen. Fla. Small Bus. Person of the Yr., SBA-C. of C., 1981. Mem. Women's Bus. Ednl. Confs. Fla. (bd. dirs. 1984-85, exec. v.p. 1985-86, pres. 1986, chmn. bd. dirs. 1987), Nat. Fedn. Ind. Bus. (guardian adv. council), Fastener Assn. (bd. dirs. 1980-84), Central Fla. Leadership Council (bd. dirs. 1984—), Greater Orlando C. of C. (chairperson N.W. regional coun. 1990), Fla. Exec. Women, Better Bus. Bur. Cen. Fla. (mem. exec. com., chmn. 1989, bd. dirs. 1989), Beta Sigma Phi (pres. Orlando 1957-59), Rotary. Republican. Episcopalian. Avocations: tennis, golf, reading. Office: Fla Threaded Products Inc 3060 Clemson Rd Orlando FL 32808-3945

GROGAN, DARE LONDON, educator, sales professional; b. Greensboro, N.C., Feb. 12, 1955; d. Charles Stokes and Rachel (Bennett) London; m. Randy Glenn Grogan, Apr. 9, 1977 (div. 1983); 1 child, Ruth Anne. BS in Early Childhood Edn., U. N.C., Greensboro, 1988. Sales staff Hitching Post, Reidsville, N.C., 1975-95; educator Bethany Sch., Reidsville, 1988—; sales assoc. Belk, Reidsville, 1995—; volleyball coach Bethany Sch., Reidsville, 1989—, Beta Club sponsor, 1990—. Youth leader St. Thomas Episcopal, Reidsville, 1986 95, vestry mem., 1993 96; crop walk organizer Crop Walk, Reidsville, 1993; mem. Reidsville Solid Waste Commn., 1993—. Mem. ASCD, NCAE, Alpha Chi. Episcopalian. Home: 7943 US 158 Reidsville NC 27320

GROGAN, SUZANN JEANETTE-WYMAN, artist; b. L.A., July 6, 1962; d. Frank Adelbert Jr. and Beverly Ann (Burge) Wyman; m. Marvin John Grogan, June 1, 1985. AA, Fullerton Coll., 1984. Drafter Cetec Corp., Southgate, Calif., 1983-85; drafter, illustrator MegaTape Corp., Duarte, Calif., 1985-94; design drafter Magellan Systems Corp., San Dimas, Calif., 1994—; writer Victorville, Calif., 1988—, artist, 1990—; dir. pub. Mojave Inst. Arts, Apple Valley, Calif., 1994. Artist (painting) Art of the West mag., 1993; contbr. articles to U.S. Art, Art Trends., Western Horseman. Charter mem. Nat. Mus. Am. Indian, Washington, 1993—; mem. Nat. Mus. Women in Arts, Washington, 1993—; signature mem. Western Acad. Women Artist; mem. High Desert Cultural Arts Found., Apple Valley, 1994—. Adopted Hon. mem. Wappo Tribe, Sonoma County, Calif., 1994. Mem. Oil Painters Am. (assoc.), Laguna Art-A-Fair Coop. Home and studio: 13840 Galaxy Way Victorville CA 92392-9385

GRONAU, CRYSTAL LYNN, accountant; b. Newton, Kans., May 27, 1957; d. Albert Earl and Patricia Ann (Ulmer) G. BA, Tabor Coll., 1977; MBA, Golden Gate U., 1984. CPA, Calif., Kans. Sr. Grant Thornton, Wichita, Kans., 1979-83; mgr. Price Waterhouse, San Jose, Calif., 1984-86, Palo Alto, 1987-88; sr. mgr. Price Waterhouse, Palo Alto, Calif., 1990-92, 94—; Price Waterhouse GmbH, Frankfurt, Germany, 1992-94; mgr. taxation Geothermal Resources Internat., San Mateo, Calif., 1986-87; sr. mgr. Berger Lewis, San Jose, 1988-89. Mem. Calif. Soc. CPAs, Am. Women's Soc. CPAs. Office: Price Waterhouse 525 University Ave Ste 200 Palo Alto CA 94301-1916

GRØNDAHL, JENNIFER JO, union organizer; b. Topeka, Sept. 20, 1971; d. Orvin Nordean and Debra Lynn (Dodson) G. BA in Art History & Polit. Sci., Washburn U., 1996. Union organizer Am. Fed. Tchrs., Topeka, 1995-96, Laborer's Internat. Union N.Am., 1996—. Vol. Kans. Dem. Party, Topeka, 1992—, Florence Crittiten Home for Abused Women, Topeka, 1992-94, Advance Team Pres. Clinton, Topeka and Kansas City, 1994; 2d dist. rep. Kansas Young Dems., 1993-94. Scholar Nat. Fedn. Women's Dem. Clubs, 1995. Mem. Kans. Fedn. Women's Dem. Clubs. Lutheran. Home: 2212 SW Morningside Rd Topeka KS 66614-1469

GRONER, KAREN HELEN, fashion designer; b. N.Y.C., Aug. 8, 1948; d. Harry Leon and Shirley Ann (Kreiswirth) G. BA magna cum laude, Hunter Coll., 1969; BFA, Parsons Sch. Design, 1976. Supr. spl. sales Met. Mus., N.Y.C., 1969-71; H.S. art tchr. N.Y. Bd. Edn., 1971-73; freelance design asst. Leo Narducci, 1975—; freelance design reporter Kmart, 1976-79; designer Stella Originals, N.Y.C., 1976-79; owner, designer Grownbeans, N.Y.C., 1980—; costumer designer Perridane, N.Y., 1992-93. Home: 110 Bank St New York NY 10014 Office: Grownbeans 41 Union Sq New York NY 10003

GRONEWOLD, SUE ELLEN, history educator; b. Peoria, Ill., Apr. 18, 1947; d. Herman J. and Eleanor J. Gronewold; m. Peter Winn, May 22, 1976; children: Ethan, Sasha. BA, U. Wis., 1969, MA, 1973; MA, Columbia U., 1980, PhD, 1996. Cert. H.S. social studies, N.J. Tchr. social studies LaFollette H.S., Madison, Wis., 1972-75, West Windsor Plainsboro H.S., Princeton Junction, N.J., 1975-77; lectr. on Asia Am. Mus. Natural History, N.Y.C., 1980-84; ednl. cons. in pvt. practice N.Y.C. and Boston, 1982-92; vis. asst. prof. Marist Coll., Poughkeepsie, N.Y., 1993—; asst. prof. Marist Coll., Poughkeepsie, 1996—; vis. lectr. Smith Coll., Northampton, Mass., 1984-85; project officer N.Y. Coun. for the Humanities, N.Y.C., 1985-86, 88; co-dir. humanities lecture series Marist Coll., Poughkeepsie, 1994—; acad. co-dir of China Identity Project, Am. Forum for Global Edn., N.Y.C., 1995—. Author: Beautiful Merchandise: Prostitution in China, 1982. Fellowship grantee Columbia U., N.Y.C., 1980; grantee Lilly Endowment, 1988; Spencer Found. grantee Woodrow Wilson Found., Princeton, N.J., 1989. Mem. Am. Hist. Assn., Assn. for Asian Studies, Com. on Tchg. About Asian, Mission Study's Group, Com. on Women' Studies. Home: 315 W 106th St 10C New York NY 10025 Office: Marist Coll 290 North Rd Poughkeepsie NY 12601

GROOM, EVA MARIE, medical social worker; b. Champaign, Ill., Aug. 9, 1962; d. Dennis Robert and Mary Ann (Polanek) G.; m. Micheal J. Medina, July 16, 1994; 1 child, Nathan Kocovsky Medina. BS, Elmhurst Coll., 1985; MSW, U. Denver, 1991. Med. social worker Denver Gen. Hosp., 1991-94; home health social worker Porter Care at Home, 1994-96, NSI Home Health, 1995—, Staff Builders Home Health, 1995—. Democrat. Home: 1977 S Urban St Lakewood CO 80228

GROOMS, SUZANNE SIMMONS, music educator; b. New Orleans, Jan. 9, 1945; d. Claude Arthur and Mary Rachel (Pierce) Simmons; m. Barton Collins Grooms, May 12, 1973; children: David Barton, Michael Claude. BS, U. Tenn., 1966; M Music Edn., So. Ill. U., 1969. Cert. Suzuki tchr. instrumental music. Mem. violin sect. Knoxville (Tenn.) Symphony Orch., 1958-66; violinist St. Louis Philharmonic Orch., 1967-68; instr. Suzuki Inst., U. Wis., Stevens Point, 1970-73; violinist Amarillo (Tex.) Symphony Orch., 1973-77; dir., coordinator Suzuki string program Amarillo Coll., 1977—; violin tchr., co-founder Amarillo Area Youth Symphony. co-author: (Suzuki handbook) How To Make Your Twinkle Brighter, 1985. Bd. dirs. March of Dimes, Amarillo, 1977-79, Greater S.W. Music Festival, 1990—, Amarillo Symphony Youth Orch., Art Force, 1988-92; mem. Amarillo Jr. League, 1977-84; cir. chmn. United Meth. Ch., Amarillo. Grantee Harrington Found., 1981. Mem. Suzuki Assn. Ams., Internat. Suzuki Assn., Symphony Guild. Home: 4908 Erik Ave Amarillo TX 79106-4703 Office: Amarillo Coll PO Box 447 Amarillo TX 79178-0001

GROSE, ELINOR RUTH, retired elementary education educator; b. Honolulu, Apr. 23, 1928; d. Dwight Hatsuichi and Edith (Yamamoto) Uyeno; m. George Benedict Grose, Oct. 19, 1951; children: Heidi Diane Hill, Mary Porter, John Tracy, Nina Evangeline. AA, Briarcliff Jr. Coll., 1948; postgrad., Long Beach State U., 1954-55; BS in Edn., Wheelock Coll., Boston, 1956; MA in Edn., Whittier Coll., 1976. Cert. tchr., Mass., N.Y., Calif. Reading tchr. Cumberland Head Sch., Plattsburgh, N.Y., 1968-70; master tchr. Broadoaks Sch., Whittier (Calif.) Coll., 1971; reading tchr. Phelan/Washington Schs., Whittier, 1971-73; elem. tchr. Christian Sorensen Sch., Whittier, 1977-94, ret., 1994; cons. Nat. Writing Projet, 1987—, South Basin Writing Project, Long Beach, 1987—; team tchr. Young Writers' Camp, Long Beach State U., 1988. Author: Primarily Yours, 1987, Angel Orchid Watercolor, 1994. First v.p. Women's League of Physicians Hosp., Plattsburgh, 1970; asst. to Christian, Jewish and Muslim pres., v.p.s of Acad. Judaic, Christian and Islamic Studies 6th Assembly World Coun. Chs., Vancouver, 1983. Named Companion of the Order of Abraham, Acad. for Judaic, Christian and Islamic Studies, 1987. Mem. NEA, Calif. Tchrs. Assn., Whittier Elem. Tchrs. Assn., English Coun. of Long Beach. Presbyterian. Home: 6085 E Brighton Ln Anaheim CA 92807

GROSHNER, MARIA STAR, nuclear engineer; b. Las Vegas, Nev., Aug. 31, 1961; d. Robert Leroy and Stepheny (Higby) G.; m. Robert Clay Singleterry Jr., May 18, 1984. BS in Nuclear Engring., U. Ariz., 1984. Engr. in tng., Idaho. Reactor operator EG&G Idaho, Inc., Idaho Falls, 1985-89, engr., 1989-90, sr. engr., 1990-91; export control reviewer EG&G Idaho Inc., Idaho Falls, 1990-91; engr. III Westinghouse Idaho Nuclear Co., Idaho Falls, 1991-92, sr. engr. I, 1992-94; sr. engr., safety analyst Lockheed Martin Idaho Techs. Co., Idaho Falls, 1994—; prin. mem. Quantum Solutions, LLC, 1995—. Mem. Citizen Energy Alert Network, Nuclear Energy Inst., Washington, 1987—, Planned Parenthood, 1992—. Mem. AAAS, AAUW, NAFE, NOW, Nat. Soc. Profl. Engrs., Am. Nuclear Soc. (media rels. chmn. Idaho chpt. 1990), Soc. Women Engrs. (chpt. sect. rep. 1990-91, treas. 1993-96, v.p. southeastern Idaho chpt. 1989, coord. young women's conf. 1990), Toastmasters Internat. (chpt. pres. 1990, adminstrv. v.p. Jack C. High unit 1989, v.p. pub. rels. 1995, Competent Toastmaster, Able Toastmaster), U.S. Golf Assn. Home: 365 Carol Ave Idaho Falls ID 83401-3176 Office: Lockheed Martin Idaho Techs Co PO Box 1625 Idaho Falls ID 83415-3210 also: Quantum Solutions LLC PO Box 484 Rigby ID 83442-0484

GROSS, ARLENE BARBARA COHEN, writer, business executive; b. N.Y.C., Dec. 3, 1931; d. Simon and Yetta (Shammes) Cohen; m. Gerald Gross, June 2, 1957; children: Alison, Adam, Seth. BA, Hunter Coll., 1954; MFA, Sarah Lawrence Coll., 1975. Cert. elem. tchr., N.Y. Exec. dir. Peekskill (N.Y.) Drama Workshop, 1975-77; group sales con. An Evening Dinner Theatre, Elmsford, N.Y., 1981-87; adminstr. vol. dept. White Plains (N.Y.) Svc. Harlem Valley Psychiat. Ctr., 1988-91; pres. Reach Out With Drama, Inc., Croton-on-Hudson, N.Y., 1994—; ptnr. Gross Assocs., Croton-on-Hudson, N.Y., 1978—. Co-author (dramatic scenarios) School Secrets, 1993. Program v.p. Women in Sales, White Plains, 1984-86; pres. Croton Children's Theatre, 1972-73. Mem. AAUW (Peekskill br. pres. 1989-93, dist. V br. coun. rep. 1991-93, Initiative for Edn. Equity award 1995). Office: Gross Assocs 63 Grand St Croton On Hudson NY 10520

GROSS, DEENA BETH, managing editor; b. Boston, Dec. 19, 1958; d. Sidney and Doris (Koren) G.; m. Mark J. Weinstein, May 26, 1991. AB, Bryn Mawr Coll., 1980. Reporter The Scranton (Pa.) Times, 1980-82, The Sun-Tattler, Hollywood, Fla., 1982-85; asst. city editor The Sun-Tattler, Hollywood, 1985-89, city editor, 1989; metro editor Burlington (Vt.) Free Press, 1989-90; copy editor York (Pa.) Dispatch/Sunday News, 1990-91, mng. editor, 1991—. Jewish. Office: York Dispatch Sundzy News 205 N George St York PA 17401

GROSS, DORINE MILES, artist; b. Detroit, Oct. 29, 1945; d. Theodore and Janet Catherine (Szymanek) Miles; m. Charles William Gross, June 17, 1966; children: Darcy Gross Dragovic, Alecia Kay. A in Fine Arts, W.R. Harper Coll., 1983; BA, Govs. State U., 1984; MFA, Northwestern U., 1986. Grad. tchr. Northwestern U., Evanston, Ill., 1984-86, instr., 1985-86; freelance artist Rye, N.H., 1986—; guest lectr. W.R. Harper Coll., Palatine, Ill., 1984-85, Acad. Fine Art & Design, Bratislava, Slovakia, 1993, J. Koniarek Gallery, Tranava, Slovakia, 1993; adj. prof. U. N.H., Durham, 1987-89, Notre Dame Coll., Manchester, N.H., 1991; panel discussionist Karl Drerup Gallery, Plymouth (N.H.) State Coll., 1990; key note spkr. Internat. Symposium on Art, Moravani, Slovakia, 1993. One woman shows include Women's Bd. Rm., Art Inst. Chgo., 1980, Paul Waggoner Gallery, Chgo., 1982, Kemper Group, Long grove, Ill., 1983, Dittmar Gallery, Evanston, Ill., 1986, Capricorn Galleries, Bethesda, Md., 1990, Notre Dame Coll., Manchester, N.H., 1993, Pierce Gallery, Portsmouth, N.H.; represented in permanent collections Brenau U., Gainesville, Ga., Butler Inst. Am. Art, Youngstown, Ohio. Commr., sec. Lake Barrington (Ill.) Park Dist., 1982-86. Recipient Muriel T. Lagasse Meml. award Springfield Art League, 1988, Pub. Art commn. State of N.H., 1995. Mem. Nat. Soc. Painters, Coll. Art Assn., N.H. Art Assn. (award 1988-89, 90-91), Seacoast Cultural Art Alliance, Rye Art Study. Home: PO Box 761 Rye NH 03870

GROSS, DOROTHY-ELLEN, library director, dean; b. Buffalo, June 13, 1949; d. William Paul and Elizabeth Grace (Hough) G. BA, Westminster Coll., 1971; MLS, Rosary Grad. Sch. Libr. Sci., 1975; MDiv, McCormick Theol. Sem., 1975. Jr. cataloger McCormick Theol. Sem., Chgo., 1972-75; head tech. svcs. Barat Coll., Lake Forest, Ill., 1975-79, head libr., 1980-82; dir. coll. libr. North Park Coll. and Theol. Sem., Chgo., 1982-87, dir. coll. and sem. librs., 1987—, assoc. dean, 1990—, prof., 1991—; cons. acad. librs.; spkr. various profl. meetings and confs. Author (chpt. in book) Managing Student Workers in College Libraries, 1986; editor: Libras Handbook and Directory; co-editor North Park Faculty Publs. and Creative Works, 1992, Pvt. Acad. Librs. in Ill. newsletter; contbr. articles to profl. jours. Vol. United Way. Mem. ALA, LIBRAS (pres. 1983-85), Am. Coun. Edn. (participant nat. identification program), Assn. Coll. and Rsch. Librs., Pvt. Acad. Librs. Ill. (pres. 1981-83, 91—), Ctr. for Scandinavian Studies (bd. dirs. 1983-94), Swedish Am. Hist. Soc., Foster Investors (pres. 1990-91). Presbyterian. Office: North Pk Coll and Theol Sem 3225 W Foster Ave Chicago IL 60625-4810

GROSS, HANNAH SARAH, lawyer; b. Boston, Aug. 12, 1950; d. Richard Leon and Muriel Elaine (Shea) Kaye; m. Mark A. Gross, June 29, 1969; children: Jason Z., Dana S. Student, Bard Coll., Annandale-on-Hudson, N.Y., 1967-69; BA, Herbert H. Lehman Coll., Bronx, 1974; JD magna cum laude, Pace U., 1981. Bar: N.Y. 1982, U.S. Dist. Ct. (so. dist.) N.Y. 1989. Assoc. Gross & Young, Mount Vernon, N.Y., 1981-84, Rosen, Hacker & Nierenberg, New Rochelle, N.Y.C., 1984-85, Hertzog, Calamari & Gleason, N.Y.C., 1985; ptnr. Gross and Gross (previously Gross & Young), Mt. Vernon, 1986—; part-time agy. counsel City of Mt. Vernon Urban Renewal Agy., 1983; part-time counsel State Senator Nicholas Spano, Yonkers, 1987-89. Vol. arbitrator Small Claims part Mt. Vernon City Ct., 1991—; 4th vice chair Westchester (N.Y.) Dem. Com., 1995—; 2d vice chair Mt. Vernon Dem. City Com., 1994-95; chair Anti-Defamation League Regional Bd., Westchester/Putnam/Rockland, 1985-87, exec. bd., 1984—; bd. dirs. Mt. Vernon Martin Luther King Jr. Commn., 1994—; bd. dirs. Police Athletic League, Mt. Vernon, 1993—; mem. Mt. Vernon Centennial Ball Com., 1993, Ronald Blackwood Inaugural Ball Com., 1992; chmn. Westchester County Blue Ribbon Panel on Bias Related Violence, 1989; chair adult edn. Free Synagogue of Westchester, 1978; life mem. nat. women's com. Brandeis U.; vol. writer campaign materials, polit. pieces, press releases. Recipient Torch of Liberty award Anti-Defamation League of B'nai B'rith, 1987; named Outstanding Woman of Achievement B'nai B'rith Women, 1989. Mem. Westchester County Bar Assn., Mt. Vernon Bar Assn. Jewish. Office: Gross and Gross 9 W Prospect Ave Mount Vernon NY 10550

GROSS, HARRIET P. MARCUS, religion and writing educator; b. Pitts., July 15, 1934; d. Joseph William and Rose (Roth) Pincus; children: Sol Benjamin, Devra Lynn. AB magna cum laude, U. Pitts., 1954; cert. in religious teaching, Spertus Coll. of Judaica, Chgo., 1962; MA, U. Tex., Dallas, 1990. Assoc. editor Jewish Criterion of Pitts., 1955-56; publs. writer B'nai B'rith Vocat. Svc., 1956-57; group leader Jewish Community Ctrs. of Met. Chgo., 1958-63; columnist Star Publs., Chicago Heights, Ill., 1964-80; pub. info. specialist Operation ABLE, Chgo., 1980-81; dir. religious sch. Temple Emanu-El, Dallas, 1983-86; freelance writer, 1986—; columnist Dallas Jewish Life Monthly, 1992—; lectr. U. Tex., Dallas, 1994—; tchr. writing Homewood-Flossmoor (Il.) Park Dist., Brookhaven Jr. Coll., Dallas; advisor journalism program Prairie State Coll., Chicago Heights, 1978-80; adv. bd. The Creative Woman quar. publ. Governors State U., Governors Park, Ill., The Mercury U. Tex., Dallas. Bd. dirs., sec. Family Svc. and Mental Health Ctr. of South Cook County, Ill., 1965-71; active Park Forest (Ill.) Commn. on Human Rels., 1969-80, chmn., 1974-76; bd. dirs. Ill. Theatre Ctr., 1977-80, Jewish Family Svc. of Dallas, 1982-95; mem. Dallas Jewish Edn. Com., 1992-95; Dallas Jewish Historical Soc., 1995—. Recipient Humanitarian Achievements award Fellowship for Action, 1974; Honor award Anti-Defamation League of B'nai B'rith, 1978; Community Service award Dr. Charles E. Gavin Found., 1978, 1st Ann. Leadership award Jewish Family Svc., 1990, Katie award Dallas Press Club, 1995. Mem. Nat. Fedn. Press Women, Tex. Press Women, Ill. Woman's Press Assn. (named Woman of Yr. 1978), Intertel (pres. Gateway Forum of Dallas 1984-85), Nat. Assn. Temple Educators, Mensa, Sigma Delta Chi, Phi Sigma Sigma. Jewish. Developed 1st community newspaper action line column, 1966. Office: 8560 Park Ln Apt 23 Dallas TX 75231-6312

GROSS, IRIS LEE, association executive; b. Bklyn., Aug. 11, 1941; d. Frank and Anne (Schecter) Goodman; children: Michael, Henry. BA, Am. U., 1963. Cert. assn. exec. Field rep. mid-Atlantic region B'Nai Brith Women, Rockville, Md., 1973-76, dir. mid-Atlantic region, 1976-81; cen. svcs. dir. Nat. Coun. Jewish Women, N.Y.C., 1981-90, exec. dir., 1990-94; exec. dir. Birmingham (Ala.) Festival of Arts, 1994—. Commr. Montgomery County Commn. for Women, 1980-81. Recipient Achievement Cert. City of Rockville, 1975, Cert. of Appreciation March of Dimes, 1980. Mem. Am. Soc. Assn. Execs., N.Y. Soc. Assn. Execs. (bd. dirs. 1987-90, Outstanding Com. Chair 1986), Soc. Non-Profit Orgns. Democrat. Home: 806 Inverness Ln Birmingham AL 35242 Office: Nat Council of Jewish Women 53 W 23rd St New York NY 10010

GROSS, KAREN CHARAL, lawyer; b. N.Y.C., Nov. 25, 1940; d. Harry B. and Adele (Hook) Charal; m. Meyer A. Gross, Aug. 16, 1964; children: Dana Leslie, Jennifer P., Pamela A. AB, Barnard Coll., 1962; JD, NYU, 1965. Bar: N.Y. 1965. Atty. Wolder & Gross, N.Y.C., 1965-78, Wolder, Gross & Yavner, N.Y.C., 1978-86; v.p. legal and bus. affairs Good Times Home Video Corp., N.Y.C., 1986—. Editor NYU Law Rev., 1963-65. Parent liaison Ramaz Sch., N.Y.C., 1980-86; del. Dem. County Com., N.Y.C., 1988—; legal mentor to students Barnard Coll., N.Y.C. John Norton Pomeroy scholar NYU, 1963-65. Mem. Copyright Soc. USA. Office: GoodTimes Home Video Corp 16 E 40th St New York NY 10016-0113

GROSS, KATHLEEN ALBRIGHT, interventional radiology nurse, educator; b. Mechanicsburg, Pa., June 10, 1951; d. Clyde Nelson and Louise Aldine (Swigert) Albright; m. Richard Joseph Gross, Oct. 15, 1972; children: David, Jonathan. Diploma in Nursing, Harrisburg Hosp. Sch. Nursing, 1972; BS summa cum laude, Pa. State U., Harrisburg, 1977; BSN summa cum laude, Coll. Notre Dame Md., 1982. Cert. med.-surg. nurse, ACLS. Staff nurse ICU M.S. Hershey (Pa.) Med. Ctr., 1972-74; rsch. asst. in dermatology Johns Hopkins Bayview Med. Ctr. (formerly Balt. City Hosps.), 1977; rsch. asst. dept. health svcs. rsch. Johns Hopkins Sch. Hygiene and Pub. Health, Balt., 1978; staff nurse crit. care unit, ICU, med.-surg. Upjohn Healthcare, Balt., 1978-81; camp nurse Friends Sch., Balt., 1985; office nurse Balt., 1982-94; instr. Greater Balt. Med. Ctr. Sch. Radiologic Tech., Balt., 1991—; staff nurse interventional radiology Greater Balt. Med. Ctr., 1988—; staff nurse Patient First, 1994—. Instr. BCLS, Am. Heart Assn., Balt., 1983—, vol. fundraiser, 1985, 87, 88; vol. Gilman Sch., Balt., 1981—; vol. naturalist Irvine Natural Sci. Ctr., Stevenson, Md., 1987-91; vol. fundraiser Leukemia Soc. Am., Balt., 1989; aux. membership chairperson Balt. City Hosps., 1976, 77. Mem. Am. Radiol. Nurses Assn.(exec. com. 1994—, ANA-nursing orgn. liaison forum), Md. Radiol. Nurses Assn. (v.p. 1991-92, pres. 1993-94, bd. dirs. 1995—, rep. to 1st nursing summit 1991), Soc. for Vascular Nursing, Balt. Interventional Radiol. Technologists Assn., Delta Tau Kappa, Sigma Theta Tau. Home: 1243 Berans Rd Owings Mills MD 21117-1641 Office: Greater Balt Med Ctr Interventional Radiology 6701 N Charles St Baltimore MD 21204-6808

GROSS, LAURA ANN, marketing and communications professional; b. Kew Gardens, N.Y., July 11, 1948; d. Melvin Fredericks and Harriette (Levy) G. BA, Boston U., 1970; MA, Columbia U., 1974. Staff writer Am. Banker, N.Y.C., 1974-82, assoc. editor, 1982-88; dir. fin. svcs., instns., communications Am. Express Travel/Related Svcs. Co., N.Y.C., 1988-89; dir. sales promotion and pub. rels. Am. Express Travelers Cheque Group/Am. Express Travel Svcs., N.Y.C., 1989-92; dir. strategic bus. comm. Am. Express Travel Related Svcs., N.Y.C., 1992-93; pres. Strategic Comm. Cons., N.Y.C., 1993—. Author, editor consumer surveys and articles; speaker in field. Recipient editorial awards Pannell Kerr Forster, 1984, N.E. Bus. Press Editors, 1986, N.Y. Bus. Press. Editors, 1987, first Boston U. Coll. of Liberal Arts Young Alumni award, 1985. Mem. Bank Mktg. Assn., Promotion Mktg. Assn. (Spire award 1991), Pub. Rels. Soc. Am. (Silver Anvil award 1990, Big Apple award 1992, Creativity in Pub. Rels. award 1993).

GROSS, LILLIAN, psychiatrist; b. N.Y.C., Aug. 18, 1932; d. Herman and Sarah (Widelitz) Gross. BA, Barnard Coll., 1953; postgrad. U. Lausanne (Switzerland), 1954-56; MD, Duke U., 1959. Diplomate Bd. Pediatrics, Am. Bd. Psychiatry and Neurology, Am. Bd. Child Psychiatry; m. Harold Ratner, Feb. 4, 1961; children: Sanford Miles, Marcia Ellen. Intern Kings County Hosp., Bklyn., 1959-60, resident, 1967-70, fellow in child psychiatry, 1969-70, psychiatrist devel. evaluation clinic, 1970-72; resident Jewish Hosp. Bklyn., 1960-62, fellow in pediatric psychiatry, 1962-63; physician in charge pediatric psychiat. clinic Greenpoint (N.Y.) Hosp., 1964-67; pvt. practice psychiatry, Great Neck, N.Y., 1970—; clin. instr. psychiatry Downstate Med. Ctr., Bklyn., 1970-74, clin. asst. prof., 1974—; lectr. in psychiatry Columbia U., 1974—; psychiat. cons. N.Y.C. Bd. Edn., 1972-75, Queens Children's Hosp., 1975—; mem. med. bd. Camp Sussex (N.J.), 1963—, Saras Ctr., Great Neck, N.Y., 1977—. Fellow Am. Acad. Pediatrics, Am. Acad. Psychiatry, Am. Acad. Child Psychiatry, Am. Soc. Clin. and Experiential Hypnosis, N.Y. Soc. Clinical Hypnosis (past pres.); mem. AMA, Am. Psychiat. Assn., Nassau Psychiat. Assn., Bklyn. Psychiat. Assn., Bklyn. Pediatric Soc. (sr. mem.), Nassau Pediatric Socs., Soc. Adolescent Psychiatry, N.Y. Coun. Child Psychiatry, Soc. Clin. and Exptl. Hypnosis, Am. Med. Women's Assn. (Nassau, pres. 1985-86, 95—), N.Y., Kings County med. socs., N.Y. Soc. Clin. Hypnosis (past pres.), Internat. Soc. for Study of Multiple Personality and Dissociation (founder, pres. L.I. component study group). Home and Office: 55 Blue Bird Dr Great Neck NY 11023-1001

GROSS, PRIVA BAIDAFF, art historian, retired educator; b. Wieliczka, Poland, June 19, 1911; came to U.S., 1941, naturalized, 1955; d. Israel and Leopolda (Friedman) Baidaff; Ph.M., Jagellonian U., Cracow, Poland, 1937; postgrad. (N.Y. U. scholar 1945-47), N.Y. U. Inst. Fine Arts, 1945-48; m. Feliks Gross, July 25, 1937; 1 dau., Eva Helena Gross Friedman. Mem. faculty Queensborough Community Coll., CUNY, 1961-81, assoc. prof. art history, 1971-81, ret., 1981, co-chmn. art and music dept., 1966-68, chmn. art dept., 1968-74, dir. coll. gallery, 1968-77. SUNY grantee, 1967. Mem. AAUW (dir. 1972-76, 1980-82), Coll. Art Assn. Am., Soc. Archtl. Historians, Gallery Assn. N.Y. State (dir. 1972-73), N.Y. State Assn. Jr. Colls., AAUP, Polish Inst. Arts and Scis. Am., Council Gallery and Exhbn. Dirs. (dir. 1970-72). Contbr. articles, revs. to profl. publs. Home: 310 W 85th St New York NY 10024-3819

GROSS, RUTH TAUBENHAUS, physician; b. Bryan, Tex., June 24, 1920; d. Jacob and Esther (Hirshenson) Taubenhaus; m. Reuben H. Gross, Jr., Aug. 22, 1942; (div. June 1952); 1 son, Gary E. BA, Barnard Coll., 1941; MD, Columbi U., 1944. Intern, Charity Hosp., New Orleans, 1944; resident in pediatrics Tulane U., New Orleans, 1945, Columbia U., N.Y.C., 1946, 47; instr. Radcliffe Infirmary, Oxford, Eng., 1949-50; instr. pediatrics Stanford (Calif.) U., 1950-53, asst. prof., 1953-56, assoc. prof., 1956-60, prof., 1973-92, prof. emerita, 1992; acting exec. pediatrics, 1957-59, assoc. dean student affairs, 1973-75, dir. div. gen. and ambulatory pediatrics, 1975-85, dir. Stanford-Children's Ambulatory Care Ctr., 1980-85, nat. study dir. Infant Health and Devel. Program, 1983-92; assoc. prof. pediatrics, co-dir. div. human genetics Albert Einstein Coll. Medicine, Yeshiva U., N.Y.C., 1960-64, prof. pediatrics, 1964-66; clin. prof. pediatrics U. Calif. Med. Ctr., San Francisco, 1966-73; dir. dept. pediatrics Mt. Zion Hosp. and Med. Ctr., San Francisco, 1966-73. Commonwealth fellow human genetics Instituto de Genetica, Pavia, Italy, 1959-60. Mem. Inst. Medicine, NAS, Am. Fedn. Clin. Rsch., Am. Pediatric Soc., Soc. Pediatric Rsch., Am. Acad. Pediatrics, Ambulatory Pediatric Assn., Soc. Rsch. in Child Devel., Phi Beta Kappa, Alpha Omega Alpha, Sigma Xi. Contbr. articles to profl. jours.

GROSS, SHARON L., finance and accounting manager; b. Tacoma Park, Md., Feb. 21, 1954; d. Karl Crowell Jr. and Mary Ann (Barringer) Hoffman; m. Marvin Bruce Gross, June 5, 1981. AA, Glendale C.C., 1984; BS in Acctg., U. Md., 1995. Jr. acct. Wilkins-Rogers, Inc., Ellicott City, Md., 1981-84; billing analyst ITT Dialcom, Rockville, Md., 1984-85; acctg. and fin. mgr. Ogden Logistics Svcs., Greenbelt, Md., 1989-94; mgr. fin. and acctg. Dynamic Sys., Inc., Alexandria, Va., 1995—; mem. organizing com. Md. Deltek Users Group, 1992—. Mem. Inst. Mgmt. Accts., Golden Key.

GROSS, SHARON RUTH, forensic psychologist, researcher; b. L.A., Mar. 21, 1940; d. Louis and Sylvia Marion (Freedman) Lackman; m. Zoltan Gross, Mar. 1969 (div.); 1 child, Andrew Ryan; m. Ira Chroman, June 1994. BA, UCLA, 1983; MA, U. So. Calif., L.A., 1985, PhD, 1991. Tech. Rytron, Van Nuys, Calif., 1958-60; computress on tetrahedral satellite Space Tech. Labs., Redondo Beach, Calif., 1960-62; owner Wayfarer Yacht Corp., Costa Mesa, Calif., 1962-64; electronics draftsperson, designer stroke-writer characters Tasker Industries, Van Nuys, 1964-65; pvt. practice cons. Sherman Oaks, Calif., 1965-75, 77-80; printed circuit bd. designer Systron-Donner, Van Nuys, Calif., 1975-76; design checker, tech. writer Vector Gen., Woodland Hills, CAlif., 1976-77; undergrad. adv. U. So. Calif., L.A., 1987-89, rsch. asst. prof., rsch. assoc. social psychology, 1991—; owner Attitude Rsch. Litig. and Orgn. Consultants. Contbr. chpts. to books. Recipient Haynes Found. Dissertation fellowship U. So. Calif., 1990. Mem. APA (student dissertation rsch. award 1991), AAAS, Computer Graphics Pioneers, Am. Psychol. Soc., Western Psychol. Assn. Democrat. Jewish. Office: U So Calif Dept Psychology Los Angeles CA 90089-1061

GROSS, SHIRLEY MARIE, artist, farm manager; b. Beardstown, Ill., Apr. 4, 1917; d. Robert Lee and Marie Elizabeth (Ellrich) Northcutt; A.A., Stephens Coll., 1936; B.A., Ill. Coll., 1938; m. Carl David Gross, Oct. 4, 1941; children—David Lee, Susan Jean Gross Conner. Med. technologist St. John's Hosp., Springfield, Ill., 1938-41, Schmidt Meml. Hosp., Beardstown, 1957-64; librarian Beardstown Public Library, 1970-76; pvt. practice farm mgmt., Beardstown, 1958—; bd. dirs. First State Bank Beardstown, Heart of Ill. Investment Clubs; exhibitor various art shows, Ill., 1969—. Co-author: Beardstown Ladies, Common Sense Investment Guide, 1995, Beardstown Ladies, Stitch-in-Time Guide to Growing Your Nest Egg, 1996. Bd. dirs. Beardstown Hosp., Head Start; trustee First Congregational Ch. Beardstown. Winner art awards various shows. Mem. Am. Soc. Clin. Pathologists (med. technologist), Beardstown Bus. and Profl. Women's Investment Club, Cass County Hist. Soc., Beardstown Restoration Soc. Jacksonville Area Artist League, Beardstown Hosp. Aux., Beardstown Woman's Club, Cass County Coun. for the Arts Club, Beardstown Bus. and Profl. Women's Club (pres. local chpt. 1968-70), Supreme Emblem Club. Democrat. Home: 15 Blvd Rd Beardstown IL 62618

GROSS, SUSAN LYNN, administrative assistant; b. Chgo., Dec. 27, 1952; d. William Theodore and Avis Dianne (Boothman) G. Sec. to asst. buyer Sears Roebuck & Co., Chgo., 1971-74, sec. to buyer, 1974-76, sec. to mktg. mgr., 1976-79, exec. sec. to asst. v.p., 1979-90, adminstrv. asst. to fin. mgr., 1990-95; adminstrv. asst. to v.p. credit fin. Sears Roebuck & Co., Hoffman Estates, Ill., 1995—. Mem. Nat. Mus. Women in Arts (charter). Office: Sears Roebuck & Co 3333 Beverly Rd Hoffman Estates IL 60179

GROSS, WENDY S., public relations consultant; b. Cleve., Oct. 6, 1942; d. Alton E. and Jeanne (Schoen) G. BA in English, U. Mich., 1963. Asst. dir. pub. relations Girl Scouts of Chgo., 1964-66; account exec. Beveridge Orgn., Inc., Chgo., 1966-70; free-lance consultant Chgo., 1970-78; acct. exec. Golin/Harris Comm., Chgo., 1978-80, acct. supr., 1980, v.p., 1981-82, sr. v.p., 1982-90; sr. v.p. Ruder Finn, Chgo., 1990-94, Manning, Selvage & Lee, Chgo., 1994—. Mem. Pub. Rels. Soc. Am., Publicity Club of Chgo. (Golden Trumpet award 1981, 87, 90, 94, 95, 96, CIPRA award 1996). Home: 1000 Lake Shore Plz Chicago IL 60611-1129 Office: Manning Selvage & Lee 303 E Wacker Dr Chicago IL 60601-5212

GROSSENBACHER, KATHERINE ANN, elementary education educator; b. Guantanamo Bay, Cuba, Nov. 20, 1947; (parents Am. citizens); d. John Daniel and Dorothy Helen (Collins) Collins; m. John Joseph Grossenbacher, Apr. 24, 1971; children: Michael Joseph, Heidi Kristin. AA in Liberal Studies with distinction, San Marcos-Palomar Coll., 1988; BS in Edn. with distinction, George Mason U., 1991. Cert. NK-4 collegiate profl. tchr., Va. Adminstrv. asst. CIA, Washington and McLean, Va., 1968-71; tchr. kindergarten Westmore Elem. Sch., Fairfax City, Va., 1991-92; tchr. Kempsville Meadows Elem. Sch., Va. Beach, 1992-94, White Oaks Elem. Sch., Burke, Va., 1994-96. Mem. ASCD, NEA, Assn. for Childhood Edn. Internat., Fairfax Edn. Assn., Golden Key, Alpha Chi, Kappa Delta Pi. Home: care COMSUB PSC 810 Box 16 FPO AE 09619-3000

GROSSET, ANNE MARIE, biophysicist, researcher; b. Pitts., June 26, 1957; d. Serge Philippe and Helen Mary (Walton) G.;m. Denis Louis Pilloud, Mar. 23, 1991; children: Hélène Marie, Aurélie Véronique. BSCE, MIT, 1980; MS in Colloids, Polymers and Surfaces, Carnegie-Mellon U., 1988, MSCE, 1989; postgrad. in Biophysics, U. Pa., 1989—. Sr. rsch. engr. Westinghouse Elec. Corp. R&D Ctr., Pitts., 1980-85; asst. in phys. chemistry Swiss Fed. Inst. Tech., Lausanne, 1989; asst. in biochemistry U. Fribourg, Switzerland, 1992-93; doctoral candidate in biophysics U. Pa., Phila., 1989-92, 93—. Contbr. articles to profl. jours. Mem. Am. Inst. Chemists, Am. Peptide Soc., Biophys. Soc.

GROSSET, JESSICA ARIANE, computer analyst; b. Paris, Aug. 31, 1952; came to U.S., 1970; d. Raymond Louis and Barbara Ann (Byrne) G.; m. Bruce Edward Kaskubar, May 23, 1986. AA, Berkshire Community Coll., Pittsfield, Mass., 1972; BS, SUNY, Potsdam, 1979; postgrad., Ariz. State U., 1980, U. Minn., 1980-81. Computer programmer Kay-Bee Toy and Hobby Shops, Lee, Mass., 1974-78; computer analyst Mayo Clinic, Rochester, Minn., 1981—. Mem. Nat. Assn. Female Execs. Office: Mayo Clinic 200 1st St SW Rochester MN 55905-0001

GROSSETETE, GINGER LEE, retired gerontology administrator, consultant; b. Riverside, Calif., Feb. 9, 1936; d. Lee Roy Taylor and Bonita (Beryl) Williams; m. Alec Paul Grossetete, June 8, 1954; children: Elizabeth Gay Blech, Teri Lee Zeni. BA in Recreation cum laude, U. N.Mex., 1974, M in Pub. Adminstrn., 1978. Sr. ctr. supr., Office of Sr. Affairs, City of Albuquerque, 1974-77, asst. dir. Office of Sr. Affairs, 1977-96; conf. coord. Nat. Consumers Assn., Albuquerque, 1978-79; region 6 del. Nat. Coun. on

Aging, Washington, 1977-84; conf. chmn. Western Gerontol. Soc., Albuquerque, 1983; N.Mex. del. White House Conf. on Aging, 1995; mem. adv. coun. N.Mex. Agy. on Aging, 1996-99. Contbr. articles to mags. Campaign dir. March of Dimes N.Mex., 1966-67; pres. Albuquerque Symphony Women's Assn., 1972; mem. exec. com. Jr. League Albuquerque, 1976; mem. Gov.'s Coun. on Phys. Fitness, 1987-91, chmn. 1990-91; mem. bd. dirs. N.Mex. Sr. Olympics, 1995—. Recipient N.Mex. Disting. Pub. Service award N.Mex. Gov.'s Office, 1983, Disting. Woman on the Move award YWCA, 1986, Outstanding Profl. award N.Mex. State Conf. on Aging, 1995, Presdl. citation S.W. Soc. on Aging, 1995. Fellow Nat. Recreation and Pk. Assn. (bd. dirs. S.W. regional coun. rep., bd. dirs. leisure and aging sect., pres. N.Mex. chpt. 1983-84, bd. dirs. N.Mex. Sr. Olympics, 1994—, Outstanding profl. award 1982); mem. ASPA (pres. N.Mex. coun. 1987-88), S.W. Soc. on Aging (pres. 1984-85, bd. dirs., Outstanding Profl. award 1991, Presdl. citation 1996), U. N.Mex. Alumni Assn. (bd. dirs. 1978-80, Disting. Alumni award 1985), Las Amapolas Garden Club (pres. 1964), Phi Alpha Alpha, Chi Omega (pres. alumni 1959-60), Pi Lambda Theta. Home: 517 La Veta Dr NE Albuquerque NM 87108-1403

GROSSETT, DEBORAH LOU, psychologist, behavior analyst, consultant; b. Alma, Mich., Feb. 16, 1957; d. Charles M. and Margaret A. (Roethlisberger) G. BS, Alma Coll., 1979; MA, Western Mich. U., 1981, PhD, 1984. Lic. psychologist, Tex.; cert. in diagnostic evaluation, Tex.; registered behavior analyst, Tex. Grad. rsch. and teaching asst. Western Mich. U., Kalamazoo, 1979-84; asst. group home supr., community outreach Residential Opportunities, Kalamazoo, 1982-84; psychologist Richmond (Tex.) State Sch., 1984-87, Shapiro Devel. Ctr., Kankakee, Ill., 1987-88; clin. coord. Monroe Devel. Ctr., Rochester, N.Y., 1988; chief psychologist Denton (Tex.) State Sch., 1989-90; dir. psychol./behavioral svcs. Ctr. for the Retarded, Houston, 1990—; behavioral cons. Ctr. for Developmentally Disabled Adults, Kalamazoo, 1984, Goodman-Wade Enterprises, Houston, 1987; instr. psychology Houston Community Coll., 1985-86, U. Houston-Clear Lake, 1987, 92, 95. Contbr. chpt. to book, articles to profl. jours. Western Mich. U. fellow, 1984. Mem. Am. Psychol. Assn., Am. Assn. on Mental Retardation, Assn. for Behavior Analysis (chair Outreach Bd. 1989-91), Tex. Assn. for Behavior Analysis (bd. dirs. 1989-91). Democrat. Presbyterian. Home: 9750 Ravensworth Dr Houston TX 77031-3130 Office: Ctr for the Retarded Inc 3550 W Dallas St Houston TX 77019-1702

GROSSMAN, AUDREY MARIE, medical/surgical nurse; b. Plymouth, Ind., Oct. 7, 1938; d. Graham Henry and Grace (Huitema) G. Diploma, Meml. Hosp., South Bend, Ind., 1960. RN, Ind.; cert. med.-surg. nurse. Staff nurse preceptor Meml. Hosp. of South Bend, 1960, 94—, charge nurse, 1961-93.

GROSSMAN, BARBARA SUSANNE, publisher; b. Phila., Apr. 22, 1951; d. Morris I. and Gladys (Yovel) G.; m. Michael Jon Gross, Dec. 31, 1978; children: Willa Rebecca, Max Lawrence, Gilda Hanna. BA, Bard Coll., 1973; MFA, U. Iowa, 1975. Teaching and writing fellow U. Iowa, Iowa City, 1974-75; editorial asst. Knopf, N.Y.C., 1975-77; asst. editor Harper & Row, N.Y.C., 1977-79; editor, sr. editor Crown, N.Y.C., 1979-88; pub. Scribners, N.Y.C., 1988-94, Viking, N.Y.C., 1994—; trustee Bard Coll. Bd. Trustees, Annandale on Hudson, 1991—. Mem. Women Media Group. Democrat. Jewish. Office: Viking 375 Hudson St New York NY 10014-3658

GROSSMAN, BETH ANN, artist; b. Mpls., June 6, 1958; d. Erwin H. and Arlis F. Grossman; m. Storrs Townsend Hoen, Oct. 15, 1995. BA, U. Minn., 1980; MA, NYU, 1987. Set designer Third World Inst. for Theatre Arts Study, N.Y.C., 1981-84; graphic designer pvt. practice, N.Y.C., 1982-87, San Francisco, 1987-90; northwest regional coord. leader NO LIMITS for Women in Arts, Oakland, Calif., 1990—; curator art exhbn. at Ellis Island, 1996. Del. to Beijing Internat. Women's Forum, Women Caucus Art, 1995; leadership trainer, group leader Project Kesher, Internat. Jewish Conf., Kiev, Ukraine, 1994, Am. Field Svc. to Norway, 1976. U. Minn. Exch. grantee to Malaysia, 1978, Jerome Found. Artist grantee, 1995; Grad. sch. scholar Paulette Goddard Performing Arts, 1985. Democrat. Home: 693 Fairmount Ave Oakland CA 94611

GROSSMAN, ELIZABETH KORN, nursing administrator, retired college dean; b. S.I., N.Y., May 15, 1923; d. George and Ethel (Elliot) Korn; m. Thomas Grossman, Feb. 23, 1952 (dec. 1987); 1 child, Thomas. BA, Hunter Coll., 1944; MN, Western Res. U., 1947; MS in Nursing Edn., Ind. U., 1960, EdD, 1972. Researcher Columbia Carbon Corp., Bklyn., 1944; staff nurse, asst. head nurse, head nurse, supr. Univ. Hosp., Cleve., 1947-52; Instr. Mt. Sinai Hosp. Sch. Nursing, Cleve., 1952-53; supr. maternity nursing Meth. Hosp., Indpls., 1953-57; instr. maternity nursing, 1957-59; instr. DePauw U., Indpls., 1959-62; asst. prof., then assoc. prof., grad. maternity Ind. U., Indpls., 1959-66, prof., chairperson grad.-undergrad. maternity nursing, 1966-73, dean Sch. Nursing, 1973-88, dean, prof. emeritus, 1988—; civilian nat. cons. emeritus USAF Nurse Corps, 1983-86. Contbr. articles to profl. jours. Elected mem. Hunter Coll. Hall of Fame, 1973. Fellow Am. Acad. Nursing; mem. Am. Nurses Assn., Nat. League Nursing (Nurse of Yr.), Ind. Citizen League for Nursing, Am. Assn. Colls. Nursing (treas. 1981-85), Nurses Assn. of Am. Coll. Ob-Gyn (4th and 7th nat. program meeting com. 1987-88, chair com. on edn. 1980-82), Midwest Alliance Nursing (treas. 1979-81), Ind. State Nurses Assn. (treas. dist. 5 1988-92), Sigma Xi, Sigma Theta Tau (Disting. Service award 1977, co-chmn. campaign for Ctr. for Nursing Scholarship), Little Red Door Soc. (bd.), Rotary, Altrusa, Julian Ctr. Bd., Delta Kappa Gamma, Alpha Xi Delta (Woman of Distinction 1988). Republican. Roman Catholic. Home: 11201 Westfield Blvd Carmel IN 46032-3551 Office: Ind U Sch Nursing 610 Barnhill Dr Indianapolis IN 46202-5117

GROSSMAN, FRANCES KAPLAN, psychologist; b. Newport News, May 28, 1939; d. Rubin H. and Beatrice (Fischlowitz) Kaplan; m. Henry Grossman, July 26, 1970; children: Jennifer, Benjamin. BA, Oberlin (Ohio) Coll., 1961; MS, PhD, Yale U., 1965. Diplomate Am. Bd. Profl. Psychology. Asst. prof. Yale U., New Haven, 1965-69; asst. prof. Boston U., 1969-71, assoc. prof. psychology, 1971-82, prof. psychology, 1982—. Author: Brothers and Sisters of Retarded Children, 1971, Pregnancy, Birth and Parenthood, 1980. Trustee Oberlin Coll., 1990-92, pres. Alumni Assn., 1979-80. Recipient Cert. of Appreciation Oberlin Coll. Alumni Assn., 1983. Fellow APA (mem. ethics com. 1994—); mem. Mass. Psychol. Assn. (chair ethics com. 1989-91, Career Contbn. award 1991), Oberlin Coll. Alumni Assn., Sigma Xi, Phi Beta Kappa. Jewish. Office: Boston Univ Dept Psychology 64 Cummington St Boston MA 02215-2407

GROSSMAN, GAEL E., humanities educator; b. Detroit, June 27; d. Louis D. and Micki H. (Sherman) G. BA, U. Mich., 1988; MA, Mich. State U., 1990, postgrad., 1990—. Cert. secondary English and social studies tchr., reading instr., Mich. Instr. Baker Coll., Owosso, Mich., 1988-90; tchg. asst. Mich. State U., East Lansing, 1989-93; assoc. prof. Reading (Pa.) Area C.C., 1993—, chair humanities, 1995—. Mem. Nat. Coun. Tchrs. English. Office: Reading Area CC 10 S 2d St Reading PA 19603

GROSSMAN, JANICE, publisher; b. Montreal, Que., Can., Nov. 3, 1949; m. Daniel Rubinstein, July 11, 1978; 1 child, Lauren Alexandra. MA, NYU, 1970; BA, New Sch. Social Research, 1971. Advt. sr. exec. recruiter Merrill, Lynch, Pierce, Fenner & Smith Inc., N.Y.C., 1976-78; advt. sales rep. Ms. mag., N.Y.C., 1978-80; N.Y. advt. mgr. Ms. Mag., N.Y.C., 1980-82, advt. dir., 1982-84; advt. dir. New Woman Mag., N.Y.C., 1984-86, assoc. pub., 1986-88, became pub., 1989; became pub. In Fashion Mag., N.Y.C., 1988, N.Y. Mag., 1991; pub. Seventeen Mag., 1992—; v.p., group pub. K-III Magazines, 1992—. Mem. Fragrance Found., Fashion Group, Advt. Women N.Y., Cosmetic Exec. Women, Advt. Club N.Y. Home: 12 Colvin Rd Scarsdale NY 10583-1408 Office: Seventeen Mag 850 3rd Ave New York NY 10022-6222*

GROSSMAN, JOANNE BARBARA, lawyer; b. Brookline, Mass., Oct. 23, 1949; d. Bernard R. and Beatrice G. (Quint) G.; m. John H. Seesel, Dec. 30, 1973; children: Benjamin P., Rebecca A. AB, Radcliffe Coll., 1971; JD, U. Calif., Berkeley, 1975. Bar: Calif. 1975, D.C. 1976, U.S. Dist. Ct. D.C. 1976, U.S. Ct. Appeals (D.C. cir.) 1976, U.S. Supreme Ct. 1979. Assoc. Covington & Burling, Washington, 1975-83, ptnr., 1983—. Office: Covington & Burling PO Box 7566 1201 Pennsylvania Ave NW Washington DC 20044*

GROSSO, PATRICIA IDA, kindergarten educator; b. Bridgeport, Conn., Aug. 26, 1944; d. Frank and Frances Ida (Altieri) G. BS, So. Conn. State U., 1966; MA, Fairfield U., 1970; postgrad., U. Bridgeport, 1977; Cert. in Advanced Study, Fairfield U., 1988. Cert. tchr. pre-sch.-8, intermediate adminstrv. cert., Conn. Primary tchr. Trumbull, Conn., 1966—. Rep. Trumbull Town Coun., 1992-93. Recipient Teaching grants for Tchrs. of Math., Bridgeport Area Found., 1980s, Outstanding Tchr. award Weller Found., 1992, Mini-Grant Program for Tchrs., Am. Brands, 1994. Mem. AAUW, Elem. and Mid. Sch. Prins. of Conn., Kindergarten Assn. of Conn., ATOMIC, Phi Delta Kappa (v.p. for mem.). Democrat. Roman Catholic.

GROTZINGER, LAUREL ANN, university librarian; b. Truman, Minn., Apr. 15, 1935; d. Edward F. and Marian Gertrude (Greeley) G. BA, Carleton Coll., 1957; MS, U. Ill., 1958, PhD, 1964. Instr., asst. libr. Ill. State U., 1958-62; asst. prof. Western Mich. U., Kalamazoo, 1964-66; assoc. prof. Western Mich. U., 1966-68, prof., 1968—, asst. dir. Sch. Librarianship, 1965-72, chief rsch. officer, 1979-86, interim dir. Sch. Libr. and Info. Sci., 1982-86, dean grad. coll., 1979-92, prof. univ. libr., 1993—. Author: The Power and the Dignity, 1966; mem. editl. bd. Jour. Edn. for Librarianship, 1973-77, Dictionary Am. Libr. Biography, 1975-77, Mich. Academician, 1990—; contbr. articles to profl. jours. Trustee Kalamazoo Pub. Libr., 1991-93, v.p., 1991-92, pres., 1992-93; pres. pro tem Kalamazoo Bach Festival, 1996. Mem. ALA (sec.-treas. Libr. History Round Table 1973-74, vice chmn., chmn-elect 1983-84, chmn. 1984-85, mem.-at-large 1991-93), Spl. Librs. Assn., Assn. Libr. Info. Sci. Edn., Mich. acad. Sci., Arts and Letters (mem.-at-large, exec. com. 1980-86, pres. 1983-85, exec. com. 1990-94, pres. 1991-93), Internat. Assn. Torch Clubs (v.p. Kalamazoo chpt. 1992-93, pres. 1993-94, exec. com. 1989-95), Phi Beta Kappa (pres. S.W. Mich. chpt. 1977-78, sec. 1994—), Delta Phi Mu, Phi Delta Epsilon, Alpha Beta Alpha, Delta Kappa Gamma (pres. Alpha Psi chpt. 1988-92), Phi Kappa Phi. Home: 2729 Mockingbird Dr Kalamazoo MI 49008-1626

GROTZINGER, LELINDA GRETCHEN, cinema executive; b. L.A., Nov. 19, 1958; d. Otto Wilhelm and Gretchen LeAnn (Moore) von Grotzinger; m. Eric Guhenhas, July 7, 1981 (dec. Feb. 1982); children: (twins) Otto and Wilhelm; m. Brian Burton Montonbatten III, May 5, 1994; 1 child, Brian Burton Montonbatten IV. BA, Calif. State U., Fresno, 1992. Filmmaker Angel Films, Fresno, 1977-86; v.p. mktg., advt. Angel Films Cos., New Franklin, Mo., 1986-90; co-owner Angel Films Cos., New Franklin, 1991-96. Dir. (film) Uttland, 1994; dir., producer Marie du Le, 1995. Lectr. Big Sisters, Columbia, 1990-96; del. head Dem. Party Mo., Columbia, 1988; pres. PTA, New Franklin, Mo., 1989; pres. restoration Save Salfield Manor, London, 1990, Glasgow (Mo.) Hist. Soc., 1993. Mem. DAR, Women in Film. Jewish. Office: Angel Films 967 Hwy 70 New Franklin MO 65274

GROUSE, JAN ELLEN, physician; b. Seattle, Apr. 14, 1947; d. John Galt and Jean Frances (Shaver) Lindtwed; m. Lawrence Douglas Grouse, Oct. 27, 1973; children: Eric, Carrie, Christopher. BS, U. Puget Sound, 1969; MD, U. Wash., 1973. Diplomate Am. Bd. Family Practice. Intern in family practice Meml. Hosp. Med. Ctr., Long Beach, Calif., 1973-74; resident in family practice Franklin Sq. Hosp., Balt., 1974-76; asst. dir. Cmty. Family Practice Residency, LaGrange, Ill., 1979-80; staff physician primary care Student Health, U. Md., College Park, 1977-79; asst. dir. Hinsdale (Ill.) Family Practice Residency, 1980-83, dir. edn., 1983-84; faculty coord. geriatrics Glendale (Calif.) Adventist Family Practice Residency, 1985-88, assoc. dir., 1986-88; columnist med. news Family Cir. mag., N.Y.C., 1988-89; asst./assoc. dir. St. Joseph Family Practice Residency, Stamford, Conn., 1989-92; v.p. Med. Comm. Resources Inc., Gig Harbor, Wash., 1992—; leader task force on elderly Hinsdale (Ill.) Hosp., 1981-83. Med. editor Women's Health Advocate newsletter, Fairfax, Va., 1994—. Fellow Am. Acad. Family Physicians; mem. Am. Geriatric Soc., Soc. Tchrs. Family Medicine, Wash. Acad. Family Physicians (mem. publs. com. 1993—). Office: Med Comm Resources Inc 8316 86th Ave NW Gig Harbor WA 98332-6747

GROVE, MYRNA JEAN, elementary education educator; b. Bryan, Ohio, Oct. 24, 1949; d. Kedric Durward and N. Florence (Stombaugh) G. Student, Bowling Green State U., 1970-71; BA in Edn., Manchester Coll., 1971; postgrad., U. No. Colo., 1974-76, Purdue U., 1977, St. Francis Coll., Ft. Wayne, Ind., 1986, Coll. Mount St. Joseph, Ohio, 1986. Cert. elem. tchr., Ohio. Tchr. elem. sch. Bryan City Schs., 1972—. Author: Asbestos Cancer: One Man's Experience, 1995; editor newspaper column Education Today, 1975-82, newsletter N.W. Ohio Emphasis, 1981-83 (award 1981). Dir., violinist Bryan String Ensemble, 1981—; organist Trinity Episc. Ch., Bryan, 1979-89; active Lancaster Mennonite Hist. Soc., Hans Herr Found.; trustee Bryan Area Cultural Assn., 1984-89; bd. dirs. William County Cmty. Concerts; regional docent P. Buckley Moss. Jennings scholar Martha Holden Jennings Found., Bowling Green State U., 1982-83. Mem. NEA (Ohio del., state contact 1986-87), Nat. Assn. Gifted Children, Am. Booksellers' Assn. (assoc. mem.), Writers Info. Network, Ohio Edn. Assn. (presenter 1984, del. global issues 1986, sec. N.W. Ohio Tchrs. Uniserv. 1975-78), Ohio Assn. Gifted Children, Bus. and Profl. Women Ohio (individual devel. com. 1986-90, speaking skills cert. 1987), N.W. Ohio Manchester Coll. Alumni Assn. (past pres.), Bryan Edn. Assn. (exec. com., pres. 1985-86), P. Buckley Moss Soc., Trees of Life (v.p. 1994—, reg. moss docent), Alpha Delta Kappa (pres. 1996—), Alpha Mu.

GROVE, NETTIE MILLS, retired educational lobbyist; b. Chgo., Apr. 28, 1930; d. Roger Sherman and Ruth Wright Mills; m. Robert Thomas Grove, July 20, 1953 (wid. May 1965). BEd, Western Coll. for Women, Oxford, Ohio, 1953. Cert. tchr., N.C. Tchr. Morehead City (N.C.) Schs., 1953-55, Havelock (N.C.) Schs., 1955-59, Mt. Pleasant (N.C.) Elem. Sch., 1959-64; ednl. lobbyist N.C. Gen. Assembly, Raleigh, 1965-94. Bd. dirs., pres. Wake County Head Start, Raleigh, 1985-90; precinct chair N.C. Dem. Party, Raleigh, 1975-80; bd. dirs., chmn. Wake County Schs., Raleigh, 1969-74; chmn. Western Coll. Alumni, Raleigh, 1970-75. Home: 312 Linden Ave Raleigh NC 27601

GROVE, SARA ANN, political science educator; b. Johnstown, Pa., Oct. 10, 1962; d. Clifford Richard and Anastasia Elizabeth (Dugan) Grove; m. Bradley Gene Stiles, June 3, 1989. BA, Pa. State U., 1983; MA, U. N.C., 1986, PhD, 1991. Rsch. asst. N.C. Bar Assn., Raleigh, 1987-88; instr. dept. polit. sci. Frostburg (Md.) State U., 1989-90, asst. prof. dept. polit. sci., 1991; asst. prof. govt. dept. polit. sci. Shippensburg (Pa.) U., 1992—. Contbr. articles to profl. jours. Cmty. adv. bd. Public Opinion, Chambersburg, Pa., 1995; dir. statewide election polls, Gannett News Svc., Chambersburg, 1994—. Mem. Women's Caucus for Polit. Sci.-South (treas. 1993—), Phi Kappa Phi (#270 treas. 1995—), Beta Sigma Phi. Office: Shippensburg Univ 1871 Old Main Dr Shippensburg PA 17257

GROVER, DOROTHY LUCILLE, education educator; b. New Zealand, Sept. 9, 1936; came to U.S., 1966; d. Kenneth Frank Russell and Lucy Dorothy (Boshier) G.; 1 child, Tony. BA, Victoria U., Wellington, New Zealand, MA, 1966; PhD, U. Pitts., 1970. Asst. prof. U. Wis., Milw., 1970-72; asst. prof. U. Ill., Chgo., 1972-75, assoc. prof., 1975-88, prof., 1988—. Author: Prosentential Theory of Truth, 1992. Fellow Inst. Humanities, U. Ill., Chgo., 1989-90; Mellon Postdoctoral fellow U. Pitts., 1980; NEH summer rsch. grantee, 1978. Mem. Am. Philos. Assn., Soc. for Women in Philosophy. Home: 1093 S Park Ter Chicago IL 60605

GROVER, IVA SUE, librarian; b. Eau Claire, Wis., June 21, 1941; d. Harvey B. and Harriette L. (Britton) G.; m. Robert W. Jahns, Nov. 18, 1974 (div. Feb. 1984). BA in Bus. Adminstrn., U. Puget Sound, Tacoma, Wash., 1964; M Librarianship, U. Wash., 1966. Cert. tchr. K-12, Wash; lic. massage practitioner, Wash. Jr. high libr. Granger (Wash.) Sch. Dist., 1966-69; sr. high libr. North Thurston Sch. Dist., Lacey, Wash., 1969-70, Libby (Mont.) Sch. Dist., 1970-71; area libr. Pierce County Rural Libr. Dist., Tacoma, Wash., 1971-74; head libr. Whatcom C.C., Bellingham, Wash., 1974-80, libr. coord., 1980-96; co-owner Friendly Books, Anacortes, Wash., 1974-84; owner Light Therapies, Bellingham, 1994—. Contbr. Writing Across the Curriculum and the Academic Library, 1995; book reviewer Western N.Y. Geneal. Soc. Jour., 1988—. Co-founder Whatcom County Post-Polio Support Group, Bellingham, 1991; bd. dirs. Cmty. Food Coop., Bellingham, 1995—. Recipient Juror's award fibers unltd. show Whatcom Mus. History and Art and Whacom Textile Guild, Bellingham, 1985. Mem. Am. Massage Therapy Assn., Assn. C.C. Adminstrs., C.C. Librs. and Media Specialists, Western N.Y. Genealogy Soc.

GROVER, ROSALIND REDFERN, oil and gas company executive; b. Midland, Tex., Sept. 5, 1941; d. John Joseph and Rosalind (Kapps) Redfern; m. Arden Roy Grover, Apr. 10, 1982; 1 child, Rosson. BA in Edn. magna cum laude, U. Ariz., 1966, MA in History, 1982; postgrad. in law, So. Meth. U., Dallas. Libr. Gahr High Sch., Cerritos, Calif., 1969; pres. The Redfern Found., Midland, 1982—; ptnr. Redfern & Grover, Midland, 1986—; pres. Redfern Enterprises Inc., Midland, 1989—; chmn. bd. dirs. Flag-Redfern Oil Co., Midland. Sec. park and recreation commn. City of Midland, 1969-71, del. Objectives for Convocation, 1980; mem., past pres. women's aux. Midland Community Theatre, 1970, chmn. challenge grant bldg. fund, 1980, chmn. Tex. Yucca Hist. Landmark Renovation Project, 1983, trustee, 1983-88; chmn. publicity com. Midland Jr. League Midland, Inc., 1972, chmn. edn. com., 1976, corr. sec., 1978; 1st v.p. Midland Symphony Assn., 1975; chmn. Midland Charity Horse Show, 1975-76; mem. Midland Am. Revolution Bicentennial Commn., 1976; trustee Mus. S.W., 1977-80, pres. bd. dirs., 1979-80; co-chmn. Gov. Clements Fin. Com., Midland, 1978; mem. dist. com. State Bd. Law Examiners; trustee Midland Meml. Hosp., 1978-80, Permian Basin Petroleum Mus., Libr. and Hall of Fame, 1989—. Recipient HamHock award Midland Community Theatre, 1978. Mem. Ind. Petroleum Assn. Am., Tex. Ind. Producers and Royalty Owners Assn., Petroleum Club, Racquet Club (Midland), Horseshoe Bay (Tex.) Country Club, Phi Kappa Phi, Pi Lambda Theta. Republican. Home: 1906 Crescent Pl Midland TX 79705-6407 Office: PO Box 2127 Midland TX 79702-2127

GROVES, BARBARA, performing company executive. Artistic dir. Martha Graham Dance Co., N.Y.C. Office: Martha Graham Dance Co 316 E 63rd St New York NY 10021-7702*

GROVES, SHARON SUE, elementary education educator; b. Springfield, Mo., Apr. 25, 1944; d. William Orin Jr. and Ruth M. (Jones) Hodge; m. Donald L. Groves, July 20, 1963. BA, Drury Coll., 1966, MEd, 1969. Cert. life elem. tchg.; Psychol. Examiners Cert. Adminstrn. Elem. tchr. Springfield Pub. Schs., 1966—; asst. instr. individual testing Drury Coll., Springfield, 1969-76; asst. instr. enhancing math. S.W. Mo. State U., Springfield, 1991-94; sr. leader MAP 2000 (Mo. Assessment Project) Class I. Author: Modeling Effective Practices: Geometry and Computation. Active Springfield's Curriculum Coun.; mem. Tchg. Cadre, Strategic Planning Team; hon. life mem. PTA; chmn. adminstrv. coun. Hood United Meth. Ch.; children's coord., math. workshops.; sr. leader Mo. Assessment Project, 1993—. Recipient Extra Mile award, 1989; named Fremont Tchr. of the Yr., 1988, 93. Mem. ASCD, Internat. Reading Assn., Assn. for Childhood Edn., Nat. Coun. Tchrs. Math., Mo. Coun. Tchrs. Math., Mo. State Tchrs. Assn. (pres. S.W. dist., Educator of Yr. 1989, Leader of Yr. 1990), Springfield Edn. Assn. (pres.), Delta Kappa Gamma (1st v.p.). Home: 8076 W Farm Rd 144 Springfield MO 65802-9555

GROWE, JOAN ANDERSON, state official; b. Mpls., Sept. 28, 1935; d. Lucille M. (Brown) Johnson; children: Michael, Colleen, David, Patrick. B.S., St. Cloud State U., 1956; cert. in spl. edn., U. Minn., 1964; exec. mgmt. program State and local govt., Harvard U., 1979. Tchr. elem. pub. schs. Bloomington, Minn., 1956-58; tchr. for exceptional children elem. pub. schs. St. Paul, 1964-65; spl. edn. tchr. St. Anthony Pub. Schs., Minn., 1965-66; mem. Minn. Ho. of Reps., 1973-74; sec. of state State of Minn., St. Paul, 1975—; mem. exec. coun. Minn. State Bd. Investment. Mem. Women Execs. in State Govt., Women's Campaign Fund, Women's Polit. Caucus, Minn. Women's Econ. Roundtable; candidate U.S. Senate, 1984; bd. dirs. Greater Mpls. coun. Girl Scouts U.S., Wayside House. Recipient Minn. Sch. Bell award, 1977, YMCA Outstanding Achievement award, 1978, Disting. Alumni award St. Cloud State U., 1979, Charlotte Striebel Long Distance Runner award Minn. NOW, 1985, The Woman Who Makes a Difference award Internat. Women's Forum, 1991, Esther V. Crosby Leadership award Greater Mpls. Girl Scout Coun., 1992. Mem. Nat. Assn. Secs. of State (pres. 1979-80), Minn. Equal Rights Alliance, LWV. Roman Catholic. Office: Sec of States Office 100 Constitution Ave Rm 180 Saint Paul MN 55155*

GRUBE, ELISABETH FRANCES, strategic and financial planning administrator; b. N.Y.C., Nov. 9, 1965; d. Heinrich and Elisabeth Klara (Leitner) M.; m. Patsy Matthew Grube, Aug. 20, 1988. BBA, Western Conn. State U., 1987; MBA, Pace U., 1993. Broker trainee Dean Witter Reynolds, Inc., N.Y.C., 1987; trust acct. Mfrs. Hanover Corp. (Chase), N.Y.C., 1987-89, trust officer, asst. mgr., 1989-90; investment, mktg. asst. Bayeriche Vereinsbank, AG, Munich, 1991; legal asst. P. Matthew Grube, Poughkeepsie, N.Y., 1991-94; cost analyst People's Bank, Bridgeport, Conn., 1993-95, mgmt. devel. cons., 1994-95; fin. and cost analyst, profitibility cons. Signet Bank Corp., Richmond, Va., 1995; mgr. strategic and fin. planning Ruesch Internat., Inc., Washington, 1995—. Home: 10725 Drumm Ave Kensington MD 20895

GRUBER, THERESA MARIE, biologist, computer technician; b. Phila., Oct. 2, 1960; d. Fred W. and Patricia A. (Webster) G. AA in Linguistics, CCAF, Maxwell AFB, Ala., 1986; BS in Biology cum laude, Rowan Coll. N.J., Glassboro, 1995. Shift supr. Air Force, Kelly AFB, Tex., 1981-92; computer technician VHHS, Mt. Holly, N.J., 1993—. Home: 201 Morgan Ave Palmyra NJ 08065

GRUBER-BALDINI, ANN LYNCH, psychologist, researcher; b. Reading, Pa., Feb. 12, 1963; d. James Henry and Rosann (Lynch) Gruber; m. J. Randall Baldini, Aug. 16, 1986. BA in Psychology and Sociology, Bucknell U., 1985; MS in Human Devel. and Family Studies, Pa. State U., 1989, PhD, 1991; postgrad., U. Mich., 1991-93. Social work intern Lewisburg United Meth. Home, 1984; rsch. asst. psychology dept. Bucknell U., 1984; rsch. asst. human devel. and family studies Pa. State U., 1985-89, pre-doctoral trainee human devel. and family studies, 1989-91; postdoctoral rsch. fellow Inst. Gerontology U. Mich., Ann Arbor, 1991-93; guest rschr. Nat. Inst. on Aging-Gerontology Rsch. Ctr., Balt., 1991-93; rsch. assoc. Rsch. Inst., Hebrew Home of Greater Washington, Rockville, Md., 1993-94; rsch. fellow/data analyst dept. epidemiology & preventive medicine U. Md. at Balt., 1994-95; rsch. assoc. dept. epidemiology & preventive medicine U. Md., Balt., 1995—; abstract reviewer Gerontol. Soc. Am., Washington, 1991—. Co-author 2 book chpts.; contbr. articles to profl. jours. Recipient Postdoctoral fellowship U. Mich., 1991-93, Predoctoral trainee award Nat. Inst. on Aging, 1989-91. Mem. APA, Gerontol. Soc. Am. Home: 7236 Life Quest Ln Columbia MD 21045-5253 Office: Dept Epidemiology and Preventive Medicine U Md at Balt 660 W Redwood St Baltimore MD 21201-1596

GRUBIN, SHARON E., federal judge; b. Newark, Feb. 9, 1949; d. Harold and Blanche (Dultz) G. AB with honors, Smith Coll., 1970; JD with honors in Legal Writing and Analysis, Boston U., 1973. Bar: N.Y. 1974, U.S. Dist. Ct. (so. and ea. dists.) N.Y. 1974, U.S. Ct. Appeals (2nd cir.) 1974. Litigator White & Case, N.Y.C., 1973-84; judge U.S. Dist. Ct. (so. dist.) N.Y., N.Y.C., 1984—; chair 2d cir. task force on gender, racial and ethnic fairness in the cts.; lectr. NYU Sch. Law, Yale Law Sch., Bklyn. Law Sch., N.Y. Law Sch.; dir., sec., exec. com. Lawyers' Com. on Violence, Inc. Author: (with others) Advocacy-The Art of Pleading a Cause, 1985, Removal, Federal Civil Practice, 1989, and supplement, 1993; spkr. seminars in field. Mem. ABA (jud. adminstrn. divsn.), Nat. Assn. Women Judges (chair fed. gender bias com., publicity com., newsletter com.), Fed. Bar Coun. (trustee, chair nominating com., v.p. 1990-94, award com. 1988-94, com. on 2d dir. cts., long-range planning com.), N.Y. State Bar Assn. (exec. com., nominations com., comml. and fed. litig. sect.), N.Y. State Assn. Women Judges (bd. dirs.), Assn. of Bar of City of N.Y. (chair nominating com. 1995—, chair spl. com. on legal history, chair spl. com. on Orison S. Marden Meml. lectrs., exec. com. 1990-94, spl. com. on gender bias in fed. cts. 1991-94, coun. on jud. adminstrn. 1986-90, prof. and jud. ethics com. 1986-89, nominating com. 1984-85, com. on jud. 1982-83, chair young lawyers com. 1979-81), Am. Judicature Soc. (editl. com. 1996—). Office: US Dist Ct US Courthouse 500 Pearl St Rm 1360 New York NY 10007

GRUEBEL, BARBARA JANE, internist, pulmonologist; b. Honolulu, May 12, 1950; d. Robert William and Elenor Jane (Perry) G.; BS, Stephen F. Austin State U., 1977; MD (Robert Wood Johnson Found. scholar, Coll. Women's Club scholar), Baylor Coll. Medicine, 1974. Intern in internal medicine U. Rochester, 1974-75, resident in internal medicine, 1975-77; pulmonary fellow U. Mich., 1977-79; mem. med. staff Anthony L. Jordan Health Center, Rochester, N.Y., 1976-77, Univ. Health Service, Ann Arbor,

Mich., 1978-79; med. dir. progressive respiratory care unit Meth. Med. Ctr., 1979-80; asst. prof. medicine U. Tex. Health Sci. Center, Dallas, 1979-80; cons. in pulmonary disease, Dallas, 1980-93; pvt. practice of pulmonary medicine, 1993—; clin. asst. prof. medicine U. Tex. Health Sci. Center, 1980—; nat. affiliate faculty Am. Heart Assn. Mem. TEXPAC. Recipient award for gen. excellence in pediatrics, 1974, Stanley W. Olson award for acad. excellence, 1974, John Richard Fox award, 1974, Stuart A. Wallace award in pathology, 1974; Welch Found. grantee, 1970; Am. Lung Assn. tng. fellow, 1977-79. Diplomate Nat. Bd. Med. Examiners. Fellow Am. Coll. Chest Physicians (named Young Pulmonary Physicians of Future 1979); mem. Am. Med. Women's Assn. (scholastic excellence award 1974), Am. Thoracic Soc., Am. Lung Assn., AMA, Am. Coll. Physicians, Dallas County Med. Soc., Tex. Med. Soc., Dallas Internist Assocs., Nat. Assn. Med. Dirs. Respiratory Care, Dallas Acad. Internal Medicine, Am. Cancer Soc., Dallas C. of C., Oak Cliff C. of C., Alpha Omega Alpha, Beta Beta Beta. Office: 221 W Colorado Blvd Ste 310 Dallas TX 75208-2310

GRUEN, DOLORES COLEN, psychologist consultant; b. Erie, Pa., Aug. 6, 1924; d. Harry and Rose (Shenker) Colen; m. Dieter M. Gruen, June 27, 1948; children: Erica, Karen, Jeffery. BS, Ohio State U., 1944, MA, 1945; PhD, U. Chgo., 1952. Lic. clin. psychologist, Ill. Instr. Roosevelt U., Chgo., 1945-51; dir. psychology svcs. Downers Grove (Ill.) Schs., 1959-81; pvt. clin. practice Downers Grove, 1981—; cons. Nahal Psychiatric Group, Downers Grove, 1995—; cons. Cath. Charities, Chgo., 1985-90. Co-author (health manual) Be Your Own Best Friend, 1994. Chair health com. sr. citizen adv. bd. Downers Grove Twp., 1989—. Named Outstanding Vol., Downers Grove Twp., 1991. Fellow Assn. Sch. Psychologists; mem. APA (diplomate), NEA (life mem.), Nat. Register of Health Care Providers. Home: 1324 59th St Downers Grove IL 60516 Office: Ste 214 6800 S Main St Downers Grove IL 60516

GRUEN, MARSHA IRENE, marketing executive; b. Bklyn., Feb. 14, 1941; d. Harold and Adele (Brooks) Aisley; m. Peter Gruen, 1959 (div. 1977); children: Arthur, Kim; m. Bernard Berch, Sept. 8, 1985. Student, U. Calif., Berkeley, 1958-62. V.p. client svcs. Stratmar Sys., Port Chester, N.Y., 1977-93; dir. ops. Smart Demo, Wilton, Conn., 1993-94; v.p. ea. region Super Mktg., Mpls., 1994-95; dir. field promotion svcs. Mktg. Force, Detroit, 1995—. Vol. Bella Abzug Reelection Com., White Plains, N.Y. Mem. LVW, NOW, NAFE, Nat. Assn. Demonstration Cos. Home and Office: 15 Rita Rd Ridgefield CT 06877

GRUFFERMAN, BARBARA HANNAH, publishing executive. Pub. Star mag.; sr. v.p. publishing Nat. Enquirer. Office: Star Magazine 660 White Plains Rd Tarrytown NY 10591*

GRUHL, ANDREA MORRIS, librarian; b. Ponca City, Okla., Dec. 9, 1939; d. Luther Oscar and Hazel Evangeline (Anderson) Morris; m. Werner Mann Gruhl, July 10, 1965; children: Sonja Krista, Diana Krista. BA, Wesleyan Coll., 1961; MLS, U. Md., 1968; postgrad., Johns Hopkins U., 1970-71, U. Md., 1968, 71-73, Oxford U., 1996. Tchr. Broward County, Fla., Dept. Def. Montgomery County (Md.), 1961-66; libr. Prince Georges County (Md.) Pub. Libr., 1966-68, 81-83, U. Md., College Park, 1970-72; art. history rschr. Joseph Alsop, Washington, 1972-74; libr. Howard County Pub. Libr., Columbia, Md., 1969-70, 74-79; European exch. staff Libr. of Congress, Washington, 1982-86; cataloger fed. documents GPO, Washington, 1986-93, supervisory libr., 1993—; mem. women's program adv. com., processing dept. rep. Libr. of Congress, 1983-86, mem. ofcl. Libr. of Congress delegation to Internat. Fedn. Libr. Assn. ann. conf., Munich, 1983, Chgo., 1985; state del. White House Conf. on Librs., 1978, 90. Indexer, editor: Learning Vacations, 3d edit., 1980; editor: Federal Librarian, 1994—; LCPA Index to Libr. of Congress Info. Bull., 1984. Trustee Howard County (Md.) C.C., 1989-95, Howard County Pub. Libr., Columbia, Md., 1979-87; publ. chmn. LWV Howard County, 1974, bd. dirs., 1996—; citizens rep. Howard County, exec. bd. Balt. Regional Planning Coun. Libr. com., 1976-79; bd. dirs. LWV of Howard County, 1996—; Friends of Libr., Howard County, pres., 1976; vol. Nat. Gallery Art Libr., Washington, 1978-80. Mem. ALA (trustee assn. 1982-87, cataloging sect. 1988—, govt. documents roundtable 1988—, fed. librs. roundtable 1988—, internat. rels. roundtable 1988—), Assn. Libr. Collections and Tech. Svcs., Libr. Info. Tech. Assn., Libr. Adminstrn. and Mgmt. Assn. (policy and evaluation com. 1996—), D.C. Libr. Assn. (co-chair mgmt. interest group 1996—), UN Assn. (Nat. Capitol area chpt., membership com., Md. telephone chair 1992-94), Art Librs. Soc. N.Am. (coord. publ. exhbn. 1980-82), Libr. Congress Profl. Assn. (coord. ann. staff art shows 1982-83, chmn. libr. sci. group 1985-87), Libr. Congress Am. Fedn. State County and Mcpl. Employees Union 1477 (program chair 1984-86), Md. Libr. Assn. (pres. trustee divsn. 1982-83), Assn. C.C. Trustees, Md. Assn. C.C. Trustees (sec. 1991-92, bd. dirs. 1992-93), Md. Assn. C.C. (bd. dirs. 1992-95). Democrat. Lutheran. Home: 5990 Jacobs Ladder Columbia MD 21045-3817 Office: Govt Printing Office Washington DC 20401

GRUHZIT-HOYT, OLGA MARGARET, author; b. Columbus, Ga., Nov. 16, 1922; d. Oswald Martin and Elfriede Victoria (Nerica) Gruhzit; m. Edwin Palmer Hoyt, III, May 24, 1947 (div. June 1992); children: Diana, Helga Berliner, Christopher. BA, U. Mich., 1943. Editor news divsn. Office of War Info., N.Y.C., 1944-45; asst. news editor Office of War Info., Beirut, Lebanon, 1945; editl. rschr. Time mag., N.Y.C., 1945-47; free lance corr. N.Am. Newspaper Alliance, 1947, 48, 75; columnist, book reviewer Denver Post, 1949-50; columnist, book editor Colorado Springs (Colo.) Free Press, 1951-55; mag. stringer Time mag., 1951-55; children's book reviewer N.Y. Times, N.Y.C., 1957-64; book rschr., editor, 1959-92. Author: If You Want a Horse, 1965, Witches, 1969, The Bedouins, 1969, American Indians Today, 1972, Demons, Devils and Djinn, 1974, Exorcism, 1978, Censorship in American (with Edwin P. Hoyt), 1970, Freedom of the News Media (with Edwin P. Hoyt), 1973, Lust for Blood: The Consuming Story of Vampires, 1984, re-issues, 1991-95, They Also Served: American Women in World War II, 1995; contbr. articles to profl. jours. including Saturday Rev., Balt. Sun, N.Am. Newspaper Alliance, Daily Press, Gazette Jour., Gloucester, Va., China Reconstructs. Founder, pres. Delhi (N.Y.) Art Group, 1993-96. Home: 17 Franklin St Delhi NY 13753

GRULING, KAY ANN, family physician; b. Merrill, Wis., Sept. 28, 1961; d. Robert Herman and Esther Martha (Schulz) G.; m. Timothy Charles Buttke, June 11, 1988; children: Calla Kay, Isaac Friederick. Student, U. Wis., Wausau, 1982, U. Wis., 1984, Rheinische Frederick-Wilhelms U., Bonn, West Germany, 1984, U. Wis., 1988. Diplomate Am. Bd. Family Practice. Intern and resident in family medicine U. Wis. Wausau Program, 1988-91; family physician Wausau Med. Ctr., 1991—; mem. edn. com., exec. com. Wausau Family Practice Ctr., 1988-91, bioethics com., 1989-91; mem. pediat. sedation task force Wausau Hosp., 1991—, edn. com., 1992— (chairperson 1993-95); mem. physician extender task force Wausau Med. Ctr., 1991—, mktg. com., 1992—, physician charging practices subcom., 1993-95, walk-in dept. task force, 1994; mem. Shadowing Program U. Wis. Stevens Point, 1992-95; vol. faculty Residency Program Wausau Family Practice, 1991—; mem. domestic abuse task force, med. dir. Marathon County Med. Soc., 1993; v.p. U. Wis. Marathon Ctr. Found., 1994-95; bd. dirs. U. Wis. Marathon Ctr. Bd. dirs., mem. public edn. com. Marathon Unit Am. Cancer Soc., 1992-95; active Trinity Lutheran Ch., 1988—; active local and regional polit. campaigns, 1988—; mem., vol. Farm Bureau. Mem. Wis. Acad. Family Physicians, 1983— (publs. and pub. rels. com. 1991—, chairperson, 1992-95), legis. affairs com., 1991, women's task force, 1991-92, access to health care task force, 1992—, newsletter editor, 1992-95, Wis. Valley Dist., 1988—, pres. 1991—). Democrat. Lutheran. Home: 620 Hwy 0 Wausau WI 54401 Office: Wausau Med Ctr 2727 Plaza Dr Wasau WI 54401

GRUMBACHER, JACQUELINE WERTIME, communications executive; b. Tarrytown, N.Y., Apr. 30, 1944; d. Gaspare and Josephine (Galiano) Giuliano; 1 child, Gregory Steven; 1 stepchild, Sara Katherine; m. Steven Grumbacher, Apr. 22, 1989. BA, Bryn Mawr Coll., 1966. Editor Harper & Row Pub., Evanston, Ill., 1968-72; freelance writer, editor Washington, 1973-77; comm. dir. ARC Nat. Hdqs., Washington, 1977-88; sr. v.p. comm. Mortgage Bankers Assn. Am., Washington, 1988—; mem. homeownership-2000 task force Dept. Housing & Urban Devel. Active AIDS Edn. Task Force, 1987-88. Mem. Nat. Press Club, Am. Soc. Assn. Execs., Jane Austen Soc. N.Am. Home: 2412 S Queen St Arlington VA 22202-1554 Office: Mortgage Bankers Assoc of Am 1125 15th St NW Washington DC 20005-2707

GRUMET, PRISCILLA HECHT, fashion specialist, consultant, writer; b. Detroit, May 11, 1943; d. Lewis Maxwell and Helen Ruth (Miller) Hecht; m. Ross Frederick Grumet, Feb. 24, 1968; 1 child, Auden Lewis. AA, Stephens Coll., 1963; student, Ga. State Coll., 1983-85. Buyer Rich's Dept. Store, Atlanta, 1963-68; instr. fashion retail Fashion Inst. Am., Atlanta, 1968-71; pres., lectr., cons. Personally Priscilla Personal Shopping Svc., Atlanta, 1971—; retail and customer svc. cons. By Priscilla Grumet, Atlanta, 1989—; instr. Cont. Edn. Program Emory U., Atlanta, 1976—; fashion merch. coord. Park Pl. Shopping Ctr., Atlanta, 1979-83; writer Altanta Bus. Mag., 1984—; cons., buyer Greers-Regensteins Store, Atlanta, 1986-87; writer Atlanta Mag., 1994—; guest lectr. Fashion Group of Am., Rancho La Puerta Resort, Tecate, Mex., 1985—; bus. cons. Atlanta Apparel Mart, 1992—; adv. bd. Bauder Fashion Col., 1986—, Atlanta Apparel Mart, 1992—; fashion panel judge Weight Watchers Internat., 1981; columnist Marquee mag., Atlanta, 1992—; lectr. on customer svc. Rhodes Furniture, Marriott Corp., So. Bell, Lady Love Cosmetics, Atlanta Retail Stores, others, 1994—. Author: How to Dress Well, 1981; reporter Women's Wear Daily, 1976-90; columnist Atlanta Scene Mag.; contbr. articles to mags. and publs. including Atlanta, Seventeen, Nat. Jeweler's (Editor's Choice award The Nat. Libr. of Poetry 1995), The Old Farmer's Almanac. Pub. rels. dir., Atlanta Jewish Home Aux., 1986-89; admissions advisor, Stephens Coll., 1979—. Mem. Fashion Group, Inc., Women in Comm., Nat. Coun. Jewish Women, Atlanta Press Club, Buckhead Bus. Assn., Temple Sisterhood (spkr., spl. events com. 1983—). Home and Office: 2863 Careygate NW Atlanta GA 30305-2821

GRUNDBERG, BETTY, state legislator, property manager; b. Woden, Iowa, Feb. 16, 1938; d. Edwin and Eva Ruth Meyer; m. Arnie Grundberg, Dec. 31, 1960; children: Christine, Julie, Michael, Susan. BA, Wartburg Coll., 1959; MA, U. Iowa, 1969; postgrad., Drake U. Cert. tchr. Property mgr. and renovator Des Moines, 1973—; with Des Moines Sch. Bd., 1975-90; legis. State of Iowa, Des Moines, 1993—. Active LWV, Des Moines, 1972—. Republican. Home and Office: 224 Foster Dr Des Moines IA 50312-2540

GRUNDY, BETTY LOU BOTTOMS, anesthesiology and pharmaceutics educator; b. Dothan, Ala., Jan. 3, 1940; d. Wilmer Rudolph and Marie Belle (Brandon) Bottoms; m. David Mather Grundy, June 3, 1963; children: Jennifer Marie, Thomas Mather. Postgrad., Huntington Coll., Montgomery, Ala., 1956-59; MD, U. Fla., 1963. Rotating intern Gen. Rose Meml. Hosp., 1963-64; gen. med. practice Homestake Gold Mine, Lead, S.D., 1964-65; resident in anesthesiology Peter Bent Brigham Hosp., Boston, 1965-67; pvt. practice, anesthesiology St. Luke's Hosp., Saginaw, Mich., 1967-75; asst. prof. anesthesiology Mich. State U., Saginaw, 1967-75, Case Western Res. U., Cleve., 1975-79, U. Pitts., 1979-82; prof., chmn. of anesthesiology Coll. of Medicine, Oral Roberts U., Tulsa, 1982-84; prof. anesthesiology U. Fla., Gainesville, 1984—; chief anesthesiology svc. VA Med. Ctr., Gainesville, Fla., 1984-92; prof. anesthesiology and pharmaceutics U. Fla., Gainesville, 1992—; assoc. examiner Am. Bd. Anesthesiology, Hartford, Conn.; vol. site visitor Residency Rev. Com. for Anesthesiology, Accreditation Coun. for Grad. Med. Edn., 1982—. Editor: The Quality of Care in Anesthesia, 1982, Evoked Potentials Intraoperative and ICU Monitoring, 1988. Recipient Spl. award for New Investigators in Anesthesiology, NIH, 1979. Mem. Am. Electroencephalographic Soc. (evoked potentials com. 1982-89). Methodist. Home: 504 NW 89th St Gainesville FL 32607-1453 Office: Univ Fla Box J 254 JHMHC Gainesville FL 32610-0254

GRUNNET, MARGARET LOUISE, pathology educator; b. Mpls., Feb. 20, 1936; d. Leslie Nels and Grace Harriet (Thomson) Grunnet; m. Irving Noel Einhorn, Mar. 10, 1972; stepchildren: Jeffrey Allan, Franne Ruth, Eric Carl, Stanley Glenn. BA summa cum laude, U. Minn., Mpls., 1958; MD, U. Minn., 1962; MS, Ohio State U., 1969. Resident in psychiatry U. Pa. Sch. Medicine, Phila., 1963-64; resident anatomic pathology Presbyn.-U. Pa. Med. Ctr., Phila., 1965-66; fellow neuropathology Phila. Gen. Hosp., 1967, Ohio State U. Hosp., Columbus, 1968-69; instr. Ohio State U., 1969; asst. prof. U. Utah Sch. Medicine, Salt Lake City, 1970-76, assoc. prof., 1976-80; assoc. prof. pathology U. Conn. Sch. Medicine, Farmington, 1980-90, prof., 1990—. Contbr. articles to profl. jours. Mem. Am. Med. Women's Assn., Internat. Soc. Neuropathology, Conn. Soc. Pathologists, Am. Assn. Neuropathologists, Phi Beta Kappa, Alpha Omega Alpha. Mem. Ch. of Christ. Home: 1550 Asylum Ave West Hartford CT 06117-2805 Office: U Conn Health Ctr Dept Pathology Farmington CT 06032

GRUSH, HELEN BUTLER, educational consultant; b. Winchester, Mass., Aug. 1, 1921; d. Horace and Helen Gretchen (Avery) Butler; m. Willard Parker Grush, Aug. 29, 1942 (dec.); children: Sandra LeFlore Bergmann, Jeffrey Willard, Kimball Warren. BS, Northeastern U., 1970; MEd, Boston U., 1974. Tchr. Smith Sch., Lincoln, Mass., 1962-64; instr., author Mass. Coun. Pub. Schs., Boston, 1963-65; supr. Community Svc. Corps-Migrant, Boston, 1965-66; ednl. dir. Perceptual Edn. Rsch., Wellesley, Mass., 1966-68; asst. prof. Lesley Coll. Grad. Sch., Cambridge, Mass., 1972-80; co-founder LEAD Ednl. Resources, Lexington, Mass., 1972; author, lectr., instr. Logical Encoding and Decoding Program, 1972-85; editorial cons. Logical Encoding and Decoding Program Ednl. Resources, Bridgewater, Conn., 1985—. Mem. founding com.Pilgrim Congl. Ch., Lexington; pres. Florence Crittenden League. Mem. AAUW (bd. dirs.), Laudholm Preserve, Fla. Ctr. for the Arts, Vero Beach ARt Club. Republican. Congregationalist. Home: 200 Greytwig Rd Apt 111 Vero Beach FL 32963-1549

GRYGUTIS, BARBARA, artist. One woman show at Scottsdale Ctr. for the Arts, 1988; exhibited in group exhibns. Internat. 94 Socrates Sculpture Park, L.I. City, N.Y., 1994, Arts Festival of Atlanta, 1993, U. Ala. Nat. Site Sculpture Invitational, 1993, The Found. for Architecture and The Clay Ctr., 1993, Quadriennal Competition, Faenza, Italy, 1989, Scottsdale Ctr. for the Arts, 1986, The Vice-Pres.'s House, 1978, Herbert Johnson Mus. of Art, Cornell U., 1978, Renwick Gallery, Smithsonian Inst., 1977, Mus. of Contemporary Crafts, 1977, Mus. of Folk Art and Crafts, 1977, Everson Mus. of Art, 1977, John Michael Kohler Arts Ctr., 1977. El Presidio Nat. Register Historic Dist. adv. coun. Architecture and Design Rev. Bd., 1978-90; artist cons. to project for pub. places Urban Design, Mgmt. and Devel. Strategies for the Tucson Arts Dist., 1988. Recipient Govs. award Ariz. Women's Partnership, 1985, Award of Merit The Albuquerque Conservations Assn., 1991, Second prize Ceramics in the Urban Setting, the Second Internat. Quadrennial Competition, 1988, Individual Project Design Arts award Nat. Endowment for the Arts, 1988, Individual Artist award, 1975; project grant Tuscon Pima Arts Coalition, 1984, Ariz. Commn. on the Arts, 1984. Home: 273 N Main Ave Tucson AZ 85701

GRZENDA-BRITE, NADINE HAZELAN, nurse, educator; b. Paris, May 10, 1954; came to U.S., 1963; d. Joseph E. Jr. and Lucie Margaret (Guichard) Bryant; m. Joseph John Grzenda, Mar 17, 1978 (div. 1981); 1 child, Adrienne Lucille; m. Charles Francis Brite, May 21, 1987 (div. 1991). Attended, Wichita State U., 1972-75, 93—; ADN, Kans. C.C., Kansas City, Kans., 1982; BSN, Ft. Hays State U., 1993. RN, Kans. Neurology staff nurse Stormont Vail Regional Med. Ctr., Topeka, Kans., 1983-87; med.-surg. staff nurse St. Francis Hosp., Topeka, 1987—; adj. instr. Highland (Kans.) C.C., 1993—. Brownie troop leader Kaw Valley Girl Scout Assn., Holton, Kans., 1985-88. Democrat. Roman Catholic. Home: 918 Forest St Holton KS 66436

GUADAGNO, MARY ANN NOECKER, social scientist, consultant; b. Springville, N.Y., Sept. 21, 1952; d. Francis Casimer and Josephine Lucille (Fricano) Noecker; m. Robert George Guadagno, Aug. 29, 1970 (div. Mar. 1981). BS in Edn. cum laude, SUNY, Buffalo, 1974; MS, Ohio State U., 1977, PhD, 1978. Grad. teaching assoc. Ohio State U., Columbus, 1974-77, grad. rsch. assoc., 1977-78; asst. prof. U. Minn., St. Paul, 1978-83; cons. Nationwide Ins. Co., Columbus, 1982-83, rsch. assoc. Corp. Rsch., 1983-86, product devel. assoc., Office of Mktg., 1986-89; adjunct prof. Coll. Bus. & Pub. Adminstrn. Franklin U., Columbus, Ohio, 1985-89; lectr. Coll. Bus. Adminstrn. and Econ. Ohio Dominican Coll., Columbus, 1986-89; scientist family econ. rsch. group USDA, Washington, 1989-93; survey statistician Nat. Ctr. for Health Stats., HHS, Washington, 1993—; chair Women's Coun., DHHS, Hyattsville, Md., 1995—; mem. women in sci., 1991-93. Author: Family Inventory of Money Management, 1982, Family Inventory, 1982; contbr. articles to profl. jours., 1978—. Com. mem. United Way, Mkt Rsch. Info. Exchange, Columbus, Ohio. Recipient Spl. Recognition award Ohio House Reps., 1987, Cert. Grad. award Columbus Area Leadership Program, 1987, Cert. Appreciation award Am. Mktg. Assn., 1987, Cert. Merit award U.S. Dept. Agr., 1991. Mem. Columbus Area Leadership Program, Ohio State U. Coll. Human Ecology Alumni. Republican. Roman Catholic. Home: 4853 Cordell Ave Apt 921 Bethesda MD 20814-3024 Office: HHS Nat Ctr for Health Stats 6525 Belcrest Rd Rm 915 Hyattsville MD 20782-2003

GUARD, PATRICIA J., federal agency administrator; b. Lafayette, Ind., June 9, 1948. BS, Purdue U., MS. Therapist speech, lang. and hearing Logansport Area Joint Spl. Svcs. Coop., 1974-76, supr. speech dept., 1976-78; dir. spl. edn. Boone-Clinton-NW Hendricks Count Joint Svcs. Spl. Edn. Coop., 1978-81; rsch. asst. U.S. Ho. of Reps., 1981-82; legis. specialist Office Legis. and Pub. Affairs, 1983-84; acting dir. Office Spl. Edn. Programs Dept. Edn., 1985-86, deputy dir. Office Spl. Edn. Programs, 1984-85, 86-87, sr. legis. analyst Office Legis. and Pub. Affairs, 1987-90, dir. policy and planning staff Office Spl. Edn. and Rehabilitative Svcs., 1990-92, dep. dir. Office Spl. Edn., 1992-93, acting dir. Office Spl. Edn. Programs, 1993-94; mem. sr. exec. svc. Office Edn. Programs, Washington, 1994—. Vice chmn., trustee Arlington Cmty. Residence, Inc., 1993, bd. dirs., 1989—. Fellow Inst. Ednl. Leadership, 1981; recipient Disting. Alumni award Purdue U., 1989, Mentor award Dept. Edn., 1994. Office: Spl Edn Programs 330 C St SW Washington DC 20202

GUARDALABENE, JEANNINE SUE, marriage and family therapist; b. Walton, N.Y., June 14, 1952; d. James Harby and Ruth Louise (Le Tourneur) Courtney; m. Anthony E. Guardalabene. AA, Citrus Coll., Azusa, Calif., 1972; BA, Azusa Pacific Coll., 1974; MA, N.W. Christian Coll., 1994. Elementary sch. tchr. Azusa Unified Schs., 1974-78; sales rep. Red Carpet Real Estate, Claremont, Calif., 1978-79; pres. Statewide Transmissin Svc., Inc., Elmira, Oreg., 1982-94; owner, cons. ReGard, Eugene, Oreg., 1992—; family therapist pvt. practice, Eugene, 1994—. Co-author: (workbook) ReGard: Men and Women Working Together, 1992. Case mgr. United Way, Eugene, 1991-93; crisis phone vol. Women Space, Eugene, 1991-93; vol., contbr. ARC, Oreg., 1994. Mem. AAUW, Women in the Arts, Women's Bus. Network. Republican. Office: Re Gard 350 E 11th Ave Apt 3 Eugene OR 97401-3226

GUASTAFESTE, ROBERTA HARRISON, cellist; b. N.Y.C., Feb. 20, 1929; d. Michael and Rena (Fish) Harrison; m. Joseph R. Guastafeste, June 21, 1953 (div. 1982); children: Camille Avellano, Manon Spadaro. Student, L.A. City Coll., 1946-49, UCLA, 1949-51. Cellist Dallas Symphony Orch., 1950-60; instr. So. Meth. U., Dallas, 1951-60; prin. cellist Arie Crown Theatre, Chgo., 1966-86, Auditorium and Schubert Theaters, Chgo., 1986-89; instr. North Park Coll., Chgo., 1975-89; sole propr. A440 String Instrument Shop, Chgo., 1982—; pvt. cello instr. Mem. ACLU, Nat. Mus. for Women in Arts, U.S. Holocaust Mus., Art Inst. Chgo., Chgo. Mus. Contemporary Art, Chamber Music Am., Greenpeace, Arts Club Chgo., Sierra Club. Democrat. Jewish. Home: 2031 N Halsted St Chicago IL 60614

GUBBIN, BARBARA ASHLEY BRENDON, librarian; b. Calcutta, India, Jan. 9, 1952; d. Richard F.B. and Rosemarie A. (Walker) G.; m. J. Sidney Cunningham, Aug. 16, 1975. BA, U. Birmingham, 1972; diploma in library sci., U. London, 1976, MA, 1977. Librarian Fawcett Library, London, 1976-77; reference librarian San Antonio Pub. Lib., 1977-79; collection devel cons. San Antonio Area Library System, 1979-80, coordinator, 1980-85; coordinator Houston Area Library System, 1985-89; asst. dir. Houston Pub. Libr., 1989-95, dir., 1995—. Bd. dirs. Tex. Coun. for the Humanities, 1993—, treas., 1996; bd. dirs. Houston READ Commn., 1995—, sec.; OCLC Users Coun. del., 1993—, mem. exec. com., 1996—. Mem. ALA, Tex. Libr. Assn. (pres. 1996, Outstanding New Libr. 1983). Office: Houston Pub Libr 500 McKinney Ave Houston TX 77002-2534

GUCIARDO, JOAN, family and consumer sciences educator; b. Centralia, Ill., Oct. 23, 1951; d. Ralph and Dorothy Margaret (Liszewski) Prusacki; m. John Edward Guciardo, Aug. 10, 1974. BS, Ea. Ill. U., 1973, MS, 1986. Tchr. family and consumer scis. Althoff Cath. H.S., Belleville, Ill., 1973-74, Assumption H.S., E. St. Louis, Ill., 1974-75, O'Fallon Twp. H.S., 1975—. Mem. NAFE, Am. Assn. Family and Consumer Scis. (cert.), Ill. Vocation Assn., Profl. Dressmakers Assn. Roman Catholic. Home: 204 Ross Ln Belleville IL 62220 Office: O'Fallon Twp H S 600 S Smiley O'Fallon IL 62269

GUDANEK, LOIS BASSOLINO, social worker; b. N.Y.C., Jan. 28, 1944; d. Frank and Anna (Scarlata) Bassolino; m. Richard Stanley Gudanek, Sept. 3, 1977. BA in Anthropology and Sociology, Queens Coll., 1973; postgrad., Hunter Coll., 1973-76, JRW Inst. Alcohol Studies, 1988-89; student Eating Disorders Inst., Rollins Coll., 1991; MSW, Fordham U., 1994. Cert. alcoholism counselor, social worker, HIV counselor, N.Y. Student intern Arms Acres, Carmel, N.Y., 1988-89; adult therapist Arms Acres, Carmel, 1989-91; vocat. counselor Westchester County Med. Ctr.-Alcoholism Treatment Svcs., Yonkers, 1991-94, Westchester County Med. Ctr.-WEST-PREP, Valhalla, N.Y., 1994-96; pvt. practice White Plains, N.Y., 1994—; social worker The Week-End Ctr., Mt. Kisco, N.Y., 1996—; lectr. JRW Inst. on Alcohol Studies, Yonkers, N.Y., 1991, St. Thomas Aquinas Coll., 1994; presenter in field. Mem. NASW, Internat. Assn. Eating Disorders Profls. (sec. tri-state region 1989-91, vice-chmn. 1991—, ednl. coord. 1992—), Nat. Assn. Alcoholism and Drug Abuse Counselors, N.Y. Fedn. Alcoholism and Chem. Dependency Counselors, N.Y. Womens Coalition on Chem. Dependency (treas. 1991-92, bd. dirs. 1994—), Adoptees' Liberty Movement Assn. Office: The Week-End Ctr 120 Kisco Ave Mount Kisco NY 10549 also: 200 Bloomingdale Rd Ste 1 White Plains NY 10605

GUDMUNDSON, BARBARA ROHRKE, ecologist; b. Chgo.; d. Lloyd Ernest and Helen (Bullard) Rohrke; m. Valtyr Emil Gudmundson, June 14, 1951 (dec. Dec. 1982); children: Holly Mekkín Leighton, Martha Rannveig. BA, U. Tenn., 1950; MA, Mankato State Coll., 1965; PhD, Iowa State U., 1969. Microbiologist Hektoen Inst. & Ill. Ctr. Hosp., Chgo., 1950-52; immunologist Jackson Meml. Lab., Bar Harbor, Maine, 1952-54; dist. ecologist Corps of Engrs., St. Paul, 1971-72; sr. ecologist North Star Rsch. Inst., Mpls., 1972-76; staff engr. Met. Waste Control Commn., St. Paul, 1976-77; pres., prin. ecologist Ecosystem Rsch. Svc./Upper Midwest, Mpls., 1978—; pvt. practice as cons. ecologist, Des Moines and Mpls., 1968-70; mem. Citizens League Task Force on the Mississippi Riverfront, 1973-74; mem. adv. com. Mpls. Lakes Water Quality, Mpls., 1974-75; field ecologist Mississippi River Canoe Expdn., Coll. of the Atlantic, Bar Harbor, 1979; mem. City of Mpls. Capital Long-Range Improvements Commn. Author: V. Emil Gudmundson: Icelandic Canadian Unitarian, A Personal Biography, 1991; editor-in-chief The Icelandic Unitarian Connection, 1984; contbr. articles to profl. jours. Mem. from 61st dist. Dem.-Farmer-Labor Ctr. Com., Minn., 1978-80; mgr. Minnehaha Creek Watershed Dist., Hennepin & Carver Counties, Minn., 1979-83; mem. Capital Long-Range Improvements Com., Mpls., 1981; mem. steering com. Nokomis East Neighborhood Assn., 1995—. River Basin Ecology grantee Iowa Acad. Scis., Cedar Falls, 1976, Mississippi River Ecology grantee Freshwater Biol. Rsch. Found., Navarre, Minn., 1979, Fulbright Sr. Rsch. grantee USA/Iceland Fulbright Commns., Washington, Reykjavik, 1986, 92; recipient Anita Hill Courage and Justice award, 1994. Mem. NOW (Minn. state bd. 1979—), Ecol. Soc. Am. (pres. Minn. chpt. 1971-75), Geol. Soc. Minn. (pres. 1981), Phycological Soc. Am., Internat. Assn. Diatom Rsch., Sigma Xi, Phi Kappa Phi, Sigma Delta Epsilon-Grad. Women in Sci. (nat. membership com. 1990-93, chmn. 1991-93). Unitarian Universalist. Home: 5505 28th Ave S Minneapolis MN 55417-1957 Office: Ecosystem Rsch Svc/Upper Midwest PO Box 17102 Minneapolis MN 55417-0102

GUDNITZ, ORA M. COFEY, secondary education educator; b. Crawfordsville, Ark., Jan. 24, 1934; d. Daniel S. and Mary (Oglesby) Cofey; children: Ingrid M. Hunt, Carl Erik, Katrina Beatrice. BA, Lane Coll., Jackson, Tenn., 1955; MEd, Temple U., 1969; student, U. Copenhagen, 1957; MA in Theol. Studies, Ea. Bapt. Theol. Sem., Pa., 1995, Eastern Bapt. Theol. Sem., Pa., 1995. Cert. permanent English, social studies and French tchr., Pa. Tchr. English, chmn. dept. Sayre Jr. High Sch., Phila.; tchr. English, Overbrook High Sch., Phila.; founder, exec. dir. Young Communicators Workshop, Inc.; lectr., Denmark. Contbr. articles to newspapers, poetry to anthologies. Recipient award Chapel of Four Chaplains, 1976, Women in Edn. award, 1988; grantee Haas Found., 1977, also others. Mem. Nat. Coun. Tchrs. English, Assn. for Ednl. Communication and Tech., Phi Delta Kappa, Delta Sigma Theta.

GUENTHER, SHEILA WALSH, sales and promotion executive; b. Hamilton, Mont., Sept. 19, 1933; d. Leo Frederick and Edith Frances (Leonard) W.; James William Guenther, June 29, 1957; children: Kurt Dennis, Kelly David, Gayla Koleen. BA cum laude, Wash. State Coll., 1955. Layout artist The Bon Marche, Spokane, Wash., 1955-56; sales promotion mgr. The Bon Marche (formally The Paris), Great Falls, Mont., 1956-57; faculty staff artist info. and pub. rels. Mont. State Coll., Bozeman, 1958-61; sales promotion mgr. David's House Name Brands, Wichita, Kans., 1961-65; writer, graphic artist Warren Printing, Chamberlain Graphics, Olympia, Wash., 1965-73; art instr. Wichita State U.; writer, graphics freelancer Prescott Co. Advt. Pub. RelS., Olympia, Wash., 1970-77; instr. Clark Coll., Vancouver, Wash., 1979-81; sales promotion dir. Vancouver Furniture, 1974-94; pres. Walsh Guenther & Assocs., Inc., Vancouver, 1982—; Printer's Ink juror; mem. adv. coun. Columbian newspaper, 1996—. Co-author: Vancouver on the Columbia Business History, 1986. Columbian People in Need Adv. Com., Ellen Goodman Project for YWCA Emergency Shelter, Hands Across Clark County Stop Hunger Campaign; co-founder Swift Charity Auction, 1977. Recipient Spokane and Wichita Newspaper and TV Advt. award, Sertoma, Benjamin Franklin Svc. award, 1984, Woman of Achievement award YWCA, 1988. Mem. Wichita Press Women, Advt. Fedn., Oreg. Women in Comms., Retail Advt./Mktg. Assn., Columbian Newspaper Adv. Coun., Delta Phi Delta. Democrat. Office: PO Box 61628 Vancouver WA 98666-1628

GUERKE, GWENDOLYN FRANKEL, columnist, editor; b. Milford, Del., Sept. 16, 1947; d. Bernard and Frances (Emory) Frankel; m. Stephen L. Guerke, June 6, 1970 (div. Aug., 1987); children: Daniel, Matthew. BA, U. Del., 1969. Editor Milford (Del.) Chronicle, 1978-79, 96—; features editor, assignment editor Del. State News, Dover, 1989-94, columnist, 1994—. Office: Del State News PO Box 737 Dover DE 19903 also: Milford Chronicle PO Box 297 Milford DE 19963

GUERRA, MARTHA C., elementary educator; b. El Paso, Tex., Dec. 20, 1950; d. Serapio Q. and Manuela (Lizardo) Chavez; m. Raymond B. Guerra, Jr., June 12, 1971; children: Raymond Gabriel, Raphael Stephen. Assoc. degree, E.P.C.C., El Paso, 1977; BS in Edn. with honors, U. Tex., El Paso, 1990. Accounts payable clk. Continental Water Supply, El Paso, 1970-72; receptionist Am. Hosp. Supplies/Converters, El Paso, 1975-77; substitute tchr. Clint (Tex.) Ind. Sch. Dist., 1972-85, Ysleta Ind. Sch. Dist., El Paso, 1986-90; tchr. Myrtle Copper Sch. Socorro Ind. Sch. Dist., El Paso, 1990—; pres., treas. PTA Clint Ind. Sch. Dist., 1983-85; pres. parent-tchr. orgn. Socorro Ind. Sch. Dist., 1991-93. Jr. & sr. v.p. VFW Ladies Aux., 1972-74. Mem. Tex. State Tchrs. Assn., Kappa Delta Pi (historian 1990). Roman Catholic. Address: PO Box 612 Clint TX 79836-0612

GUERRANT, HELEN ORZEL, artist; b. Boston, Mar. 19, 1920; d. Staley Orzel and Jo Ann Hite; m. Paul Nelson Horton (div.); m. Robert Shields Guerrant, Mar. 1, 1947; children: Somerset Orzel, David Denison, Daniel Guerin, Emerson Roy. BS, Cornell U., 1942; postgrad., U. Va., Roanoke Coll., Radford Coll., Hollins Coll., Va. Poly. Inst. Asst. geneticist Atlee Burpee Seed Co., Doylestown, Pa.; with diagnostic dept. N.Y. State Health Dept., N.Y.C.; pilot Martha Ann Woodrum Svcs., Woodrum Field, Roanoke, Va.; judge Nat. Coun. Flower Show. One woman shows include Palette Art Gallery, White House Gallery, Roanoke Fine Arts Ctr., Martinsville Fine Arts Ctr., Va. Employment Commn., Olde Eng. Frame; exhibited in group shows Valentine Mus., Richmond, Va., Empire State Bldg., N.Y.C., Reynolds Metal Co., Norfolk (Va.) Mus. Art Svc. and Art Lending, Winston-Salem (N.C.) Gallery Contemporary Art, 20th Century Gallery Contemporary Art, Williamsburg, Va., L.I. Art Show, Lynchburg Area Show, Roanoke Area Artists Show, Roanoke Coll. Ann. Shows, Wesley Found., Dominion Bank, Roanoke, Sovran Bank, United Va. Bank, Richmond, Va. Commonwealth Bankshares, Richmond, Miller and Rhoads Sidewalk Show, AAUW Heironimus Show, Roanoke Fine Arts Ctr., Lynchburg Fine Arts Ctr., Roanoke Area Shows, Lynchburg Area Shows, Radford Coll., Roanoke Coll., Bath County Regional Area Show. Active Docent Guild, Miller and Main Galleries, White House Galleries, New River Arts Coun., Arts Coun. of Blue Ridge. With USN, 1943-45. Recipient Prints Bath County Area Show award, Best Oil Bath County Regional Area Show award, Best in Show award Dogwood Festival, 1st Watercolor award Roanoke Coll. Show, Watercolor award Bath County Regional Art Show, Best in Show award Lynchburg Area Show, Watercolor award Roanoke Coll. Art Show, Watercolor award AAUW Show, Oil award Radford Coll. Show, Drawings and Graphics award Roanoke Coll. Show. Mem. Am. Legion, Va. Watercolor Soc., League of Roanoke Artists, Morning Music Club. Home: 1816 Windsor Ave SW Roanoke VA 24015-2340

GUERRINI, SUSAN CAROL, vocal music specialist; b. Phila., May 8, 1949; d. Henry Martin and Mary Agnes (Schaller) Seybold; m. Frank C. Guerrini, June 12, 1971; children: Dominic C., James P., Benjamin J. B Music Edn., Temple U., 1971, postgrad., 1991; postgrad., Rowan Coll., 1992, MA in Tchg. Music, 1995. Cert. music tchr., N.J. Vocal music specialist Mantua (N.J.) Twp., 1971-74, Moorestown (N.J.) Pub. Schs., 1974-76, Evans Sch., Marlton, N.J., 1976—; asst. choral dir. Cherokee H.S., Marlton, 1991—, pianist, 1988—; organist Assumption Ch., Atco, N.J., 1986-88. Composer children's songs; author children's plays. Mem. ASCD, Music Educators Nat. Conf. Home: 217 Dock Rd Atco NJ 08004 Office: Evans Sch Rt 73 Marlton NJ 08053

GUEST, BARBARA, author, poet; b. Wilmington, N.C., Sept. 6, 1920; d. James Harvey and Ann (Hetzel) Pinson; m. Lord Stephen Haden-Guest, 1948 (div. 1954); 1 child, Hon. Hadley; m. Trumbull Higgins, 1954 (dec.); 1 child, Jonathan van Lennep. AB, U. Calif., Berkeley, 1943. Editorial assoc. Art News, 1951-59. Author: (plays) The Ladies Choice, 1953, The Office, 1961, Port, 1965; (poems) The Location of Things, 1960, Poems, 1963, The Blue Stairs, 1968, Moscow Mansions, 1973, (with Sheila Isham) I Ching: Poems and Lithographs, 1969, The Countess from Minneapolis, 1976, The Türler Losses, 1980, Biography, 1981, Quilts, 1981, Fair Realism, 1989, (with June Felter) Musicality, 1989, (with Richard Tuttle) The Altos, 1991, Defensive Rapture, 1993, Selected Poems, 1995, Stripped Tales, 1995; (novel) Seeking Air, 1978; (biography) Herself Defined: The Poet H.D. and Her World, 1984.; (poems) Quill, Solitary Apparition, 1996. Recipient Longview award Longview Found., 1960, Laurence Lipton prize in lit., 1990, San Francisco State U. award for poetry, 1994, Fund for Poetry award, 1995, Am.'s award, 1996, Pen West Josephine Miles award, 1996; Yaddo fellow, 1958; Nat. Endowment for the Arts grantee, 1978. Address: 1301 Milvia St Berkeley CA 94709-1934

GUEST, MARILYN KAY, art gallery director; b. Los Alamos, N.Mex., Jan. 24, 1964; d. Alan Douglas Larrabee and Sandra Kay (Emmons) Dolak; m. Brian Keith Guest, Mar. 26, 1982 (dec. Oct. 1993); children: Molly K., Hannah E., Dylan M. AA in Electronic and Mech. Drafting, Pueblo (Colo.) C.C., 1986; BS in Fine Art and Sociology, U. So. Colo., 1996. Tchr.'s asst. Dist. A, Fayetteville, N.C., 1993-94; asst. dir. U. So. Colo. Art Gallery, Pueblo, 1995—; bd. dirs. Site Based Accountability, Dist. 60 Accountability. Dir. women's programs Women and Non-traditional Student's Ctr., Pueblo, 1993-94, mentor, 1994-95. Mem. Las Hermanas, Alpha Chi.

GUFFEY, BARBARA BRADEN, elementary education educator; b. Pitts., Aug. 10, 1948; d. James Arthur and Dorothy (Barrett) Braden; 1 child, William Butler Guffey III. BA in Elem. Edn., Westminster Coll., New Wilmington, Pa., 1970; MEd in Elem. Edn., Slippery Rock State Coll., 1973; postgrad., U. Pitts., Duquesne U., Westminster Coll. Cert. tchr., elem. and secondary history and govt. edn, elem. prin. Tchr. Shaler Area Sch. Dist., Glenshaw, Pa., lang. arts area specialist, 1988-91, 92-93, grad. level chmn., 1991-92, mem. instrnl. support team, curriculum support math./sci., 1994—; mem. Shaler Area Stretegic Planning Core Team, 1992-96; mem. A.S.S.E.T. Leadership Team, 1995—; condr. seminars and workshops in field. Pres. alumni coun. Westminster Coll., 1996—, v.p., 1995-96, chmn. homecoming all-alumni luncheon, 1991-93, homecoming chair, 1995, 96; active Burchfield Elem. Sch. PTA; active Glenshaw Presbyn. Ch. Mem. NEA, Children with Attention Deficit Disorders, Pa. Edn. Assn. Shaler Area Edn. Assn. (v.p., negotiator, former rec. sec., bldg. rep., editor newsletter), Wetern Pa. Geneal. Soc. (rec. sec., bd. dirs. 1992—), Perry Historians, Indiana County Geneal. and Hist. Soc., Juniata County Hist. Soc., Armstrong County Hist. and Mus. Soc., Westminster Coll. Women's Club Pitts. (treas. 1994—, former pres., v.p., sec., ways and means chair), Kappa Delta Pi. Office: Burchfield Elem Sch 1500 Burchfield Rd Allison Park PA 15101-4000

GUFFEY, EDITH A., religious organization administrator. Sec. United Ch. of Christ, Cleve. Office: United Ch of Christ 700 Prospect Ave E Cleveland OH 44115-1131*

GUGGENHEIMER, ELINOR, civic leader, writer; b. N.Y.C., Apr. 11, 1912; d. Nathan and Lillian (Fox) Coleman; m. Randolph Guggenheimer, June 2, 1932; children: Charles, Randolph Jr. Student, Vassar Coll., 1929-31; BA, Barnard Coll., 1938; DHL (hon.), Marymount-Manhattan Coll., 1987, CUNY Grad. Ctr., 1993. Dir. N.Y.C. Audio-Visual Tng. Office, 1943-44, Day Care Coun. of N.Y., N.Y.C., 1948-60; commr. City Planning, N.Y.C., 1960-67; on-air host, "Straight Talk" WOR-TV, N.Y.C., 1970-73; chmn. Def. Adv. Com. on Women in Svcs., Washington, 1963, 64; commr. N.Y.C. Dept. Consumer Affairs, 1974-78; dir. Coun. Sr. Ctrs. and Svcs., N.Y.C., 1978-83; dir., pres. Nat. Child Care Action Campaign, N.Y.C., 1983-92; lectr. Ctr. for Urban Affairs, New Sch. for Social Rsch., N.Y., 1965-70; tchr. Tchrs. Coll., Columbia U., 1969. Author: Planning for Parks, 1968, The Pleasure of Your Company, 1990; lyricist: Potholes, 1982. Bd. dirs. Community Svc. Soc., 1953—, Jewish Assn. Svcs. to the Aged, 1968—; pres. N.Y. Women's Agenda, 1991—. Recipient Finley award City Coll. Alumni, Spl. award City of N.Y. Human Resource Adminstrn., 1984; named one of 100 Most Important Women in U.S. Ladies Home Jour., 1980, 88, Louise Waterman Wise Woman of Yr. Nat. Coun. Jewish Women, 1974, One of 75 Most Influential Women in Bus. Crain's N.Y., 1966. Mem. Bus. & Profl. Women, Cosmopolitan Club, Women's City Club, City Club of N.Y. (bd. dirs. 1978-85), Lexington Democratic Club, Internat. Women's Forum (bd. dirs., founder, former pres.). Jewish. Office: New York Womens Agenda 218 W 40th St Rm 206 New York NY 10018-1509

GUGLIUZZA, KRISTENE KOONTZ, transplant and general surgery educator; b. Siloam Springs, Ark., May 2, 1956; d. Lloyd Lawson Koontz Jr. and Helen Ruth (Camfield) Smith; m. Joseph Thomas Gugliuzza III, Sept. 3, 1989. AS, Lake Land Coll., Mattoon, Ill., 1977; BS with honors, Ea. Ill. U., Charleston, 1978; MD, U. Ill., Rockford, 1982. Diplomate Am. Bd. Surgery. Intern dept. surgery Tulane U. Med. Sch. and Affiliated Hosps., New Orleans, 1982-83, resident, 1983-87, fellow divsn. transplantation, 1987-89, instr. surgery, rsch. assoc. in surgery and transplantation, 1989-90; asst. prof. U. Tex. Med. Br., Galveston, 1990—; spl. fellow in pancreas transplantation U. Minn., Mpls., 1989; courtesy staff St. Mary's Hosp., Galveston, 1991-96; recovery surgeon La. Organ Procurement Agy., New Orleans, 1989-90; presenter in field. Contbr. articles to med. jours. Fellow ACS; mem. AMA, Am. Diabetes Assn., Galveston County Med. Soc., Tex. Med. Assn., Cell Transplant Soc., Am. Med. Women's Assn., Assn. Women Surgeons, Singleton Surg. Soc., Assn. Acad. Surgery, Transplantation Soc., Tex. Transplant Soc., Tulane Surg. Soc., Southwestern Surg. Conf., N.Y. Acad. Scis., Am. Soc. Gen. Surgeons, Am. Soc. Transplant Physicians, Tex. Surg. Soc. Office: U Tex Med Br Dept Surgery 301 University Blvd Galveston TX 77555-0542

GUIDA, PAT, information broker, literature chemist; b. Highland Park, Mich., Aug. 30, 1929; d. Wilfred Bernard and Patricia Mary (Kelly) Graham; m. Alexander Bohr, 1948 (div. 1965); m. Edward Silvio Guida, Aug. 29, 1965; children: Niels Graham, Eric Alexander. Student, Regis Coll., 1946-48, Rutgers U., 1952-55; BS cum laude, Fairleigh Dickinson U., 1961. Asst. librarian Warner-Lambert Research Inst., Morris Plains, N.J., 1961-64; librarian Reaction Motors Div. Thiokol, Denville, N.J., 1964-69; mgr., info. ctr. Foster D. Snell Div., Booz Allen & Hamilton Inc., Florham Park, N.J., 1969-80; pres. Pat Guida Assocs., Fairfield, N.J.; mem. Sci. Adv. Bd. EPA, Washington, 1978-82, Library Com. Chemists Club, N.Y.C., 1983-89. Editor: Chemical Digest, 1971-74. Pres. PTA, Sparta, N.J., 1959-60. Mem. Am. Chem. Soc., Inst. Food Technologists (profl.). Office: 24 Spielman Rd Fairfield NJ 07004-3412

GUIDER, DEBORAH L., lawyer; b. Stamford, Conn., Jan. 23, 1956. AB magna cum laude, Mount Holyoke Coll., 1977; JD cum laude, Georgetown U., 1983. Ptnr. Chadbourne & Parke LLP; mem. Law and Policy Internat. Bus., 1982-83. Contbr. articles to profl. jours. Mem. N.Y. State Bar Assn., Phi Beta Kappa. Office: Chadbourne & Parke LLP 30 Rockefeller Plz New York NY 10112*

GUIDONE, HEATHER LYNN CHRISTINA, executive assistant; b. Warwick, N.Y., Sept. 15, 1970; d. John G. and Patricia L. (Kelly) Roppolo; m. Louis Michael Guidone, Oct. 19, 1991. Cert. in bus. tech., Orange-Ulster Tech. Sch., 1988. Office mgr. Inter Innovation LeFebure, Inc., N.Y.C., 1988-89; asst. to v.p. corp. fin. divsn. Security Pacific Merchant Bank Corp., N.Y.C., 1989-91; exec. asst. to mng. dir./worldwide dept. head Morgan Stanley & Co., Inc., N.Y.C., 1991—, investment banking unit adminstr., 1991—. Mem. Am.-Italian Cancer Found., 1995—. Mem. NAFE, Internat. Profl. Secs. Inc. (exec. com.), Endometriosis Rsch. Assn., Micro Soc. Inc. (asst. to bd. dirs. 1993—). Democrat. Roman Catholic. Home: 24 Belfield Ave Staten Island NY 10312 Office: Morgan Stanley & Co Inc 1585 Broadway New York NY 10036

GUIDRY, MARY LEE, nursing educator, legal consultant; b. Glenmora, La., Nov. 25, 1928; d. James Thomas and Myrtle Lillian (Young) Walker; m. James Lawrence Guidry, May 29, 1961; children: Michael Wayne, James, Stephen Edward. BS, Sacred Heart Dominican Coll., 1962; MS, Tex. Woman's U., 1970; EdD, U. Houston. RN, Tex. Staff nurse pediatrics St. Joseph's Hosp., Houston, 1950-55; staff nurse, head nurse, supr. VA Hosp., Houston, 1955-61; instr., assoc. dean Prairie View A&M Coll., 1963-70; supr., instr. M.D. Anderson Hosp., Houston, 1971-74; asst. prof. nursing U. St. Thomas, Houston, 1974—; assoc. prof. nursing Prairie View Coll. Nursing, 1985—; coordinator R.N. sect. faculty devel. in nursing project So. Regional Edn. Bd., 1977-82; legal cons. Perdue, Turner, Berry, Law firm, Houston, 1980—; expert witness med. malpractice, 1977—. Instr. breast self exam. Am. Cancer Soc., Houston, 1979; mem. Cancer awareness Black Adv. Group, Cancer Info. Service, 1981-84, cert., 1982. Mem. Tex. Nurses Assn. (chmn. council on practice 1979-84, dist. bd. mem. 1983-84), Chi Eta Phi, Sigma Theta Tau, Sigma Gamma Rho. Democrat. Baptist. Home: 2418 Oakdale St Houston TX 77004-7428

GUIGNARD, MONICA GABRIELLE, human resources administrator; b. Syracuse, N.Y., Oct. 4, 1970; d. Michael James and Susan Jessie (Andrews) G. BA, Mary Washington Coll., 1992. Receptionist AAO-HNS, Alexandria, Va., 1992-94; human resources adminstr. The Mills Corp., Arlington, Va., 1994—. Mng. editor News from the St. Mem. NAFE, Soc. Human Resources Mgmt. Office: The Mills Corp 1300 Wilson Blvd Ste 400 Arlington VA 22209

GUILL, MARGARET FRANK, pediatrics educator, medical researcher; b. Atlanta, Jan. 18, 1948; d. Vernon Rhinehart and Margaret N. (Tichenor) Frank; m. Marshall Anderson Guill III, July 6, 1974; children: Daniel Marshall, Laura Elizabeth. BA, Agnes Scott Coll., 1969; MD, Med. Coll. Ga., 1972. Diplomate Am. Bd. Pediatrics, Am. Bd. Pediatrics subbd. pulmonology, Am. Bd. Allergy and Immunology, Nat. Bd. Med. Examiners. Resident in pediatrics Kaiser Found. Hosp., San Francisco, 1976-78, fellow in allergy, 1978-79; staff physician Waipahu (Hawaii) Clinic, 1973-76; intern in internal medicine Med. Coll. Ga., Augusta, 1973, resident in pediatrics, 1974, fellow in allergy and immunology, 1979-80, from asst. prof. to prof. pediatrics, 1981—; also chief sect. pediatric pulmonology and dir. Asthma Ctr. Med Coll. Ga., Augusta, dir. Cystic Fibrosis Ctr., 1990—; spkr. in field. Host Healthwatch weekly program WJBF-TV, 1982-83; contbr. articles to profl. jours. Active Reid Meml. Presbyn. Ch.; vol. tchr. Episcopal Day Sch., 1982-85; career day participant Acad. Richmond County, 1982, 83; med. advisor Augusta Area Allergy and Asthma Support Group, 1984-86; adv. bd. East Cen. br. Am. Lung Assn. Ga., 1985—, program of work com., 1987—, bd. dirs., 1987—, program coordinating com., 1990-91, exec. bd. 1989-91, adv. bd. Asthma Ski Mates Am., 1990; med. staff Camp Breathe Easy, 1985—, med. dir. 1996. Recipient Mosby Book award, 1973; rsch. grantee BRSG, 1981-86, Del Labs., 1982, Merrell-Dow, 1983, 84, Elan Pharms., 1986, Am. Lung Assn. Ga., 1986, 87, Hollister-Stier, 1986, Fisons Corp., 1989, 91-93, 95, Med. Coll. Ga., 1989, Am. Heart Assn., 1991, Genentech, 1991-96, Miles, 1992, Clintrials, 1995. Fellow Am. Acad. Pediat., Am. Coll. Chest Physicians, Am. Acad. Allergy and Immunology, Am. Coll. Allergy, Am. Assn. Cert. Allergists; mem. Med. Assn. Ga., Richmond County Med. Soc., Allergy and Immunology Soc. Ga., S.E. Allergy Assn. (Hal Davison award 1985), Am. Assn. Clin. Immunologists and Allergists, Ga. Thoracic Soc., Am. Thoracic Soc., Assn. for Care Asthma, Alpha Omega Alpha. Home: 2247 Pickens Rd Augusta GA 30904-4462 Office: Med Coll Ga Dept Pediatrics Augusta GA 30912

GUILLEMETTE, GLORIA VIVIAN, dressmaker, designer; b. North Attleboro, Mass., June 27, 1929; d. Wilfred Anthony Roy and Sylviana (Bonnoyer) King; student Nat. Sch. Dress Design, 1976; m. Thomas William Guillemette, Mar. 24, 1963; children: Sylvia Marie, Katherine Anne, John Thomas. Machine operator dress mfg. cos., 1945-60; asst. to dressmaker and designer, Windsor, Conn., 1960-63; owner Mrs. G's Studio, Enfield, Conn., 1963-87; dir. Fashion Show, 1973, 76. Cub Scout commr. Boy Scouts Am., 1979-85; mem. Enfield Fair Rent Commn., 1979-87; justice of peace Conn., 1979—; mem. Republican Town Com., 1976-91; sec. United Meth. Women, 1977-82; mem. Enfield Fair Rent Commn., 1979-87, Presdl. Task Force, 1982-83. Club: Republican Women (pres. 1995—).

GUILLERMO, LINDA SUE, clinical social worker; b. Chgo., July 4, 1951; d. Triponio Pascua and Helen Elizabeth (Moskal) G.; B.A., U. Ill., Chgo., 1973, M.S.W., 1975, postgrad., 1980; postgrad. Jane Addams Coll. Social Work, 1980-82; Diplomate in clin. social work, 1987. Mktg. research interviewer Rabin Research Co., Chgo., 1970-73; mktg. research interviewer, coder Marcor Mktg. Research, Inc., Chgo., 1973-75; social work intern Child and Family Services, Chgo., 1973-74, Chgo. Bd. Edn., 1974-75; social worker, therapist child abuse and neglect, case investigator, case planning cons., social service program planner Ill. Dept. Children and Family Services, Chgo., 1975-78, social service program planner, contract negotiator, monitoring agt. Central Resources Contracts and Grants, 1978-79; real estate sales person Sentry Realty, Chgo., 1976—; social worker, therapist, program coordinator, casework supr. of child abuse assessment and intervention program, proposal writer Casa Central, Chgo., 1979-82, casework cons. of child abuse assessment and intervention program, proposal writer, program dir. and casework supr. of early intervention program, 1979-85; social worker, clin. supr. Chgo. Bd. Edn., 1985—; tng. specialist City Coll. of Chgo., 1980; adj. asso. researcher Asher Feren Law Office, Chgo., 1980-81. Treas. Greenleaf Condominium Assn., Chgo., 1980-81, sec., 1987-88, interim pres. 1988, regional rep. North Ill. Assn. of Sch. Social Workers, 1986-87, Lic. real estate salesperson, Ill. Mem. Nat. Assn. Social Workers (register clin. social workers), Acad. Cert. Social Workers, Ill. Cert. Lic. Social Workers, North Side Real Estate Bd.

GUILMET, GLENDA JEAN, artist; b. Tacoma, Wash., Mar. 28, 1957; d. Cody Calvin Black and Maria Isabel Rivera; m. George Michael Guilmet, May 24, 1980; children: Michelle Rene, Douglas James. Student, Clover Park Vocat. Tech. Inst., 1982-83; BA in Bus. Adminstrn., U. Puget Sound, 1981, BA in Art, 1989. Freelance photographer Tacoma, 1976—; women's sports photographer U. Puget Sound, Tacoma, 1977-78, asst. photographer, 1978-79; visual artist Tacoma, 1982—; photographic cons. Puyallup Tribe of Indians, Tacoma, 1984; on-call photographer Puyallup Tribal Health Authority, Tacoma, 1984-86, represented by Sacred Circle Gallery Am. Indian Art, Seattle, Mahler Fine Arts, Seattle, Arts Comm. Internat., Phila.; instr. sculpture Tacoma Arts Commn., 1989; guest lectr. U. Puget Sound, 1990, 94; grants juror Artist Trust, Seattle, 1990; video festival juror Tacoma Mcpl. TV, 1990; photography competition juror Washington State PTA Reflections Com., 1995. Contbr. photographs to various publs.; one woman shows include Stage Door Gallery, Tacoma Little Theatre, 1993, Seattle U. Women's Ctr., 1994, Instituto de Cultura Puertorriquena, Jayuya, Carolina and Caguana, P.R., 1994, 95, Galleria on Broadway, Tacoma, 1996; exhibited in group shows at Nat. Mus. of Women in the Arts, Washington, D.C., 1989-90, U. Puget Sound, Tacoma, 1989, Windhorse Gallery, Seattle, 1990, Chase Gallery, Spokane City Hall, 1990 Hanforth Gallery, Tacoma, 1990, 91, Washington State Capital Mus., Olympia, Washington, 1990, Foyer of the Okean Theater, Vladivostok, Russia, 1992, First Night Gallery, Tacoma, 1992, Sacred Cir. Gallery of Am. Indian Art, Seattle, 1993, 96, Cunningham Gallery, U. Wash., 1993, Western Gallery, Western Wash. U., Bellingham, 1993, Seattle Art Mus., 1993, Bibliotheque Nationale de France, 1994, Street Level Photography Gallery, Glasgow, Scotland, 1995, Tacoma Art Mus., 1995, Park Ave. Armory, N.Y.C., 1995, Westfalische Museum Fur Naturkunde, Munster, Germany, 1995, 96, others; represented in permanent collections at Steilacoom (Wash.) Tribal Mus., Bibliotheque Nat. de France, U. Puget Sound, Puyallup Tribe of Indians, also corp. collections. Recipient 1st Place Photography award, Crosscurrents Art Contest, 1988. Mem. Artist Trust, En Foco, Atlatl. Home and Studio: 1211 S Tyler St Tacoma WA 98405-1135

GUINN, JANET MARTIN, psychologist, consultant; b. Rapid City, S.D., Aug. 16, 1942; d. Verne Oliver and Carolyn Yetta (Clark) Martin; m. David Lee Guinn, Oct. 27, 1962 (div. June 1988); children: Cynthia Gail, Kevin Scott, Garrett Lee. BS in Psychology, U. Alaska, 1980, MS in Counseling Psychology, 1983; PhD in Clin. Psychology, Calif. Sch. Profl. Psychology, 1988. Lic. psychologist, Alaska, Nev. Pvt. practice Anchorage, 1988-93, Carson City and Reno, Nev., 1993—; clinician Behavior Medicine Cons., 1983-84; pvt. practice clinician, 1983-84; supr. Southcentral Counseling Ctr., Anchorage, 1984-85; cons. City/Borough of Juneau, Alaska, 1988; psychologist youth treatment program Alaska Psychiat. Inst., Anchorage, 1989-90; psychologist Nev. Mental Health Inst., Sparks, 1994—; cons. in field; cons. Alaska Small Bus. Coalition, Anchorage, 1990-92; reviewer Blors Corp. Contbr. articles to profl. jours. Active in politics. Mem. APA, Am. Coll. Forensic Examiners, Nev. Psychol. Assn., Internat. Neuropsychol. Soc., Rotary, Psi Chi. Republican. Office: 2470 Wrondel Way # 111 Reno NV 89502-3701

GUINN, SUSAN LEE, lawyer; b. Langhorne, Pa., July 22, 1965; d. Walter William and Setsuko (Yamada) G. BSN, U. N.Mex., 1988; JD, U. Denver, 1991. Bar: Calif. 1991, U.S. Dist. Ct. Calif. (so. and cen. dists.) 1991. Ptnr. Robinson, Phillips & Calcagnie, San Diego, 1993—. Mem. ATLA (poliction action mgmt. com. 1995, publ. om. 1993—), Calif. Trial Lawyers Assn. (bd. govs., chair women's caucus, edn. com. 1994—), Attys. Info. Exch. Group, Western Trial Lawyers Assn. (bd. govs., edn. chmn. 1993—), San Diego Trial Lawyers Assn., Trial Lawyers for Pub. Justice, Lawyers Club. Office: Robinson Phillips & Calcagnie 110 Laurel St San Diego CA 92101-1419

GUISEWITE, CATHY LEE, cartoonist; b. Dayton, Ohio, Sept. 5, 1950; d. William Lee and Anne (Duly) G. BA in English, U. Mich., 1972; LHD (hon.), R.I. Coll., 1979, Eastern Mich. U., 1981. Writer Campbell-Ewald Advt., Detroit, 1972-73; writer Norman Prady, Ltd., Detroit, 1973-74, W.B. Doner & Co., Advt., Southfield, Mich., 1974-75; group supr. W.B. Doner & Co., Advt., 1975-76, v.p., 1976-77; creator, writer, artist Cathy comic strip Universal Press Syndicate, Mission, Kans., 1976—. Author, artist: The Cathy Chronicles, 1978, What Do You Mean, I Still Don't Have Equal Rights??!!, 1980, What's a Nice Single Girl Doing with a Double Bed?!!, 1981, I Think I'm Having a Relationship with a Blueberry Pie!, 1981, It Must Be Love, My Face Is Breaking Out, 1982, Another Saturday Night of Wild and Reckless Abandon, 1982, Cathy's Valentine's Day Survival Book, How to Live through Another February 14, 1982, How to Get Rich, Fall in Love, Lose Weight, and Solve all Your Problems by Saying "NO", 1983, Eat Your Way to a Better Relationship, 1983, A Mouthful of Breath Mints and No One to Kiss, 1983, Climb Every Mountain, Bounce Every Check, 1983, Men Should Come with Instruction Booklets, 1984, Wake Me Up When I'm a Size 5, 1985, Thin Thighs in Thirty Years, 1986, A Hand to Hold, An Opinion to Reject, 1987, Why Do the Right Words Always Come Out of the Wrong Mouth?, 1988, My Granddaughter Has Fleas, 1989, $14 in the Bank and a $200 Face in My Purse, 1990, Reflections (A Fifteenth Anniversary Collection), 1991, Only Love can Break a Heart, but a Shoe Sale Can Come Close, 1992, Revelations From a 45-Pound Purse, 1993; TV work includes 3 animated Cathy spls. (Emmy award 1987). Recipient Reuben award Nat. Cartoonists Soc., 1992. Office: Universal Press Syndicate 4900 Main St Kansas City MO 64112-2630

GULA, LISA ANNE, financial consultant, physicist; b. Elmhurst, Ill., May 21, 1960; d. Henry Edward and Mary Frances (Clark) G. BS in Physics, U. Calif., Riverside, 1981, MS in Physics, 1983. Mem. tech. staff Hughes Aircraft Co., El Segundo, Calif., 1984; laser physicist Northrop Corp., Hawthorne, Calif., 1985-88; sci. analyst XonTech, Inc., Van Nuys, Calif., 1988-90, Space Computer Corp., Santa Monica, Calif., 1990-92; fin. advisor Am. Express Fin. Advisors, Inc., L.A., 1992—. Office: Am Express Fin Advisors Inc 11835 W Olympic Blvd #900E Los Angeles CA 90064

GULBRANDSEN, NATALIE WEBBER, religious association administrator; b. Beverly, Mass., July 7, 1919; d. Arthur Hammond and Kathryn Mary (Doherty) Webber; m. Melvin H. Gulbrandsen, June 19, 1943 (dec. Feb. 1991); children: Karen Ann Bean, Linda Jean Goldsmith, Eric Christian, Ellen Dale Williams, Kristin Jane Morgan. BA, Bates Coll., 1942, LLD (hon.), 1996; LHD, Meadville/Lombard Theol. Sch., Chgo., 1991. Social worker Bur. Child Welfare, Bangor, Maine; moderator Unitarian Universalist Assn., Boston, 1985-93. Exec. dir. Girl Scouts U.S., Belmont, Mass., 1943-45, leader 1941-44, 52-65, leadership trainer 1946-63, bd. dirs., Wellesley, Mass., 1950-63, pres. 1960-63; mem. permanent sch. accomodations com., Wellesley, 1970-76, Wellesley Youth Commn., 1968-70, Wellesley town meeting, 1967-91; trustee Wellesley Human Relations Service, 1964-76, pres. 1973-76; bd. dirs. Newton Wellesley Weston Needham Area Mental Health Assn., 1975-78, Am. Field Service, 1964-70; co-chair METCO Program of Wellesley, 1965-69; trustee Unitarian Universalist Women's Fedn., 1971-81, pres. 1977-81. Recipient Wellesley Ctr. Community award, 1981. Mem. Boston Bates Alumnae Assn. (pres. 1966-69), Internat. Assn. Religious Freedom (mem. council 1981-90, v.p. 1990-93, pres. 1993-96). Lodge: Sons of Norway. Home: 35 Riverdale Rd Wellesley MA 02181-1625 Office: Internat Assn for Religious Freedom, 2 Market St, Oxford 0X1 3EF, England

GULICK, DEBORAH JEAN, elementary education educator; b. Edenton, N.C., Oct. 21, 1953; d. Lyman Mark and Rena (Bakker) G. AA, Centenary Coll., Hackettstown, N.J., 1974; BA, Oral Roberts U., 1976; MA, Fairleigh Dickinson U., 1981. Cert. elem. and mid. sch. tchr., K-12 supr., N.J. Tchr. Mt. Olive Twp. Bd. Edn., Budd Lake, N.J., 1976—. Editor (newsletter) Mountain View News, 1986—. Mem. Chancel Choir, United Presbyn. Ch., Flanders, N.J., 1988-92, Sr. Choir, Hacketts-Town, N.J., 1993—. Recipient Gov.'s Tchr. Recognition award State of N.J., 1991. Mem. Edn. Assn. Mt. Olive (treas. 1986-88), Morris County Coun. Edn. Assn. (rep. 1987-93). Home: 663 Rockport Rd Hackettstown NJ 07840 Office: Mountain View Sch Cloverhill Dr Flanders NJ 07836

GULICK, DONNA MARIE, accountant; b. N.Y.C., Jan. 25, 1956; d. H.R. and M.G. Gulick. MBA, Fairleigh Dickinson U., 1981, MS, 1986. Programmer Wash. State U., Pullman, 1983; acctg. analyst IBM, Tarrytown, N.Y., 1983-89, program mgr., 1989-91; program mgr. long-term disability plan IBM, Purchase, N.Y., 1991-92; staff acctg. analyst labor charges IBM, Tarrytown, N.Y., 1992-94; project mgr. IBM, Somers, N.Y., 1994—. Mem. Assn. MBA Execs., ACM, Inst. of IEEE, Nat. Assn. Unknown Players, Delta Mu Delta. Roman Catholic. Home: 395 State Route 28 Bridgewater NJ 08807-2471 Office: IBM Rt 100 Somers NY 10589

GULLACE, MARLENE FRANCES, systems analyst, programmer, consultant; b. Ft. Belvoir, Va., Jan. 12, 1952; d. Amerigo Francis and Martha Arlene (Wise) Guy; m. Gerald Lynn Tolley, June 26, 1970 (div. Nov. 1974); 1 child, Gerald Lynn Tolley Jr.; m. Salvatore Gullace, Nov. 19, 1976 (div. Apr. 1991). AA in Pre-Law, Cochise Coll., 1979; BA in Polit. Sci., U. Ariz., 1982; AA in Computer Sci., Bus., Chaparral Coll., 1985. Realtor, entrepreneur, inventor Sierra Vista, Ariz., 1977-84; ADP instr. Chaparral Coll., Tucson, 1985; model Barbizon, Tucson, 1986-87; clk. HUD/FHA, Tucson, 1987-88; computer programmer DOD Inspector Gen., Arlington, 1988-89; programmer analyst U.S. Army Corps of Engrs., USAF, Washington, 1989-91, Calibre Systems Inc., Falls Church, Va., 1991; cons., systems analyst/programmer EDP, Vienna, Va., 1991-93; info. engr. Ogden Profl. Svcs. (now named Anteon Corp.), Vienna, 1993-96, Orkand Corp., 1996—. Patented toy, registered trademark. Realtor assoc. Cochise County Bd. Realtors, 1977-84. Mem. IEEE, Fed. Women's Program at SBA (sec. 1976). Methodist. Home: 3327 Piney Ridge Ct Herndon VA 20171-4019

GULLEDGE, KAREN STONE, educator, administrator; b. Fayetteville, N.C., Feb. 3, 1941; d. Malcolm Clarence and Clara (Davis) Stone; m. Parker Lee Gulledge Jr, Oct. 17, 1964. BA, St. Andrews Presbyn. Coll., Laurinburg, N.C., 1963; MA, East Carolina U., 1979; EdD, Nova U., 1986. Social worker Lee County, Sanford, N.C., 1963-64; tchr. Asheboro (N.C.) City Schs., 1964-67, Winston-Salem (N.C.)/Forsyth County Schs., 1967-70; research analyst N.C. Dept. Pub. Instrn., Raleigh, 1971-76, sch. planning cons., 1976-89, dir. sch. planning, 1989-95; dir. ednl. svcs. Peterson Assocs., Raleigh, 1995—; chmn. N.C. Elem. Commn. of So. Assn. Colls. and Schs., 1995; leader profl. seminars; spkr. in field. Trustee St. Andrews Coll. Recipient Outstanding Educator award, 1992. Mem. Coun. Ednl. Facility Planners (pres., chmn. 1995, Disting. Ednl. Achievement award 1994), Delta Kappa Gamma. Democrat. Home: 7405 Fiesta Way Raleigh NC 27615-3325 Office: Peterson Assocs PO Box 24118 Charlotte NC 28224

GULLETTE, ETHEL MAE BISHOP (ETHEL MAE BISHOP), pianist; b. St. Paul, Mar. 29, 1908; d. Clarence Eugene and Alma (Beckman) Bishop; m. William Brandon Gullette, Sept. 5, 1936; children: Ethel Mae, Charlene Ann. MusB, MacPhail Sch. Music, Mpls., 1928; BA, U. Minn., 1931; diploma, Juilliard Sch. Music, 1936; pvt. study piano with Donald N. Ferguson, James Friskin. Pianist and accompanist in concerts and radio appearances, Midwest U.S., 1925-33; voice accompanist Juilliard Sch. Music, also pvt. piano tchr., N.Y.C., 1933-47; duo-pianist, accompanist Fairfield County, Conn., 1951-89, also Hartford, Conn., N.J. and N.Y.C., 1967-89; concert pianist, Ea. U.S., 1953-89; 30 concerts Fairfield Hills Hosp., New Town, Conn., 1957-71; concerts, Savannah, Ga., Hilton Head Island and Beaufort, S.C., 1972; accompanist Darien Troupers, 1968, 69; New Canaan High Sch. Summer Theater, 1972-73; concert appearances include Dallas, 1983, Scottsdale, Ariz., 1985, Lebanon, Bridgeport, Greenwich, New Canaan, Norwalk and Darien, Conn., 1980-89; mem. New Canaan Piano Quartet, 1960-68, New Canaan Town Players, 1952-88, accompanist, 1958-63, 73; mem.; accompanist Nutmeg Music Theatre, 1957-61, Westport, Ct.; Demi-Opera Co., Brookfield Summer Theatre, Conn., 1961, many others. Bd. govs., rehearsal pianist Norwalk Symphony Orch., 1955-62; mem. New Canaan Community Concerts Assn., 1954-88, membership chmn., 1967-69, bd. dirs. 1961-69, 84-88; active fund drives charitable orgns.; co-pres. New Canaan High Sch. Parent's Coun., 1964-65; active New Canaan Congregational Ch., also mem. music com., 1994. Recipient Hon. Golden Eaglet award Southwestern Coun. Girl Scouts U.S.A., 1985; also citations for work in Am. Cancer Soc. and ARC drives. Mem. N.Y. Singing Tchrs. Assn., New Canaan Hist. Soc. (photographer gown exhibits 1968-86), Darien Community Assn. (bd. dirs. 1962-64, chmn. duo piano group 1962-64, 82-84, sec. duo piano group 1984-86), New Canaan Libr., New Canaan Audubon Soc., Norwalk Symphony Orch. Women's Assn. (mem. bd. 1976-82, life mem.), Am. Shakespeare Guild, AAUW (charter 1970—, named Outstanding Mem. Conn. chpt. 1980, life mem., nat. named Gift fellowship 1988), Friends N.Y. Philharm. Orch. (New Canaan chmn. 1968-71), Fairfield County Panhellenic Coun., Juilliard Alumni Assn., U. Minn. Alumni Assn. (past dir. N.Y.), New Canaan Community Concerts Assn. (hon. life, Membership and Svc. award 1974, citation for 25 yrs. outstanding achievements 1979), Mu Phi Epsilon (recognition as 50 yr. mem. 1977), Delta Zeta (alumni charter; pres. local alumnae chpt. 1961-63, treas. 1982-84; named Outstanding New Eng. Alumna 1980, Nat. Woman of Yr. 1982; recipient Golden Rose 50 yr. meml. award 1981, New Eng. Cert. Achievement, 1989, Very Spl. Delta Zeta Alumna award, 1990, Order of the Pearl 65 yr. meml. award 1995; ann. alumna svc. award established in her name by Fairfield County chpt. 1983). Clubs: Schubert (St. Paul); Atlantic Beach (L.I., N.Y.); Schubert of Fairfield County (duo piano group sec. 1980-82 life mem.). Home: 225 Essex Mdws Essex CT 06426-1524

GULLETTE, MARGARET MORGANROTH, cultural critic, writer; b. N.Y.C., May 13, 1941; d. Martin and Betty (Eisner) Morganroth; m. David G. Gullette, June 4, 1964; 1 child, Sean Morganroth. BA in English, Radcliffe Coll., 1962; MA in Comparative Lit., U. Calif., Berkeley, 1964; PhD in Comparative Lit., Harvard U., 1975. Vis. scholar Harvard U, Cambridge, Mass., 1993-94, 95-96, Northeastern U., Boston, 1994-95, Simmons Coll., Boston, 1995-96; asst. dir. Harvard-Danforth Ctr. for Tchg. and Learning, 1976-85; chair adv. com. Bunting Inst., Radcliffe, 1993—. Author: Safe at Last in the Middle Years, 1988, Mona Caird's Daughters of Panaaus, 1989; author essays numerous mags. Co-editor Age Studies Series, U. Press Va., 1993—. Bunting fellow Bunting Inst., 1986-87, Am. Coun. Learned Socs. fellow, 1986-87, NEH fellow, 1991-92. Home: 68 Pembroke St Newton MA 02158

GULLETTE, RHONDA YUVONNE, logistic management specialist; b. Dayton, Ohio, Nov. 25, 1962; d. Peter M. and Helen L. (Baker) G. BS, Central State U., Wilberforce, Ohio, 1986. Cert. in acquisition logistics, program mgr.; lic. real estate salesperson. Logistics mgmt. specialist Wright-Patterson AFB, Ohio, 1986—; beauty cons. Mary Kay Cosmetics, 1993; realtor Century 21, 1990. Named one of Outstanding Young Women in Am., 1991; recipient 3rd runner up prize Jocelyns Modeling Contest, 1st runner up Miss Hemisphere, Top Ten Miss Heart of Ohio; participant in beauty contests. Mem. Blacks in Govt., Federally Employed Women, Nat. Bd. Realtors, Ohio Bd. Realtors, Dayton Bd. Realtors, Kappa Alpha Psi, Delta Sigma Theta (Alpha Psi scholarship). Democrat. Baptist. Home: PO Box 33763 Dayton OH 45433-0763

GULLEY, JOAN LONG, banker; b. Balt., Sept. 10, 1947; d. Thomas F. and Florence (Waldron) Long; m. Philip Gordon Gulley, aug. 2, 1969; 1 child, Colin Jason. BA, U. Rochester, 1969; postgrad., Harvard U., 1985. Analyst U.S. Dept. Commerce, Washington, 1969-70, Fed. Res. Bd., Washington, 1970-74; sr. analyst 5, Washington, 1979-81; asst. v.p. Fed. Res. Bank Boston, 1975-79, v.p., 1981-83; sr. v.p. 5, 1983-86; exec. v.p. The Mass. Co., Boston, 1986-94, pres., CEO, 1994, also bd. dirs.; chmn., CEO PNC Bank New Eng., 1995—; bd. dirs. Mass. Housing Investment Corp. Bd. dirs. The Steppingstone Found., YMCA Greater Boston; trustee Wang Ctr. for Performing Arts. Mem. Mass. Bankers Assn. (bd. dirs.), Mass. Bus. Roundtable, Boston Econs. Club, Algonquin Club, Phi Beta Kappa. Office: PNC Bank, New England 125 High St, Oliver St Tower Boston MA 02110

GULLICKSON, NANCY ANN, art association administrator; b. Memphis, Jan. 7, 1942; d. Alfred John and Mildred Lucille (Houston) Bowen; m. John Charles Gullickson, June 25, 1966; children: Jay Weldon, Christine Lee. BFA, Miss. Univ. Women, 1964. Owner Yellow Awning Interiors, Lawrenceville, Ga., 1975-85; exec. dir. Gwinnett Coun. Arts, Inc., Duluth, Ga., 1983—; pres. Ga. Assembly Cmty. Arts Agys., 1987, Alliance Children's Theatre, Atlanta, 1982-83, Lawrenceville Jr. Women's Club, 1977; trustee Woodruff Arts Ctr., Atlanta, 1982-83. Sec., bd. dirs. Gwinnett Conv. & Vis. Bur., 1992—; bd. dirs. Gwinnett Heart Assn., 1994—, Lawrenceville Downtown Devel. Authority, 1989-96; sustainer Gwinnett North Fulton Jr. League, 1985—. Recipient Gwinnett's Exceptional Women Leaders award League Women Voters, 1995. Home: 373 Summit Ridge Dr Lawrenceville GA 30245 Office: Gwinnett Coun Arts Inc Gwinnett Coun Arts Ctr 6400 Sugarloaf Pky Bldg 300 Duluth GA 30155

GULLO, SILVANA LAFERLITA, administrator; b. Buenos Aires, Dec. 16, 1958; arrived in U.S., 1959; d. John and Maria (Gattuso) Laferlita; m. James Czernics, Dec. 30, 1977 (div. Oct. 1982); m. Philip Gullo, July 29, 1990; 1 child, Oliver. Diploma, Briarcliffe Coll. Bus. & Tech., 1977. Exec. asst. N.Y. Thoroughbred Breeders, Inc., Elmont, N.Y., 1982-93; exec. dir. Ronald McDonald House of L.I., New Hyde Park, N.Y., 1993—; fin. cons. N.Y. Thoroughbred Breeders, Inc., Elmont, 1993-96. Mem. spl. com. Garden City South Cmty. League, Franklin Sq., 1994-95. Office: Ronald McDonald House LI 267-07 76th Ave New Hyde Park NY 11040

GULYA, AINA JULIANNA, neurologist, surgeon, educator; b. Syracuse, N.Y., Feb. 3, 1953; d. Aladar and Sylvia E. Gulya; m. William R. Wilson, May 21, 1983. AB cum laude, Yale Coll., 1974; MD with distinction in rsch., U. Rochester, 1978. Intern, jr. resident in gen. surgery Beth Israel Hosp., Boston, 1978-80; resident in otolaryngology Mass. Eye & Ear Infirmary, Boston, 1980-83; fellow in otology/neurotology Bapt. Hosp. Ear Found., Nashville, 1983-84; asst. prof. surgery George Washington U., Washington, 1984-87, assoc. prof. surgery, 1987-90; assoc. prof. otolaryngology and head and neck surgery Georgetown U., Washington, 1990-94, prof. otolaryngology and head and neck surgery, 1994—; assoc. examiner Am. Bd. Otolaryngology, 1993—; adj. prof. otolaryngology-head and neck surgery Georgetown U., 1996—. Co-author: Anatomy of the Temporal Bone With Surgical Implications, 1986, 95; assoc. editor Am. Jour. Otology, 1989—. Bd. dirs. Deafness Rsch. Found., 1994—. Recipient Libr. award Rochester Acad. Medicine, 1975, Honor award Am. Acad. Otolaryngology-Head and Neck Surgery, 1991. Mem. Am. Otological Soc. (coun. 1993—, editor-libr. 1995—, trustee rsch. fund 1993—), Am. Neurotology Soc. (coord. for continuing med. edn. 1990-95), Am. Acad. Otolaryngology, Head and Neck Surgery Inc. (bd. dirs. 1995—). Office: Dept Otolaryngology-Head & Neck Surgery 3800 Reservoir Rd NW Washington DC 20007-2196

GULYAS, CAROL, advertising executive. Exec. v.p., dir. L.Am. affiliates DraftDirect Worldwide, Chgo. Office: DraftDirect Worldwide 142 E Ontario Chicago IL 60611-2818*

GUMPPERT, KARELLA ANN, federal government official; b. N.Y.C., Oct. 16, 1942; d. Leonard Lewis and Florence M. Gumppert. AB in Polit. Sci., George Washington U., 1963, postgrad., 1963-65. Lic. in real estate sales, Md., 1984. Editor to Bd. Govs. Fed. Res. Sys., Washington, 1966-67; editl. asst. Jour. of Maritime Law and Commerce, N.Y.C., 1969-71; adminstr. NYU Law Sch., N.Y.C., 1968-73; law asst. White & Case and other firms, N.Y.C., Boston, Hartford, 1974-80; vol. asst. U.S. Presdl. Inaugural Com., Washington, 1981; confidential asst. The White House Staff, Washington, 1981; publs. asst. Congressional Budget Office, Washington, 1982-84; credit summarizer Xerox Corp., Arlington, Va., 1985-86; asst. in govtl. affairs Mut. Omaha, Washngton, 1988; land law adjudicator U.S. Dept. Interior, Anchorage, 1991—. Author, illustrator: (children's book) An Adventure, 1949; founding editor lit. mag. Springboard, 1959; mem. editorial bd. newspaper Amicus Curiae, 1964-65. Charity asst. Girl Scouts U.S.A., N.Y.C., 1952-54, Christian Assn., N.Y.C., 1959-61, Wesley Found., Washington, 1962-63; vol. asst. N.Y. Rep. County Com., 1959-62, Conn. Reps. State Com., Hartford, 1979-80. Recipient numerous scholarships, 1957-60. Mem. NAFE, Nat. Trust for Hist. Preservation, Nat. Audubon Soc., Women's Nat. Rep. Club, Subscribers of Anchorage Opera Assn.

GUNDERSEN, ALLISON MAUREEN, massage therapist, intercultural consultant; b. Syracuse, N.Y., Oct. 14, 1959; d. Jerrold Paul and Rosemarie Noël (Harvey) G. AB, Cornell U., 1981; postgrad., NYU, 1982-83, Swedish Inst., 1991, Lesley Coll., 1994—. Assoc. Morgan Stanley & Co., N.Y.C., 1981-84, sr. assoc., 1985-86; project mgr. Morgan Stanley Internat., Tokyo, 1987-88; cons. Computech Cons. Svcs., Winchester, N.J., 1989-90; pres. Woman About Globe, Ltd., N.Y.C., 1990-93; assoc. Cambridge (Mass.) Myotherapy, 1992—; cons. Nomura Rsch. Inst. Am., N.Y.C., 1989-90. Mem. NAFE, NOW (dir. membership processing N.Y.C. 1990), Internat. Feminists Japan (coord. 1987-88), Am. Massage Therapists Assn., Soc. Intercultural Educators, Trainers and Rschrs. Democrat.

GUNDERSON, JUDITH KEEFER, golf association executive; b. Charleroi, Pa., May 25, 1939; d. John R. and Irene G. (Gaskill) Keefer; student public schs., Uniontown, Pa.; m. Jerry L. Gunderson, Mar. 19, 1971; children: Jamie L., Jeff S.; stepchildren: Todd G. (dec.), Marc W., Bookkeeper, Fayette Nat. Bank, 1957-59, gen. ledger bookkeeper, 1960-63; head bookkeeper First Nat. Bank Broward, 1963-64; bookkeeper Ruthenberg Homes, Inc., 1966-69; bookkeeper, asst. sec./treas. Pennisular Properties, Inc. subs. Investors Diversified Svcs. Properties, Mpls., 1969-72; comptr., pres. Am. Golf Fla., Inc., dba Golf and Tennis World, Deerfield Beach, 1972-89, stockholder, 1992—; sales assoc. Realty Brokers Internat., Inc., 1990; former sec., treas. Internat. Golf, Inc., now stockholder; dir. Mary Kay Cosmetics, 1993—; v.p. Am. Golf Unltd. Inc., 1995—; county committeewoman, Broward County, Fla., 1965-66; ind. agt. personal and family devel. seminars Slight Edge Enterprises, Inc., 1989-91; active Performing Arts Ctr. Energetic Resourceful Supporters. Mem. NAFE, Assn. Profl. Saleswomen, Internat. Platform Assn., Nat. Golf Found., C. of C., Beta Sigma Phi.

GUNDERSON, MARY ALICE, writer, educator; b. Sheridan, Wyo., Jan. 18, 1936; d. Bernard Graham and Leah Mary (Gilkeson) Wright; m. Edwin Donald Gunderson, July 16, 1964; 1 child, James Nelson. BA in Elem. Edn., U. Wyo., 1957, postgrad., 1971-86. Elem. tchr. Sweetwater County, Green River, Wyo., 1957-58, Natrona County Sch. Dist., Casper, Wyo., 1958-68; homebound instr. Natrona County Sch. Dist., Casper, 1969-73; pub. info. officer Natrona County Libr., Casper, 1976-79; artist in residence Wyo. Arts Coun., Cheyenne, 1973-88; instr. creative writing Casper Coll., 1993-96, devel. studies in English, 1986-94; freelance writer, 1968—; poetry editor/cons. High Plain Press, Glendo, Wyo., 1994—; mem. lit. adv. com. Casper Coll., 1988-92; grants panelist Wyo. Coun. on Arts, Cheyenne, 1988—. Author: Devils Tower: Stories in Stone, 1988 (Nat. Fedn. Presswomen award 1989), Land Marked: Collected Curry Stories, 1992 (Wyo. State Hist. Soc. award 1992); contbr. essays, fiction, poetry to numerous lit. mags. Dir. PressWomen H.S. Journalism Contest, 1987-88; contest dir., booklet editor Wyo. Writers, Inc., 1983; bd. dirs. Cmty. Concert Assn., Casper, 1988. Writing and Rsch. grantee Wyo. Coun. for Humanities, 1980, Individual Artist grantee Wyo. Coun. on Arts, 1995-96, Fiction fellow Wyo. Coun. on Arts, 1987, Ucross Found. resident, 1986, others. Mem. Wyo. Alumni Assn., Am. Assn. Ret. Persons. Democrat. Presbyterian. Home: 318 W 14th St Casper WY 82601

GUNDERSON, ROBERTA MOLNAR, education educator; b. N.Y.C., Apr. 21, 1935; d. Ludwig Stephen and Emma Caroline (Vitarius) Molnar; m. Robert Clifford Gunderson, Apr. 10, 1954; children: Christopher Robert, Kim Roberta, Andrew Stephen. BS in Edn. magna cum laude, Miami U., Oxford, Ohio, 1968; MEd, Wright State U., 1979. Cert. English tchr., guidance counselor, Ohio. English tchr. Fairborn (Ohio) H.S., 1968-94, chair English dept., 1977-82; lectr. H.S. Journalism Workshop, Columbia U., N.Y.C., 1982, 84, Ohio U., Athens, 1985-88; cons. The Penguin Can. Dictionary, Penguin Books/Can., 1987-89; mem. faculty S.C. Tech. Coll. of the Lowcountry, Ctrl. Tex. Coll. Tutor Reading Discovery, Beaufort County Schs., St. Helena Island, S.C., 1995—; facilitator Am. Believes in Courtesy, Beaufort County Schs., S.C., 1995—; sponsor Beaufort Chamber Orch. Recipient Excellence in Edn. award Greene County Ohio Bd. Edn., 1989, 90, 91, 92, 94. Mem. AAUW (chair Equity in Edn. 1995—), Dataw Island Garden Club (sec. 1995—), Friends of Hunting Island (bd. dirs. 1996—). Home: 518 Island Circle East Saint Helena Island SC 29920

GUNDY-REED, FRANCES DARNELL, librarian, healthcare manager; b. Muskegon, Mich., Aug. 19, 1947; d. Joseph Leo and Olaverne (Mathis) Merle; m. Russell Norman Gundy, Sept. 18, 1965 (div. 1985); 1 child, Raymond Joseph; m. Robert A. Reed, Aug. 26, 1995. AS, Aquinas Coll., 1988, BA, 1991; MLS, Wayne State U., 1993. Owner, pres. Helpmates, Inc., Muskegon, 1992—. Active Mich. Strategic Planning Com., Muskegon Cmty. Health Project. Mem. ALA (nat. chair grassroots com., Specialized Svcs. Coordination com.), AAUW, Nat. Assn. for Self-Employed, AMBUCS (2d v.p.), Network Small Bus. Owners, Intellectual Freedom Roundtable, Libr. Info. and Tech. Assn., Assn. Libr. Collections and Tech. Svcs., Mich. Libr. Assn., Pub. Libr. Assn., Women's Divsn. C of C. (bd. dirs.), Women's Expo. (bd. dirs.). Home: 629 Fruitvale Rd Montague MI 49437

GUNN, JOAN MARIE, health care administrator; b. Binghamton, N.Y., Jan. 29, 1943; d. Andrew and Ruth Antoinette (Butler) Jacoby; m. Albert E. Gunn, Jr; children: Albert E. III, Emily W., Andrew R., Clare M., Catherine A.B., Philip D. BS summa cum laude, Tex. Women's U., 1983; MSN, U. Tex., Houston, 1989. Staff nurse geriatrics St. Anthony's Ctr., Houston, 1985-86; charge nurse gero psychiatry Bellaire Gen. Hosp., Houston, 1986; head nurse gero psychiat. unit U. Tex./Harris County Psychiat. Ctr., Houston, 1986-88, asst. dir. nursing adult svcs., 1988-90, DON adult svcs., 1990-93, nurse exec., 1991-93, DON, 1993—, asst. adminstr., 1994—. Mem. Nat. Soc. Colonial Dames of the XVII Century, Daus. of Union Vets. of Civil War, Sigma Theta Tau. Roman Catholic. Home: 2329 Watts St Houston TX 77030-1139 Office: U Tex Harris County Psychiat Ctr 2800 S Macgregor Way Houston TX 77021-1032

GUNN, MARY ELIZABETH, retired English language educator; b. Great Bend, Kans., July 21, 1914; d. Ernest E. and Elisabeth (Wesley) Eppstein; m. Charles Leonard Gunn, Sept. 13, 1936 (dec. Apr. 1985); 1 child, Charles Douglas. AB, Ft. Hays State U., 1935, BS in Edn., 1936, MA, 1967. Tchr. English Unified Sch. Dist. 428, Great Bend, 1963-80; tchr. English Barton County C.C., Great Bend, 1977-84, tchr. adult edn., 1985-87, tchr. ESL, 1988-94; ret., 1994. Conf. Am. Studies fellow De Pauw U., 1969; recipient Nat. Cmty. Svc. award DAR, 1996. Mem. AAUW (Outstanding Mem. 1991), NEA, Bus. and Profl. Women (Woman of Yr. 1974), Kans. Adult Edn. Assn. (Master Adult Educator 1986), Kans. Assn. Tchrs. English, PEO, Delta Kappa Gamma, Alpha Sigma Alpha. Democrat. Mem. United Ch. of Christ. Home: 3009 16th St Great Bend KS 67530-3705

GUNN, SANDRA JOYCE, musician and church lay leader; b. Allentown, Pa., Oct. 30, 1951; d. Hilbert Guy and Joyce Marie (Mantz) Snyder; m. Bruce Myron Gunn, Oct. 17, 1981. BS in Music Edn., Lebanon Valley Coll, 1973. Cert. instrumental and vocal music tchr. Handbell dir. Calvary Presbyn. Ch., Riverton, N.J., 1983-87; dir. music (choir and instruments) Broad St. United Meth. Ch., Burlington, N.J., 1987—; part-time bookkeeper Lippincott Fuel Co., Delanco, N.J., 1985-92; ch. auditor Calvary Presbyn. Ch., Riverton, 1988, 91; chmn. Christian edn., elder Calvary Presbyn. Ch., Riverton, 1979-82, 96—, chmn. worship com., 1996—; youth advisor Broad St. United Meth. Ch., 1987, chmn. Ann. Choir Festival, 1990—; chmn. worship com. Broad St. United Meth. Ch., Burlington, 1991-93, coord. youth Sunday and Christmas Eve svcs., 1989-94; asst. dir. N.J. Meth. Chorale for Gr. Britain concert tour, 1991. Treas. Porch Club, Riverton, 1983-85; sec. Riverton Rep. Club, 1985-86; mem. Riverton Improvement Com., 1989; pres. N.J. Women's Clubs, Riverton, 1985-90, dir. chorus, 1992—; instr. music appreciation course Burlington County Continuing Edn. Program, 1991. Home: 808 Main St Riverton NJ 08077-1707 Office: Broad St United Meth Ch 36 E Broad St Burlington NJ 08016-1631

GUNNING, CAROLYN SUE, nursing educator; b. Ft. Smith, Ark., Dec. 16, 1943; d. Laurence George and Flora Irene (Garner) G. BS, Tex. Woman's U., 1965; MS, U. Colo., 1973; PhD, U. Tex.-Austin, 1981. Registered nurse, Tex. Clinician III, Bexar County Hosp., San Antonio, 1968-71; instr. U. Tex. Sch. Nursing, San Antonio, 1973-74, asst. prof., 1974-83, asst. to dean, 1977-79, assoc. prof., asst. dean undergrad. programs, 1983-84, assoc. dean, 1984-88; dean Sch. Nursing Marshall U., Huntington, W.Va., 1988-90; dean Coll. Nursing, Tex. Women's U., 1991—; accreditation site visitor Nat. League for Nursing, 1982-88 . Active Leadership San Antonio, 1978-79. Served to capt. Nurse Corps, U.S. Army, 1965-68; to lt. comdr. Army N.G., 1980-88. Decorated Army Commendation medal. Mem. ANA, Nat. League for Nursing, Sigma Theta Tau, Kappa Delta Pi. Contbr. articles to profl. jours.

GUNNOE, NANCY LAVENIA, food executive, artist; b. Southside, Tenn., Jan. 7, 1921; d. Edgar Hatton and Clara Sharp (McCurdy) Thompson; m. Raymond Glen Gunnoe, Dec. 6, 1941; children: Lynn Thompson Gunnoe Sheets, Paul Randall (dec.), Joy Virginia Gunnoe Woodrum. Student, Austin Peay Coll., 1939, U. Charleston, 1973-87, 91. Cashier Kroger Co., Charleston, W.V., 1939-40; with Superior Laundry & Cleaning, Charleston, 1940-41; file clk. Hancock Oil Co., Oakland, Calif., 1942; office clk. Office Price Adminstrn., Stockton, Calif., 1943; sec.-treas. R.G. Gunnoe Farms Inc., Charleston, 1947—. Exhibited at local orgns. Mem. Nat. League Am. Pen Women, Inc., Allied Artists W.Va., Univ. Charleston Builders, Kanawha Valley Hist. and Preservation Soc., Charleston Woman's Club, Sunrise Mus. Republican. Home: 2040 Oakridge Dr Charleston WV 25311-1112 Office: 2115 Oakridge Dr Charleston WV 25311

GUNTER, CHERYL LYNNELL, loan processor; b. Lawrenceville, Ga., July 3, 1955; d. Glenn Lester and Juanita Joyce (Wages) G. Attended, Gainesville Jr. Coll., Oakwood, Ga., 1973-75, Lanier Tech., Oakwood, 1973-75. Ins./payroll clerk Home Mission Bd. SBC, Alpharetta, Ga., 1976-81, data entry clerk, 1981-84, loan processor, 1984—. Southern Baptist. Office: Home Mission Bd SBC 4200 N Point Pky Alpharetta GA 30202

GUNTER, KAREN JOHNSON, government official; b. Pensacola, Fla., Jan. 7, 1948; d. Erskine DeWitt and Grace (Crutchfield) Johnson; m. Thomas A. Gunter, Aug. 25, 1975 (div. Dec. 1981). BS, U. So. Miss., 1970; MS, Fla. State U., 1976. Social svc. worker Fla. Bur. Blind Svcs., Pensacola, 1970-74; supervising counselor Fla. Bur. Blind Svcs., Tallahassee, West Palm,

1974-75; M.D. examiner Office Disability Determinations, Social Security Adminstrn., Tallahassee, 1976-80, M.D. rev. examiner, 1980-81, M.D. hearing examiner, 1981-82, M.D. examiner supr., 1982-86, area office program adminstr., 1986—; govt. official, Jafra; skin care cons. Vol. ARC. Recipient Director's citation Social Security Adminstrn., 1978, Commr.'s citation, 1988, Profl. Supr. of Quarter award Office Disability Determination, 1987. Mem. Nat. Assn. Disability Examiners (treas. 1982-85, pres. 1988-89, pres. S.E. region 1985-86, 91-92, S.E. regional dir. 1993—), Fla. Assn. Disability Examiners (pres. 1982, Examiner of Yr. 1984). Democrat. Baptist. Home: 812 Voncile Ave Tallahassee FL 32303-4683 Office: PO Box 7417 Tallahassee FL 32314-7417

GUNTER, NINA G., religious organization administrator; m. D. Moody Gunter; children: Dwight M., Dwayne M. BA in Edn. and Psychology, Trevecca Nazarene Coll., 1958, DD (hon.), 1989; MEd. in Counseling, U. S.C., 1970. Ordained elder Ch. of Nazarene. Tchr. various sch. dists., 1960-75; dist. pres. Nazarene World Mission Soc., S.C., 1961-76; mem. gen. coun. Nazarene World Mission Soc., 1976-85; exec. dir. Nazarene World Mission Soc., Kansas City, Mo., 1986—; spkr. convs., revivals, ch. svcs. Office: Church of the Nazarene 6401 Paseo Blvd Kansas City MO 64131-1213

GUNTHER, BARBARA, artist, educator; b. Bklyn., Nov. 10, 1930; d. Benjamin and Rose (Lev) Kelsky; m. Gerald Gunther, June 22, 1949; children: Daniel Jay, Andrew James. BA, CUNY, 1949; MA, San Jose State U., 1975. Instr. printmaking, drawing, painting Cabrillo Coll., Aptos, Calif., 1976-93; instr. lithography Calif. State U., Hayward, 1978-79; instr. studio arts Calif. State U., San Jose, summer 1977, 78, 80; co-founder San Jose Print Workshop, 1975. One-woman shows include Palo Alto (Calif.) Cultural Ctr., 1981, Smith Andersen Gallery, Palo Alto, 1981, Miriam Perlman, Inc., Chgo., 1984, D.P. Fong & Spratt Galleries, San Jose, 1991, 93, Branner/Spangenburg Gallery, Palo Alto, U. Calif., Santa Cruz, 1991, Frederick Spratt Galleries, San Jose, 1996; exhibited in numerous group shows; represented in permanent collections at San Jose Art in Pub. Places Program, Hilton Towers Hotel, GM, Found. Press, Inc. Recipient Purchase award Palo Alto Cultural Ctr., 1975, Judges' Merit award Haggin Mus., 1988. Mem. Calif. Printmakers Soc., Women's Caucus for Art, San Jose Art League. Studio: 199 Martha St No 22 San Jose CA 95122

GUNZBURGER, SUZANNE NATHAN, county commissioner, social worker; b. Buffalo, July 12, 1939; d. Lawrence Emil and Ruth Lucille (Wohl) Nathan; m. Gerard Josef Gunzburger, Apr. 10, 1960; children: Ronald Marc, Cynthia Anne, Judith Lynn. BS in Edn., Wayne State U., 1959; MSW, Barry U., 1974. Tchr. pub. schs. Detroit, 1959-63, Trumbull, Conn., 1963-66, North Miami Beach, Fla., 1967-68, Broward County, Fla., 1968-72; pvt. practice clin. social work Hollywood, Fla., 1975—; vice mayor City of Hollywood, 1983-84, 85-87, city commr., 1982-92; commr. Broward County, 1992—, chair, 1994-95. Bd. dirs. Environ. Coalition Broward County, 1982-89; chmn. Met. Planning Orgn., Broward County, 1984-87, 89, Statewide Human Rights Adv. Com., 1988-89; pres. Broward County Mental Health Bd., 1984; active on Broward County Commn. Status Women, 1978-82, White House Conf. Families, Balt., 1980; del. Broward County League Cities, 1988-92; mem. adv. bd. Broward Homebound, 1991—; mem. Broward Children's Svc. Bd., 1988-92; mem. bd. dirs. Fla. League of Counties, 1992—; mem. Broward County Water Adv., 1992-94; mem. Broward County Comty. Redevel. Agy., 1992—; mem. bd. dirs. Broward County Econ. Devel. Bd., 1992—; mem. South Fla. Regional Planning Coun., 1992-94; Broward chair Concert Assn. of Fla., Inc., 1996—. Named Broward County Woman of Yr., 1990, Humanitarian of Yr., David Posnack, Jewish Comty. Ctr., 1994, Environmentalist of Yr., Broward County Environ. Coalition, 1994; recipient Disting. Achievement award Am. Jewish Congress, 1990, Fla. Philharm. Woman of Style and Substance, 1995, Woman of Distinction award March of Dimes, 1996, Heart award Children's Consortium, 1996, Disting. Alumni award Barry U., 1996, Jesse Portis Helms Dem. of Yr. award Dolphin Dem. Club, 1996; inductee Broward County Women's Hall of Fame, 1995. Mem. Nat. Assn. Social Workers (diplomate clin. social work), Internat. Acad. Behavioral Med., Counseling and Psychotherapy (diplomate profl. psychotherapy), Am. Acad. Behavioral Med. (clin. mem.), Women in Communications (Woman of Yr. in Govt. 1983), Nat. Coun. Jewish Women (pres. 1980-82, Hannah G. Solomon award 1989), Hollywood C. of C. (leadership devel. 1990—), Kiwanis. Democrat. Office: Office Bd County Commrs Govtl Ctr Rm 412 115 S Andrews Ave Fort Lauderdale FL 33301-1801

GURINSKY, SYLVIA, journalist; b. Miami, Fla., Oct. 3, 1968. BS in Comm., Fla. Internat. U., 1990. Editl. rschr., writer WPLG-Channel 10, Miami, Fla., 1990—. Recipeitn Sch. Bell award Fla. Edn. Assn., 1991, 92, 94, Fla. AP award, 1994, 95, 2d place, 1996; Taishoff fellow. Mem. NATAS, Soc. Profl. Journalists (Miami chpt. sec. 1992-94, v.p. membership 1994—, pres.-elect 1996—).

GURKE, SHARON MCCUE, naval officer; b. Bklyn., Apr. 4, 1949; d. James Ambrose and Marion Denise (Coombs) McCue; BA, Molloy Cath. Coll., 1970; MS in Systems Mgmt., U. So. Calif., 1977; m. Lee Samuel Gurke, Apr. 16, 1977; children: Marion Dawn, Leigh Elizabeth. Commd. ensign U.S. Navy, 1970; advanced through grades to capt., 1991; aircraft maintenance duty officer Orgn.-Intermediate Maintenance Officer, Comdr. Naval Air Force U.S. Pacific Fleet, Naval Air Sta., North Island, San Diego, 1974-77; head quality assurance div. Intermediate Maintenance Dept. Supporting Aircraft, Naval Air Sta., Miramar, San Diego, 1977-78, avionics div. officer, 1978-80; officer in charge Naval Aviation Engring. Service Unit Pacific Naval Air Sta., North Island, 1980-82; aircraft Intermediate Maintenance officer Naval Air Sta., Alameda, Calif., 1982-84; aircraft Intermediate Maintenance officer Naval Sta., Rota, Spain, 1984-86, Naval Air Systems Command Aviation Maintenance Policy Br., 1986-88, asst. program mgr. NACOLMIS, 1987-88; dir. ops. Naval Aviation Depot, North Island, 1988-90, Dept. of Navy OP-514C, 1990-92; exec. officer Naval Aviation Depot, Pensacola, Fla., 1992-94; commdg. officer Naval Aviation Depot Co., Pensacola, Fla., 1994-96, chief of naval operation, indsl. facility policy head, 1996—. Interviewed by S.D. TV for Success Story. Decorated Legion of Merit, 2 Naval Commendation medals, 3 Meritorious Svc. medals. Lic. pilot; first female naval officer selected for aero. engring. tng.; recipient Capt. Winifred Q. Collins award USN, 1980. Mem. Ninety Nines, San Diego Naval Women Officers Network (chmn.). Home: 2511 London Derry Rd Alexandria VA 22308

GURNSEY, KATHLEEN WALLACE, state legislator; b. Donnelly, Idaho; d. Robert G. and Thelma (Halferty) Wallace; m. Vern L. Gurnsey, May 7, 1950; children: Kristina Johnson, Steve, Scott. BA in Bus. Adminstn., Boise State U., 1976. Mem. Idaho Ho. of Reps., Boise, 1974—. Bd. dirs. YMCA, Boise; elder, pres. Women's Assn. First Presbyn. Ch.; bd. dirs. Fundsy, St. Luke's Aux.; mem. Def. Adv. Com. Women in the Svc., Dept. Def., 1982-84. Named Disting. Citizen Idaho Statesman, Woman of Yr. Soroptimist, Woman of Achievement Altrusa Club, Outstanding Alumna Boise State U., 1991, Silver medallion Boise State U., 1996, Outstanding Legislator Nat. Rep. Legis. Assn., 1995, Woman of Yr. for Boise Boise C. of C., 1995. Mem. AAUW (Outstanding Community Svcs. award 1991), Bus. and Profl. Women, Jobs Daus. (Bethel guardian honored quenn). Republican. Presbyterian. Home: 1111 W Highland View Dr Boise ID 83702-1319

GURWITZ-HALL, BARBARA ANN, artist; b. Ayer, Mass., July 7, 1942; d. Jack and Rose (Baritz) Gurwitz; m. James M. Marshall III, Mar. 12, 1966 (div. 1973); m. William D. Hall, May 3, 1991; 1 ward: Samantha Hollinger, 1994-96. Student, Boston U., 1960-61, Katherine Gibbs Sch., Boston, 1961-63. Represented by Karin Newby Gallery, Tubac, Ariz.; represented by Wilde-Meyer Gallery, Scottsdale, Ariz.; Artist-in-residence Desert House of Prayer, Tucson, 1989-91; oblate mem. Benedictine Sisters Perpetual Adoration, 1986—. One-woman show YWCA, Bklyn., 1977, Henry Hicks Gallrey, Bkyn., 1978, Misty-Mountain Gallery, Tubac, Ariz., 1987, Karin Newby Gallery, Tubac, 1989; exhibited in group shows Becket (Mass.) Art Ctr., 1978, Winter Gallery, Tucson, 1980, Johnson Gallery, Bisbee, Ariz., Hilltop Gallery, Nogales, Ariz., 1981, Scharf Gallery, Santa Fe, 1982, Data Mus., Ein Hod, Israel, 1985, C.G. Rein Gallery, Santa Fe, 1986, Tubac Ctr. for Arts, 1985, Mesquite Gallery, Patagonia, Ariz., 1986, Beth O'Donnell Gallery, Tucson, 1989, Karin Newby Gallery, 1989—, Wilde-Meyer Gallery, Scottsdale, Ariz., 1991—, Art Collector's Gallery, Tulsa, 1992, Mountain Oyster Club, Tucson, 1994, Phoenix Mus. League, 1994, Santa Cruz Valley Art Assn., 1994, 96, Brewster Ctr., 1994, 95, Tubac Bienniel Gala, 1994, 96; represented in permanent collections Diocese of Tucson, Data Mus., Desert House of Prayer, Tucson, Ethical Cutlure Soc., Bklyn., St. Andrews Episcopal Ch., Nogales, Tubac Elem. Sch., also numerous corp. and pvt. collections in U.S. and Europe. Mem. Tubac Village Coun., 1979-86; bd. dirs. Pimeria Alta Hist. Soc., Nogales, Ariz., 1982-84; creator Children's Art Walk, Tubac Sch. Sys. and Village Coun., 1980; set designer, choreographer DeAnza Ann. Pageant, Tubac Ctr. Arts, 1982—; pastoral asst. St. Ann's Parish, Tubac, 1986-89; team mem. R.C.I.A. Our Lady of the Valley Parish, Green Valley, Ariz., 1994—. Mem. Nat. League Am. PEN Women, Inc. (Sonoran Desert br.), Santa Cruz Valley Art Assn. (hon. mention ann. juried show 19889-95, Best of Show award 1989, award for excellence 1992), Assn. Contemplative Sisters.

GUSS, SUZANNE, lawyer; b. Louisville, May 11, 1950; d. Donald and Gloria Joyce (Goldsmith) G.; m. Richard W. Hill, Aug. 30, 1987; children: Emily Rose Hill, Michael Everett Hill. BA, Colgate U., 1972; JD, Hofstra U. Sch. Law, 1980. Bar: Ky. 1980. Editl. asst. Hosp. for Joint Diseases Med. Ctr., N.Y.C., 1973-75; law clk. Middleton, Rentlinger & Baird, Louisville, 1978, 79, U.S. Dist. Ct. (ea. dist.) N.Y., Westbury, 1979; asst. atty. gen. Atty. Gen.'s Office, Frankfort, Ky., 1980-85; dir. devel. planned giving U. Louisville, 1985—; mem. Estate Planning Coun., Louisville, 1990—, Ky. Planned Giving Coun., Louisville, 1990—. Office: U Louisville Devel Office Louisville KY 40507

GUSSOW, JILL SUZANNE, photography educator; b. Colorado Springs, Colo., Mar. 29, 1951; d. Roy Lionel and Mary Eugenia (Maynard) G.; m. Robert Marcus, Dec. 3, 1989; children: Zora Gussow, Marcus. BFA, Cooper Union Adv. Sci. and Art, 1973; MFA, Rochester Inst. Tech., 1979. Photographer Margaret Woodbury Strong Mus., Rochester, N.Y., 1979-82; instr. photography Cmty. Darkroom, Rochester, N.Y., 1981—; inst. art & photography Rochester Inst. Tech., 1982-85; instr. drawing U. Rochester, 1984-85; asst. prof. art, photography SUNY, Brockport, N.Y., 1983-94; adj. asst. prof. art, painting Monroe C.C., Rochester, 1995; adj. instr. photography, design Rochester Inst. Tech., 1995-96. One-woman shows include Foto Gallery, N.Y.C., 1983, Village Gate Art Ctr., Rochester, 1985, Little Gallery, Rochester, 1988, Burchfield Art Ctr., Buffalo, 1991, Visual Studies Workshop, Rochester, 1994; group shows include Queens Mus., 1975, Project Studios One (P.S.I.) Queens Artists, L.I., N.Y., 1977; Murray (Ky.) State U., 1978, Akron-Summit County Libr., Akron, Ohio, 1979, Mus. Contemporary Crafts, N.Y.C., 1980, Link Gallery, Rochester, 1981, Gallery Contemporary Metalsmithing, Rochester, 1982, Tower Fine Arts Gallery, Brockport, 1983-93, Meml. Art Gallery, Rochester, 1985-89, The Light Factory, Charlotte, N.C., 1986, Village Gate Art Ctr., Rochester, 1987, Pyramid Art Ctr., Rochester, 1988, Dawson Gallery, Rochester, 1990, Textile Arts Internat., Inc., Mpls., 1992, Burchfield Art Ctr., Buffalo, 1993, Joseloff Gallery, HArtford, Conn., 1994, Meml. Art Gallery, 1995, Senai De Technologias De Imagens, Sao Paulo, Brazil, 1996, others; represented in permanent collections at Burchfield Art Ctr., Dawson Gallery, Rochester, Ann Havens, Rochester, Ralph Ruoff, Rochester, Museu De Arte de Sao Paulo Assis Chateaubriand. Grantee N.Y. State Creative Artist Svc., 1980-81, Monroe County & N.Y. State Coun. ARts, 1987, N.Y. Found. Arts, 1990-91, Deming Meml. Fund, 1994. Mem. Coll. Art Assn., Soc. Photographic Educators. Home: 153 Averill Ave Rochester NY 14620

GUST, JOYCE JANE, artist; b. Milw., June 5, 1952; d. Walter F. and Jane A. (Klappa) Stoelzel; m. Wayne C. Fitzner, Feb. 13, 1971 (div. 1979); 1 child, Mark Wayne; m. Melvin. R. Gust, June 24, 1983. BS, Marquette U., 1981; postgrad., U. Wis., Oshkosh, 1985-90. Registered med. technolgoist. One woman shows include Pinecotheca Gallery, Waupun, Wis., 1993, Blatz Gallery, Milw., 1994, Lazarro Signature Gallery Fine Art, Stoughton, Wis., 1994, Constance Lindholm Fine Art, Milw., 1995, Artworks Gallery, Green Bay, 1995; two person shows include Capitol Civic Ctr., Manitowoc, Wis., 1992; represented in group shows at Signature Gallery, Stoughton, 1989, 91, Cudahy Gallery of Milw. Art Mus., 1989-92, Allen Priebe Art Gallery, Oshkosh, Wis., 1990, Jura Silverman Gallery, Spring Green, Wis., 1990, Chimerical Gregg Art Gallery, La Puente, Calif., 1990, Peltz Gallery, Milw., 1991-92, Ariel Gallery, N.Y., 1990, Neville Mus., Green Bay, 1992, John Michael Kohler Art Ctr., Sheboygan, Wis., 1993, Paine Art Mus., Oshkosh, 1996, others; represented in permanent collections Carroll Coll. Art Mus., Waukesha, Wis., Very Special Arts Wis. Permananet Wis. Artists Collection, Madison, Neville Pub. Mus., Green Bay, Sister Kenny Inst., Mpls., Aid Assn. for Lutherans Ins., Paine Art Ctr., others; featured artist Artworks Gallery, Green Bay, 1993. Recipient Jurors award 1st Ann. Wis. Artists Exhbn., 1992, purchase awards Parkside Nat. Print Exhbn., 1993, Galex Nat., Galesburg, Ill., 1993. Very Spl. Arts Wis. Purchase award, 1994, 96, 1st Pl. Internat. Award in Drawing, Sister Kenny Inst., 1995. Mem. Wis. Painters and Sculptors (Jurors award 1992), Wis. Women in The Arts. Home and Studio: 7064 Jacobson Dr Winneconne WI 54986-9764

GUSTAFSON, SANDRA LYNNE, secondary education educator; b. Phila., Mar. 8, 1948; d. William Henry Gustafson and Ruth Blossom (Berger) Watson. BS in Edn., Temple U., 1969. Tchr. Lincoln H.S., Phila., 1969-78, 85-88, Germantown H.S., Phila., 1978-85; tchr. Germantown-Lankenau Motivation H.S., Phila., 1988—, dean of discipline, 1994—; asst. to vice prin. Lincoln H.S., Phila., 1970-78; sponsor Nat. Honor Soc., Phila., 1989-92, 93—, Peer Counselors and Peer Tutors, Phila., 1989—; chaperone on choir's trip to Europe, Lincoln H.S., 1973, coord. Freshman Orientation Program, Phila., 1993—. Sponsor Big Brother/Big Sister Program, 1994—. Mem. Phila. Fedn. Tchrs. (del. to state conv. 1973, del. to nat. conv. 1973, 74), Phila. Area Spanish Educators, MLA, Sigma Delta Pi, Kappa Delta Epsilon. Democrat. Jewish. Office: Germantown Lankenau Motivation HS 201 Spring Ln Philadelphia PA 19128-3914

GUSTIN, ANN WINIFRED, psychologist; b. Winchester, Mass., 1941; d. Bertram Pettingill and Ruth Lillian (Weller) G.; B.A. with honors in Psychology, U. Mass., 1963; M.S. (USPHS fellow), Syracuse U., 1966, Ph.D., 1969. Registered psychologist, Sask.; lic. psychologist, Ga.; Diplomate Am. Bd. Med. Psychotherapists. Research asst., psychology trainee U. Mass., Tufts U., Harvard U., Syracuse U., 1961-66; psychology intern VA, Canandaigua, N.Y., 1967-68; asst. prof. psychology U. Regina (Sask., Can.), 1969-74, assoc. prof. psychology, dir. counseling services, head clin. tng., 1974-78; pvt. practice psychology, Carrollton, Ga., 1978—, Atlanta, 1980—; staff tng. cons. Frobisher Bay Dept. Social Services, N.W. Territories, Can., 1979-80; cons. staff Tanner Hosp.; ancillary staff West Paces Ferry Hosp.; psychiat. cons. Social Security Adminstrn., Ga. Dept. Human Resources, 1980—. Membership chmn. Carroll County Mental Health Assn., 1979-81; mem. nat. mental health disaster response team ARC. Fellow Ga. Psychol Assn. (exec. divsn. lic. psychologists 1986-91, 92—, Nat. Red Cross disaster mental health team 1991—); mem. Am. Psychol. Assn., Can. Psychol. Assn., Sask. Psychol. Assn. (mem. exec. council 1971-72, registrar 1972-73), Nat. Assn. Disability Examiners, Ga. Assn. Disability Examiners. Office: 107 College St Carrollton GA 30117-3136 also: One Decatur Town Ctr 150 E Ponce De Leon Ave Ste 46 Decatur GA 30030-2553

GUSTINA, DONNA ELIZABETH, sign language educator, consultant; b. Waverly, N.Y., Dec. 29, 1947; d. Donald Hugh and Elizabeth (Berry) G.; divorced; children: Kevin Daniel Pocobello, Karen Marie Pocobello. BS, Nazareth Coll. Rochester, 1970; MS, Rochester Inst. Tech., 1975. Cert. N.Y. State Edn. Dept.; permanent cert. K-12, N.Y. Tchr. grades. 4, 5, 6 St. Marys Elem. Sch., Nevada, Mo., 1972-74; instr. human devel. Nat. Tech. Inst. for Deaf at Rochester Inst. of Tech., 1974-76, sign lang. rsch. assoc./ asst., 1979-80, prof. Am. sign lang., 1980—, faculty devel., 1983-84, chair dept. comm., 1984-85; dir. Comm. Resource Ctr. Ind. Living Ctr., Corning, N.Y., 1987-90; tchr., instr. Am. sign lang. Corning C.C., 1987-90; coord. comm. evaluation svcs. Nat. Tech. Inst. for Deaf, Rochester, 1991—; cons. access for deaf edn., Corning and Elmira, N.Y., 1987-90; adj. prof. Monroe C.C., Rochester, 1993—; sec. adv. bd. Deaf Women of Rochester, 1993-95. Author: Technical Signs Manual: Religion, English, Mathematics, Audiology, Career Education, 1982-85, Basic Sign Communications: Teacher's Guide and Student Maerials, 1984; contbr. articles to profl. jours. including Jour. of Deaf Studies and Deaf Education, Jour. Rehab. Audiology. Named Deaf Woman of Yr., Quota Club Internat.; featured in book Deaf Women: A Parade Through the Decades, 1989; recipient Eisenhart award for Outstanding Tchg. Rochester Inst. of Tech., 1984. Mem. Am. Sign Lang. Tchrs. Assn. (profl. level tchg. cert., mem. Lilac chpt., mem. N.Y. state chpt.), Monroe County Assn. for Hearing Impaired People (chair adv. bd. 1995—), Nat. Assn. of Deaf, Nat. Tech. Inst. for the Deaf (chair deaf profl. group 1992-94), Deaf Women United, Am. Soc. for Deaf Children. Democrat. Roman Catholic. Home: 43 Woodridge Trail Henrietta NY 14467 Office: Nat Tech Inst for Deaf 52 Lomb Memorial Dr Rochester NY 14623

GUSTITUS, LINDA, lawyer, legislative aide; b. Rockford, Ill., Dec. 29, 1947; d. Joseph Jerome and Helen Victoria (Danielson) G.;p m. Robert Oswald Johnsen, Oct. 2, 1971: children: Robert Joseph Johnsen, Sandra Satre Johnsen. BA, Oberlin Coll., 1969; JD, Wayne State U., 1975. Bar: Ill. Staff atty. Ill. Fair Employment Practices Commn., Chgo., 1975-76; asst. state's atty. Cook County State's Atty. Office, Chgo., 1976-77; trial atty. U.S. Dept. Justice, Washington, 1977-79; staff dir., chief counsel subcom. oversight of govt. mgmt. U.S. Senate, Washington, 1979—; adj. prof. George Washington U., 1993-94. Democrat. Unitarian. Office: US Senate Oversight Com 446 Hart Senate Office Bldg Washington DC 20510*

GUTCHESS, SHERRI LYNN, communications executive; b. Syracuse, N.Y., Jan. 22, 1967; d. F. Fredrick and Elizabeth P. (Peenstra) G. BS in Pub. Rels./Journalism cum laude, Utica Coll., Syracuse U., 1989. Media rels. intern Utica Coll. of Syracuse U., 1988-89, media. rels. mgr., 1989; pub. rels. exec. Concept Cons., Syracuse, N.Y., 1989-90; pubs. mgr. Sta. WCNY-TV, Syracuse, N.Y., 1990; dir. comms. Loretto, Syracuse, N.Y., 1990-94; dir. cmty. rels. Hematology-Oncology Assocs. of Ctrl. N.Y., Syracuse, N.Y., 1994-95; comms. dir. Ctrl. N.Y. Girl Scout Coun., Inc., Syracuse, N.Y., 1995-96; freelance comms. cons. Syracuse, 1996—; campaign assoc. March of Dimes, Utica, N.Y., 1989. Vol. Susan G. Komen Found. Breast Cancer Found. Ctrl. N.Y. Chpt., 1994-95. Recipient Frank E. Gannett Journalism scholarship, 1988, 89, Reader's Digest grant, 1989. Mem. Am. Cancer Soc. (mem. ctrl. N.Y. chpt. relay for life com.), United Way of Ctrl. N.Y. (mem. comms. com.), Syracuse Press Club (assoc.), Women in Comms., Inc. (chairperson membership com. ctrl. N.Y. chpt., leading edge award 1995). Presbyterian. Home and Office: 126 N Midler Ave Syracuse NY 13206

GUTENTAG, PATRICIA RICHMAND, social worker, family counselor, occupational therapist; b. Newark, Apr. 10, 1954; d. Joseph and Joan (Miller) Leflein; m. Herbert Norman Gutentag; children: Steven, Jesse. BS in Occupational Therapy, Tufts U., 1976; MSW, Boston Coll., 1979. Lic. family and marriage counselor, lic. clin. social worker, N.J.; diplomate Am. Bd. Examiners in Clin. Social Work; registered occupational therapist, N.J. Social worker Jewish Family Svc., Salem, Mass., 1979-82; pvt. practice family and marriage counselor Westfield and Red Bank, N.J., 1982—; cons. high stress, Westfield and Red Bank, 1982—. Fellow N.J. Soc. for Clin. Social Work; mem. NASW, Am. Occupational Therapists Assn., Registered Occupational Therapists Assn., Soc. for Advancement Family Therapy in N.J., Am. Anorexia-Bulimia Assn., Am. Assn. Marriage and Family Therapy. Office: 200 Maple Ave Red Bank NJ 07701-1732

GUTHRIE, DIANA FERN, nursing educator; b. N.Y.C., May 7, 1934; d. Floyd George and A. May (Moler) Worthington; m. Richard Alan Guthrie, Aug. 18, 1957; children: Laura, Joyce, Tammy. AA, Graceland Coll., 1953; RN, Independence (Mo.) Sanitarium, 1956; BS in Nursing, U. Mo., 1957, MS in Pub. Health, 1969; EdS, Wichita State U., 1982; PhD, Walden U., 1985. RN, Mo., Kans.; lic. profl. counselor, Kans.; cert. in stress mgmt. edn.; cert.clin. hypnosis; lic. holistic nursing; cert. healing touch; advanced RN practitioner; lic. marriage and family therapist. Instr. red cross U.S. Naval Sta., Sangley Point, Philippines, 1961-63; acting head nurse newborn nursery U. Mo., Columbia, 1963-64, birth defect nurse dept. pediatrics, 1964-65, nursing dir. clin. research ctr., 1965-67, research asst., 1967-73; diabetes nurse specialist Sch. Medicine U. Kans., Wichita, 1973—, asst. then assoc. prof. Sch. Medicine, 1974-85, prof. dept. pediat. and psychiatry Sch. Medicine, 1985—; prof. dept. nursing Kans. U. Med. Ctr., Wichita, 1985—; nurse cons. diabetes Mo. Regional Med. Program, Columbia, 1970-73; nat. advisor Human Diabetes Ctr. for Excellence, Lexington, Ky., 1982-90, Phoenix, 1983-92, Charlottesville, Ky., 1990-95; adj. prof. Sch. Nursing Wichita State U., 1985—. Author: Nursing Management of Diabetes, 4th edit. 1997, The Diabetes Source Book, 1990, rev. edit., 1995; contbr. articles to profl. jours. Mem. health adv. bd. Mid-Am. All Indian Ctr., Wichita, 1978-80; bd. dirs. Wichita Urban Indian Health Clinic, 1980-82; trustee Graceland Coll., Lamoni, Iowa, 1996—. Recipient Explemplary Recognition award Epsilon Gamma chpt. Sigma Theta Tau, 1996. Fellow Am. Acad. Nursing; mem. ANA, APHA, Am. Diabetes Assn. (affiliate bd. dirs. 1979-83, pres. Kans. affiliate 1980-81, 90-91, Outstanding Educator award 1979), Am. Assn. Diabetes Educators (cert., Disting. Svc. award 1984), Am. Assn. Med. Psychotherapists (profl. adv. bd. 1985—), Sigma Theta Tau (exemplar recognition award Epsilon chpt. 1996). Democrat. Mem. Reorganized LDS Ch.

GUTHRIE, GLENDA EVANS, educational company executive; b. De Funiak Springs, Fla., Aug. 10, 1945; d. Owen Clement and Vera Mae (Adams) Evans; m. Theron Asbury Guthrie Jr., June 10, 1967; children: Michael Patrick, Jennifer Leigh. BS in Elem. Edn., Samford U., 1967; MA in Elem. Edn., U. Ala., 1983; EdS in Ednl. Leadership, U. Fla., 1990. Tchr. grades 8-9 Warrington Jr. High, Pensacola, Fla., 1967; tchr. grades 4-5 Birmingham (Ala.) City Schs., 1967-69; tchr. grade 5 Faith Christian Sch., Bessemer, Ala., 1969-70; tchr. grade 4 Fairfield Highlands Christian Sch., Birmingham, 1973-74, First Bapt. Sch., Pleasant Grove, Ala., 1974-83; tchr. grade 5 Ctrl. Park Christian Sch., Birmingham, 1983-84, elem. dir., 1984-86; tchr. grades 5-6 Duval County Sch., Jacksonville, Fla., 1986-90; ednl. cons. Jostens Learning Corp., Phoenix, 1990-92; sr. ednl. cons., 1993-95; staff devel. specialist Jostens Learning Corp., Phoenix, 1995—; co-founder Success Unlimited Learning Ctr., Birmingham, 1985-86; judge Sci. Fair, Jacksonville, 1988-90; seminar/workshop leader; mem. elem. textbook com. Duval County Schs., 1988-89. Active Clearview Bapt. Ch. Named Tchr. of Yr. Livingston Sch., Jacksonville, 1989, Ednl. Cons. of Yr., 1991-92. Mem. ASCD, Internat. Reading Assn., Nat. Coun. Tchrs. Math., Kappa Delta Pi. Republican. Baptist. Home: 300 Cannonade Cir Franklin TN 37064

GUTHRIE, HELEN A., nutrition educator, consultant; b. Sarnia, Ont., Can., Sept. 25, 1925; d. David and Helen (Sweet) Andrews; m. George Guthrie, June 4, 1949; children: Barbara, Jane, James. BA, U. Western Ont., 1946, DSc (hon.), 1982; MS, Mich. State U., 1948; PhD, U. Hawaii, 1968; DSc, U. Guelph, 1996. Registered dietitian, Pa. From instr. to prof. Pa. State U., University Park, 1949-73, chair dept., 1974-89, endowed prof. nutrition, 1989-91, prof. emerita, 1991—; v.p. Heinz Inst. Nutrition Scis., 1993—; nutrition cons. to industry, govt. and academia. Chmn. Bd. of Health, State College, Pa., 1977-82. Recipient Borden award Am. Home Econs. Assn., 1976, W.O. Atwater award USDA, 1989, Pacemaker award Pa. Nutrition Coun., 1994. Fellow Am. Inst. Nutrition (councillor 1982—, pres. 1987—, Elvehjhem award for pub. svc. 1989), Soc. Nutrition Edn. (pres. 1978-79, fellow, 1992), Internat. Life Sci. Inst.-Nutrition Found. (trustee 1979-92, v.p. nutrition 1986-89, editor Nutrition Today 1987—, Philippine Assn. Nutrition and Dietetics (hon.). Home: 1316 S Garner St State College PA 16801-6328 Office: Pa State U S-125 S Human Devel University Park PA 16802

GUTHRIE, JANET, professional race car driver; b. Iowa City, Mar. 7, 1938; d. William Lain and Jean Ruth (Midkiff) G. B.S. in Physics, U. Mich., 1960. Comml. pilot and flight instr., 1958-61; research and devel. engr. Republic Aviation Corp., Farmingdale, N.Y., 1960-67; publs. engr. Sperry Systems, Sperry Corp., Great Neck, N.Y., 1968-73; racing driver Sports Car Club Am. and Internat. Motor Sports Assn., 1963-86; profl. racing driver U.S. Auto Club and Nat. Assn. for Stock Car Racing, 1976-80; pres. Janet Guthrie Racing Enterprises Inc., 1978—; highway safety cons. Met. Ins. Co., 1980-87. Recipient Curtis Turner award Nat. Assn. for Stock Car Racing-Charlotte World 600, 1976; First in Class, Sebring 12-hour, 1970; North Atlantic Road Racing champion, 1973; named to Women's Sports Hall of Fame, 1980. Mem. Madison Ave. Sports Car Driving and Chowder Soc., Women's Sports Found., Les Dames d'Aspen, Internat. Wine and Food Soc., Nat. Spkrs. Assn.

GUTHRIE, JUDITH K., federal judge; b. Chgo., July 13, 1948; d. David Curtis and Kathleen McAfee G.; m. John H. Hannah, Jr., May 9, 1992. Student, Ariz. State U., 1966-68; BA, St. Mary's U., 1971; JD cum laude, U. Houston, 1980; postgrad., Harvard U., 1990. Bar: Tex. 1981, U.S. Dist. Ct. (ea. dist.) Tex. 1982, U.S. Ct. Appeals (5th cir.) 1982, U.S. Dist. Ct.

(no. dist.) Tex. 1983, U.S. Dist. Ct. (we. dist.) Tex. 1984. Editor Am. Coun. Edn., Washington, 1972-73; exec. asst. Tex. Ho. Reps., Austin, 1973-75; lobbyist Bracewell & Patterson, Austin, 1975-80; assoc. Bracewell & Patterson, Houston, 1980-81; briefing atty. Tex. Ct. Appeals, Tyler, 1981-82; ptnr. Hannah & Guthrie, Tyler, Tex., 1982-86; magistrate judge U.S. Dist. Ct. (ea. dist.) Tex., Tyler, 1986—; instr. legal asst. program, Tyler Jr. Coll., 1986-87; apptd. Tex. Judicial Coun., 1991—, gender bias task force, 1991—; lectr. in field. Contbr. articles to profl. jours. Bd dirs. Found. Women's Resources, Leadership Am., Leadership Tex.; adv. bd. Main St. Project; former Dem. chmn. Smith County; legal asst. adv. bd. Tyler Jr. Coll., 1986—; mem. Citizens Commn. Tex. Judicial System, 1992—. Mem. ABA (fed. trial judges legis. com. 1991—), Am. Judges Assn., Assn. U.S. Magistrates, 5th Cir. Bar Assn., State Bar Tex. (dist. 2A grievance com. 1990—, chmn. 1995—, coun. mem. women and law sect. 1981-84, bd. dirs. lawyers' credit union 1983-84, citizens and law focused edn. com. 1984-85), Smith County Bar Assn. (chmn. law libr. com. 1985—). Office: US District Court 300 Federal Bldg & US Ct House 211 W Ferguson St Tyler TX 75702-7212

GUTIERREZ, PATRICIA MARIELENA, systems engineer; b. Spartanburg, S.C., Mar. 4, 1970; d. Carlos Dario and Barbara Ruth (Hoyle) G. BSME, N.C. State U., 1993; MS in Info. Sci., Pa. State U., 1996. Student trainee NASA, Wallops Flight Facility, Wallops Island, Va., 1989-90; asst. chemist No. Telecom, Inc., Research Triangle Park, N.C., 1991-92; sys. engr. Lockheed Martin, Valley Forge, Pa., 1993-96; project mgr. Blacksmith, Inc., McLean, Va., 1996—. Mem. ASME, AIAA, Alpha Delta Pi, Alpha Delta Pi. Home: 13816L Braddock Springs Rd Centreville VA 20121

GUTIN, MYRA GAIL, communications educator; b. Paterson, N.J., Aug. 13, 1948; d. Stanley and Lillian (Edelstein) Greenberg; m. David Gutin, Sept. 5, 1971; children: Laura, Sarah, Andrew. BA, Emerson Coll., 1970, MA, 1971; PhD, U. Mich., 1983. Asst. prof. communications Cumberland County Coll., Vineland, N.J., 1972-80; asst. prof. communications Rider U., Lawrenceville, N.J., 1981-88, prof., 1989—; adj. instr. Essex County Coll., Newark, 1971-72, Nassau C.C., Garden City, N.Y., 1972, Trenton (N.J.) State Coll., 1981-84; adj. asst. prof. Rider U., 1981-85; lectr. in field. Author: The President's Partner The First Lady in the 20th Century, 1989; contbr. articles to profl. jours. Oficer Emerson Coll. Nat. Alumni Bd., 1994—; mem. Kellman Acad. Sch. Bd., 1996—. Recipient Alumni Achievement award Emerson Coll., Boston, 1991. Mem. Ctr. for Study of the Presidency, Speech Comm. Assn., Ea. Comm. Assn. Home: 119 Greenvale Ct Cherry Hill NJ 08034-1701

GUTMAN, LUCY TONI, school social worker, educator, counselor; b. Phila., July 13, 1936; d. Milton R. and Clarissa (Silverman) G.; divorced; children: James, Laurie. BA, Wellesley Coll., 1958; MSW, Bryn Mawr Coll., 1963; MA in History, U. Ariz., 1978; MEd, Northwestern State U., 1991, MA in English, 1992; postgrad., U. So. Miss., 1992—. Cert. Acad. Cert. Social Workers, La. Bd. cert. social worker, sch. social work specialist, Nat. Bd. Cert. Counselor; diplomate in clin. social work; cert. secondary tchr., La. Social worker Phila. Gen. Hosp., 1963-65; sr. social worker Irving Schwartz Inst. Children and Youth, 1965-66; sr. psychiat. social worker Child Study Ctr. Phila., 1966-68; chief social worker Framingham (Mass.) Ct. Clinic Juvenile Offenders, 1968-72; cons. Nashua (N.H.) Community Coun., 1969-72; dir. clinic, supr. social work Tucson East Community Mental Health Ctr., 1972-74; coord. spl. adoptions program Cath. Social Svcs. So. Ariz., Tucson, 1974-75; social worker Met. Ministry, 1983; supr. social work Leesville (La.) Mental Health Clinic, 1984; sch. social worker Vernon Parish Sch. Bd., Leesville, 1984—; adj. instr. English, sociology, Am. and European history Northwestern State U., Ft. Polk, La., 1984—; part-time counselor River North Psychol. Svcs., Leesville, 1989-92; presenter ann. conf. NASW, 1987, 88, La. Sch. Social Workers Conf., 1986, 87, La. Spl. Edn. Conf., 1988, La. Conf. Tchrs. English, 1991, 94, So. Assn. women Historians, 1994. Contbr. articles to profl. jours. Nat. Soc. Colonial Dames scholar, 1978-79; fellow Pa. State, 1961-62, NIMH, 1962-63. Mem. NASW, AACD, MLA, LWV, Am. Coll. Pers. Assn., Acad. Cert. Social Workers (diplomate), Bus. and Profl. Women Assn., Am. Legion Aux., So. Hist. Assn., So. Assn. Women Historians, Gamma Beta Phi, Phi Alpha Theta. Home: 2004 Allison St Leesville LA 71446-5104

GUTMAN, SHARON WEISSMAN, Holocaust educator; b. Worcester, Mass., May 22, 1949; d. Max (Marcus Heine) and Syma (Sternberg) Weissman; m. Paul Jerome Gutman, June 18, 1970 (dec. Sept., 1990); children: Rachel Z., Matthew A.; m. Charles Rand Lightner, June 26, 1993. BA, Bennington Coll., 1971; rabbinic student, Hebrew Union Coll., Hebrew Union Coll., N.Y.C., 1995—. Instr. Brit. fiction Beit Brl Tchrs. Coll., Tel Aviv, Israel, 1984-86; internat. coord. Remembering for the Future Internat. Conf., Berlin, 1991-93; v.p. Phila. Ctr. on the Holocaust, Genocide and Human Rights, 1991—, The Annual Scholars' Conf. on the Holocaust and the Chs., Phila., 1992—; dir. Post Holocaust Generation in Diaglogue, N.Y.C., 1992—. Asst. U.S. dir. First Official Commemoration of Babi Yar, Kiev, Ukraine, 1992; leader Sabbath Svc., Medbridge Convalescent Home, Springfield, N.J., 1993, 94. Home: 518 Lawrence Ave Westfield NJ 07090

GUTTMAN, HELENE NATHAN, biomedical research consultant, regression therapist; b. N.Y.C., July 21, 1930; d. Arthur and Mollie (Bergovoy) Nathan. BA, Bklyn. Coll., 1951; AM, Harvard U., 1956; MA, Columbia U., 1958; PhD, Rutgers U., 1960. Chartered chemist Royal Soc. Chemistry; registered profl. animal scientist; registered and cert. profl. past-life regression therapist; bd. cert. nutrition specialist; bd. cert. and registered hypnotherapist. Rsch. technician Pub. Health Rsch. Inst., N.Y.C., 1951-52; control bacteriologist Burroughs-Wellcome, Inc., Tuckahoe, N.Y., 1952-53; vol. researcher Haskins Labs., N.Y.C., 1952-53; rsch. asst. Haskins Labs., 1953-56, rsch. assoc., 1956-60, staff microbiologist, 1960-64; lectr. dept. biology Queens Coll., N.Y.C., 1956-57; rsch. collaborator Brookhaven Nat. Labs., Upton, L.I., N.Y., 1958; guest investigator Botanisches Institut der Technisches Hochschule, Darmstadt, Germany, 1960; rsch. assoc. dept. biol. scis. Goucher Coll., Towson, Md., 1960-62; vis. asst. rsch. prof. dept. medicine Med. Coll. Va. Richmond, 1960-62; asst. prof., then assoc. prof. dept. biology NYU, 1962-67; from assoc. prof. to prof. dept. biol. scis. U. Ill.-Chgo., 1967-75, prof., 1969-75; prof. dept. microbiology U. Ill. Med. Sch., 1969-75; assoc. dir. for rsch. Urban Systems Lab. U. Ill., 1975; expert Office of Dir. Nat. Heart, Lung and Blood Inst., NIH, Bethesda, Md., 1975-77; coordinator rsch. resources Office Program Planning and Evaluation Nat. Heart, Lung and Blood Inst., NIH, 1977-79; dep. dir. Sci. Adv. Bd., Office of Adminstr., EPA, 1979-80; program coordinator, post-harvest tech., food safety and human nutrition, sci. and edn. adminstrn. USDA, 1980-83, assoc. dir. Beltsville Human Nutrition Rsch. Ctr., Agrl. Rsch. Svc., 1983-89; pres. HNG Assocs., 1983—; nat. animal care coord. Nat. Program Staff Agr. Rsch. Svc./USDA, Beltsville, Md., 1989-95; bd. advisors The Monroe Inst., 1993—. Sr. author: Experiments in Cellular Biodynamics, 1972; co-editor (procs.) First Joint USA-USSR Joint Symposium on Blood Transfusion, Moscow, 1976, DHEW Publ. No. (NIH) 78-1246, 1978; editorial bd. Jour. Protozoology, 1972-75, Jour. Am. Med. Women's Assn., 1978-81, Methods in Cell Science, 1994—; sr. editor: Science and Animals: Addressing Contemporary Issues, 1989; editor: Guidelines for Well-being of Rodents in Research, 1990, Rodents and Rabbits: Current Research Issues, 1994; (with others) Rodents and Rabbits: Addressing Current Issues, 1994; contbr. articles profl. jours. Mem. edn. com. Ill. Commn. on Status Women, 1974-75; cons. EPA, sci. adv. bd., 1974-79; bd. dirs. Du Page County Comprehensive Health Care Agy., 1974-75. Andelot fellow Harvard U., 1956, Rutgers scholar Rutgers U., 1960; recipient Thomas Jefferson Murray prize Theobald Smith Soc., 1959; spl. award for work in Germany Deutscher Forschungs Gemeinschaft, 1960; Fellow Dazian Found., 1956; research grantee. Fellow AAAS, Am. Inst. Chemists (com. chmn.), Am. Acad. Microbiology, N.Y. Acad. Scis.; mem. Soc. Am. Bacteriologists (pres.'s fellow 1957), Internat. Soc. for the Study of Subtile Energies and Energy Medicine, Assn. for Transpersonal Psychology (profl. mem.), Soc. for In Vitro Biology (chair constn. and bylaws com. 1994—, Disting. Svc. award 1995), Tissue Culture Assn. (com. chmn. Nat. Capital Area br. 1988-90), Am. Soc. Neurochemistry, Am. Soc. Biol. Chemistry and Molecular Biology, Neuroscis. Soc., Am. Soc. Microbiologists, Am. Soc. Cell Biology (past com. chmn.), Am. Soc. Clni. Nutrition, Soc. Protozoology (past mem. exec. com., past jour. editl. bd.), Assn. Women in Sci. (past mem. exec. bd., past com. chmn.), Fed. Orgn. Profl. Women (past task force chmn., past pres.), Univ. and Coll. Women Ill. (past v.p.), Am. Running and Fitness Assn. (bd. dirs., mem. editl. bd., mem. bd. advisors 1993-95), Assn. Past Life Rsch. and Therapy, Sigma Xi, Sigma Delta Epsilon (past coord. regional ctrs.). Home and Office: 5607 Mclean Dr Bethesda MD 20814-1021

GUY, JENNIFER LOUISE, nursing administrator; b. Ashtabula, Ohio, Oct. 17, 1948; d. Edward Frederick abnd Louise Arnoldia (Plagkais) Peterson; m. Donald File, Mar. 17, 1973 (div. Oct. 1978); m. Jerry Thomas Guy, Feb. 10, 1981; 1 child, Thomas Osler. BS, Ohio State U., 1970; diploma, Mt. Carmel Sch. Nursing, 1977. Lab. tech. Ashtabula (Ohio) Gene Hosp., 1964-65; rsch. specialist infectious diseases Ohio State U., Columbus, 1966-73, rsch. specialist oncology, 1973-77; dir. oncology Grant Med. Ctr., Columbus, 1977-88; adminstr. oncology Pk. Med. Ctr., Columbus, 1988—; adminstr. Columbus Cmty. Clin. Oncology Program, 1985-88; trustee Am. Cancer Soc., Columbus, 1995-96, v.p., 1995-96; pres. Assn. Cmty. Cancer Ctrs., Rockville, Md., 1991-92; grant reviewer NIH, Bethesda, Md., 1986—. Contbr. articles to profl. jours, chpts. to books. Bd. dirs. Franklin County Unit Am. Cancer Soc., 1992—; trustee Columbus Cmty. Clin. Oncology Program, 1990-94, Columbus Race for the Cure, 1994—, Pk. Found. Columbus, 1995—. Mem. Oncology Nursing Soc. Republican. Office: Pk Med Ctr 1492 E Broad Columbus OH 43206

GUY, L(EONA) RUTH, educator; b. Kemp, Tex., Mar. 17, 1913; d. Henry Luther and Minnie Elizabeth (Murphy) G. AB, Baylor U., 1934, MS, 1949; PhD, Stanford (Calif.) U., 1953. Rsch. fellow NOOO Stanford U., 1951-53, teaching asst., 1951; with U. Tex. Southwestern Med. Sch., Dallas, 1962-82, prof., 1977-82, prof. emeritus, 1982—; assoc. dir. Parkland Meml. Hosp. Blood Bank, Dallas, 1953-78; cons. VA Hosp., Dallas, 1960-80, Temple, 1964-80; vis. prof. to Far East, China Med. Bd. of N.Y., N.Y.C., 1969-70. Author: (with others) Modern Blood Banking and Transfusion Practices, 1982; editor: Technical Manual, 1966; contbr. numerous articles to profl. jours. Bd. dirs. Dallas Repertory Theater, Dallas, 1983-89. Named Disting. Alumnus Baylor U., 1994; inducted into Tex. Women's Hall of Fame, Gov.'s Commn. for Women, 1989. Fellow Am. Soc. Clin. Pathologists (hon., assoc., Disting. Svc. award 1989); mem. Bus. and Profl. Women's Club Dallas (pres. 1970-71), Baylor Women's Coun. (Woman of Distinction award 1988), Baylor Heritage Club (pres. Dallas chpt. 1991-92), Zonta (pres. Dallas chpt. 1961-62, Spirit of Zonta award 1994). Baptist. Home: 5455 La Sierra Dr Dallas TX 75231-4176

GUY, SHARON KAYE, state agency executive; b. Nashville, Apr. 5, 1958; d. Dallas Hearold and Elizabeth Jean (Towns) Gregory; 1 child, Anthony Lee. Grad. high sch., Chgo. Clk. Pub. Health dept. State of Tenn., Nashville, 1979-84, office mgr. Health Facilities commn., 1984-92; asst. Legis. Svcs., Nashville, 1992-95; rep. State Ins., Nashville, 1995—; acct. Bryant Guy Constrn., Nashville, 1984—. Blood drive coord. ARC, Nashville, 1984—; campaign vol. United Way, Nashville, 1984—; vol. State Community Coll., 1990—, Nashville Tech., 1991—. Baptist. Home: 121 Candle Woods Dr Hendersonville TN 37075 Office: Andrew Jackson State Office Bldg Ste 1400 Andrew Jackson Bldg Nashville TN 37243-0295

GUYNES, DEMI See **MOORE, DEMI**

GUZY, CAROL, photojournalist. ADN, Northampton County Area C.C., Pa.; AAS in Photography, Art Inst. Ft. Lauderdale. Staff photographer The Miami Herald, 1980-88; now staff photographer The Washington Post, 1988—. Recipient Best Portfolio award Atlanta Seminar Photojournalism, 1982, 85, 90, Robert F. Kennedy award, 1984, Excellence citation Overseas Press Club, 1986, Pulitzer Prize in spot news photography, 1986, 95, Leica Excellence medal, 1994; named Newspaper Photographer of Yr. Nat. Press Photographer Assn., 1989, 92, Photographer of Yr. White House News Photographers Assn., 1991, 93, 94, 96. Office: The Washington Post 1150 15th St NW Washington DC 20071-0001*

GUZY, MARGUERITA LINNES, secondary education educator; b. Santa Monica, Calif., Nov. 19, 1938; d. Paul William Robert and Margarete (Rodowski) Linnes; m. Stephen Paul Guzy, Aug. 25, 1962 (div. 1968); 1 child, David Paul. AA, Santa Monica Coll., 1959; student, U. Mex., 1959-60; BA, UCLA, 1966, MA, 1973; postgrad. in psychology, Pepperdine U., 1988-92; cert. bilingual competence, Calif., 1994. Cert. secondary tchr., quality review team ednl. programs, bilingual, Calif. Tchr. Inglewood (Calif.) Unified Sch. Dist., 1967—, chmn. dept., 1972-82, mentor, tchr., 1985-88; clin. instr. series Clin. Supervision Levels I, II, Ingelwood, 1986-87; clin. intern Chem. Dependency Ctr., St. John's Hosp., Santa Monica, 1988-92; lectr. chem. and codependency St. John's Hosp., Santa Monica, 1992—; tchr. Santa Monica Coll., 1975-76; cons. bilingual edn. Inglewood Unified Sch. Dist., 1975—, lead tchr. new hope program at-risk students, 1992; cons. tchr. credentialing fgn. lang. State of Calif., 1994; sch. rep. restructuring edn. for state proposal, 1991—; mem. Program Quality Rev. Team Pub. Edn., Calif., 1993; mem. Supt.'s Com. for Discrimination Resolution, 1994-95. Author: Elementary Education: "Pygmalian in the Classroom", 1975, English Mechanics Workbook, 1986. Recipient Teaching Excellence cert. State of Calif., 1986; named Tchr. of Yr., 1973, 88. Mem. NEA, Calif. Tchrs. Assn., Inglewood Tchrs. Assn. (local rep. 1971-72, tchr. edn. and profl. svcs. com. 1972-78), UCLA Alumnae Assn. (life), Prytanean Alumnae Assn. (bd. dirs. 1995-96, 1960's rep., 2d v.p. membership 1996-98). Republican. Office: Monroe Jr High Sch 10711 S 10th Ave Inglewood CA 90303-2015

GUZZETTI, BARBARA JEAN, education educator; b. Chgo., Nov. 15, 1948; d. Louis Earnest and Viola Genevive (Russell) G. BS, No. Ill. U., 1971, MS, 1974; PhD, U. Colo., 1982. Title I reading tchr. Harlem Consolidated Sch. Dist., Loves Park, Ill., 1971-72; elem. classroom tchr. Rockford (Ill.) Pub. Schs., 1972-77; diagnostic tchr. Denver Pub. Schs., 1977-78; secondary reading tchr. Jefferson County Pub. Schs., Lakewood, Colo., 1979-81, secondary reading specialist, 1983-84; rsch. and program assoc. Mid-Continent Regional Ednl. Lab., Aurora, Colo., 1983-84; evaluation specialist N.W. Regional Ednl. Lab., Denver, 1984-85; assoc. prof. Calif. State U., Ponoma, 1985-88, Ariz. State U., Tempe, 1988—; chair, tech. com. Nat. Reading Conf., 1994-96. Author: Literacy Instruction in Content Areas, 1996; mem. editl. bd. The Reading Tchr., Jour. of Reading Behavior, Nat. Reading conf. Yearbook; contbr. articles to profl. jours. Mem. Am. Ednl. Rsch. Assn., Nat. Reading Conf., Internat. Reading Assn. (chair studies and rsch. grants com. 1992-95). Democrat. Lutheran. Home: 2170 E Aspen Dr Tempe AZ 85282-2953 Office: Ariz State U Coll of Edn Tempe AZ 85287-0311

GWIN, DOROTHY JEAN BIRD, psychology educator, college dean; b. Smith, Tex., June 26, 1934; d. Joseph William and Elva Gracie (Elledge) Bird; m. Clinton Dale Gwin, Nov. 21, 1964; 1 child, Clinton Bird. BBA, East Tex. State U., 1954, MS, 1955; EdD, U. Kans., 1958. Lic. psychologist, La. Tchr. Thomas Jefferson High Sch., Port Arthur, Tex., 1954; resident dir. U. Kans., Lawrence, 1955-57; sch. psychologist Caddo Parish Schs., Shreveport, La., 1958-67, con. psychologist, 1967-70; prof. psychol., edn. Centenary Coll., Shreveport, La., 1967-79, 1996—, dean, 1979-92, dean enrollment mgmt., 1993-96, prof. edn., psychol. and dir. alumni rels., 1992-93. Bd. dirs. Vol. of Am., Shreveport, 1967-70; pres. bd. dirs. Southfield Sch., Shreveport, 1984-86, bd. dirs. 1974-87. Fulbright U.S. Ednl. Adminstrs. grantee to Germany, 1990. Mem. Am. Pers. Guidance Assn. (life). Home: 3402 Madison Park Blvd Shreveport LA 71104-4546 Office: Centenary Coll La 2911 Centenary Blvd Shreveport LA 71104-3335

GWINN, MARY ANN, newspaper reporter; b. Forrest City, Ark., Dec. 29, 1951; d. Lawrence Baird and Frances Evelyn (Jones) G.; m. Richard A. King, June 3, 1973 (div. 1981); m. Stephen E. Dunnington, June 10, 1990. BA in Psychology, Hendrix Coll., 1973; MEd in Spl. Edn., Ga. State U., 1975; MA in Journalism, U. Mo., 1979. Tchrs. aide DeKalb County Schs., Decatur, Ga., 1973-74, tchr., 1975-78; reporter Columbia (Mo.) Daily Tribune, 1979-83; reporter Seattle Times, 1983—, now internat. trade and workplace reporter; instr. ext. divsn. U. Wash., Seattle, 1990; journalism instr., Seattle U., 1994. Recipient Charles Stewart Mott Found. award for edn. reporting, 1980, C.B. Blethen award for enterprise reporting Blethen Family, Seattle, 1989, Pulitzer Prize for nat. reporting, 1990. Mem. Newspaper Guild. Office: Seattle Times PO Box 70 1120 John St Seattle WA 98111

GWINN, MARY DOLORES, philosopher, author, speaker; b. Oakland, Calif., Sept. 16, 1946; d. Epifanio and Carolina (Lopez) Cruz; m. James Monroe Gwinn, Oct. 23, 1965; 1 child, Larry Allen. Student, Monterey Peninsula Jr. Coll., 1965. Retail store mgr. Consumer's Distbg. divsn. May Co., Hayward, Calif., 1973-78; mktg. rep. Dale Carnegie Courses, San Jose, Calif., 1978-79; founder, pres. Strategic Integrations, Ariz.'s Innovative Bus. Devel. Ctr., Scottsdale, 1985—; speaker St. John's Coll. U. Cambridge, England, 1992; founder, pres. Internat. Inst. for Conceptual Edn., Scottsdale, 1993—, Gwinn Genius Inst., 1995—. Founder new fields of study Genestics and NeuroBus.; profiled the Thought Process of Genius; conceived Whole Brain Business Theory, 1985; author: Genius Leadership Secrets From The Past For the 21st Century, 1995; contbr. articles to profl. jours. Republican. Home and Office: 5836 E Angela Dr Scottsdale AZ 85254-6410

GWOZDZ, KIM ELIZABETH, interior designer; b. Spokane, Wash., June 10, 1958; d. Myron Marcus and Marilyn Kay (Alsterlund) Westerkamp; m. Edwin Eugene Gwozdz, June 14, 1981; children: Ryan Marcus, Lauren Taylor. Student, U. Florence, Italy, 1979; BFA in Graphic Design, Illustration and Art History, U. Ariz., 1980. Design asst. Morse Studio, Scottsdale, Ariz., 1982; interior designer Pat Bacon & Assocs., Scottsdale, Ariz., 1983-88; prin., interior designer Provenance, Inc., Scottsdale, Ariz., 1988-90; dir. residential design Cox, James & Assocs., Phoenix, Ariz., 1990; prin, interior designer Kim E. Gwozdz/Provenance, Phoenix, Ariz., 1991, 1993—; interior designer Brady's Interior Design and Florist, Scottsdale, 1991-93. Contbr. articles to profl. jours. Nursery dir. infant and toddler care Mt. Cavalry Luth. Ch., Phoenix, 1985, mem. youth bd., 1984-89, trustee, 1993—; mem. Jr. League of Phoenix, 1989—, HIV/AIDS com., 1994—; mem. Orpheum Theater com., 1989-94, vice chmn., 1990-91, chmn., 1992-94, Gift Mart com. Design Decorations, 1991-92, chmn., 1991, exec. com., bd. dirs. Orpheum Theatre Found., 1992—; active annual gala com. Am. Cancer Soc., 1993-94, 94-95, 95-96, March of Dimes Gourmet Gala, 1991, 93, 95; design affiliate Nat. Trust for Hist. Preservation, 1986—. Recipient First Place award Annual Wool Rug Design Competition, Edward Fields, Inc., 1989, Second Place award, 1990, Third Place award, 1991. Mem. Am. Soc. Interior Designers (assoc. Ariz. North chpt., significant interiors survery com. 1975-91, chmn. 1990-91, Phoenix Home and Garden com. 1989-90, Herberger Theatre com. 1989-91, awards com. 1989, 91, chmn. 1990, competitions com. 1991, chmn. 1989-90, Rosson House Christmas chmn. 1986-91, hist. preservation chmn. 1988-91, directory chmn. Designers Market 1991, project designer, 1996; mem. nominating com. 1991-92, mktg. com. 1995, Third Place award Ariz. North 1987, Second Place award 1987, 88, 92, 95, First Place award Nat. 1989, 94, 95). Republican. Lutheran. Home: 529 W Palm Ln Phoenix AZ 85003-1129 Office: Kim E Gwozdz/Provenance 2425 E Camelback Rd Ste 450 Phoenix AZ 85016-4236

GWYNN, CAT, photographer; b. Glendale, Calif., July 22, 1962; d. Gary Duane and Constance (Gwynn) Stevens. Student, Otis/Parsons Art Inst., L.A., 1985-89. Tchg. asst. Otis/Parsons Art Inst., L.A., 1986-87; pvt. photography tchr., 1988—; photographer, artist Gilda's Club, N.Y.C., 1995—, Women's Clinic, L.A., 1994—. Dir., animation asst. numerous music videos, TV film, commls., L.A., N.Y.C., and San Francisco, 1987-90; filmmaker short films comml. spots, music videos, N.Y.C., San Francisco, L.A., Seattle, 1987—; photographer comml. and fine art exhbns. and publs., nationwide, 1986—; photographer: (book) Forever Yes, Art of the New Tattoo, 1992; photographer, artist: (book) Rocks of Ages, 1992; dir., filmmaker: (short documentary) Forever, Yes, Art of the New Tattoo, 1992, (short film) Angels with Dirty Faces, 1992. Recipient Best of Show award L.A. Art Assn., 1995, Award of Merit Orange County AD Awards, 1994, 1st pl. portrait and documentary photography L.A. Photography Ctr., 1987, 1st pl. portrait photography, 1986. Mem. NOW. Democrat. Home: 4470 Sunset Blvd #114 Los Angeles CA 90027

GYURO, PAULA CANDICE, financial planner; b. Phillipsburg, N.J., May 23, 1947; d. Alfred Eugene Gyuro and Pauline Johanna (Tinnes) Caldwell. BA, Ohio Wesleyan U., 1969; MBA, Xavier U., 1984. CFP. Events coord. The Nestle Co., Marysville, Ohio, 1969-73; sr. technologist R&D The Kroger Co., Cinti, Ohio, 1973-88; personal fin. advisor Am. Express Fin. Advisors, Inc., Cinti, 1989—. Mem. Inst. CFPs, Miami Valley Soc. Inst. CFPs. Office: Am Express Fin Advisors Inc 11590 Century Blvd Ste 214 Cincinnati OH 45246-3317

HAAB, LUCILLE HELEN, primary school educator; b. Bakersfield, Calif., Sept. 11, 1943; d. Frank W. Haab and Lucy Haab Davis. BA, Calif. State U., San Jose, 1966, MA, 1992. Cert. kindergarten/primary tchr., Calif., gen. elem. tchr., Calif. Kindergarten tchr. Evergreen Sch. Dist., San Jose, 1966—, mentor tchr.; lectr./cons. Bur. of Edn. and Rsch., Bellevue, Wash., 1990-95; lectr./cons. Seminars for Early Childhood, San Jose, 1995—; pvt. lectr./cons. in field, 1988—. Author: The Developmentally Appropriate Classroom: A Children's Garden, 1990, Art Activities to Grow On, 1990. Mem. Saratoga Drama Group, 1974—. Democrat.

HAAG, ALANA ZOE, secondary education educatpr; b. York, Pa., Feb. 16, 1948; d. Paul R. Forry and Yaroslava L. (Langova) Kasl; m. Robert Eugene Haag, Aug. 20, 1977; children: Mariana, Michael. BS, Millersville U., 1970, MA, 1975. French tchr. Northeastern H.S., Manchester, Pa., 1970—; mem. student asst. team, Manchester, 1991—. Active Southern Dem. Club, 1970—, York Twinning Assn., 1970—. Mem. Northeastern Edn. Assn. (chairperson). Lutheran. Home: 23 W High St Windsor PA 17366-9709 Office: Northeastern H S 300 High St Manchester PA 17345-1508

HAAG, CAROL ANN GUNDERSON, marketing professional, consultant; b. Mpls.; d. Glenn Alvin and Genevieve Esther (Knudson) Gunderson; m. Lawrence S. Haag, Aug. 30, 1969; 1 child, Maren Anne. BJ, U. Mo., 1969; postgrad., Roosevelt U., Chgo., 1975—. Pub. relations writer, advt. copywriter Am. Hosp. Supply Corp., Evanston, Ill., 1969-70; asst. dir. pub. relations Rush-Presbyn. St. Luke's Med. Ctr., Chgo., 1970-71; asst. mgr. pub. and employee communications Quaker Oats Co., Chgo., 1971-72, mgr. editorial communications, 1972-74, mgr. employee communications programs, 1974-77; dir. pub. relations Shaklee Corp., San Francisco, 1978-82; pres. CH & Assocs., San Francisco, 1982-84; dir corp. communications BRAE Corp., San Francisco, 1984; dir. mktg. St. Francis Meml. Hosp., San Francisco, 1985-89, dir. mktg. and planning svcs., 1989-91; ptnr. Haag & Rohan, San Francisco, San Diego, 1991—; cons. in field. Bd. dirs. Calif. League Handicapped; mem. adv. bd. San Francisco Spl. Olympics; mem. pub. relations com. San Francisco Recreation and Parks Dept., San Francisco Vol. Bur. Recipient 1st place cert. Printing Industry Am., 1972, 74, 1st place spl. comm. award Internat. Assn. Bus. Communicators, 1974, 1st place citation Chgo. Assn. Bus. Communicators, 1974, gold award Healthcare Mktg. Reports, 1989, 90. Mem. NATAS, Indsl. Com. Coun., Pub. Rels. Soc. Am., San Francisco C. of C. (grad. leadership program 1991, bd. dirs. leadership coun.), San Francisco Press Club. Home and Office: 133 Fernwood Dr Moraga CA 94556-2315

HAAS, CAROLYN BUHAI, elementary education educator, publisher, writer, consultant; b. Chgo., Jan. 1, 1926; d. Michael and Tillie (Weiss) Buhai; m. Robert Green Haas, June 29, 1947 (dec. June 30, 1984); children—Andrew Robert, Mari Beth, Thomas Michael, Betsy Ann, Karen Sue. B.Ed., Smith Coll., Northampton, Mass., 1947; postgrad. Nat. Coll. Edn., Evanston, Ill., 1956-59; Art Inst. Chgo., 1958-59. Tchr., Francis W. Parker Sch., Chgo., 1947-49; tchr. art Glencoe Pub. Schs., Ill., 1967-68, substitute tchr., 1964-72; co-founder PAR Leadership Tng. Found., Northfield, Ill., 1969-81; pres., editor CBH Pub., Inc., Northfield, 1979-92; cons., writer, adv. bd. The Learning Line; cons. presch. sci. program Mus. Sci. and Industry, Chgo.; adv. bd. My Own Mag.; cons. in field. Author: (with Ann Cole and Betty Weinberger) I Saw a Purple Cow, 1972, A Pumpkin In A Pear Tree, 1974, Children Are Children Are Children, 1976, Backyard Vacation, 1978, Purple Cow to the Rescue, 1982, Recipes for Fun and Learning, 1982, (with A.C. Friedman) My Own Fun, 1990, The Big Book of Recipes for Fun, 1979, Look At Me: Activities for Babies and Toddlers, 1985; co-editor: Know Your Town/East Hampton League Women Voters of the Hamptons, 1993; contbr. articles to profl. jours. Pres., West Sch. PTA, Glencoe; pres. Jr. Bd. Scholarship and Guidance, Chgo.; bd. dirs. Family Counseling Service of Glencoe, Glencoe Human Relations Com.; pres., sec., bd. dirs. Glencoe Pub. Library; pres. Friends of Glencoe Pub. Library; co-founder Glencoe Patriotic Days Com.; co-chmn. Frank Lloyd Wright Bridge Com., Glencoe; pres., bd. dirs. Chgo. League Smith Coll.; mem. women's bd. Northwestern U.; bd. dirs. Chgo. chpt. Am. Jewish Com.; mem. women's com. Chgo. Symphony Orch. Clubs; bd. dirs. Art Resources in Teaching;

vol. Parish Art Mus., The Retreat. Mem. AAUW, LWV (bd. dirs.), Internat. Reading Assn., Soc. Children's Bookwriters, Children's Reading Roundtable, Nat. Assn. Edn. Young Children, Assn. Childhood Edn. Internat., NEA, Jimmy Ernst Artists Alliance (bd. dirs.), Phi Delta Kappa. Democrat. Jewish. Avocations: art, reading, sports, travel.

HAAS, ELLEN, federal agency administrator; b. N.Y.C., July 25, 1939. BA in History, U. Mich., 1961. Am. history and govt. tchr. Oklahoma City Pub. Schs., 1961-63; dir. consumer edn. County of Montgomery, Md., 1973-74; acting exec. dir. Nat. Consumers League, 1975-76; exec. dir. Pub. Voice for Food and Health Policy, Washington, 1982-93; asst. sec. agriculture food and consumer svcs. USDA, Washington, 1993—. Office: USDA Food & Consumer Svcs 14th & Independence Ave SW Washington DC 20250-0002*

HAAS, JACQUELINE CRAWFORD, lawyer; b. St. Louis, Nov. 9, 1935; d. Ernest Augustus and Nora (Fullard) Crawford; m. Karl Alan Haas, Jan. 27, 1962 (dec. Mar. 1986); children: James Andrew, Susan Jennifer, David Reid, Peter Crawford. AB, Cornell U., 1957; LLB, Harvard U., 1961. Bar: N.Y. 1962, U.S. Dist. Ct. (so. dist.) N.Y. 1963, U.S. Ct. Appeals (2d cir.) 1968, Mass. 1972. Assoc. Lord, Day & Lord, N.Y.C., 1961-63; atty. family ct. div. Legal Aid Soc., Bklyn., 1964-66; exam. atty. N.Y.C. Dept. of Investigation, 1966-68, exec. asst. to commr., 1969-71; pvt. practice Weston, Mass., 1971—; mem. Greater Boston com. Harvard U. Law Sch. Fund, Cambridge, Mass., 1976—. Del. Mass. Dem. Issues Conv., 1983, 85, 87, 89, 92, 93, 95, Mass. Dem. Nominating Conv., 1984, 86, 94; mem. Mass. Dem. Party Platform Com., 1993; mem. Dem. Town Com., Weston, 1984—, vice chmn., 1984-86; chmn. bd. Roxbury-Weston Programs, Inc., 1982-84; mem. family com. METCO, 1973-75, cmty. coord. coun., 1982-85; mem. Weston Housing Needs Com., 1991-93. Mem. ABA (civil practice and procedure of the antitrust sect.), Mass. Bar Assn., Assn. of Bar of N.Y.C., Harvard Law Sch. Assn. Mass. (v.p. 1991—). Democrat. Episcopalian. Office: 42 Partridge Hill Rd Weston MA 02193-1750

HAAS, KELLEY WEYFORTH, marketing and communications company executive; b. St. Louis, July 27, 1964; d. Francis Griffin Jr. and Mara (Kelley) Weyforth; m. Timothy John Haas, June 27, 1987. BSBA, U. Kans., 1986. Bookkeeper Mktg. Resources, Inc., Overland Park, Kans., 1983-84, prodn./traffic asst., 1984-85, media buyer, planner, 1985-86, coord. tng. programs, 1986-87, traffic mgr., 1987-89; sr. account. exec. Mktg. Resources Am., Inc., Overland Park, 1989-91, account supr., 1991-92, v.p., account supr., 1992-93, v.p. mktg. svcs., 1993-94, sr. v.p. mktg. svcs., 1994-95; sr. v.p. COO Mktg. Resources Am. Inc., Overland Park, 1995—; also bd. dirs., mem. exec. com. Mktg. Resources Am., Inc., Overland Park. Mem. Advt. Club Kansas City, Bus. Mktg. Assn. Office: Mktg Resources Am Inc 10551 Barkley St Overland Park KS 66212-1812

HAAS, SUZANNE NEWHOUSE, management consultant, human resources specialist; b. Akron, Ohio, Feb. 7, 1945; d. Earl Wallace and Bernice (Pikoski) Newhouse; m. Raymond John Haas, Feb. 8, 1975; children: Monique, John, Alexander. BA in Psychology, Kent (Ohio) State U., 1984, BA in Bus. Adminstrn., 1985; MA in Indsl. Psychology, Cleve. State U., 1991. Asst. dept. head Green Cross Gen. Hosp., Cuyahoga Falls, Ohio, 1966-73; customer svc. rep. Ohio Bell Telephone Co., Akron, 1973-75; job analyst McKinley Life Care, Canton, Ohio, 1988; mgmt. cons. Paragon Human Resource Systems, Canton, 1989—; rsch. asst. N.E. Ohio U. Coll. of Medicine, Rootstown, 1990-93; site coord. Vanderbilt U. Inst. Mental Health Policy, Nashville, Tenn., 1993—; rsch. site coord. Vanderbilt U., Nashville, 1993—. Mem. APA, ASTD, Am. Psychol. Soc., Acad. Mgmt., Ohio Psychol. Assn. Republican. Roman Catholic. Home: 115 48th St NW Canton OH 44709-1418 Office: Paragon Human Resource Sys 115 48th St NW Canton OH 44709-1418

HAASE, PATRICIA ANN THOMPSON, nursing educator; b. Franklin, Ind., Dec. 8, 1931; d. Lawrence Edmond and Dorcas Rhea (Burton) Thompson; m. William C. Haase, Sept. 4, 1957 (div. Sept., 1972). BS in Nursing, Ind. U., 1956, MS in Nursing, 1957; PhD, Purdue U., 1972. RN, Ind. Project dir. nursing curriculum So. Regional Edn. Bd., Atlanta, 1972-75, 76-82; dir. grad. studies in nursing Ga. State U., Atlanta, 1975-76; dean Sch. of Nursing U. Tenn., Chattanooga, 1982-86, prof. nursing, 1986—; asst. prof. De Pauw U., Indpls., 1965-66, asst. prof. , dir. assoc. degree program in nursing, Ind. U., Indpls., 1966-72. Author: (books) The Origins and Rise of Assoc. Degree Nursing Edn., 1990, Assoc. Degree Nursing Edn.: An Historical Annotated Bibliography, 1942-88, 1990; also contbr. numerous articles to profl. jours., presented many papers at sci. and ednl. confs. Recipient Disting. Alumni award Ind. U. Sch. of Nursing, 1980. Home: 4016 Loch Highland Pass Roswell GA 30075 Office: Univ Tenn Sch of Nursing 615 McCollie Ave Chattanooga TN 37403

HAAS-ORO, DEBRA ANN, dentist; b. Mascoutah, Ill., May 12, 1953; d. Cyril John and Elizabeth Louise (Billhartz) Haas; m. Robert John Oro, June 17, 1979; children: Philip, Anna. BS in Biology with honors, U. Ill., 1975; postgrad., Harvard U., Boston, 1975-76; DMD, U. Pa., 1979. Lic. dentist Pa., N.J., Ariz. Dentist/rschr. NIH Dental Rsch., Bethesda, Md., 1977; dentist USPHS, Kotzebue, Alaska, 1978; resident Luth. Med. Ctr., Bklyn., 1979-80; attending/lectr. Brookdale Hosp. and Med. Ctr., Bklyn., 1980-81, Hudson Valley Hosp. Ctr., Cortlandt Manor, N.Y., 1982-96; pres., dentist Hudson Valley Dental Medicine, Cortlandt Manor, 1985-96; pres., co-founder Penn Dental Cons., Oro Valley, Ariz., 1993—; lectr. in field. James scholar U. Ill., 1972, Robert Woods Johnson scholar, 1975. Fellow Acad. Gen. Dentistry; mem. ADA, Acad. Cosmetic Dentistry, N.Y. State Dental Soc., North Dist. Dental Soc., So. Ariz. Dental Soc., Peekskill-Yorktown Dental Soc. (pres. 1987-88), Kappa Delta (v.p. 1973), Alpha Lambda Delta. Home: 991 W Wheatgrass Pl Oro Valley AZ 85737

HABACHY, SUZAN SALWA SABA, development economist, foundation administrator; b. Cairo, Egypt, July 15, 1933; came to the U.S., 1952; d. Saba and Gameela (Gindy) H. BA, Bryn Mawr (Pa.) Coll., 1954; MA, Harvard U., Cambridge, Mass., 1956. Teaching fellow Ohio U., Athens, 1957-58; economist Mobil Oil Co., N.Y.C., 1959-64; reporter, editor Petroleum Intelligence Weekly, N.Y.C., 1964-65, McGraw Hill News Bur., London, England, 1965-68; program officer UN, N.Y.C., 1969-75, section chief, 1975-88; focal point for women UN Office of Pers., N.Y.C., 1988-93; exec. dir. The Trickle Up Program, N.Y.C., 1994—. Home: 1056 Fifth Ave New York NY 10028

HABER, DIANE LOIS, psychotherapist, clinical specialist; b. Bklyn., Oct. 4, 1937; d. Philip and Ida (Kleinfeld) H.; m. Paul Friedman, Sept. 27, 1959 (div. Feb. 1978); children: Philip Friedman, Andrew Friedman, Melanie Friedman; m. Robert Bruce, Mar. 29, 1992. Diploma, Mt. Sinai Hosp. Sch. Nursing, N.Y.C., 1959; BA, Marymount Manhattan Coll., 1976; MS, Yeshiva U., 1981. RN, N.Y.; cert. clin. specialist psychiat./mental health nursing cert. in gerontology, behavioral psychotherapy, hypnosis, EMDR. Clin. supr. psychiat. St. Barnabas Hosp., Bronx, N.Y., 1982-84; psychiat. nurse clinician Frances Schervier Home and Hosp., Riverdale, N.Y., 1984-88; staff devel. coord. Holliswood (N.Y.) Hosp., 1988-93; psychotherapist in pvt. practice Great Neck, N.Y., 1991—; primary psychotherapist Coney Island Hosp., Bklyn., 1993—; tchr. Bd. Edn., Queens, N.Y., 1985-88; cons. nursing homes N.Y.C. Dept. Health, 1985-87; workshop presenter. Mem. N.Y. Soc. Ericksonian Psychotherapy and Hypnosis (bd. dirs., chmn. 1991-95), Network of N.Y. Clin. specialists (rec. sec., bd. dirs.), Am. Soc. Clin. Hypnosis. Democrat. Jewish. Home: 58-46 246 Crescent Douglaston NY 11362 Office: 15 Canterbury Rd #A-4 Great Neck NY 11021-2610

HABER, FLORENCE, retired hospital administrator; b. N.Y.C., Oct. 31, 1916; d. Albert and Dora (Bernstein) Novick; m. Harry Haber, Nov. 22, 1939 (dec. Feb. 1991); children: Carol Diamond, Helen Bilgoray. BS in Health Sci. cum laude, Hunter Coll., 1971. Cert. registered record adminstr. Am. Med. Record Assn. Sec., attendance supr. Hicksville Pub. Schs., L.I. and N.Y.C.; sec., prin. Temple Sinai Religious Sch., Roslyn and L.I.; dir. med. records Sydenham Hosp.-Health and Hosp. Corp., N.Y.C., 1971-73; dir. psychiat. records Met. Hosp., N.Y.C., 1973-78; discharge planning coord. Metropolitan Hosp., N.Y.C., 1979-85. Pres. Sisterhood Temple Beth-El, North Bellmore, N.Y., 1954-55; bd. dirs. Temple Beth-El, North Bellmore, 1956-57. Recipient Svc. Achievement award Temple Beth-El, 1962; named Prime Time Vol. Area Agy. on Aging, Palm Beach, Fla., 1995. Mem. Jewish Fedn. South Palm Beach County (mem. Jewish edn. com. 1995—, chair elder hostel com. 1994—, sec. acad. Jewish studies com. 1992—, Vol. of Yr. 1996).

HABERL, VALERIE ELIZABETH, physical education educator, company executive; b. N.Y.C., July 6, 1947; d. William Anthony and Rose Mary (Hoholecek) H. BS, So. Conn. State U., 1969, postgrad., 1979. Cert. elem. tchr., Conn. Tchr. phys. edn. West Haven (Conn.) Bd. Edn., 1969—; supr. West Haven Parks and Recreation, 1980—; pres. Creative Studio, 1992—. Mem. Conn. Assn. Health, Phys. Edn., Recreation and Dance. Republican. Roman Catholic.

HABERLAND, NANCY ELLEN, sailing coach; b. Evanston, Ill., Aug. 16, 1960; d. William and Eila Marie (Taipale) H. BS in Dietetics & Mgmt., Miami U., 1984. Registered dietitian. Sailing sch. dir. J World, Newport, R.I., 1986-94; athlete USSA/U.S. Olympic Com., 1990-94; sailing coach U.S. Naval Acad., Annapolis, Md., 1994—; nutrition cons., 1990—. Author: J World Performance Handbook, 1990. Grantee Women's Sports Found., 1993. Mem. U.S. Europe Dinghy Class Assn. (founder, pres. 1992-95), U.S. Sailing Assn., Am. Dietetic Assn., Miami U. Sailing Club (pres. 1982-84), Phi Upsilon Omicron. Lutheran. Home: 437 N Neptune Dr Satellite Beach FL 32937

HABERMAN, LOUISE SHELLY, consulting company executive; b. N.Y.C.; d. Harry Martin and Rebecca (Binstock) H.; m. Gordon Joel Schochet. BA, Cornell U., 1971; PhD, Princeton (N.J.) U., 1984. Mem. faculty numerous colls. and univs.], 1975-84; researcher pub. policy U.S. Dept. Commerce, 1976; prin. investigator pub. policy study State of N.J., Trenton, 1979-80; pvt. practice cons. Highland Park, N.J., 1984-86; head regional bank svcs. Multinational Strategies, Inc., N.Y.C., 1986-90; pres. Haberman Assocs., Inc., Edison, N.J., 1990—. Author: (monograph) Regional Banks: International Strategies for the Future, 1987; editor: (with Paul Sacks) Ann. Rev. of Nations, 1988; contbr. articles to profl. jours. Issues advisor selected polit. candidates and civil liberties causes. Office: Haberman Assocs Inc 315 N 8th Ave Edison NJ 08817-2914

HABERMANN, HELEN MARGARET, plant physiologist, educator; b. Bklyn., Sept. 13, 1927. AB, SUNY, Albany, 1949; MS, U. Conn., 1951; PhD, U. Minn., 1956. Asst. botanist U. Conn., Storrs, 1949-51; asst. U. Minn., Mpls., 1951-53, asst. plant physiologist, 1953-55, head residence counselor, 1955-56; rsch. assoc. U. Chgo., 1956-57; rsch. fellow Hopkins Marine Sta. Stanford (Calif.) U., 1957-58; from asst. prof. to assoc. prof. biol. scis. Goucher Coll., Towson, 1958-70, chmn. dept. biology, 1963-66, 68, 78-79, prof., 1970-92, Lilian Welsh prof. biol. scis., 1982-92; prof. emeritus, 1992—. Co-author Biology: A Full Spectrum, 1973, Mainstreams of Biology, 1977. NIH spl. rsch. fellow Rsch. Inst. Advanced Study, Balt., 1966-67. Fellow AAAS; mem. Phytochem. Soc. N.Am. (sec. 1987-93), Am. Soc. Plant Physiologists, Am. Soc. Hort. Sci., Soc. Devel. Biology, Am. Soc. Photobiology, Am. Inst. Biol. Scis., Scandinavian Soc. Plant Physiology, Internat. Soc. Plant Molecular Biology, Japanese Soc. Plant Physiology, Soc. Exptl. Biology and Medicine, Am. Camellia Soc., Pioneer Camellia Soc. (pres. 1994-95), Am. Hort. Soc., Sigma Xi. Office: Goucher Coll Dept Biol Scis 1021 Dulaney Valley Rd Baltimore MD 21204-2753

HABERT, MARTHA JANET, psychotherapist, clinic manager; b. N.Y.C., Feb. 16, 1946; d. Harry Westler and Edna (Winisky) Rockman; m. Saleh Habert, June 7, 1964; children: Marc, Harriet, Emily. BA, Queens Coll., 1977; M in Social Work, Adelphi Sch. of Social Work, 1980; cert. in Psychoanalytic Psychotherapy, Washington Square Inst., 1986. Cert. clin. social worker, N.Y. Social worker Forest Hills (N.Y.) Comty. House, 1980-82; social worker Queensboro (N.Y.) Soc. Family LIfe Clinic, 1982-84, sr. social worker, 1984-85, coord. hotel program, 1985-88, clinic supr., 1986-88; social worker Parker Jewish Geriatric Inst. Home Care, 1988-93; sr. social worker Flushing (N.Y.) Hosp. Mental Health Clinic, 1988—, clinic mgr., 1994—; psychotherapist pvt. practice, 1984—. Mem. NOW, Nat. Assn. Social Workers, Am. Bd. Examiners in Clin. Social Work, Planned Parenthood. Office: 110 50 71st Rd Ste 1L Forest Hills NY 11375 also: Flushing Hosp 146-01 45th Ave Flushing NY 11355

HABICHT, PATRICIA T., lawyer, bank executive; d. Frank H. and Jeanne (Patrick) H. BS in Math., Purdue U., 1971; JD, Northwestern U., 1974. Sr. v.p., assoc. gen. counsel The 1st Nat. Bank Chgo., 1974—. Mem. ABA, Am. Coll. Real Estate Lawyers, Chgo. Bar Assn. Office: The 1st Nat Bank Chgo Ste 0801 1 First National Plz Chicago IL 60670

HAC, LUCILE ROSE, biochemistry educator; b. Lincoln, Nebr., May 18, 1909; d. Peter F. and Carrie E. (Orinsky) H. BA, U. Nebr., 1930, MSc, 1931; PhD, U. Minn., 1935. Microbiologist Md. State Health Dept., Balt., 1935-36; rsch. assoc. dept. Ob-gyn. U. Chgo., 1936-43; rsch. dir. Internat. Minerals & Chem., Chgo., Calif., Tex. and, Fla., 1943-61; assoc. prof. biochemistry Northwestern U. Med. Sch., Chgo., 1961-77, emeritus prof., 1977—; job counsellor North Shore Sr. Ctr., Northfield, Ill., 1978—. Patentee in field; contbr. articles to profl. jours. Bd. dirs. LWV, Wilmette, Ill., 1980-84. Recipient Kuppenheimer grant U. Chgo., 1936-45, Claude Pepper Disting. Svc. award, 1990, Clyde Murray Older Worker award Operation Able Chgo., 1991; named to Sr. Citizen Hall of Fame, Chgo., 1985. Mem. Am. Chem. Soc. (dir., bd. dirs. 1940-45), AAUW, Zonta Internat., Phi Beta Kappa, Sigma Xi, Iota Sigma Pi, Sigma Delta Epsilon. Republican. Home: 812 Oakwood Wilmette IL 60091-3318

HACKENBERG, BARBARA JEAN COLLAR, advertising and public relations executive; b. Venango County, Pa., Apr. 15, 1927; d. Guy Lamont and Marion Leona (Kingsley) Collar; m. George Richardson, June 13, 1953; children: Kurt Edward, Kim Ellen, Caroline Kingsley. BA, Grove City (Pa.) Coll., 1948; ML, U. Pitts., 1949. Advt. dir. The Halle Bros. Co., Erie, Pa., 1950-52, advt. and sales promotion dir., 1952-54; exec. dir. Wyomissing (Pa.) Inst. Fine Arts, 1970-74; dir. and community liason Freedman Gallery, Albright Coll., Reading, Pa., 1976-78; selling supr. Pomeroy's Children's Dept., Wyomissing, Pa., 1981-83; pub. relations account exec. Wentworth Assocs., Lancaster, Pa., 1983-84; exec. dir. World Affairs Coun., Reading, 1987—; owner The WRITE Place, Reading, 1979—. V.p. Harrisburg (Pa.) Foreign Policy Assn., 1964-67; various fund-raising activities, 1954-70; pub. relations chmn. Erie World Affairs Ctr., 1957-60. Mem. Women in Communications, Inc. (pub. relations chmn. ctrl. Pa. chpt., 1984-87, sec. ctrl. Pa. chpt., 1986-87).,. Methodist. Home and Office: 1334 Welsh Rd Reading PA 19607-9334

HACKENBURG, JEAN MARIE, financial executive; b. Jackson, Mich., Oct. 14, 1948; d. Kenneth Gilbert and Lorraine Marie (Bishop) VerPlanck; m. John Ray Hackenburg, June 28, 1969; 1 child, Kara Nicole. BA, Grand Valley State U., 1969; MBA, Santa Clara U., 1979. Acctg. mgr. Atari, Sunnyvale, Calif., 1974-80, dir. fin., 1980-82, v.p. fin., 1982-83; v.p. fin. and adminstrn. Mad Computer, Santa Clara, Calif., 1984, Etak, Inc., Menlo Park, Calif., 1985-87; CFO Valisys Corp., Santa Clara, 1988-94; CFO, v.p. product ops. Energy Line Sys., Inc., Berkeley, Calif., 1994—. Democrat.

HACKER, GERALDENE G., secondary school educator, counselor; b. Midland, Mich., Aug. 22, 1946; d. George Henry and Gertrude Emma (Mudd) Green; m. James Carl Hacker, Nov. 27, 1968; children: Lisa Janel, Ann Marie. BA, Ctrl. Mich. U., 1967, MA, 1983. Cert. secondary sch. tchr., Mich. Tchr. Freeland (Mich.) H.S., 1967—; co-owner The Video Stop, Freeland, 1985—, Hacker Bldg. Corp., Freeland, 1978—. Mem. Downtown Devel. Authority-Tittabawasee Twp., Freeland, 1988—; sec. Saginaw (Mich.) County Reps., 1988-92; del. Rep. State Convs., 1988-92; deacon Zion Luth. Ch. Recipient Golden Apple award Lawyers Assn., 1992. Mem. Freeland Edn. Assn. (bldg. rep., pub. rels. chair, grievance chair, pres. 1968—). Office: Freeland HS 8250 Webster Rd Freeland MI 48623-9023

HACKETT, BARBARA (KLOKA), federal judge; b. 1928. B of Philosophy, U. Detroit, 1948, JD, 1950. Bar: Mich. 1951, U.S. Dist. Ct. (ea. dist.) Mich. 1951, U.S. Ct. Appeals (6th cir.) 1951, U.S. Supreme Ct. 1957. Law clk. U.S. Dist. Ct. (ea. dist.) Mich., 1951-52; chief law clk. U.S. Ct. Appeals, Mich., 1965-66; asst. pros. atty. Wayne County, Mich., 1967-72; pvt. practice law Detroit, 1952-53, 72-73, Frasco, Hackett & Mills, 1984-86; U.S. magistrate U.S. Dist. Ct. (ea. dist.) Mich., Detroit, 1973-84, judge, 1986—; mem. Interstate Commerce Commn., 1964. Trustee U. Detroit, 1983-89, Mercy High Sch., Farmington Hills, Mich. 1984-86, Detroit Symphony Orch., Orch. Hall Assocs., Detroit Sci. Ctr., United Community Svcs. Recipient Pres.'s Cabinet award U. Detroit Mercy, 1991. Mem. ABA (spl. ct. judge discovery abuse com. 1978-79, com. on cts. in cmty. 1979-84), Am. Judicature Soc., Fed. Bar Assn. (sec. 1981-82), Fed. Judges Assn., Nat. Assn. Women Judges, Nat. Dist. Attys. Assn., Nat. Assn. R.R. Trial Counsel, State Bar Mich., Women Lawyers Assn. Mich. Pros. Attys. Assn. Mich. (Disting. Svc. award 1971), Oakland County Bar Assn., U. Detroit Law Alumni Assn. (officer 1970-75, pres. 1975-77, Alumni Tower award 1976), Women's Econ. Club (bd. dirs. 1975-80, pres. 1980-81, named Detroit's Dynamic Women 1992), Econ. Club Detroit (bd. dirs. 1979-85, 88—), Phi Gamma Nu. Office: US Dist Ct 718 Theo Levin Courthouse 231 W Lafayette Blvd Detroit MI 48226-2719

HACKETT, CAROL ANN HEDDEN, physician; b. Valdese, N.C., Dec. 18, 1939; d. Thomas Barnett and Zada Loray (Pope) Hedden; BA, Duke, 1961; MD, U. N.C., 1966; m. John Peter Hackett, July 27, 1968; children: John Hedden, Elizabeth Bentley, Susanne Rochet. Intern. Georgetown U. Hosp., Washington, 1966-67, resident, 1967-69; clinic physician DePaul Hosp., Norfolk, Va., 1969-71; chief spl. health services Arlington County Dept. Human Resources, Arlington, Va., 1971-72; gen. med. officer USPHS Hosp., Balt., 1974-75; pvt. practice family medicine, Seattle, 1975—; mem. staff, chmn. dept. family practice Overlake Hosp. Med. Ctr., 1985-86; clin. asst. prof. Sch. Medicine U. Wash. Bd. dirs. Mercer Island (Wash.) Preschool Assn., 1977-78; coordinator 13th and 20th Ann. Inter-profl. Women's Dinner, 1978, 86; trustee Northwest Chamber Orch., 1984-85. Mem. AAUW, Am. Acad. Family Practice, King County Acad. Family Practice (trustee 1993-96), King County Med. Soc. (chmn. com. TV violence), Wash. Acad. Family Practice, Wash. State Med. Soc., DAR, Bellevue C. of C., NW Women Physicians (v.p. 1978), Seattle Symphony League, Eastside Women Physicians (founder, pres.), Sigma Kappa, Wash. Athletic Club, Columbia Tower, Seattle Yacht Club. Episcopalian. Home: 4304 E Mercer Way Mercer Island WA 98040-3826 Office: 1414 116th Ave NE Bellevue WA 98004-3801

HACKETT, EILEEN ANN, human resources officer, banker; b. Jamaica, N.Y., June 22, 1958; d. William Joseph and Philomena Delores (Marziotto) H. BS, Marywood Coll., 1980; MS in Counseling, Queens Coll., 1987. Paying and receiving clk. Long Term Credit Bank of Japan, N.Y.C., 1980, FX trader, 1981-85, human resources officer, 1985—; bus. rep. N.Y. Telephone Co., 1980-81. Vol. Cabrini Hosp. Hospice, N.Y.C., 1986-88. Mem. Am. Assn. Counseling and Devel. Roman Catholic. Office: Long Term Credit Bank Japan 165 Broadway New York NY 10006

HACKETT, LINDA LEPLEY, nurse psychotherapist, consultant; b. Merced, Calif., May 21, 1943; d. Richard Wood and Della Martha (Rathmell) Lepley; m. Thomas T. Hackett, June 24, 1967; children: Gordon Clark, Matthew T. Diploma in Nursing, Williamsport Sch. Nursing, Pa., 1964; BA, Thomas Edison U., 1975; MA, Fairfield U., 1979. Cert. clin. specialist; APRN. Sr. specialty nurse, psychiat. nurse Ft. Logan Hosp., Denver, 1965-67; supr. psychiat. nursing Rancocas (N.J.) Valley Hosp., 1971-72, nurse psychotherapist, 1973-77; chief psychiat. nursing Norwalk (Conn.) Hosp., 1977-78, cons. and clin. specialist, 1978-81; nurse psychotherapist, co-owner Nurse Counseling Group, Norwalk, 1979—; cons. Action Mktg., Englewood, N.J., 1983-85, Lea Manor Nursing Home, Norwalk, 1983-84, Westport Mktg., 1982-83, Ventura Promotion, N.Y.C., 1979-82. Pres. CNA Polit. Action, Meriden, Conn., 1985-86, mem., cons. YMCA, New Canaan, Conn., 1982; mem. various coms. Congl. Ch., New Canaan. Mem. Soc. Nurse Psychotherapists, Conn. Nurses Assn. (chmn. govt. rels. com. 1985-86, Florence Wald for Outstanding Contb. to Nursing Practice award 1984). Office: Nurse Counseling Group 150 East Ave Norwalk CT 06851

HACKETT, LOUISE, personnel services company executive, consultant; b. Sheridan, Mont., Nov. 11, 1933; d. Paul Duncan and Freda A. (Dudley) Johnson; m. Lewis Edward Hackett, June 24, 1962; 1 child, Dell Paul. Student U. Oreg., 1959-61; BA, Calif. State U.-Sacramento, 1971. Legal sec. Samuel R. Friedman, Yreka, Calif., 1952-58, Barber & Cottrell, Eugene, Oreg., 1958-59; paralegal Elmer Sahlstrom, Eugene, 1959-62; legis. aide Calif. Legislature, Sacramento, 1962-72; owner Legal Personnel Services, Sacramento, 1973-78, corp. pres., 1979—; pres. Legalstaff, Inc., 1987—; curriculum adv. dept. bus. Am. River Coll., Sacramento, 1974-79; founder, adminstr. Pacific Coll. Legal Careers, Sacramento, 1973-84; cons. legal edn. Barclay Schs., Sacramento, 1984; active Sacramento Employees Adv. Coun. Designer, pub. Sacramento/Yolo Attys. Directory, 1974—. Author operations manual and franchise training textbook; contbr. articles to profl. jours. Adv. bd. San Juan Sch. Dist., 1975-84. Mem. Calif. Assn. Personnel Cons., Sacramento Council Pvt. Edn. (pres. 1976-77), Pi Omega Pi. Clubs: Sierra Sail and Trail, Soroptimist Internat. Lodge: Order of Rainbow. Avocations: skiing, sailing, gardening, horseback riding. Office: Legal Personnel Svcs 1415 21st St Sacramento CA 95814-5208 also: 433 California St Ste 904 San Francisco CA 94104-2013 also: 2103 Landings Dr Mountain View CA 94043-0839 also: 111 N Market St Ste 404 San Jose CA 95113-1101

HACKLEMAN, KATHERINE ELAINE, editor; b. El Dorado Springs, Mo., Aug. 26, 1951; d. James Paul and Della Rebecca (Black) Whitesell; m. Edward Dwayne Hackleman, June 3, 1972; 1 child, Jeremy. BS, U. Mo., 1973. Reporter McPherson (Kans.) Sentinel, 1974-86, mng. editor, 1989—; pub., owner Hackleman Publs., McPherson, 1986-89. Co-author series of articles on drug abuse McPherson Sentinel, 1991 (State PA award). Chmn., vice chair, sec. All Schs. Day Ann. Celebration, McPherson, 1981-93; sec. 125th Anniversary Com. for City of McPherson, 1996—; v.p. bd. dirs. McPherson Arts Coun.; bd. dirs., clk. Ch. of The Brethren; mem. McPherson Conv. and Visitors Bd. Named Regional Editor of Yr. Am. Pub. Co., 1995. Mem. Kans. AP Mng. Editors Assn., Kans. Press Assn. (Victor Murdock award 1992), McPherson C. of C. Republican. Office: McPherson Sentinel 301 S Main Mc Pherson KS 67460

HACKLER, JANET ANTHONY, public relations specialist; b. Piedmont, Calif., July 13, 1938. BA in Polit. Sci., U. Calif., Berkeley, 1961, MA in Edn., 1968; postgrad. in bus. adminstrn., Fordham U., N.Y.C. Tchr. English Orinda Union Sch. Dist., Calif., 1962-68; coordinator ednl. research, edn. counselor Hill & Knowlton Inc., N.Y.C., 1968-70; cons., writer Ednl. Systems & Designs, Westport, Conn., 1974; writer, producer Producers Row Inc., N.Y.C., 1975; v.p. public rels. V & J Tax Co., 1993—. Mem. championship synchronized swimming team; appearances include Australian Olympics, Brussels World Fair, Ed Sullivan Show. Recipient Helms award, 1963 (All-American 1956-61).

HACKNEY, VIRGINIA HOWITZ, lawyer; b. Phila., Jan. 11, 1945; d. Charles Rawlings and Edith Wrenn (Pope) Howitz; m. Barry Albert Hackney, Feb. 15, 1969; children: Ashby Rawlings, Roby Howison, Trevor Pope. BA in Econs., Hollins Coll., 1967; JD, U. Richmond, 1970. Bar: Va. 1970. Assoc. Hunton & Williams, Richmond, Va., 1970-77, ptnr., 1977—; pres. Am. Acad. Hosp. Attys. Chgo., 1992-93. Mem. agy. evaluation com. United Way of Greater Richmond, 1981-86; sustainer Jr. League of Richmond. Named Outstanding Woman in field of law, YWCA, Richmond, 1981. Mem. ABA (bus. law sect. 1984—, forum com. on health law 1982—), Am. Acad. Hosp. Attys. (bd. dirs. 1988-94, pres. 1992-93), Va. State Bar (long range planning com. 1985-90, chmn. standing com. lawyer discipline 1986-90, exec. com. 1988-90). Office: Hunton & Williams Riverfront Plz East Tower 951 E Byrd St Richmond VA 23219-4074

HACKWOOD, SUSAN, electrical and computer engineering educator; b. Liverpool, Eng., May 23, 1955; came to U.S., 1980; d. Alan and Margaret Hackwood. BS with honors, DeMonfort U., Eng., 1976; PhD in Solid State Ionics, DeMontfort U., Eng., 1979; PhD (hon.), Worcester Poly. Inst., 1993; DSc (hon.), DeMontfort U., 1993. Rsch. fellow DeMonfort U., Leicester, Eng., 1976-79; postdoctoral rsch. fellow AT&T Bell Labs., Homdel, N.J., 1980-81; mem. tech. staff AT&T Bell Labs., Homdel, 1981-83, supr. robotics tech., 1983-84, dept. head robotics tech., 1984-85; prof. elec. and computer engring. U. Calif., Santa Barbara, 1985-89, dir. Ctr. Robotic Systems in Microelectronics, 1985-89; dean Bourns Coll. Engring. U. Calif., Riverside, 1990-95; exec. dir. Calif. Coun. on Scis. and Tech., Riverside, 1995—. Editor Jour. Robotic Systems, 1983, Recent Advances in Rototics, 1985; contbr.

over 100 articles to tech. jours.; 7 patents in field. Mem. IEEE (sr.). Office: U Calif Riverside Campus Council on Science & Tech Riverside CA 92521-0162*

HADAS, ELIZABETH CHAMBERLAYNE, publisher; b. Washington, May 12, 1946; d. Moses and Elizabeth (Chamberlayne) H.; m. Jeremy W. Heist, Jan. 25, 1970 (div. 1976); m. Peter Eller, Mar. 21, 1984. A.B., Radcliffe Coll., 1967; postgrad. Rutgers U., 1967-68; M.A., Washington U., St. Louis, 1971. Editor U. N.Mex. Press, Albuquerque, 1971-85; dir., 1985—. Mem. Assn. Am. Univ. Presses (pres. 1992-93). Democrat. Home: 2900 10th St NW Albuquerque NM 87107-1111 Office: U New Mexico Press 1720 Lomas Blvd NE Albuquerque NM 87106-3807

HADDA, JANET RUTH, Yiddish language educator, lay psychoanalyst; b. Bradford, Eng., Dec. 23, 1945; came to U.S., 1948; d. George Manfred and Annemarie (Kohn) H.; m. Allan Joshua Tobin, Mar. 22, 1981; stepchildren: David, Adam. BS in Edn., U. Vt., 1966; MA, Cornell U., 1969; PhD, Columbia U., 1975. Prof. Yiddish UCLA; research psychoanalyst So. Calif. Psychoanalytic Inst., L.A., 1988—, tng. and supervising analyst, 1995—, Inst. Contemporary Psychoanalysis, 1993—. Author: Yankev Glatshteyn, 1980, Passionate Women, Passive Men: Suicide in Yiddish Literature, 1988; editorial bd. Prooftexts, Yivo Ann.; contbr. articles to profl. jours. Mem. Assn. Jewish Studies, MLA, Am. Psychoanalytic Assn., Inst. Contemporary Psychoanalysis, Phi Beta Kappa. Office: UCLA Dept Germanic Langs 310 Royce Hall Los Angeles CA 90024

HADDAD, MARYLOU PHYLLIS, elementary education educator; b. Bklyn., Sept. 21, 1937; d. John Jr. and Ann Marie (Garzia) Scorsone; m. Jamil Raouf Haddad, Aug. 1, 1959; children: Ralph John, John Lawrence, James Matthew. BA magna cum laude, Hunter Coll., 1982; MA, CUNY, 1985; cert. of advanced study in ednl. comm. and tech., NYU, 1991. Tchr. N.Y.C. Bd. Edn., 1984—; participant Comprehensive Sch. Improvement Planning Com., N.Y.C., 1985-87, Henry St. Settlements Arts in Education Program, N.Y.C., 1988-91, Henry St. Settlement Arts and Ptnrs. Program, N.Y.C., 1990, Sch. Based Mgmt. and Shared Decision Making Program, N.Y.C., 1993-95, The Bklyn. Mus. Tchr. Inst., 1995-96. Mem. AAUW, Nat. Mus. Women in Arts (charter mem.), Kappa Delta Pi. Home: 8801 Shore Rd Apt 5A-W Brooklyn NY 11209

HADDOCK, ANNETTE HARRISON, early childhood education educator; b. Macon, Ga., Jan. 30, 1950; d. John Jay and Sara (Hodges) Harrison; m. Robert Clark, Aug. 12, 1973; children: Tosha, Clark, Rachel. BS in Edn., Ga. So. U., Statesboro, 1972; MEd, Ga. Coll., Milledgeville, 1979, EdS, 1985. Tchr. DaKalb Bd. Edn., Chamblee, Ga., 1972-73, Bulloch County Bd. Edn., Statesboro, 1973-74, Bibb Bd. Edn., Macon, 1977—. Named Tchr. of Yr. Stephens Sch., 1983, 90. Mem. Internat. Reading Assn. (sec. Middle Ga. Coun. 1985-86), Delta Kappa Gamma (v.p. 1990-92). Baptist. Home: 101 Williamson Dr Macon GA 31210 Office: Brookdale Sch 3600 Brookdale Ave Macon GA 31204-2728

HADDOX, ARDEN RUTH STEWART, automotive aftermarket manufacturing executive; b. Wheeling, W.Va., Sept. 29, 1930; d. Oliver Shaw and Helen (Neitzel) Stewart; children: Mark, Todd. BA, Baldwin Wallace Coll., 1952. Trainee GM, Cleve., 1952-57; tchr. Elyria (Ohio) City Bd. Edn., 1967-85; pres., CEO AAR, Inc., Cleve., 1984—, also chmn. bd. dirs. Pres. Elyria Schs. PTA, 1967; treas. Homeowners Assn., North Ridgeville, Ohio, 1988-89; mem. adv. com. bus. and tech. Cuyahoga C.C. Recipient Weatherhead 100 award Case Western Res. U., 1990, 91, 92, 93, 94, 95. Republican. Episcopalian. Home: 32889 Brownstone Ln North Ridgeville OH 44039-2503 Office: AAR Inc 34999 Mills Rd North Ridgeville OH 44039

HADLEY, ALICE OMAGGIO, French educator, writer; b. Phila., Nov. 24, 1947; d. William Edward and Alice Marie (Abel) Burns; m. Henry H. Hadley. BS, Pa. State U., 1969; MA, Ohio State U., 1972, PhD, 1977. Assoc. dir. ERIC Clearinghouse on Langs. and Linguistics Ctr. for Applied Linguistics, Arlington, Va., 1977-79; asst. prof. of modern and classical langs. U. N.Mex., Albuquerque, 1979-80; asst. prof. of French U. Ill., Urbana, 1980-85, assoc. prof. French, 1985-94, prof. French, 1994—. Author: (textbook) Teaching Language in Context, 1986, 2d edit., 1993 (Kenneth W. Mildenberger prize 1987); co-author: (textbook) (with J. Muyskens and others Rendez-vous: An Invitation to French, 1982, 4th edit., 1994, (textbook) (with others) Kaléidoscope: Grammaire en contexte, 1984, 3d edit., 1993; editor: Research in Language Learning: Principles, Processes and Prospects, 1993; mem. editl. bd. Modern Lang. Jour., 1993—. Recipient Stephen A. Freeman award N.E. Conf. on Tchg. of Fgn. Langs., 1979. Mem. Am. Coun. on Tchg. of Fgn. Langs. (exec. coun. 1983-87, pres. 1986, Paul Pimsleur award 1980, Anthony Papalia award 1989), Am. Assn. Tchrs. of French, Am. Assn. Univ. Suprs., Coordinators and Dirs. of Fgn. Lang. Programs (mem. editl. bd. 1990—), Ill. Coun. on Tchg. of Fgn. Langs. Home: 1772 County Rd 1650N Urbana IL 61801 Office: Univ Ill Dept French 2090 Fgn Lang Bldg 707 S Mathews Ave Urbana IL 61801

HADLEY, CAROLYN BETH, physician, educator; b. Dallas, Nov. 22, 1945; d. Charles Franklin and Sadie Beth (Humphreys) Hadley; m. Richard G. Suchan, Dec. 28, 1985; children: Richard C., Stephen G. BA with honors in Microbiology, U. Kans., 1968; MS in Clin. Microbiology, Columbia U. Coll. Physicians and Surgeons, 1974; MD, U. Pa., 1981. Diplomate Am. Coll. Med. Examiners., Am. Bd. Ob-Gyn. Maternal-Fetal Medicine. Lab technologist St. Joseph Mercy Hosp., Ann Arbor, Mich., 1968-70; sr. technologist, diagnostic microbiology svc. Columbia Presbyn. Med. Ctr., N.Y.C., 1970-73, sr. asst. supr., 1973-75; asst. microbiologist Hosp. of U. Pa., Phila., 1975-77, resident in ob-gyn., 1981-85, fellow in maternal fetal medicine, 1985-87; teaching asst. in microbiology U. Kans., 1968; teaching fellow microbiology U. Mich. Med. Sch., 1969; asst. prof. Med. Coll. Pa., 1987-91, assoc. prof., 1991-93, dir. obstetrics, 1992, asst. prof. anesthesiology, 1993. Recipient Undergrad. Rsch. award U. Kans., 1967; Philip Williams prize in obstetrics, 1984; S. Leon Israel prize in obstetrics, 1985; Henrietta Ottinger/Huston MacFarlane scholar Med. Coll. Pa., 1978-93. Fellow Am. Coll. Ob-Gyn.; mem. AMA, Am. Soc. Microbiology (specialist in microbiology), Am. Soc. Clin. Pathologists (specialist microbiologist), Phila. Perinatal Soc., Soc. for Perinatal Obstetricians, DAR, U. Kans. Alumni Assn., Phila. Obstet. Soc., Phi Beta Kappa. Office: Med Coll Pa Dept Ob-Gyn 3300 Henry Ave Philadelphia PA 19129-1121

HADLEY, DEBRA SUE, electric company executive; b. Monett, Mo., June 9, 1956; d. R. Wayne and Robbie N. (Lawrence) Cox; m. Larry K. Reeves, Aug. 9, 1975 (div. Aug. 1991); children: Tiffany Dawn, Brittany Nicole; m. Gary Mitchell Hadley, July 17, 1993; 1 child, Chloe Jo. AS in Computer Programming, Mo. So. State Coll., 1982, BSBA in Acctg., 1991. CPA, Mo. Asst. credit mgr. ConAgra, Carthage, Mo., 1991; fuel acct. The Empire Dist. Elec. Co., Joplin, Mo., 1991-95, regulatory analyst, 1995—. Mem. Inst. Mgmt. Accts. (asst. dir. tech. programs 1995-96, dir. spl. activities and employment 1996-97), Alpha Chi. Baptist. Home: 815 N Wall Joplin MO 64801 Office: Empire Dist Electric Co 602 Joplin St Joplin MO 64801-1166

HADLEY, JANE BYINGTON, psychotherapist; b. N.Y.C., Apr. 24, 1929; d. David and Ruth (Johnson) Millar; m. Arthur Twining Hadley, Feb. 24, 1979; children: Elisabeth Jane Wheeler, Caroline Anne Thies. BA, U. Va., 1951; MA, Columbia U., 1967; analytic tng., Met. Ctr. for Mental Health, 1970-73. Intern Queens Coll., 1969; pvt. practice psychotherapy N.Y.C., 1971—. Bd. dirs. Children's All Day Sch. Mem. APA, Cosmopolitan Club, Century Assn. Democrat. Episcopalian.

HADLEY, LEILA ELIOTT-BURTON (MRS. HENRY LUCE, III), author; b. N.Y.C., Sept. 22, 1925; d. Frank Vincent and Beatrice Boswell (Eliott) Burton; m. Arthur T. Hadley, II, Mar. 2, 1944 (div. Aug. 1946); 1 child, Arthur T. III; m. Yvor H. Smitter, Jan. 24, 1953 (div. Oct. 1969); children: Victoria C. Van D. Smitter Barlow, Matthew Smitter Eliott, Caroline Allison F.S. Nicholson; m. William C. Musham, May 1976 (div. July 1979); m. Henry Luce III, Jan. 1990. MD, St. Timothy's Sch., 1943. Author: Give Me the World, 1958, How to Travel with Children in Europe, 1963, Manners for Children, 1967, Fielding's Guide to Traveling with Children in Europe,1972, rev., 1974, 84, Traveling with Children in the U.S.A., 1974, Tibet-20 Years After the Chinese Takeover, 1979, (with Theodore B. Van Itallie) The Best Spas: Where to Go for Weight Loss, Fitness Programs and Pure Pleasure in the U.S. and Around the World, 1988, rev., 1989, A Journey with Elsa Cloud, 1997; assoc. editor: Diplomat mag., N.Y.C., 1964-65, Saturday Evening Post, N.Y.C., 1965-67; editorial cons. TWYCH, N.Y.C., 1985-87; book reviewer Palm Beach Life, Fla., 1967-72; contbg. editor Spa Vacations mag., 1989—; consulting editor: Tricyle, The Buddhist Rev., 1991—; garden columnist Fishers Island Gazette; contbr. articles tovarious newspapers, mags. Bd. dirs. Tibet House, 1995, Fishers Island Conservancy, 1995, The Kitchen, Haleakala, Inc., 1995; co-founder Wings Trust, Inc. Mem. Acad. Am. Poets, Soc. Woman Geographers (exec. council 1984—), Authors Guild, Nat. Writers Union, Nat. Press Club, Explorers Club, Central Park Conservancy. Republican. Presbyterian. Home: 4 Sutton Pl New York NY 10022-3056 Office: Sterling Lord Literistic 65 Bleecker St New York NY 10012

HADLEY, PAMELA LYNN, adolescent counselor; b. Independence, Kans., Nov. 19, 1963; d. Billy Eugene and Mary Sue (Younger) Reed; m. Joe B. Hadley, Sept. 23, 1995; children: Garett Chase, Tanner Keith. BS, U. Tex., Arlington, 1987. Cert. alcohol and drug abuse counselor, compulsive gambling counselor; lic. chem. dependency counselor. Phys. therapy asst. Dr. James Elbaor, Arlington, 1980-83; supr. cashiers Target, Arlington, 1983-84; unit sec. Mansfield (Tex.) Community Hosp., 1984-85; sec. Willow Creek Hosp., Arlington, 1986-87, ednl. tester, 1987-89, student assistance counselor, 1989-90; case mgr., counselor Oak Grove Treatment Ctr., Burleson, Tex., 1990-91; drug edn. specialist Mansfield Ind. Sch. Dist., 1991-94; juvenile detention officer Tarrant County, Ft. Worth, 1994; case mgr. All Saints Episc. Hosp., Hurst, Tex., 1994—; cons. ednl. tester Carpenter & Assocs., Arlington, 1988-90, Mind Time, Arlington, 1989, Willow Creek Hosp., Arlington, 1989-90, Oak Grove Treatment Ctr., Burleson, 1990. Coach Mansfield Pee-Wee Cheerleading, 1986-90, coach adult volleyball; vol. Dallas Intertribal Ctr., 1990, Project Charlie, Kids Safe Saturday, 1990-91, AIDS Outreach Ctr., 1994, Horizons Tng. Mem. NAFE, Tex. Assn. Alcohol and Drug Abuse Counselors, Tarrant County Assn. Alcohol and Drug Abuse Counselors, Tex. Assn. Studetn Asst. Profls. Republican. Home: 1025 NCR 810 Alvarado TX 76009

HADLEY, SUSAN R., accountant; b. Boise, Idaho, Mar. 30, 1969; d. Douglas Gene and Sonja K. (Philliber) H. BA, Boise State U., 1992. CPA. Adminstrv. asst. Boise Printer Divsn. Hewlett Packard, 1988-92; audit assoc. Coopers & Lybrand, 1992-93; asst. contr. St. Mary Lodge & Resort, 1993-94; payroll/benefits mgr. Sun Valley (Idaho) Resort, 1994—. Vol. Idaho Foodbank Warehouse, Idaho Shakespeare Festival, Arts in the Park. Mem. Inst. Mgmt. Accts. (bd. dirs.). Home: PO Box 1343 Sun Valley ID 83353 Office: Sun Valley Co PO Box 10 Sun Valley ID 83353

HAEBERLE, ROSAMOND PAULINE, retired educator; b. Clearwater, Kans., Oct. 23, 1914; d. Albert Paul and Ella (Lough) H. BS in Music Edn., Kans. State U., 1936; MusM, Northwestern U., 1948; postgrad., Wayne State U., 1965, 65, 66. Profl. registered parliamentarian. Tchr. sch. dist., Plevna, Kans., 1936-37, Esbon, Kans., 1937-41, Frankfort, Kans., 1941-43, Garden City, Kans., 1943-44; music supr. sch. dist., Waterford Twp., Mich., 1944-47; tchr. sch. dist., Pontiac, Mich., 1947-80; ret. sch. dist., Pontiac, 1980. Bd. dirs., ho. chmn. Pontiac-Oakland Symphony; adv. coun. Waterford Sr. Citizens, chmn., 1990-93; pres. Oakland County Pioneer and Hist. Soc., 1992-94. Recipient Tchrs. Day award Mich. State Fair, 1963. Mem. AAUW (pres. 1970-72, founds. chair Pontiac br.), Mich. Fedn. Music Clubs (state pres. 1993-95, pres. Tuesday musicale of Pontiac 1984-86), Mich. Fedn. Bus. and Profl. Womens Club (Woman of Achievement award dist. IX 1994), Mich. DARS (state parliamentarian 1985-96), DAR (Gen. Richardson chpt., regent 1983-85, libr. and parliamentarian, Excellence in Cmty Svc. award 1995), Waterford-Clarkston Bus. and Profl. Womens Club (bylaws and parliamentarian), Pontiac Area Ret. Sch. Pers. (parliamentarian, pres. 1981-84), Mich. Assn. Retired Sch. Pers (Disting. Svc. award 1994), Pontiac Area Bus. and Profl. Women (pres. 1959-61), Pontiac Area Fedn. women's Clubs (pres. 1976-78, 81-84), Detroit Coll. Womens Club, Mich. Registered Parliamentarians, Eastern Star, Zeta Tay Alpha, Mu Phi Epsilon, Beta Sigma Phi (life). Republican. Methodist.

HAEN, JOANNE LEE, English educator; b. Iola, Kans., Dec. 25, 1943; d. Wesley Ross and Virginia Lee (Sechrest) Clendenen; m. Michael Edward Haen, June 12, 1965 (dec. 1978); children: Pier Michelle, Micah Aaron, Nichole Tennille. AA, Iola Jr. Coll., 1963; BS in Edn., Emporia State Tchrs., 1965; MS, Kans. State U., 1968. English tchr. 8th-9th grade Junction City (Kans.) Sch. Sys., 1965-67; journalism instr. Kansas City (Kans.) C.C., 1968-91, English instr., 1991—; English coord. Kansas City C.C., 1992-94, instrl. cons. humanities and fine arts divsn., 1993—, honors faculty, 1994—, honors coun. chair, 1994-95, editor coll. catalog, 1991—. Asst. softball coach Girls Softball League, 1980's. Mem. NEA, Kans. Nat. Edn. Assn., Lighthouse Preservation Soc., Nat. Coun. of Tchrs. of English. Office: Kansas City Cmty Coll 7250 State Ave Kansas City KS 66112

HAENSLY, PATRICIA A., psychology educator; b. Kronenwetter, Wis., Dec. 4, 1928; d. Paul Frank and Valeria (Woyak) Banach; m. William E. Haensly, 1954; children: Paul, Robert, Thomas, James, John, David, Mary, Katherine. BS, Lawrence U., 1950; MS in Genetics, Iowa State U., 1953; PhD in Ednl. & Devel. Psychology, Tex. A&M U., 1982. Histo technique specialist dept. vet. pathology Iowa State U., Ames, 1958-63; asst. prof. dept. ednl. psychology Tex. A&M U., College Station, 1982—; instr. Blinn Jr. Coll., College Station; prin. Investigator Project Mustard Seed, U.S.D.O.E. Javits Grant, 1993-96; assoc. dir. programs Inst. for Gifted and Talented Tex. A&M U., College Station, dir. summer presch. program Minds Alive, 1987-95; prin. investigator project mustard seed U.S. Dept. Energy, 1993-96; adj. faculty mem. Western Wash. U., 1996—. Contbd. editor Roeper Rev., 1996—; contbr. articles to profl. publs., chpts. to books on mentoring creativity and giftedness; editl. rev. bd. Gifted Child Quar., 1996—. Recipient Outstanding Woman award AAUW, 1980, Govt. Rsch. Javits grante, 1993-96, Hon. Mention Hollingworth award Intertel Found., 1993. Mem. Tex. Assn. for Gifted and Talented (1st v.p. 1988, 89, editor news mag. 1988, 89), Nat. Assn. Gifted Children (co-chmn. rsch. and evaluation com. 1985-87, John Curtis Gowan Rsch. award 1981), World Coun. for Gifted and Talented Children, Inc., Southwestern Ednl. Rsch. Assn., Soc. for Rsch. in Child Devel., Coun. for Exceptional Children, Assn. for Childhood Edn. Internat., Am. Creativity Assn. (charter), Am. Psychol. Soc., Phi Kappa Phi. Home: 3384 Northgate Rd Bellingham WA

HAFFNER, AGNES CRISTINA, legal secretary; b. Ahuachapan, El Salvador, May 22, 1948; came to the U.S., 1980; d. Ruben Guerra and Argentina (Contreras) Sarmiento; children: Patricia, Gilbert, Kristy. AA in Criminal Justice, Union County Coll., 1994; BA in Pub. Adminstrn., Kean Coll. N.J., 1996, postgrad., 1996—. Chief libr. Sch. Agrl. Scis. Nat. U. El Salvador, San Salvador, 1970-80; prodn. mgr. Inland Casket Mfg., Riverside, Calif., 1984-86; purchasing dept. sec. Harvard Industries-Elastic Stop Nut Am. Divsn., Union, N.J., 1986-89; legal sec. Almeida & Livingston, Newark, 1989-90, N.J. State Divsn. of the Ratepayer Adv., Newark, 1990—. Scholar Union County Chpt.-N.J. Assn. Legal Secs., 1993, Mountainside Women's Club, Cranford, N.J., 1993-94, Bus. and Profl. Women's Club Westfield, N.J., 1994, Bus. and Profl. Women's Club Clark, N.J., 1994. Mem. Am. Assn. for Pub. Adminstrn., Latino-Native Am. Network, Union County Coll. Alumni Assn., Pi Alpha Alpha. Roman Catholic. Home: 96 Pennington St #1 Newark NJ 07105 Office: NJ State Divsn Ratepayer Adv 31 Clinton St 11th Fl Newark NJ 07102

HAFFNER, BARBARA FRANCES HEWES, librarian; b. Oak Park, Ill., Nov. 5, 1925; d. Edgar Douglas Hewes and Inez Elizabeth Elzbeck; m. Richard Glenn Haffner, Nov. 24, 1949; children: Bruce, Mary, James, John, Russell. BA, Beloit Coll., 1947; MLS, Rosary Coll., 1967. Spl. projects libr. Suburban Libr. Sys., Burr Ridge, Ill., 1967-77; libr. dir. Bedford Park Pub. Libr., Bedford Park, Ill., 1977-91. Mem. DAR (registrar, vice regent, 1994-96), PEO (rec. sec.), Delta Delta Delta. Home: 7S061 Quincy Ct Hinsdale IL 60521

HAFFNER, MARLENE ELISABETH, internist, public health administrator; b. Cumberland, Md., Mar. 22, 1941. Student Western Res. U., 1958-61; MD, George Washington U., 1965; MPH, Johns Hopkins U., 1991. Intern, George Washington U. Hosp., Washington, 1965-66; fellow in dermatology Columbia-Presbyn. Med. Ctr., N.Y.C., 1966-67; resident in internal medicine St. Luke's Hosp., N.Y.C., 1967-69; fellow in hematology. Albert Einstein Coll. Medicine, Bronx, 1969-71, asst. clin. prof. medicine, 1971-73; vis. asst. attending Bronx Mcpl. Hosp. Ctr. (N.Y.), 1969-71; clin. assoc. in family, cmty. and emergency medicine U. N.Mex. Sch. Medicine, Albuquerque, 1974-83, clin. assoc. dept. medicine, 1974-83; acting clin. dir. Gallup Indian Med. Ctr. (N.Mex.), 1973-74, chief adult outpatient dept., 1971-74, chief dept. internal medicine, 1971-74; dir. Navajo Area Indian Health Service, Indian Health Service, Window Rock, Ariz., 1974-81; assoc. dir. for health affairs Bur. Med. Devices, FDA, Rockville, 1981-82, dir. Office Health Affairs, Ctr. for Devices and Radiol. Health, 1982-87; dir. office of orphan products devel. FDA, 1987—; MPH Johns Hopkins Sch. Hygiene and Pub. Health, 1991; assoc. clin. prof. dept. medicine Uniformed Svcs., adj. prof. preventive medicine, biometrics Univ. of Health Scis., Bethesda, Md.; asst. surg. gen., rear admiral USPHS. Home and Office: Orphan Products Devel FDA HF 35 5600 Fishers Ln Rockville MD 20857-0001

HAFFORD, PATRICIA ANN, electronic company executive; b. Springfield, Mass., Feb. 11, 1947; d. Arthur Charles and Sophie Louise (Piesyk) Rood; m. Jerry William Hafford, May 1, 1971 (div. Apr. 1993); children: Mark Dutton, Lauren Melynn. BA in Liberal Arts and Scis., U. Conn., 1968. Elem. tchr. East Granby (Conn.) Schs., 1968-69; presch. tchr. RCA-Discovery Ctr., East Hartford, Conn., 1969-70; tng. specialist Travelers Ins. Co., Hartford, 1970-73; scriptwriter ednl. TV Ednl. Satellite Tech. Demonstration Fedn. of Rocky Mt. States, Denver, 1973; with computer documentation dept., tech. writer Hewlett-Packard Corp., Ft. Collins, Colo., 1973-77, documentation mgr., 1977-82, market devel. engr., 1982-83, product mgr., 1983-92, sales devel. mgr., 1993, product mgr., 1994—. Editor: Writing and Designing Operator Manuals. Vol. Mountain Prairie Coun. Girl Scouts U.S.A., 1991-93. Mem. Soc. for Tech. Comm. (v.p. Rocky Mountain chpt. 1979-81, chmn. Art and Writing Competition 1980-81, chmn. Art and Writing Competition 1980-81, dir.-sponsor on bd. dirs. Region 8 1981-84), Ft. Collins Jr. League. Republican. Methodist. Office: Hewlett-Packard 3404 E Harmony Rd Fort Collins CO 80525-9544

HAFNER, GENEVIEVE, photographer; b. Saint-Galmier, Loire, France, June 20, 1961; came to U.S., 1986; d. André Jean Marius and Irène Marie (Massardier) H. CAP in Photography, EFET Sch. Photography, Lyon, France, 1983. Staff photographer La Tribune-Le Progres-Hebdo, Saint Etienne, France, 1984-86; photo corr. City Mag. Internat., N.Y.C., 1987-91; staff photographer News Comm., Inc., N.Y.C., 1991-96; pub., photographer Concrete Jungle images, Inc., N.Y.C., 1990—. Photographer: New York: Metropolis of the American Dream, 1995; photographer Herman Miller Ann. Report, 1993 (Merit award 1994). Office: Concrete Jungle Images Inc 42 W 29th St New York NY 10001

HAFNER-EATON, CHRIS, health services researcher, educator; b. N.Y.C., Dec. 9, 1962; d. Peter Robert and Isabelle (Freda) Hafner; m. James Michael Eaton, Aug. 9, 1986; children: Kelsey James, Tristen Lee. BA, U. Calif., San Diego, 1986; MPH, UCLA, 1988, PhD in Health Svcs., 1992. Cert. health edn. specialist; internat. bd. cert. lactation cons. Cons. dental health policy UCLA Schl. Dentistry, 1989; grad. teachng asst. UCLA Sch. Pub. Health, 1987-92; health svcs. researcher UCLA, 1987-92; cons. health policy U.S. Dept. Health & Human Svcs., Washington, 1988—; analyst health policy The RAND/UCLA Ctr. Health Policy Study, Santa Monica & L.A., 1988-94; asst. prof. health care adminstrn. Oreg. State U. Dept. Pub. Health, Corvallis, 1992-95; pres. Health Improvement Svcs. Corp., 1994—; dir. rsch. rev. La Leche League Internat., 1996—; adj. faculty pub. health Linn-Benton Coll., 1995—; bd. dirs. Benton County Pub. Health Bd., Healthy Start Bd.; mem. Linn-Benton Breastfeeding Task Force, Samaritan Mother-Baby Dyad Team. Contbr. articles to profl. jours. Rsch. grantee numerous granting bodies, 1988-94. Mem. AAUW, NOW, La Leche League Internat. (area profl. liaison for Oreg.), AM. Pub. Health Assn. (med. care sect., women's caucus), Am. Assn. World Health, Oreg. Pub. Health Assn., Oreg. Health Care Assn., Assn. Health Svcs. Rsch., Soc. Pub. Health Edn., Physicians for Social Responsibility, UCLA Pub. Health Alumni Assn., Delta Omega. Home: 1807 NW Beca Ave Corvallis OR 97330-2636

HAFT, GAIL K., pediatrician; b. N.Y.C., Mar. 5, 1938; d. Herbert and Pearl (Mittleman) Klein; m. Jacob I. Haft, Mar. 27, 1964; children: Bethanne, Ian. AB in Chemistry, Vassar Coll., 1959; MD, U. Rochester, 1963. Diplomate Nat. Bd. Med. Examiners, Am. Bd. Pediatrics. Intern Albert Einstein Coll. Medicine, N.Y.C., 1963-64, resident, 1964-65; resident Mt. Sinai Hosp., N.Y.C., 1967-68; pediatrician Dept. Health, Staten Island, N.Y., 1965-67, Head Start, Englewood, N.Y., 1969-71, Dept. Health, Hackensack, N.J., 1970-71; utilization rev. physician Hosp. Corp., N.Y.C., 1973-76; pediatrician Westchester County Health Dept., N.Y., 1974-76; sch. physician Bd. Edn., Yonkers, N.Y., 1974-76; bus. mgr. Heartronics, Newark, 1980-94; chief med. officer Bergen County Spl. Svcs., Paramus, N.J., 1984—; physician Tenafly (N.J.) Sch. Bd. Edn., 1990-94. Mem. Tenafly Bd. Edn., 1983-89, pres., 1986-88.

HAGAN, LAURA LEE, physical education educator; b. Washington, Jan. 29, 1952; d. Lawrence Percival and Evelyn Mary (Gicker) H. BS, James Madison U., Harrisonburg, Va., 1974. Cert. coach. Tchr. Annandale (Va.) H.S., 1974—, track coach, 1974-80, field hockey coach, 1979-85, softball head coach, 1984-91, basketball head coach, 1979—. Named Coach of Yr., Washington Post Jour. Newspaper, 1988. Mem. Women's Basketball Coaches Assn. (200 Win Club 1993), Va. H.S. Coaches assn. (200 Victory Club 1993), Nat. Fedn. H.S. Coaches, Vogues Basketball Assn. (coach 1987—, bd. dirs. 1994—), No. Va. Tip Off Club (bd. dirs. 1993-94). Republican. Presbyterian. Home: 7252 Glen Hollow Ct # 3 Annandale VA 22003 Office: Annandale H S 4700 Medford Dr Annandale VA 22003

HAGAN, LYNN PURNELL, social worker, recreation therapist; b. Houston, Nov. 28, 1954; d. William Bartell and Minnie Francis (Grantham) Purnell; m. Donald Frank Hagan, May 12, 1979; 1 child, Bryan Purnell Hagan. BA, Tex. A&M U., 1977; MS, U. So. Miss., 1994, MSW, 1996. Cert. therapeutic recreation specialist; lic. master social worker. Edn. coord. Audubon Inst., New Orleans, 1984-85; adminstr. space sci. La. Nature and Sci. Ctr., New Orleans, 1985-90; dir. Space and Earth Sci. Resources, Slidell, La., 1990—; tchr. St. Tammany Parish Schs., Slidell, 1990-92; cons. Inst. for Disability Studies, U. So. Miss., Hattiesburg, 1995-96; social worker, recreation therapist, dir. social svcs. Newton (Miss.) Regional Hosp., 1996—; cons. The ARC, Hattiesburg, 1996; dir. Space and Earth Resources, Slidell; cons., vol. Audubon Inst., New Orleans, Houston Zoo. Contbr. articles to profl. publs. Vol. La. Nature and Sci. Ctr., New Orleans. Maj. Civil Air Patrol, 1987—. Rsch. grant Com. on Svcs. and Resources for Women, 1994; recipient Frank Brewer Aerospace Edn. award Civil Air Patrol, 1993; named Olympic Torch Bearer U.S. Olympic com., 1996. Mem. AAUW (pres. 1986—, Career Devel. grant 1993), NASW, Am. Therapeutic Recreation Assn., Nat. Therapeutic Recreation Soc., Assn. for Exptl. Edn., Phi Kappa Phi. Home: 212 Lake Tahoe Slidell LA 70461 Office: Newton Regional Hosp 202 Main St Newton MS 39345

HAGAN, MARY ANN, lawyer; b. Phila., Feb. 18, 1935; S. Harry A. and Marie (Farrell) H. BA, Immaculata (Pa.) Coll., 1956; MA in History, U. Pa., 1958; LLB, Temple U., 1963. Bar: Pa. 1964, U.S. Dist. Ct. Pa. 1972, U.S. Ct. Appeals (3d cir.) 1980, U.S. Tax Ct. 1965. Historian U.S. Dept. Interior, Phila., 1958-60; atty. Urban Renewal Adminstrn., Phila., 1963-65; trial atty. IRS, Office of Chief Counsel, Washington & Phila., 1965-73; supervisory trial atty. U.S. Equal Employment Opportunity Commn., Phila., 1973-77; pvt. practice Phila., 1978—; arbitrator U.S. Dist. Ct., Phila., 1975—, mem. employment panel, 1989—, fed. mediator, 1991—. Mem. Nat. Employment Lawyers Assn. (co-chair 1994 regional conf.), Phila. Bar Assn. Office: 612 One East Penn Sq Philadelphia PA 19107

HAGARTY, EILEEN MARY, pulmonary clinical nurse specialist; b. Chgo., June 17, 1950; d. Lawrence C. and Eleanore R. (Mark) Pauls; m. Jon R. Hagarty, June 23, 1979; children: Patrick Michael, Rita Kristine. BSN, DePaul U., Chgo., 1974; MS, No. Ill. U., 1975. RN, Ill.; cert. clin. specialist in med.-surg. nursing. Staff nurse Edward Hines Jr. VA Hosp., Hines, Ill., 1971-75, pulmonary clin. nurse specialist, 1975—; chair membership com. of nursing assembly Chgo. Lung Assn., 1980-86; nat. recognized lectr. in the field of pulmonary nursing, funded prin. investigator. Contbr. articles to profl. jours. Recipient Excellence in Nursing award Dept. VA, 1992. Mem. ANA (task force), Ill. Nurses Assn., Respiratory Nursing Soc. Home: 7824

Mayfair Ln Darien IL 60561-4864 Office: Edward Hines Jr Hosp 111N Dept VA Hines IL 60141

HAGBERG, BETTY SUZANNE, library administrator; b. Moline, Ill., Sept. 18, 1942; d. Irvin William and Lorraine (Jamieson) McLaughlin; m. Darrel Raymond Hagberg, Nov. 25, 1967; 1 child, Darla Renee. BS in Geography, Ill. State U., 1964; MS in Mgmt., Fla. Inst. Tech., 1978. Vol. Peace Corps, Ethiopia, 1964-66; libr. Deere & Co., Moline, 1972-75, mgr. libr. svcs., 1976—; pres., bd. dirs. River Bend Libr. Sys., Coal Valley, Ill., 1994—; chair Conf. Bd. Info. Svcs. Adv. Coun., N.Y.C., 1996—. Lt. (j.g.) USN, 1968-69. Mem. Spl. Librs. Assn., Zonta (sec. 1980-81). Home: 3418-12 Street East Moline IL 61244 Office: Deere and Co John Deere Rd Moline IL 61265

HAGBERG, VIOLA WILGUS, lawyer; b. Salisbury, Md., July 3, 1952; d. William E. and Jean Shelton (Barlow) Wilgus; m. Chris Eric Hagberg, Feb. 19, 1978. BA, Furman U., Greenville, S.C., 1974; JD, U. S.C., 1978, U. Tulsa, 1978; DOD Army Logistics Sch. honor grad. basic mgmt. def. acquisition, def. small purchase, advanced fed. acquisition regulation, Fort Lee, Va., 1981-82. Bar: Okla. 1978, Va. 1979, U.S. Ct. Appeals (4th cir.) 1979. With Lawyers Com. for Civil Rights, Washington, 1979; pub. utility specialist Fed. Energy Regulatory Commn., Washington, 1979-80; contract specialist U.S. Army, C.E., Ft. Shafter, Hawaii, 1980-81; contract officer/supervisory contract specialist Tripler Army Med. Ctr., Hawaii 1981-83; supervisory procurement analyst and chief policy Procurement Div. USCG, Washington, 1983; contracts officer and chief Avionics Engring Contracting Br., 1984; procurement analyst office of sec. Dept. Transp., 1984-85; contracting officer Naval Regional Contracting Ctr., Long Beach, Calif., 1985-87; chief acquisition rev. and policy, Hdqrs. Def. Mapping Agy., Washington, 1987-92, dir. acquisition ops., Fairfax, Va., 1992-93, dir. acquisition policy, 1994—. Mem. ABA (law student div. liaison 1977-78), Nat. Contract Mgmt. Assn., Va. State Bar Assn., Okla. Bar Assn., Phi Alpha Delta, Kappa Delta Epsilon. Home: 9810 Meadow Valley Dr Vienna VA 22181-3215 Office: Def Mapping Agy (PC) 8613 Lee Hwy Fairfax VA 22031-2130

HAGEMAN, ANNA ROBBINS, writer; b. N.Y.C., May 24, 1920; d. Samuel Wolfe and Marie Lillian (Sassenhagen) Robbins; m. William Charles Hageman, July 7, 1956 (dec. Apr. 1978); children: Marie Dorothy, Anna Margaret. Student, U. Pa., 1937-38, Beaver Coll., 1939-40. Writer, rschr. coord. health and beauty aids advt. Sta. KYW, Phila., 1951-52; market analyst, asst. and acting rsch. mgr. promotion dept. Phila. Inquirer, 1952-56; assoc. rschr. Rsch. and Info. for Edn., King of Prussia, Pa., 1967-68; writer Rsch. for Better Schs., Phila., 1975; organizer, operator Robbins & Hageman Rsch., Glenside, Pa., 1956-59. Contbr. numerous articles to popular mags. and newspapers,. Pres. bd. dirs. Contact Gloucester County, 1996&, former chmn. publicity and recruitment, tel. worker, support person, asst. chmn. on-going tng.; active United Meth. chs., 1945—; ecumenical chmn. 1st United Meth. Ch., Glassboro, N.J.; vol. Gloucester County Rep. Com. Mem. South Jersey Writers, U. Pa. Alumnae Assn. (55th reunion com.).

HAGEN, UTA THYRA, actress; b. Göttingen, Germany, June 12, 1919; came to U.S., 1926; d. Oskar F. L. and Thyra A. (Leisner) H.; m. Herbert Berghof, Jan. 25, 1957 (dec. Nov. 1990); 1 child, Leticia. DFA (hon.), Smith Coll., 1978; LHD (hon.), De Paul U., 1981, Wooster Coll., 1982; DFA (hon.). Tchr. acting Herbert Berghof Studio, N.Y.C., 1947—, now chmn. Appeared as Ophelia, Dennis, Mass., 1937, as Nina in Sea Gull, N.Y.C., 1938, Key Largo, 1939, Vicki, 1942, Othello, 1943-45, Masterbuilder, 1947, Faust, 1947, Angel Street, 1948, Street Car Named Desire, 1948, 50, Country Girl, 1950, G.B. Shaw's Saint Joan, 1951-52, Tovarich, City Center, 1952, In Any Language, 1952, The Deep Blue Sea, 1953, The Magic and the Loss, 1954, The Island of Goats, 1955, A Month in the Country, 1956, Good Woman of Setzuan, 1957, Who's Afraid of Virginia Woolf, 1962-64, The Cherry Orchard, 1968, Charlotte, 1980; also univ. tour 1981-82, Mrs. Warren's Profession, Roundabout Theatre, N.Y.C., 1985—, You Never Can Tell, Circle in the Square, 1986—; (films) The Other, 1972, The Boys from Brazil, 1978, Reversal of Fortunes, 1990; TV appearances include A Month in the Country, 1956, Out of Dust, 1959; appeared in numerous TV spls. and guest star appearances including Lou Grant, 1982, A Doctor's Story, 1984, PBS Am. Playhouse prodn. The Sunset Gang, 1991; author: Respect for Acting, 1973, Love for Cooking, 1976, Sources, a Memoire, 1983, A Challenge For The Actor, 1991; appearances include numerous roles with H.B. Playwrights Found., 1965-95. Chmn. bd. HB Playwrights Found., 1991—. Recipient Antoinette Perry award, 1951, 63, N.Y. Drama Critics award, 1951, 63, Donaldson award for best actress, 1951, London Critics award for best actress, 1963-64 season, Outer Cir. award, Mayor's Liberty medal, 1986, John Houseman award for disting. svc., 1987, Campostella award for disting. svc., 1987, Living Legacy award Women's Internat. Ctr., 1994, Lucille Lortell Lifetime Achievement award, 1995, Drama Legend award, 1996; named to Theatre Hall of Fame, 1981. Office: Herbert Berghof Studio 120 Bank St New York NY 10014-2126*

HAGER, ELIZABETH SEARS, social services organization administrator; b. Washington, Oct. 31, 1944; d. Hess Thatcher and Elizabeth Grace (Harper) Sears; m. Dennis Sterling Hager, Sept. 3, 1966; children: Annie Elizabeth, Lucie Caroline. BA, Wellesley Coll., 1966; MPA, U. N.H., 1979. Prin. Philbrook Ctr., Concord, N.H., 1970-71; rep. N.H. Gen. Ct., Concord, 1973-76, 85-94; del. N.H. Constitutional Conv., Concord, 1974, 84; campaign coord. Anderson for Pres. Rep. Primary, N.H., 1980; mem. Concord City Coun., 1982-90; mayor City of Concord, 1988-90; exec. dir. United Way of Merrimack County, Concord, 1996—; bd. dirs. Chubb Investment Funds, Concord, CFX, Soc. for Protection of N.H. Forests. Commr. N.H. Commn. on the Status of Women; pres. Greater Concord United Way, 1980-81; campaign chair United Way of Merrimack County, Concord, 1986. Republican. Episcopalian. Home and Office: 5 Auburn St Concord NH 03301-3002

HAGER, JULIE-ANN, lawyer, educator; b. Kermit, Tex., Aug. 25, 1954; d. Howard Glenn and Marianne Johanne (Ratzer) H. BA magna cum laude, Baylor U., 1976; JD, U. Tex., 1979. Bar: Tex., U.S. Dist. Ct. (we. dist.) Tex., U.S. Ct. Appeals (5th cir.). Assoc. Wilson, Grosen Heider & Burns, Austin, Tex., 1979-83, ptnr., 1983-90; pvt. practice Law Offices of Julie Ann Hager, Austin, 1990—; tchr. U. Tex. Paralegal Inst., Austin, 1990—. Vol. Austin Rape Crisis Hotline, 1988—, Austin Ctr. for Battered Women, Tex. Head Injury Assn., 1987—; vol. mediator Alternative Dispute Resolution, Austin, 1988—; speaker in field. Fellow Tex. Bar Found.; mem. ABA, ATLA, AAUW, Am. Soc. Law and Medicine, Travis County Women's Law Assn., Travis County Bar Assn. Democrat. Home: 7629 Parkview Cir Austin TX 78731-1127 Office: 111 Congress Ave Ste 1060 Austin TX 78701-4043

HAGER, MARGARET CHASE, state official; b. Richmond, Va., Nov. 16, 1940; d. Clarence Ryland Chase and Sally Lewis (Dickinson) Todd; m. John Henry Hager, Feb. 27, 1971; children: John Virgil, Henry Chase. BA, Wheaton Coll., 1963. Mem. Nat. Coun. Disability, Washington, 1988-92; mem. Mayor's Commn. Disabled/Disability Svcs. City of Richmond, Va., 1984—, chmn., 1989-90; mem. U.S. Archl. and Transp. Barriers Compliance Bd., Washington, 1993—; dir. Dept. Rights Virginians with Disabilities Commonwealth of Va., Richmond, 1994—, mem. long-term care coun., 1994—; disability adv. mem., bd. dirs. Sophia House, 1993—; mem. Project Placement adv. com. Depts. Edn., Rehabilitative Svcs., 1987-89; mem. adv. com. Very Spel. Art Va., Richmond, 1991—, bd. dirs., 1987-91; exec. com. mem. City of Richmond Office Human Svcs. Advocacy, 1988-90. Mem. adv. bd. Commonwealth Girl Scout Coun. Va., Inc., 1990—, steering com. fund raising event, 1994; mem. com. Jefferson Poplar Forest Fund, 1984; bd. dirs., exec. fin. com. Richmond Eye and Ear Hosp., 1990-94; bd. dirs. Richmond Ballet, 1980-89; mem. Jr. League Richmond, 1985—; mem. parent's coun. Hampden-Sydney (Va.) Coll., 1991—, St. Christopher's Sch., 1978—; mem. jr. bd. Children's Hosp., Richmond, 1971-78. Recipient Hon. Disability Svcs. award Adult Devel. Ctr., 1989. Mem. Nat. Soc. Colonial Dames Am. (Va. chpt.), Japan-Va. Soc. (bd. dirs., exec. com., acculturation com. 1987—), Women's Club, James River Garden Club, Tuckahoe Rep. Women's Club, Bush/Quayle Alumni Assn. Presbyterian. Home: 4600 Sulgrave Rd Richmond VA 23221 Office: Dept Rights Viginians Disabilities James Monroe Bldg 17th Fl 101 N 14th St Richmond VA 23219-3684

HAGERDON, KATHY ANN (KAY HAGERDON), financial analyst, educator; b. Fremont, Ohio, Mar. 20, 1956; d. Willis Harold and Lillian Mae (Bahnsen) Lehmann; m. Michael Lee Hagerdon, Apr. 21, 1979; children: Patrick Michael, Robert Joseph, Andrew Richard. BSBA, Ohio State U., 1978; MBA, Ashland U., 1991. Budget analyst Small Motors divsn. Westing House, Bellefontaine, Ohio, 1978-80; fin. analyst Aerospace Elec. divsn. Westing House, Lima, Ohio, 1980-82, fin. cost analyst, 1982-85; sr. fin. analyst Elec. Sys. divsn. Westing House, Lima, 1985-91, lead profl., 1991-92; sr. fin. analyst Sund Strand Electric Power Sys., Lima, 1992-96; plant controller Sund Strand Electric Power Sys., Phoenix, 1996—; chmn. supervisory com. Westing House Credit Union, 1991-94; part-time prof. Tiffin U., Lima, 1994-96, Northwestern Bus. Coll., Lima, 1994-95. Mem. Inst. Mgmt. Accts. (v.p. membership 1994-96), Toastmasters Internat. (pres. 1993-95, Com. award 1991). Roman Catholic. Home: 12232 N 40th Dr Phoenix AZ 85029

HAGERTY, POLLY MARTIEL, financial analyst, construction executive; b. Joliet, Ill., Aug. 17, 1946; d. George Albert and Gene Alice (Roush) Jerabek; m. Theodore John Hagerty, Feb. 12, 1972. BS in Elem. Edn., Midland Luth. Coll., 1968; MEd in Early Childhood Edn., U. Ill., 1977; MBA in Fin., U. Tex., 1986. Elem. tchr. Madison Heights (Mich.) Sch. Dist., 1968-70, Taft Sch. Dist., Lockport, Ill., 1970-72; systems clerk U.S. Army, The Pentagon, Washington, 1972-74; psychology aide Psychology Clinic U. Ill., Urbana, 1974-75; elem. tchr. Champaign (Ill.) Sch. Dist., 1975-77; with recruitment Standard Oil of Ohio, Cleve., 1977-78; v.p. NCNB Texas-Houston, 1981-88, Citibank, Tucson, 1988-92; substitute tchr. Austin (Tex.) Ind. Sch. Dist., 1993-94; fin. analyst MK Devel. Inc., Austin, 1994—; co-owner Hagerty Constrn. Co., Austin, 1994—. Pres. Christus Victor Luth. Ch., League City, Tex., 1985-88, Luth. Ch. of the Foothills, Tucson, 1990-92; treas. Holy Cross Luth. Ch., Austin, 1996—. Recipient Golden Circle Sales and Svc. award, 1991. Mem. NAFE, AAUW, U. Ill. Alumni Club. Republican. Lutheran. Home: 7403 Callbram Ln Austin TX 78736-3119 Office: 7200 N Mo Pac Expy Ste 400 Austin TX 78731-2562

HAGGARD, JOAN CLAIRE, church musician, piano instructor, accompanist; b. Ann Arbor, Mich., July 7, 1932; d. Clifford Buell and Bertha (Woodhurst) Wightman; m. Harold Wallace Haggard, June 30, 1956; children: Alan C., Stephen T., John A., Marian E. BA, Carleton Coll., 1954; postgrad., Ecole des Beaux Arts, Fontainebleau, France, 1954, U. Mich., 1954-55; A., Am. Guild Organists, 1980. Cert. pvt. piano tchr. Organist, choir dir. St. Paul's Episc. Ch., Riverside, Ill., 1955-59; dir. of music St. Andrew's Episc. Ch., Livonia, Mich., 1960-72; organist Christ Episc. Ch., Dearborn, Mich., 1973-83; dir. of music St. Philip's Episc. Ch., Rochester, Mich., 1983-92; organist, music coord. 1st United Meth. Ch., Farmington, Mich., 1992—; pvt. piano tchr., Livonia, 1960—; piano instr. Southfield (Mich.) Sr. Adult Ctr., 1992—; accompanist Creative and Performing Arts High Sch., Livonia, 1987-90; accompanist many solo instrumental and vocal performances, 1959—. Editor Livonia Youth Symphony Soc. newsletter, 1972-77; contbr. articles to profl. jours. Pres. Livonia Youth Symphony Soc., 1973-76; program dir. Episcopal Diocese Mich. Jr. Choir Camp, 1981-84, 87-89; coord. daily worship Triennial Conv. Episcopal Ch., Detroit, 1988. Mem. Am. Guild Organists (dean Detroit chpt. 1976-79, gen. chmn. nat. conv. 1986, councillor Region V 1986-92), Nat. Guild Piano Tchrs. (judge piano auditions 1987—), Music Tchrs. Nat. Assn., Assn. Anglican Musicians, Hymn Soc. in the U.S. and Can., Assn. Diocesan Liturgy and Music Commns., Music Commn. Episcopal Diocese Mich. (chmn. 1980-81), Piano Tchrs. Forum (Livonia area, pres. 1995—), Friend of Arts, SAI, PEO. Home: 33974 N Hampshire St Livonia MI 48154-2722

HAGGER, BOBBIE, elementary education educator; b. Green Bay, Wis.; d. Robert G. and Thelma R. (Wickman) Alwin; children: Katie, Julie. BS in Elem. Edn., Wayne State U., 1971; M of Elem. Edn., Western Mich. U., 1976. Elem. tchr. Dept. Def. Dependent Schs., Strullendorf, Germany, 1985-87, Fennville (Mich.) Pub. Schs., 1971-85, 87—. Named Tchr. of Yr., Fennville Pub. Schs., 1993. Home: 6272 126th Ave Fennville MI 49408-9650 Office: Fennville Pub Schs Memorial Dr Fennville MI 49408

HAGGERTY, GRETCHEN R., petroleum and steel industry executive. V.p., treas. USX Corp., Pitts. Office: USX Corp 600 Grant St Pittsburgh PA 15219-4776

HAGLER, CAROLE COLE, elementary education educator; b. Arlington, Tex., Feb. 5, 1959; d. Bill E. and Shirley E. (Tibbit) Cole; m. Jack P. Hagler, July 18, 1981; children: Megan, Molly. BS in Edn., Baylor U., 1981. Tchr. Arlington (Tex.) Ind. Sch. Dist., 1983-94, lead tchr., 1994—; mem. textbook adoption com., Arlington, 1992-93, chpt. 1 steering com., 1986—. Mem. Internat. Reading Assn., Tex. State Reading Assn., Arlington Reading Assn. (treas. 1985-87), Assn. Tex. Profl. Educators, Assn. for Compensatory Educators of Tex. Methodist. Office: Foster Elem Sch 1025 High Point Rd Arlington TX 76015-3515

HAGLUND, BERNICE MARION, elementary school educator; b. Negaunee, Mich.; d. Paul and Bernice Cody; m. Charles Haglund; children: Christopher C., Mary. BA, No. Mich. U., 1971, MA, 1978. Tchr. Arnold Elem. Sch., Mich. Center Schs., Mich.; social sec., v.p., pres. Mich. Ctr. Jr. Child Study Group, 1979-83, com. mem. sci. com., dept. head to curriculum counsel, 1993—. V.p., treas., social sec. Commonwealth Wives, Jackson, 1971-82. Mich. State grantee U.S. Optical soc., 1993. Mem. AAUW (sec. social edn. area), ASCD, Bus. and Profl. Women (sec. 1969-71, coord. study group 1972—, sec., social, contact edn. chair, woemn's issues), Orton Soc. (workshop trainer), Mich. Dyslexia Inst., Mich. Sci. Tchrs. Assn., Nat. Sci. Tchrs., Acad. Orton Gillingham, Phi Delta Kappa. Roman Catholic. Home: 1840 Noon Rd Jackson MI 49201-9154

HAGMAN, BETTY JO, elementary education educator; b. Tonasket, Wash., Nov. 4, 1937; d. Roy Jilies and Esther Naomi (Juday) VanWoert; m. Karl Robert Hagman, Dec. 28, 1963; children: John Robert, Sandra Gail. BA in Edn., Ea. Wash. U., 1959; postgrad., Western Wash. U., 1963. Cert. tchr. K-12. 2nd grade tchr. Highline Sch. Dist., Burien, Wash., 1959-61; 4th grade tchr. DuPont-Ft. Lewis Sch. Dist., Ft. Lewis, Wash., 1962-66; tchr. various grades LaCrosse (Wash.) Sch. Dist., 1976—. Mem. NEA, Nat. Coun. Tchrs. Math., Wash. Edn. Assn., Wash. State Math. Coun., Reading Club (sec., v.p.), Alpha Delta Kappa. Home: PO Box 86 Lacrosse WA 99143-0086

HAGOOD, ANNABEL DUNHAM, speech communication educator, consultant; b. Hattiesburg, Miss., Feb. 7, 1924; d. John H. and Isabella (Smith) Dunham; m. William Knox Hagood, June 6, 1950 (div. Sept. 1969). A.B., Southwestern La. Inst., 1944; M.A., U. Wis., 1946; postgrad., 1947-49. Asst. dir. debate and drama Southwestern La. Inst., 1944-45; asst. counselor U. Wis., 1945-46; instr. U. Ala., Tuscaloosa, 1946-49; asst. prof. speech U. Ala., 1949-57, assoc. prof., 1957-63, prof., 1963-87, prof. emeritus, 1987-94, dir. forensics, 1946-77, chmn. area rhetoric and speech communication, 1973-76, chmn. dept. speech communication and theatre, 1976-79, chmn. dept. speech communication, 1979-87, chmn. student acad. affairs Coll. Arts and Scis., 1969-71; chmn. arts and scis. faculty senate (U. Ala.), 1972-73; pres. faculty senate U. Ala., 1975-77; pres. Annabel Hagood and Assocs., communication cons., Biloxi, Miss., 1989—; Mem. adv. com. contests and awards Alexander Hamilton Bicentennial Commn., 1956-57; trustee Nat. Debate Tournament Com., 1967-77, chmn., 1968-69, 74-76, treas., 1972-73. Editor: The Register, 1956, 57; Contbr. chpts. to books, articles to profl. jours. Designer Fla. Endowment for Humanities; trustee, chmn. bd. trustees Delta Sigma Rho-Tau Kappa Alpha, 1980-93, mem. long-range fin. com. Nat. Debate Tournament com., 1979-83; participant 1st Presdl. Librs. Conf. on Pub. and Pub. Policy, Gerald Ford Presdl. Libr., 1983. Recipient Outstanding Commitment to Teaching award U. Ala. Nat. Alumni Assn., 1986, Disting. Service award U. Ala. Faculty Senate, 1986, Service award U. Ala. Sch. Communication, 1987, Leadership award U. Ala. Sch. Communication, 1987. Mem. Am. Forensic Assn. (past nat. pres., 1st recipient Disting. Svc. award 1979), Speech Comm. Assn. (chmn. com. internat. discussion and debate 1953-55), Assn. Comm. Adminstrn. (exec. com. 1982-84), Ala. Speech Assn., Phi Kappa Phi, Pi Kappa Delta, Delta Sigma Rho, Tau Kappa Alpha (past nat. pres., bd. of trustees, chmn. bd. 1980-95). Home and Office: Annabel Hagood & Assocs Comm Cons 1324 Beach Blvd Biloxi MS 39530-3527

HAGY, TERESA JANE, elementary education educator; b. Bristol, Va., Nov. 1, 1950; d. Don Houston and Mary Garnett (Yeatts) Hagy. AA in Pre-Edn., Va. Intermont Coll., 1970, BA in Elem. Edn., 1972; MEd, U. Va., 1976, postgrad.; postgrad., Radford U. Cert. tchr., Va., Tenn. Tchr. 1st and 4th grades St. Anne's Demonstration Sch., Bristol, Va., 1972-75; tchr. 1st, 3d, 4th, 5th and 6th grades Washington Lee Elem. Sch., Bristol, 1975—; clin. instr. edn. Va. Intermont Coll., Bristol, 1972-75; coordinator gifted and talented program Bristol Schs., 1980-82; condr. workshops; developer tests to evaluate reading progress. Pres. women's circle Cen. Christian Ch., Bristol, Tenn., also v.p. women's fellowship, libr. chmn., mem. ch. choir, dir. music for Bible Sch., Sunday sch. tchr. 3d and 4th grades, 1979—. Recipient numerous edn. awards; named Tchr. of Yr., S.W. Va. Reading Coun., 1994, Tchr. of Quarter, Bible Sch., 1992. Mem. NEA, AAUW (sec. 1976-79, v.p. 1981-86), Va. Edn. Assn., Bristol Edn. Assn. (sec. 1978-80, chmn. Am. Edn. Week 1993, v.p.-membership chair 1994-95), Va. State Reading Assn., U. Va. Alumnae Assn., Va. Intermont Coll. Alumni Assn. (nat. pres. 1987-89), U. Va. Alumni Assn., Delta Kappa Gamma (chpt. v.p. 1986-88, pres. 1988-90, coordinating coun. chmn. 1990-92), Nat. Trust for Hist. Preservation, Phi Theta Kappa. Republican. Home: 820 Virginia Ave Bristol TN 37620-3935 Office: Washington Lee Elem Sch Washington Lee Dr Bristol VA 24201

HAHN, HELENE B., motion picture company executive; b. N.Y.C.. BA, Hofstra U.; JD, Loyola U., Calif., 1975. Bar: Calif. 1975. V.p. bus. affairs Paramount Pictures Corp., L.A., sr. v.p. bus. affairs, 1983-84; sr. v.p. bus. and legal Walt Disney Studios, Burbank, Calif., 1984-87, exec. v.p., 1987-94; with Dreamworks, 1994—. Recipient Frontrunner award in bus. Sara Lee Corp., 1991, Big Sisters Achievement award, 1992, Clairol Mentor award, 1993, Women in Bus. Magnificent Seven award, 1994.

HAHN, LUCILLE DENISE, paper company executive; b. Stony Point, N.Y., Oct. 8, 1940; d. Raymond and Catherine (Nobert) Hoyt. Lab. asst. Champion Internat. (formerly St. Regis Paper Co.), West Nyack, N.Y., 1972-74, technician, 1974-77, tech. asst., 1977-79, rsch. asst., 1979-82, technologist, 1982-84, sr. technologist, 1984-86, assoc. testing coord., 1986-89, testing engr., 1989-96, sr. quality engr., 1996—. Author: Testing Guidebook, 1990, (videos) Testing the Strength Properties of Paper, 1991, Testing the Strength Properties of Board, 1991. Fellow TAPPI (sec. process and product quality divsn. 1987-88, vice chair 1989-90, chmn. 1991-92, bd. dirs. 1993-96); mem. NAFE. Office: Champion Internat West Nyack Rd West Nyack NY 10994

HAHN, MARY DOWNING, author; b. Washington, Dec. 9, 1937; d. Kenneth Ernest and Anna Elisabeth (Sherwood) Downing; m. William Edward Hahn, Oct. 7, 1961 (div. 1977); children: Katherine Sherwood, Margaret Elizabeth; m. Norman Pearce Jacob, Apr. 24, 1982. BA in Fine Arts and English, U. Md., 1960, MA in English, 1969. Asst. libr. children's sect. Prince George's County Meml. Libr. System, Laurel, Md., 1975-91; instr. English U. Md., College Park, 1970-74; free-lance illustrator PBS/WETA, Arlington, Va., 1973-75. Author: The Sara Summer, 1979, The Time of the Witch, 1982, Daphne's Book, 1983 (William Allen White Children's Choice award 1985-86), The Jellyfish Season, 1985, Wait Till Helen Comes: A Ghost Story, 1980 (11 Children's Choice awards), Tallahassee Higgins, 1987, Following the Mystery Man, 1988, December Stillness, 1988 (Book award Child Study Assn. 1989, Calif. Young Readers' medal 1990-91), The Doll in the Garden, 1989 (Md. Children's Book award 1990-91, 7 Children's Choice awards), The Dead Man in Indian Creek, 1990 (4 Children's Choice awards), The Spanish Kidnapping Disaster, 1991, Stepping on the Cracks, 1991 (Scott O'Dell Hist. Fiction award 1992, ALA notable 1991, Joan G. Sugarman award, Hedda Seisler Mason award, Children's Choice awards), The Wind Blows Backward, 1993 (ALA Best Books for Young Adults), Time for Andrew, 1994 (4 Children's Choice awards), Look for Me by Moonlight, 1995 (Yalsa Quick Picks for Reluctant Readers), The Gentleman Outlaw and Me-Eli, 1996, Following My Own Footsteps, 1996, As Ever, Gordy, 1997. Recipient Scott O'Dell award for hist. fiction, 1992. Mem. PEN, Soc. Children's Book Writers, Washington Children's Book Guild, Authors Guild.

HAHN, SHARON LEE, city official; b. Kenosha, Wis., Sept. 22, 1939; d. Vincent B. and Mary Lee (Vaux) McCloskey; 1 child, John V. Calhoun. Student Kent State U., 1983. Cert. mcpl. clk., notary pub., Ohio. Sec., Simmons Bedding Co., Columbus, Ohio, 1960-61; exec. sec. Westinghouse, Columbus, 1962-68; legal sec. Bricker Law Firm, Columbus, 1969-70; asst. to prosecutor Whiteleather Law Firm, Columbia City, Ind., 1970-77; legal sec. Metz, Bailey & Spicer, Westerville, Ohio, 1977-80; clk. of coun., sec. to city mgr. City of Westerville, 1981-87; clk. of coun., records mgr. City of Westerville, 1981—. Deputy Registrar, Franklin County Bd. of Elections; pres. Meadowlake Assn., 1991-94. Mem. Ohio Mcpl. Clks. Assn. (bd. dirs. 1984-86, 91-94, asst. treas. 1994-95), Internat. Inst. Mcpl. Clks. (CMC award 1984, records mgmt. com. 1986-94), Am. Assn. Records Mgrs. and Adminstrs., Nat. Assn. Govt. Archives and Records Adminstrs. Presbyterian. Avocations: golf, organ, crocheting. Home: 356 Macintosh Way Westerville OH 43081-3595 Office: City of Westerville 21 S State St Westerville OH 43081-2121

HAHN, TARA LYNN, accountant; b. Iowa City, Iowa, Apr. 9, 1969; d. Donald Lee and Kathryn Jane (Hagen) Enochson; m. Marty Lee Hahn, Dec. 22, 1995. BBA in Acctg., Mt. Mercy Coll., 1991. Plant acct. Sullivan Graphics, Marengo, Iowa, 1991-94, sr. acct., 1994—. Little League coach Marengo Recreation Commn., 1992, 93, 94, 96. Mem. Inst. Mgmt. Accts.

HAHN, VIRGINIA LYNN, reporter; b. Wharton, Tex., Oct. 27, 1951; d. Conrad E. and Verna Mae (Ammons) H. Student, Sam Houston State U., 1974. Reporter Pasadena (Tex.) Citizen Newspaper, 1975—; mem. Tex. Press Women, 1976-86, Nat. Fedn. Press Women, 1976-86; condr. workshop Christian Writer's Conf., Pasadena, 1992. Bd. dirs. San Jacinto Day Found., Pasadena, 1990—; mem. pub. rels. com. Am. Cancer Soc., Pasadena, 1996—; vol. Restoration of USS Tex., Pasadena, 1992-94; former mem. Pasadena Rotary South, 1992-94, Am. Heart Assn., Pasadena, 1990-92. Recipient awards Nat. Fedn. Press Women, 1985—, Tex. Press Women, 1985-90, Harris County Med. Soc., 1991-94. Mem. Am. Cancer Soc. (com. mem.), Pasadena Kiwanis Club (hon.), Alpha Rho (sec.), Beta Sigma Phi. Democrat. Mem. Church of God. Office: Pasadena Citizen Newspaper 102 S Shaver Pasadena CA 77506

HAHNER, LINDA R. R., artist, creative director; b. Healdsburg, Calif., Dec. 4, 1952; d. Ellison and Joan (Prenderville) Ruffner; m. Thomas G. Russell, Dec. 23, 1971 (div.); 1 child, Thomas Kristian Russell, 1 foster child, Eric J. Miklas; m. Wolfgang Andreas Hahner, Dec. 21, 1989. BA Fine Art/Creative Writing with honors, Principia Coll., Elsah, Ill., 1980; MFA, Washington U., St. Louis, 1986; student, Skowhegan Sch. Painting/Sculp., 1985, Acad. Fine Art, Helsinki, Finland, 1987. Painter, prof., artist London and Helsinki, 1986-95; CEO, creative dir. Out of the Blue Design, Mill Valley, Calif., 1995—. One-person shows include The Am. Ctr., Helsinki, 1986, Helsinki Art Hall, 1987, Millikin Gallery, Decatur, Ill., 1988, Hagelstam Gallery, Helsinki, 1990, Zimmerman Gallery, Breisach, Germany, 1994; exhibited in group shows Steinberg Gallery, St. Louis, 1986, B Z Wagman Gallery, St. Louis, 1988, Rislakki Collection, Helsinki, 1991; represented in permanent collections Boatman's Bank, 1st Nat. Bank of Columbia, Finland/U.S. Ednl. Exch. Commn., Trade-off OY, KOP Bank Finland, Veikko Savolainen, Arja and Kari Antilla. Fulbright fellow and travel grantee, 1986; Skowhegan award and grantee, 1985. Mem. Women in Multimedia, Multimedia Devel. Group., ACM & Siggraph. Office: Out of the Blue Design 241 E Blithedale Ave Mill Valley CA 94941

HAIG, SUSAN, conductor. Conductor Windsor Symphnoy Orchestra, Windsor, ON. Office: Windsor Symphony Orch, 174-198 Pitt St W, Windsor, ON Canada N9A 5L4*

HAIGH, NANCY, set decorator. films include: Checking Out, 1988, Field of Dreams, 1989, Earth Girls Are Easy, 1989, The Grifters, 1990 (also set designer), Miller's Crossing, 1990, Guilty By Suspicion, 1991, Bugsy, 1991, Barton Fink, 1991, Hero, 1992, The Hudsucker Proxy, 1994, Forrest Gump, 1994 (Academy award nomination best art direction 1994). *

HAIGHT, CAROL BARBARA, lawyer; b. Buffalo, May 3, 1945; d. Robert H. Johnson and Betty R. (Walker) Hawkes; m. H. Granville Haight, May 28, 1978 (dec. Nov. 1983); children: David Michael, Kathleen Marie. BSW summa cum laude, Widener U., Chester, Pa., 1980, BA in Psychology summa cum laude, 1980; JD cum laude, Widener U., Wilmington, Del.,

1984. Assoc. Pepper, Hamilton & Scheetz, Phila., 1985-88, Hodgson, Russ, Andrews, Woods & Goodyear, Buffalo, 1988-90; pvt. practice Boca Raton, Fla., 1990—; arbitrator Am. Arbitration Assn., 1988—, mediator, 1989—, mediation instr.; founding dir. Mediation Ednl. Svc.: Coun. for Marriage Preservation and Divorce Resolution, Inc., 1992. Contbr. article to profl. jours. Mem. ABA (com. on adr), Pa. Bar Assn., Fla. Bar Assn., Phi Kappa Phi, Phi Alpha Delta, Phi Gamma Mu. Republican. Episcopalian. Home: Braemar Isle Townhouse 9 4744 S Ocean Blvd Highland Bch FL 33487-5343 Office: 370 Camino Gardens Blvd Ste 300 Boca Raton FL 33432-5826

HAIKEN, LEATRICE BROWN, periodical editor; b. Morristown, N.J., Mar. 27, 1934; d. Ellen (Liss) Schwartz; m. Martin Leslie Haiken, June 24, 1956; children: Matthew Scott, Susan Beth. Student, Douglass Coll., 1951-54; BA, Upsala Coll., 1955; postgrad., China Inst., 1960, Art of Baking, 1962, Cordon Bleu Sch. Cooking, 1974, NYU, 1976-77. Mkt. rep. Allied Stores Corp., N.Y.C., 1956-66; dir. showroom Philmaid Lingerie, N.Y.C., 1966-76; editor food and equipment div. Weight Watchers Mag., N.Y.C., 1976-85, editor in chief, 1985—; editorial dir. Weight Watchers Pub. Group, 1991—, v.p., 1992—; founder, dir. North Shore Cooking Sch., Port Washington, 1970; owner North Shore Caterers, Port Washington, 1970-76; instr. Youth Employment Services, Great Neck, N.Y., 1973, community enrichment program, 1974-75, Port Washington Adult Edn., 1982-84. Contbg. editor: Great Meals in Minutes, 1985. Nutrition cons. Port Washington community action council, 1977-87. Mem. Roundtable Women in Food Svc., Women in Comm., Am. Soc. Mag. Editors, Am. Inst. Wine and Food, Les Amis du Vin, N.Y. Hort. Soc., Hort. Alliance of the Hamptons, Oldways Preservation and Exch. Trust, Newswomen's Club, Knickerbocker Yacht Club, Chandon Club. Office: Weight Watchers Magazine WW 21st Corp 360 Lexington Ave New York NY 10017-6502

HAINES, RANDA, film director; b. L.A., Feb. 20, 1945. Studied with Lee Strasberg; student, Sch. Visual Arts, 1975, Am. Film Inst. Appeared in off-off Broadway prodns.; script writer for TV series Family, 1970's; appeared in film documentary: Calling the Shots, 1988; dir.: (TV spl.) Under the Sky, 1979, (TV series) Knots Landing, 1979, Tucker's Witch, 1982, For Love and Honor, 1983, The Family Tree, 1983, (TV movie) Something About Amelia, 1984, (Emmy award nomination for director of a limited series or spl.), (TV episodes) Learning in Focus, 1980, Hill St. Blues, 1982, Bang! You're Dead!, 1985, Judy You're Not Yourself Today, 1990, (films) Children of a Lesser God, 1986, The Doctor, 1991. Mem. Dirs. Guild Am. Office: Dirs Guild Am 7950 Sunset Blvd Hollywood CA 90046*

HAINES, VIRGINIA E., state official, former assemblywoman; b. Lakewood, N.J., June 6, 1946. Student, Ocean County C.C. Clk. N.J. Gen. Assembly, 1987-90; asst. dir. Ocean County Securities Dept., 1990-91; mem. Dover Twp. Mcpl. Utilities Authority, 1987—, chmn., 1991—; N.J. state assemblywoman 10th Legis. Dist., Brick, N.J., 1991-94; exec. dir. State Lottery Divsn., N.J., 1994—; N.J. state del. Rep. Nat. Conv., 1992; Rep. state committeewoman, Ocean County, 1985—; vice-chmn. labor com. Nat. Coun. State Legislatures; mem. Assembly Labor Com., Assembly State Govt. Com. Hon. bd. dirs. Lyons-Sambora Charity Ski Series; mem. Monmouth-Ocean Devel. Coun., Alice Paul Centennial Found., Inc.; mem. adv. bd. Ctr. for Kids and Family at Comty. Med. Ctr.; alt. mem. Regional Perinatal Consortium of Monmouth and Ocean County; bd. dirs. Ocean County Girl Scouts, Big Bros./Big Sisters of Ocean County; chmn. Ocean County Family Planning Ctr.; bd. dirs., past chmn. Local Adv. Coun. Alcohol and Drug Abuse, bd. dirs., past pres. Ocean County chpt. Am. Heart Assn. Named Citizen of Yr., Nat. Coun. Drug and Alcohol Abuse, 1990. Mem. Nat. Rep. Legislators Assn., Nat. Orgn. Women Legislators, N.J. Rep. Coalition for Choice, N.J. Rep. Women of 90s (vice chmn.), Women in the Senate and House, N.J. Assn. for Elected Women Ofcls., Women's Polit. Action Com. of N.J., Monmouth County Fedn. Rep. Women. Home: 497 Batchelor St Toms River NJ 08753-6702 Office: State Lottery Divsn State House Trenton NJ 08625-0002*

HAINING, JEANE, psychologist; b. Camden, N.J., May 2, 1952; d. Lester Edward and Adina (Rahn) H. BA in Psychology, Calif. State U., 1975; MA in Sch. Psychology, Pepperdine U., 1979; MS in Recreation Therapy, Calif. State U., 1982; PhD in Psychology, Calif. Sch. Profl. Psychology, 1985. Lic. clin. psychologist 1987, lic. ednl. psychologist 1982. Crisis counselor Calif. State U., Northridge, 1973-74; recreation therapist fieldwork Camarillo (Calif.) State Hosp.-Adolescent/Children's Units, 1974—; Intern recreation therapist UCLA Neuropsychiatric Inst., L.A., 1975-76; substitute tchr./recreation therapist New Horizons Sch. for Mentally Retarded, Sepulveda, Calif., 1976-79; intern sch. psychologist Los Nietos (Calif.) Sch. Dist., 1977-79; sch. psychologist Rialto (Calif.) Unified Sch. Dist., 1979-82; clin. psychologist field work San Joaquin County Dept. Mental Health, Stockton, Calif., 1982-83; intern clinical psychologist Fuller Theol. Sem. Psychology Ctr., Pasadena, Calif., 1984-85; clin. psychologist U.S. Dept. Justice, Terminal Island, Calif., 1985-86; cmty. mental health psychologist L.A. County Dept. Mental Health, 1987-89; clin. psychologist Calif. Dept. Corrections, Parole Outpatient Clinic, L.A., 1990—, Mary Magdeline Project, Commerce, Calif., 1992—; mem. psychiat.-psychol. panel adult and juvenile Superior Ct., L.A., 1992—; mem. psychiat. panel U.S. Dist. Ct. (cen. dist.) Calif., L.A., 1989—; clin. psychologist O. Carl Simonton Cancer Ctr., Pacific Palisades, Calif., 1993—. Adv. bd. Camarillo (Calif.) State Hosp., 1994—, vice-chmn. adv. bd., 1996; examiner Lic. Ednl. Psychologist Oral Examinations, Calif. Bd. Behavioral Sci. Examinations, Sacramento, 1985. Recipient award Outstanding Achievement Western Psychology Conf., Calif., 1974. Mem. Am. Psychol. Assn., Calif. Psychol. Assn., L.A. Psychol. Assn., Forensic Mental Health Assn. (con. planning com. 1993). Democrat. Lutheran.

HAINSWORTH, MELODY MAY, information professional, researcher; b. Vancouver, B.C., Can., May 13, 1946; m. Robert John Hainsworth, Jan. 6, 1968; children: Kaleeg William, Shane Alan. BA with honors, Simon Fraser U., Vancouver, 1968; MLS, Dalhousie U., Halifax, N.S., Can., 1976; PhD, Fla. State U., Tallahassee, 1992. Libr. Dept. Edn. of Tanzania, Mbeya, 1969-72, Dept. of Edn. of Zambia, Mwinilunga, 1972-74; law libr., deptl. libr. Dept. of Atty. Gen. of N.S., Halifax, 1975-77; regional libr. Provincial Ct. Librs. Dept. of Atty. Gen. of Alta., Calgary, 1977-80, So. Alta. Law Soc. libr., 1980-89; dir. librs. Keiser Coll., Tallahassee, 1992-93; v.p. info. resources and svcs. Internat. Coll., Naples, Fla., 1993—; adj. instr. Sch. Libr. and Info. Studies, Fla. State U., Tallahassee, 1990-91; speaker in field; active Women's Polit. Caucus. Author monographs; contbr. articles to profl. jours. Pres. Naples Free Net, 1993—; co-chair adv. com. com. on edn. and tech. Fla. State Bd. Ind. Colls. and Univs., 1993—; pres. Pvt. Coll. and Univ. Libr. Consortium Bd., 1995—; founding mem. Pub. Access to the Law of Fla., 1990—; mem. adv. bd. paralegal program Ft. Lauderdale Coll., Tallahassee, 1990-92; mem. exec. bd. Calgary Legal Guidance, 1985—, vice chmn., 1988-89, hon. life mem.; tech. grant com. Collier County Edn. Found., 1994—. Student Leader Bursaries Simon Fraser U. scholar, 1966-68; H.W. Wilson scholar Dalhousie U., 1974; Fla. State U. grad. asst., 1989-90. Mem. Spl. Librs. Assn (chair 1994—), North Fla. Libr. Assn., Fla. State, Ct. and County Librs. Assn., Tallahassee Law Librs. Assn., Fla. Libr. Assn., Assn. Libr. and Info. Sci. Edn., Alta. Legal Archives Soc. (hon. life), Collier County Bar Assn., Tempo, Naples Press Club. Office: Internat Coll 2654 Tamiami Trl E Naples FL 33962-5707

HAIRALD, MARY PAYNE, vocational education educator, coordinator; b. Tupelo, Miss., Feb. 25, 1936; d. Will Burney and Ivey Lee (Berryhill) Payne; m. Leroy Utley Hairald, May 31, 1958; 1 child, Burney LeShawn. BS in Commerce, U. Miss., 1957, M in Bus. Edn., 1963; postgrad., Miss. Coll., 1964, Miss. State U., 1970, U. So. Miss., 1986-88, 90. Bus. edn. tchr. John Rundle High Sch., Grenada, Miss., 1957-59; youth recreation leader City of Nettleton, Miss., summers 1960-61; tchr. social studies Nettleton Jr. High Sch., 1959-70; tchr.-coord. coop. vocat. edn. program Nettleton High Sch., 1970—; area mgr. World Book, Inc., Chgo., 1972-84; local coord. Am. Inst. for Fgn. Study, Greenwich, Conn., 1988—; instr. bus. Itawamba C.C., Tupelo, 1975-80; sponsor Coop. Vocat. Edn. Club, Nettleton, 1970—; advisor DECA, Nettleton, 1985—. Editor advisor State DECA Newsletter, 1987-92; contbr. articles on coop. edn. to newspapers. Co-organizer Nettleton Youth Recreation Booster Club; fundraiser Muscular Dystrophy Assn.; Sunday sch. tchr. coll. and career class Nettleton United Meth. Ch. Recipient 1st place Nat. Newsletter award Nat. DECA, 1988, 89, 90, 92, Excellence in Supervision award Am. Inst. for Fgn. Study, 1992; named Star Tchr., 1978, 95, Miss. Econ. Coun., 1995, Dist. II DECA Advisor of Yr., Miss. Assn. DECA, 1990, 93. Mem. AAUW (charter), Am. Vocat. Assn. (Region IV Coop. Vocat. Edn. Educator of Yr. 1985, Region IV Mktg. Edn. Educator of Yr. 1988, Region IV New and Related Svcs. Tchr. of Yr. 1996, Region IV Vocat. Tchr. of Yr. 1996), Coop. Work Experience Edn. Assn., Miss. Assn. Vocat. Educators (dist. sec.), Miss. Assn. Coop. Vocat. Edn. Tchrs. (v.p. 1980-83, pres. 1983-84, Miss. Tchr. of Yr. 1984, 87, 95), Mktg. Edn. Assn., Nettleton Ladies Civitan Club (charter), Phi Delta Kappa. Democrat. Methodist. Home: PO Box 166 Nettleton MS 38858-0166

HAIRE, CAROL DIANE, speech-language pathologist; b. Littlefield, Tex., June 24, 1949; d. Lloyd Fredrick and Martha Vera (Smith) H. BA, Tex. Tech. U., 1970, EdD, 1976; MA, North Tex. State U., 1971. Diplomate Am. Bd. Disability Analysts; lic. speech-lang. pathologist, counselor, marriage and family therapist, Tex.; cert. forensic examiner. Speech pathologist Cooke County Tex. Schs., Gainesville, 1972, Muleshoe (Tex.) Schs., 1973-74; instr. Tex. Tech. U., Lubbock, 1974-76; asst. prof. Howard Payne U., Brownwood, Tex., 1976-77; prof., dir. speech-lang. pathology Hardin-Simmons U., Abilene, Tex., 1977—; owner Haire Speech, Lang., and Learning Ctr., Abilene, 1986—; cons. Home Health Agencies, Abilene, 1978—, West Tex. Rehab. Ctr., Abilene, 1977—. Bd. dirs. Food Bank Abilene; profl. adv. bd. Home Health Svcs., Tex.; pres. Big Country Speech & Hearing Assn., Abilene, 1979-80. Named Outstanding Young Woman of Abilene, 1983; recipient Pathfinder award Taylor County, Tex., 1993. Mem. Am. Speech-Lang.-Hearing Assn. (cert.), Am. Psychol. Assn., Am. Coll. Forensic Examiners, Tex. Ednl. Diagnosticians Assn., Coun. for Exceptional Children, Abilene C. of C., Phi Kappa Phi (life). Office: 1925 Hospital Pl Abilene TX 79606

HAISLMAIER, PATRICIA ANNE, school psychologist; b. Lansing, Mich., Nov. 6, 1944; d. Russel Ambrose and Blanche LoDema (Barnhart) Lawler; m. Paul George Haislmaier, July 8, 1967; children: Jennifer, Kai Paul. BA, Marquette U., 1966; MA, Am. Internat. Coll., 1971; MS, U. Wis., Milw., 1991. Tchr. Longmeadow/Wilbroken Pub. Schs., Mass., 1969-71; ednl. specialist Jewish Vocat. Svc., Milw., 1971-80; tchr. St. Francis Children's Ctr., Milw., 1980-90, prin., 1990-92, sch. psychologist, program dir., 1992-94; sch. psychologist Milw. Jewish Day Sch., Elmbrook Sch. Dist., 1994—; cons. Children's Outing Assn., Milw., 1993-94, Shared Therapeutic Svcs., Milw., 1987-89; lectr. U. Wis., Milw., 1993—, Cardinal Stritch Coll., Milw., 1989-92. Com. mem., adv. bd. EXCEL program U. Wis., Milw., 1992-94; mem. speakers bur. Child Abuse Prevention Network, Milw., 1993-94; com. mem. START SMART, Milw., 1993-94. Mem. ASCD, Nat. Assn. Sch. Psychologists, Coun. for Exceptional Children, Coun. for Adminstrs. in Spl. Edn., Wis. Assn. Sch. Psychologists Assn., Wis. Divsn. for Early Childhood. Roman Catholic.

HAIZLIP, MARJORIE TORELLI, municipal official; b. Syracuse, N.Y., Sept. 10, 1951; d. Alexander John and Virginia (Tardy) Torelli; m. William Paul Haizlip, June 9, 1973; children: Virginia, Kirby. BA, William Smith Coll., 1973; MS, SUNY, Geneseo, 1978. Secondary tchr. Newark (N.Y.) Ctrl. Sch., 1975-84, East Seneca (N.Y.) Ctrl. Sch., 1984-85, Holland (N.Y.) Ctrl. Sch., 1985-86, Bloomfield Ctrl. Sch., East Bloomfield, N.Y., 1986-90; coord. pub. rels. and edn. Western Finger Lakes Solid Waste Mgmt. Authority, Lyons, N.Y., 1990—. Editor Waste Wise newsletter, 1990-95. Leader, mem. svc. unit com. Girl Scouts U.S.A., Canandaigua, N.Y., 1986—, bd. dirs. Seven Lakes coun., 1996-98. Mem. Women in Comm. Episcopalian.

HAJEK, ELLEN MAY, publishing executive, writer; b. Humboldt, Nebr., Oct. 16, 1941; d. Ernest Ray and Wilma Hazel (Wright) Hunzeker; m. Stanley Mathias Hajek, May 29, 1964 (dec. 1992); 1 child, Michael. BS in Edn., Peru (Nebr.) State Coll., 1962; MA in English, U. No. Colo., Greeley, 1970. Cert. secondary tchr., Nebr., Colo. Tchr. English and drama Humboldt (Nebr.) H.S., 1962-63; tchr. English and math. Essex (Iowa) Ind. Sch., 1963-64; typographer, compositionist The Weekly Times, Shenandoah, Iowa, 1964-65; newsroom receptionist The Greeley Tribune, 1965-66; substitute tchr. Jefferson County Schs., Golden, Colo., 1966-77; coord. pub. rels. Cleo Wallace Ctr., Broomfield, colo., 1974-75; pub. Hajek House, Golden, 1993—; freelance writer, Golden, 1966-92; asst. prof. Colo. Sch. Mines, Golden, 1991-92. Author: Willy Was a Winner, 1992, Humpties, Parts of Speech with Eggceptional Personalities, 1992, Building Sentences with Humpties, 1993, The How to Write Book, 1994, Diagramming, the Key to Understanding Grammar, 1994. Vol. tutor Adult Edn. Tutorial, Denver, 1974, Jefferson County Schs., Golden, Colo., 1977-92, City of Lakewood, Colo., 1994. Recipient 1st prize in writing contest City of Lakewood. Mem. Colo. Ind. Pubs. Assn. Roman Catholic. Home: 12750 W 6th Pl Golden CO 80401 Office: Hajek House 12750 W 6th Pl Golden CO 80401-4674

HALAS, CYNTHIA ANN, system support specialist; b. Norristown, Pa., July 24, 1961; d. George and Maria (Mitrik) H. Student, Temple U., 1979-80; AS in Bus. Adminstrn., Montgomery County Coll., Blue Bell, Pa., 1993; student, Springhouse Computer Sch., Exton, Pa., 1994-95. Columnist, corr. The Recorder, Conshohocken, Pa., 1980-81; claims supr. Liberty Mut. Ins. Co., Blue Bell, 1980-84; claims svc. rep. Met. Property & Liability Ins. Co., Wayne, Pa., 1984-87; model Frank James Assocs., Phila., 1986-87; auditor/tng. coord. Coresource, Inc., Wayne, 1987-94; sys. support analyst Del. Valley Fin. Svcs., Inc., Berwyn, Pa., 1994-95; sys. support coord. U.S. Healthcare, Blue Bell, Pa., 1995—. Active Nat. Arbor Day Found. Mem. NAFE, U.S. Fencing Assn. Byzantine Catholic. Office: US Healthcare 1425 Union Meeting Rd PO Box 3013 Blue Bell PA 19422

HALCO, LISA MARIE, academic administrator; b. Granada Hills, Calif., Oct. 5, 1965; d. Robert Henry and Ann-Marie Aldrea (Massé) H. BA, Texas Tech U., 1986, MA, 1989. Instr. Eldorado Coll., West Covina, Calif., 1989-90; asst. dean Eldorado Coll., Oceanside, Calif., 1990-91; dean Eldorado Coll., San Diego, 1991; assoc. dir. Eldorado Coll., Escondido, Calif., 1992-93; exec. dir. Eldorado Coll., Oceanside, 1993—; mem. Sch. to Career Cmty. awareness action team, San Diego, 1995—; mem. exec. com. Job Tng. Partnership Act, 1995; co-chair affirmative action adv. com. Oceanside Unified H.S. Dist. Com. mem. City of Oceanside Vision 2020. Mem. NAFE, Oceanside C. of C. Office: Eldorado Coll 2204 El Camino Real Oceanside CA 92054

HALE, ANN ELISABETH, sociometrist; b. Bluefield, W.Va., Sept. 24, 1942; d. Clarke Hudspith and Alleen Elisabeth (Walker) H. BA, Greensboro Coll., 1965; MSLS, U. Pitts., 1968; MA, Sangamon State U., 1973. Cert. trainer, educator, practitioner Am. Bd. Examiners in Psychodrama, Sociometry and Group Psychotherapy. Asst. prof. libr. Shippensburg (Pa.) State Coll., 1968-70; asst. prof. libr. instrn. Sangamon State U., Springfield, Ill., 1970-73; dir. Toronto (Ont., Can.) Ctr. for Psychodrama and Sociometry, 1975-81; resident trainer Moreno Inst., Beacon, N.Y., 1973-75; pres. Blue Ridge Human Rels. Tng. Inst., Roanoke, Va., 1981—, N.W. Action Methods Tng. Ctr., Seattle, 1987-91, Am. Sociometric Inst., Roanoke, 1994—. Author: Conducting Clinical Sociometric Explorations, 1985; editor: Who Shall Survive, 1994; cons. editor Jour. Group Psychotherapy, Psychodrama and Sociometry, 1985-90. Fellow Am. Soc. Group Psychotherapy and Psychodrama (pres. 1993-95, Hannah Wiener Profl. Svc. award 1996); mem. Fedn. Trainers and Tng. Programs in Psychodrama (pres. 1981), Inst. for Noetic Scis. Home: 2027 Windsor Ave SW Roanoke VA 24015 Office: Blue Ridge Human Rels Int Inst 824 Campbell Ave SW Roanoke VA 24016

HALE, BEVERLEE ANN, home care nurse; b. Akron, Mar. 5, 1948; m. Douglas W. Hale. Student, Kans. U., 1969. Nurse to home care Profl. Nursing, Akron, 1994—. Mobile meals vol. Mobile Meals Inc., Akron, 1990—; election poll worker Rep. Party, Akron, 1995—; nat. coord. for the ICA ICA of Am., San Diego, 1982—. Recipient Citizen of Yr. Ohio Health Dept., 1991. Mem. NOW (pub. rels. chair 1990—, sec., 1990—, chair health task force, 1990—, women of Yr. 1995), Nat. Resources (Ohio divsn.). Republican. Home: 233 Rohner Ave Akron OH 44319

HALE, CHARLOTTE, author, publishing executive; b. Jacksonville, Fla., Jan. 6, 1928; d. Anthony W. and Eleanor (Cunningham) Hale; m. Norris TeBeau Pindar III, May 23, 1986; 1 child by previous marriage, Stanley R. Smith Jr. Student, Armstrong Jr. Coll., 1947-48. Copy writer Sta. WSAV, Savannah, Ga., 1948-49, copy dir., 1949-51; copy dir. Sta. WSAV-TV, 1955-57; with advt. dept. Savannah News-Press, 1957-59; staff writer Sunday mag. Atlanta Jour.-Constn., 1960-70; free-lance writer, 1969—; founder, owner Charlotte Hale Communiqué, founder, pres. Epiphany Press, Savannah; cons. U.S. CSC, 1976-79; guest speaker various colls., schs., chs., clubs, 1969—; founder Time of Your Life mgmt. seminar, 1978, Facing Forward motivational seminar and workshop on aging, 1982, Going First Class seminar, 1984; speech writer state polit. candidates, 1959-68; news writer U.S. Army, Ft. Stewart, Ga., 1951. Author: Full-Time Living, 1978, (with Layona Glenn) I Remember, I Remember, 1968; editor and writer various books by Anita Bryaht and Bob Green, 1970-77, A New Day, 1992, Atlanta's Source Guide, 1991; editor: The Super Years, 1984; contbr. book revs. to newspapers. Vol. Savannah Symphony, 1955-59; bd. dirs. Savannah Mental Health Assn., 1957-59; co-chmn. Women's Bus. Initiative; trustee Ga. Conservancy, Inc., 1968-70. Mem. Nat. Speakers Assn., Chatham Commerce CLub (chmn. 1991-92). Home and Office: 629 E 55th St Savannah GA 31405-3617

HALE, CYNTHIA LYNETTE, religious organization administrator; b. Roanoke, Va., Oct. 27, 1952. BA, Hollins Coll., 1975; MDiv, Duke U., 1979; D in Ministry, United Theol. Sem., Dayton, Ohio, 1991. Ordained Disciples of Christ Ch., Va., 1977. Head resident Hollins (Va.) Coll., 1975-76; intern to minister St. Mark's United Meth. Ch., Charlotte, N.C., 1976; undergrad. counselor Office of Minority Affairs Duke U., Durham, N.C., 1976-77; intern to minister Staunton Meml. Ch., Pittsboro, N.C., 1977-78; coordinating counselor summer transitional program Duke U., Durham, N.C., 1978; chaplain Fed. Correctional Instn., Butner, N.C., 1978-83; chaplain, instr. staff tng. acad. Fed. Prison System, Glynco, Ga., 1983-85; pastor, developer Ray of Hope Christian Ch., Decatur, Ga., 1986—; 1st vice moderator Christian Ch. (Disciples of Christ), U.S. and Can., 1993—; bd. dirs. Coun. on Christian Unity, 1978-81; bd. trustees Disciples Nat. Convocation, 1980-86, pres. 1982-84, pres. ministers' fellowship, 1990—; task force on Renewal and Structural Reform, Disciples of Christ, 1980-87, adminstrv. com. 1982-87, gen. bd., 1982-88; bd. dirs. Disciples Divsn. Higher Edn., St. Louis, 1986-89; bd. trustees Lexington (Ky.) Theol. Sem., 1990—; bd. dirs. Disciples' Nat. Evangelic Assn., 1991—. Mem. governing bd. Nat. Coun. Chs., 1978-83, panel on bio-ethical concerns, 1980-82. Recipient Liberation award Disciples Nat. Conv., 1984, Religion award DeKalb Br. NAACP, 1990, Religious award for dedicated svc. Ninety-Nine Breakfast Club. Office: Christian Church (Disciples of Christ) 3936 Rainbow Dr Decatur GA 30034-2213

HALE, JUDY ANN, education educator; b. Tuscaloosa, Ala., Oct. 16, 1955; d. Rogene Bae and Berta Inez (Smelley) Hale. BA, David Lipscomb U., 1978; MEd, Ala. A&M U., 1989; PhD, Miss. State U., 1994. Art tchr. grades 7-8 Scottsboro (Ala.) Jr. High, 1978-81; headstart tchr. Bridgeport (Ala.) Elem. Sch., 1983-84, tchr. grade 1, 1984-87; migrant tchr. grades K-6 Stevenson (Ala.) Elem. Sch., 1987-89, kindergarten tchr., 1989-91; tchg. asst. Miss. State U., Starkville, 1991-94; asst. prof. Jacksonville (Ala.) State U., 1994—; owner, operator The Art Studio, Scottsboro, 1981-83; presenter in field. Mem. beautification coun. C. of C., Scottsboro, 1983; mem., v.p. Doctoral Student's Assn., Starkville, 1991-94. Faculty Rsch. grantee Jacksonville State U., 1994-96. Mem. AAUW (sec. 1987-89, pres. 1989-91), DAR, Am. Assn. for Edn. Young Children, Mid South Ednl. Rsch. Assn., Ala. Assn. for Young Children, Phi Delta Kappa (historian 1993-94). Office: Jacksonville State Univ Ramona Wood Bldg 700 Pelham Rd N Jacksonville AL 36265-1602

HALE, KAYCEE, research marketing professional; b. Mount Hope, W.Va., July 18, 1947; d. Bernard McFadden and Virginia Lucille (Mosley) H. AA, Compton Coll., 1965; BS, Calif. State U., Dominguez Hills, 1981. Fashion model O'Bryant Talent Agy., L.A., 1967-77; faculty mem. L.A. Trade-Tech. Coll., 1969-71, Fashion Inst., L.A., 1969-77, 1975—; pres. The Fashion Co., L.A., 1970-75; co-host The Fashion Game TV Show, L.A., 1982-87; exec. dir. Fashion Inst. Design and Merchandising Resource & Rsch. Ctr., L.A., 1975—, Fashion Inst. Design and Merchandising Mus. and Libr., L.A., 1977—; lectr. in field, internat., 1969—. Author: (brochure) What's Your I.Q. (Image Quotient)?; (tape) Image Builders; contbg. editor Library Management in Review; columnist The Public Image, 1990; contbr. Bowker Annual 1990-91, (newsletter) Northeast Library System, 1991. Adv. bd. Calif. State U., Long Beach, 1988-91. Mem. ALA, Spl. Librs. Assn. (pres. elect 1986—, pres. 1987-88, bd. dirs. So. Calif. chpt. 1985—), Spl. Librs. Adv. Coun. (pub. rels. com. 1987-89), SLA Libr. Mgmt. Div. (chmn.-elect 1987-88, chmn. 1988-89, pres.'s task force on image of libr./info. profl.), Textile Assn. L.A. (bd. dirs. 1985-87), Calif. Media and Libr. Educators Assn., Am. Mktg. Assn., Western Mus. Conf., Am. Mus. Assn., Costume Soc. Am. Office: Fashion Inst Design & Merchandising 919 S Grand Ave Los Angeles CA 90015-1421

HALE, MARCIA L., federal official. B in Polit. Sci., U. S.C., MPA. Asst. county planner Aiken County (S.C.) Planning Commn.; legis. asst. to U.S. rep. Butler Derrick of S.C. Washington; Washington dir. State of S.C.; dir. scheduling Hollings for Pres. campaign, 1984; field dir. Dem. Congl. Campaign Com.; southern field dir., conv. mgr. Dukakis Presl. Campaign; cons. Greenberg-Lake, Washington, Dem. Senatorial Campaign Com., 1990; polit. dir. Dem. Congl. Campaign Com.; asst. to Pres., dir. scheduling and advance White House, Washington, 1992-93; asst. to Pres., dir. intergovtl. affairs, 1993—. Office: The White House Office Intergovtl Affairs 1600 Pennsylvania Ave NW Washington DC 20500

HALE, MARIAN LEIGH, speech-language pathologist; b. Baton Rouge, Dec. 24, 1968; d. Ronald Eugene and Judith Annette (Marchant) H. BS in Edn. with honors, U. Ark., 1990, MS, 1992. Cert. clin. speech-lang. pathologist; lic. speech-lang. pathologist, Ark. Speech-lang. pathologist Bates Elem. Sch., Fayetteville, Ark., 1992—; chairperson comprehensive outcomes evaluation com. Bates Elem. Sch., 1994—; mem. search commn. U. Ark.; program coord. Nat. Student Speech Hearing lang. Assn., Fayetteville, 1990-91. Mem. Am. Speech and Hearing Assn., Golden Key. Office: Bates Elem Sch 601 S Buchanan Ave Fayetteville AR 72701-5611

HALE, MARIE STONER, artistic director; b. Greenwood, Miss.. Student in Piano, U. Miss., Hattiesburg; studied with Richard Ellis, Christine du Boulay, Jo-Anna Kneeland, David Howard. Tchr. Ellis/du Boulay Sch., Chgo., Jo-Anna Kneeland Imperial Studios, Palm Beach County, Fla.; co-founder Ballet Arts Found., West Palm Beach, Fla., 1973-86; co-founder, artistic dir. Ballet Fla., West Palm Beach, 1986—. Office: Ballet Fla 500 Fern St West Palm Beach FL 33401-5726

HALE, NANCY ANNETTE, kindergarten educator; b. Paris, Tex., Sept. 6, 1959; d. William Richard and Ruby Lee (Davidson) Bills; m. Roy Wayne Hale, May 6, 1983; 1 child, Christopher Wayne. BA in Elem. Edn., U. Tex., San Antonio, 1986, MEd in Early Childhood Edn., 1995. Cert. elem. tchr., early childhood specialist, kindergarten team leader, supr., Tex. Presch. tchr. Adventure Presch., San Antonio, 1986-87; 1st grade tchr. Bob Hope Elem. Sch. S.W. Ind. Sch. Dist., San Antonio, 1987-89, 1st grade tchr. Hidden Cove Elem. Sch., 1989-91, kindergarten tchr. Hidden Cove Elem. Sch., 1991—; mem. Districtwide Improvement Coun. S.W. Ind. Sch. Dist., 1990-91, instnl. coord., 1992-93, site-based mgmt. com., 1992-93, social studies instrnl. coord., 1992-93, dist. curriculum design com., 1996-98, campus improvement com., 1996-97, kindergarten team leader, 1996—, dist. curriculum designer, 1996—, mentor tchr., 1996, campus improvement com., 1996—. Mem. Neighborhood Watch, Atascosa, Tex., 1988—; sec. Macdona Heights Homeowners Assn. Mem. NEA, ASCD, ATPE, KTOT, Nat. Assn. for Edn. of Young Children, Tex. State Tchrs. Assn. Baptist. Home: 10925 Kelly Rd Atascosa TX 78002-3728

HALE, SARAH RUTH TREVATHAN, elementary school educator; b. Jonesboro, Ark., June 22, 1954; d. Lucian Henry and Ruby Karnese (Williams) Trevathan; m. Charles Edward Hale, Sept. 8, 1979; children: Matthew James, Jeremy Luke, Rebekah Elaine. AA, Freed-Hardeman U., 1974, BS, 1976; postgrad., U. Memphis, 1988—. Supr. before and after sch. care Harding Acad., Memphis, 1988-92; substitute tchr. Memphis (Tenn.) City Schs., 1992-93, Lawrence County Bd. Edn., Lawrenceburg, Tenn., 1993—. Pres. Leoma (Tenn.) Elem. Sch. PTO, 1994-95. Home: 150 Rabbit Trail Rd Leoma TN 38468-5663

HALEM, MERYL HARMON, psychotherapist; b. Manhattan, N.Y., Mar. 13, 1953; d. David H. and Elaine K. (Korman) Harmon; m. Ronald Scott Halem, Mar. 15, 1975 (div.); children: Danielle Shana, Beth Elana; life ptnr. Sharron Rhea Friedlander, Dec. 22, 1992. BA in Psychology, U. Hartford, 1975; MA in Clin. Psychology, New Sch. for Social Rsch., 1979; MSW, Adelphi U., 1985; cert. in family and couples therapy, Ackerman Inst. Family Therapy, 1993. Diplomate Am. Bd. of Examiners in Clin. Social Work; nat. cert. counselor; nat. cert. family therapist; Acad. Cert. Social Work. Instr. psychology Malverne (N.Y.) Adult Sch. Edn., 1979-82; rehab. counselor Met. Workshop for the Blind, N.Y., 1979-81; work adjustment counselor, rehab. counselor The N.Y. Assn. for the Blind Lighthouse, N.Y., 1981-83; group leader, counselor YM-YWHA, Roslyn, N.Y., 1983-86; coord., social worker Assn. Neurologically Impaired & Learning Disabled Children, N.Y., 1985-86; social worker, psychotherapist Cmty. Adv. Program for the Elderly, Little Neck, N.Y., 1986—; psychotherapist Halem Counseling Svcs., Bayside, N.Y., 1980—. Fellow Am. Orthopsychiatric Assn., N.Y. State Soc. for Clin. Social Work; mem. NOW (psychotherapy referral network), NASW (coun. on aging), Am. Assn. for Marriage and Family Therapy (clin. mem.), Nat. Bd. for Cert. Counselors, Inst. for Noetic Scis., Collaborative Family Health Care Coalition, Ackerman Inst. for Family Therapy, Alpha Chi, Psi Chi (pres. U. Hartford chpt. 1974). Mem. Ethical Humanist Society. Home: Apt 3D 4 W Mill Dr Great Neck NY 11021 Office: Halem Counseling Svcs Bayside Med Arts Ctr Ste 202 23-91 Bell Blvd Bayside NY 11360

HALES, LINDA, newspaper editor; b. Kansas City, Mo., Nov. 30, 1949; d. Samuel Dale and Erika Anne (Sitte) Hales; m. George Edward Gudauskas Jr. BA in French and Polit. Sci., U. Kans., 1971, BSJ, 1974. Copy editor Chgo. Today, 1974, Chgo. Tribune, 1974-78; asst. nat. editor Washington Star, 1978-79; news editor U.S. News and World Report, 1979-82; spl. reports editor Internat. Herald Tribune, Paris, 1983-88; sr. editor Health sect. Washington Post, 1988-89, editor Washington Home sect., 1990—. Recipient J.C. Penney Journalism award U. Mo., 1991. Office: The Washington Post 1150 15th St NW Washington DC 20071-0001*

HALES, LOUISE ANNE, health care organization administrator; b. New Castle, Pa., Jan. 5, 1951; d. Donald Michael and Phyllis Virginia (Lowery) Burke; m. George Winston Hales, Oct. 30, 1984; 1 child, Thomas Winston. BSBA, W.Va. U., 1972; MBA, St. Ambrose U., 1994. With John Deere Co., Columbus, Ohio, 1972-90; quality assurance adminstr. Deere & Co., Moline, Ill., 1990-93; mgr. quality deployment John Deere Health Care, Moline, 1993—; assoc. faculty St. Ambrose U., Davenport, Iowa, 1996. Mem. ASTD, Am. Soc. Quality Control, Internat. Soc. Performance Improvement, Windsor Crest Club (bd. dirs. 1995—), St. Ambrose U. Alumni Assn. (pres. 1995—). Office: John Deere Health Care Inc 1300 19th St East Moline IL 61244

HALEY, CAIN CALMES, computer consultant; b. Greensville, S.C., Apr. 4, 1952; d. Julius French and Melville Cain (Calmes) H.; m. John Francis Blakeslee, Jr., Oct. 24, 1983. BA, U. S.C., 1974, MA, 1975. Sch. psychologist Allendale (S.C.) County Sch., 1976-77; sch. psychologist, tchr. Beaufort (S.C.) County Sch., 1977-80; editor South World Mag., Hilton Head, S.C., 1980-82; mgr. Acctg./Mgmt. Svcs., Hilton Head, S.C., 1982-83, Computer Gazebo, Hilton Head, 1983-84; owner, prin. Entre Computer Ctr., Hilton Head, 1984-92, Calcom Ventures, Hilton Head, 1987—; ptnr. Robbins & Haley, Atlanta, 1990-92; adv. to bd. dirs. Dunes Mktg. Group, Hilton Head, 1984-86. Mem. Hilton Head Planning Commn., 1987—; bd. dirs. Gov.'s Council Vocat. Edn., Hilton Head, 1987—. Mem. LWV (chmn. 1986-87), Profl. Women (pres. 1985-86), Hilton Head C. of C. (chmn. com. 1986-87), Nat. Assn. Female Execs., Zonta. Office: Calcom Ventures 52 New Orleans Rd Hilton Head Island SC 29928-4722

HALEY, JEANNE ACKERMAN, preschool director; b. Dayton, Ohio, June 26, 1953; d. Harold John and Florence Mary (Jacobs) Ackerman; m. James Francis Haley, Feb. 28, 1975; children: J. Michael, Jason, Jamie. AB, Miami JAcobs Jr. Coll., 1972; BBA, Ft. Lauderdale Coll. Bus., 1974. Sec. to pres. Fla. Atlantic U., Boca Raton, 1974-76; tchrs. aide Meth. Early Childhood Edn., Boca Raton, 1974-83; substitute tchr., tchrs. aide Mint Hill Presbyn. Ch. Presch., Charlotte, N.C., 1984-86; tchr. St. James Episcopal Presch., Warrenton, Va., 1987-93; dir. St. John Presch. and Extended Care Program, Warrenton, Va., 1993-96, St. John Presch. Program and Parish Sch. of Religion Program, 1993—; adminstrv. asst. to propertors The Inn at Little Washington (Va.), 1993. Chairperson Diocesan Com. on Extended Day Programs, Diocesan Com. on Pre-Schs., organizer, dir.'s com., Diocese of Arlington, Va.; leader, organizer Boy Scouts Am., Charlotte, N.C., Warrenton, 1984—, asst. dist. commr., Warrenton, 1991-93, com. mem. troop 175, 1992— (Dist. award Merit 1992, Key Three award 1991); leader, organizer Girl Scouts U.S. Nat. Capital, Washington, 1991-94; v.p. Friends of Libr. Bd., Deerfield Beach, Fla., 1975-83. Mem. Assn. Childhood Edn. Internat., Nat. Assn. for Edn. of Young Children, Fauquier Cmty. Child Care Network (charter), Nat. Assn. Child Care Profls. Roman Catholic. Office: St John Presch 285 Winchester St Warrenton VA 22186

HALEY, JOHNETTA RANDOLPH, musician, educator, university administrator; b. Alton, Ill., Mar. 19; d. John A. and Willye E. (Smith) Randolph; children from previous marriage: Karen, Michael. MusB in Edn., Lincoln U., 1945; cert. cons., 1995; MusM, So. Ill. U., 1972. Vocal and gen. music tchr. Lincoln High Sch., E. St. Louis, Ill., 1945-48; vocal music tchr., choral dir. Turner Sch., Kirkwood, Mo., 1950-55; vocal and gen. music tchr. Nipher Jr. High Sch., Kirkwood, 1955-71; prof. music Sch. Fine Arts, So. Ill. U., Edwardsville, 1972—, dir. East St. Louis Campus, 1982—; adjudicator music festivals; area music cons. Ill. Office Edn., 1977-78; program specialist St. Louis Human Devel. Corp., 1968; interim exec. dir. St. Louis Council Black People, summer 1970. Bd. dirs. YWCA, 1975-80, Artist Presentation Soc., St. Louis, 1975, United Negro Coll. Fund, 1976-78; bd. curators Lincoln U., Jefferson City, Mo., 1974-82, pres., 1978-82; chairperson Ill. Com. on Black Concerns in Higher Edn.; mem. Nat. Ministry on Urban Edn., Luth. Ch.-Mo. Synod, 1975-80; bd. dirs. Council Luth. Chs. Stillman Coll; pres. congregation St. Philips Luth. Ch.; bd. dirs. Target 2000; mem. Ill. Aux. Bd., United Way, v.p. East St. Louis Community Fund, Inc. Recipient Cotillion de Leon award for Outstanding Community Service, 1977, Disting. Alumnae award Lincoln U., 1977, Disting. Service award United Negro Coll. Fund, 1979, SCLC, 1981; Community Service award St. Louis Drifters, 1979, Disting. Service to Arts award Sigma Gamma Rho, Nat. Negro Musicians award, 1981, Sci. Awareness award, 1984-85, Tri Del Federated award, 1985, Martin Luther King Drum Maj. award, 1985, Bus. and Profl. Women's Club award, 1985-86, Fred L. McDowell award, 1986, Vol. of Yr. award Inroad's Inc., 1986, Woman of Achievement in Edn. award Elks, 1987, Woman of Achievement award Suburban Newspaper of Greater St. Louis and Sta. KMOX-Radio, 1988, Love award Greeley Community Ctr., Sammy Davies Jr. award in Edn., 1990, Yes I Can award in Edn., 1990, Merit award Urban League, 1994, Legacy award Nat. Coun. of Negro Women, 1995; named Disting. Citizen, St. Louis Argus Newspaper, 1970, Dutchess of Paducah, 1973. Mem. Council Luth. Chs., AAUP, Coll. Music Soc., Music Educators Nat. Conf., Ill. Music Educators Assn., Nat. Choral Dirs. Assn., Assn. Tchr. Educators, Midwest Kodaly Music Educators, Nat. Assn. Negro Musicians, Jack and Jill Inc., Women of Achievement in Edn., Friends of St. Louis Art Mus., The Links, Inc., Las Amigas Social Club, Alpha Kappa Alpha (internat. parliamentarian, Golden Soror award 1995), Mu Phi Epsilon, Pi Kappa Lambda. Lutheran. Home: 230 S Brentwood Blvd Clayton MO 63105-1602 Office: So Ill U PO Box 1606 Edwardsville IL 62026-1500

HALEY, KARLA LORRAINE, secondary education educator; b. Mt. Kisco, N.Y., Mar. 8, 1970; d. Kenneth George and Lorraine Ann (Buzzutto) H. BEd, Cornell U., 1992, MEd, 1993. Cert. tchr. secondary sch. biology, chemistry, gen. sci., N.Y. 7th, 8th grades sci. tchr. Mildred E. Strang Middle Sch., Yorktown Heights, N.Y., 1993—; pre-freshman coll. biology tchr., Manhattanville Coll., Purchase, N.Y., 1994. Office: Mildred Strang Middle Sch 2701 Crompond Rd Yorktown Heights NY 10598

HALEY, PATRICIA ANN, psychiatric therapist, school counselor, administrator; b. Waxahachie, Tex., Jan. 17, 1951; d. Bob A. and Gertie M. (Graham) H. BA, Tex. Woman's Univ., 1973, postgrad. in deaf edn., 1978; MEdin counseling and student svcs., U. North Tex., 1994. Tchr. Ennis (Tex.) Ind. Sch. Dist., 1985-93; counselor Ferris (Tex.) Ind. Sch. Dist., 1994—; psychiat. therapist HCA Med. Ctr., Columbia-Midway Park Hosp.; owner Graham Comms., Waxahachie. Editor (poetry) Family Tributes, 1989, Therapeutic Poetry, 1990, Heroes and Heroines, 1991; contbg. poet (cassette) The Sound of Poetry, 1993. Fellow AAUW (interviewee cable TV show 1994); mem. ACA, Tex. Counseling Assn. (Ednl. Endowment award 1996), Poetry Soc. of Tex., Tex. Play Therapy Assn., Tex. Sch. Counselors Assn., Kappa Delta Pi, Phi Delta Kappa, Pi Lambda Theta.

HALFMANN, EUNICE KELLER, writer; b. Plymouth, N.H., Feb. 23, 1916; d. Carl and Pearl (Johnson) Whittemore; m. William W. Keller; children: Daniel W., Thomas W.; m. Howard Halfmann, Feb. 2, 1980. Nursing cert., Plymouth State Coll., 1933. Author: Clothespins and Calendars. Home: 28 Cold Brook Rd Millers Falls MA 01349

HALFORD, ELIZABETH NELLE, army officer; b. St. Louis, July 5, 1965; d. James David and Patricia Ellen (Arnett) Halford; m. Sean Murphy Nolan, Dec. 29, 1990. BS, U.S. Mil. Acad., 1988. Commd. 2d lt. U.S. Army, 1989, advanced through grades to capt.; exec. officer A Co., 293d Engr. Bn., Baumholder, Germany, 1990-91; instr./writer U.S. Army Engr. Sch., Ft. Leonard Wood, Mo., 1991-93; co. comdr. 515th Engr. Co., Ft. Leonard Wood, 1993—. Coach Ft. Leonard Wood Swim Team, 1991-92. Decorated Army Commendation medal, Meritorious Svc. medal. Mem. AAUW, Soc. Am. Mil. Engrs., Assn. U.S. Army, Army Engr. Assn., Am. Polit. Sci. Assn. Christian.

HALFORD, MARY ELIZABETH, librarian; b. Longthorpe, Eng., July 14, 1952; came to U.S., 1981; d. Aubrey Seymour and Giovanna Mary (Durst) Halford-Macleod; m. Peter Leroy Staffel, Dec. 18, 1980; children: Huw Matsen Staffel, Johanna Mary Kathryn Staffel. BA, U. Stirling, Scotland, 1976, PhD in German Lang. and Lit., 1981; MLS, La. State U., 1986. Asst. L.Am. Libr. Tulane U., New Orleans, 1982-84, asst. to bibliographers, 1984-85, asst. bibliographer for humanities and fine arts, 1985-90; reference libr. Bethany (W.Va.) Coll., 1991-92, reference and interlibr. loan libr., 1992-95, coord. libr. pub. svcs., 1995—. Author: Illustration and Text in Lutwin's "Eva und Adam", 1980, Lutvin's "Eva und Adam", 1984. Sunday sch. tchr., lay reader St. Matthew's Episcopal Ch., Wheeling, W.Va., 1994—. Mem. ALA, AAUW, Nat. Mus. Women in Arts, W.Va. Libr. Assn., Libr. of Congress Assocs. Home: 1313 Valley View Ave Wheeling WV 26033

HALFVARSON, LUCILLE ROBERTSON, music educator; b. Petersburg, Ill., May 17, 1919; d. Harris Morton and Lucille (Fox) Robertson; m. Sten Gustaf Halfvarson, Aug. 8, 1946; children: Laura, Eric, Linnea, Mary. BA, Knox Coll., 1941; MusM, Am. Conservatory, 1969. Cert. tchr., Ill. Tchr. music and speech Freeman Elem. Sch., Aurora, Ill., 1941-44; choral dir. Galesburg (Ill.) Sr. H.S., 1944-46; dir. of music Our Savior Luth. Ch., Aurora, Ill., 1950-63; oratorio soloist, 1952-67; dir. of music Westminster Presbyn. Ch., Aurora, 1963-84; vocal instr. Merit Music Program, Chgo., 1982-93; ret., 1993; choir dir. 1st Meth. Ch., Galesburg, 1944-46; choral-vocal instr. Waubonsee C.C., Sugar Grove, Ill., 1967-79; organizer Jr. Coll. Music Festival, Waubonsee Coll., Sugar Grove, 1972-73; pvt. practice vocal instrn., Aurora, 1979—. Conductor Messiah Concert Waubonsee Coll., Paramount Arts Ctr., 1968—, 25th Concert, 1992. Co-chair Citizens Adv. Com. Paramount Arts. Ctr., Aurora, 1977-78; founder, pres. United Arts Bd. Fox Valley, 1977-82; chair Paramount Celebration Arts, 1985-86; residency dir. Met. Life Affiliate Artist, Aurora, 1982-83; bd. dirs. YWCA, 1984-91, chair corp. award com., 1994-95. Recipient Disting. Svc. award Cosmopolitan Club, Aurora, Ill., 1983; named Woman of Year YWCA, Aurora, 1976, Disting. Alumni Knox Coll., Galesburg, Ill., 1984. Mem. AAUW, DAR, PEO, Music Educators Nat. Conf., Am. Choral Dirs. Assn., Aurora C. of C. (Image Maker 1992), Phi Beta Kappa. Home: 1105 W Downer Pl Aurora IL 60506-4821

HALL, ADRIENNE ANN, international marketing executive; b. Los Angeles; d. Arthur E. and Adelina P. Kosches; m. Maurice Hall; children: Adam, Todd, Stefanie, Victoria; adopted children: Joe Hibbitts, Joe Kwan, Carlos Moreno. B.A., UCLA. Founding ptnr. Hall & Levine Advt., L.A., 1965-80; vice chmn. bd. Eisaman, Johns & Laws Advt. Inc., L.A., Houston, Chgo., N.Y.C., 1980-94; pres., CEO The Hall Group, Beverly Hills, Calif., 1994—; founder, ptnr. Women, Inc.; chmn. Eric Bovy Inc., 1986-89, Hall Partnership, Venture Capital; bd. dirs. Calif. Mfrs. Assn. Svc. Corp., Inc. Trustee UCLA; bd. regents Loyola-Marymount U., L.A.; mem. The Founders of Music Ctr., Pres. Circle, L.A. County Commr. Mus. Art, Calif. Gov.'s Commn. on Econ. Devel., task force Rebuild L.A.; bd. dirs. United Way, ARC, Exec. Svc. Corps, The 2000 Regional Partnership, Shelter Partnership; trustee Nat. Health Found., Am. Women in Econ. Devel.; gov. Town Hall; mem. adv. coun. Girl's Clubs Am.; mem. adv. bd. girl Scouts U.S., Asian Pacific Women's Adv., Coalition of 100 Black Women, Nat. Network of Hispanic Women, Women of Color, Women in Bus., Downtown Women's Ctr. and Residence, Leadership Am., Washington, L.A. Food Bank; mem. exec. bd. Greater L.A. Partnership for Homeless. Recipient Nat. Headliner award Women in Comm., 1982, Profl. Achievement award UCLA Alumi, 1979, award for cmty. svc., 1994, Asian Pacific Network Woman Warrior award, 1994, Woman of Yr. award Am. Advt. Fedn., 1973, Ad Person of West award Mktg. and Media Decisions, 1982, Bus. Woman of Yr. award Boy Scouts Am., 1983, Women Helping Women award Soroptimists Internat., 1984, 1st ann. portfolio award for exec. women, 1985, Communicator of Yr. award Ad Women, 1986, leader award YWCA, 1986; Mem. Internat. Women's Forum (bd. dirs., Woman Who Made a Difference award 1987), Am. Assn. Advt. Agys. (bd. dirs. 1980, chmn. bd. govs. western region), Western States Advt. Agys. Assn. (pres. 1975), Hollywood Radio and TV Soc. (dir.), Nat. Advt. Rev. Bd., Overseas Edn. Fund, Com. 200 (western chmn.), Women in Communications, Orgn. Women Execs., Calif. Women's Forum (founder, chmn. The Trusteeship), Rotary (L.A. 5 chpt.), Internat. Bus. Fellows (mem. adv. bd.), Women's Econ. Alliance, Nat. Assn. Women Bus. Owners (adv. bd.), Am. Heart Assn. (adv. bd.). Clubs: Calif. Yacht; Stock Exchange, Los Angeles Advt. (pres.) (Los Angeles). Lodge: Rotary. *

HALL, ANNA CHRISTENE, government official; b. Tyler, Tex., Dec. 18, 1946; d. Willie B. and Mary Christene (Wood) H. BA in Polit. Sci., So. Meth. U., 1969. Clk.-stenographer Employment and Tng. Adminstrn., U.S. Dept. Labor, Dallas, 1970, fed. rep., 1970-80; program analyst U.S. Dept. Labor, Washington, 1980-84, div. chief, 1984-87, exec. asst., 1987-88; office dir. U.S. Dept. Labor, Dallas, 1988—. Recipient Outstanding Performance award U.S. Dept. Labor, 1972, 73, 74, 79, Meritorious Achievement award, 1986. Mem. Partnership for Employment and Tng., Nat. Honor Soc. Democrat. Presbyterian. Home: 2304 Hunters Run Dr Dallas TX 75232-4146 Office: US Dept Lab ETA 525 Griffin St Rm 315 Dallas TX 75202

HALL, BARBARA FOOTE, pilot, photojournalist; b. Memphis, Apr. 19, 1947; d. Douglas Alan and Alice Mary (Conyers) Hall; m. William Rue Gregg, Jan. 23, 1979 (div. 1986); 1 child, William Hall. Student, Rochester (N.Y.) Inst. Tech., 1965-68; BS, U. Colo., 1974. Cert. airline transportation pilot. Photographer Eastman Kodak Co., Rochester, N.Y., 1965-79; pilot Eastern Airlines, Miami, Fla., 1979-91, Delta Air Lines, Atlanta, 1991—. Photojournalist Eastman Kodak Publs., 1972-79, The Falcon, 1979-90, Delta NewsDigest, 1991—. Vol. Habitat for Humanity, Atlanta, 1991—, Nat. Park Svc., Kennesaw, Ga., 1987—, Summer Olympic Games, Atlanta, 1996. Olympic Relay Torchbearer, 1996 Summer Olympic Games, Atlanta. Mem. Soc. Women Airline Pilots, Air Line Pilots Assn. Home: 3430 Owens Pass Kennesaw GA 30152

HALL, BARBARA L., interior designer, artist; b. Tulsa, Jan. 24, 1936; d. Paul Martin and Nell (Coy) Bolley; m. Denton Lee Richey, 1955 (div. 1970); 1 child, Christina Lee Edwards; m. William Volker Longmoor, 1971 (dec. 1981); m. Robert Leroy Hall. BFA, U. Kans. Interior designer Pat O'Leary Assoc., Fairway, Kans., 1974-78, Jack Rees Interiors, Kansas City, Mo., 1978-83; interior designer, owner, pres. The Studio, Inc., Prairie Village, Kans., 1983-86; prin. Barbara Hall Interiors, Sun Lakes, Ariz., 1984—. Mem. Am. Soc. Interior Design (profl.), Ariz. Watercolor Assn. (juried mem.). Home and Office: 11006 E Sunnydale Dr Sun Lakes AZ 85248

HALL, BEVERLY ADELE, nursing educator; b. Houston, Aug. 19, 1935; d. Leslie Leo and Lois Mae (Pesnell) H. BS, Tex. Christian U., 1957; MA, NYU, 1961; PhD, U. Colo., 1974. RN, Tex., N.Y. With Ft. Worth (Tex.) Dept. Health, 1957-59; asst. prof. U. Mass., Amhurst, 1961-65; chief nurse N.Y.C. Med. Coll., 1965-67; asst. prof. U. Colo., Denver, 1967-70; assoc. prof. U. Washington, Seattle, 1974-80; prof., chmn. dept. U. Calif., San Francisco, 1980-84; Denton Cooley prof. nursing U. Tex., Austin, 1984—; mem. grad. faculty Sch. Biomed. Sci. U. Tex., Galveston; pres. med. svcs. Bd. Dir. Project Transitionss; mem. NIH Study Group. Author: Mental Health and the Elderly, 1985 (Book of Yr.); mem. editl. rev. bd. Advances in Nursing, Archives Psychiat. Nursing, Qualitative Health Rsch., Rsch. in Nursing and Health, Nursing Outlook, Jour. Profl. Nursing, Jour. of the Am. Psychiat. Nurses Assn.; contbr. articles to profl. jours., chpts. to books. Served to capt. U.S. Army, 1962-66. Recipient Tex. Excellence Teaching award U. Tex. Ex-Students Assn., 1994. Fellow Am. Acad. Nursing (governing bd., mem. fellowship selection com.), Am. Coll. Mental Health Adminstrn.; mem. ANA (divsn. gerontological practice), Coun. Nurse Rschrs., Am. Inst. Life Threatening Illness and Loss, So. Nursing Rsch. Soc. Home: 8401 Mesa Doble Ln Austin TX 78759-8028 Office: U Tex 1700 Red River St Austin TX 78701-1412

HALL, BEVERLY JOY, police officer; b. St. Paul, Minn., Dec. 31, 1957; d. Kenneth Ray and Harriet Kathleen (Fuller) H.; m. Charles Alan Neuman, Feb. 14, 1956. AAS in Law Enforcement, North Hennepin C.C., Brooklyn Park, Minn., 1977. Lic. peace officer, Minn. Community svc. officer Brooklyn Park Police Dept., 1977-79; police officer St. Paul Police Dept., 1979-86, police sgt., 1986-95, police lt., 1995—; hostage negotiator, St. Paul Police Dept., 1991-92, hostage negotiating team coord., 1992—. Mem. Internat. Assn. Women Police (regional coord. 1988-94, bd. dirs.), Minn. Assn. of Women Police (pres. 1982-86), Assn. Tng. Officers of Minn., Fed. Bur. of Investigations Nat. Acad. Assocs. Office: Saint Paul Police Dept 100 E 11 St Saint Paul MN 55101

HALL, CARLA LOUISE, English educator, consultant; b. Pasadena, Calif., Sept. 17, 1966; d. Dave Lee and Rosalee Jane (Ewing) Smith; m. James Earl Hall, Aug. 3, 1991; children: James, Jonathan. BS in English, Western Oreg. State U., 1989; MA in Edn., Calif. State U., Bakersfield, 1995. Cert. tchr., Oreg., Calif. English tchr. Pub. Sch., Lancaster, Calif., 1990-95; English and history tchr. Laurel Springs Sch., Ojai, Calif., 1995—; tennis coac jr. varsity girls tennis Pub. Sch., Lancaster, 1991-93, advisor varsity cheerleading, 1990-91, writer/creator edn. exit exam, 1992; edn. cons. Laurel Springs Sch., 1995. Author (English reading course) Reading for Pleasure, 1995, English Composition, 1996, College Writing, 1996, On-Line Creative Writing Course, 1996. Recipient scholarship Phi Theta Kappa, 1984, scholarship Soroptimist, 1984, Runner-up Miss Mont., Miss USA Pagent, 1984. Mem. Calif. Tchrs. Assn., Mom's Club. Republican.

HALL, CAROLYN VOSBURG, artist, author; b. Fenton, Mich., July 22, 1927; d. Guy Melvin and Doris Laura (Bourns) Vosburg; m. Clarence Albert Hall, July 26, 1952; children: Randall Ross, Claudia Hall Stroud, Garrett Alan. Student, Oliver Coll., 1945, Mich. State U., 1946; BFA, Cranbrook Acad. Art, Bloomfield Hills, Mich., 1949, MFA, 1951. Instr. N.D. State Coll., Fargo, 1944-50; freelance art critic Birmingham Eccentric, 1965-75; dir. writing conf. Detroit Women Writers/Oakland U., Rochester, Mich., 1980-90; exhibited art locally and nationally, 1945-95. Author: Stitched and Stuffed Art, 1972, I Love Popcorn - I Love Ice Cream, 1976, Sewing Machine Craft Book, 1980, Soft Sculpture, 1984, Teddy Bear Craft Book, 1986, A to Z Soft Animals, 1988, Friendship Quilts, 1993, Pictorial Quilts, 1993, Alphabet Stitchery, 1995; co-editor: Drawing and Coloring Book, 1980, Artists Sketch Book, 1985, Voices on Writing Fiction, 1987; contbr. articles to profl. jours. Fundraiser Planned Parenthood, 1953-60. Recipient award for art column Mich. Press Assn., 1968, grants Mich. Arts Coun., 1984-90. Mem. Detroit Women Writers (pres. 1975—), Birmingham Women Painters (pres. 1969—), Cranbrook Writer's Guild (bd. mem., v.p. 1985—), Birmingham Bloomfield Art Assn. (v.p. 1957—). Unitarian. Home: 20730 Kennoway Beverly Hills MI 48025

HALL, CHARLENE MARIE, mental health administrator, social worker; b. Hamilton, Ohio, Jan. 9, 1948; d. Charles Aaron and Mary Louise (Sprandel) Rook; m. W. Edward McGinnis, June 15, 1968 (div. Jan. 1980); children: Kevin Michael McGinnis, Kathleen Marie McGinnis, Kelly Megan McGinnis; m. Arvel J. Edward Hall, Nov. 11, 1994. BA in Human Svcs. summa cum laude, Coll. of Mount St. Joseph, 1989; postgrad., U. Cin., 1992. Lic. social worker, Ohio; cert. occupancy specialist Nat. Ctr. for Housing Mgmt., Washington, cert. mgr. housing. Office mgr. Logsdon Nursing Home, Hamilton, Ohio, 1974-77, Tri-County Extended Care Ctr., Fairfield, Ohio, 1978-79, Galbraith and Galbraith Pub. Accts., Hamilton, 1979-86; dir. mgmt. svcs. Butler County Mental Health Bd., Hamilton, 1986-91, dir. residential and mgmt. svcs., 1991—; exec. dir. New Aves., Inc., Hamilton, 1991—. Choir mem., soloist at pvt. audience with Pope John Paul II, Vatican City, 1988; patient care vol. Hospice, Hamilton, 1990-95; com. chair Mental Health Levy Campaigns, Butler County, 1987-92; mem. Disabled Am. Vets. Aux., Cold Spring, Ky., 1996. Mem. Ohio Program Evaluators Group, Comty. Mental Health Fin. Mgmt. Group. Democrat. Unitarian. Office: Butler County Mental Health 201 N Brookwood Ave Hamilton OH 45013

HALL, CHARLOTTE HAUCH, publishing executive; b. Washington, Sept. 30, 1945; d. Charles Christian and Ruthadele Bertha (LaTourrette) H.; m. Robert Lindsay Hall, June 8, 1968; 1 child, Benjamin H. BA, Kalamazoo Co., 1966, MA, U. Chgo., 1967. Reporter, news editor The Ridgewood (N.J.) Newspapers, 1971-74; copy editor, news editor The Record, Hackensack, N.J., 1975-76; asst. mng. editor The Boston Herald Am., 1977-78; dep. met. editor The Washington Star, 1979-80; news editor, Nassau County editor, Washington news editor Newsday, Melville, N.Y., 1981-87, asst. mng. editor, 1988-94; mktg. dir. Newsday, Inc., Melville, 1994—. Mem. Newspaper Assn. Am., Phi Beta Kappa. Office: Newsday Inc 235 Pinelawn Rd Melville NY 11747-4226

HALL, CYNTHIA HOLCOMB, federal judge; b. Los Angeles, Feb. 19, 1929; d. Harold Romeyn and Mildred Gould (Kuck) Holcomb; m. John Harris Hall, June 6, 1970 (dec. Oct. 1980);. A.B., Stanford U., 1951, J.D., 1954; LL.M., NYU, 1960. Bar: Ariz. 1954, Calif. 1956. Law clk. to judge U.S. Ct. Appeals 9th Circuit, 1954-55; trial atty. tax div. Dept. Justice, 1960-64; atty.-adviser Office Tax Legis. Counsel, Treasury Dept., 1964-66; mem. firm Brawerman & Holcomb, Beverly Hills, Calif., 1966-72; judge U.S. Tax Ct., Washington, 1972-81, U.S. Dist. Ct. for central dist. Calif., Los Angeles, 1981-84; cir. judge U.S. Ct. Appeals (9th cir.), Pasadena, Calif., 1984—. Served to lt. (j.g.) USNR, 1951-53. Office: US Ct Appeals 9th Cir 125 S Grand Ave Pasadena CA 91105-1621

HALL, DEBORAH MARIE, lawyer, brewing company executive; b. Oakland, Calif., Oct. 7, 1949; d. John Standish Bohannon and Mary (Swinson) H.; m. Eric Levin Meadow, Feb. 1973 (div. June 1982); 1 child, Jesse Standish Meadow Hall. Paralegal cert., Sonoma State U., Rohnert Park, Calif., 1984; JD, John F. Kennedy U., Walnut Creek, Calif., 1989. Bar: Calif. 1991. Paralegal Law Offices Marc Libarle/Quentin Kopp, Cotati, Calif., 1983-84, MacGregor & Buckley, Larkspur, Calif., 1984-86, Law Offices Melvin Belli, San Francisco, 1987-88, Steinhart & Falconer, San Francisco, 1988; mgr. Computerized Litigation Assocs., San Francisco, 1986; law clk. Morton & Lacy, San Francisco, 1989-91, assoc., 1991—; pres. Barbary Coast Brewing Co. Atty. Vol. Legal Svcs., San Francisco, 1991-95; judge San Francisco Youth Ct., 1995-96; com. chmn. Point Richmond (Calif.) coun., 1994-96. Recipient Whiley Manuel Pro Bono award State Bar Calif., 1993. Mem. Nat. Assn. Ins. Women, Def. Rsch. Inst., Bar Assn. San Francisco (del. 4th world conf. on women 1995), Internat. Com. Lawyers for Tibet (litigation com. 1991-96, co-chair women's com.), Ins. Claims Assn. (chmn. membership com. 1994-96), Hon. Order of Blue Goose Internat., Queen's Bench (chmn. employment com. 1994-96, bd. dirs. 1996). Democrat. Office: Morton & Lacy Ste 2280 Three Embarcadero Ctr San Francisco CA 94111

HALL, DOROTHY LOUISE PARZYK, curriculum coordinator; b. Worcester, Mass., Nov. 23, 1943; d. Francis Stephen and Jeanne Anita (Mathieu) Parzyk; m. Michael Stephen Hall, June 30, 1967 (separated 1989); children: Michelle Stephanie, Suzanne Marie. BS in Edn., Worcester State Coll., 1965; MEd, U. N.C., Greensboro, 1983, CAS, 1986, EdD, 1991. Cert. tchr., Mass.; cert. tchr., reading specialist, curriculum specialist, N.C. Tchr. 1st grade Town of Holden, Mass., 1965-67; tchr. 1st and 2d grades Old Richmond Elem. Sch. Winston-Salem (N.C.)-Forsyth County Schs., 1967-71, tchr. 1st grade Old Town Elem. Sch., 1971-83; vis. instr. Wake Forest U., Winston-Salem, 1983-86; reading/curriculum coord. Winston-Salem/Forsyth County Schs., 1986—; cons. various schs. N.C., S.C., 1991—, Milw. City Schs., 1994-96, Sheboygan (Wis.) Schs., 1995, St. Louis Schs., 1995-96. Author: Making Words, 1994, Making Big Words, 1994; author chpts. and articles. Mem. Internat. Reading Assn. (local pres. 1993-94), Phi Delta Kappa, Delta Kappa Gamma (local pres. 1996—). Roman Catholic. Home: 3060 Minart Dr Winston Salem NC 27106 Office: Winston-Salem/Forsyth Co Schs Winston Salem NC 27102

HALL, ELLA TAYLOR, clinical school psychologist; b. Macon, Miss., Nov. 30, 1948; d. Essex and Mamie (Roland) Taylor; children: Banyikaai Monique (dec.), Motiqua Shante. BA, Fisk U., 1971, MA, 1973; PhD, George Peabody Coll., 1978. Mental health specialist behavioral sci. div. Meharry Med. Coll., Nashville, 1976-77; assoc. psychologist Bronx (N.Y.) Psychiat. Ctr., 1979; clin. psychologist Wiltwyck Residential Treatment Ctr., Ossining, N.Y., 1979-81; clin. cons. Abbott House, Irvington, N.Y., 1982-85; sch. psychologist Abbott Union Free Sch. Dist., 1985—; cons. psychologist Youth Theater Interactions, Inc., N.Y.; rschr in the field. Author: (poetry) Double Twister, Somebody, Clinging Tears, 1994, Maple Tree at Dawn, 1995, Down My Three Rows, 1995, Mama Sis, 1995, These Times, 1995, Ordinary, 1996, Young Wilted Flower; (art) In My Mind, 1994, Picking Cotton, 1995. Lay reader, acolyte Episcopal Ch. Mem. Yonkers schs. PTA; mem. Com. on Spl. Edn. NIMH tng. grantee, Kendall grantee; Crusade fellow. Mem. Schomburg Ctr. for Rsch., N.Y. State Psychol. Assn., Coun. Exceptional Children, N.Y. Bot. Soc., Delta Sigma Theta. Avocation: photography.

HALL, GEORGIANNA LEE, special education educator; b. Greeley, Colo., Apr. 2, 1947; d. John Russell and Lois Louise (Urich) Martin; m. William James Bailey, 1970 (div. June 1972); m. Rex Henry Hall, Dec. 22, 1984; 1 stepchild, Jorri Colleen. AA, Fullerton (Calif.) Jr. Coll., 1967; BA, Calif. State U., Fullerton, 1969, elem. edn. credential, 1971, learning handicapped credential, 1976. Cert. resource specialist, lang. devel. specialist. Tutor Edn. Project for Disadvantaged Youth Savanna Sch. Dist., Stanton, Calif., 1965-69; math. tchr. Norwalk (Calif.)-LaMirada Sch. Dist., 1971-72; tchr. Cypress (Calif.) Sch. Dist., 1972-74, tchr. learning disability, 1974-80, tchr. learning handicapped, 1976, tchr. communicatively handicapped, 1981—, resource specialist, 1981—, dist. mentor tchr. for spl. edn., 1993—; dist. spl. edn. rep. for writing of Original Greater Anaheim Consortium Plan for Spl. Edn., 1980; dist. interview team for tchrs., prins., and aides, Cypress, 1985—, dist. staff devel. com., tchg. and assessment com., 1994-95; compliance program quality reviewer dist. leadership team rep. State Calif., Orange County, 1991—; Cypress dist. rep. for drug free schs. Cypress Sch. Dist.-U. Calif., Irvine, 1992—; King sch. rep. dist. drug alcohol tobacco edn.; mem. leadership team King Elem. Sch., Cypress, 1989—; lead tchr. for conflict mgr. tng., 1993—; coord. sch. intervention team, 1989—; coord. activities Svcs. for At-Risk Students, King Elem. Sch., 1990—, crisis interventino team, 1994—; dist. coord. CCR, 1994—; mem. Dist. Coord. Curriculum Com., 1994—; mem. dist. adv. com. Medi-Cal, 1994—; mem Dist. Testing and Assessment Com., 1994—; ACT tchr. rep. interview team for dir. instrn. and spl. edn., 1996, dist. interview team for instrnl. aides. Neighborhood rep. Muscular Dystrophy Assn., Huntington Beach, Calif., 1988—, Coun. for Paralyzed vets., Huntington Beach, 1989—; vol. reading tutor PLUS, Huntington Beach, 1992; publicity chmn. King Sch. PTA, 1992-93, 93-94; coord. resources needy families, King elem. sch. Recipient Hon. Svc. award PTA King Sch., Cypress, 1982; named Spl. Edn. Tchr. of Yr. Resource Specialists Calif., 1989. Mem. NEA, Calif. Tchrs. Assn., Assn. Cypress Tchrs. (sch. rep. 1974-76, 79-82, sec. 1976-77, 2d v.p. 1978-79, 1st v.p. 1979-80), Calif. Assn. Resource Specialists, Children with Attention Deficit Disorder, Learning Disability Assn., Calif. Assn. for Supervision and Curriculum Devel. Office: King Elem Sch 8710 Moody St Cypress CA 90630-2220

HALL, JANE ANNA, writer, model, artist; b. New London, Conn., Apr. 4, 1959; d. John Leslie Jr. and Jane Dezzie (Green) H. Grad. model, Barbizon Sch., 1976. Model Barbizon Agy., New Haven, 1977; employed by dir. of career planning Wesleyan U., Middletown, Conn., 1985-86; free lance writer, poet, 1986—; poetry contest judge Saybrook 25th Anniversary Celebration, Acton Pub. Libr., 1992; group poetry reader Literacy Vols. Valley Shore, Westbrook, 1995. Author: Cedar and Lace, 1986, Satin and Pinstripe, 1987, Fireworks and Diamonds, 1988, Stars and Daffodils, 1989, Sunrises and Stone Walls, 1990, Mountains and Meadows, 1991, Moonlight and Water Lillies, 1992, Sunsets and Beaches, 1993, New and Selected Poems 1986-95, 1994, Under Par Recipes, 1994, New and Selected Poems for Children 1986-95, 1995; founder, editor Poetry in Your Mailbook newsletter, 1989—; one woman shows include Westbrook (Conn.) Pub. Libr., 1989-96. Sunday sch. tchr. 1st Congl. Ch., Westbrook, 1977-90, asst. supt., bd. dirs. Christian edn., 1979-84; poetry reader Congl. Ch., Broad Brook, Conn., 1988; group poetry reader and displayer Westbrook Pub. Libr., 1989, 91, reader Night of Thousand Stars readathon, 1990; group poetry displayer Acton Pub. Libr., Old Saybrook, Conn., 1990, judge poetry contest 25th anniversary celebration, 1992. Recipient 2d prize Conn. Poetry Soc., 1983-86, chapbooks added to Soc. permanent archives at Housatonic Cmty. Tech. Coll., 1995; cert. of merit for disting. svc. to cmty., 1989, cert. world leadership, 1989. Mem. Internat. Platform Assn., Romance Writers Am. (book cover bd. designer Conn. chpt. 1991-93), Conn. Poetry Soc. (pres. Old Saybrook chpt. 1989-91, world poetry chmn. 1989; poetry reader 20th anniversary Russell Libr. Middletown, Conn. 1994). Home and Office: PO Box 629 Westbrook CT 06498-0629

HALL, JO(SEPHINE) MARIAN, newspaper editor, photographer; b. Aberdeen, S.D., July 12, 1921; d. Charles Martin Sykes and Deedie Mae (Keiser) Gruett; m. Winston Hall, Dec. 4, 1940; children: Wendy Diane, Willis Edward. Student, U. Colo., 1958, U. S.D., 1976. With advt. dept. Mobridge (S.D.) Reminder, 1955-61, columnist, 1956-61; with advt. dept., columnist Mobridge Tribune, 1961-67, news editor, photographer, 1968-81, editor people page, 1981—. Airway observer U.S. Weather Bur., Mobridge, 1939-84; sec. bd. dirs. Klein Mus., Mobridge, 1976-80; chpt. pres. Am. Field Svc., 1972-82; vol. Mobridge Regional Hosp., 1990—; organist, dir. choir, sr. warden of vestry St. James Episcopal C., Mobridge; mem. S.D. Episcopal Diocesan Coun., 1993—. Recipient numerous state and nat. awards for feature stories, news stories, coluns, obituaries, photography, spl. sects. headlines, 1959—, including Herbert Bayard Swope award, 1978; 1st place award for newspaper editing Nat. Fedn. Press Women, 1979, for spl. edit., 1982; Golden Quill award S.D. Press Women, 1988. Democrat. Home: 910 3d Ave W Mobridge SD 57601 Office: Mobridge Tribune 111 3d St W Mobridge SD 57601

HALL, JUDITH YOUNG, nurse; b. Akron, Ohio, June 29, 1948; d. Frank Marshall and Dorothy Geraldine (Patterson) Young; m. Howard Rodney Hall, Mar. 21, 1970; children: Melissa Elyse, Simon Marshall, Elizabeth Grace. BA, U. Calif., 1971; BSN, U. Akron, 1983. Patient care coord. Northridge (Calif.) Med. Ctr., 1986-87; coord. of grad. admissions U. So. Calif. Sch. of Nursing, L.A., 1989; mgr. neonatal intensive care & pediat. Ventura (Calif.) County Med. Ctr., 1990-92; dir. Perinatal Advisory Coun. of L.A. Comm., Encino, Calif., 1992-95; dir. clin. ops. & Svcs. Olsten Kimberly Quality Care, San Mateo, Calif., 1995; mgr. clin. rsch. Natus Med., Inc., San Carlos, Calif.; cons. Fetal Infant Mortality Review, L.A., 1993-94, Healthy Futures March of Dimes, L.A., 1993-94, Am. Belongs To Our Children, L.A., 1993-94, Ventura County Teen Pregnancy Coalition, 1993-94. Co-author, editor: Neonatal Protocols, 1992, Pre-Natal and Intrapartum Guidelines, 1994. Vol. nurse St. Paul's Episcopal Ch., Akron. 1983, lect. March of Dimes Speakers Bur., Burbank, Calif. 1993-94, Health Advisory Com. Early Intervention, L.A., 1993-94. Mem. Nat. Assn. of Neonatal Nurses, Am. Assn. of U. Women, Assn. of Women's Health Obstetrics & Neonatal Nurising. Episcopal. Home: PO Box 1899 El Granada CA 94018-1899

HALL, KATHRYN EVANGELINE, writer, lecturer; b. Biltmore, N.C.; d. Hugh Canada and Evangeline Haddon (Jenkins) Hall; B.A., U. N.C., M.A.; diploma Adams Sch. Music, Montreat, N.C.; postgrad. Yale, U. London, Fla. Atlantic U. Author: The Papal Tiara, History of the Episcopal Church of Bethesda-By-The-Sea, 1964, The Architecture and Times of Robert Adam, 1969, The Pictorial History of the Episcopal Church of Bethesda-By-The-Sea, 1970-71, 86, Joseph Wright of Derby, A Painter of Science, Industry, and Romanticism, 1974, A History of English Architecture, 1976-82; Sir John Vanbrugh's Palaces and the Drama of Baroque Architecture, 1982-84, History of the Episcopal Church of Bethesda-by-the Sea 1889-1989, The First One Hundred Years and Into the Second Century, 1990-93; lectr. history, art and architecture, U.S., Eng. and Scotland, 1961—. Vice pres. The Jr. Patronesses, Palm Beach, Fla., 1964. Mem. Nat. League Am. Pen Women (Owl award 1972, 76, 77, 95, pres. Palm Beach chpt. 1975-80, 2d v.p. 1994—), Palm Beach Quills (historian), Palm Beach County Hist. Soc. (gov.), Internat. Platform Assn., Nat. Soc. Arts and Letters, Soc. Four Arts, Cum Laude Soc., Palm Beach Civic Assn. Episcopalian. Clubs: Everglades (Palm Beach); English Speaking Union (Palm Beach and London). Home: Acadie PO Box 648 Palm Beach FL 33480-0648

HALL, KATHRYN O'NEIL, photographic company official; b. St. Joseph, Mo., Apr. 16, 1952; d. Monte Virgil O'Neil and Ardyce Marie (Hartman) Couch; m. Bruce Edwin Hall, June 8, 1974; children: Nathan Estes, Patrick O'Neil. BSBA, U. Denver, 1974. Master scheduler Colo. div. Kodak, Windsor, 1974-79, adminstrv. mgr., 1979-81, prodn. mgr., 1982-84, materials mgr., 1985-95. Pres. sch. bd. St. Vrain Valley Sch. Dist., Longmont, Colo. Mem. Am. Prodn. and Inventory Control Soc. (cert. in prodn. and inventory mgmt., program chmn. 1988-89), AAUW (program chmn. 1995-96). Home: 502 Collyer St Longmont CO 80501-5543

HALL, LAURA ANN, public relations manager; b. Fort Benning, Ga., Nov. 13, 1968; d. Garrett S. and Barbara A. Hall. BA in Mass Comms., U. Mass., 1990. Account coord. Cone Comms., Boston, 1990-92; sr. account exec. Hill & Knowlton, Atlanta, 1992-94; account dir. Cairns & Assocs., N.Y.C., 1994-95; account supr. DeVries Pub. Rels., N.Y.C., 1995—. Publicity chmn. Artcare, Atlanta, 1993-94. Mem. PRSA. Office: DeVries Pub Rels 30 E 60th St New York NY 10022

HALL, LINDA NORTON, reading specialist; b. Houston, Oct. 7, 1947; d. Charles E. Norton and Carol (Kirkpatrick) Allen-Poulos; m. Robert William Hall, Jan. 28, 1967; children: Christopher M., Kevin M., Michelle K. Student, Tarleton State U., 1965-67; BA with distinction, San Jose State U., 1969; postgrad., U. Florence, Italy, 1970-71; MA in Reading with honors, U. Tex., Permian Basin, 1995. Cert. tchr. life K-9, Calif., tchr. life elem. and sociology, Tex.; cert. reading recovery trained tchr., Tex., advanced reading recovery, Ohio. 4th grade math. and sci. tchr. Los Arboles Elem., San Jose, 1969; tchr. 1st and 3rd grades K.R. Smith Elem., San Jose, 1969-70; tchr. ESL Dr. Russell Elem., Garden Grove, Calif., 1972; tchr. 1st and 1st/2nd combination A. Smith Elem., Huntington Beach, Calif., 1972-75; tchr. 3rd grade Travis Elem., Midland, Tex., 1988-91; reading specialist, reading recovery tchr. Crockett Elem. Sch., Midland, 1991—, title I lead tchr., 1995—; coord. staff devel. Crockett Elem. Sch., 1995—; campus resource rep. Crockett Elem. Sch., Midland, 1991-94, compter technologist, 1992—, study group adminstr., 1994—; rep., sec. sight-based mgmt. com. Campus Ednl. Improvement Coun., Midland, 1992—; coord./liaison Mobil Oil and Midland Ind. Sch. Dist., 1991—. Photographer: Balboa Island in Zoom, 1973 (1st pl. award 1970—); seamstress: Child Busy Book: Orange County Fair, 1977 (1st pl. award 1965-77). Study group mem. Bible Study Fellowship, Calif., Tex., 1973-85; presch. tchr./leader Cmty. Bible Study, Midland, 1985-88; swim meet timer City of Midland Swim Team, 1986-92; tchr. 8th and 11th grade Sunday Sch. First Bapt. Ch., Midland, 1986—; liaison/coord. Ptnrs. in Edn., Midland, 1991—. Recipient horse tng./showing awards, 1960-65; named Parent of Yr. Midland Bapt. Schs., 1985, Tchr. of Yr. Crockett Elem., Midland C. of C., 1994; recipient Austin Meml. Tchr. Scholarship Midland PTA, 1991, Pegasus Grant awards-1st pl. Mobil Oil, Midland, 1991-94; Mobil Found. grantee schoolwide thematic unit structures, 1994, 95. Mem. Internat. Reading Assn., Tex. State Reading Assn., Midland PTA, Midland Reading Coun. (sec. 1992-93,v.p. 1993-94), Reading Recovery Coun. N.Am., Delta Kappa Gamma. Baptist. Home: 1501 W Pine Ave Midland TX 79705-6526 Office: Crockett Elem Sch Midland Ind Sch Dist 401 E Parker Ave Midland TX 79701-2724

HALL, MADELON CAROL SYVERSON, elementary education educator; b. Kerkhoven, Minn., Dec. 27, 1937; d. Reuben C. and Hattie C. (Anderson) Syverson; m. Lewis D. Hall, June 13, 1959 (dec. 1984); children: Warren L., Charmaine D. BA, Trinity Bible Coll., Chgo., 1959; MEd, U.Cin., 1973. Cert. tchr., Ohio. Dir. admissions, asst. registrar Trinity Bible Coll., 1959-62; supr. elem. music edn. Dist. 80 Cook County Schs., Norridge, Ill., 1962-65; tchr. Rockford (Ill.) City Schs., 1966-67; tchr. music elem. grades Boone County Pub. Schs., Florence, Ky., 1970-72; tchr. music elem. grades Oak Hills Local Sch. Dist., Cin., 1972—, also bldg. career coord., safety patrol sponsor. Composer: Seven Ways to Grow for Children's Mus., 1991. dir. Summer Safety Village Program, 1987-91, Cin. May Festival Chorus. Recipient Spl. Projects award Great Oaks Career Devel., 1992; named Tchr. of Yr. Oak Hills Sch. Dist, 1990-91. Mem. NEA, Ohio Edn. Assn., Music Educators Nat. Conf., Career Edn. Assn. (Tchr. of Yr. Ohio unit 1989-90), World Future Soc., The Hunger Project, Just Say No Club. Methodist. Home: 456 Happy Dr Cincinnati OH 45238-5254

HALL, MARCIA JOY, non-profit organization administrator; b. Long Beach, Calif., June 24, 1947; d. Royal Waltz and Norine (Parker) Stanton; m. Stephen Christopher Hall, March 29, 1969; children: Geoffrey Michael, Christopher Stanton. AA, Foothill Coll., 1967; student, U. Oreg., 1967-68; BA, U. Washington, Seattle, 1969. Instr. aide Glen Yermo Sch., Mission Viejo, Calif., 1979-80; market rsch. interviewer Rsch. Data, Framingham, Mass., 1982-83; adult edn. instr. Community Sch. Use Program, Milford, Mass., 1982-83; career info. ctr. coord. Milford High Sch., 1983-86; corp. rels. dir. Sch. Vols. for Milford, Inc., 1985-86; NE area coord. YWCA of Annapolis and Anne Arundel County, Severna Park, Md, 1987-89; exec. dir. West Anne Arundel County C. of C., Odenton, Md., 1989—. Pres. PTO, Mission Viejo, 1979-80, Milford, 1981-84; consumer assistance vol., Calif. Pub. Interest Rsch. Group, 1977-78. Mem. Am. Bus. Women's Assn., Internat. Platform Assn., Toastmasters (treas. 1988—, pres. 1989—). Home: 507 Devonshire Ln Severna Park MD 21146-1017

HALL, MARIAN ELLA See ROBERTSON, MARIAN ELLA

HALL, MARNY, psychotherapist; b. New Rochelle, N.Y., Aug. 9, 1943; d. Benjamin and Marjory (Belish) H. BA in English Literature, U. Mich., 1964; MSW, Hunter Coll., 1969; PhD in Psychology, Union Grad. Sch., 1981. Lic. social worker, Calif. Clin. psychotherapist N. County Mental Health Clinic, Daly City, Calif., 1970-75; assoc. staff human sexuality program U. Calif., San Francisco, 1976-82; pvt. practice, 1975—; instr. Sonoma State Coll., U. Calif. ext., 1975-80, Antioch Coll. W., San Francisco, 1975-80, John F. Kennedy U., Orinda, Calif., 1991. Author: The Lavender Couch: A Consumer's Guide to Psychotherapy for Lesbians and Gay Men, 1985; contbr. articles to profl. jours. and anthologies; appointed to editl. bd. The Cutting Edge gay and lesbian divsn. of NYU Press, 1992; prodr. (video) The Invisible Minority: Gays in Corporations, 1982. Address: 4112 24th St San Francisco CA 94114

HALL, NANCY CHRISTENSEN, publishing company executive, author, editor; b. N.Y.C., Nov. 14, 1946; d. Henry Norman and Elvira (Dugan) Christensen; m. John R. Hall Jr., June 12, 1968; children: Jonathan Scott, Kirsten Marie. B.A., Manhattanville Coll., 1968; postgrad., Old Dominion U., 1970-71. Sr. assoc. editor Cahners Pub. Co., N.Y.C., 1972-74; freelance editor N.Y.C., 1974-78; sr. editor Grosset and Dunlap, N.Y.C., 1978-81; exec. editor, asst. v.p. Macmillan Pub. Co., N.Y.C., 1981-84; assoc. pub., v.p. Simon & Schuster Pub. Co., N.Y.C., 1984-85; founder, prin. Nancy Hall, Inc., juvenile book devel co., N.Y.C., 1986—. Author: Monsters: Creatures of Mystery, 1980, Macmillan Fairy Tale Alphabet Book 1983; editor: Platt and Munk Treasury of Stories for Children, 1981, Favorite Tales from Hans Christian Andersen, 1988; prodr. series: Macmillan Jumbo Seasonal Patterns, Macmillan Manipulatives, Sesame Street Early Learning Games, Mickey's Young Readers Libr., Disney's Small World Libr., My First Hello Readers, and others. Office: Nancy Hall Inc 23 E 22d St New York NY 10010

HALL, PAMELA ELIZABETH, psychologist; b. Jacksonville, Fla., Sept. 10, 1957; d. Gary Curtiss and Ollie (Banko) H. BA, Rutgers U., 1979; MS in Edn., Pace U., 1981, PsyD in Psychology, 1984. Lic. psychologist, N.Y., N.J., Calif. Psychology extern St. Vincent's Med. Ctr., N.Y.C., 1981-82; intern in clin. psychology Elizabeth (N.J.) Gen. Med. Ctr., 1982-83, staff psychologist, 1983-85; staff psychologist J.F.K. Med. Ctr., Edison, N.J., 1985-87; pvt. practice Summit and Perth Amboy, N.J., 1985—; sr. supervising psychologist Muhlenberg Med. Ctr., Summit, N.J., 1987-90; rsch. affiliate/internat. lectr. NIMH field trials on assessment of dissociative disorders Yale U., New Haven, 1990—. Mem. Mayor's Com. on Substance Abuse, Perth Amboy, 1987. Named Henry Rutgers scholar, 1979. Mem. Am. Soc. Clin. Hypnosis, Internat. Soc. for Study of Dissociation (founder, pres. N.J. chpt. 1988—), Pace U. Alumni Assn., Rutgers U. Alumni Assn., Psi Chi. Home: PO Box 1820 Perth Amboy NJ 08862-1820

HALL, PAMELA S., environmental consulting firm executive; b. Hartford, Conn., Sept. 4, 1944; d. LeRoy Warren and Frances May (Murray) Sheely; m. Stuart R. Hall, July 21, 1967. BA in Zoology, U. Conn., 1966; MS in Zoology, U. N.H., 1969, BS summa cum laude, Whittemore Sch. Bus. and Econs., U. N.H., 1982; student spl. grad. studies program, Tufts U., 1986-90. Curatorial asst. U. Conn., Storrs, 1966; rsch. asst. Field Mus. Natural History, Chgo., 1966-67; teaching asst. U. N.H., Durham, 1967-70; program mgr. Normandeau Assocs. Inc., Portsmouth, N.H., 1971-79, marine lab. dir., 1979-81, programs and ops. mgr., Bedford, N.H., 1981-83, v.p., 1983-85, sr. v.p., 1986-87, pres., 1987—. Mem. Conservation Commn., Portsmouth, 1977-90, Wells, Estuarine Rsch. Res. Review Commn., 1986-88, Great Bay (N.H.) Estuarine Rsch. Res. Tech. Working Group, 1987-89; trustee Trust for N.H. Lands, 1990-93; trustee N.H. chpt. Nature Conservancy, 1991-96, chair, 1995-96; incorporator N.H. Charitable Fund, 1991—; bd. advisors Vivamos Mejor, USA, 1990—; bd. dirs. Environ. Bus. Coun. New England, 1995—. Graham Found. fellow, 1966; NDEA fellow, 1970-71. Mem. ASTM, Am. Mgmt. Assn., Nat. Assn. Environ. Profls., Sigma Xi. Home: 4 Pleasant Point Dr Portsmouth NH 03801-5275 Office: Normandeau Assocs Inc 25 Nashua Rd Bedford NH 03110-5527

HALL, PHOEBE POULTERER, lawyer, judge; b. Watertown, N.Y., Dec. 4, 1941; d. William Taylor, Jr., and Betty (Bennett) Poulterer; m. Franklin P. Hall, July 26, 1969; children—Kimberly Ann, Franklin P. B.A., U. Del.-Wilmington, 1963; J.D., Georgetown U., 1969. Bar: Va. Assoc., Hall & Hall, Richmond, Va., 1969—; substitute judge Gen. Dist. Cts., City of Richmond, 1983—, commr. in chancery, circuit cts., 1981—; founding dir., Cardinal Savs. & Loan Assn., Richmond, 1978—. Bd. trustees, Va. Mus. Fine Arts, 1983—; commr. Human Relations Commn., Richmond, 1972-73; dir. Family and Children's Services, Richmond, 1976-78; mem. worship com. 1st Presbyterian Ch., Richmond, 1983—; mem. state central com. Democratic Party, Va., 1974-80; pres. Women's Health Adv. Bd. Med. Coll. Va., 1989—; mem. adv. bd. Make Women Count, 1994—; trustee Presbytery of the James, 1989—; bd. dirs. Dispute Resolution Ctr., 1996—. Recipient Outstanding Citizenship award Urban League, Richmond, 1983; first woman pub. defender, City of Richmond, 1970; designer, instr. first course for paralegals, Va. State Bar, 1974. Mem. ABA, Richmond Bar Assn., Met. Richmond Women's Bar (founding 1971—), Va. Trial Lawyers Assn., Assn. Trial Lawyers Am., Bus. and Profl. Women's Assn., Am. Bus. Women's Assn. Lodge Soroptimists. Home: 9006 Cherokee Rd Richmond VA 23235-1414 Office: Hall & Hall BonAir Profl Bldg 2800 Buford Rd Ste 202 Richmond VA 23235-2453

HALL, PHYLLIS CHARLENE, therapist, counselor; b. L.A., Mar. 18, 1957; d. Clellan James Jr. and Yvonne Rayedith (Ralls) H. BA, Whittier Coll., 1979; MS in Phys. Edn., Calif. State U., Fullerton, 1985, MS in Counseling, 1988; PhD in Psychology, U.S. Internat. U., 1996. Coach varsity girls basketball, softball Calif. High Sch., Whittier, 1979-80; counselor Rio Hondo Coll., Whittier, 1980-88; coach asst. girls varsity basketball Long Beach (Calif.) Wilson High Sch., 1985-88; therapist intern Turning Point Counseling, Garden Grove, Calif., 1988-89; counselor Long Beach City Coll., 1988—, girls acad. advisor, 1989-94, asst. coach girls basketball, 1993-94; psychologist asst./intern Family Svcs. Long Beach, 1994—; bd. dirs. Long Beach City Coll. Author: Liberators from Planet Liberx, 1985. Co-sponsor African Am. in Unity Long Beach City Coll., 1990-92; com. mem. 1st Annual African Am. Achievement Conf., San Deigo, 1994. Mem. Calif. Tchrs. Assn., Long Beach City Coll. Counselors Assn., Women in Arts. Office: Long Beach City Coll 1305 E Pch Long Beach CA 90806

HALL, REBECCA ANN, executive secretary; b. Detroit, July 28, 1949; d. Henry August and Jeanne Maude (Plank) Isaacson; m. Gene Lawrence Hall, June 16, 1973; children: Mellany Anne, Leah Jayne. BS in Edn., Ctrl. Mich. U., 1971. Cert. tchr., Mich. Therapist speech and lang. Lapeer (Mich.) Cmty. Schs., 1971-77; office aide Eaton Rapids (Mich.) Pub. Schs., 1991—. Parent involvement program coord. Lockwood Elem. Sch., Eaton Rapids, 1995—. Mem. AAUW (sec. 1989-91, chair Heritage com. 1989-91, 2d v.p. 1991-93, pres.-elect 1994-95, pres. 1995—). Home: 8175 E 5 Point Hwy Eaton Rapids MI 48827 Office: Lockwood Elem Sch 300 Greyhound Dr Eaton Rapids MI 48827

HALL, ROCHELLE DENISE, elementary school educator; b. Kansas City, Kans., Jan. 3, 1956; d. Theodore and Barbara Jean (Williams) H. AA, Penn Valley C.C., Kansas City, Mo., 1976; BA, U. Mo., Kansas City, 1978, MA, 1985; Edn. Specialist Degree, U. Mo., 1992. Cert. specialist in reading, Mo. Tchr. Kansas City Sch. Dist., 1979-85, reading resource tchr., 1985-95, tchr. grade 1, 1995—; del. Literacy and Lang. Arts Instrn. Delegation to Peoples Republic of China, 1995. Supt. Sunday sch. Emmanuel Bapt. Ch., 1992—; del. lang. arts & literacy delegation People to People Citizen Amb. Progra, China, 1995; vol. for adult basic edn. program; tutor Laubach Literacy Coun. Kansas City, 1996—. Recipient IMPACT Reading award Kansas City Reading dept., 1990. Mem. ASCD, NAACP, Internat. Reading Assn. (chpt. v.p. 1994—), Phi Delta Kappa (youth advisor 1993—). Democrat. Baptist. Office: E F Swinney Applied Skills 1106 W 47th St Kansas City MO 64112-1215

HALL, SUSAN LAUREL, artist, educator; b. Point Reyes Sta., Calif., Mar. 19, 1943; d. Earl Morris and Avis Mary (Brown) H. BFA, Calif. Coll. Arts & Crafts, Oakland, 1965; MA, U. Calif., Berkeley, 1967. Mem. faculty Sch. Visual Arts, N.Y.C., 1981-92. Artist: one person shows San Francisco Mus. of Art, 1967, Quay Gallery, San Francisco, 1969, Phyllis Kind Gallery, Chgo., 1971, 98 Greene St. Loft, N.Y.C., Whitney Mus. Modern Art, N.Y.C., 1972, Nancy Hoffman Gallery N.Y.C., 1973, 75, Henderson Mus. U. Col., Boulder, 1973, U. R.I. Gallery, Kingston, 1976, Harcus Krakow Rosen Sonnabend Gallery, Boston, 1976, Hal Bromm and Getler-Pall Galleries, N.Y.C., 1978, Helene Shlien Gallery, Boston, 1978, Hamilton Gallery N.Y.C., 1978, 79, 81, 83, Ovsey Gallery, L.A., 1981, 82, 84, 87, 89, 91, Paule Anglim Gallery, San Francisco, 1975-83, Ted Greenwald Gallery, N.Y.C., 1986, Trabia Macafee Gallery N.Y.C., 1988, 89, Wyckoff Gallery, Aspen, Colo., 1990-92, Milagros Contemporary Art, San Antonio, 1995, Brendan Walter Gallery, L.A., 1995, U. Tex. San Antonio, 1996,; group shows include Whitney Mus. of Am. Art, San Francisco Mus., Oakland Mus., Balt. Mus., Inst. Contemporary Art, Phila., Hudson River Mus., Bklyn. Mus., Nat. Mus. Women in the Arts, Mus. Fine Arts, Boston, Aldrich Mus. Contemporary Art, G.W. Einstein Gallery, Blum Helman Downtown, Leo Castelli Gallery Uptown, Graham Modern, N.Y.C., Kunstmus. Luzern, Switzerland, Landesmus., Bonn, Germany; represented in pub. collections at Whitney Mus. Am. Art, San Francisco Mus., Bklyn. Mus., Carnegie Inst., St. Louis Mus., Nat. Mus. Women in the Arts and others. Nat. Endowment Arts fellow, 1979-87, Adolph Gottleib Found. fellow, 1995; grantee: Pollack Krasner Found., N.Y. State Coun. on Arts.

HALL, TELKA MOWERY ELIUM, educational administrator; b. Salisbury, N.C., July 22, 1936; d. James Lewis and Malissa (Fielder) Mowery; m. James Richard Elium III, June 20, 1954 (div. 1961); 1 child, W. Denise Elium Carr; m. Allen Sanders Hall, Apr. 15, 1967 (div. 1977). Student, Am. Inst. Banking, 1955-57, Mary-Hardin Baylor Coll., Waco, Tex., 1957; BA, Catawba Coll., Salisbury, 1967; MEd, Miss. U. for Women, Columbus, 1973; EdS, Appalachian State U., 1975; postgrad., U. N.C., Greensboro, 1977; EdD, U. N.C., Chapel Hill, 1990. Cert. early childhood, intermediate lang. arts and social studies tchr., curriculum specialist, adminstr., supr., supt., N.C.; notary pub., N.C. Bookkeeper, teller Citizens & So. Bank, Spartanburg, S.C., 1955-56; bookkeeper 1st Nat. Bank, Killeen, Tex., 1956-58; bookkeeper, savs. teller Exchange Bank & Trust Co., Dallas, 1958-61; acct. Catawba Coll., 1961-65; floater teller bookkeeping and proof depts. Security Bank & Trust Co., Salisbury, 1965-68, 71; tchr. Rowan County Sch. System, Salisbury, 1967-70, 71-72, 1973-82; asst. prin. North Rowan Elem. Sch., Spencer, N.C., 1982-94; asst. prin. Rockwell (N.C.) Elem. and China Grove Elem. Schs., 1994-96, ret., 1996; part time asst. prin. of curriculum China Grove Elem., 1996—; receptionist H & R Block, Salisbury, 1979-83; Chpt. I reading tchr. Nazareth Children's Home, Rockwell, N.C., 1979-81.

Author: The Effect of Second Language Training in Kindergarten on the Development of Listening Skills. Mem. Salisbury Cmty. Chorus, 1951-52, Hist. Salisbury Found., Inc., Salisbury Concert Choir, 1981-83; foreperson Rowan county grand jury, 1991; pianist Franklin Presbyn. Ch., Salisbury, 1952-55, choir dir., 1975-87; past pres. Women of Ch., Sunday Sch. tchr., sec., 1979-80, deacon, 1980-83, elder, 1991-92, 96-99, clk. of session, 1992, choir mem., 1947—, hand-bell choir 1996—; cons. Dial HELP, Salisbury, 1981-83; charter mem. bd. dirs. Old North Salisbury Assn., 1980—. Civitan Music scholar, 1954, Kiwanis Acad. scholar, 1966, Catawba Coll. Acad. scholar, 1965-67, Mary Morrow Ednl. scholar N.C. Assn. Educators, 1966. Mem. AAUW (v.p. 1985-87, 91-93), ASCD, N.C. Assn. Sch. Adminstrs., N.C. Assn. Educators, Tarheel Assn. Prins. and Asst. Prins., U. N.C. Gen. Alumni Assn., Rowan County Prins. Assn., Sci. Alliance (Rowan County, charter), Salisbury Hist. Assn., Kappa Delta Pi, Theta Phi (pres. 1992-93). Home: 1626 N Main St Salisbury NC 28144-2928 Office: China Grove Elem 514 Franklin St China Grove NC 28023

HALL, TENNIEBEE M., editor; b. Bakersfield, Calif., May 21, 1940; d. William Elmer and Lillian May (Otis) Hall; m. Harold Robert Hall, Feb. 20, 1965. BA in Edn., Fresno State Coll., 1962; AA, Bakersfield Coll., 1960. Cert. tchr., Calif. Tchr. Edison (Calif.) Sch. Dist., 1962-65; substitute tchr. Marin and Oakland Counties (Calif.), Berkeley, 1965-66; engring. asst. Pacific Coil Co., Inc., Bakersfield, 1974-81; editor United Ostomy Assn., Inc., Irvine, Calif., 1986-91. Co-author: Treating IBD, 1989, Current Therapy in Gastroenterology, 1989; author, designer: Volunteer Leadership Training Manuals, 1982-84; contbr. articles to Ostomy Quar., 1973—. Mem. Pacific Beach Town Coun., San Diego, 1977—; campaign worker Maureen O'Connor (1st woman mayor of city), San Diego, 1986; mem. Nat. Digestive Diseases Adv. Bd., NIH, Washington, 1986-91; mem. planning and devel. bd. Scripps Clinic and Rsch. Found. Inflammatory Bowel Disease Ctr., San Diego, 1993—; various vol. activities, 1966-74, 81-86. Recipient Outstanding Svc. award VA Vol. Svc., Bur. of Vets. Affairs, Washington, 1990. Mem. Nat. Assn. Parliamentarians, United Ostomy Assn. Inc. (regional program dir. 1980-84, pres. 1984-86, Sam Dubin award 1983, Industry Adv. award 1987), Crohn's and Colitis Found. Am. (nat. trustee 1986-95, nat. v.p. 1987-92). Home and Office: 5284 Dawes St San Diego CA 92109-1231

HALL, TERRY LEE, accountant; b. Champaign, Ill., Dec. 10, 1949; d. Albert L. and Catherine A. (Comstock) Hall; m. Thomas F. Johnston, Sept. 27, 1971 (div. Jan. 1979); 1 child, Daniel K. Johnston. BA, Barat Coll., Lake Forest, Ill., 1984. CPA, Ill., Wis. Acct. Terry Hall, CPA, Waukegan, 1985—; bd. dirs. Lake Forest (Ill.) Profl. Women's Round Table. Bd. dirs. YWCA of Lake County, Waukegan, Ill., 1987-89; bd. dirs. Women in Dir.'s Chair, Chgo., 1989—, Stage Two Theater Co., 1991—; mem. alumni coun. Lake Forest Acad., 1986—. Mem. AICPA, ABA (assoc.), Nat. Assn. Tax Preparers, Ill. Soc. CPAs (mem. faculty, mem. state litigation com. 1988—), Wis. Inst. CPAs (state litigation com. 1989-92), Chgo. Soc. Women CPAs, Lake County Estate Planning Coun., Women's Fin. Network, Am. Woman's Soc. CPAs, CPAs for the Pub. Interest (Outstanding Vol. 1991).

HALL, WANDA JEAN, mental health professional, consultant; b. Miami, Okla., July 3, 1943; d. Max Calvin Kinnaman and Dorothy D. (Peck) Fadler; m. James Marvin Hall, Apr. 10, 1964 (div. Feb. 1965); m. George Edward Hall, Mar. 21, 1973; children: Heather Renata, Samuel. AA, Stephens Coll., Columbia, Mo., 1963; BS, Kans. U., Pittsburg, 1965; MS, New Sch. for Social Rsch., N.Y.C., 1991. Asst. psychologist Parsons (Kans.) State Hosp., 1966-67; hosp. care investigator N.Y. Dept. Social Work, N.Y.C., 1968-70; social worker Drug Abuse Program, Amsterdam, The Netherlands, 1970-74; dir. Washington Park Co-op Presch., N.Y.C., 1974-75; project dir. Manhattan Devel. Ctr., N.Y.C., 1975-77; pvt. practice as human devel. specialist, N.Y.C., 1978-81; community rels. coord. Orange County Dept. Mental Health, Goshen, N.Y., 1981—; parenting cons. Teens Exploring Parenting, Inc., Middletown, N.Y., 1990-94, instr. Orange County C.C., Middletown, 1990—, Mt. St. Mary Coll., Newburgh, N.Y., 1993—. Producer, host radio talk show Conversation on Epilepsy, Radio Sta. WGNY, 1981; dir, narrator mental health skits Forum Players, 1980; producer, host 6 TV series Love from the 26, 000 Club, 1983. Bd. dirs. Orange County Coalition for Choice, Warwick, N.Y., 1981—, Orange County Task Force on Child Abuse/Neglect, 1984-89, Ct. Apptd. Spls. Assts., 1987-96, Bandwagon Cmty. Ctr., chairperson, 1990-95; mem. Planned Parenthood, Orange County, 1989—, Safe Homes, Orange County, 1987—, Middletown Coun. Cmty. Agys., 1980-96, Interagy. Coun. Child Sexual Abuse; co-founder Orange County Parenting Coalition, 1990—. Recipient DWI Alcohol Safety award N.Y. State Alcohol Bur., Albany, 1986, Cmty. Svc. award Youth Bur. Goshen, 1987, Zonta scholar award, 1989, Cmty. Svc. award Otisville (N.Y.) State Correction, 1989, Nat. Assn. Counties award Confident Parenting Program, 1993, Hospice Orange Vol. award, 1993, The Gilbert award, 1995, Human Rights award Orange County Human Rights Commn., 1995. Mem. NAACP. Methodist. Office: Orange County Dept Mental Health Drawer 471 Harriman Dr Goshen NY 10924

HALLADAY, LAURIE ANN, public relations consultant, former franchise executive; b. Monroe, Mich., Aug. 18, 1945; d. Alvin John and Florence (Lowrey) Kohler; m. Edward L. Howell, Aug. 27, 1966; m. 2d Fredric R. Halladay, May 24, 1980. BJ, U. Mo., 1967. Reporter, staff writer Copley Newspapers, L.A., 1967-69; account exec. Furman Assocs., L.A., 1969-71, v.p., 1971-74; account supr. Bob Thomas & Assocs., L.A., 1974-76, v.p., 1976-78; v.p., sr. ptnr. Fleishman-Hillard, Inc., St. Louis, 1980-84; owner, operator McDonald's, Portland, Oreg., 1984-87, McDonald's McStop of Mid.-Mo., Kingdom City, 1988-92; chmn. press ops. for Budweiser/G.I. Joe's Portland 200 Indy Car Race, 1984-87; mem. advt., promotions com. Hollywood Boosters, 1986. Bd. dirs. Waterman Place Assn., St. Louis, 1983; mem. pub. rels. com. Winston Churchill Meml., Fulton, 1988-92. Recipient Merit award Calif. Press Women, 1969, Lulu award Los Angeles Women's Ad Club, 1976, McDonald's Outstanding Store award, 1985, 86, 89, 90, 91. Mem. PRSA (Prism award 1977), Soc. Am. travel Writers (assoc. 1981-84), Women in Comm. (dir. St. Louis 1980-82), Nat. Tour Assn., Mo. Travel Coun., Delta Delta Delta (alumna adviser 1989, 90,, v.p. Delta Xi House Corp. 1991, collegiate dist. officer 1991, 94, regional program chmn. 1994, program resource team pub. rels. specialist 1995-96, nat. chmn. pub. rels. 1996). Home: 2071 Tocobaga Ln Nokomis FL 34275-5310

HALLAM, BEVERLY (BEVERLY LINNEY), artist; b. Lynn, Mass., Nov. 22, 1923; d. Edwin Francis and Alice (Linney) Hallam Murphy. BS in Edn, Mass. Coll. Art, 1945; postgrad., Cranbrook Acad. Art, Mich., 1948; MFA, Syracuse U., 1953. Chmn. dept. art Lasell Jr. Coll., Auburndale, Mass., 1945-49; assoc. prof. Mass. Coll. Art, 1949-62; bd. dirs. Barn Gallery Assocs., Inc., Ogunquit, Maine, 1970—. One-person shows include Joe and Emily Lowe Art Center, Syracuse U., 1953, DeCordova Mus., Lincoln, Mass., 1954, Shore Galleries, Boston, 1959, 62, 68, 73, 74, Witte Meml. Mus., San Antonio, 1968, U. Maine, 1969, Lamont Gallery, Exeter, N.H., 1969, Addison Gallery, Andover, Mass., 1971, Fitchburg Art Mus., 1972, Fairweather Hardin Gallery, Chgo., 1972, Hobe Sound (Fla.) Galleries, 1973, Inst. Contemporary Art, Boston, 1977, PS Galleries, Maine, 1981, Payson-Weisberg Gallery, N.Y.C., 1984, Farnsworth Mus., Rockland, Maine, 1984, Midtown Galleries, N.Y.C., 1988, Francesca Anderson Gallery, Boston, 1988, Hobe Sound Galleries North, Portland, Maine, 1988, Evansville (Ind.) Mus. Arts and Sci., 1990, Sheldon Swope Mus., Terre Haute, Ind., 1990, Art Mus. S.E. Tex., Beaumont, 1990, Bergen Mus. Art and Sci., Paramus, N.J., 1990, Polk Mus. Art, Lakeland, Fla., 1991; two-person show, Inst. Contemporary Art, Boston, 1956, numerous group shows including Barn Gallery, 1954-94, Busch-Reisinger Mus., Harvard U., 1956, 59, 60, Portland Mus., 1959, 84, 92, 93, Mus. Fine Arts, Boston, 1960, Inst. Contemporary Art, Boston, 1960, 63, 68, 77, Pace Gallery, Boston, 1962, DeCordova Mus., 1963, 64, 68, 69, 70, 71, 75, Ward-Nasse Gallery, N.Y.C., 1971-72, Ogunquit (Maine) Mus. Am. Art, 1964, 70, 71, 78, 80, 84, 89, 91-93, 95, R.I. Arts Festival, 1966, Smithsonian Instn., Washington, 1966, Am. Water Color Soc. Traveling Exhibition, 1967, Watercolor U.S.A., Springfield, Mo., 1968, Maine State Mus., 1976, Maine Coast Artists, 1974, 75, 77, 83, 89, 92, 93, Joan Whitney Payson Gallery of Art, Maine, 1980, Farnsworth Art Mus., 1982, 87, 92, 95, Bowdoin Coll. Mus. Art, 1984, 92, Midtown Payson Galleries, N.Y.C., 1985, 87, 90, 92, Expo '92, Seville, Spain, Barbara Scott Gallery, Bay Harbor Island, Fla., 1993, Fitchburg (Mass.) Art Mus., 1994; represented in permanent collections Rose Art Mus. Brandeis U., Fogg Art Mus., Cambridge, Mass.; Corcoran Gallery Am. Art, Washington, Witte Meml. Mus., San Antonio, DeCordova Mus., Lincoln, Addison Gallery, Andover, Bowdoin Coll. Mus. Art, Fitchburg Art Mus., Ogunquit Mus. Am. Art, Portland Mus., Colby Coll., U. Maine, Currier Gallery Art, Manchester N.H., Farnsworth Library and Art Mus., Rockland, Maine, U. N.H. Art Galleries, Durham, Everson Mus., Syracuse, First Nat. Bank, Boston, Ernst and Ernst, Chgo., Carnegie Corp., N.Y., Nat. Mus. Women in the Arts, Washington, Gouws Capital Mgmt., Inc., Portland, Maine, others, also, pvt. collections, U.S. Can., Paris, Switzerland; Publ. Beverly Hallam, Paintings, Drawings and Monotypes, 1956-71, 1971; subject of book and video Beverly Hallam: The Flower Paintings, 1990. Recipient Pearl Safir award Silvermine Guild Artists, New Canaan, Conn., 1955, Painting prize Boston Arts Festival, 1957, Blanche E. Colman Found. award, 1960, Hatfield awards Boston Soc. Watercolor Painters, 1960, 64, 1st prize Edwin Webster award, 1962, Am. Artist Achievement award, 1993. Mem. Ogunquit Art Assn. (past pres.), Archives of Am. Art, Artists Equity. Home: 30 Surf Point Rd York ME 03909-5053

HALLANAN, ELIZABETH V., federal judge; b. Charleston, W.Va., Jan. 10, 1925; d. Walter Simms and Imogene (Burns) H. U. Charleston, 1946; JD, W.Va. U., 1951; postgrad, U. Mich., 1964. Atty. Crichton & Hallanan, Charleston, 1952-59; mem. W.Va. State Bd. Edn., Charleston, 1955-57, Ho. of Dels., W.Va. Legis., Charleston, 1957-58; asst. commr. pub. instns. Charleston, 1958-59; mem., chmn. W.Va. Pub. Service Commn., Charleston, 1969-75; atty. Lopinsky, Bland, Hallanan, Dodson, Deutsch & Hallanan, Charleston, 1975-84; judge U.S. Dist Ct. (so. dist.) W.Va., 1983—. Mem. W.Va. Bar Assn. Office: US Dist Ct PO Drawer 5009 Beckley WV 25801-7509*

HALLBAUER, ROSALIE CARLOTTA, business educator; b. Chgo., Dec. 8, 1939; d. Ernest Ludwig and Kathryn Marquerite (Ramm) H. BS, Rollins Coll., 1961; MBA, U. Chgo., 1963; PhD, U. Fla., 1973. CPA, Ill.; cert. mgmt. acct., cost analyst, profl. estimater. Assoc. prof. acctg. Fla. Internat. U., Miami, 1972—. Mem. Am. Acctg. Assn., Am. Woman's Soc. CPAs, Ill. Soc. CPAs, Inst. Mgmt. Accts., Acctg. Historians Soc., Beta Alpha Psi, Pi Gamma Mu. Office: Fla Internat Univ N Miami Campus 3000 NE 145th St Miami FL 33181-3612

HALLBERG, AUDREY BARKER, real estate broker; b. Paterson, N.J., May 28, 1939; d. Albert C. and Ann (Downey) Barker; m. Howard V. Hallberg; children: Scot V., Liisa A. BS, U. R.I., 1961. GRI, CRS. With Munroe Realtors, Wakefield, R.I., 1968-87; owner, prin. Hallberg Realtors, Wakefield, 1987—. Chair bd. trustees Kingston Congl. Ch., 1993-94, 96, vice chair, 1995—; corp. mem. South County Hosp., Wakefield, 1988—; trustee U. R.I. Found., Kingston, 1988—; bd. dirs. Health Ctr. of South County, Wakefield, 1979-85. Mem. Kent-Washington Bd. Realtors (chair sunshine com. 1988—), Washington County Bd. Realtors (sec. 1973-74). Office: Hallberg Realtors 471 Main St Wakefield RI 02879

HALL-ELLIS, SYLVIA DUNN, educator, consultant; b. Kewanee, Ill., June 21, 1949; d. M. Orrill and Elizabeth J. (Boase) Dunn; m. J. Theodore Ellis, Dec. 24, 1989. BA, Rockford (Ill.) Coll., 1971; MLS, U. North Tex., Denton, 1972; MA, U. Tex., San Antonio, 1976; PhD, U. Pitts., 1985. Cert. pub. libr., Tex., N.Y., Pa. Sys. coord. San Antonio Pub. Libr., 1973-76; div. libr. Corpus Christi Pub. Librs., 1976-78; asst. dir. So. Tier Libr. Sys., Corning, N.Y., 1978-81; dir. libr. devel. State Libr. of Pa., Harrisburg, 1981; devel. officer PRLC, Inc., Pitts., 1981-85; pres., owner The Blue Bear Group, Inc., Central City, Colo., 1985-92; profl. cataloger Arapahoe Libr. Dist., Littleton, Colo., 1991; head libr. Rocky Mountain Coll. Art, Denver, 1992-93; asst. prof. L.S. Sam Houston State U., Huntsville, Tex., 1993-95, adj. prof., 1995—; devel. officer/grant proposal writer Region One Edn. Svc. Ctr., Edinburg, Tex., 1995—; adj. prof. libr. sci. U. Ariz., Tucson, 1995; cons. to various state govts., 1981—. Author: Grantwriting For School And Small Public Libraries, 1996; contbd. articles and tech. reports. Docent, Denver Mus. Natural History, 1992—; pres. Rocky Mountain LAN Engrs., Denver, 1993; cons., treas. Columbine Family Health Ctrs., Inc., Black Hawk, 1988-89; mem. Gilpin County Econ. Devel. Commn., Central City, 1987-89; tech. prep mem. Rio Grande Valley Inc., Tex., 1995—. Mem. ALA, Tex. Libr. Assn., Colo. Libr. Assn. Office: Region One Edn Svc Ctr 1900 W Schunior St Edinburg TX 78539

HALLEN, LYNN B., social worker; b. N.Y.C., May 18, 1948; d. Arthur and Beatrice (Jaffe) Hallen; m. Philip R. Wallas, Apr. 30, 1983; 1 child, Amanda. BA, U. Mich., 1970, MSW, 1973. Diplomate Am. Bd. Examiners in Clin. Social Work, NASW. Staff social worker Children's Psychiat. Ctr., Red Bank, N.Y., 1973-75; social worker Needham (Mass.) Youth Commn., 1975-76; chief social worker South Shore Day Care Svcs., Quincy, Mass., 1976-77; social worker Ea. Middlesex Cmty. Mental Health, Wakefield, Mass., 1977-82; pvt. practice Birchmeadow Counseling Collaborative, Reading, Mass., 1982—; lectr. Wheelock Coll., Boston, 1979; group leader abuse workshops, Wakefield, 1983-84. Mem. Sch. Coun., Newton, Mass., 1995-96; pres. After-Sch. Day Care Bd., Newton, 1990-96. Mem. Am. Soc. for Reproductive Medicine. Office: Birchmeadow Counseling Coll 18A Woburn St Reading MA 01867

HALLER, IRMA TOGNOLA, secondary education educator; b. Bainbridge, N.Y., Aug. 25, 1937; d. Tullio and Margaretha (Fuchs) Tognola; m. Hans R. Haller, July 11, 1964. BA, SUNY, Albany, 1959; MEd in Teaching of Social Studies, Boston U., 1962. Tchr. social studies Chenango Valley Jr.-Sr. High Sch., Binghamton, N.Y., 1959-64; tchr. social studies and English Sidney (N.Y.) High Sch., 1964—, chair dept. social studies, 1986—; mem. tchr. edn. adv. bd. SUNY, Oneonta, chair, 1985-88, 93-94; active local sch. improvement coms. Mem. steering com. Sidney Ctrl. Schs. Bus. Edn. Cmty. Partnership, 1992—; active local sch. improvement coms. N.Y. State Electric and Gas Corp. grantee, 1985; Catskill Regional Tchr. Ctr. grantee, 1985, 87, 89. Mem. Nat. Coun. Social Studies, N.Y. State Social Studies Coun., N.Y. State United Tchrs., Catskill Area Social Studies Coun. (newsletter editor 1989-90), Sidney Tchrs. Assn., Phi Delta Kappa. Office: Sidney H S 95 W Main St Sidney NY 13838-1601

HALLER, KAREN SUE, writer; b. St. Louis, Apr. 25, 1935; d. Frank Michael and Frieda Catherine (Hartmann) Kratoville; m. Albert John Haller; children: Christopher Karl, Debra Lynn. BS in Edn., U. Mo., 1956. Tchr. elem. sch. Ladue (Mo.) Sch. Dist., 1956-60; hearing testing tech. Spl. Sch. Dist. St. Louis County, 1975, 76. Author, photographer: Walking with Wildflowers, 1994; contbg. photographer: Wildflowers of Arkansas, 1984, Sensitive Plants of St. Francis National Forests, 1984, Wildflowers of North America, 1987. Asst. leader, leader brownie troop Girl Scouts Am., 1969, 70, jr. girl scouts troop, 1970, 71; advisor Co-ed explorer post Boy Scouts Am., 1976-80; bus tour guide, chmn. St. Louis Vis. Ctr., 1966-70; mem. mortar bd. U. Mo., Columbia, 1955. Mem. Nat. Audubon Soc. (program chmn. 1987-90, awards chmn. 1990, Dorr scholar 1989), Mo. Native Plant Soc. (pres. 1991-93, Erna R. Eisendrath Edn. award 1994), Webster Groves Nature Study Soc. (pres. 1978-80, conservation chmn. 1983-86), Sierra Club, Naiads (v.p., pres., treas., sec.). Home and Office: 618 Spring Meadows Dr Ballwin MO 63011

HALLINGER, JANE STURGIS, English educator; b. Woodbury, N.J., Aug. 31, 1938; d. Bernard Miller and Elizabeth (Simokat) Sturgis; m. Donald E. Hallinger, Dec. 30, 1962; children: Kimberly Anne, Deborah Lynn, Christopher. BA in Speech, DePauw U., 1960; AM in Comm., Ind. U., 1964; MA in English, Calif. State U., L.A., 1982. Writer, newscaster Sta. KSWS-TV, Roswell, N.Mex., 1962-64; writer Sta. KRBC-TV, Abilene, Tex., 1964-66; tutor, reader Pasadena (Calif.) City Coll., 1971-78, assoc. prof. English and comm., 1978—, v.p., pres. senate, 1986-89, mem. found. bd., 1987-89; mem. accreditation teams, Santa Rosa, Calif., 1991—, Solano, Calif., 1993, Cabrillo, Calif., 1995, Orange Coast, 1996; mem. Calif. Chancellor's Consultation, 1993—; rep. to the Gt. Tchrs. Conf. Contbr. short stories to various mags. Treas. Pasadena Sister Cities, 1992-94; v.p. Californians, 1993, pres., 1994. Recipient resolution Calif. Assembly, 1996; faculty scholar Pasadena City Coll., 1986. Mem. Faculty Assn. Calif. C.C.'s (bd. dirs. 1990—, pres. 1993-96), Omicron Mu Delta. Democrat. Home: 1300 New York Dr Altadena CA 91001 Office: Pasadena City Coll 1570 Colorado Blvd Pasadena CA 91106

HALL-JIRAN, KRISTI, social services administrator; b. Jamestown, N.D., July 6, 1967. BA in Psychology and Health, Concordia Coll., 1989; MA in Counseling, U. N.D., 1990. Lic. profl. counselor, N.D. Bd. Counselor Examiners. Violence intervention adv. Cmty. Violence Intervention Ctr., Grand Forks, N.D., 1990-92; dir. svcs. coord. Cmty. Violence Intervention Ctr., Grand Forks, 1992-94, exec. dir., 1995—; family therapist, counselor Village Family Svc. Ctr., Grand Forks, 1992-94. Active Sharon Luth. Ch., Grand Forks, 1995. Mem. N.D. Counseling Assn., N.D. Mental Health Counselors Assn. (sec., v.p., pres. N.E. region 1993-95), N.D. Coun. on Abused Women's Svcs. (v.p. 1995—). Lutheran. Office: Cmty Violence Intervention Ctr 111 S 4th St Grand Forks ND 58201

HALLMAN, VICTORIA STELLA, athletic director; b. Phila., May 3, 1952; d. John Betchel Hallman and Elizabeth (Rita) Di Gregorio Ford. BA, San Diego State U., 1975; MA, S.W. Tex. State U., 1981, postgrad., 1987, 91. Cert. mgmt., supt., Tex. Tchr., coach San Antonio Ind. Sch. Dist., 1978-82; women's track coach, instr. S.W. Tex. State U., San Marcos, 1982-83; tchr., coach Westlake H.S. Eanes Ind. Sch. Dist., Austin, Tex., 1983-90; asst. prin. Jr. H.S. Del Valle (Tex.) Ind. Sch. Dist., 1990-93, athletic dir., 1993—; mem. rsch. com. Tex. Athletic Equality Project, Austin, 1987-88; curriculum cons. Concordia Luth. Coll., Austin, 1987-88. Mem. AIDS care team St. Austin's Cath. Ch., Austin, 1993—, mem. Landings, 1991—. Mem. Tex. H.S. Coaches Assn., Tex. H.S. Women's Coaching Assn., Tex. Coun. Women Sch. Execs. (pres. local chpt. 1988-90), San Diego State U. Aztec Varsity Club, Phi Delta Kappa. Democrat. Home: 4001 Stonecroft Dr Austin TX 78749-3165 Office: Del Valle Ind Sch Dist 2407 Shapard Ln Del Valle TX 78617-2257

HALLMARK, R. ELAINE, lawyer, mediator, consultant; b. Pasadena, Calif., Dec. 9, 1942; d. James Steele Temple and Ruth Evelyn (Cordill) Raabe; m. William Lewis Hallmark, Apr. 2, 1961; children: William Royce, Kimberly Anne. Student, Stanford U., 1960-61; BA in Polit. Sci., George Washington U., 1965; JD, Lewis and Clark U., 1976. Bar: Oreg. Caseworker State of Oreg. Welfare and Children's Svcs., Eugene, Salem, Portland, 1966-73; sole practitioner of law Portland, 1976-78, 86-88; educator, adminstr. Creative Initiative Found., Portland, 1977-81; trainer, adminstr. Beyond War Found., Palo Alto and Portland, 1981-83; atty. Bonneville Power Adminstrn., Portland, 1984-85; mediator Confluence N.W., Portland, 1988—; with Oreg. Dispute Resolution Com., Salem, 1989-93, chair, 1989-92. Author legal articles. Mem. Oreg. State Bar (exec. com. ADR sect. 1989-94), Multnomah Bar Assn. (chair ADR com. 1988-91, award of merit 1989), Soc. Profls. in Dispute Resolution (co-chair environ. and pub. disputes sector 1992-94). Office: Confluence NW Hallmark Assocs 10th Fl 1220 SW Morrison St Portland OR 97205

HALLOCK-MULLER, PAMELA, oceanography educator, biogeologist, researcher; b. Pierre, S.D., June 2, 1948; d. Graydon B. and Marjorie L. (Millard) H.; m. Robert Glenn Muller, Aug. 22, 1969. BA in Zoology, U. Mont., 1969; MSc in Oceanography, U. Hawaii, 1972, PhD in Oceanography, 1977. Asst. prof. earth scis. U. Tex. of Permian Basin, Odessa, 1978-83; assoc. prof. marine sci. U. South Fla., St. Petersburg, 1983-88, prof., 1988—. Assoc. editor Jour. Foraminiferal Rsch., Washington, 1985—; mem. editl. bd. Marine Micropaleontology jour., 1990—, Geology, 1996—; contbr. articles to sci. jours., chpt. to books. Vol. speaker Pinellas County (Fla.) Schs. Speaker Bur., 1984—, U. South Fla.-St. Petersburg Speakers Bur., 1989—; judge local, regional, and state sci. fairs, Fla., 1989—; vol. Pinellas County Dems., St. Petersburg, 1988, 92. Deutscher Akademischer Austanschdienst rsch. fellow, Kiel, Germany, 1978; summer faculty fellow NASA Goddard Space Flight Ctr., 1987; NSF rsch. grantee, 1981, 85, 87, 89, 92. Fellow Cushman Found. for Foraminiferal Rsch. (bd. dirs. 1989—, v.p. 1992, 94, pres. 1995-96), Geol. Soc. Am. (W. Storrs Cole Rsch. award 1994); mem. Paleontol. Soc. Assn. Woman Geoscientists, Soc. Sedimentary Geology (v.p. Permian Basin sect. 1982-83), Am. Littoral Soc. (sci. advisor Coral Reefs 1988—), N.Am. Micropaleontol. Soc., Am. Acad. Underwater Scis. Democrat. Office: U South Fla Dept Marine Sci 140 7th Ave S Saint Petersburg FL 33701-5016

HALLSTRAND, SARAH LAYMON, denomination executive; b. Nashville, Oct. 25, 1944; d. Charles Martin and Lillian Christina (Stenberg) Laymon; m. John Peter Hallstrand, July 6, 1974; 1 child, Lillian Johanna. BA cum laude, Fla. So. Coll., 1966; ThM, Boston U., 1971; D of Ministry, McCormick Theol. Sem., 1985; grad., Coll. for Fin. Planning, Denver, 1990. Ordained Am. Baptist Ch., 1976. Dir. Christian edn. Trinity United Meth. Ch., Bradenton, Fla., 1968-70, Univ. United Meth. Ch., Syracuse, N.Y., 1971-73; assoc. min. First Bapt. Ch., Syracuse, 1973-78; pastor Oneida (N.Y.) Bapt. Ch., 1978-80; midwest rep. Mins. and Missionaries Benefit Bd., Am. Bapt. Chs., Oak Park, Ill., 1981—; leader retirement planning seminars Am. Bapt. Assembly, Green Lake, Wis., 1985—; mem. rep. Midwest Commn. on the Ministry, Valley Forge, Pa., 1985—; adj. prof., pastoral care McCormick Theol. Sem., Chgo., 1986—; adj. prof. retirement planning The Divinity Sch., Rochester, N.Y., 1994; vis. scholar Am. Bapt. Bd. Ednl. Ministries, Valley Forge, 1986-87; bd. dirs. Midwest Career Devel. Svc., Chgo., 1987—, chair, 1993—; bd. dirs. The Gathering Place Retreat Ctr., Gosport, Ind., 1988-95; mem. program com. and women in ministry rep. Roger Williams Fellowship, 1988-95; mem. nat. continuing edn. team Am. Bapt. Chs., Valley Forge, Pa., 1991—; conf. leader for women's spiritual renewal weekends; speaker in field. Contbg. author: Songs of Miriam: A Women's Book of Devotions, 1994; contbr. articles to profl. jours. Mem. Am. Bapt. Chs. Mins. Coun., Inst. Cert. Fin. Planners (cert.), Internat. Soc. Retirement Planners, Alpha Gamma Delta. Democrat. Office: Mins and Missionaries Benefit Bd PO Box 549 Oak Park IL 60303-0549

HALLYBURTON, CAROLE-ANNE, entertainment critic; b. Salisbury, N.C., Jan. 13, 1970; d. Charles Bennett and Ruth Carole (Painter) H. BA in English, U. N.C., Chapel Hill, 1992. Lifestyle asst. Salisbury Post, 1992-95, entertainment and book critic, 1992—, news asst., 1995—; cons. Harlequin Romance, N.Y.C., 1995; entertainment cons. Daily Tar Heel, Chapel Hill, N.C., 1989-91. Contbr. articles to lit. mags. Salisbury Woman's Club scholar, 1988. Mem. N.C. Press Assn., N.C. Working Press. Episcopalian. Office: Salisbury Post Newspaper Box 4639 131 W Innes St Salisbury NC 28145

HALM, NANCYE STUDD, foundation executive; b. Jamestown, N.Y., Mar. 26, 1932; d. Thomas Howerton and Margaret Hazel (LeRoy) Neathery; m. David Philip Mack, Aug. 25, 1951 (div. 1972); children: Margaret, Jennifer, Geoffrey, Peter; m. Loris L. Studd, July 6, 1974; m. James Richard Halm, Aug. 30, 1991. BS in Edn., SUNY, Fredonia, 1954, postgrad.; postgrad., St. Bonaventure U. Tchr. Morning Sun (Iowa) Consolidated Schs., 1956-57, Panama (N.Y.) Cen. Schs., 1958-65, Jamestown (N.Y.) Pub. Schs., 1967-69, Olean (N.Y.) Pub. Schs., 1969-72, Jamestown Pub. Schs., 1972-73; pers. mgr. F.W. Woolworth Co., Lakewood, N.Y., 1972-79; dir. Nat. Conf. Christians & Jews, Jamestown, 1979-86; counselor N.Y. State Div. for Youth, Jamestown, 1979-89; exec. rep. Am. Bapt. Found., Valley Forge, Pa., 1989-94; adminstr. New Castle Christian Acad., 1996—. Nat. bd. dirs. Am. Bapt. Chs. U.S.A., Valley Forge, Pa., 1988-89; v.p. Chautauqua County Am. Bapt. Women, 1981-90; pres. Falconer Bapt. women, 1986-90; love gift chmn. Pitts. Bapt. Assn., 1990-91. Recipient Cert. of Merit Cassadaga Job Corp, 1984. Mem. Rebekah. Republican. Home: 1702 W Washington St New Castle PA 16101-1360

HALONEN, JANE SIMMONS, psychology educator, author; b. South Bend, Ind., July 14, 1950; d. Harold Franklin and Dixie Dell (Sewell) Simmons; m. Brian T. Halonen, May 21, 1976. BA, Butler U., Milw., 1972; MS, U. Wis., Milw., 1975, PhD, 1980. Lic. clin. psychologist, Wis. Dir. Shore Sch., Evanston, Ill., 1979-81; prof. Alverno Coll., Milw., 1981—; therapist Wellspring Com/ Assm/, Wanwatosa, Wis., 1983-88; therapist, co-founder Phoenix Clinic, Wanwatosa, Wis., 1988-95; cons. Family Svc. Milw., 1991-96, ETS, Princeton, N.J., 1994-96. Author: (textbooks) Teaching Social Interaction, 1994, Critical Thinking Companion, 1995, Psychology: Contexts of Behavior, 1996. Fellow APA; mem. Am. Assn. Higher Edn., Coun. Tchrs. Undergrad. Psychology (pres. 1990-92), Midwestern Psychol. Assn. Home: 14420 50th Rd Sturtevant WI 53177 Office: Alverno Coll 3401 S 39th St Milwaukee WI 53234-3922

HALPERIN, ESTHER WAITZ, clothing company executive; b. Allentown, Pa., Aug. 17, 1925; d. Abraham and Sadie (Ostrow) Waitz; m. Marvin Goldberg, 1947 (div. 1957); m. Bernard Halperin, June 15, 1963 (dec. 1964); children—Richard Goldberg, Jonathan Halperin; m. Abe Krantz, June 19, 1974 (div. dec. 1985). B.A., Moravian coll., 1948; M.S., Temple U., 1962. Pre-sch. tchr. Jewish Community Ctr., Allentown, 1955-63, summer camp tchr. 1955-63; kindergarten tchr. Jewish Day Sch., Allentown, 1962; pres. Halsen Products, Inc., Slatington, Pa., 1964—. Chmn. Allentown United Way, 1966-81; subscriber Met. Opera, N.Y.C., 1974—. Mem. Atlantic Apparel Assn., Lehigh Valley Needle Trades (bd. dirs. 1964-80, chmn. Pa. apparel week 1969), Pi Delta Epsilon. Republican. Clubs: Hadassah, ORT (Allentown). Lodge: Shriners. Avocations: opera; ballet; dancing; travel. Home: 3717 W Congress St Allentown PA 18104-2645

HALPERIN, KRISTINE BRIGGS, insurance sales and marketing professional; b. Pocatello, Idaho, July 25, 1947; d. Fergus J. and Shirley (Tanner) Briggs; m. Michael Lauren Halperin, Aug. 5, 1995; children: Anthony Ted Rojas, Nancy Kristine Rojas. Student, Idaho State U., 1965-66. Tech. coord. Farmers Ins. Group, Pocatello, 1971-81; svc. rep. All Seasons Ins. Agy., Ventura, Calif., 1982; sr. comml. underwriting asst. Royal Ins. Co., Ventura, 1982-85; sr. comml. lines underwriter Andreini & Co., Ventura, 1985-88; large comml. account unit coord. Frank B. Hall, Inc., Oxnard, Calif., 1988-93; comml. lines supr. Fox Ins. Agy. Inc., Camarillo, Calif., 1993—. Editor (bulletin) News Waves, 1985-87; artist various works specializing in charcoal portraits. Mem. NAFE, Ins. Women Ventura County (treas. 1987-88, v.p. 1988-90, 96—, pres. 1990-91, corr. sec. 1991-92, bd. dirs. 1986, Woman of Yr. 1989-90), Nat. Assn. Ins. Women. Republican. Baptist. Home: 2197 Brookhill Dr Camarillo CA 93010-2107 Office: Fox Ins Agy Inc 2301 Daily Dr Ste 200 Camarillo CA 93010-6613

HALPIN, ANNA MARIE, architect; b. Murphysboro, Ill., July 24, 1923; d. John William and Anna Christina (Weilmuenster) H. B.S. in Architecture, U. Ill., 1948. Designer, project architect various firms,, San Francisco, Rome, N.Y.C., 1948-67; editorial dir. Sweet's div. McGraw-Hill, Inc., N.Y.C., 1967-88; ret. Sweet's div. McGraw-Hill, Inc.; freelance cons., 1988—; rep. to Constrn. Industries Coordination Com., Am. Nat. Metric Council, 1974-80. Mem. AIA (treas., dir. N.Y. chpt. 1974-78, coll. fellows 1976, nat. dir. 1977-79, nat. v.p. 1980, dir. Found. 1980, Richard Upjohn fellow 1991), Women's Equity Action League (pres. N.Y. state orgn. 1976-77), Constrn. Specifications Inst., Alliance Women in Architecture, City Club N.Y. Home: 519 E 86th St New York NY 10028-7541

HALPIN, MARY ELIZABETH, psychologist; b. Oak Park, ILl., June 4, 1951; d. Thomas Joseph and Rita Helen (Foley) H. BA, Marquette U., 1973, MEd, 1975, PhD, 1983. Lic. psychologist, Ill., Calif. Staff psychologist Milw. Children's Hosp., 1975-83; postdoctoral intern El Dorado County Mental Health Ctr., Placerville, Calif., 1983-84; psychologist Inst. for Motivational Devel., Lombard, Ill., 1985-88; psychologist, founder, gen. ptnr. Assocs. for Adolescent Achievement, Deerfield, Ill., 1989-94; psychologist pvt. practice, 1995—; appeared on Oprah Winfrey Show, 1995. T.v. appearance Oprah Winfrey Show, 1995. Chmn., mem. peer rev. com. Charter Barclay Hosp., Chgo., 1991-93. Mem. APA, AAUW, Ill. Psychol. Assn. (standing hearing panel ethics com. 1993, pub. rels. com. 1994). Office: 420 Lake Cook Rd Ste 109 Deerfield IL 60015-4914

HALSBAND, FRANCES, architect; b. N.Y.C., Oct. 30, 1943; d. Samuel and Ruth H.; m. Robert Michael Kliment, May 1, 1971; 1 child, Alexander H. B.A., Swarthmore Coll., 1965; M.Arch., Columbia U., 1968; Registered architect, N.Y., N.J., Mass., Conn., Ohio, Va., N.H., Cert. Nat. Coun. Archtl. reg. bds.; Architect Mitchell/Giurgola Architects, N.Y.C., 1968-72; ptnr. R.M. Kliment & Frances Halsband Architects, N.Y.C., 1972—; vis. critic archtl. design Columbia U., 1975-78, N.C. State U., 1978, Rice U., 1979, U. Va., 1980, Harvard U., 1981, U. Pa., 1981, Columbia U., 1987; dean, Sch. of Architecture, Pratt Inst., 1991-94; mem. N.Y.C. Landmarks Preservation Commn., 1984-87; lectr. U. So. Calif., U. Va., Temple U., Washington U., Tulane U., Harvard U., U. Oreg., U. Washington Projects include: Computer Sci. Bldg., Columbia U. (AIA Nat. Honor award 1987), Gilmer Hall addition U. Va., Town Hall, Salisbury Conn., Computer Sci. Bldg., Princeton U. (AIA Nat. Honor award 1994), Case Western Reserve Adelbert Hall restoration (AIA Nat. Honor award 1994), Alvin Ailey Am. Dance Theater Found., N.Y.C. hdqs. Marsh & McLennan Co, Ind. Bank Hdqs., Bklyn. Coll. Master Plan, Entrance Pavillion L.I. Rail Rd. Penn. Sta.; works exhibited in Cooper-Hewitt Mus., Bklyn. Mus., Nat. Acad. Design, Deutsches Architekturmuseum, Frankfurt; author: Annotated Bibliography of Technical Resources for Small Museums, 1983. Trustee Nat. Inst. Archtl. Edn., 1988-93; mem. archtl. rev. panel Fed. Res. System, 1993—. Fellow AIA (exec. bd. N.Y.C. chpt. 1979, pres. N.Y.C. chpt., 1991-92), Century Assn.; mem. Archtl. League N.Y. (exec. bd. 1975—, v.p. arch. 1981-85, pres. 1985-89), Assn. Collegiate Schs. Architecture (northeast regional dir. 1993-95). Office: R M Kliment & Frances Halsband 255 W 26th St New York NY 10001-8001

HALSEY, EUGENIA GRIFFIN, news correspondent; b. Richmond, Va., May 17, 1956; d. John Selden and Judith Cary (Burnett) H.; m. David Kent Jenkins Jr., May 14, 1988. BA in English, U. Va., 1978. Anchor, reporter Va. Network WINA Radio, Charlottesville, Va., 1977-78, WRVA Radio, Richmond, Va., 1978-79; reporter WDBJ-TV, Roanoke, Va., 1979-82; state capitol corr. WDBJ-TV, Richmond, Va., 1982-85; corr. CNN, Chgo., 1985-87; freelance corr. CNN, Washington, 1987-94, corr., 1994—. Recipient Spot News TV award UPI, Va., 1980, MS Pub. Edn. award Nat. Multiple Sclerosis Soc., Washington, 1993.

HALSEY, MARTHA TALIAFERRO, Spanish language educator; b. Richmond, Va., May 5, 1932; d. James Dillard and Martha (Taliaferro) H. AB, Goucher Coll., 1954; MA, U. Iowa, 1956; PhD, Ohio State U., 1964. Asst. prof. Penn State U., University Park, 1964-70, assoc. prof., 1970-79, prof. Spanish, 1979-95, prof. emerita, 1995—; vis. Olive B. O'Connor prof. lit. Colgate U., Hamilton, N.Y., 1983. Author: Antonio Buero Vallejo, 1973; editor: Madrugada, 1969, Hoy es fiesta, 1978, Los inocentes de la Moncloa, 1980, El enganao, Caballos desbocaos, 1981, (with Phyllis Zatlin) The Contemporary Spanish Theater: A Collection of Critical Essays, 1988, Dictatorship to Democracy: The Recent Plays of Buero Vallejo (La Fundación to Música cercana), 1994; editor: Estreno, 1992—; gen. editor Estreno Contemporary Spanish Plays, 1992—; mem. editorial bd. Modern Internat. Drama, 1968-75, Ky. Romance Quar., 1970-76, Annals of Contemporary Spanish Liturature, 1991—; contbr. articles to profl. jours. Am. Philos. Soc. grantee, 1970, 78; Inst. for Arts and Humanistic Studies grantee, 1977, Program Cultural Cooperation Between Spain's Ministry of Culture and U.S. Univs. grantee, 1992, 94, 95. Fellow Hispanic Soc. Am. (hon.); mem. MLA, South Atlantic MLA, Am. Assn. Tchrs. Spanish and Portuguese, N.E. Modern Lang. Assn., Hispanic Soc. of Am. (hon. assoc. 1995), Phi Beta Kappa, Phi Sigma Iota, Sigma Delta Pi. Democrat. Episcopalian. Clubs: Fellowship of Reconciliation, Episcopal Peace Fellowship, Nuclear Freeze Group, War Resisters League. Home: 151 W Prospect Ave State College PA 16801-5248 Office: Penn State U Dept Spanish State College PA 16802

HALTERMAN, KATHLEEN, elementary school educator; b. St. Louis, July 10, 1959; d. Thomas Ray Halterman and Nancy Corine (Dexheimer) Rutsaert. BS in Edn., Ill. State U., 1984; MA in Edn., Chapman U., 1996. Elem. tchr. St. Mary's Sch., Cheyenne, Wyo., 1984-89, Earlimart (Calif.) Elem. Sch., 1989—; coord. sch. wide Book It!, Earlimart, 1989—, mem. leadership team, 1995—. Camp dir. San Francisco Girl Scout Coun., 1988; music dir. church choir, Tulare, Calif., 1990—. Recipient Anna Keaton scholarship Assn. Residence Halls, Ill. State U., 1984. Mem. ASCD. Democrat. Roman Catholic. Home: 236 E Merritt Ave Tulare CA 93274-1912 Office: Earlimart Elem Sch PO Box 11970 Earlimart CA 93219-1970

HALTOM, CRISTEN EDDY, psychologist; b. Albion, N.Y., Oct. 22, 1948; d. Arthur Benedict and Susan (Cooper) Eddy; m. Maurice Haltom Jr., Apr. 5, 1980; children: Jhakeem, Ajemo, Rebecca. BA, Albion Coll., 1970; MS, Cornell U., 1974, PhD, 1978. Lic. psychologist, N.Y. Instr. Eisenhower Coll., Seneca Falls, N.Y., 1976, Elmira (N.Y.) Coll., 1976-77, Cornell U., Ithaca, N.Y., 1977-78; clin. psychology intern Benjamin Rush Ctr. Mental Health and Mental Retardation, Phila., 1978-79; assoc. psychologist Elmira Psychiat. Ctr., 1979-84; pvt. practice Ithaca, 1984—. Co-editor: Women and Problem Drinking, 1980; contbr. articles to profl. jours. Panelist Cable Channel 7 TV, Ithaca, 1988, arts & scis. career ctr. Cornell U., 1994. Mem. APA, Ctrl. N.Y. Psychol. Assn., World Fedn. Mental Health, Internat. Assn. Eating Disorders Profls., Christian Assn. Psychologists. Office: 215 N Geneva St Ithaca NY 14850-4135

HALVORSEN, DOROTHY C., counselor, consultant, real estate broker; b. N.Y.C., June 27, 1932; d. James Joseph Clark and Antonia (Sembritzki) Robidoux; m. Halvor Halvorsen (div. 1975); children: Karen Loebe, Ingrid Halvorsen, Brenda Halvorsen, Erik Halvorsen; m. John Dickson. BA in English magna cum laude, North Adams State Coll., 1973; MA in Guidance Counseling, Castleton State Coll., 1982. Cert. guidance counselor, tchr. English. Real estate broker Bennington, Vt., 1965-73; tchr. English Mt. Anthony Union H.S., Bennington, Vt., 1973-88, guidance counselor, 1988—; tchr. English Adult Edn. Program, Bennington, Vt., 1990-95; cons. Koby Larz Assocs., Bennington, Vt., 1993—; presenter in field. Guardian ad Litem Vt. State Family Ct., Bennington, 1994—. Mem. Am. Counseling Assn., Am. Sch. Counselor Assn., Am. Vocat. Assn. Congregationalist. Home: 11 Stonehedge Dr Bennington VT 05201 Office: Mt Anthony Union HS Park St Bennington VT 05201

HALVORSON, JUDITH ANNE (JUDITH ANNE DEVAUD), elementary education educator; b. Bethesda, Md., Apr. 28, 1943; d. Henri J. and Mary L. (Baumgart) Devaud; m. Peter L. Halvorson, Feb. 4, 1964; 1 child, Peter Chase. BS in Edn., U. Cin., 1965; MA in Edn., U. Conn., 1974, Cert. Advanced Grad. Study in Edn., 1980. Tchr. Greenhills-Forest Park (Ohio) City Schs., 1965-67, Weld County Schs., Greeley, Colo., 1969-70, Chaplin (Conn.) Elem. Sch., 1970—; mentor Beginning Educator Support program State of Conn. and Chaplin Elem. Sch., 1988—; supr. student tchrs. East Conn. State U., U. Conn., U. No. Colo., 1969—. Past vice-chmn., past chmn., past sec. Coventry (Conn.) Bd. Edn., 1981-95; chmn. Coventry Sch. Bldg. com., 1981-92, Coventry Parks and Recreation Com., 1980-82, chmn., 1982; mem. Dem. Town Com. Coventry, 1973—. Grantee, Nat. Sci. Edn. project, 1977-78; named Outstanding Elem. Tchr. Am., 1974; recipient Citation for Cmty. Leadership, Nat. Women's History Month, 1991; recognized for svc. to pub. edn. in Conn., Conn. Assn. Bds. of Edn., 1993, 94, 95, for contbns. to Conn., Beginning Educator Support and Tng. program Conn. State Dept. Edn., 1991-93, for svc. to cooperating tchr. programs Ea. Conn. State U., 1993, 95, for Outstanding Svc. to Pub. Edn., State of Conn., 1995. Mem. NEA, Conn. Edn. Assn., Chaplin Edn. Assn. (past pres., v.p., chmn. negotiations 1970—), Pi Lambda Theta (past pres., v.p., chmn. membership Beta Sigma chpt. 1974—), Phi Delta Kappa. Episcopalian. Home: 90 David Dr Coventry CT 06238-1320

HALVORSON, M. CADY, clothing designer, entrepreneur; b. Devils Lake, N.D., Sept. 21, 1958; d. Glen David and Lois Rae Kirk; m. Chris Matthew Halvorson, Aug. 10, 1986; children: Lydia, Alissa. BS, N.D. State U., 1980. Interpretive naturalist, nat. park ranger Theodore Roosevelt Nat. Park, Mandora, N.D., 1977; recruiter, mgr. Personell Brokers, Boulder, Colo., 1980-82; engrng. adminstr. Boulder Steel, 1982-88; profl. artist Boulder, 1988-90; couture Papion, Boulder, 1990-93; pres. Solonia, Inc., Boulder, 1993—. Artist: (poker face) Colorful Colorado, 1992 (2d Place award 1992); designer: (children's collection) Conservation Fair, 1995. Vol. emergency room Am. Red Cross, Boulder, 1980-83; leader Girl Scouts of Am., Boulder, 1993-96. Mem. Am. Bus. Women. Office: Solonia 195 S 33d St Boulder CO 80303

HALVORSON, MARY ELLEN, education educator, writer; b. Salem, Ohio, Apr. 23, 1950; d. Robert J. and Betty June (Bear) Batzli; m. Thomas Henry Halvorson, June 10, 1972; children: Christine Lynn, Matthew Thomas, Rebecca Lynn. BS in Edn. with distinction, No. Ariz. U., 1972, postgrad., 1973-92; postgrad., U. Ariz., 1974-76, Ariz. State U., 1975-76, U. Phoenix, 1989-90; Calif. Coast U., 1994—. Cert. elem. tchr., libr., Ariz. Tchr. Prescott (Ariz.) Unified Schs., 1972-77, dir. community nature ctr., 1978, reading tutor, 1985-88, family math. tchr., 1989-90, part-time libr., 1991-92; dir. Prescott Study Ctr., 1987-90; writer ednl. materials Herald House, Independence, Mo., 1994—; instr. Yavapai C.C., 1994—; guest speaker Abia Judd Young Authors, Prescott, 1992; math. enthusiast instr. Ariz. Dept. Edn., Prescott, 1989-92; asst. instr. outdoor edn. Ariz. State U., Prescott, 1977-78; tutor English grammar No. Ariz. U., Flagstaff, 1971-72. Co-author: Arizona Bicentenial Resource Manual, 1975; contbr. book rev. column to Prescott Courier, 1993, also articles to profl. publs. Cert. adult instr. Temple Sch., Independence, Mo., 1985—; sec., bd. dirs. Whispering Pines, Prescott, 1989-93; music docent Prescott Symphony Guild, 1982-85; state Christian edn. dir. Cmty. of Christ. Ch., Ariz., 1977-82, elder, counselor to pastor, 1993—; spokesperson Franklin Heights Homeowners, Prescott, 1985; leader Prescott Pioneers 4-H Club, 1989—, Christian Youth Group, 1985—; fundraiser Graceland Coll., 1993; craft demonstrator Sharlott Hall Mus.; master of ceremonies Prescott Summer Pops Symphony, 1995. Recipient 4-H Silver Clover Svc. award, 1995; named Outstanding Young Educator, Prescott Jaycees, 1976, Outstanding Young Women of Am., 1985. Mem. Phi Kappa Phi, Kappa Delta Pi, Sigma Epsilon Sigma. Home: 2965 Pleasant Valley Dr Prescott AZ 86301-7116

HALWIG, NANCY DIANE, banker; b. Rochester, N.Y., Sept. 17, 1954; d. Norman Charles and Elizabeth Marie (Callemyn) Graupman; m. John Michael Halwig, June 14, 1975; children: Courtney Elizabeth, John Christopher. BA in Elem. Edn. with honors, Goucher Coll., 1975; M. Mgmt. in Fin., Northwestern U., 1979. Br. adminstrv. mgmt. trainee Md. Nat. Bank, Balt., 1975-76; comml. banking officer Am. Nat. Bank Chgo., 1976-80; v.p. relationship mgr. Citicorp USA-Chgo., 1980-85; v.p., team leader Citicorp N.Am., Atlanta, 1985-89, v.p. region credit officer, 1986-90; v.p., regional mgr. Kredietbank-Atlanta, 1990-95; regional v.p. Bank of Am., FSB, Atlanta, 1995-96, sr. v.p., 1996—; mem. contbns. com. Citicorp, Chgo., Atlanta, 1984-90; sec., bd. dirs. S.E. Cobb Allergy and Asthma, P.C. Mem. fin. com. Big Bros./Big Sisters, Atlanta, 1987-91; mem. leadership forum Scottish Rite Hosp., Atlanta, 1988-92; contbns. contact Scitrek Mus., Atlanta, 1988-90, mem. pres.'s coun., 1990-91; mem. steering com. N.W. Ga. Girl Scouts Friendship Ctr., 1993, mem. Friendship Circle, 1996; troop treas. Girl Scouts U.S., 1994-96; sustainer Atlanta Women's Fund, 1995-96. Named one of Atlanta Women to Watch, Atlanta Bus. Chronicle, 1988. Mem. Fin. Women Internat. (Paragon Cir., future com. 1996—), Nat. Assn. Bank Women (found. trustee 1984-85, treas. found. 1985-86, bd. dirs. and chmn. fin. com. 1987-88, chmn. task force on child care financing alternatives, restructuring task force 1988-89, nat. conf. program chmn. 1991-92), Women's Fin. Exch. (founding bd. dirs.), Atlanta C. of C., Atlanta Venture Forum, Assn. Corp. Growth, Northwestern Univ. Club of Atlanta, Phi Beta Kappa. Republican. Home: 4400 Woodland Brook Dr NW Atlanta GA 30339-5365 Office: Bank of Am FSB 1230 Peachtree St Ste 3600 Atlanta GA 30309

HAM, STEPHANIE ANN, interior architect; b. Elgin, Ill., Oct. 29, 1950; d. Erwin Joseph and Adele Lou (Wagner) Seyk; m. Arthur Daniel Vermeire, Aug. 14, 1970 (div. 1978); 1 child, Holly Ann Vermiere; m. Jay Todd Ham, Jan. 1, 1987. BS in Interior Architecture, Ariz. State U., 1987. Interior designer United Bank, Phoenix, 1987-88, Architecture One, Phoenix, 1988-89, CBS Property Svcs. Inc., Phoenix, 1989-93; interior designer, sr. planner McCarthy Nordburg, Ltd., Phoenix, 1993-94; facilities project planner City of Phoenix, 1994—. Mentor Ariz. Womens' Found., Phoenix, 1990. Recipient First Place Elderly Care Housing award Del Webb Corp., 1986. Mem. NAFE, Assn. of U. Women. Republican. Roman Catholic. Office: City of Phoenix 200 W Washington St Fl 14 Phoenix AZ 85003-1611

HAMAN, PAMELA ANN, neonatal nurse practitioner; b. Johnstown, Pa., Aug. 16, 1960; d. Dale William and Frances (Oyaski) Harris; m. Dean Wayne Haman, Dec. 12, 1981; children: Kirsten Leigh, Aubree Ann, Abigail Susanne. BSN, Pa. State U., 1981; cert. neonatal nurse practitioner, Georgetown U., 1989. RN, Pa.; cert. nurse practitioner. Nurse clinician Pa. State U., Hershey, 1981-89, neonatal nurse practitioner, 1989—; item writer Nat. Cert. Corp., Chgo., 1992, 93; counselor Nursing Mothers Counselors, Harrisburg, Pa., 1985-89, co-coord., 1986-87. Contbr. articles to profl. jours. Mem. devel. com. Middletown Christian Sch., 1992—. Mem. Nat. Assn. Neonatal Nurses, Nurse Practitioners of Ctrl. Pa., Susquehanna Valley Assn. Neonatal Nurses (pres.-elect 1990-92, pres. 1992-94). Methodist. Home: 115 Providence Cir Middletown PA 17057-3490 Office: Pa State U Childrens Hosp PO Box 850 Hershey PA 17033

HAMARSTROM, PATRICIA ANN, director, animation/multimedia specialist; b. Kans. City, Mo., Aug. 13, 1952; d. Harold Melchor and Nettie Ann (Wussow) H.; m. John D. Williams, Mar. 10, 1972 (div. 1980): 1 child, Jeffrey D. MFA, U. Mo., Kansas City, Mo., 1981; PhD, U. Tex., Richardson, Tex, 1988. Dir., actress Mo. Repertory Theatre, Kansas City, Mo., 1978-81; exec. prodr. video and prodn. mgr. Multi-Image Resources, Inc., Dallas, 1982-85; pres., CEO Hamar Prodns., Inc., Dallas, 1985—; mem. sr. faculty in computer animation/multimedia Art Inst. Dallas, 1993—; guest lectr./dramaturg Dallas Theatre Ctr., 1985-91; lectr. U. Tex., Richardson, 1985-88; dir. Playwrighting Program New Arts Theatre, Dallas, 1983-85; cons. play selection Addison (Tex.) Ctr. Theatre, 1986; guest dramaturg/dir. S.T.A.G.E., Dallas, 1985-89. Playwright: Stone Child, 1979; dir. plays, including: The King and I, 1985, Possessed for Romance, 1985, Landscape of the Body, 1986, Othello, Shakespeare in the Pk., 1988, Long Day's Journey Into Night, Nat. Theatre Yugoslavia, 1988-92; assoc. prodr. R, 1988; prodr., translator, adapter play: A Tomb for Boris Davidovich, 1986; prodr., dir., screenwriter films: Long Day's Journey Into Night, 1988, Tom, Dick and Harry, 1990, A Tomb for Boris Davidovich, 1991, Dance of the Tigers, 1992, Texas Women, 1992; organizer, artistic dir. Women's Herstory Celebration, 1991-92. Del. Dem. Nat. Conv., Kansas City, Mo., 1976, Dem. State Conv., Houston, 1992; bd. dirs. Addison Ctr. Theatre, 1984-88; mem. Adv. Bd. Humanities Forum, Dallas Theatre Ctr., 1986-87; chairperson tech. com. Art Inst. Dallas; U.S. cultural rep. to Yogoslavia USIA, 1988. Mem. AAUW, Dramatists Guild, Inc. Soc. of Theatrical Artists Guidance and Enhancement, Women in Film, Assn. of Theatre In Higher Edn., Assn. of Ind. Video and Film Makers, Dallas Artists Rsch. & Exhbn., Dallas Comm. Coun., Video 8 Users. Home and Office: Hamar Prodns Inc 912 Whitehall Dr Plano TX 75023-6737

HAMBLEN, L. JANE, lawyer; b. Edna, Tex., June 16, 1949; d. William Herbert and Lillian Gertrude (Hotman) H. BA, Rice U., 1971; JD, U. Tex., 1976; LLB, Cambridge (Eng.) U., 1977. Assoc. Davis Polk & Wardwell, N.Y.C., 1977-84; assoc. O'Melveny & Myers, N.Y.C., 1984-86, ptnr., 1987—. Mem. devel. com. Planned Parenthood N.Y., 1990—; alumni dist. dir. U. Tex. Law Sch., N.Y., 1991-94, dir. alumni bd., 1994—. Office: O Melveny & Myers Citicorp Ctr 153 E 53rd St Fl 54 New York NY 10022-4611

HAMBLET, CAROLE ORR, artist; b. Alexandria, Ind., June 10, 1933; d. Carl Victor and Marian Martha (Long) Coonse; m. Larry D. Ribble (dec. July 1953); m. Thomas LeRoy Orr, Nov. 10, 1950 (div. Oct. 1979); children: Karen Sue, Terri Ribble, David Thomas; m. Lev C. Hamblet Jr., Feb. 5, 1982; stepchildren: James, Jean, Laura, Anne. Cert., Famous Artist Sch., Westport, Conn., 1956, Art Instrn. Schs., Mpls., 1962. Asst. art dir. La Gallerie du Mall, Houston, 1975-78; free lance fine artist Lantern Ln. Gallery, Houston, 1968-81, ast. mgr., design cons., 1979-81; artist Artist Showroom, Houston, 1982—; participating artist numerous fine art galleries including Assistance Guild, Houston, 1968, Beaux Arts, Houston, 1968-70, Houston Gamma Phi Gallery, 1971-72, Houston Delta Gamma Found., 1978-81, Glassell Sch. of Art Houston, 1983. One-woman shows at Nobler Gallery, Houston, 1967, Art Gallery, Pasadena, Tex., 1968, Gallarie La Rue, Austin, Tex., 1971, Gallery 12, Houston, 1972, Main St., Houston, 1974, La Galerie de Mall, Houston, 1976-78, Triumvirate Gallery, Santa Fe, N.Mex., 1980, Latern Ln. Gallery, Houston, 1968-81, Houshang's Gallery, Dallas, 1980-82, Battle Horn Galleries Ltd., Santa Fe, 1984, New Trends Inc., Santa Fe, 1985-88, Horizons Galleries, Houston, 1990-93, Houston C.C., Heinen Theatre, 1992, Windsor Gallery, Ft. Lauderdale, Fla., 1994. Art instr. adults Ch. of the Advent, Houston, 1968-70; adult edn. instr. arts Ch. Sch. Conf., Dept. Christian Edn., Trinity Ch., Diocese of Tex., Houston, 1969. Recipient Profl. Best Ann. Competition Art Instrn. Schs., Mpls., 1965. Studio: Artist Showroom DBA 880 Tully Rd Townhouse # 29 Houston TX 77079

HAMBRICK, ERNESTINE, colon and rectal surgeon; b. Griffin, Ga., Mar. 31, 1941; d. Jack Daniel and Nannie (Harper) Hambrick Rubens. BS, U. Md., 1963; MD, U. Ill., 1967. Diplomate Am. Bd. Colon and Rectal Surgery, Am. Bd. Surgery. Intern surgery Cook County Hosp., Chgo., 1967-68, resident gen. surgery, 1968-72, fellow colon and rectal surgery, 1972-73, attending surgeon, 1973-74, part-time attending surgeon, 1974-80; pvt. practice colon and rectal surgery Chgo., 1974—; chief of surgery Michael Reese Hosp., Chgo., 1993-95. Contbr. articles to profl. jours. Trustee Rsch. & Edn. Found., Michael Reese Med. Staff, Chgo., 1994—. Mem. ACS, Am. Soc. Colon and Rectal Surgeons (v.p. 1992-93, trustee Rsch. Found. 1992—), Am. Coll. Gastroenterology. Office: 30 N Michigan Ave Ste 1118 Chicago IL 60602-3503

HAMBURG, BEATRIX ANN, medical educator, researcher; b. Jacksonville, Fla., Oct. 19, 1923; d. Francis Minor and Beatrix McCleary; married, May 25, 1951; children: Eric N., Margaret A. A.B., Vassar Coll., 1944; M.D., Yale U., 1948; DHL (hon.), Northwestern U., 1994. Diplomate: Nat. Bd. Med. Examiners. Intern Grace-New Haven Hosp., 1948-49; resident Yale Psychiat. Inst., New Haven, 1949-50; resident in pediatrics Children's Hosp., Cin., 1950-51; resident in psychiatry Inst. Juvenile Research, 1951-53; research assoc. Stanford U. Med. Sch. (Calif.), 1961-71, assoc. prof. psychiatry, 1976-80; assoc. prof. Harvard Med. Sch., Boston, 1980-83; exec. dir. Div. Health Policy Research, 1981-83; prof. psychiatry and pediatrics Mt. Sinai Med. Sch., N.Y.C., 1983—, dir. div. child and adolescent psychiatry, 1988-92; pres. William T Grant Found, NYC, 1992—; assoc. dir. Lab. of Stress and Conflict, Stanford U. Med. Sch., 1974-76; sr. research psychiatrist NIMH, Bethesda, Md., 1978-80; dir. studies Pres.'s Commn. Mental Health, 1977-78; mem. vis. com. Sch. Pub. Health, Harvard U., 1977-80, commn. on behavior and soc., Nat. Acad. Scis., 1983—. Author: Behavioral and Psychosocial Issues in Diabetes, 1980, School Age Pregnancy and Parenthood, 1986; contbr. numerous sci. articles to profl. jours. Trustee W.T. Grant Found., 1978—; bd. dirs. New World Found., 1978-83, Bush Found., Revson Found., Greenwall Found., 1986—; mem. Pub. Health Coun. State of N.Y., 1978-80. Vis. scholar Ctr. Advanced Study Behavioral Scis., 1967-68; recipient Outstanding Achievement award Alcohol, Drug Abuse and Mental Health Adminstrn., 1980. Fellow Am. Acad. Child Psychiatry; mem. AAAS (bd. dirs. 1987-91), NIMH (nat. adv. mental health coun.), Inst. of Medicine of NAS, Soc. Profs. Child Psychiatry (program com. 1972-74), Am. Acad. Child Psychiatry (adolescent com. 1977-81), Soc. Adolescent Medicine, APHA (adolescent com. 1978-80), Soc. Study of Social Biology, Acad. Rsch. in Behavioral Medicine (exec. coun. 1980), N.Y. Acad. Medicine (bd. trustees 1992), Century Club, Phi Beta Kappa. Office: William T Grant Found 515 Madison Ave New York NY 10022-5403

HAMBURG, MARGARET ANN (PEGGY HAMBURG), city commissioner; b. Chgo., July 12, 1955; d. David Alan and Beatrix Ann (Mc Cleary) H.; m. Peter Fitzhugh Brown, May 23, 1992; children: Rachel Ann Hamburg Brown, Evan David Addison Brown. BA magna cum laude, Harvard/Radcliffe Coll., 1978; MD, Harvard, 1983. Diplomate Am. Bd. Internal Medicine, Nat. Bd. Med. Examiners. Intern, resident in internal medicine The N.Y. Hosp., Cornell Med. Coll., N.Y.C., 1983-86; spl. asst. to the dir., office of disease prevention and health promotion, office of the asst. sec. for health U.S. Dept. Health and Human Svcs., Washington, 1986-88; spl. asst. to the dir. Nat. Inst. Allergy and Infectious Diseases, NIH, Bethesda, Md., 1988-89, asst. dir., 1989-90; deputy commr. Family Health Svcs., N.Y.C. Dept. Health, N.Y.C., 1990-91; commr. of health N.Y.C. Dept. Health, N.Y.C., 1991—; guest investigator The Rockefeller U., N.Y.C., 1985-86; clin. instr. dept. medicine Georgetown U. Sch. Medicine, Washington, 1986-90; asst. prof. clin. pub. health Columbia U. Sch. Pub. Health, N.Y.C., 1991—; adj. asst. prof. medicine Cornell U. Med. Coll., N.Y.C., 1991—; scholar Pub. Health Leadership Inst. Ctr. for Disease Control U. Calif., 1992; bd. dirs. N.Y.C. Health Systems Agy., Med. and Health Rsch. Assn., Health Hosps. Corp, Nat. Coun. on Women's Health, Primary Care Devel. Corp.; steering com. women and aids NIH, 1991; bd. govs. Greater N.Y. Hosp. Assn., 1991—; mem. bd. sci. advisors. Nat. Pub. Radio, 1992—; com. mem. on substance abuse mental health issues in aides rsch., 1993—; advisory bd. mem. Medunsa Trust, Inc., Med. U. So. Africa, 1993—; mem. defense sci. bd. task force on Gulf War Syndrome U.S. Dept. Defense, 1993—; bd. mem. sci. counselors Nat. Ctr. Infectious Diseases, U.S. Ctrs. for Disease, 1994—. Editorial bd. mem. Jour. N.Y. Acad. Sci., 1992—, The Bull. of N.Y. Acad. Medicine, 1992—, Current Reviews in Pub. Health, 1993—; contbr. to numerous profl. jours. Vol. attending physician The Washington Free Clinic, Washington, 1988-90. Recipient commendation Pub. Health Svc., 1988, 90, Spl. Recognition award Pub. Health Svc., 1990, cert. of Honor The Women's Club of N.Y., 1993, N.Y. Rotary Club award, 1993, Robert F. Wagner Pub. Svc. award NYU, 1993. Fellow AAAS (med. scis. section com. 1989—); mem. ACP, APHA, Am. Med. Women's Assn., Coun. on Fgn. Rels., Health Care Exec. Forum, N.Y. Acad. Medicine, Pub. Health

Assn. N.Y.C., Inst. Medicine, Soc. Social Biology, Women in Health Mgmt. Office: NYC Dept Health 125 Worth St New York NY 10013-4006

HAMBURGER, MARY ANN, medical management consultant; b. Newark, Aug. 25, 1939; d. Herman and Sylvia (Strauss) Marcus; div. June 1966; children: Bruce David, Marc Laurence. AA, U. Bridgeport (Conn.), 1960. Office mgr. Millburn, N.J., 1970-84; propr., mgr. Mary Ann Hamburger, Assocs., med. mgmt. cons. co., Maplewood, N.J., 1984-; tchr. adult edn. South Orange Maplewood Bd. Edn., 1975-83; cons. Wellcare of N.Y.; profl. physician recruiter, N.Y., N.J.; broker med. practices. Mem. NAFE. Democrat. Jewish. Home and Office: 74 Hudson Ave Maplewood NJ 07040-1403

HAMBY, BARBARA JEAN, writer, poet; b. Chico, Calif., Apr. 20, 1929; d. Frank Llewellyn Fairfield and Grace Ellen Mann; separated; children: Gail D. Wilson Anderson, Kurt E. Deutscher. Student, U. Wash., 1947-48, Clark Coll., 1990—. Author: My Muse Has Many Moods, 1995. Named Golden Poet, World of Poetry, 1987, 91, Silver Poet, 1989. Mem. NOW, Older Women's League, Oreg. State Poetry Assn. (2nd prize 1995), Wash. State Poets (sec., 3rd prize 1995), Southwest Wash. Writers, Clark Poets (1st prize 1990). Democrat. Unitarian. Office: Drummer Pub PO Box 65996 Vancouver WA 98665

HAMBY, JEANNETTE, state legislator; b. Virginia, Minn., Mar. 15, 1933; d. John W. and Lydia M. (Soderholm) Johnson; m. Eugene Hamby, 1957; children—Taryn Rene, Tenya Ramine. BS, U. Minn., 1956; MS, U. Oreg., 1968, PhD, 1976. Vice chmn. Hillsboro High Sch. Dist. Bd., 1973-81; mem. Washington County Juvenile Services Com., 1980—; mem. suggested legis. com. Council State Govts., 1981—, Oreg. state rep., 1981-83; mem. Oreg. State Senate from 5th dist., 1983—. Mem. Oreg. Mental Health Assn., Am. Nurses Assn., Oreg. Nurses Assn., Am. Vocat. Assn., Oreg. Vocat. Assn., Oreg. Vocat./Career Adminstrs., Phi Kappa Phi, Phi Delta Kappa. Lutheran. Republican. Home: 952 NE Jackson School Rd Hillsboro OR 97124-2314 Office: Oreg State Senate State Capital Salem OR 97310*

HAMEL, ELIZABETH CECIL, volunteer, educator; b. Altoona, Pa., June 13, 1918; d. Francis Anthony and Charlotte Margaret (Devine) Murphy; m. William Rogers Hamel, Mar. 2, 1943; children: Michele Ferencsik, Deirdre, Anthony, Cecily Charlyn Houston. BArt, Villa Maria Coll., 1939; MA, Pa. State U., 1940; cert. approval, U. Cambridge, Eng., summer 1986. Tchr. English, head Spanish dept. East High Sch., Erie, Pa., 1940-43; prof. lit. Vernon Ct. Jr. Coll., Newport, R.I., 1966-69. Mem. Francestown (N.H.) Improvement Assn., 1958—, Peterborough (N.H.) Hist. Soc., 1987—, Art and Hist. Soc. East Martello Tower Mus., Key West, Fla., 1987—, Founders' Soc. Tennessee Williams Fine Arts Ctr., Key West, 1986—; bd. dirs. Old Island Restoration Found., Key West, 1990—; bd. dirs. Friends of Libr., 1985-86, 93—, sec., 1986-87, 92—; mem. White House Vol. Group, Washington, 1972-74; trustee Newport County Preservation Soc. Mem. Gen. Fedn. Women's Club (bd. dirs. Key West chpt. 1986—), Key West Woman's Club (bd. dirs., parliamentarian 1986—, del. state con. 1988—), Peterborough Woman's Club, Garden Club, Greenfield Woman's Club (pres. 1979-80). Republican. Roman Catholic. Home: Blacksmith Shop Main St Francestown NH 03043

HAMILL, JUDITH ELLEN, municipal government administrator; b. Chgo., Mar. 8, 1953; d. William Patrick and Dolores Jean (Lhamon) H.; m. Thomas A. Jaconetty, Aug. 3, 1991; 1 child, Nicole Alicia Jaconetty. MusB, Roosevelt U., 1975; M of Urban Planning and Policy, U. Ill., Chgo., 1979; M of Pub. Adminstrn., Harvard U., 1982. Staff asst. Thomas H. Miner & Assocs., Chgo., 1972-75; project dir. Chgo. Council on Fine Arts, 1977-78; project planning dept. planning City of Chgo. Dept. Planning, Ill., 1978-81; research staff Stevenson/Stern for Ill., Chgo., 1982; ind. cons. Chgo., 1982-86; city planner Dept. Aviation, Chgo., 1986-87; dir. noise abatement office Dept. of Aviation, Chgo., 1987-95; program dir. first dep. comm. office O'Hare Internat. Airport, Chgo., 1995—. Vice chairperson Ill. Women's Polit. Caucus, Chgo., 1975-82; active Women in Govt. Rels., Chgo., 1977-82, Ill. Dem. Women, Springfield, Ill., 1981—, Cook County Dem. Women, Chgo., 1982—; mem. jr. gov. bd. Chgo. Symphony Orch., 1981-89; mem. Bus. and Profl. Assn. Chgo. Symphony Orch., 1990—; bd. dirs. Rogers Park Cmty. Coun., 1990-93. Recipient Community Svc. award S.W. Parish and Neighborhood Fedn., 1993; Harvard U. scholar, Cambridge, Mass., 1981-82. Club: Harvard of Chgo. Home: 4801 N Harlem Ave Chicago IL 60656-3505

HAMILTON, ANTONIA WALLACE, foundation administrator; b. Phila., July 12, 1940; d. James Magee and Christine Ann (Klesius) Wallace; children: Jennifer W., Colin J. AB, Smith Coll., 1962; MA, U. VA., 1968; MLS, U. Mich., 1971. Program dir. mus. of art U. Iowa, Iowa City, 1975-77; pres. Back Room Graphics, Iowa City, 1977-79; dir. pub rels. Hansen Lind Meyer, Iowa City, 1982-86; corp. devel. dir. U. Iowa Found., Iowa City, 1987-91; mem. Bd. Realtors, Ann Arbor, Mich. 1974, dir. corp. and found. devel. Swarthmore Coll. 1991-92; dir. devel. Chester County Historical Soc. 1992—; mem. bd. Chester County Estate Planning Coun. 1994—; mem. bd. Chester County Tourist Bur. 1995—. Editor: Bonding, 1983, Parent-Infant Bonding, 1981, "Small Pleasures", 1980. Contbr. articles to profl. jours. Mem. Friends Devel. Coun., Mus. of Arts, Iowa City, 1985-87, Friends of Univ. Libr., Iowa City, 1979-84, Resources Conservation Commn., Iowa City, 1980-83, Airport Commn., Iowa City, 1990-91. Mem. AIA, Soc. Mktg. Profl. Svcs. (Ann. Design award, Washington, 1985, jury), Iowa City C. of C. (bd. dirs. 1989-91), Phi Beta Kappa, Beta Phi Mu. Home: 358 N Church St West Chester PA 19380-3209 Office: Chester County Hist Soc 225 N High St West Chester PA 19380

HAMILTON, BEVERLY LANNQUIST, investment management professional; b. Roxbury, Mass., Oct. 19, 1946; d. Arthur and Nancy Lannquist. BA cum laude, U. Mich., 1968; postgrad., NYU, 1969-70. Prin. Auerbach, Pollak & Richardson, N.Y.C., 1972-75; v.p. Morgan Stanley & Co., N.Y.C., 1975-80, United Techs., Hartford, Conn., 1980-87; dep. comptr. City of N.Y., 1987-91; pres. ARCO Investment Mgmt Co, L.A., 1991—; also v.p. Atlantic Richfield Co., L.A.; also v.p. Atlantic Richfield Co., L.A.; bd. dirs. Conn. Natural Gas Co., Conn. Mut. Investment Mgmt., TWA Pilots; dir. acctg. plan Emerging Markets Growth Fund. Trustee Hartford Coll. for Women, 1981-87, Stanford Univ. Mgmt. Co., 1991—; bd. dirs. Inst. for Living, 1983-87. Mem. NCCJ (bd. dirs. 1987-91). Office: ARCO Investment Mgmt Co 515 S Flower St Los Angeles CA 90071-2201

HAMILTON, CINDA RAE, customer service executive; b. Paris, Ill., Mar. 22, 1963; d. Raymond B. and Jean Ann (Powers) Cottle; m. Bradford Allen Hamilton, June 6, 1981; children: Jonathan, Jocelyn. BSBA, U. Toledo, 1985. CPA, cert. mgmt. acct. Auditor Arthur Andersen, Toledo, 1985-89; auditor Cummins Engine Co., Columbus, Ind., 1989-91, mgr. dept. treasury, 1991-94, svc. contr., 1994-95; mgr. customer svc./material planning Cummins Engine Co., Memphis, 1995—. Mem. Inst. Mgmt. Accts. (dir. program book 1991), AICPAs. Office: Cummins Engine Co Inc 4155 Quest Way Memphis TN 38115

HAMILTON, DAGMAR STRANDBERG, lawyer, educator; b. Phila., Jan. 10, 1932; d. Eric Wilhelm and Anna Elizabeth (Sjöström) Strandberg; A.B., Swarthmore Coll., 1953; J.D., U. Chgo. Law Sch., 1956; J.D., Am. U., 1961; m. Robert W. Hamilton, June 26, 1953; children: Eric Clark, Robert Andrew Hale, Meredith Hope. Admitted to Tex. bar, 1972; atty., civil rights div. U.S. Dept. Justice, Washington, 1965-66; asst. instr. govt. U. Tex.-Austin, 1966-71; lectr. Law Sch. U. Ariz., Tucson, 1971-72; editor, researcher Assoc. Justice William O. Douglas, U.S. Supreme Ct., 1962-73, 75-76; editor, research Douglas autobiography Random House Co., 1972-73; staff counsel Judiciary Com., U.S. Ho. of Reps., 1973-74; asst. prof. L.B. Johnson Sch. Pub. Affairs, U. Tex., Austin, 1974-77, assoc. prof., 1977-83, prof., 1983—, assoc. dean, 1983-87; vis. prof. Washington U. Law Sch., St. Louis, 1982; vis. fellow Univ. London, 1987-88, vis. prof. U. Maine Portland, 1992. Mem. Tex. Bar Assn., Am. Law Inst., Assn. Pub. Policy Analysis and Mgmt., Kappa Beta Phi (hon.), Phi Kappa Phi (hon.). Democrat. Quaker. Contbr. to various publs. Home: 403 Allegro Ln Austin TX 78746-4301 Office: U Tex LBJ Sch Pub Affairs Austin TX 78712

HAMILTON, DIANE BRONKEMA, nursing educator; b. Fulton, Ill., Sept. 24, 1946; d. Peter and Blanche (Hoogheem) Bronkema. Diploma, Northwestern U. Sch. Nursing, 1967; BSN, West Tex. State U., 1978; MA, U. Iowa, 1980; PhD, U. Va., 1987. RN. Instr. Mt. Mercy Coll., Cedar Rapids, Iowa, 1980-82; asst. prof. nursing U. Va., Charlottesville, 1985-87, Med. U. S.C., Charleston, 1988-92, U. Rochester, N.Y., 1992-94; assoc. prof. Western Mich. U., 1994—; cons. in field. Author: Pharmacology in Nursing, 1988, 2d edit., 1993; editl. bd. mem. Nursing History Review, 1991-95; contbr. articles to profl. jours. Bd. dirs. Heritage Coun., Cedar Rapids, 1980-82. Capt. USAF, 1970-75. Fellow U. Pa. 1991, Lillian Brunner post doc fellowship, 1992; grantee DuPont scholar, 1984, NIH, 1982; recipient Lavinia Dock award for hist. scholarship, 1991, Nat. Rsch. Svc. award NIH, 1983, Best of Image award, 1993. Mem. ANA, Am. Assn. History Medicine, Am. Assn. History Nursing (bd. dirs. 1991-95), Women's Club, Sigma Theta Tau Internat. (heritage com.). Home: 2370 Mansfield St Kalamazoo MI 49009 Office: Western Mich U Sch of Nursing Kalamazoo MI 49008

HAMILTON, DOROTHY JEAN, nursing educator; b. Gaffney, S.C., Oct. 17, 1954; d. J.C. and Martha Jean (Long) Phillips; m. Moses Marshall, May 20, 1989 (div.); children: Doricia, Maurice Jr., Angelina, Michelle, Melissa. ADN, Cuyagoga C.C., Cleve., 1979; BSN, Cleve. State U., 1988; MSN, Case Western Res. U., 1996. RN, Ohio; CCRN; charge nurse practitioner; cert. ACLS provider and instr. Staff nurse Cleve. Clinic Found., 1979-86, asst. nurse mgr., 1986-93, clin. instr. cardiac, 1993—. Mentor John Haye H.S., Cleve., 1993—. Mem. AACN, ANA, Soc. Critical Care Medicine. Home: 3975 Colony Rd Cleveland OH 44118-2305 Office: Cleve Clinic Found 9500 Euclid Ave Cleveland OH 44195

HAMILTON, JACQUELINE, art consultant; b. Tulsa, Mar. 28, 1942; d. James Merton and Nina Faye (Andrews) H.; m. Richard Sanford Piper, Jan. 2, 1968 (div. June 1976). BA, Tex. Christian U., 1965; grad., Stockholm U., 1967; postgrad., Harvard U., 1972-73, Tufts U., 1971, Rice U., 1982-83, Houston C.C., 1986-87. Pvt. practice art cons. Houston, 1979—. Contbr. articles to profl. publs. Active Cultural Arts Council of Houston. Mem. Assn. Corp. Art Curators, Nat. Assn. Corp. Art Mgmt., Rice Design Alliance, Tex. Arts Alliance, The Houstonian Club, The Forum Club, L'Alliance Francaise, Swedish Club. Presbyterian. Office: PO Box 1483 Houston TX 77251-1483

HAMILTON, JEAN CONSTANCE, judge; b. St. Louis, Nov. 12, 1945; d. Aubrey Bertrand and Rosemary (Crocker) H. A.B., Wellesley Coll., 1968; J.D., Washington U., St. Louis, 1971; LL.M., Yale U., 1982. Bar: Mo. 1971. Atty. Dept. of Justice, Washington, 1971-73, asst. U.S. atty., St. Louis, 1973-78; atty. Southwestern Bell Telephone Co., St. Louis, 1978-81; judge 22d Jud. Circuit, State of Mo., St. Louis, 1982-88; judge Mo. Ct. Appeals (ea. dist.), 1988-90; U.S. dist. judge U.S. Dist. Ct. (ea. dist.) Mo., 1990—, chief judge, 1995—. Mem. ABA, Bar Assn. Met. St. Louis, Women Lawyers Assn. Met. St. Louis, Nat. Assn. Women Judges, Am. Law Inst. Episcopalian. Office: US Court and Custom House 1114 Market St Fl 1 Saint Louis MO 63101-2043

HAMILTON, JUDITH ANN, human resources professional; b. Humboldt, Nebr., Nov. 19, 1946; d. Donald Leonard and Betty June (Warner) Stalder; m. Rodney Gene Hamilton, Mar. 23, 1973; 1 child, Russell Allen. BBA, U. Denver, 1990; cert. mgmt. devel., U. Colo., 1984. Cert. sr. profl. in human resources, 1991. V.p. adminstrn. Particle Measuring Systems Inc., Boulder, Colo., 1979-85; dir. human resources Access Graphics, Inc., Boulder, 1990-93; prin. Solutions Resource Group, Santa Fe, 1994—; speaker Colo. Bus. Educators Conf., Denver, 1991; event judge Future Bus. Leaders Am., Colo., 1991. Chairperson Bus. Adv. Com., Adams County Sch. Dist. 12, Colo. Named Bus. Person of Yr., Future Bus. Leaders Am., 1991. Mem. Soc. Human Resource Mgmt., Colo. Human Resource Assn., No. N.Mex. Human Resource Assn. (basic reading tutor Santa Fe literacy program, v.p. of pub. rels.), Human Resource Mgmt. Assoc. Albuquerque, N. Mex. (state dir. SHRM of N.Mex. State coun. 1996), Boulder Area Human Resource Assn. (dir. 1992, 93), program Com. for N. Mex. State Conf. of SHRM (chair). Office: PO Box 22790 Santa Fe NM 87505-6503

HAMILTON, JUDITH HALL, computer company executive; b. Washington, June 15, 1944; d. George Woods and Jane Fromm (Brogger) Hall; m. David Hamilton, Oct. 2, 1970 (div. 1980); m. Stephen T. McClellan, Oct. 29, 1988. BA, Ind. U., 1966; postgrad., Boston U., 1966-68; postgrad. Exec. Sch. Mgmt., UCLA, 1980-81. Programmer System Devel. Corp., Santa Monica, Calif., 1968-69, dir. programming, 1975-80; systems analyst Daylin, Inc., Beverly Hills, Calif., 1969-71; systems mgr. Audio Magnetics, Gardena, Calif., 1971-73; pres. Databasics, Inc., Santa Monica, 1973-75; v.p. Computer Scis. Corp., El Segundo, Calif., 1980-87; ptnr. Ernst & Young, L.A., 1987-89, Manhattan, N.Y., 1989-91; sr. v.p., gen. mgr. Locus Computing Corp., L.A., 1991-92; pres., CEO Dataquest, Inc., a Dun & Bradstreet Corp., San Jose, Calif., 1992-95, First Floor Software, Mountain View, Calif., 1996—; bd. dirs. The Application Group, Com. Econ. Devel.; bd. advisors Perot Systems. Active World Affairs Coun. L.A.; mem. bus. bd. N.Y. Zool. Soc. Mem. Assn. Data Processing Svc. Orgns. (bd. dirs., chmn.), Information Tech. Assn. Am., Orgn. Women Execs., Calif. C. of C. (bd. dirs. 1994—, Dept. of Commerce Dist. Export Coun. No. Calif.), Kappa Alpha Theta. Office: First Floor Software 444 Catro St Mountain View CA

HAMILTON, JUDY LYNN, counselor; b. West Point, Miss., May 31, 1958; d. Charlie Mattice and Ruth (Jones) Graves; m. Bernard Hamilton Jr.; children: Julie, Jasmine, Bernard S. BS, U. So. Miss., 1980; MS, Memphis State U., 1982; ednl. specialist, Miss. State U., 1996. Therapist Mid South Hosp., Memphis, 1980-83; engr. intern Reynolds Elec. and Engring. Co., Las Vegas, 1984-85; counselor Nev. Dept. pf Prisons, Las Vegas, 1985-88; counselor intern Millsaps Vocat., Starkville, Miss., 1994-95. Mem. Nat. Civil Rights Mus., Memphis, 1994—, Black Cmty. Network Organ., Las Vegas, 1996. Mem. NAACP (life), ACA, Am. Sch. Counseling Assn., Phi Delta Kappa.

HAMILTON, LINDA, actress; b. Salisbury, Md., Sept. 26, 1956; m. Bruce Abbott (div.). Appeared in plays Looice, 1975, Richard III, 1977; films include T.A.G.: The Assassination Game, 1982, Children of the Corn, 1984, The Stone Boy, 1984, The Terminator, 1984, Black Moon Rising, 1986, King Kong Lives!, 1986, Mr. Destiny, 1990, Terminator 2: Judgment Day, 1991, Silent Fall, 1994, The Shadow Conspiracy, 1996; TV series include The Secrets of Midland Heights, 1980-81, King's Crossing, 1982, Beauty and the Beast, 1987-90 (Golden Globe award nomination 1988, 89); TV movies include Reunion, 1980, Rape and Marriage - The Rideout Case, 1980, Country Gold, 1982, Secrets of a Mother and Daughter, 1983, Secret Weapons, 1985, Club Med, 1986, Go Toward the Light, 1988. Office: Internat Creative Mgmt 8942 Wilshire Blvd Beverly Hills CA 90211-1934*

HAMILTON, LINDA HELEN, clinical psychologist; b. N.Y.C., Dec. 2, 1952; d. Peter and Helen (Casey) Homek; m. Terrence White, Aug. 10, 1974 (div. 1983); m. William Garnett Hamilton, Dec. 29, 1984. BA summa cum laude, Fordham U., 1984; MA, Adelphi U., 1986, PhD, 1989. Lic. psychologist, N.Y. Dancer N.Y.C. Ballet, 1969-88; clin. psychologist Fair Oaks Hosp., Summit, N.J., 1989-90, Miller Inst. for Performing Artists, N.Y.C., 1989-95; pvt. practice N.Y.C., 1991—; rsch. assoc. Miller Inst. Performing Artists, N.Y.C., 1987-95; chair dance com. MedArt U.S.A., N.Y.C., 1990-92; cons. psychologist Sch. Am. Ballet, N.Y.C., 1991—, Women's Ctr. Health and Social Issues, St. Luke's-Roosevelt Hosp. Ctr., N.Y.C., 1996—; advice columnist Dance Mag., 1992—; co-leader Performing Arts Medicine Delegation to Russia and Ea. Europe, 1992; dir. eating disorders program Performing Arts Psychotherapy Ctr., N.Y.C., 1996—. Contbr. articles to profl. jours. and popular mags. Miller Inst. Performing Artists grantee, 1987. Mem. APA (Daniel E. Berlyne award 1993), Ea. Psychol. Assn., Soc. for Exploration Psychotherapy Integration. Office: 30 W 60th St New York NY 10023-7902

HAMILTON, LORRAINE REBEKAH, adult education consultant; b. York, Pa., Jan. 17, 1960; d. Robert Stephen Sheely and Emma Estella (Taylor) Ford; m. Ronald Dana Hamilton, Apr. 14, 1990. Diploma in Drafting and Design Tech., Cumberland-Perry Tech. Sch., Mechanicsburg, Pa., 1978; BS in Psychology, U. Houston, 1992, MA in Gen. Behavioral Scis., 1994. Drafter aluminum products Capitol Products, Camp Hill, Pa., 1978-81; drafter oil field equipment Continental Emsco, Houston, 1981-82; coll. prof. Coll. of the Mainland, Texas City, Tex., 1983-87; contract drafter/piping Astech Svcs., Houston, 1985-86; computer specialist Amoco Oil Co., Texas City, 1986-92; ind. cons. Sage Learning Method, 1994—; owner Synergy Sys., 1994-95, E-Three, 1996—; founder EntertaiNET Networking Party, 1996—. Convenor Women's Studies Student Assn., Houston, 1994; treas., forum rep. NOW, Houston, 1992; vol. Landmark Edn. Corp., Houston, 1992-94. Mem. Omicron Delta Kappa. Home: PO Box 22653 Houston TX 77227-2653

HAMILTON, NANCY BETH, business executive; b. Lakewood, Ohio, July 22, 1948; d. Edward Douglas and Gloria Jean (Blessing) Familo; m. Thomas Woolman Hamilton, June 10, 1970; children: Susan Elizabeth, Catherine Anne. BA, Denison U., 1970. Cert. secondary edn. tchr., Fla. Tchr. Orange County (Fla.) Bd. Edn., 1970-71; registrar Jones Coll., Orlando, Fla., 1971-72; mgr. service dept. Am. Lawyers Co., Cleve., 1972-79, mgr. data processing dept., 1980-95, corp. sec.-treas., 1995—. Mem. bd. editors Comml. Law Jour., 1991—. Trustee, treas. Westshore Montessori Assn., Rocky River, Ohio, 1984-88; bd. dirs. Holly Ln. PTA, Westlake, Ohio, 1988-94, treas., 1992-94; bd. dirs. Parkside PTA, Westlake, 1991—, treas., 1994—; treas. Westlake H.S. PTA, 1995—. Mem. Comml. Law League Am. (chmn. com. 1989-94, membership chmn. 1994—), Alpha Phi (pres. Cleve. Westshore chpt. alumnae 1986-88). Republican. Methodist. Clubs: Westwood Country, Cleve. Yachting (Rocky River). Office: Am Lawyers Co 853 Westpoint Pky Ste 710 Cleveland OH 44145-1532

HAMILTON, PAMELA J., chemicals executive. Sr. v.p. human resources W.R. Grace & Co., Boca Raton, Fla. Office: WR Grace & Co One Town Center Rd Boca Raton FL 33486-1010*

HAMILTON, PHYLLIS JEAN, judge; b. Jacksonville, June 12, 1952. BA, Stanford Univ., 1974; JD cum laude, Univ. of Santa Clara Sch. of Law, 1976. Bar: Calif. 1976. Dep. state pub. defender San Francisco, Calif., 1976-80; adminstrv. judge U.S. Merit Systems Protection Bd., San Francisco, Calif., 1980-85; court commr. Oakland Mcpl. Ct., Oakland, Calif., 1985-91; magistrate judge U.S. Dist. Ct. (Calif. no. dist.), 9th circuit, San Francisco, 1991—. Mem. Nat. Assn. of Women Judges, Calif. Women Lawyers Assn., Women Lawyers of Alameda County, Charles Houston Bar Assn., Alameda County Bar Assn. Office: US Courthouse PO Box 36105 450 Golden Gate Ave Rm 15-5408 San Francisco CA 94102

HAMILTON, PHYLLIS MAE, educator; b. Negley, Ohio, Apr. 25, 1933; d. W.R. Earl and Margaret Matilda (Keeney) H. BS, Kent State U., 1968; MEd, Duquesne U., 1976. Tchr. elem. sch. So. Local Sch. Dist., Salineville, Ohio, 1963, United Local Sch. Dist., Hanoverton, Ohio, 1963-67, Broward County Sch. Dist., Ft. Lauderdale, 1968-69, Keystone Oaks Sch. Dist., Pitts., 1969—. Vol. Am. Cancer Soc., Pitts., 1996—, Am. Heart Assn., Pitts., 1992-95. Mem. AAUW, Dormont Coll. Club (pres., sec., treas. numerous coms.), Delta Kappa Gamma (pres., treas. chmn. scholar fund), Kappa Delta Pi. Presbyterian. Home: 2856 Glenmore Ave Pittsburgh PA 15216

HAMILTON, RHODA LILLIAN ROSEN, language educator, consultant; b. Chgo., May 8, 1915; d. Reinhold August and Olga (Peterson) Rosen; grad. Moser Coll., Chgo., 1932-33; BS in Edn., U. Wis., 1953, postgrad., 1976; MAT, Rollins Coll., 1967; postgrad. Ohio State U., 1959-60; postgrad. in clin. psychology Mich. State U., 1971, 76, 79, 80; postgrad. Yale U., 1972, Loma Linda U., 1972; postgrad. in computer mgmt. systems U. Okla., 1976; postgrad. in edn. U. Calif., Berkeley, 1980; m. Douglas Edward Hamilton, Jan. 23, 1936 (div. Feb. 1952); children: Perry Douglas, John Richard. Exec. sec. to pres. Ansul Chem. Co., Marinette, Wis., 1934-36; personnel counselor Burneice Larson's Med. Bur., Chgo., 1954-56 adminstrv. asst. to Ernst C. Schmidt, Lake Geneva, Wis., 1956-58; asso. prof. fin. aid Ohio State U., 1958-60; tchr. English to speakers of other langs., Istanbul, Turkey, 1960-65; counselor Groveland (Fla.) H.S., 1965-68; guidance counselor and psychol. cons. early childhood edn. Dept. Def. Overseas Dependents Sch., Okinawa, 1968-85; pres. Hamilton Assocs., Groveland, Fla., 1985—; vis. lectr. Okla. State U., 1980; co-owner plumbing, heating bus., Marinette, 1943-49; journalist Rockford (Ill.) Morning Star, 1956-58, Istanbul AP, 1960.; lectr. Lake Sumter C.C., 1989—, Lake Sumter Jr. Coll., 1989. Vol. instr. U.S. citizenship classes, Okinawa, 1971-72; judge Gold Scholarships Okinawa (Japan) Christian Schs., 1983, 84. Mem. Fla. Retired Educators, Am. Fedn. Govt. Employees, Phi Delta Gamma. Episcopalian. Clubs: Order Eastern Star (organist), Shuri chpt. One Japan, (life mem. Trillium No. 208 Wis., dual mem.), Marinette Woman's Club (Wis., pres. 1949-51), Groveland Woman's Club (Fla.). Author poetry on Middle East, 1959-64; Career Awareness, 1978. Office: Hamilton Assocs Cons 2408 Ellsworth Way #1A Frederick MD 21702

HAMILTON, RUTH HELLMANN, design company owner; b. Millboro, S.D., Oct. 15; d. Walter Otto and Laura Ethel (King) Hellmann; m. Gordon Eugene Hamilton, June 11, 1950; children: Kristin Goodnight, Bret Hamilton, Lori O'Toole, Lynnelle Anderson. AB, Nebr. Wesleyan U., Lincoln, 1948; MEd and Humanities, So. Meth. U., 1952. Owner, chief exec. officer Sonoran Desert Designs, Tucson, 1976-95; lectr. Ariz. Desert Mus., Tucson, 1985-86, Tohono Chul Mus., Tucson, 1986-95, Prescott Coll., Tucson, 1987, Tucson Bot. Gardens, 1985-95, Elderhostel, 1991-92; tchr. design student classes. Exhibited displays for Old Pueblo Mus. at Foothills Mall, 1987-90; demonstrations of desert designs Ariz. State Conv. Garden Clubs N.Mex., 1987, 89; one-woman shows at Tucson Garden Club, 1988, 90; original designs published by Nat. Coun. Garden Clubs Calendars, 1984, 87, 89, 95. Mem. pub. svcs. bd. KVOA-TV, 1969-74. Mem. Los Cerros Garden Club (pres. 1984-85, 94-95). Home: 7720 N Sendero De Juana Tucson AZ 85718-7517

HAMILTON, SHIRLEY SIEKMANN, arts administrator; b. South Bend, Ind., Aug. 31, 1928; d. George F. and Clarice B. (Rapp) Burdick; m. Max R. Siekmann, June 23, 1951; children: Sheryl, Pamela, David; m. Keith L. Hamilton, Sept. 3, 1983. Student St. Mary's Coll., 1946-47; BA, DePauw U., 1950; postgrad. Ind. U., South Bend. Tchr. public schs., St. Joseph County, Ind., 1950-51, Greencastle, Ind., 1951-52, Ft. Lauderdale, Fla., 1952-53; exec. dir. Michiana Arts and Scis. Council, Inc., South Bend, Ind., 1973-86; tech. asst. cons., adv. panelist Ind. Arts Commn.; treas. Ind. Alliance Arts Councils, 1982. Mem. St. Joseph County Parks and Recreation Bd., 1971-81, park found. bd., 1988-95; pres. Mental Health Assn. of St. Joseph County, 1972; St. Joseph County Scholarship Found., 1977-82; Community Found. of St. Joseph County, 1979-95, bd. dirs. and grant chmn.; pres., bd. dirs. United Way St. Joseph County, 1981-82; bd. dirs., spl. events chmn. Internat. Summer Spl. Olympics Games, 1986-88; bd. dirs. Firefly, 1987—, Meml. Hosp. Found., 1990—, South Bend Regional Mus. Art, 1988-95, Friends of Snite Mus. Art, Notre Dame Ind., 1989-95, Logan Ctr. Found., 1990—, Morris Civic Auditorium Bd., 1995—. Recipient Community Service award Michiana Arts and Scis. Council, 1968, Arts award, 1987, Arts Service award, Ind. Assembly of Local Arts Agys., 1987. Mem. Ind. Arts Advs., Ind. Alliance Arts Councils, Nat. Assn. Arts Councils. Club: Jr. League South Bend (pres.). Producer 13 week TV series: Inside Our Schools (Jr. League of South Bend Outstanding Community Service award 1964).

HAMILTON, VIRGINIA (MRS. ARNOLD ADOFF), author; b. Yellow Springs, Ohio, Mar. 12, 1936; d. Kenneth James and Etta Belle (Perry) H.; m. Arnold Adoff, Mar. 19, 1960; children: Leigh Hamilton, Jaime Levi. Student, Antioch Coll., 1952-55, Ohio State U., 1957-58, New Sch. for Social Research; LLD (hon.), Wright State U., Ohio. May Hill Arbuthnot honor lectr., 1992. Author: Zeely, 1967 (Nancy Block Meml. award Downtown Community Sch. Awards Com.), The House of Dies Drear, 1968 (Edgar Allan Poe award for best juvenile mystery 1969), The Time-Ago Tales of Jadhu, 1969, The Planet of Junior Brown, 1971 (John Newbery Honor Book award 1971), W. E. B. DuBois: A Biography, 1972, Time-Ago Lost: More Tales of Jahdu, 1973, M. C. Higgins, the Great, 1974 (Lewis Carroll Shelf award 1974, Boston Globe/Horn Book award 1974, John Newbery medal 1975, Nat. Book award 1975), Paul Robeson: The Life and Times of a Free Black Man, 1974, Arilla Sun Down, 1976, Illusion and Reality, 1976, Justice and Her Brothers, 1978, Jahdu, 1980, Dustland, 1980, The Gathering, 1981, Sweet Whispers, Brother Rush, 1982 (John Newbery Honor Book award 1983, Coretta Scott King award 1983, Boston Globe/Horn Book award 1983, Am. Book award nomination 1983), The Magical

Adventures of Pretty Pearl, 1983, Willie Bea and the Time the Martians Landed, 1983, A Little Love, 1984 (Horn Book Fanfare award 1985), Junius Over Far, 1985, The People Could Fly: American Black Folktales, 1985 (Coretta Scott King award 1986, N.Y. Times Best Illustrated Children's Book award 1986), The Mystery of Drear House, 1987, A White Romance, 1987, In the Beginning: Creation Stories from Around the World, 1988 (John Newbery Honor Book award 1989), Anthony Burns: The Defeat and Triumph of a Fugitive Slave, 1988 (Boston Globe/Horn Book award 1988, Coretta Scott King award 1989), The Bells of Christmas, 1989, The Dark Way: Stories from the Spirit World, 1990, Cousins, 1990, The All Jahdu Storybook, 1991, Many Thousands Gone, 1992, Plain City, 1993, Jaguarundi, 1994, Her Story: African American Folktales. 1995; editor: The Writings of W. E. B. DuBois, 1975. Recipient Ohioana Lit. award, 1969, 84, Ohioana Lit. award for body of work, 1981, Regina medal Cath. Libr. Assn., 1990, Hans Christian Andersen award nomination, 1992, Laura Ingalls Wilder medal ALA, 1995, John D. and Catherine T. MacArthur Genius award fellow, 1995. Address: care Arnold Adoff Agy PO Box 293 Yellow Springs OH 45387-0293

HAMIN, AMY LYNN, speech and language pathologist; b. Stevens Point, Wis., Nov. 6, 1961; d. David John and Marilyn C. (Dorn) Jacobs; m. Jody Arthur Hamin, July 13, 1985; 1 child, Cody Jacob. BS, U. Wis., Stevens Point, 1984, MS, 1985. Cert. in speech and lang. pathology. Speech/lang. pathologist Marshfield (Wis.) Sch. Dist., 1986-92, Wisconsin Rapids (Wis.) Pub. Schs., 1992—; varsity cheerleader coach John Edwards H.S., Port Edwards, Wis., 1995—; evaluator, diagnostician, cons. Augmentative Comm. Tech. Team, Wisconsin Rapids, 1992—; provider speech/lang. svcs. Mem. Am. Speech/Lang./Hearing Assn. Lutheran. Home: 1454 A County JJ Nekoosa WI 54457

HAMLER, SHELLEY JEFFERSON, administrator; b. Cin., Oct. 22, 1951; d. Browne Elliott and Elizabeth Sanfré (Showes) Jefferson. BS in Edn., Ohio State U., 1972; MEd, Xavier U., 1974; EdD, U. Cin., 1995. Tchr. Cutter Jr. High Sch., Cin., 1972-76, Woodward High Sch., Cin., 1976-82; coord. Cin. Pub. Schs., 1982-86, local sch. evaluator, 1986, asst. prin., 1986-88, prin., 1988-94, dir. career paths, 1994—. Mem. NAACP (life), Nat. Alliance of Black Sch. Educators (life), Urban League, The Links Inc. (Cin. chpt.), Delta Sigma Theta, Delta Kappa Gamma (scholar 1994-95). Office: Cin Pub Schs PO Box 5381 Cincinnati OH 45201-5381

HAMLIN, LISA KATHLEEN, librarian; b. Nashville, Mar. 8, 1962; d. James William Hamlin and Louise Margaret (Reid) Cox. BS, Belmont U., 1983; MLS, Vanderbilt U., 1985; PhD in Metaphys. Sci., Progressive Universal Life Ch., 1995; PhD in Parapsychology, P.U.L.C., 1995, DD (hon.), 1995; BMSc., U. Metaphysics, 1995, MMSc, 1996. Ordained metaphys. minister Internat. Metaphys. Ministry, 1995. Grad. asst. to dir. edn. libr. Vanderbilt U., Nashville, 1984-85; cataloging libr. Shiloh Regional Libr., Jackson, Tenn., 1985-86; various temp. positions Nashville, 1986; sch. libr. Mt. Juliet (Tenn.) Elem. Sch., 1987-89; tech. svcs. libr. Brentwood (Tenn.) Libr., 1990—. Contbr. poetry to anthologies At Water's Edge, 1995 (Editor's Choice award), The Best Poems of 1996, 1996, Poetic Voices of America, 1996. Ch. pianist, asst. choir dir., Sunday sch. tchr. Nashville Bapt. Temple, 1977-84. Mem. ALA (mem. audivisual roundtable 1985-86), Tenn. Libr. Assn., Chronic Fatigue and Immune Dysfunction Syndrome Soc., Interstitial Cystitis Assn., Assn. Rsch. and Enlightenment, Nat. Wildlife Fedn., Humane Soc. U.S., Nature Conservancy, People for Ethical Treatment of Animals, Sierra Club, Am. Heart Assn., Nat. Audubon Soc., AMFAR. Home: 4853 Cimarron Way Antioch TN 37013 Office: Brentwood Libr 5055 Maryland Way Brentwood TN 37027

HAMLIN, SONYA B., communications specialist; b. N.Y.C.; d. Julius and Sarah (Saltzman) Borenstein; m. Bruce Hamlin (dec. 1977); children: Ross, Mark (dec. 1992), David. BS, MA, N.Y.U.; HLD (hon.), Notre Dame Coll., 1970. Host arts program Sta. WHDH-TV, Boston, 1963-65; host, prodr., writer (syndicated PBS program) Meet the Arts Sta. WGBH-TV, Boston, 1965-68; cultural reporter Sta. WBZ-TV, Boston, 1968-71, TV host, producer The Sonya Hamlin Show, 1970-75; host, producer Sunday Open House program Sta. WCVB-TV, Boston, 1976-80; host, producer, writer Speak Up and Listen program Lifetime Cable Network, N.Y.C., 1982-84; pres. Sonya Hamlin Communications, Boston and N.Y.C., 1977—, Different Drummer Prodns., N.Y.C., 1982-86; pvt. comm. cons., U.S., Can., and Europe, 1977—; adj. lectr. Harvard Grad. Sch., Edn., Cambridge, Mass., 1974-76, Harvard Law Sch., 1977-81, Kennedy Sch. Govt., Harvard U., 1978-79; adj. asst. prof. Boston U. Med. Sch., 1977-80; mem. faculty Nat. Inst. Trial Advocacy, South Bend, Ind., 1977—, U.S. Dept. Justice, Washington, 1979-87, ABA, Chgo., 1979—; chmn. Law/Video Co., N.Y.C. and Waltham, Mass., 1987-92; comm. cons., weekly and weekend performer Today in NY (NBC), 1995—; daily panelist O.J. Today (Fox), 1995-96. Author: What Makes Juries Listen, 1985, How to Talk So People Listen, 1988, What Makes Juries Listen Today, 1996; prodr., dir., writer (films) China" Different Path, 1979 (Emmy nominee), Paul Revere: What Makes a Hero, 1976, others; contbr. articles to numerous profl. jours. Active Gov. Commn. Status of Women, Mass., 1973-83; campaign co-chair Mass. ERA Campaign, 1975-76; cons. Gov. Michael Dukakis, 1978, Dem. Nat. Party, Washington, 1979; bd. dirs. mem. Nat. Vol. Action com. United Way, Washington, 1986-91; bd. dirs. Taubman Ctr. Kennedy Sch. Harvard U., 1989-95. Recipient Best Program award for Meet the Arts Internat. Ednl. TV Assn., Tokyo, 1969, Ohio State Cultural Reporting award, 1970; named Outstanding Broadcaster New Eng. Broadcasters, Boston, 1973; Sonya Hamlin Day named in her honor Mayor of Boston, 1974.; archive of her works established Boston U. Library, 1983. Mem. Am. Fedn. TV and Radio Artists, Nat. Acad. TV Arts and Scis. (two Emmy nominations).

HAMM, MARIEL MARGARET, soccer player; b. Selma, Ala., Mar. 17, 1972; m. Christian Corry. BS in Polit. Sci., U. N.C., 1994. Named U.S. Soccer Female Athlete of Yr., 1994-95, MVP of U.S. Women's Cup, 1995; recipient Gold medal Atlanta Olympics, 1996. Office: US Soccer Fedn US Soccer House 1801-1811 S Prairie Ave Chicago IL 60616*

HAMMACK, GLADYS LORENE MANN, reading specialist, educator; b. Corsicana, Tex., Nov. 15, 1923; d. John Elisha and Maude (Kelly) Mann; m. Charles Joseph Hammack; Sept. 4, 1949;children: Charles Randall, Cynthia Lorain, Kelly Joseph. B in Journalism, U. Tex., 1953; elem. tchr. cert., U. Houston, 1970, MEd, 1974, cert. reading specialist, 1974. Cert. profl. reading specialist, Tex. Tchr. Zion Luth. Sch., Pasadena, Tex., 1964-68, Housman Elem. Sch., Houston, 1970-74, Pine Shadows Elem. Sch., Houston, 1975-76; reading lab. tchr. Spring Br. High Sch., Houston, 1976-82; tchr. St. Mark Luth. Sch., Houston, 1982-88, pvt. tutor and homework study hall tchr., 1988—; mem. Spring Br. Ind. Sch. Dist. Textbook Selection Com., Houston, 1973; field rep. to. student tchrs., U. Houston, 1974; presenter reading workshop, U. Tex., Austin, 1983. Author: (guide) Evaluation of Textbooks, 1974. Del. Tex. Dem. Conv., Austin, 1960. Recipient scholarship, U. Tex. Sports Assn., Austin, 1947. Mem. Tex. State Tchrs. Assn., Tex. Ret. Tchrs. Assn. Lutheran. Home: 8926 Theysen Dr Houston TX 77080-3023

HAMMACK, JULIA DIXON, music educator; b. Sturgis, Ky., Oct. 11, 1913; d. Augustus Rees and Ethel Lisle (McKeaig) H. B Music Edn., Murray State U., 1937; M Music Edn., Am. Conservatory Music, 1943. Cert. tchr. (life). Vocal and instrumental dir. grades 1-12 Dixon (Ky.) Schs., 1937-41; vocal supr.-dir. grades 1-12 Claksville (Tenn.) Schs., 1941-45; piano tchr., choir dir. Union U., Jackson, Tenn., 1945-47; piano tchr. Tift Coll. Women, Forsyth, Ga., 1947-51; program dir. U.S. Army, Stutgart, Germany, 1952-54; asst. prof. Wis. State U., 1955-59; pvt. piano tchr., 1937-93; ch. choir dir. Salem Luth. Ch., Indpls., 1983-90, 1st Bapt. Ch., Forsyth, 1947-51. Fin. supporter Am. Pianist Assn., 1992-95, Indpls. Symphony Orch., 1980-96. Mem. Matinee Musicale (profl. assoc.), St. Teresa's Guild (corr. sec. 1990-96), Sigma Alpha Iota (Indpls. alumnae chpt., life, corr. sec., editor 1986-96, Rose of Honor 1990). Democrat. Episcopalian. Home: Apt 408 2625 N Meridian St Indianapolis IN 46208-7701

HAMMARGREN, MARJORIE DOLORES, printing company executive; b. Watertown, S.D., July 6; d. Edward Richard and Elizabeth Christina (Mach) H. Student, U. Minn., 1983-85. Clk.-treas. City of Kilkenny, Minn., 1970-84; sec. Hammargren Printing Co., Kilkenny, 1956-70, gen. mgr., owner, 1970—; designer floral arrangements Waseca (Minn.) Greenhouse, 1956-68. Author: History of Church of St. Canice, 1954; exhibited art, photography, crafts, 1968—, including Sister Kenny Internat. Arts Fair for People with Disabilities, Mpls., Le Sueur County Fair, Le Center, Minn. Del. Rep. county, dist. and state convs., Minn., 1976—; vice chmn. Le Sueur County Rep. Com., 1988—; mem. bd. Minn. Coun. on Disability, St. Paul, 1993—, Faribault deanery Coun. Cath. Women, 1964-75, S.W. deanery, 1975—; speaker on Ams. with Disabilities Act and spl. needs of people with disabilities. Recipient U.S. Bicentennial citation Gov. of Minn., 1976, leadership award St. Paul and Mpls. Archdiocesan Coun. Cath. Women, 1978, award S.W. Deanery Coun. Cath. Women, 1978, cert. and pin Minn. Clks. and Fin. Officers Assn., 1985, social justice disability award Archdiocesan Cath. Charities, 1994, Good Neighbor award Sta. WCCO, 1994; named one of 59 Minnesotan "Community Heros" Torchbearers for the Olympic Flame, Rochester, 1996. Mem. Am. Legion Aux. (pres. Kilkenny 1993-94), St. Canice Rosary Soc. (pres. 1988-89), Le Sueur County Old Settlers Assn., Le Sueur County Hist. Soc. (life), Daus. Union Vets. Civil War, Caths. United for Spiritual Action, Cmty. and Sportsman Club.

HAMMER, BARBARA JEAN, film maker, media artist; b. L.A., May 15, 1939; d. John Wilber and Marian (Kusz) H. BA in Psychology, UCLA, 1961; MA in English Lit., San Francisco State U., 1963, MA in Film, 1975. Cert. jr. coll. tchr., Calif. Mem. grad. faculty media studies New Sch. for Social Rsch., N.Y.C., 1994—; mem. documentary jury Sundance Film Festival, Park City, Utah, 1994; pres. jury The Yamagata Internat. Documentary Film Festival, Japan, 1995. Documentary films include: Dyke Tactics, 1974, Jane Brakhage, 1975, Double Strength, 1978, Women I Love, 1976, Arequipa, 1981, Pools, 1981, Sync Touch, 1981, Pond and Waterfall, 1982, Audience, 1983, Bent Time, 1984, Optic Nerve, 1985 (Ann Arbor Film Festival First prize, Bucks County Film Festival First prize, Onion City Film Festival award), No No Nooky T.V., 1987 (Ann Arbor Film Festival award 1987, Humboldt Film Festival Arcata award 1987), Place Mattes, 1988, Endangered, 1988 (Black Mariah Film Festival First prize, Bucks County Film Festival First prize), Still Point, 1989, Sancutus, 1990 (San Francisco Internat. Film Fest award 1991, Ann Arbor Film Festival award 1991, Balt. Film/Video Festival 2d prize 1991), Vital Signs, 1991 (Video Art award Soc. Encouragement of Contemporary Art-San Francisco, Utah Film/Video Festival Best Exptl. Film 1991, Calif. State Fair Award of Excellence 1992, Black Mariah Film/Video Festival Juror's award 1992), Nitrate Kisses, 1995 (Audience award Madrid Internat. Women Dirs. Festival), Tender Fictions, 1996 (Isabella Liddell Art award Ann Arbor Film Festival 1996, Dir.'s Choice award Charlotte Film and Video Festival 1996). Western Media Regional grantee Film Prodn., 1988, 90, Film Prodn. grantee NEA, 1990, Film Prodn. grantee Am. Film Inst., 1992; recipient John D. Phelan award for experimental filmmaking, 1988, John D. Phelan award for video art, 1990. Mem. Assn. Ind. Film/Video N.Y.C. (bd. dirs. 1990—, advocacy chair 1990—). Democrat. Office: 55 Bethune St # 114G New York NY 10014

HAMMER, BONNIE, broadcast executive. V.p. current programs USA Networks, N.Y.C. Office: USA Networks 1230 Avenue of the Americas New York NY 10020*

HAMMER, DEBORAH MARIE, librarian; b. Bronx, N.Y., Nov. 16, 1947; d. Ben and Helen (Lorenz) Halprin; m. Mark Stewart Hammer, May 30, 1976; 1 child, Joshua Robert. BA, CCNY, 1968; MLS, Rutgers U., 1969. Cert. libr. N.Y. Gen. asst. info., tel. ref. div. Queens Borough Pub. Libr., 1969-71, gen. asst. popular libr., 1972-80; asst. div. head history, travel & biography Queens Borough Pub. Libr., Jamaica, N.Y., 1972-81; div. head history, travel & biography Queens Borough Pub. Libr., 1981-92, div. mgr. social scis., 1992—. Libr. Temple Emanuel, New Hyde Park, N.Y., 1987. Democrat. Office: Queens Borough Pub Libr 89-11 Merrick Blvd Jamaica NY 11432-5200

HAMMER, KATHERINE GONET, software company executive; b. Shreveport, La., Jan. 5, 1946; d. Joseph Peter and Bernice Evelyn (Post) Gonet; m. Gael Warren Hammer, May 25, 1965 (div.); children: Katherine Elizabeth, Evelyn Alice; m. Ronald R. Scott, Feb. 14, 1982. BA in English, U. Iowa, 1967, MA in Linguistics, 1969, PhD in English Linguistics, 1973. Asst. prof. Coe Coll., Cedar Rapids, Iowa, 1973-75; assoc. prof. in linguistics Wash. State U., Pullman, 1975-80; vis. scholar Ctr. for Cognitive Sci. U. Tex., Austin, 1980-81; software devel. mgr. Tex. Instruments, Austin, 1981-84; mem. tech. staff Microelectronics and Computer Tech. Corp., Austin, 1984-90; pres., chief exec. officer Evolutionary Techs. Internat., Inc., Austin, 1991—. Office: Evolutionary Techs Inc 4301 Westbank Dr Ste 100 Austin TX 78746-6546

HAMMER, MARION PRICE, association administrator; b. Columbia, S.C., Apr. 26, 1939; 3 children. Chmn. legis. policy com. NRA, Fairfax, Va., pres. Registered lobbyist for pro-gun issues. Recipient Harlon B. Carter Legis. Achievement award, 1992, SCOPE ann. 2d Amendment award, 1987, Roy Rogers Man of Yr. award, Outstanding Cmty. Svc. award Nat. Safety Coun., 1993, Nat. Edn. award Am. Legion. Mem. NRA (life, cert. firearms instr., chmn. task force on hunter safety legislation, vice chmn. women's policies com., mem. nominating com., pub. affairs com., ethics com., membership coms.), Unified Sportsmen of Fla. (exec. dir. 1978—). Office: NRA 11250 Waples Mill Rd Fairfax VA 22030

HAMMER, SIGNE, writer, editor, consultant; b. Indpls., Aug. 31, 1940; d. John Jacob and Agnes Gudrun Hammer. BA, Wellesley Coll., 1963. Editl. asst. Atlantic Monthly Press, Boston, 1963-65; asst. editor Harper & Row, N.Y.C., 1965-69; freelance journalist, writer, N.Y.C., 1969-84; sr. editor Sci. Digest, N.Y.C., 1984-86; freelance writer, editor, cons. Readers Digest, MetLife, N.Y.C., 1986—; adj. assoc. prof. creative writing NYU, N.Y.C., 1976-88. Author: Women: Body and Culture: Essays on the Sexuality of Women in a Changing Society, 1975, Daughters and Mothers: Mothers and Daughters, 1975, paperback edit., 1976, reissued 1979 (Lit. Guild alt.), Passionate Attachments: Fathers and Daughters in America Today, 1982, By Her Own Hand: Memoirs of a Suicide's Daughter, 1991, paperback edit., 1992 (N.Y. Times Book Rev. Notable Book of Yr. 1991, New and Noteworthy Book); contbg. author: Pleasures: Women Write Erotica, 1984, Erotic Interludes: Tales Told by Women, 1986, Strange Stories, Amazing Facts of America's Past, 1989, Practical Problem Solver, 1991; contbr. articles to Travel/Holiday, Harper's Bazaar, McCall's, Mademoiselle, Playgirl, Working Woman, Ms., Parade, Perspectives on Tech., Sci. Digest, Health, Fiction, New Eng. Rev., Rapport, also newspapers. Active Angry Arts, N.Y.C., 1966-68, N.Y. Radical Feminists, N.Y.C., 1968-71, Get Smart, N.Y.C., 1991-92. Mem. Authors Guild, PEN Am. Ctr., Writers Room. Democrat. Office: care The Writers Room 10 Astor Pl New York NY 10003

HAMMER, SUSAN W., mayor; b. Monrovia, Calif., Dec. 21, 1938; d. James Nathan and Katrine (Krutzsch) Walker; m. Philip Hammer, Sept. 4, 1960; children: Philip, Hali, Matthew. BA in History, U. Calif., Berkeley, 1960. Svc. rep. Pacific Telephone Co., Berkeley, 1960-61; staff asst. Peace Corps, Washington, 1962-63; councilwoman City of San Jose, Calif., 1980-81, 83-90, spl. asst. to mayor, 1981-82, vice mayor, 1985-87, mayor, 1991—. Bd. dirs. San Jose Mus. Art, 1971-90, pres., 1978-80; mem. governing bd. NCCJ, 1978—; mem. adv. bd. Cmty. Found. Santa Clara County, 1978—; mem. Santa Clara County Transp. Com., 1976-77, Santa Clara County Juvenile Justice Commn., 1980, Victim-Witness Adv. Bd., 1977-90, Children's Health Coun., San Jose, 1981-89, Santa Clara Valley Leadership Program, 1986-90, Childrens Shelter Project, 1991—, Am. Leadership Forum, 1992—; past chmn. parents adv. com. Trace Sch.; chair Pres.' Adv. Com. on Trade Policy and Negotiation; mem. San Jose Fine Arts Commn., 1980. Recipient Rosalie M. Stern Community Svc. award U. Calif., 1975, Disting. Citizen of San Jose award Exch. Club, 1979, Investment in Leadership award Coro Found., 1985, Tzedek award for honor, compassion and community svc. Temple Emanu-El, 1987, Recognition award YWCA, Santa Clara County, 1989, resolution of commendation Assn. for Responsible Alcohol Control, 1990, Woman of Achievement award The Women's Fund, 1990, Dox Quixote award Nat. Hispanic U., 1991, Friends of Bay Area Mcpl. Elections Com. award, 1991. Democrat. Office: Office of Mayor 801 N 1st St Rm 600 San Jose CA 95110-1704

HAMMERSCHMIDT, MARILYN KAY, health services administrator; b. Belpre, Kans., Mar. 28, 1944; d. Lawrence Ferdinand and Frances Elizabeth (Schmitt) Koett; m. Harold Francis Hammerschmidt, Dec. 1, 1973; children: Kevin Frances, Brian James. BSN, St. Mary of the Plains Coll., 1969. RN, Colo., Kans. Staff nurse Great Bend (Kans.) Med. Ctr., 1967-68; relief charge nurse St. Anthony's Hosp., Dodge City, Kans., 1968-69; county health nurse Pawnee County Health Dept., Larned, Kans., 1969-71; pub. health nurse Wichita (Kans.) Sedge County Health Dept., 1971-72; relief charge nurse orthopaedics Wesley Med. Ctr., Wichita, 1972-73; home health nurse St. Frances Home Health, Grand Island, Nebr., 1976-77; evening charge nurse orthopaedics-pediats. Ft. Hamilton Hughes Hosp., Hamilton, Ohio, 1984-88; nursing supr. home health Am. Nursing Care, Cin., 1988-92; dir. health svcs. Lakewood (Colo.) Meridian Retirement Comty., 1992—; mem. nursing adv. bd. Red Rocks C.C., Denver, 1994, 95. Author: (tape) Care of Death and Dying, 1991. Democrat. Roman Catholic. Home: 8970 W Portland Ave Littleton CO 80123-8011

HAMMERSTROM, BEVERLY SWOISH, state representative; b. Mineral Wells, Tex., Mar. 28, 1944; d. William Graham and Marjorie Wirth (Lillis) Swoish; m. Don Preston Hammerstrom, June 25, 1966 (div. Oct. 1976); children: Todd Preston, Rory Scott. BA, Adrian Coll., 1966; MPA, U. Toledo, 1994. Cert. mcpl. clk. Tchr. Geneva (N.Y.) Pub. Schs., 1966-69; substitute tchr. Darien (Wis.) Pub. Schs., 1970-71; tchr. Bedford Coop. Nursery Sch., Lambertville, Mich., 1975; retail mgr., buyer Gallerie, Toledo, 1975-78, Personal Touch, Toledo, 1978-80; clk. Bedford Township, Temperance, Mich., 1980-92; state rep. State of Mich., Lansing, 1993—; bd. dirs. Family Med. Ctr., Temperance; emergency mgmt. bd. Washtenaw County, Ypsilanti, Mich., 1993—, Monroe (Mich.) County, 1993—. Mem. IIMC Found. (bd. dirs. 1996), Mich. Assn. Clks. (life, pres. 1990-91), Am. Legis. Exch. Coun. (transp. task force), Coun. State Govt. (med. policies com., del. 1995—), Women in Govt. Republican. Roman Catholic. Home: 1183 Oakmont Dr Temperance MI 48182-9563 Office: Mich Ho Rep PO Box 30014 Lansing MI 48909-7514

HAMMERT, DOROTHY SAVAGE, investment company executive; b. Hartshorne, Okla.; d. Eugene Bertrand and Lillian Vivian (Graves) Savage; m. Walter Scott Hammert Jr., Sept. 2, 1972; children: Diane Welker, Cindy Heinze, Warren, June. BA in English, U. Okla., 1951. Cert. profl. sec. Sr. sec. Stanolind Oil and Gas Co., Oklahoma City, Okla., 1951-58, Pan Am. Petroleum Corp., Oklahoma City, Okla., 1963-67; exec. sec. to chmn. of bd., chief exec. officer Benham-Blair and Affiliates, Oklahoma City, Okla., 1967-81; dist. mgr., area ednl. cons. World Book Ednl. Products, Oklahoma City, Okla., 1987-95; owner Practical Publishing Co., Oklahoma City, Okla., 1991—. Author: Rights are Responsibilities, 1991. V.p. Oklahoma City chpt. Freedoms Found. at Valley Forge, 1991-92; pres. Okla. Mother's Assn., 1996. Named Sec. of Yr. Nat. Secs. Assn., 1979, Okla. Mother's Assn. Mother of Yr., 1994. Mem. Am. Bus. Women's Assn. (yearbook chmn. 1991), Synergy Bus. Group (pres. 1987-88, 94-95), Women's Bus. Network (membership chmn. 1991), Joie de Vie Club (pres. 1993-94), Psi Psi Psi (pres. 1979-80, 93-95), Alpha Chi Omega (sect. chmn. 1987-88). Republican. Episcopalian. Home: 1616 Westminster Pl Oklahoma City OK 73120-1230 Office: Practical Pub Co 1616 Westminster Pl Oklahoma City OK 73120-1230

HAMMES, THERESE MARIE, advertising, public relations and marketing executive; b. Chgo., Mar. 27, 1955; d. Howard John and Lorna Marie (Jeans) H. BFA with honors, U. Miami, Coral Gables, Fla., 1976; MBA in Internat. Bus., St. Thomas U., Miami, 1992. Lic. real estate broker, Fla. Pres. Hammes Advt. Agy., Coral Gables, Fla., 1978—; pres., broker Hammes Realty Mgmt. Corp., Coral Gables, 1986—; pres. Pro-Motion Media, Inc., Coral Gables, 1990-92; external bank dir. 1st Fla. Savings, FSB, 1990-93; v.p. Ponce de Leon Devel. Assn., Coral Gables, 1990-91, bd. dirs. One-woman show includes U. Miami, Fla., 1975; juried art show Lowe Art Mus., 1976, Internat. Erotic Art Show, Miami Beach, 1995. Bd. dirs. Young Dems., Dade County, 1982-86; del. Fla. Dem. Conv., 1995; mem. fin. com. Dade County Dem. Party Exec. Com., 1995; landlord Dade County Dem. Party, 1995—; trustee Miami Youth Mus., 1990-94, bd. dirs., 1994—; mem. Leadership Miami, 1988—, mem. exec. com., co-chair commn., 1990—, chair pub. rels. and comms. com., 1991-93; bd. dirs. Crime Stoppers, 1992—; mem. home enthusiast panel Home & Gardens Remodeling Ideas mag. Named Miss Minn. Coun. of State Socs., 1975, Valley Forge Freedom Found. scholar, 1971; recipient Fla. award for mktg. excellence in best print campaign Best Corp. Campaign, Best Print Ad, Best Spl. Event, Best Collateral, 1989, 1991 Up and Comer award for advt. Price Waterhouse/South Fla. Mag., 1991. Mem. Nat. Assn. Women Bus. Owners (pub. rels. chmn. 1985-89), Builders Assn. South Fla. (editor, publisher 1986-87), Advt. Fedn. Greater Miami, Coral Gables C. of C., Greater Miami C. of C., Orange Key, Alpha Lambda Delta. Democrat. Home: 460 Hardee Rd Coral Gables FL 33146-3555 Office: Hammes Advt Inc 896 S Dixie Hwy Coral Gables FL 33146-2604

HAMMETT, CHARLOTTE KAYE, communications educator; b. Glasgow, Ky., Mar. 4, 1952. BA in Speech and Theatre, Western Ky. U., 1974, MA in Speech and Theatre, 1979; MFA in Acting, U. Louisville, 1987; postgrad., U. Ky., 1991. Tchr., chair dept. speech & theatre Lindsey Wilson Coll., Columbia, Ky., 1981-83; tchr. basic pub. speaking, acting U. Louisville, 1984-87; endl. theatre leader, acting intern Ark. Repertory Theatre, Little Rock, 1988; adj. faculty Spalding U., Louisville, 1989—; assoc. prof., program coord. comms. dept. Jefferson C.C., Louisville, 1989—; profl. trainer Group W Comm., 1990—, Hammett Comms. Ky. Found. for Women grantee; Devel. grantee Ky. Arts Coun. Cmty. Arts, 1996. Mem. NOW, ASTD, AFTRA, Speech Comm. Assn., South East Theatre Conf., Actors Equity (cand.), Performing Arts League Louisville, U. Louisville Coll. Arts and Scis. Alumni, Pleiades Theatre Co. (founder, bd. dirs., actor, dir.).

HAMMOND, ANNA JOSEPHINE, nurse practitioner; b. Cumberland, Md., Sept. 16, 1938; d. Ernest Morton and Helen Grace (Hamilton) Wolford; m. Harold Allan Hammond, Oct. 3, 1959; 1 child, Norma Lee. Diploma, Sacred Heart Hosp. Sch. Nsg., 1959; postgrad., U. Md., 1979. RN, Md.; cert. nurse practitioner. Office nurse Ralph W. Ballin, MD, Cumberland; staff nurse Sacred Heart Hosp., Cumberland, 1963-67, head nurse ICU, critical care nurse, 1967-70, nurse practitioner emergency dept., 1978-90; nurse practitioner Seton Med. Clinic, 1990-93, Hampshire Meml. Hosp. and Elk Garden Rural Health Clinic, 1993—. Mem. ANA, Md. Nurses Assn., Coun. Nurse Practitioners, Am. Acad. Nurse Practitioners, Sacred Heart Hosp. Alumni Assn. Home: 5 Lakeside Loop Ridgeley WV 26753-9730

HAMMOND, DEANNA LINDBERG, linguist; b. Calgary, Alta., Can., May 31, 1942; d. Albin William and Emma Lou (Thompson) Lindberg; m. Jerome J. Hammond, 1968 (div. 1980). B.A., Wash. State U., 1964; M.A., Ohio U., 1968; Ph.D., Georgetown U., 1977; student summer sch., U. Ariz., Guadalajara, Portland State U. With Peace Corps., Colombia, 1964-66; prof. English Universidad Industrial, Bucaramanga, Colombia, 1966-67; tchr. English, Spanish Pullman High Sch., Wash., 1969-74; lectr. Georgetown U., Washington, 1974-77; dir. summer sch. program Georgetown U., Quito, Ecuador, 1977; head lang. services Congl. Research Services Library of Congress, Washington, 1977—; part-time faculty George Mason U.; mem. adv. bd. traduction, terminologie, redaction U. Que., Can.; pres. Interlingua Inst., Westchester, N.Y. Translator: Psychological Operations in Guerrilla Warfare. Active Friends of Colombia. Recipient Community Service award Sec. Califano, 1978. Mem. Am. Translators Assn. (guest editor ATA Scholarly Monograph series 1994, Gode medal 1992, past pres.), Nat. Peace Corps Assn., Returned Peace Corps Vols. Washington, Libr. Congress Profl. Assn., Libr. Congress Hispanic Cultural Soc., Assn. for Machine Translation in Ams. (bylaws com., edn. com.), Am. Assn. Tchrs. Spanish and Portuguese, Mid-Am. Translators Assn. (life, chmn. nominating com. 1994), Zonta Internat. (former pres. Alexandria club, mem. scholarship com., internat. rels. com., bd. dirs., del. internat. conv. Detroit 1994, dist. 3 internat. rels. com. chmn. 1996—), Carolina Assn. Translators and Interpreters, Phi Beta Kappa. Democrat. Home: 3560 S George Mason Dr Alexandria VA 22302-1034 Office: Libr of Congress Congl Rsch Lang Svcs Washington DC 20540

HAMMOND, DEBBIE JOHNSON, computer analyst; b. Shelbyville, Ky., June 21, 1957; d. Shirley De Rice Johnson and Charlotte Jane (White) Groves; m. Fred Franklin Hammond, June 27, 1987. BA in Polit. Sci., Ky. State U., 1987. Program coord. Commonwealth of Ky., Frankfort, 1976—. Mem. Ky. Human Svcs. Agy., TenUre (nominating com. 1982—).

Democrat. Baptist. Home: 433 Inman St Harrodsburg KY 40330 Office: Commonwealth of Ky 275 E Main St Frankfort KY 40621

HAMMOND, DEBORAH ELLEN, health facility administrator; b. Cleve., July 15, 1951; d. Edward James and Virginia (Dommermuth) H.; m. David Lawrence Emanuel, Nov. 24, 1979; 1 child, Leah Helen. BS, Emory U., 1973; MD, U. Okla., 1977. Diplomate Am. Bd. Internal Medicine. Staff physician Cmty. Health Plan Suffolk, Hauppauge, N.Y., 1980-82; med. dir. Take Care of Okla., Tulsa, 1983-86; from med. dir. to v.p. med. svcs. Prudential Ins. Co. Am., Houston, 1986-93; exec. dir. PruCare of N.Y., PruCare of N.J., Suffern, 1993-96, v.p. med. sys., 1996—. Home: 668 Alanon Rd Ridgewood NJ 07450-5326

HAMMOND, DEBORAH LYNN, lay worker; b. Olney, Md., Feb. 12, 1958; d. Cornelius Dennis Sr. and Beverly Laura (Dunn) H. AA in Gen. Studies, Catonsville C.C. Sec. Mt. Zion United Meth. Ch., Ellicott City, Md., 1980—; with Balt. Gas Electric Co., Pasadena, Md.; sec. The Md. Correctional Instn. for Women, Jessup, Md., 1995—. Chaplain, vol. activity coord. sec. Md. Correctional Instn. Women, 1995; choir dir. Falls Road AME Ch., 1995—; instr. adult edn. Milford Mill H.S. Home: 3668-D Mount Ida Dr Ellicott City MD 21043-4537 Office: Md Correctional Instn Women 7943 Brockbridge Rd Jessup MD 20794-9999

HAMMOND, DEBRA A., accountant; b. Worcester, Mass., Nov. 23, 1966; d. Robert Daniel and Janet Madeline (Ferrandino) H. BSBA, Worcester State Coll., 1989; MBA, Nichols Coll., 1995. Office mgr. Hall Bros., Inc., West Boylston, Mass., 1989-91; asst. contr. Worcester Regional Transit Authority, 1991-93, grants/contracts coord., 1993—. Mem. Inst. Mgmt. Accts. (dir. Worcester chpt. 1994, v.p. Worcester chpt. 1995, pres.-elect Worcester chpt. 1996).

HAMMOND, JANE LAURA, retired law librarian, lawyer; b. nr. Nashua, Iowa; d. Frank D. and Pauline (Flint) H. BA, U. Dubuque, 1950; MS, Columbia U., 1952; JD, Villanova U., 1965, LHD, 1993. Bar: Pa. 1965. Cataloguer Harvard Law Libr., 1952-54; asst. libr. Sch. Law Villanova (Pa.) U., 1954-62; libr. Sch. Law, Villanova (Pa.) U., 1962-76, prof. law, 1965-76; law libr., prof. law Cornell U., Ithaca, N.Y., 1976-93; adj. prof. Drexel U., 1971-74; mem. depository libr. coun. to pub. printer U.S. Govt. Printing Office, 1975-78; cons. Nat. Law Libr., Monrovia, Liberia, 1989. Fellow ALA; mem. ABA (coun. sect. legal edn. 1984-90, mem. com. on accreditation 1982-87, mem. com. on stds. rev. 1987-95), PEO, Coun. Nat. Libr. Assn. (sec.-treas. 1971-72, chmn. 1979-80), Am. Assn. Law Librs. (sec. 1965-70, pres. 1975-76). Episcopalian. Office: Cornell Law Sch Myron Taylor Hall Ithaca NY 14853

HAMMOND, KAREN SMITH, marketing professional, paralegal; b. Baton Rouge, Dec. 20, 1954; d. James Wilbur Smith and Carolyn (May) Carper; m. Ralph Edwin Hammond, Dec. 17, 1985. Student, La. State U., 1973-75, Colo. Women's Coll., 1976; BJ, U. Colo., 1978; cert. paralegal, U. Tex., 1981. Newspaper reporter Lakewood (Colo.) Sentinel, 1978; paralegal Office U.S. Atty. No. Dist. Tex.; sales rep. Arlington Citizen Jour. newspaper, 1979-80; legal asst. Oscar H. Mauzy Atty.-at-Law, Dallas, 1981; editor Ennis (Tex.) Press, 1981-82; sales rep. VEU Subscription TV, Dallas, 1983-84; comml. account rep. U.S. Telecom, Dallas, 1984; with The Movie Channel/ Showtime, 1985; mktg. rep. Allnet Comm., Dallas, 1985-87, ChemLawn Svcs. Inc., Plano, Tex., 1992, Accuroof, 1994, Diversified Info. Svcs., Plano, 1994, Elite Roofing, Plano, 1994—; owner Smith, Hammond & Assocs., Dallas, 1986; advt. sales rep. Legal Asst. Today Mag., 1987; sales rep. Telecable Inc., Richardson, Tex., 1988-91; account exec. Brewer Comm., Carrollton, Tex., 1988-89, Plano (Tex.) Cellular, 1989-90; triex agt. Pkwy. Pontiac, Dallas, 1983-86; free lance writer Dallas Metro mag., 1991—. Bus. writer Mid-Cities Daily News, 1981. Campaign mgr. Mark Bielamowicz for Mayor, Cedar Hill, Tex., 1979; active campaigns Martin Frost for U.S. Congress, Dallas, 1978, Jimmy Carter for Pres., Ft. Worth, 1980, Ann Richards for Gov., Tex., 1990. Mem. NAFE, Women in Comms. (fin. com. 1979), Dallas Assn. Legal Assts., Soc. Profl. Journalist, Dallas C. of C. Democrat. Home: 3500 Hillridge Dr Apt 118 Plano TX 75074-4367 Office: Elite Roofing 1209 Ave N Plano TX 75074

HAMMOND, KATHLEEN ANN, nutrition support nurse; b. Lowell, Mass., Jan. 18, 1960; d. Louis D. and Vera M. (Scalph) Pesce, m. Maxwell Hammond, May 25, 1991; children: Matthew Scott, Mark Lee. Diploma, Piedmont Hosp. Sch. Nursing, 1981; BS, U. Ga., 1985, MS, 1987; BSN, 1994. RN, Ga.; cert. nutrition support nurse. Staff nurse med.-surg. and ICU Clayton Gen. Hosp., Riverdale, Ga., 1981-85; staff nurse Piedmont Hosp., Atlanta, 1987-90; nutrition support nurse DeKalb Med. Ctr., Decatur, Ga., 1988-92; dir. clin. edn. Home Nutritional Svcs., Marietta, 1992-94; cons. in field Lilburn, Ga., 1994—; clin. instr. nutrition support U. Ga., Athens, 1987—; lectr. nursing Shallowford Ctr., Dunwoody, Ga., 1992—; course dir. nutrition physician asst. program Emory U.; nursing edn. coord. Nations Healthcare, 1996. Contbg. author: (booklet) Groshong, Kickman and Port Catheters, 1991, Transitional Feedings in Nursing Core Curriculum, Am. Soc. Parenteral and Enteral Nutrition, 1995, Guidelines for Nutrition Care, 1996, Contemporary Nutrition Support Practices, 1996. Mem. Am. Soc. Parenteral and Enteral Nutrition, Ga. Area Soc. Parenteral and Enter Nutrition (pres. 1992-93), Sigma Xi. Home: 4063 Deerbrook Way SW Lilburn GA 30247-3220

HAMMOND, KRISTINE LIND, publications manager; b. Seattle, Aug. 6, 1953; d. John Church Lind Sr. and Arlene Marie (Grundstrom) Tocantins; m. Patrick D. Hammond, June 23, 1979; children: Matthew Patrick, Elizabeth Siri. BA, U. Wash., 1977. Program asst. U. Wash., Seattle, 1973-77; tech. editor Flow Industries, Inc., Kent, Wash., 1978-90; publs. mgr. QUEST Integrated, Inc., formerly Flow Industries Inc., Kent, 1990—; sole proprietor publs. cons. Kirstine L. Hammond Publs., Buckley, 1990—. PTA newsletter editor White River Elem., Buckley, 1989-94; strategic planning com. mem. White River Sch. Dist., Buckley, 1994-95; v.p., exec. bd. mem. Buckley Plateau Coalition, 1994—; mem. comprehensive plan commn. City of Buckley. Recipient Wash. State PTA Outstanding Newsletter award Wash. PTA, 1991, 92, 94. Mem. Buckley Plateau Coalition (exec. bd., v.p., pres., 1994—). Home: 26224 112th St E Buckley WA 98321 Office: QUEST Integrated Inc 21414 68th Ave S Kent WA 98032

HAMMOND, LOU RENA CHARLOTTE, public relations executive; b. Muenster, Tex., Sept. 3, 1939; d. Louis Martin and Regina L. (Schoech) Wolf; m. Christopher Weymouth Hammond, Sept. 6, 1964; 1 child, Stephen. BA, U. Houston, 1962. Rep. pub. rels. Pan Am. Airways, N.Y.C., 1968-76, mgr. pub. rels., 1977-79, dir. pub. rels., 1980-81, dir. pub. affairs, 1981; pres., ptnr. Taylor and Hammond, N.Y.C., 1981-84; prin., pres. Lou Hammond and Assocs., N.Y.C., 1984—. Editor: (calendar) Avenue mag., 1976-79. Mem. Women's Bd. of Madison Sq. Boys and Girls Club, N.Y.C. Opera Guild. Recipient Matrix award in pub. rels., 1992, Winthrop W. Grice award Hotel Sales and Mktg. Assoc. Internat., 1992, Inside PR Mag.'s All-Star award, 1992. Mem. Soc. Am. Travel Writers, Fashion Group, Assn. Better N.Y., Les DAmes de Escoffier, Women's Forum, Women Execs. in Pub. Rels., Doubles Club. Roman Catholic. Office: Lou Hammond & Assocs Inc 39 E 51st St New York NY 10022-5901

HAMMOND, MARGARET C., physiatrist; b. 1953. MD, Med. Coll. Sic., 1979. Cert. in Phys. Med. Rehab. Mem. staff Seattle VA Hosp. Office: Seattle VA Hosp 1660 S Columbian Way # 128 Seattle WA 98108

HAMMOND, MARY SAYER, art educator; b. Bellingham, Wash., Oct. 1, 1946; d. Boyd James and Jacqueline Anna (Thurston) Sayer; m. Lester Wayne Hammond, Aug. 26, 1967 (div. Feb. 1972); m. Wiley Devere Sanderson, Jan. 13, 1983. BFA in Art Edn., U. Ga., 1967, MFA in Photo Design, 1977; PhD in History of Photo/Art Edn., Ohio State U., 1986. Art supr. Madison County Pub. Schs., Danielsville, Ga., 1968-71; art instr. U. Ga., Athens, 1971-73, instr. photo design, 1975-76; instr. in art edn. North Ga. Coll., Dalonega, 1975; instr. in art Valdosta (Ga.) State Coll., 1976-77, asst. prof. art, 1979-80; asst. prof. art, Am. Studies George Mason U., Fairfax, Va., 1980-87, assoc. prof. art, Am. Studies, 1987-94, prof. art, Am. studies, 1995—, dir. divsn. art studio; adminstrv. assoc. Ohio State U., Columbus, 1978-79, tchg. assoc., 1977-78; co-dir. Saturday program U. Ga., 1966-76, tchg. asst., 1974. Photographs represented in permanent collections at Ctr. for Creative Photography, Ariz., Internat. Mus. Photography, N.Y.C., Nat. Gallery of Art, Washington, Nat. Mus. Women in Arts, Washington. Treas. Faculty Senate of Va., 1991-96. Grantee Fulbright Hays Commn., 1973-74; travel grantee Samuel H. Kress Found., 1986, George Mason U., 1993, 91—; photographer's fellow NEA, 1982-84. Mem. Soc. Photo Edn. (mid-Atlantic bd. dirs. 1990—), Phi Kappa Phi (hon.). Office: George Mason U MS1C3 Art Studio Fairfax VA 22030-4444

HAMMOND, PATRICIA FLOOD, lawyer; b. Racine, Wis., Aug. 29, 1948; d. Francis James Flood and Shirley (Osterholt) Erickson; children: Bradley D. Mortensen, Erin N. Mortensen. Student, Wis. State U., Oshkosh, 1966-69, Alverno Coll., West Allis, 1973-74. Bar: Va.1985, U.S. Dist. Ct. (ea. dist.) Va. 1988. Br. dir. Am. Heart Assn., Manassas, Va., 1977-85; attorney Manassas, Va., 1985--; ptnr. Smith, Hudson, Hammond and Alston, Manassas, Va.; mem. VBA-VSB joint com. on alternative dispute resolution. Contbr. articles to newspapers. Mem. ABA, ACLU, ATLA, Nat. Abortion and Reproductive Rights Action League, Va. State Bar Assn., Prince William County Bar Assn. (treas., pres. 1991). Democrat. Episcopalian. Office: Smith Hudson Hammond & Alston 9403 Grant Ave Manassas VA 22110-5509

HAMMOND, SHIRLEY EANES, boutique owner; b. Halifax, Va., July 16, 1933; d. Coleman Taft and Nan Beth (Wyatt) Eanes; m. Giles Lawrence Parrish, Nov. 1, 1952 (div. Nov. 1958); 1 child, Constance Dawn Parrish Beekman.m. John Insley Hammond, June 18, 1985. Student, Southwestern Coll., 1950-51, Va. Western Cmty. Coll., 1973-76. Cert. color/image cons., body and wardrobe cons., style cons. Adminstrv. asst., office mgr. Graham-White Sales Corp., Salem, Va., 1960-76, 78-83; fgn. svc. sec. Dept. of State, U.S. Embassy, Santo Domingo, Dominican Republic, 1976-78; part owner, v.p. Colors and You, Inc., Roanoke, Va., 1983-91; owner, pres. Colors Too, Inc., Roanoke, 1992—; cons. Beauty for All Seasons, Inc., Idaho Falls, Idaho, 1983—, internat. career instr., 1985-90. Trustees com., Sunday sch. tchr. Raleigh Ct. United Meth. Ch., Roanoke; vol., mem. S.W. Va. Emmaus Cmty., Roanoke. Office: Colors Too Inc Towers Mall Roanoke VA 24015

HAMMOND, SUSAN GAIL, school counselor; b. White Salmon, Wash., Mar. 6, 1959; d. William Edward and Juanita Minnie (Coffman) H. BS in Edn., Eastern Oreg. State Coll., 1982; MS in Psychology, Ctrl. Wash. U., 1989. Cert. continuing tchr., Wash., continuing counselor, Wash. Tchr. Wamic (Oreg.) Grade Sch., 1982-86; tchr., counselor Cle Elum Roslyn Sch. Dist., Roslyn, Wash., 1989-95; counselor Ellensburg (Wash.) Sch. Dist., 1995—; bd. dirs. Kittitas County Youth Safety Bd., Ellensburg; mem. Strategic Planning Team, Ellensburg, 1995. Bd. dirs. Kittitas County Wash. Citizens for Fairness, Ellensburg, 1994—; sch. dist. rep. Cmty. Health & Safety Network Bd., Ellensburg, 1994—. Mem. Am. Sch. Counseling Assn., Am. Assn. Counseling & Devel. Democrat. Home: 81 Wheeler Rd Ellensburg WA 98926 Office: Morgan Mid Sch 400 E 1st Ellensburg WA 98926

HAMMOND-KOMINSKY, CYNTHIA CECELIA, optometrist; b. Dearborn, Mich., Sept. 1, 1957; d. Andrew and Angeline (Laorno) Kominsky; m. Theodore Glen Hammond, Sept. 21, 1985. Student Oakland U., Rochester, Mich., 1976-77; OD magna cum laude, Ferris Coll. Optometry, 1981. Lic. optometrist, Mich.; cert. diagnostic and therapeutic pharm. agt. Intern, Optometric Inst. and Clinic of Detroit, 1980, Ferris State Coll., Big Rapids, Mich., 1980, Jackson Prison (Mich.), 1981; assoc. in pvt. practice, Warren, Mich., 1981-82; optometrist Pearle Vision Ctr., Sterling Heights, Mich., 1982-87, K-Mart Optical Ctr., Sterling Heights, 1982-87, Royal Optical, Sterling Heights, 1988—; provided eye care to nursing homes, Mt. Clemens, Mich. Inventer binocular low vision aid device. Avocations: music, sports, clogging, gardening, antique crystal. Home: 47626 Cheryl Ct Shelby Township MI 48315-4708 Office: Royal Optical Lakeside Mall 14300 Lakeside Cir Sterling Heights MI 48313-1326

HAMMONDS-WHITE, SUSAN ELISABETH, counselor; b. Nashville, May 25, 1946; d. R. Glenn and Virginia (McBunnett) Hammonds; m. Ivan Ignacio Botero-Paramo (div. 1978); m. Walter H. White III, Mar. 9, 1985; 1 child, Christiana Marie Hammonds. BA, Wellesley Coll., 1968; MAT, Harvard U., 1972; MA, Lesley Coll., 1982; EdD, Vanderbilt U., 1989. Lic. profl. counselor; nat. cert. counselor. Tchr. Colegio Nueva Granada, Bogotá, Colombia, 1974-77; prin. mid. sch. Colegio Nuevo Granada, Bogota, Colombia, 1977-80; social worker II Dept. Social Svcs., Newton, Mass., 1982-84; clin. therapist Luton Mental Health, Nashville, 1984-88; owner Life Cycles Counseling Svcs., Nashville, 1990—; adj. asst. prof. human resources Vanderbilt U., Nashville, 1990—; cons. Lic. Profl. Counseling Bd., Nashville, 1995—; bd. dirs., editor Nashville Psychotherapy Inst. Sunday sch. tchr. Woodmont Christian Ch., Nashville, 1993—. Mem. Mid. Tenn. Counseling Assn. (Member of Yr. 1994-95), Tenn. Counseling Assn. (licensure chair 1994—, lobbyist 1994, 95). Democrat. Office: Life Cycles Counseling Svcs Ste 205 5819 Old Harding Pike Nashville TN 37205

HAMMONTREE, MARIE GERTRUDE, writer; b. Jefferson County, Ind., June 19, 1913; d. Harry Clay and Hattie Agnes (Means) H. BA, Butler U., 1949. Sec. Bobbs-Merrill Co., Indpls., 1934-42, Ind. U. Med. Ctr., Indpls., 1942-48, Travel Enterprises, Inc., N.Y.C., 1949-50, U.S. Dept. Justice (FBI), Indpls., 1950-75; bookkeeper, purchasing agt. Office of William H. Hudnut, III/ Mayor of Indpls., 1978-92. Author: (children's books) Will and Charlie Mayo: Doctor's Boys, 1954, A.P.Giannini: Boy of San Francisco, 1956, Albert Einstein: Young Thinker, 1961, Mohandas Gandhi: Boy of Principle, 1966, Walt Disney: Young Movie Maker, 1969. Active in campaigns of Mayor William H. Hudnut, III and Ind. State Reps., Indpls., 1975-92. Mem. Nat. League Am. Pen Women (pres. Indpls. chpt. 1978-80), Women in Comms., Soc. of FBI Alumni, Inc. (treas. Indpls. chpt. 1990—), Sigma Tau Delta, Phi Kappa Phi. Republican. Presbyterian. Home: 8140 Township Line Rd # 5213 Indianapolis IN 46260-5832

HAMNER, ELIZABETH FLOURNOY, education consultant; b. Richmond, Va., June 1, 1943; d. Laurance Davis and Susan Nelson (Mooers) H. BA, Longwood Coll., 1965, MS, 1971. English and drama tchr. Huguenot Acad., Powhatan, Va., 1965-70; asst. prin., tchr. Manchester Ind. Shc., Richmond, 1971-74; spl. edn. tchr., tennis coach Huguenot Acad., 1974-76; from exec. dir. to prodr., dir. Heritage Prodns., Richmond, Strasburg, Va., 1976-86; cons. in field Richmond, 1990—. Republican. Episcopal. Home: 1512 Sharpsburg Ct Richmond VA 23228

HAMNER, SUZANNE LEATH, history educator; b. Ft. Worth, Feb. 29, 1940; d. Roland Martin and Mabel Lois (Hall) Leath; m. W. Easley Hamner, June 18, 1961; children: Janine Suzanne, Michael Edward. BA summa cum laude, Meredith Coll., Raleigh, N.C., 1961; MA, Tulane U., New Orleans, 1964. Teaching asst. Tulane U., New Orleans, 1963-64, 65-66; instr. history Coll. Liberal Arts Northeastern U., Boston, 1966-71, lectr. history Univ. Coll., 1972-73, 74-75; lectr. history Coll. Arts and Scis. and Univ. Coll. Coll. Arts and Scis., Boston, 1985—; sr. lectr. U. Coll., 1985—. Contbg. editor Reclaiming Our Global Heritage, Vol. I and Vol. II, 1990. Mem. adv. com. Follow Through Program, Cambridge (Mass.) Sch. Dept., 1977-79; treas., v.p. adv. bd. Buckingham Browne and Nichols Sch., Cambridge, 1980-86; clk., bd. dirs., adv. bd. Cambridge Civic Assn., 1976-95; treas. Alice Wolf Election Com., City Coun., Cambridge, 1979-96; advisor Wolf Campaign for State Rep., 1996; overseer Handel and Haydn Soc., Boston, 1989—; trustee Chorus pro Musica, 1993-95; mem. adv. com. Meml. Ch., Harvard U., 1992-94. Woodrow Wilson Found. fellow, Princeton, N.J., 1961-62; Tulane U. scholar, 1962-64. Mem. Am. Hist. Assn., New Eng. Hist. Assn., Phi Alpha Theta. Democrat. Home: 3 Ellery Sq Cambridge MA 02138-4227 Office: Northeastern U History Dept 360 Huntington Ave Boston MA 02115-5005

HAMOR, KATHY VIRGINIA, consultant; b. Port Jervis, N.Y., Aug. 2, 1957; d. John Barry and Grace Marion (Carpenter) H. BA, Elmira Coll., 1979; MPA, U. S.C., 1983. Paralegal Bergson, Borkland, Margolis & Adler, Washington, 1979-81; presdl. mgmt. intern U.S. Customs Svc., Washington, 1983-85, project mgr., 1986-88, pub. affairs officer, 1989-90, chief press ops. br., 1991-92; cons., lobbyist Mehl & Pickens Assocs., Inc., Washington, 1992-94; pres. Capital Concepts, Washington, 1994—. Home: 4535 28th Rd S # A Arlington VA 22206-3372

HAMOVITCH, SUSAN REBECCA, documentary filmmaker, communications educator; b. Buffalo, Oct. 28, 1952; d. William and Mitzi (Berger) H.; m. Albert Auster, Sept. 6, 1992. BA, U. Chgo., 1974; MFA, CUNY, 1990. Media cons. N.Y.C. Bd. Edn., 1991—; dir. Wonderland Prodns., Bklyn., 1993—; instr. comm. Coll. of S.I., N.Y., 1994, Bklyn. Coll., CUNY, 1995—; participating mem. children's studies program Bklyn. Coll., CUNY, 1996; instr. comm. Nassau C.C., Garden City, N.Y., 1995—; cons. Young Audiences, N.Y.C., 1994—. One-woman shows Key Gallery, N.Y.C., 1978, 79; exhibited in group show Gettler-Pall Gallery, N.Y.C., 1978; producer, dir. film On The Road to Choice, 1990; assoc. producer The Housing Rights Series, 1985; contbr. articles and revs. to profl. publs. Mem. adv. bd. Women's Housing Coalition, N.Y.C., 1986-90, Welfare League (Letchworth Village), Thiells, N.Y., 1993—. Mem. Univ. Film and Video Assn., Assn. Ind. Film and Videomakers, Women Make Movies, N.Y. State Art Tchrs. Assn., Assn. for Help Retarded Children.

HAMOY, CAROL, artist; b. N.Y.C., May 22, 1934; d. Morris David and Selma (Essex) Cohen. Student, Newark (N.J.) Sch. Fine Art, Art Students League, N.Y.C. Lectr., spkr. in field. One-woman shows include Viridian Gallery, N.Y.C., 1977, USMA/West Point, N.Y., 1978, Katonah (N.Y.) Gallery, 1983, Lower Manhattan Cultural Coun., N.Y.C., 1986, May Mus./ Lawrence, N.Y. Ceres, N.Y.C., 1992, MTA-Arts for Transit, N.Y.C., 1993, Robert Kahn Gallery, Houston, 1993, Temple Judea Mus., Elkins Park, Pa., 1993, Univ. Art Ctr., Shreveport, La., 1993, Ceres, N.Y.C., 1994, Goldman Art Gallery, Rockville, Md., 1995, Nat. Mus. Am. Jewish History, Phila., 1995, Broadway Windows, N.Y.C., 1996, Ellis Island Immigration Mus., N.Y.C., 1996; group shows include JRC Gallery, Evanston, Ill., 1992, AIR, N.Y.C., 1992, SUNY, New Paltz, 1992, Judah Magnes Mus., Berkeley, Calif., 1992, Abrons Art Ctr., N.Y.C., 1992, Ceres, 1992, 93, ArtLab, S.I., N.Y., 1992, Walsh Gallery, Fairfield, Conn., 1993, Soho 20, N.Y.C., 1993, Janice Charach-Epstein Mus., West Bloomfield, Mich., 1994, Klutznick Mus., Washington, 1995, Newhouse Ctr. for Contemporary Art, S.I., 1995, Fine Arts Gallery, Ft. Lauderdale, Fla., 1995, Nat. Mus. Women in the Arts, Washington, 1995, Ctrl. YWHA, Queens, N.Y., 1995, Firehouse Gallery, Garden City, N.Y., 1995, Prince St. Gallery, N.Y.C., 1995, Phoenix Gallery, N.Y.C., 1995, Krasdale Gallery, Fairfield, 1995, Hastings (N.Y.) Gallery, 1995, SW Tex. U., 1995, Arthur Ross Gallery, Phila., 1996, St. Marks Gallery, N.Y.C., 1996, Contemporary Art Gallery, Santa Fe, 1996, others; permanent collections include Nat. Mus. Women in the Arts, Kluznick Nat. Jewish Mus., Washington, others. Recipient grants VCCA, Sweet Briar, Va., 1980, Artists' Space, N.Y.C., 1981, Hillwood Art Mus., NYSCA, 1992, MTA-Arts for Transit, N.Y.C., 1993. Home: 340 E 66 St New York NY 10021

HAMPL, MARY NOTERMANN, materials agent; b. Mpls., Feb. 3, 1945; d. Joseph and Fern Irene (Ladwig) Little; m. Richard L. Notermann, Aug. 2, 1968 (div. July 1981); children: Jennifer Anne, Jason Richard; m. Werner Heinz Hampl, July 6, 1985; stepchildren: Matthew H., Carrie Elizabeth. BA, U. Minn., 1974; cert. spl. studies, Harvard U. Ext., 1989. Caseworker Outreach Ctr. Retarded Citizens, Mpls., 1974-75; exec. dir. South Side Svc. Retarded Citizens, Mpls., 1975-79; material control adminstr. Honeywell, Inc., Mpls., 1979-81; sr. buyer, planner NBI, Inc., Boulder, Colo., 1981-85; materials mgr. Zymacom, Inc., Westford, Mass., 1985-88; materials purchasing Roll Sys., Inc., Burlington, Mass., 1989-91; purchasing mgr. Medisense, Inc., Bedford, Mass., 1991—; sec. Reubin Lindh Day Care Ctr., Mpls., 1977-79. Mem. LWV, Am. Assn. Purchasing Mgmt., Am. Prodn. and Inventory Control Soc. (cert.), Mensa. Home: 17 Arborwood Dr Burlington MA 01803-3816 Office: Medisense Inc 4A Crosby Dr Bedford MA 01730

HAMPTON, CAROL MCDONALD, religious organization administrator, educator, historian; b. Oklahoma City, Sept. 18, 1935; d. Denzil Vincent and Mildred Juanita (Cussen) McDonald; m. James Wilburn Hampton, Feb. 22, 1958; children: Jaime, Clayton, Diana, Neal. BA, U. Okla., 1957, MA, 1973, PhD, 1984. Postulant Episcopal Diocese of Okla., 1996. Tchg. asst. U. Okla., Norman, 1976-81; instr. U. of Sci. and Arts of Okla., Chickasha, 1981-84; coord. Consortium for Grad. Opportunities for Am. Indians, U. Calif., Berkeley, 1985-86; trustee Ctr. of Am. Indian, Oklahoma City, 1981—; vice chmn. Nat. Com. on Indian Work, Episc. Ch., 1986; field officer coun. Native Am. Ministry, 1986-94, sec., co-chmn., advising elder, prin. elder 1994-96; field officer for Congl. Ministries, 1994—; mem. nat. coun. Chs. Racial Justice Working Group, 1990—, co-convenor, 1991-93, convenor, 1993-95; officer Multicultural Ministries, 1994—. Contbr. articles to profl. jours. Trustee Western History Collections, U. Okla., Okla. Found. for the Humanities, 1983-86; mem. bd. regents U. Sci. and Arts Okla., 1989-95; bd. dirs. Okla. State Regents for Higher Edn., mem. adv. com. on social justice; mem. World Coun. of Chs. Program to Combat Racism, Geneva, 1985-91; bd. dirs. Caddo Tribal Coun., Okla., 1976-82; accredited observer Anglican Consultative Coun. 4th World Conf. on Women, 1995. Recipient Okla. State Human Rights award, 1987; Francis C. Allen fellow, Ctr. for the History of Am. Indian, 1983. Mem. Western History Assn., Western Social Sci. Assn., Orgn. of Am. Historians, Am. Hist. Assn., Okla. Hist. Soc., Assn. Am. Indian Historians (founding mem. 1981—). Democrat. Episcopalian. Club: Jr. League (Oklahoma City). Avocation: travel. Home: 1414 N Hudson Ave Oklahoma City OK 73103-3721 Office: Episcopal Ch Congl Ministry 924 N Robinson Ave Oklahoma City OK 73102-5814

HAMPTON, MARGARET FRANCES, international trade and finance professional; b. Gainesville, Fla., May 12, 1947; d. William Wade and Carol Dorothy (Maples) H.; m. Kenneth Lee Kauffman (dec.); 1 child, Robert Lee. BA in French summa cum laude, Fla. State U., 1969; postgrad. U. Nice (France), summer 1969; MBA in Fin. (Alcoa Found. fellow), Columbia U., 1974. Fin. analyst, economist Bd. of Govs. of Fed. Res. System, Washington, 1974-75; v.p. corp. fin. Mfrs. Hanover Trust Co., N.Y.C., 1975-76; v.p., dir. corp. planning and fin., asset and liability mgmt. and strategic planning coms. Nat. Bank of Ga., Atlanta, 1976-81; sr. v.p. corp. planning and devel. Bank South Corp., Atlanta, 1981-85; mng. ptnr. Hampton Mgmt. Cons., Atlanta, 1985—; pres., bd. dirs. Accent Enterprises, Inc., Atlanta, 1993—; pres., CEO Accent Global Mktg., Inc., Atlanta, 1993—; registered rep. Rockwell Investments, Inc., Evergreen, Colo., 1994-96, offshore commodities trader, 1995—; broadcast affiliate TPN, 1995; v.p. Internat. Friendship City, 1996—. Nat. trustee Leukemia Soc. Am., 1986-90; trustee Ga. chpt. Leukemia Soc., 1980-94, treas., 1981-82, 1st v.p., 1982-84, sec., 1991-92, hon. bd. dirs.; dir. Combined Health Appeal Ga., 1991—, sec., 1992—. Named Trustee of Yr., Leukemia Soc., 1982, 85; recipient Gold Key, Fla. State U. Hall of Fame. Mem. Planning Execs. Inst., Atlanta Venture Forum, Am. Inst. Banking, Inst. of Fin. Edn., Am. Fin. Assn., Downtown Atlanta C. of C., (govt. affairs subcom. 1976-77) Atlanta C. of C. (high tech. task force 1982-83), Ga. Women's Forum (sec./treas., bd. dirs. 1985-86), Ga. Exec. Women's Network (sec. 1982-83, dir. 1982-84), Bus. and Tech. Alliance, Mortar Bd., Alliance Française, Kappa Sigma Little Sisters (pres., treas., sweetheart), Phi Beta Kappa, Beta Gamma Sigma, Phi Kappa Phi, Alpha Lambda Delta, Pi Delta Phi, Alpha Delta Pi. Episcopalian. Clubs: Women's Commerce (charter mem., steering com. 1985-86), Northside Athletic.

HAMRE, MARETA CATHERINE, lawyer; b. Fort Collins, Colo., Nov. 30, 1963; d. Robert Henry Hamre and Faith Mary (Weis) Harder; m. Mark Bruce Abbott, Sept. 22, 1990; children: Madeline Hamre, Nicholas Jack. AB, Harvard U., 1985; JD, U. Calif. Berkeley, 1990. Bar: Calif. 1991. Rshc. assoc. Policy Studies in Edn., Great Neck, N.Y., 1985-87; atty. Stutman, Treister & Glatt P.C., L.A., 1990—. John Harvard scholar, 1985; recipient Elizabeth Carey Aggasiz award Radcliffe Coll., 1985. Mem. Am. Bar Assn. Methodist. Office: Stutman Treister & Glatt PC 3699 Wilshire Blvd Ste 900 Los Angeles CA 90010

HAMROCK, MARGARET MARY, retired educator, writer; b. Campbell, Ohio, Apr. 2, 1910; d. Louis Francis and Mary (Augustin) H. BS in Edn., Kent State U., 1946. Tchr. Campbell (Ohio) Bd. Edn., 1927-75; ret., 1975. Author: Tell Me I'm Somebody, 1994; composer of songs; over 100 letters to editor pub. in Cleve. Plain Dealer, Youngstown Vindicator, nat. mags. Mem. Ohio Ret. Tchrs. Assn. (life), Kent State U. Alumni Assn.

HAN, SOO J., governmental administrator; b. Suwon, Korea, Sept. 2, 1970; came to U.S., 1974.; d. Hui Yul and Sung Ok (Kim) H. BA, Boston U., 1992, BSBA, 1992. Staff asst. Office of the V.P. of U.S., Washington, 1993-96; assoc. dep. dir. vice presdl. advance Clinton/Gore '96, Washington, 1996—.

HANAWAY, ANDREA STEIN, emergency physician; b. Phila., Feb. 26, 1947; d. Raymond Oscar and Phyllis (Pomcranz) Stein; divorced; children: Jaime Karen, Stacy Alix. BA, U. N.C., 1969; MD, Med. Coll. Pa., 1973. Diplomate Am. Bd. Emergency Medicine, Nat. Bd. Med. Examiners; cert. ACLS provider and instr., BLS instr. Intern Med. Coll. Pa., Phila., 1973-74, resident in ob-gyn., 1974-75, resident, then chief resident emergency medicine, 1975-77; clin. instr. dept. medicine U. Pa. Med. Sch., Phila., 1977-79; attending physician emergency dept. Presbyn.-U. Pa. Med. Ctr., 1977-79; dir. emergency unit Albert Einstein Med. Ctr. Mt. Sinai-Daroff Divsn., 1979-85; clin. instr. dept. emergency medicine Thomas Jefferson U. Med. Sch., Phila., 1984—; dir. emergency dept. John F. Kennedy Meml. Hosp., Phila., 1985-88, 89—; attending physician emergency medicine and indsl. medicine St. Luke's Hosp., Bethlehem, Pa., 19988-89; co-chmn. med. panel Pa. Bd. Pensions and Retirement; small group seminar instr. dept. psychiatry Thomas Jefferson U. Med. Sch., 1982-85; adj. asst. prof. emergency Med. Coll. Pa./Hahnemann U., Phila., 1995; pres. med. staff John F. Kennedy Meml. Hosp., 1993-95, chair credentials com., 1995. Fellow Am. Coll. Emergency Physicians; mem. AMA, Pa. Emergency Physicians Soc., Phila. C. of C., Psi Chi. Office: John F Kennedy Meml Hosp Langdon St & Cheltenham Ave Philadelphia PA 19124

HANBACK, HAZEL MARIE SMALLWOOD, management consultant; b. Washington, Sept. 19, 1918; d. Archibald Carlisle and Mary Louise (Mayhugh) Smallwood; m. William B. Hanback, Sept. 26, 1942; 1 child, Christopher Brecht. AB, George Washington U., 1940; MPA, Am. U., 1968. Archivist, U.S. Office Housing Expediter, 1948-50; mgmt. engr. U.S. Archives, 1950-51; spl. asst.-indsl. specialist Sec. Def., 1951-53; dir. documentation div. Naval Facilities Engring., Alexandria, Va., 1953-81; mgmt. cons., 1981—. Author: Military Color Book, 1960—, Status of Women in a Cybernetically Oriented Soc., 1968—, (newsletter) Worms Eye View, 1982—, The Military Industrial Complex, 1982—. Pres., West End Citizens Assn., Washington, 1956-58; trustee George Washington U., 1979—. Nominee Rockefeller Pub. Service award, 1969, Fed. Woman's award, 1969; recipient cert. of merit Dep. Def., 1965. Mem. Mortar Bd., Phi Delta Gamma, Sigma Kappa. Democrat. Episcopalian. Clubs: George Washington U. (chmn. bd. 1971-75), Columbian Women (pres. George Washington U. Club 1967-69), Order Ea. Star. Home: 2152 F St NW Washington DC 20037-2712

HANCHETT, SUZANNE LORRAINE, anthropologist, consultant; b. Salinas, Calif., June 17, 1941; d. Edward Lorraine and Clara Louise (Walldow) H.-McDonald; m. Stanley Regelson, June 21, 1964 (div. May 1979); 1 child, Moira Ellen; m. Michael Munk, Nov. 27, 1992. BA, Reed Coll., 1962; PhD, Columbia U., 1970. Instr. anthropology Bard Coll, Annandale-on-Hudson, N.Y., 1969-70; asst. prof. Queens Coll. City Univ. N.Y., 1971-78; dir. govt. and found grants Bedford Stuyvesant Restoration Corp., Brooklyn, N.Y., 1979-83; dir. resource devel. Cmty. Family Planning Coun., N.Y.C., 1983-86; sr. planner Office Svcs. Planning, Human Resources Adminstrn. City of N.Y., 1986-88, project dir. cmty. planning for teens Bur. Maternity Svcs. and Family Plannig Dept. Health, 1988, coord. Office Adolescent Pregnancy and Parenting Svcs. Office of the Mayor, 1988-90, coord. kinship and foster care program N.Y.C. Child Welfare Adminstrn., 1990-91; devel. cons. Rsch. Planning for Soc. and Health Consulting Svcs., Portland, 1991—; sr. adv. Bangaldesh Flood Action Plan U.S. Agy. for Internat. Devel., 1991-93, cons. tech. assistance program West Bank, Gaza, 1994; cons. World Bank Bangladesh, 1995. Author: Coloured Rice: Symbolic Structure in Hindu Family Festivals, 1988; contbr. articles to profl. jours. Past mem. bd. dirs. Manhattan (N.Y.) Teen Pregnancy Network. Fellow Am. Inst. Indian Studies, 1977, rsch. fellow NIMH, 1966-67, Ogden Mills Fellow Am. Mus. Natural History, 1970-71; writing grantee Am. Coun. Learned Soc., Fulbright faculty rsch. abroad grantee, 1976. Fellow Am. Anthropol. Assn., Soc. Applied Anthropology; mem. Am. Pub. Health Assn., Nat. Coun. Internat. Health, Assn. Asian Studies, Assn. Women in Devel., Soc. South India Studies (past pres.). Democrat. Jewish. Office: RPSH Consulting Svcs 5119 SE 44th St Portland OR 97206

HANCOCK, SANDRA OLIVIA, secondary and elementary school educator; b. Jackson, Tenn., Oct. 22, 1947; d. Carthel Leon and Thelma (Thompson) Smith; m. Jerome Hancock, Aug. 1, 1969; children: Casey Colman, Mandy Maria. BS, U. Tenn., 1969, MS, 1973; grad. safety seminar, Universal Cheerleaders Assn., 1989. Cert. educator. Educator Lexington (Tenn.) High Sch., 1969-70, Clarksburg (Tenn.) High Sch., 1970-78, 83-90, Dresden (Tenn.) Jr. H.S., 1994-95; instr. Camden (Tenn) Elem. Sch., 1995—; instr. Very Spl. Arts Festival, Carroll County, Tenn., 1994, Camden (Tenn.) Elem. Sch., 1995-96; GED instr. Contbr. poetry to various publs. Cub scout leader Boy Scouts Am., Clarksburg, 1982-84; assoc. mem. St. Labre Indian Sch. and Home Arrow Club, Ashland, Mont., 1988-89; former vol. March of Dimes; vol. Leukemia Soc. Am.; mem. fund raising com. Project Graduation, Huntingdon H.S., 1992-95; dir. presch. 1st United Meth. Ch., Huntingdon, 1992-93; art edn. asst. Huntingdon Spl. Sch. Dist., 1993-94. Recipient various poetry awards. Mem. U.S. Olympic Assn., Nat. Cheerleaders Assn. (Superior Advisor Performace award 1988), Am. Assn. Cheerleading Coaches and Advisors, Jackson Writer's Group (rec. sec. 1993-94), Poetry Soc. Tenn. (rec. sec. 1993-94, guest spkr. 1994), Haiku Soc. Am., Phi Delta Kappa (N.W. Tenn. chpt. sec. 1993-94). Republican. Home and Office: 435 Timber Ln Huntingdon TN 38344-1625 Office: Camden Elem Sch Washington St Camden TN 38320

HAND, VIRGINIA SAXTON, home health nurse; b. Phila., July 21, 1956; d. John Grant and Grace Marie (Palermo) Saxton; m. Arthur L. Hand III, June 2, 1979; children: Arthur IV, Katherine, Ryan, Sean. RN, St. Agnes Med. Ctr. Sch., Nursing, Phila., 1977. RN, Pa. Staff nurse St. Agnes Med. Ctr., Phila., 1977-78, head nurse, 1979-81; staff nurse Frankford Hosp., Phila., 1985-93; home health nurse Phila., 1993—. Vol. meals to shut-ins St. Matthew Outreach, Phila., 1989—; group facilitator St. Matthew's Mothers of PreTeens, Phila., 1994—; mem. Precana team St. Matthew's Ch., 1990—. Roman Catholic. Home: 3212 Cottman Ave Philadelphia PA 19149-1511

HANDELMAN, ALICE SAMUELS, public relations professional, freelance writer; b. Bklyn., Mar. 17, 1943; d. Ned Harlan and Margaret (Isaacs) Samuels; m. Howard Talbot Handelman, Aug. 29, 1965; children: Karen Handelman Hirshman, Patricia Handelman Bloom, Marjorie Lynn Handelman. BJ, U. Mo., 1965. Intern reporter Miami (Fla.) News, summer 1964; staff feature writer St. Louis Blues, 1968-77; freelance writer, St. Louis, 1967—; also community rels. assoc. Jewish Ctr. for Aged of Greater St. Louis, Chesterfield, Mo., 1981-85, dir. community rels., 1985—; instr. hockey for women Meramec C.C., St. Louis, 1976-77; pub. rels. cons. Jewish Family and Children's Svc., St. Louis, 1983, 89; adv. com. vis. prof. program JCA Assocs., 1981-83, Gerontol. Inst., St. Louis, 1981-83. Author, photographer: LaSalle Street--A History of the St. Louis Wholesale Flower Market, 1987; freelance writer, contbr. to St. Louis Globe-Dem., St. Louis Post-Dispatch, N.Y. Times, St. Louis Jewish Light, St. Louis Blues Goal Mag., Hockey News, Hockey World, Ladue News, Sporting News, Nat. Hockey League, Hockey Pictorial, Suburban Jour. Newspapers; writer copy for Knight's Catalogue, 1983. Pub. rels. chmn. Nat. Coun. Jewish Women, 1981-83, publicity chmn. fashion sale, 1985; pres. Weber Sch. PTA, Creve Coeur, Mo., 1982; mem. Women's Am. ORT, 1965—; life mem. Jewish Hosp. Aux., 1965—, Jewish Ctr. for Aged Aux., 1986—; pres. Young Women's Coun. on Edn. of Jewish Fedn. St. Louis, 1969; mem. cen. advancement team Pkwy. Central High Sch., 1985-89; photographer Tour de Cure bicycle ride to benefit Am. Diabetes Assn., 1992, 93. Recipient William Randolph Hearst award Hearst Found., Columbia, Mo., 1965, United Way Graphic Design award, 1986, United Way Photography award, 1987, 95, Star Communicator Photography award, 1987, 89, 2d place award Guide to Jewish Life in St. Louis photo contest, 1989, 2d place award Jewish Hosp. St. Louis Generations of Women photo contest, 1989, Star Communicator comm. program award United Way Greater St. Louis, 1990, Bronze Photography award, 1995; Besse Marks Meml. scholar, 1964-65. Mem. Nat. Fedn. Press Women (1st place award comm. contest, 3rd place photo feature 1989, 3rd place award advt. photography 1993, hon. mention advt. photo, 2d place mktg. new svc. award, 2nd place mag. advt., 1996, 3rd place direct mail mktg. fundraising lit., 2nd place direct mail advt.- fund raising Ann. NFPW Comm. Contest 1996, 3rd place Color Mag. Advt. 1996), Jewish Ctr. for Aged Aux., Fellows of Jewish Hosp., Mo. Press Women (1st place corp. newsletter category state feature writing comm. contest, 1988, 93, 1st place advt. photography, 2nd place feature article, 3 1st place awards, 1994, 1st place not for profit newsletter, 1994, 5 1st place awards, 1995, 1st place award Mo. Assn. of Homes for the Aging, 1994, planning com. Fair St St. Louis Srs. Day 1995, 96, planning com. Srs. Day VP Fair 1994), Mo. Assn. Homes for the Aging (publicity com., Outstanding 1st Place Newsletter award), Nat Fedn. Press Women (1st place feature photo 1994), Mo. Press Women (pub. chmn. 1994), Women in Communications (Ruth Philpott Collins award 1984, Best in the Midwest, 2d place feature writing, 1992), Meadowbrook Country Club (Ballwin, Mo.). Jewish. Home: 12 Terry Hill Ln Saint Louis MO 63131-2422 Office: Jewish Ctr for Aged of Greater St Louis 13190 S Outer 40 Rd Chesterfield MO 63017

HANDLER, ENID IRENE, health care administrator, consultant; b. N.Y.C., Oct. 17, 1932; d. Solomon and Fran S. (Bernstein) Ostrov; m. Murry Raymond Handler, Nov. 22, 1952; children: Lowell S., Lillian Handler Koch, Evan Elliott. BS, Queens Coll., 1968; MS in Adminstrv. Medicine, Columbia U., 1973. Adminstrv. dir. Phelps Mental Health Ctr., North Tarrytown, N.Y., 1973-85; cons. to health care providers Cortland Manor, N.Y., 1986-92; mgmt. cons. Durham County (N.C.) Mental Health/Devel. Disabilities Svc., Chapel Hill, N.C., 1993-94; mem. bd. dirs. Orange County (N.C.) AIDS Svc. Agy., 1992-94, Inst. for Parapsychology, 1996—; presenter to profl. orgns. Contbr. articles and book revs. to profl. jours. Mem. adv. bd. Marymount Coll., North Tarrytown, 1983, Iona Coll., New Rochelle, N.Y., 1983; mem. adv. bd. Search for Change, Inc., White Plains, 1987-90; bd. dirs. Keon Sch., Montrose, N.Y., 1986-88; chair North Westchester County Mental Health Coun., 1974-80; pres. Westchester Assn. Vol. Agys., 1981-82; mem. Westchester County Community Svcs. Bd., 1980-86. NIH fellow Columbia U., N.Y.C., 1971-72. Fellow Am. Orthopsychiat. Assn.; mem. NAFE, Columbia U. Alumni Assn. Home and Office: Enid Handler Cons 9318 Laurel Springs Dr Chapel Hill NC 27516-5649

HANDLER, JANICE, lawyer; b. Newark, July 9, 1945; d. Lester Robert and Rose Mildred (Reider) Handler; m. Norman Harry Ilowite, June 4, 1978. BA, Douglass Coll., 1967; JD, Rutgers Law Sch., 1970; LLM, NYU, 1980. Bar: N.Y. Law clk. to presiding justice U.S. Dist. Ct. (so. dist.), N.Y.C., 1970-71; assoc. Fried, Frank, Harris, Shriver & Jacoboon, N.Y.C., 1971-72; atty. SEC, N.Y.C., 1972-74; counsel Thomas J. Lipton, Englewood Cliffs, N.J., 1974-77; mktg. counsel Lever Brothers Co., N.Y.C., 1977-83, asst. gen. counsel, 1983-87; sr. counsel Chesebrough-Ponds, Inc., Greenwich, Conn., 1987-90; gen. counsel Elizabeth Arden Co., N.Y.C., 1990—. Reviewer N.Y. Law Jour., N.Y.C., 1982—. Bd. dirs. Douglass Coll. Assoc. Alumnae, 1972-74. Mem. ABA (sect. on litigation's com. on corp. counsel), N.Y. State Bar Assn. (Corp. Counsel Sect.), Assn. Bar City N.Y. (advt. industry subcom. 1982—).*

HANDLER, MIMI, editor, writer; b. Boston, Sept. 16, 1934; d. Eli and Josephine (Bronstein) Richman; m. Jack G. Handler, June 11, 1956 (div. 1981); children—Jessica, Susannah, Sarah. B.A., Brandeis U., 1956. Staff corr. Ladies' Home Jour., Phila., 1956-59; sec. law jour. Emory U., Atlanta, 1970-71; free-lance ct. reporter Atlanta, 1971-73; projects editor Early Am. Life, Harrisburg, Pa., 1979-80, mng. editor, 1980-88, sr. editor, 1988-90; editor New England, 1990-93; editor in chief Early Am. Life, Harrisburg, Pa., 1993—; speaker Old Sturbridge Village conf., 1986, 87, Strawbery Banke Antiques Symposium, 1992. Democrat. Jewish. Office: Early American Life PO Box 8200 Harrisburg PA 17105-8200*

HANDLEY, MARGIE LEE, business executive; b. Bakersfield, Calif., Sept. 29, 1939; d. Robert E. and Jayne A. (Knoblock) Harrah; children: Steven Daniel Lovell, David Robert Lovell, Ronald Eugene Lovell; m. Leon C. Handley, Sr., Oct. 28, 1975. Grad. high sch., Willits, Calif. Lic. gen. engring. contractor. Owner, operator Shasta Pallet Co., Montague, 1969-70; owner, operator Lovell's Tack 'n Togs, Yreka, Calif., 1970-73; v.p. Microphor, Inc., Willits, 1974-81; pres. Harrah Industries, Inc., Willits, 1981—, Hot Rocks, Inc., Willits, 1983-89; gen. ptnr. Madrone Profl. Group, Willits, 1982—; co-ptnr. Running Wild Ostriches, 1994—; bd. dirs. Nat. Bank of the Redwoods, NBR Mortgage Co., Howard Found.; active State of Calif. Employment Tng. Panel, 1993-95, coord. State Calif. Timber Transition, 1994-95, State of Calif. Econ. Strategy Panel, 1995—; apptd. mem. Sate of Calif. Econ. Strategy Panel, 1995—. Sec. Willits Cmty. Scholarships, Inc., 1962; trustee Montague Meth. Ch., 1966-73; sec. Montague PTA, 1969; clk. bd. trustees Montague Sch. Dist., 1970-73; del. Calif. State Conf. Small Bus., 1984; alt. del. Rep. Nat. Conv., Kansas City, Detroit, 1976, 80; 3d dist. chmn. Mendocino County Rep. Ctrl. Com., 1978-84; mem. Calif. State Rep. Ctrl. Com., 1985, 86, 87; Rep. nominee for State Senate Calif. 2nd Senate Dist., 1990, 93; mem. Rep. Congl. Leadership Coun., 1980-82; Mendocino County chmn. Reagan/Bush, 1980, 84; Mendocino County co-chmn. Deukmejian for Gov., 1982; mem. Region IX Small Bus. Adminstrn. Adv. Coun., 1982-93; mem. Gov.'s Adv. Coun., 1983-90; Rep. nominee State Assembly 1st Assembly dist.; del., asst. sgt. of arms Rep. Nat. Conv., Dallas, 1984, del., New Orleans, 1988, San Diego, 1996; vice chmn. Mendocino County Rep. Ctrl. Com., 1985; mem. Willits C. of C. (hon.), Calif. Transp. Commn., 1986-90; state dir. North Bay Dist. Hwy. Grading and Heavy Engring. divsn. 1986; dir. Lit. Vols. Am. Named Mendocino 12th Dist. Fair Woman of the Year, 1987. Mem. No. Coast Builders Exch., Soroptimist Internat. Home: PO Box 1329 Willits CA 95490-1329 Office: Harrah Industries Inc 42 Madrone St Willits CA 95490-4249

HANDLEY, MARILYN WHEAT, journalist; b. Grove Hill, Ala., Jan. 29, 1959; d. Gary Cunningham and Florence Lorraine (Urquhart) Wheat; m. Michael Alan Handley, Feb. 7, 1981 (div. July 1993); children: Michael Adam (dec.), Jared Thomas, Miranda Lorraine. BA, Livingston U., 1980. Asst. news dir. WHOD-Radio, Jackson, Ala., 1980-81; sports editor SHelby County Reporter, Columbiana, Ala., 1981-82; pub. rels. dir. Livingston (Ala.)-Tombigbee Med. Ctr., 1984-85, Rush-Hill Hosp., York, Ala., 1986; editor Sumter County Jour., York, 1986-91; asst. editor Monroe Jour., Monroeville, Ala., 1991, editor, 1992—, part owner, 1996—; exec. dir. Greenville (Ala.) C. of C., 1992. Bd. dirs. Ala. Press Assn. Journalism Found., Birmingham, 1994—, Sumter County Bd. Edn., Livingston, 1986-91, Leadership Now!, Monroeville, 1992—; founding mem. The Ala. Solution, Birmingham, 1995. Recipient Torch award Ala. Federated Women's Clubs, 1989, Douglas L. Cannon Med. Journalism award Ala. Med. Assn., 1995. Mem. Monroeville Bus. and Profl. Women (v.p. 1995, pres. 1996), Monroeville Area C. of C. (bd. dirs. 1996—), Monroeville Kiwanis (bd. dirs.), Beta Sigma Phi (pres. 1996—). Home: 508 Todd St Monroeville AL 36460 Office: Monroe Jour 126 Hines St PO Box 826 Monroeville AL 36461

HAND WRIGHT, LAURA BELLA, broadcast executive; b. Petersburg, Va., Jan. 25, 1950; d. Clifton Earl and Libera Elisa Hand; m. Ronald H. Wright, May 26, 1979; children: Kyle Randall, Carinne Alissa. BA, Syracuse U., 1971. Newscaster Sta. WFBL, Syracuse, N.Y., 1970-72; reporter Sta. WSYR, Syracuse, N.Y., 1972-76; cmty. rels. dir., anchor/prodr. Sta. WSTM, Syracuse, N.Y., 1976—; columnist Community Newspapers, Manlius, N.Y., 1990-93; adj. instr. colls. and univs., 1979-82. Adv. bd. Syracuse Salvation Army, 1986—, Am. Lung Assn. Ctrl. N.Y., 1994—. Named Woman of the Yr. Syracuse AAUW, 1985, Syracuse U. Alumna of the Yr., 1992; recipient numerous media awards. Mem. Syracuse Press Club (bd. dirs. 1986-88, 1990—), Syracuse Univ. Alumni Assn. (bd. dirs. 1989—), Newhouse Alumni Assn., Sedgwick Farm Tennis Club, Chi Omega. Office: WSTM-TV 1030 James St Syracuse NY 13203-2704

HANDY, ALICE WARNER, state agency administrator; b. Wilmington, Del., Apr. 17, 1948; d. Carleton Thomas and Ruth Francis (Lees) H.; m. Peter A. Stoudt; children: Nicholas Lyon Gerow, Jennifer Lees Gerow, Abigail Hurst Gerow. BA, Conn. Coll., 1970; postgrad., U. Va., 1975-78. Asst. investment officer Travelers Ins. Co., Hartford, Conn., 1970-74; investment officer U. Va., Charlottesville, 1974-81, asst. v.p., investment officer, 1981-88, univ. treas., 1988, 90—; treas. Commonwealth of Va., Richmond, 1988-90; bd. dirs. First Union Bank of Va., 1995—; chmn. state coun. local debt, state treasury bd.; commr. Va. Agrl. Devel. Authority, Va. Port Authority; treas. Va. Coll. Bldg. Authority; mem. Va. Edn. Loan Authority, Va. Resources Authority, Va. Small Bus. Financing Authority; sec.-treas. Va. Pub. Bldg. Authority, Va. Pub. Sch. Authority, all 1988-90; cons. various U. Va. founds., 1985—; vice chair investment adv. com. Va. Retirement System, 1994—. Trustee Va. Outdoors Found., 1988-90, Va. Hist. Preservation Found., 1989-90; troop leader Girl Scouts U.S., Charlottesville, 1985-88; bd. dirs. Va. Discovery Mus., Charlottesville, 1988, Conn. Mut. Property Mgmt., 1991-94, Investment Fund for Founds., 1991—, Charlottesville chpt. Am. Heart Assn., 1991-93; mem. fin. com. Thomas Jefferson Ch., Charlottesville, 1987-95; treas. Preservation Alliance, 1990-93, U. Va. Real Estate Found., 19916; mem. Mcpl. Securities Rulemaking Bd., 1993—, chmn., 1995-96. Democrat. Unitarian. Office: U Va PO Box 9012 Charlottesville VA 22906-9012

HANDY, DRUCILLA, public relations executive; b. Lynchburg, Va., Aug. 21, 1924; d. John Bryant and Allen (Steele) H.; m. Robert M. Redinger, Oct. 30, 1954. Student, Swarthmore Coll., 1941-43. Publicist Metro-Goldwyn-Mayer, Washington, 1943-45; editor house organ Du Pont, Richmond, Va., 1945-47; account exec. Rosemary Sheehan Publicity, N.Y.C., 1947-50; pub. rels. dir. Helene Curtis Industries, Inc., Chgo., 1950-54; account supr. Gardner & Jones (name now Hill & Knowlton), Chgo., 1954-56; pres. Drucilla Handy Co. div. L.C. Williams & Assocs., Inc., Chgo., 1956—. Bd. dirs. various civic and cultural orgns., Chgo. Mem. NAFE, Nat. Assn. Women Bus. Owners, Pub. Rels. Soc. Am. (accredited), Counselors Acad., Chgo. Network, Arts Club Chgo., Execs. Club Chgo. *

HANDY, KRISTINA, writer; b. Gunnison, Utah, Oct. 18, 1968; d. Alonzo Hazelton and Carolyn (Jones) H. BA in Internat. Rels. and Spanish, Brigham Young U., 1990; postgrad., U. Md., 1994—. Graphic illustrator U.S. Dept. Labor/Vocat. Tng. and Constrn., Riyadh, Saudi Arabia, 1984; mail clk. U.S. Army Post Office, Riyadh, 1985; office clk. Sci. Application Internat. Corp., Denver, 1987; intern Can. Embassy, Madrid, 1988; with Hill AFB, Ogden, Utah, 1989-90; assoc. editor Internat. Studies Assn., Provo, Utah, 1990-91; writer, program asst. The Cottage Program Internat., Salt Lake City, 1991—. Vol. trainer, crisis worker Salt Lake Rape Crisis Ctr., 1992—; vol. Utah AIDS Found., 1992; bd. dirs. Mormon Women's Forum, Salt Lake City, 1992—. David M. Kennedy Ctr. for Internat. and Area Studies scholar, 1990-91, Leadership scholar, 1986-87. Democrat. Mormon. Home: 4816 Erie St College Park MD 20740

HANEY, JILL LESLIE, educator; b. Bellevue, Wash., Dec. 2, 1968; d. Richard C. and Lois J. (Kilde) H.; m. Antonio K. Osborn, June 20, 1992. BA, Trinity U., 1991, MAT, 1992. Tchr. reading San Antonio Ind. Sch. Dist., 1992—; facilitator summer sch. San Antonio Ind. Sch. Dist., 1993; reading styles trainer Nat. Reading Styles Inst., Syosset, N.Y., 1994—; local mgr. regional conv. Nat. Sci. Tchrs. Assn., San Antonio, 1995. Coun. mem. House of Prayer Luth. Ch., San Antonio, 1994—; bd. dirs. Trinity U. San Antonio Alumni Chpt., 1994-96. Murchison scholar Trinity U., 1987-91. Mem. ASCD, Nat. Coun. Tchrs. English, Nat. Mid. Sch. Assn., Internat. Reading Assn. Office: Mark Twain Mid Sch 2411 San Pedro San Antonio TX 78212

HANFORD, MONA TANIA, fundraiser; b. N.Y.C., May 24, 1943; d. Frederick Marich and Vera (Merejko) Mooney; m. William Edward Hanford Jr., June 14, 1963; children: William Edward III, Tania Hanford Neild. BA, Mount Holyoke Coll., 1964; MA, Vanderbilt U., 1968. Capital campaign coord. St. Patrick's Episcopal Day Sch., Washington, 1983-85, dir. devel., 1985—; cons. Christ Ch., Washington, 1991-94, Friends Com. on Nat. Legis., Washington, 1993-96; mem. philantropy commn. Coun. for Advancement and Support of Edn., Washington, 1992-94; pres. Elixir, Inc., Consulting Firm. Bd. mem. Jr. League Washington, 1978-80; mem. commn. Diocese of Washington, 1986-90. Recipient Heavy Hitters award Coun. for Advancement and Support of Edn., Washington, 1992, 96. Mem. Nat. Soc. Fund Raising Execs. (cert. fund raising exec.), Planned Giving Study Group, Jr. League (bd. mem.). Home: 5613 Overlea Rd Bethesda MD 20816 Office: St Patricks Episcopal Day Sch 4700 Whitehaven Pkwy NW Washington DC 20007

HANFT, RUTH S. SAMUELS (MRS. HERBERT HANFT), health care consultant, educator, economist; b. N.Y.C., July 12, 1929; d. Max Joseph and Ethel (Schechter) Samuels; m. Herbert Hanft, June 17, 1951; children: Marjorie Jane, Jonathan Mark. BS, Cornell U., 1949; MA, Hunter Coll., 1963; PhD, George Washington U., 1989; ScD (hon.), U. Osteo. Med & Health Scis., 1993. Cons. Urban Med. Econs. Project, Hunter Coll., N.Y.C. and D.C. Dept. Health, 1962-63; health economist Office of Rsch. and Stats., Social Security Adminstrn., Washington, 1964-66; chief grants mgmt. health div. Office Econ. Opportunity, Washington, 1966-68; sr. health analyst Office of Asst. Sec. Planning and Evaluation HEW, Washington, 1968-71, spl. asst., asst. sec. health, 1971-72; dep. asst. sec. for health policy, rsch. and stats. Office of Asst. Sec. for Health HEW, 1977-79, dep. asst. sec. for health rsch., stats. and tech., 1979-81; health care cons., 1981-88; cons., rsch. prof. dept. health svcs. mgmt. and policy George Washington U., Washington, 1988-91, prof., 1991-95; cons., 1995—; vis. prof. Dartmouth Med. Sch., 1976—; sr. rsch. assoc. Inst. Medicine-NAS, Washington, 1972-76. Contbr. articles to profl. jours. Mem. Med. Assistance Svc. Bd. Commonwealth Va., 1984-89, Meharry Med. Coll. Bd. Trustees, 1989-94. Fellow Hastings Ctr.; mem. Inst. of Medicine, Nat. Acad. Sci. Jewish. Home: 3609 Cameron Mills Rd Alexandria VA 22305-1107

HAN-GROSE, GRACE SERINA, violinist, educator; b. Chgo., Jan. 28, 1963; d. David and Janet (Chou) Han; m. Michael David Grose, Sept. 1, 1990. MusB magna cum laude, Columbus Coll., 1986; MusM magna cum laude, Fla. State U., 1989. Violinist Savannah (Ga.) Symphony Orchestra, 1990—, violinist string quartet, 1993. Columbus (Ga.) Coll. scholar, 1983-86; recipient grad. assistantship Fla. State U., 1987-90. Mem. Am. Fedn. of Musicians, Chamber Music Am. Presbyterian. Home: 418 E 52d St Savannah GA 31405

HANKA, DEBORAH RAE, secondary education educator; b. Washington, Apr. 24, 1950; d. Raymond Lawrence and Ann Elizabeth (Shillingburg) Heironimus; m. Edward Alan Hanka, May 24, 1975. BA in Social Scis., Towson State U., 1972. Cert. tchr., Md. Tchr. Prince George's County Bd. Edn., Upper Marlboro, Md., 1972—. Co-author: How to Use the Community as a Resource, 1983 (Notable Children's Trade Book in Social Studies 1983). Poll judge Bd. Election Suprs., Anne Arundel County, Md., 1984-87; active NOW. Named Outstanding Tchr. Historian for Prince George's County, U.S. Capitol Hist. Soc., 1988. Mem. NEA, Md. Edn. Assn., Prince George's County Educators Assn. (faculty rep. 1981-83). Office: Martin Luther King Jr Acad Ctr 4545 Ammendale Rd Beltsville MD 20705

HANKES, JENNIFER ELIZABETH, civil engineer; b. St. Paul, June 30, 1969; d. James Thomas and Diane (Kirwin) H.; m. Scott Edward Painter, June 5, 1996. BS, U.S. Mil. Acad., 1991. Engr. platoon leader 34th Engring. Bn. U.S. Army, Ft. Riley, Kans., 1992-94; tng. officer 24th Prime Power Bn. U.S. Army, Ft. Belvoir, Va., 1994-95; project mgr. corps. of engring. USACG-L.A. dist. U.S. Army, L.A., 1995—. Capt. U.S. Army, 1991—. Mem. NAFE, Soc. Am. Mil. Engrs. (sec. L.A. post 1996—). Democrat. Roman Catholic. Home: Box 24 1223 Wilshire Blvd Santa Monica CA 90403 Office: USACE-L A Dist 300 N Los Angeles St Los Angeles CA 90012

HANKINS, MARY DENMAN, elementary school educator; b. Roane County, Tenn., Jan. 31, 1930; d. Elmer Hoyle and Lela Emiline (Cox) Denman; m. Charles Russell Hankins, Mar. 23, 1951; children: Jennifer, Susan, Charles Thomas, Amy. BS, Montreat (N.C.) Coll., 1950; postgrad., East Tenn. State U., Tusculum Coll., Greeneville, Tenn. Cert. elem. tchr., Tex., Tenn. Tchr. elem. Greene County (Tenn.) Schs., 1955-87; tchr. adult basic edn. Greeneville (Tenn.) Schs., 1978-85; elem. tchr. Cedar Hill (Tex.) Ind. Sch. Dist., 1987-95. Contbg. author of sci. and math. home activities for children for textbook cos. Mem. NEA, Tex. Tchrs. Assn., Tenn. Edn. Assn., Tenn. Tchrs. Study Coun., Greene County Edn. Assn. (past editor newsletter), Delta Kappa Gamma.

HANKS, AMY ELIZABETH, artist; b. N.Y.C., Dec. 2, 1966. BFA in Studio Art, U. Tex., 1987; MFA in Ceramics, U. Mich., 1994. Owner Clayworks, Chgo., 1989-92; artist-in-residence Urban Gateways, Chgo., 1990-92, Ox-Bow Sch. of Arts, Saugatuck, Mich., 1994; educator Ann Arbor (Mich.) Art Ctr., 1995-96; cons. Art Train, Ann Arbor, 1996. Works featured in mag. Generator, 1995. Recipient Best of Show award Scarab Club, 1996; Nanette Finger scholar Anderson Ranch, 1993; Individual Artist fellow Ill. Arts Coun., 1989, Rackham Merit fellow U. Mich., 1992. Mem. Nat. Coun. for Edn. in Ceramic Arts (presenter conf. 1996), Coll. Art Assn., Ann Arbor Art Ctr., Detroit Artist Market. Home: 438 W Main St Cary IL 60013

HANLEY, PATRICIA LYNN, school system administrator; b. Syracuse, N.Y., Jan. 29, 1950; d. William Benedict and Louise Morgan (Frasch) H. BS in Elem. and Spl. Edn., Bowling Green State U., 1972, MS in Spl. Edn., 1975; Reading Specialist, No. Ariz. U., 1982; Sch. Dist. Adminstrn. Cert., SUNY, Cortland, 1993. Cert. sch. dist. adminstr., spl. edn. tchr., N.Y. Learning disabilities specialist Wood County (Ohio) Schs., 1974-75; cons. Mishawaka (Ind.) City Schs., 1975-78; coord. spl. edn. Bur. of Indian Affairs, Tuba City, Ariz., 1978-82; faculty Onondaga C.C., Syracuse, N.Y., 1982-87; dir., counselor, advisor spl. svcs. project SUNY, Plattsburgh, 1984-87; ednl. cons. Syracuse Area Schs., 1987-89; core tchr. N.Y. State Divsn. for Youth, Albany, 1989-90; dir. spl. programs Enfield (N.Y.) Elem., 1992-93; owner I Am - I Can, Ithaca, N.Y., 1991—; cons. N.Y. State Commn. of Corrections, Albany, 1995, N.Y. State Commn. for Reform of Juv. Justice System, N.Y.C., 1994. Speaker Women's Info. Assn., Ithaca, 1994, Gov.'s Task Force on Sexual Harrassment, Albany, 1992. Recipient Cavallo prize for moral courage in govt., Cavallo Found., Washington, 1994. Mem. Assn. for Children with Learning Disabilities, Women in Higher Edn., N.Y. State Guidance and Personnel Assn., Ams. with Disabilities Act Assn. Home: 165 Horton Rd Newfield NY 14867

HANNA, EMMA HARMON, architectural designer, business owner, official; b. Sharpsville, Pa., Apr. 29, 1939; d. James McKerney Supplee and Anne (Woods) Thompson; m. William Hayes Harmon, Sept. 1, 1962 (div. 1984); 1 child, James McKarney Harmon; m. Hugh Allen Hanna, Mar. 21, 1992. BArch, Kent (Ohio) State U., 1962. Drafter W.H. Harmon Architects, Orlando, Fla., 1970-73; pres., owner The Plan Shop, Inc., Orlando and Palm Bay, Fla., 1973-87, The Plan Place, Inc., Palm Bay, 1987—; pres. Engring. & Design Concepts, Palm Bay, 1986—; vice chmn. Palm Bay Utility Corp.; vice chmn. substance abuse program Broken Glass, Valkaria, Fla. Mem. coun. City of Palm Bay, 1989-91, dep. mayor, 1991-92; treas. League of Cities, Brevard County, Fla., 1989-92, East Ctrl. Fla. Planning Coun., Orlando, 1989-90; mem. Federated Rep. Women, South Brevard County, 1989-91; mem. exec. com. Brevard County Reps.; mem. Panther Athletic Assn. bd. Fla. Inst. Tech., 1990—, pres., 1995-96; mem. open campus adv. coun. Brevard C.C., Holmes Regional Hosp. Devel. Coun., 1991—. Mem. Home Builder and Contractors Brevard County (assoc., bd. dirs. 1993—, 2nd v.p. 1994-95, Assoc. of Yr. 1995), Bldg. Ofcls. Assn. Brevard County (assoc., Assoc. of Yr. 1989), Drafters Guild (organizer), Palm Bay C. of C., Greater South Brevard C. of C. (mem. govt. affairs com., bd. dirs. 1991-93), Exch. Club (chpt. pres., charter pres.), Zonta Club Melbourne. Home: 1482 Meadowbrook Rd NE Palm Bay FL 32905-5007 Office: The Plan Place 1398 Palm Bay Rd NE Palm Bay FL 32905-3837

HANNA, MARY ANN, education educator; b. Sumter, S.C., Apr. 16, 1947; d. Ernest Lee and Lucile (Horton) Kluttz; m. Dixon Boyce Hanna, June 21, 1994; children: Patrick D., Nathon Lee. BA, Furman U., Greenville, S.C., 1969; MA, Va. Tech., Blacksburg, 1975; PhD, 1979. Lic. prof. counselor, Va.; cert. mental health counselor. 1st grade tchr. N.C. Pub. Schs., Gastonia, Raleigh, N.C., 1969-70; kindergarten tchr. Pitts. Pub. Schs., 1970-71; lead tchr., program coord. A. Leo Weil Elem. Sch., Pitts., 1971-72; curriculum supr. Montgomery County Schs., Christiansburg, Va., 1974-76; ednl. cons. pvt. practice, 1979-91; asst. prof. Coll. Human Resources Va. Tech., Blacksburg, 1978-80; counselor dept. psychology Radford (Va.) U., 1992; specialist assessment Dept. Edn. Commonwealth of Va., 1992-93; asst. prof. Coll. Edn. Radford U., Va., 1993—; cons., instr. U. Va., Charlottesville, 1976-78; cons. Neonatal Assessment Roanoke (Va.) Meml. Hosp., 1980-92; cons. Assessment CTB/McGraw Hill, Monterey, Calif., 1993—; cons., asst. prof. Continuing Edn. Va. Tech., Blacksburg, 1994—. Author: The Open Classroom: A Practical Guide for the Elementary School teacher, 1974, Your Child's Development Scrapbook, 1986; contbr. articles to profl. jours. Bd. dirs. NRV Childcare Program Dublin, Va., 1982-84; Sunday Sch. tchr. Lutheran Meml. Ch., Blacksburg, Va., 1991—; vol. Gilbert Linkous Elem. Sch. Blacksburg, Va., 1988-92. Named Outstanding Student Tchr. Furman U., Greensville, S.C., 1969. Fellow Orthopsychiatry; mem. ACA, Chi Sigma Iota. Lutheran. Home: 3700 W Ridge Dr Blacksburg VA 24060-8564 Office: Radford University PO Box 6994 Radford VA 24142-6994

HANNA, NOREEN ANELDA, adult education administrator, consultant; b. Napa, Calif., Nov. 28, 1939; d. Thomas James and Eileen Anelda (Jordan) H.; m. Leon O'bine Gotcher, Aug. 14, 1971 (div. Nov. 1980); children: John Allen, Tamara Kay. BA, San Francisco State U., 1963; postgrad., Sonoma State U., 1974-81, Ctr. for Leadership Devel., 1982-83; MA, U. San Francisco, 1989. Cert. gen. elem., specialist in reading, gen. adminstrv. svcs. Classroom tchr. Ullom Elem. Sch., Las Vegas, Nev., 1963; classroom tchr. J. L. Shearer Elem. Sch., Napa, 1963-78, reading resource tchr., 1978-80; asst. prin. Napa Valley Adult Sch., Napa, 1980-81, acting prin., 1981-82; prin. El Centro Elem. Sch., Napa, 1982-83; adminstr. J.T.P.A./Gain Programs, Napa, 1983-90; prin. Napa Valley Adult Sch., Napa, 1983—; commn. mem. Calif. Post Secondary Edn., 1987-89; cons. Calif. Dept. Edn., Sacramento, 1988—; adv. bd. dir. Ctr. for Adult Edn., San Francisco (Calif.) State U., 1988-95; adv. bd. mem. Immigration Reform & Control Act, Sacramento, 1989-92; presenter and cons. in field. Exec. bd. dirs. Leadership Napa Valley, 1985-93; sec. Leadership Napa Valley Found., 1988—. State Edn. scholar Calif. PTA, 1976, Grad. Edn. scholar Delta Kappa Gamma, Napa, 1977; recipient Cmty. Leadership award Napa Valley Unified Sch. Dist., 1988, Assn. Calif. Adminstrs. Adult Edn. Adminstr. of yr. award, 1992, George C. Mann Disting. Svc. award Calif. Coun. for Adult Edn., 1994. Mem. ASCD, Am. Assn. for Adult and Continuing Edn., Assn. Calif. Sch. Adminstrs. (chair to state adult edn. com. 1988-89, 93—, state rep. assembly del. 1989-92, state adult edn. com. chairperson 1989-92, others), Calif. Coun. for Adult Edn. (North Coast chpt. bd. dirs. 1988—), Napa C. of C. (bd. dirs. 1985-88, edn./bus. com. 1985—, others), Correctional Educators Assn., Soroptimist Internat. of Napa, Phi Delta Kappa, Delta Kappa Gamma. Republican. Roman Catholic. Office: Napa Valley Adult Edn 2425 Jefferson St Napa CA 94558-4931

HANNA, SHARON LYN, social science educator and author; b. Cozad, Nebr., Oct. 7, 1940; d. Eldred Reynolds and Lorane Mae (Casselman) H.; m. Larry Luther Patterson, June 17, 1962 (div. June 1977); children: Lisa Ann, Lyn Kathleen; m. Robert George Dinkel, Dec. 26, 1978. BA, Nebr. Wesleyan U., 1962; MS, U. Nebr., 1980. Tchr. Lincoln (Nebr.) Pub. Schs., 1962-65, 79-80, Fair Lawn (N.J.) Pub. Schs., 1965-66; dir., tchr. Early Childhood Edn. Ctr., Freeport, Ill., 1970-76; dept. chair and instr. social sci. S.E. Cmty. Coll., Lincoln, 1980—; presenter numerous city, state and nat. groups. Author: Person to Person, 1995; contbr. articles to profl. jours. State pres. Stepfamily Assn. Am., 1980-88, nat. chmn. nat. conf., 1987, nat. v.p., 1988-90, nat. pres., 1990-92. Recipient Disting. Internat. Citizen award Alpha Gamma Delta, 1993. Mem. APA, AAUW, Nat. Coun. Family Rels., Midwest Sociol. Assn., Faculty Assn. Home: 6020 Rosebud Cir Lincoln NE 68516 Office: SE Cmty Coll 8800 O St Lincoln NE 68520

HANNAFAN, KAY H. PIERCE, lawyer; b. Wilmington, Del., Nov. 6, 1952; d. Clifton and Monica Harvey; m. Christopher J. Hannafan, Aug. 21, 1993; children: John Harvey Pierce, Stephen Harvey Pierce. BS in Engring., U. Tenn., 1974, JD, 1979. Bar: Ill. 1980. Patent agt. Union Carbide Corp., Oak Ridge, Tenn., 1974-77; patent atty. Gould Inc., Rolling Meadows, Ill., 1980-85; corp. atty. Baxter Healthcare Corp., Deerfield, Ill., 1985—. Pro bono atty. Lake County, Ill. Vol. Lawyers Program, 1993-94. Office: Baxter Healthcare Corp 1435 Lake Cook Rd Deerfield IL 60015-5213

HANNAH, BARBARA ANN, nurse, educator; b. Pawnee, Okla., Sept. 25, 1943; d. Harold Ray and Betty Jean (Newport) Norris; m. Charles Bush Hannah, Mar. 25, 1971; children: Charles Douglas, Harry William. AS, Rogers State Coll., Claremore, Okla., 1974; BS in nursing, Tulsa U., 1976; MS, Okla U., 1985; postgrad., Okla. State U., 1989. RN, Okla.; cert. BLS, ACLS, PALS. Nurse St. Francis Hosp., Tulsa, 1968-77, edn. specialist, 1986-90, clin. mgr. post-anesthesia care unit, 1991—; dir. clin. prodn. CSI Prodns. for Medcom Inc., Tulsa, 1977-86; asst. adminstr. nursing Cleveland (Okla.) Area Hosp., 1990-91; cons. St. Anthony Hosp., Oklahoma City, 1985; mem. affiliate faculty, chmn. emergency cardiac care com. Am. Heart Assn., 1986, mem. nat. faculty, 1990—; bd. dirs. Citizen CPR, 1986-91, chmn. comprehensive monitoring com., 1990-91. Producer audio-visual programs for nursing edn., 1977-86. Mem. Food & Refreshment Com. Channel 8 fund raising drive, Tulsa, 1985, 86. Recipient spl. awards and honors All Heart Vol., 1988. Mem. NAFE, Acute Care Nurses Assn. (seminar dir., treas. Greater Tulsa area chpt.), Okla. Nurses Assn. (dist. 2 com. on profl. practice), Am. Heart Assn. (v.p. program com. 1990—, chmn. faculty BLS task force Woman of Yr., Okla. affiliate 1993, chmn. Okla. affiliate 1994, 95-96), Am. Soc. Post Anesthesia Nurses (1st pl. poster award Nat. Ann. Conf. 1993, alt. del. from Okla. 1994), Okla. Soc. Post Anesthesia Nurses (pres. Tulsa chpt. 1993), Am. Soc. Peri Anesthesia Nurses (Okla. del. to bd. 1996—), Sigma Theta Tau. Home: PO Box 112 Skiatook OK 74070-0112 Office: St Francis Hosp 6161 S Yale Ave Tulsa OK 74136-1902

HANNAH, DARYL, actress; b. Chgo., 1960; d. Don and Sue Hannah. Student, U. So. Calif., Goodman Theater Co., Chgo. Ind. actress, 1978—. Films include The Fury, 1978, The Final Terror, 1981, Hard Country, 1981, Summer Lovers, 1982, Blade Runner, 1982, Reckless, 1984, Splash, 1984, The Pope of Greenwich Village, 1984, The Clan of the Cave Bear, 1986, Legal Eagles, 1986, Roxanne, 1987, Wall Street, 1988, High Spirits, 1988, Steel Magnolias, 1989, Crimes and Misdemeanors, 1989, Crazy People, 1990, At Play in the Fields of the Lord, 1991, Memoirs of an Invisible Man, 1992, Grumpy Old Men, 1993, The Little Rascals, 1994, A Hundred and One Nights, 1995, The Tie that Binds, 1995, Grumpier Old Men, 1995, Two Much, 1996, The Last Days of Frankie the Fly, 1996; TV film Paper Dolls, 1982, Attack of the 50 Foot Woman, 1993. *

HANNAH, MARY-EMILY, university consultant, educator; b. Denver, Mar. 14, 1936; d. Stewart Whistler and Emily (Wight) H. AB, Grinnell Coll., 1958, LLD (hon.), 1981; MA, U. Iowa, 1962; PhD, U Ill., 1967; postgrad., U. Denver, U. Colo., U. Fla., Harvard. Instr. Arvada High Sch., Denver, 1958-61; prof. speech St. Cloud (Minn.) State U., 1962-64, 67-78, dept. chmn., 1968-72; asst. prof. speech Sacramento State U., 1966-67; asst. v.p. Met. State U., St. Paul, 1975, acting. pres., 1977; vice chancellor acad. affairs Minn. State Univ. System, St. Paul, 1976-80; chancellor U. Wis.-Eau Claire, 1980-84; vice chancellor Pa State System of Higher Edn., Harrisburg, 1984-93; faculty Carnegie Mellon Acad. Leadership Inst., 1991-93; leader People to People Delegation to USSR, 1991, South Africa, 1995. Trustee The Sage Colls., 1988-96. Named Disting. Alumna Grinnell Coll., 1980; Princeton U. rsch. fellow, 1966. Mem. Am. Assn. Higher Edn., Pa. Acad. Profession of Teaching (chair bd. dirs.), Am. Assn. State Colls. and Univs. (mission to Brazil 1983), Phi Kappa Phi, Delta Sigma Rho-Tau Kappa Alpha, Omicron Delta Kappa, PEO. Home: PO Box 1036 South Orleans MA 02662

HANNAN, BRADLEY, educational publishing consultant and executive; b. Rochester, N.Y., Apr. 24, 1935; d. Jack Seymour MacArthur and Alice E. (Knapp) Staley; m. William J. Hannan, Jr., June 15, 1957 (div. 1977); children: Megan, Timothy, Patrick, Moira. BA, Ariz. State U., 1957. Tchr. various sch. dists. Ariz., 1957-62; English language cons. Evanston (Ill.) Twp. High Sch., 1963-65; editor, then sr. editor Harper & Row Pubs., Evanston, 1965-75; sr. reading text editor Scott, Foresman & Co., Glenview, Ill., 1975-78, sr. editor lang. arts, 1982-87; dir. reading McDougal Littell & Co., Evanston, 1978-81; project dir. spelling Ednl. Challenges, Alexandria, Va., 1981-82; dir. curriculum and product mgmt. for reading and lang. arts texts Open Court Pub. Co., Chgo. and Peru, Ill., 1987-88; cons., project dir. lang. arts texts Harcourt Brace, Orlando, Fla., 1988-89; sr. mng. editor reading, lang. arts, social studies Sci. Rsch. Assocs., Chgo., 1989; cons. ednl. pub. Chgo., 1989-90; dir. reading, lang. arts, social studies Proof Positive/Farrowlyne Assocs., Chicago, 1990—; speaker Internat. Reading Assn., New Orleans, 1981, Chgo. Women in Publishing, 1981, Childrens' Reading Roundtable, Chgo., 1985; developer reading textbook series. Mem. Internat. Reading Assn., Nat. Council Tchrs. English, Chgo. Book Clinic. Home: 800 Judson Ave Apt 301 Evanston IL 60202-2451 Office: 1620 Central St Evanston IL 60201-1506

HANNAWAY, PATRICIA HINMAN, art scholar, historian, poet; b. Mpls., Jan. 25, 1929; d. Ira Perry and Florence Elizabeth (Montgomery) Hinman; m. Glenn H. Altland, June 12, 1948 (div. 1968); children: David Lee, Roger Dean, Stanley William (dec.), Glenn H. III (dec.); m. Walter F. Hannaway, Feb. 7, 1972 (dec. 1985). Grad. high sch., Mpls., 1947. Freelance writer Mpls., 1953-59; advt. copywriter Boutell's Inc., Mpls., 1958-59, Colle McVoy, Mpls., 1959, Knox-Reeves Advt., Mpls., 1960-62; woman's page editor Key West (Fla.) Citizen, 1963-65; creative dir. Grant Advt., Miami, 1967-68; info. specialist Fla. Dept. Commerce, Tallahassee, 1968-69; creative dir. Daniels Rainey Advt., Clearwater, Fla., 1970-72, Profl. Bus. Assocs., Lutz, Fla., 1988-90; freelance researcher/author. Author: Winslow Homer in the Tropics, 1974. Pres. Friends of Libr., Clearwater, 1975-76, Friends of Tampa Hills Libr.; adv. bd. mem. Pasco Libr. System, 1991-93; coord. New River Poets and Writers, 1995-96. Democrat. Lutheran. Office: Agape Unlimited PO Box 7112 Wesley Chapel FL 33543-7112

HANNEKEN, KATHRYN ANN, school superintendent; b. Shelbyville, Ill., Jan. 19, 1949; d. Neil R. and Nelda Jean (Wharton) Balding; m. Hank Hanneken, Nov.28, 1970; 1child, Alexis Suzanne. BS in Edn., Eastern Ill.U., 1970, MS in Edn., 1973, Specialist in Edn., 1987. Cert. in ednl.adminstrn.-supt., elem., spl. edn. tchr. Tchr. Mattoon (Ill.) Cmty. Unit Dist. 2, 1970-80, prin., 1980-89; supt. Jasper Cmty. Consol. Dist. #17, Fairfield, Ill., 1989—; ednl. cons. Ill. sch. dists. and orgns.,1988—. Officer, mem. Amicum, Fairfield,1989—; adv. bd. I-Search, Mattoon,1986-89. Named Outstanding Young Educator, Ill. Jaycees, 1977; recipient Those Who Excel award for ednl. excellence Ill. State Bd. Edn., 1979, Nat. Sch./Bus. Partnership award ASBO Internat., 1986. Mem. Ill. Assn. Sch. Adminstrs., Ill. Prins. Assn. (officer, dir., Ill. Nat. Disting. Prin. award1988), Kiwanis, Epsilon Sigma Alpha, Alpha Gamma Delta. Roman Catholic.

HANNEMAN, ELAINE ESTHER, salesperson; b. Waupaca, Wis., Aug. 28, 1928; d. Martin Fred Strey and Laura Rucks; m. Alfred Adam Hanneman, Feb. 14, 1948; children: Karen, Dale, Sally, Sandra. High sch. grad., 1946. Acct. AAL Life Ins. Co., Appleton, Wis., 1946-48; salesperson Cinderella Cosmetics, 1948-60; sales Artex Paint, Milw., 1960-74, Car Ins. and Memberships (AAA), Appleton, Wis., 1974-78, Am. Family Life, Columbus, Ga., 1979—. Mem. Gold Century Club, Pres. Club, Am. Family Life. Lutheran. Home: PO Box 244 103 W St Weyauwega WI 54983-0244 also: 1842 Edgewater Dr Amherst WI 54407

HANNER, DAWNA MELANSON, medical/surgical nurse, analyst; b. Boston, June 4, 1947; d. Frank O. and Patricia C. (Sears) Melanson; m. David M. Hanner, Sept. 1984; children: Daniel Thompson, Scott Thompson. RN Sch. Nursing, Cooley-Dickinson Hosp., Northampton, Mass., 1968. RN, Tex., Mass., N.Y. Staff nurse Columbia Presbyn. Hosp., N.Y.C., St. Elizabeth's Hosp., Boston; triage nurse Children's Med. Ctr., Austin, Tex.; pediatrics charge nurse S.W. Tex. Med. Ctr. Hosp., San Antonio; pediatrics office nurse Dr. Robert A. Wymer, M.D., San Antonio; internat. med. triage supr./mgr. Southboro (Mass.) Med. Group; unit coord. insvc. implementation, nurse mgr. HMO unit Austin Regional Clinic, 1983-84; nurse auditor cost containment svcs. TSSF, Austin, Tex., 1985-88; nurse IV analyst Recipient Utilization Control Tex. Dept. Human Svcs., Austin, 1988-95; quality assessment nurse Tex. Dept. Health Managed Care Bur., 1995—. Mem. NAFE, Tex. Med. Auditors Assn., Exec. Women Tex. Govt. Home: 1004 Alegria Rd Austin TX 78757-3404 Office: Tex Dept of Human Svcs PO Box 149030 Austin TX 78714-9030

HANNI, GERALDINE MARIE, therapist; b. Salt Lake City, Nov. 14, 1930; d. John Henry and Theresa Justine (Keirce) Gold; m. Kenneth J. Hanni, Mar. 14, 1951; children: Debra, Valerie, Kathleen, Cynthia, Kristine. BS, U. Utah, 1951, MSW, 1983. Lic. clin. social worker. Tchr. Hillside Jr. High Sch., Salt Lake City, 1970-73; intern Davis County Schs., Farmington, Utah, 1981-82, Westside Mental Health, Salt Lake City, 1982-83; group leader LDS Social Services, Salt Lake City, 1985; therapist ISAT, Salt Lake City, 1983-90, clin. dir., 1987-90; clin. instr. U. Utah, Salt Lake City, 1986-90; pvt. practice, 1990—; mem. bd. Salt Lake County Sexual Abuse Task Force, Salt Lake City; cons. LDS Social Services, Salt Lake City, 1984-86. Contbg. author: Abuse and Religion, Confronting Abuse—an LDS Perspective. Sect. dir. Mortar Bd. Honor Soc., western U.S., 1970; pres. Highland High PTA, Salt Lake City, 1980; chairperson Highland High Community Sch. Orgn., Salt Lake City, 1981. Mem. Nat. Assn. Social Workers (Utah chpt.). Democrat. Mormon.

HANOWER, SANDRA L., financial analyst, portfolio manager. BA in Bus. Adminstrn., U. Wash., Seattle, 1982. CFA. Money market trader Old Nat. Bank, Seattle, 1982; instnl. equity sales asst. Merrill Lynch Capital Markets, Seattle, 1982-84; equity trader, systems mgr. Kunath Karren Rinne & Atkin, Seattle, 1984-90; asst. v.p. and portfolio mgr. Security Pacific Bank, 1990-92, Seafirst Bank, Seattle, 1992-93; fin. advisor Sigma Kappa Sorority, Seattle, 1985-87. Chmn. fin. com. Seattle Art Mus.-Met. Guild, 1989-90, chairperson exec. com. 1990-92. Mem. Assn. Investment Mgmt. and Rsch., Seattle Soc. Fin. Analysts (chmn. edn. com. 1989-91, sec. 1991-92, v.p. 1992-93, pres. 1993-94), Houston Soc. Fin. Analysts, Wash. Athletic Club, Univ. Club, Lakeside Country Club. Home: 415 Shadywood Rd Houston TX 77057-1419

HANRATTY, CARIN GALE, pediatric nurse practitioner; b. Dec. 31, 1953; d. Burton and Lillian Aleskowitz; m. Michael Patrick Hanratty, May 22, 1983; 1 child, Tyler James. BSN, Russell Sage Coll., 1975; postgrad., U. Calif., San Diego, 1980. Cert. CPR instr.; cert. NALS; cert. specialist ANA. PNP day surgery unit Children's Med. Ctr., Dallas, 1981-85; clin. mgr. pediatrics Trinity Med. Ctr., Carrollton, Tex., 1985-86; pediatric drug coord. perinatal intervention team for substance abusing women and babies Parkland Meml. Hosp., Dallas, 1990—. Guest talk show Morning Coffee, Sta. KPLX-FM, various TV programs. Rep. United Way, 1988—, blood donor chair Parkland Hosp., 1990—, chair March of Dimes, 1992—; bd. dirs., med. cons. KIDNET Found. Mem. ARC (profl., life), Nat. Assn. PNPs (v.p. Dallas chpt. 1982-83), Tex. Nurses Assn. Office: Parkland Meml Hosp PNP 5201 Harry Hines Blvd Dallas TX 75235-7708

HANSARD-WEINER, SONJA, English educator, art gallery owner, editor; b. Wichita Falls, Tex., June 4, 1944; d. S. Lester Hansard and Zylpha F. (Rogers) Sullivan; m. Andrew D. Weiner Jan. 1, 1974; children: Heather, Adam, Holly, Joshua. BA, U. St. Thomas, Houston, 1966; MA, U. Tex., El Paso, 1972; postgrad., U. Wis., Madison, 1972-76. Acad. counselor Coop. Program for Ednl. Opportunity, Chgo., 1968-69; childcare worker Lake County Dept. Pub. Welfare, Gary, Ind., 1970-71; tchg. asst. U. Wis., Madison, 1972-76; owner Spaightwood Galleries, Madison, 1980—; instr. Madison Area Tech. Coll., Madison, 1978—; program chair midwest region MRC, 1985-86. Author: (jour.) Graven Images, 1995-96; co-author: (catalogue) Gérard Titus-Carmel: Forging the Real, 1992; assoc. editor: (jour.) Graven Images, 1994—. Mem., former officer Marquette Neighborhood Assn., 1974—. Recipient Summer Seminar fellow NEH, Madison, 1995. Mem. Shakespeare Assn. Am., Midwest Regional Coun. of Tchrs. of English, Sixteenth Century Studies. Democrat. Roman Catholic. Home: 1150 Spaight St Madison WI 53703 Office: MATC 211 N Carroll St Madison WI 53703

HANSEN, BARBARA CALEEN, physiology educator, scientist; b. Boston, Nov. 24, 1941; d. Reynold L. and Dorothy (Richardson) Caleen; m. Kenneth Dale Hansen, Oct. 8, 1976; 1 son, David Scott. B.S., UCLA, 1964, M.S., 1965; Ph.D., U. Wash., 1971. Asst. prof. then assoc. prof. U. Wash., Seattle, 1971-76; prof., assoc. dean U. Mich., Ann Arbor, 1977-82; assoc. v.p. acad. affairs and research, dean grad. sch. So. Ill. U., Carbondale, 1982-85; v.p. for grad. studies and research U. Md., Balt. and Baltimore County, 1985-90; prof. physiology, dir. obesity and diabetes rsch. ctr. U. Md., 1990—; mem. adv. com. to dir. NIH, Washington, 1979-83; mem. joint health policy com. Assn. Am. Univs., Nat. Assn. State Univs. and Land-Grant Colls., Am. Coun. on Edn., Washington, 1982-86; mem. nutrition study sect. NIH, 1979-83; mem. program com. Inst. Medicine-NAS, Washington, 1982-84; mem. Armed Forces Epidemiology Bd., 1991-95, Bd. Sci. Counselors, Nat. Toxicology Bd., NIEHS, NIH, 1992-94; mem. search com. Office of Rsch. Integrity, NIH, 1992-93. Contbr. articles to profl. jours.; editor: Controversies in Obesity, 1983; chpts. on physiology. Mem. adv. com. Am. Bur. Med. Advancement China, N.Y.C., 1982-85, Robert Wood Johnson Found., Princeton, N.J., 1982-91; mem. adv. bd. African-Am. Inst. 1987-91. U. Pa. Inst. Neuroscis. fellow, 1966-68; Arthur Patch McKinley scholar of Phi Beta Kappa, 1964. Mem. Am. Physiol. Soc., Inst. Medicine of NAS, Am. Inst. Nutrition, Am. Soc. for Clin. Nutrition (v.p., pres.-elect 1994-95, pres. 1995-96), Internat. Assn. for Study of Obesity (pres. 1986-90), N.Am. Assn. for Study of Obesity (pres. 1984-85, 86—), Nat. Assn. State Univs. and Land Grant Colls. (chaiperson coun. on rsch. policy and grad. edn. 1986-87), Phi Beta Kappa. Republican. Presbyterian. Office: U Md Sch Medicine Obesity and Diabetes Rsch Ctr 10 S Pine St MSTF6-00 Baltimore MD 21201-1192

HANSEN, CAROL LOUISE, English language educator; b. San Jose, Calif., July 17, 1938; d. Hans Eskelsen and Thelma Josephine (Brooks) Hansen; m. Merrill Chris Davis, July 17, 1975 (div. 1978). BA in English, San Jose State U., 1960; MA in English Lit., U. Calif., Berkeley, 1968; PhD in English Lit., Ariz. State U., 1975. Asst. prof. English City Coll. San Francisco, Calif., 1985—, Coll. San Mateo, Calif., 1987—. Author: Woman as Individual in English Renaissance Drama, 1993, 2nd edit., 1995. Active Grace Cathedral, San Francisco. NDEA fellow, English-Speaking Union fellow for rsch. in Eng. Ariz. State U., 1972. Mem. MLA (exec. com. discussion group on two-yr. colls.), Virginia Woolf Soc. Episcopalian. Office: City Coll San Francisco 50 Phelan Ave San Francisco CA 94112

HANSEN, DONNA LAUREE, court reporting educator; b. Concordia, Kans., Dec. 25, 1939; d. Peter August and Lynda Bernice (Carlson) H. BA, Bethany Coll., 1961; MS, Kans. State U., 1986. Cert. tchr., Kans., notary pub., Kans. Tchr. Munden (Kans.) High Sch., 1961-64; instr. typing Brown Mackie Coll., Salina, Kans., 1964-74, instr. ct. reporting, 1974-77, chairperson ct. reporting, 1977-88, cons., instr., 1989—; instr. shorthand workshop Pittsburg (Kans.) State U., 1978, Emporia (Kans.) State U., 1978; adminstr. social work spl. project City of Camden, N.J., summers 1962, 63. Compiler (books) Court Reporting Procedures, 1981, Court Reporting Theory Review Books 1, 2, 3, 1983, Court Reporting Advanced Theory Review, Vols. I, II, III, 1984. Bd. dirs. YWCA, Salina, 1991-93, membership chair, 1992-93; mem. alumni bd. Bethany Coll., Lindsborg, Kans., 1979-81. Mem. AAUW (pres 1995-97, numerous offices, Outstanding Mem. 1980), Kans. Bus. Tchrs. Assn., Nat. Bus. Tchrs. Assn., Kans. Shorthand Reporters Assn., Nat. Shorthand Reporters, Delta Kappa Gamma (numerous offices). Republican. Lutheran. Office: Brown Mackie Coll 126 S Santa Fe Ave Salina KS 67401-2810

HANSEN, ELISA MARIE, art historian; b. Sarasota, Fla., July 14, 1952; d. Gotfred and Barbara (Ham) Hansen; m. Flemming Sogaard, 1987; children: Inga Marie, Anna Sofia. BA in Art History, Fla. State U., 1974; MA in Art History, So. Meth. U., 1982; MA, U. So. Fla., 1984. Edn. specialist Pinellas County Art Coun., Clearwater, Fla., 1977-78; curator of edn. Mus. Fine Arts, St. Petersburg, Fla., 1978-80; asst. prof. Eckerd Coll., St. Petersburg, 1985-88, adj. prof., 1988—; dir. adult and ed. programs, acting curator The John & Mable Ringling Mus. Art, Sarasota, 1989-95; adj. instr. Ringling Sch. Art and Design, 1992—. Contbr. articles and book reviews to profl. jours. Mem. Am. Assn. Mus., Coll. Art Assn. Republican. Lutheran.

HANSEN, HEIDI NEUMANN, advertising executive; b. N.Y.C., Feb. 2, 1955; d. Roy G. and Carolyn (Holmes) Neumann; m. Bruce Alan Hansen, Sept. 1, 1984. Student MIT, 1975-76; A.B., Colby Coll., Waterville, Maine, 1977. Benefits adminstr. Gen. Host Corp., Stamford, Conn., 1977-78; pres. Letterworks Internat., Portland, Maine, 1981—; bd. dir. SALT Ctr. Documentary Studies, 1993-95; bd. advisors Docktrap River Fish Farm, 1992—. Dir., Maine Handicapped Skiing, Portland, 1984-92; vol. Maine Med. Ctr., Portland, 1982—; bd. dir. Portland Concert Assn., 1992—; trustee Portland Mus. Art, 1993—; corporator Maine Med. Ctr., 1993—. Mem. Maine Audubon Soc, Nature Conservancy, Ad Club of Greater Portland (dir. 1983-85, v.p. 1985-87, pres. 1987-88), Portland C. of C. (bd. dir. 1990-92). Avocations: travel, hiking, sailing. Home: 313 Fowler Rd Cape Eliz ME 04107-2501 Office: Letterworks Internat 18 Ashmont St Portland ME 04103-4412

HANSEN, JEAN MARIE, math and computer educator; b. Detroit, Mar. 8, 1937; d. Harvey Francis and Ida Marie (Hay) Chapman; m. Donald Edward Hansen, Aug. 29, 1968; children: Jennifer Lynn, John Francis. BA, U. Mich., 1959, MA, 1960. Cert. Secondary Sch. Tchr. Tchr. Detroit Pub. Schs., 1959-60, Newark (Calif.) Sch. Dist., 1960-65, Dept. Def., Zweibruken, Germany, 1965-67, Livonia (Mich.) Pub. Schs., 1967-69; instr. Ford Livonia Transmission Plant, 1990—; trustee/pres. Northville (Mich.) Bd. Edn., 1981—. Author: California People and Their Government, 1965, Voices of Government, 1969-70. Named Disting. Bd. Mem., Mich. Assn. Sch. Bds., 1991, Citizen of Yr., Northville C. of C., 1991. Mem. AAUW (v.p. Northville bd. 1982-86, pres. 1987-89, Mich. chpt. Agt. of Change award, edn. area 1985), LWV, Kiwanis, Northville Women's Club. Republican. Home: 229 Linden St Northville MI 48167-1426

HANSEN, JO-IDA CHARLOTTE, psychology educator, researcher; b. Washington, Oct. 2, 1947; d. Gordon Henry and Charlotte Lorraine (Helgeson) H.; m. John Paul Campbell. BA, U. Minn., 1969, MA, 1971, PhD, 1974. Asst. prof. psychology U. Minn., Mpls., 1974-78, assoc. prof., 1978-84, prof., 1984—, dir. Ctr. for Interest Measurement Rsch., 1974—, dir. counseling psychology program, 1987—. Author: User's Guide for the SII, 1984, 2d edit., 1992, Manual for the SII, 1985; editor: Measurement and Evaluation in Counseling and Development, 1993—; contbr. numerous articles to profl. jours., chpts. to books. Recipient early career award U. Minn., 1982, E.K. Strong, Jr. gold medal Strong Exec. Bd., 1984. Fellow APA (coun. reps. 1990-93, pres. divsn. counseling psychology 1993-94, chmn. joint com. testing practices 1989-93, com. to revise APA/AERA.NCME testing stds. 1993—, Lema Tyler award for rsch. and profl. svc. 1996), Am. Psychol. Soc.; mem. ACA (extended rsch. award 1990, rsch. award 1996), Assn. for Measurement and Evaluation (pres. 1988-89, Exemplary Practice award 1987, 90). Office: U Minn Dept Psychology Ctr Interest Measurement 75 E River Rd Minneapolis MN 55455-0280

HANSEN, KAREN THORNLEY, accountant; b. Chgo., June 1, 1945. BA, Marycrest Coll., Davenport, Iowa, 1967. CPA, N.Y.; cert. M.T. Med. staff tech. Mercy Hosp., Davenport, Iowa, 1967-68, St. Joseph Hosp., Chgo., 1968, Spl. Hematology, Wilford Hall, USAF Hosp., Lackland AFB, Tex., 1973-78; staff acct. Lewittes & Co., Poughkeepsie, N.Y., 1980-81; sr. acct. Urbach, Kahn & Werlin, Poughkeepsie, 1981-82; ptnr. Hansen & Dunn, CPA's, Poughkeepsie, 1982-94, Hansen & Arnold, Poughkeepsie, 1995—. Bd. dirs., sec. United Way Dutchess County, Poughkeepsie, 1988—; bd. dirs. YMCA Dutchess County, Girl Scouts U.S.A., 1983-87, Mid-Hudson Civic Ctr., Inc., 1993-95; mem. Jr. League Poughkeepsie, 1979—, Civic Properties, Inc., 1992—; mem. membership com. and econ. devel. com. Poughkeepsie Partnership, Inc.; trustee St. Martin de Porres Ch. Mem. AICPA, N.Y. State Soc. CPAs, Greater Poughkeepsie Area C. of C. (bd. dirs. 1986—, 1st vice chair 1991—, sec. exec. com. 1991, v.p. exec. com. 1993—), Amrita Club (bd. dirs. 1982-92, pres. 1990), Poughkeepsie Tennis Club. Republican. Roman Catholic. Office: Hansen & Arnold 309 Main Mall Poughkeepsie NY 12601-3116

HANSEN, KATHRYN GERTRUDE, former state official, association editor; b. Gardner, Ill., May 24, 1912; d. Harry J. and Marguerite (Gaston) Hansen; BS with honors, U. Ill., 1934, MS, 1936. Sec., U. N.C., 1936-37; sec., U. High Sch., U. Ill., 1937-44; Personnel asst. U. Ill., Urbana, 1944-46, supr. tng. and activities, 1946-47, personnel officer, instr. psychology, 1947-52, exec. sec. U. Civil Service System Ill., also sec. for merit bd., 1952-61, adminstrv. officer, sec. merit bd., 1961-68, dir. system, 1968-72; lay asst. firm Webber, Balbach, Theis and Follmer, P.C., Urbana, Ill., 1972-74. Bd. dirs. U. YWCA, 1952-55, chmn., 1954-55; bd. dirs. Champaign-Urbana Symphony, 1978-81; sec. Presbyn. Women 1st Presbyn. Ch., Champaign, 1986-90, mem. coordinating team, 1986-91. Mem. Coll. and Univ. Personnel Assn. (hon., life mem., editor jour. 1955-73, newsletter, internat. pres. 1967-68, nat. publs. award named in her honor 1987, Ill. State award 1996), Annuitants Assn. State Univs. Retirement System Ill. (state sec.-treas. 1974-75), Pres.'s Council U. Ill. (life), U. Ill. Alumni Assn. (life), Friends of the Library (bd. dirs. 1987-91), U. Ill. Found., Nat. League Am. Pen Women, AAUW (state 1st v.p. 1958-60, hon., life), Secretariat U. Ill. (life, named scholarship 1972—), Grundy County Hist. Soc. (life), Delta Kappa Gamma (state pres. 1961-63), Phi Mu (life), Kappa Delta Pi, Kappa Tau Alpha. Presbyterian. Clubs: Fortnightly (Champaign-Urbana), U. Ill. Women's Club, Evening Etude-Mozart Club (hon.). Lodge: Order Eastern Star. Author: (with others) A Plan of Position Classification for Colleges and Universities; A Classification Plan for Staff Positions at Colleges and Universities, 1968; Grundy-Corners, 1982; Sarah, A Documentary of Her Life and Times, 1984, Ninety Years with Fortnightly, Vols. I and II, an historical compilation, 1986, Vol. III, 1995, Whispers of Yesterday, 1989, Through the Years with the Champaign-Urbana Business and Professional Women's Club, 1912-1993, 1993, My Heritage, 1995, Presbyterian Women of First Presbyterian Church, Champaign, Illinois, An Historical Documentary, 1870-1995, 1996; editor: The Illini Worker, 1946-52; Campus Pathways, 1952-61; This is Your Civil Service Handbook, 1960-67; author, cons., editor publs. on personnel practices. Home: 1004 E Harding Dr Apt 307 Urbana IL 61801-6346

HANSEN, LORRAINE SUNDAL (SUNNY HANSEN), counselor, educator; b. Albert Lea, Minn.; d. Rasmus O. and Cora B. Sundal; m. Tor Kjaerstad Hansen, Dec. 15, 1962; children: Sonja, Tor S. BS, U. Minn., 1951, MA, 1957, PhD, 1962; postgrad., U. Oslo, Norway, 1959-60. Nat. cert. counselor; cert. career counselor. English tchr. St. Louis Park, Minn., 1951-53, Lab. Sch. U. Chgo., 1953-54; tchr. English and journalism Univ. High Sch., U. Minn., Mpls., 1954-57, counselor, dir. counseling, 1957-70; asst. prof., assoc. prof., prof. ednl. psychology U. Minn., Mpls., 1962—; founder, dir. project BORN FREE; cons. schs. and colls.; lectr. throughout U.S. and 16 countries; dir. workshops on career devel. and career counseling, gender roles, integrative life planning; co-dir. MICI Internat. Counseling Inst., 1989, 91, 93, 95. Author: Career Guidance Practices in School and Community, 1970, An Examination of Concepts and Definitions of Career Education, 1976, Integrative Life Planning, 1996, (with others) Educating for Career Development, 1975, 80, Career Development and Planning, 1982, Eliminating Sex Stereotyping in Schools, 1984; editor: Career Development and Counseling of Women, 1978, Career Patterns of Selected Women Leaders, 1987, Integrative Career Planning, 1994, (with others) Growing Smart: What's Working for Girls in Schools, 1995, Gender Issues: Multicultural counseling, 1995, Career Development Trends and Issues in U.S., 1993; mem. editl. bd. Intern. Jour. Advancement Counseling, 1980-88, Minn. Jour. for Counseling and Human Devel., 1984-95. Fulbright scholar U. Oslo, 1959-60; named Outstanding Leader in Edn. Mpls. YWCA, 1984; recipient Career Devel. Profl. Award S.E. Minn. chpt. ASTD, 1986. Fellow APA; mem. AAUW, Am. Coun. Assn. (pres.-elect 1988-89, pres. 1989-90, Best Video award 1980, Nat. Profl. Devel. award 1995), Minn. Psychol. Assn., Minn. Assn. for Counseling and Devel. (recipient cert. recognition 1976, Nat. Disting. Achievement award 1990), Am. Sch. Counselors Assn., Am. Coll. Pers. Assn., Am. Coll. Counselors Assn., Assn. for Counselor Edn. and Supervision (Nat. Disting. Mentor award 1985), Nat. Career Devel. Assn. (pres.-elect 1984-85, pres. 1985-86, Eminent Career award 1990), Minn. Career Devel. Assn. (pres. 1982-83, Rsch. award 1980, Outstanding Achievement award 1986), Internat. Assn. Ednl.-Vocat. Guidance, Internat. Round Table for Advancement of Counseling (exec. coun. v.p. 1986-88), Assn. for Multicultural Counseling and Devel., Assn. for Adult Devel. and Aging, Minn. Women's Consortium, Upper Midwest Norwegian-Am. C. of C. (bd. dirs. 1988—), Phi Delta Kappa, Chi Sigma Iota. Democrat. Congregationalist. Office: U Minn Dept Ednl Psychology 139 Burton Hall 178 Pillsbury Dr SE Minneapolis MN 55455-0296

HANSEN, NANCY KAY, psychologist, educator; b. Indpls., Apr. 24, 1956; d. Frank Ewart and Alberta Arlene (Montgomery) Spencer; m. Curtis Jay Hansen, July 18, 1981. BS in Gen. and Exptl. Psychology, Ball State U., 1979; MA in Gerontol. Counseling, U. Notre Dame, 1985, MA in Counseling Psychology, 1988, PhD in Counseling Psychology, 1992. Neuropsychology extern Meml. Regional Rehab. Inst., South Bend, Ind., 1987-88, 89-90; clin. intern Martinez (Calif.) VA Med. Ctr., 1990-91, clin. fellow, 1991-92; rsch. fellow U. Mich., Ann Arbor, 1992-94; asst. prof. Saginaw Valley State U., University Center, Mich., 1994—; adj. faculty St. Mary's Coll., South Bend, 1988-90. Contbr. articles and abstracts to profl. publs. Vol. cons., rschr. U. Mich. Med. Ctr., Ann Arbor, 1994—; group facilitator Widow to Widow, St. Joseph's County Mental Health Assn., South Bend, 1987-88; group facilitator caregiver's support group Nat. Assn. for Alzheimers and Related Disorders, South Bend, 1986-89; vol. instr. class to early retirees Bendix Corp./Forever Learning Inst., South Bend, 1988. Recipient Rsch. award Retirement Rsch. Fund, 1988; rsch. fellow NIH, 1992-94; tng. stipend NIMH, 1985-87; tuition scholar U. Notre Dame, 1985-90. Mem. APA, Am. Assn. Spinal Cord Injury Psychologists (presenter rsch. posters 1994, 95), Soc. Behavioral Medicine, Am. Congress Rehab. Medicine, Ea. Paralyzed Vets. Assn. (rsch. com. mem. 1994—). Democrat. Office: Saginaw Valley State U Brown 166 7400 Bay Rd University Center MI 48710

HANSEN, ROBYN L., lawyer; b. Terre Haute, Ind., Dec. 2, 1949; d. Robert Louis and Shirley (Nagel) Wieman; m. Gary Hansen, Aug. 21, 1971 (div. 1985); children: Nathan Ross Hansen, Brian Michael Hansen; m. John Marley Clarey, Jan. 1, 1986. BA, Gustavus Adolphus, 1971; JD cum laude, William Mitchell Coll. Law, 1977. Bar: Minn. 1977, U.S. Dist. Ct. Minn. 1977. Atty. Briggs and Morgan P.A., St. Paul, 1977-93, Leonard, Street & Deinard, Mpls., 1993—. Trustee Actors Theatre St. Paul, 1980-88, Minn. Mus. Am. Art, 1994—; bd. dirs. St. Paul Downtown Coun., 1985-93, Met. State U. Found., 1993—; exec. dir. Minn. Inst. Pub. Fin., 1987-93, bd. dirs., 1993-95, pres., 1995. Mem. ABA, Minn. Bar Assn., Ramsey County Bar Assn., Nat. Assn. Bond Lawyers. Office: Leonard Street & Deinard 2270 World Trade Ctr Saint Paul MN 55101

HANSEN, ROSANNA LEE, publishing executive; b. Huron, S.D., July 11, 1947; d. Walter Noble and Leanna Grace (Dickinson) Parmeter; m. Corwith Randall Hansen. BA, Oberlin (Ohio) Coll., 1969; MA, Johns Hopkins U., Balt., 1970. Vol. U.S. Peace Corps, Iligan, Philippines, 1970-72; editor Boating Industry Mag., N.Y.C., 1973-76; mng. editor Pub. Affairs Com., N.Y.C., 1976-81; sr. editor Grosset & Dunlap, N.Y.C., 1981; exec. editor Macmillan Pub., N.Y.C., 1982-85; editor-in-chief Golden Books, Western Pub., N.Y.C. and Racine, Wis., 1985-87; v.p., pub. Grolier Enterprises, Danbury, Conn., 1987-93, Troll Assocs., Inc., Mahwah, N.J., 1993-95; pres. Hansen Assocs., Tuckahoe, N.Y., 1995—. Author: Gymnastics: The New Era, 1979, Fairy Tale Book of Ballet, 1980, Wolves and Coyotes, 1981, My First Book of Space, 1985, Horses and Ponies, 1988, A Day in the Life of a Baby Dinosaur, 1996. Violinist Westchester Symphony, Scarsdale, N.Y., 1978-82. Mem. Authors Guild, Soc. Children's Book Writers. Office: 149 Crestwood Ave Tuckahoe NY 10707-2208

HANSEN, RUTH LUCILLE HOFER, business owner, consultant; b. Wellman, Iowa, Feb. 8, 1916; d. Harve Hiram and Frances Ada (Fitzsimmons) Hofer; m. Donald Edward Hansen, June 26, 1937 (dec. Feb. 1996); children: James Edward, Sandra Kaye. Student, Upper Iowa U., 1958, U. Northern Iowa, 1959. Co-founder, v.p. H & H Distbg. Co., West Union, Iowa, 1946-59; cons. H & H Distbg. Co.; v.p., gen. ptnr., sec., treas. Don E. Hansen Family Partnership Ltd. Pres. United Presbyn. Women of Bethel Presbyn. Ch., West Union, Iowa, 1967—, mem. comty. planning and devel. commn.; pres. Lakes & Prairies Presbyterial, Cedar Rapids, Iowa, 1972-75; elder Bethel Presbyn. Ch., West Union, 1960-63; v.p., program chmn., camp dir., leader Camp Wyo. Ch. Camp; dist. Wapsipinicon coun. Girl Scouts, 1972-75; tchr. Vacation Bible Sch., Ch. Sch. for Adults, 1970; rep. John Knox Presbytery. Mem. Bus. and Profl. Women (pres.). Home: 704 N Vine St West Union IA 52175 Home (winter): 10549 Bayside Rd Sun City AZ 85351

HANSEN, SALLY JO, school system coordinator; b. San Fernando, Calif., Sept. 8, 1937; d. Kenneth Morris Sr. and Carmen (Woods) High; m. Mark Herman Hansen, June 14, 1958; children: Laurie Jo, Mark. BA, U. Redlands, 1959. Cert. lang. devel. specialist, Calif., cert. crosscultural lang. and acad. devel. specialist, Calif. Tchr. elem. Covina (Calif.) Unified Sch. Dist., 1959-60; tchr. remedial reading Newport-Mesa Unified Sch. Dist., Newport Beach, Calif., 1965-80, tchr. ESL, 1980-88; title VII coord. Newport-Mesa Unified Sch. Dist., Newport Beach, 1988—, ESL bilingual project coord., 1990—, coord. Healthy Start, 1992—; presenter and staff trainer in field. Author and editor: ESL Guide for Classroom Teachers, 1992. Pres. PTA, Newport Beach/Costa Mesa, 1965-70 (bd. dirs. 1965-80); legis. rep. Orange County Tchr. of Speakers of Other Langs., 1985-87. Mem. Nat. Assn. Bilingual Edn., Calif. Assn. Bilingual Edn., Nat. Charity League (past officer), Rep. Women, U. Redlands Alumni Assn. Presbyterian. Office: Newport Mesa Unified Sch Dist 1050 Arlington Dr Costa Mesa CA 92626-5626

HANSEN, SUSAN ELIZABETH, mental health counselor, forensic consultant; b. Mesa, Ariz., Aug. 12, 1949; d. Robert Paul and Gwendolyn (Gaddis) H.; children: Heather Lyn, Meredith Clark. BA, La. State U., 1971; MA, Ga. State U., 1977. Lic. mental health counselor. Mental health counselor intern Altamonte Springs, Fla., 1987-89; counselor, psychometrician Ctr. for Life Mgmt., Orlando (Fla.) Regional Med. Ctr., 1989, Glenbeigh Hosp., Orlando, 1989-93; psychometrician Ctrl. Fla. Psychol. Svcs., Sanford, Fla., 1992-93; mental health counselor Psychol. Affiliates Inc., Winter Park, Fla., 1993-94; pvt. practice Maitland, Fla., 1994—; trainer Divided Loyalties, Winter Park, 1993-94; cons., trainer Inst. Profl. Youth Ministry, Orlando, 1993—; cons. Family Svcs. Planning Team, Orlando, 1993—, Parent Network of Fla., Orlando, 1995—. Mem. ACA, Orange County Counseling Assn. Office: 500 N Maitland Ave # 306 Maitland FL 32751

HANSEN, ZANDRA DAWN, pricing analyst; b. Van Nuys, Calif., Nov. 15, 1963; d. William David Jr. and Mary Louise (Ashford) Jordan; m. Robert Alan Hansen, Dec. 2, 1989. BS in Microbiology, San Diego State U., 1984; postgrad., Kennesaw State U. Pricing analyst Rockwell Internat., El Segundo, Calif., 1984-86; sr. pricing analyst Northrop Corp., Pico Rivera, Calif., 1986-90; corp. cost analyst Sci. Rsch. Corp., Atlanta, 1992-94; sr. pricing analyst Nat. Data Corp., Atlanta, 1996—. Mem. Inst. Mgmt. Accts., Cobb County Bus. and Profl. Women's Group. Home: 610 Creekwood Dr Marietta GA 30068

HANSEN-RACHOR, SHARON ANN, conductor, choral music educator; b. Omaha, Nebr., Aug. 22, 1954; d. Joseph Anthony Busch and Helen Marie Prokop Krustev; m. David John Rachor, May 27, 1991; 1 stepchild, Stephanie Rachor. BM, U. Nebr., Omaha, 1975; MM, U. Nebr., Lincoln, 1978; postgrad., U. Ill., 1981-82; DMA, U. Mo., Kansas City, 1986. Pub. sch. music tchr. Millard and Springfield (Nebr.) schs., 1975-83; grad. teaching asst. U. Ill., 1981-82, U. Mo., Kansas City, 1983-86; assoc. prof. choral music and conducting U. No. Iowa, Cedar Falls, 1986-94; assoc. prof. choral music and conducting, dir. choral activities U. Wis., Milw., 1994—; vis. prof. orchestral studies U. Regensburg, Germany, 1993; cons. in field. Contbr. articles to profl. jours.; mem. editl. bd. Choral Jour. U. No. Iowa grantee, Amsterdam, 1991, Stuttgart, Germany, 1993-94; Kemper fellow U. Mo., Kansas City, 1986. Mem. Am. Choral Dirs. Assn., Internat. Fedn. Choral Music, Gachinger Kantorei Stuttgart, Phi Kappa Lambda, Mu Phi Epsilon, Pi Kappa Pi, Alpha Lambda Delta. Home: 4340 N Woodburn Shorewood WI 53211 Office: U Wis Milw Dept Music Fine Arts Music Box 413 Milwaukee WI 53201

HANSON, ANN ELLIS, classics educator; b. Kalamazoo, June 24, 1935; d. Marion Dickson and Jessica Elizabeth (Jamieson) Ellis; widowed; 1 child, Mary Elizabeth. AB in Classics, U. Mich., 1957, MA in Ancient History, 1964; MA in Classics, U. Pa., 1967, PhD in Classics, 1971. Assoc. prof. classics Fordham U., Bronx, 1968-85; prof. classics U. Mich., Ann Arbor, 1995—. Contbr. articles to profl. jours. MacArthur Found. fellow, 1992—. Mem. APA (bd. dirs. 1994—). Home: 1914 Old Orchard Ct Ann Arbor MI 48103 Office: U Mich Dept Classical Studies 435 S State St Ann Arbor MI 48109-1003

HANSON, ANNE COFFIN, art historian; b. Kinston, N.C., Dec. 12, 1921; d. Francis Joseph Howells and Annie Roulhac (Coffin) Coffin; m. Bernard Alan Hanson, June 27, 1961; children by previous marriage: James Warfield Garson, Robert Coffin Garson, Ann Blaine Garson. B.F.A., U. So. Calif., 1943; M.A. in Creative Arts, U. N.C., 1951; Ph.D., Bryn Mawr Coll., 1962. Instr. Albright Art Sch., U. Buffalo, 1955-58; vis. asso. prof. art Cornell U., 1963; asst. prof. Swarthmore Coll., 1963-64, Bryn Mawr Coll., 1964-68; dir. Internat. Study Center, Mus. Modern Art, N.Y.C., 1968-69; adj. assoc. prof. NYU, 1969-70; prof. history art Yale U., New Haven, 1970-92; chmn. dept. Yale U., 1974-78, acting dir. Art Gallery,, 1985-87, John Hay Whitney prof. emeritus, 1992—; vis. Clark prof. Clark Art Inst., Williams Coll., fall 1990; Samuel H. Kress prof. (hon.) Ctr. Advanced Study Visual Arts Nat. Gallery Art, Washington, 1992-93. Author: Jacopo della Quercia's Fonte Gaia, 1965, Edouard Manet, 1966, Manet and the Modern Tradition, 1977, The Futurist Imagination, 1983, Severini: Futurista 1912-1917, 1995; also articles in profl. jours.; mem. editl. bd. The Art Bull., 1971-91; editor monograph series Coll. Art Assn., 1968-70; mem. governing bd. Yale U. Press, 1977-90; mem. editl. com. Art Jour., 1979-83. Mem. governing bd., v.p. Hillstead Mus., Farmington, Conn., 1989-92, v.p., 1991-92; adv. bd. Swann Found. for Cartoon and Caricature, N.Y.C., 1988-93. NEH fellow, 1967-68; Am. Coun. Learned Socs. grantee, summer 1963, fellow, 1983-84; resident Am. Acad. Rome, spring, 1974; fellow Inst. Advanced Study, fall, 1983. Mem. Coll. Art Assn. Am. (pres. 1972-74), Comité Internationale de l'histoire de l'Art (nat. mem. 1975-92). Office: Yale U Dept History Art PO Box 208272 New Haven CT 06520-8272

HANSON, CATHERINE IRENE, lawyer; b. Oakland, Calif., Apr. 18, 1955; d. Hobart and Adele Frances (Brooks) H.; m. Theodore E. Lobman, Setp. 6, 1981; children: Alexander Theodore, Zachary William. BA, U. Calif., Berkeley, 1978, JD, 1982. Assoc. Hassard Bonnington, San Francisco, 1982-86; chief atty. Calif. Med. Assn., San Francisco, 1986—, v.p., gen. counsel, 1992—. Co-author: Peer Review Law, 1991, 93, California Physicians Legal Handbook, 1990-96. Mem. ABA, Am. Soc. Law and Medicine, Am. Soc. Med. Assn. Attys. (past pres. 1994—), Nat. Health Lawyers Assn., Calif. Soc. Health Care Attys. (past pres. 1994—). Office: Calif Med Assn PO Box 7690 221 Main St San Francisco CA 94120-7690

HANSON, DIANE CHARSKE, management consultant; b. Cleve., May 15, 1946; d. Howard Carl and Emma Katherine (Lange) Charske; m. William James Hanson, June 30, 1973. BS, Cornell U., 1968; MS, U. Pa., 1989. Home service rep. Rochester Gas and Electric, N.Y., 1968-70; home economist U. Conn., Storrs, 1970-72; job analyst personnel dept. State of Conn., Hartford, 1972-73; sales rep. Ayerst Labs., Waterbury, Conn., 1973-80, sales trainer, 1979-80; dist. sales mgr. Phila., 1980-87; pres. Creative Resource Devel., W. Chester, Pa., 1986—; developer, pres. Womens Referral Network, West Chester, 1987-89. Vice-pres., bd. dirs., aux. pres. Chester County Soc. for Prevention Cruelty to Animals, 1986-91, pres. bd. dirs., 1992-94, mem. exec. com., 1994—. Mem. ASTD (v.p. comm. 1991-92), Internat. Soc. for Performance Improvement (v.p. programs Great Valley chpt. 1993-94, pres.-elect 1995, pres. 1996), Pa. State Tech. Devel. Ctr. (bd. dirs. 1991-92), Assn. Quality and Participation, Phila. Soc. for Human Resources, Phila. Human Resources Planning Group, Phila. Orgn. Devel. Network, Chester County Human Resources Assn. (program chair 1991-92). Home and Office: 824 W Strasburg Rd West Chester PA 19382-1927

HANSON, HEIDI ELIZABETH, lawyer; b. Portsmouth, Ohio, Nov. 13, 1954. BS, U. Ill., 1975, JD, 1978. Bar: Ill. 1978, U.S. Dist. Ct. (no. dist.) Ill., U.S. Ct. Appeals (7th cir.). Atty. water, air and land pollution divs. Ill. EPA, Springfield, Ill., 1978-85; atty. water pollution div. Ill. EPA, Maywood, Ill., 1985-86; assoc. Ross & Hardies, Chgo., 1987-89, ptnr., 1990-94; founder H.E. Hanson Law Offices, Western Springs, Ill., 1994—. Mem. Chgo. Bar Assn., Air and Waste Mgmt. Assn., Indsl. Water, Waste and Sewer Group. Office: 4721 Franklin Ave Ste 1500 Western Springs IL 60558-1720

HANSON, KAREN, philosopher, educator; b. Lincoln, Nebr., Apr. 11, 1947; d. Lester Eugene and Gladys (Diessner) H.; m. Dennis Michael Senchuk, Aug. 22, 1970; children: Tia Elizabeth, Chloe Miranda. BA summa cum laude, U. Minn., 1970; MA, Harvard U., 1980, PhD, 1980. Lectr. to assoc. prof. Ind. U., Bloomington, 1976-91, prof. philosophy, 1991—, adj. prof. Am. studies, women's studies, and comparative lit., 1991—; mem. governing bd. Ind. U. Inst. for Advanced Study, Bloomington, 1992-95; mem. editorial bd. Peirce Edition Project, Indpls., 1982-89, 90—. Author: The Self Imagined, 1986; co-editor: Romantic Revolutions, 1990; assoc. editor Jour. Social Philosophy, 1982-86; edtl. bd. Philosophy of Music Edn. Rev., 1992—; edtl. cons. Am. Philos. Quar., 1995—; contbr. articles to profl. books and jours. Del. Am. Coun. Learned Socs., 1993— (exec. com., 1994—); officer John Dewey Found., 1989—. Office of Women's Affairs disting. scholar, 1995. Mem. Am. Philos. Assn. (exec. officer 1986-91, program com. 1984-91, nominating com. 1993-94, 95-96), Am. Soc. for Aesthetics (program com. 1989-90), Soc. for Women in Philosophy, Phi Beta Kappa (exec. com. Gamma of Ind. chpt. 1993—, officer 1995—, pres. 1996—). Home: 1606 S Woodruff Ln Bloomington IN 47401-4448 Office: Ind U Dept of Philosophy Sycamore 026 Bloomington IN 47405

HANSON, MARIAN W., state legislator; b. Santa Maria, Calif., Jan. 17, 1933; m. Darrel Hanson; 4 children. Rancher; mem. Mont. Ho. of Reps., 1983—, spkr. of the ho. pro tempore, 1993; county mem. Local Govt. Study Commn. Republican. Home: PO Box 237 Ashland MT 59003-0237 Office: Mont Ho of Reps State Capitol Helena MT 59620*

HANSON, OLIVIA NADINE, physical science technician, secretary, counselor; b. Dott, W.Va., Mar. 21, 1943; d. Ewell Blake and Eleanor Ruth (Breeden) Bailey; m. Walter Wayne Radford (dec. Mar. 1989); children: Donald Wayne Radford, Donna Jayne Radford-Baez, Adam Keith Radford; m. John Winton Radford (dec. July 1990); 1 child, John Blake Radford; m. John Charles Hanson, Feb. 10, 1995. Grad., The Exec. Sec. Sch., Bluefield, Va., 1973. Legal asst. Edwin Wiley, Princeton, W.Va., 1973-74; typesetter Princeton Times, 1973-74; inspection recording clk. Dept. Labor, Princeton, 1974-86, phys. sci. technician, 1974-95; bookkeeper DAR, Washington, 1961-62; aerobic instr. Figure Trim, Princeton, 1980-86; sales rep. Shaklee Chrp., San Francisco, 1982-95, Sarah Coventry, N.Y.C., 1974-80; counselor Civil Rights, Princeton, 1990-95. Chmn. for St. Jude Children's Rsch. Hosp., Memphis, 1986; tutor Lit. Vol. Am., Princeton, 1988-95; counselor Equal Employment Opportunity, Pitts., 1990-95; sec. Fed. Women's Program, Mt. Hope, W.Va., 1993-95. Named Mother of Yr., Willowbrook Bapt. Ch., 1973. Democrat. Home: 1032 Miles Standish Ct Virginia Beach VA 23455

HANSON, PATTI LYNN, human resources director; b. Kennewick, Wash., Apr. 21, 1953; d. Lyle Harry and Ellene Lavonne (McGrath) Morgan; m. Dale R. Hanson, Jan. 18, 1995. AS, El Paso C.C., Colorado Springs, Colo., 1972; BS, Regis Coll., 1982; M in Human Resources Devel., Webster U., 1994. Sec. Adams County Sch. Dist., Thornton, Colo., 1972-73; sec. Montgomery Ward & Co., Denver, 1973-77, computer operator, 1977-79, sec., 1979-83, pers. supr., 1983-84; pers. mgr. Montgomery Ward & Co., Shawnee Mission, Kans., 1984-86; govt. funds coord. Montgomery Ward & Co., Kansas City, Mo., 1986; div. tng. mgr. Montgomery Ward & Co., Kansas City, 1986-88; regional human resource mgr. KFC Nat. Mgmt. Co., Irving, Tex., 1988-90; human resources dir. Businessland, Inc./JWP, Lenexa, Kans., 1990-91; dir. Entex Info. Svcs., Lenexa, Kans., 1992—. Active Big Sisters Am., Denver, 1984. Mem. Human Resource Mgmt. Assn. Republican. Home: 11978 Connell Shawnee Mission KS 66213 Office: Entex 10509 W 84th Ter Lenexa KS 66214-1643

HANSON, PAULA E., state legislator; b. Jan. 21, 1944; m. Jim Hanson; 3 children. Mem. Minn. State Senate, 1992—, mem. various coms. Democrat. Home: 2428 Bunker Lake Blvd NE Ham Lake MN 55304-7129 Office: Minn State Senate State Capital Building Saint Paul MN 55155-1606*

HANSON, TRUDY L., speech communications educator; b. Magnolia, Miss., June 12, 1950; d. Truett Carr and Marie (Green) Lewis; m. Michael D. Hanson, Aug. 19, 1972; children: Leah, Chad, Ashley, Tori. BS in Speech/English Edn., La. State U., 1971, MA Speech, 1973; EdD Higher Edn., Tex. Tech U., 1994. Tchg. asst. La. State U., Baton Rouge, 1971-73; asst. prof. West Tex. A&M, Canyon, 1989—; instr. Thomas Nelson C.C., Hampton Roads, Va., 1974, Amarillo Coll., 1981-89. chmn. rhetoric and communication theory, Tex., 1994-95. Dir. West Tex. A&M U. Storytelling Festival, 1991—; parent chair Amarillo Coll. Suzuki Strings, 1985—, Amarillo Coll. Symphony Youth Orch., 1993—, Amarillo Symphony Youth Orch., 1993-96. Mem. Speech Comm. Assn., So. States Comm. Assn. (vice chair gender studies divsn. 1996), Tex. Speech Comm. Assn. (v.p. elect), Tejas Storytelling Assn., Tex. Assn. Gifted and Talented, Tex. Assn. Comm. Adminstrn. (pres. 1994-95). Democrat. Mem. LDS Ch. Home: 6209 Estacado Ln Amarillo TX 79109-6922 Office: WTAMU Box 747 ACT Dept Canyon TX 79016

HANSON, WENDY KAREN, chemical engineer; b. Mpls., May 29, 1954; d. Curtis Harley Hanson and Patricia Lou (Vogler) Schweiger. BS, U. Minn., 1976; BA, U. Colo., Denver, 1984; postgrad., U. Calif., La Jolla, 1984-87. Chem. technician Shasta Beverages, Mpls., 1977-78, Conwed, Roseville, Minn., 1978-80; geologist Century Geophys. Corp., Grand Junction, Colo., 1980, Tooke Engring., Grand Junction, 1980-82; sr. scientist Sci. Ventures, San Diego, 1987-96; engr. Parker-Hannifin Corp., San Diego, 1996—. Patentee magnesium separation from Dolomitic phosphate by sulfuric acid leaching. Judge San Diego (Calif.) Sci. and Engring. Fair,

1987—; leader, publs. editor San Diego (Calif.) Wilderness Assn., 1989—. Mem. Am. Chem. Soc. Office: Parker-Hannifin Corp 7664 Panasonic Way San Diego CA 92173

HANTMAN, SARAH ANN, health professional; b. Wyandotte, Mich., Oct. 19, 1952; d. Paul Reginald and Betty Elaine (Wilson) Longfield; m. Barry Mark Hantman, Dec. 27, 1970; 1 child, Bryan Jonathan. BA in Journalism, Rider U., 1975. Bur. chief United Artists-Columbia CATV-NJ, Oakland, N.J., 1976-77; offset and sr. offset machine operator N.J. Dept. Labor, Trenton, 1980-88; tng. technician div. of AIDS prevention and control N.J. Dept. Health, Trenton, 1988-90, clearinghouse coord. div. of AIDS prevention and control, 1990-91, health profl. divsn. family health svc. WIC program, 1991-92, health profl., div. mgmt. and adminstrn., 1992—; co-owner Sabar Internat., West Trenton, N.J., 1984—. Community activist Grand Ave. Hist. Assn., West Trenton, 1989—. Recipient Letter and Plaque designating her house as hist. Ewing Twp. Hist. Commn. and Zoning Bd., West Trenton, 1989. Mem. NAFE, Nat. Trust and Hist. Preservation (preservation forum 1976—), Nat. Geog. Soc., The Wilderness Soc., Nat. Parks and Conservation Assn., Environ. Def. Fund, World Wildlife Fund. Presbyterian. Office: NJ Dept Health CN 350 John Fitch Plz Trenton NJ 08625-0360

HANTON, SHARON ELEANOR, social worker; b. Superior, Wis., Mar. 23, 1939; d. Earl Richards and Eleanor Dungan; m. John P. Hanton, June 12, 1970; children: Marjorie (dec.), Katherine, Patricia. BA in Social Work, Coll. St. Catherine, 1961; MSW, Cath. U., 1976. Program dir. Urban Life Inst., San Francisco, 1967-70; instr. U. San Francisco, 1967-70, Mont. State U., Bozeman, 1971-81; exec. dir. Mont. Chpt. NASW, Bozeman, 1981—, Galnatin Coun. on Health & Drugs, Bozeman, Mont., 1981-82; social worker pvt. practice, Bozeman, Mont., 1983—; cons. Mount View Care Ctr., Bozeman, Mont., 1990-91, Mt. View Nursing Home, White Sulphur Springs, Mont., 1986—, Wheatland Meml. Nursing Home, Harlowton, Mont., 1990—; founder, dir. One Family Assessment Program, 1994—; tchr. in field. Contbr. articles to profl. jours. Founder Daycare Ctr. U. Mont., Bozeman, Mont., 1975, Rural Generalist Soc. Work Office, gardiner, Mont., 1976, Career Transition Program For Women, 1981; lobbyist Licensing of Social Workers/Vendorship for Social Workers, 1983-85. Recipient Social Workers of Yr. award Nat. Assn. Soc. Workers Mont. chpt., 1992. Mem. NASW, Am. Bd. Examiner in Clin. Social Work. Democrat. Roman Catholic. Home: 9440 Hodgeman Canyon Dr Bozeman MT 59715-8322 Office: 13 S Willson Ave Bozeman MT 59715-4610

HANZAK, JANICE CHRISMAN, accountant; b. Cleve., Mar. 20, 1944; d. William Patrick and Helen (Mulvich) Chrisman; m. Henry Stanley Hanzak, July 18, 1964; 1 child, Kevin. BBA, Ursuline Coll., 1979. CPA, CFP; cert. mgmt., cert. valuation analyst. Clk. Prudential Ins. Co., East Cleveland, Ohio, 1962-63; bookkeeper White Motor Co., Cleve., 1963-68; CPA, tax mgr. Heiser & Assocs., Willoughby, Ohio, 1974-85; CPA, tax supr. Bond Sippola & DeJoy, Willoughby, 1985-91; CPA, pres. J.C. Hanzak & Co., Willoughby Hills, Ohio, 1991—; tax cons. Lake County Realtors Assn., Mentor, Ohio, 1992; speaker seminars in field. Treas. Highland Heights (Ohio) Mayoral Com., 1983; mem. Highland Heights Legis. Com., 1982, St. Paschal Bull. Com., Highland Heights, 1978; charter mem. Willoughby Hills Bus. Assn., 1992; founding pres. Network Profls. of Lake County, 1993; pres. Lake County Estate Planning Coun., Mentor, 1990-92; v.p. Women Bus. Owners of Western Res., Mentor, 1990-92; exec. bd. Ursuline Coll., Pepper Pike, Ohio. Recipient scholarship Bus. and Profl. Women's Assn., Washington, 1973. Mem. AICPA, Ohio Soc. CPAs, Am. Women's Soc. CPAs, Tax Club of Cleve., Internat. Bd. CFPs, Wildwood Yacht Club, Entrepreneurial Roundtable Assn. (founding mem.). Roman Catholic. Office: JC Hanzak & Co 2860 Bishop Rd Wickliffe OH 44092

HANZALEK, ASTRID TEICHER, public policy consultant; b. N.Y.C., Jan. 6, 1928; d. Arthur Albin and Luise Gertrude (Funke) Teicher; m. Frederick J. Hanzalek, Nov. 11, 1955. A, Concordia Coll., 1947; BA, U. Pa., 1949. Cons. Suffield, Conn., 1960—; state rep. Conn. Gen. Assembly, Hartford, 1970-80, asst. majority leader, 1973-74, asst. minority leader, 1975-80; corporator Conn. Childrens Med. Ctr, 1986—; bd. dirs. Conn. Water Co., Clinton. Contbr. articles to profl. jours.; comment features Sta. WSFB-TV and Sta. CP-TV,Hartford, 1975—. Trustee Priscilla Maxwell Ednicott Scholarship Fund, 1972—; chmn. Conn. Energy Found., Hartford, 1986—; vice-chmn. Bradley Internat. Airport Commn., 1972—, Greater Hartford chpt. ARC, 1975-82; mem. Conn. Inter Agy. Libr. Planning Com., Hartford, 1975-85, Conn. State Coun. Environ. Quality, Hartford, 1980-93; chmn. Conn. River Watershed Coun., Easthampton, Mass., 1980-92; pres. Conn. Sr. Intern Program, Bridgeport, 1980-90; chmn. Conn. State Ethics Commn., Hartford, 1985-93; sec. Conn. Humanities Coun., Middletown, 1980-92; commr. New England Interstate Water Pollution Control Commn., 1993—; mem. Conn. Greenways Commn., 1992—. Recipient Man of Yr. award Conn. Jaycees, 1972, Panelist of Yr., Auto. Consumer Action Panel, 1975-85. Mem. Antiquarian and Landmarks Soc. (v.p. 1974—), Conn. Forest and Park Assn. (v.p., bd. dirs. 1975—), Conn. Coun. Environ. quality, Suffield Land Conservancy (bd. dirs. 1965—, founder), Nat. Order Woman Legislators. Republican. Lutheran. Home: 155 S Main St Suffield CT 06078-2238

HAPNER, ELIZABETH LYNN, lawyer, writer; b. Cleve., May 15, 1957; d. William Ralph Hapner and Anita F. (Thomas) Gillen; 1 child, Kyle William. BA in English, U. Fla., 1978, JD, 1980. Bar: Fla. 1981, U.S. Dist. Ct. (mid. dist.) Fla. 1986. Atty. Pub. Defender's Office, Bartow, Fla., 1981, State Atty.'s Office, Tampa, 1981-86; prin./pres. Elizabeth L. Hapner, P.A., Tampa, 1986—; dir. DUI Counterattack Sch., Tampa, 1985—, Prevention, Rehab., Edn. Program, Inc., Tampa, 1990—; adv. Children's Bd Task Force for Judiciary, Tampa, 1991-93. Author: Texas Probate Manual, 1983, Georgia Probate, 1985, Virginia Probate, 1987, Florida Juvenile Procedure, 1986, Florida Civil Procedure, 1990. Mem. Hillsborough County Democratic Adv. Coun., 1988—; trustee Carrollwood Recreation Dist., 1989-91; chair sr. pastor nom. com., Forest Hills Presbyn. Ch., 1989-91, 93-94, elder, 1995—; active mem. Jr. League of Tampa, Inc. Named Victim's Voice, Hillsborough County Victim Assistance Coun., 1991; recipient Pro Bono Svc. award Guardian Ad Litem's Office, Tampa, 1989-95. Mem. ABA, Fed. Bar Assn., Nat. Assn. Female Execs., Internat. Platform Assn., Fla. Bar Assn. (juvenile ct. rules com. 1991—, chair 1994-95, family law special needs of children com. 1992—, chair 1996—, bar fee arbitration com., 1989—, family law juvenile com. 1993—, vice chair 1995—), Fla. Acad. Trial Lawyers, Hillsborough County Bar Assn., Mensa. Democrat. Presbyterian. Home: PO Box 272998 Tampa FL 33688-2998 Office: 101 S Franklin St Ste 100 Tampa FL 33602-5327

HAPNER, MARY LOU, securities trader/dealer; b. Fort Wayne, Ind., Nov. 9, 1937; d. Paul Kenneth Brooks and Eileen (Summers) H. BS with honors, Ariz. State U., 1966, MS, 1967. Stockbroker Young, Smith & Peacock, Phoenix, Ariz., 1971-76, v.p., 1976-89; v.p. Peacock, Hislop, Staley & Given, Phoenix, 1989-90, 1st v.p., 1990—. Author: Career Courage, 1984. Chmn. March of Dimes, Sun City, Ariz., 1983; trustee St. Lukes, Phoenix, 1978; mem. fin. com. YWCA, Phoenix, 1975; chair budget com. Ch. of Beatitudes, Phoenix, mem. exec. coun., 1991. Mem. Charter 100 (chair membership 1979-81, pres. 1980, pres. 1982, v.p. 1981, treas., membership chair 1995). Republican. Lutheran.

HAQUE, MALIKA HAKIM, pediatrician; b. Madras, India; came to U.S., 1967; d. Syed Abdul and Rahimunisa (Hussain) Hakim; MBBS, Madras Med. Coll., 1967; m. C. Azeez Haque, Feb. 5, 1967; children: Kifizeba, Masarath Nashr, Asim Zayd. Diplomate Am. Bd. Pediatrics. Rotating intern Miriam Hosp., Brown U., Providence, 1967-68; resident in pediatrics Children's Hosp., N.J. Coll. Medicine, 1968-70; fellow in devel. disabilities Ohio State U., 1970-71; acting chief pediatrics Nisonger Ctr., 1973-74; staff pediatrician Children and Youth Project, Children's Hosp., Columbus, Ohio, also clin. asst. prof. pediatrics Ohio State U., 1974-80; clin. assoc. prof. pediatrics Ohio State U., 1981—, clin. assoc. prof. dept. internat. health Coll. Medicine, 1993—; pediatrician in charge cmty. Children's Hosp. Cmty. Hlth Ctrs. Children's Hosp., Columbus, 1982—, dir. pediatric acad. assoc., Columbus Children's Hosp., Ohio State U., 1992—; cons. Central Ohio Head Start Program, 1974-79; med. cons. Bur. Rehab. and Devel. Disabilities for State of Ohio, 1990—. Contbr. articles to profl. jours. and newspapers. Charter mem. Rep. Presdl. Task Force, 1982—, Nat. Rep. Senatorial Com., 1985—, U.S. Senatorial Club; charter founder Ronald Reagan Rep. Ctr.; trustee Asian Am. Health Alliance Network, Columbus, 1994—. Recipient Physician Recognition award AMA, 1971-86, 88-91, 92—, Gold medals in surgery, radiology, pediatrics and ob/gyn; Presdl. medal of Merit, 1982. Fellow Am. Acad. Pediatrics; mem. Islamic Med. Assn., Am. Assn. of Physicians of Indian Orgin, Ambulatory Pediatric Assn., Cen. Ohio Pediatric Soc., Islamic Med. Assn. Muslim. Research on enuresis. Home: 5995 Forestview Dr Columbus OH 43213-2114 Office: 700 Childrens Dr Columbus OH 43205-2666

HARAGA, LIANA T., biologist, researcher; b. Yassy, Romania, June 28, 1952; came to U.S., 1991; d. Theodor and Maria (Lemnaru) Economu; m. Dan Haraga, Aug. 27, 1982. B of Biology, Al. I. Cuza U., Yassy, 1978; grad. with honors, Debrecen (Hungary) U., 1976. Tchr. biology, asst. dir. Sch. No. 142, Bucharest, Romania, 1978-81; rsch. scientist Sera and Vaccines Cantacuzino Inst., Bucharest, 1981-91; lab. coord. Mt. Sinai Med. Ctr., N.Y.C., 1991-92; scientist Immunomedics, Inc., Newark, 1992-94; rsch. assoc. Wyeth-Lederle Vaccines & Pediatrics, Pearl River, N.Y., 1994—; mgr. prodn. Tissue Culture Dept. Cantacuzino Inst., Bucharest, 1989-91. Contbr. sci. papers to profl. jours. Biology scholar Debrecen U., 1976. Mem. AAAS, N.Y. Acad. Sci.

HARA-ISA, NANCY JEANNE, graphic designer; b. San Francisco, May 14, 1961; d. Toshiro and Masaye Hara; m. Stanley Takeo Isa, June 15, 1985. Student, UCLA, 1979-82; BA in Art and Design, Calif. State U., L.A., 1985. Salesperson May Co., L.A., 1981; svc. rep. Hallmark Cards Co., L.A., 1981-83; prodn. artist Calif. State U., L.A., 1983, Audio-Stats Internat. Inc., L.A., 1983; prodn. asst. Auto-Graphics Inc., Pomona, Calif., 1984-85, lead supr., 1985-86; art dir., contbg. staff writer CFW Enterprises, Burbank, Calif., 1987-88; graphic designer, prodn. mgr. Bonny Jularbal Graphics, Las Vegas, Nev., 1988-90; graphic designer Weddle Caldwell Advt., Las Vegas, 1990-92; owner Nancy Hara-Isa Designs, 1992—; graphic artist Regional Transp. Commn. of Clark County, Las Vegas, 1993—; freelance designer Caesar's Palace. Writer Action Pursuit Games mag. Parade asst., mem. carnival staff Nisei Week, L.A., 1980-84; asst., mem. Summit Orgn., L.A., 1987—; participant Clark County Leadership Forum. Mem. NAFE, Women in Profl. Graphic Svcs. (acting 1st v.p. 1990, 2d v.p. 1991), Women in Comms. Republican. Presbyterian. Home: 367 Cavos Way Henderson NV 89014-3555

HARALSON, LINDA JANE, communications executive; b. St. Louis, Mar. 24, 1959; d. James Benjamin and Betty Jane (Myers) N.; married. BA summa cum laude William Woods Coll., 1981; MA, Webster U., 1982. Radio intern Stas.-KFAL/KKCA, Fulton, Mo., 1981; paralegal Herzog, Kral, Burroughs & Specter, St. Louis, 1981-82; staffing coordinator, then mktg. coordinator Spectrum Emergency Care, St. Louis, 1982-85, mktg. mgr., 1985-87; dir. mktg. and recruitment Carondelet Rehab. Ctrs. Am., Culver City, Calif., 1987—; mktg. dir. outpatient and corp. services Calif. Med. Ctr., Los Angeles, 1987-88; mktg. dir. Valley Meml. Hosp., Livermore, Calif., 1988-89; account exec. Laurel Communications, Medford, Oreg., 1989-91; community rels. dir. Rogue Valley Med. Ctr., Medford, 1991-95; pub. rels. dir. Rogue Valley Manor, Medford, 1995—; Party chmn. Heart Assn., St. Louis, 1982—; bd. dirs. Am. Lung Assn. Oreg. Recipient Flair award Advt. Fedn. St. Louis, 1984, Hosps. award Hagen Mktg. Research and Hospitals mag., 1984; presdl. acad. scholar William Woods Coll., Fulton, 1977-81. Mem. IABC, NAFE, Am. Mktg. Assn., So. Oreg. Advt. Profls., Britt Music Festivals, Alpha Phi Alumnae Assn. (pres. chpt. 1985-87). Republican. Presbyterian. Avocations: running, travel, sports, French, needlepoint. Home and Office: 48 Indian Shores Lincoln City OR 97367

HARASTA, CATHY ANN, journalist; b. Glens Falls, N.Y., July 1, 1952; d. Guy J. and Margaret C. (Daly) Luciano; m. Joe P. Harasta, Aug. 24, 1974; children: Lindsey Anne, Valerie M. BA in English, SUNY, Oswego, 1974; MA in English, SUNY, Binghamton, 1977. Cert. secondary tchr., N.Y. Ref. libr. asst. Dallas Times Herald, 1976-78, asst. ref. editor, 1978-81; sports copy editor Dallas Morning News, 1981-83, sports media columnist, 1983-85, sports writer, reporter, 1985-90, sports columnist, 1990—. Recipient Charles E. Green Journalism award, Headliners Found. Tex., 1994, 2d pl. award for column writing, Tex. Assoc. Press Mng. Editors Assn., 1993. Mem. Assn. Women in Sports Media. Office: Dallas Morning News POB 655237 Dallas TX 75265

HARAYDA, JANICE, newspaper book editor, author; b. New Brunswick, N.J., July 31, 1949; d. John and Marel (Boyer) H. BA cum laude, U. N.H., 1970. Editorial asst. Mademoiselle mag., N.Y.C., 1970; asst. to travel editor Saturday Rev., N.Y.C., 1971; sr. editor, contbg. editor Glamour mag., N.Y.C., 1971-78; editorial dir. Boston mag., 1978-81; freelance writer, Boston, 1981-87; book editor Plain Dealer, Cleve., 1987—; lectr. Radcliffe Pub., Cambridge, Mass., 1979, 80, Cath Conf., among others; instr. writing Marymount Coll., N.Y.C., 1977; instr. journalism Boston U. Sch. Pub. Comm., 1979; freelance writer for numerous nat. mags., newspapers, including N.Y. Times, Wall Street Jour., Washington Post. Author: The Joy of Being Single, 1986; contbg. author: Rooms with No View, 1974, Titters, 1979, Women: A Book for Men, 1979. Mem. adminstrv. bd. Park Ave. United Meth. Ch., N.Y.C., 1975-78, active civic, corp. and religious groups, 1988—. Recipient award for Excellence in Journalism Cleve. Press Club, 1994; named guest editor Mademoiselle mag., 1970. Mem. Am. Soc. Journalists and Authors, Nat. Book Critics Cir., Royal Scottish Country Dance soc., English Speaking Union, Clan Donald USA, Internat. Platform Assn. Office: The Cleve Plain Dealer 1801 Superior Ave E Cleveland OH 44114-2107

HARBOUR, PATRICIA ANN MONROE, poet; b. Winchester, Ind.; d. Cecil James and Opal (Crouse) Monroe; m. James Claude Harbour, July 29, 1972; children: Eric Arif Monroe Khan, Reneé Ann Monroe Harbour. A in Bus., Ball State U., 1956. Typist Lincoln Life Ins. Co., Ft. Wayne, Ind., 1957; office sec. Lincoln Life Ins. Co., Dallas, 1957; legal exec. sec. Russell E. Wise Law Firm, Union City, Ind., 1958-63; sales assoc., sr. sales assoc. Palais Royal (SRI Retailers, Inc.), Katy, Tex., 1993, sr. sales assoc., cosmetician, cons., 1994; instr. tap dancing, swimming. Contbr. poems World of Poetry (honorable award 1991), Sparrowgrass Poetry Forum, Inc., 1992, The Poetry Center Anthology, Arcadia Poetry Anthology (honorable award 1992), On the Threshold of a Dream. Vol. III (Outstanding Poets of 1994: Nat. Libr. of Poetry, Editor's Choice Outstanding Achievement award 1994). Mem. Internat. Soc. Poets (Poet of Merit award, 1992, 93), Sigma Sigma Sigma. Home: 310 Buckeye Dr Katy TX 77450-1633

HARCUM, LOUISE MARY DAVIS, retired elementary education educator; b. Salisbury, Md., May 1, 1927; d. E. Linwood and Dora Ellen (Shockley) Davis; m. W. Blan Harcum, Sr., Sept. 5, 1944; children: W. Blan, Jr., Angie E., Lee P., R. Linwood. BS, Salisbury State U., 1962, MEd, 1969; grad., Inst. Children's Lit., 1995. Cert. tchr., Md. Tchr. Wicomico County Bd. Edn., Salisbury, Md., 1962-93, subs. tchr., 1996—; columnist Daily Times, 1985-87; tchr. cons. Eastern Shore Md. Writing Project. Co-author: Wicomico County History, 1981; author: Behavior Modification, 1989-92. Co-coord. Rep. Party Campaign, Wicomico County, Md., 1992; vice chmn. Zoning Appeals Bd.; pres. Wicomico County Farm Bur. Women, 1993, leader Olympians-Mardela 4-H Club; mem. New Cmty. Singers, 1975-95, Sen. Richard Colburn's Scholarship Com.; chmn. senatorial com. for Colburn, 1996—. Mem. AAUW (pres. 1968-70, 74-75, 2d time pres. Salisbury Branch 1995-96), Third Time Around-Salisbury Studio of Dance, Eastern Shore Writers Assn., Wicomico County Rep. Women, Wicomico Rep. Club, Retired Tchrs. of Wicomico County (pres. 1996-97). Republican. Methodist. Home: 10720 Snethen Church Rd Mardela Springs MD 21837-2246

HARDACRE, JOY LYNN, nurse; b. Muncie, Ind., Feb. 12, 1952; d. Frank Doyle and Edna J. (Kaelin) Wright; m. Roger Ellis Hardacre, May 19, 1995; children: Candice, Carrisa. LPN, Muncie (Ind.) Sch. Practical Nursing, 1977. LPN, Ind. Staff nurse Ball Meml. Hosp., Muncie, Ind., 1978-82; asst. DON Chateau Conv. Ctr., Muncie, 1983; pvt. nurse Muncie, 1984; Tb outreach nurse Madison County Health Dept., Anderson, Ind., 1985-91, Tb regional coord., 1991—; exec. dir. Delaware County Tc Assn., Muncie, 1991, migrant nurse, 1991-93. Recipient Merit award Am. Lung Assn., 1994. Methodist. Office: Shalico Ctr 3336 N St Rd 9 Anderson IN 46012

HARDAGE, PAGE TAYLOR, health care administrator; b. Richmond, Va., June 27, 1944; d. George Peterson and Gladys Odell (Gordon) Taylor; m. Thomas Brantley, July 6, 1968; 1 child, Taylor Brantley. AA, Va. Intermont Coll., Bristol, 1964; BS, Richmond Profl. Inst., 1966; MPA, Va. Commonwealth U., Richmond, 1982. Cert. tchr. Competent toastmaster, dir. play therapy svcs. Med. Coll. Va. Hosps., Va. Commonwealth U., Richmond, 1970-90; dir. Inst. Women's Issues, Va. Commonwealth U., U. Va., Richmond, 1986-91; adminstr. Childhood Lang. Ctr. at Richmond, Inc., 1991—; bd. dirs. Math. and Sci. Ctr. Found., Richmond, Emergency Med. Svcs. Adv. Bd., Richmond. Treas. Richmond Black Student Found., 1989-90, Leadership Metro Richmond Alumni Assn.; bd. dirs. Richmond YWCA, 1989-91; group chmn. United Way Greater Richmond, 1987; bd. dirs. Capital Area Health Adv. Coun.; commr. Mayors Commn. of Concerns of Women, City of Richmond. Mem. NAFE, ASPA, Adminstrv. Mgmt. Soc., Internat. Mgmt. Coun. (exec. com.), Va. Recreation and Park Soc. (bd. dirs.), Va. Assn. Fund Raising Execs., Rotary Club of Richmond. Unitarian. Office: Childhood Lang Ctr at Richmond Inc 4202 Hermitage Rd Richmond VA 23227-3755

HARDCASTLE, BERNADETTE ROLLINS, accountant; b. Corpus Christi, Tex., Oct. 2, 1947; d. Woodrow Jarrett and Marjorie Anne (Williams) R.; m. William Wayne Hardcastle, Apr. 24, 1965; children: Nicholas Wayne, Camille Colette, Lia Therese. AA, Del Mar Coll., 1973; BA summa cum laude, Corpus Christi State U., 1978. CPA, Tex., 1983. Mgr. KPMG Peat MArwick, Corpus Christi, Tex., 1981-86; shareholder Collier Johnson & Woods, Corpus Christi, Tex., 1986-95; acct. pvt. practice, Corpus Christi, Tex., 1996—; founder, 1st chair Com. Women CPAs, Corpus Christi. Bd. dirs., treas. YWCA, Corpus Christi, 1991—; treas. Vol. Coun.-State Sch., Corpus Christi, 1990-91; mem. South Tex. Women's Forum, Corpus Christi, 1983-88. Mem. AICPA (tax practice sect.), AAUW (Corpus Christi chpt.), Tex. Soc. CPAs (treas., bd. dirs. 1986-90), Exec. Women Internat., Phi Theta Kappa. Roman Catholic. Home: 5416 Stonegate Way Corpus Christi TX 78411 Office: 5151 Flynn Pky Ste 412F Corpus Christi TX 78411

HARDCASTLE, MARCIA E., newspaper editor; b. Oakland, Calif., Nov. 28, 1945; d. Charles Frederick and Lillian Callita (Johnson) Temme; children: Glenn Arthur Hardcastle, Jason Roger Hardcastle. BA, San Jose State U. Society editor Los Altos (Calif.) News, 1967-70; reporter, lifestyle editor Santa Maria (Calif.) Times, 1979-82; adminstrv. asst. sr. Diablo Canyon Nuclear Power Plant, Calif., 1983-86; lifestyle editor 5-Cities Times Press Recorder, Arroyo Grande, Calif., 1987—; cons. pub. rels., Pismo Beach, Calif., 1977—; chair bd. dirs. publicity Am. Heart Assn., San Luis Obispo, Calif. Press sec. Assemblyman Eric Seastrand, Calif., 1982; campaign mgr. Tris Colman for State Assembly, Calif., 1994; founder Five Cities Women's Network, 1987—; worthy advisor Girl Scouts Am. Recipient Cmty. Svc. award Santa Maria Mental Health Assn., 1980, Media award Calif. Mental Health Assn., 1980, Hon. Mention award Nat. Newspaper Assn., 1989, 2d Place award Best Lifestyle/Family Life Pages Calif. Newspaper Assn., 1991. Republican.

HARDEN, KAREN ENTSMINGER, curriculum specialist; b. Covington, Va., Oct. 1, 1949; m. Franklin Delano Harden; children: John, Steven, Jami, Amity. BA in English, N.C. State U., 1974; AA in Journalism, Jefferson State Coll., Birmingham, Ala., 1981; MEd in Secondary Edn., James Madison U., 1994. Cert. tchr. secondary English, journalism, gifted edn., Va. English tchr. So. Christian Acad., Knightdale, N.C., 1975-78; English tchr. (summer session) Wm. G. Enloe H.S., Raleigh, N.C., 1976, 77; English Tchr. East Cary (N.C.) Jr. H.S., 1979; GED, homebound interim tchr. Oneonta (Ala.) City Schs., 1980-81; English tchr., dept. chair Luray (Va.) H.S., 1982—; workshop instr. Va H.S. League, Charlottesville, 1985-92, Jostens Publishing Co., State College, Pa., 1989-91; mem. publs. adv. com. Va. H.S. League, Charlottesville, 1986-91; scholastic publn. evaluator, Columbia U., N.Y.C., 1989, 90. Author: (handbook for new tchrs.) A Practical Guide for Survival in the LHS Classroom, 1994 (sch. bd. citation 1994). Named tchr. of yr. Shenandoah Valley Folklore Soc., Harrisonburg, Va., 1985, Luray H.S. Student Coop. Assn., 1989, 90, Page News & Courier, 1994; recipient Ray Kroc Tchr. Achievement award, McDonald's, Inc., 1991, 94, 96; recipient VFW citation for cmty. svc., 1993; named outstanding tchr. of gifted, No. Va. Coun. Gifted and Talented Edn. Mem. Alpha Delta Kappa (pres. 1996-98), Phi Delta Kappa. Home: 18 Canaan St Luray VA 22835-9734

HARDEN, MARY LOUISE, human resources management specialist; b. Natchez, Miss., Mar. 27, 1942; d. John Charles and Dorothy Louise (Reynolds) Brown; m. Billy Gene Redd, Mar. 12, 1957 (div. 1961); children: Andre Ranier, Allison Lawanda, Robin Yvette; m. Percy Lawrence Harden Jr., Aug. 31, 1968; children: Darrell Lawrence, Craig Robison. Student, Ball State U., 1975-76, Ind. U., Purdue U., 1983-88; BSBA, Ind. Wesleyan U., 1989; postgrad., U. S.C., 1990; MA, Ball State U., 1995. Editor-in-chief U.S. Army Fin. and Acctg. Ctr., Indpls., 1974-81, pers. mgmt. specialist, 1981-87, pub. affairs officer, 1987-91; personnel mgmt. specialist Def. Fin. and Acctg. Svc., 1991—; fed. women's program mgr. U.S. Army Fin. and Acctg. Ctr., Indpls., 1981-85; course mgr. Dept. Army, Indpls., 1982-85. Bd. dirs. Nat. Coalition of 100 Black Women, Indpls., 1986—, Indpls. YWCA, 1989—; minority advisor United Way of Cen. Ind., Indpls., 1985—. Named Madame C.J. Walker Outstanding Woman of Yr., Ctr. for Leadership Devel. and Indpls. C. of C., 1988. Fellow Dept. Def. Exec. Leadership Program; mem. Federally Employed Women (bd. dirs. 1978—), Am. Soc. Mil. Comptrs., Fed. Exec. Assn. (Fed. Employee of Yr. award 1978). Presbyterian. Office: Def Fin and Acctg Svc Human Resources DFAS-HQ Indianapolis IN 46249-2501

HARDEN, OLETA ELIZABETH, English educator, university administrator; b. Jamestown, Ky., Nov. 22, 1935; d. Stanley Virgil and Myrtie Alice (Stearns) McWhorter; m. Dennis Clarence Harden, July 23, 1966. BA, Western Ky. U., 1956; MA in English, U. Ark., 1958, PhD, 1965. Teaching asst. U. Ark., Fayetteville, 1956-57, 58-59, 61-63; instr. S.W. Mo. State Coll., Springfield, 1957-58, Murray (Ky.) U., 1959-61; asst. prof. English Northeastern State Coll., Tahlequah, Okla., 1963-65; asst. prof. Wichita (Kans.) State U., 1965-66; asst. prof. English Wright State U., Dayton, Ohio, 1966-68, assoc. prof., 1968-72, prof., 1972—, asst. chmn. English dept., 1967-70, asst. dean, 1971-73, assoc. dean, 1973-74, exec. dir. gen. univ. services, 1974-76, pres. of faculty, 1984-85. Author: Maria Edgeworth's Art of Prose Fiction, 1971, Maria Edgeworth, 1984. Wright State U. rsch. and devel. grantee, 1969, 78, Ford Found. grantee, 1971, Wright State U. sabbatical grantee Oxford U., Eng., 1978-79, 86-87; recipient Presdl. award for Outstanding Svc. Wright State U., 1986, Alumni Teaching Excellence award, 1993. Mem. MLA, Coll. English Assn., AAUP, Women's Caucus for Modern Langs., Am. Com. Irish Studies. Home: 2618 Big Woods Trl Fairborn OH 45324-1704 Office: Wright State U Dept English 7751 Colonel Glenn Hwy Dayton OH 45431-1674

HARDEN, PAMELA IRIS, artist, printmaker, researcher; b. Jacksonville, Fla., Dec. 14, 1954; d. Denton and Helen Althea (Batchelor) H.; m. Robert Sidney Chesick, Apr. 17, 1977; (div. June, 1991); m. Ian Davis Johnson, June 3, 1994. BFA in Art with distinction, U. N.C., 1994. Artist wardrobe dept. Last of the Mohicans (film), Asheville, N.C., 1991; artist-printmaking Fulbright Exchange Grant, Lima, Peru, 1995-96. Solo exhbns. include Instituto Cultural Peruana Norteamericano, Arequipa, Peru, 1996, Instituto Cultural Peruana Norteamericano, Lima, Peru, 1996; group shows include Zone 1 Contemporary, Asheville, N.C., 1994, U. N.C. Juried Exhbn., 1994, Sr. Exhbn., 1994; represented in permanent collections at Instituto Cultural Peruanao Norteamericano, Lima, Pontificia Universidad Catolica, Lima, Fulbright Commn., Lima. Home and Office: 93 Dorchester Ave Asheville NC 28806

HARDER, JANET FAY, special education educator; b. Fulton, N.Y., Feb. 16, 1929; d. Ward Keefe and Hazel Neola (King) Donovan; widowed; children: Katherine Biss, John R., William L., Jennifer Ott, Victoria K. BS in Psychology, St. Lawrence U., 1951; postgrad., Hunter Coll., 1955-56, Syracuse U., 1962-66. Tchr. blind Suffolk BOCES, Patchogue, L.I., 1954-62, N.Y. Schs., Syracuse, 1962-66. Author: Letters from Carrie, 1986. Sch. Bd. pres. Phoenix Ctrl. Schs., 1972-80; village bd. trustee Phoenix, 1980-89; organizer, pres. Phoenix Coop. Nursery Sch., 1964—, Village Players, Phoenix, 1968-76; commr. Schroeppel Pres. Commn., chair 1987—; mem., pres. Greater Phoenix Improvement, 1985, 95; bd. dirs. Heritage Found.,

1992—, Oswego County Tourism Coun., 1986—; organizer, chair Phoenix Indsl. Mus., 1996—. Recipient Preservation award Pres. Assn. of Ctrl. N.Y., 1987, Heritage Found., 1988, 90, DeWitt Clinton Masons, 1988, Planning award Oswego County, 1993. Mem. C. of C. (Woman of Yr. 1987). Home: 25 Church St Phoenix NY 13135

HARDER, WENDY WETZEL, communications executive; b. Oceanside, Calif., Feb. 14, 1951; d. Burt Louis and Marjorie Jean (Evans) W.; m. Peter N. Harder, Dec. 1, 1984; 1 child, Jonathan Russell. AA, Palomar Coll., 1971; BA in Communications, U. So. Calif., 1973; MBA, Pepperdine U., 1988. Pub. rels. dir. Orange County Community Devel. Coun., Santa Ana, Calif., 1975-76; assoc. producer Sta. KOCE-TV, Huntington Beach, Calif., 1976-77, reporter, 1977-79, anchor, assoc. producer, 1979-82; sr. adminstr. communications Mission Viejo (Calif.) Co., 1983-84, mgr. corp. affairs, 1984-85, dir. corp. affairs, 1985-91, v.p. corp. affairs, 1991-93, v.p. mktg. and corp. comm., 1993—. 1st v.p. Aliso Viejo (Calif.) Cmty. Found., 1988-93, pres., 1993—, Saddleback Coll. Found., Mission Viejo, 1989-94; co-chmn. The Ctr. on Tour-Schs. Com., Orange County, Calif., 1989-92; v.p. Found. for Vocat. Visions, 1996—, Found. for Vocat. Visions, 1996—; bd. dirs. Dunaj Internat. Dance Ensemble, Orange County, 1985—. Recipient Golden Mike award Radio & TV News Assn., 1981; co-recipient Best Spl. Event award, Pub. Rels. Soc. Am., 1986, Golden Mike award Radio & TV News Assn., 1979. Mem. Orange County Press Club (Best Feature Release award 1983), Royal Scottish Country Dance Assn., Orange County Folk Dancers. Republican. Lutheran. Office: Mission Viejo Co 26137 La Paz Rd Mission Viejo CA 92691-5309

HARDESTY, BARBARA LYNNE, revenue agent, auditor; b. Encino, Calif., Nov. 22, 1966; d. Charles Conrad Hardesty and Patricia Lynne (Weaver) Lane; m. Adrian Dale Haupt, Aug. 254, 1985 (div. May 1992); children: Nicholas Scott Haupt, Jeremy Julian Zavala; m. Jesus Jose Zavala, Jr., Mar. 18, 1994. BSBA with honors, U. Tex., El Paso, 190. Revenue agent IRS, El Paso, 1991—; security technician, computers, IRS, 1994—, outreach and small bus. workshop presenter, IRS, 1993—. Den leader Boy Scouts of Am., El Paso, 1994, 95; legis. com. chair, PTA Rosa Guerrero Elem. Sch., El Paso; tutor, mentor Helping One student to Succeed, Beall Elem. Sch., El Paso, 1993-95; team mother Am. Youth Soccer Orgn., El Paso, 1995—. Recipient Mgr.'s award IRS, 1994, cert. of appreciation Vol. in Pub. Schs., 1993. Mem. Boy Scouts of Am., PTA. Home: 7253 Imperial Ridge El Paso TX 79912

HARDIMAN, THERESE ANNE, lawyer; b. Chestnut Hill, Pa., Mar. 2, 1956; d. Edward Joseph and Grace Joan (Shaw) Hardiman; m. David J.P. Malecki, Feb. 3, 1990; 1 child, Christine Mary; BA in History, BA in Psychology, Mt. St. Mary's Coll., 1978; JD, Thomas M. Cooley Law Sch., 1983. Bar: Pa. 1983, U.S. Dist. Ct. (ea. dist.) Pa. 1983, U.S. Ct. Appeals (3d cir.) 1984, U.S. Dist. Ct. (mid. dist.) Pa. 1989. Staff rsch. asst. Internat. Brotherhood of Teamsters, Washington, 1978-79; law clk. Richard R. Rashid, Atty. at Law, Lansing, Mich., 1981-82; law clk. Pearlstine, Salkin, Hardiman & Robinson, Landsdale, Pa., 1981; staff asst. Employment Rels. Bd., Mich. Dept. Civil Svc., Lansing, 1982; mem. Pearlstine, Salkin, Hardiman & Robinson, Landsdale, 1983-86; v.p. Edward J. Hardiman & Assocs. P.C., 1986-94; sole practitioner, 1995—. Editor-in-chief Pridwin, 1978, layout editor, 1977. Recipient Golden Key award, Delta Theta Phi, 1981; Outstanding Student award Student Bar Assn., Thomas M. Cooley Law Sch., 1982. Mem. ABA, Assn. Trial Lawyers Am., Pa. Assn. Trial Lawyers, Pa. Bar Assn., Monroe County Bar Assn., Montgomery County Bar Assn., Delta Theta Phi. Republican. Roman Catholic. Office: PO Box 66 Pocono Pines PA 18350

HARDIN, ELIZABETH ANN, academic administrator; b. Charlotte, N.C., Nov. 21, 1959; d. William Gregg and Ann (Astin) H. BBA magna cum laude, U. Ga., 1981; MBA, Harvard U., 1985. Spl. project coord. NCNB Corp., Charlotte, 1981-82, investment officer, 1982-83; cons. Booz, Allen & Hamilton, Atlanta, 1985-86; asst. placement dir. Harvard U. Bus. Sch., Boston, 1986-87, dir. MBA program adminstrn., 1987-89, acting placement dir., 1988-89; mgr. employment Sara Lee Hosiery, Winston-Salem, N.C., 1990-92, mfg. mgr., 1992-93; dir. product devel. Sara Lee Hosiery, Winston-Salem, 1993-94; mng. cons. Info. Sci. Assocs., Charlotte, N.C., 1994-95; assoc. vice chancellor for bus. planning U. N.C., Charlotte, 1995—; cons., developer adminstrv. policy guide Chelsea (Mass.) Pub. Schs., 1989-90. Mem. adv. bd. Harvard Non-Profit Fellowship, 1986—; chmn. Harvard Non-Profit Mgmt. Fellowship, 1989-96; active AIDS Action Com. Mass., Holy Comforter, Charlotte; mem. total quality edn. task force N.C. Bus. Com. on Edn., 1992-93; troop leader Girl Scouts U.S.A.; mem. Leadership Charlotte, 1996—. Fellow State Farm Co. Found., 1980, Delta Gamma Found., 1983. Mem. Assn. for Corp. Growth (bd. advisors 1996—), Harvard Bus. Sch. Assn., Phi Kappa Phi, Delta Gamma (pres. alumnae Charlotte 1982-83). Republican. Office: U of NC at Charlotte Charlotte NC 28223

HARDIN, J. LYNNE, small business owner, consultant; b. Santa Ana, Calif., Nov. 6, 1946; d. Robert S. and Ann (Fleming) H.; divorced; 1 child, Blakemore Edward,. Student, Pensacola Coll., 1964-66. Agt., broker T.M.I., Tiburon, Calif., 1970-72; founder, owner Key West (Fla.) Tennis, Inc., 1972-79; v.p. Maritime Internat., Ft. Lauderdale, Fla., 1979-82; pres. J.K. Fin.-Pinellas Co., St. Petersburg, Fla., 1982-88; dir. devel. Okla. Sch. Sci. and Maath., Oklahoma City, 1982-86; pres. Hardin Internat., Oklahoma City, 1982—. Bd. dirs. Kirkpatrick Ctr., Oklahoma City, 1987—, Integrated Food Technologies, Emmaus Pa. and Oklahoma City, 1992—, Okla. Ind. Coll. Assn., Oklahoma City, 1994—; founder Concerned Women, Oklahoma City, 1992; originator Breast Cancer Bill, Oklahoma City, 1994; mem. Okla. Internat. Women Forum, Oklahoma City, 1994—. Decorated knight Ordo Byzantinus Sancti Sepulchri (Malta). Mem. AAUW, Nat. Soc. Fund Raising Execs., Rotary. Home and Office: 1616 Norwood Pl Oklahoma City OK 73120

HARDIN, SHERRIE ANN ASFOURY, commercial photographer; b. Saratoga Springs, N.Y., May 28, 1950; d. Edward Asfoury and Olivia Dorethea (Rehm) Melrose; m. Lin Hardin, Feb. 13, 1972. Student, Polk Community Coll., Winter Haven, Fla., 1968-69, 77, La Harbor Coll., Wilmington, Calif., 1984-85, El Camino Coll., Hawthorne, Calif., 1985-87. Dep. Polk County Sheriff's Office, Bartow, Fla., 1975-78; freelance comml. artist Winter Haven, Fla., Sacramento, Fla., 1978-84; photographer Nissan Motor Corp. in USA, Gardena, Calif., 1985-86; gen. mgr. Awards-Rex Group, Hawthorne, 1986-88; photog. coord. Meisel, Atlanta, 1988-89; owner, mgr. Sherrie Hardin, Photographer, 1985—; mentor Cartersville Md. Sch., 1996—. Photog. work includes stock, indsl., environ. and nature photography, restorations of old damaged photographs and fiine art photography. Mem. Etowah Creative Art Coun. (bd. dirs.), Rockmart Art Coun., Environ. Def. Fund, Nat. Trust for Hist. Preservation, High Mus. of Art, Cartersville-Bartow County C. of C. Office: 844 Terry White Rd Aragon GA 30104

HARDING, ILO-MAI, program director; b. Parnu, Estonia, Apr. 4, 1944; d. Ants and Aino (Liidak) Soots; m. Imre Lipping (div.); children: Arno Timo, Mark Eero, Tuuli Mai; m. Jordan Lee Harding, Oct. 21, 1986. BA, U. Toronto, 1966. Program asst. Office of Symposia and Seminars Smithsonian Instn., Washington, 1979-80, Nat. Mus. Am. Art, Washington, 1980-81; internat. radio broadcaster (Estonian svc.) Voice of Am., Washington, 1981-84; internat. visitor exch. specialist USIA, Washington, 1984-85, acad. exch. specialist, 1985-88, sr. program officer Fulbright Tchr. Exchange office acad. programs, 1988—. Vol. Am. Cancer Soc., Chevy Chase, Md. Home: 4719 Merivale Rd Chevy Chase MD 20815-3705 Office: USIA Office Acad Programs Bur Ednl and Cultural Affai Washington DC 20547-0001

HARDING, MARIE, ecological executive, artist; b. Glen Cove, N.Y., Nov. 13, 1941; d. Charles Lewis and Marie (Parish) H.; m. John P. Allen, Jan. 29, 1965 (div. Oct., 1991); 1 child, Eden A. Harding. BA, Sarah Lawrence Coll., 1964; postgrad., Arts Students League, N.Y.C., 1965. Founder Synergia Ranch, Santa Fe, N. Mex., 1969; founding mem., actress Theater of All Possibilities, Santa Fe, 1971-86; founding mem., dir. Inst. Ecotechnics, Santa Fe, London, U.S., Eng., 1974—; bd. dirs. Synopco Corp., N. Mex., 1974-81; bd. dirs., founding mem. Substantia Planetary Inc., London, Santa Fe, 1976-80, Savannah Systems Pty., Ltd. and Outback Sta. Pty. Ltd., Kimberly region, Australia, 1976—; chairperson, dir. EcoWorld, Inc., Santa Fe, 1982-94; dlr., founding mem., CFO Space Biospheres Ventures, Biosphere 2, Ariz., 1984-94; chairperson, CEO Oceans Expeditions, Inc., 1986-92; pres. EcoFrontiers Co. Ecol. Devel. and Implementation, Santa Fe, 1994—, Decisions Team, Inc. Ecol. Project Mgmt., Santa Fe, 1994—; participant in constrn. and fin. Capt. R. Heraclitus rsch. vessel, Oakland, Calif., 1974; bd. dirs. Hotel Vajra, Kathamdu, Tibet, 1976-94, Caravan of Dreams Performing Arts Ctr., Ft. Worth, 1983-94, Synergetic Press, London and Ariz., 1984—. Artist: paintings shown in exhibitions San Francisco, London, Ft.Worth, Santa Fe, Biosphere 2, Ariz., 1982-83, Biosphere & Paintings Exhbn., London, 1996; project dir., artist mural project History of Jazz, Dance, Theater, Ft. Worth, 1982-83; producer, dir. (films) Bryon Gysin Loves ya, Project Charlie, The Search, Synergia History, Planet Earth Conf. Vol. Swallows, Madras, India, 1964, Project Concern, Vietnam, Hong Kong, 1964-65; artist, founder, trustee October Gallery Trust, internat. artists forum, London, 1979; mem. Planetary Coral Reef Found., Inc., 1993—. Mem. NOW, Friends of Tibet, N. Mex. Black Belt Club, Tae Kwon Doe Inst. N. Mex. Home and Office: Synergia Ranch 28 Synergia Rd Santa Fe NM 87505

HARDINGER, ANN NAOMI, community health nurse, home health nurse; b. Cumberland, Md., Oct. 23, 1942; d. John B. and Margaret N. (Ferguson) H. Student, Frostburg State Coll., 1960-61; RN diploma, Meml. Hosp., Cumberland, Md., 1963; student, Allegany C.C., 1966-70; BSN magna cum laude, N.C. Ctrl. U., Durham, 1972; MS, PH Tchr. Preparation, U. N.C. Sch. Pub. Health, Chapel Hill, 1975; cert. maternal and gynecological tng. course, U. N.C. Sch. Pub. Health, Greensboro, 1974. Cert. community health nurse. Med.-surg. nurse, 3-11 charge nurse Meml. Hosp., Cumberland, Md., 1963-70; acute respiratory care unit nurse Duke U. Med. Ctr., Durham, N.C., 1971; home care nurse Meml. Hosp., Cumberland, Md., 1972; profl. nurse traineeship USPHS, 1972-74; migrant health project nurse Tyrrell-Hyde-Washington Counties N.C. State Bd. Health, Raleigh, 1973; pub. health nurse Durham County Health Dept., N.C., 1974-75; nursing instr. Eastern Mennonite Coll., Harrisonburg, Va., 1975-78, asst. prof. nursing, 1978-84; pub. health nurse Thomas Jefferson Health Dist., Charlottesville, N.C., 1984-87; staff devel. coord., infection control nurse, employee health nurse Charter Hosp., Charlottesville, N.C., 1987-93; clin. supr. Martha Jefferson Hosp. Home Care, Charlottesville, N.C., 1993-94, staff educator, 1994—; lectr., presenter, workshop leader numerous univs.; mem. infection control com. Charter Hosp. of Charlottesville, Va., 1987-93 (acting dir. nurses 1991, mem. safety com. 1987-93, mem. wellness com. 1987-93, AIDS monthly lecture to adult CDU, 1988-91). Contbg. author: Women's Health Nursing Examination Book, 1984, How to Achieve Quality and Accrediation in Hospital Infection Control Programs, 1990; editor newsletters: Orgelwerke des Tales g., 1977-82. Bd. dirs., med. adv. com. chair Shenandoah Valley chpt. March of Dimes, 1976-82; bd. mem., awards com. chairperson Charlottesville-Albemarle Mental Health Assn., 1995—; mem. health promotion com. Thomas Jefferson Health Dist., 1986; BLS instr. Am. Heart Assn., 1988—; mem. Am. Guild Organists (editor newsletter 1977-82, sec. Rockingham chpt. 1977-82, mem. Rockingham County chpt. 1977-84, mem. Charlottesville-Albemarle chpt. 1984—, mem program com. Charlottesville-Albemarle chpt. 1988-89, 93-95, sub-dean Charlottesville-Albemarle chpt., 1993-95, dean Charlottesville-Albemarle chpt. 1995—), First United Meth. Ch., Charlottesville, Va. (mem. adminstrv. bd. 1988-94, mem. coun. ministries 1988-94, mem. worship commn. 1986-94, others), Asbury United Meth. Ch., Harrisonburg, Va. (chairperson worship commn. 1980-84, mem. adminstrv. bd. 1980-84, mem. coun. ministries 1980-84, others), others. Mem. Va. Soc. Profl. Nurses (info. coord., past newsletter editor), Am. Pub. Health Assn., Am. Nurses Assn., Va. Nurses Assn. (past v.p., del. dist. 9, editor of newsletters 1985-86), U. N.C. Gen. Alumni Assn., Sigma Theta Tau. Home: 1612 Cambridge Cir # A Charlottesville VA 22903-1316 Office: Martha Jefferson Hosp HomeCare 2409 Ivy Rd Charlottesville VA 22903

HARDRICK, MARIA DARSHELL, government official, accountant; b. Milw., Feb. 5, 1966; d. Dorotha G. Hardrick. BS, Wilberforce U., 1988. CPA, Ohio. Revenue agt. IRS, Cleve., 1988—. Vol. Project Friendship. Mem. Nat. Assn. Black Accts., Black Profl. Assn. Baptist. Home: 5382 Lee Rd Apt 203 Cleveland OH 44137-2569 Office: IRS 5990 W Creek Rd Independence OH 44131

HARDWICK, ELIZABETH, author; b. Lexington, Ky., July 27, 1916; d. Eugene Allen and Mary (Ramsey) H.; m. Robert Lowell, July 28, 1949 (div. Oct. 1972); 1 child, Harriet. A.B., U. Ky., 1938, M.A., 1939; postgrad., Columbia U., 1939-41. Adj. assoc. prof. Barnard Coll. Author: novels The Ghostly Lover, 1945, The Simple Truth, 1955, Sleepless Nights, 1979; essays A View of My Own, 1962; Seduction and Betrayal, 1974; Bartleby in Manhattan, 1983. Editor: The Selected Letters of William James, 1960; adv. editor: N.Y. Rev. Books. Recipient George Jean Nathan award for dramatic criticism, 1966, gold medal for criticism Am. Acad. Arts and Letters, 1993; Guggenheim fellow, 1947. Mem. Am. Acad. and Inst. Arts and Letters. Home: 15 W 67th St New York NY 10023-6226

HARDY, BETH BENITA, nurse; b. Vallejo, Calif., Sept. 11, 1964; d. Agre Abaloc Sanchez and Benita (Licopit) Ionin; m. Troy Allen Hardy, Dec. 16, 1983; children: Tylina Marie, Darryl Allen. AA in Vocat. Nursing, Merced Coll., 1991, ASN, 1993; BSN, Ea. N.Mex. U., 1995. LVN, Calif.; RN, N.Mex., Tex. Float pool LVN Mercy Hosp., Merced, Calif., 1991; staff Anberry Health Care, Atwater, Calif., 1991, Chowchilla (Calif.) Dist. Meml. Hosp., 1991-92; staff RN Plains Regional Med. Ctr., Clovis, 1993-95; staff Clovis Vets. Primary Care Clinic, 1994—. Asst. troop leader Girl Scouts U.S.A., Atwater, 1990-92, troop leader, Clovis, 1994-95. Mem. ANA, Nat. League Nursing, N.Mex. Nurses Assn., Sigma Veta Ni (pres. 1989-90).

HARDY, DORCAS RUTH, government relations and public policy consultant; b. Newark, N.J., July 18, 1946; d. Colburn and Ruth (Hart) H. B.A., Conn. Coll., 1964-68; M.B.A., Pepperdine U., 1976. Legis. rsch. asst. U.S. Senator Clifford P. Case, Washington, 1970; spl. asst. White House Conf. Children and Youth, Washington, 1970-71; exec. dir. Health Svcs. Industry Commn., Cost of Living Coun., Washington, 1971-73; asst. sec. Calif. Dept. Health, Sacramento, 1973-74; assoc. dir. U. So. Calif. Ctr. Health Svcs. Rsch., 1974-81; asst. sec. human devel. svcs. HHS, Washington, 1981-86; commr. Social Security HHS, Washington, DC, 1986-89; pres. Dorcas R. Hardy & Assocs., Spotsylvania, Va., 1989—; chmn. bd. dirs., pres. and CEO (acting) Work recovery, Inc., Tucson, Ariz. Author: Social Insecurity: The Crisis in America's Social Security System and How to Plan Now for Your Own Financial Survival, 1992. Mem. Girl Scouts USA; bd. dirs. Wolf Trap Found. for Performing Arts, Com. on Developing Am. Capitalism; former chmn. Pres.'s Task Force on Legal Equity for Women. Mem. Nat. Fedn. Rep. Women, Exec. Women in Govt. Office: Washington Metro Office 11407 Stonewall Jackson Dr Spotsylvania VA 22553-4608

HARDY, JANE ELIZABETH, communications educator; b. Fenelon Falls, Ont., Can., Mar. 27, 1930; came to U.S., 1956, naturalized, 1976; d. Charles Edward and Augusta Miriam (Lang) Little; m. Ernest E. Hardy, Sept. 3, 1955; children: Edward Harold, Robert Ernest. BS with distinction, Cornell U., 1953. Garden editor and writer Can. Homes Mag., Maclean-Hunter Pub. Co., Ltd., Toronto, Ont., 1954-55, 56-62; contbg. editor Can. Homes, Southam Pub. Co., Toronto, Ont., 1962-66; instr. Cornell U., 1966-73, sr. lectr. in comm., 1979-96; mem. Cornell U. Provost's Adv. Com. on Status of Women, 1977-81; lectr., condr. workshops on writing. Author: Writing for Practical Purposes, 1996; editor pro-tem Cornell Plantations Quar., 1981-82; author numerous publs. including brochures, slide set scripts, contbr. numerous articles in mags. Mem. Women in Comms. Inc. (faculty advisor 1977-95, liaison 1986-94, chair, adv.mem. 1988-90), Royal Hort. Soc., Ithaca Garden Club, Ithaca Women's Club, Pi Alpha Xi, Phi Kappa Phi, Alpha Omicron Pi. Home: 215 Enfield Falls Rd Ithaca NY 14850-8797 Office: Cornell U Dept Communication 328 Kennedy Hall Ithaca NY 14853-4203

HARDY, LINDA LEA STERLOCK, media specialist; b. Balt., Aug. 15, 1947; d. George Allen and Dorothy Lea (Briggs) Sterlock; m. John Edward Hardy III, Apr. 25, 1970; 1 child, Roger Wayne. BA in History, N.C. Wesleyan Coll., 1969; MEd in History, East Carolina U., 1972, MLS, 1990. Cert. tchr., N.C. History tchr. Halifax (N.C.) County Schs., 1972-83, learning lab tchr., 1983-91, computer lab tchr., 1990-95; media specialist Nash-Rocky Mount (N.C.) Schs., 1995—; part-time history instr. Nash C.C., 1993. Mem. AAUW (pres. Rocky Mount br. 1993-95, Named Gift award 1987), Bus. and Profl. Women (pres. Rocky Mount chpt. 1986-87, 90-91, treas. 1992—, sec.-treas. dist X 1989-90, state election chmn. 1989-90, 93-95, Girl Friday award 1981, Woman of Yr. award 1986), Nat. Assn. Educators, N.C. Assn. Educators, Nash/Rocky Mount Assn. Educators (raculty rep. 1995—), Phi Delta Kappa, Pi Gamma Mu. Republican. Methodist. Office: Nash-Rocky Mount Schs Benvenue Mid Sch 1571 Benvenue Rd Rocky Mount NC 27804-1846

HARDY, LOIS LYNN, educational training company executive; b. Seattle, Aug. 20, 1928; d. Stanley Milton and Helen Berniece (Conner) Croonquist; m. John Weston Hardy, July 29, 1951 (div. 1974); children: Sarah Lynn, Laura Lynn; m. Joseph Freeman Smith, Jr., Apr. 18, 1981; stepchildren: Nancy Smith Willis, Martha Smith Dahlquist. BA, Stanford U., 1950, MA, 1952; postgrad., U. Calif., Berkeley, 1957-78, U. San Francisco, 1978-81. Cert. life secondary tchr., life counselor, adminstr., Calif.; lic. career and ednl. counselor, Calif. Tchr., counselor Eastside Union High Sch. Dist., San Jose, Calif., 1951-55; dir. Lois Lynn Hardy Music Studio, Danville, Calif., 1955-69; high sch. tchr. San Ramon Unified Sch. Dist., Danville, 1969-71, counselor, 1971-83; dir. Growth Dynamics Inst., Alamo, Calif., 1976—; instr. Fresno (Calif.) Pacific Coll., 1976-79, Dominican Coll., San Rafael, Calif., 1979—; cons., trainer Personal Dynamics Inst., Mpls., 1976—, Performax Internat., Mpls., 1979—, San Jose Unified Sch. Dist., 1986-86, Novato (Calif.) Unified Sch. Dist., 1985-86, IBM, San Francisco, 1984, corp. and ednl. cons., 1951—. Author: How To Study in High School, 1952, 3d edit., 1973; (with B. Santa) How To Use the Library, 1954; How To Learn Faster and Succeed: A How to Study Workbook For Grades 1-14, 1982, rev., 1985; author various seminars; contbr. numerous articles to profl. jours. Choir dir., organist Community Presbyn. Ch., Danville, 1966-68, elder, 1974-75; speaker to numerous orgns., 1955—. Named Musician of Yr., Contra Costa County, 1978, Counselor of Yr., No. Calif. Personnel and Guidance Assn., 1980; Olive S. Lathrop scholar, 1948, AAUW scholar, 1950; recipient Colonial Dames prize in Am. History, 1950. Mem. Am. Assn. Counseling and Devel., Calif. Assn. Counseling and Devel., Calif. Tchrs. Assn., Calif. Career Guidance Assn., Nat. Speakers Assn., Am. Guild Organists, Stanford U. Alumni Assn., Calif. Assn. for the Gifted, Delta Zeta. Democrat. Presbyterian. Office: Growth Dynamics Inst PO Box 1053 Alamo CA 94507-7053

HARDY, SUE PENNINGTON, family nurse practitioner; b. Sumter, S.C., Dec. 14, 1956; d. Charles Richard and Wanda Fay (Bolton) Pennington; m. Timothy Leon Hardy, May 27, 1979; 1 child, Taylor Scott Hardy. BSN, Miss. U. for Women, Columbus, 1979; MSN, U. Ala., Birmingham, 1984, postgrad., 1989. RN, Ala.; cert. family nurse practitioner. Charge nurse U. Ala. Birmingham Med. Ctr., 1979-81; LPN instr. Birmingham Skills Ctr., 1981-82; family nurse practitioner Jefferson County Health Dept., Birmingham, 1984-85; nurse practitioenr U. Ala., Birmingham, 1985-92; dir. clin. svcs. Cardiovascular Assocs., Birmingham, 1992—; v.p. Hardy Engring., Inc., Trussville, Ala., 1995—. Named to Outstanding Young Women of Am., 1985. Mem. NAFE, ANA, Ala. State Nurses Assn. (Outstanding Nursing Coun. chair 1989), Ala. Nurse Practitioner Coun. (pres. 1988-89), Sigma Theta Tau. Republican. Baptist. Office: Cardiovascular Assocs 880 Montclair Rd Birmingham AL 35213

HARDY, VICKI, elementary school principal; b. Dallas, Dec. 12, 1949; d. Charles Preston and Bertha Frances (Wynne) Sheldon; m. Howard Lawrence Hardy, Jan. 22, 1972. BS, U. Tex., 1971; MEd, U. North Tex., 1977, 81. Tchr. Pearland (Tex.) Ind. Sch. Dist., 1972-73; tchr., asst. prin. Hurst Euless Bedford Ind. Sch. Dist., Bedford, Tex., 1973-86; curriculum cons. Irving (Tex.) Ind. Sch. Dist., 1986-89; prin. Schertz-Cibolo-Universal City Sch. Dist., Schertz, Tex., 1989-92, Cedar Hill (Tex.) Ind. Sch. Dist., 1992-96, Northwest Ind. Sch. Dist., Trophy Club, Tex., 1996—; evaluator So. Assn. of Schs., 1987; TSII mem. Tex. Edn. Agy., Austin, 1990—. Mem. ASCD, Internat. Reading Assn., Nat. Coun. Tchrs. English, Tex. Elem. Prins. and Suprs. Assn., Ex-Students Assn. of U. Tex., Women in the Major Leagues, Delta Kappa Gamma (v.p. 1985-86, Friendship award 1985), Phi Delta Kappa (2d v.p. 1988-89, pres. 1989-90). Office: Lakeview Elem Sch 100 Village Trail Trophy Club TX 76262

HARDY, VICTORIA ELIZABETH, management educator; b. Marion, N.C., Feb. 26, 1947; d. Milton Victor Roth and Bertha Jean (Norris) R.; m. Michael Carrington Hardy, June 19, 1983 (div. 1993); 1 child, Christopher. BS in Edn., U. Mo., 1970; postgrad., So. Ill. U., 1974-75; postgrad. Mgmt. Devel. Program, Stanford U., 1980-81. Pub. sch. tchr. English and Theater, 1970-75; gen. mgr. Miss. River Festival, Edwardsville, Ill., 1975-77; dir. events and svcs. Stanford (Calif.) U., 1977-83; exec. dir. Meadowlands Ctr. for the Arts, Rutherford, N.J., 1983-87; pres., chief exec. officer Music Hall Ctr. for the Arts, Detroit, 1987-89; prin. AMS Planning & Rsch., Conn., 1989-94; prof. facility mgmt. Ferris State U., Big Rapids, Mich., 1994—; mem. faculty CUNY, 1986-88. Pres., bd. dirs. New Performance Gallery, San Francisco, 1977-83; mem. Wingspread Conf. Johnson Found., Milw., 1983; mem. USICA study team People's Republic of China, 1981; state bd. dirs. Arts Found., Mich., 1987-95. Recipient Gold medal for Community Programs Coun. for Advancement and Support of Edn., Stanford, 1985; named in Creativity in Business Doubleday, 1986. Mem. League of Hist. Am. Theaters (pres. bd. dirs. 1987-89), Nat. Trust for Hist. Preservation, Assn. of Coll. Univ. and Community Arts Adminstrs. (exec. bd. dirs. 1977-83), Internat. Facility Mgmt. Assn. (bd. dirs. 1994—). Democrat. Office: Ferris State Univ Coll of Tech Swan 312 915 Campus Dr Big Rapids MI 49307-2291

HARE, ELEANOR O'MEARA, computer science educator; b. Charlottesville, Va., Apr. 6, 1936; d. Edward King and Eleanor Worthington (Selden) O'Meara; m. John Leonard Ging, Feb. 4, 1961 (div. 1972); 1 child, Catherine Eleanor Ging Huddle; m. William Ray Hare, Jr., May 24, 1973. BA, Hollins Coll., 1958; MS, Clemson U., 1973, PhD, 1989. Rsch. asst. cancer rsch. U. Va. Hosp., Charlottesville, 1957-58; rsch. specialist rsch. labs. engring. sci. U. Va., Charlottesville, 1959-64; tchr. Pendelton (S.C.) High Sch., 1964-65; vis. instr. dept. math. Clemson (S.C.) U., 1974-79, instr. dept. computer sci., 1979-83, lectr. dept. computer sci., 1983-90, asst. prof. dept. computer sci., 1990—. Contbr. articles to profl. jours. Bd. dirs. LWV of the Clemson Area, 1988-96; chmn. nursing home study LWV of S.C., 1988-92; oboe and English horn player Anderson (S.C.) Symphony, 1980—. Fellow Inst. Combinatories and its Applications; mem. AAUP, Assn. for Computing Machinery. Office: Clemson U Dept Computer Sci Clemson SC 29634-1906

HARF, PATRICIA JEAN KOLE, syndicated columnist, educational consultant, lecturer; b. Berea, Ohio, Oct. 14, 1937; d. Paul Frederic and Mena (Labordes) Kole; m. Fredric Henry Harf, June 21, 1969. BS in Edn., Baldwin-Wallace Coll., Berea, Ohio, 1959; MS in Edn., U. Akron, 1966; Dr. in Edn., Ariz. State U., 1972; PhD, London Inst. Applied Rsch., 1995; HHD, World Acad., 1994; PhD, London Inst. Applied Rsch., 1995. Rsch. Ednl. Rsch. Coun. Am., 1967-69; tchr. Berea City Schs., Cleve. and Parma, Ohio, 1969-73; asst. prof. Cleve. State U., 1975—; corr., columnist, freelance writer, syndicated columnist Chronicle-Telegram, Elyria, Ohio, 1986-89; owner Harf's Comms. Inc., Berea, Ohio, 1993—; ednl. cons. State of Ohio; syndicated columnist Universal Press, Cleve. Plain Dealer; diagnostician of reading difficulties; cons. learning disabilities; guest lectr.; TV guest appearances. Author teaching materials and tchr. and children's texts; contbr. articles to profl. jours. ; also advisor to book pubs. and magazines. Pres. Berea Hist. Soc., World Found. Successful Women; mem. Cleve. Orch. Women's Com.; advisor Cleve. Radio and TV Coun.; tutor Project Learn, Cleve.; mem. Berea Rep. Precinct Com.; founder Preventive Parenting; dep. senator Internat. Parliament Safety & Peace Italy. Named Intellectual Woman of Yr., 1991-92, Emminent fellow in Universe of Mankind, 1994, Ohio Ednl. Woman of Yr., Ohio Educator of Yr. and Outstanding Educator, Outstanding Citizen Berea C. of C., Ohio Edn. Woman of Yr., 1991, Most Admired woman of Yr., 1993, Lifetime Fellow and Hon. Prof. Australian Inst. for Coordinated Rsch., 1995; recipient Women's Inner Cir. of Achievement award, 1992, Woman of Yr. commemorative medal Order of Internat. Fellowship, 1994, Excellence in Journalism award 1990-93, World Lifetime Achievement award, 1996; named baroness Royal Order Bohemian Crown, 1994. Mem. NEA, NOW, Soc. Profl. Journalists (Excellence in Journalism award 1990), Berea C. of c. (Outstanding Citizen 1965), Berea Hist. Soc., Berea Bus. and Profl. Women, Internat. Reading Assn. (cons. and writer for reading tchrs.), Ohio Edn. Assn. (Woman of Yr. in Comms. 1991), Internat. Platform Assn., World Found. of Successful Women, Nat. Assn.

Women, Profl. Educators Assn., Learning Disability Assn., Nat. Assn. Psychologists, Ohio Assn. Psychologists, Nat. Assn. Women in the Arts, Western Res. Rep. Women's Assn., Kiwanis (sec., v.p.), Berea Rep. Club (Mayoral Volunteerism award 1987), Press Club of Cleve. Republican. Methodist. Home: 323 Westbridge Dr Berea OH 44017-1562

HARGRAVE, SARAH QUESENBERRY, marketing, public relations company executive; b. Mt. Airy, N.C., Dec. 11, 1944; d. Teddie W. and Lois Knight (Slusher) Quesenberry. Student, Radford Coll., 1963-64, Va. Poly. Inst. and State U., 1964-67. Mgmt. trainee Thalhimer Bros. Dept. Store, Richmond, Va., 1967-68; Cen. Va. fashion and publicity dir. Sears Roebuck & Co., Richmond, 1968-73; nat. decorating sch. coord. Sears Roebuck & Co., Chgo., 1973-74, nat. dir. bus. and profl. women's programs, 1974-76; v.p., treas., program dir. Sears-Roebuck Found., Chgo., 1976-87, program mgr. corp. contbns. and memberships, 1981-84, dir. corp. mktg. and pub. affairs, 1984-87; v.p. personal fin. svcs. and mktg. Northern Trust Co., Chgo., 1987-89, Hargrave Consulting, 1989—. Bd. dirs. Am. Assembly Collegiate Schs. Bus., 1979-82, mem. vis. com., 1979-82, mem. fin. and audit com., 1980-82, mem. task force on doctoral supply and demand, 1980-82; mem. Com. for Equal Opportunity for Women, 1976-81; chmn., 1978-79, 80-81; mem. bus. adv. coun. Walter E. Heller Coll. Bus. Adminstrn., Roosevelt U., 1979-89; co-dir. Ill. Internat. Women's Yr. Ctr., 1975. Named Outstanding Young Women of Yr. Ill., 1976; named Women of Achievement State Street Bus. and Profl. Woman's Club, 1978. Mem. Eddystone Condominium Assn. (v.p. 1978-86), Am. Mktg. Assn., Profl. Women's Network. Home and Office: 34 Fairlawn Ave Daly City CA 94015-3425

HARING, ELLEN STONE (MRS. E. S. HARING), philosophy educator; b. L.A., 1921; d. Earl E. and Eleanor (Pritchard) Stone; m. Philip S. Haring, Dec. 1942 (div. June 1951). BA, Bryn Mawr Coll., 1942; MA, Radcliffe Coll., 1943, PhD (AAUW fellow), 1959. Adminstrv. worker ARC, Boston, 1943; mem. faculty Wheaton Coll., Norton, Mass., 1944-45; mem. faculty Wellesley Coll., 1945-72, assoc. prof., 1958-64, prof. philosophy, 1964-72; prof. philosophy U. Fla., Gainesville, 1972-93, prof. emerita, 1993—; chmn. dept. U. Fla., 1972-80. Mem. Am. Philos. Assn., Metaphys. Soc. Am. Office: U Fla Griffin-Floyd 330 Gainesville FL 32611-8545

HARING, MARILYN JOAN, academic dean; b. Jerome, Ariz., Aug. 29, 1941; d. Earl Austin and Genevieve Theresa (Defilippi) S. BA in Edn., Ariz. State U., 1963, MA in Edn., 1966, PhD, 1978. Vis. asst. prof. Ariz. State U., Tempe, 1978-80, asst. prof., 1980-84; assoc. dean for edn. U. N.C., Greensboro, 1984-88; dean Sch. Edn. U. Mass., Amherst, 1988-91, Purdue U., West Lafayette, Ind., 1991—; sr. rsch. assoc. Ctr. for Evaluation and Rsch., Greensboro, 1985-88; dir. Commonwealth Acad. for Mentoring, Amherst, 1989-91. Contbr. articles to profl. jours., book chpts. Carnegie Corp. grantee, 1989-90. Mem. Am. Ednl. Rsch. Assn., Am. Psychol. Assn., Women Educators (nat. coord. 1987-89), Am. Coun. on Edn. (state coord. nat. identification project 1987-88). Office: Purdue U Sch Edn 1440 LAEB West Lafayette IN 47907-1440

HARIRI, GISUE, architect, educator; b. Abadan, Iran, May 16, 1956; came to U.S., 1974; d. Karim Hariri and Behjat (Isphahani) Saboonchi. BArch, Cornell U., 1980. Apprentice Jennings and Stout, San Francisco, 1980-82; Paolo Soleri, Arcosanti, Ariz., 1982-83; apprentice Paul Segal Assocs. Architects, N.Y.C., 1983-85; ptnr. Hariri & Hariri, N.Y.C., 1986—; lighting and furniture designer, 1993—; participant in Urban Housing Festival, The Hague, The Netherlands, 1991; lectr. in field. Work exhibited in Storefront for Art and Architecture, N.Y.C., 1988, Parson Sch. Design, N.Y.C., 1988, Princeton (N.J.) U., 1988, Archtl. League N.Y., 1990, Kent (Ohio) State U., 1991, Richard Anderson Gallery, N.Y.C., 1993, Cornell U., Ithaca, N.Y., 1993, Contemporary Arts Ctr., Cin., 1993, others, also in various profl. publs.; Monograph: Hariri & Hariri Work in Progress, 1996. Recipient Young Architects Forum award Archtl. League N.Y., 1990. Office: Hariri & Hariri 18 E 12th St New York NY 10003-4458

HARKIN, RUTH R., federal agency administrator, lawyer; b. Vesta, Minn.; d. Walter Herman and Virginia (Coull) Raduenz; m. Tom Harkin, July 6, 1968; children: Amy, Jenny. BA in English, U. Minn., 1966; JD, Cath. U., 1972. With Dept. Army, Korea, 1966-67, Polk County Social Svcs., Des Moines, 1968; clk. Lawyers Com. Civil Rights under Law; elected county atty. Story County, Iowa, 1972-76; spl. prosecutor Polk County, 1977-78, dep. gen. counsel Dept. Agriculture, Washington, 1979-81, Akin, Gump, Strauss, Hauer & Feld, LLP, Washington, 1983-93; pres., chief exec. officer Overseas Pvt. Investment Corp., Washington, 1993—. Mem. Iowa Bar Assn., D.C. Bar Assn. Democrat. Lutheran. Office: Overseas Pvt Investment Co Office of the President 1100 New York Ave NW Washington DC 20527-0001

HARKINS, LIDA E., state legislator, educator; b. Jersey City, Jan. 24, 1944; d. Paul Vincent and Lida Cecelia (Higgins) McMahon; children: Michael, Julie, Joseph. BA, Regis Coll., 1966; cert. in pub. policy mgmt., Boston Coll., 1986. Tchr. Mass. Pub. Schs., 1966-68; dir. sch. bus. tng. partnership The Edn. Co-op., Wellesley, Mass., 1988-89; state legislator 13th Norfolk Dist., Needham, Dover and Medfield, Mass., 1989—; bd. dirs. Charles River Workshop for Retarded Citizens, Needham, 1989. Mem. com. Needham Sch., 1976-82, chmn., 1979-80; mem. Needham Town Meeting, 1976—; chmn. Needham Dem. Town Com., 1983-85; bd. dirs. Needham area Boy Scouts Am., 1989. Recipient Alumnae Achievement award Boston Coll., 1989, Golden Donkey award Rendon Report Annual Polit. awards, 1989. Mem. Women Dems. of Dover and Needham. Roman Catholic. Home: 14 Hancock Rd Needham MA 02192-1926 Office: Mass Ho of Reps State Capitol Boston MA 02133

HARKINS-CARTER, ROSEMARY KNIGHTON, anatomy educator, scientist; b. Amarillo, Tex., Aug. 5, 1938; d. Herbert Curtis Knighton and Pauline Cloteal (Jones) Knighton-Young; m. Clarence Harkins, Nov. 24, 1964 (Oct. 1977); m. Elmer Bud Carter, Nov. 18, 1994. BS in Biology and English, West Tex. State U., 1964; MS in Anatomy, U. Okla., 1971, PhD in Anatomy, 1972; BS in Mortuary Sci., U. Cen. Okla., 1976. Registered med. technologist Am. Soc. Clin. Pathologists. Med. technologist U. Tex. Med. Br., Galveston, 1958-62, St. Anthony's Hosp., Amarillo, 1962-66, VA Hosp., Oklahoma City, 1968-70, Bapt. Med. Ctr., Oklahoma City, 1970-72; assoc. dean Coll. Allied Health U. Okla. Health Scis. Ctr., Oklahoma City, 1972-88; dean Coll. Allied Health Howard U., Washington, 1988-91; coord. for allied health Langston (Okla.) U., 1991—; Cons. health edn. Fla. State Univ. Sys. Bd. Regents, Tallahassee, 1983, 87; mem. nat. adv. com. on accreditation and instnl. eligibility U.S. Dept. Edn., Washington, 1981-83; cons. Am. Phys. Therapy Assn., Washington, 1983; mem. exec. coun. Nat. Inst. on Disability and Rehab. Rsch., Office of Spl. Edn., U.S. Dept. Edn., 1991-92. Author: (jours.) Anatomical Record, 1972, Jour. Heredity, 1974. Mem. adv. bd. Eastside Environ. Coalition region VI U.S. EPA, Oklahoma City, 1995-96. Col. USAR, 1981—. Ford Found. fellow for advanced studies, 1971-72. Fellow Am. Soc. Allied Health Professions; mem. Okla. Soc. for Clin. Lab. Scis. (chair edn. com. 1995-96), Sigma Xi, Delta Sigma Theta. Episcopalian. Home: 1001 Dean Pl Oklahoma City OK 73117 Office: Langston U Sch Nursing/Health Profess Langston OK 73050

HARKLEROAD, JO-ANN DECKER, special education educator; b. Wilkes-Barre, Pa., Oct. 22, 1936; d. Leon Joseph Sr. and Beatrice Catherine (Wright) Decker; m. A. Dwayne Harkleroad; 1 child, Leon Wade. AS, George Washington U., 1960, BS in Health, Phys. Edn. and Recreation, 1968, MA in Spl. Edn. and Ednl. Diagnosis and Prescription, 1969, also postgrad. Recipient Appreciation cert. Fairfax County (Va.) Police Dept., 1987, Meritorious Svc. medal Pres. Com. on Employment of People with Disabilities, 1988. Instr. Cath. U. Am., Washington, 1960-61; tchr. Bush Hill Day Sch., Franconia, Va., 1961-63; ednl. diagnostician Prince William County Schs., Manassas, Va., 1969-71, supr. title I, 1971-72; writer, editor Sta. WNVT-TV, Fairfax, Va., 1980-82; dir. spl. edn. Highland County Schs., Monterey, Va., 1987-90. Author: (novel) Horse Thief Trail, 1981, 83, 86; columnist op-ed page The Recorder; radio broadcaster Sta. WVMR, Frost, W.Va. Elder Presbyn. Ch., McDowell, Va., Clifton, Va.; former mem. comm. com. Shenandoah Presbytery; dir. McDowell Presbyn. Ch. Choir; rotating dir. Highland County Cmty. Choir; pres. Highland County Pub. Libr. Bd. Home: Windy Ridge Farm HCR 33 Box 60 Mc Dowell VA 24458

HARKNESS, MABEL GLEASON, retired librarian; b. Oil City, Pa., Jan. 20, 1913; d. Charles Wilcox and Mabel Amy (Fulton) Gleason; m. Benjamin Olney, Mar. 23, 1946 (dec. 1963); m. Bernard Emerson Harkness, Sept. 5, 1964 (dec. 1980). AB, U. Rochester, 1935, MA, 1962. Cert. libr., N.Y. Libr. Stromberg-Carlson Co., Rochester, N.Y., 1942-51, Garden Ctr. Rochester, 1953-67, Monroe County (N.Y.) Bookmobile, 1952-53; now ret.; vol. cataloger Geneva (N.Y.) Hist. Soc.; editor Gleam mag., Rochester Poetry Soc., 1945, Engr.'s Notebook, Stromberg-Carlson Co., 1946-50, Garden Ctr. Bull., 1955-67; co-founder, past pres. Western N.Y. chpt. Spl. Libr. Assn., 1945. Compiler: Harkness Seedlist Handbook 1986 (Worth award for bot./hort. writing Am. Rock Garden Soc.), 2d edit., 1993; contbr. articles on horticulture and local history to various publs. Trustee Keuka Coll., Keuka Park, N.Y., 1971-80, now emeritus. Mem. AAUW (life), Am. Rock Garden Soc. (life), Alpine Garden Soc. (Eng.), Scottish Rock Garden Club (life). Republican. Episcopalian. Home: 5169 Pre Emption Rd Geneva NY 14456-9736

HARKNESS, MARY LOU, librarian; b. Denby, S.D., Aug. 19, 1925; d. Raleigh Everette and Mary Jane (Boyd) Barker; m. Donald R. Harkness, Sept. 2, 1967. B.A., Nebr. Wesleyan U., 1947; A.B. in L.S, U. Mich., 1948; M.S., Columbia U., 1958. Jr. cataloger U. Mich. Law Library, 1948-50; asst. cataloger Calif. Poly. Coll., 1950-52; asst. cataloger, then head cataloger Ga. Inst. Tech., 1952-57; head cataloger U. S.Fla., Tampa, 1958-67; dir. libraries U. S.Fla., 1967-87, dir. emeritus, 1987—; cons. Nat. Library Nigeria, 1962-63. Bd. dirs. Southeastern Library Network, 1977-80. Recipient Alumni Achievement award Nebr. Wesleyan U., 1972. Mem. Am., S.E., Fla. library assns., Fla. Women's Alliance, Athena Soc. Democrat. Mem. United Ch. Christ. Home: 13511 Palmwood Ln Tampa FL 33624-4409

HARKNESS, SARAH PILLSBURY, architect; b. Swampscott, Mass., July 8, 1914; d. Samuel Hale and Helen (Watters) Pillsbury; m. John C. Harkness, June 14, 1941; children: Sara, Joan, Nell, Timothy, Alice, Frederick, John P. M.Arch., Smith Coll., 1940; M.F.A. (hon.), Bates Coll., 1974. Registered architect, Mass. Prin. The Architects Collaborative, Cambridge, Mass., 1945-87; profl. adviser ecol. architecture Oberlin Coll., 1993; participant "Design-In" Coll. of the Atlantic, 1991; vis. critic U. Ariz. Sch. Architecture, 1990, MIT Sch. Architecture, 1986, 87; adv. bd. U. Tenn., 1982-85, Princeton U. Sch. Architecture, 1976-84; faculty rep. Boston Architecture Ctr., 1989; rev. com. in architecture La. Bd. Regents, 1978; selection com. U. Va. Sch. Architecture Thomas Jefferson Meml. Found., 1975-76; juries AIA design awards; lectr. schs. architecture and AIA chpts. Author: (with James N. Groom, Jr.) Building Without Barriers, 1976, The Architects Collaborative Encyclopedia of Architecture, 1986; editor: Sustainable Design for Two Maine Islands, 1985, Visions of Sustainability, 1991, and others. Recipient honor award for Bates Coll. Library AIA-ALA, 1976, Louis I. Kahn citation for Olin Arts Ctr., Bates Coll., 1987, AIA honor award for Chase Learning Ctr., Eaglebrook Sch., 1967, Am. Assn. Sch. Adminstrs. award Fox Lane Middle Sch., Bedford, N.Y., 1961. Fellow AIA (bd. dirs. 1972-75, v.p. 1978); mem. Boston Soc. Architects (bd. dirs. 1979-80, pres. 1985, award of honor 1991, Honor award in edn. and rsch. 1994). Address: 34 Moon Hill Rd Lexington MA 02173-6113

HARLAN, KATHLEEN T. (KAY HARLAN), business consultant, professional speaker and seminar leader; b. Bremerton, Wash., June 9, 1934; d. Floyd K. and Rosemary (Parkhurst) Troy; m. John L. Harlan, Feb. 16, 1952 (div. 1975); children: Pamela Kay, Kenneth Lynwood, Lianna Sue; m. Stuart Friedman, Nov. 10, 1991. Chair Kitsap-North Mason United Way, 1968-70; owner, operator Safeguard N.W. Systems, Tacoma, 1969-79; devel., mgr. Poulsbo (Wash.) Profl. Bldg., 1969-75; pres. Greenapple Graphics, Inc., Tacoma, 1976-79; owner, mgr. Iskrem Hus Restaurant, Poulsbo, 1972-75; pres. Bus. Seminars, Tacoma, 1977-82; owner, mgr. Safeguard Computer Ctr., Tacoma, 1982-91; owner Total Systems Ctr., Tacoma, 1983-88; mem. Orgnl. Renewal, Inc., Tacoma, 1983-88; assoc. mem. Effectiveness Resource Group, Inc., Tacoma, 1979-80; pres. New Image Confs., Tacoma, 1979-82; speaker on mgmt. and survival in small bus.; CEO Manage Ability, Inc., profl. mgmt. firm, 1991—; bus. mgr. Another Door to Learning, 1993-96, exec. dir., 1996—. Contbg. author: Here is Genius!, 1980; author small bus. manuals. Mem. Wash. State br. Boundary Rev. for Kitsap County, 1970-76, Selective Svc. Bd. 19, 1969-76; co-chair Wash. State Small Bus. Improvement Coun., 1986; del. White House Conf. on Small Bus., 1986; chair Wash. State Conf. on Small Bus., 1987; mem. exec. bd. Am. Leadership Forum, 1988-94; dir. Bus. Leadership Week, Wash. State, 1990-96; chair Pro-Tech Pierce County, 1992-94; chair Allenmore Hosp., 1993-96; founding mem. Multicare Health Found., 1995—. Recipient Nellie Cashman award; named Woman Entrepreneur of Yr. for Wash. State, 1986, 87. Mem. Tacoma-Pierce County C. of C. (lifetime exec. bd. 1985—, chair spl. task force on small bus. for Pierce County 1986-89, treas. 1987-88, chair-elect 1988-90, chair 1990-91).

HARLAN, NANCY MARGARET, lawyer; b. Santa Monica, Calif., Sept. 10, 1946; d. William Galland and Betty M. (Miles) Plett; BS magna cum laude, Calif. State U., Hayward, 1972; JD, U. Calif., Berkeley, 1975; m. John Hammack, Dec. 1, 1979; children: Laryssa Maria Rebello, Leea Elyce Harlan. Admitted to Calif. bar, 1975, Fed. bar, U.S. Dist. Ct. for Central Dist., 9th Circuit, 1976; assoc. firm Poindexter & Doutré, Los Angeles, 1975-80; residential counsel Coldwell Banker Residential Brokerage Co., Fountain Valley, Calif., 1980-81; sr. counsel for real estate subs. law dept. Pacific Lighting Corp., Santa Ana, Calif., 1981-87; sr. v.p., gen. counsel The Presley Cos., 1987—. Exec. v.p. student body U. Calif., Berkeley, 1974-75; bd. dirs. La Casa. Mem. ABA, State Bar Calif., L.A. County Bar Assn., Orange County Bar Assn. (dir. corp. counsel sect. 1982—), Calif. Women Lawyers Assn., Orange County Women Lawyers Assn., L.A. Women Lawyers Assn., Nat. Assn. Female Execs., Bus. and Profl. Women. Office: Presley Homes 19 Corporate Plaza Dr Newport Beach CA 92660

HARLASS, SHERRY ELLEN POOL, writer, aquatics instructor; b. Bourne, Mass., Jan. 2, 1961; d. Sydney Smith and Shirley Ruth (Fisher) Pool; m. Mark Paul Harlass, July 17, 1982; children: Rachel Miranda, Mark Daniel. Student, S.W. Tex. State U., 1979-80; BA in Journalism, Midwestern State U., Wichita Falls, Tex., 1982. Reporter Wichita Falls Record News, 1980-82, Wichita Falls Times, 1982-83; staff writer Branch-Smith, Inc., Ft. Worth, 1984-85, prodn. editor, 1986-88, mng. editor, 1988-91; freelance writer, editor, photographer Arlington, Tex., 1991-94, Hurst, Tex., 1994—; instr. aquatic fitness, 1993—, arthritis aquatic, 1994—. Contbr. articles to newspapers and mags. Named one of the Notable Women of Tex., 1983. Mem. Internat. Assn. Fitness Profls., Women in Comms. Inc. (v.p. membership Ft. Worth chpt. 1994-95, treas. Ft. Worth chpt. 1996—), Nat. Fedn. Press Women, Tex. Press Women, Nat. Assn. Women in Horticulture, Mary/Martha Soc. (sec. 1986-88, pres. 1992-94), Tex. Rangers Women's Club (sec. 1986-88), Mothers of Little Lambs (MOLLIES, co-coord. 1995-96), Aquatic Exercise Assn., Arthritis Found., Immanuel Luth. Sch. PTO (key coord. 1996—). Lutheran. Home and Office: 852 Park Forest Dr Hurst TX 76053-7100

HARLE, NICKI, non-profit administrator; b. Columbus, Tex., Oct. 15, 1948; d. Wilton Elwood and Lillian Patricia (Pratka) Stallman; m. Robert P. Harle, June 29, 1974; children: J.W., Kirt, Lee. BA in Speech, S.w. Tex. State U., 1971. Alumni dir. S.W. Tex. State U., San Marcos, 1972-74; owner/instr. Harle Dance Studio, Baird, Tex., 1975-89; instr. aerobics/drill Cisco (Tex.) Jr. Coll., 1982-89; talk show hostess, prodr. KRBC-TV, Abilene, Tex., 1989-92; exec. dir. Tex. Midwest Cmty. Network, Baird, 1974—. Editor/pub.: West Texas Travel Guide, 1991-94. Bd. dirs. Abilene Conv. and Visitors Bur., Abilene, 1991-96, Tex. Rural Leadership Program, Austin, 1996—; econ. devel. dir. City of Baird, 1996—; customer adv. bd. Contel Telephone Co., Dallas, 1991; elder, clk. of session Presbyn. Ch., Baird, 1977-80, 92-95. Mem. Leadership Tex., C. of C. (bd. dirs. 1976-78, 90-95, Citizen of the Yr. 1993). Presbyterian. Home: PO Box 605 Baird TX 79504 Office: Texas Midwest Community Network PO Box 605 Baird TX 79504

HARLEM, SUSAN LYNN, librarian; b. L.A., Oct. 1, 1950; d. Frank Joseph and Esther Frances (Bomell) H.; m. Anthony Stephen Hacsi, Aug. 31, 1990. BA, UCLA, 1972, MLS, 1976. Libr. U. Md., College Park, 1976-79, U.S. Dept. Edn., Washington, 1979-82, GSA, Washington, 1982-87, NLRB, Washington, 1988—; tutor Washington Lit. Coun., 1992—. Coauthor: Washington on Foot, 1984. Office: NLRB Libr 1099 14th St NW Washington DC 20570-3419

HARLEMAN, ANN, English educator, writer. BA in English, Douglass Coll., 1967; PhD in Linguistics, Princeton U., 1972; MFA in Creative Writing, Brown U., 1988. Asst. prof. dept. English Rutgers U., New Brunswick, N.J., 1973-74; asst. prof. dept. English U. Wash., Seattle, 1974-79, assoc. prof., 1979-84; vis. assoc. prof., rsch. affiliate writing program MIT, Cambridge, 1984-86; vis. scholar program in Am. civilization Brown U., Providence, 1986—; Cole disting. prof. Wheaton (Mass.) Coll., 1992-93; prof. English, RISD, Providence, 1994—; Fulbright-Hays lectr., 1980-81; lectr. R.I. Coun. Arts, 1989. Author: Graphic Representation of Models in Linguistic Theory, 1976, (with Bruce A. Rosenberg) Ian Fleming: A Critical Biograhy, 1989, Happiness, 1994, Bitter Lake, 1996; translator: Mute Phone Calls, 1992; contbr. over 50 articles to scholarly publs., transls. and revs., poems and short stories to lit. mags. Recipient Raymond Carver prize, 1986, Nelson Algren runner-up award Chgo. Tribune, 1987, 3d prize Judith Siegal Pearson award, 1988, Chris O'Malley fcition prize Madison Rev., 1990, Judith Siegal Pearson award, 1991, syndicated fiction award PEN, 1991, Iowa short fiction award, 1993; Guggenheim fellow, 1976-77, fellow Huntington Libr., 1979-80, MacDowell Colony, 1988, Am. Coun. Learned Socs., 1992, Wurlitzer Found., 1992; sr. scholar Am. Coun. Learned Socs./IREX, 1976-77; grantee Fockefeller Found., 1989, NEH, 1988. Mem. PEN Am. Ctr. Home: 55 Summit Ave Providence RI 02906-2709 Office: Brown U Program In Am Civilization Providence RI 02912

HARLEMAN, KATHLEEN TOWE, museum administrator, art historian; b. Boston, Feb. 6, 1953; d. Donald Robert Ferguson and Martha Jane (Havens) H. BA, Middlebury Coll., 1975; MA, The Johns Hopkins U., 1977; MBA, U. Ottawa, 1981. Chief of registration Nat. Gallery Can., Ottawa, 1985-88; registrar Art Gallery of Ontario, Toronto, 1988-89, acting dir. art support, 1989-90, mgr. collection and exhibn. projects, 1990-92, dir. exhibns. and facilities, 1992-94; assoc. dir. Davis Mus. and Cultural Ctr. Wellesley Coll., Mass., 1994—, lectr., 1996. Fellow Gilman Found., 1975-78; travel grantee Kress Found., 1977. Mem. Am. Assn. Muss. Office: Davis Mus and Cultural Ctr Wellesley Coll 106 Ctrl St Wellesley MA 02181

HARLESTON, GWENDOLYN PATRICE, federal agency administrator; b. Opa Locka, Fla., Dec. 8, 1957; d. Roy and Willie Artis (Jackson) Boone; children: Darrick, Lavisia Thomas, Markenya; m. Alan Wayne Harleston, Feb. 28, 1991; children: Yvette, Gregory, Renee. BS in Bus. Mgmt., Fla. Meml. Coll., 1989. Dept. mgr. Jordan Marsh, Miami, Fla., 1978-83; asst. store mgr. Casual Corner, Miami, 1984; ops. mgr. Dean Witter Reynolds, Miami, 1984-89; fed. investigator EEOC, N.Y.C., 1989—. Mem. NAFE, Local 3555 AFGE AFL-CIO (v.p. N.Y. chpt. 1993—). Republican. Baptist. Home: 52 Mountbatten Dr Old Bridge NJ 08857

HARLETT, CHRISTINA LEE, obstetrics nurse; b. Evanston, Ill., May 28, 1949; d. Edward Robert and Betty Jane (Larison) Esdale; m. John Michael Harlett, Oct. 3, 1970; children: Aaron Michael, Alex Michael. Diploma, Maumee Valley Hosp., Sch. of Nursing, 1971. RN, Ind. Staff nurse Toledo Hosp., 1971-77; evening charge nurse Ind. U. Med. Ctr., Indpls, 1977-80, staff devel. profl., 1980-83; sect. mgr. obstet. and newborn unit Women's Hosp., Indpls., 1983-94, sect. mgr. labor and delivery, obstet. and newborn units, 1994-95; dir. maternal child svcs. Columbia Women's Hosp., Indpls., 1995—; co-chair 5th ann. perinatal Wyeth Labs., Charleston, S.C., 1991, co-chair 6th ann. perinatal, New Orleans, 1993, com. mem. perinatal adv. bd. Phila, 1989, 90, early discharge com.; adv. bd. Wyeth Labs, 1994, 95. Adv. bd. Photo-Atlas of Nursing Procedures, 1984; co-editor (newsletter) Perinatal Nursing Link, 1992, 93. Mem. Assn. Women's Health, Obstet. and Neonatal Nursing (planning com. dist. V and Indpls. chpt. 1989-91). Roman Catholic. Home: 10 Wildwood Ct Brownsburg IN 46112-1961

HARLEY, RUTH, artist, educator; b. Phila., July 24, 1923; children: Peter Wells Bressler, Tori Angela. Student, Pa. State U., 1941; BFA, Phila. Coll. Art, 1945; postgrad., U. N.H., 1971, Hampshire Coll., 1970. Former instr. Phila. Mus. Art, 1946-59; former art supt. Ventnor (N.J.) City Bd. Edn., 1959-61; art tchr. The Print Club, Phila., Allens Lane Art Ctr., Phila., Suburban Ctr. Arts, Lower Merion, Pa., Radner (Pa.) Twp. Adult Ctr., 1949-59, Atlantic City Adult Ctr., 1959-60. One-woman shows include Dubin-Lush Galleries, Phila., 1956, Pa. Acad. Fine Arts, Phila., 1957, Contemporary Art Assn., Phila., 1957, Vernon Art Exhbns., Germantown, Pa., 1958, Detroit Inst. Arts, 1958, Phila. Mus. Art, 1957, 59, Moore Inst., Phila., 1962-68, Greenhill Galleries, Phila., 1974, Phila. Civic Ctr., 1978, Natal Rio Grande du Norte, Brazil, 1979, Galerie Novel Esprit, Tampa, Fla., 1992-95, Mind's Eye Gallery, St. Petersburg, Fla., 1993; exhibited in various group shows, including Group 55, Phila., 1955, Print Club, Phila., 1955, Nat. Tours 1956-59, Pa. Acad. Fine Arts, 1957, Vernon Art Exhbns., 1958, Detroit Inst. Arts, 1958, Phila. Mus. Art, 1959, Moore Inst., 1962, Phila. Civic Ctr. Mus., 1975, Galerie Nouvel Esprit Assemblage Russe, 1992, Kenneth Raymond Gallery, Boca Raton, 1992-93, Mind's Eye Gallery, 1993, Polk Mus. Art, Lakeland, Fla., 1993, Don Roll Gallery, Sarasota, Fla., 1994-95, Las Vegas (Nev.) Internat. Art Expo, 1994, Heim Am. Gallery, Fisher Island, Fla., 1996, Galerie Nouvel Esprit, 1996; represented in permanent collections at U. Villanova (Pa.) Mus., Temple U. Law Sch., Pa., Wynnerwood Mus. Art, Woodmere Mus., Phila.; included in Art in America Ann. Guide, 1993-97; 1973 photo sculpture commd. through Phila. ReDevel. Authority. Address: PO Box 433 Melrose FL 32666-0433

HARLIN, ALTHEA L., lawyer; b. Oakland, Calif., Oct. 27, 1961. BS magna cum laude, Tulane U., 1982; JD cum laude, Harvard U., 1986. Bar: Pa. 1987, D.C. 1988. Law clk. to Hon. John Pratt U.S. Dist. Ct. D.C., 1986-87; ptnr. Arnold & Porter, Washington. Office: Arnold & Porter 555 12th St NW Washington DC 20004-1202*

HARLIN, MARILYN MILER, marine botany educator, researcher, consultant; b. Oakland, Calif., May 30, 1934; d. George T. and Gertrude (Turula) Miler; m. John E. Harlin II, Oct. 25, 1955 (dec. Feb. 1966); children: John E. III, Andrea M. Harlin Cilento. AB, Stanford U., 1955, MA, 1956; PhD, U. Wash., 197l. Instr. Am. Coll. Switzerland and Leysin, 1964-66; asst. prof. Pacific Marine Sta., Dillon Beach, Calif., 1969; asst. prof. marine biology U. R.I., Kingston, 197l-75, assoc. prof., 1975-83, prof., 1983—, chair botany dept.; guest scientist Atlantic Regional Lab., Halifax, N.S., Can., 1973-78; hon. vis.prof. LaTrobe U., Bundoora, Victoria, Australia, 1984; resource person R.I. Coastal Resource Mgmt. Coun., 1980—, R.I. Dept. Environ. Mgmt., 1980; cons. Applied Sci. Assocs., Narragansett, R.I., 1988—, Western Australia Water Authority, Perth, 1994; rsch. assoc. U. Calif., Santa Cruz, 1993. Co-editor: Marine Ecology, 1976, Freshwater and Marine Plants of Rhode Island, 1988. Bd. dirs. Westminster Unitarian Ch., East Greenwich, R.I., 1987; bd. govs. Women's Ctr., Kingston, 1989-90. Grantee NOAA, 1975-81, Dept. Environ. Mgmt./EPA, 1989-91, U.S. Fish and Wildlife, 1995. Mem. Internat. Phycological Soc., Phycological Soc. Am. (editor newsletter 1982-84, editorial bd. 1988-90), N.E. Algal Soc. (exec. com.), Sigma Xi (pres., sec. 1979-82). Office: U RI Dept Botany Kingston RI 02881

HARLIN-FISCHER, GAYLE C., elementary education educator; b. Fort Worth, Mar. 27, 1950; d. Noble Eugene and Myrtle Mildred (Aycock) Chandler; m. Roger William Harlin, May 23, 1979 (div. 1987); children: Jesse Chandler Harlin, Laura Claire Harlin; m. Terry Wayne Fischer, Mar. 18, 1990. BS in Edn., U. Ga., 1973; MS in Edn., U. Okla., 1990, postgrad., 1991-94. Cert. tchr., Tex., Okla.; cert. elem. prin. Okla. Tchr. Cobb County Dist., Marietta, Ga., 1973-75; tchr. of emotionally disturbed Spring Br. Acad., Houston, 1976-78; 4th grade tchr. Aldine Sch. Dist., Houston, 1979-81; tchr. of emotionally disturbed Mid-Del Schs., Midwest City, Okla., 1979-81; 3d grade tchr. Mid Del Schs., Midwest City, Okla., 1989—; 6th and 8th grade tchr. Norman (Okla.) Sch. Dist., 1988-89; trainer behavioral mgmt. Mid-Del Schs., 1990-95; chmn. adminstrv. com. Okla. Commn. on Tchr. Preparation, Oklahoma City, 1991-95. Mem. NEA, ASCD, Coun. for Exceptional Children, Coun. for Children with Behavioral Disorders, Coun. Adminstrs. in Spl. Edn., Okla. Assn. Colls. Tchr. Edn. (presenter winter conf. 1993), Assn. Classroom Tchrs., Okla. Edn. Assn. Home: 6028 SE 104th St Oklahoma City OK 73165-9606

HARLOW, ELIZABETH MARY, music educator; b. Boston; d. William Joseph and Elizabeth Frieda (Binnig) H.; 1 child, William Harlow Gunn. MusB, Danbury State Tchrs. Coll., Conn., 1959. Music tchr. Guilford Bd. Edn., Conn., 1959-62, North Haven Bd. Edn., Conn., 1962-65,

Hamden Bd. Edn., Conn., 1976—. Mem. Conn. Ednl. Assn., Nat. Music Educators, Am. Choral Dirs. Assn. Hamden Edn. Assn.

HARMAN, JANE FRANK, congresswoman, lawyer; b. N.Y.C., June 28, 1945; d. A. N. and Lucille (Geier) Lakes; m. Sidney Harman, Aug. 30, 1980; children: Brian Lakes, Hilary Lakes, Daniel Geier, Justine Leigh. BA, Smith Coll., 1966; JD, Harvard U., 1969. Bar: D.C. 1969, U.S. Ct. Appeals (D.C. cir.) 1972, U.S. Supreme Ct. 1975. Spl. asst. Commn. of Chs. on Internat. Affairs, Geneva, Switzerland, 1969-70; assoc. Surrey & Morse, Washington, 1970-72; chief legis. asst. Senator John V. Tunney, Washington, 1972-73; chief counsel, staff dir. Subcom. on Rep. Citizen Interests, Com. on Judiciary, Washington, 1973-75; adj. prof. Georgetown Law Ctr., Washington, 1974-75; chief counsel, staff dir. Subcom. on Constl. Rights, Com. on Judiciary, Washington, 1975-77; dep. sec. to cabinet The White House, Washington, 1977-78; spl. counsel Dept. Def., Washington, 1979; ptnr. Manatt, Phelps, Rothenberg & Tunney, Washington, 1979-82, Surrey & Morse, Washington, 1982-86; of counsel Jones, Day, Reavis & Pogue, Washington, 1987-92; mem. 103rd Congress from 36th Calif. dist., 1992—; mem. vis. coms. Harvard Law Sch., 1976-82, Kennedy Sch. Govt., 1990—. Counsel Dem. Platform Com., Washington, 1984; vice-chmn. Ctr. for Nat. Policy, Washington, 1981-90; chmn. Dem. Nat. Com. Nat. Lawyers' Coun., Washington, 1986-90. Mem. Phi Beta Kappa. Democrat. Office: US House Reps 325 Cannon House Office Bldg Washington DC 20515-0536 Office: 5200 W Century Blvd Ste 960 Los Angeles CA 90045-5900 also: 3031 Torrance Blvd Torrance CA 90503-5015*

HARMAN, NANCY JUNE, elementary education educator; b. WaKeeney, Kans., June 23, 1954; d. Don Raymond and Ida Berdena (Hildebrand) Legere; m. Roger Dean Harman, May 24, 1975; children: Michael James, Jennifer Legere. BS in Elem. Edn., Ft. Hays State U., 1975, MS in Edn. Adminstrn., 1993. Cert. early childhood, elem. tchr., elem. adminstr., Kans. Tchr. Catherine Elem. Sch., Hays, Kans., 1975-76, Dodge Elem. Sch., Wichita, Kans., 1977-80, Franklin Elem. Sch., Wichita, 1981-82, Felten Mid. Sch., Hays, 1987-90, O'Loughlin Elem. Sch., Hays, 1990—; mem. nat. leadership team Operation Primary Phys. Sci., 1996—. Parent coord. Hays Striders Track Club, 1987-92; mem. com. Sternberg Discovery Rm., Hays, 1993-94; mem. Hays Book Guild, 1987—; past mem. bd. dirs. Hays Arts Coun. Mem. ASCD, PEO, Nat. Coun. Tchrs. English, Kans. Reading Assn., Kans. Assn. Tchrs. English (state bd. dirs. 1993—, Kans. comm. arts standards writers com.), Kans. Assn. Tchrs. of Math., Phi Delta Kappa, Alpha Delta Kappa (pres. 1988-93). Presbyterian. Home: 2306 Plum St Hays KS 67601-3035 Office: O Loughlin Elem Sch 1401 Hall St Hays KS 67601-3753

HARMEL, HILDA HERTA *See* **PIERCE, HILDA**

HARMLESS, ANN ELIZABETH, psychotherapist, social worker; b. Kansas City, Mo., Sept. 10, 1962; d. Roy Jr. and Mary Louise (Brettel) H.; m. Keith Scott Dubanevich, June 17, 1995. BS in Bus., Kans. State U., Manhattan, 1984; MSW, Smith Coll., 1989. Lic. master social worker; lic. profl. counselor. Pharm. sales rep. Marion Labs., Houston, 1984-85; corporate lender Texas Commerce Bank, Houston, 1985-87; psychotherapist Southwest Psychol., Houston, 1990-91; pvt. practice Houston, 1991—; social work fellow The Menninger Found., Topeka, Kans., 1989-90; cons. Vitalizing, Houston, 1991—, Fluor Daniel, Houston, 1992—, Mental Health Mental Retardation, Houston, 1992-94, Wellmill, Houston, 1995—. Active Jr. League, Houston, 1985-93, Mus. Fine Arts, Houston, 1993—, Nat. Abortion Rights Activist League, Houston, 1993—, NOW, Houston, 1994—. Social Work fellow Menninger Found., 1990; scholar Brown Found., 1987-89. Mem. Houston Group Psychotherapy Soc. (editor 1991-94), Houston Assn. Social Work, Tex. Bd. Profl. Counselors, Employee Assistance Program Assn. Democrat. Unitarian. Office: 12603 Southwest Fwy # 310 Stafford TX 77477

HARMON, CLARA CHOKENEA, public relations/marketing executive; b. Cleve., Feb. 5, 1953; d. Arthur Charles and Clara Ann (Sinagra) Chokenea; m. John Clifford Harmon, July 21, 1979; children: Anna Grace, Gail Frances. BS in Journalism, Bowling Green State U., 1975; MBA, Rochester Inst. Tech., 1979. Employee info. editor, news svcs. editor, sales rep. Eastman Kodak Co., Rochester, N.Y., 1975-79; mgmt. asst. South Ctrl. Bell/AT&T, Louisville, 1979-81; account exec. Caldwell Van Riper Inc., Indpls., 1981-82; editl. staff writer Sherman-Eckert Visual and Verbal Comms., Webster, N.Y., 1993; dir. comms. Pers. Works Inc., Pittsford, N.Y., 1993-95, dir. mktg., 1995-96; group leader corp. commn.; vis. nurse svc. of Rochester and Monroe County, 1996—. Loaned exec. United Way, Rochester, 1979; chair cmty. rels. com., bd. dirs. Girls Clubs of Greater Indpls., 1982-84; mem. mktg./publ rels. com. ARC, Rochester, 1984-86; mem. bldg. mgmt. team, parent rep. shared decision-making team Thornell Rd. Elem. Sch., Pittsford, 1993-95; various com. chair positions Plank South Sch. PTSA, Webster, N.Y., 1991-92, chair family to family program, 1990-92; founder Plank Rd. South Pub. Ctr., Webster, 1991-92. Mem. Women in Comms. (pres. Rochester chpt. 1978-79, membership v.p. 1994-95, nat. nominations chair 1982-82), Soc. for Human Resource Mgmt. (newsletter editor 1994-96). Mem. United Ch. of Christ. Home: 58 Cambric Cir Pittsford NY 14534 Office: Visiting Nurse Svc 2180 Empire Blvd Webster NY 14580

HARMON, GAIL MCGREEVY, lawyer; b. Kansas City, Kans., Mar. 15, 1943; d. Milton and Barbara (James) McGreevy; m. John W. Harmon, June 11, 1966; children: James, Eve. BA cum laude, Radcliffe Coll., 1965; JD cum laude, Columbia U., 1969. Bar: Mass. 1970, D.C. 1976, U.S. Dist. Ct. D.C. Assoc. Gaston Snow & Ely Bartlett, Boston, 1970-75, Steptoe & Johnson, Washington, 1975-76, Roisman, Kessler & Cashdan, Washington, 1976-77; ptnr. Harmon, Curran & Tousley, Washington, 1977-90, Harmon, Curran & Spielberg, Washington, 1990—. Pres. Women's Legal Def. Fund, 1982-84; mem. steering com. Emily's List, 1985—. Democrat. Episcopalian.

HARMON, JACQUELINE BAAS, librarian, infosystems specialist; b. Kalamazoo, Oct. 23, 1934; d. Jacob and Ethyl (Zuidema) Baas; m. Robert E. Davis, Aug. 21, 1955 (div. July 1979); children: Robert J., Sarah Jane, James E.; m. W.R. Harmon, Jan. 5, 1985. BS, Western Mich. U., 1955; postgrad., U. Iowa, 1961; MLS, U. Tex., Austin, 1978. Cert. tchr., Mich., Tex., Iowa. Dir. info. svcs. Motorola, Inc., Austin, 1978-83; mgmt. and systems specialist Lockheed Missiles and Space Corp., Austin, 1983-84; corp. librarian Microelectronics and Computer Tech. Corp. (MCC), Austin, 1984—. Contbr. articles to profl. jours. Pres. Austin Library Comm., City of Austin, 1978-89, Cen. Tex. Library Systems Bd., Austin, 1986-88, Sta. KLRN Adv. Bd., Austin, 1979; v.p. Internat. Hospitality Commn., Austin, 1976-88; mem. U. Tex. Adv. Coun. Library Sch., 1984-89. Mem. IEEE, Am. Assn. for Artificial Intelligence, ALA, Tex. Library Assn. Home: 10997 County Road 653 Gobles MI 49055-9282 Office: Asbury Theol Sem 210 N Lexington Ave Wilmore KY 40390-1129

HARMON, JANE ELLEN, occupational therapist, writer; b. Muskegon, Mich.; d. Robert Junior and Edith (Boven) H. BS in Occupational Therapy, Western Mich. U., 1974; postgrad., Cleve., 1977. Registered occupational therapist; licensed occupational therapist, Tex.; cert. CPR/BCLS instr.-trainer. From vol. to staff therapist Hackley Hosp., Muskegon, 1972-75; head occupational therapy dept. Mercy Hosp., Muskegon, 1975-79; pvt. practice, 1976-79; with Mary Free Bed Hosp. & Rehab. Ctr., Grand Rapids, 1979; free-lance writer, 1979—; cons. Tri-City Health Ctr./Hosp., Dallas, 1993. Author: At Home with MS, 1996; contbg. writer Inside MS, 1996; contbr. articles to profl. jours.; contbg. editor, cons. Occupational Therapy Forum, 1993—. Active Arthritis Vol. Action Com., 1975-79; founder Vols. Against Multiple Sclerosis Mich. chpt. Nat. Multiple Sclerosis Soc., 1973 (recipient Individual Vol. of the Yr. award, 1994), co-chair Govtl. Rels. Com., mem. profl. adv. com. North Tex. chpt., mem. patient svc. com., MS Tex. CAN, 1996—; mem. HIV/AIDS Com. Bethel Ch., Dallas, 1992—, prayer chain coord., 1990-96, editor Bethel News, 1989-90; editor, cage bird cons. pet-facilitated therapy program Baylor Inst. for Rehab., Dallas, 1992-93; founder, dir. Project HAVEN Dallas Cage Bird Soc., 1991-93; vol. Dallas Ctr. for Ind. Living, 1990—; liaison Classis Pella Com. on Disability Concerns; founder, dir. Ecology Ministries, 1987—; rep. com. disability concerns Classis Pella, Christian Reformed Ch. N.Am., 1994—; mem. Nat. Svcs. Adv. Coun. Nat. Multiple Sclerosis Soc., 1996—; bd. dirs. Northeast Tex. chpt. Am. Parkinson Disease Assn., 1996—; mem. Greater Dallas/Ft. Worth chpt. Myasthenia Gravis Found., 1994—; mem. Dallas County CLASS adv. bd., 1996—; resource person MS & Degenerative Neurol. Diseases, 1991—. Mem. Tex. Occupational Therapy Assn., Environ. Health Assn. Dallas, Am. Occupational Therapy Assn., Write Shop Writer's Assn. Office: 14232 Marsh Ln Ste 320 Dallas TX 75234-3865

HARMON, MARCI JANET, controller; b. Newark, Mar. 6, 1960; d. Harold E. and Lorraine G. (Schulte) Jayson; m. Brian Stewart Harmon, May 6, 1984. BS in Acctg., Pa. State U., 1982; MBA in Fin., Fairleigh Dickinson U., Madison, N.J., 1987. CPA, N.J. Auditor Arthur Andersen & Co., Houston, 1982-83; sr. fin. analyst Kidde, Inc., Saddle Brook, N.J., 1983-85; asst. controller Maritz Communications Co., Parsippany, N.J., 1985-88; contr. Lamar Cos., Morristown, N.J., 1988-91; mem. fin. adv. com. City of Mt. Arlington, N.J., 1986-88. V.p. Long Valley PTA. Fellow N.J. State Soc. CPAs (dir.); mem. AICPA, NAFE, Nat. Assn. Accts., Pa. State U. Alumni Assn., Long Valley Area Jr. Women Club (v.p.), Washington Twp. Newcomers Club, Alpha Phi. Jewish.

HARMON, MARIAN SANDERS, writer, sculptor; b. Detroit, Jan. 16, 1916; d. Joseph and Anne (Stern) Sanders; m. Edward Stein, Jan. 15, 1950 (dec. 1960); m. Leonard Byron Harmon, 1963. BA, U. Mich., 1937. Dir. radio and TV Simons Michelson, Detroit, 1948-60; editor Table Talk Bridge Newspaper, 1954-62; writer ABC-TV, N.Y.C., 1960-65; organizer, pres. Visual Arts Forum, 1981-93. Author: (poems) The Hourglass, 1982; editor AAUW, East Hampton, 1984-87, various newspapers, 1945-65; first editor Northwest Detroiter, 1947; freelance writer for newspapers and mags.; computer art in invitational art shows, 1995, 96. Recipient Best Sculpture in Show award Guild Hall East Hampton, 1989. Home: PO Box 1547 East Hampton NY 11937-0795

HARMON, MELINDA FURCHE, federal judge; b. Port Arthur, Tex., Nov. 1, 1946; d. Frank Cantrell and Wilma (Parish) Furche; m. Frank G. Harmon III, Oct. 16, 1976; children: Mary Elizabeth, Phelps, Francis. AB, Harvard U., 1969; JD, U. Tex., 1972. Bar: Tex. 1973, U.S. Dist. Ct. (so. dist.) Tex. 1974, U.S. Dist. Ct. (no. dist.) Tex. 1975, U.S. Dist. Ct. (ea. dist.) Tex. 1978, U.S. Ct. Appeals (5th and 11th cirs.) 1981, U.S. Supreme Ct. 1982, U.S. Ct. Claims 1987. Law clk. to presiding judge U.S. Dist. Ct. (so. dist.) Tex., Houston, 1973-75; atty. Exxon Co., Houston, 1975-88; judge 280th Jud. Dist. Ct. Tex. State Trial Ct., ctrl. jurisdiction, 1988-89; judge U.S. Dist. Ct. (so. dist.) Tex., Houston, 1989—. Mem. Tex. Bar Assn., Houston Bar Assn., Harvard Radcliffe Club. Roman Catholic. Office: US Dist Ct US Courthouse 515 Rusk St Ste 9114 Houston TX 77002-2605*

HARMON, SHARON GRANHOLM, special education educator; b. Sewickley, Pa., June 13, 1948; d. Walter Alex and Bertha Louise (Jones) Granholm; m. Charles Ellis Harmon, June 6, 1969; 1 child, Brad Vann. BS, Ga. State U., 1970, MEd, 1974. Cert. T-5 spl. edn. tchr., K-12 mental retardation, learning disabilities tchr., Ga. Tchr. spl. edn. DeKalb County Bd. Edn., Decatur, Ga., 1970-75, Rockdale County Bd. Edn., Conyers, Ga., 1976-77, 82-93, Lowndes County Bd. Edn., Valdosta, Ga., 1993—; cons. Gwinnett, Newton, Rockdale Early Intervention Program, summer 1993; mem. 21st Century Consortium for Edn., Athens, Ga., 1990. Co-chmn. host com. Friendship Force, Atlanta, 1977. Fellow Am. Wilderness Leadership Sch., Granite, Wyo., 1988. Mem. NEA, Coun. for Exceptional Children, Ga. Assn. Educators, Lowndes County Assn. Educators. Baptist. Home: 2600 Pebblewood Dr Valdosta GA 31602 Office: Hahira Elem Sch 350 Claudia Dr Hahira GA 31632

HARMON BROWN, VALARIE JEAN, hospital laboratory director, information systems executive; b. Peoria, Ill., June 21, 1948; d. Donald Joseph and Frances Elizabeth (Classen) Harmon; m. James Roger Brown, Aug. 21, 1982 (dec. May 1994). BSMT, Northwestern U., Chgo., 1970. Med. tech. Evanston (Ill.) Hosp., 1970-71, chief tech., 1971-75; med. tech. II M.D. Anderson Hosp., Houston, 1975-76; dir. lab. Physicians Ref. Lab., Houston, 1978-81, Med. Ctr. Hosp., Conroe, Tex., 1981-91, Palo Pinto Gen. Hosp., Mineral Wells, Tex., 1993-94; sales mgr. Long Beach (Calif.) Meml. Med. Ctr., 1995-96; quality assurance/regulatory affairs mgr. Consol. Med. Labs., Lake Bluff, Ill., 1996—; lab. cons. Texaco Chem. Wellness Program, Conroe, 1989; health career sponsor Willis Ind. Sch. Dist., Tex., 1989, 90; mem. adv. bd. Med. Lab. Technician program Weatherford Coll., 1994. Coord. blood drive Gulf Coast Region Blood Ctr., 1986-91; sponsor colon cancer screening Montgomery County Health Fair, 1986; sponsor Camp Sunshine/Lions Club, 1988; sponsor cholesterol screening Med. Ctr. Hosp. Health Fair, 1989. Mem. NAFE, Am. Soc. Clin. Pathologists, Am. Soc. Med. Technologists, Clin. Lab. Mgmt. Assn. Republican. Roman Catholic. Home: 1050 E Martingale Ln Round Lake Beach IL 60073 Office: Consol Med Labs Ste 1200 101 Waukegan Rd Lake Bluff IL 60044-1669

HARMS, DEBORAH GAYLE, psychologist; b. Ft. Worth; d. Raymond O. Smith and Billie (Allen) Greenwade; m. Joel Randall Harms; children: J. Christopher, Ryan R., Catherine R. BA with honors with high distinction, Wayne State U., 1977; MA in Clin. Psychology, U. Detroit, 1979, PhD in Clin. Psychology, 1984. Lic. psychologist. Trainee in psychology Henry Ford Hosp., Troy, Mich., 1978-79; intern in psychology Detroit Psychiat. Inst., 1979-82; staff psychologist Eastwood Clinic, Harper Woods, Mich., 1983-86; pvt. practice Harms and Harms, PC, Birmingham, Mich., 1985—; staff psychologist Dominican Consultation Ctr., Detroit, 1986-89; sr. psychologist Oakland County Probate Ct., Pontiac, Mich., 1990. Teaching fellow U. Detroit, 1978-79. Mem. APA, Nat. Register Health Care Providers in Psychology, Mich. Psychol. Assn., Mich. Women Psychologists, Mensa, Phi Beta Kappa. Home: 21783 Corsaut Ln Beverly Hills MI 48025-2607 Office: Harms and Harms PC 199 W Brown St Birmingham MI 48009

HARNAGE, KRISTINE ANDREA, newspaper editor; b. Heidelberg, Germany, Jan. 28, 1968; came to U.S., 1968; d. Thomas Addison and Nancy Janes (Bowles) H. BA, Valdosta State U., 1991. Editor-in-chief The Press Advantage, Adel, Ga., 1991-92; lifestyles reporter The Valdosta Daily Times, 1992-95; lifestyles editor Thomasville (Ga.) Times-Enterprise, 1995—. Pub. rels. coord. Valdosta Jr. Women's Club, 1992-95; pub. rels. rep. Valdosta Civic Round Table, 1992-95; vol. ARC, 1992-95, March of Dimes, 1993-95, Am. Cancer Soc., 1994-95; bd. dirs. parish coun. St. John's Ch., Valdosta, 1994-95. Recipient 3rd Place award Ga. Press Assn. for Lifestyle Coverage, 1995-96. Mem. Women's Forum of Thomasville (mentor upward bound program Thomas Coll. 1996—). Roman Catholic. Home: 121 Covington Ave #67 Thomasville GA 31792-5245 Office: Thomasville Times-Enterpris 106 S St Thomasville GA 31792

HARNETT, LILA, publisher; b. Bklyn., Oct. 4, 1926; d. Milton Samuel and Claire S. (Merahn) Mogan; m. Joel William Harnett. BA, CUNY, 1946; postgrad., New Sch. for Social Rsch., 1950. Pers. exec. Walter Lowen Agy., N.Y.C., 1947-52; pub. Bus. Atomics Report, N.Y.C., 1953-63; weekly columnist N.Y. State Newspapers, 1964-74; fine arts editor Cue Mag., N.Y., 1975-80; founder, contbg. editor Phoenix Home & Garden mag., 1980—, assoc. pub., 1988—, editor, 1996—; pub. Scottsdale (Ariz.) Scene mag., 1992—. Home: 4523 E Clearwater Pky Paradise Vly AZ 85253-2815 Office: Phoenix Home & Garden 4041 N Central Ave Phoenix AZ 85012

HARNSBERGER, THERESE COSCARELLI, librarian; b. Muskegon, Mich.; d. Charles and Julia (Borrell) Coscarelli; B.A. cum laude, Marymount Coll., 1952; M.L.S., U. So. Calif., 1953; postgrad. Rosary Coll., River Forest, Ill., 1955-56, U. Calif., Los Angeles Extension, 1960-61; m. Frederick Owen Harnsberger, Dec. 24, 1962; 1 son, Lindsey Carleton. Free-lance writer, 1950—; librarian San Marino (Calif.) High Sch., 1953-56; cataloger, cons. San Marino Hall, South Pasadena, Calif., 1956-61; librarian Los Angeles State Coll., 1956-59; librarian dist. library Covina-Valley Unified Sch. Dist., Covina, Calif., 1959-67; librarian Los Angeles Trade Tech. Coll., 1972—, mem. acad. senate, 1996—; med. librarian, tumor registrar Alhambra (Calif.) Community Hosp., 1975-79; tumor registrar Huntington Meml. Hosp., 1979—; pres., dir. Research Unltd., 1980—; free lance reporter Los Angeles' Best Bargains, 1981—; med. library cons., 1979—; reviewer various cookbooks, 1991—. Author numerous poems. Chmn. spiritual values com. Covina Coordinating Council, 1964-66; chmn. Neighborhood Watch, 1976—. Winner poetry contest Pasadena Star News, 1993. Mem. ALA, Internat. Women's Writing Guild, Calif. Assn. Sch. Librarians (chmn. legis. com.), Acad.Com. Partimers Rep., 1996 Covina Tchrs. Assn., AAUW (historian 1972-73), U. So. Calif. Grad. Sch. Libr. Sci. (life), Am. Nutrition Soc. (chpt. Newsletter chmn.), Nat. Tumor Registrars Assn., So. Calif. Tumor Registrars Assn., Med. Libr. Assn., So. Calif. Libr. Assn., So. Calif. Assn. Law Libr., Book Publicists So. Calif., Am. Fedn. Tchrs. (exec. bd. parttimers 1994, alt. exec. bd. local # 1521 coll. guild 1994—, acad. senate parttimers rep. 1996—), Coll. Guild, Calif. Libr. Assn., Assn. Poetry Bibliographers, Faculty Assn. Calif. Community Colls., Immaculate Heart Coll. Alumnae Assn., Assistance League Pasadena, Loyola Marymount Alumnae Assn. (coord. 1986), Pi Lambda Theta. Author: (poetry) The Journal, 1982, To Julia: in Memoriam; contbr. articles to profl. jours., poems to newspapers. Office: 2809 W Hellman Ave Alhambra CA 91803-2737

HARP, TONI N., state legislator; b. San Francisco. BA, Roosevelt U.; MEd, Yale U. Mem. New Haven Bd. Aldermen, 1988-92, Commn. Affirmative Action, 1990-92; Conn. state senator, 1993—; project coord. health svcs. Democrat. Address: 26 Lynwood Pl New Haven CT 06511-4713 Office: Conn State Senate State Capitol Hartford CT 06106*

HARPER, AUDREY MCCORMICK, multimedia company executive; b. Muncie, Ind., Dec. 30, 1934; d. Cassius D. and Olive M. (Allen) McCormick; m. John Christian Harper, Dec. 20, 1958; children: Brenda C., Olivia A., John Christian Jr. BA, Vassar Coll., Poughkeepsie, N.Y., 1957. Econ. analyst Harvard Grad. Sch. Econs., Cambridge, Mass., 1958-60; gen. mgr., ptnr. Monaco, Bethel, Conn., 1976—. Mem. Vassar Club (Fairfield County chpt. pres. 1975-76), Harvard Club (N.Y.C.), Fairfield County Hunt Club. Republican. Episcopalian. Home: 16 Old Weston Rd Weston CT 06883

HARPER, CHRISTINE JOHNSON, psychiatric clinical nurse, administrator; b. Tyler, Tex., June 26, 1952; d. Reinhold P. and Alice G. (Levingston) Johnson; m. James H. Harper, Sept. 4, 1982; 1 child, Timothy Wright. BSN, U. Tex., 1974; MS, U. Tex., Tyler, 1981; MSN, Tex. Woman's U., 1992. RN, Tex.; cert. clin. nurse specialist in psychiat. mental health. Instr. Tyler Jr. Coll., 1976-87; sr. lectr. U. Tex., Tyler, 1987-91, adj. nursing faculty, 1994—; clin. specialist Rusk (Tex.) State Hosp., 1992-94, dir. nursing svcs., 1994—. Mem. Tex. Nurses Assn. (bd. dirs. dist. 19, ho. of dels., past pres., Exemplary Leadership in Tex. Nursing award 1988), Am. Psychiat. Nurses Assn. (Tex. rep. 1995), Sigma Theta Tau (chmn. nominations Iota Nu chpt.). Home: PO Box 921 Rusk TX 75785-0921

HARPER, DELPHINE BERNICE, health administrator; b. Boston, Sept. 6, 1947; d. James Albert and Bernice (Bell) Garnett; m. John Henry Redd III, Dec. 31, 1966 (div. May 1972); 1 child, John; m. Morris Harper, Aug. 18, 1975; children: Michele, Kimberly. Cert. acctg., Boston Sch. Bus., 1966; BS, Northeastern U., 1973; postgrad., L.I. U., 1975-76. Lic. real estate agt., D.C., Md. Asst. Admissions Office Northeastern U., Boston, 1968-71; adminstrv. asst. to dir. Assn. for Better Housing, Boston, 1971; community organizer Roxbury Multi Svc. Ctr., Boston, 1971-72; unit mgr. Peter Bent Brigham Hosp., Boston, 1972-74; mgmt. analyst State of Mass., Boston, 1974-75; proprietor Kimele's Wine & Cheese, Cambridge, Mass., 1978-79; real estate agt. Bd. Realtors, D.C., Md., 1983-86; program officer, asst. dir. resident svcs. Dept. Housing, 1986-88; v.p. ops., mgmt. officer Health Care Systems Corp., Silver Spring, Md., 1988—. Author: Beyond, 1994. Bd. dirs. Dem. Nat. Com., Washington, 1988; mem. Kennedy Ctr., 1989—. John F. Kennedy scholar Northeastern U., Boston, 1971-73, Martin Luther King scholar, 1970-71. Mem. Am. Mgmt. Assn., Greater Washington Edn. Telecommunication Assn., Women in Arts, Smithsonian Assocs., Nat. Trust for Hist. Preservation, Nat. Geog. Soc., Nat. Assn. Investors Corp., N.Y. Met. Opera Guild, Archaeol. Inst. Am., N.Y. Mus. Natural History, Phi Beta Kappa.

HARPER, DIANE MARIE, resolution analyst; b. Harrisburg, Pa., Oct. 22, 1938; d. Paull Harry Rineard and Berneice Marie (Westhafer) Gerhardt; m. William Irvin Harper, Nov. 17, 1957 (div. Aug. 1981); children: Dawn Michelle, Steven Lee, William Madison. Student, Harrisburg Area C.C., 1992—. Telephone operator United Telephone Pa., Carlisle, 1956-59; keypunch operator United Telephone Pa., Harrisburg, 1960-61, Safety Sales & Svc., Harrisburg, 1967-70; keypunch operator, lead data entry operator Kinney Shoe Corp., Camp Hill, Pa., 1970-84; data entry operator First Health, Harrisburg, 1984-92; resolution analyst Electronic Data Systems, Camp Hill, 1992—; Stephen minister; reporter, writer pubs. com. Electronic Data Systems, 1996—, human resources coord. corrective action com., 1993—, social coord. 2d shift Pa. XIX staff, 1993—. Com. woman 4th Ward, Carlisle, Pa., 1959-61; minority inspector polls, Carlisle, 1959-61; pres. Mother's of DeMolay, Carlisle, 1976-78. Mem. NOW, Nat. Abortion and Reproductive Rights Action League, Nat. Pks. and Conservation Assn., Nat. Resources Def. Coun., Nat. Arbor Day Found., Pa. Sheriff's Assn. (hon.), Pa. Chiefs of Police Assn., Mechanicsburg Mus. Assn., Legal Assts. Club, Friends Harrisburg Uptown Libr., Friends Mechanicsburg Libr., Little Theatre Mechanicsburg (v.p. 1962-63, pres. 1963-67), Nat. Trust for Hist. Preservation. Democrat. Lutheran. Home: 306 S Market St Mechanicsburg PA 17055 Office: Electronic Data Systems 275 Grandview Ave Camp Hill PA 17011

HARPER, (VESTA) DIANNE, educator; b. Santa Fe, N.Mex., July 9, 1942; d. Donald Franklin Hervey and Bettie Ellen (Culbertson) Wilcox; m. James K. Harper, June 8, 1963; children: Anne Elizabeth, Erin Lane. BA, Colo. State U., 1964. Tchr./counselor West Yuma R-J1 Sch. Dist., Yuma, Colo., 1964-80, 88—; owner Harper's Ltd., Yuma, 1982-88; task evaluator New Stds. Project, Colo.; co-chair Stds. Assessment Implementation and Devel. Coun., Colo., 1993—; adv. bd. U. No. Colo. English dept., 1992—; presenter in field. Trustee Yuma Hosp. bd. dirs., 1978—; mem. Yuma County Child Protection Team, Colo., 1984—; bd. dirs. Yuma Theater Co., 1983—. Grantee Gates Co., Santa Fe, 1992. Mem. PEO, NEA, Colo. Edn. Assn. Home: 36550 County Road G Yuma CO 80759-7803

HARPER, DOROTHY GWYN, principal; b. Durham, N.C., Feb. 11, 1953; d. Julius Johnston and Patricia (Wright) Gwyn; m. Joseph Stanway Harper, Nov. 29, 1975; children: Willard Russell, Christopher Colman. BA in Psychology and Anthropology, U. N.C., 1975; EdD in Ednl. Leadership, U. N.C., Greensboro, 1994; MS in Spl. Edn., Fla. State U., 1981. Cert. tchr., N.C. Handicapped presch. tchr. Orange County Devel. Ctr., Chapel Hill, N.C., 1975-77; respite care coord. Orange County ARC, Chapel Hill, N.C., 1977-78; tchr. Gretchen Everhart Trainable Ctr., Tallahassee, 1981-82; spl. edn. tchr. Reidsville (N.C.) Sr. H.S., 1983-88; asst. prin. Reidsville Mid. Sch., 1988-91; prin. Moss St. Elem. Sch., Reidsville, 1991-95, J.E. Holmes Middle Sch., Eden, N.C., 1995—. Mem. Rockingham County Tomorrow, 1994-95, Leadership Rockingham, 1994. Named Prin. of Yr., Wachovia Bank, 1993; fellow Edn. Policy Fellowship Program, 1990-91. Mem. ASCD, Coun. for Exceptional Children. Office: JE Holmes Middle Sch 211 N Pierce St Eden NC 27288-3532

HARPER, GLADYS COFFEY, health services adviser; b. Pitts.; d. Clarence William and India Anna (James) Jackson; BA, U. Pitts., 1970, MPA, 1972, MSH, 1973; m. Thomas A. Harper, Jan. 21, 1968. With Allegheny County (Pa.) Health Dept., 1958—, chief office tng. and edn. adminstrn., 1975-76, adv. curriculum devel. and health adminstrn., 1976—; health technician specialist office health affairs OEO, Washington, 1965; vis. lectr. Grad. Sch. Public and Internat. Affairs, U. Pitts., 1970—; bd. dirs. Heritage Nat. Bank, 1988—; panelist Sta. WQED-TV White House Conf. Food, Nutrition and Health; trustee Mayview State Hosp., 1975-96, v.p. bd. trustees, 1978, trustee clin. pastoral edn. program, 1979-80; bd. dirs. United Mental Health, Inc. Co-producer documentary: What's Buggin' The Blacks?, Sta. KDKA-TV, 1968; host Weekly News Notes, Sta. KDKA-Radio, 1989—. Program chmn. Law Day, Allegheny County Assn. Lawyers' Wives, 1980; program chmn. Pa. Bar Assn. Wives Program, 1978; trustee Louis Little Meml. Fund, Allegheny County Bar Assn., 1979; founder Judge Thomas A. Harper Meml. Scholarship, Howard U. Sch. Law, 1984. Active Allegheny County Bicentennial Com., 1987, Afro-Am. Heritage Day Parade Com., 1987; exec. v.p. Afro-Am. Heritage Parade Assn., chmn. judging com., 1988; v.p. Hist. Soc. of Western Pa., 1988; pres. Tri-Rivers African Am. Archives, Inc., 1991. Named Woman of Yr., Greyhound Corp., 1967, 1 of 25 Outstanding Pittsburghers, Wayfarer Mag., Chrysler Corp., 1967; recipient Health Services award Pitts. Club United, 1970, Harold B. Gardner award-Md. Citizen Health award, Allegheny County Med. Soc., 1973, Drug Edn. recognition Pitts. Press, 1971, citation for environ. health curriculum devel. and supervision Chatham Coll., 1976, award African Meth. Episcopal Zion Ch., 1984, Trailblazer award Renaissance Publs, 1992, Outstanding Citizen award Hand in Hand, 1992, Black History Month citation Bur. Surface Mining, U.S. Dept. Interior, 1992; crowned Bahamas Princess Christmas Queen, Freeport, 1976. Mem. APHA, Royal Soc. Health, Am. Soc. Pub. Adminstrn., Conf. Minority Pub. Adminstrs., Legis. Council Western Pa. (dir., v.p. elect 1982), Western Pa. Genealogy Soc. (pres. 1983), Legis. Council Western Pa. (pres. 1983), League Community Health Workers, AAUW, NAACP (Isabel Strickland Youth Advisor award 1967, Daisy E. Lampkin Human Rights award 1969), Hist. Soc. Western Pa. (trustee 1984, v.p. bd. trustees 1988), U. Pitts. Alumnae Assn. (Bicentennial scholarship com.), Program to Aid Citizen Enterprises (commr., treas. 1968-76). Home: 5260 Centre Ave Pittsburgh PA 15232-1334

HARPER, GLORIA JANET, artist, educator; children: Dan Conyers, Jan Girvan. Student, Famous Artists Sch., 1967-69, 69-71; BA in Comml. Art, Portland C.c., 1981; postgrad., Valley View Art Sch., 1982-89, Carrizzo Art Sch., 1983-89, Holdens Portrait Sch., 1989; studied with Daniel Greene, 1989, postgrad. in paralegal studies. Cert. art educator. Artist, art instr. Art By Gloria, 1980—; owner Art By Gloria Art Sch. and Gallery, Pendleton, Oreg., 1991—; lectr., workshop presenter in field, 1980—. Paintings and prints included in various mags. Mem. NAFE, Nat. Assn. Fine Artists, Water Color Soc. Am., Nat. Mus. Women in Arts, So. Career Inst. Profl. Legal Assts. (area rep.), Profl. Legal Assts., Pendleton C. of C. Home: PO Box 1734 Pendleton OR 97801-0570 Office: Art By Gloria 404 SE Dorion Ste 204 Pendleton OR 97801-2214

HARPER, JANET SUTHERLIN LANE, educational administrator, writer; b. La Grange, Ga., Apr. 2, 1940; d. Clarence Wilner and Imogene (Thompson); m. William Sterling Lane, June 28, 1964, (div. Jan. 1981); children: David Alan, Jennifer Ruth; m. John F. Harper, June 9, 1990. BA in English and Applied Music, LaGrange Coll., 1961; postgrad., Auburn U., 1963; MA in Journalism, U. Ga., Athens, 1979. Music and drama critic The Brunswick News, Brunswick, Ga., 1979—; info. asst. Glynn County Schs., Brunswick, 1979-82; adj. prof. Brunswick Coll., Ga., 1981-87; dir. pub. info. and publs. Glynn County Schs., Brunswick, 1982—; media relations Ga. Assn. of Ednl. Leaders, 1983—. Contbg. editor Ga. Jour., 1981-84; editor, writer GAEL Conf. Jours., 1987-89. Organist St. Simons United Meth. Ch., 1981—; pres. Jekyll Island Music Theater Bd., 1994—. Recipient award of excellence in sch. and community rels. Ga. Bd. Edn., 1984, 92, Edn. Leadership award, Ga., 1989. Mem. Nat. Sch. Pub. Rels. Assn. (Golden Achievement award 1985, 2 awards 1988, 90, 3 awards 1991, 92, 94), Ga. Sch. Pub. Rels. Assn. (Disting. Svc. award 1991), Brunswick Press-Advt. Club (award of excellence in pub. rels. 1992), Brunswick Golden Isles C. of C., Mozart Soc., Phi Delta Kappa, Phi Kappa Phi, Sigma Delta Chi. Office: Glynn County Schs 1313 Egmont St Brunswick GA 31520-7244

HARPER, KAREN BEIDELMAN, elementary school educator; b. Des Moines, June 27, 1952; d. Oliver Jason and Luana Margery (Wills) Beidelman; m. Doyle Ray Harper, Aug. 6, 1977; children: Jenny, Abby. B in music edn., Drake U., 1974; MM in Music Therapy, Loyola U., 1977; cert. in elem. edn., U. Iowa, 1990. Cert. tchr. Iowa; cert. music tchr. Iowa; registered music therapist, cert. infant edn. and massage therapist. Elem. tchr. J.J. Finley Elem. Sch., Gainesville, Fla., 1977-78, W.H. Beasley Mid. Sch., Palatka, Fla., 1978-79, Lincoln Elem. Sch., Iowa City, 1991, Community Edn. Ctr. Secondary Sch., Iowa City, 1991-92, St. Anthony Sch., Des Moines, 1992-95; substitute tchr., 1996—; child life specialist Schoitz Med. Ctr., Waterloo, Iowa, 1980-83; activity coord. The Carney Hosp., Boston, 1984-85; child life coord. South Shore Hosp., Weymouth, Mass., 1985-88; infant massage instr. Infant Sensory Enrichment Edn., Grimes, Iowa, 1984—, parent-infant instr., 1984—. Recipient Outstanding Svc. award Beta Phi Zeta, 1974. Mem. Internat. Assn. Reading, Nat. Mid. Sch. Assn., Pi Lambda Theta, Mu Phi Epsilon (sec., historian 1973-74). Home: 716 Dolan Dr Grimes IA 50111-1085

HARPER, MARY SADLER, banker; b. Farmville, Va., June 15, 1941; d. Edward Henry and Vivien Morris (Garrett) Sadler; m. Joseph Taylor Harper, Dec. 21, 1968; children by previous marriage: James E. Hatch III, Mary Ann Hatch Czajka. Cert. Fla. Trust Sch., U. Fla., 1976. Registered securities rep., Fla., gen. securities prin., fin. and ops. prin., options prin., mcpl. securities prin. Dep. clk. Polk County Cts., Bartow, Fla., 1964-67; rep. Allen & Co., Lakeland, Fla., 1967-71; with First Nat. Bank, Palm Beach, Fla., 1971-89, sr. v.p., 1984-86, sr. v.p. S.E. Bank N.A., Palm Beach, 1986-89; pres., CEO Palm Beach Capital Svcs., Inc., 1986-88, mng. dir. Investment Svcs., Palm Beach Capital Svcs. Div., 1988; v.p. investments, trustee J.M. Rubin Found., Palm Beach, 1983—; sr. v.p. investment div. Island Nat. Bank & Trust Co., 1989—; chmn., dir., pres. CEO Island Investment Svcs., Inc., Palm Beach, 1989—, also bd. dirs.; mem. adv. coun. Nuveen, 1987-96. Mem. adv. panel Palm Beach County YWCA, 1984—; Jupiter Hosp. Found.; life mem. June Beach Civic Assn. Mem. YWCA (adv. panel 1985, endowment com. 1990-93), Nat. Assn. Securities Dealers (registered dist. com. mem. 1995—), Fin. Women Internat., Fla. Securities Dealers Assn., Exec. Women of Palm Beaches (mem. fin. com. 1985-92), Internat. Soc. Palm Beach (treas., trustee 1986—), Jupiter Hosp. Med. Assn. (pres.'s club 1989—), Loxahatchee Hist. Soc. (bd. dirs. 1991-93, chmn. devel. com. 1992-93), Sebring, Fla. Hist. Soc. (life), Jupiter/Tequesta C. of C. (assoc.), United Daus. of Confederacy, Gov.'s Club, Pub. Securities Assn. (exec. rep.), Jonathans Golf Club, Rotary (Palm Beach found. com. 1990—, bd. dirs. 1992, 93-94), Lighthouse Gallery Art (life), Norton Gallery Art (patron). Democrat. Baptist. Avocations: reading, history. Home: 630 Ocean Dr Apt 103 Juno Beach FL 33408-1916 Office: Island Investment Svcs Inc Island Nat Bank Palm Beach 180 Royal Palm Way Palm Beach FL 33480-4254

HARPER, NANCY EUDORA HAMLETT, critical care nurse; b. Prince Edward County, Va., Dec. 17, 1940; d. Daniel Lee and Pearle Imogene Hamlett; children: Russell Lee, Keith Hamlett, Gaynell Arlington. Diploma in nursing, Lynchburg Gen. Hosp. Sch., 1970; AA, Ctrl. Va. C.C., 1978; BA, Randolph-Macon Women's Coll., 1980; MEd, Lynchburg Coll., 1991. Nurse various hosps., nursing homes, pub. schs., Amherst, Va., 1970-90, Lynchburg (Va.) Gen. Hosp., 1990—, Strooband's Heart Ctr. Va., Lynchburg, 1990—; substitute tchr. Amherst County Pub. Schs., Va., 1980—. Leader literary support group Women's Resource Ctr., Lynchburg, 1987; vol. Va. Bapt. Hosp. Adult Day Care, 1987; teen leader Oakdale Bapt. Ch., 1970. Mem. James River Writers Guild, Phi Theta Kappa. Democrat.

HARPER, PAMELA SOLVITH, management consultant; b. Cleve., May 18, 1953; d. Marvin and Jean M. (Charney) Solvith; m. D. Scott Harper, May 8, 1976; children: Jason, Rebecca. Student, U. Mich., 1976-78; PhB, Northwestern U., 1982. Pers. asst. Films Inc., Wilmette, Ill., 1983-84; asst. mgr. human resources Infolink Corp., Northbrook, Ill., 1984-85; recruiting coord. Timeplex Inc., Woodcliff Lake, N.J., 1985-86; employment mgr. Simon & Schuster Inc., Englewood Cliffs, N.J., 1987-89; mgr. staffing ABB Power Generation Inc., North Brunswick, N.J., 1989-91; ptnr. Paradigm Assocs. TQ, Glen Rock, N.J., 1991-93; pres. Bus. Advancement Inc., Glen Rock, N.J., 1994—; instr. divsn. continuing edn. Bergen C.C., Paramus, N.J., 1993—, SUNY/Westchester C.C., Valhalla, N.Y., 1994-95; spkr. in field. Columnist/panelist The Record N.J., 1993—. Mem. ASTD, Total Quality Inst. (charter), Soc. Human Resource Mgmt., Alpha Sigma Lambda. Office: Bus Advancement Inc 178 Sycamore Ter Glen Rock NJ 07452-1907

HARPER, PATRICIA M., state legislator; b. Cresco, Dec. 4, 1932; d. Patrick Mullaney and Martha Gossman; 1 child, Susan. BA, U. No. Iowa, MA. Tchr. secondary math. and sci., 1955-86; mem. Iowa Ho. of Reps. Bd. dirs. Independence Haven. Mem. AAUW, LWV, Waterloo Edn. Assn., Alliance for Mentally Ill. Democrat. Home: 3336 Santa Maria Dr Waterloo IA 50702-5334 Office: Iowa Ho of Reps State Capitol Des Moines IA 50319

HARPER, PATRICIA NELSEN, psychiatrist; b. Omaha, July 25, 1944; d. Eddie R. and Marjorie L. (Williams) Nelsen. BS, Antioch Coll., Yellow Springs, Ohio, 1966; MD, U. Nebr., 1975. Cert. psychiatrist. Psychiatric residency Karl Menninger Sch. of Psychiatry, Topeka, 1975-78; staff psychiatrist The Menninger Clinic, Topeka, 1978--; faculty mem. Karl Menninger Sch. of Psychiatry, Topeka, 1982--, candiate Topeka Inst. for Psychoanalysis, 1982--. Program dir. Alcohol and Drug Abuse Recovery Program C.F. Menninger Meml. Hosp., Topeka, 1987--. Mem. Am. Psychiatric Assn., Am. Med Women Assn., Am. Psychoanalytic Assn. Office: The Menninger Clinic PO Box 829 Topeka KS 66601-0829

HARPER, PAULA, art history educator, writer; b. Boston, Nov. 17, 1938; d. Clarence Everett and Maura (Lee) Fish. BA in Art History magna cum laude, Hunter Coll., 1966, MA in Art History, 1968; postgrad., U. N.Mex., 1968-69; PhD in Art History, Stanford U., 1976. Dancer Munt-Brooks Modern Dance Co., N.Y.C., 1963-65; teaching fellow U. N.Mex., 1968-69; asst. prof. Calif. Inst. Arts, Valencia, 1971-72; dir. Hunter Arts Gallery CUNY, 1977-78; vis. asst. prof. Mills Coll., Oakland, Calif., spring 1979, 80-81, Stanford (Calif.) U., 1979-80; assoc. prof. art history U. Miami, Coral Gables, Fla., 1982—; art critic Miami News, 1982-88; frequent lectr. mus., art galleries and univs.; project advisor TV series on Camille Pissarro, PBS Channel 10, St. Thomas, V.I., 1992—. Author: (with R.E. Shikes) Pissarro: His Life and Work, 1980 (transl. into French, German, and Romanian), Daumier's Clowns, 1981; author (catalogues) "Powerplay" Paintings by Judy Chicago, 1986, Contemporary Sculpture from the Martin Z. Margulies Collection, 1986, Visions from Brazil-The Drawings of Paolo Gomes Garcez, 1993; contbr. articles to profl. jours., books, exhbn. catalogues. Bd. trustees Ctr. for Fine Arts, Miami, 1990-93; mem. Art in Pub. Places Com., Miami Beach, 1991—. Recipient Film Inst. fellowship CUNY, 1966, Tuition fellowship Hunter Coll., 1966-67, Ford Found. grant Stanford U., 1969-73, Rsch. grant French govt., 1973-74, Rockefeller Found. Residency at Bellagio, 1991, Ailsa Mellon Bruce Vis. Sr. fellowship, CASVA, Nat. Gallery of Art, 1990-91. Mem. Coll. Art Assn. (founder Women's Caucus for Art 1972, pres. N.Y. chpt. 1977-78, nat. adv. bd. 1977-80), Internat. Assn. Art Critics, Soc. Mayflower Descs., Foundlings Club, Art Table.

HARPER, SANDRA STECHER, university administrator; b. Dallas, Sept. 21, 1952; d. Lee Roy and Carmen (Crespo) Stecher; m. Dave Harper, July 6, 1974; children: Justin, Jonathan. BS in Edn., Tex. Tech. U., 1974; MS, U. N. Tex., 1979, PhD, 1985. Speech/reading tchr. Nazareth (Tex.) High Sch., 1974-75; speech/English tchr. Collinsville (Tex.) High Sch., 1975-77, Pottsboro (Tex.) High Sch., 1977-79; communication instr. Austin Coll., Sherman, Tex., 1980-82; rsch. asst. U. N. Tex., Denton, 1982-84; vis. instr. communication Austin Coll., Sherman, 1985; asst. prof. communication McMurry Coll., Abilene, Tex., 1985-89; assoc. prof. comm. McMurry U., Abilene, Tex., 1989-95, dean Coll. Arts and Scis., 1990-95; v.p. for acad. affairs Oklahoma City U., 1995—; asst. dir. NEH univ. core curriculum project McMurry U., Abilene, Tex.; critic judge Univ. Interscholastic League, Austin, 1980-93; mem. adv. bd. Univ. Rsch. Consortium, Abilene, 1990-95. Contbr. articles to profl. jours.; author: To Serve the Present Age, 1990; co-author U.S. Dept. Edn. Title III Grant. Planner TEAM Abilene, 1991; del. Tex. Commn. for Libr. and Info. Svcs., Austin, 1991; chair Abilene Children Today: Life and Cmty. Skills Task Force, 1994-95. Named Outstanding Faculty Mem., McMurry U., 1988, Outstanding Adminstrv., 1993; Media Rsch. scholar, Ctr. for Population Options, 1989. Mem. Internat. Communication Assn., Speech Communication Assn., So. Speech Communication Assn., Film and Video Assn., Council Coll. of Arts and Sciences. Democrat. Roman Catholic. Office: Oklahoma City U 2501 N Blackwelder Oklahoma City OK 73106

HARPER, SHIRLEY FAY, nutritionist, educator, consultant; b. Auburn, Ky., Apr. 23, 1943; d. Charles Henry and Annabelle (Gregory) Belcher; m. Robert Vance Harper, May 19, 1973; children: Glenda, Debra, Teresa, Suzanna, Cynthia. BS, Western Ky. U., 1966, MS, 1982. Cert. nutritionist and lic. dietitian, Ky. Dir. dietetics Logan County Hosp., Russellville, Ky., 1965-80; cons. Western State Hosp., Hopkinsville, Ky., 1983-84, instnl. dietetic adminstr., 1984-88; dietitian Rivendell Children's Psychiat. Hosp., Bowling Green, Ky., 1988-90; instr. nutrition Western Ky. U., Bowling Green, 1990-92; cons. Auburn (Ky.) Nursing Ctr., 1976-95, Belle Meade Home, Greenville, Ky., 1980—, Brookfield Manor, Hopkinsville, Ky., 1983—, Sparks Nursing Ctr., Central City, Ky., 1983—, Muhlenberg Cmty. Hosp., Greenville, 1989—, Russellville (Ky.) Health Care Manor, 1978-83, 92—, Westlake Cumberland Hosp., Columbia, Ky., 1993—, Franklin-Simpson Meml. Hosp., Franklin, Ky., 1993—; nutrition instr. Madisonville (Ky.) Cmty. Coll., 1995—. Mem. regional bd. dirs. ARC of Ky., Frankfort, 1990-96; vice chair ARC of Logan County, 1992-93, chmn., 1993-96; bd. dirs. Logan County ARC United Way, 1993—; co-chair adv. coun. devel. disabilities Lifeskills, 1992-93, adv. coun. Lifeskills Residential Living Group Home, 1993-96, human rights adv. coun., 1994-96; chair Let's Build our Future Campaign; nutrition del. Citizen Am. Program to USSR, 1990; adv. chair for vocat. edn., Russellville; mem. adv. coun. for home econs. and family living, We. Ky. U., 1990-93; bd. dirs. ARC of Logan County for United Way, 1993—. Recipient Outstanding Svc. award Am. Dietetic Assn. Found., 1993, Outstanding Svc. award Barren River Mental Health-Mental Retardation Bd., 1987, Svc. Appreciation award Logan-Russellville Assn. for Retarded Citizens, 1987, Internat. Woman of Yr. award for contribution to Nutrition and Humanity, Internat. Biographical Assn., 1993-94, World Lifetime Achievement award Am. Biographical Inst., 1995; inaugurated Lifetime Dep. Gov., Am. Biographical Rsch. Bd., 1995, Pres.'s award ARC of Logan County, 1996. Mem. Am. Dietetic Assn., Nat. Nutrition Network, Ky. Dietetic Assn. (pres. Western dist. 1976-77, Outstanding Dietitian award 1984), Bowling Green-Warren County Nutrition Coun., Nat. Ctr. for Nutrition and Dietetics (charter), Ky. Nutrition Coun., Logan County Home Economist Club (sec. 1994-95, v.p. 1995-96, pres. 1996-97), Internat. Biog. Assn., Internat. Platform Assn., Gerontol. Nutritionist, Oncology Nutrition, Diabetes Care and Edn., Dietitians in Nutrition Support, Dietitians in Gen. Clin. Practice, Cons. Dietitians in Health Care, Dietetic Educators of Practice Nutrition, Edn. of Health Profls., Nutrition Rsch. and Nutrition Edn. for Pub. Practice Groups, Phi Upsilon Omicron (pres. Beta Delta alumni chpt. 1994-96). Home and Office: 443 Hopkinsville Rd Russellville KY 42276-1286

HARR, LUCY LORAINE, professional society administrator; b. Sparta, Wis., Dec. 2, 1951; d. Ernest Donald Harr and Dorothy Catherine (Heintz) Harr Vetter. B.S., U. Wis.-Madison, 1976, M.S., 1978. Lectr. U. Wis., Madison, 1977-82; asst. editor Everybody's Money Everybody's Money Credit Union Nat. Assn., Madison, 1979-80, assoc. editor Everybody's Money, 1980-82, editor Everybody's Money, 1982-84, mgr. ann. report, 1984-92, v.p. pub. rels., 1984-93, sr. v.p. credit union devel., 1993-96, sr. v.p. consumer rels. and corp. responsibility, 1996—; dir. consumer appeals bd. Ford Motor Co., Milw., 1983-87. Bd. dirs. Madison Area Crimestoppers, 1982-84. Recipient Clarion award, 1982. Mem. Women in Communications (pres. Madison profl. chpt. 1982-83, nat. v.p. programs 1986-87), Internat. Assn. Bus. Communicators (program chmn. dist. meeting 1981), Am. Soc. Assn. Execs. (Gold Circle award 1984). Home: 514 Westmorland Blvd Madison WI 53711-1639 Office: Credit Union Nat Assn Inc 5710 Mineral Point Rd Madison WI 53705-4454

HARR, MARTHA A., English educator; b. Canton, Ill., May 5, 1952; d. Charles E. and Joan (Simpson) Smith; m. Robert L. Harr, Aug. 5, 1972; children: Derek R., Tawny L. AA, Spoon River Coll., 1972; BA, Western Ill. U., 1974, MA, 1991. Instr., chair dept. English Cuba (Ill.) H.S., 1985—; instr. English Spoon River Coll., Canton, Ill., 1991—. Pres. United Meth. Women, 1996—, chair pastor-parish com., 1996—. Named Spoon River country's favorite educator Canton Daily Ledger, 1995. Mem. Nat. Coun. Tchrs. English, Ill. Assn. Tchrs. English. Home: 21245 N Winship Rd Cuba IL 61427

HARRELL, BARBARA JOY SPIER, retired school librarian; b. Bastrop, La., Oct. 5, 1931; d. Maurice Hugo and Ida Avis (Smith) Spier; m. John Frederick Harrell Sr. (dec.); children: John F. Jr., Susan E. Harrell Fogleman. AD, N.E. Jr. Coll., Monroe, La., 1950; BS in English Edn., La. State U., 1952, MS in Libr. Sci., 1955. Asst. libr. Iberville Parish Libr., Plaquemine, La., 1952-55; libr. Evangeline Parish Libr., Ville Platté, La., 1955-59, Oak Hill H.S.-Rapides Parish Sch. Bd., Alexandria, La., 1959-92; ret., 1992. Mem. sr. citizens choir God's Recycled Angels. Mem. La. Ret. Tchrs. Assn. Home: 6449 Boeuf Trace Alexandria LA 71301

HARRELL, IRIS FAYE, general contractor; b. Franklin, Va., Apr. 1, 1947; d. Alton Joseph and Evelyn Pearl (Goodwin) H.; life ptnr.: Anne Elizabeth Benson, May 12, 1979. BA, Mary Washington Coll., 1969; M in Edn. Adminstrn., Va. Commonwealth U., 1975. Tchr. Henrico County Schs., Varina, Va., 1969-71, Richmond (Va.) City Schs., 1972-73, Rough Rock Navajo Reservation, Ariz., 1974-75; tribunal adminstr. Am. Arbitration Assn., Dallas, 1979-80; regional dir. Women in Cmty. Svc., Dallas, 1980-81; owner, gen. contractor Harrell Remodeling, Dallas, 1981-84, Harrell Remodeling, Inc., Menlo Park, Calif., 1984—. Named female entrepreneur of the year Nat. Assn. Women Bus. Owners, 1996. Mem. Nat. Assn. Remodelers (nat. contractor of yr. award-bathrooms 1995), Nat. Kitchen & Bath Assn., Menlo Park C. of C. Democrat. Mem. Christian Sci. Ch. Office: Harrell Remodeling 108 Gilbert Ave Menlo Park CA 94025

HARRELL, JOAN MARIE, nurse; b. Billings, Mont., June 28, 1953; d. William and Dorothy Jean (Turnquist) Clemens; m. Anthony Frank Lippold, May 10, 1976; 1 child, Bonnie Jean Lippold; m. Daniel Edgar Harrell, June 7, 1986; children: Amanda and Melissa Harrell. AAS, Casper Coll., 1980; BS in Nursing, U. Phoenix, Fountain Valley, Calif., 1992. RN, Ky.; CCRN, cert. registered nurse hospice. Med. - surg. staff nurse Natrona County Meml. Hosp., Casper, Wyo., 1980-82; pediat. staff nurse Indian Health Svc. - Whiteriver (Ariz.) Apache Tribe, 1982-84; intensive care staff nurse VA Med. Ctr., Tucson, 1984-89, Loma Linda, Calif., 1989-92; sr. clin. nurse U.S. Pub. Health Svc., Fed. Bur. Prisons, Lexington, Ky., 1993-96; with 28th Med. Ops. Squadron, Ellsworth AFB, S.D., 1996—; health educator Fed. Bur. Prisons parents and children class, 1993-96—. Vol. Hospice of Blugrass, Lexington, 1993-96, Woodford County Health Dept., Versailles, Ky., 1995; spkr., presenter Ky. State Foster Parents Assn. conf., Bowling Green, 1996. Mem. Children and Adults with Attention Deficient Disorders, Hospice Nurse Assn., Ky. Breast Cancer Coalition, Sigma Theta Tau. Democrat. Roman Catholic. Home: PO Box 253 Box Elder SD 57719 Office: Federal Med Ctr 28th Medical Operations Sqd Ellsworth AFB SD 57706

HARRIETT, JUDY ANNE, medical equipment company executive; b. Walterboro, S.C., July 22, 1960; d. Billy Lee and Loretta (Rahn) H. BS in Agrl. Bus./Econs., Clemson U., 1982. Sales rep. III Monsanto Corp., Atlanta, 1982-85; surg. stapling rep. Ethicon, Inc., Johnson & Johnson Corp., Somerville, N.J., 1985-87; dist. sales mgr. Imed Corp., San Diego, 1987—, regional tng. coord., 1992-93; mem. pres. adv. panel, 1991, 92, mem. pres. club, 1993. Author: Time and Territory Management, 1984. Com. mem. Multiple Sclerosis Fund Raising Benefit, Knoxville, Tenn., 1988, 89, Women's Ctr. Benefit, Knoxville, 1990. Mem. NAFE. Republican. Home: 21620 Mayhew Rd Mooresville NC 28115-8661 Office: Imed Corp 9775 Businesspark Ave San Diego CA 92131-1642

HARRIFF, SUZANNA ELIZABETH, advertising consultant; b. Vicksburg, Miss., Dec. 30, 1953; d. David S. and F. Suzanna (McElwee) Bahner; m. James R. Harriff, Sept. 10, 1977; 1 child, Michael James. B.A. summa cum laude, SUNY-Fredonia, 1976; postgrad. Cornell U. Law Sch., 1981; MDiv with distinction Colgate Rochester Divinity Sch., 1995. Ordained to ministry Bapt. Ch., 1995. Media asst. Comstock Advt., Syracuse, N.Y., and Buffalo, 1976-77; media buyer/planner G. Andre Delporte, Syracuse, 1979-81; media dir. Roberts Advt., Syracuse, 1982; dir. media services Signet Advt., Syracuse, 1982-84; owner, pres. MediaMarCon, Syracuse, 1984—. Music dir., pianist Manlius United Methodist Ch., N.Y., 1983-92, youth dir., 1983-85; dir. music First Bapt. Ch., Manlius, 1993-96; assoc. pastor Andrews Meml. UMC, 1996—; tchr. Am. Bapt. Chs. N.Y. state lay studies program, Bethel Bible Sem., Syracuse; co-chair St. Nicholas Ecumenical Festival, 1992-96; Pheresis donor ARC, 1987—; vol. Sta. WCNY-TV pub. TV auction drive, co-chair media div., chair media div., 1986—, gen. chair, 1994; accompanist musicals and chorus Manlius-Pebble Hill Sch.; resource devel. chair Winterfest, Syracuse, 1992. Mem. NAFE, Syracuse Advt. Club (dir. 1985-88, program chair 1986-88, pres. 1988-89), Irish-Am. Cultural Inst. Syracuse, Phi Beta Kappa. Democrat. Avocations: music; theatre. Home: 8180 Bluffview Dr Manlius NY 13104-9740

HARRIGAN, LAURA G., newspaper editor; b. Newark, Nov. 29, 1953; d. Michael Charles and Sarah Ellen (Hutchinson) Guarino;. BA, Wagner Coll., 1975. Reporter/columnist S.I. (N.Y.) Advance, 1975-79, Sunday editor, 1979-84; asst. news editor Courier-News, Bridgewater, N.J., 1984-85, news editor, 1985-86, spl. projects editor, 1986-87, exec. news editor, 1987-90, asst. mng. editor, 1990-91, mng. editor, 1991—. Recipient hon. mention Charles Stewart Mott nat. edn. writing award, 1978, Equality, Dignity & Independence award Nat. Easter Seals, 1994. Mem. AAUW, AP Mng. Editors Assn. (pres. N.J. chpt. 1992-94), N.J. Press Assn. (editl. com. 1995—). Office: The Courier-News PO Box 6600 1201 Route 22 Bridgewater NJ 08807

HARRIGAN, ROSANNE CAROL, nursing educator; b. Miami, Feb. 24, 1945; d. John H. and Rose (Hnatow) Harrigan; children: Dennis, Michael, John. BS, St. Xavier Coll., 1965; MS in Nursing, Ind. U., 1974, EdD, 1979. Staff nurse, recovery rm. Mercy Hosp., Chgo., 1965, evening charge nurse, 1965-66; head nurse Chgo. State Hosp., 1966-67; nurse practitioner Health and Hosp. Corp. Marion County, Indpls., 1975-80; assoc. prof. Ind. U. Sch. Nursing, Indpls., 1978-82; nurse practitioner, developmental follow-up program Riley Hosp. for Children, Indpls., 1980-85; chief, nursing sect. Riley Hosp. Child Devel. Ctr., Indpls., 1982-85; prof. Ind. U. Sch. Nursing, Indpls., 1982-85; chmn., prof. maternal child health Niehoff Sch. Nursing, Loyola U. of Chgo., 1985-92; dean U. Hawaii, 1992—; lecturer Ind. U. Sch. Nursing, 1974-75, chmn. dept. pediatrics, family and women's health, 1980-85; adj. prof. of pediatrics Ind. U. Sch. Med., 1982-85; editorial bd. Jour. Maternal Child Health Nursing, 1984-86, Jour. Perinatal Neonatal, 1985—, Jour. Perinatology, 1989—, Loyola U. Press, 1988—; adv. bd. Symposia Medicus, 1982-84, Proctor and Gamble Rsch. Adv. Com. Blue Ribbon Panel; scientific review panel NIH, 1985; cons. in field. Contbr. articles to profl. jours. bd. dirs. March of Dimes Cen. Ind. Chpt., 1974-76, med. adv., 1979-85; med. and rsch. adv. March of Dimes Nat. Found., 1985—, chmn. Task Force on Rsch. Named Nat. Nurse of Yr. March of Dimes, 1983; faculty research grantee Ind. U., 1978, Pediatric Pulmonary Nursing Tng. grant Am. Lung Assn., 1982-85, Attitudes, Interests and Competence of Ob-Gyn Nurses Rsch. grant Nurses Assn. Am. Coll. Ob-Gyn., 1986, Attitudes, Interests and Priorities of Neonatal Nurses Rsch. grant Nat. Assn. Neonatal Nurses, 1987, Biomedical Rsch. Support grant, 1988; Doctoral fellow Am. Lung Assn. Ind. Tng. Program, 1981-86. Mem. AAAS, ANA (Maternal Child Nurse of Yr. 1983), AWONN (chmn. com. on rsch. 1983-86), Am. Nurses Found., Nat. Assn. Neonatal Nurses, Nat. Perinatal Assn. (bd. dirs. 1978-85, rsch. com. 1986), Midwest Nursing Rsch. Soc. (theory devel. sect.), Ill. Nurses Assn. (commn. rsch. chmn. 1990-91), Ind. Nurses Assn., Hawaii Nurses Assn., Ind. Perinatal Assn. (pres. 1981-83), N.Y. Acad. Sci., Ind. U. Alumni Assn. (Disting. Alumni 1985), Sigma Xi, Pi Lambda Theta, Sigma Theta Tau (chpt. pres. 1988-90). Home: 44-345 Kaneohe Bay Dr Kaneohe HI 96744-2663

HARRIMAN, CONSTANCE BASTINE, lawyer; b. Palo Alto, Calif., Oct. 9, 1948; d. John Howland and Barbara (Brunmark) H.; m. W. Edward Whitfield, Sept. 22, 1990. BA cum laude, Stanford U., 1970, MA, 1973; JD, UCLA, 1980. Bar: Calif. 1980, D.C. 1985, U.S. Dist. Ct. (no., ctrl. and ea. dists.) Calif. 1980, U.S. Ct. Appeals (9th cir.) 1983. Assoc. Sheppard, Mullin, Richter & Hampton, 1980-85; atty. advisor Office Legal Policy, Dept. Justice, Washington, 1982; spl. asst. to solicitor Dept. Interior, Washington, 1985-86, assoc. solicitor for energy and resources, 1986-87, asst. sec. for fish, wildlife and parks, 1989-91; assoc. Steptoe & Johnson, Washington, 1987-89; dir. Export-Import Bank of U.S., Washington, 1991-94; pvt. practice, 1994—. Mem. UCLA Law Rev. Apptd. commr. Gt. Lakes Fishery Commn., 1989; mem. Adv. Coun. Hist. Preservation. Mem. Nat. Planning Assn. (bd. trustees), The Met. Club (Washington), The Beach Club (Santa Monica, Calif.), Phi Beta Kappa.

HARRIMAN, PAMELA DIGBY CHURCHILL, diplomat, philanthropist; b. Farnborough, Eng., Mar. 20, 1920; came to U.S., 1959, naturalized, 1971; d. Edward Kenelm and Constance Pamela Alice (Bruce) Digby; m. Randolph Churchill, 1939; 1 son, Winston Spencer; m. Leland Hayward, May 4, 1960; m. W. Averell Harriman, Sept. 27, 1971. B in Domestic Sci.-Economy, Downham (Eng.) Sch., 1937; postgrad. Sorbonne, Paris, 1937-38; JD (hon.) Columbia U., Coll. William & Mary. With Ministry of Supply, London, 1942-43; with Churchill Club for Am. Servicemen, 1943-46; journalist Beaverbrook Press, Europe, 1946-49; U.S. amb. to France, Paris, 1993—; chmn., founder Democrats for the 80s, 1980-90 and Democrats for the 90s, 1991; nat. co-chair Clinton-Gore Presdl. Campaign, 1992; bd. dirs. Commn. on Presdl. Debates, 1987-93; mem. Nat. Com. Dem. Party, 1989-93; past hon. trustee, past hon. mem. exec. com. Brookings Instn.; mem. Council on Fgn. Rels.; past trustee Rockefeller U., Coun. Nat. Gallery Art, Winston Churchill Found. U.S.; past adv. council W. Averell Harriman Inst. for Russian Studies; past mem. bd. friends Kennan Inst. for Advanced Russian Studies; past vice chmn. Atlantic Council, past bd. dirs. Mary W. Harriman

Found., also various philanthropic founds. Named Dem. Woman of Yr., Woman's Nat. Dem. Club 1980; Commandeur Arts & Lettres. Office: American Embassy Paris Psc 116 APO AE 09777-9998

HARRINGTON, ANNE, science historian; b. N.Y.C., June 15, 1960; d. Gerard Jr. and Sue Leia (Sayer) H.; m. Godehard Oepen, Sept. 10, 1989. BA summa cum laude, Harvard U., 1982; PhD, Oxford U., 1985. Rsch. fellow Wellcome Inst., London, 1985-86; Humboldt rsch. fellow Freiburg (Germany) U., 1986-88; asst. prof. Harvard U., Cambridge, Mass., 1988-91, Morris Kahn assoc. prof., 1991-95, prof., 1995—; cons. Network on Mind-Body Interactions, MacArthur Found., Chgo, 1992—; fellow Mind-Brain-Behavior Initiative, Harvard U., Cambridge, 1993—, governing bd., 1994—, assoc. dir., 1996—. Author: Medicine, Mind and the Double Brain, 1987, Reenchanted Science, 1996; editor: So Human A Brain, 1992, "Just" a Placebo?, 1996. Recipient Capt. Jonathan Fay prize Radcliffe Coll., 1982, Bowdoin prize Harvard U., 1982, Marshall Trust scholarship, 1982-85, Wellcome Trust Postdoctoral Rsch. fellowship at Oxford and London, 1985-86, Alexander von Humboldt Postdoctoral Rsch. fellowship Freiburg U., 1986-88; grantee Nat. Libr. Medicine, 1991, NSF, 1991, Spencer Found., 1993. Mem. AAAS, History of Sci. Soc. Office: Harvard U Dept History of Sci Sci Ctr 235 Cambridge MA 02138

HARRINGTON, ANNE WILSON, medical librarian; b. Phila., June 18, 1926; d. Edgar Myers and Jean Gould (DeHaven) Wilson; m. James Paul Harrington, June 11, 1948; children: Barbara Gould Harrington Murphy, Ian Edgar, Eric Bradley. BA, U. Pa., Phila., 1948; MS in Libr. Sci., Villanova U., 1977. Clk. Princeton U., 1948-51; CEO, ptnr. Teesdale Co., West Chester, Pa., 1954—; libr. asst. Franklin Inst., Phila., 1974-76; med. staff libr. The Chester County Hosp., West Chester, 1977—; mem., treas., chmn. sub-com. Consortium Health Info., Chester, 1977—. Trustee, sec., com. chmn. Wilmington (Del.) Friends Sch., 1963-72, 89; treas. com. on edn. Phila. Yearly Meeting Soc. Friends, 1980-91; mem., rep. Friends Coun. on Edn., Phila., 1991-96; overseer Quaker Info. Ctr., Phila., 1992-96; bd. mem., subcom. chmn. cmty. bd. Kendal Corp. CCRC, Kennett Square, Pa., 1973—. Mem. Med. Libr. Assn., Acad. Health Info. Profls. (sr.), Phila. Area Med. Library Assn., Lake Paupac Club (chmn. environ./ecol. com.), Friends Med. Soc. Democrat. Home: 1117 Talleyrand Rd West Chester PA 19382-7416 Office: Chester County Hosp West Chester PA 19380

HARRINGTON, BETTY BYRD, entrepreneur; b. Longview, Tex., July 11, 1936; d. William Henry Byrd and Minnie Lee Tidwell; 1 child, Randy Lee Harrington. AA, Cedar Valley DCCCD, Dallas, 1988. Adminstrv. asst. Conf. Coun. on Ministries United Meth. Ch., Dallas, 1983-86; pres., actress, model, entertainer Kathy King Entertainment Agy., DeSoto, Tex., 1956—; pres. Gateway to Success/Resume Writing and Career Counseling, DeSoto, Tex., 1987—; Career Devel. and Placement, 1982—. Author: The Dallas Dazzler, Job Search and Interview Techniques, (poetry) She Has Been Faithful, 1996, Pity the Children, 1996. Mem. AFTRA, AGVA, DeSoto C. of C., Greater Dallas C. of C. Republican. Baptist. Home and Office: 1338 E Parkerville Rd De Soto TX 75115-6421

HARRINGTON, CAROL A., lawyer; b. Geneva, Ill., Feb. 13, 1953; d. Eugene P. and M. Ruth (Bowersox) Kloubec; m. Warren J. Harrington, Aug. 19, 1972; children: Jennifer Ruth, Carrie Anne. BS summa cum laude, U. Ill., 1974, JD magna cum laude, 1977. Bar: Ill. 1977, U.S. Dist. Ct. (no. dist.) Ill. 1977, U.S. Tax Ct. 1979. Assoc. Winston & Strawn, Chgo., 1977-84, ptnr., 1984-88; ptnr. McDermott, Will & Emery, 1988—; speaker in field. Co-author: The New Generation Skipping Tax, 1986, Generation Skipping Tax BNA Management, 1991, Generation-Skipping Transfer Tax, Warren, Gorham & Lamont, 1995; contbr. articles to profl. jours., Trustee and Estate mag. Fellow Am. Coll. Trusts and Estate Coun.; mem. ABA (chmn. B-1 generation skipping transfer com. 1987-92, coun. real property, probate and trust law sect. 1992—), Ill. State Bar Assn., Chgo. Bar Assn. (trust law com. divsn. 1), Chgo. Estate Planning Coun. Office: McDermott Will & Emery 227 W Monroe St Chicago IL 60606-5016

HARRINGTON, CAROLYN MARIE, accountant, artist; b. Pasadena, Calif., Oct. 19, 1938; d. Walter and Laina (Kallio) Hingula; m. William Harrington, July 12, 1971; 1 child, Christina. AA in Acctg., Bklyn. Coll., 1960; BS in Acctg., CUNY, 1962; MPA, L.I. Univ., 1991. Internal auditor Tchrs. Ins. and Annuities, N.Y.C., 1960-62; jr. acct. Goldfein & Goldfein, CPA, N.Y.C., 1962-63; field auditor Guardian Life Ins., N.Y.C., 1963-67; chief acct. Careers Inc., N.Y.C., 1967-69; sr. acct., dept. head Grolier Internat., N.Y.C., 1969-73; acct. Suffolk County Govt., Yaphank, N.Y., 1984-96; sr. auditor Suffolk County Govt., Haupauge, N.Y., 1996—; ptnr., artist Bellport Lane Art Gallery, 1994—, v.p. Wet Paints Studio Group, Sayville, N.Y., 1992-94, treas. East of Broadway Show Group, East Islip, N.Y., 1982-83. Leader Girl Scouts of Am., East Islip, 1979-83. Recipient Holbein award of excellence for painting "Three Amigos" East Islip Arts Coun., 1993, Pub. Adminstrn. award L.I. Univ., 1991, Spl. Opportunity stipend N.Y. Found. for the Arts and East End Coun., 1995. Mem. South Bay Art Assn., Babylon Arts Coun., Huntington Twp. Art League, Smithtown Twp. Art Coun. Republican. Roman Catholic. Home: 122 Keswick Dr East Islip NY 11730 Office: Suffolk County Dept Human Svcs 395 Oser Ave Hauppauge NY 11788

HARRINGTON, ELLEN M., film curator; b. Boston, Oct. 30, 1963; d. Joseph A. Harrington and Ellen (Collins) Philie. BA, Dartmouth Coll., 1985; MA, NYU, 1991. Program asst. N.Y. Shakespeare Festival/Film at the Pub. Theater, N.Y.C., 1988-89; rsch. coord. Punch Prodns., N.Y.C., 1989-91; spl. events and exhbns. coord. Acad. Motion Picture Arts & Scis., Beverly Hills, Calif., 1993—. Office: Acad Motion Picture Arts & Scis 8949 Wilshire Blvd Beverly Hills CA 90211

HARRINGTON, LAMAR, curator, museum director; b. Guthrie Center, Iowa, Nov. 2, 1917; d. Arthur Sylvester and Anna Mary (Landkamer) Hannes; m. Stanley John Harrington, 1938 (div. 1972); 1 dau., Linda Harrington Chace. Student music, Cornish Sch. Fine Arts, Seattle, 1945-50; B.A. in History of Art, U. Wash., 1979. Mem. staff Henry Art Gallery, U. Wash., Seattle, 1957-75; assoc. dir. Henry Art Gallery, U. Wash., 1969-75; curator, research assoc. Archives Northwest Art, U. Wash. Libraries, 1975-77; dir., chief curator Bellevue Art Mus., Wash., 1985-90; cons. in arts, 1977—; mem. panel visual arts divsn. NEA, 1976-78; juror fellowships Western States Arts Fedn., 1989; pres. Western Assn. Art Mus., 1973-75; trustee Pacific N.W. Arts Ctr., 1971-74; exec. com. Pacific N.W. Arts Coun. of Seattle Art Mus., 1976, mem. steering com. photography coun., 1977-78; v.p. Pottery Northwest, 1977-78; participant 1st Symposium on Scholarship and Lang., Nat. Endowments for Humanities and Arts, 1981; mem. adv. com. N.W. Oral History Project, Archives Am. Art, 1981; mem. Pilchuck adv. coun., 1992-95; trustee, chmn. archives Pilchuck Glass Sch., 1981-87, Internat. Coun., 1987-92; trustee Seattle bd. Santa Fe Chamber Music Festival, 1981-87, adv. bd. Santa Fe, 1985-89; trustee Puget Sound Chamber Music Soc., 1987-88; lectr. in field, organizer exhbns., leader seminars, mem. art juries, appearances on TV, 1963-73. Author: Ceramics in the Pacific Northwest: A History, 1979, Washington Craft Forms: an Historical Perspective, 1981; founder: Archives of N.W. Art, U. Wash., 1969, Index of Art in Pacific N.W., U. Wash. Press, 1970; curator Third Wyoming Biennial Exhbn., 1988-89, James W. Washington Jr.; The Spirit in the Stone Bellevue Art Mus., 1989; resident curator, mgr. Frank Lloyd Wright: In the Realm of Ideas Bellevue Art Mus., 1989; curator: Between Night and Morning: The Work of Guy Anderson, 1990, Eternal Laughter: A Sixty-Yr. Retrospective of George Tsutakawa Bellevue Art Mus., 1990; contbr. author, curator The History of Twentieth Century Am. Craft, Am. Craft Mus., 1996—. Recipient Friends of Crafts award Seattle, 1972, Woman of Achievement award Women in Communications, 1974, Gov. Writer's award, 1980, Arts Svc. award King County Arts Commn., 1987, Gov. Wash. Art award, 1988, Bellevue Art Commn. Arts award, 1989, Community Svc. award Am. Inst. Interior Designers, 1990, Pyramid award Corp. Coun. for Arts, 1990; establishment of LaMar Harrington endowment Bellevue Art Mus., 1991. Fellow Am. Crafts Coun. (hon.); mem. AIA (hon.), Pacific N.W. Arts and Crafts Assn. (pres. 1957-59), Allied Arts Seattle (trustee 1962-81), Japan-Am. Soc. Wash. (trustee 1986-88), U. Washington Retirement Assn. (exec. com. 1992-94, chair art collection Univ. House at Wallingford 1995—). Home: 1707 Water St # 7 Port Townsend WA 98368

HARRINGTON, MARY EVELINA PAULSON (POLLY HARRINGTON), religious journalist, writer, educator; b. Chgo.; d. Henry Thomas and Evelina (Belden) Paulson; m. Gordon Keith Harrington, Sept. 7, 1957; children: Jonathan Henry, Charles Scranton. BA, Oberlin Coll., 1946; postgrad., Northwestern U., Evanston, Ill., Chgo., 1946-49, Weber State U., Ogden, Utah, 1970s, 80s; MA, U. Chgo.-Chgo. Theol. Sem., 1956. Publicist Nat. Coun. Chs., N.Y.C., 1950-51; mem. press staff 2d assembly World Coun. Chs., Evanston, Chgo., 1954; mgr. Midwest Office Communication, United Ch. of Christ, Chgo., 1955-59; staff writer United Ch. Herald, N.Y.C., St. Louis, 1959-61; affiliate missionary to Asia, United Ch. Bd. for World Ministries, N.Y.C., 1978-79; freelance writer and lectr., 1961—; corr. Religious News Svc., 1962—; prin. lectr. Women & Family Life in Asia series to numerous librs., Utah, 1981, 81-82; pub. rels. coord. Utah Energy Conservation/Energy Mgmt. Program, 1984-85; tchr. writing Ogden Community Schs., 1985-89; adj. instr. writing for publs. Weber State U., 1986—; instr. Acad. Lifelong Learning, Ogden, 1992—, Eccles Community Art Ctr., Ogden, 1993—; dir. communication Shared Ministry, Salt Lake City, 1983—; chmn. communication Intermountain Conf., Rocky Mountain Conf., Utah Assn. United Ch. of Christ, 1970-78, 82—, Ind. Coun. Chs., 1960-63; chmn. communication Ch. Women United Utah, 1974-78, Ogden rep., 1980—. Editor: Sunshine and Moonscapes: An Anthology of Essays, Poems, Short Stories, 1994, (booklet) Family Counseling Service: Thirty Years of Service to Northern Utah, 1996; contbr. numerous articles and essays to religious and other publs. Pres. T.O. Smith Sch. PTA, 1976-78, Ogden City Coun. PTA, 1983-85; assoc. dir. Region II, Utah PTA, Salt Lake City, 1981-83, mem. State Edn. Commn., 1982-87; chmn. state internat. hospitality and aid Utah Fedn. Women's Clubs, 1982-86; v.p. Ogden dist., 1990-92, pres. Ogden dist., 1992-96, state resolutions com., 1996—; trustee Family Counseling Svc. No. Utah, Ogden, 1983-95, emeritus trustee, 1995—; Utah rep. to nat. bd. Challenger Films, Inc., 1986—; state pres. Rocky Mountain Conf. Women in Mission, United Ch. of Christ, 1974-77, sec., 1981-84, vice moderator Utah Assn., 1992-94. Recipient Ecumenical Svc. citation Ind. Coun. Chs., 1962, Outstanding Local Pres. award Utah PTA, 1978, Outstanding Latchkey Child Project award, 1985, Cmty. Svc. award City of Ogden, 1980, 81, 82, Celebration of Gifts of Lay Woman Nat. award United Ch. of Christ, 1987, Excellence in the Arts in Art Edn. award Ogden City Arts Commn., 1993, Spirit of Am. Woman in Arts and Humanities award Your Cmty. Connection, Ogden, 1994; Utah Endowment for Humanities grantee, 1981, 81-82. Mem. Nat. League Am. Penwomen (chmn. Utah conv. 1973, 11 awards for articles and essays 1987-95, 1st pl. news award 1992), AAUW (state edn. rep. 1982-86). Democrat. Home and Office: 722 Boughton St Ogden UT 84403-1152

HARRINGTON, MICHAELE MARY, art educator, graphic designer, consultant; b. Boston, June 27, 1946; d. William Gerard and Jadwiga (Jerasonek) H.; m. Jeffrey Fancher Nicoll, Sept. 12, 1970; children: Heather Anne, James Craig William. BFA cum laude, Mass. Coll. Art, 1968. Prodn. mgr. R.H. Stearns Co., Boston, 1968-69; layout artist Grossman's, Braintree, Mass., 1971-72, Bradlee's, Braintree, 1973; asst. art dir. Canton (Mass.) Advt. Agy., 1973-78; watermedia and collage artist, graphic designer, illustrator Hyattsville & Darnestown, Md., 1978—; represented by The Franklin St. Gallery, Hagerstown, Md.; mem. faculty Rockville Arts Place, 1990-92; demonstrator, studio and workshop tchr., 1988—; design cons. KBL Group, Silver Spring, Md., 1986-92; book illustrator Denlinger Publs., Ltd., Fairfax, Va., 1986. Exhibited in group shows So. Watercolor Soc., Pensacola, Fla., 1982, Am. Watercolor Soc., N.Y.C., 1983, 90, Catherine Lorillard Wolfe Arts Club, N.Y.C., 1983, 84, Midwest Watercolor Soc., Davenport, Iowa, 1983, Mid-Atlantic Regional, Balt., 1983, 84, 86, 87, 89, 91, New Orleans Art Assn., 1984, Dundalk Coll., Md., 1985, San Diego Watercolor Soc., 1990, North Coast Collage Soc., Pitts., Watercolor Soc., Rocky Mountain Nat., 1991, Rock Creek Gallery, Washington, 1993, The Art Barn, Washington, 1993, Ariz. Aqueous IX, Tubac, 1994 (Merit award), Three Rivers Art Festival, Pitts., 1994, Strathmore Hall, Rockville, Md., 1995, 96, Kensington (Md.) Gallery, 1996; one-person shows Montpelier Cultural Arts Ctr., Laurel, Md., 1982, Friendship Gallery, Chevy Chase, Md., 1990, Artshowcase Gallery, Balt., 1991, 92; represented in permanent collections including Washington Health Ctr., Coast Guard Art Collection of Smithsonian Instn., Washington. Juror art in pub. places program Md.-Nat. Capital Parks and Planning Commn., Hyattsville, Md., 1980-91, also assorted Washington area art assns.' regional exhbns., 1990—. Recipient Jurors Choice award Md. Fedn. Art, 1982, 2d Place award New Orleans Art Assn., Gold medal Catherine Lorillard Wolfe Arts Club, 1984, Abstract award Md. Nat. Found., 1989, Zeber Exptl. award North Coast Collage Soc., 1991, award of merit Ariz. Aqueous IX, 1994. Mem. Potomac Valley Watercolorists (juried, v.p. 1993-96), Strathmore Hall Artists, Coast Guard Artists Program.

HARRINGTON, NANCY REGINA O'CONNOR, volunteer; b. Chgo., Oct. 28, 1928; d. John Roland and Ethel Catherine (Constable) O'Connor; m. James Edward Harrington, Sept. 8, 1951; children: Mary Beth Grayson, Janet Gaines, Gail, Nancy Chartier. BA in art edn., Rosary Coll., River Forest, 1946-50. Cert. art tchr., Ill. Artist Chgo. Park Dist., 1949; art tchr. Chgo. elem. schs., 1951-52; color coord. homes Palos Park (Ill.) Builder, 1957-58; vol. Art Inst. of Chgo., 1980-86. Exhibited in Loyola Ramble, 1970s, Wilmette, 1960s, Palos Park, Ill., Evergreen Park, Ill., Chgo., Osprey, Fla., 1990s, Glenview, Ill., 1980s, 1990s. Pres. Mothers Club, v.p. Parents Club Regina Dominican H.S., Wilmette, Ill., 1972-73; vol. Judge Robert Downing Dem. Party, Glenview, Ill., 1974; 1st forelady of criminal ct. Cook County Ct. Sys., Chgo., 1980s; vol. Resurrection House Daycare Ctr. for Homeless, Sarasota, Fla., 1993—; gen. chair Beaux Arts Festival, The Oaks C.C., 1996; mem. women's bd. Rosary Coll., 1990—. Recipient Kemeny Lion medallion Art Inst. Chgo., 1980s; Honored vol. Sarasota Arts Coun., 1992. Mem. AAUW, Natl. Heritage Soc., North Shore Country Club (gen. chairperson 9-hole golf, gen. chairperson art festival, 1996), Oaks Country Club (mem. garden club, 1991—, ad hoc archtl. rev. bd., 1991-92, women's bd., 1993; gen. chairperson art festival, 1995—, gen. chairperson Oaks Celebrates Arts, 1994, chairperson Art Club, 1993-94; founder Art Appreciation Club, 1993, Artist of Month Column (author) 1994—); founding mem. Nat. Women's Art Museum. Roman Catholic. Home: 210 St James Pk Osprey FL 34229

HARRINGTON-JOHNSON, DIANE GAIL, religious studies educator; b. Miami, Fla., Aug. 5, 1963; d. James Thomas and Eva Mae (Stephens) H. BBA, U. Miami, 1985, MBA, 1987. Mktg. rep. John Hancock Mut. Life Ins. Co., Boston, 1985-86; pres. Fla. Gold Seal Inc., Miami, 1986—; ext. agt., entrepreneurial educator USDA, Washington, 1994—; prof. religious studies Trinity Internat. U., Miami, 1994—; adj. prof. entrepreneurial edn., small bus. devel. U. Fla., 1994—. Leader Bible Bapt. Ch., 1989. Mem. NAFE, Nat. Assn. Life Underwriters, Internat. Platform Assn. Nat. C. of C., Ctr. Fine Arts, Nat. Assn. Hist. Preservation, Smithsonian Inst., Am. Inst. Researchers. Republican. Baptist. Home: 7899 NW 181st St Miami FL 33015

HARRIS, ANN BIRGITTA SUTHERLAND, art historian; b. Cambridge, Eng., Nov. 4, 1937; came to U.S., 1965; d. Gordon B.B.M. and Gunborg Elizabeth (Wahlström) Sutherland; m. William Vernon Harris, July 13, 1965; 1 son, Neil William Orlando Sutherland. B.A. with 1st class honours, Courtauld Inst., U. London, 1961, Ph.D., 1965. Asst. lectr. U. Leeds, 1964-65; asst. prof. art history Columbia U., N.Y.C., 1965-71, Hunter Coll., N.Y.C., 1971-73; asso. prof. SUNY, Albany, 1973-77; chmn. for acad. affairs Met. Mus. Art, N.Y.C., 1977-80; part-time faculty Juilliard Sch., N.Y.C., 1978-84; prof. U. Pitts., 1984—; a founder, 1st pres. Women's Caucus for Art, 1973-76; disting. vis. prof. U. Tex.-Arlington, fall 1982; Mellon prof. history of art U. Pitts., spring 1984; vis. prof. history of art So. Meth. U., Dallas, fall 1993. Author: Andrea Sacchi, 1977, Selected Drawings of Gian Lorenzo Bernini, 1977; co-author: Die Zeichnungen von Andrea Sacchi und Carlo Maratta, 1967, Women Artists: 1550-1950; exhbn. catalogue, 1977. Fellow Guggenheim Found., 1971, Ford Found., 1975-76, NEH, 1981-82, rsch. fellow Getty Mus. Art, 1988. Mem. Coll. Art Assn., Women's Caucus for Art. Office: U Pittsburgh Dept Art Pittsburgh PA 15260

HARRIS, ANNE M., writer; b. Albany, N.Y., Dec. 31, 1965; d. Edward C. and Anna Mae (Loehrlein) H.; life ptnr. Vanessa Agnew. BFA, NYU, 1994, MFA, 1995. Editor Books of Wonder, N.Y.C., 1991-94; teaching artist, reader Young Playwrights, Inc., N.Y.C., 1993-96; lit. intern, script reader New Dramatists, N.Y.C., 1995-96; co-founder, artistic dir. Lesbian Exch. of New Drama, N.Y.C., 1993—. Author: (play) Coming In, 1994; editor quar. LEND Newsletter, 1993—; author articles. Vol. Gay/Lesbian Anti-Violence Project, N.Y.C., 1996. Jean Stein scholar NYU, 1993. Mem. Dramatists Guild Inc. (moderator 1994-96, mem. women playwrights com. 1996). Democrat. Office: LEND 559 3rd St Brooklyn NY 11215

HARRIS, B. MARIE, newspaper editor; b. West Point, Miss., June 13, 1949; d. William Henry and Wanda Marie (West) H.; m. John Edward Lambeth, Nov. 27, 1980. BS cum laude, Miss. U. for Women, 1971. Advt. rep. Daily Herald, Biloxi, Miss., 1971-73; advt. mgr. Daily Times Leader, West Point, 1973-75, mng. editor, 1975-81; copy/city/graphics editor Sun Herald, Biloxi, 1981-86, assoc. editor, 1989-94, editl. dir., 1994—. Pres. Clay County C. of C., West Point, 1975; bd. dirs. Miss. Press Assn., Jackson, 1976-80, pres., 1980-81. Mem. Gulfport Rotary Club. Baptist. Office: Sun Herald PO Box 4567 Biloxi MS 39535

HARRIS, BERNICE LEE, educator; b. Emmett, Idaho, Apr. 3, 1946; d. Orville Lee and Aloisia W. (Odermott) H.; 1 child, Peregrin Harris-Marshall. BA in English Edn., U. Wyo., 1974, MA in English, 1981; PhD in English, U. Tulsa, 1993. Freelance film producer San Francisco, 1969-71; media cons. Anchorage Sch. Dist., 1973-77; lectr. media and edn. U. Alaska, Anchorage, 1973-78; tchr. English, women's history and film history Anchorage Sch. Dist., 1977-78; dir. humanities, cons. women's studies Wyo. Coun. for Humanities, Laramie, 1981-84; lectr. women's studies and English U. Wyo., Laramie, 1984-85; mem. humanities faculty Alaska Pacific U., Anchorage, 1985-86; instr. humanities Tulsa Jr. Coll., 1988; grad. asst. U. Tulsa, 1987-93; asst. prof. English, 1993-95; asst. prof. Lewis Clark State Coll., Lewiston, Idaho, 1995—; co-dir. Wyo. Women's Oral History Project, Laramie, 1979-81; co-founder, pres. Wyo. Oral History Assn., Laramie, 1980-84; coord. lecture series Alaska Pacific U., 1985-86; cons. in field. Author of short stories and poems. Bd. dirs. Alaska Women's Resource Ctr., Anchorage, 1976-78, Women's Ctr., Laramie, 1978-79, 82-85; bd. dirs. Call Rape Inc., Tulsa, 1988, crisis line vol., 1987-91. U. Wyo. scholar, 1973, 79; Coe fellow, U. Wyo., 1973. Mem. MLA, Shakespeare Assn. Am., Renaissance Soc. Office: Lewis Clark State Coll 500 8th Ave Lewiston ID 83501

HARRIS, DALE HUTTER, judge, lecturer; b. Lynchburg, Va., July 10, 1932; d. Quintus and Agnes (Adams) Hutter; m. Edward Richmond Harris Jr., July 24, 1954; children—Mary Fontaine, Frances Harris Russell, Jennifer Harris Haynie, Timothy Edward. BA, Sweet Briar Coll., 1953; MEd in Counseling and Guidance, Lynchburg Coll., 1970; JD, U. Va., 1978; LLD (hon.), Wilson Coll., 1988. Bar: Va. 1978, U.S. Dist. Ct. (we. dist.) Va. 1978, U.S. Ct. Appeals (4th cir.) 1978. Admissions asst. Sweet Briar Coll. (Va.), 1953-54; caseworker Winchester/Frederick Dept. Welfare, Va., 1954-55; vis. lectr. Lynchburg Coll. (Va.), 1971; assoc. Davies & Peters, Lynchburg, 1978-82; substitute judge 24th Dist. Gen. Dist. and Juvenile and Domestic Relations Dist. Cts. Va., 1980-82; judge Juvenile and Domestic Relations Dist. Ct., Lynchburg, 1982—; lectr. law U. Va. Law Sch., 1986—; pres. VA Coun. of Juvenile and Family Ct. Judges, 1994-96; panel of experts, adv. com. Child Protection and Custody Resource Ctr., 1994—; mem. commn. on Future Va's Jud. system, 1987-89; adv. bd. mem. Hilton project on model state laws about family violence. Vice chmn. bd. dirs. Sweet Briar Coll., 1976-86; vol. coordinator vols. in probation with Juvenile and Domestic Ct., 1971-73; chmn. steering com. for establishment Youth Service Bur., Lynchburg, 1972-73; chmn. bd. dirs. Lynchburg Youth Services, 1973-75; mem. adv. bd. Juvenile Ct., 1957-60, 62-68, sec., 1966-68; bd. dirs. Family Service Lynchburg, 1967-69; Lynchburg Fine Arts Ctr., 1965-67, Seven Hills Sch., 1966-73, Greater Lynchburg United Fund, 1963-65, Lynchburg Assn. Mental Health, 1960-61, Miller Home, 1980-82, Lynchburg Gen.-Marshall Lodge Hosps., Inc., 1980-82; v.p. Lynchburg Mental Health Study Commn., 1966; bd. dirs. Lynchburg Sheltered Workshop for Mentally Retarded Young Adults, 1965-69; bd. dirs. Lynchburg Guidance Ctr., 1959-61, v.p., 1970, pres., 1961; bd. dirs. Hist. Rev. Bd. Lynchburg, 1978-82; adv. bd. study of effectiveness of civil protection orders Nat. Ctr. State Cts., 1994—. Mem. Nat. Council Juvenile and Family Ct. Judges, ABA, Va. State Bar (bd. govs. criminal law sect. 1988—, bd. govs. family law section 1989—, child custody edn. com., 1993—), Va. Trial Lawyers Assn., Va. Bar Assn., Lynchburg Bar Assn., Am. Prosecutors Rsch. Inst. and NCJFCJ (adv. com. 1992-94), Phi Beta Kappa. Office: Juvenile and Domestic Relations Dist Ct PO Box 757 Lynchburg VA 24505-0757

HARRIS, DEANNA JEAN, editor; b. Waterloo, Iowa, June 17, 1947; d. Eugene Hildred and Marynette (Roberts) H. BA, U. Iowa, 1969; MFA, U. N.C., 1971. Asst. editor D.C. Heath & Co., Lexington, Mass.; prodn. mgr. Alan Guttmacher Inst., N.Y.C.; editor Learning Internat., Stamford, Conn.; project specialist Purity Supreme, Billerica, Mass.; publs. editor U. Tulsa, Okla., 1990—; freelance writer Zenger-Miller, 1990-91, Sterling Winthrop, N.Y.C., 1993; project writer U.S. Dept. Transp., Boston, 1992. Editor Dialog Mag. of the U. Tulsa; writer of short stories and plays. Active First Bapt. Ch. North Tulsa, Okla., 1992, Vol. Ctr. Adv. Bd., Tulsa, 1992, Hillcrest Women's Health Adv. Bd., Tulsa, 1993. Recipient Poetry writing award U. Iowa, Iowa City, 1968, Book-of-the-Month Club Regional award Book-of-the-Month Club, 1969. Mem. Women in Comm., Inc. (newsletter editor 1992-93, sec. 1993-94), Delta Sigma Theta. Democrat. Office: Univ Tulsa 600 S College Ave Tulsa OK 74104-3189

HARRIS, DEBRA BRIGHT, director of admissions; b. N.Y.C., Nov. 25, 1969; d. Keith Anthony and Gwendolyn Veronica (Ghee) B. BS, Syracuse U., 1991; MEd, Harvard U., 1993. Sta. rels. coord. Ind. TV Network, N.Y.C., 1991-92; admissions com. mem. Harvard Grad. Sch. of Edn., Cambridge, Mass., 1992-93; program coord. Harvard Career Office, Cambridge, Mass., 1992-93; dir. admissions George Washington U., Washington, 1993—. Advisor tutorial program Reid Temple African Meth. Episc. Ch., Lanham, Md., 1994—. Mem. Nat. Assn. Women in Edn., Nat. Assn. Grad. Admissions Profls., Delta Sigma Theta Sorority, Inc. (workshop facilitator 1995). Office: The George Washington U Grad Sch Edn 2134 G St NW Washington DC 20052

HARRIS, DIANA KOFFMAN, sociologist, educator; b. Memphis, Aug. 11, 1929; d. David Nathan and Helen Ethel (Rotter) Koffman; student U. Miami, 1947-48; BS, U. Wis., 1951; postgrad. Tulane U., New Orleans, 1951-52; MA, U. Tenn., 1967; postgrad. U. Oxford (Eng.), 1968-69; m. Lawrence A. Harris, June 24, 1951; children: Marla, Jennifer. Advt. and sales promotion mgr. Wallace Johnston Distbg. Co., Memphis, 1952-54; welfare worker Tenn. Dept. Pub. Welfare, Knoxville, 1954-56; instr. sociology Maryville (Tenn.) Coll., 1972-75; instr. sociology Fort Sanders Sch. Nursing, Knoxville, 1971-78; instr. sociology U. Tenn., Knoxville, 1967—; series editor Garland Pub., Inc. 1989—. Chmn. U. Tenn. Coun. on Aging, 1979—; organizer Knoxville chpt. Gray Panthers, 1978; mem. Gov.'s Task Force on Preretirement Programs for State Employers, 1973; mem. White House Conf. on Aging, 1981; bd. mem. Knoxville-Knox County Council on Aging, 1976, Sr. Citizens Info. and Referral, 1979, Sr. Citizens Home-Aide Svc., 1977; del. E. Tenn. Coun. on Aging, 1977. Recipient Meritorious award Nat. U. Continuing Edn. Assn., 1982, Pub. Svc. award Nat. Alumni Assn., 1992, Nat. Alumni Assn. Pub. Svc. award, 1992, Appreciation award Assn. Gerontology in Higher Edn., 1994. Mem. Am. Sociol. Assn., AAAS, Gerontol. Soc. Am., Popular Culture Assn., So. Sociol. Soc., So. Gerontol. Soc. (Pres.'s award 1984), N. Central Sociol. Assn. Clubs: London Competitor's, Nat. Contest Assn., Knoxville Kontestars. Author: Readings in Social Gerontology, 1975, (with Cole) The Elderly in America, 1977, The Sociology of Aging, 1980, 2d edit., 1990; co-author: Sociology, 1984, Annotated Bibliography and Sourcebook: Sociology of Aging, 1985, Dictionary of Gerontology, 1988, Teaching Sociology of Aging, 3d edit., 1991; aging series editor Garland Pub., Inc., 1989—; contbr. articles to profl. jours. Home: PO Box 50546 Knoxville TN 37950-0546 Office: U Tenn Dept Sociology PO Box 50546 Knoxville TN 37950-0546

HARRIS, DIANE CAROL, merger and acquisition consulting firm executive; b. Rockville Centre, N.Y., Dec. 25, 1942; d. Daniel Christopher and Laura Louise (Schmitt) Quigley; m. Wayne Manley Harris, Sept. 30, 1978. BA, Cath. U. Am., 1964; MS, Rensselaer Poly. Inst., 1967. With Bausch & Lomb, Rochester, N.Y., 1967-96, dir. applications lab., 1972-74, dir. tech. mktg. analytical systems div., 1974-76, bus. line mgr., 1976-77, v.p. planning and bus. programs, 1977-78, v.p. planning and bus. devel. Soflens div., 1978-80, corp. dir. planning, 1980-81, v.p. corp. devel., 1981-96; v.p. RID-N.Y. State, 1980-83; pres. Hypotenuse Enterprises, Inc., 1996—; mem.

adv. bd. Merger Mgmt. Report, 1986-92; internat. bd. dirs. Assn. Corp. Growth, v.p. corp. mem. affairs, 1993-94, v.p. internat. expansion, 1994-95, pres. elect, 1996; bd. dirs. Delta Labs., Inc., Duriron Co. Contbr. articles to profl. jours. Pres. Rochester Against Intoxicated Driving, 1979-83, chmn. polit. action com., 1983, 86; bd. dirs., chmn. long-range planning com. Rochester area Nat. Council on Alcoholism, 1980-84; bd. dirs. Rochester Rehab. Ctr., 1982-84, Friends of Bristol Valley Playhouse Found., 1983-87; mem. Stop DWI Adv. panel to Monroe County Legislature, 1982-87, N.Y. State Coalition for Safety Belt Use, 1984-85; mem. key exec. group Rensselaer Poly. Inst., 1993-96; mem. Com. 200, 1993—; mem. ACG skrs. bur., 1993—; mem. catalyst adv. com., 1995. Recipient Disting. Citizen's award Monroe County, 1979, Tribute to Women in Industry and Service award YWCA, 1983, Pres.'s 21st Century Leadership award-Women's Hall of Fame, 1995; NSF grantee, 1963; selected as one of 50 Women to Watch in Corp. Am., Bus. Week mag., 1987, 92, one of 100 Women To Watch, Duns Bus. Rev., 1988; Assn. For Corp. Growth Meritorious Svc. award, 1995. Mem. Am. Mgmt. Assn., Fin. Execs. Inst., Assn. Corp. Growth, C. of C. (pub. safety com. Rochester Area chpt., task force on hwy. safety and legis. 1981-86, high tech. Rochester adv. panel 1989—), Phi Beta Kappa, Sigma Xi, Delta Epsilon Sigma. Home: 60 Mendon Center Rd Honeoye Falls NY 14472-9363 Office: Hypotenuse Enterprises, Inc 1 Lincoln First Sq PO Box 54 Rochester NY 14601-0054

HARRIS, DIXIE LEE, former corrections educator; b. Paragould, Ark., Feb. 22, 1926; d. Elmer Henderson and Alice (Cothern) H. BS in Math. and Chemistry, Ark. State U., 1946; MA in Sci. Tchg., Columbia U., 1955; PhD in Comparative Edn., Syracuse U., 1970; labor studies diploma, Cornell U., 1989. Cert. tchr. secondary scis. and math.; secondary supr./prin., N.Y. Qualitative analyst Tenn. Eastman Corp., Oak Ridge, 1946-47; chemist The Tex. Co., Beacon, 1947-55; tchr. math. and chemistry Bur. Indian Affairs, Mt. Edgecumbe, Alaska, 1957-60; corrections tchr. Matteawan State Hosp., Beacon, N.Y., 1967-91, Fishkill Correction Facility Pub. Employees Fedn., 1983-91. Author: Twenty (fictional) Stories of Bible Women, 1980. Elected union rep., steward, exec. bd. Pub. Employees Fedn., Albany, N.Y., 1983-91; bd. dirs., trails com. chair Environ. Planning Lobby (now named Environ. Advocates), Albany, 1967-83; mem. numerous environ. and civic orgns. Mem. ACLU, NOW, Americans United for Seperation of Ch. and State, Soc. Bib. Lit., Bib. Arch. Soc., Pub. Employees Fedn. Retirees, Am. Mensa, Am. Youth Hostels, Religious Coalition for Reproductive Choice, Scenic Hudson, N.Y. State Labor-Religion Coalition. Democrat. Methodist. Home: 1 Schenck Ave Beacon NY 12508

HARRIS, EMILY LOUISE, special education educator; b. New London, Conn., Nov. 16, 1932; d. Frank Sr. and Tanzatter (McCleese) Brown; m. John Everett Harris Sr., Sept. 10, 1955; children: John Everett Jr., Jocelyn E. (dec.). BS, U. Conn., 1955; MEd, Northeastern U., 1969. Cert. tchr. elem. spl. subject sci., Mass., spl. subject reading; cert. secondary prin. Tchr. New Haven Sch. Dept., 1957-59, Boston Sch. Dept., 1966-68, Natick (Mass.) Sch. Dept., 1969-72; cert. nurse's asst. The Hebrew Rehab. Ctr., Roslindale, Mass., 1973-75; spl. edn. educator Boston Sch. Dept., 1975-76, 78—, support tchr., 1976-78; site coord. Tchr. Corps., 1977-81. Editor, compiler: Cooking With the Stars, 1989. Mem.-del. Mass. Fedn. Tchrs., Boston, 1993-96; elected rep. AFL-CIO (Boston Tchrs. Union), 1986-96; registrar of voters Dorchester (Mass.) H.S., 1986—; adv. bd. New England Assn. Schs. and Colls., 1980-93; 1st v.p., bd. dirs. League of Women for Comty. Svcs., Boston, 1976-80, Cynthia Sickle-Cell Anemia Fund, Boston, 1976-80. Recipient Tchg. award Urban League Guild Mass., 1993. Mem. AAUW (mem. Washington chpt.), Zeta Phi Beta (grad. mem., Zeta of Yr. 1994), Alpha Delta Kappa, Kappa Delta Pi, Order Ea. Star (past worthy matron Prince Hall chpt. 1983-84). Home: 36 Dietz Rd Hyde Park MA 02136

HARRIS, EMMA EARL, nursing home executive; b. Viper, Ky., Nov. 6, 1936; d. Andrew Jackson and Zola (Hall) S.; m. Ret Haney Marten Henis Harris, June 5, 1981; children: Debra, Joseph, Wynona, Robert Walsh. Grad. St. Joseph Sch. Practical Nursing. Staff nurse St. Joseph Hosp., Bangor, Maine, 1973-75; office nurse Dr. Eugene Brown, Bangor, 1975-77; dir. nurses Fairborn Nursing Home, Ohio, 1977-78; staff nurse Hillhaven Hospice, Tucson, 1979-80; asst. head nurse, 1980. Author: Thoughts on Life, 1988. Vol. Heart Assn., Bangor, 1965-70, Cancer Assn., Bangor, 1965-70. Mem. NAFE. Democrat. Avocations: theatre, opera. Home: 530 E Flores St Tucson AZ 85705-5723

HARRIS, EMMYLOU, singer; b. Birmingham, Ala., Apr. 2, 1947; children: Hallie, Meghann. Student, U.N.C.-Greensboro. Singer, 1967; assisted Gram Parsons on album GP, Grievous Angel, 1973; toured with Fallen Angels Band, performed across Europe and U.S.; recording artist on albums for Reprise Records, Warner Bros. Records., Electra/Asylum Records; appeared in rock documentary The Last Waltz, 1978; albums include The Gliding Bird, 1969, Pieces of the Sky, 1975, Elite Hotel, 1976 (Grammy award), Luxury Liner, 1977, Quarter Moon In A Ten Cent Town, 1978, Profile: Best of Emmylou Harris, 1978, Blue Kentucky Girl, 1979, Light of the Stable, 1979, Evangeline, 1981, Last Date, 1982, White Shoes, 1983, Profile II: Best of Emmylou Harris, 1984, The Ballad of Sally Rose, 1985, Thirteen, 1986, Trio (with Dolly Parton, Linda Ronstadt), 1987 (Grammy award), Angel Band, 1987, Bluebird, 1988, Duets, 1990, At Cowgirl's Prayer, 1993, Songs Of The West, 1994, Wrecking Ball, 1995 (Grammy award 1996); co-writer, co-prodr.: (with Paul Kennerley) The Ballad of Sally Rose, 185. Pres. Country Music Found., 1983—. Recipient of 7 Grammy awards, 1979, 80, 81, 84, 87, 92, 96; named Female Vocalist of Yr., Country Music Assn., 1980; co-recipient (with Dolly Parton and Linda Ronstadt) Album of Yr. award Acad. Country Music, 1987. Office: M Hitchcock Mgmt PO Box 159007 Nashville TN 37215-9007

HARRIS, FRANCES ALVORD (MRS. HUGH W. HARRIS), retired radio and television broadcaster, consultant; b. Detroit, Apr. 19, 1909; d. William Roy and Edith (Vosburgh) Alvord; m. Hugh William Harris, Sept. 24, 1932; children: Patricia Anne (Mrs. Floyd A. Metz), Hugh William, Robert Alvord. AB, Grinnell Coll., 1929; LHD (hon.), Ferris State Coll., 1980. With advt. dept. Himelhoch Bros. & Co., Detroit, 1929-31; broadcaster as Julia Hayes Robert P. Gust Co., 1931-34; tng. and pers. dept. Ernst Kern Co., 1935-36; broadcaster as Nancy Dixon Young & Rubicam, Inc., 1939-42; women's editor Sta. WWJ, Detroit, 1943-64, Sta. WWJ-TV, 1947-64; spl. features coord. Sta. WWJ-TV-AM-FM, 1964-74; treas. I.C. Harris & Co., Detroit, 1963-82, pres., chief exec. officer, 1982-84, chmn. bd., 1984-85; creator 1st ct. show Traffic Ct., 1949. Author, editor: Focus: Michigan Women, 1977. Mem. exec. bd. Wayne County chpt. Mich. Soc. for Mental Health, 1953-63; chmn. Mental Health Week, 1958-59; mem. Wayne County Com. on Aging, 1975-85, chmn., 1976-77; publicity com. YWCA, 1945, 2d v.p., 1963; mem. publicity com. Tri-County League for Nursing, 1956-61; publicity chmn. Met. Detroit YWCA Bd. Dirs., 1961-66, exec. com., 1962-67; campaign dist. chmn. United Found., 1959, unit chmn., 1960-61, chmn. speakers bur., 1974; exec. bd. United Fund. Women's Orgn., 1962-64; governing bd. United Community Svcs. Women's Com., 1961-66; bd. dirs. United Community Svcs., 1964-67; bd. dirs. Homemaker Svc. Met. Detroit, pres., 1969-70, co-founder, 1965; bd. dirs. Vis. Nurse Assn., pres., 1974-76; bd. dirs. Camp Fire Girls of Detroit, mem. nat. coun., 1967-72, mem. nat. bd., exec. com., 1970-72, pres., 1978-80; bd. dirs. Well Being Svc. Aging, 1969-74, Sr. Ctr., 1971-76, Friends Detroit Pub. Libr., 1972—, Friends Children's Museum, 1972-74, 83—; trustee Detroit Com. Alcoholism, 1961-64; mem. Mayor's Com. for Freedom Festival, 1959, chmn. women's activities, 1965; mem. Mayor's Com. for UN Week, 1959; mem. Gov.'s Commn. Status of Women, 1962-69, Mich. State Women's Commn., 1969-77; mem. nat. coun. Homemaker Svc., 1970-73; mem. adv. com. to trustees Grinnell Coll.; mem. bd. control Ferris State Coll., 1968-78; mem. def. adv. com. Women in the Svcs., 1970-73, chmn., 1973; program chmn. Met. Detroit YMCA, 1973-75; sec.-treas. Mich. Assn. Governing Bds. State Colls. and Univs., 1975, v.p., 1976-77, pres., 1977-78; bd. dirs. United Community Svcs., Detroit, 1973-75, mem. assembly, 1984-90; mem. communications com. local congregation and Episc. Diocese of Mich., 1965-66. Recipient Grinnell Coll. Alumni award, 1959, Mental Health Soc. Mich. award, 1958, Theta Sigma Phi Headliner award for Mich., 1951, nat., 1952, Heart of Gold award, 1976, Women's Advt. Club of Detroit Civic award, 1957, Gov. award NATAS, 1987, Mich. award NATAS, 1994; named Advt. Woman of Year, Detroit, 1958, 73, Soroptimist Woman of Yr., 1965, Fran Harris Day in her honor, Detroit, 1960, Vol. State of Mich., 1975; inducted into the Mich. Jouralism Hall Fame, 1986, Mich. Women's Hall of Fame, 1988; commendation service award Mich. Assn. Bus. Owners; 1st woman comml. newscaster, Detroit, 1943. Mem. Am. Women in Radio and TV (pres. Detroit chpt. 1957-58, gen. chmn. nat. conv. 1966, Outstanding Community Svc. award 1972, Life Achievement award 1991), Women's Advt. Club of Detroit (pres. 1959-60, mem. bd. 1974-77), UN Assn. U.S.A. (dir. Detroit chpt. 1962-65, Mich. div. bd. 1963-65), Advt. Fedn. (nat. v.p. women's activities 1964-67), Nat. Fedn. Press Women (hon.), 1973, Women in Communications (pres. Detroit 1950-51; del. to Asian-Am. Women in Broadcasting Conf. 1966, nat. 1st v.p. 1968-71, nat. pres. 1971-73, chmn. Communications Conf. Ams., 1968, del. III World Congress Women Journalists 1973), Women's Econ. Club (charter mem., dir. 1975-82, membership chmn. 1975, program chmn. 1976, pub. rels. co-chmn. 1977, treas. 1978, sec. 1979, 1st v.p. 1980, pres. 1981), Pi Epsilon Delta. Home: 34601 Elmwood St Apt 241 Westland MI 48185-3079

HARRIS, JANE URSULA, art gallery director; b. Buffalo, Aug. 4, 1965; d. William Patrick and Ursala Margaerite (Raidler) H. BA in Anthropology, SUNY, Buffalo, 1987, BA in Women Studies magna cum laude, 1987, MA in Humanities, 1990. Instr. Am. studies dept. SUNY, Buffalo, 1989-91; housing specialist Belmont Shelter Corp., Buffalo, 1990-93; gallery dir. Soho 20, N.Y.C., 1995-96, Amos Eno, N.Y.C., 1996—; intern New Mus. Cont. Art, N.Y.C., fall 1993, Whitney Mus. Am. Art, N.Y., summer 1994; rsch. assn. Pub. Art Fund, N.Y.C., spring 1994. Contbr. Rev. mag. Chair housing com. Western N.Y. Coalition for the Homeless, Buffalo, 1992-93. Mem. Phi Beta Kappa. Home: 12 John St # 11 New York NY 10038 Office: Amos Eno Gallery 594 Broadway #404 New York NY 10012

HARRIS, JANIE TWARDOWSKY, construction contractor; b. Dallas, Dec. 1, 1958; d. Thomas Chester and Janie Louise (Chandler) Hearring; m. Thomas W. Twardowsky, Oct. 25, 1980 (div. Dec. 1985); children: Reba Lynn, James David; m. Roger Lynn Harris, June 24, 1989; 1 child, Kathryn E. Twardowsky. Student, U. Houston, 1978-82. Cert. grad. remodeler Nat. Assn. Home Builders. Sherrif's dep. Harris County Sherrif's Dept., Houston, 1977-88; pres., owner Harris Constrn., Humble, Tex., 1988—. Bd. mem. Humble Area PTA, Atascocita United Meth. Ch., Humble; committeeman Houston Women's Bus. Coun. Named Houston 100, Greater Houston Partnership, 1995, Woman of Achievement (Bus.) Family Time, Humble, 1995, 1st runner up Woman Bus. Owner of Yr., 1995. Mem. Profl. Connection, Greater Houston Builders Assn. (v.p., membership chmn. remodeler's coun. 1995—), Humber Area C. of C. (bd. dirs.).

HARRIS, JEAN LOUISE, physician; b. Richmond, Va., Nov. 24, 1931; d. Vernon Joseph and Jean Louise (Pace) H.; m. Leslie John Ellis Jr., Sept. 24, 1955; children: Karen Denise, Pamela Diane, Cynthia Suzanne. BS, Va. Union U., 1951; MD, Med. Coll. Va., 1955; ScD (hon.), U. Richmond, 1981. Intern Med. Coll. Va., Richmond, 1955-56, resident internal medicine, 1956-58, fellow, 1958-60; fellow Strong Meml. Hosp.-U. Rochester (N.Y.) Sch. Medicine, 1958-60; rsch. assoc. Walter Reed Army Inst. Rsch., Washington, 1960-63; pvt. practice medicine specializing in internal medicine allergy Washington, 1964-71; instr. medicine Howard U. Coll. Medicine, Washington, 1960-68, asst. prof. dept. community health practice, 1969-72; prof. family practice Med. Coll. Va., Va. Commonwealth U., 1973-78; also dir. Center Community Health, 1973-78; sec. Human Resources Commonwealth of Va., 1978-82; v.p. state mktg. programs Control Data Corp., 1982-84, v.p. state govt. affairs, 1984-86, v.p. bus. devel., 1986-88; pres., chief exec. officer Ramsey Found., 1988-92; sr. assoc. dir., dir. med. affairs U. Minn. Hosp. and Clinic, Mpls., 1992—; lectr. dept. med. care and hosps. Johns Hopkins, Balt., 1971-73; asst. clin. prof. dept. community medicine Charles R. Drew Postgrad. Med. Sch., L.A., 1970-73; adj. asst. prof. dept. preventive and social medicine UCLA, 1970-72; chief bur. resources devel. D.C. Dept. Health, 1967-69; exec. dir. Nat. Med. Assn. Found., Washington, 1969-72; Cons. div. health manpower intelligence HEW, 1969; mem. recombinant DNA adv. com. HEW USPHS-NIH, 1979-82; vice chmn. Nat. Commn. on Alcoholism and Alcohol Related Diseases, 1980-81; mem. Pres.'s Pvt. Sctor Initiatives Task Force, 1981-82, Def. Adv. Com. on Women in the Service, 1985-88, Eden Prairie City Council, 1987—. Trustee U. Richmond, 1982-90; bd. dirs. United Way St. Paul; mem. Greater Mpls. coun. Girl Scouts U.S. Recipient award East End Civic Assn. Richmond, Va., 1955, 1st Ann. Serwa award Va. Commonwealth chpt. Nat. Coalition of 100 Black Women, 1989, Leadership award S.W. Suburban Twin Cities chpt. NAACP, 1989; named one of Top 100 Black Bus. and Profl. Women, Dollars and Sense mag., 1985. Mem. Nat. Med. Assn., Inst. Medicine of NAS, Am. Coll. Physician Execs., NAACP, Women's Econ. Roundtable, Rotary, Sigma Xi, Beta Kappa Chi, Alpha Kappa Mu, Delta Sigma Theta. Home: 10860 Forestview Cir Eden Prairie MN 55347-2022 Office: U Minn Hosp and Clinic Harvard St at E River Rd Minneapolis MN 55455

HARRIS, JEANNETTE FRANCES, artist; b. Mountain Grove, Mo., Nov. 17, 1938; d. Solon Francis and Mary Elizabeth (Roper) Manchester; m. James Partsch Harris, Mar. 18, 1965; children: James Patrick, Amy Elizabeth. BS in Edn. with honors, Southwest Mo. State U., 1962. judge Sandbridge Art Show, Virginia Beach, Va., 1976-77; bd. mem. Textile Designer's Assn., 1978-79; founding bd. mem. Children's Art Ctr., Norfolk, Va., 1977; scholarship chmn. Marianas O'Wives, 1984, 85, 86, Kitsap Quilters Guild, 1993-96; bd. mem. North Kitsap Arts and Craft Guild, 1989-92; mem. scholarship bd. North Kitsap Arts and Crafts, 1990-92; co-founder The Clay People, 1996. One-woman shows include Shoreline (Wash.) Coll., 1990, 91; exhibited in group shows at Virginia Beach (Va.) Art Ctr., 1975-76, Folk Arts Festival, Virginia Beach, 1975-76, Sandbridge Beach Art Show, Virginia Beach, 1976-77, Carlyle House, Alexandria, Va., 1978, Azalea Festival, Norfolk, Va., 1978, Textile Designer's Assn. Ann. Show, Norfolk, 1978, 79, Studio Northwest Mem. Shows, London, 1980-83, Guam Visual Arts Guild, Agana, 1984, Quad-A Guild Ann. Fine Art Show, Seattle, 1987, 88, Southwest Mo. State U. Alumni Art Show, 1988, Kitsap Arts and Crafts Show, Poulsbo, Wash., 1989, 90, 91, 92, Am. Assn. Cmty. and Jr. Colls. Nat. Conv., Seattle, 1990, Shoreline Arts Coun., Seattle, 1990, Artworks '92, Silverdale, Wash., 1992, Bainbridge (Wash.) Island Parks and Recreation Arts and Crafts Show, 1992, Hale Koa Internat. Christmas Fair, Honolulu, 1992, Artworks '93, 1993, Sidney Mus. and Arts Assn., Port Orchard, Wash., 1993, Cultural Arts Found., Poulsbo, 1993, Washington Potters' Assn., Portland, Oreg., 1993, Seattle, 1993, 94, 95, 96, Seattle Pacific U., 1993, Arts Coun. of Snohomish County Gallery, Everett, Wash., 1993, 94, 95, Fiberworks '94, Port Townsend, Wash., 1994, Kitsap Regional Libr., Bremerton, Wash., 1995, Kitsap Quilters' Ann. Show, Poulsbo, 1995, 96; pub. art commn. Arness Park, Kingston, Wash., 1992.

HARRIS, JILL, writer, editor; b. Phila., Sept. 10, 1943; d. S. Miller and Mary Louise (Snellenburg) H.; m. John H. Herman, Sept. 23, 1972 (div. Dec. 1994); children: Margaret Harris Herman, Anthony Harris Herman. BA in English, U. Pa., Phila., 1965. Asst. dir. alumni relations U. Pa., Phila., 1965-67; editl. asst. The New Yorker, N.Y.C., 1967-72; assoc. editor Avon Books, N.Y.C., 1973-75; travel and food writer D Mag., Dallas, 1980, 95, restaurant critic, 1980; dir. The Mostly French Cooking Sch., Dallas, 1981-82; freelance writer The Dallas Morning News, Dallas, 1996—, Dallas Family, Dallas, 1994; writer, copy editor The Art Squad, Dallas, 1994—. Author: (mag.) D Mag., 1980, 95, Dallas Family, 1994; writer: (newspaper) The Dallas Morning News, 1996—; co-author: (cookbook) A Mostly French Food Processor Cookbook, 1977, rev. edit. 1982; artist, designer: (furniture models and sketches) The Arlington Mus., 1992, The Dallas Morning News, 1996—. Artist, participant in fund raising exhibits E.A.S.L., Dallas, 1993—; mem. Choice, Dallas, 1993-95. Mem. Women in Communications (chair 1995—).

HARRIS, JOAN WHITE, foundation officer, arts administrator; b. New Haven, Mar. 9, 1931; d. Louis and Martha (Rahm) White; m. Gerald Baumann Frank, Feb. 12, 1953 (div. 1974); children: Daniel Bruce, Jonathan White, Louise Blanche; m. Irving Brooks Harris, June 19, 1974. BA, Smith Coll., 1952. Editorial asst. Oxford U. Press, N.Y.C., 1952-53, Ency. Brit., Chgo., 1953-54; TV producer, Chgo., 1976, 78, 80; pres. Chgo. Opera Theater, 1977-84, chair, 1984-87, bd. dirs., 1975-80; panelist, cons. Nat. Endowment for the Arts, 1980—; chair nat. bd. Aspen Music Festival, Colo., 1984-85, trustee, 1990—; mem. adv. bd. U.S.-China Arts Exchange, 1985-93. Pres. Harris Found., Chgo., 1976—; bd. dirs./trustee Mus. Contemporary Art, Chgo., 1976—, vice chmn., 1989—, Hampshire Coll., Amherst, Mass., 1977-84, Chgo. Symphony Orch., 1978—, Nat. Inst. Music Theater, Washington, 1982-87, Ind. Sector, Washington, 1983-89; pres. Ill. Art Alliance, 1990—; pres. Chgo. Music and Dance Theater, 1992—; trustee Columbia Coll., 1994—; bd. dirs. Ill. Ctr. for the Book, 1990-94, Northwestern Program for Performing Artists, 1986—, Am. coun. for the Arts, 1990-94, Nat. Cultural Alliance, 1991—, Sculpture Chgo., 1991—, Chgo. Inst. Architecture & Urbanism, 1992-94; commr. cultural affairs City of Chgo., 1987-89; pres. Ill. Arts Alliance, 1990—, Chgo. Music & Dance Theater, 1992. Clubs: Arts, Saddle and Cycle, Lake Shore, Standard (Chgo.), Lotos (N.Y.C.). Home and Office: Harris Found Ste 400 2 N LaSalle St Chicago IL 60602-3703

HARRIS, JOSEPHINE STEVENSON, health educator; b. Jackson, Miss., Sept. 19, 1947; d. Arvesta and Addie Boddie (Davis) Kelly; m. Lee Stevenson, June 17, 1976 (div. 1986); children: George A., Michael Lawrence; m. Johny L. Harris, Apr. 1995. BS in Health, Phys. Edn., Jackson State U., 1971, MS in Health Edn., 1974, cert. edn. adminstrn., 1994. Instr. phys. edn. Langston (Okla.) U., 1971-73; instr. health edn. Ctrl. H.S., St. Paul, Minn., 1974-77; instr. health, coll. prep. MS Jobs Corps Ctr., Crystal Springs, Miss., 1977-79; instr. phys. edn. Lanier H.S., Jackson, Miss., 1979-80, asst. prin., 1996—; instr. health edn., dept. chmn. Blackburn Middle Sch., Jackson, Miss., 1980-96; trainer C.O.A. U. So. Miss.; mem. adv. bd. J.C.P.T.S.A., Jackson, 1994-95; choreographer Cotillion Links, Debutantes Ball. Mem. Women for Progress of Miss., Jackson; dir. sanctuary choir Pine Grove Bapt. Ch., Jackson, 1991—; designer beautification circle, 1984—. Mem. NEA, AAUW, AAHPERD, Miss. Edn. Assn., Delta Sigma Theta. Democrat. Baptist. Home: 251 Valley Ridge Jackson MS 39206 Office: Blackburn Middle Sch 1311 W Pearl Jackson MS 39203

HARRIS, JULIE (ANN), actress; b. Grosse Pointe Park, Mich., Dec. 2, 1925; d. William Pickett and Elsie (Smith) H.; m. Jay I. Julien, Aug. 12, 1946 (div. 1954); m. Manning Gurian, Oct. 21, 1954 (div. 1967); 1 child, Peter; m. Erwin Carroll, Apr. 1977, (div. 1982). Student, Perry Mansfield Theatre Work Shop,, 1941-43, Yale Drama Sch.,, 1944-45. Theater debut in It's a Gift, N.Y.C., 1945; appeared in plays Playboy of the Western World, 1946, Oedipus, 1946, Henry IV-Part II, 1946, Alice in Wonderland, 1947, We Love A Lassie, 1947, Macbeth, 1948, Sundown Beach, 1948 (Theatre World award 1949), The Young and Fair, 1948-49, Magnolia Alley, 1949, Montserrat, 1949, The Member of the Wedding, 1950-51 (Donaldson award 1950), I Am a Camera, 1951-52 (Tony award 1952, Donaldson award 1952, Variety-N.Y. Drama Critics Poll 1952), Mademoiselle Colombe, 1954, The Lark, 1955 (Tony award 1956), The Country Wife, 1957, The Warm Peninsula, 1959, Little Moon of Alban, 1960, Romeo and Juliet, 1960, King John, 1960, A Shot in the Dark, 1961, Marathon 33, 1964 (Tony nomination 1964), Hamlet, 1964, Ready When You Are, C.B, 1964, The Hostage, 1965, Skyscraper, 1965 (Tony nomination 1969), A Streetcar Named Desire, 1967, Forty Carats, 1968 (Tony award 1969), The Women, 1970, And Miss Reardon Drinks A Little, 1971-72, Voices, 1972, The Last of Mrs. Lincoln, 1972 (Tonyaward 1973), The Au Pair Man, 1973 (Tony nomination 1974), In Praise of Love, 1974, Break a Leg, 1979, On Golden Pond, 1980, Mixed Couples, 1980, Under the Ilex, 1983, Tusitala, 1988, (nat. co.) Driving Miss Daisy, Love Letters, 1989; one-woman theater presentations include The Belle of Amherst, 1977 (Grammy award 1977, Tony award 1977), Currer Bell, Lucifer's Child, 1991, Glass Menagerie, 1994; film debut in The Member of the Wedding, 1952 (Acad. award nomination); other films include The East of Eden, 1955, I Am a Camera, 1955, The Truth About Women, 1958, Poacher's Daughter, 1960, Requiem for a Heavyweight, 1962, The Haunting, 1963, The Moving Target, 1966, You're a Big Boy Now, 1966, Reflections in a Golden Eye, 1967, The Split, 1968, Journey into Midnight, 1968, The People Next Door, 1970, The Hiding Place, 1975, Voyage of the Damned, 1976, The Bell Jar, 1979, The Prostitute, 1980, The Nutcraker: The Motion Picture, 1986, Gorillas in the Mist, 1988, Housesitter, 1992, The Dark Half, 1993; TV series include Thicker Than Water, 1973, The Family Holvak, 1975, Knots Landing, 1979-87; TV movies include Wind From the South, 1955, The Good Fairy, 1956, The Lark, 1957, Johnny Belinda, 1968, Little Moon of Alban, 1958 (Emmy award 1959), A Doll's House, 1959, Victoria Regina, 1961 (Emmy award 1962), The Power and the Glory, 1961, Pygmalian, 1964, Hamlet, 1964, The Holy Terror, 1965, Anastasia, 1967, The House on Green Apple Road, 1970, How Awful About Alan, 1970, Home for the Holidays, 1972, The Greatest Gift, 1974, Backstairs at the White House, 1979, The Gift, 1979, The Christmas Wife, 1979, Too Good To Be True, 1988, Single Women, Married Men, 1989, They've Taken Our Children: The Chowchilla Kidnapping Story, 1993, When Love Kills: The Seduction of John Nearn, 1993, One Christmas, 1994, Scarlett, 1994; author: (with Barry Tarshis) Julie Harris Talks to Young Actors, 1971. Recipient Antoinette Perry award for best actress in Forty Carats, 1969, The Last of Mrs. Lincoln, 1973; Nat. Medal of the Arts, 1994. Office: William Morris Agy 1325 Ave of the Americas New York NY 10019-4702*

HARRIS, KATHERINE SAFFORD, speech and hearing educator; b. Lowell, Mass., Sept. 3, 1925; d. Truman Henry and Katherine (Wardwell) Safford; m. George Harris, Oct. 2, 1952; children: Maud White, Louise. BA, Radcliffe Coll., 1947; PhD, Harvard U., 1954. Rsch. assoc. Haskins Labs., New Haven, 1952-85, v.p., 1985—; prof. speech and hearing CUNY, N.Y.C., 1970—, Disting. prof., 1982—; active U.S./Israeli Speech Program Littauer Found., N.Y.C., 1986. Author: (with Borden and Raphael) Speech Science Primer, 1980, 3d edit., 1985, (with Baer and Sasaki) Phonatory Control, 1986. Nat. Inst. Neurol. Diseases and Stroke grantee. Fellow AAAS, Acoustical Soc. Am., Am. Speech Hearing Assn., N.Y. Acad. Scis. Office: CUNY Grad Sch 33 W 42nd St New York NY 10036-8003

HARRIS, LENORE ZOBEL, school nurse; b. Shoemaker, Calif., Nov. 1, 1944; d. Jerome Fremont and Louise Maxine (Purwin) Zobel; m. Robert Thomas Harris, June 19, 1966; children: Rebecca Louise, Grant Thomas. BSN, Stanford U., 1967; postgrad., Calif. State U., San Diego, 1969-72; MA, Calif. State U., Stanislaus, 1993. RN, Calif. Staff nurse Stanford (Calif.) Univ. Hosp., 1967-68; pediatric nurse to pvt. practice physician San Diego, 1968-73; sch. nurse Oak Park Unified Sch. Dist., Agoura, Calif., 1978-79, Simi Valley (Calif.) Unified Sch. Dist., 1975-85; camp nurse Kennolyn Camps, Aptos, Calif., 1982, 83, 84; sch. nurse Ventura (Calif.) Unified Sch. Dist., 1984-87; coord. health svcs., Lincoln Unified Sch. Dist., Stockton, Calif., 1987—; originator, chmn. Disaster Preparedness Com., 1985-87; chmn. health advc. com. Lincoln Unified Sch. Dist., 1987—, fmaily life edn. adv. com., 1988—, trainer S.J. County teen advs., 1992—; organizer, adviser Mid. Sch. "Just Say No" Club, 1988-91; spkr. on health issues to sch. nurses and educators. Writer Calif. Office of AIDS Manual; contbr. articles to profl. jours. Bd. dirs. Tri-County chpt. Am. Lung Assn., 1994—; troop leader San Diego and Ventura area Girl Scouts U.S., 1963, 78-81; officer Ventura Parent Coop. Nursery Sch., 1976-81; pres. Poinestia PTA, Ventura, 1985-87; officer Pacific Mid. Sch. PTSA, Stockton, 1988-90, Lincoln H.S. PTSA, Stockton, 1990-94. Named Calif. Health Educator of the Yr., 1996, Calif. Sch. Nurse of Yr., No. Sect., 1996. Mem. AAUW, Nat. Assn. Sch. Nurses, San Joaquin County Sch. Nurse Orgn. (chmn. 1990-92), Calif. Sch. Nurse Orgn. (nominating com. 1991-92, chair pub. rels. sect.), San Joaquin County Health Edn. Com. (speaker on health issues). Office: Lincoln Unified Sch Dist 2010 W Swain Rd Stockton CA 95207-4055

HARRIS, LINDA RUTH, obstetrician and gynecologist; b. Clarkfield, Minn., June 22, 1954; d. Harold Francis Harris and Darlene Irene (Vik) Shaw. BA summa cum laude, Luther Coll., 1975; MD, U. Iowa, 1978. Diplomate Am. Bd. Ob-Gyn. Physician Feminist Women's Health Ctr., L.A., 1980-82, Eldonna Christine, M.D., Napa, Calif., 1983-85, Ob-Gyn. Health Ctr., Medford, Oreg., 1985—. Cons. Planned Parenthood, Medford, 1990-94; bd. dirs. Crossroads, Medford, 1985-87. Mem. ACOG (sect. chair 1982), AMWA, Oreg. Med. Assn., N.Am. Soc. of Pediatric and Adolescent Gynecology, Am. Soc. for the Study of Colposcopy and Cervical Pathology. Democrat. Office: Ob-Gyn Health Ctr 777 Murphy Rd Medford OR 97504

HARRIS, LISA ELLYN, art specialist, photographer; b. Oceanside, N.Y., Feb. 22, 1965; d. John Keith and Pamela (Patton) H. AA, U. Fla., 1987; BA in Art History, U. N.C. Greensboro, 1990, cert art specialist, 1992. Art specialist Guilford County Schs., Greensboro, 1992—; photography tchr. UNC, Greensboro, 1992-96; photography tchr., photographer Withrop Coll., Rock Hill, S.C., 1994-96; photography tchr. William and Mary, Williamsburg, Va., 1995, staff photographer, 1995; drawing instr. Guilford County PTA, Greensboro, 1995. Vol. Ea. Music Festival Guilford Coll., 1996. Mem. Am. Crafts Coun., N.C. Art Educators Assn., N.C. Assn. of Educators, United Arts Coun. Fund. Home: 1326 W Friendly Ave Greensboro NC 27403 Office: Guilford County Sch Southeast HS Greensboro NC 27403

HARRIS, LISA GAEL, English language educator; b. Kingsville, Tex., Nov. 9, 1958; d. Dudley Michael Harris and Barbara Wilkes (Burton) Jett; m. A.J. Van Omme, Dec. 14, 1982 (div. 1984); 1 child, Callia Antonia; m. Kevin M. Centlivre, Dec. 2, 1990; 1 child, Jakob Parker. BA in Comparative Lit., San Francisco State U., 1983; postgrad., U. South Fla., 1996—. Cert. tchr. English 6-12, ESOL, Fla. Editor, translator Amsterdam, The Netherlands, 1983-87; substitute tchr. Pinellas County, Fla., 1987-88; ESOL tchr. Pinellas County Sch. Bd., Fla., 1989-93; ESOL tchr. Lakewood H.S., Pinellas County, 1993—, chair ESOL dept., 1996—; sponsor Nat. Honor Soc., St. Petersburg, Fla., 1993—. leader Girl Scouts U.S.A., St. Petersburg, Fla., 1988-89, 94-95. Mem. NEA, Sunshine State Tchrs. of English as Second or Other Lang., Pinellas County Tchrs. Assn. Democrat. Office: Lakewood HS 1400 54th Ave S Saint Petersburg FL 33705

HARRIS, LUCY BROWN, accountant, consultant; b. Ft. Smith, Ark., Feb. 25, 1924; d. Joseph Real and Lucy (McDonough) Brown; m. Clyde B. Randall, June 10, 1944 (div. Aug. 1970); children: Clyde B. III, Bradford, Sara, Lucy, Mark R.; m. Mack C. Harris, Aug. 1, 1980. Student, Holton Arms Jr. Coll., 1943, U. Mo., 1944; BA, U. Ark., 1970; grad., U. Tex., 1982. CPA. Comptroller Rebmar, Inc., Dallas, 1974-78; acctg. mgr. Republic Bank, Dallas, 1978-80; ptnr. Lucy B. Harris Ltd. Co., CPAs, Dallas, 1981—; cons. Discipleship Counseling Svcs., Dallas, 1987-90. Mem. Better Bus. Bur.; bd. dirs. Ethel Daniels Found., Dallas, 1987-90, NAWBO. Mem. AICPA, Nat. Assn. Women Bus. Owners, Tex. Soc. CPAs, CPA Club, Jr. League of Dallas, Brookhollow Golf Club, Kappa Alpha Theta. Episcopalian. Office: 3710 Rawlins St Ste 810 Dallas TX 75219-4237

HARRIS, MARCELITE JORDAN, air force officer; b. Houston, Jan. 16, 1943; d. Cecil Oneal and Marcelite Elizabeth (Terrell) Jordan; m. Maurice Anthony Harris, Nov. 29, 1980; children: Steven Eric, Tenecia Marcelite. BA, Spelman Coll., 1964; postgrad., Ctrl. Mich. U., 1976-78, Chapman Coll., 1979-80; BS, U. Md., Okinawa, Japan, 1986. Tchr. Head Start, Houston, 1964-65; commd. 2d lt. USAF, 1965, advanced through grades to brig. gen., 1965—; student Squadron officers Sch., 1975; with Hdqrs. USAF, Pentagon, 1975; comdr. 39 Cadet Squadron, USAF Acad., Colorado Springs, Colo., 1978, Air Refueling Wing, McConnell AFB, Kans., 1980, Avionics Maintenance Squadron, McConnell AFB, 1981, Field Maintenance Squadron, McConnell AFB, 1982; dir. maintenance Pacific Air Forces Logistics Support Ctr., Kadena Air Base, Japan, 1982; student Air War Coll., 1983; dep. chief maintenance Tech. Tng. Ctr., Keesler AFB, Miss., 1986, wing comdr., 1988; student Harvard U.Sr. Officers Course, 1988, Capstone Flag and Gen. Officers Course, 1990; vice comdr. Oklahoma City Air Logistics Ctr., Tinker AFB, 1990—; dir. tech. tng. USAF, Randolph AFB, Tex., 1993—; dir. of maintenance USAF, 1994. Cabinet mem. United Way, Oklahoma City, 1991; mem. adv. bd. Salvation Army, Oklahoma City, 1991—; bd. dirs. U.S. Automobile Assn., 1993—, 5 Who Care, 1992, Urban League. Decorated Bronze star, 1972; named one of Top 100 Afro-Am. Bus. and Profl. Women, Dollars and $ense Mag., 1989, named Most Prestigious Individual, 1991. Mem. Fed. Mgrs. Assn., Nat. Contract Mgmt. Assn., Tinker Mgmt. Assn., Air Force Assn. *

HARRIS, MARGARET, pianist, conductor, composer; b. Chgo., 1943; d. William and Clara Harris. BS, Juilliard Sch. Music, 1964, MS, 1965. Am. mus. specialist, cons. Porgy and Bess Bolshoi Theater of Opera and Ballet, Uzbekistan, 1995; music and artistic dir. United Negro Coll. Fund Chorale, N.Y.C., 1995—; adj. lectr. and prof. Bronx Cmty. Coll. of CUNY, 1991—; adjudicator, lectr. Unisys Symposium for African-Am. Composers Detroit Symphony Orch., 1993; keynote spkr. 30th anniversary conf. Mo. Arts Coun., 1995; music dir., founder New Millieum Chorale, N.Y.C., 1996. Debut as pianist at age 3; toured as child prodigy; debut with Chgo. Symphony Orch., 1953; condr., pianist Black New World ballet prodn.; toured Europe twice as mus. dir. Black New World and Negro Ensemble Co. N.Y.; debut Town Hall, 1970; pianist, condr. prodn. Hair; musical dir., condr. Two Gentlemen of Verona, Guys and Dolls; made debut as symphonic condr. with Grant Park and Chgo. Symphonies, 1971; soloist original piano concerto L.A. Philharmonic, 1972, 73; condr. St. Louis, Minn., San Diego, Detroit symphonies, L.A. Philharmonic, Wolf Trap Park, Opera Ebony, N.Y.C., 1977, Winston-Salem, N.C. Symphony, 1988; mus. dir. One More Time, Israel, Europe, N.Y.; mus. dir./pianist I Love New York, Europe, 1984; mus. dir. Amen Corner, Broadway, 1984; artist-in-residence Hillsborough Coll., Tampa, Fla., 1984; mus. dir., condr. nat. TV spls.; mus. dir., condr. Raisin on Broadway and nat. tour; exec./music dir. Newark Boys Chorus; panelist Nat. Endowment Arts, Nat. Opera Inst. Affiliate Artists, N.Y.C., Dame Knights of Malta; composer of musical (with Ruby Dee), 1988; former artistic dir., condr. N.Y. Boys Choir; vis. disting. prof. U. West Fla., 1989—; pres. Margaret R. Harris Enterprises; condr. Dayton Philharm., 1991; apptd. permanent artistic and music dir. Olympus Music Soc., N.Y.C., 1994; pianist European Concert tour, Germany, 1994; guest condr. Bklyn. Philharmonic, 1994; other compositions include David, Cycle of Psalms, Spiritual Suite, Stabat mater, Mass in A, the Lord's Prayer, We are D.C.'s Future, Christ is Alive Here, 1994; European concept tour as pianist, 1994; Am. cultural specialist for U.S.I.A., Porgy & Bess in Russian, 1995; numerous commissioned compositions for chorus, orch., voice and piano, 1994.

HARRIS, MARGARET ELIZABETH, writer; b. Bridgeton, N.J., May 31, 1968; d. F. Warren and Jean Elizabeth (Grosscup) H. BA, Rutgers Coll., 1990. Info. asst. Bristol-Myers Squibb, Princeton, N.J., 1990-93; info. mgr., writer, editor Emron, Inc., Warren, N.J., 1993-95; sr. copywriter Ferguson Comms. Group, Parsippany, N.J., 1995-96, Harriston, Star, Wiener & Beitler - N.J., Parsippany, N.J., 1996—. Mem. Am. Med. Writers Assn. Home: 18 Court St Flemington NJ 08822 Office: HSWB NJ Morris Corp Ctr III Bldg D 400 Interpace Pkwy Parsippany NJ 07054

HARRIS, MARGARET RENÉ (PEGGY HARRIS), medical/surgical nurse; b. Chgo., June 4, 1959; d. Ludalph Edward and Josephine (Antoinette (Dinolfo) H. Diploma, Evang. Sch. Nursing, Oak Lawn, Ill., 1982; BSN, Elmhurst Coll., 1985. Staff nurse Christ Hosp. and Med. Ctr., Oak Lawn, 1982-88, Mercy Home Healthcare, Chgo., 1988-91, Ventilator Support Ctr., Hinsdale, Ill., 1988-89, North Ctrl. Dialysis Ctrs., Chgo., 1991—. Mem. Am. Lung Assn. Met. Chgo. (vol. RN Camp Action 1988—, edn. chairperson 1993-95). Democrat. Roman Catholic.

HARRIS, MARIA LOSCUTOFF, special education educator, consultant; b. Rahmet Abad, Iran, Jan. 25, 1940; came to U.S., 1949; d. Vasiliy Vasilivitch and Esfir Alexsevna (Samadouroff) Loscutoff; m. Bernard Harris, Sept. 30, 1972; children: William, Richard, Lynn, Clifford, Robert, Bernard, Peter, Steven, Barbara. AA, Sierra Coll., Rocklin, Calif., 1960; BS, San Francisco State U., 1963; MS, Manhattan Coll., 1985. Cert. in spl. edn. and field of dyslexia, N.Y., Calif. Tchr. bus. edn. Westmoor H.S., Daly City, Calif., 1963-66, Coll. San Mateo, Calif., 1964, 65, Amador Sch. Dist., Pleasanton, Calif., 1967-69; adminstrv. asst. LTV, Inc., Anaheim, Calif., 1969-71; office mgr. Western div. Ocean & Atmospheric Sci. Inc., Santa Ana, Calif., 1971-72; office mgr., asst. to adminstr. Ocean & Atmospheric Sci. Inc., Dobbs Ferry, N.Y., 1972-79; officer mgr., adminstr. Harris Sci. Svcs., Dobbs Ferry, 1979-84; reading and classroom tchr. Windward Sch., White Plains, N.Y., 1984-88; learning specialist Irvington (N.Y.) Union Free Sch. Dist., 1988—; cons., tutor Harris Sci. Svcs., Dobbs Ferry, 1993—; mem. Westchester Reading coun. Supporter, contbr. Midnight Run for Homeless, 1985—; vol. Census Bur., 1990, Dobbs Ferry, 1989. Mem. Orton Dyslexia Soc., Internat. Reading Assn., Kappa Delta Pi. Home: 15 Overlook Rd Dobbs Ferry NY 10522-3209 Office: Irvington Union Free Schs 6 Dows Ln Irvington NY 10533-2102

HARRIS, MARILYN, retired academic administrator; b. N.Y.C.; d. Bernard and Rose (Block) Hochberg; m. Seymour J. Harris; children: Randall (dec.), April. AB summa cum laude, Hunter Coll., 1945; MS, Iowa State U., 1947. Faculty dept. math and stats. Hunter Coll., N.Y.C., 1946-48; systems analyst, statistician market research services Gen. Electric Co., N.Y.C., 1962-67; biostatistician comprehensive child care project Einstein Med. Sch., N.Y.C., 1967-69; asst. to dean, acting dir. computer ctr. Baruch Coll. CUNY, 1969-72; dir. data collection and evaluation office univ. mgmt. data Cen. Office, CUNY, 1972-74; dir. mgmt. info. systems Bklyn. Coll., CUNY, 1974-79, dir. personnel services, 1979-85, asst. v.p. human resources and adminstrv. services, 1985-89, bd. dirs. Bklyn. Ctr. Performing Arts, 1982-89, chair seat campaign, 1984-86; Docent Pollock/Krasner House, East Hampton, L.I., 1995—. Bd. dirs. Project Greenhope, 1988-93; vol. mgmt. cons. Women in Need, 1988—, bd. dirs., 1989-92, sec. exec. com., 1990-92; bd. dirs. Women's City Club, 1990—, active homeless project, 1989-91, mem. emergency task force, 1992-93, v.p. ops., 1993-94; active Womanspace of Gt. Neck, 1989, mem. exec. com.-at-large, 1990-94, mem. adv. bd., 1994-96; adv. bd. Omsbudservice of Nassau County, 1991—. Recipient Excellence award Art League Nassau County, 1994, Helen Nobel award of merit Nat. Art League, 1996. Mem. Artists Network Great Neck, Jimmy Ernst Artist Alliance, Phi Beta Kappa, Phi Kappa Phi, Pi Mu Epsilon. Home: 9 Knightsbridge Rd Great Neck NY 11021-4569

HARRIS, MARILYN LOUISE, educator; b. Hutchinson, Kans., July 29, 1950; d. Willard E. Wallace and Ruby V. (Coffey) O'Mara; m. Robert B. Harris, Mar. 6, 1982; children: Matt, Ted, Emily. BS, U. Nebr., 1971, MEd, 1975, PhD, 1984. Cert. elem. tchr., counselor, adminstr., Nebr. Elem. tchr. Lincoln (Nebr.) Pub. Schs., 1973-74, elem. counselor, 1974-77, elem. coord., 1977-82, staff devel. instr., 1982-83; grad. asst. U. Nebr., Lincoln, 1982-83, supr. student tchrs., 1985-87; dir. corp. tng. and devel. Harris Labs., Lincoln, 1987—; bd. dirs. Nebr. Job Tng. Coun., Lincoln, 1988-91. Bd. dirs. ARC, Lincoln, 1989-91, Jr. League Lincoln, 1989-92, Lincoln Cmty. Playhouse, 1988-91, Lincoln Children's Mus., 1987-92, 1st Plymouth Ch. Bd. Music/Fine Arts, Lincoln, 1990-92; bd. dirs. St. Elizabeth Cmty. Health Ctr., Lincoln, 1989—, bd. sec., 1991-92, bd. vice chairperson, 1992-95, bd. pres., 1995—; pres. St. Elizabeth Aux., Lincoln, 1989-91; mem. devel. com. Lincoln Pub. Schs. Found., 1989—, found. chairperson, 1995—; mem. adv. com. Inst. Lifelong Learning, Nebr. Wesleyan U.; mem. adult basic studies adv. com. S.E. C.C.; mem. planning com. Sisters of Charity, Cin., 1993—; bd. dirs. Nebr. Pub. TV, 1993, Nebr. Arts Coun., 1993—. Mem. ASTD (sec. 1988-89, pres. 1990-91), Phi Delta Kappa. Republican. Home: 2829 S 31st St Lincoln NE 68502-5201 Office: Harris Labs PO Box 80837 Lincoln NE 68501-0837

HARRIS, MARION HOPKINS, former government official; b. Washington, July 27, 1938; d. Dennis Cason and Georgia (Greenleaf) Hopkins; m. Charles E. Harris, July 1957 (div. 1964); 1 child, Alan E. MPA, U. Pitts., 1971; M in Mgmt. Sys., U. So. Calif., 1984, DPA, 1985. Dir. program planning Rochester Urban Renewal Agy., N.Y., 1971-72; exec. dir. Fairfax County Redevel. and Housing Authority, Fairfax, Va., 1972-73; dep. dir. housing mgmt. HUD, Detroit, 1973-75; pres., prof. dept. bus. and pub. adminstrn. Bowie State U., Md.; mng. auditor GAO, Washington, 1979-80; sr. field officer for housing, Washington, 1979-89, dir. evaluation divsn. adminstrn., 1989-91. Bd. dirs. S.W. Neighborhood Assembly, Washington, 1979-80; commr. S.W. Adv. Neighborhood Commn., Washington, 1986; mem. pub. adv. com. Washington Coun. Govts., 1985-87; Wash. Suburban Sanitary Com.; mem. consumer adv. bd. Wash. Suburban Sanitary Com., 1989—; bd. dirs. Bowie State U. Found., 1991—; mem. transition team Gov. State of Md., 1995; mem. Md. Gov.'s Workforce Investment Bd., 1996—. Maj. USAMC. Recipient Outstanding Performance award HUD, 1984; Carnegie-Mellon mid-career fellow, 1970; Ford Found. travel-study awardee, 1970. Mem. Am. Acad. Soc. and Polit. Sci., U. So. Calif. Doctoral Assn., LWV (exec. bd. Washington 1983-84). Roman Catholic. Avocations: ballroom dancing, foreign travel, swimming. Home: 12306 Sea Pearl Ct Laurel MD 20708-2848

HARRIS, MARY HOWARD, accountant, educator; b. Riverside, N.J., Oct. 2, 1965; d. Henry Robert and Lois Jean (Frank) Howard; m. Stephen Andrew Harris, Nov. 7, 1992; children: Stephen Andrew, Jr, Shannon Lois. BA in Econs., Ursinus Coll., Collegeville, Pa., 1987; MBA in Acctg., St. Joseph's U., Phila., 1993. Cert. mgmt. acct., Pa. Mgmt. trainee Meridian Bank, Phila., 1987-88, asst./br. mgr., 1988-90, credit analyst, 1990-92, sr. auditor, 1992-94; sr. acct. Meridian Securities, Reading, Pa., 1994-95; staff acct. Rhone Poulenc Rorer, Inc., Collegeville, Pa., 1995—; adj. prof. Alvernia Coll., Reading, 1994, Muhlenberg Coll., Allentown, 1995. Mem. Inst. Mgmt. Accts. Republican. Roman Catholic. Home: 1315 New Philadelphia Rd Pottstown PA 19465

HARRIS, MERLE WIENER, college administrator, educator; b. Hartford, Conn., July 25, 1942; d. Irving and Leah (Glasser) Wiener; m. David R. Harris, June 23, 1963; children: Jonathan, Rebecca. BS, Cen. Conn. U., 1964, MS, 1973; EdD, U. Mass., 1988. Clk., edn. com. Conn. Gen. Assembly, Hartford, 1971-72; career edn. coordinator Bloomfield (Conn.) Pub. Schs., 1973-78; asst. to commr. Dept. of Higher Edn., Hartford, Conn., 1978-82, asst. commr., 1982-88, deputy commr., 1988-89; pres. Charter Oak State Coll., Newington, Conn., 1989—; exec. dir. Bd. for State Acad. Awards, Hartford, Conn., 1989—; interim pres. Cen. Conn. State U., 1995-96; cons. U.S. Dept. Edn. Career Edn., Washington, 1974; fellow Inst. for Ednl. Leadership, 1980; bd. dirs. Old State House, Conn. Ctr. for Edn. and Tng. Techs., Conn. Literacy Vols., Conn. Humanities Coun.; chmn. Joint Com. Ednl. Tech., 1991—. Democrat. Jewish.

HARRIS, MICALYN SHAFER, lawyer; b. Chgo., Oct. 31, 1941; d. Erwin and Dorothy (Sampson) Shafer. AB, Wellesley Coll., 1963; JD, U. Chgo., 1966. Bar: Ill. 1966, Mo. 1967, U.S. Dist. Ct. (ea. dist.) Mo. 1967, U.S. Supreme Ct. 1972, U.S. Ct. Appeals (8th cir.) 1974, N.Y. 1981, N.J. 1988, U.S. Dist. Ct. N.J., U.S. Ct. Appeals (3rd cir.) 1993. Law clk. U.S. Dist. Ct., St. Louis, 1967-68; atty. The May Dept. Stores, St. Louis, 1968-70, Ralston-Purina Co., St. Louis, 1970-72; atty., asst. sec. Chromalloy Am. Corp., St. Louis, 1972-76; pvt. practice, St. Louis, 1976-78; atty. CPC Internat., Inc., 1978-80; divsn. counsel CPC N.Am., 1980-84, asst. sec., 1981-88, gen. counsel S.B. Thomas, Inc., 1983-87; corp. counsel, CPC Internat. Englewood Cliffs, N.J. 1984-88; assoc. counsel Weil, Gotshal & Manges, N.Y.C., 1988-90; pvt. practice, 1991; v.p., sec., gen. counsel Winpro, Inc., 1991—; arbitrator Am. Arbitration Assn., NYSE, NASD, The Aspen Ctr. for Conflict Mgmt. Mem. ABA (bus. law section, chair corp. counsel com., past chair subcom. counseling the mktg. function, securities law com., tender offers and proxy statements subcom., task force on computer software contracting, task force on bus. ethics of lawyers, task force on conflicts of interest, ad hoc com. on tech.), N.Y. State Bar Assn. (securities regulation com. computer law com., task force on shrink-wrap licensing, sablaw, exec. com. bus. law sect.), Bar Assn. Met. St. Louis (past chmn. TV com.), Mo. Bar Assn. (past chmn. internat. law com.), Ill. Bar Assn., Am. Corp. Counsel Assn. N.J. (past bd. dirs. and chmn. bus. law com.), Am. Corp. Counsel Assn. N.Y. (mergers and acquisitions com., corp. law com.), N.J. Bar Assn., Computer Law Assn. Address: 625 N Monroe St Ridgewood NJ 07450-1206

HARRIS, NATHOLYN DALTON, food science educator, researcher; b. Calvary, Ga., Feb. 26, 1939; d. Martin Luther and Elvie (Clinard) Dalton; m. Ronald A. Harris, June 15, 1967; children: Rhonda Lynn, Scott Eaton. BS, Berry Coll., Mt. Berry, Ga., 1961; MS, Ohio State U., 1962; PhD, U. Wis., 1967. Instr. Berry Coll., 1962-63; rsch. asst. U. Wis., Madison, 1963-66, lectr., 1966-71; asst. prof. food sci. Fla. State U., Tallahassee, 1971-74, assoc. prof., 1975-86, prof., 1986—. Co-author: Meal Management, 1984; contbr. rsch. articles to profl. jours. Named an Outstanding Young Woman Am., 1961; Helena Chamberlain fellow Ohio State U., 1961. Mem. Inst. Food Technologists, So. Assn. Agrl. Scientists (exec. bd. 1974-83), Fla. Assn. Milk, Food and Environ. Scientists (exec. bd. 1988—), Southeastern Tchrs. Food and Nutrition (pres. 1983-84), Springtime Tallahassee, Sigma Xi (pres local chpt. 1985-86), Alpha Chi. Democrat. Baptist. Office: Fla State U Dept Nutrition & Food Sci Tallahassee FL 32312-9797

HARRIS, RHONDA ELAINE, environmental engineer, consultant; b. Oklahoma City, Feb. 20, 1957; d. James Raymond and Bobbye (Richey) H.; m. Paul Alton Roach, Mar. 13, 1993. BS in Civl Engring., U. Tex., 1984; MBA, So. Methodist U., 1989. Environ. engr. Camp Dresser & McKee Inc., Dallas, 1984-91, EPA, Dallas, 1991-93; mgr. KPMG Peat Marwick, Dallas, 1993-94; pres. Profl. Opers., Inc., Plano, Tex., 1994—. Contbr. articles to profl. jours. Mem. Plano (Tex.) 1000, 1992, Trinity River Corridor Improvement Com., Dallas, 1996. Recipient Jack Huppert award Soc. Mexicana de Agua, A.C., 1994. Mem. Am. Water Works Assn., Water Environment Assn. Tex. (pres. 1996—), Water Environment Fedn. (bd. dirs. 1990-93, v.p. 1996-97, svc. award 1989, 93). Home: 1509 Livingston Dr Plano TX 75093

HARRIS, ROBERTA LUCAS, social worker; b. St. Louis, Nov. 13, 1916; d. Robert Joseph and Clara Louise (Mellor) Lucas; AB, St. Louis U., 1955, MSW, 1964; m. William F. Sprengnether Jr., Aug. 21, 1937 (dec. 1951); children: Robert Lucas, Madelon Sprengnether Littlejohn, Ronald John; m. Victor B. Harris, Sept. 13, 1955 (dec. June 1960). Field instr. Sch. Social Work St. Louis U., 1967-70; chief of domestic rels. City of St. Louis, 1966-86. Dir., Citizens' Housing Coun., 1956-60; del. to Community Family Life Clinic, 1957; dir. Landmarks Assn., 1957-63; pres. Compton Heights Improvement Assn., 1973, bd. dirs., 1994—; hon. mem. Normandy Hist. Assn., 1995; bd. mem. Compton Heights Assn., 1995—. NIMH grantee. Mem. NASW, Mo. Assn. Social Workers, Assn. Family Conciliation Cts. (dir. 1968-86), Greater St. Louis Probation and Parole Assn. (sec. 1976), St. Louis U. Sch. Social Svc. Alumni Assn. (sec. 1973), LWV (dir. 1956-61), Wednesday Club. Methodist. Home: 3137 Longfellow Blvd Saint Louis MO 63104-1609

HARRIS, ROSEMARY ANN, actress; b. Ashby, Eng., Sept. 19, 1930; d. Stafford Berkley and Enid (Campion) H.; m. Ellis Rabb, Dec. 4, 1959 (div. 1967); m. John Ehle, Oct. 21, 1967; 1 child, Jennifer. Student, Royal Acad. Dramatic Art, 1951-52; hon. doctorate, Smith Coll., 1969, Wake Forest U., 1978. Theater debut in Winter Sunshine, Bognar Regis, Eng., 1948; Broadway debut in Climate of Eden, N.Y.C., 1952; other theatrical appearances include Seven Year Itch, London, 1953, various Shakespearean and other roles, Bristol Old Vic, 1954-55, London Old Vic, 1955-56, 1963, 1964, Interlock, N.Y.C., 1957, The Disenchanted, N.Y.C., 1958; with Group 20 Players, Wellesley, Mass., in Pygmalion, Much Ado About Nothing, Man and Superman, Peter Pan, 1958-59; The Tumbler, N.Y.C., 1960; Assn. Producing Artists Repertory Company, U. Mich., 1962-63, 1964, N.Y.C., 1964-67; Chichester (Eng.) Festival, 1963, 64; A Streetcar Named Desire, Merchant of Venice, N.Y.C., 1973, The Royal Family, N.Y.C., 1975, The New York Idea (Obie award), Three Sisters, 1977; The Seagull, N.Y. Shakespeare Festival, 1981; All My Sons, London, 1981; Heartbreak House, London, 1982, N.Y.C., 1983; A Pack of Lies, 1984; Hay Fever, Broadway, 1985-86, ; film appearances include Beau Brummell, 1954, The Shiralle, 1956, A Flea in Her Ear, 1967, Camelot, The Boys from Brazil, 1978, The Ploughman's Lunch, 1983; To the Lighthouse (Locarno Film Festival award 1983), Crossing Delancy, 1988, Tom and Viv, 1994 (Acad. award nominee for Best Supporting Actress 1995); TV appearances include series the Chisholms, 1979-80, Holocaust, 1978 (Golden Globe award), Profiles in Courage, A Dickens Chronicle, Athens Where The Theater Began, Blithe Spirit, Strange Interlude, 1988, Great Appearances: Old Reliable, 1988. Recipient Antoinette Perry award, 1966, for A Lion in Winter, 1984, for A Pack of Lies; Vernon Rice award, 1962; Theatre World award, 1953; Delia Austrian Drama League award, 1967; Obie award, 1961, 65; Whitbread award, 1965-67; London Evening Standard award, 1969; Outer Circle Critics award, 1972; Drama Desk award, 1971, 72, 76; Emmy award, 1976; Golden Globe award, 1978. Mem. Actors Equity Assn., AFTRA, Screen Actors Guild. Address: William Morris 1325 Ave of the Americas New York NY 10019-4001*

HARRIS, RUBY LEE, realtor; b. Booneville, Miss., Mar. 5, 1939; d. Carl Jackson and Gladys (Downs) Hill; m. Lee Kelly Harris, Apr. 21, 1962; children: Lee Kelly Jr., Bradford William. Student, N.E. Miss. Jr. Coll., Booneville, 1957-58, U. Ala., Tuscaloosa, 1958-59. Lic. real estate agt., Calif. Agt. Forest E. Olson, El Toro, Calif., 1974-76, Coldwell Banker, Mission Viejo, Calif., 1976-78, Associated Realtors, Mission Viejo, 1978—. Mem. Children's Home Soc. Calif., Mission Viejo, 1985-88, Boys and Girls Club Am., San Clemente, Calif., 1989-91, Capistrano, 1994-95; mem. election com. Orange County, Mission Viejo, 1974—. Mem. Nat. Assn. Realtors, Calif. Assn. Realtors, Saddleback Valley Bd. Realtors (bd. dirs. 1989). Republican. Office: Associated Realtors 25350 Marguerite Pky Mission Viejo CA 92692-2908

HARRIS, SHARI LEA, mathematics educator; b. Macon, Mo., May 17, 1964; d. Walter Edward and Darlene (Tipton) H. BSE in Math. Edn. cum laude, N.E. Mo. State U., 1986; MS in Applied Math., U. Mo., 1991. Cert. secondary math. tchr., Mo. Cons. micromputer lab. Northeast Mo. State U., Kirksville, 1982-84, tutor coll. algebra, 1984-85, instr. math. lab., 1985; teaching asst. U. Mo., Columbia, 1986-87, 89-91; math. tchr. Highland High Sch., Ewing, Mo., 1987-88; substitute tchr. Quincy (Ill.) Sr. High Sch., 1988-89; math. tchr. Kemper Mil. Acad., Boonville, Mo., 1990; instr. math. S.E. Mo. State U., Cape Girardeau, 1991—. John J. Pershing scholar Northeast Mo. State U., Kirksville, 1982-86. Mem. Math. Assn. Am., Nat. Coun. Tchrs. of Math., Kappa Mu Epsilon, Alpha Phi Sigma.

HARRIS, SHARON DENISE, writer, technical; b. Pine Bluff, Ark., Oct. 13, 1966; d. Ed Willie and Leola Brenetta (Jackson) H. BA, Ouachita Bapt. U., 1988. Sales svc. corr. Ctrl. Moloney Components, Pine Bluff, 1988-89; tech. writer I, II Alltel Info. Svcs., Little Rock, 1989-93; sr. tech. writer Alltel Info. Svcs., Atlanta, 1993—. Author: (play) Mama Bear, 1995; contbr. articles to profl. jours. Office: PO Box 922489 Norcross GA 30092

HARRIS, SHELLEY FOLLANSBEE, contracts administrator; b. Quantico, Va., Oct. 20; d. Lawrence Peyton and June Maynard (Trout) H. BS in Fine Arts, Towson State U., 1973. Surgeon's asst. Drs. Bennett, Johnson & Eaton, P.A., Balt., 1979-82; pers. adminstr., human resources specialist Legent, Vienna, Va., 1983-88; pers. cons. Snelling & Snelling, Vienna, 1988-89; acct. exec. Forbes Assocs., Inc., Annandale, Va., 1989-90; spl. projects adminstr. for dep. gen. counsel, contracts and legal divsn. Electronic Data Systems Corp., Herndon, Va., 1991—. Vol. scuba instr. asst., EDS Mentor Program, In Touch-EDS Friends of Viet Nam Vets, emergency rm. vol. Reston Hosp.; team capt. Walk for Wealth; cmty. rels. ambassador Bowl for Bus. Jr. Achievement; active Holiday LINCS family project, Holiday 1994-96. Recipient regional awards for paintings, regional and nat. awards for sales and mktg., also awards for community contbns. Mem. Artist's Equity. Episcopalian. Home: 851 Dogwood Ct Herndon VA 22070-5446

HARRIS, SHERYL O., nutritionist, consultant; b. Waco, Tex., Mar. 24, 1957; d. Alton C. and Ruth (Howlett) Olivero; m. James Edgar Harris, Aug. 29, 1955; 1 child, Crystel. BS, Tex. Christian U., 1979; MS, U. North Tex., 1996. Registered dietitian Commn. on Dietetic, registered sanitarian Tex. Bd. of Licensure Registration; lic. dietitian Tex. State Bd. Licensure of Dietitian. Pres. Nutrition Consulting Assoc., Ft. Worth, 1980—; regional mgr. Am. Med. Inter, Houston, 1982-86; corp. dietitian Nat. Heritage, Inc., Dallas, 1986-89; dir. corp. svcs. Retirement Corp. Am., Dallas, 1989-90; dir. nutrition svcs. Health Care Capital, Shreveport, La., 1990-94; coord. procurement Ft. Worth Ind. Schs., 1994—. Mem. Tex. Dietetic Assn., Ft. Worth Dietetic Assn. (dir. pub. rels. 1980-82), Alpha Kappa Alpha (pres. 1979-81), Phi Upsilon Omicron. Home: 124 Meadows Burleson TX 76028

HARRIS, SONDRA TRAXLER, auditor; b. Magee, Miss., Apr. 21, 1966; d. Windell Thellis and Barbara Ann (Gaskin) Traxler; m. Ronald Lane Harris, June 8, 1984; children: Rosha Diane, Dakota Ann. BSBA in Acctg., U. So. Miss., 1992. CPA. Tax auditor Miss. State Tax Commn., Jackson, 1993—; purchasing agt. Performance Evaluation & Expenditure Rev./Com. Miss. Legis., Jackson, 1993; owner Harris Acctg. Svcs., Forest, Miss., 1993—. Bd. dirs. Burns Comm. Ctr., Raleigh, Miss., 1992—.

HARRIS, STACY, print and broadcast journalist; b. Mpls.; d. LLoyd and Francine H. Student, Coll. of Emporia, Kans., 1969, Vanderbilt U., 1972; BA, U. Md., 1973. Regular contbr. Country Song Roundup, Derby, Conn., 1976-92; interim Nashville editor Country Song Roundup, Derby, 1978-79, Newsweek mag., N.Y.C., 1983—; writer Sta. ABC Radio News, N.Y.C., 1986—, SDX Gridiron Show, Nashville, 1990—. Author: (children's books) Comedians of Country Music, 1978, The Carter Family, 1978, The Best of Country, 1993; editor Country Spirit 1990—; contbg. author, rschr. Country Music Stars and the Supernatural, 1978-79; contbg. editor Inside Country Music, 1981-83; columnist Stacy on Line, for Country on Line, Internet, 1995—; contbr. articles to Nashville Banner, US, New Woman, Entertainment Weekly and other publs. Arbitrator Better Bus. Bur., Nashville, 1988. Recipient Voice of Democracy award VFW, 1969, Outstanding Teenager award, 1970. Mem. Nat. Entertainment Jounalists Assn. (pres. 1989), Country Music Assn., Soc. Profl. Journalists, Nat. Press Club, Music Country PC Users Group, Williamson County Human Assn. (now Animaland) (vol. 1988—), Am. Mensa Ltd. Home and Office: The Windsor Tower 4215 Harding Rd Nashville TN 37205-2016

HARRIS, STEPHANIE FRANCES, health educator; b. Port Jefferson Station, N.Y., Feb. 27, 1967; d. Edmund Anthony and Barbara Elaine (Grodman) Franchi; m. Craig Matthew Murphy-Harris, Sept. 27, 1992. BA in Health Psychology, Pa. State U., 1989; MS in Health Edn., Am. U., 1991. Aerobics instr. Pa. State Health Club, State College, 1987-89; promotion dir. Pa. State Student Health Ctr., State College, 1988-89; health fitness specialist U.S. Postal Svc. Wellness Ctr., Washington, 1989-90; program mgr. Wellness Ctr. The Am. U., Washington, 1990-91; asst. dir. Wellness Coun. of the Piedmont, Greensboro, N.C., 1991-93; site supr. Wellness Ctr. Glaxo-Wellcome, Inc., Research Triangle Park, N.C., 1993-94; corp. health rep. Rex Wellness Ctr., Raleigh, N.C., 1994-96; asst. dir. Wellness Coun. N.C., 1996—; bus. and industry com. mem. Pres. Coun. on Phys. Fitness and Health, Raleigh, 1991—; planning com. mem. N.C. Health Promoters Network, Chapel Hill, N.C., 1994-95; cons., instr. Orange County Sch. Dist.-Dept. Continguing Edn., Chapel Hill, 1995—. Vol. Coun. for Sr. Citizens, Durham, N.C., 1993—. Mem. Assn. for Worksite Health Promotion (chairperson 1994—), Nat. Wellness Assn. Home: 181 Wendover Rd Asheville NC 28806

HARRIS, SUSAN LOUISE, financial services company executive. AB, UCLA, 1978; JD, U. So. Calif., 1981. Bar: Calif. 1981. Assoc. Lillick, McHose & Charles, 1981-85; sr. v.p., gen. counsel corp. affairs, sec. SunAmerica, Inc., L.A., 1985—. Office: SunAmerica Inc 1 Sun America Ctr Los Angeles CA 90067-6121

HARRIS, TERESA MARIA, visual artist; b. St. Louis, Dec. 20, 1957; d. Singleton Levi and Josie Bernice (Watkins) H. BFA, Washington U., St. Louis, 1975; MA, Fontbonne Coll., 1981; MFA, Pratt Inst., 1990. Cert. elem. and secondary sch. tchr., Mo. Art tchr. Christensted Bd. of Edn., St. Croix, V.I., 1975-76, St. Louis Bd. of Edn., 1976-87, 88-89; art tcht. Newark Mus./Rutgers U., 1995—, Jersey City (N.J.) State Coll., 1996—; prof. art Passaic County Cmty. Coll., Paterson, N.J., 1996—; art tchr., cons. Jamaica Arts Ctr., 1992—, Bronx Coun. on the Arts, 1990-95, Children's Arts Carnival, N.Y.C., 1991-92, Bklyn. Arts and Cultural Assn., Bklyn., 1990-91. One-woman shows include Sunshine Inn Restaurant, 1980, Vaughn Cultural Ctr., 1989; exhibited in group shows at Kimberly Gallery, 1976, Fontbonne Coll., 1981, U. Mo., 1982, Webster Coll., 1984, Florissant Valley Cmty. Coll., 1984, Ridge Street Gallery, 1991, L.I. City Artlofts, 1992, Citicorp Bldg., Cmty Showcase Gallery, 1992, Art in General, 1994; contbr. articles to profl. jours. Individual artist grant N.Y. Dept. of Cultural Affairs, 1995; fellowship Nat. Endowment for the Humanities, 1980. Mem. Jamaica Co-op, Coll. Arts Assn. Home: 24 Mill St Apt 111 Paterson NJ 07501

HARRIS, VERA EVELYN, personnel recruiting and search firm executive; b. Watson, Sask., Can., Jan. 11, 1932; came to U.S., 1957; d. Timothy and Margaret (Popoff) H.; student U. B.C. (Can.), Vancouver; children—Colin Clifford Graham, Barbara Cusimano Page. Office mgr. Keglers, Inc., Morgan City, La., 1964-67; office mgr., acct. John L. Hopper & Assos., New Orleans, 1967-71; office mgr. Elite Homes, Inc., Metairie, La., 1971-73; comptroller Le Pavillon Hotel, New Orleans, 1973-74; controller Waguespack-Pratt, Inc., New Orleans, 1974-76; adminstrv. controller Sizzler Family Steak Houses of So. La., Inc., Metairie, 1976-79; dir. adminstrn. Sunbelt, Inc., New Orleans, 1979-82, sec., dir., 1980—; exec. v.p. Corp. Cons., Inc., 1980-83, pres., 1984-86; pres. Harris Personnel Resources, Arlington, Tex., 1986—, Harris Enterprises, Arlington, 1986—, Harris Personnel Resources Health Staff, Arlington, 1990—; exec. dir. Nat. Sizzler Franchise Assn., 1976-79. Mem. NAFE, Am. Bus. Women's Assn., La. Assn. Personnel Consultants (treas. 1985-86), Indep. Recruiters Group, Soc. Exec. Recruiters. Home: 3110 Waterside Dr Arlington TX 76012-2123 Office: Harris Personnel Resources 2201 N Collins St Ste 260 Arlington TX 76011-2653

HARRIS, VIRGINIA SYDNESS, publisher, educator; b. Fargo, N.D., Oct. 24, 1945; d. Kenneth Jeffries and Jeanette Lucille (Dunkirk) Sydness; m. Granville Reed Harris, Dec. 29, 1966; children: G. Richard, Donald Thomas, Steven Jeffrey. BS in Polit. Sci. and Edn., Moorhead State U., 1967; CSB (hon.), Mass. Metaphysical Coll., 1982; postgrad., Principia Coll., Elsah, Ill., Mills Coll. Owner Edgewater Inn & Marina, Detroit Lakes, Minn., 1966-70; asst. to presdl. interpreter U.S. Dept. State, Washington, 1967-68; sec. sch. tchr. Fargo (N.D.) Pub. Schs., 1968-70; TV host, prodr. Pub. Broadcast Sys., Fargo, 1968-70; Christian Sci. tchr., 1982—, Christian Sci. lectr., 1983-89; faculty mem. Healing & Spirituality Symposium Harvard Med. Sch. and New Eng. Deaconess Hosp., Boston, 1995—. Contbr. articles to profl. jours.; spkr. in field. Bd. dirs. LWV, Fargo, 1968-73, YWCA, Fargo, 1969-73; clk. Christian Sci. Ch., Boston, 1986-90, bd. dirs., 1990—; treas., bd. dirs. Nat. Found. Women Legislators, Inc., Washington, 1994—. Mem. AAUW, PEO, Jr. League Boston (cmty. chmn.), Wellesley Coll. Club, City Club Washington. Home: 111 Bogle St Weston MA 02193 Office: The First Ch of Christ Scientist 175 Huntington Ave A253 Boston MA 02115

HARRIS-OFFUTT, ROSALYN MARIE, psychotherapist, counselor, nurse anesthetist, educator, author; b. Memphis; d. Roscoe Henry and Irene Elnora (Blake) Harris; 1 child, Christopher Joseph. R.N., St. Joseph Catholic Sch. Nursing, Flint, Mich., 1965; B.S. in Wholistic Health Scis., Columbia-Pacific U., 1984, postgrad., 1985—. RN; cert. registered nurse in anesthesia; nat. bd. cert. addiction counselor; cert. psychiat. nursing Kalamazoo State Hosp.; lic. profl. counselor, N.C.; cert. detoxification acupuncturist; Staff nurse anesthetist, clin. instr. Cleve. Clinic Found., 1981-82; pvt. practice psychiat. nursing and counseling; Assoc. Counselor in Human Services, Shaker Heights, Ohio, 1982-84; ind. contractor anesthesia Paul Scott & Assocs., Cleve., 1984, Via Triad Anesthesia Assocs., Thomasville, N.C., 1984-85; sec. Cons., Psychology and Counseling, P.A., pvt. practice psychiat. nursing and counseling, Greensboro, N.C., 1984-86, pvt. practice psychiat. nursing, counseling and psychotherapy UNA Psychol. Assocs., 1986—, staff cons. Charter Hills Psychiat. Hosp. in Addictive Disease, 1991—; nat. resource cons. Am. Assn. Nursing Anesthetists on Addictive Disease; cons. Ctr. for Substance Abuse Prevention, also adviser to assoc. and clin. med. dir. Ctr. Substance Abuse Prevention. Co-sponsor adolescent group Jack and Jills of Am., Inc., Bloomfield Hills, Mich., 1975; co-sponsor Youth of Unity Ctr., Cleveland Heights, Ohio, 1981-84; vol. chmn. hospitality Old Greensboro Preservation Soc., 1985; bd. dirs. Urban League, Pontiac, Mich., 1972; apptd. mem. gov's. coun. on alcohol and other drug abuse State of N.C., 1989—, gov's. coun. women's issues of addiction, 1991—; apptd. adviser to assoc. clin., med. dir. Ctr. for Substance Abuse Prevention, Dept. Health and Human Svcs. U.S., 1991—, nat. speakers bureau, 1991—, cons.; apptd. legis. com., mental health study commn. on child and adolescent substance abuse State of N.C., 1992—; lay speaking min. United Meth. Ch.; mem. Triad United Meth. Native Am. Ch. Mission . Columbia-Pacific U. scholar, 1983. Contbr. chpt. to book, also articles and columns in health field. Fellow Soc. Preventitive Nutritionists; mem. Am. Assn. Profl. Hypnotherapists (registered profl. hypnotherapists, adv. bd.), Am. Assn. Nurse Anesthetists (cert.), Nat. Alaska Native Am. Indian Nurses Assn., Assn. Med. Educators and Rsch. in Substance Abuse, Nat. Acupuncture Detoxification Assn., Am. Assn. Counseling and Devel., Assn. for Med. Edn. and Rsch. in Substance Abuse, Am. Assn. Clin. Hypnotists, Am. Assn. Wholistic Practitioners, Am. Nurse Hypnotherapy Assn. (state pres. 1992—), Am. Nurse Assn., Am. Holistic Nurses Assn. (charter mem.), Guilford Native Am. Assn., Negro Bus. and Profl. Women Inc. (v.p., parliamentarian 1961-83), Oakland County Council Black Nurses (v.p. 1970-74), Assn. Med. Educators (researcher substance abuse, ad hoc com. mem. cultural diversity 1994—), Zeta Phi Beta (Nu Xi Zeta chpt. 2d anti-basilevs 1992-93). Republican. Avocations: music, nature, reading, Egyptian history, metaphysics. Office: UNA Psychol Assocs 620 S Elm St Ste 371 Greensboro NC 27406-1371

HARRISON, ANNA JANE, chemist, educator; b. Benton City, Mo., Dec. 23, 1912; d. Albert S.J. and Mary (Jones) H. Student, Lindenwood Coll., 1929-31, L.H.D. (hon.), 1977; A.B., U. Mo., 1933, B.S., 1935, M.A., 1937, Ph.D., 1940, D.Sc. (hon.), 1983; D.Sc. (hon.), Tulane U., 1975, Smith Coll., 1975, Williams Coll., 1978, Am. Internat. Coll., 1978, Vincennes U., 1978, Lehigh U., 1979, Hood Coll., 1979, Hartford U., 1979, Worcester Poly. Inst., 1979, Suffolk U., 1979, Eastern Mich. U., 1983, Russell Sage Coll., 1984, Mt. Holyoke Coll., 1984, Mills Coll., 1985; L.H.D. (hon.), Emmanuel Coll., 1983; D.H.L., St. Joseph Coll., 1985, Elms Coll., 1985, R.I. Coll., 1990. Instr. chemistry Newcomb Coll., 1940-42, asst. prof., 1942-45; asst. prof. chemistry Mt. Holyoke Coll., 1945-47, asso. prof., 1947-50, prof., 1950-76, prof. emeritus, 1979—, chmn. dept., 1960-66, William R. Kenan, Jr. prof., 1976-79; Mem. Nat. Sci. Bd., 1972-78; Disting. Vis. prof. U.S. Naval Acad., 1980. Author: (textbook with Edwin S. Weaver) Chemistry: A Search to Understand, 1989; contbr. articles to profl. jours. Recipient Frank Forrest award Am. Ceramic Soc., 1949; James Flack Norris award in chem. edn. Northeastern sect. Am. Chem. Soc., 1977; AAUW Sarah Berliner fellow Cambridge U., Eng., 1952-53; Am. Chem. Soc. Petroleum Research Fund Internat. fellow NRC Can., 1959-60; recipient Coll. Chemistry Tchr. award Mfg. Chemists Assn., 1969. Mem. AAAS (dir. 1979-85, pres. 1983, chmn. bd. 1984-85), Am. Chem. Soc. (chmn. divsn. chem. edn. 1971, pres. 1978, dir. 1976-79, award in chem. edn. 1982), Internat. Union Pure and Applied Chemistry (U.S. nat. com. 1978-81), Vols. in Tech. Assistance (bd. dirs. 1990-94), Sigma Xi (bd. dirs. 1988-91). Address: 14 Ashfield Ln South Hadley MA 01075-1321

HARRISON, BETTINA HALL, biology educator; b. Foxboro, Mass.; d. Malcolm Bridges and Rita Louise (Busiere) Hall; m. John W. Harrison, July 12, 1941 (dec.); children: John W., Deborah, Christine. BS, U. Mass., 1939; AM, Radcliffe Coll., 1940; PhD, Boston U., 1968. Faculty Lasell Jr. Coll., Auburndale, Mass., 1940-41, 52-56, Maine Mills Lab., 1941-43, 49-51; with Cen. Main Hosp., 1943-45; faculty biology U. Mass., Boston, 1967—. Contbr. articles to profl. jours. Named Outstanding Tchr., U. Mass./Boston, 1986. Mem. Am. Soc. Cell Biology, N.Y. Acad. Sci., New Eng. Soc. Electron Microscopy (pres. 1963-64), AAAS, Internat. Soc. for Development and Comp. Immunology. Home: 19 Priscilla Ln Medford MA 02155

HARRISON, BETTY CAROLYN COOK, vocational educator, administrator; b. Cale, Ark., Jan. 11, 1939; d. Denver G. and Minnie (Haddox) Cook; m. David B. Harrison, Dec. 31, 1956; children: Jerry David, Phyllis Lynley. BSE, Henderson State Tchrs. Coll., Arkadelphia, Ark., 1961; MS, U. Ark., 1971; PhD, Tex. Agrl. and Mech. U., 1975. Tchr. secondary schs., McCrory, Ark., 1962-64, Taylor, Ark., 1964-69, Shongaloo, La., 1969-73, Minden, La., 1974-76, 77-80; adminstrv. intern La. Dept. Edn., 1974; cooperating tchr., supr. student tchrs. Grambling (La.) State U., 1974-76, La. Tech. U., Ruston, 1974-76, 78-80; asst. prof. vocat. edn. Va. Poly. Inst. and State U., Blacksburg, 1976-77; asst. prof. vocat. edn. Coll. Agr., La. State U., Baton Rouge, 1980-85, assoc. prof. Sch. Vocat. Edn., 1985-90, prof. vocat. edn., 1990—, sect. leader home econs. edn., 1982-85, head dept. home econs. edn. and bus. edn., 1985-87, dir. La. Job Link Ctr., 1988-91; dir. Sch. of Vocat. Edn., 1993-94, grants U.S. Office of Edn., La. Dept. of Edn., U.S. Dept. of Labor-Job Tng. Ptnrship. Act, La. Dept. of Employment and Tng., Va. Dept. of Edn.; mem. La. State U. Grad. Coun., 1990—, courses and curriculum sch. and coll., 1989-92. Contbr. articles to profl. jours. HEW fellow, 1973; grantee Future Homemakers Am., 1956, Coll. Acads., 1956, Ark. Edn. Assn., 1966-69, Internat. Paper Co., 1966-68, La. Dept. Edn., 1972. Mem. Assn. Tng. Devel. (v.p. communication 1991-92, sec. 1993-94), Am. Vocat. Assn. (regional pub. rels. voting del.), Nat. Assn. Vocat. Spl. Needs Personnel, Am. Vocat. Edn. Rsch. Assn., Am. Home Econs. Assn., La. Home Econs. Assn. (bd. dirs., pres.-elect), La. Vocat. Assn. (bd. dirs.), La. Assn. Vocat. Home Econs. Tchrs. (pres.), Nat. Assn. Vocat. Home Econs. Tchrs., Nat. Assn. Vocat. Home Econs. Tchr. Educators (newsletter editor), Home Econs. Edn. Assn. (regional dir., nat. v.p., editor and chair publs. 1987-93), NEA (nat. assembly del.), Family Relations Council La. (edn. chmn. officer), Phi Delta Kappa, Delta Kappa Gamma (chpt. v.p., rsch. chair 1978-86), Gamma Sigma Delta (historian, sec., treas. 1984-93). Democrat. Baptist. Home: 2100 College Dr Apt 157 Baton Rouge LA 70808-1810 Office: La State U Sch Vocat Edn Baton Rouge LA 70803

HARRISON, BRENDA ENGLISH, newspaper editor; b. Florence, S.C., Mar. 13, 1951; d. Ernest Rob and Christine Rosetti (Jackson) English; m. Daniel Joe Wells, July 25, 1969 (div. Aug. 1986); m. Henry Edward Harrison, May 1, 1994; 1 stepchild, Allison Harrison. Librarian Florence (S.C.) Morning News, 1967, reporter, 1980-86, society editor, 1986-88; editor The News Journal, Florence, S.C., 1988—. Bd. dirs. Florence Area Literacy Coun., 1981-90, Florence Civic Ballet Co., 1991-93, Florence Little Theatre, 1988-94; treas. Area Rescue Mission, 1991-96. Named Newspaper Reporter of the Yr., Francis Marion Coll., Florence, 1989; recipient S.C. Media awards, S.C. Alliance for the Mentally Ill, 1992, 93. Home: 1774 Woods Dr Florence SC 29505

HARRISON, CAROL LOVE, fine art photographer; b. Washington, Mar. 4, 1950; d. Hunter Craycroft and Margaret Varina (Edwards) H.; m. Gregory Grady, Feb. 25, 1978; children: Olivia Love Harrison, Blake McGregor, Harrison Edwards. BS in Fgn. Svc., Georgetown U., 1973; MFA, U. Md., 1983. guest lectr. art George Mason U., 1986, 87; participant creative program Fairfax County Coun. of Arts, 1990-92; participant artist workshop program Va. Mus. Fine Arts, Richmond, 1988-89. One-woman shows include Rizzoli Internat. Bookstore and Gallery, Washington, 1982, Arnold and Porter, Washington, 1983, Covington and Burling, Washington, 1983, Crowell and Moring, Washington, 1984, Nat. Strategy Info. Ctr., Washington, 1984, Swidler and Berlin, Washington, 1985, Reynolds Minor Gallery, Richmond, Va., 1987, Peninsula Fine Arts Ctr., Newport News, Va., 1989, Georgetown U., Washington, 1994; represented in permanent collections at Corcoran Gallery Art, Washington, Va. Mus. Fine Arts, Richmond, Arnold and Porter, Williams Cos., Tulsa, Covington and Burling, United Va. Bank; photographs exhibited in Art Gallery of U. Md., Smithsonian Instn., Washington Women's Art Ctr., pub. in Antietam Rev., Washington Rev., Photo Rev., Washingtonian, Profiles; represented by Reynolds Gallery. Vol. Woods Acad., Bethesda, Md., 1995-96, Our Lady of Victory Sch., Washington, 1995-96. Mem. Congl. Country Club, Langley Swim and Tennis Club. Episcopalian. Home and Office: 666 Live Oak Dr Mc Lean VA 22101

HARRISON, CHRISTINE DELANE, educational administrator; b. Dearborn, Mich., July 22, 1947; d. Walter Frederick and Marguerite Elaine (Champagne) Hancock; m. Charles Richard Bashawaty, Aug. 31, 1968 (div. 1972); 1 child, Brett Charles; m. Andrew David Harrison, June 14, 1980; 1 child, Andrew David, II. BS, Ea. Mich. U., 1969. Cert. early elem. tchr., Mich. Tchr. Westland Schs., Mich., 1969-71, Dept. Army, Ansbach, Germany, 1971-72; prin. sec. chemistry dept. U. Mich., Ann Arbor, 1973-78; word processing mgr. Great Copy Co., Ann Arbor, 1978-79; dir., v.p. Great Lakes Sch., Madison Heights, Mich., 1979-92; v.p., adminstrn. asst., Good Herbs, Inc., 1992—. Editor: Thorne's Guide to Herbal Extracts, 1992, A Practical Guide to Herbal Extracts, 1995; editl. asst. Herbal Extracts, 1984; Bull. of Thermodynamics and Thermochemistry, 1973-78. Bd. dirs. Perry Nursery Sch., Ann Arbor, 1976-77. Recipient Prodn. award and Dedication award Los Feliz Apple Sch. Mem. Nat. Trust for Hist. Preservation, Greenpeace, Sierra Club. Avocations: reading, bicycling, aerobics, sailing. Office: Good Herbs Inc 1875 Woodslee Dr Troy MI 48083-2234

HARRISON, DENISE LEE, editor; b. Washington, Aug. 3, 1960; d. David Ellis and Marlene Ann (Robertson) Lee; m. Charles Robert Harrison Jr., June 29, 1985. BA, U. Md., 1983; MLA, Johns Hopkins U., 1995. Editor Johns Hopkins U., Balt., 1986—, sr. publs. editor, 1990-94; writing intern TRAC, Washington, 1983; writing intern adviser Inst. Internat. Programs, Sch. Hygiene and Pub. Health Johns Hopkins U., 1986-94, internat. visitor and workshop coord. Book reviewer The Daily Record Newspaper, 1986. English tutor U. Md., Catonsville, 1980-83; newsletter editor Kensington Improvement Assn., Balt., 1991-93. Mem. Johns Hopkins Women's Forum, Omicron Delta Kappa (sec. 1981), Sigma Pi Tau (sec. 1982). Office: Johns Hopkins U Ctr Human Nutrition Sch Hygiene & Pub Health 615 N Wolfe St Baltimore MD 21205-2103

HARRISON, ELIZABETH ANN, elementary school educator; b. Iola, Kans., Nov. 10, 1948; d. Ed Lee and Thelma Lorraine (Cheney) Honeycutt; m. Charles Edward Harrison, July 7, 1979; children: Candace Leeann, Mary Elisabeth. AA, Allen County C.C., Iola, 1968; BS, Kans. State Tchrs. Coll., 1970, MS, 1971. Tchr. reading Boys Indsl. Sch., Topeka, Kans., summer 1971; tchr. 4th grade Shawnee Mission Schs., Shawnee, Kans., 1971-74, tchr. 2d grade, 1974-75, Title I reading tchr., 1975-78; dist. reading tchr. Shawnee Mission Schs., Lenexa, Kans., 1978-79, tchr. 3d grade, 1983-87, tchr. 5th grade, 1987—; cons. Reading and Lang. Coun., Shawnee Mission, Kans., 1993-95, Team Approach to Better Schs., Lenexa, 1987-94. Youth advisor NAACP, Shawnee Mission, 1994—; tutoring coord. Saturday Sch., Second Bapt. Ch., Argentine, Kans., 1974-94; tchr. rep. PTA, Lenexa, 1983-94; prin. Sch. Christian Edn., 1974—. Recipient Excellence in Edn. award Commerce Bank, Lenexa, 1992, Cmty. Svc. award U.S. Dept. Health and Human Svcs., 1991, Don Bosco Ctr., Kansas City, Mo., 1993, USMCR Toys for Tots, Shawnee Mission, 1994; named nominee for Phoebe Apperson Hearst Outstanding Educator award Nat. PTA, 1994-96. Mem. NEA, Alpha Delta Kappa (v.p. 1996—). Home: 5102 Mansfield Ln Shawnee KS 66203 Office: Mill Creek Elementary Sch 13951 W 79th St Lenexa KS 66215-2410

HARRISON, H. SHIRLEY, retired social worker; b. McKeesport, Pa., Dec. 7, 1925; d. Jacob and Esther (Zolten) Perlstein; widowed; children: Michael Barry Rubin (dec.), Laurance Richard Rubin. BA, Duquesne U., 1963; MSW, U. Pitts., 1966. Rsch. asst. Alleghany County United Way, Pitts., 1966-67; social work cons. Pa. Dept. Health, Pitts., 1967-68; dir. spl. project Commn. on Alcohol and Drugs Abuse, Edmonton, Alta., Can., 1968-72; regional program specialist Divsn. Alcohol and Drug Abuse, St. Louis, 1973-77; West region mgr. Divsn. Alcohol and Drug Abuse, Kansas City, Mo., 1983-87; freelance cons. various agys. Kansas City, 1987-94. Mem. mayor's task force City of Kansas City, Mo., 1987-89; mem. alcohol adv. bd. Mo. Divsn. Alcohol and Drug, Kansas City, 1988-90, chair Nat. Coun. on Alcohol and Drug, 1992-93; chair state legis. com. Am. Assn. Ret. Persons, Mo., 1994-95, nat. legis. com., 1994-95, women's issues specialist, 1996—; chair Mo. Patient Care Rev. Found. Bd., Mo., 1995—; mem. Jackson County Mental Health Levy Bd., 1995—. Democrat. Home: # 317 210 W 100th Ter Kansas City MO 64114

HARRISON, HELEN RAY GRIFFIN, educator; b. Enterprise, Ala., Oct. 13, 1936; d. A. D. and Ethel (Hitchcock) Griffin; m. Burt P. Redmon, June 3, 1956 (div.); children: John Patrick, Michael Lee; m. Dan Albert Harrison, Nov. 19, 1982. BS in Edn., Troy State U., 1975, MS in Elem. Edn., 1979. Tchr. Enterprise (Ala.) Pub. Schs., 1975—. Dir. ch. baby nursery; sponsor guide dog for the sight-impaired. Mem. NEA, Ala. Edn. Assn., Enterprise Edn. Assn. Baptist. Home: 115 Kate St Enterprise AL 36330 Office: Rucker Blvd Elem Sch 209 Regency Dr Enterprise AL 36330

HARRISON, JOAN LYNN, art educator; b. Rockville Center, N.Y., Oct. 11, 1950; d. William T. and Vera A. (Hart) H.; m. Michael E. Ach, May 31, 1983; children: Emily, Chloe. BA in Fine Art, C.W. Post U., 1972, MA in Fine Arts, 1980. Graphic artist Sta. WPIX TV, N.Y.C., 1973, Sta. WOR TV, N.Y.C., 1974-75; adminstr. L.I. U. (C.W. Post U.), Brookville, N.Y., 1975-76, assoc. prof., 1986—; mem. media adv. bd. Pt. Washington (N.Y.) Pub. Libr.; interviewer; curator Photojournalism in the 80s catalog exhbn., 1985, Montage catalog exhbn., 1987; artist-in-residence Visual Studies Workshop, Rochester, 1988, Polaroid 20X24 Studio, N.Y.C., 1990, Kodak-Ctr. for Creative Imaging, Maine, 1991. Photographs exhibited in numerous shows. Faculty release grantee L.I. U., 1992-97. Mem. Friends of Photography, Photographic Resource Ctr. Democrat. Office: LI U CW Post Campus Art Dept Northern Blvd Brookville NY 11548

HARRISON, LOIS SMITH, hospital executive, educator; b. Frederick, Md., May 13, 1924; d. Richard Paul and Henrietta Foust (Menges) Smith; m. Richard Lee Harrison, June 23, 1951; children: Elizabeth Lee Boyce, Margaret Louise Wade, Richard Paul. BA, Hood Coll., 1945, MA, 1993; MA, Columbia U., 1946; LHD (hon.), Hood Coll., 1993. Counselor CCNY, 1945-46; founding adminstr., counselor, instr. psychology and sociology Hagerstown (Md.) Jr. Coll., 1946-51, registrar, 1946-51, 53-54, instr. psychology and orienta, 1954-56; registrar, instr. psychology, Balt. Jr. Coll., 1951-54; bus. mgr., acct. for pvt. med. practice Hagerstown, 1953—; trustee Washington County Hosp., Hagerstown, 1975—; chmn. bd. Washington County Hosp., 1986—; bd. dirs. Home Fed. Savs. Bank, Hagerstown, 1983—; speaker ednl. panels, convs. hosp. panels and seminars. Author: The Church Woman, 1960-65. Trustee Hood Coll., Frederick, 1972—, chmn. bd., 1979—; mem. Md. Gov.'s Commn. to Study Structure and Ednl. Devel. Commn., 1971-75; pres. Washington County Coun. Ch. Women, 1970-72; appointee Econ. Devel. Commn., County Impact Study Commn. Bd.; bd. dirs. Md. Hosp. Assn., Md. Chs. United, 1975—; chmn. bd. dirs. Md. Hosp. Edn. Inst., 1988—; pres. Ch. Consistory; chmn. Chesapeake Healthcare Forum, 1995—. Recipient Alumnae Achievement award Hood Coll., 1975, Washington County Woman of Yr. award, AAUW, 1984, Md. Woman of Yr. award, 1984, Md. Woman of Yr. award Francis Scott Key Commn. for Md.'s 350th Anniversary, 1984; named one of top 10 women Tri-State area, Herald-Mail Tri-State newspaper, 1990, Zonta Internat. Woman of Yr., 1994. Mem. Hagerstown C. of C. Republican. Home: 12835 Fountain Head Rd Hagerstown MD 21742-2748 Office: Washington Cty Hosp Off Chmn Bd Hagerstown MD 21740

HARRISON, MARSHA YARBERRY, volunteer; b. Pine Bluff, Ark., Feb. 12, 1949; d. Randle A. and Sara Ann (Lee) Yarberry; m. Preston E. Harrison Jr., June 24, 1971; children: Kristofer Lee, Robert Randle. BS in Therapeutic Recreation, Tex. Woman's U., 1970. Cert. recreation therapist. Activities dir. Treemont, Dallas, Albert Schweitzer Homes, Mpls. Bd. mem. East Tex. Symphony, Tyler, Jr. League Tyler, ARC, Tyler, Discovery Sci. Pl., Tyler, 1986—, United Way Tyler, 1992—, Boy Scouts of East Tex., Tyler, 1993—; pres. City Coun. PTA, Tyler, 1996—. Named Outstanding Vol., Jr. League of Tyler, 1990, Vol. of Yr., Tyler City, 1991. Mem. Tyler City Coun. PTAs (life). Home: 2104 Parkway Pl Tyler TX 75701

HARRISON, PATRICIA DE STACY, public relations consulting company executive; b. N.Y.C.; m. Emmett Bruce Harrison; 3 children. BA, Am. U., 1968; MA, George Mason U. V.p. Holly Realty Co., Arlington, Va., 1965-69; co-founder, ptnr. E. Bruce Harrison Co., Washington, 1973—; pres. AEF/Harrison Internat., Washington, 1973—; keynote spkr. U.S. Dept. Labor del. to Israel and Greece, Indsl. Devel. Authority of Ireland Conf./Women Execs. in Mgmt., U.S. Info. Agy./WorldNET program for entrepreneurs via satellite to 7 countries, Export Expo '90, Seattle, Nat. Govs. Conf., U.S. SBA Fin. Mgmt. Conf. in 9 states, mgmt. and tng. program for women entrepreneurs Budapest, Hungary (Alliance Decade for Democracy series); guest lect. Thomas Colloquium on Free Enterprise, 1989; trustee Guest Svcs., Inc.; mem. adv. coun. Avon Products, Inc. Author: Inside and Out: The Story of a Hostage, 1981, (with Margaret Mason, editor) The Washington Post Pocket Style Plus, 1983-84, America's New Women Entrepreneurs, 1986. Bd. dirs. Med. Coll. Pa. Recipient Librs.' and Tchrs.' award for play produced at Kennedy Ctr., 1980, Del. award Insieme per La Pace, Rome, 1988, Disting. Woman award Northwood Inst., 1991; named Washington Woman of Yr., Washington Women Mag., 1985, Entrepreneur of Yr., Washington, Arthur Young Co. and Venture mag., 1988, Women of Enterprise award. Mem. Nat. Women's Econ. Alliance Found., Pres.'s Export Coun., SBA Nat. Adv. Coun. (co-chmn., exec. com.), SBA Women's Network for Entrepreneurial Tng. (adv. coun.), Nat. Coal Coun. (exec. com.), Women in Internat. Trade, Nat. Fedn. Press Women (ex-officio, communication award 1979, bus. communicator of yr. 1988), Capital Press Women (ex-officio, named bus communicator of yr. 1988, journalist award for non-fiction 1988), Pub. Rels. Soc. Am. (counsellors acad.), Internat. Pub. Rels. Assn. Office: E Bruce Harrison Co 1440 New York Ave NW Ste 300 Washington DC 20005-2111*

HARRISON, SALLY LOUISE, educator, administrator, consultant; b. Wisconsin Rapids, Wis., May 7, 1951; d. Jackson and Lorraine Barbara Evelyn (Bishop) Burt; m. David John Harrison, June 12, 1972 (div. Feb. 1990); children: Jeffry, Bryan; m. Joseph Eugene Miller, July 22, 1992; children: Michael Miller, Jennifer Miller, Andrew Miller. BA in Edn., Ctrl. Wash. U., Ellensburg, 1972, MA in Edn., 1977; postgrad., Walden U., Mpls., 1995—. Cert. tchr., prin., Wash. Tchr. elem. and middle sch. West Valley Sch. Dsit., Yakima, Wash., 1973-86, gifted coord./adminstr., 1986-88; prin. South Whidbey Intermediate Sch., Langley, Wash., 1988-91, Dutch Hill Elem. Sch., Snohomish, Wash., 1991-93; performance standards mgr. Edmonds Sch. Dist., Lynnwood, Wash., 1993-94, dir. standards and assessment, 1994—; sr. assoc. Inst. for Peak Performing Schs., Greeley, Colo., 1992—; mem. grad. faculty Lesley Coll., Cambridge, Mass., 1995—; dir. Wash. Alliance Assessment Ctr., Shoreline, 1996—; mem. U.S. team to Internat. Systems Thinking Conversation, 1994. Contbr. Snohomish Edn. found., 1996, United Way, Seattle, 1990—. Goals 2000 grantee, 1995-96; Rachel Royston Found. scholar, 1996. Mem. ASCD, Internat. Reading Assn., Wash. Ednl. Rsch. Assn., Nat. Staff Devel. Coun. Office: Edmonds Sch Dist 20420 68th Ave W Lynnwood WA 98036

HARRISON, VIRGINIA FLORENCE, retired anatomist and educator, philanthropist; b. St. Louis, Mar. 15, 1918; d. George Benjamin and Florence Gertrude (McManus) H.; m. William Hector Marsh, Dec. 1, 1963 (dec. Dec.

1986); m. George William Elliott, Oct. 27, 1991; stepchildren: Carolyn Frances Roberts, George William II, Robert Bonner (dec. Apr. 1995), Cathrine Susan Dimino. BS, U. Wis., 1940, PhD, 1959; MA, Columbia U., 1944. Lectr. Columbia U., N.Y.C., 1943-46; asst. prof. Mary Washington Coll. of U. Va., Fredericksburg, 1946-48; asst. prof. Oreg. State U., Corvallis, 1948-50, assoc. prof., 1950-59; instr. Army Med. Acad./Brooks Army Med. Ctr., San Antonio, 1959-60, assoc. prof., 1960-64; vis. prof. U. Wash., Seattle, 1961; lectr. U. Tex. Med. Sch., Galveston, 1962-64, Hadassah Med. Sch., Hebrew U. of Jerusalem, 1965; lectr. grad. sch. U. Wis., Madison, 1964; pvt. practice stock mkt. investment lectr. Washington, 1969-83; cons. U. Tex. Med. Sch., 1962-64, U.S. Pentathlon Team, San Antonio, 1960-64, Dentists for Treatment of Pain from Muscular Tension, San Antonio, 1960-64. Contbr. articles to profl. jours. Bd. visitors Sch. Edn., U. Wis., Madison. Recipient Civilian Meritorious Svc. award U.S. Civil Svc., 1965; Amy Morris Homans fellow, 1958; hon. fellow U. Wis., 1956, 58, 59. Fellow AAHPERD, Tex. Acad. Sci.; mem. Am. Assn. Anatomists divs. Fedn. Am. Socs. for Exptl. Biology, Cosmos Club, Sigma Delta Epsilon, Pi Lambda Theta. Home: 6333 Cavalier Corridor Falls Church VA 22044-1301

HARRISON, WENDY JANE MERRILL, realtor; b. Waterbury, Conn., Dec. 4, 1961; d. David Kenneth and Jane Joy (Nevius) Merrill; m. Aidan T. Harrison; children: Christopher, Charlotte. BA in Journalism, George Washington U., Washington, 1981; MBA in mgmt., Cornell U., 1992. Intern in edn. HEW, Washington, summer 1978, writer, summer 1979; rsch. asst. dep. health svcs. adminstrn. George Washington U., Washington, 1979-81; sec. Nat. Assn. Beverage Importers, Washington, 1981; account exec. Staff Design, Washington, 1982; adminstrv. aide Internat. Food Policy Rsch. Inst., Washington, 1983-86; program assoc. Acad. for Ednl. Devel., Washington, 1986-87; pvt. practice cons. Washington, 1987-88; adminstrv. mgr. food and nutrition policy program Cornell U., Ithaca, 1988-92; cons. in mgmt. of med. practices Med. Bus. Mgmt., Ithaca, 1994-95; realtor Century 21 Alpha, 1995—; cons., editor George Washington U., 1986; cons., rapporteur Internat. Food Policy Restaurant Inst., Washington and Copenhagen, Denmark, 1987; cons., adminstr. Hansell & Post, Washington, 1987-88, Cornell U., Washington and Ithaca, 1988. Sponsor Worldvision, Tanzania, 1988-91. George Washington U. scholar, 1979-81. Mem. Milpitis Host Lions Club (2d v.p.), Sigma Delta Xi (scholar 1980). Democrat. Episcopalian. Home: 785 Heflin St Milpitas CA 95035

HARRISON-JONES, LOIS, school superintendent; b. Westmoreland County, Va., Apr. 30, 1934; widowed. BS in Elem. Edn., Va. State Coll., 1954; MS in Reading, Temple U., 1962; postgrad., Columbia U., 1964; postgrad. in adminstrn. and supervision, U. Va., 1967-68; EdD, Va. Tech., 1982; LLD (hon.), Mt. Ida Coll., 1992, New England Sch. of Law, 1994. Cert. elem. and middle sch. tchr., elem. supr., gen. supr., dir. instrn., asst. supt. instrn., Va., supt., Va., Mass. Tchr. Woodville Elem. Sch., 1954-59; consulting tchr. Richmond (Va.) Pub. Schs., 1959-61; asst. prin. Baker Elem. Sch., Richmond (Va.) Pub. Schs., 1961-67, prin., 1967-70; coord. student teaching and summer programs Richmond (Va.) Pub. Schs., 1970-73, dir. area II, 1973-76, asst. supt. elem. edn., 1976-81, asst. supt. elem. and secondary edn., 1981-83, asst. supt. elem. edn., 1983-85, supt., 1985-88; assoc. supt. ednl. svcs. Dallas Ind. Sch. Dist., 1988-90, dep. supt., 1990-91; supt. Boston Pub. Schs., 1991—; assoc. prof. grad. sch. edn. Harvard U., Cambridge, 1991—; mem. adjunct faculty U. Mass., Boston. Contbr. articles to profl. jours. Former chair bd. dirs. Math & Sci. Ctr., Richmond; former mem. Polit. Congress African-Am. Women, Dallas, Coalition of 100 Black Women, Richmond, Alpha Bettes, Richmond, Urban League, Richmond; former bd. dirs. YWCA, Richmond, United Way Greater Richmond, chmn. pers. com., Communities in Schs., Dallas, St. John Missionary Bapt. Ch., Dallas; past chmn. city/county govt. divsn. United Way Richmond, Henrico, Chesterfield, Hanover; former trustee Va. State U.; past chairperson bd. trustees Ebenezer Bapt. Ch., Richmond; alumna Dallas Opportunity; trustee Mus. Fine Arts, Boston; overseer Boston Sci. Mus. Recipient citation Newton (Mass.) Rotary Club, 1991, Proclamation award Tex. State Senate, 1991, Support citation Sarah Gorham Women's Missionary Soc. Charles St. AME Ch., 1991, Boston City Coun. Resolution, 1991, Ofcl. citation Senate Commonwealth Mass., 1991, Ofcl. citation Ho. Reps. Commonwealth Mass., award Congress Exemplary Supts., 1992, Disting. Women Leader Lecture Series award Greater Dallas C. of C., 1992, Pres. citation Alpha Kappa Alpha Sorority, 1992, ciation Mt. Zion Lodge, 1992, Appreciation award Project 2000 Boston Coll., 1992, citation Italian-Am. Com. Mass. Quincentennial Commn., 1992, cert. recognition Fed. Exec. Bd. Women's Opportunity Com., 1992, award Parent's and Children's Svcs., 1992, award Exec. Club Greater Boston C. of C., 1993, Outstanding Black Women of Yr. award Big Sister Assn. Greater Mass., 1993, Women of Courage and Conviction award Nat. Coun. Negro Women, 1993, citation Boston Urban Bankers Forum, 1993, Truth award Nat. Sojourner, 1993, Dr. Martin Luther King, Jr. Leadership award, citation for commitment to Engring. Workforce for Future, 1993, Boston Urban Bankers edn. award, 1995; named Woman of Yr. Boston Network for Women in Politics and Govt., 1993. Mem. ASCD (former bd. dirs., former pubs. com., urban edn. adv. bd. critical issues com.), NAACP (former exec. com. Dallas and Richmond brs., Disting. Svc. award 1992), Va. Assn. Supervision and Curriculum Devel. (past pres.), Am. Assn. Sch. Adminstrs., Nat. Alliance Black Sch. Adminstrs. (pres. supts. commn.), Coun. Great City Schs., Mass. Assn. Sch. Supts. (Pres.'s award), Mass. Assn. Law Enforcement Officers (hon.), Richmond Travelers Aid Soc. (past pres., bd. dirs.), Continental Socs., Inc. (past pres.), Alpha Kappa (Alpha Xi Omega chpt.). Office: Boston Public Schools Office of Superintendent 26 Court St Boston MA 02108-2505

HARRSCH, PATRICIA EILEEN, nursing consultant; b. Niagara Falls, N.Y., Sept. 14, 1951; d. William Joseph and Jane Marie (Taylor) Russell; m. Keith Alan Harrsch, Aug. 13, 1988. ADN, Madison Area Tech. Coll., Wis., 1985; BSN, Edgewood Coll., 1987; BA Journalism, U. Wis., 1987, MSN, 1994. Nurse clin. II Mendota Mental Health Inst., Madison, 1986-91, U. Wis. Hosp. and Clins., 1991-94; diabetes support group leader U. Wis. Hosp. and Clinics, Madison, 1992-95; nurse cons. I Dept. Health and Social Svcs., Madison, 1994—. Mem. Am. Coll. Legal Medicine (Hirsch award 1993), ANA, Am. Diabetes Assn., Alliance for the Mentally Ill, Sigma Theta Tau (rsch. award 1992). Democrat. Unitarian Universalist. Home: 1151 Jenifer St Madison WI 53703 Office: Dept of Health and Family Svcs 111 West Wilson St Madison WI 53701

HARSIN, S(USAN) JILL, history educator; b. Indpls., Feb. 10, 1951; d. Charles Duane and Mary Margaret (Graham) H.; m. Briton Cooper Busch, June 4, 1985. BA, S.W. Mo. State U., 1973; MA, U. Iowa, 1975, PhD in History, 1982. Vis. asst. prof. Oberlin (Ohio) Coll., 1982-83; asst. prof. history Colgate U., Hamilton, N.Y., 1983-87, assoc. prof. history, 1988—, chmn. history, 1988-94. Author: Policing Prostitution in 19th Century Paris, 1985; contbr. articles to profl. jours. Mem. Am. Hist. Assn., French Hist. Soc., Western Soc. for French History, 18th Century Studies Assn., Soc. for Cinema Studies.

HART, CYNTHIA FAYE, elementary education educator; b. Orange, N.J., July 26, 1938; d. James Benjamin and Elizabeth (Massey) Kelly; m. Lionel DePau Hart, June 18, 1960 (div. Oct. 1975); 1 child, Kevin Blair. BS, Fairleigh Dickinson U., 1961; MA in Early Childhood, Kean Coll., 1996. Cert. elem. tchr., N.J. Tchr. Newark Bd. Edn., 1963—; mentor Camden St. Sch., Newark, 1994-95. V.p. Martin Luther King Jr. Civic, N.J., 1994—; lifetime mem. NAACP, Urban League. Recipient Recognition Resolution award City Coun. City Newark, 1992, 2d place Newark Bd. Edn. Math. Fair, 1992; named Outstanding Tchr. Martin L. King Jr. Civic, 1992. Mem. ASCD, ACEI, Assn. for Childhood Edn. Internat., Nat. Edn. Assn., Nat. Assn. of Colored Women's Clubs, Inc., N.J. State Fed. of Colored Women's Clubs, Inc., N.J. Chpt. Nat. Com. for Prevention of Child Abuse, Newark Early Childhood Educators Assn., N.J. Edn. Assn., Newark Tchrs' Assn., Federated Clubs Am., Kappa Delta Pi. Home: 55 Hillcrest Ter East Orange NJ 07018-2357

HART, ELLEN, writer; b. Mpls., Aug. 10, 1949; d. Herman Charles and Marjory Rowena (Anderson) Boehnhardt; life partner Kathleen Linda Kruger; children: Shawna Kruger Gibson, Bethany Kruger. BA, Ambassador U., 1972. tchr. The Loft, Mpls., 1995-96. Author: Hallowed Murder, 1989, Vital Lies, 1991, Stage Fright, 1992, A Killing Cure, 1993, A Small Sacrifice, 1994, This Little Piggy Went to Murder, 1995, For Every Evil, 1995, Faint Praise, 1995, Robbers Wine, 1996, The Oldest Sin, 1996. Mem. Sisters in Crime.

HART, ELSIE FAYE, elementary education educator; b. Shelbyville, Ill., Oct. 15, 1920; d. James Ray and Maude May (Allison) Cain; m. Harold Delbert Bible, June 15, 1941 (div. Apr. 1948); children: Gary H., Rex. E. (dec.); m. Frederick Christopher Hart, July 28, 1950 (dec. Dec. 1994); children: Susan Hart Eichman, Pamela L. Elem. teaching cert., Ea. Ill. U., 1942; BS in Edn., No. Ill. U., 1968; postgrad., Rockford Coll., 1972-73. Cert. elem. tchr., Ill. Tchr. Findlay (Ill.) Elem. Sch., 1942-47; tchr. Winnebago County Schs., Rockford, Ill., 1948-52, Rockford Parochial Schs., 1957-63; tchr. Rockford Pub. Schs., 1964-82, substitute tchr., 1982—. Author: The On and the Under Dog, 1992; contbr. articles to profl. jours. Pres. Assn. for Childhood Edn. Internat., Rockford, 1968-76; sec.-treas. Ill. Assn. for Supervision & Curriculum Devel., Rockford, 1970-80; mem. NEA, Ill. Edn. Assn., Rockford Edn. Assn., 1964-82; mem. Rockford Art Assn., 1968, Beta Sigma Phi, Rockford, 1950, Rockford Creative Dramatics Assn., 1968, Mauh-Nah-Tee See Country Club, Rockford, 1982; vol. tchr. Rockford Parochial schs. Recipient Cert. of Commendation in recognition of meritorious svc. Ill. Supt. Pub. Instrn., 1974; nominated Ill. Retired Tchrs. Hall of Fame. Mem. AAUW (historian Rockford chpt. 1970—), Ill. Ret. Tchrs. Assn., Winnebago/Boone Ret. Tchrs. Assn., Women of the Moose, Holy Family Women's Guild, Rockford Women's Club (sec. 1970, publicity com. 1971, membership com. 1972, ways/means com. 1988-91, bd. dirs. 1993-94, long-range planning com. 1994—, program com. 1994-95, dir. 1995-98), Nat. Women's Hall of Fame. Republican. Roman Catholic. Home: 1507 Al Crest Rd Rockford IL 61107-2125

HART, JANE SMITH, music educator; b. Rockwell City, Iowa, Sept. 4, 1913; d. Aleck Lewis and Jane Laura (Lewis) Smith; m. Leslie Alexander Hart, Nov. 21, 1942; children: Sara Jane, David Meade. Degree in music edn., Juilliard, 1938; MA in Music Edn., Columbia U., 1958. Music tchr. N.Y.C. Schs., 1941-42, Juliarichman H.S., 1941-42, H.S. of Homemaking, Bklyn., 1942-43, Trinity Elem. Sch., New Rochelle, N.Y., 1964-66, Barnard Sch. for Boys, Riverdale, N.Y., 1966-77, Horace Mann, Riverdale, N.Y., 1966-77, New Rochelle Pub. Libr. Concerts, 1978-90. Author: Singing Bee, 1982 (Parents' Choice Mag. award 1985). Mem. Westchester Musicians Guild, publicity chmn., 1981-96. Mem. LWV, Nat. League American Pen Women, N.Y. Women Composers, Authors of Am. Democrat. Unitarian. Home: 120 Pelham Rd Apt 6-C New Rochelle NY 10805

HART, JEAN HARDY, international business operations systems specialist, consultant; b. Cleve., Jan. 19, 1942; d. Gilbert Elliott and Jessie (Peterson) Brown; m. Richard Pierpont Thomas, June 16, 1962 (div. Sept. 1974); children: Perry Glenn, Geb Weller, Hans Richard; m. Howard Phillips Hart, Jan. 19, 1988; stepsons: Colin, Guy. BA, Goddard Coll., 1973. Tech. communications specialist The Mitre Corp., Boston, 1973-75; site adminstr., tech. communications expert The Mitre Corp., Madrid, 1975-77; mgr. internat. programs Honeywell Info. Systems, Newton, Mass., 1977-78; account mgr. sales and contracts Honeywell Info. Systems, 1978-79, tech. analyst, 1979-81; dist. mgr. Europe Honeywell Info Systems, 1981-84; mgr. third party svc. Honeywell Info. Systems, Boston, 1984-85, 85-86; resident mgr. Honeywell Info. Systems, Beijing, 1985; dir. fed. accounts Honeywell Info. Systems, McLean, Va., 1986-88; bus. advisor CIA, McLean, Va., 1989-90; dir. Hartwell Mgmt., Ltd. Internat. Strategic Info. Group, London and, Va., 1991—; internat. bus. cons. U.S. Govt., Washington, 1991—; info. profl. various cos., Washington, 1991—; lectr. numerous worldwide colls. and govt. orgns., 1968—; strategy cons. to provost Coll. Integrated Sci. and Tech., James Madison U., Harrisonburg, Va., 1992; cons. internat. bus. ops. Author, prodr. videotape Chief Justice Warren Burger, 1987; exec. prodr. videotape Exec. V.p. Reynolds Metals, 1993; editor-in-chief Bus. of Edn., 1995; contbr. articles to profl. jours. Mem. NAFE, AAUW, Am. Assn. Info. Profls., Am. Mgmt. Assn. Episcopalian. Home and Office: Hart Consultancy HCR 1 Box 131B Free Union VA 22940-9530

HART, JOAN LOUISE, adult education educator; b. Morristown, N.J., Jan. 22, 1949; d. Chauncey Edward and Elizabeth Louise (Laubenstein) H. BA in History/Art History, Hood Coll., Frederick, Md., 1971; MFA in Art History, Syracuse U., 1974. Park technician Morristown (N.J.) Nat. Park, 1971-72; with Employers Overload, Washington, 1975-78, 79-80; adminstrv. asst. Cultural Alliance, Washington, 1978-79, Signal Cos., Washington, 1980-81; adminstrv. asst. pers. Am. Coll. Obstetricians, Washington, 1981-82; exec. dir. Museum One, Inc., Washington, 1982—; rschr. hist. books Smithsonian Instn., Washington, 1975-76; rschr. edn. Am. Cmty. Svc. Network, Washington, 1990-94. Author: Beyond the Tunnel: Arts and Aging in America, 1992, Step by Step: Creating for Life, 1994. Syracuse U. Fine ARts Grad. fellow, 1973. Mem. Pilot Club (v.p. 1986-87). Home and Office: 35 Dover Chester Rd Randolph NJ 07869-1233

HART, KAREN JEAN, special education educator; b. Elizabeth, N.J., July 6, 1952; d. Santo Joseph and Florence (Machrone) Materia; m. Thomas Raymond Hart, June 28, 1975; children: Brian, Kimberly. BA, Kean Coll. of N.J., 1974, MA, 1981. Cert. elem. tchr. of reading, reading specialist, tchr. of handicapped and learning disabilities. Elem. tchr. Harding Sch., Kenilworth, N.J., 1970-74; adj. faculty Kean Coll., Union, N.J., 1981-87; supplemental instr. Bridgewater (N.J.) -Raritan, 1987-91; tchr. of the handicapped Somerset County Vo-Tech, Bridgewater, 1991—; yearbook fin. advisor Sch. Yearbook, 1993-95. Den leader Boy Scouts Am., Bridgewater, 1989-91, cubmaster, 1991-92, advancement chair, Martinsville, 1993-95; sec., cultural arts chair PTO, Bridgewater, 1991—. Recipient Citation State Legis., State of N.J., 1992. Mem. Coun. of Exceptional Children, Kappa Delta Pi, Phi Delta Kappa. Home: 282 Carber St Bround Brook NJ 08805 Office: Somerset County VoTech HS North Bridge and Vogt Bridgewater NJ 08807

HART, KITTY CARLISLE, arts administrator; b. New Orleans, Sept. 3, 1917; d. Joseph and Hortence (Holtzman) Conn; m. Moss Hart, Aug. 10, 1946 (dec. 1961); children: Christopher, Cathy. Ed., London Sch. Econs., Royal Acad. Dramatic Arts; DFA (hon.), Coll. New Rochelle; DHL (hon.), Hartwick Coll.; LHD (hon.), Manhattan Coll., Amherst Coll. Chmn. emeritus N.Y. State Council on the Arts. Former panelist: TV show To Tell the Truth; actress on stage and in films including The Marx Brothers A Night at the Opera, 1936; Broadway theatre appearance in On Your Toes, 1983-84; singer, Met. Opera, TV moderator and interviewer; author: (autobiography) Kitty, 1988; contbr. book revs. to jours. Assoc. fellow Timothy Dwight Coll. of Yale U.; bd. dirs. Empire State Coll.; formerly spl. cons. to N.Y. Gov. on women's opportunities; mem. vis. com. for the arts MIT. Recipient Nat. medal of Arts from Pres. Bush, 1991. Office: Arts Coun 915 Broadway Fl 8 New York NY 10010-7106

HART, LAUREN L., marketing executive; b. Providence, Jan. 30, 1952; d. Giovanni and Ruth Elsie (Schultheis) Luongo. BS, U. R.I., 1975, MS, 1981. Mktg. asst. Agawam Creative Mktg., Rowley, Mass., 1977-79; asst. sales & mktg. Ocean State Jobbers Inc., North Kingstown, R.I., 1979-81; rsch. assoc. U. R.I., Kingston, 1979-81; mktg. rep. lab supply & chem. sales Ea. Scientific Co., Providence, 1981-82; mktg. mgr., v.p. mktg., v.p. corp., ops. officer Alan's Bus. Machines Inc., Barre, Vt., 1983-89; chief exec. officer Continental Resource Group, Ltd., Barre, Vt., 1989—. Mem. NAFE, Women Bus. Owners Vt., Nat. Women Bus. Owners, AAUW (nat. and local), Inst. Food Technologists (Z John Ordahl award 1981), Advt./Image/Mktg. Assn. (pres. 1985-86, 92—), Ptnrs. of the Cornell Fine Arts Mus. (founding mem., chmn. pub. rels. 1990-91, pres. 1991-92),. Home: 7629 Hanover Way # 201 Oklahoma City OK 73132

HART, MARGARET ROGENE, journalist, consultant; b. Amsterdam, N.Y., Dec. 26, 1913; d. Edmond James and Rogene Margaret (Dougherty) H. BA, U. Albany, 1934; MA, Syracuse U., 1935. Lic. tchr. h.s., N.Y. Instr. Collegiate Ctr. Syracuse U., Rome, N.Y., 1936; tchr. Rome Pub. Schs., 1937-45; reporter Daily Sentinel, Rome, 1946-51, copyeditor, 1952-79, libr. cons., 1981-94; editing cons. 5 books on harness horse racing, 1969-81; editing cons. book on Adirondacks, 1982. Playwright: Wednesday Is the Best Day of the Week, 1992; author: (book sect.) Centennial History of Rome, N.Y., 1970; contbr. poetry to anthologies. Bd. dirs. United Way, Rome, 1985-88, Dollars for Scholars, Rome, 1990-96; trustee Rome Hist. Soc., Rome, 1984-87; tutor Literacy Vols. of Am., Utica and Rome, 1988-94. Recipient Gold award for svc. Rome United Way, 1989, commendation Civil Def. Coun., 1967. Mem. Nat. League Am. Pen Women (nat. chmn. grants for mature women 1992), Bus. and Profl. Women's Club (charter, Rose of Challenge 1977), Wednesday Morning Club Rome (pres. 1987-89). Roman Catholic. Home: 611 E Garden St Rome NY 13440-5305

HART, MARIAN GRIFFITH, retired reading educator; b. Bates City, Mo., Feb. 5, 1929; d. George Thomas Leon and Beulah Winiferd (Hackley) Griffith; m. Ashley Bruce Hart, Dec. 23, 1951; children: Ashley Bruce Hart II, Pamela Cherie Hart Gates. BS, Cen. Mo. State Coll., 1951; MA, No. Ariz. U., 1976. Title I-Chpt. I reading dir. Page (Ariz.) Sch. Dist.; Title I dir. Johnson O'Malley Preschool, Page Sch. Dist.; dist. reading dir. Page Sch. Dist.; bd. dirs. Lake Powell Inst. Behavioral Health Svcs., sec., 1993-95, mem. fin. com., 1995—. Author: Calculateurs Analogiques Répétitifs, 1968, Introduction to Nonlinear Automatic Control, 1966, (with others) High-Speed Analog Computers, 1962, General Sensitivity Theory, 1971, Control Aspects of Biomedical Engineering, 1987, Intelligent Robotic Systems, 1991, Nonanalytical Methods for Motor Control, 1995. Vol., organizer, mgr., instr. Page Cmty. Adult Lit. Program, Page Cmty. Adult Literacy Program, 1986-91, Marian's Literacy Program, 1991-95; lifetime mem. Friends of Page Pub. Libr., sec. bd., 1990-91. Mem. Lake Powell Inst. Behavioral Health Svcs. (bd. dirs., sec. 1993-95, chmn. fin. com. 1995, fin. com. 1995—, Page Main St. Vol. of Yr. 1992), Delta Kappa Gamma (pres. chpt. 1986-90, historian 1990-92, Omicron state coms., scholarship 1988-89, nominations 1991, Omicron State Coms. comms. 1995-97), Beta Sigma Phi (pres. chpt., v.p. chpt.). Home and Office: 66 S Navajo Dr PO Box 763 Page AZ 86040

HART, MELISSA A., state senator; b. Pitts., Apr. 4, 1962; d. Donald P. and Albina Simone Hart. BA, Washington and Jefferson Coll., 1984; JD, U. Pitts., 1987. Pa. state senator, atty.; chmn. Sen. Fin. Com.; vice chmn. Sen. Pub. Health & Welfare Com. Mem. Pa. Bar Assn., Allegheny County Bar Assn., Women's Bar Assn. Western Pa., North Suburban Builders Assn. Republican. Office: Pa State Senate State Capitol Harrisburg PA 17120

HART, NETT, community organizer; b. St. Paul, Dec. 9, 1948. BA, Augsburg Coll., 1971; MA, Northwestern/Luther U., 1978. Educator art dept. Richfield, Minn., 1970-76; designer Jensen Hart Design, Mpls., 1976-92; educator United Theol., St. Paul, 1979; adminstr. Lesbian Natural Resources, Mpls., 1989—; organizer Creating a Lesbian Future, Mpls., 1990-93; pub. Word Weavers, Mpls., 1979—. Author: Spirited Lesbians, 1989; co-author: (with Lee Lanning) Ripening, 1981, Dreaming, 1983, Awakening, 1987; contbr. numerous essays to publs. and anthologies. Office: Lesbian Natural Resources PO Box 8742 Minneapolis MN 55408

HART, PAMELA HEIM, banker; b. Chgo., July 14, 1946; d. Gordon Theodore and Leah Almira (Gardner) Heim; m. William Richard Hart, July 8, 1972 (div. 1979); 1 child, Elizabeth Alyson. BA, DePauw U., 1968; MA in Teaching, Washington U., St. Louis, 1970; M in Mgmt., Purdue U., 1982. Chartered bank auditor; cert. bank compliance officer. Tchr. history University City (Mo.) High Sch., 1969-74; teaching asst. Purdue U., Hammond, Ind., 1980-82, guest faculty, 1983-84; auditor Continental Bank NA, Chgo., 1984-86, legal and regulatory compliance specialist, 1986-88, asst. auditor, 1988-92, sr. portfolio risk analyst, 1992-94; with asset securitization group Bank of Am. (formerly Continental Bank NA), Chgo., 1994—; v.p. Capital Raising Products, 1994—. Trustee Forest Ridge Acad., Schererville, Ind., 1987-88; mem. vestry St. Paul Episc. Ch., Munster, Ind., 1982-92; active LWV. Mem. Chartered Bank Auditors Assn., Chicagoland Compliance Assn. (bd. dirs., treas. 1987-88), Cert. Bank Compliance Officer Assn. (exam. com. mem. 1992-96), P.E.O. Home: 8936 Southmoor Ave Hammond IN 46322-1808 Office: Bank of Am 231 S La Salle St Chicago IL 60604-1407

HART, PATRICIA A., public health officer; b. Pitts., Dec. 7, 1954; d. Charles Richard and Dorothy Mary (Froehlich) Dagnall; m. James A. Hart III, July 23, 1988. BS in Environ. Sci., Rutgers U., 1976, MPH, 1987. Lic. health officer, sanitary inspector, N.J.; registered environ. health specialist, N.J. Sanitarian Burlington County Health Dept., Mt. Holly, N.J., 1977-78, Hunterdon County Health Dept., Flemington, N.J., 1978-80; sanitarian East Winsdor Twp. (N.J.) Health Dept., 1980-82, sr. sanitarian, 1982-84; health officer East Windsor Twp. (N.J.) Health Dept., 1989—; prin. sanitarian East Winsdor Twp. (N.J.) Health Dept., 1984-87; health officer West Winsdor Twp. (N.J.) Health Dept., 1987-89; sec. Hazardous Waste Adv. Coun., Trenton, N.J., 1982-89; mem. conflict resolution bd. Ctrl. Jersey Maternal and Child Health Consortium, New Brunswick, N.J., 1992—. Co-author: The Role of the Local Health Official in Hazardous Material Response, 1983. Recipient Pub. Health Leadership award Western Consortium for Pub. Health, 1995-96; RADON coord. grantee Nat. Environ. Health Assn., 1994. Mem. APHA, N.J. Health Officers Assn., N.J. Pub. Health Assn., N.J. Environ. Health Assn., Mercer County Health Officers Assn. (v.p. 1995—). Office: East Windsor Twp Health Dept 16 Lanning Blvd East Windsor NJ 08520

HART, VIRGINIA WADE, elementary education educator; b. Rolla, Mo., Nov. 20, 1943; d. Clifford Neil and Nellie Z. (Jaggers) Wade; m. Edward F. Hart, Oct. 12, 1968 (div. June 1994); children: Edward S., Clifford T., James R., Deborah J., Sarah E. BA in Sociology, Mary Washington Coll., Fredericksburg, Va., 1965; MA in Elem. Edn., Adelphi U., Garden City, N.Y., 1973; MA in Reading, U. Ala., Birmingham, 1988, student, 1990. Cert. in elem. edn., reading, early childhood edn., Ala. Tchr. 1st grade Nassakegg Elem. Sch., Setauket, N.Y., 1966-68, Blue Point (N.Y.)-Bayport Schs., 1968-69; ednl. outreach Discovery Place Children's Mus., Birmingham, 1986-87; tchr. developmental kindergarten Hall Kent Elem. Sch., Birmingham, 1989-90, tchr. kindergarten, 1990-91, tchr. 2d grade, 1991—; clin. master tchr. U. Ala., Tuscaloosa, 1993—; mem. curriculum adv. com. Hoover Pub. Sch., 1989-91. Bd. dirs. Grace House Ministries, Fairfield, Ala., 1993-96. Mem. Internat. Reading Assn., Nat. Coun. Tchrs. English, Whole Lang. Umbrella, Nat. Sci. Tchrs. Assn., Kappa Delta Pi. Baptist. Office: Hall Kent Elem Sch 213 Hall Ave Homewood AL 35209

HARTE, REBECCA ELIZABETH, computer scientist, consultant; b. Camp LeJeune, N.C., Jan. 28, 1967; d. Franklin James and Rebecca Irene (Adams) H. BA in Maths., Hollins Coll., 1989; MS in Info. Mgmt., George Washington U., 1994. Cert. netware engr., 1996. Math. asst. Hollins Coll., Roanoke, Va., 1987-89; chief information officer BRTRC, Vienna, Va., 1989—. Mem. AAAS, IEEE, Math. Assn. Am., Am. Math. Soc., Assn. for Computing Machinery, Phi Beta Kappa, Sigma Xi. Home: 5200 Olley Ln Burke VA 22015-1747 Office: BRTRC Ste 800 8260 Willow Oaks Corporate Dr Fairfax VA 22031-4513

HARTE, SHERRI JEAN, technical writer; b. Dallas, Mar. 17, 1954; d. Dalton Eugene and Margie Marie (High) Brockway; m. Larry J. Key, Oct. 6, 1972 (div. June 1991); 1 child, Jason J. BA in English, Southern Meth. U., 1995. Tech. writer Pro Consultants, Dallas, 1994-95, Electronic Form Systems, Carrollton, Tex., 1995-96, Micrograyx, Inc., Richardson, Tex., 1996—. Reading instr. Literary Vols. of Am., Dallas, 1991; vol. Genesis Women's Shelter, Dallas, 1995. Recipient numerous writing awards Southern Meth. U., 1993-95. Mem. Phi Beta Kappa, Golden Key, Sigma Tau Delta. Home: 10316 Linkwood Dallas TX 75238 Office: Micrografx Inc 1303 E Arapaho Rd Richardson TX 75081

HARTER, CAROL CLANCEY, university president, English language educator; m. Michael T. Harter, June 24, 1961; children: Michael R., Sean P. AB, SUNY, Binghamton, 1964, MA, 1967, PhD, 1970; LHD, Ohio U., 1989. Instr. SUNY, Binghamton, 1969-70; asst. prof. Ohio U., Athens, 1970-74, ombudsman, 1974-76, v.p., dean students, 1976-82, v.p. for adminstrn., assoc. prof., 1982-89; pres., prof. English SUNY, Geneseo, 1989-95; pres. U. Nev., Las Vegas, 1995—. Co-author: (with James R. Thompson) John Irving, 1986, E.L. Doctorow, 1990; author dozens of presentations and news columns; contbr. articles to profl. jours. Office: U Nev Las Vegas Office of Pres 4505 Maryland Pkwy Box 1001 Las Vegas NV 89154-9900

HARTFORD, ANN MARIE, accountant, controller; b. Methuen, Mass., Mar. 7, 1961; d. John Michael and Stephanie Mary (Bajor) Kaminski; m. Allen Edward Hartford Jr., Sept. 17, 1989; children: Meredith Lynne, Victoria Ann, Stefanie Marie. BS in Acctg., Bentley Coll., 1982, MS in Taxation, 1990. CPA, Mass. Staff acct. James, Turonis & McLeod, PC, Lawrence, Mass., 1982-85; sr. acct. Martin D. Braver & Co., Chestnut Hill,

Mass., 1985-87; acct. Tofias, Fleishman, Shapiro, Cambridge, Mass., 1987-89; contr. CJ McCarthy Ins. Agy., Wilmington, Mass., 1989—; acct. Hartford Assocs., Methuen, Mass., 1992—; student mentor Bentley Coll. Career Devel., 1992—. Scholar Bentley Coll., 1979, 80, 81. Fellow Nat. Assn. Accts. (dir. community responsibility 1983-86), Mass. Assn. Pub. Accts. Republican. Roman Catholic. Office: CJ McCarthy Ins Agy Inc 229 Andover St Wilmington MA 01887-1080

HARTFORD, CAROL, nursing administrator; b. Rockland, Maine, Dec. 8, 1941; m. Thomas Hartford, July 3, 1965; children: Michael, Betsy. BSN, U. Maine, 1965. Cert. nursing adminstr. ANA. Staff nurse Ctrl. Maine Gen. Hosp., Lewiston, 1965, Ireland Army Hosp., Ft. Knox, Ky., 1966; nurse educator Augusta (Maine) State Hosp., 1967-68; dir. home health Leisure Lodge Home Health, Lampasas, Tex., 1983-84; RN coord. Brown County Mental Health Ctr., Green Bay, Wis., 1984-94, nursing svcs. adminstr., 1994—. Recipient Marne Vol. award 3d Inf. Divsn., Wurzburg, Germany, 1981. Mem. Wis. Nurses Assn. (bd. dirs., 2d v.p. 1994-96), N.W. Wis. Psychiat. Nurses Assn. (bd. dirs., 1st v.p. 1992-96). Home: 2080 W Vista Cir DePere WI 54115 Office: Brown County Mental Health 2900 St Anthony Dr Green Bay WI 54311

HARTH, ERICA, French language and comparative literature educator; b. N.Y.C. B.A., Barnard Coll., 1959; M.A., Columbia U., 1962, Ph.D. in French, 1968. Instr. French, NYU, 1964-66; from instr. to asst. prof. Columbia U., 1967-71; lectr. Tel-Aviv U., Israel, 1971-72; asst. prof. Brandeis U., 1972-75, assoc. prof. French, 1975-85, prof. French and comparative lit., 1985-92, prof. humanities and women's studies, 1992—. NEH fellow, 1970; Am. Council Learned Socs. fellow, 1978, 1990, Bunting Inst. fellow, 1989, NEH fellow, 1989. Mem. MLA. Author: Cyrano de Bergerac and the Polemics of Modernity, 1970; Ideology and Culture in Seventeenth Century France, 1983, Cartesian Women: Versions and Subversions of Rational Discourse in the Old Regime, 1992; contbr. articles to profl. jours. Office: Brandeis U MS 024 Dept Romance & Languages Waltham MA 02254

HARTIG, SANDI BERMAN, legal secretary; b. Houston, Sept. 4, 1948; d. Morris Leon and Helen O. (Houston) Berman; m. Robert L. Hartig, Nov. 28, 1992; children: Rebecca Lowe, Jonathan Lowe. Student, U. Houston, 1966-69, Houston C.C., 1979-82. Cert. legal sec. Sec. Houston, 1981-85; owner The Source, Houston, 1981-84; legal sec. Contract, Houston, 1985-91, Weil, Gotshal & Manges, Houston, 1991—; cons. Fed. Litigation Handbook, 1994. Contbr. article to profl. jour. Tchr. Helfman Religious Sch. Congregation Emanu El, Houston, 1988-95. Mem. Am. Organ Transplant Assn. (mem. bd. 1986-93, pres. 1993—), Houston Assn. Legal Secs. (mem. bd. 1988—, recording sec. 1992-93, 96—), La Leche League (area dir. 1971-78), Sisterhood of Congregation Emanu El (mem. bd. 1972-81). Jewish. Office: Weil Gotshal & Manges 700 Louisiana Ste 1600 Houston TX 77002-2784

HARTIGAN, GRACE, artist; b. Newark, Mar. 28, 1922; d. Matthew A. and Grace (Orvis) H.; m. Robert L. Jachens, May 1941 (div. 1948); 1 son, Jeffrey A.; m. Robert Keene, Dec. 14, 1959 (div. 1960); m. Winston H. Price, Dec. 24, 1960 (dec. 1981). Student pvt. art classes. Dir. Md. Inst. Grad. Sch. Painting, 1965—. One-woman shows Tibor de Nagy Gallery, N.Y.C., 1951-55, 57-59, Vassar Coll. Art Gallery, 1954, Martha Jackson Gallery, N.Y.C., 1962, 64, 67, 70, U. Chgo., 1967, Gertrude Kasle Gallery, Detroit, 1968, 70, 72, 74, Robert Keene Gallery, Southampton, N.Y., 1957-59, Gres Gallery, Washington, 1960, U. Minn., 1963, William Zierler Gallery, N.Y.C., 1975—, C. Grimaldis Gallery, Balt., 1979, 81, 82, 84, 86, 87, 89, 90, 93, Hamilton Gallery, N.Y.C., 1981, Gruenebaum Gallery, N.Y.C., 1984, 86, 88, Kouros Gallery, N.Y.C., 1989, ACA Gallery, N.Y.C., 1991, 92, 94; exhibited in numerous group shows including Modern Art in U.S., 1955-56, 3d Internat. Contemporary Art Exhbn., 1957, 4th Internat. Art Exhbn., Japan, 1957, IV Biennial, Sao Paulo, 1957, New Am. Painting Show, Europe, 1958-59, World's Fair, Brussels, 1958, The Figure Since Picasso, Mus. Ghent, Belgium, Moca in Moca Chicago, Hand Painted Pop Moca L.A., Whitney Mus. Am. Art, N.Y.C., 1992-93; represented in permanent collections Mus. Modern Art, Walker Art Center, Whitney Mus. Am. Art, Art Inst. Chgo., Met. Mus. Art, Raleigh Mus., Providence Mus., Bklyn. Mus., Mpls. Mus., Albright-Knox Gallery, Buffalo, numerous others. Recipient Merit award for art Mademoiselle Mag., 1957, Nat. Inst. Arts and Letters purchase award, 1974. Address: 1701 1/2 Eastern Ave Baltimore MD 21231-2420

HARTIGAN, JACQUELINE RENEÉ, investigator; b. San Francisco, Mar. 10, 1961; d. Charles Allen and Lucille Avra (Miller) Ramsey; m. Daniel William Hartigan, Apr. 23, 1988; children: Daniel Albert, Rachel Aron. BS, Calif. State U., Chico, 1983. Cert. peace officer, Calif. Youth counselor Calif. Youth Authority, Chino, 1985-89; job developer Goodwill Industries, San Bernardino, Calif., 1989-90; licensing analyst Cmty. Care Licensing, Riverside, Calif., 1990-95; investigator Dept. Social Svcs., Carlsbad, Calif., 1995—; pres. sch. site coun. Riverside Unified Sch. Dist., 1995-96; advisor Dayton-Hudson Target Family to Family Project, 1993-94. Vol. Children's Advocacy Coun., Riverside, 1994-96, Harrison Elem. PTA, Riverside; treas. St. Thomas Baseball, Riverside, 1995-96. Mem. Calif. Fraud Investigators. Jewish. Office: State Dept Social Svcs 5962 La Place Ct Ste 185 Carlsbad CA 92008

HARTLEY, CORINNE, painter, sculptor, educator; b. L.A., July 24, 1924; d. George D. and Marjorie (Fansher) Parr; m. Thomas L. West, Sept. 3, 1944 (div. 1970); children: Thomas West III, Tori West, Trent West; m. Clabe M. Hartley, Aug. 27, 1973 (separated). Attended, Chouinard Art Inst., L.A., 1942-44, Pasadena (Calif.) Sch. Fine Arts, 1952-54. Paste up artist Advt. Agy., L.A., 1944; fashion illustrator May Co., L.A., 1944-45; freelance fashion illustrator Bullock's, L.A., 1946-76; art tchr. Pasadena Sch. Fine Arts, 1965-71; pvt. art tchr., owner studio, Venice, Calif., 1971—; presenter art workshops; art provider to Art in Motion Prints and Cards. Exhbns. include Dassin Gallery, L.A., 1981—, Legacy Gallery, Scottsdale, Ariz., 1989—, G. Stanton Gallery, Dallas, 1990—, Coda Gallery, Palm Desert, Calif., 1993—, Huntsman Gallery, Aspen, Colo., 1995—. Recipient Purchase award Nat. Orange Show, San Bernardino, Honor award All City Art Festival, Barnsdall Park, L.A. Mem. Nat. Watercolor Soc., Oil Painters Am., Calif. Art Club, L.A. Art Assn., Laguna Beach Art Assn., Women Painters West. Republican. Studio: 411 N Venice Blvd Venice CA 90291

HARTLEY, HELEN ROSANNA, business educator; b. Hannibal, Mo., May 6, 1947; d. Roger Chase and Rose Evelyn (Peterson) Higgins; m. William Clarence Hartley, Aug. 17, 1969; children: Nathan William, Andrew Chase. BS in Edn., Ctrl. Mo. State U., 1969; MA, Appalachian State U., 1988. Cert. tchr., N.C., Mo. Spanish instr. Ctrl. H.S., Argyle, Iowa, 1969-70; modern langs. instr. Burke County Pub. Schs., Morganton, N.C., 1974-81; ednl. computing instr. Appalachian State U., Boone, N.C., 1988-91; bus. computing instr. Western Piedmont C.C., Morganton, 1990—, sec. faculty/staff coun., 1993-96; mem. tech. adv. com. Burke County, N.C., 1991-93, mem. chpt. II adv. com., 1992-94; sponsor computer club Salem Elem. Sch., Burke County, 1989-91; mem. Info. Tech. Task Force, 1995—, N.C. Curriculum Improvement Project, 1994-96. Contbr. articles to profl. jours. Mem., treas. Burke Soccer Assn., 1989—; mem. past officer Morgan Jr. Woman's Club, 1975-86; advisor Explorer Scout Post, Morganton, 1990-93. Mem. State Employees Assn. N.C., Computer Instrs. Assn., Bus. Instrs. Assn. Office: Western Piedmont CC 1001 Burkemont Ave Morganton NC 28655-4504

HARTLEY, KAREN JEANETTE, lawyer, mediator; b. Oakland, Calif., Aug. 2, 1950; d. Samuel Louis and Jean Iris (Beven) Ostrow; m. Terry Van Hook, Aug. 29, 1970 (div. Mar. 1976); m. William Headley, Jan. 22, 1977 (div. Mar. 1988). BA in Psychology with highest honors, UCLA, 1972; DMin, Sch. of Theology, Claremont, Calif., 1976; JD cum laude, U. San Diego, 1982. Bar: Calif. 1982, U.S. Dist. Ct. (9th cir.), 1983, Hawaii 1991, Oreg. 1996; ordained to ministry, Meth. Ch., 1973. From intern to asst. United Meth. Ch., 1969-71; asst. minister St. Paul's United Meth. Ch., San Bernardino, Calif., 1973-74; assoc. minister Claremont United Meth. Ch., 1974-76; sr. minister Santee (Calif.) United Meth. Ch., 1977-79; clk. Calif. Supreme Ct., San Francisco, 1981; cons. Regional Dept. Edn., San Diego, 1979-81; assoc. atty. Duke, Gerstel, Shearer & Bregante, San Diego, 1983-84, Finley, Kumble, Wagner et al, San Diego, 1984-87; prin. atty., mediator Hartley & Assocs., San Diego, 1987-95, Eugene, Oreg., 1996—; mediator San Diego Mediation Ctr., 1990-95; adj. instr. mediation clinic Sch. Law U. Oreg., Eugene; instr. bus. devel. Lane C.C., Eugene. Mem. ABA, Oreg. Bar Assn. Democrat. Office: Hartley & Assocs 2884 Chambers St Eugene OR 97405

HARTLEY, MARY CAROL, interior designer; b. Waco, Tex., Feb. 6, 1941; d. Laddie Earl and Mary Elizabeth (McMillan) Broadway; m. Ted Lowe Hartley; children: Tana Lizabeth, Timothy Lowe, Taylor Lowe. BBA, Baylor U., 1965. Dir. Clovis (N.Mex.) Women's Shelter, 1987-88, Cities in Sch., N.Mex., 1993-94, N.Mex. First, 1993-96; sec. N.Mex. Gov.'s Found., 1994-96. Bd. dirs. Clovis/Curry County C. of C., 1994-96, pres. 1995-96, Mem. of Yr. 1995. Mem. Lubbock (Tex.) Jr. League, Tri Delta Alumni Assn. (pres. 1970-86). Democrat. Methodist.

HARTLEY, MAXINE TINA, executive search and management consultant; b. N.Y.C.; d. Philip Edward and Mollie (Adler) Morgaman; divorced; children: Heather Brooke, Erin Lindsey. BA with honors, Hunter Coll., 1966. Pres. Bader Hartley & Assocs., Inc., N.Y.C., 1979-88, New Paradigms Inc., N.Y.C., 1988-93; sr. v.p./mng. dir. Skott Edwards Cons., N.Y.C., 1993-95; pres. diversity resources Earley Kielty & Assocs. Inc., N.Y.C., 1995—; adv. bd. dirs. Nat. Assn. Women Bus. Owners; mentor Women Unlimited, N.Y.C., 1995. Speaker for various orgns. Mem. NAFE, TRENDS (pres.), Soc. Human Resources Mgmt.

HARTMAN, DEBRA LEE, artist; b. Chgo., June 7, 1944. Student, Bradley U., 1962, Northwestern U., 1963, U. Wis., 1981-84, Northeast Ill. U., 1990—. bd. dirs. Chgo. Artists Coalition, Chgo. Artists Month; founder, dir. Artists Quadrant, 1992-95; founder, exec. dir. NomadCtrl., Evanston, 1994. Solo exhbns. include Beverly Art Ctr., Chgo., 1995, Espresso Pacific Gallery, Chgo, 1995, Deerpath Gallery, Lake Forest, Ill., 1995, Seebeck Gallery, Kenosha, Wis., 1996; group exhbn. include: Flora '88, '92 Chgo. Botanic Soc., The Northern Nat., 1989, The Annual Alice and Arthur Baer Competition, Chgo., 1989, 91-93, Westmoreland Art Nat., 1996, 39th Chautauqua Nat. Exhibit, 1996, the Rocky Mountain Nat. Water Media Exhibit, 1996.

HARTMAN, JOAN EDNA, English educator; b. Bklyn., N.Y.C., Oct. 5, 1930; d. H. Graham and Edna (Kuebler) H. Student, Mt. Holyoke Coll., 1951; postgrad., Duke U., Durham, 1952, Oxford U., 1958-59; PhD, Radcliffe Coll., Cambridge, 1960. Instr. Washington Coll., Chestertown, Md., 1952-54; instr. Wellesley Coll., 1959-62, asst. prof., 1962-63; asst. prof. Conn. Coll., New London, 1963-66, CUNY-Queens Coll., Flushing, 1967-70; asst. prof. CUNY-S.I. C.C., 1970-72, assoc. prof., 1972-76; prof. CUNY-Coll. S.I., 1976—, acting dean humanities and social scis., 1995—. Editor: Women in Print I, II, 1982, (En)Gendering Knowledge, 1991, The Norton Reader, 1996, Concerns; contbr. articles to profl. jours. Fellow, AAUW, NEH, Mellon Found., Folger Shakespeare Libr. Mem. MLA, Nat. Coun. Tchrs. English, Soc. for the Study of Women in the Renaissance, Women's Caucus for the Modern Langs., Nat. Arts Club. Office: Coll Staten Island 2800 Victory Blvd Staten Island NY 10314-6635

HARTMAN, LEE ANN WALRAFF, educator; b. Milw., Apr. 21, 1945; d. Emil Adolph and Mabelle Carolyn (Goetter) Walraff; m. Patrick James Hartman, Oct. 5, 1968; children: Elizabeth Marie, Suzanne Carolyn. BS, U. Wis., 1967; postgrad., U. R.I., 1972-73, Johns Hopkins U., 1990, Trinity Coll., 1996. Cert. tchr., Wis., Md. Secondary educator Port Wash. Bd. Edn., Wis., 1967-68; instr. ballet YWCA, Wilmington, Del., 1977-78; tutor Md. Study Skills Inst., Columbia, 1984-86; tchr. Howard County Bd. Edn., Columbia, 1985—. Contbr. articles to profl. jours. Bd. dirs. Columbia United Christian Ch., 1980-83; mem. Gifted and Talented Com., Columbia, 1980—, Lang. Arts Com., 1985—, USCG Officers Wives Club, 1970-72, Hosp. Aux. Bay St. Louis, 1970-72; troop leader Girl Scouts U.S., Columbia, 1980-91, Hospice; mem. exec. bd. PTA, 1990—. Recipient World Life Achievement award Internat. Biog. Ctr., 1994, Woman of Yr. award Am. Biog. Inst., 1994. Mem. AAUW (exec. bd. 1985—), NAFE, Home Hosp. Tchrs. Assn. Md. (chair pub. rels., sec., citizen adv. com. 1995—), Internat. Platform Assn., Beaverbrook Homemakers Assn. (citizens adv. com. 1995, pres. 1994). Home: 5070 Durham Rd W Columbia MD 21044-1445 Office: Howard County Bd Edn Rte 108 Columbia MD 21044

HARTMAN, LENORE ANNE, physical therapist; b. Cleve., May 27, 1938; d. Howard Andrew and Emma Elizabeth (Beck) H. BS in Agriculture, Ohio State U., 1960, MS in Agriculture, 1963; postgrad., Kans. State U., 1963-67; cert. in phys. therapy, U. Kans., 1968. Staff phys. therapist R.J. Delano Sch. for the Handicapped, Kansas City, Mo., 1969-74; chief phys. therapist Children's Mercy Hosp., Kansas City, 1974-78; relief staff Mass Gen. Hosp., Boston, 1969-70; staff phys. therapist Menorah Med. Ctr., Kansas City, 1979-87; clin. instr. phys. therapy St. Louis U., 1974-78, U. Ky., 1974-78, U. Mo., Columbia, 1973-78, U. Kans. Med. Ctr., Kansas City, 1974-87; mem. med. adv. com. Hospice Care of Mid Am., Kansas City, 1984-87; staff phys. therapist S.W. Gen. Hosp., 1992—; phys. therapy cons. Rocky River Riding Therapeutic Riding Program, 1994—; chapel organist St. Luke's Hosp., Kansas City, 1978-87. Contbr. articles to profl. jours. Ohio del. Internat. Farm Youth Exch., Brazil, 1962. Mem. Internat. Farm Youth Exch. Assn. (life), Am. Phys. Therapy Assn. (del. to nat. 1975-76), Mo. Phys. Therapy Assn. (chmn. northwest dist. 1974-76), Am. Guild of Organists (chmn. profl. concerns com. Greater Kansas City chpt. 1983), Japan Am. Soc., Ohio State U. Alumni Assn. (life), Ohio Phys. Therapy Assn., Cleve. All-Breed Tng. Club, Western Res. Kennel Club, Pembroke Welsh Corgi Club of Western Res., Am. Morgan Horse Assn., N.Am. Riding Assn. for Handicapped, U.S. Dressage Fedn., North Ohio Dessage Assn., Omicron Delta Epsilon, Phi Delta Gamma. Office: Southwest Gen Health Ctr Dept Physical Therapy Middleburg Heights OH 44130

HARTMAN, MARY LOUISE, information services librarian; b. Toledo, Ohio, Mar. 18, 1942; d. Carl Leo and Marie Louise (Weis) Campbell; m. Charles Martin, June 27, 1964; children: Christine, Katherine, Jeffrey, John. BA in History, Rosary Coll., River Forest, Ill., 1964; MLS, Rutgers U., 1980. Info. svcs. librarian Princeton (N.J.) Pub. Libr., 1983—; on-line rsch. svcs. cons. East Windsor, 1987—. Bd. dirs. New Grange Sch., Trenton, N.J., 1996; co-founder Pax Christi N.J., Middletown, 1981; pres. Assn. for Rights of Catholics in the Ch., Delran, N.J., 1989—, editor newsletter, 1988. Mem. Women's Ordination Conf., Call to Action, Corpus. Roman Catholic. Office: Assn for Rights of Cath PO Box 912 Delran NJ 08075-0756

HARTMAN, MARY S., historian; b. Mpls., June 25, 1941; married. BA, Swarthmore Coll., 1963; MA, Columbia U., 1964, PhD, 1970. Instr. to asst. prof. Rutgers U., 1968-75; assoc. prof. to prof. history Douglass Coll., Rutgers U., 1975—; dean Douglass Coll. Rutgers U., 1982-94; dir. Inst. for Women's Leadership Douglass Coll., 1994—; Univ. prof. Rutgers U., 1994—. Author: Clio's Consciousness Raised, 1974, Victorian Murderesses, 1978. Office: Inst for Women's Leadership Wood Lawn Carriage House 86 Clifton Ave New Brunswick NJ 08901

HARTMAN, PATRICIA JEANNE, lawyer, educator; b. Redding, Calif., Apr. 24, 1956; d. Gary Mac and Rosemary Catherine (Aldrich) H. BS in Bus. Adminstrn., Calif. State U., Sacramento, 1978, BA in Econs., 1978, MBA with honors, 1979; JD with distinction, U. of Pacific, Sacramento, 1983. Bar: Calif. 1983, U.S. Dist. Ct. (ea. dist.) Calif. 1983. Adminstrv. analyst Dist. Attys. Office, Sacramento, 1976-80; assoc. prof. Calif. State U., Sacramento, 1979—; assoc. Van Camp & Johnson, Sacramento, 1983-85; assoc. Diepenbrock, Wulff, Plant & Hannegan, LLP, Sacramento, 1985-89, ptnr., 1989—; mem. County Bar Sects., Sacramento, 1983—. Contbr. articles to profl. jours. Trustee Sutter Hosps. Found., Sacramento, 1988—. Fellow AAUW; mem. ABA, LWV (steering com. 1994), Calif. State Bar, Women Lawyers of Sacramento, Med.Group Mgmt. Assn., Sacramento C. of C. Office: Diepenbrock Wulff Plant & Hannegan LLP 300 Capitol Mall 17th Fl Sacramento CA 95814

HARTMAN, ROSEMARY JANE, special education educator; b. Gainesville, Fla., Aug. 24, 1944; d. John Leslie and Irene (Bowen) Goddard; m. Alan Lynn Gerber, Feb. 1, 1964 (div. 1982); children: Sean Alan, Dawn Julianne Silva, Lance Goddard; m. Perry Hartman, June 27, 1992. BA, Immaculate Heart Coll., 1967; MA, Loyola U., 1974. Cert. resource specialist. Tchr. L.A. Unified Schs., 1968-78; resource specialist Desert Sands Unified Sch. Dist., Palm Desert, 1978-83, Palm Springs Unified Schs., 1983—. Co-author: The Twelve Steps of Phobics Anonymous, 1989, One Day At A Time in Phobics Victorious, 1992; founder Phobics Victorious, 1992. Mem. Am. Assn. Christian Counselors (charter), Internat. Platform Assn. Office: Phobics Victorious PO Box 695 Palm Springs CA 92263-0695

HARTMAN, RUTH ANN, educator; b. Galion, Ohio, Aug. 18, 1938; d. Richard Lewis and Florence Evelyn (Ireland) Campbell; m. Richard Louis Hartman, Jan. 14, 1956; children: Jeffery Lee, Marsha Elaine, Jerry Steven. BS, Ohio State U., 1970; MEd, U. LaVerne, 1976, postgrad., 1985—; postgrad., U. Akron, 1977-85. cert. tchr., Ohio. Tchr. Willard (Ohio) City Schs., 1964-65; educator Mansfield (Ohio) City Schs., 1966—, home tutor, 1971-81, educator, 1977—, faculty advisory com., 1990-92, young authors coord., 1991-92, co-coord. career edn., 1991-92; cons. Ohio State U., Ashland (Ohio) Coll., Mt. Vernon (Ohio) Nazarene Coll., 1976—. Co-author: Handbook for Student Teachers, 1983; contbr. to Norde News. Mem NEA, Ohio Edn. Assn., North Cen. Ohio Tchrs. Assn., Mansfield Edn. Assn. Republican. Methodist. Home: RR 1 Plymouth OH 44865-9801 Office: Mansfield City Schs 1138 Springmill St Mansfield OH 44906-1525

HARTMAN, RUTH GAYLE, rancher; b. San Francisco, Apr. 17, 1948; d. William James and Doris June (Reinhold) Nixon; m. Marcus Max Hartman, Dec. 14, 1968; children: William Marcus Hartman, Alicia Marlene Hartman. Grad. high sch., Sunnyvale, Calif. Cert. cosmetologist. Cosmetologist Palo Alto, Calif., 1966-68; engring. clk. Pacific Telephone, San Francisco, 1968-69, traffic data clk., 1969-76; owner, mgr. Coffee Creek (Calif.) Ranch Inc., 1976—. Appointed parent mem. Act Testing Secondary Adv. Bd., Sacramento, 1988-90; mem. Trinity High Sch. Curriculum Com., Weaverville, Calif., 1984, 85. Mem. Dude Ranch Assn., Trinity County C. of C., U.S. C. of C., Calif. Hotel and Motel Assn. (bd. dirs. 1992—, mem. ednl. com., mem. govtl. affairs com.), Internat. Platform Assn. Episcopalian. Home and Office: HC 2 Box 4940 Trinity Center CA 96091-9505

HARTMAN, VICTORIA, book designer; b. N.Y.C., July 8, 1942; d. Leo and Doris (Eichler) H.; m. Joseph Gomez, June 20, 1965 (div. 1983). BFA, Cooper Union. Art asst. juvenile books Random House, N.Y.C., 1964-66; art dir. juvenile books Lothrop Lee & Shepard, N.Y.C., 1967-74; book designer Southampton, N.Y., 1974—. Author: The Silly Jokebook, 1987, The Silliest Ever Jokebook, 1993, Westward Ho Ho Ho!, 1992, Too Cool Jokes for School, 1996. Mem. Authors Guild, Graphic Artists Guild. Home: 164 Halsey St Southampton NY 11968

HARTMAN-ABRAMSON, ILENE, adult education educator; b. Detroit, Nov. 8, 1950; d. Stuart Lester and Freda Vivian (Nash) Hartman; m. Victor Nikolai Abramson, Oct. 24, 1941. BA, U. Mich., 1972; MEd, Wayne State U., 1980, PhD in Higher Edn., 1990. Cert. continuing secondary tchr., Mich. Program developer and instr. William Beaumont Hosp., Royal Oak, Mich., 1972-74; vocat. counselor for emigres Jewish Vocat. Svc. and Cmty. Workshop, Detroit, 1974-81; program developer and cons. Detroit Psychiat. Inst., 1982; instr. for foreign students Oakland C.C., Farmington Hills, Mich., 1983—, acad. coord. overseas info. program, 1995—; mem. adv. bd. Mich. Dept. Edn., Detroit, 1981; lectr. Internat. Conf. Tchrs. English to Speakers of Other Langs., 1981; guest presenter Wayne State U., Lawrence Tech. U., 1991, U. Mich. Anxiety Disorders Program, 1993; presenter rsch. presentations Nat. Coalition for Sex Equity in Edn., Ann Arbor, Mich.; presenter at seminar on learning anxiety Interdisciplinary Studies program Wayne State U., 1995; chair profl. stds. and measures com. Mich. Devel. Edn. Consortium; mem. rehab. adv. coun. State of Mich. Mem. editl. bd. Mensa Rsch. Jour.; contbr. articles to prof. jours. Am. Arabic and Jewish Friends, Detroit, 1988—. Mem. Am. Anthropol. Assn., Am. Mensa Ltd. (rsch. rev. com.), Math. Assn. Am., Nat. Assn. Fgn. Student Affairs, Mich. Coun. on Learning for Adults, Assn. for Women in Math., TESOL, Nat. Assn. for Devel. Edn. Jewish. Office: Oakland Community Coll 27055 Orchard Lake Rd Farmington Hills MI 48334

HARTMAN-GOLDSMITH, JOAN, art historian; b. Malden, Mass., June 3, 1933; d. Hyman and Ruth (Hadler) Lederman; m. Alan Hartman, Jan. 10, 1952 (div.); 1 dau., Hedy Hartman; m. 2d Robert Goldsmith, Aug. 12, 1976. Instr., coordinator, initiator art history program China Inst. in Am., N.Y.C., 1967-77; lectr. Sch. Continuing Edn. NYU, 1967-77; exec. officer Jewish Mus., N.Y.C., 1976-77, dir. pub. info., 1977-80; founder, dir. Inst. for Asian Studies, Inc., N.Y.C., 1981—; lectr. Cooper-Hewitt Mus. of Design (Smithsonian Inst.), 1976, 83; lectr. museums Los Angeles, St. Louis, Pitts., Indpls., Buffalo, Rochester, N.Y., Toronto, Can., Denver Art Mus., Seattle Art Mus., Asian Art Mus. San Francisco; lectr. museums Oriental Ceramic Soc., Tokyo, Hong Kong; spl. lectr. tour Archaeol. Inst. Am., 1977; condr. seminars on Chinese jade Met. Mus. Art, N.Y.C., 1977, 81, 83; fellow in perpetuity, mem. vis. com. slide and photograph library Met. Mus. Art; trustee Indpls. Mus. Art; mem. art com. China House Gallery, N.Y.C.; program chmn. ann. conf. MAR-Assn. Asian Studies, Buchnel U., 1974. Am. corr.: Oriental Art mag., London, 1963-81; contbr. feature articles to profl. publs.; guest curator, author catalogs; author: Chinese Jade of Five Centuries, 1969, slide survey Introduction to Chinese Art, 1973, Chinese Jade, 1986; contbr. book revs. to learned jours. Nat. Endowment grantee, vis. specialist Buffalo Mus. Sci., 1972, Indpls. Mus. Art, 1971, reviewer NEH div. pub. programs, 1978—. Mem. Am. Oriental Soc., Assn. for Asian Studies (founding mem. Mid-Atlantic Region 1972, sec.-treas. 1973, adv. council 1974-75), Oriental Club of N.Y., Oriental Ceramic Soc. Office: Inst for Asian Studies 141 E 44th St Ste #802 New York NY 10017

HARTMAN-IRWIN, MARY FRANCES, retired language professional; b. Portland, Oreg., Oct. 18, 1925; d. Curtiss Henry Sabisch and Gladys Frances (Giles) Strand; m. Harry Elmer Hartman, Sept. 6, 1946 (div. June 1970); children: Evelyn Frances, Laura Elyce, Andrea Candace; m. Thomas Floyd Irwin, Apr. 11, 1971. BA, U. Wash., 1964-68; postgrad., Seattle Pacific, 1977-79, Antioch U., Seattle, Wash., 1987, Heritage Inst., Seattle, Wash., 1987. Lang. educator Kennewick (Wash.) Dist. # 17, 1970-88; guide Summer Study Tours of Europe, 1971-88. Sec. Bahai Faith, 1971-94, libr., Pasco, Washington, 1985-88; trustee Mid. Columbia Coun. Girl Scouts U.S.; mem. Literacy Coun. Fulbright summer scholar, 1968. Mem. NEA, Wash. Edn. Assn., Kennewick Edn. Assn., Nat. Fgn. Lang. Assn., Wash. Fgn. Lang. Assn., Literacy Coun. Home: P O Box 247 Netarts OR 97143-0247

HARTMANN, RUTH ANNEMARIE, health care education specialist; b. Naumburg, Saale, Germany, Mar. 16, 1936; came to U.S., 1957; d. Kurt and Anna (Jöesch) H.; m. Karl-Heinz Falatyk (div. 1983); children: Ulrich, Ute; m. Franklin J. Herzberg, 1987. Diploma in nursing, Medizinische Fachschule, Potsdam, German Dem. Republic, 1956; BA in German summa cum laude, U. Wis., Milw., 1978, MLS, 1979; EdD in Adult Edn., Nova U., 1987. Info. specialist Fluid Power Assn., Milw., 1980-81; asst. librarian Miller Brewing Co., Milw., 1979-82; patient edn. librarian VA Med. Ctr., Milw., 1982-85, health care edn. specialist, 1986—; adj. prof. (part-time) grad. health-care scis. Cardinal Stritch Coll. Mem. editl. bd. Jour. Healthcare Edn. and Tng., 1993-95; contbr. articles to profl. jours. Bd. dirs. Concord Chamber Orch., Milw., 1982-91; vol. Cancer Soc., Milw., 1985—; reviewing bd. for program certification Am. Diabetes Assn., 1990-94; chairperson pub. edn. com. Am. Cancer Soc., 1993-94, mem. exec. bd. dirs., editl. bd. Jour. Healthcare Edn. and Tng. Mem. Am. Assn. Adult Continuing Edn., Am. Soc. Healthcare Edn. and Tng., Spl. Libr. Assn. (treas. 1981-83), Libr. Community Milw., Area Coun. Health Educators (chairperson 1986-88), Nat. Wellness Coun., U. Wis. Alumni Assn., Phi Kappa Phi. Office: Clement J Zablocki VA Med Ctr Milwaukee WI 53295

HARTNER, MICHELLE CHRISTINE, forensic technologist; b. Miami, Fla., Nov. 4, 1968; d. William Joseph and Georgette (Schur) H. BS in Polit. Sci. and Social Sci., Fla. State U., 1990; postgrad., U. South Fla. City clk. intern North Miami (Fla.) City Hall, 1985-96; crime lab. technician Fla. Dept. Law Enforcement, Tampa, 1990-93, crime lab. tech. supr., pub. records custodian, 1993-96, forensic technologist, 1996—; aide legal unit forfeiture sect. Metro Dade Police Dept., Miami, 1986-90. Sec. steering com. Campaign to Elect Mark Hanisee to Ho. of Reps., Tampa. Mem. Am. Soc. Pub. Adminstrn. Republican. Russian Orthodox. Office: Fla Dept Law Enforcement 4211 N Lois Ave Tampa FL 33614

HARTNESS, SANDRA JEAN, venture capitalist; b. Jacksonville Fla., Aug. 19, 1944; d. Harold H. and Viola M. (House) H. AB, Ga. So. Coll., 1969; postgrad., San Francisco State Coll., 1970-71. Researcher Savannah (Ga.) Planning Commn., 1969, Environ. Analysis Group, San Francisco, 1970-71; dir. Mission Inn, Riverside, Calif., 1971-75; developer Hartness Assocs., Laguna Beach, Calif., 1976—; ptnr. Western Neuro-Care Ctr., Tustin Calif., 1983-89; pres. Asset Svcs., Inc., 1981—. V.p., mem. bd. dirs. Evergreen Homes, Inc., 1986-90. Recipient numerous awards for community svc. Democrat. Office: Hartness Assocs 32612 Adriatic Dr Monarch Beach CA 92629-3510

HARTNETT, ELIZABETH A., trade association executive; b. Metuchen, N.J., June 28, 1952; d. John J. and Rita (Hackett) Kirwan; m. Raymond T. Hartnett, July 16, 1977; children: Kathleen E., John T. BS, Wheeling Coll., 1974. CPA, Pa. Jr. acct. Deloitte Haskins & Sells, Pitts., 1974-76; sr. acct. Deloitte Haskins & Sells, Washington, 1976-81, mgr., 1981-84; contr. Electronic Industries Assn., Washington, 1984-86, v.p. fin., 1986—; treas. Electronic Industries Found., Washington, 1984—. Mem. Am. Soc. Assn. Execs., Greater Washington Soc. Assn. Execs., Pa. Inst. CPA's, D.C. Inst. CPA's. Republican. Roman Catholic. Office: Electronic Industries Assn 2500 Wilson Blvd Arlington VA 22201-3834

HARTNETT, KOULA SVOKOS, English language and literature educator, author, playwright; b. Uniontown, Pa., Oct. 25, 1938; d. Charles Notias and Thelma (Pagonis) Svokos; m. Richard A. Hartnett, Oct. 3, 1968; children: Mark, Chris. BA in English, W.Va. U., 1960, MA, 1969, EdD in Higher Edn. Adminstrn., 1979. Instr. English W.Va. U., Morganton, 1967-68, vis. asst. prof., 1980-81; English instr. Prince George's County C.C., Largo, Md., 1969-70; dir. pub. rels., English asst. prof. Kirkland Hall Coll., Easton, Md., 1969-72; English instr. Waynesburg (Pa.) Coll., 1988-89; part-time faculty English Fairmont (W.Va.) State Coll., 1989—; founding mem. exec. bd. Ctr. for Women's Studies, W.Va. U.; vis. scholar Peking U., Fudan U.; dir. Natural Way Orgn. for Promotion of Complementary/Preventative Healthcare, 1993—. Author: Zelda Fitzgerald and the Failure of the American Dream for Women, 1991, The Occidental Tourist: A Journey Through China, 1988-91; writer, dir. Miss Zelda, 1994; co-editor Eureka! Wellness Newsletter, 1994—, East/West Healing Jour., 1996; contbr. articles and lectures on China and women's issues to profl. jours., articles on recovery/self-help issues to holistic publs. Mem. MLA, Am. Popular Culture Assn., Popular Culture Assn., Women in Communications, South Atlantic MLA, AAUP, So. Popular Culture Assn., Morgantown Music Club, Beau Monde Club, Cotillion Club, Phi Delta Kappa (newsletter editor 1976-77), Delta Delta Delta (alumna). Greek Orthodox.

HARTSE, DENISE YVONNE, society editor; b. Miles City, Mont., Nov. 5, 1951; d. Wayne Edwin and Lola Marion (Shipman) Durfee; m. Marcus R. Hartse, June 16, 1979. AA, Miles C.C., 1972; BA, U. Mont., 1975. Typesetter H & T Quality Printing, Miles City, Mont., 1975-76, 79-81; layout Larson Publs., Miles City, Mont., 1976-78, Sagebrush Publs., Miles City, Mont., 1978-79; soc. editor Miles City Star, Miles City, Mont., 1981—. Precinct committeewoman Dem. Party, Custer County, Mont., 1970-72; asst. Bills Coord., Mont. State Ho. of Reps., 1975; Mont. Dem. Exec. Bd., pres. New Dem. Coalition; mem. Miles City Concert Assn. Bd.; sec./treas. Miles City Arts, Cultural and Hist. Preservation Commn., 1991—. Mem. AAUW (liaison officer), Nat. Fedn. Press Women, Mont. Press Women (past pres., pres., treas.), Barn Players, Inc. (bd. dirs.), Rainbow Girls (bd. dirs. 1981-94), Miles City Centennial Quilters (pres. 1987-90, 92-93), Custer County Art Ctr., Quilters Art Guild No. Rockies (bd. dirs. 1992—). Presbyterian. Home: 615 Yellowstone Ave Miles City MT 59301-4230 Office: Miles City Star PO Box 1216 Miles City MT 59301-1216

HARTSOCK, PAMELA ELAYNE, intermediate school educator; b. San Marcos, Tex., July 3, 1956; d. Dwight Edward Beery and Nancy Louise (Snyder) Collert; m. Paul David Billiat, Aug. 18, 1975 (div. May 1982); 1 child, Korinne Elayne; m. Donald Jay Hartsock, Oct. 31, 1993. BA in Music Edn., Ohio Wesleyan U., 1978; MA in Edn., Ohio State U., 1988. Tchr. music Westover Elem. Sch., Stamford, Conn., 1978-80, Oak Ridge Elem. Sch., Darien, Conn., 1980-81; tchr. lang. arts, music Willis Intermediate Sch., Deleware, Ohio, 1983—; instr. Ashland U., Columbus, Ohio, 1990—. Bd. dirs. Ctrl. Ohio Symphony, Deleware, 1994—, prin. flutist, 1982—. NEH grantee, 1992. Mem. Nat. Coun. Tchrs. English, Ohio Coun. Tchrs. English Lang. Arts, Internat. Reading Assn. Office: 78 W William St Delaware OH 43015

HARTUNG, ROCKELLE RANN, vocational educator; b. Denver, July 19, 1964; d. Rolla Reginald Jr. and Jewel Maurine (Parker) R.; m. Philip H. Hartung III, June 15, 1990. AS in Bus., Aurora (Coll.) Cmty. Coll., 1990; BS in Computer Systems Analysis/Design, Met. State U., 1992; MA in Spl. Edn., U. No. Colo., 1996. Cert. tchr., Colo. Adminstrv. asst. Paychex, Inc., Chgo. and Aurora, Colo., 1984-87; asst. plant engr. Electromedics, Inc., Aurora, Colo., 1987-88; paraprofl.-spl. edn. Aurora Pub. Schs., 1988-90; advisor level III Met. State Coll., Denver, 1989-91; vocat. tchr. coord. Cherry Creek Pub. Schs., Aurora, Colo., 1992—; adv. bd. Aurora Pub. Schs., 1991-92, Cherry Creek Schs., Aurora, 1992—. Mem. AAUW (bd. dirs.). Office: Cherry Creek Schs 4360 S Pitkin St Aurora CO 80015

HARTWIG, MARLENE L., real estate broker; b. Marshalltown, Iowa, Dec. 17, 1938; d. Leland F. and Gladys P. (Gilmore) Turner; m. Clair E. Hartwig, Mar. 24, 1956; children: Dirk, Lezli, Ross. GRI, CRS; lic. broker. Sales assoc. Marshalltown, 1968-84; broker ERA Concept III, Marshalltown, 1984—, owner, 1985—; mem. Housing Task Force, Marshalltown, 1994-95, Bd. Rev., Marshalltown, 1985-94, Bd. Appeals, Marshalltown, 1987-95, Marshalltown Condemnation Commn., 1994-95; pres. Marshalltown Bd. Realtors, 1988-89. Named Broker of Yr., ERA MidAm., 1989, Realtor of Yr., Marshalltown Bd. Realtors, 1991. Mem. TTT (chpt. pres. 1983-84), Kiwanis, Elmwood Country Club. Office: ERA Concept III 204 E LinnSt Marshalltown IA 50158

HARTY, SHEILA THERESE, theologian, writer, editor; b. Nurnberg, Germany, Jan. 24, 1948; came to U.S., 1951; d. Gerald Aloysius and Rosella Therese Harty. BA in Theology, U. South Fla., 1970; MA in Theology, Fla. State U., 1973. Lectr., counselor in drug sci. and drug edn. U.S. Army, Nurnberg, Fed. Republic Germany, 1974-75; personal adminstr. to campaign mgr. Ramsey Clark Senate Race, N.Y.C., 1976-77; personal adminstr. to Ralph Nader Ctr. for Study of Responsive Law, Washington, 1977-84; lectr. bus. ethics Faculty of Commerce Univ. Coll. Cork, Ireland, 1982-83; dir. corp. initiatives div. Nat. Wildlife Fedn., Washington, 1984-86; free lance writer, editor Washington, 1986-89; editor Congl. Budget Office, Washington, 1989-91; communication dir. Project 2061 AAAS, Washington, 1991-93; sr. editor,project mgr. Fed. Program Directories, Carroll Pub. Co., 1993-96; cons. Internat. Orgn. Consumers Unions, Hague, Netherlands, 1982-88. Author: Hucksters in the Classroom, 1979 (George Orwell award 1980); Consumer Initiatives, 1983; The Corporate Pied Piper, 1984; contbr. articles to profl. jours. Mem. Nat. Writers Union. Democrat. Roman Catholic. Home and Office: 2032 Belmont Rd NW Washington DC 20009-5426

HARTZ, LUETTA BERTHA, insurance agent; b. Stevens Point, Wis., Sept. 29, 1947; d. Alfred Bernard Carl and Bertha Martha (Stauffer) Janz; m. James Patrick Hartz, Dec. 31, 1975 (dec. 1995). Student Madison (Wis.) Bus. Coll., 1965-66. With Employers Ins. of Wausau (Wis.), 1966-68; casualty rater Sentry Ins. Co., Stevens Point, Wis., 1968-70, casualty supr., 1970-71, casualty trainor, 1971-72, customer service corr., 1972-74, bur. technician, 1974-75, customer service and acctg. mgr., Concord, Mass., 1975-79, personal lines property processing mgr., 1979-81, personal lines casualty processing mgr., 1981-83, comml. lines underwriting services mgr., 1983-85, comml. lines ops. mgr., 1985-87; agent Lewis P. Bither Ins. Agy., Inc., Tewksbury and Tyngsboro, Mass., 1988-90; acct. rep. Brewer & Lord, Acton, Mass., 1990—. Campaign treas. Reps., county clk. candidate, Portage County, Wis., 1972. Mem. U.S. Golf Assn. (asso.), Nat. Assn. Ins. Women, Mass. Assn. Ins. Women. (Middlesex chpt. 1984-96). Roman Catholic. Clubs: Emblem (1st asst. marshall 1980-81, treas. 1981-83). (Concord, Mass.); Maynard Country (bd. govs. 1984-86) (Mass.). Home: 40 Drummer Rd Acton MA 01720-5202

HARTZ, MICHELLE R., advertising executive. MBA, U. Calif. Rschr., account exec. Ogilvy & Mather, N.Y.C., 1977-79; account exec. Hill & Knowlton Pub. Rels., Washington, 1979-81; dir. mktg. Bethesda (Md.) Research Labs., 1981-85; sr. v.p. Burson-Marsteller, Washington, 1985-91, Powell Tate, A Cassidy Co., Washington, 1991—. Office: Powell Tate A Cassidy Co 700 13th St NW Ste 1000 Washington DC 20005-3960*

HARTZ, RENEE SEMO, cardiothoracic surgeon; b. Bessemer Twp., Mich., Dec. 7, 1946; d. Rita Ann Semo; children: Tyler Joseph, Colin Wilson. BA, Western Mich. U., 1969; MD, Northwestern U., 1974. Diplomate Am. Bd. Surgery, Am. Bd. Thoracic Surgery. Intern pediatrics Children's Meml. Hosp., Chgo., 1974-75; intern gen. surgery Northwestern Meml. Hosp., Chgo., 1975-76, resident gen. surgery, 1976-79; chief resident cardiothoracic surgery Northwestern Meml. Hosp., 1979-81; instr. dept. surgery Northwestern U. Med. Sch., Chgo., 1978-81, assoc. in surgery, 1981-85; asst. prof. surgery med. sch. Northwestern U., Chgo., 1985-87, assoc. prof. surgery med. sch., 1987-92; prof. surgery, chief div. cardiothoracic surgery U. Ill. Hosp. & Clinics, Chgo., 1992—; apptd. to Northwestern Meml. Hosp., Chgo., Children's Meml. Hosp., Chgo., VA Lakeside Hosp., Chgo., Evanston (Ill.) Hosp., Columbus Hosp., Chgo.; laser researcher Northwestern U. Med. Sch., 1984—, U. of Ill. Hosp., West Suburban Hosp., Ill. Masonic Hosp. Contbr. articles to profl. jours.; contbr. chpts. to Perioperative Cardiac Dysfunction II, 1985, General Thoracic Surgery, 1989, New Technology in Vascular Surgery, 1988. Mem. Am. Coll. Chest Physicians, Am. Coll. Surgeons, Am. Heart Assn., Am. Women's Med. Assn., Assn. for Acad. Surgery, Chgo. Heart Assn., Chgo. Surg. Soc., Ill. Surg. Soc., Laser Inst. Am., Soc. Thoracic Surgeons, Soc. Univ. Surgeons, Am. Assn. Thoracic Surgeons, Sigma Xi. Office: U Ill Chgo 1740 W Taylor St # C 959 Chicago IL 60612-7232

HARTZELL, IRENE JANOFSKY, psychologist; b. L.A. Vor-Diplom, U. Munich, 1961; BA, U. Calif., Berkeley, 1963, MA, 1965; PhD, U. Oreg., 1970. Lic. psychologist, Wash., Ariz. Psychologist Lake Washington Sch. Dist., Kirkland, Wash., 1971-72; staff psychologist VA Med. Ctr., Seattle, 1970-71, Long Beach, Calif., 1973-74; dir. parent edn. Children's Hosp., Orange, Calif., 1975-78; clin. psychologist Kaiser Permanente, Woodland Hills, Calif., 1979—; clin. instr. dept. pediatrics U. Calif. Irvine Coll. Medicine, 1975-78. Author: The Study Skills Advantage, 1986; contbr. articles to profl. jours. Intern Oreg. Legislature, 1974-75. U.S. Vocat. Rehab. Adminstrn. fellow U. Oreg., 1966-67, 69. Mem. APA, Pi Lambda Theta.

HARTZLER, GENEVIEVE LUCILLE, physical education educator; b. Hammond, Ind., June 19, 1921; d. Lewis Garvin and Effie May (Orton) H. BS in Edn., Ind. U., 1944; MEd, U. Minn., 1948. Tchr. phys. edn. Griffith (Ind.) Pub. Schs., 1944-45, Northrup Collegiate Sch., Mpls., 1945-47; supr. student tchrs., 1947-79; tchr. phys. edn. Marquette (Mich.) Pub. Schs., 1948-50, Albion (Mich.) Pub. Schs., 1951-56; tchr. phys. edn. Jackson (Mich.) Pub. Schs., 1957-79, supr. student tchrs., 1950-80, coord., project dir., tchr., coach, 1979-83; chair equity workshop Jackson Pub. Schs., 1979-83; chair various convs., 1964-70. Mem. Am. Heart Assn., Jackson, 1977-83; mem., chair Women in Mgmt., Jackson, 1981-83; mem. Bus. and Profl. Women, Jackson, 1980-90. Recipient Honor awards Young Woman's Christian Assn. and Mich. Divsn. Girls and Women's Sports. Mem. AAHPERD, NEA, Mich. Assn. Health, Phys. Edn. and Recreation (Honor award), Mich. Edn. Assn. (Women's Cultural award), Delta Kappa Gamma (Woman of Distinction award). Home: 703 Bay Meadows Cir Lady Lake FL 32159-2285

HARVEY, ANNE REYNOLDS, retired social worker, civic worker; b. Clarksburg, W.Va., Nov. 25, 1924; d. Moore Martin and Alma Vera (Engle) Reynolds; m. Charles Victor Dauenheimer, Nov. 4, 1945 (div. 1965); m. John Jackson Harvey, Dec. 31, 1967 (div. 1971). AB in Sociology, Antioch Coll., 1946; MA in Sociology, W.Va. U., 1967. Elem. tchr. Monongalia County Bd. Edn., Osage, W.Va., 1947-48; reporter Clarksburg Telegram, 1948-49; exec. asst. Placement Office, W.Va. U., Morgantown, 1949-51, tng. asst. Appalachian Ctr., 1965-66, edn. and tng. specialist, 1966-68; sec. Union Carbide Corp., Clarksburg, 1951-53; supr., staff asst. Union Carbide Corp., N.Y.C., 1953-64; cons. Union Carbide Africa, Kenya, 1968-70; employment specialist W.Va. Job Svc., Clarksburg, 1971-75; social svc. worker W.Va. Dept. Human Svcs., Clarksburg, 1975-87; ret., 1987; with Egerton Coll., Njoro, Kenya, 1968-70. Contbr. articles on local environ. issues Clarksburg Exponent-Telegram, 1980—. Former pres. and current v.p. Foster Grandparents Adv. Coun., Clarksburg; leader Citizens' Referendum for County-Wide Recycling, Harrison County, W.Va., 1989-90, Citizens United Against Landfill Increase, Harrison County, 1991—; a founder Harrison Environ. Citizens Orgn., 1992; state sec. W.Va. Civil Liberties Union, Charleston, 1991-95; Dem. candidate for W.Va. Ho. of Dels., 1992; chmn. conservation Clarksburg Women's Club, 1992-96; past sect., bd. dirs. Clarksburg Art Ctr.; mem. W.Va. Environ. Coun., Citizens Action Group, W.Va. Population Issues Forum. Mem. LWV, Sierra Club (Laurel award for environ. initiative W.Va. chpt. 1994). Home: Hill Girt Farm Rt 3 Box 72 Clarksburg WV 26301

HARVEY, BRENDA S., literature educator; b. Mt. Gilead, Ohio, Nov. 19, 1963; d. Paul Walter and Marjory Joan (Dearth) McChesney; married. BA, Ohio No. U., 1986, MA, 1989, PhD, 1993. Tchr. Worthington (Ohio) City Schs., 1986-91; tchg. assoc. Ohio State U., Columbus, 1991-93; asst. prof. Mt. Vernon (Ohio) Nazarene Coll., 1993—; presenter papers in field. Co-chmn. Mansfield Art Ctr. Activities Coun., 1993—. Recipient Cynthia Cook scholarship, Ohio State U., Columbus, 1994. Mem. Nat. Coun. Tchrs. of English, Internat. Reading Assn. Republican. Methodist. Office: Mt Vernon Nazarene Coll 800 Martinsburg Rd Mount Vernon OH 43050-9509

HARVEY, CYNTHIA, ballet dancer; b. San Rafael, Calif.. Studied with Christine Walton, The Novato Sch. Ballet; student, San Francisco Ballet Sch., Marin Ballet Sch., Sch. Am. Ballet Theatre, N.Y.C., Am. Ballet Theatre Sch., N.Y.C., Nat. Ballet Sch. Can., Toronto. With Am. Ballet Theatre, N.Y.C., 1974, soloist, 1978-82, prin. dancer, 1982-86, 1988—; prin. dancer Royal Ballet, London, 1986-88; Guest artist, The Royal ballet, The Birmingham Royal Ballet. Creator: role of Gamzatti in La Bayadere; appeared in Swan Lake, Don Quixote, Sleeping Beauty, Giselle, Raymonda, Ballet Imperial, Coppelia, Etudes, Manon, Romeo and Juliet, La Sylphide, Les Sylphides, Symphony Concertante, Symphonic variations, Theme and Variations. Recipient John Anthony Bitson award, 1973. Office: care Am Ballet Theatre 890 Broadway New York NY 10003-1211

HARVEY, DENISE ELAINE, secondary education educator; b. Marceline, Mo., Aug. 26, 1959; d. Wayne Lee and Karen Beth (Jones) Drake; m. Timothy Edward Harvey, July 25, 1981; children; Joshua Timothy, Cierra Denise. BS in English Edn., N.E. Mo. State U., 1981, MA, 1986. Cert. tchr. and libr., Mo. Tchr. LaPlata (Mo.) High Sch., 1981-82, Macon (Mo.) R-I High Sch., 1982—; instr. Moberly Area (Mo.) C.C., 1992—; libr. Macon Elem. Sch., 1992, 94. Active tchr., youth sponsor Clarence (Mo.) Christian Ch., 1982—, dir. vacation Bible sch., 1990-91. Named one of Outstanding Young Women Am., 1984; recipient Tchr. Appreciation award Mo. Scholars Acad., 1994. Mem. Nat. Coun. Tchrs. English, Mo. Coun. Tchrs. English, Mo. State Tchrs. Assn., Macon Cmty. Tchrs. Assn., Delta Kappa Gamma. Republican. Home: 208 N Center St # 125 Clarence MO 63437 Office: Macon R-I High Sch S Missouri St # 63 Macon MO 63552-1314

HARVEY, ELINOR B., child psychiatrist; b. Boston, Jan. 11, 1912; d. William and Florence (Maysles) H.; m. Donald K. Freedman, July 2, 1936; children: Peter, F. Kenneth. BS cum laude, Jackson Coll., 1933; MD, Tufts U., 1936. Diplomate Am. Bd. Psychiatry and Neurology, Nat. Bd. Med. Examiners. Intern New Eng. Hosp. Women and Children, Roxbury, Mass., 1936-37; resident Sea View Hosp., Staten Island, N.Y., 1937-39; adminstrv. and indsl. physician Assoc. Hosp. Svc. N.Y., 1939-41; house physician, resident Henry St. Settlement House, N.Y.C., 1939-41; pvt. practice Arlington, Va., 1941-43; pvt. practice as pediatrician Newport News, Va., 1943-46; clinician Westchester County Health Dept., White Plains, N.Y., 1947; pediatrician Arrowhead Clinic, Duluth, Minn., 1947-48; resident in psychiatry VA Hosp., Palo Alto, Calif., 1949-52; resident in child psychiatry child guidance clinic Children's Hosp. San Francisco, 1952-53, fellow in child psychiatry, 1953-54; pvt. practice as child and family psychiatrist Berkeley, Calif., 1954-68, Juneau, Alaska, 1968-77; instr. Am. U., Washington, 1941-43; clinician prenatal clinics Arlington County Health Dept., Arlington, 1941-43; clinician Planned Parenthood, Washington, 1941-43; mem. adv. com. emergency maternal and infant care program Children's Bur., Washington, 1942-48; instr. pediatrics schs. nursing Buxton and Riverside Hosps., 1943-46; consulting pediatrician Cmty. Hosp. & Clinic, Two Harbors, Minn., 1947-48; mem. courtesy staff Herrick Hosp., Berkeley, Calif., 1955-68, Bartlett Meml. Hosp., Juneau, 1968-77; cons. U.S. Bur. Indian Affairs Dept. Edn., Alaska, 1968-76, S.E. Regional Mental Health Clinic, Juneau, 1975-77, Mars & Kline Psychiat. Clinic and Hosp., Port-Au-Prince, Haiti, 1977-78, Navajo Area Indian Health Svc., Gallup, N.Mex., 1980—, Brookside Hosp., San Pablo, Calif., 1984—; instr. mental health and mental illness Alaska Homemaker-Home Health Aide Svcs., Juneau C.C., 1968-77; coord. State of Alaska Program Continuing Edn. Mental Health, 1974-76; clin. assoc. prof. dept. psychiatry and behavioral scis. U. Wash., Seattle, 1976-77; vol. child and family psychiatrist Bapt. Mission, Fermathe, Haiti, 1977-79; instr. child devel. Mars & Kline Psychiat. Clinic and Hosp., 1977-78; mem. hosp. staff Gallup (N.Mex.) Indian Med. Ctr., 1980—; cons. Brazelton neonatal behavioral assessment Navajo Area Indian Health Svc., 1982—, infant-parent program Brookside Hosp., 1984—; demonstrator, trainer Brazelton neonatal behavioral assessment scale Ctr. de Recursos Educatius per a Deficients Visuals a Catalunya, Barcelona, Spain, 1992; active Child Protection Agy., Juneau; mem. planning bd. Coordinated Child Care Ctr., Juneau; mem. grant writing com. of planning bd. Cmty. Mental Health Ctr., Juneau; presenter in field. Author: (with others) Annual Progress in Child Psychiatry and Child Development, 10th ann. edit., 1977, Expanding Mental Health Intervention in Schools, Vol. I, 1985, Psychiatric House Calls, 1988, The Indian Health Service Primary Care Provider, 1991; contbr. articles to profl. jours. Mem. comprehensive health planning coun. City and Borough of Juneau. Grantee NIMH, 1958-63. Fellow Am. Psychiat. Assn. (life), Am. Acad. Child and Adolescent Psychiatry (life, mem. task force Am. Indian children); mem. No. Calif. Psychiat. Assn., Internat. Assn. Child Psychiatry, World Fedn. Mental Health, Internat. Assn. Circumpolar Health, Soc. Reproductive and Infant Psychology. Home and Office: 1547 Buckeye Ct Pinole CA 94564-2124

HARVEY, GENEVIEVE, special education educator; b. Oak Harbor, Wash., Mar. 14, 1970; d. John Charles and Dianee (Neu) H.; 1 child, Kayleigh Blaine Harvey. BS in Edn., Ohio U., 1992. Tchr. special edn. middle sch. Centerville (Ohio) Schs., 1993-94; tchr. presch. special edn. West Carrollton (Ohio) Schs., 1994—. Home: 120 Bethel Rd Centerville OH 45458

HARVEY, HILDA RUTH, special education educator; b. Kingsville, Tex., Sept. 6, 1950; d. Nicolas Guerra and Maria de Jesus (Sanchez) Montalvo; m. Steve Allen Harvey, Oct. 20, 1978 (div. Nov. 1991); children: John, Kristy. BA, Tex. Wesleyan Univ., 1982; cert., Univ. Mary Hardin Baylor, 1985. Cert. secondary edn. educator. Tchr. adult edn. Ctrl. Tex. Coll., Killeen, 1985-86; tchr. homebound Fort Worth Ind. Sch. Dist., 1986-87, psychoednl. instr., 1987-91, adult ESL instr., 1988-90; spl. educator Killeen (Tex.) Ind. Sch. Dist., 1991—; fgn. lang. chmn. Manor Mid. Sch., Killeen, Tex., 1995—; cons. Fort Worth Ind. Sch. Dist., 1990-91. With USAF, USAFR, U.S. Army Res., 1975—. Recipient Outstanding Coach-Girls Softball Dependent Youth Activity Ctr., 1983. Fellow ASCD; mem. AAUW, Tex. State Tchrs. Assn., Disabled Am. Vets., Century Club, Sigma Delta Pi. Republican. Southern Baptist. Office: Manor Mid Sch 1700 S WS Young Dr Killeen TX 76543

HARVEY, JANE HULL, religious organization administrator. Student, Vanderbilt Div. Sch., 1956-57, George Peabody Coll. Tchrs., 1956-58; BA with high honors, Scarritt Coll., 1958; grad., Tokyo Sch. Japanese Lang., 1966; tchg. cert., Sogetsu Japanese Ikebana Inst., 1969; MA with highest honors, Columbia U., 1972. Tchr. remedial English lang. arts Englewood, N.J.; tchr. head start, learning disabled children Ctrl. Harlem, N.Y.C.; asst. prof. English and print journalism Tsuda Women's Coll., Tokyo; adminstrv. sec. Bishop-Korean Meth. Ch., Seoul; tchr. ESL Ewha Women's U. Ext., Seoul; office mgr. ednl. TV office Pub. Broadcasting Svc., Washington, 1980-81; program coord., asst. dir. dept. social and econ. justice Gen. Bd. of Ch. and Soc.-The United Meth. Ch., 1981-86, program coord. justice for women project, 1986-88, dir. dept. human welfare, 1988-92, asst. gen. sec. Ministry of God's Human Cmty., 1992—; leader internat. exch. program of Japanese U. students to visit U.S. univs. and chs.; coord. ch.'s involvement UN Decade of Women End of Decade Conf., Vienna, Austria and Nairobi, Kenya; founding mem., advisor Co-Madres, 1982; chair Washington Interreligious Staff Cmty., 1983-85, 89-91; leader Bd. of Ch. and Soc. Multi-Ethnic Del., UN Conf. on Women, Nairobi, 1985, Gen. Bd. Ch. and Soc. del. to UN Conf. on Population and Devel., Cairo, 1992, UN World Conf. on Women in Beijing, 1995; liaison Gen. Commn. on the Status and Role of Women, 1988—; co-chair Interreligious Coalition on Smoking or Health, 1992—; pres. Interfaith Impact for Justice and Peace, chair bd. dirs., 1995—; rep. Inter-religious Coalition on Smoking and Health; chair Nat. Coun. of Chs. Health and Welfare Work Group; coach Tsuda Coll. English Debate team, Tokyo; spkr. in field. Asst. to editor Japan Christian Activity News, 1975-79; editl. asst. AMPO Mag., 1975-79; contbr. articles to profl. jours. co-dir. McGovern for Pres. Campaign, Englewood, N.J., 1972; campaign coord., speech writer Dem. Mayoral Campaign, Englewood, 1972; co-coord. United Farm Workers Boycott, Englewood, 1972-74; vol. adminstrv. asst. Greater Englewood Housing Authority, 1972-74; adult counselor Youth March Against Hunger, Englewood, 1972-74; co-founder Judson Health Project for Working Women, N.Y.C., 1973-75; mem. bd. dirs. Ctr. for Reproductive and Sexual Health, N.Y.C., 1973-75; advisor Korean Legal Aid Ctr. for Family Rels., 1980-87; bd. mem. Ptnrs. for Global Justice, 1982-87; co-chair religion and race com. Dumbarton United Meth. Ch., Georgetown, 1986-88; chief staff Infant Formula Task Force, 1988—; founding mem. The World Alliance for Breast-feeding Action Internat. Conf., Penang, Malaysia, 1990—. Home: 10414 Hayes Ave Silver Spring MD 20902

HARVEY, JANE R., investment company executive; b. Tarrytown, N.Y., Oct. 13, 1945; d. Fred W. and Margaret (White) Rosenbauer. Student, U. Ariz., Iona Coll., Coll. Fin. Planning; grad., Pace U. Lic. ins. counselor; registered fin. cons. Registered rep. KMS Fin. Svcs., Inc., Tucson, acct. exec., 1994—. Contbr. articles to profl. jours. Active Resources for Women. NAFE, Internat. Assn. Fin. Planning (past bd. dirs., v.p. membership So. Ariz. chpt., pres. 1994—), Internat. Assn. Registred Fin. Planners (bd. govs., speaker conv.), Internat. Assn. Registered Financial Cons. (bd. dirs. 1995—), Am. Bus. Womens Assn., Am. Assn. Individual Investors, Tucson C. of C., Nat. Assn. WOmen Bus. Owners. Office: KMS Financial Svcs Inc 4525 E Skyline Dr Ste 105 Tucson AZ 85718

HARVEY, JOANN MARIE, physical education specialist, consultant; b. Lapwai, Idaho, Feb. 4, 1938; d. Jesse and Anna (Jackson) H.; children: Bradley, Jeffrey, Jennifer, Joel, Rosalyn. BA in Edn., Phys. Edn., Natural Sci., Ea. Wash. U., 1978; M in Orgnl. Leadership, Gonzaga U., 1993. Res./d.c. N.W. Airlines, Washington, 1957-59; fitness dir. Y.M.C.A., Coeurd Alene, Idaho, 1973-81; owner, mgr. Fitness Ctr., Hayden, Idaho, 1981-86; phys. edn. specialist Coeurd'Alene Sch. Dist., Hayden, Idaho, 1986—; wellness cons. hosp. and sch., Coeurd Alene, 1981-86. Author poetry. mem. North Idaho Dem. Party, Coeurd Alene, 1994—. Mem. AAHPERD, Coeurd 'Alene Edn. Assn. (human/civil rights chair 1994-95), Idaho Coun. Cath. Women (bd. dirs. 1991-95, past pres.). Home: 6015 N Mount Carrol St Coeur D Alene ID 83814-9606 Office: Hayden Elem Sch North Government Way Hayden ID 83835

HARVEY, JUDITH GOOTKIN, elementary education educator, real estate agent; b. Boston, May 29, 1944; d. Myer and Ruth Augusta (Goldstein) Gootkin; m. Robert Gordon Harvey, Aug. 3, 1968; children: Jonathan Michael, Alexander Shaw. BS in Edn., Lesley Coll., Cambridge, Mass., 1966; MS in Edn., Nazareth Coll., Rochester, N.Y., 1987. Kindergarten tchr. Williams Sch., Chelsea, Mass., 1966-69; owner, tchr. Island Presch., Eleuthera, Bahamas, 1969-70; substitute tchr. Brighton Cen. Schs., Rochester, N.Y., 1985—; agt. The Prudential Rochester Realty, Pittsford, N.Y. Author, dir.: (play) The Parrot Perch, 1991. Bd. dirs. in charge pub. rels. George Eastman House Coun., mem. award steering com honoring Lauren Bacall, 1990, chmn. gala celebration honoring Audrey Hepburn, 1992, mem. steering com. honoring Ken Burns, 1995; mem. art in bloom steering com. for fashion show Meml. Art Gallery, 1994; co-chmn. Fashionata, Rochester Philharm. Orch., 1990; mem. steering com. of realtors Ambs. to Arts; mem. steering com. Reels and Wheels-George Eastman House, 1995, 96; mem. steering com. Reel and Wheels Antique Car Festival,

1995, 96. Mem. Chatterbox Club, Genesee Valley Club, Million Dollar Producer's Club. Home: 14 Whitestone Ln Rochester NY 14618-4118 Office: The Prudential 11 State St Pittsford NY 14534

HARVEY, JUDY CAROL, accountant, tax preparer; b. Cassville, Mo., Aug. 22, 1944; d. Charles Turner and Bonita (Vanzandt) Edmondson; m. Raymond Lowell Harvey, Sept. 30, 1972 (div. Mar. 1995); children: Angela Lynn Harvey, step-children: Michael Peck, Clifford Ray Harvey. BS, Southwest Mo. State U., Springfield, 1990. Tax preparer H&R Block, Springfield and Aurora, Mo., 1975-85; kennel owner and operator Harvey's Kennel, Marionville, Mo., 1975-82; tax preparer and mem. support staff Baird, Kurtz & Dobson, CPA, Springfield, Mo., 1985-90; staff acct. Zurcher, Sturhahn & Co., CPA, Cassville, Mo., 1991; tax preparer and acct. Caviness & Co., CPA, Monett, Mo., 1993-94; substitute tchr. Cassville Schs., 1992-94; acctg. specialist Daisy Mfg. Co., Rogers, Ark., 1994-96; assoc., tax dept. Wal-Mart, Bentonville, Ark., 1996—. Leader, judge 4-H, Barry & Lawrence County, Mo.; group leader FBLA Ethics Conf., Aurora, Mo., 1993; pres. Nichols Elem. PTA, Springfield, 1975-77. Mem. DAR (mem. chair 1994-96). Republican. Mem. Ch. of Christ. Home: 129 Robinhood Dr Cassville MO 65625 Office: Wal-Mart Corp Offices 702 SW Eighth St Bentonville AR 72716-8013

HARVEY, KATHERINE ABLER, civic worker; b. Chgo., May 17, 1946; d. Julius and Elizabeth (Engelman) Abler; student La Sorbonne, Paris, 1965-66; AAS, Bennett Coll., 1968; m. Julian Whitcomb Harvey, Sept. 7, 1974. Asst. libr. McDermott, Will & Emery, Chgo., 1969-70; librarian Chapman & Cutler, Chgo., 1970-73, Coudert Freres, Paris, 1973-74; adviser, organizer library Lincoln Park Zool. Soc. and Zoo, Chgo., 1977-79, mem. soc.'s women's bd., 1976—, chmn. libr. com., 1977-79, sec., 1979-81, mem. exec. com., 1977-81; mem. jr. bd. Alliance Francaise de Chgo., 1970-76, treas., mem. exec. com., 1971-73, 75-76, mem. women's bd., 1977-80, 95—; mem. Fred Harvey Fine Arts Found., 1976-78; hon. life mem. Chgo. Symphony Soc., 1975—; mem. Phillips Acad. Alumni Coun., Andover, Mass., 1977-81, mem. acad.'s bicentennial celebration com. class celebration leader, 1978, co-chmn. for Chgo. acad.'s bicentennial campaign, 1977-79, mem. student affairs and admissions com., 1980-81; mem. aux. bd. Art Inst. Chgo., 1978-88; mem. Know Your Chgo. com. U. Chgo. Extension, 1981-84; mem. guild Chgo. Hist. Soc., 1978—, bd. dirs., 1993—; mem. women's bd. Lyric Opera Chgo., 1979—, chmn. edn. com., 1980, mem. exec. com., 1980-84, 88—, treas. women's bd., 1983-84, 1st v.p. 1988-90; mem. women's bd. Northwestern Meml. Hosp., 1979—, treas., chmn. fin. com., 1981-84, 92-94, mem. exec. com., 1981-88, 92—, devel. com. 1995—, 2d v.p. 1996—, founding chair pres. com. 1993—; vis. com. Sch. Music Northwestern U., 1995—; bd. dirs. Found. Art Scholarships, 1982-83; bd. dirs. Glen Ellyn (Ill.) Children's Chorus, 1983-90 , founding chmn. pres.'s com., 1983—; mem. women's bd. Chgo. City Ballet, 1983-84; trustee Chgo. Acad. Scis., 1986-88; adv. coun. med. program for performing artists Northwestern Meml. Hosp., 1986-94, mem. exec. com., 1992—, bd. treas., 1992—; pres., bd. dirs. William Ferris Chorale, 1988-89; chmn. pres. com. Chgo. Children's Choir, 1991-93. Mem. Antiquarian Soc. of Art Inst. Chgo. (life); bd. dirs. Grant Park Concerts Soc., 1986-92, Guild of the Chgo. Historical Soc., 1994-96, Antiquarian Soc. Art Inst. Chgo., 1994—. Mem. Arts Club of Chgo. (dir. 1996—), Friday Club (corr. sec. 1981-83), Casino Club (gov. 1982-88, sec. 1984-85, 1987-88, 1st v.p. 1985-86, 2d v.p. 1986-87), Cliff Dwellers CLub. Home: 1209 N Astor St Chicago IL 60610-2300

HARVEY, LYNNE COOPER, broadcasting executive, civic worker; b. nr. St. Louis; d. William A. and Mattie (Kehr) Cooper; A.B., Washington U., St. Louis, 1939, M.A., 1940; m. Paul Harvey, June 4, 1940; 1 son, Paul Harvey Aurandt. Broadcaster ednl. program KXOK, St. Louis, 1940; broadcaster-writer women's news WAC Variety Show, Fort Custer, Mich., 1941-43; gen. mgr. Paul Harvey News, ABC, 1944—; pres. Paulynne Prodns., Ltd., Chgo., 1968—, exec. producer Paul Harvey Comments, 1968—; pres. Trots Corp., 1989—; editor, compiler The Rest of the Story. Pres. woman's bd. Mental Health Assn. Greater Chgo., 1967-71, v.p. bd. dirs., 1966—; pres. woman's aux. Infant Welfare Soc. Chgo., 1969-71, bd. dirs., 1969—; mem. Salvation Army Woman's Adv. Bd., 1967; reception chmn. Community Lectures; Woman's com. Chgo. Symphony, 1972—; pres. Mothers Council, River Forest, 1961-62; charter bd. mem. Gottlieb Meml. Hosp., Melrose Park, Ill.; mem. adv. bd. Nat. Christian Heritage Found., 1964—; mem. USO woman's bd., 1983, woman's bd. Ravinia Festival, 1972—; trustee John Brown U., 1980—; bd. dirs. Mus. Broadcast Communications, 1987—; mem. adv. coun. Charitable Trusts, 1989—; mem. Joffrey Ballet Com. Recipient Religious Heritage of Am. award, 1974, Little City Spirit of Love award, 1987, Salvation Army Others award, 1989. Mem. Phi Beta Kappa, Kappa Delta Pi, Phi Sigma Iota, Eta Sigma Phi. Clubs: Chicago Golf, Woman's Athletic, Nineteenth Century Woman's, Press (Chgo.); Oak Park Country. Home: 1035 Park Ave River Forest IL 60305-1307

HARVEY, MICHELLE MAUTHE, foundation administrator; b. Bethesda, Md., Dec. 29, 1954; d. Benjamin Camille and Lelia Anne (Webre) Mauthe; m. Don Warren Harvey, Mar. 31, 1979; children: Elise Brandner, Benjamin Casimir. BS in Forestry, U. South, 1976; MBA, Duke U., 1989. Forester Internat. Paper Co. Inc., Natchez and Brandon, Miss., 1976-80; framer, mgr. Frame Workshop, Lexington, Ky., 1981-83; mgr., dir. Country Stitchery Frameshop, Raleigh, N.C., 1984; dir. found. rels., placement and internship Sch. Forestry & Environ. Studies Duke U., Durham, N.C., 1984-90; dir. Am. Forest Found., Washington, 1990-92; mgr. planning and devel. Am. Forest Coun., 1990-92; dir. Environ. Partnership Initiative-MEB, Washington, 1993; v.p. programs Nat. Environ. Edn. and Tng. Found., Washington, 1994—; mem. N.Am. Waterfowl Mgmt. Plan Implementation Bd., 1990-92; chair Animal Inn Nat. Partnership, 1992. Bd. dirs. Wake County Literacy Coun., Raleigh, 1984-88, Soc. Preservation Hist. Oakwood City Lights Ball, 1988, Ctr. Children's Environ. Literature, 1994—. Mem. Soc. Internat. Practical Tng. (regional com. 1985-90), Soc. Am. Foresters (nat. task force on forestry edn. 1991-93, sec. human resources working group rep. social scis. to Forest Sci. and Tech. Bd. 1995—, chair nat. capital chpt. 1995-96, 1993-94, nat. leadership conf. steering com. 1990-93, nat. com. on women and minorities 1984-88), Assn. Found. Group (co-chair program planning 1991-93, dean tng. workshops 1991-93), Washington Ethical Soc. (steering com. nat. helping hands craft sale 1992, teen youth leader 1993—). Democrat. Office: NEETF 734 15th St NW Ste 420 Washington DC 20005-2302

HARVEY, NANCY MELISSA, media specialist, art teacher; b. Atlanta, Mar. 31, 1934; d. Alfred Alonzo and Helen Rosella (Puntney) Ettinger; m. Dale Gene Harvey, Aug. 23, 1957; children: Howard Russell, Andrew Dale, Renee Jeannine. BA, U. Mont., 1957; M in Human Svcs., Coll. of Gt. Falls, Mont., 1987. Cert. tchr., Mont. Media specialist, libr. Flathead H.S., Kalispell, Mont., 1971-79; libr., art tchr. Cut Bank (Mont.) H.S., 1979-94. Contbr. poetry to Arts in Mont., Mont. Arts mag., Poetry Today quar., Today's Poets anthology. Recipient Mary Brennan Clapp Poetry awrd Mont. Arts Found., 1973; grantee Mont. Com. for the Humanities, 1985, 87. Mem. AAUW (life), Mont. Genealogy Soc. (treas. Tangled Roots chpt. 1990—), Delta Kappa Gamma (chpt. pres. 1994-96), Phi Kappa Phi. Democrat. Presbyterian.

HARVEY, REBECCA SUZANNE, accountant, business analyst; b. Somerville, N.J., July 21, 1971; d. Ronald Glen H. and Susan Lynn (Hagenbuch) Gerwer. BS in Accounting, Susquehanna U., 1993. Asst. to acct. pay clk. Akzo Engring. Plastics, Neshanic Station, N.J., 1990; asst. to mgr. Wilson Color Inc., Neshanic Station, N.J., 1990-92, asst. to peronnel dir., 1993, acct., 1993-95; SAP R/3 fin. bus. analyst M.A. Hanna Color, Suwanee, Ga., 1995—. Mem. Inst. Mgmt. Accts. Home: 286 Barbertown Point Breeze Rd Frenchtown NJ 08825 Office: MA Manna Color 800 Satellite Blvd Sunwanee GA 30174-2878

HARVEY, WILHELMINA GOEHRING, county and municipal official; b. Key West, Fla., Feb. 7, 1912; d. Edward Goehring and Annie Bromhall (Carey) Page; m. Cornelius B. Harvey II, Feb. 19, 1936 (dec.); 1 child, Cornelius B. Harvey III (dec. 1981). BA, Fla. State U., 1935; MA, Nova U., 1985. Sch. tchr. Monroe County Sch. Bd., Key West, 1934-36, mem. sch. bd., 1968-76; indsl. rels. officer USN, 1940-58; county commr., mayor Monroe County Govt., Key West, 1980-86, 88—. Recipient Oldsmobile Athena award Key West C. of C., Disting. Svc. award NCOA. Mem. NAACP, BPW (pres. Fla. chpt.), Am. Legion Aux. (pres., Disting. Svc. award), Monroe County Vet. Coun., Key West Bus. & Profl. Coun., Zonta (hon.), Key West Women's Club (hon.), Dist. Fedn. Women's Clubs, Polit. Action Women's Club, Martello County Fine Arts Coun., Greater Key West C. of C., Cuban Club, Beta Sigma Phi. Democrat. Episcopalian. Home: PO Box 93 1800 Atlantic Blvd 104A Key West FL 33041 Office: County Monroe 310 Fleming St Key West FL 33040

HARVILL, MELBA SHERWOOD, university librarian; b. Bryson, Tex., Jan. 22, 1933; d. William Henry and Delta Verlin (Brawner) Sherwood; m. L. E. Harvill Jr., Feb. 2, 1968; children: Sherman T. III, Mark Roling. BA, North Tex. State Coll., 1954; MA, North Tex. State U., 1968, MLS, 1973, PhD, 1984. Tchr. Graham (Tex.) Ind. Sch. Dist., 1966-68; reference libr. Midwestern U., Wichita Falls, 1968-73; dir. librs. Midwestern State U., Wichita Falls, 1973—; presenter in field. Vol. Boy Scouts Am., Wichita Falls, 1969-74, Conv. and Visitors Bus. Falls Fifty, 1993—; vol. Wichita Falls Sr.-Jr. Forum, 1978, mem. exec. bd. girls club, ways and means com., sec., asst. treas.; chmn. United Way, Midwestern State U., 1975-76; mem. talent coordinating com. Wichita Falls Centennial Celebration; mem. U. North Tex. Advancement Adv. Coun.; vol. Conv. and Vis. Bur., Lone Stars, 1993—; bd. dirs. YWCA Wichita Falls, 1987-94, pres. bd. dirs., 1989-91, 94-95; grad. Leadership Wichita Falls, 1990. Recipient Svc. award Sr.-Jr. Forum, Wichita Falls United Way Community Svc. award, 1975, Svc. award YWCA Bd. Dirs., 1991; named Met. BPW Woman of Yr., 1980. Mem. ALA, LWV (program v.p., pres. 1991-92), Tex. Libr. Assn. (mem. planning com., mem. membership com., mem. legis. com., mem. rsch. and grants com., chairperson dist VII, chairperson adminstrn. round table), Tex. Coun. State U. Librs. (sec.-treas. 1990-92), Wichita Falls Rotary North (sec. 1993—), U. North Tex. Alumni Assn. (bd. dirs. 1992-94), Phi Alpha Theta, Pi Sigma Alpha, Phi Delta Phi, Gamma Theta Upsilon, Alpha Chi, Beta Phi Mu, Phi Delta Kappa. Democrat. Home: 4428 BUS 287J Iowa Park TX 76367 Office: Midwestern State U 3410 Taft Blvd Wichita Falls TX 76308-2095

HARWARD, VALERIE PIERCE, property consultant; b. Brigham City, Utah, 1940; d. Julian M. Pierce and Bonnie B. (Jeppesen) Jurgensmeier; m. Thomas O. Harward, Jan. 14, 1986; children: George, Allison, Russell, Laura, Lisa, Rachel, Mick, David. Degree, Long Beach (Calif.) City Coll., 1959, postgrad., 1959; postgrad., Utah State U., 1985. State cert. appraiser gen. Adminstrv. asst. Med. Ctr., Long Beach, 1958-60; pres. Creative Cons., Orange County, Calif., 1970-73; owner Color Me Beautiful, 1973—; real estate sales exec. Cache Enterprises and Realty, Logan, Utah, 1980-85; residential sales mgr. Bus. Capital Inc., Logan, 1986; real estate sales agent Preferred Real Estate Investments, Logan, 1986; real estate and bus. cons. McKinley Inst., Orem, Utah, 1986-89; owner Assoc. Property Cons., Murray, Utah, Denver, and Nev., 1986—, Color Me Beautiful. Active Mormon Ch., Long Beach, 1957-71, PTA, Pleasant Grove, Utah; precinct capt. Rep. Central Com., Long Beach, 1959-60; chmn. Nat. Save Children Air Lift, Virginia Beach, Va., 1976. Recipient Svc. award ARC, 1975. Mem. Logan Bd. Realtors (chmn. multiple listing svc. 1985, svc. award 1985, chmn. polit. action com. 1984-86), Utah County Bd. Realtors, Cypress C. of C. (chmn. 1971), Cypress Jr. Women's Club (chmn. 1970). Home and Office: Assoc Property Cons 4253 Sumac Ct Pleasant Grove UT 84062-9456

HARWICK, BETTY CORINNE BURNS, sociology educator; b. L.A., Jan. 22, 1926; d. Henry Wayne Burns and Dorothy Elizabeth (Menzies) Routhier; m. Burton Thomas Harwick, June 20, 1947; children: Wayne Thomas, Burton Terence, Bonnie Christine Foster, Beverly Anne Carroll. Student, Biola, 1942-45, Summer Inst. Linguistics, 1945, U. Calif., Berkeley, 1945-52; BA, Calif. State U., Northridge, 1961, MA, 1965; postgrad., MIT, 1991. Prof. sociology Pierce Coll., Woodland Hills, Calif., 1966-95, pres. acad. senate, 1976-77, pres. faculty assn., 1990-91, chair dept. for philosophy and sociology, 1990-95, co-founder, faculty advisor interdisciplinary religious studies programcreator, 1988-95; chmn. for sociology L.A. C.C. Dist., 1993-95. Author: (with others) Introducing Sociology, 1977; author: Workbook for Introducing Sociology, 1978. faculty rep. Calif. C.C. Assn., 1977-80. Alt. fellow NEH, 1978. Mem. Am. Acad. Religion, Soc. Bibl. Lit., Am. Sociol. Assn. Presbyterian. Home: 19044 Superior St Northridge CA 91324-1845 Office: LA Pierce Coll 6201 Winnetka Ave Woodland Hills CA 91371-0001

HARWOOD, ELEANOR CASH, librarian; b. Buckfield, Me., May 29, 1921; d. Leon Eugene and Ruth (Chick) Cash; B.A., Am. Internat. Coll., 1943; B.S., New Haven State Tchrs. Coll., 1955; m. Burton H. Harwood, Jr., June 21, 1944 (div. 1953); children—Ruth (Mrs. William R. Cline), Eleanor, James Burton. Librarian, Rathbun Meml. Library, East Haddam, Conn., 1955-56; asst. librarian Kent (Conn.) Sch., 1956-63; cons. to Chester (Conn.) Pub. Library, 1965-71. Served from ensign to lt. (j.g.) USNR, 1944-46. Mem. Am., Conn. library assns., Chester Hist. Soc. (trustee 1970-72), D.A.V., Am. Legion Aux., Soc. Mayflower Descs., Appalachian Mountain Club. Mem. United Ch. Author: (with John G. Park) The Independent School Library and the Gifted Child, 1956; The Age of Samuel Johnson, (essay) Remember When, 1987, (essay) Growing Up in Chester, 1993, (novel) Moosley Yours, 1996. Home: 10 Maple St # 255 Chester CT 06412-1316

HARWOOD, LYNNE, artist, book designer; b. Boston, Nov. 16, 1944; d. Reed and Faith (Garrison) H.; m. Roland Louis Gilbert, Aug. 1, 1979 (div. Aug. 1982); children: Curtis Gilbert, Sarah Gilbert. BA, Sarah Lawrence Coll., 1968. self-employed artist, Anson, Maine, 1972—; pres. Union of Maine Visual Artists, 1988. Author, illustrator: Honeybees at Home, 1994. Maine Green Party. Home: RR 1 Box 2060 Anson ME 04911-9742

HARWOOD, VIRGINIA ANN, retired nursing educator; b. Lawrenceville, Ohio, Nov. 5, 1925; d. Warren Leslie and Ruth Ann (Wilson) H.; m. Kenneth Dale Juillerat, Dec. 21, 1946 (div. 1972); children: Rozanne Augsburger, Vicki Sue Terry, Carol Mann, Karen Juillerat. RN, City Hosp. Sch. Nursing, Springfield, Ohio, 1946; BSN, Ind. U., 1968; MS in Edn., Purdue U., 1973, PhD, 1982. Cert. psychiat./mental health nurse, ANA. Staff nurse various hosps., 1946-60; pub. health nursing supr. Whitley County Health Dept., Columbia City, Ind., 1960-65; nursing supr., coordinator staff devel. Ft. Wayne (Ind.) State Hosp., 1965-69; faculty sch. nursing Parkview Hosp., Ft. Wayne, 1969-74; faculty dept. nursing Ball State U., Muncie, Ind., 1974-77; dir. nursing program Thomas More Coll., Ft. Mitchell, Ky., 1977-79; faculty sch. nursing Purdue U., West Lafayette, Ind., 1979-80; dean sch. nursing Ashland (Ohio) Coll., 1980-83; retired, 1983-86; charge nurse admission psychiat. unit VA Med. Ctr., Marion, Ind., 1986-93, ret., 1994—. Active Rep. Nat. Com., 1978—, U.S. Senatorial Club, 1984—, Rep. Pres. Task Force, 1982—; mem. ch. coun. Grace Luth. Ch., Gas City, Ind., 1993-96; bd. dirs. Luth. Ctr., Ball State U., Muncie, Ind. Mem. Am. Nurses Found., Mensa, Sigma Theta Tau. Home: 6611 Quail Ridge Ln Marion IN 46804

HASBROOK, ROSE A., accountant; b. Owatonna, Minn., Apr. 6, 1948; d. Carl Raymond and Ethel Mae (Farka) Quimby; m. Clarence J. Hasbrook, June 30, 1968; children: Brian Paul, Heidi Mae, Christopher Erik. Grad. in Acctg., Hennepin Tech. Coll., 1996. Telephone operator Honeywell, Mpls., 1967-69; receptionist WR Nammon & Co., Mpls., 1969-72; asst. mgr. White Castle, Mpls., 1972-75; mgr. The Smok Haus, Mpls., 1975-77; asst. bookkeeper Superior Plating Inc., Mpls., 1977-79; bookkeeper Bros. Restaurants, St. Louis Park, Minn., 1979-81; premium and commn. technician Prudential Ins. Co., Mpls., 1995; contr. Devin Lane Collections, Mpls., 1995—. Recipient scholarship NSP Co., 1995. Mem. Minn. Truck Driving Championship, Inst. Mgmt. Accts. Home: 1030 24th Ave NE Minneapolis MN 55418 Office: Devin Lane Collections 510 First Ave N Ste 802 Minneapolis MN 55403

HASELTINE, FLORENCE PAT, research administrator, obstetrician, gynecologist; b. Phila., Aug. 17, 1942; d. William R. and Jean Adele Haseltine; m. Frederick Cahn, Mar. 12, 1964 (div. 1969); m. Alan Chodos, Apr. 18, 1970; children: Anna, Elizabeth. BA in Biophysics, U. Calif., Berkeley, 1964; PhD in Biophysics, MIT, 1964-69; MD, Albert Einstein Coll. of Medicine, 1972. Diplomate Am. Bd. Ob-Gyn, Am. Bd. Reproductive Endocrinology. Asst. prof. dept. ob-gyn. and pediatrics Yale U., New Haven, 1976-82, assoc. prof. dept. ob-gyn. and pediatrics, 1982-85; dir. Ctr. for Population Research, Nat. Inst. Child Health and Human Devel. NIH, Bethesda, Md., 1985—; founder Haseltine Systems, Inc., Products for the Disabled, 1995—. Co-author: Woman Doctor, 1976, Magnetic Resonance of the Reproductive System, 1987; co-editor 25 books on reproductive scis. Fellow Am. Coll. Ob-Gyn.; mem. AAAS (bd. dirs.), Inst. of Medicine, Am. Fertility Soc., Soc. Gynecol. Investigation, Soc. for Advancement Women's Health Rsch. (founder, bd. dirs.), Soc. Cell Biology. Office: NIH/NICHD Ctr Population Rsch 9000 Rockville Pike 6100/8B07 Executive Blvd Bethesda MD 20892

HASHIMOTO, CHRISTINE L., physician; b. Chgo., June 29, 1947; d. Shigeru and Kiyo (Sato) H. BA, Oberlin Coll., 1968; MD, Med. Coll. of Pa., 1973. Clin. instr. internal medicine, emergency medicine Med. Coll. and Hosp. of Pa., Phila., 1976-77; asst. prof. medicine Health Service Ctr. U. Colo., Denver, 1977-80, clin. asst. prof. medicine, 1980-87; staff physician emergency dept. St. Joseph Hosp., Denver, 1980-88, Rose Med. Ctr., Denver, 1988-91, Luth. Med. Ctr., Wheatridge, Colo., 1991—. Mem. Colo. Med. Soc., Denver Med. Soc., Am. Coll. Emergency Physicians. Office: Luth Med Ctr 8300 W 38th Ave Wheat Ridge CO 80033-6005

HASKELL, MOLLY, author; b. Charlotte, N.C., Sept. 29, 1939; d. John Haskell and Mary Clark; m. Andrew Sarris, May 31, 1969. BA, Sweet Briar Coll.; student, U. London, England, Sorbonne, Paris. Pub. rels. assoc. Sperry Rand; writer, editor French Film Office, New York; film critic Village Voice, Viva, New York Magazine, Vogue; film reviewer "Special Edition" Pub. TV; film reviewer "All Things Considered" Nat. Pub. Radio; adj. prof. film Columbia U., New York, 1996; writer; artistic dir. Sarasota French Film Festival. Author: From Reverence to Rape: The Treatment of Women in the Movies, 1973, rev. edit., 1987, Love and Other Infectious Diseases: A Memoir, 1990, Holding My Own in No Man's Land, 1996; (plays) The Last Anniversary, 1990; contbr. articles and essays to jours. Recipient Nat. Bd. Review of Motion Pictures award, 1989, Chevalier de l'Ordre des Artes et des Lettres, 1989, Disting. Alumna award Stweet Briar Coll., 1994. Mem. Nat. Soc. of Film Festival Selection Critics, N.Y. Film Critics Circle, N.Y. Film Festival Selection Com., N.Y. Inst. for the Humanities, The Century Club, Phi Beta Kappa.

HASKINS, LINDA L., English educator; b. Beaver Falls, Pa., Aug. 31, 1947; d. Henry Griffin and H. Elizabeth Haskins. BA in English, Del. State U., 1969; MA in English, Seton Hall U., 1971; MA in Film, West Chester State U., 1983. Instr. Capitol Sch. Dist., Dpver, Del., 1971-72, U. Del., Newark, 1972-75; asst. prof. Del. State U., Dover, 1975—. Contbg. editor: Succeeding Despite the Odds. Recipient NEH award, 1983. Mem. AAUP, AAUW, Nat. Coun. Tchrs. of English, NAACP, Alpha Kappa Mu, Alpha Kappa Alpha. Office: Del State U 1200 N DuPont Hwy Dover DE 19901-2277

HASSAN, BARBARA JEAN, banker; b. Boise, Idaho, Jan. 20, 1947; d. Carl L. and Marilyn R. (Carson) Sparks; m. James Feldman, June 25, 1968 (div. Nov. 1972); m. Nabil M. Hassan, June 30, 1973; children: Sharif M., Adham C. Grad. H.S., Yakima, Wash. Lic. notary pub., Wash. Head teller Seattle Trust & Savs., 1966-71; customer svc. supr. Lloyds Bank, San Francisco, 1971-77; customer svc. officer Wells Fargo Bank, San Francisco, 1977-82; br. mgr., asst. v.p. Yakima (Wash.) Fed. Savs., 1985—; chmn. adv. bd. Stanton Alternative Sch., Yakima, 1990-92. Mem. Fin. Women Internat. (treas. 1993-94, v.p. 1994-95, pres. 1995-96). Democrat. Presbyterian. Home: 1112 S 32nd Ave Yakima WA 98902 Office: Yakima Fed Savs 3910 Tieton Dr Yakima WA 98902

HASSELBALCH, MARILYN JEAN, state official; b. Omaha, Jan. 2, 1930; d. Paul William and Helga Esther (Nodgaard) Campfield; m. Hal Burke Hasselbalch, June 13, 1954 (div. 1973); children: Kurt Campfield, Eric Burke, Peter Nels, Ane Catherine. BA with high distinction, U. Nebr., 1951. Cert. secondary tchr., Nebr. Pub. sch. tchr. Omaha and Long Beach, Calif., 1951-55; staff asst. U.S. Congressman Charles Thone, Lincoln, Nebr., 1973-78, Gov. of Nebr., Lincoln, 1978-82; exec. asst. Nebr. State Treas., Lincoln, 1983-86; sr. asst. Nebr. Gov. Kay A. Orr, Lincoln, 1987-91; exec. dir. Nebr. Appraiser Licensing Bd., Lincoln, 1991—. Mem. camp bd. dirs. YMCA, Nebr., 1969-70; mem. Nebr. Edn. Policies Commn., 1982; state conv. del. Rep. Party Nebr., 1986, 88; gov.'s rep. Nebr. State Hist. Soc., Lincoln, 1987-89; del. Edn. Commn. on States, Balt., 1988; participant strategic leadership for gubernatorial execs. Duke U., 1988; sec. Mission bd. Christ Luth. Ch., 1993—; treas. Danish Sisterhood # 90, 1995—. Named to Outstanding Young Women Am., 1961. Mem. Nat. Fedn. Rep. Women, Lancaster County Rep. Women (exec. bd. 1988), Am. Legion Aux., Assn. Appraiser Regulatory Ofcls. (bd. dirs. 1995—), Danish Sisterhood Am., Phi Beta Kappa, Theta Sigma Phi, Kappa Tau Alpha. Lutheran. Home: 4705 South St Lincoln NE 68506-1257 Office: Real Estate Appraiser Bd Nebr State Office Bldg Lincoln NE 68509

HASSELL, PAMELA SUSAN, photography educator; b. Rockville Centre, N.Y.; d. Edwin Robert and Pauline (Malone) H. Student, Sch. Visual Arts, N.Y.C., 1969-71; BA in Art History with honors, Stony Brook U., 1974; MA in Art History, Goddard Coll., 1978. Picture rschr. Connoisseur Mag., N.Y.C., 1984, asst. picture editor, 1985-86, assoc. picture editor, 1986-88, picture editor, 1988-90, dir. photography, 1990-92; dir. photography Buzz Mag., L.A., 1992-95; photography instr. UCLA Ext., L.A., 1995—, Otis Coll. Art and Design, L.A., 1996—. Active NOW-S.W. Chpt., Calif., 1995-96. Recipient cert. of excellence for picture editor Comm. Arts Photography, 1990, cert. of excellence for dir. of photography Comm. Arts Photography, 199, cert. of distinction for mag. cover design Creativity, 1991, cert. of merit for photography Soc. of Publ. Designers-29th Annual Competition, 1993. Mem. Women in Film.

HASSENBOEHLER, DONALYN, principal. Prin. McMain Magnet Secondary Sch.; evaluator FIRST grants U.S. Dept. Edn. Recipient U.S. Dept. Edn. Blue Ribbon award, 1990-91. Office: McMain Magnet Secondary Sch 5712 S Claiborne Ave New Orleans LA 70125-4908

HASSERT, ELIZABETH ANNE, transportation executive; b. Joliet, Ill., July 28, 1956; d. Wilbur Clarence and Frances Romayne (McLaughlin) H. BA, St. Mary's Coll., Notre Dame, Ind., 1978. Dept. mgr. Lord & Taylor, Aurora, Ill., 1978-79, Oak Brook, Ill., 1979-80; account exec. Cast (N.Am.) Ltd., Rolling Meadows, Ill., 1980-82; sales mgr. Cast (UK) Ltd., London, 1982-83, Sofati Container (UK), Birmingham, Eng., 1983-84; account exec. Sea-Land Svc., Inc., Rolling Meadows, 1984-88, sales mgr., 1988-90, sales exec., 1990—; recognition sponsor Quality Mgmt. Sea-Land Svc., Inc., 1989-92. Recipient of CSX award of Excellence, 1993. Mem. Ocean Freight Agts., World Trade Club, Midwest Fgn. Freight Club, Hinsdale Jr. Women's Club, Detroit Ocean Freight Agy., St. Mary's Coll. Alumnae Assn. Republican. Roman Catholic. Home: 625 N County Line Rd Hinsdale IL 60521-2406 Office: Sea-Land Svc Inc 3501 W Algonquin Rd Ste 600 Rolling Meadows IL 60008-3132

HASSETT, MARY RUTH, nursing educator; b. San Bernardino, Calif., July 20, 1944; d. Raymond Vernon and Mary Elizabeth (Rudolph) Mortorff; m. Roland Warren Coleman, Dec. 26, 1964 (div. Feb. 1977); 1 child, Timothy James Coleman; m. C. Michael Hassett, Feb., 1977; stepchildren: Deborah Kay Hassett Riffel, Vicki Lynn Hassett Ellis. BSN, Pacific Luth. U., 1971; M of Nursing, UCLA, 1974; PhD in Nursing, U. Tex., 1990. CNS, Kans. Staff nurse med.-surg. Mercy Hosp., San Diego, 1964; charge nurse well-care unit Whittier (Calif.) Presbyn. Intercom. Hosp., 1964; staff nurse med.-surg. Tacoma (Wash.) Gen. Hosp., 1969-70; staff nurse oper. rm. & med.-surg. Providence Hosp., Washington, 1965; staff nurse oper. rm./PAR & med.-surg. Whittier Hosp., 1968-69; charge nurse oper. rm./PAR Beverly Hosp., Montebello, Calif., 1970-72; staff nurse mental health D.E. Brotman Meml. Hosp., Culver City, Calif., 1973-74; instr. psychiat. tech. Rio Hondo C.C., Whittier, 1974-75; instr. registered nursing Cypress (Calif.) Coll., 1975-77; prof., dir. grad. studies Ft. Hays State U., Hays, Kans., 1979-94, chair, prof. dept. nursing, 1994—; cons. sex and disability U. Calif.-San Francisco Sch. Medicine, 1976; cons. computer-based instrn. Kans. State Bd. Nursing, Topeka, 1992—. Contbr. book chpts.: Computer applications in nursing education and practice, 1992 (AJN award 1993), Procs. of Fourth Internat. Conf. on Nursing Use of Computers and Info. Sci., 1991; contbr. book abstracts: Dissertation Abstracts International, 1991, Procs. Fifth Internat. Conf. on Nursing Use of Computers and Info. Sci., 1994; contbr. articles to nursing jours.; script cons. (videotapes) Spiritual Care practicua, 1981. Chair bd. dirs. Comty. Day Care Ctr., Inc., Hays, 1981-82; chair com. on grants, rep. Care Network, Inc., Hays, 1986-88; mem. human resources devel. com. Kans. Dept. Social and Rehab. Svcs., Mental Health & Retardation Svcs.,

Topeka, 1991-92, co-chair Healthcare subcom. Hays Info., 1995-96. Dept. Health, Edn. & Welfare Mental Health Tng. grantee, 1976-78, grantee Ellis County, Kans., 1988, IBM, 1989-92, 90, U.S. Dept. Health & Human Svcs. Tng. grantee, 1992-95. Mem. ANA (coun. on computer applications in nursing, coun. nurse rschrs.), Nat. League for Nursing (coun. nursing informatics), Assn. for Devel. Computer-Based Instrnl. Sys. (interactive video-audio SIG chair 1992-94, bd. dirs. 1993-94, editl. rev. bd. 1994-95), Am. Med. Informatics Assn. (assoc., nursing informatics working group), Kans. State Nurse's Assn. (coun. on edn. 1985-87, steering com. 1986-88, pres. dist. 16 1986-88, editl. bd. 1992, 93, Excellence in Continuing Edn. award 1992). Republican. Mem. Assemblies of God. Home: 2910 Roosevelt Hays KS 67601-2033 Office: Ft Hays State U STH 122 C 600 Park St Hays KS 67601-4009

HASTINGS, DEBORAH, bass guitarist; b. Evansville, Ind., May 11, 1959; d. Mortimer Winthrop Hastings and Margaret Hooper (Smith) Zimmerman. Student music, U. Wis. Bass guitarist N.Y.C. and Madison, Wis., 1975—; freelance photographer Madison, 1976-81; band leader Bo Diddley, 1992—; founder A/Prompt Computer Telepromting Svcs., Inc., 1994—; performed Inauguration Pres. George Bush, 1989; performed with Billy Preston, Dr. John, Koko Taylor, Willie Dixon, Albert Collins, Joe Cocker, Carla Thomas, Eddie Floyd, Ron Wood, Steve Cropper, Bo Diddley, Jerry Lee Lewis, George Gobel, Chuck Berry, Joe Louis Walker, Ben E. King, Sarah Dash, Little Anthony and the Imperials, Sam Moore, Chuck Jackson, John Lee Hooker, Mick Fleetwood, Al Kooper, Huey Lewis, James Cotton; TV shows include Legends of Rock and Roll Live from Rome performed with Bo Diddley, BB King, James Brown, Little Richard, Ray Charles, Fats Domino, others. Author: Photographers Market, 1981; bass player TV shows Joan Rivers, 1987, Classsics of Rock and Roll, 1988, Gunslingers tour Live from the Ritz with Ron Wood & Bo Diddley, 1988, Live from the Ritz, 1989, Legends of Rock and Roll (live from Australia), Legends of Guitar from Seville, Spain, 1991, Showtime at the Apollo, 1992, N.Y. at Night, 1992; performed Into The Night, 1991 (TV show) Nashville Now, 1991, American Musicshop, 1991, Greece, Johnny Carson Show, 1990, Pat Sajak Show, 1990, Carla Thomas, 1991, Arts & Entertainment Revue, 1990, (Madison Sq. Garden) Tribute to John Lee Hooker, 1990, Richard Nader's 25th Anniversary Show, 1994, Conan O'Brien Show, 1996; recordings include Bo Diddley's 40th Anniversary Album A Man Amongst Men, 1996; performer in concert video A Man Amongst Men, 1996; 89 tours in Europe, Australia and Japan. Fundraiser, bassist polit. campaigns, Madison; bass player Pres. Bush inauguration, 1989. Recipient numerous awards for pottery, award Arts Coun., Madison, Arts Coun., Ann Arbor, Mich. Mem. Musicians Union (local 802). Democrat. Office: Talent Cons Internat 1560 Broadway Ste 1308 New York NY 10036-1525

HASTINGS, L(OIS) JANE, architect, educator; b. Seattle, Mar. 3, 1928; d. Harry and Camille (Pugh) H.; m. Norman John Johnston, Nov. 22, 1969. B.Arch., U. Wash., Seattle, 1952, postgrad. in Urban Planning, 1958. Architect Boeing Airplane Co., Seattle, 1951-54; recreational dir. Germany, 1954-56; architect (various firms), Seattle, 1956-59, pvt. practice architecture, 1959-74; instr. archtl. drafting Seattle Community Coll., part-time 1969-80; owner/founder The Hastings Group Architects, Seattle, 1974—; lectr. design Coll. Architecture, U. Wash., 1975; incorporating mem. Architecta (P.S.), Seattle, 1980; pres. Architecta (P.S.), from 1980; mem. adv. bd. U. Wash. YWCA, 1967-69; mem. Mayor's Com. on Archtl. Barriers for Handicapped, 1974-75; chmn. regional public adv. panel on archtl. and engring. services GSA, 1976; mem. citizens adv. com. Seattle Land Use Adminstrn. Task Force, from 1979; AWIU guest of Soviet Women's Con., 1983; speaker Pacific Rim Forum, Hong Kong, 1987; guest China Internat. Conf. Ctr. for Sci. and Tech. of the China Assn. for Sci. and Tech., 1989; mem. adv. com. Coll. architecture and urban planning U. Wash., 1993; mem. accreditation team U. Oreg. Coll. Architecture, 1991, N.J. Inst. Tech. Sch. Architecture, 1992. Design juror for nat. and local competitions, including Red Cedar Shingle/AIA awards, 1977, Current Use Honor awards, AIA, 1980, Exhibit of Sch. Architecture award, 1981; Contbr. to: also spl. features newspapers, articles in profl. jours. Sunset mag. Mem. bd. Am. Women for Internat. Understanding, del. to, Egypt, Israel, USSR, 1971, Japan and Korea, 1979, USSR, 1983; mem. Landmarks Preservation Bd. City of Seattle, 1981-83; mem. Design Constrn. Rev. Bd. Seattle Sch. Dist., 1985-87; mem. mus. con. Mus. History and Industry, 1987—; leader People to People del. women architects to China, 1990. Recipient AIA/The Seattle Times Home of Month Ann. award, 1968; Exhbn. award Seattle chpt. AIA, 1970; Environ. award Seattle-King County Bd. Realtors, 1970, 77,; AIA/House and Home/The American Home Merit award, 1971, Sp. Honor award Wash. Aggregates and Concrete Assn., 1993, Prize bridge Am. Inst. Steel Contrn., 1993; Honor award Seattle chpt. AIA, 1977, 83; Women Achievement award Past Pres. Assembly, 1983, Washington Women and Trading Cards, 1983; Nat. Endowment for Arts grantee, 1977; others; named to West Seattle High Sch. Hall of Fame, 1989, Woman of Achievement Matrix Table, 1994; named Woman of Distinction, Columbia River Girl Scout Coun., 1994. Fellow AIA (pres. Seattle chpt. 1975, pres. sr. coun. 1980, state exec. bd. 1975, N.W. regional dir. 1982-87, Seattle chpt. found. bd. 1985-87, Bursar Coll. Fellows 1989-90, Coll. of Fellows historian 1994—, internat. rels. com. 1988-92, vice chancellor 1991, chancellor 1992, Seattle chpt. medal 1995), Internat. Union Women Architects (v.p. 1969-79, sec. gen. 1985-89, del. UIA Congress, Montreal 1990), Am. Arbitration Assn. (arbitrator 1981—), Coun. of Design Professions, Assn. Women Contrs., Suppliers and Design Cons., Allied Arts Seattle, Fashion Group, Tau Sigma Delta, Alpha Rho Chi (medal). Office: The Hastings Group-Architects 603 Stewart St #915 Seattle WA 98101

HASTINGS, MARY LYNN, real estate broker; b. Carthage, N.Y., Jan. 16, 1943; d. Floyd Albert and Mary Frances (Schack) Neuroth; m. Ronald Anthony Casel, Nov. 28, 1963 (div. Nov. 1977); children: Mark, Steven, Glen; m. Charles F. Hastings, Apr. 27, 1991. Grad. Harper Method, Rochester, N.Y., 1961. Lic. real estate broker. Owner M. L. Salon, Rochester, N.Y., 1962-72; specialty tchrs.-aide Broward County, Ft. Lauderdale, Fla., 1973-77; office mgr. Broward County Voter Registration, Margate, Fla., 1977-82; real estate salesperson Pelican Bay, Daytona Beach, Fla., 1982-84, broker, 1984—, broker; owner Mary Lynn Realty, 1989—. Mem. adv. bd. Dem. Club, Margate, Fla., 1977-82. Mem. Nat. Assn. Realtors, Fla. Home Builders Assn., Nat. Home Builders Assn., Daytona Beach Home Builders Assn., Daytona Beach Bd. Realtors, Ft. Lauderdale Bd. Realtors, Nat. Assn. Women in Constrn. (v.p. 1988-89, pres.-elect 1989—, pres. 1990—), NAFE, Sales and Mktg. Council. Avocations: travel, dancing, theater, real estate investments. Democrat. Roman Catholic. Home: 1301 Beville Rd Daytona Beach FL 32119 Office: Mary Lynn Realty 1301 Beville Rd # 20 Daytona Beach FL 32119

HASTINGS, SALLY ANN, historian, educator; b. Framingham, Mass., Mar. 21, 1945; d. Dana Bowers and Florence Mary (Ames) H.; m. H. Reid Nolte, June 25, 1988. BA magna cum laude, Tufts U., 1967; MA in East Asian Studies, Yale U., 1969; PhD in Japanese History, U. Chgo., 1980. From instr. to assoc. prof. Northeastern Ill. U., Chgo., 1979-90; from asst. prof. to assoc. prof. history Purdue U., West Lafayette, Ind., 1990—; postdoctoral fellow Japan Inst. Harvard U., Cambridge, Mass., 1983-84; vis. asst. prof. U. Iowa, Iowa City, 1984-85; vis. assoc. prof. history U. Mich., Ann Arbor, 1995. Author: Neighborhood and Nation in Tokyo, 1995; co-editor U.S.-Japan Women's Jour., 1995—. Committeeman Whiteside County (Ill.) Dem. Com., 1994-96. Mem. Assn. for Asian Studies (coun. of confs. 1995—), Am. Hist. Assn., Midwest Conf. on Asian Affairs (exec. sec. 1990-93), Midwest Japan Seminar (chair 1984-88), Phi Beta Kappa. Episcopalian. Home: 304 W 14th St Sterling IL 61081 Office: Purdue Univ History Dept University Hall West Lafayette IN 47907

HASTINGS, TRISH D., counselor; b. Atlanta, Nov. 4, 1960; d. Richard W. and Dorothy I. (Ingram) H. BS in Psychology, Ga. State U., 1983; MA in Counseling, Regent U., 1993, cert., 1993. Lic. profl. counselor. Libr. prin. assoc. Fulton County, Atlanta, 1983-91; intern counselor Regent U., Va. Beach., 1992-93; PRN social worker Brawner Mental Health, Smyrna, Ga., 1993-94; acting dir. of counseling svcs. Toccoa Falls (Ga.) Coll., 1995-96; pvt. practice Toccoa, 1996—; mem. Toccoa Falls Coll. Counseling Com., 1995-96. Inreach/outreach leader 1st Bapt. Ch. of Sandy Springs, Atlanta, 1982-91, vol. Feed the Hungry Found., Atlanta, 1985-87. Mem. ACA, Am. Assn. of Christian Counselors, Lic. Profl. Counselors Assn. of Ga. Office: PO Box 724 Toccoa GA 30577

HATCH, DOROTHY LEBAKER, writer, actress; b. L.A., Apr. 6, 1920; d. Edwin Harrison and Estelle (Saff) LeBaker; m. William Edward Hatch, June 22, 1941 (dec. Oct. 1977); children: Dorothea Lee, William Edward, Jr. BA, Stanford U., 1943; studied at Breadloaf and with Robert Fro, Ripton, Vt., 1955; student, Inst. Advanced Studies in The Theatre Arts, N.Y.C., 1964, Bodleian, Oxford, Eng., 1982. Performer The Harvard Dames, Cambridge, Mass., 1946-57; prin. actress Adelphi Summer Stock, N.Y., 1964-65, Greenwich Mews, N.Y.C., 1966; character actress Children's Theater Internat., Inc., N.Y.C., 1967-69; prin. actress The Westchester Theater Co., N.Y., 1968; film actress Forman, Crown Hausman, Inc., 1970, Frank Perry Films, Inc., 1970, Rollins & Joffe Prodns., 1970; cons. poetry Stone House Press, Roslyn, N.Y., 1983—, devel. adv. com. Libr. Assocs., Stanford U., 1993; vis. com. to pres. on librs., Stanford, 1984-87. Author: Waking to the Day, 1985, The Curious Act of Poetry, 1991; appeared in Racine's Phèdre, Comédie Française, N.Y., 1966. V.p. LWV, Hempstead-Garden City, N.Y., 1948-50; co-founder Free Assn. Libr., Garden City, 1952; chmn. AAUW, Garden City, 1962-65; reader, recorder Recording for the Blind, N.Y.C., 1970; pres. Hofstra U. Libr. Assocs. Rare Books, 1975; leader Poetry Readers' Workshop Garden City Adult Edn., 1975-77; bd. dirs. Adelphi U. Friends, Garden City, 1978; mem. exec. bd. Friends of Garden City Pub. Libr., 1989—. Recipient Svc. award Pres. Payton Hofstra U., 1975. Mem. SAG, AFTRA, Actors' Equity Assn., The Grolier Club N.Y., Poets & Writers, Inc. (listed writer), Pen and Brush Inc. (Candace Stevenson Poetry award 1983), Poetry Soc. Am. (life) (award 1977), The Actors' Fund Am. (life), Hist. Socs. Garden City and L.I. (life).

HATCH, KELLEY MARIE, journalist, television news anchor, writer; b. Balt., June 16, 1958; d. Roland W. and Ava Marie (Jackson) Marsh; m. James R. Johnson II (div.); children: Jeremiah Shawn, Joshua Adam; m. Brett Wilder Hatch, Feb. 22, 1992. Student, Lincoln Meml. U., 1976-77, U. Mich., Flint, 1987-88, N.Mex. State U., 1989. Mktg.cons. Sta. KPSA, Alamogordo, N.Mex., 1989-90; dir. mktg. Temporarily Yours, Inc., Farmington, N.Mex., 1991; account exec. Sta. KOBF-TV, Farmington, 1991-92, news anchor, 1992-96; freelance writer, 1996—. Pres. Am. Heart Assn., 1994, bd. dirs., sec., 1991-92; bd. dirs. Childhaven, 1992—, San Juan Stage Co., 1991—; bd. dirs., fin. devel. com. ARC, 1992—. Recipient Best Investigative News award, AP, 1993, 95, Honorable Mention Gen. News award, AP, 1994, Top Story of Yr. award N.Mex. Broadcasters, 1995. Mem. Am. Bus. Women's Assn. (pres. 1991). Republican.

HATCH, MARIA ANNA, restaurant owner; b. Las Cruces, N.Mex., July 17, 1959; d. Fred F. and Rosa Christopherson (DeVargas) Christopherson; m. Harry J. Hatch, Nov. 27, 1982; children: Lauren D., Derek J. BA in Edn., N.Mex. State U., 1995. Exec. sec. N.Y. Life Ins., Las Cruces, 1978-82; owner, mgr. Dairy Queen Restaurants, Las Cruces, 1982—. Mem. ways and means com. Jr. League Las Cruces, 1993-95. Crimson scholar N.Mex. State U., Las Cruces, 1992-93. Home: 2245 Sunrise Point Las Cruces NM 88011

HATCH, WILDA GENE, broadcast company executive; b. Ogden, Utah, Nov. 28, 1917; d. Abraham Lincoln and Edris Alida (Toombs) Glasmann; m. George Clinton Hatch, Dec. 24, 1940; children: Michael Zbar, Diane G. Orr, Jeffrey B., Randall C., Deepika Ogsbury. BA, Stanford U., 1939; HHD (hon.), Weber State U., 1981. Pres. The Std. Corp., Ogden, 1955—; v.p. Sta. KUTV, Salt Lake City, 1956-94. Pres. Women's State Legis. Coun., Salt Lake City, 1967-69; active LWV, Salt Lake City, 1965—. Democrat. Home: 1537 Chandler Dr Salt Lake City UT 84103-4220

HATCHER, LUCILLE ROBINSON, science educator; b. Prairie Point, Miss., July 28, 1951; d. Eddie D. and Lucille (White) Robinson; m. Levi Mark Hatcher, Dec. 27, 1994; children: Christopher, Ayatti, Lavetta. BSBA, Alcorn State U., 1973; BS in Secondary Sci., Miss. State U., 1976, BS in Biology, 1993. Data processor Sparatus Corp., Louisville, Miss., 1973-74; tchr. gen. sci., earth sci., biology, bus. math. Noxubee County Schs., Macon, Miss., 1974—; co-owner Pineywood Quik Shop, Macon, 1985-90, Airport Food Mart, Macon, 1987—, Corner Quick Stop, 1987-92, Our Restaurant, 1995—; coord. reading and GED program, 1992-93. Advisor, editor: (newsletter) The Energy Educators, 1988 (1st pl. award 1988). Mem. NAACP, Jackson, Miss., 1987; del. Young Dems. of Miss., Jackson, 1979, Young Dems. of Am., St. Louis, 1980; scout leader Girl Scouts Am., Macon, 1976; ch. adminstr. Fellowship of Hope Comty. Ch., 1990-94. Recipient Miss. State award of excellence Miss. Dept. of Energy, 1987, Miss. Gov.'s award, 1988; grantee Noxubee County Edn. Fund, 1987-91. Mem. Nat. Assn. Biology Tchrs., Nat. Mid. Sch. Tchrs., Miss. Sci. Tchrs. Assn., Miss. Assn. Edn. and Nat. Dels., Noxubee County Assn. Edn. Pres. (past pres.). Home: 202 E North St Macon MS 39341-2810

HATELEY, LYNNETTE SUE, telecommunications, cable and multimedia analyst; b. Burns, Wyo., May 12, 1949; d. Raymond Ervin and Ethel Vivian (Stagner) Woolery; m. James Wilbur Hateley Jr., Aug. 19, 1971; children: Rae Lynn Woolery, James Trevor Woolery, Shannon Layne Woolery, William Sterling Stagner. BS in Bus. Adminstrn. with honors, U. Wyo., 1971; MS in Fin. with honors, U. Ariz., 1975; postgrad., U. Denver, 1974-75. CFA. Ops. asst. Mountain Bell Operator Svcs., Phoenix, 1973-74; fin. analyst Mountain Bell Treasury and Revenue Requirements, Denver, 1974-79; mgr. product forecasting Mountain Bell Bus. Mktg., Denver, 1979-82; mktg. and fin. analyst Mountain Bell New Ventures, Denver, 1982-85; staff mgr. opportunity analyses U.S. West Mktg./Bus. Devel., Denver, 1985-87; staff mgr. fin. strategies U.S. West Comms. and Treasury, Denver, 1987-89; mgr. fin. analysis and modeling Info. Providers Market, Denver, 1989-91; fin. analyst-telecomms. carriers fin. analyst-telecomms. carrier, Denver, 1991-93; mgr. market analysis and bus. devel. U.S. West Multimedia Comms., Inc., Englewood, Colo., 1993—; investment cons. Market Navigators Inc., Denver, 1991—. Mem. Voice of Many Feathers, Denver, 1994. Mem. Assn. for Investment Mgmt. and Rsch. (exam. staff 1991—), Denver Soc. Security Analysts, Beta Gamma Sigma, Phi Kappa Phi, Phi Gamma Nu (pres. 1967-71). Episcopalian. Office: US West Multimedia Comms 9785 S Maroon Cir Englewood CO 80112-5919

HATFIELD, JANICE LEE (FORD), secondary education educator; b. Washington, Jan. 23, 1941; m. William F. Hatfield. BS, Concord Coll., Athens, W.Va., 1962; MA in English, Bowling Green State U., 1964; postgrad., W.Va. U., 1977-80. Tchr. Alderson (W.Va.) H.S., 1963-64, Beverly (W.Va.) H.S., 1964-65, Charles Town (W.Va.) Sch., 1965-67; instr. W.Va. U., Morgantown, 1967-69, Marshall U., Huntington, W.Va., 1969-70, King's Coll., Raleigh, N.C., 1974-75, N.C. State U., Raleigh, 1975-76; teaching fellow W.Va. U., 1977-80; tchr. English West Greene H.S., Waynesburg, Pa., 1981—. We. Pa. Writing Project fellow, 1993. Mem. ASCD, nat. Coun. Tchrs. English, We. Pa. Coun. Tchrs. English. Home: PO Box 353 Mount Morris PA 15349-0353 Office: West Greene Schs RR 5 Box 36-a Waynesburg PA 15370-8600

HATFIELD, JULIANA, vocalist; b. Duxbury, Mass., 1968. Student, Berklee Sch. Music. Recording and performing artist, 1987—; singer, bass guitarist Blake Babies, 1987-91. Albums (solo) include Hey Babe, 1992, Become What Your Are, 1993, Only Everything, 1995, (with Blake Babies) Nicely, Nicely, 1987, Earwig, 1989, Sunburn, 1990, (with Lemonheads) It's a Shame About Ray, 1992, Come On Feel the Lemonheads, 1993. Office: Atlantic Records 75 Rockefeller Plaza New York NY 10019 also: 9229 Sunset Blvd Los Angeles CA 90069*

HATFIELD, JULIE STOCKWELL, journalist, newspaper editor; b. Detroit, Mar. 22, 1940; d. William Hume and Ruth Reed (Palmer) Stockwell; m. Philip Mitchell Hatfield, Aug. 1, 1964 (div. 1979); children—Christian Andrew, Juliana, Jason David; m. Timothy Leland, Nov. 23, 1984; stepchildren—Christian Bourso, London Chamberlain. B.A., U. Mich, 1962. Staff reporter Women's Wear Daily, NYC, 1962-64; freelance feature writer Bath-Brunswick Times, Wis. State Jour., 1964-68, Quincy Patriot Ledger, Mass., 1968-77; freelance music critic, fashion editor Boston Herald, 1977-79; fashion editor Boston Globe, 1979-95, living/arts writer, 1995-96, soc. columnist, 1996—. Author: (with others) Guide to the Thrift Shops of New England, 1982. Recipient Lulu award Men's Fashion Assn., 1985, Atrium award for Outstanding WRiting on Fashion U. Ga., 1987, 92; Nat. Endowmend Arts grantee, 1973. Episcopalian. Office: Boston Globe Newspaper 135 Morrissey Blvd Dorchester MA 02125-3310

HATHAWAY, LYNN MCDONALD, education advocate, administrator; b. N.Y.C., Mar. 28, 1939; d. William Douglas IV and Dorothy Edna (Homan) McDonald; m. Earl Burton Hathaway II, July 7, 1962; children: Earl Burton III, Amanda McDonald. BA, Bryn Mawr Coll., 1960. Editorial asst. Mademoiselle mag., N.Y.C., 1960-61; adminstrv. asst. Peace Corps office Nat. Coun. Chs., N.Y.C., 1961-62; vice chmn. community rsch. N.Y. Jr. League, 1969-70; editor, chmn. N.Y. Entertains cookbook, 1973-74; edn. chair London Svc. League, 1979-80; pres., dir. London Svc. League, Jr. League, 1980-82; ind. writer, editor London, 1983. Bd. dirs. Friends of Ferguson Libr., Stamford, Conn., 1988, mem., rec. sec., v.p., pres., 1988-95, trustee, 1995—; trustee, mem. exec. com., chair student life com. Conn. State U. Sys., 1991—. Mem. Bryn Mawr Alumnae Assn. (pres. London 1983-86, internat. councillor 1988-90). Episcopalian. Home: 50 Old North Stamford Rd Stamford CT 06905-3961

HATLER, PATRICIA RUTH, lawyer; b. Las Vegas, Nev., Aug. 4, 1954; d. Houston Eugene and Laurie (Danforth) Hatler; m. Howard A. Coffin II; children: Sloan H. D. Coffin, Laurie H. M. Coffin. BS, Duke U., 1976; JD, U. Va., 1980. Bar: Pa. 1980. Assoc. Dechert, Price & Rhoads, Phila., 1980-83; assoc. counsel Independence Blue Cross, Phila., 1983-86, sr. v.p., gen. counsel, corp. sec., 1987—. Home: 116 Millcreek Rd Ardmore PA 19003-1504 Office: Independence Blue Cross 1901 Market St Philadelphia PA 19103-1400

HATLEY, AMY BELL, elementary education educator, broadcast journalist; b. Concord, N.C., May 5, 1940; d. Austin H. and Frances Louise (Norris) Bell; m. Wayne Douglas Hatley, Aug. 27, 1961; 1 child, Adam Douglas. BA, Meredith Coll., 1962; MEd, Converse Coll., 1986. Cert. tchr. N.C., S.C. Tchr. grades 1-3 Thomasboro Elem., Charlotte, N.C., 1962-67; tchr. grade 3 Thomasboro Elem., Charlotte, 1968-71; tchr. grade 2 Allenbrook Elem., Charlotte, 1966-67, Charlotte (N.C.) Latin, 1971-72, Carmel Acad., Charlotte, 1972-75, Spartanburg (S.C.) Day Sch., 1977—; broadcast journalist, assignment editor WSPA AM-FM Radio & TV, CBS Affiliate, Spartanburg, 1984—. Author, producer: (broadcast documentary series) The Unraveling of the American Teacher, 1989 (1st pl. award AP 1989), Standardized Testing: Has It Failed the Grade?, 1990 (1st pl. award AP 1990), Illiteracy: S.C.'s Abiding Legacy, 1991 (1st pl. award AP 1991). Com. chmn. Bd. Spartanburg (S.C.) Little Theater, 1990; mem. pub. rels. com. United Way of the Piedmont, Spartanburg, 1991-94; bd. regents Leadership Spartanburg, 1992-94; bd. dirs. Spartanburg County Literacy Orgn.; edn. com. Spartanburg CCounty Consensus Project, 1991-94; strategy com. Spartanburg County Am. 2000 Project, 1992-94. Mem. Nat. Press Fedn., Palmetto Assn. Ind. Schs., Spartanburg Speakers Bur., S.C. Media Women. Methodist. Home: 2581 Moore Duncan Hwy Moore SC 29369-9453 Office: WSPA-TV Communications Park Spartanburg SC 29304

HATTAN, SUSAN K., legislative staff member; b. Lincoln, Nebr., Jan. 11, 1951; d. Hubert Curtis and Margaret Marie H. BA summa cum laude, Washburn U., 1973; MA with distinction, Am. U., 1977. Legis. aide to Senator Robert J. Dole, Washington, 1973-77; policy analyst, special asst. Adminstrn. of Food Safety and Quality Svc., Dept. Agrl., Washington, 1977-78; legis. dir. to Senator Nancy L. Kassebaum, Washington, 1978-89; minority staff dir., sub-committee on edn., arts and humanities Senate Com. on Labor and Human Resources, Washington, 1989-92, minority staff dir., 1993-94, staff dir., 1995—. Mem. Phi Kappa Phi, Zeta Tau Alpha. Office: Labor & Human Resources Rm 835 Senate Hart Office Bldg Washington DC 20510

HATTON, BRENDA SHIRLEY, writer; b. Winchester, Ky., Apr. 28, 1945; d. Benjamin Marion and Minnie (Rice) Huff; m. Wallace Glen Hatton, Feb. 8, 1964; children: Carolyn, Sherry Lynn, Connie Gail and Ronnie Dale (twins). Student, Ea. Ky. U., 1995. Contbr. poems to books. Mem. Ch. of God. Home: 1011 Bethel Rd Lancaster KY 40444

HATZENBELLER, ALICE MARIE, religious organization administrator; b. South Milwaukee, Wis., Jan. 30, 1950; d. Victor Joseph and Theresa Lorraine (Retzke) Romanak; m. Garold Edwin Hatzenbeller, Aug. 8, 1970 (div. 1992); children: Jeffrey, Victoria, Theresa. BA in Bus. and Mgmt. with honors, Alverno, Milw., 1988. Cert. pastoral bereavement counselor. Program. asst. religious formation office St. John Parish, South Milwaukee, 1982-83; dir. religious formation St. Matthew Parish, Oak Creek, Wis., 1988-90, pastoral assoc., 1990—; cons. Archdiocese of Milw., 1989—; chair bd. dirs. Mathaetai: Inst. of Disciplineship, Milw., 1990—; vice-chair South Milw./Oak Creek Interfaith for the Elderly Bd., 1992—. Mem. Pastoral Assocs. Milw. Archdiocese (mem. planning core group 1993—). Roman Catholic. Office: St Matthew Parish 9303 S Chicago Rd Oak Creek WI 53154

HAUBERT, ALAINE, ballet dancer, educator; b. Flushing, N.Y.. Student, Sch. Am. Ballet, San Francisco Ballet Sch. Dancer Pacific Ballet; soloist, prin. dancer Am. Ballet Theatre, N.Y.C., 1965-69, ballet mistress, 1993—; prin. dancer The Joffrey Ballet, N.Y.C., 1969-79; ballet mistress N.J. Ballet, Ballet Hispanico, Ballet Concierto de San Juan; mem. dance faculty U. Hawaii; dance tchr. in N.Y., Europe, P.R.. Performed in dances including The Green Table, The Moor's Pavane, The Three-Cornered Hat, Le Beau Danube, The Dream. Office: Am Ballet Theatre 890 Broadway New York NY 10003-1211

HAUCH, VALERIE CATHERINE, historian, educator, researcher; b. Washington, May 20, 1949; d. Charles Christian and Ruthadele Bertha (LaTourrette) H. BA in History, Kalamazoo Coll., 1971; MA in Medieval Studies, Western Mich. U., 1977; grad. cert. C.C. Teaching, U. St. Thomas, St. Paul, 1995. Social sci. analyst Congl. Rsch. Svc. Libr. Congress, Washington, 1971-72; ind. contractor Minn. Hist. Soc., St. Paul, 1987-88, adminstrv. asst., 1990—; mus. asst. John H. Stevens House Mus., Mpls., 1990; teaching intern Normandale C.C., Bloomington, Minn., 1995; cmty. edn. tchr. Mpls. Pub. Schs., 1990—. Mem. AAUW, Am. Assn. Mus., Am. Hist. Assn., Phi Beta Kappa. Home: 2609 Morgan Ave N Minneapolis MN 55411

HAUGAN, GERTRUDE M., clinical psychologist; b. New Richland, Minn.; d. Henry Albert and Ella Pauline (Gardson) H. BA, George Washington U., 1952, MA, 1956; PhD, U. Md., 1970. Lic. psychologist, D.C., Md. Research psychologist New Eng. Med. Ctr., Boston, 1959-62; intern clin. psychology Hall Psychiat. Inst., Columbia, S.C., 1968-69; fellow in pediatrics Sch. Medicine Johns Hopkins U., Balt., 1970-71; clin. psychologist adloescent program Devel. Services Ctr., Washington, 1971-72, chief children's unit, 1972-85; chief Devel Services Ctr., Washington, 1986-94; cons. in psychology Ea. Shore State Hosp., Cambridge, Md., 1969-71, in child psychology Ctr. for Spl. Edn., Annapolis, Md., 1972-76; instr. in child psychology Montgomery Coll., Rockville, Md., 1977-78. Contbr. articles to profl. jours. Mem. profl. adv. council Easter Seal Soc. for Disabled Children and Adults, Washinton, 1987. Mem. APA, D.C. Psychol. Assn., Am. Assn. on Mental Retardation, Phi Beta Kappa. Home: 4720 S Chelsea Ln Bethesda MD 20814-3720

HAUGER, JANET LOUISE, mathematics educator, computer administrator; b. Morris, Ill., Apr. 11, 1944; d. Harvey Norman and Lila Virginia (Hare) Vaksdal; m. Steven Edward Hauger, Aug. 21, 1965; children: Bryan Edward, Erin Suzanne. BS, Ill. State U., Normal, 1966, MS in Edn., 1970. Cert. 6-12 phys. edn. and math. tchr., elem. tchr., K-12 phys. edn. tchr., Ill. Tchr. Bloomington (Ill.) Jr. H.S., 1966-67; faculty asst. Ill. State U., Normal, 1969-72; tchr. Ottawa (Ill.) Twp. H.S., 1979-80, Ottawa Elem. Schs., 1980-82, Grand Ridge (Ill.) Sch., 1983-84, Shepherd Jr. H.S., Ottawa, 1984—; co-athletic dir. Shepherd Jr. H.S., 1987-94, computer coord., 1992—, math. dept. head, 1994—, vol. coord., 1994—. Liaison/co-founder Shepherd Parents Club, Ottawa, 1994. Recipient Edn. grant Ill. Power Co., 1995. Mem. AAUW (gender equity chair 1993-95), Nat. Tchrs. Math., Delta Kappa Gamma (membership chair 1994-95). Lutheran. Office: Shepherd Jr HS 701 E McKinley Rd Ottawa IL 61350

HAUGLAND, BRYNHILD, retired state legislator, farmer; b. Ward County, N.D., July 28, 1905; d. Nels and Sigurda (Ringoen) H.; BA, Minot State Coll., 1956; LLD (hon.), N.D. State U., 1984. Mem. N.D. Ho. of Reps., 1938-90, chmn. com. social services and vets. affairs, mem. com.

industry, bus. and labor. Mem. Def. Adv. Com. Women in Services, 1955-58. Vice chmn. N.D. Gov.'s State Health Planning Com., 1944-75; past mem. Ward County Zoning Commn., Minot City Planning Commn., N.D. Bicentennial Commn. Bd. dirs. Internat. Peace Garden, 1953—, Minot State Coll. Found., Minot Commn. on Aging; mem. N.D. Legislature, 1938-90; mem. adv. com. Women in Svcs. Nat. Defense, Washington, 1953-56; past mem. adv. coun. N.D. Employment Security Bur., Ward County Zonin Commn., Minot Planning Commn., N.D. Bicentennial Commn., 1976—. Named Outstanding Legislator, Nat. Assembly Govt. Employees, 1979; recipient Golden award for Outstanding Service, Minot State Coll. Alumni, 1968, Genie award Minot C. of C., 1973, award Nat. Coun. Advancement and Support Edn., 1988 ; Hon. Mem. Uniformed Fire Fighters N.D., 1976; recipient Milky Way award Dairy Industry N.D., 1977, Disting. Service award Western N.D. Health Systems Agy., 1977-78, N.D. Water Wheel N.D. Water Users Assn./N.D. Water Mgmt. Dists. Assn., 1981, Service to Mankind award Sertoma Clubs, 1983, Merit award Pub. Health Assn. N.D., 1983, Liberty Bell award State Bar Assn., 1983, Disting. Service award Mental Health Assn. N.D., 1983, award Minot Assn. Home Builders, 1984, Good Citizen Scouting award, 1984, Disting. Service award Am. Protestant Health Assn., 1985; recognized state conv. Rep. Party for Half Century of Dedicated Pub. Service, longest serving legislator in nation on date of retirement, elected 26 terms-52 yrs., Woman of Distinction award Minot YWCA, 1993, Theodore Roosevelt Rough Rider award, 1995; numerous others; inducted into Scandinavian Hall of Fame, 1984; com. rm. named for her N.D. State Capital Bldg., Bismarck, 1987; Paul Harris fellow Rotary, 1993. Mem. Bus. and Profl. Women's Club (named Woman of Yr. 1956, 71, 89), Am. Assn. Ret. Persons, Nat. Ret. Tchrs. Assn., Farmers Union and Farm Bur., Minot State Coll. Alumni Assn. (dir., award for 50 yrs. svc. bd. dirs. 1993), Eureka Homemakers Club, Quota Club, Delta Kappa Gamma. Lutheran. Home: RR 6, Box 362A Minot ND 58703-9265

HAUGLAND, SUSAN WARRELL, education educator; b. Portland, Oreg., Aug. 29, 1950; d. George William and Commery Wallace (Coleman) Warrell; m. Jerry Lee Haugland, July 24, 1982; children: Charles, Michael. BS in Child Devel., Oreg. State U., 1972; PhD in Psychology, Saybrook Inst., 1976. Cert. family and consumer scis. Dir., head tchr. Lafayette Co-op Nursery Sch., Detroit, 1973-75; handicapped svcs. coord. OutWayne County Head Start, Wayne, Mich., 1975-76; asst. prof. child devel. Va. Poly. Inst. and State U., Blacksburg, 1976-79; prof. child devel. S.E. Mo. State U., Cape Girardeau, 1979—; dir. Ctr. for Child Studies, Cape Girardeau, 1979—, Kids Interacting with Devel. Software, Cape Girardeau, 1985—; chair Human-Environ. Studies, Cape Girardeau, 1990-93; judge Developmental Software Awards, 1991—, Child Mag. Awards, 1992—. Author: Developmental Evaluations of Software for Young Children, 1990, Helping Young Children Grow, 1980; dept. editor Day Care and Early Education, 1992-94; editl. bd. Jour. Computing in Childhood Edn. Sec. steering com. Technology & Young Children Caucus. Grantee numerous orgns. Mem. Nat. Assn. for Edn. Young Children, Nat. Assn. for Early Childhood Tchr. Educators, Tech. and Young Children Caucus (sec.), Nat. Assn. Family and Consumer Scis., Omicron Nu, Phi Kappa Phi. Democrat. Methodist. Office: Ctr for Child Studies SE Mo State U Cape Girardeau MO 63701

HAUKENESS, HELEN, journalist; b. Fortuna, N.D.; d. O.J. and Ella Pauline (Norum) H.; m. James Byrne Ranck Jr., July 9, 1961; 1 child, Mary Haukeness Ranck. AB, Augsburg Coll. Editl. asst. Am. Jour. Microbiology, Ann Arbor, Mich., 1964-67; editor Applied Dynamics News, Ann Arbor, 1969-72; reader, copy and line editor Avon Books, N.Y.C., 1976-80; copy editor Warner Publs., N.Y.C., 1980-84; freelance journalist, writer, 1984—. Contbr. travel essays to various newspapers, short stories and essays to periodicals. Mem. Village Dems., N.Y.C., 1990—. Fellow N.Y. Coun. for Arts, 1995, MacDowell Colony, 1971, 73, 75, 78, 82, Yaddo, 1984, Va. Ctr. Creative Arts, 1983, 87, Millay Colony for Arts, 1980; recipient Hopwood award in fiction U. Mich., 1971. Mem. Am. Soc. Journalists and Authors, Authors Guild. Home: 100 Bank St New York NY 10014

HAUNER, PHYLLIS MARIE, systems analyst; b. Bronx, N.Y., Feb. 1, 1954; d. William Joseph and Dolores E. Hauner. AAS in Bus. Adminstrn., N.Y. Inst. Tech., 1978, BS in Mgmt., 1981; MBA, Adelphi U., 1987. From inventory analyst to systems analyst Grumman Corp., Bethpage, N.Y., 1979-86; sr. systems analyst Grumman Aircraft, Bethpage, N.Y., 1986-89; from adminstr. III to adminstr. sr. GPU Nuclear Corp., Parsippany, N.J., 1989-95, staff mem., 1995—. Roman Catholic. Home: 28 Laurel Ridge Rd East Stroudsburg PA 18301-8945 Office: GPU Nuclear Corp 1 Upper Pond Rd Parsippany NJ 07054

HAUPTLI, BARBARA BEATRICE, environmental specialist; b. Glenwood Springs, Colo., Sept. 20, 1953; d. Frederick James and Evelyn June (Rood) H.; m. Curtis Scott Bostian, July 4, 1992. BBA, Western State Coll., 1975. Contract specialist USA-TACOM, Warren, Mich., 1981-86; contract buyer Martin Marietta Orlando (Fla.) Aerospace, 1986; purchasing expediter Moog, Inc., Clearwater, Fla., 1986-89; subcontract adminstr. Olin Ordnance, St. Petersburg, Fla., 1989-91; sr. subcontract adminstr. Olin Ordnance, 1991-93; reimbursement specialist Tod. K. Allen, Inc., 1993—. Mem. Nat. Contract Mgmt. Assn.

HAUPTMAN, BETTY, hospital official, fundraiser; b. Bklyn., Nov. 26, 1936; d. Herman Paul and Regina (Greenberg) Holzman; m. Michael Hauptman, Nov. 28, 1957; children: James, William. BBA, CUNY, 1958. Dir. devel. Greenwich (Conn.) Libr., 1986-89, Ctr. for Non Profit Corps., Princeton, N.J., 1990-91, Windward Sch., White Plains, N.Y., 1992-93; dir. individual gifts Greenwich Hosp., 1993—; justice of peace, Greenwich, 1984—. Trustee, pres. Greenwich Libr., 1984-86; vice chmn. Greenwich Bd. Health, 1981-84; co-chmn. cmty. forum United Way Greenwich, 1987-89; bd. dirs. Shelter for Homeless Stamford, Conn., 1990—; dist. leader Greenwich Dem. Town Com., 1990-95. Mem. Nat. Soc. Fund Raising Execs., LWV (pres. Greenwich 1974-76). Home: 13 Carriage Rd Cos Cob CT 06807 Office: Greenwich Hosp 5 Perryridge Rd Greenwich CT 06830-4608

HAUPTMAN, MARJORIE ANNE LEAHY, communications executive; b. Jackson, Tenn., Aug. 31, 1938; d. John Solinsky and Marjorie Elizabeth (Aylor) Solinsky; m. Edward J. Leahy, July 2, 1960 (div. Mar. 19, 1991); children: James Peter, Laura Marjorie, John Edward; m. John Andrew Hauptman, Sept. 18, 1991; stepchildren: Skye, Tara, Kyle. BS, Syracuse U., 1960; MA in English/Creative Writing, SUNY, Stony Brook, 1996. TV editor, reporter Rome (N.Y.) Daily Sentinel, 1961-62; freelancer Croton-on-Hudson, N.Y., 1966-74; editor The Navigator, Poughkeepsie, N.Y., 1974-76; staff writer Gannett Westchester Newspapers, Tarrytown, N.Y., 1978-81; pres. Five String Prodns., Croton-on-Hudson, 1981-89, Corp. Editions, Inc., Bellport, N.Y., 1989—; cons. in field. Mem. Water Control Commn., Croton-on-Hudson, 1989-90, Conservation Adv. Coun., Croton-on-Hudson, 1978-90; environ. instr. Westchester County Pks., White Plains, N.Y., 1988-91; coord. Clearwater Hudson River Revival, Poughkeepsie, N.Y., 1978-95. Mem. Women in Comms. (v.p. pub. rels. 1982-84), Nat. Writers Union (Westchester Fairfield chpt., workshop speaker writers' conf. 1990, 94). Office: Corporate Editions Inc PO Box 14 Bellport NY 11713-0014

HAUSE, EDITH COLLINS, college administrator; b. Rock Hill, S.C., Dec. 11, 1933; d. Ernest O. and Violet (Smith) Collins; m. James Luke Hause, Sept. 3, 1955; children—Stephen Mark, Felicia Gaye Hause Friesen. B.A., Columbia Coll., S.C., 1956; postgrad. U. N.C.-Greensboro, 1967, U. S.C., 1971-75. Tchr. Richland Dist. II, Columbia, 1971-74; dir. alumnae affairs Columbia Coll., 1974-82, v.p. alumnae affairs, 1982-84, v.p. devel., 1984-89, v.p. alumnae rels., 1989—. Named Outstanding Tchr. of Yr., Richland Dist. II, 1974. Mem. Columbia Network for Female Execs., Council for Advancement and Support Edn., Nat. Soc. Fund Raising Execs., S.C. Assn. Alumni Dirs. (pres. 1995—). Republican. Methodist. Home: 92 Mariners Pointe Rd Prosperity SC 29127-9386 Office: Columbia Coll Alumnae Office Columbia SC 29203

HAUSELT, DENISE ANN, lawyer; b. Wellsville, N.Y., Oct. 12, 1956; d. John Donald and Maureen (Whelan) H. BS, Cornell U., 1979, JD, 1983. Bar: N.Y. 1984, Ill. 1984, U.S. Dist. Ct. (we. dist.) N.Y. 1984, U.S. Bankruptcy Ct. 1984. Summer assoc. Wildman, Harrold, Allen & Dixon, Chgo., 1982; assoc. Nixon Hargrave Devans & Doyle, Rochester, N.Y., 1983-86; asst. counsel Corning (N.Y.) Inc., 1986—; Bd. dirs. So. Tier Legal Svcs., Bath, N.Y., 1986-89, Home Health Svcs., Inc., Corning, 1986—. Recipient Am. Jurisprudence Constl. Law prize, Cornell U., 1981, others. Mem. ABA, N.Y. State Bar Assn., Cornell Law Assn., Keuka Yacht Club. Republican. Home: 164 Delevan Ave Corning NY 14830-3224 Office: Corning Inc Riverfront Plz MP-HQ-E2 Corning NY 14831

HAUSER, CAROL ANN, organizational development specialist; b. Cin., Mar. 28, 1949; d. Harold C. Hauser and Mary Rita (Oehler) Scheidt. BS, Xavier U., 1971; M in Pastoral Studies, Loyola U., 1983, MA, 1985. Tchr. Ursuline Acad., Cin., 1973-81; dir. univ. ministry Loyola U., Chgo., 1981-86; strategist Neighborhood Reinvestment, Cin., 1990-93; dir. continuous improvement Dayton (Ohio) Pub. Schs., 1993—; cons. Sisters of Mercy, Cin., 1984-90, St. Gregory Coll., Campbelltown, Australia, 1985-88, Franciscan Health Care N.Y./N.J., 1985-86, Coll. Mount St. Joseph, Cin., 1988-92. Author: (program manual) Youthworks: A Manual for Developing Neighborhood Based Programs, 1991 (One of 10 Best in Nation 1992); editor, contbr.: Turning: Parables and Paradigms, 1986. Bd. mem. Chatfield Coll., St. Martin, Ohio, 1985-89, Ursuline Acad., Cin., 1985-89, Arts and Humanities Resource Ctr., Cin., 1985-87, Cmty. Info. Exch., Washington, 1992. Grantee NSF, 1978. Mem. ASCD, Am. Mgmt. Assn., Am. Soc. for Quality Control. Democrat. Roman Catholic. Home: 3221 Ridge Ave Dayton OH 45414 Office: Dayton Pub Schs 348 W 1st St Dayton OH 45402

HAUSER, RITA ELEANORE ABRAMS, lawyer; b. N.Y.C., July 12, 1934; d. Nathan and Frieda (Litt) Abrams; m. Gustave M. Hauser, June 10, 1956; children: Glenvil Aubrey, Ana Patricia. AB magna cum laude, CUNY Hunter Coll., 1954; D in Polit. Economy with highest honors, U. Strasbourg, France, 1955; Licence en Droit, U. Paris, 1958; student law sch., Harvard U., 1955-56; LLB with honors, NYU, 1959; LLD (hon.), Seton Hall U., 1969, Finch Coll., 1969, U. Miami, Fla., 1971, Colgate U., 1995. Bar: D.C. 1959, N.Y. 1961, U.S. Supreme Ct. 1967. Atty. U.S. Dept. Justice, 1959-61; pvt. practice N.Y.C., 1961-67; ptnr. Moldover, Hauser, Strauss & Volin, 1968-72; sr. ptnr. Stroock & Stroock & Lavan, N.Y.C., 1972-92, of counsel, 1992—; pres. The Hauser Found., N.Y.C., 1990—; Handmaker lectr., Louis Brandeis Lecture Series, U. Ky. Law Sch.; lectr. on internat. law Naval War Coll. and Army War Coll.; Mitchell lectr. in law SUNY, Buffalo; USIA lectr. constl. law Egypt, India, Australia, New Zealand; bd. dirs. The Eisenhower World Affairs Inst.; U.S. chmn. Internat. Ctr. for Peace in Middle East, 1984-92; bd. dirs. Internat. Peace Acad., 1990—, chair 1993—; U.S. pub. del. to Vienna follow-up meeting of Conf. on Security and Cooperation in Europe, 1986-88; mem. adv. panel in internat. law U.S. Dept. State, 1986-92, Am. Soc. Internat. Law Award to honor Women in Internat. Law. Contbr. articles on internat. law to profl. jours. U.S. rep. to UN Commn. on Human Rights, 1969-72; mem. U.S. del. to Gen. Assembly UN, 1969; vice chmn. U.S. Adv. Com. on Internat. and Cultural Affairs, 1973-77; mem. N.Y.C. Bd. Higher Edn., 1974-76, Stanton Panel on internat. info., edn., cultural rels. to reorganize USIA and voice of Am., 1974-75, Mid. East Study Group Brookings Inst., 1975, 87-88, U.S. del. World Conf. Internat. Women's Yr., Mexico City, 1975; co-chair Com. for Re-election Pres., 1972, Presdl. Debates project LWV, 1976, Coalition for Reagon/Bush; adv. bd. Nat. News Coun., 1977-79; bd. dirs. Bd. for Internat. Broadcasting, 1977-80, Catalyst, Internat. Peace Acad., The Aspen Inst., U.S. Coun. Germany; trustee, exec. com. N.Y. Philharm. Soc.; adv. bd. Ctr. for Law and Nat. Security, U. Va. Law Sch., 1978-84; vis. com. Ctr. Internat. Affairs Harvard U., 1975-81, John F. Kennedy Sch. Govt., Harvard U., 1992—; mem. bd. advisors Middle East Inst., Harvard U.; bd. of visitors Georgetown Sch. Fgn. Svc., 1989-94; chmn. adv. panel Interna. Parliamentary Group for Human Rights in Soviet Union, 1984-86; mem. Lawyers Com. for Human Rights, 1995—; mem. spl. refugee adv. panel Dept. State, 1981; bd. fellows Claremont U. Ctr. & Grad. Sch., 1990-94; former trustee Internat. Legal Ctr., Legal Aid Soc. N.Y., Freedom House. Fulbright grantee U. Strasbourg, 1955; Intellectual Exch. fellow Japan Soc.; recipient Jane Addams Internat. Women's Leadership award, 1996, women in internat. law award Am. Soc. Internat. Law, 1995. Fellow ABA (life, mem. standing coms. on law and nat. security 1979-85, standing com. on world order under law 1969-78, standing com. on jud. selection, tenure, compensation 1977-79, coun. sect. on ind. rights and responsibilities 1970-73, advisor bd. jour. 1973-78); mem. Am. Soc. Internat. Law (v.p. 1988—, mem. exec. com. 1971-76), Am. Fgn. Law Assn. (bd. dirs.), Am. Arbitration Assn. (past bd. dirs.), Ams. Soc. (bd. dirs. 1988—), Coun. Fgn. Rels. (bd. dirs.), Internat. Inst. for Strategic Studies (London, bd. dirs. 1994—), Am. Coun. on Germany, Friends of the Hauge Acad. Internat. Law (bd. dirs.), Assn. of Bar of City of N.Y., Catalyst (bd. dirs. 1989-96). Republican. Office: Stroock & Stroock & Lavan 7 Hanover Sq New York NY 10004-2616 also: The Hauser Found 712 5th Ave New York NY 10019-4108

HAUSER, SARA N., writer, educator; b. Jacksonville, Fla., Feb. 19, 1919; d. Austin Thomas and Camilla (Raulerson) Nooney; m. Thomas Allan Smith, Apr. 20, 1946 (dec. Aug. 1977); children: Thomas Allan Jr., Linda Smith Bates, Sean Patrick Smith; m. Elmer Leonard Hauser, June 19, 1978. BA, Fla. State U., 1941; MA, U. South Fla., 1972. Math. educator Duval County Schs., Jacksonville, Fla., 1941-46; librarian Brownsville Children's Libr., Bklyn., 1946-47; educator U.S. Navy Base, Port Lyautey, Morocco, 1948-53; media specialist Hillsborough County Schs., Plant City, Fla., 1954-79; established ctrl. media ctrs. in elem. schs., Plant City, 1956-60. Author: Scattered Leaves, 1994; contbr. feature articles to Lakeland (Fla.) Ledger, 1970-73. Mem. AAUW, DAR (registrar 1992—), Friendship Force (sec. 1992-93), Federated Woman's Club (treas. 1992-93), New Eng. Hist. Geneal. Soc., Fla. State Geneal. Soc., Alpha Chi Alpha, Delta Kappa Gamma. Home: 4444 Saxon Dr New Smyrna Beach FL 32169-4135

HAUSLER, SARA FINCHAM, learning disabilities specialist, educator; b. Pratt, Kans., Aug. 3, 1940; d. Donald Arthur and Lois (Figge) Farmer; m. Robert Kent Fincham, Sept. 2, 1962 (div. Aug. 1978); children: Amy Lynn Fincham Keller, Anne Elisabeth Fincham Marshall, Sara Kimberly Fincham; m. William Hausler, June 29, 1991. BS in Secondary Edn., Kans. U., 1962; MEd, Wichita State U., 1985. Cert. learning disabilities, French, social studies tchr. French, civics tchr. Richlands (N.C.) H.S., 1965-66; substitute tchr. Wichita (Kans.) Pub. Schs., 1967-72; learning disabilities resource tchr. Newton (Kans.) H.S., 1980-81; substitute tchr. Wichita Pub. Schs., 1981-82; learning disabilities resource tchr. Horace Mann Mid. Sch., Wichita, 1982; Derby (Kans.) 7-8 Ctr., 1982-83, Valley Center (Kans.) H.S., 1983-93; substitute tchr. Wichita Pub. Schs., 1993—; learning support tchr. Wichita Collegiate Sch., 1994—. Mem. Eastminster Presbyn. Ch. Women's Circle, Wichita, 1984-91; home room mother Andover (Kans.) Elem. Sch., 1974-78; laymem. gifted com. Andover H.S., 1976. Recipient Big Sister award Kans. U., 1959. Mem. Learning Disabilities Assn., Kans. U. Alumni, Wichita State U. Alumni, Kappa Alpha Theta (editor, sec. 1966—), Phi Kappa Phi.

HAUSS, DEBORAH, marketing communications consultant, magazine writer; b. Elizabeth, N.J., Sept. 5, 1955; d. Henry and Beatrice Susan (Manasse) H.; m. David B. Baron, June 19, 1994. BA in Journalism and English Lit., U. Del., 1977; postgrad., U. Oreg., 1976. Local news reporter Wilmington (Del.) News-Jour., 1976; advt. prodn. asst. Ladies Home Jour., N.Y.C., 1977-78; asst. editor Gralla Publs., N.Y.C., 1978-79, assoc. editor, 1979-80, sr. assoc. editor, 1980, mng. editor, 1980-84, editor-in-chief, 1984-87, assoc. pub., 1987-89; editor-in-chief, assoc. pub. Premium/Incentive Bus., 1984-89; pres. In-Hauss Strategies, Inc., Hillside, N.J., 1989—. Editor: Incentive Travel Case Study Book, 1990. Reading tutor Lit. Vol. Am., Newark, 1993—. Mem. Soc. Incentive Travel Execs. (past bd. dirs. 1988-90), Premium Merchandising Club N.Y. (past bd. dirs. 1989-93). Democrat. Jewish. Home: 26 Carter Rd West Orange NJ 07052-4612 Office: In-Hauss Strategies Inc 100 Central Ave Hillside NJ 07205-2306

HAUSSLER, SUSAN CURRAN, nursing educator. BSN, Cornell U.-N.Y. Hosp., N.Y.C., 1965; MS, Boston U., 1980; EdD, Vanderbilt U., 1986. RN, N.H., Mass. Staff nurse Elliot Hosp., Manchester, N.H.; asst. prof. U. Lowell, Mass.; assoc. dean, assoc. prof. U. Mass., Boston. Contbr. articles to profl. jours. Mem. Nat. League Nursing (Coun. of Baccalaureate and Higher Degree Programs program evaluator), Sigma Theta Tau (Rsch. award 1985). Home: 89 Gilcreast Rd Londonderry NH 03053-3514

HAVENS, CANDACE JEAN, planning consultant; b. Rochester, Minn., Sept. 13, 1952; d. Fred Z. and Barbara Jean (Stephenson) H.; m. Bruce Curtis Mercier, Feb. 22, 1975 (div. Apr. 1982); 1 child, Rachel; m. James Arthur Renning, Oct. 26, 1986; children: Kelsey, Sarah. Student, U. Calif., San Diego, Darmouth Coll., 1970-72, Am. U., Beirut, 1973-74; BA in Sociology, U. Calif., Riverside, 1977; MPA, Harvard U., 1994. Project coord. social svc. orgn. Grass Roots II, San Luis Obispo, Calif., 1976-77; planning enforcement technician City San Luis Obispo, 1977-81, asst. planner, 1981-83; assoc. planner City of San Luis Obispo, 1983-86, coord. parking program, 1986-88, spl. asst. to city adminstr., 1989, planning cons., 1991—; mgmt. rsch. specialist Bank of Boston, 1995-96. Past pres. Nat. Charity League, Riverside; mem. San Luis Obispo Med. Aux., 1986-93, San Luis Obispo Arts Coun., 1986—; pres. bd. dirs. San Luis Obispo Children's Mus., 1990-91, CFO, 1993; mediator in Newton (Mass.) Cts., 1996. Mem. AAUW, Am. Inst. Cert. Planners, Toastmasters (sec. 1986-87, v.p. 1987-88, pres. 1989-90, treas. 1991-92), Am. Planning Assn., Mass. Assn. Mediation Profls. and Practitioners. Office: 1555 Higuera St San Luis Obispo CA 93401

HAVENS, CAROLYN CLARICE, librarian; b. Nashville, Sept. 11, 1953; d. Charles Buford and Iris Mae (Anderson) H.; m. Hilton Harris Huey, June 9, 1990; children: Heather Louise, Quentin Harris. AA, Sue Bennett Coll., 1973; BA in English, U. West Fla., 1974; MLS, U. Ky., 1981. Tchr. Escambia High Sch., Pensacola, Fla., 1974-75; salesperson Univ. Mall, Pensacola, 1975-77; libr. tech. U. Ky., Lexington, 1978-82; libr. Auburn (Ala.) U., 1982—. Contbr. articles to profl. jours. and newspapers; editorial bd.: A Dynamic Tradition, 1991. Bd. dirs. Nat. Kidney Found. Ala., Opelika, 1986-89; active Conscientious Alliance for Peace, Auburn, 1989—. Clergy and Laity Concerned, Atlanta, 1991—. Mem. ALA, Southeastern Libr. Assn., Ala. Libr. Assn., North Am. Serials Interest Group, Ala. Assn. Coll. and Rsch. Librs., Studio 218. Democrat. Methodist. Office: Auburn U Ralph Draughon Libr Auburn AL 36849-5606

HAVENS, GAIL ANN DELUCA, nurse ethicist; b. Jamaica, N.Y., July 13, 1938; d. Francis Joseph and Ethel Mildred (Livingston) DeLuca; m. Donald Campbell Havens, Jr., Apr. 23, 1960; children: Donald Campbell III, Andrew Livingston. Diploma, St. Vincent's Hosp. Med. Ctr., 1959; BSN, Vt. Coll. Norwich U., 1991; MS, U. Md., 1993, PhD, 1995. RN Pa., Vt., N.Y. Staff nurse St. Vincent's Hosp. and Med. Ctr., N.Y.C., 1959-61; pvt. duty Muhlenberg Hosp., Plainfield, N.J., 1962-63; staff nurse Overlook Hosp., Summit, N.J., 1971-74; from float nurse to dir. nursing svcs. The Dartmouth-Hitchcock Med. Ctr., Hanover, N.H., 1975-91; rsch. asst. U. Md. Balt. Sch. Nursing, 1991-94; rsch. assoc. Pa. State U. Sch. Nursing, State College, 1996—; content expert N.H. Senate Com. on Pub. Instns. and Health, Concord, 1991, N.H. House Com. on Health Care, Concord, 1991, Execution of Advance Directives, 1996. Mem. ANA, APHA, Sigma Theta Tau, Ea. Nursing Rsch. Soc., Soc. for Health & Human Values. Home: 1352 Sandpiper Dr State College PA 16801 Office: Pa State U Sch Nursing 307 F Health/Human Devel E University Park PA 16802

HAVENS, PAMELA ANN, college official; b. Plattsburgh, N.Y., Nov. 30, 1956; d. Thomas L. and MaryAnn (Zalen) Romeo; m. Stephen L. Havens, Aug. 9, 1986; 1 child, Stephanie Leigh. BA, Eisenhower Coll., 1978; MA summa cum laude, SUNY, Plattsburgh, 1987. VISTA vol. Retired Sr. Vol. Program, Plattsburgh, 1978-79; copywriter, newsperson Stas. WEAV-AM/WGFB-FM, Plattsburgh, 1979-83; traffic clk. Sta. WCFE-TV, Plattsburgh, 1983-84, pub. info. coord., 1984-85; coll. rels. officer Clinton Cmty. Coll., Plattsburgh, 1985-89; dir. publs. and comm. Cayuga C.C., Auburn, N.Y., 1989—. Bd. dirs. Auburn Players Cmty. Theatre, 1991-93. Named Young Careerist Alternate Bus. and Profl. Women's Club, 1986. Mem. NAFE, AAUW, Eisenhower Coll. Alumni Assn. (bd. dirs. 1990-97, chmn. bd. 1992-95), Auburn Kiwanis Club (bd. dirs. 1995—, 2d v.p. 1996—). Office: Cayuga Community Coll 197 Franklin St Auburn NY 13021-3011

HAVESON, BARBARA MARCIA, retired elementary education educator; b. Wharton, Tex., Aug. 4, 1934; d. Jack and Bertha (Kreitstein) Roth; m. Robert Franklin Haveson, Nov. 25, 1956; children: Celia Hannah (dec.), Judy. BS, U. Houston, 1956. V.p. Fort Bend Tchr. Assn., 1972-73; pres. Fort Bend Tchrs. Assn., Sugarland, Tex., 1973-75; mem. exec. bd. region 4 TSTA, Houston, 1978-80; mem. Kinneret Group-Houston Chpt. of Hadassah, 1991—; v.p. Kinneret Group, 1992-93. Recipient Hadassah Nat. Leadership award, 1996. Mem. Kinneret Group-Houston Chpt. of Hadassah (pres. 1992-95), Delta Kappa Gamma. Jewish. Home: 201 Vanderpool #102 Houston TX 77024

HAVILAND, CAMILLA KLEIN, lawyer; b. Dodge City, Kans., Sept. 13, 1926; d. Robert Godfrey and Lelah (Luther) Klein; m. John Bodman Haviland, Sept. 7, 1957. AA, Monticello Coll., 1946; BA, Radcliffe Coll., 1948; JD, Kans. U., 1955. Bar: Kans. 1955. Assoc. Calvert & White, Wichita, Kans., 1955-56; sole practice, Dodge City, 1956—; probate, county and juvenile judge Ford County (Kans.), 1957-77; mem. Jud. Coun. Com. on Probate and Juvenile Law. Mem. adv. bd. Salvation Army, U. Kans. Sch. Religion, Sch. Anthropology Wichita State U. Recipient Nathan Burkan award ASCAP, 1955. Mem. Ford County Bar Assn. (pres. 1980), S.W. Kans. Bar Assn. (pres. 1968, bd. dirs. 1994—), Kans. Bar Assn., ABA, C. of C., Order of Coif, PEO, Phi Delta Delta. Democrat. Episcopalian. Clubs: Prairie Dunes Country (Hutchinson, Kans.); Soroptimists. Contbr. articles to profl. jours. Home: 2006 East Lane Ave Dodge City KS 67801-2828 Office: PO Box 17 203 W Spruce St Dodge City KS 67801-4426

HAVILAND, MARLITA CHRISTINE, elementary school educator; b. Moses Lake, Wash., Sept. 4, 1952; d. Marvin Curtis and Delita F. (Grout) McCully; m. James A Haviland, June 18, 1971. BS in Edn., So. Nazarene U., Bethany, Okla., 1973; MA in Edn., No. Ariz. U., 1987. Cert. elem. tchr., Ariz., Colo., ESL, basic edn., spl. edn. tchr., c.c., Ariz., early childhood edn., Colo,. Elem. tchr. St. Paul (Ark.) Pu. Sch., Twin Wells Indian Sch., Sun Valley, Ariz., Navajo Gospel Mission, Kykotsmovi, Ariz., Shonto (Ariz.) Boarding Sch.; instr. Northland Pioneer Coll.; coord. Sch. Wide Book Fair. Mem. Nat. Fedn. Fed. Employees (local sec., treas., steward), Ariz. CADRE, Alpha Nu, Phi Kappa Phi. Home: PO Box 7427 Shonto AZ 86054

HAVILAND, MARTHA BALLIET, geneticist; b. Boston, Aug. 21, 1965; d. Randolph T. and Jeannette M. (Jones) H.; m. John Warren Schrum Jr., June 24, 1989; 1 child, Nicolaus Balliet. BA in Biology, Genetics, Rutgers U., 1987; MS in Human Genetics, U. Mich., 1989, MA in Stats., 1991, PhD in Human Genetics, 1993. Teaching asst. U. Mich., Ann Arbor, 1989, rsch. asst., 1992-93, rsch. fellow, 1993-96, rsch. investigator, 1996—. Vol. U. Mich. Women in Sci. Program, 1991—, Sci.-By-Mail, Boston, 1995—. Douglass Coll. scholar, 1983-87; NSF fellow, 1987-90, Rackham Predoctoral fellow U. Mich., 1991-92. Mem. AAAS, Am. Soc. Human Genetics. Office: U Mich Dept Human Genetics Med Sci Bldg II Rm 4708 Ann Arbor MI 48109-0618

HAVLICEK, SARAH MARIE, small business owner, educator; b. N.Y.C., Jan. 29, 1950; d. Raymond Joseph and Rosalie Maria (Zona) Havlicek; m. william Gabriel Tortora, Sept. 16, 1972 (div. 1995); children: Nina-Gabrielle, Eva-Juliet. BS, NYU, 1972; MA, San Francisco State U., 1976. Cert. tchr., N.Y. Co-owner, mgr., instr. Sound Universe Inc., N.Y.C., 1972-74; customer rels. Chartered Bank, San Francisco, 1974-76, Standard Chartered Bank, N.Y.C., 1976-78; co-owner, mgr. Design Constrn. Co., N.Y.C., 1978-94; edn. coord. Internat. Automotive Parts & Accessories Assn., Bethesda, Md., 1994—. Painting exhibits include Daughters, Patterns; poetry collections include Lines of Evidence, Coney Island Games, Quid Pro Quo, Air Circles. Mem. Internat. Platform Assn., Am. Soc. Assn. Execs. Home: Kenwood Pl 5301 Westbard Cir Apt 337 Bethesda MD 20816-1427 Office: 4600 East-West Hwy Bethesda MD 20814

HAWES, SUE, lawyer; b. Washington, Mar. 30, 1937; d. Alexander Boyd and Elizabeth (Armstrong) H.; m. James E. Brodhead, June 21, 1963; children: William James Pusey Brodhead, Daniel Alexander Hawes Brodhead. BA, Sarah Lawrence Coll., 1959, MA, 1963; JD, Whittier (Calif.) Sch. of Law, 1983. Bar: Calif. 1988, U.S. Dist. Ct. (cen. dist.) Calif. 1990. Dancer and choreographer N.Y.C., Washington, Latin Am., Europe, 1959-62; instr., dir. dance program dept. theatre and phys. edn. Smith Coll., Northampton, Mass., 1963-65; instr. dept. dance UCLA, 1973-75; freelance script supr. L.A., 1976-80; prin. Law Office of Sue Hawes, L.A., 1988-96. Articles editor Whittier Law Rev., 1982-83. Active Santa Barbara Symphony League. Mem. AAUW, State Bar Calif., Santa Barbara County Bar Assn., Actors' Equity Assn. Democrat.

HAWKE, MARY ANGELA, lawyer; b. Hackensack, N.J., June 6, 1965. BBA, Coll. William and Mary, 1987; JD, Fordham U., 1992. Bar: N.J. 1992, U.S. Dist. Ct. N.J. 1992, N.Y. 1993, U.S. Dist. Ct. (so. and ea. dists.) N.Y. 1994. Ptnr. Anderson Kill Olick & Oshinsky, P.C., N.Y.C. Mem. ABA, N.Y. State Bar Assn., Assn. of Bar of City of N.Y. Office: Anderson Kill Olick & Oshinsky PC 1251 Ave of the Americas New York NY 10020-1182*

HAWKEN, PATTY LYNN, nursing educator, dean of faculty; b. Wheaton, Ill., July 13, 1932; d. Leonard William and Betty (Stock) H. BSN, U. Mich., 1956; MSN, Case Western Res. U., 1962, PhD, 1970. Instr. U. Mich., Ann Arbor, 1956-57, Highland Hosp., Oakland, Calif., 1957-59; instr. Case Western Res. U., Cleve., 1960-63, asst. prof., 1963-67, assoc. prof., 1967-69, assoc. prof., assoc. in adminstrn., 1969-71; assoc. prof. Emory U., Atlanta, 1971-72, prof., dir., 1972-74; dean, prof. U. Tex. Health Sci. Ctr. Sch. Nursing, San Antonio, 1974—. Contbr. articles to nursing jours. Bd. dirs. Wesley Community Ctr., San Antonio, 1986, 89; mem. United Way Allocation Com., San Antonio, 1987; mem. adv. com. Trinity U. Health Care Adminstrn., San Antonio, 1984—, VA Dean's Com., San antonio, 1982—. Recipient Nurse of Yr. award Tex. Nursing Assn., San Antonio chpt., 1985, Disting. Alumni award Case Western Res. U., 1991; named to Women's Hall of Fame, Mayor's Commn. on Women, San Antonio, 1986. Mem. ANA (cabinet on edn. 1986-88), Nat. League Nursing (pres. 1989-91, Disting. Svc. award 1991), Am. Assn. Colls. of Nursing (com. on edn. 1986-88), Commns. Grads. Fgn. Nursing Schs. (trustee, pres. 1983-85), Am. Acad. Nursing (bd. govs. 1994—), San Antonio 100 Club, Internat. Women's Forum (San Antonio pres. celebration, Hall of Fame 1994—). Home: 1826 Fallow Run San Antonio TX 78248-2000 Office: U Tex Health Sci Ctr 7703 Floyd Curl Dr San Antonio TX 78284-6200

HAWKEY, PENELOPE J., advertising agency executive; b. Morristown, N.J., Sept. 17, 1942; d. William R. and Jeanne Elizabeth (Haas) Sharp; m. William Stevenson Hawkey, May 26, 1968; children: Adam Stewart, Robin Davidge, Renn McDonnell, Timothy Schuyler, Molly Driscoll; stepchildren: Elizabeth Martin, William Stevenson. BA, Ohio U., Athens, 1964. Jr. writer Grey Advt., N.Y.C., 1966; jr. writer, then v.p. J. Walter Thompson Co., N.Y.C., 1966-73; v.p., assoc. creative dir. McCann-Erickson, N.Y.C., 1973-74, sr. v.p., group creative dir., 1975-76; ptnr., exec. v.p. Dillon, Gordon, Hawkey, Short, N.Y.C., 1977-85; past pres., exec. creative dir. Bloom/FCA, N.Y.C.; vice chmn., chief creative dir. Publicis/Bloom Inc., N.Y.C.; mem. N.Y. Bd. Govs. Mem. Ad Coun., Advertising Women of N.Y. (Ad Woman of Yr. 1990, Matrix award 1991). Office: Publicis/Bloom Inc 304 E 45th St New York NY 10017-3425*

HAWKINS, BRENDA L., psychologist, educator. BS in Secondary Edn., Frostburg State Coll., 1972; MS in Counseling and Guidance, Ind. U., 1977, EdD in Counseling and Counselor Edn., 1981. Lic. psychologist; cert. Nat. Bd. Cert. Counselors. Intern, acting counselor Ctr. for Human Growth & Career Ctr. Ind. U., Bloomington, 1980-81; counselor Counseling Ctr. SUNY, Fredonia, 1981-83; psychologist Karuna Counseling, Atlanta, 1984-87; asst. prof., psychologist Dept. Psychiatry Sch. Medicine Emory U., Atlanta, 1988-93; pvt. practice, 1985—; trainer paraprofessionals Women's Crisis Svc., Bloomington, Ind., 1975-77; site visitor accreditation tng. Internat. Assn. Counseling Svcs., 1983; mem. spkrs. bur. Mental Health Assn. Met. Atlanta, 1983—; group facilitator Adult Survivors of Phys. and Emotional Child Abuse Ga. Coun. on Child Abuse, Atlanta, 1990-91. Contbr. articles to profl. jours.; presenter in field. Recipient Md. Senatorial scholarship, 1968-72, Md. Congress of Parents and Tchrs. scholarship, 1968-72, Delta Theta Tau scholarship, 1977-80. Mem. APA, Am. Soc. Clin. Hypnosis (cert. cons. in clin. hypnosis, cert. in clin. hypnosis), Assn. for Women in Psychology, Am. Counseling Assn., Assn. for Specialists in Group Work (mem. awards com. 1982-83), Internat. Soc. for the Study of Dissociation, Ga. Psychol. Assn. (sr. mem.-at-large divsn. F exec. coun. divsn. of women psychologists 1990-92, divsn. F rep. ann. meeting com. 1991-92), Atlanta Hypnosis Soc., Pi Lambda Theta.

HAWKINS, CYNTHIA, artist, educator; b. N.Y.C., Jan. 29, 1950; d. Robert D. Hawkins and Elease Coger; m. Steven J. Chaiken, Feb. 5, 1977 (div. Aug. 1985); m. John Edward Owen, Aug. 24, 1985; children: Ianna, Zachary. BA, Queens Coll., 1977; MFA, Md. Inst. Coll. Art, 1992. tchg. asst. Md. Inst. Coll. of Art, Balt., 1990, 91, 92; adj. instr. Rockland C.C., Suffern, N.Y., 1993, 94, 95, 96, Parsons Sch. Design, N.Y.C., 1996; mentor Empire State Coll., Nyack, N.Y., 1994; artist-in-residence The Studio Mus. Harlem, N.Y., 1987-88, Va. Ctr. for Creative Arts, Sweet Briar, Va., 1995-96; vis. artist Round House Press, Hartwick Coll., Oneonta, N.Y., 1994; curator Rockland Ctr. for Arts, art dept. Rockland C.C., Nyack, 1994-95, The Rotunda, 1994, 95; vis. lectr. Forman Gallery, Hartwick Coll., Oneonta, 1994, Rockland C.C., Suffern, 1994, 95; presenter in field. One-person shows include Paul Klapper Libr., Queens Coll., N.Y., 1974, Just Above Midtown/Downtown Gallery, N.Y.C., 1981, Frances Wolfson Art Ctr., Miami (Fla.)-Dade C.C., 1986, Cinque Gallery, N.Y.C., 1989, Essex (Md.) C.C., 1991, Trinity Luth. Ch., New Milford, Conn., 1993; exhibited in group shows Queens Coll. Gallery, N.Y.C., 1973, Emily Lowe Gallery, Hempstead, N.Y., 1979, Jamie Szoke Gallery, N.Y.C., 1984, Grace Borgenicht Gallery, N.Y.C., 1986, Aljira Gallery, Newark, 1989, Dome Gallery, N.Y.C., 1990, Decker Gallery, Balt., 1991, Kromah Gallery, Balt., 1992, Arts Alliance Haverstraw, N.Y., 1993, Nabisco Gallery, East Hanover, N.J., 1994, Artist Space, N.Y.C., 1993, Bronx Mus. Arts, 1994, U. Notre Dame at Balt., 1995, No. Westchester Ctr. for Arts, Mt. Kisco, N.Y., 1996, Hopper House, Nyack, 1996; represented in permanent collections The Bronx Mus. of Arts, N.Y.C., Trinity Luth. Ch., New Milford, Dept. of State, Washington, The Printmaking Workshop; represented in corp. and pvt. collections Chevron Corp., Calif., Cameron and Colby, N.Y.C., C.D. Walsh Assocs., Conn.; works featured in publs. including N.Y. Times, Village Voice, 25 Years of African American Women Artist, Home Mag. Recipient 2d pl. award for mixed media Atlanta Life Ins. Co. exhbn. and competition, 1984; fellow Va. Ctr. for Creative Arts, 1996, The Studio Mus. in Harlem, 1987-88, Patricia Robert Harris fellow U.S. Dept. Edn., 1990-92. Democrat. Episcopalian.

HAWKINS, ELINOR DIXON (MRS. CARROLL WOODARD HAWKINS), retired librarian; b. Masontown, W.Va., Sept. 25, 1927; d. Thomas Fitchie and Susan (Reed) Dixon; AB, Fairmont State Coll., 1949; BS in Libr. Sci., U. N.C., 1950; m. Carroll Woodard Hawkins, June 24, 1951; 1 child, John Carroll. Children's libr. Enoch Pratt Free Libr., Balt., 1950-51; head circulation dept. Greensboro (N.C.) Pub. Libr., 1951-56; libr. Craven-Pamlico Libr. Svc., New Bern, N.C., 1958-62; dir. Craven-Pamlico-Carteret Regional Libr., 1962-92; storyteller children's TV program Tele-Story Time, 1952-58, 63—; bd. dirs. Triangle Bank of New Bern. Mem. New Bern Hist. Soc., 1973—, Tryon Palace Commn., 1974—; mem. adv. bd. Salvation Army. Authority. Mem. N.C. Assn. Retarded Children, Pilot Club (pres. 1957-58, v.p. 1962-63). Baptist. Home: PO Box 57 Cove City NC 28523-0057

HAWKINS, ELIZABETH BARD, communications product manager; b. Washington, Apr. 4, 1969; d. Fred Weaver and Sallie (Bard) H. BA in Govt. and Internat. Rels., Georgetown U., 1991; postgrad., U. N.C., 1996—. Asst. to prodr. Walt Disney Pictures, Prague, Czech Republic, 1992; asst. mgr. Internat. Family Entertainment, Prague, Czech Republic, 1992; prodn. asst. ABC News, Washington, 1993; project mgr. Jahn, Bayer & Assocs., San Francisco, 1993-95, Kid Soft, Calif., 1995-96.

HAWKINS, IDA FAYE, educator; b. Ft. Worth, Dec. 28, 1928; d. Christopher Columbus and Nannie Idella (Hughes) Hall; m. Gene Hamilton Hawkins, Dec. 22, 1952; children: Gene Agner, Jane Hall. Student Midwestern U., 1946-48; BS, N. Tex. State U., 1951; student Lamar U., 1968-70; MS, McNeese State U., 1973.Tchr. DeQueen Elem. Sch., Port Arthur, Tex., 1950-54, Tyrrell Elem. Sch., Port Arthur, 1955-56, Roy Hatton Elem. Sch., Bridge City, Tex., 1967-68, Oak Forest Elem. Sch., Vidor, Tex., 1968-91, ret. 2d v.p. Travis Elem. PTA, 1965-66, 1st v.p., 1966-67; corr. sec. Port Arthur City coun. PTA, 1966-67; Sunday sch. tchr. Presbyn. Ch., 1951-53, 60-66. Named Tchr. of Yr., Oak Forest Elem., 1984-85. Mem. NEA, Tex. State Tchrs. Assn., Am. Psychol. Assn. Home: 6315 Central City Blvd Apt 619 Galveston TX 77551-3807

HAWKINS, JACQUELYN, elementary and secondary education educator; b. Russell Springs, Ky., Apr. 30, 1943; d. J.T. Hawkins and Maudie Bell Crew. BS, Andrews U., 1969; MEd, Xavier U., 1976. Cert. elem. tchr., Ohio, reading tchr. elem. and high sch., Ohio. Tchr. Cin. Pub. Schs., 1969—, Cummins Sch., Cin., 1971-81; tchr. Windsor Sch., Cin., 1982-83; tchr. Windsor Sch., 1983-89, acting contact tchr. chpt. 1 reading program, 1989-93; reading recovery tchr. Windsor Sch., Cin., 1993—; rep. Cin. Coun. Educators, 1986-89, 91-92, 92-93, mem. book com.; mem. sch. improvement program Windsor Sch., 1982-84; mem. Sch. Improvement Program Cin. Chairperson United Way at Windsor Sch. Cin., 1986-89, 90-92, United Negro Coll. Fund Cin., 1986-89, ARC, Windsor Sch., Cin., 1986-89, 90-92; rep. Fine Arts Fund Cin., 1986-88; co-leader 4-H Club, Cin., 1987-88; leader Girl Scouts U.S., Cin., 1988-93; tutor Tabernacle Bapt. Ch., 1989; co-chairperson Windsor ARC, 1991-92. Recipient Cert. Achievement Cummins Sch. Cin., 1978. Democrat.

HAWKINS, JANICE EDITH, medical/surgical clinical nurse specialist; b. Greer, S.C., Sept. 12, 1950; d. Theron Gibson and Christine Edith (Bright) H. Diploma, Greenville (S.C.) Gen. Hosp. Sch. Nursing, 1971; BSN, Med. U. of S.C., 1974; MN, Emory U., 1977. RN, Ga.; CS; cert. nutrition support nurse. Staff nurse Emory U. Hosp., Atlanta, 1974-76; instr., staff nurse Med. U. of S.C., Charleston, 1978-79; instr. nursing edn., staff nurse Wilford Hall Med. Ctr. Lackland AFB, San Antonio, 1979-83; clin. nurse specialist med.-surg./nutrition support VA Med. Ctr., Decatur, Ga., 1983—; affiliate faculty BCLS Am. Heart Assn., 1989—; presenter in field. Contbr. chpts. to books and articles to profl. jours. Lt. col. USAF, 1979-83, USAFR, 1983—. Mem. ANA (chairperson coun. clin. nurse specialists 1989-91, chairperson coun. nurses in advanced practice 1991-92, task force to delineate the substructure of the Congress Nursing Practice 1990-91), Nurses Orgn. Vets. Affairs, Am. Soc. Parenteral and Enteral Nutrition (nurses com., stds. com. 1988-90, 96—, nominating com. 1992), Res. Officers Assn., Ga. Soc. Parenteral and Enteral Nutrition (bd. dirs. 1992-94), Ga. Nurses Assn. (cabinet on govtl. affairs 1989-93, chairperson 1995—), Sigma Theta Tau. Home: 1750 Clairmont Rd # 21 Decatur GA 30033-4030

HAWKINS, JOELLEN MARGARET BECK, nursing educator; b. Harvey, N.D., Dec. 15, 1941; d. Charles Joel and Gertrude Adelaide (Waits) Beck; m. Charles Albert Watson, June 27, 1964 (div. 1978); children: John Charles, Andrew Bruce; m. David Gene Hawkins, Oct. 4, 1978. Student, Oberlin Coll., 1959-61; Diploma, Chgo. Wesley Meml. Hosp., Sch. of Nursing, 1964; BS in Nursing, Northwestern U., Chgo., 1964; MS, Boston Coll., 1969, PhD, 1977. Cert. women's health nurse practitioner. Staff nurse Sheboygan (Wis.) Meml. Hosp., 1964-65; instr., staff Boston Lying in Hosp., 1965-66, 68-69; staff nurse Brookline (Mass.) Vis. Nurse Assn., 1968, Guy's Hosp., London, 1968; campus nurse Roger Williams Coll., Bristol, R.I., 1969-70; instr. Salve Regina Coll., Newport, R.I., 1970-74; mem. faculty Roger Williams Coll., Bristol, 1974-75; prof. U. Conn., Storrs, 1978-83; assoc. prof. Boston Coll., Chestnut Hill, Mass., 1975-78, prof., 1983—; women's health nurse practitioner Crittenton Hastings House, 1984—. Author, co-author over 25 books; editor: Linking Nursing Education and Practice, 1987 (Book of Yr. award Am. Jour. Nursing 1988), Dictionary of American Nursing Biography, 1988; contbr. numerous articles to profl. jours. and chpts. to books. Recipient Disting. Alumni award North H.S., 1989; named Nurse Practitioner of Yr. Am. Acad. of Nurse Practitioners, 1995. Fellow Am. Acad. Nursing; mem. ANA, Mass. Nurses Assn. (Disting. Nurse Rschr. award 1984, Lucy Lincoln Drown Nursing History award 1994), Internat. Coun. Women's Health, Nat. Acad. Practice, Am. Assn. for History Nursing (nominating chmn. 1989), Assn. Women's Health Obstetric and Neonatal Nurses, Sigma Theta Tau (Elizabeth Russell Belford Founder's award for excellence in edn. 1993). Democrat. Unitarian. Home: 151 Stanton Ave Auburndale MA 02166-3005 Office: Boston Coll Chestnut Hill MA 02167

HAWKINS, JULIA C. ESTES, elementary school educator; b. Hackleburg, Ala., Jan. 7, 1942; d. Clarence Boyd and Nealie Clementine (Green) Estes; m. Leslie Benjamin Hawkins, June 1, 1968; children: John Michael, Jeffrey Benjamin. BA, Harding Coll., 1964; BA in Edn., No. Ariz. U., 1989. Cert. elem. and mid. sch. tchr.; cert. high sch. English and social studies. English and sociology tchr. Trumann (Ark.) H.S., 1964; phys. edn. tchr. Morenci (Ariz.) Jr. H.S., 1964-65; English tchr. Morenci H.S., 1965-68; 11th grade English tchr. Jacksonville (N.C.) Sr. H.S., 1968-70; tchr. Dixon Elem. Sch., Holly Ridge, N.C., 1970; 7th and 8th grade reading tchr. Morenci Pub. Schs., 1972-73, elem. sch. tchr., 1980—; elem. sch. tchr. Hyder Sch. Dist., Dateland, Ariz., 1977-80; mem. curriculum-assessment steering com. Morenci Pub. Schs., 1994-95. Mem. NEA (cluster del. 1991), Ariz. Edn. Assn. (del.), Morenci Edn. Assn. (past pres., membership chair, chair book fair 1993-94, 94-95, 95-96), Internat. Reading Assn., Phi Kappa Phi. Mem. Ch. of Christ.

HAWKINS, KATHERINE ANN, hematologist, educator; b. Teaneck, N.J., Oct. 25, 1947; d. Howard Robert and Helen Ann (Foley) Hawkins; m. Paul Jonathan Chrzanowski, June 29, 1974; children: Eric, Brian. AB, Manhattanville Coll., Purchase, N.Y., 1969; MD, Columbia U., 1973. Intern Presbyn. Hosp., N.Y.C., 1973; intern Roosevelt Hosp., N.Y.C., 1974-75, resident, 1975-77; fellow NYU, 1977-79; attending hematologist Sickle Cell Ctr. St. Luke's Hosp., N.Y.C., 1985-87; assoc. attending physician St. Luke's - Roosevelt Hosp. Ctr., N.Y.C., 1989; asst. clin. prof. medicine Columbia U., N.Y.C., 1987-94, assoc. clin. prof., 1994—; assoc. dir. dept. medicine, dir. med. edn. St. Luke's Hosp., N.Y.C., 1991—; mem. attending staff Beth Israel Hosp., N.Y.C., Calvary Hosp., N.Y.C., 1991. Contbr. articles to profl. jours. Fellow ACP; mem. AMA, Am. Soc. Hematology. Roman Catholic. Office: 200 W 86th St New York NY 10024-3303

HAWKINS, LINDA PARROTT, school system administrator; b. Florence, S.C., June 23, 1947; d. Obie Lindberg Parrott and Mary Francis (Lee) Evans; m. Larry Eugene Hawkins, Jan. 5, 1946; 1 child, Heather Nichole. BS, U. S.C., 1969; MS, Francis Marion Coll., 1978; EdS in Adminstrn., U. S.C., 1994. Tchr. J.C. Lynch High Sch., Coward, S.C., 1973-80; tchr. Lake City (S.C.) High Sch., 1980-89, coord. alternative program, 1989-90, asst. prin., 1990-94; assoc. prin. Lake City H.S., 1994—; chair dept. Lake City H.S., 1980-89; mem. Williamsburg Tech. Adv. Coun., Kingstree, S.C., 1985-90; mem. adv. coun. Florence-Darlington (S.C.) Tech., 1981-87; co-chair Florence-Darlington-Marion counties preparation for the technologies consortia steering com.; co-chmn. allied health adv. com., 1990-93; spkr., presenter leadership workshops. Editor: Parliamentary Procedure Made Easy, 1983; contbr. articles to profl. jours. State advisor Future Bus. Leaders of Am., Columbia, S.C., 1978-86; treas. S.C. State Women's Aux., 1983-93; sec.-treas. J.C. Lynch Elem. Sch. PTO. Named Outstanding Advisor S.C. Future Bus. Leaders of Am., 1985, Tchr. of Yr., S.C. Bus. Edn. Assn., 1988-89, Secondary Tchr. of Yr., Nat. Bus. Edn. Assn., 1989-90, Educator of Yr. S.C. Trade & Indsl. Edn. Assn., 1993, S.C. Asst. Prin. of Yr., 1995. Mem. Profl. Secs. Internat., Nat. Bus. Assn. (S.C. chpt. membership dir. 1986-89, so. region membership dir. 1989-92, secondary program dept. dir. 1991-92), S.C. Bus. Edn. Assn. (jour. editor 1985-86, v.p. for membership 1986-87, treas. 1987-88, pres. elect 1988-89, pres. 1989-90), Am. Vocat. Assn., S.C. Vocat. Assn. (parliamentarian 1985-86, v.p. 1989-90, treas. 1991-92), Internat. Soc. Bus. Educators, Lake City C. of C., Kappa Kappa Iota, Delta Kappa Gamma. Democrat. Baptist. Office: Lake City High Sch PO Drawer 1569 Lake City SC 29560-1157

HAWKINS, LORETTA ANN, secondary school educator, playwright; b. Winston-Salem, N.C., Jan. 1, 1942; d. John Henry and Laurine (Hines) Sanders; m. Joseph Hawkins, Dec. 10, 1962; children: Robin, Dionne, Sherri. BS in Edn., Chgo. State U., 1965; MA in Lit., Governor's State U., 1977, MA in African Cultures, 1978; postgrad, U. Chgo., 1994—. Cert. tchr., Ill. Tchr. Chgo. Bd. Edn., 1968—; lectr. Chgo. City Colls., 1987-89; tchr. English Gage Park H.S., 1988—; Mem. steering com. Mellon Seminar U. Chgo., 1990; tchr. adv. com. Goodman Theatre, Chgo., 1992, mem. cmty. adv. coun., 1996—. Author: (reading workbook) Contemporary Black Heroes, 1992, (plays) Of Quiet Birds, 1993 (James H. Wilson award 1993), Above the Line, 1994, Good Morning, Miss Alex; contbr. poetry, articles to profl. publs. Santa Fe Pacific Found. fellow, 1988, Lloyd Fry Found. fellow, 1989, Andrew W. Mellon Found. fellow, 1991, Ill. Arts Coun. fellow, 1993; Cmty. Arts Assistance Program Award grantee Chgo. Dept. Cultural Affairs; recipient Feminist Writers 3d pl. award NOW, 1993, Zora Neale Hurston-Bessie Head Fiction award Black Writer's Conf., 1993, numerous others. Mem. AAUW, Nat. Coun. Tchrs. English, Am. Fedn. Tchrs., Women's Theatre Alliance, Dramatists Guild of Am., Internat. Women's Writing Guild. Home: 8928 S Oglesby Ave Chicago IL 60617 Office: Gage Park HS 5630 S RockwellAve Chicago IL 60629

HAWKINS, MARY ELLEN HIGGINS (MARY ELLEN HIGGINS), former state legislator, public relations consultant; b. Birmingham, Ala.; student U. Ala., Tuscaloosa, 1945-47; m. James H. Hawkins, Feb. 13, 1960 (div., 1971); children: Andrew Higgins, Elizabeth, Peter Hixon. Congl. aide to several mems. U.S. Ho. Reps., 1950-60; art instr. Sumter County Schs., Americus, Ga., 1971-72; staff writer Naples (Fla.) Daily News, 1972-74; prin. Daniels-Hawkins, Naples, 1982-84; mem. Fla. Ho. of Reps., Tallahassee, 1974-94; vice chmn. BancFlorida Fin. Corp., Naples, 1979-91, chmn., 1991-93, pres., CEO, 1991-92, also bd. dirs. Columnist, contbr. articles to local newspapers. V.p. Naples Philharmonic, 1984-91; numerous offices Rep. Party of Ga., Americus, 1965-71. Recipient numerous awards for work in Fla. Legislature. Mem. Zonta Internat. Avocation: painting.

HAWKINS, MELINDA FRANCIS, principal; b. Carlsbad, N.Mex., Oct. 23, 1946; d. William Harold and Wanda B. (Hellyer) Pixler; m. Frank Gary Hawkins, Aug. 6, 1966; children: Leesa Gretchen, Andrew Gary. BA, Stephen F. Austin State U., 1971; MEd, Tarleton State U., 1982. Tchr. Nacogdoches (Tex.) Ind. Sch. Dist., 1971-72, Mart (Tex.) Ind. Sch. Dist., 1973; tchr., adminstr. Robinson (Tex.) Ind. Sch. Dist., 1974-89, prin., 1989—. Mem. ASCD, Tex. Assn. Secondary Sch. Prins., Tex. Assn. Mid. Schs., Tex. Mid. Sch. Network, Tex. PTA (life). Home: 778 E Leona Pky Lorena TX 76655-4207 Office: Robinson Ind Sch Dist 500 W Lyndale Ave Waco TX 76706-5505

HAWKINS, NAOMI RUTH, nurse; b. Ft. Smith, Ark., Mar. 8, 1947; d. William Oscar and Sallie Inez (Reynolds) H. BS in Nursing, U. Cen. Ark., 1974. RN, Ark.; cert. pediatric nurse practitioner, Ark. Nurse practitioner Booneville (Ark.) Med. Clinic, 1975-78; lic. practical nurse Greenhurst Nursing Home, Charleston, Ark., 1967-73, RN, 1973-75; pediatric nurse practitioner Ark. Dept. Health, Paris, Ark., 1978—. Fellow Nat. Assn. Pediatric Nurse Assocs. and Practitioners; mem. Ark. Assn. Pediatric Nurse Assocs. and Practitioners, Am. Assn. Christian Counselors, Pub. Health Nurses Assn. Ark., Ark. State Employees Assn. Democrat. Baptist. Home: RR 2 Box 93 Charleston AR 72933-9418 Office: 102 E Academy St Paris AR 72855-4432

HAWKINS, PAULA, federal official, former senator; b. Salt Lake City; m. Walter Eugene Hawkins; children: Genean, Kevin Brent, Kelley Ann. Student, Utah State U., 1944-47, HHD (hon.), 1982; PhD (hon.), Nova U., St. Thomas Villa Nova, Bethune-Cookman, 1986, Rollins Coll., 1990. Dir. Southeast First Nat. Bank, Maitland, Fla., 1972-76; del. Rep. Nat. Conv., Miami, 1968, 72, 76, 80, 84, 88, 92; mem. rules com. Rep. Nat. Conv., 1972, co-chmn. rules com., 1980, co-chmn. platform com., 1984; bd. dirs. Fla. Fedn. Rep. Women, 1968—; elected mem. Fla. Pub. Svc. Commn., Tallahassee, 1972-79, chmn., 1977-79; mem. Rep. Nat. Com. for Fla., 1968-87, mem. rule 29 com., 1973-75; U.S. senator from Fla., 1981-87; mem. labor and human resources com., agrl. com., banking com., fgn. rels. com., drug free sch. com. U. S. Senate, chmn. subcom. on drug abuse, chmn. family and children subcom., 1982-86, chmn. drug enforcement caucus, 1981-87; apptd. permanent subcom. on narcotics control and terrorism OAS, 1981—; apptd. chmn. Nat. Commn. on Responsibilities for Financing Post Secondary, 1990-92; pres. Paula Hawkins and Assocs., Winter Park, Fla., 1988—; v.p. Air Fla., 1979-80; bd. dirs. Philip Crosby Assocs., Alexander Proudfoot; del. UN Narcotic Conv., Austria, 1987, Spain, 1993, N.Y.C., 1994. Author: Children at Risk, 1986. Charter mem. bd. dirs. Fla. Americans Constl. Action Com. of 100, 1966-68, sec.-treas., 1966-68; mem. Fla. Gov.'s Commn. Status Women, 1968-71; mem. Pres.'s Commn. White House Fellowships, 1975; bd. dirs. Freedom Found., 1981—; del. UN Narcotic Conv., Seville, Spain, 1993; U.S. del. UN Conv., N.Y.C., 1994—. Recipient citation for service Fla. Rep. Party, 1966-67, award for legis. work Child Fund Inc, 1982, Israel Peace medal, 1983, Tree of Life award Jewish Nat. Found, 1985, Nat. Mother of Yr. award, 1984, Grandmother of Yr.award, 1985, Albert Einstein Good Govt. award, 1986, Good Govt. award Maitland Jaycees, 1976, Outstanding award Am. Acad, Pediatricians, 1986; named Guardian of Small Bus. Nat. Fedn. Ind. Bus., 1982, 83, 84, 86, Rep. Woman of Yr. N.Y. Women's Nat. Rep. Club, 1981, Outstanding Woman of Utah, 1985, Outstanding Woman of Yr. in Govt. Orlando C. of C., 1977, Woman of Yr., KC, 1973. Mem. Maitland C. of C. (chmn. congl. action com. 1967). Mem. Ch. Jesus Christ of Latter-day Saints (pres. Relief Soc., Orlando Stake 1960-64. Club: Capitol Hill (Washington), Interlaken Country (Winter Pk.). Office: PO Box 193 Winter Park FL 32790-0193*

HAWKINS, PORTIA SHULER, musician; b. Orangeburg, S.C., Aug. 18, 1948; d. John Milton and Edna (Williamson) Shuler; m. William Pruden Hawkins, Jr., June 4, 1977; 1 child, John Marvin. BA, Fisk U., Nashville, 1970; MusM in Piano Performance, Yale U., 1972. Cert. music tchr. Nat. Music Tchrs. Assn. Instr. music Claflin Coll., Orangeburg, 1972-73, S.C. State Coll., Orangeburg, 1973-74, So. U., Baton Rouge, 1974-76, Norfolk (Va.) State Coll., 1976-77; artist affiliate Emory U., 1979-81; pvt. piano instr. Roswell, Ga., 1983—; part-time instr. music Spelman Coll., Atlanta, 1989, 1995—, DeKalb Coll., Clarkston, Ga., 1993—. Mem. Pro Mozart Soc., Nat. Fedn. Musicians, Nat. Guild Piano Tchrs., Ga. Music Tchrs. Assn. (state chmn. student chmn. 1994—, adjudicator 1990—, v.p. North DeKalb chpt. 1991-92), Atlanta Music Club, Atlanta Music Tchrs. Assn., Mu Phi Epsilon. Home: 885 Greenvine Trace Roswell GA 30076 Office: DeKalb Coll 555 N Indian Creek Clarkston GA 30021 also: Agnes Scott Coll 141 E College Ave Decatur GA 30030

HAWKINS, TERESA ANN, vocational education educator; b. Staunton, Ill., Mar. 6, 1956; d. James C. and Catherine C. (Dover) H. BS in Edn., U. Mo., 1979; MEd, No. Ariz. U., 1994. Cert. secondary tchr. (life) Mo., C.C. vocat. tchr. Ariz. Sports agate clk. Ariz. Daily Star, Tucson, 1986-87; med. transcriptionist Carondelet Transcription Svc., Tucson, 1987-89, U. Physicians, Inc., Tucson, 1989-92; vocat. tchr. Pima C.C., Tucson, 1992—, mem. adj. faculty, 1994-95; ednl. intern Telesvcs. Industry Group, Tucson, 1994, mem. ednl. task force, 1994-95. Active Planned Parenthood So. Ariz., Tucson, 1988—. Mem. AAUW, Am. Assn. C.C. Women, Mo. Alumni Assn., Phi Kappa Phi. Home: 463 S Camino Seco Tucson AZ 85710 Office: Pima CC Ctr Tng & Devel 5901 S Calle Santa Cruz Tucson AZ 85709-6310

HAWKS, PATRICIA KATHLEEN, psychological therapist; b. Guam, Feb. 11, 1948; d. James Lawrence Sr. and Mary Helen (Keefe) Seale; divorced; children: Robert Wade, Steven Pryor. BS, U. Tenn., Martin, 1970, MS, 1974; EdD, U. Memphis, 1994. Alcohol and drug counselor, trainer Memphis Fed. Correctional Instn., 1992-94; pvt. practice Bartlett (Tenn.) Family Counseling Ctr., 1994-95; exec. counselor Second Chance Ministries, Memphis, 1994-95; behavioral specialist Peabody Residential Treatment Ctr., Memphis, 1994—; domestic violence counselor Memphis Police Dept., 1996—; therapist Midtown Mental Health, Memphis, 1996—; expert witness Memphis Juvenile Ct., 1995; mem. student adv. com. Office of Dean of Edn., U. Memphis, 1992-93, mem. grad. student assn. com., 1991-93; presenter in field. Active local PTA, Memphis, 1992—. Mem. NAFE, ACA, Tenn. Assn. for Gifted (v.p. 1996—), Am. Correctional Assn., Kappa Delta Pi. Episcopalian. Home: 7557 Wheatley Dr Germantown TN 38138 Office: Peabody Residential Treatment Ctr 1242 Peabody Ave Memphis TN 38104

HAWLEY, LINDA DONOVAN, advertising executive; b. Bryn Mawr, Pa., Nov. 1, 1946; d. John Donovan and Ann (Durnall) H.; diploma in advt. Charles Morris Price Sch. Advt., Phila., 1965. Sr. writer The Bulletin Co., Phila., 1968-72, The Advt. People, Inc., Bala Cynwyd, Pa., 1973-75, Elkman Advt. Co., Inc., Bala Cynwyd, 1975-77; sr. copywriter Mel Richman Inc., Bala Cynwyd, 1977-80; pres., creative dir. Hawley & Matthews Inc., Exton, 1980—; instr. Charles Morris Price Sch., Pa. State U. Recipient various advt. awards including Neographics award, 1970, Addy award, 1976, 93, Addy awards 2d Dist., 1980, Phila., 1981, 89; Charles Morris Price Sch. Disting. Alumni Award, 1977; TRAC award, 1983, 84, Billy award, 1985. V.p. bd. Pa. Lupus Found., pres. 1993-94; mem. adv. bd. Joseph J. Peters Inst., 1991-93. Mem. Phila. Club Advt. Women (pres. 1978-80), Phila. Women's Network (pres. 1983-84, dir. 1984-85), Am. Advt. Fedn. (Pa. lt. gov. 1979-84, 87-88, lt. gov. 1990-92, 2d dist. sec. 1981-82, Crystal Prism award), TV and Radio Advt. Club, Phila. Advt. Club (bd. dirs.). Roman Catholic. Office: Hawley & Matthews Inc 661 Exton Commons Exton PA 19341-2446

HAWLEY, LUCRETIA MARLENE, retired accounting educator; b. Stillwater, Okla., Nov. 19, 1932; d. Owen Hartman Schneider and Maudee Dessie (Callicoat) Bearg; m. Robert Paul Hawley, Nov. 27, 1955; children: James Owen, Kathleen Francis Jeschke, John Robert. BS in Econs., Ctrl. Mo. State U., 1955, BSBA in Acctg., 1955, MA in Acctg., 1970. CPA, cert. mgmt. acct. Payroll clk. Westinghouse, Kansas City, Mo., 1951; internal auditor Spencer Chem., Kansas City, 1955-56; bus. skills and Am. history tchr. J.C. Penney H.S., Hamilton, Mo., 1965-67; bus. skills and speech tchr. Breckenridge (Mo.) H.S., 1967-70; bus. skills and acctg. tchr. various bus. schs., 1970-77; instr., asst. prof. acctg. Mo. Western State Coll., St. Joseph, Mo., 1970-71, 77-95; ret., 1995; mem. acad. computing com. Mo. Western State Coll., St. Joseph, 1988-95. Co-pastor, treas. RLDS Ch. Mem. Inst. Mgmt. Accts. (bd. dirs., CMA dir., student dir.), Sr. Citizens Found. (treas., bd. dirs. 1980-95), Gen. Fedn. Women's Clubs Monday Club (pres.), Phi Delta Kappa, Delta Kappa Gamma (v.p., pres. 1984-88, 96—). Republican. Home: Rt 2 Box 34 Hamilton MO 64644

HAWLEY, MARY KATHLEEN, writer, editor; b. Milw., Sept. 10, 1957; d. Patrick William and Cecilia Mary (Lemberger) Hawley; m. Thomas Alan Miecznikowski, May 9, 1992; 1 child, Nadia Hawley Miecznikowski. BA in Theology, U. Notre Dame, 1980; MA in Interdisciplinary Arts Edn., Columbia Coll., Chgo., 1987. Migrant resource asst. South Bend (Ind.) Cmty. Sch. Corp., 1981-82; theology instr. St. Joseph's H.S., South Bend, 1982-85; interim editor Chgo. Catolico newspaper, 1986-87; freelance writer, editor and translator Chgo., 1987-88; editor integrated lang. arts Scott Foresman and Co., Glenview, Ill., 1988—; mem. lit. bd. Tia Chucha Press, Chgo., 1995—; editor, bd. dirs. Letter Ex, Chgo., 1988-93. Author: (poetry) Double Tongues, 1993, (children's books) The Adventures of Max and Ned, 1996, Annie's Secret Diary, 1996; editor: Star Wallpaper: The Neutral Turf Anthology of Young Chicago Poets, Vols. I, II, III, 1992-95; recordings include Sounds From Chicago Girls' Night Out, 1989; contbr. to poetry anthologies and poetry jours. Recipient 1st prize in spring poetry contest Rambunctious Rev., 1995; Chgo. Dept. Cultural Affairs awardee, 1993. Mem. Nat. Coun. Tchrs. English, Acad. Am. Poets, Phi Beta Kappa. Roman Catholic. Home: 6635 N Glenwood # 2 Chicago IL 60626-4709

HAWLEY, NANCI ELIZABETH, public relations and communications professional; b. Detroit, Mar. 18, 1942; d. Arthur Theodore and Elizabeth Agnes (Fylling) Smisek; m. Joseph Michael Hawley, Aug. 28, 1958; children: Michael, Ronald, Patrick (dec.), Julie Anne. Pres. Tempo 21 Nursing Svcs., Inc., Covina, Calif., 1973-75; v.p. Profl. Nurses Bur., Inc., L.A., 1975-83; cons. Hawley & Assocs., Covina, 1983-87; exec. v.p. Glendora (Calif.) C. of C., 1984-85; dir. membership West Covina (Calif.) C. of C., 1985-87; exec. dir. San Dimas (Calif.) C. of C., 1987-88; mgr. pub. rels. Soc. for Advancement of Material and Process Engrs., Covina, 1988-92; small bus. rep. South Coast Air Quality Mgmt. Dist., 1992-94; bus. counselor Commerce and Trade Agy., Small Bus. Devel. Ctr., 1994; exec. v.p. Ont. (Calif.) C. of C., 1994—. V.p. Sangabriel valley chpt. Women in Mgmt. Recipient Youth Motivation award Foothill Edn. Com., Glendora, 1987. Mem. NAFE, Pub. Rels. Soc. Am., Soc. Nat. Assn. Publs., Am. Soc. Assn. Execs., Nat. Assn. Membership Dirs., Profl. Communicators Assn. So. Calif., Western Assn. Chamber Execs. (Spl. merit award for mag. pub. 1995), Kiwanis Internat. (sec. 1989-90, pres. West Covina 1990-91, Kiwanian of Yr. 1989), Rotary Internat. Office: Ontario C of C 2151 East D St Ste 203A Ontario CA 91764

HAWLEY, SANDRA SUE, electrical engineer; b. Spirit Lake, Iowa, May 7, 1948; d. Byrnard Leroy and Dorothy Virginia (Fischbeck) Smith; m. Michael John Hawley, June 7, 1970; 1 child, Alexander Tristin. BSEE, U. Dayton, 1981; BS in Math. and Stats., Iowa State U., 1970; MS in Stats., U. Del., 1975. Rsch. analyst State of Wis., Madison, 1970-71; rsch. asst. Del. State Coll., Dover, 1972-73; asst. prof. math. and statis. Wesley Coll., Dover, 1974-81, chmn. dept. math. and computer sci., 1978-80; elec. engr. Control Data Corp., Bloomington, Minn., 1982-85, sr. elec. engr. Custom Integrated Circuits, 1985-89; sr. lead engr. Cardiac Pacemakers, Inc., 1989-90; mgr. Tech. Rosemount Inc., 1990-94; prin. cons. Tri-Ess, Mpls., 1994—. Contbr. articles to profl. jours. Elder Presbyn. Ch. U.S.A., 1975—, mem. session Oak Grove Presbyn. Ch., Bloomington, 1985-88; moderator Presbyn. of Twin Cities Area, 1996—, chair Presbyn. Coun., 1994, chair Coun. United Action, 1989-92, adminstrv. comm., 1989-91, commr. to Synod of Lakes & Prairies, 1990, Gen. Assembly Coun., 1992—, com. on coun., 1992, commr. Gen. Assembly, 1991, chair Nat. Ministries divsn. Gen. Assembly, 1996—. NSF scholar U. Dayton, 1981. Mem. IEEE, Soc. Women Engrs. Office: Tri-Ess 7724 W 85th St Minneapolis MN 55438-1382

HAWLEY, THERESA ANNE LAWTON, developmental psychologist; b. Syracuse, N.Y., June 13, 1966; d. John F. and Anne M. (Perkins) Lawton; m. Michael Joseph Hawley, Sept. 26, 1992. BA, U. Notre Dame, 1988; PhD, U. Mich., 1992. Program and rsch. analyst Ounce of Prevention Fund, Chgo., 1993—. Contbr. articles to profl. jours. Bd. dirs. Christmas in April, Aurora, Ill., 1992-94. Fellow NSF, 1989-92. Mem. APA, Am. Orthopsychatric Assn., Soc. for Rsch. in Child Devel., Phi Beta Kappa. Roman Catholic. Office: Ounce of Prevention Fund 122 S Michigan #2050 Chicago IL 60603

HAWN, GOLDIE, actress; b. Washington, Nov. 21, 1945; d. Edward Rutledge and Laura (Steinhoff) H.; m. Gus Trinkonis, May 16, 1969 (div.); m. Bill Hudson (div.); children: Oliver, Kate Garry, Wyatt Russell. Student, Am. U. Profl. dancer, 1965; profl. acting debut in Good Morning, World, 1967-68; mem. company TV series Laugh-In, 1968-70; appeared in TV spl. Pure Goldie, 1971; films include: The One and Only Genuine Original Family Band, 1968, Cactus Flower, 1969 (Acad. award best supporting actress 1969), There's A Girl In My Soup, 1970, $, 1971, Butterflies Are Free, 1971, The Sugarland Express, 1974, The Girl from Petrovka, 1974, Shampoo, 1975, The Duchess and the Dirtwater Fox, 1976, Travels with Anita, 1978, Foul Play, 1978, Seems Like Old Times, 1980, Lovers and Liars, 1981, Best Friends, 1982, Swingshift, 1984, Overboard, 1987, Bird on a Wire, 1989, Deceived, 1991, Housesitter, 1992, Death Becomes Her, 1992, Crisscross, 1992, The First Wives Club, 1996, Everybody Says I Love You, 1996; exec. producer and star films Private Benjamin, 1980, Protocol, 1984, Wildcats, 1986, My Blue Heaven (co-exec. prodr. only), 1990, Something to Talk About, 1995 (exec. prodr. only); host TV spl. Pure Goldie, 1970, Goldie Hawn Special, 1978, Goldie and Liza Together, 1980, Goldie and Kids: Listen to Us!, 1982. Office: care ICM Ed Limato 8942 Wilshire Blvd Beverly Hills CA 90211*

HAWN, MICAELA (MICKI HAWN), mathematics educator; b. Mobile, Ala., July 13, 1945; d. Lowell Oliver Hawn and F. Lemoine (Williams) Brummitt; child from previous marriage: Douglas S. McKay, Jr.; m. Ivan Lee Gordon, Jr. BS, U. South Ala., 1967, MA, 1972; EdS, Barry U., 1995. Tchr. Murphy H.S., Mobile, 1967-69; tchr., dept. chair Hillsdale Mid. Sch., Mobile, 1969-87; tchr. Deerfield Beach (Fla.) Mid. Sch., 1987-88; tchr., team leader, competitions coord. Parkway Mid. Sch., HiTech Magnet, Ft. Lauderdale, 1988-96; tchr. Pompano Beach (Fla.) Broadcast & Communications Magnet Sch., 1996—; Tchr. Dauphin Way Methodist Ch., Mobile, 1970-87. Mem. ASCD, AAUW, Internat. Soc. Tech. in Edn., Nat. Coun. Tchrs. Math., Fla. Assn. Computer Educators, Mensa, Alumni Assn., Phi Delta Kappa. Methodist. Home: 7604 SW 8th Ct North Lauderdale FL 33068

HAWTHORNE, SHELBY MYRICK, reading specialist; b. Washington, June 20, 1945; d. James Franklin and Mildred Elizabeth (Myrick) Smith; m. Randall Stone Hawthorne, June 17, 1967. BA Elem. Edn., Coll. William and Mary, 1967, MA in Edn., 1975. Tchr. Norge (Va.) Elem. Sch., 1967-75, reading specialist, 1975-89; reading specialist Clara Byrd Baker Elem. Sch., Williamsburg, Va., 1989—. Bd. dirs. Spiked Shoe Soc., Williamsburg, Va., 1976—; participant People to People Internat., 1993. Mem. Nat. Coun. Tchrs. English, Internat. Reading Assn., Delta Kappa Gamma (chpt. pres. 1988-90), Phi Delta Kappa (chpt. v.p. 1994-95, pres. 1995—). Home: 101 Braddock Rd Williamsburg VA 23185 Office: Clara Byrd Baker Elem Sch 3131 Ironbound Rd Williamsburg VA 23185

HAY, BETTY JO, civic worker; b. McAlester, Okla., June 6, 1931; d. Duncan and Kathryn Myrtle (Albert) Peacock; m. Jess Thomas Hay, Aug. 3, 1951; children: Deborah Hay Spradley, Patricia Lynn Daibert. BA, So. Meth. U., 1952. Bd. dirs. White House Preservation Fund, 1980-87, Nat. Parents as Tchrs., 1991-94; bd. dirs. Nat. Mental Health Assn., 1978-87, pres., 1986, mem. fin. com. and child adolescent com., 1978-79, mem. resource devel. com., 1980-83; v.p. fundraising Mental Health Assn. Tex., 1980, bd. dirs., 1974-90, pres., 1983-84; bd. dirs. Mental Health Assn., Dallas County, 1972-88, pres., 1981-82; bd. dirs. United Way Met. Dallas, 1983-94, treas., 1989; bd. dirs. Assn. Higher Edn. North Tex., 1980-82, vice chmn., 1982-83, chmn., 1984-85; mem. adv. bd. Sch. Social Work, U. Tex., Arlington, 1983-94; mem. Nat. Commn. on Children, 1989-92, Dallas Coun. on World Affairs, Woman's Div., March of Dimes Aux., 1982—; bd. dirs. Baylor Coll. Dentistry, 1987-94. mem. exec. com., 1989, vice chmn., 1992; mem. Tex. Commn. on Children and Youth, 1994-95; pres. Tex. Mental Health Found., 1982—; many past involvements in charitable orgns. Address: 7236 Lupton Cir Dallas TX 75225-1737

HAY, ELIZABETH DEXTER, embryology researcher, educator; b. St. Augustine, Fla., Apr. 2, 1927; d. Isaac Morris and Lucille (Lynn) H. AB, Smith Coll., 1948; MA (hon.), Harvard U., 1964; ScD (hon.), Smith Coll., 1973, Trinity Coll., 1989; MD, Johns Hopkins U., 1952, LHD (hon.), 1990. Intern in internal medicine Johns Hopkins Hosp., Balt., 1952-53; instr. anatomy Johns Hopkins U. Med. Sch., Balt., 1953-56, asst. prof., 1956-57; asst. prof. Cornell U. Med. Sch., N.Y.C., 1957-60; asst. prof. Harvard Med. Sch., Boston, 1960-64, Louise Foote Pfeiffer assoc. prof., 1964-69, Louise Foote Pfeiffer prof. embryology, 1969—, chmn. dept. anatomy and cellular biology, 1975-93; prof. dept. cell biology, 1993—; cons. cell biology sect. NIH, 1965-69; mem. adv. coun. Nat. Inst. Gen. Med. Sci., NIH, 1978-81; mem. sci. adv. bd. Whitney Marine Lab., U. Fla., 1982-86; mem. adv. coun. Johns Hopkins Sch. Medicine, 1982—; chairperson bd. sci. counselors Nat. Inst. Dental Rsch., NIH, 1984-86; mem. bd. sci. counselors Nat. Inst. Environ. Health Sci., NIH, 1990-93. Author: Regeneration, 1966; (with J.P. Revel) Fine Structure of the Developing Avian Cornea, 1969; editor: Cell Biology of Extracellular Matrix, 1981, 2d edit., 1991; editor-in-chief Developmental Biology Jour., 1971-75; contbr. articles to profl. jours. Mem. Scientists Task Force of Congressman Barney Frank, Massach, 1982-92. Recipient Disting. Achievement award N.Y. Hosp.-Cornell Med. Ctrl. Alumni Coun., 1985, award for vision rsch. Alcon, 1988, Excellence in Sci. award Fedn. Am. Socs. Exptl. Biology. Mem. Soc. Devel. Biology (pres. 1973-74), Am. Soc. Cell Biology (pres. 1976-77, legis. alert com. 1982—, E.B. Wilson award 1989), Am. Assn. Anatomists (pres. 1981-82, legis. alert com. 1982—, Centennial award 1987, Henry Gray award 1992), Am. Acad. Arts and Scis., Johns Hopkins Soc. Scholars, Nat. Acad. Sci., Inst. Medicine, Internat. Soc. Devel. Biologists (exec. bd. 1977), Boston Mycol. Club. Home: 14 Aberdeen Rd Weston MA 02193-1733 Office: Harvard Med Sch Dept Cell Biology 220 Longwood Ave Boston MA 02115-5701

HAY, ELOISE KNAPP, English language educator; b. Chgo., Nov. 19, 1926; d. G. Prather and Lucy (Norvell) Knapp; m. Stephen Northup Hay, June 11, 1954 (dec. Apr. 1996); children: Catherine, Edward. BA, Elmira Coll., 1948; PhD, Radcliffe Coll., 1961; DLitt (hon.), Elmira Coll., 1994. Tchg. fellow Harvard U., Cambridge, Mass., 1950-54; asst. prof. English U. Ill., Chgo., 1961-64; lectr. dept. English U. Calif., Santa Barbara, 1967-70, acting assoc. prof., religious studies, 1975-77, asst. prof. English, 1977-80, assoc. prof. English, 1980-82, prof., 1982-96; prof. English U. Delhi, India, 1970-71; mem. English lit. adv. com. Coun. for Internat. Exch. of Scholars, Washington, 1983-85, 88. Author: The Political Novels of Joseph Conrad, 1963, 2d edit., 1981, T.S. Eliot's Negative Way, 1982; contbr. articles on other lit. subjects including Hawthorne, Dickens, James, Kipling, Forster, and Proust. Mem. U. Calif. Santa Barbara Sr. Women's Coun. Radcliffe (Bunting) Inst. fellow, 1964-66; sr. fellow NEH, 1974-75; recipient Disting. Teaching award U. Calif.-Santa Barbara Alumni, 1981. Mem. MLA Am. (mem. exec. com. on late 19th-early 20th-century lit. 1979-84, chmn. com. 1984), Phi Bet Kappa. Democrat. Roman Catholic. Home: 3310 Los Pinos Dr Santa Barbara CA 93105-2630 Office: U Calif Dept English Santa Barbara CA 93106 *Died Apr. 30, 1996.*

HAY, HEATHER, securities analyst; b. Balt., May 30, 1966; d. Barbara Jean (Brown) Lambdin; m. James Joseph Murren; 1 child, Jack Hurst Murren. BA, Johns Hopkins U., 1988. CFA. Analyst Salomon Bros. Inc., N.Y.C., 1989-93; v.p. J.P. Morgan Securities, N.Y.C., 1993—. Mem. NOW, Inst. CFAs, N.Y. Soc. Securities Analysts.

HAYCOX, ROLANDA MOORE, lawyer, nurse; b. Indpls., July 19, 1964; d. Richard Roland and Roberta Joyce (Wood) Moore; m. James William Haycox, Aug. 7, 1986. BSN with honors, Ind. U., Indpls., 1986, JD magna cum laude, M in Health Adminstrn., 1992. Bar: Ind. 1992, U.S. Dist. Ct. (no. and so. dists.) Ind. 1992; RN, Ind. Nurse Cmty. Hosp. East, Indpls., 1986-91, St. Francis Hosp., Beech Grove, Ind., 1990; rsch. asst. Ind. U. Sch. Law, 1990-92; assoc. Baker & Daniels, 1992-95; mgr. clin. and reimbursement regulation NovaCare, Inc., Carmel, Ind., 1995-96; legal counsel Admina Star Fed., Inc., Indpls., 1996—; condr. seminars in nursing and legal fields; mentor M Health Adminstrn. mentorship program Ind. U. Sch. Pub. and Environ. Affairs. Editor-in-chief Ind. Law Rev., 1991-92; contbr. articles to profl. jours. Bd. dirs. Alpha Home Assn. Greater Indpls., 1993-96; vol. Meth. Hosp. Hospice of Indpls., 1993-95. Lloyd G. Balfour scholar, 1991, alumni scholar Eli Lilly & Co., 1992. Mem. ABA, Ind. Bar Assn., Indpls. Bar Assn., Am. Coll. Healthcare Execs., Nat. Health Lawyers Assn., Med. Group Mgmt. Assn., Am. Acad. Healthcare Attys., Am. Soc. Writers on Legal Subjects, Pi Alpha Alpha, Phi Delta Phi. Republican. Episcopalian. Office: Adnina Star Fed Inc 8115 Knue Rd Indianapolis IN 46250

HAYDEN, DIANE LEISERSON, artist, art educator; b. New Haven, Conn., June 27, 1955; d. Mark Whittlesey and Jean Gardner (Oliver) Leiserson; m. Paul Thomas Hayden, Aug. 2, 1980; children: Olivia Grace, Dorothy Jean, Rose Alice. Maturité Fédérale Suisse, Nouvelle Ecole Moser, Geneva, 1974; BA, Yale U., 1978; MFA, Parsons Sch. Design, 1981. Instr. L.A. County H.S. for the Arts, 1987; instr. Otis Art Inst. Parsons Sch. Design, L.A., 1987-88; assoc. faculty Herron Sch. Art, Indpls., 1989-92; instr. Indpls. Mus. Art, 1993, Otis Coll. Art and Design, L.A., 1996—; panelist, discussant Am. Culture Assn. annual meeting, San Antonio, 1991; mem. steering com. Women and Art in Ind. Conf., Indpls., 1990; spkr. in field. One woman exhbns. include Ruschman Gallery, Indpls., 1995; group exhbns. include Nat. Art Mus. Sport, Indpls., 1993, Am. States Arts Competition, Indpls., 1994. Grantee City of L.A. Cultural Affairs, 1987, Individual Artist Tech. grantee Arts Coun. Indpls., 1991; recipient 1st prize Painting Pacific Art Guild, 1986, 3rd prize Am. States Arts Competition, 1994. Office: 6538 La Garita Dr Palos Verdes Peninsula CA 90275

HAYEK, CAROLYN JEAN, retired judge; b. Portland, Oreg., Aug. 17, 1948; d. Robert A. and Marion L. (DeKoning) H.; m. Steven M. Rosen, July 21, 1974; children: Jonathan David, Laura Elizabeth. BA in Psychology, Carleton Coll., 1970; JD, U. Chgo., 1973. Bar: Wash. 1973. Assoc. firm Jones, Grey & Bayley, Seattle, 1973-77; sole practice law, Federal Way, Wash., 1977-82; judge Federal Way Dist. Ct., 1982-95; ret., 1995. Task force mem. Alternatives for Wash., 1973-75; mem. Wash. State Ecol. Commn., 1975-77; columnist Tacoma News Tribune Hometown Sect., 1995—; bd. dirs. 1st Unitarian Ch. Seattle, 1986-89, vice chair 1987-88, pres., 1988-89; den leader Cub Scouts Mt. Rainier coun. Boy Scouts Am., 1987-88, scouting coord., 1988-89; bd. dirs. Twin Lakes Elem. Sch. PTA. Recipient Women Helping Women award Federal Way Soroptimist, 1991, Martin Luther King Day Humanitarian award King County, 1993, Recognition cert. City of Federal Way Diversity Commn., 1995. Mem. AAUW (br. pres. 1978-80, 90-92, chmn. state level conf. com. 1986-87, mem. diversity com. 1991—, state bd. mem. 1995—), ABA, Wash. Women Lawyers, Wash. State Bar Assn., King County Dist. Ct. Judges Assn. (treas., exec. com. 1990-91, 92-93, com. chmn., chair and rules com. 1990-91, 92-94), Elected Wash. Women (dir. 1983-87), Nat. Assn. Women Judges (nat. bd. dirs., dist. bd. dirs. 1984-86, chmn. rules com. 1988-89, chmn. bylaws com. 1990-91), Fed. Way Women's Network (bd. dirs. 1984-87, 88-91, 95—, pres. 1985, program co-chair 1989-91, co-editor newsletter), Greater Fed. Way C. of C. (dir. 1978-82, sec. 1980-81, v.p. 1981-82), Sunrise Rotary (com. svc. chair, bd. dirs., membership com., Federal Way chpt. 1991-96, youth exchange officer 1994-95), Washington Women United (bd. dirs. 1995—), Unitarian Universalist Women's Assn. (chair bylaws com. 1996—). Republican. Address: PO Box 24494 Federal Way WA 98093-1494

HAYES, ALBERTA PHYLLIS WILDRICK, retired health service executive; b. Blakeslee, Pa., May 31, 1918; d. William and Maude (Robbins) Wildrick; diploma Wilkes Barre Gen. Hosp. Sch. Nursing, 1938-41; student Wilkes Coll., 1953-54, Pa. State U., 1969—; m. Glenmore Burton Hayes, Oct. 9, 1942; children: Glenmore Rolland, William Bruce. Nurse, Monroe County Gen. Hosp., East Stroudsburg, Pa., 1941-44; pvt. duty nurse, 1944-56; with White Haven (Pa.) Center, 1956-82, dir. residential services, 1966-82, ret., 1982. Pres. Tobyhanna Twp. Sch. PTA, 1948-49, Top-o-Pocono Women of Rotary, 1975-76; nurse ARC, 1955; adv. council Luzerne County Foster Grandparent Program, 1977—, Health Services Keystone Job Corps, Drums, Pa., 1977—; active Tobyhanna Twp. Zoning Hearing Bd., Pocono Pines, Pa.; coord. Pocono Mountain Chpt. Choral Group, 1993—; chmn. bd. trustees Blakeslee United Meth. Ch. Mem. Am. Assn. Mental Deficiency, Am. Legion Aux. (unit pres. 1946-47), Ea. Star (Lehigh chpt.). Club: Pocono Mountains Women's (Blakeslee, sec. 1993, past pres.). Home: PO Box 11 Blakeslee PA 18610-0011

HAYES, ALICE BOURKE, university official, biology educator; b. Chgo., Dec. 31, 1937; d. William Joseph and Mary Alice (Cawley) Bourke; m. John J. Hayes, Sept. 2, 1961 (dec. July 1981). B.S., Mundelein Coll., Chgo., 1959; M.S., U. Ill., 1960; Ph.D., Northwestern U., 1972; DSc (honoris causa), Loyola U., Chgo., 1994. Researcher Mcpl. Tb San., Chgo., 1960-62; faculty Loyola U., Chgo., 1962—, chmn. dept., 1968-77, dean natural scis. div., 1977-80, asso. acad. v.p., 1980-87, v.p. acad. affairs, 1987-89; provost, exec. v.p. St. Louis U., 1989-95; pres. U. San Diego, 1995—; mem. space biology program NASA, 1980-86; mem. adv. panel NSF, 1977-81, Parmly Hearing Inst., 1986-89; del. Bot. Del. to South Africa, 1984, to People's Republic China, 1988, to USSR, 1990; reviewer Coll. Bd. and Mellon Found. Nat. Hispanic Scholar Awards, 1985-86; bd. dirs. Pulitzer Pub. Co. Co-author books; contbr. articles to profl. publs. Campaign mem. Mental Health Assn. Ill., Chgo., 1973-89; trustee Chgo.-No. Ill. divsn. Nat. Multiple Sclerosis Soc., 1981-89, bd. dirs., 1980-88, com. chmn., sec. to bd. dirs., vice chmn. bd. dirs.; trustee Regina Dominican Acad., 1984-89, Civitas Dei Found., 1987-92, Rockhurst Coll.; trustee St. Ignatius Coll. Prep. Sch., bd. dirs., 1984-89, sec., vice chmn.; bd. dirs. Urban League Met. St. Louis, St. Louis Sci. Ctr., 1991-95, Cath. Charities St. Louis, 1992-95, St. Louis County Hist. Soc., 1992-95. Named to Teachers' Hall of Fame Blue Key Soc.; fellow in botany U. Ill., 1959-60; fellow in botany NSF, 1969-71; grantee Am. Orchid Soc., 1967; grantee HEW, 1969, 76; grantee NSF, 1975; grantee NASA, 1980-85. Mem. AAAS, AAUP (corp. rep. 1980-85), Am. Assn. for Higher Edn., Am. Assn. Univ. Adminstrs. (mem. program com. nat. meeting 1988), Am. Soc. Gravitational and Space Biology, Assn. Midwest Coll. Biology Teachers, Am. Soc. Plant Physiology, Bot. Soc. Am., Am. Inst. Biol. Scis. Acad., Chgo. Network, Soc. Ill. Microbiologists (edn. com. 1969-70, Pasteur award com. 1975, pub. rels. com. 1974, chair speakers' bur. 1974-79), Chgo. Assn. Tech. Socs. (acad. liaison 1982-85, awards com. 1984-89), Am. Coun. on Edn. (corp. rep. higher edn. panel), Ctr. Rsch. Librs. (nominating com. 1986), North Ctrl. Assn. Colls. and Schs. (cons., evaluator Commn. on Higher Edn. 1984-95, commr.-at-large 1988-94), Mo. Women's Forum Club, Sigma Xi, Delta Sigma Rho, Sigma Delta Epsilon, Phi Beta Kappa, Alpha Sigma Nu. Democrat. Roman Catholic. Office: U San Diego 5998 Alcala Park San Diego CA 92110-2492

HAYES, ALLENE VALERIE FARMER, government executive; b. Washington, Sept. 23, 1958; d. Thomas Jonathan and Allena V. (Joyner) Farmer; m. Thomas Gary Hayes; 1 child, Tommia Chanel. Student, Richmond Coll., London, 1980; BA, Clark U., 1980; cert., U. Oxford, Eng., 1981; M.L.S., U. Md., 1986. Libr. asst. NUS Corp., Gaithersburg, Md., 1981-82; cataloger Libr. of Congress, Washington, 1982-84, copyright specialist, 1984-85; congl. fellow Ho. of Reps. Com. on D.C., Washington, 1985—; English tutor, writer Natural Motion, Washington, 1983-84; intern, archivist Howard U., Washington, 1985; intern Libr. Congress Intern Program, 1991-92. Compiler: Single Mother's Resource Directory, 1984. Compiler, editor: Policy Research, 1985. Author booklet: D.C. Statehood Issue, 1986. Mem. U. Md. College Park Black Women's Coun., 1984, NAACP; vol. Congl. Black Caucus Found., Washington, 1985. Recipient Fgn. Study award Am. Inst. for Fgn. Study, 1981; Congl. Black Caucus fellow, 1985. Mem. ALA, Libr. of Congress Profls. Assn., Daniel A.P. Murray Afro-Am. Culture Assn. of Libr. of Congress (mem. exec. bd., newsletter editor, pres. 1994—), Delta Sigma Theta (tutor 1986). Avocations: travel; writing; dance; drama; tennis. Home: 1120 K St NE Washington DC 20002-7110 Office: Libr of Congress 101 Independence Ave SE Washington DC 20540-0001

HAYES, ANN LOUISE, English educator, consultant, poet; b. Los Angeles, May 13, 1924; d. George Henry and Bernice (Derby) Bowman; m. Frank A. Hayes, Oct. 29, 1943 (dec. Oct. 1968). B.A. summa cum laude, Stanford U., 1948, M.A., 1950. Instr. Stanford U., Calif., 1950; teaching assoc. Ind. U., Bloomington, 1953-55; instr. Coe Coll, Cedar Rapids, Iowa, 1955-57; instr. English Carnegie-Mellon U., Pitts., 1957-60, asst. prof., 1960-65, assoc. prof., 1965-74, prof., 1974—; cons. Coll. Bd., N.Y.C., 1964—. Author: The Dancer's Step, 1973, The Living and the Dead, 1975, Witness: How All Occasions, 1977, Progress, Dancing, 1986, Circle of the Earth, 1990, Letters At Christmas and Other Poems, 1995; contbr. poems and essays to mags. Recipient Borestone Mountain Poetry award, 1969, Elliott Dunlap Smith prize Carnegie-Mellon U., 1991. Mem. Phi Beta Kappa. Democrat. Office: Carnegie-Mellon Univ Dept English Pittsburgh PA 15213

HAYES, BERNARDINE FRANCES, computer systems analyst; b. Boston, June 29, 1939; d. Robert Emmett and Mary Agnes (Tague) H. BA in Edn., St. Joseph Coll., 1967; MA in Urban Affairs and Pub. Policy, U. Del., 1973, PhD in Pub. Policy, 1978. Elem. tchr. St. Dominick Sch., Balt., 1960-63; tchr. sci., math. and art St. Mary's Sch., Troy, N.Y., 1963-65, Our Lady Queen of Peace Sch., Washington, 1965-68, St. Patrick Sch., Richmond, Va., 1968-69, St. Peter Cathedral Sch., Wilmington, Del., 1969-71; planner health and social svcs. Model Cities Program, Wilmington, 1971-72; dir. rsch. Del. State Dept. Mental Health, Wilmington, 1972-75; dir. planning and evaluation Mental Health, Mental Retardation Svcs., West Chester, Pa., 1976-78; instr. Boston U., 1978; div. dir. Systems Architects, Inc., Randolph, Mass., 1979-81; group mgr. Unisys Corp., Cambridge, Mass., 1981—; cons. in field; pres., founder Hayes Assocs., a communication firm, 1989—; developed Project Helplink, 1990-92; instr. Radcliffe Seminars, Cambridge, 1994—. Contbr. numerous articles to profl. jours. Bd. sec. Model Cities, 1969-70; chairperson bd. State Service Ctr., Wilmington, 1972-75; mem. Human Rels. Commn., Washington, 1965-68; co-chmn. State-wide Coalition for Human Svcs., Del., 1972-74; activist Vietnam protest, Del., 1970-74, Civil Rights Movement, 1965—, numerous polit. campaigns, 1972—; alt. del. Mass. Dem. Conv., 1985; bd. v.p. Women's Action for Nuclear Disarmament, Arlington, Mass., 1982-91, fin. com. chmn., 1983-85, 88-90, treas., 1988-90, chmn. polit. action com., 1983-84, dir. nat. voter registration campaign, 1984.; active Mondale for Pres., 1984, John Kerry for Senator campaign, Mass., 1984, Clinton for Pres., 1992, Studds for Congress, 1992; del. Com. for an Enduring Peace, Soviet Peace Commn., Moscow, 1987; bd. trustees Mass. Assn. for the Blind, 1989—, Children's Justice Ctrs., Tulsa, 1994—; coord. Women's Acad. Group, 1995—. Fellow NSF, 1966. Mem. NAACP, NOW, Women's Inst. Housing and Econ. Devel. (bd. dirs. 1985-88), Boston Mus. Fine Arts. Roman Catholic. Home: 49 Crane Rd Quincy MA 02169-2621

HAYES, BRENDA SUE NELSON, artist; b. Rockford, Ill., May 26, 1941; d. Reuben Hartvick and Mary Jane (Pinkston) Nelson; m. John Michael Hayes, Jan. 26, 1964; 1 child, Amy Anne. BFA in Graphic Design, U. Ill., 1964. Exec. officer JMH Corp., Indpls., 1971—. Exhibited at Art Source, Bethesda, Md., The Corp. Collection, Kansas City, Mo., The Hang Up Gallery, Sarasota, Fla., Susan Musleh-Art By Design, Inc., Indpls., Swan Coach House Gallery, Atlanta, Arnot Art Mus., Elmira, N.Y., Indpls. Mus. Art, Pindar Gallery, Soho, N.Y.; represented in permanent collections at Holy Family Hosp., Des Plaines, Ill., Lilly Endowment, Dow Venture Ctr. Internat. Hdqs., Wishard Hosp., Indpls., Deloitte Touche, Inc., Indpls. Art Ctr., IBM, AT&T, U.S. Sprint, NWS Corp., Chgo., Meth. Hosp., Indpls., Eli Lilly Corp. Offices, Hewlett-Packard, Trammell Crow, Dow Consumer Products, Melvin Simon & Assocs., Dow Elanco Corp. Hdqs., CopyRite Inc., Support Net, NBD Bank Processing Ctr. Lobby, Indpls., Cellular One Regional Offices, Nat. City Plaza, others. Bd. dirs. Contemporary Art Soc. for Indpls. Mus. Art, 1993—, sec., 1992-94; charter mem. Nat. Mus. Women in Arts. Lydia Bates scholar U. Ill., 1961-63, Ill. Found. of Study scholar, 1963-64, resident schoar, 1960-64; recipient Panhellenic award for Study U. Ill., 1963-64, Gallery Exhbn. awards. Mem. Nat. Mus. Women in the Arts (charter), Gamma Alpha Chi (Outstanding Woman in Journalism 1964). Home: 157 E 71st St Indianapolis IN 46220-1011 Studio: 921 E 66th St Indianapolis IN 46220-1137

HAYES, CAROL JEANNE, physical education educator; b. Cambridge, Mass., Apr. 18, 1942; d. Joseph Raymond and Gertrude Marie (Poitras) Boudreau; m. James Anthony Hayes, Oct. 24, 1964 (wid. Mar. 1978); children: James Anthony, Sharon Marie. BSEd, Boston State Coll., 1963, MEd, 1978, postgrad., 1980; postgrad., Boston State Coll./Salem State, 1986—. Cert. CPR and first aid provider. Phys. edn./health instr. Wilmington (Mass.) Pub. Schs., 1963-65, 72—; part-time phys. edn. tchr. Concord (Mass.) Pub. Schs., 1968-69; trainer Spl. Olympics participants, Wilmington, 1983-86; Little League mgr., LExington, 1974-76; bike safety com. Wilmington Police Dept., 1983-85; coord. After Sch. Tournaments, North Intermediate Sch., Wilmington, 1986-91; mem. adv. coun. Woburn St. Sch., 1992—, mem. crisis team, 1993—. Author: (curriculum) Elementary/Adaptive/Kindergarten, 1986. Badge counselor Boy Scouts Am., Lexington, 1978-84; vol./minister of comfort St. Brigid, 1978—, care eucharistic minister, 1993—; mem. Lexington Hist. Soc.; coord. Heart Week Activities for Intermediate Students, 1990—; others. Mem. AAHPERD, NEA, Wilmington Tchrs. Assn. (exec. bd. 1972, bargaining team 1992, greivance com. 1991, pres. 1995—), Mass. Tchrs. Assn., Mass./AHPERD. Roman Catholic. Home: 9 Farmcrest Ave Lexington MA 02173-7112 Office: Wilmington Pub Schs Wilmington MA 01887

HAYES, CAROLINE M., computer scientist; b. Nicols, S.C., Aug. 20, 1966; d. Dehugh Nathaniel Pasiley and Katrina (Hayes) McKay; m. Hondree Nance, Nov. 18, 1988 (div. 1992). BS, S.C. State U., 1988; MS in Computer Sci., Howard U., 1992. Mem. tech. staff AT&T Bell Labs., Columbus, Ohio, 1989-92; assoc. Sears, Fair Oaks, Va., 1994-95; sales assocs. Woodworth & Lothrop, Fair Oaks, 1993-94; tchr. Lake View (S.C.) Schs. Dist., 1994; missionary Union AME, Lake View, S.C., 1994-95, Fairfax, Va., 1994-95. Debutante Criterion Club, Dillon, S.C., 1988; mem. Young Dems., 1987. Mem. NAFE, Alpha Kappa Mu. Methodist. Home: 632 Racetrack Rd Nichols SC 29581

HAYES, CHRISTINE MIRIAM, art educator; b. Pittsfield, Mass., May 7, 1969; d. Charles Lauchlan and Miriam Ann (Flanagan) H. BA in English, Providence (R.I.) Coll., 1991; postgrad., So. Conn. State U., 1996. Asst. to Robert Conway Artistic Estate of Woodengraver Fritz Eichenberg, Narragansett, R.I., 1991—; art tchr. Lisbon Pub. Schs., Conn., 1996, Turn-of-River Mid. Sch., Stamford, Conn., 1996—; intern Mus. of Art R.I. Sch. of Design, Providence, 1991. Exhibited in group shows at Changing Tastes Cafe, Hartford, Conn., 1993, New Britain Mus. of Am. Art, 1993, Perry's Coffee House, 1994, New Britain Pub. Libr., 1995, A Gathering Place, 1996, A Reader's Feast, 199, So No Festival, 1996, Radillac Cafe, 1996. Scholarship So. Conn. State U., 1995-96. Mem. Coll. Art Assn., Nat. Art Edn. Assn., New Britain Mus. of Am. Art, The Vicious Cir. Home: 111 Mitchell St New Britain CT 06053

HAYES, CONSTANCE J., pediatric cardiologist; b. Cortland, N.Y., July 16, 1937; d. John Burns and Anna Marie (McGuire) H.; m. Edward William Lewison, Nov. 8, 1980. RN, BS, Coll. St. Rose, 1959; MD, Loyola U., Chgo., 1965. Diplomate Am. Bd. Pediatrics, Am. Bd. Pediatric Cardiology, Nat. Bd. Med. Examiners. Resident in pediatrics St. Vincent's Hosp., N.Y.C., 1965-68; fellow in pediatric cardiology Columbia U., N.Y.C., 1968-71, assoc. pediatrics coll. p. & s., 1971-72, asst. prof. clin. pediatrics, 1972-80, assoc. clin. prof. pediatrics, 1980—. Contbr. articles to profl. jours. Fellow Am. Acad. Pediatrics, Am. Coll. Cardiology; mem. Am. Heart Assn., N.Y. Heart Assn., Pediatric Cardiology Soc. Greater N.Y. (pres. 1987-88). Office: Columbia Presbyn Med Ctr 3959 Broadway New York NY 10032-1537

HAYES, CONSTANCE MARY, artist, painter, educator; b. Gardiner, Maine, Sept. 17, 1952; d. Philip Edward and Yvette Alice (Charette) H. BA, U. Maine, 1974; BFA, Maine Coll. Art, 1980; MFA, Tyler Sch. Art, 1982. Cert. K-12 tchr. Pub. sch. tchr. Waldoboro and Union Jr. H.S., Maine, 1975-77; asst. dir. admissions Maine Coll. Art, Portland, 1982-84, drawing instr., 1987-92, interim dean, 1992; painter, artist N.Y.C., 1992—; found. program coord. Maine Coll. Art, 1991-92; Monhegan Island artist-in-residence, 1991; mem. Art in Embassies program, Sanaa, Yemen, 1995. Vis. artist/lectr. Bowdoin Coll., Brunswick, Maine, 1989, Alfred (N.Y.) U., 1993, San Francisco State U., 1995, U. Maine, Augusta, 1995. Skowhegan (Maine) Sch. Painting and Sculpture scholar, 1989. Mem. Graphic Artists Guild, Artist Equity, Art Dirs. Club. Democrat. Roman Catholic. Home and Office: 301 E 21st St 13D New York NY 10010

HAYES, DIANA LYNN, theology educator, consultant; b. Buffalo, May 30, 1947; d. Leonard L. and Helen L. (Dodson) H. BA, SUNY, Buffalo, 1969; JD, George Washington Nat. Law Ctr., 1973; PhD, STD, Catholic U. Louvain, Belgium, 1988. Bar: Nebr., Nebr. Supreme Ct. Atty. Dept. Labor, Washington, 1973-75, N.Y. State, Albany, 1978-80; legis. cons. Archdiocese of Washington, 1983-85; asst. prof. theology Georgetown U., Washington, 1988-94, assoc. prof., 1994—; adj. faculty mem. Xavier U. Inst. Black Catholic Studies, New Orleans, 1991—, St. Bernard's Sem., Albany, 1991, 96. Author: Hagar's Daughters: Womanist Ways of Being in the World, 1995, Trouble Don't Last Always: Soul Prayers, 1995, And Still We Rise: An Introduction to Black Liberation Theology, 1996. Bd. dirs. Woodstock Theol. Ctr., Washington, 1993—, Nat. Ctr. Pastoral Leadership, Washington, 1994—. Mem. Catholic Theol. Soc. Am., Am. Acad. Religion, Coll. Theology Soc., Soc. for Study of Black Religion. Office: Georgetown U Dept Theology Box 571135 Washington DC 20057-1135

HAYES, GLADYS LUCILLE ALLEN, state community care official, poet, writer; b. Havelock, Nebr., Nov. 29, 1913; d. Harry Arthur and Louise (Vogel) Allen; m. James Franklin Hayes, Oct. 5, 1943; children: J. Allen, Warren Andrew. Secretarial diploma, Lincoln (Nebr.) Sch. Commerce, 1932; student, Santa Clara U., 1950-60; BS in Media Studies, Sacred Heart U., Fairfield, Conn., 1989, exec. MBA, 1991. Cert. profl. religion tchr. Archdiocese of San Francisco. Exec. tech. sec. McCormick-Selph divsn. Teledyne Corp., Hollister, Calif., 1960-65; adminstrv. asst. to v.p. Greater Bridgeport Regional Narcotics Program, Inc., Bridgeport, Conn., 1979-81; adminstrv. asst. to scientists and engrs. CBS Lab. div. CBS Inc., Stamford, Conn., 1968-76; sec. to Nobel laureate and physicist Dennis Gabor, Dsc, FRS U. London, U.S., 1971-79; corp. sec. Automated Power Systems, Inc., Bridgeport, 1976-90; owner, mgr. GA Secretarial Svc., Stratford, Conn., 1980-91; med. sec. Conn. Community Care, Inc., Stratford, Conn., 1986-91; sec., environ. resources U.S. Army Corps Engrs., Elmendorf AFB, Anchorage, Alaska, 1992-93; substitute tchr. Anchorage Sch. Dist., 1992-93, Juneau (Alaska) Sch. Dist., 1994-95; cmty. svc. rep. Alaska Dept. Corrections, Juneau, 1994-95; radio broadcaster Fairfield U., 1985-91; owner, mgr. G A Secretarial Svc., 1985-96. Former residential fund raising chmn. ARC, Gilroy, Calif.; former motion picture chmn. St. Mary's Sch., Gilroy, also past pres. Mothers' Guild, former mem. Edn. Commn.; former fundraiser March of Dimes; mem. various choirs and choral groups, Calif., Conn., Alaska; mem. Nat. Coun. on Aging; tchr. religion Archdiocese of San Francisco, Diocese of Lincoln, 1933-67, Archdiocese of Bridgeport, 1968-72. Recipient Excellence in Aging award Conn. Community Care, Inc., 1989, prize for photograph City of Bridgeport, 1987, Pope Pius X Medal of Honor, 1959. Mem. Nat. Honor Soc. Republican. Roman Catholic.

HAYES, JANET GRAY, retired business manager, former mayor; b. Rushville, Ind., July 12, 1926; d. John Paul and Lucile (Gray) Frazee; A.B.. Ind. U., 1948; M.A. magna cum laude, U. Chgo., 1950; m. Kenneth Hayes, Mar. 20, 1950; children: Lindy, John, Katherine, Megan. Psychiat. caseworker Jewish Family Service Agy., Chgo., 1950-52; vol. Denver Crippled Children's Service, 1954-55; vol. Adult and Child Guidance Clinic, San Jose, 1958-59; mem. San Jose (Calif.) City Council, 1971-75, vice-mayor, 1973-75, mayor, 1975-82; co-chmn. com. urban econs. U.S. Conf. Mayors, 1976-78, co-chmn. task force on aging, mem. sci. and tech. task force, 1976-80, bd. trustees, 1977-82; bd. dirs. League Calif. Cities, 1976-82, mem. property tax reform task force, 1976-82; chmn. State of Calif. Urban Devel. Adv. Com., 1976-77; mem. Calif. Commn. Fair Jud. Practices, 1976-82, client-community relations dir. Q. Tech., Santa Clara, Calif., 1983-85, bus. mgr. Kenneth Hayes MD, Inc., 1985-88; pres. bd. trustees San Jose Mus. Art, 1987-89; founder, adv. bd. Calif. Bus. Bank, 1982-85. Mem. Dem. nat. campaign com., 1976; mem. Calif. Dem. Commn. Nat. Platform and Policy, 1976; del. Dem. Nat. Conv., 1980; bd. dirs. South San Francisco Bay Dischargers Authority; chmn. Santa Clara County Sanitation Dist.; mem. San Jose/Santa Clara Treatment Plant Adv. Bd.; chmn. Santa Clara Valley Employment and Tng. Bd. (CETA); past mem. EPA Aircraft/Airport Noise Task Group; bd. dirs. Calif. Center Rsch. and Edn. in Govt., Alexian Bros. Hosp., 1983-92; bd. dirs., chmn. adv. council Public Tech. Inc.; mem. bd. League to Save Lake Tahoe, 1984—. AAUW Edn. Found. grantee. Mem. Assn. Bay Area Govts. (exec. com. 1971-74, regional housing subcom. 1973-74, regional housing subcom. 1973-74), LWV (pres. San Francisco Bay Area chpt. 1968-70, pres. local 1966-67), Mortar Bd., Phi Beta Kappa, Kappa Alpha Theta.

HAYES, JOYCE MERRIWEATHER, secondary education educator; b. Bay City, Tex., Aug. 29, 1943; d. Calvin and Alonia (Harris) Merriweather. BS, Wiley Coll., Tex., 1967; postgrad., U. N.Y., Stony Brook, 1968; MS in Guidence Counseling, Ea. Mich. U., 1974; postgrad., Mercy Coll., 1991-92, Ea. Mich. U., 1991-92; MEd, U. Detroit, 1992. English tchr. Terrance Manor Mid. Sch., Augusta, Ga., 1968-69, Longfellow Jr. H.S., Flint, Mich., 1969-81; English tchr. No. H.S., Flint, 1981—, chmn. English dept., 1992—; English and speech tchr. Jordan Coll., Flint, 1989-91; adult edn. tchr. Mott Adult H.S., Flint, 1978-80; presenter workshops in field. Composer 3 gospel songs. Vol. Second Ward City Coun., Flint, 1989, Cmty. Coun., Flint, 1992-93, Cmty. Wide Assn. Coun., Flint, 1993; intercessory prayer warrior, asst. head greeter, kitchen com. worker Family Worship Ctr. Ch., Flint, 1993—. Mem. NEA, Nat. Coun. Tchrs. English (chair workshops 1992-93, mem. nominating com. 1994), Mich. Edn. Assn., United Tchrs. of Flint (in-svc. com., Flares-English tchrs.), Phi Delta Kappa (past pres.). Home: 621 Thomson St Flint MI 48503-1942

HAYES, JUDITH, psychotherapist, educator; b. Lumberton, N.C., June 28, 1950; d. Eugene Lennon and Ada Margaret (Regan) Hayes; m. Jonathan Lafayette II Cutrell (div. Jan. 1979); 1 child, Jonathan L. Cutrell III; m. William Evans Hannon. BA, Augusta Coll., 1973; MA summa cum laude, U. N.C., Charlotte, 1996. Cert. tchr. midl sch. exceptional children. Tchr. Horry County (S.C.) Schs., 1973-77, Alexander County Schs., Taylorsville, N.C., 1978-83, Iredell County Schs., Statesville, N.C., 1983-94; with Charter Pines Behavioral Health, Charlotte, N.C., 1996—. Bd. dirs. Statesville Dogwood Festival, 1981-82; ch. organist Fair Bluff (N.C.) Bapt., 1974-78. Fellow Phi Kappa Phi; mem. ACA (rep. N.C. Assn. Educators 1993-94), Mu Tau Beta chpt. Chi Sigma Iota.

HAYES, LAURA JOANNA, psychologist; b. Winnebeau, N.C., Mar. 26, 1943; d. Victor Wilson and Pansy Lorraine (Springsteen) Hayes; m. Jerry Allen Gladson, June 20, 1965 (div. Mar. 1992); children: Joanna Kaye, Paula Rae. BA, So. Coll., 1965; MEd, U. Tenn., Chattanooga, 1977; EdD, Vanderbilt U., 1985. Lic. psychologist, Ga. Psychol. intern Lakeshore Mental Health Inst., Knoxville, Tenn., 1985-86; counselor, psychologist Tara Heights Enterprises, Atlanta, 1986—; psychologist, owner Assoc. Psychol. Svcs., Inc., Ringgold, Ga., 1990—. Mem. APA, Christian Assn. for Psychol. Studies, Ga. Psychol. Assn. Democrat. Home: 327 Homestead Cir Kennesaw GA 30144-1335 Office: Assoc Psychol Svcs Box 700 5476 Battlefield Pkwy Ringgold GA 30736

HAYES, MARY ESHBAUGH, newspaper editor; b. Rochester, N.Y., Sept. 27, 1928; d. William Paul and Eleanor Maude (Seivert) Eshbaugh; B.A. in English and Journalism, Syracuse (N.Y.) U., 1950; m. James Leon Hayes, Apr. 18, 1953; children—Pauli, Eli, Lauri Le June, Clayton, Merri Jess Bates. With Livingston County Republican, Geneseo, N.Y., summers, 1947-50, mng. editor, 1949-50; reporter Aurora (Colo.) Advocate, 1950-52; reporter-photographer Aspen (Colo.) Times, 1952-53, columnist, 1956—, reporter, 1972-77, assoc. editor, 1977-89, editor in chief, 1989-92, contbg. editor, 1992—; contbg. editor Destinations Mag., 1994—. tchr. Colo. Mountain Coll., 1979. Mem. Nat. Fedn. Press Women (1st prizes in writing and editing 1976-80), Colo. Press Women's Assn. (writing award 1974, 75, 78-85, sweepstakes award for writing 1977, 78, 84, 85, 91, 92, 93, also 2d place award 1976, 79, 82, 83, 94, 95, Woman of Achievement 1986). Mem. Aspen Community Ch. Photographer, editor: Aspen Potpourri, 1968, rev. edit., 1990. Home: PO Box 497 Aspen CO 81612-0497 Office: Box E Aspen CO 81612

HAYES, MARY JOANNE, special education educator; b. Bloomington, Ind., Feb. 3, 1944; d. John and Marie (Van Buskirk) Reeves; m. Jack Lee Hayes, June 25, 1983. BA, Olivet U., Kankakee, Ill., 1968; MA, Ind. U., 1972; postgrad., Ind. U., South Bend, 1987, Ind. State U., 1989. Lic. tchr., Ind. Tchr. 3rd grade Saulk View Sch., Steger, Ind., 1968-69; tchr. 1st grade Break-O-Day Sch., New Whiteland, Ind., 1969-83; tchr. emotionally handicapped David Turnham Edn. Ctr., Dale, Ind., 1987—. Mem. Coun. Exceptional Children, Coun. Behavorial Disorders, Ind. Reading Coun. Home: PO Box 191 Dale IN 47523-0191 Office: David Turnham Ednl Ctr Dale IN 47523

HAYES, MARY PHYLLIS, savings and loan association executive; b. New Castle, Ind., Apr. 30, 1921; d. Clarence Edward and Edna Gertrude (Burgess) Scott; m. John Clifford Hayes, Jan. 1, 1942 (div. Oct. 1952); 1 child, R. Scott. Student, Ball State U., 1957-64, Ind. U. East, Richmond, 1963; diploma, Inst. Fin. Edn., 1956, 72, 76. Teller Henry County Savs. and Loan, New Castle, 1939-41, loan officer, teller, 1950-62, asst. sec., treas., 1962-69, sec., treas., 1969-73, corp. sec., 1973-84; v.p., sec. Ameriana Savs. Bank (formerly Henry County Savs. and Loan), New Castle, 1984-91; exec. sec. Am. Nat. Bank, Nashville, 1943-44; corp. sec. Ameriana Fin. Svcs., 1984-91. Treas. Henry County Chpt. Am. Heart Assn., New Castle, 1965-67, 76-87, vol. Indpls. chpt. 1980—; membership sec. Henry County Hist. Soc., New Castle, 1975-90; sec. Henry County chpt. ARC, New Castle, 1976-91; elected mem. Found. Inst. Fin. Edn., 1991—; mem. Internat. Platform Assn., 1974—, Woman's Club 1992—; vol. Ind. Basketball Hall of Fame, 1993—. Mem. Inst. Fin. Edn. (sec.-treas. East Ctrl. Ind. chpt. 1973-91), Ind. League Savs. Insts. (25 Yrs. award 1975, 40 Yrs. Cert. award 1988), Internat. Platform Assn., Henry County Hist. Soc. (mem. sec.), Altrusa (past officer, bd. dirs. New Castle chpt.), PEO (past chaplain, sec., past pres. 1994-95), Woman's Club, New Castle Henry County C. of C., Guyer Opera House Guild, Art Ctr. of Henry County, Psi Iota Xi (past sec.-treas.). Mem. Christian Ch.

HAYES, MARYLEE, editor, writer, nurse; b. Allegan, Mich., Nov. 14, 1949; d. Gay F. and Anna Marie (Swanty) H. Cert., Famous Writer's Sch., 1971; BA cum laude in English, U. Alaska, 1988; RN, Mercy Ctrl. Sch. of Nursing, Grand Rapids, Mich., 1970. RN, Colo., Wis., Wash., Mich., Alaska. Bedside nurse Anchorage, 1970—; with Alaska Native Med. Assn., Anchorage. Author: (book) My Life is a Rainbow, 1977; editor: (jour.) Alaska Women Speak, 1992—, Women's Feminist Jour., 1992—; contbr. articles to jours. and mags. Active Take Back the Night, Anchorage, 1995—; camp host Alaska State Park Svcs., Eagle River, 1993. Lt. USAF, 1975-77. Mem. NOW, Sierra Club, Greenpeace, Easter Seal Soc. Home: HC 85 Box 9337 Eagle River AK 99577 Office: Alaska Women Speak PO Box 92842 Anchorage AK 99509

HAYES, NANCY EVEYLIN, anthropologist, geographer, researcher; b. N.Y.C., Dec. 7, 1941; d. Anatoli Nikolai Peres and Anna Katrina Rodrigues. BSED, U. Ga., 1970, postgrad., 1973. Elem. tchr. Kingsland (Ga.) Elem. Sch.; cash audit clk. Nat. Shirt Shops, N.Y.C.; paymaster St. Gillians/A.J. Bari, N.Y.C.; asst. bookkeepr Panorama Press, N.Y.C.; expense acct. Finlay, N.Y.C.; owner, mgr. S.D. Problem Shoppe, N.Y.C., 1990-96; owner Second Dollar Group subs. S.D. Problem Shoppe, Dead Weight Exch.; sec. Internat. Students Orgn. U. Ga., Athens, 1968. Mem. NOW, N.Y. Acad. Scis., N.Y. State Archael. Assn., Nat. Writers Union, Internat. Healers, Gen. Inst. Semantics, W.M.S.A., Spiritual Frontiers Fellowship. Democrat. Jewish. Home: 100 Cooper St New York NY 10034

HAYES, PATRICIA ANN, university president; b. Binghamton, N.Y., Jan. 14, 1944; d. Robert L. and Gertrude (Congdon) H. BA in English, Coll. of St. Rose, 1968; PhD in Philosophy, Georgetown U., 1974. Tchr. Cardinal McCloskey High Sch., Albany, N.Y., 1966-68; teaching asst. Georgetown U., Washington, 1968-71; instr. philosophy Coll. of St. Rose, Albany, 1973-75, instr. bus., spring 1981, adminstrv. intern to acad. v.p., 1973-74, dir. admissions, 1974-78, dir. adminstrn. and planning, 1978-81, v.p. adminstrn. and fin., treas., 1981-84; pres. St. Edward's U., Austin, Tex., 1984—; bd. dirs. Tex. Bus./Edn. Coalition. Bd.dirs. Sta. KLRU Pub. TV, United Way, Seton Med. Ctr. Mem. Ind. Colls. and Univs. Tex., So. Assn. Colls. and Schs. (commn. on colls.), Tex. Assn. Bus. and C. of C. (bd. dirs.). Roman Catholic. Office: St Edwards U Office of the President 3001 S Congress Ave Austin TX 78704-6489

HAYES, PRISCILLA ELLEN, environmental educator; b. Abington, Pa., Oct. 13, 1953; 2. Stuart Fleming and Louise Day (Baldwin) H.; m. Peter Douglas Patterson, June 20, 1986; children: Daniel Edwin Hayes-Patterson, Douglas Lester Hayes-Patterson. AB, Princeton U., 1975; JD, Duke U., 1979. Bar: N.J. Staff atty. N.J. Pub. Interest Rsch. Group, Newark, Camden, Trenton, 1979-80; dep. atty. gen. civil rights State of N.J., Newark, 1980-84; dep. atty. gen. environ. protection State of N.J., Trenton, 1984-87; coord. clean cmtys. edn. program Washington Twp., Robbinsville, N.J., 1986—. Author: Deodorant Blues, 1994 (2d prize); contbr. articles, revs. to profl. publs. Environ. commr. Washington Twp., Robbinsville, 1990-93, recycling coord., 1991—. Recipient Clean and Proud award N.J. Dept. Environ. Protection, 1994, Commendation for Recycling Edn. award Mercer County Improvement Auth., 1994; grantee N.J. Dept. Environ. Protection, 1993-95. Mem. Lawrenceville Writers Group, Master Gardeners of Mercer County (chair publicity 1993—, co-chair newsletter, cert.). Office: Moon Moth Prodns 3 Trellis Way Robbinsville NJ 08691-1617

HAYES, SHARON LARUE (SHARI HAYES), clinical medical assistant, travel agent; b. Eugene, Oreg., Nov. 12, 1943; d. Lawrence Earl and Marjorie Ann (Smith) Crook; m. Lorin Donald Lewis (div. 1977); children: Kevin Earl Lewis, Randall Bruce Lewis, Gregory Steven Lewis; 1 foster child, Deborah Jo Bull-Plume; m. Richard David Hayes, Mar. 17, 1984; 1 child, David Sean Gregory; stepchildren: Heidi O'Malley, Heather Angela. Student, U. Oreg., 1962-63, Chemeketa C.C., Salem, Oreg., 1972, Lane C. C., Eugene, Oreg., 1981, 83. Cert. med. asst.-clin., 1973; ltd. radiology permit holder, Oreg., 1982. Med. asst., office mgr. Daniel DiIaconi, MD, Surgeon, Carl H. Matthey, MD, family practice, 1970-79, Daniel Usdin, MD, Cardiologist, Jacksonville, Fla., 1979-80; med. asst., ltd. x-ray permit holder Clifford Bre Miller, MD, family practice, Eugene, Oreg., 1980-85; med. asst., limited x-ray tech. Terry Copperman, MD, family practice, Eugene, Oreg., 1981-95; med. asst., clinical office mgr., transcriptionist R. Garr Cutler, MD, plastic/reconstructive and hand surgeon, Eugene, Oreg., 1985-95; adminstrv. asst., med. asst. Lewis Thompson, MD, plastic/reconstructive and hand surgeon, Tulsa, Okla., 1995—; travel agent Uniglobe Magic Carpet, 1989—; crafter jewelry Shari's Original Designs, Eugene, 1990-93. Appeared in Eugene Opera, 1983-85, Main Stage Theater, Eugene, 1982. Host U. Oreg. fgn. student program, 1982-95; bd. dirs. Oreg. Repertory Theatre, Eugene, 1984-85, Plan Loving Adoptions Now Internat. Adoption Agy., McMinnville, Oreg., 1994-95; foster parent to 19 foster children, 1968-72; spkr., counselor foster parent support groups, Lane County, Oreg., 1967-70; dir. children's choir Liberty Gardens Bible Ch., Salem, Oreg., 1970-72, tchr. Sunday sch., 1960-95; dir. Jet Cadets children's group, Salem, 1969-72; mem. PTA, 1970—. Named Med. Asst. Yr. Marion and Polk Chpt. of Medical Assistants, 1977, Lane County, 1990, State of Oreg., 1991. Mem. Assn. Plastic Surgery Assts., Am. Assn. Med. Assts. (mem. edn. com., house of dels. State of Oreg. 1971-72, 89, v.p. Lane chpt. med. assts. 1988, pres. 1989), Doll Dreamers UFDC (sec. 1993-94). Home: 3939 So 125 E Ave Tulsa OK 74146

HAYLETT, MARGARET WENDY, television director, engineer; b. Ravenna, Ohio, Jan. 11, 1953; d. James Edward and Edith Marie (Campbell) H. Tech. cert., WIXY Sch. Broadcasting, Cleve., 1973; student, Empire State Coll., 1988—. FCC 1st class/gen. radio telephone lic. Engr. Sta. WJKW-TV, Cleve., 1973-81; engr. Sta. WOKR-TV, Rochester, N.Y., 1981-87, dir., 1987—. Home: 26 Harvest Rd Fairport NY 14450-2849

HAYLING, MARVA DELORES THOMAS, primary school educator; b. Madison, Fla., Nov. 10, 1951; d. Samuel Nokey and Ethel Rosalee (Mason) Thomas; m. Charles Cleaver Hayling Jr.; children: Carney, Jason, Roderick, Robert, Saná, Marla. Attended, Fla. Jr. Coll., Jacksonville, 1970-71; BS in Early Childhood and Elem. Edn., Edwards Waters Coll., Jacksonville, 1976; postgrad, Fla. A&M U., 1976; attended, Indian River C.C., Fort Pierce, Fla., 1995. Cert. devel. edn. ESOL, early childhood, elem. edn., ESOL. Tchr. 3d grade Chester A. Moore, 1977-78; tchr. 2d and 3d grade Fort Pierce Elem., 1978-86; tchr. 3d grade Windmill Point, 1986-88, Frances K. Sweet, 1988-91; tchr. 3d grade Manatee Elem., 1991-94, reading specialist, 1994—; instr. gen. edn., allied health Indian River C.C., 1994. Mem. AAUW, NAACP (St. Lucie branch), Classroom Tchrs. Assn., Jack and Jill of Am., Inc., Zeta Phi Beta (sec.). Home: 1815 N 17th St Fort Pierce FL 34950 Office: Manatee Elem 1450 SW Heatherwood Blvd Port Saint Lucie FL 34986

HAYLOR, JANE T., lawyer; b. Cin., Dec. 30, 1946. BS, Case Western Res. U., 1968, JD, 1986. Bar: Ohio 1986. Ptnr. Baker & Hostetler, Cleve. Mem. Case Western Res. U. Law Rev., 1984-85, articles editor, 1985-86. Mem. ABA, Ohio State Bar Assn. Office: Baker & Hostetler 3200 Nat City Ctr 1900 E 9th St Cleveland OH 44119-3485*

HAYMAN, CAROL ANNE, anthropology educator, photographer; b. Ft. Walton Beach, Fla., Feb. 18, 1953; d. William Paul and Thomasina Maude (Garbutt) Hayman; m. Robert Rayford White; 1 child, Brandon Paul White. BFA, U. Tex., 1975, BA, 1977, MA, 1989. Peace Corps vol., instr. Jamaica Sch. Art, Kingston, 1978-80; instr. Austin (Tex.) C.C., 1990—; instr. Tex. Luth. U., 1994—. Recipient Arts Week Vol. award City of Austin, 1994. Home: 1001 Eason St Austin TX 78703 Office: Austin CC 1212 Rio Grande Austin TX 78701

HAYMAN, LINDA C., lawyer; b. Morgantown, W.Va., 1947. BS, Ohio State U., 1969; MA, U. Colo., 1973; JD, Capital U., 1979. Bar: Ohio 1979, N.Y. 1982. Ptnr. Skadden, Arps, Slate, Meagher & Flom, N.Y.C. Office: 919 3rd Ave New York NY 10022*

HAYMON, SANDRA WAUTHENA, psychologist; b. Dothan, Ala., Oct. 3, 1949; d. Christopher Columbus Haymon and Mildred (Reeder) Williamson; m. Kedrick Earl Durden, Feb. 20, 1982 (div. Apr. 1989). BS magna cum laude, Troy State U., 1977, MS, 1978; PhD in Counseling Psychology and Human Syss., Fla. State U., 1992. Asst. mgr. Avco Fin. Svcs., Dothan, 1975-76; salesperson Gunter Dunn Furniture, Ozark, Ala., 1976-78; mktg. mgr. Bishop Uniform and Linen Co., Dothan, 1978-79; tng. dept. mgr. Michelin Tire Corp., Dothan, 1979-84; psychology intern Fed. Bur. Prisons, 1991-92; psychology resident Apalachee Ctr. Mental Health, Tallahassee, 1993-94; owner, pres. Hayman Consulting and Rsch., Tallahassee, 1994—; owner Magnolia Prodns., Tallahassee, 1996—; instr. Fla. State U., Tallahassee, 1988, 91. Mem. ednl. com. So. Ala. Symphony Guild, Dothan, 1984-88; vol. Young Reps. Party, Dothan, 1984-88, vol. work with young women, Dothan, 1984-88. Named to Outstanding Young Women of Am., 1979. Mem. Am. Assn. Counseling and Devel., Am. Mental Health Counselors Assn., ASTD, Am. Psychol. Assn., Zonta Internat., Tallahassee C. of C. (women's forum), Gamma Beta Phi. Home and Office: 3038 O'Brien Dr Tallahassee FL 32380-2751

HAYNE, HARRIET ANN, state legislator, rancher; b. Puget Island, Washington, Sept. 11, 1922; d. Albert Greger and Angeline Marie (Benjaminsen) Danielsen; m. Jack McVicar Hayne, Apr. 3, 1946; children: Mary Joan, John David, Alice Sue, Nancy Ann. Student, Healds Bus. Coll., San Francisco, 1941-42, Wash. State U., 1946-47. Rep. Mont. Legis. Assembly, 1979-80, 84—. Precinct, then state committeewoman, vice-chmn., active various campaigns Mont. Reps., Pondera County, 1963. Served as staff sgt. USMC, 1943-45. Mem. Am. Nat. Cattlewomen, Nat. Order Women Legislators, Am. Farm Bur., Am. Legion Aux., Am. Legion, Women Marines Assn., Nat. Fedn. Rep. Women. Lutheran.

HAYNER, JEANNETTE CLARE, state legislator; b. Jan. 22, 1919; m. Herman H. Hayner, 1942; children: Stephen A., James K., Judith A. BA, U. Oreg., 1940, JD, 1942, PhD (hon), Whitman Coll., 1992. Atty. Bonneville Power Co., Portland, Oreg., 1943-47; mem. Wash. Ho. of Reps., 1972-76, Wash. Senate from Dist. 16, 1977-92, minority leader, 1979-80, 83-86, majority leader, 1981-82, 87-92; dist. chmn. White House Conf. on Children and Youth, 1970; dir. Standard Ins. Co. Portland, 1974-90. Mem. Walla Walla Dist. 140 Sch. Bd., 1956-63, chmn. bd., 1959-61; mem. adv. bd. Walla Walla Youth and Family Svc. Assn., 1968-72; active YWCA, 1968-72; chmn. Walla Walla County Mental Health Bd., 1970-72; former mem. Wash. Coun. on Crime and Delinquency, Nuclear Energy Coun., Bonneville Power Regional Adv. Coun., State Wash. Organized Crime Intelligence Adv. Bd.; mem. Coun. State Govts. Governing Bd.; former asst. whip Republican Caucus. Mem. Wash. State Centennial Commn.; bd. dir. Washington Inst. for Policy Studies, 1992—; bd. dir. chmn. bd. TV Washington. Recipient Merit award Walla Walla C. of C., Pres's. award Pacific Luth. Univ., 1982, Pioneer award U. Oreg., 1988, Lifetime Achievement award Wash. State Ind. Colls., 1991, Washington Inst. Columbia, 1991; named Legislator of Yr. Nat. Rep. Legislators' Assn., 1986, Chairman's award, 1989, Wash. Young Rep. Citizen of Yr., 1987, Legislator of Yr. Nat. Rep. Legislators Assn., 1989. Mem. Oreg. Bar Assn., Delta Kappa Gamma (hon.), Kappa Kappa Gamma. Lutheran. Home: PO Box 454 Walla Walla WA 99362

HAYNES, BARBARA JUDITH, language educator; b. Trenton, N.J., Apr. 6, 1942; d. Harry G. and Doris M. (Leigh) Horne; m. Joseph A. Haynes, Dec. 11, 1965; children: Joseph III, Jennifer, Charles R. III. Student, Douglass Coll., 1960-62; diploma propeudétique, U. Paris, 1965; MAT, Fairleigh Dickinson U., 1979. Cert French, ESL, elem. tchr., supervision, N.J. ESL tchr. Magnet Ctr., Orange, N.J., 1979-86, River Edge (N.J.) Bd. Edn., 1986—; ESL/bilingual stds. com. Nat. Bd. for Profl. Teaching Stds., 1994—; presenter in field. Author: Classroom Teacher's E.S.L. Survival Kit for Begining Students, 1996; co-author: Classroom Teacher's E.S.L. Survival Kit #1, 1994, Classroom Teacher's E.S.L. Survival Kit #2, 1995. Pres. Bergan County ESL/Bilingual Tchrs., Paramus, N.J., 1990-93. N.J. Govs. Tchr. grant, 1989. Mem. TESOL (elem. spl. interest group sec. 1994-96, noms. com. 1996, Newbury House award for excellence in tchg. 1994), N.J. TESOL-BE (bd. dirs., chair elem. spl. interest group rep. 1994-96, ESL Tchr. of Yr. 1993). Home: 18 Oakwood Rd Allendale NJ 07401-2117 Office: River Edge Bd Edn 410 Bogert Rd River Edge NJ 07661-1813

HAYNES, CAROLINE HOPPER, preschool administrator; b. Cheyenne, Wyo., May 28, 1959; d. George William and Sally (Hunter) Hopper; m. Mark F. Haynes, Aug. 24, 1985. BA in Econs. and Polit. Sci. cum laude, U. of South, 1981; MBA in Internat. Bus., George Washington U., 1987. Legis. aide to Senator Alan K. Simpson, U.S. Senate, Washington, 1982-83, legis. asst., 1983-87; legis. mgr. legis. affairs U.S. Treasury Dept., Washington, 1987-88, sr. legis. mgr., 1988-89, dep. asst. sec. for legis. affairs, 1989-91, prin. dep. asst. sec. for legis. affairs, 1991-92; v.p. Arlington Unitarian Coop. Pre-sch., Arlington, 1993-94, pres., 1994—. Office: Arlington Unitarian Coop Pre-sch Arlington VA 22203

HAYNES, CHERYL ETTORA, healthcare industry marketing representative; b. Washington, Oct. 13, 1948; d. Joseph Harvey Jr. and Rosalie Elizabeth (Brown) F.; m. Leon Haynes Jr., Feb. 15, 1988 (dec. Feb. 1989); 1 child, Aisha Nia Ruffin-Haynes. BS, Wayland Bapt., 1991; MA, Webster U., 1993. Clk. typist Dept. Def., Battle Creek, Mich., 1971-76, USDA, Howell, Mich., 1976-78; acctg. tech. dept. mgmt. and budget State of Mich., Lansing, 1978-80; enlisted U.S. Army, 1980; served as med. lab. tech. Walter Reed Army Med. Ctr., Washington, 1981-84; student adv. lab. Acad. Health Scis., St. Sam Houston, Tex., 1984-85; med. lab. non-commd. officer dept. pathology Brooke Army Med. Ctr., Ft. Sam Houston, 1985-87, 89-91; med. lab. non-commd. officer 121st Evacuation Hosp., Seoul, Republic of Korea, 1987-88, 41st Combat Support Hosp., Ft. Sam Houston, 1988-89; mgr. Supply Ctr. Logistics div., Ft. Sam Houston, 1991-94; faculty Wayland Bapt. U., 1994—; mktg. rep. Consolidated Care Crew Home Health Agy., Inc., San Antonio, 1995—. Mem. Nat. Coun. Negro Women, Washington, 1966-70, Bapt. Tng. Union, Washington, 1975-70. Mem. Am. Coll. Healthcare Execs., Nat. Assn. Health Svc. Execs. Home: 6868 Columbia Rdg Converse TX 78109-3419 Office: North Star Healthcare Mgmt Ste 200 7550 IH 10W San Antonio TX 78229

HAYNES, DEBORAH GENE, physician; b. York, Neb., Feb. 18, 1954; d. Gene Eldridge and Margaret Lucille (Manchester) Haynes; m. Russell Larry Beamer, Mar. 3, 1979; children: Staci E. Beamer, Lindsay M. Beamer, Stephanie L. Beamer. BA in Biology cum laude, Wichita State U., 1976; MD, U. Kans., Wichita, 1979. Diplomate Am. Bd. Family Practice; cert. Added Qualifications-Geriatrics. Resident St. Joseph Hosp., Wichita, 1979-82; instr. dept. family and community medicine St. Joseph Family Practice Residency, U. Kans., Wichita, 1982-84, asst. prof. dept. family and community medicine, 1984-85; pvt. family practice Northeast Family Physicians, Wichita, 1985—; clin. asst. prof. U. Kans. Sch. Medicine, Witchita, 1985—; bd. govs. endowment assn. Wichita State U., 1995—; bd. dirs. Via Christi Regional Med. Ctr., Physicans Med. Assocs., chmn. Trustee Wichita Collegiate Sch., 1993—. Recipient P.G. Czarlinsky award for Disting. Clin. Svc., U. Kans., 1979, Wichita State U. Gore scholarship, 1992. Fellow Am. Acad. Family Physicians (del. 1991—, commn. on edn. 1991-96, task force on procedures, Mead Johnson award 1990-91, chair COD credential com. 1994), Kans. Acad. Family Physicians (pres. elect 1988-89, pres. 1989-90), Kans. Med. Soc., Med. Soc. Sedgwick County (del. 1990-91, chair profl. investigation com. 1993-95), Alpha Omega Alpha. Presbyterian. Home: 1015 N Linden Cir Wichita KS 67206-4075 Office: 8100 E 22nd St N Bldg 2200 Wichita KS 67226-2301

HAYNES, JEAN REED, lawyer; b. Miami, Fla., Apr. 6, 1949; d. Oswald Birnam and Arleen (Wiedman) Dow. AB with honors, Pembroke Coll., 1971; MA, Brown U., 1971; JD, U. Chgo., 1981. Bar: Ill. 1981, U.S. Ct. Appeals (7th cir.) 1982, U.S. Dist. Ct. (no. dist.) Ill. 1983, U.S. Dist. Ct. (cen. dist.) Ill., 1988, N.Y. 1991, U.S. Dist. Ct. (so. dist.) N.Y. 1991, U.S. Dist. Ct. (no. and ea. dists.) N.Y. 1992, U.S. Ct. Appeals (10th cir.) 1993, U.S. Ct. Appeals (11th cir.) 1995. Tchr. grades 1-4 Abbie Tuller Sch., Providence, 1971-72; tchr./facilitator St. Mary's Acad., Riverside, R.I., 1972-74; tchr./head lower sch. St. Francis Sch., Goshen, Ky., 1974-78; law clk. U.S. Ct. Appeals (7th cir.), Chgo., 1981-83; assoc. Kirkland & Ellis, Chgo., 1983-87, ptnr., 1987—. Governing mem. Art Inst. Chgo., 1982-90, mem. aux. bd., 1986-90, membership com. aux. bd., 1987-90, v.p. for devel., 1988-90; vis. com. U. Chgo. Law Sch., 1990-92. Mem. ABA (com. on affordable justice litigation sect. 1988—), Ill. Bar Assn. (life), Assn. Bar City N.Y., Internat. Bar Assn., Am. Judicature Soc. (life, chmn., membership com. 1991—, v.p. 1994—, mem. exec. com. 1992—, bd. dirs. 1991—), Three Lincoln Ctr. Condominium Assn. (pres. 1995—), Law Club Chgo., Mid-Am. Club. Office: Kirkland & Ellis Citicorp Ctr 153 E 53rd St New York NY 10022-4602

HAYNES, KAREN SUE, university president, social work educator; b. Jersey City, July 6, 1946; d. Edward J. and Adelaide M. (Hineson) Czarnecki; m. James S. Mickelson; children: Kingsley Eliot, Kimberly Elizabeth, David. AB, Goucher Coll., 1968; MSW, McGill U., 1970; PhD, U. Tex., 1977. Cons. Inst. Nat. Planning, Cairo, 1977-78; asst. prof. Ind. U., Indpls., 1978-81, assoc. prof., 1981-85; prof. social work U. Houston, 1985-95, dean, 1985-95, pres., 1996—; pres. Ind. Coalition Human Services, Indpls., 1984-85. Author: Sage Publications, 1984; Longman, 1986, 91, 93, 96, Springer, 1989, also articles. Mem. Nat. Assn. Social Workers, Council Social Work Edn., Internat. Assn. Schs. Social Work, Nat. Aliance Info. and Referral (pres. 1983-87), Leadership Houston, 1986, Leadership Tex., 1990, Leadership Am., 1996. Avocation: poetry. Office: U Houston-Victoria 2506 Red River Victoria TX 77901

HAYNES, MARCIA MARGARET, insurance agent; b. Bay City, Mich., June 28, 1931; d. Frederick O. and Margaret M. (Oakes) Rouse; m. N. Fred Haynes, July 20, 1957;children: Carol M. Krashen, David F. Haynes, Julie A. Haynes. BA, Denison U., Granville, Ohio, 1953. With advt.-sales dept. Birmingham (Mich.) Eccentric, 1953-55; tchr. Port Huron (Mich.) Area Schs., 1955-58; student tchr. coord. Mich. State U., Port Huron, Mich., 1967-70; insurance agent Northwestern Mut. Life Ins. Co., Port Huron, Mich., 1981—. Leader, Girl Scout U.S., Port Huron, 1956-57; treas. and bus. mgr., Port Huron Little Theater, Port Huron, 1959-1961; sec., v.p., and pres., Mus. of Arts and History, 1968-69, 74-80; sec., v.p. bd. dirs., Port Huron Hosp. Aux., 1960-70; trustee, Hist. Soc. of Mich., Ann Arbor, 1975-81; coord. of preservation Round Island Lighthouse, Straits Mackinac, Mich., 1972-76; chmn. Horizons, Port Huron Bicentennial Com., Port Huron, 1976; active in Rep. State Bicentennial Com, Lansing, Mich. 1976; trustee, St. Clair County C.C., Port Huron, 1981-99, vice chmn., 1985-95; bd. dirs., Stuart House Mus., Mackinac Island, Mich., 1978, Internat. Symphony, Port Huron and Sarnia, Ont., Canada, 1983-86; sec., treas., and bd. dirs., Blue Water Area Tourism Bureau, Port Huron, 1985-87; adv. bd., Cmty. Found. of St. Clair County, Port Huron, 1986-91, 94—; vestry Grace Episcopal Ch., 1990-93; bd. dirs. Am. Heart Assn. St. Clair County, 1994—; v.p. fin. Blue Water Found. Boy Scouts Am., 1995—. Mem. Nat. Life Underwriters, Port Huron Life Underwriters, Port Huron Estate Planning Coun. (pres. 1985-86), Mich. Mus. Assn. (bd. dirs. 1984-86), Rotary, Port Huron Golf Club. Home: 813 Lakeview Ave Port Huron MI 48060-2103

HAYNIE, ANNA MAE DOWDELL, psychologist; b. Tampa, Fla., Feb. 9, 1944; d. Richard Samford and Ida Belle (Appleby) Dowdell; m. Lorenzo Morris Haynie, Sept. 4, 1965 (div. Feb. 1985); children: Deborah Leigh, Richard Morris. BS in Psychology, U. Tenn., Chattanooga, 1978, MS in Clin. Psychology, 1982. Lic. psychol. examiner. Practicum Orange Grove Ctr., Chattanooga, 1980; intern Marshal Jackson Mental Health Ctr. and Jackson County Hosp., Scottsboro, Ala., 1980-81; resident Marshal Jackson Mental Health Ctr. and Jackson County Hosp., Scottsboro, 1981; team leader, counselor Joe Johnson Mental Health Ctr., Chattanooga, 1981-84; day treatment supr., primary therapist Chattanooga Psychiat. Clinic, 1984-85; pvt. practice Monteagle, Tenn., 1985—; speaker in field; cons. to Moscow Pers. Tng. Ctr., 1991, '92. Contbr. articles, short stories, poetry to Russian jours. Com. mem. Very Spl. Arts Festival, Franklin County, 1988. Mem. AACD, Am. Mental Health Counselors Assn., Assn. for Measurement and Evaluation, Tenn. Assn. Psychol. Examiners, Mountain Assn. Community Svcs. (bd. dirs. 1987—, v.p. 1989, pres. 1990-92), Monteagle Mountain Devel. Assn. (bd. dirs. 1986—), Optimist Internat. (charter mem. 1987, pres. 1989), Psychol. Cons. (pres. 1987—, del. to Soviet Union, 1991). Republican. Episcopalian. Office: Psychological Cons PO Box 785 1 Central Ave Monteagle TN 57356

HAYNOR, PATRICIA MANZI, nursing educator, consultant; children: Kelly Christine, Craig; m. Donald C. Maaswinkel. Diploma in nursing, Grasslands Hosp., Valhalla, N.Y.; BSN, Fairleigh Dickinsn U., 1967; MSN in Nursing Adminstrn., U. Pa., 1969; D Nursing Sci., Widener U., 1989. RN, Pa., N.J., N.Y., Del. Asst. dir. surg. nursing Thomas Jefferson U. Hosp., Phila., 1972-74; asst. dir. nursing care depts. Our Lady of Lourdes Hosp., Camden, N.J., 1974-76; assoc. dir. nursing West Jersey Hosp., Camden, 1976-79; dir. nursing West Jersey Health System, Camden, 1979-81, corp. dir. nursing, 1981-82; v.p. nursing Crozer-Chester (Pa.) Med. Ctr., 1982-85; coord. nursing adminstrn. program, asst. prof. Widener U., Chester, 1985-87; v.p. for nursing St. Francis Med. Ctr., Trenton, N.J., 1987-90; asst. prof. U. Del. Coll. Nursing, 1990-92; assoc. prof. Villanova (Pa.) U. Coll. Nursing, Phila., 1992—; cons. Nurse Assocs., Haddon Heights, N.J., 1985—; spkr. in field; abstractor Am. Orgn. Nurse Execs. Leadership Perspectives. Contbr. articles to profl. publs. Mem. adv. bd. Camden County unit Am. Cancer Soc. Mem. AAUP, Am. Orgn. Nurse Execs., Am. Coll. Healthcare Execs., S.E. Pa. Orgn. Nurse Leaders (bd. dirs., chair by-laws). Home: 201 9th Ave Haddon Heights NJ 08035-1632 Office: Villanova U Coll Nursing Villanova PA 19085

HAYS, CYNTHIA L., internal auditor; b. Phoenix, Mar. 22, 1969; d. Richard Kelly and Barbara Anne (Weible) Shields; m. Timothy David Hays, Feb. 27, 1988; children: Stephanie, Christina. B in Acctg., U. San Diego, 1991. CPA, Calif.; cert. internal auditor. Sr. ops. analyst San Diego Gas and Electric, 1991—. Recipient Outstanding Student award Wall St. Jour., 1991. Mem. Inst. Mgmt. Accts. (scholarship recipient 1989, edn. projects dir. 1991-93, newsletter dir. 1993-94, v.p. comm. 1994-95, v.p. membership 1995-96), Inst. Internal Auditors, U. San Diego Acctg. Alumni (chairperson/co-founder).

HAYS, DIANA JOYCE WATKINS, consumer products company executive; b. Riverside, Calif., Aug. 29, 1945; d. Donald Richard and Evelyn Christine (Kolvoord) Watkins; m. Gerald N. Hays, Jan 30, 1964 (div. Jan. 1970), 1 child, Tad Damon. BA, U. Minn., 1975, MBA, 1982. Dir. environ./phys. sci. Sci. Mus. Minn., St. Paul, 1972-76; dir. mktg. rsch. No. Natural Gas Co., Omaha, 1977-78; mktg. asst., asst. product mgr. Gen. Mills, Inc., Mpls., 1978-81; product mgr. ortho pharms. Consumer Products div. Johnson & Johnson, Raritan, N.J., 1981-82, product dir. home diagnostics, 1982-86; mktg. dir. new market devel. Consumer Products div. Becton Dickinson & Co., Franklin Lakes, N.J., 1986-90; dir. home diagnostics worldwide program Becton Dickinson Advanced Diagnostics Div. Becton Dickinson & Co., Balt., 1990-93; founder, pres. Exec. Computing Solutions, Inc., Vista, Calif., 1991—; product mktg. mgr. Jostens Learning Corp., San Diego, 1994-95; mgr. MIS Circus Distbn., Inc., Vista, Calif., 1995—; chmn. energy exhibit com. Assn. Sci.-Tech. Ctrs., Washington, 1974-75. Producer Ecologenie, 1975. Recipient Tribute to Women and Industry award YWCA, 1989. Mem. Am. Mktg. Assn., NAFE, Twin Mgmt. Forum, Am. Assn. of Health Svcs. Mktg., Capital PC User Group, Beta Gamma Sigma (life). Republican. Roman Catholic. Office: Circus Distbn Inc 1333 Keystone Way Vista CA 92083

HAYS, HOLLY MARY, editor, freelance photojournalist; b. L.A., Nov. 28, 1952; d. Herschel Martin and Mary Catherine (Miller) H. Cert. in art history, Fla. State U., 1971; cert. in computer sci., Fla. Atlantic U., 1979; BS in Journalism, U. Fla., 1974. Layout editor Ind. Fla. Alligator, Gainesville, 1974; reporter Gainesville Sun, 1974; computer specialist Gilbert Law Printing, Gardena, Calif., 1975; copy editor Hartford (Conn.) Courant, 1976-78; mech. artist CRC Press, Inc., Boca Raton, Fla., 1980-85; asst. editor Fla. Living mag., Gainesville, 1986-92, mng. editor, 1993-94, editor-in-chief, 1994-95; asst. editor Ga. Living mag., Gainesville, 1989-91; owner Cross Creek Wilderness Safaris, 1995—; writer Womans World Mag., Englewood, N.J., 1987-89; writer, photographer Fla. Sportsman Mag., Miami, 1988. Vol. Marjorie K. Rawlings State Hist. Site, Cross Creek, Fla., 1987—; lic. master capt. USCG. Mem. Outdoor Writers Am., Internat. Group for Hist. Aircraft Recovery (expedition mem.). Republican. Home and Office: PO Box 96 Lochloosa FL 32662-0096

HAYS, KATHY ANN, elementary education educator; b. Council Bluffs, Iowa, Sept. 29, 1955; d. Leo P. and Monica G. (Schwery) Kenkel; m. Dan P. Hays, Aug. 20, 1988; children: Caitlin Leigh, Patrick Joseph. BS in Elem. Edn., Creighton U., 1977, MS in Elem. Edn., 1984. Cert. elem. tchr., Nebr. 6th grade tchr. Treynor (Iowa) Pub. Schs., 1977-79; from 6th grade tchr. to gifted cons. Ralston (Nebr.) Pub. Schs., 1979-86, 5th grade tchr., 1986-88; 5th grade tchr. Blue Valley Pub. Schs., Overland Park, Kans., 1988-91, Elkhorn (Nebr.) Pub. Schs., 1991—; lang. arts chair Elkhorn Pub. Schs., 1994—; leadership acad. Blue Valley Pub. Schs., Overland Park, 1991-92; presenter in field. Cantor St. Vincent De Paul Ch., Omaha, 1991—. Named Educator of Yr. Ralston Pub. Schs., 1988. Mem. Nebr. Assn. for Gifted Children, Nat. Coun. Tchrs. English, Phi Delta Kappa. Democrat. Roman Catholic. Home: 519 S 215th St Elkhorn NE 68022 Office: Elkhorn Pub Schs 400 S 210th St Elkhorn NE 68022-2103

HAYS, KAY ANN, elementary counselor, educational diagnostician; b. Dallas, June 5, 1949; d. John Gilford and Billie Grace (Minter) Reynolds; m. Thomas Michael Hays, Sr., Dec. 28, 1975; children: Allison Ann, Thomas Michael. BS, East Tex. State U., Commerce, 1971, MEd, 1974; student, Tex. Woman's U., Denton, 1982-88. Cert. edn. counselor, ednl. diagnostician, Tex.; lic. prof. counselor, lic. marriage and family therapist, Tex. Tchr. Yantis (Tex.) Ind. Sch. Dist., 1971-72, Duncanville (Tex.) Pub. Schs., 1972-74; tchr. Birdville Ind. Sch. Dist., Ft. Worth, 1974-79, counselor, 1979-84, counselor, ednl. diagnostician, 1984-95. Mem. Tex. Counseling Assn. (presenter 1993, 94, 95), Tex. Tchrs. Assn., Women's Club Ft. Worth, Pi Kappa Phi. Democrat. Methodist. Office: Birdville Ind Sch Dist 3001 Layton St Fort Worth TX 76117-3930

HAYS, MARY KATHERINE JACKSON (MRS. DONALD OSBORNE HAYS), civic worker; b. Flora, Miss.; d. Rufus Lafayette and Ada (Collum) Jackson; student U. Miss., 1925-26, Millsaps Coll., 1926-27, 43-44; grad. Clark Bus. Sch., 1934; student Columbia U., 1935, Strayer Bus. Coll., 1951; m. Halbert Puffer Oliver, Aug. 9, 1927 (dec. 1934); m. 2d, Donald Osborne Hays, Aug. 30, 1937. Sec. to pres. McCullough Box and Crate Co., Pharr, Tex., 1934-36; sec. to field supr. Miss. Unemployment Compensation Commn., 1936-37; rep. Homes of Tomorrow, 1940 N.Y. World's Fair; sec. to head interior design Lord & Taylor, N.Y.C., 1940; sales dept. Knabe Piano Co., N.Y.C., 1941-43. Active, Little Theatre, Wilkes Barre, Pa., 1937-39; charter mem. and incorporator Conf. State Socs., Washington, 1952; vol. worker Am. Cancer Soc., Washington, 1957; mem. Center City Residents Assn., Phila., 1956; mem. women's com. Nat. Symphony Assn., vol. worker USO, 1945-48, symphony sustaining com. drives, 1957; mem. women's com. Corcoran Gallery Art, Washington, 1957-62; mem. Pierce-Warwick Adoption Assn. of Washington Home for Foundlings; vol. Washington Heart Assn., 1959-66; mem. Nat. Capital Area chpt. United Ch. Women, 1957-72; mem. D.C. Episcopal Home for Children, 1961-86, D.C. Salvation Army Aux., 1962—. Mem. Miss. State Soc. D.C. (sec. 1950-53), Miss. Women's Club D.C., DAR (vice regent chpt. 1970-72, regent chpt. 1972-74, vice chmn. D.C. com. celebration Washington's birthday 1972-76, state libr. 1974-76, state officers club 1976—), chpt. chmn. DAR Svc. for Vet. Patients Com., 1986-88, 90-95, UDC (chpt. historian 1982-84, 86—, chaplain 1984-86), Johnstone Clan Am. (exec. coun. 1976-81, nat. chmn. membership com. 1976-81), First Families of Miss., Women's Club of Flora, Miss. Episcopalian. Club: The Washington. Home: 200 Dominican Dr Apt 3212 Madison MS 39110

HAYS, RUTH, lawyer; b. Fukuoka, Japan, Sept. 20, 1950; d. George Howard and Helen Jincy (Mathis) H. AB, Grinnell Coll., 1972; JD, Washington U., 1978. Bar: Mo. 1978. Law clk. U.S. Ct. Appeals (8th cir.), St. Louis, 1978-80; assoc. Husch & Eppenberger, St. Louis, 1980-87, ptnr., 1987—. Articles editor Urban Law Annual, 1977-78. Bd. dirs. Childhaven, St. Louis, 1982-93, pres. 1987-88. Olin fellow Monticello Coll. Found., St. Louis, 1975-78; recipient Spl. Svc. award Legal Svs. Ea. Mo., 1993. Mem. ABA, Mo. Bar Assn., Bar Assn. Met. St. Louis, Employee Benefits Assn. (pres. 1995), Working in Employee Benefits, Order of Coif, Phi Beta Kappa. Office: Husch & Eppenberger 100 N Broadway Ste 1300 Saint Louis MO 63102-2706

HAYS, SORREL (DORIS), composer; b. Memphis, Aug. 6, 1941; d. Walter Ernest and Christina Doris (Fair) Hays. MusB, U. Chattanooga, 1963; master diploma, Munich Sch. for Music, 1966; MusM, U. Wis., 1968. Lectr. piano U. Wis., Madison, 1967-68; asst. prof. Converse Coll., Mt. Vernon, Iowa, 1969-70; asst. prof. music theory CUNY-Queens Coll., 1975-76; lectr. women's music New Sch. for Social Rsch., N.Y.C., 1976-77; concert pianist U.S. and Europe, 1971-85; rec. artist Atlantic Records; rec. artist other labels, including Folkways, Opus One, New World, and Tellus; cons. new music, author, composer contemporary music text projects Silver Burdett Pub., Morristown, N.J., 1974-84; cons. women's programming Nat. Pub. Radio, Washington, 1980-82. Writer, composer (mus. theater prodns.) including Something (To Do) Doing, 1984 (1st audio exhibit prize Whitney Festival 1990), Love in Space, 1986, Sound Shadows, 1990 (Whitney Mus. award 1990), (opera in 3 acts) The Glass Woman, 1989, (opera for radio) Dream in Her Mind, 1995; premiered Henry Cawell piano concerto in U.S.; keyboard rec. artist Dutch and German broadcasting orgns., 1983—. Lobbyist to Washington-and N.Y.-based instns. for equity and parity at nat. levels for women in music Nat. Music Coun., Rockefeller Found., Nat. Endowment for Arts. N.Y. Found. for Arts artist fellow, 1985. Mem. ASCAP (ann. awards 1980—), Frau und Musik. Home: 697 West End Ave New York NY 10025

HAYWARD, PATRICIA LYNN, communications company executive; b. Santa Ana, Calif., Mar. 22, 1961; d. Benjamin Neff Hayward and Angela (Shiner) TenBroeck; m. Jeffrey S. Depew. BS, Pa. State U., 1983; MBA, Columbia U., 1987. Sales rep. Bus. Info. Svcs. divsn. Control Data Corp., Greenwich, Conn., 1983-86; mgr. bus. devel. Black & Decker Corp., Shelton, Conn., 1987-88; assoc. Booz Allen & Hamilton, N.Y.C., 1988-90; cons. to sr. cons. to ptnr. Mktg. Corp. of Am., Westport, Conn., 1990-95; v.p. client and market devel. Turner Broadcasting Sales, Inc., N.Y.C., 1995—. Vol. Women's Crisis Ctr., Norwalk, 1992—. Office: Turner Broadcasting Sales Inc 420 Fifth Ave New York NY 10018

HAYWARD, TERESA CALCAGNO, foreign language educator; b. N.Y.C., Jan. 28, 1907; d. Vito and Rosalie (Amato) Calcagno; m. Peter Hayward, Feb. 6, 1932; children: Nancy, Peter. BA, Hunter Coll., 1929; MA, Columbia U., 1931. Tchr. romance langs. Jr. High Sch. 164, N.Y.C., 1936-57, Jr. High Sch. 141, Riverdale, N.Y., 1957-71; tchr. English to Japanese women Nichibei Fujinkai, Riverdale, 1972—, chmn. Riverdale chpt., 1976-92, Manhattan, 1992—. Bd. dirs. Riverdale chpt. UN Assn., 1973—; mem. Hunger and Social Outreach com. Christ Ch., Riverdale. Democrat. Episcopalian. Avocations: concerts, piano, art lectures, travel. Address: c/o Nancy Hayward 371 Flat Shoals Rd Salem SC 29676

HAYWOOD, ANNE MOWBRAY, pediatrics, virology, and biochemistry educator; b. Balt., Feb. 5, 1935; d. Richard Mansfield and Margaret (Mowbray) H. BA in Chemistry, Bryn Mawr Coll., 1955; MD, Harvard U., 1959. Cert. Am. Bd. Pediatrics. Intern pediatrics U. Calif. Med. Ctr., San Francisco, 1959-60; postdoctoral fellow biochemistry dept. Columbia U., N.Y.C., 1961-62; postdoctoral fellow div. biology Calif. Inst. Tech., Pasadena, 1960-61, 62-64; asst. prof. microbiology, microbiology dept. Northwestern U. Med. Sch., Chgo., 1964-66, Yale U. Med. Sch., New Haven, 1966-73; resident pediatrics U. Wash., Seattle, 1974-75, pediatric infectious disease fellow, 1975-76; pediatric infectious disease fellow Vanderbilt U., Nashville, 1976-77; assoc. prof. pediatrics and microbiology U. Rochester, N.Y., 1977—; vis. asst. prof. Rockefeller U., N.Y.C., 1971-72; vis. scientist biophysics unit Agrl. Rsch. Coun., Cambridge, Eng., 1972-74, Inst. for Immunology and Virology, U. Zürich (Switzerland), 1987; vis. assoc. prof. dept. zoology U. Calif., Davis, 1986. Co-author: Practice of Pediatrics, 1977, Infections in Children, 1982, Liposome Letters, 1983, Practice of Pediatrics, 1987, Molecular Mechanisms of Membrane Fusion, 1988, Membrane Fusion, 1991, Encyclopedia of Human Biology, 1991, Cell and Model Membrane Interactions, 1991. Fogarty Internat. Ctr. Sr. fellow NIH, 1987, European Molecular Biology Orgn. fellow, 1973-74, NIH Spl. fellow, 1971-73, Am. Cancer Soc. Postdoctoral fellow, 1960-62; Harvard Med. Sch. scholar, 1955-59, Harriet Judd Sartain scholar, 1955-59, N.Y. Alumnae scholar Bryn Mawr Coll., 1951-55. Mem. Biophys. Soc., Am. Soc. for Biochem. and Molecular Biology, Infectious Diseases Soc. Am. Democrat. Office: U Rochester Med Ctr PO Box 777 Rochester NY 14642-8777

HAYWOOD, B(ETTY) J(EAN), anesthesiologist; b. Boston, June 1, 1942; d. Oliver Garfield and Helen Elizabeth (Salisbury) H.; m. Lynn Brandt Moon, Aug. 29, 1969 (div. Aug. 1986); children: Kaylin, Kris Lee, Kelly, Kasy R. BSc, Tufts U., 1964; MD, U. Colo., 1968; MBA, Oklahoma City U., 1993. Intern Wilford Hall AFB, San Antonio, Tex., 1968-69; resident in pediatrics U. Ariz., Tucson, 1971-72, resident in anesthesiology, 1972-74; dir. anesthesia dept. Pima County Hosp., Tucson, 1975-76; staff anesthesiologist South Community Hosp., Oklahoma City, 1977—; staff anesthesiologist Moore (Okla.) Mcpl. Hosp., 1981-94, chief of anesthesia, 1990-94; staff anesthesiologist St. Anthony Hosp., Oklahoma City, 1982—; chief of ethics com. S.W. Med. Ctr., 1996—. Bd. dirs. N.Am. South Devin Assn., Lynnville, Iowa, 1978-86; mem. med. com. Planned Parenthood Okla., 1992—. Lt. col. USAFR, 1968—. Mem. AMA, NAFE (co-dir. Oklahoma City chpt. 1996—), World South Devon Assn. (U.S. rep. 1985, 88—), Tufts U. Alumni Assn. (rep.), Chi Omega (treas. 1963-64). Republican. Presbyterian. Home: 6501 Hunting Hill Oklahoma City OK 73116-3523

HAZAN, MARCELLA MADDALENA, author, educator, consultant; b. Cesenatico, Italy, Apr. 15, 1924; d. Giuseppe and Maria (Leonelli) Polini; m. Victor Hazan, Feb. 24, 1955; 1 child, Giuliano. Dr. in Natural Scis., U. Ferrara, 1952, Dr. in Biology, 1954. Researcher Guggenheim Inst., 1955-58; prof. math. and biology Italian State schs., 1963-66; founder Sch. of Italian Cooking, N.Y.C., 1969-94, Marcella Hazan Sch. of Classic Italian Cooking, Bologna, Italy, 1976-94, Master Classes in Classic Italian Cooking, Venice, Italy, 1986—; pres. Hazan Classic Enterprises, Inc., 1978—. Author: The Classic Italian Cookbook, 1973, More Classic Italian Cooking, 1978, Marcella's Italian Kitchen, 1986, Essentials of Classic Italian Cooking, 1992. Roman Catholic. Address: PO Box 285 Circleville NY 10919-0285

HAZARD, PEGGY JEAN, curator; b. Elizabeth City, N.C., May 13, 1954; d. Bernard Thomas and Carole June (Vaclavek) Burba; m. J. Michael Hazard, Aug. 6, 1977; children: Megan, Nathan. BA in Edn., Ariz. State U., 1976; MA in Art History, U. Ariz., 1993. Cert. tchr., Ariz. Asst. exhibit curator Tohono Chul Park, Tucson, 1990—; bd. dirs. Assocs. of Art History, Tucson, 1994—. Mem. Am. Assn. Museums, Mus. Assn. Ariz., Tucson Assn. Museums (rep., v.p. 1993-94, pres. 1994-95), Am. Quilt Study Group. Home: 8902 N Riviera Dr Tucson AZ 85737

HAZEEM, KATHRYN A., legislative counsel; b. Pitts., Sept. 10, 1959. BA, Oral Roberts U., 1982; JD, Cath. U. Am., 1985. Dir. legal affairs Coalition Religious Freedom, 1985-87; assoc. Coale, Kananack &

Murgatroyd, 1987-89; minority counsel Subcom. Civil and Constl. Rights Com. Judiciary, 1989-94; chief counsel Subcom. to the Constn. Com. Judiciary, 1995—. Office: Subcom Constn Ford House Office Bldg Washington DC 20515

HAZEKAMP, PHYLLIS WANDA ALBERTS, library director; b. Chgo.; d. John Edward and Mary Ann (Demski) Wojciechowski. BA, De Paul U., 1947; MSLS, La. State U., 1959; postgrad., Santa Clara U., U. Chgo. Cert. tchr., Calif., Ariz. Libr. Agrl. Experiment Sta., U. Calif., Riverside, 1959-61; tech. libr. Lockheed Tech. Libr., Palo Alto, Calif., 1962-63; asst. law libr. Santa Clara (Calif.) U. Law Sch., 1963-72; libr. dir. Carmelite Seminary, San Jose, Calif., 1973-78; reference libr. San Jose State U., 1978-79; libr. dir. SAI Engrs., Santa Clara, 1980-81, Palmer Coll. Chiropractic, San Jose, 1981-90, Camp Verde (Ariz.) Community Libr., 1990—; mem. Cultural Commn., Santa Clara, 1968-72; pres. Santa Clara Art Assn., 1973-74. Mem. Kiwanis Internat., House of Ruth (bd. dirs. 1995—). Office: Camp Verde Community Libr 130 Black Bridge Loop Rd Camp Verde AZ 86322

HAZEL, JOANIE BEVERLY, elementary education educator; b. Medford, Oreg., Jan. 20, 1946; d. Ralph Ray Lenderman and Vivian Thelma (Holtane) Spencer; m. Larry Aydon Hazel, Dec. 28, 1969. BS in Edn., So. Oreg. Coll., Ashland, 1969; MS in Edn., Portland State U., 1972; postgrad., U. Va., 1985. Elem. tchr. Beaverton (Oreg.) Schs., 1972-76, Internat. Sch. Svcs., Isfahan, Iran, 1976-78; ESL instr. Lang. Svcs., Tucker, Ga., 1983-84; tchr. Fairfax (Va.) Schs., 1985-86; elem. tchr. Beaverton (Oreg.) Schs., 1990—. Mem. Nat. Trust for Hist. Preservation, Hist. Preservation League of Oreg., Portland. Mem. AAAS, U.S. Hist. Soc., Platform Soc., Smithsonian Instn., Am. Mus. Natural History, Nat. Mus. Women in Arts, U.S. Hist. Soc., The UN, The Colonial Williamsburg Found., Wilson Ctr., N.Y. Acad. Sci., Nat. Trust for Hist. Preservation, Hist. Preservation League of Oreg. Home: 4920 NW Salishan Dr Portland OR 97229

HAZELTINE, JOYCE, state official; b. Pierre, S.D.; m. Dave Hazeltine; children: Derek, Tara, Kirk. Student, Huron (S.D.) Coll., No. State Coll., Aberdeen, S.D., Black Hills State Coll., Spearfish, S.D. Former asst. chief clk. S.D. Ho. of Reps.; former sec. S.D. State Senate; sec. of state State of S.D., Pierre, 1987—. Adminstrv. asst. Pres. Ford Campaign, S.D.; Rep. county chmn. Hughes County S.D. Mem. Nat. Assn. Secs. of State (exec. bd., pres.). Office: Sec of State's Office 500 E Capitol Ave Ste 204 Pierre SD 57501-5077

HAZELTON, PENNY ANN, law librarian, educator; b. Yakima, Wash., Sept. 24, 1947; d. Fred Robert and Margaret (McLeod) Pease; m. Norris J. Hazelton, Sept. 12, 1971; 1 dau., Victoria MacLeod. BA cum laude, Linfield Coll., 1969; JD, Lewis and Clark Law Sch., 1975; M in Law Librarianship, U. Wash., 1976. Bar: Wash. 1976; U.S. Supreme Ct. 1982. assoc. law libr., assoc. prof. U. Maine, 1976-78, law libr., assoc. prof., 1978-81; asst. libr. for rsch. svcs. U.S. Supreme Ct., Washington, 1981-85, law libr., 1985; law librarian U. Wash., Seattle, 1985—, prof. law, 1985—; tchr. legal rsch., law librarianship, Indian law; cons. Maine Adv. Com. on County Law Librs., Nat. U. Sch. Law, San Diego, 1985-88, Lawyers Cooperative Pub., 1993-94. Author: Computer Assisted Legal Research: The Basics, 1993; contbr. articles to legal jours. Recipient Disting. Alumni award U. Wash., 1992. Mem. ABA (sect. legal edn. & admissions to bar, chair com. on librs. 1993-94, vice chair 1992-93, 94-95), Am. Assn. Law Schs. (com. law librs. 1991-94), Law Librs. New Eng. (sec. 1977-79, pres. 1979-81), Am. Assn. Law Librs. (cert., program chmn. ann. meeting 1984, exec. bd. 1984-87, v.p., pres.-elect 1989-90, pres. 1990-91, program co-chair Insts. 1983, 95), Law Librs' Soc. Washington (exec. bd. 1983-84, v.p., pres.-elect 1984-85), Law Librs. Puget Sound, Wash. State Bar Assn. (chair editl. adv. bd. 1990-91), Wash. Adv. Coun. on Librs., Westpac. Office: U Wash Marian Gould Gallagher Law Libr 1100 NE Campus Pky Seattle WA 98105-6617

HAZELTON, VINA JANE, retired claims representative, artist; b. Toppenish, Wash., Mar. 18, 1931; d. Dow Lefield and Ruth Gladys (Jenks) Ashford; m. Melbourne Eugene Jenks, Dec. 25, 1952 (dec. Nov. 1987); 1 child, William Randall; m. Byron W. Hazelton, May 1991. Student, Chemeketa C.C., 1978—. With ID bur. Oreg. State Police Dept., Salem, 1949-55, supr. clerical dept., 1953-55, clk. typist patrol office, 1956-59; sec. pers. dept. Boeing Airplane Co., Seattle, 1952-53; lithographer Moore Bus. Forms, Salem, 1959-65; clk. Marion County Dist. Ct., Salem, 1965; with Social Security Adminstrn., 1965-91; telephone svc. rep. Social Security Adminstrn., San Diego, 1976-77; claims rep. Social Security Adminstrn., Salem and Albany, Oreg., 1978-91; ret., self employed artist, author, 1991—. With USNR, 1950-54. Mem. Am. Fedn. Govt. Employees (union rep.). Democrat. Methodist. Home and Office: 3792 Augusta National Dr S Salem OR 97302-9716

HAZEN, ELIZABETH FRANCES, retired special education educator; b. Lamar, Colo., May 27, 1925; d. Otis Garfield and Cora B. (Baker) McDowell; children: H. Ray, Bobby D., Anita K. Iezza, Gloria G. Gill. AA, Lamar Jr. Coll., 1946; BS in Edn., Southwestern Okla. U., 1967, MS in Edn., 1969; postgrad., Ea. Ky. U., 1983. Cert. speech-hearing therapist, reading specialist, learning and behavior disorders, Ky. Elem. tchr. Granada (Colo.) Sch., 1946-51, South Ctrl. Elem. Sch., Lamar, Colo., 1951-52; lead tchr. Tom Thumb Pre-Sch., Ellsworth AFB, S.D., 1961-62; math. and sci. tchr. Elk City (Okla.) Elem. Sch., 1966-67; beginning speech tchr. Sayer Jr. Coll., Okla., 1967-68; speech and hearing therapist Burns Flat (Okla.) Schs., 1967-69, Maconaqueh Sch. Corp., Bunker Hill, Ind., 1969-72; reading specialist Myers Mid. Sch., Louisville, Ky., 1972-76; tchr. Core Westport Jr. H.S., Louisville, 1977-79, chmn. Core dept., 1978-79; learning disabled resource tchr. Jeffersontown H.S., Louisville, 1979-80, Waggoner Mid. Sch., Louisville, 1980-81, Westport Mid. Sch., Louisville, 1981-94; ret., 1994; chmn. exceptional children's edn. dept. Westport Mid. Sch., Louisville, 1983-91; speech and hearing therapist Burns Flat (Okla.) Bd. Edn., 1967-69. Bd. dirs. Westport Middle Schs. PTA/Student Assn., 1989-90. Named Outstanding Tchr. of Disadvantaged, State of Okla., 1969. Mem. NEA, Ky. Mid. Sch. Assn., Ky. Edn. Assn., Jefferson County Tchrs. Assn. Home: 3130 Hewitt Ave Louisville KY 40220-2226

HAZLEWOOD, JUDITH EVANS, retired librarian; b. McKenzie, Tenn., Mar. 30, 1930; d. Henry Bascom and Bertie (Harvey) Evans; m. Bob J. Hazlewood, June 11, 1955; children: Jeffrey E., Amy H. McAtee. BS in English, Memphis State U., 1952; MA in English, Vanderbilt U., 1954; MA in Libr. Sci., George Peabody Coll., 1959. Sec. bus. office Memphis State U., 1951-53; tchr. English and home econs. Messick High Sch., Memphis, 1954-57; statis. clk. office v.p. U. Fla., 1957-58; English tchr. Hume-Fogg High Sch., Nashville, 1958-59; cataloger Nashville Pub. Libr., 1962-63; acquisitions libr. Lambuth U., Jackson, Tenn., 1964-74, libr. dir., 1974-95; part-time English instr. Bethel Coll., McKenzie, 1960-62. Mem. Tenn. Libr. Assn. (sec. for educators, nominating com., chair honors awards com., chair staff devel./recruitment com., membership com.), West Tenn. Libr. Assn., West Tenn. Acad. Libr. Consortium, Tenn. Archivists, Delta Kappa Gamma, Kappa Delta Pi. Methodist. Office: Lambuth U 705 Lambuth Blvd Jackson TN 38301-5280

HAZUDA, HELEN PAULINE, sociologist, educator; b. San Francisco, Oct. 20, 1943; d. Alexander William and Dolores Underwood (Green) H.; children: Ann Elizabeth Richter, Sean. BA in Sociology and Philosophy, Incarnate Word Coll., 1965, MA in Edn. and History, 1968; PhD in Sociology, U. Tex., 1975. Asst. prin. Incarnate Word H.S., San Antonio, 1967-71; discipline head for curriculum, instrn., dir. bilingual edn. Our Lady the Lake U., San Antonio, 1976-79; asst. prof. clin. medicine in medicine and psychiatry U. Tex. Health Sci. Ctr., San Antonio, 1980-88, assoc. prof. medicine dept. medicine and psychiatry, 1988—; del. Gov's White House Conf. Children and Youth, Austin, 1970; admissions com. med. sch. U. Tex. Health Sci. Ctr., San Antonio, 1986-91, med. humanities curriculum planning com., 1989-91, tech. adv. panel for clin. and epidemiological rsch., 1991—; doctoral dissertation com. Sch. Nursing, 1992-93, adj. asst. prof. medicine and psychiatry, 1979-80; lectr. Incarnate Word Coll., San Antonio, 1971-72; cons. San Luis Valley Health and Aging Study/U. Colo. Health Sci. Ctr., Denver, 1992—; mem. nat. adv. panel RMC Rsch. Corp., 1977-81; mem. ad hoc study section NIH, 1988, mem. clin. applications and prevention adv. com. divsn. epidemiology and clin. applications Nat. Heart, Lung and Blood Inst., 1991-94, chair behavioral medicine working group, 1993-94, task force on rsch. in epidemiology and prevention cardiovascular disease, 1993-94; reviewer grants and proposals; mem. working group on epidemiology of hypertension in Hispanic-Ams., Native Ams., and Asian/Pacific Islanders-Ams., 1993-94; co-chair NHLBI Conf. socioeconomic status and cardiovascular health and disease, 1995; cons. McDonnell-Douglas Automation Co., St. Louis, 1969-78, Devel. Assocs., 1975-77; speaker and presenter in field. Contbr. articles to profl. jours. Panelist San Antonio Cmty. Symposium on the Changing Role Women in Personal and Profl. Life, 1976; resource person Leadership San Antonio, 1976; co-chair Working Women in Am.: Where Are They and Why are They There?, 1976-77; judge Hobby Middle Sch. Sci. Fair, San Antonio, 1984, John Jay H.S. Sci. Fair, San Antonio, 1987, Alamo Area Regional Sci. Fair, San Antonio, 1987; alumnae bd. dirs. Incarnate Word H.S., San Antonio, 1986-89; pledge vol. Womens Faculty Assn., San Antonio, 1991. U.S. Seminar on the Epidemiology and Prevention Cardiovascular Disease fellow, Lake Tahoe, Calif., 1983; instl. rsch. grantee U. Tex. Health Scis. Ctr./Hogg Found. for Mental Health, Austin, 1981-82; grantee Am. Heart Assn., 1983-84, Morrison Trust Found., 1986-87, NIH, 1979—, Nat. Cancer Inst., 1985-89. Mem. Am. Sociol. Assn., Soc. for Behavioral Medicine, Am. Diabetes Assn., Soc. for Epidemiol. Rsch., Am. Heart Assn. (mem. coun. on cardiovasc. epidemiology), Acad. Behavioral Medicine Rsch., Phi Kappa Phi, Kappa Gamma Phi, Alpha Chi, Alpha Lambda Delta. Office: U Tex Health Sci Ctr Dept Medicine/Epidemiology 7703 Floyd Curl Dr San Antonio TX 78284-7873

HAZZARD, SHIRLEY, author; b. Sydney, Australia, Jan. 30, 1931; d. Reginald and Catherine (Stein) H.; m. Francis Steegmuller, Dec. 22, 1963 (dec. Oct. 1994). Ed., Queenwood Sch., Sydney, to 1946. With Combined Services Intelligence, Hong Kong, 1947-48, U.K. High Commr.'s Office, Wellington, N.Z., 1949-50, UN (Gen. Service Category), N.Y.C., 1952-62; Boyer lectr., Australia, 1984, 88. Author: Cliffs of Fall and Other Stories, 1963; novel The Evening of the Holiday, 1966; fiction People in Glass Houses, 1967; novel The Bay of Noon, 1970; History Defeat of an Ideal: A Study of the Self-Destruction of the United Nations, 1973; novel The Transit of Venus, 1980, History Countenance of Truth, 1990; contbr. short stories to New Yorker mag. Trustee N.Y. Soc. Library. Recipient 1st prize O. Henry Short Story awards, 1976, Lit. award Nat. Inst. Arts and Letters, 1966; Guggenheim fellow, 1974; recipient Nat. Book Critics Circle award for Fiction, 1981. Mem. Nat. Acad. Arts and Letters, Century Club (N.Y.C.). Address: 200 E 66th St New York NY 10021-6728

HEACKER, THELMA WEAKS, retired elementary school educator; b. Lakeland, Fla., Nov. 27, 1927; d. Andrew Lee and Stella Dicy (Hodges) Weaks; m. Howard V. Heacker, Aug. 21, 1947; children: Victor, Patricia, Paula, Jonathan, Johannah; m. V.L. Brown, Mar. 31, 1991. BA, Carson-Newman Coll., Jefferson City, Tenn., 1949; MA, Tenn. Technol. U., 1980; postgrad., U. Tenn. Cert. elem. and secondary tchr., Tenn.; cert. secondary tchr., Ga. Elem. tchr. Hamblen County Pub. Schs., Morristown, Tenn., 1949; secondary tchr. Morgan County-Coalfield High Sch., Coalfield, Tenn., 1986-87, Roane County-O. Springs High Sch., Oliver Springs, Tenn., 1949-71; elem. tchr. Morgan County-Petros-Joyner Sch., Oliver Springs, 1975-93. Named Tchr. of Yr., 1986. Mem. NEA, Tenn. Edn. Assn., Ea. Tenn. Edn. Assn., Morgan County Edn. Assn., RCTA, HCTA. Home: 102 Ulena Ln Oak Ridge TN 37830-5237 Office: Petros Joyner Elem Sch Petros-Joyner Rd Oliver Springs TN 37840-9700

HEAD, ELIZABETH, lawyer; b. Rochester, Minn., Dec. 17, 1930; d. Walter Elias and Ruth Winnogene (Evesmith) Bonner; m. C.J. Head, Dec. 30, 1950; 1 child, Alison Elizabeth. BA, U. Chgo., 1949, JD, 1952. Bar: Ill. 1952, Calif. 1955, N.Y. 1958, U.S. Supreme Ct. 1963, D.C. 1978. Atty. Nat. Labor Rels. Bd., Washington, 1953-54; assoc. Johnston & Johnston, San Francisco, 1954-56; atty. Aminoil Inc., San Francisco, 1956-57; teaching assoc. Law Sch. Columbia U., N.Y., 1957-58; assoc. Skadden Arps, N.Y., 1958-60; atty. The Coca-Cola Corp., N.Y., 1961-65; assoc. Kaye Scholer, N.Y., 1965-72, ptnr., 1973-82; ptnr. Hall & Estill, Tulsa, 1983-87; vis. fellow antitrust analysis Fed. Energy Regulatory Commn., Washington, 1987-89; gen. counsel Columbia U., N.Y.C., 1989—. Trustee Philbrook Mus., Tulsa, 1983-87, Mary Baldwin Coll., Staunton, Va., 1983-87. Mem. ABA (standing com. on dispute resolution 1983-90), Assn. of Bar of City of N.Y. (non-profit orgns. com. 1989-90, chair 1992-95), Century Assn., Order of Coif, Phi Beta Kappa. Office: Columbia U Office Gen Counsel 110 Low Memorial Libr New York NY 10027

HEAD, MELVA ANN, artist; b. St. Louis, July 9, 1937; d. Melvin G. and Muriel J. (Hall) Irwin; m. Fred L. Head, Dec. 15, 1956; children: Allan L., Shawn M. Studied with, Thelma DeGoede Smith, 1973-83, Kwok Wai Lau, 1983—. V.p. gallery La Habra (Calif.) Art Assn., 1986-88, v.p. membership, 1988-89, v.p. programs, 1989-91, pres., 1991-92, dir., 1992-95. Exhbns. include Long Beach (Calif.) Arts, 1994, 95, 96, Palm Springs (Calif.) Desert Mus., Gallery 825, L.A., 1995-96, Pasadena (Calif.) Presbyn. Ch., 1995, L.A. Art Assn., Chevron Oil and Field Rsch., La Habra, Calif., 1991. Mem. Artists Coun. Palm Springs, L.A. Arts, Long Beach Arts, La Habra Art Assn.

HEADDEN, SUSAN M., editor. Formerly reporter Indianapolis Star, Indianapolis; now assoc. editor U.S. News & World Report, Washington. Recipient Pulitzer Prize for investigative reporting, 1991. Office: US News and World Report 2400 N St NW Washington DC 20037-1153*

HEADDING, LILLIAN SUSAN (SALLY HEADDING), writer, forensic clairvoyant; b. Milw., Jan. 1, 1944; d. David Morton and Mary Davis (Berry) Coleman; m. James K. Hill (div. 1976); children: Amy Denise; m. John Murray Headding (div. 1987). BA, U. Nev., 1975; MA, U. Pacific, 1976. With Gimbels, Milw., 1963-65; spl. assignment G2 USAPIC U.S. Womens Army Corp., 1963; retail mgr. Frandisco Corp., N.Y.C., 1965-66; dist. mgr. Anita Shops, Los Angeles, 1966-68; store mgr. Clothes Closet, Sunnyvale, Calif., 1969-70; owner Lillian Headding Interiors & Comml. Design, Pittsburg, Calif., 1976-88; mfrs. rep. and assoc. J.G. West, San Francisco, 1989-91; Karate instr. Sch. of the Tiger, Pleasant Hill, Calif., 1988-94, 1st degree black belt, 1973; clairvoyant, psychic cons. on numerous crime and missing persons cases, U.S., Can., Eng. and France, 1972—. Author: (as Sally Davis): When Gods Fall; author short stories, poetry. Bd. dirs. and co-founder Cmty. Action Against Rape, Las Vegas, 1972-75; self-def. expert Las Vegas Met. Police Dept., 1972-75, North Las Vegas (Nev.) Police Dept.; co-supr. Family & Children's Svcs., Contra Costa County, Calif., 1985-86. Mem. AAUW, People for Ethical Treatment of Animals, Walnut Creek Writers Group (pres.), Berkeley Women's Writers Group, Philippine Hawaiian Black Belters Assn., Humane Farming Assn., Am. Assn. Profl. Psychics. Democrat. Jewish. Office: 5333 Park Highlands Blvd #33 Concord CA 94521-3718

HEADLEY, ANNE RENOUF, technology commercialization financier; b. N.Y.C., Apr. 3, 1937. Diploma, Emma Willard Sch., 1954; student, Inst. World Affairs, 1957; AB magna cum laude, honors in Anthropology, Columbia U., 1959; MA, Yale U., 1962, PhD, 1966; JD with honors, Am. U., 1978; postgrad., Duke U. Sch. Law. Asst. prof. U. N.C., Chapel Hill, 1966-71; sr. profl. cons. U.S. Govt., Washington, 1972-75; pvt. practice fin. cons. Washington, 1976—; vis. assoc. prof. George Washington U. Sch. Bus. Adminstrn., Washington, 1983-84; gen. ptnr., v.p. Tech. Mgmt. Corp., Montgomeryville, Pa., 1986-88; chmn. Pivot, Inc., 1988—; founding prin. SaraTech Fin. Inc., 1990-92; sr. v.p., head internat. bus. Hectron Inc., Washington, 1992-93; corp. dir.; dir. fin. devel. Ctr. for Space and Advanced Tech., 1990; cons. The Brookings Instn., Washington, 1966, U.S. Dept. State, Washington, 1967, World Bank, 1992—; mem. Pres.'s Commn. Grad. Edn., 1967-68, Nat. Chamber Found. Task Force on Space Commercialization, Washington, 1983-86; vis. scholar Carnegie Endowment for Internat. Peace, N.Y.C., 1968-69; fellow U.S. Dept. State, EUR/RPE, 1967; bd. dirs. Advanced Tech. Orgn. of Md., 1985-88; northeastern dir. Va. Advanced Tech. Assn., 1984-88; fin. and tech. speaker. Contbr. articles on tech. commercialization and fin. to profl. jours. Co-char, charter mem. U.S./China Capital Cities Coun., Washington, 1985-95; advisor Greater Washington D.C. Bd. Trade, 1985-86, Internat. Red Cross, 1987-90; mem. Mayor's Adv. Coun. on Trade and Investment, 1987-91; mem. adv. coun. Ctr. for Internat. Bus. Edn. U. Alaska, Fairbanks, 1990-91, co-chmn. World Trade Day, 1989; bd. dirs. Nat. Symphony Orch., 1990—, Greater Washington Met. Boys and Girls Clubs, 1992—. Woodrow Wilson fellow, 1958, Bushnell fellow, Yale U., 1964, Hon. Officer-Faculty fellow U.S. Dept. State, 1967; recipient citation Washington D.C. Mayor's Office, 1986. Fellow Washington Acad. Scis.; mem. Am. Soc. Internat. Law, Internat. Forum U.S. C. of C., Internat. Energy Seminar-Johns Hopkins Sch. for Advanced Internat. Study, Corcoran Gallery of Art (nat. coun.), Washington Internat. Trade Assn., Assn. for Corp. Growth, Phi Beta Kappa.

HEADLY, GLENNE AIMÉE, actress; b. New London, Conn., Mar. 13, 1959. Mem. of ensemble Steppenwolf Theatre. Appeared on stage in Curse of Starving Class, Balm in Gilead, Arms and the Man; films: Making Mr. Right, 1987, Nadine, 1987, Dirty Rotten Scoundrels, 1988, Paperhouse, 1989, Dick Tracy, 1990, Mortal Thoughts, 1991, Mr. Holland's Opus, 1994; TV miniseries: Lonesome Dove, 1989 (Emmy nomination for best supporting actress); TV films include Seize the Day, 1986, And The Band Played On, 1994. Recipient three Joseph Jefferson awards for best supporting actress, Chgo.; named Best Newcomer Theatre World Award Com., N.Y. Office: Internat Creative Mgmt 8942 Wilshire Blvd Beverly Hills CA 90211-1934

HEALEY, ANN RUSTON, diaconate program director; b. Havana, Cuba, Dec. 29, 1939; d. Homer Max and Elizabeth Dillon (Rea) H. BA in Spanish, French, Ohio Wesleyan U., 1961; MA in Religious Studies, Mundelein Coll., 1975; cert. pastoral leadership, St. Louis U., 1982; MDiv, Assn. for Clin. Pastoral Edn., Atlanta, 1983; PhD, Columbia Pacific U., 1991. Cert. social worker, Ill. Mental health social worker Dept. Mental Health, Chgo., 1964-68; hosp. social worker St. Joseph Hosp., Chgo., 1968-73; social work progam dir. Sr. Ctrs. Met. Chgo., 1973-75; retreat and spiritual dir. Cenacle Retreat House, Chgo., 1975-80; hosp. chaplain Barnes Hosp., St. Louis, 1981-82, Mercy Med. Ctr., Bakersfield, Calif., 1982-83; chaplain tng. supr. Immanuel Med. Ctr., Omaha, 1983-84; program dir. permanent deacon formation program Catholic Diocese Ft. Worth, 1984—; resident in clin. pastoral edn. Assn. for Clin. Pastoral Edn., Atlanta, 1981-82, 83-84; exec. bd. dirs. S.W. Career Devel. Ctr., Arlington, Tex., v.p. 1990-93, pres. 1993-95, chair search com., 1993-95; mem. adj. faculty Inst. for Pastoral Life, Kansas City, Kans., 1988-92, Inst. for Religious and Pastoral Studies, U. Dallas, 1989-90; chmn. 2d Ecumenical Consultation on Deacons and Diaconate, Nat. Coun. Chs., Ft. Worth, 1988; mem. exec. bd. Tarrant Area Community Chs., 1991-93; retreat and spiritual dir., 1982—; dir. Twelve Step Journey to Wholeness Workshop, 1986-92; mem. Bishop's Task Force on Women's Concerns, 1987-93; mem. Tex. Cath. Conf. Task Force for Priest Shortage, 1984-85. Mem. Nat. Assn. Permanent Diaconate Dirs. (sec. 1987-89, region X rep. 1990-92, exec. bd. 1992-95, pres.-elect 1992-93, pres. 1993-94, past pres. 1994-95), Nat. Assn. Cath. Chaplains (cert.), Assn. for Clin. Pastoral Edn. (clin.), Spiritual Dirs. Internat., Coll. Chaplains (assoc.), Am. Assn. Pastoral Counselors (profl. affiliate 1990—), Charles A. Lindbergh N-X-211 Collectors' Soc. (curator 1988-90, archivist 1990—, charter mem.). Democrat. Home: 210 Mountainview Dr Hurst TX 76054-3068 Office: The Catholic Center 800 W Loop 820 S Fort Worth TX 76108-2936

HEALEY, DEBORAH LYNN, education administrator; b. Columbus, Ohio, Sept. 15, 1952; d. James Henry and Marjorie Jean Healey; 1 child, Jesse Healey Winterowd. BA in German/Religion, Queen's U., 1974; MA in Linguistics, U. Oreg., 1976, PhD in Edn., 1993. Instr. Lane C.C., Eugene, Oreg., 1976-77; instr., materials developer Rogue C.C., Ashland, Oreg., 1977-79; instr. Chemeketa C.C., Salem, Oreg., 1979-80; instr., computer ops. English Lang. Inst. Oreg. State U., Corvallis, 1979-85, 88-93; instr., computer ops. Yemen-Am. Lang. Inst., Sana'a, Yemen, 1985-88; programmer, cons. Internat. Soc. for Tech. in Edn., Eugene, 1989-91; coord. instr. English Lang. Inst. Oreg. State U., Corvallis, 1993-95, tech. coord., 1995—; Macintosh support Computer-Enhanced Lang. Instrn. Archive, 1993—; computer cons. in field. Author: (book) Something To Do On Tuesday, 1995; editor, author Computer-Assisted English Lang. Learning Jour., 1990—; co-editor (ann. publ.) CALL Interest Sect. Software List, 1990—; co-author (software) The House, At The Zoo, 1993. Mem. TESOL (interest sect. chair 1992-92), Oreg. TESOL (newsletter editor 1981-84), Nat. Assn. Fgn. Student Advisors-Assn. Internat. Educators, Am. Ednl. Rsch. Assn., Computer Assn. Lang. Instrn. Consortium. Office: ELI Oreg State Univ 301 Snell Hall Corvallis OR 97331-8515

HEALEY, LYNNE KOVER, editor, writer, broadcaster, educator; b. L.I., N.Y.; d. Richard Frederick Bascom and Margaret Harriet (Fuchs); div.; children: Christine Josepha, Lauren Teresa. AA in Journalism and Psychology, Middlesex County Coll., 1979; BA in Comm., Rutgers U., 1983; MA in English, Drew U., 1987. Editor A.M. Best Co., Oldwick, N.J., 1985-91; communications cons. MetLife Ins. Co., 1992—; free-lance cons. Sea-Land Corp., Menlo Park, N.J., 1984-85; free-lance writer, 1977—; adj. prof. English Middlesex County Coll., Edison, N.J. Mem. Meeting Planners Internat. (bd. dirs. N.J. chpt., co-chairperson com. for Give Kids the World project), Rutgers U. Alumni Assn. (exec. com.), Alpha Sigma Lambda (grad. sch. scholar 1986, bd. dirs. Rutgers chpt.). Office: MetLife Bridgewater NJ 08807

HEALY, ALICE FENVESSY, psychology educator, researcher; b. Chgo., June 26, 1946; d. Stanley John and Doris (Goodman) Fenvessy; m. James Bruce Healy, May 9, 1970; 1 dau., Charlotte Alexandra. AB summa cum laude, Vassar Coll., 1968; PhD, Rockefeller U., 1973. Asst. prof. psychology Yale U., New Haven, 1973-78, assoc. prof. psychology, 1978-81; assoc. prof. psychology U. Colo., Boulder, 1981-84, prof. psychology, 1984—; rsch. assoc. Haskins Labs., New Haven, 1976-80; mem. com. NIMH, Washington, 1979-81; co-investigator rsch. contract USAF, U. Colo., 1985-86; prin. investigator rsch. contract U.S. Army Rsch. Inst., U. Colo., 1986—, Naval Tng. Systems Ctr., 1993-94. Co-author: Cognitive Processes, 2d edit., 1986; editor: Memory and Cognition, 1986-89, (with S.M. Kosslyn and R.M. Shiffrin) From Learning Theory to Connectionist Theory: Essays in Honor of William K. Estes, Vol. I, 1992, From Learning Processes to Cognitive Processes: Essays in Honor of William K. Estes, Vol. II, 1992, (with L.E. Bourne Jr.) Learning and Memory of Knowledge and Skills: Durability and Specificity, 1995; assoc. editor Jour. Exptl. Psychology, 1982-84; contbr. more than 100 articles to profl. jours., chpts. to books. Recipient Sabbatical award James McKeen Cattell Fund, 1987-88; NSF Rsch. grantee, 1977-86, Spencer Found. Rsch. grantee, 1978-80. Fellow APA (exec. com. divsn. 3 1989-92, chair membership com. 1992-93), AAAS (nominating com. 1988-91, chair 1991, chair-elect psychology sect. 1994, chair psychology sect. 1995-96, retiring chair psychology sect. 1996—); mem. Psychonomic Soc. (governing bd. 1987-92, publs. com. 1989-93), Soc. Math. Psychology, Rocky Mountain Psychology Assn. (pres.-elect 1993-94, pres. 1994-95, past pres. 1995-96), Cognitive Sci. Soc., Univ. Club, Phi Beta Kappa, Sigma Xi. Home: 840 Cypress Dr Boulder CO 80303-2820 Office: U Colo Dept Psychology Campus Box 345 Boulder CO 80309-0345

HEALY, GWENDOLINE FRANCES, controller; b. Brighton, Sussex, Eng., Nov. 25, 1940; came to U.S., 1971, naturalized, 1995; d. Frank William Barnes and Violet May (Kelly) Billingham; m. John Francis Healy, Sept. 1, 1972; children: Robert Charles, Jennifer Diane. BA, Brighton (Eng.) Poly. Inst., 1958. Acct. Comstock Internat., N.Y.C., 1972-73, Burgdorff Realtors, Summit, N.J., 1973-75; artist Athens, 1976-79; acct. Temple B'nai, Morristown, N.J., 1985-88; contr. W.H. Collins, Inc., Whippany, N.J., 1988—; dir. mktg. Healy Fin. Svcs., Morristown, 1989—. Leader MCC Commerce, Morristown, 1994-95; mem. Morristownship Task Force, 1995. Mem. Morris County Mental Health Assn. (bd. dirs., sec.-treas. 1995—), Daus. Brit. Empire (past treas. J. Elliot Langstaff chpt.). Republican. Home: 1 Barnstable Ct Morristown NJ 07960 Office: Healy Fin Svcs PO Box 16 Convent Station NJ 07961

HEALY, MARGARET MARY, retail marketing executive; b. Bklyn., Dec. 31, 1938; d. Nicholas Joseph and Margaret Marie (Ferry) H.; m. Robert L. Parker, 1979 (div. 1988); 1 child, Nicole Parker. BA, Manhattanville Coll., 1961; cert., NYU, 1967, Columbia U., 1971. Account exec. Geer, DuBois & Co., Inc., N.Y.C., 1965-71; dir. mktg. comm. Dry Dock Savs. Bank, N.Y.C., 1971-72; operating v.p. Bloomingdales, N.Y.C., 1972-79; owner, pres. Healy & Pratts, Inc., N.Y.C., 1979-88, PH Network, Dallas, 1992—; mgr. corporate pub. rels. J.C. Penney Co., Dallas, 1988-92; bd. dirs. North Side Savs. Bank, Floral Park, N.Y. Co-author: Salute to Italy Celebrity Cookbook, 1984, Salute to America Celebrity Cookbook, 1986. Bd. dirs. Dallas Children's Theatre, 1989—. Recipient Cmty. Svc. award VFW, 1978. Roman Catholic. Home: 5435 Mercedes Ave Dallas TX 75206-5819 Office: PH Network 2811 Mckinney Ave Ste 356E Dallas TX 75204-2547

HEALY, MARY (MRS. PETER LIND HAYES), singer, actress; b. New Orleans, Apr. 14, 1918; d. John Joseph and Viola (Armbruster) H.; m. Peter Lind Hayes, Dec. 19, 1940; children: Peter Michael, Cathy Lind. Student parochial schs., New Orleans; hon. degree, St. Bonaventure U. With 20th Century Fox, Hollywood, Cal. Author: Twenty-five Minutes from Broadway, 1961; pictures and others, 1937-40; Broadway prodns. Around the World, 1943-46; (with husband) TV series Inside U.S.A, 1949, Peter and Mary Show, Star of the Family, 1952, Peter Lind Hayes Radio show, CBS, 1954-57; Broadway prodn. Who Was That Lady, 1957-58, Peter Lind Hayes show, ABC-TV, 1958-59, Peter and Mary, ABC-Radio, 1959—, Peter and Mary in Las Vegas; TV-film; Star (with husband) WOR radio show, 6 yrs; TV film series Fin. Planning for Women; (with husband) Film The 5000 Fingers of Dr. T, 1953; Appeared in: (with husband) Film Peter Loves Mary, 1960, When Television Was Live, 1975; films: You Ruined My Life, 1986, Looking To Get Out with Jon Voight, 1985. Roman Catholic. Club: Pelham Country. Home: 3538 Pueblo Way Las Vegas NV 89109-3339

HEALY, PATRICIA COLLEEN, social worker; b. Denver, Aug. 24, 1935; d. Cecil John and Gracia Maude (Walker) Schulte; m. John Patrick Healy III, Aug. 3, 1957 (div. Jan. 1972); 1 child, Sean Patrick. BA, Sacred Heart Coll., Wichita, 1957; MSW, U. Kans., 1983; postgrad., Wichita State U., 1974, 75, 89, Emporia (Kans.) State U., 1990. Lic. specialist clin. social worker, Kans.; cert. in spinal cord injury medicine. Proofreader Wichita Pub. Co., 1953; clk. typist Nat. Sales, Inc., Wichita, 1954-58, Dept. of Army, Ft. Leavenworth, Kans., 1958-60, Air Force, McConnell AFB, Kans., 1962-63; clk., typist VA Regional Office, Wichita, 1963-66; self-employed typist Wichita, 1966-70; ward clk., typist VA Regional Office and VA Med. Ctr., Wichita, 1970-73; vets. benefits counselor VARO, Wichita, 1973-83; social worker VA Med. Ctr., Wichita, 1983—. Author filmstrip, columns, book revs., feature stories and poetry. Former mem. Ctrl. Plains AAA Coun. on Aging; bd. dirs. Ind. Living Ctr. South Ctrl. Kans., 1990-96. Recipient Eddy L. Sutton award, Sunflower Subchapter, Paralyzed Vets. Am., 1992. Mem. Kans. Soc. Clin. Social Workers (mem. editl. bd. 1986-87), Paralyzed Vets. Am., Wichita Assn. of Visually Handicapped (bd. dirs. 1989-92), Kans. Authors Club. Roman Catholic. Office: VA Med Ctr 5500 E Kellogg Dr Wichita KS 67218-1607

HEALY, PHYLLIS M. CORDASCO, school social worker; b. Newark, Oct. 2, 1939; d. Carl and Mae (Seritella) Cordasco; married, Dec. 22, 1966. BA, Caldwell Coll., 1978; MS, Columbia U. Sch. Social Work, 1981; MA, Fairleigh Dickinson U., 1989. Cert. social worker, N.Y.; sch. social work specialist; diplomate in clin. social work; qualified clin. social worker; lic. clin. social worker, N.J. Social worker United Cerebral Palsy of North N.J., East Orange, 1982-84, Cerebral Palsy Assn. Middlesex County, Edison, N.J., 1985-90; sch. social worker, mem. presch. child study team Newark Bd. Edn., 1992, coord. presch. handicapped program Office Child Guidance, 1990-92, coord. presch. hand. prog. Office Child Guidance Placement, 1992, social svcs. coord. N.J. Goodstarts prog. curr. svcs., 1992—; cons. in field. Founding mem. sr. citizen ctr. Borough of Caldwell, chair rent review bd. Recipient Alumna of Yr. award Caldwell Coll., 1985-86, Marion award, 1991. Mem. AAUW (legis. chair 1982-84), Acad. Cert. Social Workers, Coun. for Exceptional Children (N.J. divsn. early childhood pres. 1992-94, Mideast regional coord. for the internat. divsn. for early childhood 1994—), Caldwell Coll. Alumni Assn. (scholar chair 1982-87), Columbia U. Alumni Assn. Roman Catholic. Home: Westover House 519 Bloomfield Ave Caldwell NJ 07006-5550 Office: Newark Bd Edn 2 Cedar St Newark NJ 07102-3015

HEANUE, ANNE ALLEN, librarian; b. Ft. Oglethorpe, Ga., Feb. 7, 1940; d. James Edward and Mary (Dennean) Allen; m. Kevin E. Heanue, July 20, 1963; children: Mary, Brian, Patricia. BA cum laude, Dunbarton Coll., 1962; MA, Georgetown U., 1966; MS in Libr. Sci., Cath. U. Am., 1976. Libr. Deloitte Haskins and Sells, Washington, 1977-79; asst. to dir. Am. Libr. Assn., Washington, 1979-81, asst. dir., 1981-84, assoc. dir., 1984—. Bd. dirs. Alexandria (Va.) LWV, 1967-78; chmn. Alexandria Spl. Edn. adv. com., 1978-79; mem. Alexandria Gypsy Moth Control Commn., 1991—. Recipient Fed. Librs. Round Table Achievement award, 1988. Mem. ALA, Am. Soc. Assn. Execs., D.C. Libr. Assn. (bd. dirs. 1994—), Beta Phi Mu, Pi Gamma Mu. Roman Catholic. Home: 610 Pullman Pl Alexandria VA 22305-1226 Office: ALA 1301 Pennsylvania Ave NW Washington DC 20004

HEAP, SUZANNE RUNDIO, elementary school educator; b. Long Beach, Calif., June 10, 1935; d. George Lionel and Jennie Bolton (Rundio) Heap; children: Katharine Trent, Cecily Gullett. BA, Mary Washington Coll., Fredericsburg, Va., 1957; MA in Edn., Azua-Pacific U., 1978; student, Calif. Western-USIU, San Diego, 1970. Cert. elem. tchr. K-8, Calif., Level I Orff-Schulwerk nat. cert; cert. in master gardening, Calif. Tchr. 5th and 6th grades Chula Vista (Calif.) Elem. Sch. Dist., kindergarten tchr., ret., 1991; cons. bargaining team Chula Vista Edn. Assn. Vol. with U. Calif. Cooperative Extension/U.S. Dept. Agr. Vol. numerous civic orgns.; exec. com. bd., recording sec. U. Calif. Coop. Ext. Master Gardener, San Diego County. Recipient Instruction grant, ORFF Instrumentarium, We Honor Ours award San Diego county svc. ctr. coun. Calif. Tchrs. Assn., 1991. Mem. Calif. Ret. Tchrs. Assn., NSF Math. Inst. Univ. Calif. San Diego, Am. ORFF-Schulwerk Assn. (bd. sec. San Diego chpt. 1991-93). Home: 620 1st St Coronado CA 92118-1202

HEAP, SYLVIA STUBER, civic worker; b. Clifton Springs, N.Y., Sept. 25, 1929; d. Stanley Irving and Helen (Hill) Stuber; BA cum laude, Bates Coll., 1950; postgrad. U. Conn. Sch. Social Work, 1952-54, Boston U. Sch. Social Work, 1953-54, SUNY, Brockport, 1979, SUNY-Potsdam, 1980, MS in Adult Edn., Syracuse U., 1989; m. Walker Ratcliffe Heap, June 9, 1951; children: Heidi Anne, Cynthia Joan, Walker Ratcliffe III. Dir. Y-Teens, YWCA, Holyoke, Mass., 1950-51; social group worker West Haven (Conn.) Community House, 1951-54; program dir. YWCA, Ann Arbor, 1954-55, part-time, 1955-59; mem. adv. bd. div. continuing edn. Jefferson Community Coll., 1965—, chmn. adv. bd., 1968—; pres. Jefferson County Med. Soc. Aux., 1971-72; bd. dirs. St. Lawrence Valley Ednl. TV, 1973-83, sec., 1976-80, treas., 1980-82; v.p., 1982-83, dir. Chem. People Project, 1983; bd. dirs. Watertown Lyric Theatre, 1973-83; bd. dirs. N.Y. State Med. Soc. Aux., 1974-85, 2d v.p. bd., 1979-80; fitness instr. Jefferson Community Coll., Watertown, 1977-86; chmn. health projects N.Y. State Med. Soc. Aux., 1981-85. Named Citizen of Yr. Greater Watertown C. of C., 1975, Friend of Community Colls. N.Y. State Bd. Trustees, 1988. Mem. AAUW, Friends of Pub. TV, Coll. Women's Club Jefferson County, Phi Beta Kappa. Unitarian Universalist. (UN office envoy 1978—, St. Lawrence dist. envoy 1992—).

HEARN, JOYCE CAMP, retired state legislator, educator; b. Cedartown, Ga., d. J.C. and Carolyn (Carter) Camp; m. Thomas Harry Hearn (dec.); children: Theresa Hearn Potts Bailey, Kimberly Ann Johnson, Carolyn Lee Becker. Student, U. Ga.; BA, Ohio State U., 1957; postgrad, U. S.C. Former high sch. tchr.; dist. mgr. U.S. Census, 2d Congl. Dist., 1970; mem. S.C. Ho. of Reps., 1975-89, asst. minority leader, 1976-78, 86-89; chmn. commn. alcohol beverage control, 1989-91; pres., cons. Hearn & Assocs., Columbia, S.C., 1995—. Mem. Richland County Planning Commn., 1974-76; bd. dirs. Meml. Youth Ctr. and Stage South; chmn. Sexual Assault Awareness Week; vice chmn. Dist. Republican Com., 1968; Rep. chmn. 2d Congl. Dist., 1969; Rep. chmn. Richland County, 1972; del., platform com. Rep. Nat. Conv., 1980, 84; moderator Kathwood Bapt. Ch., 1979-80, former asst. Sunday Sch. tchr.; bd. dirs. Small Bus. Devel. Ctr. S.C., Columbia Coll. Bd. Vis., Columbia Urban League, Fedn. of Blind; trustee Columbia Mus. Art; apptd. to Alcohol Beverage Control Bd., 1989, apptd. chmn. commn., 1990-92, commr., 1991-94; bd. dirs. Lupus Found., 1990—; chair nat. adv. com. Occupational Safety and Health, 1980-88. Recipient Outstanding Citizen award Columbia Rape Coalition, 1977, Disting. Service award Claims Mgmt. Assn. S.C., 1977, Nat. Fedn. Blind S.C., 1978, Columbia Urban League, 1983, MADD, 1985, Outstanding Legislator of Yr. award Alcohol and Drug Abuse Assn., 1980, Retarded Citizens Assn., 1982, S.C. Rehab. Assn., 1984, S.C. Assn. of Deaf, 1987, Legislator of Yr., Fedn. of Blind, 1988, Disting. Legislator, DAV, 1989; Honoree, Easter Seals, 1989; numerous other awards. Mem. Nat. Order of Women Legislators (v.p., pres.), Order of the Palmetto, S.C. Women's Club, Columbia Women's Club (bd. dirs.), Larkspar Garden Club.

HEARN, KATHLEEN K. (KATHLEEN KLOTZ CROSHAL), judge, lawyee; b. Sandusky, Ohio, Mar. 21, 1947; d. Earl A. and Mary W. (Donahue) Klotz; m. Dane P. Winters, Nov. 14, 1964 (div. Feb. 1972); children: Lisa C. Winters, Timothy D. Winters; m. Bruce L. Hearn, Apr. 18, 1981 (div. Dec. 1986); 1 child: Cassandra; m. James M. Croshal, May 3, 1987. BA Communications and Theatre, U. Colo., 1973, JD, 1979. Gen. mgr. Goldenrod Showboat, St. Louis, 1975; asst. mgr. box office, adminstrv. asst. Heritage Sq. Opera House, Golden, Colo., 1974-75, box office mgr., bus. mgr., 1976, bookkeeper, adminstrv. asst., 1975-76; bookkeeper Internat. Sports Distbrs., Boulder, Colo., 1978-79; student atty. Legal Aid and Defender Program, 1977-78; dep. dist. atty. 10th Jud. Ct., Pueblo, Colo., 1979-81; assoc. J.E. Losavio Jr., Pueblo, 1981; pvt. practice Pueblo, 1981-87; asst. to county atty. Pueblo County Dept. Social Svcs., 1982-88; assoc. Petersen & Fonda, P.C., Pueblo, Colo., 1987-91; ptnr. Petersen & Fonda, P.C., Pueblo, 1992-95; judge Pueblo (Colo.) County Ct., 1995—. Mem. ABA, Colo. Bar Assn. (bd. govs. 1994—), Pueblo County Bar Assn. (exec. com., v.p., pres. elect 1992-93, pres. 1993-94), Colo. Trial Lawyers Assn., Pueblo C. of C., Kiwanis Internat. Club, Phi Delta Phi (outstanding grad. region X), others. Office: Pueblo County Ct 10th Judicial Dist 320 W 10th St Pueblo CO 81003

HEARN, MARY ROSAMOND, accountant; b. Meriden, Conn., July 22, 1957; d. Robert James Jr. and Rosamond Gertrude (Ernst) H. BS, U. N.C., 1986. CPA, Md. Bus. mgr. Allegro Music Svc., Silver Spring, Md., 1986-93; acct. Foxx & Co., CPAs, Bethesda, Md., 1993-95; pres. Mary R. Hearn & Assocs., 1995—. Vol. Friends of the Nat. Zoo, Washington, 1991, The Nature Conservancy, Chevy Chase, Md., 1994-95, Whitbread Chesapeake, 1996. Mem. NAFE, AICPA, Md. Assn. CPAs, Women's Sailing Assn. (co-founder Chesapeake Bay 1996). Home: PO Box 6366 Annapolis MD 21401

HEARN, SHARON SKLAMBA, lawyer; b. New Orleans, Aug. 15, 1956; d. Carl John and Marjorie C. (Wimberly) Sklamba; m. Curtis R. Hearn. BA magna cum laude, Loyola U., New Orleans, 1977; JD cum laude, Tulane U., 1980. Bar: La. 1980, Tex. 1982; cert. tax specialist. Law clk. to presiding judge U.S. Ct. Appeals Fed. Cir., Washington, 1980-81; assoc. Johnson & Swanson, Dallas, 1981-84, Kullman Inman Bee & Downing, New Orleans, 1984—. Recipient Am. Legion award, 1970. Mem. ABA, La. State Bar Assn., Tex. State Bar Assn., Dallas Women Lawyers Assn. Democrat. Roman Catholic. Home: 44 Swallow St New Orleans LA 70124-4404 Office: Kullman Inman Bee & Downing 615 Howard Ave New Orleans LA 70130-3917

HEARNE, CAROLYN FOX, art and history educator, artist; b. Brownwood, Tex., June 15, 1945; d. Marshal D. and Lena May (Parson) Fox; m. Roy Nicholas Hearne, Apr. 14, 1968; children: Jason Nicholas, Angela Della. BA in Spanish, Art, So. Meth. U., 1967; MA in Fine Arts, U. Tex., Tyler, 1985. Astrology lady, commls. K-BUY Radio, Ft. Worth, 1970-71; decorator, exec. dir. Holiday Inns, Inc., Houston, 1971-73; exec./bilingual sec. Kennecott Copper Corp., Houston, 1973-74; owner Fox-Hearne Studio, Kilgore, Tex., 1977—; art/music, history tchr. LeTourneau U., Longview, Tex., 1988—; co-chmn. LeTourneau Fine Arts Week, Longview, 1992—; demonstrator, lectr. mus. and art groups, Longview and Tyler, 1979—; judge East Tex. art groups, Longview, Kilgore, and Henderson, 1990—; invited participant Master Artists Workshop, L.I. U., 1990. Prin. works include book cover, Gory Days, 1987, bronze sculpture, Frontier Spirit, 1983 (Citation 1983), sculpture for dedication, Gussie Nell Davis, 1983, commnd. A Race Against Time, 1978 (Spl. award 1978), model for catalouge, TV commls. for Strictly Petites, 1987—; exhbns. incl. Tex. Art Gallery, 1990-92. Bd. dirs. Kilgore Hist. Preservation Found., Kilgore, 1989—, past sec., past pres.; chmn. art fest Kilgore Improvement and Beautification Assn., 1981-86; chmn. Kilgore Civic Ball, 1980; decorator Jr. League Charity Ball, Longview, 1992; pres. Kilgore Garden Club, 1982-83; chmn. Theatre Restoration Kilgore, 1989-92; life mem. Tex. PTA, 1978—; bd. dirs., 1st v.p. Longview Art Mus., 1994—, exhbns. and acquisitions chmn., 1995-97. Recipient 5 Citation awards East Tex. Classics, 1981, Outstanding Achievement award Artitudes mag., 1989. Mem. East Tex. Fine Arts Assn. (pres. 1981-83, Top Citation award 1984), Tex. Fine Arts Assn., LeTourneau Faculty Orgn., Coterie Club (pres. 1990). Republican. Presbyterian. Home: 8 Briar Ln Kilgore TX 75662-2201 Office: LeTourneau Univ Mobberly Ave PO Box 7001 Longview TX 75607-7001

HEARTT, CHARLOTTE BEEBE, university official; b. N.Y.C., Nov. 12, 1933; d. Stacey Kile and Charlotte Beebe; BA, Wellesley Coll., 1954; m. William Hollis Peirce, 1954; children: Daniel Converse, William Kile; m. Stephen Heartt, 1962; children: Thomas Beebe, Sarah Lincoln. Intern Office of V.p. Richard Nixon, Washington, 1953; asst. in Computing Numerical Analysis Lab. U. Wis., Madison, 1954-56; dir. fund raising Boston Arts festival, 1961; sec. to dean coll. rels. Radcliffe Coll., Cambridge, Mass., 1961-62; sec. to chmn. dept. city planning Harvard U., Cambridge, 1962; Fulbright program adviser, study abroad adviser Brandeis U., 1966-71, dir. office internat. programs, 1971-75, dir. found. and corp. rels., 1976-79; dir. corp. rels., asst. dir. devel. Smith Coll., Northampton, Mass., 1979-81, dir. devel., 1981-95, dir. prin. gifts, 1995—. Mem. Commonwealth Task Force on the Open Univ., 1973; bd. dirs. Council on Internat. Ednl. Exchange, 1973-77, mem. exec. com., 1975-77; bd. dirs. Boston Area Seminar for Internat. Students, 1973-76; mem. Sect. on U.S. Study Abroad (nat. sec., regional rep. 1972-74), Nat. Assn. Fgn. Student Affairs (nat. commr. liaison), Nat. Assn. Women Deans, Adminstrs. and Counselors (internat. students and programs com. 1974-76), Nat. Soc. Fund Raisers, Council for Advancement and Support Edn.; mem. adv. com. New England Colls. Fund, 1981-95; trustee Berkshire Sch., 1989—. Home: 51 Belmont Ave Northampton MA 01060-3705 Office: Smith Coll Devel Office Clark Hall 50 Elm St Northampton MA 01060-2935

HEATH, MARIWYN DWYER, writer, legislative issues consultant; b. Chgo., May 1, 1935; d. Thomas Leo and Winifred (Brennan) Dwyer; m. Eugene R. Heath, Sept. 3, 1956; children: Philip Clayton, Jeffrey Thomas. BJ, U. Mo., 1956. Mng. editor Chemung Valley Reporter, Horseheads, N.Y., 1956-57; self-employed freelance writer, platform speaker, editor Tech. Transls., Dayton, Ohio, 1966—; cons. Internat. Women's Commn., 1975-76; ERA coord. Nat. Fedn. Bus. and Profl. Women's Clubs, 1974-82; mem. polit. and mgmt. cons. ERAmerica, 1976-82, exec. dir., 1982-88; pres. Miami Valley Regional Transit Authority, 1986-88, bd. dirs. 1984-91; chair Regional Transit Coalition, 1991-94. Author: 75 Years and Beyond-BPW/USA, 1994. Mem. Gov. Ohio Task Force Credit for Women, 1973; mem. Midwest regional adv. com. SBA, 1976-82; mem. Ohio Women's Commn., 1990—, vice chair, 1993-96, chair 1996—; pres. Dayton Pres.'s Club, 1973-74; chmn. Ohio Coalition ERA Implementation, 1974-75; appt. joint civilian orientation conf., U.S. Dept. Def., 1988. Recipient Legion of Honor award Dayton Pres.'s Club, 1987, Keeper of Flame award Ohio Sec. of State, 1990; named One of 10 Outstanding Women of World Soroptimist Internat., 1982; named to Ohio Women's Hall of Fame. Mem. AAUW (dir. Dayton 1965-72, Woman of Year award Dayton 1974), Nat. Fedn. Bus. and Profl. Women's Clubs (pres. Dayton 1967-69, Ohio 1976-77, nat. polit. action com. 1985—, chmn. 1988—), Miami Valley Mil. Affairs Assn. (bd. dirs.), Ohio Women (v.p. 1983-86, bd. dirs. 1977-89), Assn. Women Execs., Women in Communications. Republican. Roman Catholic. Address: 10 Wisteria Dr Dayton OH 45419-3451

HEATH, MARY ELIZABETH, elementary education educator; b. Tampa, Fla., Nov. 19, 1947; d. Ernest Paul and Bessie (Black) Maney; m. Richard Edwin Heath, Dec. 21, 1968; children: Taliver B., Forrest J. BS in Human Devel., U. N.C., 1980; MEd, Coastal Carolina U., 1987; postgrad., Harvard U., 1996. Cert. early childhood edn. tchr., cert. elem. sch. prin. Kindergarten tchr. Horry County Schs., Myrtle Beach, S.C., 1982-96; asst. prin. Myrtle Beach Primary Sch. and Elem. Sch. Contbr. articles to profl. jours. Sec. Rep. Precinct, Garden City, S.C., 1982. Named 1st Runner-up Tchr. of Yr., Horry County, 1993. Mem. Phi Delta Kappa (newsletter editor 1993—), Alpha Delta Kappa (pres. 1991-93). Republican. Methodist. Home: 818 River Oak Dr Murrells Inlet SC 29576 Office: Myrtle Beach Elem Oak St Myrtle Beach SC 29577

HEATHERLEY, MELODY ANN, nursing administrator; b. Dallas, Apr. 15, 1957; d. Harold Ray and Barbara Ann (Roebuck) Jones; m. James Lawrence Heatherley, July 21, 1982. BSN, U. Tex., Arlington, 1979; postgrad., Amber U. RN, Tex., Fla. Surg. nurse St. Paul Hosp., Dallas, 1979, Mesquite (Tex.) Meml. Hosp., 1979-80; charge nurse All Saints Hosp.-Main, Ft. Worth, 1980-87; house supr., charge nurse All Saints Cityview Hosp., Ft. Worth, 1987-88; staff nurse ICU, critical care coord. Hosp. Corp. Am. Med. Plz. Hosp., Ft. Worth, 1986-89; staff nurse ICU, CCU Harris Meth. Hurst, Euless, Bedford, Bedford, Tex., 1989-91; staff nurse rehab. unit Harris Meth. HEB, Bedford, 1991; charge nurse surg. ICU, cardiovascular recovery Humana Hosp.-Lucerne, Orlando, Fla., 1991-93, relief house supr., 1991-93; divsn. supr. nursing adminstrn. St. Paul Med. Ctr., Dallas, 1993-94; adminstrv. supr Baylor Med. Ctr. Ellis County, Waxahachie, Tex., 1994—. Mem. AACN, ANA, NAFE, Assn. Rehab. Nurses, Tex. Orgn. Nurse Execs., Tex. Nurses Assn. Episcopalian. Office: Baylor Med Ctr Ellis County Waxahachie Campus 1405 W Jefferson St Waxahachie TX 75165-2231

HEATLEY, CONNIE LA MOTTA, association executive; b. Bronx, N.Y., Oct. 10, 1942; d. Salvatore Charles and Mary Moscatiello LaMotta; children: Raphael, Peter, David. BA, SUNY, Albany, 1969; postgrad., Fordham U., 1974. Activities coord. San Diego Assn. for the Retarded, 1970-72; edn. program dir. Edn. Ctrs. of Newark Archdiocese, 1973-79; dir. comm. tng. Riverside Eating Disorder Clinic, Secaucus, N.J., 1979-84; comm. coord. Sun Chem. Corp., N.Y.C., 1984-86; pub. rels. dir. Nat. Coffee Assn., N.Y.C., 1986-87; v.p. pub. rels. Direct Mktg. Assn., N.Y.C., 1987-96, sr. v.p. pub. rels., 1987. Mem. Pub. Rels. Soc. Am., Women in Communications, Am. Soc. Assn. Execs. (assoc.). Episcopalian. Office: Direct Mktg Assn 1120 Ave of Americas New York NY 10036-6700

HEATON, HELEN TURNER, media specialist; b. Teague, Tex., July 31, 1940; d. James Roy and Beatrice Ione (Beaver) Turner; children: Brent Turner Heaton, Lori Anne Heaton. BS, Stephen F. Austin State U., Nacogdoches, Tex., 1962; MLS, Sam Houston State U., Huntsville, Tex., 1988. Tchr. English Lufkin (Tex.) Ind. Sch. Dist., 1978-84; media specialist Zavalla (Tex.) Ind. Sch. Dist., 1984-91, Hudson Ind. Sch. Dist., Lufkin, 1991—. Mem. AAUW, Tex. Libr. Assn., Tex. Assn. Sch. Librs., Tex. State Tchrs. Assn., Tex. Computer Educators Assn., Delta Kappa Gamma. Baptist. Office: Hudson Ind Sch Dist RR 12 Box 8600 Lufkin TX 75904-9329

HEATON, JANET NICHOLS, artist, art gallery director; b. Miami, Fla., May 27, 1936; d. Wilmer Elwood and Katherine Elizabeth (Rodgers) Nichols; m. Wendell Carlos Heaton, Apr. 14, 1956; children: Benjamin Nichols Heaton, Nancy Elizabeth Breedlove. Student, Fla. State U., 1954-56. Artist Heaton's Studio & Gallery, Lake Park, Fla., 1976—, dir., 1979—. Exhibited in group shows at Leight Yawkey Woodson Art Mus., Wausau, Wis., 1988-89, 91-93, 95, 96, Norton Gallery Art, West Palm Beach, Fla., 1989, Mt. Kenya Safari Club, Kenya, East Africa, 1989, Prestige Gallery, Toronto, Can., 1989, Kimball Art Ctr., Park City, Utah, 1990-91, Grand Cen. Gallery, N.Y.C., 1990, Gallery Fine Arts, Ft. Myers, Fla., 1990, Cornell Fine Art Mus., Winter Park, Fla., 1990, Cen. Park Zoo Gallery, N.Y.C., 1991, Norton Art Gallery, Palm Beach, Fla., 1992, The Art League Marco Island, Fla., 1993, 96, Washington State Hist. Soc. Mus., Tacoma, 1993, Leigh Yawkey Woodson Art Mus., Wausau, 1993, Old Sch. Sq. Cultural Arts Ctr., Delray Beach, Fla., 1993, 94, The Salmagundi Club, N.Y.C., 1994, J.N. Bartfield Galleries, N.Y.C., 1994, Pt. Royal Gallery, Naples, Fla., 1994, Brookfield Zoo, Chgo., 1994, Ward Mus. Wildfowl Art, Salisbury, Md., 1995, Easton (Md.) Waterfowl Festival, 1995, Sarasota (Fla.) Visual Art Ctr., 1995, Art League Maro Island, Fla., 1996, Shenandoah Art Ctr., North Wainsboro, Va., 1996, Wendell Gilley Mus., Southwest Harbour, Maine, 1996; represented in permanent collections Leigh Yawkey Woodson Art Mus., State House, Nairobi, Kenya; numerous pvt. collections; subject numerous art jours. Mem. Soc. Animal Artists, Pastel Soc. Am., Fla. Watercolor Soc., Outdoor Writers Assn. Am., Catherine Lorillard Wolfe Art Club, Inc. Home: 11680 Lake Shore Pl North Palm Beach FL 33408 Office: Heatons Studio and Gallery 1169 Old Dixie Hwy Lake Park FL 33403-2330

HEATON, JEAN, early childhood educator; b. Equality, Ill., Feb. 27, 1933; d. Lytle and Loretta (Drone) Mossman; m. Fred T. Heaton, June 10, 1954 (div. Dec. 1979); children: Fred T., Laura, Sheri; m. Michael Marticorena, Mar. 14, 1987. BS in Home Econs., Southern Ill. U., 1955, MS in Edn., 1958; PhD in Child Devel., Early Childhood Edn, Fla. State U., 1971. Cert. secondary educator Ill., Fla., Calif. Tchr. Corham (Ill.) High Sch., 1955-57; rsch. asst. Southern Ill. U., Carbondale, 1957-58; tchr. Jefferson High Sch., Tampa, Fla., 1958-60, Hamilton Jr. High Sch., Oakland, Calif., 1960-61; prof. San Francisco State U., 1961-94; ednl. cons. Dept. Home and Cmty. Devel., U. Monrovia, Liberia, 1982, Calif. State Dept. Edn., 1974-76; mem. adv. bd. Skyline Coll., 1973-94, coord. Study Tours; presenter at profl. confs. Contbr. articles to profl. jours. and newsletters. Recipient Meritorious Performance award SFSU, 1986 and 1989. Mem. Infant/Toddler Consortium San Francisco Bay Area (exec. com. 1988-93), San Francisco/San Mateo Child Care Consortium (exec. com. 1987-93), Calif. Coun. on Children and Youth (exec. com. Region II 1982-90), San Francisco Assn. for Edn. Young Children (pres. 1990-92), AAUW (exec. com. San Mateo br. 1981-83), Pi Lambda Theta, Omicron Nu.

HEBEL, DORIS A., astrologer; b. Chgo., Jan. 1, 1935; d. Erich and Anna Dorothea (Hircy) H.; m. Leon L. Bram, Apr. 29, 1961 (div. Dec. 1973); 2 children. Libr. Campbell-Mithun, Chgo., 1958-61, Kenyon & Eckhardt, Chgo., 1961-64; pres. Astro-Technic Forecasting, Chgo., 1965—. Author: Contemporary Lectures, 1975, Celestial Psychology, 1985; contbr. various articles in astrological jours. and magazines. Mem. Am. Fedn. Astrologers (life), Nat. Coun. for Geocosmic Rsch. (life, nat. bd. dirs. 1975-80), Nat. Astrol. Soc., Assn. for Astrol. Networking, Internat. Soc. for Astrol. Rsch. Home and Office: 151 N Michigan Ave Apt 1001 Chicago IL 60601-7543

HEBENSTREIT, JEAN ESTILL STARK, religion educator, practitioner; d. Charles Dickey and Blanche (Hervey) Stark; student Conservatory of Music, U. Mo. at Kansas City, 1933-34; AB, U. Kans., 1936; m. William J. Hebenstreit, Sept. 4, 1942; children: James B., Mark W. Authorized C.S. practitioner, Kansas City, 1955—; bd. dir. 3d Ch., Kansas City, 1952-55, chmn. bd. 1955, reader, 1959-62; authorized C.S. tchr., C.S.B., 1964—; bd. dirs. First Ch. of Christ Scientist, Boston, 1977-83, chmn. bd., 1981-82; mem. Christian Sci. Bd. of Lectureship, Christian Sci. Bd. Edn. Bd. trustees The Christian Sci. Pub. Soc. Mem. Art of Assembly Parliamentarians (charter, 1st pres.), Pi Epsilon Delta, Alpha Chi Omega (past pres.), Carriage Club. Contbr. articles to C.S. lit. Home: 310 W 49th St Ste A-2 Kansas City MO 64112-2401 Office: 310 W 49th St Ste A-1 Kansas City MO 64112

HEBER, RUTH R., psychologist, consultant; b. Lodz, Poland, June 27, 1935; came to U.S., 1957; d. Moses Zwi and Ryna (Glucklich) Borenstein; m. Jacob Heber, 1955 (div. 1982); children: Ron, Sheldon, Lorraine; m. Lawrence Walter Kullman, 1987. BA in Psychology, CUNY, 1972; MS in Ednl. Psychology and Guidance, Yeshiva U., 1974, PhD in Devel. Psychology, 1979. Lic. psychologist, N.Y. Staff psychotherapist North Suffolk Mental Health Ctr., N.Y., 1980-82; supervising psychologist, clinic and program coord. Creedmoor Psychiat. Ctr., N.Y., 1982-88; dir. East Side Consultation Ctr., N.Y.C., 1988—; adj. asst. prof. psychology Queens Coll., CUNY; cons., lectr. Humanistic Psychology Ctr., N.Y., 1983-93; lectr. psychiatry Mt. Sinai Sch. Medicine, CUNY, 1990-9 5, asst. clin. prof., 1995—; supr. psychiat. residents Mt. Sinai Med. Ctr., N.Y.C., 1989—; adj. prof. The Union Inst. Grad. Sch. Cin., 1991—; participant, supr. Holocaust Survivors Treatment Program, 1993—; pvt. practice; presenter, guest spkr., workshop leader. Mem. APA (program chmn. humanistic psychology divsn. 1988-89, treas. 1989-92, pres. 1993-94, 95—), Am. Acad. Psychotherapists, Internat. Coun. Psychologists, Internat. Assn. Applied Psychology, Internat. Assn. Cross-Cultural Psychology, Am. Group Psychotherapy Assn., Ea. Group Psychotherapy Assn., N.Y. State Psychological Assn. (disaster/crisis response network 1993—, colleague assistance program com. 1992—), Assoc. Alumni Mt. Sinai Med. Ctr., Phi Beta Kappa, Psi Chi, Kappa Delta Pi, Delta Phi Alpha. Office: 200 E 33rd St Apt 4I New York NY 10016-4826

HEBERLE, JANET MAXINE, business educator; b. Pitts., Nov. 22, 1940; d. Mathew Elmer and Gladys Irene (Pritts) Miller; m. Raymond Russell Heberle, Aug. 22, 1964; 1 child, Sarah Ashley. BS in Bus Edn., Indiana U. Pa., 1962, MS in Bus. Edn., 1967. Cert. supervisory and secondary sch. adminstrn. Bus. tchr. Sharpsburg (Pa.) Schs., 1962-64; bus. tchr., dept. head Shaler Area Sch. Dist., Glenshaw, Pa., 1964—. Mem. NEA, Pa. State Edn. Assn., Shaler Area Edn. Assn. Home: 472 Old Mill Rd Pittsburgh PA 15238-1916 Office: Shaler Area Sch Dist 1800 Mt Royal Blvd Glenshaw PA 15116

HEBERT, DONNA MARIE, food product executive; b. Worcester, Mass., June 20, 1951; d. Charles George and Lena Marie (Diliddo) Olson; m. Raymond Louis Hebert, June 17, 1972; children: Wendy Ann, Daniel Raymond. Student, Quinsigamond C.C., Worcester, 1969-70, Assumption Coll., Worcester, 1970-72. Sales person F.W. Woolworth, Worcester, 1967-69; rschr. State Mut. Life Ins., Worcester, 1969-70; bus. office pers. Assumption Coll., Worcester, 1970-73; pres. Stage Stop Candy, Ltd., Dennis Port, Mass., 1982—. Treas. troop 82 Boy Scouts Am., South Dennis, Mass., 1988-93; Eucharistic Min. Recipient Bronze Pelican, Diocesan Scout Office, Fall River, 1990. Mem. Dennis C. of C. (mem. govt. affairs com.), Cape Cod Pers. Assn., D-Y Band Parents. Roman Catholic. Office: Stage Stop Candy Ltd 411 Main St Dennis Port MA 02639-1308

HEBERT, ELLEN JAYNE, casino supervisor; b. Jersey City, N.J., Nov. 9, 1956; d. William Henry and Margene Emma (Garrison) Scheurle; m. Joseph Edward Scarlatella, June 9, 1979 (div. 1987); children: Amy Jo, Joseph William, David Gene; m. Glenn Melvin Hebert, Nov. 8, 1991. Grad. h.s., Ventura, Calif. Owner, operator Joe's Mountain Copy, Running Springs, Calif., 1983-88; gaming dealer Sam's Town Goldriver, Laughlin, Nev., 1988-90; dual rate floor person Flamingo Hilton, Laughlin, 1990-95; supr. casino pit Avi Hotel & Casino, Laughlin, 1995—; instr. Mohave C.C., Bullhead City, Ariz., 1994—. Leader Girl Scouts Am., Needles, Calif., 1988; founder Sheriff's Safety Kids, Needles, 1989. Lutheran. Home: 2047 Carty Way Needles CA 92363 Office: Avi Hotel & Casino 10000 Aha Macav Pkwy Laughlin NV 89028

HEBERT, JANICE ELAINE, lawyer; b. Morgan City, La., Jan. 16, 1957; d. Earl Joseph and Nelwyn Elaine (Shepherd) H.; m. Arthur Joseph Cormier III, Oct. 2, 1987; children: Stephan Williams, Carlin Anne, Lillian Elaine. BA, U. Southwestern La., 1987; JD, La. State U., 1990. Bar: La., U.S. Ct. Appeals (5th cir.), U.S. Dist. Ct. (we. dist.) La. Law clerk Hon. Michael J. McNulty 16th J.D.C., La., 1990-92; sr. law clerk Hon. Richard T. Haik U.S. Dist. Ct., 1992-95; asst. U.S. atty. we. dist. La. U.S. Atty.'s Office, Lafayette, 1995—. Mem. Dem. Nat. Party, Spouse's Assn. Lafayette Police Dept., 1987-93; charter mem. Rape Crisis Ctr. Lafayette, 1982-87; pres., charter mem. Women's Legal Alliance, 1988-90. Recipient John Marshall Alternate Dispute Resolution award U.S. Atty. Gen. Janet Reno, 1996; La. State U. scholar, 1987-88; recipient Liaison award Rape Crisis Ctr., 1985. Mem. La. Bar Assn., Lafayette Parish Bar Assn., Lafayette Assn. Women Attys., ACLU. Office: US Attys Office 600 Jefferson St Ste 1000 Lafayette LA 70501

HEBERT, MARY OLIVIA, retired librarian; b. St. Louis, Nov. 11, 1921; d. Arthur Frederick and Clara Marie (Golden) Meyer; certificate librarianship, Washington U., St. Louis, 1972; m. N. Hal Hebert, Sept. 9, 1943 (dec. Mar. 1969); children—Olivia, Stephen (dec.), Christina, Deborah, Beth, John, James. Secretarial positions in advt., 1942-43; v.p. Hebert Advt. Co., 1955-66; adminstrv. asst. communications Blue Cross, St. Louis, 1966-69, librarian, 1969-91, ret., 1991. Mem. Spl. Libraries Assn. (pres. St. Louis Metro chpt. 1984), St. Louis Med. Librs., St. Louis Regional Libr. Network (coun. 1986-89). Roman Catholic.

HECETA, ESTHERBELLE AGUILAR, anesthesiologist; b. Cebu City, Philippines, Jan. 1, 1935; came to U.S., 1962, naturalized, 1981; d. Serafin Aquilar and Elsie (Nichols) Aguilar; m. Wilmer G., Heceta, Apr. 5, 1962; children: W. Cristina, W. Elgine, Wuela E. BS Chemistry cum laude, Silliman U., Dumaguete City, Philippines, 1955, BS cum laude, 1956; MD cum laude, U. East Ramon Magsaysay Meml. Med. Center, Quezon City, Philippines, 1961. Diplomate Am. Bd. Anesthesiology, Philippine Bd. Anesthesiology. Intern, Youngstown (Ohio) Hosp. Assocs., 1962-63, resident in anesthesiology, 1963-66; anesthesiologist Salem (Ohio) City Hosp., 1967, St. Joseph's Hosp., Manapla, Philippines, 1967-72; instr. dept. anesthesiology U. Tenn., Memphis, 1972-74; staff anesthesiologist Ohio Valley Med. Ctr., Wheeling, W.Va., 1974—; anesthesiologist Bellaire (Ohio) City Hosp., 1975—; staff anesthesiologist East Ohio Regional Hosp., Martins Ferry, Ohio, 1989—; Joint Conf. Comm. for Profl Affairs, Ohio Valley Med. Ctr., 1992—, mem. exec. comm., sec.-treas. med. dental staff, 1992—, pres.-elect, 1993-94, pres. med. dental staff, 1994-95, physician reviewer Anesthesiology W. Va. Med. Inst., 1992—, mem. Claims Review Panel W. Va. Med. Assn., 1990—; Vol. med.-surg. mission to Philippines, 1982-90. Fellow Am. Coll. Anesthesiology; mem. AMA, Am. Soc. Anesthesiologists, Ohio Valley Philipine Med. Assn. (pres. 1988-90), Tri-State Phillipine-Am. Assn. (pres. 1991-92), Assn. Philippine Physicians in Am., Philippine Soc. Anesthesiologists in Am., W.Va. Soc. Anesthesiologists, Internat. Anesthesia Research Soc., Am. Med. Women's Assn. (organizer, pres. 1983, regional gov. Region IV 1987-89), W.Va. Med. Soc., Ohio County Med. Soc. Presbyterian. Home: 15 Holly Rd Wheeling WV 26003-5656 Office: Ohio Valley Med Ctr Dept Anesthesiology 2000 Eoff St Wheeling WV 26003-3871

HECHLER, ELLEN ELISSA, elementary education educator; b. Detroit, May 20, 1954; d. Mark and Rose (Rifkin) H. BS, Wayne State U., 1976, MEd, 1980, EdD in Curriculum and Instrn., 1995. Math. tchr. Detroit Pub. Schs., 1977—; presenter workshops in field. Author: (book) Simulated, Real-Life Experiences Using Classified Ads in the Classroom, 1991, A Mathematical Word Search Puzzle Book, 1996, (card game) Mental Math, 1991, Mental Math Series II, 1992; developer in field. Bd. dirs. Orgn. for Rehab. Through Tng., Southfield, 1980—. Recipient scholarship Stephen Bufton Meml. Educators Fund, 1992-93. Mem. ASCD, Detroit Area Coun. Tchrs. of Math. (pres. 1988-89), Mich. Coun. Tchrs. of Math. (exec. bd. dirs. 1980-90, presenter workshops), Nat. Coun. Tchrs. of Math. (presenter workshops), Nat. Coun. Suprs. Math., Mich. Assn. Computer Users in Learning, Southwest Ont. Math. Educators (presenter workshops), Am. Bus. Women's Assn. Office: MidMath PO Box 2892 Farmington MI 48333-2892

HECHT, MARIE BERGENFELD, retired educator, author; b. N.Y.C., Oct. 21, 1918; d. Frank Falle and Marie (Trommer) Bergenfeld; BA, Goucher Coll., 1939; MA, New Sch. for Social Research, 1971; m. Morton Hecht, Jr., Dec. 17, 1937 (div.); children: Ann (Mrs. David Bloomfield), Margaret, Laurence, Andrew. Tchr. Am. history Mineola High Sch., Garden City Park, N.Y., 1960-80. Mem. Am. Hist. Assn., Orgn. Am. Historians. Author (with Herbert S. Parmet): Aaron Burr: Portrait of an Ambitious Man, 1967; Never Again: A President Runs for a Third Term, 1968; John Quincy Adams: A Personal History of An Independent Man, 1972; The Women, Yes, 1973; Beyond the Presidency: The Residues of Power, 1976; Odd Destiny: The Life of Alexander Hamilton, 1982, The Church on the Hill, 1987. Address: 5 Hewlett Pl Great Neck NY 11024-1605

HECHT, MARJORIE MAZEL, editor; b. Cambridge, Mass., Dec. 21, 1942; d. Mark and Theresa (Shuman) Mazel; m. Laurence Michael Hecht, July 2, 1972. B.A. cum laude, Smith Coll., 1964; postgrad., London Sch. Econs., 1964-65; M.S.W, Columbia U., 1967. Dir. Forest Neighborhood Service Ctr., N.Y.C., 1967-70, Wiltwyck Sch. for Boys, Bronx Center, N.Y., 1970-73; mng. editor Fusion Mag., Washington, 1977-87, 21st Century Sci. & Technol. Mag., Washington, 1987—. Co-author: Beam Defense: An Alternative to Nuclear Destruction, 1983 (Aviation and Space Writers award 1983); editor: Colonize Space! Open the Age of Reason, 1985, The Holes in the Ozone Scare: The Scientific Evidence That the Sky Isn't Falling, 1992. Press rep. LaRouche Campaign, N.Y.C., 1984. Democrat. Jewish. Office: 21st Century Sci & Technol Mag PO Box 16285 Washington DC 20041-6285

HECHT, SYLVIA LILLIAN, pianist, educator; b. Jacksonville, Fla., Feb. 2, 1920; d. Samuel and Florence (Rabinowitz) Haimowitz; m. Erwin Hecht, June 18, 1945 (div. 1950); 1 child, Francia De Beer. BMus, Rollins Coll., 1942; student with Carl Friedberg, Juilliard Sch., 1940; student with Isidor Philipp, Paris Conservatory, N.Y.C., 1942-44. Mem. piano faculty N.Y. Coll. Music, N.Y.C., 1943-69, chmn. preparatory divs., 1967-69; dir. Sci. Devel. Programs Inc. Bank St. Coll., N.Y.C., 1976-78, Fordham U., N.Y.C., 1978—; vendor ESEA Title II Eisenhower Profl. Devel. Program N.Y. Bd. Edn., Bklyn., 1990—; cons. after sch. sci. programs pub. and ind. schs., N.Y.C., 1976—, La Guardia H.S. Performing Arts (Piano), N.Y.C., 1980—. Active sci. scholarships to Fordham U. programs N.Y.C. Pub. Schs., 1978—, free in-house sci. programs and auditoriums Inner City Pub. Schs. of Manhattan, 1986—. Recipient Young Artists award Nat. Fedn. Music Clubs, L.A., 1941; grantee Richard Lounsbery Found., 1987-89, Chase Manhattan Bank, 1992-95, Citibank, Chem. Bank, others. Mem. Assoc. Music Tchrs. League of N.Y. (bd. dirs. 1977-80), Phi Beta, Pi Kappa Lambda. Democrat. Jewish.

HECKART, EILEEN, actress; b. Columbus, Ohio, Mar. 29, 1919; d. Leo Herbert and Esther (Stark) Purcell; m. John Harrison Yankee Jr., June 26, 1943; children: Mark Kelly, Philip Craig, Luke Brian. BA, Ohio State U., 1942, LHD (hon.), 1981; postgrad., Am. Theatre Wing, 1944-48; LLD, Sacred Heart U., Bridgeport, Conn., 1973; DFA (hon.), Niagara U., 1981. Broadway plays include Voice of the Turtle, 1944, Brighten the Corner, 1946, They Knew What They Wanted, 1948, Stars Weep, 1949, The Traitor, 1950, Hilda Crane, 1951, In Any Language, 1953, Picnic, 1953, Bad Seed, 1955 (Tony nomination), A View From the Bridge, 1956, Dark at the Top of the Stairs, 1958 (Tony nomination), Invitation to a March, 1960 (Tony nomination), Everybody Loves Opal, 1961, Family Affair, 1962, Too True to Be Good, 1963, And Things That Go Bump in the Night, 1965, Barefoot in the Park, 1965-66, You Know I Can't Hear You When the Water's Running, 1967, The Mother Lover, 1968, Butterflies Are Free, 1969 (Tony nomination), Veronica's Room, 1973, The Effect of Gamma Rays on Man-in-the-Moon Marigolds, 1971, Remember Me, 1975, Mother Courage and Her Children, 1975, Mrs. Gibbs in Our Town, 1976, Elemosynary, 1987, Northeast Local, 1995; one-woman shows: Eleanor, 1976, Ladies at the Alamo, 1977, Margaret Sanger-Unfinished Business, 1989, The Cemetery Club, 1990, Love Letters, 1991, Driving Miss Daisy, 1991; movies include Miracle in the Rain, Bad Seed (Oscar nomination), Bus Stop, Hot Spell, Daily Citation, 1956 (Oscar nomination, Drama Critics award), My Six Loves, 1962, Up the Down Staircase, 1966, Save Me a Place at Forest Lawn, 1967 (Emmy award), No Way to Treat a Lady, 1968, Butterflies Are Free, 1972 (Acad. award, Straw Hat award 1973, 75, 77), Zandy's Bride, 1974, The Hiding Place, 1975, Burnt Offerings, 1975, Wedding Band, 1975 (Emmy nomination), Heartbreak Ridge, 1986, The Cemetery Club, 1990, Love Letters, 1990, Driving Miss Daisy, 1991; TV movies, 1947—; TV series Trauma Center, Annie McGuire, 1988-89, Partners in Crime, Mary Tyler Moore Show, 1976, 77 (2 Emmy nominations), Back Stairs at the White House, 1979 (Emmy nomination), FDR's Last Year, 1987, The Cosby Show, 1987 (Emmy nomination), (daytime show) One Life to Live, 1987 (Emmy nomination), Love and War (Emmy award, Guest Actress - Comedy Series, 1994), The Five Mrs. Buchanans, 1994. Recipient Outer Circle award, 1953, Daniel Blum award, 1953, Sylvania TV award, 1954, Donaldson award, 1955, Hollywood Fgn. Press award, 1956, March of Dimes award, 1970, Aegis award, 1970, Ohio State U. Centennial award, 1970, Gov.'s award of Ohio, 1977, Ohiana Libr. award, 1978, Emmy award, 1994, Lichtenberg award Pi Beta Phi, 1994; named to Theatre Hall of Fame, 1995. Mem. Pi Beta Phi.

HECKEL, SALLY, independent filmmaker; b. Rochester, N.Y., Sept. 26, 1945; d. George Philip and Ethel Morley (Gage) H. MFA in Film, N.Y.U., 1973. Ind. filmmaker, 1973—. Producer, adaptor, dir. editor: (film) A Jury of Her Peers, 1980 (Acad. Award nom. Best Dramatic Live-Action Short, Blue Ribbon Am. Film Festival 1981, Cine Golden Eagle 1981, ATOM award Australian Tchrs. of Media Best Dramatic Film 1982, Santa Fe Film Expo Judges award Sinking Creek Film Celebration 1982, Chris award Columbus Film Festival 1982, Best Language Arts Film Birmingham Internat. Edn. Film Festival 1982); prodr., dir., animator, editor: (film) The Bent Tree, 1979 (Judge's award Sinking Creek Film Celebration 1980, Cine Golden Eagle 1980); co-dir., cinematographer, editor: (film) It's Not A One Person Thing, 1977 (Judges award Sinking Creek Film Celebration 1977); prodr., writer, dir., editor: (film) Ordinary Days, 1974 (Silver Hugo award Chgo. Internat. Film Festival 1974, First prize for Narrative Film Womanview 1974, Judges award Wash. Nat. Student Film Festival 1974, Directing and Cinematography awards N.Y.U. Film Festival 1974, Cine Golden Eagle 1974). Recipient Abraham Schneider award N.Y.U. Grad. Inst. Film/TV, 1972, Leo Jaffe award, 1972, Film Prodn. awards N.Y.S. Coun. for the Arts, 1982, 86, 89; Post-Grad. Fellow in Film grant N.Y.U. Nat. Endowment For the Arts with N.Y.U. Grad. Inst. Film/TV, 1975; artist grant Creative Artists Pub. Svc. N.Y.S. Coun. for the Arts, 1975, Film Prodn. grantee Women's Fund-Joint Found. Support, 1977, Film Prodn. grantee Beard's Fund & Cowan Found., 1978, 79, 80, Ind. Filmmaker grantee Am. Film Inst., 1981, Film Prodn. grantee Jerome Found., 1982, Film Prodn. grantee Nat. Endowment For the Arts, 1990. Home: 52 E 1st St New York NY 10003

HECKER, KARYN JANE, principal; b. Dayton, Ohio, Aug. 21, 1947; d. Edward Joseph and Ruth Loraine (Kochendoerfer) Makley; m. William Earl Hecker, June 20, 1970; children: Moira, Brent, Alana. BS in Edn., U. Dayton, 1969, MS in Edn., 1990. Cert. secondary edn., supervision, elem. prin. Substitute tchr. Dayton Pub. Schs., 1968-69; tchr. Beavercreek (Ohio) Pub. Schs., 1969-71, substitute tchr., 1988-89; substitute tchr. St. Luke Sch., Beavercreek, 1987-89; tchr. Dayton Cath. Elem. Sch., 1991—, prin., 1994—; presenter Ohio Cath. Edn. Assn., Cin., 1993, Holy Angels Sch., Dayton, 1992; asst. grad. studies U. Dayton, 1989-90. Strategic planner Beavercreek Schs., 1990; CASE mem. Carroll H.S., Dayton, 1994. Mem. ASCD, Nat. Cath. Edn. Assn. Roman Catholic. Office: Dayton Cath Elem Sch 3805 Kings Hwy Dayton OH 45406-3517

HECKERT, CONNIE K., writer; b. Jefferson, Iowa, Nov. 5, 1948; d. Leland M. and LaVone J. Delp; m. John W. Heckert, June 20, 1970; 1 child, Stephanie Gevone. Med. asst. cert. program, Career Acad., 1968; BA, Augustana Coll., 1976; MA, U. Iowa, 1984. Med. records libr. Iowa State U. Veterinary Clinics, Ames, 1968-73; proofreader Peoria Engring., East Moline, Ill., 1975; asst. health planner Iowa Health Sys. Agy., Davenport, Iowa, 1977-78; instr. Blackhawk Coll., Moline, Ill., 1985; adj. asst. prof. English St. Ambrose U., Davenport, 1985-93; keynote spkr. and tchr. of numerous conferences and workshops. Author: Miss Rochelle and the Lost Bell, 1985, Dribbles, 1993, Lyons: 150 Years North of the Big Tree, 1985, The Swedish Connections, 1986 (3d place award in nonfication Nat. League of Am. Pen Women, Inc. 1987), The First 100 Years: A Pictorial History of Lindsay Park Yacht Club, 1987, (with others) To Keera with Love: Abortion, Adoption or Keeping the Baby, 1987 (faculty devel. grant St. Ambrose U. and state, reg. and nat. awards from respective branches of the Nat. League of Am. Pen Women, Inc. 1987, 1988), Roots & Recipes: Six Generations of Heartland Cookery, 1995; contbr. to numerous periodicals; frequently writes for Des Moines Register. Writer of the Year Quad Cities Writers Club, 1982; First Place Writing awards Miss. Valley Writers Conf., 1986, Super Friend award Friends of Davenport Pub. Libr., 1988, cert. of appreciation Student Government Assn., St. Ambrose U., 1988, Hist. Preservation Achievement award Scott County Hist. Preservation Soc., Inc., 1989. Mem. Nat. League of Am Pen Women, Inc. (past pres., Quad Cities chpt.), Soc. of Children's Book Writers and Illustrators, Children's Reading Roundtable of Chgo. (assoc.). Republican. Lutheran. Home: 16 Oakbrook Dr Bettendorf IA 52722*

HECKMAN, CAROL A., biology educator; b. East Stroudsburg, Pa., Oct. 18, 1944; d. Wilbur Thomas and Doris (Betts) H. BA, Beloit (Wis.) Coll., 1966; PhD, U. Mass., Amherst, 1972. Rsch. assoc. Yale U. Sch. Medicine, New Haven, 1973-75; staff mem. Oak Ridge (Tenn.) Nat. Lab., 1975-82; adj. assoc. prof. U. Tenn.-Oak Ridge Biomed. Grad. Sch., 1980-82; assoc. prof. Bowling Green (Ohio) State U., 1982-86, prof. biology, 1986—; cons. NSF, Washington, 1977-80; dir. EM facility Bowling Green State U., 1982—; NSF trainee, Amherst, 1967-70. Contbr. articles to profl. jours., chpts. to books. Internat. Cancer Rsch. Tech. fellow Internat. Union Against Cancer, 1980, Heritage Found. fellow, 1982, guest rsch. fellow, Uppsala, Sweden, 1989-90; grantee NSF, 1981-84, 90-92, NIH, 1987-88. Mem. AAAS, Am. Soc. Cell Biology, Microscopy Soc. Am., N.W. Ohio Microscopy (sec.-treas. 1986-90, pres. 1990-94), Tissue Culture Assn., Ohio Drug Devel. (pres. 1993—), Ohio Acad. Sci., Sigma Xi. Episcopalian. Home: 861 Ferndale Ct Bowling Green OH 43402-1609 Office: Bowling Green State U Dept Biol Scis Bowling Green OH 43403

HECKMAN, CAROL E., judge; b. Clinton, Iowa, Oct. 18, 1952; children: Tyler, Ethan. BA magna cum laude, Lawrence Univ., Wis., 1974; JD magna cum laude, Cornell Law Sch., 1977. Bar: N.Y., U.S. Supreme Ct., U.S. Tax Ct., U.S. Dist. Ct. (we. dist.) N.Y. Law clk. to Chief Judge John T. Curtin U.S. Dist. Ct. (we. dist.) N.Y., Buffalo, 1977-79, asst. U.S. atty., 1981-85, magistrate judge, 1992—; trial atty. Dept. of Justice, Civil Rights Div., D.C., 1979-81; assoc. Albrecht, Maguire, Heffern & Gregg, P.C., Buffalo, 1985-86, ptnr., 1986-89; ptnr. Lippes, Kaminsky, Silverstein, Mathias & Wexler, Buffalo, 1989-92; mem. adv. com. for adminstrv. office U.S. Cts. Bd. dirs. Children's Hosp. Buffalo, 1995—. Recipient Farley prize in philosophy Lawrence Univ., Fraser prize for outstanding scholarship and character Cornell Law Review, Achievement award N.Y. State Women's Bar Assn., 1992. Mem. Cornell Law Sch. Advisory Coun., Nat. Assn. of Women Judges, Fed. Magistrate Judges Assn., Erie County Bar Assn., Women's Bar Assn. of the State of N.Y., Women Lawyers of We. N.Y., N.Y. State Bar Assn., Nat. Assn. of Women Judges. Office: US Courthouse 68 Court St Rm 418 Buffalo NY 14202-3405

HECTOR, SARA ELAINE, education consultant; b. Waco, Tex., Sept. 14, 1941; d. Lindon Burton and Ella Louise (Barnes) Tomlin; m. Robert Tully Neill, May 23, 1963 (div. Dec. 1983); children: James, Nancy; m. Garland Dean Hector, June 13, 1987. AA, Temple Jr. Coll., 1961; BS in Edn., S.W. Tex. U., 1963, MEd, 1968; mid mgmt. cert., U. Houston, Clear Lake, 1983. Cert. elem. tchr., secondary tchr. History/English tchr. Harlandale Ind. Sch. Dist., San Antonio, 1962-63, San Marcos (Tex.) Jr. H.S., 1963-64; history tchr., dept. chair Seabrook (Tex.) Interm-Clear Creek, 1965-85; asst. prin. League City (Tex.) Interm-Clear Creek, 1985-92; field svc. specialist Region IV ESC, Houston, 1992-95; edn. cons. Nat. Edn. Svc. "Discipline With Dignity", 1995—; tour coord. Lakeland Tours, Charlottesville, Va., 1978-85; nat. faculty USA Today, Arlington, Va., 1994—; adj. prof. U. Houston, Clear Lake, 1989-92; proctor San Marcos Bapt. Acad., 1961-63. Mem. Grand Jury, Galveston County, Tex., 1970; drama dir. U. Bapt. Ch., Houston, 1982-85, children's choir dir., 1980-85, Friendswood Bapt. Ch., 1985-87. Fellow Inst. for Devel. of Ednl. Activities; mem. ASCD, Nat. Staff Devel. Coun., Phi Delta Kappa. Home and Office: 2220 Marina Way # 219 Kemah TX 77565

HEDEMAN, FRANCES ILENE, secondary education educator; b. Rutland, Iowa, Dec. 16, 1946; d. Garnie Clopton and Florine Mabel (Collicott) Hood; m. Donald Lee Hedeman, May 31, 1969. BA, U. No. Iowa, Cedar Falls, 1969, MA, 1992. Cert. profl. tchr., Iowa. Tchr. Reinbeck (Iowa) Cmty. Sch., 1969-70; tchr., dir. speech and theatre Dubuque (Iowa) Sr. H.S., 1970—. Communion steward Grandview United Meth. Ch., Dubuque, 1984-94. Recipient Disting. Alumni Recognition award U. No. Iowa, 1980; named Tchr. of Yr., Dubuque Cmty. Schs., 1989-90. Mem. Speech Comm. Assn., Iowa Comm. Assn. (editor newsletter 1994-95), Nat. Fedn. State H.S. Assns., Nat. Stds./Curriculum Frameworks Cadre, Phi Delta Kappa, Delta Kappa Gamma. Office: Dubuque Sr HS 1800 Clarke Dr Dubuque IA 52001-4101

HEDGE, JEANNE COLLEEN, health physicist; b. Scottsburg, Ind., May 30, 1960; d. Paul Russell and Barbara Jean (Belshaw) H. BS in Environ. Health, Purdue U., 1983. Chemistry and health physics technician Marble Hill Nuclear Generating Sta., Pub. Svc. Ind., Madison, 1983-84; radiation protection asst. Pub. Svc. Electric and Gas Co., Hancock's Bridge, N.J., 1984-85, radiation protection technician, 1985-89, engr., 1989-90, lead engr., 1990-91, sr. staff engr., 1991-95, sr. staff health physicist, 1995—; mem. People to People Internat. Citizen Amb. Exch., People's Republic of China, 1988; del. Internat. Environ. Conf., Moscow, 1994. Mem. NOW, Am. Nuclear Soc., Health Physics Soc.

HEDGECOUGH, REBECCA J., nurse; b. Dayton, Ohio, Dec. 17, 1963; d. Opie L. and Margaret L. (Henry) Hedgecough; 2 children, Jaime Nicole, Jordan Nicholas. LPN, Livingston (Tenn.) Tech., 1983; ASN, SUNY, Albany, 1991. RN, Tenn.; cert. ACLS, Tenn.; CCRN. Critical care nurse Cookeville (Tenn.) Gen. Hosp., 1983-91, CCRN cardiac cath. lab., 1994—; nurse cardiology Dr. J.B. Arnstine, Cookeville, 1991-93. Recipient Cmty. Leadership award Am. Biog. Inst., 1986, Internat. Biog. Achievement award, 1984, Tenn. Gov.'s award for Vocat. Edn., 1983. Mem. AACN (cert.), Coun. Cardiovascular Nursing, Am. Heart Assn., Am. Kennel Club, Upper Cumberland Kennel Club (sec.). Mem. Ch. of God. Home: 969 Indian Hills Rd Cookeville TN 38506 Office: Cookeville Gen Hosp 142 W 5th St Cookeville TN 38501-1760

HEDGEMAN, LULAH M., secondary education educator; b. Memphis, Jan. 30, 1938; d. A.B. and Joanne (Wells) McEwen; m. Herbert L. Hedgeman, Sept. 1962 (div. 1967); 1 child, Denita J. BA, Fisk U., 1959; MusM, Memphis State U., 1970; cert., No. Ill. U., 1976; DFA (hon.), Rhodes Coll., 1991. Tchr. Melrose Jr. High Sch., Memphis, 1960-63, Chgo. Pub. Schs., 1963-66, Hamilton High Sch., Memphis, 1966-70, Treadwell High Sch., Memphis, 1970-76, Overton High Sch., Memphis, 1976—. Mem. Opera Memphis Guild, 1974—, NAACP, 1970—, Memphis Symphony Guild, 1976—; music cons. Miss. Blvd. Christian Ch., Memphis, 1989. Named Most Outstanding Condr. World Music Festivals, 1982, Most Outstanding Performing Arts Tchr. The Disney Co., 1990; recipient Gov's. award NARAS, 1991. Mem. NARAS (asst. condr. All-Am. h.s. grammy jazz choir 1994, Mr. Holland award 1996), NEA, Memphis Edn. Assn., tenn. Edn. Assn., Tenn. Music Educators Assn. (bd. dirs. 1970), Nat. Black Music Caucus (bd. dirs. 1990), West Tenn. Vocal Assn. (pres. 1968-70), Am. Choral Dirs. Assn. (pres. Tenn. chpt. 1980-82), Music Educators Nat. Conf., Rotary (Tchr. Excellence award Memphis chpt. 1984), Delta Sigma Theta (Arts and Letters award 1991). Office: Overton Performing Arts High Sch 1770 Lanier Ln Memphis TN 38117-7006

HEDGES, ELAINE R., retired literature educator; b. Yonkers, N.Y., Aug. 18, 1927; d. John Aloyisius and Catherine Mary Ryan; m. William Leonard Hedges, June 28, 1956; children: Marietta, James. BA, Barnard Coll., 1948; MA, Harvard U., 1950, PhD, 1970. Instr. Wellesley (Mass.) Coll., 1954-56, San Francisco State Coll., 1957-58, Goucher Coll., Balt., 1964; asst. prof. English Towson State U., Balt., 1967-71, assoc. prof. English, 1971-73, dir. women's studies, 1972-94, prof. English and Am. lit., 1973-95, prof. emerita, 1996—; vis. prof. Am. studies Free U. Berlin, 1979, 81; adv. bd. The Feminist Press, N.Y.C., 1985—; cons. in field. Author: Hearts and Hands, 1987; author, editor: In Her Own Image, 1980, Ripening: Selected Writings of Meridel le Sueur, 1982; editor: Heath Anthology of American Literature, 1990, 2nd edit., 1994, Listening to Silences, 1994; contbr. articles to profl. jours., chpts. to books. Co-dir. curriculum transformation projects Ford Found., FIPSE, Md., 1983-90; co-dir. Nat. Ctr. Curriculum Transformation Resources on Women, Balt., 1992—. Fellow AAUW, 1954-55, Am. Coun. Learned Socs., 1978-79, Nat. Endowment for the Humanities, 1988-89. Mem. MLA, Am. Studies Assn., Nat. Women's Studies Assn., Charlotte Perkins Gilman Soc. (pres. 1990—). Home: 317 Hawthorn Rd Baltimore MD 21210 Office: Towson State U Inst Tchg and Rsch on Women Baltimore MD 21252

HEDGES, KAMLA KING, library director; b. Covington, Va.; d. John Wilton and Rhoda Alice (Loughrie) K.; m. Harry George Hedges, July 24, 1988. AB, Coll. of William and Mary, 1968; MLS, Vanderbilt U., 1969. Law and legis. reference libr. Conn. State Libr., Hartford, 1969-74; dep. law libr. Steptoe and Johnson, Washington, 1974-78; law libr. Wilkinson, Cragun and Barker, Washington, 1978-83; corp. libr. The Bur. of Nat. Affairs, Inc., Washington, 1983-94, dir. libr. rels., 1995—. Compiler: (directories) BNA's Directory of State and Federal Courts, Judges, Clerks, 1995, BNA's State Administrative Codes and Registers, 1995; contbr. chpt. to law manual. Mem. Am. Assn. Law Librs. (exec. bd. dirs. 1984-87), Spl. Libr. Assn. Episcopalian. Home: 4331 Embassy Park Dr NW Washington DC 20016-3607 Office: Bur Nat Affairs Inc 1231 25th St NW Washington DC 20037-1157

HEDGES, SARA JO, English educator; b. Lancaster, Ohio, Apr. 1, 1950; d. Joseph and Ruth (Johnson) Fraker; m. Charles Michael Henderly, June 25, 1971 (div. Nov. 1978); children: Amy Beth, Virginia Anne; m. Lawrence Keith Hedges, June 16, 1984. BS Edn., Ohio State U., 1972; MS Edn., U. Dayton, 1992. Cert. English and speech edn. Tchr. English Lancaster (Ohio) City Schs., 1973—; Coll. Edn. advisory Ohio U., Athens, 1992-93; liaison com. Lancaster City Schs., 1991-93, leadership team, 1989—, North Ctrl. steering com., 1994—. host family Rotary, Lancaster, 1990-92; vol. Cancer Soc., Lancaster, 1986-90, Heart Fund, Am. Heart Assn., Lancaster, 1987-91. Recipient Golden Apple Achiever award Ashland Oil, 1991; named Rotary Outstanding Tchr. of Yr. Mem. ASCD, NEA, Nat. Coun. Tchrs. English, Ohio Edn. Assn., Lancaster Edn. Assn. (bldg. rep. 1990—). Republican. Methodist. Home: 2700 Wittenberg Dr NW Lancaster OH 43130-8832 Office: Lancaster HS 1312 Granville Pike Lancaster OH 43130-1033

HEDMAN, JANICE LEE, business executive; b. Elmhurst, Ill., Feb. 7, 1938; d. George Marion Hickman and Vera Beryl (Olsen) Sample; m. Daryl F. Hedman, Aug. 29, 1971 (div. Aug. 1983); children: Kevin G., Gregory Scott, Danny L., Shelly L.. Wolanski. Student, U. Puget Sound, 1970, Tacoma (Wash.) Community Coll., 1980. Head teller Puget Sound Nat. Bank, Tacoma, 1970-75; real estate agt. Shorewood Realty, Gig Harbor, Wash., 1975-80; mktg. rep. Western Fin. Planning, Inc., Tacoma, 1981-83; co-owner Schatz Avant Garde, Gig Harbor, 1984-86; asst. mgr. Classic Restaurant, Gig Harbor, 1984; co-owner Hedman Enterprises, Gig Harbor, 1976-93; owner, property mgr. Hedman Enterprises, 1993—; v.p. adminstrn. Teardrop Am., Inc., Wenatchee, Wash., 1986-90; pres. Teardrop N.W. Inc., Wenatchee, 1988-90; co-owner J&R Mktg., Wenatchee, 1989-90; mktg. specialist John L. Scott, Inc., Gig Harbor, 1991—; mktg. rep. sr. r&d Excel Telecomms., 1996—. Asst., Women's Task Force, Tacoma, 1980-81; asst. in fund raising events Am. Cancer Soc., 1992—. Mem. Epsilon Sigma Alpha (pres. 1980-81, v.p. 1981-82). Home: 5109 Point Fosdick Dr NW # 235E Gig Harbor WA 98335-1716 Office: John L Scott Inc 5500 Olympic Dr Apt H-106 Gig Harbor WA 98335-1487

HEDRICK, JOAN DORAN, writer; b. Balt., May 1, 1944; d. Paul Thomas and Jane (Connorton) Doran; m. Travis K. Hedrick, Aug. 26, 1967; children: Jessica, Rachel. AB, Vassar Coll., 1966; PhD, Brown U., 1974. Instr. Wesleyan U., Middletown, Conn., 1972-74, asst. prof. English, 1974-80; prof. history Trinity Coll., Hartford, Conn., also dir. women's studies program; vis. asst. prof. Trinity Coll., Hartford, 1980-81, vis. assoc. prof., 1981-82. Author: Solitary Comrade: Jack London and His Work, 1982, Harriet Beecher Stowe: A Life, 1994 (Pulitzer Prize for biography 1995). Mem. MLA, Am. Studies Assn., Org. Am. Historians, Soc. Am. Historians. Office: Trinity College Dept of History 300 Summit St Hartford CT 06106-3100

HEDSTROM, SUSAN LYNNE, maternal women's health nurse; b. Dowagiac, Mich., Jan. 17, 1958; d. Clinton J. and Gloria Anna (Hyink) Moore. ADN, Southwestern Mich. Coll., 1978. RN, Mich., Ind., Calif., Ga., Fla. Staff nurse obstetrics unit Lee Meml. Hosp., Dowagiac, Mich., 1979-81, Meml. Hosp., South Bend, Ind., 1981-90; with MRA Staffing Systems, Inc., Ft. Lauderdale, Fla., 1990-93; staff nurse traveler MUSC, Charleston, S.C., 1990-91; nurse Desert Hosp., Palm Springs, Calif., 1991, Ind. U. Hosp., Indpls., 1992, Valley Med Ctr., Fresno, Calif., 1992; staff nurse post partum/nursery Tallahassee Meml. Regional Med. Ctr., 1993-95, asst. head nurse post partum, 1995—. Mem. Am. Women's Health, Obstetrics and Neonatal Nurses. Office: Tallahassee Meml Reg Hosp Magnolia Dr & Miccosukee Rd Tallahassee FL 32308

HEEBNER, MARY DORETTA, artist, writer; b. L.A., Apr. 19, 1951; d. Walter Shussler and Claire Lucille (Menei) Heebner; m. Steven Everett Craig, Mar. 11, 1971 (div. Apr. 1984); 1 child, Sienna Radha; m. Macduff Everton, Aug. 12, 1989. BFA, U. Calif., Santa Barbara, 1973, MFA, 1977. Exhibited in group shows at Cheney Cowles Mus., Spokane, Wash., 1981, L.A. County Mus. Art, 1981, 84, 85, 92, U.S.A. Today Exhbn., Washington, 1983, Hodges-Banks Gallery, Seattle, 1983, U. Calif.-Santa Barbara, 1984, 87, Allrich Gallery, San Francisco, 1979, 81, 83, 84, 85, 86, 88, Contemporary Arts Forum, Santa Barbara, 1985, 87, 89, , Santa Barbara Mus. Art, 1980, 85, 90, 93, Linda Hodges Gallery, Seattle, 1987, 89, 92, 94, 96, U. Oreg. Mus. Art, Eugene, 1986-88, Casa de Cultura, Oaxaca, Mex., 1988, Markel/Sears, N.Y.C., 1990, Lone Pine Gallery, Irvine, Calif., 1990, De la Guerra Gallery, Santa Barbara, Calif., 1990, 92, Kay Kimpton Gallery, San Francisco, 1991, Anne Reed Gallery, 1992, Karpeles Manuscript Mus., Santa Barbara, Calif., 1993, Conejo Valley Mus. Art, Thousand Oaks, Calif., 1993, Ro Snell Gallery, Santa Barbara, 1993, 95, Antiken Mus., Basel, Switzerland, 1996, Nat. Mus. Women in the Arts, Washington, 1996; works in permanent collections at U. Art Mus., U. Calif. Santa Barbara, La. State Mus., Baton Rouge, Visa Corp., Calif., San Francisco Mus. Modern Art, USA Today, Washington, IBM, N.Y.C., L.A., Pacific Telecom., N.Y.C., TMS Entertainment, L.A., AT&T, N.Y.C., The Gap, San Francisco, U.S. Embassy, Eritrea, Africa, Hewlett Packard, Palo Alto, Calif., Tanoan, Albuquerque, Security Pacific Nat. Bank, L.A.; contbr. articles to profl. jours. including Travel Holiday, Conde Nast Traveler, Santa Barbara Mag., San Francisco Focus Mag. Patent Fund Travel grantee, U. Calif.-Santa Barbara, 1978, Pres.'s Undergrad. fellow, 1972, Regents Scholar fellow, 1969-72, Calif. State scholar, 1969-72. Democrat. Office: 914 Santa Barbara St Santa Barbara CA 93101

HEENAN, BARBARA ELAINE, medical laboratory administrator; b. Oakland, Calif., May 19, 1947; d. Arnold Peter and Josephine LaVina (Lee) Andersen; m. William Donald Heenan, Nov. 22, 1969. BS, N.D. State U., 1969; postgrad., U. St. Thomas, St. Paul, 1993—. Rsch. asst. Housefly Genetics Lab. USDA, Fargo, N.D., 1966-68; student technologist St. Joseph Hosp., St. Paul, 1968-69; rsch. technician Mayo Clinic, Rochester, Minn., 1969-70; med. technologist Unity Hosp., Fridley, Minn., 1970-74; spl. chemist St. Vincent Hosp., Green Bay, Wis., 1975-77; supr., dir. mktg. Kallestad Ref. Lab SERA, Chaska, Minn., 1977-82; lab. dir. Coon Rapids (Minn.) Med. Ctr., Allina Med. Group, 1983—; mem. adv. bd. St. Paul Tech. Coll. Med. Lab. Technician Program, 1989—, chair, 1990-92; safety officer Coon Rapids Med. Ctr., 1983—; chair safety couns. Allina Med. Group, 1996—, mem. fin. steering com.; mem. safety steering com. Allina, 1994—. Mem. task force infectious waste, Minn., 1988-89; foster parent cats Animal Humane Soc., Hennepin County, Minn., 1993—; fishing & ecology educator Dept. Natural Resources, Minn., 1990—; vol. naturalist Hennepin Parks, 1990—. Recipient Disting. Vol. award Hennepin Parks, 1996; nat. Merit Letter Commendation scholar, 1965. Mem. Am. Soc. Clin. Lab. Sci. (nat. program chair biochemistry 1980, chair biochemistry stds. rev. 1980-81, reg. V biochemistry scientific assembly chair 1977-80), Minn. Soc. Med. Tech. (chair biochemistry sect. 1974-75, recording sec. 1979-81, chair exhbts. and social ann. meeting 1980, alt. rep. coun. allied healthcare providers state PSRO 1980-81, rep. coun. 1981-83, mem. devel. com. 1981-83, pres. 1982-83, past pres. 1983-84, chair govt. affairs 1984-86, Minn. atty. gen. task force infectious waste 1988-89), Clin. Lab Mgmt. Assn., Toastmasters Internat. (pres. 1994-95, Quality award 1993, Toastmaster of Yr. 1992-95, Able Toastmaster 1996), Women Anglers Minn., Mensa. Home: 8401 32nd Ave N Minneapolis MN 55427-2503 Office: Coon Rapids Med Ctr 9055 Springbrook Dr Minneapolis MN 55433-5842

HEEP, LISA MASTERS, city planner; b. Rye, N.Y., Dec. 30, 1958; d. Donald Smith and Eleanor Isabel (Egan) Masters; m. Donald James Heep, Nov. 16, 1985; children: Samantha Allison Heep, Eric William Heep. BA, Wellesley (Mass.) Coll., 1980; MA in Urban and Regional Planning, U. So. Calif., L.A., 1983. Planning technician City of Santa Fe Springs, Calif., 1982-84; asst./assoc. planner City of Long Beach, Calif., 1986-89, sr. planner, 1989-90; prin. planner City of Irvine, Calif., 1992-93; zoning adminstr. City of Long Beach, 1993-94; planning mgr. City of West Hollywood, Calif., 1994—. Mem. Am. Planning Assn., Am. Assn. Environ. Planners. Democrat. Home: 3311 Lees Ave Long Beach CA 90808 Office: City of West Hollywood 8300 Santa Monica Blvd West Hollywood CA 90069

HEER, CAROL LYNNE, special education educator; b. Wauseon, Ohio, Dec. 8, 1948; d. Richard and Lois (Gentit) H. BA in Edn., Adrian Coll., 1970; MEd, Bowling Green State U., 1987. Cert. elem. tchr., Ohio. Tchr. Millcreek-West Unity (Ohio) Schs., 1970—, Title I tchr., 1987—; admissions dir. Sauder Farm and Craft Village, Archbold, Ohio, 1978—. Supt. United Meth. Ch., West Unity, 1992-94, lay reader, 1989-90, Sunday sch. tchr., 1986-95, style show coord., 1993-95. Mem. Ohio Reading Assn., Internat. Reading Assn. Methodist. Office: Millcreek West Unity Schs S Defiance St West Unity OH 43570

HEERE, KAREN R., astrophysicist; b. Teaneck, N.J., Apr. 9, 1944; d. Peter N. and Alice E. (Hall) H. BA, U. Pa., 1965; MA, U. Calif., Berkeley, 1968; PhD, U. Calif., Santa Cruz, 1976. Rsch. assoc. NRC NASA Ames Rsch. Ctr., Moffett Field, Calif., 1977-79; rsch. astronomer U. Calif., Santa Cruz/NASA Ames Rsch. Ctr., 1979-86; assoc. prof. San Francisco State U., 1986-87; scientist Sci. Applications Internat. Corp., Los Altos, Calif., 1974-76, 87-93; rsch. specialist Sterling Software, Palo Alto, Calif., 1993—; vis. scientist TATA Inst. for Fundamental Rsch., Bombay, India, 1984; adj. prof. San Francisco State U., 1987—. Author numerous articles in field. Mem. Am. Astron. Soc. Home: PO Box 2427 El Granada CA 94018-2427

HEERKENS, MARIE FRANCES, artist; b. Rochester, Apr. 4, 1963; d. Gerrit N. and Frances Louise (Renner) H. BA, SUNY, Geneseo, 1985. Profl. picture framer Light Impressions Corp., Rochester, N.Y., 1985-87; artist computer graphics Teach Yourself by Computer Software, Rochester, N.Y., 1986-90, Mercier Publs., Inc., Rochester, N.Y., 1989-90; mgr. framing dept. Graystone Artists Supply, Webster, N.Y., 1990-93; freelance artist, owner Flora & Fauna, Victor, N.Y., 1995—. Illustrator: (book) As I Write This Letter, 1982, (newsletter) The Peace Network, 1989-95. Mem. N.Am. Mycological Assn., Ontario County Arts Coun., Genesee Region Orchid Soc., Rochester Area Mycological Assn. (sec./treas. 1996), The Nature Conservancy (vol.), Citizens for United Earth.

HEESZEL, KATHRYN PAULINE, library clerk; b. San Diego, Feb. 27, 1949; d. Edwin Herman and Virginia Elisabeth (Meixner) H.; m. Patrick Colglazier, Aug. 4, 1975 (div. 1992); children: Elizabeth, Deborah, Vernon, Rebecca. BA, Calif. State U., Hayward, 1982. Tchrs. aide Fremont (Calif.) Unified Schs., 1988-90; substitute tchr. Fremont Unified Schs., Newark, Calif., 1993-96; libr. clk. Alameda County Libr., Newark, Calif., 1990-96. Mem. Smithsonian Assocs., Nat. Wild Life Assn. Democrat. Lutheran. Home: 48348 Davis St Fremont CA 94538 Office: Alamada County Libr Network 6300 Civic Terr Ave Newark CA 94560

HEFFERAN, COLIEN JOAN, economist; b. Mpls., May 13, 1949; d. Bernard and Rosemary Arnsdorf; m. Hollis Spurgeon Summers, Oct. 14, 1987; 1 child, Margaret Vimont Summers. BS, U. Ariz., 1971; MS, U. Ill., 1974, PhD, 1976. Asst. prof. Pa. State U., University Park, 1975-79; econ., rsch. leader Agrl. Rsch. Svc., USDA, Hyattsville, Md., 1979-88; assoc. adminstr. Coop. State Rsch., Edn. and Ext. Svc., 1988—; adj. prof. U. Md., University Park, 1982-88; chmn. Ctr. for Family, Washington, 1985-87; vis. fellow Australian Nat. U., Canberra, NSW, 1989-91. Mem. editl. bd. Jours.-Family Econ. Issues, 1987—. Recipient Outstanding Citizen award U. Ariz., 1985, Outstanding Alumni award U. Ill., 1986. Mem. Am. Econ. Assn., Am. Coun. on Consumer Interests. Democrat. Roman Catholic.

HEFFERNAN, PATRICIA CONNER, management consultant; b. N.Y.C., Oct. 11, 1946; d. Arthur S. and Catherine (Center) Conner; B.A., U. Va., 1968; M.B.A., Suffolk U., 1980; m. John Joseph Heffernan, Sept. 13, 1969 (dec. June 1996). Cert. mgmt. cons. office mgr. Wobbly Barn, Killington, Vt., 1968-72; bus. mgr. Woodstock Country Sch., Vt., 1972-74; assoc. dean Vt. Law Sch., Royalton, Vt., 1974-83; mgmt. cons. Heffernan & Assocs., Killington, 1982-87; mgmt. cons., v.p. Sandage Inc., Burlington, Vt., 1987-92; mgmt. cons., ptnr. Mktg. Ptnrs., Inc., Burlington, 1992—. Vt. del. White House Conf. on Small Bus.; mem. region 1 adv. coun. U.S. Small Bus. Adminstrn.; mem. Gov.'s Commn. on Women; bd. dirs. Rutland div. Chittenden Bank, 1975-92, Rutland Regional Med. Ctr., 1986-91, New England Bus. for Social Responsibility, 1990-93. Trustee, pres. Killington Mountain Sch., 1978-85; mem. Killington Planning Commn., 1975-87; mem. Killington Zoning Bd., 1979-84, Vt. Epilepsy Assn., 1977—, Vt. Telecommunications Commn., Vt. Econ. Devel. Adv. Coun.; mem. Vt. steering com. for ACE Nat. Identification Program for Women in Higher Edn., 1978-83. Named Outstanding Leader Vt. YWCA, 1985, Woman of Yr. Vt. Bus. and Profl. Women Found., 1986, Women in Bus. Adv. Small Bus. Adminstrn., 1993. Mem. Inst. Mgmt. Cons. (v.p. New Eng. region, nat. dir. 1991-93), Vt. Bus. Assn. for Social Responsibility (dir., pres. 1991—), Women Bus. Owners Vt. (dir. 1983—, founder, pres. 1984-86), Nat. Assn. Women Bus. Owners. Office: Mktg Ptnrs Inc 176 Battery St Burlington VT 05401-5296

HEFFERON, LAUREN JEANINE, tour operator, business owner; b. Lawrence, Mass., May 24, 1961. BA in Anthropology, Cornell U., 1983. Owner, founder Ciclismo Classico-Italian walking and biking vacations, Arlington, Mass., 1988—. Author: (book) Cycle Food, 1983. Named Rotary scholar Rotary Found., 1983; recipient Gen. Excellence Entrepreneurial Prize Home Office Computing Mag., 1994. Office: Ciclismo Classico 13 Marathon St Arlington MA 02174-6940

HEFNER, CHRISTIE ANN, publishing and marketing executive; b. Chgo., Nov. 8, 1952; d. Hugh Marston and Mildred Marie (Williams) H. BA summa cum laude in English and Am. Lit., Brandeis U., 1974. Freelance journalist, Boston, 1974-75; spl. asst. to chmn. Playboy Enterprises, Inc., Chgo., 1975-78, v.p., 1978-82, bd. dirs., 1979—, vice chmn., 1986-88, pres. 1982-88, COO, 1984-88, chmn., CEO, 1988—; bd. dirs. Playboy Found.-Playboy Enterprises, Inc., Ill. chpt. ACLU, Mag. Pubs. Assn., Sealy Corp. Bd. dirs. Nat. Coalition on Crime and Delinquency, Goodman Theatre, Chgo., Brandeis U., Rush-Presbyn.-St. Lukes Med. Ctr. Recipient Agness Underwood award L.A. chpt. Women in Communications, 1984, Founders award Midwest Women's Ctr., 1986, Human Rights award Am. Jewish Com., 1987, Harry Kalven Freedom of Expression award ACLU, Ill., 1987, Spirit of Life award City of Hope, 1988, Eleanor Roosevelt award Internat. Platform Assn., 1990, Will Rogers Meml. award Beverly Hills C. of C. and Civic Assn., 1993. Mem. Brandeis Nat. Women's Com. (life), Com. of 200, Young. Pres. Orgn., Chgo. Network, Voters for Choice, Phi Beta Kappa. Democrat. Office: Playboy Enterprises Inc 680 N Lake Shore Dr Chicago IL 60611-4402*

HEFT, CAROL BETH, artist, rehabilitation counselor; b. Phila., Mar. 11, 1954; d. Charles B. and Leeba R. (Melmed) H.; m. William L. Warfield Jr., 1986. BFA, R.I. Sch. Design, 1976; MS Edn., Hunter Coll., N.Y.C., 1995. Cert. rehab. counselor. Artist, tchr. Studio in a Sch. Assn., N.Y.C., 1987-88; recreation worker Office of Aging, N.Y.C. Housing Authority, 1989-90; program dir. Park Slope Sr. Citizens Ctr., Bklyn., 1990-92; rehab. assoc. Fedn. Employment and Guidance Svc., N.Y.C., 1992; rehab. counselor Areba Casriel Inst., N.Y.C., 1993; sr. rehab. counselor Employment Program for Recovered Alcoholics, N.Y.C., 1993—; pvt. career devel. specialist, N.Y.C., 1995—. One-woman shows include Gallery 120, N.Y.C., 1982, Ten Worlds Gallery, N.Y.C., 1989; exhibited in group shows at Columbia Coll. and Mo. Arts Coun., 1992, PSA Art Showcase, 1994, St. Johns U. Gallery, 1996, Blue Mountain Gallery, 1995-96, St. Johns U. Nat. Exhbn., 1996. Mem. ACA, N.Y. Fedn. Alcoholism and Chem. Dependency Counselors, Coll. Art Assn., Am. Assn. Museums. Office: Employment Program for Recovered Alcoholics 225 W 34th St # 410 New York NY 10122

HEGE, MELISSA CARRIER, brewing company executive; b. Largo, Fla., Feb. 15, 1968; d. Richard Patrick and Patricia Marie (Owens) C.; m. Alan Lee Hege, Dec. 15, 1992. AA, St. Petersburg Jr. Coll., Clearwater, Fla., 1988; BS in Chem. Engring., U. South Fla., Tampa, 1992. Supr. brewing Anheuser Busch, St. Louis, 1992-95, process specialist in brewing, 1995—. Office: Anheuser Busch 1 Busch Pl Bldg 174-2 Saint Louis MO 63118

HEGEL, CAROLYN MARIE, farmer, farm bureau executive; b. Lagro, Ind., Apr. 19, 1940; d. Ralph H. and Mary Lucile (Rudig) Lynn; m. Tom Lee Hegel, June 3, 1962. Student pub. schs., Columbia City, Ind. Bookkeeper Huntington County Farm Bur. Co-op, Inc. (Ind.), 1959-67; office mgr., 1967-70; twp. woman leader Wabash County Farm Bur., Inc. (Ind.), 1970-73, county woman leader, 1973-76; dist. woman leader Ind. Farm Bur., Inc., Indpls., 1976-80, 2d v.p., bd. dirs., 1980—, chmn. women's com., 1980—, exec. com. 1988—; farmer, Andrews, Ind., 1962—; dir. Farm Bur. Ins. Co., Indpls., 1980—, exec. com., 1988; mem. rural task force Great Lakes States Econ. Devel. Commn., 1987-88, Ind. Farm Bur. Svc. Co., 1980—, bd. dirs. Ind. Farm Bur. Found., Indpls., 1980—, Ind. Inst. Agr., Food and Nutrition, Indpls., 1982—, Ind. 4-H Found., Lafayette, 1983-86; mem. Ind. Rurual Health Adv. Coun., 1993—; com. mem. Hoosier Homestead Award Cert. Com., Indpls., 1980—; speaker in field. Women in the Field columnist Hoosier Farmer mag., 1980—. Named one of Outstanding Farm Woman of Yr. Country Woman Mag., 1987. Organizer farm div. Wabash County Am. Cancer Soc. Fund Dr. (Ind.), 1974; Sunday sch. tchr., bd. dir. childrens' activities Bethel United Meth. Ch., 1965—, pres. Bethel United Methodist Women, Lagro, 1975-81; bd. dirs. N.E. Ind. Kidney Found., 1984—, Nat. Kidney Found. of Ind., 1985-89, v.p., 1986—; active Leadership Am. Program, 1988. Recipient State 4-H Home Econs. ward Ind. 4-H, 1960; named Farm Woman of 1987 Country Woman mags. Mem. Women in Comm., Inc., Ind. Agrl. Mktg. Assn. (bd. dirs. 1980-94), Producers Mktg. Assn. (bd. dirs. 1980-94), Am. Farm Bur. Fedn. (midwest rep. to women's com. 1986-93). Republican. Home: 3330 N 650 E Andrews IN 46702-9616 Office: Ind Farm Bur Inc PO Box 1290 225 S East St Indianapolis IN 46202-4042

HEGEL, PAMELA RENE, elementary school educator; b. Fargo, N.D., July 9, 1958; d. James and Delores (Fisher) Booke; m. Darwin George Hegel, Aug. 3, 1984. BA, Dickinson (N.D.) State U., 1989. Office mgr. Farmers Ins. Group, Dickinson, N.D., 1974-77, Kukowski Land Co., Dickinson, 1981-88; real estate agt. Joe LaDuke Real Estate, Dickinson, 1977-81; tchr. Banning (Calif.) Unified Schs., 1988-94, Palm Springs (Calif.) Sch. Dist., 1994—. Recipient cert. of appreciation Ednl. Testing Svc., 1991. Mem. Calif. Tchrs. Assn.

HEGENDERFER, JONITA SUSAN, public relations executive; b. Chgo., Mar. 18, 1944; d. Clifford Lincoln and Cornelia Anna (Larson) Hazzard; m. Gary William Hegenderfer, Mar. 12, 1971 (dec. 1978). BA, Purdue U., 1965; postgrad. Calif. State U.-Long Beach, 1966-67, Northwestern U., 1969-70. Tchr. English, Long Beach schs., Calif., 1965-68; editorial asst. Playboy Mag., Chgo., 1968-70; communications specialist Am. Med. Assn., Chgo., 1970-72; v.p. Home Data, Hinsdale, Ill., 1972-75; mktg. mgr. Olympic Savs. & Loan, Berwyn, Ill., 1975-79; sr. v.p. Golin/Harris Communications, Chgo., 1979-89; pres. JSH & A, Chgo., 1989—; bd. dirs. Chgo. Internat. Film Festival, 1989, 90. Editor directory, Fin. Info. Nat. Directory, 1972; author: Slim Guide to Spas, 1984, (video) PR Guide for Chgo. LSCs, 1991; contbr. articles to profl. jours. Co-chmn. pub. rels. com. Am. Cancer Soc., Chgo., 1984; com. mem. March of Dimes, Chgo., 1986; mem. pub. rels. com. Girl Scouts Chgo., 1989-90, mem. bd. dirs. 1994-95; bd. dirs. Greater DuPage Women's Bus. Coun., 1992-93, Girl Scouts Am. DuPage County, 1994-95; vol. ctr. adv. com. United Way, Chgo., 1990-93, mem. community svc. com. Publicity Club Chgo., 1990—. Recipient 5 Golden Trumpet awards Publicity Club Chgo., 1983, 86, 94, Silver Trumpet awards, 1984, 86, 88, Spectra awards Internat. Assn. Bus. Communicators, 1984, 85, 87, Gold Quill award, 1985, Bronze Anvil award Pub. Rels. Soc. Am., 1985. Mem. Am. Mktg. Assn., Publicity Club of Chgo., Pub. Rels. Soc. Am., Chgo. Women in Pub. Clubs: Council on Fgn. Relations, Metropilitan Womens Forum, Cinema Chgo. (bd. dirs. 1988-89). Avocations: travel, photography. Office: JSH & A Comms 1311 Butterfield Rd Ste 312 Downers Grove IL 60515-5605

HEGSTED, EVELYN PHILLIPS, elementary education educator; b. Aberdeen, Idaho, Apr. 7, 1935; m. Dan Wray Hegsted; children: Daniel Mark, Vivian Bowman. BA, Idaho State U., 1960. cert. elem. tchr., Idaho. Classroom tchr. Dist. #25, Pocatello, Idaho, 1962-94. Recipient Golden Apple award J.R. Simplot Co., 1995. Mem. Pocatello Edn. Assn., Internat. Reading Assn. (sec., past pres.), Delta Kappa Gamma (local pres. 1980-82, state cons. chmn. 1988, 93-95). LDS. Home: 924 Meadowbrook Ln Pocatello ID 83201-3628 Office: Syringa Elem Sch 388 E Griffith Rd Pocatello ID 83201-3510

HEID, LISA MICHELLE, controller; b. Appleton, Wis., Nov. 6, 1966; d. Richard M. and Yvonne M. (Herbst) H. BA in Acctg., Lakeland Coll., 1988; postgrad., U. Wis., Oshkosh, 1993—. CPA, CMA, Wis. Sr. acct. Schumaker Romenesko and Assoc., Appleton, 1986-92; asst. contr. Plexus Corp., Neenah, Wis., 1992—; evening instr. Fox Valley Tech. Coll., Appleton, 1990-94. Treas. Tri County Recreation Assn., Neenah, 1989-95. Mem. Inst. Mgmt. Accts., Wis. Inst. CPAs (chair acctg. careers com. 1993-95). Home: 589 Chestnut St Neenah WI 54956 Office: Plexus Corp 55 Jewelers Park Dr Neenah WI 54956

HEIDELBERGER, KATHLEEN PATRICIA, physician; b. Bklyn., Apr. 13, 1939; d. William Cyprian and Margaret Bernadette (Hughes) H.; m. Charles William Davenport, Oct. 8, 1977. B.S. cum laude, Coll. Misericordia, 1961; M.D. cum laude, Woman's Med. Coll. Pa., 1965. Intern Mary Hitchcock Hosp., Hanover, N.H., 1965-66, resident in pathology, 1966-70; mem. faculty U. Mich., Ann Arbor, 1970—, assoc. prof. pathology, 1976-79, prof., 1979—. Mem. Am. Soc. Clin. Pathologists, U.S.-Can. Acad. Pathology, Soc. for Pediatric Pathology, Coll. Am. Pathologists. Office: U Mich Box 0054 Dept of Pathology UH 2G/332 Ann Arbor MI 48109

HEIDEMANN, MARY ANN, community planner; b. Detroit, Feb. 17, 1950; d. O.K. and Mary Elizabeth (Berry) Rodewald; m. Karl Werner, June 19, 1982; children: Heather Lisa, Karl Kristoffer. BA in Archtl. History, Reed Coll., Portland, Oreg., 1970; postgrad., U. Pa., Phila., 1972-75; MA in Pub. Adminstrn., U. Wis., 1985, PhD in Land Resources, 1989. Profl. cmty. planner, Mich. Apprentice Paolo Soleri, Architect, Scottsdale, Ariz., 1970-71; staff planner Jack McCormick & Assocs., Devon, Pa., 1972-74; natural resource planner Brown County Planning Commn., Green Bay, Wis., 1976-78; planning cons. Champ, Parish, Raasch, De Pere, Wis., 1978-80; policy analyst U.S. EPA, Chgo., 1980-81; cmty. svc. specialist Wis. Dept. Natural Resources, Madison, 1981-85; chief environ. analysis Wis. Dept. Transp., Madison, 1985-86; project mgr. Wade-Trim/Impact, Taylor, Mich., 1987-88; owner, prin. planner Mary Ann Heidemann & Assocs., Rogers City, Mich., 1988—; lectr. U. Wis., Green Bay, 1977-78; asst. prof. Kans. State U., Manhattan, 1975-76; exec. dir. East Mich. Environ. Action, West Bloomfield, 1986-87; adj. prof. Lake Superior State U., Sault Ste. Marie, 1988—; mem. planner lic. bd. Gov. State Mich., Lansing, 1990-94. Founding mem. Bay Renaissance, Green Bay, 1979-80; mem. Orion Twp. Planning Commn., Mich., 1986-87; county commr. Presque Isle County Bd., Rogers City, Mich., 1992-93; bd. dirs. Presque Isle Harbor Assocs., 1993-96. Dean Webster Meml. scholar Reed Coll., Portland, Oreg., 1968-69; fellow NEH, San Diego, 1978. Mem. AAUW, Am. Inst. Cert. Planners (planning exam. com. 1992), Am. Planning Assn., Mich. Soc. Planning Ofcls. (tng. workshop instr.), Harmony Choraleers, Mich. Historic Preservation Network, Presque Isle Lighthouse Assn. Democrat. Presbyterian. Office: Mary Ann Heidemann & Assocs 150 S 3rd St Rogers City MI 49779-1710

HEIDISH, LOUISE ORIDGE-SCHWALLIE, transportation specialist, marketing professional; b. Cin., May 21, 1938; d. Leslie Jacob and Louise (Oridge) Schwallie; m. William Edward Heidish, Sept. 2, 1961; children: Sara Louise, Amy Jean. BA in History, Denison U., 1960; MA in History, Miami U., Oxford, Ohio, 1962; MS in Urban Studies, Ala. A&M U., 1994. Secondary tchr. Fox Chapel Sch. Dist., Pitts., 1962-69; part-time instr. U. Ala., Huntsville, 1976-78; substitute history tchr. City of Huntsville Schs., 1977-79; dir. comm. svcs. Heidish Enterprises, Huntsville, 1979-83; transp. specialist City of Huntsville, 1981—; regional 5 state coord. AAUW and NEH, Huntsville, 1981-83. Author: Biography: Alexander Long 1816-86, 1962, Marketing Ride Sharing, 1994. Mem., project chair Huntsville Symphony Orch. Guild, 1974—; bd. dirs. Huntsville-Madison County Sr. Ctr., 1980-86, sec. 1981, v.p. 1982, pres. 1983; bd. dirs. Huntsville High Sch. PTA, 1983-88, v.p. 1985-86, pres. 1986-88; com. chmn. Panoply of the Arts Festival, Huntsville, 1985-87. Mem. AAUW (local pres. 1979-81, state v.p. 1981-83, regional coord. 1981-83), Pub. Rels. Coun. No. Ala. (newsletter editor 1993, conf. treas. 1994, coun. treas. 1995, coun. sec. 1996), S.E. Assn. for Commuter Transp. (regional conf. chair 1995, chpt. treas. 1996), Kappa Kappa Gamma (alumnae officer, local pres., regional officer 1958—). Presbyterian. Office: Pub Transp City Huntsville 100 Church St SW Huntsville AL 35801-4908

HEIDLAGE, KATHARINE SANDERSON, lawyer; b. Geneva, N.Y., Mar. 16, 1951; d. Francis Thayer and Adele Julie (Owens) Sanderson; m. Richard Clemens Heidlage, May 31, 1975; children: Benjamin Frederick, Charles Jackson, William Richard. AB, Smith Coll., 1973; JD, Boston U., 1978, LLM in Taxation, 1983. Bar: Mass. 1978, U.S. Dist. Ct. (1st cir.) 1979, U.S. Tax Ct. 1979, U.S. Ct. Appeals (1st cir.) 1979. Assoc. Gaston & Snow and predecessor firms, Boston, 1978-82, Peabody & Brown, Boston, 1982-85; gen. counsel, mng. dir., v.p. New England Funds L.P., Boston, 1982-93, 1988—. Bd. dirs. Underwood After Sch. Program, Inc., 1990-94. Mem. ABA, Mass. Bar Assn., Boston Bar Assn., Mass. Women's Bar Assn. Democrat. Episcopalian. Office: New England Funds L P 399 Boylston St Boston MA 02116-3305*

HEIER, MARILYN KAY, elementary education educator; b. Oakley, Kans., Nov. 22, 1939; d. Vincent M. and Ferne (Beckman) Dickman; m. Linus B. Heier, June 15, 1961; children: Donita Bozarth, Michael, Beverly, Christina Shaheen, Lawrence. BS in Home Econs., Marymount Coll., Salina, Kans., 1960; MS in Elem. Edn., Ft. Hays State U., Hays, Kans., 1980. Cert. in elem. and secondary edn., Kans. Tchr. home econs., English and phys. edn. Bethune (Colo.) Pub. Schs., 1960-62; tchr. 5th grade Unified Sch. Dist. 291, Grinnell, Kans., 1974—, head tchr., 1990—; mem. Quality Performance Edn. Com., Grinnell, 1992-95; mem. Profl. Devel. Coun.,

Grinnell, 1990-95. Mem. St. Mary's Altar Soc., Immaculate Conception Ch. Jennibelle Watson scholar, 1979. Mem. NEA, Kans. Edn. Assn., Grinnell Tchrs. Assn. (pres. 1984 86, head negotiator 1994-95), Delta Kappa Gamma (pres 1988-90), Phi Delta Kappa. Democrat. Roman Catholic. Home: Box 191 206 S Harrison Ave Grinnell KS 67738 Office: USD 291 of Grinnell PO Box 126 202 S Monroe Grinnell KS 67738

HEIFETZ, SONIA, retired pharmacist; b. Rowne, Poland; came to U.S., 1929, naturalized, 1934; d. Zise and Toiba (Ehrlich) Heifetz. PhG, Temple U., 1933. Asst. chief pharmacist Grad. Hosp. U. Pa., Phila., 1937-49, dir. pharmacy svcs., 1949-77; formerly pharmacist-mgr. Rite-Aide Corp., now ret. Cert. tchr. of Russian, Phila. Bd. of Edn. div. sch. extension; asst. dir. pharmacy Eastern State Sch. and Hosp., Trevose, Pa., 1982-92, ret., 1992. Mem. AAUW, Am. Soc. Hosp. Pharmacists, Del. Soc. Hosp. Pharmacists (hon.), Pa. Soc. Hosp. Pharmacists (hon.), Phila. Guild Hosp. Pharmacists (v.p. 1966, treas. 1967-77). Home: 2665 Willits Rd Apt 324 Philadelphia PA 19114-3470

HEIGHT, DOROTHY I., association executive. Mem. nat. staff YWCA of the U.S.A., 33 yrs. Pres. Nat. Coun. Negro Women, 1957—; hon. mem. nat. bd. dirs. YWCA of the U.S.A. Recipient Ambassador award YWCA of the U.S.A., 1993.

HEILBRUN, CAROLYN GOLD, English literature educator; b. East Orange, N.J., Jan. 13, 1926; d. Archibald and Estelle (Roemer) Gold; m. James Heilbrun, Feb. 20, 1945; children: Emily, Margaret, Robert. B.A., Wellesley Coll., 1947; M.A., Columbia U., 1951, Ph.D., 1959; D.H.L. (hon.), U. Pa., 1984, Bucknell U., 1985, Russell Sage Coll., 1987, Smith Coll., 1989, Berea Coll., 1991, New Sch. for Social Rsch., 1993, Lewis & Clark Coll., 1993; D.F.A. (hon.), Rivier Coll., 1986; DHL, Lewis and Clark U., 1993; DFA, U. St. Thomas, 1994. Instr. Bklyn. Coll., 1959-60; instr. Columbia U., N.Y.C., 1960-62, asst. prof., 1962-67, assoc. prof., 1967-72, prof. English lit., 1972—; Avalon Found. prof. humanities Columbia U., 1986-93; prof. emerita Columbia U., N.Y.C., 1986-93; vis. prof. U. Calif., Santa Cruz, 1979, Princeton U., N.J., 1981, Yale Law Sch., 1989. Author: The Garnett Family, 1961, Christopher Isherwood, 1970, Towards Androgyny, 1973, Reinventing Womanhood, 1979, Writing a Woman's Life, 1988, Hamlet's Mother and Other Women, 1990, The Education of a Woman: The Life of Gloria Steinem, 1995; 11 novels as Amanda Cross, 1964 (recipient Nero Wolfe award 1981—). Guggenheim fellow, 1966; Rockefeller fellow, 1976; Sr. Rsch. fellow NEH, 1983; recipient Alumnae Achievement award Wellesley Coll., 1984, award of excellence Grad. Faculty of Columbia Alumni, 1984. Mem. MLA (pres. 1984), Mystery Writers Am. (exec. bd. 1982-84), Phi Beta Kappa. Office: Ellen Levine Literary Agy Ste 1801 15 East 26th St New York NY 10010

HEILBRUNN, BERNICE A., lawyer, educator; b. N.Y.C., Jan. 2, 1949; m. D. Joseph Petvin, Aug. 20, 1978. BA, Harvard U., 1970, MA, 1971, JD, 1974. Bar: N.Y. 1975, Tex. 1976, N.J. 1981. Assoc. Trubin Sillcocks Edelman & Knapp, N.Y.C., 1974-75; corp. counsel Exxon Co. USA, Houston and Linden, N.J., 1976-82; ptnr. Friedman Siegelbaum, Roseland, N.J., 1985-90; counsel environment, health and safety Lyondell - Citgo Refining Co., Ltd., Houston, 1992—. Mem. ABA, State of Tex. Bar Assn., Houston Bar Assn., Am. Corp. Counsel Assn. (Houston chpt. bd. dirs. 1995—, chmn. environ. law com. 1994—). Office: Lyondell-Citgo Refining Co. Ltd. 12000 Lawndale Houston TX 77017

HEILEMAN, SANDRA MARIE, health facility administrator, educator; b. Chgo., Jan. 28, 1959; d. Stanley Vincent and Angeline Sajkiewicz. BS, Rush U., 1988, MS, 1989; postgrad., U. Ill., Chgo., 1992—. RN, Ill.; cert. BLS instr. Am. Heart Assn.; cert. oncology nurse; cert. breast health awareness instr. Acct., comptr. McKinsey Steel Co., Inc., Forest Park, Ill., 1976-79; exec. dir. Adolescent Youth Svcs., Village of Stone Park, Ill., 1979-81; coord. Midwest Therapeutic Assocs., Morton Grove, Ill., 1981-83, adminstr., 1983-86; in-outpatient oncology nurse Rush North Shore Med. Ctr., Skokie, Ill., 1988-89; oncology resource nurse West Suburban Hosp. Med. Ctr., Oak Park, Ill., 1989-90; oncology clin. nurse specialist Holy Family Hosp., Des Plaines, Ill., 1990-92; oncology clin. specialist, dir. autologous transplant program N.W. Oncology, Hematology S. C., Elk Grove Village, Ill., 1992-95; dir. Breast Ctr. The Dr.'s Hosp., Dallas, 1996—; asst. prof. Wright Coll., Chgo., 1990-95; mem. profl. adv. bd. Rainbow Hospice, Park Ridge, Ill., 1990-93; profl. educator Ill. Cancer Pain Initiative, N.W. Suburban Cook County, Ill., 1991—. Author: (ednl. program) AIDS-Facts & Myth, 1988, (audio cassettes-patient edn.) Chemo-Induced Sequelae, 1989. Bd. dirs. Am. Cancer Soc. Unit 113, 1992—. Rush U. scholar, 1987-88; recipient Luther Christman award and scholarship Rush U./Rush Presbyn. St. Lukes Med. Ctr., 1988, Excellence in Gerontol Nursing award, 1988, Spl. Project award, 1988. Mem. Oncology Nursing Soc. (pres. elect local chpt., chmn. mem. com.), Am. Cancer Soc. (mem. nurses ednl. com. 1990—, profl. educator 1990—, Grad. scholar 1988-89, bd. dirs. unit 113 1992—), Soc. Otolaryngology and Head-Neck Nurses (treas. 1990-93, legis com. 1991, editor newsletter 1991), Gamma Phi chpt. Sigma Theta Tau. Republican. Roman Catholic. Home: 1317 Alexis Ave #309 Fort Worth TX 76120 Office: The Dr's Hosp Breast Ctr Ste 210 9330 Poppy Dr Dallas TX 75218

HEILER, LYNN, publishing executive. Pub. Bon Appetit, N.Y.C. Office: Bon Appetit NY Bur 360 Madison Ave New York NY 10007*

HEILIG, MARGARET CRAMER, nurse, educator; b. Lancaster, Pa., Jan. 17, 1914; d. William Stuart and Margaret White (Snader) Cramer; m. David Heilig, June 1, 1942; children: Judith, Bonnie, Barbara. BA in Psychology, Wilson Coll., 1935; MSW, U. Pa., 1940; AAS in Nursing Delaware County C.C., 1970. Registered nurse. Caseworker Children's Bur., Lancaster, Pa., 1935-37, Phila., 39-42; group worker Ho. of Industry Settlement Ho., Phila., 1937-39; curriculum chmn. Upper Darby Adult Sch. (Pa.), 1958-68; health asst., camp mother Paradise Farm Camp, Downington, Pa., 1960-70, camp nurse, 1970-78, infirmary dir., 1978-86; med. surg. nurse Crozer-Chester Med. Ctr., Chester, Pa., 1970; out-patient nurse Maternal Infant Care, Chester, 1971; coll. nurse Delaware County C.C., Media, Pa., 1971-76, dir. health svcs., 1976-84, health cons., 1984—, writer bi-weekly health newsletter Life Lines, 1973—, Health Svcs., 1988—, mem. spkrs. bur., 1975-93, dir. health fair, 1979—; cons. Coll. Health Svc. for Middle States Evaluation, 1988. Author: First Aid Booklet, 1976; also articles and columns in health field. Nurse for health screening children's program Tyler Arboretum, Media, 1982-93, Update on Personal Health, Broadmeadows Women's Prison, 1973, 82; former leader Delaware County Council Girl Scouts U.S.; clk. Lansowne Friends Meeting, 1987-91, active newsletter, 1990-94; mem. Upper Darby Recreation Bd., 1956-58, Upper Darby Adult Sch. Bd., 1956-68, curriculum chmn., 1958-68; provider host home for fgn. exchange students, 1965-75; participant Audubon Ann. Bird Count, 1970—; coord., dir. Bi-Ann. Soc. of Friends Ch. Retreat, 1970-92; ARC Speakers' Bur.-AIDS; tchr. Beginning Birding course Del. County C.C.; bd. dirs. Ret. Sr. Vol. Program Del. County, 1991—. Recipient Ollie B. Moten award Am. Coll. Health Assn., 1987, Disting. Nursing Alumni award Del. County C.C., 1995; inducted into Legion of Honor Chapel of Four Chaplains, 1980; honored by dedication Park Area on Campus Del. County C.C.; team leader homeless advocacy, Upper Darby, Pa., 1990—; vol. Coun. Bd. Tyler Arboretum, 1989-94. Mem. ANA, Pa. Nurses Assn., Delaware County Nurses Assn. (membership chmn. 1977-78), Southeastern Pa. Coll. Health Nurses Assn. (co-founder, pres. 1983-85), Middle Atlantic Coll. Health Assn., Delaware Valley Soc. for Adolescent Health, Family Svc. Assn. Delaware County (bd. dirs. 1989-91), LWV, Women's Internat. League for Peace and Freedom, Brandywine Conservance. Quaker. Avocations: piano and choral music, nature walking, handicrafts (craft participant Pa. Renaissance Faire 1985—, writer health and safety column in Shire Chronicle for participants, 1993—). Home: 605 Mason Ave Drexel Hill PA 19026-2429 Office: Del County Community Coll Health Ctr Media PA 19063

HEIM, DIXIE SHARP, family practice nurse clinician; b. Kansas City, Kans., Feb. 28, 1938; d. Glen Richard and Freda Helen (Milburn) Stanley; m. Theodore Eugene Sharp, Aug. 12, 1960 (dec. Apr., 1972); children: Diane Yvonne Price, Andrew Kirk, Bryan Scot; m. Roy Bernard Heim, June 14, 1979. Diploma nursing, St. Luke's Hosp. Sch. Nursing, Kansas City, Mo., 1959; family practice nurse clinician, Wichita State U., 1974. Cert. advanced registered nurse practitioner, Kans. Nurse surgical ICU Staff Kaiser Found. Hosp., San Francisco, 1959-61; operating room supr. St. Luke's Hosp., Kansas City, Mo., 1962-63; emergency room, operating room supr. Lawrence (Kans.) Meml. Hosp., 1963-72; nurse clinician various doctors, Lawrence, 1973-81; nursing supr. spl. projects St. Francis Hosp. and Med. Ctr., Topeka, Kans., 1981-94; primary health care giver Health Care Access, Lawrence, 1992-94; nurse practitioner Dr. Glen Bair, Topeka, 1990-94; advanced registered nurse practitioner Dr. Jerry H. Feagan, Topeka, 1994, McLouth (Kans.) Med. Clinic, 1994—, Jefferson County Meml. Hosp., Winchester, Kans., 1995-96; family practice nurse practitioner Robert E. Jacoby II., M.D., Topeka, 1996—; preceptor nurse practitioner program U. Kans., 1993—; primary health care provider Jefferson County Law Enforcement Ctr., Oskaloosa, Kans., 1995—. V.p. Am. Bus. Women. Assn. Lawrence chpt., 1969, sec. 1968; vol. Children's Hour, Lawrence, 1965-72, Comty. Resource for Career edn., 1975-76; adv. bd. E. Ctrl. Kans. Econs. Opportunity Corp., Lawrence, 1993-95; mem. Rep. Women Douglas County, Lawrence, 1994. Recipient Nursing the Heart of Health Care award Kaiser Permanente, 1994. Mem. ANA, Kans. State Nurses Assn. (v.p. 1958, chairperson fund raising campaign 1994, bd. dirs. 1996). Address: 540 Arizona St Lawrence KS 66049-2100 Office: Robert E Jacoby II MD 901 SW Garfield Topeka KS 66606-1695

HEIM, KATHRYN MARIE, psychiatric nurse, author; b. Milw., Sept. 29, 1952; d. Lester Sheldon Wilcox and Laura Dora (Corpie) Wilcox Sears; m. Vincent Robert Gouthro, June 30, 1970 (div. 1976); 1 child, Robert Vincent; m. George John Heim, Sept. 17, 1977 (div. 1988). AS in Nursing, Milw. Area Tech. Coll., 1983; BS in Nursing, NYU, 1986; MS in Mgmt., Cardinal Stritch Coll., 1988; postgrad., Newport U., 1989—. Cert. psychiatric and mental health nurse, AMA. Staff geriatric nurse Clement Manor, Greenfield, Wis., 1983; nurse, health educator Milw. Boys Club, 1983-84; nurse mgr. Milw. County Mental Health Complex, Milw., 1984—, mem. gero-psychiat. inpatient adv. com., 1986-87; RN Psychiat. Acute Care Day Hosp., 1992—; mem. nursing rsch. com. Milwaukee County Mental Health Complex, 1986—; research on loneliness as it relates to mental health, 1989-92. Mem. wellness task force Milw. County Mental Health Complex, 1988-89, chairperson sensory deficit com. Geropsychiatry, 1989-90; active Boy Scouts Am., Milw., 1978-80. Mem. ANA (cert. gerontol. nurse), NAFE (network dir. Milw. chpt. 1982-92), Wis. Nurses Assn., NYU Alumni Assn., Cardinal Stritch Alumni Assn. (class rep. 1986-88), Milw. Area Tech. Coll. Alumni Assn. Home: 351 N 62rd St Milwaukee WI 53213 Office: Milw County Mental Health 9455 W Watertown Plank Rd Milwaukee WI 53226-3559

HEIM, MARCY LYNN SCHULTZ, foundation executive; b. Theresa, Wis., Nov. 15, 1957; d. Robert Julius and Irene Laura (Wecker) Schultz; m. Kenneth J. Heim; stepchildren: Carly, Elliott; 1 child, Robert James. BS in Natural Scis. with distinction, U. Wis., 1979. Exec. asst. Wis. Phys. Therapy Svcs., Madison, 1975-80; dir. pub. rels. Wis. DHI Coop., Madison, 1980-83; sr. dir. devel. U. Wis. Found., Madison, 1983—; lead singer Marcy & The Highlights, 1980—; cons. Marks Entertainment and Pub. Rels., 1985—. Vol. United Way of Dane County, 1987, Salvation Army, 1990—; treas. Van Hise Elem. PTO, 1994-95; participant Leadership Greater Madison, 1996—. Mem. Nat. Agr. Alumni and Devel. Assn. (bd. dirs. 1994—, edn. com. 1992-93, chair edn. com. 1994-96, pres.-elect 1996), Nat. Agr. Mktg. Assn., Pub. Rels. Soc. Am., Assn. Women Bus. Coalition (bd. dirs. 1988-91), Women in Comm. Inc. (bd. dirs. 1988-91, pres. Madison chpt. 1990-91), Daus. of Demeter (bd. dirs. 1995—, pres.-elect 1996), Kiwanis (chair/co-chair agr. conservation and environ. com. Downtown Madison chpt. 1991—, bd. dirs. 1996), Alpha Zeta. Republican. Lutheran. Home: 471 Presidential Ln Madison WI 53711-1153 Office: U Wis Found 1848 University Ave PO Box 8860 Madison WI 53708-8860

HEIM, TONYA SUE, nurse, small business owner; b. Huntingburg, Ind., Nov. 9, 1948; d. Harold William and Marjorie Elouise (Buse) Rothert; m. James Frederick Heim, Sept. 6, 1969; children: Brian Christopher, Andrea Christine. Diploma, Deaconness Sch. Nursing, Evansville, Ind., 1969. RN, Ind.; cert. HIV/AIDS instr.; cert. in infection control. Oper. rm. staff nurse St. Joseph's Hosp., Huntingburg, 1969-71, emergency rm. staff nurse, 1969-71, staff nurse obstetrics dept., 1971-73, supr. obstetrics dept., 1973-85, dir. obstetrics oper. rm., 1985-88, dir. nursing, 1988-89, dir. obstetrics, oper. rm., infection control sterilizing, 1989-95, dir. surg. svcs., 1995—; owner, operator Holland (Ind.) Toning and Tanning Ctr., 1987—; co-owner Heim Hardware, 1989—. Instr., trainer ARC So. Ind., 1970-92; chmn. health profl. adv. com., mem. exec. com. So. Ind./Ill. chpt. March of Dimes, 1978-92; v.p., chmn. program com., bd. dirs. So. Hills Counseling Ctr., Jasper, Ind., 1988—; event coord. Hoosiers for Safety Belts, Dale, Ind., 1987; troop coleader Girl Scouts Am., Holland, 1986-88; active Southridge Band Boosters, Huntingburg, 1986-91; mem. AIDS coun. S.W. Dubois County Sch. Corp., 1988-94; mem. adv. coun. Prenatal Substance Use Prevention Program, 1989-93; mem. HIV prevention community planning com., Ind. State Dept. Health, 1994-95; chmn. schs. com., chmn. Midwest AIDS Tng. and Edn. Ctr. com., founding co-chmn. Dubois County AIDS Community Action Group, Huntingburg, 1991—; mem. S.W. Dubois County Sch. Bd., 1992—, pres., 1996; active March of Dimes, 1978-90; mem. legis. com. Ind. StateSch. Bd. Assn., 1996. Mem. ANA (bd. dirs.), NAACOG, Ind. Coun. Nurse Mgrs., Assn. for Practitioners in Infection Control (Amelia K. Sloan lectureship Ind. 1992), Assn. Oper. Rm. Nurses, Huntingburg C. of C., Beta Sigma Phi (v.p.). Republican. Lutheran. Home: PO Box 88 403 2nd Ave Holland IN 47541-9757 Office: St Josephs Hosp 1900 Medical Arts Dr Huntingburg IN 47542-9375

HEIMANN, JANET BARBARA, volunteer trail consultant; b. Santa Cruz, Calif., Dec. 18, 1931; d. John Louis and Charlotte Lucina (Burns) Grinnell; m. Richard Frank Gustav, July 10, 1953; children: David Robert, Gary Alan, Kathleen Janet. BS, U. Calif., Berkeley, 1954. Vol. trail rschr. Monterey County Pks. Dept.; appointee Carmel Valley Trail Adv. Com., 1993—. Pres. Folsom Freedom Trails, Placer County, Calif., 1980-83; chmn. Adopt-a-Trail, Folsom Lake Trail Patrol, Placer County, 1986-88; bd. dirs. Loomis Basin Horseman Assn., Placer County, 1986-87. Mem. AAUW. Republican. Home: 11565 Mccarthy Rd Carmel Valley CA 93924-9239

HEIMANN-HAST, SYBIL DOROTHEA, language arts and literature educator; b. Shanghai, May 8, 1924; came to U.S., 1941; d. Paul Heinrich and Elisabeth (Halle) Heimann; m. David G. Hast, Jan. 11, 1948 (div. 1959); children: Thomas David Hast, Dorothea Elizabeth Hast-Scott. BA in French, Smith Coll., 1946; MA in French Lang. and Lit., U. Pitts., 1963; MA in German Lang. and Lit., UCLA, 1966; diploma in Spanish, U. Barcelona, Spain, 1972. Cert. German, French and Spanish tchr., Calif. Assoc. in German lang. UCLA, 1966-70; asst. prof. German Calif. State U., L.A., 1970-71; lectr. German Mt. St. Mary's Coll., Brentwood, Calif., 1974-75; instr. French and German, diction coach Calif. Inst. of Arts, Valencia, 1977-78; coach lang. and diction UCLA Opera Theater, 1973-93, ret., 1993, lectr. dept. music, 1973-93; interviewer, researcher oral history program UCLA, 1986-93; dir., founder ISTMO, Santa Monica, Calif., 1975—; cons. interpreter/translator L.A. Music Ctr., U.S. Supreme Ct., L.A., J. Paul Getty Mus., Malibu, Calif., Warner New Media, Panorama Internat. Prodn., Sony Records, 1986—; voice-over artist; founder, artistic dir. Westside Opera Workshop, 1986—. Author of poems. UCLA grantee, 1990-91. Mem. AAUP, AFTRA, MLA, SAG, Sunset Succulent Soc. (v.p., bd. dirs., reporter, annual show chmn.), German Am. C. of C., L.A. Home and Office: 1022 17th St Apt 7 Santa Monica CA 90403-4339

HEIMARK, SONDRA ANDERSON, clinical social worker; b. Mt. Vernon, Ill., Jan. 15, 1944; d. Kenneth A. Anderson and Grace (Sawyer) Weber. AA in Social Welfare, Coll. of the Desert, Palm Desert, Calif., 1976; BA in Sociology & Psychology, San Bernardino State U., 1978; MSW, San Diego State U., 1980. Lic. clin. social worker Calif.; cert. clin. hypnotist. Clin. social worker Riverside County Mental Health, Indio, Calif., 1978-80; owner, therapist Las Adelfas Counseling, Indio, Calif., 1980-83; co-owner, therapist The Next Step, Palm Desert, Calif., 1981-87, trim-life group leader, 1984-86; owner, therapist Your Time, Bermuda Dunes, Calif., 1987-89, Arroyo Grande, Calif., 1989-93, Nipomo, Calif., 1993—; tchr. Assertiveness & Stress Mgmt. Annenberg Ctr. for the Scis., 1983-89; social work cons. Care West Convalescent, Palm Springs, Calif., 1984-89. Author, narrator, performer health oriented audio clin. hyponosis tapes, 1991—. Fellow Calif. Soc. Clin. Social Work; mem. Nat. Assn. Social Workers, Western Gerontological Assn., Nipomo C. of C., Better Bus. Bur., Soroptimists Internat. (woman of distinction 1989). Democrat. Baptist. Office: "Your Time" 1010 Upper Los Berros Rd Nipomo CA 93444

HEIMBOLD, MARGARET BYRNE, publisher, educator, consultant; b. Tullamore, Ireland, June 24; came to U.S., 1966, naturalized, 1973; d. John Christopher and Anne (Troy) Byrne; m. Arthur Heimbold, Feb. 26, 1984; 1 child, Eric Thomas Gordon. BA, Queens Coll. Recipient cert. Dale Carnegie, 1977, Psychol. Corp. Am., 1981, Wharton Sch., 1983, Stanford U., 1989. Group advt. mgr. N.Y. Times, N.Y.C., 1978-85; pub. Am. Film, Washington, 1985-86, v.p., pub. Nat. Trust for Hist. Preservation, Washington, 1986-90; pres. Summerville Press, Inc., Washington, 1990—; pub. Metro Golf, 1992—; advisor Mag. Pubs. Bd. dirs. Anchor Ctrs. Ireland; bd. trustees Nat. Mus. Women in Arts. Mem. NAFE, Am. Soc. Assn. Execs., Women's Econ. Alliance, Soc. Nat. Assn. Publs. (chmn. editl. com., bd. dirs.), D.C. Preservation League. Avocations: golf, writing, volunteering.

HEIMBURGER, ELIZABETH MORGAN, psychiatrist; b. Atlanta, Apr. 23, 1932; d. Henry Durand and Lillian Elizabeth (Palmour) Morgan; div.; children: Elizabeth Morgan Whitaker, Homer Aggie Whitaker III, Margaret Diane Heimburger, Richard Ames Heimburger Jr., Katherine Durand Heimburger. BS, Ga. State U., 1963; MD, Med. Coll. Ga., 1967. Diplomate Am. Bd. Psychiatry and Neurology. Intern in internal medicine Med. Coll. Ga., Augusta, 1967-68, resident in gen. psychiatry, 1968-70; fellow in child and adolescent psychiatry U. Tex., Galveston, 1970-72; asst. prof. dept. psychiatry U. Tex. Med. Br., Galveston, 1972-73, assoc. prof., dir. residency tng., 1980-87; asst. prof., assoc. prof., dir. psychosomatic svcs. U. Mo. Sch. Medicine, Columbia, 1973-80, clin. assoc. prof. dept. psychiatry, 1987—; pvt. practice specializing in adolescent psychiatry Columbia, 1987—; examiner Am. Bd. Psychiatry and Neurology, Chgo., 1977—; specialist, site visitor residency rev. Coun. Grad. Med. Edn., Washington, 1983—; exec. bd. Am. Assn. Dirs. Psychiat. Residency Tng., 1982-90; exec. coun. Tex. Psychiat. Soc., Austin, 1983-86; dir. confs., workshops on orgnl. and group dynamics. Editorial cons. bd. Am. Psychiat. Assn. Press., Inc., Washington,1 987-90; contbr. articles, scholarly papers to profl. publs. Bd. dirs. Mental Health Assn., Galveston, 1984-87, YMCA, Columbia, 1987-89. Grantee NIMH, 1978-80, 80-83. Fellow Am. Psychiat. Assn.; mem. Am. Soc. Adolescent Psychiatry, Am. Assn. Child and Adolescent Psychiatry (com.), A.K. Rice Inst. (bd. dirs. 1979-85, pres. Cen. States Ctr. 1979-88, bd. dirs. 1979-95), Am. Horticulture Soc. Episcopalian. Home and Office: 814 Hulen Dr Columbia MO 65203-1472

HEINE, KRISTINE E., public relations consultant; b. Spencer, Iowa, Aug. 1, 1950; d. Russell C. and Ellen C. (Johnson) H.; m. Albert T. Yamada. BA in Comms., U. S.D., 1972; MBA, George Washington U., 1982. Sr. v.p. Edelman Worldwide, Washington, 1977-83; v.p. Gray and Co., Washington, 1983-84; mgr. pub. rels. Control Data Corp., Mpls., 1984-86; dir. pub. affairs Leighton and Regnery, Washington, 1986-90; pres. KEH Comms., Washington, 1988-90, 93-95; dir. pub. liaison U.S. Agy. for Internat. Devel., Washington, 1990-93; sr. v.p. Ruder-Finn, Inc., Washington, 1995—; pub. rels. adv. Asian Am. Arts and Media, Washington, 1986-90, bd. dirs.; pub. rels. adv. Asian Am. Film Festival, Washington, 1988-90; press sec. rep. Charles Grassley, Washington, 1976-77; congl. intern rep. Wiley Wayne, Washington, 1971. Contbr. articles to profl. jours. Vol. Bush-Quayle campaign, Washington, 1988, Bush for President, 1987-88; singer Nat. Festival Choir, 1990—. Phi Beta Kappa. Republican. Lutheran. Office: Ruder-Finn Inc 1440 New York Ave NW Washington DC 20005

HEINEMANN, KATHERINE (KAKI HEINEMANN), author; b. St. Louis; d. Herbert N. and Elsa S. (Straus) Arnstein; BS, Washington U., St. Louis, 1950, MA (Arts and Scis. Faculty award 1950), 1956; m. Morton D. May, 1937; children: David A., Philip F.; m. Sol Heinemann, July 8, 1950; 1 child, Kate Heinemann Taucher. Freelance writer, poet, 1960—; prof. English, U. Tex., El Paso, 1968-74; condr. poetry readings, workshops, 1968—; mem. El Paso Art Resources Dept. Bd., 1980-81; author: Brandings, 1968; Some Inhuman Familiars, 1983; taping for Poetry Collection of Library of Congress, 1982. Mem. PEN, Nat. Soc. Arts and Letters. Home: 111 Emerson St #1423 Denver CO 80218

HEINRICHS, MARY ANN, former dean; b. Toledo, Mar. 28, 1930; m. Paul Warren Heinrichs, Jan. 26, 1952; children: Paul, John, Nancy, James. PhD, U. Toledo, 1973. Prof. English, U. Toledo, Ohio, 1965-77, dean, 1977-93; prof. emeritus Coll. Edn. Contbr. articles to profl. jours. Mem. Community Planning Coun. Rsch. Project Employed Women, Ohio, 1982-84; mem. Coun. Family Violence, Toledo, 1981—; com. chmn. St. Joseph Sch. Bd., Toledo, 1976-79. Recipient Outstanding Scholarship award U. Toledo, 1965; AAUW scholar, 1984, Humanities scholar, 1987—; named One of Foremost Women 20th Century, 1987, Outstanding Woman U. Toledo, 1991; inducted into Notre Dame Acad. Hall of Fame, 1991. Mem. AAUW (corp. rep. 1978-84), Internat. Tech. Communications Soc. (chmn. 1979-80), Zonta, Pi Lambda Theta (chpt. pres. and del. 1974-76), Phi Kappa Phi (chpt. pres. and del. 1969). Roman Catholic. Avocations: hiking, travel, music. Office: U Toledo 2801 W Bancroft St Toledo OH 43606-3328

HEINS, ESTHER, botanical artist, painter; b. Bklyn., Nov. 10, 1908; d. Israel and Margaret (Brown) Berow; m. Harold Heins; Sept. 8, 1929 (dec. 1987); children: Marilyn, Judith Leet. BS in Edn., Mass. Coll. Art, 1929. Freelance artist Boston, 1930-60; bot. artist Arnold Arboretum, Boston, 1960—. Contbr. bot. illustrations to profl. jours.; one-woman shows include Graham Arader Gallery, N.Y.C., Harvard Radcliffe Hilles Libr., Arnold Arboretum, Boston Pub. Libr.; group shows include Arnold Arboretum, Munich, Germany, Smithsonian, Washington, Oakland, Calif., Pitts., others; represented in permanent collections at Mus. Fine Arts, Boston, Hunt Inst. for Bot. Documentation, Arnold Arboretum, Boston Pub. Libr., Fogg Mus., Cambridge, and numerous others in pvt. collections; illustrator, contbr. essay: (book) Flowering Trees and Shrubs: The Botanical Paintings of Esther Heins, 1987. Mem. Guild of Natural Sci. Illustrators. Home and Studio: 8 Mitchell Rd Marblehead MA 01945

HEINTZ, CAROLINEA CABANISS, retired home economics educator; b. Roanoke, Va., Jan. 19, 1920; d. Luther Bertie and Emblyn Bird (Jennings) Cabaniss; m. Howard Elmer Smith, Dec. 19, 1942 (div. Aug. 1975); children: Emblyn Davis, Cynthia Shannon, Cheryl Peterson, Melyssa Sexton; m. Raymond Walter Heintz, May 21, 1977; 1 stepchild, James. BS in Home Econ. Edn., U. Ala., Tuscaloosa, 1941; vocat. home econ. degree, Montevallo Coll., 1941. Cert. vocat. home econs. tchr. Swimming instr. Camp Mudjekeewis, Centerlovel, Maine, summer 1940; home econs. tchr. Roanoke Pub. Schs., 1941-43; dietitian U. Va., Charlottesville, 1943; nutrition edn. specialist Liberty Health Ctr. Svcs., Liberty Center, Ohio, 1974-80; home economist Dayton Hudson Dept. Store, Toledo, 1980-84; splty . food instr., continuing edn. U. Toledo, 1984-85; pres., mem. Greater Toledo Nutrition Coun., 1966-92, 94-96; bd. dirs. Sunset House Aux., 1996. Spkr. United Way, Toledo, 1965-90; founder, pres. Mobile Meals Toledo, Inc., 1968-71, mem. adv. bd., 1988-95, bd. dirs., chmn. pub. rels., 1996—; affiliate mem. Arts Commn., Toledo, 1976-77; chmn. Sapphire Ball, Toledo Symphony Orch., Toledo Opera, 1978; adminstrv. coord. Feed Your Neighbor program Met. Chs. United, Toledo, 1979-86; deacon Collingwood Presbyn. Ch., 1969-71, elder, 1972-74, 77-79, trustee, 1984-86, elder, clk. of session, 1991-94, elder, stewardship chmn., 1996—, del. to Maumee Valley Presbytery, 1991-96; mem. steering com. Interfaith Hospitality Network, 1992-94, bd. dirs., 1993-94; alt. del. Gen. Assembly Presbyn. Ch. U.S.A., 1993, del.-commr., 1994. Recipient Woman of Toledo award St. Vincent Hosp. and Med. Ctr. Guild, 1967, 80, Outstanding Community Svc. award United Way, 1987. Mem. AAUW (bd. dirs. 1974-76, 94-96, chmn. mem. gourmet group 1972-80, 92-96, edn. found. chmn. 1994-96, book sale chmn.), Ohio Med. Aux. (1st v.p. 1973-74), Aux. Acad. Medicine (pres. 1967-68, chmn. med. gourmet group 1966, 92-94, 95-96, Health Care award 1974), Sigma Kappa (various alumni offices). Republican. Home: 3407 Bentley Blvd Toledo OH 43606-2860

HEINTZ, MARGARET CURETON, accountant; b. Mooresville, N.C., Jan. 6, 1970; d. David Junior and Rebecca Ann (Griffin) Honeycutt; m. Stephen Scott Heintz, May 20, 1995. AAS in Acctg., Mitchell C.C., Statesville, N.C., 1990; BS in Acctg. magna cum laude, Gardner-Webb U., Statesville, 1995. Sales assoc. Revco Drugs, Inc., Mooresville, 1986-90; asst. acct. Toter, Inc., Statesville, 1990-92, gen. acct., 1992-94, cost acct., 1994—. Mem. choir Beulah Bapt. Ch., 1995—. Republican. Home: 160 Cotton Wood Rd Cleveland NC 27013

HEISE, MARILYN BEARDSLEY, public relations company executive; b. Cedar Rapids, Iowa, Feb. 26, 1935; d. Lee Roy and Angeline Myrtle (Knudson) Beardsley; m. John W. Heise, July 9, 1960; children: William Earnshaw, Steven James, Kathryn Kay Heise Benninghoff. BA, Drake U., 1957. Account exec. The Beveridge Orgn., Chgo., 1958-60; editor, pub. The Working Craftsman mag., Northbrook, Ill., 1971-78; columnist Chgo. Sun-Times, 1973-78; pres. Craft Books, Inc., Northbrook, 1978-84; v.p. Sheila King Pub. Rels., Chgo., 1984-87, Aaron D. Cushman, Inc., Chgo., 1987-88; pres. Creative Cons. Assocs., Inc., Glencoe, Ill., 1989—, Charity Cards, 1991—; mem. adv. panel Nat. Crafts Project, Ft. Collins, Colo., 1977; mem. adv. panel and com. Nat. Endowment for Arts, Washington, 1977; mem. adv. bd. The Crafts Report, Seattle, 1978-86. Recipient achievement award Women in Mgmt., 1978. Mem. Pub. Rels. Soc. Am. (accredited). Office: Creative Cons Assocs Inc 854 Grove St Glencoe IL 60022-1568

HEISEN, JOANN HEFFERNAN, health care company executive; b. Silver Spring, Md., Jan. 25, 1950; d. Milton F. and Jeanne (Berger) Heffernan; childen: Douglas, Gregory, Cynthia, Courtney. BA, Syracuse U., 1972; postgrad., NYU, 1978. Comml. lending officer Chase Manhattan Bank, N.Y.C., 1972-77; chief fin. officer Kenmill Textile Corp., N.Y.C., 1977-82; v.p. corp. affairs Primerica Corp., Greenwich, Conn., 1982-89; asst. treas. Johnson & Johnson, New Brunswick, N.J., 1989-90, v.p., mem. corp. staff, 1990-91, treas., corp. officer, 1991-94, contr., 1994—; bd. trustees Princeton Med. Ctr. Bd. dirs., v.p., corp. adv. chmn. Abbott House, Westchester, N.Y., 1983-91; bd. dirs. Women's Rsch. and Edn. Inst., Washington, 1990—, Rec. for Blind, Princeton, N.J., 1990—; bd. dirs. vis. com. MIT Sloan Sch. Mgmt.; bd. dirs. adv. com. Maxwell Sch. Citizenship & Pub. Affairs. Recipient Women Achiever award YWCA N.Y., 1983, TWIN award Nat. YMCA, 1987. Mem. Fin. Women's Assn. (pres. 1980-81), Nat. Investor Rels. Inst. (bd. dirs. N.J. chpt. 1991—), Pharm. Mfg. Treas. Group, N.Y. Treas. Group, Econ. Club N.Y. Office: Johnson & Johnson One Johnson & Johnson Pla New Brunswick NJ 08933

HEISLER, EILEEN, television producer. Student, Ind. U.; diploma in film and TV, NYU. Exec. prodr. TV sitcom "Ellen" Touchstone TV, L.A., 1994—. Co-writer: (with DeAnn Heline) (episodic TV) Doogie Howser, M.D.; co-writer, co-prodr. (with Heline) Roseanne, Murphy Brown. Office: Walt Disney World 500 S Buena Vista St Burbank CA 91521-1884

HEISLER, VICKI LYNN, elementary school educator; b. Indpls., Sept. 29, 1952; d. Robert Edward and Melba Jean (Cass) Gray; m. Charles Eric Heisler, June 10, 1972; children: Jason Erik, Aaron Nicholaus. BA in Teaching Spl. Edn., U. No. Colo., 1974, postgrad., 1984—. Cert. tchr K-12 EMH, K-6 elem. edn. Tchr. mentallyhandicapped Greeley-Weld (Colo.) Dist. 6, 1974-77, 78-79, insvc. coord., 1977-78, tchr. severe and profound multi-handicapped, 1979-82, tchr. intermediate/elem. sch., 1982-86, tchr. kindergarten/1st grade, 1986-92, tchr. spl. assignment for instructional support/insvc., 1988-92, tchr. elem. intermediate, 1992—; tchr. outreach edn. courses U. No. Colo., Greeley, 1975-92; tchr. family and life edn. AIMS C.C., 1981-90; cons. Julesberg (Colo.) Pub. Schs., 1975, Aurora (Colo.) Pub. Schs., 1975, Julesberg Assn. for Retarded, 1977; parent educator AIMS C.C., 1981-83; presenter to local, state and regional presentations at convs. Author bi-mo. edn. col. Greeley Tribune, 1993—; author/curriculum specialist (parenting TV shows) First and Foremost series, 1992—; author: (young adult fiction) A Matter of Two Minds, 1994. Adv. bd. Greeley Coll. for Living, 1976-78; pres. Assn. for Retarded Citizens, Greeley, 1976; lay ministries chair Our Savior's Luth. Ch., Greeley, 1980; historian Greeley Children's Chorale, 1990-92; vice chair sch. improvement com. Brentwood Mid. Sch., 1991—; sec. Colo. Dance Theatre, Inc., 1995—. Named Jefferson Elem. Tchr. of the Yr., Greeley, 1984, Outstanding Tchr., Phi Delta Kappa, 1991, Feature Tchr. of Gifted, Assn. for Talented and Gifted, 1989; recipient Forward in Tech. award Meeker Elem. Sch., 1996; Hewlet-Packard Creative Teaching grantee, 1989, STAR Grant-Dist. Six grantee, 1990. Mem. ASCD, Nat. Assn. for Edn. Young Children, Nat. Coun. Tchrs. English, Internat. Reading Assn. Lutheran. Office: Greeley-Weld District Six 811 15th St Greeley CO 80631-4625

HEISS, CLAIRE DEYOUNG, manufacturing executive; b. Oak Park, Ill., Dec. 1, 1946; d. Frederick H. and Ruth E. (DeYoung) H. BSIE, U. Ill., 1970. Quality mgr. X-Ray products GE, Milw., 1970-76; mfg. mgr. Home laundry GE, Louisville, 1977-79; new plant start-up mgr. Aircraft Engine GE, Wilmington, N.C., 1980-82; mfg. mgr. Aerospace Simulation Systems GE, Daytona Beach, Fla., 1982-87; mfg. dir. X-Ray Bus./Med. Systems GE, Milw., 1989-93; ops. dir. Motorola Tactical Electronics, Scottsdale, Ariz., 1987-89; v.p. consumer loans Bank Am., Brea, Calif., 1993-94; v.p., gen. mgr. cooking products Frigidaire Co., Springfield, Tenn., 1994—. Malcolm Baldrige Nat. Quality award Examiner, U.S. Dept. Commerce, 1992-93. Home: 114 Pembroke Dr Hendersonville TN 37075

HEITKAMP, HEIDI, state attorney general; b. Breckenridge, Minn.; m. Darwin Lange; children: Alethea Lange, Nathan Lange. BA, U. N.D., 1977; JD, Lewis and Clark Coll., 1980. Intern asst. Environ. Study Conf., Washington, 1976; legis. intern N.D. Legis. Coun., Bismarck, 1977; exec. dir. Northwestern Environ. Def. Ctr., Portland, 1978-79; rsch. asst. Nat. Resources Law Inst., Portland, 1979; atty. enforcement divsn. EPA, Washington, 1980-81; asst. atty. gen. Office of N.D. State Tax Commr., Bismarck, 1981-85, adminstrv. counsel, 1985-86, tax commr., 1986-92; atty gen. State of N.D., Bismarck, 1993—; del. Am. Coun. Young Polit. Leaders, UK Internat. Def. Conf., 1988; trustee Fedn. Tax Adminstrs., 1991. N.D. State Crusade chmn. Am. Cancer Soc., 1988—. Recipient Young Achiever award Nat. Coun. Women, 1987; named One of 20 Young Lawyers Making a Difference, ABA Barrister mag., 1990; Toll fellow Coun. State Govts., 1986. Mem. Nat. Assn. Atty. Gens. Office: Attorney General State Capitol 600 E Boulevard Ave Bismarck ND 58505-0040

HEITKAMP, MILLIE MARIE, nursing administrator; b. Celina, Ohio, Nov. 15, 1946; d. Herbert Raymond and Velma Mary (Prenger) Bergman; m. John Edward Heitkamp, July 23, 1966; children: Cynthia, Tim, Mark. AD AS, Edison State C.C., 1985. RN, Ohio. Nurses' aide Upper Valley Med. Ctr., Troy, Ohio, 1979-85, staff nurse, 1985-90; staff nurse Upper Valley Family Care, New Carlisle, Ohio, 1990-91; nursing supr. Upper Valley Family Care, Troy, 1991—; dir. Office Networking and Continuing Edn., Troy, 1991—. Co-author, editor manual: Telephone Triage for the Family Physician's Office, 1993. Mem. Am. Assn. Office Nurses, Ohio Soc. Office Nurses. Home: 5218 S Worley Rd Tipp City OH 45371 Office: Upper Valley Family Care 23 S Weston Rd Troy OH 45373

HEITMANN, CHERYL, psychotherapist; b. St. Joseph, Mo., May 31, 1945; d. Harold and Emma (Clark) Smalley; m. Dennis Heitmann, May 11, 1974; children: Erin, Lyndsay, Greg. BA, DePauw U., 1967; MSW, Calif. State U., Sacramento, 1971. Lic. clin. social worker, Calif.; diplomate clin. social work NASW. Probation officer County of Cook, Chgo., 1967-68; social worker Children's Bapt. Home, Inglewood, Calif., 1971-74; psychiat. social worker L.A. County/U. So. Calif. Med. Ctr., 1974-75; emergency room social worker Los Robles Hosp., Thousand Oaks, Calif., 1978; pvt. practice Pasadena, Calif., 1979-86, Agoura, Calif., 1986—; polit. cons. D.C. Cons., Agoura, 1995; mem. adv. bd. Conejo Free Clinic, Thousand Oaks, 1992-95; leader workshops on self-esteem and communication, 1988-95. Bd. dirs., founder Nat. Women's Polit. Caucus, Conejo Valley, 1990-95; chairperson Commn. on Status of Women, Pasadena, 1978-82; mem. edn. adv. com. Assemblyman Takasugi, 1994-95; mem. adv. bd. Creative Options' Woman's Day Conf., 1990-95; 2d v.p. Westlake High Sch. PTA, 1995—. Named Woman of Distinction Soroptimist Internat. Conejo, 1994; recipient Gold award for Outstanding Citizen Calif. Tchrs. Assn., 1995. Mem. AAUW (chair pub. policy 1990-92, chair edn. 1993-95). Democrat. Episcopalian.

HEITNER, KERI LYNN, psychology writer, researcher; b. N.Y.C., Mar. 9, 1957; d. Kenneth A. and Sylvia (Kaminsky) H.; m. George S. Lipkowitz, July 3, 1978; children: Adam, Joshua. BA in Psychology, SUNY, Stony Brook, 1978; MA in Psychology, New Sch. for Social Rsch., N.Y.C., 1982; MPhil in Psychology, CCNY, 1985, PhD in Psychology, 1986. Adjunct prof. various colls., N.J., 1982-88; project evaluator Union County Coll., Cranford, N.J., 1987-88; freelance writer/editor Amherst, Mass., 1988—; rsch. specialist Hampden County Employment and Tng. Consortium, Springfield, Mass., 1989-90; project mgr. U. Mass. Donahue Inst., Amherst, 1990-96; writer/researcher, owner All Aspects Rsch., Amherst, 1995—; bd. dirs. The Care Ctr., Holyoke, Mass., Capacidad, Amherst. Editor conf. proc. The Univ. of Mass. and the Bldg. of a Pluralistic Sys. of Higher Edn., 1993; author social and polit. commentary The Amherst Bull., 1993—; author, editor rsch. publs. Chair Amherst Dem. Town Com., 1993-96; mem. Amherst Zoning Bd. of Appeals, 1994—; elected mem. Amherst Dem. Town Com., 1990—. Recipient grant Mass. Dept. Med. Security, 1990-96. Mem. AAAS, APA (divsn. consulting psychology, divsn. media psychology, divsn. psychology of women), Soc. for Psychol. Study of Social Issues, Am. Ednl. Rsch. Assn., Assn. Women in Psychology, N.Y. Acad. Scis., Mass. Assn. for Women in Edn. (chair social policy, exec. com. mem., 1994—). Democrat. Jewish. Office: All Aspects Research PO Box 1195 Amherst MA 01004-1195

HEITZ, CAROLE ANN, secondary education educator; b. Marshfield, Wis., June 28, 1941; d. John Wilson and Fidelia Charlotte (Schmitt) Atwood; m. John Milton Heitz, Sept. 16, 1965; children: Michael Robert, Andrew John. BA English, Okla. City Univ., 1963; MA English, Cen. State U., 1974. Cert. secondary edn. tchr., Okla. Tchr. English McGuinness High Sch., Oklahoma City, 1963-65, St. Cloud (Fla.) Mid. Sch., 1967-70; tchr. English and social studies John Carroll Sch., Oklahoma City, 1978-79; tchr. English Hefner Jr. High Sch., Oklahoma City, 1979-91; tchr. English/journalism Edmond (Okla.) Meml. High Sch., 1990—; adj. faculty U. Md., European Divsn., 1977-78, Oklahoma City U., 1990—; dist. coord. Edmond Pub. Schs., Edmond Evening Sun Newspaper, 1990—. Liaison Bapt. Med. Ctr. Putnam City Ptnrs. in Edn., Oklahoma City, 1989-91. Recipient Eloise Rees Writing Mentorship Edmond Ednl. Endowment, 1994; named to 5-Alive Oklahoma's Best, KOCO-TV, Oklahoma City, 1990-91. Mem. Nat. Coun. of Tchrs. of English, NEA, Okla. Edn. Assn., Edmond Assn. Classroom Tchrs., Okla. Interscholastic Assn., Delta Kappa Gamma.

HEITZENRODER, WENDY ROBERTA, elementary school educator; b. Erie, Pa., Nov. 14, 1948; d. Robert Walfred and Ruth Wilhelmena (Sandberg) Gustavson; m. Frederick Charles Heitzenroder, June 20, 1970; 1 child, Matthew Frederick. BA, Thiel Coll., Greenville, Pa., 1970; MA, W.Va. U., 1980, EdD, 1988. Caseworker Philadelphia County, Phila., 1970-71; spl. edn. tchr. John E. Davis Sch., East. Pa. Psychiat. Inst., Phila., 1971-77, Marion County Schs., Fairmont, W.Va., 1977-90, Fox Chapel Area Schs., Pitts., 1990—; instr. spl. edn. W.Va. U., Morgantown, 1989-90; cons. Marion County Bd. Edn., Fairmont, 1989-90. Mem. Jr. League of Fairmont, 1980s; mem. choir Salem Luth. Ch., 1990—, mem. bell choir, 1990—. Jr. League of Fairmont grantee, 1989; Excellence for Edn. grantee, Pitts., 1991, 92; Thanks to Tchrs. finalist Giant Eagle award, 1994-95. Mem. Phi Delta Kappa. Home: RR 9 Box 543 Greensburg PA 15601-9255 Office: Fox Chapel Area Sch Dist 611 Field Club Rd Pittsburgh PA 15238-2406

HEIZER, IDA ANN, retired real estate broker; b. Oxford, Colo., Mar. 14, 1919; d. Albert Henry and Ella (Engbrook) Ordener; m. Donald Heizer, Apr. 7, 1947; children: Robert John. Diploma, Brown's Bus. Coll., 1939; student Otero Jr. Coll., 1946-47, U. So. Colo., 1962; grad. Realtors Inst., Nat. Assn. Real Estate Bds., 1972. Cert. closer real estate, cert. residential specialist. Clk., Montgomery Ward Co., LaJunta, Colo., 1935-37; bookkeeper Colo. Bank & Trust Co., LaJunta, 1937-38; cashier/bookkeeper Fox Theatre, LaJunta, 1939-40; clk. Civil Service, LaJunta, 1940-45; stenoabstractor Deaf Smith Abstract Office, Hereford, Tex., 1948-50; sec. Otero County Agt. Office, Rocky Ford, Colo., 1953-55; real estate broker Pueblo Realty & Service Co., Inc., Colo., 1958-86; ret., 1988. Mem. Pueblo Bd. Realtors, Nat. Assn. Real Estate Appraisers, Nat. Assn. Realtors, Colo. Assn. Realtors, Women's Council Realtors, Daus. of the Republic Tex., Beta Sigma Phi. Home and Office: 331 Van Buren St Pueblo CO 81004-1807

HELBERG, KRISTIN VAUGHAN, artist; b. Syracuse, N.Y., Aug. 7, 1947; d. Burton Edward and Shirley Adelaide (Holden) H. Student, Boston U., 1965-67, Gerritt Rietvald Acad., Amsterdam, The Netherlands, 1969. Dress designer India Imports R.I., Providence, 1967-68, 70-71; costume designer Ctr. Stage, Balt., 1972; owner, pub. Rainy Day Press, Sausalito, Calif., 1972-84; gallery artist Gene Reed Galerie, Nyack, N.Y., 1987—, Toad Hall Gallery, Cooperstown, N.Y., 1990—, Gallery Americana, Houston, 1991—, Frank Miele Gallery, N.Y.C., 1992—, Galerie Black, Lausanne, Switzerland, 1995—. One-woman shows include Toad Hall Gallery, Saratoga Springs, N.Y., 1991, Very Spl. Arts, Washington, 1993, NIH, Bethesda, Md., 1994, Embassy of Switzerland, Washington, 1995, Children's Nat. Med. Ctr., Washington, 1996; exhibited in groups shows at Toad Hall Gallery, 1992, Gallerie Pro Arte Kaspar, Morges, Switzerland, 1994; represented in permanent collections NIH, Children's Nat. Med. Ctr. Scholar Ford Found., 1972; artist-in-residency grantee Md. State Arts Coun., 1989—, Howard County Arts Coun., 1993—, grantee Montgomery County Arts Coun., 1989-93. Home and Studio: 206 S Washington St Baltimore MD 21231

HELBERG, SHIRLEY ADELAIDE HOLDEN, artist, educator; b. Solvay, N.Y., Mar. 9; d. Isaac Edgar and Gladys Evelyn (Tucker) Holden; student Syracuse U.; m. Burton Edvard Helberg; children: Keir Holm Helberg, Kristin Vaughan Helberg, Kecia Tucker Lau, Kandace Holden Mead, Kraig Brownlee Helberg. BE, Johns Hopkins U., 1969; MFA, Md. Inst. Art, 1975. Tchr. various schs. in N.J. and Pa.; tchr. Manchester (Pa.) Pub. Schs., 1965-84, Balt. City Schs., 1988-92; demonstration tchr., Balt. City Schs., O'Donnell Heights Sch., 1992. One-woman art show U. Va., Charlottesville, 1974, Cayuga Mus. Art and History, Auburn, N.Y., 1974, Hist. Soc. York Mus., Pa., 1977, York Coll., 1984, Country Club of York; paintings in many private collections including Pres. Richard Nixon. Bd. dirs. York (Pa.) Arts Coun., 1964-66. Mem. NEA, Nat. League Am. Pen Women (Pa. State art chmn. 1972-74, pres. Pa. orgn. 1974-76, nat. scholarship chair 1976-1996, 96—, registrar 1986-88, 5th v.p. 1988-90, chmn. nat. sch. com. 1992-94, 1994-96; Disting. Svc. award 1978, 80, 82, 84, 86, 88, 90, 92. Disting. Achievement award 1988, 1994), NEA, named Outstanding Elem. Tchr. Supt. and Bd. Edn. NE sch. dist., Manchester, Pa., 1974. Pa. State Edn. Assn., Internat. Platform Assn., Harrisburg and York Art Assns., Pa. Watercolor Soc., Johns Hopkins Faculty Club. Republican. Methodist. Home: RR 4 Spring Grove PA 17362-9804 also: 727 S Ann St Baltimore MD 21231-3402

HELD, BARBARA KAY, pediatric nurse; b. Sandusky County, July 23, 1938; d. Kenneth M. and Mary Elizabeth (Bower) Stokes; m. Donald J. Held, Jan. 3, 1960; children: Elizabeth Marie, Theodore Joseph, John Merl. Student, Capital U., 1956-57; diploma, Riverside Hosp. Sch. Nursing, 1965. Cert. PALS. Team leader, pediatrics Riverside Hosp., Toledo; nurse, emergency rm. Riverside Hosp.; presenter in field. Mem. Riverside Alumni Assn. (pres. 1990—).

HELD, LILA M., art appraiser; b. Cleve., Oct. 5, 1925; d. Mark and Edythe H. (Dobrin) Bloomberg; m. Jacob Herzfeld, Oct. 20, 1946 (div. 1964); children: Garson, Michael; m. Merle Donald Held, Feb. 19, 1966; children: Joanne, Barbara. Student, Coll. William and Mary, 1945-46, Ohio State U., 1943-44, Case Western Res. U., 1944-45; postgrad., Case Western Res. U., 1962-66; student, Akron U., 1960-61; BS in Art Edn., Kent State U., 1961-62; M in Valuation Sci., Lindenwood Coll., 1989. Instr. art Canton (Ohio) YMCA, 1965, Beachwood (Ohio) Bd. Recreation, 1967-68; substitute tchr. art, art history Cleveland Heights, Ohio, 1967-68; freelance artist, writer, researcher, 1940—; art cons., appraiser Art Consultants Assocs., Englewood, Colo., 1985—; curatorial aid Denver Art Mus., 1985-89; fine arts appraiser, Cleve., 1989—. Works exhibited in museums and galleries in Cleve., Akron, Richmond, Va., St. Louis; speaker in field; judge at numerous art shows. Bd. dirs. Cleve. Artists Found.; mem. Akron (Ohio) Art Mus., Butler Inst. of Am. Art, Cleve. Mus. Natural History, Western Res. Hist. Soc., Toledo Mus. of Art; sec. Coun. of Cleve. Ctr. of Contemporary Art; active Continuing Edn. Assn. Case-Western Res. U., Allen Meml. Art Mus. Mem. Am. Soc. Appraisers (sr. mem., cert. in fine arts), Cleve. Mus. Art, Cleve. Ctr. for Contemporary Art (vol.), Cleve. Soc. for Contemporary Art, Nat. Coun. Jewish Women, Ohio Contemporary Glass Alliance, Art Alliance for Contemporary Glass, Temple Mus., Mus. of Am. Folk Art, Allbright-Knox Mus. (Buffalo, N.Y.). Home and Office: 13800 Shaker Blvd Apt 804 Shaker Heights OH 44120-1574

HELD, NANCY B., perinatal nurse, lactation consultant; b. Winchester, Mass., Sept. 4, 1957; d. Ann and Laurence Babine; m. Lew Held, May 22, 1976; children: David, Jessica. BSN, NYU, 1979; MS, U. Calif., San Francisco, 1992. Cert. lactation and childbirth educator, Am. Soc. Psychoprophylaxis Obstetrics. Labor/delivery nurse Pascack Valley Hosp., Westwood, N.J., 1979-83; obstetrics educator Drs. Pinski, Wiener & Grasso, Westwood, N.J., 1982-85; ob/gyn office nurse Drs. Power Hagbom Holter & Clark, San Francisco, 1986-87; asst. to dir. maternity svcs. Women's Health Assn., Greenbrae, Calif., 1987-89; perinatal edn. and lactation ctr. clin. coord. Calif. Pacific Med. Ctr., San Francisco, 1989—; owner North Bay Lamaze, 1988—; speaker and cons. in field. Recipient Founders Day award, NYU. Fellow Am. Coll. Childbirth Educators; mem. Assn. Women's Health Obstetric and Neonatal Nursing (spkr. nat. con. 1993, nat. rsch. utilization team 1993), Am. Soc. Psychoprophylaxis (chpt. co-pres.), Nurses Assn. of Am. Coll. Ob/Gyn, Internat. Childbirth Educators Assn., Internat. Lactation Cons. Assn., Sigma Theta Tau.

HELD, VIRGINIA, philosophy educator; b. Mendham, N.J., Oct. 28, 1929; d. John Howard Nott and Margaretta (Wood) Potter; m. Hans W. Held, Sept. 1950 (div. 1981); children: Julia, Philip. A.B., Barnard Coll., 1950; Ph.D., Columbia U., 1968. Mem. staff Reporter mag., 1954-65; lectr. philosophy Barnard Coll., 1964-66; mem. faculty Hunter Coll., CUNY, 1965—, prof. philosophy CUNY Grad. Sch., 1977—, disting. prof., 1996—; vis. lectr. Yale U., 1972; dir. NEH summer seminar, Stanford U. Law Sch., 1981; vis. scholar Harvard U. Law Sch., 1981-82; vis. prof. Dartmouth Coll., 1984, UCLA, 1986; Truax vis. prof. Hamilton Coll., 1989. Author: The Bewildered Age, 1962, The Public Interest and Individual Interests, 1970, Rights and Goods, Justifying Social Action, 1984, 89, Feminist Morality: Transforming Culture, Society and Politics, 1993; also more than 80 articles or chpts. in books; editor: Property, Profits and Economic Justice, 1980, Justice and Care: Essential Readings in Feminist Ethics, 1995; co-author: Women's Realities, Women's Choices, 1983, 2d edit., 1995; co-editor: Philosophy and Political Action, 1972, Philosophy, Morality and International Affairs, 1974; mem. editorial bd. Am. Philos. Quar., 1993-96, Ethics, 1982-91, Hypatia, Philosophy and Phenomenological Rsch., 1990-96, Polit. Theory, Pub. Affairs Quar., 1990-93, Social Theory and Practice, Jour. Ethics. Fulbright fellow, 1950; Rockefeller Found. fellow, 1975-76; fellow Ctr. for Advanced Study in Behavioral Scis., 1984-85. Mem. Am. Philos. Assn. (exec. com. Eastern divsn. 1979-81, Eastern divsn. rep. 1992-95), Columbia U. Seminars (Assoc.), Conf. Methods (exec. com. 1971—), Internat. Assn. Philosophy Law and Social Philosophy (pres. Am. sect. 1981-83), Soc. for Philosophy and Pub. Affairs (chmn. 1972), Soc. Women in Philosophy. Office: CUNY Grad Sch Dept Philosophy 33 W 42nd St New York NY 10036-8003

HELDRICH, ELEANOR MAAR, publisher; b. Hagerstown, Md, Nov. 4, 1929; d. Richard and Sara (Mish) Maar; m. Frederich Joseph Heldrich; children: Sarah, Susan, Frederick, Philip. Grad. high sch., Balt. Editor Federated Garden Clubs of Md., Balt., 1975—; pub., founder Prospect Hill Press, Balt., 1981—, Prospect House, Balt., 1996—. Pres. Beautiful Balt., Inc., 1985-89; founder Prospect House, 1996—. Recipient Publ. award Nat. Coun. State Garden Clubs, 1984, 86. Mem. Pub. Mktg. Assn., Balt. Pubs. Assn., Internat. Assn. Ind. Pubs. (com. small mag. editors and pubs.), Md. Assn. for Dyslexic Youth and Adults. Office: Prospect Hill Press 216 Wendover Rd Baltimore MD 21218-1837

HELFAT, LUCILE, social services professional; b. N.Y.C., Apr. 6, 1919; d. Morris and Anna (Katz) Podell; m. Bernard Helfat, June 27, 1943; children: Jonathan, Mark. BS, U. Mich., 1942; MS, Columbia U., 1944. Cert. social worker, psychiatric social worker. Mem. faculty Queens Coll. CUNY, N.Y.C., 1966-76; supr. social work L.I. Jewish Hosp., N.Y.C. Co-author: Child Psychology, 1981; contbr. articles to profl. jours. Chmn. State of N.Y. Northeastern Queens Nature and Hist. Preserve Commn.; mem. Ft. Tolten Redevel. Auuthority, 1996—. Home: 26-18 West Dr Douglaston NY 11363-1049

HELFGOTT, GLORIA VIDA, artist; b. N.Y.C., May 25, 1928; d. Charles and Anna (Cohen) Wolff; m. Roy B. Helfgott; 1 child, Daniel Andrew. Grad. in fine arts, Cooper Union, 1948. faculty mem. Ctr. for Book Arts, N.Y.C., 1989-96, Brookfield (Conn.) Craft Ctr., 1988-96, Art New Eng. at Bennington (Vt.) Coll., 1992, Womens Studio Workshop, Rosendale, N.Y., 1992. Group exhbns. include P.S.I., L.I., N.Y., 1979, Handin Hand Gallery, N.Y.C., 1985, Grad. Ctr. for the Arts, W.Va. U., Morgantown, 1988, Berkshire Mus., Pittsfield, Mass., 1988, Ctr. for the Arts, Avado, Colo., 1989, Hoffman Gallery, Portland, Oreg., 1990, Granary Books, N.Y.C., 1990, Ted Cronin Gallery, N.Y.C., 1990, Boca Raton (Fla.) Mus., 1991, Sazama Gallery, Chgo., 1992, Harper-Collins Exhbn. Space, N.Y.C., 1993, Istvan Kiraly Mus., Hungary, 1994, Meml. Art Mus., Ormond Beach, Fla., 1994, Brown U., 1995, Nexus Gallery, Phila., 1995, Ctr. for Book Arts, 1996; represented in permanent collections Ruth and Marvin Sackner Archive of Concrete and Visual Poetry, Miami Beach, Fla., Nat. Mus. Women in the Arts, Washington, Victoria and Albert Mus., London. Mem. Guild of Book Workers. Home and Office: 1784 Pallisades Dr Pacific Palisades CA 90272

HELGANZ, BEVERLY BUZHARDT, counselor; b. Tampa, Fla., June 7, 1941; d. M. O. Buzhardt and Jeanne M. Buzhardt Crabb; m. Charles F. Helganz Jr., June 26, 1964 (dec. Dec. 1977). AA, Jacksonville U., 1962, BA, 1974; MEd, U. North Fla., 1993. Customer contact So. Bell, Jacksonville, Fla., 1959-66, supr., 1966-80, staff mgr., 1980-91; assessment counselor Charter Hosp., Jacksonville, 1995; sr. counselor River Region Human Svcs., Jacksonville, 1995—; past pres. Am. Bus. Women's Assn., Jacksonville, 1969-70. Mem. women's aux. U. Med. Ctr., Jacksonville, 1994—, Hospice of N.E. Fla., Jacksonville, 1994—; panel mem. foster care citizen's rev. bd. 4th Jud. Cir. Ct., Jacksonville, 1993—; docent Mus. Sci. and History, 1993—; past pres. Jacksonville Alumnae Panhellenic Assn., 1982. Recipient Merit award Am. Bus. Women's Assn., 1966, Woman of Yr. award, 1969, Honor Ring Alumnae's cert of merit Zeta Tau Alpha, 1975, 76, Girl of Yr. award Beta Sigma Phi. Mem. ACA, Fla. Counseling Assn., N.E. Fla. Mental Health Counselors Assn., Mental Health Assn., Telephone Pioneers of Am. (life), Pilot Club Jacksonville (bd. dirs., past pres.), Club Continental, Phi Kappa Phi. Home: # 97 5000 San Jose Blvd Jacksonville FL 32207

HELGENBERGER, MARG, actress; m. Alan Roseberg; 1 child, Hugh. Appeared in TV series Ryan's Hope, 1984-86, The Shell Game, 1987, China Beach, 1988-91 (Emmy award; named Primetime Programming Individual Outstanding Supporting Actress in Drama Series, 1990, 91); co-host of New Year's Rockin' Eve, 1988, Home, 1989, (TV movies) Blind Vengence, 1990, Death Dreams, 1991, In Sickness and In Health, 1992, Through the Eyes of a Killer, 1992, When Love Kills: The Seduction of John Hearn, 1993, Stephen King's The Tommyknockers, 1993, Where Are My Children?, 1994, Lie Down with Lions, 1994, Partners, 1994; appeared in films Always, 1989, After Midnight, 1989, Crooked Hearts, 1991, Desperate Motive, 1993, The Cowboy Way, 1994, Bad Boys, 1995, Species, 1995. *

HELIN, JACQUELYN M., classical musician, music educator; b. Chgo., Sept. 24, 1951; d. Rudolph A. and Janet M. (Wallin) H.; m. Robert A. Glick, May 13, 1989; children: Kathryn Tyra Helin-Glick, William David Helin-Glick. MusB, U. Oreg., 1973; MA, Stanford U., 1976; D of Musical Arts, U. Tex., Austin, 1982. Tchg. musician Lincoln Ctr. Inst., N.Y.C., 1987-91; tchr. 92nd St Y Performing Arts Dept., N.Y.C., 1990-91; faculty mem. 92d St Sch. Music, N.Y.C., 1987-91; classical musician, tchr. N.Y.C., 1979-91, Sante Fe, 1991—; cons. in field. Solo performer The Corcoran Gallery, Washington, 1982, Dumbarton Oaks, Washington, 1982, The Chagall Mus., Nice, France, 1984, Merkin Concert Hall, N.Y.C., 1986, the 92d St Y., N.Y.C., 1992, Caltech, Pasadena, 1993, Onthe Horowitz Piano, Los Alamos, N.Mex., 1993, others; pianist Redwood Symphony, 1994, Santa Fe Symphony, 1994, Mesa Symphony, 1994, Richmond Symphony, 1995, Greenwich Symphony, 1996; live radio appearances include Peformance Today on NPR, WFMT, Chgo., WNCN, N.Y.C., WNYC, N.Y.C., WBAI, N.Y.C., WGBH, Boston, WGMS, Washington, numerous others. Recipient Lucy Moses award Outstanding Promise Yale U. Sch. Music, New Haven, Conn., 1974; named winner Artists in Competition, N.Y.C., 1984. Mem. Western State Arts Fedn. (performing arts touring roster 1993-96), Northwest Arts Alliance, Western Alliance Arts Adminstrs., N.Mex. Touring & Residency Roster, The Bohemians. Home: 2327 Santa Barbara Dr Santa Fe NM 87505

HELIN, YVETTE MARIE, artist, costume designer; b. Kansas City, Mo., Feb. 27, 1963; d. Arthur F. and Charlotte Anne H. BFA, Kansas City Art Inst., 1985. guest spkr. Parsons Sch. Design, N.Y.C., 1996, art dept. Yale U., New Haven, 1996; guest artist Washington U., St. Louis, 1991; guest vis. artist U. Del., Newark, 1996. Exhbns. include Nelson Atkins Mus. Art, Kansas City, 1985, WIndow Installation, Hartford, Conn., 1986, Barney's N.Y. Sculpture, N.Y.C., 1989, Cucaracha Theater, N.Y.C., 1989, 1991, Flytrap Art Event, Blkyn., 1991, Green Rm., Bklyn., 1992, Pub. Theater, N.Y.C., 1992, Herron Test Site Gallery, Bklyn., 1992, PS1 Mus., Queens, N.Y., 1993, Krannert Art Mus., Champaign, Ill., 1993, Angus + Art, N.Y.C., 1993, Seafirst Gallery, Seattle, 1994, Barucha Coll., Bklyn., 1995; creator Pedestrian Project, 1990—. Franklin Furnace grantee, 1990, 92, Puffin Found. grantee, 1992, 96, Margolis-Brown Adaptors grantee, 1992, Lower Manhattan Cultural Coun. grantee 1993-95, grantee Gunk Found. 1996; Kansas City Art Inst. scholar, 1981. Home: 258 Wythe Ave Brooklyn NY 11211

HELINE, DEANN, television producer. Student, Ind. U.; diploma in film and TV, NYU. Exec. prodr. TV sitcom "Ellen" Touchstone TV, L.A., 1994—. Co-writer: (with Eileen Heisler) Doogie Howser, M.D.; co-writer, co-prodr. (with Heisler) Roseanne, Murphy Brown. Office: Walt Disney World 500 S Buena Vista St Burbank CA 91521-1884

HELKE, CINDA JANE, pharmacology and neuroscience educator, researcher; b. Waterloo, Iowa, Feb. 27, 1951; d. Gerald and Lorna (Smith) Pieres; m. Joel Edward Helke, Aug. 10, 1974. BS in Pharmacy, Creighton U., 1974; PhD, Georgetown U., 1978. Staff fellow NIH, Bethesda, Md., 1978-80; asst. prof. dept. pharmacology Uniformed Svcs. Univ. of the Health Scis., Bethesda, 1980-85, assoc. prof. dept. pharmacology, 1985-88; prof. dept. pharmacology Uniformed Svcs. Univ. Health Scis., Bethesda, 1988—, prof. neurosci. program, 1991—, dir. neurosci. program, 1993—; mem. adv. panel Am. Heart Assn., 1984-87, NIH, Bethesda, 1987-91; mem. oversight rev. panel NSF, 1986, pharmacology test com. Nat. Bd. Med. Examiners, 1992-94. Author chpts. in books; mem. editl. bd. Synapse, Pharmacology, Jour. Comparative Neurology; contbr. numerous articles to profl. jours. NIH grantee, 1981—. Mem. AAAS, Am. Soc. Pharmacology and Exptl. Therapeutics, Soc. for Neurosci. Women in Sci., Women in Neurosci., Soc. for Neurosci. (sec., treas. Washington chpt. 1985-87). Office: Uniformed Svcs U Health Sci 4301 Jones Bridge Rd Bethesda MD 20814-4712

HELLER, AMANDA, editor; b. Washington, D.C., Apr. 6, 1946; d. Leo and Shirley (Stein) Young; m. Richard Benjamin Heller, Aug. 13, 1972; 1 child, Benjamin David. AB, Mt. Holyoke Coll., 1968. Editor Atlantic Monthly, Boston, 1969-76, Art New England, Boston, 1980-85; freelance editor, 1976—; book rev. columnist Boston Globe, 1980—. Co-author: Storm Across Asia, 1979. Mem. Dem. City Com., Newton, Mass., 1993—.

HELLER, DOROTHY, artist; b. N.Y.C., June 15, 1926; d. Samuel and Rebecca (Cohn) H. Studied with, Hans Hofman, N.Y.C., 1942. One-person shows include Betty Parsons Gallery, N.Y.C., 1972, 76, 78, U. Pa., 1976, Cathedral St. John the Divine, N.Y.C., 1976, East Hampton Gallery, N.Y.C., 1963, Galerie Facchetti, Paris, 1955, Tibor De Nagy, N.Y.C., 1953, Poindexter Gallery, 1956, 57; exhibited in group shows at Denver Art Mus., 1953, Whitney Mus. Ann., 1957, Mus. Modern Art Traveling Show, 1963, Betty Parsons Gallery, 1972-81, U. Calif. Art Mus., 1974, Met. Mus. Art, N.Y.C., 1979, Otis Art Inst., 1979, Bklyn. Coll. Art Gallery, 1990; represented in permanent collections Met. Mus. Art, N.Y.C., U. Calif. Art Mus., Berkeley, Cornell U. Johnson Mus., Ithaca, N.Y., Wadsworth Atheneum, Hartford, Conn., Smithsonian Instn. Archives, Washington, Zimmerli Mus., New Brunswick, N.J., Alexandria (La.) Mus., Auburn (Ala.) U., Whitney Communications, N.Y.C., Chase Manhattan Bank, N.Y.C., many others. Recipient Internat. Woman of Yr. award, 1976.

HELLER, ELEANOR, artist; b. Phila., Mar. 28, 1918; d. m. Edward Eugene Heller (dec.), May 30, 1947. BA, Bryn Mawr Coll., Bryn Mawr, 1939; MA, Bryn Mawr Coll., 1941, MSS, 1941; postgrad., U. Penn., Phila., 1939-40; student, Art Students League, Woodstock, 1967, SUNY, New Paltz, 1967. Caseworker Family Svc., Grand Rapids, Mich., 1941-42, Am. Red Cross (mil. hosp.), 1942-44, Jewish Family Svc., Cleve., 1944-46, VA, N.Y.C., 1946-49, Ctrl. Bur. for the Aged, N.Y.C., 1949-52; pvt. practice potter, sculptor Kerhonkson, N.Y., 1955-67; pvt. practice abstract artist Sarasota, Fla., 1968—; vol., advisor in art Women's Resource Ctr., Sarasota, 1979-82; vol., one of founders Women's Caucus for Art, Sarasota, 1985. Author: Art of Ceramics (slide-tape lecture for state-wide use), 1973, Ringling Art Mus.; contbr. articles on art; one woman shows include Bethlehem Art Gallery, Vail's Gate, N.Y., 1963, Hilton Leech Gallery, Sarasota, Fla., 1973, 75, Manatee Cmty. Coll., Bradenton, Fla., 1985, Women's Resource Ctr., Sarasota, 1990; exhibited in group shows Longboat Key Art Ctr., Fla., 1970, Arvida Show, Sarasota Art Assn., Sarasota, 1982, Statewide Invitational, Longboat Key Art Ctr., 1983, Sarasota Centennial Invitational, 1986, Fla. Women Artists-Womens Studio Workshop, Binnewater Arts Ctr., Rosendale, N.Y., 1988, Sarasota Art Assn. (Award winner 1989), Women's Caucus for Art, Sarasota, 1993, Voorhees Gallery, Sarasota, 1994; represented in permanent collection Nat. Mus. of Women in the Arts, Washingto n. Recipient Best of Show award Woodstock Craftmens Guild, Woodstock, 1963; first prize Longboat Key Art Ctr., Sarasota, 1970; first Fla. artist admitted to permanent collection National Museum of Women in the Arts, Washington, 1987.

HELLER, LOIS JANE, physiologist, educator, researcher; b. Detroit, Jan. 4, 1942; d. John and Lona Elizabeth (Stockmeyer) Skagerberg; m. Robert Eugene Heller, May 21, 1966; children: John Robert, Suzanne Elizabeth. BA, Albion Coll., 1964; MS, U. Mich., 1966; PhD, U. Ill., Chgo., 1970. Instr. med ctr. U. Ill., Chgo., 1969-70, asst. prof., 1970-71; asst. prof. U. Minn., Duluth, 1972-77, assoc. prof., 1977-89, prof., 1989—. Author: Cardiovascular Physiology, 3d edition, 1989; contbr. numerous articles to profl. jours. Mem. Am. Physiol. Soc., Am. Heart Assn., Soc. Exptl. Biology and Medicine, Internat. Soc. Heart Rsch., Sigma Xi. Home: 311 Halsey St Duluth MN 55803-2535 Office: Univ Minn Sch of Medicine Duluth MN 55812

HELLER, MARYELLEN, special education educator; b. Mt. Kisco, N.Y., Apr. 9, 1957; d. Michael Joseph and Ellen Agnes (O'Grady) Romano; m. Robert Edward Heller, Dec. 22, 1979; children: Kerry, Rob, Kathleen. BA Psychology, Elem. Edn., Spl. Edn., Coll. of New Rochelle, 1979; MS Reading, Western Conn., 1989. Second grade tchr. St. Patrick's Grammar Sch., Yorktown, N.Y., 1979-82; art instr. Newtown (Conn.) Continuing Edn., summer 1992; resource rm. tchr. City Hill Mid. Sch., Naugatuck, Conn., 1992-93, spl. edn. tutor, 1993; reading cons. Community Scch., Prospect, Conn., 1993-94; reading specialist Broadview Mid. Sch., Danbury, Conn., 1994—; lang. arts specialist Roberts Ave. Sch., Danbury, Conn., 1995—; art instr. Southbury (Conn.) Parks and Recreation, 1992; dried flower instr. for adults, Newtown Adult Edn., 1992; profl. devel. instr. Community Sch., Prospect, Conn., 1994, Danbury Schs., Conn., 1995; reading cons. Broadview Mid. Sch., 1996—. Pageant dir. Sacred Heart Ch., Southbury, 1991-94, CCD tchr., 1992-94; PTA program dir. Pomperaug Elem. Sch., Southbury, 1991-92; com. to select a site for group home for mentally retarded adults, Town Bd. of Somers, N.Y., 1978-79. Mem. Conn. Edn. Assn., Danbury Tchrs. Assn., ACES Alternat. Edn. Ctr. Home: 75 Stonegate Dr Southbury CT 06488 Office: Broadview Middle Sch 72 Hospital Ave Danbury CT 06810-6021

HELLER, NADINE VERDAN, artist, writer, educator; b. Bklyn., Feb. 26, 1959; d. Irving and Vera (Resnikoff) Heller; m. Scott Pellnat; 1 child, Saskia Vera Heller Pellnat. BA in Comparative Lit., Bklyn. Coll., 1984; Masters Diploma, N.Y. Acad. Art, 1987; MFA, Columbia U., 1989. Adj. prof. fine arts and English Boricua Coll., N.Y.C., 1993-95, Touro Coll., N.Y.C., 1994—; mem. adv. bd. Discoveries, N.Y.C., 1994. Exhibited works at 450 Gallery, N.Y.C., N.Y. Acad. Art, Grace Harkin Gallery, N.Y., Fourth World/A.W.O.W., N.Y.C., 1996, Gallery 313, N.Y.C., numerous others; artist-curator N.Y. Soho Biennial '95; contbr. articles to profl. jours. Involved in campaign for a pilot crisis ctr. to serve people affected by episodic forms of mental illness. Recipient Jakobson award for fiction Wesleyan U./Wesleyan Writers Conf., 1995; Elizabeth Found. for arts grantee, 1994-95; Artists' Fellowship fellow, 1995. Mem. N.Y. Artists Equity, Nat. Aliance for the Mentally Ill, Friends of Alliance for the Mentally Ill, Phi Beta Kappa, Sigma Delta Lambda. Home: 1747 E 3rd St Apt B14 Brooklyn NY 11223 Office: 470 Prospect Ave # 1D Brooklyn NY 11215

HELLER, NANCY GALE, art historian, educator; b. L.A., Apr. 21, 1949; d. Jules and Gloria (Spiegel) H. AB, Middlebury Coll., 1970; MA, Rutgers U., 1975, PhD, 1982. Part-time instr./tchg. asst. Rutgers U., New Brunswick, N.J., 1974-77; instr. East Tex. State U., Commerce, 1977-79; asst. prof., then assoc. prof. Univ. of the Arts, Phila., 1990-96, prof., 1996—; editor Nat. Gallery of Art, Washington, 1981; adj. asst. prof. Georgetown U., Washington, 1990, 93, 94, 96; asst. prof. U. Md., 1982-85, 87-88; chair art history panel Southeastern Conf. Art Colls., Washington, 1995; panelist 1st Ann. Conf. on Liberal Edn. of Performing Arts, Winston-Salem, N.C., 1994; juror Greater Norristown (Pa.) Art League, 1995. Author: Women Artists: An Illustrated History, 1st edit. 1987, rev./expanded edit. 1991; co-author: The Regionalists, 1976, An Age of Grandeur, 1995; co-editor: North American Women Artists of the 20th Century, 1995. NEH fellow, 1995, Smithsonian Instn. fellow, 1979-81. Mem. Spanish Dance Soc. (vice chair 1984—), North Am. Catalan Soc., Soc. Dance History Scholars, Coll. Art Assn. Avocation: Spanish Dance. Office: U of the Arts Humanities Dept 320 S Broad St Philadelphia PA 19102

HELLER, PATRICIA ANN, container company executive; b. Summit, N.J., Sept. 16, 1946; d. Henry August and Mary Eugenia (McDonough) Cubberley; m. Frank Joseph Miskewitz, Sept. 23, 1967 (div. Feb. 1982); children: Thomas, Tammy; m. Jerome Heller, Feb. 26, 1991 (dec. Aug. 1991). Diploma, All Souls Hosp. Sch. Nursing, Morristown, N.J., 1967; BS in Pub. Adminstrn., St. Josephs Coll., North Wyndam, Maine, 1983. RN, N.J. Nurse Overlook Hosp., Summit, 1967-69, 71-78, U.S. Army Hosp., Bad Caanstatt, Germany, 1969-70; nurse, office mgr., surg. asst. Morey Wosnitzer, M.D., Springfield, N.J., 1982-86; nurse, office mgr. Drs. Malcolm Schwartz and Bernard Lehrhoff, Westfield, N.J., 1986-87; adminstrv. asst. Champion Container Corp., Avenel, N.J., 1987-89, fin. contr., treas., 1989-91, pres., 1991—; mem. editl. adv. bd. Closures and Containers mag., 1995—. Mem. Springfield Dem. Com., 1970-90, Union County Dem. Com.; vol. Emanuel Cancer Found., 1993—, mem. adv. bd., 1995—; vol. N.J. Spl. Olympics, 1994—. Mem. NAFE, Nat. Assn. Fruit Flavors and Syrups, Nat. Assn. Container Distbrs., N.J. Bus. and Industry Assn., N.J. Assn. Women Bus. Owners (awards chmn. 1993-94, sec. 1994-95, pres. 1996-97, Teal Heart award 1995), Union County C. of C. (bd. dirs. 1996—). Republican. Roman Catholic. Home: 12 Cowperthwaite Pl Westfield NJ 07090 Office: Champion Container Corp 180 Essex Ave Avenel NJ 07001

HELLER, PEGGY OSNA, poetry therapist, psychotherapist; b. Bklyn., Nov. 21, 1936; d. Charles S. and Miriam (Mendelson) Freundlich; m. Eugene Paul Heller, Aug. 3, 1957 (div. 1986); children: Elise Karen, Meredith Leslie. BA, Bklyn. Coll., 1958; MSW, Cath. U. Am., 1983; PhD, Pacific Western U., 1995. Diplomate Acad. Cert. Social Workers (lic. clin. social worker); registered clin. poetry therapist. Speech correction tchr. N.Y.C. Bd. Edn., 1958-60; program dir., instr., writer test courses Stanley H. Kaplan Ednl. Ctrs., N.Y.C., Washington, 1959-81; clin. social worker D.C. Therapy Group, Washington, 1983-85; bibliotherapist Psychiat. Inst. Washington, 1985-87; pvt. practice Potomac, Md., 1985—; lectr. Create Ctr. for Therapy, Growth and Tng., Bethesda, Md., 1984-92, Cath. U. Am., Washington, 1984-89, Lesley Coll., Cambridge, Mass., 1992, Fla. Internat. U., Miami, 1992; poetry therapy cons. Mt. Vernon Hosp., Alexandria, Va., 1987-90, Dominion Hosp., Falls Church, Va., 1990-92, Psychiat. Inst., Washington, 1992-95; dir. Nat. Ctr. Poetry Therapy Edn., 1993—, Poetry Therapy Tng. Inst., 1995. Mem. editl. staff Jour. Poetry Therapy, 1986—, Jour. Arts in Psychotherapy, 1988—; contbr. articles to profl. jours. Former program dir. Beverly Farms PTA, Potomac, Md., Hoover Cmty. Sch., Potomac; founder Last Friday Playreading Club, Potomac, 1983—. Mem. NASW, Am. Group Psychotherapy Assn., Nat. Assn. Poetry Therapy (pres. 1991-93, Disting. Svc. award 1993), Nat. Assn. Poetry Therapy Found. (v.p. 1993-96, pres. 1996—), Nat. Fedn. Biblio/Poetry Therapy (treas. 1987—), Bibliotherapy Round Table (treas. 1984—), Greater Washington Soc. Clin. Social Work, Mensa. Home and Office: 7715 Whiterim Ter Potomac MD 20854-1775

HELLMANN, RENE BRAUN, English as a Second Language educator; b. Hammond, Ind., July 13, 1967; d. Philip Leo and Suellen Ann (Thiel) Braun; m. Anthony Lawrence, June 29, 1991; children: Alexander, Nicholas. BA, Ind. U., 1989, MA, 1990. ESL tchr. Henry Abbott RVT Sch., Danbury, Conn., 1990-92, Danbury Adult Edn., 1990—; adj. prof. Western Conn. State U., Danbury, 1991—. Mem. TESOL. Home: 31 Pocono Ln Danbury CT 06810

HELLYER, CONSTANCE ANNE, communications executive, writer; b. Puyallup, Wash., Apr. 22, 1937; d. David Tirrell and Constance (Hopkins) H.; m. Peter A. Corning, Dec. 30, 1963 (div. 1977); children: Anne Arundel, Stephanie Deak; m. Don W. Conway, Oct. 12, 1980. BA with honors, Mills Coll., 1959. Grader, researcher Harvard U., Cambridge, Mass., 1959-60; researcher Newsweek mag., N.Y.C., 1960-63; author's asst. Theodore H. White and others, N.Y.C., 1964-69; freelance writer, editor Colo., Calif., 1969-75; writer, editor Stanford (Calif.) U. Med. Ctr., 1975-79; communications dir. No. Calif. Cancer Program, Palo Alto, 1979-82; comm. dir. Stanford Law Sch., Palo Alto, 1982—. Founding editor (newsletters) Insight, 1978-80, Synergy, 1980-82, Stanford Law Alum, 1992-95; editor (mag.) Stanford Lawyer, 1982—; contbr. articles to profl. jours. and mags. Recipient silver medal Coun. for Advancement and Support Edn., 1985, 89, award of distinction dist. VII, 1994. Mem. No. Calif. Sci. Writers Assn. (co-founder, bd. dirs. 1979-93), Phi Beta Kappa. Democrat. Home: 2080 Louis Rd Palo Alto CA 94303-3451 Office: Stanford Law Sch Stanford CA 94305-8610

HELM, JOCELYN B., gerontologist; b. Boston, Sept. 20, 1928; d. George Warrin and Helen Elizabeth (Nathan) Bird; m. Carl Edward Helm, June 10, 1950; children: Carla Jean, Curtis Warrin, Christopher Evan, Kimberly. BA in Edn., Duke U., 1950; MA in Edn., NYU, 1974. Asst. dir. phys. edn. YWCA, Detroit, 1951-53; tchr. phys. edn. Stuart Sch. Secred Heart, Princeton, N.J., 1969-73; intern St. Vincent's Hosp., N.Y.C., 1973-74; exec. dir., founder Princeton Sr. Resource Ctr., 1974—; adj. asst. prof. Stockton State Coll., Pomona, N.J., 1975. Mem. Princeton Cmty. Housitn, 1983—; mem., sec. Mercer City Alcohol & Drug Abuse Adv. Com., Trenton, 1990—; bd. dirs. Am. Heart Assn., Princeton, 1994; transp. com. ARC, Princeton, 1991—; chair Salvation Army Svc. Group, Princeton, 1986—. Recipient Delta Phi Rho Alpha Athletic award, 1950; Woman of Yr. Soroptimist Internat., 1996, Ethical Svc. award Ethical Humanist Soc., 1996. Mem. Am. Dance Therapy Assn., Am. soc. Aging, Nat. Assn. Sr. Eating Disorders (trustee 1989—), Older Women's League, Sigma Phi Omega. Home: 207 Mt Lucas Rd Princeton NJ 08540 Office: Princeton Sr Resource Ctr Spruce Cir Princeton NJ 08540

HELM, JUNE, anthropologist, educator; b. Twin Falls, Idaho, Sept. 13, 1924; d. William Jennings and Julia Frances (Dixon) H.; m. Pierce Erwin King, Aug. 15, 1967. PhB, U. Chgo., 1944, AM, 1950, PhD, 1958. Lectr. Carleton U., Ottawa, Ont., Can., 1949-59; asst. prof. anthropology U. Iowa, Iowa City, 1960-63, assoc. prof., 1963-66, prof., 1966—; adviser Indian Brotherhood for N.W.T. Can. 1974; cons. Mackenzie Valley Pipeline Inquiry, Govt. of Can., 1975-76. Author: The Lynx Point People: The Dynamics of a Northern Athapaskan Band, 1961, Indians of the Subarctic, 1976; editor: Subarctic: Vol. VI Handbook of North American Indians, 1981, Social Contexts of American Ethnology, 1840-1984, 1985; contbr. numerous articles to profl. jours. Fellow AAAS, Am. Acad. Arts and Scis. (chmn. sect. H 1978); mem. Am. Anthrop. Assn. (pres. 1985-87), Am. Ethnol. Soc. (pres. 1982-83, editor publs. 1964-68), Ctrl. States Anthrop. Soc. (pres. 1970-71). Office: U Iowa Dept Anthropology Iowa City IA 52242

HELM, PHALA ANIECE, physiatrist; b. Ft. Worth, 1931. MD, U. Tex., Dallas, 1966. Diplomate Am. Bd. Phys. Medicine and Rehab. Intern Baylor U. Med. Ctr., Dallas, 1966-67, resident in phys. med. and rehab., 1967-70; mem. staff Parkland Meml. Hosp., Dallas; prof. physiatry U. Tex. S.W. Med. Ctr., Dallas. Mem. ABA, ADA, Am. Acad. Phys. Medicine and Rehab., Am. Congress Phys. Medicine and Rehab. Office: U Tex Health Sci Ctr 51-104 Sprague Clin Sci Bldg 5323 Harry Hines Blvd Dallas TX 75235-9055

HELMAR-SALASOO, ESTER ANETTE, literacy educator, researcher; b. Subiaco, W.A., Australia, Oct. 26, 1956; came to U.S., 1987; d. Harald R. and Liana M. (Kikas) H.; m. Lembit Salasoo, Jan. 2, 1988; children: Imbi, Markus, Kristjan. BA, U. W. Australia, Perth, Australia, 1977; Diploma in Edn., U. W. Australia, Perth, 1978; MS, SUNY, Albany, 1988; postgrad. studies in Edn., 1989—. Tchr. English, lit. Pub. Schs. W. Australia, 1978-85, ESL tchr. Tuart Coll., W. Australia, 1986; teaching asst. SUNY, Albany, 1988, rsch. asst., 1989-90; cons. Nat. Javits Project for Lang. Arts Rsch., Washington, 1992. Home: 2280 Berkley Ave Schenectady NY 12309

HELMER, CAROL A., psychologist, school psychologist; b. Newport News, Apr. 24, 1946; d. Frederick Otto and Phyllis Amelia (Calf) Helmer; 1 child, Shannon Helmer Ducey. BA, Roanoke Coll., Salem, Va., 1967; MS, Radford U., Va., 1968; PhD, Hofstra U., 1985. Lic. psychologist, N.Y. Tchr. math. Brentwood (N.Y.) pub. schs., 1968-70, psychologist, 1970-72; psychotherapist Bi-County Cons. Ctr., Amityville, N.Y., 1970-78; psychologist BOCES II, Patchogue, N.Y., 1972-73, Middle Country Schs., Centereach, N.Y., 1973—; psychotherapist North Shore Cons., Smithtown, N.Y., 1978-82; pvt. practice psychology Coram, N.Y., 1986—; supr. interns, Hofstra U., 1980—, Adelphi U., 1985-86, Queens Coll., 1986-87, St. John's U., 1987—. Bd. dirs. Community House, Centreach, 1986-87. Redford U. grad. assistantship, 1967-68. Mem. APA (cert. in treatment of alcohol and other psychoactive substance user disorders), EMDRIA, N.Y. State Psychol. Assn. (pres. sch. divsn. 1994), Suffolk County Psychol. Assn. (sch. psychology com. chmn., exec. bd. mem. 1990-94), Rotary. Office: 1 Freemont Ln Coram NY 11727-3234

HELMER, DONA JEAN, librarian; b. Miles City, Mont., Aug. 25, 1948; d. William Charles and Eleanor Grace (McDonagh) Klar; m. Roger Burton Helmer, Nov. 27, 1967; 1 child, Elizabeth Ann. BS, U. Wis., Whitewater, 1970; MA, No. Ill. U., DeKalb, 1972; MLS, 1975; EdSpec, U. So. Miss., 1983. Dir. Libr. Svcs. Jordan Valley (Oreg.) Union H.S., 1974-78; head Children's Svcs. Missoula (Mont.) City-County Libr., 1978-80; dir. Tri Valley Sch. Libr., Healy, Alaska, 1980-83; instr. U. So. Miss., Hattiesburg, 1983-86; head Youth Svcs. Anchorage Pub. Libr., 1986-89; dir. Libr. Svcs. Yupiit Sch. Dist., Akiachak, Alaska, 1989-90; libr. Adak (Alaska) Region Schs., 1990-92; assoc. prof. Mont. State U., Billings, 1992—, 1992—; bd. mem. KUSM- Pub. TV, Bozeman, Mont., 1994—, ALAN, 1978-82. Editor: Selecting Materials for School Library Media Centers, 1990. Grantee carnegie Found., 1988; recipient JMRT award 3M/JMRT, 1981. Mem. ALA, Media Roundtable Alaska Libr. Assn., Children's and Young Adult Group, Assn. Libr. Svc. to Children, Internat. Reading Assn. Office: Montana State Univ Library 1500 N 30 Billings MT 59101

HELMER, M. CHRISTIE, lawyer; b. Portland, Oreg., Oct. 8, 1949; d. Marvin Curtis and Inez Bahl (Corwin) H.; m. Joe D. Bailey, June 23, 1979; children: Tim Bailey, Bill Bailey, Kim Easton. BA in English magna cum laude, Wash. State U., 1970; JD cum laude, Lewis & Clark, 1974. Bar: Oreg. 1974, U.S. Supreme Ct. 1975, U.S. Ct. Appeals (9th cir.) 1975. Assoc. Miller, Nash, Wiener, Hager & Carlsen, Portland, 1974-81, ptnr., 1981—; mem. Oreg. Bd. Bar Examiners, Portland, 1978-81; del. 9th Cir. Jud. Conf., 1984-87, mem. exec. com., 1987-90. Author: Arrest of Ships, 1985. Mem. ABA, FBA (bd. dirs. 1994—), Oreg. Bar (bd. govs. 1981-84, treas. 1983-84), Maritime Law Assn., Internat. Bar Assn., Founder's Club (v.p., bd. dirs., sec. 1986-92), Multnomah Athletic Club, Phi Beta Kappa. Office: Miller Nash Wiener Hager & Carlsen 111 SW 5th Ave Ste 3600 Portland OR 97204-3639

HELMOND, KATHERINE, actress; b. Galveston, Tex., July 5, 1934; d. Patrick Joseph and Thelma Louise (Malone) H.; m. David Christian, Dec., 1968. Pres. Taur Can Prodns., Hollywood, Calif., 1979—. Appeared as Jessica Tate in TV series Soap, 1978-81 (Emmy award best actress, 1978, 79, 80, 81, Golden Globe award 1980); co-star TV series Who's The Boss?, 1984-92, Coach, 1995—; guest star appearances in TV series and in TV movies including Dr. Max, 1974, Larry, 1974, Locusts, 1974, The Autobiography of Miss Jane Pittman, 1974, The Legend of Lizzie Borden, 1975, The Family Nobody Wanted, 1975, Cage Without a Key, 1975, The First 36 Hours of Dr. Durant, 1975, James Dean, 1976, Wanted: The Sundance Woman, 1976, Little Ladies of the Night, 1977, Getting Married, 1978, miniseries Pearl, 1978, Diary of a Teenage Hitchhiker, 1979, Scout's Honor, 1980, miniseries World War III, 1982, For Lovers Only, 1982, Rosie: The Rosemary Clooney Story, 1982, When Will I Be Loved, 1990, The Perfect Tribute, 1991, Deception: A Mother's Secret, 1991, Grass Roots, 1992, Liz: The Elizabeth Taylor Story, 1995; film appearances include: The Hospital, 1971, The Hindenberg, 1975, Baby Blue Marine, 1976, Family Plot, 1976, Time Bandits, 1981, Brazil, 1986, Shadey, Overboard, 1987, Lady in White, 1988, Inside Monkey Zetterland, 1993, Amore!, 1993, The Spy Within, 1995; stage appearences include House of Blue Leaves, 1971 (N.Y. Drama Critics Variety award 1971, Clarence Derwent award 1971, L.A. Drama Critics award 1972), Great God Brown, 1973, Quartermaine's Terms, 1984, Mixed Emotions, 1993; appeared with numerous repertory theatres including Associated Producing Artists, N.Y.C., Trinity Sq. Repertory Co., R.I., Hartford Stage, Phoenix Repertory, N.Y.C. Mem. Screen Actors Guild, AFTRA. Roman Catholic. Office: William Morris Agy care Lee Stollman 151 S El Camino Dr Beverly Hills CA 90212-2704*

HELMS, FRANCES CRESWELL, editor, columnist; b. Blacksburg, S.C., Sept. 18, 1944; d. Bruce Jackson Creswell and Betty Jean (Moss) McDaniel; m. Steven Hoyt Upchurch, Apr. 21, 1967 (div. June 1989); children: Alan, Karen, Susan, Joel; m. Vance Elbert Helms Jr., Jan. 15, 1990. Student, Limestone Coll., 1976, Converse Coll., 1985-87; MA in Journalism, U. S.C., 1993. Account rep. Gaffney (S.C.) Ledger, 1968-72; dir. advt. Sta. WFGN, Gaffney, 1972-75; reporter Spartanburg (S.C.) Herald-Jour., 1976-83, editor lifestyles, 1983-89; columnist N.Y. Times Regional Newspapers, 1984-90; adj. prof. U. S.C., Spartanburg, 1989; editor Richmond (Va.) Mag., 1989—. Sec. Am. Cancer Soc., Gaffney, 1974-77; bd. dirs. ARC, Gaffney, 1988-89. Named Writer of Yr. S.C. Assn. Retarded Citizens, 1979, Newspaper Woman of Yr., S.C. Press Assn., 1981, Woman of Achievement Media Women S.C., 1988; recipient Sch. Bell award S.C. Edn. Assn., 1982. Mem. Va. Press Women (bd. dirs. 1989—, Sweepstakes winner 1991-92, 95, 5 1st pl. writing-editing awards 1991), Nat. Fedn. Press Women. Republican. Lutheran. Home: 1713 Hungary Rd Richmond VA 23228-2334

HELMS, LISA MARIE, pediatric intensive care unit nurse, military officer, air force flight nurse; b. Sioux City, Iowa, Nov. 24, 1962; d. Dean Edward and Betty Lou Victora (Guenther) H. BA in Nursing, Carroll Coll., Helena, Mont., 1986; postgrad., Calif. State U., Sacramento, 1990-92; MSN, Incarnate Word Coll., 1996. Cert. pediatric nurse. Enlisted U.S. Army, 1981, advanced through grades to capt., 1990; nurse U.S. Army, San Francisco, 1986-90, Calif. Nat. Guard, San Francisco, 1990-92, Rio Linda (Calif.) Union Sch. Dist., 1990-92; enlisted USAF, 1992; mem. A.F. Nurse Corps Wilford Hall Med Ctr., Lackland AFB, Tex., 1992—; deployed to Guantanamo Bay, Cuba, July to Oct. 1994 for Operation Sea Signal, Operation Safe Haven; provider med. care to Haitian/Cuban migrants. Vol. Big sister/Big brother program United Way. Decorated Humanitarian Svc. medal, Army Commendation medal. Mem. AACN, Nat. Assn. Flight Nurses and Aerospace Med. Assn., Assn. Nurses in AIDS Care. Roman Catholic.

HELMS-VANSTONE, MARY WALLACE, anthropology educator; b. Allentown, Pa., Apr. 15, 1938; d. Samuel Leidich and Mary (Wallace) Helms; divorced. BA, Pa. State U., State College, 1960; MA, U. Mich., 1962, PhD, 1967. Instr. Wayne State U., Detroit, 1965-67; asst. prof. Syracuse (N.Y.) U., 1967-68; lectr. Northwestern U., Evanston and Chgo., Ill., 1969-79; prof. U. N.C., Greensboro, 1979—, head dept. anthropology, 1979-85. Author: Asang: A Miskito Community, 1971, Middle America, 1975, Ancient Panama, 1979, Ulysses' Sale, 1988, Craft and the Kingly Ideal, 1993, Creations of the Rainbow Serpent, 1995; contbr. articles to profl. jours. Fellow Am. Anthrop. Assn.; mem. Am. Soc. Ethnohistory (pres. 1976), Am. Ethnological Soc., So. Anthrop. Soc. (pres. 1980-81, proceedings editor 1982-94). Office: Univ NC Dept Anthropology Greensboro NC 27412

HELOISE, columnist, lecturer, broadcaster, author; b. Waco, Tex., Apr. 15, 1951; d. Marshal H. and Heloise K. (Bowles) Cruse; m. David L. Evans, Feb. 13, 1981. B.S. in Math. and Bus, S.W. Tex. State U., 1974. Owner, pres. Heloise, Inc. Asst. to columnist mother, Heloise, 1974-77, upon her death took over internationally syndicated column, 1977; author: Hints from Heloise, 1980, Help from Heloise, 1981, Heloise's Beauty Book, 1985, All-

New Hints from Heloise, 1989, Heloise: Hints for a Healthy Planet, 1990, Heloise from A to Z, 1993, Household Hints for Singles, 1993, Hints for All Occasions, 1995; contbg. editor Good Housekeeping mag., 1981, Speaker for the House; co-founder, 1st co-pilot Mile Pie in the Sky Balloon Club. Mem. Good Neighbor Coun. Tex.-Mex.; sponsor Nat. Smile Week. Recipient Mental Health Mission award Nat. Mental Health Assn., 1990, The Carnegians Good Human Rels. award, 1994. Mem. AFTRA, SAG, Women in Comm. (Headliner 1994), Tex. Press Women, Internat. Women's Forum, Women in Radio and TV, Confrerie de la Chaine des Rotisseurs (bailli San Antonio chpt.), Ordre Mondial des Gourmets De'Gustateur de U.S.A., Death Valley Yacht and Racket Club, Zonta. Home: PO Box 795000 San Antonio TX 78279-5000 Office: care King Features Syndicate 235 E 45th St New York NY 10017-3305

HELSTEDT, GLADYS MARDELL, vocational education educator; b. Forest City, Iowa, May 7, 1926; d. Gordon Ingeman and Pearl Gertrude (Hauan) Field; m. Lowell Lars Helstedt, Aug. 26, 1950; children: Mardell Lynn, David Lowell, Marilee Pearl, Marcia Kay. AA, Waldorf Coll., 1945; BS, Mankato State U., 1969. Bus. tchr. Crystal Lake (Iowa) H.S., Crystal Lake, Iowa, 1945-47; parish sec. St. Paul's Lutheran Ch., Mpls., 1949-51; bus. tchr. Sioux Valley High Sch., Lake Park, Iowa, 1969-70, Radcliffe (Iowa) High Sch., 1970-76; activity dir. Marinuka Manor Care Ctr., Galesville, Wis., 1976-79; bus. tchr. Galesville High Sch., 1979-80; asst. dir. Ret. Sr. Vol. Program, Whitehall, Wis., 1981-83; coord., instr. Western Wis. Tech. Inst., La Crosse, 1984; sr. instr. Tex. State Tech. Coll., Sweetwater, 1985-92; ret., 1992. Dir. music Salem Luth. Ch., Roscoe, Tex., 1985-90. Mem. Philos. Edn. Orgn. (pres. 1982-84), Tex. State Tech. Coll. Women (sec. 1991-92), Bus. Profls. Am. (advisor 1986-92). Home: 570 Quant Ave N Lakeland MN 55043-9545

HELTERLINE, MARILYN, sociology educator; b. Syracuse, N.Y., Oct. 18, 1947; d. Frederick William and Mary Ellen (Gaffney) Helterline; m. Charles J. Buehler, June 14, 1969 (dec. Dec. 1976); m. Peter Friedman, Oct. 9, 1981; children: Willa Helterline Friedman, Samuel Helterline Friedman. BA, LeMoyne Coll., 1969; MA, U. Notre Dame, 1971, PhD, 1974. Prof. sociology SUNY, Oneonta, 1973—. Contbr. articles to profl. jours. Mem. Am. Sociol. Assn. Democrat. Home: 69 Maple St Oneonta NY 13820 Office: SUNY College at Oneonta Oneonta NY 13820

HELTON, LUCILLE HENRY HANRATTIE, academic administrator; b. Ft. Worth, Mar. 2, 1942; d. P.D. and Virginia (Clark) Henry; m. Wayne Hanrattie, June 26, 1965 (div. Apr. 1986); children: Clark, Chris; m. William M. Helton, Jr., Mar. 19, 1988. BA, So. Meth. U., 1964; MEd, U. Pitts., 1968; cert. in adminstrn., William Paterson Coll., 1984; cert. in mid-mgmt., Tex. Christian U., 1987. Cert. elem. tchr. N.J., Pa., Tex. Nat. field sec. Kappa Kappa Gamma Sorority, Columbus, Ohio, 1964-65; elem. tchr. Pitts. Bd. Edn., 1965-69; co-dir, chmn. dept. maths. Assn. Children with Learning Disabilities Sch., Pitts., 1969-72; tchr. elem., secondary, gifted and remedial and home instrn. programs West Milford (N.J.) Bd. Edn., 1976-84; prin., exec. dir. Hill Sch., Ft. Worth, 1984—; mem. exec. bd. Tex. Assn. Non-pub. Schs. Mem. ASCD, Tex. Ind. Sch. Consortium, Learning Disabilities Assn. Am., Leadership Tex., Coalition for Spl. Needs Students, Orton Dyslexia Soc., Forum Ft. Worth, Rotary (bd. dirs.). Democrat. Methodist. Office: Hill Sch of Ft Worth 4817 Odessa Ave Fort Worth TX 76133-1640

HELTON, SANDRA LYNN, finance executive; b. Paintsville, Ky., Dec. 9, 1949; d. Paul Edward and Ella Rae (Van Hoose) H.; m. Norman M. Edelson, Apr. 15, 1978. BS, U. Ky., 1971; MBA, MIT, 1977. Capital budget adminstr. Corning (N.Y.) Glass Works, 1978-79, fixed assets mgr., 1979-80, contr. electronics divsn., 1980-82, mgr. customer fin. svcs., 1982-84, dir. fin. svcs., 1984-86, asst. treas., 1986-91, v.p., treas., 1991-94, sr. v.p., treas., 1994—. Vol. Mass. Gen. Hosp., Boston, 1976; treas. Corning Mus. of Glass; treas pres. bd. dirs. Chemung Valley Arts Coun., Corning, 1981-87; bd. dirs. Corning Summer Theatre, 1987-91, Arnot Hosp. Found., 1988—; mem. fin. com. Clemens Performing Arts Ctr., Elmira, N.Y., 1985-92; mem. adv. bd. Chase Lincoln, 1988-91; mem. bus. com. Met. Mus. Art, 1992—; pres. bd. dirs. Rockwell Mus., 1992—; mem. Regional Cultural Adv. Com., 1992—; mem. FEI com. on Corp. Fin., 1995—; bd. dirs. Arnot Ogden Meml. Med. Ctr., Arts of the So. Finger Lakes. Mem. Nat. Assn. Corp. Treass., Fin. Women's Assn., Soc. Internat. Treas., Fin. Execs. Inst.

HELWICK, CHRISTINE, lawyer; b. Orange, Calif., Jan. 6, 1947; d. Edward Everett and Ruth Evelyn (Seymour) Hailwood; children: Ted C., Dana J. BA, Stanford U., 1968; MA, Northwestern U., 1969; JD, U. Calif., San Francisco, 1973. Bar: Calif., U.S. Supreme Ct. U. S. Ct. Appeals (9th cir.), U.S. Dist. Ct. (no., ctrl., so. and ea. dist.) Calif. Tchr. history New Trier Twp. High Sch., Winnetka, Ill., 1968-69; sec. to the producer Flip Wilson Show, Burbank, Calif., 1970; rsch. assoc. Bingham, Summers, Welsh & Spilman, Indpls., 1973; assoc. Crosby, Heafey, Roach & May, Oakland, Calif., 1973-78; asst. counsel litigation U. Calif., Oakland, 1978-84, mng. univ. counsel, 1984-94, counsel Berkeley campus, 1989-94; gen. counsel Calif. State U. Sys., 1994—; lectr. in field. Mem. instnl. review bd. Devel. Studies Ctr., Oakland, 1990—; DECIDE project instr. Wildwood Elem. Sch., Peidmont, Calif., 1989-91; cub scout leader Piedmont, 1988-91; leader Camp Fire Girls Club, Piedmont, 1990-93; bd. dirs. Wildwood Sch. Parents' Club, 1987—, col. coord., 1987-89, parent edn., 1989-90, membership com., 1990-91, bd. edn. rep., 1991-94. Mem. Nat. Assn. Coll. and Univ. Attys. (bd. dirs. 1995 , publs. com. 1993-94, arrangements coms. 1992-93, ann. cong. program com. 1992-94), State Bar Calif. (exec. com. 1980-83), Alameda County Bar Assn. (exec. com. trial practice sect. 1994, minority access program com. 1989, bd. dirs. 1977), Alameda County Bar Found. (adv. trustee 1988-90, bd. dirs. 1991), Alameda County Fee Arbitration Panel, order of Coif. Episcopalian. Office: Calif State U 400 Golden Shore St Long Beach CA 90802-4209

HELZNER, JUDITH FRYE, association administrator; b. Salem, Mass., Sept. 13, 1951; d. Albert and Audrey (Frye) Helzner; m. Robert Bernstein, Aug. 1, 1993. BA in French, Tufts U., 1973; MA in Internat. Rels., U. Pa., 1975, MA in Demography, 1976. Assoc. in women's program Pathfinder Fund, Boston, 1977-82; program rep. Pvt. Agys. Collaborating Together, N.Y.C., 1982-84; ind. cons. N.Y.C., 1985; program officer Internat. Women's Health Coalition, N.Y.C., 1985-87; dir. program coordination Internat. Planned Parenthood/Western Hemisphere Region, Inc., N.Y.C., 1987—. Translator: (French to English) Human Fertility: The Basic Components, 1976; mem. editorial adv. bd. Reproductive Health Matters, 1992—; contbr. chpts. to books, articles to profl. jours. Univ. fellow U. Pa., 1973-74, NIH fellow, 1975-76. Mem. APHA, Assn. for Women in Devel., Population Assn. Am., Am. Soc. for Pub. Adminstrn. (exec. com. and elections officer sect. for internat. comparative adminstrn. 1988-94), Internat. Union for Sci. Study of Population, Phi Beta Kappa. Office: Internat Planned Parenthood Western Hemisphere Region Inc 902 Broadway 10th Fl New York NY 10010

HEMINGWAY, BETH ROWLETT, author, columnist, lecturer; b. Richmond, Va., May 6, 1913; d. Robert Archer and Evelyn Lucille (Doggett) Rowlett; B.Mus., Hollins Coll., 1934; m. Harold Hemingway, Apr. 2, 1938; children—Ruth Hartley, Martha Scott. Writer, Richmond-Lifestyle mag.; columnist Artistry in Bloom, Richmond Times-Dispatch; author: A Second Treasury of Christmas Decorations, 1961; Flower Arrangement with Antiques, 1965; Christmas Decorations Say Welcome, 1972; Antiques Accented by Flowers, 1975; Beth Hemingway's No Kin to Ernest, 1980; Holidays with Hemingway, 1985; lectr. numerous states, also Australia, 1966, Eng., 1977. Vol., Hermitage Meth. Home, 1977-79. Mem. Nat. League Am. Pen Women, Va. Writers Club, Richmond Hort. Assn., Va. Fedn. Garden Clubs (book rev. chmn.), Richmond Council Garden Clubs (flower arrangement chmn.), Clay Spring Garden Club (pres. 1953-55), Barton Garden Club (pres. 1959-61, 74). Republican. Methodist. Home: 1900 Lauderdale Dr Apt E-103 Richmond VA 23233-3942

HEMINGWAY, MARIEL, actress; b. Mill Valley, Calif., Nov. 21, 1961; d. John Hadley and Byra Louise (Whittlesey) H.; m. Steven Douglas Crisinan, Dec. 9, 1984; children: Dree, Langley. Studies with Harold Guskin. Owner, sec. Clear Water Pictures, 1986; co-owner Sam's Cafe Restaurant, N.Y. Actress: (stage prodns.) The Palace of Amateurs, California Dog Flight, 1985, (feature films) Lipstick, 1976, Manhattan, 1979 (Acad. award nomination 1979), Personal Best, 1982, Star '80, 1983, Creator, 1985, The Mean Season, 1985, Superman IV: The Quest for Peace, 1987, Sunset, 1988, The Suicide Club, 1988, Delirious, 1991, Falling From Grace, 1992, (TV movies) I Want to Keep My Baby, 1977, Amerika, 1987, Into the Bad Lands, 1991, Desperate Rescue: The Cathy Mahone Story, 1993, (TV series) Civil Wars, Storytime, Central Park West. Office: care ICM 8942 Wilshire Blvd Beverly Hills CA 90211-1934*

HEMISH, CAROL MARIE, liturgist/spiritual director, musician; b. Canby, Minn., June 12, 1950; d. Richard Joseph and Mathilda Rose (Mihm) H. BA in Music Edn., Piano Performance, Mt. Mary Coll., Milw., 1973; MA in Liturgical Studies, St. John's U., Collegeville, Minn., 1985. Cert. spiritual dir. Dir. music, liturgy and spiritual renewal St. Mary's Parish, Willmar, Minn., 1981-84; dir. music ministries Epiphany Parish, Coon Rapids, Minn., 1984-87; liturgy dir. Marquette U., Milw., 1987-90, St. Benedict Ctr., Madison, Wis., 1990-92; assoc. dir. Archdiocesan Spirituality Ctr., New Orleans, 1992-93; coord. Ctr. for Liturgy at St. Louis U., 1994—; retreat dir. Sacred Heart Retreat House, Sedalia, Colo., 1989—; liturgy cons. various religious congregations, dioceses, parishes, 1980—. Mem. Sch. Sisters Notre Dame, Nat. Pastoral Musicians, Assn. Contemplative Sisters, Spiritual Dirs. Internat. Home: 3933 Fillmore St Saint Louis MO 63116 Office: Ctr for Liturgy at St Louis U 3745 W Pine Mall Saint Louis MO 63108

HEMMINGSEN, BARBARA BRUFF, microbiology educator; b. Whittier, Calif., Mar. 25, 1941; d. Stephen Cartland and Susanna Jane (Alexander) Bruff; m. Edvard Alfred Hemmingsen, Aug. 5, 1967; 1 child, Grete. BA, U. Calif., Berkeley, 1962, MA, 1964; PhD, U. Calif., San Diego, 1971. Lectr. San Diego State U., 1973-77, asst. prof., 1977-81, assoc. prof., 1981-88, prof., 1988—; vis. asst. prof. Aarhus U. Denmark, 1971-72; cons. AMBIS, Inc., San Diego, 1984-85, Woodward-Clyde Cons., 1985, 87-91. Author: (with others) Microbial Ecology, 1972; contbr. articles to profl. jours. Mem. Planned Parenthood, San Diego. Mem. AAAS, Am. Soc. Microbiology, Am. Women in Sci., San Diego Assn. for Rational Inquiry (newsletter co-editor 1996—). Democrat. Office: San Diego State U Dept Biology San Diego CA 92182-4614

HEMMY, MARY LOUISE, social work administrator; b. Mpls., Nov. 14, 1914; d. Albert H. and Mary (Scott) H. BS, U. Minn., 1936, MA in Social Wk., 1941. Caseworker Washington U. Med. Ctr., St. Louis, 1937-40, Ill. Svcs. for Crippled Children, Springfield, 1941-42; instr., asst. prof. Sch. Social Wk., Washington U., 1942-45; dir. social wk. dept. Washington U. Med. Ctr., 1945-52; assoc. prof., dir. social wk. Coll. Medicine, U. Ill., Chgo., 1952-53; exec. dir. Am. Assn. Med. Social Workers, Washington, 1953-55; prof. sch. medicine sch. social work U. Pitts., 1956-59; exec. dir. Benjamin Rose Inst., Cleve., 1959-77; mem. spl. med. adv. group VA, 1963-68; mem. Ohio Bd. Examiners Nursing Home Adminstrs., 1973-77. Mem. Nat. Assn. Social Workers (bd. dirs. 1961-63), Am. Assn. Homes for Aging (bd. dirs. 1963-70). Home: 13505 SE River Rd Portland OR 97222-8038

HEMPEL, KATHLEEN JANE, paper company executive; b. Monroe, Wis., Nov. 10, 1950; d. Francis H. and Mary Joan (Martin) Mottley; m. Rolf R. Hempel, Aug. 1, 1970; children: Michelle, Patricia. Student, U. Wis., Platteville; grad., U. Wis., Stevens Point, 1972; MBA, Ariz. State U., Tempe, 1984. V.p. Ft. Howard Corp., Green Bay, Wis., 1973-82, 1st v.p., 1986-87, also bd. dirs.; sr. exec. v.p. Ft. Howard Corp., Green Bay, 1988-92, vice chmn., CFO, 1992—, also bd. dirs.; cons. Hewitt Assocs., Phoenix, 1985-86. Office: Ft Howard Corp 1919 S Broadway Green Bay WI 54304-4905

HEMPERLY, REBECCA S., publishing manager; b. Reading, Pa., June 17, 1966; d. Kenneth Jay and Ann Rebecca (Riehl) H. BA, Wheaton Coll., 1988; MA, Emerson Coll., 1992. Editl. asst. Coll.-Hill Press/Little, Brown, Boston, 1988-90; editl. asst. Little, Brown and Co., Boston, 1990, contracts coord., 1990-92, asst. mgr. contracts, 1992—; spkr. rights and permissions Assn. Am. Pub., Washington, 1996; mem. diversity task force Little, Brown and Co., Boston, 1993—. Contbr. essays: The Book Group Book, 2d edit., 1995, Teaching Contemporary Theory to Undergraduates, 1995. Team capt. AIDS walk-a-thon Little, Brown and Co./AIDS Action Com., Boston, 1995, 96; phone coord. GLOW, Watertown, Mass., 1989—; mem. Rails to Trails Conservancy, 1995—. Mem. Women in Publishing, Nat. Writers' Union, Bookbuilders of Boston, Phi Beta Kappa (scholar 1988). Office: Little Brown and Co 34 Beacon St Boston MA 02108

HEMPFLING, LINDA LEE, nurse; b. Indpls., July 28, 1947; d. Paul Roy and Myrtle Pearl (Ward) H. Diploma Meth. Hosp. Ind. Sch. Nursing, 1968; postgrad. St. Joseph's Coll. Charge nurse Meth. Hosp., Indpl., 1968; staff nurse operating room Silver Cross Hosp., Joliet, Ill., 1969; charge nurse operating room Huntington (N.Y.) Hosp., 1969-73; night supr. oper. rm., post anesthesia care unit Hermann Hosp., Houston, 1973-76; unit. mgr., purchasing coord. oper. rms., 1976-83; RN med. auditor, quality improvement and tng. coord. Nat. Healthcare Rev., Inc., Houston, 1984—. Future Nurses Am. scholar, 1965, Nat. Merit scholar, 1965. Mem. Assn. Oper. Rm. Nurses, Tex. Med. Auditors Assn., Nat. Med. Cost Containment Assn. Office: 6565 Fannin MS MBI-04 Houston TX 77030

HEMPHILL, JEAN HARGETT, college dean; b. Pollocksville, N.C., Aug. 21, 1936; d. Robert Franklin and Frances (Hill) Hargett; m. Raymond Arthur Hemphill, Feb. 28, 1964; 1 child, Gerald Franklin. BS, East Carolina U., 1958; MEd, U. Nev.-Las Vegas, 1968; student N.C. State U., 1993. Sec.-treas. Five Points Milling Co., Inc., New Bern, N.C., 1968-77; instr. Craven C.C., New Bern, 1973-80, dean service techs., 1980—; mem. New Bern-Craven County Tech. Prep, steering com. New Bern-Craven County Sch., 1990-95; supervisor rep. curriculum improvement project N.C. C.C. Sys., 1992-96. Scholarship chmn. continuing edn. div. Woman's Club, New Bern, 1981—, treas. continuing edn. div., 1986—. Mem. N.C. Assn. C.C. Instrnl. Adminstrs., Phi Kappa Phi. Democrat. Methodist. Office: Craven Community Coll 800 College Ct New Bern NC 28562-4900

HEMPHILL, NORMA JO, special event planning and tour company executive; b. Enid, Okla., Nov. 25, 1930; d. Wyatt Warren and Wanda Markes (Parker) Stout; m. Benjamin Robert Hemphill, June 21, 1952; children: Susan Colleen, Robert Gary. Student, Okla. State U.; BA, U. Calif., Berkeley, 1955. Former acct. Better Bus. Bookkeeping, Lafayette, Calif.; tchr., Head Start tchr. Chino (Calif.) Elem. Sch., 1966-68; pres., founder Calif. Carousel and Carousel Tours, Lafayette, 1972—; spkr. in field; cons., dir. various orgns. Past bd. dirs. PTA, Moraga, Calif., Lafayette; bd. dirs. Children's Home Soc., Upland, Calif., 1965-69; past demonstation tchr. Presbytery of Bay Area, San Francisco; past supt. 1st Presbyn. Ch., Oakland, Calif., elder, 1977—, trustee, 1980; mem. hon. adv. com. Festival of Lake, Oakland, 1982; bd. govs. Goodwill Industries, 1978-79; founder, chmn. Joint Svc. Clubs Foster Children's Ann. Christmas Party; mem. adv. com. for William Penn Mott Jr. Visitors Ctr., Presidio of San Francisco Nat. Park, 1995—. Named Person of Yr. award Advt.-Mktg. Assn. East Bay, 1978; co-recipient Event of Yr. award, Am. Pub. Rels. Assn., 1984. Mem. Lake Merritt Breakfast Club (Oakland, spl. events com., bd. govs., named Citizen of Community 1992), Lake Merritt Inst. (hon.), Soroptomist (very important women honor roll Diablo Valley 1990, keynote speaker 1991), Pi Beta Phi (bd. dirs., spl. events com. Contra Costa County chpt., Founder's Day speaker at U. Calif.-Berkeley, 1993). Office: Calif Carousel & Carousel Tours PO Box 537 Lafayette CA 94549-0537

HENARD, ELIZABETH ANN, controller; b. Providence, Oct. 9, 1947; d. Anthony Joseph and Grace Johanna (Lokay) Zorbach; m. Patrick Edward Mann, Dec. 18, 1970 (div. July 1972); m. John Bruce Henard Jr., Oct. 19, 1974; children: Scott Michael, Christopher Andrew. Student, Jacksonville (Fla.) U., 1966. Sec. So. Bell Tel.&Tel., Jacksonville, 1964-69; office mgr. Gunther F. Reis Assocs., Tampa, Fla., 1969-71; exec. sec. Ernst & Ernst, Tampa, 1971-72; exec. sec. to pres. Lamalie Assocs., Tampa, 1972-74; exec. sec. Arthur Young & Co., Chgo., 1975; adminstrv. asst. Irving J. Markin, Chgo., 1975; contr., v.p., corp. sec. Henard Assocs., Inc., Dallas, 1983-92. Mem. Dallas Investors Group (treas. 1986-91), Tampa Palms Country Club. Republican. Roman Catholic. Home: 15705 Mifflin Ct Tampa FL 33647-1120

HENDERSHOT, CAROL MILLER, physical therapist; b. Lancaster, Pa., July 24, 1959; d. Richard Horace and Joan Marie (Nonnenmocher) Miller; m. Richard A. Hendershot, Dec. 29, 1989; 1 child, Scott Michael. BS in Physical Therapy, Quinnipiac Coll., 1981. Staff phys. therapist Easter Seal Rehab. Ctr., Lancaster, 1981-85, phys. therapy dept. head, 1986-89; staff phys. therapist Community Hosp. of Lancaster, 1985-86, Guilds' Sch. & Neuromuscular Ctr., 1990—. Dir. publicity and pub. rels. Lancaster Dist. United Meth. Women, 1988-89, chmn. ch. and soc. com., 1987, 88, mem. chancel choir, 1981-89, mem. adminstrv. bd., 1975-88; trustee Audubon Pk. United Meth. Ch., 1990-93, mem. chancel choir 1990-92, mem. staff parish rels. com. 1993-94, mem. Jubilee Bell Choir, 1990—; dir. Bethlehem and Joy Bells Handbell Choirs, 1994—. Mem. Neuro-Devel. Treatment Assn., Visiting Nurse Assn. (profl. adv. com. 1987-89), Beta Beta Beta. Democrat. Methodist. Home: 6007 W Hopi Ct Spokane WA 99208-9046

HENDERSHOTT LOVE, ARLES JUNE, television news director; b. Rockford, Ill., Oct. 22, 1956; d. Eugene Bourden and Rose Marie (Erickson) Hendershott; m. Joseph William Love, Sept. 20, 1986. BS with high honors, Ill. State U., 1979. Reporter Sta. WTVO-TV, Rockford, 1979-82, news producer, 1982-83; news assignment editor Sta. WIFR-TV, Rockford, 1983-86, news dir., 1986—; speaker Rockford Pub. Schs., 1980-83. Producer news story Pee Wee Explosion, 1985 (AP award 1986). Bd. dirs. Rockford Airshow, 1994-95; mem. com. YWCA, Rockford, 1987, Westminister Presbyn. Ch., Rockford, also tchr. Sunday Sch.; bd. dirs. No. Ill. chpt. March of Dimes, 1980-84, NW Ill. chpt. Spl. Olympics, Rockford, 1986—, Discovery Ctr. Mus., Rockford, 1987—, N.W. Ill. Alzheimer & Related Disorder Assn., 1991, Rockford CrimeStoppers, 1992—; active YMCA Luncheon Coun., 1992-93, leader Rockford Lunch Coun., 1994-95. Recipient Leadership award Ken-Rock Community Ctr., Rockford, 1980, Presidential award of honor Rockford Jaycees, 1986, Dist. award Zonta Pub. Rels. Campaign, 1990, Leader Luncheon award YWCA, 1991. Mem. AAUW (bd. dirs. 1982-84), NAFE, Radio-TV News Dirs. Assn. (TV state coord. for Ill. 1989—), Ill. News Broadcasters Assn., Soc. Profl. Journalists, Am. Mgmt. Assn., Archeology Inst. Am., Rockford C. of C. (pres. club 1993—), Univ. Chgo. Oriental Inst., Ill. Assoc. Press (exec. com. 1989—, pres.-elect 1990, pres. 1991), Lens & Shutter Club (pres. 1983-85, others), Zonta. Office: Sta WIFR-TV 2523 S Meridian Rd Rockford IL 61102

HENDERSON, CONNIE CHORLTON, city planner, artist and writer; b. Cedar Rapids, Iowa, July 16, 1944; d. Robert Brown and Lorraine Madeline (Marquardt) Chorlton; m. Dwight Franklin Henderson, Dec. 24, 1966; 1 child, Patricia. BA, Anderson U., 1966; MA in Edn., St. Francis Coll., Ft. Wayne, Ind., 1972; MPA, U. Tex. San Antonio, 1987. Art coord. Ft. Wayne Comty. Schs., 1966-67; art tchr. East Allen County Schs., New Haven, Ind., 1968-71, 74-79; instr. Manchester Coll., N. Manchester, Ind., 1971-72; rsch. assoc. Tremar Real Estate Rsch., San Antonio, 1983-84; planning asst. (vol.) City of San Antonio, Tex., 1985-88; planner I City of San Antonio, 1988-89, project mgmt. specialist, 1990, conservation edn. coord., 1990-91; Planner II San Antonio Water System, 1990-96, water edn. coord., 1996—; docent (vol.) San Antonio Mus. Assn.; rsch. mgr. N. San Antonio C. of C., 1988. Artist: numerous paintings and fiber sculptures in juried and invitational shows, 1966-80; poetess: (2d prize Iowa Poetry Day Assn., 1961). Bd. dirs. Tex. Soc. to Prevent Blindness, San Antonio, 1981-83; v.p. U. Tex. at San Antonio Women's Club, 1981-82, pres. 1983-84; mem. San Antonio Conservation Soc., 1985—, mem. Assistance League of San Antonio, 1988—, liason Thrift House, San Antonio, 1995-96; co-pres. River Gardens Family and Friends, 1993-94, sec., 1995-96. Mem. Am. Planning Assn. (cert. planner, asst. dir. San Antonio sect. 1990, dir., 1991-93, Am. Water Works Assn., Univ. of Tex. at San Antonio Alumni Assn. Home: 2410 Shadow Cliff San Antonio TX 78232 Office: San Antonio Water System 1001 E Market St San Antonio TX 78205

HENDERSON, DIANE V., therapist, consultant, speaker, author; b. Charlottesville, Va., Oct. 23, 1943; d. Francis Joseph and Eva Leonora (Wood) Valenti; m. Stephen Henderson, June 7, 1964 (div. Feb. 1979); children: David R., Jeffrey Paul; m. Fred William Holdsworth, June 21, 1991. BA in Psychology, N.C. State U., 1978; MSW, U. N.C., 1982. Cert. clin. social worker, N.C. Dir. family svcs. Luth. Family Svcs., Raleigh, N.C., 1973-75; therapist Psychol. Svcs., Raleigh, 1983-85; pres., founder Tng. Assocs., Rocky Mount, N.C., 1985—; therapist Carsten's Psychol. Svc., Rocky Mount, 1994—; bd. advisor N.C. Women's Mag., Rocky Mount, 1995. Author: Coping With Grief—A Self Help Booklet, 1979. Bd. dirs. YWCA, Rocky Mount, 1993-96. Home and Office: Tng Assocs 230 Villa St Rocky Mount NC 27804

HENDERSON, ELIZABETH ANN, farmer; b. N.Y.C., Jan. 13, 1943; d. Sydney and Laura (Rosenbaum) Berliner; m. Harry Brinton Henderson III, Sept. 23, 1966 (dec. Jul. 1972); 1 child, Andrew Melville. BA, Barnard Coll., 1964; MA, Yale U., 1966, PhD, 1975. Asst. prof. Russian lit. Boston U., 1975-81; organic farmer Unadilla Farm, Gill, Mass., 1981-88, Rose Valley Farm, Rose, N.Y., 1988—; adminstrv. coun. N.E. Sustainable Agr. Rsch. and Edn. Program, Burlington, Vt., 1993—, mem. tech. com., 1990-93; mem. adv. coun. to dean Coll. Agr. and Life Scis., cornell U., Ithaca, N.Y., 1995—; lectr. in field. Author/editor: The Real Dirt: Farmers Tell About Organic and Low-Input Practices, 1994; author: Food Book for a Sustainable Harvest, 1994; contbr. articles to profl. jours. Mem. exec. com. Nat. Sustainable Agr. Coord. Coun., Washington, 1993—; chmn. Wayne County Agrl. and Farmland Protection Bd., N.Y., 1993—; adv. com. Farming Alterantives Program, Cornell U., 1993—; bd. dirs. Genesee-Finger Lakes Food Sys. Project, 1994—. Named Conservation Farm of the Yr., Wayne County Soil and Water Conservation Disst., 1991, Honoree of the Yr., North Rose Wolcott Profl. Bus. Women's Assn., 1994; AAUW Jr. Faculty grantee, 1978. Mem. N.E. Organic Farming Assn. (founding pres. 1982-84, governing coun. 1988—, Outstanding Mem. Yr. 1990), N.Y. Sustainable Agr. Working Group (steering com. mem. 1992—), N.Y. Grange (gatekeeper 1995-96). Home and Office: PO Box 149 4209 Covell Rd Rose NY 14542

HENDERSON, GERALDINE THOMAS, retired social security official, educator; b. Luling, Tex., Jan. 7, 1924; d. Cornelius Thomas and Maggie (Keyes) Thomas; m. James E. Henderson, Feb. 9, 1942 (dec. Apr. 1978); children—Geraldine, Jessica, Jennifer. BS, Fayetteville State U., 1967. Tchr. Cumberland County Schs., Fayetteville, N.C., 1966-67, Fayetteville City Schs., 1967-68; with Social Security Adminstrn., Fayetteville, 1968-87; substitute tchr. Cumberland County Sch. System, 1987—; claims rep. Pres. Fayetteville State U. Found., 1981-82; pres. NAACP, Fayetteville br., 1983-86. DeaconColl. Heights Presbyn. Ch., 1965-79, ruling elder, 1980-91; bd. dirs. Fayetteville Art Coun., 1984—, Cumberland County United Way, 1993—, chmn. div. corp. mission Fayetteville Presbytery, 1986, mem. personnel review bd. City of Fayetteville, 1987—; inductee Nat. Black Coll. Alumni Hall of Fame, 1988; bd. dirs. Habitat for Humanity, Fayetteville, N.C., 1989, Share, Heart of the Carolinas, 1991; moderator Presbytery of Coastal Carolina, 1989; vice chair Cape Fear Food Bank, 1991. Recipient Life Membership Chmn. award NAACP Nat. Conv., Chgo., 1994, Essence of Freedom award NAACP State Conf., Goldsboro, N.C., 1995. Mem. LWV, Nat. Assn. Equal Opportunity in Higher Edn. (disting. alumni 1989), Legion Aux. (treas. 1981-83), Zeta Phi Zeta (Woman of Yr. 1984), Omega Psi Phi (Citizen of Yr. 1985). Democrat. Presbyterian. Avocations: creative dress design; gardening; travel.

HENDERSON, GLORIA FORTE, school system administrator; b. Winston-Salem, N.C., Oct. 13, 1944; d. Allan U. and Bertha E. (Barber) F.; m. Frank H. Henderson Jr., Aug. 27, 1965; children; April Michelle, Frank H. III. BA, U. Md., 1966, MA, 1979. Cert. adminstr., supr., and tchr., D.C. Tchr. D.C. Pub. Schs., Washington, 1968-89, asst. prin., 1989-93, dep. dir. lang. minority affairs br., 1993-95, prin., 1995—; chairperson edn. com. Grace Episcopal Day Sch., Silver Spring, Md., 1980-83. Mem. adv. bd. Montgomery County Pub. Schs., Silver Spring, 1970-72. Fellow Cafritz, Inst. Devel. Ednl. Adminstrs., Inst. Ednl. Devel.; mem. Delta Kappa Gamma (pres., v.p.), Phi Delta Kappa. Home: 1207 N Belgrade Rd Silver Spring MD 20902

HENDERSON, HARRIET, librarian; b. Pampa, Tex., Nov. 19, 1949; d. Ervin Leon and Hannah Elizabeth (Yoe) H. AB, Baker U., 1971; MLS, U. Tex., 1973. Sch. libr. Pub. Sch. System, Pampa, Tex., 1971-72; city libr. City of Tyler, Tex., 1973-80, City of Newport News, Va., 1980-84; dir. librs. and info. svcs. City of Newport News, 1984-90; dir. Louisville Free Pub. Libr.; del. White House Conf. Librs. and Info. Svcs.; bd. mem. Tex. Libr. Systems Act Adv. Bd., 1979-80. Budget panel chmn. Peninsula United Way, Hampton, Va., 1984-85; mem. bd. Peninsula coun. Boy Scouts Am., 1982-84,

Peninsula Womens Network, Newport News, 1983-85; mem. Leadership Louisville, 1991—, Alliant Health System Adult Oper. Bd., 1991—; mem. adv. com. dept. edn. Spalding U., 1991—; diaconate Hidenwood Presbyterian Ch., Newport News, 1983-85; del. White House Conf. Librs. and Info. Svcs., 1991. Recipient Tribute to Women in Bus. and Industry, Peninsula YWCA, Newport News, 1984. Mem. ALA, Ky. Libr. Assn. (vice chair pub. libr. sect. 1994), Va. Libr. Assn. (chmn. legis. com. 1981-84, v.p. 1985, pres. 1986), Rotary Club Louisville (chair youth svc. com. 1994—), Jr. League Louisville. Office: Louisville Free Pub Libr Office of Dir 301 York St Louisville KY 40203-2257

HENDERSON, JANA L., federal agency administrator, infosystems specialist; b. Anamosa, Iowa, Feb. 19, 1944; d. H. Dean and Rosetta I. (Lyon) H.; m. Steven J. Reinking, June 18, 1966 (div. June 1971). BA cum laude, U. Iowa, 1966, MBA, 1975. Cert. secondary edn. tchr., math. Systems analyst Iowa Nat. Mut. Ins. Co., Cedar Rapids, 1966-73; sr. systems analyst Westinghouse Learning Corp. div. Westinghouse Corp., Iowa City, Iowa, 1973-77, sr. computer specialist, 1977-88; sr. program mgr. U.S. Dept. Edn., Washington, 1988—, also cons., 1976. Mem. NAFE, Beta Gamma Sigma. Methodist. Lodge: Order Eastern Star. Office: US Dept Edn ROB3 # 4621 600 Independence Ave Washington DC 20202-0001

HENDERSON, KAREN LECRAFT, federal judge; b. 1944. BA, Duke U., 1966; JD, U. N.C., 1969. Ptnr. Wright & Henderson, Chapel Hill, N.C., 1969-70, Sinkler, Gibbs & Simons, P.A., Columbia, S.C., 1983-86; asst. atty. gen. Columbia, 1973-78; sr. asst. atty. gen., dir. of spl. litigation sect., 1978-82, deputy atty. gen., dir. of criminal div., 1982; judge U.S. Dist. Ct. S.C., Columbia, 1986-90, U.S. Ct. Appeals (D.C. cir.), Washington, 1990—. Apptd. Dist. Ct. Adv. Com. Mem. ABA (litigation sect. and urban, state and local government law sect.), N.C. Bar Assn., S.C. Bar (government law sect., trial and appellate practice sect., fed. judges assn.). Office: US Ct Appeals DC Cir US Courthouse 3rd & Constitution Ave NW Washington DC 20001*

HENDERSON, LOIS TERRY FEATHERSTONE, elementary education educator; b. Irvington, N.J., Nov. 13, 1944; d. Charles and Geraldine (Jefferson) Featherstone. BS, St. John's U., Jamaica, N.Y., 1966; postgrad., Columbia U., 1970; postgrad in Arts Adminstrn., NYU, 1996—. Cert. elem. tchr., N.Y. Tchr. N.Y.C. Bd. Edn., 1966—, tchr. human rels., 1970—; fieldsite coord. Youth Employment Tng. Program, N.Y.C., 1978; pvt. tutor Spike Lee Prodns.: Tutoring Plus, N.Y.C., 1993; tchr. advisor Scholastic Publs., N.Y.C., 1994-95. Docent Mus. for African Art, N.Y.C., 1994—; bd. dirs. Lincoln Square Neighborhood Ctr., N.Y.C., 1995—. Mem. Alpha Kappa Alpha. Home: 435 E 65th St New York NY 10021 Office: Bd Edn 2365 8th Ave New York NY 10037

HENDERSON, MARLO DELENE, elementary school educator; b. Lynchburg, Va., Sept. 20, 1966; d. Webb Ferlow and Joyce Ann (Woodall) H. BS in Psychology, Va. Poly. Inst. and State U., 1988; MEd in Curriculum and Instrn., Lynchburg Coll., 1992. Cert. tchr. K-4, 4-8. Mental health case mgr. Ctrl. Va. Cmty. Svcs., Lynchburg, 1989-90; tchr. 2d grade Appomattox (Va.) County Schs., 1990—. Mem. Piedmont Area Reading Coun. (pres., Tchr. of the Yr.), Internat. Reading Assn., Va. State Reading Assn., Va. Coun. Tchrs. Math., Kappa Delta Pi. Democrat. Baptist. Home: RR 1 Box 99c5 Lynch Station VA 24571-9732

HENDERSON, MARY ELIZABETH, journalist, newspaper editor; b. Jackson, Miss., Oct. 29, 1967; d. Thomas Dent and Nora Natalie (Hutchings) James; m. James William Henderson, Aug. 12, 1989; children: Wade Bradford, Molly Elizabeth. Student in pub. rels./journalism, Miss. State U., Starkville, 1985-90. Pub. rels. rep. Digicon Plastics, Pensacola, Fla., 1989-90; escrow rep. Barnett Mortgage Co., Jacksonville, Fla., 1991-93, sr. escrow specialist, 1993-94, internal bankruptcy and foreclosures dir., 1994-95; family living and lifestyles editor The Greenwood (Miss.) Commonwealth, 1995—; Adv. bd. Leflore County Extension Svc., Greenwood, 1995—; news feature and photography editor, Greenwood Commonwealth, 1995-96. Mem. Altrusa Internat. (pres.-elect 1996—), LeBonte Woman's Club (com. chair 1995—). Republican. Baptist. Office: The Greenwood Commonwealth 329 US 82 West PO Box 8050 Greenwood MS 38935

HENDERSON, MARY LOUISE, civic worker; b. Windsor, Ont., Can., Apr. 24, 1928; came to U.S., 1932; d. Kenneth Charles and Florence McGie (Morton) Campbell; m. Ernest Flagg Henderson III, Dec. 31, 1953; children: Ernest Flagg IV, Roberta C. BA, Bard Coll., 1950. V.p. Ruse & Urban, Inc., advt., Detroit, 1950-53; v.p., bd. dirs. Henderson House Am., Sudbury, Mass., 1969—. Pres. Wellesley (Mass.) Friendly Aid Assn., 1970-75, Newton (Mass.) Wellesley Hosp. Aid, 1980-82, 88-89; co-founder Wellesley Community Ctr., 1972, pres., 1983-85; bd. dirs., mem. exec. com. Norumbega Coun. Boy Scouts Am., 1974—, pres., 1989-91; trustee Newton-Wellesley Hosp., 1982—, mem. exec. com., 1990—; bd. dirs., mem. exec. com. Greater Boston adv. bd. Salvation Army, 1985—; mem. nat. adv. bd. Officers Tng. Sch. Salvation Army, 1994—; bd. dirs. Newton-Wellesley Vis. Nurse Assn., 1974—; corporator Boston Bio-Med. Inst., 1990—; also others. Mem. Mensa, Am. Needlepoint Guild (founder, pres. Mass. chpt. 1974-77, bd. dirs. 1974—, nat. historian 1989—). Republican. Episcopalian. Home: 171 Edmunds Rd Wellesley MA 02181-1331

HENDERSON, MAUREEN MCGRATH, medical educator; b. Tynemouth, Eng., May 11, 1926; came to U.S., 1960; d. Leo E. and Helen (McGrath) H. MB BS, U. Durham, Eng., 1949, DPH, 1956. Prof. preventive medicine U. Md. Med. Sch., 1968-75, chmn. dept. social and preventive medicine, 1971-75; assoc. epidemiology Johns Hopkins U. Sch. Hygiene and Pub. Health, 1970-75; prof. epidemiology and medicine U. Wash. Med. Sch., 1975-96, prof. emeritus, asst. v.p. and assoc. v.p. health scis., 1975-81, head cancer prevention rsch. program Fred Hutchinson Cancer Rsch. Ctr., 1983-94; mem. Nat. Inst. Environ. Health Scis. Adv. Coun., 1994 ; chmn. epidemiology and disease control study sect. NIH, 1969-82; chmn. clin. trial rev. com. Nat. Heart Lung and Blood Inst., 1975-79; mem. Nat. Cancer Adv. Bd., 1979-84; mem. bd. Robert Wood Johnson Health Policy Fellowship, 1989-93; bd. on radiation effects rsch. NRC, 1991—. Assoc. editor jour. Cancer Rsch., 1987-88; mem. editorial bd. Jour. Nat. Cancer Inst., 1988—; mem. editorial adv. bd. Cancer Detection and Prevention, 1992—. Recipient John Snow award Am. Pub. Health Assn., 1990; Luke-Armstrong scholar, 1956-57; John and Mary Markle scholar acad. medicine, 1963-68. Mem. Inst. Medicine of NAS (coun. 1981-85), Am. Coll. Epidemiology, Assn. Tchrs. Preventive Medicine (pres. 1972-73), Soc. Epidemiol. Rsch. (chmn. 1969-70), Internat. Epidemiol. Assn. (exec. officer 1971-76), Internat. Coun. Cancer Rsch. (sci. adv. bd. 1989—), Am. Epidemiol. Soc. (pres. 1990-91). Home: 5309 NE 85th St Seattle WA 98115-3915 Office: Fred Hutchinson Cancer Ctr Cancer Prevention Rsch Program 1124 Columbia St Seattle WA 98104-2015

HENDERSON, MAXINE OLIVE BOOK (MRS. WILLIAM HENDERSON, III), association executive; b. Rush, Colo., Apr. 22, 1924; d. Jesse Frank and Olive (Booth) Book; BA, U. Colo., 1945; m. William Henderson III, Apr. 10, 1948 (dec. May 1983); children—William IV, Meredith. Personnel adminstr. Gen. Electric Co., Schenectady and N.Y.C., 1945-54; asst. dir. placement Katherine Gibbs Sch., N.Y.C., 1967-70; v.p., dir. William Henderson Cons., Inc., N.Y.C., 1969-83, pres., dir., 1983-86; dir. recruitment Girl Scouts U.S.A., N.Y.C., 1973-78, dir. human resources, 1978-82, dir. career devel., 1982-91, administr. human resources 1991-93; pres., adminstr. World Found., 1993—. Pres., Goddard-Riverside-Trinity Sch. Thrift Shop, N.Y.C., 1964-65, Trinity Sch. Mothers' Orgn., N.Y.C., 1965-66; treas. Brearley Sch. Parents Assn., N.Y.C., 1966-67; mem. The Museums at Stony Brook, Smithtown Arts Coun., Mus. Modern Art. Mem. Am. Portuguese Soc., 1983—. Episcopalian. Clubs: North Suffolk Garden, Nissequogue Beach, Nissequogue Platform Tennis Assn. (St. James, L.I., N.Y.). Home: 606 W 116th St New York NY 10027-7011 also: PO Box 174 Saint James NY 11780 Office: 420 Fifth Ave New York NY 10018-2798

HENDERSON, NANCY GRACE, marketing and communications executive; b. Berkeley, Calif., Oct. 23, 1947; d. John Harry and Lorraine Ruth (Johnson) H. BA, U. Calif., Santa Barbara, 1969; MBA, U. Houston, 1985; teaching credential, U. Calif., L.A., 1971. Chartered Fin. Analyst. Tchr. Keppel Union Sch. Dist., Littlerock, Calif., 1969-72, Internat. Sch. Prague, Czechoslovakia, 1972-74, Sunland Luth. Sch., Freeport, Bahamas, 1974-75; tchr., dept. head Internat. Sch. Assn., Bangkok, Thailand, 1975-79; exec. search Diversified Human Resources Group, Houston, Tex., 1979-82; data processing analyst Am. Gen. Corp., Houston, 1982-83, personnel and benefits dept., 1983-85, investment analyst, 1985-86, equity security analyst/quantitative portfolio analyst, 1986-87; dir. mktg. and communications Vestek Systems Inc., San Francisco, 1987-90, dir. technical publs., 1990—; tchr. English as Second Language program Houston Metro. Ministries, 1980-81. Pres., bd. dirs. Home Owners Assn., Walnut Creek, Calif., 1988-90; tchr. English to refugees Houston Metro Ministries, 1982; exec. dir. Internat. Child Abuse Prevention Found., 1989; ch. choir, session, fundraising and com. chmn. Presbyn. Ch.; active Crisis Hotline, 1978-79, 92-93; dir. project Working in Networks for Good Shelter, 1993-95. Named a Notable Woman of Tex., 1984-85. Mem. Assn. for Investment Mgmt. and Rsch., Toastmasters (pres. Houston chpt. 1983, v.p. 1982-83). Office: Vestek Systems 388 Market St Ste 700 San Francisco CA 94111-5314

HENDERSON, ROBBYE ROBINSON, library director; b. Morton, Miss., Nov. 10, 1937; d. Robert and Aljuria (Myers) R.; 1 child, Robreka Aljuria. BA in Lang. Arts, Tougaloo Coll., 1960; MSLS, Atlanta U., 1968; PhD in Ednl. Leadership, So. Ill. U., 1976. Librarian Patton Lane High Sch., Basteville, Miss., 1960-66, Utica (Miss.) Jr. Coll., 1966-67, Miss. Indsl. Coll., Hollysprings, 1967-68; acquisition librarian Miss. Valley State U., Itta Bena, 1968-72, acting librarian, 1972-73, dir. James Herbert White Library, 1973—; cons. Office of Health Resources Opportunity, Washington, 1977-79, Miss. Assn. of Colls., Jackson, 1970-79. Vol. Teen Parenting Project State of Miss., 1987. Mem. Miss. Library Assn., Alpha Kappa Alpha (pres. Kappa Alpha Omega chpt. 1984-86, coordinator 1987, Baseilus award 1985). Home: MVSU Box 5042 14000 Highway 82 W Itta Bena MS 38941-1400 Office: Mississippi Valley State U James Herbert White Libr Itta Bena MS 38941

HENDERSON, SUSAN ELLEN FORTUNE, lawyer, educator; b. Bluefield, W.Va., Dec. 21, 1957; d. William Edward and Gladys Ellen (Scott) Fortune. Student, Randolph-Macon Woman's Coll., 1976-78; BS summa cum laude, Bluefield State Coll., 1986; JD cum laude, Washington & Lee U., 1994. Bar: Va. 1994, W.Va. 1995. Legal sec., paralegal, office mgr. Katz, Kantor & Perkins, Bluefield, 1979-86; paralegal, office mgr. David Burton, Atty. at Law, Princeton, W.Va., 1986-91; assoc. Burton & Kilgore, Princeton, W.Va., 1994-95; sole practice Bluefield, 1995—; instr. Bluefield State Coll., 1996—; tchr. Legal Learning Inst., Manassas, Va., 1995-96. Nat. Merit scholar, 1976, Disting. scholar Randolph-Macon Woman's Coll., 1976, Law scholar Washington & Lee U., 1991. Mem. ABA, ATLA, Va. Trial Lawyers Assn., Main St. Bluefield Bd. of Dirs. Home: 105 South Ln Bluefield VA 24605 Office: Atty at Law 308 North St Bluefield WV 24701

HENDLER, ROSEMARY NIELSEN, business owner, computer artist; b. Sydney, Australia, Oct. 18, 1946; came to U.S., 1954, naturalized, 1970; d. Robert Stanley McFarlane and Joyce Elizabeth (Annetts) Nielsen; m. Joel Arnold Hendler, June 1, 1977; 1 child, Stewart Maxwell. BA, U. Calif., Berkeley, 1968; postgrad., Acad. Art San Francisco, 1974-76, UCLA, 1985-87. Buyer linens Breuners Home Furnishings, Oakland, Calif., 1969-71; buyer textiles Liberty House, San Francisco, 1971-73, Bullock's, Palo Alto, 1973-75; graphic artist Montclarion Pubs., Oakland, 1975-77; pres., owner Cordeaux River Trading Co., L.A., 1986-93; owner, ptnr. Moon Star Design Studio, Orinda, Calif., 1995—. Advisor (CD-ROM) Visionary Stampede, Multimedia Project, San Francisco; exhibited computer art in numerous one-woman shows, 1994, 95, 96. Bd. dirs. docent coun. L.A. County Mus. Art, 1981—; VIP hostess Olympic Games, L.A., 1984; bd. dirs. Young Audiences, L.A., 1985-87; exec. bd. Orinda Arts Coun., 1991—, pres., 1993-94; mem. art guild Oakland Mus., 1991—; mem. task force Arts and Cultural Coun. of Contra Costa County, 1994—. Recipient Design award Levi Strauss, 1975, Honorable Mention awrd Manhattan Arts Internat., 1996, others. Mem. NAFE, Nat. Assn. Local Arts Agys., Nat. Assn. Desktop Pubs., Calif. Assn. Local Arts Agys., Jr. League L.A., Costume Coun., L.A. County Mus. Art, Lamorinda Arts Alliance, Artists in Tech., Orinda C. of C. Republican. Office: 16 El Verano Orinda CA 94563-1912

HENDLEY, EDITH DI PASQUALE, physiology and neuroscience educator; b. N.Y.C., Sept. 5, 1927; d. Michael and Rose (Parillo) Di Pasquale; m. Daniel Dees Hendley, Apr. 21, 1952; children: Jane Alice, Joyce Louise, Paul Daniel. AB, Hunter Coll. City N.Y., 1948; MS, Ohio State U., 1950; PhD, U. Ill., Chgo., 1954. Instr. U. Chgo., 1954-56; asst. lectr. U. Sheffield (Eng.), 1956-57; instr., rsch. assoc. Johns Hopkins U. Sch. Medicine, Balt., 1963-72; sr. investigator Friends Med. Sci. Rsch. Ctr., Balt., 1972-73; assoc. prof. U. Vt. Coll. Medicine, Burlington, 1973-83, prof., 1983-94; prof. emeritus, 1994—. Co-author 6 books; contbr. over 60 articles to profl. jours. Rsch. grantee NIH, 1974—, NSF, 1986-89, Vt. affiliate Am. Heart Assn., 1982-83, The Sugar Assn. Inc., 1984-85. Mem. AAAS, Am. Physiol. Soc., Am. Soc. Pharmacology and Exptl. Therapeutics, Soc. for Neurosci. (exec. com., treas. Vt. chpt. 1978—), Assn. for Women in Sci. (treas. 1972-74, exec. com., long-range planning com. 1974-76). Home: 10 Highland Ter S Burlington VT 05403-7601 Office: U Vt Coll Medicine Dept Molecular Phys Bi Burlington VT 05405

HENDLEY, SHIRL ELAINE, accountant; b. Havana, Fla., Apr. 29, 1959; d. Clarence and Gennett (Johnson) Graham. BA in Polit. Sci., U. Fla., 1981, MA in Pub. Adminstrn., 1983; MS in Mgmt. Info. Sys., George Washington U., 1994, Cert. in African Studies. Cert. govt. fin. mgr. Evaluator U.S. Gen. Acctg. Office, Atlanta, 1983-85, Washington, 1985-87; sr. evaluator U.S. Gen. Acctg. Office, Boston, 1987-88, Washington, 1988-92; sr. sys. acct. USIA, Washington, 1992—; owner Collectible Classics Antiques and Collectibles, St. Leonard, Md. Elections judge Prince Georges County, Md., 1990-92; bd. dirs. cable TV City of Takoma Park, Md., 1986-87; mem. Prince George's chpt. LWV, 1991-92; active combined fed. campaign U.S. Info. Agy., Washington, 1996; vol. Urban League, Nat. Park Svc., others. Recipient Pres.'s Leadership award U. Fla.; named to Outstanding Young Women of Am., 1988; Fgn. Lang. Area fellow U.S. Office of Edn., U. Fla., 1981-83. Mem. Am. Women Econ. Devel. Corp. Home: 8671 Ritchboro Rd Forestville MD 20747

HENDRA, BARBARA JANE, public relations executive; b. Watertown, N.Y., July 14, 1938; d. Frederick R. and Irene J. (Rotundo) H. BA, Vassar Coll., 1960. Publicity dir. Fawcett World Library, N.Y.C., 1961-69; v.p., dir. publicity and pub. relation Pocket Books-Simon & Schuster, N.Y.C., 1969-77; corp. dir. publicity and pub. relations Putnam Pub. Group, N.Y.C., 1977-79; pres. Barbara J. Hendra Assocs., Inc., N.Y.C., 1979-91, The Hendra Agy. Inc, Bklyn., 1991—; adj. prof. NYU, 1981. Contbg. author: Trade Book Marketing, 1983, The Encyclopedia of Publishing, 1995. Mem. Pubs. Publicity Assn. (bd. dirs. 1977-81, pres. 1979-81), Vassar Club, Regency Whist Club, Women's Media Group. Mem. Pubs. Publicity Assn. (bd. dirs. 1977-81, pres. 1979-81), Women's Media Group, Book Critics Cir., Vassar Club, Regency Whist Club. Home: 140 Sterling Pl Brooklyn NY 11217-3307 Office: The Hendra Agy Inc 142 Sterling Pl Brooklyn NY 11217-3307

HENDREN, MERLYN CHURCHILL, investment company executive; b. Gooding, Idaho, Oct. 16, 1926; d. Herbert Winston and Annie Averett Churchill; student U. Idaho, 1944-47; B.A. with honors, Coll. of Idaho, 1986. m. Robert Lee Hendren, June 14, 1947; children—Robert Lee, Anne Aleen. With Hendren's Furniture Co., Boise, 1947-69; co-owner, v.p. Hendren's Inc., Boise, 1969-87, pres. 1987—. Bd. dirs. Idaho Law Found., 1978-84; chmn. Coll. of Idaho Symposium, 1977-78, mem. adv. bd., 1981—; bd. dirs. SW Idaho Pvt. Industry Council, 1984-87; pres. Boise Council on Aging, 1959-60, mem. adv. bd., 1986—; mem. Gov.'s Commn. on Aging, 1960, Idaho del. to White House Conf. Aging, 1961; trustee St. Luke's Regional Hosp., 1981-92; mem. adv. bd. dirs. Boise Philharm. Assn., Inc., 1981—, Ballet Idaho; bd. dirs. Children's Home Soc. Idaho, 1988; founding pres. Idaho Congl. Award Program, 1993—; sustaining mem. Boise Jr. League. Mem. Boise C. of C. (bd. dirs. 1984-87), Gamma Phi Beta. Episcopalian. Home: 3504 Hillcrest Dr Boise ID 83705-4503 Office: 1109 Main St Ste 230 PO Box 9077 Boise ID 83702

HENDREY, TARA LOUISE, financial analyst, financial systems analyst; b. Huntingburg, Ind., July 4, 1964; d. Charles C. and Ruth A. (Finney) H. BS, U. Evansville, 1986. Cost acct. Metco divsn. Perkin Elmer, Westbury, N.Y., 1987-89, fin. acct., 1989-91, fin. analyst, 1991-93; fin. analyst Am. Air Filter Internat., Louisville, 1994—. Mem. Inst. Mgmt. Accts. United Methodist. Home: HC 64 Box 74 Leopold IN 47551 Office: Am Air Filter Internat 215 Ctrl Ave Louisville KY 40208

HENDRICKS, FLORA ANN, former special education educator; b. Cape Girardeau, Mo., Apr. 3, 1955; d. James Philbert and Bessie Geraldine (Mason) Joyce; m. Norman Harold Hendricks, Oct. 5, 1985; stepchildren: Theresa Lynn Ramirez, David Lane Hendricks. BS in Edn., S.E. Mo. State U., 1978; postgrad., U. Mo., 1994. Lifetime cert. tchr., Mo. Warehouse and prodn. line worker Procter and Gamble Corp., Jackson, Mo., summer 1973-78; tchr. spl. edn. I and II Poplar Bluff (Mo.) Regional Ctr., 1979-83; social svc. worker Jefferson County divsn. Family Svcs., Hillsboro, Mo., 1983; case mgr. I, II, III St. Louis Regional Ctr., 1983-94. Mem. Baby Boomer's Club, St. Luke's United Meth. Ch., civic activities vol., 1988-89, vol. ch. nursery, 1988-89. Mem. NOW, AAUW (vol. Elf's Workshop Kirkwood br., mem. bd. dirs., edn. area chair Kirkwood/Webster Groves Mo. br., mem. banquet com. Kirkwood-Webster bd. officers and com. chairs 1996-97), S.E. Mo. State U. Alumni Assn. Democrat. Home: 6339 Treeridge Trail Oakville MO 63129-4640

HENDRICKS, IDA ELIZABETH, mathematics educator; b. Roanoke, Va., Aug. 13, 1941; d. Samuel Jarboe and Nannie Virginia (Needy) Hodges; m. William Hampton Hendricks, Aug. 10, 1963; 1 child: William Hodges. BS in Math. & BA in Secondary Edn., Shepherd Coll., 1963; MA in Devel. Studies/Leadership Edn., Appalachian State U., 1992, cert. devel. edn. specialist, 1988. Faculty Harpers Ferry (W.Va.) High Sch., 1963-72, Jefferson High Sch., Shanandoah Junction, W.Va., 1972-78; mem. math. faculty, devel. math. specialist, adminstr. Shepherd Coll., Shepherdstown, W.Va., 1981-94; ret., 1994; creator, implementor devel. math. program Shepherd Coll.; tutor. Contbr. articles to profl. jours. Elder, organist, supt. Sunday sch., mem. Christ Reformed Ch., Shepherdstown, 1950—; organist Shepherdstown Presbyn. Ch., 1957—. Mem. AAUW (past treas.), Nat. Assn. Devel. Edn., W.Va. Assn. Devel. Edn. (sec. 1993—, v.p. 1994-95), W.Va. Coun. Tchrs. Math., Shepherdstown Hist. Soc. Home: PO Box 123 Shepherdstown WV 25443-0123

HENDRICKS, SUSAN MCCURDY, art educator, artist; b. Buffalo, Jan. 12, 1941; d. Robert C. and Gladys C. (Deel) McCurdy; m. Thomas C. Hendricks, June 17, 1961; children: Jennifer Ann, Julie Lynn. AA, Montgomery Coll., 1987; BS, U. Md., 1989, MA, 1992, PhD, 1995. Cert. K-12 art edn. tchr., Md. Proprietor Ceramic Studio, Olney, Md., 1970-85; art specialist Howard (Md.) Bd. Edn., 1989—; grad. asst. U. Md., College Park, 1992-95; instr. art Montgomery Coll., Rockville, Md., 1995—; cons. in field. Author: A Cross Discipline Approach for Developing Cultural Literacy in the Arts, 1990, Convergence on the Roles and Guidelines for Designing, Implementing and Teaching a Multicultural Elementary Art Education Curriculum, 1995; contbr. articles to profl. jours. Chairperson Williamsburg Civic Assn., 1973—; active Md. Multicultural Coalition. Mem. NAEA, Seminar for Rsch. in Art Edn., Golden Key, Phi Theta Kappa. Home: 3601 John Carroll Dr Olney MD 20832

HENDRICKSON, LOUISE, retired association executive, retired social worker; b. Lansdowne, Pa., Sept. 14, 1916; d. Norman and Gertrude (Powers) H. AA, Long Beach Jr. Coll., 1936; BA, U. Calif., Berkeley, 1938, gen. secondary tchr.'s cert., 1939; MS in Social Work, Columbia U., 1952. Cert. secondary tchr., Calif.; registered social worker, Calif. Dir. young adult program YWCA, Oakland, Calif., 1944-48; dir. group work and informal edn. svcs. YWCA, Bklyn., 1948-53; exec. dir. YWCA, Spokane, Wash., 1953-58; field cons. Nat. Bd. YWCA, Chgo., 1958-63; assoc. exec. community divsn. Nat. Bd. YWCA, N.Y.C., 1963-66, exec. community divsn., 1966-71, dir. orgn. devel., 1971-74, dep. exec. dir., 1974-82, ret., 1982. Contbr. articles to profl. jours. Pres. Cmty. Welfare Coun., Spokane, 1956-57; mem. majority coun. Emily's List, Washington, 1994-96; mem. Common Cause, LWV. Mem. NASW (charter 1958-62).

HENDRICKSON, NORMA KAREN, librarian; b. Morris, Minn., Sept. 13, 1936; d. Ernest A. and Caren Helene (Jensen) Reitan; m. Robert Francis Hendrickson, Aug. 6, 1961 (div. nov. 8, 1991; children: Jill Eileen, Nancy Ellen, Mark Robert, David Brian. BA, Concordia Coll., Moorhead, Minn., 1958; MALS, U. mich., 1959. Jr. libr. Okla. State U., Stillwater, 1959-62; circulation libr. U. Chgo. Edn. Libr., 1962-63; cataloger U. Chgo. Law Libr., 1964-66; cataloger Libr. of Congress, Washington, 1966-74, 80, supr., 1981-90, team leader, 1990; law cataloger Cook County Law Libr., chgo., 1974-79; catalog liaison Northwestern U., Evanston, Ill., 1979-80; team leader Libr. of Congress, Washington, 1990. Bd. dirs. C&O Canal Assocs., Glen Echo, Md., 1991—. Mem. ALA, Potomac Tech. Processing Librs. (rep. from D.C. 1985-96), D.C. Libr. Assn. Home: 9106 Kingsbury Dr Silver Spring MD 20910 Office: Libr of Congress Spl Materials 1st and Independence SE Washington DC

HENDRIE, ELAINE, public relations executive; b. Bklyn., d. David and Pearl Kostell; m. Joseph Mallam Hendrie; children: Susan, Barbara. Asst. account exec. Benjamin Sonnenberg Public Relations firm, N.Y.C., 1953-57; pub. relations cons., writer, editor, dir. pub. relations and media Religious Heritage of Am., Washington, 1973-75; producer, interviewer radio program, sta. WRIV and stas. WALK-AM and -FM, L.I., N.J., Westchester County, N.Y., Conn., 1974-77; exec. dir. Women in New Directions, Inc., Suffolk County, N.Y., 1974-77; nat. media coordinator NOW, Washington, 1978; media dir. Am. Speech-Lang.-Hearing Assn., Washington, 1979-80; pub. info. officer, head media and mktg. Dept. Navy, Washington, 1980-81; pres. Hendrie & Pendzick, 1982-92, Elaine Hendrie Pub. Rels., 1992—; resource person for media Nat. Commn. on Observance of Internat. Women's Yr., 1977; cons. Multi-Media Prodns. Inc., N.Y.C., 1978—, Women in New Directions, Inc., 1981—. Mem. adv. bd. Women's Edn. and Counseling Ctr., SUNY-Farmingdale. Home: 50 Bellport Ln Bellport NY 11713-2736

HENDRIX, BONNIE ELIZABETH LUELLEN, elementary school educator; b. Corry, Pa., July 21, 1942; d. Francis Wilson and Frances (Welch) Luellen; m. E. Lindsey Hendrix, Aug. 24, 1963; children: Lance Adair, Djuana Sue, Shane René. BEd, Anderson Coll., 1965; MEd, Berry Coll., 1986. 1st grade tchr. Madison County Bd. Edn., Anderson, Ind.; kindergarten tchr. Walker County Bd. Edn., LaFayette, Ga., 1994—; mentor tchr. Continuous Quality Instructions Sys; pvt. practice piano tchr. Active community and ch. orgns. Mem. NEA, ASCD, PAGE, Ga. Assn. Edn., Walker Assn. Edn. Home: 76 Old Trion Rd La Fayette GA 30728-3714

HENDRIX, SUSAN CLELIA DERRICK, civic worker; b. McClellanville, S.C., Jan. 19, 1920; d. Theodore Elbridge and Susan Regina (Bauknight) Derrick; m. Henry Gardner Hendrix, June 5, 1943; children: Susan Hendrix Redmond, Marilyn Hendrix Shedlock. BA, Columbia Coll., 1941; MA, Furman U., 1961; EdD (hon.) Columbia Coll., 1985. Cert. tchr., S.C. Tchr. Whitmire Pub. Schs., 1941-43, Greenville Pub. Schs., S.C., 1944-46, 58-63, dir. Reading clinic, 1965-68; counselor Greenville Pub. Schs., 1963-65; supr. Greenville County Sch. Dist., S.C., 1965-68, dir. pub. rels., 1968-83; grad. instr. Furman U., 1967-69; cons. Nat. Seminar on Desegregation, 1973. Author: (with James P. Mahaffey) Teaching Secondary Reading, 1966; Communicating With the Community, 1979, History of Robert Morris Class, 1995; editor: Communique, 1968-83; mem. editl. staff Book of Discipline, 1996; contbr. articles to profl. jours. and mags. Chmn. bd. trustees Columbia Coll., 1969-70; chmn. Greenville County Rehab. Bd., S.C., 1974-76; vice chmn. bd. Jr. Achievement, Greenville, 1978-79; chmn. S.C. Commn. on Women, Columbia, 1982-88; pres. United Meth. Women, Buncombe St. Ch., Greenville, 1956-57; mem. adminstrv. bd. Buncombe St. Ch., 1968—, bd. trustees, 1980-88, lay del. to S.C. Ann. Conf., 1986—; mem. United Meth. Ch. Southeastern Jurisdictional Coun. on Ministries, 1984-88; chmn. S.C. Conf. Coun. on Ministries United Meth. Ch., 1980-88, del. gen. conf., 1980, 84, 88, 92, S.C. Conf. Comm., 1995—; mem. Bd. Global Ministries United Meth. Ch., 1972-80, mem. commn. study of ministry, 1984-92, mem. gen. ch. coun. ministries, 1988—, mem. gen. conf. agys. staff and site location com., 1988—, rschr. missions project, West Africa, 1986, chmn. com. legis., 1992—, chmn. com. on inter-agency legis, 1992—, mission agy. site location com., 1993—, structure com., 1992—. Recipient Medallion Columbia Coll., 1980, Alumnae Disting. Svc. award Columbia Coll., 1983, Disting. Achievement award Women's History Week, Greenville, 1984, S.C. Woman of Achievement award, 1988. Mem. S.C. PTA (life), Columbia Coll. Alumnae Assn. (life), Democratic Women, S.C. Women in Govt. (bd. dirs.

1985-87), Alpha Delta Kappa (pres. 1970-72, 90-91). Home and Office: 309 Arundel Rd Greenville SC 29615-1303

HENDRIX-WARD, NANCY KATHERINE, environmental energy professional; b. Russellville, Ala., Nov. 28, 1944; d. Raymond Clyde and Mattye Lou (Kimbrough) Smith; m. Adrian Dale Hendrix, Jan. 8, 1963 (div. Mar. 1982); children: David Wayne, Amy Kathleen, Susan Gayle; m. Robert Lawrence, Feb. 22, 1986. AA, Draughon's Bus. Coll., Jackson, Miss., 1963; student, East Miss. Jr. Coll., Scoobe, 1978-79; AA, Anchorage Community Coll., 1981; BBA, U. Alaska, 1982-84. Dir. Retired Sr. Vol. Program, Big Springs, Tex., 1974-76; adminstr. USAF, Adana, Turkey, 1977-79; environ. specialist Minerals Mgmt. Svc. Dept. of Interior, Anchorage, 1980-85; tech. editor Intelligence and Threat Analysis Ctr. U.S. Army, Washington, 1985-87; editor Inst. Def. Analyses, Alexandria, Va., 1987-88; writer, editor minerals mgmt. svc. U.S. Dept. Interior, Herndon, Va., 1988-89; environ. protection specialist, program mgr. U.S. Dept. Energy, Oak Ridge, Tenn., 1989—; coordinator Equal Opportunity com., Anchorage, 1983-85. Vol. counselor The Women's Ctr., Vienna, Va., 1987, Parent's Aid, Child Advocacy com., Anchorage, 1981-85; counselor Suicide Prevention Ctr., Anchorage, 1982-85. Mem. NAFE, LWV, Soc. for Tech. Communication, Federally Employed Women.

HENG, SIANG GEK, communications executive; b. Singapore, Singapore, Dec. 4, 1960; came to U.S., 1984.; m. G.J. Sturgis, 1991. BSEE with honors, Nat. U. Singapore, 1983; MSEE in Computer Engring., U. So. Calif., 1985; MS in Engring. Mgmt., Nat. Technol. U., 1993. Rsch. engr. Nat. Univ. Singapore, 1983-84; sys. mgr. LinCom Corp., L.A., 1985-87; fin. planner N.Y. Life Ins. Co., L.A., 1987-88; tech. staff AT&T, Holmdel, N.J., 1988-96; sr. tech. staff AT&T, Holmdel, 1996—; freelance computer and comm. cons., N.J., 1987-94. Contbr. articles to profl. jours. Office: AT&T Rm 2M-617 PO Box 3030 101 Crawfords Corner Rd Holmdel NJ 07733-3030

HENGESBACH, ALICE ANN, public relations consultant; b. Camp Lejeune, N.C., Aug. 26, 1949; d. Robert Williams and Barbara Ann (Wilson) H. BA in English, St. Xavier Coll., 1971; cert. secondary edn., Lake Erie Coll., 1972. Cert. tchr. English, N.Y., subs. tchr., Ohio. Tchr. secondary English and reading Painesville and Mentor, Ohio, 1972-74; dir. mktg. Tri-Con, Inc., Cleve., 1974-83; asst. account exec. The Urda Co., Akron, Ohio, 1983-85; dir. Marketspan Internat., U.S. and U.K., 1986-89; prodn. mgr. Edward Howard & Co. (formerly David A. Meeker & Assoc. Inc.), Akron, 1985-87, account exec., 1987-88; instr. media rels. Kent (Ohio) State U., 1990; pub. rels./mktg. comms. cons. Hengesbach & Assocs., Phillipsport, N.Y., 1988—; coord., on-site facilitator Nat. Golf Found.'s Golf Summit, Westchester, N.Y., 1986; developer ann. promotional program greater Akron area Pvt. Industry Coun.; co-chair promotion Nat. Inventors Hall of Fame, Akron, 1990. Past bd. dirs. YWCA, Akron, Summit County Drug Bd., Akron; bd. dirs., cert. tutor Literacy Vols. of Am.; active Nature Conservancy, Ohio and N.Y.; cons. pub. rels. N.Y. Spl. Olympics, Lathan, 1991; vol., life mem. Sarah Wells coun. Girl Scouts U.S.A. Mem. Pub. Rels. Soc. Am. (accredited pub. rels. counselor). Roman Catholic. Home and Office: Hengesbach & Assocs PO Box 836 Red Hill Rd Phillipsport NY 12769-0836

HENIG, ROBIN MARANTZ, journalist; b. Bklyn., Oct. 3, 1953; d. Sidney S. and Clare (Stern) Marantz; m. Jeffrey R. Henig, June 17, 1973; children: Jessica, Samantha. BA, Cornell U., Ithaca, N.Y., 1973; MSJ, Northwestern U., Evanston, Ill., 1974. Assoc. editor Comprehensive Therapy Mag., Chgo., 1974-75; asst. editor, writer The New Physician Mag., Chgo., 1975-77; asst. mng. editor The Blue Sheet, Washington, 1977-78; features and news editor Bio Science Mag., Washington, 1978-80; freelance writer Takoma Park, Md., 1980—; mem. bd. dirs. D.C. Science Writers' Assn., 1996—. Author: How A Woman Ages, 1985, The Myth of Senility, 1988, Being Adopted, 1993, A Dancing Matrix, 1994, The People's Health, 1996. Pres. PTA, Silver Spring, Md., 1986-87. Recipient Nat. Media award Am. Coll. Allergy & Immunology, 1993; Science Writer fellow Marine Biological Lab., 1990. Mem. Am. Soc. Journalists & Authors (pres. D.C. chpt. 1992-94, June Roth award for Medical Writing 1993, 94, Author of the Yr. 1994), Nat. Assn. Science Writers, The Authors Guild. Jewish.

HENKE, JANICE CARINE, educational software developer and marketer; b. Hunter, N.D., Jan. 28, 1938; d. John Leonard and Adeline (Hagen) Hanson; children: Toni L., Tom L., Tracy L. BS, U. Minn., 1965; postgrad., misc. schs., 1969—. Cert. elem. tchr., Minn., Iowa. Tchr. dance, 1953-56; tchr. kindergarten Des Moines Pub. Schs., 1964-65; tchr. elem. Ind. Sch. Dist. 284, Wayzata, Minn., 1969-93; pvt. bus. history Wayzata, 1978—; marketer, promoter health enhancement Jeri Jacobus Cosmetics Aloe Pro, Am. Choice Nutrition, Multiway, KM Matol, Wayzata, 1978—; developer ednl. software, marketer of software Computer Aided Teaching Concepts, Excelsior, Minn., 1983—; authorized rep. Minn. Edn. Assn. with Midwest Benefit Advisers, Excelsior, Minn., 1993—; developer, author drug edn. curriculum, Wayzata, 1970-71; mem. programs com. Health and Wellness, Wayzata, 1988-93; chmn. Wayzata Edn. Assn. Ins. Com., 1991-93; mem. Staff Devel. Adv. Bd., Wayzata, 1988-93; coach Odyssey of the Mind, 1989-93. Author, developer computer software; contbr. articles to newspapers. Fundraiser Ind. Reps. Wayzata, 1976-79; mem. pub. rels. com. Lake Minnetonka (Minn.) Dist. Ind. Reps., 1979-81, fundraising chmn., 1981-82; chmn. Wayzata Ind. Reps., 1981-82; sec. PTO, Wayzata, 1981-82. Mem. NEA, Minn. Edn. Assn., Wayzata Edn. Assn. (bd. mem., ins. chairperson). Lutheran. Office: Computer Aided Teaching 20380 Excelsior Blvd Excelsior MN 55331-8733

HENKE, SUSAN KAY, elementary education educator; b. Berwyn, Ill., Aug. 7, 1949; d. Henry Edward and Joan Ellen (Bangston) Roberts; m. Donald A. Henke; 1 child, Charles Roberts Even. BS in Edn., No. Ill. U., 1971; MEd, Nat. Louis U., 1996. Cert. in elem. edn., mental retardation, behaviorally/emotionally disturbed. Tchr. jr. h.s. mentally handicapped Dekalb (Ill.) Spl. Edn., 1971-73; tchr. mentally handicapped, dir. behavioral disturbed, coord. student svcs. Speed Devel. Ctr., Chicago Heights, Ill., 1973-76; tchr. kindergarten and presch. Alpha Presch. and Kindergarten, Homewood, Ill., 1980-82; tchr. behaviorally disturbed Hoover Elem. # 157, Calumet City, Ill., 1982-89, tchr. 4th grade, sci., 1989—; cons. Curriculum Reform Bus., Lansing, Ill., 1996; mem. sch. improvement steering com. Hoover # 157, Calumet City, 1996, curriculum devel./assessment chair, 1996. Docent Lincoln Park Zoo, Chgo., 1992-96. Adaptor grantee Ill. Math. and Sci. Acad., 1992, 93, grantee U. Calif., Berkeley, 1988-89. Mem. ASCD, AAUW, Nat. Sci. Tchr. Assn., Ill. Sci. Tchrs. Assn., Ill. Fedn. Tchrs. Home: 18242 Roy St Lansing IL 60438 Office: Hoover Elem Sch # 157 1259 Superior Ave Calumet City IL 60409

HENKEL, CATHY, newspaper sports editor. Office: The Seattle Times 1120 John St Seattle WA 98109-5321

HENKEL, JENNY SAUCIER, neurovirologist; b. Athens, Ga., Dec. 28, 1955; d. John Harmond and Sara Ernestine (Saucier) H.; m. Michael Andrew Tigges, Sept. 6, 1981 (div. 1991); m. David Robert Beers, July 7, 1994. BS magna cum laude, U. Ga., 1980, MS, 1983; PhD, Baylor Coll. Medicine, 1996. Rsch. asst. Baylor Coll. Medicine, Houston, 1983-87. Contbr. articles to profl. publs. Wolcott scholar. Mem. AAUW (Am. Fellows award 1994-95), AAAS, Am. Soc. Virology, Am. Soc. Microbiology, Am. Soc. for Neurosci. Home: 6015 Portal Dr Houston TX 77096 Office: Baylor Coll Medicine Dept Virology One Baylor Plz Houston TX 77030

HENKENIUS-KIRSCHBAUM, JOANNE, nursing administrator; b. Perth Amboy, N.J., Nov. 24, 1959; d. Glenn Joseph and Catherine Regina (Higgins) Henkenius; m. Myron Richard Kirschbaum, Jr., June 8, 1984; children: Tyler Joseph Kirschbaum, Logan Richard Kirschbaum. BSN, Ariz. State U., 1981; MS, Champman Coll., 1990; MSN, U. Tex., San Antonio, 1994. RN, Tex. Nurse intern USAF, Keesler AFB, Miss., 1982; staff nurse obstet. unit USAF, Robins AFB, Ga., 1982-85; staff nurse neonatal intensive care USAF, Clark AFB, The Philippines, 1985-87, clin. edn. coord., 1987-88; nurse staff devel. officer USAF, Cannon AFB, N.Mex., 1988-92; asst. nurse mgr. USAF, Lackland AFB, Tex., 1994-95, nurse mgr. pediat. intensive care, 1995—; cert. instr., trainer CPR Am. Heart Assn., 1984—, instr. neonatal resuscitation, 1990—; instr. advanced pediats. Am. Acad. Pediats., 1995—. Mem. adv. bd. High Risk Infant Program, San Antonio, 1995—; mentor Students Taking All the Right Steps Lackland AFB Elem. Sch., 1996—; vol. Salvation Army, San Antonio, 1996—. Recipient Nat. Collegiate Nursing award, 1994; Grad. scholar Nursing Alumni Assn., 1994, All-Am. scholar U.S. Achievement Acad., 1994. Mem. Nat. Assn. Neonatal Nurses (edn. com. 1994—), Assn. Women's Health, Obstet. and Neonatal Nurses (edn. com. Lonestar chpt. 1995—), Sigma Theta Tau.

HENKIND-JOSLOW, JANICE VERONICA, family nurse practitioner; b. N.Y.C., Feb. 3, 1951; d. William I. and Veronica A. Benjamin; BA, Mercy Coll., 1972; MS, U. Bridgeport, 1977; BSN U. Mass., 1993, MSN, 1995; postgrad. Yale U., 1995—; m. Paul Henkind, May 22, 1977 (dec. 1986); 1 child, Aaron Samuel; m. David L. Joslow, May 6, 1988 (dec. 1995); 1 child, Sarah Edith. Electron microscopist Boyce Thompson Inst. for Plant Rsch., 1972-74, dept. ophthalmology Montefiore Hosp. and Med. Ctr., 1974-76; exec. adminstr. Assn. for Rsch. in Vision and Ophthalmology, New Rochelle, N.Y., 1977-87, mng. editor Ophthalmology, Jour. Am. Acad. Ophthalmology, 1979-87, also XXIV Internat. Congress Opthalmology; pres. Med. Dialogues, Inc., N.H. Inn Mgmt. Co., Inc.; corporator Inn at Amherst Corp. Trustee Old Sturbridge Village, Mass., 1988-93, mem. fin. com., 1987-88, mem. long range planning com. 1988-93, bd. overseers, 1984—; mem. corp. N.Y. Bot. Garden, 1984—. Winner Martha Stone award in floriculture, 1983, 84. Mem. Assn. Women in Sci., Nat. Assn. Female Execs. Am., Assn. for Rsch. in Vision and Ophthalmology (hon.), Sigma Theta Tau, Alpha Sigma Lambda. Author: (with Keith Zinn) chpt. The Retinal Pigment Epithelium, 1979, Biomedical Foundations of Ophthalmology; contbr. articles to profl. jours. Address: 58 Sunset Ave Amherst MA 01002

HENLINE, CHARLOTTE ANN, social service administrator; b. Rochester, N.Y., July 10, 1946; d. Richard Eugean and Rita Virginia (McGrath) Graney; m. George Dexter Henline, Aug. 23, 1964; children: Edward Allen, Timothy Wayne, Richard Bea. BA, Glenville State Coll., 1983. Lic. social worker, W.Va.; ordained min. Ch. of the Ams., 1996. Domestic violence counselor Women's Aid in Crisis, Buckhannon, W.Va., 1985-90; dir. Women's Aid in Crisis, Elkins, W.Va., 1990-91; cmty. resource specialist, HIV/AIDS educator MT CAP of WV, Inc., Buckhannon, 1991—; owner Bait-Master Inc., French Creek, W.Va., 1990-96, C&G Taxi, Buckhannon, 1995—. Recipient Susan B. Anthony award W.Va. NOW, 1991. Mem. W.Va. NOW (pres.), Upshur County Christmas Store (bd. dirs. 1990-96), Women of Moose (chaplain 1995-96), Stockyard Youth Com. (bd. dirs. 1994-96). Democrat. Home: PO Box 7 French Creek WV 26218 Office: Mountain CAP WVa Inc 26 N Kanawha St Buckhannon WV 26201

HENN, JO ALLISON, judge, lawyer; b. Troy, Ohio, May 11, 1960; d. Dwight C. and Diane C. (Snyder) H. BS, Juniata Coll., 1982; JD, U. Toledo, 1984. Bar: Ohio 1985, N.Y. 1990. Staff atty. Legal Aid Soc., Dayton, Ohio, 1985-88, Prisoner's Legal Svcs., Poughkeepsie, N.Y., 1988-92; adminstrv. law judge unemployment ins. appeal bd. N.Y. State Dept. Labor, Albany, 1992—; pvt. practice as pro bono atty. Cohoes, N.Y., 1992—. Recipient Family Svc. award Battered Women's Project, Dayton, 1986. Democrat. Office: N Y State Dept Labor Rm 288 State Office Campus Bldg 12 Albany NY 12240

HENN, SHIRLEY EMILY, retired librarian; b. Cleve., May 26, 1919; d. Albert Edwin and Florence Ely (Miller) H.; AB, Hollins Coll., 1941; MS, U. N.C., 1966; m. John Van Bruggen, July 14, 1944 (div. May 1947); 1 child, Peter Albert (dec.). Libr. asst. Hollins (Va.) Coll., 1943-44, 61-64, reference libr., 1965-84, ret., 1984; advt. mgr. R.M. Kellogg Co., Three Rivers, Mich., 1946-47; exec. sec. Hollins Coll. Alumnae Assn., 1947-55; real estate salesman Fowlkes & Kefauver, Roanoke, Va., 1955-61. Pres. Soc. for Prevention Cruelty to Animals, 1959-61, 69-72, bd. dirs., 1972-81; donor Mary Williamson award in Humanities Hollins Coll., 1947—; endowed fund for purchase books children's lit. collection Fishburn Libr. Hollins Coll., 1986-93; donor, patron Women's Ctr. Hollins Coll., 1993—, Scholarship Aids, 1994, Children's Lit. Masters Program, 1993-95; active Nat. Trust for Historic Preservation, 1994—, Roanoke Valley Hist. Soc., 1984—, Roanoke Valley Hist. Mus., Roanoke Valley Sci. Mus., Cystic Fibrosis Found., 1995—, Nat. Audubon Soc., 1995—, MADD, 1995—; donor Va. Tech. Found. for restoration Hotel Roanoke, 1992—; ptnr. Spl. Olympics, 1995—. Recipient Rath award, 1984, Critical Scholarship award, 1995, Creative Achievement award, 1995—. Mem. ALA, MADD, Am. Alumni Council (dir. 1952-54, dir. women's activities 1952-54), Va. Libr. Assn., Nat. DAR (libr. Nancy Christian Fleming chpt. Roanoke 1977-84, regent 1984-88, chair Good Citizenship award 1990-92, Am. Essay awards 1991—), Poetry Soc. Va. Clubs: Quota Internat. (chpt. pres. 1958-60) (Roanoke), Antique Automobile Club Am., Roanoke Valley Antique Auto Club, Roanoke Valley Mopar Club, Children's Lit. Assn., Am. Mus. Nat. History, Blue Ridge Zool. Soc., Cystic Fibrosis Found., Poetry Soc. Va., Nat. Audubon Soc. Author, illustrator: Adventures of Hooty Owl and His Friends, 1953; editor: Hollins Alumnae Bull., 1947-56. Avocations: collecting teddy bears, antique French and English plates, bells, pewter. Home: 6915 Tinkerdale Rd Roanoke VA 24019-1530

HENNECY, BOBBIE BOBO, English language educator; b. Tignall, Ga., Aug. 11, 1922; d. John Ebb and Lois Helen (Gulledge) Bobo; student, Wesleyan Conservatory, 1943-44; AB summa cum laude, Mercer U., Macon, Ga., 1950; postgrad. Oxford (Eng.) U. English-Speaking Union Scholar, 1961; MA, Emory U., 1962; postgrad. Cambridge U., Eng., 1987; m. James Howell Hennecy, Dec. 28, 1963; 1 child, Erin. Sec. Tattnall Sq. Bapt. Ch., 1943-48; sec., adminstrv. asst. to pres., instr. Mercer U., 1950-61, instr. English, 1961-76, asst. prof., 1976-89, emeritus assoc. prof. and adj. prof., 1989—; founder Tattnall Sq. Acad., Macon, 1968, sec. acad. corp., 1968-73, dir., 1968-78; Bobbie Bobo Hennecy scholarship named in her hon. Tattnall Sq. Acad., Mercer U.; NDEA fellow Emory U., 1962; named outstanding Psi Gamma Chi Omega, 1995. Mem. AAUW (chpt. v.p. 1959, pres. 1964), AAUP, MLA, S. Atlantic MLA, So. Comparative Lit. Assn., Am. Comparative Lit. Assn., Internat. Comparative Lit. Assn., Nat. Assn. Tchrs. English, Ga. Assn. Tchrs. English, English Speaking Union, LWV, Collegiate Press (adv. bd.), Am. Acad. Poets, Pres. Club of Mercer U., YWCA (life), Mid. Ga. Art Assn., Hereditary Register, Soc. Genealogists London, Nat. Soc. So. Dames, Nat. Soc. Magna Charta, UDC (pres. 1994-96), DAR (registrar 1980-82), Daus. of 1812, Descendants, Colonial Clergy, Daus. of Am. Colonists, Jamestowne Soc., Colonial Dames XVII Century (chpt. 1st v.p. 1988-91), Colonial Order of the Crown (descendants of Charlemagne), Ams. of Royal Descent, Mid. Ga. Hist. Soc., Coosa County Ala. Hist. Soc., Friends of the Cannonball House, Cardinal Key, Sigma Tau Delta, Sigma Mu (pres., v.p., sec.-treas.), Phi Delta (advisor), Phi Kappa Phi, Alpha Psi Omega, Chi Omega (alumnae pres. 1953, advisor 1953-83). Baptist. Home: 1347B Adams St Macon GA 31201-1515

HENNENFENT, MARY LOUISE, science educator; b. Granite City, Ill., Dec. 2, 1963; d. William Lewis and Sarah Dean (Watts) Metcalf; m. Gregory Clark Hennenfent, May 21, 1983; 1 child, Samantha Grace. BS in Biology, Lindenwood Coll., 1985, MA in Edn., 1994. Sci. educator Hamilton (Mo.) R-II Schs., 1985-87, Morgan County R-I Schs., Stover, Mo., 1987-89, Francis Howell North H.S., St. Charles, Mo., 1989—. Choir mem. United Meth. Ch. the Shepard, St. Charles, 1994-95. Mem. NEA, Nat. Biology Tchrs. Assn., Sci. Tchrs. Mo. Methodist. Home: 20 Stone Mill Ln Saint Peters MO 63376-7036 Office: Francis Howell North HS 2549 Hackmann Rd Saint Charles MO 63303

HENNER, MARILU, actress; b. Chgo., Apr. 6, 1952; m. Frederic Forest, 1980 (div.); m. Rob Lieberman, 1990. Attended, U. Chgo. Appearances include (TV series) Taxi, ABC, 1978-82, NBC, 1982-83, Evening Shade, CBS, 1990-94, Marilu, 1994-95, (TV movies) Dream House, 1981, Stark, 1985, Love With A Perfect Stranger, 1986, Ladykillers, 1988, Chains of Gold, (films) Between the Lines, 1977, Blood Brothers, 1978, Hammett, 1983, The Man Who Loved Women, 1983, Johnny Dangerously, 1984, Cannonball Run II, 1984, Perfect, 1985, Rustler's Rhapsody, 1985, L.A. Story, 1991, Noises Off, 1992; Broadway debut in Over Here; other Broadway prodns. include Pal Joey, Social Security; stage performances include Grease (nat. co.), Carnal Knowledge, Grown-Ups, Super Sunday.

HENNESS, SUSAN LAUBER, small business owner; b. Oak Park, Ill., Feb. 13, 1945; d. Robert Raymond and Alyce (Kloos) Lauber; m. Charles Parker Henness, Nov. 8, 1969; children: Alyce Braddock, Charles Parker. BSJ, Northwestern U., 1966. Asst buyer Carson Pirie Scott & Co., Chgo., 1966-67; sys. engr. IBM, Chgo., 1967-69, mktg. rep., 1969-71; asst. dir. series WQLN, Erie, Pa., 1975; treas., owner Thompson Maple Products, Inc., Corry, Pa., 1982-94, CFO, owner, 1994—. Pres. Erie Area Fund for the Arts, 1984-86, bd. dirs., 1980—; bd. dirs. Citizens Arts. Pa., Harrisburg, 1986—; pres. Erie Summer Festival of the Arts, 1984; founding bd. dirs. Coun. of One Hundred, Northwestern U., Evanston, Ill., 1993—, co-chair internship com., 1996—.

HENNESSEY, ALICE ELIZABETH, forest products company executive; b. Havenhill, Mass., May 24, 1936; d. H. Nelson and Elizabeth E. (Johnson) Pingree; A.B. with honors, U. Colo., 1957; cert. with distinction Harvard-Radcliffe Program in Bus. Adminstrn., 1958; m. Thomas M. Hennessey, June 13, 1959; children—Shannon, Sheila, Thomas N. With Boise Cascade Corp. (Idaho), 1958—, sec. to pres., 1958-60, adminstrv. asst. to pres., 1960-61, 65-71, corp. sec., 1971—, v.p., 1974-82, sr. v.p., 1982—. Dir. First Interstate Bank of Idaho. Bd. dirs. Boise Pub. Libr. Found., U. Idaho Found.; sustaining mem. Boise Jr. League; mem. exec. bd. U S WEST Communications, Idaho. Mem. Am. Soc. of Corp. Secs., Nat. Investor Relations Inst., Pub. Relations Soc. of Am., Phi Beta Kappa, Alpha Chi Omega. Office: Boise Cascade Corp PO Box 50 Boise ID 83728-0001*

HENNESSEY, AUDREY KATHLEEN, educator; b. Fairbanks, Apr. 4, 1936; d. Lawrence Christopher and Olga Virginia (Strandberg) Doheny; m. Gerard Hennessey, Mar. 10, 1963; children: Brian, Kate. BA, Stanford U., 1957; HSA, U. Toronto, Ont., Can., 1968; PhD, U. Lancaster, Eng., 1982. Asst. dir. European sales Univ. Soc., Heidelberg, Fed. Republic Germany, 1959-61; landman's asst. Union Oil Co. Calif., Anchorage, 1962-63; adminstr. group pension Mfgs. Life Ins., Toronto, 1963-65; instr. office systems Adult Edn. Ctr., Toronto, 1965-68; lectr. office systems Salford Coll. Tech., Lancashire, Eng., 1968-70; sr. lectr. data processing Manchester (Eng.) Polytechnic, 1970-79; lectr. computation U. Manchester, Eng., 1979-82; assoc. prof. computer sci. Tex. Tech. U., Lubbock, 1982-86, assoc. prof. info. systems, 1987-94, prof. info. systems, 1994—; dir. Inst. for Studies of Organized Automation, Lubbock, 1987-95; pres. ISOA Inc., 1994—; dir. Internat. Ctr. Informatics Rsch., 1996—; vis. instr. Fed. Law Enforcement Tng. Ctr., Glynco, Ga., 1984-88; adj. prof. West Tex. A&M U., Canyon, 1994-95, U. Alaska, Anchorage, 1995, U. Tex., Dallas, 1995—. Author: Computer Applications Project, 1982; editor procs.: Office Document Architecture Internat. Symposium, English version, 1991; contbr. articles to profl. jorus.; patentee in field. Organizer Explorer Scouts Computer Applications, Lubbock, 1983-85. Recipient various awards Tex. Instruments, 1982-86, 94-95, Xerox Corp., 1985, Halliburton, 1986, Sys. Exploration, 1987, State of Tex., Tex. Advanced Tech. Project, 1988-93, 96—, Knowledge-based Image Analysis award USN Space Sys., 1991—, Immunization Tracking Sys. award Robert Wood Johnson Found., 1993, Leica, 1994, Sematech ADC awards, 1994. Mem. IEEE, Soc. Mfg. Engrs., Assn. Computing Machinery, Data Processing Mgmt. Assn. (pres. chpt. 1989, Disting. Info. Sci. award 1992, pres. SIGAI 1996—), Sigma Xi (pres. Tex. Tech. chpt. 1996—). Office: ICIR MS #2101 Tex Tech U Lubbock TX 79409 also: U Tex Dallas Richardson TX 75083-0688 also: OICIR 1221 W Campbell Rd Ste 231 Richardson TX 75080

HENNESSY, ELLEN ANNE, lawyer, educator; b. Auburn, N.Y., Mar. 3, 1949; d. Charles Francis and Mary Anne (Roan) H.; m. Frank Daspit, Aug. 27, 1974. BA, Mich. State U., 1971; JD, Cath. U., 1978; LLM in Taxation, Georgetown U., 1984. Bar: D.C. 1978, U.S. Ct. Appeals (D.C. cir.) 1978, U.S. Supreme Ct. 1984. Various positions NEH, Washington, 1971-74; atty. office chief counsel IRS, Washington, 1978-80; atty.-advisor Pension Benefit Guaranty Corp., Washington, 1980-82; assoc. Stroock & Stroock & Lavan, Washington, 1982-85; assoc. Willkie Farr & Gallager, Washington, 1985-86, ptnr., 1987-93; dep. exec. dir. and chief negotiator Pension Benefit Guaranty Corp., Washington, 1993—; adj. prof. law Georgetown U., Washington, 1985—. Mem. ABA (supervising editor taxation sect. newsletter 1984-87, mem. standing com. on continuing edn. 1990-94, chairperson joint com. on employee benefits 1991-92), Am. Law Inst./ABA (mem. com. on continuing profl. edn. 1994—), Women in Employee Benefits (pres. 1987-88), D.C. Bar Assn. (mem. steering com. tax sect. 1988-93, chairperson continuing legal edn. com. 1993-95). Democrat. Home: 1926 Lawrence St NE Washington DC 20018-2734 Office: Pension Benefit Guaranty Corp 1200 K St NW Ste 210 Washington DC 20005-4025

HENNESSY, MARGARET BARRETT, health care executive; b. Oak Park, Ill., Apr. 16, 1952; d. Bernard Leo and Frances (Madigan) H. BA in Sociology and Psychology, St. Norbert Coll., DePere, Wis., 1974; MS, Rush U., Chgo. Communications specialist Ill. Cancer Coun., Chgo., 1983-84; adminstrv. asst. Rush-Presbyn./St. Luke's Med. Ctr., Chgo., 1984-85; adminstrv. intern Cook County Hosp., Chgo., 1985-86; fin. analyst Loyola U. Med. Ctr., Maywood, Ill., 1986-89; operating officer Howard Brown Meml. Clinic, Chgo., 1989-93; hematology-oncology adminstr. Loyola U. Med. Ctr., Maywood, Ill., 1993-96; assoc. dir. primary care svcs. Lake County Health Dept., Waukegan, Ill., 1996—; guest lectr. Loyola U. Law Sch., 1989-90. Contbr. articles to profl. jours. Tchr. English as a second lang. World Relief Orgn., Chgo., 1989; cons. United Charities Camps, Chgo., 1989. Recipient Foster G. McGaw scholar, Am. Coll. health Care Execs., 1985. Mem. Rush U. Alumni Assn. (pres.), Chgo. Health Execs. Forum, Am. Coll. Healthcare Execs., Assn. Ambulatory Care Adminstrs. Office: Lake County Pub Health Dept 2400 Belvedere Rd Waukegan IL 60085

HENNING, JUDITH LOUISE, secondary school educator; b. Scranton, Pa.; d. Richard Leland Van Fleet; m. George Frederick Henning III, Jan. 22, 1972; children: Adam, Aaron, Susan. Student, Johns Hopkins Hosp., 1970; BS, Pa. State U., 1971; MS, U. Wis., 1972. Cert. tchr., Pa., N.Y. Home economist Pa. State Extension Svc., Honesdale, 1971; home econs. tchr. Upper Darby (Pa.) H.S., 1973, Chichester Jr. H.S., Boothwyn, Pa., 1973-76; tchr. family and consumer scis. Montrose (Pa.) Area H.S., 1977—, dept. chair, 1978—; adult sch. tchr. Chichester H.S., 1974-76. Vol. ARC, Montrose, 1978—. Mem. AAUW, Pa. State Edn. Assn., Am. Assn. Family and Consumer Scis., Pa. Assn. Family and Consumer Scis., Omicron Nu. Democrat. Methodist. Home: 7 Hillendale Dr Montrose PA 18801-9006 Office: Montrose Area Sch Dist RR 3 Box 28 Montrose PA 18801-9507

HENNING, KARLA ANN, molecular biologist, research scientist; b. Oakland, Calif., May 31, 1960; d. Karl Bruno and Barbara Jean (Harris) H. AB in Biochemistry, U. Calif., Berkeley, 1982; PhD in Genetics, Stanford U., 1993. Biomed. scientist Lawrence Livermore (Calif.) Nat. Lab., 1982-85; predoctoral fellow U. Tex. Southwestern Med. Ctr., Dallas, 1990-93, postdoctoral fellow, 1993-95; postdoctoral fellow Nat. Ctr. for Human Genome Rsch., Bethesda, Md., 1995—. Contbr. chpt. to book. Calif. Alumni scholar Calif. Alumni Assn., Berkeley, 1978. Mem. AAAS, AAUW, Am. Soc. Human Genetics. Home: 208 Congressional Ln #T2 Rockville MD 20852 Office: NCHGR/NIH Bldg 49 Rm 3B19 9000 Rockville Pike Bethesda MD 20892-4442

HENNINGER, POLLY, neuropsychologist, researcher and clinician; b. Pasadena, Calif., Apr. 1, 1946; d. Paul Bennett and Mary (MacNair) Johnson; m. Richard Henninger Jr., 1966 (div. 1983); children: Marguerite, Nathan; m. Clyde Pechstedt, 1985 (div. 1992). BA, Ind. U., 1967, Pomona Coll., 1977; MA, U. Toronto, 1969, PhD, 1982; PhD (respecialization), Fuller Theol. Sem., 1995. Registered psychologist, Ont., Can. Postdoctoral fellow Calif. Inst. Tech., Pasadena, 1982-84; doctoral respecialization in clin. psychology Fuller Theol. Sem., Pasadena, 1991-95; asst. prof. Pitzer Coll., Claremont, Calif., 1984-87, Brock U., St. Catharines, Ont., 1987-91; vis. assoc. divsn. biology Calif. Inst. Tech., Pasadena, 1984-94; asst. dir. neuropsychol. svcs. Ctr. for Aging Resources, Fuller Theol. Sem., Pasadena, 1991-92; psychology intern Boston VA Med. Ctr. and New Eng. Med. Ctr., 1994-95; neuropsychology fellow Tufts Med. Sch., Boston, 1995-96; staff neuropsychologist Fall River Outpatient Clinic Braintree Rehab. Hosp., 1995—; rsch. assoc. Harvard Med. Sch., Boston, 1996—. Contbr. chpts. to books, articles to profl. jours. Recipient fellowships and grants. Mem. APA (div. 40 chair rsch. selection 1986-89), Nat. Acad. Neuropsychology, Can. Psychol. Assn., Internat. Neuropsychol. Soc. Democrat. Episcopalian. Home: 220 Jamaica Way 16 Jamaica Plain MA 02130 Office: VA Med Ctr Psychology Svc 116B 150 S Huntington Dr Boston MA 02130

HENNION, CAROLYN LAIRD (LYN HENNION), investment executive; b. Orange, Calif., July 27, 1943; d. George James and Jane (Porter) Laird; m. Reeve L. Hennion, Sept. 12, 1964; children: Jeffrey Reeve, Douglas Laird. BA, Stanford U., 1965; grad. Securities Industry Inst., U. Pa., 1992.

CFP, fund specialist; lic. ins. agt.; registered gen. securities prin. Portfolio analyst Schwabacher & Co., San Francisco, 1965-66; adminstrv. coord. Bicentennial Commn., San Mateo County Calif., 1972-73; dir. devel. Crystal Springs Uplands Sch., Hillsborough, Calif., 1973-84; tax preparer Household Fin. Corp., Foster City, Calif., 1982, freelance, 1983-87; sales promotion mgr. Franklin Distbrs., Inc., San Mateo, 1984-86, v.p. and regional sales mgr. of N.W., 1986-91, Mid-Atlantic, 1991-94; v.p. Viatech, Inc., 1986-92; v.p. Keypoint Svcs. Internat., 1992—; pres. Brock Rd. Corp., 1993—; v.p. Strand, Atkinson, Williams & York, Medford, Oreg., 1994—. Editor: Lest We Forget, 1975. Pres. South Hillsborough Sch. Parents' Group, Calif., 1974-75; sec. Vol. Bur. of San Mateo County, Burlingame, Calif., 1975; chmn. Community Info. Com., Town of Hillsborough, 1984-86, mem., subcom. chmn. fin. adv. com., 1984-86; mem. coun. Town of Buncom, Oreg., 1990—; bd. dirs. Pacific N.W. Mus. Natural History, 1995-96; chmn. Jackson County Applegate Trail Sesquicentennial Celebration, 1995—; treas. Sesquicentennial Wagon Train, 1995—; v.p. and sec. So. Oreg. Hist. Soc. Found., 1995—; trustee Oreg. Shakespeare Festival Endowment Fund, 1996—. Recipient awards Coun. for Advancement and Support of Edn., 1981, Exemplary Direct Mail Appeals Fund Raising Inst., 1982, Wholesaler of Yr. Shearson Lehman Hutton N.W Region, 1989, Golden Mic award Frederic Gilbert Assocs., 1993. Mem. Securities Industry Assn. (chmn. state membership 1989-91), Internat. Assn. Fin. Planners (sec. Oreg. chpt. 1988-89, bd. dirs.), So. Oreg. Estate Planning Coun., Buncom Hist. Soc., Oreg. Shakespeare Festival, Britt Festivals, So. Oreg. Hist. Soc., Arts Coun. So. Oreg., Jr. League. Republican. Home: 3232 Little Applegate Rd Jacksonville OR 97530-9303 Office: Strand Atkinson Williams & York 1 North Holly Medford OR 97501

HENRIKSEN MACLEAN, EVA HANSINE, former anesthesiology educator; b. Petaluma, Calif., Jan. 1, 1929; d. Peder Henrik Boas and Karen (Nielsen) Henriksen; m. Daniel Edward MacLean, Aug. 25, 1957 (dec. Dec. 1981); children: Elizabeth, Mary Ann. AA, U. Calif., Berkeley, 1948, BA, 1950; MD, Yale U., 1954. Diplomate Am. Bd. Anesthesiology. Intern, resident Los Angeles County Hosp., L.A., 1954-57; from instr. to asst. prof. anesthesia Loma Linda U. (formerly Coll. Med. Evangelists), L.A., 1957-68; from instr. to assoc. prof. surgery anesthesiology Sch. Medicine U. So. Calif., L.A., 1957-94, assoc. prof. anesthesiology emeritus, 1994—; anesthesia cons. L.A. Coroner's Office, 1992-94. Mem. governing coun. Angelica Luth. Ch., 1992-96. Democrat. Home: 957 Arapahoe St Los Angeles CA 90006-5703

HENRIKSON, LOIS ELIZABETH, photojournalist; b. Lytton, Iowa, Nov. 10, 1921; d. Daniel Raymond and Cora Elizabeth (Thomson) Wessling; m. Arthur Allen Henrikson, July 3, 1943; children: Diane Elizabeth, Janet Christine, Michele Charlene Henrikson Smetana. BS, Northwestern U., 1943. Adminstrv. asst. to v.p., dir. ops. bus. communications div. ITT Telecommunications Corp., Des Plaines, Ill., 1980-82; adminstrv. asst. to exec. v.p. Wholesale Stationers' Assn., Des Plaines, 1982-84, membership svcs. coord., editor membership roster, 1984-88; field editor Office World News, BUS Publ. Group, Jericho, N.Y., 1988-92. Contbg. editor: Home World Bus. ICD Publs., Today's Office, FM Bus. Publs., Inc., Office Tech. Mgmt., Bus. Tech. Comms. Inc.; project editor: Dyna Search, Inc., Wallace Offutt Cons. Chair safety com. Cumberland Sch. PTA, Des Plaines, 1957-58, publicity 1960-61; bd. dirs. Maine West High Sch. Music Boosters, Des Plaines, 1967-69; capt. fin. dr. YMCA, Des Plaines, 1964; mem. diaconate bd., visitation coord., growth and membership bd. 1st Congl. Ch., Des Plaines; mem. Art Inst. Chgo., Peal Ctr. for Christian Living. Mem. NAFE, AAUW (chair social com. 1983-84, editor newsletter 1984-85, 88-94, newsletter 1st pl. award 1993, membership com. 1988-94, N.W. Suburban Ill. br. Ednl. found. contbn. made in honor 1992, 95), DAR, Am. Soc. Assn. Execs. (cert. membership mktg. 1986), Am. Soc. Profl. Execs. Women, Am. Assn. Editl. Cartoonists, Aux. Chgo. Soc. Assn. Execs. (registrar 1984-85), Soc. Profl. Journalists, Am. Bus. Editors and Writers, Nat. Soc. Magna Carta Dames, Am. of Royal Descent, Alpha Gamma Delta. Home and Office: 27 N Meyer Ct Des Plaines IL 60016-2243

HENRIQUES, DIANA BLACKMON, journalist; b. Bryan, Tex., Dec. 17, 1948; d. Lawrence Ernest and Pauline (Webb) Blackmon; m. Laurence Barlow Henriques, Jr., June 7, 1969. BA with distinction, George Washington U., 1969. Editor Lawrence Ledger, Lawrenceville, N.J., 1969-71; reporter Asbury Park (N.J.) Press, 1971-74; copy editor Palo Alto (Calif.) Times, 1974-76; investigative reporter Trenton (N.J.) Times, 1976-82; bus. writer The Phila. Inquirer, 1982-86; writer Barron's Fin. Weekly, N.Y.C., 1986-89, The New York Times, 1989—; vis. fellow, cons. Woodrow Wilson Sch., Princeton U., N.J., 1981-82, Guggenheim Found., N.Y., N.J., 1981-82. Author: (book) The Machinery of Greed, 1986; contbr. articles to profl. jours. Recipient Bell Prize N.J. Press Assn., 1977, numerous writing awards, 1970-77. Mem. N.Y. Fin. Writers Assn., Reporter's Com. for Freedom of the Press, Phi Beta Kappa. Office: The New York Times 229 W 43rd St New York NY 10036-3913*

HENRIQUEZ-FREEMAN, HILDA JOSEFINA, fashion design executive; b. Palmarito de Cauto, Oriente, Cuba, June 18, 1938; came to U.S., 1960; d. Matias and Isabel Beatrice (Freeman) Henriquez. BA, Bethune-Cookman Coll., 1963; postgrad., Tchrs. Coll., 1965-66, Roosevelt U., 1966, Northwestern U., 1969-70; cert., No. Ill. U., 1975; postgrad., Loop Coll., 1972-84. Modiste/couturier Fina Modas, Habana, Cuba, 1952-59; instr. English Habana Pub. Sch., Cuba, 1956-58; ct. reporter Govt. La Cabana, Habana, Cuba, 1959-60; language instr. Ft. Lauderdale Sch. Dist., Fla., 1963-64; custom design Freeman's Fashion Atelier, Chgo., 1965-68; pres. dir. Acad. for Fashion Art Design, Chgo., 1968—; head designer Eur-Am. Creations, Chgo., 1978-81; cons. Freeman's Enterprise, Chgo., 1982—. Mentor Spanish coalition, Youth Career Awareness Program, Chgo., 1987. Mem. Cuban C. of C., Cuban Liceo, Ill. Assn. Trade and Tech. Schs., NAFE. Office: Acad for Fashion Art Design 410 S Michigan Ave Chicago IL 60605-1302

HENRY, ANN RAINWATER, education educator; b. Okla., Nov. 2, 1939; d. George Andrew and Opal Norma (Cohea) Rainwater; m. Morriss M. Henry, Aug. 1, 1964; children: Paul, Katherine, Mark. BA, U. Ark., 1961, MA, 1964, JD, 1971. Bar: Ark. 1971. Pvt. practice law Fayetteville, Ark., 1971-72; instr. Coll. Bus. Adminstrn. U. Ark., Fayetteville, 1976-78, asst. prof., 1978-84, assoc. prof., 1984—, asst. dean, 1984-86, assoc. dean, 1986-89, faculty chair, 1989-91. Bd. dirs. City of Fayetteville, 1977-83, 91-92, McIlroy Bd., Fayetteville, 1986—; chmn. cert. com. Ark. Tchrs. Evaluation, 1984-85; mem. Ark. Local Svcs. Adv. Bd., 1980-88, Ark. Gifted and Talented, 1989—, Ark. State Bd. Edn., 1985-86. Mem. Ark. Alumni Assn. (bd. dirs., asst. treas. 1989-93), Fayetteville C. of C. (bd. dirs. 1983-85), Ark. Bar Assn. (chmn. ethics com. 1986-87). Democrat. Methodist. Home: 2465 Township Common Dr Fayetteville AR 72703-3568 Office: U Ark BA 204 Fayetteville AR 72701

HENRY, CATHERINE THERESA, insurance company executive; b. N.Y.C., June 25, 1934; d. John Patrick and Bridie (Hartnett) H. Student, Queens Coll., 1960-63. With Equitable Life Assurance Soc., N.Y.C., 1952—, systems analyst, 1965-74, adminstrv. mgr., 1974-76, personnel mgr., 1976-80, asst. v.p., personnel officer, 1980-83, v.p., human resources officer, 1983-90, v.p. ins. svcs., 1990-94, v.p. tech. mgmt., 1994—. Exec. com. W. 89th St. Park Block Assn., N.Y.C., 1986—. Named to Acad. Women Achievers, YWCA, 1985. Mem. Am. Soc. Quality and Participation, Orgnl. Devel. Network, Orgnl. Devel. Network of Greater N.Y., N.Y. Human Resource Planners, Human Resource Planning Soc. (bd. dirs. 1990-93, sec. 1993-95, pres. 1995—). Office: The Equitable 787 7th Ave New York NY 10019

HENRY, DIANE J., financial planner, tax consultant; b. L.A., Oct. 22, 1933; m. David W. Henry, June 18, 1955; children: Rebecca, Christine, Matthew. BS, UCLA, 1956. Owner, mgr. Horizon Gallery, Durham, N.C., 1986-88; tax cons. Encinitas, Calif., 1992—; fin. planner Sentra Securities Corp., La Jolla, Calif., 1993—. Mem. Internat. Assn. for Fin. Planning, Nat. Assn. Enrolled Agts., Calif. Soc. Enrolled Agts., Inland Soc. Tax Cons. Office: 187 Calle Magdalena Encinitas CA 92024

HENRY, FRANCES ANN, journalist, educator; b. Denver, July 23, 1939; d. Lewis Byford and Betsy Mae (Lancaster) Patten; m. Charles Larry, June 28, 1963 (div. May 1981); children: Charles Kevin, Tracy Diane. BA in English, Carleton Coll., 1960; MA in Social Sci., U. Colo., Denver, 1988; MA in Journalism, Memphis State U., 1989. Cert. tchr. Lang. arts tchr. Rolla (Mo.) Pub. Schs., 1963-66; journalism tchr. Douglas County Pub. Schs., Castle Rock, Colo., 1976—, chmn. English dept., 1993—; mng. editor Douglas County News-Press, Castle Rock, 1986-87, editor Fourth World Bulletin, 1988; exec. editor Daily Helmsman Memphis State U., 1988-89, gen. mgr. Daily Helmsman, 1991-92. Contbr. articles to profl. jours. Mem. ACLU, Colo. H.S. Press Assn. (sec. 1981-83, pres. 1983-91, bd. dirs., named Colo. Journalism Tchr. of Yr. 1985), Assn. for Edn. in Journalism and Mass Comm., Mensa, Kappa Tau Alpha. Democrat. Episcopalian. Office: Douglas County High Sch 2842 Front St Castle Rock CO 80104-9427

HENRY, GINA MARIE, special education educator, lawyer; b. Phila., July 20, 1963; d. James Edwin Jr. and Ruth T. (Russell) H. BA, U. Pa., 1985; JD, U. Va., 1988; MEd, Coll. William and Mary, 1991; postgrad., U. Mich., 1992—. Bar: Pa.; cert. tchr., Va. Rsch. asst. Coll. William and Mary, Williamsburg, Va., 1989-91; rsch., tng. asst. U. Mich., Ann Arbor, 1992—. Co-chair womens divsn. Little Rock Bapt. Ch., Detroit, 1994. Rackham Minority fellow U. Mich., 1992—, Minority fellow, 1992—. Mem. NAACP, Am. Ednl. Researchers Assn., Coun. for Exceptional Children. Democrat. Office: Univ Mich Sch Edn 610 E University Ave Ann Arbor MI 48109-1259

HENRY, GISÈLE BYRD, publishing executive, book designer; b. Dothan, Ala., June 10, 1956; d. John Edwin and Yvonne Caroline (Mertz) B.; married. BS in Journalism, U. Md., 1979; Diplome, U. Sorbonne, Paris, 1986. Design mgr. Nat. Telephone Coop. Assn., Washington, 1980-83; freelance designer Paris, 1983-87; art dir. Univ. Press Am., Lanham, Md., 1987-89, v.p. design, 1991—. Mem. organizing com. Mardi Gras Masquerade Ball for charity, Balt., 1992, 93, 94. Mem. Washington Book Pubs. (book jacket design award 1992, 93). Democrat. Office: Univ Press Am 4720 Boston Way Lanham Seabrook MD 20706-4310

HENRY, KAREN LEE, writer, lecturer; b. Grand Rapids, Mich., Feb. 20, 1944; d. Leo John and Mary Alice (Mallick) H.; m. Richard John Kamel, Mar. 5, 1990. AS with high honors, Davenport Coll., 1983; BA, U. Mich., 1989. Writer Palestine Human Rights Campaign, Chgo., 1984-85; journalist Al Fajr, Jerusalem, 1985-86; dir. activities Villa Maria Retirement Cmty., Grand Rapids, Mich., 1990-93; libr. asst. Grand Rapids Pub. Libr., 1994—; freelance writer, lectr. Grand Rapids; ednl. cons. on Mid. East Inst. for Global Edn., Grand Rapids, 1983—, bd. dirs., 1995—. Contbr. articles to profl. jours. Apptd. Housing Bd. Appeals, Grand Rapids, 1984; spl. projects dir. Econ. Devel. Corp., Grand Rapids, 1983; active Grand Rapids AIDS Task Force, 1986-92, Coop Am., Feminist Majority, Am. Ednl. Trust, New Jewish Agenda, Am. Arab Anti-Discrimination Com., YWCA, Nat. Humane Soc., Expressions for Women; bd. dirs. YWCA, Grand Rapids, 1996—, Am. Friends Svc. Com. of Great Lakes Region, 1996—; pres., founding mem. Women's Action Network, Grand Rapids, 1993—. Recipient Appreciation cert. Econ. Devel. Corp., 1983, Housing Appeal Bd., 1985, Chicago House, 1987. Mem. AAUW, Nat. Assn. Arab Am. Women, Nat. Mus. Women in Arts, Am. for Mid. East Understanding, Union Palestinian Women's Assn. Home and Office: 1617 Oswego NW Grand Rapids MI 49504

HENRY, KATHERINE SAVAGE, physician; b. Marietta, Ga., Aug. 30, 1944; d. James Ernest and Audrey Louise (Armstrong) Savage; BA, Birmingham-So. Coll., 1966; MD, Emory U., 1971. Intern, resident in internal medicine Ga. Bapt. Hosp., Atlanta, 1971-73; emergency room physician Baylor Med. Ctr., Dallas, 1973-74; family physician The Family Clinic, Garland, Tex., 1974; family practice medicine, Richardson, Tex., 1974—; chmn. dept. family practice Richardson Gen. Hosp., 1975; cons. health care Richardson YWCA; exec. com. Richardson Med. Ctr., 1975-78; first physician, designer health service U. Tex., Dallas, 1974-76; chairperson med. adv. com. Dallas Hospice, Inc.; asst. clin. prof. Dept. Community Medicine and Family Practice Southwestern Med. Sch. Diplomate Am. Bd. Family Practice. Columnist The Texas Woman's News. Recipient Physicians Recognition award AMA. Fellow Am. Acad. Family Physicians, Am. Coll. Cryosurgery, Am. Soc. Sports Medicine; mem. AAUW, Am. Coll. Physician Execs., Am., Tex. acads. family practice, Dallas County Med. Soc., Tex. Soc. Sports Medicine, Tex. Med. Assn., Am. Med. Women's Assn. (charter pres. Dallas chpt. 1980). Home: 16007 Ranchita Dr Dallas TX 75248-3834 Office: 721 W Arapaho Rd Ste 2 Richardson TX 75080-4155

HENRY, KRISTEN GAE, chemistry educator; b. Lemmon, S.D., May 13, 1959; d. Jack Martin and Barbara Harriet (Olson) Wanstedt; m. Bruce G. Henry, May 22, 1982 (div. Aug. 1995); children: Karissa, Kelli. BS, S.D. State U., 1980; MS, Tex. A&M U., 1982. Chemistry tchr. A&M Consol. H.S., College Station, Tex., 1985—; cons. in advanced placement chemistry, 1992—. Contbr. articles to profl. jours. Recipient S.W. Regional award in H.S. Chemistry Tchg., Am. Chem. Soc., 1993, AP award S.W. Region Coll. Bd., 1995. Mem. Sci. Tchr.'s Assn. of Tex., Assn. Chemistry Tchrs. of Tex. Lutheran. Home: 4603 Colonial Cir College Station TX 77845 Office: A&M Consol HS 701 FM 2818 College Station TX 77840

HENRY, LETUS KAY, elementary education educator, hair designer; b. Pocola, Okla., July 29, 1942; d. Joe L. and Edna Marie (Williams) Howard; m. Thomas O. Henry, Mar. 31, 1962 (div. 1987); 1 child, Tommy Dewayne. Diploma, Millies Beauty Coll., 1961; AA, Carl Albert Jr. Coll., 1981; BS in Edn., Northea. Okla. State U., 1982, MEd, 1987. Hair designer owner Kay Styling Salon, Pocola, Okla., 1965-75; tchr. elem. Pocola Sch., 1982-95; hair designer J.C. Penney Styling Salon, Fort Smith, Ark., 1990-95; tchr. tutor, 1990-95; tchr. cons. Northeastern State Coll., Tahlequah, Okla., 1990-91, Westark Coll., Fort Smith, Ark., 1991-93. Tchr. Am. Heart Assn., Pocola, 1991-92, chair Am. Cancer Soc., Fort Smith, 1992-95, St. Jude Children Hosp., 1992-94. Mem. NEA, Okla. Edn. Assn., Pocola Classroom Tchr. Assn., United Teaching Profession. Republican. Methodist. Home: 124 N 53 Fort Smith AR 72903

HENRY, MADELEINE MARY, classics educator; b. Mpls., Dec. 14, 1949; d. Arthur Claude and Florence Frances (Tonrich) H. BA, U. Minn., 1971, MA, 1973, PhD, 1983. Assoc. prof. classical studies, women's studies Iowa State U., Ames, 1992—. Author: Prisoner of History: Aspasia of Miletus and Her Biographical Tradition, 1995; contbr. articles to profl. jours. Mem. APA (edn. com. 1993-96), Women's Classical Caucus (co-chair 1989-90), Phi Beta Kappa. Office: FLL 300 Pearson Hall Ames IA 50011

HENRY, MARGUERITE, author; b. Milw.; d. Louis and Anna (Kaurup) Breithaupt; m. Sidney Crocker Henry. Author: Auno and Tauno: A Story of Finland, 1940, Dilly Dally Sally, 1940, Birds at Home, 1942, Geraldine Belinda, 1942, (with Barbara True) Their First Igloo on Baffin Island, 1943, A Boy and a Dog, 1944, Little Fellow, 1945, Justin Morgan Had a Horse, 1945 (Newbery Honor award 1948, Jr. Scholastic Gold Seal award 1948, Friends of Lit. award 1948), Robert Fulton: Boy Craftsman, 1945, Misty of Chincoteague, 1947 (Boys' Club of Am. award, Lewis Carroll Shelf award, Newbery Honor award), Benjamin West and His Cat, Grimalkin, 1947, Always Reddy, 1947, King of the Wind, 1948 (John Newbery medal 1949), Sea Star: Orphan of Chintoteague, 1949, Little-or-Nothing from Nottingham, 1949, Born to Trot, 1950, Album of Horses, 1951, Portfolio of Horses, 1952, Brighty of the Grand Canyon, 1953 (William Allen White award 1956), Wagging Tails: An Album of Dogs, 1955, Cinnabar: The One O'Clock Fox, 1956, Black Gold, 1957 (Sequoyah Children's Book award 1959), Muley-Ears, Nobody's Dog, 1959, Gaudenzia: Pride of the Palio, 1960 (Clara Ingram Judson award Soc. Midland Authors 1961), Misty, the Wonder Pony, by Misty, Herself, 1961, All About Horses, 1962, Five O'Clock Charlie, 1962, Stormy, Misty's Foal, 1963, White Stallion of Lipizza, 1964, Portfolio of Horse Paintings, 1964, Mustang, Wild Spirit of the West, 1966 (Western Heritage award Nat. Cowboy Hall of Fame 1967, Sequoyah Children's Book award 1969), Dear Readers and Riders, 1969, Album of Dogs, 1970, San Domingo: The Medicine Hat Stallion, 1972 (Clara Ingram Judson award Soc. Midland Authors 1973), Stories From Around the World, 1974, Pictorial Life Story of Misty, 1976, One Man's Horse, 1977, The Illustrated Marguerite Henry, 1980, Marguerite Henry's Misty Treasury, 1982, Our First Pony, 1984, Misty's Twilight, 1992, (pop-up book) Marguerite Henry's Album of Horses, 1993; "pictured geographies" series Alaska, 1941, Argentina, 1941, Brazil, 1941, Canada, 1941, Chile, 1941, Mexico, 1941, Panama, 1941, West Indies, 1941, Australia, 1946, Bahamas, 1946, Bermuda, 1946, British Honduras, 1946, Dominican Republic, 1946, Hawaii, 1946, New Zealand, 1946, Virgin Islands, 1946; films: Brighty, 1967, Justin Morgan Had a Horse, 1971, Peter Lundy and the Medicine Hat Stallion, 1977, King ofthe Wind, 1990; documentary: The Story of a Book, 1979. Recipient Lit. for Children award So. Calif. Coun., 1973, Kerlan award Univ. of Minn., 1975; named Author of Diamond Jubilee Yr. Ill. Assn. of Tchrs. of English, 1982. Office: care Macmillan Pub Co div of Simon & Schuster 1230 Avenue of the Americas New York NY 10020*

HENRY, PAULA LOUISE (PAULA LOUISE HENRY COOVER), association executive; b. White Plains, N.Y., Mar. 5, 1947; d. Raymond Francis and Carolyn Louise (Landis) Henry; m. John David Coover, Nov. 18, 1967 (div. Jan. 1992); children: Jeffrey Darren, Robert Benson, Jennifer Danielle (dec.). AA in Psychology, Monmouth U., 1967; student, Pace U., 1972-76; BA in Psychology, Monmouth U., 1993. Chair gifted and talented com., then pres. Hunterdon County (N.J.) Coun. PTAs, 1980-86; chmn. county pres. group, nat. conv. del., gen. conv. chmn. N.J. Congress Parents & Tchrs., Trenton, 1985-87, field svc. chmn., 1985-89, pres., 1989-91, immediate past pres., 1991-93, hon. v.p., 1991-95; asst. to dean Faculty of Mgmt. Rutgers U., Newark, 1995—. Mem. sch. bd. Union Twp. Bd. Edn., Hampton, N.J., 1983-86, assembly del., 1984-86, legis. chmn. 1984-86, policy chmn. 1986, edn. chmn. 1984-85; trustee Jennie M. Haver Scholarship Fund, 1984-89; mem. Hunterdon County Edn. Coalition, 1984-88, Child Abuse and Missing Children Com., Hunterdon, 1987—, Hunterdon County Youth Svcs. Commn., Flemington, 1987—, N.J. Gov.'s Commn. on Quality Edn., 1991-93; treas. Fannie B. Abbott Student Loan Found., 1985-90, trustee, 1985—; v.p. Hunterdon County Child Assault Protection Program, 1986-90; mem. strategic planning com. United Way of Essex and West Hudson, 1994-95. Republican. Methodist. Home: PO Box 5228 Clinton NJ 08809-0228 Office: Rutgers Univ Faculty of Mgmt Newark NJ 01102

HENRY, SHERRYE, federal agency administrator. Grad. magna cum laude, Vanderbilt U.; MBA, Fordham U. Dir. outreach programs Dana Alliance for Brain Initiatives; asst. adminstr. Office Women's Bus. Ownership SBA; vice-chair interagy. com. on women's bus. enterprise. Author of 2 books including The Deep Divide: Why American Women Resist Equality; contbr. numerous articles to profl. jours.; creator, host Woman program on Sta. WCBS-TV, N.Y.C.; ind. prodr., broadcaster Sherrye Henry Program WOR Radio, N.Y.C. Active Group for the South Fork, eastern end of L.I., N.Y., Fedn. Protestant Welfare Agys. N.Y., The Retreat, East Hampton, N.Y. Mem. Women's Forum N.Y. (founder). Office: Office of Women's Bus Ownership 409 3rd St SW Washington DC 20416*

HENRY-THIEL, LOIS HOLLENDER, psychologist; b. Phila., Jan. 19, 1941; d. Edward Hubert and Frances Lois (Nesler) Hollender; m. Charles L. Henry, Oct. 24, 1964 (div. 1971); children: Deborah Lee, Randell Huitt, Andrew Edward; m. Brian L. Thiel, Jan. 1, 1989. BA, Thomas A. Edison Coll., 1979; MSW, Fordham U., 1981; PhD in Psychology, City U. L.A., 1992. Diplomate cert. neurofeedback provider; cert. social worker, Ariz., N.Y., N.J.; lic. svc. profl., career counselor, Ariz. Pers. asst., sec. IBM, Paterson, N.J. and St. Louis, 1964-66; min.'s asst. Grace Luth. Ch., St. Cloud, Fla., 1966-68; adminstr./tchr. Fla. Finishing Acad., St. Cloud, 1968-70; adminstrv. asst. Newark Book Ctr., 1972-77; intern, med. social worker Jersey City Med. Ctr., 1979-80; intern, psychiatric/med. social worker VA Med. Ctr., Lyons, N.J., 1980-81; sch. social worker Lakeview Learning Ctr., Budd Lake, N.J., 1981-82; mgr. human resources Terak Corp., Scottsdale, Ariz., 1982-85; v.p. counseling and bus. devel. Murro & Assocs., Phoenix, 1985-88, exec. v.p. cons., 1988-91; prin. career cons. Henry & Assocs., Scottsdale, 1982—; staff psychologist Nelson O'Connor & Assocs., Phoenix, 1993—; cert. neurotherapist Forensic Psychol. Svcs., Phoenix, 1995—; career cons., individual/family counselor/psychotherapist/neurotherapist, spkr., Henry & Assocs., Scottsdale, 1982—; adj. prof. Ottawa U.; staff psychologist Nelson O'Connor & Assocs.; mem. employers com. Ariz. Dept. Econ. Security; cons. in field. Coordinator-vol. Job-A-Thon, Phoenix, 1983. Fellow Am. Orthopsychiat. Assn., Internat. Assn. Outplacement Profls. (treas. Ariz. region 1992-95, assoc. editor Internation Jour. Neuronal Regulation), Nat. Registry of Soc. Neuronal Regulation (diplomate); mem. NASW, Soc. Human Resource Mgmt., Am. Assn. Psychophysiology. Office: 8628 E Granada Rd Scottsdale AZ 85257-2943

HENS, VIRGINIA (DOROTHY), emergency medical system executive; b. Buffalo, Sept. 9, 1938; d. Edward Pochopin; m. Daniel F. Hens; children: Mark, David, Robert, Peter. Nursing diploma, U. Rochester, N.Y., 1959. RN, N.Y. Staff nurse Roswell Park Cancer Inst., Buffalo, 1959-60; staff nurse Millard Fillmore Hosp., Buffalo, 1964-70, emergency nurse, 1970-74, supr. nursing, 1974-78, patient care coord., 1978-85; dir. patient svcs. Millard Fillmore Suburban Hosp., Williamsville, N.Y., 1985-87; exec. dir. Western Regional EMS, Buffalo, 1987—. Co-chmn. All Am. City-Civic Empowerment Com., Buffalo, 1994, 95, 96; co-chair Buffalo Ambassadors, 1994-95, chair, 1995-96. Named Nurse of Distinction N.Y. State Legislature, 1992. Mem. NAFE, Emergency Nurses Assn. (pres. western N.Y. chpt. 1983-84, pres. N.Y. state 1984-86, chair nat. resolutions com., nat. pub. edn. com., Ena Anita Dorr award 1990). Office: Western Regional EMS 462 Grider St Buffalo NY 14215-3075

HENSCHEL, SHIRLEY MYRA, licensing agent; b. N.Y.C., Dec. 18, 1932; d. Joseph and Leah Rose (Cooper) H. BA, Barnard Coll., 1954. Pub. rels., sales promotion exec. Louis Marx & Co., Inc., N.Y.C., 1954-59; acct. exec. Harold J. Siesel Co., N.Y.C., 1959-62; pres. U.S. Motor Sport Promotions, Inc., N.Y.C., 1962-66; v.p. Flora Mir Candy Corp., N.Y.C., 1966-71, Marden-Kane, Inc., N.Y.C., 1971-79; pres. Alaska Momma, Inc., N.Y.C., 1979—. Mem. Licensing Industry and Merchandisers Assn. (charter mem. Achievement award 1988, nominated for Hall of Fame 1994), Women Inc., Women in Toys (charter mem.), Am. Bookseller's Assn. (assoc.). Democrat. Jewish. Office: Alaska Momma Inc 303 Fifth Ave New York NY 10016

HENSELER, SUZANNE MARIE, state legislator, social studies educator, majority whip; b. Brookline, Mass., Dec. 7, 1942; d. Paul R. and Evelyn (Warren) McGoldrick; m. John L. Henseler, June 26, 1965; children: Sean Patrick, Warren Paul, Timothy Brian. BS in History Edn., Boston Coll., 1964. Tchr. Pilgrim High Sch., Warwick, 1964-66; clk. house labor com. R.I. Ho. Reps., Providence, 1977-82; tchr. St. Rocco Sch., Johnston, R.I., 1984—; mem. R.I. Ho. of Reps., Providence, majority whip, 1992—. Former mem., bd. mem. North Kingstown (R.I.) Soccer Assn., 1974-89; mem. North Kingstown Dem. Town Com., 1974—; mem. sch. com., Kingstown, 1974-76; co-chair pay equity commn., 1995—; co-chair Legis. Women's Health Commn., 1995—; chmn. R.I. Mobile Home Commn., 1988—; chmn. Legis. Commn. to Study the Solid Waste Mgmt. Corp. Named Outstanding Young Women of Yr., North Kingstown Jaycettes, 1977, Nat. Environ. award 1993. Mem. Nat. Orgn. Women Legislators, Women in Govt. Home: 210 Edmond Dr North Kingstown RI 02852-2416 Office: Majority Whip State House # 303 Providence RI 02903

HENSELMEIER, SANDRA NADINE, training and development consulting firm executive; b. Indpls., Nov. 20, 1937; d. Frederick Rost Henselmeier and Beatrice Nadine (Barnes) Henselmeier Enright; m. David Albert Funk, Oct. 2, 1976; children: William H. Stolz, Jr., Harry Phillip Stolz II, Sandra Ann Stolz. AB, Purdue U., 1971; MAT, Ind. U., 1975. Exec. sec. to dean Ind. U. Sch. Law, Indpls., 1977-78; adminstrv. asst. Ind. U.-Purdue U., Indpls., 1978-80, assoc. archivist, 1980-81; program and communication coordinator Midwest Alliance in Nursing, Indpls., 1981-82; tng. coordinator Coll./Univ. Cos., Indpls., 1982-83; pres. Better Bus. Communications, Indpls., 1983—; adj. lectr. lectr. U. Indpls. Center Continuing. Mgmt. Devel. and Edn., Indpls., 1984—. Author: Successful Customer Service Writing, Winning with Effective Business Grammar, Successful Telephone Communication and Etiquette, Management Writing; contbr. articles to profl. jours. Bus. adv. com. computer programmer tng. Crossroads Rehab. Ctr.; exec. adv. bd. Profl. Secs. Internat. 500 chpt. Mem. Am. Soc. Indexers Soc., Soc. Tech. Comms., Indpls. Computer Soc., Indpls. C. of C., Econ. Club Indpls. Republican. Presbyterian. Avocations: traveling, walking, reading, learning new ideas. Office: Better Bus Communications PO Box 20309 Indianapolis IN 46220-0309

HENSHAW, JULIA PLUMMER, publishing executive; b. Charlottesville, Va., June 4, 1941; d. Herbert Plummer and Elizabeth (Magruder) H.; children: Andrew Nevil Wise, Jeremy Henshaw Wise. AB, Wellesley Coll., 1962; MA, Wayne State U., 1967. Asst. editor Macmillan Co., N.Y.C., 1963-65; asst. prof., assoc. prof. Ctr. for Creative Studies, Detroit, 1973-81; editor Detroit Inst. Arts, 1981-84, dir. publs., 1984—; bd. dirs. Assn. Art

Editors, N.Y.C. Editor: The Detroit Institute of Arts: A Visitor's Guide, 1995. Office: Detroit Inst Arts 5200 Woodward Ave Detroit MI 48202

HENSON, (BETTY) ANN, media specialist, educator; b. Tampa, Fla., Dec. 20, 1944; d. James (Jim) and Beth (Tabb) H. BA, U. South Fla., 1966; MEd, U. Fla., 1980, EdS, 1985. Cert. tchr., Fla. English tchr. Hillsborough County Schs., Tampa, 1967-68; drama tchr. Cultural Enrichment Ctr., Gainesville, Fla., 1969-70, Title II Grant, Gainesville, 1970-72; lang. arts tchr. Alachua County Schs., Gainesville, 1972-74; team leader humanities ESAA Grant Alachua County, Gainesville, 1975-82; media specialist Alachua County Schs., Gainesville, 1982—, tech. coord., 1993—; adj. faculty Nova U., Gainesville, 1988-91, Ctr. for Distance Learning, Ocala Ctr., St. Leo's Coll., 1994-95. Presenter in field; slide show prodr. (Fla. ctr. for children and youth award 1984). Recipient First Liberty Inst. award Ams. United Rsch. Found., Washington, 1991; grantee Fla. Ctr. Tchrs. Resident Scholar, 1993, grants in field. Mem. Nat. Coun. for the Social Studies, Profl. Assn. Libr. and Media Specialists (sec. 1991-92, 94-95), Fla. Assn. Media in Edn. (tech. coord. 1993—), Alpha Delta Pi. Home: 203 SW 41st St Gainesville FL 32607-2778 Office: Westwood Middle Sch 3215 NW 15th Ave Gainesville FL 32605-5053

HENSON, ANNA MIRIAM, otolaryngology researcher, medical educator; b. Springfield, Mo., Nov. 7, 1935; d. Bert Emerson and Esther Miriam (Crank) Morgan; m. O'Dell Williams Henson, Aug. 1, 1964; children: Phillip, William. BA, Park Coll., Parkville, Mo., 1957; MA, Smith Coll., 1959; PhD, Yale U., 1967. Instr. Smith Coll., Northampton, Mass., 1960-61; rsch. assoc. Yale U., New Haven, 1967-74; instr. U. N.C., Chapel Hill, 1975-78, rsch. asst. prof., 1978-83, rsch. assoc. prof., 1983-86, rsch. prof. dept. surgery Sch. Medicine, 1986—; mem. study sect. on hearing rsch. NIH, Bethesda, Md., 1990-93. Contbr. articles to profl. jours. Fulbright scholar, Australia, 1959-60; NIH grantee, 1975—. Mem. Assn. for Rsch. in Otolaryngology, Sigma Xi. Office: U NC Cb 7090 Taylor Hall Chapel Hill NC 27599

HENSON, GENE ETHRIDGE, retired legal administrator; b. Lawrenceville, Ga., Sept. 26, 1924; d. Fred Golden and Cora Jewell (Smith) Ethridge; student public schs., Lawrenceville; m. James Arthur Henson, May 2, 1948 (dec.); diploma Interior Design Gwinnett Tech. Inst., 1991. 1 child, Gena Arlene. With Smith, Currie & Hancock, Atlanta, 1959-90, adminstr., 1965-90; chair fashion & design adv. com. Gwinnett Tech. Inst., 1992-93; owner Gene Henson Interiors. Ofcl. hostess for State of Ga., So. Gov.'s Conf., Atlanta, 1971; past adult tchr. First Bapt. Ch., Lawrenceville; mem. adv. coun. Ctr. for Profl. Edn., Ga. State U., 1980-84; bd. dirs., v.p. County Seat Players Theatre Group; actress Steel Magnolias, The Foreigner, Harvey, Our Town; bd. dirs. Gwinnett Coun. for the Arts, Vines Botanical Gardens. Mem. Assn. Legal Adminstrs. (nat. v.p. 1979—, dir. 1979-83), Internat. Interior Design Assn., Atlanta Assn. Legal Execs. (1st pres. 1975), Assn. Legal Adminstrs. (v.p. Atlanta chpt., pres.-elect 1986-87, pres. 1987-88, life mem. 1991). Home and Office: 74 Scenic Hwy Lawrenceville GA 30245-5729

HENSON, GLENDA MARIA, newspaper writer; b. Marion, N.C., June 17, 1960; d. Douglas Bradley and Glenda June (Crouch) H. BA in English cum laude, Wake Forest U., 1982. Reporter Ark. Dem., Little Rock, 1982-84; bur. reporter Tampa Tribune, Crystal River, Fla., 1984; statehouse reporter Ark. Gazette, Little Rock, 1984-87; bur. chief Ark. Gazette, Washington, 1987-89; editorial writer Lexington (Ky.) Herald-Leader, 1989-94; editorial writer, columnist The Charlotte (N.C.) Observer, 1994—. Mem. Wake Forest Presdl. Scholarship Com., Ky., 1992, Wake Forest Bd. Visitors, 1995—; Pulitzer Prize juror, 1994, 95. Recipient Pulitzer prize, 1992, Walker Stone award Scripps Howard Found., 1992, award Ky. Press Assn., 1992, N.C. Press Assn., 1995, Leadership award Duke U., 1995, Nat. Headliner award, 1996; named Wake Forest Woman of Yr., 1992. Mem. Soc. Profl. Journalists (Sigma Delta Chi award 1991, Green Eyeshade award Atlanta chpt. 1992), Nat. Conf. Editorial Writers, Omicron Delta Kappa. Home: 1527 Cleveland Ave # B Charlotte NC 28203-4515 Office: The Charlotte Observer PO Box 32188 Charlotte NC 28232-2188

HENSON, LISA, motion picture company executive; b. 1960; d. Jim Henson. Attended, Harvard U. Exec. asst. to head prodn. Warner Bros., 1983-85, dir. creative affairs, 1985-92, v.p. prodn., 1992-93, exec. v.p. prodn., 1993; pres. worldwide prodn. Columbia Pictures. Office: Columbia Pictures 10202 W Washington Blvd Culver City CA 90232*

HENSON, MICHELE, state legislator; b. Boston, Aug. 29, 1946; m. Doug Henson. AA, LaSalle U., 1966; BA, U. Miami. Adminstr. Metro Dental Svcs., 1985—; mem. Ga. Ho. of Reps. from dist. 57, 1990-92, Ga. Ho. of Reps. from dist. 65, 1993—; mem. health and ecology com., industry com., vice-chair ins. com.; co-chair Ga. Gen. Assembly Women's Caucus, 1995-96. Democrat. Jewish. Office: Ga House of Reps State Capitol Atlanta GA 30334

HENSON SCALES, MEG DIANE, artist, writer, publisher; b. Portland, Oreg., Oct. 16, 1953; d. Kenneth Jack and Jessie Louise (Mott) Henson; m. Jeffrey Charles Henson Scales, Dec. 16, 1985; 1 child, Coco Tigre Roja. Student, San Francisco State U., 1972-73, 74-75, Friends' World Coll., Guatemala, 1974. Founding mem. Black Edn. Ctr., Portland, Oreg., 1970-71; mng. editor Woman's Bldg., L.A., 1979-81; pvt. investigator Kleinbauer Investigations, L.A., 1981-83; tchr. CUNY, N.Y.C., 1987-89, Mindbuilders, Bronx, N.Y., 1987-89; painter, writer, strategist Henson Scales Prodns., N.Y.C., 1989; founder Com. for Rational African Americans Against the Parade, N.Y.C., 1995; pub., editor The Harlem Howl, N.Y.C., 1995-96. Author: The Book of Love, 1988, Melisma, 1989 (Deming award 1989); co-creator, performer Tragedy in Black and White/A Race Record in One Act, 1981; dir., prodr. video documentary Class, 1989. Founding mem. African Am. Against Violence, N.Y.C., 1995. Recipient N.Y. Found. Arts fellowship, N.Y.C., 1989. Home: 1945 7th Ave #4N New York NY 10026

HENTZ, MARIE EVA, real estate investor and developer; b. Detroit, Sept. 27, 1920; d. Charles and Eva (Follman) Hentz. Student Detroit Bus. U., Wayne State U. Draftsman, Cadillac Motor Co., Detroit, 1941-44; stenographer Great Lakes Steel Co., River Rouge, Mich., 1945-46, Can. Nat. R.R., Detroit, 1946-49; sec. UNOCAL, L.A., 1950-72; real estate investor, mgr., developer, Thousand Oaks, South El Monte, and Coto de Caza, Calif., 1950—; gen. ptnr. Hentz & Christensen, Ltd., South El Monte, Calif., 1953-86, Hentz Properties, Ltd., Burbank, 1971—. Mem. Union Oil Alumni, Coto Valley Country Club, Women's League of Coto de Caza. Republican. Avocations: gardening, reading, travel.

HENZLER, CAROLYN JEAN, artist; b. Bryan, Tex., Dec. 29, 1944; d. Melvin Charles and Mildred Pearl (Novosad) H.; m. Terrence Day, Oct. 19, 1974. AB, U. Calif., Berkeley, 1974. One-woman shows include The New Gallery of the Ednl. Alliance, N.Y.C., 1990, 91, 92, Ernest Rubenstein Gallery, N.Y.C., 1995; two-person shows include The New Gallery of the Ednl. Alliance, N.Y.C., 1988, 93; exhibited in group shows at 80 Washington Sq. East Gallery, N.Y.C., 1985, Circlework Visions Gallery, N.Y.C., 1987; internet on-line show, 1995. Recipient Exhibition grants Artists Space, 1988, 90, 91. Mem. Artists Equity, Dieu Donne, Manhattan Graphics Ctr. Democrat.

HEPBURN, KATHARINE HOUGHTON, actress; b. Hartford, Conn., May 12, 1907; d. Thomas N. and Katharine (Houghton) H.; m. Ludlow Ogden Smith (div.). AB, Bryn Mawr Coll., 1928; LHD (hon.), Columbia U., 1992. Actress: (films) A Bill of Divorcement, 1932, Christopher Strong, 1933, Morning Glory, 1933 (Acad. award for best performance by actress 1934), Little Women, 1933, Spitfire, 1934, The Little Minister, 1934, Alice Adams, 1935, Break of Hearts, 1935, Sylvia Scarlett, 1936, Mary of Scotland, 1936, A Woman Rebels, 1936, Quality Street, 1937, Stage Door, 1937, Bringing up Baby, 1938, Holiday, 1938, The Philadelphia Story, 1940 (N.Y. Critic's award 1940), Woman of the Year, 1941, Keeper of the Flame, 1942, Stage Door Canteen, 1943, Dragon Seed, 1944, Without Love, 1945, Undercurrent, 1946, Sea of Grass, 1946, Song of Love, 1947, State of the Union, 1948, Adam's Rib, 1949, The African Queen, 1951, Pat and Mike, 1952, Summertime, 1955, The Rainmaker, 1956, The Iron Petticoat, 1956, The Desk Set, 1957, Suddenly Last Summer, 1959, Long Day's Journey into Night, 1962 (Best Actress, Cannes Internat. Film Festival), Guess Who's Coming to Dinner, 1967, (Acad. award for best actress 1968),The Lion in Winter, 1968 (Acad. award for best actress 1969), Madwoman of Chaillot, 1969, Trojan Women, 1971, A Delicate Balance, 1973, Rooster Cogburn, 1975, Olly, Olly, Oxen Free, 1978, On Golden Pond, 1981 (Acad. award for best actress 1981), George Stevens: A Filmmaker's Journey, 1984, The Ultimate Solution of Grace Quigley, 1985, Love Affair, 1994; (plays) The Czarina, 1928, The Big Pond, 1928, Night Hostess, 1928, These Days, 1928, Death Takes a Holiday, 1929, A Month in the Country, 1930, Art and Mrs. Bottle, 1930, The Warrior's Husband, 1932, Lysistrata, 1932, The Lake, 1933, Jane Eyre, 1937, The Philadelphia Story, 1939, Without Love, 1942, As You Like It, 1950, The Millionairess, Eng. and U.S.A., 1952, The Taming of the Shrew, The Merchant of Venice, Measure for Measure,, Eng. and Australia, 1955, Merchant of Venice, Much Ado about Nothing, Am. Shakespeare Festival, 1957, toured later, 1958, Twelfth Night, Antony and Cleopatra, Am. Shakespeare Festival, 1960, Coco, 1969-70, toured, 1971, The Taming of the Shrew, 1970, A Matter of Gravity, 1976-78, West Side Waltz, 1981, (TV movies) The Glass Menagerie, 1973, Love among the Ruins, 1975, The Corn Is Green, 1979, Mrs. Delafield Wants to Marry, 1986; Laura Lansing Slept Here, 1988, The Man Upstairs, 1992, This Can't Be Love, 1994, One Christmas, 1994; narrator, co-writer documentary Katharine Hepburn: All About Me, 1993; author: The Making of the African Queen, 1987, (autobiography) Me, 1991. Recipient gold medal as world's best motion picture actress Internat. Motion Picture Expn., Venice, Italy, 1934, ann. award Shakespeare Club, N.Y.C., 1950, award Whistler Soc., 1957, Woman of Yr. award Hasty Pudding Club, 1958, outstanding achievement award for fostering finest ideals of acting profession, 1980, lifetime achievement award Coun. Fashion Designers Am., 1986, award Kennedy Ctr. Awards, 1990. Address: William Morris Agy 151 S El Camino Dr Beverly Hills CA 90212-2704*

HEPBURN, ROSANNA LEVINE (ROSANNE LEVINE), artist; b. N.Y.C., May 31, 1954; d. Archie and Gilda (Stecher) Levine. BFA, U. Miami, 1975; 2-yr. degree in Textile Design, Fashion Inst. Tech., N.Y.C., 1978; student, Art Students League, 1984-89. Textile designer In-Materials, N.Y.C., 1978-79; owner costume jewelry co. La Vie En Rose, N.Y.C., 1979-90; jewelry designer Melmar, N.Y.C., 1990-92; artist N.Y.C., 1992—. Work represented in Charlene Cody Gallery, Santa Fe, Mark Humphrey Gallery, Southampton, N.Y., Norton Gallery, Darien, Conn., Main St. Gallery, Nantucket, Mass., Salmagundi Club, 1996. Recipient Rose Parsons Meml. award, Washington Sq. Art Show, N.Y.C., 1995, Manhattan Arts Internat. Showcase award, 1996. Mem. Larchmont Artist Guild, Copley Soc. Boston, Catherine Lorillard Art Club, Allied Artists of Am., Art Students League (working scholarship 1993, in-class competition award 1993). Studio: 41 Union Sq West Rm 1118 New York NY 10003

HEPPE, KAROL VIRGINIA, lawyer, educator; b. Vinton, Iowa, Mar. 14, 1958; d. Robert Henry and Audry Virginia (Harper) H. BA in Law and Society, U. Calif., Santa Barbara, 1982; JD, People's Coll. of Law, 1989. Cmty. organizer Oreg. Fair Share, Eugene, 1983; law clk. Legal Aid Found. L.A., summer 1986; devel. dir. Ctrl. Am. Refugee Ctr., L.A., 1987-89; exec. dir. Police Watch-The Police Misconduct Lawyer Referral Svc., L.A., 1989-94; prof. law People's Coll. of Law, L.A., 1992-94; dir. alternative sentencing project Ctr. Juvenile and Criminal Justice, 1994-95; with Bay Area Police Watch, 1996; vol. law clk. Legal Aid Found. L.A., 1984-86, Lane County Legal Aid Svc., Eugene, 1983. Editor (newsletters) Law Studies in Action, Ctrl. Am. Refugee Ctr., 1986, Prison Break, 1994. Bd. dirs. People's Coll. of Law, 1985-90, Law Student Civil Rights Rsch. Coun., N.Y.C., 1986; bd. dirs., law student organizer Nat. Lawyers' Guild, L.A., 1984-87; mem. Coalition for Human Immigrants Rights, 1991-92, So. Calif. Civil Rights Coalition, 1991-92. Scholar, Kramer Found., 1984-88, Law Students' Civil Rights Rsch. Coun., 1986, Davis-Putter Found., 1988, Assn. for Cmty.-Based Edn. Prudential, 1988.

HEPPLER, ROBIN LEE, science administrator; b. Detroit, Aug. 12, 1953; d. Warren G. and Maurida (Tillie) H. Student, Glendale Community Coll., 1971-74, 82, Ariz. State U., 1975, 81, U. Wis., 1981. Various positions Valley Nat. Bank, Phoenix, Ariz., 1971-78; project bus. regional dir. Jr. Achievement, Inc., Phoenix, San Jose, Atlanta, 1978-81; asst. v.p., ctr. mgr. 1st Tenn. Bank, Memphis, 1981-83; customer svc. mgr., ops. analyst Wells Fargo Credit Corp., Phoenix, 1983-84; officer Citibank, Ariz., Phoenix, 1984-85; ops. mgr., asst. v.p. MeraBank, Phoenix, 1985-89; lending officer, policy analyst 1st Interstate Bank, Phoenix, 1989; project mgr. Colo. Nat. Bank, 1991-93; project mgr. Ctr. of Excellence for Project Mgmt. US West Techs., Denver, 1993—. Precinct bd. Maricopa County Election Dept., Phoenix, 1990; fundraiser Fiesta Bowl Com., Tempe, Ariz., 1990-92; bd. sec. Ariz. Easter Seal Soc., Phoenix, 1989-90; bd. dirs. Cen. Ariz. Arthritis Found., Phoenix, 1989-90, chmn. jingle bell run, 1989, active Fiesta Bowl Parade Com., 1983-92; chmn. jail-athon Am. Cancer Soc., 1989; coord. Andre House Diocese of Phoenix, 1987-90; sec. bd. dirs. Human Svcs. Inc., Denver, 1991-95; chmn. Festival of Kites, Denver, 1992, chmn. champagne and chocolate black tie silent auction, 1994, Denver Jr. League, 1994-96; chair holiday mart solicitations, 1996, safehouse Denver 5K run, corporate teams chair, 1994, 95. Named one of Outstanding Young Women Am., 1979; recipient award for outstanding contbn. Arthritis Found., 1990, award for outstanding achievement Am. Cancer Soc., Phoenix, 1989. Mem. Fin. Women Internat. (bd. dirs. 1988-90), Soc. Tech. Communicators. Home: 3635 S Carr St Denver CO 80235-1801

HEPPNER, GLORIA HILL, science administrator; b. Gt. Falls, Mont., May 30, 1940; d. Eugene Merrill and Georgia M. (Swanson) Hill; m. Frank Henry Heppner, June 6, 1964 (div. 1975); 1 child, Michael Berkeley. BA, U. Calif., Berkeley, 1962, MA, 1964, PhD, 1967. Damon Runyon postdoctoral fellow U. Wash., Seattle, 1967-69; asst. and assoc. prof. Brown U., Providence, 1969-79, Herbert Fanger meml. lectr., 1988; chmn. dept. immunology, dir. labs., sr. v.p. Mich. Cancer Found., Detroit, 1979-91; dir. breast cancer program Karmanos Cancer Inst., 1991—, dep. dir., 1994—; assoc. chairperson for rsch. dept. internal medicine Wayne State U. Sch. Medicine, Detroit, 1991—; mem. external adv. com. basic sci. program M.D. Anderson Hosp. and Tumor Clinic, Houston, 1984-94; mem. external adv. com. Case Western Res. U. Cancer Ctr., Cleve., 1988—, Roswell Park Meml. Inst., Buffalo, 1991—; Sarah Stewart meml. lectr. Georgetown U., Washington, 1988; bd. sci. counselors Nat. Inst. Dental Rsch., 1993—. Editor: Macrophages and Cancer, 1988; mem. editorial bd. Cancer Rsch., 1989-93, Jour. Nat. Cancer Inst., 1988, Sci., 1988-92; contbr. over 200 articles to sci. jours. Bd. dirs. Lyric Chamber Ensemble, 1996—. Recipient Mich. Sci. Trail-Blazer award State of Mich., 1987; fellow Damon Runyon-Walter Winchell Found., 1967-69. Mem. AAAS, Am. Assn. for Cancer Rsch. (bd. dirs. 1983-86, chmn. long-range planning com. 1989-91), Am. Assn. Immunologists, Metastasis Rsch. Soc. (bd. dirs. 1985-89), Women in Cancer Rsch. (nat. pres.), Internat. Differentiation Soc. (v.p. 1990-92, pres. 1992-94), LWV (bd. dirs. Grosse Pointe, Mich. 1989-95). Democrat. Office: Karmanos Cancer Inst. 110 E Warren Ave Detroit MI 48201-1312 Office: John R Harper Hosp Dept Internal Medicine Detroit MI 48201

HERALD, CHERRY LOU, research educator, research director; b. Beeville, Tex., Dec. 23, 1940; d. Edwin Sherley and Margaret Lucille (Caron) Bell; m. Delbert Leon Herald, Jr., July 31, 1964; children: Heather Amanda, Delbert Leon, III. BS, Ariz. State U., 1962, MS, 1965, PhD, 1968. Faculty rsch. assoc. Cancer Rsch. Inst. Ariz. State U., Tempe, 1973-74, sr. rsch. chemist Cancer Rsch. Inst., 1974-77, asst. to dir. and sr. rsch. chemist Cancer Rsch. Inst., 1977-83, asst. dir., assoc. rsch. prof. Cancer Rsch. Inst., 1984-88, assoc. dir., rsch. prof. Cancer Rsch. Inst., 1988—. Co-author: Biosynthetic Products for Cancer Chemotherapy, vols. 4, 5, & 6, 1984, 85, 87, Anticancer Drugs from Animals, Plants & Microorganisms, 1994, sci. jours. Mem. Am. Soc. Pharmacognosy, Am. Chem. Soc. Office: Ariz State U Cancer Rsch Inst Tempe AZ 85287-2404

HERB, JANE ELIZABETH, banker; b. Pottsville, Pa., Nov. 26, 1959; d. Wallace Lamar and Arlene Grace (Miller) Kimmel; m. David Glenn Herb, Dec. 22, 1978; 1 child, Jennifer Marie. Student, ICS, 1995—. Adminstrv. asst., customer svc. rep. Pa. Nat. Bank and Trust Co., Valley View, 1977-85; cosmetic salesperson Mary Kay Cosmetics, Dallas, 1980-84; fin. svc. salesperson for various firms, 1985-88; acct. supr., customer svc. rep. Jetson Direct Mail Svcs. Inc./Time Warner Inc.-N.Y.C., St. Clair, Pa., 1988-94; compliance mgr., asst. to pres. Gratz (Pa.) Nat. Bank, 1994—. Republican. United Methodist. Home: PO Box 565 Valley View PA 17983 Office: Internat Correspondence Schs The Gratz Nat Bank PO Box 159 Gratz PA 17030

HERBERT, BARBARA, editor, public relations consultant; b. Passaic, N.J., Nov. 10, 1960; d. William James and Beatrice (Payne) H. BA in Journalism, Rutgers U., 1983. Devel. asst. Theatre of Universal Images, Newark, 1983-86; office mgr. Seton Hall U., South Orange, N.J., 1991-92; scriptwriter Bundy Prodns., Newark, 1992-93; editor The Prudential, Roseland, N.J., 1993—; cons. Bundy Prodns., Newark, 1992—. Cons. Project 2000, Newark, 1991—, Louisville, 1992—. Sgt. USAF, 1986-91, Korea. Decorated Air Force Commendation medal. Mem. Minority Interchange (pub. rels. chairperson), Roseland Cmty. Svcs., N.J. Citizens for Change. Office: Prudential Healthcare Group 56 Livingston Ave Roseland NJ 07068

HERBERT, CAROL SELLERS, farming executive, lawyer; b. Durham, N.C., Mar. 2, 1943; d. George Grover and Mae (Savage) Sellers; m. James Keller Herbert, Nov. 13, 1980; children: John, Katherine, Paul, Barry. BA, Duke U., 1964; JD cum laude, Whittier Coll., 1976. Bar: Calif. 1976, U.S. Dist. Ct. (cen. dist.) Calif. 1976. Tchr. h.s. Wasatch Sch. Dist., Heber, Utah, 1964-67; dir., tchr. Pinedale (Mont.) Sch. Dist., 1967-71; adminstr. Whittier Law Sch., L.A., 1971-76; lawyer Katz Granof Palarz, Beverly Hills, Calif., 1976-79; exec. dir. MBJ Legal and Profl. Pub., Inc., L.A., 1979-83; dean San Joaquin Coll. Law, Fresno, Calif., 1981-85; pres., co-founder Barrister Project, L.A., 1985-90, Herbert Found., Fresno and Lindsay, Calif., 1990—; dir., CFO HerCal Corp., Lindsay, Calif.; trustee Domus Mitus Found., Fresno, 1994-96; founder Beverly Hills Bar Assn. Com. on Women and Law, 1977; dir. CLI DreamWeavers Divsn., Lindsay, Calif., 1995. Prodr. Lang. of Dreams (video series), 1994—. Mem. ABA, Calif. State Bar Assn.

HERBERT, MARY KATHERINE ATWELL, freelance writer; b. Grove City, Pa., Dec. 9, 1945; d. Stewart and Luella Irene (Brown) Atwell; m. Roland Marcus Herbert; children: Stephen Todd, Amy Elizabeth, Jill Anne. BA, Ariz. State U., 1968, MA, 1973; film cert., U. So. Calif., 1978. Film writer Scottsdale Daily Progress, 1976-79; dir. pub. relations Phoenix Theatre, 1980-85; script analyst, 1985-86; exec. asst. to v.p. prodn. DeLaurentiis Entertainment Group, 1986; producer's assoc. film TRAXX, 1986-87; devel. dir. Devin/DeVore Prodns., 1988-89; free-lance script analyst and writer Glendale, Calif., 1989—. Script writer: (TV shows) Trial By Jury, Dick Clark Prodn., Dry Heat, Blind Desire, others; author: Writing Scripts Hollywood Will Love, 1994. bd. mgrs. Hollywood-Wilshire YMCA. Mem. Women in Comms., Ariz. Forum, Kappa Delta Pi, Pi Lambda Theta.

HERBOLSHEIMER, HENRIETTA, physician, consultant; b. Peru, Ill., Feb. 10, 1913; d. George Leonard III and Catherine Carolyn (Neureuther) H. SB, U. Chgo., 1936, MD, 1938; MPH, Johns Hopkins U., 1948. Diplomate Am. Bd. Preventive Medicine. Maternal and child health physician Ill. Dept. Pub. Health, Springfield, 1941-44; dir. Hill Bureton Hosp. Program Hill Burton Hosp. Program, Springfield, 1044-48; dir. maternal and child health Ill. Dept. Pub. Health, Springfield, 1945-48, med. adminstrv. asst. to dir., 1948-51, dir. civil def. program-med. aspects, 1950-51; mem. faculty of medicine U. Chgo., 1951-80, assoc. prof. medicine emeritus, 1980—; dir. adult health/occ. medicine City of Chgo., Dept. Pub. Health, 1981-83; physician cons. Ill. Dept. Pub. Aid, Springfield, 1984—. Contbr. numerous articles to profl. jours. Bd. dirs. Vis. Nurse Assn., Chgo., 1960-74; mem. vis. com. Oriental Inst. U. Chgo., 1994—. Recipient Alumni award medicine U. Chgo., 1994. Fellow Am. Coll. Preventive Medicine; mem. AMA (del. 1977-92, Benjamin Rush award 1985), Am. Pub. Health Assn., Ill. State Med. Soc. (trustee 1975-84), Chgo. Med. Soc. (councillor 1977—), Am. Inst., Phi Beta Kappa, Alpha Omega Alpha, Sigma Xi. Home: 1700 E 56th St Ste 3507 Chicago IL 60637-1936

HERBST, MARIE ANTOINETTE, former state senator; m. Paul Herbst. BA, Albany State Tchr.'s Coll.; Masters, Columbia U.; postgrad. secondary sch. adminstrn., U. Conn. Pub. sch. tchr. East Windsor, Conn.; mem., asst. majority leader Conn. State Senate from 35th Dist.; 7th-9th grade tchr. E.W. H.S.; chmn. pub. safety com.; asst. minority leader, 1989-92; mem. fin., revenue, bonding com., 1989; mem. edn. com. Lector Sacred Heart Ch.; past chmn. H.S. DDC; past mem. Ladies of Sacred Heart; past mem. Tri-Town Disabled Com., Vernon Town Coun., 1975-79; past mem. Vernon Bd. Edn.; mem. Adult Edn. Adv. Commn., 1985; active New Rockville Youth Studies, 1995—; activities corporator Rockville Cen. Hosp., 1994—; bd. dirs. Tolland Health Inc.; apptd. to Vernon Town Coun., 1995; elected by dep. mayor to Vernon Town Coun., 1995. Mem. Internat. Edn. Assn., Nat. Edn. Assn., Conn. Edn. Assn., Phi Delta Kappa, Gamma Kappa Rho. Democrat. Roman Catholic. Home: 245 Brandy Hill Rd Vernon Rockville CT 06066-5609

HERBST, PATRICIA CARLISLE, lay worker; b. Pitts., July 21, 1933; d. Burton Samuel and Katherine (Schiffhauer) Carlisle; m. Richard Joseph Herbst Sr.; children: Patricia Rae, Tracy Lynn, Karen Kay, Gregory Paul, Richard Joseph Jr. BA in Theology, Allentown Coll. St. Francis deSales, 1993; MA in Holistic Spirituality/Spiritual Direction, Chestnut Hill Coll., 1994. Dir. of vols. Presbyn. Homes We. N.Y., 1978-82; dir. religious edn. Holy Ghost Ch., Bethlehem, Pa., 1982-89; pvt. practice spiritual dir. Bethlehem, Pa., 1986—; pastoral minister Ch. Assumption Blessed Virgin Mary, Bethlehem, Pa., 1990—; spiritual dir. Ch. Renewal Ctr., Allentown, Pa., 1993—; cons. Diocesan Exec. Youth Bd., Allentown, Pa., 1985-89; chair, bd. Ea. Pa. Dir. Religious Edn. Conf., Allentown, 1983-89; chair vol. seminar U. Buffalo, 1980; organizer charter office Vol. Adminstrs. We. N.Y., 1979-82. Judge elections GOP, Chgo., 1960-64. Mem. Am. Counseling Assn., Assn. Transpersonal Psychologists, Spiritual Dirs. Internat. Roman Catholic. Home: 1290 Sycamore Ave Bethlehem PA 18017-1040

HERBSTMAN, LORETTA, sculptor; b. Bklyn., June 14, 1939; d. Berardino and Sabina (Senelli) Guicciardini; m. Martin Herbstman, Aug. 28; children: Jason, Dana. Instr. stone sculpture J. Reid Sch. Art, Buford, Ga., 1996—. Sculptor in stone, cast bronze, cast resins and wire mesh; group exhibits in galleries throughout Manhattan, L.I., Staten Island and shown on Joe Franklin TV Show, as well as Smithtown Art Coun. Mill Pond House, C.W. Post U. Hutchins Gallery, Gallery North, Suffolk County Bald Hill Cultural Ctr., Falconaire's Gallery, N.Y. Design Ctr.; jewelry designer/maker. Founder, pres. Farmingville (N.Y.) Improvement Coun.; mem. East End Arts Coun., Huntington Town Art League, Smithtown Art League, Westhampton Cultural Consrotium. Recipient 1st prize for sculpture in a mixed-media juried show East Islip Arts Coun., numerous others. Mem. Nat. Sculpture Soc., Ga. Artists Registry.

HERBSTREITH, YVONNE MAE, primary education educator; b. Wayne County, Ill., Aug. 18, 1942; d. Daniel Kirby and Rizpah Esther (Harvey) Smith; m. Bobbie L. Cates, Oct. 18, 1964 (div. 1969); 1 child, Shawn L.; m. Jerry Carrol Herbstreith, Sept. 15, 1979. BS, So. Ill. U., 1964. Cert. elem. tchr., Ill. Kindergarten tchr. Beardstown (Ill.) Elem., 1964-65, Pekin (Ill.) Pub. Schs. # 108, 1966-94. V.p. Pekin Friends of 47, 1986-91, pres. 1991-93, pres. Rebecca-Sarah Cir. 1st United Meth. Ch., Pekin, 1988—; trustee Sta. WTVP-TV, Peoria, Ill., 1990-91; active PTA, 1965-94, treas. 1992-93. Recipient Louise Alloy award Sta. WTVP, 1995. Mem. NEA (life), AAUW, Ill. Edn. Assn., Pekin Edn. Assn., Pekin Friends of Libr., Tazewell County Ret. Tchrs., Alpha Delta Kappa, Alpha Theta (chpt. pres. 1986-88, state sgt. at arms 1990-92, state chaplain 1992-94, state pres.-elect 1994-96, state pres. 1996—). Democrat. Methodist. Home: 1922 Quail Hollow Rd Pekin IL 61554-6351

HERD, CHARMIAN JUNE, singer, actress; b. Waterville, Maine, June 1, 1930; d. Samuel Braid and Jennie May (Lang) Herd; B.A., Colby Coll., 1950; postgrad. Boston U., 1951, EdM, U. Maine, 1965; ednl. cert. No. Conservatory, Bangor, Maine, 1954; also study voice with Roger A. Nye. Dir. music State Sch. for Girls, Hallowell, Maine, 1950-51; head English, French, dramatics depts. St. George High Sch., Tenants Harbor, 1951-52; dir. music pub. schs. Albion and Unity, 1952-54, Troy, Freedom, Maine, 1953-54; dir. music pub. sch. system Belgrade, Maine, Waterville Jr. High Sch., 1954-55; dir. vocal music Waterville Jr. and Sr. high schs., 1954-58; head English and dramatics depts. Besse High Sch., Albion, 1959-62; tchr. French, Skowhegan Jr. High Sch., 1962-63; tchr. French, English, Skowhegan Sr. High Sch., 1963-69; tchr. French, Lawrence Sr. High Sch., Fairfield, Maine, 1969-71, chmn. drama and speech dept., 1972-79; instr. dramatics U. Maine, Farmington, 1969-70; tchr. conversational French, Skowhegan Adult Edn. Sch.,

1963-69, drama instr., 1965-69; dance asst. Plaza Studio; producer, appeared in role of Vera, Mame, Waterville; soloist various churches, Maine, 1951—; mus. dir. children's sect., performing mem. Theater at Monmouth, Maine, 1970—, mem. exec. bd., 1976—, sec. bd. trustees, 1977—; performing mem. Augusta Players, Camden Civic Theatre, Portland Lyric Theatre, Waterville Players, Titipu Choral Soc., Waterville Community Ballet, Choral Arts Soc., Portland, Maine, 1980—, Treasure Coast Opera Soc., Ft. Pierce, Fla., 1986—, Riverside Theatre Co., Vero Beach, Indian River Ctr. for Arts, New Lyric Opera, Port St. Lucie, Fla.; theatre chmn. ann. Maine Festival Arts, Bowdoin Coll., 1978—; soloist Vero Beach Chorale Soc., 1986—, numerous club, ch., conv., coll. concerts, oratorios; performing mem. Vero Beach Solo Gates, Encore Alley Theatre, 1987-91, Esprit des Amis, Vero Beach, Ft. Pierce City Ballet, Fla.; treas. Coast Opera Co., Ft. Pierce, Fla., 1986—, New Lyric Opera, Port Saint Lucie, Fla., 1995—; hostess, prodr. TV show Lively Arts of the Treasure Coast with Charmian Herd, Ft. Pierce, Fla., 1994—. Bd. dirs. Opera New Eng., 1980—, Portland Lyric Theatre, 1982—Mem. Waterville Friends Music, DAR, Waterville Theatre Guild (charter mem., pres. 1967——), Vero Beach Theatre Guild (Fla.), Encore Alley Theatre, Vero Beach, Waterville Bus. and Profl. Women's Club (program chmn. 1957-58, v.p. 1958-59, pres. 1959-61, chmn. drama dept. 1961, drama and music chmn. 1961—), Fla. Profl. Theatre Assn., Ednl. Speech and Theatre Assn. Maine (mem. exec. bd., pres. 1972-74), Maine Profl.-Community Theatre Assn. (mem. organizing com.), Actors Equity Assn., Albion-Burnham Tchrs. Club (sec. 1960-61), NEA, Maine Tchrs. Assn., New Eng. Theatre Conf. (exec. bd. 1976—, 1st v.p. 1976-77, conf. chmn. 1977), Theatre Assn. Maine (membership chmn. 1972-73, 2d v.p. 1973-74, exec. bd. 1972—, exec. sec. 1975—, state pres. 1976—), Internat. Platform Assn., Nat. Assn. Tchrs. of Singing (sec. Maine chpt. 1980—), Pine Tree Post Card Club (exec. bd., Spring show chmn. 1979-80, pres. 1982-84), Maine Hist. Soc., Bay State Post Card Club, R.I. Post Card Club. Club: Cecilia (Augusta, Maine). Composer sacred music: Babylon, 1959, The Greatest of These is Love, 1961, Pan; Keep Not Thy Silence, O God, Remember Now Thy Creator, Slow, Slow, Fresh Fount, A Witch's Charm, Hymn to God the Father. Avocations: acting, singing, oil painting, collecting opera and operetta scores. Home and Office: 601 Seaway Dr E 2 Fort Pierce FL 34949

HEREDIA-SUÁREZ, PAULA PATRICIA, filmmaker, artist; b. San Salvador, El Salvador, Oct. 13, 1957; came to U.S., 1982; d. Leonardo Heredia and Mercedes Suarez; m. Larry Garvin, June 1, 1987. Pres. Mamboreta, Inc., N.Y.C., 1989—; instr. film prodn. New Sch. Social Rsch., N.Y.C. Prodr. films The Marriage Dinner, 1987, Beyond the Window/Tras la Ventana, 1988, Chile, 1989, Slings and Arrows, 1996, editor American Heroes series, Finding Christa (Sundance Jury award for best documentary 1992), Unzipped (Sundance audience award 1995, Am. Cinema Editors award (Eddie), 1996); TV and videos include (dir., editor) Inspirational Woman: Frida Kalho, Inspirational Woman, Oseola McCarter, The School of the Americas, creative cons.) Philip Johnson, Portrait of an Eccentric Artist, (creative dir.) The Tee Ridder Miniature Museum, (dir.) The Couple in the Cage, 1993, Teniendo un Bebe, 1996; work has appeared on TV series Frontline, Am. Playhouse, POV-The Am. Documentary, Vanguard-Cinemax, Bravo Performance, BBC Fine Cuts. Mem. Women Make Movies, Lincoln Ctr. Film Soc., Latino Collaborative. Home and Office: 245 E 40th St Apt 23C New York NY 10016

HERGENHAN, JOYCE, public relations executive; b. Mt. Kisco, N.Y., Dec. 30, 1941; d. John Christopher and Goldie (Wago) H. B.A., Syracuse U., 1963; M.B.A., Columbia U., 1978. Reporter White Plains Reporter Dispatch, 1963-64; asst. to Rep. Ogden R. Reid Washington, 1964-68; reporter Gannett Newspapers, 1968-72; with Consol. Edison Co. of N.Y., Inc., N.Y.C., 1972-82, v.p., 1977-79, sr. v.p. pub. affairs, 1979-82; v.p. corp. pub. relations General Electric Co., Fairfield, Conn., 1982—. Office: GE 3135 Easton Tpke Fairfield CT 06431-0002

HERING, DORIS MINNIE, dance critic; b. N.Y.C., Apr. 11, 1920; d. Harry and Anna Elizabeth (Schwenk) H. B.A. cum laude, Hunter Coll., 1941; M.A., Fordham U., 1985. Freelance dance writer, 1946-52; assoc. editor, prin. critic Dance mag., N.Y.C., 1952-72; exec. dir. Nat. Assn. for Regional Ballet, N.Y.C., 1972-87; adj. assoc. prof. dance history NYU, 1968-78; freelance dance writer, lectr., cons., 1987—; mem. dance panel NEA, 1972-75, cons., 1991—; mem. dance panel N.Y. State Coun. Arts, 1992-96; bd. dirs. Walnut Hill Sch., 1975—, Internat. Ballet Competition, 1981—; hon. bd. dirs. Phila. Dance Alliance, 1980—; cons. Regional Dance Am.; adj. assoc. prof. dance history NYU Grad. Sch. Edn. Author: 25 Years of American Dance, 1950, Dance in America, 1951, Wild Grass, 1965, Giselle and Albrecht, 1981; sr. editor Dance mag., 1989—. Howard D. Rothschild Rsch. fellow Harvard U., 1991-93; recipient 33d ann. Capezio Dance Found. award for lifetime svc., 1985, Award of Distinction Dance mag., 1987, Sage Cowles Land Grant chair in dance U. Minn., 1993; named to Hunter Coll. Alumni Hall of Fame, 1986. Mem. Dance Critics Assn., Assn. Dance History Scholars, Phi Beta Kappa, Chi Tau Epsilon (hon.).

HERMAN, ALEXIS M., federal official; b. Mobile, Ala.. Grad., Xavier U. Founder, CEO A.M. Herman & Assocs., Washington; nat. dir. Minority Women's Employment Program, Washington, until 1977; dir. Women's Bur. Dept. Labor, Washington, 1977-81; chief staff, then dep. chair Dem. Nat. Conv. Com., Washington, until 1991, CEO, 1991-92; dep. dir. Clinton-Gore Presdl. Transition Office, Washington, 1992-93; asst. to President U.S., Pub. Liason dir. White House, Washington, 1993—. Mem. Nat. Coun. Negro Women, Delta Sigma Theta. Office: White House Office Pub Liaison 1600 Pennsylvania Ave NW Washington DC 20500*

HERMAN, ANDREA MAXINE, newspaper editor; b. Chgo., Oct. 22, 1938; d. Maurice H. and Mae (Baron) H.; m. Joseph Schmidt, Oct. 28, 1962. BJ, U. Mo., 1960. Feature writer Chgo.'s Am., 1960-63; daily columnist News Am., Balt., 1963-67; feature writer Mainichi Daily News, Tokyo, 1967-69; columnist Iowa City Press-Citizen, 1969-76; music and dance critic San Diego Tribune, 1976-84; asst. mng. editor features UPI, Washington, 1984-86, asst. mng. editor news devel., 1986-87; mng. editor features L.A. Herald Examiner, 1987-91; editor/culture We/Mbl Newspaper, Washington, 1991—. Recipient 1st and 2d prizes for features in arts James S. Copley Ring of Truth Awards, 1982, 1st prize for journalism Press Club San Diego, 1983. Mem. Soc. Profl. Journalists, Am. Soc. Newspaper Editors, AP Mng. Editors, Women in Communications. Office: We/Mbl Newspaper 1350 Connecticut Ave NW Washington DC 20036-1701

HERMAN, BARBARA ROSE, interior decorator; b. Worcester, Mass., Feb. 14, 1938; d. Albert H. and Mary Margaret (Convery) Garnache; children: Diane G. Herman Johnson, Mary E. Herman Thurston, Tracy A., Barry J. Cert., N.Y. Sch. Interior Design, N.Y.C., 1972, RISD, Providence, 1974. Owner Decorating Barn, Auburn, Pa., 1970-79, Barbara Herman Ineriors, Worcester, Mass., 1979—; tchr. Worcester Night Life Continuing Edn., Worcester, 1970-89, Becker Jr. Coll., Worcester, 1982; lectr. in field. Work appeared in Womens Day Mag., 1987, Condo Media Cover, 1989, Condo Media Cover, 1992. Mem. Worcester Exec. Assn. (pres. 1984). Roman Catholic. Home: 73 Pointe Rok Dr Worcester MA 01604-1466 Office: Barbara Herman Interiors 104 June St Worcester MA 01602-2950

HERMAN, ELIZABETH MULLEE, elementary educator; b. N.Y.C., May 1, 1939; d. Raymond Garrett and Theresa (Lang) Mullee; m. Paul Herman, Feb. 10, 1962; children: Susan, Christina, Andrew, Marianne Schell, Jane (dec.). BA, Manhattanville Coll., Purchase, N.Y., 1960; MA, Columbia U., 1962; Cert. Advanced Study, Sacred Heart U., Fairfield, Conn. Tchr. Birch Wathen Sch., N.Y.C., 1960-61, Madison Jr. High Sch., Trumbull, Conn., 1978-79, Holy Rosary Sch., Bridgeport, Conn., 1979-82, St. Teresa Sch., Trumbull, 1982-88, Roosevelt Sch., Bridgeport, 1988-94, Maplewood Annex Sch., Bridgeport, 1994—. Baptism tchr. St. Theresa Ch., Trumbull, 1980—, reader, 1980—; mem. Secular Order Franciscans. Chase Bank mini grantee, 1993, Bridgeport Bus. Coun. mini grantee, 1994; Pimms scholar, 1993; mem. Italian Ctny. Club. Mem. NEA, APA, Bridgeport Edn. Assn., Conn. Edn. Assn., Candlewood Lake Club. Roman Catholic. Home: 144 Plymouth Ave Trumbull CT 06611-4152 Office: Maplewood Annex Sch 322 Wells St Bridgeport CT 06606

HERMAN, JOAN ELIZABETH, insurance company executive; b. N.Y.C., June 2, 1953; d. Roland Barry and Grace Gales (Goldstein) H.; m. Richard M. Rasiej, July 16. 1977. AB, Barnard Coll., 1975; MS, Yale U., 1977. Actuarial student Met. Life Ins. Co., N.Y.C., 1978-82; asst. actuary Phoenix Mut. Life Ins. Co. (now Phoenix Home Life Mut. Ins.), Hartford, Conn., 1982-83; assoc. actuary, dir. underwriting research Phoenix Mut. Life Ins. Co., Hartford, Conn., 1983-84, 2d v.p., 1984-85, v.p., 1985-89, sr. v.p., 1989—; bd. dirs. PM Holdings, Inc., Phoenix Am. Life Ins. Co., Integrated Healthcare Resources Group, Inc., Phoenix Life and Reins. of N.Y. Contbr. articles to profl jours. Capt. fundraising team Greater Hartford Arts Coun., 1986; bd. dirs. Hadassah, Glastonbury, Conn., Temple Beth Hillel, South Windsor, Conn., 1983-84, Children's Fund Conn., 1992—, My Sister's Place, Shelter, Hartford, 1989-94, Western Mass. Regional Nat. Conf. Conn., 1995—; bd. dirs. Hartford Ballet, 1989-95, corporator, 1995—; bd. dirs. Leadership Greater Hartford, 1989-94, chmn. bd. dirs., 1993-94; mem. bd. founders Am. Leadership Forum of Hartford, 1991—; corporator Hartford Sem., 1994—. Fellow Soc. Actuaries (chairperson health sect. coun. 1994-95); mem. Am. Acad. Actuaries (bd. dirs. 1994—), Am. Leadership Forum, Home Office Life Underwriters Am. Jewish. Office: Phoenix Home Life One American Row Hartford CT 06102

HERMAN, MAJA See HERMAN-SEKULICH, MAYA B.

HERMAN, MARY MARGARET, neuropathologist; b. Plymouth, Wis., July 26, 1935; d. Elmer Fredolein and Esther Lydia (Bross) H.; m. Lucien Jules Rubinstein, Jan. 31, 1969. BS in Med. Sci., U. Wis., 1957, MD, 1960. Diplomate Nat. Bd. Med. Examiners, Am. Bd. Anatomic Pathology, Am. Bd. Neuropathology. Rotating intern Mary Hitchcock Meml. Hosp., Hanover, N.H., 1960-61; resident in neurology U. Wis. Hosps., 1961-62; intern in pathology Yale U., New Haven, 1962-63, asst. resident in pathology, 1963-64, fellow neuropathology, 1964-65, rsch. assoc. pathology, 1967-68; fellow neuropathology Stanford U., Palo Alto, Calif., 1965-66, fellow, acting instr. neuropathology, 1966-67, asst. prof. pathology, 1967-74, assoc. prof. (with tenure), 1974-81; prof., co-dir. div. neuropathology U. Va. Sch. Medicine, Charlottesville, 1981-91, prof. div. clin. pathology, 1991-92; spl. expert neuropathology in clin. brain disorders br. NIMH, Washington, 1991—; neuropathologist NIMH Brain Collection, 1992—, Stanley Fund Brain Collection, 1992—; vis. asst. prof. Albert Einstein Coll. Medicine, Bronx, N.Y., 1971-72; mem. program project rev. com. Nat. Inst. Neurol. and Communicative Diseases, NIH, 1973-77; cons. lab. svc. VA Hosp., Salem, Va., Ctrl. Va. Tng. Ctr., Lynchburg, 1982-92, ad hoc mem. pathology A study sect., 1986-91; cons. neuropathologist D.C. Med. Examiner's Office, Washington, 1992—, D.C. Gen. Hosp., 1992—. Mem. edit. bd. Jour. Neuropathology and Exptl. Neurology, 1989-93; contbr. over 130 articles to profl. jours. Recipient Rsch. Career Devel. award NIH, 1967-72, Faculty Devel. award Merck Found., 1969. Mem. AAAS, Am. Assn. Neuropathologists (Weil award 1974), Am. Soc. for Investigative Pathology, Soc. for Devel. Biology, Internat. Soc. Neuropathology, Am. Soc. Cell Biology (rsch. fellowship program, mentor scientist summer tchr. 1994), Internat. Acad. Pathology, Am. Tissue Culture Assn., Soc. Neurosci. Home: 125 S Reynolds St J-501 Alexandria VA 22304-3152 Office: NIMH Neurosci Ctr at St Elizabeths Clin Brain Disorders Br Washington DC 20032

HERMAN, SHIRLEY YVONNE, accountant, financial planner; b. Jersey City, Nov. 22, 1941; d. Otto and Mary (Erde) H. BA, CCNY, 1963. IRS enrolled agt. Pvt. practice N.Y.C., 1984—. Mem. Nat. Assn. Pub. Accts., Nat. Assn. Tax Practioners, Nat. Assn. Enrolled Agts, Am. Assn. Women Accts. Office: 853 Broadway Ste 1101 New York NY 10003-4703

HERMAN, SUSAN N., legal educator; b. Bklyn., Feb. 16, 1947; d. Nathan H. and Frances (Pickus) H.; m. Paul A. Gangsei, June 16, 1978; 1 child, Erica Herman Gangsei. AB, Barnard Coll., 1968; JD, NYU, 1974. Bar: N.Y. 1975, U.S. Dist. Ct. (so., ea., we. and no. dists.) N.Y. 1975, U.S. Ct. Appeals (2d cir.) 1975. Law clk. to presiding justice U.S. Ct. Appeals (2d cir.), N.Y.C., 1974-76; assoc. dir. Prisoners' Legal Services N.Y., N.Y.C., 1976-80; from asst. prof. to prof. Bklyn. Law Sch., 1980—; reporter, criminal procedure com. U.S. Dist. Ct. (ea. dist.) N.Y., Bklyn., 1986—, coord. tng. program civil litigation fund, 1984. Contbr. articles to profl. jours. Mem. due process com. ACLU, 1982—, chmn., 1985—. Mem. ABA, N.Y.C. Bar Assn., ACLU (nat. bd. dirs. 1988—), Order of Coif. Office: Bklyn Law Sch 250 Joralemon St Brooklyn NY 11201-3798

HERMAN-DUNN, RUTH ANN, psychologist; b. Salem, Oreg., Jan. 18, 1963; d. Peter Shaw and Theresa Eileen (Little) H. BA, U. Calif., Santa Barbara, 1987; MA, Ohio State U., 1990; PhD in Counseling Psychology, U. Fla., 1993. Fellow in substance abuse Seattle VA, 1993-94, psychotherapist, cons., 1992—; clin. supr. U. Wash., 1995—; ind. rschr. U.Fla., Gainesville, 1989—. Author and presenter in field. Mem. APA, Wash. Stae Psychol. Assn., Phi Beta Kappa. Democrat. Unitarian Universalist. Office: 4850 California Ave SW #102 Seattle WA 98116

HERMANN, MARY, advertising executive. Exec. v.p., exec. dir. accts. svcs. Ammirati & Puris/Lintas, N.Y.C. Office: Ammirati & Puris Lintas One Dag Hammarskjold Plz New York NY 10017*

HERMANN, NAOMI BASEL, librarian, interior decorator; b. N.Y.C., Feb. 12, 1918; d. Alexander and Rebecca (Deinard) Basel; m. Henry I. Almour, June 26, 1938 (dec.); 1 child, Jay Alexander; m. Stanford Leland Hermann, Dec. 20, 1951. BS in Edn., NYU, 1937, MS in Psychology, 1939; MLS, Columbia U., 1963; postgrad., Vassar Coll., Cornell U., Hunter Coll. Newspaper reporter Times Picayune, New Orleans, 1935; tchr. gifted children N.Y.C. Schs., 1946-58; libr. supr. 22 elem., jr. and sr. high schs., N.Y.C., 1958-72; libr. Brandeis High Sch., 1972-75; interior decorator, pvt. practice, N.Y.C., 1946—; instr. Children's Literature, N.Y.C. Bd. Edn., 1969-73; libr. examiner, N.Y.C. Bd. of Edn., 1967-72. Pres. Hadassah, N.Y.C., 1939-41, life mem.; life mem. Coun. Jewish Women, 1974—; charter mem. Eleanor Roosevelt Fund for Women and Girls; established adult library Temple Beth El, Boca Raton, Fla. Mem. AAUW (pres. Boca Raton chpt. 1987-89), Boca Raton Noontime Ladies Club (pres.). Home: 550 S Ocean Blvd Boca Raton FL 33432-6264

HERMAN-SEKULICH, MAYA B. (MAJA HERMAN), poet, essayist, editor; b. Belgrade, Serbia, Yugoslavia, Feb. 17, 1959; came to U.S., 1980, naturalized, 1992; d. Bogomir Herman and Lily (Strauss) Tišma; m. Milosh Sekulich. MA, Belgrade U., 1977; PhD in Comparative Lit., Princeton U., 1986. Fulbright lectr. Rutgers U., New Brunswick, N.J., 1982-84; cons. Novo Arts, N.Y.C., 1988-90; vis. lectr. Princeton (N.J.) U., 1985, 88; lectr., reader in field. Author: (poems) Camerography, 1990, Cartography, 1992, Sketches for Portraits, 1992, (essays) Literature of Transgression, 1986, rev. edit., 1994, The Jade Window: Images from Southeast Asia, 1994, English lang. edit., 1996 ; editor/translator: Anxiety of Influence (Harold Bloom), 1981, Cathedral (Raymond Carver), 1991, Myth and Structure (Northrop Frye), 1991, Poems of Our Climate (Wallace Stevens), 1995; contbg. editor Night, 1990-91; edited and translated intros. to 10 books; contbr. to scholarly jours.; correspondant (weekly) VREME, Belgrade, 1995—. Princeton U. fellow, 1980-85, Fulbright fellow, 1982-84. Fellow AAUW; mem. PEN (Am. chpt., Serbian chpt.), Poetry Soc. Am. Home: 69 Fifth Ave Apt 11A New York NY 10003

HERMEY, CYNTHIA LOUISE, critical care nurse, clinical nurse specialist; b. Somerville, N.J., June 5, 1963; d. James Madison and Beverly Annette (Scruggs) Horton; m. Lowell Kevin Hermey, Feb. 3, 1990; children: Megan Annette, Kaitlin Elizabeth. BA in Psychology, BSN, Trenton State Coll., 1986; M of Nursing, La. State U., New Orleans, 1989. CCRN; cert. ACLS, PALS, BCLS, BCLS instr. Charge nurse burn ICU West Jefferson Med. Ctr., Marrero, La., 1987-88, charge nurse surg. cardiac ICU, 1988-89; ind. nurse contractor Trauma Nurses, Inc., Trenton, 1990; charge nurse shock/trauma Cooper Med. Ctr., Camden, N.J., 1990-91; adj. faculty Old Dominion U., Norfolk, Va., 1992-95; adj. assoc. prof. Norfolk State U., 1992-95; critical care clin. specialist DePaul Med. Ctr., Norfolk, 1991-95; critical care nurse mgr. Oconee Meml. Hosp., Seneca, S.C., 1995—. Author: Quick IV Therapy Pocket Guide, 1995, (booklet) Mosby's Medical-Surgical Nursing Video Series, 1994-95; contbr. Handbook of Critical Care Nursing, 1996. Mem. AACN (vol. adv. team 1995-96, speaker and panelist 1992-94, pres. Tidewater chpt. 1993-95, CCRN chmn. 1991-93), Sigma Theta Tau. Episcopalian. Home: 305 S Catherine St Walhalla SC 29691

HERNANDEZ, ALICIA C., elementary school educator; b. N.Y.C., Oct. 22, 1967; d. Elsie (Toro) Romero. AA, Miami (Fla.) Dade C.C., 1988; BS, Fla. Internat. U., 1991, MS, 1995. Cert. tchr., Fla.; cert. elem. edn., early childhood and ESOL endorsed. Tchr., tutor Our Lady of Charity, Hialeah, 1990, Dade County Pub. Schs., Miami, 1991—. Vol. Camillus House, Miami, 1990; peer advisor FIU Coll. Edn., Miami, 1990-91. Recipient scholarship Adolph Coors Corp., 1989; Sallie Mae Beginning Tchr. of Yr. Region III finalist. Mem. Future Educators Am., Kappa Delta Pi (pres. 1990-91, Membership award 1990), Chi Alpha Theta (pledge pres. 1990), Omicron Delta Kappa. Democrat. Roman Catholic. Home: #105 8311 SW 5th St Hollywood FL 33025 Office: Ernest R Graham Elem Sch 7330 W 32d Ave Hialeah FL 33016

HERNANDEZ, ANN MARGARET, education educator; b. Williamsport, Pa., Feb. 19, 1939; d. Adam E. and Helen A. (McMunn) Sieminski; m. Jorge E. Hernandez, June 20, 1970; children: James, Natalia, David. BS in Edn., Ohio U., 1961; MEd in Adminstrn., Pa. State U., 1969; EdD in Instrnl. Leadership, U. Ala., 1984. Tchr. Greenwich (Conn.) Sch. Sys., 1961-65, L.A. (Calif.) City Schs., 1965-66, Colegio Bolivar, Cali, Colombia, 1966-68; elem. prin. Colegio Bolivar, Cali, 1968-88; dir. early childhood and lower sch. Canterbury Sch., Ft. Wayne, Ind., 1988-95; asst. prof. edn. St. Francis Coll., Ft. Wayne, 1995—; adj. prof. Ind. Vocat. Tech. Coll., Ft. Wayne, 1989-95, Ind. U.-Purdue U., Ft. Wayne, 1993-95; bd. dirs. WFWA-TV Pub. Broadcasting, Ft. Wayne, 1995—; presenter and cons. in field. Named Nat. Disting. Prin., U.S. Dept. Edn., 1987. Mem. ASCD, Nat. Assn. for the Edn. of Young Children, So. Assn. Colls. and Schs. (evaluator for overseas schs.), Phi Delta Kappa, Kappa Delta Pi. Home: 7012 Blake Dr Fort Wayne IN 46804 Office: St Francis Coll 2701 Spring St Fort Wayne IN 46808

HERNANDEZ, CHRISTINE, educational consultant; b. San Antonio, July 23, 1951; d. Joe and Aurora (Zapata) H. BA, Our Lady of the Lake Coll., 1973; MA, U. Tex., 1981. Cert. elem. tchr. Tchr. San Antonio Ind. Sch. Dist., 1973-83; pres. San Antonio Fedn. of Tchrs., 1983-86; ednl. cons. Bexar County Fedn. Tchrs., San Antonio, 1986-90. Mem. Dist. 124 Tex. Ho. of Reps., 1991—, mem. legis. budget bd., 1994—, mem. appropriations com., 1993—, mem. pub. edn. com., 1993—; bd. edn. San Antonio Ind. Sch. Dist., 1986-91; pub. mem. bd. dirs. State Bar Tex., 1989-92; bd. dirs. So. Regional Coun., 1990—, mem. exec. com., 1993-95, v.p., 1995—; bd. dirs. Target '90 Goals for San Antonio, 1987-91, Providence High Sch., 1987-90; bd. dirs. Tex. Lyceum, sec., 1991-93, v.p. 1993-94; exec. com. San Antonio River Corridor com. 1987-89, Govs. Commn. for Women, 1985-87, Tex. Task Force on Indigent Health Care, 1983-84; bd. mgrs. Bexar County Hosp. Dist., 1982-84; bd. review Hist. Dists. and Landmarks, 1981-82; task force Southland Corps. Coll. Program, 1985; mem. San Antonio Commn. on Literacy, 1987-89; trustee United Way, 1988—; parliamentarian Nat. Found. Women Legislators, 1995—. Named Hispanic Woman of Yr., 1984, Young Woman of Promise, Good Housekeeping Mag., 1985, Sunday's Woman, S.A. Light, 1985, Alumnus of Yr., U. Tex., San Antonio, 1993, Friend of Bus., Tex. C. of C., 1993; recipient Outstanding Leadership award YWCA, 1989, others. Mem. Tex. Assn. Sch. Bds. (bd. trustees 1989-90), Leadership Am. Alumnae Assn., Hispanic Women's Network of Tex. (bd. dirs.), Leadership San Antonio Alumni Assn., Tex. Women's Forum (v.p.), Any Baby Can Alliance, Leadership Tex. Alumnae Assn., San Antonio 100 (charter), Labor Coun. for Latin Am. Advancement (nat. exec. bd.), San Antonio AFL-CIO Coun., Am. Fedn. Tchrs. (v.p. 1978-81, treas. 1981-83, pres. 1983-86). Democrat. Roman Catholic. Office: 301 S Frio St Ste 152 San Antonio TX 78207-4423

HERNANDEZ, JACQUELINE LEE, insurance agent; b. Traverse City, Mich., July 2, 1951; d. Lawrence E. and Marguerite A. (Eagle) Cochrane; m. Jack D. Lyon, Aug. 2, 1969 (div. Jan. 1976); children: Julie Ann, Jason Duane; m. John R. Hancock, Nov. 5, 1983 (div. 1984); m. Juan Carlos Hernandez, Feb. 1992 (div. Dec. 1994). BA in Bus. Adminstrn., Ctrl. Mich. U., 1975. Exec. sec. Redman Agy., Lake City, Mich., 1979-80; adminstrv. asst. Northwestern Mutual Life Ins. Co., Cadillac, Mich., 1980-82; dist. agy. office mgr. Northwestern Mutual Life Ins. Co., Traverse City, Mich., 1982-92; office mgr. fin. svcs. GHA Ins., Traverse City, Mich., 1992-94, sr. account exec., 1995—. Mem. NAFE, Nat. Assn. Health Underwriters (Am. Enterprise award 1995), Northern Mich. Assn. Health Underwriters (charter, sec. 1993-94, treas. 1994-95). Office: GHA Ins 415 Munson Ave Traverse City MI 49686

HERNANDEZ, JO FARB, museum and curatorial consultant; b. Chgo., Nov. 20, 1952. BA in Polit. Sci. & French with honors, U. Wis., 1974; MA in Folklore and mythology, UCLA, 1975; postgrad., U. Calif., Davis, 1978, U. Calif., Berkeley, 1978-79, 81. Registration Mus. Cultural History UCLA, 1974-75; Rockefeller fellow Dallas Mus. Fine Arts, 1976-77; asst. to dir. Triton Mus. Art, Santa Clara, Calif., 1977-78, dir., 1978-85; adj. prof. mus. studies John F. Kennedy U., San Francisco, 1978; grad. advisor arts adminstrn. San Jose (Calif.) State U., 1979-80; dir. Monterey (Calif.) Peninsula Mus. Art, 1985-93, cons. curator, 1994—; prin. Curatorial and Mus. Mgmt. Svcs., Watsonville, Calif., 1993—; lectr., panelist, juror, panelist in field USIA, Calif. Arts Coun., others; vis. lectr. Am. Cultural Ctr., Jerusalem, 1989, Binat. Ctr., Lima, Peru, 1988, Daytona Beach Mus. Art, 1983, Israel Mus., 1989, U. Chgo., 1981, Oakland Mus., 1996, others; guest curator San Diego Mus. Art, 1995—; guest on various TV and radio programs. Contbr. articles to profl. publs.; author: (mus. catalogs) The Day of the Dead: Tradition and Change in Contemporary Mexico, 1979, Three from the Northern Island: Contemporary Sculpture from Hokkaido, 1984, Crime and Punishment: Reflections of Violence in Contemporary Art, 1984, The Quiet Eye: Pottery of Shoji Hamada and Bernard Leach, 1990, Alan Shepp: The Language of Stone, 1991, Wonderful Colors: The Paintings of August Francois Gay, 1993, Jeannette Maxfield Lewis: A Centennial Celebration, 1994, Armin Hansen, 1994, Jeremy Anderson: The Critical Link/A Quiet Revolution, 1995, among others. Bd. dirs. Bobbie Wynn and Co. of San Jose, 1981-85, Santa Clara Arts and Hist. Consortium, 1985; bd. dirs. Non-Profit Gallery Assn., 1979-83, v.p., 1979-80. Recipient Golden Eagle award Coun. Internat. Non-theatrical Events, 1992, Leader of Decade award Arts Leadership Monterey Peninsula, 1992. Mem. Am. Assn. Mus. (mus. assessment program surveyor 1990, 94, lectr. 1986, nat. program com. 1992-93), Calif. Assn. Mus. (chair ann. meeting 1990, chair nominating com. 1988, 90, 93, bd. dirs. 1985-94, v.p. 1987-91, pres. 1991-92), Artable, Am. Folklore Soc., Western Mus. Conf. (bd. dirs., exec. com. 1989-91, program chair 1990), Nat. Coun. for Edn. in Ceramic Arts, Phi Beta Kappa. Office: Curatorial and Mus Mgmt Svcs 345 White Rd Watsonville CA 95076-0429

HERNANDEZ, MARISSA, physicist; b. Manila, Dec. 26, 1964; came to the U.S., 1989; d. Juan and Josefina (Timbol) H. BS in Physics, Ateneo de Manila U., 1985; MS in Physics, Tex. Tech. U., 1992; MS in Radiol. Physics, Wayne State U., 1993. Physics instr. U. Philippines, Manila, 1985-89; teaching asst. Tex. Tech. U., Lubbock, 1989, rsch. asst., 1990-92; rsch. asst. Wayne State U., Detroit, 1992-93; med. physicist Allegheny U. of the Health Scis., Phila., 1994—. Contbr. articles to profl. jours. Scholar Philippine VA Office, 1981-85; fellow Robert A. Welch Found., 1990-92; scholarship grantee PEO, 1993. Mem. Ateneo Physics Soc. (pres. 1984-85), Biophys. Soc., Am. Phys. Soc., Am. Assn. Physicists in Medicine, Sigma Pi Sigma. Office: Allegheny U of the Health Scis Radiation Physics Safety 3300 Henry Ave Philadelphia PA 19129-1121

HERNDON, ALICE PATTERSON LATHAM, public health nurse; b. Macon, Ga.; d. Frank Waters and Ruby (Dews) Patterson; m. William Joseph Latham, July 21, 1940 (dec. Apr. 1981); children: Jo Alice Latham Miller, Marynette Latham, Lauruby Cathleen Beach; 1 adopted child, Courtney Marie Herndon; m. Sidney Dumas Herndon, Apr. 26, 1985. diploma, Charity Hosp. Sch. Nursing, New Orleans, 1937; student George Peabody Coll. Tchrs., 1938-39; BS in Pub. Health Nursing, U. N.C., 1954; MPH, Johns Hopkins U., 1966. Staff pub. health nurse assigned spl. venereal disease study USPHS, Darien, Ga., 1939-40; county pub. health nurse Bacon County, Alma, Ga., 1940-41; USPHS spl. venereal disease project, Glynn County, Brunswick, 1943-47; county pub. health nurse Glynn County, 1949-51, Ware County, Waycross, 1951-52; pub. health nurse supr. Wayne-Long-Brantley-Liberty Counties, Jesup, 1954-56 dist. dir. pub. health nursing Wayne-Long-Appling-Bacon-Pierce Counties, Jesup, 1956-70; dist. chief nursing S.E. Ga. Health Dist., 1970-79, organizer mobile health services, 1973—. Exec. dir. Wayne County Home Health Agy., 1968-80; exec. dir. Ware County Home Health Agy., 1970-79, mem. exec. com., 1978-85;

mem. governing bd. S.E. Ga. Health Systems Agy., 1975-82; mem. governing bd. Health Dept. Home Health Agy., 1978—, also author numerous grant proposals. Bd. dirs. Wayne County Mental Health Assn., 1959, 60, 61, 81, 82, Wayne County Tb Assn., 1958-62; a non-alcoholic organizer Jesup group Alcoholics Anonymous, 1962-63; mem. adv. coun. Ware Meml. Hosp. Sch. Practical Nursing, Waycross, Ga., 1958; mem. Altar Guild, St. Paul's Episc. Ch., 1979-86, vestrywoman, 1981-82; mem. Altar Guild St. Marks Episcopal Ch., Brunswick, Ga., 1994—. Recipient recognition Gen. Service Bd., Alcoholics Anonymous, Inc. Fellow APHA; mem. ANA, 8th Dist. (pres. 1954-58, sec. 1958-60, dir. 1960-62, 1st v.p. 1962), GA. Nurses Assn. (exec. bd. 1954-58, program rev. continuing edn. com. 1980-86, Dist. 21 Excellence in Nursing award 1994), Ga. Pub. Health Assn. (chmn. nursing sect. 1956-57), Ga. Assn. Dist. Chiefs Nursing (pres. 1976). Contbr. to state nursing manuals, cons. to Home Health Svc. Agys. Home: 192 Bluff Dr Brunswick GA 31523

HERNDON, ANNE HARKNESS, sales executive; b. Knoxville, Tenn., July 21, 1951; d. Alexander Jones and Mary Belle (Lothrop) Harkness; m. David S. Egerton, Apr. 21, 1972 (div. 1979); children: David, Mary; m. Morris Herndon, Nov. 26, 1993. Student, Agnes Scott Coll., Decatur, Ga., 1969-71, U. Tenn., 1971-73. Mktg., advt. mgr. Volunteer Realty, Knoxville, 1975-77; adminstrv. asst. nat. sales Creative Displays, Knoxville, 1977-81; salesperson Sta. WJXB Radio, Knoxville, 1981-86, sales mgr., 1988—; sales and mktg. mgr. Cellular One, Knoxville, 1986-87; cons. nat. ourdoor advt. Berkline Corp., Morristown, Tenn., 1978-81, Knoxville C. of C.; speaker nat. convs. Contbr. articles to profl. jours. Bd. dirs. Knoxville Polit. Action Com., Knoxville Arts Coun., Knoxville Beautification Bd., Boy Scouts Fin. Com.; com. mem. Dogwood Arts Festival, United Way. Recipient Pres.'s award South Ctrl. Comm. Corp., 1991, 92, 93. Mem. Ad Club. Republican. Presbyterian. Home: 605 Westborough Rd Knoxville TN 37909-2132 Office: WJXB 1100 Sharps Ridge Knoxville TN 37917-7122

HERNDON, CATHY CAMPBELL, artist, art educator; b. Richmond, Va., Sept. 25, 1951; d. Kenneth Holcomb and Grace (Brooks) Campbell. BS in Art and Drama, Radford (Va.) Coll., 1973; MS in Art Edn., Va. Commonwealth U., 1980. Art cons., tchr. Hanover County Schs., Ashland, Va., 1973-76; art tchr. Stafford County Schs., Stafford, Va., 1976-86; artist, signmaker Woodford, Va., 1986-92; artist, tchr. Fredericksburg (Va.) City Schs., 1992—; neon artist, mixed media constrn. artist; artist, tchr. Rappahannock Security Ctr., Fredericksburg, 1989-91; artist, tchr. Fredericksburg Ctr. for Creative Arts, 1984—, curator, 1991-94, bd. dirs., 1984—; exchange tchr. Kingston U., Eng., 1995—. One-person shows include Fredericksburg Ctr. for Creative Arts, 1986, Southside Va. C.C., Alberta, 1992, Art First Gallery, Fredericksburg, 1992, 94, Shenandoah Valley Art Ctr., Waynesboro, Va., 1993, Geico Corp. Hdqs., Fredericksburg, 1994, others; exhibited in group shows at Exposure Unltd., Fredericksburg, 1985—, Art in Greece, Helios, 1992, Montross Galleries, Fredericksburg, 1992, Va. Ctr. Creative Arts, Sweetbriar, Rocquebrune, France, 1995; executed various murals. Historian, Fredericksburg Sister City Assn., 1992—. Recipient numerous awards for works; named Best in Show, Hanover Arts Festival, 1995. Mem. Nat. Art Edn. Assn., Washington Projects for the Arts, Va. Mus. Fine Arts, Va. Watercolor Soc. Home: PO Box 7955 408 Frederick St Fredericksburg VA 22401 Office: FCCA 813 Sophia St Fredericksburg VA 22401-5823

HERNDON, DONNA RUTH GROGAN, educational administrator; b. Murray, Ky., Aug. 14, 1942; d. E. Leon and Virgil (Childress) Grogan; m. Clarence W. Herndon Jr., Jan. 31, 1963; children: Melissa Herndon Graves, Roger Allan (dec.). BS summa cum laude, Murray State U., 1960; MA, Western Ky. U., 1975. Tchr. biology Calloway County High Sch., Murray, 1964-66, dir. project COPE, 1978-81; coord. of vols. Army Community Svc., Berlin, Fed. Republic of Germany, 1972; vol. supr. Army Community Svc., Ft. Knox, Ky., 1974-75; mayor Van Voorhis Community, Ft. Knox, Ky., 1975-76; plant mgr. Lin-Val Garden Ctr., Penn Hills, Pa., 1977; admissions rep. Art Inst. Pitts., 1978; dir. alumni affairs Murray (Ky.) State U., 1981-92; coord. Family Resource Ctr., Calloway County Schs., Murray, 1992—. Bd. dirs., co-founder CHAMP, Murray, 1986-93; rep edn Ky Juvenile Justice Commn., 1982-92; mem. adv. coun., mem. social work dept.; adv. bd. Murray State U. Coll. Industry and Tech.; mem. rural health adv. bd. U. Ky.; bd. dirs. Murray United Way; bd. dirs. Murray-Calloway C. of C., Leadership Ky. Found. Recipient Recognition award Murray State U. Black Alumni, 1989, Humanitarian of Yr. award Murray Rotary Club, 1994; named Vol. of Yr., United Way of Ky., 1993; Donna Herndon scholarship established Murray State U. Student Alumni Assn., 1988; state winner Ky. Fedn. Women's Clubs Poetry Contest. Mem. Ky. Alliance for Exploited and Missing Children (bd. dirs. 1982-92), Ky. Ctr. Pub. Issues (bd. dirs. 1990-92), Nat. Coun. for Advancement and Support Edn. (achievement award 1984, bronze award 1987, Dist. III Outstanding Advisor award 1992), Nat. Assn. Parents and Tchrs. (hon. life), Leadership Ky. (bd. dirs. 1990-95), Leadership Ky. Alumni Assn. (trustee 1989-95), Murray Woman's Club. Mem. Ch. of Christ. Office: Calloway County Schs Family Resource Ctr RR 6 Box 57 AA Murray KY 42071-9104

HERNDON, LYDIA RAINEY, education educator; b. Atlanta, May 27, 1950; d. Joseph Sistrunk and Mary Adelaide (Wright) Rainey; m. Robert K. Herndon, Feb. 14, 1976; children: Nicolette Burton Herndon, Robert K. II. BA in Psychology, Duke U., 1972; MEd, Ga. State U., Atlanta, 1981; PhD in Ednl. Adminstrn. and Supervision, Ga. State U., 1994. Cert. paralegal, tchr. K-8, Alaska, level III tchr. tng. Precepts Ministries, Chattanooga. Fulltime adj. U. Alaska, Anchorage, 1992-93; coord. kid's coll. Clayton State U., Morrow, Ga., 1994—; adj. prof. West Ga. Coll., Carrollton, 1994—; cons. Character Edn. Inst., San Antonio, 1994—; motivational speaker in field. Contbr. chpt. to book. Bd. dirs., pres. Protestant Women of the Chapel, Ft. Wainwright, Alaska, 1990-92, Ft. Richardson, Alaska, 1992-93. Mem. ASCD, Phi Delta Kappa. Home: 125 Heritage Lake Dr Fayetteville GA 30214-7345

HERNREICH, NANCY, federal official; b. State College, Miss., July 27, 1946; d. Bernard Francis and Nancy Davis (Martin) McAvoy; m. Robert Eastman Hernreich, Feb. 28, 1977 (div. 1979); 1 child, Ashley Proulx. BA, Webster Coll., 1968; postgrad., Ark. State U. Social worker Jonesboro (Ark.) Sch. Dist., 1970-76; scheduling sec. Gov. of Ark., Little Rock, 1985-92; dep. asst. to pres., dir. Oval Office White House, Washington, 1993—. Mem. Ft. Smith Jr. League, Little Rock Jr. League; chmn. bd. Ft. Smith Pride; social worker, Jonesboro; bd. dirs. Big Bros./Big Sisters Ft. Smith, Spl. Olympics; mem. state steering com. Mondale for Pres.; mem. state Dem. Exec. Com.; del. Dem. Nat. Conv., 1980; election commr. Sebastion County; coord. Sebastion County Clinton Campaign, 1980, 82, 84; dir. March of Dimes Telethon, 1985; head state pub. affairs com. Jr. League. Democrat. Office: White House 1600 Pennsylvania Ave NW Washington DC 20500*

HERO, BARBARA FERRELL, visual and sound artist, writer; b. L.A., Jan. 3, 1925; d. Paul C. and Lucile (Evans) Ferrell; children: Alfred O. III, Barbara Ann, Michelle Claire, David Evans. BA in Art, George Washington U., 1950; EdM in Math., Boston U., 1980; cert. in techniques of computer sound Synthesis, MIT, 1981. Art tchr. Marjory Webster Jr. Coll., Washington, 1953-54; printmaker, painter, 1948—; vis. artist, lectr. U. Mass., Amherst, 1970s, Rochester (N.Y.) Inst. Tech., 1970s, U.S. Psychotronics Assn., Chgo., 1981-89; mus. sound creator Acoustic Brain Rsch., N.C., 1989; founder, dir. Internat. Lambdoma Rsch., Wells, Maine, 1994. Inventor Lambdoma Harmonic Keybd.; exhibited in Contemporary Am. Artist series Corcoran Gallery of Art, 1950; paintings represented in collections at Chase Manhattan Bank, N.Y.C., 1960s, Miami (Fla.)-Dade U., 1960s; author: Lambdoma Unveiled (The Theory of Relationships), The Glass Bead and Knot Theory of Relationships, The Lambdoma Resonant Harmonic Scale (P, Q, R, S, T, U, V and W); contbr. articles to profl. jours. Recipient Davina Winslow Meml. prize Nat. Soc. Painters in Casein, 1964, Cert. of Achievement, Interant. Assn. Colour Healers, London, 1982, J.A. Gallimore cert. for tech. R&D in psychotronics U.S. Psychotronics Assn., Chgo., 1994. Mem. Math. Assn. Am., N.Y. Acad. Scis. Office: Internat Lambdoma Rsch Inst 496 Loop Rd Wells ME 04090

HEROLD, ROCHELLE SNYDER, early childhood educator; b. Bklyn., Oct. 6, 1941; d. Abe and Anna (Chazen) Snyder; m. Frederick S. Herold, May 7, 1966; children: David Marc, Caryn Michele. BA, Bklyn. Coll., 1963; MS, CCNY, 1968. Cert. tchr., N.Y.; cert. child-care provider, Fla. Tchr. N.Y.C. Pub. Schs., 1963-68; tchr., adminstr. Chanute AFB Pvt. Sch., Rantoul, Ill., 1970-72; dir. early childhood edn. Temple Solel, Hollywood, Fla., 1974—, dir. social and ednl. programs for young couples, families and singles, 1995—; cons. bd. dirs. Temple Solel, 1982-93; nursery sch. com. PTO, 1982—; lectr., co-coord. at tchr. seminars, parenting lecture series. Author, illustrator: A Family Seder Through a Child's Eyes, 1984, Celebrating Shabbat in the Home, 1992, Perfect Parenting, 1994. Mem. So. Assn. on Children Under Six, Fla. Assn. Children Under Six, Broward Assn. Children Under Six, Cen. Agy. Jewish Edn., AMA Aux., Fla. Med. Assn. Aux., Temple Solel Sisterhood. Office: Temple Solel Nursery Sch 5100 Sheridan St Hollywood FL 33021-2827

HERR, EVE MARIE, food service executive; b. Buffalo, Sept. 29, 1956; d. Slavko Stanislaus Lavtar and Johanna Mary (McMullen) Croft; m. Robert John Herr, Sept. 9, 1977. Grad. H.S., Lackawanna, N.Y., 1975. Cert. scuba diver, N.Y. Gen. mgr. Pine Hill Food Svc., Orchard Park, N.Y., 1977-95; info. provider Strauss Comm., Carmel, Calif., 1995—. Author: (poetry) Walk Through Paradise, 1995 (editor's award 1995). Vol. Compeer, Buffalo, 1995. Mem. The Cousteau Soc., Children Internat. Democrat. Roman Catholic. Home: 2423 W Church St Eden NY 14057

HERR, PAMELA STALEY, author, historian; b. Cambridge, Mass., July 24, 1939; d. A. Eugene and Phyllis (Parker) Staley; divorced; children: Christianna, Robin Elizabeth. BA magna cum laude, Harvard U.-Radcliffe Coll., 1961; MA, George Washington U., 1971. Writer, historian Field Ednl. Publs., Palo Alto, Calif., 1973; editor Sullivan Assocs., Palo Alto, 1973-74; project mgr. Sullivan Assocs., Menlo Park, Calif., 1974-76; mng. editor Am. West mag., Cupertino, Calif., 1976-79; author, historian, 1980—. Author: Jessie Benton Frémont, 1987, paperback edit., 1988 (Spur award for best western nonfiction book Western Writers Am. 1987); editor: (with Mary Lee Spence) The Letters of Jessie Benton Frémont, 1992; bd. editors Western Hist. Quar., 1993-96. Grantee Nat. Hist. Publs. and Records Commn., Nat. Archives, 1989-91. Mem. Western History Assn., Inst. for Hist. Studies, Phi Beta Kappa. Home: 559 Seale Ave Palo Alto CA 94301

HERRANEN, KATHY, artist, graphic designer; b. Zelienople, Pa., Dec. 22, 1943; d. John and Helen Elizabeth (Sayti) D'Biagio; m. John Warma Herranen, Dec. 31, 1974 (div. Feb. 1994); 1 child, Michael John. Student, Scottsdale Cmty. Coll., 1990—. Cert. tchr. art, State Bd. Dirs. for Cmty. Coll. of Ariz. Horseback riding instr. Black Saddle Riding Acad., Lancaster, Calif., early 1960's; tel. company supr. Bell Tel., Bishop, Calif., 1965; reporter, part-time photographer Ellwood City (Pa.) Ledger, 1967-70; backcountry guide and cook Mammoth Lakes (Calif.) Pack Outfit, 1970; motel mgr. Mountain Property Mgmt., Mammoth Lakes, 1970-72; reporter, bookkeeper Hungry Horse (Mont.) News, 1973-74; pig farmer Columbia Falls, Mont., 1973-75; fine artist, illustrator, graphic designer Mont., Calif., and Ariz., 1980—; fine arts cons. Collector's Gallery, Galleri II, Yuma, Ariz., 1983-84; wind chime designer, creator Phoenix, 1995—; guest lectr. Paradise Valley Tchrs Acad., Phoenix, 1993, Sr. Adult Edn. Program, Scottsdale (Ariz.) Cmty. Coll., 1994, pastel painting instr., 1996; guest demonstrator Binder's Art Ctr., Scottsdale, 1995, Backstreet Furniture and Art, Phoenix, 1995; guest lectr., demonstrator Summer Edn. Program Paradise Valley Sch. Dist. Solo shows include Pinnacle, Phoenix, 1993, Villas of Sedona, Ariz., 1995. Sec. Young Dems., Ellwood City, late 1960's, Vistas Home Owners Assn., Phoenix, 1995—; troubleshooter Maricopa County Elections Dept., Phoenix, 1994-96. Recipient 1st place award Potpourri Artists, Yuma, Ariz., 1981, Subscriber award Butte (Mont.) Arts Coun., 1981, 2nd place award Desert Artists, Yuma, 1982, honorable mention Yuma County Fair, Yuma, 1983, Wildlife Painting Exhibit, Scottsdale, 1993, honorable mention Scottsdale Studio 13, 1991, 92, Special award, 1993, Merit award, 1993, 94 (2). Mem. Nat. Assn. Sr. Friends Fine Artists (chmn. 1995-96, honorable mention 1993, People's Choice award 1996), Nat. and Ariz. chpts. of Women's Caucus for Art, Phoenix Artists Guild, Ariz. Pastel Artists Assn. (charter mem., membership chmn. 1995-96, 2d v.p., show chmn. 1996—, guest demonstrator 1995, Merit award 1995), Artists and Craftsmen of Flathead Valley (founder, charter mem., pres. 1981-82), Phi Theta Kappa. Republican. Lutheran.

HERRERA, ANA LUISA, news anchor; b. Lima, Peru, Dec. 1, 1956; came to U.S., 1986; d. Alberto and Luisa (Jefferson) H.; m. Bruce Michael Baur, Sep. 12, 1993; children: Ana Jadira, José Alfredo. Masters in Journalism, Catholic U., Lima, 1975. Radio producer and anchor CIEN-FM, Lima, 1986; cultural reporter La Prensa newspaper, Lima, 1976-80; free-lance columnist El Comercio, Lima, 1984-86; news anchor Panamericana T.V., Lima, 1980-86; reporter El Nuevo Herald, Miami, Fla., 1987, Sta. WSCV, Miami, Fla., 1987-89; corr. Latin Am. and Carribbean Telemundo Network, Miami, Fla., 1989-91; news anchor Sta. KVEA, Los Angeles, 1992; news anchor internat. NBC Canal do Noticias, Charlotte, N.C., 1993—.

HERRERA, CAROLINA, fashion designer; b. Caracas, Venezuela, Jan. 8, 1939. Founder, head designer Carolina Herrera, 1981—, introduced CH line, 1986—. Office: 501 7th Ave Fl 17 New York NY 10018-5903*

HERRERA, LIANA ESPERANZA, secondary education educator; b. Bluefields, Zelaya, Nicaragua, Apr. 3, 1956; came to U.S. 1971; d. Leonides Solòrzano and Esperanza (Moody) Centeno; m. Mark Patterson, June 18, 1977 (div. Feb. 1984); children: Tani Patterson, Mark A. Patterson, Christopher, Jason; m. Joaquin Herrera, May 26, 1984 (div. May 1991). BA, Utah State U., 1991. tchg. cert., Utah, Ariz. Tchr. Spanish Clark County Sch. Dist., Las Vegas, Nev., 1991-92, Uintah Sch. Dist., Vernal, Utah, 1992-93, Lake Havasu (Ariz.) Unified Sch. Dist. # 1, Lake Havasu H.S., 1993—; tech. prep. Mohave C.C., Lake Havasu City, 1995, 96. Mem. AAUW (ednl. equity chmn. 1995—), Assn. of Sisters Cities. Republican. Mormon. Home: 2361 Tee Dr Lake Havasu City AZ 86406 Office: Lake Havasu City H S 2675 Palo Verde Blvd Lake Havasu City AZ 86403

HERRERA, MARY CARDENAS, education educator, music minister; b. Sugar Land, Tex., Feb. 21, 1938; d. Jose Chavez and Juanita (Lira) Cardenas; m. Saragosa Martin Herrera, Sept. 20, 1960 (dec.); children: Michael (dec.), Patricia Ann Zagrzecki, Aaron Martin, Katherine Ann Nava. Grad., Patricia Stevens Bus. Sch., 1960; student, Houston C.C., 1991, 92. Sec. William Penn Hotel, Houston, 1959-66; payroll clk. Peakload, Inc., Houston, 1967-69; acctg. clk. Am. Gen., Inc., Houston, 1970-73; nurse asst. Ft. Bend Ind. Sch. Dist., Stafford, Tex., 1973-88; tchr.'s asst. Ft. Bend Ind. Sch. Dist., Sugarland, Tex., 1988—; numerous offices Holy Family Cath. Ch., Missouri City, Tex., 1981-90, Hispanic choir dir., 1981-89; Hispanic choir dir. Notre Dame Cath. Ch., 1990-91; Hispanic del. Galveston-Houston Diocese, 1987-89; regional del. Encuetro Diocesceno Conf., San Antonio, 1983, 84, 85; dir., coord. Diocesan Hispanic Choir, 1982-86, music workshops, 1982-88. Songwriter in field. Mem., tchr. PTO, 1973—; mem. Holy Family Hispanic Com.; mem. choir Iglesia del Pueblo, Pasadena, Tex., 1991, 92, asst. Sunday sch. tchr., 1992-93, coord. monthly Women's Praise Gathering, 1994—; music minister local prayer groups Houston area, 1990—. Mem. Women's Aglow (praise and worship music minister Pasadena chpt. 1988-90), Nat. Assn. Pastoral Musicians, Iglesia del Pueblo. Democrat. Home and Office: 4506 Ludwig Ln Stafford TX 77477-5219

HERRERA, PALOMA, dancer; b. Buenos Aires, Dec. 21, 1975; d. Alberto Oscar and Diana Lia (Rube) H. Attended, Olga Ferri Studio, 1982, Ballet Sch. of Minsk, 1987, English Nat. Ballet, London, 1990, Sch. Am. Ballet, N.Y.C., 1991; diploma, Inst. Superior Art at The Colon Theatre, Buenos Aires, 1991. Soloist Am. Ballet Theatre, N.Y.C., 1992-95, prin. dancer, 1995—. Dancer (ballets) Don Quixote, 1987, 88, soloist La Bayadere, The Sleeping Beauty, Don Quixote, Met. Opera, N.Y.C., 1992, Etudes, The Sleeping Beauty, Swan Lake, Symphonie Concertante, Voluntaries, 1993, prin. Symphonic Concertatne, Symphonic Variations, 1993; prin. Peasant Pas de Deux in Giselle, Colon Theatre, Buenos Aires, 1992, La Bayadere, 1993; prin. Don Quixote, soloist Etudes, Voluntaries, Theme and Variations, Kennedy Ctr., Washington, 1993; prin. The Nutcracker, Dorothy Chandler Pavilion, L.A.., 1993, Palace Theatre, Stamford, Conn., 1993; repertoire Met. Opera House Symphonic Variations, Theme and Variations, The Nutcracker, Cruel World, Symphonie Concertante, Gala Performance, 1994, La Bayadera, Don Quixote, Paquite, How Near Heaven, Les Sylphides, Cruel World, Tchaikovsky Pas de Deux, Romeo and Juliet, 1995; guest artist Ballet Gala, Toronto, 1993, Colon Theatre, Buenos Aires, 1993, Gala Ballet of Aix-En-Provence, France, 1993, New Generation Ballet, Moscow, Gala Tribute to Nureyev, Toronto, Le Gala des Etoiles, Montreal, Internat. Evenings of Dance, Vail, Colo., Don Quixote, Kremlin Palace, Moscow, 1995. Recipient First prize Latino Am. Ballet Contest, Lima, Peru, 1985, Coca-Cola Contest of Arts and Scis., 1986, Finalist diploma XIV Varna (Bulgaria) Internat. Competition of Ballet, 1990; scholar Colon Theatre Found., 1989; Dance scholar Antorchas Found., 1991. Home: One Lincoln Plz 20 W 64th St Apt F New York NY 10023-7129 also: Billinghurst 2553 1o Piso Dto, CP 1425 Buenos Aires Argentina Office: American Ballet Theatre 890 Broadway Fl 3 New York NY 10003-1211

HERRERA, SANDRA JOHNSON, school system administrator; b. Riverside, Calif., June 21, 1944; d. William Emory Johnson and Mildred Alice (Alford) Wimer; m. Wynn Neal Huffman, Feb. 19, 1962 (div. May 1967); 1 child, Kristen Lee; m. Steven Jack Herrera, June 21, 1985. AA in Purchasing Mgmt., Fullerton Coll., 1983; BSBA, U. Redlands, 1985, MA in Mgmt., 1988. Sr. purchasing clk Fullerton (Calif.) Union High Sch. Dist., 1969-77, buyer, 1977-79, coord. budgets and fiscal affairs, 1979-83; asst. dir. fin. svcs. Downey (Calif.) Unified Sch. Dist., 1983-85; dir. acctg. Whittier (Calif.) Union High Sch. Dist., 1985-89; asst. supt. bus. Whittier City Sch. Dist., 1989-91, Oxnard Elem. Sch. Dist., 1991—; cons. Heritage Dental Lab., El Toro, Calif, 1981—. Spl. dep. sheriff Santa Barbara (Calif.) County Sheriff's Mounted Posse, 1986-90; spl. dep. marshal U.S. Marshals Posse, Los Angeles, 1987-95. Mem. Calif. Assn. Sch. Bus. Ofcls. (treas. S.E. sect. 1985, mem. acct. R & D com. 1983-89, mem. chief bus. officials com. 1989—), So. Calif. Paraders Assn. (exec. sec. 1976—), Calif. State Horsemens Assn. (regional v.p. 1986-87, sec. 1988), Alpha Gamma Sigma. Home: 5688 La Cumbre Rd Somis CA 93066-9783 Office: Oxnard Elem Sch Dist 1051 S A St Oxnard CA 93030-7442

HERRERA, SHIRLEY MAE, personnel and security executive; b. Lynn, Mass., Apr. 5, 1942; d. John Baptiste and Edith Mae Lagasse; m. Christian Yanez Herrera, Apr. 30, 1975; children: Karen, Gary, Ivan, Iwonne. AS in Bus., Burdette Bus. Coll., Lynn, 1960; student, Wright State U., 1975-78. Cert. facility security officer, med. asst. in pediatrics. Med. asst. Christian Y. Herrera, M.D., Stoneham, Mass., 1972-74; human resource adminstr. MTL Systems, Inc., Dayton, Ohio, 1976-79; dir. pers. and security Tracor GIE, Inc., Provo, Utah, 1979—; cons. on family dynamics family enrichment program Hill AFB, Utah, 1980-82; cons. on health care mgmt. Guam 7th Day Adventist Clinic, 1983; cons. on basic life support and CPR, Projecto Corazon, Monterrey, Mex., 1987—; faculty mem. Inst. for Reality Therapy, 1991—. Contbg. editor Inside Tractor, 1991—. Chmn. women's aux. YMCA Counselling Svcs., Woburn, Mass., 1970; chmn. youth vols. ARC, Wright-Patterson AFB, Dayton, 1974-76; trustee Quail Valley Homeowner's Assn., Provo, 1988-89; rep. A Spl. Wish Found., Provo, 1989. Recipient James S. Cogswell award Def. Investigative Svc., Dept. Def., 1987. Mem. Inst. for Realty Therapy (cert.), Pers. Assn. Ctrl. Utah, Women in Mgmt. (coun. mem. 1991-95), Nat. Classification Mgmt. Soc. (chairperson Intermountain chpt. 1992-94). Republican. Home: 3824 Little Rock Dr Provo UT 84604-5234

HERRERA, VICTORIA MARGARET, speech and language pathologist, special education educator; b. Colorado Springs, Colo., June 5, 1958; d. Eliseo Beltran Pacheco and Juanita Bersabe (Ruiz) Maestas; m. Macario Juan Herrera, Mar. 19, 1991; children: Mike, Matthew, Mark, Joshua. BA summa cum laude, N.Mex. Highlands U., 1991; MS summa cum laude, Ea. N.Mex. U., 1995. Spl. edn. tchr. West Las Vegas (N.Mex.) Schs., 1989-94; speech-lang. pathologist Pecos (N.Mex.) Ind. Schs., 1994—; cons. Tchr. Assistance Team, Pecos Schs., 1995—. Author numerous grant proposals, 1993—. Guest spkr. Marriage Enrichment Program, Las VEgas, 1993, 94, 96; coach Spl. Olympics, Las Vegas., 1990, 91, 92. Recipient Bus. Women's scholarship Clairol Found., 1989, Nat. Hispanic scholarship Nat. Hispanic Scholarship Found., 1990, 91, 92, 93, 94, Exemplary Dedication award N.Mex. Sec. of State, 1993. Mem. Phi Kappa Phi. Home: 3301 Luna Dr Las Vegas NM 87701

HERRERIAS, CARLA TREVETTE, epidemiologist, manager; b. Chgo., Apr. 8, 1964; d. Ludvik Frank and Carlotta Trevette (Walker) Koci; m. Jesus Herrerias, Feb. 25, 1989; children: Elena Mikele, Coco Trevette. BS in Med.Tech., Ea. Mich. U., 1987; MPH in Molecular and Hosp. Epidemiology, U. Mich., 1991. Med. clk. hydramatic divsn. GM, Ypsilanti, Mich., 1983-86; researcher, staff dept. human genetics U. Mich., Ann Arbor, 1987-91; program mgr. Am. Acad. Pediatrics, Elk Grove Village, Ill., 1991—. Project mgr., contbr.: Clinical Practice Guideline: Otitis Media with Effusion in Young Children, 1994. Mem. APHA, Ill. Pub. Health Assn., Assn. for Health Svcs. Rsch., U. Mich. Alumni Soc., U. Mich. Club Chgo. Office: Am Acad Pediatrics 141 Northwest Point Blvd Elk Grove Village IL 60007

HERRES, VALERIE ANN, community health educator; b. Buffalo, May 25, 1943; d. John S. and Antonina M. (DiPasquali) Lopez; m. David S. Herres, June 6, 1964 (div. Sept. 1995); children: Ajilla, Albion. BA in English/Philosophy, William Smith Coll., 1965; MEd, Lyndon State U., 1992. Cert. guidance counselor, N.H., Vt. Art tchr. Colebrook (N.H.) Acad., 1973-75; site coord. Coos County Family Health, Colebrook, N.H., 1976-91; cmty. health educator Coos County Family Health, Berlin, N.H., 1991—; mental health bd. mem. Upper Conn. Valley, Colebrook, N.H., 1974-75, mem. hosp. adv. bd.; trainer, facilitator Human Svcs. Coos County, N.H., 1990—; vol. coord., trainer Hospice North, Colebrook, 1990—; adj. faculty Lyndon State Coll., Lyndonville, Vt., 1992-94, Coll. Lifelong Learning U. N.H., 1993—. Author numerous poems. Mem., staff Com. for Non-violent Action N.Y., 1965-67; vista vol. N.H. Assn. for the Elderly, Penacook, 1971-73; com. mem. KIDSCOUNT, Lancaster, N.H., 1995—. Mem. Am. Counseling Assn., Sexuality Info. and Edn. Coun. of the U.S., Phi Beta Kappa. Democrat. Buddhist. Home: PO Box 536 Lancaster NH 03584 Office: Coos County Family Health Svcs PO Box 170 Colebrook NH 03576

HERRICK, KATHLEEN MAGARA, social worker; b. Mpls., Oct. 18, 1943; d. William Frank and Mary Genevieve (Gill) Magara; m. John Middlemist Herrick, Feb. 5, 1966; children: Elizabeth Jane, Kathryn Mary. BA in Social Work and French, Coll. St. Benedict, St. Joseph, Minn., 1965; MSW (Mildred B. Erickson fellow 1975), Mich. State U., E. Lansing, 1976. Social worker II, Carver County Social Services, Chaska, Minn., 1965-70; therapist St. Lawrence Community Mental Health Center, Lansing, Mich., 1974-75; sch. social worker Ingham Intermediate Sch. Dist., Mason, Mich., 1975-76; home/sch. coordinator Eaton Intermediate Sch. Dist., Charlotte, Mich., 1976-81, sch. social worker, 1994—; caseworker St. Vincent Home for Children, Lansing, 1979-80; tchr. cons. for severely emotionally impaired, 1981-83; behavior disorder cons., 1983-85; sch. social work cons., 1985-87, prevention specialist profl. and program svcs., 1987-94. Chairperson bd. dirs. Eaton County Child Abuse and Neglect Prevention Council, 1986—; Democratic precinct del.; bd. dirs. Catholic Social Services, Lansing; specialist substance abuse prevention region XIII SAPE, 1987-94. Mem. NEA, Nat. Platform Assn., Mich. Edn. Assn., Nat. Assn. Social Workers, Nat. Assn. Retarded Citizens, Am. Orthopsychiat. Assn., Mich. Assn. Sch. Social Workers, Mich. Assn. Emotionally Disturbed Children, Eaton County Assn. Retarded Citizens, Nat. Platform Assn., NOW, Nat. Women's Health Network, Amnesty Internat., Mich. Assn. Suicidology, Glasser Inst. for Reality Therapy and Choice Theory, Phi Kappa Phi, Phi Alpha. Democrat. Roman Catholic. Home: 2113 Long Leaf Trl Okemos MI 48864-3210 Office: 1790 E Packard Hwy Charlotte MI 48813

HERRICK, SYLVIA ANNE, health service administrator; b. Minot, N.D., Oct. 5, 1945; d. Sylvester P. and Ethelina (Harren) Theis; m. Michael M. Herrick, Nov. 8, 1989; children: Leo J., Mark A. BSN, U. N.D., 1967; MS in Pub. Health Nursing, U. Colo., Denver, 1970; sch. nurse credential, San Jose State U., 1991; postgrad., Golden Gate U. RN, Calif.; cert. pub. health nursing, health svc. Pub. health nurse Dept. Pub. Health City of Mpls.; instr. nursing San Francisco State U.; cons. exec. search Med-Power Resources, Alameda; coord. health svcs. Alameda Unified Sch. Dist.; team mgr. home care nursing and program devel. coord. Vis. Nurse Assn. and Hospice of No. Calif.; spkr. in field. Mem. Nat. Nurses Bus. Assn., Calif. Sch. Nurses Orgn. (bd. dirs., chair edn Bay Coast sect.), Delta Kappa Gamma. Home: 1711 Encinal Ave Alameda CA 94501-4020

HERRIN, FRANCES SUDOMIER, retired volunteer social worker; b. Hamtramck, Mich., Dec. 1, 1914; d. Wesley Valentine and Anna Theresa

(Langowski) Sudomier; widowed. Grad., high sch., 1933. Sec. Parke Davis & Co., Detroit, 1946-47; assembler Gen. Motors, Detroit, 1947, Chrysler Corp., Hamtramck, 1950-57; vol. social worker, mem. adv. com. Detroit Area Agy. on The Aging, Detroit, 1981-92; spkr. St. Theresa Guild, 1981-92, Golden Agers, 1981-92, Polish-Am. Sr. Citizens, 1981-90; precision-tool tested parts of B-29 bomber planes in World War II, Henry Ford Aircraft Bldg., River Rouge Plant. Active in Dem. and Rep. election campaigns; mem. St. Florian's Hist. Commn., Hamtramck, 1985—; sr. citizen activist several sr. orgns., Washington; mem. ret. sr. vol. program Cath. Social Svcs., Wayne County, 1986-87; mem. Presdl. Task Force for Pres. Reagan; patron Cath. orgns. where missionaries provide relief of food, clothing and edn. to children, especially orphaned children of devasted countries. Recipient Medal of Merit from Pres. Reagan. Mem. St. Theresa's Guild. Roman Catholic.

HERRIN, JENNIE I., newspaper editor; b. Nowata, Okla., Sept. 13, 1934; d. Charles R. and Ora O. (McMahan) McGrew; m. Dwaine Eldon Herrin, Oct. 7, 1955; children: Bradley Edward, Brent Eric. Student, U. Wichita, Kans., 1955. Lic. real estate agent, Mo. Sports editor Barry County Advertiser, Cassville, Mo., 1975-94, editor, 1994—. Mem. Cassville C. of C. (dir. 1995-96, v.p. 1996), Mo. Press Assn., S.W. Mo. Bd. Realtors, Soroptimist Internat. (women making a difference chair 1995-96, publicity com. 1994-96, SOLT com. 1995-96). Office: Barry County Advertiser 904 West St Cassville MO 65625

HERRING, SUSAN WELLER, dental educator, oral anatomist; b. Pitts., Mar. 25, 1947; d. Sol W. and Miriam (Damick) Weller; m. Stephen E. Herring, Nov. 18, 1967 (div. Oct. 1983); m. Norman S. Wolf, May 27, 1995. BS in Zoology, U. Chgo., 1967, PhD in Anatomy, 1971. NIH postdoctoral fellow U. Ill., Chgo., 1971-72, from asst. prof. to prof. oral anatomy and anatomy, 1972-90; prof. orthodontics U. Wash., Seattle, 1990—; vis. assoc. prof. biol. sci. U. Mich., Ann Arbor, 1981; cons. NIH study sect., Washington, D.C., 1987-89; sci. gov. Chgo. Acad. Sci., 1982-90; mem. pub. bd. Growth Pub. Inc., Bar Harbor, Maine, 1982—. Mem. editl. bd. Acta Anatomica, 1989—, Jour. Dental Rsch., 1995—; contbr. articles to profl. jours. Predoctoral fellow NSF, 1967-71; rsch. grantee NIH, 1975-78, 81—, NSF, 1990-92, 94-95. Fellow AAAS; mem. Internat. Assn. Dental Rsch. (dir. craniofacial biology group 1994-95, v.p. 1995-96, pres.-elect 1996-97), Am. Soc. Zoologists (chmn. vertebrate zoology 1983-84, exec. com. 1986-88), Am. Soc. Biomechanics, Am. Assn. Anatomists (chmn. Basmajian com. 1988-90), Soc. Vertebrate Paleontology, Am. Soc. Mammalogists, Internat. Soc. Vertebrate Morphology (convenor 4th congress 1994, pres. 1984—), Sigma Xi. Office: U Wash Box 357446 Seattle WA 98195-7446

HERRINGTON, DALE ELIZABETH, lay worker; b. Logansport, La., Feb. 1, 1913; d. Charles Ross and Ola Delnorte (Tillery) Currie; m. Cecil Doyle Herrington, June 25, 1939; 1 child, Jo Earle Herrington Hartt. BS, Stephen F. Austin Univ., 1932, MA, 1948, MEd, 1948. Cert. tchr., Tex. Min. edn. First Bapt. Ch., Garrison, Tex., 1947-81, organist, 1947—, lay worker, 1947—, tchr. Sunday sch. Bible, 1947—, woman's missionary union dir., 1990-92; tchr. Garrison Pub. Schs., 1940-76; dir./asst. dir. Vacation Bible Sch., Garrison, 1950-92; vol. local newspaper, nursing home and sch., city libr., ch. libr. Named Mother of Yr., First Bapt. ch., Garrison, 1988, Citizen of Yr., Garrison, 1992. Mem. Nat. Ret. Tchrs. Assn., Tex. Ret. Tchrs. Assn. (life), Stephen F. Austin Alumni Assn. (life), Lions (Sweetheart), Heritage Soc., Genealogy Soc., Order Eastern Star (past Matron, organist), Delta Kappa Gamma. Home: 319 N Avenue A Garrison TX 75946

HERRINGTON, VICTORIA LEE, manufacturing company administrator; b. Cloquet, Minn., Apr. 7, 1952; d. Lawrence Gerald and Inez Emily (Ott) Drouillard; m. Michael Ray Herrington, May 20, 1972. BS in Acctg., Quincy U., 1978; MBA, Western Ill. U., 1984. CPA, Ill.; cert. compensation profl. Internal auditor Moorman Mfg. Co., Quincy, Ill., 1978-86, payroll mgr., 1987-91, dir. compensation, 1991—. Loaned exec. United Way, Quincy, 1989-90, bd. dirs., 1994—; bd. dirs. Moorman Employees Credit Union, Quincy, 1986-88. Mem. Am. Compensation Assn., Compensation and Benefits Network, Ill. CPA Soc., Am. Payroll Assn., Toastmasters (v.p. pub. rels. 1994-95). Republican. Lutheran. Office: Moorman Mfg Co 1000 N 30th St Quincy IL 62305-3115

HERRINGTON-BORRE, FRANCES JUNE, sign language school director; b. Austin, Tex., June 14, 1935; d. George Wilmas Neill and Mildred Lucille (Alexander) Williamson; m. Harold M. Herrington, June 6, 1953 (dec. Dec. 1978); children: Harold M. (dec.), Cheryl Anne Herrington; m. Thomas Raymond Borre, Apr. 5, 1985. Student, U. Tex., 1967-71. With Tex. Dept. Human Services, Austin, 1961-90, adminstrv. technician, 1967-71, field rep., 1971-81, asst. personnel dir., 1981-88, labor relations dir., 1988-89, judge adminstrv. law, 1989-90; free-lance profl. interpreter for deaf, 1964—; dir. Austin Sign Lang. Sch., 1964—; legis. liaison symposium Deaf and Hard-of-Hearing Texans, 1991—; cons. in field; project dir. Gov.'s Office, 1980. Gov.'s appointee Joint Adv. Com. on Ednl. Services to Deaf, Austin, 1976-78; chmn. Tex. Commn. for Deaf Bd. Eval. of Interpreters, 1981-84; chmn. Tex. State Agy. Liaisons to Gov.'s Commn. for Women, 1985. Recipient Tex. Rehab. Commn. Merit award, 1977, Gov.'s citation, 1978; co-recipient Lyndon B. Johnson award Tex. Assn. for the Deaf and the Gallaudet U. Regional Ctr., 1992; named An Outstanding Woman Central Tex., AAUW, 1982, Significant and Meritorious Service to Mankind award Capitol Sertoma Club, 1976, Disting. Service as Adv. and Interpreter award Dal-Tar Lions Club, 1977. Mem. Nat. Assn. of Deaf (Golden Hand award 1987), Tex. Assn. of Deaf (Service citation 1967, Vol. Svc. award 1971, 93, 95, Interpreter of Decade award 1981, Presdl. citation for Outstanding Svc. to symposium on deafness 1989, Friendship award 1994, Gratitude for Vol. Svcs. award 1993-95, Appreciation award 1996), Nat. Registry Interpreters for Deaf, Tex. Soc. Interpreters for Deaf (pres. 1969-70), Austin Interpreters for Deaf. Mem. Ch. of Christ. Home: 2404 Laramie Trl Austin TX 78745-3664

HERRMANN, CAROL, university administrator; b. Mt. Kisco, N.Y., Dec. 23, 1944; d. Eugene C. and Anne M. McGuire; m. Robert O. Herrmann; children: John Martin II, Nell Elizabeth. AB, Bucknell U., 1966; MA, Pa. State U., 1970. Bus. editor, writer Centre Daily Times Newspaper, State College, Pa., 1980-82; with Pa. State U., University Park, 1982—, exec. asst. to pres. for adminstrn., 1986-88, v.p. for adminstrn., 1988-94, sr. v.p. for adminstrn., 1994—; mem. ctrl. region bd. Mellon Bank, 1994—; bd. dirs. Woolrich, Inc. Bd. trustees Pa. Coll. Tech., 1989—; mem. Centre Regional Planning Commn., State Coll., 1973-80, chmn., 1974-76, borough planning commn., 1973-80; media coord. Common Cause 23d Congl. Dist., 1977-80; bd. dirs. United Way, Centre County, Pa., 1989-91. Mem. AAUW, Women in Communications, Kappa Tau Alpha, Phi Delta Kappa. Home: 568 Ridge Ave State College PA 16803-3441 Office: Pa State U Old Main # 205 University Park PA 16802

HERRMANN, DEBRA MCGUIRE, chemist, educator; b. Ft. Benning, Ga., Dec. 28, 1955; d. Delbert Wayne and Twyla Pauline (Moran) McGuire; m. David Read Herrmann, Aug. 2, 1980; children: Adam James, Jesse Read, Aaron Matthew. BS in chemistry, U. Tex., 1979, U. Ark., 1989. Rsch. chemist Dow Chem., Oyster Creek, Freeport, Tex., 1980-84; chemist Aluminum Co. Am., Bauxite, Ark., 1984-87; tchr. Little Rock (Ark.) Sch. Dist., 1987-90. Pres., bd. dirs. Little Peoples Acad. Sch. Montessori, Ottumwa, Iowa, 1990-93. Mem. PEO, Phi Beta Kappa. Democrat. Presbyterian. Home: 1349 Lakeview Dr Southlake TX 76092

HERRMANN-LUKOMSKI, JANET CAMILLE, management and educational consultant; b. Herkimer, N.Y., Nov. 13, 1947; d. Edward John and Amelia (Catroppa) Lukomski; m. Siegfried Edwin Herrmann, June 7, 1969; children: Ingrid Kay, Heidi Jay. BM, SUNY, Fredonia, 1969; MM, Syracuse U., 1971; PhD, Union Inst., 1994. Cert. tchr., N.Y. Music tchr. Syracuse (N.Y.) City Sch. Dist., 1971-76; humanities prof. World U., San Juan, P.R., 1976-77; humanities prof. Miami-Dade C.C., 1982-85, dir. advt.-mktg., 1985-90; dir. music edn. Dade County Pub. Schs., Miami, 1991-94; pres., CEO Jan Herrmann Assocs., Inc., Miami, 1994—; pub. Internat. Bus. News, Herrmann Assocs., Inc., 1982-85. Mem. AAUW (pres. 1983-85, v.p. 1981-83, Edn. Found. Named Gift 1985). Recipient Membership award Women in Comm., 1987, Excellence in Advt. Fla. Assn. of C.C., 1987, Admissions Mktg. Report, 1989.

HERROLD, REBECCA MUNN, music educator, writer; b. Warren, Pa., Sept. 29, 1938; d. Gordon Clifford and Edith Esther (Lind) Munn; m. Stephen Herrold, 1959. MusB, U. Miami, 1960; MA, San Jose State U., 1968; D Mus. Arts, Stanford U., 1974. Asst. prof. Youngstown (Ohio) State U., 1974-75, Oreg. State U., Corvallis, 1975-80; assoc. prof. music San Jose State U., 1980-84, prof. music, 1984—. Author: (textbook) New Approaches to Elementary Classroom Music, 1984, 2nd edit., 1991, Mastering the Fundamentals of Music, 1996, Computer Programs for Music Instruction, Tutor Software, Inc., arranger Shawnee Press Inc., 1974—, pianist in Santa Clara Trio, Santa Clara U., 1987—. Grantee Apple Computer Co., 1981, Atari Computer Co., 1982, Bell and Howell. Mem. Coll. Music Soc., Nat. Consortium for Computer Based Music Instrn., Am. Assoc. for Gifted Children, Calif. Coun. on Computers in Music, Calif. Coun. Music Tchr. Educators (se.c 1985-86), Stanford Alumni, Music Educators Nat. Conf., League of Am. Pen Women, Woodland Hills Country Club. Democrat. Home: 1530 Montalban Dr San Jose CA 95120-4829 Office: San Jose State U School of Music and Dance San Jose CA 95192

HERRON, CAROLIVIA, novelist, English educator; b. Washington, July 22, 1947; d. Oscar Smith and Georgia Carol (Johnson) H. AB in English Lit., Ea. Bapt. Coll., 1969; MA in English Lit., Villanova (Pa.) U., 1973; MA, PhD, U. Pa., 1985; student, MIT, 1995. Asst. prof. Afro-Am. studies and comparative lit. Harvard U., Cambridge, Mass., 1986-90; assoc. prof. English Mt. Holyoke Coll., South Hadley, Mass., 1990-92; bd. dirs. curriculum devel. program NEH, Cambridge, Study Group in Afro-Asiatic Roots of Classical Civilization, Cambridge; vis. fellow Folger Shakespeare Libr., Washington, 1989—; Benedict vis. prof. Carleton Coll., Northfield, Minn., 1989-90; dir. Epicenter for the Study of Epic Lit.; vis. scholar Hebrew Coll., Mass., 1994-96, Harvard Div. Sch., 1995—; tech. assoc. Harvard Grad. Sch. Edn., 1996—; dir. conf. on African-Am. Jews, Hebrew Coll., 1995—; coord. African-Am. electronic texts devel. Howard U. Author: (novel) Thereafter Johnnie, 1991, (scholarly books) Selected Works of Angelina Weld Grimke, 1991, Afrekete/The Old Lady, 1995, Beginning Anew: Jewish Women/ Chamisa, 1996; (children's fiction) Nappy Hair, 1996; (feminist writing) Beginning Anew: Jewish Women/Chamisa, 1996; contbr. articles to profl. jours. Fulbright scholar, 1985-86; Bunting fellow Radcliffe Coll., 1988—. Mem. Classical Assn. New Eng. Home: 11 Dana St Revere MA 02151

HERRON, CINDY, vocalist, actress; b. San Francisco, 1966; m. Glenn Braggs; 1 child, Donovan Andrew. Vocalist En Vogue, Atco/Eastwest Records, N.Y.C. Albums include Born to Sing (Platinum 1990), Funky Divas, Remix to Sing, Runaway Love; actress (motion picture) Juice, 1992. Recipient Soul Train Music award, 1991; nominated Grammy award, 1990. Office: care En Vogue Atco Eastwest Records 75 Rockefeller Plz New York NY 10019-6908*

HERRON, ELLEN PATRICIA, retired judge; b. Auburn, N.Y., July 30, 1927; d. David Martin and Grace Josephine (Berner) Herron; A.B. Trinity Coll., 1949; M.A., Cath. U. Am., 1954; J.D., U. Calif.-Berkeley, 1964. Asst. dean Cath. U. Am., 1952-54; instr. East High Sch., Auburn, 1955-57; asst. dean Wells Coll., Aurora, N.Y., 1957-58; instr. psychology and history Contra Costa Coll., 1958-60; dir. row Stanford, 1960-61; assoc. Knox & Kretzmer, Richmond, Calif., 1964-65. Bar: Calif., 1965. Ptnr. Knox & Herron, 1965-74, Knox, Herron and Masterson, 1974-77 (both Richmond, Calif.); judge Superior Ct. State of Calif., 1977-87; pvt. judge, 1987-90; pvt. judge Jud. Arbitration and Mediation Svc., Inc. (JAMS- Endispute), 1990—; ptnr. Real Estate Syndicates, Calif., 1967-77; owner, mgr. The Barricia Vineyards, 1978—. Active numerous civic orgns. Democrat. Home: 51 Western Dr Richmond CA 94801-4011

HERRON, JANET IRENE, industrial manufacturing engineer; b. Zanesville, Ohio, Oct. 14, 1949; d. Lincoln and Freda Louise (Nolan) Estep; m. Wade Harold Herron, June 10, 1967; children: Toni Renee, Dawnise Renee. AAS, Muskingum Area Tech. Coll., 1978; BS, Ohio U., 1990. Elec., mech. designer Nat. Cash Register, Cambridge, Ohio, 1978-83; restructuring engr. Cooper Ind., Zanesville, 1983-87; sr. product engr., quality mgr. Tomkins Ind., Malta, Ohio, 1990-93; pres., owner Herron Engring. & Design, Chandlersville, Ohio, 1993—; engring. instr. Mid-East Ohio Joint Vocat. Sch., 1987-88, Ctrl. Ohio Tech. Coll., 1987-88, Muskingum Area Tech. Coll., 1990—; mfg. outreach engr. Edison Welding Inst. Columbus, Ohio, 1996—. Mem. NAFE, AAUW, Inst. Indsl. Engrs., Soc. Mfg. Engrs., Soc. Engrs. in Mfg., Soc. Women Engrs., Mid-East Ohio Women's Entrepreneurs. Democrat. Presbyn. Home: 9945 Claysville Rd Chandlersville OH 43727

HERRON, LEDA ESTHER, civic volunteer; b. Middlesboro, Ky., Sept. 12, 1915; d. Garrett and Laura Jalane (Wilson) Barnett; widowed; 1 child, Daniel Ferrell. Diploma, Evans Hosp., 1939. Nurse Carbon Carbide Corp., Oak Ridge, Tenn., 1942-46; dir., health coord. Head Start, Rockwood, Tenn., 1965-83; exec. dir. United Way Roane County, Harriman, Tenn., 1983—. East Tenn. campaign mgr. Dem. Women, Harriman., 1950-82; vol. Salvation Army, ARC; hon. mem. Roane County Rescue Squad, 1995; election commr. Roane County. Boy Scout of Am., Silver Faun award. Mem. Kiwanis. Home: 1116 Fairground Ct Kingston TN 37763 Office: United Way Roane County PO Box 317 Harriman TN 37748

HERRON, LORI S., special education educator; b. Sherman, Tex., Nov. 19, 1967; d. Darrell James and Doris Laverne (Miller) H. BBA, U. Okla., 1990. Cert. tchr., Okla. Spl. edn. tchr. Madill (Okla.) Pub. Schs., 1993—; presenter Okla. Fedn. Coun. for Exceptional Children, 1994. Grantee: Assistive Tech. grant Idea-B discretionary grant, Madill Schs., 1993. Mem. Coun. for Exceptional Children (pres. Texoma chpt. 1993-94). Home: 1829 Red Fox Rd Durant OK 74701 Office: Madill Middle Sch 601 W McArthur Madill OK 73446

HERRUP, BECKY SPECTOR, healthcare consultant; b. Miami Beach, Fla., Dec. 20, 1955; d. Sheldon Marvin and Ethyl (Cohen) Spector; m. Laurence Allan Herrup, Aug. 27, 1977; children: Bradley Spector, Lindsey Blair. AS in Nursing, ADN, Miami (Fla.) Dade C.C., 1978, AA in Fine Arts, 1978; accreditation cert., Am. Inst. Med. Law, Miami, 1993. Lic. healthcare risk mgr., Fla.; RN, Fla.; diplomate Am. Bd. Healthcare Risk Mgmt., Am. Bd. Risk Mgmt. Neonatal nurse, maternal-child educator Cedars of Lebanon, Miami, 1978-81; pediat. staff nurse Golden Glades Regional Med. Ctr., Miami, 1988-89, utilization rev. case mgr./quality improvement coord., 1989-92, acting dir. quality mgmt., 1993-94, risk mgr., 1993-95; pvt. practice healthcare cons. Miami, 1995—. Founding pres. Second Generation Deed Club Cancer Clinic, Miami, 1985-87; founding mem. Ann Weinstein Koch Bone Marrow Donor Registry, Miami, 1987—; donor advocate-liaison Am. Bone Marrow Donor Registry, 1993—. Recipient Cabinet Svc. award U. Miami Sch. Medicine, 1988, Woman of the Yr., 1989. Mem. Am. Bd. Healthcare Risk Mgmt., Am. Soc. Healthcare Risk Mgmt., Fla. Soc. Utilization Rev./Quality Improvement Assn., Fla. Med. Malpractice Rev. Assn., Fla. Med. Malpractice Claims Coun., South Fla. Soc. Healthcare Risk Mgrs. Office: 326 71st St Miami Beach FL 33141

HERSCHEDE, JOAN ROTH, holding company executive; b. Portsmouth, Ohio, Jan. 14, 1940; d. Albert Joseph Roth and Leona Agnes Simon; m. Mark Paul Herschede, June 22, 1970 (dec. May 1991); children: Donald Lee Huffman II, Deborah Leona Huffman. Exec. Frank Herschede Co., Cin.; bd. dirs. Fifth Third Bank, Cin. Trustee U. Cin.; chmn. WCET-TV, Cin.; bd. dirs. United Way, Cin.

HERSEY, MARILYN ELAINE, performing company executive; b. N.Y.C., June 28, 1943; d. Charles Kenneth Hersey and Ella Margaret (Morgan) Decker; m. David William Orange, Nov. 17, 1972 (div. Dec. 1984); 1 child, Kristin Eleanor. BA, SUNY, Binghamton, 1965. Mng. dir. Boston Post Rd. Stage Co. (dba Fairfield County Stage Co.), Westport, Conn., 1985-93; exec. dir. Westport Arts Ctr., 1994—. Actress-singer, 1965-72; freelance writer, 1972-84; columnist The Westport News. Mem. Westport Arts Adv. Coun.; mem. Fairfield County Arts Alliance; mem. arts adv. com. Westport Schs. Mem. Am. Fedn. TV and Radio Artists, Actors' Equity Assn. Office: Westport Arts Ctr 17 Morningside Dr S Westport CT 06880-5432

HERSH, JENNIFER NEWTON, art history educator, artist; b. Lawrence, Kans., Sept. 26, 1961; d. Robert Tweed and Sally Newton (Six) H.; m. David Andrew Seideman, July 3, 1992. BA, Carleton Coll., 1983; MFA, Pratt Inst., 1985; MA, Hunter Coll., 1988; PhD, CUNY, 1996. Curatorial asst. Bklyn. Mus., 1989-90; asst. prof. Pratt Inst., Bklyn., 1990—; rschr. Mus. Modern Art, N.Y.C., 1990-91; adj. lectr. Hunter Coll., N.Y.C., 1992-93. Author: The Brooklyn Museum's Paintings, 1996; exhibitions include Hunter Thomas Gallery, 1989, 450 Broadway Gallery, 1994; illustrator, photographer Tuff Stuff Mag., 1995. Recipient Art Excellence award RCA, 1980; Kristie Jayne fellow Grad. Ctr., 1993-94, Dominic J. Madormo fellow, 1994. Mem. Am. Assn. Muss., Am. Hist. Soc., Coll. Art Assn., Sci. and Lit. Soc., Graphic Artists Guild. Home: 57 Sherman St Brooklyn NY 11215

HERSH, KRISTIN, vocalist, musician; b. Atlanta, 1965. Represented by 4AD, 1985-91, Sire Records, 1987—; lead singer Throwing Muses, late 1970s—; solo vocalist, 1994—. Albums include Throwing Muses, 1986, The Fat Skier, 1987, House Tornado, 1988, Hunkpapa, 1989, The Real Ramonoa, 1991, Red Heaven, 1992, Hips and Makers, 1994, Strings, 1994, University, 1995. Office: Sire Records 3300 Warner Blvd Burbank CA 91505-4694*

HERSHATTER, ANDREA SILVER, university official; b. N.Y.C., Jan. 19, 1960; d. K. David and René Eileen (Kirsch) Silver; m. Bruce Warren Hershatter, Oct. 1, 1983; children: Jessica René, Justin Ross. BS in Mgmt., Tulane U., 1981; MBA, Duke U., 1983. Promotions and mktg. dir. WBAG, The Village Cos., Burlington, N.C., 1983-84; asst. dir. admissions and fin. aid Fuqua Sch. Bus. Duke U., Durham, N.C., 1984-86, assoc. dir. admissions, 1986-87; dir. admissions and student affairs Emory Bus. Sch. Emory U., Atlanta, 1988-90, asst. dean Emory Bus. Sch., 1990-94, assoc. dean for acad. programs Goizueta Bus. Sch., 1994-96, assoc. dean undergrad. edn., 1996—, adj. instr., rep. grad. mgmt. admissions coun., chmn. MBA curriculum task force; mem. reaccreditation task force So. Assn. Colls. and Schs., Am. Assn. Collegiate Schs. Bus.; trustee Grad. Mgmt. Admissions Coun., 1996—; mem. bd. trustees nominating group, rsch. adv. group GMAC; MBA/MPH curriculum rep. Rollins Sch. Pub. Health, FLAS scholarship selection com. Soviet programs, Emory U., mem. career svcs. adv. bd.; advisor MBA Enterprise Corps. and Free Mkt. Devel. Adv. Program., mem. MBA roundtable steering com. Editor-in-chief Emory Bus. Mag., 1993, contbg. editor, 1993—. Pres. Mt. Paran Neighborhood Assn., Atlanta, 1991-94. Democrat. Jewish. Home: 4400 Mount Paran Pky NW Atlanta GA 30327-3722 Office: Emory Univ Goizueta Bus Sch Atlanta GA 30322

HERSHEY, BARBARA (BARBARA HERZSTEIN), actress; b. Hollywood, Calif., Feb. 5, 1948; d. William H. Herzstein; 1 child, Tom; m. Stephen Douglas, Aug. 8, 1992. Student public schs., Hollywood. Appearences include (TV series) The Monroes, 1966-67, From Here to Eternity, 1979, (mini-series) A Man Called Intrepid, 1979, Return to Lonesome Dove, 1993, Abraham, 1994; other TV appearances include Gidget, 1965, The Invaders, 1967, Daniel Boone, 1967, Love Story, 1973, Bob Hope Chrysler Theatre, 1967, High Chaparral, 1967, Kung Fu, 1973, CBS Playhouse, 1967, (TV movies) Flood, 1976, In the Glitter Palace, 1977, Just a Little Inconvenience, 1977, Sunshine Christmas, 1977, Angel on My Shoulder, 1980, The Nightingale, 1985, My Wicked, Wicked Ways... The Legend of Errol Flynn, 1985, Passion Flower, 1986, Killing in a Small Town, 1990 (Emmy award 1990, Golden Globe award 1991), Paris Trout, 1991 (Emmy award nomination), Stay the Night, 1992, Abraham, 1994, (films) With Six You Get Egg Roll, 1968, Last Summer, 1969, Heaven with a Gun, 1969, The Liberation of L.B. Jones, 1970, The Baby Maker, 1970, The Pursuit of Happiness, 1971, Dealing, 1971, Boxcar Bertha, 1972, Angela (Love Comes Quietly), 1974, The Crazy World of Julius Vrooder, 1974, Diamonds, 1975, You and Me, 1975, Dirty Night's Work, 1976, The Stunt Man, 1980, Take This Job and Shove It, 1981, The Entity, 1982, The Right Stuff, 1983, Americana, 1983, The Natural, 1984, Hoosiers, 1986, Hannah and Her Sisters, 1986, Tin Men, 1987, Shy People, 1987 (Best Actress Cannes Film Festival, 1987), A World Apart, 1988 (Best Actress Cannes Film Festival, 1988), The Last Temptation of Christ, 1988, Beaches, 1988, Tune in Tomorrow, 1989, Defenseless, 1991, The Public Eye, 1992, Falling Down, 1993, Swing Kids, 1993, Splitting Heirs, 1993, A Dangerous Woman, 1993, Last of the Dogmen, 1995, Portrait of a Lady, 1996, The Pallbearer, 1996; (theatre, Broadway) Einstein and the Polar Bear, 1981. Recipient Golden Palm award for best actress Cannes Film Festival, 1987, 1988. Office: CAA care Kevine Huvane 9830 Wilshire Blvd Beverly Hills CA 90212-1804*

HERSHEY, LINDA ANN, neurology and pharmacology educator; b. Marion, Ind., Jan. 15, 1947; d. Matthew John and Janice Elaine (Moody) Kwolek; m. Charles Owen Hershey, May 1, 1976; children: Edward, William, Erin. BS, Purdue U., 1968; PhD, Washington U., St. Louis, 1973, MD, 1975. Diplomate Am. Bd. Psychiatry and Neurology. Resident in neurology Barnes Hosp., St. Louis, 1976-78; fellow in clin. pharmacology Strong Meml. Hosp., Rochester, N.Y., 1978-80; asst. prof. neurology Case Western Res. U., Cleve., 1980-86; assoc. prof.neurology and pharmacology SUNY, Buffalo, 1986-94, prof. neurology and pharmacology, 1994—; chief neurology svc. Buffalo VA Med. Ctr., 1986—; mem. neurology adv. group VA, Washington, 1994—. Co-author: Handbook of Dementing Illnesses, 1994; mem. editl. bd. Clin. Pharmacology and Therapeutics, 1993—, Stroke, 1995—; contbr. articles to profl. jours. Co-dir. Alzheimers Disease Assistance Ctr., Buffalo, 1994—; elder Univ. Presbyn. Ch., Buffalo, 1995-96. Grantee Sterling-Winthrop Co., 1992-96, Lorex Pharms., 1995-96, Nat. Inst. Neurol. and Communicative Disorders and Stroke, 1994—, Parke-Davis, 1996—. Fellow Am. Acad. Neurology, Am. Neurol. Assn.; mem. Ctrl. Soc. for Neurol. Rsch., Am. Soc. Clin. Pharmacology and Therapeutics, Am. Heart Assn. (mem. exec. com. stroke coun. 1993—, chmn. program com. 1995—). Office: Buffalo VA Med Ctr 3495 Bailey Ave Buffalo NY 14215

HERSHEY, SUSAN LOUISE, social services administrator; b. Steubenville, Ohio, Aug. 11, 1949; d. George J. and S. June Granatir; m. Adrian V. Hershey, July 10, 1971; children: John, Brian. BSBA in Mgmt., Franciscan U . of Steubenville, 1987. Exec. dir. United Way of Jefferson County, Steubenville, 1989—. Bd. mem. Upper Ohio Valley Adult Literacy Coun., Steubenville, 1987-89; bd. mem., sec. Fed. Emergency Mgmt. Assn., Steubenville, 1990—; sponsor Steubenville H.s. Beta Club, 1994-96. Recipient Social Svc. award Quinn Meml. A.M.E. Ch., Steubenville, 1995. Mem. Rotary Club of Steubenville. Office: United Way Jefferson County 630 Market St Steubenville OH 43952

HERSHFIELD, LOTTE CASSEL, writer, editor; b. Breslau, Germany, Jan. 20, 1931; came to U.S., 1946, naturalized, 1952; d. Isidor Lippman and Sabine (Leser) Cassel; m. Nathan Hershfield, Apr. 7, 1951; children—Leonie, Joel. A.A., McCoy Coll. Johns Hopkins U., 1951. Library asst. Enoch Pratt Free Library, Balt., 1948-51; copywriter, proof reader Jewish Times, Balt., 1947-48; copywriter, food editor Catholic Transcript, Hartford, Conn., 1970-86; personnel dir. adminstrv. office Mercyknoll, Inc., West Hartford, Conn., 1986—; library substitute West Hartford Pub. Schs., 1964-70; lectr. in field. Mem. Temple Emanuel, West Hartford, Conn. Editor: Of Loaves and Fishes and Other Dishes, 1978, 2d edit., 1980. Contbr. articles to profl. jours., food section Hartford Courant, recipes in cookbooks. Mem. Arthritis Found. Conn., Mothers Against Drunk Driving. Democrat. Jewish. Lodge: Mercyknoll Aux. Avocations: researching recipes; knitting; reading; writing; foreign traveling. Office: Mercyknoll Inc 243 Steele Rd West Hartford CT 06117-2741

HERSON, ARLENE RITA, producer, journalist, television program host; b. N.Y.C.; d. Sam and Mollie (Friedman) Hornreich; m. Milton Herson, June 16, 1963; children: Michael, Karen. Student, Queens Coll., 1957, New Sch. for Social Rsch., N.Y.C., 1960. Exec. sec. Tex McCrary, Inc., N.Y.C., 1958-60; asst. to William L. Safire Safire Pub. Rels., N.Y.C., 1960-62; columnist The Advisor, Inc., Middletown, N.J., 1974-78; prodr., host The Arlene Herson Show, N.Y.C., 1978—; syndicated nationally on Tempo TV, 1988, Channel Am., 1989-93; spokesperson Storer Cable TV, Monmouth County, 1989-91, Nutri/Systems, Monmouth and Ocean Counties, 1989-90; news anchor Nostalgia Cable TV Network at Rep. Nat. Conv., 1993; cons., talent coord. Super Annuities, 1993-94. Contbg. writer The Washington/Hampton Connection Dan's Papers, 1993—, The Hill Newspaper, 1994—; exec. producer The Magic Flute, conductor Victor Borge, Constitution Hall, Washington, 1995; exec. producer, casting dir. (musical) 1776, Constitution Hall, Washington, 1996; interviewer Steven Spielberg's Shoah Found., 1996.

Bd. dirs. women's activities campaign for Sen. Jacob J. Javits, N.Y.C., 1968, Monmouth (N.J.) Mus., 1982-86, Will Rogers Inst., 1992—, Washington Symphony Orch., 1994—, v.p., 1994; mem. 92d St. Y Benefit com., Variety-The Children's Charity; mem. Women's Project and Prodns., 1992; com. mem. Children's Psychiat. Ctr., 1971-90, Monmouth Park Charity Fund, 1980-90; mem. corp. exec. bd. Family and Childrens' Svcs., 1985-90, Ctrl. Park Conservancy, Women of Washington, also mentor program Women's Econ. Devel. Coun.; life mem. N.Y. chpt. Brandeis U. Libr. Fund; mem. dir.'s resource coun. Nat. Women's Econ. Alliance; mem. social com. Westbridge Condominium; fin. chmn. Mike Herson for Congress, 19994, fin. com. March of Dimes, 1995; mem. profl. women's coun. Nat. Mus. of Women in the Arts, 1994; com. mem. Vincent T. Lombardi Cancer Rsch. Ctr., 1994-96, Parkinson's Action Network, 1996. Recipient CAPE award for best talk show on Cable TV Network, 1984-93, Woman of Achievement in Comm. award Adv. Commn. on Status of Women, 1986, Pub. and Leased Access award for best talk show Paragon Cable TV, N.Y.C., 1988, spl. resolution N.J. Assembly, 1988, Willie award for outstanding svc. Will Rogers Inst., 1992; nominee Cable ACE award for best talk show series nationwide. Mem. NAFE, NATAS, Nat. Acad. Cable Programming, Nat. Assn. Profl. Women, Women in Commn., Women in Cable, Women in Film and Video, Am. Women in Radio and TV, Internat. Radio and TV Soc., Internat. Newswoman's Assn., Nat. Press Club, Friars Club, Bethesda Country Club, Lotos Club, East River Tennis Club.

HERTE, MARY CHARLOTTE, plastic surgeon; b. Milw., May 31, 1951. BS, Mt. Mary Coll., Milw., 1973; MD, U. Wis., 1977. Diplomate Am. Bd. Plastic Surgery. Research fellow in plastic surgery Grad. Sch. Medicine Ea. Va. U., Norfolk, 1978; resident in gen. surgery Univ. Hosps., Madison, Wis., 1978-81, resident in plastic surgery, 1981-83; pvt. practice specializing in cosmetic plastic surgery Las Vegas, Nev., 1983—; chief of surgery Humana Sunrise, Las Vegas, 1989-92; chief of plastic surgery Sunrise Children's Hosp., Las Vegas, 1990-96. Recipient Woman of Promise award Good Housekeeping Mag., 1985. Fellow ACS, Am. Acad. Pediatrics; mem. Am. Cleft Palate Assn., Assn. Women Surgeons, Am. Med. Women's Assn., Am. Soc. Plastic and Reconstructive Surgeons, Nev. State Med. Soc. (del. 1986-88), Clark County Med. Soc. (trustee 1986-88), Nev. Soc. Women Physicians (v.p. 1991-93, pres. 1994—), Soroptimist Internat. (treas., fin. sec. Greater Las Vegas chpt. 1985-87). Office: 3006 S Maryland Pky Ste 415 Las Vegas NV 89109-2235

HERTEL, SUZANNE MARIE, personnel administrator; b. Hastings, Neb., Aug. 8, 1937; d. Louis C. Hertel and W. Lenore (Cross) Budd. BA, Doane Coll., Crete, Neb., 1959; MSM, Union Theol. Sem., 196l; postgrad., U. Hartford, 1966, U. Conn., 1975; MA, Merrill Palmer Inst., 1977; EdD, Boston U., 1982. Music tchr. Pub. Sch., Wethersfield, Conn., 1962-63; serials libr. Hartford (Conn.)Sem. Found., 1963-64; elem. tchr. Pub. Sch., Glastonbury, Conn., 1965-79; asst. prof. Univ. Northern Iowa, Cedar Falls, Iowa, 1979-81; training mgr. Focus Research Systems Inc., W. Hartford, Conn., 1982-89; pers. adminstr. City of Hartford, 1989—; mem. Human Resource Mgmt. Delegation, Russia and Estonia, 1992; mem. Initiative for Edn., Sci. and Tech., South Africa, 1995. Recipient Maria Miller Stewart award, 1992. Mem. Am. Soc. Training and Devel., Am. Guild Organists. Democrat. Office: City of Hartford Mcpl Bldg Main St Hartford CT 06103

HERTENSTEIN, MYRNA LYNN, publishing executive; b. Detroit, July 19, 1937; d. Bernard Franklin and Alice Agnes (Stewart) Aller; m. George Ronald Hertenstein, June 21, 1958 (div. July 1979); children: Dale Ronald, Robert Mark. AS in Bus., Wayne State U., 1957; student, Huntingdon Coll., 1980-84. Departmental sec. Sch. of Bus. Wayne State U., Detroit, 1957-59; county and vol. coord. Montgomery (Ala.) Area Coun. on Aging, 1977-80; admissions counselor Coastal Tng. Inst., Montgomery, 1981-83; rural volunteerism coord. State of Ala., Montgomery, 1983-84; account exec. Ala. Bus. Rev., Montgomery, 1984-85, Sta. WRJM-FM, Montgomery, 1985-86; asst. local sales mgr. Sta. WCOV-TV Fox Affiliate, Montgomery, 1986-90; owner, assoc. pub. TRAVELHOST of Cen. Ala., Montgomery, 1990—; mem. Dirs. of Vols. in Agys., Montgomery, 1978-82, Montgomery County Health Coun., 1979-81, Area Agy. on Aging Adv. Coun., Montgomery, 1981-83, Pres.' Coun. Montgomery, 1983, 84; asst. to instr. Dale Carnegie & Assocs., Montgomery, 1978-83. Editor (newsletter) Montgomery Area Coun. on Aging, 1978-80; dir., writer (commls.) Sta. WCOV-TV, 1986-90; writer (commls.) Sta.WRJM-FM, 1985-86. Mem. adminstrv. coun. Whitfield United Meth. Ch., Montgomery, 1977, coord. Meals-on-Wheels, 1978-86; mem. pub. rels. coun. First United Meth. Ch., Montgomery, 1992-94; den leader, coach Boy Scouts Am., Bellevue, Nebr., 1969-71; editor Capitol Jr. Woman's Club. Montgomery, 1975-82; pres. Parents Without Ptnrs., 1983-85; bd. dirs. Arthritis Found., 1992—, vice chair 1995, chair Ala. chpt. exec. com., 1996; exec. com. Ala. Dance Theatre, 1996—. Recipient Emerging 30 award Montgomery Area C. of C., 1992, small business of yr. award, 1994, corp. vol. of yr. award Voluntary Action Ctr., Montgomery, 1992, award Montgomery Com. for Arts, 1993. Mem. Pub. Rels. Coun. Ala., Ala. Travel Coun., Montgomery Restaurant Assn., Montgomery Hotel/Motel Assn. (bd. dirs. 1992-94), Sales and Mktg. Execs. (editor newsletter 1995-96), Montgomery Assn. Bus. Communicators, Montgomery Advt. Fedn. (bd. dirs. 1985-92, 96—), Montgomery C. of C. (vice chmn. ambs. 1992, chmn. ambs. 1993, chmn. advt. promotions and pubis. 1994, hospitality devel. and mktg. task force 1995—, chmn. spl. projects com. 1996), Montgomery Civitans. Home: 3005 Baldwin Brook Dr Montgomery AL 36116-3803 Office: Travelhost of Cen Ala PO Box 20666 Montgomery AL 36120-0666

HERTOG, MARY KAY, career officer; b. Bossier City, La., July 9, 1956; d. Donald Edward and Mary (Skocich) Reeves; m. Herman Mark Hertog III, July 14, 1979. BA in Sociology, Miami U., Oxford, Ohio, 1978; MA in Human Rels., Webster U., 1985; postgrad., Air Command and Staff Coll., 1990-91. Commd. 2d lt. USAF, 1978, advanced through grades to lt. col., 1994; security police shift comdr. 1608 Security Police Squadron, Kirtland AFB, Albuquerque, N.Mex., 1979-81; security police ops. officer 63d Security Police Squadron, Norton AFB, San Bernardino, Calif., 1981-83; security police exec. officer HQ Mil. Airlift Command, Scott AFB, Belleville, Ill., 1983-84; security police ops. officer 554 Security Support Squadron, Nellis AFB, Las Vegas, Nev., 1984-86; security police comdr. 554 Security Support Squadron, Nellis AFB, Las Vegas, 1986-87; security police staff officer HQ Pacific Air Forces, Hickam AFB, Honolulu, 1987-90; staff officer HQ USAF/Security Police, Pentagon, Washington, 1991-95; cmdr. 377th Security Police Squadron, Kirtland AFB, N.Mex., 1996—. Mem. Air Force Security Police Assn. (charter mem.), Air Force Assn., Miami Tribe. Roman Catholic. Home: 377 Security Police Squad Kirtland AFB NM 22202-4124

HERTWECK, ALMA LOUISE, sociology and child development educator; b. Moline, Ill., Feb. 6, 1937; d. Jacob Ray and Sylvia Ethel (Whitt) Street; m. E. Romayne Hertweck, Dec. 16, 1955; 1 child, William Scott. A.A., Mira Costa Coll., 1969; B.A. in Sociology summa cum laude, U. Calif.-San Diego, 1975, M.A., 1977, Ph.D., 1982. Cert. sociology instr., multiple subjects teaching credential grades kindergarten-12, Calif. Staff research assoc. U. Calif.-San Diego, 1978-81; instr. sociology Chapman Coll., Orange, Calif., 1982-87; instr. child devel. MiraCosta Coll., Oceanside, Calif., 1983-87, 88-89; instr. sociology U.S. Internat. U., San Diego, 1985-88 ; exec. dir., v.p. El Camino Preschools, Inc., Oceanside, 1985—. Author: Constructing the Truth and Consequences: Educators' Attributions of Perceived Failure in School, 1982; co-author: Handicapping the Handicapped, 1985. Mem. Am. Sociol. Assn., Am. Ednl. Research Assn., Nat. Council Family Relations, Nat. Assn. Edn. Young Children, Alpha Gamma Sigma (life). Avocations: foreign travel; sailing; bicycling. Home: 2024 Oceanview Rd Oceanside CA 92056-3104 Office: El Camino Preschs Inc 2002 California St Oceanside CA 92054-5673

HERTZ, ELLEN SHAPIRO, mathematical statistician; b. N.Y.C., Apr. 5, 1937; d. Max and Rose (Sandlow) Shapiro; m. René Daniel Hertz, July 3, 1963 (div. 1989); children: Joseph, Julia Hertz Davidson. BS, CCNY, 1958; AM, Columbia U., 1960, PhD, 1970. Lectr. in math. CCNY, N.Y.C., 1966-68; ops. rsch. analyst U.S. Dept. of Army, Ft. Monmouth, N.J., 1979-83; math. statistician U.S. Dept. Transp., Washington, 1988—. Mem. Am. Statis. Assn., Assn. for Women in Math., Math. Assn. Am., Washington Statis. Soc. Office: US Dept Transp NRD31 400 7th St SW Washington DC 20590

HERTZ, HEATHER KAY, small business owner; b. Bismarck, N.D., Nov. 13, 1969; d. Milton John and Carol Ann (Ormiston) H.; m. Stanley William Blickensderfer, July 3, 1994. BA in Eng., French, Magazine Journalism, Syracuse U., 1991. Cert. emergency med. technician and instr.; cert. CPR instr. Owner H Writing and Photography, Mott, N.D., 1992—, Hertz Studio of Music, Mott, 1992—. Contbr. articles to farming publs. Organist 1st Congl. Ch., Mott, 1994—; training officer Mott Ambulance Svc., 1995—. Mem. AAUW (sec. 1993—), Nat. Fedn. Music Clubs, Music Tchrs. Nat. Assn. (Badlands ch., pres. 1995—), N.D. EMS Assn., N.D. Instr./coord. Soc., N.D. Advanced Life Support Soc. Home & Office: 606 E 4th St Mott ND 58646

HERTZ, LAURIE ANNE, database programmer, artist; b. Milw., Nov. 23, 1968; d. William Russell Hertz and Barbara Marion (Guenter) Kasik. BFA, U. Wis., Milw., 1991. Data processing mgr. MGIC, Milw., 1988-93; list mgr. B&I Furniture, Milw., 1993-94; rsch. data mgr. Milw. Health Dept., 1994—. Illustrator, writer: (book) I Like Your Hair (Best of Show U. Milw. Fine Arts Gallery, 1992); illustrator: (books) Jane, 1994, Harsh, 1996. Democrat. Roman Catholic. Office: Milw Health Dept 841 N Broadway Rm 102 Milwaukee WI 53202

HERTZOG, ARDITH ELYSE, federal agency administrator; b. Washington, Aug. 26, 1964; d. Robert Leon and Ardith Elspeth (Hay) Beadles; m. Scott Lisle Hertzog, Oct. 12, 1991. BSChE, N.C. State U., 1987, postgrad., 1987-88; postgrad., George Mason U., 1991, 92. Acting asst. dept. head sales La Vogue, Durham, N.C., 1981-82; sales assoc. Collections, Durham, 1983; co-op student chem engring. E.I. duPont de Nemours & Co., Wilmington, N.C., 1985-86; rsch. asst. in astrophysics N.C. State U., Raleigh, 1987; sales assoc. Leather 'N' Wood, Raleigh, 1988-89; patent examiner chem. group U.S. Patent & Trademark Office, Washington, 1989-91, 93—. NSF fellow, 1987.

HERZECA, LOIS FRIEDMAN, lawyer; b. N.Y.C., July 7, 1954; d. Martin and Elaine Shirley (Rapoport) Friedman; m. Christian S. Herzeca, Aug. 15, 1980; children: Jane Leslie, Nicholas Cameron. BA, SUNY-Binghamton, 1976; JD, Boston U., 1979. Bar: N.Y. 1980, U.S. Dist. Ct. (so. and ea. dist.) N.Y. 1980. Atty. antitrust div. U.S. Dept. Justice, Washington, 1979-80; assoc. Fried, Frank, Harris, Shriver & Jacobson, N.Y.C., 1980-86, ptnr., 1986—. Editor Am. Jour. Law and Medicine, 1978-79. Mem. ABA, N.Y.C. Bar Assn. Office: Fried Frank Harris Shriver Jacobson 1 New York Plz New York NY 10004

HERZENBERG, CAROLINE STUART LITTLEJOHN, physicist; b. East Orange, N.J., Mar. 25, 1932; d. Charles Frederick and Caroline Dorothea (Schulze) L.; m. Leonardo Herzenberg, July 29, 1961; children: Karen Ann, Catherine Stuart. SB, MIT, 1953; SM, U. Chgo., 1955, PhD, 1958; DSc (hon.), SUNY, Plattsburgh, 1991. Asst. prof. Ill. Inst. Tech., Chgo., 1961-66, research physicist ITT Research Inst., 1967-70, sr. physicist, 1970-71; lectr. Calif. State U., Fresno, 1975-76; physicist Argonne (Ill.) Nat. Lab., Ill., 1977—; prin. investigator NASA Apollo Returned Lunar Sample Analysis Program, 1967-71; producer and host TV sci. series Camera on Sci.; disting. vis. prof. SUNY, Plattsburgh, 1991; mem. final selection com. 1993 Bower award and Prize for Achievement in Sci.; bd. adv. the Bower award and Prize for Achievements in Sci.; mem. nat. panel of advisors PBS TV sci. series Bill Nye the Sci. Guy; steering com. mem. Midwest Consortium for Internat. Security Studies. Author: Women Scientists from Antiquity to the Present: An Index, 1986. Contbr. articles to profl. jours. Candidate for alderman, Freeport, Ill., 1975; past chmn. NOW chpt., Freeport. Am. Phys. Soc. Congl. Scientist fellow finalist, 1976-77; recipient award in sci. Chgo. Women's Hall of Fame, 1989. Fellow AAAS, Am. Phys. Soc. (past chmn. com., past sec.-treas. forum on Physics and Soc., exec. bd. Forum on the History Physics, panel pub. affairs); mem. Assn. Women in Sci. (nat. sec. 1982-84, pres. 1988-90), Sigma Xi. Home: 1700 E 56th St Ste 2707 Chicago IL 60637-1935 Office: Argonne Nat Lab DIS Divsn Argonne IL 60439

HERZFELD-KIMBROUGH, CIBY, mental health educator; b. Mobile, Ala., Oct. 10, 1941; d. Julius Sr. and Nettie (Fraizer) Herzfeld; m. Charles C. Kimbrough, Nov. 28, 1964; children: Carolos R., Choron F. BS, U. Mo., 1970; MA, Wash. U., 1980; MAT, AGC, Webster U., 1982. Cert. tchr., Mo. Coord. children-adolescent svcs. Metro Comprehensive Mental Health Ctr., St. Louis; cons. C. Kimbrough and Assocs.; instr. minority mental health Wash. U., St. Louis; founder, exec. dir. Creative Inovative and Behavioral Experences, CIBE; mng. dir. CKAN Ltd., Nigeria; project coord. Children's Devel. Ctr., Lagos, Nigeria; intervention specialist, counselor Ferguson Florissant Schs.; adj. instr. St. Louis U.; developer Children's Treatment Program; established Metroties Day Treatment Sch., 1987. Knoxville Coll. acad. scholarship, 1961; NIMH fellow, 1979; recipient Outstanding Leadership award Woman's Collaboration Conf., 1985, Exceptional Tchr. award INROADS Pre-Coll. Inst., 1986, Devel. award MTS, Lagos, Nigeria. Mem. Nat. Black Child Devel. Inst. (pres. St. Louis affiliate, Outstanding Svc. award), St. Louis Assn. of Black Psychologists (membership chair), St. Louis Mental Health Assn. (children's svcs. coun., membership chair), Mo. Psychol. Assn. (St. Louis network for women psychologists sec.), Nigerian Field Soc. (membership chair), Internat. Platform Soc., 100 Black Women, Nigerian Federated Women, Am. Woman's Club. Home: 11752 Russet Meadow Dr Saint Louis MO 63146-4231

HERZL, JUDY LYNN, artist; b. N.Y.C., June 18, 1957; d. Theodore and Felice Rachel (Freund) H. BFA, Boston Mus. Sch. Fine Art, 1979. Visual artist, designer Western States Arts Fedn., Santa Fe, 1990-95; designer Judy Herzl Design, Santa Fe, 1992—; lectr. in field. Exhibited in group shows at Provincetown (Mass.) Mus. and Art Assn., 1985 (2nd place), Santa Fe Festival Arts, 1987, State Fine Arts Gallery, Albuquerque, 1987, 89, Ctr. Contemporary Art, Santa Fe, 1987, 96, Soc. Photographic Edn., Albuquerque, 1987, No. Ariz. State Univ., Flagstaff, 1988, Santa Fe Ctr. Photography, 1988, 90, N.Mex. Coun. Photography, Santa Fe, 1988, Sena Galleries East, Santa Fe, 1989, 90, Carnegie Cultural Ctr., North Tonawanda, N.Y., 1990, Coll. Santa Fe Fine Arts Gallery, 1991, Mus. Fine Arts, Santa Fe, 1991, Judah L. Magnes Mus., Berkley, Calif., 1992, Copeland Rutherford Fine Arts, Ltd., Santa Fe, 1992, Cheekwood Mus. Art, Nashville, 1993, Roswell (N.Mex.) Mus., 1993, Govs. Gallery, Santa Fe, 1994, Jewish Mus., San Francisco, 1995, Cloudcliff Artspace, Santa Fe, 1995, Eidolon Gallery, Santa Fe, 1995, Univ. N.Mex. Continuing Edn. Conf. Ctr., 1995, Dartmouth St. Gallery, Albuquerque, 1996; represented in permanent collections Mus. Fine Arts, Santa Fe, N.C. Ctr. Advancement Tchg., Cullowhee. Artist in Residence fellow Mass. Coun. on Arts and Humanities, Boston, 1986, Artpark, Lewiston, N.Y., 1990, Dorland Mountain Arts Colony, Temecula, Calif., 1992; Willard Van Dyke Meml. grantee N.Mex. Coun. Photography, Santa Fe, 1987. Home & Office: 1804 Tewa Rd Santa Fe NM 87505

HERZSTEIN, BARBARA See HERSHEY, BARBARA

HESLIN, CATHERINE M., information scientist; d. Thomas C. and Marie A. (Bruno) H. BA, U. Pa., 1971; MS, Drexel U., 1973; BS, St. Joseph's U., 1983. Med. libr. Phila. Gen. Hosp., 1973-74; info. specialist Rhone Pulenc Rorer, Collegeville, Pa., 1974-90, Info. Solutions, Norristown, Pa., 1991-92, Heslin Info. Svc., Norristown, 1993—. V.p. Patrician Soc. of Ctrl. Norristown, 1984—; chmn., treas. Montgomery County Women's Conf., Blue Bell, Pa., 1988—; mem. chmn. Zoning Hearing Bd., Norristown, 1993—. Mem. NAFE, Spl. Libr. Assn., Bus. and Profl. Women's Club. Home: 1819 Locust St Norristown PA 19401

HESS, DARLA BAKERSMITH, cardiologist, educator; b. Valparaiso, Fla., June 4, 1953; d. James Barry and Irma Marie (Baker) Bakersmith; m. Leonard Wayne Hess, July 20, 1988; 1 child, Ever Marie. BS, Birmingham So. Coll., 1975; MD, Tulane U., 1979. Diplomate Am. Bd. Internal Medicine, Am. Bd. Cardiovascular Disease. Commd. ensign USN, 1979, advanced through grades to lt. comdr., 1988; resident in internal medicine Portsmouth (Va.) Naval Hosp., 1979-82, cardiologist, head non-invasive cardiology, 1986-88; fellow in cardiology San Diego Naval Hosp., 1982-84; cardiologist, head med. officer in charge ICU Camp Lejeune (N.C.) Naval Hosp., 1984-85; asst. prof. medicine U. Miss. Med. Ctr., Jackson, 1988-91, asst. prof. ob/gyn., 1990-91; dir. adult echocardiography, co-dir. fetal echocardiography U. Mo., Columbia, 1991—, co-dir. Adult Cogenital Heart Disease Clinic, 1991—, asst. prof. medicine, asst. prof. ob/gyn., 1991—. Author: (with others) Obstetrics and Gynecology Clinics, 1992, Clinical Problems in Obstetrics & Gynecology, 1993, General Medical Disorders During, 1991; contbr. articles to So. Med. Jour., Ob/Gyn. Clinics N.Am., So. Med. Assn. Annual Meeting, Soc. Perinatal Obs., Jour. Reproductive Medicine; co-editor Fetal Echocardiography, 1997. Fellow Am. Coll. Cardiology; mem. Am. Heart Assn. (fellow stroke coun.), Am. Soc. Echocardiography, Am. Assn. Nuclear Cardiology, Phi Beta Kappa, Alpha Omega Alpha. Republican. Episcopalian. Home: PO Box 10200 Columbia MO 65205-4003 Office: U Mo Health Sci Ctr 1 Hospital Dr Columbia MO 65212-5276

HESS, DOLORES J., elementary education educator; b. North Charleroi, Pa., July 11, 1940; d. George and Sarah (Tatalovich) Vranges; m. Clarence K. Hess, July 29, 1961; children: Susan Elaine Nickler, Todd Isaac, Dianne Faye Dish, Scott Michael. BS, Calif. (Pa.) U., 1974, MS, 1977, reading supr. cert., 1980. Reading specialist Bethlehem Ctr. Schs., Fredericktown, Pa., 1975-78; lang. arts educator Bethlehem Ctr. Schs., Fredericktown, 1978-80, reading supr., 1980-82, reading tchr., 1982-89, lang. arts tchr., 1989—; field test participant Nat. Bd. for Profl. Tchg. Stds., Pitts., 1991-93; strategic planning mem. Bethlehem-Ctr. Schs., Fredericktown, 1991-93, presenter, 1992-93; New Zealand trip participant. Presdl. scholar Calif. (Pa.) U., 1980. Mem. AAUW, Internat. Reading Assn., Keystone State Reading Assn., Nat. Coun. Tchrs. English, Pa. State Edn. Assn. (local treas., sec., v.p., county chpt. sec.), Delta Kappa Gamma. Home: 2732 Main St Box 67 Beallsville PA 15313-0067 Office: 136 Crawford Rd Fredericktown PA 15333

HESS, EVELYN VICTORINE (MRS. MICHAEL HOWETT), medical educator; b. Dublin, Ireland, Nov. 8, 1926; came to U.S., 1960, naturalized, 1965; d. Ernest Joseph and Mary (Hawkins) H.; m. Michael Howett, Apr. 27, 1954. MB, BChir BA in Obstetrics, U. Coll., Dublin, 1949; MD, 1980. Intern West Middlesex Hosp., London, Eng., 1950; resident Clare Hall Hosp., London, 1951-53, Royal Free Hosp. and Med. Sch., London, 1954-57; rsch. fellow in epidemiology of Tb Royal Free Med. Sch., London, 1955; asst. prof. internal medicine U. Tex. Southwestern Med. Sch., 1960-64; assoc. prof. dept. medicine U. Cin. Coll. Medicine, 1964-69, McDonald prof. medicine, 1969—, dir. div. immunology, 1964-95; sr. investigator Arthritis and Rheumatism Found., 1963-68; attending physician Univ. Hosp., chief clinician Arthritis Clinic, 1965—; attending physician VA Hosp.; cons. Children's Hosp., Cin., 1967—, Jewish Hosp., Cin., 1968—; mem. various coms., mem. nat. adv. coun. NIH; mem. various coms. FDA, Cin. Bd. Health. Contbr. articles on immunology, rheumatic diseases to jours., chpts. to books. Active Nat. Pks. Assn., Smithsonian Instn., others. Recipient Arthritis Found., 1973, 78, 83, Am. Lupus Soc., 1979, Am. Acad. Family Practice, 1980, award for AIDS work State of Ohio, 1989, Spirit of Am. Women award, 1989; travel fellow Royal Free Med. Sch., Scandinavia, 1956, Empire Rheumatism Coun., 1958-59. Master ACP; fellow Am. Acad. Allergy, Royal Soc. Medicine; mem. Heberden Soc., Am. Coll. Rheumatology, Pan-Am. League Assns. for Rheumatology, Ctrl. Soc. Clin. Rsch., Am. Fedn. Clin. Rsch., Am. Assn. Immunologists, Am. Soc. Nephrology, Am. Soc. Clin. Pharmacology and Therapeutics, Transplantation Soc., Reticuloendothelial Soc., N.Y. Acad. Scis., Soc. Exptl. Biology and Medicine, Rheumatological Soc. Colombia (hon.), Rheumatological Soc. Peru (hon.), Rheumatological Soc. Italy (hon.), Clin. Immunol. Soc. Japan (hon.), Alpha Omega Alpha. Home: 2916 Grandin Rd Cincinnati OH 45208-3418 Office: U Cin Med Ctr Cincinnati OH 45267

HESS, HELEN ELIZABETH, retired secondary school educator, musician; b. Elkader, Iowa, Feb. 22, 1930; d. James Dale and Helen Louise (Wahl) Welsch; m. Roger Merle Hess, Dec. 18, 1966. BA, U. So. Miss., 1952, MA, 1955. Tchr. Natchez (Miss.) Pub. Schs., 1952-54; tchr. Bakersfield (Calif.) City Schs., 1955-89, ret., 1989; staff mem. Bakersfield Symphony Orch., 1989—. Life mem. Washington Jr. H.S. PTA; mem. Assistance League Bakersfield, 1990—; bd. dirs. Bakersfield Masterworks Chorale. Named Outstanding Classroom Tchr., Bakersfield Rotary Club, 1970. Mem. Local and State Ret. Tchrs. Assn. Republican. Presbyterian. Office: Bakersfield Symphony Orch 1401 19th St Ste 130 Bakersfield CA 93301-4400

HESS, IRMA, academic program director, translator; b. Frankfurt, Germany, Feb. 5, 1939; came to U.S., 1957, naturalized, 1960; d. Frederick and Martha (Mahlert) Alban; 1 child, Harold Alban Hess. B.A., New Sch. for Social Research, 1977; B.S., SUNY-Albany, 1976; M.A., NYU, 1979, M.P.A., 1984, advanced profl. cert., grad. of bus., 1986. Asst. to spl. psychol. testing Bd. Edn., Mt. Vernon, N.Y., 1959-65, health chmn., 1959-66; ind. practice bookkeeping, 1959-65; translator N.Y.C. cts. and agys., 1959—, interpreter, 1959-77; counselor Family Ct., Criminal Ct. Youth Div., N.Y.C., 1976-78; tchr. New Rochell Bd. Edn., 1976-78; adminstr. NYU, N.Y.C., 1978—. Vice pres. PTA, Mt. Vernon, 1968-70; chmn. Mt. Vernon Community Chest, 1971-73; sec. N.Y.C. br. ARC, 1975-77. Recipient Mayor of N.Y. accomplishment cert., 1978; scholar State of N.Y., 1976, NYU, 1978. Mem. Am. Soc. Pub. Adminstrs., U.S. Exec. Women, Am. Translators Assn., Am. Pub. Health Adminstrs., Am. Polit. Sci. Assn., N.Y. Acad. Scis., New Sch. for Social Research Alumni Assn., NYU Alumni Assn. Avocations: golf; ballet; tennis; folk music. Office: NYU D'Agostino Hall 110 W 3rd St New York NY 10012-1012

HESS, LISA DIANE, artist; b. Harrisburg, Pa., Nov. 7, 1958; d. Gunther Alfred and Kala (Capln) H.; m. Mark Stacy Hesselgrave, June 4, 1989; 1 child, Sophie Eve. BFA, Phila. Acad. Fine Arts, 1981; MFA, Yale U., 1985. Tchg. asst. Yale U., New Haven, 1984; lectr. in drawing SUNY, Purchase, 1986-87, Paire Coll. Art, Hamden, Conn., 1989; lectr. in life drawing, painting U. Conn., Storrs, 1989. One-woman shows include Erector Sq. Gallery, New Haven, 1994, Kent (Conn.) Gallery, 1995, Lukacs Gallery, Fairfield U., 1996; group exhbns. include Pa. Acad. Fine Arts, Phila., 1981, Phila. Art Alliance, 1982, Yale Sch. of Art Gallery, New Haven, 1985, Pleiades Gallery, N.Y., 1987, Munson Gallery, New Haven, 1988, Artspace, 1994, Tatistcheff & Co., N.Y.C., 1993, 94, 95. Awarded residency Millay Colony for the Arts, 1992, Seaside Inst., 1996.

HESS, MARCIA WANDA, retired educator; b. Cin., Mar. 15, 1934; d. Edward Frederick Lipka and Rose (Wirtle) Lipka Stanley; m. Edward Emanuel Grenier, Aug. 9, 1952 (div.); m. Thomas Benton Hess, Mar. 25, 1960; children: Kathleen Ann, Cynthia Jean, Thomas Allen. Grad. high sch., Cin. Instr. asst. Cin. Pub. Schs., 1970-95, also mem. staff desegregation workshop and unified K-12 reading communication arts program staff tng. com.; ret., 1995. Contbr. tchr.-instr. asst. handbook, instr. asst. tng. film. Mem. Winton Place Vets of World War II Women's Aux. (pres. 1982-84, bd. dirs. 1982-86, 89-91). Republican. Roman Catholic. Home: 765 Derby Ave Cincinnati OH 45232-1836

HESS, MARGARET JOHNSTON, religious writer, educator; b. Ames, Iowa, Feb. 22, 1915; d. Howard Wright and Jane Edith (Stevenson) Johnston; B.A., Coe Coll., 1937; m. Bartlett Leonard Hess, July 31, 1937; children—Daniel, Deborah, John, Janet. Bible tchr. Cmty. Bible Classes Ward Presbyn. Ch., Livonia, Mich., 1959-96, Christ Ch. Cranbrook (Episcopalian), Bloomfield Hills, Mich., 1980-93, Lutheran Ch. of the Redeemer, Birmingham, Mich., 1993—. Co-author: (with B.L. Hess) How to Have a Giving Church, 1974, The Power of a Loving Church, 1977, How Does Your Marriage Grow?, 1983, Never Say Old, 1984; author: Love Knows No Barriers, 1979; Esther: Courage in Crisis, 1980; Unconventional Women, 1981, The Triumph of Love, 1987; contbr. articles to religious jours. Home: 16845 Riverside Dr Livonia MI 48154-2428

HESS, MARILYN ANN, state legislator; m. Dennis J. Hess; children: Christine, Craig. AA, NYU, 1977; BBA in Mgmt. cum laude, Pace U., 1980. Assoc. Merrill Lynch, N.Y.C., 1972-77; home improvement contractor Conn., 1982-90; mem. Conn. Ho. of Reps., 1993—; state rep. 150th Assembly Dist., Conn., 1993—; chmn. Conn. Internat. Trade Coun., 1995—; mem. Rep. Roundtable of Greenwich, 1993—, Amb. and Roundtable, 1994—, Conn. Reps. for Choice, 1992—; dir. Rep. Town Com., 1989—. Organizer pack 516 Boy Scouts Am., N.Y.C., 1976; fund raiser, chmn. Lewisboro Neighbor's Club, South Salem, 1979; sec. Ridgefield HIst. Dist. Commn., 1984-85, Greenwich Hist. Dist. Commn., 1988-90, Friends of the Byram Shubert Libr. Bd., 1989-93; del. Parents Together, 1980; underwriting com. Bruce Mus. Ball, 1990-91; alternate Greenwich Planning and Zoning Commn., 1990-93; founding trustee Byram Scholarship fund, 1991—. Named Mother of Yr. Town and Village Newspaper, 1974. Home: 61

Byram Shore Rd Greenwich CT 06830-6906 Office: Ho of Reps State Capitol Hartford CT 06106

HESS, SUZANNE HARRIET, newspaper administrator, photographer, editor; b. Steubenville, Ohio, Nov. 8, 1941; d. Roswell J. and Ruth R. (Feuer) Caulk; m. Richard Robert Hess, Aug. 28, 1960 (div. Oct. 1989); children: Richard, Rebecca. Student, Lane C.C., 1961. Cert. radiologist, Oreg. Med. asst. Dr. John Burket, Medford, Oreg., 1970-72; sec. receptionist Dr. Paul Saarinen, Eugene, Oreg., 1982-84; office mgr. Europcar Internat., Sicily, Italy, 1989-91; visitor svcs. mgr. Conv. and Visitors Assn. Lane County, Eugene, Oreg., 1991-94; office mgr. Nat. Masters News, Eugene, Oreg., 1994—; bd. dirs. U.S. Amateur Track and Field, Oreg., Photographer Nat. Masters News, 1994—. Sec. Oreg. Track Club, Eugene, 1993-96, com. person for preservation of Prefontaine Rock, 1995; protester Preservation of Old Growth Timber, Eugene, 1994. Recipient Appreciation award Oreg. Track Club, 1995, 2 Nat. Championship awards U.S. Amateur Track and Field, 1995, Silver medal 16# and 25# weight throw U.S. Amateur Track and Field Nat. Masters Indoor Championship, 1995, Bronze medal discus and hammer U.S. Amateur Track and Field Nat. Masters Outdoor Championships, 1995, Gold medal 16# weight throw and 25# superweight throw U.S. Amateur Track and Field Nat. Masters Weight and Superweight Championships, 1995, Gold medal U.S. Amateur Track and Field Nat. Masters Weight Pentathlon, 1995; named All Am. U.S. Amateur Track and Field, 1995. Democrat. Office: Nat Masters News 1675 Willamette St Eugene OR 97401

HESSE, CAROLYN SUE, lawyer; b. Belleville, Ill., Jan. 12, 1949; d. Ralph H. Hesse and Marilyn J. (Midgley) Hesse Dierkes; m. William H. Hallenbeck. B.S., U. Ill., 1971, M.S., U. Ill.-Chgo., 1977; J.D., DePaul U., 1983. Bar: Ill. 1983, U.S. Dist. Ct. (no. dist.) Ill. 1983. Research assoc. U. Ill., Chgo., 1974-77; tech. adviser Ill. Pollution Control Bd., Chgo., 1977-80; environ. scientist U.S. EPA, Chgo., 1980-84; assoc. Pretzel & Stouffer, Chartered, Chgo., 1984-87, Coffield Ungaretti Harris & Assocs., Chgo., 1987-88, ptnr. McDermott, Will & Emery, 1988—. Contbr. articles on environ. sci. to profl. jours. Mem. ABA, Chgo. Bar Assn. Office: McDermott Will & Emery 227 W Monroe St Chicago IL 60606-5016

HESSE, MARIAN K., musician; b. Denver, June 5, 1960; d. Eugene Joseph Hesse and Theresa Donalea Davis; m Bruce Christopher Barrie, May 12, 1991. BMus, U. No. Colo., 1982; MMus, Yale U., 1985. Asst. prin. horn player New Haven Symphony, 1982-86; horn player, pres. Chestnut Brass Co., Phila., 1986—; affiliate mem. faculty Temple U., Phila., 1990-96; 2nd horn player Peter Britt Festival, Jacksonville, Oreg., 1990—. Performer: (recs.) Listen to the Mockingbird, 1991, For God & Country, 1992, Tippecanoe & Tyler, Too, 1992, Opening Night, 1993, A Renasisance Noel, 1995. Mem. Am. Fedn. Musicians, Internat. Horn Soc. Office: Chestnut Brass Co PO Box 30165 Philadelphia PA 19103

HESSE, MARTHA O., natural gas company executive; b. Hattiesburg, Miss., Aug. 14, 1942; d. John William and Geraldine Elaine (Ossian) H. B.S., U. Iowa, 1964; postgrad., Northwestern U., 1972-76; M.B.A., U. Chgo., 1979. Research analyst Blue Shield, 1964-66; dir. div. data mgmt. Am. Hosp. Assn., 1966-69; dir., chief operating officer SEI Info. Tech., Chgo., 1969-80; assoc. dep. sec. Dept. of Commerce, Washington, 1981-82; exec. dir. Pres.' Task Force on Mgmt. Reform, 1982; asst. sec. mgmt. and adminstrn. Dept. of Energy, Washington, 1982-86; chmn. FERC, Washington, 1986-89; sr. v.p. 1st Chgo. Corp., 1990; now pres. Hesse Gas, Houston; bd. dirs. Am. Nat. Resources Pipeline Co. subs. Coastal Corp., Pinnacle West Capital Corp., Ariz. Pub. Svc. Co., Sithe Energies, Inc., Mut. Trust Life, Laidlaw. Office: # 129 6524 San Felipe Houston TX 77057

HESSELBEIN, FRANCES RICHARDS, foundation executive, consultant, editor; b. South Fork, Pa.; d. Burgess Harmon and Anne Luke (Wicks) Richards; widowed, 1978; 1 child, John Richards. DHL (hon.), Buena Vista Coll., 1987, Juniata Coll., 1990, Hood Coll., 1991; D Mgmt. (hon.), GM Inst., 1990; LLD (hon.), Wilson Coll., 1991; LHD (hon.), Marymount-Tarrytown Coll., 1993; DHL (hon.), Boston Coll., 1994, U. Nebr., Kearney, 1994, Lafayette Coll., 1995, Carroll Coll., 1996, Fairleigh Dickinson U., 1996, Muhlenburg Coll., 1996. CEO Talus Rock Girl Scout Coun., Johnstown, 1970-74, Penn Laurel Girl Scout Coun., York, Pa., 1974-76, Girl Scouts U.S., N.Y.C., 1976-90; pres., CEO Peter F. Drucker Found. Nonprofit Mgmt., N.Y.C., 1990—; bd. dirs. Mut. of Am. Ins. Co., N.Y.C.; mem. nat. bd. visitors Peter F. Drucker Grad. Mgmt. Ctr., Claremont (Calif.) Grad. Sch., 1987—; chmn. bd. govs. Josephson Ethics Inst.; mem. adv. com. to bd. dirs. N.Y. Stock Exch., 1988-91; bd. govs. Ctr. for Creative Leadership, Greensboro, N.C., 1992—; mem. adv. bd. Harvard Buus. Sch.'s Initiative on Social Enterprisem, Harvard's Kennedy Sch. Govt. Nonprofit Policy and Leadership Program. Mem. edit. adv. bd. Nonprofit Mgmt. and Leadership; editor-in-chief Leader to Leader; co-editor The Leader of the Future, Drucker Found. Future Series. Dir. Youth for Understanding, Washington, 1984—; trustee Juniata Coll., Huntingdon, Pa., 1988—, Allentown (Pa.) Coll., 1988—; mem. Pres.'s Adv. Com. on Points of Light Initiative Found., 1989; bd. dirs. Nat. Exec. Svc. Corps., N.Y., Commn. on Nat. and Cmty. Svc., 1991-94; mem. adv. bd. The Leadership Inst., U. So. Calif., 1991, Harvard Bus. Sch.'s Initiative on Social Enterprise, Harvard U.'s John F. Kennedy Sch. Govt. Nonprofit Policy and Leadership Program; mem. Kellogg Found. Nat. Task Group on African-Am. Men and Boys. Recipient Outstanding Achievement award Inter-Svc. Club Coun., Johnstown, 1976, Entrepreneurial Woman award Women Bus. Owners of N.Y., 1984, Nat. Leadership award United Way of Am., Washington, 1985, Disting. Cmty. Svc. award Mut. of Am. Ins. Co., 1985, Dir.'s Choice-award Nat. Women's Econ. Alliance, 1989, Pa. Soc. Disting. Citizen award, 1991, Wilbur M. McFeeley award Internat. Mgmt. Coun. YMCA, 1993; inducted into the Bus. Hall of Fame, Johnstown, 1995; named Outstanding Exec., Savvy Mag., 1985; on cover BusinessWeek, 1990; featured in Chief Exec. mag., 1995, Fortune, 1995, 96. Mem. Sky Club, Pa. Soc. Club, Marco Polo Club. Office: Peter F Drucker Found Nonprofit Mgmt 320 Park Ave 3d Fl New York NY 10022

HESSEN, MARGARET TREXLER, internist, educator; b. Allentown, Pa., Jan. 6, 1956; d. John Peter and Virginia Ruth (Hamilton) Trexler; m. Scott Edward Hessen, Aug. 15, 1981; 1 child, Scott Trexler, David Hamilton. AB, Mt. Holyoke Coll., 1978; MD, Jefferson Med. Coll., 1982. Diplomate Am. Bd. Internal Medicine. Resident in internal medicine Laukenau Hosp., 1982-85; fellow in infectious diseases Med. Coll. Pa., Phila., 1985-87, instr. medicine, 1987-88, asst. prof., 1988-89, clin. asst. prof., 1989—; pvt. practice Drexel Hill, Pa., 1989—; dir. med. edn. Jefferson Park Hosp., Phila., 1987-89. Contbr. articles to Am. Jour. Medicine, Jour. Infectious Disease, Antimicrobial Agts. and Chemotherapy, also chpt. to books. Grantee Am. Fedn. for Aging Rsch., 1988, Allegheny Singer Rsch. Inst., 1988; Mary Dewitt Petit fellow Alumni Assn. Med. Coll. Pa., 1988. Fellow ACP; mem. AMA, AAAS, Infectious Disease Soc. Am., Am. Soc. for Microbiology, Alpha Omega Alpha.

HESSER, HELEN ELIZABETH, elementary and secondary school educator; b. Gladerwater, Tex., Dec. 12, 1935; d. Milton Dysert and Katie Matilda (Durham) Brewer; m. Garland Wayne Hesser, Jan. 1, 1956 (dec. Apr. 1987); children: Sheila Carol, Sheena Sue (dec.), Marvin Ray. AA, Tyler (Tex.) Jr. Coll., 1977; BS in Edn., U. Tex., Tyler, 1979; MEd, Stephen F. Austin State U., Nacogdoches, Tex., 1985. Cert. tchr., Tex., S.D., Alaska. Kindergarten tchr. Tyler Pub. Schs., 1980-86; spl. edn. tchr. Brownsboro (Tex.) Pub. Schs., 1986-91, Little Wound Sch., Pine Ridge Reservation, Kyle, S.D., 1991-95; tchr. mid. sch. history and lang. arts, h.s. lang. arts Heritage Christian Sch., Cadillac, Mich., 1995-96; naturalist Custer State Park, S.D., 1990; selected participant The Mammoth Trek, Chadron (Nebr.) State Coll., 1991, 92. Sunday sch. tchr. Sharps Corner Bapt. Ch., Porcupine, S.D., 1992-95. Mem. Coun. for Exceptional Children, Internat. Reading Assn., S.D. Indian Edn. Assn., Alpha Delta Kappa. Home: 440 Allen St Cadillac MI 49601

HESSION, EILEEN MELIA, educational publishing company representative; b. Rockaway, N.Y., July 22, 1949; d. John G. and Marguerite (Rourke) Melia; 1 child, Amanda. BS, Plattsburgh U., 1971; MS, Hofstra U., 1975, Tchr. Cert., 1989. Cert. elem. tchr., elem. adminstr. Freelance writer, 1977—; tchr. New Hyde Park (N.Y.) Schs., 1971-83; rep. Harcourt Brace jovanovich, Orlando, Fla., 1983-88, Silver Burdett Ginn, Parsippany, N.J., 1988—; ednl. cons. Contbr. articles to mags. Mem. ASCD. Office: Silver Burdett Ginn Simon & Schuster Edn Group 516 W Beech St Long Beach NY 11561-3010

HESSON, DONNA D., librarian; b. Oakland, Calif., Oct. 11, 1956; d. Wallace Eugene and Harriett Rose (Vascou) Derryberry; m. Thomas Gwinn Hesson, June 22, 1985; 1 child, Brian Christopher. BA in History and Librarianship, Fla. State U., 1978, MLS, 1979. Reference libr. Balt. County Pub. Libr., Catonsville, Md., 1979-80; nursing sch. libr. Md. Gen. Hosp., Balt., 1981-85; libr., cataloger Welch Med. Libr. Johns Hopkins U., Balt., 1985-86, reference libr., 1989-91; reference libr. Lilienfeld Meml. Libr. Johns Hopkins Sch. Pub. Health, Balt., 1986-88; asst. dir. Lilienfeld Meml. Lib Johns Hopkins Sch. Pub. Health, Balt., 1993—; info. specialist DAKKRO Corp., Edgewood, Md., 1991-93. Mem. Md. Assn. Health Sci. Librs., Med. Libr. Assn. (mid-Atlantic chpt.), Sigma Alpha Iota, Zeta Tau Alpha. Office: Johns Hopkins Sch Pub Healt Abraham M Lilienfeld Meml 624 N Broadway 9th Fl Baltimore MD 21205-1901

HESTENES, ROBERTA RAE, college president, minister; b. Huntington Park, Calif., Aug. 5, 1939; d. Robert James and Besse Rae (Nipp) Louis; m. John D. Hestenes; children: Joan Hestenes Lehnen, Eric Magnus, Stephen Eastvold. BA, U. Calif., Santa Barbara; M in Divinity, Fuller Theol. Sem., 1979, D.Min., 1983; DHL (hon.), Houghton Coll.; DD (hon.), Seattle Pacific U. Ordained to ministry Presbyn. Ch., 1979. Dir. adult edn. and small group ministries United Presbyn. Ch., Seattle, 1967-74; assoc. in ministry LaCanada (Calif.) Presbyn. Ch., 1974-84; assoc. prof., dir. Christian Formation and Discipleship program Fuller Theol. Sem., Pasadena, Calif., 1975-87; bd. dirs., chmn. strategic planning com. World Vision U.S., 1980—; bd. dirs. World Vision Internat., 1982—, chmn. bd. dirs., 1985—; pres., prof. Christian spirituality Eastern Coll., St. Davids, Pa., 1987—; assoc. Wayne (Pa.) Presbyn. Ch., 1991—; cons. numerous Presbyn. orgns.; minister Kenya, Australia, South Africa, Singapore, Hong Kong, South Korea, Philippines, Cen. am. Author: (books) Using the Bible in Groups, 1985, 92, Discovering II Corinthians/Galatians, 1986, Turning Committees Into Communities, 1991, Mastering Teaching, 1991, Growing The Church Through Small Groups, 1993; author: (with Earl Palmer) Mastering the Art of Teaching, 1992; (taped courses) Building Christian Communicty Through Small Groups, 1985, Helping Christians Grow: Adult Formation and Discipleship in the Local Church, 1987; co-editor: Women and the Ministries of Christ, 1979; contbr. articles to profl. jours.;. Fellow Case Methods Inst.; mem. Am. Acad. Religion, Religious Edn. Assn., Nat. Assn. of Profs. of Christian Edn. Office: Ea Coll Office of the President 10 Fairview Dr Saint Davids PA 19087-3696*

HESTER, KARA-LYN ANNETTE, software engineer; b. Phila., Feb. 27, 1963; d. Javis Leon and O. Elizabeth (Seals) W. BS in Computer Sci., Drexel U., 1986, MS in Computer Sci., 1992. Intake worker Wheel's Inc., Phila., 1983; staff cons. computer ctr. Drexel U., Phila., 1984, sr. cons., 1984-85; programmer E. I. duPont, Phila., 1985; sr. programmer, computer scientist RMS Techs., Inc., Marlton, N.J., 1986-94, tech. mgr. Geophys. Scis. Lab.; sys. engr. SHL Systemhouse, Inc., Robbinsville, N.J., 1994—. Author manual: AFCAD Revisited, 1984; co-designer, implementor software. Recipient Letter of Commendation, U.S. Naval Acad., 1990. Mem. IEEE, Assn. for Computing Machinery. Home: 204 Centaurian Dr Berlin NJ 08009 Office: SHL Systemhouse Inc Ste 560 500 Horizon Dr Robbinsville NJ 08691

HESTER, LINDA HUNT, university dean, counselor; b. Winston-Salem, N.C., June 16, 1938; d. Hanselle Lindsay and Jennie Sarepta (Hunt) H. BS with honors, U. Wis., 1960, MS, 1964; PhD, Mich. State U., 1971. Lic. ednl. counselor, Wis. Instr. health and phys. edn. for women U. Tex., Austin, 1960-62; asst. dean women U. Ill., Urbana, 1964-66; dean of women, asst. prof. sociology and phys. edn. Tex. Woman's U., Denton, 1971-73; rsch. assoc. bur. higher edn. Mich. Dept. Edn., Lansing, 1969-70; counselor Dallas Challenge and Dallas Ind. Sch. Dist., 1989-90. Bd. dirs. Dallas Opera, 1986—; Stradivarious mem. Dallas Symphony, 1991—; assoc. mem. Dallas Mus. Art, 1991—. Fellow coll. edn. Mich. State U., 1968. Mem. Am. Counseling Assn., Am. Coll. Pers. Assn., Nat. Assn. Women in Edn., Brookhaven Country Club, Delta Kappa Gamma, Alpha Lambda Delta. Republican. Presbyterian. Home and Office: 7606 Wellcrest Dr Dallas TX 75230-4857

HESTER, NANCY ELIZABETH, county government official; b. Miami, Fla., Jan. 20, 1950; d. George Temple and Lorraine Patricia (Cluney) Hester; BA, Bucknell U., 1972; MIA, Columbia U., 1974; MBA, Fla. Internat. U., 1979. Treasury rep. Westinghouse Elec. Co., N.Y.C., 1974-76; adminstrv. officer serving in bldg. and zoning, gen. services, and corrections and rehab. depts. Metro Dade County, Fla., 1979—, bur. comdr. corrections and rehab. dept., 1990—; adj. prof. Fla. Internat. U., Miami, 1980-83. Bd. dirs. YWCA Greater Miami, 1988-92, LWV Dade County, 1993—, pres. bd. dirs., pres. bd. trustees edn. fund, 1994-96; mem. adv. bd. SafeSpace, 1995—. Mem. Zool. Soc. Fla., Miami City Ballet Guild.

HETFELD, ELIZABETH ANN, industrial engineer; b. Oshkosh, Wis., Feb. 28, 1954; d. Frederick Damler and Connie Steiger Dempsey; children: Hunter H. Student, U. Autonima, Guadalajara, Mex., 1974; BA in Architecture, U. N.Mex., 1979. Project mgr. drafting Hutchinson, Brown & Ptnrs., Architects, Albuquerque, 1978-80; engr. facilities constrn. mgmt. divsn. Albuquerque Ops. Office, 1982-90, engr. quality engrng. divsn., 1982-90, engr. budget and resources mgmt., 1982-90, site mgr. uranium mill tailings remedial action project, 1982-90; sect. chief indsl. tech. Bonneville Power Adminstrn., Portland, Oreg., 1990—; mem. employee support sounding bd. Bonneville Power Adminstrn., Portland, 1990-91, mem. women's resource group, 1990-93. Mem. City Club Portland, 1990-91.

HEUER, LAURA MARIE, auditor; b. Racine, Wis., June 1, 1966; d. Donald George and Kay Edith (Smigun) Hiller; m. J. Joseph, June 23, 1990; 1 child, Brent Thomas. BBA in Acctg., U. Wis., 1988. CPA. Audit supr. Henshue, Hall & Assocs., Madison, Wis., 1988-92, Valley Bancorp., Appleton, Wis., 1992-94; gen. auditor Old Nat. Bancorp., Evansville, Ind., 1994—. Bd. dirs. Chrysalis, Evansville, 1996—; mem. Jr. Svc. League, Madison, 1991-92. Mem. AICPA, Wis. Soc. CPAs. Office: Old Nat Bancorp PO Box 718 420 Main St Evansville IN 47705

HEUER, MARGARET B., retired microcomputer laboratory coordinator; b. Juneau, Alaska, Sept. 12, 1935; d. William George and Flora (Rusk) Allen; m. Joseph Louis Heuer; children: Leilani, Joseph (dec.), Daniel, Suzanne, Karen, Mark, Jerina. AA, San Bernardino Valley Coll., 1980. Cert. data processing, computer repair and maintenance, microcomputer support specialist. Coord. microcomputers lab. Oakton Community Coll., Skokie, Ill., 1981-93; ret., 1993.

HEUMANN, JUDITH, federal agency administrator; m. Jorge Pineda. BA Speech and Theatre, Long Island U., 1969; MPH, U. Calif., Berkeley, 1975. Spl. edn. and 2d grade tchr. N.Y.C. Pub. Schs., 1970-73; legis. asst. to chair Senate Com. Labor and Pub. Welfare, Washington, 1974; sr. dep. dir. Ctr. Independent Living, Berkeley, 1975-82; spl. asst. to exec. dir. State Dept. Rehab., Sacramento, Calif., 1982-83; v.p., co-founder, dir. Rsch. Tng. Ctr. Pub. Policy in Independent Living, Berkeley, Calif., 1983-93; co-founder World Inst. Disability, Berkeley, Calif.; U.S. asst. sec. U.S. Dept. Edn., Washington, 1993—; also chair, vice chair Archtl. & Transp. Barriers Compliance Bd., Washington. Office: Dept of Edn Spl Edn & Rehabilitative Svcs 330 C St SW Ste 3006 Washington DC 20202-2500 also: Archtl & Transp Barriers Compliance Bd 1331 F St NW Ste 100 Washington DC 20004-1111*

HEUPEL, CYNTHIA LOU, principal; b. Fargo, N.D., Apr. 7, 1955; d. Thomas Herald and Gladys Bernice (Weber) Kelly; m. Kenneth Wayne Heupel, June 26, 1976; children: Joshua Kenneth, Andrea Lou. BS, No. State U., 1979, M of Secondary Edn., 1984. Coord., tchr. gifted edn. Aberdeen (S.D.) Pub. Schs., 1979-86; asst. prin. Ctrl. High Sch., Aberdeen, 1987-90, prin., 1990—. Mem. ASCD, NAt. Assn. Secondary Sch. Prins., Sch. Adminstrs. S.D., S.D. Assn. Secondary Sch. Prins., Phi Delta Kappa, Delta Kappa Gamma. Office: Ctrl HS 225 3d Ave SE Aberdeen SD 57401

HEUSCHELE, SHARON JO, university program director; b. Toledo, Ohio, July 12, 1936; 1 child, Brent Philip. BE, U. Toledo, 1965, MEd, 1969, PhD, 1973. Cert. elem., secondary tchr., Ohio. Asst. prof. Ohio Dominican Coll., Columbus, 1970-73, St. Cloud U., Minn., 1973-74; assoc. prof. Ohio State U., Columbus, 1974-79; dean instl. planning Lourdes Coll., Sylvania, Ohio, 1980—, chmn. sociology, econs. and polit. sci. dept.; cons. U. Hawaii, 1979, others. Bd. dirs. Trinity-St. Paul Inner City Program, Toledo, 1968; cons. Ohio Civil Rights Commn., 1972; active Dem. campaigns. U. Toledo fellow, 1967-69; recipient Citation, U. Toledo, 1979, Journalistic Excellence award Columbia Press Assn., N.Y.C., 1954. Mem. Am. Council Edn., Ohio Conf. Coll. and Univ. Planning, Soc. Coll. and Univ. Planning (com. 1984-85), Phi Theta Kappa, Phi Kappa Phi (Citation 1973), U. Toledo Alumni Assn., U.S. Coast Guard Aux. Lutheran. Avocations: fossil and mineral collecting, poetry, novel writing, horseback riding. Office: Lourdes Coll 6832 Convent Blvd Sylvania OH 43560-2853

HEUSEL, BARBARA STEVENS, English scholar and educator; b. Louisville, Jan. 12, 1935; d. Jay T. and Ruth L. (Wiesman) Stevens; children: Heidi Heusel Freeman, Lisa Gillig, Gretchen Heusel. BA, Heidelberg Coll., 1957; MA, U. Louisville, 1967; PhD, U. S.C., 1983. Instr. dept. of English U. Louisville, 1965-68, Furman U., Greenville, S.C., 1968-84; vis. asst. prof. English Wake Forest U., Winston-Salem, N.C., 1985-88; lectr. in English U. N.C., Chapel Hill, 1984-85, 88-89; assoc. prof. English N.W. Mo. State U., Maryville, 1990—; dir. of curriculum The ArtSchool, Carrboro, N.C., 1988-90; cons. PENULTIMA, Chapel Hill, N.C., 1988—; lectr. in field. Author: Patterned Aimlessness: Iris Murdoch's Novels of the 1970s and 1980s, 1995; contbr. articles to profl. jours. Mellon grant Furman U., 1979-80, grant Nat. Endowment for the Humanities, 1989. Mem. AAUW, Iris Murdoch Soc. (founder, sec.-treas. 1986-93, pres. 1993—), MLA, James Joyce Soc., South Atlantic MLA. Office: Dept of English NW Mo State U Maryville MO 64468

HEWETT, JOAN, writer; b. N.Y.C., May 3, 1990; d. Jack Leeds and Edith Rolland; m. Richard Ridgely Hewitt, July 1960; children: Angela Lee, Christopher R. Student, U. Chgo. Author: The Mouse and the Elephant, 1977, Watching Them Grow, Inside a Zoo Nursery, 1979 (Notable Children's Book citation ALA), Fly Away Free1980, When You Fight the Tiger, 1984, Motorcycle on Patrol: The Story of a Highway Officer, 1986 (So. Calif. Coun. on Literature for Children and Young People award for notable achievement in photojournalism), On Camera: The Story of a Child Actor, 1987, Getting Elected: The Diary of a Campaign, 1989, Laura Loves Horses, 1990, Hector Lives in the United States Now, 1990, (Notable Children's Trade Book in the Social Studies citation and Carter G. Woodson Book award for outstanding merit - elem., Nat. Coun. for the Social Studies, 1991), Public Defender: Lawyer for the People, 1991, (Notable Children's Trade Book in the Social Studies citation, and ALA's Recommended Book for Reluctant Readers citation, 1992) Tiger, Tiger, Growing Up, 1990, Tunnels, Tracks and Trains: Building a Subway, 1995, Rosalie, 1987 (Notable Children's Trade Book in the Social Studies citation, 1988). Mem. Soc. of Children's Book Writers and Illustrators. Home: 5725 Buena Vista Terr Los Angeles CA 90042*

HEWITT, FRANKIE LEA, theater producer; b. Roger Mills Cty, Okla., June 17, 1931; d. Frank David and Mary Lou (Wood) Teague; m. Alonzo Robert Childers, Dec. 10, 1951 (div. 1955); m. Don S. Hewitt, June 8, 1963 (div. 1974); children: Jilian, Lisa. Grad., Napa (Calif.) High Sch., 1949. Women's editor Napa Daily Register, 1949-51; asst. advt. dir. Rose Marie Reid Swim Suits, L.A., 1951-52; writer Calif. Inst. Social Welfare, L.A., 1954-55; writer, legis. aide Nat. Inst. Social Welfare, Washington, 1956-58; staff dir. U.S. Senate Subcom. to Investigate Juvenile Deliquency, Washington, 1959-61; pub. affairs advisor U.S. Mission to UN, N.Y.C., 1961-63; founder, producing dir. Ford's Theatre Soc., Washington, 1967—. Recipient Congl. Arts Caucus award, 1993; named Washingtonian of Yr., Washingtonian Mag., 1978, Woman of Yr., Women's Equity Action League, 1981, YWCA, 1986. Office: Ford's Theatre 511 10th St NW Washington DC 20004-1402

HEWITT, VIVIAN ANN DAVIDSON (MRS. JOHN HAMILTON HEWITT, JR.), librarian; b. New Castle, Pa.; d. Arthur Robert and Lela Luvada (Mauney) Davidson; m. John Hamilton Hewitt, Jr., Dec. 26, 1949; 1 son, John Hamilton III. AB with honors, Geneva Coll., 1943, LHD, 1978; BSLS, Carnegie Mellon U., 1944; postgrad., U. Pitts., 1947-48. Sr. asst. libr. Carnegie Libr., Pitts., 1944-49; instr., libr. Sch. Libr. Sci. Atlanta U., Atlanta U., 1949-52; with Readers Reference Svc., Crowell-Collier Pub. Co., N.Y.C., 1953-55; libr. Rockefeller Found., N.Y.C., 1955-63; librarian Carnegie Endowment Internat. Peace, N.Y.C., 1963-83; librarian Mexican Agrl. Program, Rockefeller Found., summer 1958; dir. libr. and info. svcs. Katherine Gibbs Sch., N.Y.C., 1984-86; reference asst. Coun. on Fgn. Rels., 1986-89; lectr. spl. librarianship at grad. schs. of L.S. and info. throughout U.S. and Can., 1968—; condr. profl. seminars Am. Mgmt. Assn., 1968-69, UN Inst. Tng. and Rsch., 1973, 74, Grad. Sci. Libr. and Info. Sci., Rutgers U., 1986; SLA rep. to Internat. Fedn. Libr. Assns., 1970-73, 73-75, 75-77; mem. nat. adv. com. Ctr. for the Book, Libr. of Congress, 1979-84; mem. adv. bd. Who's Who in Black Am., 1990—. Contbr. chpt. to: The Black Librarian in America, 1970, What Black Librarians Are Saying, 1972, New Dimensions for Academic Library Service, 1975, A Century of Service, 1976, Handbook of Black Librarianship, 1977, The Black Librarian in America Revisited, 1994. Bd. dirs. Graham-Windham, 1967, sec., 1980-87; bd. dirs. Laymen's Club, Cathedral Ch. of St.John the Divine, 1975—, sec., 1986-93. Recipient Outstanding Cmty. Svc. awards United Fund N.Y., 1965-77, Disting. Alumna award U. Pitts.-Carnegie Libr. Schs. Alumni Assn., 1978, Merit award Carnegie Mellon U. Alumni Assn., 1979. Mem. ALA (Disting. Svc. to Librarianship award Black Caucus 1978, Leadership in Profession award Black Caucus 1992), Spl. Librs. Assn. (pres. N.Y. chpt. 1970-71, nat. pres. 1978-79, named to Hall of Fame, condr. seminar 1969, rep. to Pacem In Terris Convocation 1965, rep. to White House Conf. Internat. Cooperation Yr. 1965), Jack and Jill Am., Inc. (ea. regional dir. 1967-69), Alpha Kappa Alpha. Democrat. Episcopalian. Home: 862 W End Ave New York NY 10025-4959

HEWLETT, GLORIA LOUISE, rancher, retired educator, civic volunteer; b. Clifton, Tex., Nov. 28, 1930; d. Dock Simpson and Leona Martha (Fricke) Martin; m. Robert Eckhart Hewlett, Jr., Sept. 3, 1950; children: Robert Eckhart, III, Jeffrey Martin Hewlett. BA, U. Corpus Christi, 1962; MEd, Northwestern State U., Natchitoches, La., 1974; DEd, East Tex. State U., 1988. Tchr. Terrebonne Parish Sch. Dist., Houma, La., 1962-69, Natchitoches (La.) Parish Sch. Dist., 1970-76, Mesquite (Tex.) Sch. Dist., 1977-91; ret., 1991. Author: A Descriptive Study of Textbook Preparation Programs and State Level Textbook Adoption in Texas, 1988. Mem. sr. affairs commn. Dallas City Coun., 1995-97; pres. Eta Zeta chpt. of Delta Kappa Gamma, Dallas, 1992-94. Named Gift to the Ednl. Found. of AAUW, 1992-93, 94-95. Mem. AAUW (pres. Dallas br. 1991-93, v.p. Tex. 1994-96), The Women's Found., Dallas Hist. Soc., Am. Legion Aux. Presbyterian. Home and Office: 9402 Mill Hollow Dallas TX 75243-6338

HEWSON, CAROLYN ANNE SECHREST, counselor, educator, psychotherapist; b. Greenville, S.C., July 31, 1927; d. Ernest Cornell and Carrie (Pollard) Sechrest; m. Donald Frederick Hewson, Aug. 23, 1958; children: Anne Lila, Kim Elizabeth. BA, Furman U., 1948; MA, Columbia U., 1953, EdD, 1955. English tchr. St. George H.S., S.C., 1949-50; English tchr., counselor Parker H.S., Greenville, 1950-52; dir. guidance White Plains (N.Y.) H.S., 1955-58; sch. psychologist, guidance cons. Pelham (N.Y.) Schs., 1958-60; faculty Tchrs. Coll., Columbia U., N.Y.C., 1958-64; prof. edn. C.W. Post Campus, L.I. U., Brookville, N.Y., 1965—; chair dept. counseling C.W. Post Campus, L.I. U., Brookville, 1968-92; pvt. practice psychotherapy, Northport, N.Y.; bd. mem., publicity chair Pederson-Krag Ctr., Tng. Ctr., 1986—. Author: New Dimensions in Counseling, 1958, (with others) Interns in Guidance, 1960. Named Woman of Yr., N.Y. Pers. and Guidance Assn., 1975. Mem. ACA, Am. Sch. Counselors Assn., Assn. Counselor Educators and Suprs., Am. Mental Health Counselors Assn. Office: CW Post Campus Northern Blvd Brookville NY 11548

HEWSON, MARY MCDONALD, civic volunteer; b. Larned, Kans., Nov. 5, 1922; d. William Michael and Bernice Ulata (Gregory) McDonald; m. Kenneth Dean Hewson, June 21, 1946; children: Rebecca Hewson Lewis, Roberta Hewson Grogan, Margaret Hewson Smith. BS in Edn. cum laude,

Kans. State U., 1948, BS in Psychology, 1948. Cert. secondary edn. tchr. Freshman counselor Kans. State U., 1948-49; substitute tchr. Larned Unified Sch. Dist., 1958—, tchr. gifted program, 1988; at home tutor, 1938—; spkr. Nat. Fraternity Blue Key Kans. State U., 1995—. Trustee Kans. State U. Found., Manhattan, 1980—; mem. Kans. Farmers Union, McPherson, 1982—, Help Eliminate Abuse Locally, Larned, 1982—, Mental Helath Assn., Larned, 1982—; spokesperson 8 counties Pawnee County Health Resource, Kans., 1992—, Ctrl. Kans. Environ. Resource Planning Group, 1992—; chmn. Swims for Kids; mem. Pawnee County Fair Growth Com., 1995; vol. gifted tchr. aide, 1996—. Recipient Medallion award Kans. State U., 1986, Nat. Vol. of Yr. award Coun. for Advancement and Support of Edn., 1983; named to Nat. Women's Hall of Fame, 1996. Mem. AAUW (charter), DAR (officer), Kans. Press Women (life mem., patron ednl. support 1988), YMCA (bd. dirs.), Philanthropic Ednl. Orng., Kans. State U. Alumni Assn. (strategic planning com., student rels. com.), Phi Alpha Mu. Home: PO Box 102 Larned KS 67550-0102

HEXT, KATHLEEN FLORENCE, internal audit college adminstrator; b. Bellingham, Wash., Oct. 7, 1941; d. Benjamin Byron and Sarah Debell (Youngquist) Gross.; m. George Ronald Hext, June 13, 1964 (div. 1972); m. William H. Lewis, Nov. 14, 1992. BA magna cum laude, Lewis & Clark Coll., Portland, Oreg., 1963; MA, Stanford U., 1964; MBA, UCLA, 1979. CPA; chartered bank auditor; cert. info. systems auditor. Chief exec. officer Internat. Lang. Ctr., Rome, 1970-77; sr. auditor Peat, Marwick, Mitchell & Co., L.A., 1979-81; mgr. fin. audit Lloyds Bank, L.A., 1981-83, mgr. EDP audit, 1983-85; dir. corp. audit First Interstate Bancorp, L.A., 1985-89, sr. v.p., gen. auditor, 1989-91, sr. v.p., chief compliance officer, 1991-94; compliance cons. Proactive, Inc., 1993—; dir. internal audit Calif. State U., Long Beach, 1996—; treas., Arcadia H.O. Assoc., El Monte, Calif., 1982-84, 86-88, pres., 1985. Recipient Edward W. Carter award UCLA, 1979. Mem. AICPA, Calif. Soc. CPA. Republican. Avocations: photography, microcomputers, reading. Home: 1226 Upland Hills Dr S Upland CA 91786-9173

HEY, NANCY HENSON, educational administrator; b. Cleve., Apr. 1, 1935; d. Henry Brumback Henson and Isabelle (Smock) Selverstone; m. Robert Pierpont Hey, July 4, 1959; 1 child, Julie Dean. AB, Bates Coll., 1957; MS in Edn., Bank St. Coll. of Edn., 1961. Cert. advanced profl. in early childhood nursery thru grade 3, Md. 1st grade tchr. Concord (Mass.) Pub. Schs., 1958-59; tchr. The Potomac Sch., McLean, Va., 1959-60, Galloway Sch., Atlanta, 1968-69; head tchr. Beauvoir Sch. Nursery Dept., Washington, 1969-70; supr. student tchrs. U. Md. Coll. of Edn., College Park, 1973-76, Tufts U., Medford, Mass., 1978-79; head tchr. Newton Ctr. (Mass.) Day Care Ctr., 1980-81, Community Child Devel. Ctr., Peabody, Mass., 1981-82; dir. Greater Lawrence (Mass.) YWCA Children's Ctr., 1982-86; tchr. Prince George's County (Md.) Pub. Schs., 1986-88; dir. Child Devel. Ctr., Fed. Trade Commn., Washington, 1988-92, Chevy Chase Plaza Children's Ctr., Washington, 1992-93; specialist/adminstr. in early childhood Ctr. for Young Children, U. Md., 1994—; supr. student tchrs. Simmons Coll., Boston, 1965-67; teaching asst. to head of lower sch.Shady Hill Sch., Cambridge, Mass., 1960-61; mem. task force com. Region III Dept. of Social Svcs., Middleton, Mass., 1984-86; bd. dirs. Greater Lawrence Coun. for Children, 1984-86. Mem. Nat. Coalition for Campus Childcare. Mem. Nat. Assn. for Edn. of Young Children, World Org. Early Childhood Edn., Congl. and Fed. Child Care Dirs. Assn. (sec. 1990-92), Dirs. Exch., Nat. Coalition for Campus Child Care. Home: 10908 Candlelight Ln Potomac MD 20854-2756 Office: U Md Ctr for Young Children Valley Dr College Park MD 20742

HEYDE, MARTHA BENNETT (MRS. ERNEST R. HEYDE), psychologist; b. New Bern, N.C., Jan. 31, 1920; d. George Spotswood and Katherine (McIntosh) Bennett; AB, Barnard Coll., 1941; MA, Columbia, 1949, PhD, 1959; m. Ernest R. Heyde, Aug. 17, 1946. Instr. psychol. founds. and services Tchrs. Coll., Columbia U., N.Y.C., 1953-60, research asst., career pattern study Horace Mann-Lincoln Inst., Tchrs. Coll. Columbia U., 1957-59, research assoc., 1960-70, cons., 1970-73. Mem. Barnard Coll. Alumnae Council, 1956-61, 69—, pres. class, 1956-61. Trustee, Barnard Coll., 1974-78, hon. vice-chmn. Barnard Coll. Centennial, 1987-89. Mem. Am. Psychol. Assn., Sigma Xi, Kappa Delta Pi, Pi Lambda Theta. Contbr. to research monograph The Vocational Maturity of Ninth Grade Boys, 1960, Floundering and Trial After High Sch, 1967; co-author: Vocational Maturity During the High School Years, 1979. Home: 530 E 23rd St Apt 8E New York NY 10010-5030

HEYDE, NORMA LEE, singer, music educator; b. Herrin, Ill., Dec. 31, 1927; d. Charles LaRue and Callie (Logan) Swinney; m. John Bradley Heyde, Aug. 24, 1947. MusB, U. Mich., 1949, MusM, 1950; grad. cert. in lieder and oratorio, Mozarteum, Salzburg, Austria, 1956. Mem. voice faculty U. Mich. Sch. Music, Ann Arbor, 1950-54, Eastern Mich. U., Ypsilanti, 1954-57; instr. music lit. York Coll. Pa., 1969; artist, tchr. in residence Transylvania Music Camp, Brevard, N.C., 1950-54; assoc. prof. music Salisbury (Md.) State U., 1971-87; dir. music 1st Presbyn. Ch., Milford, Del., 1958-66; artist, tchr. voice Franklin and Marshall Coll., Lancaster, Pa., 1988—; soprano artist various orchs. and choral socs. Nat. Gallery of Art, Washington, 1950-88. Benefit recitalist Meml. Hosp., Civic Ctr., Marion, Ill., Milford Libr., York Symphony Assn., 1960-90, Habitat for Humanity Project, York, Pa., 1993. Oliver Ditson scholar U. Mich., 1946-50, James L. Babcock scholar, 1946-50. Mem. Nat. Assn. Tchrs. Singing, Music Tchrs. Nat. Assn. (adjudicator music competitions), Music Educators Nat. Conf., AAUP, PEO, Phi Kappa Phi (emeritus life), Pi Kappa Lambda, Mu Phi Epsilon. Home: 940 Clubhouse Rd PO Box 2365 York PA 17405

HEYDRICK, LINDA CAROL, consulting company executive, editor; b. Pomona, Calif., July 25, 1947; d. Robert Bruce and Wanda Georgine (Wellman) Middough; m. Stephen R. Bova, Jan. 20, 1968 (div. May 1981); children: Karen E., Lori L.; m. Allen L. Heydrick, Mar. 15, 1995. Student, El Camino Coll., Gardena, Calif., 1965-66. Sec. TRW, Inc., Manhattan Beach, Calif., 1967-68, USAF NCO Clubs, Mildenhall, Eng., 1968-70; adminstrv. asst. Prudential-Bache Securities, N.Y.C., 1970-73, Tex. Instruments, Inc., Dallas, 1980-83; asst. to pres. Acclivus Corp., Dallas, 1983-85, mgr. design and prodn., 1985-88, mgr. ops., 1988-89, v.p. ops., 1989—; cons. Digital Equipment Corp., Boston, 1984-89, internat. translations of books, audiotapes and videotapes. Editor: (books and videotapes) BASE for Sales Performance, 1984, Acclivus Sales Negotiation, 1985, The New BASE for Sales Excellence, 1989, Major Account Planning and Strategy, 1993, rev., 1996, Building on the BASE (award for best new tng. products Human Resource Exec.), 1993. Organizer Meals on Wheels, Denton, Tex., 1977; editor, pub Denton Bible Ch., 1993—. Mem. ASTD, Instructional Systems Assn., Nat. Soc. for Performance and Instrn., Soc. for Aplied Learning Tech., Soc. for Acceleractive Learning and Tchg., Internat. Listening Assn., Womens Ctr. Dallas. Republican. Home: 3301 Santa Monica Denton TX 76205-8245 Office: Acclivus Corp 14500 Midway Rd Dallas TX 75244-3109

HEYEN, BEATRICE J., psychotherapist; b. Chgo., June 23, 1925; d Carl Edwin and Anna W. (Carlson) Lund; m. Robert D. Heyen, June 16, 1950 (dec. Feb. 1981); children: Robin, Jefferson, Neil; m. Robert Christiansen, Nov. 24, 1984. BS, U. Chgo., 1949. Instr. Boone (Iowa) Jr. Coll., 1959-64, Rochester (Minn.) Jr. Coll., 1967-68, Winona (Minn.) State Coll., 1965-68; dir. social svc. State Clinic, Kirksville, Mo., 1968-71; supr., dir. Family Counseling Agy., Joliet, Ill., 1971-85; pvt. practice Muskegon, Mich., 1985—; cons. Homes for Aged, Programs for Aged, Winona, 1965-68, Spl. Programs and Individuals in Psychotherapy, Muskegon, 1984—; dir. Christiansen Fine Art Gallery, North Muskegon. Mem. Gov.'s Com. on Status of Women, Iowa, 1957-62, Gov.'s Com. on Aging, Minn., 1966-68. Grantee for Pilot Projects in Svc. to Women 1971-84. Mem. NASW, Acad. Cert. Social Workers, C.G. Jung Inst. (Chgo.). Methodist. Home: 1610 N Weber Rd Muskegon MI 49445-9629

HEYER, ANNA HARRIET, retired music librarian; b. Little Rock, Aug. 30, 1909; d. Arthur Wesley and Harriet Anna (Gage) H. A.B., B.Mus., Tex. Christian U., 1930; B.S. in L.S., U. Ill., 1933; M.S. in L.S., Columbia U., 1939; M.Mus. in Musicology, U. Mich., 1943. Elem. sch. music tchr. Ft. Worth Pub. Schs., 1931-32; high sch. librarian, 1934-38; cataloguer library, U. Tex.-Austin, 1939-40; music librarian, asst. prof. L.S., N. Tex. State U. (name now U. N. Tex.), Denton, 1940-65, librarian emeritus, 1976; cons. music library materials Tex. Christian U., Ft. Worth, 1965-79; ret., 1979. Author: A Check-List of Publications of Music, 1944; A Bibliography of Contemporary Music in the Music Library, North Texas State College, 1955; Historical Sets, Collected Editions and Monuments of Music: A Guide to Their Contents, 1957, 2d edit., 1969, 3d rev. edit., 1980; contbr. articles to profl. publs. Recipient citations for contbn. to music librarianship Music Library Assn., 1980, to music librarianship in Tex., 1983. Mem. ALA, Tex. Library Assn., Music Library Assn., AAUW, DAR. Mem. Disciples of Christ Ch. Clubs: Altrusa, Woman's Club Ft. Worth, Colonial Country. Home: 5334 Premier Ct Fort Worth TX 76132-4016

HEYER, LAURA MIRIAM, special education educator; b. L.A., Jan. 6, 1967; d. William Ronald and Miriam Harriet (Muedeking) Heyer. BA, U. Va., 1990, M of Tching., 1990. Lic. tchr. Va. Asst. tchr. Sch. for Contemporary Edn., Annandale, Va., 1991-93, classroom tchr., 1993—. Support group facilitator, Sexual Minority Youth Assistance League, Washington, 1995—. Mem. Coun. for Children with Behavioral Disorders, Coun. for Exceptional Children. Office: Sch for Contemporary Edn 7010 Braddock Rd Annandale VA 22003

HEYER, VERONICA JEAN, publishing executive; b. Fond du Lac, Wis., Mar. 3, 1966; d. Neil William and Kathleen Ann (Lorenz) Kibler; m. Mark Jay Heyer, Nov. 23, 1991. BA in Journalism with honors, U. Wis., 1989. Asst. Lowe & Partners, N.Y.C., 1990; exec. asst. Nat. Cable Advertising, N.Y.C., 1990-91; sales asst. Fairchild Pubs., N.Y.C., 1991, bus. coord., 1991-92, office mgr., 1992-94, asst. pub., 1995, asst. pub., bus. mgr., 1995—. Capt. United Way, ABC, capital cities, Fairchild Pubs., N.Y.C., 1994, 95. Scholar AAUW, Fond du Lac chpt., 1985, journalism scholar U. Wis., Madison, 1989. Mem. Phi Beta Kappa. Republican. Catholic. Home: 22 Orient Ave Brooklyn NY 11211 Office: Fairchild Publs 7 West 34th St New York NY 10001

HEYMOSS, JENNIFER MARIE, librarian; b. Detroit, Apr. 14, 1958; d. John Joseph and Virginia Marie (Kern) H. BA in English and German, Wayne State U., 1980, MS in Libr. Sci., 1981. Libr. asst. Wayne State U. Librs., Detroit, 1982-83; asst. libr. Plunkett & Cooney, Detroit, 1983-86, Henry Ford Mus. & Greenfield Village Rsch. Ctr., Dearborn, Mich., 1986-90; libr. Henry Ford Mus. & Greenfield Village Rsch. Ctr., Dearborn, 1990-92; asst. head tech. svcs. Flint (Mich.) Pub. Libr., 1992—. Literacy vol., 1987—. Mem. ALA. Spl. Librs. Assn. (various coms. 1988-92), Mich. Libr. Assn., Pub. Librs. Assn., Phi Beta Kappa, Beta Phi Mu. Democrat. Methodist. Office: Flint Pub Libr 1026 E Kearsley St Flint MI 48503-1923

HEYN, ELA FREDERICA, executive assistant; b. Bloomington, Ind., May 12, 1966; d. Udo Eberhard Gunnar and Ela (Tkacz) H. BBA, James Madison U., 1990; postgrad., U. Phoenix, San Francisco, 1993-95. Mktg. rschr. Smithsonian Mag., N.Y.C., 1990-91; asst. to v.p. Guest Informant, N.Y.C., 1991-92, The Conf. Bd., N.Y.C., 1992-95, Ogilvy & Mather, N.Y.C., 1996—. Author, reviewer PCM Mag., 1991—. With U.S. Army, 1984-87. Mem. Mensa. Republican. Roman Catholic. Office: Ogilvy & Mather 309 W 49th St New York NY 10019

HEYNEN, DIANNE SCHLANGEN, psychotherapist; b. Watertown, S.D., Sept. 22, 1962; d. Leonard John and Joyce Ione (Johnson) Schlangen; m. Glen Allen Heynen, Sept. 29, 1990; children: Heather, Paul, Tonya. AA, Dakota State U., 1982; BS, U. S.D., 1985; MS, S.D. State U., 1995. Lic. profl. counselor, S.D.; nat. cert. counselor. Programmer analyst Citibank, Sioux Falls, S.D., 1985-88, sr. programmer analyst, 1988-90, data ctr. mgr., 1990-91, requirements analyst, 1991-94; counselor Luth. Social Svcs., Sioux Falls, S.D., 1995—. Contbr. articles to profl. jours. Vol. Sioux Valley Hospice, Sioux Falls, 1994—. Mem. Am. Counselors Assn., Internat. Assn. Family & Marital Therapists, S.D. Counselor Assn., Chi Sigma Iota. Lutheran. Home: 211 E 9th St Dell Rapids SD 57022 Office: Luth Social Svcs 705 E 41st St Sioux Falls SD 57105

HIATT, CARRIE SMITH, elementary education educator; b. Colfax, N.C., Sept. 3, 1933; d. Hugh Patrick and Jenny Blanche (Crutchfield) Smith; m. W. Reid Hiatt, Sept. 1, 1974, 1 stepchild, Hilda. Ab, High Point (N.C.) U., 1954. Elem. sch. tchr. Sedge Garden Elem., Kernersville, N.C. Tchr. Sunday sch. Shady Grove Wesleyan Ch., Colfax, 1954-92, asst. organist, 1980—, ch. sec., 1980-82. Mem. NEA, N.C. Assn. Educators, Internat. Reading Assn., Ladies Aux. VFW Post (sec. 1988-92). Home: 1124 Peabody Rd Colfax NC 27235-9742

HIATT, JANE CRATER, arts agency administrator; b. Winston-Salem, N.C., May 26, 1944; d. Howard Rondthaler Jr. and Irene (Sides) Crater; m. K.W. Everhart Jr. (div. June 1973); m. Wood Coleman Hiatt, May, 1978; 1 child, Jonathan David. BA, U. N.C., 1966; MA, Wake Forest U., 1972. Eng. tchr. Winston-Salem (N.C.)/Forsyth County Schs., 1966-70; exec. dir. Tenn. Com. for the Humanities, Nashville, 1973-77; cons. various ednl. and cultural agys. Ocean Springs, Miss., 1978-80; asst. dir. Miss. Humanities Coun., Jackson, Miss., 1981-85; exec. dir. Arts Alliance of Jackson and Hinds County, Miss., 1985-89, Miss. Arts Commn., Jackson, 1989-95; participant Arts Leadership Inst. of Humphrey Inst. for Pub. Affairs, Mpls., 1986, Leadership, Jackson, 1987. Co-editor Peoples of the South, 1976; exec. producer (TV series) The South with John Siegenthaler, 1976; host, reporter Miss. Ednl. TV, Jackson, 1981-87. Mem. Miss. Econ. Coun., 1986-87, Miss. R & D Coun., 1984-88; pres. Mental Health Assn. of Hinds County, Jackson, 1986; treas. Miss. for Ednl. Broadcasting, 1987, 88, 89, Premier Class Leadership, Jackson, 1987, 88. Recipient Heritage award City of Biloxi, 1984. Mem. Nat. Assembly of Local Arts Agys., Nat. Coun. on Arts, Nat. Assembly State Arts Agys. (bd. dirs. 1992-95, 2d v.p. 1995), So. Arts Fedn. (bd. dirs. 1989-95), Miss. Ctr. for Nonprofits (vice chmn., bd. dirs. 1993—), Pub. Edn. Forum (bd. dirs. 1993—), Greater Jackson Found. (bd. dirs. 1996—), Phi Beta Kappa. Home: 507 Roses Bluff Dr Madison MS 39110-9690

HIATT, MARJORIE MCCULLOUGH, service organization executive; b. Cin., July 12, 1923; d. Robert Stedman and Mildred (Rogers) McCullough; m. Homer E. Lunken, Apr. 15, 1944 (dec. 1970); children: Karen (dec. 1948), Kathryn Lunken Summers, Margo Lunken Yesner; m. William McLeod Ittmann, Mar. 17, 1972 (dec. 1982); m. Harold Hiatt, Apr. 14, 1984. Student, U. Cin., 1941-43. Active Girl Scouts U.S., 1962—, chmn. conv. com., 1972, del. world convs., 1969, 72, 75, 78, 81, 84, 87, 93, chmn. pub. relations com., 1963-66, mem. nat. exec. com., 1963-75, mem. nat. bd., 1962—, 4th v.p., 1966-69, 1st v.p., 1969-72, nat. pres., 1972-75, chmn. nat. adv. council, 1975-82, mem. birthplace adv. com., 1980—; vice chmn. world conf., Orleans, France, 1981; mem. world com. World Assn. Girl Guides and Girl Scouts, 1978-87, vice chmn., 1984-87. Regional dir. Assn. Jr. Leagues Am., 1958-60, nat. pres., 1960-62; mem. br. Jr. League Cin., 1944-58, Nat. Tng. Labs., 1963-66, Nat. Assembly for Social Policy and Devel., 1968-71; mem. exec. com. Council Nat. Orgns. for Children and Youth, 1960-62, 68-72; bd. dirs. United Way Am., 1962-67, sec., 1965-66, v.p., 1966-67, 1989—; mem. policy com. Center Vol. Soc., 1971-72; bd. dirs. Coll. Prep. Sch., Cin., 1962-69, pres., 1964-69; bd. dirs. Cin. Speech and Hearing Center, 1955-66, v.p., 1958-62, pres., 1963-66, trustee emeritus, 1966—; mem. bd. Children's Theatre, Cin., 1948-58, pres., 1948-50; bd. dirs. Community Health and Welfare Council Cin., 1957-63, Hamilton County (Ohio) Research Found., 1963-65, Cancer Family Care, Cin., 1971-72, Boys Clubs Greater Cin., Marjorie P. Lee Home for Aged, Music Hall Assn., Cin. Symphony Orch.; bd. dirs. Beechwood Home for Incurables, 1975-87; bd. dirs. St. Margaret Hall, 1991—, Cin. Civic Garden Ctr., 1992-95; mem. Ohio Citizens Coun., 1956-58; mem. bd. 7th Presbyterian Ch., 1967-74, 85—, ruling elder, 1976-78, 95—, chmn. bd. trustees, 1992-94; sr. warden St. Martin's in the Field, Biddeford Pool, Maine; bd. dirs. Greater Cin. Found., 1979-87; bd. dirs. U. Cin. Found., 1979—, pres. 1986-88, vice chmn. 1988—, trustee emeritus, 1993—; pres. Garden Club Cin., 1984-86, co-chmn. zone X meeting, 1989, zone X chmn. pub.; bd. dirs. Friends Cin. Parks, 1987—, corr. sec., 1989-92; trustee Cin. Assn. Performing Arts, Inc.; founding bd. dirs. Emery Soc. Children's Hosp; pres. protem Cin. Parks Found., 1995. Mem. Olave Baden-Powell Soc. (v.p. 1991-93, pres. 1993—), World Found. for Girl Guides and Girl Scouts (v.p. 1989—), Garden Club Am. (vice chmn. founder's fund 1991-92), Am. Psychiat. Assn. Aux. (bd. dirs., rec. sec. 1991-92). Home: 2353 Bedford Ave Cincinnati OH 45208-2656

HIBLER, JUDE ANN, photojournalist; b. Portland, Oreg., Apr. 6, 1943; d. William Eliot and Myrtle Winifred (Johnson) Henderson; m. Jeffrey Charles Hibler, Jan. 27, 1962; 1 child, Beth Karen. Student, Portland State Coll., 1960-61, Pima C.C., 1980, U. Colo., Boulder, 1982, Antioch U. West, 1981-82. Exec. sec., office mgr. Campus Christian Ctr., Tucson, 1979-80; alcohol counselor Whole Person Health Ctr., Boulder, 1984; adminstrv. mgr. Nordstrom, San Diego, 1985-88; publ., editor, owner Jazz Link Mag., San Diego, 1988-91; co-owner, photojournalist Jazz Link Enterprises, Longmont, Colo., 1991—; cons. El Cajon (Calif.) Jr. High Sch., 1989, Long Beach (Calif.) High Sch., 1990. Co-author: Joe Pass: Improvising Ideas, 1994; contbg. writer: Encyclopedia of Jazz, 1995, The Dale Bruning Jazz Guitar Series Vol. 1: Phrasing & Articulation, 1995; co-prodr. CD: Dale Bruning Quartet's Tomorrow's Reflections, 1995; co-prodr., leader, author: Jazz Music & Media Clinic Book, 1996; publ./editor: Jazz Link Mag., 1988 (best jazz pub. 1988); editor The Gift of Jazz mag., 1995-96; photographer: (book covers) Joe Pass Note by Note, 1994, Improvising Ideas, 1994; photojournalist Jazzscene of Oreg., JazzNow Mag., 1992-94, Concord Jazz. Named Outstanding Svc. Nat. Assn. Jazz Educators, 1989, First Friend of Jazz Dr. Billy Taylor's Soundpost, 1991. Mem. San Diego Musicians Union (hon. mem.). Democrat. Home and office: 3721 Columbia Dr Longmont CO 80503-2117

HICKCOX, LESLIE KAY, health educator, counselor; b. Berkeley, Calif., May 12, 1951; d. Ralph Thomas and Marilyn Irene (Stump) H. BA, U. Redlands, 1973; MA, U. of the Pacific, 1975; MEd, Columbia U., 1979; MEd, EdD, Oreg. State U., 1987, 88, 91. Cert. state C.C. instr. (life), Calif. Instr. health curriculum and supervision Concordia Coll., Portland, Oreg.; health and phys. edn. instr. Portland C.C.; instr. human studies and comm. Marylhurst (Oreg.) Coll.; edn. supr., instr. Oreg. State U., Corvallis; phys. edn. instr., dir. intramurals SUNY, Stony Brook; coord., instr. dept. health, phys. edn. and recreation Rogue C.C., Grants Pass, Oreg., 1995-96; founder Experiential Learning Inst., 1992—. Contbr. articles to profl. jours. Mem. ASCD, Nat. Ctr. for Health Edn., Assn. for Advancement of Health Edn., Higher Edn. R & D Soc. Australasia, Coun. for Adult and Exptl. Learning, Kappa Delta Phi, Phi Delta Kappa. Office: Rogue CC Dept Health Phys Edn Recrn Grants Pass OR 97526

HICKERSON, PATRICIA PARSONS, military officer; b. Louisville, Sept. 15, 1942; d. John Millard and Rose (Brill) Parsons; m. Dennis Fogarty, Dec. 18, 1974. MusB, Converse Coll., 1964, MusM, 1966; student, Women's Army Corps Officer Basic Course, 1968, Infantry Officer Advanced Course, 1973, U.S. Army Command and General Staff Coll., 1978, Nat. War Coll., 1986-87; D of Pub. Svc., Converse Coll., 1989. 1st lt. U.S. Army, 1968, advanced through grades to Brig. Gen., 1991; asst. manpower control officer to manpower control officer Manpower Control Divsn., Military Dist. Washington, 1968-69; comdr., 14th Army Band U.S. Women's Army Corps. Ctr., Ft. McClellan, Ala., 1970-72; br. advisor Combat Svc. Support Br., Readiness Group Atlanta, Ft. Gillem, Ga., 1973-75; admissions officer U.S. Military Acad., West Point, N.Y., 1975-77; personnel mgmt. officer U.S. Army Military Personnel Ctr., 8th U.S. Army, Korea, 1978-79; deputy G-1 (personnel) 2d infantry divsn. Korea, 1979-80; pers. staff officer, assignment procedures office U.S. Army Mil. Pers. Ctr., Alexandria, Va., 1980-82; mil. asst. Office of Asst. Sec. of Army for Manpower & Res. Affairs, Washington, 1982-83; chief pers. actions div. VII Corps-U.S. Army, Europe, 1984; commdr. 38th Pers. and Adminstrn. Battalion, VII Corps-U.S. Army, Europe, 1984-86; adminstrv. asst. to chmn. of joint chiefs of staff Office of the Joint Chiefs of Staff, Washington, 1987-89; commdr. ctrl. sector U.S. Mil. Entrance Processing Command, North Chicago, Ill., 1989-91; adj. gen. U.S. Total Army Pers. Command, Alexandria, 1991—; commdr. U.S. Army Phys. Disability Agy., Alexandria, 1991—; Commanding General U.S. Army Soldier Support Inst., Fort Jackson, SC; dir. Pentagon Fed. Credit Union, 1992-94. Decorated Def. Superior Svc. medal with one oak leaf cluster, Legion of Merit, Meritorious Svc. medal with four oak leaf clusters, Army Commendation medal, Joint Chief of Staff Identification badge, Army Gen. Staff Identification badge, Order of the Horatio Gates Gold medal. Mem. Andrews Air Force Golf Club. Office: U S Army Soldier Support Institute Fort Jackson SC 29207-7025*

HICKEY, ANNE JANICE, social services administrator; b. Quincy, Mass., Sept. 30, 1943; d. Joseph and Anne Frances (Mulligan) Wall; m. Peter Hickey, Sept. 12, 1964; children: Patricia, Kristen, Erin, Lauren. Assoc. Gen. Studies, Manchester (Conn.) C.C., 1991; B Gen. Studies, U. Conn., 1993, cert. in gerontology, 1996. Decorator Sears Roebuck Co., Manchester, 1980-88; resident svcs. coord. Hartford East Assn., East Hartford, Conn., 1994—. Host TV program for srs. Accent on Aging. Mem. East Hartford Eldercare Com., 1994—; election coord. Groark for Gov., Conn. Party, 1994. Mem. NOW, Am. Soc. Aging, Older Women's League, Cameo, Golden Key, Phi Kappa Phi, Alpha Sigma Lambda, Phi Theta Kappa. Democrat. Roman Catholic. Home: 92 Butternut Rd Manchester CT 06040 Office: Hartford East Assoc 886 Main St East Hartford CT 06108

HICKEY, DELINA ROSE, education educator; b. N.Y.C., Mar. 25, 1941; d. Robert Joseph and Marie (Ripa) H.; m. David Andrews, 1 child by previous marriage, Jon Robert. BS in Edn., SUNY, Oneonta, 1963; MA, Manhattan Coll., 1967; EdD in Counselor Edn. and Psychology, U. Idaho, 1971; attended Inst. Ednl. Mgmt. (IEM) Harvard U., 1995. Elem. sch. tchr., counselor, Westchester, N.Y., 1963-68; part-time instr. psychology St. Thomas Aquinas Coll., Sparkhill, N.Y., 1971-72; asst. prof. edn. Nathaniel Hawthorne Coll., Antrim, N.H., 1972-75; prof. faculty Keene (N.H.) State Coll., 1975—, assoc. prof. edn., 1978—, prof. edn., coordinator faculty, 1987—; interim dean profl. studies 1987; mem. N.H. Legislature from 13th Dist., 1981-85; mem. adv. council Title IV, 1979-82; fellow Nat. Ctr. Research in Vocat. Edn., 1984-85; assoc. in edn. Harvard U., 1984-85, Inst. Ednl. Mgmt., 1995; interim v.p. student affairs Keene State U., 1990, apptd. v.p. student affairs, 1991. Trustee, Big Bros./Big Sisters, Keene, 1978-80, Family Planning Services S.W. N.H., 1976-85, Monadnock Hospice, 1994—, chair pers. com.; mem. bd. trustees Monadnock Family Svcs., 1995—; mem. N.H. Juvenile Conf. Com., 1976-81; pres. bd. dirs. CHESCO. Mem. Nat. Assn. Student Pers. Adminstrs. (adv. com. region I), N.H. Order Women Legislators, New Eng. Research Orgn., Am. Vocat. Assn., N.H. Pers. and Guidance Assn., N.H. Nat. Assn. Student Personnel Adminstrs. (adv. bd.), New Eng. Assn. of Tchrs. and Educators. Democrat. Author articles in edns. Office: Student Ctr Keene State Coll Keene NH 03431

HICKINBOTHAM, LETHA BELLE, real estate broker, business owner; b. New Haven, Mo., Feb. 8, 1935; d. Clarence Virgil and Gladine Louise (Helling) Laubinger; m. Floyd E. Hickinbotham, May 3, 1953; children: Floyd, Marjean, Twila, Scott. Student, East Ctrl. Coll., Union, Mo., 1970, 77, 79 86. Grad. Realtors Inst., Mo. Assn. Realtors. With acctg. and billing dept. Fed. Res. Bank, St. Louis, 1952-53; restaurant hostess Snell's Family Restaurant, Sullivan, Mo., 1958-61; with acctg. and billing dept. Crawford Electric Co-op, Bourbon, Mo., 1961-63, Authorized Investor Group, Inc., St. Clair, Mo., 1966-76; dist. clk., sec. Anaconda Sch. Dist. 87, St. Clair, 1966-76; real estate broker Hickinbotham Real Estate, Inc., St. Clair, 1976—; developer, owner Budget Lodging, St. Clair, 1989—, Subway Sandwich and Salad Restaurant, St. Clair, 1992—; pres. Franklin County Women's Coun. Realtors, St. Clair, 1980. Contbr. articles to profl. jours. Mem. Internat. Real Estate Policy Com., 1986-87; mem. bldg. and grounds com. Mt. Zion Bapt. Ch., St. Clair, 1990; bd. dirs. Sullivan Bapt. Hosp. Coun. Named to Honor Soc., Mo. Assn. Realtors, 1986, 87, 88, to Nat. Honor Soc., Nat. Assn. Realtors, 1987. Mem. Tri-County Bus. and Profl. Women's Club (pres. 1981-82, Women of Yr. 1982), Franklin County Bd. Realtors (pres. 1985, Realtor of Yr. 1983), Mo. Women's Coun. Realtors (pres. 1983, Mo. Woman of Yr. 1985), Mo. Indsl. Devel. Coun., St. Clair C. of C. (bd. dirs. 1985, chair 1990), St. Clair Rotary (sec. and guide for Rotary Internat. team annual), East Ctrl. Coll. Found. (pres. 1994-96). Democrat. Baptist. Office: Hickinbothm Real Estate Inc 862 S I 44 Outer Rd W Saint Clair MO 63077

HICKMAN, DARLENE, sports association executive; b. Vancouver, Wash., Oct. 13, 1943; m. William Hickman; two children. V.p. USA Track and Field; pvt. practice track and field and cross country coach. mem. Pacific Northwest Assn. USA Track and Field (pres. 1989—, race walk com., youth athletics com., women's track and field com.). Office: USA Track and Field PO Box 120 Indianapolis IN 46206-0120

HICKMAN, ELIZABETH PODESTA, retired counselor, educator; b. Livingston, Ill., Sept. 30, 1922; d. Louis and Della (Martin) Podesta; BE summa cum laude, Eastern Ill. State U.; MA, George Washington U., 1966; postgrad. U. Chgo., 1945, U. Va., 1964-66, (fellow) Northeastern U., 1967-68;

EdD (Exxon Found. grantee, Raskob Found grantee), George Washington U., 1979; m. Franklin Jay Hickman, Mar. 17, 1944 (dec.); children: Virginia Hickman Hellstern, Franklin. Tchr. public schs., Ill., Ohio, Va., Naples, Italy, 1944-64; dir. coll. transfer guidance Marymount Coll. of Va., Arlington, 1964-67, dir. Counseling Center, 1974-81, assoc. dean counseling and residence life, 1981-84; community counselor div. Mass. Employment Security, Newton, 1968-69; tchr. English conversation, Fuchu, Japan, 1969-73; placement dir., career counselor Coll. Great Falls (Mont.), 1973-74; assoc. researcher George Washington U., 1986; lectr. Far East di v. U. Md., Fuchu, 1971-73; spl. adv. Internat. Ranger Camps, Denmark and Switzerland, 1974-81; spl. cons. Internat. Quaker Sch., Wekhoven, Netherlands, 1959-63; mem. steering com. Pres.'s Com. on Employment of Handicapped, 1974-95. Vol., ARC, 1967-78, Family Services, 1954-75, White House Agy. Liaison, 1986—, Kennedy Ctr. Adminstrn., Washington, 1984—. Served with WAVES, 1943-44. Recipient Disting. Alumnus award Eastern Ill. U., 1984. Lic. counselor, Va. Mem. Am. Personnel and Guidance Assn., Nat. Assn. Women Deans, Adminstrs. and Counselors, Nat. Vocat. Guidance Assn., Am. Coll. Personnel Assn., No. Va. Counselors Assn., Delta Epsilon Sigma, Pi Lambda Theta. Roman Catholic. Home: 4708 38th Pl N Arlington VA 22207-2915

HICKMAN, MARGARET CAPELLINI, advertising agency executive; b. Hartford, Conn., Sept. 21, 1949; d. Anthony Serafino Capellini and Mary Magdelan (Budash) Zanardi; m. Richard Lonnie Hickman, Nov. 6, 1982; children: Wilder A., Langdon B. BA, U. Conn., 1971. Mktg. asst. Advo Sys., Inc., Hartford, 1971-72, mktg. analyst, 1972-75; mktg. asst. Cinamon Assocs. Inc., Brookline, Mass., 1975-77, prodn. supr., 1977-81, v.p. prodn., 1981-84, v.p. client svcs., 1984-85; dir. client svcs. Bozell, Jacobs, Kenyon & Eckhardt, Boston, 1985-86, v.p. client svcs. Cinamon Assocs., 1986; ptnr. Hickman & Hickman, Merritt Island, Fla., 1987; prodn. mgr. Direct Mktg. Agy., Stamford, Conn., 1988-90; v.p. prodn. Martin Direct, Glen Allen, Va., 1990-96; v.p. prodn. Martin Agy., Richmond, Va., 1996—. Mem. Direct Mktg. Assn. (past sec., treas., v.p.), Cape Ann Child Devel. Programs (past dir.), Ctrl. Fla. Direct Mktg. Assn. (past mem.), Am. Legion Aux. Democrat. Roman Catholic. Home: 10717 Wellington St Fredericksburg VA 22407-1272

HICKMAN, MARSHA WILSON, admissions counselor; b. Clinton, Ind., May 1, 1957; d. Claude Derrill and Bessie Faye (Brown) Wilson; m. Danny Ray Hickman, May 10, 1975; children: Matthew Dustin, Jessica Faye. BS in Mgmt. of Human Resources, Oakland City (Ind.) Coll., 1991; postgrad., Ind. U. S.E., New Albany. Asst. dist. mgr. Avon Products, Cin., 1978-87; asst. to English and math. profs. Oakland City U., Bedford, 1987-89; admissions counselor Bedford (Ind.) Coll. Ctr., 1994-96; adminstrv. asst. Orange County Child Care Cooperative, Paoli, Ind., 1988-90, dir. youth svcs., 1990-93; dir. Lawrence County First Steps and Step Ahead, 1996—; mem. svc.-learning adv. com. Middle Grades Improvement, Paoli, 1992-93; mem. gifted and talented adv. com. Paoli Schs., 1990—. Actor, singer, dancer Orange County Players, Paoli, 1985—; mem. youth adv. coun. Ctrl. Bapt. Ch., Paoli, 1984—. Named one of Outstanding Young Women Am., 1986; Youth as Resources grantee Nat. Crime Prevention Coun., 1992, 91, Cmty. Guidance for Youth grantee Lilly Endowment, 1993; recipient Gov.'s Voluntary Action award State of Ind., 1992, 93. Mem. Ind. Assn. Coll. Admissions Counselors (legis. com. 1994-95). Baptist. Home: 314 Sycamore Paoli IN 47454 Office: Hoosier Uplands Econ Devel Corp 710 6th St Bedford IN 47421

HICKMAN, MAXINE VIOLA, social services administrator; b. Louisville, Miss., Dec. 24, 1943; d. Everett and Ozella (Eichelberger) H.; m. William L. Malone, Sept. 5, 1965 (div. 1969); 1 child, Gwendolyn. BA, San Francisco State U., 1966; MS, Nova U., 1991; postgrad., Calif. Coast U., 1991—. Lic. State of Calif. Dept. Social Svcs. IBM profl. mechanic operator Wells Fargo Bank, San Francisco, 1961-65; dept. mgr. Sears Roebuck & Co., San Bruno, Calif., 1966-77; adminstr. Pine St. Guest House, San Francisco, 1969-88; fin. planner John Hancock Fin. Svcs., San Mateo, Calif., 1977-81; chief exec. officer Hickman Homes, Inc., San Francisco, 1981—; cons. BeeBe Meml. Endowment Found., Oakland, Calif., 1990—, Calif. Assn. Children's Home-Mems., Sacramento, 1989—. Mem. NAACP, San Francisco. Named Foster Mother of Yr., Children's Home Soc. Calif., 1985, Woman of Yr., Gamma Nu chpt. Iota Phi Lambda, 1991. Mem. Foster Parents United, Calif. Assn. Children's Homes, Nat. Bus. League, Order of Ea. Star, Masons (worthy matron), Alpha Kappa Alpha. Democrat. Baptist. Office: Hickman Homes Inc 67 Harold Ave San Francisco CA 94112-2331

HICKMAN, TERRIE TAYLOR, administrator; b. Rapid City, S.D., Dec. 2, 1962; d. William Adrian and Carolyn Gene (Habben) T. BS, Okla. State U., 1985; MEd, Cen. State U., 1988. Mktg. dir. Tealridge Manor, Edmond, Okla., 1989-90; owner Oxford Pointe Jazzercize, Edmond, Okla., 1989-90; adminstr. Retirement Inn at Quail Ridge, Oklahoma City, Okla., 1991-92, Country Club Square, Edmond, 1992-93; planner Areawide Aging Agency, Oklahoma City, 1992—; co-chmn. Okla. Bus. and Aging Leadership Coalition, newsletter Networker editor; presenter in field; adv. coun. sr. companion planning com. State of Okla. Conf. on Aging. Co-editor Sage Age; contbr. articles to various pubs. Co-chmn. media hosting party Olympic Festival, Norman, Okla., 1989; co-coord. jazzercize for hope Benefit for Hope Ctr., Edmond, The McGruff Safe House Program, Stillwater, Okla.; com. chmn. Coalition for Elderly Concerns, Oklahoma City; vol. Stillwater Domestic Violence Shelter, Payne County Employment Svcs., Stillwater; mem. renter's adv. bd. Okla. State U. Student Senate. Mem. Women in Bus., Edmond Area C. of C., Okla. Bus. and Aging Leadership Coalition, Phi Kappa Delta, Alpha Gamma Delta, Sigma Phi Omega. Republican. Lutheran.

HICKMAN, TRAPHENE PARRAMORE, library director, storyteller, library and library building consultant; b. Dallas, Jan. 31, 1933; d. Redden Travis and Stella (Moore) P.; m. John Robert Hickman, June 9, 1950; children—Lynn Kleifgen, Laurie Ward. A.A., Mountain View Community Coll.; B.A., U. Tex-Arlington; M.L.S., U. North Tex. Cert. librarian, Tex. Librarian Cedar Hill Pub. Library, Tex., 1959-77; dir. Dallas County Library System, Dallas, 1977-93; libr. cons. Dallas County, 1993—. Editor: History and Directory of Cedar Hill, 1976; editor News and Views newsletter Dallas county Employees, 1986-92. Chmn. Bicentennial Com., Cedar Hill, 1976; del. Dem. Nat. Conv. 9th Senate Dist., Tex., 1976; chmn. Sesquicentennial Com., Cedar Hill, 1984-86; Dallas County Dem. Forum; mem. Electoral Coll., 1988; chairperson Women's Bd. Northwood Inst., Cedar Hill; active Dallas County Sesquicentennial Com., 1996—. Recipient Newsmaker of Yr. award Cedar Hill Chronicle, 1976; named Ambassador of Goodwill, State of Tex., 1976. Mem. ALA, Tex. Libr. Assn. (legis. com. 1984-95, councillor 1982-83, trustee com. 1987—, pub. info. com. 1987—), Pub. Libr. Adminstrs. of North Tex. (sec., v.p., pres. 1980, 87), Dallas County Libr. Assn., N.E. Tex. Libr. Sys. (legis. commn. 1978-95, Libr. of Yr. 1987), U. North Tes. Sch. Libr. and Info. Scis. Alumni Assn. (pres. 1987-88), Cedar Hill C. of C., Cedar Summit Book Club (officer), Dallas Area Storytelling Guild (pres. 1995—). Democrat. Methodist. Home and Office: 421 Lee St Cedar Hill TX 75104-2697

HICKS, ALISA REY, editor, newspaper; b. Hayward, Calif., Oct. 17, 1968; d. Arthur Wayne and Judith Mildred (Patterson) H. B in English, Mills Coll., 1991. Reporter, news editor Daily Sparks (Nev.) Tribune, 1991-94; news editor Moscow (Idaho)-Pullman Daily News, 1994-95, Hi-Desert Star, Yucca Valley, Calif., 1995—. Democrat. Home: 7264 Olympic Rd #101 Joshua Tree CA 92252 Office: Hi-Desert Star 56445 29 Palms Hwy Yucca Valley CA 92284

HICKS, BETHANY GRIBBEN, lawyer, commissioner; b. N.Y., Sept. 8, 1951; d. Robert and DeSales Gribben; m. William A. Hicks III, May 21, 1982; children: Alexandra Elizabeth, Samantha Katherine. AB, Vassar Coll., 1973; MEd, Boston U., 1975; JD, Ariz. State U., 1984. Bar: Ariz. 1984. Pvt. practice Scottsdale and Paradise Valley, Ariz., 1984-91; law clk. to Hon. Kenneth L. Fields Maricopa County Superior Ct. (S.E. dist.), Mesa, 1991-93, judge pro tem, 1993—; commr. Maricopa County Superior Ct., Mesa, 1994-95; Phoenix; magistrate Town of Paradise Valley, Ariz., 1993-94. Mem. Jr. League of Phoenix, 1984-91; bd. dirs. Phoenix Children's Theatre, 1988-90; parliamentarian Girls Club of Scottsdale, Ariz., 1985-87, 89-90, bd. dirs., 1988-91; mem. exec. bd., sec. All Saints' Episcopal Day Sch. Parents Assn., 1991-92, pres., 1993-94; mem. Nat. Charity League, 1995—. Mem. ABA, State Bar Ariz., Maricopa County Bar Assn. Republican. Episcopalian. Club: Paradise Valley Country. Office: 9th Flr 101 West Jefferson Phoenix AZ 85003-2205

HICKS, DOLORES KATHLEEN (DE DE HICKS), association executive; b. Mount Vernon, Iowa, Sept. 22, 1932; d. Edward M. and Olga Marie (Hekl) Staskal; m. Roswell Allen Hicks, Sept. 5, 1952; children: Thomas, Gregory, Bryan, Kevin. Student, Colo. Coll., 1950-52. Exec. women's wardrobe cons. Bullock's, Torrance, Calif., 1985-86; exec. dir. The Vol. Ctr., Torrance, 1986—; pres. Vol. Ctrs. So. Calif., 1988; coord. First Lady of Calif. Outstanding Vol. Awards, Sacramento, 1993; nat. bd. dirs. Vol. Ctrs.-Points of Light Found., Washington, 1993-96. Pres. LWV, Palos Verdes Peninsula, Calif., 1981-83; chair Year of the Coast, Calif. LWV, Sacramento, 1984; active in state and local polit. campaigns. Named YWCA Woman of the Yr., YWCA, Torrance, 1986, Woman of Distinction, Soroptomist, Torrance, 1988. Mem. Pvt. Industry Coun. (bd. mem. 1994-96), Cmty. Assn. of the Peninsula (life, pres. 1984-87, Palos Verdes Peninsula Citizen of Yr. 1987, Outstanding Vol. award 1988), So. Bay Prodrs. Guild (Outstanding Interviewer 1995), Vol. Ctrs. of Calif. (bd. mem. 1988—, Founders award 1991), Gamma Phi Beta (alumni mem., Internat. Carnation award 1992, Achievement award 1993). Democrat. Roman Catholic.

HICKS, DOROTHY JANE, obstetrician and gynecologist, educator; b. Cleve., Apr. 18, 1919; d. Arnell R. and Marvel M. (Hale) H. AB, Case Western Reserve U., 1941; MD, Temple U., 1944. Diplomate Am. Bd. Obstetrics and Gynecology. Asst. prof. dept. ob-gyn. U. Miami, 1967-85, prof., 1985—; bd. dirs. rape treatment ctr. Jackson Meml. Hosp., Miami, med. dir., 1974-93, cons., 1993—; dir. pedigyn clinic Jackson Meml. Hosp. Contbr. articles to profl. jours. Fellow Am. Coll. Ob-Gyn., N.Am. Soc. Pediatric and Adolescent Gynecology, South Atlantic Ob-Gyn. Soc., Fla. Soc. Ob/Gyn, Miami Ob/Gyn Soc. Office: U Miami Sch Medicine Dept Ob-Gyn PO Box 016960 Miami FL 33101

HICKS, HERALINE ELAINE, environmental health scientist, educator; b. Beaufort, S.C., Sept. 27, 1951; d. Heral and Ophelia Lillie (Albergottie) H. BA, Ohio Wesleyan U., 1973; MS, Atlanta U., 1978, PhD, 1980; postgrad., U. N.C., 1980-84. Rsch. assoc. Chapel Hill Dental Rsch. Ctr. U. N.C., 1980-81; NIH postdoctoral fellow Chapel Hill Dental Rsch. Ctr. Chapel Hill Dental Rsch. Ctr. and Dept. Surgery, 1982-84; guest scientist Naval Med. Rsch. Inst., Bethesda, Md., 1985-87; asst. prof. Chapel Hill Sch. Dentistry U. N.C., 1985-88; prof., dir. electron microscopy Morris Brown Coll., Atlanta, 1988-90; sr. environ. health scientist, dir. Cts. for Disease Control and Prevention/Agy. for Toxic Substances and Disease Registry, Atlanta, 1990—; program dir. Gt. Lakes Human Health Effects Rsch. Program, Agy. for Toxic Substances and Disease Registry; mem. health profls. task force adv. bd. Internat. Joint Commn., Washington, 1995—. Author: (chpt.) Development and Diseases of Cartilage and Bone Matrix, 1987, Birth Defects and Reporductive Disorders, 1993; contbr. articles to profl. jours. Predoctoral traineeship NIH, 1977-79, Barnett F. Smith award for outstanding achievement Atlanta U., 1978; Acad. scholar Ohio Wesleyan U., 1969-73, Josiah Macy Jr. scholar Woods Hole Marine Biol. Lab., 1979, Tuition scholar Atlanta U., 1979-80; postdoctoral fellow NIH, 1982-84, Notable Alumnus of Clark U., 1995; named one of Outstanding Young Women of Am., 1980. Mem. Am. Soc. for Cell Biology (Young Investigator fellowship 1990), Teratology (Young Investigator fellowship 1987), Microscopy Soc. Am., Biology Honor Soc., Beta Kappa Chi. Presbyterian. Office: Ctrs for Disease Control and Prevention Mail Stop E29 1600 Clifton Rd NE Atlanta GA 30333

HICKS, LUCILE P., state legislator; b. Greenwood, Miss., May 11, 1938; m. William Hicks, 1960. BS, Millsaps Coll.; MPA, Harvard U., 1986. High sch. sch. tchr.; mem. Mass. Ho. of Reps., 1980-90, Mass. Senate, 1990-96; mem. Wayland Rep. Town Com. Mem. LWV, Jr. League Boston, Sudbury Valley Trustees. Home: 5 Wildwood Rd Wayland MA 01778-2121 Office: State House State Capitol Boston MA 02133

HICKS, NANCY BENNETT, social services administrator; b. Covington, Va., Sept. 18, 1936; d. James Gordon and Margaret Ida (Dickerson) Bennett; m. Jackson Earl Hicks, July 3, 1958; 1 child, Margaret Elizabeth Hicks Sargent. BA, Erskine Coll., Due West, S.C., 1958; MA, East Tenn. State U., 1975, EdD, 1979. Tchr. Greene County Schs., Stanardsville, Va., 1958-61; tchr. City of Covington, 1961-63, Clayton County Schs., Jonesborough, Ga., 1963-67; grad. student East Tenn. State U., Johnson City, 1972-80; chair, edn. dept. Va. Intermont Coll., Bristol, 1981-89; chair undergrad. edn. dept. Carson-Newman Coll., Jefferson City, Tenn., 1989-90; mgr. sr. ctr. City of Kingsport (Tenn.), 1990—; mem. srs. task force Kingsport Tomorrow, 1990—, Sr. Ctr. dirs. Area Agy. on Aging, Johnson City, 1990—. Editor: (poem collection) By the Sea, 1985. Pres. Woodland Garden and Art Club, Kingsport, 1978; pres. Kingsport Music Club, 1980; chair Srs. Task Force, 1991-93. Mem. Nat. Recreation & Pks. Assn., Nat. Coun. on Aging, Phi Kappa Phi. Republican. Presbyterian. Home: PO Box 3153 Kingsport TN 37664 Office: Senior Citizens Center 225 W Center St Kingsport TN 37660-4237

HICKS, PHYLLIS ANN, medical, surgical nurse; b. Croghan, N.Y., July 4, 1935; d. Leonard B. and Doris A. (Schack) Bush; m. Patrick Clare, Aug. 1, 1953 (dec. Jan. 1976); m. Charles L. Hicks, May 26, 1979; children: Michael Clare, Maureen (dec.), Martin (dec.); stepchildren: Lynn, Melinda, Kevin. ADN, St. Elizabeth's Hosp., Utica, N.Y., 1988; cert. pharmacology, Bd. Coop. Ednl. Svcs., Verona, N.Y., 1989, phlebotomy cert., 1994; student, Mercy Hosp. Sch. Nursing, Watertown, N.Y., 1952-53. RN, N.Y. Nurse med.-surg. unit Rome (N.Y.) Murphy Meml. Hosp., 1988-90; head nurse geriatrics Stonehedge Nursing Home, Rome, N.Y., 1990; nurse I Mohawk Valley Psychiatric Ctr., Utica, N.Y., 1990-91; charge nurse ventilator unit Oneida (N.Y.) City Hosp., 1993—. Home: 10276 State Rt 26 Ava NY 13303 Office: Oneida Health Care Assn 321 Genesee St Oneida NY 13421

HICKS, ROBIN WELLS, nurse; b. Ft. Oglethorpe, Ga., Jan. 16, 1955; d. Marvine Eugene and Opal Evelyn (Edmonds) Wells; m. Dennis Ray Hicks, Nov. 19, 1976 (div. 1994); 1 child, Amy Nicole. Diploma in nursing, J.F. Drake Tech., 1974; degree in nursing, John C. Calhoun, Decatur, Ala., 1979; BSN magna cum laude, U. Ala., 1991. RN, Ala.; ACLS. Office nurse Cromeans Clinic, Scottsboro, Ala., 1974-76; charge nurse Huntsville (Ala.) Nursing Home, 1976-78; operating rm. nurse Huntsville Hosp., 1980-81, Jackson County Hosp., Scottsboro, 1981-85; hemodialysis charge nurse BMA Dialysis, Scottsboro, 1985-90; asst. dir. blood svc. No. Ala. ARC, Huntsville, 1991—; part-time charge nurse Jackson County Nursing Home, Scottsboro, 1978-80. Vol. Madison chpt. ARC, Huntsville, EMT, Woodville, Ala. Democrat. Home: 1202 Birchwood Dr Scottsboro AL 35768-3006

HICKS, VICKI JEAN, lawyer; b. Woodward, Okla., Dec. 30, 1955; d. Morris E. and Betty J. (Hicks) H. BS, Phillips U., 1978; JD, U. Okla., 1981. Bar: Okla. 1981, D.C. 1982, U.S. Dist. Ct. D.C. 1982. Assoc. Balsamo & Dominquez, Washington, 1983-84; internat. cons. Nebr. Wheat Bd., Washington, 1984; policy analyst Office Antiboycott Compliance Internat. Trade Adminstrn., Washington, 1984-87; legis. counsel Sen. Quentin N. Burdick, Washington, 1987-92; chief of staff rep. Karan English Washington, 1993; asst. dep. adminstrv. cmty. ops. Dept. Agr., 1993—. Pres., Georgetown North Unit Owner's Assn., 1986. Recipient scholarship U. Okla., 1980. Mem. D.C. Bar, Okla. Bar Assn., Okla. State Soc. Washington (pres. 1994, trustee 1995—).

HIEATT, CONSTANCE BARTLETT, English language educator; b. Boston, Feb. 11, 1928; d. Arthur Charles and Eleonora (Very) Bartlett; m. Allen Kent Hieatt, Oct. 25, 1958. Student, Smith Coll., 1945-47; AB, Hunter Coll., 1953, AM, 1957; PhD, Yale U., 1959. Lectr. City Coll., CUNY, 1959-60; from asst. prof. to assoc. prof. English Queensborough Community Coll., CUNY, 1960-65; assoc. prof., then prof. St. John's U., Jamaica, N.Y., 1965-69; prof. English U. Western Ont., London, Can., 1969-93, prof. emeritus, 1993—. Author: (with A.K. Hieatt) The Canterbury Tales of Geoffrey Chaucer, 1964, rev. edit., 1981, Spenser: Selected Poetry, 1970; The Realism of Dream Visions, 1967, Beowulf and Other Old English Poems, 1967, rev. edit., 1983, Essentials of Old English, 1968, The Miller's Tale By Geoffrey Chaucer, 1970; (with Sharon Butler) Pleyn Delit: Medieval Cookery for Modern Cooks, 1976, rev. edit., 1979, (with Brenda Hosington) rev. 2d edit., 1996, Karlamagnus Saga, Vols. I and II, 1975, Vol. III, 1980; (with Sharon Butler) Curye on Inglysch, 1985; An Ordinance of Pottage, 1988, (with Robin F. Jones) La Novele Cirurgerie, 1990; (with Minnette Gaudet) Guillaume de Machaut's Tale of the Alerion, 1994; (with Brian Shaw and Duncan Macrae-Gibson) Beginning Old English, 1994; also children books (with Hieatt) The Canterbury Tales of Geoffrey Caucer, 1961, Sir Gawain and the Green Knight, 1967, The Knight of the Lion, 1968, The Knight of the Cart, 1969, The Joy of the Court, 1971, The Sword and the Grail, 1972, The Castle of Ladies, 1973, The Minstrel Knight, 1974. Yale U. fellow, and Lewis-Farmington fellow, 1957-59; Can. Council and Social Sci. and Humanities Rsch. Coun. grantee; Yale U. vis. fellow, 1985-86, 89-93. Fellow Royal Soc. Can.; mem. MLA, Medieval Acad. Am., Internat. Saga Assn., Internat. Soc. Anglo-Saxonists, Soc. for Advancement Scandinavian Studies, Assn. Can. Univ. Tchrs. English, New Chaucer Soc., Anglo-Norman Text Soc. Episcopalian. Home: 304 River Rd Deep River CT 06417-2120

HIEBEL, JOANN HELEN, advertising executive; b. Hinckley, Minn., Dec. 7, 1936; d. Joseph Nicholas and Lillian Anna (Korbel) Williams; m. Kenneth John Hiebel, Sept. 5, 1959 (div. Apr. 1981); children: Caroline Kathleen, Michael John. Student Coll. of St. Benedict; BA, U. Minn., 1958. Adminstrv. asst. Admiral-Merchants, St. Paul, 1958-63; tchr. piano, Mpls., 1964-74; adminstrv. asst. Minn. Opera Co., St. Paul, 1974-77; advt. assoc. Coulter & Assocs., Mpls., 1977-79; mgr. pub. relations Profl. Instruments, Mpls., 1979-81; owner, pres., CEO Jo Ann Hiebel & Assocs., Mpls., 1981—; exec. dir. Minn. Tooling and Machining Assn. (now Minn. Precision Mfg. Assn.), 1981—; advt. rep. and pub. assoc. Bolger Publs., Mpls., 1982-85. Bd. dirs. Exec. Manor Condominium Assn., Mpls., 1980-81, Kidney Found. of Upper Midwest, St. Paul, 1983-86; del. Minn. Conf. on Small Bus., Mpls., 1981, 87; mem., pres. Mrs. Jaycees, St. Anthony, Minn., 1963-70; founder Group IV Assn. Mgmt., Inc., 1988. Mem. Nat. Assn. Women Bus. Owners, Advt. Fedn. Minn., Sales and Mktg. Execs.-Mpls., Minn. Soc. Assn. Execs., Minn. Assn. Commerce and Industry, Gamma Phi Beta. Republican. Home: 110 Bank St # 1105 Minneapolis MN 55414 Office: Hiebel & Assocs Inc 3300 Bass Lake Rd Minneapolis MN 55429

HIEMIER, PAIGE DANA, nurse; b. N.Y.C., May 11, 1954; d. Stanley Richard and Faith Mae (Dow) H. AS, Bergen Community Coll., 1985; student, William Paterson Coll., 1989, New Sch., N.Y.C., 1990. RN, N.Y. Nurse neonatal ICU St. Luke's Hosp., N.Y.C., 1986-90, nurse emergency and pediat. emergency rm., 1990—, nurse pediatric AIDS Clinic, 1991-93; nurse emergency rm. Kennedy Meml. Hosp., Saddlebrook, N.J., 1991-93; chairperson St. Luke's Collective Bargaining Unit, N.Y.C., 1989-91. Author: Another Side of Innocence, 1989; contbr. poetry to various publs. Mem. citizen's adv. com. Bergen C.C., 1985-86; RN organizer Local 1199, N.Y., 1993—. Home: PO Box 375 Ridgefield Park NJ 07660-0375

HIERONYMUS, CLARA BOOTH WIGGINS, journalist; b. Drew, Miss., July 25, 1913; d. Bruce Charles and Maude (Watson) Wiggins; m. Senator Cleo Hieronymus, Apr. 24, 1937 (dec. Mar. 1995); children: Bruce Lee, Jane (Mrs. David Piller). BA cum laude, U. Tulsa, 1932; MSW, U. Okla., 1936; DFA, R.I. Coll., 1984. Employment sec. and counselor YWCA, Tulsa, 1936-38; labor market analyst Okla. Employment Service, also instr. sociology U. Tulsa, 1938-50; free-lance writer Nashville, Tennessean, 1951-56; art and drama critic, 1956-90, drama critic, 1990—, home furnishings editor, 1956-83; mem. rotating faculty Nat. Critics Inst., 1975—; adj. instr. theatre criticism Belmont Univ., 1989-90; book review radio sta. KFMJ, Tulsa, 1938-45; speaker before groups, 1950—; arts clinician Tenn. Arts Acad. of Tenn. Dept. Edn., 1993. Author: (with Barbara Izard) Requiem for a Nun: On Stage and Off, Scholar's Catalog for Retrospective Exhibit of Lee and Pup McCarty, potters and designers, 1991, 95; editor City of Forest Hills quar. newsletter, 1992—. Mem. panel jurors for selection Am. Children's Theaters to perform at Internat. Conf. U.S.A., 1972; bd. dirs. Samaritans, Inc., 1967-76, pres., 1967-69; bd. dirs. Middle Tenn. chpt. Nat. Arthritis Found., 1967-70; charter mem. bd. Middle Tenn. Historic Sites Fedn., 1968-70; mem. Tenn. Fine Arts Ctr. and Bot. Gardens, 1959—; mem. adv. bd. O'More Coll. Design, 1970-91, bd. dirs., 1991-94; adv. bd. Nashville Ballet Soc., 1977-79; founder, life mem. O'More Design Guild, 1970—. Recipient Dorothy Dawe award Am. Furniture Mart, 1960, 63, 66, 69, Dallas Market Ctr. award, 1965, Disting. Achievement in Arts awards Tenn. Art League, 1987, 89, Gov.'s award in arts, 1980, Humanitarian award Fisk U., 1983, Disting. Achievement award Tenn. Theater Assn., 1987; named Woman of Year in Communications, Bus. and Profl. Women's Club, Nashville, 1966; named to Mayor's Com. Community Excellence, 1982; honored by Links, Inc., 1982; honored by Tenn. State U. for disting. svc. in art for students, 1986, 89, honored in "Accolade to Clara" Tenn. Performing Arts Ctr., 1986, 87, honored by O'More Coll. Design, 1990, Intermus. Coun. Nashville for disting. svc., 1990; named Pride of Tenn., 1982, Disting. Alumna U. Tulsa, 1988; named among 10 best and most rep. women in critical professions today in Women in Am. Theater, 1981; Metro Arts Commn. honoree, 1991, Botanical Gardens and Fine Arts Ctr. honoree, 1990; award from Stages monthly theater review publ. for lifetime achievement in theater, 1991. Mem. Am. Soc. Interior Designers (press assoc., 20 Yrs. Disting. Svc. award Nashville chpt.), Nashville Children's Theatre, Assn. Internationale du Theatre pour L'Enfance et Jeunesse, Am. Theater Critics Assn. (founding mem., governing bd. 1974—, nat. chmn. 1980-84, exec. sec. 1984—). Democrat. Methodist. Clubs: Centennial (Nashville), Le Petit Salon (Nashville). Office: The Tennessean Am Theatre Critics Assn 1100 Broad St Nashville TN 37203

HIESTAND, EMILY LUCILLE, artist, writer; b. Chgo., July 15, 1947; d. Orris Sidney and Frances Emily (Watkins) H.; m. Peter Niels Dunn, Oct. 8, 1995. BFA, Phila. Coll. Art, 1970; MA in Writing, Boston U., 1988, PhD, 1991. Designer Edn. Devel. Ctr., Cambridge, Mass., 1970-73; creative dir. Hiestand Design Assoc., Watertown, Mass., 1973-88, The Artemis Ensemble, Cambridge, 1988-92; artist, poet, essayist Cambridge, 1980—; vis. poet Boston U., 1991, 92. Author: Green the Witch Nazel Wood, 1988 (NP series award 1988), The Very Rich Hours, 1992; lit. and poetry editor: Orion Mag., 1992—; contbr. essays and poetry to popular mags. and revs.; painting exhibits include Van Buren Brazelton Cutting Gallery, 1983, 84, 86, The Blue Diner, Boston, 1987, Off The Wall Gallery, 1985. Co-founder, co-dir. Communicators for Nuclear Disarmament, Boston, 1980-85; founder, dir. Friends of Sandcastles, Cambridge, 1973-93; bd. dirs. Assocs. of Boston Pub. Libr., 1995—. Recipient Whiting Writers award Mrs. Giles Whiting Found., 1990, Nat. Poetry Series award, 1988, Discovery/The Nation award The Nation/92d St. Poetry Program, 1988; video grantee Mass. Cultural Coun., 1992. Mem. Acad. Am. Poets. Democrat.

HIESTAND, SHARON DILORENZO, real estate professional, architect; b. Jennings, La., Oct. 11, 1946; d. Garland and Annabelle (Carter) H.; m. Frank Clifford DiLorenzo, Feb. 5, 1965; children: Anthony Garland, Michael Russell. B Archtl. Design, U. Hartford, 1968; MFA in Design Comms., Sch. Art Inst. Chgo., 1972; PhD in Indsl. Psychology, U. Conn., 1980; CFP, Roosevelt U., 1990. Registered investment real estate profl. Assoc. prof. interior architecture Sch. of Art Inst. Chgo., 1971-76; vis. prof. archtl. history Barat Coll., Lake Forest, Ill., 1979-80; tenant coord. new constrn. Taubman Devel., Bloomfield Hills, Mich., 1980-84; capital constrn. facilities mgr. U. Chgo. Hosps. and Clinics, Chgo., 1984-92; mgmt. cons. bus. svcs. Ameritech, Barrington, Ill., 1992-94; mktg. editor Clark Reports, Lake Bluff, Ill., 1993; constrn. estimator, Barrington, 1968; downtown rehab. specialist Yale Grad. Sch. Arch., New Haven, New Haven Cmty. Investment Corp., 1968-70; multi-family rehab. specialist Handy-Help Svcs., Barrington, 1990-96; tech. writer Clark Bus. Svcs., Clark Assocs., Lake Bluff, 1994. Artist/architect serigraph Hartford Atheneum, 1968; printmaker, architect, artist lithograph for Prudential Ins., 1969, Metropolis, 1970. Recipient Supermarket of 1973, Enviro-Technics Ltd., Cert. Grocers Ind., Ill., Wis. and Mich., 1969, Home Design award Frank Lloyd Wright Home and Studio Found., 1972, Indsl. Renovation award AIA. Mem. AAUW, LWV, Barrington C. of C., Nat. Trust for Hist. Preservation, Architecture Soc. of Art Inst. Chgo., Graham Found. for Advanced Studies in Fine Arts. Roman Catholic. Address: Business Services Ste 1285 254 Steeplechase Rd Barrington IL 60011-1285 Home: 254 Steeplechase Rd Barrington Hills IL 60010 Office: Clark Reports 925 Sherwood Dr Lake Bluff IL 60010

HIGBEE, ANN G., public relations executive, consultant; b. Newark, May 6, 1942; d. Roger Herald German and Charlotte May (Ryan) Wentzell; m. James Lyman Higbee, June 25, 1965; 1 child, Travis James. BS, U. Md., 1964. Field rep. Am. Field Svc., N.Y.C., 1964-65; from acct. exec. to v.p.

Rath Orgn., Syracuse, N.Y., 1965-71, T.A. Best Co., Skaneateles, N.Y., 1971-75; dir. devel. Manlius Pebble Hill Sch., Jamesville, N.Y., 1975-79; dir. pub. rels., mng. ptnr. Eric Mower and Assocs., Syracuse, 1980—. Chair Pub. Broadcasting Coun./CNY, Syracuse, 1977-84; dir. Crouse Health, Syracuse, 1983—; trustee Coll. Environ. Sci. and Forestry Found., Syracuse, 1991—. Named Women of Achievement by Post-Standard, Syracuse, 1973, Outstanding Young Woman by Jaycees, Syracuse. Mem. Pub. Rels. Soc. Am. (accredited, counselors sect.), Am. Assn. Advt. Agys. (pub. rels. com.). Office: Eric Mower & Assocs 500 Plum St Syracuse NY 13204-1401

HIGDON, BARBARA J., college president; b. Independence, Mo., May 18, 1930; m. 1950; 3 children. B.A., U. Mo., 1951, M.A., 1952, Ph.D. in Speech, 1961. Assoc. prof. English, speech, Tex. So. U., 1958-62; prof. Graceland Coll., Lamoni, Iowa, 1962-75, pres., 1984-91, pres. emerita, 1992—; dean, v.p. acad. affairs Park Coll., 1975-84; bd. SS. Cyril and Methodius Found., Bulgaria 1992—; chair Iowa Peace Inst., 1992. Author: Good News for Today, 1981, Committed to Peace, 1994. Office: Graceland Coll Office of the President Lamoni IA 50140

HIGDON, BERNICE COWAN, retired elementary education educator; b. Sylva, N.C., Feb. 26, 1918; d. Royston Duffield and Margaret Cordelia (Hall) Cowan; m. Roscoe John Higdon, Aug. 12, 1945; children: Ronald Keith, Rodrick Knox, Krista Dean. BS, Western Carolina U., 1941; cert. tchr., So. Oreg. Coll., 1967; student, Chapman Coll., 1971. Cert. tchr., Calif. Prin., tchr. Dorsey Sch., Bryson City, N.C., 1941-42; expeditor Glenn L. Martin Aircraft Co., Balt., 1942-45; tchr. elem. sch. Seneca, S.C., 1945-46, Piedmont, S.C., 1946-47; tchr. elem. sch. Columbia, S.C., 1950-51, Manteca, Calif., 1967-68; kindergarten tchr. 1st Bapt. Ch., Medford, Oreg., 1965-67; tchr. elem. sch. Marysville (Calif.) Unified Sch. Dist., 1968-83; tchr. Headstart, Manteca, 1968. Past counselor Youth Svc. Bur., Yuba City, Calif.; troop leader Girl Scouts U.S.A., Medford, 1962-63; past Sunday sch. tchr. 1st Bapt. Ch., Medford; bd. dirs. Christian Assistance Network, Yuba City, 1984-85; aux. vol. Fremont Med. Ctr., Yuba City, 1984-94; deaconess Evang. Free Ch., Yuba City, 1991-93. Recipient cert. of appreciation Marysville Unified Sch. Dist., 1983, Christian Assistance Network, 1985; cert. of recognition Ella Elem. Sch., Marysville, 1983. Mem. Calif. Ret. Tchrs. Assn., Nat. Ret. Tchrs. Assn., Sutter Hist. Soc., AAUW, Am. Assn. Ret. Persons. Home: 1264 Charlotte Ave Yuba City CA 95991-2804

HIGDON, POLLY SUSANNE, federal judge; b. Goodland, Kans., May 1, 1942; d. William and Pauline Higdon; m. John P. Wilhardt (div. May 1988); 1 child, Liesl. BA, Vassar Coll., 1964; postgrad., Cornell U., 1967; JD, Washburn U., 1975; LLM, NYU, 1980. Bar: Kans. 1975, Oreg. 1980. Assoc. Corley & Assocs., Garden City, Kans., 1975-79, Kendrick M. Mercer Law Offices, Eugene, Oreg., 1980-82; pvt. practice law Eugene, 1983; judge U.S. Bankruptcy Ct., Eugene, 1983-95, Portland, Oreg., 1995—. Active U.S. Peace Corps, Tanzania, East Africa, 1965-66. Mem. Am. Bankruptcy Inst., Nat. Conf. Bankruptcy Judges, Oreg. Women Lawyers. Office: US Bankruptcy Ct 1001 SW 5th Ave 7th Fl Portland OR 97204

HIGGINBOTHAM, EDITH ARLEANE, radiologist, researcher; b. New Orleans, Sept. 14, 1946; d. Luther Aldrich and Ruby (Clark) H.; m. Terry Lawrence Andrews (div. 1979); m. Donald Temple Ford (div. 1989). BS, Howard U., 1967, MS, 1970, MD, 1974. Diplomate Am. Bd. Radiology, Am. Bd. Nuclear Medicine. Intern St. Vincent's Hosp., N.Y.C., 1974-75, resident in diagnostic radiology, 1975-78, resident in nuclear radiology, 1978-79; asst. prof. radiology, chief nuclear Medicine Howard U., Howard U. Hosp., Washington, 1979-82; assoc. prof. clin. radiology, dir. nuclear medicine U. Medicine and Dentistry N.J., Newark, 1982-90; locum tenens radiologist Sterling Med., Cin., 1991—, Med. Nat., San Antonio, 1990-91; diagnostic radiologist Diagnostic Health Imaging Systems, Lanham, Md., 1994—; cons. Biotech. Rsch. Inst., Rockville, Md., 1989-94; profl. assoc. Ctr. for Molecular Medicine and Immunology, Newark, 1984-90, asst. prof. radiology George Washington U., Washington, 1990; presenter in field. Contbr. articles and abstracts to med. jours. Named Outstanding Working Woman, Glamour mag., 1981, Hon. Dep. Atty. Gen., State of La., 1982. Mem. Am. Coll. Radiology, Radiol. Soc. N.Am., Soc. Nuclear Medicine, Sigma Xi, Phi Delta Epsilon. Roman Catholic. Home: PO Box 1066 Clarksville TN 37041-1066 also: # A-25 300 Greenwwood Ave Clarksville TN 37040 also: 3926 Chestnut St New Orleans LA 70115

HIGGINBOTHAM, WENDY JACOBSON, political adviser, writer; b. Salt Lake City, Oct. 23, 1947; d. Alfred Thurl and Virginia Lorraine (LaCom) Jacobson; m. Keith Higginbotham, July 12, 1969; children: Ann Elizabeth, Ryan Keith, Laura Carol. Student, Occidental Coll., 1965-66, U. Grenoble, France, 1967; BA cum laude with highest honors, Brigham Young U., 1969. Teaching instr. Brigham Young U., Provo, Utah, 1969-70, editor univ. press, 1970-71; freelance editor Camarillo, Calif., 1971-78; freelance newspaper writer Vienna, Va., 1983-85; mem. profl. staff U.S. Senate Labor Com., Washington, 1985-86; exec. asst. U.S. Senator Orrin G. Hatch, Washington, 1986-88, legis. dir., 1988-91, chief of staff/adminstrv. asst., 1991-94, chief policy adviser, 1994-95; polit. adviser, freelance writer Washington, 1996—. Pres. Parent-Tchr. Assn., Vienna, 1981-82. Mem. Profl. Rep. Women, Phi Kappa Phi. Mormon. Home: 2022 Willow Branch Ct Vienna VA 22181-2972

HIGGINS, CONSTANCE DALKE, education educator; b. Denver, Oct. 21, 1950; d. Phillip George and Anna Evelina (Carlson) Logan. BA, U. Colo., 1972; MA, U. Denver, 1974, PhD, 1984. Tchr. spl. edn. Farmington (N.Mex.) Schs., 1974-78, 80-81, Aztec (N.Mex.) Schs., 1978-80; assoc. prof. edn. support program students with disablities U. Wis., Whitewater, 1984-94; prof. U. Wis., 1994—; ednl. cons. in field. Author: Access for All, 1991, Life Works, 1994, Positeens, 1996. Recipient award Assn. Handicapped Student Svc. Programs in Postsecondary Edn., 1988, Outstanding Rsch. award Coll. Edn., U. Wis., Whitewater, 1989; grantee State of Wis., 1985-86, 87-88, 89, 91-92, U.S. Govt. 1985-90. Mem. ASCD, Coun. for Exceptional Children, Coun. for Learning Disabilities, Internat. Assn. Spl. Edn. Home: 16 Birchbrook Rd Bronxville NY 10708

HIGGINS, DOROTHY MARIE, academic dean; b. Lawrence, Mass., May 1, 1930; d. John Daniel and Mary Jane (Herbertson) H. AB, Emmanuel Coll., 1951; MS, Cath. U., 1961; PhD, Boston Coll., 1966. Assoc. prof. chemistry Emmanuel Coll., Boston, 1966-88, chair chemistry dept., 1974-85; div. chair math., sci., tech. Roxbury Community Coll., Roxbury Crossing, Mass., 1988-90; dean arts and scis. Teikyo-Post U., Waterbury, Conn., 1990—; grant cons. N.E. coll. Optometry, Boston, 1986; faculty cons. Zymark Corp., Hopkinton, Mass., 1982; rsch. assoc. U. Mass., Boston, 1975-84. Editor: (workbook) Geometry: Development Students, 1989; editor sci. newsletter, 1989; editorial adv. bd. Jour. Coll. Sci. Teaching, 1984-88. Instrumentation grantee NSF, 1985, Chautauqua grantee NSF, 1981-82, Instrumentation grantee George Alden Trust, 1985, Boston Globe Found., 1985, Extramural Assoc. grantee NIH, 1984. Mem. Am. Chem. Soc., Nat. Sci. Tchrs. Assn., New Eng. Chem. Tchrs., Soc. Coll. Sci. Teaching, Am. Assn. Higer Edn., Sigma Xi. Democrat. Roman Catholic. Office: Teikyo Post U 800 Country Club Rd Waterbury CT 06708-3200

HIGGINS, HANNAH B., art historian, educator; b. N.Y.C., Aug. 21, 1964; d. Richard Carter Higgins and Alison Knowles; m. Joseph Bernard Reinstein, Oct. 20, 1990. BA, Oberlin Coll., 1988; MA, U. Chgo., 1990, PhD, 1994. Gallery lectr. The Art Inst. of Chgo., 1990-91; course asst. U. Chgo., 1992, writing intern, 1993; adj. faculty Columbia Coll., Chgo., 1993; asst. prof. U. Ill., Chgo., 1994—; cons. Hermann Braun Fluxus Collection, Germany, Fluxus Festival Chgo., 1993. Contbr. articles to profl. jours. Office: U Ill Chgo Dept Art History 935 W Harrison St Chicago IL 60607-7039

HIGGINS, ISABELLE JEANETTE, librarian; b. Evanston, Ill., Dec. 13, 1919; d. Frank LeRoy and Ada Louise (Wilcox) Heck; m. George Alfred Higgins, Jan. 23, 1945 (dec. Sept. 1994); children: Alfred Clinton, Donald Quentin, Heather Higgins Aanes, Laura Higgins Palmer, Carol Higgins. BS, Northwestern U., 1940; MLS, U. Md., 1971. Cert. libr., Md. With Liebermann Waelchli Co., Tokyo, 1940-41, Shanghai Evening Post, 1941-42; editorial asst. Newsweek mag., N.Y.C., 1944; wire editor FBIS/FCC, Washington, 1944-46; rsch. and analysis China desk CIA, Washington, 1946-49; supr. library vols. Westbrook Sch., Bethesda, Md., 1965-69; reference librarian Montgomery County Pub. Libraries, Bethesda, 1969-83; librarian Brooks Inst. Photography, Santa Barbara, Calif., 1984—; treas. Friends of Santa Barbara Pub. Library, 1987-88. Mem. AAUW (bd. dirs. Santa Barbara br. 1988-94, del. nat. conv. 1989), Spl. Librs. Assn., Calif. Libr. Assn., Santa Barbara Little Gardens Club (pres. 1987-89), Floriade Garden Club (pres. 1990-91). Congregationalist. Home: 1128 Garcia Rd Santa Barbara CA 93103-2128 Office: Brooks Inst Photography 801 Alston Rd Santa Barbara CA 93108-2309

HIGGINS, JOAN MARIE, freelance writer, producer; b. Shamokin, Pa.; d. Leon Francis and Anna (Kiewlak) H. Student, Middlesex County Coll., Edison, N.J., 1971-73, The New Sch. for Social Rsch., N.Y.C. Mem. staff Eyewitness News/ABC-TV, N.Y.C., 1972-86; planning unit editor, field producer Eyewitness News/ABC-TV, 1985-86; freelance producer, writer, publicist N.Y.C., 1986-87, Children's Television Workshop, N.Y.C., 1986-87, Dino DeLaurentis Entertainment Co., N.Y.C., 1987; publicist Zarem Pub. Rels., N.Y.C., 1987, Self Mag., 1986-87; sr. publicist Avon Books/The Hearst Corp., N.Y.C., 1987-89; freelance writer, publicist Dances with Wolves TIG/Orion Pictures, NBC-TV, Universal TV, 1990-91; freelance writer, publicist St. Martin's Press, 1992—. Recipient Emmy award cert. of recognition for rsch. on TV spl., NATAS, 1981. Mem. Writers Guild Am. Home: 301 St James Ave Woodbridge NJ 07095-1609

HIGGINS, KATHLEEN K., landscape foreman; b. Sharon, Conn., July 4, 1964; d. George Robert and Doris May (Sprague) H.; 1 child, Kyla Cherie. B of Tech., SUNY, Cobleskill, 1992. Landscape foreman Kent (Conn.) Greenhouse, 1986-88; landscape designer Adams Nurseries, Alden, N.Y., 1992; greenhouse worker Angle Acres Greenhouse, Orchard Park, N.Y., 1991-92; landscape foreman Kent Horticultural Svc., 1992—. Mem. NOW, Sierra Club. Home: RR 1 Box 55A Kent Rd Wassaic NY 12592

HIGGINS, KATHRYN O'LEARY, government official; b. Sioux City, Iowa, Oct. 11, 1947; d. Paul C. and Mary Kathryn (Callaghan) O'Leary; widowed; children: Liam James, Kevan Paul. BS, U. Nebr., 1969. Manpower specialist U.S. Dept. Labor, Washington, 1969-78; asst. dir. employment policy White House Domestic Policy, Washington, 1978-81; staff dir. minority U.S. Senate Labor & Human Resources Com., Washington, 1981-86; chief of staff U.S. Representative Sander Levin, Washington, 1986-93, Sec. of Labor Robert Reich, Washington, 1993—; cabinet sec. Cabinet Affairs, Washington. Vol. Gonzaga Mother's Club, Washington, 1988—; vol., host parent Project Children, Washington, 1987—. Democrat. Roman Catholic. Home: 6915 Ridgewood Ave Chevy Chase MD 20815-5149 Office: Office of the Sec Dept of Labor 200 Constitution Ave NW Washington DC 20210-0001 Office: The White House Office Cabinet Affrs Old Executive Bldg Washington DC 20500*

HIGGINS, MARGARET MURPHY, special education educator; b. Phila., Oct. 25, 1947; d. John Patrick and Rose (Scullin) Murphy; m. John Joseph Higgins, Feb. 21, 1969; children: Erin, John, Cara, Kevin. BA, Temple U., 1969; MA, Beaver Coll., 1979; EdD, Nova U., 1994. Cert. elem. and gifted tchr., Pa., Fla. Elem. tchr. Archdiocese of Phila., 1966-79; gifted edn. specialist Colonial Sch. Dist., Plymouth Meeting, Pa., 1979-81, Seminole County (Fla.) Schs., 1984—; presenter Fla. Assn. Gifted, Orlando, 1991-92, Stetson U., Deland, Fla., 1991, Fla. Edn. Tech. Conf., 1995, FDLRS Gifted Day, 1996; regional dir. Odyssey of Mind, Fla., 1989-92. Vol. publ. info. World Cup Soccer, Orlando, 1994, Atlanta Olympics, 1995-96. Recipient Tchr. Merit award Walt Disney Found., 1990, 93. Republican. Roman Catholic. Home: 130 Hunters Trl Longwood FL 32779-3052 Office: Seminole County Schs Indian Trails Middle Sch 555 Tuskawilla Rd Winter Springs FL 32708-3706

HIGGINS, MARIKA O'BAIRE, nursing educator, writer, entrepreneur, ontological coach; b. Manila, The Philippines, Oct. 3, 1947; d. Gerald John and Giovanna (BelForti) Barry; m. Dean. J. P. Higgins, July 1, 1978; children: Matthew, Alexei, Rita, Dean Patrick. Student, U. Conn., 1964-65; diploma, Ellis Hosp. Sch. Nursing, 1977; BSN, Russell Sage Coll., 1980, postgrad., 1983, 94; student, 3-yr. ontological design course, Logonet Inc., 1987-93; postgrad. in humanities, Calif. State U., Dominguez Hills, 1995—; postgrad., Calif. State U., 1995—; Grad. in Ontological Design, Logonet, Inc., Alameda, Calif., 1993; postgrad., Calif. State U., 1995. RN. Team leader, staff RN Samaritan Hosp. Acute Psychiatry, Troy, N.Y.; staff RN, pediatric ICU Albany (N.Y.) Med. Ctr.; rsch. RN Commn. on Quality Care for Mentally Disabled, Albany; staff RN Columbia-Greene Med. Ctr., Catskill, N.Y.; night charge nurse Conifer Park, Scotia, N.Y.; nursing educator St. Clare's Hosp., Schenectady, N.Y.; founder, designer Future Design & Co., 1995—; English tchr. Lang. Inst., Taipei, Taiwan. Novelist, publ. poet, lit. writer; comml. artist Echo Mag. Vol. curriculum designer in gifted and talented programs; mem. Red Cross Disaster Team. Mem. Internat. Women Writers Guild, Childreach Plan Internat. Home: 166 Lincoln Ave Saratoga Springs NY 12866-4629

HIGGINS, MARY ELLEN See HAWKINS, MARY ELLEN HIGGINS

HIGGINS, NANCY BRANSCOME, management and counseling educator; b. New Castle, Pa.; d. Otis and Ola May (Vaughn) Branscome; m. Bernard F. Higgins, Nov. 15, 1969; 1 child, Bernard F. II. BBA, Westminster Coll., 1967, MEd, 1970; MA, Pepperdine U., 1979; EdD, Vanderbilt U., 1990. Cert. counselor; full life cmty. coll. cert. in bus. mgmt. and indsl. human resources mgmt., psychology, office svcs. and related technologies. Counselor U. Md., College Pk., 1976-77; prof. part-time Hartnell Coll., Salinas, Calif., 1977-80; prof. mgmt. Monterey (Calif.) Peninsula Coll., 1977-80; coord., adminstr. Pepperdine U., Ft. Ord, Calif., 1977-80; prof. part-time Park Coll., Ft. Myer, Va., 1980-82, No. Va. C.C., Annandale, 1980-82, Prince George's Coll., Largo, Md., 1980-82; prof. mgmt. and mktg., coord. Montgomery Coll., Rockville, Md., 1982—, chairperson mgmt. dept., 1993—; mem. Faculty Congress, Montgomery Coll., 1985-87, diversity, com., 1994—, advising com. student devel., 1994—, critical literacy com. mem., 1994—, mgmt. adv. com., 1982—, tech. prep. com., 1994, 50th anniversary com., 1996—; mem. task forceNat. Coun. for Occupational Edn., 1994. Vol. ARC, Washington, Lakeside Hosp., Cleve., 1990; mem. WETA-Edn. TV, Fairfax, Va. Recipient Student Devel. award Montgomery Coll., 1982, Svc. award, 1982; grantee Montgomery Coll., 1990. Mem. AAUW, ASTD (membership com. and career devel. 1994—), Soc. Human Resources Mgmt., Nat. Soc. Exptl. Edn., Am. Assn. Women in C.C.'s, Pepperdine U. Alumni Assn., Vanderbilt U. Alumni Assn., Westminster Coll. Alumni Assn., Chi Omega (rush chairperson 1994—). Home: 7764 Heatherton Ln Potomac MD 20854-3212

HIGGINS, SISTER THERESE, English educator, former college president; b. Winthrop, Mass., Sept. 29, 1925; d. James C. and Margaret M. (Lennon) H. AB cum laude, Regis Coll., 1947; MA, Boston Coll., 1959, DHL, 1993; PhD, U. Wis., 1963; DHL, Emmanuel Coll., 1977, Lesley Coll., 1991; postgrad. in lit. and theology, Harvard U., 1965-66; LLD (hon.), Northeastern U., 1982, Bentley Coll., 1992, Regis Coll., 1994. Joined Congregation of Sisters of St. Joseph, Roman Cath. Ch., 1947; asst. prof. English, Regis Coll., Weston, Mass., 1963-65, asst. prof., 1965-67, assoc. prof. English lit., 1968—, pres., 1974-92, also trustee; book reviewer Boston Globe, 1965—. Trustee Waltham (Mass.) Hosp., 1978-85, Cardinal Spellman Philatelic Mus., 1976-92; mem. Mass. Gov.'s Commn. on Status Women, 1977-79, Nat. Com. Ecclesial Role Women, Archdiocesan Fin. Coun., 1991—. U. Wis. research grantee Eng. Mem. Nat. Cath. Ednl. Assn., AAUW, MLA, AAUP, Assn. Ind. Colls. and Univs. Mass. (exec. com.), New Eng. Colls. Fund, NEASC (commn.). Office: Regis Coll 235 Wellesley St Weston MA 02193-1505

HIGGS, BEVERLY WHITE, broadcast journalist; b. Frankfurt, West Germany, Aug. 4, 1960; d. Freeman and Modesta (Brown) White; m. Xavier Tyrone Higgs, May 30, 1993. JB, U. Tex., 1981. Reporter, editor, photographer KCEN-TV NBC, Waco, Tex., 1981-84; reporter KENS-TV CBS, San Antonio, 1984-85; reporter, anchor WKRC-TV ABC, Cin., 1985-89; reporter, substitute anchor WTVJ-TV NBC, Miami, 1989-92; reporter KNBC-TV NBC, L.A., 1992—. Bd. dirs. Bottomless Closet, L.A., 1996—. Recipient Peabody award for coverage of Hurricane Andrew U. Ga./WTVJ-TV, Miami, 1993. Office: KNBC-TV 3000 W Alameda Ave Burbank CA 91523

HIGHSMITH, ANNA BIZZELL, executive secretary; b. Richmond, Va., May 31, 1947; d. John Lee and Jacquelyn Frances (Miller) Bizzell; m. Jack Francis Starkey, Jan. 25, 1970 (div. Apr. 1972); 1 child, Mary Cathereine; m. Lemuel Martin Highsmith, May 25, 1974; 1 child, Lemuel Tayloe. Student, N. Fla. Jr. Coll., 1965-66, Armstrong State Coll., 1966-71. Sec. Seaboard Coastline RR, Savannah, Ga., 1966-76; sec., bookkeeper Highsmith Enterprises, Savannah, 1976—; Centennial Olympic vol. Yachting-Sports Info. Desk, Olympic Village, Savannah, Ga., 1996. Pres., chmn. of bd. Ballet South, Inc., Savannah, 1982-89, bd. dirs., advisor to pres., 1989—. Mem. Nat. Assn. Women in Constrn. (bd. dirs. 1982-87, 90-92, v.p. 1987-88, pres. 1989-90, 90-91, 94-95), Rinky Dink Sailing Club (sec., editor newsletter 1990-93, liaison 1989-93, prin. race officer 1993, cert. club race officer 1994), Geechee Sailing Club (editor newsletter 1990-91, sec. 1993), Savannah Yacht Club.. Republican. Episcopalian. Home: 519-A Whitfield Ave Savannah GA 31406-8207 Office: Highsmith Enterprises 615 Stiles Ave Savannah GA 31401-5322

HIGHSMITH, WANDA LAW, retired association executive; b. Cleveland, Mo., Oct. 25, 1928; d. Lloyd B. and Nan (Sisk) Law; student U. Mo., 1954-56; 1 child, Holly. Legal sec., firms in Mo. and D.C., until 1960; various staff positions Am. Coll. Osteopathic Surgeons, 1960-72, asst. exec. dir., conv. mgr., Alexandria, Va., 1974-94; ret., 1994. Mem. NAFE, Profl. Conv. Mgmt. Assn., Washington Soc. Assn. Execs., Am. Soc. Assn. Execs. Republican. Methodist. Home: 4835 Martin St Alexandria VA 22312-1838

HIGMAN, SALLY LEE, company executive; b. Hinsdale, Ill., Sept. 12, 1945; d. Lee Fulton and Freda Margaret (Doehle) H. AB in Social Scis., Shimer Coll., Mt. Carroll, Ill., 1967; MA in Govt., Claremont (Calif.) Grad. Sch., 1969; M of Planning, U. So. Calif., 1973; Cert. in Higher Studies in Ekistics, Athens Tech. Orgn., Athens Ctr. of Ekistics, 1970. Cons. Doxiadis Assocs., Athens, Greece, 1971; rsch. asst. U. So. Calif., 1971-72; cons. Republic of Ecuador, Quito, 1973-75, UN Devel. Prog., Quito, 1975-76; environ. analyst Tetra Tech Inc., Pasadena, Calif., 1976-78; sr. environ. planner Nus Corp., Sherman Oaks, Calif., 1978-81; project mgr. ACT, Inc., Westminster, Calif., 1981-87; owner Higman Doehle Environ. Cons., L.A., 1987-88; pres. Higman Doehle Inc., L.A., 1988—. Contbr. articles to profl. jours. Ford Found. scholar U. So. Calif., 1971-73, jr. rsch. fellow Athens Ctr. of Ekistics, 1969-71; intern Social Sci. Rsch. Coun., Ford Found., 1973-75. Mem. Shimer Coll. Scholastic Soc. Democrat. Episcopalian.

HILBERG, ROSEMARY H., human resource specialist; b. Elmhurst, Ill., Feb. 28, 1922; d. Michael and Gertrude H. (Heegard) Kross; m. Albert W. Hilberg, Aug. 22, 1944; children: Jeffrey, Eric, David, Kristin, Susan. BS in Biology, Elmhurst Coll., 1944; MA in Developmental Clin. Psychology, Antioch U., Columbia, Md., 1978; LLD (hon.), Elmhurst Coll., 1971. Lab. asst. Kegerreis Med. Clinic, Elmhurst, Ill., 1946-47; substitute tchr. Montgomery County (Md.) Pub. Schs., 1965-66; elected mem. Montgomery County Bd. Edn., 1966-74; legis. aide Md. Ho. of Dels., Annapolis, 1976-77; employee assistance specialist Montgomery County Pub. Schs., 1979—; planner/dir. 1st Network Symposium on Family Therapy Practice, D.C. Met. Area, 1978; adult edn. instr. Montgomery County Pub. Schs., 1981. Editor voters guide/bd. dirs. LWV of Montgomery County, 1950-54, 1st v.p., sec. Montgomery County Coun. of PTAs, 1964-66, elected precinct chair Dem. Party of Montgomery County, 1964-66. Recipient Life Membership award Md. Congress of Parents and Tchrs., 1976. Democrat. Unitarian. Home: 12512 Davan Dr Silver Spring MD 20904 Office: MCPS/EAP Ctr/Maryvale Elem 1000 First St Rockville MD 20850

HILBERMAN, ELAINE See CARMEN, ELAINE

HILBERT, VIRGINIA LOIS, computer consultant and training executive; b. Detroit, June 4, 1935; d. Howard G. and Lois (Garner) Swaggerty; m. James R. Hilbert, Nov. 24, 1958; children: James Jr., Jennifer, Douglas, Alexandra. BA with honors, U. Mich., 1957. Govt. analyst dept. pers. City of Detroit, 1957-60; owner, dir. Profl./Tech. Devel., Inc. dba Lansing (Mich.) Computer Assn. and Lansing Computer Inst., 1978—; participant, del. work group Gov.'s Small Bus. Conf. Contbr. articles to profl. jours. Mem. adv. com. Capital Area Sci. and Math. Challenge Grant; mem. tech. bd. Capital Region Cmty. Found., mem. accrediting comn. career schs. and Colls. of tech., Bus. Edn. Alliance for progress, adv. com.Capital Area Sci. & Math, Capital Area Health Alliance; sec. Tennis Patrons Bd., Lansing, 1984-89, Pro Symphony, 1984—; active Lansing Art Gallery, 1978-84. Mem. ASTD, ASCD, Nat. Fedn. Ind. Bus. (guardian), CEO Network, Women Bus. Owners Assn., Mich. Tech. Coun., Nat. Bus. Edn. Assn., Gov.'s Small Bus. Conf. (del. gov.'s work group), Mich. Opportunity Card, Accrediting Commn. of Career Schs. and Colls. of Tech., Bus. Edn. Alliance for Progress, Capital Area Sci. and Math. Challenge Grant Adv. Com., U.S. C. of C., Lansing C. of C. (small bus. coun., co-chair info. and seminar Small Bus. Edn., Cmty. Health Info. Network-Tech. Adv. Group com. Capital Area Health Alliance, del. White House Conf. on Small Bus. 1995, state chmn. Human Capital 1995, chair Human Capital region V for implementation 1996, mem. bd. physician health plan 1996), Rotary, Zonta, Alpha Phi (pres. heart equip. fund bd. 1975-96, alumnae pres.). Episcopalian. Home: 938 Wildwood Dr East Lansing MI 48823-3050 Office: Lansing Computer Inst 501 N Marshall St Lansing MI 48912-2306

HILBUN, HENRIETTA RESWEBER, mathematics educator; b. St. Martinville, La., May 11, 1958; d. Francis Thomas and Ellen Cecile (Campbell) Resweber; m. Joel D. Hilbun, June 30, 1988; children: David Thomas, Michael Patrick. BS in Math. Edn., U. Southwestern La., 1979, MEd in Adminstr. and Supervision, 1982, computer sci. cert., 1988. Tchr. high sch. math. Lafayette (La.) Parish Sch. Bd., 1979—; mem. Carencro High Sch. Discipline Com., Lafayette, 1993—; supervising tchr. La. State U., 1996—. La. State U. Geometry Software grantee, 1994. Mem. NEA, Nat. Coun. Tchrs. Math., La. Assn. Educators, Lafayette Parish Assn. Educators (pres. 1988-89, treas. polit. action com. 1990—), St. Peter and St. Paul Ladies Altar Soc., Phi Kappa Phi. Democrat. Roman Catholic. Office: Carencro High Sch 721 W Butcher Switch Rd Lafayette LA 70507-2303

HILDEBRAN, FRANCES ELAINE, municipal clerk; b. Shelby, N.C., Nov. 8, 1954; d. James Pinkney and Margaret Ellen (Mull) Sain; m. Dennis Alan Hildebran, June 26, 1976; 1 child, Curtis Alan. AAS, Western Piedmont C.C., 1975. Cert. mcpl. clk., N.C. Adminstrv. sec. Burke County Health Dept., Morganton, N.C., 1975-80; adminstrv. asst. to city mgr. City of Valdese, N.C., 1980—. Loaned exec. Burke County United Way, Morganton, 1990, bd. dirs., 1991—; mem. Burke County Libr. Bd., Morganton, 1995—; mem. indsl. adv. bd. Valdese Gen. Hosp., 1994—; sec., advocate Heritage Mid. Sch. Advocates, 1996; pres. Rutherford Coll. Elem. Sch. PTO, 1993; mem. Leadership Burke, Burke County C. of C., Morganton, 1991. Mem. Internat. Inst. Mcpl. Clks., N.C. Assn. Mcpl. Clks., Valdese Pilot Club (pres. 1981). Baptist. Office: City of Valdese 121 Faet St Valdese NC 28690

HILDEBRAND, CAROL ILENE, librarian; b. Presho, S.D., Feb. 15, 1943; d. Arnum Vance and Ethel Grace (Cole) Stoops; m. Duane D. Hildebrand, Mar. 21, 1970. BA, Dakota Wesleyan U., Mitchell, S.D., 1965; M in Librarianship, U. Wash., 1968. Tchr. Watertown (S.D.) H.S., 1965-67; libr. dir. Chippewa County Libr., Montevideo, Minn., 1968-70, The Dalles (Oreg.)-Wasco County Libr., 1970-72; libr. Salem (Oreg.) Pub. Libr., 1972-73; libr. dir. Lake Oswego (Oreg.) Pub. Libr., 1973-82; asst. city libr. Eugene (Oreg.) Pub. Libr., 1982-91, acting city libr., 1991-92, libr. dir., 1993—; cons., condr. workshops in field. Vice chmn. LWV, Lane County, 1987; bd. dirs. People for Oreg. Librs. Polit. Action Com., 1986—; sec. Citizens for Lane County Libr., 1985-88. Named Woman of Yr., Lane County Coun. of Orgns., 1995. Mem. ALA (chpt. councilor 1990-94), AAUW (bd. dirs. 1986, sec. 1995-96), Pacific N.W. Libr. Assn. (pres. 1989-90), Oreg. Libr. Assn. (pres. 1976-77), Rotary, Phi Kappa Phi. Methodist. Office: Eugene Public Library 100 W 13th Ave Eugene OR 97401-3433

HILDEBRAND, CHRISTA, lawyer; b. Warstein, Germany, Dec. 27, 1945; came to U.S., 1970; d. Fritz and Hilde (Pothoff) H.; m. Jeffrey Abrams; 1 child. Grad., Acad. Sci. and Tech., Isny, Germany, 1970; BA, BS, U. Wis., 1972, MA, 1973, PhD, 1980, JD, 1983. Bar: Wis. 1983, N.Y. 1985, Patent Bar 1986. Assoc. David Hoxie Faithful & Hapgood, N.Y.C., 1983-85, Fish & Neave, N.Y.C., 1985-90; with Egli Internat., N.Y.C., 1990-94; assoc., resident atty. Cohen Pontani Lieberman & Pavane, N.Y.C., 1994—. Mem.

ABA, Am. Intellectual Property Law Assn., N.Y. Patent Law Assn. Office: Cohen Pontani Et Al 551 Fifth Ave New York NY 10176

HILDEBRANDT-WILLARD, CLAUDIA JOAN, banker; b. Inglewood, Calif., Feb. 12, 1942; d. Charles Samual and Clara Claudia (Palumbo) H.; m. I. LeRoy Willard, Nov. 5, 1993. BBA, U. Colo. Head teller First Colo. Bank & Trust, Denver, 1969-70; asst. cashier First Nat. Bank, Englewood, Colo., 1975-79, asst. v.p., 1979-83, v.p., 1983-92; owner CJH Enterprises, Inc., Breckenridge, Colo., 1980—, Garden Tea Shop, Georgetown, Colo., Laudiac, Inc., Breckenridge, 1993—. Mem. Nat. Assn. Bank Women, Fin. Women Internat. (pres. elect. 1989-92), Am. Soc. for Pers. Adminstrn., Am. Inst. Banking, Mile High Group. Roman Catholic. Home: PO Box 5714 Breckenridge CO 80424-5714 also: PO Box 665 Georgetown CO 80444-0665 Office: 612 A 6th St Georgetown CO 80444

HILDERLEY, JERIANN GERTRUDE, novelist, educator; b. Saginaw, Mich., July 17, 1937; d. Clifton Tabor and Gertrude (Volz) Hilderley. Student, Smith Coll., 1955-57; BA, U. Calif., Berkeley, 1959; MA, U. Mich., 1961; M Spl. Edn., CUNY, 1988. Lic. spl. edn. tchr., N.Y. Dir. cmty.-based theaters Burning City Theater and Women's Ritual Theater, N.Y.C., 1962-74; dir. Sea Wave Record Co., N.Y.C., 1978-81; coord. data conversion BRS Med. Inc., N.Y.C., 1982-83; exec. sec. Nat. Coun. Chs., N.Y.C., 1983-84; tchr., curriculum developer, grants writer N.Y.C. Pub. Sch. 721, 1994—; juror in music C.A.P.S., N.Y.C., 1979-80; cons. Computer Arts Mgmt., N.Y.c., 1994—. Author: Mari, 1990; contbr. articles to profl. publs. Fundraiser, mem. Upper West Side Dem. Party, N.Y.C., 1986—; mem. adv. bd. Soho Women Artists, N.Y.C., 1992—; mem. West End Ave. Block Assn., N.Y.C., 1991—. Grantee N.Y. coun. Arts, 1971-73, CEC, Impact, Am. Heart Assn., 1985-89, N.Y. Found. for Arts, 1991-93, Art Ptnrs. Dewitt Wallace grantee N.Y. Fund for Pub. Edn., 1991-93. Fellow Blue Mountain Artists Ctr. (writer in residence 1994), Va. Creative Ctr. Arts (writer in residence 1993), Cummington Cmty. of Arts (writer in residence 1992); B.M.I. (composer, reviewer 1979—), Lady Slipper Inc. (contbg. composer 1979-84). Home: 711 W End Ave GGN New York NY 10025

HILDRETH, SANDRA JEAN, secondary school art educator; b. Milw., Oct. 15, 1946; d. Henry John and Jacqueline Marie (Marquardt) Tutino; children: Jennifer, David. BFA, tchg. cert., Western Ky. U., 1969; post-grad., SUNY, Potsdam, 1973—. Cert. art K-12, N.Y. Tchr. art DuPont Manual Jr./Sr. H.S., Louisville, 1969-70; libr. clk. Pratt Inst., Bklyn., 1970-71; tchr. art Franklin County B.O.C.E.S., Malone, N.Y., 1971-72, Madrid (N.Y.)-Waddington Ctrl. Sch., 1972—; instr. art methods St. Lawrence U., Canton, N.Y., 1990—. One-woman show Maxfield's Restaurant, Potsdam, 1986; exhibited in group show Brainard Art Galley, SUNY, Potsdam, 1976, 85, Mus. Natural History, Cin., 1980, 82, Ark. Wildlife Fedn., 1980, S.E. Ark. Arts and Sci. Ctr., Pine Bluff, 1980, 81, Spencer Crest Nature Learning Ctr. and Mus., Corning, N.Y., 1983, Tchrs. Learning Ctr., Canton, N.Y., 1988, Gibson Gallery, SUNY, Potsdam, 1994, Adirondack Vis. Interpretive Ctr., Paul Smith, N.Y., 1995, Ctr. for the Visual Arts, Inc., Wausaw, Wis., 1995. Recipient Multimedia in Edn. award SONYTHE Jour., 1993; named Outstanding Supr. Tchr. local chpt. Phi Delta Kappa, 1994; Christa McAuliffe fellow U.S. Dept. Edn., 1988; Excellence in Edn. grantee Reynolds Metals, 1990, 91, 93, 95. Mem. N.Y. State United Tchrs., N.Y. State Art Tchrs. Assn. Home: 2 Crescent Dr Norwood NY 13668-9784 Office: Madrid-Waddington Ctrl Sch PO Box 67 Madrid NY 13660-0067

HILER, MONICA JEAN, reading and sociology educator; b. Dallas, Sept. 3, 1929; d. James Absalom and Monica Constance (Farrar) Longino; m. Robert Joseph Hiler, Nov. 1, 1952; children: Robert, Deborah, Michael, Douglas, Frederick. BA, Agnes Scott Coll., Decatur, Ga., 1951; MEd, U. Ga., Athens, 1968, EdS, 1972, EdD, 1974. Social worker Atlanta Family and Children's Services, 1962-63; tchr. Hall County pub. schs., Ga., 1965-67; mem. faculty Gainesville Jr. Coll., Ga., 1968-87, prof. reading and sociology 1975-87, chmn. devel. studies program, 1973-85, acting chmn. div. social scis., 1986-87, prof. emeritus reading and sociology, 1987—; cons. So. Regional Edn. Bd., 1975-83, Gainesville Coll., 1987-95; apptd. spl. advocate Juvenile Ct. Union County, Ga., 1994-96. Mem. ASCD, Internat. Reading Assn., Ga. Sociol. Assn., Gainesville Music Club, Phi Beta Kappa, Phi Delta Kappa, Phi Kappa Phi. Avocations: piano, painting, sewing.

HILEY, VICKY ELAINE, art educator, professional cook; b. Pattonsburg, Mo.; d. John Richard and Florence Leota (Mooney) Mikes; div. 1993; children: Hobart Ray Jr., Christopher Quetin, Michael Joshua Edward, Jacqueline Stella Mae. BA in Edn., Art, Mo. Western State Coll., St. Joseph, 1976; tchg. cert. K-6, Northwest Mo. State, Maryville, 1978. Art educator grades K-12 Southwest RI, Ludlow, Mo., 1976-77; tchr. 2d grade Winston (Mo.) RVI, 1977-80; tchr. 1st grade Tri-County Elem., Jamesport, Mo., 1980-85; art educator K-12 Breckenridge, Mo., 1985-90; cook McDonald Tea Room, Gallatin, 1991—; educator "Parents as Tchrs.", Winston, Mo., 1994—. Troop leader Girl Scouts, Winston, 1989—. Home: Rt 1 Box 114A Winston MO 64689

HILFSTEIN, ERNA, science historian, educator; b. Krakow, Poland; came to U.S., 1949, naturalized, 1954; d. Leon and Anna (Schornstein) Kluger; BA, CCNY, 1967, MA, 1971, PhD, City U. N.Y., 1978; m. Max Hilfstein; children: Leon, Simone Juliana. Tchr. secondary schs., N.Y.C., 1968-84, 86-92; collaborator Polish Acad. Scis., 1968-85; vis. prof. Queens Coll., 1973; affiliate Grad. Sch./Univ. Ctr., City U. N.Y. NEH grantee, 1984-85; recipient Rector's medal Univ. M. Kopernik, Torun, 1989, Order of Merit Silver medal Republic of Poland, 1991. Mem. History Sci. Soc., Polish Inst. Arts and Scis. in Am., CUNY Acad. for the Humanities and Scis., N.Y. Acad. Scis., Kościuszko Found., United Fedn. of Tchrs. (chpt. chmn. 1978-84, 86-92, del. 1980-92), Am. Mus. Nat. History, Libr. of Congress; mem. Nat. Commn. Am. Fgn. Policy. Democrat. Jewish. Author: Starowolski's Biographies of Copernicus, 1980; collaborator English version of Nicholas Copernicus Complete Works, vol. 1, 1972, vol. 2, 1978, vol. 3, 1985, vols. 2 & 3, 2d edit., 1992; co-translator: The State Theory of Thomas Hobbes Leviathan, 1996; contbr. articles and revs. to profl. jours. Editor: Science and History, 1978, Copernicus and His Successors, 1995; co-author: The Leviathan in the State Theory of Thomas Hobbes, 1996. Home: 1523 Dwight Pl Bronx NY 10465-1121

HILGARTNER, MARGARET WEHR, pediatric hematologist, educator; b. Balt., Nov. 6, 1924; d. Andrew Henry and Margaret Elizabeth (Wehr) H.;m. Albert Milton Arky; children: George, Elizabeth, John. AB, Bryn Mawr Coll., 1946; MA, Duke U., 1951, MD, 1955. Diplomate Am. Bd. Pediatrics, Am. Bd. Pediatric Hematology/Oncology. Intern Bellevue Hosp., N.Y., 1955-56; resident in pediatrics N.Y. Hosp.-Cornell Med. Ctr., 1956-58, fellow in hematology/oncology, 1958-61, instr. in pediatrics, 1961-67, physician-in-charge pediatric coagulation, 1965—, asst. prof., 1967-73, dir. hemophilia comprehensive treatment, 1970—, assoc. prof., assoc. attending pediatrician outpatient dept., 1973-78, prof., dir. pediatric hematology/oncology div., attending pediatrician, 1978—, Harold Weill prof. pediatric hematology, 1988; assoc. attending pediatrician N.Y. Hosp., 1974—; adj. attending physician Sloan-Kettering Cancer Ctr., N.Y., 1979—; bd. dirs., mem. exec. com. N.Y. Blood Ctr.; cons. Bur. Handicapped Children, N.Y., 1971, Factor VIII Inhibitor Study Group, 1974, Ho. Reps. Ways and Means Com., 1977, Senate and Ho. Reps. Health Subcom. on Health, 1978-80, Fgn. and Interstate Commerce Com.-Ho. Reps. Subcom. on Pub. Health and Environment, 1979, N.Y. State Com. on Transfusion, 1979—, Ad Hoc Com. Rev. Rsch. in Edn., 1981-82; cons. in medicine Englewood (N.J.) Hosp., 1974—, in pediatric hematology, 1982—; lectr.-in-medicine Mt. Sinai Hosp., N.Y., 1979—; vis. prof. Rochester (Minn.) Hemophilia Ctr. 1979, 1980, Marshfield (Wis.) Clinic, 1979, Oakland Children's Hosp., 1981, Hangchow, Beijing, Kian, Peoples Republic of China, 1981, Johns Hopkins U. 1982, Rochester Strong Meml., 1985, Duke U., 1985.; chmn. Gov.'s adv. coun. to N.J. Dept. Health Hemophilia Program, 1973-80; mem. task force Factor VIII-Inhibitors Nat. Heart Lung Inst., 1975-80; mem. adv. com. publ. health #94-63 Health Svcs. Adminstrn., 1976lbood disease and resources Nat. Heart Lung Inst. NIH, 1985-89; chmn. Feiba Study Com., U.S. chpt., 1981—, pediatric working group World Fedn. Hemophilia, 1982; mem. ad hoc AIDS adv. com. Nat. Heart Lung Blood Inst. NIH, 1985—;. Mem. profl. adv. bd. mag. Baby Talk, 1987—; contbr. numerous articles to profl. jours. Mem. Am. Acad. Pediat. (chmn. sect. program oncology/hematology), Am. Heart Assn., Am. Med. Women's Assn., Am. Pediatric Soc., Am. Soc. Hematology, Assn. Women in Sci. (treas. 1974-76), Harvey Soc., Internat. Soc. Blood Transfusion, Internat. Soc. Thrombosis and Hemostasis, Nat. Hemophilia Found. (bd. dirs. met. chpt. 1965-69, trustee 1968-88, med. dir. met. chpt. 1970—, mem. med. and sci. bd. 1973-87, v.p. 1979-84, mem. edn. resources project 1979—), N.Y. Acad. Sci., N.Y. Soc. Study Blood, World Fedn. Hemophilia (chmn. child care com. 1990), Am. Soc. Pediatric Hematology/Oncology, Children's Blood Found. (med. dir. 1978—, bd. dirs. 1987—, pres. 1995—), Cooley's Anemia Found. (bd. dirs. 1987—). Office: Cornell U Med Coll Dept of Pediatrics 525 E 68th St New York NY 10021-4873

HILL, ALICE LORRAINE, history, genealogy and social researcher, educator; b. Moore, Okla., Jan. 15, 1935; d. Robert Edward and Alma Alice (Fraysher) H.; children: Debra Hrboka, Pamela Spangler, Eric Shiver, Lorraine Smith. Grad., Patricia Stevens Modeling Sch., Orlando, Fla., 1963; student, Draughton Sch. Bus., Oklahoma City, 1968-69, Troy State U., 1970-71, Ventura Coll., 1974; AA in Gen. Edn., Rose Coll., Midwest City, Okla.; BS in Bus. and Acctg., Ctrl. State U., 1977; student, U. Okla., 1977-78; postgrad., Calif. Luth. U., 1988; ed. Sch. Edn., UCLA, 1990. Cert. cmty. coll. life instr. acctg., bus. and indsl. mgmt., computer and related techs., and real estate, Calif.; ordained min., Gospel Ministry, 1982; lic. in real estate sales. Former model, 1990-95; with L.A. Unified Sch. Dist., 1990-95; founder A. Hill & Assocs. (formerly America, We Love You), Oxnard, Calif., 1993—; co-founder Law of Moses Common Law Legal Assn., Kingfisher, Okla., with Internat. Hdqs. at Brussett, Mont., 1994; founder The Los Artistas for creative activities for young people, 1996; rschr. Americana 2000. Author: America, We Love You (Congl. Record Poem), 1975; ghost writer book for Shafenberg Rsch. Found., 1981; author: (lyrics) Come Listen to the Music, 1996, Someday John, 1996; contbr. various articles and poems to profl. publs. Named hon. grad. Patricia Stevens Modeling Sch. (fla.); recipient scholarship Leadership Enrichment Program, Okla., 1977, Hon. recognition Okla. State Bd. of Regents for Higher Edn., 1977, Presdl. citations for Pres. Ford, 1975, 76, Admired Woman of the Decade award, 1994, Life Time Achievement award, 1995, Most Gold Record award, 1995, Key award for Rsch., Internat. Cultural Diploma of Honor, 1995, Woman of Yr. award, 1995, Internat. Woman of Yr. award Order Internat. Fellowship, 1994/95, Disting. Mem. Internat. Poetry Soc.. Mem. NAFE, NEA, AAUW, Internat. Platform Assn., Ventura County Profl. Women's Networking. Home: 1646 Lime Ave Oxnard CA 93033-6897

HILL, ALICIA CLEMMONS, accountant; b. Baton Rouge, Dec. 27, 1963; d. William Ray and Laura Lane (Brian) Clemmons; m. Lancy Edward Hill III; 1 child, Robert Lance. BS in Acctg., Southeastern La. U., 1988. Acct. TCI, Baton Rouge, 1986-88; auditor Premier Bank, N.A., Baton Rouge, 1988-91; CFO ENTECON Internat., Baton Rouge, 1986-91; comptr. Baton Rouge Title Co., 1991—; Recipient Presdl. citation Am. Bankers Assn., 1985. Mem. Inst. Mgmt. Accts., La. Assn. Bus. and Industry. Home: 2615 Stonewood Dr Baton Rouge LA 70816

HILL, ANITA CARRAWAY, retired state legislator; b. Chatfield, Tex., Aug. 13, 1928; d. Archie Clark and Martha (Butler) Carraway; BA in Journalism, Tex. Woman's U., 1950; m. Harris Hill, Sept. 20, 1952; children: Stephen Victor, Virginia Evelyn. Reporter Garland (Tex.) Daily News, 1950-51; ednl. dir. First Meth. Ch., Garland, 1951-53; chemist Kraft Foods Co., Garland, 1953-56; legis. aide, Tex. Legislature, 1975-77; mem. Tex. Ho. of Reps., 1977-92, mem. mcpl. bond and revenue sharing coms., 1971-74; ret., 1992. Awards chmn. City of Garland Environ. Council; mem. City of Garland Park and Recreation Bd., 1971-77, chmn., 1976-77; life mem. PTA; mem. Dallas County Mental Health Mental Retardation bd. trustees. Named Disting. Alumna, Tex. Woman's U., 1981. Mem. Garland C. of C., Rowlett C. of C., Bus. and Profl. Women's Club (Garland Woman of Year, 1980), AAUW, Tex. Assn. Elected Women. Republican. Methodist.

HILL, ANNA MARIE, manufacturing executive; b. Great Falls, Mont., Nov. 6, 1938; d. Paul Joseph and Alexina Rose (Doyon) Ghekiere. AA, Oakland Jr. Coll., 1959; student, U. Calif., Berkeley, 1960-62. Mgr. ops. OSM, Soquel, Calif., 1963-81; purchasing agt. Arrow Huss, Scotts Valley, Calif., 1981-82; sr. buyer Fairchild Test Systems, San Jose, Calif., 1982-83; materials mgr. Basic Test Systems, San Jose, 1983-86; purchasing mgr. Beta Tech., Santa Cruz, Calif., 1986-87; mgr. purchasing ICON Rev., Carmel, Calif., 1987-88; materials mgr. Integrated Components Test System, Sunnyvale, Calif., 1988-89; mfg. mgr. Forte Comm., Sunnyvale, 1989-94; new products mgr. Cisco Sys., San Jose, 1994—; cons., No. Calif., 1976—. Counselor Teens Against Drugs, San Jose, 1970, 1/2 Orgn., Santa Cruz, 1975-76. Mem. Am. Prodn. Invention Control, Nat. Assn. Female Execs., Nat. Assn. Purchasing Mgmt., Am. Radio Relay League. Democrat. Home: 733 Rosedale Ave # 4 Capitola CA 95010-2248 Office: Cisco Systems 110 W Tasman Dr San Jose CA 95134-1700

HILL, BETTI CHRISTIE, government executive; b. Bozeman, Mont., Feb. 11, 1954; d. Douglas P. and Ruth M. (Bristow) Christie; married; children: Todd, Corey, Mike. BA, Western Mont. Coll., 1976. Sch. tchr. Chester and Townsend, Mont., 1976-78; pub. info. officer Office of Pub. Instrn., Helena, Mont., 1980-84; with Hill Pub. Rels., Helena, 1984-89; field rep. U.S. Sen. Conrad Burns, Helena, 1989-91; chief of staff Lt. Gov.'s Office, Helena, 1991—. Fin. dir. County Rep. Party, Helena, 1991—; mem. WMC Found. Bd., Dillon, 1989-93, Mont. House Bd., Helena, 1989-92. Home: PO Box 4717 Helena MT 59604

HILL, BETTY JEAN, nursing educator, academic administator; b. Ishpeming, Mich., Nov. 27, 1937; d. Azarius William and Evelyn (Herring) Parsons; m. Edwin E. Hill, Nov. 27, 1959 (dec. 1979); children: Cheryl, Kenneth; m. Harold Ralph Pawley, June 27, 1981. B in Nursing, No. Mich. U., Marquette, 1972, MEd, 1974; M in Nursing, Wayne State U., 1977, PhD, 1979. RN, Mich. Staff nurse St. Luke's Hosp., Marquette, 1958-60; supr. Meadowbrook Hosp., Bellaire, Mich., 1959-60; head nurse St. Luke's Hosp., Marquette, 1960-62, clin. instr., 1868-70; asst. prof. No. Mich. U., Marquette, 1972-75, assoc. prof., 1978-80, asst. dean, 1980-82, dean, prof., 1982—. Contbr. articles to jours.; author: (with others) Theory Construction, 1981. Fund Chairperson Hospice, Marquette, 1988. Fellow AASCU Acad. Leadership, 1991-93, Harvard Inst. for Ednl. Mgmt., 1992, No. Econ. Initiatives Corp., 1992—. Mem. Mich. and Nat. League for Nursing, Mich. Assn. Colls. of Nursing (treas. 1986-90), Midwest Alliance in Nursing, Am. Assn. State Coll. and Univs., Am. Assn. Colls. and Nursing, Marquette Econ. Club (pres. 1989-90), Rotary Club, Planned Parenthood, Sigma Theta Tau. Methodist. Home: 643 Lakewood Ln Marquette MI 49855-9517 Office: No Mich U Nursing Magers Hall Marquette MI 49855

HILL, BONNIE GUITON, dean; b. Springfield, Ill., Oct. 30, 1941; d. Henry Frank and Zola Elizabeth (Newman) Brazelton; m. Walter Hill Jr.; 1 child, Nichele Monique. BA, Mills Coll., 1974, MS, Calif. State U., Hayward, 1975; EdD U. Calif., Berkeley, 1985. Adminstrv. asst. to pres.'s spl. asst. Mills Coll., Oakland, Calif., 1970-71, adminstrv. asst. to asst. v.p., 1972-73, student svcs. counselor, adv. to resuming students, 1973-74, asst. dean of students, interim dir. ethnic studies, lectr., 1975-76; exec. dir. Marcus A. Foster Ednl. Inst., Oakland, 1976-79; adminstrv. mgr. Kaiser Aluminum & Chem. Corp., Oakland, 1979-80, v.p., gen. mgr. Kaiser CTR Inc., 1980-84, vice chmn. Postal Rate Commn., Washington, 1985-87, asst. sec. for vocat. and adult edn. U.S. Dept. of Edn., 1987-89; sec. State and Consumer Svcs. Agy. State of Calif.; spl. adviser to the Pres. for Consumer Affairs, dir. U.S. Office Consumer Affairs, 1989-90; pres., CEO Earth Conservation Corps, Washington, 1990-91; sec. State and Consumer Svcs. Industry, State of Calif., 1991-92; dean McIntire Sch. Commerce, U. Va., Charlottesville, 1992—; bd. dirs. La.-Pacific Corp., Niagara Mohawk Power Corp., Rreef-Reit, San Francisco, Hershey Foods Corp., AK Steele Corp., Crestar Fin. Corp. Office: Office of Dean McIntire Sch Commerce U Va Monroe Hall Charlottesville VA 22903

HILL, CARLOTTA J.H., physician; b. Chgo., Apr. 8, 1948; d. Clarence Kenneth and Vlasta (Cizek) Hayes; m. Chester James Hill III, June 10, 1967 (div. 1974); m. Carlos Alberto Rotman, July 31, 1980; children: Robin Mercedes. BA magna cum laude, Knox Coll., 1969; MD with honors, U. Ill., 1973. Diplomate Nat. Bd. Med. Examiners, 1974, Am. Bd. Dermatology, 1978. Intern Mayo Sch. Medicine, Rochester, N.Y., 1973-74; resident U. Ill., Chgo., 1975-78, asst. prof. clin. dermatology Coll. Medicine, 1978-93, assoc. prof. clin. dermatology Coll. Medicine, 1993—; sen. U. Ill. Senate, Chgo., 1986-91; councilor Chgo. Med. Soc., 1990—. Contbr. articles to profl. jours. Bd. dirs. Summerfest St. James Cathedral, Chgo., 1986-91, YWCA, Lake Forest, Ill., 1995—; master gardner Chgo. Botanic Garden, Glencoe, Ill., 1994—. Recipient Janet Glasgow award Am. Women's Med. Assn., 1973. Mem. AMA, Am. Acad. Dermatology, Herb Soc. Am. (chmn. ways and means No. Ill. unit 1994-96, treas. N. Ill. unit 1996—), Ill. State Med. Assn., Ill. State Dermatologic Soc., Chgo. Med. Soc., Chgo. Dermatologic Soc., Phi Beta Kappa, Alpha Omega Alpha. Episcopalian. Office: Dept Dermatology 808 S Wood St Chicago IL 60612-7300

HILL, CHARLOTTE SEVIER, hypnotherapist; b. Hot Springs, Ark., Mar. 2, 1939; d. Charles W. and Doris Dean (Sevier) Hill; m. Geary A. Fraley, Jan. 1967 (div. Nov. 1969); m. Roy L. Richardson, Nov. 24, 1969 (div. Nov. 1977); 1 child, Joshua. BA, U Mo., 1962, MA, 1979. Registered hypnotherapist, 1991. Tchr. speech, English Raytown (Mo.) South Jr. H.S., 1962-67; tchr. English lit. Zama (Japan) Am. Sch., 1968-69; tchr. English, English lit., speech McLouth (Kans.) H.S., 1970-71; developer speech, comm. dept. Eudora (Kans.) H.S., 1971-74; instr. U. Mo., Kansas City, 1977-81; subs. tchr. Center H.S., Kansas City, 1979-80; asst. v.p. Tenenbaum-Hill Assoc., Kansas City, 1981-87; tchr. English and speech Raymore-Peculiar H.S., Peculiar, Mo., 1980-81; nat. sales mgr. The Larson Co., Tucson, 1987-88; exec. dir., prin. The Laurel Group, Kansas City, 1988-89; hypnotherapist UNUS, Kansas City, 1991—; dir. Kenneth C. Hill Found., Kansas City, 1993—. Co-founder Religious Sci. Ch. of Kansas City; mem. steering com. Clinton/Gore '96, 1995—; mem. adv. bd. Citizens Assn., Kansas City, 1995—; bd. dirs. Westport Hist., Kansas City, 1995—; v.p. Renaissance West, Kansas City, 1995-96, pres., 1996—; mem. exec. com. The AIDS Coun. of Greater Kansas City, 1996—; pres. Hope Care Ctr., Kansas City, 1996—, sec. founding bd., 1994-95; candidate Kansas City City Coun., 1995. Recipient Religious Soc. Founders award, 1991, Optimists award for tchg. Optimists Club, 1966. Mem. Am. Counseling Assn., Internat. Assn. of Counselors & Therapists, Labor's Ednl. and Polit. Club (founding mem.). Democrat. Home and Office: 446 W 56th St Kansas City MO 64113

HILL, CHRISTINE LUCILLE, secondary education educator; b. Washington, Aug. 19, 1964; d. John Henry Jr. and Carol Pearl (Halverson) Schuster; m. David Wayne Hill, June 16, 1990. AA, Iowa Lakes C.C., 1984; BS, Iowa State U., 1987; postgrad., U. Conn., 1994—. Substitute tchr. Des Moines Pub. Schs., 1987-88; tchr. elem. sch. Island Paradise Schs., Honolulu, 1988-89; counselor adult edn. Halawa (Hawaii) Correctional Facility, 1989; tchr. elem. sch North Little Rock (Ark.) Schs., 1990-92; facilitator gifted and talented Lawton (Okla.) Pub. Schs., 1992-94; tchr. jr. high sch. Beauregard Schs., DeRidder, La., 1994—; tchr. of gifted grades K-8 East Beauregard H.S., DeRidder, La., 1995—. Mem. Officer's Wives Club, 1990—, mem. scholar com., 1994; Jr. Svc. League, Lawton, 1994—. Mem. AAUW, ASCD, Nat. Assn. Gifted Children, Delta Kappa Gamma, Beta Sigma Phi. Republican. Lutheran. Home: PO Box 4057 Fort Polk LA 71459-1057 Office: East Beauregard 5364 Hwy 113 Deridder LA 70634

HILL, CLARA EDITH, psychology educator; b. Shivers, Miss., Sept. 13, 1948; d. Fletcher Von and Anna (Teich) H.; m. James Gormally, May 25, 1974; children: Kevin, Katherine. BA, So. Ill. U., 1970, MA, 1972, PhD, 1974. Lic. psychologist, Md. Asst. prof. dept. psychology U. Md., College Park, 1974-78, assoc. prof. dept. psychology, 1978-85, prof. dept. psychology, 85—. Author: Therapist Techniques and Client Outcomes, 1989, Working With Dreams in Psychotherapy, 1996; editor Jour. Counseling Psychology, 1994—; contbr. articles to profl. jours. Grantee NIMH, 1983-92. Fellow Am. Psychol. Assn.; mem. Soc. Psychotherapy Rsch. (pres. N.Am. chpt. 1990, pres. internat. orgn. 1994-95). Office: U Maryland Dept Psychology College Park MD 20742

HILL, CLAUDIA ADAMS, tax consultant; b. Long Beach, Calif., Oct. 14, 1949; d. Claude T. Adams and Geraldine (Jones) Crosby; m. W. Eugene Hill, Sept. 14, 1968 (div. Oct. 1983); children: Stacia Heather, Jonathan Eugene; m. Larry C. Enoksen, June 4, 1988. BA, Calif. State U., Fullerton, 1972; MBA, San Jose State U., 1978. Systems analyst quality assurance group United Technology Ctr., 1972-73; with Commrs. Adv. Group IRS, 1987; prin., owner Tax Mam, Inc., 1974—; noted lectr. in field of taxation; tax advisor to Rsch. Inst. Am., also pubs., Nev., tax analysts, Va. Contbr. articles to profl. jours. Mem. Nat. Soc. Pub. Accts. (accredited tax advisor, liaison to profl. assns. IRS, Franchist Tax Bd., v.p. tax standards bd. accreditation coun. acctg. and taxation), Nat. Assn. Enrolled Agts., Calif. Soc. Enrolled Agts. Republican. Office: TAX MAM Inc 10680 S De Anza Blvd Cupertino CA 95014-4446

HILL, DAWN DAWIN BATTS, elementary music educator; b. Charlotte, N.C., July 21, 1967; d. David Dwight and Judy Kay (McKinney) Batts; m. Milton Dale Hill, July 6, 1991; 1 child, Noah Dale. MusB, Meredith Coll., 1989; MusM, East Carolina U., 1992. Music tchr. Carver Elem. Edgecombe County Schs., Tarboro, N.C., 1989-90; music tchr. Bulluck Elem. Edgecombe County Schs., Tarboro, 1989-91, music tchr. Southwest Edgecombe, 1989-91; music tchr. Speight Middle Sch. Wilson (N.C.) County Schs., 1991-92, music tchr. Winstead Elem., 1991—; guest spkr. Bedding Field H.S., Wilson, 1992, 95, Meredith Coll, Raleigh, N.C., 1992. Composer musical works. Ch., mem., pianist, choir mem., soloist, substitute Sunday tchr. Tabernacle Bapt. Ch., Wilson; piano tchr. and cmty. pianist, Wilson. Grantee Tain County Edn. Found., Edgecombe County, 1990. Mem. Pi Kappa Lambda. Republican. Home: 1650 Bloomery Rd Bailey NC 27807-9523 Office: Winstead Elem Sch 1713 Downing St SW Wilson NC 27893-5711

HILL, DEBORA ELIZABETH, author, journalist, screenwriter; b. San Francisco, July 10, 1961; d. Henry Peter and Madge Lillian (Ridgeway-Aarons) H. BA, Sonoma State U., 1983. Talk show host Rock Jour. Viacom, San Francisco, 1980-81; interviewer, biographer Harrap Ltd., London, 1986-87; editor North Bay Mag., Cotati, Calif., 1988; guest feature writer Argus Courier, Petaluma, Calif., 1993-95; concept developer BiblioBytes, Hoboken, N.J., 1994-95, White Tiger Films, San Francisco, 1995—; feature writer The Econs. Press, 1996—; assoc. prodr. White Tiger Films, 1995—. Author: CUTS from a San Francisco Rock Journal, 1982, Punk Retro, 1986, Gale Research—Resourceful Woman, 1994, St. James Guide to Fantasy Writers, 1995, St. James Guide to Famous Gays and Lesbians, 1996, A Ghost Among Us, 1996; co-writer, cons. producer The Danger Club; contbr. stories and articles to profl. jours. Democrat. Home: 110 Grant Ave Petaluma CA 94952 Office: care Ellen Steele PO Box 447 Organ NM 88052 also: care Scott Ferguson 1779 43d Ave San Francisco CA 94112

HILL, DIANE SELDON, corporate psychologist; b. Mpls., Sept. 17, 1943; d. Earl William and Geraldine (Le Veille) Seldon; m. David Reuben Hill, May 14, 1986 (div. Feb. 1988); children: Anna Marion, Jason David. BA, Mt. Holyoke Coll., 1965; MA in Psychology, U. Minn., 1968, PhD in Psychology, 1974; Advanced Mgmt. Program, U. Pa. Wharton Sch., 1992. Lic. psychologist, Colo; diplomate in clin. psychology Am. Bd. Profl. Psychologists. Instr., counselor Student Counseling Bur. U. Minn., Mpls., 1968-70, advisor women's programs, Student Activities Bur., 1970-71; instr. psychology Augsburg Coll., Mpls., 1970-71; counselor, tchr. humanities Emma Willard Sch., Troy, N.Y., 1972-75; dir. counseling and re-engagement Colo. Women's Coll., Denver, 1976-77; clin. field supr., Sch. Profl. Psychology U. Denver, 1977—; asst. clin. prof. psychology U. Colo. Health Scis., Denver, 1981-89, Ctr. for Creative Leadership, Colorado Springs, 1981—; pvt. practice Denver, 1977-89; mgmt. and organizational cons. Somerville and Co., Inc., Denver, 1989—; dir. Profl. Exams. Svc., N.Y.C., 1991—; presenter at profl. meetings; expert witness on psychology ethics; presenter testimony before Colo. legis. hearing coms. and Colo. Ins. Commn.; lobbyist for psychology licensure Parliament of Finland, 1989. Named NDEA IV fellow U. Minn., 1967-68. Fellow Am. Psychol. Assn.; mem. Colo. Psychol. Assn. (bd. dirs. 1979-82, dir. polit. action com.), Am. Assn. State Psychology Bds. (del. 1982-83, mem.-at-large exec. com. 1983, pres. 1988-91), Colo. Bd. Psychologist Examiners (bd. dirs. 198-187, chmn. 1983-88), Women's Forum Colo. (mem. com. 1979—). Episcopalian. Home: 2052 Bellaire St Denver CO 80207-3722 Office: Somerville End Co Inc The Cairn Bldg 1625 Broadway 727 E 16th Ave Denver CO 80203

HILL, DONNA MARIE, communications executive; b. Amesbury, Mass., July 25, 1957; d. Robert and Marie Doris (Lucier) Menzigian. BS in Math., U. Lowell, 1979, MBA in Ops., 1983. Material control analyst AVCO

Corp., Wilmington, Mass., 1979-81; ops. analyst Blue Cross & Blue Shield, Boston, 1981-83, risk analyst, 1983-84; systems analyst Bell Atlantic Corp., Bethesda, Md., 1984-86; cons. internal Bell Atlantic Corp., Bethesda, 1986-89, project mgr., 1989-91, new tech. strategic planning mgr., 1992—; speaker FUSE Nat. and Regional Confs., 1988, 91. inventor (software) User-assisted Adhoc Reporting, 1988, Natural English Report Access, 1988. Vol. Montgomery County Vol. Assn., Montgomery, Md., 1983—, PALS Montgomery County, 1984—; chair spl. events New Mem. Svcs. John F. Kennedy Ctr. Performing Arts, Washington, 1985—, mem. vol. adv. com., 1991, 92; chair vol. adv. com. Kennedy Ctr., 1992—; bd. dirs. Sister City Corp., Rockville, 1992—, v.p., 1993-95, pres.-elect, 1994-95, pres., 1995—. Mem. NAFE, Ops. Rsch. Sco., Intelligent Computer Rsch. Inst., Focus User Troup (co-chmn. artificial intelligence group 1989, leader, coord. spl. interest groups for Nat. Com., 1989, nat., regional spkr. 1988, 91), Rockville Jr. C. of C. (sec. 1992-93), Md. State Jr. C. of C. (program mgr. internat. involvement 1992-93, dist. dir. 1993-94, cmty. devel. v.p. 1994-95, USJCC internat. affairs commn. 1995—, JCI individual devel. commn. 1996), Internat. Spkrs. Platform. Republican. Roman Catholic. Office: Bell Atlantic 6701 Democracy Blvd Bethesda MD 20817-1572

HILL, DOROTHY MONROE, retired educator; b. Portsmouth, Va., Oct. 8, 1923; d. Elmer Sylvester and Dorothy Fleet (Barkley) Monroe; m. Gladstone Middleton Hill, June 19, 1945; children: Dorothy Fleet Hill, Robert M. Hill, Brooke Hill Weber, Thomas Wyatt Hill. BA, Westhampton Coll., 1944; MA, U. Va., 1973. Cert. tchr. K-12, Va. H.s. tchr. Va. Beach (Va.) Pub. Schs., 1944-45; elem. and middle sch. tchr., dept. head Ports Pub. Schs., Portsmouth, Va., 1969-90, ret., 1990; mem. strategic action com. Portsmouth Pub. Schs., 1993-94, grant writer John Tyler Sch., 1994. Bd. dirs. Planned Parenthood of S.E., Va. 1992-96, Cmty. Concert Assn., 1988-96, Va. Coun. of Chs., 1992-96; com. Portsmouth Dem. Com., 1991-93; resource mother Child and Family Svc., Portsmouth, 1991-92. Recipient Outstanding Social Studies Tchr. Va. Coun. for Social Studies, 1985. Mem. AAUW (pres., v.p., mem. state bd. dirs., Ednl. Found. Named grant 1985), The Students Club (pres. 1994-96), World Affairs Coun., Nat. Woman's Polit. Caucus, Delta Kappa Gamma. Democrat. Methodist. Home: 405 Shenandoah St Portsmouth VA 23707

HILL, EARLENE HOOPER, state legislator; b. Balt., Oct. 22; d. Otis Barnett Hooper and Thelma E. (Richardson) Young; 1 child, Charisse E. BA, Norfolk State U.; MSW, Adelphi U. Mgr. N.Y. State Dept. Social Svcs., N.Y.C.; mem. N.Y. State Assembly, 1988—; mem. women's program, shop steward Pub. Employees Fedn., 1980-88, mem. exec. bd. Mem. exec. bd. Jack & Jill of Am., Inc., Nassau County, N.Y., 1985—; mem. Nat. Women's Polit. Caucus, N.Y.C., 1987—. Mem. Negro Bus. and Profl. Women (Cen. Nassau chpt.), Delta Sigma Theta. Democrat. Office: NY State Legislature State Capitol Albany NY 12224

HILL, EDITH MARIE, medical/surgical nurse; b. Wailuku, Maui, Hawaii, June 10, 1947; d. John Arthur and Sally Ayako (Oda) Pratt; m. Michael Eliott Hill, Mar. 29, 1969; children: Laura Marcienne, Adam Jeffrey. Diploma in nursing, Rochester (N.Y.) State Hosp., 1968; BSN, Nazareth Coll. Rochester, 1981; postgrad., U. Rochester. RN, N.Y. Staff nurse Strong Meml. Hosp., Rochester, 1968-69, various facilities, Tex., Calif., Ala., Ohio, 1969-73; staff nurse Genesee Hosp., 1973-93, perioperative nurse clinician, 1993—. Contbg. author of chpt. in book Core Curriculum in Perioperative Nursing, 1995; contbr. articles to profl. publs. Mem. ANA, Nat. Assn. Orthop. Nurses, Assn. Oper. Rm. Nurses (cert., sec. Upstate N.Y. chpt. 1994-96). Office: Genesee Hosp Operating Rm 224 Alexander St Rochester NY 14607-4002

HILL, ELEANOR JEAN, lawyer; b. Miami Beach, Fla., Dec. 19, 1950; d. Elbert Cray and Florence Louise (Strzycki) Hill; m. Thomas Paul Gross, April 7, 1990; 1 child, Bryan Michael Gross. BS, Fla. State U., 1972, JD, 1974. Bar: Fla. Asst. atty. U.S. Atty's Office, Tampa, Fla., 1975-78; spl. atty. Organized Crime Strike Force, U.S. Dept. Justice, Tampa, Fla., 1978-80; asst. counsel U.S. Senate Permanent Subcommittee on Investigations, Washington, 1980-82, chief counsel to minority, 1982-87, staff dir., chief counsel, 1987-95, inspector gen. U.S. Dept. Defense, Arlington, Va., 1995—. Mem. Fla. Bar Assn., Phi Beta Kappa, Phi Kappa Phi. Office: Office of the Ispector General 400 Army Navy Dr Arlington VA 22202-2884

HILL, ELIZABETH GOODWIN, legislative analyst; b. Modesto, Calif., Jan. 16, 1950; d. Judson Norton Stone Jr. and Beverly Jean (Goodwin) Winger; m. Laurence Arden Hill, June 22, 1974; children: Erik G., Kristina M. BA with honors, Stanford U., 1973; M in Pub. Policy, U. Calif., Berkeley, 1975. Program analyst Legis. Analyst's Office, Sacramento, 1976-79, prin. program analyst, 1979-86, legis. analyst, 1986—; adv. bd. mem. Ctr. for Calif. Studies, Sacramento, 1988—, Govt. Tech. Conf., Sacramento, 1993—, Pub. Policy Inst. Calif., San Francisco, 1995—; mem. Calif. Constn. Revision Commn., Sacramento, 1994-96. Author (newsletter) Ballot-Box Budgeting, 1990; contbr. chpt. to book. Legis. chair United Way Campaign, Sacramento, 1988, 96; scout leader Boy Scouts Am., Sacramento, 1990-93. Fulbright scholar Royal Inst. Tech., Stockholm, 1976; named Outstanding Young Women of Am., 1986; recipient Disting. Svc. award Calif. Assn. of Counties, 1995. Mem. Nat. Assn. Legis. Fiscal Officers, Western States Legis. Fiscal Officers Assn. (pres. 1990), Assn. for Pub. Policy and Mgmt., Stanford Alumni Assn., Calif. Alumni Assn. Office: Legis Analysts Office Ste 1000 925 L St Sacramento CA 95814

HILL, ELIZABETH MARIE, research scientist; b. Tuscaloosa, Ala., Oct. 26, 1954; d. William Taylor and Kathleen (Jordan) H. AB in Psychology, U. Mich., 1977; MS in Exptl. Psychology, Tulane U., 1979, PhD in Exptl. Psychology, 1983; MS in Biometry, La. State U., 1986. Instr. dept. psychology Furman U., Greenville, S.C., 1981-82; rsch. fellow dept. psychiatry Albert Einstein Coll. Medicine, N.Y.C., 1982-84; rsch. fellow dept. biometry and genetics La. State U. Med. Ctr., New Orleans, 1985-87; rsch. fellow dept. psychiatry U. Mich., Ann Arbor, 1987-88, asst. rsch. scientist dept. psychiatry, 1990—; dir. biometrics divsn. dept. psychiatry U. Mich., Ann Arbor, 1989-94; dir. data mgmt. and analysis U. Mich. Alcohol Rsch. Ctr., Ann Arbor, 1989—. Contbr. articles to profl. jours. Active So. Poverty Law Ctr., Montgomery, Ala., 1990—. Grantee Nat. Inst. on Alcoholism and Alcohol Abuse, 1995, 96. Mem. NOW, Rsch. Soc. on Alcoholism, Human Behavior and Evolution Soc. (treas. 1989-90, newsletter editor 1992—), Animal Behavior Soc., Biometric Soc. Office: Univ Mich Alcohol Rsch Ctr Ste 2A 400 E Eisenhower Pkwy Ann Arbor MI 48108

HILL, ELIZABETH STARR, writer; b. Lynn Haven, Fla., Nov. 4, 1925; d. Raymond King and Gabrielle (Wilson) Cummings; m. Russell Gibson Hill, May 28, 1949; children: Andrea van Waldron, Bradford Wray. Student, Finch Jr. Coll., 1941-42, Columbia U., 1970-73. Freelance writer; past dir. Princeton Creative Ctr.; tchr. writing Princeton Adult Sch. Author: (juvenile books) The Wonderful Visit to Miss Liberty, 1961, The Window Tulip, 1964, Evan's Corner, 1967, 91 (ALA Notable Book for Children), Master Mike and the Miracle Maid, 1967, Pardon My Fangs, 1969, Bells: A Book to Begin On, 1970, Ever-After Island, 1977, Fangs Aren't Everything, 1985, When Christmas Comes, 1989, The Street Dancers, 1991, Broadway Chances, 1992 (ABA Pick of the Lists), The Banjo Player, 1993, Curtain Going Up!, 1995; contbr. articles to mags. including Reader's Digest, many others. Mem. Authors Guild, Authors League Am., Univ. Club Winter Park. Office: Harold Ober Assn Inc 425 Madison Ave New York NY 10017-1110

HILL, EMITA BRADY, academic administrator; b. Balt., Jan. 31, 1936; d. Leo and Lucy McCormick (Jewett) Brady; children: Julie Beck, Christopher, Madeleine. BA, Cornell U., 1957; MA, Middlebury Coll., 1958; PhD, Harvard U., 1967. Instr. Harvard U., 1961-63; asst. prof. Western Reserve U., 1967-69; from asst. prof. to v.p. Lehman Coll. CUNY, Bronx, N.Y., 1970-91; chancellor, grad. faculty Ind. U., Kokomo, Ind., 1991—. Mem. Am. Assn. Higher Edn., Assn. Am. Coll., Am. Soc. for 18th Century Studies, Am. Assn. State Colls. and Univs., Internat. Assn. Univ. Pres., Internat. Soc. for 18th Century Studies, Phi Beta Kappa. Office: Ind U PO Box 9003 2300 S Washington St Kokomo IN 46902-9003

HILL, FAY GISH, librarian; b. Rensselaer, Ind., Sept. 19, 1944; d. Roy Charles and Vergie (Powell) Gish; m. John Christian Hill, May 20, 1967; 1 child, Christina Gish. BA, Purdue U., 1967; MLS, U. Tex., 1971. Asst. librarian basic reference dept. Tex. A&M U., College Station, 1972, assoc. librarian sci. ref. dept., 1972-74, acting head librarian sci. reference dept., 1975; reference librarian Cen. Iowa Regional Library, Des Moines, 1984—. Troop leader Girl Scouts U.S., Ames, Iowa, 1983-88; bd. dirs. Friends of Fgn. Wives, Ames, 1982-86. Mem. ALA, Iowa Libr. Assn., Iowa Libr. Assn. Found. (bd. dirs. 1990-95). Presbyterian. Home: 5604 Thunder Rd Ames IA 50014-9448 Office: Cen Iowa Regional Libr Reference 515 Douglas Ave Ames IA 50010-6215

HILL, GRACE LUCILE GARRISON, education educator, consultant; b. Gastonia, N.C., Sept. 26, 1930; d. William Moffatt and Lillian Tallulah (Tatum) Garrison; m. Leo Howard Hill, July 24, 1954; children: Lillian Lucile, Leo Howard Jr., David Garrison. BA, Erskine Coll., 1952; MA, Furman U., 1966; PhD, U. S.C., 1980. Lic. sch. psychologist, S.C. Tchr. Bible, Clinton (S.C.) Pub. Schs., 1952-53; tchr. English Parker High Sch., Greenville, S.C., 1953-55; elem. tchr. Augusta Circle Sch., Greenville, 1955-57; tchr. homebound children Greenville County Sch. Dist., Greenville, 1961-64, psychologist, 1966-77; adj. prof. grad. studies in edn. Furman U., Greenville, 1977—, U. S.C., Columbia, 1982—; ednl. cons. Ednl. Diagnostic Svcs., Greenville, 1980—; exec. dir. Camperdown Acad., Greenville, 1986-87; cons. learning disability program Erskine Coll., Due West, S.C., 1978—. Contbr. articles to profl. jours. Pres. Lake Forest PTA, Greenville, 1970-71; pres. of Women A.R. Presbyn. Ch., Greenville, 1973-75, adult Bible tchr., 1978—; sec. bd. trustees Erskine Coll., 1982-88; bd. dirs. Children's Bur. S.C., Columbia, 1981-87, YWCA, Greenville, 1984-88; bd. advisors for adoption S.C. Dept. Social Svcs., Columbia, 1987-92. Recipient Order of the Jessamine, Greenville News award, 1994-95. Mem. Am. Edn. Rsch. Assn. (southeastern rep. 1982-84, editor newspaper for SIG group 1982-83), Jean Piaget Soc., Assn. for Supervision and Curriculum Devel., Orton Dyslexia Soc. (pres. Carolinas br. 1984-88), Ea. Ednl. Rsch. Assn., S.C. Psychol. Assn., Order of the Jessamine, Delta Kappa Gamma. Democrat. Home and Office: 28 Montrose Dr Greenville SC 29607-3034

HILL, HELEN MOREY WILLIAMS, English literature educator; b. Bklyn., Mar. 26, 1915; d. Arthur Herbert and Sophie Weston (Baker) Williams; children: Rebeca, Anthony, Richard, Alan. AB, Wheaton Coll., Norton, Mass., 1936; AM, Brown U., Providence, R.I., 1937. Grad. tchg. asst. U. Ill., Urbana, 1939-42, 1945-48; editl. asst. U. Mich., Ann Arbor, 1959-63; instr., prof. English Ea. Mich. U., Ypsilanti, 1963-83. Co-editor: New Coasts and Strange Harbors: Discovering Poems, 1974, Straight on Till Morning: Poems of the Imaginary World, 1977, Dusk to Dawn: Poems of Night, 1980; (author) A Proud and Fiery Spirit: Journals of Captain Edward Baker, 1846-1895; Memoirs of Crooked Lane, Duxbury and Marshfield, Massachusette, 1995; contbr. articles to profl. jours. Founder Alliance For the Mentally Ill Wastenaw County, 1984, Trailblazers of Wasttenaw, Ann Arbor, 1989. Rsch. grantee Nat. Hist. Records and Publs. Commn. (Nat. Archives), 1972. Home: 928 Olivia Ave Ann Arbor MI 48104

HILL, I. KATHRYN, professional certification agency administrator; b. Phila., Apr. 6, 1950; d. Joseph Anthony and Irma Lorraine (Walther) Piehs; m. John Patrick McElwain, May 17, 1969 (div. Aug. 1979); children: John Charles, Brian Patrick; m. David Terence Hill, Sept. 27, 1980. BA, Widener Coll., 1979; MEd, Temple U., 1982. Cert. secondary tchr., Pa. Translator, transcriber Sci-Tech, Inc., Phila., 1970-77; tchr. West Chester (Pa.) East High Sch., 1978, Garnet Valley Jr.-Sr. High Sch., Concordville, Pa., 1979; asst. to dir. Nat. Bd. Med. Examiners, Phila., 1980-81, evaluation program asst., 1981-82, evaluation program assoc., 1982-84, sr. program assoc., 1984-85; asst. exec. v.p. Fedn. State Med. Bds., Ft. Worth, 1985-86, asst. exec. v.p., exec. dir. of the examination bd., 1986-94, sr. v.p., exec. dir. examination bd., 1995-96; exec. v.p. Nat. Commn. on Cert. of Physician Assts., Atlanta, 1996—. Editor: FLEX/SPEX Guidelines, 1985, 87, 90, FLEX/SPEX Info. Bull., 1987-94; co-editor Fedn. Exchange, 1986-95; contbr. articles to profl. jours. Mem. Am. Ednl. Rsch. Assn., Nat. Coun. on Measurement in Edn., Assn. of Am. Med. Colls. Republican. Lutheran. Office: NCCPA 6849-B2 Peachtree Dunwoody Atlanta GA 30328

HILL, JANICE BROWN, communications specialist; b. Memphis, Jan. 23, 1953; d. Chester Norman and Jennie Belle (McGinnis) Brown; m. Scott Pyron Hill, Apr. 30, 1977; children: Jennie McGinnis, Susan Rebecca. BA in Journalism, U. Ill., 1975. Reporter The Evansville (Ind.) Courier, 1975-77; cmty. affairs mgr. Mead Johnson Co., Evansville, 1977-80; comm. mgr. Am. Cancer Soc., Memphis, 1980-81; comm. supr. Holiday Inns, Inc., Memphis, 1981-84; comm. cons. Memphis, 1984-92; dir. comm. YWCA of Greater Memphis, 1992-96. Trustee 1st Congl. Ch., Memphis, 1992-94; site coord. Memphis Interfaith Hospitality Network; mem. capital campaign com. Balmoral Presbyn. Ch., Memphis. Mem. Women in Comm. Presbyterian. Home: 2349 Ridgeland St Memphis TN 38119 Office: Organ Transplant Fund 1102 Brookfield Rd Ste 201 Memphis TN 38119

HILL, JUDITH DEEGAN, lawyer; b. Chgo., Dec. 13, 1940; d. William James and Ida May (Scott) Deegan; children: Colette M., Cristina M. BA, Western Mich. U., 1960; JD, Marquette U., 1971; cert. U. Paris, Sorbonne, 1962; postgrad. Harvard U., 1984. Bar: Wis. 1971, Ill. 1973, Nev. 1976, D.C. 1979. Tchr., Kalamazoo (Mich.) Bd. Edn., 1960-62, Maple Heights (Ohio), 1963-64, Shorewood (Wis.) Bd. Edn., 1964-68; corp. atty. Fort Howard Paper Co., Green Bay, Wis., 1971-72; sr. trust adminstr. Continental Ill. Nat. Bank & Trust, Chgo., 1972-76; atty. Morse, Foley & Wadsworth Law Firm, Las Vegas, 1976-77; dep. dist. atty., criminal prosecutor Clark County Atty., Las Vegas, 1977-83; atty. civil and criminal law Edward S. Coleman Profl. Law Corp., Las Vegas, 1983-84; pvt. practice law, 1984-85; atty. criminal div. Office of City Atty., City of Las Vegas, 1985-89, pvt. practice law, 1989—. Bd. dirs. Nev. Legal Svcs., Carson City, 1980-87, state chmn., 1984-87; bd. dirs. Clark County Legal Svcs., Las Vegas, 1980-87; mem. Star Aux. for Handicapped Children, Las Vegas, 1986-96; Greater Las Vegas Women's League, 1987-88; jud. candidate Las Vegas Mcpl. Ct, 1987, Nev. Symphony Guild, Variety Club Internat., 1992-93, Las Vegas Preservation Group. Recipient Scholarship, Auto Specialties, St. Joseph, Mich., 1957-60, St. Thomas More Scholarship, Marquette U. Law Sch., Milw., 1968-69; juvenile law internship grantee Marquette U. Law Sch., 1970. Mem. Nev. Bar Assn., So. Nev. Assn. Women Attys., Ill. Bar Assn., Children's Village Club (pres. 1980) (Las Vegas, Nev.). Home: 521 Sweeney Ave Las Vegas NV 89104-1436 Office: Ste 211 726 S Casino Center Blvd Las Vegas NV 89101-6700

HILL, JUDITH SWIGOST, business analyst, information systems engineer; b. Harvey, Ill., Dec. 31, 1942; d. J.W. and M.J. (Kuczaik) Swigost; m. Wallace H. Hill, May 16, 1982; stepchildren: Scott, Amy, Molly, Elizabeth. BA in English/Theater, U. Ill., 1964; postgrad., Am. U., 1967-69, New Sch. for Social Research, N.Y.C., 1977-82, 83-85. Vol. U.S. Peace Corps, Philippines, 1964-66; recruiter U.S. Peace Corps, Washington, 1966-67; program mgr. U.S. Peace Corps, Micronesia, 1968; dir. corr. U.S. Peace Corps, Washington, 1969; editor, prin. Congl. Monitor, Inc., Washington, 1970-76; legis. analyst Philip Morris, Inc., N.Y.C., 1976-77; tech. analyst, writer Jesco, Inc., N.Y.C., 1978-79; assoc. pub. Thomas Pub. Co., N.Y.C., 1980-84; bus. analyst AGS, Inc. Ind. Cons., N.Y.C., 1984-93; dir. MIS N.Y.C. Sch. Constrn. Authority, 1993-94; ind. cons. in project mgmt. N.Y.C., 1994—; ind. cons. on expert systems design and devel., N.Y.C., 1987—. Contbr. articles to profl. jours. Active Murray Hill Com., N.Y.C., 1986—. Mem. IEEE, ACM, Assn. Systems Mgmt., Am. Assn. for Artificial Intelligence, Spl. Interest Group on Artificial Intelligence, Internat. Assn. Knowledge Engrs., Nat. Assn. Returned Peace Corps Vols., Returned Peace Corps Vols. Greater N.Y. (by-laws com. 1985-86, spkrs. bur. 1987). Jewish. Home and Office: 155 E 34th St Apt 12C New York NY 10016-4751

HILL, KATHERINE ANN, county auditor; b. Seattle, Aug. 7, 1945; d. Reinhold and Mary Odell (Zimmer) Sell; m. James Stanford Swanson, Aug. 12, 1963 (div. Jan., 1979); children: James Stanford Jr., Margaret Ann, William Arnold, Matthew John; m. Warren A. Hill, JUne 30, 1979; step children: Warren A. Jr., Kenneth Earl, June Elizabeth. BA in Acctg. magna cum laude, Western Wash. U., 1987. Acct. Mobil Oil. Corp., Ferndale, Wash., 1988; staff acct., office mgr. Nelbro Packing, Anacortes, Wash., 1989-90; tax acct. pvt. practice Bow, Wash., 1990-91; acct. sherrif's office County of Skagitt, Mt. Vernon, Wash., 1991-94; auditor County of Skagitt, Mt. Vernon, 1995—; as auditor, also head of county elections, 1995—. Mem. Mt. Vernon Rep. Women, 1995—, treas. 1996—. Mem. Am. Assn. Women Accts., Wash. Fin. Officers Assn., Govt. Fin. Officers Assn., Wash. Assn. County Auditors. Office: Skagit County Auditor 700 S Second Rm 201 Mount Vernon WA 98273

HILL, KAY CARRICK, banker; b. Memphis, Feb. 12, 1935; d. Laban Frank and Mary (Tynes) Carrick; divorced; children: Susan Hill Pfau, Laban Carrick. Student, Rhodes Coll., 1953-54. Bank loan officer 1st Tenn. Bank, Memphis, 1972-77; loan officer United Am. Bank, Memphis, 1977-80; v.p. United Am. Fin. Corp., Knoxville, Tenn., 1980-83; sr. v.p. United Am. Bank, Memphis, 1983—. Past treas., mem. Corp. Vol. Coun., Memphis, 1985—; dir. Grace House, Memphis, 1994—; dir., sec., chmn., mem. fin. com. St. Marys Manasas Ala. Redevel. Team, Memphis, 1993—. Mem. Am. Inst. Banking (dir. 1994—). Republican. Episcopalian. Home: Apt 2 5480 Poplar Ave Memphis TN 38119

HILL, LA JOYCE CARMICHAEL, marketing professional; b. Tifton, Ga., Nov. 14, 1952; d. Ralph Eugene and Vista Eloise (Dooley) Carmichael; m. Bobby Wayne Hill, Jan. 1, 1972. AS, Abraham Baldwin Agrl. Coll., Tifton, 1971. With R.E. Carmichael Co. Inc., 1970-89, sec./treas., 1978-88, pres., chmn. bd., 1988-89; gen. mgr. J & B Power Equipment, Inc., 1989-95; v.p. J&B Power, 1995—. Mem. Chula Charge United Meth. Women (sec.-treas. 1986—), Tifton Exch. Club (pres. 1994-95). Methodist. Home: PO Box 947 Tifton GA 31793-0947

HILL, LARKIN PAYNE, real estate company data processing executive; b. El Paso, Tex., Oct. 30, 1954; d. Max Lloyd and Jane Olivia (Evatt) H. Student Coll. Charleston, 1972-73, U. N.C., 1973. Lic. real estate broker, N.C. Sec., property mgr. Max L. Hill Co., Inc., Charleston, S.C., 1973-75, sec., data processor, 1979-82, v.p. adminstrn., 1982—; resident mgr. Carolina Apts., Carrboro, N.C., 1975-77; sales assoc., Realtor, Southland Assocs., Chapel Hill, N.C., 1977-78; cons. specifications com. Charleston Trident Multiple Listing Service, 1985. Bd. dirs. Charleston Area Arts Coun., 1992-93. Mem. Royal Oak Found., Scottish Soc. Charleston (bd. dirs. 1989-91), Preservation Soc., Charleston Computer Users Group, N.C. Assn. Realtors, Spoleto Festival USA (chmn. auction catalog com. 1990-92); co-chair Beaux Arts Ball, Sch. Arts. Republican. Methodist. Avocations: reading, crossword puzzles, Am. Staffordshire Terriers, T'ai Chi. Home: 7 Riverside Dr Charleston SC 29403-3217 Office: Max L Hill Co Inc 824 Johnnie Dodds Blvd Mount Pleasant SC 29464

HILL, LORIE ELIZABETH, psychotherapist; b. Buffalo, Oct. 21, 1946; d. Graham and Elizabeth Helen (Salm) H. Student, U. Manchester, Eng., 1966-67; BA, Grinnell Coll., 1968; MA, U. Wis., 1970, Calif. State U., Sonoma, 1974; PhD, Wright Inst., 1980. Instr. English U. Mo., 1970-71; adminstr., supr. Antioch-West and Ctr. for Ind. Living, San Francisco, Berkeley, 1975-77; dir. tng. Ctr. for Edn. and Mental Health, San Francisco, 1977-80, exec. dir., 1980-81; pvt. practice Berkeley and Oakland, Calif., 1976—; instr. master's program in psychology John F. Kennedy U., Orinda, Calif., 1985, 94—; founder group of psychotherapists against racism; speaker on cross-cultural psychology; creater Jump Start, a violence prevention and unlearning racism program for youth; trainer for trainers 3rd Internat. Conf. Conflict Resolution, St. Petersburg, Russia; sr. facilitator Color of Fear; chair-elect Calif. Psych. Assn. Pub. Interest Divsn. Organizer against nuclear war; founding mem. Psychotherapists for Social Responsibility; psychologist Big Bros. and Big Sisters of the East Bay, 1986-88; vol. instr. City of Oakland Youth Skills Devel. Program; active Rainbow Coalition for Jesse Jackson's Presdl. Campaign, Ron Dellums Re-election Com.; campaigner for Clinton-Gore; founder, chair Psychotherapists against Violence; creator JumpStart program. Recipient Helen Margulies Mehr Pub. Svc. award. Mem. Calif. Psychol. Assn. (chair-elect pub. interest divsn., pub. interest divsn. Helen Margulies Mehr award for pub. svc. 1996). Democrat-Socialist. Office: 2955 Shattuck Ave Berkeley CA 94705-1808

HILL, LORRAINE K., addictions administrator, counselor; b. Salamanca, N.Y., Sept. 26, 1943; d. Charles B. and Betty May (Krise) H.; m. James P. Bentley Sr., Mar. 22, 1962 (div. Oct. 1983); children: James P. Jr., Betty Lu Bentley Lindberg, Cherie Renee Bentley. AA, Jamestown C.C., 1976; BS, Empire State Coll., 1983; M of Profl. Studies, Alfred U., 1988. Cert. alcoholism counselor, substance abuse counselor, addiction counselor. Psych technician Jamestown (N.Y.) Gen. Hosp., 1978-79; mental health counselor Chautauqua County Mentlah Health, Jamestown, 1979-81; substance abuse counselor Chautauqua County Clinic, Jamestown, 1981-85, program coord., 1988-89; program dir. Wyoming County Alcoholism Program, Warsaw, N.Y., 1988-89; clinic dir. Cattaraugus County Coun., Olean, N.Y., 1989-91; exec. dir. Cattaraugus County Coun. on Alcoholism and Substance Abuse, Olean, N.Y., 1991—; mem. N.Y. State CAC Credentials Bd.; chairperson Office of Alcoholism and Substance Abuse Svcs. Office: Cattaraugus Coun Alcoholism and Substance Abuse 201 S Union Olean NY 14760

HILL, MARY LOU, accountant, business consultant; b. Phila., July 8, 1936; d. Norman Findlay and Gladys Louise (Weigand) Tompkins; m. Ernest Clarke Hill Jr., Mar. 15, 1958; children: Sally, Holly, Randy, Chuck, Jim. Student, U. Miami, 1954-55, U. Okla., 1955-57; BBA, Portland State U., 1979, M in Taxation, 1982. CPA, Oreg. Staff acct. Fordham & Fordham, Hillsboro, Oreg., 1982-84; instr. Portland (Oreg.) State U., 1984-85; owner The Bookshelf, Sunriver, Oreg., 1985-88; instr. Cen. Oreg. Community Coll., Bend, 1986, 88-89; small bus. cons., 1988—; staff acct. Richard Rocci CPA, Portland, Oreg., 1990-91, Scribner & Scribner, PC, Portland, 1992-94, Alten & Sakai & Co., Portland, 1994-95. Mem. AAUW, Oreg. Soc. CPAs, Kappa Kappa Gamma. Democrat. Christian Scientist. Home and Office: 9172 SW Wilshire St Portland OR 97225-4059

HILL, PAMELA, television executive; b. Winchester, Ind., Aug. 18, 1938; d. Paul and Mary Frances (Hollis) Abel; m. Tom Wicker, Mar. 9, 1974; 1 son, Christopher Hill; stepchildren: Cameron Wicker, Grey Wicker, Lisa Freed, Kayce Freed. B.A., Bennington Coll., 1960; postgrad., Universidad Autonoma de Mexico, 1961, U. Glasgow, 1958-59. Fgn. affairs analyst Nelson A. Rockefeller Presdl. Campaign, 1961-64; researcher, assoc. producer, dir., producer NBC News, 1965-73, dir. White Paper series, 1969-72, producer Edwin Newman's Comment, 1972; producer Closeup documentary series ABC News, N.Y.C., 1973-78, exec. producer, 1978-89; v.p. ABC News, 1979-89; v.p., exec. producer CNN Special Assignment, Cable News Network, N.Y.C., 1989—; sr.v.p. sr. exec. CNN Special Assignment, Cable News Network, 96—; mem. Coun. on Fgn. Relations. Author: United States Foreign Policy, 1945-65, 1968; Contbr. photographs to Catching Up With America, 1969. Trustee Bennington Coll., Fund for Free Expression, Media and Soc. Columbia U. Recipient (with CNN special assignment staff) 4 Cable Ace awards, 8 CINE awards, 6 Chris awards, 2 Clarion awards, 2 Emmy awards, 4 Headliner awards, 5 Internat. Film & TV Festival of N.Y. awards, 7 Worldfest Houston Film Festival, 8 Unity awards; recipient Joan Sorenstein Barone award, 1993; recipient (with ABC Closeup staff) 24 Emmy awards, 10 DuPont awards, 10 Christopher awards, 19 CINE Golden Eagle awards, 5 Headliner awards, 2 Peabody awards, 10 Am. Film Festival awards, 9 Clarion awards, 3 Gabriel awards, 3 Overseas Press Club awards, Edward R. Murrow prize, 4 Edward R. Murrow Brotherhood awards. Mem. Dirs. Guild (mem. coun. on fgn. rels.), Writers Guild, Nat. Acad. Television Arts and Scis. *

HILL, PAMELA JEAN, middle school educator; b. Oxford Junction, Iowa, Jan. 6, 1964; d. Ronald Eugene and Marlene Joyce (Bright) Hansen; m. Bradley John Hill, July 25, 1987. BA, Luther Coll., 1986. Tchr. 5th and 6th grades Monroe (Iowa) Elem. Sch., 1986-87; tchr. 6th grade PCM Mid. Sch., Prairie City, Iowa, 1987—; head dept. math., PCM Cmty. Schs., 1992—, mem. instrnl. coun., 1992-96. Mem. NEA, Iowa Edn. Assn., Prairie Care/Monroe Edn. Assn., PEO (corr. sec. BH chpt.), Delta Kappa Gamma. Democrat. Lutheran. Office: PCM Mid Sch PO Box 530 Prairie City IA 50228-0530

HILL, PATRICE S., journalist, economist; b. Taipei, Taiwan, Oct. 27, 1954; parents Am. citizens; d. Robert John Jr. and Gladys (Evers) H. BA, Oberlin Coll., 1976. Reporter Inside Washington, 1982-85, Bond Buyer, Washington, 1986-93; chief econs. corr. Washington Times, 1993—. Mem. Nat. Press Club. Home: 1661 Crescent Pl NW # 304 Washington DC 20009 Office: Washington Times 3600 New York Ave NE Washington DC 20002

HILL, PATRICIA LISPENARD, insurance educator; b. N.Y.C., June 25, 1937; d. George Joseph and Elizabeth (Lispenard) H.; children: George, Christopher, Susan, Daniel, Frederic, Elizabeth. Student Barnard Coll., 1954-55, Pace U., 1972-74, Coll. of Ins., 1980. Lic. ins. broker, 1961—; owner, dir. Hill Sch. of Ins., N.Y.C., 1978—; also ptnr. Hill & Co. Ins. Brokers. Office: 139 Fulton St New York NY 10038-2594

HILL, RUTH FOELL, language consultant; b. Houston, Sept. 13, 1931; d. Ernest William and Florence Margaret (Kane) Foell; children: Linden Ruth, Andrea Grace. Student, Principia Coll., 1950; BA, U. Calif., Berkeley, 1952; postgrad., San Diego State, 1955, Cen. Piedmont, 1981. Cert. tchr., Calif. Owner, dir. Art Gallery of Chapel Hill (N.C.), 1966-75; ecumenical bd. Campus Ministry, Charlotte; with referral svc. Charlotte (N.C.) Bed and Breakfast Registry, 1980-90; lang. cons. Berlitz Internat., Raleigh, N.C., 1988-91; cert. cons. Performax Internat.; rep. UN Decade for Women Conf., NGO Forum, Nairobi, Kenya, 1985, Women and Global Security Conf., 1986; rep. emerging issues forum N.C. State U., 1987-93; presenter in field. Bd. dirs., chmn. natural resources com. LWV; coord. USIA grant region 6, Internat. Exch. Network; mem. N.C. Leadership Forum, N.C. Citizens Assembly, 1989; chmn. Week of Edn. Pub. Forum on Energy, Union Concerned Scientists, 1990-93; bd. dirs. Nat. Women's Conf. Commn., 1994—; mem. edn. subcom. Mayor's Internat. Cabinet, 1995; mem. Congress House Spkr.'s Citizen Task Force, 1995—; mem. Rep. Platform Com. and Nat. Presdl. Task Force, 1995, Rep. Inner Cir., 1995. Named Outstanding Athlete Women's Athletic Assn., Woman of the Yr., Am. Biog. Inst., 1994; Hewlett Found. scholar. Mem. AAUW (v.p. membership com., bd. dirs.), Ams. for Legal Reform (adv. bd.), Am. Farm Land Trust, UN Assn. U.S.A. (chpt. pres. 1991-93, co-chair UN Day Queens Coll. 1992, N.C. divsn. sec. 1993-94, UN50 chair 1995), Am. Biog. Inst. Rsch. Assn. (nominated to bd. govs.), Carolina Coun. on World Affairs, Chapel Hill-Carrboro Sch. Art Guild (pres.), Midwest Acad., World Wide Women in Environment, N.Y. Acad. Sci. Republican. Christian Scientist. Office: PO Box 220802 Charlotte NC 28222-0802

HILL, SHIRLEY ELIZABETH (DIETZ), nurse; b. Leominster, Mass., Jan. 14, 1921; d. George Albert and Alta (Conrey) Dietz; m. Albert Seymour Hill; children: Jeffrey Albert, Jordan Roy, Joy Alta. RN diploma, Katherine McQueen Meml. Sch., 1958; BSN, U. Nebr., 1968; MSN, U. R.I., 1974. RN, Md., R.I., Nebr., N.J., Mass., Vt. Staff nurse med.-psychiat. Prison Hosp., Framingham, Mass., 1948-54; charge nurse med.-surg. Kent and Queen Anne's Hosp., Chestertown, Md., 1958; staff nurse med. R.I. Hosp., Providence, 1958-59; head nurse med.-surg. Kent County Hosp., Warwick, R.I., 1959-60; charge nurse psychiat. R.I. Med. Ctr., Howard, 1960-63; head nurse psychiat. St. Joseph's Hosp., Omaha, 1963-64; staff nurse Vis. Nurse's Assn., Combined Agy., Omaha, 1964-66; instr. student nurse diploma program psychiat. nursing Greystone Park State Hosp., Morristown, N.J., 1966-67; sr. instr. med.-surg. nursing diploma program St. Luke's Hosp. Sch. Nursing, New Bedford, Mass., 1967-74; instr. The Newport (R.I.) Coll., 1974-77, asst. prof., 1977-78; instr. Bristol C.C., Fall River, Mass., 1978-80; dir. case mgmt., exec. staff Corrigan Mental Health Ctr. Mass. State Dept. Mental Health, Fall River, 1979-82, dir. cmty. health Corrigan Mental Health Ctr., 1982-86; small bus. owner Edgeview Antique Rose Garden and Gift Shop, 1986—; chmn. dist. III legis. com. Mass. Nurses' Assn.; legis. del. Mass. Health Coun.;em. Mental Health and Gerontology Adv. Bd. Mem. editl. adv. The Mass. Nurse, 1977. Town Meeting Rep., Natick, Mass., 1948; cons., organizer Women's Ctr., New Bedford, Mass., 1968-69; chmn. social action com., budget and fin. com. North Dartmouth Quaker Meeting, Soc. Friends, 1973-75, chmn. peace and social concerns com., 1975-77, mem. cemetary com., 1975—, clk. of Quaker meeting, 1975-78; town auditor Brandon, Vt., 1995—. Mem. ANA, Nat. League for Nursing, State Nurses' Assn. Democrat. Mem. Soc. of Friends. Home: 27 Marble St Brandon VT 05733

HILL, SUSAN EILEEN, auditor; b. Toledo, Ohio, Aug. 13, 1948; d. Kenneth Allen and Doris Eileen (Baker) H. BA, Morehead State U., 1972. Pressman Daily Sentinal, Grand Junction, Colo., 1980-81; janitor City Market, Grand Junction, Colo., 1981-92, auditor, 1992—. Inventor (patent pending) Heart Felt Trash Can.

HILL, SUSAN SLOAN, safety engineer; b. Quincy, Mass., June 1, 1952; d. Ralph Arnold and Grace Elenore (Sloan) Crosby; m. William Loyd Hill, Dec. 16, 1973 (div. July 1982); m. William Joseph Graham, Sept. 10, 1983 (div. Feb. 1985). Assoc. Sci. in Gen. Engring., Motlow State C.C., Tullahoma, Tenn., 1976; BS in Indsl. Engring., Tenn. Technol. U., 1978. Intern, safety engr. Intern Tng. Ctr., U.S. Army, Red River Army Depot, Tex., 1978-79, Field Safety Activity, Charlestown, Ind., 1979, system safety engr. Comm.-Electronics Command, Ft. Monmouth, N.J., 1979-84, gen. engr., 1984-85; chief system safety Arnold Air Force Sta., USAF, Tullahoma, 1984; system safety engr. U.S. Army Safety Ctr., Ft. Rucker, Ala., 1985-91; medically retired; ind. cons. system safety, 1991—; founder Fibromyalgia Support Group; leader Arthritis Found. Support Group; active Arthritis Found. Recipient 5 letters of appreciation U.S. Army. Mem. NAFE, Assn. Fed. Safety and Health Profls. (regional v.p. 1980-84), Soc. Women Engrs., Nat. Safety Mgmt. Soc., Am. Soc. Safety Engrs., System Safety Soc., Order Engr. Republican. Episcopalian. Avocations: bowling, needlework, sewing, cooking, golf. Home and Office: PO Box 1075 Tullahoma TN 37388-1075

HILLARD, CAROLE, state official; b. Deadwood, S.D., Aug. 14, 1936; m. John M. Hillard; children: David, Sue Ellen, Todd, Eddie, Lonnell. BA in Edn., Univ. of Ariz., 1957; MA in Edn., S.D. State Univ., 1982; MA in Polit. Sci., Univ. of S.D., 1984. State rep. State of S.D., 34th dist., 1991-95; lt. gov. State of S.D., 1995—; dir. Mich. Nat. Bank., Black Hills Regional Eye Inst., YMCA; mem. exec. bd. Nat. Crime Prevention Coun. Active Rapid City Common Coun., Rapid City C. of C., S.D. Bd. of Charities and Corrections, McGruff Crime Prevention Coun. (exec. bd.), S.D. Corrections Commn., Cmty. Care Ctr., S.D. Children's Home Soc., S.D. Assurance Alliance, Nat. Child Protection Partnership, First United Methodist Ch. (exec. bd.), Rapid City Econ. Devel. Partnership, F.L.A.G.S. Found.; mem. exec. bd. Bog Bros./Big Sisters. Recipient Pub. Svc. award, 1987, Gov.'s Outstanding Citizen award, 1988, George award Rapid City C. of C., 1994; named Outstanding Chirperson, United Way, 1986, S.D. Guardian Small Bus., 1994. Mem. LWV, Women's Network, Mt. Rushmore Soc., Indian-White Coun., Toastmasters, Ninety-niners, Rapid City Fine Arts Coun. Republican. Methodist. Office: Office of Lt Governor State Capitol 500 E Capitol Ave Ste 204 Pierre SD 57501-5070

HILLEBRAND, GAIL K., lawyer; b. Oakland, Calif., July 25, 1956; d. John J. and Elizabeth May Hillebrand; m. Hugh S. Barroll, Aug. 20, 1983; 2 sons. BA, U. Calif., San Diego, 1977; JD, U. Calif., Berkeley, 1981. Bar: Calif. 1981. Judicial law clk. to Hon. R. Boochevar U.S. Ct. Appeals (9th cir.), 1981-82; assoc. McCutch, Doyle, Brown & Enerser, San Francisco, 1982-85; mem. litigation counsel Consumers Union U.S., Inc., San Francisco, 1985—; mem. Savings Assn. Ins. Fund Adv. Coun., Washington, 1989-91; mem. consumer adv. coun. Fed. Res. Bd., Washington, 1995—. Contbr. articles to profl. jours. Bd. dirs. Calif. Reinvestment Com., San Francisco, 1992—; bd. dirs., vice chair Nat. Cmty. Reinvestment Coalition, Washington, 1990-92. Mem. ABA. Office: Consumers Union US 1535 Mission St San Francisco CA 94103

HILLEGASS, CHRISTINE ANN, psychologist; b. Lancaster, Pa., July 13, 1952; d. Michael and Ann Christine (Wolf) H.; m. E. Cornelius Kocsis, Aug. 6, 1983. BA, Bard Coll., 1975; MA in Forensic Psychol., John Jay Coll. Criminal Justice, 1979; PsyD, Rutgers U., 1993. Staff psychologist Dept. Corrections, Adult Diagnostic Treatment Ctr., Avenel, N.J., 1979-84; dir. Monmouth County Sexual Abuse Treatment and Prevention Program, Ocean, N.J., 1984-87; cons., trainer, therapist various mental health, social svc., correctional and law enforcement agys., 1981—; mem. Monmouth County Sexual Abuse Coalition, 1983—, chair, 1986-87, co-chair, 1987-88; mem. N.J. Statewide Sexual Abuse Network, 1984-89, Monmouth Prosecutor's Task Force on Child Abuse, Freehold, N.J., 1985-86. Recipient Woman of Achievement award Monmouth County Adv. Commn. on Status of Women, 1987. Mem. Am. Psychol. Assn., N.J. Psychol. Assn., Am. Profl. Soc. on Abuse of Children, Am. Assn. of Applied and Preventive Psychol. Office: 500 N Bridge St Bridgewater NJ 08807-2135

HILLER, DEBORAH LEWIS, long term care and retirement facility executive; b. Philipsburg, Pa., Nov. 8, 1947; d. Edward Trumble and Margaret Grace France (Bates) Lewis; m. Alan John Ross, Jan. 20, 1979; 1 child: Edward Simpson Ross. Bar: Ohio. Law clk. to Hon. Robert Krupansky U.S. Dist. Ct., Cleve., 1975-76; trial atty. antitrust divsn. U.S. Dept. Justice, Cleve., 1977-81; ptnr. Calfee, Halter & Griswold, Cleve., 1981-93; pres., CEO The Eliza Jennings Group, Cleve., 1993—. Mem. ABA, Ohio Bar Assn. (chmn. antitrust law sect. 1991-93, bd. govs. 1986-93), Fed. Bar Assn., Cleve. Bar Assn. Democrat. Episcopalian. Home: 427 Bassett Rd Bay Village OH 44140-1815

HILLER, JOAN VITEK, sociologist; b. Mpls., Apr. 4, 1960; d. Thomas Mark and Louanne (Howard) Vitek; m. James G. Hiller, Aug. 28, 1987; 1 child, Thomas Joseph. BA, Coll. St. Catherine, 1982; MS, Tex. A&M U., 1985; PhD, Northwestern U., 1996. Lic. independent social worker, Minn. Statistician Ctr. Health Studies and Policy Rsch./Northwestern U., Evanston, Ill., 1985-87; sr. program evaluation specialist Minn. Dept. Human Svcs., St. Paul, 1987-89; dir. nonprofit svcs. Willowbrooke Orgn. Devel., Burnsville, Minn., 1990—; adj. instr. U. St. Thomas, St. Paul, 1989-95, Hamline U., St. Paul, 1988-91, Coll. St. Catherine, 1994-95, Inver Hills C.C., 1988—; rep. Gov.'s Com. Drug-Free Schs., 1987-89; ex-officio Minn. Juvenile Justice Adv. Com., St. Paul, 1986-87. Bd. dirs. Open Your Heart to the Hungry and Homeless, St. Paul, 1989-94, v.p., 1991-93. Mem. NAFE, Am. Sociol. Assn. (cert. applied social rsch., mem. com. on pub. affairs 1992-93), Mensa (v.p. Minn. chpt. 1992-94, pres. chpt. 1994-96), Sociologists Minn. (bd. dirs. 1991-93). Roman Catholic. Home: 3206 Red Oak Cir N Burnsville MN 55337-3307

HILLERS, ELLEN MARSH, film-television production coordinator; b. Syracuse, N.Y., Feb. 19, 1961; d. Robert Stilphen and Eleanor Hunter (Marsh) H. BA, Wells Coll., 1983. Production coord.: (films) Scrooged, Paramount Pictures, N.Y.C., 1987, Reversal of Fortune, Pressman Film, N.Y.C., 1989, Lorenzo's Oil, Universal City Studios, Pitts., 1991, Quiz Show, Disney, N.Y.C., 1993, Little Big League, Castlerock Entertainment, L.A./Mpls., 1993, Twelve Monkeys, Universal City Studios, Phila./Balt., 1995, Men in Black, Columbia Pictures, N.Y., 1996; (TV) Miami Vice, 911; (other) The Super, Funny About Love, A Kiss Before Dying, The Accidental Tourist, Beaches, True Love. Mem. Internat. Alliance Theatrical Stage Employees and Moving Picture Machine Operators of U.S. and Can. Republican. Episcopalian. Home: 124 Rim Rock Dr Durango CO 81301-8603

HILLERT, GLORIA BONNIN, anatomist, educator; b. Brownton, Minn., Jan. 25, 1930; d. Edward Henry and Lydia Magdalene (Luebker) Bonnin; m. Richard Hillert, Aug. 20, 1960; children: Kathryn, Virginia, Jonathan. BS, Valparaiso (Ind.) U., 1953; MA, U. Mich., 1958. Instr. Springfield (Ill.) Jr. Coll., 1953-57; teaching asst. U. Mich., Ann Arbor, 1957-58; instr., dept. head St. John's Coll., Winfield, Kans., 1958-59; asst. prof. Concordia Coll., River Forest, Ill., 1959-63; vis. instr. Wright Jr. Coll., Chgo., 1974-76, Ill. Benedictine Coll., Lisle, 1977-78, Rosary Coll., River Forest, 1976-81; prof. anatomy and physiology Triton Coll., River Grove, 1982-92, prof. emeritus, 1992—; vis. asst. prof. Concordia U., 1993—; vis. instr. Wheaton (Ill.) Coll., 1988; advisor Springfield Jr. Coll. Sci. Club, 1953-57, Concordia Coll. Cultural Group, 1959-62; program dir. Triton Coll. Sci. Lectr. Series, 1983-87; participant Internat. Educators Workshop in Amazonia, 1993. Dem. campaign asst., Maywood, Ill., 1972, 88; vol. Mental Health Orgn., Chgo., 1969-73, Earthwatch, St. Croix, 1987, Costa Rica, 1989, Internat. Med. Care Team, Guatemala, 1995. Mem. AAUW, Ill. Assn. Community Coll. Biol. Tchrs., Nat. Assn. Biol. Tchrs. Lutheran. Home: 1620 Clay Ct Melrose Park IL 60160-2419 Office: Triton Coll 2000 N 5th Ave River Grove IL 60171-1907

HILLERY, MARY JANE LARATO, columnist, producer, television host, reserve army officer; b. Boston, Sept. 15, 1931; d. Donato and Porzia (Avellis) Larato; Asso. Sci. (scholar), Northeastern U., 1950; BS, U. Mass. Harvard Extension, 1962; grad. Command and Gen. Staff Coll., 1982; m. Thomas H. Hillery, Feb. 25, 1961; 1 son, Thomas H. Sales agt., linguist Pan Am. Airways, Boston, 1955-61; interpreter Internat. Conf. Fire Chiefs, Boston, 1966; tchr. Spanish, YWCA, Natick, Mass., 1966-67; cmty. rels. cons., adv. bd. dirs., lectr. for migrant edn. project div. Mass. Dept. Cmty. Affairs, Boston, 1967-69; editor-in-chief Sudbury (Mass.) Citizen, 1967-76; assoc. editor The Beacon, 1976-79, contbg. editor, 1979-83; area editl. adviser Beacon Pub. Co., Acton, Mass., 1970-80, editor, 1976-80; columnist Town Crier, 1987—; contbg. editor Towne Talk, 1975-79, Citizens' Forum, 1975-81; editor Spl. Forces Ann. History, 1990; dir. pub. affairs Mass. Dept. Environ. Quality Engring., 1981-83; prodr., host TV interview show For the Record, 1985—; pub. affairs officer Fed. Emergency Mgmt. Agy., 1995—. Mem. Bus. Adv. Com., 1972-77, Sudbury Sch. Com., 1976-77; mem. Meml. Day Celebration Com., 1972—, master of ceremonies, 1973-96; chmn. Sudbury WWII Commemorative Cmty., 1992—; mem. Sudbury Town Report, 1967-72, 85-88, chmn., 1969-72; chmn. Sudbury Vets. Adv. Com., 1986-92; panelist Internat. Women's Year Symposium, 1975, Women in Politics, 1987, Women In Mil., 1987; mem. congl. 5th dist. Mass. nomination bd. West Point, apptd. mil. aide-de-camp to Mass. Gov. Wm. Weld, 1992—; Veterans' agent Town of Sudbury, 1992—. Served with USN, 1950-54; lt. col. USAR; Persian Gulf, 1991-92; liaison officer U.S. Mil. Acad. West Point, 1976-89; pub. affairs officer 94th USAR Command, 1982-83, Office of Sec. of Def., The Pentagon, Washington, 1989-93. Editor Hansconian, 1983-85. Decorated Meritorious Svc. medal 1985, Joint Svc. Achievement medal, 1991, Nat. Def. medal-Bronze Stars, 1991, Outstanding Svc. award Sec. Def. Pub. Affairs, 1992, Joint Meritorious unit award, 1992, Def. Superior Svc. medal, 1993; Named Editor of Year, Beacon Pub. Co., 1970; recipient medal of appreciation Internat. Order DeMolay, 1969, certificates of appreciation U.S. Def. Civil Preparedness Agy., 1975, Mass. Bicentennial Commn., 1976, Appreciation award U.S. Mil. Acad., 1976-86, Res. Officers Assn., 1976-86; citations Mass. State Senate, 1979, 82; Newswriting award Media Contest, Air Force Sys. Command, 1984, Outstanding Svc. award Sec. Def. Pub. Affairs, 1991. Mem. LWV (dir. 1964-68), Nat. Editl. Assn., Nat. Newspaper Assn., Nat. Press Club, Rotary Internat. (mem. Sudbury chpt. scholarship com. 1993—, bd. dirs. 1994-95, 96-97, pub. rels. chmn. 1995-96, assoc. editor The Bulletin, 1996—), New Eng. Press Assn., Bus. and Profl. Women's Club (Sudbury 1st v.p. 1973-74, pres. 1974-76, parliamentarian 1978-88, 90-92, legis. chair, 1990-92, state bylaws com. 1977-78, 79-81, 86-88, state legis. chmn. 1979-81, 86-88, state polit. action com. chmn. 1988-89, Woman of Yr. 1979, Woman of Achievement 1982), Nat. League Am. Pen Women (exec. bd. Boston 1974-76, 78-88, pres. 1976-78, 94—, state exec. bd. 1994—, publicity chmn. 1979-80, chmn. bylaws com. 1979-80, 86-88, parliamentarian 1978-80, 82-88, auditor 1980-82, 84-88, 1st v.p. 1988-92, nat. editor Achievements, The Pen Woman 1992-94), Res. Officers Assn. (life, state sec. 1978-79, state army v.p. 1992-95, pres. Boston chpt. 1986-88, dept. state pres. 1996—, army v.p. 1995-96, army coun. rep. 1989-92, budget com., 1990-91, state publicity chmn. 1988-92, editor Advisor 1991-95, Outstanding Svc. award 1978-79, co-chair Nat. Conv., 1995—, state pres.-elect 1995, pres. 1996-97), Omega Sigma. Home: 66 Willow Rd Sudbury MA 01776-2663

HILLESTAD, DONNA DAWN, nurse; b. Merrill, Wis., May 13, 1938; d. Martin T. and Edna (Frederick) Dietrich; m. John Curtis Hillestad, July 18, 1959; children: Dori Jean, David Jeffrey. BSN, Mankato U., 1962. RN, Minn. Office nurse Fairmont (Minn.) Clinic, 1963-65, pvt. duty, pub. health nurse, 1965-67; charge nurse, supr. Lakeview Meth. Health Care Ctr., Fairmont, 1967—; nurse ins. phys. for numerous ins. cos., 1980—. Active Fairmont Community Concert Assn.; host fgn. exch. students, 1989, 90, 91, 92. Mem. AAUW (pub. rels. com. 1986-87, historian 1982-84, bull. editor 1985-86, chmn. hospitality 1987-88, mem. cultural interests com. 1980-81, Internat. Rels. award 1991), Bus. and Profl. Women (chmn. internat. rels. 1986, emblem chmn. 1982-83, pub. rels. com. 1984-85, found. com. 1990, historian 1976, nominating sunshine com. 1989-90, auditing com. 1986-87, sec. 1985-86, 88-89), Holiday Travel Club (founder), Friendship Force (So. Minn. chpt. sec. 1995—), Tourist Club, Cmty. Club, Garden Club. Lutheran. Home: 803 S Hampton St Fairmont MN 56031-4308

HILLGREN, SONJA DOROTHY, journalist; b. Sioux Falls, S.D., May 17, 1948; d. Ralph Oliver and Priscilla Adaline (Mannes) Hillgren; m. Ralph Lee Hill (dec.). BJ, U. Mo., 1970, MA, 1972; postgrad. (Nieman fellow), Harvard U., 1982-83. Washington corr. Ohio-Washington News Svc., 1972-73; reporter UPI, Annapolis, Md., 1974-76; reporter/editor UPI, Washington, 1976-78; farm editor UPI, 1978-88; Washington corr. Knight-Ridder, Washington, 1988-90; Washington editor Farm Jour., 1990-95, editor, 1995—. Recipient J.R. Russell award Newspaper Farm Editors Am., 1985, Reuben Brigham award Agrl. Communicators in Edn., 1988; named Old Master, Purdue U., 1992, Agrl. Communicator of Yr., Nat. Agri-Mktg. Assn., 1996; Woodrow Wilson vis. fellow, 1993—. Mem. Nat. Assn. Agrl. Journalists (pres. 1987-88), Nat. Press Club (bd. govs. 1991—, chair 1993-94, v.p. 1995, pres. 1996), Soc. Profl. Journalists, Investigative Reporters and Editors, Am. Soc. of Mag. Editors, Am. Agrl. Editors' Assn., Farm Found., Coun. on Fgn. Rels., Congl. Country Club, Pi Beta Phi. Lutheran. Home: 2800 29th Pl NW Washington DC 20008-3501 Office: Farm Jour 1325 G St NW Ste 200 Washington DC 20005

HILL-HULSLANDER, JACQUELYNE L., nursing educator and consultant; b. Melrose Park, Ill., Jan. 9, 1940; d. Richard C. and Marian L. (Hamlin) Hill; m. Gale Franklin Hulslander, June 5, 1993; children: Daryl, Gary. Diploma, Evanston (Ill.) Hosp. Assn., 1961; BS, Elmhurst (Ill.) Coll., 1977, BSN, 1981; MS, Nat.-Louis U., Evanston, 1986; PhD, U. Ill., 1990. Cons. in course devel. Ill. Bell Telephone Co., Chgo.; cons. for employee devel. Glen Oaks Med. Ctr., Glendale Hts., Ill.; prof. Triton Coll., River Grove, Ill.; staff nurse OB Evanston (Ill.) Hosp. Assn., 1961-62; staff and charge nurse OB Gottlieb Mem. Hosp., Melrose Park, Ill., 1962-65; faculty OB Proviso Sch. Practical Nursing, Maywood, Ill., 1965-67; charge nurse OB Gottlieb Meml. Hosp., Melrose Park, 1970-75; grad. rsch. asst. dept. vocat. edn. U. Ill., Champaign-Urbana, Ill., 1988-89; faculty prof. basic med. surg. nursing and obstetrics Triton Coll., River Grove, Ill., 1976—; cons. Dawson Tech. Inst., Chgo. City Coll.; cons. Engring. Systems Inc., Aurora, Ill.; presenter in field. Multicompetencies for Practical Nurses grantee, 1986. Mem. Chateau Lorraine Homeowners Assn. (sec., v.p., pres. 1992-96), U. Ill. Alumn Assn., Phi Delta Kappa, Phi Kappa Phi. Home: 222 Lorraine Cir Bloomingdale IL 60108-2546 Office: Triton Coll 2000 N 5th Ave River Grove IL 60171-1907

HILLIARD, PAULINE ELAINE, librarian; b. Gainesville, Tex., June 21, 1945; d. Loyd George and Ruby Evelyn (Wilson) H. BS, Tex. Woman's U., 1968, postgrad., summers 1988,89; MA, Ohio U., 1975. Cert. tchr. English, bus., ESL, learning resources, Tex. Tchr. English Edinburg (Tex.) H.S., 1968; grad. tchg. asst. English Okla. State U., Stillwater, 1968-69; English/ESL/reading tchr. Peace Corps, The Philippines, 1969-72; jr. high reading tchr. Edinburg Jr. H.S., 1973; grad. tchg. asst. Ohio U., Athens, 1973-75, ESL instr., 1975-78; reading tchr. Jr. H.S., Garden City, Kans., 1978-80; English/ESL tchr. Boswell H.S., Ft. Worth, Tex., 1980-88; libr. Brackett Ind. Sch. Dist., Brackettville, Tex., 1989—. With USAR, 1979-85. Named to Outstanding Young Women of Am., 1977. Mem. NOW, Returned Peace Corps Assn., Alpha Chi, Sigma Tau Delta. Democrat. Home: PO Box 564 Brackettville TX 78832 Office: Brackett Ind Sch Dist 400 Ann St Brackettville TX 78832

HILLIARD, WENDY, sports foundation administrator. Mem. U.S. Nat. Rhythmic Gymnastics Team; owner Rhythmic Gymnastics N.Y. Mem. Women's Sports Found. (pres., trustee, travel and tng. fund grantee). Office: Eisenhower Park East Meadow NY 11554

HILLIS, MARCIA LOUISE, sculptor, art educator; b. San Antonio, Mar. 13, 1964; d. Robert Edmund Hillis and Margaret Susan (Lowry) Bland. BA, U. Va., 1986. Exhibited in group shows at One Main St., Bklyn., 1993, Silvermine Art Guild, New Canaan, Conn., 1993, Bronx Mus. of Arts, 1993, L.I. Univ., Bklyn., 1994, PS 122, N.Y.C., 1994, OIA, N.Y.C., 1994, Paula Cooper Gallery, N.Y.C., 1995, Snug Harbor Cultural Ctr., S.I., 1995, Maria Feliz Gallery, Jim Thorpe, Pa., 1996; artist: (artist's books) Crossings, 1985, 86, Promotional Copy, 1994, Time Capsule, 1995. Fundraiser, educator Greenpeace, N.Y.C., 1989-90; vol. Cmty. Bd. # 2, Bklyn., 1996. Recipient Jurists' award Anthropology Mus. of People of N.Y., 1991, Artists in the Marketplace award Bronx Mus. of Arts, 1993. Mem. Bklyn. Waterfront Artists' Coalition. Democrat. Home: 39 Pearl St 3F Brooklyn NY 11201

HILLIS, MARGARET, conductor, musician; b. Kokomo, Ind., Oct. 1, 1921; d. Glen R. and Bernice (Haynes) H. MusB, Ind. U., 1947; grad. student choral conducting, Juilliard Sch. Music, 1947-49; MusD (hon.), Temple U., 1967, Ind. U., 1972, Carthage Coll., 1979, Wartburg Coll., 1981, Adrian Coll., 1990, U. Mo., Kansas City, 1996, U. Ill., 1996; DFA (hon.), St. Mary's Coll., 1977, Lake Forest Coll., 1980, North Park Coll.; DHL (hon.), St. Xavier Coll., 1988; LittD (hon.), St. Mary of the Woods Coll., 1990. Dir., Met. Youth Chorale, Bklyn., 1948-51; asst. condr., Collegiate Choral, N.Y.C., 1952-53; mus. dir., condr., Am. Concert Choir, N.Y.C. from 1950, Am. Concert Orch. from 1950; condr., instr., Union Theol. Sem., 1950-60, Juilliard Sch. Music, 1951-53; dir. choral dept., Third St. Music Sch. Settlement, 1953-54; founder, music dir., Am. Choral Found., Inc., from 1954; choral dir., N.Y.C. Opera Co., 1955-56, Chgo. Mus. Coll. of Roosevelt U., 1961-62; condr., choral dir., Santa Fe Opera Co., 1958-59, Chgo. Symphony Chorus, 1957-94; music dir., N.Y. Chamber Soloists, 1956-60; choral condr., Am. Opera Soc., N.Y.C., 1952-68; mus. asst. to music dir., Chgo. Symphony Orch., 1966-68; music dir., condr., Kenosha Symphony Orch., 1961-68; condr., choral dir., Cleve. Orch. Chorus, 1969-71; prof. conducting, dir. choral orgns., Northwestern U. Sch. Music, 1970-77; vis. prof. conducting, Ind. U. from 1978; resident condr. Chgo. Civic Orch., 1967-90; music dir. Choral Inst., 1968-70, 75; mus. dir., condr., Elgin (Ill.) Symphony Orch., 1971-85; condr. Chgo.'s Do-It-Yourself Messiah, 1976—; dir. choral activities San Francisco Symphony Orch., 1982-83; guest condr., Chgo. Symphony, Cleve. Orch., Minn.Orch., Nat. Symphony Orch., others. Artists' adviser Nat. Fedn. Music Clubs Youth Auditions, 1966-70; mem. vis. com. dept. music U. Chgo., 1971—; chmn. choral panel Nat. Endowment for Arts, 1974-82; hon. mem. Roosevelt U. Coun. of 100, 1976—; adv. bd. Cathedral Choral Soc. Washington Cathedral, 1976—; mem. Nat. Coun. Arts, 1985-90. Civilian flight instr. USA CAA, WTS, World War II. Recipient Grammy awards for best choral performances: Verdi's Requiem, 1978, Beethoven's Missa Solemnis, 1979, Brahm's Ein Deutsches Requiem, 1980, Berlioz' La Damnation de Faust, 1983, Haydn's Creation, 1984, Brahm's Ein Deutsches Requiem, 1985, Orff's Carmina Burana, 1987, Bach's B-Minor Mass, 1991, Bartok's Cantata Profana, 1993, Grand Prix du Disque for Berlioz' La Damnation de Faust, 1982, Golden Plate award Am. Acad. Achievement, 1967, Alumnus of Year award Ind. U. Sch. Music Alumni, 1969, Steinway award, 1969, Chgo. YWCA Leader Luncheon I award, 1972, Friends of Lit. award, 1973, SAI Found. Circle of 15 award, 1974, Woman of Yr. in Classical Music award Ladies Home Jour., 1978, Leadership for Freedom award Women's Scholarship Assn. Roosevelt U., 1978, Dushkin award, 1992, Gov.'s award, Chgo. Chpt. Nat. Acad. Recording Arts Scis., 1992. Mem. Nat. Fedn. Music Clubs (hon., citation for contbns. to musical life of nation 1981), Am. Choral Dirs. Assn., Assn. Choral Condrs., Am. Music Center, P.E.O., Sigma Alpha Iota (hon.), Pi Kappa Lambda (hon.), Kappa Kappa Gamma (Alumni Achievement award 1978), Chorus America (formerly Assn. Profl. Vocal Ensembles), Am. Symphony Orch. League, Nat. Soc. Lit. and Arts. Office: Chgo Symphony Orch 220 S Michigan Ave Chicago IL 60604-2508

HILLMAN, BARBARA HALL, elementary school educator; b. Summit, N.J., Dec. 5, 1947; d. Ralph Charles and Dorothy Jane (Young) Hall; m. Robert John Hillman, Dec. 21, 1969; children: Eric, Greg. BA in Elem. Edn., Kean Coll., 1974. Cert. elem. and early childhood tchr., N.J. Tchr. St. Rose of Lima Sch., Freehold, N.J., 1968-73; tchr. Wall Twp. Bd. Edn., Wall, N.J., 1974—, whole lang. tchr. trainer, 1989—; whole lang. tchr. trainer Manalapan (N.J.)-Englishtown Bd. Edn., 1992, 93. Mem. commn. Sea Girt (N.J.) Recreation, 1991—; cub scout pack master Boy Scouts Am., Sea Girt, 1984-91; treas. West Belmar PTA, Wall, 1982—; active Sea Girt Sch. PTO, 1982-94; rep. in children's lit. exch. with China, Citizens Ambassador Program, 1994. Wall Found. for Ednl. Excellence grantee, 1993; named Life Mem., PTA, 1991. Mem. NEA, Internat. Reading Assn., Monmouth County Reading Assn., N.J. Edn. Assn., Monmouth County Edn. Assn., Wall Twp. Edn. Assn. Home: 411 Chicago Blvd Sea Girt NJ 08750-2010 Office: West Belmar Sch 925 17th Ave Wall NJ 07719-3102

HILLMAN, CAROL BARBARA, communications executive; b. N.Y.C., Sept. 6, 1940; d. Joseph Hoppenfeld and Elsa (Spiegel) Hoppenfeld Resika; m. Howard D. Hillman, May 25, 1969. BA with honors, U. Wis., 1961; Fulbright scholar U. Lyon (France), 1961-62; MA, Cornell U., Ithaca, N.Y.,

1966. Asst. editor Holt Rinehart & Winston, Pubs., 1965-66; staff assoc. pub. rels. Ea. Airlines, N.Y.C., 1966-74; pub. affairs mgr. Squibb Corp., N.Y.C., 1974-75; asst. dir. corp. pub. rels. Burlington Industries, N.Y.C., 1975-77, dir. corp. pub. rels., 1977-80, v.p. pub. rels., 1980-82; v.p. corp. communications Norton Co., Worcester, Mass., 1982-89, sr. cons. 1989-90; nat. dir. pub. rels. and communications Deloitte & Touche, Wilton, Conn., 1990-91; v.p. Univ. Rels. Boston U., 1991-95; prin. Hillman & Kersey Strategic Comms., 1995—; mem. Pub. Affairs Coun., Machinery & Allied Products Inst., 1982-89; mem. dep. policy com., agenda com. Mass. Bus. Roundtable, 1982-89; bd. dirs. Mass. Econ. Stabilization Trust, 1987—. Mem. Cornell Coun., Ithaca, 1981-85, pub. rels. com. 1981-88; mem. adv. coun. Coll. Human Ecology, Cornell U., Ithaca, 1982-84; mem. adv. bd. Ct. Apptd. Spl. Advocates, Worcester, 1983-87; voting mem. Wis. Union Trustees, U. Wis., Madison, 1982-90, trustee, 1990—; mem. board vistors, college letter sci., U. Wis., 1996—, Clark U. Assocs., Worcester, 1983-89; bd. dirs. Planned Parenthood League Mass., 1986-90, pub. affairs com. 1991—; trustee Quinsigamond Community Coll., Worcester, 1987—. Cornell Grad. fellow Cornell U., 1962. Mem. Pub. Rels. Soc. Am., Internat. Women's Forum, Mass. Women's Forum, Arthur Page Soc., The Wisemen, Phi Beta Kappa, Phi Kappa Phi. Home: 299 Belknap Rd Framingham MA 01701-4716 Office: Hillman & Kersey 222 Berkeley St Ste 1930 Boston MA 02116

HILLMAN, CAROL ELIZABETH, real estate broker; b. Monticello, Ark., July 29, 1947; d. Horace Lavon McManus and Leathel Jeanette (Higgins) Losh; m. William Carlton Hillman, Oct. 21, 1967; 1 child, Carol Lynn. Grad. high sch., Monticello, 1965. Lic. real estate broker. Exec. sec. Hamburg (Ark.) Shirt Co., 1965-67; office and payroll mgr. Glamorise Founds., Inc., Dermott, Ark., 1967-69; cashier, customer svc. rep. Main Dept. Store, Rolla, Mo., 1975-77; office mgr., chiropractic asst. Dr. J.W. Moffett Chiropractic, Bolivar, Mo., 1977-80; salesperson Sta. KYOO Radio, Bolivar, 1980-83, sales mgr., 1983-91, gen. mgr., 1991-93; real estate broker-salesperson Perkins Realtors, Bolivar, 1993-94; owner Carol E. Hillman Real Estate Co., Bolivar, 1994—; bd. dirs. bus. adv. bd. students S.W. Bapt. U., Bolivar, 1992-93. Co-chair entertainment Bolivar Country Days, 1992—. Recipient High Series awards Outreach League, 1991. Mem. Bolivar Bd. Realtors, Ozark Bd. Realtors, Bolivar Area C. of C. (Sta. KYOO rep. 1983-93). Home: 1301 E 420th Rd Bolivar MO 65613-9803 Office: Carol E Hillman Real Estate Co 1301 E 420th Rd Bolivar MO 65613

HILLMAN, CAROLYNN M., psychotherapist, writer; b. Hartford, Conn., Oct. 29, 1942; d. Nathan and Lillian Leah (Leibert) H.; m. Ulysses Stephen Harrigan, Jan. 22, 1978; children: Nurelle, Robyn. BA, Barnard Coll., 1964; MSW, Hunter Coll./CUNY, 1968. Cert. social worker; cert. psychoanalyst; cert. sex therapist; lic. clin. social worker. Social worker Goddard Riverside Head Start, N.Y.C., 1968-70, Soundview-Throgs Neck Cmty. Mental Health Ctr., N.Y.C., 1970-71, Jewish Family Svc., N.Y.C., 1971-78; pvt. practice N.Y.C., 1978—. Author: Recovery of Your Self-Esteem, 1992, Love Your Looks, 1996. Mem. com. that investigated instl. racism in Teaneck Pub. Sch. Sys., N.J., 1993-94; exec. bd. mem. PTA, Teaneck, N.J., 1995—. Fellow Soc. Clin. Social Work Psychotherapists; mem. NASW, Am. Soc. Sex Educators & Counselors & Therapists, Soc. Sex Therapists & Rechrs., Feminist Therapy Collective. Office: 300 W 72d St # 2F New York NY 10023

HILLMAN, CHARLENE HAMILTON, public relations executive; b. Akron, Ohio; d. Charles Edward and Maeton (Anderson) Hamilton; m. Robert Edward Hillman; 1 child, Robert Edward (dec.). Student, Youngstown Coll., Ind. U. Extension. Mem. Bob Long Assocs., Indpls., 1959-62; pub. relations dir. Paul Lennon Advt. Agy., Indpls., 1962-63, Clowes Meml. Hall, Indpls., 1963-64; owner, pres. Charlene Hillman Pub. Rels. Assocs., Indpls., 1964-75; sr. v.p., dir. pub. rels. Caldwell-van Riper, Inc., Indpls., 1975-90, also dir.; pvt. practice. Editor: Hoosier Ind. quar. mag., 1966-95. (Frances Wright award 1984), Pub. Rels. Soc. Am (pres. Hoosier chpt. 1967, nat. bd. dirs. 1974-75, inducted to coll. fellows, 1992), Ind. Pub. Rels. Soc. (past pres.), Small Bus. Coun. (bd. dirs.), Ind. C. of C. Home and Office: 2216 Oak Run Pl Indianapolis IN 46260-5123

HILLMAN, JENNIFER ANNE, ambassador, trade negotiator; b. lawyer, Toledo, Jan. 29, 1957; d. Charles Winchell and Anne Sylvia (Mossberg) H.; m. Mitchell Rand Berger, Oct. 20, 1990; 1 child, Benjamin Stanley Berger. BA, Duke U., 1978, MEd, 1979; JD, Harvard U., 1983. Bar: D.C., U.S. Ct. Internat., U.S. Mil. Appeals. Asst. to chancellor Duke U., Durham, N.C., 1979-80; freshman Proctor Harvard U., Cambridge, Mass., 1981-83; assoc. Patton, Boggs & Blow, Washington, 1983-87; legis. asst. Senator Terry Sanford, Washington, 1987-88, legis. dir., 1988-92; dep. cluster coord. for fin. instns. U.S. Presdl. and Vice Presdl. Transition Team, Washington, 1992-93; ambassador, chief textile negotiator Office of U.S. Trade Rep., Exec. Office of Pres., Washington, 1993-95; gen. counsel Office of the U.S. Trade Rep., 1995—; trustee Duke U., 1977-80. Mem. N.C. Dems., Raleigh, 1986—, Georgetown Presbyn. Ch., 1988—; tchr. adult learning Sacred Heart, Washington, 1983-92; adviser Terry Sanford for Senate Campaign, 1986, 92. Mem. Coun. on Women's Studies Duke U., Phi Beta Kappa. Office: US Trade Rep 600 17th St NW Washington DC 20506-0200

HILLMAN, JOYCE, state legislator; b. Deshler, Nebr., June 10, 1936; m. Kenneth Hillman, 1954; children: Janine Hergenreder, Shari Johnston, Terry. Mem. Nebr. Legislature from 48th dist. Bd. dirs. Old West Trail Found., Family Preservation Team. Democrat. Lutheran. Office: Nebr State Legislature State Capitol Lincoln NE 68509*

HILLMAN, RITA, investor; b. N.Y.C., May 16, 1912; d. Rudolf and Bertha (Goodman) Kanarek; m. Alex L. Hillman, Aug. 23, 1932 (dec. 1968); children: Richard Alan (dec.), Alex L. Student NYU, 1929-32. Mem. Met. Mus. Art (mem. vis. com. 20th century art dept.), Am. Friends Israel Mus. (exec. com.), Bklyn. Acad. Music (vice chmn.), Internat. Ctr. Photography (hon. chmn.), Alex Hillman Family Found. (pres.). Home: 895 Park Ave New York NY 10021-0327 Office: 630 5th Ave New York NY 10111-0001

HILLS, BEVERLY DIANNE, librarian; b. Honolulu, Feb. 10, 1955; d. Robert Elliot and Ruth Shirley (Glenn) H. AA in Edn., Tidewater C.C., Virginia Beach, Va., 1977, AS in Bus., 1977; BS in Bus. Mgmt., Old Dominion U., 1979; MSLS, Cath. U. of Am., 1992. Interior decorater, owner, cofounder Coverage Upholstery, Virginia Beach, Va., 1979-88; learning lab asst. Tidewater C.C., Virginia Beach, 1980-87, libr. asst., 1988-92, libr., 1992—. Mem. ALA, Va. Libr. Assn. Methodist. Office: Tidewater CC 1700 College Crescent Virginia Beach VA 23456

HILLS, CARLA ANDERSON, lawyer, former federal official; b. Los Angeles, Jan. 3, 1934; d. Carl H. and Edith (Hume) Anderson; m. Roderick Maltman Hills, Sept. 27, 1958; children: Laura Hume, Roderick Maltman, Megan Elizabeth, Alison Macbeth. A.B. cum laude, Stanford U., 1955; student, St. Hilda's Coll., Oxford (Eng.) U., 1954; LL.B., Yale U., 1958; hon. degrees, Pepperdine U., 1975, Washington U., 1977, Mills Coll., 1977, Lake Forest Coll., 1978, Williams Coll., 1981, Notre Dame U., 1993. Bar: Calif. 1959, DC 1974, U.S. Supreme Ct. 1965. Asst. U.S. atty. civil div. Los Angeles, 1958-61; ptnr. Munger, Tolles, Hills & Rickershauser, Los Angeles, 1962-74; asst. atty. gen. civil div. Justice Dept., Washington, 1974-75; sec. HUD, 1975-77; ptnr. Latham, Watkins & Hills, Washington, 1978-86, Weil, Gotshal & Manges, Washington, 1986-88; U.S. trade rep. Exec. Office of the Pres., 1989-93; chmn., CEO Hills & Co., 1993—; bd. dirs. Corning Glass Works, Am. Airlines, Fed. Nat. Mortgage Assn., Am. Internat. Group, Time-Warner, Lucent Techs., Inc.; adj. prof. Sch. Law, UCLA, 1972; mem. Trilateral Commn., 1977-82, 93—, Am. Com. on East-West Accord, 1977-79, Internat. Found. for Cultural Cooperation and Devel., 1977-89, Fed. Acctg. Standards Adv. Council, 1978-80; mem. corrections task force Los Angeles County Sub-Regional; adv. bd. Calif. Council on Criminal Justice, 1969-71; mem. standing com. discipline U.S. Dist. Ct. for Central Calif., 1970-73; mem. Adminstrv. Conf. U.S., 1972-74; mem. exec. com. law and free soc. State Bar Calif., 1973; bd. councillors U. So. Calif. Law Center, 1972-74; trustee Pomona Coll., 1974-79; trustee Brookings Instn., 1985; mem. at large exec. com. Yale Law Sch., 1973-78; mem. com. on Law Sch. Yale Univ. Council; Gordon Grand fellow Yale U., 1978; mem. Sloan Commn. on Govt. and Higher Edn., 1977-79; mem. advisory com. Princeton U., Woodrow Wilson Sch. of Pub. and Internat. Affairs, 1977-80; trustee Am. Productivity and Quality Ctr., 1988; council mem. Calif. Gov. Coun. Econ. Policy Adv., 1993—, Coun. on Fgn. Rels., 1993—; vice-chair Nat. Com. on U.S.-China Rels., 1993—; bd. dirs., U.S.-China Bus. Coun., vice-chair, 1995—. Co-author: Federal Civil Practice, 1961; co-author, editor: Antitrust Adviser, 1971, 3d edit., 1985; contbg. editor: Legal Times, 1978-88; mem. editorial bd. Nat. Law Jour., 1978-88. Trustee U. So. Calif., 1977-79, Norton Simon Mus. Art, Pasadena, Calif., 1976-80; trustee Urban Inst., 1978-89, chmn., 1983-89; co-chmn. Alliance to Save Energy, 1977-89; vice chmn. adv. coun. on legal policy Am. Enterprise Inst., 1977-84; bd. visitors, exec. com. Stanford U. Law Sch., 1978-81; bd. dirs. Am. Coun. for Capital Formation, 1978-82, Inst. for Internat. Econs., 1993—; mem. adv. com. MIT-Harvard U. Joint Ctr. for Urban Studies, 1978-82. Fellow Am. Bar Found.; mem. Los Angeles Women Lawyers Assn. (pres. 1964), ABA (chmn. publs. com. antitrust sect. 1972-74, council 1974, 77-84, chmn. 1982-83), Fed. Bar Assn. (pres. Los Angeles chpt. 1963), Los Angeles County Bar Assn. (mem. fed. rules and practice com. 1963-72, chmn. issues and survey 1963-72, chmn. sub-com. revision local rules for fed. cts. 1966-72, mem. jud. qualifications com. 1971-72), Am. Law Inst., Am. China Soc. Clubs: Yale of So. Calif. (dir. 1972-74); Yale (Washington). Office: 1200 19th St NW Ste 201 Washington DC 20036-2412

HILLS, LINDA LAUNEY, advisory systems engineer; b. New Orleans, June 21, 1947; d. Edgar Sebastien and Isabel (James) Launey; m. Marvin Allen Hills Sr. Jan. 29, 1977 (div. July 1982); 8 stepchildren. Student, Navy Avionics Schs., Memphis and San Diego, 1979-89; certs. in IBM Tech. Tng., System Mgmt. Schs., Chgo. and Dallas. Cert. disaster recovery planner. Sec. Calhoun and Barnes Inc. Co., New Orleans, 1965; clk. typist Social Security Adminstrn., New Orleans, 1965-67, U.S. Marshal's Office, New Orleans, 1967-69; supr. U.S. Atty.'s Office, New Orleans, 1969; with clk.'s office U.S. Dist. Ct. (ea. dist.) La., New Orleans, 1969-73; steno, sr. sec. Kelly Girl and Norrell Temp Services, New Orleans, 1974; aviation electronic technician, PO2 USN, Memphis and San Diego, 1974-78; customer engr. trainee IBM, Dallas, 1979; customer engr., systems mgmt. specialist IBM, San Diego, 1979-84; system ctr. rep. NSD Washington System Ctr. IBM, Gaithersburg, Md., 1984-87; ops. specialist mktg. dept. IBM, San Diego, 1987—, adv. systems engr., 1988-91; lectr., cons. in field. Author 5 books. Vol. Touro Infirmary, Dialysis Unit, New Orleans, 1965-67, New Orleans Recreation Dept. 1964-68, PALS-Montgomery County Mental Health Orgn., Bethesda, Md., 1984-87, various polit. candidates, 1963—; mem. Calif. Gov.'s Subcom. on Disaster Preparedness. Mem. NAFE, ACP, DAV, Info. System Security Assn., Women Computer Profls. San Diego, Data Processing Mgmt. Assn., San Diego Zoolog. Soc., Assn. System Mgmt., Smithsonian Instn. (resident assoc.), Nat. Trust Hist. Preservation. Office: PO Box 261806 San Diego CA 92196-1806

HILLS, PATRICIA GORTON SCHULZE, curator; b. Baraboo, Wis., Jan. 31, 1936; d. Hartwin A. Schulze and Glennie Gorton Baker; m. Frederic W. Hills, Jan. 17, 1958 (div. Feb. 1974); children: Christina, Bradford; m. Guy Kevin Whitfield, Jan. 3, 1976; 1 child, Andrew. BA, Stanford U., 1957; MA, Hunter Coll., 1968; PhD, NYU, 1973. Curatorial asst. Mus. Modern Art, N.Y.C., 1960-62; guest curator Whitney Mus. Am. Art, 1971-72, assoc. curator 18th and 19th Century art, 1972-74; vis. asst. prof. art dept. Hunter Coll., 1973; adj. assoc. prof. fine arts Inst. Fine Arts NYU, 1973-74; assoc. prof. fine arts and performing arts York Coll. CUNY, 1974-78; assoc. prof. dept. art history Boston U., 1978-88, prof., 1988—, chmn. dept., 1995—; adj. assoc. prof. Grad. Sch. Arts and Scis., Columbia U., 1974-75; adj. curator Whitney Mus. Am. Art, 1974-87. Author: Eastman Johnson, 1972, The American Frontier: Images and Myths, 1973, The Painters' America: Rural and Urban Life, 1810-1910, 1974, Turn-of-Century America: Paintings, Graphics, Photographs, 1890-1910, 1977, Social Concern and Urban Realism: American Painting of the 1930s, 1983, Alice Neel, 1983, John Singer Sargent, 1986, Stuart Davis, 1996; co-author: The Figurative Tradition and the Whitney Mus. Am. Art, 1980, Jacob Lawrence: Thirty Years of Prints: 1963-93. Danforth Found. grad. fellow for women, 1968-72, John Simon Guggenheim Meml. Found. fellow, 1982-83, Charles Warren Ctr. for Studies in Am. History fellow, 1982-83, W.E.B. DuBois Inst. for Afro-Am. Rsch. fellow, Harvard U., 1991-92, NEH fellow, 1995. Mem. Coll. Art Assn., Women's Caucus for Arts, Am. Studies Assn. Home: 238 Putnam Ave Cambridge MA 02139-3767 Office: Boston U Dept Art History Boston MA 02215

HILLS, REGINA J., journalist; b. Sault Sainte Marie, Mich., Dec. 24, 1953; d. Marvin Dan and Ardithanne (Tilly) H.; m. Vincent C. Stricherz, Feb. 25, 1984. B.A., U. Nebr., 1976. Reporter UPI, Lincoln, Nebr., 1976-80, state editor, bur. mgr., 1981-82; state editor, bur. mgr. UPI, New Orleans, 1982-84, Indpls., 1985-87; asst. city editor Seattle Post-Intelligencer, 1987—; panelist TV interview show Face Nebr., 1978-81; vis. lectr. U. Nebr., Lincoln, 1978, 79, 80; columnist weekly feature Capitol News, Nebr. Press Assn., 1981-82. Recipient Outstanding Coverage awards UPI, 1980, 82. Mem. U. Nebr. Alumni Assn., Zeta Tau Alpha. Office: Seattle Post-Intelligencer 101 Elliott Ave W Seattle WA 98119-4220

HILLYARD, SYLVIA JO, drama/theatrical designer, educator; b. Phillipi, W.Va., Jan. 12, 1945; d. William David and Forest (Stewart) H.; m. Clifton Wyndham Pannell, Dec. 9, 1994; stepchildren: Alexander, Richard, Charles, Thomas. AA, Ocala Jr. Coll., 1965; BS, Fla. State U., 1967, MFA, 1970. Instr. drama S.W. Mo. State U., Springfield, 1970-74; asst. prof. U. New Orleans, 1974-77; drama prof. U. Ga., Athens, 1977—, assoc. dept. head, 1979-95; costume designer Asolo State Theater, Sarasota, Fla., 1968, Coll. Light Opera Co., Falmouth, Mass., 1970, ABC-TV Breaking Away, Athens, 1979, Highlands (N.C.) Playhouse, 1989-95; costume designer, theater mgr. Jekyll Island (Ga.) Musical Comedy Fest, 1984-88, Highlands Playhouse, 1989. Co-author: Varieties of Theatrical Art, 1985; contbr. articles to profl. jours.; book review editor Theater Design & Tech., 1991—. Bd. mem. Helios Arts Found., 1993-95, Torch Club Internat., 1992—. Recipient Creative Rsch. aard U. Ga. Rsch. Found., 1985, Sandy Beaver Teaching award Franklin Coll. Arts and Sci., 1982, award for costume designs for HMS Pinafore, 1986. Fellow U.S. Inst. for Theatre Tech. (bd. dirs. 1979-85, 90—); mem. Costume Soc. Am., Canadian Inst. Theater Tech., U.S. Inst. for Theater Tech., U. & Coll. Theater Assn. (v.p. design & tech. 1982-84), Southeastern Theater Conf., Phi Kappa Phi, Delta Sigma Gamma. Home: 520 W Cloverhurst Ave Athens GA 30606 Office: U Ga Dept Drama Baldwin St Athens GA 30602

HILTABRAND, LINDA MAE, state official; b. La Salle, Ill., Jan. 7, 1953; d. Lyndon Dean and June Catherine (Schafer) H. AS, Illinois Valley C.C., Oglesby, Ill., 1973; BS in Agr., U. Ill., 1975. County mgr. Ill. Farm Bur., Greenville, 1975-78; reclamation specialist Ill. Dept Mines and Minerals, Springfield, 1978-95; environ. protection specialist Ill. Dept. Natural Resources, Ottawa, 1995—. Mem. Nat. Assn. State Reclamationists (pres. 1989-90, 96—), Ill. Fedn. Bus. and Profl. Women (pres. 1992-93), Ill. Fedn. Square and Round Dance Clubs (pres. 1996—), Ill. Square Dance Assn. (rec. sec. state coun. 1995-96), Peoria Area Square Dance Assn. (pres. 1993-95), U. Ill. Agrl. Alumni (country coord. 1988-90), Zonta (pres. La Salle-Peru 1983-85, area bd. dirs. 1986-88, parliamentarian dist. VI 1988-90, internat. environ. com. 1992-94). Home: 1825-A Baker Ln Peru IL 61354 Office: Ill Dept Natural Resources Office Mines and Minerals 424 W Main St St 3 Ottawa IL 61350

HILTS, RUTH, artist; b. Sparks, Nev., Dec. 4, 1923; d. William and Nellie Elisa (DeGoosh) Gonzales; m. Robert Norton Hilts, Sept. 28, 1942; children: Robert Norton, Jr., Deirdre Lynn. BA, U. Nev., 1962. Grad. teaching asst. dept. English U. Nev., Reno, 1962-63, editor-interviewer dept. oral history, 1967-74; profl. artist Reno, 1975—. One-woman shows include Sierra Nev. Mus. Art, 1987-88, Nev. Gallery, Reno, 1990, River Gallery, Reno, 1995, Red Mountain Gallery at Truckee Meadows C.C., Reno, 1995; exhibited in group shows at Watercolor West XIV, Riverside, Calif., 1982, Nev. Mus. Art Biennial, Reno, Las Vegas, 1990, 96, Sierra Nev. Coll., Tahoe, 1992-93, Stremmel Gallery, Reno, 1992-94, River Gallery, 1993-94, Sierra Arts Found. Gallery, Reno, 1994-95; represented in permanent collections including Nev. Mus. Art, Kafoury, Armstrong & Co., Reno, First Interstate Bank, Reno, Helms Constrn. Co., Reno, Dean Witter, Reynolds, Inc., Reno, Tournament Players Club, Las Vegas, Comstock Bank, Reno; contbr. art to publs. Nev. Mag., 1988, Encore, 1995, Neon, 1995. Mem. Nat. Mus. Women in the Arts, Nev. Mus. Art, Sierra Arts Found. (grantee for excellence 1995), Phi Kappa Phi. Home and Office: 1895 Wren St Reno NV 89509-2334

HIMELSTEIN, SUSAN, psychologist; b. Norwalk, Ohio, Feb. 27, 1951; d. Warren and Frances (Jenkins) Holzhauser. BS, Miami U., Oxford, Ohi, 1973; MA, UCLA, 1981, PhD with honors, 1987. Lic. psychologist, sch. psychologist, counselor, tchr., Calif. Staff psychologist Verdugo Psychotherapy Inst., Glendale, Calif., 1987-88; counselor, psychologist Beverly Hills (Calif.) Unified Schs., 1988—; pvt. practice Santa Monica, Calif., 1989—; psychologist, cons., sr. faculty mem. Reiss-Davis Child Study Ctr., 1987—; adj. prof. Pepperdine U., Culver City, 1989—, vis. prof., 1996—; supr. interns for various univs.; spkr. UCLA Ext. Confs., 1994—. Acad. scholar Calif. State Fellowship, 1981-83. Mem. APA, L.A. County Psychol. Assn., Calif. Psychol. Assn. Office: 233 Wilshire Blvd Ste 910 Santa Monica CA 90401-1211

HIMES, DAWN MICHELLE, dietitian, consultant; b. Poplar Bluff, Mo., Jan. 17, 1969; d. Jimmie Royal and Sandra Kay (Ashby) Joiner; m. Gary Lloyd Himes, Oct. 8, 1994. BS, S.E. Mo. State U., 1990; MS, Eastern Ill. U., 1991. Registered dietitian; cert. nutrition support dietitian. Clin. dietitian Drs. Regional Med. Ctr., Poplar Bluff, 1991-93; cons. dietitian Lucy Lee Hosp., Poplar Bluff, 1992-93; adminstrv. dietitian Healthcare Hospitality Svcs., Phila., 1994-96; ind. cons. Knoll Pharms., Mt. Olive, N.J., 1994—; adj. faculty Eastern Coll., St. Davids, Pa., 1994-95; regional dietitian Culinary Svc. Network, Blue Bell, Pa. Mem. Am. Dietetic Assn., Pa. Dietetic Assn., Phila. Dietetic Assn., Am. Soc. Parenteral and Enteral Nutrition, Kappa Omicron Nu. Home: 706 Pearl St Birdsboro PA 19508

HIMM, EMILIE GINA, records and information manager; b. Huntington, N.Y., July 12, 1946; d. Joseph Pratte and Constance Delores (Carioli) Walker; m. Thomas Robert Himm, Apr. 23, 1966; 1 child, Thomas Francis II. Student, Thomas Edison State Coll., 1990-93, 96—. Cert. Pub. Mgr., Rutgers State U. Acct. corr. McGraw Hill, Inc., Hightstown, N.J., 1966-68; various supervisory and adminstrv. positions various state agencies, Trenton, N.J., 1973-85; mcpl. court adminstr. Pemberton (N.J.) Twp., 1985-86; records and info. mgr. N.J. Dept. Transp., Trenton, 1986—; co-chair Industry Action Com., Prairie Village, Kans., 1989, chair, 1990-92, 95—; mem. impact study group N.J. Dept. State, Trenton, 1991. Bd. dirs. Soroptimists Internat., 1986-88; publicity chair Little League Aux., Pemberton Twp., 1982-84; post-prom com. Bordentown (N.J.) Residents Against Drugs, 1991-93; mem. Prin.'s Adv. Coun., Bordentown, 1992. Named Employee of Yr., N.J. Dept. Transp., 1993. Mem. ASPA, Nat. Assn. State Info. Resource Execs., Assn. Records Mgrs. and Adminstrs. (co-founder so. N.J. chpt., sec. 1981, 82, bd. dirs. ctrl. N.J. chpt. 1990-92, pres. 1993-95). Democrat. Roman Catholic. Office: NJ Dept of Transportation CN 600 Trenton NJ 08625

HIMMELBERG, BARBARA TAYLOR, controller; b. Schenectady, N.Y., Aug. 17, 1951; d. Robert Arthur and Maureen (Balhoff) Taylor; m. Jerome Paul Himmelberg Jr., Feb. 14, 1985. BS in Math., U. Mass., 1973. Account rep. GE Info. Svc. Co., Schenectady, 1973-78; fin. mgr. GE, Bridgeport, Conn., 1978-79, Dallas, 1979-80, Rome, Ga., 1980-81, Portland, Oreg., 1982-83; fin. mgr. Tektronix Inc., Portland, 1983-88; chief fin. officer Am. Guarantee Fin. Corp., Portland, 1988-89; contr. Lasco Shipping Co., Portland, 1990—. Treas. Mothers Against Drunk Driving, Portland Bradley-Angle House Shelter, Portland; bd. dirs. Komen Breast Cancer Found., Portland, Cascade AIDS Project, Portland. Office: Lasco Shipping Co 3200 NW Yeon Ave Portland OR 97210-1524

HINDERLING, KAREN MARIE CIANFROCCO, elementary education educator; b. Rome, N.Y., Aug. 17, 1969; d. Dominick A. and Janet L. (Clough) C. BS in Elem. Edn. cum laude, SUNY, Oswego, 1991; M in Reading, SUNY, Cortland, 1994. Cert. tchr. elem. edn. 1-6, math. ext. 7-9, nursery, kindergarten, reading tchr. Third and fourth grade looping program tchr. Oriskany (N.Y.) Cen. Sch., 1991-94; 4th grade tchr. N.A. Walbran Elem. Sch., Oriskany, 1994—; tchr. asst. spl. edn., Rome (N.Y.) Sch. Dist., 1991, tchr. TLC Day Care, Whitesboro, N.Y., 1988; mem. multiage com., Oriskany, 1992—, lang. arts com., 1991—, tech com., 1991. Organized Explore, Discover, Connect Family Fun Night, N.A.Walbran Elem. Sch., fall 1994, 95. Recipient Beautification grant Nat. Gardening Assn., Burlington, Vt., 1993, Excellence in Tchg. award Oriskany Tchrs. Assn., 1993. Mem. PTA (treas. 1994-95). Office: Oriskany Sch Dist Rte 69 Oriskany NY 13424

HINDES, JANICE YOW, artist, educator; b. Poteet, Tex., Mar. 29, 1947; d. Rees Glen and Marjorie B. (McDonald) Yow; m. Billy R. Hindes; children: Rhonda, Wes. BS in Edn., Tex. A&I, 1969; MS in Art, Tex. A&M, 1995. Girls coach Charlotte (Tex.) Pub. Sch., 1971-72, spl. edn. tchr., 1972-73; founder Hindes Studio & Gallery, Tex., 1974; instr. Hill Country Arts Found., Ingram, Tex., 1989—, Verner Fine Art Sch., McAlester, Okla., 1990—; instr. Coppini Acad. Fine Art, San Antonio, 1990—, program chmn., 1994-95; instr. Schreiner Coll., Kerrville, Tex., 1995; founder San Antonio Art Sch., 1995. Recipient Copini Adult scholarship Coppini Mus., 1974, Purchase award Scottsdale Artist Sch., Ariz., 1991, Best of Show Tex. Regional award Oil Painter's Am., Chgo., 1994. Mem. Oil Painter's Am. Regional (best of show award 1994, show chmn. 1995), Western Acad. Women Artist, Brush Country Art Club (pres. 1985). Home and Office: PO Box 309 Charlotte TX 78011

HINDLE, PAULA ALICE, nursing administrator; b. Cambridge, Mass., Feb. 26, 1952; d. Edward Adam and Geraldine Ann (Donahue) H. BSN, Fitchburg State Coll., 1974; MSN, Duke U., 1980; MBA, Simmons Coll., 1988. Staff nurse Mt. Auburn Hosp., Cambridge, Mass., 1974-75; staff nurse U. Hosp., Boston, 1975-77, head nurse, 1977-79; staff nurse Duke U. Med. Ctr., Durham, N.C., 1979-80, clin. instr., 1980-81, area mgr., 1981; nurse leader, clin. dir. New Eng. Med. Ctr., Boston, 1981-87; cons. Ctr. for Nursing Case Mgmt., Boston, 1984-87; v.p. nursing Faulkner Hosp., Boston, 1987-94; v.p. nursing and support svcs. Alexandria (Va.) Hosp., 1994—; mem. adv. com. Regis Coll. Nursing, 1993; mem. planning and resource com. Simmons Coll., 1993-94; mem. affiliate faculty George Mason U., 1994-95. Active Am. Heart Assn. Mem. Am. Orgn. Nurse Execs., Va. Orgn. Nurse Execs., Mass. Orgn. Nurse Execs. (treas. 1991-93), Humane Soc., Simmons Coll. Grad. Sch. Mgmt. Alumni Assn. (bd. dirs. 1991-93, pres. 1992-93), Sigma Theta Tau. Democrat. Roman Catholic. Home: 5908 Munson Ct Falls Church VA 22041-2444 Office: Alexandria Hosp 4320 Seminary Rd Alexandria VA 22304-1500

HINDS, BARBARA MARIE, corporate secretary; b. Lynwood, Calif., Jan. 17, 1949; d. Tildo and Louise Maxine (Duff) Bartoletti; m. Hubert H. Hinds Jr., Apr. 16, 1976 (div. June 1989). Grad. high sch., South Gate, Calif. Various positions Atlantic Richfield Co., L.A., 1969-77, asst. corp. sec., 1977—. Mem. Am. Soc. Corp. Secs. Republican. Office: Atlantic Richfield Co 515 S Flower St Bldg 4589 Los Angeles CA 90071-2201

HINDS, GAYLE LYNN, design engineer; b. Detroit, Sept. 7, 1968; d. Joseph Charles and Sandra Mae (Shene) Gamrat; m. Brett S. Hinds, April 4, 1992, 1 child, Noah. BSME, Lawrence Technol. U., 1991. Teller, clk. St. Mark's Credit Union, Warren, Mich., 1984-89; design engr. Hoechst Tech. Polymers, Auburn Hills, Mich., 1991—. Mem. Soc. Automotive Engrs. (assoc.), Soc. Plastics Engrs. (assoc.). Office: Hoechst Celanese Corp 1195 Centre Rd Auburn Hills MI 48326

HINER, ELIZABETH ELLEN, pharmacist; b. Balt., Aug. 11, 1943; d. Samuel Joseph and Zola Mae (Hedrick) Bracken; m. William O. Hiner (div.); children: Christine Ellen, Oliver Joseph; m. Ray Danforth Crosley, Aug. 3, 1985. BS in Pharmacy, W.Va. U., 1966; postgrad., Johns Hopkins U., 1984-87; cert. in pub. health pharmacy, Royal Soc. Health, London, 1996. Registered pharmacist, W.Va., Md., Va. Staff pharmacist U. Va. Hosp., Charlottesville, 1965-66; pharmacy supr. Andrew Rader Army Health Clinic, Ft. Meyer, Va., 1977; pharmacist NIH, Bethesda, Md., 1977-78; consumer safety officer Bur. Biologics FDA, Bethesda, 1978-80, freedom of info. officer, 1980-81, biologics adverse reaction coord., 1981-84, sr. regulatory officer divsn. bacterial products, 1984-92; dir. health promotion fed.-state rels. FDA, Rockville, Md., 1992—; mem., chairperson pharmacy adv. com. USPHS, Rockville, 1991—; ad hoc mem. Bur. Voluntary Compliance, Nat. Assn. Bds. of Pharmacy, Chgo., 1993, 94, 95. Contbr. articles to sci. jours. Mem. parent adv. bd. Beaver Coll., Glenside, Pa., 1993—; mem. Olney (Md.) Women's League, 1986—. Capt. USPHS, 1978—. Recipient Cert. of Recognition, Nat. Assn. Bds. of Pharmacy, 1993, 94, 95. Mem. Am. Pharm.

Assn., Am. Soc. Health Sys. Pharmacists, Commd. Officers Assn., Lambda Kappa Sigma Alumni.

HINER, GLADYS WEBBER, psychologist; b. Mt. Park, Okla., Mar. 10, 1907; d. Santford and Erie Emma (Rose) Webber; m. Wayman Hiner, Aug. 11, 1927 (dec. Mar. 1967); children: Waynel Cook, Sandra Homer. BS, U. Okla., 1934, MS, 1955, PhD, 1962; HHD (hon.), Wagon Wheel Found., McCloud, Okla., 1973. Bd. cert. devel. psychologist. Tchr. Okla. City Pub. Schs., 1953-61; dir. Dale Rogers Tng. Ctr., Okla. City, 1962-63; prof. Okla. City U., 1963-72, Rose State Coll., Okla. City, 1972-86; cons. Wagon Wheel Sch. McLoud, Okla., 1962-82, pvt. practice, Okla. City, 1986—. Supr. Sunday Sch. Trinity Baptist Ch., Okla. City, 1940-72; bd. dirs. Okla. State Assn. for Mentally Retarded Children, 1963-67, Youth and Child Coun. Okla. U. Med. Sch., 1966-69, Bridge Builders, Okla. City; Dem. state del., 1986. Fellow Okla. Psychol. Assn., Am. Assn. on Mental Deficiency; mem. The Acad. Ret. Profls., Okla. Hist. Soc., DAR, Colonial Dames, Psi Chi, Phi Theta Kappa. Home: 400 Canadian Trails Dr Apt #3 Norman OK 73072

HINERFELD, LEE ANN, veterinarian; b. San Francisco, Apr. 24, 1955; d. Norman Martin and Ruth Jean (Gordon) H. BA, Vassar Coll., 1977; DVM, Tufts U., 1986; MS, U. Wyo., 1987. Lic. Conn., Mass. Sr. rsch. technician U. Mass. Med. Ctr., Worcester, 1977-80; small animal clinician, assoc. vet. Mt. Pleasant Hosp. for Animals, Newtown, Conn., 1987, Shakespeare Vet. Hosp., Stratford, Conn., 1988-90, New London (Conn.) Vet. Hosp., 1990—. Fellow Conn. Acad. Vet. Practice, Am. Vet. Med. Assn., Conn. Vet. Med. Assn., Assn. Women Vets; mem. Defenders of Wildlife, Population Comm. Internat., Common Cause, New Forests Project, Phi Kappa Phi. Office: New London Vet Hosp 122 Cross Rd Waterford CT 06385-1204

HINERFELD, RUTH J., civic organization executive; b. Boston, Sept. 18, 1930; m. Norman Hinerfeld, children: Lee, Thomas, Joshua. A.B., Vassar Coll., 1951; grad., Program in Bus. Adminstrn., Harvard-Radcliffe Coll., 1952. With LWV, 1954—, UN observer, 1969-72, chairperson internat. relations com., 1972-76, 1st v.p. in charge legis. activities, 1976-78, pres., 1978-82; dir. LWV Overseas Edn. Fund, 1975-76, trustee, 1975-86; chairperson LWV Edn. Fund, 1978-82; mem. White House Adv. Com. for Trade Negotiations, 1975-82; sec. UN Assn. of U.S., 1975-78, vice chmn., 1983—, bd. govs., 1975—, mem. econ. policy coun., 1976-93; vice chair Overseas Devel. Coun.; mem. U.S. del. auspices of Nat. Com. on U.S.-China Rels. and Chinese People's Inst. Fgn. Affairs, 1978. Mem. coun. Nat. Mcpl. League, 1977-80, 83-86. del.-at-large Internat. Women's Year Conf., Houston, 1977; mem. exec. com. Leadership Conf. on Civil Rights, 1978-82; trustee Citizens Research Found., 1978—; mem. Nat. Petroleum Coun., 1979-82; mem. U.S. del. to World Conf. on UN Decade for Women, 1980; mem. adv. com. Nat. Inst. for Citizen Edn. in the Law, 1981-91; mem. North South Roundtable, 1978-88; mem. nat. gov. bd. Common Cause, 1984-90; vice chmn. U.S. com. UNICEF, 1986-90, treas., 1990-91; mem. Nat. Adv. Coun.; mem. vis. com. Harvard U. Bus. Sch., 1984-90; mem. Bretton Woods Com.; bd. dirs. Com. for Modern Cts. Recipient Disting. Citizen award Nat. Mcpl. League, 1978; Outstanding Mother award Nat. Mother's Day Com., 1981; Aspen Inst. Presdl. fellow, 1981. Mem. Council on Fgn. Relations, Phi Beta Kappa. Office: 11 Oak Ln Larchmont NY 10538-3917

HINES, ANNA GROSSNICKLE, author, illustrator; b. Cin., July 13, 1946; d. Earl Stanton and Ruth Marie (Putman) Grossnickle; m. Gary Roger Hines, June 19, 1976; children: Bethany, Sarah, Lassen. Art major, San Fernando Valley St, 1964-67, 72; BA in Human Devel., Pacific Oaks Coll., 1974, MA in Human Devel., 1978. Tchr. L.A. City Day Care Ctrs., 1967-70, Columbia Elem. Sch., Calif., 1975-78. Author: Taste The Raindrops, 1983, Come To The Meadow, 1984, Maybe A Band-Aid Will Help, 1984, Bethany For Real, 1985, All By Myself, 1985, Cassie Bowen Takes Witch Lessons, 1985, Don't Worry I'll Find You, 1986, Daddy Makes The Best Spaghetti, 1986, I'll Tell You What They Say, 1987, Keep Your Old Hat, 1987, It's Just Me, Emily, 1987, Grandma Gets Grumpy, 1988, Boys Are Yucko!, 1989, They Really Like Me, 1989, Sky All Around, 1989, Big Like Me, 1989, Mean Old Uncle Jack, 1990, The Secret Keeper, 1990, Remember The Butterflies, 1991, The Greatest Picnic In The World, 1991, Jackie's Lunch box, 1991, Tell Me Your Best Thing, 1991, Moon's Wish, 1992, Rumble Thumble Boom!, 1992, Moompa, Toby and Bomp, 1993, Gramma's Walk, 1993, Even If I Spill My Milk?, 1994, What Joe Saw, 1994, BIG HELP!, 1995, When the Goblins Came Knocking, 1995; illustrator: A Ride in the Crummy, 1991, Flying Firefighters, 1993, Day of the High Climber, 1994. Children's Book Coun., 1988. Mem. Soc. of Children's Book Writers and Illustrators, Internat. Reading Assn. Office: care Greenwillow Books 105 Madison Ave New York NY 10016-7418 also: Clarion Books 215 Park Ave S New York NY 10003-1603

HINES, DAISY MARIE, writer; b. Hanna City, Ill., Dec. 31, 1913; d. Frank W. and Edith Earl (Folger) Humphrey; m. Herbert Waldo Hines, Jr., Dec. 20, 1958; children: Grace Consuelo, Ruby Marie. Student Western Ill. U., 1955-57, So. Ill. U., 1956. Mem. staff advt. dept. Macomb Daily Jour. (Ill.), 1943-47; writer, exec., dir., promoter McDonough County Tb Assn., 1949-58; sec. U.S. Dept. Agr., Macomb, 1955-58; researcher, writer 1st Nat. Bank, Springfield, 1963; adminstrv. asst. to state legislator, 1964-69; with Sentinel Printing Co., Illiopolis, Ill., 1965; newspaper columnist, free-lance writer, mem. survey staff Prairie Farmer Pub. Co., Oak Brook, Ill., 1965-79, Successful Farming, Des Moines, 1982; Springfield corr. Automotive News div. Crain Communications, Inc. Active Altar Soc. Blessed Sacrament Cath. Ch., Springfield; freelance writer Springfield Cath. Times newspaper, 1991, Decatur (Ill.) Herald and Review newspaper, 1991; corr. Ill. State Jour.-Register, Springfield; chmn. Illiopolis unit Univ. Ill. Home Extension; pub. relations dir. Springfield chpt. Am. Cancer Soc., 1961-68; 2d v.p. Ill. Conf. Tb Workers, 1952-53; mem. Sangamon County Farm Bur. (women's com., chmn. health and safety), St. John's Hosp. Auxiliary. Mem. Nat. League Am. Pen Women (pres. Springfield chpt. 1972-73, sec. Ill. br. 1974), Western Ill. U. Alumni Council (sec.; Disting. Alumni award 1982; com. mem. Coll. Applied Scis. Agr. rep. Alumni Council), Illiopolis Am. Legion (aux. unit 521), Ill. Press Assn. USAF Air Def. Team (hon. life), Ill. Women for Agr., Civil War Round Table, Sangamon County Hist. Soc. Club: Republican Women's. Address: 2504 Holmes Ave Springfield IL 62704-4635

HINES, LINDA MARIE, educational and community service agency executive; b. Denver, Dec. 20, 1940; d. Laurence Gerald and Betty Marie (Fish) Arnold; m. Donald Merrill Hines, June 10, 1961; children: Warren Donald, Eric Daniel, Alan Bennett. BA summa cum laude, Lewis & Clark Coll., 1962; MA, Ind. U., 1967. Tchr. Eisenhower High Sch., Yakima, Wash., 1962-65; teaching assoc. Ind. U., Bloomington, 1965-67; rsch. assoc. Wash. State U., Pullman, 1973-74, editor Coll. Vet. Med., 1974-76, dir. Info. & Rsch. Svcs., 1977-79, dir. Vet. Pub. Rels. & Devel., 1979-83; exec. dir. Delta Soc., Renton, Wash., 1983—; cons. sci. & tech. com. Holden Village, Chelan, Wash., 1978-83; planning com. mem. NIH Workshop, Bethesda, Md., 1987. Author: Community People-Pet Programs That Work, 1985, Pets in Prison: A New Partnership, 1983; co-author: Guidelines: Animals in Nursing Homes, 1983; co-editor: Phi Kappa Phi Jour., 1986. Co-founder Fish Vols., Pullman, 1970-72; bd. dirs. Elderhostel Planning Com., Pullman, 1977-79, N.Am. Riding for Handicapped, Denver, 1980-81; cons. Seattle Housing Authority-Pets, 1984; co-founder People-Pet Partnership, Pullman, 1979-83; sec. Internat. Assn. Human-Animal Interaction Orgns., 1989—; mem. social concerns com. Luth. Ch. Recipient Recognition award Seattle Kennel Club, 1988; grantee major founds. and corps. Mem. AAUW, Am. Soc. Assn. Execs., Wash. Soc. Assn. Execs., Am. Luth. Ch. Women (pres., libr.), Book Club, Issaquah Alps Trail Club. Office: Delta Soc 289 Perimeter Rd East Renton WA 98055-1329

HINES, MARION LOUISE See DEXHEIMER, MARION LOUISE

HINES, MELISSA A., chemist; b. Galveston, Tex., Dec. 27, 1962; d. Robert L. and Mary Lou (Johnston) H. BS, MIT, 1984; PhD, Stanford U., 1992. Postdoc. mem. tech. staff AT&T Bell Labs., Murrey Hill, N.J., 1992-94; asst. prof. Cornell U., Ithaca, N.Y., 1994—. Recipient Beckman Young Investigator award Beckman Found., 1995. Mem. Am. Physical Soc., Am. Chemical Soc. Office: Cornell U Dept Chemistry Baker Lab Ithaca NY 14853

HINES, PATRICIA, social worker; b. Watertown, N.Y., Nov. 4, 1947; d. Arthur and Bella (O'Neil) Hines; BS, SUNY, Oswego, 1969; MSW, SUNY, Buffalo, 1975; M in Pub. Adminstrn., Fairleigh Dickinson U., 1982. Lic. clin. social worker. Supr. social work Ocean County Bd. Social Services, Toms River, N.J., 1973-77, adminstrv. supr. social work, 1977-83, dep. dir., 1983—; social work cons. Ocean County Vis. Homemaker Svc., Inc., Toms River, 1975-80, Cmty. Meml. Hosp., Toms River, 1978-79, Manchester Manor, Lakeview Manor, Bartley Manor Convalescent Ctr., Ocean Convalescent Ctr., Barnegat Nursing Facility, Burnt Tavern Convalescent Ctr., Jackson Health Care Ctr., Logan Manor, Medicenter, Freehold Convention Ctr., Emery Rehab., So. Ocean; prin. in Sr. Care Planning Assocs.; instr. social work Georgian Court Coll., Lakewood, 1975—. Chmn. Ocean County Title XX Coalition, 1977-82; bd. dirs. Ocean County Family Planning Program, Toms River, 1969-73, Mental Health Bd., 1983-84; mem. exec. bd. United Way, 1983-96; mem. Aging Network Svc., 1992—. Cert., Dr. Thomas Gordon Parent Effectiveness Trainer. Mem. Acad. Cert. Social Workers, Nat. Assn. Social Workers (nat. register clin. social workers, diplomate clin. social work, lic. clin. social worker). Home: 13 Bay Harbor Blvd Brick NJ 08723-7303 Office: 1027 Hooper Ave Toms River NJ 08754

HINES, THEADOSHIA MITCHELL, emergency nurse; b. New Haven, Sept. 4, 1955; d. Robert Lee and Gladys (Fields) Mitchell; m. Barry Roderick Hines, Oct. 1, 1989; 1 child, Ilyse Victoria. ADN, U. Bridgeport, 1975, BS, 1983; MSN, U. Conn., 1992. Cert. BLS, ACLS instr., CCRN, CEN, TNCC. Staff nurse St. Joseph's Manor, Trumbull, Conn., 1975-77; staff/charge nurse emergency dept., insvc. coord. St. Vincent's Med. Ctr., Bridgeport, Conn., 1977-95; mgmt./emergency dept. Moses Cone Meml. Hosp., Greensboro, N.C., 1995—. Christian edn. dir. Olivett Congl. Ch., Bridgeport, 1994; health history interviewer ARC, Milford, Conn., 1986—. Mem. AACN, Emergency Nurses Assn. Home: 4001 Stillbrook Ln High Point NC 27265

HINES, TINA LOREE, video producer, writer, publicist; b. Orlando, Fla., Apr. 26, 1955; d. William and Dorothy Virginia (Martin) H.; m. Stephen Lynn Collins, June 21, 1994; stepchildren: Kevin Lynn, Tracy Edwards. Student, U. Nebr., 1973-76; BA in Journalism, Ea. Wash. U., 1988; Cert. in Film and Video, U. Wash., 1989; MS in Mass Comm., Miami U., Oxford, Ohio, 1995. Race horse exerciser Ak-sar-Ben Race Track, Omaha, 1973-77, Belmont Park Race Track, Elmont, N.Y., 1978-83; jockey Hialeah, Gulfstream, Calder, Miami, 1983-85; pub. asst. Playfair Race Track, Spokane, Wash., 1986-88, Longacres Park, Renton, Wash., 1988-92; sr. staff writer Turfway Park, Florence, Ky., 1992-95; pub. asst. Keeneland Racing Assn., Lexington, Ky., 1993-95; prodn. support ABC Sports, N.Y.C., 1995—; owner, prodr. Fast Horses Prodns., Burlington, Ky., 1995—; mem. notes team Jim Beam Stakes Turfway, Florence, Ky., 1993-95, Preakness Pimlico, Balt., 1993-94; media asst. Ky. Derby Churchill Downs, Louisville, 1993-94; dir. sta. rels. Breeders' Cup Newsfeed, Louisville, 1994. Prodr.: (video documentary) Five Women Jockeys, 1995, Faulkner's Old Colonel, 1995; prodr., writer (video/book) Women Jockeys History, 1996—; writer (screenplay) Sand Tracks, 1995—. Vol., asst. leader Boy Scouts, Burlington, Ky., 1993—; vol. Cable One of No. Ky., Florence, 1996. Recipient Grad. assistantship Miami U., Oxford, Ohio, 1994. Mem. Women in Comms., Inc., Turf Publicists of Am., Ky. Thoroughbred Media, Cin. Film Commn. (vol. 1993—). Office: Fast Horses Prodns 5873 Green Acres Ln Burlington KY 41005

HINES, VONCILE, special education educator; b. Detroit, Dec. 1, 1945; d. Raymond and Cleo (Smith) H. AA, Highland Park Community Coll., 1967; BEd, Wayne State U., 1971, MEd, 1975; MA, U. Detroit, 1978. Tchr. primary unit Detroit Bd. Edn., 1971-79, spl. educator, 1979-94; tchr. trainee Feuerstein's Instrumental Enrichment, 1988—; cons. Queen's Community Workers, Detroit, 1977—; evaluator Teen Profl. Parenting Project, New Detroit Inc., 1986-87; guest educator, critic "Express Yourself", Sta. WQBH 1400 AM, 1989. Author: I Chose Planet Earth, 1988; inventor in field. Recipient cert. of merit State of Mich., 1978, 88, cert. of appreciation Queen's Cmty. Workers, 1980, Wayne County Bd. Commrs., 1988, award of recognition Detroit City Coun., 1984, 88. Mem. Assn. for Children and Adults with Learning Disabilities, Assn. Supervision and Curriculum Devel., Nat. Thinking Skills Network, NAFE, Nat. Council Negro Women (presenter 1987), Met. Detroit Alliance of Black Sch. Educators. Democrat.

HINES-MARTIN, VICKI PATRICIA, nursing educator; b. Louisville, Aug. 18, 1951; d. William Adolphus Hines and Mary Iris Bailey; m. Kenneth Wayne Martin, Dec. 30, 1978; 1 child, Michelle Hines Martin. BSN, Spalding Coll., 1975; MA in Edn., Spalding U., 1983; MSN, U. Cin., 1986; PhD, U. Ky., 1994. Cert. clin. specialist in adult psychiat. mental. Staff nurse Norton Hosp., Louisville, 1978-81; instr. critical care Sts. Mary & Elizabeth Hosp., Louisville, 1981-82; asst. chief nursing svcs. VA Med. Ctr., Cin., 1983-85; nursing instr. Jefferson Community Coll., Louisville, 1985-87; head nurse mgr. VA Med. Ctr., Louisville, 1987-88; asst. prof. nursing Ind. U. S.E., New Albany, 1989-95, U. Ky., Lexington, 1995—; bd. dirs. Seven Counties Mental Health Svcs.; mem. steering com. on practice parameters Ky. Health Policy Bd. Contbr. articles to profl. jours. Nurses Scholar/Fellow, Lucy Zimmerman scholar, 1982, Estelle Massey Osborne Meml. scholar, 1983-84, trainee U. Cin., 1983, grad. scholar, 1983; named to Outstanding Young Women of Am., 1986; recipient Rsch. award Ky. Nurses Found., 1992, Nursing Excellence award Jefferson County Ky., 1995, Psychiatric Mental Health Nurse of the Year Ky. Nurses Assn., 1995; Elizabeth Carnegie scholar, 1991, Am. Nurses Found. scholar, 1992; Fellow U. Ky., 1988, grad. fellow, 1992,; postdoctoral fellowship in Health Policy ANA Ethnic Minority fellowship program, 1996. Mem. ANA (minority clin. fellow 1991-93), Ky. Nurses Assn. (mental health coun. sec. 1986-88, psych. mental health nurse of yr. award 1995), Kyanna Black Nurses, Inc. (co-founder, past pres.), Nat. Black Nurses Assn., Soc. Edn. and Rsch. Psychiat. Nursing, Sigma Theta Tau. Office: Univ of Kentucky College of Nursing 537 CON Lexington KY 40536

HINKEL, PAMELA EYRE, retired army officer; b. Chgo., Nov. 3, 1948; d. Francis Thomas and Jane (Burd) Eyre; m. Thomas S. Hinkel, Jr., Mar. 6, 1995. BA, Ctrl. State U. Okla., 1972; MPA, U. Okla., 1976. Commd. 2d lt. U.S. Army, 1973, advanced through grades to lt. col., 1991; test and evaluation officer Ft. Gordon, Ga., 1982-85, rsch. and devel. coord. Ft. Monmouth, N.J., 1985-88, with army gen. staff Pentagon, Washington, 1988-91, acquisition policy staff officer Army Secretariat Pentagon, 1991-94; asst. project mgr. Def. Telecomm. Svc., Washington, 1994-95; test & evaluation officer Army Secretariat, Pentagon, 1995-96, ret., 1996. Fellow Armed Forces Communications Electronics Assn. Home: 942 Creek Dr Annapolis MD 21403

HINKELMAN, LAURA M., meterologist, researcher; b. Rochester, N.Y., June 14, 1965; d. Robert Charles and Carol Grace (Vogt) H. Student, Oberlin Coll., 1984-85; BA in Physics, Earlham Coll., 1988. Profl. summer intern Eastman Kodak Co. Rsch. Labs., Rochester, N.Y., 1985-87, rsch. asst., 1988-89; summer intern Nat. Weather Svc., Washington, 1988; lab. engr. Ultrasound Rsch. Lab., U. Rochester, 1990-96; rsch. asst. meteorology Pa. State U., University Park, 1996—. Contbr. articles to profl. jours. Mem. Am. Meteorol. Soc. (assoc.), Acoustical Soc. Am. (assoc.). Office: Pa State U Dept Meteorology 503 Walter Bldg University Park PA 16802-5013

HINKELMAN, RUTH AMIDON, insurance company executive; b. Streator, Ill., June 4, 1949; d. Olin Arthur and Marjorie Annabeth (Wright) Amidon; m. Allen Joseph Hinkelman, Jr., Oct. 28, 1972; children: Anne Elizabeth, Allen Joseph III. AB in Econs., U. Ill., 1971. Underwriter Kemper Ins. Group, Chgo., 1971-75; acct. exec. Near North Ins. Agy., Chgo., 1975-76; underwriter Gen. Reinsurance Corp., Chgo., 1976-78, asst. sec., 1978-79, asst. v.p., 1979-83, 2nd v.p., 1983-87, v.p., 1987—. Home: 133 Linden Ave Wilmette IL 60091-2838 Office: Gen Reinsurance Corp 233 S Wacker Dr Ste 4100 Chicago IL 60606

HINKLE, BARBARA CONAWAY, higher education administrator, educator; b. Elkins, W.Va., Dec. 8, 1947; d. Charles C. Conaway and Fay E. (Evans) Cooper; m. Carl E. Hinkle, Dec. 30, 1967 (div. 1996); children: Tracy, Toby, Tara. BA, W.Va. U., 1968, MS, 1969. Grad. tchg. asst. W.Va. U., Morgantown, 1968-69, sys. analyst, 1969-71; math. instr. North Va. C.C., Alexandria, 1971-73; math. instr. Seton Hill Coll., Greensburg, Pa., 1976-82, asst. prof. math., dept. chair, 1982-88, dean enrollment, 1987-90, v.p., registrar, 1990—. Bd. dirs., pres. Greensburg Salem Sch. Dist., 1981—; bd. dirs. Westmoreland Intermediate Unit, Greensburg, 1983—, Greensburg Recreation Bd., 1983—; pres. PTA, East Pgh. St. Sch., Greensburg, 1976-84. Named Most Outstanding Woman, AAUW, 1981. Democrat. United Methodist. Home: 219 Tremont Ave Greensburg PA 15601 Office: Seton Hill Coll Greensburg PA 15601

HINKLE, BETTY RUTH, educational administrator; b. Atchison, Kans., Mar. 18, 1930; d. Arch W. and Ruth (Baker) Hunt; m. Charles L. Hinkle, Dec. 25, 1950 (div.); children: Karl, Eric. B.A., U. Corpus Christi, 1950; M.S., Baylor U., 1956; M.A., U. North Colo., 1972, Ed.D., 1979. Cert. tchr. Tex., 1950, Mass., 1961, Colo., 1966; cert. adminstr., Colo., 1976. Mem. faculty Alice (Tex.) Independent Sch. Dist., 1950, Waco (Tex.) Ind. Sch. Dist., 1951-52, 1953-58; Hawaii Pub. Schs., Oahu, 1952-53, Newton Pub. Schs., Newtonville, Mass., 1962-63; Colorado Springs (Colo.) Pub. Schs., 1966-78; cons., exec. dir. spl. projects unit Colo. State Dept. Edn., Denver, 1978—; exec. dir. Office Fed./State Program Svcs., 1992-94; asst. commr., 1995; retired, 1995; rep. fed. rels. office of the commr. edn., 1995—; cabinet Colorado Dept. Edn., mem. Quality Coun., fed. liaison rep. to chief state sch. officers, Washington, chmn. 1996; alt. foreman Denver Grand Jury, 1983. Recipient Dept. of Edn. Specialists award Colo. Assn. Sch. Execs., 1979, Employee Yr. award Colo. Dept. Edn., 1986, Fed. Ednl. Program Adminstrv. Coun. Ann. award for Distinctive Svc. to Colo. Children, 1988. Mem. Am. Assn. School Adminstrs, Colo. Assn. Sch. Execs (coordinating council, 1976-79, v.p. dept. of edn. specialists 1974-75, pres. 1975-76), Assn. for Supervision and Curriculum Devel., Phi Delta Kappa. Home: 3329 E Bayaud Ave #710 Denver CO 80209 Office: Colo Dept Edn 201 East Colfax Denver CO 80203

HINKLEY THOMPSON, CAROL JOYCE, philanthropy consultant, motivational speaker; b. Detroit, Oct. 28, 1939; d. Carl O. and Vivial Louise (Hoover) Hinkley; m. Keith Francis MacKechnie Thompson, Oct. 5, 1962 (div. Aug. 1979); children: Kathryn M. Thompson Timms, Gregory R., Rebecca E. Thompson Cecin, Gwendolynne Thompson Lyon, Monica Clare. Student, Mercy Coll. Sch. Nursing, Detroit, 1960-62; BS magna cum laude, Tex. Woman's U., Denton, Tex., 1988. Office nurse Miller & Shore, Boston, 1962; pvt. perinatal educator Cambridge, Dallas, Tulsa, Mass., 1965-90; S.W. regional dir. Am. Soc. Psychoprophylaxis in Obs., Inc., Dallas, 1967-71; exec. dir. Family Life Info. Ctr., Dallas, 1973-81; mgr., co-founder Dallas Chamber Orch., 1979-82; major gifts officer U. North Tex., Denton, 1989-92; pvt. cons. nationwide, 1992—; chmn., exec. producer LORAC, Inc., Dallas, 1994—. Author: Childbirth Today: Prepared and Positive, 1978; columnist Grapevine Sun, 1980-81; contbr. articles to profl. jours. Originator, lobbyist for passage Child Safety Act U.S. Congress, Washington, 1965-66; co-founder Stop the Hwy., Tulsa, 1966, Family Life Info. Ctr., Dallas, 1973, 1977; trustee Family Counseling and Children's Svcs., Big Bros., Big Sisters; founder Project-Abandoned Mother and Child, Dallas, 1978, Leadership Dallas. Mem. AAUW, Internat. Platform Assn., Nat. Soc. Fund Raising Execs., Internat. Trade Assn., Dallas, Ind. Colls. Advancement Assn., The Dallas 40, Dallas Coun. World Affairs, Univ. Ind., Ctr. on Philanthropy, Greater Dallas Hispanic C. of C. (trustee). Office: LORAC Inc 5025 B Winder North Richland Hills TX 76180

HINMAN, ROSALIND VIRGINIA, storyteller, drama educator; b. London, May 5, 1938; d. Frederick and Gladys Molly (Seabrook) Ellam; m. Richard Leslie Hinman, Sept. 23, 1967; children: Katherine, Jeremy, Adrian, Isabel. Diploma in Dramatic Art, U. London, 1958; cert. in Edn., Cen. Sch. Speech and Drama, London, 1959. Lectr. Ministere d'Edn. Nat. U. France, Tourcoing, Albi, 1960-63, U. de Caen, France, 1960-63; domestic & overseas exhibit adminstr. The Design Coun., London, 1963-66; artist Boces, Westchester, N.Y., 1968-70, Eugene O'Neill Theater Ctr., Waterford, Conn., 1980—; freelance performer Old Lyme, Conn., 1982—; performing artist Conntours Conn. Commn. on the Arts, Hartford, 1988—; artistic dir. Conn. Student Performing Arts Festival, Middletown, 1988—. Author: Three Hairs From The Devil's Beard and Other Tales, 1990. Sec., bd. mgrs. Old Lyme (Conn.) Phoebe Griffin Noyes Libr., 1987-92, pres., 1992—; pres. Conn. Storytelling Ctr., 1994—. Home and Office: 1 Smith Neck Rd Old Lyme CT 06371-2617

HINMAN-SWEENEY, ELAINE MARIE, aerospace engineer; b. Lincoln Park, Mich., Nov. 18, 1960; d. John Edward and Florence Emelie (Langouse) H.; m. Joseph Lee Sweeney, May 24, 1992. BS in Aero. Engring., U. Mich., 1983; MS in Aerospace Engring., U. Tenn., 1989; PhDME, Vanderbilt U., 1993. Engr. Marshall (Ala.) Space Flight Ctr. NASA, 1983-94, Oceaneering Space Sys., Houston, 1995—; mem. Global Environ. Inst. Curriculum Devel. Com.; mem. Masters of Space studies curriculum planning working group Internat. Space U., 1993. Safety diver Neutral Bouyancy Simulator, Extravehicular Mobility Unit suit, 1987. Recipient performance award NASA, 1987, 90-93, tech. innovation award, 1989, cert. of appreciation, 1988. Mem. AIAA (sr., space ops. support tech. com. 1991—, Outstanding Young Aero. Engr. of Yr. award 1986), Soc. Mfg. Engrs. Robotics Internat. (chmn. 1989-90, sec. 1987, mem. nat. adv. bd. 1994-96, chmn. nat. adv. bd. 1996, Outstanding Engr. award 1988). Home: 2703 Shady Ln Webster TX 77598-6001 Office: Oceaneering Space Sys 16665 Space Center Blvd Houston TX 77058-2253

HINOJOSA, LETITIA, vocalist; b. San Antonio, Dec. 6, 1955; d. Felipe and Maria H.; m. Craig Barker, 1982; children: Adam, Maria, Christina. Singer Mel Tillis Prodn. Co., Nashville, 1983-85; performer locally and on radio, 1973, gubernatorial inauguration Ann Richard's, 1991, presdl. inauguration Bill Clinton, 1993. Recordings include Taos to Tennessee, 1987, Homeland, 1989, Aquella Noche, 1991, Memorabilia Navidena, 1991, Culture Swing, 1992 (Folk Album of Yr., Nat. Assn. Ind. Record Distbrs. 1992), Destiny's Gate, 1994, Frontéjas, 1995; TV appearances include CBS This Morning, 1993; radio appearances include Prairie Home Companion, All Things Considered, 1994. Recipient First prize Kearville Folk Festival, 1979. Office: Manazo Music Mgmt PO Box 3304 Austin TX 78764*

HINOJOSA, MARIA L., news correspondent; b. Mexico City, July 2, 1961; d. Raul and Berta (Ojeda) H.; m. German E. Perez, July 20, 1991. BA magna cum laude, Barnard Coll., 1984. Reporter Enfoque Nacional, San Diego, 1985, prodr., 1987; asst. prodr. weekend edit. NPR, Washington, 1986; freelance reporter, prodr. NPR, N.Y.C., 1989, correspondent, 1990—; prodr. CBS News Radio, N.Y.C., 1988; asst. prodr. CBS This Morning, N.Y.C., 1988; reporter Sta. WNYC Radio, N.Y.C., 1990; host radio Latino USA, N.Y.C., 1993—; host TV show Visiones Sta. WNBC, N.Y.C., 1993—; lectr. in field. Mem. editl. bd. NACLA, N.Y. Bd. dirs. Columbia U. Coun. on Urban Affairs, N.Y.C., 1994. Recipient Unity award for radio feature Lincoln U., 1992, Cindy award Assn. Visual Communicatoes, 1993, Best Radio Feature award Soc. Profl. Journalists, 1993, Robert F. Kennedy Journalism award, 1995. Mem. Nat. Assn. Hispanic Journalists (Best Radio Report 1992), Nat. Alliance Third World Journalists, Newswoman's Club of N.Y. Office: Nat Pub Radio 801 2nd Ave New York NY 10017-4706

HINSCH, GERTRUDE WILMA, biology educator; b. Chgo., Oct. 20, 1932; d. Hans Rudolph and Gertrude (Kalb) H. BSEd, No. Ill. U., 1953; MS, Iowa State U., 1955, PhD, 1957. Instr. Mt. Holyoke Coll., South Hadley, Mass., 1957-60; asst. prof., then assoc. prof. Mt. Union Coll., Alliance, Ohio, 1960-67; assoc. prof. U. Miami (Fla.), 1966-74; assoc. prof. U. South Fla., Tampa, 1974-80, prof., 1980—. Office: U S Fla Dept Biology Tampa FL 33620

HINSHAW, ADA SUE, health facility administrator; b. Arkansas City, Kans., May 20, 1939; d. Oscar A. and Georgia Ruth (Tucker) Cox; children: Cynthia Lynn, Scott Allen Lewis. BS, U. Kans., 1961; MSN, Yale U., 1963; MA, U. Ariz., 1973, PhD, 1975; DSc (hon.), U. Md., 1988, Med. Coll. of Ohio, 1988, Marquette U., 1990, U. Nebr., 1992; D Sci. (hon.), Mount Sinai Med. Ctr. Instr. Sch. Nursing U. Kans., 1963-66; asst. prof. U. Calif., San Francisco, 1966-71; prof. U. Ariz., Tucson, 1975-87; dir. nursing rsch. U. Med. Ctr., Tucson, 1975-87; dir. Nat. Inst. Nursing Rsch. Pub. Health Svc., Dept. Health and Human Svcs., NIH, Washington, 1987—. Contbd. articles to profl. jours. Recipient Kay Schilter award U. Kans., 1961, Lucille Petry Leone award Nat. League for Nursing, 1971, Wolanin Geriatric Nursing Rsch. award U. Ariz., 1978, Alumni of the Yr award Sch. Nursing U. Kans., 1981, Disting. Alumni award Sch. Nursing Yale U., 1981, Alumni Achievement award U. Ariz., 1990, Disting. citation Kans. Alumni Assn., 1992, Health Leader of the Yr. award PHS, 1993, Centennial award Columbia Sch. Nursing, 1993. Mem. ANA (Nurse Scientist of the Yr. award

1985), Coun. on Nursing Rschrs. (Nurse Scientist of the Yr. award 1985), Md. Nurses Assn., Western Soc. for Rsch. in Nursing, Am. Acad. Nursing, Nat. Acad. Practice, Inst. Medicine, Sigma Xi, Sigma Theta Tau (Beta Mu Chpt. award of Excellence in Nursing Edn., 1980, Elizabeth McWilliams Miller award, 1987), Alpha Chi Omega.

HINSON, JANE PARDEE HENDERSON, lactation consultant; b. Durham, N.C., Mar. 17, 1947; d. Harvey Constantine and Sarah Lodge (Pardee) Henderson; m. Malcolm Douglas Fyfe, July 11, 1971 (div.); m. James Travis Hinson, June 7, 1974; children: Jane Pardee, James Travis Jr., Sarah MacQueen. BA, U. N.C., 1969, MPH, 1992. Cert. lactation cons. Tchr. English Orleans Parish Sch., New Orleans, 1969-72, Charlotte(N.C.)-Mecklenburg Schs., 1972-76; lactation cons. Charlotte, 1986-92; lactation cons., mgr. Mercy Lactation Ctr. Mercy Hosp. South, Charlotte, 1992—. Bd. dirs. Breastfeeding Peer Counselor Program, Charlotte, 1994—; bd. dirs., sec. Mecklenburg Coun. on Adolescent Pregnancy, Charlotte, 1989-94; mem. adv. bd. to county commrs. Mecklenburg County Human Svcs. Coun., Charlotte, 1992—; mem. Jr. League, Charlotte. Mem. Am. Coll. Healthcare Execs., Metrolina Healthcare Execs., Internat. Lactation Cons. Assn. (treas. bd. dirs. 1993-95), Mid-South Lactation Cons. Assn. (treas. bd. dirs. 1990-92). Democrat. Presbyterian. Home: 2915 Houston Branch Rd Charlotte NC 28270 Office: Mercy Lactation Support Ctr 10628 Park Rd Charlotte NC 28210

HINTGEN, SHARON VOIGT, mathematician, educator; b. Perham, Minn., May 3, 1950; d. Irvin Cyrus and Delores Mae (Lange) Voigt; m. Thomas LeRoy Hintgen, July 12, 1975; children: Mark Thomas, Paul Michael. BA, U. Minn., 1972; BS, Moorhead State U., 1991; MS, Bemidji State U., 1996. Tchg. asst. U. Minn., Morris, 1970-72; adminstr. Otter Tail County Hist. Soc., Fergus Falls, Minn., 1973-78; personnel asst. Lake Region Hosp., Fergus Falls, 1983-95; instr. math. Fergus Falls C.C., 1992—. Vol. Peace Corps, Senegal, West Africa, 1992. Mem. AAUW (treas. 1996, found. chair 1993-94, edn. chmn. 1993-94), Nat. Coun. Tchrs. Math., Am. Heart Assn., Lake Region Toastmasters (sec./treas. 1991-93, edn. v.p. 1993-94, pres. 1994-95). Home: 111 W Vasa Ave Fergus Falls MN 56537 Office: Fergus Falls CC 1414 College Way Fergus Falls MN 56537

HINTHORN, MICKY TERZAGIAN, volunteer, retired; b. Jersey City, N.J., July 5, 1924; d. Bedros H. and Aznive (Hynelian) Terzagian; m. Wayne L. Hinthorn, Aug. 11, 1957. BS in Occupational Therapy, U. So. Calif., 1953; MBA, Coll. Notre Dame, Belmont, Calif., 1984. Registered occupational therapist. Gen. office worker Drake Secretarial Coll., Jersey City, 1941-42; sec., expediter Western Electric Co., Kearny, N.J., 1943-45; sec. div. edn. CBS, NYC, 1945-46; sec. to v.p. sales Simon and Schuster, Inc., NYC, 1947-51; gen. office worker in Sch. of Edn. U. So. Calif., L.A., 1951-52; occupational therapist Palo Alto (Calif.) Clinic, 1954-55; chief occupational therapist Children's Health Coun., Palo Alto, 1954-56; sec. to chief mil. engr. Lenkurt Electric Co., San Carlos, Calif., 1956-58; sr. sec. re-entry program Bank of Am., Redwood City, Calif., 1979-80; ret., 1980; organizer occupational therapy dept. Children's Health Coun., Palo Alto, Calif., 1954, chief 1954-56. Author, editor numerous newsletters and orgns.' papers. Charter mem., membership chair U. So. Calif. Pres. Cir., San Francisco, 1978-80; treas. North Peninsula chpt. San Francisco Opera Guild, San Mateo, Calif., 1979; vol. pub. info. chair re-election San Mateo County Supr., Redwood City, Calif., 1978; founder, charter pres. Friends of Belmont (Calif.) Libr., 1974-75; mem. Coastside Fireworks Com., 1989-94, chair corp. sponsorship, 1992-93. Recipient Hon. Mem., Friends of San Francisco Pub. Libr., 1974. Mem. AAUW (pres. San Mateo br. 1976-77; Half Moon Bay br. chair local scholarships 1992, historian 1992-94, corr. sec. 1995—); name grant honoree Edn. Found. Jodi Gordon Endowment 1991-92), Half Moon Bay Coastside C. of C. (coastside bus. edn. scholarships 1992, 93), Seton Med. Ctr. Coastside Aux. (assoc.), U. So. Calif. Alumni Assn. (life), Friends of Filoli. Home: PO Box 176 Half Moon Bay CA 94019-0176

HINTON, ANGELA LYON, primary education educator; b. Shelby, N.C., Dec. 6, 1965; d. Thurman and Amaryllis (Blalock) Lyon; m. Donald Everett Hinton Jr., Aug. 1, 1992. BS in Edn. cum laude, Western Carolina U., 1990; MEd, U. S.C., 1992, EdS in Guidance & Counseling, 1995, postgrad., 1995—. Cert. elem., early childhood, guidance and counseling edn. Kindergarten tchr. Blacksburg (S.C.) Primary, 1990-91; tchr. grade 2 Limestone Elem., Gaffney, S.C., 1991-92; tchr. grade 4 Goucher Elem., Gaffney, 1992-93, tchr. grade 3, 1993-94, part-time compensatory instr. afterschool program, 1993-94; kindergarten tchr. J. Paul Beam Elem., Gaffney, 1994—; guidance counselor Daniel Morgan Elem. and Macedonia Elem., 1995—; cons. and workshop condr. in field. Mem. coordinating com. Tast of Gaffney, S.C., 1993—. Mem. ASCD, ACA, NEA, S.C. Edn. Assn., Internat. Reading Assn., S.C. Internat. Reading Assn., Cherokee Reading Coun. (sec. 1994-95), Gaffney Jr. Woman's Club. Home: 308 Hampton Blvd Gaffney SC 29341-3513 Office: Daniel Morgan Elem 210 Daniel Morgan Sch Rd Gaffney SC 29341-3435

HINTON, PAULA WEEMS, lawyer; b. Gadsden, Ala., Dec. 5, 1954; d. James Forrest and Juanita (Weems) H.; m. Steven D. Lawrence, Mar. 31, 1984; 1 child, David Hinton Lawrence. BA, U. Ala., 1976, MPA, 1979, JD, 1979. Bar: Ala. 1979, Tex. 1982, U.S. Dist. Ct. (so. dist.) Ala. 1980, U.S. Dist. Ct. (so. dist.) Tex. 1981, U.S. Dist. Ct. (no. dist.) Tex. 1988, U.S. Dist. Ct. (ea. and we. dists.) Tex. 1989, U.S. Dist. Ct. (no. and mid. dists.) Ala. 1993, U.S. Ct. Appeals (5th and 11th cirs.) 1981. Law clk. to magistrate U.S. Dist. Ct. Ala., Mobile, 1979-80; assoc. Vinson & Elkins, Houston, 1981-88; ptnr. Akin Gump Strauss Hauer & Feld, L.L.P., Houston, 1989—. Rotary fellow U. Sevilla, Spain, 1980-81. Mem. State Bar Tex. (women in the profession com.), Houston Bar Found. (bd. dirs., chmn. 1996). Office: Akin Gump Strauss Hauer & Feld LLP 711 Louisiana St Houston TX 77002-2716

HINTON, SHARON TONYA CURTIS, nursing educator; b. Chgo., Aug. 2, 1958; d. Robert Garrett and Mamie Ruth (McMillan) Curtis; m. James Fred Hinton, Dec. 17, 1989; children: Katie Ruth, Matthew James. Diploma in nursing, East Tenn. Bapt. Hosp., Knoxville, 1986. RN, Tex., Tenn., Ariz., N.C., Fla., Hawaii, Wyo.; cert. EMT-Paramedic, Tex.; cert. BCLS, ACLS, Advanced Burn Life Support, CPR instr., cert. first aid, back injury prevention HIV/AIDS edn., first response. Nurses aide Sevier Med. Ctr., Sevierville, Tenn., 1984; rehab.-clin. nurse technician Patricia Neal Rehab.-Ft. Sanders Med. Ctr., Knoxville, 1984-86; staff nurse ICU, East Tenn. Bapt. Hosp., 1986-88; staff nurse neurol. ICU, St. Mary's Med. Ctr., Knoxville, 1987-88; staff nurse trauma ICU, Barrows Neurol. Inst., Phoenix, 1988; staff critical care nurse Traveling Nurse Corps, Malden, Mass., 1987-89; dir. staff edn., coord. disaster svcs. Caprock Hosp. Dist., Floydada, Tex., 1990; pres., instr. Rural Nurse Resource, Inc., Floydada, 1990—, dir. tng. ctr., 1995—; chmn., mgr. Floyd County chpt. ARC, Floydada, 1990-94, liaison disaster svcs., dir., instr., 1994-95; bd. dirs. Hale County ARC, Panhandle Plains chpt. ARC, 1994-95; dir. South Plains Health Provider Orgn., 1996—. Guest speaker Meth. Men's Assn., Rotary, Floydada, 1990. Recipient Nat. Nursing Pin, ARC, 1987, cert. of appreciation Am. Heart Assn., 1990, 95. Mem. Emergency Nurses Assn., Order of Ea. Star. Methodist. Office: Rural Nurse Resource Inc RR 4 Box 123 Floydada TX 79235-9223

HINTON, S(USAN) E(LOISE), author; b. Tulsa, 1948; m. David Inhofe, 1970; 1 child, Nicholas David. BS, U. Tulsa, 1970. Author (teen-age fiction) The Outsiders, 1967 (N.Y. Herald Tribune Best Teenage Book list 1967, Chgo. Tribune Book World Spring Festival Honor Book 1967, Media and Methods Maxi award 1975, Mass. Children's Book award 1979), That Was Then, This Is Now, 1971 (ALA Best Books for Young Adults list 1971, Chgo. Tribune Book World Spring Festival Honor Book 1971, Mass. Children's Book award 1978), Rumble Fish, 1975 (ALA Best Book for Young Adults list 1975, Sch. Libr. Jour. Best Books of Yr. list 1975, Land of Enchantment award N.Mex. Libr. Assn. 1982), Tex, 1979 (ALA Best Books for Young Adults list 1979, Sch. Libr. Jour. Best Books of Yr. list 1979, Am. Book award nominee 1981, Calif. Young Reader medal nominee 1982, Sue Hefly award 1983), Taming the Star Runner, 1988, Big David, Little David, 1994; (screenplay, with Francis Ford Coppola) Rumble Fish, 1983; film appearances Tex, 1982, The Outsiders, 1983, The Puppy Sister, 1995. Recipient Golden Archer Award, 1983; Author award ALA Young Adult Svcs. Divsn./Sch. Libr. Jour., 1988. Office: Delacorte Press Press Rels 1540 Broadway # Bdd New York NY 10036-4039*

HINZ, DOROTHY ELIZABETH, writer, editor, international corporate communications and public affairs specialist; b. N.Y.C.. AB, Hunter Coll.; postgrad., Columbia U. Asst. to dir. devel. Columbia U., N.Y.C., 1953-55; mng. editor, econs. rschr.-analyst, writer speeches, position papers W.R. Grace & Co., N.Y.C., 1955-64; staff writer Oil Progress, fgn. news media, speeches, films, internat. petroleum ops., pub. rels. dept. Caltex Petroleum Corp., N.Y.C., 1964-69; fin. editor Merrill Lynch, Pierce, Fenner & Smith, 1969-74; mgr. publs., mgr. speakers' bur., assoc. speech writer mktg. and corp. comm. dept. Mfrs. Hanover Corp., N.Y.C., 1974-88; mem. Internat. Seminars, Columbia U., N.Y.C., 1988—; mem. internat. seminars Columbia U., 1988—. Contbr. articles on multinat. corps., developing nations, trade and fin. to various publs.; researcher of policy proposals for J.P. Grace's book, It's Not Too Late in Latin America. Mem. N.Y. Press Club, Americas Soc., Spanish Inst., Bolivarian Soc. Home and Office: ste 104 600 W 115th St New York NY 10025-7720

HIPP, KRISTINE A., educator; b. Duluth, Minn., Sept. 17, 1949; d. Neil Timothy Sullivan and Evelyn Marie (Chartier) Kiefer; m. John A. Hipp, Nov. 25, 1972. BS, U. Wis., Whitewater, 1971, MS, 1975; PhD, U. Wis., Madison, 1995. Tchr. spl. edn. Janesville (Wis.) Sch. Dist., 1971-80, 80-90; edn. cons. pvt. practice, Wis., Ind., 1987—; coord. staff devel. Jonesville Sch. Dist., 1988-92; rsch. assoc. U. Wis., Madison, 1992-95; asst. prof. Ball State U., Muncie, Ind., 1995—; adj. grad. instr. U. Wis., Whitewater, 1975-90. IDEA fellow, 1990. Mem. NOW, AAUW, ASCD, Am. Ednl. Rsch. Assn., Nat. Staff Devel. Coun., U. Wis. Alumni Assn. Democrat. Office: Ball State U Dept Edn Leadership Tchrs Coll 915B Muncie IN 47306

HIPPLE, SAUNDRA JEANNE, newspaper publisher; b. Balt., Nov. 12, 1942; d. Lester Elliott and Julia Olive (Redd) Lumpkin; m. Robert Bruce Hipple, Dec. 31, 1960; children: Robert, Donna, Lori, Michael, Richard. Circulation Balt. Observer, 1974-77; assembly worker Dupree, El Monte, Calif., 1978-81; from bookkeeper to owner Voice of the Valley, Maple Valley, Wash., 1981—. bd. dirs. Cmty. Ctr., Maple Valley, Wash., 1981-86. Home: PO Box 482 Maple Valley WA 98038 Office: Voice of the Valley PO Box 307 Maple Valley WA 98038

HIRN, DORIS DREYER, health service administrator; b. N.Y.C., Dec. 3, 1933; d. James Howard and Dorothy Van Nostrand (Young) Dreyer; student Colby Jr. Coll., 1950-51, Hofstra U., 1953-56; m. John D. Hirn, Oct. 27, 1956; children—Deborah Lynn, Robert William. Owner, Dutchlands Farm, Albany, N.Y., 1957-62, Hickory Hill Farm, Galena, Ill., 1965-75; adminstr. Home Health Service, Chgo., 1972-74, exec. dir. Suburban Home Health Service, 1974-87; exec. dir. Home Health Svc. Chgo. North, 1987-95; exec. dir. Columbia Home Care, 1995-96; v.p., pub. Caregivers Inc., 1995—; ptnr. Candor Assocs.; pres. Hirn Assocs. Ltd.; dir. Nat. Health Delivery Systems, Serengeti Prodns., Inc.; bd. dirs. Lifeline Pilots, Inc., NAHC, Fin. Mgrs. Forum, Ill. Long Term Task Force, Ill. Homecare Coun., BBH Assocs., Inc.; pub. Caregivers Resource Directory. Author: Survey Process in Home Health Manual; contbr. nat. seminars on quality assurance, rehab., long term care, reimbursement legislation; also articles to Caring Mag., Elder Svcs. Directory, Jour. Am. Geriatric Soc.; editor, pub. Caregivers Inc. Served with WAVES, 1951-52. Recipient Ill. Govs. award for Excellence Home Care Agy., 1989. Mem. ICHA, Nat. Assn. Home Care. Clubs: Chgo. Yacht. Home: 5747 N Sheridan Rd Chicago IL 60660-4755

HIRONO, MAZIE KEIKO, state official; b. Fukushima, Japan, Nov. 3, 1947; came to U.S., 1955, naturalized, 1957; d. Laura Chie (Sato) H. B.A., U. Hawaii, 1970; J.D., Georgetown U., 1978. Dep. atty. gen., Honolulu, 1978-80; house counsel INDEVCO, Honolulu, 1982-83; sole practice, Honolulu, 1983-84, Shim, Tam, Kirimitsu & Naito, 1984-88; mem. Hawaii Ho. of Reps., Honolulu, 1980-94; elected lt. gov., 1994. Del., State Democratic Party Conv., Honolulu, 1972-82; bd. dirs. Nuuanu YMCA, Honolulu, 1982-84, Moiliili Community Ctr., Honolulu, 1984. Mem. U.S. Supreme Ct. Bar, Hawaii Bar Assn., Phi Beta Kappa. Democrat. Office: State Capitol Lt Governors Office PO Box 3226 Honolulu HI 96801

HIRSCH, ANN ULLMAN, retired academic administrator; b. N.Y.C., Feb. 12, 1929; d. Julian S. and Louise (Levien) Ullman; m. James E. Galton, Aug. 22, 1948 (div. 1962); children: Beth, Jean; m. David I. Hirsch, Mar. 22, 1963; stepchildren: Peter, Amanda. BS, NYU, 1950; postgrad., Queens Coll., Flushing, N.Y., 1955-57. Music tchr. Herricks (N.Y.) Sch., 1950-52, East Meadow (N.Y.) Pub. Schs., 1952-53; exec. dir. Ea. Suffolk Sch. Music, Riverhead/Southampton, N.Y., 1977-88; self-employed piano tchr., N.Y., 1950-95; dir. music edn. Unitarian Sunday Sch., Freeport, N.Y., 1956-63; singer Oratorio Socs., Levittown and Bridgehampton, N.Y., 1950-85, L.I. Philharm. Chorus, Westbury, N.Y., 1989—; violinist Sound Symphony, Shoreham, Wading River, N.Y., 1980—, orch. pianist, 1980—. Author: Basic Guide to the Teaching of Piano, 1974. Mem. Arts in Edn. Task Force, BOCES, Westhampton, N.Y., 1977-87; planning mem., panelist Nat. Guild Cmty. Schs. of the Arts, 1980-88; tchr. Literacy Vols. Am., Riverhead/Mastic, 1988-91; bd. mem. L.I. Masterworks Chorus, Commack, N.Y., 1992—. Named East End Woman of Yr. in Edn., East End Mag., Suffolk County, N.Y., 1979. Mem. LWV, Peconic Land Trust, Westhampton Beach Hist. Soc., Bay Area Friends of the Fine Arts (bd. mem.), Southampton Twp. Wildfowl Assn. Home: Box 304 Remsenburg NY 11960

HIRSCH, BETTE G(ROSS), college administrator, foreign language educator; b. N.Y.C., May 5, 1942; d. Alfred E. and Gladys (Netburn) Gross; m. Edward Raden Silverblatt, Aug. 16, 1964 (div. Feb. 1975); children: Julia Nadine, Adam Edward; m. Joseph Ira Hirsch, Jan. 21, 1978; stepchildren: Hillary, Michelle, Michael. BA with honors, U. Rochester, 1964; MA, Case Western Res. U., 1967, PhD, 1971. Instr. and head French dept. Cabrillo Coll., Aptos, Calif., 1973-90, divsn. chair fgn. langs. and comms. divsn., 1990-95, interim dir. student devel., 1995-96, dean, transfer edn., 1996—; mem. steering com. Santa Cruz County Fgn. Lang. Educators Assn., 1981-86; mem. liaison com. fgn. langs. Articulation Coun. Calif., 1982-84, sec., 1983-84, chmn., 1984-85; workshop presenter, 1982—; vis. prof. French Mills Coll., Oakland, Calif., 1983; mem. fgn. lang. model curriculum stds. adv. com. State Calif., 1984; instr. San Jose (Calif.) State U., summers 1984, 85; reader Ednl. Testing Svc. Advanced Placement French Examination, 1988, 89; peer reviewer for div. edn. programs, NEH, Washington, 1990, 91, 93; grant evaluator, NEH, 1995; mem. fgn. lang. adv. bd. The Coll. Bd., N.Y.C., 1986-91. Author: The Maxims in the Novels of Duclos, 1973; co-author (with Chantal Thompson) Ensuite, 1989, 93, Moments Litteraires, 1992 (with Chantal Thompson and Elaine Phillips) Mais Oui! workbook, lab. manual, video manual, 1996; contbr. revs. and articles to profl. jours. Pres. Loma Vista Elem. Sch. PTA, Palo Alto, Calif., 1978-79; bd. dirs. United Way Stanford, Palo Alto, 1985-90, mem. allocations com., 1988. Grantee NEH, 1980-81, USIA, 1992; Govt. of France scholar, 1982. Mem. Am. Coun. on Teaching of Fgn. Langs., Am. Assn. Tchrs. French (exec. coun. No. Calif. chpt. 1980-85), Assn. Calif. Community Coll. Adminstrs., Assn. Depts. Fgn. Langs. (exec. com. 1985-88, pres. 1988), Modern Lang. Assn. (mem. adv. com. on fgn. langs. and lits. 1995—). Democrat. Jewish. Home: 4149 Georgia Ave Palo Alto CA 94306-3813 Office: Cabrillo College 6500 Soquel Dr Aptos CA 95003-3119

HIRSCH, GILAH YELIN, artist, writer; b. Montreal, Quebec, Can., Aug. 24, 1944; came to U.S., 1963; d. Ezra and Shulamis (Borodensky) Y. BA, U. Calif., Berkeley, 1967; MFA, UCLA, 1970. Prof. of art Calif. State U., Dominguez Hills, L.A., 1973—; adj. prof. Internat. Coll., Guild of Tutors, L.A., 1980-87, Union Grad. Sch., Cin., 1990. Founding mem. Santa Monica (Calif.) Art Bank, 1983-85; bd. dirs. Dorland Mountain Colony, Temecula, Calif., 1984-88. Recipient Disting. Artist award Calif. State U., 1985, Found. Rsch. award, 1988-89; grantee Nat. Endowment for the Arts, 1985; Dorland Mountain Colony fellow, 1981-84, MacDowell Colony fellow, N.H., 1987, Banff Ctr. for the Arts fellow, Can., 1985; named artist-in-residence RIM Inst., Payson, Ariz., 1989-90, Tamarind Inst. of Lithography, Albuquerque, 1973, Rockefeller Bellagio Ctr., Italy, 1992, Tyrone Guthrie Ctr. for the Arts, Annamahkerrig, Ireland, 1993. Home: 2412 Oakwood Ave Venice CA 90291-4908 Office: Calif State Univ Dominguez Hills 1000 E Victoria St Carson CA 90747-0001

HIRSCH, IRMA LOU KOLTERMAN, nurse, association administrator; b. Clay Center, Kans., June 11, 1934; d. Arthur Henry and Mildred (Peterson) Kolterman; m. William A. Hirsch, June 8, 1958; children: David William, Brian Duane. BS in Nursing, U. Kans., 1957; M in Nursing, U. Washington, Seattle, 1961. R.N. Mo. Instr. Duke U., Durham, N.C., 1961-64; nurse clinician U. Kans. Med. Ctr., Kansas City, 1968-70; project dir., cons. Mo. Regional Med. Program, Kansas City, 1970-74; project dir., program coordinator Am. Nurses' Assn., Kansas City, 1974-79, policy devel., 1981-92; supr. VA Med. Ctr., Kansas City, 1979-81; dept. dir., 1981-83, policy devel., 1983-92; cons. nursing edn. Joint Commn. on Accreditation of Hosps., Chgo., 1973; cons. for project devel. Am. Nurses Found., Kansas City, 1974; cons. nursing standards Health Standards Directorate, Ottawa, Ont., Can., 1978, Mid-Am. Coalition on Health Care, 1993—, Sch. Nursing U. Mo., Kansas City, 1996—. Editor: Guidelines for Review of Nursing Care at the Local Level, 1976, Nursing Quality Assurance Management/Learning System, 1982, Peer Review in Nursing, 1982, Issues in Professional Practice, 1985, Classification Systems for Describing Nursing Practice, 1989. Mem. Friends of Art, Kansas City, 1975—, Internat. Relations Council, Kansas City, 1980—, 2d Presbyn. Ch., Kansas City, elder, deacon, strategic planning chmn.; chpt. pres. Am. Field Svcs., Kansas City, 1978-79; mem. adv. com. Nancy Whalen Nursing Found., 1992—; mem. evaluation com. Heart Am. United Way, 1993—; trustee Presbyn. Manors Mid-Am., 1979-86, Kansas City Manor, 1992—, chair adv. com., 1995—, Nursing Heritage Found., 1994—, pres. 1995—. Mem. ANA (pres. Mo. dist. 1980-81), Kans. U. Nurses Alumni Assn. (pres. 1964-66), Sigma Theta Tau. Home: 1035 W 57th Ter Kansas City MO 64113-1163

HIRSCH, KATHLEEN L., realtor; b. St. Louis, Apr. 8, 1944; d. Lawrence William and Lucille Ann (Swanson) Loptien; m. Peter Leander Hirsch, July 14, 1968 (div. June 1981). Student, U. Chgo., 1962-63, No. Ill. U., 1963-64; BA in Biology magna cum laude, Lone Mountain Coll., 1975. Reservation agt. Ea. Airlines, Chgo., 1964-66, Pan Am. Airways, Chgo., 1966-68; traffic clk. Heublein Inc., San Francisco, 1970-72; circulation libr. Lone Mountain Coll., San Francisco, 1974-77; supr. Blue Shield, San Francisco, 1977-80; mktg. rep. Cetus Corp., Emeryville, Calif., 1980-84; realtor Mason McDuffie R.E., Alameda, Calif., 1985-88, Harbor Bay Realty, Alameda, 1988—. Mem. Calif. Assn. Realtors (grad. Realtor Inst. 1995, bd. dirs. 1990, 91), Alameda Assn. Realtors (past pres. 1991, bd. dirs. 1988-92, chair, membership v.p. 1988), Realtor Inst., Women's Coun. Realtors (relocation and referral cert. 1992). Democrat. Unitarian. Office: Harbor Bay Realty Ste 200 885 Island Dr Alameda CA 94502

HIRSCH, LENORE ANN, elementary school principal; b. Bridgeport, Conn., Aug. 5, 1946; d. Felix Adler and Anne Marie (Stoff) H. BA, U. Mass., 1968; MS in Tchg., U. Chgo., 1971. Cert. elem. and secondary tchr., resource specialist, sch. adminstrn., tchr. of learning handicapped, Calif. Tchr. various bay area schs., Calif., 1971-81; resource specialist Pleasanton (Calif.) Joint Elem. Sch. Dist., 1981-85, vice prin., 1985-86; asst. prin. Castro Valley (Calif.) Unified Sch. Dist., 1986-88; prin. Fremont (Calif.) Unified Sch. Dist., 1988-92, Napa (Calif.) Valley Unified Sch. Dist., 1992—; cons. Berkeley (Calif.) Unified Sch. Dist., 1976. Treas., v.p., pres. Pi Lambda Theta, Berkeley, 1972-75. Recipient Lucy Dewey award Castro Valley Unified Women, 1988, Outstanding Adminstr. award Fremont Assn. Counselors and Psychologists, 1991. Mem. ASCD, Assn. Calif. Sch. Adminstrs., Mensa, Sierra Club, Rotary (bd. dirs. 1994-95). Office: Browns Valley Elem Sch 1001 Buhman Ave Napa CA 94558-5202

HIRSCH, LORE, psychiatrist; b. Mannheim, Fed. Republic of Germany, July 8, 1908; came to U.S., 1940; d. Erwin Hirsch and Marie Kiefe; m. Eugene Hesz, Jan. 25, 1958 (div. Oct. 1968). MD, Karl Ruprecht U., Heidelberg, Fed. Republic Germany, 1937. Diplomate Am. Bd. Neurology and Psychiatry. Intern Greenpoint Hosp., Bklyn., 1942-43; resident Bellvue Hosp., N.Y.C., 1943-48; sect. chief VA Hosp., Bronx, N.Y., 1949-54; dir. psychiatry Wayne County Gen. Hosp., Mich., 1954-55; dir. outpatient services Northville (Mich.) Regional Hosp., 1955-58; practice medicine specializing in psychiatry Dearborn, 1958—. Contbr. numerous articles to profl. jours. Fellow Am. Psychiat. Assn. (life); mem. AMA (life), Mich. Med. Soc., Wayne County Med. Soc., Mich. Psychiat. Soc. Unitarian-Universalist. Home: 212 S Melborn St Dearborn MI 48124-1455 Office: 2021 Monroe St Dearborn MI 48124-2926

HIRSCH, ROSEANN CONTE, publisher; b. N.Y.C., Feb. 5, 1941; d. Frank and Anna (Burzycki) Conte; m. Barry Jay Hirsch, Oct. 1, 1967; children: Brian Christopher, Nicholas Benjamin, Jonathan Alexander. Student, Boston U., 1958-61. Editorial asst. Grolier, Inc., 1962-64; editor Ideal Pub. Corp., N.Y.C., 1968-74; editorial dir. Sterling's Mags., Inc., N.Y.C., 1975-78, Hearst Spl. Publs., Hearst Corp., N.Y.C., 1978-84; v.p. Ultra Communications, Inc., N.Y.C., 1984-89; pub., pres. Dream Guys, Inc., N.Y.C., 1986—; pres. Lamppost Press, Inc., N.Y.C., 1989-. Author: Super Working Mom's Handbook, 1986; editor: Young & Married Mag., 1976-77, 100 Greatest American Women, Good Housekeeping's Moms Who Work; contbr. articles to various mags. Home: 1172 Park Ave New York NY 10128-1213 Office: Lamppost Press Inc 1172 Park Ave # 8 B New York NY 10128-1213

HIRSCHFELD, ARLENE F., civic worker, homemaker; b. Denver, Apr. 6, 1944; d. Hyman and Gertrude (Schwartz) Friedman; m. A. Barry Hirschfeld, Dec. 17, 1966; 2 children. Student, U. Mich., 1962-64; BA, U. Denver, 1966. English tchr. Abraham Lincoln High Sch., Denver, 1966-70. Pres. Jr. League of Denver, 1986-87, v.p. ways and means, 1985-86, v.p. mktg., 1982-83, chmn. Colo. Cache mktg. com., 1978-79, chair holiday mart, 1981, 85-87, participant in Nat. Jr. League Mktg. Conf.; trustee Graland Country Day Sch., 1988-97, bd. sec., 1990-95, chmn. edn. com., 1989-95, pres. parent coun., 1982-83, auction chmn., 1980, 81; bd. dirs. Allied Jewish Fedn., 1988-96; chair Allied Women's Camp, 1993; co-chmn. collector's choice event Denver Art Mus., 1989, 94, bd. trustees, 1995-98; co-chmn. benefit luncheon Pub. Edn. Coalition, 1990, mini grants selection com., 1985-87; mem. bd. Minoru Yasui Comty. Vol. award, 1986-87; mem. Greater Denver C. of C. Leadership Denver, class of 1987-88; bd. dirs. Women's Found. Colo., 1992—, Anti-Defamation League, 1994-96, Colo. Spl. Olympics, 1994—; mem. dean's coun. Harvard Div. Sch., 1992—; exec. com. Children's Diabetes Found., Denver, 1993—. Named Humanitarian of Yr. Nat. Jewish Ctr., 1988, named to Colo. Women's Econ. Devel. Coun. by Gov. of Colo., 1989—, Sustainer of Yr. Jr. League, 1992; recipient Nat. Women's Mus. of the Arts. Colo. Chpt. award, 1991, U. Denver Founder's Day Alumni Community Svc. award; recipient Woman of Distinction award Rocky Mtn. News and Hyatt Beaver Creek, 1993, Colo. I Have A Dream Found. award, 1992. Mem. Colo. Women's Forum. Office: 5200 Smith Rd Denver CO 80216-4525

HIRSCHFELD, SUE ELLEN, geological sciences educator; b. Ossining, N.Y., Jan. 12, 1941; d. Ira Bertram and Helen Caroline (Rieser) H. BS, U. Fla., 1963, MS, 1965; PhD, U. Calif., Berkeley, 1971. Prof. Calif. State U., Hayward, 1971—, chair dept. geol. scis., 1988-94. Co-author videotapes in field, 1985, 92, 95, 96; contbr. articles to profl. jours. Grantee Calif. State U., 1976, 78, 93, 95. Mem. AAAS, Geol. Soc. Am., Soc. for Sedimentary Geology, Assn. for Women Geoscientists (founder). Office: Calif State U Hayward CA 94542

HIRSCHFIELD, RONNI JOAN, retired elementary educator, actress; b. N.Y.C., Mar. 21, 1940; f. Benjamin and Dorothy (Dopkin) Sharaga; m. Jack H. Hirschfield, Aug. 3, 1963; children: Rina Michele, Amie Danielle, Scot Jonathan. BS, Hoffstra U., 1962, MS, 1965. Cert. elem tchr., 1962, reading tchr., 1965, social studies tchr., 1990. Tchr. Syosset Pub. Schs., N.Y., 1962-63, Massapequa Pub. Schs., N.Y., 1963-64; reading specialist Bellmore-Merrick Pub. Schs., N.Y., 1965-90, tchr. social studies, 1991-95. Appeared in Gilbert and Sullivan L.I. Opera Co. plays H.M.S. Pinafore, Mikado, Pirates of Penzance (in Yiddish). Choir mem., purveyor, primary vendor Congregation B'Nai Israel, Freeport. Mem. Ret. Tchrs. Assn.. Jewish.

HIRSCHHORN, ROCHELLE, genetics educator; b. Bklyn., Mar. 19, 1932; d. Hyman and Anna Reibman; m. Kurt Hirschhorn; children: Melanie D., Lisa R., Joel N. BA, Barnard Coll., 1953; MD, NYU, 1957. Intern NYU-Bellevue Med. Divsn., N.Y.C., 1958-59; rsch. fellow, teaching asst. NYU Sch. Medicine, N.Y.C., 1963-65, assoc. rsch. scientist, 1965-66, instr. in medicine, 1966-69, asst. prof. medicine, 1969-74, assoc. prof. medicine, 1974-79, prof. medicine, 1979—, head divsn. med. genetics, 1984—; hon. fellow Galton Lab. Human Genetics & Biometry Univ. Coll., London, 1971-72; assoc. attending physician in medicine Bellevue Hosp., N.Y.C., 1969-80, Univ. Hosp., NYU Sch. Medicine, 1974-81; attending physician Bellevue

Hosp., 1980—, Univ. Hosp., 1981—; mem. numerous NIH coms. & study sects., 1973—; vis. prof. Harvard U., 1995, U. Calif. San Francisco, 1995. Senator NYU Senate, mem. pediatrics search com., 1987-89, human subjects instl. rev. bd., 1989-94, co-dir. second year med. genetics course, 1989-93, NYU appointments and promotions com. 1995—; trustee AIDS Med. Found./AMFAR; judge Westinghouse Nat. Sci. Talent Search; founding mem. Village Cmty. Sch. Fellow AAAS, Am. Coll. Rheumatology, Am. Coll. Med. Genetics (founder); mem. NAS, Inst. Medicine, Am. Soc. for Clin. Investigation, Assn. Am. Physicians, Am. Assn. Immunologists, Am. Soc. Human Genetics (cert. 1987), Interurban Clin. Club (pres. 1987-88), Peripatetic Soc., Soc. for Inherited Metabolic Diseases, Harvey Soc. (coun. 1989-92), Alpha Omega Alpha (councillor Delta of N.Y. 1982—). Office: NYU Med Ctr 550 1st Ave New York NY 10016-6481

HIRSH, CRISTY J., school counselor; b. Dallas, Oct. 3, 1952; d. Bernard and Johanna (Cristol) H. BS in Early Childhood and Elem. Edn., Boston U., 1974; MS in Spl. Edn., U. Tex., Dallas, 1978; MEd in Counseling and Student Svcs., U. North Tex., 1991. Nat. cert. counselor; lic. profl. counselor, Tex.; cert. tchr., Tex., Mass. Dir., learning specialist Specialized Learning, Dallas, 1981-93; counselor, mem. adj. faculty Eastfield Coll., Mesquite, Tex., 1992-95; counselor Grapevine (Tex.)-Colleyville Ind. Sch. Dist., 1995—; mem. adj. faculty Richland Coll., Dallas, 1991-92. Mem. Am. Counseling Assn., Coun. for Exceptional Children, Coun. for Learning Disabilities, Pi Lambda Theta, Phi Delta Kappa. Office: VISTA Alternative Campus c/o 3051 Ira E Woods Ave Grapevine TX 76051

HIRSHFIELD, JANE B., poet; b. N.Y.C., Feb. 24, 1953; d. Robert L. and Harriet Esther (Miller) H. AB magna cum laude, Princeton U., 1973. Lectr. U. San Francisco, 1991—; vis. assoc. prof. U. Calif. Berkeley, 1995; adv. bd. Marian Arts Coun., San Rafael, Calif., 1988—; steering com. Pen Am. Ctr. West Coast br., Berkeley, 1991-94; adj. prof. No. Mich. U., Marquette, 1994, U. Minn., Duluth, 1995. Author: (book) Alaya, 1982, Of Gravity & Angels, 1988, The October Palace, 1994; editor: (book) The Ink Dark Moon, 1988, Women in Praise of the Sacred, 1994. Recipient Guggenheim fellowship Guggenheim Found., 1985, Rockefeller Found. Bellagio fellowship, 1995, Commonwealth Club Poetry medal Commonwealth Club of Calif., 1988, 94, Poetry Ctr. Book award San Francisco State Poetry Ctr., 1994, Bay Area Book Reviewers award, 1994.

HIRSHMAN, LINDA REDLICK, law educator, writer; b. Cleve., Apr. 26, 1944. BA in Govt. with Honors, Cornell U., 1966; JD, U. Chgo., 1969; PhD in Philosophy, U. Ill., Chgo., 1995. Bar: Ill. 1969, U.S. Supreme Ct. 1975. Assoc. Isham, Lincoln & Beale, Chgo., 1969-71; legal specialist Project SAFE, 1971-72; assoc., then ptnr. Jacobs, Burns, Sugarman & Orlove, 1972-82; assoc. prof. Ill. Inst. Tech. Chgo.-Kent Coll. Law, 1983-89, prof., 1989—; vis. prof. Brandeis U., Mass., 1966; Lewis scholar Washington and Lee U., Va., 1995; mem. nat. bd. Women's Studies program Brandeis U., Waltham, Mass. Mem. law rev. U. Chgo., 1967-68; contbr. articles to profl. publs. Mem. ABA, Am. Law Inst. Home: PO Box 217 Cave Creek AZ 85331 Office: Ill Inst Tech Kent Coll Law 565 W Adams St Chicago IL 60661-3601

HIRST, NANCY HAND, retired legislative staff member; b. L.A., Feb. 24, 1926. BA magna cum laude, Stanford U., 1947. Staff dir. Spl. Subcom. on Traffic Safety, Washington, 1957-58; legis. asst., speechwriter Rep. John C. Watts, 1962-71; adminstrv. aide to chmn. Ho. Com. on Edn. and Labor, Washington, 1975-77. Contbr. photographs to Rio Rimac, Ency. Britannica, 1965. Trustee Va. Mus. Fine Arts, Richmond; active Va. Bd. Historic Resources; chmn. Citizens Adv. Coun. on Furnishing and Interpreting the Exec. Mansion, 1988-93; active 175th Anniversary Commn. for Va.'s Exec. Mansion, 1987-88; trustee Am. Friends of Attingham Summer Sch., G.B., 1988-91; chmn. Woodlawn Plantation Coun., 1974-86; trustee, v.p., pres. Woodlawn Found., 1987-88; bd. visitors George Mason U., 1982-90; mem. Stanford in Washington Coun.; vice chair Mid-Atlantic region Stanford Centennial. Mem. Phi Beta Kappa. Home: 1001 Basil Rd Mc Lean VA 22101-1819

HIRST, WILMA ELIZABETH, psychologist; b. Shenandoah, Iowa; d. James H. and Lena (Donahue) Ellis; m. Clyde Henry Hirst (dec. Nov. 1969); 1 child, Donna Jean (Mrs. Alan Robert Goss). AB in Elementary Edn., Colo. State Coll., 1948, EdD in Ednl. Psychology, 1954; MA in Psychology, U. Wyo., 1951. Lic. psychologist, Wyo. Elem. tchr., Cheyenne, Wyo., 1945-49, remedial reading instr., 1949-54; assoc. prof. edn., dir. campus sch. Nebr. State Tchrs. Coll., Kearney, 1954-56; sch. psychologist, head dept. spl. edn. Cheyenne (Wyo.) pub. schs., 1956-57, sch. psychologist, guidance coordinator, 1957-66, dir. rsch. and spl. projects, 1966-76, also pupil personnel, 1973-84; pvt. cons., 1984—; vis. asst. prof. U. So. Calif., summer 1957, Omaha U., summer 1958, U. Okla., summers 1959, 60; vis. assoc. prof. U. Nebr., 1961, U. Wyo., summer 1962, 64, extension divsn., Kabul, Afghanistan, 1970, Cath. U., Goias, Brazil, 1974; investigator HEW, 1965-69; prin. investigator effectiveness of spl. edn., 1983-84; participant seminar Russian Press Women and Am. Fedn. Press Women, Moscow and Leningrad, 1973. Sec.-treas. Laramie County Coun. Community Svcs., 1962; mem. speakers bur., mental health orgn.; active Little Theatre, 1936-60, Girl Scout Leaders Assn., 1943-50; mem. Adv. Coun. on Retardation to Gov.'s Commn.; mem., sec. Wyo. Bd. Psychologist Examiners, 1965-71 vice chmn., 1971-74; chmn. Mayor's Model Cities Program, 1969; mem. Gov.'s Com. Jud. Reform, 1972; adv. council Div. Exceptional Children, Wyo. Dept. Edn., 1974; mem. transit adv. group City of Cheyenne, 1974; bd. dirs. Wyo. Children's Home Soc., 1968, treas., 1978-84; rsch. on women's prisons State of Wyo., 1989; bd. dirs. Goodwill Industries Wyo., chmn., 1981-83; mem. Wyo. exec. com. Partners of Americas, 1970-86; del. Internat. Conv. Ptnrs. of Ams., Jamaica, 1987; del., moderator pers. com. Presbytery of Wyo., 1987-90, mem. mission program com., 1991-95, spl. gifts com. 1994—; bd. dirs. workforce opportunities adv. com. AARP, 1992-94; Friendship Force ambassador to Honduras, 1979; chmn. bd. SE Wyo. Mental Health Center, 1969; elder 1st Presbyn. Ch., Cheyenne, 1978—, also bd. deacons; chmn. adv. assessment com. Wyo. State Office Handicapped Children, 1980, 81; mem. allocations com. United Way of Laramie County, active People to People Internat., Child Welfare Project, 1992; participant People to People Internat. Citizen Amb. Program, child welfare project assist Lithuania, Latvia, Estonia, 1992. Named Woman of Year, Cheyenne Bus. and Profl. Women, 1974. Diplomate Am. Bd. Profl. Psychology. Fellow Am. Acad. Sch. Psychology; mem. APA, ASCD, Internat. Council Psychologists (chmn. Wyo. div. 1980-85), AAUP, Am. Assn. State Psychology Bds. (sec.-treas. 1970-73), Wyo. Psychol. Assn. (pres. 1962-63), Laramie County Mental Health Assn. (bd. mem., corr. sec. 1963-69, pres.), Wyo. Mental Health Assn. (bd. mem.), Internat. Platform Assn., Am. Ednl. Research Assn., Assn. for Gifted (Wyo. pres. 1964-65), Am. Personnel and Guidance Assn., Am. Assn. Sch. Adminstrs., NEA (life, participant seminar to China 1978), AAUW, Cheyenne Assn. Spl. Personnel and Prins. (pres. 1964-65, mem. exec. bd. 1972-76), Nat. Fedn. Press Women (dir. 1979-85), DAR (vice regent Cheyenne chpt. 1975-77), AARP (state coordinator 1988—, preretirement planning specialist 1986-88, state coord. work force program, 1992—, leadership coun., state del. nat. conv. 1990, pilot project Wyo. state delivery for retirement planning 1990—, AARP Works, op. project state govt. edn. assn. and AARP work force vols. video for retirement planning statewide 1993, master trainer retirement planning 1993—, employment planning master trainer, 1994—, planning com. Area 8 Conf., leadership meeting 1994, mem. adv. coun. Laramie County Widowed Persons Svcs. 1995—, bd. dirs. 1996—), Psi Chi, Kappa Delta Pi, Pi Lambda Theta, Alpha Delta Kappa (pres. Wyo. Alpha 1965-66). Presbyn. Lodge Soc. Colonial Dames XVII Century, Order Eastern Star, Daus. of Nile. Clubs: Wyo. Press Women, Zonta (pres. Cheyenne 1965-66, treas. dist. 12 1974). Author: Know Your School Psychologist, 1963, Effective School Psychology for School Administrators, 1980. Home and Office: 3458 Green Valley Rd Cheyenne WY 82001-6124

HIRVELA-ABERLE, HELEN DEREE, administrator, lawyer; b. Jesup, Ga., Apr. 6, 1952; d. David Andrew and Glenna DeRee (O'Quinn) Hirvela; m. Robert Kenneth Aberle, Aug. 21, 1982 (div. Feb. 1995); children: Alexis DeRee, Julianne Allocca. BS, Ga. So. U., 1974; JD, John Marshall Law Sch., 1979. Bar: Ga., 1979; U.S. Dist. Ct. (so. dist.) Ga. 1980. Econ. devel. specialist Altamaha Ga. So. Area Planning and Devel. Commn., Baxley, 1974-76; paralegal Gibbs, Leephart & Smith, P.G., Jesup, Ga., 1976-79, assoc., 1979-81; sr. ct. clk. State Ct. of Fulton County, Atlanta, 1981-83; caseworker II S.D. Dept. Social Svcs., Rapid City, 1983-85; paralegal instr. Barclay Career Sch., L.A., 1986-88; dir. of adminstrn. Broadcast Tng., Ing./Columbia Sch. Broadcasting, Hollywood, Calif., 1990-91; adminstrv. atty. Nev. Pub. Svc. Commn., Las Vegas, 1991-93; asst. adminstr. State of Nev./Dept. Bus. Industry, Divsn. Indsl. Rels., Las Vegas, 1993—. Contbr. various Altamaha Ga. So. Area Planning and Devel. Commn. publs. Mem. Comm. Leadership Class, Wayne County C. of C., 1987; panel speaker Emerging Leadership Conf., South Ga. Coll., Douglas, 1973. Mem. DAR, Bus. and Profl. Women, Zeta Tau Alpha, Pi Kappa Phi. Democrat. Methodist. Office: Nev Divsn Indsl Rels 2500 W Washington Ste 100 Las Vegas NV 89106

HIRZEL, KATHY RENEE, telecommunications consultant, photographer; b. Toledo, Oct. 2, 1962; d. Alfred Ernest and Eleanor Theresa (Hotchkiss) H. BBA in Econs., Ohio U., 1984; MA in Geography, San Francisco State U., 1996. Internat. telecom. cons. AT&T, San Francisco, 1993—; photo historian East Marin Island Archaeol. Project, Marin County, Calif., 1992; field supr. Sunol Archaeol. Project, 1993; photo curator San Francisco State U. Bayside Archaeology, 1992. Photo editor: (book) Personal Videoconferencing, 1996. Mem. Assn. Am. Geographers, Soc. for Calif. Archaeology. Office: 2371 25th Ave San Francisco CA 94116

HISEY, LYDIA VEE, educational administrator; b. Memphis, Tex., July 10, 1951; d. Murray Wayne Latimer and Jane Kathryn (Grimsley) Webster; m. Gregory Lynn Hisey, Oct. 4, 1975; children: Kathryn Elizabeth, Jennifer Kay, Anna Elaine. BS in Edn., Tex. Tech U., 1974, MEd, 1990. Cert. tchr., mid-mgmt., Tex.x. Tchr. phys. edn. Lubbock (Tex.) Ind. Sch. Dist., 1975-79, tchr., 1982-91, asst. prin., 1991-95, prin., 1995—. Recipient Way-To-Go award Lubbock Ind. Sch. Dist., 1989, Impact II grantee, 1991. Mem. Tex. Elem. Prins. and Suprs. Assn., Delta Kappa Gamma, Phi Delta Kappa. Baptist. Home: 4613 94th St Lubbock TX 79424-5015

HITCHCOCK, CHRISTINA ANN, company official, columnist; b. Lawrence, Mass., Apr. 20, 1949; d. Henry A. and Charlotte T. (Jastrzebska) Dobrzynski; m. Alton Ward Hitchcock, May 15, 1970; children: Melanie Susannah, Andrew Alton. Assoc. B.A., Merrimack Coll., 1976; BA in English summa cum laude, U. N.H., 1996. Bus. mgr. Apple Valley Electric, Derry, 1986-96, Robert Frost Sch., Derry, N.H., 1987-89; columnist Lawrence Eagle-Tribune, 1994—. Treas. Friends of Derry Libr., 1993—. Mem. Nutfield Exch. Club (sec. 1993-94). Home: PO Box 285 Derry NH 03038

HITCHCOCK, JANE STANTON, playwright; b. N.Y.C., Nov. 24, 1946; d. Robert Tinkham Crowley and Joan (Alexander) Stanton; m. William Mellon Hitchcock, Oct. 10, 1975 (div. Jan. 1991); m. Jim Hoagland, July 14, 1995. BA, Sarah Lawrence Coll., Bronxville, 1964-68. Author: Trick of the Eye, 1992 (Edgar award nominee, Hammett prize nominee), The Witches' Hammer, 1994; screenwriter Our Time, 1974, First Love, 1976; producer Stalking Immortality (documentary) 1978; playwright Grace, 1981, Bhutan or Black Tie in the Himalayas, 1983, The Custom of the Country, 1986, Vanilla, 1990. Mem. PEN, The Dramatists' Guild, The Writers' Guild.

HITCHCOCK, KAREN RUTH, biology educator, university dean, academic administrator; b. Mineola, N.Y., Feb. 10, 1943; d. Roy Clinton and Ruth (Wardell) H. BS in Biology, St. Lawrence U., 1964; PhD in Anatomy, U. Rochester, 1969. Postdoctoral fellow in pulmonary cell biology, Webb-Waring Inst. Med. Rsch., 1968-70; asst. prof. dept. anatomy Tufts U. Sch. Medicine, Boston, 1970-75, assoc. prof. dept. anatomy, 1975-80, assoc. prof., acting chmn. dept. anatomy, 1976-78, assoc. prof., chmn. dept. anatomy, 1978-80, prof., chmn. dept. anatomy and cellular biology, 1980-82, George A. Bates prof. histology, chmn. dept. anatomy and cellular biology, 1982-85; prof. dept. cell biology and anatomy Tex. Tech U. Health Scis. Ctr., assoc. dean Tex. Tech U. Sch. Medicine, Lubbock, 1985-87; vice chancellor rsch., dean grad. coll., prof. cell biology, anatomy and biol. scis. U. Ill., Chgo., 1987-91, v.p. acad. affairs, prof. biol. scis. U. at Albany, SUNY, 1991-95, interim pres., 1995-96, pres., 1996—; mem. nat. adv. rsch. resources coun. NIH, 1992-96, Nat. Bd. Med. Examiners, 1983-85; bd. dirs. N.Y. Capital Region Ctr. Econ. Growth, 1996—; mem. steering com. Assn. Colls. & Univs. State N.Y., 1995—; mem. N.Y. State Senate Higher Edn. com. adv. com., 1995—; pres. bd. dirs. Capital Region Info. Svc., N.Y., 1995—. Mem. Am. Assn. Anatomy (chmn., exec. council 1979-81), Am. Assn. Anatomists (exec. com. 1981-85, v.p. 1986-88, pres. 1990-91), Nat. Bd. of Med. Examiners, Nat. Assn. for Biomed. Rsch. (bd. dirs. 1990), Nat. Assn. State Univs. and Land-Grant Colls. (chair coun. acad. affairs com. 1994-95), Ill. Soc. Med. Rsch. (pres. 1990). Home: 286 Riverview Rd Rexford NY 12148-1649 Office: U at Albany Office of Pres 1400 Washington Ave Albany NY 12222-0001

HITCHCOCK, LILLIAN DOROTHY STAW, educator, actress, artist; b. Detroit, Dec. 19, 1922; d. Charles Stawowczyk And Mary Waligora; m. Richard Elmer Hitchcock, June 28, 1952; children: Charles, Harriet, Roger, Stephen. BA in Edn., Wayne State U., 1946, MA in Interpretative Speech, 1952; postgrad., U. Wis., 1948; cert. in art, Inst. for Am. Univs., Avignon, France, 1981; cert. in French, Cath. U. Paris, 1983; postgrad., Inst. for Am. Univs., Aix-en-Provence, France, 1991. Speech and English tchr. Lakeview High Sch., St. Claire Shores, Mich., 1947-49; speech and journalism tchr. Mercy Coll., Detroit, 1949-52; substitute tchr. in speech and English Birmingham (Mich.) Pub. Schs., 1960-88; speech and English tchr. Bloomfield Hills (Mich.) Pub. Schs., Detroit Pub. Schs., 1960-70; tchr. French, Montessori Sch., Bloomfield Hills, 1988—; performer, dir. Civic Theatre, Wayne State U., Cath. Theatre, Detroit, 1943-46; chmn. Detroit Theatre Olympiade for World Cmty. Theatre, 1979; mem. St. Dunstan's Theatre, Bloomfield Hills; docent Cranbrook Mus. Modern Art, Bloomfield Hills, 1988—. Performer Festival Original One-Act Plays, Ann Arbor, Mich., 1994. Del. People to People-Health Care, China, 1984. Mem. AAUW (bd. dirs. children's theatre Birmingham 1960-80), UN rep. and del. 1970-73), Tuesday Musicale. Mem. Internat. Platform Assn. (1st Place and Silver Bowl award 1994). Roman Catholic. Home: 6140 Westmoor Rd Bloomfield Hills MI 48301-1355

HITCHENS, MARY ANN, athletic administrator; b. Dover, Del., Aug. 12, 1945; d. E. Dallas and Elizabeth F. (Gordy) H.; m. Bruce Ian Campbell, July 17, 1976 (div. Mar. 1983). BS in Phys. Edn. with honors, U. Del., 1967, MEd in Guidance and Counseling, 1971. Tchr., coach Springer Jr. H.S., Wilmington, Del., 1967-68, Brandywine H.S., Wilmington, 1968-69; mem. faculty U. Del., Newark, 1969—, assoc. prof. phys. edn., 1969—, head coach women's basketball, 1969-79, head coach women's field hockey, 1973-89, coord. women's athletics, assoc. dir. athletics. Mem. U. Del. Commn. on Status of Women, chair, 1985-86. Recipient Josten's Svc. award Ea. Coll. Athletic Conf., 1993, E. Arthur Trabant Instnl. Equity award U. Del., 1994, Women's Sports and Fitness award, 1994, Pathfinder award Nat. Assn. for Girls and Women in Sport, 1994; named Field Hockey Coach of Yr., East Coast Conf., 1983, 85, 87, 88. Mem. AAHPERD, Del. Assn. for Health, Phys. Edn., Recreation and Dance (Profl. Honor award 1978), Nat. Assn. Collegiate Women's Athletic Adminstrs., Nat. Coll. Athletic Assn. (field hockey com. 1989-90, chair field hockey com. 1990-91, pres. North Atlantic Conf. 1992-94). Office: U Del Delaware Field House S College Ave Newark DE 19716

HITE, CATHARINE LEAVEY, orchestra manager; b. Boston, Oct. 1, 1924; d. Edmond Harrison and Ruth Farrington Leavey; m. Robert Atkinson Hite, Aug. 28, 1948; children: Charles Harrison, Patricia Hite Barton, Catharine Hite Dunn. BA, Coll. William and Mary, 1945. Restoration guide Williamsburg Restoration, 1944-45; asst. edn. dept. Honolulu Acad. Arts, 1945-46; sec., tour guide edn. dept. office chief curator Nat. Gallery Art, 1946-48; opera liason/coord. Honolulu Symphony, 1972-73, asst. to gen. mgr., 1973-75, community devel. dir./opera coord., 1975-77, dir. ops./opera prodn. coord., 1977-79, orch. mgr., 1979-84, mem. exec. com., 1965-69, pres. women's assn., 1965-66; com. chmn., opera assn. chmn. Hawaii Opera Theatre, 1966-69. Mem. W. R. Farrington Scholarship Com., 1977—, chmn., 1982-94; mem. community arts panel State Found. Culture and the Arts, 1982, State Found. Music and Opera, 1984; docent Iolani Palace, 1990—; docent Honolulu Acad. Arts, 1996—. Mem. Jr. League, Alliance Française, Hawaii Watercolor Soc. Mem. Phi Beta Kappa. Episcopalian.

HITE, ELINOR KIRKLAND, oil company human resources manager; b. Abington, Pa., Sept. 28, 1942; d. Bryant Mays and Bernice Eleanor (Tanis) Kirkland; m. Anthony L. Hite, July 7, 1967 (div. 1974); 1 child, Juddson Kirkland. BA in English, Denison U., Granville, Ohio, 1964; MA in Counseling, Princeton Theol. Sem., 1966. Asst. dir. pers. Edwards Bros. Printing Co., Ann Arbor, Mich., 1973-74; asst. dir. career counseling/placement U. Ill., Chgo., 1975-81; human rels. assoc. Amoco Corp., Chgo., 1981-82, sr. human rels. rep., 1982-85, staff human rels. rep., 1985-87, human rels. cons., 1987—; vol. career employment lectr., Chgo., 1985—. Chair clin. mgmt. com. Lorene Replogle Counseling Ctr., Chgo., 1981—; trustee, officer 4th Presbyn. Ch., Chgo., 1985—, elder, officer, 1985-91, chair pers. com., 1989—; pres. 200 S. Home Condo Assn., Oak Park, Ill., 1982-91, 93—; bd. dirs. Frank Lloyd Wright Mus., 1994—; chair human resources policies com., bd. trustees McCormick Theol. Sem., 1996—. Presbyterian.

HITE, SHERE D., author, cultural historian; b. St. Joseph, Mo., Nov. 2, 1942; m. Friedrich Hoericke, 1985. BA cum laude, U. Fla., 1964, MA, 1968; postgrad., Columbia U., 1968-69. Dir. feminist sexuality project NOW, N.Y.C., 1972-78; dir. Hite Rsch. Internat., N.Y.C., 1978—; instr. female sexuality NYU, 1977—; lectr. Harvard U., McGill U., Columbia U., Cambridge U. (Eng.), The Sorbonne, Paris, Oxford U., 1995-96, also numerous women's groups; internat. lectr., 1977-90; mem. adv. bd. Am. Found. Gender and Genital Medicine, Johns Hopkins U. Author: The Hite Report: A Nationwide Study of Female Sexuality, 1976, The Hite Report on Male Sexuality, 1981, Women and Love: A Cultural Revolution in Progress, 1987, Fliegen mit Jupiter, 1993, The Hite Report on the Family: Icons of the Heart, 1994, Women as Revolutionary Agents of Change: The Hite Reports and Beyond, 1994, The Divine Comedy of Ariadne and Jupiter, 1994, The Hite Report on the Family: Growing Up Under Patriarchy, 1994, The Hite Report on Hite (on Herself): A Sexual & Political Autobiography, 1996; co-author: Good Guys, Bad Guys: The Hite Guide to Smart Choices, 1991; cons. editor: Sexual Honesty: By Women for Women, 1974, Jour. Sex Edn. and Therapy, Jour. Sexuality and Disability. Mem. NOW, AAAS, Am. Hist. Assn., Am. Sociol. Assn., Acad. Polit. Sci., Soc. for Women in Philosophy, Internat. Women Writer's Orgn. (v.p.). Office: 2 Soho Sq, London W1V, England

HITT, GWEN KEYS, school counselor, minister of music; b. Laurel, Miss., June 10, 1944; m. Irving Hitt, June 21, 1966; children: Oliver Irving, Carter Clifton. AA, Jones Jr. Coll., 1964; BA in Music Edn., Miss. U. for Women, 1968; MA in Christian Edn., So. Bapt. Theol. Sem., 1969; cert. in gifted edn., William Carey Coll., 1985; MEd, U. So. Miss., Hattiesburg, 1987, cert. in guidance and counseling, 1988; postgrad., Jackson State U., 1988, U. Miss., Oxford, 1991. Min. of music Salem Bapt. Ch., Collins, Miss., 1963-64, 74-76, 1986-94; min. of music Big Level Bapt. Ch., Wiggins, Miss., 1976-82, Williamsburg Bapt. Ch., Collins, 1983-85, First Bapt. Ch., Braxton, Miss., 1995—; girls activity dir. YMCA, Louisville, 1966-67; med. asst. So. Bapt. Theol. Sem. Clinic, Louisville, 1967-68; music tchr. du Pont Manual H.S., Louisville, 1968-74; mental health worker Pine Belt Regional Mental Health Ctr., Hattiesburg, 1974-76; spl. edn. tchr. Hopewell Elem. Sch., Collins, 1984-85; tchr. of gifted Collins Mid. Sch., 1985-87, counselor, 1987—; contract cons. music dept. Miss. Bapt. Conv., 1976-84; news dir., talk show host WIGG Radio, Wiggins, 1977-82; news corr. Daily Herald, Biloxi, Miss., 1977-82; mem. ASTROTECH tng. for tchrs. program Stennis Space Ctr., 1985; presenter at workshops in field. Conbtg. editor Church Music RFD, 1979; author: We Shall Come Rejoicing, A History of Baptist Church Music in Mississippi, 1984, Covington Crossroads, The History of Covington County, Mississippi, 1984, Dinner on the Ground, 1987, Middle School Munchies, 1988; co-author: Happiness is Homemade, A Parenting Handbook for Middle School Families, 1989; organizing editor Patchwork newsletter, 1989-92; co-editor: Reflections of Childhood and Youth, 1990; contbr. articles to profl. publs.; dir., writer musical presentations, 1983-96. Dir. Cmty. Youth Chorus, 1991-96; dir. choir Opryland, Nashville, 1991; mem. Brit. sch. studies St. Mary's Boy's Choir Sch., Reigate, Eng., 1992; mem. constrn. team to build Univ. Bapt. Ch., Fairbanks, Alaska, 1994; organizer, co-dir. Singing Christmas Tree, 1992-93; organizer Cmty. Resource Day, 1991, County Wide Parents for Pub. Schs., 1991; vol. with youth and adult groups on mission activities, W.Va., Tenn., La., N.C., Miss. Gulf Coast, 1986-96; dir. Okatoma Dinner Theater, 1992-96; mem. organizing com. ann. Walk America, March of Dimes, 1994-95; mem. craft adv. com. for gender equity Jones Jr. Coll., 1994-96; mus. dir. ground breaking Miss. VA Nursing Ctr., Collins, 1994; dir. bell choirs for performance for Miss. Gov. Kirk Fordice, 1993, and at White House, Washington, 1993. Grantee Miss. Power Found., 1987, 89, Bell South Found., 1989, 92, Miss. Arts, 1989, Dept. Hwy. Safety, 1989-92, Children's Trust Fund of Miss., 1989-92, 4-H, 1994, Met. Life, 1994, 95, Covington County Edn. Found., 1995, Chisholm Found., 1995; recipient Recognition award Miss. Bapt. Conv., 1984, Vol. of Yr. award Covington County C. of C., 1989; Paul Harris fellow Rotary Internat., 1990. Mem. AAUW, Miss. Counselor's Assn. (Sch./Cmty. Program of Yr. award 1994), Miss. Profl. Educators, Covington County Tchr.'s Assn., Covington County Tchrs. of English, Covington County Tchrs. of Reading, Covington County C. of C. (chmn. cultural arts com. 1993-96, pres. 1991-92, edn. chmn. 1990-91), Miss. State Alumni Assn., Pine Belt Regional Counselor's Assn. (sec. 1995-96), Okatoma Golf Club. Home: 110 Herrin Dees Rd Rt 4 Box 255 Collins MS 39428 Office: PO Box 757 Collins MS 39428

HIXON, ANDREA KAYE, healthcare quality specialist; b. Clifton Forge, Va., Jan. 15, 1955; d. Leon Malcolm and Mary Ruth (Bowyer) Whitmer; m. Charles L. Hixon Jr., Sept. 11, 1976. ADN, Frederick (Md.) Community Coll, 1974; BSN, George Mason U., Fairfax, Va., 1981; MS, U. Md., Balt., 1986. Cert. profl. for healthcare quality, 1993. Staff ambulatory care VA Med. Ctr., Martinsburg, W.Va., 1974-82; nursing home adminstr. VA Med. Ctr., 1982-86; quality assurance coord. nursing James A. Haley VA Hosp., Tampa, Fla., 1987-93; coord. med. ctr. CQI Program, Tampa, 1993—. Mem. Am. Assn. Spinal Cord Injury Nurses, Nat. Assn. for Healthcare Quality. Home: 2610 Bridle Dr Plant City FL 33567-6742

HIXON, EMILY EARL, artist, educator; b. Auburn, Ala., July 30, 1919; d. Charles Robert and Hassie Earl (Terrell) H.; m. Paul David Sturkie, June 19, 1940 (div. Oct. 1962); children: David Paul Sturkie, Margaret Anne Sturkie Mitchell; m. Frank Beasley Gunter, July 4, 1974 (dec. July 1979). BA, Auburn U., 1940; MA, Rutgers U., 1966. Illustrator Ala. Ext. Svc., Auburn, 1942-44; art dir. Rutgers Prep., Somerset, N.J., 1961-74; founding and exhibiting mem. Amos Eno Gallery, N.Y.C., 1974—. One-person shows include Edinburgh, Princeton, N.Y.C., New Brunswick, N.J.; exhibited in group shows at Coburg, Germany, Windsor, Can., Phila., Boston, Calif., Chgo., East Hampton, Sag Harbor, Montclair Coll., Montclair Mus., N.J. State Mus., Trenton, N.J.; represented in permanent collections at Bristol-Meyers Squibb, Johnson & Johnson, Rutgers U. Monmouth Coll, also pvt. collections. Mem. H.S. Task Force, Franklin Twp., N.J., 1968, mem. human rels. commn., 1968-72; bd. dirs. Hamilton Pk. Youth Devel., Franklin Twp., 1970-74, Intercounty Cmty. Devel. Corp., Franklin Twp., 1975-82. Recipient 1st prize in oils Monmouth Coll., 1964, Printmaker's prize N.J. Painters and Sculptor's Soc., 1965, Purchase prize Monmouth Coll., 1973. Mem. Jimmy Ernst Artists Alliance, Guild Hall (East Hampton), Parrish Art Mus., Amos Eno Gallery. Democrat.

HIXON, STEPHANIE ANNA, religious organization administrator, clergywoman. Grad. in music edn. and music therapy, Shenandoah U.; MDiv, Luth. Theol. Sem., Gettysburg, Pa. Ordained to ministry United Meth. Ch. Former tchr. pub. schs.; pastor United Meth. Ch., Pa., W.Va.; mem. Gen. Secretariat, Gen. Commn. on Status-Role of Women United Meth. Ch., Evanston, Ill.; mem. various bds. and task forces, including Coll. of Women, subcom. on support for clergywomen, racial and ethnic clergy and clergy couples of bd. ordained ministry Ctrl. Pa. Ann. Conf., United Meth. Ch.; mem. gen. bd. Nat. Coun. Chs. of Christ in U.S.A., mem. sexuality study group; pub. spkr., retreat facilitator, workshop leader in field. Prodr. video Ask Before You Hug: Sexual Harassment in the Church. Bd. dirs. Better Exisence with HIV, Evanston and Chgo.; active women's orgns. Office: United Meth Ch Gen Secretariat 1200 Davis St Evanston IL 60201

HIXSON, DORIS KENNEDY, secondary education educator; b. Sweetwater, Tenn., Mar. 24, 1944; d. Warren Harding and Orinda Eugenia (Wood) Kennedy; m. Virgil Lee Hitson, Dec. 31, 1963 (dec. July 1973); m. Luther Terrell Hixson, Feb. 14, 1974; children: Rindi, Elaine,

Liana. Student, Less-McRae Jr. Coll., 1962-63, Vanderbilt U., 1963-64; BA in English, Tenn. Wesleyan Coll., 1967; postgrad., U. Tenn., Chattanooga, 1983-85; MA in Liberal Studies, Hollins Coll., 1985. Secondary English tchr. Cleveland (Tenn.) City Schs., 1967—; faculty rep. United Tchg. Profession, Cleveland, 1976-86, Tchrs. Study Coun., Cleveland, 1983-87; English instr. Cleveland (Tenn.) State C.C., 1986-89. Bd. dirs. YMCA, Cleveland, 1978-81; pres. SNB Women's Book Club, Cleveland, 1992-94; chmn. Christian edn., 1995-96, Sunday Sch. supt. Wesley Meml. Meth. Ch., Cleveland, 1994-96. Fellow in Bible Lit. NEH, Bloomington, Ind., 1977, fellow in Lit. of Alienation NEH, Hollins, 1983, fellow in English Romantics NEH, Chgo., 1987, fellow in Holocaust Lit. NEH, Boston, 1993. Mem. Nat. Coun. Tchrs. English, Tenn. Coun. Tchrs. English, United Tchg. Profession (rep. 1976-86), Delta Kappa Gamma (rec. sec. 1987-90, parliamentarian 1990-94). Home: PO Box 8 Calhoun TN 37309 Office: Cleveland High 850 Raider Dr Cleveland TN 37312

HIXSON, SHEILA ELLIS, state legislator; b. L'Anse, Mich., Feb. 9, 1933; divorced; children: Denise, Lynn, Andy, Todd. AB, No. Mich. U., 1953. Tchr. Head Start; campaign mgr., aide Congressman William Ford, Mich., 1963-64; adminstrv. aide to state senator, 1965-66, legal aide to sec. of Dem. Nat. Conv., 1966-76; mem. Md. Ho. of Dels., Annapolis, 1976—, mem. ways and means com., environ. matters com., budget and audit com., house rules and exec. nominations com., procurement com., lottery com., others, chair joint com. fed.-state rels., chair task force on child abuse and neglect; chmn. Ways and Means com.; mem. Gov. Work Force Investment Bd. Mem. Montgomery County Dem. State Cen. Com. Mem. Nat. Assn. Sunday Sch. Instrs., Nat. Profl. and Bus. Women's Orgn., Women's Polit. Caucus, Plowmen and Fishermen, NOW. Home: 1008 Broadmore Cir Silver Spring MD 20904-3108 Office: Md Gen Assembly Ways and Means Com Rm 100 Lowe House Office Bl Annapolis MD 21401-1991

HIZER, MARLENE BROWN, library director; b. Shattuck, Okla., Mar. 29, 1940; d. Marvin Ira and Geneva Marie (Wright) Brown; m. Ammon M. Hizer, Mar. 19, 1960; children: Lori Marie Hizer Hunt, Holly Dot Hizer Caldwell. BS in Edn., N.W. Mo. State U., 1962; MS in Edn. emphasizing Libr. Sci., Ctrl. Mo. State U., 1966. Cert. tchr. libr. sci. Stenographer Butler Mfg., Kansas City, 1958-59; tchr., libr. Eastgate Jr. High Sch., Kansas City, 1962-69; dir. Nevada (Mo.) Pub. Libr., 1985—; lit. tutor, Nevada, Mo., 1992—; del. Mo. Gov.'s Conf., Jefferson City, 1990. Editor (newspaper) NEWSMAT, 1962-69, Northwest Missourian, 1958-62. Core communicator Mo. Citizen's Coun., Nev., 1980—; edn. counselor LDS Relief Soc., Nev., 1973-77; Sunday sch. tchr. LDS Ch., 1990—, sem. tchr., 1975-78, pub. affairs dir., 1990—; mem. Friends of Nev. Pub. Libr. Recipient Albert B. Fuson Meml. award for Highest Contbns., 1958, Scholastic award AAUP, 1962, Star award Nat. Scholastic Press Assn., 1962; named one of Outstanding Young Women of Am., 1970; Curator scholar U. Mo., 1958, scholar Bus. and Profl. Women's Assn., 1959. Mem. AAUW (cultural interest com. 1990-91), DAR (vice regent 1991-93, yearbook com., friends of the libr. com. 1995-97), ALA, Mo. Libr. Assn., Pub. Libr. Assn., Pub. Libr. Dirs., Mo. State Libr. Inst., Mo. Pub. Libr. Coun. (recorder 1991-93), Vernon County Hist. Soc., Soroptimist Internat. (chair Internat. Goodwill and Understanding, parliamentarian 1996-97). Democrat. Home: RR 2 Box 158 Nevada MO 64772-9674 Office: Nevada Pub Libr 225 W Austin Blvd Nevada MO 64772-3343

HLAVAY, SARAH INEZ, fundraising executive; b. Corvallis, Oreg., Dec. 10, 1942; d. Samuel Sidney and Mary Eleanor (Grantham) Wood; m. Joseph Francis Hlavay, Aug. 3, 1985. BS, U. Ga., 1964; MA in Tchg., Emory U., 1965; MBA, Pepperdine U., 1979. Social studies coord. Holy Innocents Parish Day Sch., Atlanta, 1965-68; adminstrv. asst. Dorothy Freedman & Assoc., N.Y.C., 1969; regional sales mgr. Milliken, Inc., L.A., 1969-74; acct. exec. Clinique Labs., Inc., L.A., 1974-75; area mgr. Orlane, L.A., 1975-79; ESL tchr. Beverly Hills (Calif.) Adult Sch., 1980-81; regional rep. St. Jude Childrens Rsch. Hosp., Arlington, Va., 1982-83; assoc. dir. alumni rels. Emory U., Atlanta, 1983-85; mgmt. cons. S.I. Wood and Assoc., Calgary, Can., 1979—. State treas. Nat. Soc. Fund Raising Execs., Atlanta, 1984-85; bd. dirs. Learning Ctr., Calgary, 1988-94, Juvenile Diabetes Found., L.A., 1979-81; state cen. com. Calif. Rep. Party, L.A., 1973—; active Nat. Charity League, L.A., 1978—. Ford Found. fellow Emory U., 1964. Mem. N.S. Daus. of the Am. Revolution (past regent), Colonial Dames of Am., Colonial Dames XVII Century (organizing pres. 1968—), N.S. Daus. of Colonial Wars (state chaplain 1993—), N.S. Sons and Daus. of the Pilgrims (nat. chair 1995—), Alpha Gamma Delta (internat. ext. com. 1960—). Episcopalian. Home: 94 Willow Park Green SE, Calgary, AB Canada T23 3 L1 Office: Chief Constrn Co Ltd, Calgary, AB Canada

HLOZEK, CAROLE DIANE QUAST, securities company administrator; b. Dallas, Apr. 17, 1959; d. Robert E. and Bonnie (Wootton) Quast. BS, Tex. A&M U., 1982, BBA, 1982. CPA, Tex. Internal auditor Brown & Root Inc., Houston, 1982-84; asst. contr. Wilson Supply Co., Houston, 1984-86, sr. acctg. supr., Hydro Conduit Corp., Houston, 1986-87; fin. analyst Am. Capital, Houston, 1989-94; dir. adminstrn. CFO Am. Gen. Securities, Inc. 1994—. chmn. bd. dirs. On Our Own Inc. 1987-91. Mem. MENSA, Houston Zool. Soc., Tex. Soc. CPAs, Houston Livestock Show and Rodeo. Lutheran. Home: 15405 Mauna Loa Ln Houston TX 77040-1344 Office: Am Gen Securities Inc 2727 Allen Pky Ste 290 Houston TX 77019-2115

HO, BETTY CHUENYÜ YULIN, physiological educator, researcher; b. Nanking, China, Nov. 20, 1930; came to U.S., 1947; d. William Tien-Hu and Gwei-Hsin (Wang) Ho; m. Lajos Rudolf Elkan, Feb. 27, 1958 (div. Aug. 1967); children: Amanda, Anita, Julien (dec.), Raoul. Student, Western Coll., Oxford, Ohio, 1947-48; BS, Columbia U., 1952; postgrad., Conservatoire de Musique, Lausanne, Switzerland, 1956-58, CCNY, 1966-67, 73-75. Lab. technician Columbia U., N.Y.C., 1953-54; ct. report typist Palais de Justice, Lausanne, Switzerland, 1956-57; pianist, accompanist Ecole de Ballet Mara Dousse, Lausanne, Switzerland, 1958-60; English tchr. Montcalme Inst., Lausanne, Switzerland, 1960-61; piano tchr. Le Manoir Inst., Lausanne, Switzerland, 1960-61, N.Y.C., 1964-65; rsch. dir. Juvenescent Rsch. Corp., N.Y.C., 1963—. Author: The Living Function of Sleep, Life & Aging, 1967, The Origin of Variation of Races of Mankind & The Cause of Evolution, 1969, A Scientific Guide to Peaceful Living, 1972, How to Stay Healthy A Lifetime Without Medicines, 1979, A Chinese & Western Daily Practical Health Guide, 1982, Immediate Hints to Health Problems, 1991, 101 Ways to Live 150 Years Young and Healthy, 1992, Una Guia Unica para la salud, la juventud y la longevidad, 1994, A Unique Health Guide for Young People, 1994, The Body Bible, 1996, Vive Napoleon, 1997. Named Citizen of Yr. Principality of Hutt River Province, Queensland, Australia, 1994, awarded royal patronage status for life, 1995. Home: 807 Riverside Dr Apt 1F New York NY 10032

HO, WEIFAN LEE, merchandise executive; b. N.Y.C., Mar. 11, 1951; d. Ho chee and Kwan Fong Lui. Student, Middlebury Coll.; BA, CCNY, 1972. Buyer Bloomingdales, N.Y.C., 1989-92; divsnl. mdse. mgr. Conran's-Habitat, N.Y.C., 1992-93; buyer Abraham and Straus/Jordan Marsh, N.Y.C., 1994, Macy's East, N.Y.C., 1995—, Gimbels, N.Y.C. Mem. NAFE. Office: Macy's East 151 W 34th St New York NY 10001

HOADLEY, IRENE BRADEN (MRS. EDWARD HOADLEY), librarian; b. Hondo, Tex., Sept. 26, 1938; d. Andrew Henry and Theresa Lillian (Lebold) Braden; m. Edward Hoadley, Feb. 21, 1970. BA, U. Tex., 1960; AMLS, U. Mich., 1961, PhD, 1967; MA, Kans. State U., 1965. Cataloger Sam Houston State Tchrs. Coll. Library, Huntsville, Tex., 1961-62; head circulation dept. Kans. State U. Library, Manhattan, 1962-64; grad. asst. U. Mich. Dept. of Library Sci., 1964-66; librarian gen. adminstrn. and research Ohio State U. Libraries, Columbus, 1966-73; asst. dir. libraries adminstrv. services Ohio State U. Libraries, 1973-74; dir. of libraries Tex. A&M U. Library, College Station, Tex., 1974-92; dir. Evans Libr. Capital Campaign, 1993-95; dir. Higher Edn. Act Inst. Quantitative Methods in Librarianship, Ohio State U., summer 1969; instr. inst. U. Calif. at San Diego, 1970, summer; Mem. steering com. Gov's. Conf. on Library and Info. Services, Ohio, 1973-74, joint chairperson, 1974; mem. adv. com. Library Services and Constrn. Act Cuyahoga County Pub. Library, Cleve., 1973. Author: (with others) Physiological Factors Relating to Terrestrial Altitutes: A Bibliography, 1968; Editor: (with Alice S. Clark) Quantitative Methods in Librarianship: Standards, Research, Management, 1972; chair editorial adv. bd. National Forum, 1992—; contbr. (with Alice S. Clark) articles to profl. jours. Co-chair program com. Tex. Conf. Librs. and Info. Svcs., 1989-91. Recipient Scarecrow Press award for libr. lit., 1971, Disting. Alumnus award Sch. Libr. Sci., U. Mich., 1976; named Assn. Coll. and Rsch. Librs. Acad. Rsch. Libr. of Yr. 1994. Mem. ALA (coun. 1990-94, legis. com. 1990-92), Am. Librs. (edtl. bd., Ohio Libr. Assn. (chmn. constn. com. 1967-68, chmn. election tellers com. 1969, asst. gen. chmn. local conf. com. 1969-70, sec. 1970-71, v.p., pres.-elect 1971-72, pres. 1972-73, bd. dirs. 1970-75), Tex. Libr. Assn. (com. on White House conf. 1975-77, vice chmn., chmn. coll. and univ. divsn. 1977-78, exec. bd. 1978-81, legis. com. 1987-89, chair nominating com. 1994, Tex. Libr. of Yr. 1994), Assn. Rsch. Librs. (bd. dirs. 1978-81, search com. for exec. dir. 1980, stats. com. 1991-93, Acad. Libr. of Yr. 1994), Midwest Fedn. Libr. Assns. (exec. bd. 1973-74, chairperson program com. 1974), Online Computer Libr. Ctr. (pres. User's Coun., 1983-84, 84-85, trustee 1984-90, chmn. pers. and compensation com. 1987-89), Tex. Conf. Librs. and Info. Svcs. (co-chair program com.), Coll. and Rsch. Librs. (edtl. bd. 1991-96), Phi Kappa Phi (chair nat. forum com. 1993-96), Phi Alpha Theta, Pi Lambda Theta, Beta Phi Mu, Phi Delta Gamma. Home: 5835 Raymond Stotzer Pky College Station TX 77845-8060

HOAGLAND, CHRISTINA GAIL, occupational therapist, industrial drafter; b. Long Beach, Calif., July 18, 1954; d. Joseph Richard and Dorothy Marian (Bell) H. BS in Occupl. Therapy, Loma Linda U., 1975; AS in Indsl. Drafting Tech., Mt. San Antonio Coll., 1985. Registered occupl. therapist. Occupl. therapist Yuka Mission Hosp., Zambia, Africa, 1976-77; staff occupl. therapist Glendale (Calif.) Adventist Med. Ctr., 1978-79; indsl. drafter Amerex Co., Riverside, Calif., 1985-88; re-entry occupl. therapist Rancho Los Amigos, Downey, Calif., 1989-90; staff occupl. therapist Corona (Calif.) Cmty. Hosp., 1990-92; occupl. therapist Linda R. Brown, Visalia, Calif., 1992; floating staff occupl. therapist St. Mary's Rehab. Ctr., Grand Junction, Colo., 1992—. Mem. Am. Occupl. Therapy Assn., Occupl. Therapy Assn. Colo. Nat. Mus. Women in Arts, Western Colo. Ctr. for the Arts. Democratic Socialist. Seventh-Day Adventist. Home: 578 N 26th St Grand Junction CO 81501-7961 Office: St Mary's Rehab Ctr 1100 Patterson Rd Grand Junction CO 81506

HOAGLAND, JENNIFER HOPE, accountant; b. N.Y.C., Nov. 29, 1955; d. John Joseph and Winifred Adele (Strohmann) Vetter; m. John Grinnell Hoagland, Jr., Jan. 24, 1983; 1 child, John Grinnell III. BS in Acctg., Case We. Res. U., 1977; postgrad., U. Tex., El Paso, 1989—. CPA, Tex.; cert. internal auditor; cert. in mgmt. acctg. Rsch. analyst Predicasts, Inc., Cleve., 1977-79; internal auditor El Paso Electric Co., 1979-80; acct. Exxon Corp., Houston, 1980-81; sr. acct. Colton, Starr, Pena & Co., El Paso, 1981-83, Paul J. Ellenburg Corp., El Paso, 1983-85; dir. of acctg. Life Mgmt. Ctr., El Paso, 1985—. Mem. AICPA, Inst. Mgmt. Accts. Office: Life Mgmt Ctr 8929 Viscount Blvd El Paso TX 79925-5823

HOAR, MARY MARGRETTE, gifted education educator; b. Yonkers, N.Y., Dec. 28, 1948; d. Thomas Aquinas and Margaret Agnes (Delapp) H. BS, Cornell U., 1970; MS, Fordham U., 1973. Cert. tchr. early childhood edn., N.Y., kindergarten, N.Y. Tchr. elem. edn. Sch. # 12, Yonkers, N.Y., 1970-76; tchr. elem. edn. Sch. # 6, Yonkers, N.Y., 1976-81, tchr. gifted and talented edn., 1982-86; tchr. computer King Elem. Summer Sch. King Elem. Summer Sch., Yonkers, 1986—; tchr. early childhood gifted and talented edn. Dr. Martin Luther King Jr. Sch. Computer Sci. and High Tech., Yonkers, 1986—; mem. sch. improvement plan com. Yonkers Bd. Edn., 1987—, United Way rep., 1974-81, mem. tchr.'s interest com., 1972-81, 82—; mem. newspaper staff Yonkers Fedn. Tchrs. Svcs., 1980—, bldg. rep., 1972-81, 87—; trainer Am. Fedn. Tchrs., N.Y. State United Tchrs. Leadership Effectiveness Tng. Workshops, N.Y. State United Tchrs. Officer Yonkers Jay-n-Cees, 1973-83, mem. goals com., golden age com., Outstanding Young Teenager chair; mem. Mayor's Community Rels. Com., 1975—, exec. chair, 1980-82; chair pub. rels. com., exec. com., salute to bus. and industry com., program com.; mem. Westchester exec. bd. No. Metro chpt. March of Dimes, 1974—, walkathon coord. com., reading olympics chair, pub. affairs com.; advisor Mayor's Youth Adv. Com., 1976-79; br. chair Yonkers Red Cross Svc. Ctr., 1975—, chair centennial com., bd. dirs., chair youth svcs.; youth coord. Senator John F. Flynn Sr. Citizens Youth Conf. Day, 1976; bd. dirs. Untermeyer Performing Arts Coun., 1976—, also treas., antique show chairperson, chairperson Art in the Park, chairperson nominating com., chairperson Eileen O'Connor Performing Arts Scholarship, charter mem.; bd. dirs. Family Svc. Yonkers, 1978—, chairperson, 1987—, also mem. exec. com., chairperson ho. com., chairperson homemakers com., mem. vol. com., mem. Nearly New Shop com.; bd. dirs. Enrico Fermi Scholarship Breakfast com., Yonkers Hist. Soc.; mem. steering com. Cornell Women's Club of Westchester, Yonkers Marathon Com. Recipient Janet Hopkins Meml. award for Outstanding Vol. Svc., 1987, Key to City of Yonkers, Mayor Angelo Martinelli, 1977. Mem. Cornell Women's Club of Westchester. Democrat. Roman Catholic. Home: 29 Marshall Rd Yonkers NY 10705-2531 Office: Yonkers Bd Edn 135 Locust Hill Ave Yonkers NY 10701-2917

HOART, GLADYS GALLAGHER, English educator; b. N.Y.C., June 27, 1914; d. Martin and Edna (Parker) Gallagher; m. Francis Xavier Hoart, June 25, 1939; children: Robert, Helen, Andrew. AB cum laude, NYU, 1967, MA, 1970; MA in Liberal Studies, New Sch. for Social Rsch., 1975. Cert. mem. N.Y. Stock Exchange. Adj. prof. English Nassau C.C., Garden City, N.Y., 1970—; dir. Career Seminars for Teenage Girls, Flushing, N.Y., 1963-64; tutor Black Studies Program, Manhasset, N.Y., 1968-69. Pres., co-founder Broadway Homeowners' Assn., Flushing, N.Y., 1964-65; committeewoman Dem. Party, Manhasset, N.Y., 1970; organizer Parkchester (N.Y.) Golden Age Club, 1953. Mem. AAUW, Alliance Floor Brokers, Musicians Club (bd. dirs. 1993—). Roman Catholic.

HOBAN, LILLIAN, author, illustrator; b. Phila., May 18; d. Jules and Fanny (Godwin) Aberman; children: Phoebe, Abrom, Esmé, Julia. Student, Phila. Mus. Sch., Hanya Holm Sch. Dance, N.Y.C., Martha Graham Sch. Dance. Author, illustrator: (children's books) I Can Read, Arthur Series, 1972—; illustrator: (children's books) Frances Series, 1964— (Notable Book award), First Grade Series, 1967—, Jim Books, Charlie the Tramp (Christopher award). Mem. PEN, Authors Guild, Soc. Children's Book Writers. Democrat. Jewish.

HOBART, BILLIE, education educator, consultant; b. Pitts., Apr. 19, 1935; d. Harold James Billingsley and Rose Stephanie (Sladack) Green; m. W.C.H. Hobart, July 20, 1957 (div. 1967); 1 child, Rawson W. BA in English, U. Calif., Berkeley, 1967, EdD, 1992; MA in Psychology, Sonoma State U., 1972. Cert. tchr., Calif. Asst. prof. Coll. Marin, Kentfield, Calif., 1969-78; freelance cons., writer, 1969—; asst. prof. Contra Costa Coll., San Pablo, Calif., 1986—. Author: (cookbook) Natural Sweet Tooth, 1974, (non-fiction) Expansion, 1972, Purposeful Self: Coherent Self, 1979, (non-fiction) Talking to Dead People, 1996; contbr. articles to profl. jours. Served with WAC, 1953-55. Mem. No. Calif. Coll. Reading Assn. (pres. 1996—), Mensa, Phi Delta Kappa, Commonwealth Club San Francisco. Home and Office: PO Box 1542 Sonoma CA 95476-1542

HOBBS, AVANEDA DORENZA, management company executive, minister, singer; b. Charlottesville, Va., July 23, 1955; d. Frederick Douglass and Viola Marie H. BS in Sociology, Va. Wesleyan, 1976; MA in Edn. Adminstrn., Spirit of Truth Inst., Richmond, Va., 1994, EdD in Edn. Adminstrn., 1994; PhD in Comm. and Counselling, Spirit of Truth Inst., 1995. Ordained minister, Charismatic Ch., 1990. Lead singer Gospel Equattes, Washington, 1971; vocalist Mighty Clouds of Joy, 1972, various orgns., 1975—; bus. mgr. Rev. Demond Wilson., Washington, 1990-91; CEO World Resource Outreach Co., Forestville, Md., 1991—; bd. dirs. Solid Rock Records, In The Beginning Ministries, Inc., CAPublishing; i nat. dir. pub. rels. Gospelrama conv., 1985-88; internat. comm. and ednl. cons. Idahosa World Outreach, Nigeria, 1990-93. vocalist: popular gospel singer since early 1970's, concert, TV and radio appearances; author: Guide to Black Religious and Supporting Orgns., 1990. Participant in Congl. and White House Briefings as influential religious leader in D.C., 1992. Recipient Outstanding Svc. award Christian Music Conf., 1980, D.C. Mayoral commendation, 1990. Mem. NAFE, Broadcast Music, Inc. (assoc.), Christian Mgmt. Assn., Christian Believers United, Ministerial Fellowship of Christian Believers United, Black Nat. Religious Broadcasters, Christian Mgmt. Assn., Uniformed Code Coun., Traditional Values Coalition. Republican.

HOBBS, CATHERINE LYNN, English language and literature educator; b. Guymon, Okla., Feb. 13, 1951; d. Dan Stewart and Betty Jean (Ray) H. m. Cecil L. Peaden, Mar. 23, 1975 (div. Feb. 15, 1994). Carin Journalism, U. Okla., 1973; MA in Modern Letters, U. Tulsa, 1983; PhD in English, Purdue U., 1989. Instr. Rogers State Coll., Tulsa, Okla., 1983-84; vis. lectr. comms. U. Tulsa, 1984-85; teaching asst. English dept. Purdue U., West Lafayette, Ind., 1985-89; asst. prof. English Ill. State U., Normal, 1989-92; asst. prof. English dept. U. Okla., Norman, 1992-95, assoc. prof., 1995—; mem. bd. history of rhetoric discussion group, 1993—. Editor: Nineteenth-Century Women Learn to Write, 1995; mem. editl. bd. jour. Genre, 1992—; contbr. articles to profl. jours. NEH fellow, 1990, 93. Mem. AAUW, MLA, Am. Soc. Eighteenth Century Studies, Internat. Soc. History of Rhetoric, Nat. Coun. Tchrs. of English, Rhetoric Soc. Am., Soc. Critical Exch., Tchrs. for Democratic Soc., Phi Kappa Phi. Democrat. Office: U Okla English Dept Norman OK 73019

HOBBS, VIVIAN LEE, lawyer; b. Washington; d. Moses Edward and Frances Ann (Scribner) Hobbs; children: Jason Michael, Gregory James, Jennifer Ann. BS summa cum laude, U. Md., 1978; JD summa cum laude, Georgetown U., 1981. Bar: D.C. 1981. Ptnr. Arnold & Porter, Washington, 1981—; mem. adv. coun. on employee welfare U.S. Dept. Labor; mem. steering com. D.C. chpt. W.E.B. Mem. ABA (employee benefits com. 1985—, chair new welfare benefits legis. subcom. 1992-94), D.C. Bar Assn. (chmn. welfare plan subcom. 1988-90). Office: Arnold & Porter 555 12th St NW Washington DC 20004

HOBEN, SALLY, human resources consultant; b. Detroit, Mar. 9, 1951; d. John David and Evelyn Jane (Krause) H.; m. James Hinkle, Aug. 1976 (div. Mar. 1981); 1 child, Brandon Hinkle. BS in Bus. Edn., Western Mich. U., 1972; MA in Guidance Counseling, Ea. Mich. U., 1973; cert. employee benefits specialist, Wharton Bus. Sch., 1993. Lic. profl. counselor, Mich. With human resources mgmt. dept. Henry Ford Health Sys., Detroit, 1975-95; human resources mgmt. cons., owner Hoben & Assocs., Inc., Bloomfield Hills, Mich., 1993—. Author seminar workbooks, 1994. Mem. ACA, Mich. Counselors Assn., Mich. Mental Health Counselor's Assn., Mich. Mental Health Counselors Assn. (bd. dirs. 1995). Home and Office: Hoben & Assocs Inc 1234 S Timberview Tr Bloomfield Hills MI 48304

HOBER, NADINE M., pediatric nurse; b. Norman, Okla., Aug. 21, 1957; d. Francis Andrew and Lorena Jean (Pristash) H. BSN, U. Okla., 1980, MSN, 1993; Cert. Pediat. NursePractitioner, U. Colo., 1984. Cert. Controlling Aggression in Patients Environment; BLS AHA, Pediat. ALS; cert. pediat. nurse practitioner ANA; Tex. advanced nurse practitioner; advanced RN, Okla. Intern Aurora (Colo.) Humana Hosp., 1983, Plan de Salud, Fort Lupton, Colo., 1983; intern adolescent clinic Children's Hosp. Okla., Oklahoma City, 1984, intern cardiovascular clinic, 1992; intern health promotion disease prevention Brookwood Med. Ctr., Oklahoma City, 1984-85; pediat. nurse practitioner Brookwood Pediatrics, Oklahoma City, 1984-85; registered relief charge nurse II maternal-child health unit, asst. in-patient daycare facility, preceptor osteopathic residency program Hillcrest Med. Ctr., Oklahoma City, 1984-86; pediat. nurse practitioner Pediat. and Adolescent Medicine, Oklahoma City, 1986-87, Pediat. Assocs., Oklahoma City, 1987-88; assoc. pediat. faculty, pediat. nurse practitioner Children's Hosp. Okla., pub. health nurse practitioner Okla. State Dept. Health State of Okla., Oklahoma City, 1988-93; pediatric nurse practitioner Pediatrics, Yukon, Okla., 1993; quality assurance, employee health nurse, clin. nurse mgr., personnel privileging com., supr. LPN licensure probationary period, coord. adminstrv. tng Drug Recovery, Inc., Oklahoma City, 1994-95; pediatric nurse practitioner Med-Nat., Inc., San Antonio, 1995—; pub. health nurse practitioner Cmty. Coun. Ctrl. Okla. pediat. program Variety Health Ctr., Hope Ctr. Health Clinic, Emerson Alternative Teen Parent Program, 1988-95; pub. health nurse practitioner WIC/Nutrition Svcs. program nurse cons., 1988-95, mem. com. Women's, Infant, Children Fed. Supplemental Food & Nutrition Program State Fed. Regulation Plan FYY, 1991; vol. pediat. nurse practitioner Health for Friends, Norman, Okla., 1994-95; preceptor physician's asst. Gen. Leonard Wood Army Commd. Hosp., Fort Leonard, Mo., mem. audit com., chairperson med. forms Okla. Dept. mental Health and Substance Abuse Svcs., 1995; mem. pediat. high risk com. Okla. State Dept. Health; chairperson English/Spanish medication label com. Cmty. Coun. Ctrl. Okla. Pediat. Program, 1992, ambulatory pediat. clinic policies and procedures com., 1991-92, chariperson patient handout com., 1990-92, mem. infant and pediat. high-risk/at-risk com., 1990-92, quality improvement com., 1990-92, chairperson infant and pediat. high-risk/at-risk tracking program, 1991-92; mem. primary care task force com. Children's Hosp. Okla., Oklahoma City, 1988-89, chairperson pediat. out-patient telephone triage, 1988-89; presenter in field. Mem. Nat. Assn. Clin. Nurse Specialists, Nat. Assn. Pediat. Nurses and Assoc. Practitioners (nat. chpt., officer nominating com. 1990 Okla. chpt.), Okla. Nurse Practitioner Assn., Sigma Theta Tau (Beta Delta chpt.). Democrat. Episcopalian. Home: 700-B Curtis Dr Rolla MO 65401 Office: Gen Leonard Wood Army Commd Hosp 10 Freedom Dr Fort Leonard Wood MO 65473

HOBERECHT, REYNOTTA, school system administrator; b. Mattoon, Wis., Mar. 26, 1938; d. Laurence Herman and Magdalena Evelina (Waidelich) Jahnke; m. Hal G. Hoberecht, Sept. 19, 1970; 1 child, Marc. BS, U. Wis., 1961; MA, U. San Francisco, 1978. Tchr. Travis (Calif.) Unified Schs., 1971-95, adminstrv. asst., 1995—; participant Unidad de Paleontologia Expdn., Las Hoyas, Spain, 1992. Ecosystems project award Travis Sch. Bd., 1993. Mem. Calif. Tchrs. Assn. (treas. 1994-96, sec. 1967-68).

HOBERMAN, RUTH SARAH, English literature educator; b. New Haven, Conn., Aug. 30, 1951; d. Henry Don H. and Miriam (Schine) Elkin; m. Richard Sylvia, Feb. 25, 1986; 1 child, Madeline. BA, Oberlin Coll., 1973; MA, Columbia U., 1977, PhD, 1984. Prof. English Ea. Ill. U., Charleston, 1984—. Author: Modernizing Lives, 1987; co-author: The McGraw Hill Guide to World Literature, 1987. Chair Women's Studies Coun., Ea. Ill. Coun., 1988-89. Mem. Modern Lang. Assn., Soc. for Study of Narrative Lit., Midwest Modern Lang. Assn., LWV (bd. dirs. Coles County chpt. 1995—). Office: Ea Ill U English Dept Charleston IL 61920

HOBSON, KAREN, textiles executive; b. L.A., Feb. 28, 1950; d. Robert James and Jean Marion (Shaw) Waller; m. Stephen Lee Hobson, June 28, 1970; children: Matthew F., Andrew S. BA, Calif. State U., 1974. Mgr. Bullocks, Calif., 1974-77; buyer Kling Kinsler, Calif., 1979-81; sales and merch. Traci Lynn, Calif., 1981-87; nat. sales mgr. Little Trotter, Calif., 1987-89, Great Escape, Calif., 1989-93; v.p. merch. Cherokee Apparel, Calif., 1993-94; owner KGB Clothing Co., Huntington Beach, Calif., 1995—. Home: 319 18th St Huntington Beach CA 92648 Office: KGB Clothing Co 18281 Gothard St #110 Huntington Beach CA 92648

HOCHBERG, AUDREY G., state legislator; b. Stamford, Conn., June 26, 1933; m. Herbert Hochberg; children: Carol, Brenda, Judith. BA in Econs. magna cum laude, Radcliffe Coll., 1955. Legislator dist # 8 Westchester County, 20 yrs.; mem. N.Y. State Assembly, 1992—, mem. edn., social svcs., energy, local govts., transp. coms.; minority leader Westchester County Bd. Legislators, 1976-79; chair Westchester County Criminal Justice Coord. Council, 1980-82; mem. Westchester County Task Force on Jail Overcrowding, 1980-92; co-chair Spl. Commns. Additional Revenues and Reducing Expenditures, 1990-92; bd. dirs. Hudson Valley Health Sys. Agy.; mem. task force on Corrections Overcrowding, Westchester Health Planning Coun., Westchester County Bd. of Health; mem. adv. bd. N.Y. State Cmty. Affairs. Bd. dirs. Boy's and Girls' Glub New Rochelle, WESCOP. Recipient Woman of Yr. award NOW, 1973. Mem. Phi Beta Kappa. Office: NY State Assembly State Capitol Albany NY 12224

HOCHLERIN, DIANE, pediatrician, educator; b. N.Y.C., Feb. 4, 1942; d. William J. and Bertha Hochlerin. BS, Bklyn. Coll., 1958; MD, Med. Coll. Pa., 1962. Diplomate Am. Bd. Pediats. Intern Albert Einstein Hosp., Phila., 1966-67; resident Phila. Gen. Hosp., 1967-69; attending pediatrician St. Luke's Roosevelt Hosp., N.Y.C., 1969—; clin. assoc. prof. pediats. Columbia U., N.Y.C., 1969—; asst. attending physician Cath. Med. Ctr., N.Y.C., 1993—; mem. courtesy staff Beth Israel, 1995—; faculty advisor Adelphi U., N.Y.C., 1994. Fellow Am. Acad. Pediats.; mem. N.Y. State Med. Soc., County Med. Soc. Home and Office: 305 E 86th St Apt 20rw New York NY 10028-4754

HOCHSCHILD, CARROLL SHEPHERD, medical equipment and computer company executive, educator; b. Whittier, Calif., Mar. 31, 1935; d. Vernon Vero and Effie Corinne (Hollingsworth) Shepherd; m. Richard Hochschild, July 25, 1959; children: Christopher Paul, Stephen Shepherd. BA in Internat. Rels., Pomona Coll., 1956; Teaching credential U. Calif., Berkeley, 1957; MBA, Pepperdine U., 1985; cert. in fitness instrn., U. Calif., Irvine, 1988. Cert. elem. tchr., Calif. elem. tchr. Oakland (Calif.) Pub. Schs., 1957-58, San Lorenzo (Calif.) Pub. Schs., 1958-59, Pasadena (Calif.) Pub. Schs., 1959-60, Huntington Beach (Calif.) Pub. Schs., 1961-63, 67-68; adminstrv. asst. Microwave Instruments, Corona del Mar, Calif., 1968-74; co-owner Hoch Co., Corona del Mar, 1978—. Rep. Calif. Tchrs. Assn., Huntington Beach, 1962-63. Mem. AAUW, P.E.O. (projects chmn. 1990-92, corr. sec. 1992-94, chpt. pres. 1994-95), Internat. Dance-Exercise Assn., NAFE, ASTD (Orange County chpt.), Assistance League Newport-Mesa. Republican. Presbyterian. Clubs: Toastmistress (corr. sec. 1983), Jr. Ebell (fine arts chmn. Newport Beach 1966-67).

HOCK, JOANNE MEANS, film director, cinematographer; b. Charlotte, N.C., Sept. 11, 1958; d. William Edward and Bonnalyn (Means) H.; m. Randy Fulp, Aug. 31, 1985 (div. July 1990). BA, U. N.C., 1981. Promotions dir. WCHL Radio, Chapel Hill, N.C., 1981-82; creative dir. Highland Advt., Winston Salem, N.C., 1982-83; prodr., dir. WCNC-TV - Group W, Charlotte, N.C., 1983-87; writer, prodr. Archdale Advt., Charlotte, 1987-90, creative dir., 1990-92; dir., cinematographer Bridge Prodns., Charlotte, 1993—. Recipient Addy award Advt. Club, Charlote, 1989, Telly award TV Advt., 1994. Mem. Charlotte Film and Video Assn. (bd. dirs., info. dir. 1993—). Home: 2015 Club Rd Charlotte NC 28205 Office: Bridge Prodns 420 W 5th St Charlotte NC 28202

HOCKETT, SHERI LYNN, radiologist; b. Cleburne, Tex., Apr. 20, 1953; d. Dale and Rosamond (Prater) Hockett; BA, So. Meth. U., 1974; MD, Southwestern Med. Sch., 1978; m. David Alexander Campbell, Apr. 22, 1978; children: Courtney Michelle, Jonathan David. Resident diagnostic radiology St. Paul Hosp., Dallas, 1978-81, chief resident, 1980-81; fellow, 1981-82; chmn. dept. radiology Baylor Med. Ctr. Garland, Tex. Diplomate Am. Bd. Radiology. Mem. Am. Assn. Women Radiologists, Am. Coll. Radiology, Radiol. Soc. N.Am., Tex. Radiol. Soc., AMA, Dalls-Ft. Worth Radiol. Soc. Office: 2300 Marie Curie Dr Garland TX 75042-5706

HODAPP, SHIRLEY JEANIENE, curriculum administrator; b. Uniontown, Pa., July 10, 1934; d. James Sylvester and Nellie Mae (Kennedy) Amos; children: Holly Hodapp Vining, Curtis, David, Gordon. BS in Elem. Edn., Otterbein Coll., 1956; MEd, Wright State U., 1973; EdS, U. Toledo, 1990. Cert. elem. tchr., local supt., Ohio. Tchr. 3d grade Elyria (Ohio) City Schs., 1955-56; tchr. 2d grade Beavercreek Local Schs., Xenia, Ohio, 1956-57; tchr. elem. Xenia City Schs., 1965-73; ednl. facilitator Wright State U., Dayton, Ohio, 1973-74; adminstr. Marion S. Kinsey PreSch., Xenia, 1974-79; adminstr. elem. Northeastern Local Schs., Defiance, Ohio, 1979-85; supr. elem. Defiance County Bd. Edn., 1985-92, dir. curriculum and related svcs., 1992-94; nat. cons. ITE Ednl. Consulting, 1995—; adj. prof. Defiance Coll., 1985-93, U. Toledo, 1989, N.W. Tech. Coll., Archbold, Ohio, 1989-90, Bowling Green State U., 1994; dir. Little Gnat Kindergarten Readiness program, Babson Park Elem. Sch., 1996—; cons. in field. Author: Learning About Our World-Germany, 1993, Integrated Thematic Experiences, Implementation Guide, 1994; author and editor: Solving The Puzzles of Early Childhood, 1986, Integrated Thematic Experiences, Vol. I, 1993; contbr. articles to profl. jours. Chmn. Tng. Ohio's Parents for Success Program, Defiance County, 1989-92; mem. Early Childhood Intervention Collaborative, Defiance County, 1988-92, Four County Early Childhood Adv. Coun., Archbold, 1986-90; host Ohio Coop. Ext. Svc. Internat. Exch. Program, Defiance, 1990; chmn. Defiance 2000 Sch. Readiness Fair, 1994; coord. Lake Wales Pub. Libr. Time to Rhyme Presch. Summer Program, 1995; bd. dirs. Lake Wales Cmty. Theatre, 1995—; presch. planning com. Babson Park Elem. Sch., 1995—; corr. sec. Fla. Fedn. Music Clubs, 1995—; vol. dir. Little Gnat Program, Babson Park Elem. Sch. Martha Holden Jennings grantee; named Early Childhood Advocate of Yr., Defiance Assn. for Edn. Young Children, 1988, Leader of Lang. Arts Support Groups in Ohio, Ohio Dept. Edn., 1990. Mem. ASCD, AAUW, Nat. Coun. Tchrs. Social Studies, Nat. Coun. Tchrs. Math., Nat. Assn. for Edn. of Young Children, Polk Coun. for Edn. of Young Children, Assn. Childhood Edn. Internat., Nat. Fedn. Music Clubs. Home: 48 W Johnson Ave Lake Wales FL 33853

HODEL, MARY ANNE, library director; b. St. Louis, Aug. 12; d. William George and Florence Marie (Betz) H.; children: Courtney Hodel Denham, Christian Hodel Denham. BA, U. Wis., 1968; MLS, Catholic U., 1973. Project libr. TRACOR-JITCO, Rockville, Md., 1973-74; from project mgr. to database mgr. Nat. Resources Libr. U.S. Dept. of Interior, Washington, 1974-77; cataloger USAF Base Libr., Ramstein, Germany, 1977-79; from project libr. to automation libr. Law Libr. Georgetown U., Washington, 1984-85, automation libr. Law Libr., 1985-91; chief state libr. resource ctr. Enoch Pratt Free Libr., Balt., 1991-95; dir. Ann Arbor (Mich.) Dist. Libr., 1995—; mem. Network Coord. Coun. Md. Librs., 1991-95; mem. Sailor implementation group, 1992-95, grants and devel. task force liaison, 1993-95. Mem. ALA, Am. Assn. Law Librs. (chair innovative interfaces users com. 1988-89, editor innovative interfacers survey 1989, program coord. ann. meeting 1987), Pub. Libr. Assn. (sys. sect. v.p./pres.-elect 1994-95, pres. 1995—), Md. Assn. Profl. Libr. Adminstrs., Md. Libr. Assn. (del. to ALA legis. day 1992, co-chair tech. interest group 1994, conf. planning com. 1993, 94, program coord. 1994), Law Librs. Soc. Washington (program coord. 1989, 90, chair innovative interfaces users workshop 1989, pres. acad. spl. interest sect. 1988-89, rec. sec. 1989-91). Home: 1881 Snowberry Ridge Rd Ann Arbor MI 48103 Office: 343 S 5th Ave Ann Arbor MI 48104

HODGE, ANN LINTON, artist; b. Long Beach, Calif., Aug. 24, 1934; d. Mills Schuyler and Irma Jean (Linn) Hodge; m. Quentin Conitz Becker, Dec. 19, 1968 (dec. May 1978); children: Susan Jean Becker Pedersen, Kathryn Ann Becker Michlitsch, Deborah Rena Becker Lippert, Naomi Ruth, David Mills, Sharon Elizabeth Becker Glutting; m. Glenn Julian Erickson, Dec. 3, 1994. Student, U. So. Calif., Long Beach, Carroll N. Jones Jr.'s Sch. Fine Arts, Stowe, Vt., 1990-92. Fine arts portrait artist individual commns. Whittier and Long Beach, Calif., 1958-68; mural artist for local businesses Whittier and Long Beach, 1958-68; fine arts portrait artist individual commns. Mandan & Bismarck, N.D., 1968—; instr. basic drawing and advanced portraiture The Renaissance Palette Sch. Fine Arts, Mandan, 1970—; adj. prof. basic drawing Bismarck State Coll., Mandan, 1996—; ofcl. state portrait artist Rough Rider Hall of Fame, N.D. State Capital, Bismarck, 1994—; judge art show Glen Ullin (N.D.) Art Assn., 1995; guest lectr. art Shiloh Christian Sch., Bismarck, 1988, Hughes Jr. H.S., Bismarck, 1996. Portraits on display on Internet, 1995—; represented at Gary's Gallery II, Scottsdale, Ariz., 1994—. Bible tchr., Bismarck, 1980's. Address: The Renaissance Pallette 1008 6th Ave NW Mandan ND 58554-2407

HODGE, KATHERINE RHODES, retired school guidance counselor; b. Norfolk, Va., Oct. 17, 1928; d. E. Weldon and Mary (Eaton) Rhodes; m. Kenneth D. Hodge, June 13, 1949; children: Jeffrey M., Judith M. BA, Coll. William and Mary, 1948; MEd, SUNY, Buffalo, 1970. Cert. secondary tchr., Va.; cert. secondary tchr. guidance counselor, N.Y. Tchr. French and English, Norfolk County Schs., Norfolk, 1948-53; tchr. English Clarence (N.Y.) Sch. Sys., 1966-68, guidance counselor, 1969-86; ret., 1986; co-writer Western N.Y. Vocat. Guidance Program, Buffalo, 1982-84. Edn. dir., observer chmn. LWV Moore County, N.C., 1988—, pres., 1991-93; budget chmn. LWV N.C., 1994; vol. guardian ad litem Moore County, 1989—; clk. of session West End (N.C.) Presbyn. Ch., 1994-96; bd. dirs. Ruth Pauley Lecture Series, 1995—. Mem. AAUW, Moore County Hist. Assn., Keep Moore County Beautiful, PEO, Phi Beta Kappa, Kappa Delta Pi, Alpha Delta Kappa, Pi Beta Phi. Home: 1066 Seven Lakes N West End NC 27376

HODGE, KATHLEEN DEVAULT, artist; b. Providence, Nov. 25, 1956; d. Philip Allan and Elizabeth Ann (Flynn) H.; m. John Spencer DeVault, May 19, 1990. AA, RI Jr. Coll., 1976; student, RI Sch. Design, 1976-78; BFA, Swain Sch. Design, 1980. Artist in residence Rocky Mountain Nat. Park, 1994. One person exhbns. include Sarah Doyle Gallery Brown U., Providence, 1992, Gallery 401 Jewish Cmty. Ctr., Providence, 1992, Cavanagh Gallery, Providence Coll., Providence, 1992, Po Gallery, Providence, 1994; executed mural Hasbro Children's Mus., Providence, 1995. Home: 47 Washington St Warren RI 02885

HODGE, KATHLEEN O'CONNELL, academic administrator; b. Balt., Dec. 26, 1948; d. William Walsh and Loretto Marie (Wittek) O'Connell; m. Vern Milton Hodge, Apr. 8, 1972; children: Shea, Ryan. BS, Calif. State U., Fullerton, 1971, MS, 1975; postgrad., U. So. Calif., 1974, U. Calif., Irvine, 1977-84. Cert. marriage and family therapist. Counselor Saddleback Coll., Mission Viejo, Calif., 1975-87, prof. of psychology, speech, 1975-87, dean of continuing edn., cmty. svcs., dean emeritus inst., 1987-95, vice chancellor, 1995—; accreditation liaison officer Saddleback Coll., 1986; mem. adv. bd. Nat. Issues Forum, Calif., 1985, 87, Saddleback Coll. Community Services, 1984, Access and Aspirations U. Calif., Irvine, 1979. Author: (workbook) Assessment of Life Learning, 1978; editor emeritus: Flavors in Time Anthology of Literature, 1992. Mem. Calif. Community Coll. Counselors Assn. (region coord. 1987), Calif. Tchrs. Assn., Am. Assn. Women Community and Jr. Colls., Assn. Marriage Family Therapists, C.C. Educators of Older Adults (pres. 1990-92). Democrat. Roman Catholic. Home: 4011 Calle Juno San Clemente CA 92673-2616 Office: Saddleback Coll 28000 Marguerite Pky Mission Viejo CA 92692-3635

HODGE, MARTHA ELIZABETH (BETSY HODGE), investment company executive; b. Phila., Dec. 30, 1950; d. Harry Colvin and Jeannette M. (Hartwell) Taylor; m. Thomas H. Hodge, July 2, 1971; 1 child, Jeannette E. Student, Phila. Coll. of Textiles & Science, Phila., 1990—. Telecommunications mgr. Miller Anderson & Sherrerd, West Conshohocken, Pa., 1985-89; asst. treas./sec., mgr. gen. affairs LTCB-MAS Investment Mgmt., Inc., West Conshohocken, Pa., 1989—. Office: LTCB-MAS Investment Mgmt Inc 1 Tower Brg Ste 1000 West Conshohocken PA 19428

HODGE, MARY GRETCHEN FARNAM, manufacturing company distributor, manager and executive; b. DeFuniak Springs, Fla., Sept. 24, 1943; d. Thomas Dewey and Mary Catherine (Mixon) Farnam; m. Spessard L. Hodge, Apr. 28, 1962; children: Jennifer Robin, Monica Leigh Hodge Schulz, Stephanie Lea Hodge Glascock. Student, Orlando Coll.; grad., Citizens' Police Acad., Maitland, Fla., 1996. Adminstrv. asst. The Cameron and Barkley Co., Orlando, Fla., 1961-68, office mgr. Machine Tool div., 1975-76; mgr. Frazer Machinery and Supply Co., Orlando, 1976—, sec.-treas., 1988—. Pioneered effort to establish parent support groups for gifted edn., Seminole County, 1979; sec. Parent of Gifted Edn., Seminole County, 1980-87; mem. adv. bd. Exceptional Student Edn., Seminole City, Fla., 1980-87; chairperson Maitland (Fla.) Centennial Founders Bd., 1985; tour guide Orlando Opera Guild, Winter Park, Fla., 1985; celebrity waitress Leukemia Soc. Am., Orlando, 1986; co-chairperson Project Graduation Lyman High Sch., Seminole County, 1986—; chairperson Alzheimers Resource Auction Dinner, Winter Park, 1987, 88, pres., bd. dirs. 1988-89, ex-officio bd. dirs. 1989-90, 96—; v.p. bd. dirs. Maitland Civic Ctr., 1993-94, pres. bd. dirs. 1994-95, 95-96; v.p. Maitland Woman's Club, 1994-95, 95-96, 96-97, mem. Cultural Corridor Com., Maitland, 1994, 95, 96; bd. dirs. non-profit Showcase Group, Maitland Hist. Soc.; co-chair Am. Heart Assn. Lock-up Vol., 1995-96; vol. Golden Orch. and Chorus Aux., Maitland/So. Sem. C. of C., Over the Rainbow Auction, 1995, 96. Recipient appreciation plaque Dividends, Seminole City, 1974-75, cert. appreciation Maitland Civic Ctr., 1986, Alzheimer Resource Ctr., Winter Park, 1987, Pres.'s Gavel, 1989, 96, Northam award, 1995. Mem. Am. Machine Tool Ditbrs., Soc. Mfg. Engrs., Maitland Woman's Club (several offices 1970—). Democrat. Methodist.

HODGE-MOHR, J. RENEA, marketing communications professional; b. Cleburne, Tex., Nov. 16, 1959; d. W. H. and Francea G. (Winnett) H.; 1 child, Daniel Stallings. BS in Graphic Design, Lamar U., 1981. Designer Helena Labs., Beaumont, Tex., 1982-87; sales assocl Computer Dimensions, Beaumont, 1987-90; publs. dir. Enviro Contractors, Beaumont, 1990-91; self-employed JR & Assocs., Nederland, Tex., 1991-92; dir. mktg. comms. CDR Environ., Houston, 1992-94; dir. investor rels. N-Viro/Synagro, Houston, 1992-94; proprietor JR & Assocs., Houston, 1995—; cons. Animal Transp. Assn., 1995-96; newsletter pub. Covenant House Tex., Houston, 1995-96. Mem. Am. Bus. Women's Assn. (pres. 1995-96), Profl. Environ. Mktg. Assn. (newsletter editor 1995-96), Bus. Mktg. Assn. (newsletter editor 1995-96). Office: JR & Assocs PO Box 11084 Spring TX 77391

HODGEN, LAURIE DEE, geologist, editor; b. Portland, Oreg., July 28, 1949; d. Charles Donald and Verla Lucille (Walker) H.; m. Malcolm Mallory Clark, Sept. 1, 1979; 1 child, Kelly Donald. BA, U. of the Pacific, 1971; cert. continuous improvement/qual. mgmt., U. Calif., Santa Cruz, 1994. Geologic field asst. U.S. Geol. Survey, Menlo Park, Calif., 1972, geologist, 1972-75, geologic map editor, 1975-85, supervisory geologist, 1985-91, asst. br. chief, 1991-95, geologic map editor, 1995—. Arch., builder personal residence, 1981-88. Asst. handicapped riders Westwind 4H, Los Altos Hills, Calif., 1987—. Recipient Blue Pencil award Nat. Assn. Govt. Communicators, 1991, Cert. Recognition Br. Western Tech. Reports, 1995; alumni fellow U. of the Pacific, 1983. Mem. Assn. Earth Sci. Editors. Home: 26135 Altadena Dr Los Altos Hills CA 94022 Office: US Geol Survey 345 Middlefield Rd Menlo Park CA 94025

HODGES, ANN, television editor, newspaper columnist; b. McCamey, Tex., Sept. 7, 1928; d. Ernest Cornelius and Margaret Isabel (Wood) Haynes; m. Cecil Ray Hodges, July 2, 1954 (div. Nov. 1974); children: Craig McNeley, Elizabeth Ann. B.J., U. Tex., 1948. Reporter, Houston Chronicle, 1948-51; society editor The News, Mexico City, 1951-52; reporter Houston Chronicle, 1952-54, TV editor, columnist, 1962—; mem. adv. bd. U. Miami TV Ctr. for Advancement of Modern Media, 1994—; U.S. Juror Banff TV Festival, 1995. Mem. Critics Consensus (dir. 1965-75), TV Critics Assn. (founder, exec. bd., v.p., pres.). Club: Houston Press (pres. 1967-68). Office: Houston Chronicle Texas And Travis St Houston TX 77002

HODGES, ELIZABETH SWANSON, educator; b. Anoka, Minn., Apr. 7, 1924; d. Henry Otto and Louise Isabel (Holiday) Swanson; m. Allen Hodges, June 27, 1944; children: Nancy Elizabeth, Susan Kathleen, Jane Ellen, Sara Louise. BA cum laude, Regis Coll., Denver, 1966; postgrad., U. No. Colo., 1966-79, Valdosta State U., 1979-81. Cert. secondary edn., hosp./homebound, learning disabilities, Colo., Ga., Ariz. Vol. emergency St. Anthony's Hosp., Denver, 1960-64; v.p., tutor St. Elizabeth's Adult Tutorial, Denver, 1964-69; hosp./homebound tchr. Liberty County Sch. System, Hinesville, Ga., 1979-87; ednl. tutor Colo. River Indian Tribes, Parker, Ariz., 1986-87; vol. Twin Cities Community Hosp., Templeton, Calif., 1987-89, Guardian Ad Litem Cir. Ct. 5th Dist. Fla., 1992—, Munroe Regional Med. Ctr., Ocala, Fla., 1991-92; cons., tutor Sylvan Learning Ctr., Ocala, 1990—. Reporter Trinity Triangle Newsletter, Ocala, 1992—. Mem. AAUW (chmn. internat. affairs 1991-92). Democrat. Roman Catholic. Home and Office: 4544 SE 13th St Ocala FL 34471-3241

HODGES, KAREN CAPRILES, museum curator; b. Willemstad, The Netherlands Antilles, Nov. 4, 1941; came to U.S., 1958; d. Edwin Capriles and Florence (Halpern) Delvalle; m. Robert Mitchell Hodges, Dec. 22, 1962; children: Allison Edwina, Patrick Christopher. BA, Wellesley Coll., 1962; MSW, Simmons Sch. Social Work, 1964; MA in Art History, Ariz. State U., 1988. Tutor, lectr. Math. Learning Ctr., Ariz. State U., Tempe, 1981-83; curatorial asst. Phoenix Art Mus., 1983-86, asst. curator, 1986-91, assoc. curator, 1992—, acting curator fashion design, 1996—; panel mem. Phoenix Art Commn., 1990, 95, Ariz. Commn. on Arts, 1992. Wellesley Coll. scholar, 1962. Mem. Am. Assn. Mus., Coll. Art Assn. Office: Phoenix Art Mus 1625 N Central Ave Phoenix AZ 85004-1624

HODGE-SPENCER, CHERYL ANN, orthodontist; b. Dorchester, Mass., Apr. 1, 1952; d. Herbert Thomas and Edwina Catherine (Morey) Hodge; m. John Lawrence Spencer, June 10, 1978; children: Devin Thomas, Ian Nicholas. BS in Biology cum laude, Boston Coll., 1974; DMD, Tufts Sch. Dental Medicine, 1977; MPH, Harvard U. Sch. Pub. Health, 1981; Cert. in Orthodontics, Harvard Dental Sch., 1983. Orthodontist Brockton/Bridgewater, Mass., 1984—; orthodontic cons. Mass. Hosp. Sch., Canton, Mass., 1990—; vice chmn. Bd. of Investment, Bridgewater Savs. Bank, 1989-92; asst. coach Duxbury Youth Hockey Bantam Team, 1993-94. Lt. Dental Corps USN, 1977-80. Recipient Johnson & Johnson Dentistry award, 1977. Mem. Am. Assn. Orthodontists, Mass. Dental Soc., South Shore Dist. Dental Soc. (sec. 1990-92, peer rev. bd. 1990-92), Northeastern Soc. Orthodontists, Harvard Club Boston, Harvard Soc. Advancement Orthodontics, Metro South C. of C., Rotary (bd. dirs. charitable and ednl. fund 1989-92), Pierre Fouchard Acad., Ma. Amateur Hockey Assn. (intermediate patched hockey coach). Roman Catholic. Office: 572 Pleasant St Brockton MA 02401-2515

HODGES-ROBINSON, CHETTINA M., nursing administrator; b. Roosevelt, N.Y., Mar. 12, 1963; d. Clifford and Janice (Revis) Hodges-Jones; m. Darrell K. Robinson, Mar. 17, 1991. BSN, NYU, 1986. Cert. med.-surg. nurse basic life support and advanced cardiac life support. Staff nurse NYU Med. ctr., N.Y.C., 1986-87, Christ Hosp., Jersey City, 1986-87; cardiothoracic recovery rm. and post-anesthesia nurse, staff nurse Lenox Hill Hosp., N.Y.C., 1987-94; asst. nurse mgr. critical care/intensive/coronary care unit Good Samaritan Hosp., West Islip, L.I., N.Y., 1994—; staff nurse cardiovasc. ICU U. Hosp. at Stony Brook, N.Y., 1995—; field nurse Staff Builders, Medford, N.Y., 1995—; asst. head nurse Jewish Home and Hosp. for the Aged, Bronx, N.Y., 1996—. Mem. Luth. Ch. of the Good Shepherd, Roosevelt, N.Y. Mem. ANA, N.J. Nurses Assn., Black Nurses Assn. (L.I. chpt.), Zeta Alpha Beta. Home: 119 S 28th St Wyandanch NY 11798-2813

HODGESS, ERIN MARIE, statistics educator; b. Pitts., Nov. 12, 1960; d. Edwin E. and Justine J. (Plazak) H. BS in Econs., U. Dayton, 1981; MA in Econs., U. Pitts., 1987; MS in Stats., Temple U., 1989, PhD in Stats., 1995. Econ. rsch. analyst Mellon Bank, NA, Pitts., 1981-85; programmer Techalloy Co., Inc., Rahns, Pa., 1985-86; programmer analyst The Linpro Co., Berwyn, Pa., 1986-87, Jones Apparel Group, Bristol, Pa., 1987-88; programming cons. various cos., Phila., 1988-89; teaching asst. Temple U., Phila., 1990-92, adj. instr., 1992-94, group leader grad. asst. tng. workshop, 1992; asst. prof. U. Houston-Downtown, 1994—; spkr. Temple U.-Rutgers U. Stats. Day, Brunswick, N.J., 1988; presenter Statis. Sci. Conf., Rider U. Lawrenceville, N.J., 1995. Contbr. articles to profl. jours., including Jour. Statis. Sci., Linear Algebra and Its Applications. Fellow Temple U., 1988-90, grantee, 1994. Mem. Am. Statis. Assn. (presenter winter meeting Raleigh, N.C. 1995), Soc. Indsl. and Applied Math., Inst. Math. Stats. (presenter 4th matrix workshop McGill U., Montreal Que., Can. 1995), Intertel Internat., Mensa. Democrat. Roman Catholic. Home: 9449 Briar Forest Dr Apt 3544 Houston TX 77063-1048 Office: U Houston-Downtown One Main St Houston TX 77002

HODGSON, JANE ELIZABETH, obstetrician and gynecologist, consultant; b. Crookston, Minn., Jan. 23, 1915; d. Herbert and Adelaide (Marin) H.; m. Frank Walter Quattlebaum, Feb. 22, 1940; children: Gretchen, Nancy. BS, Carleton Coll., 1934, DSc (hon.), 1994; MD, U. Minn., 1939, MS in Ob-Gyn., 1947. Diplomate Am. Bd. Ob.-Gyn. Fellow Mayo Clinic, Rochester, Minn., 1941-44; pvt. practice in ob-gyn. St. Paul, 1947-72; med. dir. Preterm Clinic, Washington, 1972-74; med. dir. fertility control clinic St. Paul Ramsey Med. Ctr., 1974-79; med. dir. Planned Parenthood Minn., St. Paul, 1980-82, Midwest Health Ctr. Women, Mpls., 1981-83, Women's Health Ctr., Duluth, Minn., 1981-84; mem. staff Women's Health Ctr., Duluth, 1986—, also bd. dirs.; ostetrician/gynecologist Project Hope, Grenada, West Indies, 1984; vis. prof. ob-gyn. project hope Zheijiang Med. Sch., Hangzhou, People's Republic of China, 1985-86; clin. assoc. prof. ob-gyn. U. Minn., Mpls., 1986—; vis. med. educator Project Hope, Cairo, 1979-80; vis. prof. dept. ob-gyn. U. Calif., San Francisco, 1983. Editor: Abortion & Sterilization, 1981; contbr. 54 articles to profl. jours. Bd. dirs. Genesis II Women, Mpls., 1988—, Pro Choice Resources, Mpls., 1991—, Wellstone Alliance, Mpls., 1992—. Recipient Ann. Humanitarian award Nat. Abortion Fedn., 1981, Woman Physician of Yr. award Med. Women Minn. Med. Assn., 1983, Ann. Jane Hodgson Reproductive Freedom award Nat. Abortion Rights Action League, 1989, Hanah G. Solomon award Nat. Coun. Jewish Women, 1990, Margaret Sanger award Planned Parenthood Fedn. of Am., 1995, Harold Swanberg award Am. Med. Writer's Assn., 1996. Fellow Am. Coll. Ob-Gyn. (founding); mem. Am. Med. Women's Assn. (E. Blackwell award 1992, Reproductive Health award 1994), Minn. Ob-Gyn. Soc. (pres. 1967), Minn. Med. Assn. (So. Minn. Med. award 1952), Minn. Women's Polit. Caucus (16th Ann. Founding Feminist award 1988), Mayo Clinic Alumni Assn. Home and Office: 1537 Fisk St Saint Paul MN 55117-3415

HODGSON, LYNN MORRISON, marine biologist; b. Atlanta, July 30, 1948; d. Fred Grady Jr. and Florence Kimball (Morrison) H. BS, Coll. of William and Mary, 1970; MS, U. Wash., 1972; PhD, Stanford U., 1979. Asst. rsch. scientist U. Fla., Gainesville, 1979-81; vis. asst. prof. U. Ark., Fayetteville, 1981-82; asst. rsch. scientist Harbor Br. Found., Ft. Pierce, Fla., 1982-85; asst. prof. biology Northern State U., Aberdeen, S.D., 1985-88, chair dept. math. and natural scis., 1988-92, prof. biology, 1989-92; assoc. prof. biology U. Hawaii at West Oahu, Pearl City, 1992-95, prof. biology, 1995—. Contbr. articles to Botanica Marina, Marine Biology, Jour. of Phycology and others. Grantee S.D. Dept. of Water and Natural Resources, 1987-88, Hawaii Natural Areas Reserves, 1990-91, Ednl. Improvement Fund, 1992-93, Hawaii Dept. of Health, 1993-94. Mem. Internat. Phycological Soc., Brit. Phycological Soc., Phycological Soc. of Am. (nominations chair 1986-87), S.D. Acad. Scis. (pres. 1992), Sigma Xi, Kappa Mu Epsilon. Office: U Hawaii at West Oahu 96-043 Ala Ike St Pearl City HI 96782-3366

HODGSON, MARGARET ELLEN, counselor; b. Norwich, Conn., Jan. 3, 1961; d. Joseph C. and Patsy R. (Hayley) Yanish; m. Darryl S. Hodgson, June 4, 1983; children: Joshua D., Trisha L. AA in Psychology, Broward C.C., Hollywood, Fla., 1981; BS in Psychology, Miami Christian Coll., 1983; MA in Counseling, W.Va. Grad. Coll., 1994. Lic. prof. counselor, N.C. Child care counselor Pembroke Christian Acad., Miramar, Fla., 1979-83; sci. tchr. grades 7-12 Pembroke Christian Acad., Miramar, 1983-84; activities asst. Freeport (Ill.) Manor Nursing Ctr., 1985-87; child caregiver T.L.H. Care, Freeport, Ill., 1988-89, South Charleston, W.Va., 1989-92; child therapist YWCA Resolve Family Abuse Program, Charleston, W.Va., 1994-95; tchg. asst. counseling W.Va. Grad. Coll., South Charleston, 1994-95; counselor Youth Focus, Inc., High Point, N.C., 1995—. Mem. ACA, Assn. for Specialists in Group Work, Internat. Assn. for Addictions and Offenders Counselors. Office: Youth Focus Inc 305 N Main St High Point NC 27260

HODGSON, MARY LAPP, counselor; b. Buffalo, N.Y., Apr. 19, 1929; d. John C. and Marjorie B. (Broas) Lapp; m. John Hyland Hodgson, July 21, 1951 (dec. July 1960); children: John M., David C.; m. Edward C. Morin, May 27, 1979 (dec.). BA cum laude, Mt. Holyoke Coll., 1951; MA, Syracuse U., 1962; PhD, SUNY, Buffalo, 1978. Cert. clin. mental health counselor, sex. therapist, clin. hypnotherapist; diplomate Bd. Sexology. Sch. counselor Penfield (N.Y.) Jr. H.S., 1962-64, Jefferson Rd. Elem. Sch., Pittsford, N.Y., 1968-76; counselor Boike Counseling Inc., Rochester, N.Y., 1976—; founder, chair Sexual Abuse Treatment Providers Network, Rochester, 1986-91; bd. dirs. Parent & Child Svcs., Rochester, 1986-92; pres., bd. dirs. Safe Space, Inc., Rochester, 1993—; speaker and lectr. in field, 1975—. Author: (with others) Perspectives on Work and the Family, 1984. Pres. PTA, Lowville, N.Y., 1960-61; co-pres. Home Sch. Coun., Penfield, 1966-67; bd. dirs. YMCA, Webster, N.Y., 1982-86. Mem. ACA, NOW, Rochester Women's Network. Democrat. Office: Boike Counseling Inc 120 Linden Oaks Rochester NY 14625

HODNICAK, VICTORIA CHRISTINE, pediatric nurse; b. Detroit, Dec. 29, 1960; d. Roderick Lewis and Beverly Caroline (Backus) Turner; m. Mark Michael Hodnicak, Sept. 20, 1986; children: Christopher Alan and Matthew Lewis (twins). ADN, Henry Ford C.C., Dearborn, Mich., 1982. RN, Mich., Tenn. Charge nurse, surg. nurse Harper Grace Hosp., Detroit, 1982-86; neonatal nurse St. John Hosp., Detroit, 1986; home care nurse, coord. med. mgmt. Bloomfield Nursing Svcs., Clawson, Mich., 1986-88; coord. pediatric endocrine growth study So. Health Sys., Memphis, 1988-92; nurse specialist, growth study coord. U. Tenn. Med. Group/St. Jude Children's Rsch. Hosp., Memphis, 1992—; home care pediatric nurse Personal Pediatric Nursing Profls., Pontiac, Mich., 1987-88; staff nurse Nancy Kissick's Profl. Nursing Svc., Mt. Clemens, Mich., 1988. Inventor Growth Hormone; new dose form, 1991, Hydrocortisone dose and stress dosing card, 1990; contbr. articles to profl. jours. Mem. Pediatric Endocrinology Nursing Soc. (membership com. 1992), Endocrine Nursing Soc., Human Growth Found., Neurofibromatosis Found., Turner Syndrome Soc., MAGIC Found. Lutheran. Office: Univ Tenn Med Group 50 N Dunlap St Memphis TN 38103-4909

HODNICKI, JILL ANN, historian, researcher; b. Holyoke, Mass., June 22, 1957; d. Edward and Mona H. (Peterhansel) H. BA, Coll. Our Lady of Elms, 1979; MA, U. Mass., 1981. Prospect researcher Mount Holyoke Coll.,

South Hadley, Mass., 1981-92, dir. prospect resch., 1992—, curator South Hadley Canal at 200 Yrs./Art Mus., 1996; instr. art history U. Mass., Amherst, 1981. Curator exhibit Mount Holyoke Coll. Art Mus., 1996. Active Holyoke Hist. Commn., 1991—, chmn., 1992—. Mem. Soc. Archtl. Historians, New England Soc. Archtl. Historians, New England Devel. Rsch. Assn., New England Historic Geneal. Soc., Assn. Profl. Rschrs. Advancement. Roman Catholic. Office: Mount Holyoke Coll Mary Woolley Hall South Hadley MA 01040

HODSON, NANCY PERRY, real estate agent; b. Kansas City, Mo., Nov. 19, 1932; d. Ralph Edward Perry and Juanita (Youmans) Jackman; m. William K. Hodson, Oct. 4, 1974 (div. Jan. 1985); children: Frank Tyler, Lisa Thompson, Suzanne Desforges, Robert Hodson. Student, Pine Manor Jr. Coll., 1950-51, Finch Coll., 1951-53. Cert. real estate agt., Calif.; cert. interior designer. Owner Nancy Perry Hodson Interior Design, L.A. and Newport Beach, Calif., 1974-82; agt. Grubb and Ellis, Newport Beach, 1990, Turner Assocs., Laguna Beach, Calif., 1990-92. Founder U. of Calif. Arboretum, Irvine, 1987, Opera Pacific, Costa Mesa, Calif., 1987; mem. U. of Calif. Rsch. Assocs., Irvine, 1986; pres. Big Canyon Philharm., Newport Beach, 1990; bd. dirs. Jr. Philharm., L.A., 1975-78. Mem. Big Canyon Country Club, L.A. Blue Ribbon 400 (1975-78), Jr. League Garden Club (pres. 1990-91), Big Canyon Garden Club (pres. 1989-91), Inst. of Logopedics (chmn. 30th Anniversary 1965), Guilds of Performing Arts Ctr. Presbyterian.

HOELSCHER, MICHELLE DENISE, accountant; b. Corpus Christi, Tex., July 6, 1970; d. Norbert Dennis and Barbara Annette (Najvar) H. BBA in Acctg., S.W. Tex. State U., 1992. CPA, Tex. Acctg. trainee United Svcs. Automobile Assn., San Antonio, 1993; fin. acct. USAA Life Ins. Co., San Antonio, 1994—. Mem. AICPAs, Tex. Soc. CPAs (San Antonio chpt.). Office: USAA USAA Bldg San Antonio TX 78288

HOELTERHOFF, MANUELA VALI, newspaper editor, critic; b. Hamburg, Germany, Apr. 6, 1949; came to U.S., 1957; d. Heinz Alfons and Olga Christine (Goertz) H. B.A., Hofstra U., 1971; M.A., NYU, 1973. Assoc. editor Arete Pub. Co., Princeton, N.J., 1977-80; editor-in-chief Art and Auction Mag., N.Y.C., 1979-81; arts editor Wall Street Jour., N.Y.C., 1981-89, books editor, 1989—; sr. cons. editor Smart Money Mag., N.Y.C., 1989—. Recipient Pulitzer prize Columbia U., 1983; recipient citation for disting. commentary Am. Soc. Newspaper Editors, 1982, 83. Office: Wall St Jour 200 Liberty St New York NY 10281-1003*

HOELTKE, BETH JUNE, graphic design educator, consultant; b. Columbus, Ind., Dec. 22, 1958; d. William Richard and June Ann (Gilbert) H. BS in Indsl. Tech. Graphic Arts, U. Wis., Stout, 1982, MS in Indsl. Tech. Mng. Edn., 1994. Mgr. Savoy Dixie Press, Lafayette, La., 1982-83; estimating/prodn. mgr. Satterwhite Printing Co., Richmond, Va., 1983-88; customer svc. rep. Printery, Inc., Milw., 1989-91; residential home instr. Willowglen Acad. East, Milw., 1992; instr., cons. John Marshall H.S., Milw., 1992-93; instr., course designer Shorewood (Wis.) H.S., 1993-95; instr., learning disabilities cons. Al Collins Graphic Design Sch., Tempe, Ariz., 1995-96; tchr. Anderson Jr. H.S., 1996—; tech. edn. cons. various high schs., Milw., 1990-95. Vol. caretaker Ronald McDonald House, Milw., 1990-93. Office: Al Collins Graphic Design Sch 1140 S Priest Tempe AZ 85281

HOENICK, RUTH ANN, elementary education educator; b. Sheboygan, Wis., June 1, 1950; d. John C. and Lorraine M. (Manthey) Huige; m. John E. Hoenick, May 31, 1969; children: Kim Katherine, J. Robert. BS in Elem. Edn., U. Wis., Oshkosh, 1978; MEd, Cardinal Stritch Coll., Milw., 1985. Cert. elem. edn. K-6. 1st grade tchr. Shorewood (Wis.) Pub. Schs., 1980-89, 2nd grade tchr., 1989—; dir., pres. Sherman House, Inc., Milw., 1991—; instr. Cardinal Stritch Coll., Milw., 1985—; facilitator, cons. Roots & Wings Parent Workshop, Milw., 1993—; chairperson staff devel., peer coaching, sci. com., mem. instrnl. planning coun. Shorewood Schs., 1989—; facilitator recovering person group Sherman House, Inc., Milw., 1991—. Author, dir. (ptnr. program) Neighborhood Ptnrs., 1989-91; author: (play for children) The Odd Mystery, 1991; composer: We're All the Same, 1993. Com. mem. Sherman Park Cmty. Assn., Milw., 1989—, N.W. Cmty. Assn., Milw., 1991—. Tchr. World candidate Wis. Dept. Instrn., Madison, 1994, 95. Mem. NEA, Wis. Educators Assn., North Shore Educators Assn., Assn. Curriculum and Instrn., Kappa Delta Pi.

HOEY, RITA MARIE, public relations executive; b. Chgo., Nov. 4, 1950; d. Louis D. and Edith M. (Finnemann) Hoey; m. Joseph John Dragonette, Sept. 4, 1982. BA in English and History, No. Ill. U., 1972. Asst. dir. Nat. Assn. Housing and Human Devel., Chgo., 1975; public relations account exec. Weber Cohn & Riley, Chgo., 1975-76; publicity coordinator U.S. Gypsum Co., Chgo., 1976-77; with Daniel J. Edelman, Inc., Chgo., 1977-84, sr. v.p., 1981-84; exec. v.p. Dragonette, Inc., Chgo., 1984-91, pres., 1991—. Mem. Pub. Rels. Soc. Am., Women in Communications. Home: 3416 Cherry Valley Rd Woodstock IL 60098-8173 Office: Dragonette Inc 205 W Wacker Dr Ste 2200 Chicago IL 60606-1215

HOFER, JUDITH K., retail company executive. b. Feb. 16, 1940, Hillsboro, Oreg. d. Frank E. Hofer and Helen K. Cook. BA Oreg. State. U., 1959, BS, Portland State U., 1961. Trainee, buyer, Meier & Frank Dept. Store, Portland, Oreg., 1961-65; v.p., gen. mgr., Clark Jr., Portland, 1966-72; v.p., gen. merchandising mgr. Meier & Frank, Portland, 1972-76; gen. mgr. Emporium-Capwell, San Francisco, 1976-78; exec. v.p. Famous-Barr Stores (subs. The May Co.), 1978-81; pres., CEO Meier & Frank, Portland, Oreg., 1981-83; pres., CEO, May Co., L.A., 1983-86, Famous-Barr Co. (div. May Department Stores Co.), St. Louis, 1986-87, Meier & Frank (div. May Department Stores Co.), Portland, 1988-96; pres., CEO Filene's, Boston, 1996—; bd. dirs. Dial Corp., Phoenix, Key Bank of Oreg., Portland. Bd. dirs. Assn. Portland Progress, 1988-931; bd. Trustees Nat. 4-H 1991, Boy Scouts Am., St. Louis, 1986-88, Downtown St. Louis, 1986-88; trustee Nat. Jewish Hosp. & Asthma Ctr., Denver, 1983-87, City of Hope Hosp., Duarte, Calif., 1984-88, Nat. 4-H Coun., 1990—; bd. counselors Sch. Bus. Administrn. U. So. Calif., L.A., 1984-86. Named one of ten Women of Achievement City of St. Louis, 1980; recipient Spirit of LIfe award City of Hope, L.A., 1985. Mem. Nat. Women's Forum, Fashion Group, Com. of 200, Assn. U. Women, Young Pres.' Orgn. Avocation: antique doll collecting. Office: 426 Washington St Boston MA 02108*

HOFF, ANN M., sales professional; b. Morrison, Ill., June 12, 1958; d. Elmer Boyed and marion (Grill) H. BS in Studio Art, U. Wis., Platteville, 1980; MS in Animal Sci., U. Ariz. Asst. tchr. U. Wis., Platteville, 1978-80; rsch. asst. U. Ariz., Tucson, 1980-83; pharm. salesperson Bristol Myers-Squibb, Tucson, 1983-86; exec. sales rep. Smith Kline Beecham, Tucson, 1986—; staff Primavera Fundraiser, Tucson, 1995; chmn. So. Ariz. Ceramic Artists, Tucson, 1995; main instr. East Side Tae Kwon Do. Ceramics sculptor with numerous exhbns., including: juried shows by So. Ariz. Ceramics Assn., Impressions Gallery, Tucson, 1991 (1st place award), 1992, and 1995; group shows: Invisible Theater, Tucson, 1995, Phoenix Ctr. Visual Arts Gallery, 1995, Art Forms Gallery, Tucson, 1994, 95, Alamo Gallery, Tucson, 1994, 95, U. Ariz. Student Union Gallery, 1992, So. Ill. U., 1991, others. Awards include riding the Res. World Champion Am. Paint Horse, Ft. Worth, 1993, 94, named 6th Novice Amatuer for 1993, Ft. Worth, 1993. Mem. Am. Paint Horse Assn., So. Ariz. Ceramic Artists. Democrat. Presbyterian. Home: 9142 E Indian Hills Tucson AZ 85740

HOFF, JEANNE BRANDT, accounting educator; b. San Francisco, June 30, 1955; d. John Elwood and Mary Helen (Fay) Brandt; divorced; 1 child, Kristin. BS, Golden Gate U., 1978, MBA, 1986. CPA, W.Va., Calif. Staff acct. Hood & Strong CPAs, San Francisco, 1978-79, Blanding & Buchanan, Walnut Creek, Calif., 1979-81; lectr. acctg. Sonoma State U., Rohnert Park, Calif., 1987-93; prof. acctg. Bethany (W.Va.) Coll., 1993—; adj. prof. acctg. Golden Gate U., San Francisco, 1979-87. Mem. Am. Acctg. Assn., W.Va. Soc. CPAs (recruiting & opportunity com. 1995—, edn. com. 1994, 96—), Inst. Internal Auditors (coll. rels. com. 1996—), Inst. Mgmt. Accts., Alpha Xi Delta (faculty advisor 1996—).

HOFFER, ALMA JEANNE, nursing educator; b. Dalhart, Tex., Sept. 15, 1932; d. James A. and Mildred (Zimlich) Koehler; m. John L. Hoffer, Oct. 7, 1954; children: John Jr., James Leo, Joseph V., Jerome P. BS, Bradley U., 1970; MA, W. Va. Coll. Grad. Study Inst., 1975; EdD, Ball State U., 1981, MA, 1986. Reg. Nurse. Staff nurse St Joseph Hosp., South Bend, Ind., 1958-59, Holy Cross Cen. Sch., St Joseph Hosp., South Bend, 1959-63; sch. nurse South Bend Sch. Corp., 1970-72; faculty staff Morris Harvey Coll., Charleston, W.Va., W.Va. Inst. Tech., Montgomery, 1975-76; asst. prof. Ball State U., Ind., 1976-77, Ind. U.-Purdue U., Ft. Wayne, 1977-81; assoc. prof. U. Akron, Ohio, 1981-83, 91—, asst. dean, grad. edn., 1983-90, assoc. prof., 1991-93; prof., chair Dept. of Nursing St. Francis Coll., Fort Wayne, Ind., 1993—; trustee Akron Child Guidance, 1983-88, 89—, chair planning com., 1988; nursing Blick Clin., Akron, 1988; rsch. cons. St. Joseph Hosp., Ohio, 1989; researcher, presenter in field. Contbg. author: Family Health Promotion Theories and Assessment, 1989, Nursing Connections, 1992. Task force mem. Gov. Celeste's Employee Assistance Program for State U. Campuses, Ohio, 1983-84, del. People to People Citizen Amb. Program to Europe, 1988. Mem. ANA, Nat. League for Nursing, Midwest Nursing Rsch. Soc., Transcultural Nursing Assn., Portage Country Club, Tippecanoe Country Club, Sigma Theta Tau. Republican. Roman Catholic. Office: Saint Francis Coll Dept of Nursing Fort Wayne IN 46808

HOFFER, DEBRA HUMES, performing company executive. Exec. dir. Louisville Ballet. Office: Louisville Ballet 315 E Main St Louisville KY 40202*

HOFFER, SHARON MARIE, secondary education educator; b. Dallas, Oct. 18, 1941; d. Bates Lowry and Marie E. (Grady) H. BA in Secondary Edn., U. Mo., Kansas City, 1971, MA in Secondary Edn. (Math), 1976; PhD in Adult and Extension Edn., Tex. A&M U., 1986. Tchr. 7th grade St. Peter's Prince Sch., San Antonio, 1962-64, St. Catherine of Siena Sch., Metairie, La., 1964-66; tchr. 7th, 8th grades Holy Trinity Sch., Kansas City, Mo., 1966-69; tchr. math., music, reading Guardian Angels Sch., Kansas City, 1969-70, St. Peter's Sch., Kansas City, 1971-77; dept. chair, tchr. math. St. Mary's High Sch., Independence, Mo., 1977-80; tchr. math. St. Teresa's Acad., Kansas City, Mo., 1980-81; instr. math. Tex. A&M U., College Station, 1982-86; curriculum-grant writer Pan-Ednl. Inst., Independence, 1987; tchr. math. East Environ. and Agribusiness Magnet High Sch., Kansas City, 1987—. Mem. ASCD, Nat. Coun. Tchrs. Math., Mensa. Roman Catholic. Home: 2819 Campbell St Kansas City MO 64109-1125

HOFFLEIT, ELLEN DORRIT, astronomer; b. Florence, Ala., Mar. 12, 1907; d. Fred and Kate (Sanio) H. A.B., Radcliffe Coll., 1928, M.A., 1932, Ph.D., 1938; D.Sci. (hon.), Smith Coll., 1984. From research asst. to astronomer Harvard Coll. Obs., 1929-56; mathematician Ballistic Research Labs., Aberdeen Proving Ground, Md., 1943-48; tech. expert, 1948-62; lectr. Wellesley Coll., 1955-56; mem. faculty Yale U., 1956—, sr. research astronomer, 1974—; dir. Maria Mitchell Obs., Nantucket, Mass., 1957-78; mem. Hayden Planetarium Com., N.Y.C., 1975-90; editor Meteoritical Soc., 1958-68. Author: Some Firsts in Astronomical Photography, 1950, Yale Bright Star Catalogue, 4th edit., 1982, Astronomy at Yale, 1701-1968, 1992; also rsch. papers. Recipient Caroline Wilby prize Radcliffe Coll., 1938, Grad. Soc. medal, 1964, cert. appreciation War Dept., 1946, alumnae recognition award Radcliffe Coll., 1983, George van Biesbroeck award U. Ariz., 1988, Glover award Dickinson U., 1995; asteroid Dorrit named in her honor, 1987. Fellow AAAS, Meteoritical Soc.; mem. Internat. Astron. Union, Am. Astron. Soc. (Annenberg award 1993), Am. Geophys. Union, Astron. Soc. New Haven (hon.), Am. Assn. Variable Star Observers (hon.), Am. Def. Preparedness Assn., N.Y. Acad. Scis., Conn. Acad. Arts and Scis., Nantucket Maria Mitchell Assn. (hon.), Nantucket Hist. Soc., Yale Peabody Mus. Assocs., Astron. Soc. Pacific, Phi Beta Kappa, Sigma Xi, Harvard Club of So. Conn. Office: Yale U Observatory PO Box 208101 New Haven CT 06520-8101

HOFFMAN, ALEXANDRA, writer; b. Chgo., Dec. 1, 1934; d. Harry and Fay (Elin) H. BA, U. Mich., 1956. Dep. dir. pub. info., publs. mgr. Montefiore Med. Ctr., Bronx, N.Y., 1966-84; freelance writer N.Y.C., 1984—. Contbg. author: (book) Magic and Medicine of Plants, 1986. Mem., bd. dirs. Lexington Dem. Club, N.Y.C., 1965-75. Mem. Nat. Assn. Sci. Writers, Internat. Assn. Bus. Communicators, Editl. Freelancers Assn., N.Y. Healthcare Pub. Rels. and Mktg. Soc. Home: 501 E 87th St 9G New York NY 10128 Office: 501 E 87th St 9G New York NY 10012-8000

HOFFMAN, ANN FLEISHER, labor union official, lawyer; b. Phila., June 1, 1942; d. Willis Jr. and Mary (Leffler) Fleisher; m. Charles Stuart Hoffman Jr., June 7, 1964 (div. 1979); m. Arnold Perry Rubin, Jan. 1, 1985 (div. 1993). BA, Barnard Coll., 1964; JD, U. Md., 1972. Bar: Md., 1972, N.Y., 1978. Reporter, producer Sta. WBAL-TV, Balt., 1965-68; assignment editor, producer Sta. WJZ-TV, Balt., 1968-69; assoc. Edelman, Levy and Rubenstein, Balt., 1972-77; assoc. gen. counsel Internat. Ladies' Garment Workers Union, N.Y.C., 1977-79, dir. Profl. And Clerical Employees div., 1987-91; asst. dir. legis. dept. Internat. Ladies' Garment Workers Union, Washington, 1991-94, assoc. dir., 1994-95; exec. asst. to Atty Gen. U.S. Dept. Justice, Washington, 1979-81; counsel Dist. 1 Communications Workers Am., N.Y.C., 1981-85; adminstrv. asst. to v.p. Communications Workers Am., N.Y.C. and Cranford, N.J., 1985-87; assoc. legis. dir. Union of Needletrades, Indsl. and Textile Employees, 1995—; lectr. U. Md. Sch. of Law, Balt., 1972-77; adj. faculty Cornell U. Trade Union Women's Studies Program, N.Y.C., 1979-85; trustee Botto House Am. Labor Mus., Haledon, N.J., 1986-89. Author: (with others) Legal Status of Homemakers in Maryland, 1978, Bargaining for Child Care, 1985, 2d edit., 1991. Founding mem. Women's Law Ctr., Balt., 1971-77; mem. Balt. City Charter Review Commn., 1973-76; bd. dirs. ACLU Md. Chpt., Balt., 1975-77, Campfire Girls Chesapeake Council, Balt., 1976-77; co-chair Sachs for Atty. Gen., Md., 1976-77; pub. mem. N.Y. State Banking Bd., N.Y.C., 1984-85. Mem. ABA, Coalition of Labor Union Women (treas. N.Y.C. chpt. 1981-83), Nat. Network of Women Union Lawyers (founder), Lawyers and Legal Workers for Working Women (founder), Cornell U. Adj. Faculty Fedn., Friends of Earth (bd. dirs. 1996—), Order of Coif. Home: 2810 Mckinley St NW Washington DC 20015-1216 Office: Internat Ladies Garment Union 815 16th St NW Washington DC 20006-4104

HOFFMAN, ANN ZEGOB, volunteer; b. Alamosa, Colo., Aug. 29, 1953; d. Nesrala Jr. and Mary Jane (Eichman) Zegob; m. David Gardner Hoffman, Oct. 9, 1977; children: Sarah Zegob, Rachel Gardner, Hannah Kasden. BSBA cum laude, U. Denver, 1975, MBA, 1976. Mktg. mgr., officer United Bank of Denver, 1976-83; asst. v.p. United Bank of Littleton, Colo., 1983-86; fin. cons. Englewood, Colo., 1986—. Mem. bd. dirs., past pres. U. Denver Alumni, 1980—, Cherry Hills Village Elem.; mem. bd. dirs. Nat. Jewish Hosp. Assn., Denver, 1985-88. Recipient Outstanding Svc. to Alumni award U. Denver, 1989. Mem. AAUW, NOW, 20/20 Investment Club. Home: 1500 E Layton Englewood CO 80110

HOFFMAN, ARLENE FAUN, podiatric medicine educator, physiologist; b. N.Y.C., Nov. 23, 1941; d. Abraham S. and Pearl Tootsie (Weiss) H. BS, CUNY, 1962; PhD in Physiology, SUNY, Bklyn., 1966; D of Podiatric Medicine, Calif. Coll. Podiatric Medicine, San Francisco, 1976. Instr. CUNY, N.Y.C., 1964-66; assoc. prof. basic scis. Calif. Coll. Podiatric Medicine, 1967-68, prof., 1969—, asst. dir. basic scis., 1967-69, dir., 1969-75, assoc. dean curricular affairs, 1972-75, assoc. prof. podiatric medicine, 1978-81, prof., chief non-invasive vascular lab., 1981—; postdoctoral fellow immunophysiology Stanford U. Med. Sch., Palo Alto, Calif., 1966-67; mem. physiology sect. Nat. Bd. Podiatry Examiners, 1967-76; mem. tng. grant rev. com., heart and cardiovascular sect. Nat. Heart, Lung and Blood Inst., 1976-77; cons. Vascular Evaluation Cos., 1986—; mem. Bd. Podiatric Medicine, 1985-92; bd. dirs. Am. Bd. Podiatric Orthopedics and Primary Medicine, 1992—. Editor: Yearbook of Podiatric Medicine & Surgery, 1979, Lower Extremity, 1994—; editor, mem. adv. bd. Jour. Am. Podiatric Med. Edn., 1971-75, editor (adv. bd.) Jour. Am. Podiatric Med. Assn., 1971-92; author: The Podiatry Curriculum, 1970; contbr. articles to profl. jours. Bd. dirs. Lyon-Martin Womens Alternative Med. Svcs., San Francisco, 1980-82, Nat. Ctr. for Lesbian Rights, San Francisco, 1989-93. USPHS fellow, 1962-66. Fellow Am. Assn. Podiatric Dermatology, Am. Soc. Podiatric Medicine, Am. Coll. Foot and Ankle Orthopedics and Primary Podiatric Medicine, Nat. Acad. Practice; mem. Am. Podiatric Med. Assn. (editor jour. 1970—, Meritorious Svc. citation 1996). Office: Calif Coll Podiatric Medicine 1835 Ellis St San Francisco CA 94115-4003

HOFFMAN, BARBARA A., state legislator; b. Balt., Mar. 8, 1940; d. Sidney Wolf and Eve (Simonoff) Marks; m. Donald Edwin Hoffman, 1960; children: Alan Samuel, Michael Stuart, Carolyn Mara. B.S., Towson State U., 1960; M.A., Johns Hopkins U., 1966. Secondary sch. tchr., Balt., 1960-63; supr. student tchrs. Morgan U., Balt., 1968-73; exec. dir. Md. Democratic party, 1979-84; mem. Md. State Senate from 42d Dist., 1983—, chair budget and tax com. Bd. dirs. Kennedy Inst.; mem. com. for children U. Md. Med. Sys., Nat. Jewish Dem. Coun. Co-author: Journeys in English, 1968. Recipient Outstanding Contbns. to Party award Md. Dem. party, 1984, Disting. Svc. award Va./Md. Coll. Vet. Medicine, 1994, Appreciation award MICUA, 1995, Balt. Jewish Coun., 1995, Legis. award Balt. County Commn. on Disabilities, 1995. Mem. Md. Assn. Elected Women (exec. bd. 1985), Nat. Order Women Legislators, Balt. Blews Coalition Blacks and Jews, Md. Com. for Children (pres. 1983), Hadassah (group pres. 1980-82). Jewish. Office: Md State Senate State Capitol Annapolis MD 21401 Other: 2905 W Strathmore Ave Baltimore MD 21209-3810

HOFFMAN, BARBARA ANN, English language educator; b. Rochester, N.Y., Dec. 19, 1941; d. Joseph George and Lucy Rose (Voelkl) H. Student, Nazareth Coll., Rochester, N.Y., 1959-62; BA, D'Youville Coll., 1963; MA, Cath. U. Am., 1965; postgrad., Duquesne U., 1966-69. Instr. English Marywood Coll., Scranton, Pa., 1969-72, asst. prof., 1972-90, prof., 1990—; catechist U. Scranton, 1987-92. Author (poetry) Cliffs of Fall, 1979; contbr. poetry to various publs. Student of Japanese Tea Ceremony. Recipient Excellence in Teaching award Sears Roebuck and Co., 1990; Marywood Scholarship named in her honor, 1991. Mem. AAUP, Urasenke Chanoyu Soc. Democrat. Roman Catholic. Home: 1749 Jefferson Ave Scranton PA 18509-1754 Office: Marywood Coll PO Box 814 Scranton PA 18501-0814

HOFFMAN, CATHY, lawyer; b. Nyack, N.Y., Dec. 10, 1959. BA, Colgate U., 1981; JD magna cum laude, U. Minn., 1987. Bar: D.C. 1989. Law clk. to Hon. Donald P. Lay U.S. Ct. of Appeals (8th cir.), 1987-88; ptnr. Arnold & Porter, Washington. Articles editor Minn. Law Rev., 1986-87. Mem. Order of the Coif. Office: Arnold & Porter 555 12th St NW Washington DC 20004*

HOFFMAN, DARLEANE CHRISTIAN, chemistry educator; b. Terril, Iowa, Nov. 8, 1926; d. Carl Benjamin and Elverna (Kuhlman) Christian; m. Marvin Morrison Hoffman, Dec. 26, 1951; children: Maureane R., Daryl K. BS in Chemistry, Iowa State U., 1948, PhD in Nuclear Chemistry, 1951. Chemist Oak Ridge (Tenn.) Nat. Lab., 1952-53; mem. staff radiochemistry group Los Alamos (N.Mex.) Sci. Lab., 1953-71, assoc. leader chemistry-nuclear group, 1971-79, divsn. leader, chem.-nuclear divsn., 1979-82, div. leader isotope and nuclear chem. div., 1982-84; prof. chemistry U. Calif., Berkeley, 1984-91, prof. emerita, 1991-93, prof. grad. sch., 1993—; faculty sr. scientist Lawrence Berkeley (Calif.) Lab., 1984—; dir.'s fellow Los Alamos Nat. Lab., 1990—; dir. G.T. Seaborg Inst. for Transactinium Sci., 1991-96; panel leader, speaker Los Alamos Women in Sci., 1975, 79, 82; mem. subcom. on nuclear and radiochemistry NAS-NRC, 1978-81, chmn. subcom. on nuclear and radiochemistry, 1982-84; titular mem. commn. on radiochem. and nuclear techniques Internat. Union of Pure and Applied Chem., 1983-87, sec., 1985-87, chmn., 1987-91, assoc. mem. 1991-93; organizer symposium Pacifichem Confs., 1984, 89, 95; lectr. Japan Soc. Promotion Sci., 1987; mem. com. 2d Internat. Symposium on Nuclear and Radiochemistry, 1988; planning panel Workshop on Tng. Requirements for Chemists in Nuclear Medicine, Nuclear Industry, and Related Fields, 1988, radionuclide migration peer rev. com., Las Vegas, 1986-87, steering com. Advanced Steady State Neutron Source, 1986-90, steering com., panelist Workshop on Opportunities and Challenges in Research with Transplutonium Elements, Washington, 1983; mem. energy rsch. adv. bd. cold fusion panel, Dept. Energy, 1989-90; mem. NAS separations subpanel of separations tech. and transmutation systems panel, 1992-94, NAS-NRC Bd. on Radioactive Waste Mgmt., 1994—. Contbr. numerous articles in field to profl. jours. Sr. postdoctoral fellow NSF, 1964-65, fellow Guggenheim Found., 1978-79; recipient Alumni Citation of Merit Coll. Scis. and Humanities, Iowa State U., 1978, Disting. Achievement award Iowa State U., 1986, Berkeley citation U. Calif. Berkeley, 1996. Fellow AAAS, Am. Inst. Chemists (pres. N.Mex. chpt. 1976-78), Am. Phys. Soc.; mem. Am. Chem. Soc. (chmn. nuclear chemistry and tech. divsn. 1978-79, com. on sci. 1986-88, exec. com. divsn. nuclear chemistry and tech. 1987-90, John Dustin Clark award Ctrl. N.Mex. sect. 1976, Nuclear Chemistry award 1983, Francis P. Garvan-John M. Olin medal 1990), Am. Nuclear Soc. (co-chmn. internat. conf. Methods and Applications of Radioanalytical Chemistry 1987), Norwegian Acad. Arts and Scis., Sigma Xi, Phi Kappa Phi, Iota Sigma Pi (nat. hon. mem.), Pi Mu Epsilon, Sigma Delta Epsilon, Alpha Chi Sigma. Methodist. Home: 2277 Manzanita Dr Oakland CA 94611-1135 Office: Lawrence Berkeley Lab MS70A-3307 NSD Berkeley CA 94720

HOFFMAN, EDITH DENISE, marketing professional; b. N.Y.C.; d. Jack L. and Roslyn (Illions) Birn; m. Martin J. Hoffman; children: Elyse, David, Mara. AS, SUNY, 1978. Pres. Edith D. Hoffman & Co., N.Y.C., 1980—; trainer, field rep. Arbitron Secaucus, N.J., 1980-83; social and med. rsch. Westat, Rockville, Md., 1985—; social rschr. Rsch. Triangle Inst., Research Triangle Park, N.C., 1994—; rschr. Response Analysis, Princeton, N.J., 1995—. Contbr. articles to profl. jours. Pres. Sweet Hollow PTA, Dix Hills, N.Y.; v.p. Half Hollow PTA Coun., Dix Hills; advisor N.Y.C. Sea Gypsies Scuba Club, N.Y.C., 1987—; rep. Citizens Adv. Coun. L.I. Sound Study, 1990—. Mem. L.I. Divers Assn. (bd. dirs. 1980—, pres. 1984-86, Viking Diver of the Yr. award 1986). Office: Edith D Hoffman Co 33 Briarwood Rd Wheatley Heights NY 11798-1048

HOFFMAN, GWENDOLYN L., emergency medicine physician, educator; b. Muskegon, Mich., 1942. MD, Mich. State U., 1976. Diplomate Am. Bd. Emergency Medicine (bd. dirs.). Intern Butterworth Hosp., Grand Rapids, Mich., 1976-77, resident, 1977-79, mem. staff, 1979—; assoc. prof. Mich. State U., East Lansing. Mem. AMA, SAEM, Am. Coll. Emergency Physicians. Office: Am Bd Emergency Medicine 3000 Coolidge Rd East Lansing MI 48823*

HOFFMAN, JANET N., psychic counselor; b. New Somerset, Ohio, Dec. 16, 1936; d. Charles Kennith and Jenny (Douds) Speedy; m. A. William Anderson, May 19, 1956: children: William, Robert, James; m. Sherwin Joseph Hoffman, Nov. 30, 1985. Student, Asbury Coll., 1953-54, Harvard U., 1971. Clk. Higbee Co., Cleve., 1955-56; adminstrv. asst. GE, Cleve., 1956-58, Hardware Mut., Boston, 1958-60; owner, operator Pantry Rest Motel, Toronto, Ohio, 1975-80; pvt. practice psychic counselor Toronto, 1980—; guest talk show Sta. WEIR, Weirton, W.Va., 1980-81, Sta. WLIT, Steubenville, Ohio, 1980-81, Sta. WSTV, 1988-90, 92, 96; lectr. various women's clubs, Steubenville. Home: 1303 N 4th St Toronto OH 43964-1807

HOFFMAN, JENNIFER ISOBEL, librarian; b. Washington, Sept. 13, 1948; d. Robert Gustavus and Maureen (May) Moll; m. Melvin Jacob Hoffman, Aug. 21, 1971; children: Robert, William. BA in English, SUNY, 1971, MS in Edn., 1973, M in Library Sci., 1978. Librarian Buffalo and Erie County Pub. Libr. Extension Svcs. Br. Libr., 1981-88; librarian Elma Pub. Libr. Buffalo and Erie County Pub. Libr. Contracting Librs., 1988-91; librarian City of Lackawanna Pub. Libr. Buffalo and Erie County Pub. Libr., 1991—. Mem. Am. Library Assn. Democrat. Episcopalian. Office: Lackawanna Pub Libr 560 Ridge Rd Buffalo NY 14218-1320

HOFFMAN, JUDY GREENBLATT, preschool director; b. Chgo., June 12, 1932; d. Edward Abraham and Clara (Morrill) Greenblatt; m. Morton Hoffman, Mar. 16, 1950 (div. Jan. 1983); children: Michael, Alan, Clare. BA summa cum laude, Met. State Coll., Denver, 1972; MA, U. No. Colo., 1976, MA in Spl. Edn. Moderate Needs, 1996. Cert. tchr., Colo. Presch. dir. B.M.H. Synagogue, Denver, 1968-70, Temple Emanuel, Denver, 1970-85, Congregation Rodef Shalom, Denver, 1985-88; tchr. Denver Pub. Schs., 1988—; bilingual tchr. adults in amnesty edn. Denver Pub. Schs., 1989-90. Author: I Live in Israel, 1979, Joseph and Me, 1980 (Gamoran award), (with others) American Spectrum Single Volume Encyclopedia, 1991. Coord. Douglas Mountain Therapeutic Riding Ctr. for Handicapped, Golden, Colo., 1985—; dir. Mountain Ranch Summer Day Camp for Denver Pub. Schs., 1989-91. Mem. Nat. Assn. Temple Educators. Democrat.

HOFFMAN, KIT, director; b. Grosse Pointe, Mich., Sept. 30, 1951; d. Andrew W. and Elizabeth M. (Campbell) H.; m. Peter F. Dittner, Dec. 15,

1980; children: Marissa Elise, Marshall Hoffman; step-children: Amy Elizabeth Morris, Steven Michael Dittner. BA in Speech and Theatre, Mercy Coll. Detroit, 1973; postgrad., Oakland U., 1974, U. Tenn., 1982. Tchr. theatre Frazer (Mich.) H.S., 1973-74, St. Agatha H.S., Redford, Mich., 1974-75; founder, dir. Bijou Theatre, Knoxville, Tenn., 1978-84; workshop facilitator Sexual Assault Crisis Ctr., Knoxville, 1990-93; dir. Civic Theatre of Orlando, Fla., 1996—; cons. U.S. Govt., others, 1990-96. Author: (poem) Survivor, 1993. Home: 512 Mansfield Dr Altamonte Springs FL 32714-3141

HOFFMAN, LINDA R., social services administrator; b. New Haven, Conn., July 23, 1940; d. Bernard Harry and Sylvia (Paul) Rosenfield; m. Peter A. Hoffman, Sept. 25, 1965; 1 child, Tracie Lee. BA, Russell Sage Coll., 1962; MSW, Columbia U., 1968. Cert. social worker, N.Y. Case worker Conn. Dept. Welfare, New Haven, 1962-63; case worker N.Y.C. Bur. Child Welfare, 1963-65, supr., 1965-66; asst. to commr. program planning N.Y.C. Dept. Social Svcs., 1968-70; spl. asst. to commr. N.Y.C. Spl. Svcs. for Children, 1972-79; pres. N.Y. Found. Sr. Citizens, N.Y.C., 1979—; cons. USIA, Teheran, Iran, summer 1975; adj. prof., mem. dean's adv. coun. Columbia Sch. Social Work. Mem. Cmty. Bd. # 8, N.Y.C., 1981—, legis. com. N.Y.C. Commn. Status of Women, 1981—; mem. exec. com. policy on aging N.Y. Cmty. Trust's Ctr.; mem. pub. programs and policy com. United Jewish Appeal Fedn. N.Y., N.Y.C., 1982—; mem. YWCA/N.Y.C. Acad. Women Achievers, 1994, bd. dirs., 1995—. Recipient Presdl. Recognition award for Community Svc., 1983, East Manhattan C. of C. award for Disting. Civic Svc., 1990. Mem. Nat. Assn. Social Workers (cert.), Women's City Club of N.Y. Office: NY Found Sr Citizens 150 Nassau St Ste 1730 New York NY 10038-1516

HOFFMAN, M. KATHY, graphic designer, packaging designer; b. Sidney, Nebr., Aug. 30, 1956; d. Norman and Irline (Dillon) Barnica; m. Jeffrey W. Hoffman, Apr. 16, 1988. BA, U. Nebr., Kearney, 1978, BFA, 1984, MA, 1987. Product quality assurance Baldwin Filters, Kearney, Nebr., 1978-88, product technician, 1988-90, product devel. technician, 1990-92, product identification coord., 1992—, packaging and graphics designer, 1993—. Mem. Inst. Packaging Profls., Assn. Corel Artists and Designers, Women in Packaging. Office: Baldwin Filters 4400 Highway 30 E Kearney NE 68847-9797

HOFFMAN, MARGARET ANN HOVLAND, artist, activist; b. Seattle, Feb. 20, 1930; d. Harold Kenneth and Gertrude Anne (Maxson) Hovland; m. Lee Harold Hoffman, Sept. 11, 1993 (div.); children: Lori, Lee. Student, U. Wash., 1948-51; B of Profl. Arts, Art Ctr. Coll. Design, 1955. Interior designer Bon Marché, Seattle, 1948-49; interior designer, coord. Paul Siegal, Seattle, 1949-51; asst. designer Seattle Design Ctr.; indsl. designer Olsen/Spencer, L.A., 1955-57; freelance artist L.A., 1957-61, 85—; designer, asst. Don Hoffman Jewelry, Beverly Hills, Calif., 1975-85; activist, creator, founder Oceanside Beach Restoration Assn., San Diego County, Calif., 1988—; mem. grad. and alumni adv. bd. Art Ctr. Sch. Coll. Design, L.A. and Pasadena, Calif., 1956-80. Designer logos and pamphlets for Shell Oil, 1953, AEC, 1953-55, Owl/Rexall Drugs, 1954, Pegasus/Tidewater Oil, 1955-57, Atomic Energy Commn. Mem. Women in Arts (charter). Home: 270 Tavistock Ave Los Angeles CA 90049

HOFFMAN, MARIANNE MACINA, nonprofit organization administrator; b. N.Y.C., Apr. 29, 1951; d. Vito William Jr. and Frances (Florio) Macina; m. Neil Richard Hoffman, April 29, 1995. BS in Journalism, U. Fla., 1973; postgrad., U. London, 1973; AA in Advt. ARt, Inst. Atlanta, 1975. Writer Clearwater (Fla.) Sun, 1965-69; pub. rels., graphics specialist Hensley-Schmidt Engts., Atlanta, 1975-76; creative dir. Mackey Green & Assocs., Atlanta, 1976; assoc. editor So. Banker Mag., Atlanta, 1977-78; managing editor Pension World Mag., Atlanta, 1978-79; communications writer No. States Power Co., Mpls., 1979-80; advt. dir. Carlton Celebrity Dinner Theater, Bloomington, Minn., 1980-82; coord., mktg. svcs. St. Paul Cos. Inc., 1982-87; regional mgr. Western Ins. Info. Svc., Portland, Oreg., 1987—; bd. dirs. Ins. Edn. Found. Oreg., Portland, 1989—. Exec. prodr.: (consumer videos) Preventing Home Burglary, 1988 (Gold medal 1990), Don't Give a Thief a Free Ride: Preventing Auto Theft, 1990, Bon Voyage: Tips for a Safe Vacation, 1993. Mem. task force Oreg. Juvenile Firesetter Edn., Salem, 1988-92; mem. Oreg. Coun. Against Arson, 1988—, v.p., 1994, 95; mem. exec. bd. Crime Prevention Assn. Oreg., 1992-94, treas., 1995—; bd. dirs. Oreg. Traffic Safety NOW, 1988-91. Recipient Merit award Ins. Info. Inst., N.Y.C., 1989, Commendation award Oreg. Coun. Against Arson, 1989, Crime Prevention award Crime Prevention Assn. Oreg., 1990, Media award, 1989. Mem. Soc. Chartered Property Casualty Underwriters (Oreg. chpt. bd. dirs. 1990-92, new designee rep. we. region 1989-90, cert.). Republican. Roman Catholic. Office: Western Ins Info Svc 11855 SW Ridgecrest Dr Ste 107 Beaverton OR 97008-6356

HOFFMAN, MARY CATHERINE, nurse anesthetist; b. Winamac, Ind., July 14, 1923; d. Harmon William Whitney and Dessie Maude (Neely) H.; R.N., Methodist Hosp., Indpls., 1945; cert. obstet. analgesia and anesthesia, Johns Hopkins Hosp., 1949, grad. U. Hosp. of Cleve. Sch. Anesthesia, 1952; Staff nurse Meth. Hosp., 1945-49; research asst., then staff anesthetist Johns Hopkins Hosp., 1949-62; staff anesthetist Meth. Hosp., 1962-64, U. Chgo. Hosps., 1964-66; chief nurse anesthetist Paris (Ill.) Community Hosp., 1966-80; staff anesthetist Hendricks County Hosp., Danville, Ind., Ball Meml. Hosp., Muncie, Ind., 1981-86; instr.-trainer CPR, 1975-81; mem. Terr. 08 CPR Coordinating Com., 1975-80. Mem. Am. Assn. Nurse Anesthetists, Am. Heart Assn., Ind. Fedn. Bus. and Profl. Women's Clubs (Ill. dist. chmn. 1977-78, state found. chmn. 1978-79; found. award 1979). Republican. Presbyterian. Home: 1700 N Maddox Dr Muncie IN 47304-2674

HOFFMAN, MAVIS WANDA, business official; b. New Hampton, Iowa, Apr. 8, 1929; d. Sjur Getinus and Bertha (Njus) Saanderson; m. Donald Nordness Hoffman, Dec. 30, 1960; children: Keith Donald, Robert Craig. BA, U. Calif., Berkeley, 1951, MA, San Francisco State U., 1958. Tchr. LaVista Sch. Dist., Hayward, Calif., Irvington (Calif.) Sch. Dist., 1951-52, LaVista Sch. Dist., Hayward, Calif., 1952-54, Richmond (Calif.) Sch. Dist., 1954-55, U.S. Mil. Schs., Erlangen, Germany, 1955-56, San Leandro (Calif.) Sch. Dist., 1956-61; adminstr. San Ramon Engrs., Dublin, Calif., 1975—. Membership chmn. Eugene O'Neill Found., Danville, Calif., 1996—; mem. Dublin Ptnrs. in Edn., 1995-96; mem. Nightowls Aux., Mt. Diablo Rehab. Ctr., 1991—; chmn. workshop monitors Math.-Sci. Conf. for Girls, Tri-Valley Area, 1993-95. Mem. AAUW (life, various offices), World Affairs Coun., U. Calif. Alumni Assn., Dublin C. of C., San Francisco Mus., Oakland Mus., Blackhawk Mus., St. Mary's Mus., Diablo Country Club.

HOFFMAN, NANCY YANES, medical author, editor, health care consultant, lecturer; b. Boston, July 2, 1929; d. William Phillip and Edith Sara (Bernstein) Yanes; m. Marvin J. Hoffman, Feb. 15, 1948; children: William Yanes, Holly Hoffman Brookstein, Jennifer Yanes Hirshorn. Student, Conn. Coll., 1946-48; BS with high distinction, U. Rochester, 1950, MS, 1968. Lectr., editor, educator, healthcare comm. cons. Rochester, 1970—; asst. prof. English St. John Fisher Coll., Rochester, N.Y., 1969-79; assoc. prof. English St. John Fisher Coll., Rochester, 1979-86; dir. Am. Guardian Life Ins. Co., Jenkintown, Pa., 1979-85; pub. relations con. Ochsner Med. Insts., New Orleans, 1978-82; pres. NYH Healthcare Assocs., Rochester, 1985—; Spl. clin. investigator Walter Reed Army Med. Ctr., Washington, 1983-85; vis. prof of med. humanities, U. New England Med. Sch., 1985; mem. breast cancer detection awareness task force Am. Cancer Soc., Syracuse, N.Y., 1986—; guest prof. St. Catherine's Coll., Oxford U., 1996; lectr. on health care comm. U.S., Can., U.K., France, South Africa, Spain, Australia, New Zealand. Author: Change of Heart: The Bypass Experience, 1985; co-author: Breast Cancer: A Practical Guide to Diagnosis, 1995; columnist Jour. AMA, 1972-85; contbr. numerous articles to profl. and popular jours., 1970—. Named Instr. of Excellence N.Y. State English Council, 1982; recipient scholarship Nat. Endowment for Humanities, 1978. Mem. Am. Med. Writers Assn., Nat. Assn. of Sci. Writers, Am. Soc. Journalists and Authors, Authors Guild, N.Y. Acad. Scis., Am. Diabetes Assn. (profl. sect.), Coun. of Am. Diabetes, Soc. of Diabetes Educators, AAAS, Soc. for Tech. Comm., Women in Comms., MLA, Am. Heart Assn., Nat. Coun. Tchrs. English, Am. Culture Assn. Home and Office: 16 San Rafael Dr Rochester NY 14618-3702

HOFFMAN, SHARON LYNN, research editor; b. Chgo.; d. David P. and Florence (Soifer) Seaman; m. Jerry Irwin Hoffman, Aug. 25, 1963; children: Steven Abram, Rachel Irene. BA, Ind. U., 1961; M Adult Edn., Nat.-Louis Univ., 1992. High sch. English tchr. Chgo. Pub. Schs., 1961-64; tchr. Dept. of Def. Schs., Braconne, France, 1964-66; tchr. ESL Russian Inst., Garmisch, Fed. Republic Germany, 1966, 67; tchr. adult edn. Monterey Peninsula Unified Schs., Ft. Ord, Calif., 1977-79; tchr. ESL MAECOM, Monmouth County, N.J., 1979-80; lectr., tchr. adult edn. Truman Coll./Temple Shalom, Chgo.; tchr. homebound Fairfax County Pub. Schs., Fairfax, Va., 1976; entry operator Standard Rate & Data, Wilmette, Ill., 1986-87; rsch. editor, spl. projects editor Marquis Who's Who, Wilmette, 1987-92; mem. adj. faculty Nat.-Louis U., Evanston and Wheeling, Ill., 1993—; tutor coord., then coord. learning specialist Nat.-Louis U., 1993—; pres. Cultural Transitions, Highland Park, Ill., 1992—. Mem. AAUW, LWV, ASTD, TESOL, Nat. Coun. Tchrs. English, Chgo. Drama League. Home and Office: 2270 Highmoor Rd Highland Park IL 60035-1702

HOFFMAN, SUE ELLEN, elementary education educator; b. Dayton, Ohio, Aug. 23, 1945; d. Cyril Vernon and Sarah Ellen (Sherer) Stephan; m. Lawrence Wayne Hoffman, Oct. 28, 1967. BS in Edn., U. Dayton, 1967; postgrad., Loyolla Coll., 1977, Ea. Mich. U., 1980; MEd, Wright State U., 1988. Cert. reading specialist and elem. tchr., Ohio. 5th grade tchr. St. Anthony Sch., Dayton, Ohio, 1967-68, West Huntsville (Ala.) Elem. Sch., 1968-71; 6th grade tchr. Ranchland Hills Pub. Sch., El Paso, Tex., 1973-74; 3rd grade tchr. Emerson Pub. Sch., Westerville, Ohio, 1976, St. Joan of Arc Sch., Aberdeen, Md., 1976-78, Our Lady of Good Counsel, Plymouth, Mich., 1979-80; 5th grade tchr. St. Helen Sch., Dayton, 1980—. Selected for membership Kappa Delta Pi, 1988. Mem. Internat. Reading Assn., Ohio Internat. Reading Assn., Dayton Area Internat. Reading Assn., Nat. Cath. Edn. Assn. Roman Catholic. Home: 2174 Green Springs Dr Kettering OH 45440-1120 Office: St Helen Sch 5086 Burkhardt Rd Dayton OH 45431-2043

HOFFMAN, SUSAN E. SLADEN, medical nurse, case manager; b. Washington, Mar. 3, 1949; d. Burt Deale and Lisette B. (Ridgeway) Sladen. AA, Montgomery Coll., Takoma Park, Md., 1978; BA, U. Md., 1971; postgrad., Fla. Internat. U., Miami. RN, Fla.; CRRN; cert. rehab. provider, case mgr. Homecare supr., dir. in-svc. edn., dir. health care svcs. Med. Pers. Pool, Miami; rehab. specialist Comprehensive Rehab. Assocs., Inc., Ft. Lauderdale, Fla.; ind. cons. Pompano Beach, Fla. Contbr. articles to newsletter. Mem. Am. Rehab. Nurses Assn., Broward Assn. Rehab. Nurses, Fla. Assn. Rehab. Nurses, Case Mgmt. Assn., U. Md. Alumni Assn., Alpha Omicron Pi. Home: 239 SE 3rd Ter Pompano Beach FL 33060-7130

HOFFMAN, VALERIE JANE, lawyer; b. Lowville, N.Y., Oct. 27, 1953; d. Russell Francis and Jane Marie (Fowler) H.; m. Michael J. Grillo, Apr. 4, 1996. Student, U. Edinburgh, Scotland, 1973-74; BA summa cum laude, Union Coll., 1975; JD, Boston Coll., 1978. Bar: Ill. 1978, U.S. Dist. Ct. (no. dist.) Ill. 1978, U.S. Ct. Appeals (3rd cir.) 1981, U.S. Ct. Appeals (7th cir.) 1983. Assoc. Seyfarth, Shaw, Fairweather & Geraldson, Chgo., 1978-87, ptnr., 1987—; adj. prof. Columbia Coll., 1985. Contbr. articles to legal publs. Dir. Remains Theatre, Chgo., 1981-95, pres., 1991-93, v.p., 1991-95; dir. The Nat. Conf., Chgo. Region, 1993—, nat. trustee, 1995—; bd. advisors Union Coll. Trustees, 1996—. Mem. ABA, Chgo. Bar Assn., Law Club Chgo., Chgo. Yacht Club, Univ. Club Chgo. (bd. dirs. 1984-87), Phi Beta Kappa. Office: Seyfarth Shaw Et Al 55 E Monroe St Ste 4400 Chicago IL 60603-5702

HOFFMANN, ELINOR R., lawyer; b. N.Y.C., Apr. 18, 1954. BA magna cum laude, NYU, 1974, LLM in Antitrust and Trade Regulation, 1984; JD cum laude, Bklyn. Law Sch., 1977. Bar: N.Y. 1978, U.S. Dist. Ct. (so. and ea. dists.) N.Y. 1978, U.S. Supreme Ct. 1982, U.S. Ct. Appeals (2nd cir.) 1991, U.S. Ct. Appeals (5th cir.) 1994. Ptnr. Coudert Bros., N.Y.C. Mng. editor Bklyn. Law Rev., 1976-77; contbr. articles to profl. jours. Mem. ABA, N.Y. State Bar Assn., Phi Beta Kappa. Office: Coudert Bros 1114 Avenue Of The Americas New York NY 10036-7703*

HOFFMANN, FRANCES LEE, sociology educator; b. Pensacola, Fla., Apr. 14, 1946; d. Conrad Edmund and Margaret (Daniels) H.; m. Richard Bruce Rosenfeld, Dec. 20, 1976; children: Jake, Sam. BA, Cornell U., 1968; MA, U. Ky., 1971; PhD, U. Oregon, 1976. Asst. prof. sociology Skidmore Coll., Saratoga Springs, N.Y., 1976-86; dean of student affairs Skidmore Coll., Saratoga Springs, 1978-88, assoc. prof. sociology, 1987-89; from vis. assoc. prof. to assoc. prof. of sociology U. Mo., St. Louis, 1990—; dir. Inst. for Women's and Gender Studies, U. Mo., St. Louis, 1992—; vis. scholar Four Winds Saratoga Hosp., Saratoga Springs, 1989-90, cons. Four Winds Saratoga Hosp., Saratoga Springs, 1990—. Contbr. articles to profl. jours. including Jour. of Coll. Student Psychotherapy, Harvard Ednl. Rev., Am. Jour. Ortho Psychiatry, Nat. Women's Studies Assn. Jour. Bd. edn. Charlton (N.Y.) Sch., 1986-89; bd. dirs. Planned Parenthood Saratoga, N.Y., 1987-89. Recipient award for disting. svc. to higher edn. Coll. Student Pers. Assn. N.Y., 1985. Mem. AAUW (mem. awards panel fellowships 1995-97), Nat. Women's Studies Assn. (conf. site coord., 1996-97). Home: 7217 Princeton Saint Louis MO 63130 Office: Inst for Women's & Gender Studies 8001 Natural Bridge Rd Saint Louis MO 63121

HOFFMANN, FRANCES PORTER, librarian, development coordinator; b. Louisville, Dec. 27, 1927; d. Robert Hugh and Frances (Pfeffer) Porter; m. John F. Hoffmann, Sept. 14, 1948; children: Frances H. Stains, Amy H. Aird. BA in History, Trinity U., San Antonio, 1949; MSLS, Our Lady of the Lake U., San Antonio, 1978. Office mgr. acad. libr. St. Mary's U., San Antonio, 1975-77, library assoc., 1977-79, tech. svcs. librarian, 1979-84; coord. tech. svcs. & automated systems Palo Alto Coll., San Antonio, 1986-90, spl. project librarian, 1990-95; devel. coord. I Care San Antonio, 1995—. 1st v.p. Nueces County Pharm. Assn. Auxiliary, Corpus Christi, Tex., 1965; chaplain Tom Brown Middle Sch. PTA, Corpus Christi, 1966; troop leader Girl Scouts of Am., Corpus Christi, 1960-65; docent San Antonio Mus. Assn., 1968-69; v.p. Tech. Svcs. Int. Group, 1992-93; pres. Coun. Rsch. Acad. Librs., 1993-94. Mem. ALA, Nat. Soc. Daughters of the Am. Revolution, San Antonio Genealogical & Hist. Soc. Presbyterian.

HOFFMANN, JOAN CAROL, retired academic dean; b. Cedarburg, Wis., Feb. 20, 1934; d. Frank Ernst and Althea Wilhelmina (Behm) H. Nursing diploma Michael Reese Hosp., 1955; BS in Zoology, U. Wis., Madison, 1959; PhD in Physiology, U. Ill., Chgo., 1965. RN, Wis., Ariz. Sci. instr. Michael Reese Hosp., Chgo., 1959-62; USPHS trainee U. Ill., Chgo., 1962-64; NSF postdoctoral fellow Coll. de France, Paris, 1964-65; asst. prof. U. Rochester, N.Y., 1965-70; assoc. prof., prof. U. Hawaii, Honolulu, 1970-83; dean of students U. Mass. Med. Sch., Worcester, 1983-94; ret., 1994; chmn. anatomy U. Hawaii, 1973-80. Contbr. articles to sci. jours. NIH rsch. grantee, 1966-75. Mem. Endocrine Soc., Soc. for Study of Reprodn., Am. Assn. Anatomists, Women in Endocrinology (sec. 1978-79, pres. 1987-88), Am. Coun. Edn. (bd.dirs., Mass. chpt., network identification program 1993-94), Phi Beta Kappa, Sigma Xi. Avocations: gardening, needlework, wood turning, reading. Home: 30 Homestead Rd Sedona AZ 86336-3236

HOFFMANN, KATHRYN ANN, humanities educator; b. Rockville Centre, N.Y., Oct. 26, 1954; d. Manfred and Catherine (Nanko) H.; m. Brook Ellis, Nov. 25, 1987. BA summa cum laude, SUNY Buffalo, 1975; MA, The Johns Hopkins U., 1979, PhD, 1981. Asst. prof. French lit. and lang. U. Wis.-Madison, 1981-88, U. Hawaii-Manoa, Honolulu, 1992—; mng. ptnr. Yuval Design Partnership, Chgo., 1988-92. Assoc. editor Substance, 1982-87; contbr. articles to profl. jours.; designer clothing accessories. Grantee NEH, 1993, 95; fellow Inst. Rsch. in Humanities, 1984-85, Am. Coun. Learned Socs., 1984-85. Mem. MLA, Hawaii Assn. Lang. Tchrs., N.Am. Soc. for 17th Century French Literature, Soc. for Interdisciplinary French 17th Century Studies (exec. com. 1994-96), Soc. for Interdisciplinary Study of Social Imagery, Phi Beta Kappa. Home: 3029 Lowrey Ave Apt Q2224 Honolulu HI 96822 Office: U Hawaii Manoa Dept European Languages & Lit 1890 E West Rd # 483 Honolulu HI 96822-2318

HOFFMANN, MELANE KINNEY, marketing and public relations executive, writer; b. Baton Rouge, Jan. 25, 1956; d. Kenneth Lee and Louise (Walker) Kinney; m. R. Thomas Hoffmann, Oct. 10, 1981; children: Robert James II, Halloran Kinney, Richard Walker. BA, Am. U., 1977. Gen. mgr. Dance Project, Inc., Washington, 1979-81; account exec. J. Walter Thompson Advt., Washington, 1981-84; v.p., account supr. Ketchum Advt., Washington, 1984-88, Demaine Vickers Advt., Alexandria, Va., 1988-89; sr. counsel Porter/Novelli Pub. Rels., Washington, 1989—. Dir. Resolve, Washington, 1992-93; bd. dirs. nat. capital area YWCA, Washington, 1980-82. Mem. Am. Mktg. Assn. (mem. program com. 1990-92, co-chair), Ad Club Washington (mem. membership com. 1985-90, Addy award 1987). Presbyterian. Office: Poter/Novelli 1120 Connecticut Ave NW Washington DC 20036-3902

HOFFMANN, NANCY LARRAINE, state senator; b. Needham, Mass., Sept. 22, 1947; d. Elmer and Juanita (Chauncey) Roth; m. (separated); children: Eva, Anna, Gustav. BA, Syracuse U., 1970; MS, U. Md., 1972. Prof. English and Journalism Onondaga C.C., Syracuse, 1974-76; mem. N.Y. State Senate, Albany, 1985—; prodr. TV Sta. WIXT-TV, Syracuse, 1972-76; pub. rels. cons. Benson Media, Syracuse, 1986—. City councilor Common coun., Syracuse, 1980-84. Named Legislator of Yr. N.Y. State Rifle and Pistol Assn., 1994, Womens Press Club N.Y. State, 1992; recipient Pres. award Madison County Assn. Retarded Citizens, 1992, Circle of Friends award N.Y. State Farm Bur., 1990-95, Golden Trumpet award Firemens Assn. State of N.Y., 1995. Mem. LWV, NRA, Nat. Orgn. Women Legislators (treas. 1990, corres. sec. 1991), Nat. Cattlemen's Beef Assn., Nat. Womens Polit. Caucus, N.Y. State Cattlemens Assn., N.Y. State Cattlewomens Assn., Women in Govt. Democrat. Office: 333 E Washington St 813 State Office Bldg Syracuse NY 13202

HOFFMEISTER, JANA MARIE, cardiologist. MD, SUNY Upstate Med. Ctr., Syracuse, 1976. Diplomate Am. Bd. Internal Medicine, Am. Bd. Cardiovascular Diseases. Intern Albany (N.Y.) Med. Ctr., 1976-78, resident, 1978-80, fellow div. cardiology, 1981-83; fellow div. cardiology Emory U., Atlanta, 1984; fellow coronary angioplasty and interventional cardiology Emory U. Hosp., 1985-86; presenter numerous cardiology confs. Contbr. numerous articles to profl. jours. Mem. ACP, AMA, Cardiac Soc. Upstate N.Y., N.Y. State Soc. Internal Medicine, Am. Soc. Cardiovascular Intervention. Home: 7 Reddy Ln Albany NY 12211-1632

HOFFNER, MARILYN, university administrator; b. N.Y.C., Nov. 16, 1929; d. Daniel and Elsie (Schulz) H.; m. Albert Greenberg, May 29, 1949; children: Doren Roe, Peter Cooper. BFA, Cooper Union. Art dir. Printers' Ink mag., N.Y.C., 1953-63; art dir. Print mag., N.Y.C., 1960-62; corp. art dir. Vision, Inc., Latin Am., 1963-75, 92-95; dir. alumni rels. and devel. Cooper Union, 1975-96m exec. dir. instnl. advancement, 1996—; project dir. Nat. Graphic Design Archives, 1990—. Bd. dirs. Art Dirs. Club N.Y., 1973-75, 79-82, exec. sec., 1973-75, exec. treas., 1979-82; mem. Citizens Adv. Cultural Arts Com. Dutchess County, 1978-80. Named Alumnus of Yr., Cooper Union, 1968; recipient Gold medal Art Dirs. Club, 1979, N.Y. State Coun. of the Arts award, 1995. Mem. Cooper Union Alumni Assn. (editor-in-chief 1971-74, 1st v.p. 1974-75), Council Advancement and Support of Edn., Type Dirs. Club (numerous awards), Nat. Arts Club (exhbn. com.). Contbg. editor Print mag., Art Direction, Graphis mag.; designer mags., advt., books, exhbns. Home: 51 5th Ave New York NY 10003-4320 Office: 30 Cooper Sq New York NY 10003-7120

HOFFNUNG, AUDREY SONIA, speech and language pathologist, educator; b. N.Y.C., Mar. 15, 1928; d. Nathan and Gussie (Karp) Smith; BA cum laude, Bklyn. Coll., 1949; MA, Columbia U., 1950; PhD, City U. N.Y., 1974. Cert. and lic. speech pathologist, N.Y.; m. Joseph Hoffnung, Nov. 26, 1950; children: Bonnie Fern, Tami Lynn. Rehab. therapist Ridgewood Cerebral Palsy Ctr., 1949-50; dir. speech therapy Kingsbrook Med. Ctr., Bklyn., 1950-55; therapist and cons. Morris J. Solomon Clinic, Bklyn., 1956-58; therapist Speech and Hearing Ctr. Bklyn. Coll., 1958-62, 63-64; pvt. practice speech therapy Hewlett (N.Y.) Med. Ctr., 1961-63; pvt. practice speech therapy, Oceanside, N.Y., 1964-71; cons. on staff for aphasic patients Phys. Medicine and Rehab. Ctr., South Nassau Cmtys. Hosp., 1964-65; part-time lectr. Speech and Hearing Ctr., Queens (N.Y.) Coll., 1970-72; adj. lectr. dept. speech Bklyn. Coll., 1973-74, asst. prof. speech and lang. pathology, 1974-77; asst. prof. dept. speech comm. and theatre St. John's U., Jamaica, N.Y., 1977-80, assoc. prof., 1980-91, prof., 1991—, chair, 1992-95; guest lectr. N.Y. Orton Soc., 1979, Brookdale Med. Ctr., 1978; mem. profl. adv. bd. Vis. Home Health Svcs. of Nassau County, 1973—. Author: (with Valletutti and McKnight) Facilitating communication in young children with handicapping conditions; (with Valletutti and Bender) A Functional Curriculum for Teaching Students With Disabilities Noverbal and Verbal Communication, 1996. Mem. Am. Speech-Lang.-Hearing Assn., N.Y.C. Speech, Hearing and Lang. Assn., N.Y. State Speech Lang. and Hearing Assn. (chairperson student activities 1978-79), L.I. Speech, Lang. and Hearing Assn., Nat. Student Speech-Lang.-Hearing Assn. (hon. advisor 1988), Aphasia Study Group of N.Y.C., N.Y. Acad. Scis. Contbr. articles on speech pathology to profl. jours. Home: 3282 Woodward St Oceanside NY 11572-4527 Office: St John's U Dept Speech Comm Scis and Theatre 800 Utopia Pkwy Jamaica NY 11439

HOFMAN, ELAINE D., state legislator; b. Sacramento, Sept. 20, 1937; d. Willard Davis and Venna (Gray) Smart; m. Cornelius Adrianus Hofman, Dec. 14, 1956; children: Catharina, John, Casie, Cornelius. BA, Idaho State U., 1974. Tchr. music edn. Sch. Dist. 25, Pocatello, Idaho, 1977-84; spl. asst. to Gov. Evans State of Idaho, Pocatello, 1984-87; field rep. to Congressman Stallings 2d Dist. Congressional Office, Pocatello, 1987-89; mem. Idaho Ho. of Reps., Pocatello, 1990—. Recipient Elect Lady award Lambda Delta Sigma, 1991; named Idaho Mother of Yr., Am. Mother's Assn., 1992, S.E. Idaho Family of the Yr., 1980. Democrat. Mem. Ch. of Jesus Christ of Latter-day Saints. Home: 216 S 16th Ave Pocatello ID 83201-4003

HOFMANN, KAY JOYCE, sculptor, artist; b. Green Bay, Wis., Dec. 3, 1932; d. Walter and Marie (Vandersteen) H.; m. Carl E. Schwartz, June 18, 1955, (div. 1980); children: Dawn, Carilee. Grad., Art Inst. Chgo., 1955; postgrad, Acad. de Grande Chaumiere, Paris, 1955-56. Tchr. North Shore Art League, Winnetka, 1957-90, Suburban Fine Arts Ctr., Highland Park, Ill., 1965-92, Blackhawk Mountain Sch. of Arts, Colo., 1985-93. Recipient Ryersson fellowship Art Inst. Chgo., 1955, Nat. award Nat. Soc. Arts and Letters, Louisville, Ky., 1963; named Best of Show Artist Guild of Chgo., 1970. Democrat. Home: 3140 N 77th Ave Elmwood Park IL 60707

HOFRICHTER-WATTS, SUSAN DIANE, art educator; b. Pitts., May 19, 1957; d. James Francis and Marilyn Jean (Sica) H.; m. Robert Delano Watts, July 11, 1981; children: Jeremiah Robert, Leah Nicole. BA, Carlow Coll., Pitts., 1979; M, U. Pitts., 1996. Art therapist Mayview State Hosp., Pitts., 1980-87, Woodville State Hosp., Pitts., 1981-85; art therapist, educator Wesley Acad., Pitts., 1989-90; curriculum coord., educator South Arts, Pitts., 1988-90; art educator Upper St. Clair Sch. Dist., Pitts., 1990—; bd. dirs. South Arts, Pitts., 1988-90; com. chair Cmty. Found. Upper St. Clair, Pitts., 1993—. Mem. Nat. Art Edn. Assn., Pa. Art Edn. Assn., 1830 Log House Assn., Trotwood Garden Club (pres. 1995). Home: 2554 Lindenwood Dr Upper Saint Clair PA 15241 Office: Upper St Clair Sch Dist McLaughlin Run Rd Pittsburgh PA 15241

HOFT, LYNNE ANN, educator, remedial specialist, educational consultant; b. Carroll, Iowa, Mar. 1, 1945; d. Norman North and Dorothy Mae (Dean) Hoft; 1 child, Timothy D. Cochran. BA, Briar Cliff Coll., 1971; MA in Spl. Edn., Ariz. State U., 1979; postgrad., U. Minn., 1989-92, U. St. Thomas, 1993—. Cert. elem. and spl. edn. tchr., Ariz., Minn. Tchr. St. Edward Sch., Waterloo, Iowa, 1968-70; tchr. Chino Valley Sch., Ariz., 1971-77, program developer, 1974-76; spl. edn. tchr. Tuba City Pub. Jr. H.S., Ariz., 1978-82; spl. edn. tchr., dept. chmn. Tuba City H.S., 1983-86, curriculum developer, 1984-85; remedial specialist Eagles' Nest Mid-Sch., 1986-88; spl. edn. coord. chpt. 1 Epsilon and Nexus programs Hopkins (Minn.) Pub. Schs., Hennepin County Home Sch., 1988—; founder, pres. Unltd. Learning Enterprises, Inc., Tuba City, 1983-85; trainer Empowering People/Positive Discipline, 1990—; invitational cons. Aim for Excellence, Mpls., 1990-91; cons./trainer Keys Programs, 1994—. Probation aide Waterloo Juvenile Ct., 1970-71; vol. instr. Prescott Spl. Olympics 1977-78; local coord. Tuba City Spl. Olympics, 1978-80; cons. in field 1988—. Recipient U.S. Dept Edn. Sec. award, 1991. Mem. NEA, Minn. Edn. Assn., Hopkins Edn. Assn., Tuba City Unified Edn. Assn. (pres. 1985-86). Avocations: reading, piano, parenting, hiking, writing, travel.

HOGAN, BONITA LOUISE, secondary education educator; b. Troy, N.Y., May 27, 1950; d. Edward Steven and Betty Marie (Bell) H. BS in Edn., SUNY Coll., Buffalo, 1972, MS in Edn., 1975, CAS in Ednl. Adminstrn., 1994. Cert. tchr. spl. edn., Spanish, cert. ednl. adminstr., N.Y. Tchr. 6th grade Diocese of Buffalo, Lackawanna, N.Y., 1973-74; resources rm. tchr.

BOCES Erie # 1, Lancaster, N.Y., 1974-79; tchr. English Hamburg (N.Y.) Ctrl. Sch. Dist., 1979-80, 82; tchr. Enlgish and reading Buffalo State Coll. Learning Lab., 1980-81; substitute tchr. Clarence (N.Y.) Ctrl. Sch. Dist., 1981; tchr. Spanish, English and writing Orchard Park (N.Y.) Ctrl. Sch. Dist., 1982-88; tchr. Spanish Buffalo Bd. Edn., 1988-90; tchr. Spanish, adminstrv. asst. Frontier Ctrl. Sch. Dist., Hamburg, 1990—; adj. assoc. prof. English Hilbert Coll., Hamburg, 1981—. ind. cons., Buffalo, 1990—; tchr. ESL, UNESCO and Kosciusko Found., Bydgoszcz, Poland, summer 1991. MCES scholar N.Y. State Edn. Dept., Salamanca, Spain, summer, 1990; Fulbright grantee, Mexico City, 1992. Mem. ASCD, We. N.Y. Women in Adminstrn., N.Y. State Assn. Fgn. Lang. Tchrs. (bd. dirs., officer), We. N.Y. Fgn. Lang. Educators Coun. (v.p. 1989), Phi Delta Kappa, Delta Kappa Gamma. Home: 220 Rebecca Park Buffalo NY 14207-1834

HOGAN, ILONA MODLY, lawyer; b. Erlangen, Fed. Republic of Germany, Nov. 23, 1947; came to U.S., 1951, naturalized, 1960; d. Stephen Bela and Gunda Pauline (Gastiger) Modly; m. Lawrence J. Hogan, Mar. 16, 1974; children: Matthew Lawrence, Michael Alexander, Patrick Nicholas, Timothy Stefan. Student, Marymount Coll., 1965-67; A.B. in Internat. Affairs, George Washington U., 1969; J.D., Georgetown U., 1974. Bar: D.C. 1975, Md. 1975. Intern and clk. AID, 1965-69; adminstrv. and legis. asst. to mem. Ho. of Reps., 1969-72; editor Legis. Digest, Ho. of Reps., Washington, 1972-73; asso. and law clk. firm Trammell, Rand, Nathan and Lincoln, Washington, 1972-74; mng. ptnr. firm Hogan and Hogan, Washington, Md., 1974-93; of counsel Venable, Baetjer, Howard & Civiletti, Washington, 1989-91; pres. Amcom Inc., 1978—; of counsel Salisbury & McLister, Frederick, Md., 1993—. Mem. Prince George's (Md.) Bd. Libr. Trustees, 1976-78, Prince George's County Econ. Devel. Adv. Com., 1979-82; co-chmn. Greater S.E. Cmty. Hosp. Ctr. for Aging, 1979-82; mem. Lawyers Steering com. for Reagan-Bush, 1980; nat. vice-chmn. Assn. Execs. for Reagan-Bush, 1984; mem. bus. and industry adv. com. 50th Am. Presdl. Inaugural, 1985; mem. Md. steering com. Bush for Pres., 1988, Gov.'s Higher Edn. Transition Team, 1988, Presdl. Personnel Adv. Com., 1989; v.p. St. John's Sch. Bd., 1987-88, pres., 1989; treas. U. Md. Bd. Regents, 1988-95; trustee St. James Sch., 1989-90; mem. County Commrs. of Frederick County, Md., 1994—. Mem. ABA, Md. Bar Assn., D.C. Bar. Republican. Roman Catholic. Home: 5614 New Design Rd Frederick MD 21703 Office: Winchester Hall 12 E Church St Frederick MD 21701

HOGAN, MAURA JEAN, new media specialist, artist; b. Scott AFB, Ill., May 25, 1969; d. John Edward and Lynne Marie Hogan. BA in English, George Mason U., 1991, MA in English, 1996. Tech. info. specialist U.S. Geol. Survey, Reston, Va., 1989-95, 1995—; hypertext cons. George Mason U., Fairfax, Va., 1994-95; conf. presenter in field. Designer (cover designs): Poets Anonymous, 1993-95, Several Sides of Sam, 1995 U.S. geol. Survey Ann. report, 1994, 95. Mem. Poets Anonymous, Poetry Soc. Va. Home: 5952 Bridgetown Ct Burke VA 22015 Office: US Geol Survey Mailstop 801 12201 Sunrise Valley Dr Reston VA 20192

HOGAN, NANCY KAY, elementary education educator; b. Auburn, Wash., Oct. 5, 1947; d. Henry Grant and Medora Ione (Elder) Kessner; m. David Allan Hogan, June 27, 1970; children: Jeffrey Allan, Jason Patrick, Jennifer Ann. BA in Edn., Western Wash. U., 1969; postgrad., U. Wash., 1973; M Ednl. Tech., City U., 1996. Cert. K-12 tchr., Wash. Tchr. kindergarten Kent (Wash.) Sch. Dist., 1970; elem. tchr. North Thurston Sch. Dist., Lacey, Wash., 1970-73; tchr. McLane Elem. Sch., Olympia, Wash., 1986-93, McKenny Elem. Sch., Olympia, 1993-94; tchr. Hansen Elem. Sch., Olympia, 1994—, also mem. tchr. support team. Mem. NEA, Internat. Reading Assn., Whole Lang. Umbrella, Wash. Edn. Assn., Olympia Edn. Assn., Dist. Inclusion Forum, Hansen Title I Team, Nat. Coun. Tchrs. English. Home: 3030 Aspinwall Rd NW Olympia WA 98502-1531 Office: Hansen Elem Sch 1919 Rd Sixty Five Olympia WA 98502

HOGAN, ROSEMARY, elementary school educator; b. Pitts., Sept. 3, 1946; d. Paul Nicholas and Alice Jane (Leonard) H.; life ptnr. Joanne McCloskey. BA in French and Elem. Edn., Mount Mercy Coll., 1969. Cert. tchr., Pa. Tchr. Shaler Area Sch. Dist., Glenshaw, Pa., 1972—; founding mem. No. Area Gifted Consortium, Allison Park, Pa., 1985—. Mem. NEA, Pa. State Edn. Assn. (newsletter editor 1979-84), Renaissance & Baroque Soc. Pitts. (bd. dirs. 1993—). Home: 3934 Gibsonia Rd Gibsonia PA 15044 Office: Shaler Area Sch Dist 1800 Mt Royal Blvd Glenshaw PA 15116

HOGAN, SHARON KLOSS, lawyer, planned giving director; b. Detroit, July 29, 1956; d. John Kloss and Marlene Patricia (Zatyko) Vargas; m. Scott Alan Hogan, May 29, 1993; 1 child, Allison. BA, U. Laverne, 1979; JD, Northwestern U., 1988. Bar: Oreg. 1988, Wash. 1989. Asst. treas. Caffall Bros. Forest Products, Inc., Wilsonville, Oreg., 1979-84; intern Pub Defenders Office, Portland, Oreg., 1987-88; judicial clk. Cir. Ct., Portland, Oreg., 1985-87; atty. Blair, Schaefer et al, Vancouver, Wash., 1989-91, Warren, Allen & Brookeshire, Portland, 1988-89, Gevurtz, Menashe et al, Portland, 1991-92; dir. planned giving The Salvation Army, Portland, 1992—. Chmn. adv. bd. Parents Anonymous, Vancouver, 1989-91. U. Mich. Women scholar, Ann Arbor, 1975. Mem. NSFRE, Am. Trial Lawyers Assn., Northwest Planned Giving Roundtable, Oreg. State Bar Assn., Wash. State Bar Assn., Multnomah County Bar Assn., Women in Action. Home: 1821 NW Terrace St Vancouver WA 98685

HOGE, GERALDINE RAJACICH, elementary education educator; b. Eveleth, Minn., Apr. 8, 1937; d. Robert and Dora (Tassi) Rajacich; m. Gregg LeRoy Hoge, Sept. 15, 1963 (div. Feb. 1972); 1 child, Sheryl Maurine. BS, U. Minn., 1959; MA with honors, Pepperdine U. Cert. elem. tchr., Calif. Tchr. Chaska (Minn.) Pub. Schs., 1959-60, Minnetonka (Minn.) Pub. Schs., 1960-62, Norwalk (Calif.) La Mirada Pub. Schs., 1962-64, Culver City (Calif.) Unified Sch. Dist., 1966—. Fellow Culver City Guidance Clinic Guild, 1981-89; mem. Calif. State Rep. Ctrl. Com., Sacramento, 1986-90, 92-94, L.A. County Rep. Ctrl. Com., 1987—; vice chmn. 49th Assembly Dist. Ctrl. Rep. Com., Culver City, 1988—; bd. dirs. Selective Svc. Sys., Culver City, 1993—. Named Tchr. of the Yr. Elks Lodge, 1982; grantee, 1988-89. Fellow Am. Fedn. Tchrs.; mem. Internat. Platform Assn., Calif. Fedn. Tchrs., Culver City Fedn. Tchrs. (v.p. 1978-79), Alpha Delta Pi (historian 1956-59), Delta Kappa Gamma. Republican. Office: Culver City Unified Sch 4034 Irving Pl Culver City CA 90232-2810

HOGELAND, LISA MARIA, English educator; b. Glendale, Calif., Aug. 16, 1959; d. Richard Albert and Sharon Maria (Meade) H. AB, Stanford (Calif.) U., 1981, PhD, 1992. Asst. prof. English U. Cin., 1990—. Contbr. articles to profl. jours. Democrat. Office: Dept of English U Cin Cincinnati OH 45221-0069

HOGENSEN, MARGARET HINER, librarian, consultant; b. Ottawa, Kans., Oct. 11, 1920; d. Hebron Henry and Nellie Evelyn (Godard) Hiner; widowed. BA, U. Wichita, 1942; BS in Library Sci., U. Denver, 1945. Circulation librarian Boise (Idaho) Pub. Library, 1945-49, Pomona (Calif.) Pub. Library, 1950-51; reference librarian WFIL-TV, Phila., 1963-69; rsch. dir. Concept Films, Washington, 1969-72; ind. researcher, cons. Greenbelt, Md., 1973—. Bd. dirs. Greenbelt Homes, Inc., 1977-93, pres., 1983-88; past mem. bd. dirs. Greenbelt Consumer Coop., Nat. Coop. Bank, Nat. Coop. Bus. Assn.; pres. Ea. Coop. Housing Orgn., 1992-95. Mem. Nat. Assn. Housing Coops (bd. dirs. 1986-87, 1990-94). Democrat. Christian Scientist. Home: PO Box 218 Greenbelt MD 20768-0218

HOGG, JUDITH E., neurologist, educator; b. Binghamton, N.Y.; d. Edwin Charles and Virginia Anne (Pettinato) H. AB, MD, Boston U., 1970. Diplomate Am. Bd. Psychiatry and Neurology. Intern Lenox Hill Hosp., N.Y.C., 1970-71, resident in internal medicine, 1971-72; resident in neurology Mt. Sinai Hosp., N.Y.C., 1972-75; pvt. practice, 1975-77; neuro-epidemiology rschr. NIH, Bethesda, Md., 1977-79; asst. clin. prof. neurology George Washington U., Washington, 1979-88; staff neurologist Santa Clara Valley Med. Ctr., San Jose, Calif., 1988-91; assoc. prof. sch. medicine Tex. Tech. U., Lubbock, 1991—. Mem. Am. Acad. Neurology, Am. Assn. Electrodiagnostic Medicine (assoc.), Phi Beta Kappa.

HOGG, KAREN SUE, telecommunications and information systems executive; b. Bay City, Tex., Jan. 12, 1952; d. Ernest Bascom Hogg and Allene (Bishop) Watson; m. Wesley Ray Tucker, Mar. 10, 1989. BS in Indsl. Engring., Tex. Tech. U., 1974; MBA, Washington U., 1982. Profl. engr. Tex. Computer ops. supr. Southwestern Bell, Houston, 1974-75; computer ops. supr. Southwestern Bell, St. Louis, 1975-76, from mgr. installation to staff mgr., 1976-83; prin. cons. AT&T Internat., Basking Ridge, N.J., 1983-85; nat. sales mgr. AT&T Network Systems, Morristown, N.J., 1986; mgr. telecom. Goldman Sachs & Co., N.Y.C., 1986-90, v.p. info. tech., 1990—; mem. indsl. adv. bd. Tex. Tech U., Lubbock, 1980-86. Judge YWCA Tribute to Women, Knoxville, Tenn., 1992; active Livingston Cmty. Players. Named Disting. Engr., Tex. Tech. U., 1994. Mem. Acad. Indsl. Engring. (sec./treas. 1994, vice chmn. 1995, chmn. 1996), Inst. Indsl. Engrs., Maplewood Strollers (trustee, treas. 1996), Maplewood Club (trustee 1995-96), Beta Gamma Sigma, Tau Beta Pi, Phi Kappa Phi, Alpha Pi Mu. Republican. Methodist.

HOGG, ROZALIA CRUISE, genealogist; b. Bluefield, W.Va., Dec. 31, 1931; d. George Mortimer and Beulah Grove (Fleshman) Cruise; m. Edward Welford Hogg, Jr., June 20, 1953 (dec. 1972); children: Gayle Hogg Wells, Alice Ann Hogg Conaty, Nancy Hogg Pingry. Student, Madison Coll., Harrisonburg, Va., 1951-53; BA in History, Mary Baldwin Coll., 1978. Kindergarten tchr. Ft. Meade, Md., 1953-54; tour guide Woodrow Wilson Birthplace, Staunton, Va., 1978-80, P. Buckley Moss Mus., Waynesboro, Va., 1990; genealogist Patrick County, Va., 1985—; bd. advisors Bluefield State Coll. Pres. Women of Ch., 1st Presbyn. Ch., Waynesboro, 1983-85; bd. dirs. Augusta County Hist. Soc., 1987-91, Bluefield State Coll., 1992—; vice chmn. Waynesboro Hist. Commn., 1986-91. Mem. Rosecliff Garden Club (pres. 1973-74), Va. Mus. Fine Arts, Sigma Sigma Sigma, Phi Alpha Theta. Presbyterian. Home: 272 Littletown Quarter Williamsburg VA 23185

HOHENBERGER, PATRICIA JULIE, fine arts and antique appraiser, consultant; b. Holyoke, Mass., Aug. 9, 1928; d. Ambrose Harrington and Irene Leo (Ducharme) Reynolds; m. John H. Hohenberger, June 27, 1953; children: Lisa Maria, Julie Suzanne, John Henry, James Reynolds, Patricia Antonia. BA in English, Coll. of New Rochelle, N.Y., 1950; MA in Folk Art Studies, NYU, 1983. Cert. elem. edn. tchr., Mass. Tchr. Hadley (Mass.) Pub. Schs., 1950-52, Springfield (Mass.) Pub. Schs., 1952-54; owner, dir. The Brown House Nursery Sch., Williamstown, Mass., 1962-64; tchr. Coindra Hall, Huntington, N.Y., 1970-71, St. Edward the Confessor, Syosset, N.Y., 1971-81; pres. Patricia Reynolds Hohenberger Appraisals, Northport, N.Y., 1983—; cons. Alexander-Benwood Co., Inc., Huntington, N.Y., 1986-91; lectr. Folk Art Inst., N.Y., 1985, Symposium-Gen. Accident Ins., N.Y., 1994. Author: (monograph) Gentle Reminders of the Past, 1984. Recipient Recognition for Achievement award Alexander-Benwood Co., Inc., Huntington, N.Y., 1995. Mem. Nat. Trust for Historic Preservation, Nat. Mus. Women in the Arts (charter), New England Appraisers Assn., Northport Hist. Soc. Roman Catholic. Home: 72 Burt Ave Northport NY 11768

HOLADAY, SUSAN MIRLES, editor; b. Batavia, N.Y., Nov. 2, 1938; d. Norman and Sada Jule (Jacobson) Goldberg; m. William C. Holaday, Dec. 25, 1968 (dec. Feb. 1977). BA, Syracuse U., 1960; MA, U. Chgo., 1963. Equipment editor Instns. Mag., Chgo., 1964-65; co. editor Wyman-Gordon Co., Worcester, Mass., 1968-69; writer Profile Communications, Maynard, Mass., 1969-71; assoc. editor Lodging & Food-Service News, Boston, 1972-75, mng. editor, 1975-83; editor Foodservice East (formerly Lodging & Food Svc. East), Boston, 1983—. Co-founder Navy Yard Neighborhood Assn.; mem. Boston Area A-1 Police Neighborhood Adv. Coun. Mem. Boston Computer Soc. Club: Alfa Owners NE (Boston) (founder, sec. 1970-77). Office: Foodservice East 76 Summer St Boston MA 02110

HOLAN, JERRI-ANN, architect; b. Madison, Wis., May 17, 1959; d. Edward Raymond and Gail J. (Wold) H. BArch with high honors, U. Fla., 1980; MArch with honors, U. Calif., Berkeley, 1983. Lic. architect, Calif. Fellow Arkitekturhøgskolen, Oslo, 1983-84; author Rizzoli Internat. Publs., N.Y.C., 1987—; project mgr. R.H. Lee & Assocs., Larkspur, Calif., 1985-87, Rosekrans & Assocs., San Francisco, 1988; architect Christopherson & Graff, Architects, Berkeley, 1988-91, Abrams & Millikan Assocs., Berkeley, 1991—. Author: Norwegian Wood-A Tradition of Building, 1990. Fulbright grantee, 1983-84, Marshall Fund scholar Marshall Assn., Washington, 1984, Am. Scandinavian fellow Am. Scandinavian Assn., N.Y.C., 1983-84. Mem. AIA (vol. 1987—, photography award, 1990), Fulbright Assn. Alumni, U. Calif.-Berkeley Alumni. Democrat. Home: 833 Carmel Ave Albany CA 94706-1811

HOLBA, CARRIE ANNE, librarian; b. Moline, Ill., Dec. 6, 1950; d. Robert Thomas and Frances Margaret (Cirricione) Hillmer; m. Martin Sylvester Holba, Aug. 28, 1971 (dec. Aug. 1983); children: Katie Rebecca, Jodie Theresa. BS, U. Wis., 1978, MLIS, 1988. Asst. libr. Hughes, Thorsness, Gantz, Powell & Brundin, Anchorage, Alaska, 1988-90; pub. svcs. libr. Oil Spill Pub. Info. Ctr., Anchorage, 1991-92, libr. dir., 1992—; steering com. Anchorage Libr. Info. Network, 1992—. Svc. unit dir. Susitma Coun. Girl Scouts U.S., Anchorage, 1984-89. Mem. ALA, Spl. Librs. Assn., Alaska Libr. Assn. Home: 8421 Blackberry St Anchorage AK 99502 Office: Oil Spill Pub Info Ctr 645 G St Anchorage AK 99501

HOLBERT, SUE ELISABETH, archivist, writer, consultant; b. Denver, Jan. 24, 1935; d. Roger Dean and Beth Helen (Bryant) Ramey; children: Virginia S., Roger Frederick. BA, U. Nebr., 1956; postgrad., U. Minn., 1975-79. Editor Nebr. Edn. News Nebr. Edn. Assn., Lincoln, 1956-58; advt. asst. Augsburg Pub. House, Mpls., 1961-62; edit. asst. publs. div. Minn. Hist. Soc., St. Paul, 1965-69, asst. curator manuscripts, 1972-75, curator, 1975-76, dep. state archivist, 1976-79, state archivist, 1979-92; grants officer Macalester Coll., St. Paul, 1969-72; owner Annotators 2, Used and Rare Books, St. Paul.a. Author: (with June D. Holmquist) A History Tour of 50 Twin City Landmarks, 1966, Archives and Manuscripts: Reference and Access, 1977; compiler: (with June D. Holmquist and Dorothy D. Perry) History Along the Highways, 1967; contbr. Women in Minnesota, 1977; contbr. articles to profl. jours. Mem. Women Historians of Midwest, Soc. Am. Archivists (pres. 1988), Midwest Archives Conf., Acad. Cert. Archivists, Assn. of Records Mgrs. and Adminstrs. Democrat. Unitarian. Home: 807 Saint Clair Ave Apt 3 Saint Paul MN 55105-3317

HOLBROOK, DONNA JOYCE, pulmonary clinical nurse specialist; b. Paintsville, Ky., July 15, 1950; d. Charles Wilson and Dorothy Irene (Adams) H. BA, Morehead State U., 1974; ADN, U. Ky., 1983; BSN, Ohio U., 1988; MSN, Bellarmine Coll., 1993. RN, Ky., Ohio; cert. ACLS instr./provider and PALS instr./provider, Am. Heart Assn. Health care inspector Divsn. Licensing and Regulations, State of Ky., Frankfort, 1973-78; office mgr. Holbrook & Runyon Electronics, Flatwoods, Ky., 1978-83; reporter, photographer Greenup (Ky.) County News, 1980-81; tech. nursing asst. Our Lady Bellefonte Hosp., Ashland, Ky., 1983-84; critical care staff nurse Our Lady Bellefonte Hosp., Ashland, 1984-89, pulmonary clin. nurse specialist, 1989—; vitality ctr. adv. bd. Our Lady Bellefonte Hosp., Ashland, 1993—. Guest spkr., coord. Better Breathers Club, Ashland, 1989—; Sunday sch. tchr. Flatwoods (Ky.) First Bapt. Ch., 1992—. Recipient Nat. Nurse's Day award Commonwealth of Ky., Louisville, 1994. Mem. AACN (CCRN), Am. Assn. Cardiovascular and Pulmonary Rehab., Nat. Assn. Clin. Nurse Specialists (charter mem.), Ky. Cardiopulmonary Rehab. Assn., Ky. Thoracic Soc., Respiratory Nursing Soc. Home: RR 1 Box 232 Flatwoods KY 41139-9702 Office: Our Lady Bellefonte Hosp St Christophers Dr Ashland KY 41101

HOLBROOK, MARJORIE LUCILLE, manufacturing executive; b. Noble, Ky., Aug. 21, 1948; d. Reeve Lloyd and Pherbia D. (Miller) Hudson; m. Charlie Holbrook, Dec. 24, 1966; children: 1 child, Jeffrey Steven. AS in Acctg., U. Cin., 1982; B of Gen. Studies, Xavier U., 1990. Acctg. clk. Golden Foundry, Columbus, Ind., 1966-67; payroll master Bonds Clothing, Cin., 1967-68; office mgr. Valley Industries, Inc., Cin., 1969-86; comptr. Colorpac, Inc., Franklin, Ohio, 1986; v.p., sec., treas. Valley Industries Co., Cin., 1986-96, elected pres., 1996—; adv. bd. acctg. Clermont Coll., Batavia, Ohio, 1988—; adv. bd. Ctr. for Organizational Resources, Cin., 1995—. Mem. NAFE (spkr., workshop leader, recruiter 1989—, midwest region coord. 1996—), Am. Payroll Assn. (Greater Cin. and No. Ky. chpt. v.p. 1981, programs, newletter 1993-95), Greater Cin. Women's Network (programs mgr. 1991-93, dir. 1993—, apptd. women's group liaison 1996). Home: 2743 Case Rd New Richmond OH 45157 Office: Valley Industries Co Ste 206 8280 Montgomery Rd Cincinnati OH 45236

HOLBROOK, NORMA JEANNETTE, nursing educator; b. Napton, Mo., Oct. 26, 1939; d. R. Milton and Thelma M. (Miller) Cochran; m. Ralph E. Holbrook, June 30, 1961; children: Tamara M., Jennifer L. BS in Nursing, Cen. Mo. State U., 1965; M of Nursing, Kans. U., 1982. Staff nurse Menorah Med. Ctr., Kansas City, Mo., 1965-66, head nurse, 1966-67; instr. nursing Met. Community Coll., Kansas City, 1967-68; staff nurse Independence (Mo.) Med. Ctr., 1971-73; staff nurse St. Francis Hosp., Topeka, 1975-80, 84-89, mem. continuing edn. com., 1988—; instr. nursing Washburn U., Topeka, 1981-85, asst. prof., 1986-89; edn. coord. St. Francis Hosp. and Med. Ctr., 1989-91, 93—, clin. nurse specialist in gerontology, 1991-93; chair nursing rsch. com., 1990-96; mem. nursing quality assurance com. Stormont Vail Regional Med. Ctr., Topeka, 1982-83, mem. task force for improved implementation nursing care plans, 1983, mem. nursing svc. stds. com., chair procedures com., mem. std. care plan com., 1989—, mem. editorial bd. Kansas Nurse, 1990-95. Mem. nursing adv. com. ARC, Capital area chpt., Topeka, 1980-90, chmn. 1982-83, 88-89. Presentor ednl. programs on nursing process and care planning, gerontology, stress mgmt. for caregivers, positive communicating with patients with Alzheimer's Disease. Contbr. articles to profl. jours. Mem. ANA (Kansas State Nurses Assn. coun. continuing edn. 1987-89), Nat. Gerontol. Nursing Assn., Alzheimer's Assn. (bd. dirs. Topeka chpt., mem. edn. com. 1994-96), Sigma Theta Tau Internat. (pres. Eta Kappa chpt. 1990-92, Excellence in Writing award 1993). Republican. Methodist. Office: St Francis Hosp and Med Ctr 1700 SW 7th St Topeka KS 66606-1674

HOLCOMB, ALICE WILLARD POWER, diversified investments executive; b. Franklin County, Ga., Sept. 11, 1922; d. William McKinley and Flora Sarah (Cash) Cantrell; m. Fleming Mitchell Power, May 6, 1941 (dec. Sept. 1967); children: Susan Cantrell, Fleming Michael; m. George Waymon Holcomb, June 4, 1982. Student, Toccoa (Ga.) Falls Coll., 1939-40; BS, Perry Bus. Sch., 1941. Owner Power Poultry Co., Toccoa, 1950-61, Fleming Mitchell Power Properties, Toccoa and Athens, Ga., 1962—, Power's (retail shops), Athens, 1968-85; ptnr. Power Constrn. Co., Athens, 1972—, Athens Indsl. Electric, Athens, 1973—. Active Ga. Hist. Soc. Mem. DAR. Republican. Baptist. Home and Office: 199 Avalon Dr Athens GA 30606-3234

HOLCOMB, CARAMINE KELLAM, volunteer worker; b. Painter, Va., Jan. 23, 1941; d. Emerson Polk and Amine (Cosby) Kellam; m. Isaac Somers White, Nov. 25, 1961 (div. 1975); children: Kellam White, Caramine White, Virginia Somers White; m. Harry Sherman Holcomb III, May 12, 1979. AA, St. Mary's Coll., Raleigh, 1960; Cert., Richmond Bus. Coll., Va., 1961. Bd. dirs. Kellam Energy, Inc., Belle Haven, Va., 1980—, AUto Plus, Inc., Belle Haven, 1980-89, Shore Stop, Inc., Bele Haven, 1981-89. Contbr. articles to profl. jours. Trustee Northampton-Accomack Meml. Hosp., Nassawadox, Va., 1986—, v.p. aux., 1986-88, pres., 1988-90, sec. bd. trustees, 1989-91, vice chmn., 1991-94, chair, 1994-96; bd. dirs. Ea. Shore Hist. Soc., Onancock, Va., 1987-92; bd. dirs. Med. Soc. Va. Alliance, Richmond, 1984-94, v.p., 1989-91, pres., 1992-93; treas. E. Polk Kellam Found., 1991—. Mem. AMA Alliance Bd. (ERF com. 1994, AMA-ERF com. chmn. 1994-95), Med. Soc. Va. Trust, Garden Club Ea. Shore (pres. 1973-75, 85-87, field dir. 1995—). Home: PO Box 40 Franktown VA 23354-0040

HOLCOMB, CONSTANCE L., sales and marketing management executive; b. St. Paul, Oct. 28, 1942; d. John E. Holcomb and Lucille A. (Westerdahl) Hope. BS, U. Minn., 1965; MA in Intercultural Edn., U. of the Americas, Puebla, Mex., 1975. Rsch. analyst U.S. Dept. Def., Washington, 1965-66; br. gen. mgr. Berlitz Lang. Schs., Mexico City, 1966-68; pres., gen. mgr. Centro Lingüistico, Puebla, 1968-72; gen. mgr., prof. Lang. Ctr. Am. Sch. Found., Puebla, 1972-74; assoc. prof., dir. lang. programs U. of the Americas, Puebla, 1974-76; prof., dean faculty of langs. Nat. Autonomous U. Mex., Mexico City, 1976-78; dir. sales & mktg. Longman Pub. Co., N.Y.C., 1978-80, dir. internat. sales & mktg., 1980-84; mng. dir. ESL Pub. Div. McGraw-Hill Book Co., N.Y.C., 1984-85; dir. mktg. mgmt. McGraw-Hill Tng. Systems and Book Co., N.Y.C., 1985-86; dir. mktg. electronic bus. McGraw-Hill Book Co., N.Y.C., 1986-87; info. industry mgmt. cons., career mgmt. cons., ind. contractor, N.Y.C., 1987-91; mktg. cons. Sarasota, Fla., 1991—; v.p. MexTESOL, Mexico City, 1977-78. Editor: English Teaching in Mexico, 1975; contrb. articles to profl. jours. Bd. trusteess, devel. com. mem. John and Mable Ringhive Mus., 1993—. Mem. Assn. Am. Pubs. (com. chmn. internat. div. 1980-84, exec. com. 1980-84), Info. Industry Assn., Nat. Assn. Women Cons., Am. Soc. Profl. and Exec. Women. Office: 3555 Mistletoe Ln Longboat Key FL 34228-4103

HOLCOMB, ESTHER LEE, contractor; b. Eureka, Calif., Feb. 23, 1944; d. William Lee Foxworthy and Treasa Agnes (Cunningham) Foxworthy Knights; m. Henry Samson Holcomb, June 25, 1966; children: Deborah Lynn, Timothy Lee. Student, U. Calif., Berkeley, 1961-64, U. Calif., San Francisco, 1964-66. Lic. gen. contractor. Contractor, owner Holcomb's Home Repair, San Leandro, Calif., 1988—. Human resources commr. City of San Leandro, 1986-88, pks. and recreation commr., 1988-92; trustee San Leandro Unified Sch. Dist., 1992-96, bd. pres., 1996; bd. dirs. Peralta dist. Calif. State PTA, 1985-96, membership chmn., 1995-97, pres., 1993-95. Democrat. Mem. Assembly of God. Home: 694 Douglas Dr San Leandro CA 94577

HOLDEN, CAROL H., state legislator; b. Boston, Nov. 6, 1942; m. Donald B. Holden; 4 children. BA, Trinity Coll., 1964; MAT, Boston Coll., 1965. Intern U.S. Senate, 1963-64; N.H. state rep., 1984—, vice chair children, youth and juvenile justice com., mem. state-fed. rels. com.; mem. Amherst Ways and Means Commn., 1983-86; tchr., vol. coord. Del. N.H. Constl. Conv., 1984; pres. Amherst Women's Rep. Club, 1986-88; v.p. N.H. Fed. Rep. Women's Club, 1989—; mem. Amherst Sch. Dist. Mod., 1990—; dir. N.H. Ptnrs. in Edn., 1987—, sec., 1989—, vice chair, 1990—, chair, 1992—; mem. Gov.'s Steering Com. on Volunteerism, 1991—; mem. N.H. Alliance for Effective Schs., 1991—; v.p. N.H. Congress Parents and Tchrs., 1984-86, 90—. Mem. Trinity Coll. Alumni Assn. (bd. dirs. 1980-87). Home: PO Box 13 Amherst NH 03031-0013 Office: NH Ho of Reps 33 N State St Rm 210 Concord NH 03301*

HOLDEN, LEAH R., social services executive; b. Akron, Ohio, Oct. 5, 1947; d. James B. Holden and Eleanor M. (Jackson) Humphrey; children: Zachary Melragon, Anna Yeager. BA, Smith Coll., 1968; MA, Ohio U., 1975. Social worker Los Angeles County DPSS, L.A., 1968-70, Fallsview Mental Health Ctr., Cuyahoga Falls, Ohio, 1970-72, Residential, Inc., New Lexington, Ohio, 1978-81; consultation and edn. coord. Muskingum Cmty. Mental Health Ctr., Zanesville, Ohio, 1977-78; dir. Family Advocacy, New Lexington, 1981-83; assoc. dir. The Arc of Ohio, Columbus, 1983—. Co-author: On This Journey Together, 1993; author curriculum materials Choosing a Life, 1994; co-prodr. video series On This Journey Together, 1991. Founding bd. dirs. Ohio Schs. Are for Everyone, Columbus, 1989—, Ohio Safeguards, Chillicothe, Ohio, 1982-85; bd. dirs. Main St. Mediation Svc., New Lexington, 1993—; co-chair Perry County Family and Children First, New Lexington, 1992-94. NIMH fellow, 1975-77. Democrat. Presbyterian. Home: 320 Eastern Ave New Lexington OH 43764 Office: The Arc of Ohio 1335 Dublin Rd # 205-C Columbus OH 43215

HOLDEN, LISA ROSE, physical therapist; b. Pitts., Jan. 17, 1962; d. William Thomas and Dorothy Rita (Palombo) H. BA in Human Movement, Lake Erie Coll., Painesville, Ohio, 1983; AS in Phys. Therapist Asst., C.C. Allegheny County, Monroeville, Pa., 1990; M in Phys. Therapy, Duquesne U., 1994. Lic. phys. therapist, Pa. Mental health and mental retardation specialist Sifrin Assn., Canton, Ohio, 1983-84, Idlewood Ctr., Pitts., 1985-90; phys. therapy aide The Phys. Therapy Ctr., Pitts., 1986-90, phys. therapist asst., 1990-94, phys. therapist, 1994—; instr. N.E. C.C., Canton, 1983-85. Mem. Am. Phys. Therapy Assn., Pa. Phys. Therapy Assn., Phi Theta Kappa.

HOLDEN, REBECCA LYNN, artist; b. Monterey, Calif., Nov. 29, 1952; d. Derrel Wayne and Zella Fay (Reed) H.; m. Mark Stuart Bales, June 3, 1971 (div. Nov. 1983); children: Shelly Dawn, Matthew Gregory; m. David Strong Taylor, Dec. 27, 1995. BA, U. Ark., 1995. Potter/owner Rebecca Holden Studio, Searcy, Ark., 1984-94; artist/owner Rebecca Holden's Red Lick Mountain Studio, Clarksville, Ark., 1994—. Recipient Art scholarship Susan Jones Rand Foun., 1992, 93. Mem. Ark. Craft Guild.

HOLDER, ANGELA RODDEY, lawyer, educator; b. Rock Hill, S.C., Mar. 13, 1938; d. John T. and Angela M. (Fisher) Roddey; 1 child, John Thomas Roddey Holder. Student, Radcliffe Coll., 1955-56, B.A., Newcomb Coll., 1958; postgrad., Faculty of Law-King's Coll., London, 1957-58; J.D., Tulane U., 1960; LL.M., Yale U., 1975. Bar: La. 1961, S.C. 1960, Conn. 1981. Counsel Roddey, Sumwalt & Carpenter, Rock Hill, S.C., 1960-91; atty. criminal div. New Orleans Legal Aid Bur., 1961-62; counsel York County Family Ct., S.C., 1962-64; asst. prof. polit. sci. Winthrop Coll., Rock Hill, 1964-74; research assoc. Yale U. Law Sch., 1975-77, exec. dir. program in law, sci. and medicine, 1976-77; lectr. dept. pediatrics Yale U. Sch. Medicine, 1975-77, asst. clin. prof. pediatrics and law, 1977-79, assoc. clin. prof., 1979-83, clin. prof., 1983—; counsel for medicolegal affairs Yale-New Haven Hosp. and Yale Med. Sch., 1977-89. Author: The Meaning of the Constitution, 1968, 2d edit., 1987, Medical Malpractice Law, 1975, 2d edit. 1978, Legal Issues in Pediatrics and Adolescent Medicine, 1977, 2d edit., 1985; contbg. editor: Prism mag.; contbg. editor., AMA; mem. editorial bd.: IRB; Law, Medicine and Health Care, Jour. Philosophy and Medicine; contbr. articles to profl. jours. Mem. Rock Hill Sch. Bd., 1967-68; bd. dirs. Family Planning Clinic, chmn. 1970-73; bd. trustees Ednl. Commn. for Fgn. Med. Grads., 1990—; bd. dirs. Conn. Planned Parenthood, 1993—, exec. com. 1996—; mem. lawyers' rev. group Health Care Task Force, The White House, 1993; bd. trustees Cushing/Whitney Med. Libr. at Yale U., 1996—; ethics com. Leeway AIDS Hospice, New Haven, Conn., 1996—. Mem. ABA, S.C. Bar Assn. (medico-legal com. 1973—), La. Bar Assn., New Haven County Bar Assn., Am. Soc. Law and Medicine (treas. 1981-83, sec. 1983-85, pres. 1986-88, bd. dirs. 1977-91). Democrat. Episcopalian. Home: 23 Eld St New Haven CT 06511-3815 Office: Yale U School of Medicine 333 Cedar St New Haven CT 06510-3206

HOLDER, ANNA MARIA, holding company executive; b. Key West, Fla., Feb. 22, 1966; d. James Paul Yaccarino, Sr. and Carol (Joskey) McInerny; m. Harold D. Holder, 1996. AA, St. Petersburg Jr. Coll., 1989; BS, Eckerd Coll., 1991; MA, U. South Fla., 1994, postgrad., 1995—. Adminstr. Chase Bank Fla., Pinellas Park, 1989-91; substance abuse adminstr. Centurion Hosp., Tampa, 1992; staff writer, asst. features editor The Oracle, Tampa, 1992-93; v.p. The Holder Group, Inc., Tampa, 1994—; pres. Sun-Suns Trading Co., Inc., Tampa, 1996—. Author: Relationships Among Six Business Variables in the Black Press, 1994. Bd. dirs. Hillsborough County HealtCare Adv. Bd., 1996—. Mem. LWV (pres. Hillsborough County (Fla.) chpt. 1995-96). Republican. Home: 5210 Interbay Blvd # 8 Tampa FL 33611

HOLDER, BETH D., ballet company administrator. Bd. dirs. Atlanta Ballet, 1993—, chmn. Ballet Ball, 1993, artistic dir., 1994—. Co-chair adv. com. City of Atlanta Bur. Cultural Affairs, 1991; head com. Mayor Maynard Jackson's Arts Blueprint for Action; bd. dirs. North Ga. area March of Dimes, Ga. Ctr. for Children; vol. Lovett Sch. Office: 1400 W Peachtree St NW Atlanta GA 30309

HOLDER, HOLLY IRENE, lawyer; b. Albuquerque, May 16, 1952; d. Howard George and Dorothy Evelyn (Doll) Holzum; m. William B. Holder Jr., June 4, 1974; 1 child, Eric James. BA with honors, U. Colo., 1974; JD with honors, U. Denver, 1980. Bar: Colo. 1980, U.S. Ct. Appeals (10th cir.) 1980. Chemist Indsl. Labs., Denver, 1974-76; law clk. to presiding justice Colo. Supreme Ct., Denver, 1979; assoc. Calkins, Kramer, Grimshaw and Harring, Denver, 1980-82, 84-88, McKenna, Conner & Cuneo, Denver, 1988-90, Saunders, Snyder, Ross & Dickson, Denver, 1990-93; pvt. practice Denver, 1993—. Mem. adv. com. Regional Coun. Govts. Water Resources Mgmt., 1984—; chmn. Chatfield Basin Assn., Denver, 1987, Chatfield Basin Master Plan Task Force, Denver, 1986—. Recipient Disting. Svc. award Denver Regional Coun. Govts., 1987. Mem. Colo. Bar Assn., Denver Bar Assn., Mensa, Denver Rotary. Republican. Office: Holly I Holder PC 17th St Ste 1500 Denver CO 80202-1202

HOLDER, KATHLEEN, elementary education educator; b. Peoria, Ill., Jan. 19, 1942; d. Clifford B. and Margaret Anne (Bowker) Bourne; m. James Sherman Holder, Dec. 29, 1962; children: Laurie Lynn, Cheryl Anne. BS, Bradley U., 1965; MEd, Regents Coll., 1981; postgrad., SUNY, Cortland, 1990-91. Cert. elem. tchr., Ky., N.Y., Ga.; cert. tchr. ages birth-6 yrs., Am. Montessori Soc. Tchr. St. Philomena Sch., Peoria, Ill., 1962-63, Garfield Sch., Danville, Ill., 1964-67, St. David's Sch., Willow Grove, Pa., 1972-74, St. Austin Sch., Mpls., 1974-75, Knoxville (Tenn.) City Schs., 1977-79, Chenango Forks (N.Y.) Schs., 1985-92, Fayette County Schs., Lexington, Ky., 1992-96, Glynn County Schs., Brunswick, Ga., 1996—; team coord. sci. impact project SUNY, Cortland, 1987-90, presenter tchrs. teaching tchrs., 1988, sci. insvc. workshops for tchrs. Fayette County Schs., 1994-95; team coord. Broom-Tioga Boces Coop. Regional Curriculum Devel. Project, Binghamton, N.Y., 1989;. Author: Science Curriculum Resource Guide K-3, 1989. Hoyt Found. grantee, 1988. Mem. Nat. Reading Assn., Knoxville Reading Assn. (treas. 1978-79), Delta Zeta (Sec. 1977-79, Rose of Honor 1979), Sigma Alpha Iota. Methodist. Home: 96 Marsh Oak Dr Brunswick GA 31525

HOLDER, KATHLEEN ANN, artist, art educator; b. Milw., Mar. 12, 1947; d. Boleslaus Jacob Szmanda and Gladys Cecelia (Bomske) Lehmann; m. Patrick William Holder, Jan. 21, 1967 (div. May 1976); m. James Desmond Hilton, Jan. 13, 1996. BFA, U. Wis., Milw., 1970, MFA, 1981. Tchr. Milw. Pub. Schs., 1970-79; asst. prof. U. Ark, Little Rock, 1981-87, assoc. prof., 1988-96, prof., 1996—; vis. artist Memphis Coll. Art, 1992, Purdue U., West Lafayette, Ind., 1993, Wroclaw (Poland) Acad. Art, 1995, Saint Mary's Coll., Notre Dame, 1993. Solo exhbns. include Purdue U./Salisbury State U., 1993, Perimeter Gallery, 1986, 87, 90, 92, 94, 97, Bingham Kurts Gallery, Memphis, 1986, 91, Ark. Arts Ctr., 1989, Franz Bader Gallery, Washington, 1991, Ledbetter Lusk Gallery, 1997; pub. collections include Microsoft Corp., Seattle, Scarle Collection of Contemporary Art, Chgo., McKinsey & Co., Chgo., Salisbury (Md.) State U., Skadden, Arps, Slate, Maegher & Flom, N.Y., L.A., Chgo., Piper, Jaffray & Hopwood, Mpls., Ark. Arts Ctr., Little Rock, Stephens, Inc., Little Rock, Systematics Corp., Little Rock, U. Ark. at Little Rock; rep. by Perimeter Gallery, Chgo., Ledbetter/Lusk Gallery, Memphis, New Gallery, Houston. Recipient NEA fellow MidAm. Arts Alliance, 1984, Residence fellow Va. Ctr. for the Creative Arts, 1990, 91. Democrat. Home: 400 Fountain Little Rock AR 72205 Office: U Ark 2801 S University Little Rock AR 72204

HOLDER, MARGARET CHERVENAK, secondary school educator; b. Pitts., Oct. 16, 1956; d. Stephen W. and Margaret R. (Lis) Chervenak; m. Robert Holder, Oct. 28, 1978. BS in English, Duquesne U., 1978, MS in Edn., 1984. Cert. tchr., Pa. Tchr., pub. rels. dir. Keystone Oaks Schs., Pitts., 1984; substitute tchr. various schs., 1984-85; tchr. Pitts. Pub. Schs., 1985-86, Elizabeth (Pa.) Forward Schs., 1986—; part-time instr. Chatham Coll., Pitts., 1984-85; curriculum writer Pa. Youth Apprenticeship, 1991-93; presenter Jobs for the Future, Boston, 1991-95; cons. Kennywood, West Mifflin, Pa., 1993-96; practitioner-in-residence Duq. U. Sch. Edn., fall 1995, summer 1996. Recipient Great Tchr. award St. Vincent Coll., 1991. Mem. Nat. Coun. Tchrs. English. Democrat. Roman Catholic. Office: Elizabeth Forward HS 1000 Weigles Hill Elizabeth PA 15037

HOLDER, SALLIE LOU, training and meeting management consultant; b. Cin., Jan. 25, 1939; d. David Clifford Austin and Ruth Margaret (Higby) Haver; m. Norman Horace Derwyn Holder, July 14, 1964 (div. Oct. 1975). Student, Duke U., 1957-59; BS in Home Econs. Edn., U. Md, 1962; MA in Human Resource Devel. and Edn., George Washington U., 1982. Tchr. Prince Georges County Schs., Md., 1962-66; home econs. tchr. La Reine Sr. High Sch., Suitland, Md., 1966-68; adult edn. Home econs. tchr. Suitland Sr. High Sch, 1969-73; mgr./asst. area sales mgr. The Fabric Tree, Hyattsville, Md., 1972-75; trainer Woodward & Lothrop, Washington and Prince Georges County, Md., 1975-79; conf. coord., non-credit short course coord. Univ. Coll. U. Md., College Park, 1979-87; analyst SYSCON, Washington, 1987-88; meeting mgmt. and tng. cons. Holder & Assocs., College Park, Md., 1988—; tng. specialist Fed. Deposit Ins. Corp., Washington, 1990; instr. Marymount U., Arlington, Va., 1990, Goucher Coll., Balt., 1991-93; facilitator New Beginnings, Takoma Park, Md., 1983-90, chmn. planning com., facilitator co-trainer, bd. dirs., 1983-84, chmn. facilitators, 1985-86; monitor Smithsonian Resident Assocs. Program, 1993—. Mem. alumni bd. Coll. Human Ecology, U. Md., College Park, 1971-93, pres., 1973-74, 77-80, sec., 1985-86, v.p., 1988-90; bd. dirs. Pastoral Counseling and Consultation Ctrs., 1977-86 mem., cons. lay edn. com., community edn. com.; mem. seminarian com., chmn. retreat com., vestry mem. Ch. of the Nativity, Camp Springs, Md., 1977-82; vestryman St. Andrews Episc. Ch., College Park, 1990-93; usher Arena Stage, 1990—. Recipient Disting. Svc. award Alumni Bd. of Coll. Human Ecology, U. Md., 1981, Vol. award, 1991. Mem. ASTD (Washington chpt. employer coord. 1984-85, co-chmn. program com. 1986, chmn. meeting arrangements 1987-88, treas. 1989, ASTD day chmn., nat. issues chair 1990, chair scholarship com. 1992, coord. spl. interest group 1993, Spl. Achievement award 1987, 88, 90, Pres.'s award 1993), Soc. Govt. Meeting Planners (program commn. 1987-88, communication com., ann. conf. com. 1988-89, chmn. nominating com. 1990, ann. conf. presenter 1990, 93, 94, bd. dirs. 1991-92, 95—, chmn. edn. com. for 1992 ann. conf. 1995-96, newsletter editor), U. Md. Coll. Park Alumni Assn. (bd. govs. 1989-93), Assn. Meeting Profls., Profl. Conv. Mgrs. Assn., Md. P.G. Alumni assn. (v.p. 1994—), Coll. Park Bus. and Profl. Women, Del Marva Depression Glass Club, Washington Met. Glass Club, Prince Georges Hist. Soc., Toastmasters. Episcopalian. Home and Office: 9715 48th Pl College Park MD 20740-1404

HOLDER, SUSAN MCCASKILL, computer company executive, small business owner; b. Tulsa, July 8, 1956; d. Allan Murdock McCaskill and Kathryn Irene (Padgett) Dolan; m. Robert Newton Holder, Jr., Nov. 30, 1985; children: Tara Susan, Abigail Megan. BA in Bus. Mgmt., Upsala Coll., East Orange, N.J., 1978; MBA in Fin., Fairleigh Dickinson U., 1985. Comml. underwriter State Farm Ins. Cos., Wayne, N.J., 1978-81, svc. supr., 1981-83; adminstrn. mgr. Digital Equipment Corp., Piscataway, N.J., 1983-85; project mgr. Digital Equipment Corp., Princeton, N.J., 1985-87, area adminstrv. svcs. mgr., 1987-88, area adminstrv. support mgr., 1988-89; bus. analyst U.S. Hdqrs. Digital Equipment Corp., Alpharetta, Ga., 1989-91, Westboro, Mass., 1989-91; project mgr. U.S. Desktop Svcs., Digital Equipment Corp., Alpharetta, 1991-92; co-owner Basket Innovations, Inc., Roswell, Ga., 1992-94; co-owner, tng. cons., corp. officer Asphodel Assocs., Inc., Roswell, 1994—. Mem. pastor-parish rels. Christ United Meth. Ch., Roswell, Ga., 1990-91, chair pastor-parish rels., 1992, mem. nurture com., tchr. Sunday sch. elem. grades, 1990—. Mem. AAUW (br. sec. Point Pleasant, N.J. 1986-89), Internat. Soc. for Performance Improvement. Home: 1810 Azalea Springs Trl Roswell GA 30075-1857 Office: Asphodel Assocs Inc Ste 203-231 4651 Woodstock Rd Roswell GA 30075-1640

HOLDRIDGE, BARBARA, book publisher; b. N.Y.C., July 26, 1929; d. Herbert L. and Bertha (Gold) Cohen; m. Lawrence B. Holdridge, Oct. 9, 1959; 2 children. A.B., Hunter Coll., 1950. Asst. editor Liveright Pub. Corp., N.Y.C., 1950-52; co-founder Caedmon Records, Inc., N.Y.C., 1952; partner Caedmon Records, Inc., 1952-60, pres., 1960-62, treas., 1962-70, pres., 1970-75; founder Stemmer House Pubs. Inc., Owings Mills, Md., 1975; pres. Stemmer House Pubs. Inc., 1975—; co-founder, v.p. Shakespeare Rec. So., Inc., N.Y.C., 1960-70, Theatre Rec. Soc., Inc., N.Y.C., 1964-70; founder BEDE Prodns., 1984; co-founder History Rec. Soc., Inc., N.Y.C., 1964, pres., 1964-70; lectr. on Ammi Phillips, 1959; lectr. on book pub., 1992—; adj. prof. writing media Loyola Coll., Balt., 1987-91. Author: Ammi Phillips, 1968, Aubrey Beardsley Designs from the Age of Chivalry, 1983, Chinese Cut-Out Designs of Costumes, 1989; articles on Am. paintings. Recipient Am. Shakespeare Festival award, 1962, N.Y.C. certificate appreciation, 1972; named to Hunter Coll. Hall of Fame, 1972. Mem. Phi Beta Kappa Assn. of Greater Balt. (bd. dirs.). Office: 2627 Caves Rd Owings Mills MD 21117-2919

HOLDSWORTH, JANET NOTT, women's health nurse; b. Evanston, Ill., Dec. 25, 1941; d. William Alfred and Elizabeth Inez (Kelly) Nott; children: James William, Kelly Elizabeth, John David. BSN with high distinction, U. Iowa, 1963; M of Nursing, U. Wash., 1966. RN, Colo. Staff nurse U. Colo. Hosp., Denver, 1963-64, Presbyn. Hosp., Denver, 1964-65, Grand Canyon Hosp., Ariz., 1965; asst. prof. U. Colo. Sch. Nursing, Denver, 1966-71; counseling nurse Boulder PolyDrug Treatment Ctr., Boulder, 1971-77; pvt. duty nurse Nurses' Official Registry, Denver, 1973-82; cons. nurse, tchr. parenting and child devel. Teenage Parent Program, Boulder Valley Schs., Boulder, 1980-88; bd. dirs., treas. Nott's Travel, Aurora, Colo., 1980—; nurse Rocky Mountain Surgery Ctr., 1996—; instr., nursing coord. ARC, Boulder, 1979-80, instr., nursing tng. specialist, 1980-82. Mem. adv. bd. Boulder County Lamaze Inc., 1980-88 ; mem. adv. com. Child Find and Parent-Family, Boulder, 1981-89; del. Rep. County State Congl. Convs., 1972-96, sec. 17th Dist. Senatorial Com., Boulder, 1982-92; vol. Mile High ARC, 1980; vol. chmn. Mesa Sch. PTO, Boulder, 1982-92, bd. dirs., 1982-95, v.p., 1983-95; elder Presbyn. ch. Mem. ANA, Colo. Nurses Assn. (bd. dirs. 1975-76, human rights com. 1981-83, dist. pres. 1974-76), Coun. Intracultural Nurses, Sigma Theta Tau, Alpha Lambda Delta. Republican. Home: 1550 Findlay Way Boulder CO 80303-6922 Office: Rocky Mountain Surgery Ctr 2405 Broadway Boulder CO 80304

HOLEC, ANITA KATHRYN VAN TASSEL, civic worker; b. Rahway, N.J., Nov. 11, 1947; d. Edward T. and Irene Eleanor (Barna) Van Tassel; m. Sidney W. Holec, Oct. 26, 1968. BS, U. Houston, 1969. Stockbroker Drexel Burnham Lambert, Inc., Miami, Fla., 1976-78, Merrill Lynch, Venice, Fla., 1979-80; fin. cons. Shearson Lehman Bros., Venice, 1981-87; owner, mgr. Closet Stretchers, Venice, 1987-89. Bd. dirs. Safe Place and Rape Crisis Ctr., Sarasota, 1987—, Womens Resource Ctr., Sarasota, 1981-86, 90-94, Friends Venice Libr., 1992-94, New Coll. Libr., 1991-94; mem. Leadership Sarasota, 1991-95, Jr. League of Sarasota, 1982—, Argus Found., 1982—. Home: 1708 Casey Key Rd Nokomis FL 34275-3370

HOLEN, ARLENE S., federal commissioner; b. N.Y.C., July 5, 1938; m. Sheldon Holen, Sept. 10, 1960; children: Jacqueline, Margaret. Student, Syracuse U., 1956-57; BA with distinction, Smith Coll., 1960; MA in Econs., Columbia U., 1963. Economist Bur. Internat. Labor Affairs, 1979-82; economist office of policy Dept. Labor, 1982-83, economist office of mgmt. and budget, 1983-85; sr. staff economist Pres. Coun. Econ. Advisers, 1985-88; assoc. dir. for human resources, vets. and labor Office of Mgmt. and Budget, 1988-90; commr., retiree health benefits Adv. Commn. on United Mine Workers of Am., Dept. Labor, 1990; commr. Fed. Mine Safety and Health Review Commn., Dept Labor, 1990-92; chmn. Fed. Mine Safety and Health Review Commn., Dept Labor, Washington, 1992—. Author: Immigration, Winners and Losers, 1987. Columbia U. fellow, Woodrow Wilson fellow. Mem. Phi Beta Kappa. Office: Fed Mine Safety & Health Commn Rm 604 1730 K St NW Ste 604 Washington DC 20006-3868

HOLEYFIELD, MARY ANNETTE, health and physical education educator; b. Harrison, Ark., June 20, 1955; d. Leo Dale and Etta Ruth (Petree) Borland; m. Robert Lee Holeyfield, May 18, 1974; 1 child, Ashlyn Elizabeth. BS in Health and Phys. Edn., Ark. Tech. U., Russellville, 1976, MEd in Phys. Edn., 1977. Cert. ARC instr. trainer. Elem. phys. edn. specialist Russellville Pub. Schs., 1979-85; instr. health and phys. edn. Ark. Tech. U., Russellville, 1985-92, asst. prof. health and phys. edn., 1992—. Pres. Russellville Jr. Aux., 1992. Mem. AAHPERD, Ark. Assn. Health, Phys. Edn., Recreation and Dance (past elem. sect. chair), Zeta Tau Alpha (past dist. pres., past alumnae chpt. officer). Office: Ark Tech U Hwy 7 North Russellville AR 72801

HOLGERS-AWANA, RITA MARIE, electrodiagnosis specialist; b. Chgo., Nov. 24, 1933; d. Joseph Theodore and Kathleen (Cooney) Konecny; m. Alan Miles Holgers, Aug. 8, 1960 (div. Sept. 1986); children: Dale, Ross; m. Benedict E.C. Awana, June 13, 1989 (dec. Feb. 1995). BS, N.Am. U., 1984, M Nutripathic Sci., 1988, D Nutripathy, 1988, D Nutritional Philosophy, 1990. Nutritional cons. Vitality Testing, Phoenix, 1982-84; pres., CEO Vitality Testing, Glendale, Ariz., 1984-86, Zac Engring. Inc., Lombard, Ill., 1986—; provider rels. clk. Prin. Health Care, Oakbrook Terrace, Ill., 1995—. Author: Me and My Non-Disease, 1983, Radiation, The Hidden Enemy, 1995; invention electronic water filter unit. Pres., v.p. S.W. Herbal Edn. Assn., Phoenix, 1984-85; sec. Better Breathers Club, Chula Vista, Calif., 1992-93, Concerned Citizens, Biggsville, Ill., 1975; co-founder, charter mem. Exec. Women's Coun., Moline, Ill., 1974; cub scout den leader Boy Scouts Am., Eldridge, Iowa, 1973; treas. food coop., Asuncion, Paraguay, 1958. With U.S. Fgn. Svc., 1956-61. Recipient Internat. Golf Trophy, U.S. Dept. of State, 1959, Championship Golf trophy Hend-Co-Hills, 1974, 75, 77, Tai Chi Black Belt, Shingumatsu Martial Arts, 1993. Mem. Women in the Arts, Nat. Health Fedn. (conv. spkr. 1996). Mem. Unity Ch. Home and Office: 239 S Westmore Meyers Apt E Lombard IL 60148

HOLIDAY, EDITH ELIZABETH, former presidential adviser, cabinet secretary; b. Middletown, Ohio, Feb. 14, 1952; d. Harry Jr. and Kethlyn (Watson) H.; m. Terrence B. Adamson, June 8, 1985; children: Kathlyn Holiday Adamson, Elizabeth Holiday Adamson; 1 stepchild, Terrence Morgan Adamson. Student, Miami U., Oxford, Ohio, 1970-71; BS with honors, U. Fla., 1974, JD, 1977. Bar: Fla. 1977, D.C. 1978, Ga. 1984. Assoc. Read Smith Shaw & McClay, Washington, 1977-83, Dow Lohnes & Albertson, Atlanta, 1983-84; exec. dir. Commn. on Exec. Legis. and Jud. Salaries, Washington, 1984-85; spl. counsel polit. action com. Fund for Am. Future, Washington, 1985-87; dir. ops. George Bush for Pres., Inc., Washington, 1987-88; chief counsel, nat. fin. and ops. dir. Bush-Quayle 88, Washington, 1988; with legal svcs. staff George Bush for Pres. Compliance Com., Washington, 1988; asst. sec. for pub. affairs and pub. liaison, counselor to sec. Departmental Offices, U.S. Dept. Treasury, Washington, 1988; gen. counsel U.S. Dept. Treasury, Washington, 1989-90; asst. to U.S. pres., sec. of cabinet Washington, 1990-93; legis. asst. to U.S. Sen. Nicholas F. Brady, Washington, 1982-83; bd. dirs. Amerada Hess Corp., H.J. Heinz Co., Hercules, Inc., Bessemer Trust Co., N.A., Bessemer Trust Co. of N.J., Beverly Enterprises, Inc. Recipient Alexander Hamilton award Sec. of Treasury, 1991, spl. citation John Marshall Bar Assn. Mem. Phi Delta Phi, Kappa Tau Alpha.

HOLIFIELD, ANN MARIE LEE, school system administrator; b. Columbus, Ga., Aug. 27, 1959; d. James Charles and Emily Ima Jean (Worthington) Lee; m. Thomas Lynn Holifield, May 25, 1991. Student, Columbus Area Vocat. Tech. Sch., 1977-78. Asst. mgr., mgr. Nationwide Studios, Columbus, 1983-88; exec. sec. to asst. supr. Muscogee County Sch. Dist., Columbus, 1978-93, exec. sec. to acting deputy supt., 1993-94, exec. sec. to dep. supt., 1994, exec. sec. to supt. of ed., 1995—. Mem. Muscogee Assn. Ednl. Office Profls. (sec., mem. exec. bd.), Ga. Assn. Ednl. Office Profls. Baptist. Home: 5045 3rd Ave Columbus GA 31904 Office: Muscogee County Sch Dist 1200 Bradley Dr Columbus GA 31904

HOLL, DEE LYNN, career counselor, psychotherapist, management consultant; b. Lima, Ohio, Mar. 8, 1949; d. James Adam Holl and Eileen (Gross) Parker; m. David William Dingledine (div. 1974); children: Jeffrey, Jennifer Holl Flowers. BA, U. Houston, 1985; MA, Amber U., 1993. Lic. profl. counselor. Human resources generalist Omniplan, Houston, 1986-87; plant pers. mgr. Digital Equipment, Greenville, S.C., 1987-90; sr. human resources cons. Digital Equipment, Dallas, 1990-93; cons. Drake, Beam, Morin, Dallas, 1993-95; sr. human resources mgr. Stream Internat., Dallas, 1995; site mgr., career counselor CDS/Mobil Oil, Dallas, 1995—; conf. spkr. IACMP, Dallas, 1996, Visions, Dallas, 1995. Vol. counselor AIDS Interfaith Coun., Dallas, 1994. Recipient plaque Johnson Space Ctr., 1984. Mem. ACA, IACMP (pres.-elect), ASTD. Office: Career Devel Svcs Mobil Pl 3000 Pegasus Park Dr Dallas TX 75247

HOLLAND, ALLISON DENMAN, writing and film educator; b. Stuttgart, Ark., Oct. 21, 1946; d. Floyd Allison Denman and Vergie Alice (Dumond) McCollum; children: Allison Brooks Holland, Anne Denman Holland. BS in Edn., Ark. State U., 1968; MEd, La. State U., 1969, MA in English, 1972. Tchr. Stuttgart (Ark.) H.S., 1970-71, Pearl H.S., Nashville, 1972-75, Mt. St. Mary's Acad., Little Rock, 1975-78; tchr. writing U. Ark., Little Rock, 1984—, assoc. dir. Writing Ctr., 1993-96. Columnist Ark. Women's Jour., 1993—. Marketing chmn. Jr. League Little Rock, 1980-81, edn. com. chmn., 1981-82; founder 7 on Your Side program Channel 7, Little Rock, 1982-83. Mem. Internat. Tchg. Soc. (program chmn.), Writing Program Adminstrs., Coll. Conf. on Composition and Comm., Nat. Coun. Tchrs. English, Delta Kappa Gamma (2d v.p., program chair 1994—). Office: U Ark Little Rock 2801 S University Little Rock AR 72204

HOLLAND, BETH, actress; b. N.Y.C.; d. Samson and Florence (Liebman) Hollander; m. Louis L. Friedman, Aug. 28, 1953; children: Ellen Lynn, Cathy Jayne. Pvt. studies in acting, voice tng. Arts funding cons. N.Y. State Senate, 1974-89. Appeared in various roles on TV, film and theatre, also comedy video Your Favorite Jokes, 1988. Mem. AFTRA (pres. N.Y. chpt. 1989-91, bd. dirs., trustee Health and Retirement Funds, past treas.), SAG, N.Y. TV Acad. (past bd. dirs.), Actors Equity Assn., Twelfth Night Club (bd. dirs.), Episcopal Actors Guild, Cath. Actors Guild, Players Club, Lambs Club. Home winter: 4300 N Ocean Blvd Fort Lauderdale FL 33308-5944

HOLLAND, CECELIA, writer; b. Henderson, Nev., Dec. 31, 1943; d. William Dean and Katharine (Schenck) H.; children: Julie, Bonnie, Karen, Debora. BA, Conn. Coll., 1965. Author: (novels) The Firedrake, 1966, 5th edit., 1975, Rakossy, 1967, 4th edit., 1969, Kings in Winter, 1968, 2d edit., 1969, Until the Sun Falls, 1969, 3d edit., 1970, Antichrist, 1970, as Wonder of the World, 1981, The Earl, 1971, 2d edit., 1972, as A Hammer for Princes, 1973, The Death of Attilla, 1973, 3d edit., 1992, Spanish edit., 1992, Great Maria, 1974, 5th edit., 1993, Floating Worlds, 1975, 6th edit., 1984 (also translated into Spanish), Two Ravens, 1977, 3d edit., 1979, City of God, 1979, as Die Kerkermeister Gottes:, 1995, Home Ground, 1991, ed edit., 1982, The Sea Beggars, 1982, 3d edit. 1984 (Doubleday Book Club selection), The Belt of Gold, 1984, 3d edit., 1986, Spanish edit., 1993, Pillar of the Sky, 1985, 4th edit., 1988 (alternate selection of Lit. Guild), Swedish, Dutch edits., 1986, The Lords of Vaumartin (God's Gambols), 1988, 3d edit., 1990, The Bear Flag, 1990, 3d edit., 1992, Pacific Street, 1991, 2d edit., 1991, Jerusalem, 1996, (as Elizabeth Eliot Carter) The Valley of the Kings, 1975, (as Julie Rood) Lucky Lady, 1974, also Japanese edit., (juvenile books) Ghost on the Steppe, 1969, The King's Road, 1970; contbr. articles to popular mags. Recipient Irving Stone prize, 1979, medal Conn. Coll., 1980; Guggenheim Found. fellow, 1981.

HOLLAND, DIANNA GWIN, real estate broker; b. Pueblo, Colo., Mar. 9, 1948; d. Everett Paul Gwin and Ava Mariea (Calvert) Johnson. Staff asst. The White House, Washington, 1971-77, exec. asst. to counsel, 1981-89; sales agt. Rand Real Estate, Alexandria, Va., 1977-79, Pagett Real Estate, Alexandria, 1979-81; assoc. broker WJD & Assocs., Alexandria, 1985-93; assoc. broker, asst. mgr. adminstrn. Long & Foster Realtors, 1993-96; prin. broker, v.p. Century 21 Campaign, 1996—; exec. aide to chmn. Edward Lowe Industries, Inc., 1990-91. Del. Va. Republican Conv., 1981, 82, 84. Roman Catholic. Home: 311 Park Rd Alexandria VA 22301-2737

HOLLAND, GENE GRIGSBY (SCOTTIE HOLLAND), artist; b. Hazard, Ky., June 30, 1928; d. Edward and Virginia Lee (Watson) Grigsby; m. George William Holland, Sept. 22, 1950; 3 children. BA, U. S. Fla., 1968; pupil of Ruth Allison, Talequah, Okla., 1947-48, Ralph Smith, Washington, 1977, Clint Carter, Atlanta, 1977, R. Jordan, Winter Park, Fla., 1979, Cedric Baldwin Egeli Workshop, Charleston, S.C., 1984. Various clerical and secretarial positions, 1948-52; news reporter, photographer Bryan (Tex.) Daily News, 1952; clk. Fogarty Bros. Moving and Transfer, Tampa and Miami, Fla., 1954-57; tchr. elem. Schs., Hillsborough County, Fla., 1968-72; salesperson, assoc. real estate, 1984—; owner, operator antique store, 1982-87. One-woman and group shows include Tampa Woman's Clubhouse, 1973, Cor Jesu, Tampa, 1973, bank, Monks Corner, S.C., 1977, Summerville Artists Guild, 1977-78, Apopka (Fla.) Art and Foliage Festival, 1980, 81, 82, Fla. Fedn. Women's Clubs, 1980, 81, 82; numerous group shows, latest being: Island Gifts, Tampa, 1980-82, Brandon (Fla.) Station, 1980-81, Holland Originals, Orlando, Fla.; represented in permanent collections including Combank, Apopka, also pvt. collections. Vol. ARC, Tampa, 1965-69, United Fund Campaign, 1975-76; pres. Mango (Fla.) Elem. Sch. PTA, 1966-67; pres. Tampa Civic Assn., 1974-75; vol. Easter Seal Fund Campaign, 1962-63; art chmn. Apopka Art & Foliage Festival, 1990; deaconness Ctrl. Christian Ch. of Orlando, 1992-94, chmn. bible study 1993-94. Recipient numerous art awards, 1978-82. Mem. AARP (parlimentarian Apopka chpt.), Internat. Soc. of Artists, Coun. of Arts and Scis. for Cen. Fla., Fedn. Women's Clubs (pres. Hillsborough County 1974-75, v.p. Tampa Civic 1974-75), Meth. Women's Soc. (sec. 1976-77), Nat. Trust Hist. Preservation, Nat. Hist. Soc., Fla. Geneal. and Hist. Soc., Am. Guild Flower Arrangers, The Nat. Grigsby Family Soc. (mem. SW chpt., assoc. sec. 1991-92, corp. sect. 1992—, dir. 1995—), Internat. Inner Wheel Club (past chmn. dist. 696, pres. Tampa 1972-73), Musicale Club (1st v.p. bd. incorporators Tampa 1974-75), Apopka Woman's Club (pres. 1981-82, bd. dir. 1983-85, Woman of Yr. 1991, 92), Apopka Tennis Over 50's Group Club (pres. 1988-90), Federated Garden Club Plant City Fla. Home: 1101 W Mahoney St Plant City FL 33566-4437 also: PO Box 2213 Plant City FL 33564-2213

HOLLAND, ISABELLE CHRISTIAN, writer; b. Basel, Switzerland, June 16, 1920; d. Philip Edgar and Corabelle (Anderson) H. BA, Tulane U., 1942. Censor U.S. War Dept., New Orleans, 1942-44; corr. sec. Life Mag., N.Y.C., 1944-47; editorial asst. Nat. Coun. Protestant Episcopal Chs., N.Y.C., 1947-48; asst. editor Tomorrow Mag. Creative Age Press, N.Y.C., 1948-49; advt. copywriter Franklin Spier Advt. Agy., N.Y.C., 1949-53; assoc. editor McCall's Mag., N.Y.C., 1953-55; publicity dir. Crown Pubs., Lippincott Co., Delacorte Press, Harper's Mag., G.P. Putnam, Pubs., N.Y.C., 1956-69; writer, 1969—. Author: Cecily, 1967, Amanda's Choice, 1970, The Man Without a Face, 1972, (under name Francesca Hunt) The Mystery of Castle Renaldi, 1972, Heads You Win, Tails I Lose, 1973, Kilgaren, 1974, Journey of Three, 1974, Trelawny, 1976, Moncrieff, 1975, Of Love and Death and Other Journeys, 1975 (nominated Nat. Book award 1976), Darcourt, 1976, Grenelle, 1976, Alan and the Animal Kingdom, 1977, Hitchhike, 1977, The de Maury Papers, 1977, Dinah and the Green Fat Kingdom, 1978, Tower Abbey, 1978, The Marchington Inheritance, 1979, Counterpoint, 1980, Now Is Not Too Late, 1980, Summer of My First Love, 1981, The Lost Madonna, 1981, A Horse Named Peaceable, 1982, Abbie's God Book, 1982, Perdita, 1983, God, Mrs. Musket and Aunt Dot, 1983, The Empty House, 1983, Kevin's Hat, 1984, The Island, 1984 Green Andrew Green, 1984, A Death at St. Anselm's, 1984, Flight of the Archangel, 1985, Jenny Kiss'd Me, 1985, A Lover Scorned, 1986, Henry and Grudge, 1986, Toby the Splendid, 1987, Love and the Genetic Factor, 1987, The Christmas Cat, 1987, Bump in the Night, 1988, A Fatal Advent, 1989, Thief, 1989, The Easter Donkey, 1989, The Unfrightening Dark, 1989, The Journey Home, 1990, The Long Search, 1990, The Search, 1991, The House in the Woods, 1991, Behind the Lines, 1994, Family Trust, 1994. Mem. PEN, Authors Guild, Cosmopolitan Club (N.Y.C.). Address: care Elaine Markson Lit Agy 44 Greenwich Ave New York NY 10011-8347

HOLLAND, KATHIE KUNKEL, university official, educator; b. Lake Worth, Fla., Jan. 4, 1949; d. John Alfred and Annetta (Wellman) K.; m. James Carson Holland, Dec. 15, 1968 (div. Mar. 1987); children: J. Wesley, J. Wyatt. MBA, U. Cen. Fla., 1980, BSBA, 1978. Teller 1st Fed. Savs. and Loan, West Palm Beach, Fla., 1969-70; head teller Tallahassee Fed. Savs. and Loan, 1970-71; br. mgr. Orlando (Fla.) Fed. Savs. and Loan, 1971-75; instr. Orlando Coll., 1982-85; grad. asst. U. Cen. Fla., Orlando, 1978-80, instr., 1986—, asst. dir. Small Bus. Devel. Ctr., 1986—; dir. profl. devel. Fla. Small Bus. Devel. Ctr. Network, Orlando, 1992—; bd. dirs. Ctr. for Continuing Edn. for Women, Orlando, 1987; co-founder Women Bus. Owners' Network, Orlando, 1988; mgmt. cons., Orlando. Co-author: Starting and Managing a Business in Central Florida, 1989, Professional Development Manual, 1994; contbr. articles to profl. jours. Com. mem. Jr. Achievement Ctr., Entrepreneur Task Force, Orlando, 1989; speaker Greater Brevard C. of C., Melbourne, Fla., 1989. Mem. ASTD, Nat. Coalition Bldg. Inst., Nat. Assn. Women Bus. Owners, Platform Speakers Assn., Women's Bus. Ednl. Coun. (bd. dirs. 1987—), Greater Orlando C. of C. (com. chmn. 1987), Inst. Mgmt. Cons., Omicron Delta Kappa. Republican. Presbyterian. Office: U Cen Fla Small Bus Devel Ctr Alafaya Trail Orlando FL 32816

HOLLAND, MARTHA KING, primary and secondary education educator; b. Charlottesville, Va., Jan. 20, 1965; d. Frederick Conrad Jr. and Martha King (Abbott) Holland; m. Russell Frost Shipman, Aug. 7, 1993. BA Studio Art, Mt. Holyoke Coll., 1987; MA English, U. Va., 1988-90. Cert. secondary English tchr. English tchr., coach, head grades 7 and 8 The Rivers Sch., Weston, Mass., 1990-95; English and lang. arts tchr., coach Out-of-Door Acad., Sarasota, Fla., 1995—. Author poetry, (novel) The Mangrove Legacy. Named to Terrific Tchrs. Making A Difference, Edward F. Calesa Found., Mass., 1993. Mem. Nat. Coun. Tchrs. English. Home: 1175 52d St Sarasota FL 34234 Office: The Out Of Door Acad 444 Reid St Sarasota FL 34242

HOLLAND, NANCY JEAN, philosophy educator; b. Pomona, Calif., Sept. 3, 1947; d. Glen Allen and Marjorie Jean (Stanfield) H.; m. Jeffrey Wynter Koon, Aug. 18, 1981; children: Gwendolyn Rose, Justis Vincent. BA, Stanford U., 1969; PhD, U. Calif., Berkeley, 1981. Prof. philosophy Hamline U., St. Paul, 1981—; women's studies coord. Associated Colls. Twin Cities, Mpls./St. Paul, 1993-95. Author: Is Women's Philosophy Possible, 1990. Mem. Am. Philos. Assn., Soc. Phenomenology and Existential Philosophy, Soc. for Women in Philosophy. Office: Hamline U 1536 Hewitt Ave Saint Paul MN 55104

HOLLAND, NOY, writer; b. Dayton, Ohio, Dec. 3, 1960; d. James Read and Elizabeth (Collings) H.; m. Sam Michel, June 5, 1993. Student, U. Ala., Columbia U.; BA (cum laude), Middlebury Coll., 1983; MFA, U. Fla., 1994. Instr. The Hotchkiss Sch., Lakeville, Conn., 1983; editl. asst. Esquire, N.Y.C., 1984-85; asst. to sr. editor Charles Scribner's Sons, N.Y.C., 1986-87; instr. N.Y. Assn. for New Ams., N.Y.C., 1990, U. Fla., Gainesville, 1992-94; writer-in-residence Phillips Acad., Andover, Mass., 1994—. Author: The Spectacle of the Body, 1994; contbr. articles to profl. jours. Recipient Bread Loaf scholar, 1983, U. Fla., Porter fellow, 1992, Grinter fellow, 1992-94; John Gardner fellow, Bread Loaf Colony, 1994. Episcopalian. Home: 75 Salem St # 2 Andover MA 01810 Office: Phillips Acad Rte 28 Main St Andover MA 01810*

HOLLEB, DORIS B., urban planner, economist; b. N.Y.C., Oct. 26, 1922; m. Marshall M. Holleb, Oct. 15, 1944; children: Alan, Gordon, Paul. BA magna cum laude, Hunter Coll., 1942; MA, Harvard U., 1947; postgrad. U. Chgo., 1959-60, 65-66. Economist Fed. Res. Bd., Washington, 1943-44; freelance journalist, 1945-63, econ. cons. Chgo. Dept. City Planning, 1963-66; rsch. assoc. Ctr. Urban Studies, U. Chgo., 1966-78, sr. rsch. assoc., 1978-88, dir. Met. Inst., 1973-84, professorial lectr., 1979—; chmn., Francis W. Parker Sch. Ednl. Coun., 1963-80; cons., 1980-92; bd. dirs. Adlai E. Stevenson Inst., 1972-79; mem. adv. coun. Ctr. for the Study Democratic Inst., 1975-79; bd. dirs. Inter. Am. Found., 1980-84, Pacific Basin Inst., 1981—; mem. nat. adv. com. White House Conf. on Balanced Nat. Growth and Econ. Devel., 1978; mem. Northeastern Ill. Planning Commn., 1973-77; mem. Chgo. Met. Area Transp. Coun., 1980-84; mem. adv. coun. to Nat. Ctr. Rsch. on Vocat. Edn., Dept. Edn., 1979-82, Dept. State adv. com. internat. investment, tech. and devel., 1979-81; commr. Chgo. Plan Commn., 1986—; bd. dirs. Internat. Ctr. for Rsch. on Women, 1985-91, Nat. Coun. Humanities, 1996—. Author: Social and Economic Information for Urban Planning, 1968, Colleges and the Urban Poor, 1972; contbr. articles to profl. jours.; mem. editorial bd. Illinois Issues, 1977—, v.p. 1992—. Mem. Am. Inst. Cert. Planners, Am. Planning Assn., Am. Econ. Assn., Arts Club, Univ. Club, Quadrangle Club, Harvard Club N.Y.C., Phi Beta Kappa, Lambda Alpha.

HOLLEIN, HELEN CONWAY, chemical engineer, educator; b. Fort Bragg, N.C., Mar. 21, 1943; d. Arthur Conway and Helen Vann (Parker) Faris; m. Leo Bernard Hollein, Sept. 10, 1966; children: Mary, Kathleen, Michael. BS Chem. Engring., U. S.C., 1965; MS, N.J. Inst. Tech., 1979, D Engring. Sci., 1982. Registered profl. engr., N.J. Process engr. Exxon Rsch. and Engring. Co., Florham Park, N.J., 1965-67; tchr. Livingston (N.J.) High Sch., 1967-69; substitute tchr. Singapore Am. High Sch., 1970-71; teaching asst. N.J. Inst. Tech., Newark, 1977-78, adj. intr., 1978-81; asst. prof. chem. engring. dept. Manhattan Coll., Riverdale, N.Y., 1982-88, assoc. prof., 1988-94; prof., 1994—; head dept. chem. engring. Manhattan Coll., Riverdale, N.Y., 1989—. Contbr. articles to profl. publs., chpts. to books. Recipient Teetor Ednl. award SAE, 1984; NSF grantee, 1983-92. Mem. AIChE, Am. Chem. Soc., Am. Soc. Engring. Edn., Sigma Xi (pres. Manhattan Coll. chpt. 1989-90). Office: Manhattan Coll Chem Engring Dept Riverdale NY 10471

HOLLEMAN, MARGARET ANN, library director; b. Uniontown, Pa., Dec. 5, 1933; d. Robert L. and Elizabeth V. Phillippi; m. Robert W. Holleman Jr., Dec. 20, 1953; children: David, Linda, Christopher. BA, U. South Fla., 1967; MA in English, Ariz. State U., 1971; MLS, U. Ariz., 1973. Libr. dir. Pima C.C., Tucson, 1976—. Mem. ALA, Nat. Coun. for Learning Resources, Assn. of Coll. & Rsch. Librs. (jour. editor cmty. & jr. coll. librs. sect. 1981-92), Beta Phi Mu, Pi Lambda Theta. Episcopalian. Home: 6545 Camino de Michael Tucson AZ 85718 Office: Pima CC 2202 W Anklam Tucson AZ 85709-0250

HOLLEMAN, SANDY LEE, religious organization administrator; b. Celina, Tex., June 6, 1940; d. Guy Lee and Gustine (Kirby-Sheets) Luna; m. Allen Craig Holleman, June 5, 1959. Cert., Eastfield Coll., 1979. Intern Walter Reed Gen. Hosp., Washington, D.C., 1972-73; resident Parkland Meml. Hosp., Dallas, 1973-75; with Annuity Bd. So. Bapt. Conv., Dallas, 1958—, mgr. personnel, 1983-85, dir. human resources, 1985-91, v.p. human resources, 1991—. Mem. Am. Mgmt. Soc. (dir. salary surveys local chpt. 1986—, v.p. chpt. svcs. 1987—), Dallas Soc. Human Resource Mgmt., Soc. Human Resource Mgmt., Diversity Club Dallas (program chmn. 1976, v.p. 1977), Order Ea. Star, Daus. of Nile. Baptist. Home: 4524 Sarazen Dr Mesquite TX 75150-2348 Office: Annuity Bd So Bapt Conv 2401 Cedar Springs Rd Dallas TX 75201-1407

HOLLEN, SISTER EILEEN, cardiopulmonary clinical nurse specialist; b. Phila., Apr. 28, 1951; d. Harold S. and Mildred E. (Chant) H. BSN, Holy Family Coll., 1976; MSN, U. Del., 1985. RN, Pa.; CCRN. Staff nurse in surg. unit, supr. ICU-CCU Nazareth Hosp., Phila., coord. cardiac rehab.; cardiopulmonary clin. nurse specialist Presbyn. Med. Ctr., Phila. Contbr. articles to profl. jours. Mem. AACN. Home: 8015 Moro St Philadelphia PA 19136-2617

HOLLENBECK, KAREN FERN, foundation executive; b. Snover, Mich., Mar. 30, 1943; d. Glenn Lee and Ada Gertrude (Robinson) Roberts; m. Marvin Allan Hollenbeck, June 18, 1966. AA, Kellogg Community Coll., 1980; BSBA, Nazareth Coll., 1987. Dir. fellowships W.K. Kellogg Found., Battle Creek, Mich., 1979-85, asst. v.p. adminstrn., 1985-88, v.p. adminstrn., 1988—; Bd. dirs. Cutting Edge Designs, Denver. Bd. dirs. Arc Ministries, Allegan, Mich., 1982—, Vol. Bur., Battle Creek, 1984-86, ARC, Calhoun County, Mich., 1985—. Recipient Outstanding Young Women of Am. award. Mem. NAFE, Am. Mgmt. Assn., Soc. Human Resource Mgmt., Positive Employee Practices Inst. Home: 1713 Bridle Creek St SE Grand Rapids MI 49508-4934 Office: WK Kellogg Found One Michigan Ave East Battle Creek MI 49017-4058

HOLLENBECK, MARYNELL, municipal government official; b. Nashville, May 2, 1939; d. Lee B. and Beulah B. (Bradley) Reifel; children: Braeson, Danelle. BA, Iowa State U., 1976, MS, 1980; PhD, ABD, 1981. Cert. regulatory mgr. EPA, DOT, OSHA regulation. Dir. environ. svcs. Bd. Pub. Utilities, Kansas City, Kans.; prof. Southwest Mo. State U., Springfield, Mo.; instr. Iowa State U., Ames; profl. cons. to Springfield Newspapers, Inc., Victims of Domestic Violence, Springfield Health Dept., 1984-86, Southwest Ctr. for Ind. Living, 1986-88. Contbr. articles to profl. jours. Advisor Gamma Sigma Sigma, 1984-86; mem. Hazardous Materials Ctr. Rsch. Inst., Kansas City (Kans.) Hazardous Materials Adv. Bd.; mem. Greene County Ctrl. Dem. Com., 1981-86, Story County Ctrl. Dem. Com., 1977-81; v.p. bd. dirs. Battered Women's Program, 1985-86; bd. dirs., sec. Sherwood Ctr. for Exceptional Children. Recipient Bus. and Profl. Women award for Leadership and Service, 1976. Mem. Air & Waste Mgmt. Assn. (dir. midwest sect.), Am. Pub. Power Assn. (past chair environ. sect.), Nat. Assn. Hazardous Waste Generators, Gamma Sigma Delta, Phi Kappa Phi, Alpha Kappa Delta, Sigma Xi (E.A. Ross award for sci. rsch. 1977, Von Tungeln award for leadership, rsch. and svc. 1980). Unitarian. Office: 1211 N 8th St Kansas City KS 66101-2129

HOLLEY, SYLVIA A., state legislator; b. Rutland, Vt., Apr. 7, 1942; married; 2 children. Student, Rivier Coll., 1983. Ret. video teleconf. specialist Digital Corp.; mem. N.H. Ho. of Reps.; exec. dept. and adminstrn. com. Bd. dirs. ARC, Nashua, state rels. officer; sec. LWV; cons. Everywoman's Ctr. YWCA, Manchester; gift shop vol. Cath. Med. Ctr. Office: NH Ho of Reps State Capitol Concord NH 03301

HOLLIDAY, CAROLYN PAMELA, government agency administrator; b. Washington, Aug. 26, 1952; d. Willie B. and Sybil Virginia (Thornton) Garrett; m. Richard Malcom Holliday, Apr. 12, 1970; Carolyn Patrice, Richard William. AAS cum laude, U. D.C., 1983, BA, 1985. Day camp counselor D.C. Recreation Dept., Washington, 1970; clk.-typist, clk. Washington Region U.S. Dept. State, Washington, 1971-74, data entry clk. med. records, 1974, passport specialist Washington Region, 1974-79, night shift supr. passport files, 1979-83, consular officer emergency ctr., 1983-87, consular officer fraud office, 1987-92; regional dir. Washington Passport Agy., 1992—; real estate salesperson J. Jenkins & Co. Real Estate, Lanham, Md., 1980-94. Commr. D.C. Housing Commn., Washington, 1985-86; youth counselor children's choir Glendale Bapt. Ch., 1986-92, dir., tutor, 1987—, asst. payroll clk., 1996—, dir., tutor, 1987—; den leader, coach Boy Scouts Am., 1987-92, 95; mem. Thursday Luncheon Group, 1996. Recipient fellowship Southeastern U., Washington, 1986. Democrat. Baptist. Office: Washington Passport Agy 1111 19th St NW Washington DC 20522-1705

HOLLIDAY, POLLY DEAN, actress; b. Jasper, Ala., July 2, 1937; d. Ernest Sullivan and Velma Mabell (Cain) H. B. Music Edn., Ala. State Women's Coll. (now U. Montevallo), 1959; postgrad., Fla. State U., 1960; D.H.L. hon., Mt. St. Mary's Coll., 1982. Tchr. music Sarasota (Fla.) public schs., 1961. Appeared with Asolo Theatre Repertory Co., Sarasota, 1962-72; appeared in Off-Broadway, Wedding Band, 1972; Quarrel of Sparrows, 1993, Broadway shows All Over Town, 1975, Arsenic and Old Lace, 1986-87, Cat on a Hot Tin Roof, 1990 (Tony nomination), Picnic, 1994; appeared in plays The Glass Menagerie, Tyrone Guthrie Theatre, Mpls., 1988; appeared as Flo on CBS-TV series Alice, 1976-80 (4 Emmy nominations), Flo, 1981; appeared in CBS-TV series The Client, 1995-96, Golden Girls, 1986, Amazing Stories, 1986, Home Improvement, 1993, 94; appeared in TV movies You Can't Take It With You, 1981, The Shadyhill Kidnapping, 1981, All the Way Home, 1981, Missing Children, 1982, A Gift of Love, 1983; PBS Wonderworks series Konrad, 1985, (TV movies) Triumph of the Heart, 1991; appeared in feature films All The Pres.'s Men, 1975, The One and Only, 1977, Gremlins, 1984, Moon Over Parador, 1987, Mrs. Doubtfire, 1993, Mr. Wrong, 1996. Recipient Golden Globe award for best supporting actress on TV series, 1978, 79. Episcopalian. Office: Lantz Office 888 7th Ave New York NY 10106

HOLLIEN, PATRICIA ANN, small business owner, scientist; b. N.Y.C., May 11, 1938; d. Leon and Sophia (Biernacki) Milanowski; m. Harry Hollien, Aug. 26, 1969; children: Brian, Stephanie, Christine. AA, Sante Fe Jr. Coll., 1969; ScD (hon), Marian Coll., 1983; student, U. Fla., 1977—. Rsch. asst. Marineland Rsch. Labs., 1965-69; co-owner, exec. v.p. Hollien Assocs., 1969—; owner, dir. Forensic Communication Assocs., Gainesville, Fla., 1981—, The Eden Group, Gainesville, 1995—; vis. assoc. Royal Inst. Spl. Transmission Lab., Stockholm, 1970, Wroclaw Tech. U., Poland, 1974; asst. in research Inst. Advanced Study Communication Scis. U. Fla., 1977-83, assoc. in research, 1983—; adj. asst. prof. Communication Sci. Lab., N.Y., 1982—. Co-author: Current Issues in the Phonetic Sciences, 1979; editor The Phonetician, 1991—; contbr. articles to profl. jours. Bd. dirs. Ann. Retirement Village, Waldo, Fla., 1981-93. Fellow Am. Acad. Forensic Scis., Internat. Soc. Phonetic Scis. (coun. reps. 1983—); mem. Am. Assn. Phonetic Scis., Acad. Forensic Application of the Comm. Sci., Internat. Assn. Forensic Phonetics (sec. gen. 7th ann. congress 1995). Home: 229 SW 43rd Ter Gainesville FL 32607-2270 Office: Forensic Communication Assocs PO Box 12323 Gainesville FL 32604-0323

HOLLIMON ATKINS, STEPHANIE CAROL, principal; b. Kansas City, Kans., June 18, 1949; d. Lee Edward and Dorothy Lee (Tucker) Atkins; m. Michael L. Holliman, July 7, 1973; children: LeBaron, Michael L. II. BA, Wichita U., 1971, BS, 1971, M in Adminstrv. Supervision, 1990. Cert. tchr., adminstr. Tchr. Lawrence Elem. Sch., Wichita, Kans., 1971-91; asst. prin. Benton Elem. Sch., Lawrence Elem. Sch., McCollom Elem. Sch., Wichita, 1991-92; prin. Harry St. Elem. Sch., Wichita, 1992—; truancy bd. mem. Juvenile Ct., Wichita, 1992-93. Mem. Jr. League, Wichita, 1992—. Mem. Wichita Assn. Elem. Sch. Prins., United Sch. Adminstrs., Wichita Ednl. Adminstrs. Assn., Women in Ednl. Leadership, Nat. Honor Soc., Black Hist. Soc., Sigma Gamma Rho, Phi Delta Kappa. Home: 617 Karren Ct Wichita KS 67212-4735

HOLLINBECK, ETHEL LINDELL, sculptor; b. Kewanee, Ill., Feb. 1, 1910; d. Gustav (Lindstrom) and Hilda Louise (Gustafson) Lindell; m. Richard Oftebro Hollinbeck, Mar. 27, 1928; children: Marilyn, David, Richard Jr. Grad., Mpls. Sch. of Arts, 1948. Exhibited in group shows at Met. Mus., N.Y.C., Walker, Mpls. on Com., Minn. First Outdoor Sculpture Show, Woman's Club of Mpls., Swedish Mus. of Art, St. Paul Gallery of Arts, Mpls. Inst. of Arts; works include many portraits. Recipient many awards. Mem. Soc. of Minn. Sculptors, Profl. Artists' Equity Assn. Home: 6109 Tingdale Ave Minneapolis MN 55436

HOLLINGER, PAULA COLODNY, state senator; b. Washington, Dec. 30, 1940; d. Samuel and Ethel (Levy) Colodny; m. Paul Hollinger, Sept. 16, 1962; children: Ilene, Marcy, David. RN, Mt. Sinai Hosp., N.Y.C., 1961. Mem. Md. Ho. of Dels., 1978-86; mem. Md. Ho. of Dels. Md. State Senate, Annapolis, 1987—; vice chair econ. and environ. affairs com.; chair adminisrtv., exec., legislative review com. Md. State Senate, Annapolis, 1987-94, Md. ho. dels., 1995—; mem. Gov.'s Adv. Coun. on AIDS; senate chair, 1995; senate joint com. on Health Care Delivery and Financing, 1994—; mem. Joint Com. on Health Care Cost Containment, Gov.'s Task Force to Study Nursing Crisis; vice-chair health com. Nat. Conf. State Legis., 1990, chair, 1992, past chair sci. and resources tech. com., chair health com., 1992. Bd. dirs. Nat. Coun. Jewish Women, Safety First, 1990; past pres. Women Legislators of Md., 1986, 87, 88. Recipient Murry Guggenheim award, 1961, Edith Rosen Strauss award, 1987, Verda Welcome award for outstanding polit. achievements and pub. svc., 1989, Legislator of Yr. award Md. Nurse's Assn., 1984. Mem. B'nai Brith Women, Chi Eta Phi (hon.). Office: Rm 206 Md State Senate Office Bldg Annapolis MD 21401-1991

HOLLINGSWORTH, JANE CANNON, art education educator; b. Elizabeth, N.J., Sept. 21, 1947; d. James Patterson and Laura Gordon (Peter) Cannon; m. Morris Elbert Hollingsworth, May 5, 1944; children: Leslie Suzanne, James Morris. BFA, U. Ga., 1968, MA in Edn., 1978. Cert. T-5 State Dept. Edn. Art tchr. Marietta (Ga.) H.S., 1968-70, Bowman H.S., Wadesboro, N.C., 1970-71, East Hall H.S., Gainesville, Ga., 1971-74, Gainesville (Ga.) Middle Sch., 1978—; mem. Ga. Assessment Project, Ga. State U., Atlanta; pop art curriculum Brenau U., Gainesville, 1993—. Author (lesson plan) School Arts Mag., 1982. Recipient Monetary award Chromacryl Corp., N.J., 1984. Mem. Nat. Education Assn., Ga. Assn. Educators, Gainesville Assn. Educators (sec. 1992), Ga. Art Edn. Assn. (middle grades divsn. chair 1994—, Chas. McDaniel Youth Art Month award 1986, Middle Grades Art Educator of Yr. 1994-95), Phi Delta Kappa. Methodist. Home: 3727 Windy Hill Cir Gainesville GA 30504-5737 Office: Gainesville Middle Sch 715 Woodsmill Rd Gainesville GA 30501-3020

HOLLINGSWORTH, MARGARET CAMILLE, financial services administrator, consultant; b. Washington, Feb. 20, 1929; d. Harvey Alvin and Margaret Estelle (Head) Jacob; m. Robert Edgar Hollingsworth, July 14, 1960 (div. July 1980); children: William Lee, Robert Edgar Hollingsworth Jr., Barbara Camille, Bradford Damion. AA, Va. Intermont Coll., 1949. Bookkeeper Fred A. Smith Real Estate, Washington, 1949-53; adminstrv. mgr. Airtronic, Inc., Bethesda, Md., 1953-61; pers. adminstr. Sears Roebuck, Washington, 1973-74; adminstrv. mgr., communication mgr. Garvin GuyButler Corp., San Francisco, 1980-88, exec. sec., pers. mgr., 1989-95, adminstrv. cons., ret., 1996; assoc. Robert Hollingsworth Nuclear Cons., Walnut Creek, Calif., 1975-79. Mem., bd. dirs. Civic Arts, Walnut Creek, 1975. Recipient Spl. Recognition award AEC, 1974. Mem. Internat. Platform Assn., Commonwealth Club, Beta Sigma Phi (pres. 1954). Democrat. Presbyterian. Home: 1108 Limeridge Dr Concord CA 94518-1923

HOLLINGSWORTH, MARTHA LYNETTE, educator; b. Waco, Tex., Oct. 9, 1951; d. Willie Fredrick and Georgia Cuddell (Bryant) J.; m. Roy David Hollingsworth, Dec. 31, 1971; children: Richard Avery, Justin Brian. A.A., McLennan Community Coll., 1972; B.B.A., Baylor U., 1974, MS in Ednl. Administrn., 1992. Tchr., Connally Ind. Sch. Dist., Waco, 1974—; with Adult Edn. Night Sch., 1974-78; chairperson for Area III leadership conf. Vocat. Office Careers Clubs Tex., Waco, 1985—; active Lakeview Little League Booster Club, 1985—. Mem. PTA (hon. life), Vocat. Office Edn. Tchr.'s Assn. Tex., Assn. Tex. Profl. Educators (v.p. local chpt. 1988-90), Future Homemakers Am. Area VIII (hon.), Tex. Future Farmers Am. (hon.), Delta Kappa Gamma. Baptist. Office: Connally Vocat Dept 715 N Rita St Waco TX 76705-1140

HOLLINGSWORTH, MEREDITH BEATON, enterostomal therapy clinical nurse specialist; b. Danvers, Mass., Oct. 5, 1941; d. Allan Cameron and Arlene Margaret (Jerue) Beaton; m. William Paul Hollingsworth, Nov. 19, 1983; stepchild, Brendon R. Diploma, R.I. Hosp. Sch. Nursing, Providence, 1968; BS in Nursing, U. Ariz., 1976; MS in Human Resource Mgmt., Golden Gate U., 1984; postgrad., U. Tex., 1988; EdD, U. N.Mex., 1995, postgrad., 1996—. Cert. enterostomal therapy nurse, health edn. specialist. Commd. ensign USN, 1968, advanced through grades to lt. comdr., 1979; charge nurse USN, USA, PTO, 1968-88; command ostomy nurse, head ostomy clinic Naval Hosp. Portsmouth, Va., 1985-88; pres., chief exec. officer Enterostomal Therapy Nursing Edn. and Tng. Cons. (ETNetc), Rio Rancho, N.Mex., 1989—; mgr. clin. svcs. we. area Support Systems Internat., Inc., Charleston, S.C., 1990-92; pres., CEO Paumer Assocs. Internat., Inc., Rio Rancho, N.Mex., 1992—; sr. cons. enterostomal therapy nursing, edn., & tng. cons.; provost N.Mex. Sch. Enterostomal Nursing, Rio Rancho, 1996—; enterostomal therapy nurse, clin. nurse specialist, educator Presbyn. Health Care Svcs., Albuquerque, 1992-95; sr. cons. Enterstomal Therapy Nursing Edn. & Tng. Cons. A Divsn. of Paumer Assocs., Rio Rancho, N. Mex., 1995—. Mem. adminstrv. bd. Baylake United Meth. Ch., Virginia Beach, 1980-83; chmn. bd. deacons St. Paul's United Ch., Rio Rancho; active Am. Cancer Soc. Mem. Wound, Ostomy and Continence Nurses Soc. (nat. govt. affairs com., govt. affairs com. Rocky Mountain region, pub. rels. com., regional pres. 1989-93, nat. sec. 1994-95), United Ostomy Assn., World Coun. Enterstomal Therapists, N. Mex. Health Care Assn., N. Mex. Assn. for Home Care, N. Mex. Assn. for Continuity of Care. Republican. Office: PO Box 44395 Rio Rancho NM 87174-4395

HOLLINSHEAD, ARIEL CAHILL, research oncologist; b. Allentown, Pa., Aug. 24, 1929; d. Earl Darnell and Gertrude Loretta (Cahill) H.; m. Montgomery K. Hyun, Sept. 27, 1958; children: William C., Christopher C. Student, Swarthmore Coll., 1947-48; AB, Ohio U., 1951, DSc (hon.), 1977; MS, George Washington U., 1955, PhD, 1957. Asst. prof., fellow in virology Baylor U. Med. Ctr., 1958-59; asst. prof. pharmacology George Washington Med. Ctr., 1959-61, asst. prof. medicine, 1961-64, assoc. prof. medicine, head lab. virus and cancer rsch., 1964-73, prof., dir. lab. virus and cancer rsch., 1974-89; on sabbatical leave 1990, prof. medicine emeritus, 1991—; pres. HT Virus and Cancer Rsch., 1991—; clin. rschr. trials in oncology and virology; cons. to biotech. cos. Contbr. over 250 articles on active immunotherapy and immunochemotherapy of cancer and virus diseases to sci. jours. Bd. dirs. Nat. Women's Econ. Alliance, Ohio U., Med. Coll. Pa., Nat. Arthritis Found.; mem. bd. The Women's Inst., 1994—. Named Med. Woman of Yr. Joint Bd. Am. Med. Colls., 1975-76, one of Outstanding Woman of Am., 1987, Outstanding Alumnus of Yr., Ohio U., 1990; recipient Cert. merit Med. Coll. Pa., 1975-76; decorated Star of Europe, 1980. Fellow Washington Acad. Sci., Am. Acad. Microbiology, AAAS; mem. N.Y. Acad. Sci., Am. Acad. Microbiology, Grad. Women in Sci. (nat. pres. 1985-86, bd. dirs. 1986-92), Internat. Soc. Preventive Oncology, Nat. Soc. Exptl. Biology and Medicine (Disting. Scientist award 1985), Am. Soc. Microbiology, Am. Assn. Cancer Research, Am. Assn. Immunologists, Clin. Immunology Soc., Internat. Soc. Antiviral Research, Am. Soc. Clin. Oncology, Internat. Assn. Study Lung Cancer, Internat. Union Against Cancer, Am. Med. Writers Assn., Phi Beta Kappa (alumnus 1990). Clubs: Kenwood Country, Blue Ridge Mountain Country, Washington Forum (pres. 1987, 91). Home: 3637 Van Ness St NW Washington DC 20008-3130

HOLLIS, LOUCILLE, risk control administrator, educator; b. Ft. Myers, Fla., Feb. 16, 1949; d. Luke Sr. and Louise (Wilcox) Black; m. Benjamin L. Hollis, Jr., Sept. 26, 1985. BS, N.Y. Inst. Tech., 1982, MBA, 1984. Staff asst. Equitable, N.Y.C., 1977-79, budget analyst, 1979-81, fin. analyst, 1981-85, mgr. operational planning, 1985-87, mgr. expense control, 1987-88; project leader L.I. R.R. Co., Jamaica, N.Y., 1988-91, asst. risk mgr., 1991—; comml. arbitrator Am. Arbitration Assn. Bronx fundraiser Cancer Fund Am., Knoxville, Tenn., 1991, 92; mem. bd. placement project United Way Linkage; literacy vol. Recipient Psychology award N.Y. Inst. Tech., 1981, acad. scholarship Ft. Myers Bd. Edn., 1977; honoree LIRR Women's History Celebration. Mem. NAFE, Nat. Black MBA Assn., Risk and Ins. Mgmt. Soc., RR Ins. Mgmt. Assn., Conf. Minority Transp. Ofcls., Psi Nat. Honor Soc. Democrat. Office: LI RR Co Jamaica Sta Ste 1435 Jamaica NY 11435

HOLLIS, MARY FRANCES, aerospace educator; b. Indpls., Sept. 18, 1931; d. Lucian Albert and Clara Frances Coleman; divorced; 1 child, Booker Albert Hollis. BS, Butler U., 1952, MS, 1962; postgrad., Stanford U., 1975, San Francisco State U., 1980-81. Cert. elem. tchr., Ind., Calif. Kindergartern tchr. Lockerbie Nursery Sch., Indpls., 1952, Indpls. Pub. Schs., 1952-69; tchr. K-6 San Mateo (Calif.) City Sch. Dist., 1969-91; summer sch. prin. San Mateo City Sch. dist., Foster City, Calif., 1983-91; aerospace educator, 1982—; bd. dirs. Coun. of Math./Sci. Educators of San Mateo County, Belmont, Calif. Editor: San Mateo County Math./Sci. Coun. quarterly newsletter, 1988-90. Bd. dirs. Arts Coun. of San Mateo County, 1986-91, Mid-Peninsula chpt. ACLU, San Mateo, 1990—, Unitarian-Universalist Ch. San Mateo, 1996—, Peninsula Funeral and Meml. Planning Soc., 1996—; office mgr. Roger Winston Campaign for San Mateo Union H.S. Dist. Bd. Trustees, 1993; mem. adv. com. USAF-Pacific Liaison Region-CAP, 1988-94. Recipient Life Down to Earth award NASA, Moffet Field, Mt. View, Calif., 1985-86, Earl Sams Tchr. of Yr. award Calif. Assn. Aerospace Educators, 1989, award of merit Am. Legion, San Bruno, Calif., 1989, citation Air Force Assn., Mountain View, Calif., 1991, Aviation Summer Sch. cert. of appreciation Am. Legion Dept. Calif. Aerospace Commn., 1994. Mem. NEA (life), AAUW (bd. dirs. San Carlos chpt. 1993-95), NAACP, Am. Bus. Women's Assn. (rec. sec. Foster City chpt. 1985), World Aerospace Edn. Orgn. Democrat. Unitarian-Universalist. Office: PO Box 625 Belmont CA 94002-0625

HOLLIS, SUSAN TOWER, college dean; b. Boston, Mar. 17, 1939; d. James Wilson and Dorothy Parsons (Moore) Tower; m. Allen Hollis, Nov. 10, 1962 (div. Feb. 1975); children: Deborah Durfee, Harrison. AB, Smith Coll., 1962; PhD, Harvard U., 1982. Cert. cmty. coll. instr. history and humanities. Asst. prof. Scripps Coll., Claremont, Calif., 1988-91; prof. Coll. of Undergrad. Studies The Union Inst., L.A., 1991-93; dean of the college and prof. humanities Sierra Nev. Coll.-Lake Tahoe, Incline Village, Nev., 1993-95; ind. scholar, cons. Reno, 1995-96; assoc. dean, dir. Ctrl. N.Y. Ctr. SUNY Empire State Coll., Syracuse, 1996—. Author: The Ancient Egyptian " Tale of Two Brothers", 1990; editor: Hymms, Prayers and Songs: Anthology of Ancient Egyptian Lyrics & Poetry, 1996; asst. editor: Working With No Data, 1987; co-editor: Feminist Theory and the Study of Folklore, 1994; mem. adv. bd. KMT, A Modern Jour. of Ancient Egypt, 1991—; contbr. articles to profl. publs. Music vol. Open Readings, Belmont, Mass., 1982-88; vol. Sierra Club, 1988—; problem capt. Odyssey of the Mind, Nev., 1994, 95; crew chief Tahoe Rim Trail, 1994—. Mem. Am. Acad. Religion, Am. Assn. Higher Edn., Am. Folklore Soc., Am. Oriental Soc., Am. Rsch. Ctr. Egypt, Internat. Assn. Egyptologists, Soc. Bibl. Lit. (co-chair Egyptology and History and Culture of Ancient Israel Group 1995—), Appalachian Mountain Club (co-leader 1987—), N.Y. Acad. Scis., Incline Village/Crystal Bay C. of C. (sec. and bd. dirs. 1994-95). Democrat. Home: 48-A Ponderosa Dr Syracuse NY 13215-1607 Office: SUNY Empire State Coll 219 Walton St Syracuse NY 13202

HOLLIS-ALLBRITTON, CHERYL DAWN, retail paper supply store executive; b. Elgin, Ill., Feb. 15, 1959; d. L.T. and Florence (Elder) Saylors; stepparent Bobby D. Hollis; m. Thomas Allbritton, Aug. 10, 1985. BS in Phys. Edn., Brigham Young U., 1981; cosmetologist, 1981. Retail sales clk. Bee Discount, North Riverside, Ill., 1981-82, retail store mgr., Downers Grove, Ill., 1982, Oaklawn, Ill., 1982-83, St. Louis, 1983; retail tng. mgr. Arvey Paper & Office Products (divsn. Internat. Paper), Chgo., 1984, retail store mgr., Columbus, Ohio, 1984—. Republican. Mem. LDS Ch. Avocations: writing, reading, travel. Office: Arvey Paper & Office Products 431 E Livingston Ave Columbus OH 43215-5533

HOLLISTER, JULIET GARRETSON, educator; b. Forest Hills, L.I., N.Y., Oct. 30, 1916; d. James and Dorothy Sewell (Baldwin) Garretson; m. Dickerman Hollister, June 17, 1939; children: Clay, Catharine de Rapalye, Dickerman Jr. Degree in early edn., Froebel League, N.Y.C., 1937; Hon. degree, The New Sem., N.Y.C., 1990. Founder, chmn. bd. dirs. Temple of Understanding, Cathedral of St. John the Divine, N.Y.C., 1960—; co-founder Peace Pyramid Found., Washington, 1993, 94; bd. dirs. Teilhard de Chardin, N.Y.C., Peace Works, Charleston, S.C., Pathways to Peace, Larkspur, Calif., World Peace Prayer Soc., N.Y.C.; women of vision hon. com. mem. Internat. Citizens Assembly to Stop the Spread of Weapons. Recipient Gov. Grasso Meritorious Svc. award Gov. Conn., 1979, All Faiths award Integral Yoga Internat. Soc., N.Y.C., 1986, Eleanor Roosevelt award Ctr. for Internat. Dialogue, 1994, Internat. Albert Schweitzer prize for humanities, 1995; fellow The Ctr. for World Thanksgiving, 1988. Mem. Cosmopolitan Club. Home: 661 Steamboat Rd Greenwich CT 06830-7140 Office: Temple of Understanding care Cathedral St John the Divine 1045 Amsterdam Ave New York NY 10025-1702

HOLLISTER, NANCY, state official. Lt. gov. State of Ohio, 1995—. Office: Office of Lt Governor Riffe Tower 77 S High St 30th Fl Columbus OH 43215-6108*

HOLLOWELL, JAN BENNETT, adult education educator; b. Valdosta, Ga., Nov. 11, 1951; d. Charles Leonard Bennett and Mitzi Brewton Driggers; m. Monte Jerry Hollowell, Nov. 19, 1972; children: Jerel Brett, Matt Jared. BS in Edn., Ouachita Bapt. U., Arkadelphia, Ark., 1973; MEd, U. Tex., El Paso, 1978. Cert. in adult edn., Ala., elem. edn., Tex., Ark.; cert. reading specialist, Ala., Ark., Tex. Elem. tchr. Pforzheim (West Germany) Elem. Sch., 1974-75; basic skills instr. Edn. Ctr., Ft. Bliss, Tex., 1978; Title I lang arts English tchr. El Paso Ind. Sch. Dist., 1978-80; GED/adult basic edn. instr. Region XIX Edn. Ctr., Wichita Falls, Tex., 1980-83; tutor The Reading Ctr., Huntsville, Ala., 1983; adult edn. instr. North Ala. Skills Ctr., Huntsville, 1984-88; mgr. Individualized Prescribed Instrn. Lab. J.F. Drake State Tech. Coll., Huntsville, 1988—. Mem. ASCD, NEA, Ala. Edn. Assn., Am. Vocat. Assn., Internat. Reading Assn., Drake Edn. Assn., Vocat. Indsl. Clubs Am. (advisor). Baptist. Office: JF Drake State Tech Coll 3421 Meridian St N Huntsville AL 35811-1544

HOLLYMAN, STEPHENIE, photojournalist; b. Norwalk, Conn., Dec. 19, 1952; d. Tom and Jean Hollyman. BFA, Bennington Coll., 1974. Photojournalist affiliated with Gamma-Liaison, 1982—; photo editor AP, N.Y.C., 1992; videographer Video News Internat., a N.Y. Times Co., 1993—; prof. photography Bennington (Vt.) Coll., 1992-93. Photographer: We the Homeless: Portraits of America's Displace People, 1988; producer videos Guns Hearts and Minds, Fallen Feathers, Plan De Sanchez, Behind the Bean, The Dogon: People of the Cliff, Mothers of the Missing, The View From Hanoi; photojournalist for Time, UN NGO Forum for Women, Ford Found., UNICEF, others. Recipient Book Show award Am. Inst. for Graphic Arts, 1988; Fulbright sr. rsch. fellow, 1990. Mem. Fulbright Assn., Am. Soc. Media Photographers, Coll. Art Assn., Photog. Adminstrs. Internat. Democrat. Home: 85 South St New York NY 10038 Office: Digital Journalist 85 South St New York NY 10038

HOLM, CELESTE, actress; b. N.Y.C., Apr. 29, 1919; d. Theodor and Jean (Parke) H.; m. Wesley Addy, May 22, 1966; children: Theodor Holm Nelson, Daniel Schuyler Dunning. Ed., Univ. Sch. for Girls, Chgo., Lycee Victor Durui, Paris, Francis W. Parker Sch., Chgo., Adelphi Acad., Bklyn.; DHL (hon.), Centenary Coll., 1980, Northwood U., 1981; AA (hon.), Middle Ga. Coll., 1982; ArtsD (hon.), Ea. Mich. U., 1984; DHL (hon.), Kean Coll. of N.J., 1984, Felician Coll., 1985, Jersey City State Coll., 1986; DFA (hon.), Monmouth Coll., 1987; D Liberal Arts (hon.), Fairleigh Dickinson U., 1988; D Pub. Svc. (hon.), Ea. Ill. U., 1989; DFA (hon.), Seton Hall U., 1990. Appeared in Broadway shows Gloriana, 1938, The Time of Your Life, 1939, Another Sun, 1940, Return of the Vagabond, 1940, Eight O'Clock Tuesday, 1941, My Fair Ladies, 1941, Papa Is All, 1941-42, All the Comforts of Home, 1942, The Damask Cheek, 1942-43, Oklahoma!, 1943-44, 48, Bloomer Girl, 1944-45, She Stoops to Conquer, 1949, Affairs of State, 1950-51, Anna Christie, 1952, The King and I, 1952, His and Hers, 1954, Interlock, 1958, Third Best Sport, 1958, Invitation to a March, 1960-61, Mame, 1967, Candida, 1970, Habeas Corpus, 1975-76, The Utter Glory of Morrissey Hall, 1979, I Hate Hamlet, 1991; appeared in films Three Little Girls in Blue, 1946, Gentleman's Agreement, 1947 (Acad. Award for Best Supporting Actress), Carnival in Costa Rica, 1947, The Snake Pit, 1948, Road House, 1948, Chicken Every Sunday, 1948, Come to the Stable, 1949 (Acad. Award nomination for Best Supporting Actress), Everybody Does It, 1949, Champagne for Caesar, 1950, All About Eve, 1950 (Acad. Award nomination for Best Supporting Actress), The Tender Trap, 1955, High Society, 1956, Bachelor Flat, 1961, Doctor, You've Got to be Kidding, 1966, Tom Sawyer, 1972, Three Men and a Baby, 1987; other stage appearances include (tours) Hamlet, 1937, The Women, 1937-38, Back to Methuselah, 1957, Finishing Touches, 1974, Light Up the Sky, 1975, (one-woman show) Paris Was Yesterday, 1978, (other prodns.) A Month in the Country, 1963, Madly in Love, 1964, Night of the Iguana, 1964, Captain Brassbound's Conversion, 1966, Mame (nat. tour), 1967-68 (Sarah Siddons award), Hay Fever, 1979-83, Lady in the Dark (Eng.), 1981, The Trojan Women, 1985, The Road to Mecca, 1989, Love Letters, 1990, 94, The Cocktail Hour, 1990, 94, Allegro, 1994, 50th Anniversary of The Glass Menagerie, Chgo., 1994; numerous supper club appearances, N.Y.C., Chgo., San Francisco, Washington, L.A., 1943-59; U.S.O. entertainer, ETO, 1945; 21,000 mile tour of U.S. Army bases, 1949; TV appearances include (spls. & TV movies) Cinderella, 1965, The Shady Hill Kidnapping, 1979, Backstairs at the White House, 1979 (Emmy nomination), Nora's Christmas Gift, 1989, Polly, 1989, Polly, One Mo' Time, 1990; regular roles (series) Archie Bunker's Place, 1980-81, Falcon Crest, 1985, Loving, 1986 (Emmy nomination), 91-92, Christine Cromwell, 1989-90, PBS Great Performances Talking With..., 1994; guest starring roles on Trapper John, M.D., The F.B.I., Disney's Wide World of Color, The Streets of San Francisco, Columbo, Medical Center, Captains and the Kings, Spencer For Hire, Magnum P.I., The Underground Man, Fantasy Island, The Love Boat; radio interviewer People at the UN, 1963-65; toured with theatre-in-concert program Interplay, 1963-74; appeared in The Cole Porter 100th Birthday Celebration, Carnegie Hall, 1991. Past mem. gov. bd. U.S. Com. for UNICEF; mem. Nat. Mental Health Assn., 1965—, chmn., 1969-70; v.p. Arts and Bus. Coun.; mem. Nat. Arts Coun., 1982-88; chmn. bd. dirs. N.J. Film Commn., 1983—; bd. dirs. Mayor's Midtown Com., 1975—, Actor's Fund Am., 1988—; pres. bd. Creative Arts Rehab. Ctr., 1978—; mem. nat. vis. coun. for health scis. faculties Columbia U., N.Y.C., 1989—; mem. adv. bd. N.J. Sch. for the Arts, 1989—, adv. coun. UN Assn. of N.Y.C., 1992—; chmn. Stage South Supporting Players, S.C. State Theatre, 1977. Decorated Dame King Olav of Norway; recipieerhood award Nat. Conf. Christians & Jews, 1952, Disting. Svc. award United Jewish Appeal, 1953, Award of Merit, 1954, Achievement award Israel Bonds, 1958, Award of Appreciation March of Dimes, 1959, Hadassah, 1960, Nat. Assn. for Retarded Children award, 1961, Disting. Alumni award Francis W. Parker Sch., 1964, U.S. Com. for World Fedn. of Mental Health award, 1965, Performer of Yr. award Variety Clubs Am., 1966, Edward Strecker Meml. Medal for outstanding contbns. to mental health movement, rehab. of mentally disabled, 1971, Woman of Yr. award Anti-Defamation League, 1972, Golden Needle award Am. Home Sewing Coun., 1972, Woman of Yr. award N.Y. Variety Club, 1973, Woman of Yr. nomination Ladies Home Jour., 1975, Spirit of Am. award VFW, 1976, Woman of Yr. award Westchester Fedn. Women's Clubs, 1977, Woman of Yr. award Creative Arts Rehab. Ctr., 1977, Disting. Woman award Northwood Inst., 1977, Golden Scroll award Mayor's Midtown Citizens Com., 1979, Achievement in Arts award Northwood Inst./IASTA, 1979, Actor's Studio award, 1980, Mental Health Assn. Greater Chgo. award, 1982, Zonta Internat. Humanitarian award, 1984, Compostella award, 1984, Town Hall Friend of the Arts award, 1985, Humanitarian award Creative Arts Rehab. Ctr., 1988, Internat. Platform award, 1989, The Coalition of Arts Therapy Assn. Cert. Appreciation, 1990, Edwin Forrest award for Outstanding Contbn. to Theatre, Walnut St. Theatre, Phila., 1991, The Cardinal's Com of Laity Cardinal's award, 1991, The Ellis Island Medal of Honor, 1992, Gold medal Holland Soc. N.Y., 1994, Dorothea Dix award Mental Illness Found., 1995; named to The Theatre Hall of Fame, 1992; rsch. scholar in semiotics, Claremont Grad. Sch., Calif., 1988-89. *

HOLM, JEANNE MARJORIE, author, consultant, government official, former air force officer; b. Portland, Oreg., June 23, 1921; d. John E. and Marjorie (Hammond) H. BA, Lewis and Clark Coll., 1956. Commd. 2d lt. U.S. Army, 1943; transferred to USAF, 1948, advanced through grades to maj. gen., 1973; chief manpower and mgmt. Hdqrs. Allied Air Forces So. Europe, Naples, Italy, 1957-61; congl. liaison officer, directorate manpower and orgn. Hdqrs USAF, Washington, 1961-65; dir. Women in the Air Force, 1965-73, Sec. Air Force Personnel Council, Washington, 1973-75; ret., 1975; cons. Def. Manpower Commn., Washington, 1975, undersec. air force, Washington, 1979-81; spl. asst. to Pres., 1976-77; advisor United Services Life Ins. Co., Washington; lectr. on manpower and women in mil., Presideo Press, Novato, Calif. Author: Women in the Military: An Unfinished Revolution, 1982, rev. edit., 1992; contbr. Encyclopedia of the American Military, 1994; contbr. articles to profl. jours. Chmn. adv. com. women vets. VA, Washington, 1986-88; adv. com. USCG Acad., 1983-89; dir. U.S. com. for UN Fund for Women; trustee Air Force Aid Soc.; mem. nat. adv. com. Women in Mil.Svc. Meml. Found.; mem. hon. coun. Vietnam Women's Meml. Project. Decorated D.S.M. with oak leaf cluster, Legion of Merit, medal for Human Action (Berlin Airlift), Nat. Def. Svc. medal with Bronze Star; recipient Disting. Achievement award Alumni Assn. Lewis and Clark Coll., Eugene Zuckert Leadership award Arnold Air Soc., Citation of Honor, Air Force Assn., Living Legacy award Women's Internat. Ctr., 1985; named Woman of Yr. in Govt. and Diplomacy, Ladies Home Jour., 1975; inducted into Women's Hall of Fame, Internat. Women's Forum, 1992. Mem. Air Force Assn., Ret. Officers Assn., Exec. Women in Govt. (founder, 1st chmn.). Home: 2707 Thyme Dr Edgewater MD 21037-1120

HOLM, JOY ALICE, psychology educator, art educator, artist, goldsmith; b. Chgo., May 21, 1929; d. Alvin Herbert and Willette Eugenia (Miller) H. BFA, U. Ill., 1952; MS in Art Edn. Inst. Design, Ill. Inst. Tech., 1956; PhD in Edn., U. Minn., 1967. Tchr. art, Eng. West Chgo. H.S., 1952-54; instr., tchr. art J.S. Morton H.S. & Jr. Coll., Cicero, Ill., 1954-65; asst. prof. art & design Mankato (Minn.) State U., 1965-66; asst. prof. art Ill. State U., Normal, 1966-69; assoc. prof. art & design So. Ill. U., Edwardsville, 1969-71; assoc. prof. art, art edn. Winona (Minn.) State U., 1971-75; assoc. prof., chmn. dept. art St. Mary's Coll. of Notre Dame, Ind., 1975-76; assoc. prof. art & design, secondary, continuing edn. U. Wis., Eau Claire, 1976-78; assoc. prof. art & design Sch. Art & Design Kent (Ohio) State U., 1978-80; lectr. Jungian studies C.G. Jung Inst., Evanston, Ill., 1980-82; adj. assoc. prof. art edn. Sch. Art and Design, Sch. Edn. U. Ill., Chgo., 1981-82; lectr. U. Calif. Ext., Santa Cruz, 1983—; adj. prof. art edn., design San Jose (Calif.) State U., 1983-84; owner bus. designer-goldsmith Oak Park, Ill., 1980-82, Carmel, Calif., 1982-87; owner bus. designer-goldsmith Atelier XII, Winona, 1988—; curriculum cons. North Ctrl. Assn. Accreditation Team State of Ill., Edwardsville, 1970; regional cons. Supt. Pub. Instrn., Springfield, Ill., 1970; juror exhbns.; panelist, spkr., presenter confs., meetings. Contbr., cons. Alternative Medicine: A Definitive Guide, 1994; contbr. articles to profl. jours; one-woman shows: J. Sterling Morton H.S. & Jr. Coll., 1963, Russell Art Gallery, Bloomington, 1968, Owatonna (Minn.) Art Ctr., 1980, 86; exhbns. include La Grange (Ill.) Art League (Best of Show, 1st Place award prints), 1963, 64, Minn. Mus. Art, 1974, 75, Craft & Folk Art Mus., L.A., 1978, The Gallery Kent State U., 1978, 79, Saenger Nat. Small Sculpture and Jewelry Exhibit, 1978, Diamonds Internat., N.Y., 1978, Inst. Design Alumni, 1988, Internat. Biographical Ctr. Congress Exhbn., Edinburgh, Scotland, 1994, others. Fellow World Lit. Acad.; mem. AAUP, Nat. Art Edn. Assn. (rep. Wis. Women's Caucus Houston Conf. 1978, higher edn. divsn. 1961—), Am. Assn. Higher Edn., Coll. Art Assn., Soc. N.Am. Goldsmiths, Internat. Sculpture Ctr., Gemological Inst. Am., C.G. Jung Inst. (Chgo., San Francisco), Hon. Soc. Illustrators (hon.), Internat. Soc. Study of Subtle Energies and Energy Medicine, Assn. Transpersonal Psychology, Inst. Noetic Scis., Alpha Lambda Delta (hon.), Phi Kappa Phi (hon.). Methodist. Home: PO Box 183 Winona MN 55987-0183 Office: Atelier XII PO Box 183 Winona MN 55987-0183

HOLM, VANJA ADELE, developmental pediatrician, educator; b. Kiruna, Sweden, Oct. 5, 1928; came to U.S. 1955.; d. C.V. Hjalmar and Elma Adele (Nystrom) H.; m. Carl Holm, June 15, 1952; children: Ingrid Adele, Erik Carl Anders. Med. Kand., Karolinska Inst., Stockholm, 1950, MD, 1955. Intern Swedish Hosp., Seattle, 1955-56; resident in pediatrics U. Wash. Sch. Medicine, Seattle, 1956, 62-64, fellow in devel. pediatrics, 1964-65, instr. pediatrics, 1965-69, asst. prof. pediatrics, 1969-81, assoc. prof. pediatrics, 1981—; attending pediatrician Children's Orthopedic Hosp., Univ. Hosp; med. dir. Boyer Children's Clinic and Presch. Editor: Early Intervention: A Team Approach, 1978 (Am. Med. Writers award 1979), The Prader Willi Syndrome, 1981; contbr. some 60 articles to profl. jours. Fellow Am. Acad. Pediatrics, Am. Acad. Cerebral Palsy and Devel. Medicine, Am. Assn. Mental Retardation; mem. Soc. Devel. Pediatrics, Wash. State Med. Assn. (Aesculapius award 1979), Soc. Behavioral Pediatrics. Democrat. Office: U Wash CHDD Box 357920 Seattle WA 98195-7920

HOLMAN, DIANE ROSALIE, lawyer; b. South Bend, Ind., Oct. 5, 1939; d. Raymond Francis and Ann Marie (Batsleer) Paczesny; divorced; children: Paul III, John Adam, Joseph, Felicity. BA, St. Mary's Coll., 1961; MS, St. Francis Coll., 1968; JD, Loyola U., L.A., 1976. Bar: Calif. 1976. Assoc. O'Melveny & Myers, L.A., 1976-81; assoc., ptnr. Manatt, Phelps & Phillips, L.A., 1981-85; of counsel Kindel & Anderson, L.A., 1985-87; dep. city atty. City of El Monte, Calif., 1987-89; asst. gen. counsel Family Restaurants, Inc., Irvine, Calif., 1989—. Avocations: feminist theory, reading and writing, Lakers basketball, beach walking. Mem. State Bar Calif., Orange County Bar Assn., Orange County Women Lawyers Assn. Democrat. Home: 31907 Crestwood Pl Laguna Beach CA 92677-3222 Office: Family Restaurants Inc 18831 Von Karman Ave Ste 400 Irvine CA 92715-1537

HOLMAN, KAREN MARIE, purchasing agent; b. Anchorage, Sept. 6, 1962; d. Joseph Willie and Rose Millicent (Watson) Anderson; m. Robert L. Holman Jr., Nov. 27, 1982. AA in Bus. Adminstrn., Anchorage Community Coll., 1984; BA in Orgnl. Adminstrn., Alaska Pacific U., 1991. Cert. purchasing mgr. Sr. office clk. Bur. of the Census, Anchorage, 1980; premium audit clk. Providence Wash. Ins., Anchorage, 1981-82; info. systems clk. G.A Ltd., Anchorage, 1982-83; purchasing agt. State of Alaska, Anchorage, 1984-89, U. Alaska, Anchorage, 1989-92, ATU Telecommunications, 1992—. Del. Dem. Group State Caucuses, Anchorage, 1989; mem. Greater Friendly Temple Ch. of God in Christ, state dir. pub. rels. Alaska Ecclesiastical Jurisdiction; bd. dirs. Alaska Women's resource Ctr., 1989-91. Mem. Nat. Assn. Purchasing Mgmt. Home: 3722 Randolph St Anchorage AK 99508-4529

HOLMER, JANE ANN, nursing administrator; b. Willard, Ohio, July 17, 1959; d. Ellsworth H. and Carol Sue (Armstrong) DeVaughn; m. Harold Alan Holmer, Apr. 26, 1986; children: Jennifer Rose, Daniel Robert. Student, Terra Tech. Coll., 1988-93; diploma, Owens C.C., 1996. LPN, Ohio; cert. CPR instr. Staff nurse Rehab. Hosp. St. Francis Health Care Ctr., Green Springs, Ohio, 1980-83, clin. coord. 11-7, 1983-85, staff nurse ICF 7-3, 1985-86, staff nurse skilled nursing 7-3, 1986-90, LPN nurse mgr., 1990—; sec. ethics com. St. Francis, Green Springs, Ohio, 1993—. Roman Catholic. Office: St Francis Health Care Ctr 401 N Broadway St Green Springs OH 44836-9653

HOLMES, ANITA SCHULZE, instructional resource consultant; b. Georgetown, Tex., Nov. 28, 1945; d. Gilbert Edwin and Jewel Evelyn (Dewald) Schulze; children: James Jay Holmes, Wendy Gaye Holmes. BS, S.W. Tex. State U., 1968; MEd, Sul Ross State U., 1985. Cert. mid-mgmt. adminstr., elem. edn. tchr., secondary English tchr., secondary lang. arts tchr., secondary reading tchr., home econs. tchr. Home econs. tchr. Copperas Cove (Tex.) Ind. Sch. Dist., 1968-73, Killeen (Tex.) Ind. Sch. Dist., 1973-74, Carbon (Tex.) Ind. Sch. Dist., 1975-76; elem. edn. tchr. Belton (Tex.) Ind. Sch. Dist., 1976-84; elem. and mid. sch. edn. tchr. Killeen Ind. Sch. Dist., 1984-92, instrnl. resource cons., 1992—; tchr. alternative tchr. cert. program Region XII Edn. Svc. Ctr., Waco, Tex., 1994—. Mem., Sunday sch. substitute thcr., chmn. higher edn. com., v.p. coun. on ministries First United Meth. Ch., Killeen. Named one of Outstanding Young Women of Am., 1968, 71. Mem. ASCD, Nat. Coun. for Social Studies, Internat. Reading Assn., Tex. State Reading Assn., Tex. Assn. for Supervision and Curriculum Devel. (curriculum fellow, project ABCD), Coalition for Reading and English Suprs. and Tchrs., Tex. Coun. for Social Studies, Tex. State Tchrs. Assn. (life), Tex. Coun. Tchrs. Math. Home: RR 2 Box 86J Killeen TX 76542-9602 Office: Killeen Ind Sch Dist 902 N 10th St Killeen TX 76541-4829

HOLMES, ANN HITCHCOCK, journalist; b. El Paso, Apr. 25, 1922; d. Frederick E. and Joy (Crutchfield) H. Student, Whitworth Coll., 1940, So. Coll. Fine Arts, 1944. With Houston Chronicle, 1942—, fine arts editor, 1948-89, critic-at-large, 1989—. Author: Presence, The Transco Tower, 1985, Joy Unconfined—Robert Joy in Houston: A Portrait of Fifty Years, 1986, Alley Theater: Four Decades in Three Stages, 1986. Mem. Houston Mcpl. Art Commn., 1965-74; mem. fine arts adv. coun. U. Tex., Austin, 1967—; bd. dirs. Rice Design Alliance, Houston, 1988-91, Alliance Francaise, Houston, 1989-93, Bus. Arts Fund, Houston. Recipient Ogden Reid Found. award for study of arts in Europe, 1953; Guggenheim fellow, 1960-61; recipient Ford Found. award, 1965, John G. Flowers award archtl. writing Tex. Soc. Architects, 1972, 74, 77, 80. Mem. Am. Theater Critics Assn. (exec. com. 1975—, co-chmn. 1987-88). Home: 10807 Beinhorn Rd Houston TX 77024-3008 Office: Houston Chronicle 801 Texas St Houston TX 77002-2906

HOLMES, ANN S., artist; b. Chgo., Oct. 16, 1935. BA, Sarah Lawrence Coll., 1957; D in Arts, NYU, 1982. Solo exhbns. include Silvermine (Conn.) Guild Arts Ctr., Landmark Gallery, Stamford, Conn., 1988, New Britain (Conn.) Mus., Rye (N.Y.) Art Ctr., 1989, Stamford Mus., 1989; group exhbns. include Katonah (N.Y.) Mus., 1980-90, Silvermine Guild Arts Ctr., Wadworth Atheneum, Hartford, Conn., Aldrich Mus., Ridgefield, Conn., Bridgeport (Conn.) Mus., others. Mem. Silvermine Guild Arts Ctr., Westport Art Ctr., Weston Art Ctr.

HOLMES, BARBARA DEVEAUX, college president; b. Miami, Fla., Nov. 26, 1947; d. Robert Eugene and Lula Mae (Stewart) Deveaux; m. Roosevelt Leon Holmes, June 19, 1970; children: Michael, Courtney. BA, Stetson U., 1969, MEd, 1972; PhD, U. Conn., 1974. Tchr. English, Seabreeze Sr. High Sch., Daytona Beach, Fla., 1969-72; dir. instnl. rsch. and planning Fayetteville (N.C.) State U., 1974-77, asst. to chancellor, 1977-79; dir. rsch. and planning Mo. Dept. Higher Edn., Jefferson City, 1979-81; v.p. adminstrv. svcs. Hillsborough Community Coll., Tampa, Fla., 1981-85; provost No. Va. Community Coll., Annandale, 1985-89; provost, v.p. acad. affairs Va. State U., Petersburg, 1989-90; pres. Milw. Area Tech. Coll., 1990—. Mem. Greater Milw. Com., Pvt. Industry Coun.; bd. dirs. Sinai Samaritan Med. Ctr. Fellow U. Conn. Grad. Sch., 1971-74. Mem. Am. Assn. Community and Jr. Colls., Nat. Coun. on Black Am. Affairs, Presidents Roundtable, Tempo, Rotary. Home: PO Box 10411 Conway AR 72033-2003

HOLMES, BARBARAANN KRAJKOSKI, secondary education educator; b. Evansville, Ind., Mar. 21, 1946; d. Frank Joseph and Estella Marie (DeWeese) Krajkoski; m. David Leo Holmes, Aug. 21, 1971; 1 child, Susan Ann Sky. BS, Ind. State U., 1968, MS, 1969, specialist cert., 1976; postgrad. U. Nev., 1976-78. Acad. counselor Ind. State U., 1968-69, halls dir., 1969-73; dir. residence halls U. Utah, 1973-76; sales assoc. Fidelity Realty, Las Vegas, Nev., 1977-82. cert. analyst Nev. Dept. Edn., 1981-82; tchr. Clark County Sch. Dist., 1982-87, computer cons., adminstrv. specialist instructional mgmt. systems, 1987-91, chair computer conf., 1990-92, adminstrv. specialist K-6, 1990-93, dean of students summer sch. site adminstr. Eldorado H.S., 1991—. Named Outstanding Sr. Class Woman, Ind. State U., 1969; recipient Dir's. award U. Utah Residence Halls, 1973, Outstanding Sales Assoc., 1977; Tchr. of Month award, 1983, Dist. Outstanding Tchr. award, 1984, Dist. Excellence in Edn. award, 1984, 86, 87, 88. Mem. Nev. Assn. Realtors, AAUW, Am. Assn. Women Deans, Adminstrs. and Counselors, Am. Personnel and Guidance Assn., Am. Coll. Personnel Assn., Nevadans for Equal Rights Amendment, Alumnae Assn. Chi Omega (treas. Terre Haute chpt. 1971-73, pres., bd. officer Las Vegas 1977-81), Clark County Panhellenic Alumnae Assn. (pres. 1978-79), Computer Using Educators So. Nev. (sec. 1983-86, pres.-elect 1986-87, pres. 1987-88, state chmn. 1988-89, conf. chmn. 1989-92, sec. 94—, Hall of Fame 1995), Job's Daus. Club (guardian sec. 1995—), Order Ea. Star, Phi Delta Kappa (Action award 1990-96, newspaper editor 1992-93). Developed personal awareness program U. Utah, 1973-76. Home: 2531 E Oquendo Rd Las Vegas NV 89120-2413 Office: Eldorado High Sch 1139 Linn Ln Las Vegas NV 89110-2628

HOLMES, CECILE SEARSON, religion editor; b. Columbia, S.C., Jan. 6, 1955; d. James Gadsden and Anne Keene (Searson) Holmes. BA in Journalism magna cum laude, U. S.C., 1977; fellow, U. N.C., 1982; postgrad., U. N.C., Greensboro, 1984-87. Religion writer Greensboro News and Record, 1984-87; religion writer Houston Chronicle, 1987-89, sect. editor, 1989—; mem. faculty summer journalism workshop Houston Chronicle, 1988-92; co-dir. minority journalism workshop News and Record, 1988. Author: Witnesses to the Horror: North Carolinians Remember the Holocaust, 1988; contbr. articles, book revs. to profl. jours. Mem. N.C. Episcopal Diocese Hunger Commn., 1980s; vol. Greensboro Urban Ministry, 1983-86; moderator NCCJ Forum, 1985, Ethics of Humane Care, Greensboro, 1986; mentor Edn. for Ministry, Houston, 1989—; advisor United Way Campaign for Homeless, Houston, 1991. Recipient award Piedmont Bapt. Assn., 1984, Community Journalism award N.C. A&T State U., 1984, Pub. Svc. award N.C. Press Assn., 1985, Wilbur award Religious Pub. Rels. Coun., 1986, others. Mem. Soc. Profl. Journalists (chpt. pres. and v.p., coord. registration nat. conv. 1989), Religion Newswriters Assn. (treas. 1990-92, 2d v.p. 1992-94, 1st v.p. 1994—, 2d place award ann. contest 1989, 92), Houston Press Club, Beta Sigma Phi (past v.p. Greensboro chpt., Woman of Yr. award), Kappa Tau Alpha, Omicron Delta Kappa. Office: Houston Chronicle 801 Texas St Houston TX 77002-2906*

HOLMES, GRACE ELINOR, pediatrician; b. Crookston, Minn., Mar. 27, 1932; d. William August and Anne Erika (Ermisch) Foege; m. Frederick Franklin Holmes, June 26, 1955; children: Heidi, Cindy, Lisa, Theodore, Julia, Andrew. BA, Pacific Luth. U., 1953; MD, U. Wash., 1957. Diplomate Am. Bd. Family Practice. Missionary physician Luth. Ch. Clinics, Malaysia, 1959-63; pediat. cons. Kilimanjaro Christian Med. Ctr., Tanzania, 1970-72; instr. pediat. Med. Ctr. U. Kans., Kansas City, 1967-69, asst. prof., 1969-70, 72-80, asst. prof. preventive medicine, 1978-80, assoc. prof. depts. pediat. & preventive medicine, 1980-87, prof., 1987—. Author: Whither Thou Goest, I Will Go, 1992. Recipient Humanitarian Svc. award Med. Alumni Assn. U. Wash. Sch. Medicine, 1995; named Alumna of Yr. Pacific Luth. U., 1988. Home: 4701 Black Swan Dr Shawnee KS 66216 Office: U Kans Med Ctr 4004 Robinson Hall 3901 Rainbow Blvd Kansas City KS 66160-7313

HOLMES, JENNIFER CASSIEL SPIRES, mental health nurse; b. Alamo, Ga., Feb. 2, 1953; d. Deron J. and Marie (Johnson) Spires; m. James Holmes, Aug. 27, 1984; stepchildren: Christopher, Richard, Jay. AD with honors, Mid. Ga. Coll., Cochran, 1976; BSN, Ga. Coll., Milledgeville, 1991; MSN, Ga. Coll., 1995. RN, Ga.; cert. hypnotherapist. Asst. head nurse ICU Fairview Park Hosp., Dublin, Ga., operating room nurse; office nurse Larry Grant, M.D., Macon, Ga.; nurse mgr. child and adolescent unit Charter Lake Hosp., Macon, 1985-91, asst. program adminstr. child and adolescent unit, 1991-94; prin. Total Wellness Concepts, Inc., Jeffersonville, Ga., 1995—. Mem. ANA (cert. psychiat. and mental health nursing, cert. nursing adminstrn.), Inter-Assn. Counselors and Therapists, Sigma Theta Tau. Home: RR 2 Box 19A Jeffersonville GA 31044-9406

HOLMES, KATHLEEN, artist; b. Monroe, La., Dec. 27, 1953; d. Zell and Sybil Joyce (Edwards) Smith; m. Louis Smadbeck, Feb. 5, 1982. AA, U. Fla., 1979. One-woman shows include Palm Beach C.C., Lake Worth, Fla., 1987, Corp. Art Source, Chgo., 1987, Clayton Galleries, Chgo., 1988, Bonwit Teller, Miami, Fla., 1988, Governor's Club, West Palm Beach, 1988, United Techs. of Fla., West Palm Beach, 1990, Clayton Galleries, Tampa, Fla., 1990, 92, Palm Beach County Jud. Ctr., West Palm Beach, Fla., 1992, Northwood Inst., West Palm Beach, 1992, Riverside Ctr., Palm Beach Gardens, Fla., 1993, Walter Wickiser Gallery, N.Y.C., 1994, 95, Casements Ctr., Ormond Beach, Fla., 1994, Gallery at Roundabout, N.Y.C., 1995, Art Network, Atlanta, 1996, Albers Gallery, Tex., Artisti en Viaggio, Italy, 1996; exhibited at numerous group shows, including Zuck Shuster Gallery, Boca Raton, Fla., 1990, Martin County Coun. for Arts, Stuart, Fla., 1990, Peter Drew Gallery, Boca Raton, 1991, Colorado Springs (Colo.) Fine Art Ctr., 1991, Boca Raton Mus. Art, 1991, Margaret Lipworth Fine Art, Boca Raton, 1991, Clayton Galleries, 1991, 92, Chattahoochee Valley Art Mus., LaGrange, Ga., 1992, Huntsvile (Ala.) Mus. Art, 1992, Armory Art Ctr., West Palm Beach, 1992, Soc. of Four Arts, Palm Beach, 1992, Ft. Lauderdale (Fla.) Mus. of Art, 1992, Mus. Hispanic and L.Am. Art, Miami, 1993, Pitts. Ctr. for Arts, 1993, Edith McAshan Visual Arts Ctr., Ingram, Tex., 1993, The Culture Ctr., N.Y.C., 1994, Fla. State U. Gallery and Mus., Tallahassee, 1994, Armory Art Ctr., 1994, Gallery of Living Artists, N.Y.C., 1994, 95, shidoni Galleries, Tesuque, N.Mex., 1995, Walter Wickiser Gallery, 1995, Alexander Brest Gallery, Jacksonville, Fla., 1995, A.I.R. Gallery, N.Y.C., 1996; represented in pub. and pvt. collections. Bd. dirs. Pope Theatre Co., Manalapan, Fla., 1986—, Armory Art Ctr., West Palm Beach, Fla., 1994—. Recipient award Nat. Women's Caucus for Art, Met. Mus. and Art Ctr., 1987, Ann. All Fla. Exhbn. award Boca Raton Mus. Art, 1991, Ubertalli award Palm Beach County Coun. for Arts, 1995. Home and Studio: # 4 17th Ave South Lake Worth FL 33460

HOLMES, KATHLEEN LOUISE, security executive; b. Greenfield, Mass., Aug. 16, 1958; d. Russell Alwyn and Margaret Ella (Rowles) H. BS, Northeastern U., 1980; BA, U. Mass., 1991, MA, 1995. Police officer Amherst (Mass.) Coll., 1983-85; shipping/receiving mgr. Kostiner Photographic, Leeds, Mass., 1985-87; maintainer U. Mass., Amherst, 1987-90, instr., 1992-94; campus security coord. World Learning, Brattleboro, Vt., 1994—. Mem. Vt. Colls. and Univs. Security Assn., N.E. Security Dirs. Home: 7 Millers Falls Rd Turners Falls MA 01376 Office: World Learning Sch Internat Tng Kipling Rd Brattleboro VT 05301

HOLMES, LAURA ANN, principal; b. Regensburg, Germany, Sept. 12, 1958; d. Landon and Shizuko (Jono) Hipkins; m. David Holmes, May 15, 1977. AA in Interdisciplinary Studies, Empire State Coll., 1989, BA in Ednl. Studies, 1993. Cert. social studies tchr. grades 7-12, N.Y. Vice prin., tchr. Redemption Christian Acad., Troy, N.Y., 1979—; camp dir. RCA Nature Camp, Troy. Allocations vol. United Way, Albany, N.Y., 1994-95; trustee Redemption Ch. of Christ, Troy, 1978—. Home: 192 9th St Troy NY 12180 Office: Redemption Christian Acad 192 9th St Troy NY 12180

HOLMES, MARJORIE ROSE, author; b. Storm Lake, Iowa; d. Samuel Arthur and Rosa (Griffith) H.; m. Lynn Mighell, Apr. 9, 1932; children—Marjorie Mighell Croner, Mark, Mallory, Melanie Mighell Dimopoulos; m. George P. Schmieler, July 4, 1981. Student, Buena Vista Coll., 1927-29, D.Litt. (hon.), 1976; B.A., Cornell Coll., 1931. Tchr. writing Cath. U., 1964-65, U. Md., 1967-68; mem. staff Georgetown Writers Conf., 1959-81. Free-lance writer short stories, articles, verse for mags. including McCall's, Redbook, Reader's Digest; bi-weekly columnist: Love and Laughter, Washington Evening Star, 1959-75; monthly columnist: Woman's Day, 1971-77; author: World By the Tail, 1943, Ten O'Clock Scholar, 1946, Saturday Night, 1959, Cherry Blossom Princess, 1960, Follow Your Dream, 1961, Love is a Hopscotch Thing, 1963, Senior Trip, 1962, Love and Laughter, 1967, I've Got to Talk to Somebody, God, 1969, Writing the Creative Article, 1969, Who Am I, God?, 1971, To Treasure Our Days, 1971, Two from Galilee, 1972, Nobody Else Will Listen, 1973, You and I and Yesterday, 1973, As Tall as My Heart, 1974, How Can I Find You God?, 1975, Beauty in Your Own Back Yard, 1976, Hold Me Up a Little Longer, Lord, 1977, Lord, Let Me Love, 1978, God and Vitamins, 1980, To Help You Through the Hurting, 1983, Three from Galilee—The Young Man from Nazareth, 1985, Writing the Creative Article Today, 1986, Marjorie Holmes' Secrets of Health, Energy and Staying Young, 1987, The Messiah, 1987, At Christmas the Heart Goes Home, 1991, The Inspirational Writings of Marjorie Holmes, 1991, Gifts Freely Given, 1992, Writing Articles From the Heart, 1993, Second Wife, Second Life!, 1993; contbg. editor Guideposts, 1977—; bd. dirs. The Writer, 1975—. Bd. dirs. Found. Christian Living, 1975—. Recipient Honor Iowans award Bucna Vista Coll., 1966, Alumni Achievement award Cornell Coll., 1963, Woman of Achievement award Nat. Fedn. Press Women, 1972; Celebrity of Yr. award Women in Communications, 1975; Woman of Yr. award McLean Bus. and Profl. Women, 1976; award Freedom Found. at Valley Forge, 1977; gold medal Marymount Coll. Va., 1978. Mem. Am. Newspaper Women's Club, Nat. Fedn. Press Women, Author's Guild, Washington Nat. Press Club. Home: Lake Jackson Hills 8681 Cobb Rd Manassas VA 22111

HOLMES, MARY LYNNE, corporate communications specialist; b. Columbus, Ohio, May 3, 1948; d. Andrew Jackson and Claribel Louise (Hanna) Tweed; m. Robert Alfred Holmes, Oct. 31, 1970; children: Kathryn Clare, Daniel Robert, Sarah Elizabeth. BA in Journalism, Ohio State U., 1977. Intern reporter Newark (Ohio) Adv., 1969; pub. info. asst. Chem. Abstracts Svc., Columbus, 1970; asst. to dir. devel. Columbus Parcel Svc., Columbus, 1971-76; asst. editor Fraternal Monitor, Indpls., 1978-80; freelance writer Today mag., Charlotte, N.C., 1984-85; coord. comm. St. Gabriel Ch., Charlotte, 1985-87; dir. devel., alumni and pub. rels. Charlotte Cath. H.S., 1987-93; editor Classroom Tchr., Charlotte, 1993-94; coord. comm. Duke Engring. & Svcs., Inc., Charlotte, 1995—. Mem. Women in Comm. Republican. Roman Catholic.

HOLMES, NANCY ELIZABETH, pediatrician; b. St. Louis, Aug. 3, 1950; d. David Reed and Phyllis Anne (Hunger) Holmes; m. Arthur Erwin Kramer, May 15, 1976; children: Melanie Elizabeth Kramer, Carl Edward Kramer. BA in Psychology, U. Kans., 1972; MD, U. Mo., 1976. Diplomate Am. Acad. Pediatrics. Intern., resident in pediatrics St. Louis Children's Hosp., Washington U., St. Louis, 1976-81; pediatrician Ctrl. Pediatrics, St. Louis, 1981—; sch. physician Sch. Dist. Clayton, Mo., 1985-92; asst. prof. clin. pediatrics Washington U., St. Louis, Mo., 1993—; cons. 1st. Congregational Preschool, Clayton, 1984-86, Jewish Hosp. Daycare Ctr., St. Louis, 1993—, Flynn Park Early Edn. Ctr., Un.iv. City, Mo., 1994—, community outpatient experience Preceptor Hosp., St. Louis Children's Hosp., 1991-93, 94—; mem. med. exec. com. St. Louis Children's Hosp., 1992-94. Elder Trinity Presbyn. Ch., University City, 1989-92, 96—; vol. reading tutor Flynn Park Sch., University City, 1992—; cub scout leader Flynn Park Sch., 1993—; bd. dirs. Children's Hosp. Care Group. Fellow Am. Acad. Pediatrics; mem. AMA, Mo. State Med. Assn., St. Louis Metro. Med. Soc, St. Louis Pediatric Soc. Presbyterian. Office: Ctrl Pediatrics Inc 8888 Laduc Rd #130 Saint Louis MO 63124

HOLMES, RACHEL ELLEN FLYNN, sculptor; b. Patomic River, Md., May 24, 1968; d. Richard E. Flynn and Diana Reynolds; m. Bryan K. Holmes, May 26, 1989. AA, Fla. Jr. Coll.; postgrad., U. Fla., 1996—. Exhibited in group shows Alexander Breast Gallery, Jacksonville, Fla., 1995, Beaches Fine Art Guild and Gallery, 1996, South Bank Gallery. Vol. adult studies Jacksonville Literacy Coalition, Inc., 1996. Home and Studio: 2087 Cortez Rd Jacksonville FL 32246

HOLMES, SUSAN G., educator; b. Kansas City, Mo., Mar. 7, 1955; d. Burton E. and Gloria A. (Spencer) H. BA, U. Kans., Lawrence, 1980. Cert. music therapy, education. Tchr. Dade County Schs., Miami, Fla.; entertainment coord. And More Music Corp., Miami, Fla.; music therapist, tchr. ESOL Miami; tchr. ABE Sunrise Retirement Cmty.; tchr. ESOL Miami-Palmetto Adult Edn. Ctr., Bapt. Hosp.; music therapist Shands Home Health Care. Tchr. ESOL to newly-arrived immigrants. Recipient Honor for TV series CBS News. Mem. Nat. Orgn. for Exec. Women.

HOLMES, SUZANNE MCRAE, nursing supervisor; b. Birmingham, Ala., June 23, 1952; d. Paul Bickman and Mabel E. (Tyler) McRae; m. Bryan Thomas Holmes, Jan. 14, 1989; 1 child, Meredith Rae. ADN, Jefferson State Coll., Birmingham, 1988. RN, Ala.; cert. BCLS instr. Staff nurse burn unit The Children's Hosp., Birmingham, 1988-89; staff nurse dept. medicine The Kirklin Clinic at U. Ala.-Birmingham, 1989-90, head nurse gen. medicine clinic, 1990-91, head nurse allergy clinic, 1991—; facilitator and spkr. on nursing edn. at asthma workshops Rorer Pharms., Collegeville, Pa., 1994—; mem. faculty Genecom, N.Y.C., 1994—; operator 1-800 Allergy Info. Svc., 1991-92. Editor Allergy Update, 1991-92. Mem. Am. Coll. Allergy and Immunology, Am. Acad. Allergy, Asthma and Immunology. Presbyterian. Office: The Kirklin Clinic Allergy Clinic 2d Fl 2000 6th Ave S Birmingham AL 35233-2110

HOLMES-CALVERT, JACQUELIN ANN, workers compensation administrator; b. Balt., Sept. 5, 1947; d. Paul Chester and Ethel Marie (Parker) Bianchi; m. Larry Lee Lockman, Nov. 29, 1963 (div. Oct. 1972); children: Carole Jean, Gregory Stephen; m. John Stephen Holmes, July 27, 1974 (div. May 1993); m. Stephen W. Calvert, May 19, 1995. AA in Psychology, Community Coll. of Denver, 1975; BSBA, Regis Coll., 1988; postgrad., U. Colo., Denver, 1991—. Cert. personnel classification, examinations and rules interpretation, Colo.; lic. claims adjuster. With staff support/counseling div. Community Coll. of Denver North Campus, 1973-74, asst. to dir. community services div., 1974-77; claims adjuster State Compensation Ins. Fund, Denver, 1978-80, 82-84; owner day care ctr. Littleton, Colo., 1980-82; personnel analyst Colo. Dept. Labor & Employment, Denver, 1984-88; adminstr. EEO and affirmative action Colo. Dept. Natural Resources, Denver, 1988-90; adminstr. spl. funds Colo. Div. Labor, Denver, 1990-91; dep. dir. Colo. Div. Workers Compensation, Denver, 1991—; mem. adv. bd. Colo. Health Elec. Data Interchange. Student govt. rep. Community Coll. of Denver, 1973-74; organizer Classified Employees Council, Denver, 1975; vol. orgn. support Arapahoe County Family Day Care, Littleton, 1981-82; coach Teen Quiz Team (Champions 79-83), Littleton, 1979-83; marriage enrichment cons. Littleton Ch. of the Nazarene, 1986-87; Sunday sch. tchr., 1980-87. Named an Outstanding Employee Gov.'s Office Colo. State Govt., 1986. Mem. Internat. Pers. Mgrs. Assn., Internat. Assn. Accident. Bds. and Commns. (electronic data interchange med. subcom.), Colo. EEO and AFfirmative Action Coalition, Colo. Coun. Mediators Assn., Pilot Club. Home: 4445 Hooker St Denver CO 80211 Office: Colo Div of Workers Compensation 1515 Arapahoe St Tower 2 Ste 510 Denver CO 80202

HOLMGREN, JANET L, college president; b. Chgo., Dec. 1, 1948; d. Kenneth William and Virginia Ann (Rensink) H.; m. Gordon A. McKay, Sept. 7, 1968 (div. 1990); children: Elizabeth Jane, Ellen Katherine. BA in English summa cum laude, Oakland U., Rochester, Mich., 1968; MA in Linguistics, Princeton U., 1971, PhD in Linguistics, 1974. Asst. prof. English studies Federal City Coll. (now U. D.C.), Washington, 1972-76; asst. prof. English U. Md., College Park, 1976-82, asst. to chancellor, 1982-88; assoc. provost Princeton (N.J.) U., 1988-90, vice-provost, 1990-91; pres. Mills Coll., Oakland, Calif., 1991—; mem. external adv. bd. English dept. Princeton U. Bay Area Biosci. Ctr. Author: (with Spencer Cosmos) The Story of English: Study Guide and Reader, 1986, Narration and Discourse in American Realistic Fiction, 1982; contbr. articles to profl. jours. Faculty rsch. grantee U. Md., 1978; fellow NEH, 1978, Princeton U., 1968-69, 70-72, NSF, 1969-70; recipient summer study aid Linguistic Soc. Am., Ohio State U., 1970. Mem. Assn. Ind. Caif. Colls. and Univs. (exec. com.), Nat. Assn. Ind. Colls. and Univs., Am. Coun. on Education (chair office of women in higher edn.), Calif. Acad. Sci. (coun.). Democrat. Episcopal. Office: Mills Coll Office Pres 5000 Macarthur Blvd Oakland CA 94613-1000*

HOLSTON, ANNA RHYNES, English language educator; b. Macon, Ga., Oct. 22, 1946; d. Johnny Mack and Anna Christian (Cooper) Rhynes; m. Joe Holston, June 15, 1968; children: Beverly Joyce, Kevin Cornell. BA, Paine Coll., 1968; MA, Pepperdine U., 1978; 2d MA, Baylor U., 1990. Cert. tchr., Ga., Tex. Tchr. adult edn. Fayetteville (N.C.) Tech. Inst., 1973-75, Dona Ana br. N.Mex. State U., Las Cruces, 1975-76; trainee in ednl. adminstrn. Army Edn. Ctr., White Sands Missile Range, N.Mex., 1977-80; tchr. lang. arts Killeen (Tex.) Ind. Sch. Dist., 1980-83; instr. English Ctrl. Tex. Coll., Killeen, 1983-85, 88—, McLennan C.C., Waco, Tex., 1986-88; mem. task force for fin. and resources devel. Ctrl. Tex. Coll., 1991, mem. self study com., 1992-94. Named Acad. Educator of Yr., Ctrl. Tex. Exch. Club, 1990; recipient Profl. Development award Ctrl. Tex. Coll. Found., 1993. Mem. Conf. Coll. English Tchrs., Nat. Coun. Negro Women, S.W. Regional Coun. English, Tex. C.C. Tchrs. Assn. (pres.-elect 1996), Delta Sigma Theta (mem. social action com. 1994, chair arts and letters 1994, mem. sr. citizen com. 1994—). Office: Ctrl Tex Coll Dept Comm PO Box 1800 Killeen TX 76540-1800

HOLSTON, SHARON SMITH, government official; b. Cleve., Dec. 15, 1945; d. Charles Coolidge and Eva Mae (Hall) Smith; m. Joseph Holston, Jr., Dec. 22, 1973; children: Joseph Ikaweba, Eve Denise. AB, Columbia U., 1967; M in Pub. Adminstrn., Harvard U., 1986. Personnel mgmt. specialist U.S. Commn. Civil Rights, 1967-70, HEW, 1970-72; EEO officer FDA, Rockville, Md., 1972-74, personnel mgmt. specialist, 1975-77, acting exec. officer, 1977-79, spl. asst. to assoc. commr. mgmt. and ops., 1979-80, dep. assoc. commr. mgmt. and ops., 1980-88, acting assoc. commr. mgmt. and ops., 1986-88, assoc. commr. mgt. and ops., 1988-93, assoc. commr. mgmt. and sys., 1993—. Recipient Award of Merit, FDA, 1982, 87, also commr.'s spl. citation, 1985-94; Sr. Mgmt. citation HHS, 1988, Presdl. Meritorious Rank award, 1992. Rec. sec., mem. Jack & Jill of Am.; active Mt. Calvary Bapt. Ch. Office: FDA Mgmt and Sys 5600 Fishers Ln Rockville MD 20857-0001

HOLT, BERTHA MERRILL, state legislator; b. Eufaula, Ala., Aug. 16, 1916; d. William Hoadley and Bertha Harden (Moore) Merrill; m. Winfield Clary Holt, Mar. 14, 1942; children: Harriet Wharton Holt Whitley, William Merrill, Winfield Jefferson. AB, Agnes Scott Coll, 1938; LLB, U. Ala., 1941. Bar: Ala., 1941. With Treasury Dept., Washington, 1941-42, Dept. Interior, Washington, 1942-43; mem. N.C. Ho. of Reps. from 22d Dist., 1975-80, 25th Dist., 1980-94, chmn. select com. govtl. ethics, 1979-80, chmn. constl. amendments com., 1981, 83, mem. joint commn. govtl. ops., 1982-88, chmn. appropriation com. justice and pub. safety, 1985-88, co-chair House appropriation sub-com. transp., 1991-92, co-chair appropriation sub-com. Justice and Pub. Safety, 1993—. Pres., Democratic Women of Alamance, 1962, chmn. hdqrs., 1964, 68; mem. N.C. Dem. Exec. Com., 1964-75 95—; pres. Episcopal Ch. Women, 1968; mem. coun. N.C. Episcopal Diocese, 1972-74, 84-87, 95— chmn. budget com. 1987; chmn. fin. dept., 1973-75, parish grant com., 1973-80, mem. standing com., 1975-78; chmn. Alamance County Social Svcs. Bd., 1970; mem. N.C. Bd. Sci. and Tech., 1979-83; chair Legis. Women's Caucus, 1991-94; past bd. dirs. Hospice N.C.; bd. dirs. State Coun. Social Legis., pres. SCSL 1996—, State Conf. Social Work, N.C. Epilepsy Assn., N.C. Pub. Sch. Forum. 1989, U. N.C. Sch. Pub. Health Adv. Bd., Salvation Army Alamance County, N.C., Nursing Found, 1989, Epilepsy Found., 1989; bd. Alternatives for Status Offenders Burlington, N.C., Sch. Pub. Health Adv. Bd. Recipient Outstanding Alumna award Agnes Scott Coll., 1978, Legis. award for svc. to elderly Non-Profit Rest Home Assn., 1985, health, 1986, ARC, 1987, Faith Active in Pub. Affairs award N.C. Coun. of Chs., 1987, Ellen B. Winston award State Coun. For Social Legis., 1989, Disting. Svc. award Alamance County, 1992, 1st ann. Hallie Ruth Allen Dem. Women award Alamance County, 1992; named One of 5 Distinguished Women of N.C. (Govt.), 1991. Mem. N.C. Women's Forums, Law Alumni Assn. U. N.C. Chapel Hill (bd. dir. 1978-81), N.C. Bar Assn., NOW, English Speaking Union, N.C. Hist. Soc., Les Amis du Vin, AAUW, Pi Beta Phi, Phi Kappa Gamma (hon.), Century Club. Address: PO Box 1111 Burlington NC 27216-1111

HOLT, DORENE K., pediatrics and community health nurse; b. Xenia, Ohio, Sept. 15, 1958; d. Emil J. and Alberta M. (Cavender) Martin; m. Keith A. Holt, Apr. 18, 1979; 1 child, Jessica A. BSN, Wright State U., 1985. Cert. in community health nursing. Edn. coord. Born Free Program Miami Valley Hosp., Dayton; early intervention pub. health nurse Clark County Health Dept., Springfield, Ohio, 1986-90, pub. health nurse, 1990-93; family advocacy nurse specialist Wright-Patterson AFB, Dayton, Ohio, 1993—. Mem. Ohio Soc. for Pub. Health Edn., Nat. Perinatal Assn., Ohio Perinatal Assn., Nat. Assn. for Perinatal Addiction Rsch. and Edn. Office: 74 MDOS SGOHF 5030 Pearson Rd Bldg 6219 Wright Patterson AFB OH 45433

HOLT, FRIEDA M., nursing educator, former academic director. BSN with honors, U. Colo., Boulder, 1956; MS in cmty. health nursing, Boston U., 1969, EdD, 1973. RN, Ariz., Calif., Colo., Mass., Md., Pa., Wash., Liberia, W. Africa. Instr., dir. of nursing Cuttington Coll., Liberia, Africa, 1964-67; teaching fellow sch. of nursing Boston U., 1969, asst. prof. sch. of nursing, 1969-74; assoc. prof. sch. of nursing U. Md., 1975-77, assoc. prof., assoc. dean for grad. studies sch. of nursing, 1975-77, dean's dep. sch. of nursing, 1975-86, prof., assoc. dean for grad. studies sch. of nursing, 1977-86, acting dean sch. of nursing, 1978, acting asst. dean sch. of nursing, 1981-82, acting chmn. sch. of nursing, 1983-84, acting dean sch. of nursing, 1986-87, prof., assoc. dean for grad. studies, dean's dep. sch. of nursing, 1987-88, prof., exec. assoc. dean. sch of nursing, 1988-89, acting dean, prof. sch. of nursing, 1989-90, prof. sch. of nursing, 1990-91, dir. sch. of nursing, 1992-94, prof. sch. of nursing, 1994—; project dir. Primary Care Adult Nurse Practitioner Leadership grant, 1976-82, Preparation for Tchrs. in Maternal Child Nursing, judge U. Md. grad. sch. rsch. awards, 1979-84; NLN vis. for Accreditation of Baccalaureate and Masters Nursing Program, SREB/SCCEN Task Force on Grad. Edn., presenter of numerous seminars, conferences and workshop. Contbr. of articles to profl. jours. Recipient Vet. Administrn. Commendation award, 1990, Charter Trustee award Found. for Nursing of Md., 1990, Martin Luther King, Jr. Humanitarian award, 1990. Mem. ANA, ANA Coun. of Nurse Rschr., Nat. League for Nursing, Am. Pub. Health Assn., Am. Edn. Rsch. Assn., Am. Edn. Rsch. Assn., Am. Assn. U. Prof., Md. Assn. for Higher Edn., Md. Nurses Found. Bd. Dirs. (v.p. 1988—), Soc. for Rsch. in Nursing Edn., Sigma Theta Tau. Home: 328-B Sellers Ln RD 1 Port Matilda PA 16870 Office: Pa State Univ 303A Health and Human Devel E University Park PA 16802-1503

HOLT, ISABEL RAE, radio program producer; b. Vineland, N.J., Oct. 5, 1946; d. Frederick Rae and Isabella A. (Foley) Steinborn; m. Robert Eugene Darby, Aug. 13, 1977; children: Rachel Elisabeth Darby, Nora Odette Darby. Student, Glassboro State Coll., 1968. Prodr. music program Sta. WGTB Georgetown U., Washington, 1972-74; prodr. music program Sta. WMGM, Atlantic City, N.J., 1974, Sta. KJAZ, Alameda, Calif., 1974-76, Sta. KPFA, Berkeley, Calif., 1974-76, Sta. KCRW, Santa Monica, Calif., 1977-88, Sta. KPCC, Pasadena, Calif., 1989—, ind. concert prodr., L.A. and Washington, 1973—; prodr. solo piano concerts for radio, 1980-88, jazz, rock and piano concerts for radio, 1980-88; interviewer radio programs, 1980—. Dir., coord. Washington Area Free U., 1972-74. Mem. ACLU, Amnesty Internat. Democrat. Roman Catholic. Office: Sta KPCC Pasadena City Coll 1570 E Colorado Blvd Pasadena CA 91106-2003

HOLT, LINDA HUGHEY, physician, consultant; b. Chgo., Apr. 13, 1951; d. Merle Stanley and Elaine (Cartmell) Hughey; m. John Arthur Holt; children: Matthew, Elizabeth, Eugenie. BA, Yale U., 1973; MD, U. Chgo., 1977. Diplomate Am. Bd. Ob/Gyn. Staff physician Northcare Med. Group, Evanston, Ill., 1981-87; attending staff Evanston/Glenbrook Hosp., 1981-96; dir. Inst. Women's Health Evanston Hosp., 1994—; chmn. dept. ob/q gyn. Rush North Shore Hosp., Skokie, Ill., 1989-94; pres. Women's Med. Group, Skokie, Ill., 1987-96; asst. prof. Rush Pres St. Luke's Med. Ctr., Chgo., 1989-94, Northwestern U., Evanston, 1994-96, mem. adv. bd. YME Breast Cancer Support, Chgo., Ill., 1995—, Chgo. group Nat. Osteoporosis Found. Author: AMA Guide to Woman Care, Midlife Health, Birth Tech, A-Z Women's Sexuality, 50 Hints to Help With Menopause. Fellow: Am. Coll. Ob-Gyn. Presbyterian. Office: Evanston Hosp Inst Women's Health 2650 Ridge Rd Evanston IL 60201

HOLT, MARJORIE JENSEN, artist; b. Salt Lake City, Nov. 3, 1919; d. Peter Joseph and Artimesia (Snow) Jensen; m. Robet Lewis Holt, Oct. 3, 1942; children: Karen Anne, Katherine, Robert, Elida, Peter. BS, U. Utah, 1941. Tchr. art Granite Sch. Dist., Salt Lake City, 1967-68, 68-69; tchr. graphic design Salt Lake Cmty. Coll., Salt Lake City, 1991—. Mem. Utah Water Color Soc. (pres. 1993-94). Republican. Mem. LDS Ch.

HOLT, MARJORIE SEWELL, lawyer, retired congresswoman; b. Birmingham, Ala., Sept. 17, 1920; d. Edward Rol and Juanita (Felts) Sewell; m. Duncan McKay Holt, Dec. 26, 1946; children: Rachel Holt Tschantre, Edward Sewell, Victoria Holt Schumaker. Grad., Jacksonville Jr. Coll., 1945; J.D., U. Fla., 1949. Bar: Fla. 1949, Md. 1962. Practiced in Annapolis Md., 1962; clk. Anne Arundel County Circuit Ct., 1966-72; mem. 93d-99th Congresses from 4th Dist. of Md., 1973-86; mem. armed services com.; vice chmn. Office Tech. Assessment, 1977; chmn. Republican Study com., 1975-76; of counsel Smith, Somerville & Case, Balt., 1986-90; supr. elections Anne Arundel County, 1963-65; del. Rep. Nat. Conv., 1968, 76, 80, 84, 88; mem. Pres.'s Commn. on Arms Control and Disarmament; mem. ind. commn. USAR; bd. dirs. Annapolis Fed. Savs. Bank; mem. adv. bd. Crestar. Coauthor: Case Against The Reckless Congress, 1976, Can You Afford This House, 1978. Bd. dirs. Md. Sch. for the Blind, Hist. Annapolis Found. Recipient Disting. Alumna award U. Fla., 1975, Trustees award U. Fla. Coll. Law, 1984. Mem. Am., Md., Anne Arundel bar assns., Phi Kappa Phi, Phi Delta Delta. Presbyterian (elder 1959).

HOLT, MILDRED FRANCES, educator; b. Lorain, Ohio, July 30, 1932; d. William Henry and Rachel (Pierce) Daniels; B.S., U. Md., 1962, M.Ed., 1967, Ph.D., 1977; m. Maurice Lee Holt, Sept. 11, 1949 (dec.); children—Claudia, Frances, William, Rudi. Tchr. spl. edn. St. Mary's (Md.) County Public Schs., 1962-64, coordinator Felix Johnson Spl. Edn. Center, 1964-66; demonstration tchr. spl. edn. U. Md., College Park, summer 1970, instr. spl. edn. dept. Coll. Edn., 1969-73; supr. spl. edn. Calvert and St. Mary's (Md.) Counties, 1968-69; asso. prof. spl. edn. W. Liberty (W.Va.) State Coll., 1973-75; asst. prof. Eastern Ill. U., Charleston, 1975-77; supr. spl. edn. Warren County Public Schs., Front Royal, Va., 1977-85; spl. edn. tchr. Dallas Ind. Sch. Dist., 1985—. Mem. NEA, Warren County Edn. Assn., Council Exceptional Children, Assn. for Gifted, Assn. Supervision and Curriculum Devel., Va. Edn. Assn., Va. Council Exceptional Children, Blue Ridge Orgn. Gifted and Talented, Assn. Children with Learning Disabilities, Nat. Assn. Gifted Children, Phi Theta Kappa, Kappa Delta Pi. Contbr. articles to profl. jours.; author: Reach Guidebook, 1979. Home: 2916 Sidney Dr Mesquite TX 75150-2253 Office: Joseph J Rhoads Elem Sch Dallas TX 75260

HOLT, PATRICIA LESTER, book review editor; b. Corona del Mar, Calif., Jan. 18, 1944; d. George William and Leah Beryl (Lester) H. B.A., U. Oreg., 1965. Publicity mgr. Houghton Mifflin Co., N.Y.C. and Boston, 1969-71; sr. editor San Francisco Book Co., San Francisco, 1971-77; western corr. Publishers Weekly, N.Y.C., 1977-82; book rev. editor San Francisco Chronicle, 1982—; originator The Yr. of the Reader, Library of Congress nat. campaign, 1987, The Yr. of the Young Reader, 1989; bd. dirs., v.p. Nat. Book Critics Circle, 1991—. Author: The Bug in the Martini Olive, 1992, reprinted The Good Detective, 1994. Recipient Hilly award No. Calif. Publs. Assn., 1983, Grolier Found. award ALA, 1990; named Woman of Yr. Women's Nat. Book Assn., San Francisco chpt., 1982.

HOLT, ROBIN BURNHAM, career counselor; b. Berkeley, Calif., Oct. 25, 1938; d. Clark James Burnham and Grace (Chapman) McKenney; m. Richard Watkins Holt, Nov. 3, 1962; children: Sarah Stanley, Tyler Chapman, Spencer Mahon. BA in History, U. Calif., Berkeley, 1960; MA in Career Devel., John F. Kennedy U., 1987. Cert. Calif. Registry for Profl. Counselors. Dir. counseling and corp. svcs. Alumnae Resources, San Francisco, 1987—. Co-chmn. chancellor's millenium fund U. Calif., Berkeley, 1996—. Mem. Internat. Assn. Career Mgmt. Profls, Calif. Assn. Counseling and Devel. Office: Alumnae Resources 120 Montgomery St # 600 San Francisco CA 94104

HOLT, TERESA JAN, community health nurse; b. Birmingham, Ala., Dec. 25, 1957; d. Coy Eugene and Elizabeth Jeanette (Vann) Estes; m. Thomas G. Holt, Oct. 7, 1977. AAS in Nursing, Wallace State C.C., Hanceville, Ala., 1986; BBA, Faulkner U., 1994. Staff nurse in surg. ICU Walker Regional Med. Ctr., Jasper, Ala., 1986-87; staff nurse in cardiovascular intensive care U. Ala. Hosp., Birmingham, 1987-88, circulating RN for cardiovascular oper. rm., 1987-88; staff devel. coord. with dept. edn. 1st Am. Home Care, Inc. (formerly ABC Home Health Svcs.), Cullman, Ala., 1988—; owner, founder Jan Holt and Assocs., 1992—. With Army N.G., 1982-84.

HOLTE, DEBRA LEAH, investment executive, financial analyst; b. Madison, Wis.; d. Daniel Kenneth and Marian Anne Reitan. BA, Concordia Coll., Moorhead, Minn., 1973. CFA. Capital markets specialist 1st Bank Mpls., 1981-83; v.p. Allison-Williams Co., Mpls., 1983-86, Nelson, Benson & Zellmer, Denver, 1986-90; exec. v.p. Hamil & Holte Inc., Denver, 1990-93; pres. Holte & Assocs., Denver, 1993—. Active Denver Jr. League, Western Pension Com., 1986—; bd. dirs. Denver Children's Home, 1987—, treas., 1987-91, chmn. fin. com., 1987-91, v.p., 1990—, chmn. nominating com., 1991—, pres.-elect, 1994-95, bd. pres., 1995—; adv. bd. Luth. Social Svcs., 1987; co-chair U.S. Ski Team Fundraiser; bd. dirs. Minn. Vocat. Edn. Fin., Mpls., 1984-86; bd. dirs. Colo. Ballet, 1988-93, chair nominating com., 1991-93, v.p., 1992-93, chmn. bd., 1993; mem. Fin. Analyst Nat. Task Force in Bondholder Rights, 1988-90; bd. dirs. Ctrl. City Opera Guild, 1994-95, Western Chamber Ballet, 1994-96; social co-chmn. The Arapahoe Fox Hunt, 1993-94. Mem. Fin. Analysts Fedn., Denver Soc. Security Analysts (bd. dirs. 1990—, chair ethics and bylaws com. 1987—, chair edn. com. 1988, chair membership com. 1989, rec. sec. 1990, sec. 1991, treas. 1992, program chair 1993, pres. 1994-95, dir. 1995-96). Office: Holte & Assocs 191 University Blvd Ste 244 Denver CO 80206-4613

HOLTER, PATRA JO, artist, art education consultant; b. Ashland, wis., Mar. 6, 1936; d. Percival and Sigrid Eugenia (Gadda) H. BS, U. Wis., 1958; MA, U. Calif., Berkeley, 1962; student, Nat. Acad. Art-U. Oslo, 1963; cert. in adminstrn., Fairfield U., 1983; postgrad., New Sch. Social Rsch., UCLA, U. Colo., Pratt Inst. Cert. tchr., N.Y., Wis., adminstr., N.Y. Art tchr. Herricks Jr. H.S., New Hyde Park, N.Y., 1958-60; assoc. art U. Calif., Berkeley, 1961-62; adult art tchr. U. Calif. Alumni Camp, Pinecrest, summer 1961; elem. art tchr. Ctrl. Sch., Mamaroneck, N.Y., 1964, Edgewood Sch., Scarsdale, 1971-82; elem. and jr. H.S. art tchr. Quaker Ridge Sch., Scarsdale, N.Y., 1964-70; art tchr. Scarsdale Sr. H.S., 1982-84, chmn. art dept., 1984-93; dist. visual arts supr. Scarsdale Sch. Sys., 1989-93; art tchr. workshops, curriculum developer, cons. in field, liaison Scarsdale; visual arts coord. Lincoln Ctr. Inst., N.Y.C., 1978-80; liaison art tchr. Westchester Coun. for Arts, Scarsdale, 1970's. Author, artist: Photography Without a Camera, 1972, reprinted 1980; contbr. articles, photographs to profl. publs.; group and solo exhbns. include Wis. Salon of Art, Madison, 1958, Worth Ryder Gallery, Berkeley, 1962, Am. Embassy, Oslo, 1963, Pocket Gallery, New Canaan, Conn., 1978, Mount Mercy Coll. Gallery, Cedar Rapids, Iowa, 1988, Kitchen Gallery, Scarsdale, 1993, Art Exhbn. XVIII, Ashland, Wis., 1994, Silvermine Galleries, 1994-96, Waveny Carriage Barn, New Canaan, 1995-96, Washburn (Wis.) Hist. Mus. and Cultural Ctr., 1995, Northland Coll., Ashland, 1996. Fulbright scholar, Norway, 1962-63, ext., summer 1963; recipient Exemplary Media award N.Y. Regents Adv. Coun., 1968; Scarsdale Sch. Sys. grantee, 1972. Mem. Fulbright Assn., Norwegian Fulbright Assn., Silvermine Guild of Art, N.Y. State United Tchrs. Assn., Am. Fedn. Tchrs., Nat. Mus. Women in Arts, N.Y. State Ret. Tchrs., Nat. Art Edn. Assn., Ashland Hist. Soc., Ashland Alliance for Sustainability, Chequamegon Bay Area Arts Coun., New Canaan Soc. for Arts, Wilton Garden Club, Nat. Coun. State Garden Clubs, Royal Horticultural Soc. (London), Kappa Delta.

HOLTHAUS, JOAN MARIE, elementary school educator; b. Wichita, Kans., June 3, 1964; d. Wilbur Ferdinand and Mary Teresa (Armstrong) Kruse; m. William Paul Holthaus, July 18, 1987; 1 child, Paul Thomas. BS in Edn., English, Kans. State U., 1986. 2nd grade and kindergarten tchr. Most Pure Heart Parochial Sch., Topeka, Kans., 1986—; guardian Kans. Assn. Protective Svcs., 1991—; cons. Christ the King Daycare, 1995. Author: (resource guide) Guide for Students with Diabetes (Kans. State U.), 1985. Camp dir. Am. Diabetes Assn., Rock Springs, Kans., 1990—, chmn. bd. dirs. Shawnee County chpt., 1995-96, mem. bd. dirs. Kans., 1993—. Mem. Am. Mothers (Kans. Mother of Yr. 1995-96), Topeka Area Parochial Kindergarten Tchrs. (founder), Alpha Delta Pi (mem. at large alumnae assn.). Roman Catholic.

HOLTHAUSEN, MARTHA ANNE, interior designer, painter; b. Columbus, Ohio, Oct. 28, 1934; d. Clyde Aloysius and Olive Letitia (Marlowe) Gloeckner; m. Don Trudeau Allensworth, Aug. 14, 1960 (div. 1976); 1 child, Karen Ayn; m. Ernest Arthur Holthausen, Dec. 9, 1989. BFA cum laude, Ohio State U., 1956; postgrad., Baldwin-Wallace Coll., 1959, Mt. Vernon Coll., Washington, 1980, 81. Fashion illustrator The Marston Co., San Diego, 1956-57, The Higbee Co., Cleve., 1957-58; instr. art Lakewood (Ohio) Pub. Schs., 1958-60; tchr. Princes Georges County (Md.) Pub. Schs., 1960; account exec. Stansbury Design, Inc., Prince Georges County, Md., 1975-76; interior designer Berwin Interiors, Bethesda, Md., 1977-79, W. & J. Sloane, Inc., Washington, 1980-84; pres., interior designer Martha Allensworth Interior Design, Inc., Falls Church, Va., 1984—; guest artist-in-residence Nat. Park Svc., Yosemite Nat. Park, Calif., summer 1988, 89, 91, 95. Watercolor and oil paintings in pvt. collections. Bd. dirs. C. of C. Herndon, Va., 1985-86; v.p. Montgomery County (Md.) Art Assn., 1962-63. Mem. AAUW, Internat. Furnishings and Design Soc., Vienna (Va.) Arts Soc. Episcopalian. Office: Martha Allensworth Interior Design Inc 7799 Leesburg Pike Ste 900 Falls Church VA 22043-2413

HOLTKAMP, SUSAN CHARLOTTE, elementary education educator; b. Houston, Feb. 23, 1957; d. Clarence Jules and Karyl Irene (Roberts) H. BS in Early Childhood Edn., Brigham Young U., Provo, Utah, 1979, MEd, 1982. Cert. tchr., Utah. 2d grade tchr. Nebo Sch. Dist., Spanish Fork, Utah, 1979-84, kindergarten tchr., 1984-85; tchr. 2d grade DODDS, Mannheim, Fed. Republic Germany, 1985-86; tchr. 3d grade Jordan Sch. Dist., Salt Lake City, 1987-92, tchr. 5th grade, 1992—. Mem. NEA, JEA, Utah Edn. Assn., ASCD.

HOLTON, GRACE HOLLAND, accountant; b. Durham, N.C., Sept. 14, 1957; d. Samuel Melanchthon and B. Margaret (Umberger) H. BS in Math., Univ. N.C., Greensboro, 1978; MBA, Univ. N.C., Chapel Hill, 1984; M.Acctg. Sci., U. Ill., 1993. CPA N.C.; cert. mgmt. acct. Indsl. engr. Burlington Industries, Inc., Mayodan, N.C., 1978-79; plant indsl. engr. Burlington Industries, Inc., Stoneville, N.C., 1979-80; methods indsl. engr. Blue Cross and Blue Shield of N.C., Durham, 1980-82; fin. analyst R.J. Reynolds, Inc., Winston-Salem, N.C., 1984-85; accounting cons. Ryder Truck Rental, Inc., Miami, Fla., 1985-88; controller Ryder Jacobs (div. Ryder Distbn. Resources), Jessup, Md., 1988-90; grad. asst. in acctg. U. Ill., Urbana, 1990-93; contr. Salem NationaLease, Winston-Salem, N.C., 1993-94; dir. fin. Chapel Hill-Carrboro City Schs., 1994—. KPMG-Peat Marwick scholar, 1991-92. Mem. AICPAs, Inst. Mgmt. Accts., N.C. Soc. CPAs. Democrat. Methodist.

HOLTZ, JANE KAY, special education educator; b. Ashley, N.D., Nov. 8, 1963; d. Sylvester and Florence (Feist) Meier; m. Robert A. Holtz, Nov. 13, 1993; children: Kassandra Jo, Robert Stanley. BS in Mental Retardation, Elem. Edn., Minot (N.D.) State U., 1986, MS in Spl. Edn., 1988. Tchr. educable mentally handicapped Denseith (N.D.) Pub. Sch., 1986-87; multiple handicapped tchr. Oliver Mercer Spl. Edn./Hazen (N.D.) Pub. Schs., 1988-91; tchr. educable mentally handicapped Oliver Mercer Spl. Edn./Beulah (N.D.) Pub. Schs., 1991-93; MSMI tchr. Moorhead (Minn.) Pub. Schs. #152, 1993—. Coach Minot Spl. Olympics, 1984-86, Hazen Spl. Olympics, 1988-91. Dept. Pub. Instrn. scholar, 1987-88. Mem. NEA, Coun. for Exceptional Children, Kappa Delta Pi. Roman Catholic. Home: 1941 55th Ave S Fargo ND 58104-6368 Office: George Washington Elem Sch 901 14th St N Moorhead MN 56560-1602

HOLTZ, JENNIFER KAY, medical researcher, educator; b. Chicago Heights, Ill., Nov. 20, 1961; d. Arthur Frederick Peters; m. Issam Khder Samarah, Dec. 31, 1982 (div. Jan., 1992); m. William Henry Holz, Apr. 9, 1994; 1 child, William Theodore. AA, Kansas Newman Coll., 1981, BA, 1983; MA, Wichita State U., 1992; postgrad. studies toward PhD, Emporia State U., 1995—. Medicare rep. St. Francis Regional Med. Ctr., Wichita, Kans., 1984-89; vol. and activity dir. Presbyn. Manors of Mid-Am., Wichita, 1989-90, adminstrv. intern, 1990-91; Alzheimer spl. care unit dir. Manor Health Care Corp., Wichita, 1991-92; rsch. assoc. and instr. U. Kans. Sch. of Medicine Wesley Med. Ctr., Wichita, 1992—; mem. rsch. com., U. Kansas, Sch. of Medicine, Wichita, chair rsch. edn. subcom., 1993—. Contbr. article to Jour. of Family Practice, Kansas Medicine; presenter poster U. Kans. Sch. of Medicine Wichita Rsch. Forum, 1994, 95. Tutor Literacy Vols. of Am., Wichita, 1990-92; bd. dirs. Alzheimer's Assn. S. Ctrl. Kans., 1992-95. Mem. NAFE, AAAS, Assn. for Health Svcs. Rsch. Home: 646 N Fountain Wichita KS 67208 Office: U Kans Sch Medicine Wesley Med Ctr Med Edn 550 N Hillside Wichita KS 67214

HOLTZ, SARA, lawyer, mediator, consultant; b. L.A., Aug. 7, 1951. BA, Yale U., 1972; JD, Harvard U., 1975. Bar: Calif. 1982. Assoc. Brownstein, Zeidman & Schomer, Washington, 1975-77; dep. asst. dir. FTC, Washington, 1977-82; divsn. counsel Clorox Co., Oakland, Calif., 1982-90; v.p., dep. gen. counsel Nestle U.S.A., Inc., San Francisco, 1990-94; mediator Mediation Offices of Sara Holtz, 1994—; prin. Client Focus, 1996—. Mem. Am. Corp. Counsel Assn. (bd. dirs. 1986-95, chmn. 1994-95). Office: 28 Heilmann Ct Nevada City CA 95959-2935

HOLTZ, TOBENETTE, aerospace engineer; b. Rochester, N.Y., June 20, 1930; d. Marcus and Leah (Cohen) H.; m. Joseph Laurinovics, Dec. 25, 1964. BS in Aeronautical Engring., Wayne State U., 1958; MS in Aero/Astro Engring., Ohio State U., 1964; PhD, U. So. Calif., L.A., 1974. Sr. engr. North Am. Aviation, Columbus, Ohio, 1954-59; rsch. assoc. Ohio State U., Columbus, 1959-60; sr. engr. U. So. Calif. Rsch. Found., Pt. Mugu, 1960-62, Northrop Corp., Hawthorne, Calif., 1962-67; engring. specialist McDonnell Douglas Corp., Huntington Beach, Calif., 1967-75; staff engr. Acurex Corp., Mountain View, Calif., 1975-76; project mgr. Aerospace Corp., El Segundo, Calif., 1976-82; tech. mgr. TRW, Inc., San Bernardino, Calif., 1982—. Contbr. articles to profl. jours. Assoc. fellow AIAA (sect. vice chair 1980-82, 91-92, nat. tech. mom. 1991-96, organizer nat. confs. 1979, 86, 88, 94, 96, Disting. Svc. award 1983). Office: TRW Inc PO Box 1310 San Bernardino CA 92402

HOLTZ-BORDERS, KAREN LYNN, police officer; b. Glendale, Calif., Mar. 10, 1960; d. Denison Lee and Diane Arlyce (Shapiro) Baldwin; m. Steven Henry Holtz, June 1, 1985 (div. Dec. 1992); m. Donald Eugene Borders, Apr. 29, 1995; children: Ashley, Stacey. AS, Coll. of the Desert, 1985; BS, U. Redlands, 1992. Police officer Palm Springs (Calif.) Police Dept., 1982—, explorer advisor, 1985-89, detective, 1989-94, field tng. officer, 1994-96, domestic violence detective, 1996—. Recipient Medal of Valor, Am. Legion, 1989. Republican. Roman Catholic. Office: Palm Springs Police Dept 200 S Civic Dr Palm Springs CA 92262-7201

HOLTZCLAW, DIANE SMITH, elementary education educator; b. Buffalo, May 26, 1936; d. John Nelson and Beatrice M. (Salisbury) Smith; m. John Victor Holtzclaw, June 27, 1959; children: Kathryn Diane, John Bryan. BS in Edn. magna cum laude, SUNY, Brockport, 1957, MS with honors, 1961; postgrad., SUNY, Buffalo, 1960-65, Canisus Coll., 1979, Nazareth Coll., 1981-82. Tchr. Greece Cen. Sch., Rochester, N.Y., 1957-60; supr. SUNY, Brockport, 1960-64, assoc. prof. edn., 1960-64; dir. Early Childhood Ctr., Fairport, N.Y., 1968-80; tchr. Fairport Cen. Schs., 1971—; edni. cons. in field; specialist child devel. Ch. music dir. , Rochester, N.Y., 1983—; pres. bd. dirs. Downtown Day Care Ctr., Rochester, 1974-83; mem. exec. bd. Rochester Theatre Organ Soc., 1988—. Mem. Fairport Edn. Assn. (exec. bd. 1982-83, del. 1983), N.Y. State United Tchrs., AAUW (exec. bd. 1973-74, 77-79, 83-84, pres. Fairport br. 1971-73), Internat. Platform Assn., Kappa Delta Pi. Home: 1455 Ayrault Rd Fairport NY 14450-9301 Office: Fairport Cen Schs 38 W Church St Fairport NY 14450-2130

HOLTZENDORF, STEPHANIE ELAINE, accountant; b. Rome, Ga., Sept. 13, 1960; d. Jack Clinton and Sara Mildred (Logan) S. m. Carey Preston Holtzendorf, Feb. 14, 1988; 1 child, Clinton Forrest. B in Liberal Studies Acctg., St. Edward's U., 1988. CPA, Tex. Computer clk. J Supply Co., Rome, Ga., 1979-81; acctg. clk. Butterworth Legal Publishers, Austin, Tex., 1982-86, Tex. Med. Liability Trust, Austin, 1986-88; controller Tex. Food Industry Assn., Austin, 1989-93; tech. asst. I Tex. Worker's Compensation, Austin, 1993-94, acct. II, 1994-95; budget analyst III Tex. Worker's Compensation Ins. Fund, Austin, 1995—. Mem. Inst. Mgmt. Accts., Nat. Soc. Pub. Accts., Tex. Soc. CPAs, Kyle (Tex.) C. of C. Republican. Home: 3420 Galesburg Dr Austin TX 78745 Office: Texas Workers Comp Ins Fund 221 W 6th St Ste 300 Austin TX 78701-3403

HOLTZMAN, KAREN ELAINE, art curator; b. Washington, Mar. 29, 1952; d. Max and Elsie (Loube) H. BA, U. Md., 1974, MA in Art History, 1984. Art historian Nat. Portrait Gallery, Smithsonian Inst., Washington, 1982-86; pvt. practice curator, fine art appraiser, art advisor Washington, 1986—; fine-art pub. Petra Holtzman Multiples, Inc., Washington and L.A., 1993-95. Author, curator (art catalog and exhbn.) Home?, 1990, Surveillance, 1992, Burnt Whole: Contemporary Artists Reflect on the Holocaust, 1994-95. Bd. mem. Home for Contemporary Theater and Art, N.Y.C., 1990-94, Washington Project for the Arts, 1992-96. Grantee Smithsonian Instn., London, 1981; fellow Victorian Soc., London, 1981. Mem. Am. Soc. Appraisers (cert. sr. appraiser), Art Table. Home: Apt 707E 4201 Cathedral Ave NW Washington DC 20016-4904

HOLTZMAN, ROBERTA LEE, French and Spanish language educator; b. Detroit, Nov. 24, 1938; d. Paul John and Sophia (Marcus) H. AB cum laude, Wayne State U., 1959, MA, 1973; MA, U. Mich., 1961. Fgn. lang. tchr. Birmingham (Mich.) Sch. Dist., 1959-60, Cass Tech. High Sch., Detroit, 1961-64; from instr. to prof. of French and Spanish Schoolcraft Coll., Livonia, Mich., 1964-84; chair French and Spanish depts. Schoolcraft Coll., 1984—. Trustee Cranbrook Music Guild, Ednl. Community, Bloomfield Hills, Mich., 1976-78. Recipient Fulbright-Hays award, Fulbright Commn., Brazil, 1964. Mem. AAUW, NEA, MLA, Nat. Mus. Women in Arts (cofounder 1992), Am. Assn. Tchrs. of Spanish and Portuguese, Am. Assn. Tchrs. of French, Mich. Edn. Assn. Office: Schoolcraft Coll 18600 Haggerty Rd Livonia MI 48152-3932

HOLUB, BARBARA ANN, rehabilitation nurse; b. South Euclid, Ohio, Mar. 29, 1961; d. Peter Cyril Anthony Dominic and Kathleen Theresa (Horner) McHale; m. Thomas John Joseph Holub, June 1, 1991; children: Colleen Marie, Ryan Thomas. ASN, Mattatuck C.C., 1985, Assoc. Liberal Arts, 1983. RN, Conn.; cert. rehab. nurse; cert. ins. rehab. specialist. Rehab. nurse Yale New Haven Hosp., 1985-89, Hosp. St. Raphael, New Haven, 1989-96, Grant St. Health and Rehab. Ctr., Bridgeport, Conn., 1996—. Mem. Assn. Rehab. Nurses (v.p. 1992-93, pres. 1993-94, bd. dirs. 1995—). Republican. Roman Catholic. Home: 1 Farrell Dr Ansonia CT 06401-2809 Office: Grant Street Health Rehab Ctr 425 Grant St Bridgeport CT 06604

HOLUBEC, EDYTHE JOHNSON, educational consultant; b. Muncie, Ind., July 25, 1944; d. Roger Winfield and Frances Elizabeth (Pierce) Johnson; m. James Frank Holubec, Feb. 28, 1973. BS, Ball State U., 1966; MA, U. Minn., 1976; PhD, U. Tex., 1991. VISTA vol. Vols. in Svc. to Am., N.Y.C., 1966-67; English and Reading tchr. Stevenson H.S., Livonia, Mich., 1967-69; instr., tchg. asst. U. Minn., Mpls., 1969-72; reading specialist Austin (Tex.) Ind. Sch. Dist., 1972-73, Granger (Tex.) Ind. Sch. Dist., 1976-77; English and Reading tchr. Taylor (Tex.) Ind. Sch. Dist., 1977-80; instr. U. Tex., Austin, 1981-87; ednl. cons. Coop. Learning Inst., Edina, Minn., 1987—. Co-author: Circle of Learning, 1994, Cooperation in the Classroom, 1993, Advanced Cooperative Learning, 1992, The Nuts and Bolts of Cooperative Learning, 1994. Mem. ASCD, Am. Ednl. Rsch. Assn., Internat. Reading Assn., Nat. Coun. of the Tchrs. of English, Nat. Staff Devel. Coun., Phi Delta Kappa. American Baptist. Home and Office: Box 552 Taylor TX 76574

HOLUBKA, JACQUELIN PICKFORD, physician, educator; b. Detroit, Sept. 13, 1957; d. Verne Melvin and Virginia Ruth (Fleming) Pickford. BS, Wayne State U., 1980; MD, Mich. State U., 1986. Diplomate Am. Bd. Internal Medicine. Sr. rsch. asst. Mich. Cancer Found., Detroit, 1982-84; med. resident Henry Ford Hosp., Detroit, 1986-89; dir. ambulatory edn., physician St. John Hosp., Detroit, 1989-95; dir. outpatient med. edn. St. Barnabas Med. Ctr., Livingston, N.J., 1995—, asst. program dir. internal medicine, 1995—; dir. outpatient med. edn. St. John Hosp., 1990-95; clin. asst. prof. Wayne State U., Detroit, 1993-95. Del. Citizen Amb. Program. Med. & Cultural Exch., China, 1991, Russia, 1993. Mem. ACP (Clin. Vignette award 1994), Am. Med. Women's Assn. (Janet Glascow Meml. Achievement citation 1986), Am. Soc. Internal Medicine.

HOLVICK, PATRICIA VALERIE JEAN, property manager, financial planner; b. Seattle, Nov. 10, 1921; d. Henry Carlos Houck and Peggy Dorothy Jacobsen (Houck) Hardwick; m. Carl Andrew Holvick; children: Valerie Ann, Christine Lynn, Debra Jean. BA, U. Washington, Seattle, 1944. Mem. bd. dirs. San Mateo Indsl. Corp., 1950-60, Peninsula Associated Real Estate Devel., 1960-78; v.p. Bay Area Indsl. Corp. Co., Palo Alto, Calif., 1978—; pilot Women Flyers of Am., 1948-54; fin. adv. Ventures Unlimited, 1949-55; pre-sch. tchr. Menlo Park Presbyn. Ch., 1980—. Established and funded six endowments for fellowships at Fuller, Gordon-Conwell & Princeton Seminaries, 1961—, endowment Am. Fellowship for Juvenile Diabetes & Immunology AAUW, 1994; pres. Peninsula Alpha Gamma Delta Sorority Alumnae Club, San Mateo County, Calif., 1948-50; mens' program com. Internat. Fedn. Univ. Women, Stanford, Calif., 1992. Mem. AAUW (pres. Menlo-Atherton branch 1989-91, 96—, citizen amb. Soviet Union 1991, Japan 1995, interbranch coun. chair 1991-92), DAR (chair good citizen's com. 1981—, vice-regent Gaspar De Portola chpt. 1996—), Mortar Board Alumni/Tolo Assn., Toastmasters Internat., Presbyn. Women. Democrat. Presbyterian. Home: 34 Barry Ln Atherton CA 94027

HOLZENDORF, BETTY SMITH, state senator; b. Jacksonville, Fla., Apr. 5, 1939; d. Fannie Holmes; m. King Holzendorf II; children: Kim, King III, Kevin, Kessler. BS in Biology, Edward Waters Coll., Jacksonville, 1965; MS in Biochemistry, Atlanta U., 1971; MEd, U. Fla., 1973; LLD (hon.), Edward Waters Coll., 1994. Tchr. Duval County Sch. Bd., Jacksonville, 1965-70; asst. prof. Edward Waters Coll., Jacksonville, 1971-72, dir. rsch., 1972-74, dir. fin. aid, 1974-75; with affirmative action com. City of Jacksonville, 1975-78; adminstrv. aide Mayor's Office, Jacksonville, 1979-87; field rep. Dept. Transp., Jacksonville, 1987-88; state rep. State of Fla., Jacksonville, 1988-92; state senator State of Fla., Tallahasse, 1992—; chmn., Duval County Legis. Del., 1992-93, Jacksonville C. of C. Outstanding Legislator award, 1994, chairperson, Fla. Conf. of Black State Legislators, 1994. Recipient Outstanding Educator award, 1972, Govtl. Svc. award Jacksonville C. of C., 1989, Pres.'s award Fla. A&M U., 1990, Disting. Svc. award Fla. A&M U., 1990, African Am. Heritage award for support of edn. Fla. A&M U., 1991, Human Svcs. Outstanding Leadership award, Brotherhood award, Appreciation award Nat. Coun. Negro Women, 1988, Governmental award Northwest Coun. Area Community, 1989, Quality Legislative award Fla. League of Cities, 1991, 92, Fraternal Order of Police award, 1992, Putnam County Sch. Bd. Outstanding Legislator award, 1993, Fla. Assocn. Administrators, Raymond B. Stewart Gavel award for work in edn., others. Mem. Nat. Coun. Negro Women (life), Nat. Conf. Black State Legis., Fla. Ins. Commmn., 1993, award for excellence, Alpha Kappa Alpha (life). Democrat. Mem. African Meth. Episcopal Ch. Office: State Senate State Capitol Tallahassee FL 32399-1300*

HOLZER, HELEN D., journalist; b. St. Paul, Apr. 15, 1951; d. Michael and Bertha (Shilkrot) Dorr; m. Charles B. Holzer, Dec. 20, 1970; 1 child, Julie. BA in Journalism, U. Minn., 1972. Reporter Murray Eagle, Salt Lake City, 1972; editor Goleta Valley Sun, Santa Barbara, Calif., 1973; assoc. editor Bell Pub., Denver, 1974-75; reporter, layout artist Sun Newspapers, Kansas City, Kans., 1975-78; layout artist Graphic Assocs., Hapeville, Ga., 1980-81, Associated Grocers Advt., College Park, Ga., 1982-83; mgr. advt. Brownell Electro Inc., Atlanta, 1983-89; calendar editor Atlanta Jour.-Constitution, 1990—. Dem. precinct committeewoman, Denver, 1974-75. Mem. Atlanta Press Club. Office: Atlanta Journal Constitution Features Desk 72 Marietta St NW Atlanta GA 30303-2804

HOLZINGER, JAN K., lawyer; b. St. Louis, 1956. BA, U. Tex., 1978, JD, 1981. Bar: Tex. 1981. Ptnr. Andrews & Kurth L.L.P., Houston. Assoc. editor Rev. of Litig., 1980-81. Mem. ABA, State Bar Tex. Office: Andrews & Kurth LLP 600 Travis Ste 4200 Houston TX 77002*

HOLZMAN, ESTHER ROSE, perfume company executive; b. Frankfurt, Germany; d. Fred and Anna Marie (Zell) Wetmore; m. Nicholas J. Holzman; 1 child, Stephanie Maria. M Organic Chemistry, Pvt. Sch. Dr. Binder, Stuttgart, Germany. Exec. asst. Bosch G.M.B.H., Stuttgart; owner, chief exec. officer Holzman & Stephanie Perfumes, Inc., Lake Forest, Ill., 1986—; normal control, pioneering rsch. studies in nuclear medicine under Phillip H. Henneman, M.D., Seton Hall U., Jersey City, N.J.; normal control, diabetes rsch. under Phillip H. Henneman, M.D. Organizer campaign to rescind cutbacks in fed. funding for med. rsch., 1969, 70. Recipient award for historic restoration of residential bldgs., Village of Oak Park, Ill., 1974, 76. Roman Catholic. Office: PO Box 921 Lake Forest IL 60045-0921

HOM, THERESA MARIA, osteopathic physician; b. Detroit, Oct. 25, 1957; d. Richard Gay and Elizabeth Marie (Moye) H.; m. Rick L. Anderson, June 30, 1990 (dec. Dec., 1994). BS in Biology, U. Mich., 1979; DO, Mich. State U., 1984. Diplomate Am. Osteo. Bd. Gen. Practice; cert. of proficency in med. acupuncture. Intern Oakland Gen. Hosp., Madison, Mich., 1984-85; resident, gen. practice Doctors Hosp., Columbus, Ohio, 1985-86; family physician Madison Clinic, 1986-87, Community Family Health Ctr. and ECCO Family Health Ctr., Columbus, 1987-95; clin. prof. Ohio U. Coll. Osteo. Medicine, Columbus, 1989—; apptd. osteo. mem. Ohio State Med. Bd., 1990-93, supervisory mem., 1993, v.p., 1993; bd. dirs. Asian Am. Cmty. Svcs. Physician Columbus Free Clinic, 1990. Featured poet Larry's Poetry Forum, Columbus, 1991. Mem. Am. Osteo. Assn., Am. Med. Women's Assn., Ohio Osteo. Assn. (del. 1989, 93), Pax Christi Columbus (coord. program 1989-91), Am. Coll. Osteo. Gen. Practice, Am. Acad. Med. Acupuncturists. Roman Catholic. Office: The Doctor's Office 3409 E Main St Columbus OH 43213

HOMESTEAD, SUSAN E. (SUSAN FREEDLENDER), psychotherapist; b. Bklyn., Sept. 20, 1937; d. Cy Simon and Katherine (Haas) Eichelbaum; m. Robert Bruce Randall, 1956 (div. 1960); 1 child, Bruce David; m. George Gilbert Zanetti, Dec. 13, 1962 (div. 1972)); m. Ronald Eric Homestead, Jan. 16, 1973 (div. 1980); m. Arthur Elliott Freedlender, Apr. 1, 1995. BA, U. Miami-Fla., 1960; MSW, Tulane U., 1967. Diplomate Am. Bd. Clin. Social Work; Acad. Cert. Social Workers, 1971, LCSW, Va., Calif. Psychotherapist, cons., Richmond, Va., 1971—, Los Altos, Calif.; pvt. practice, Piedmont Psychiatric Ctr., P.C. (formerly Psychol. Evaluation Rehab. Cons., Inc.), Lynchburg, Va., 1994—; cons. Family and Children's Svcs., Richmond, 1981—, Richmond Pain Clinic, 1983-84; Health Internat. Va., P.C., Lynchburg, 1984-86, Franklin St. Psychotherapy & Edn. Ctr, Santa Clara, Calif., 1988-90; pvt. practice, 1971—; Santa Clara County Children's

Svc., 1973-75, 86-88; co-dir. asthma program Va. Lung Assn., Richmond, 1975-79, Loma Prieta Regional Ctr.; chief clin. social worker Med. Coll. Va., Va. Commonwealth U., 1974-79; field supr. 1980 Census, 1981-87. Contbr. articles to profl. jours. Active Peninsula Children's Ctr., Morgan Ctr., Coun. for Community Action Planning, Community Assn. for Retarded, Comprehensive Health Planning Assn. Santa Clara, Mental Health Commn., Children and Adolescent Target Group Calif., Women's Com. Richmond Symphony, Va. Mus. Theatre, mem. fin. com. Robb for Gov.; mem. adv. com. Va. Lung Assn.; mem. steering com. Am. Cancer Soc.(Va. div.), Epilepsy Found., Am. Heart Assn. (Va. div.), Cen. Va. Guild for Infant Survival. Mem. NASW, Va. Soc. Clin. Social Work, Inc. (charter mem., sec. 1975-78), Internat. Soc. Communicative Psychoanalysis & Psychotherapy, Am. Acad. Psychotherapists, Internat. Soc. for the Study of Dissociation, Am. Assn. Psychiatric Svcs. for Children.

HOMMO, HARUMI, translator; b. Kameda-machi, Niigata, Japan, July 10, 1956; came to U.S., 1990; BA, Tokyo U., 1980; MS in acct., Pace U., 1995. CPA. Sr. translator Goldman Sachs, Tokyo, 1985-86, Nat. West County Securities, Tokyo, 1986-89, Morgan Stanley, Tokyo, 1989-90, Daiwa Inst. Rsch., N.Y.C., 1990—. MEm. Am. Translators Assn. Home: 280 Park Ave S #11D New York NY 10010

HOMSTAD, TORILD M., summer school administrator, language educator; b. Roseau, Minn., Dec. 17, 1949; d. Torliff Paul and Ella Valborg (Rolvaag) T.; m. Keith Everett Homstad, May 26, 1969; children: Hans Erik Edvart, Maia Marie Valborg. BA, St. Olaf Coll., 1971; MA, U. Minn., 1990, postgrad., 1996—. Tchg. asst. dept. Norwegian U. Minn., Mpls., 1981-95; assoc. adminstr. internat. summer sch. U. Oslo, 1981—; co-founder. lead tchr. Camp Little Am. Sons of Norway, Oslo, 1986-96. Co-editor: The Northfield Magazine, 1980-93; translator: (book sect.) An Everyday Story. Precinct chair Northfield (Minn.) Dem. Party, 1976-86; dir. City Libr. Bd., Northfield, 1985-91. Fulbright scholar, Oslo, 1995-96. Mem. Am. Coun. Tchg. Fgn. Langs., Soc. Advancement of Scandinavian Studies. Democrat. Lutheran. Home: 311 Manitou St Northfield MN 55057-1512

HONEA, JOYCE CLAYTON, critical care nurse; b. San Antoino, Oct. 4, 1952; d. Leslie James and Shirley Louis (Steinfeldt) Clayton; m. Bertrand N. Honea III, May 1, 1982; children: Matt Baker, Elissa Baker. BS in Nursing, Loretto Heights Coll., 1976; MS, Cen. Mich. U., 1990. Nurse mgr. Ivinson Meml. Hosp., Laramie, Wyo., 1982-89; nursing faculty Front Range C.C., Ft. Collins, Colo., 1990—; emergency staff nurse North Colo. Med., Greeley, 1990—. Mem. ANA (sec. 1985-87).

HONEA, NANCE, artist, educator; b. Tampa, Fla., Feb. 4, 1945; d. Hiram James and Vadie Kathryn (Fleming) H.; m. Thomas T. Bragg, Jr., Aug. 16, 1964 (div. 1973); children: Elisabeth Paige, Kristen Fleming. Student, Mercer U., 1963-64, Emory U., 1978, Art Students League, N.Y.C., 1995. Adminstrv. asst. for leukemia rsch. Emory U., Atlanta, 1973-80; owner Honea Fine Art Studio, Stone Mountain, Ga., 1980—; instr. portrait workshops, 1982—; instr. portrait painting Spruill Ctr. for Arts, Atlanta, 1985—, Internat. Workshop, Italy, 1996; instr. portrait painting Atlanta Coll. Art, 1993—, advisor Shute scholarship fund, 1993—; resident portrait painter Grand Hotel, Mackinac Island, Mich., 1981, The Lodge at Vail, Colo., 1982. One-woman shows Ga. Inst. Tech. Art Gallery, Atlanta, 1979, Am. Nat. Bank, Chattanooga, 1983, Hunter Mus. Art, Chattanooga, 1983, Macon (Ga.) Little Theater, 1988, Picasso Cafe, Atlanta, 1988, Brown & Spiegel, Atlanta, 1991; exhibited in group shows Birmingham (Ala.) Mus. Art, 1978, North Tex. State U. Art Gallery, Denton, 1979, Asheville (N.C.)) Mus., 1983, Shenandoah Coll. and Conservatory, Winchester, Va., 1985, Bellarmine Coll., Louisville, 1985, George Walter Vincent Smith Art Mus., Springfield, Mass., 1986, Macon Mus. Arts and Scis., 1986, Okla. Art Ctr., Oklahoma City, 1986, North Arts Gallery, Atlanta, 1988, Portrait Soc. Ann., 1987—, SE Pastel Soc. Internat., 1989, 90, 92, 96, Ritz-Carlton Hotel, Atlanta, 1988, Ga. Mountains Srt Mus., Gainesville, 1992, So. Bell Ctr., Atlanta, 1993, Atlanta Coll. Art, 1996, Am. Coll. Art, Atlanta, 1996, Avery Gallery, Marietta, 1996, also others; represented in over 200 corp. and pvt. collections throughout U.S. and fgn. countries. Recipient Best in Show awards La. Tech U., 1984, 1st merit award, 1986; purchase award Ga. Coun. for Arts, 1986, also others; named Artist of Yr. Atlanta br. Nat. League Am. Pen Women, 1995. Mem. Nat. Mus. Women in Arts (charter), So. Watercolor Soc., Pastel Soc. Am., Ga. Watercolor Soc. (merit award 1984), Ky. Watercolor Soc., Portrait Soc. Atlanta (charter, pres. 1985-87, exec. bd., bd. dirs., merit mem. 1991—), Ala. Watercolor Soc. (juried mem.), Southeastern Pastel Soc. (Mem. of Excellence award 1992, Merit award 1992, Honorable Mention 1990, 96), Alpha Delta Pi. Studio: 361 Navarre Dr Stone Mountain GA 30087

HONIG, ETHELYN, artist; b. N.Y.C., July 9, 1933; d. Samuel and Sophie (Brody) Blinder; m. Lester Jerome Honig, July 29, 1955 (dec. July 1992); children: Hillary Wynn Honig Ensminger, Deirdre Lynn Honig. Attended, Bennington Coll.; BA, Sarah Lawrence Coll., Bronxville, N.Y. chair adv. bd. Sculpture Ctr. Battery Park Maritime Bldg., N.Y.C., 1987; curator art exhbn. for patients Manhattan Psychiatric Ctr., N.Y.C.; pub. Art Editions, Kenneth Noland Sol Lewitt, Chgo. 7 Portfolio. One person exhbns. include Benson Gallery, Bridgehampton, L.I., N.Y., 1968, 55 Mercer Gallery, N.Y.C., 1972, 74, 83, 84, 85, 86, 87, 89, 91, 94, 96, Franklin Furnace Archive, N.Y.C., 1977, Mus. of Modern Art, 1974, 75, Rosa Esman Gallery, N.Y.C., 1975, South East Mus., Brewster, N.Y., 1978, Katonah (N.Y.) Gallery, 1981; group exhbns. include 55 Mercer Gallery, N.Y.C., 1975, 76, 78, 91, 93, U. Ariz. Mus., Tucson, 1980, So. Allegheny Mus. Art, 1981, Keene Coll. Art Gallery, Union, N.J. Foxworth Gallery, N.Y.C., 1985, Kenkelaba Gallery, N.Y.C., 1985, Somerstown Gallery, Somers, N.Y., 1985, Katonah (N.Y.) Gallery, 1987, Art Initiatives at Tribeca 148 Gallery, 1994, 95, Paula Cooper Gallery, N.Y.C., 1970, represented in permanent collections Mus. Modern Art, N.Y.C., Wadsworth Atheneum Mus., Patrick Lannon Found., Citi-Corps, Smith Coll. Mus., Northampton, Mass.; patentee in field. Founder and chairperson Clozapine Family Info. for the Alliance for the Mentally Ill, N.Y.S., 1990-96. Recipient Svc. awards Alliance for the Mentally Ill N.Y.S., Albany, 1990, Friends and Advocates for the Mentally Ill, 1990-91. Mem. Nat. Alliance for the Mentally Ill, Art Students League, 55 Mercer Artists (founding mem., treas.). Home: 137 E 95th St New York NY 10128

HONNER SUTHERLAND, B. JOAN, advertising executive; b. N.Y.C., Oct. 23, 1952; d. William John and Mary Patricia (Edwards) H.; m. Donald J. Sutherland, Oct. 3, 1987; children: Chelsea Lauren, Whitney Devon. Student, Endicott Coll., 1970-71. Art dir. Kerrigan Studio, Darien, Conn., 1971-73, Foote Cone and Belding, Phoenix, 1973-77; sr. art dir. Foote Cone and Belding, Chgo., 1977-81; v.p., assoc. creative dir. J. Walter Thompson, Chgo., 1982-86; v.p., exec. art dir. BBDO Chgo., 1986-91; creative dir. Knautz & Co., Sarasota, Fla., 1992-93; co-owner X-L Advt., Sarasota, Fla., 1993-94; owner Beyond Design, Sarasota, 1994—; cons. J. Walter Thompson, Toronto and San Francisco, 1983-84; owner Fla. Antiques, Geneva, Ill., 1986-90. Introduced Discover card, 1985. Tchr. elem. sch. art; mem. Southside Sch. PTA Bd., Sarasota, 1996—. Recipient 1st pla. TV local campaign WGN, 6th dist. Addy, 1980, Kemp. Corp. Addy, 1990; Best Internat. TV campaign Pepsi Clio, 1985. Roman Catholic. Home: 4941 Commonwealth Dr Sarasota FL 34242-1421

HONNOLD, DIERDRE WOLOWNICK, publisher, writer; b. N.Y.C., Sept. 23, 1951; d. Joseph Stanley and Stasia (Zola) Wolownick; m. Charles Forest Honnold, July 7, 1979; children: Stasia, Alexander. BA Langs., Edn., magna cum laude, CUNY, 1973, MA in French, 1981; cert. TESL, UCLA, 1981. Cert. tchr. N.Y., single substitute tchr., Calif. C.C. credentials, Calif. H.s. tchr. French, Spanish, Italian, music Various Schs., Bklyn., Bronx, and, Calif., 1973-79; instr. ESL UCLA, L.A., 1980-81, Glendale (Calif.) C.C., 1981-82; lectr. English Tokai U., Hiratsuka, Japan, 1982-85; instr. current devels. Learning Exchange, Sacramento, Calif., 1987-90; instr. ESL Sacramento (Calif.) City Coll., 1988-90; instr., coord. ESL, French Am. River Coll., Sacramento, 1990—; free lance writer Numazu, Carmichael, Calif., Japan, 1982—; mng. editor, publisher Wordwrights Internat., Carmichael, Calif., 1993—. Author: (Books) Sacramento with Kids, 1994 (Best, Travel Dir. 1994), English with Ease, 1994, '96, San Jose with Kids, 1995 (Best, Travel Dir. 1995). Founder, conductor, West Sacramento (Calif.) Cmty. Orch., 1990-93. Grantee: Polish Nat. Govt., Warsaw, 1975; recipient cert. of merit Writers' Digest, Cin., 1994. Mem. Sacramento Publishers Assn. (bd. dirs., past pres., v.p. 1995-96), Calif. Writers Club, Women Fiction Writers, Writers Connection, C. of Cs, (W. Sacramento, Sacramento, Carmichael, Calif.), Mensa, Phi Beta Kappa, Pi Delta Phi. Office: Wordwrights Internat PO Box 1941 Carmichael CA 95609

HONOR, NOËL EVANS, social services supervisor; b. Indpls., Apr. 11, 1948; d. Fredrick Harris and Shirley (Richardson) Evans; m. Herbert Lincoln Martin, Aug. 18, 1972 (div. Aug. 19, 1982); 1 child, Lisa Rochelle Martin; m. Alan Thompson Honor, Sept. 14, 1990. BA in Psychology, Fisk U., 1970; MSW, Ind. U.-Purdue U., 1972. Cert. social worker; lic. social worker, Ind.; diplomate Am. Bd. Examiners in Social Work. Social worker Wis. Dept. Health & Social Svcs., Madison, 1972-75; ct. svcs. social worker Mental Health Ctr. of Dane County, Madison, 1976-85; field practicum supr. in social work U. Wis., Madison, 1983-84; lead group facilitator, social worker Multi Resource Ctr., Inc., Mpls., 1985-86; coord. teen incest program Parental Stress Ctr., Madison, 1986; psychiat. social work case mgr. Goodwill Industries, Madison, 1986-87; outreach therapist BOOST Program of Mental Health Ctr. of Dane County, Madison, 1987-88; outreach social worker St. Elizabeth's, Indpls., 1988-91, supr. social svcs., 1991—; psychiat. social worker, group therapist for incest victims Wishard Hosp. Midtown Mental Health, Indpls., 1988—; field placement instr. Ind. U., Indpls., 1992, 94—. Active Holy Angels Cath. Ch., Indpls., 1988—, ladies aux. Knights of St. Peter Claver, 1993—, Grand Lady, 1994-96, ret., 1996. Mem. Alpha Kappa Alpha. Democrat. Roman Catholic. Office: Saint Elizabeth's 2500 Churchman Ave Indianapolis IN 46203-4613

HONOUR, LYNDA CHARMAINE, research scientist, educator, psychotherapist; b. Orange, N.J., Aug. 9, 1949; d. John Henry, Jr. and Evelyn Helena Roberta (Pietrowski) H. BA, Boston U., 1976; MA, Calif. State U., Fullerton, 1985, UCLA, 1989; postgrad., U. So. Calif., 1995—. Cert. marriage, family and children psychotherapist, Calif. Prof. psychology Pepperdine U., Malibu, Calif., 1989-95; pvt. practice psychotherapy, West Los Angeles, Calif., 1991—; clin. and vis. prof. throughout so. Calif., including Calif. Sch. Profl. Psychology, Calif. State U., L.A., 1989—; rsch. scientist in neuroendocrinology and neurochemistry in numerous labs.; condr. rsch. Neuropsychiat. Inst., Brain Rsch. Inst., Mental Retardation Rsch. Ctr., UCLA, Tulane U. Med. Sch., V.A. Med. Ctr., New Orleans, Salk Inst. Biol. Studies; rsch. cons. U. Calif. Med. Ctr., Irvine; cons. in rsch. or psychotherapy, 1976—. Contbr. articles to Hosp. Practice, Peptides, Physiology and Behavior, Pharmacology, Biochemistry and Behavior, also others. Rsch. grantee Organon Internat. Rsch. Group, The Netherlands, 1984-88. Mem. AAAS, AAUP, Am. Psychological Assn. (assoc.), Am. Psychological Soc., Calif. Assn. Marriage, Family and Child Psychotherapists, N.Y. Acad. Scis., Sons and Daus. of Pearl Harbor Survivors, Psi Chi, Sigma Delta Epsilon. Roman Catholic.

HOOD, ANTOINETTE FOOTE, dermatologist; b. Honolulu, 1941. MD, Vanderbilt U., 1967. Cert. dermatology. Intern Vanderbilt Affiliated Hosps, 1967-68; resident dermatology Harvard U., 1975-76; resident dermatology-pathology Mass. Gen. Hosp., Boston, 1976-78; fellow dermatology Harvard U., 1973-75. Office: Ind U Outpatient Ctr 3240 Dept Dermatology 550 N University Blvd Indianapolis IN 46202-5267

HOOD, DENISE PAGE, federal judge; b. 1952. BA, Yale Univ., 1974; JD, Columbia Sch. of Law, 1977. Asst. corp. counsel City of Detroit, Law Dept., 1977-82; judge 36th Dist. Ct., 1983-89, Recorder's Ct. for the City of Detroit, 1989-92, Wayne County Circuit Ct., 1993-94; district judge U.S. Dist. Ct. (Mich. ea. dist.), 6th circuit, 1994—. Recipient Judicial Service award Black Women Lawyers Assn., 1994. Mem. Am. Bar Assn., State Bar of Mich., Detroit Bar Assn. (Chmn. of Yr. award 1988), Assn. of Black Judges of Mich., Mich. Dist. Judges Assn., Am. Inns of Ct., Wolverine Bar Assn. (bd. of dirs.), Women Lawyers Assn. of Mich., Fed. Bar Assn., Nat. Assn. of Women Judges, Nat. Bar Assn. Judicial Coun., Mich. Judicial Inst. Office: US Courthouse 235 US Courthouse 231 W Lafayette Blvd Rm 235 Detroit MI 48226-2799*

HOOD, GLENDA E., mayor; m. Charles M. Hood III; 3 children. BA, Rollins Coll.; postgrad., Harvard U., Ga. State U. Commr. City of Orlando, Fla., 1982-92, mayor, 1992—; pres Glenda E. Hood & Assocs., Inc. vice chmn. mcpl. planning bd. City of Orlando, mem. nominating bd., chmn. task force bd. and commn. restructure; past chmn., founding mem. bd. dirs. Found. Orange County Pub. Schs.; co-chmn. Orlando Fights Back-Coalition for a Drug-Free Cmty.; bd. dirs. U. Ctrl. Fla. Found., Met. Orlando Urban League; past pres. exec. bd. Ctrl. Fla. Coun. of Boy Scouts; bd. overseers Rollins Coll. Crummer Grad. Sch. of Bus.; mem. adv. bd. Valencia C.C., Fla.- Costa Rica Inst.; past co-chmn. United Negro Coll. Fund; pres. Jr. League Orlando-Winter Park, Vol. Svc. Bur.; mem. Orange County Commn. on Children. Named Mcpl. Leader of Yr., Am. City and County Mag., 1992, one of Ten Outstanding Young Americans, U.S. Jaycees, one of Seven Outstanding Youth Floridians, Fla. Jaycees, Woman of Yr., Downtown Orlando Inc., one of Ten People to Watch, Fla. Trend, one of 100 Young Women of Promise, Good Housekeeping; recipient Willie J. Bruton award for cmty. svc. Met. Orlando Urban League, Summit award Women's Resource Ctr., Svc. to Mankind award Leukemia Soc. Am. Ctrl. Fla. chpt. Mem. Nat. League of Cities (past pres.), Fla. League of Cities (past pres.), Fla. C. of C. (past pres.), Greater Orlando C. of C. (past v.p.). Office: 400 S Orange Ave Orlando FL 32801-3302*

HOOD, HEATHER ANNE, minister of music; b. Royal Oak, Mich., Nov. 30, 1957; d. Samuel J. and Beatrice L. (Brewster) H. BA, Judson Coll., Elgin, Ill., 1979; MusM, No. Ill. U., 1981. Assoc. dir. music 1st Presbyn. Ch., Springfield, Ill., 1982-85; assoc. dir. music Christ Presbyn. Ch., Edina, Minn., 1986-87, min. music, 1987—; adj. instr. music Lincoln Land C.C., Springfield, 1981-85. Contbr. articles to profl. mag.; composer: Festival of Joy, 1979. Mem. Am. Choral Dirs. Assn., Am. Guild Organists, Fellowship Am. Bapt. Musicians (exec. bd. 1993-96), Choristers Guild, Presbyn. Assn. Musicians. Home: 11247 Oregon Cir Bloomington MN 55438 Office: Christ Presbyn Ch 6901 Normandale Rd Edina MN 55435

HOOD, LUANN SANDRA, special education educator; b. Bklyn., Jan. 10, 1955; d. Louie A. and Sylvia M. (Hall) Mayo; m. Stephen J. Hood. BA, St. Joseph's Coll., Bklyn., 1976; MS in Edn., Bklyn. Coll., 1979. Cert. tchr. N, K, 1-6, spl. edn., N.Y.C. lic. Edn. counselor adolescents Am. Indian Comty. House, Inc., N.Y.C., 1977-79; tchr. children with retarded mental devel. Pub. Sch. 273, Bklyn., 1979-83; tchr. early childhood Pub. Sch. 128, Bklyn., 1983-94; tchr. emotionally handicapped Pub. Sch.215, Bklyn., 1994-95; tchr. learning disabled Pub. Sch. 101, Bklyn., 1995—. Exec. sec. bd. trustees Am. Indian Comty. House, Inc., N.Y.C., 1980-91. Recipient Regents scholarship N.Y. State Edn. Dept., 1972; grantee: Indian League of the Americas, Inc. 1972, 73, 74, 75, Thunderbird Am. Indian Dancers, Inc., 1972, 73, 74, 75, Internat. Order of King's Daughters and Sons, 1976. Mem. N.Y. State Tchrs. of Handicapped. Democrat. Roman Catholic.

HOOD, MABEL HINES, social worker, retired; b. Richmond, Va., Oct. 6, 1928; d. Kenneth E. and Mabel (Satterwhite) Hines; m. Harold Parks, June 5, 1954 (div. 1958); 1 child, Patti; m. H. Bert Hood, Oct. 25, 1969; 1 child, Robert W. AB, DePauw U., 1950; MSW, Va. Commonwealth, 1967. Lic. social worker, W.Va. Social worker, supr., county dir., asst. divsn. dir. Dept. Human Svcs., Charleston, W.Va., 1950-71; supr. case workers Family Svc., Charleston, 1969-71; dir. social svc. St. Francis Hosp., Charleston, 1971-79, Arthur B. Hodges Ctr., Charleston, 1981-90; ret., 1990. Bd. dirs. YWCA, Charleston. Democrat. Presbyterian. Home: 1407 Summit Dr Charleston WV 25302

HOOD, MARY BRYAN, museum director, painter; b. Central City, Ky., July 5, 1938; d. Irving B. and Mary Louise (Anderson) Cayce; m. Ronnie L. Hood, Oct. 16, 1960. Student Ky. Wesleyan Coll., 1956-59, 68-73. Exec. dir. Owensboro Arts Commn., Ky., 1974-76; founding dir. Owensboro Mus. Fine Art, 1976—. Author/editor exhbn. catalogues. Mem. exec. com. Ky. Citizens for Arts, 1980-86, Owensboro Arts Commn., 1977—, Owensboro Bicentennial Commn., 1990—, Ky. Arts Commn., 1974-76; bd. dirs. Japan/Am. Soc. Ky., 1987-89, Owensboro Symphony, 1975-76, Owensboro Area Mus., 1970-72, Theatre Workshop Owensboro, 1968-70; chair Owensboro Mayor's Arts Com., 1970-75; me. Cmty. Appearance Planning Bd., 1988-92, Davies County Bicentennial Commn., 1990-92, Owensboro Bicentennial Commn., 1996; mem. steering com. Yr. of the Am. Craft, Ky., 1991-93, Mayor's Adv. Coun. on Arts, 1996. Mary Bryan Hood Day named in her honor, Owensboro, 1974. Mem. Southeastern Mus. Conf., Am. Assn. Mus., Ky. Assn. Mus. (pres. 1980-82). Office: Owensboro Mus Fine Art 901 Frederica St Owensboro KY 42301-3052

HOOD, OLLIE RUTH, health facilities executive; b. San Francisco, Nov. 26, 1947; d. Rodger Brown and Lucile Brooks (Reid); m. McKinley Hood, Aug. 27, 1969 (div. 1987); children: Antoinette Brown, Kirk Stewart, Seancy Hood. BA, San Francisco State U., 1971. Asst. sec., v.p. Weyerhauser Mortgage Co., L.A., 1971-80; asst. supr. Plaza Mortgage Co., L.A., 1980-84; data entry supr. Western Standard Truck, L.A., 1984-85; mgr. Kaiser Hosp., San Francisco, 1985-92; with Emory Clinic, Atlanta, 1995—. Patentee in field. Mem. Calif. Assn. Hosp. Admitting Mgrs., Nat. Assn. Hosp. Admitting Mgrs., NAFE, Kaiser Permanente Club (2d v.p. 1987), Nat. Assn. Women (v.p. 1989—). Jehovah's Witness. Home: PO Box 87117 College Park GA 30337-0117

HOOD, SANDRA DALE, librarian; b. Edmond, Okla., Nov. 28, 1949; d. Rufus Gustav and Hope Louvica (Hutton) Farber; m. Frank D. Hood Jr., May 17, 1971; 1 child, Charles Richard. BA, U. Okla., 1971, MLS, 1972; postgrad., U. Tex., San Antonio, 1992—. Libr. South Oklahoma City Jr. Coll., 1973, Daus. of Republic of Tex. Libr. at the Alamo, San Antonio, 1980-88; access coord., automation and libr. sys. libr. Palo Alto Coll. Learning Resources Ctr., San Antonio, 1988—. Pres. tech. svcs. spl. interest group Coun. Rsch. and Acad. Librs., San Antonio, 1991-92; sec., mem. exec. bd. Timberwood Park Property Owners Assn., San Antonio, 1991-94. Mem. ALA, Tex. Libr. Assn. (conf. planning com. 1992-93), Bexar Libr. Assn. (exec. bd., dir. editor 1988-90), Tex. Jr. Coll. Tchrs. Assn. Democrat. Lutheran. Home: 27030 Foggy Meadows San Antonio TX 78260 Office: Palo Alto Coll Learning Resources Ctr 1400 W Villaret San Antonio TX 78224

HOOK, VIRGINIA MAY, marketing executive; b. Balt., Mar. 11, 1932; d. Arthur M. Monroe McClelland and Margaret (Shipley) McClelland Warfield; m. Donald F. Hook, Aug. 25, 1951 (dec. Dec. 1978); children: Donald F., Jr., Donna J. Hook Kellner. Grad. high sch. Teller, Cen. Savs. Bank, Balt., 1950-68, tng. dir., 1968-71; ops. mgr. Mature Temps, Inc., Balt., 1971-81; pres. VMH Mktg. Ltd., Laurel, Md., 1982—. Mem. adv. coun., sr. aides program D.C. Dept. Labor, 1980-81; active local Democratic Party; bd. dirs., 1st v.p. Balt./Washington Grocery Mfrs. Retailers. Mem. Bank Pers. Assn. Md. (sec. 1969-71), Pers. Assn. Md. (sec. 1979-80), Exec. Women's Network, Market Rsch. Assn., Am. Mktg. Assn., Nat. Assn. Women Bus. Owners, Nat. Assn. Demonstration Cos. (bd. dirs.), Field Mktg. Svcs. Assn. Methodist. Lodge: Order Eastern Star. Home: 3 Southerly Ct Baltimore MD 21286-2776 Office: 8566 Laureldale Dr Laurel MD 20724-2008

HOOKER, ELAINE NORTON, news executive; b. Rockville Center, N.Y., Dec. 4, 1944; d. Henry Gaither and Ann Lou (Allen) Norton; m. Ronald Wayne Johnson (div.); m. Kenneth Ward Hooker Jr. (div.); children: Alisa, Miranda, Nora, Emily. Student, Wilson Coll., 1962-64, U. Hartford, 1965, Trinity Coll., 1974, Andover Newton Theol. Sch., 1988-89. Reporter, editor The Hartford (Conn.) Courant, 1969-74; newswoman AP, Hartford, 1974-75, Conn. news editor, 1975-79; western Mass. corr. AP, Springfield, Mass., 1979-80; Mass. day news supr. AP, Boston, 1981-84, Mass. news editor, 1984; Conn. bur. chief AP, Hartford, 1984-88; dep. dir. corp. comm. AP, N.Y.C., 1990, gen. exec. newspaper membership, 1991—; spkr. in field. Active various coms. at chs. in Concord, Mass., Hartford, Briarcliff, N.Y., Greenwich, Conn., N.Y.C. Recipient Sigma Delta Chi award, 1974. Mem. Soc. Profl. Journalists (mem. Freedom Info. coun. 1984-87), New Eng. Soc. Newspaper Editors (rep. Soviet journalists conf. 1985). Home: 81 Prospect St Greenwich CT 06830-5606 Office: AP 50 Rockefeller Plz New York NY 10020-1605

HOOKER, NANCY LYNN, banker; b. Des Moines, June 7, 1952; d. Alfred Daniel and Joyce Pearl (Burd) Foster; m. Terry Lee Hooker, Nov. 29, 1974; 1 child, Adam Terry. Student, Mid-America Nazarene Coll., Olathe, Kans., 1971-74. Ops. clk. State Bank and Trust, Council Bluffs, Iowa, 1970-71; clk. to office of v.p. Mid-America Coll., Olathe, 1971-73; teller First Nat. Bank of Olathe, 1973-76, 1984-88, student loans, new account rep., 1988-89, adminstrv. asst., 1989-90, asst. cashier, 1990-95, asst. v.p., 1995—, children's banking coord., 1990—. Participant/mem. Leadership Olathe, 1993; mem. ch. bd. Nall Ave. Ch. of the Nazarene, Shawnee, Kans., 1983-85. Recipient Cert. of Excellence Am. Bankers Assn., 1992-93, 94-95, 95-96. Mem. Acappella Choral Group, Choral Group/Celebration. Republican. Office: First Nat Bank of Olathe 444 E Santa Fe Olathe KS 66061

HOOKER, RENÉE MICHELLE, perinatal nurse; b. Kansas City, Mo., June 26, 1965; d. Roland Edward and Loretta Mae (Rathbun) Woods; m. Joel Thomas Hooker, Sept. 17, 1988; children: Andrew, Catherine, Rebekah. BSN, U. Kans., 1987. RN, Tex., Calif.; cert post anesthesia nurse, inpatient obstetric nurse ANCC; cert. ACLS, neonatal resuscitation. Staff med.-surg. nurse Desert Hosp., Palm Springs, Calif., 1987-88; staff nurse neonatal ICU Santa Rose Children's Hosp., San Antonio, 1988; staff obstetrics nurse, supr. post anesthesia care unit McKenna Meml. Hosp., New Braunfels, Tex., 1988—. Mem. Assn. Women's Health, Obstet. and Neonatal Nursing, Tex. Assn. Post Anesthesia Nurses, Am. Soc. Post Anesthesia Nurses, Assn. Oper. Room Nurses. Republican. Roman Catholic. Office: McKenna Meml Hosp 143 E Garza New Braunfels TX 78130

HOOKS, LONNA R., state official. Sec. State of N.J. Office: NJ Dept State State Capitol Bldg CN 300 Trenton NJ 08625*

HOOKS, VANDALYN LAWRENCE, educator; b. Dyersburg, Tenn., Feb. 26, 1935; d. James Bridges and Mary Lucille (Anderson) Lawrence; m. Floyd Lester Hooks, June 15, 1952; children: Lawrence James, Steven Lester. BA, Ky. Wesleyan U., 1967; MA, Western Ky. U., 1970, Edn. Specialist, 1976; postgrad. U. Tenn., 1975. Tchr., Owensboro Bd. Edn., Ky., 1967-71, adminstr., 1976-85; dir. career experience Western Ky. U., Bowling Green, 1971-73; dir. career edn. Owensboro Daviess County Sch. Dist., elem. tchr., 1967-71, elem. prin. 1974-78, 83-85, adminstr., elem. prin. dir. career experience, 1976-85; curriculum developer Career Experience Voc. Edn., Frankfort, Ky., 1971-76; cons. Motivation Workshop, Bowling Green, 1971-76, Decision and Goal Setting, 1971-76. Editor: Ky. Assn. Elem. Prin. Jour., 1977-81; editor, pub. Ednl. Alert, 1985-90, A Crash Course In Ednl. Reform, 1989, A Dangerous Liaison A Tax Exempt Foundation and Two Teacher Unions, 1990, The Alphabet Books, 1991, Caution! Change Agents at Work, 1992, A System for Control PPBS, 1994; contbr. articles to profl. jours. Organizer, Ky. Council for Better Edn., Owensboro, 1984; legis. advisor Eagle Forum, leadership forum, Washington, 1985, 86-87, 88-92; Rep. legis. researcher . Recipient Presdl. award, Ky. Wesleyan Coll., 1966. Mem. Concerned Edn. of Am., Nat. Council for Better Edn., Pro Family Forum, Eagle Forum, Plymouth Rock Found., Nat. Council Christian Educators. Republican. Baptist. Address: 1302 Waverly Pl Owensboro KY 42301-3683

HOOPER, ANNE DODGE, pathologist, educator; b. Groton, Mass., July 16, 1926; d. Carroll William and Bertha Sanford (Wiener) Dodge; m. William Dale Hooper, June 17, 1952; children: Elizabeth Anne, Joan Elaine, Caroline Mae. AB, Washington U., St. Louis, 1947, MD, 1952. Diplomate in pathologic anatomy, clin. pathology and forensic pathology Am. Bd. Pathology. Rotating intern Virginia Mason Hosp., Seattle, 1952-53; resident in internal medicine St. Francis Hosp., Hartford, Conn., 1953-54; resident in pathologic anatomy and clin. pathology New Britain (Conn.) Gen. Hosp., 1954-57, Presbyn. Hosp., Phila., 1957-58; resident in forensic pathology Office Med. Examiner, Phila., 1958-60; from pathologist to acting chief lab svc. VA Hosp., Coatesville, Pa., 1960-66; dir. lab. St. Albans (Vt.) Hosp., 1966-69, Kerbs Hosp., St. Albans, 1966-71, Williamson Appalachian Regional Hosp., South Williamson, Ky., 1971-73, Beckley (W.Va.) Appalachian Regional Hosp., 1974-76; asst. prof. pathology W.Va. Sch. Osteo. Medicine, Lewisburg, 1977, assoc. prof. pathology, 1978—; lab. accreditation insp. CAP, 1992, 94. Am. Osteo. Assn., 1996. Contbr. articles to profl. jours. Pres. local elem. sch. PTA, St. Albans, 1967-68; pres. Greenbrier unit Am. Cancer Soc., Lewisburg, 1989-93, bd. dirs. W.Va. div., Charleston, 1987-94, profl. edn. com. W.Va. div., 1982-94. Fellow Coll. Am. Pathologists, Am. Acad. Forensic Scis.; mem. AMA, W.Va. Med. Soc., Raleigh County Med. Soc., Am. Soc. Clin. Pathologists, Internat. Acad. Pathologists, Nat. Assn. Med. Examiners, Am. Osteo. Coll. Pathologists (assoc.). Office: WVa Sch Osteo Medicine 400 N Lee St Lewisburg WV 24901-1128

HOOPER, CASSANDRA LEE, artist, educator; b. Bklyn., June 20, 1964; d. Edward Carroll and Gail Austin (Whitaker) H. BFA, Calif. State U., Long Beach, 1988; MFA, SUNY, Purchase, 1991. Art dir. Goathill Printing Co., Costa Mesa, Calif., 1985-89; art tchr., cons. Bd. Coop. Edn. Svcs., Elmsford, N.Y., 1989—; printer, studio mgr. Josely Carvalho, N.Y.C., 1992-93; adj. asst., prof. art Bronx Cmty. Coll., N.Y.C., 1993; printmaking instr. Kansas City (Mo.) Art Inst., 1993-94; adj. lectr. SUNY, Purchase, 1995; adj. instr. art Bergen C.C., Paramus, N.J., 1995—; adj. asst. prof. art County Coll. Morris, Randolph, N.J., 1993—. Solo exhbns. include Gallery B, Long Beach, 1989, Visual Arts Gallery, N.Y.C., 1991, The Print Club, Phila., 1994; other exhbns. include Mus. Photographic Arts, San Diego, 1985, Orange Coast Libr., Costa Mesa, 1986, 87, Orange Coast Coll. Art Gallery, 1986, 87, 88, Hippodrome Gallery, Long Beach, 1989, Main Photography Gallery, 1989, SUNY Arts Gallery, Purchase, 1989, 90, 91, Islip Art Mus., N.Y.C., 1991, Dome Gallery, N.Y.C., 1991, The Dana Gallery, Dana Point, Calif., 1991, Long Beach Arts Gallery, 1991, N.J. Ctr. for Visual Arts, Summit, 1991, Internat. Ctr. for Photography, France, 1992, The Print Club, Phila., 1992, Humphrey Fine Arts, N.Y.C., 1992, Keystone Jr. Coll., La Plume, Pa., 1993, Oreg. State Libr., 1993, Formal Gallery, Canyon, Tex., 1993, Alexandria (La.) Mus. of Art, 1993, Art Ctr. Gallery, Warrensburg, Mo., 1992, Printworks Gallery, Hartford, Conn., 1994, Works Gallery, Alta., Can., 1995, Heuser & Hartman Gallery, Peoria, Ill., 1995. Grantee Puffin Found., 1993. Mem. So. Graphics Coun., Coll. Art Assn.

HOOPER, CATHERINE EVELYN, developmental engineering senior; b. Bklyn., Nov. 10, 1939; d. Frederick Charles Jr. and Catherine Veronica (Heaney) Podeyn; m. Melvyn Robert Lowney, Nov. 30, 1957 (div. 1970); children: Denise Lowney Andrade, Michele Lowney Budris; m. William White Hooper, Sept. 21, 1974. Student, San Jose (Calif.) City Coll., 1969, De Anza Coll., 1980. Insp. Amelco Semiconductor, Mountain View, Calif., 1966-68; lab. technician Fairchild R & D, Palo Alto, Calif., 1968-73; sr. lab. technician Varian Cen. Rsch., Palo Alto, 1973-84; sr. devel. engr. Hughes Rsch. Labs., Malibu, 1984—. Contbr. articles to profl. jours. Pres. Conejo Valley chpt. Nat. Women's Polit. Caucus., 1994—. Mem. Am. Vacuum Soc., Materials Rsch. Soc., Grad. Women in Sci. (L.A. pres. 1990-92), Internat. Soc. Optical Engrs., Sigma Xi (sec. 1987-90, 94). Office: Hughes Rsch Labs 3011 Malibu Canyon Rd Malibu CA 90265-4737

HOOPER, KELLEY RAE, delivery service executive; b. Tulsa, Aug. 24, 1960; d. Kenneth Roe Sharp and Beverly Jane (Phillips) Jenkins; m. John Patrick Hooper, Apr. 30, 1988 (dec. Oct. 1990). BS, Okla. State U., 1982; postgrad., So. Nazarene U., 1991—. Ter. mgr. Am. Fidelity Ins. Co., Oklahoma City, 1982-87; account exec. United Parcel Svc., Inc., Oklahoma City, 1987-89, customer svc. office supr., 1991, next day air letter ctr. coord., 1990, dist. office mgr., 1991-92, dist. area mgr.; dist. sales mgr. ctrl. Ohio United Parcel Svc., Inc., Columbus, 1994—. Dist. region grant com. United Parcel Svc. Found., Oklahoma City, 1992; mem., donor Omniplex Sci. Mus., Oklahoma City, 1990—, Ballet Okla., Oklahoma City, 1992—, Oklahoma City Arts Mus., 1992—. Mem. NAFE, Nat. Trust for Historic Preservation, Art Inst. Chgo., Sierra, Okla. State U. Alumni Assn., Pi Sigma Alpha, Internat. Wine Club. Democrat. Home: 948 S Remington Rd Bexley OH 43209-2459 Office: United Parcel Svc 5101 Trabue Rd Columbus OH 43228-9613

HOOPER-PERKINS, MARLENE, technical editor, educator; b. Jersey City, N.J., Jan. 26, 1955; d. Arthur L. and Ethel M. (Coleman) Hooper; m. James A. Perkins; children: Joy J., Samantha A. BA, Rutgers U., 1977; MS, N.J. Inst. Tech., 1994. Acct. exec. Bruno Assocs., Bloomfield, N.J., 1984-87; adj. prof. dept. humanities N.J. Inst. Tech., Newark, 1995—, technical editor, media svcs., 1987—; pres. (consulting firm) M.H. Perkins & Assocs., Elizabeth, N.J., 1995—. Bd. dirs. YWCA of Eas. Union County, Elizabeth, N.J., 1990-92; founding mem., mentor TGIF, N.J. Inst. Tech., 1995—. Mem. Douglass Assoc. Alumnae. Office: NJ Inst Tech Media Svcs 218 Central Ave Newark NJ 07102

HOOSIN, JANICE, social worker; b. Chgo., June 22, 1942; d. Herbert and Ruth Jean (Rubenstein) Lapine; B.A., U. Ill., 1964; M.S.W., Jane Addams Grad. Sch. Social Work, 1966; postgrad. U. Utah, summer, 1977. Cert. mental health adminstr., psychiat. social worker, Ill., lic. clin. social worker. Psychiat. social worker New Trier Twp. High Sch., East Winnetka, Ill., 1966-70; dir. day hosp. St. Vincent's Hosp., N.Y.C., 1970-73; psychotherapist (part-time) New Trier East High Sch., Winnetka, 1973-74; dir. psychiat. day hosp. dept. psychiatry Evanston (Ill.) Hosp., 1974-78, dir. partial hospitalization, 1978-88; pvt. practice, 1988—; clin. assoc., field work supr. U. Chgo. Sch. Social Svc. Adminstrn., 1974—; cons. in field; pvt. practice marital and individual psychotherapy, specializing in co-dependency and additions, 1975—. NIMH fellow, 1964-66. Mem. Nat. Assn. Social Workers, Assn. Mental Health Adminstrs. Jewish. Home: 2638 N Burling St Chicago IL 60614-1514 Office: 636 Church St Ste 715 Evanston IL 60201-4587

HOOVER, BETTY-BRUCE HOWARD, educator; b. Wake County, N.C., Mar. 20, 1939; d. Bruce Ruffin and Mary Elizabeth (Brown) Howard; m. Herbert Charles Marsh Hoover, Sept. 3, 1961; children: David Andrew, Howard Webster, Lorraine VanSiclen. B.A., Wake Forest U., 1961; M.A., U. S. Fla., 1978. Tchr. English, Greensboro Sr. High Sch., N.C., 1961-62, Lindley Jr. High Sch., Greensboro, 1963, Berkeley Prep. Sch., Tampa, Fla., 1976—, chmn. English dept., 1977-85, dir., dean upper div., 1984—, chmn. curriculum com., 1982-86 . Author: Resources in Education, 1992. Pres., Suncoast Midshipmen Parents Club, Tampa Bay Area, 1983-84. Mem. Assn. Supervision Curriculum Devel., Nat. Council Tchrs. English, Sociedad Honoraira Hispanica, The Nat. Coun. States, Wake Forest U. Alumni Assn., DAR, Hillsborough County Bar Aux., Cum Laude Soc. (sec. 1981—), Nat. Honor Soc., Phi Beta Kappa, Phi Sigma Iota, Sigma Tau Delta, Kappa Kappa Gamma. Republican. Episcopalian. Avocations: sewing; gardening. Home: 4504 W Beachway Dr Tampa FL 33609-4234 Office: Berkeley Preparatory Sch 4811 Kelly Rd Tampa FL 33615-5020

HOOVER, DAVONNA MARIA, primary education educator; b. Hagerstown, Md., Aug. 5, 1937; d. David Hildebrand and Frances Elizabeth (Moore) H. BEd in Elem. Edn., Coll. Notre Dame Md., 1970; MEd in Elem. Edn., Loyola Coll., Balt., 1985. Joined Sch. Sisters of Notre Dame, Balt., 1955-86; profl. cert. in religion. Tchr. grades 1-2 St. Gerard's Cath. Sch., Ft. Oglethorpe, Ga., 1957-58; tchr. grades 2-3 Sacred Heart of Jesus, Balt., 1958-68; tchr. grade 3 Our Lady of Perpetual Help Acad., Ybor City, Tampa, Fla., 1968-75; tchr. phys. edn. and art grades 1-5 Holy Spirit Cluster-Lower, Balt., 1975-79; tchr. grade 3 St. Augustine's Sch., Elkridge, Md., 1979-82; tchr. grade 3 Madonna Cath. Sch., Balt., 1982—, vice prin., 1990-94. Volleyball City Tampa (Fla.) Recreation Dept., 1971-75, softball, 1974-75. Named Outstanding Elem. Tchr. Am., Washington, 1975; Valley Forge (Pa.) Freedom Found. grantee, 1975. Mem. ASCD, Nat. Cath. Edn. Assn., Va. Geneal. Soc., Germanna Colony Va. (life). Roman Catholic. Office: Madonna Cath Sch 3601 Old Frederick Rd Baltimore MD 21229-3650

HOOVER, ETTA ELAINE, business owner; b. McMinnville, Tenn., Nov. 24, 1953; d. Austin Peay and Berchie M. (Billings) Hudson; m. Ronnie L. Hoover, Feb. 18, 1971; children: Naomi Frances, Megan Leigh. Owner Shoe Shack Inc., McMinnville, 1980—. Tchr. Sunday sch. Ch. of Christ at Earleyville, McMinnville, 1985—. Office: She Shack Inc 1100 Smithville Hwy McMinnville TN 37110

HOOVER, KATHERINE LACY, composer; b. Elkins, W.Va., Dec. 2, 1937; d. Samuel Randolph and Katherine F. (Lacy) Hoover; m. J. Christopher Schwab, July 14, 1964 (div. Aug. 1972); 1 child, Norman Daniel; m. Richard V. Goodwin, May 18, 1985. BMus Theory, perf. cert. in flute, Eastman Sch. of Music, Rochester, N.Y., 1959; MMus in Theory, Manhattan Sch. of Music, N.Y.C., 1974; student, Conductors Inst., Columbia, S.C., 1989-91. Tchr. of flute The Juilliard Sch. Prep., N.Y.C., 1962-69; tchr. of theory Manhattan Sch. of Music, N.Y.C., 1969-84; theory, composition lessons Tchrs. Coll., Columbia, N.Y., 1984-89; free-lance flutist Lincoln Ctr., Broadway, others, N.Y.C., 1962-85; composer, 1975—; originator/dir. Festivals of Women's Music, I-IV, N.Y.C., 1978-81; ptnr. Papagena Press, N.Y.C., 1989—; guest lectr. in field. Composer numerous compositions, including: Night Skies, 1994, Quintet (Da Pacem), 1989, Eleni: A Greek Tragedy, 1986, Medieval Suite, 1984 (NFA award 1987), numerous chamber pieces including Trio, Op. 14, 1978, Lyric Trio, Op. 27, 1983, Sonata, Op. 44, 1991, others; numerous other orchestral compositions, including Two Sketches, Op. 42, 1989, Clarinet Concerto, Op. 38, 1987, Double Concerto, Op. 40, 1989, Summer Night, Op. 34, 1985, others; composer solo instrumental music, including Kokopeli, 1990, Reflections, 1982, Set for Clarinet, 1978, piano pieces, 1977-82; composer choral music, including The Last Invocation, 1984, Sweet Thievery, 1985, Songs of Celebration, 1983, others; composer solo voice with instruments, including From the Testament of Francois Villon, 1982, Central American Songs, 1995, others. Recipient numerous awards including Acad. award in composition, Am. Acad. of Arts and Letters, N.Y., 1994, Composers Fellowship, Nat. Endowment for Arts, Washington, 1979, numerous ASCAP awards, 1979—; winner award for Newly Pub. Music, Nat. Flute Assn., 1987, 91, 93, 94; named Composer of the Yr., N.Y. Music Tchrs. Assn., 1989; grantee Alice M. Ditson Fund, 1984, Meet the Composer, 1976—; commd. N.Y. Flute Club, 1995, Ind. U., Pa., 1995, W. Dobbs and Marshall U., 1994, Vinland Ensemble, 1991, Duologue, 1991, N.J. Chamber Music Soc., others. Mem. ASCAP, Internat. Alliance Women in Music, N.Y. Women Composers, Nat. Flute Assn., Conductors Guild, Am. Music Ctr.

HOOVER, POLLY RUTH, classics educator; b. Yokosuka, Japan, Aug. 28, 1956; came to U.S., 1957; d. Dwight Wesley and Nannie Elizabeth (Crosby) H.; m. Thomas Hoffer, July 12, 1986. BA in Classics, Beloit Coll., 1978; MA in Philosophy, U. Chgo., 1984; MA in Classics, U. Wis., 1990, PhD in Classics, 1995. Tchr. Keith Sch., Rockford, Ill., 1985-88; lectr. U. Wis., Madison, 1993-94; sr. lectr. Ohio State U., Columbus, 1995—. Office: Ohio State U 414 University Hall 230 North Mall Columbus OH 43202

HOPE, AMMIE DELORIS, computer programmer, systems analyst; b. Washington, Nov. 28, 1946; d. Amos Alexander and Amanda Irene (Moore) H. BA cum laude, Howard U., 1976; postgrad., Am. U., 1976-84. Police officer Met. Police Dept., Washington, 1972-73, officer, 1972; tchr. St. Benedict the Moor Cath. Sch., Washington, 1979; adminstrv. asst. Coun. of D.C., Washington, 1979-81; computer programmer, systems analyst IRS, Washington, 1984—. Honoree Civic Assn.; Trustees scholar; Pub. Svc. fellow. Mem. Alpha Kappa Delta, Kappa Delta. Home: 1904 D St NE Washington DC 20002-6720

HOPE, GERRI DANETTE, telecommunications management executive; b. Sacramento, Feb. 28, 1956; d. Albert Gerald and Beulah Rae (Bane) Hope. AS, Sierra Coll., Calif., 1977; postgrad. Okla. State U., 1977-79. Instructional asst. San Juan Sch. Dist., Carmichael, Calif., 1979-82; telecomm. supr. Delta Dental Svc. of Calif., San Francisco, 1982-85; telecomm. coordinator Farmers Savs. Bank, Davis, Calif., 1985-87; telecomm. officer Sacramento Savs. Bank, 1987-95; owner GDH Enterprises, 1993—; telecomm. analyst II dept. ins. State Calif., 1995—; sr. telecomms. engr. Access Health, Inc., 1996—; founder Custom Label Designer, Sacramento; mem. telecomm. adv. panel Golden Gate U., Sacramento; lectr. in field. Mem. NAFE, Telecomm. Assn. (v.p. membership com. Sacramento Valley chpt., 1993), Am. Philatelic Soc., Sacramento Philatelic Assn., Errors, Freaks and Oddities Club, Philatelic Collectors. Republican. Avocations: writing, computers, philately, animal behavior, participating in Christian ministry. Home: 3025 U St Antelope CA 95843-2513

HOPE, JOYCE MORTENSEN, nurse, educator; b. Bklyn.; d. Daniel Theodore and Helen Irene (Maloney) Mortensen; BSN, Hunter Coll., MS, 1969; postgrad. CUNY,. Dir. edn. Jersey Shore Med. Center Sch. Nursing, 1963-65; dir. inservice edn. Metro. Hosp., N.Y.C., 1966-68; asst. prof./dir. Baccalaureate program Hunter Coll., Nursing, CUNY, 1969-74, chmn. Dept. Nursing, 1974-77, acting dean, Hunter-Bellevue Sch. Nursing, 1977-82, 82-84, assoc. prof., 1979—; faculty Brookdale Ctr. on Aging, N.Y.C., 1978—; advisor Mt. Sinai-Hunter Coll. Long Term Care Gerontology Ctr., 1980-85. Adv. com. Cmty. Svc. Soc. N.Y., 1978-86; mem. Nat. Conf. on Aging, 1975-80; participant White House Conf. on Aging, 1981. Title II traineeship, USPHS, 1968-69; Fin. awardee, Brookdale Ctr. on Aging, 1978. Mem. Gerontol. Soc. Am., Am. Geriatrics Soc., Aging in Higher Edn., Am. Nurses Assn., Nat. League Nursing, N.Y. Acad. Sci., Hunter-Bellvue Sch. Nursing Alumni Assn. (pres. 1992—), Sigma Theta Tau, Pi Lambda Theta. Office: 425 E 25th St New York NY 10010-2547

HOPE, MARGARET LAUTEN, civic worker; b. N.Y.C.; privately educated; 1 son, Frederick H., III. Mem. ball coms. various charity fund raising events. Mem. Jr. League N.Y.C., Everglades Club, Sailfish Club (Palm Beach), Women's Nat. Rep. Club (N.Y.C.), St. James Club (London). Address: Box # 601 236 Dunbar Rd Palm Beach FL 33480-3715

HOPE, MELANIE PRINTUP, graphic designer; b. Lewiston, N.Y ., Mar. 1, 1960; d. Quintin Charles and Edith Katherine (Crogan) Printup; m. Robert James Hope, Oct. 27, 1984; children: Erin Celeste, Meghan Ashley, Thomas Mark. AAS, Rochester Inst. Tech., 1980, BFA, 1982; MFA, Rensselaer Poly. Inst., 1994. Graphic artist Excalibur Group, Loudonville, N.Y., 1982-84, GE, Schenectady, N.Y., 1984-88; computer artist, designer Corp. Graphic Resource, Albany, N.Y., 1988-89; propr., designer Printup Graphic Design, Schenectady, 1989—; artists' project N.Y. State Regional Initiative-NEA, Rockefeller Found., Andy Warhol Found., Jerome Found., 1996. Author: The Chronicle of Higher Education/End Paper/We Are Alll Endangered!, 1995. Artists' fellow N.Y. Found. for Arts, 1995, intercultural film/video/multimedia fellow The Rockefeller Found., 1996. Mem. Iroquois Indian Mus. Office: Printup Graphic Design 16 Hampshire Way Schenectady NY 12309-1935

HOPKINS, CECILIA ANN, business educator; b. Havre, Mont., Feb. 17, 1922; d. Kost L. and Mary (Manaras) Sofos; B.S., Mont. State Coll., 1944; M.A., San Francisco State Coll., 1958, M.A., 1967; postgrad. Stanford U.; Ph.D., Calif. Western U., 1977; m. Henry E. Hopkins, Sept. 7, 1944. Bus. tchr. Havre (Mont.) High Sch., Mateo, Calif., 1942-44; sec. George P. Gorham, Realtor, San Mateo, 1944-45; escrow sec. Fox & Cars 1945-50; escrow officer Calif. Pacific Title Ins. Co., 1950-57; bus. tchr. Westmoor High Sch., Daly City, Calif., 1958-59; bus. tchr. Coll. of San Mateo, 1959-63, chmn. real estate-ins. dept., 1963-76, dir. div. bus., 1976-86, coord. real estate dept., 1986-91; cons. to commr. Calif. Div. Real Estate, 1963-91, mem. periodic rev. exam. com.; chmn. C.C. Adv. Com., 1971-72, mem. com., 1975-91; projector direction Calif. State Chancellor's Career Awareness Consortium, mem. endowment fund adv. com., c.c. real estate edn. com., state c.c. adv. com.; mem. No. Calif. adv. bd. to Glendale Fed. Savs. and Loan Assn.; mem. bd. advisors San Mateo County Bd. Suprs., 1981-82; mem. real estate edn. and rsch. com. to Calif. Commr. Real Estate, 1983-90; mem. edn., membership, and profl. exchange coms. Am. chpt. Internat. Real Estate Fedn., 1985-92. Recipient Citizen of Day award KABL, Outstanding Contbns. award Redwood City-San Carlos-Belmont Bd. Realtors, Nat. Real Estate Educators Assn. award emeritus, 1993; named Woman of Achievement, San Mateo-Burlingame br. Soroptimist Internat., 1979. Mem. AAUW, Calif. Assn. Real Estate Tchrs. (state pres. 1964-65, life hon. dir. 1962—, Outstanding Real Estate Educator of Yr. 1978-79), Real Estate Cert. Inst. (Disting. Merit award 1982), Calif. Bus. Edn. Assn. (certificate of commendation 1979), San Francisco State Coll., Guidance and Counseling Alumni, Calif. Real Estate Educators' Assn. (dir. emeritus, hon. dir. 1990), Real Estate Nat. Educators Assn. (award emeritus for outstanding contributions, 1993), San Mateo-Burlingame Bd. Realtors (award emeritus Outstanding Contbrs. to Membership), Alpha Delta, Pi Lambda Theta, Delta Pi Epsilon (nat. dir. interchpt. rels. 1962-65, nat. historian 1966-67, nat. sec. 1968-69), Alpha Gamma Delta. Co-author: California Real Estate Principles; contbr. articles to profl. jours. Home: 504 Colgate Way San Mateo CA 94402-3206

HOPKINS, JAN, journalist, news anchor; b. Warren, Ohio, May 22, 1947; d. Walter Charles and Lois Avelene (Botroff) Reed; m. Walter Hopkins, June 14, 1969 (div. Nov. 1981); m. Richard Trachtman, Nov. 8, 1986. Dir. news Sta. WTCL, Warren, Ohio, 1973-75; reporter, anchor Sta. WERE, Cleve., 1975-77; reporter Sta. WKBN-TV, Youngstown, Ohio, 1977-80; reporter, anchor Sta. WLWT-TV, Cin., 1980-82; assignment editor CBS News, N.Y.C., 1983; reporter, prodr. ABC News, N.Y.C., 1983-84; anchor bus. news CNN, N.Y.C., 1984—. Author: (chapter) Knight Bagehot Guide to Business Journalism, 1990. Trustee Hiram Coll., 1988-94; adv. bd. Knight Bagehot program journalism Columbia U., N.Y.C., 1994. Recipient Peabody award U. Ga., 1988, Front Page award Newswomen Club N.Y., 1988; Knight Bagehot fellow Columbia U. Sch. Journalism, 1982-83; named to Hall of Excellence Ohio Found. Ind. Colls., 1993. Mem. Econ. Club N.Y. Office: CNN Bus News 5 Penn Plz Fl 20 New York NY 10001-1810

HOPKINS, JEANNE M., communications executive. B in Comms., No. Ill. U. Radio prodr., dir. pub. info. U. Mass., Amherst; dir. media rels. WGBH Ednl. Found., Boston, 1989-94, developer govt. rels. dept., 1991, v.p. corp. comms., 1994—. Office: 125 Western Ave Boston MA 02134

HOPKINS, JEANNETTE ETHEL, book publisher, editor; b. Camden, N.J., Dec. 7, 1922; d. Carleton Roper and Gladys Eugenia (Hull) H. BA, Vassar Coll., 1944; MS, Columbia Sch. Journalism, 1945. Asst. to Sunday editor New Haven Register, 1945-46; reporter Providence Evening Bull., 1946-50, Oklahoma City Times, 1950-51; sr. editor Beacon Press, Boston, 1951-56, Harcourt Brace, N.Y.C., 1956-64, Harper & Row, N.Y.C., 1964-73; v.p. Met. Applied Res. Ctr., N.Y.C., 1970-72, cons. editor, 1973-80, 89—; dir. Wesleyan Univ. Press, Middletown, Conn., 1980-89; adj. prof. English Wesleyan U., 1987-89, U. N.H., 1989; propr. Portsmouth Athenaeum, 1991. Author: Books That Will Not Burn, 1952, 14 Journeys to Unitarianism, 1951, (with K.B. Clark) Relevant War Against Poverty, 1968, Legacy: A History of the South Church Endowment, 1995. Mem. coun. Inst. Religion in an Age of Sci., 1968-72, 80-82, 88-91; mem. bd. Unitarian UN Office, 1977-80; mem. Commn. on Appraisal, Unitarian Universalist Assn., 1976-78; bd. dirs. ACLU, 1970-79, mem. nat. adv. coun., 1986—; bd. govs. Cmty. Ch. N.Y., 1960-66, Unitarian-Universalist Ch., Portsmouth, 1990-93, lay min., 1991-95; trustee South Ch. Endowment Fund, 1996—; v.p. Unitarian Fellowship for Social Justice, 1958-62. Louise Hart Van Loon fellow, Vassar Coll., 1944; recipient Disting. Alumni award Columbia Sch. Journalism, 1981. Democrat. Unitarian. Home and Office: 39 Pray St Portsmouth NH 03801-5226

HOPKINS, KATHARINE JANE, marine policy analyst; b. Atlanta, Jan. 20, 1969; d. John David and Evelyn Ann (Harry) H. BA, U. Va., 1991; M in Pub. Policy, Coll. William and Mary, 1996; MA in Marine Resource Mgmt., Va. Inst. Marine Sci., 1996. Rsch. asst. Coll. William and Mary, Williamsburg, 1993-94, Va. Inst. Marine Sci., Gloucester Point, 1994—. Editor, photographer: A Road to the Sun, 1991. Vol. emergency med. tech. Abingdon Rescue Squad, Gloucester Point, 1995—. Thomas Jefferson fellow Coll. William and Mary, 1993-94. Mem. ACLU, Nat. Resource Def. Coun., Sierra Club, Alpha Omicron Pi (social chmn. 1987-88). Democrat. Episcopalian. Office: Va Inst Marine Sci Dept Resource Mgmt Policy Gloucester Point VA 23062

HOPKINS, LINDA ANN, school psychologist; b. Bristol, Va., Aug. 23, 1937; d. James Robert and Trula Mae (Mink) Broce; AB, King Coll., 1959; MA, East Tenn. State U., 1977, postgrad., 1977-79; postgrad. Radford U., 1978-79, U. Va., 1980-89; m. James Edwin Hopkins, Oct. 8, 1960; children: James Edwin, David Lawrence. Nat. cert. sch. psychologist. Social worker Washington County Welfare Dept., Abingdon, Va., 1959-61; social worker Bristol (Va.) Welfare Dept., 1963-65, Washington County Welfare Dept., 1965-68, Bristol Meml. Hosp., 1968-72; psychologist Washington County Public Schs., Abingdon, 1978-87; pvt. practice sch. psychology, Abingdon, 1987-91; sch. psychologist Georgetown (S.C.) Dist. Pub. Schs., 1991—; adj. prof. East Tenn. State U., 1989-91. Active Pawleys Island Rescue Squad Midway Fire Dept., Swamp Fox Players Mem. Nat. Assn. Sch. Psychologists, Phi Kappa Phi. Methodist. Home: 64 Osprey Way Georgetown SC 29440-8504 Office: Georgetown County Pub Sch Dist 305 Front St Gegetown SC 29440-3733

HOPKINS, MAUREEN MURIEL, labor union official; b. Oceanside, N.Y., June 8, 1945; d. Joseph William and Muriel Helen (Bennett) Murphy; m. Martin Conrad Ruane, July 15, 1967 (div. May 1992); m. Donald Michael Hopkins Jr., June 29, 1996. Grad. high sch., Valley Stream, L.I., N.Y. Sec. Local 854 IBT, H&W Benefits Plan, Valley Stream, N.Y., 1971-81; fund mgr. Local 854 Pension Fund Health & Welfare Benefits Plan, Valley Stream, N.Y., 1981-89; bus. agt. Local 854 I.B. of T., Valley Stream, N.Y., 1989, pres., 1990—; dir. Labor Edn. and Community Svc. Agy. Inc., Westbury, N.Y., 1988—; trustee Local 854 Health and Welfare and Pension Fund, Valley Stream, 1990—; del. Eastern Conf. Teamsters, Bethesda, Md., 1990—, Joint Coun. #16, N.Y.C., 1990—, indsl. trade divsn. Internat. Brotherhood of Teamsters, 1992—; area v.p. Internat. Teamsters' Women's Caucus, 1992—; adv. bd. Nat. Conf. Unions and Employees Benefit Funds, 1992—; commr. Teamsters Human Rights Com. and Joint Coun. 16 (rep. women's issues). Mem. Internat. Found. of Employee Benefits Plans, Assn. Benefit Adminstrs., N.Y. Inst. Technol., Indsl. Rels. Rsch. Assn., Ednl. Conf. Health and Welfare and Pension Plans. Lutheran.

HOPKINS, PAMELA SUE, school counselor; b. Ft. Scott, Kans., Jan. 16, 1968; d. Larry Wayne and Eula Kathleen (Fink) Gilliland; m. Michael Lee Hopkins, Jan. 16, 1993. AS, Ft. Scott C.C., 1988; BS, Kans. State U., Manhattan, 1991, MS, 1994. Math. and computer tchr. Lost Springs (Kans.) H.S., 1991-92; adult Word Perfect tchr. Manhattan Tech. Ctr., 1993; substitute tchr. Manhattan Sch. Dist., 1992-93; acad. advisor edn. office Kansas State U., Manhattan, 1993-94; elem. sch. counselor Missouri City (Mo.) Elem., 1994-95; H.S. counselor St. Thomas Aquinas-Mercy H.S., Florissant, Mo., 1995—. Mem. ACA, Am. Sch. Counseling Assn., Am. Volleyball Coaches Assn., Nat. Coun. Tchrs. Math., Mo. Sch. Counseling Assn. Home: 111 Pheasant Pt O'Fallon MO 63366

HOPKINS, PATRICIA ANN, personnel professional; b. Pine Bluff, Ark., Nov. 15, 1955; d. Albert and bessie Mae (Jones) Richmond; children: Ronald Jr., Patrick Deshon. AS in Gen. Studies, Pikes Peak C.C., 1988; BA in Mgmt., So. Nazarene U., 1993; MS in Mgmt., Nat. Louis U., 1995. Jr. programmer, libr. ITT Telec Svcs. Inc., Colorado Springs, Colo., 1980-87; author, authoring asst. Infotec Devel., Colorado Springs, 1987-89; curriculum developer McDonnel Douglas Tng. System, Norman, Okla., 1989-91, instructional designer, 1991-93; instructional designer McDonnel Douglas Tng. System, Hazelwood, Mo., 1993-94; tng. mgr. Maritz Performance Improvement Co., Fenton, Mo., 1994—. Mem. program bd. Black Jack Sports, coord. Boys & Girls; mem. spl. events com. Black Jack Bus. Revitalization Com.; mem. devel. com. Matthew Dickey Boys Club. With USN, 1974-80. Mem. NAFE, Am. Bus. Womens Assn. (pres. 1995—, co-chmn. St. Louis metro area coun.). Office: Maritz Performance Improvement Co 1355 N Highway Dr Fenton MO 63099

HOPKINS, SHIRLEY MAY, former educator, real estate broker; b. Detroit, Oct. 4, 1928; d. Jake Henry and Grace Mildred (Armbruster) Spiller; m. Richard Glenn Hopkins, June 7, 1949 (div. July 1955); children: Richard Reid, Leslie Lee, Scott Henry. BA, Wayne State U., 1959; MA, Calif. State U., Fullerton, 1969; PhD with honors, UCLA, 1976. Tchr. Hilltop Jr. H.S., Chula Vista, Calif., 1959-64, Santa Fe H.S., Santa Fe Springs, Calif., 1964-74; asst. prin. Fern Sch., Rosemead, Calif., 1974-76; staff adminstr. Downey (Calif.) H.S., 1976-79; realtor Creative Real Estate, Santa Barbara, Calif., 1980-84; real estate broker Allegro Realty, Santa Barbara, 1984-88; mem. Assn. Women Sch. Adminstrs., Downey, 1976-79, Women in Ednl. Leadership, L.A., 1976-79; pres. Santa Barbara Real Estate Exchangors, 1983-84. Commr., vice-chair Santa Barbara County Affirmative Action, 1995—; forewoman Santa Barbara County Grand Jury, 1992-93; membership dir. 1st United Meth. Ch., Santa Barbara, 1996—. Mem. AAUW, NAACP, Leadership Santa Barbara County, Golden State Mobilhome Owners (chair 1988-96), Pi Sigma Alpha, Phi Delta Kappa. Democrat. Methodist. Home: 205 Oceano Ave #5 Santa Barbara CA 93109

HOPKINSON, SHIRLEY LOIS, library science educator; b. Boone, Iowa, Aug 25, 1924; d. Arthur Perry and Zora (Smith) Hopkinson; student Coe Coll., 1942-43; AB cum laude (Phi Beta Kappa scholar 1944), U. Colo., 1945; BLS, U. Calif., 1949; MA (Honnold Honor scholar 1945-46), Claremont Grad. Sch., 1951; EdM, U. Okla., 1952, EdD, 1957 Tchr. pub. sch. Stigler, Okla., 1946-47, Palo Verde High Sch., Jr. Coll., Blythe, Calif., 1947-48; asst. librarian Modesto (Calif.) Jr. Coll., 1949-51; tchr., librarian Fresno, Calif., 1951-52, La Mesa, Cal., 1953-55; asst. prof. librarianship, instructional materials dir. Chaffey Coll., Ontario, Calif., 1955-59; asst. prof. librarian ship, San Jose (Calif.) State Coll., 1959-64; assoc. prof., 1964-69, prof., 1969—; bd. dirs. NDEA Inst. Sch. Librs., summer 1966; mem. Santa Clara County Civil Service Bd. Examiners. Recipient Master Gardner cert. Oreg. State U. Extension Svc. Book reviewer for jours. Mem. ALA, Calif. Library Assn., Audio-Visual Assn. Calif., NEA, AAUP, AAUW (dir. 1957-

58), Bus. Profl. Women's Club, Sch. Librs. Assn. Calif. (com. mem., treas. No. sect. 1951-52), San Diego County Sch. Librs. Assn. (sec. 1945-55), Calif. Tchrs. Assn., LWV (bd. dirs. 1950-51, publs. chmn.), Phi Beta Kappa, Alpha Lambda Delta, Alpha Beta Alpha, Kappa Delta Pi, Phi Kappa Phi (disting. acad. achievement award 1981), Delta Kappa Gamma (sec. 1994—). Author: Descriptive Cataloging of Library Materials; Instructional Materials for Teaching the Use of the Library. Contbr. to profl. publs. Editor: Calif. Sch. Libraries, 1963-64; asst. editor: Sch. Library Assn. of Calif. Bull., 1961-63; book reviewer profl. jours. Office: 1340 Pomeroy Ave Apt 408 Santa Clara CA 95051-3658

HOPP, MAGGIE (MARGARET RUTH HOPP), photographer, psychologist; b. Poughkeepsie, N.Y., Apr. 21, 1945; d. Robert Ewing and Harriet (Spitzer) H.; m. William Toney Edwards, Apr. 24, 1995. BA, Bard Coll., 1967. One-woman shows include Cathedral Mus. Cathedral St. John the Divine, N.Y.C., 1981-82, 82-83, Borough Pres.'s Gallery, N.Y.C., 1989, Urban Ctr. Gallery Mcpl. Art Soc., N.Y.C., 1990, Lobby 1133 Ave. of Ams., N.Y.C., 1991, Lobby 675 3d Ave., N.Y.C., 1993-94, Princeton U. Program in Women's Studies, 1994, Richart, N.Y., 1995, Met. Transit Auth. Arts for Transit Exhbn. Ctrs. Program, N.Y.C., 1995-96; group exhbns. include 380 Gallery, N.Y.C., 1979, 345 Gallery, N.Y.C., 1980, UN Gen. Assembly Pub. Gallery, N.Y.C., 1980, The Whitney Mus., N.Y.C., 1981, Ctrl. Pa. Festival of Arts Pa. State U., 1982, Soho Photo Gallery, N.Y.C., 1989, Perkins Ctr. for Arts, N.J., 1990, Forum Gallery Jamestown (N.Y.) C.C., 1990, Nat. Inst. Archtl. Edn., N.Y.C., 1991, The Continental Art Gallery Continental Ins. Co., N.Y.C., 1991, Robin Rice Gallery, Ltd., N.Y.C., 1991, Marine Midland Bank, N.Y.C., 1993-94, 42d St. Art Project, N.Y.C., 1993-94, Frumkin/Adams Gallery, N.Y.C., 1994, Nat. Arts Club, N.Y.C., 1994, Michael Ingbar Gallery Archtl. Art, N.Y.C., 1994, Urban Ctr. Gallery Mcpl. Art Soc., N.Y.C., 1995; contbr. photographs to numerous pubs.; represented in numerous pvt. and pub. collections. Canon Materials grantee, 1978, Polaroid Materials grantee, 1979, Eastman Kodak Profl. Imaging grantee, 1993, Met. Transp. Auth. Arts for Transit Exhbn. Ctrs. Program grantee, 1994-96. Mem. Entertainment Com. Bard Coll. (chair 1987—, bd. govs., exec. com.). Office: 103 Charles St Apt 1RE New York NY 10014-2655

HOPPER, ANITA KLEIN, molecular genetics educator; b. Chgo., Sept. 24, 1945; d. Irving and Rose (Warshawsky) Klein; m. James Ernest Hopper, Jan. 3, 1971; 1 child, Julie Victoria. BS, U. Ill., Chgo., 1967; PhD, U. Ill., 1972. Postdoctoral researcher genetics U. Wash., Seattle, 1971-75; asst. prof. microbiology U. Mass. Med. Sch., Worcester, 1975-78, assoc. prof. microbiology, 1978-79; assoc. prof. biochemistry Hershey Med. Sch., Pa. State U., Hershey, 1979-87, prof. biochemistry, molecular biology, 1987—; genetic biology panel NSF, Washington, 1981-85; mem. genetic study sect. NIH, Bethesda, 1985-89; organizer RNA processing Cold Spring Harbor meetings, 1989, 90; co-chmn. 5th Summer Symposium in Molecular Biology: The Nucleus, Pa. State U., 1986. Editor Molecular & Cellular Biology, 1989—, editl. bd., 1986-90; mem. editl. bd. RNA, 1995—; contbr. articles and symposium papers to profl. jours. Grantee NIH, 1979—, NIH U. Louisville Med. Sch., 1989, NSF, 1988-91; postdoctoral fellow NIH, 1971-73. Fellow Am. Acad. Microbiology; mem. AAAS, Am. Soc. Microbiology (chair-elect genetics & molecular biology div. 1987, chair genetics & molecular biology div. 1988), Am. Assn. Biochemists. Office: Pa State U Med Sch Dept Biochemistry & Molecular Biology Hershey PA 17033

HOPPER, RUBY LOU, clergy member; b. Harrison, Ark., May 21, 1950; d. George C. and Ethel M. (Bethany) Eddings; m. Alfred Hopper, Aug. 1, 1970. Diploma, Berean Bible Coll., Springfield, Mo., 1989. Cert. technician class III, Nat. Assn. Radio and Telecomm. Engrs., 1986; ordained minister Evangelistic Messengers, 1986. Youth leader Sycamore Log Ch., Branson, Mo., 1984—; ins. office sec. Mo. Farm Bur., Hollister, 1990-93; sec. Foxen Comm., Hollister, 1993; prodn. dept. Applied Digital, Inc., Branson, 1996; freelance writer, Hollister, 1996. vol. ARC, Branson, 1986-87; emergency coord. Amateur Radio Emergency Svc., Branson, 1988. Recipient Vol. Svc. award Pt. Lookout Health Care Ctr., 1991. Mem. Nat. Assn. Female Execs., Nat. Assn. Radio Telecomm. Engrs. (technician class III), Tri-Lakes Amateur Radio Club (v.p. 1984-88). Republican. Pentacostal. Home and Office: PO Box 332 Hollister MO 65673

HOPPER, SALLY, state legislator; widowed; children: Nancy, Joan, Caroline, Anne. BA, U. Wyo., 1956. Mem. Colo. Senate, Denver, 1987—; chair Senate Health, Environ., Welfare and Insts. com.; chair Criminal Justice Commn, mem. Judiciary com. Mem. nat. bd. Physically Challenged Access to the Woods; mem., past chair bd. Spalding Rehab. Hosp.; bd. dirs. Easter Seals of Colorado. Mem. Kappa Kappa Gamma. Republican. Episcopalian. Home: 21649 Cabrini Blvd Golden CO 80401-9487

HOPSON, JANET LOUISE, writer, educator; b. St. Louis, Oct. 22, 1950; d. David Warren and Ruth H.; m. Gerald Dommer, May 1994. BS, So. Ill. U., 1972; MS, U. Mo., 1975. Biology editor Sci. News Mag., Washington, 1974-76; nature columnist Outside Mag., San Francisco and Chgo., 1977-82; lectr. dept. natural scis. U. Calif., Santa Cruz, 1983—; reviewer NSF Grant Rev. Panel for Undergrad. Sci. Edn., Washington, 1991. Author: Scent Signals, 1979; co-author: (coll. textbooks) Biology, 1988, Nature of Life, 1989, 2d edit., 1992, 3d edit., 1995, Essentials of Biology, 1990, Biology! Bringing Science to Life, 1991; contbr. articles to profl. jours. Recipient Russell L. Cecil award Arthritis Found., 1980; NIH/Coun. for Advancement of Sci. Writing fellow, 1976, Frank Luther Mott fellow U. Mo., 1973; grad. fellow So. Ill. U., 1972. Mem. Am. Inst. Biol. Scis., Nat. Assn. Sci. Writers, Textbook Authors Assn., No. Calif. Sci. Writers Assn. (pres. 1983-86).

HOPSON, SUSANNE MAE, elementary school educator; b. Trenton, N.J., Mar. 19, 1941; d. James Cox and Martha Ann (Tindall) Fenimore; m. Robert W. Bausum, Sept. 29, 1962 (div. June 1980); children: Robert Jr., Lauren Jean, Kimberly Ann; m. William A. Hopson, Apr. 18, 1981. Student, Maryville Coll., 1958-59; BA, Grove City Coll., 1962; MA in Elem. Edn., Georgian Ct. Coll., 1981. 3d grade tchr. Washington Twp. Bd. Edn., Budd Lake, N.J., 1962-64; chpt. 1 tchr. Lavallette (N.J.) Bd. Edn., 1972-79; basic skills instr. Brick (N.J.) Twp. Bd. Edn., 1979—. Evaulation Ocean County (N.J.) Literacy Vols., 1991—. Named Tchr. of Yr., Ocean County Supt. of Schs., 1989-90. Mem. NEA, N.J. Edn. Assn., Ocean County Edn. Assn., Brick Twp. Edn. Assn. (award 1979), Internat. Reading Assn., N.J. Reading Assn. (bd. dirs. 1994—, state chair parents and reading com.), Ocean County Reading Coun. (v.p. 1987-88, pres. 1989-91, Disting. Svc. award 1993), Phi Delta Kappa. Home: 117 Poplar Way Brick NJ 08724-2501 Office: Drum Point Rd Elem Sch 41 Drum Point Rd Brick NJ 08723-6021

HOPWOOD, CHERYL J., accountant; b. Phila., Dec. 14, 1962; David A. Crispi and Dorothy J. (Hedges) Hill; m. Paul Carsley, May, 1984 (div. Mar. 1986); m. Eric R. Hopwood, May 3, 1986; children: Tara Ann, Erica Nicole. AA, Montgomery County C.C., Blue Bell, Pa., 1986; BS in Acctg., Calif. State U., 1988. CPA, Calif. Staff acct. Deloitte, Haskins & Sells, Sacramento, 1988-89, Gilbert Accy, Sacramento, 1989-90; sr. acct. Finton, Foley & Rose, Sacramento, 1990-91, Gloria Arecchi, CPA, San Antonio, 1993-95. Mem. AICPA, Beta Alpha Psi, Beta Gamma Sigma, Phi Kappa Phi. Republican. Roman Catholic. Home: 8712 Hayshed Ln Apt 101 Columbia MD 21045

HORN, KAREN NICHOLSON, banker; b. Los Angeles, Sept. 21, 1943; d. Aloys and Novella (Hartley) Nicholson; m. John T. Horn, June 5, 1965; 1 child. B.A., Pomona Coll., 1965; Ph.D., Johns Hopkins U., 1971. Economist bd. govs. FRS, Washington, 1969-71; v.p., economist First Nat. Bank, Boston, 1971-78; treas. Bell of Pa., Phila., 1978-82; pres. Fed. Res. Bank, Cleve., 1982-87; chmn. and chief exec. officer Bank One Cleveland NA, Cleve., 1987—; bd. dirs. TRW, Inc., Eli Lilly Co., Rubbermaid, Brit. Petroleum, Coun. Fgn. Rels. Chmn., trustee Case Western Res. U., Cleve.; trustee Rockefeller Found., Cleve. Clinic Found., Cleve. Orch., Cleve. Tomorrow. Office: Bank One Cleve NA 600 Superior Ave E Cleveland OH 44114-2611

HORN, MARIAN BLANK, federal judge; b. N.Y.C., June 24, 1943; d. Werner P. and Mady R. Blank; m. Robert Jack Horn; children: Juli Marie, Carrie Charlotte, Rebecca Blank. AB, Barnard Coll., 1962; student, Cornell U., Columbia U., 1965, NYU, 1965-66; JD, Fordham U., 1969. Bar: N.Y. 1970, D.C. 1973, U.S. Supreme Ct. 1973. Asst. dist. atty. Bronx County, N.Y., 1969-72; assoc. Arent, Fox, Kintner, Plotkin & Kahn, 1972-73; project mgr. Am. U. Law Sch. study on alts. to conventional criminal adjudication U.S. Dept. Justice, 1973-75; litigation atty. Fed. Energy Adminstrn., 1975-76; sr. atty. office gen. counsel strategic petroleum res. br. Dept. Energy, 1976-79, dep. asst. gen. counsel for procurement and fin. incentives, 1979-81; dep. assoc. solicitor div. surface mining Dept. Interior, 1981-83, assoc. solicitor div. gen. law, 1983-85, prin. dep. solicitor, acting solicitor, 1985; judge U.S. Ct. of Federal Claims, 1986—; adj. prof. law Washington Coll. Law, Am. U., 1973-76. Office: US Claims Ct 717 Madison Pl NW Washington DC 20005-1011*

HORN, PATRICIA SOLOMON, technology curriculum facilitator; b. Quincy, Fla., Oct. 17, 1944; d. Thomas William and Mary Margaret (Lecky) Solomon; m. Phillip W. Horn Jr., May 14, 1965; children: Phillip W. III, Thomas W. BA, Jacksonville U., 1965; MEd, U. North Fla., 1988-91, EdD, 1996. Cert. elem. tchr., Fla. Tchr. 2d and 3d grades Newberry (Fla.) Sch., 1965-68; tchr. kindergarten Dept. of Def. Schs. Overseas, Madrid, Spain, 1969-79, Lackawanna Elem. Sch., Jacksonville, Fla., 1979-85; tchr. kindergarten, sch. improvement chair Webster Sch., St. Augustine, Fla., 1987-93; facilitator for integrated curriculum and tech. St. Johns County Sch. Dist., St. Augustine, Fla., 1993—; technology cons. Fulbright Commn., Eqyptian Ministry Edn., 1996. Contbr. chpts. to Handbook of Literacy Assessment and Evaluation, and articles to profl. jours. Den leader Cub Scouts Am., Jacksonville, Fla., 1978-84; bd. dirs. Boy Scouts Am., Jacksonville, 1979-84; pres., sec. St. Johns County Med. Aux., 1987-94; bd. dirs. Childbirth and Parenting Edn. Assn. (1991-94), mem. Tech. Resource Com. for Fla. Accountability Commn., Tallahassee, 1994. Mem. ACSD (Tech. Futures Commn. 1994-95), Fla. League Tchrs. (charter, adv. bd. 1992—), Fla. Assn. Computers in Edn. (Fla. Instrnl. Tech. Tchr. of Yr. award 1994), Internat. Reading Assn., Internat. Soc. for Tech. in Edn. (Internat. Tech. Tchr. of Yr. award 1994, cons. to Fulbright Commn. of the Middle East and Egyptian Ministry of Edn. 1996), Nat. Coun. Tchrs. English and Lang. Arts, Alpha Delta Kappa, Phi Kappa Phi. Democrat. Roman Catholic. Home: 6 Versaggi Dr Saint Augustine FL 32084-6926 Office: St Johns County Sch Dist 40 Orange St Saint Augustine FL 32084-3633

HORN, ROBERTA CLAIRE, psychotherapist, photographer; b. New Brunswick, N.J.; d. John and Ruth (Holden) Teitscheid. BA cum laude, U. Calif., Berkeley, 1985; MA in Psychology, New Sch. for Social Rsch., N.Y.C., 1992; postgrad., Mass. Sch. Profl. Psychology, 1993—. Owner Roberta Horn Photography, Kennebunkport, Maine, 1983-93; exec. dir. Hospice Vols. of Saco Valley, Biddeford, Maine, 1988-90; psychology intern Wayland (Mass.) Mid. Sch., 1993-94, Boston U. Mental Health Ctr., 1994-95, Mass. Gen. Hosp./Chelsea Meml. Health Ctr., 1995-96, Mass. Gen. Hosp./Shriners Burns Inst., 1996; mental health worker Cambridge Hosp./Fresh Pond Day Treatment Ctr., 1995; counselor Rehoboth McKinley House of Hope, N.Mex., 1996; cons. History of Print exhbn. Xerox Corp., 1978. One-woman show (photography) Portraits of Serenity, Manchester, N.H., 1988. Mem. acquisition bd. for Am. Collection, Am. Sch. in London Libr., 1976-78; mem. condominium bd. San Francisco, 1981-84; bd. dirs. Caring Unltd. Family Violence Shelter, Sanford, Maine, 1986-88; student trainee Headstart, South Bronx, N.Y., 1990-91, Bensonhurst Day Hosp. Bklyn., 1991-92; program specialist children's summer camp Bishopswood, Camden, Maine, 1990. Recipient awards for photography. Mem. APA, N.Y. State Psychol. Assn., Dirs. of Vol. Orgns., Maine State Hospice Assn., York Art Assn., Art Guild of the Kennebunks (former v.p.), Maine Women in the Arts (former pres.), Psi Chi. Office: 5 Mendum St Roslindale MA 02131-1613

HORN, SUSAN DADAKIS, statistics educator; b. Cleve., Aug. 30, 1943; d. James Sophocles and Demeter (Zessis) Dadakis; m. Roger Alan Horn, July 24, 1965; children: Ceres, Corinne, Howard. BA, Cornell U., 1964; MS, Stanford U., 1966, PhD, 1968. Asst. prof. Johns Hopkins U., Balt., 1968-76, assoc. prof., 1976-86, prof. stats. and health svcs. rsch. methods, 1986-92; sr. scientist Intermountain Health Care, Salt Lake City, 1992-95; prof. dept. med. informatics Sch. Medicine U. Utah, Salt Lake City, 1992—; sr. scientist Inst. for Clin. Outcomes Rsch., Salt Lake City. Fellow Am. Statist. Assn.; mem. Am. Pub. Health Assn., Biometric Soc., Assn. for Health Svcs. Research, Sigma Xi, Phi Beta Kappa, Phi Kappa Phi. Presbyterian. Home: 1793 Fort Douglas Cir Salt Lake City UT 84103-4451 Office: Inst Clin Outcomes Rschrs 2681 Parleys Way Ste 201 Salt Lake City UT 84109

HORNAK, ANNA FRANCES, library administrator; b. College Station, Tex., June 3, 1922; d. Josef and Anna (Drozd) H. B.A., U. Tex., Austin, 1944; B.L.S., U. Ill., Champaign-Urbana, 1945; Ed.M., U. Houston, 1956. Children's librarian Schenectady Pub. Library, N.Y., 1945-47; children's librarian Pasadena Pub. Library, Calif., 1947-49; supr. Juvenile Div. Houston Pub. Library, 1949-57, asst. dir., 1957-89, ret., 1989. Named Outstanding Woman, YWCA of Houston, 1977; Outstanding Houston Profl. Woman, Fed. Houston Profl. Women, 1982. Home: 2217 Woodhead St Houston TX 77019-6820

HORN-ALSBERGE, MICHELE MARYANN, school psychologist; b. Jersey City, Feb. 27, 1952; d. Charles Joseph Jr. and Beverly Theresa (Wackar) Horn; m. Edward John Rausch, Aug. 4, 1973 (div. June 1981); m. Gary Roy Alsberge, May 16, 1987; children: Kristen, Eric. AA, Harriman (N.Y.) Coll., 1971; BA, St. Peter's Coll., Jersey City, 1972; MA, Montclair (N.J.) State Coll., 1975; postgrad., St. John's U., Jamaica, N.Y., 1986—. Cert. sch. psychologist, N.J., social studies tchr., N.J. and N.Y., English tchr., N.J. Social studies tchr. Middletown (N.Y.) Bd. Edn., 1979-80, Monroe-Woodbury Bd. Edn., Central Valley, N.Y., 1980-82; English tchr. Vernon (N.J.) Twp. Bd. Edn., 1982-84; mktg. support rep. Computer Entry Systems, Fair Lawn, N.J., 1984-88; clin. specialist Ctr. for Mental Health, Newton (N.J.) Meml. Hosp., 1990-94; sch. psychologist North Warren Regional Bd. Edn., Blairstown, N.J., 1994—; clin. specialist Prime Care, Newton, 1991-94; clinician St. John's U. Psychol. Svcs. Ctr., Jamaica, N.Y., 1986-90; clin. extern St. Clares/Riverside, Boonton, N.J., 1989-90; rsch. and clin. extern North Shore U. Hosp., Manhasset, N.Y., 1987-89. Com. mem. ctrl. planning commn. Pleasant Valley Sch. Dist., Brodheadsville, Pa., 1994—. Named Outstanding Alumna Harriman (N.Y.) Coll., 1976. Mem. APA (student affiliate), N.J. Psychol. Assn., N.J. Edn. Assn. Roman Catholic. Home: RD 3 Box 3231 Saylorsburg PA 18353 Office: North Warren Regional HS PO Box 410 Blairstown NJ 07825

HORNBAKER, ALICE JOY, author; b. Cin., Feb. 3, 1927; children: Christopher Albert, Holly Jo, Joseph Bernard III. BA cum laude and honors in Journalism, U. Calif., San Jose, 1949. Asst. woman's editor San Jose Mercury-News, 1949-55; columnist "Life After 50" Cin. Post Newspaper, 1993—; free-lance writer Cin.; owner, mgr. Frisch's Big Boy Restaurant, Cin., 1955-68; dir. pub. relations Children's Home Soc. Calif., Santa Clara, 1968-71; asst. dir. pub. relations United Fund Calif., Santa Clara, 1971—; editor Tristate Sunday Enquirer mag., 1986-89, columnist Generations Tristate mag.; editorial dir. Writers Digest Sch., Cin., 1971-75; columnist, critic, mag. writer, reporter, copy editor Tempo sec. Cin. Enquirer, 1975-93, also book editor and critic, columnist for Aging, feature writer Tempo sect.; reporter news segments on aging WKRC-TV; tchr. adult edn. Forest Hills Sch. Dist., Thomas More Coll., 1973—; reporter, specialist on aging for Cin. Enquirer, 1989-93, commentator on aging Sta. WMLX-AM, 1991-93. Author: Preventive Care: Easy Exercise Against Aging, 1974; byline in People, Modern Maturity, St. Anthony Messenger, N.Y. Times Sun. mag., and others; contbr. fiction to Enquirer mag.; freelance mag. writer. Recipient Bronze award in Am. health journalism Am. Chiropractic Assn., 1977, 78, Golden Image award Assn. Ohio Philanthropic Homes, 1989; 1st pl. for feature writing Cin. Editors Assn., 1983, 1st and 3d pl. feature writing awards Ohio Profl. Writers, Inc., 1992, Journalist of Yr. award Ohio chpt. Am. Coll. Health Care Adminstrs., 1993, Journalism award Greater Cin. Joint Coun. on Geraitric Care, 1993. Mem. Blue Pencil of Ohio State U. (pres. 1981-82), Women in Comm., Ohio Newspaper Women's Assn. (v.p. 1981-83, 1st pl. human interest story 1977-85, 2d pl. column award 1979, Tops in Ohio award 1982, M.M. McMullen 2d pl. award, 1982, Recognition award 1985, 4th pl. on aging Nat. Legacies contest 1994), Soc. Profl. Journalists (treas. 1981-82), Ohio Press Women, Inc. (1st and 3d pl. awards for feature writing 1992). Office: CW Post 125 E Court St Cincinnati OH 45202-1211

HORNBECK, NITA LOU, university and secondary school educator; b. Macamey, Tex., Feb. 16, 1929; d. Major McKinley and Eupha Addie (Todd) McLennan; m. Carlton Wayne Hornbeck; children: Rebecca Diane Cudak, Susan Dawn Treese, Cynthia Jayne Chandler, Robert Carlton. BA, Southwestern U., Georgetown, Tex., 1950; MA, Tex. A&I U., 1973. Cert. tchr., supr. Tng. dir. Scarbrough's Dept. Store, Austin, 1950; sec. Sec. of State's Office, Austin, 1950-51; dental healthr educator, counselor State Health Dept., Austin, 1951; tchr. Alice (Tex.) H.S., 1964-80; instr. Bee County C.C., 1974-76, Tex. A&I U., Kingsville, 1977-79; tchr. Round Rock (Tex.) H.S., 1981-90, ret., 1990; cons. Nat. Evaluation Sys., Austin, 1989—; presenter Using Computers in English Classrooms, 1989. Mem. AAUW (mentor for Austin 1990, outstanding woman of br. Austin 1991-92, 92-93, 95, newsletter editor Austin 1992-94, conv. dir. 1994, ctrl. Tex. dir., state bd. dirs. 1994—, pub. policy chair Austin 1994—, state program dir. 1996—, outstanding women of Tex. award 1996, organizer, co-chair Voice of Reason 1995—, grant 1995, program v.p. Tex. 1996—, grantee 1996, dir. voter's edn. campaign 1996), Tex. Retired Tchrs. Assn., (mem. pub. policy 1994—, award of distinction 1995), Williamson County Retired Tchrs. (pres. 1992-94). Democrat. Methodist. Home: 600 Parkview Dr Round Rock TX 78681 Office: Nat Evaluation Sys 2621 Ridgepoint Dr Austin TX 78754

HORNBY-ANDERSON, SARA ANN, metallurgical engineer, marketing professional; b. Plymouth, Devon, Eng., Apr. 17, 1952; came to U.S., 1986; d. Foster John and Joanna May (Duncan) Hornby; m. John Victor Anderson, Sept. 2, 1978 (div. May 1987). BSc in Metallurgy with honors, Sheffield (Eng.) City Poly., 1973, PhD in Indsl. Metallurgy, 1980. Chartered engr. Metallurgist Joseph Lucas Rsch., Solihull, Eng., 1970, William Lee Maleable, Dronfield, Eng., 1972; tech. sales specialist Applied Rsch. Labs, Luton, Beds, Eng., 1973-74; quality assurance metallurgist Firth Brown Tools, Sheffield, 1974-75, rsch. metallurgist high speed steel, 1975; lectr. Sheffield City Poly., 1975-78; grad. metallurgist, strip devel. metallurgist British Steel Corp., Rotherham, Eng., 1978-80; program mgr. Can. Liquid Air, Montreal, 1980-85; group mktg. mgr. Liquid Air Corp., Countryside, Ill., 1986-90; tech. mgr. Liquid Air Corp., Walnut Creek, Calif., 1990-93; bus. devel. mgr.-metals and materials Can. Liquid Air, Toronto, Ont., 1993—, N.Am. steel tech. mgr., 1995—; bd. dirs., chmn. R & D com., mem. publs. com., chmn. promotions and mktg. com. INvestment Casting Inst., Dallas; presenter to confs. in field. Contbr. articles to profl. jours.; patentee in field of metallurgy. Mem. AIME, Inst. Metals (young metallurgists com. 1974-80), Sheffield Metall. Soc. Inst. Metals (sec. 1978-80), Am. Soc. Metals, Am. Foundry Soc., Powder Metals Soc., Am. Iron & Steel Soc. (steering com. 1987—, chmn. topics com. 1988—, sec. 1992, vice chair 1993, chmn. 1994, bd. dirs.). Mem. Ch. of Eng. Office: Can Liquid Air, 20 York Mills Rd # 400, Toronto, ON Canada M2C 2P2

HORNE, LENA, singer; b. Bklyn., June 30, 1917; d. Gail Lumet Buckley; m. Lennie Hayton, Dec. 1947 (dec. 1971). Dancer, Cotton Club, 1934; toured, recorded with Noble Sissle Orch., 1935-36, Charlie Barnet's Band, 1940-41; became cafe soc. singer; starred in: motion pictures Cabin in the Sky, Stormy Weather, Death of a Gunfighter, Thousands Cheer, I Dood It, Swing Fever, Broadway Rhythm, Two Girls and a Sailor, Ziegfeld Follies, Panama Hattie, Till the Clouds Roll By, Words & Music, Duchess of Idaho, Meet Me in Las Vegas, others; singer popular music ; TV appearances include spl. Harry and Lena, 1970, series Cosby Show, Sanford and Son; theatrical appearances in Dance with Your Gods, Blackbird, The Lady & Her Music, 1984; albums: Lena Goes Latin, 1987, Stormy Weather, The Men in My Life, 1989, Greatest Hits, 1992, At Long Last Lena, 1992, Best of Lena Horne, 1993, We'll Be Together Again, 1994; author: (with Richard Schickel) Lena, 1965. Recipient Kennedy Ctr. honor for lifetime contributions to the arts, 1984, Paul Robson award Actor's Equity, 1985. *

HORNE, LITHIA BROOKS, finance executive; b. Troy, N.C., Nov. 2, 1951; d. Tom Stewart and Anne Grace (Ward) Brooks; 1 child, Leslie Grace Hahn. AS in Bus. Adminstrn. Acctg., Wingate U., 1972. Cert. govtl. acctg. and fin. reporting, county adminstrn., acctg. and fiscal control, budgeting and fin. planning, effective mgmt.; cert. local govtl. fin. officer. Fin. officer Stanly County, Albemarle, N.C., 1972-86; dir. fiscal ops. Brunswick County, Bolivia, N.C., 1986—. Participant conf. Nat. Assn. Counties, Anaheim, Calif., 1988-89, Miami, Fla., 1990-91, legis. conf. NACO, Washington, 1987-88, GFOA Nat. Conf., Orlando, Fla., 1992-93, 1995-96. Named N.C. Outstanding Fin. Officer, 1991-92. Mem. Govt. Fin. Officers Assn., N.C. Assn. County Finance Officers (sec.-treas. 1988-89, 2nd v.p. 1989-90, 1st v.p. 1990-91, pres. 1991-92, chmn. legis. com. 1992-93, mem. nom. com. 1994—), N.C. Cash Mgmt. Trust (chmn., adv. bd. 1987-88), NAFE, Nat. Assn. County Finance Officers and Treasurers, Carolinas Assn. Govt. Purchasers. Home: PO Box 249 Bolivia NC 28422-0249

HORNE, MARILYN, mezzo-soprano; b. Bradford, Pa., Jan. 16, 1934; d. Bentz and Berneice H.; m. Henry Lewis (div.); 1 child. Ed., U. So. Calif.; MusD (hon.), Rutgers U., 1970, Jersey City State Coll., 1973, Brown U., 1984, Juillard Sch. Music, 1994; DLitt (hon.), St. Peter's Coll.; LHD (hon.), Kean Coll., 1977. Operatic debut as Hata in The Bartered Bride, Los Angeles Guild Opera, 1954; La Scala debut in Oepidus Rex, 1969; Met. Opera debut as Adalgisa in Norma, 1970; other roles include Rosina in Barber of Seville, Cleonte in The Siege of Corinth, Isabella in L'Italiana in Algieri, Carmen at Met. Opera, 1972-73, Laura in Harvest, Chgo. Lyric Opera, Marie in Wozzeck, San Francisco Opera; also appeared in Phigenie en Tauride, Semiramide, Samson et Dalila at Met. Opera, 1987, The Ghost of Versailles, 1991, Pelléas et Mélisande, 1995; other appearances include Venice Festival by invitation of Igor Stravinsky, Am. Opera Soc., N.Y.C., for several seasons, Vancouver Opera, Philharm. Hall, N.Y.C., Paris, Dallas, Houston, Covent Garden, London, roles at La Scala, Italy, Rossini Opera Festival, Pesaro, Italy, Met. Opera, 1987; recital debuts in Madrid, Dresden, East Berlin, 1987, performed at inauguration of U.S. President Clinton, 1993; ann. recital at Carnegie Hall, European tour with husband for Dept. State, 1963; rec. artist for London, Columbia, Deutsche Grammaphon and RCA records; recs. include sountrack Carmen Jones. Founder Marilyn Horne Found. Recipient Grammy awards, 1964, 81, 83, 94., Handel medallion, 1980, Premio d'Oro, Italian Govt., 1982, Commendatore al merito della Repubblica Italiana, 1983, Gold Merit medal Nat. Soc. Arts and Letters, 1987, Fidelio Gold medal, 1988, George Peabody award, 1989, Silver medal Covent Garden Royal Opera House, 1989, Disting. Dau. of Pa. Silver medal San Francisco Opera, 1990, Nat. Arts medal, 1992; named to Harold C. Schonberg's N.Y. Times' list of 9 All-Time, All-Star Singers in Met. Opera's 100 Years, 1984, Musician of Yr. Musical Am., 1995. Office: care Columbia Artists Mgmt Inc Wilford Divsn 165 W 57th St New York NY 10019-2201 also: care Met Opera Assoc Lincoln Ctr New York NY 10023 also: BGM Classics/RCA 1540 Broadway New York NY 10036-4039*

HORNER, ALTHEA JANE, psychologist; b. Hartford, Conn., Jan. 13, 1926; d. Louis and Celia (Newmark) Greenwald; children: Martha Horner Hartley, Anne Horner Benck, David, Kenneth. BS in Psychology, U. Chgo., 1952; PhD in Clin. Psychology, U. So. Calif., 1965. Lic. psychologist, N.Y., Calif. Tchr. Pasadena (Calif.) City Coll., 1965-67; from asst. to assoc. prof. Los Angeles Coll. Optometry, 1967-70; supr. Psychology interns Pasadena Child Guidance Clinic, 1969-70; pvt. practice specializing in psychoanalysis and psychoanalytic psychotherapy, N.Y.C., 1970-83; supervising psychologist dept. psychiatry Beth Israel Med. Ctr., N.Y.C., 1972-83, coordinator group therapy tng., 1976-82, clinician in charge Brief Adaptation-Oriented Psychotherapy Research Group, 1982-83; assoc. clin. prof. Mt. Sinai Sch. Medicine, N.Y.C., 1977-91, adj. assoc. prof., 1991—; mem. faculty Nat. Psychol. Assn. for Psychoanalysis, N.Y.C., 1982-83; sr. mem. faculty Wright Inst. Los Angeles Postgrad. Inst., 1983-85; pvt. practice specializing in psychoanalysis and psychoanalytic psychotherapy L.A., 1983—; clin. prof. dept. Psychology UCLA, 1985-95. Author: (with others) Treating the Neurotic Patient in Brief Psychotherapy, 1985, Object Relations and the Developing Ego in Therapy, 1979, rev. edit., 1984, Little Big Girl, 1982, Being and Loving, 1978, 3d edit. 1990, Psychology for Living (with G. Forehand), 4th edit., 1977, The Wish for Power and the Fear of Having It, 1989, The Primacy of Structure, 1990, Psychoanalytic Object Relations Therapy, 1991; mem. editorial bd. Jour. of Humanistic Psychology, 1986—, Jour. of the Am. Acad. of Psychoanalysis; contbr. articles to profl. jours. Mem. AAAS, APA, Calif. State Psychol. Assn., Am. Women Sci., Am. Acad. Psychoanalysis (sci. assoc.), So. Calif. Psychoanalytic Soc. and Inst. (hon.). Home: 3579 E Foothill Blvd # 256 Pasadena CA 91107

HORNER, JENNIE LINN, retired educational administrator, nurse; b. Memphis, Tex., Feb. 27, 1932; d. Lester C. and Cecil T. (Knight) Linn; m. Billy A. Gooch, June 4, 1951 (dec.); children: Brenda Michael, Patricia Lynn Magneson, Robert Allen; m. 2d Donald M. Horner, July 26, 1975. RN, U. Tex., 1955; BS, No. Ariz. U., 1977, MA, 1978, EdD, 1984. Cert. tchr., registered nurse, Ariz., Tex. Indsl. nurse Lipton Tea Co., Galveston, Tex., 1955-56; head nurse U. Tex. Med. Br., Galveston, 1956-58; sch. nurse Wash. Sch. Dist., Phoenix, 1970-77; tchr. middle sch., 1977-80; asst. prin. Murphy Sch. Dist., Phoenix, 1980-82; assoc. prin. middle sch. Madison Sch., Phoenix, 1982-84; lang. arts coordinator Madison Sch. Dist., Phoenix; prin. Dysart Unified Sch. Dist., El Mirage, Ariz., 1984-87; adminstr. for ednl. svcs., 1987-91, ret., 1991; med. cons. Medahab, Phoenix. Mem. Assn. Supervision and Curriculum Devel., Sch. Nurses Orgn. Ariz. (past pres.), Am. Vocat. Assn., Am. Sch. Health Assn., Nat. Assn. Sch. Nurses, Nat. Assn. Elem. Sch. Prins., Nat. Sch. Health Assn., Ariz. Sch. Health Assn. (bd. dirs.), Ariz. Adminstrs. Assn., Aware West, Phi Delta Kappa. Democrat. Home: 14239 N 50th Ln Glendale AZ 85306-4447

HORNER, LEE, foundation executive, speaker, consultant, computer specialist; b. Sault Ste. Marie, Ont., Can., Mar. 18, 1944; came to U.S., 1976; d. William E. and Gladys (Boomhower) H.; m. Claude Lavallee, Jan. 21, 1960 (div. Sept. 1969); children—Kevin Lauren Lavallee/Petalos, Cynthia Lee Lavallee; m. James G. Petalos, Jan. 9, 1970 (dec. Jan. 1977). Student Concordia U., Montreal, Que., Can., 1975-76, U. Nev.-Las Vegas, 1977, 90. Pres., LHP Investments, Inc., Las Vegas, 1978—; v.p. Casa Mobile Corp., real estate, San Francisco, 1979—; founder, chmn. bd. PMS Research Found., Las Vegas, 1982—; pub. speaker Premenstrual Syndrome, health, wellness, cycles. Author: How to Chart Your Course to Freedom, 1983; Mini-Nutrition and Exercise Manual, 1983; PMS Minder, 1983; PMS Wellness Workbook, 1985, PMS Support Group Manual, 1985. Mem. Am. Soc. Fund Raising Execs., Am. Bus. Women's Assn., Nat. Speakers Assn. (founding pres. Las Vegas chpt. 1984-85, 88—). Club: Windjammer, Toastmasters (ednl. v.p. 1980, adminstrv. v.p. 1983, 88, pres. 1989—). Home: 2754 El Toreador St Las Vegas NV 89109-1710 Office: LHP Investments Inc PMS Rsch Found PO Box 14574 Las Vegas NV 89114-4574

HORNER, MATINA SOURETIS, retired college president, corporate executive; b. Boston, July 28, 1939; d. Demetre John and Christine (Antonopoulos) Souretis; m. Joseph L. Horner, June 25, 1961; children: Tia Andrea, John, Christopher. AB cum laude, Bryn Mawr Coll., 1961; MS, U. Mich., 1963, PhD, 1968; LLD (hon.), Dickinson Coll., 1973; LLD, Mt. Holyoke Coll., 1973; LLD (hon.), U. Pa., 1975, Smith Coll., 1979, Wheaton Coll., 1979, U. Mich., 1989; LHD (hon.), U. Mass., 1973, Tufts U., 1976, U. Hartford, 1980, U. New Eng., 1987, Bentley Coll., 1989, New Eng. Coll., 1989, Pine Manor Coll., 1989, Am. Coll. Greece, 1990; DLitt (hon.), Claremont U. Ctr. and Grad Sch., 1988, Hellenic Coll., 1990; LHD (hon.), Colby Sawyer Coll., 1991. Teaching fellow U. Mich., Ann Arbor, 1962-66, lectr. motivation personality, 1968-69; lectr. social relations Harvard U., Cambridge, Mass., 1969-70, asst. prof. clin. psychology, 1970-72, assoc. prof. psychology, 1972-89, cons. univ. health svcs., 1971-89; pres. Radcliffe Coll., Cambridge, 1972-89, pres. emerita, 1989—; exec. v.p. TIAA-CREF, N.Y.C., 1989—; bd. dirs. Neiman Marcus Group, Boston Edison Co. Co-author: The Challenge of Change, 1983; contbr. psychol. articles on motivation to profl. jours. and chpts. to books. Mem. adv. coun. NSF, 1977-87, chair, 1980-86; bd. trustees Twentieth Century Fund, 1973—, Am. Coll. of Greece, 1983-90, Mass. Eye and Ear Infirmary, 1986-90, Com. for Econ. Devel., 1988—, vice-chmn., 1992; bd. trustees Mass. Gen. Hosp., Inst. Health Professions, 1988—, vice chmn., 1994, chair, 1995, bd. dirs., 1995; bd. dirs. Coun. for Fin. Aid to Edn., 1985-89, Beth Israel Hosp., 1989-95; bd. dirs. Revson Found., 1986-92, chmn., 1992; bd. dirs. Women's Rsch. and Edn. Inst., 1979—, chair rsch. com., 1982—; mem. Coun. on Fgn. Rels., 1984—; exec. com. ACE Bus. Higher Edn. Forum, 1984-86; exec. com. New Eng. Colls. Fund, 1980—, 2d v.p., 1984-85, 1st v.p., 1985-88, pres., 1988-89; mem. nat. panel to study declining test scores Coll. Entrance Exam. Bd., 1976-77; exec. com., chair task force Pres.'s Commn. for Nat. Agenda for 1980s, 1979-80; adv. com. Women's Leadership Conf. on Nat. Security, 1982—; exec. com. Coun. on Competitiveness, 1986-89; chair task force on health care Challenge to Leadership Conf., 1987-89. Recipient Roger Baldwin award Mass. Civil Liberties Union Found., 1982, citation of merit Northeast Region NCCJ, 1982, Career Contbn. award Mass. Psychol. Assn., 1987, Disting. Bostonian award, 1990, Ellis Island medal, 1990. Mem. NOW (nat. corp. adv. bd. of legal def. and edn. fund 1984—), Am. Laryngol. Voice Rsch. and Edn. Found. (pres.), Nat. Inst. Social Scis. (medal for outstanding svc. 1973), Phi Beta Kappa, Phi Delta Kappa, Phi Kappa Phi.

HORNER, MAXINE EDWYNA CISSEL, state legislator; b. Tulsa, Jan. 17, 1933; d. Earl Henry Sr. and Corrine (Burton) Cissel; m. Donald Montell Horner Sr., 1954; children: Shari, Donald Montell Jr. BS in Pers. Mgmt., Langston U. Personnel adminstr. Tulsa Job Corps Ctr., 1971-75; dir. minority women's employment U.S. Dept. Labor, 1975-81; staff asst. U.S Rep. James Jones, Tulsa, 1984-86; mem. Okla. State Senate, 1986—; vice chmn. human resources com. 1987—; mem. bus. and labor, criminal jurisprudence, fin. coms., 1987—; chmn. govt. ops. & agy. oversight com., 1989—; mem. appropriations com., 1989—. Vol. VIP Read Aloud Program; v.p. North Tulsa Heritage Found., 1984—; pres. adv. bd. North Tulsa YMCA, 1985-86; active Corp. Membership Dr. Okla. Sickle Cell Anemia Found., Gov.'s Task Force on Affirmative Action, Simon Estes Scholarship Found., Health and Human Svcs. Com. for Nat. Conf. State Legislators, Children, Families and Social Svcs. Com., Dem. Nat. Platform Com.; chair Okla. Legis. Black Caucus; co-chair 1988 Nat. Black Caucus State Legislators Conf. Tulsa. Recipient spl. recognition Okla. Say No To Hate Crime Coalition, academic scholarship Wiley Coll., Marshall, Tex., 1951, Outstanding Community Svc. awards Tulsa Urban League, North Tulsa Bus. and Profl. Women, Tulsa Job Corps, Sunray DX Oil Co., Omega Psi Phi, grant Harvard U., MPA Program, Mid-Career Profession. Mem. NAACP, LWV, Nat. Assn. Black Social Workers, Dem. Women Action Group, Delta Sigma Theta. Baptist. Home: 3917 N Elgin Ave Tulsa OK 74106-1515 Office: State Capitol Senate House Oklahoma City OK 73105*

HORNER, SALLY MCKAY MELVIN, academic administrator; b. Fayetteville, N.C., Nov. 17, 1935; d. John Stephen and Lila Williams (Chesnutt) Melvin; m. William Wesley Horner, June 9, 1953 (div. 1983); children: Stephanie McKay Horner Toney, John Wesley Horner. BS in Chemistry, U. N.C., 1957, PhD in Inorganic Chemistry, 1961. Rsch. assoc., instr. U. N.C., Chapel Hill, 1961-67; prof. chemistry Meredith Coll., Raleigh, N.C., 1967-78, chmn. dept. chemistry and physics, 1972-78, asst. to pres., dir. instnl. rsch., 1975-78; dean arts and scis. U. Charleston, W.Va., 1978-81, provost, 1978-81, v.p. adminstrn. and fin., 1981-83, acting pres., 1984; vice chancellor planning, adminstrn., and fin. U. S.C.-Coastal Carolina Coll., Myrtle Beach, 1984-93; exec. v.p. Coastal Carolina U., Myrtle Beach, S.C., 1993—; physics cons. Rsch. Triangle Park (N.C.) Inst., 1967; cons. gen. adminstrn. U. N.C., 1977-78, bd. regents, Charleston, 1983-87; spkr. in field; nat. forum Am. Coun. on Edn. Women Adminstrs., Phoenix, 1980; chmn. statewide com. on planning S.C. Commn. on Higher Edn., 1993-96; mem. accreditation teams So. Assn. Colls. and Schs., Atlanta, 1983—; chmn. Fin. Study Com., 1993-95; commr. Commn. Colls. So. Assn. Colls. and Schs., 1994—. Contbr. articles to profl. jours. Exec. com., bd. dirs. YWCA, Charleston, 1983-84; trustee Kanawha Players Theatre, Charleston, 1983-84; bd. of trustees, Tara Hall Home for Boys, S.C., 1993-95, bd. dir., Waccamaw Mental Health Region, S.C., 1993-95; treas. Wheelwright Coun. for Arts, Conway, S.C., 1986—. Mem. Am. Chem. Soc. (section officer 1975-78), S.C. Assn. Women in Higher Edn. (bd. dirs. 1987-92), Myrtle Beach C. of C. (fin. com. 1988-91), Soc. Sigma Xi, Order of Valkyries, Phi Beta Kappa. Home: 608D N 35th Ave Myrtle Beach SC 29577-2856 Office: Coastal Carolina U PO Box 1954 Myrtle Beach SC 29578-1954

HORNER, SANDRA MARIE GROCE (SANDY HEART), educator, poet, songwriter, lyricist; b. Dallas; d. Larnell and Lee Ella (Lacy) Groce; divorced; 1 child, Danielle Marie. BA in Sociol./Philosophy with honors, Calif. State U., Dominguez Hills, 1980; postgrad., UCLA, 1978, 82-83, Consumnes River Coll., 1987, Nat. U., 1991, So. Utah U., 1993. Cert. elem. edn. K-8, Nev., K-A Occ. Std.: Bus. and Office Occupations; cert. instr. credential Calif.; cert. lifetime tchg. credential bus., Calif. Prodn. asst., sec. Paramount Pictures Corp., Hollywood, Calif., 1968-74; instr. L.A. C.C. Dist., 1976-78; tchr. Verbum Dei H.S., L.A., 1977-79; tchr., dept. chair L.A. Unified Sch. Dist., 1975-83; tchr. Sacramento (Calif.) City Unified Sch. Dist., 1985-87; editor, pub. Multi-Family Publs., Sacramento, 1986-89; tchr. Clark County Sch. Dist., Las Vegas, Nev., 1991—; adj. instr. C.C. So. Nev., Las Vegas, 1988-95. Editor: (book/newsletters) Groce Family Newsletter, 1986. Recipient Nat. History award, 1988, Editor's Choice award for poetry, 1996. Mem. AAUW, AAUP, NEA, Internat. Soc. Poets (Disting. Mem.), Am. Bus. Women's Assn., Nev. State Edn. Assn. Democrat. Office: PO Box 36452 Las Vegas NV 89133-6452

HORNER, SHIRLEY JAYE, columnist, writing and publishing consultant; b. N.Y.C., Nov. 15, 1926; d. John and Selma (Sosna) Quentzel; m. Robert George Horner (dec. Nov. 1984); children: Charles Bruce, Neil Brian. BA, NYU, 1946; MA, Columbia U., 1948, MPhil, 1976. Instr. English L.I. U., Bklyn., 1948-49, Seton Hall U., Newark, 1949-51, Queens Coll., L.I., 1953-54, Rutgers U., Newark, 1975-76; prodr. preservation experience programs Middlesex County Cultural and Heritage Commn., North Brunswick, N.J., 1980-81; editor fedn. reports Nat. Fedn. State Humanities Couns., Mpls., 1981-84; columnist, writer About Books The N.Y. Times' N.J. Weekly, N.Y.C., 1979—; lectr. for writing workshops Trenton (N.J.) State Coll., 1984, Seton Hall U., South Orange, N.J., 1990-91, N.J. Libr. Assn., Trenton, 1990-93; book review panelist WOR-TV, 1986; moderator, panelist Holocaust Rescuers in Italy Day Program, 1995; NEH-funded lectr. Seton Hall U., 1991. Co-editor: Ladies at the Cross-roads, 1978 (AAUW award 1978); editor: Conserving Communities: Urban and Suburban, 1979 (N.J. Inst. Tech. award of excellence 1980), (series of booklets) The Preservation Experience in Middlesex County, 1981 (Middlesex County award of distinction 1981; prodr. (TV program) Political Debate for '79 on Suburban Cable, 1979 (Union County award of achievement 1980). Co-chmn. Bicentennial Program for Mountainside, Union County, N.J., 1974-77; del. Union County Rep. Party, Linden, N.J., 1982-88; chmn. evaluation N.J. Com. for Humanities/NEH, New Brunswick, 1979-81; chmn. Union County Planning Bd., 1981-84; mem., publs. advisor N.J. Hist. Commn.; trustee N.J. Lit. Hall of Fame, 1987—, N.J. Ctr. for the Book, Opera at Florham Fairleigh Dickinson U., Madison, N.J., 1992—; mem. historic site com. Soc. Profl. Journalists, 1989; counsellor N.J. Cath. Hist. Records Commn. Recipient 1st Pl. Journalism award N.J. Press Women, 1980, 81; NEH grantee, 1980, 90. Mem. N.J. Literary Hall of Fame, Nat. Book Critics Cir. (bd. dirs. 1990-93, judge for NBCC awards), Images '95 Com. N.J. Ctr. for Visual Arts, Nat. Arts Club, Soc. Profl. Journalists (hist. site com. 1989). Office: care NY Times NJ Weekly 1575 Brookside Rd Mountainside NJ 07092-1601

HORNER, WINIFRED BRYAN, Humanities educator, researcher, consultant, writer; b. St. Louis, Aug. 31, 1922; d. Walter Edwin and Winifred (Kinealy) Bryan; m. David Alan Horner, June 15, 1943; children: Winifred, Richard, Elizabeth, David. AB, Washington U., St. Louis, 1943; MA, U. Mo., 1961; PhD, U. Mich., 1975. Instr. English U. Mo., Columbia, 1966-75, asst. prof. English, 1975-80, chair lower div. studies, dir. composition program, 1974-80, assoc. prof., 1980-83, prof., 1984-85, prof. emerita, 1985—; prof. English, Radford chair rhetoric and composition Tex. Christian U., Ft. Worth, 1985-93, Cecil and Ida Green disting. prof. emerita, 1993-97. Editor: Historical Rhetoric: An Annotated Bibliography of Selected Sources in English, 1980, The Present State of Scholarship in Historical Rhetoric, 1983, Composition and Literature: Bridging the Gap, 1983, Rhetoric and Pedagogy: It's History, Philosophy and Practice, 1995, Rhetoric in a Classical Mode, 1987, Nineteenth-Century Scottish Rhetoric: The American Connection, 1993. Inst. for the Humanities fellow U. Edinburgh, 1987; NEH grantee, 1976, 87. Mem. Internat. Soc. for History Rhetoric (exec. coun. 1986), Rhetoric Soc. Am. (bd. dirs. 1981, pres. 1987), Nat. Coun. Writing Program Adminstrs. (v.p. 1977-85, pres. 1985-87), Coll. Conf. on Composition and Communication (exec. com.), Modern Lang. Assn. (mem. del. assembly 1981). Home: 1904 Tremont Ct Columbia MO 65203 Office: Tex Christian U English Dept Fort Worth TX 76129

HORNICK, KATHERINE JOYCE KAY, artist, small business owner; b. Chelan, Wa., Jan. 2, 1940; d. Donald Dale and Dorothy Eleanor (Tilton) Shipton; m. Dan Lewis Hornick, Apr. 6, 1959; children: Tod A. and Daniel D. Student, Kinman Bus. U., Spokane, 1957-58, Shoreline Community Coll., Bothell, 1972-74. Owner The Traveling Gallery, Bothell, Wa., 1969-74; juror NW Pastel Soc., Redmond, Wa., 1978; resident artist Qraz Gallery, Seattle, 1968-70; represented by Bainbridge Arts & Crafts, Bainbridge Island, Wash., 1989—, Oceanlake Studio Gallery, Lincoln City, Oreg., 1989-92, Ho. of Wyo. Jade and Art, Casper, 1993, 94; Foothills Gallery Sheridan, Wyo., 1993, 94; Sticks and Stones Gallery, Seattle, 1993-94, 95, The Landing, Bainbridge Island, Wash., 1994; owner, operator Katherine J. Hornick Bus. Svcs., Bainbridge Island, 1990—; condr. Bainbridge Island Studio Tour, 1988-92; lectr. Community Groups & Sch. Puget Sound Area, 1969-92; tchr. Kay Hornick Studios Bothell, 1972-75. Exhibited in group shows Kursten Gallery, 1995; represented by Sticks and Stones Gallery, Pioneer Sq., Seattle, 1993-94, 95, Ryan Gallery, Lincoln City, Oreg., 1994, 95; art work appeared on video Earth Day Celebration, 1996. Recipient Hon. Mention Charles & Emma Frye Museum Seattle, 1988, Dorothy Dolph Jensen Meml. award Women Painters of Washington Annual Juried Show. Mem. Nat. League Am. PEN Women (apptd. auditor Seattle 1994), Nat. Mus. Women in Arts (chpt.), Nat. Western Art Assn., Bainbridge Arts and Crafts (bd. dirs. 1989-90).

HORNICKEL, CINDY, film company executive. Sr. v.p. TV prodn. New Line Prodns./New Line Cinema, L.A. Office: New Line Prodns 116 N Robertson Blvd 2d Fl Los Angeles CA 90048*

HORNY, KAREN LOUISE, library administrator; b. Highland Park, Ill., Apr. 22, 1943; d. Hugo O. and Margaret L. (Bailey) H. AB in French Lit. magna cum laude with honors, Brown U., 1965; MLS, U. Mich., 1966. Asst. core libr. Northwestern U., Evanston, Ill., 1966-68, head core collection, 1968-71, asst. univ. libr., 1971-95; dean lib. svcs., prof. libr. sci. S.W. Mo. State U., Springfield, 1995—; pres. U. Mich. Libr. Sci. Alumni Soc., 1985-86; nat. chair U. Mich. Info. and Libr. Studies Fund, 1988-90, rep. Info. and Libr. Sci. U. Mich. Alumni Bd., 1991-94; mem. alumni scholarship coun. Sch. Info. U. Mich., 1996—; mem. adv. coun. U. Ill. Grad. Sch. Libr. Sci., 1975-77; chmn. NOTIS Network Adv. Com. Northwestern U., 1988-95; prof. libr. sci.. Bd. editors Jour. Acad. Librarianship, 1978-81, Advances in Librarianship, 1993—; contbr. chpts. to books, articles to profl. jours. Recipient Disting. Alumnus award U. Mich., 1983. Mem. ALA (coun. 1983-87, div. pres. 1980-81, chmn. div. 1973-74, 76-78, chmn. various com. 1981—, rep. White House conf. com. 1990—), Mo. Libr. Assn., Ill. Libr. Assn. (coms.), Freedom to Read Found., Brown U. Club, U. Mich. Club, Phi Beta Kappa, Phi Kappa Phi, Beta Phi Mu. Episcopalian. Home: 1228 W Beekman Pl Springfield MO 65810 Office: S W Mo State U 901 S National # 175 Springfield MO 65804

HOROWITZ, BEVERLY PHYLLIS, occupational therapist, clinician, consultant, educator; b. N.Y.C., Jan. 10, 1949; d. Abe Joseph and Blanche (Reich) Postman; m. Stuart Daniel Horowitz, July 15, 1973; children: Elizabeth, Sharon, Amy. BA, SUNY, Stony Brook, 1971; MS, Columbia U., 1975; DSW, Fordham U., 1995. Lic. occupational therapist, N.Y. Tchr. English, Thomas Alva Edison High Sch., Jamaica, N.Y., 1972-73; occupational therapist St. Charles Hosp., Port Jefferson, N.Y., 1975-79, Vis. Nurse Svc., Northport, N.Y., 1980—, Gurwin Jewish Geriatric Ctr., Commack, N.Y., 1988-90; pvt. practice Huntington Station, 1980—; occupl. therapist, cons. Hilaire Farm Nursing Home, Huntington Sta., 1980-94, Muscular Dystrophy Assn., Hauppauge, N.Y., 1980-83, 88-89, Brookhaven Health Care Facility, Patchogue, N.Y., 1988; profl. adv. bd. Nat. Multiple Sclerosis L.I. chpt.; co-chair occupl. therapy dept. Touro Coll., Dix Hills, N.Y. Recipient Scholarship Am. Occupational Therapy Found., 1992. Mem. Am. Occupational Therapy Assn., Nat. Coun. on Aging, Gerontol. Soc. Am., N.Y. State Occupational Therapy Assn. (cert. appreciation 1980, 82, 83), N.Y. State Soc. on Aging. Office: Touro College Sch of Health Sci O.T. Dept 1350 Carman Rd Dix Hills NY 11746

HOROWITZ, DIANA J., artist; b. N.Y.C., Sept. 26, 1958; d. Paul and Brenda (Stone) H.; m. Paul G. Conrad, May 21, 1989; 1 child, Julia. BFA, SUNY, Purchase, 1980; postgrad., Tyler Sch. Art/Temple Abroad, Rome, 1983-84; MFA, Bklyn. Coll., 1987. adj. prof. Sch. of Art Inst. Chgo., 1987-89, Tyler Sch. Art, Rome, 1989-90, Bklyn. Coll., 1992-94. Grantee Ingram-Merrill Found., 1988, Pollock-Krasner Found., 1989. 93; recipient Rosenthal Found. award Am. Acad. Arts and Letters, 1996.

HOROWITZ, FRANCES DEGEN, academic administrator, psychology educator; b. Bronx, N.Y., May 5, 1932; d. Irving and Elaine (Moinester) Degen; m. Floyd Ross Horowitz, June 23, 1953; children: Jason Degen, Benjamin Meyer. BA, Antioch Coll., 1954; EdM, Goucher Coll., 1954; PhD, U. Iowa, 1959. Tchr. elem. sch. Iowa City, 1954-56; grad. rsch. asst. Iowa Child Welfare Sta., U. Iowa, 1956-59; asst. prof. psychology So. Oreg. Coll., Ashland, 1959-61; asst. prof. home econs. U. Kans., Lawrence, 1961-62, USHPS rsch. fellow, 1962-63, assoc. prof. dept. human devel. and family life, 1964-69, prof. dept. human devel. and family life, psychology, 1969—, chmn. dept., 1969-75, rsch. assoc., 1964-75, assoc. dean, 1975-78, vice chancellor rsch., grad. studies and pub. svc., also dean grad. sch., 1978-91, dir. Infant Rsch. Lab., 1964-91; pres. Grad. Sch. and Univ. Ctr. CUNY, 1991—; bd. dirs. Feminist Press; guest rsch. assoc. Bur. Child Rsch. U. Kans., and Parsons (Kans.) State Hosp. and Tng. Ctr., summer 1960; vis. prof. dept. psychology Tel Aviv U., 1973-74; guest rschr. dept. pediat. Kaplan Hosp., Rehovot, Israel, 1973-74; vis. lectr. dept. psychology Hebrew U., Jerusalem, 1976, cons. rsch. programs in early edn., 1980—; pres. Ctr. for Rsch., Inc., Lawrence, 1978-91; cons. OAS, 1971, U.S. Office Edn., 1969-73, NIMH, 1979; cons. to early infant stimulation program, Caracas, Venezuela, 1976; lectr. infant devel., day care to local and regional cmty. groups, 1966—; mem. adv. com. Carolina Inst. on Early Edn. of the Handicapped, 1978-83; reviewer NSF, 1978-91; mem. U. Kans. del. to Peoples Republic China, 1980; guest lectr. various profl. groups, univs., 1964—; exch. scholar Chinese Acad. Scis., People's Republic China, 1982; mem. Office Sci. Integrity Rev. Adv. Com. PHS, 1991-93; nominating com. Weizmann Women in Sci. award Am. Com. Weizmann Inst. Sci., 1994; mem. Nat. Task Force Grad. Edn., 1994—; mem. workforce devel. subcom. N.Y.C. Partnership, 1994—; mem. U.S. Nat. Com. for the Internat. Union of Psychol. Sci., 1995-97. Co-editor science watch sect. Am. Psychologist, 1993—; mem. editorial bd. Jour. Devel. Psychology, 1969-75, Early Childhood Edn. Quar., 1974—, Devel. Rev., 1981—; contbr. articles to profl. jours. Trustee L.I. Univ., 1992—; bd. dirs. Cmty. Children's Ctr., 1965-68, Douglas County Vis. Nurse Assn., 1968-69; mem. workforce devel. subcom., N.Y.C. Partnership; mem. coun. advisors, Nat. Ctr. for Children in Poverty. Recipient Trustees award medal Cherry Lawn Sch., Conn., 1971, Outstanding Educator of Am. award, 1973, Disting. Psychologist in Mgmt. award Soc. for Psychologists in Mgmt., 1993; named to Women's Hall of Fame U. Kans., 1974; Ford Found. fellow, 1954, Ctr. for Advanced Studies Behavioral Scis. fellow, Stanford U., 1983-84. recipient Rebecca Rice Alumni award Antioch Coll., 1996. Fellow APA (pres. divsn. devel. psychology 1977-78, chief sci. adviser 1989-93, pres. 1991-94, Centennial award 1992, pres. 1991-94), AAAS; mem. Soc. Rsch. in Child Devel. (editor monographs 1976-83, pres.-elect 1995—), Am. Assn. on Mental Deficiency, North Ctrl. Accrediting Assn. (bd. commrs. 1977-80), Am. Psychol. Found. (pres. 1991-94), Soc. Rsch. in Child Devel. (pres.-elect 1995—), N.Y. Women's Forum (bd. dirs. 1995—), Nat. Assn. of State Univs. and Land-Grant Colls. (chair-elect commn. on human resources and social change 1996), Sigma Xi, Phi Beta Kappa (hon.). Home: 145 Central Park W Apt 4A New York NY 10023-2004 Office: CUNY Grad Sch and U Ctr 33 W 42nd St New York NY 10036-8003

HOROWITZ, LISA BETH, lawyer; b. N.Y.C., May 12, 1954. BA summa cum laude, Tufts U., 1976; JD with honors, George Washington U., 1979. Bar: D.C. 1979. Law clk. to Judge Harry Wood U.S. Ct. Claims, 1979-80; ptnr. Finley, Kumble, Wagner et al, Washington; spl. counsel Arnold & Porter, Washington. Contbr. articles to profl. jours. Office: Arnold & Porter 555 12th St Washington DC 20004-2102*

HOROWITZ, MARY CURTIS See CURTIS, MARY ELLEN

HOROWITZ, WINONA LAURA See RYDER, WINONA

HORRELL, KAREN HOLLEY, insurance company executive, lawyer; b. Augusta, Ga., July 10, 1952; d. Dudley Cornelius and Eleanor (Shouppe) Holley; m. Jack E. Horrell, Aug. 14, 1976. B.S., Berry Coll., 1974; J.D., Emory U., 1976. Bar: Ohio 1977, Ga. 1977. Corp. counsel Great Am. Ins. Co., Cin., 1977-80, v.p., gen. counsel, sec., 1981-85; sr. v.p., gen. counsel, sec., bd. dirs. Great Am. Ins. Co., 1985—; counsel Am. Fin. Corp., 1980-81; gen. counsel numerous subsidiaries Great Ins. Co.; sec., asst. sec. numerous other fin. and ins. cos. Trustee Community Chest, 1987-91, Seven Hills Schs., 1991—, v.p., 1995—; mem. cabinet United Appeal, 1984; bd. dirs. YWCA, 1984-90, v.p. fin., 1986-89; mem. Hamilton County Blue Ribbon Task Force on Child Abuse and Neglect Svcs., 1989-91; trustee Ohio Ins. Inst., 1994—; chair Ohio Joint Underwriting Assn., 1992—. Mem. ABA, Ohio Bar Assn., Cin. Bar Assn. (admissions com. 1978-91, nominating com. 1987-90), Am. Corp. Counsel Assn. Democrat. Home: 3733 Vineyard Pl Cincinnati OH 45226-1728 Office: Great Am Ins Co 580 Walnut St Cincinnati OH 45202-3110

HORSLEY, PAULA ROSALIE, accountant; b. Smithfield, Nebr., Sept. 7, 1924; d. Karl and Clara Margaret (Busse) Fenske; m. Phillip Carreon (dec.); children—Phillip, James, Robert, David, Richard; m. Norby Lumon, Apr. 5, 1980. Student AIB Bus. Coll., Des Moines, 1942-44, YMCA Coll., Chgo., 1944-47, UCLA Extension, 1974. Acctg. mgr. Montgomery Ward & Co., Denver, 1959-62; acct. Harman & Co., C.P.A.s, Arcadia, Calif., 1962-67; controller, officer G & H Transp., Montebello, Calif., 1967-78; comptroller Frederick Weisman Co., Century City, Calif., 1978-80; chief fin. officer Lutheran Shipping, Madang, Papua, New Guinea, 1980-82; prin. Village Bookkeeper, acctg. cons., Monreno Valley, Calif., 1982—; chief fin. officer Insight Computer Products and Tech., Inc., Carlsbad, 1988—. Vol. crises counselor, supr. and instr. Melodyland Hotline, Anaheim, Calif., 1976-79. Mem. NAFE, Riverside Tax Cons., Nat. Soc. Tax Profls., Internat. Platform Assn. Republican. Lutheran. Avocations: church activities, reading, cooking, phys. fitness. Home: 1440 Brentwood Way Hemet CA 92545-7774 Office: Insight Computer Products and Techs Inc 171 Hazel Way San Gabriel CA 91776

HORSLEY, TERI LYNNE, advertising sales representative; b. Hamilton, Ohio, Nov. 23, 1961; d. James Murray and Margaret Jean (McDowell) Hoel; m. Michael Anthony Horsley, Aug. 11, 1984 (div. 1991). BA in Radio/TV/Film, No. Ky. U., 1984; postgrad., Wright State U., 1992—. With Vaughn Auctioneers, Hamilton, Ohio, 1982-85; news reporter/anchor D.J. Sta. WMOH Radio, Hamilton, Ohio, 1983-85; weather graphics asst. Sta. WKRC-TV, Cin., 1984-85; disc jockey Sta. WING Radio, Dayton, Ohio, 1985; news anchor/reporter Sta. WLW Radio, Cin., 1985-87; news stringer ABC News, 1985-87; pres., owner T.J.'s Dee-Jays - D.J. Svc., Fairfield, Ohio, 1987-89; intake interviewer Butler County Forensic Ctr., Hamilton, 1989-90; news dir., talk host Sta. WMOH Radio, Hamilton, 1989-95; news stringer Sta. WCKY News, 1989-94; stringer Sta. WSAI News, 1994-95; adv. sales rep. Thomson Newspapers/Directories, Middletown, Ohio, 1995—; instr. Conn. Sch. Broadcasting, Cin., 1990; radio news anchor Cinn. Newswatch, 1995—. Mem. panel Civitan Cmty. Disaster Team, Fairfield, 1990-91; judge Rotary Sci. Fair, Hamilton, 1991; bd. dirs. Greater Hamilton Safety Coun., 1989—, Family Svcs., 1991-94; lobbyist Arthritis Found., 1993; bd. dirs. Nat. Butler County Mental Health Ctr., 1993-95,local emergency planning com. bd., 1994-95. Mem. Soc. for Human Resources Mgmt., Lions (pres. Hamilton club 1992-93). Republican. Office: Thomson Newspapers/Directories 52 S Broad St Middletown OH 45042-0490

HORSNELL, MARGARET EILEEN, historian; b. St. Paul, Jan. 3, 1928; d. Kenneth George and Mary Elizabeth (Dowd) H. B.A., U. Minn., 1961, M.A., 1963, Ph.D. (Tozer Found. award 1966), 1967. Instr. history U. Minn., 1966-67; mem. faculty Am. Internat. Coll., Springfield, Mass., 1967—, assoc. prof. history, 1976-84, prof., 1984-96, dept. chmn., 1987-96. Recipient McKnight Found. award, 1968; alternate fellow AAUW, 1974-75; Am. Internat. Coll. summer grantee, 1970. Mem. Soc. History Edn., Inst. Early Am. History and Culture, So. Hist. Assn., Am. Legal Studies Assn., Phi Alpha Theta. Author: Spencer Roane: Judicial Advocate of Jeffersonian Principles, 1986; mem. editorial bd. This Constn., 1986-88; contbr. Encyclopedia of American Political Parties and Elections. Mem. adv. panel 500 Yrs. of Am. Clothing, 1989-92. Home: 15 Atwood Rd South Hadley MA 01075-1601

HORST, PAMELA SUE, medical educator, family physician; b. Hershey, Pa., Jan. 23, 1951; d. Ralph H. and Helen (Fry) H.; m. Thomas H. Dennison, Feb. 6, 1982; 1 child, Elizabeth Dennison. BS, Pa. State U., 1972; MD, Pa. State U., Hershey, 1976. Diplomate Am. Bd. Family Practice, Am.

Bd. Emergency Medicine. Resident in family practice Shadyside Hosp., Pitts., 1979; family physician North Jefferson Health Svcs., Clayton, N.Y., 1979-82; physician emergency rm. Geisinger Med. Ctr., Philipsburg, Pa., 1982-84; asst. prof. family medicine Albany (N.Y.) Med. Coll., 1984-88; assoc. prof. health sci. ctr. SUNY, Syracuse, 1988—; med. dir. family practice ctr. St. Joseph's Hosp. Health Ctr., Syracuse, 1989—, assoc. residency dir. family practice residency, Syracuse, 1990—. Author: (with others) Ambulatory Medicine, 1993, Manual of Family Practice, 1996; reviewer Am. Family Physician, Jour. Family Practice. Mem. pub. issues com., bd. dirs. ctrl. N.Y. chpt. Am. Cancer Soc.; past v.p. bd. dirs. Home Aides Ctrl. N.Y., Syracuse. Mem. Am. Acad. Family Physicians (instr. advanced life support in obstetrics 1992—), Soc. Tchrs. Family Medicine. Office: St Joseph's Health Ctr Family Practice Residency 301 Prospect Ave Syracuse NY 13203-1807

HORSTMAN, FREDRIKA A. (FRITZI HORSTMAN), writer; b. Chgo., Dec. 11, 1962; d. James Richard Horstman and Dorothy Ann Bernis. BA, Vassar Coll., 1984. Profl. rollerskater Coca Cola, Tokyo, 1989. Author: Oliver Stone: A Biography, 1993, The Book of B'Goos, 1996, The PMS Cookbook, 1996; dir.: (short film-documentary) Downtown, 1993 (award USA Film Festival 1993), (short dramatic film) Split, 1993, (documentary film) Huctwa Integwa, 1994; writer, dir.: (feature dramatic film) Take A Number, 1996. Mem. The Group.

HORSTMAN, SUZANNE RUCKER, financial planner; b. Coral Gables, Fla., June 27, 1945; d. Thomas John, Jr. and June Ethel Agusta (Stones) R.; m. James Winter Horstmen, Dec. 28, 1989. BBA, Fla. Atlantic U., 1971, MBA, 1975. CFP; lic. real estate agt. Assoc. dir. Am. Soc. Cons. Pharmacists, 1971-73; chpt. specialist Epilepsy Found. Am., 1973-74; assoc. dir. devel. Fairfax Hosp. Assn. Found., Springfield, Va., 1974-81; dir. devel. Arlington (Va.) Hosp. Found., 1982-86; prin. Suzanne June Rucker, Cert. Fin. Planner, Falls Church, Va., 1986-90; dir. devel. Phoexixville Healthcare Found., 1990-94, Tri-County TEC Found., 1994-96, cons., 1996—; instr. George Washington U., Washington; seminar spkr. in field. Bd. dirs. Ronald McDonald House, Wilmington and Washington, Salvation Army Aux. Washington, Rep. Working Women's Forum. Fellow Assn. Health Care Philanthropy. Republican.

HORSTMANN, DOROTHY MILLICENT, physician, educator; b. Spokane, Wash., July 2, 1911; d. Henry J. and Anna (Hunold) H. AB, U. Calif., 1936, MD, 1940; DSc (hon.), Smith Coll., 1961; MA (hon.), Yale, 1961; D Med. Scis. (hon.), Women's Med. Coll. of Pa., 1963. Intern San Francisco City and County Hosp., 1939-40, asst. resident medicine, 1940-41; asst. resident medicine Vanderbilt U. Hosp., 1941-42; Commonwealth Fund fellow, sect. preventive medicine Sch. Medicine, Yale U., New Haven, 1942-43; instr. preventive medicine Sch. Medicine, Yale U., 1943-44, 45-47, asst. prof., 1948-52, assoc. prof., 1952-56, assoc. prof. preventive medicine and pediatrics, 1956-61, prof. epidemiology and pediatrics, 1961-69, John Rodman Paul prof. epidemiology, prof. pediatrics, 1969-82; John Rodman Paul prof. epidemiology, prof. pediatrics emeritus, sr. research scientist Sch. Medicine Yale U., 1982—; instr. medicine U. Calif., San Francisco, 1944-45. Recipient Albert Coll. award, 1953, Gt. Heart award Variety Club Phila., 1968, Modern Medicine award, 1974; James D. Bruce award ACP, 1975, Thorvald Madsen award State Serum Inst. (Denmark), 1977, Maxwell Finland award Infectious Disease Soc.-Am., 1978, Disting. Alumni award U. Calif. Med. Sch., 1979, NIH fellow Nat. Inst. Med. Rsch., London, 1947-48. Master ACP; fellow Am. Acad. Pediatrics (hon.); mem. NAS, Infectious Disease Soc. Am. (pres. 1975), Am. Soc. Clin. Investigation, Am. Epidemiol. Soc. (v.p. 1974-75), Am. Pediatric Soc., Am. Soc. Virology (coun. 1983-84), Soc. Epidemiol. Rsch., Internat. Epidemiol. Assn., Royal Soc. Medicine (hon., epidemiology/preventive medicine sect.), Conn. Acad. Sci. and Engring., European Assn. Against Virus Diseases, South African Soc. Pathologists (hon.), Cuban Soc. Hygiene & Epidemiology (hon.), Sigma Delta Epsilon (hon.). Home: 11 Autumn St New Haven CT 06511-2220 Office: Yale U Sch Medicine Epidemiology and Pub Health PO Box 208034 New Haven CT 06520-8034

HORTON, GWENDOLYN, nursing educator emeritus; b. Moose Jaw, Sask., Can., June 7, 1914; came to U.S., 1919; d. Orville A. and Myrtle (King) H. AA, L.A. City Coll.; BS, Calif. State U., L.A., 1968, MS, 1974. RN; cert. pub. health. Policewoman L.A. Police Dept., 1940-45; prof. nursing L.A. City Coll., Trade Teck Coll., East L.A. Coll., Harbor Coll.; prof. nursing L.A. Pierce Coll., 1972-83, prof. emeritus, 1983—. Mem. Descanso Gardens Guild, LaCanada, Calif., 1953-56, San. Fernando Valley Bd. Realtors, Van Nuys, Calif., 1980-91; bd. dirs. Owners of Subsidized Housing; pres. L.A. Garden Club, 1988-90. Mem. Water and Power Assocs. L.A. (bd. dirs. 1989-94), Apt. Assn. Greater L.A. (v.p. 1990-91, bd. dirs.), Calif. Nurses Assn., L.A. Cinema Club, L.A. Breakfast Club (emergency aid com.), Los Feliz Rep. Women Federated, So. Calif. Rep. Women, Calif. Rep. Women. Home: 2041 N Vermont Ave Los Angeles CA 90027-1952

HORTON, JUNE CAROL, lawyer; b. L.A., June 18, 1957. BA, Mt. Holyoke Coll., 1979; JD, U. So. Calif., 1983. Atty. Metro-Goldwyn-Mayer, Culver City, Calif., 1983-86; v.p. William Morris Agy., Beverly Hills, Calif., 1986—. *

HORTON, LAUREN MALPICA, elementary school educator; b. Little Rock, July 31, 1968; d. Lawrence Payne and Hilda (Hancock) Malpica; m. Timothy Eldridge Horton, June 20, 1992. BS in Elem. Edn., U. Ark., 1990; MSEd in Reading, U. Ctrl. Ark., 1994. Cert. elem. tchr., K-12 reading tchr., N.C. 3d grade tchr. Greenbrier (Ark.) Elem. Sch., 1990-92; interim tchr. Johnson County Schs., Mountain City, Tenn., 1992-93; substitute tchr. Watauga County Schs., Boone, N.C., 1993, tchr.'s asst., 1993-96; 3d grade tchr. Blowing Rock (N.C.) Sch., 1996—. Bd. dirs. ASU Wesley Found., Boone, 19946: children's ch. coord. and tchr. Boone United Meth. Ch., 1993—. Mem. Internat. Reading Assn., PEO Sisterhood (v.p. 1992), STAR Reading Coun., Boone Svc. League, Kappa Kappa Gamma (corr. sec. 1990—, alumna). Home: 171 Ivy Dr # 8 Boone NC 28607 Office: Blowing Rock Sch Sunset Dr Blowing Rock NC 28605

HORTON, MADELINE MARY, financial planner, consultant; b. Chgo., Mar. 1, 1939; d. James P. and Priscilla Mary (Caruso) Fiduccia; m. Richard J. Dickman, July 7, 1962 (div. 1981); children: James Earl, Suzanne Dickman Noel; m. Larry B. Horton, June 30, 1984 (dec. 1993). BA in Math. cum laude, Rosary Coll., River Forest, Ill., 1960; MS in Math., U. Miami, Coral Gables, Fla., 1962; postgrad., U. Va., 1974-78. Cert. fin. planner. Instr. in math. U. Miami, Coral Gables, 1962-63, Miami Dade C.C., 1964-65, St. Patrick's High Sch., 1968-69; prin. Dickman Deductions, Charlottesville, Va., 1974-77; instr. devel. math. Piedmont Community Coll., Charlottesville, Va., 1974-78; health affairs planner U. Va. Med. Ctr., Charlottesville, 1978-80; zone mgr. Investors Diversified Svcs., Inc., Charlottesville, 1980-83; fin. cons. Merrill Lynch, Charlottesville, 1983-86; mgr., fin. cons. Prudential-Bache Securities, Inc., Charlottesville, 1986-87; investment broker Wheat First Securities Inc., Charlottesville, 1987; pres., fin. cons., founder Horton Fin. Svcs. Inc., Charlottesville, 1987—. Humor columnist Charlottesville Daily Progress, 1971; featured in article Va. Bus. monthly mag., 1988. Mem. Internat. Mgmt. Coun. (sec. Charlottesville chpt. 1986-88, v.p. 1988-89), Inst. Cert. Fin. Planners, Internat. Platform Assn., Kappa Gamma Pi. Republican. Roman Catholic. Home: 3346 Arbor Terrace Charlottesville VA 22901-7227 Office: Horton Fin Svcs Inc 1160 Pepsi Pl Ste 300 Charlottesville VA 22901-0807

HORTON, PATRICIA MATHEWS, violist and violinist, artist; b. Bklyn., Mar. 6, 1932; d. Edward Joseph and Margaret (Briggs) Mathews; m. Ernest H. Horton Jr., Mar. 6, 1982; 1 stepchild, Carol Horton Tremblay. Student in viola, William Primrose Master Class, 1980; student, Glendale (Calif.) C.C., 1981-90, 93, Art Ctr. Coll. Design, Pasadena, Calif., 1988-93; student in painting composition, Peter Liashkov, L.A., 1993—. Profl. musician on violin and viola, 1951-86. Played with New Orleans Philharm., 1959-61, U.S. Tour of San Francisco Ballet, 1965, L.A. Civic Light Opera, 1974-80, Harlem Ballet, 1984; played L.A. engagements of Bolshoi Ballet Co., 1975, Am. Ballet Theatre, 1974-80, N.Y.C. Opera, 1974-80, Royal Ballet of London, 1978, Alicia Alonzo's Cuban Balet, 1979, Deutsche Oper Berlin, 1985; played on motion picture and TV soundtrack recs., through 1986. Active Dem. Nat. Com., Women's Caucus for Art. Mem. Am. Fedn. Musicians (life), Alpha Gamma Sigma.

HORTON, ROBERTA LAZARUS, lawyer; b. Washington, Feb. 22, 1961. BA summa cum laude, Yale U., 1983, JD, 1986. Bar: Ill. 1988. Law clk. to Hon. Sam J. Ervin III Dist. Ct. Appeals (4th cir.), 1986-87; ptnr. Arnold & Porter, Washington. Mem. Phi Beta Kappa. Office: Arnold & Porter 555 12th St NW Washington DC 20004-1202*

HORTON, THELMA WHITE, educational administrator, author; b. Blyesville, Ark., Feb. 7, 1949; d. William Soloman and Corrine (Carrigans) White; m. Charles D. Horton, May 20, 1970 (div. 1991); children: Corrine Daniel, Tiffany Louise, Charles William. student Fla. Internat. U., BSW, Boise State U., 1975; hon. doctorate degree, World U. Lead tchr. Dade County Elem. Schs., Miami Dade C.C., Miami, 1980—; owner, dir. Hi School Day Care and Learning Ctr., Cutler Ridge, Fla., 1981—; lead tchr. gifted Naranja Elem. Sch.; owner Charisma, Fla.; tutor English, Perrine, Fla., 1982—; cons. WESTAT Rsch., Barr Industries, Perrine, 1981—, The Rand Co., Student Travel Svc. student placement, temp. Dade County Pub. Schs., Peskoe Elem. Active Boy Scouts U.S., PTSA, ARC; mem. usher bd. Martin Meml. Meth. Ch.; st. capt. Neighborhood Crime Watch; advocate for Nat. Tchr. Cert., 1995-96. Recipient Equity and Excellence award Magnet Innovative Programs. Mem. The Exec. Female, Children's Advocates (pres. 1975-83), United Tchrs. Dade County, Alumni Assn. Boise State U., Inst. Children's Lit., Miami C. of C., Fla. Assn. for the Gifted, Kappa Delta Pi. Home: 15905 SW 105th Ct Miami FL 33157-1571 Office: 13990 SW 264th St Homestead FL 33033

HORVATH, CAROL MITCHELL, home health administrator; b. Cleve., Aug. 7, 1940; d. Ralph Douglas and Hazel (Carpenter) Mitchell; m. William R. Horvath, Aug. 2, 1958; children: Kenneth R., Rosalie C. Stallcup. AS, Tulsa Jr. Coll., 1977, AD Nursing, 1977; BS in Profl. Arts, St. Joseph Coll., 1992; MPH, Okla. U., 1995. Cert. Gerontological Nurse. Cons. home health McCurtain Meml. Hosp., Idabele, Okla., 1989; dir. home health Okla. Home Health, Cleveland, Okla., 1980-1985; regional adminstr. Okla. Home Health, Cleveland, 1985-96; home health adminstr. Cleveland Area Hosp., 1985-96; dir. Helping Hands Program COEDD Grant Program for Aging, 1990-96; CPR instr. trainer AHA, 1990-91; nursing cholesterol trainer, 1990-96, home health nursing aide instr., 1990-96; cons. home health Mission Hill Hosp., Shawnee, Okla.; dir. home health East Tex. Med. Ctr., Mt. Vernon, 1996—. Mem. profl. adv. com. Area Agy. on Aging; active Cleve. Sch. Edn. coalition, Elderly Edn. coalition, Health Promotion coalition, Okla. Bus. and Aging Leadership coalition. Mem. Home Health Assn., Rehab. Assn., Am. Heart Assn., Pawnee County Svc. Network, Am. Coll. Healthcare Execs., Pub. Health Assn., Okla. Nurses Assn., Okla. Health and Welfare Assn. Home: 113 Oak St Mount Vernon TX 75457 Office: East Tex Med Ctr Mt Vernon Home Health Box 477-500 Hwy 37 South Mount Vernon TX 75457-3033

HORVATH, FRANCES LOUISE, dean; b. Cleve., Mar. 1, 1940; d. Florian Al and Walburga Marie (Wolf) H. BS, Marygrove Coll., 1962; MD, St. Louis U., 1967. Intern St. Louis U. Hosp., 1967-68; resident in pediat. Cardinal Glennon Hosp., St. Louis, 1968-70; pediatrician City of St. Louis Dept. Health & Hosp., 1971-73; chmn. dept. physician asst. edn. St. Louis U. Sch. Allied Health Professions, 1973-80, prof., dean, 1980—; commr. Commn. on Accreditation for Allied Health Ednl. Programs, Chgo., 1994—; cons. in field. Mem. editl. bd. Jour. Allied Health, 1983-91; contbr. articles to profl. jours. Chmn. com. on cmty. health and edn. ARC, St. Louis, 1989-90, emergency tng. com., 1982-89. St. Louis U. fellow, 1969-71; recipient Disting. Svc. award Assn. Physician Asst. Programs, 1988. Fellow Assn. Schs. Allied Health Professions; mem. AMA (chmn. com. on allied health edn. and accreditation 1990-92), Am. Acad. Physician Assts. (hon.). Office: St Louis Univ 1504 S Grand Blvd Saint Louis MO 63104

HORVATH, LYNDA, mortgage company executive. V.p., prod. acquisition Federal Nat. Mortgage Assn., Washington, D.C., now sr. v.p., capital markets. Office: Fed Nat Mortgage Assn 4000 Wisconsin Ave NW Washington DC 20016-2806*

HORWITZ, KATHRYN BLOCH, molecular biologist; b. Sosua, Dominican Republic, Feb. 20, 1941; came to U.S., 1952; d. Werner Meyerstein and Olga (Schlesinger) Bloch; m. Lawrence David Horwitz, June 14, 1964; children: Phillip Andrew, Carolyn Anita. BA, Barnard Coll., 1962; MS, NYU, 1966; PhD, U. Tex. Southwestern Med. Sch., Dallas, 1975; postdoctoral, U. Tex. Sch. Medicine, San Antonio, 1978. Instr. U. Tex. Sch. Medicine, San Antonio, 1978-79; asst. prof. U. Colo. Med. Sch., Denver, 1979-84, assoc. prof., 1984-89, prof. of medicine, pathology and molecular biology, 1989—; cellular physiology panel NSF, 1985-88; biochem. endocrinology study sect. NIH, 1989-93; mem. Pres.'s Cancer Panel Spl. Commn. on Breast Cancer, 1992, Breast Cancer Task Force, NIH, 1981-84. Author over 150 breast cancer and steroid receptors research papers, books; assoc. editor, editl. bd. for several scientific jours. Chair, sci. adv. bd. Cancer League of Colo., 1987-91; organizer Keystone Symposium on Steroid Receptors. Recipient Nat. Bd. award Med. Coll. Pa., 1986, Wilson Stone award M.D. Anderson Hosp. and Tumor Inst., 1976, Rsch. Career Devel. award Nat. Cancer Inst., 1981-86, MERIT award NIH, 1992, The U. Helsinki medal and Second Siltravouri Lectr., Finland, 1993; grantee NSF, Am. Cancer Soc., Nat. Found. Cancer Rsch. Dept. of the Army. Mem. Endocrine Soc. (program com. 1989-91, nominating com. 1989-91, chair 1991, coun. 1992-95), Am. Fedn. Clin. Rsch., Am. Soc. Cell Biology, Am. Assn. Cancer Rsch. (program com. 1994-95, state legis. com. 1993—), Western Soc. Clin. Investigation, AAAS, Am. Soc. Biochemistry and Molecular Biology. Democrat. Jewish. Office: U Colo Dept Medicine PO Box B151 Denver CO 80201-0151

HORWITZ, MARY ANN, bank executive. Sr. v.p. consumer bank Calif. Fed. Bank, L.A. Office: Calif Fed Bank 5700 Wilshire Blvd Los Angeles CA 90036*

HOSHIELD, SUSAN LYNN, pediatric nurse practitioner; b. Grand Rapids, Mich., Nov. 15, 1952; d. Edmund George and Barbara Ann (Malec) Brochu; m. Robert D. Williams (div.); 1 child, Amy Marie; m. Dennis Frank Hoshield; stepchildren: Audrey, Sherrie, Eric. AA, North Cen. Mich. Coll., 1972, ADN, 1978; BSN, Lake Superior State U., 1990; MSN, U. Mich., 1993. RN, PNP. Sales mgr. Petoskey Floral & Bridal, Petoskey, Mich., 1968-77; staff nurse NICU No. Mich. Hosp., Petoskey, 1978-88, primary nurse II/NICU, 1989-90, regional perinatal coord., 1990-95, infant apnea nurse coord., 1990-95; nursing faculty Lake Superior State U., Sault Ste. Marie, Mich., 1995-96; pediatric nurse practitioner Burns Clinic Med. Ctr., Petoskey, Mich., 1996—; adv. bd. Mich. SIDS Alliance, Lansing, 1993—; chairperson Children's Health Fair, Petoskey, 1991-95; adj. faculty Lake Superior State U., Sault Ste Marie, Mich., 1994. Author: (pamphlet) Infant Apnea Clinic, 1994. Adv. bd. sex edn. curriculum Harbor Springs, Mich., 1992—; mem. Immunization Task Force, Charlevoix, Mich., 1994; adv. com. Mich. State U. Coop. Ext., Petoskey, 1992-95, Adolescent Health, Charlevoix, 1990-93. Vol. Spotlight, Mich. SIDS Alliance, 1994; hon. chairperson March of Dimes WalkAmerica, 1994, 95. Mem. AWHONN, Perinatal Assn. of Mich. (bd. dirs., sec. 1993-95), Mich. Assn. Apnea Profls., Nurses Assn. Pediat. Nurses and Practitioners, Mich. Nurses Assn. of Pediat. Nurses and Practitioners. Home: 421 Emmet St Petoskey MI 49770-2603

HOSKINS, MABLE ROSE, secondary education educator, English language educator; b. Natchez, Miss., May 23, 1945; d. Johnny and Josephine (Jones) Reynolds; m. Charles Hoskins, Dec. 23, 1973 (div. Dec. 5, 1989). BA in English, Jackson State Coll., 1967; MED, Miss. State U., 1979, Ednl. Specialist, 1982. Tchr. English Natchez (Miss.) Pub. Schs., 1968-70, Quitman (Miss.) Consol. Schs., 1971-81, Meridian (Miss.) Schs., 1981—; bd. dirs. Pub. Employee's Retirement Sys., Jackson, 1988-92, Meridian Bonita Lakes Authority. Co-author: (teaching units) Miss. Writers Teaching Units for Secondary English, 1988; consulting editor: (book) Mississippi Writers-An Anthology, 1991. Newsletter editor, co-editor Assn. of Meridian Educators, 1988-92; mistress of ceremonies Alpha Kappa Alpha Sorority, Meridian, 1985-90; Children's Discovery, vol. coord. Meridian Coun. for the Arts, 1990. Named S.T.A.R. tchr. Miss. Econ. Coun., 1980, Tchr. of Yr., Meridian Pub. Schs., 1988, 94, finalist Miss. Hall of Master Tchrs., 1994. Mem. NEA, Miss. Assn. Educators (Mem. of Yr. 1988, bd. dirs. 1990-93), Miss. Coun. Tchrs. English, Nat. Coun. Tchrs. English, Phi Kappa Phi, Phi Delta Kappa. Baptist. Home: 1409 37th Ave Meridian MS 39307-6004 Office: Meridian H S 2320 32nd St Meridian MS 39305-4657

HOSKINS, SUSAN BONARD, writer; b. Orange, N.J., Jan. 10, 1947; d. Ralph Peter and Susan Jane (Peabody) Bonard; m. Charles John Tiensch 3d, Aug. 9, 1971; children: Christian D., Justin T.; m. Amos Earl Hoskins, Feb. 17, 1979; 1 child, Melissa K. Cert. Dental Asst., Wayne U., Chgo., 1965; student, Long Ridge Writers Group, 1995. Lic. real estate salesperson, N.H. Dental asst. Dr. Robert Eskow, Livingston, N.J., 1972-74; edn. program dir., tchr., actress Brundage Park Playhouse, Randolph, N.J., 1986-90; real estate salesperson Prudential-Marsha Foster Realtors, Milford, N.H., 1994—. Author: A Blink of an Eye, 1993, Journey's End, 1994, Descent into Hell, 1994, Luce, 1994, Adrian Wolf, 1995, The Enchantress, 1995, Black Wolf, 1995, The Reckoning, 1996. Mem. Amherst Hist. Soc., 1993—; dance chairperson Milford Pumpkin Festival, 1992; active Long Ridge Writers Group, West Redding, Conn., 1995—. Mem. Mystery Writers of Am. Republican. Presbyterian. Home: Journey's End 23 Old Manchester Rd Amherst NH 03031

HOSKINSON, CAROL ROWE, educator; b. Toledo, Mar. 10, 1947; d. Webster Russell and Alice Mae (Miller) Rowe; m. C. Richard Hoskinson, June 8, 1969; 1 child, Leah Nicole. BS in Edn., Ohio State U., 1968; MEd, Ga. State U., 1972. Tchr. Whitehall City Schs., Columbus, Ohio, 1968-69; tchr. DeKalb County Schs., Decatur, Ga., 1969-74, Mt. Olive (N.J.) Twp. Schs., 1974-75, DeKalb County Schs., Decatur, 1975-79; Fulton County Schs., Atlanta, 1991—; substitute tchr. DeKalb County Schs., Decatur, 1980-91, Fulton County Schs., Atlanta, 1989-91. Pres. Esther Jackson PTA, Roswell, Ga., 1988-89; treas. Women of the Ch., Roswell, 1983-84; chairperson local sch. adv. Esther Jackson, Roswell, 1989-91; del. Women and Constn. Conv., Atlanta, 1988; mem. Supt.'s Adv. Com.; local sch. adv. Holcomb Bridge Mid. Sch.; active Chattahoochee H.S. Booster Club; corr. sec. Chattahoochee H.S. PTSA, v.p. Cheers Club; VIP dedicated hostess Olympic Games, Atlanta, 1996. Named Vol. of Yr. Fulton County Schs., 1988-89. Mem. AAUW (v.p. Atlanta chpt. 1970-89, edn. scholarship honoree 1984, 86), Atlanta Lawn Tennis Assn., Roswell Hist. Soc., Roswell Hist. Preservation Commn., Ga. Sci. Tchrs. Assn., Nat. Mid. Sch. Assn., Zoo Atlanta, High Mus. Art, Ga. PTA, Ohio State Alumni Assn., Ga. State Alumni Assn., Profl. Assn. Educators. Democrat. Presbyterian. Home: 1670 Branch Valley Dr Roswell GA 30076-3007

HOSLER, BARBARA LEE, principal; b. Waterloo, Iowa, Nov. 7, 1955; d. Kenneth Bourdeaux and MaryLee (Meewes) Kuttler. BA, U. No. Colo., 1978, MA, 1985. Lic. tchr., prin., Colo. Tchr. Jefferson County Schs., Golden, Colo., 1978-89, asst. prin., 1989-91, prin., 1991—; instr. Aims Coll., Greeley, Colo., 1985; trainer QuickPen Internat., Englewood, Colo., 1991-96. Vol. coord. March of Dimes, Denver, 1987-90; vol. Am. Cancer Soc., Denver, 1992-96. Mem. Nat. Assn. Elem. Sch. Prins., Colo. Assn. Sch. Execs., U. No. Colo. Alumni Assn. (amb. 1991-96). Office: Coronado Elem Sch 7922 S Carr St Littleton CO 80123

HOSLEY, MARGUERITE CYRIL, volunteer; b. Houston, July 29, 1946; d. Frederick Willard and Marguerite Estella (Arisman) Collister; m. Richard Allyn Hosley II, July 18, 1968; children: Richard A. III, Sean Frederick, Michelle Cyril. BS in Edn., U. Houston, 1968; postgrad., Tex. A&M U., 1970-71. Cert. tchr., Tex. Tchr. Sharpstown High Sch., Houston, 1968-69, Bryan (Tex.) High Sch., 1969-71; ins. asst. Farmers Ins., Stafford, Tex., 1981-83; adminstrv. asst., fin. asst. Christ United Meth. Ch., Sugarland, Tex., 1984-92; mem. Planning and Zoning Commn. City of Sugarland, 1995—. Pres. bd. dirs. Ft. Bend Boys Choir, 1984-85; docent Bayou Bend Collection and Gardens, Houston Mus. Fine Arts, 1994—; bd. dirs. Am. Cancer Soc., 1990—; pres. Am. Cancer Soc. League, 1993-94; mem. Lone Staar Stomp com. Ft. Bend Mus. Assn., 1991-96; parent vol. Ft. Bend Ind. Schs., 1980-94; raffle chmn. Ft. Bend Drug Alliance Gala, 1989; newsletter chmn. Am. herat Asn. Guild, 1990-91, v.p., 1992-93. Named Ft. Bend Outstanding Woman, Ft. Bend County, 1992. Mem. Houston Ladies' Tennis Assn. (team capt.), Ft. Bend Mus., Sweetwater Country Club (bd. govs. 1990-93), Sweetwater Women's Assn. (treas. 1985-87, pres. 1987-88), Friends of Casa (charter mem.), Aggie Moms Club, Chi Omega Alumnae. Republican. Methodist. Home: 427 W Alkire Lake Dr Sugar Land TX 77478-3527

HOSMER, MICHELLE STERN, special education educator; b. St. Paul, Oct. 28, 1955; d. Alvin Fredrick and Osk Joyce (Johnson) Stern; divorced; children: Banjamin Lee, Christopher Michael. AA, Brevard C.C., 1993; BS cum laude, U. Ctrl. Fla., 1995. Exceptional edn. tchr. specific learning disabilities Brevard County Sch. Bd., Melbourne, Fla., 1990—. Active Roger Dobson Re-election for County Commr., Merritt Island, Fla.; advancement chair Boy Scouts Am., 1987—; fundraising chair Brevard County Apple Corp., 1987—; asst. youth worker Faith Luth. Ch., 1993—. Mem. Student Coun. Exceptional Children, Phi Theta Kappa, Kappa Delta Pi. Home: 5315 Broad Acres St Merritt Island FL 32953

HOSPY, PATRICIA L., chiropractor; b. Chgo.; d. Joseph F. and Verna M. H. DC cum laude, Life Chiropractic Coll. West, 1992. Ins. agt. Automobile Club So. Calif., Torrance, 1981-87; regional sales mgr. Sebastian No. Calif., Walnut Creek, 1993-94; chiropractor pvt. practice, San Mateo, Calif., 1992—; asst. prof. Life Chiropractic Coll. West, San Lorenzo, Calif., 1995—. Columnist Modern Salon Mag., Lincolnshire, Ill., 1995—. Mem. Foster City (Calif.) Fitness Resource Group, 1995—. Mem. Am. Chiropractic Assn., Calif. Chiropractic Assn., Sigma Chi Psi, Pi Tau Delta. Office: 1407 S B St San Mateo CA 94402

HOTCHKISS, ANDRA RUTH, lawyer; b. Beloit, Wis., Aug. 6, 1946; d. Hilton Delos and Katherine Ruth (Huffer) H.; m. Robert K. Byron, May 31, 1977 (dec. 1978); m. Gerald Thomas Marsischky, Feb. 25, 1990. BA cum laude, Oberlin Coll., 1968; JD, Harvard U., 1971. Bar: Mass. 1971, Calif. 1982, U.S. Dist. Ct. Mass. 1975, U.S. Ct. of Fed. Claims 1987. Dep. gen. counsel Mass. Dept. Pub. Health, Boston, 1971-78; asst. atty. gen. Mass. Dept. Atty. Gen., Boston, 1978-85; assoc. Behar & Kalman, Boston, 1985-88; assoc. Sullivan & Worcester, Boston, 1989-92, ptnr., 1992—; instr. legal writing Harvard U., Cambridge, Mass., 1984, 85. Mem. adv. com. Robert K. Byron Pub. Svc. award, 1978—; elected rep. Oberlin Coll. Nat. Alumni Coun., 1973-83, reunion gift com. co-chair, 1993, 96—. Mem. ABA, Mass. Bar Assn., Boston Bar Assn., Nat. Health Lawyers Assn., Women's Bar Assn. Mass., Civil Liberties Union Mass. Office: Sullivan & Worcester One Post Office Sq Boston MA 02109

HOTELLING, BARBARA ANTHONY, women's health nurse, educator; b. Greensboro, N.C., Nov. 14, 1949; d. William Thomas and Audree Faye (Dodson) Anthony; m. Harold Hotelling, May 4, 1974; children: Harold, George, James, Claire, Charles. BSN, U. N.C., 1972. RN Mich. Staff nurse N.C. Meml. Hosp., Chapel Hill, 1972-73; instr. Durham (N.C.) Tech. Inst., 1974-76; instr., coord. Lexington (Ky.) Assn. for Parent Edn., 1980-84; childbirth instr. Crittenton Hosp., Rochester Hills, Mich., 1984-89; dir. Birth and Parenting Educators, Rochester, Mich., 1989—; maternal, child, gynecol. nurse Anthony Nehra, MD, Rochester Hills, Mich., 1991—; perinatal coach, birth companion Oakland Family Svcs., Pontiac, Mich., 1985-92; teen childbirth educator Pontiac Northern H.S., 1985-92; childbirth educator, doula trainer, Oakland Family Svcs., Pontiac, 1985—; adv. bd. Nat. Assn. Childbirth Assts., San Jose, Calif., 1989—. Contbg. journalist Internat. Childbirth Ednl. Assn. Jour. Educator, activities supporter, Rochester Comty. Schs., 1984—. Vol. of Month Oakland Press, Pontiac, 1991. Fellow Am. Coll. Childbirth Educators; mem. Doulas of N. Am. (cert. doula, pres.-elect, 1994, pres. 1995—), Assn. Women's Health, Obstetric and NeoNatal Nurses, Internat. Childbirth Edn. Assn., Am.Soc. for Psychoprophylaxis in Obstetrics. Episcopalian. Home: 2112 Bretton Dr S Rochester Hills MI 48309-2952

HOTHERSALL, LORETTA ANNE, maternal/child health nurse; b. Bklyn., July 13, 1952; d. Edward Alfred and Rose (Laurino) O'Donnell; m. John Hothersall, Mar. 11, 1972; children: Margaret, John, Colleen. Diploma in nursing, Kings County Hosp. Ctr., Bklyn., 1972; paralegal cert., L.I. U., 1989; BS in Profl. Arts, St. Joseph's Coll., Windham, Maine, 1993; grad., Simmons Coll., Boston, 1996. RN; cert. BLS, Maine; RN, N.Y., Maine; cert. bereavement counselor, N.Y., cert. inpatient obstetrics. Staff nurse premature nursery Kings County Hosp., 1972-76; staff nurse NICU Maimonides Med. Ctr., Bklyn., 1979-86; staff nurse maternal child Luth. Med. Ctr., Bklyn., 1987-88, staff nurse spl. care nursery, 1988-90; staff nurse maternity Maine Med. Ctr., Portland, 1990-91, clin. level III nurse, 1991-92, asst. head nurse, 1992-94, coord. H.O.M.E. care early discharge program,

1994-95, staff nurse maternity, 1995—, nurse practitioner-diabetes, 1996—; instr. obstet. teen clinic Maine Med. Ctr., 1990—, BLS instr., 1991—, coord. antepartum support group, 1991—; with bereavement group-maternity Maine Med. Ctr. and Luth Med. Ctr., 1990—. Vol. blood drive ARC, Maine, 1992. Mem. AWHONN (legis. chairperson), Coalition Maine Nurses Orgn. (rep. from AWHONNsec.), Profl. Prospectives Com. Home: 4 Scabbard Rd Scarborough ME 04074-9332 Office: Maine Med Ctr 22 Bramhall St Portland ME 04102-3134

HOTTENDORF, DIANE V., dance educator; b. New London, Conn., May 17, 1947; d. Henry August and Frances D. (Babrowicz) Hottendorf. BS magna cum laude, Calif. State U., Northridge, 1970; MA summa cum laude, U. So. Calif., L.A., 1972, PhD, 1976. Teaching asst. U. So. Calif., L.A., 1972-74; asst. prof. Calif. State U., Northridge, 1973-76; head dance program Moorpark (Calif.) Coll., 1976-77; cruise staff mem. teen program Royal Caribbean Cruise Line, 1976-77; dance cons. Dept. Parks, Alexandria, Va., 1980-81; prof. dance Gallaudet U., Washington, 1981—; vis. asst. prof. World Campus Afloat, Seaboard Edn., Chapman Coll., Fall 1975; lectr. in field. Co-prodr.: (video tape) Fundamental Dance Signs, 1989, Sign 'n Sweat, 1987, Celebration of Deaf Dance, 1996; contbr. articles to profl. jours. Sponsor AA, Falls Church, Va., 1995—. Recipient Performing Arts award in dance Cultural and Fine Arts, Oxnard, 1988; grantee Gannett Found., 1983, 87, Delta Zeta and Rotary Club, 1983, May's Scholarship Fund, 1984, Delta Zeta, 1991, Psi Xota Xi, 1993; NDEA fellow, 1972-76. Mem. AAHPERD, NOW, Am. Dance Guild, Nat. Dance Assn., Sacred Dance Guild, Friends of Nat. Zoo, Nat. Mus. of Women in the Arts. Democrat. Home: 3705 S George Mason Dr Falls Church VA 22041 Office: Gallaudet Univ 800 Florida Ave NE Washington DC 20002

HOTZ, MARTHA PAULINE, artist; b. Looogootee, Ind., July 11, 1927; d. Francis Orval and Ethel Beatrice (Bradley) Summers; m. Donald Leo Hotz, Nov. 5, 1949; children: Donald Frederick, Daniel Richard, Anthony Francis, Timothy Lee, Jeffery Alan. Student, Art Instrns., Mpls., 1962-65, Art Acad., Ferdinand, Ind., 1965-67. Sec. Schwitzer-Cummins, Indpls., 1946-49; bookkeeper Reliance Mfg. Co., Loogootee, Ind., 1950-53; paste-up artist Loogootee Tribune, 1963-65, 71-86; v.p., buyer Hotz & Sons Corp., Loogootee, 1964-70; free lance artist, instr. Polly's Paintings, Loogootee, 1986—. Illustrator: (bookcover) Echoes from the Mountains,m 1990, (book) Around the Clock in Rhyme and Time, 1991, (bookcover) When God Stepped In, 1992; 14 postcards, 1986-96. Pres. Tri County Art Guild, Loogootee, 1965-75, Daviess County Art League, Washington, Ind., 1991-92, adv. bd., 1992-96. Mem. VFW Aux., KC Aux., Legion of Mary. Roman Catholic. Home: PO Box 244 Loogootee IN 47553

HOUCK, CHARLEEN MCCLAIN, education educator; b. Huntington, Pa., Dec. 1, 1944; d. Charles Lewis and Eunice C. (Keim) McClain; ; children: Michael C., Christopher R. BS in Edn., Secondary Edn., Math., Millersville U., 1968; cert. in mentally and/or physically handicapped, Kutztown U., 1986; postgrad., Allentown Coll., 1990—. Adult edn. supr. secondary math. Orrville (Ohio) City Schs., 1969-74; substitute tchr. math., sci. Hamburg (Pa.) Area Schs., 1974-76; instructional aide SR/TMR, Reading, Pa., 1976-85; tchr. learning support Conrad Weiser High Sch., Robesonia, Pa., 1985—; cons. Sci. Rsch. Assocs., Chgo., 1991—; instr. Berks County Intermediate Unit, Reading, 1989—. Contbr. articles to profl. jours. Recipient Sam Kirk award Pa. Assn. for Learning Disabilities, Annie Sullivan award Pa. Assn. Intermediate Units, Salute to Teaching award Pa. Acad. for Profession of Teaching, Outstanding Educator award Berks County Learning Disabilities Assn. Mem. ASCD, Internat. Soc. Tech. Edn., Pa. Assn. Ednl. Computing & Tech., Coun. Exceptional Children, Assn. Direct Instrn., Order of Ea. Star, VFW Aux., Am. Legion Aux., Phi Delta Kappa. Office: Conrad Weiser HS 347 E Penn Ave Robesonia PA 19551-8900

HOUGH, EDYTHE S. ELLISON, dean. BS in Nursing cum laude, U. Conn., 1961; MS in Psychiat. Nursing, Yale U., 1963; EdD in Early Childhood & Devel. Studies, UCLA, 1979; cert., Harvard U., 1984, Albert Einstein Med. Sch. Leadership Inst., 1984. Instr. sch. nursing U. Conn., Storrs, 1964-65; instr. sch. nursing UCLA, 1965-68, asst. prof., 1968-69; asst. prof. dept. nursing Mt. St. Mary's Coll., L.A., 1972-75; asst. prof. dept. psychosocial nursing U. Wash., Seattle, 1978-84, assoc. prof. dept. psychiatry & behavioral sci., 1984-85; fellow Harborview Med. Ctr., Seattle, 1984-85; assoc. prof., head dept. psychiat. nursing U. Ill., Chgo., 1985-86, chief psychiat. clin. svcs., 1985-86, assoc. dean acad. affairs Coll. Nursing, 1986-87, assoc. prof., 1987-88; assoc. v.p., assoc. dean Coll. Nursing Rush-Presbyn.-St. Luke's Med. Ctr., Chgo., 1988-92; assoc. dean edn. Coll. Nursing Rush Univ., 1991, prof. dept. med. nursing, 1992-93; dean, prof. Coll. Nursing Wayne State U., Detroit, 1993—; cons. Brentwood VA Hosp., L.A., 1969, Martin Luther King Hosp., L.A., 1973, Am. Inst. Rsch. Behavioral Scis., Palo Alto, Calif., 1977, YMCA Latchkey Child program, Seattle, 1978, King's Fund Ctr. King Edward's Hosp. Fund, London, 1983, Coll. Nursing Rush U., 1987; presenter in field. Contbr. articles to profl. jours. Mem. gov. bd. Cmty. Psychiat. Clinic, 1979-84, v.p., 1983-84, chair long-range planning com., 1983-84; gov. bd. Keystone Resources, 1982-84, Arbor Housing Assocs., 1983-84; mem. Wash. State Social Skills Consortium, 1983-85, Fourth Presbyn. Ch. Literacy Tutoring project, 1986-89, Women's Health Exec. Network, 1991-92, Sch. Medicine Charter Com. Ctr./Inst. Health Care Effectiveness, 1994—; bd. trustees Detroit Visiting Nurses Assn.; bd. dirs. Visiting Nurse Assn. Southeast Mich., 1993—, Greater Detroit Area Health Coun., Inc., 1993—. Recipient Nat. Rsch. Svc. award, 1978, Child Mental Health Faculty Devel. award NIMH, 1984, Women's Action New Direction award Women Healing the World, 1995; UCLA grantee, 1977. Fellow Am. Acad. Nursing; mem. NOW (Chgo. chpt.), ANA (coun. nurse rschrs., coun. nursing adminstrn.), Am. Psychiat. Nurses Assn., Ill. Orgn. Nurse Execs., Mich. Assn. Colls. Nursing (treas. 1993—), Mich. Nurses Assn., Midwest Nursing Rsch. Soc., Sigma Theta Tau, Soc. Edn. Rsch. Psychiat. Nursing, Transcultural Nursing Soc. Home: 1012 Audubon Grosse Pointe Park MI 48230 Office: Wayne State Univ Sch Nursing 112 Cohn Bldg 5557 Cass Ave Detroit MI 48202*

HOUGH, JANET GERDA CAMPBELL, research scientist; b. Glen Ridge, N.J., Dec. 22, 1948; d. Ralph William and Gerda Lydia (Baarck) Campbell; m. John Harrison Hough, Oct. 1, 1966 (div.); 1 child, Laura Leigh. Student Temple U. and Tyler Sch. Art, Phila., 1970-72, Pa. Acad. Fine Arts, 1972, Camden County Coll., Blackwood, N.J., 1973-75; B.S., Thomas Jefferson U., 1977. Lab. animal technician Inst. Med. Rsch., Camden, N.J., 1972-75; rsch. technician dept. biochemistry Thomas Jefferson U., Phila., 1976, phlebotomist, hematology technician, 1976-78, med. technologist spl. hematology, 1978-79, rsch. technician dept. med. genetics, 1979-80; with micromedic systems Rohm & Haas, Horsham, Pa., 1981-85; micromedic Internat. Clin. Nuclear Inc., Costa Mesa, Calif., and Horsham, 1985-91. Collaborator, editor textbook Hematology for Medical Technologists, 1983; poet, illustrator Thought Progressions, 1984. Charter mem. Nat. Rep. Presdl. Task Force, 1984—, Nat. Rep. Senatorial Com., 1984—, Rep. Presdl. Citizen's Adv. Commn., 1989-91, Nat. Rep. Congl. Com., 1992—. Mem. Internat. Soc. Poets, N.J. Hos. Assn., Am. Poetry Assn. (pub. anthologies 1986-90), Nat. Libr. Poetry (pub. anthology 1992). Roman Catholic. Avocations: drawing, painting, long-distance walking.

HOUGHTON, BERNADETTE ANNE, health facility administrator; b. Phila., Nov. 18, 1948; d. Walter William and Bernadette Anne (Fierko) H.; m. Joseph Michael Dever, (Dec. 27, 1975); 1 child, Joseph Walter Dever. BS with honors, Chestnut Hil Coll., 1970; PhD, Boston U., 1978, MBA with honors, 1982. Info. analyst Franklin Inst., Phila., 1971-72; rsch. tech. Wistar Inst., Phila., 1972-74; rsch. assoc. Boston U. Sch. of Medicine, 1978-80; fin. adminstr. Boston U., 1980-83; divsn. adminstr. Dana-Farber Cancer Inst., Boston, 1983—. Libr. Vol. Roosevelt Sch., Melrose, Mass., 1991-95, Cub Scout Den Leader Boy Scout of Am., Melrose, 1995—. Recipient fellow Boston U., 1974-78. Mem. NAFE, Am. Mgmt. Assn. Democrat. Roman Catholic. Office: Dana-Farber Cancer Inst 44 Binney St Boston MA 02115

HOUGHTON, KATHARINE, actress; b. Hartford, Conn., Mar. 10, 1945; d. Ellsworth Strong and Marion Houghton (Hepburn) Grant. BA, Sarah Lawrence Coll., Bronxville, N.Y., 1965. Founding mem. Pilgrim Repertory Co. (Shakespeare touring co. sponsored by Ky. Arts Commn.), 1971-72, S.C. Arts Commn., 1972, Miss. Arts Commn., 1973, Conn. Arts Commn., St. Joseph Coll., 1974. Debut on Broadway stage in A Very Rich Woman, 1965; appeared in stage plays Charley's Aunt, New Orleans Repertory, 1966, The Front Page, Broadway, 1968, Ten O'Clock Scholar, Royal Poinciana Playhouse, Fla., 1969, The Private Ear/The Public Eye, Sullivan, Ill., 1969, Sabrina Fair, Ivoryton Playhouse, 1968, The Miracle Worker, Sullivan, Ill., A Scent of Flowers (Theatre World award), Off Broadway, 1969, Misalliance, Hartford Stage Co., 1970, The Taming of the Shrew, Actors Theatre, Louisville, 1970, Poor Richard, Tartuffe, 1970, Ring Around the Moon, Hartford Stage Co., 1970, Major Barbara, The Glass Menagerie, Actors Theatre of Louisville, 1971, Play It Again Sam, Actors Theatre of Louisville, 1971, Suddenly Last Summer, Ivanhoe, Chgo., 1973, The Prodigal Daughter, Kennedy Center, Washington, 1973, Bell, Book and Candle, Pensacola, Fla., 1974, The Rainmaker, Ind. Repertory Co., 1975, Spiders Web, Atlanta, 1977, Hedda Gabler, Nashville, 1978, Dear Liar, Dayton, Ohio, 1978, 13 Rue de L'Amour, Ind. Repertory Co., 1978, Antigone, Nashville, 1979, Uncle Vanya, Acad. Festival Theatre, Lake Forest, 1979, Forty Carats, Radford U. Theatre, Va., 1979, A Doll's House, St. Edward's U. Theatre, Tex., 1979, The Sea Gull, Pitts. Public Theatre, 1979, The Glass Menagerie, Pa. Stage Co., 1980, Taming of the Shrew, Pa. State Festival, 1980, Terra Nova, Actors Theatre of Louisville, 1980, The Merchant of Venice, South Coast Repertory, Costa Mesa, Calif., 1981, A Touch of the Poet, Yale Repertory Theatre, 1983, To Heaven in a Swing, Am. Place Theatre, N.Y.C., tour various theaters, 1983-85, Sally's Gone She's Left Her Name, Am. Festival Theatre, N.H., 1984-86, Vivat, Vivat Regina, Mad Woman of Chaillot, The Time of Your Life, Children of the Sun, Mirror Repertory Co., N.Y.C., 1985, A Bill of Divorcement, Westport Country Playhouse, Conn., 1985, One Slight Hitch, Charlotte Repertory Co., 1986, To Heaven in a Swing, Amherst Coll., Bowdoin Coll., 1986, and Bronson Alcott Centennial Celebration, 1988, The Hooded Eye, West Bank Downstairs Theatre Bar, 1987, Ivoryton Playhouse, 1987, Murder in the Cathedral, West Point Cadet Chapel, 1987, The Leaves of Vallombrosa, 1988, Our Town, Broadway, 1988-89, Love Letters, Ivoryton Playhouse, 1989, To Kill A Mockingbird, Paper Mill Playhouse, N.J., 1991; motion pictures include Guess Who's Coming to Dinner, 1967, The Gardener, 1972, Eyes of the Amaryllis, 1981, Mr. North, 1987, Billy Bathgate, 1990, Ethan Frome, 1992, The Night We Never Met, 1992, Kalamazoo, 1993, Let It Be You, 1994; TV series The Adams Chronicles, 1975; TV mini-series I'll Take Manhattan, 1986; appeared on TV in Legacy of Fear, 1974, The Color of Friendship, 1981, (daytime serials) One Life to Live, 1989, All My Children, 1992; toured in Sabrina Fair, 1975, The Mousetrap, Arms and the Man, Dear Liar, 1976, The Streets of New York, Westport, Conn., Guildford, N.H., Dennis, Mass., Denver, 1980; appeared in To True to Be Good, Acad. Festival Theatre, Lake Forest, Ill., 1977, Spingold Theatre, Waltham, Mass., 1977, Annenberg Center, Phila., 1977; author: (plays) To Heaven in a Swing, 1982, Merlin, 1984, (1 act plays) Buddha, On The Shady Side, The Right Number, 1986, (book) The Marry Month of May, 1988, (stage prodns.) Phone Play, 1988, Good Grief, 1988, Mortal Friends, 1988 (stage prodn. premiere 1988), The Lick Penny Lover, 1988, (screenplays) The Heart of the Matter, 1989, Journey to Glasnost, 1990, Good Grief, 1991, Motherman, 1993, Acting in Concert, 1994, Spot, 1996; co-author: Two Beastly Tales, 1975; editor: MHG: A Biography, 1989. Mem. Dramatists Guild.

HOULE WESSEL, CAROLINE LOUISE, geographer, researcher, writer; b. Forest Lake, Minn., Feb. 22, 1965; d. Joseph Michael and Carla Jean (Wessel) Houle; m. Stephen Craig Stringall, May 21, 1988. BA in Geography, Humboldt State U., 1988, postgrad. in social sci., 1993. Hydrologic technician U.S. Forest Svc. Pacific S.W. Rsch. Sta., Arcata, Calif., 1986-93; coll. instr. history of women explorers So. Oreg. State Coll. Cmty. Edn. Program, Ashland, Oreg., 1994; asst. mgr. Pacific N.W. Mus. of Natural Hist. Aspen Grove Gift Shop, Ashland, Oreg., 1994-95; writer, rschr. internat. travel maps and guide books Sojourn Cartograpic Svcs., Blaine, Wash., 1994—; temp. employee rep. on sta. civil rights com., U.S. Forest Svc., Arcata, Calif., 1990-92; temp. employee chair and sta. rep. for temps., 1990-93, temp. employee rep. on Fed. Women's Program, 1992-93. Chair Humboldt State U. Students for Choice, Arcata, Calif., 1990-93. Mem. , AAUW, NOW (rep. reproductive rights rep. Oreg., 1995, recorder Rogue Valley chpt., 1994-95), Planned Parenthood (pub. affairs com., Eureka, Calif. 1990-93). Home and Office: Sojourn Cartographic Svcs 4780 Lora Ln Blaine WA 98230

HOURANI, LAUREL LOCKWOOD, epidemiologist; b. Carmel, Calif., Sept. 10, 1950; d. Eugene Franklin and Katherine Ruth (Miller) Betz; m. Ghazi Fayez Hourani, Feb. 28, 1984; children: Nathan, Danna, Lisa. BA, Chico State U., 1977; MPH, Am. Univ. Beirut, 1983; PhD, U. Pitts., 1990. Prog. evaluator Community Hosp. Monterey Peninsula, Carmel, Calif., 1978-81; instr./researcher Am. Univ. Beirut, 1981-85; predoctoral fellow U. Pitts., 1985-89; researcher, cons. V.A. Med. Ctr., Pitts., 1988-90; dir., tumor registry Med. Ctr. U. Calif. Irvine, Orange, 1990-92; epidemiologist Naval Health Rsch. Ctr., San Diego, 1993-95; head divsn. health scis., 1995—; cons. Nat. Devel. Commn. South Lebanon, 1981-83. Author: No Water, No Peace, 1985; contbr. articles to profl. jours. Bd. dirs. Am. for Justice in Middle East, Beirut, 1982-85, Nat. Devel. Com., South Lebanon, 1983-85. Recipient grant V.A., Pitts., 1989, rsch. grant U. Rsch. Bd., Beirut, 1985. Mem. Am. Psychol. Assn., Am. Pub. Health Assn., Soc. for Epidemiologic Rsch. Office: Naval Health Rsch Ctr Divsn Epidemiology PO Box 85122 San Diego CA 92186-5122

HOUSE, BONNIE KAY, graphic design educator, artist; b. Phila., Apr. 2, 1944; d. Benjamin and Gloria (Seltzer) H. BFA, Kutztown U., 1984; MFA, Rochester Inst. Tech., 1987. Advanced cert. electronic and optical storage applications. Assoc. prof. Fitchburg (Mass.) State Coll., 1987—. Illustrator: Las Desobedientes; Mujeres de Muestra America, 1995; exhibited in group and solo shows, 1974—. Chair Cultural Coun., Phillipston, Mass., 1990-94; mem. Zoning Bd. Appeals, Phillipston, 1990-94. Grantee Mass. Arts Lottery Coun., 1989, 90, 96. Mem. Mass. State Coll. Assn. (sec. 1994—, mem. exec. bd. 1992—), Phi Kappa Phi. Democrat. Office: Fitchburg State Coll 160 Pearl St Fitchburg MA 01420

HOUSE, KAREN ELLIOTT, company executive, former editor, reporter; b. Matador, Tex., Dec. 7, 1947; d. Ted and Bailey Elliott; m. Arthur House, Apr. 5, 1975 (div. Sept. 1983); m. Peter Kann, June 4, 1984; children: Hillary, Petra, Jason, Jade. B.J., U. Tex., 1970; postgrad. Inst. Politics, Harvard U., Y. Edn. reporter Dallas Morning News, 1970-71, with Washington bur., 1971-74; regulatory corr. Wall Street Jour., Washington, 1974-75, energy and agr. corr., 1975-78, diplomatic corr., 1978-84; fgn. editor Wall Street Jour., N.Y.C., 1984-89; v.p., Internat. Group Dow Jones & Co., 1989-95, pres. Internat. Group, 1995—; dir. German-Am. Coun., 1988—; bd. dirs. Coun. Fgn. Rels.; trustee Boston U.; mem. adv. bd. Ctr. Strategic Internat. Studies; mem. vis. com. Harvard U. Ctr. Internat. Affairs. Recipient Edward Weintal award for Diplomatic Reporting, Georgetown U., 1980-81, Edwin Hood award for Diplomatic Reporting Nat. Press Club, 1982, Disting. Achievement award U. So. Calif., 1984, Pulitzer prize for Internat. Reporting, 1984, Overseas Press Club Bob Considine award, 1984, 88; Harvard fellow, 1982. Fellow Nat. Acad. Arts and Scis. Home: 58 Cleveland Ln Princeton NJ 08540 Office: Dow Jones & Co 200 Liberty St New York NY 10281-1003

HOUSE, KAREN SUE, nursing consultant; b. San Francisco, July 16, 1958; d. Mathas Dean and Marilyn Frances (Weigand) H. Casa Loma Coll., 1985; AS in Nursing, SUNY at Albany, 1987. Psychiat. charge nurse Woodview Calabasas (Calif.) Hosp., 1985-87, Treatment Ctrs. Am., Van Nuys, Calif., 1987-88; cons., RN Valley Village Devel. Ctr., Reseda, Calif., 1988; plastic surg. nurse George Sanders, M.D., Encino, Calif., 1986—; nurse New Image Found., 1989—, Mid Valley Youth Ctr., 1991—; dir. nursing Encino Surgicenter (Sanders), 1992—; dir. nursing Devel. Tng. Svcs. for Devel. Disabled, 1988—; nurse cons. New Horizons for Developmentally Disabled, 1993. Instr., vol. ARC. Recipient Simi Valley Free Clinic Scholarship. Mem. Encino C. of C. Home: 29748 Saguaro St Santa Clarita CA 91384-3567 Office: 16633 Ventura Blvd Ste 110 Encino CA 91436-1834

HOUSE, KATHRYN ALINE, accountant, insurance adjuster; b. Castro Valley, Calif., Jan. 2, 1966; d. Robert and Majorie Ann (Carlson) Kocins; m. Michael Bret House, Nov. 11, 1989. BA in Acctg., Wash. State U., 1988. Cert. mgmt. acct. Fixed asset acct. Chevron Corp., San Ramon, Calif., 1988-90; acct. Lease Disclosures, Honolulu, 1990-91; staff acct. Viacom Cablevision, Pleasanton, Calif., 1991-92; acct. Honolulu Cellular, 1992-94; v.p. M & K House, Inc., Honolulu, 1994—. Wash. State U. scholar, 1984-88. Mem. Hawaii Yacht Club.

HOUSEHOLDER, BONNIE MOYER, human resources executive; b. Cleve., Jan. 22, 1947; d. John Welsh Moyer and Louise Smith; m. Daniel Reid Householder, June 23, 1972; children: William J., Dawn J. Arthur. Student, Bowling Green State U., 1965-72. Sec. Bowling Green (Ohio) State U., 1969-77; adminstrv. asst. to pres. F.W. Uhlman & Co., Bowling Green, 1977-81; exec. asst. Ernst & Young LLP, Cin., 1981-91; mgr. sales adminstrn. Clopay Corp., Cin., 1991-94; corp. sec., dir. human resources U.S. Fin. Life Ins. Co., Cin., 1994—; adv. bd. U. Cin.-Clermont Coll., 1995—. Mem. Profl. Secs. Internat. (bd. dirs. Cin. chpt. 1989-94, past pres.), Soc. for Human Resource Mgmt. Methodist. Office: US Fin Life Ins Co 201 E Fourth St 18th Fl Cincinnati OH 45202

HOUSEMAN, ANN ELIZABETH LORD, educational administrator, state official; b. New Orleans, Mar. 21, 1936; d. Noah Louis and Florence Marguerite (Coyle) Lord; m. Evan Kenny Houseman, June 25, 1960; children: Adrienne Ann, Jeannette Louise, Yvonne Elizabeth. BA, Barnard Coll., 1957; MA, Columbia Univ., 1962; PhD, Univ. Del., 1969. Cert. elem. prin., secondary sch. prin. State supr. reading Dept. Pub. Instrn., Del., 1977-79; prin. M.L. King Jr. Elem. Sch., Wilmington, Del., 1979-80; adminstr., exec. dir. Del. State Arts Coun., Wilmington, 1980-84; acting dir. Div. Hist. and Cultural Affairs State of Del., Wilmington, 1983-84, prin. P.S. du Pont Intermediate Sch., Wilmington, 1984-91; dir. Mid-Atlantic States Arts Consortium, Balt., 1980-84. Mem. adv. bd. Rockwood Mus., Wilmington, 1981-94; bd. dirs. Opera Del., Inc., Wilmington, 1984-94, pres., 1991-93, dir. devel., 1994-95; coord. adv. bd. Opera Del., Inc., Wilmington, 1995—; bd. dirs. Del. Theatre Co., Wilmington, 1984-90. Contbr. articles to profl. jours. Mem. Phi Delta Kappa. Republican. Presbyterian. Office: Opera Del 4 S Poplar St Wilmington DE 19801-5009

HOUSER, KAREN LOUISE, swim and aquatic fitness instructor, lifeguard; b. Stamford, Conn., Nov. 29, 1968; d. William Hull and Mary Ann (Yedinak) H. BS in Justice and Law Adminstrn., Western Conn. State U., 1991, BA in Sociology, 1991. Lifeguard, aquatic fitness instr. Regional YMCA Western Conn., Danbury, 1987—; asst. mgr. Gingiss Formalwear, Danbury, 1991-93; shift supr. Consumer Value Stores, Woonsocket, R.I., 1993-96; head lifeguard Ridgefield (Conn.) Recreation Ctr., 1994—; owner AQUApros, the aquativ profls., 1995—. Assoc. advisor Danbury Police Explorers, 1992—; advisor Boy Scouts Am., Norwalk, 1984—; mem. Girl Scouts, Wilton, Conn., 1974—. Mem. Aquatics Exercise Assn., U.S. Water Fitness Assn. Roman Catholic. Home and Office: 10 Clapboard Ridge Rd # 33E Danbury CT 06811

HOUSER, RUTH GERTRUDE, telecommunications company official, certified public accountant, former local government official, intellectual property manager; b. Virginia Beach, Va., Feb. 25, 1953. BS in Acctg. cum laude, Wheeling Coll., 1975. CPA, Fla., Ga., W.Va. Sr. acct. Price Waterhouse, Pitts., 1975-79; mgr. internal control Lockheed Space Opers. Co., Cape Canaveral, Fla., 1980-84; mgr. info. systems AT&T, Orlando, Fla., 1984-85; mgr. data systems group AT&T, Morristown, N.J., 1985-86, mgr., CFO systems architecture, 1986-87; fin. dir. France and Italy AT&T, Paris, 1987-89; mgr. acctg. policy AT&T, Morristown, 1989-90; dir. billing svcs. AT&T, Bridgewater, N.J., 1990-92; controller, Network Wireless Systems AT&T, Morristown, N.J., 1992-93; fin. mgr., leader billing team World Ptnrs./World Source AT&T, Bridgewater, N.J., 1993-95; cons. AT&T Solutions, 1995; dist. mgr. Lucent Techs., Inc., Intellectual Property, Coral Gables, Fla., 1995—; tax cons., Atlanta, 1979-83; fin. cons. Wheeling Coll., 1975; dir. CPA forum AT&T Chief Fin. Orgn., Morristown, 1988-90. Vol. C. Dillon Libr., Bedminster, N.J., 1985, v.p. bd. trustees, 1988-92; sec., trustee Friends of C. Dillon Libr., 1992-95; committeewoman Somerset County Reps. Dist. 5, Bedminster, 1993-95, Bedminster Twp., 1995. Mem. AICPA. Home: PO Box 1002 Pembroke Pines FL 33082 Office: Lucent Technologies Ste 511 2333 Ponce de Leon Coral Gables FL 33134

HOUSMAN, B. JANE, secondary education educator; b. N.Y.C., Oct. 15, 1937. BS, Syracuse U., 1959, MA in Edn., 1961; postgrad., C.W. Post coll., 1985; EdD, Hofstra U., 1991. Cert. elem. edn. tchr., tchr. math., sch. dist. adminstr., sch. adminstr. and supr., N.Y. Tchr. math./computer Roosevelt Jr./Sr. H.S.; grant writer, presenter in field. Mem. West Islip (N.Y.) Bd. Edn., 1978-81; mem. Family Svc. League, West Islip, 1990-93. Mem. ASCD, Internat. Soc. for Tech. in Edn., N.Y. State Assn. for Computers and Tech. in Edn., Nat. Coun. Tchrs. Math., Nassau-Suffolk Coun. Adminstrv. Women in Edn., Nassau Reading Coun., Phi Delta Kappa (v.p. membership 1992—). Home: 15 Barberry Rd West Islip NY 11795-3910

HOUSNER, JEANETTE ANN, jeweler, artist; b. Richland Center, Wis., Oct. 9, 1940; d. Richard Edward and Ardyce Evelyn (Kotvis) H.; m. Christos John Papadopoulos, Oct. 12, 1964 (div. Aug. 1988); children: Rachel, Sarah. BA, Milw.-Downer Coll., 1962; MFA, Cranbrook Acad. Art, 1964. Instr., office clk. Indian Arts and Crafts Bd., Sitka, Alaska, 1965-66; instr. jewelry Cen. Wash. U., Ellensburg, Wash., 1967-78; bus. mgr. Laughing Horse Summer Theatre, Ellensburg, 1992-93; owner, artist Jewelry, Metalsmithing, Ellensburg, 1966—. Jewelry represented on slides in permanent collection, Cranbrook Acad. Art; evening bag Art to Wear, Larson Gallery, Yakima, Wash., 1990 (Best of Accessories award), pendant 21st Kittitas County Show, Gallery One, Ellensburg, 1991 (Outstanding 3-Dimensional award), pin 40th Cen. Wash. Exhbn., Larson Gallery, Wash., Yakima, 1996 (Hon. mention); exhibited in numerous group shows, 1962—. Office worker Habitat for Humanity, Ellensburg, 1994—. Mem. NOW, LWV, Soc. N.Am. Goldsmiths, Coll. Art Assn., Am. Craft Coun. Home and Office: PO Box 636 Ellensburg WA 98926

HOUSTON, CAROLINE MARGARET, editor; b. Harrogate, Eng., May 8, 1964; came to U.S., 1975; d. William H. and Sylvia (Fineron) H. BA in Internat. Studies and Mid East Studies, George Mason U., 1989, postgrad., 1990—. Cert. fluency in Farsi and French; Gemological Inst. Am. cert. diamontologist and gemologist; lic. pvt. pilot. Editor Maxim Techs., Vienna, Va., 1988-89; sec. Am. Near East Refugee Aid, Washington and Israel, 1989-90; asst. sec., treas. World Resources Inst., Washington, 1990-91; asst. dir. client svcs. Britches of Georgetowne, McLean, Va., 1991-92; reference copyright sr. clk., preservation technician Libr. Congress, Washington, 1992-95, copyright office automation asst., 1995—; devel. cons. Legacy Internat., Jerusalem, 1990-91. Violinist with semi-profl. orchs., 1972-84. Mem. NOW, Amnesty Internat.; chmn., treas. Episcopal Ch. of Va., No. Va. Chpt. Holy Land Com. Mem. NAFE, Internat. Studies Assn., Mid. East Inst., Libr. Congress Profl. Assn. (chair membership com., co-chair pub. affairs com.), Atlantic Coun. U.S. Home: 1300 S Army Navy Dr Unit 1010 Arlington VA 22202

HOUSTON, CATHERINE JEANNETTE, artist; b. Gainesville, Tex., Sept. 10, 1946; d. Lenard Arlington and Nanalou (Elkins) Durrett; m. 1968 (dec.1976); children: Michele A. Houston, Scott D. Houston; m. Frank Alan Whiteside, 1984. BFA, U. Tex., San Antonio, 1977; MA, U. Dallas, 1979, MFA, 1981. instr. Dallas County C.C., 1980-86. Exhibited in group shows at U. Tex. at San Antonio, 1977, U. Dallas, 1979, Arlington (Tex.) Juried Art Show, 1980, City Hall Juried Art Show, 1980, Smith Coll. Exch. Exhbn., 1980, David Andersen Gallerie, Plaza of the Americas, 1981, Northlake Coll. Faculty Show, 1981, Tex. Christian U., 1983, 84, First Juried Regional Exhbn., D-W Gallery, 1984, The Art Walk German Exchange Exhibit, Dallas City Hall, 1993, Studio 12 Gallery, 1993, Tenth Ann. Nat. Juried Art Exhbn., Corsicana, Tex., 1993 (First Place Water Media 1993), Tex. Visual Arts Assn. 18th Nat. Open Exhbn., Dallas, 1993, Eleventh Ann. Nat. Juried Art Exhbn., Corsicana, 1994, Nat. Open Exhbn. Tex. Visual Arts Assn., 1994, Bucking the Tex. Myth: A Contemporary Redefinition of Who We Are, 1994, D'Art Ann. Membership Exhbn., 1994, Dishman Art Gallery, 1995, 12th Ann. Nat. Juried Art Exhbn. Navarro Coun. of the Arts, 1995, Amarillo Art Competition Mus. of Contemporary Art, 1995, DWCA Nat. Juried Show, Timespan, 1995, Laguna Meml. Mus., Austin, Tex., 1996, 13th Ann. Nat. Juried Art Exhbn., Corsicana, Tex., 1996, DVAC Ann. Membership Exhbn., Dallas, 1996, Eck Summer Festival, Montreal, 1996; one-woman show includes Northlake Gallery, 1995; contbr. articles to profl. jours. Founding pres., v.p. Coppell (Tex.) Garden Club, 1992—; mem. Tex. Master Gardeners Assn., Dallas, 1993—. Mem. Dallas Visual Artists, Tex. Visual Artists, Dallas Women Caucus for the Arts.

HOUSTON, GERRY ANN, oncologist; b. Baldwyn, Miss., July 16, 1953; d. Jeff Davis and Frances Holland (Agnew) Goodson; m. Terry L. Houston, Dec. 18, 1976 (dec. May 1987); 1 child, Claire Holland; m. Abe John Malouf, July 23, 1988. BA, U. Miss., 1974, MD, 1978. Diplomate Am. Bd. Internal Medicine, Am. Bd. Medical Oncology. Intern U. Med. Ctr., Jackson, Miss., 1978-79, resident, 1979-81, fellow oncology, 1981-83; ptnr. Jackson (Miss.) Oncology Assocs., 1987—; staff physician Miss. Bapt. Med. Ctr., Jackson, 1983—, Meth. Med. Ctr., Jackson, 1983—, St. Dominic Hosp., Jackson, 1983—, River Oaks Hosp., Jackson, 1983—, Univ. Med. Ctr., Jackson, 1983—; med. dir. Hospice of Ctrl. Miss., Jackson, 1989—; mem. exec. com. Baptist Med. Ctr., 1994. Contbr. articles to profl. jours. Chmn. exec. com. Miss. divsn. Am. Cancer Soc., 1993-95, pres., bd. dirs., 1989-93. Clin. rsch. fellow Am. Cancer Soc. Fellow ACP; mem. AMA, Nat. Hospice Orgn., Acad. Hospice Physicians, So. Assn. Oncology, Am. Soc. Clin. Oncology, Alpha Omega Alpha. Episcopalian. Office: Jackson Oncology Assocs 1190 N State St Ste 501 Jackson MS 39202-2413

HOUSTON, MELISSA MICHELLE, accountant; b. Montgomery, Ala., Oct. 1, 1966; d. Lee Christian and Louvenia (Fort) H. Student, Auburn U., 1992. Acct. Max Fed. Credit Union, Montgomery, 1993-95, BellSouth Advt. and Pub., Tucker, Ga., 1995—. Active Will's Guild Ala. Shakespeare Festival, 1993—. Recipient Cert. of Appreciation 15th Jud. Cir. Ct., 1993. Mem. Am. Soc. Women Accts., Inst. Mgmt. Accts. Democrat. Office: BellSouth Advt and Pub 2245 Northlake Pkwy Tucker GA 30084

HOUSTON, PENELOPE, singer, songwriter, recording artist; b. L.A., Dec. 17, 1957; d. David Brown Houston and Penelope Helen Vrachopoulos; m. Meletios Christos Peppas, May 17, 1993 (div. Apr., 1994); m. Patrick John Roques, June 9, 1995. Singer, songwriter Avengers, San Francisco, 1977-79; singer, songwriter, bandleader Penelope Houston and Her Band, San Francisco, 1983—; video dir., San Francisco, 1986—. Singer, songwriter (recordings) Avengers, 1983, Birdboys, 1988, The Whole World, 1993, Karmal Apple, 1994, Cut You, 1996. Named Best Folk Artist, San Francisco Weekly Music Awards, 1990, Best Singer Spex Mag., Hamburg, Germany, 1993, Outstanding Female Vocalist, Bay Area Music Awards, San Francisco, 1995. Office: PO Box 422163 San Francisco CA 94142-2163

HOUSTON, WHITNEY, vocalist, recording artist; b. East Orange, N.J., Aug. 9, 1963; d. John R. and Cissy H.; m. Bobby Brown, July 18, 1992; 1 child, Bobbi Kristina Houston Brown. HHD (hon.), Grambling U. Trained under direction of mother; mem. New Hope Bapt. Jr. Choir, 1974; background vocalist Chaka Khan, 1978, Lou Rawls, 1978, Cissy Houston, 1978, appeared in Cissy Houston night club act; record debut (duet with Teddy Pendergrass) Hold Me, 1984; albums include Whitney Houston, 1985, Whitney, 1986, I'm Your Baby Tonight, 1990; songs include Greatest Love of All, Saving My Love For You, Didn't We Almost Have It All, You're Still My Man, I'm Your Baby Tonight, 1991; appeared in HBO TV spl. Welcome Home, Heroes, With Whitney Houston, 1991; fashion model Glamour Mag., Seventeen mag., 1981; actress (movie) The Bodyguard, 1992. Recipient Grammy award, 7 Am. Music awards, 4 #1 Single Record awards; named Artist of Yr. Billboard mag., 1986. Grammy award for Best Female Pop Performance, 1985, 4 nominations, 1994, 87; Winner Am. Music award, 1985 (2), 1986 (5), 1988 (2). Office: care John Houston Nippi Inc 2160 N Central Rd Fort Lee NJ 07024-7547*

HOUTZ, FLORENCE EMILY, poet, playwright, literary-historical researcher; b. Andreas, Pa., May 9, 1923; d. Harry Daniel and Anne Priscilla (Steiner) H. BA, Susquehanna U., 1944; postgrad., U. Pa., 1944-45, Ohio State U., 1945-46; MA, U. Pa., 1946, postgrad., 1946-47. Grad. asst. in English, Ohio State U., Columbus, 1945-46; asst. instr. U. Pa., Phila., 1946-47; asst. prof. Lebanon Valley Coll., Annville, Pa., 1948-50; instr. Cedar Crest Coll., Allentown, Pa., 1957-59, Hartwick Coll., Oneonta, N.Y., 1959-62; freelance poet and playwright, lit. and hist. rschr., Phila., 1950-55, 73—, Oneonta, 1962-73. Author: (poetry) Button Briefs, 1991, Bardic Briefs, 1993, Bonbon Briefs, 1993. Vol. Dem. campaign, Washington, 1972. Recipient Katherine Tyndall Meml. prize Poetry Soc. Va., 1966, Louise Bogan Meml. prize N.Y. Poetry Forum, 1972. Mem. AAUW, Am. Assn. Ret. Persons. Home: 1324 Locust St Apt 622 Philadelphia PA 19107

HOUX, SHIRLEY ANN, personal and business services company executive, consultant, researcher; b. Claremore, Okla., Nov. 1, 1931; d. George Warren and Alta Zena (Starkweather) Pritchard; m. William Dean Munson, June 1, 1951 (div. June 1962); children—Debra Kay, Diana Sue, Donna Lynn; m. Leonard Houx, June 22, 1963 (div. Oct. 1989); 1 child, David Leonard. Student in bus. Okla. State U., 1949-50. Sec. Jack Gordon, P.A., Claremore, Okla., 1947-48; sec., personnel mgr. Gulf Oil Corp., Tulsa, 1950-51; exec. sec. to wing comdr. U.S. Air Force, Cocoa Beach, Fla., 1951-53; exec. sec. to gen. counsel Houston So., P.A., Stillwater, Okla., 1957-60; exec. sec. to exec. v.p. and sr. v.p. Williams Cos., Tulsa, 1962-64; owner, chief exec. officer Hallmark Exchange, Inc., Tulsa, 1981—; cons. small bus., Tulsa, 1981—; mem. small bus. adv. bd. Tulsa Jr. Coll., 1983—. Author: (drama) Wedding Rehearsal for the Bride of Christ, 1985. Contbg. editor The Chronicle, 1984. Co-creator, producer foot health program, 1967 (Am. Podiatry Assn. Outstanding award 1968); creator, advt. campaign for Cystic Fibrosis Found.: I'm One...Be One, 1978. Pres. women's aux. Okla. Podiatry Assn., Tulsa, 1966-82; sec.-treas. Okla. bd. examiners Okla. Podiatry Assn., 1969-76; nat. audio-visual chmn. women's aux. Am. Podiatry Assn., 1976; pres. Tulsa Cerebral Palsy Assn., 1977, Cystic Fibrosis Found. Aux., Tulsa, 1979. Named Miss Claremore, Claremore Bus. and Profl. Women, Okla., 1949; recipient Two-Star award Pure D'Lite Co., 1982. Mem. Nat. Assn. Female Execs. Democrat. Avocations: fashion design; the arts; writing.

HOVEL, ESTHER HARRISON, art educator; b. San Antonio, Tex., Jan. 12, 1917; d. Randolph Williamson and Carrie Esther (Clements) Harrison; m. Elliott Logan Hovel, Sept. 30, 1935; children: Richard Elliott, Dorothy Auverne. BA, Incarnate Word Coll., 1935; postgrad., Oxford U., 1979, British Inst. Art, Florence, Italy, 1980. Civil svc. auditor U.S. Govt. Office of Price Adminstrn., San Antonio, 1942-44; interior decorator Parkway Interior Design Studio, El Paso, Tex., 1968-72; instr. stained glass and sculpture El Paso Mus. Art, 1972-78; tchr. sculpture Albuquerque Sr. Ctrs., 1983-85; docent El Paso Mus. Art, 1972-82. Exhibited sculpture Museo De Artes, Juarez, Mexico, 1981 (1st place 1981). Bd. dirs. YMCA, Albuquerque, 1963-64 (plaque 1964); charter mem. and bd. dirs. Contact Lifeline Internat., Albuquerque, 1982-92 (2 plaques 1986, 90); mem. Com. on Bicentennial of U.S. Constitution, Washington and N.M., 1987-89. Recipient 2 medals Exxon Corp., 1986, 89, Medal of Merit Pres. Ronald Reagan, 1987; grantee Exxon Corp., 1986, 90. Mem. Jr. League Internat. (various offices 1948-93), Rotary "Anns" (various offices). Republican. Mem. Christian Ch. Home: 7524 Bear Canyon Rd NE Albuquerque NM 87109-3847

HOWARD, A. LAVERNE, bank executive. V.p. Boatman's BancShares, St. Louis. Office: Boatman's BancShares One Boatman Plz 800 Market St Saint Louis MO 63101*

HOWARD, BARBARA ANN, medical technologist; b. Centralia, Mo., Oct. 7, 1932; d. Samuel Lee and Twila Lynn (Houghton) Harshbarger; m. Edward N. Howard, Oct. 11, 1952 (div. Dec. 1962); children: Ralph Neal (dec.), LeeAnn, David Mark, Donald Edward. Cert. med. technologist, Blessing Hosp., 1958; BA in Biology, Lindenwood Coll., 1966; postgrad., U. Mo., St. Louis, 1979-81. Med. technologist St. Joseph Health Ctr., St. Charles, Mo., 1959-65, 68-77, lab. evening supr. med. technologist, 1977-85; med. technologist supr. Boonslick Med. Group, St. Charles, 1965-76, med. technologist, 1987-94; blood bank med. technologist De Paul Health Ctr., Bridgeton, Mo., 1985-87; rsch. technologist CDIC Monsanto Corp., Chesterfield, Mo., 1987; med. technologist Barnes St. Peters (Mo.) Hosp., 1994—; part-time med. technologist Barnes St. Peters (Mo.) Hosp., 1988-94, Boonslick Med. Group, 1994—. Sunday sch. tchr. 1st Meth. Ch., St. Charles, 1970, 90, 91, mem. worship com., 1992, mem. adminstrv. bd., 1990—, mem. chancel choir, 1970—; co-chmn. Grief Support Group Conf. Ctr., St. Charles, 1987-88; mem. St. Charles Choral Soc., 1970's. PEO grantee, 1977. Mem. AAUW (treas. 1990-92). Home: 719 N 5th St Saint Charles MO 63301-1934

HOWARD, BARBARA ANN, obstetrical/gynecological nurse practitioner; b. Palestine, Tex., Nov. 22, 1952; d. Pink and Pearlene Delois (Green) Sanders; m. Troy W. Simmons (div.); 1 child,Troy W. Jr.; m. Gardner B. Howard, Jr., Dec. 23, 1978; 1 child, Tiri Chantréal. AS in Nursing, Tarrant County Jr. Coll., Fort Worth, Tex., 1975; Nursing Practitioner Women's Health, U. Tex Southwestern Med. Sch., Dallas, 1992. RN, Tex.; cert. ob-gyn. nurse practitioner. Student nurse emergency room and ICC Ft. Worth Osteopathic Hosp., Ft. Worth, Tex., 1973-75; supr. emergency room Newburn Meml. Hosp., Jacksonville, Tex., 1975-77; part time staff nurse Newburn Meml. Hosp., Jacksonville, 1979-80; staff for labor and delivery Doctor's Meml. Hosp., Tyler, Tex., 1977-79; staff nurse med.-surg. Woman's Hosp. of Tex., Houston, 1982-84; nurse, PMS counselor Women's Health Inst. Baylor U., Houston, 1984-89; ob-gyn. nurse practitioner, cons. Smith County Health Dist. and Family Care Ctr., Tyler, 1990-95; pvt. practice, Henderson, Tex., 1995—; counselor PMS Support Group, Houston, 1984-89; 1st v.p. Women's Hosp. Employee Adv. Bd., Houston, 1984-88; cons. Smith County Health Dist., Tyler, 1990—. Mem. Spkrs. Bur., Women's Hosp. Tex., Houston, 1985-90; mem. Houston Regional Coun. for Alcohol and Drug Abuse, 1984-86; cons. on teen pregnancy Jr. League Tyler, 1995-97. Mem. Tex. Nursing Assn., Tex. Nurse Practitioners Assn., East Tex. Black Nurses Assn., Teenage Parent Program Adv. Com., Nat. Black Leadership Initiative Against Cancer, Profl. Black Womens Assn. Baptist. Home: 10778 County Road 2219 Tyler TX 75707-9794 Office: 815 N Marshall Henderson TX 75652

HOWARD, BARBARA BYERS, public policy consultant; b. Seattle, Mar. 9, 1930; d. Orva Oliver and Florence Viano (Soderback) Byers; m. Richard Wayne Howard, Aug. 15, 1959 (dec. Dec. 1970). BA, U. Wash., 1950; PhD, Ind. U., 1964. Reporter Bainbridge Rev., Winslow, Wash., 1950-51; publs. dir. Wash. State Assn. County Commrs., Olympia, 1951-56; rsch. cons. Inst. Pub. Adminstrn. Ind. U., Bloomington, 1956-58; instr., asst. prof. dept. govt. Ind. U., Bloomington, 1960-66; rsch. cons. Bur. Govtl. Rsch. & Svcs. U. Wash., Seattle, 1967-69; policy analyst Joint Com. on Higher Edn. Wash. State Legis., 1971-73; sr. policy analyst Com. on Govt. Ops. Wash. State Senate, Olympia, 1973-93; cons. in field Olympia, 1993—; pub. mem. Warren Featherstone Reid award adv. com., Olympia, 1995—. Author: County Government in Washington State, 1957, Accounting Practices in County Road Departments in Illinois, 1957, Gaining Government Support for Your Arts Project: A Primer for Political Advocacy, 1995. Mem. LWV (bd. dirs., newsletter editor Thurston County 1995—), Am. Soc. Pub. Adminstrn., Women in Communications, Seattle Opera Assn., Olympia Opera Guild, Seattle Art Mus.

HOWARD, BETTIE JEAN, surgical nurse; b. Balt., Sept. 26, 1926; d. Milton James and Elizabeth Maria (Morgan) Knight; m. Stanley Lewis Howard; children: Amanda J. Scott, Sarah L. Howard, Mary McK. Strobel, Elizabeth M. Shanner, Roderick S. Diploma, Church Home and Hosp., Balt., 1947. RN, Md.; cert. bd. gastroenterology nurse. Head nurse med.-surg. unit Church Home & Hosp., Balt., 1947-48; surg. pediat. staff nurse Johns Hopkins Hosp., Balt., 1948-51, surg. pediat. acting head nurse, 1951-52, otolaryngology endoscopy head nurse, 1952-56; pediat. emergency rm. triage nurse U. Md. Hosp., Balt., 1966-68; head nurse surg. endoscopy nurse U. Md. Med. Ctr., Balt., 1968—. Contbr.: (book chpt. sect.) Policy and Politics for Nurses, 1993; contbr. articles to profl. jours. Chmn. Digestive Disease Nat. Coalition, Washington, 1993-95; mem. coord. exec. panel Nat. Digestive Disease Info. Clearinghouse, NIH, Bethesda, Md., 1992-95; mem. adminstrv. bd. Grace United Meth. Ch., Balt., 1993-95. Mem. Soc. Gastroenterology Nurses and Assocs., Inc. (pres. 1988-89, Gabriele Schindler award 1991), Soc. Internat. Gastroenterol. Nurses and Endoscopy Assocs. (charter), Chesapeake Soc. Gastroenterology Nurses and Assocs. (charter, pres. 1981-83), Certifying Bd. Gastroenterology Nurses and Assocs. Inc. (pres. 1992-93). Republican. Home: 905 Saxon Hill Dr Cockeysville MD 21030-2905 Office: U Md Med Ctr 22 S Greene St Baltimore MD 21201-1544

HOWARD, CARLA GAIL, librarian; b. Sterling, Colo., Aug. 22, 1945; d. Carl G. and Christine Alice (Hoffart) Betz; m. Jerry Eldon Howard, Aug. 25, 1968; children: Justin Carl, Jason Jon. BA, Colo. State Coll., 1967; MA, San Jose State Coll., 1970; EdS, U. No. Colo., 1980. Cert. tchr. libr. media, bus. edn., math., psychology. Office occupations instr. Livermore (Calif.) High Sch., 1967-69, Chabot Coll., Hayward, Calif., 1969-72, Holy Names High Sch., Oakland, Calif., 1970-72, Colo. State U., Ft. Collins, 1972-73; libr. media specialist East Grand Sch. Dist., Granby, Colo., 1974-77; dist. libr. media coord. Natrona County Sch. Dist., Casper, Wyo., 1981—; ann. author visit Natrona County Sch. Dist., Casper, 1983—; Co-author: Relevance in the Education of Today's Business Student, 1973; contbr. articles to profl. jours. Chmn. Casper and Wyoming Centennial Edn. Com., 1988-90; assn. rep. Natrona County Edn. Assn., Casper, 1981—; chmn. bd. lay ministry Our Savior's Luth. Ch., Casper, 1991-93, vice-chmn. presch. bd., 1990-92. Mem. Am. Assn. Sch. Librs., Wyo. Libr. Assn. (recording sec. 1993—, chmn. Indian Paintbrush Book award Comm. 1991-93, chmn. Soaring Eagle Book award Comm. 1989-91), Wyo. Ednl. Media Assn. (pres. 1991-93), Internat. Reading Assn., Phi Delta Kappa, Beta Epsilon, Delta Kappa Gamma (sec. 1996—). Lutheran. Home: 4024 Somerset Cir Casper WY 82609 Office: Libr Svcs/Natrona Cty Schs 970 North Glenn Rd Casper WY 82601

HOWARD, CAROLE MARGARET MUNROE, public relations executive; b. Halifax, N.S., Can., Mar. 5, 1945; came to U.S., 1965; d. Frederick Craig and Dorothy Margaret (Crimes) Munroe; m. Robert William Howard, May 15, 1965. BA, U. Calif., Berkeley, 1967; MS, Pace U., 1978. Reporter Vancouver (Can.) Sun, 1965; editorial assoc. Pacific N.W. Bell, Seattle, 1967-70, employee info. supr., 1970-72, advt. supr., 1972, project mgr. EEO, 1972-73, mktg. mgr., 1973, info. mgr., 1974-75; dist. mgr. media relations AT&T, N.Y.C., 1975-77, dist. mgr. planning, 1977-78, dist. mgr. advt., 1978-80; media relations mgr. Western Electric, N.Y.C., 1980-83; div. mgr. regional pub. relations AT&T Info. Systems, Morristown, N.J., 1983-85; v.p., dir. pub. relations and communications policy The Reader's Digest Assn., Inc., Pleasantville, N.Y., 1985-1995;mem. summer faculty profl. publishing course Stanford U., 1993-95; bd. dirs. Andrew Corp. Author: (with Wilma Mathews) On Deadline: Managing Media Relations, 1985, 2nd edit., 1994; contbg. author: Communicators' Guide to Marketing, 1987, Experts in Action: Inside Public Relations, 2d edit., 1988, Travel Industry Marketing, 1990 The Business Speakers Almanac, 1994; editor newsletters: Wash. State Rep. Cen. Com., 1973-74; contbg. editor Pub. Relations Quar.; pres. The Reader's Digest Found.; adv. bd. Pub. Rels. News, Pub. Rels. Review, 2nd Jour. of Employee Comm. Mngr. Mem. corp. adv. bd. Caramoor Ctr. for Music and the Arts; bd. dirs. The Hundred Club of Westchester, Inc., The Lila Acheson Wallace Fund for Met. Mus. of Art, Madison Square Boy's and Girl's Club of N.Y.C. Mem. Women in Communications (bd. dirs. Wash. state 1973), Internat. Assn. Bus. Communicators, Pub. Relations Soc. Am., Nat. Press Women, Wash. Press Women (bd. dirs. 1972), Issues Mgmt. Assn., Pub. Rels. Seminar, Am. Cancer Soc., Arthur Page Soc., Wisemen, Pi Beta Phi. Angelican. Clubs: The Aspen, La Paloma Country. Home: PO Box 5499 Pagosa Springs CO 81147 Office: Reader's Digest Assn Inc Pleasantville NY 10570

HOWARD, CHRISTY J., actuary; b. Evanston, Ill., Oct. 6, 1954; d. Coydel Sandford and Ethel Marie (Franklin) Howard; children: Raymond Christopher Gunn, Justin Howard Gunn. BA, Oberlin Coll., 1976; MS in Stats., Carnegie Mellon U., 1979, MS in Pub. Policy and Mgmt., 1979. Analyst CNA, Chgo., 1979-83, mgr. comml. property pricing, 1983-85, mgr. profl. liability res. and ops. analysis, 1985-92, asst. v.p. splty. lines reserving and ops. analysis, 1993-96, v.p. and chief actuary property/casualty valuation and fin. analysis, 1996—. Trustee Prairie State Coll., 1992-95. Fellow Casualty Actuarial Soc.; mem. Am. Acad. Actuaries. Office: CNA CNA Plaza Chicago IL 60685

HOWARD, CONSTANCE ADAIR, financial advisor; b. Savannah, Ga., Oct. 2, 1964; d. Frank Roy and Bette Adair (Moore) Hurst; m. Joseph Michael Howard, May 19, 1990; children: Justin Michael, Joseph Hunter Howard. Student, South Coll., Savannah, 1985, Armstrong State Coll., 1988. Cert. fin. advisor series 7, 63 licenses. Office mgr. Millie Lewis Modeling, Savannah, 1983-86; ops. clk. Johnson, Lane, Space, Smith, Savannah, 1986-88; adminstrv. asst. Merrill Lynch, Savannah, 1988-91; fin. advisor Prudential Securities, Savannah, 1991-94; registered rep. A.G. Edwards & Sons, Inc., Savannah, 1994-96; investment adv. mktg. dir. Cornerstone Fin., Atlanta, 1996—; fin. instr. Savannah Tech. Inst., 1993—; fin. guest spkr. Sta. WSAV-TV, Savannah, 1993—; find. spkr., instr. to pub. sch. students, Savannah, 1992—; fin. spkr. to local bus. orgns., Savannah, 1992—; stock market report announcer Pub. Radio Sta. 91, Savannah, 1992; instr. fin. classes Carroll Tech., 1996. Fin. columnist: The Richmond Hill Bryan County News, 1993—, The Ga. Guardian, 1993—, The Savannah Parent, 1993, The Knowledge Exch., 1993, Times-Georgian, 1996; co-prodr., host fin. talk show Money Talks, Savannah, 1994—; prodr., host radio program Community Closeup WBMQ talk radio, WIXV I-95, Savannah. Internship mentor Savannah H.S. Program, 1993. Mem. Am. Bus. Women's Assn., Small Bus. Chamber (bd. dirs., treas. 1993—). Office: Investment Adv Mktg Dir 7411 Perimenter Ctr Atlanta GA 30346

HOWARD, CORDELIA, library director. Dir. Long Beach (Calif.) Pub. Lib. Office: Long Beach Pub Libr & Info Ctr 101 Pacific Ave Long Beach CA 90822-1097*

HOWARD, CYNTHIA STOTTS, technical writer; b. Mountain View, Calif., Mar. 25, 1964; d. Franklin Dee and Marjorie Opal (McCorkle) Stotts; m. John Avery Howard, Sept. 14, 1985; children: Amanda, Laurel. BS, Stanford U., 1985, MS, 1987, PhD, 1993. Software engr. ASK Computer Sys., Los Altos, Calif., 1984-86; teaching asst. Stanford (Calif.) U., 1987-88, rsch. asst., 1987-93; freelance tech. writer Palo Alto, Calif., 1996—. Mem. Child Care Adv. Com., Palo Alto, 1994—; leader LaLeche League, Menlo Park/Palo Alto, 1996—. Mem. ASCE (assoc.), Assn. Computing Machinery, Cap and Gown (alumnae bd. dirs.), Tau Beta Pi, Phi Beta Kappa.

HOWARD, DARCIE SHEILA, special education educator; b. Kingston, Ont., Can., Aug. 20, 1946; came to U.S., 1964; d. Gard Shaw Forrester and Mary Elizabeth (Nunn) Pike; m. Norman D. Howard, Sept. 18, 1966; children: Aaron, Matthew. BA, U. Calif., Berkeley, 1968; edn. credential, Calif. State U., Hayward, 1969; paralegal degree, Rancho Santiago Coll., 1987; spl. edn. credential, Chapman U., Orange, Calif., 1996, MEd, 1996. Cert. tchr., Calif., spl. edn. Svc. rep. Pacific Bell Telephone Co., Berkeley, 1966; tchr. Oakland (Calif.) Pub. Schs., 1969-73; tchr., tutor Calvary Christian Sch., Santa Ana, Calif., 1980-86; owner ABCaDE Computers, Santa Ana, 1986-93; spl. edn. tchr. Orange (Calif.) Unified Sch. Dist., 1990—; owner Calif. Sweet-Briar, 1991-93. Republican. Home: 1513 E Franzen Ave Santa Ana CA 92701-1641

HOWARD, DORIS MARIE, fine arts educator; b. Oyster Bay, N.Y., Feb. 24, 1946; d. Henry Seymore and Marie Mildred (Hsapray) Duncan; m. Andrew Joseph Howard, Sept. 10, 1988, 1 child, Emily Elizabeth. BFA, Syracuse U., 1968; MFA, Boston U., 1975. Cert. art tchr. Summer art dir. Thayer Acad., Braintree, Mass., 1969; art tchr. Norwood (Mass.) Schs., 1969—, adult edn. program instr., 1970-78, 80, pupil pers. svc. instr. Project Enhance, 1988-89; fine arts dept. head Norwood Jr. H.S., 1980—; artist in residence instr. Ariz. Western Coll., Yuma, 1978; bd. dirs. Mass. Cultural Coun., Norwood. Illustrator portraits, 1980—; sculpture exhbns. include Cooper and French Gallery, Newport, R.I., 1977, Brockton (Mass.) Arts Ctr., MTA Fine Arts Festival, Boston, 1978, 79, Brockton (Mass.) Cmty. Schs., 1979, Worcester (Mass.) Crafts Ctr., 1979, Ten Members Show of New Works, Boston, 1980, Artisan's Gallery, Great Neck, N.Y., 1980, Brockton Art Mus., 1988-92. Dir., designer town mural Norwood Jr. H.S., 1981, 94, pool mural Beautification Com., Norwood, 1993; initiator, dir. Japan Internat. Intern Program, Norwood, 1993-94. Recipient 1st and 2d place awards New Eng. Ceramic League, 1977, Outstanding Tchr. award Mass. Alliance for Arts Edn., 1989, Gov.'s citation for ednl. excellence Gov. Michael Dukakis, Boston, 1989. Mem. Mass. Cultural Coun., Nat. Art Edn. Assn., Mass. Alliance for Arts Edn., Mus. Fine Arts, Brocton Fuller Mus. (mems. exhibit purchase 1989). Episcopalian. Home: 103 Maple St Norwood MA 02062-2027 Office: Norwood Jr HS Endean Park Norwood MA 02062

HOWARD, ELIZABETH, corporate communications and marketing executive; b. Littleton, N.H., Apr. 24, 1950; d. Ellis Woodruff and Elizabeth (Millar) H. BA, U. N.H., 1972; MS, Pratt Inst., 1985. Dir. corp. comm. Nat. Distillers Chem. Corp, N.Y.C., 1978-85; dir. pub. rels. Transway Internat Corp., White Plains, N.Y., 1985; pres. Corp. Communications Group Millennium Inc., N.Y.C., 1986; pres. Elizabeth Howard & Co., N.Y.C., 1987—; Publ. and editor-in-chief Observations. Contbr. articles to profl. mags. Pres. Katharine Gibbs Sch. Scholarship Found., 1987-88, 94—, bd. dirs.; bd. dirs. Brenda Daniels Dance Com., 1993—, Hamilton-Madison Settlement House, N.Y.C., 1984-89, pres., 1987-89; mem. com. YMCA Greater N.Y., 1993-94. Mem. Global Econ. Action Inst., Women Execs. Pub. Rels. (bd. dirs. 1984-87), Fin. Women's Assn. (bd. dirs. 1994), Carnegie Coun., Women's Fgn. Policy Assn., Urban Land Inst. Home: 152 E 94th St Apt 8B New York NY 10128-2575 Office: 99 Park Ave New York NY 10016

HOWARD, ELSIE STERLING, marketing executive; b. Phila., June 30, 1946; d. Julian Alexander and Reba (Shaffer) S.; m. Eugene Jay Howard, Mar. 9, 1969; children: Heidi, Elizabeth. BA, U. Pa., 1968. Mgr. spl. events Miami Heart Assn., Miami Beach, Fla., 1986-91; mktg. cons. Temple Beth Sholom, Miami Beach, 1991-92, Women's Healthcare Svc., Miami Beach, 1992-93; spl. events cons. Sylvester Comp. Cancer Ctr., Miami, Fla., 1991-92; pres. Sterling Pub. Rels., Miami Beach, 1993 ; bd. dirs. Bankers Trust Co. of Fla., Children's Home Soc., 1996—. Active Citizens Commemorative Coin Adv. Com., U.S. Mint, 1994—; founding mem. Trustees' Coun. of Penn Women, 1986—, chair, 1994—; assoc. trustee U. Pa., 1987-91, founding mem. pres.'s coun., 1983—, so. regional alumni trustee, 1991—, overseer Sch. of Veterinary Medicine, 1992—, dir. Inst. Contemporary Arts, 1991—, trustee, 1990—, pres. Gen. Alumni Soc., 1995—; mem. Commn. on Status of Women, City of Miami Beach, 1992—, vice chair, 1993; founding mem. devel. coun. Sylvester Comprehensive Cancer Ctr., U. Miami Sch. Medicine, 1993—, chair spl. events task force, 1993—, vice chair devel. coun., 1995—; mem. Police Sub-Com. Task Force, City of Miami Beach, 1993—. Recipient Ivory Lady award NFIC, 1986, Women of Charity award Am. Cancer Soc., 1986, Love and Hope Rose award Juvenile Diabetes, 1985. Mem. Am. Numismatic Assn. (Pres. award 1995), Brickell Ave. Literary Soc., U. Pa. Gen. Alumni Soc. (mem. exec. com. 1991—), U. Pa. Dade Alumni Club (founding pres. 1982-85, secondary sch. chmn. 1988-90), U. Pa. Faculty Club, Westview Country Club, Foundlings Club. Democrat. Home: 4825 Lakeview Dr Miami FL 33140

HOWARD, FRANCES ESTELLA HUMPHREY, government official; b. Wallace, S.D., Feb. 18, 1914; d. Hubert Horatio and Christine (Sannes) H.; m. Ray Howard, Dec. 7, 1942 (dec. Jan. 1967); children: William, Anne. BA in Sociology, George Washington U., 1937, MA, 1941; HHD (hon.), Lane Coll., 1967; LHD, Seton Hill Coll., 1993, U. Md., Balt., 1993. With U.S. Office Civilian Def., Washington, 1941-43; liaison officer various vol. agys. for fgn. relief, Washington, 1942-60; commd. fgn. service officer Dept. State, Washington, 1960; chief liaison officer vol. agys. AID, Washington, 1960-67; chief spl. project div. Office War Hunger, Washington, 1968; liaison officer vol. health orgns., spl. asst. to assoc. dir. Office Asst. Sec. Health and Sci. Affairs HEW, Washington, 1969-70; spl. asst. to assoc. dir. for extramural programs Nat. Library Medicine, NIH, USPHS, Health and Human Services, Bethesda, Md., 1970—; lectr. to various orgns. Contbr. articles to nat. periodicals. V.p. U.S. Com. for Refugees, 1975-82; bd. dirs. Universalist-Unitarian Service Com., 1975-80, Mus. African Art, Smithsonian Instn., 1962—, Washington Opera, 1977—, Nat. Theatre Corp., 1980—, Capitol area Chpt. CARE, 1980—, Washington Ctr., 1982, Capitol Children's Mus., 1982—, Hubert H. Humphrey Inst. Pub. Affairs, U. Minn., 1983—, U.S. Capital Hist. Soc., 1984—, Environics Found. Internat., 1972—, U.N.A. (Capital Area divsn.), 1984-96, Woodrow Wilson Coun., 1994—. Recipient Disting. Service award Grand Chpt. Delta Sigma Theta, 1966; Women's Honor award Howard U., 1967; No. Va. service award Altrusa Club, 1967; Emblem of Honor award 6th Ann. Pan Am. Congress Conf. on Social Services, 1968. Mem. AAUW, Am. Polit. Sci. Assn., UN Assn., AAAS, The Royal Soc. Arts (London), Cosmos Club. Office: NIH Nat Library of Medicine 8600 Rockville Pike Bethesda MD 20894-0001

HOWARD, JANE LESLIE, business owner; b. Dayton, Ohio, Oct. 25, 1955; d. Leslie Leonard and Esther Marie (Taylor) Howard; m. Richard Dean Slade, Aug. 16, 1986 (div. July 1991). Student, U. Ky., 1973-75, Colo. Women's Coll., 1977-78; Design Diploma with highest honors, McGraw Hill Pub. Edn., 1994. Cert. desktop pub. specialist. Owner Design Works

Desktop Pub., Cin., 1991—. Mem. Nat. Assn. Desktop Pubs., Greater Cin. C. of C., Am. Mktg. Assn., Internat. Assn. Bus. Communicators, Am. Inst. Graphic Arts. Office: Design Works Desktop Pub 6024 Harrison Ave Ste 24 Cincinnati OH 45248

HOWARD, JEAN ELLIOTT, physician; b. Pomona, Calif., Apr. 23, 1941; divorced; 1 child, Crystal A. BA in Biochemistry with highest honors, U. Calif., Berkeley, 1962; MS in Biochemistry, Yale U., 1964; MD, U. Calif., San Francisco, 1969. Diplomate Am. Bd. Internal Medicine. Intern Pacific Med. Ctr., San Francisco, 1969-70, resident internal medicine, 1970-73, chief resident, 1972; chief resident Harkness Cmty. Hosp., San Francisco, 1972; fellow hematology U. Calif., San Francisco, 1973-75; rsch. fellow blood banking Irwin Meml. Blood Bank, San Francisco, 1973-74; NIH rsch. fellow ARC Blood Rsch. Lab., Bethesda, Md., 1975-76; project officer divsn. blood diseases and resouces Nat. Heart, Lung, and Blood Inst., NIH, Bethesda, 1976-77; asst. clin. prof. medicine in hematology George Washington U., Washington, 1976-77; asst. med. dir. transfusion svc., asst. clin. prof. pathology Stanford (Calif.) U., 1977-79; pvt. practice internal medicine Burlingame, Calif., 1979-80; hematologist USPHS, San Francisco, 1980-81; hematologist hematology-oncology svc. Fitzsimons Army Med. Ctr., Aurora, Colo., 1981-85; pvt. practice internal medicine, hematology and oncology Yuba City, Calif., 1985-90; med. officer, weight control, profile officer U.S. Army Hosp., Novato, Calif., 1985-91; oncologist, hematologist 9th Strategic Hosp., Beale AFB, Calif., 1987-90; mem. active staff Fremont Med. Ctr. and Rideout Meml. Hosp., Yuba City, 1985-92; oncologist, internist Evans Army Cmty. Hosp., Ft. Carson, Colo., 1990-91; chief profl. svcs. 808th Sta. Hosp., Uniondale, N.Y., 1992-93, 356th Field Hosp., Rocky Point, 1993-95; chief profl. svcs. 4420th USHA, 1995—; scientist med. dept., staff physician Occupational Medicine Clinic Brookhaven Nat. Lab., Upton, N.Y., 1991—, asst. med. dir. Marshall Island Med. Program, 1991-92, med. dir. Marshall Island Med. Program, 1993—; chief of staff Clin. Rsch. Ctr., Upton, N.Y., 1993—; chairperson tumor conf. Fremont Med. Ctr. and Rideout Meml. Hosp. Consortium, 1986-88, pharmacy and therapeutics com. United Cmty. Med. Svcs., 1990, exec. com. med. dept., Brookhaven Nat. Lab., 1993—. Author: (with others) Cryopreservation of Granulocytes in the Granulocyte: Function and Clinical Utilization, 1977; contbr. articles to med. jours. Lt. col. M.C., U.S. Army, 1981-85, 90-91, Pursian Gulf; lt. col. M.C., USAR, 1985—. NSF fellow, 1962-63. Fellow Am. Coll. Physicians; mem. Am. Soc. Hematology, Am. Soc. Clin. Oncology, Am. Coll. Occupational and Environmental Medicine, Assn. Mil. Surgeons U.S., Phi Beta Kappa. Office: Brookhaven Nat Lab Medical Dept Upton NY 11973

HOWARD, JOAN ALICE, artist; b. N.Y.C., Apr. 28, 1929; d. John Volkman and Mary Alice Devlin; m. Robert Thornton Howard, June 26, 1949; children: Barbara Jo, Robert Thornton Jr., Gregory Lyon, Brian Devlin. Student, Hunter Coll., 1947-48, UCLA, 1967-68, Los Angeles Valley Coll., 1970-71. Dir., choreographer Acad. Dance, Floral Park and Forest Hills, N.Y., 1947-57; dir. dance. Cath. Parochial schs., N.Y.C., Bklyn., and Floral Park, N.Y., 1948-55; chmn. dept. dance Molloy Coll., 1958-67; artist sta. KNBC-TV, Los Angeles, 1967-74, NBC, N.Y.C., 1974-78, sta. WNBC-TV, N.Y.C., 1978-79; artistic dir. Brookville (N.Y.) Sch., 1980-85; tchr. adult continuing edn. Lewisboro (N.Y.) Sch. Sys., 1995-96; dir. dance N.Y.C. YMCA, 1948; founder, dir. Queens-Nassau Regional Dance Theatre, 1950-55; choreographer Molloy Coll. Dance Theatre, 1959-67; cons. pre-natal exercise, L.I., N.Y., 1980—; judge art show Westbury (N.Y.) Mural Project, 1979; art cons., curator Chase Manhattan Bank, Cross River, N.Y., 1993-94; instr. Lewisboro Continuing Adult Edn., 1995-96; instr., speaker in field. One-woman shows include Dime Savs. Bank, Manhasset, N.Y., 1986-87, Ridgefield (Conn.) Guild Gallery, 1989-90, 91, 92, 93, Nardin Gallery Fine Arts, 1990, Chase Manhattan Bank, 1990-95, Manhasset Libr. Gallery, 1990-91, Hutchinson Gallery L.I. U., 1991, Rose Gallery, Kent, Conn., 1991, 92, 93, 94, Chelsea House, N.Y., 1991, Plandone Gallery, L.I., 1991, Sacco's, Ridgefield, 1991, Great Neck (N.Y.) Libr. Gallery, 1991, N.Y. Inst. Tech., Greenvale, N.Y., 1992, 93, Chase Manhattan Bank, Cross River, N.Y., 1992-93, 95-96, Hicksville (N.Y.) Gallery, 1993, Chase Manhattan Bank, N.Y., 1995-96, Aldrich Mus., 1995; exhibited in group shows at Valley Ctr. Arts Gallery, L.A., 1968-72, Home Savs. & Loan Art Exhibits, L.A., 1969-70, Westwood Art Gallery, L.A., 1972, Onion Gallery, L.A., 1972, North Ridge Women's Ctr. Gallery, L.A., 1972, Great Neck (N.Y.) Ctr. Gallery, 1976, A&S Gallery, Manhasset, 1976, Gloria Vanderbilt Designers Showcase, 1978, Ridgefield (Conn.) Guild Artists, 1983, Manhasset Libr. Gallery, 1985-89, Great Neck House Gallery, 1986-87, Hutchins Gallery C.W. Post Coll., L.I., 1986-90 (awards 1986, 87, 88, 89, 90), Dime Savs. Bank, Manhasset, N.Y., European Am. Bank, 1988, Nardin Fine Arts, Cross River, N.Y., 1989, Plandome Gallery, N.Y.C., 1990, Aldrich Mus., 1992-93, Hicksville (N.Y.) Gallery, 1993, Ridgefield (Conn.) Guild of Artists Gallery, 1993, Rose Gallery, Hicksville Gallery, 1993, Chase Manhattan Bank, N.Y.C., 1993-94, Tchr. Cont. Edn. Lernsboro Sch. Dist., N.Y., 1995-96, Adam Broderick Image Group, Ridgefield, Conn., 1995-96, Navden Gallery, N.Y., 1996; exhibited in juried shows Nassau County Mus. Fine Arts, Roslyn, N.Y., 1985, Plandome Gallery, 1987-88, Great Neck House Gallery, 1986-89 (hon. mention), East Meadow Libr. Gallery, 1988, Freeport Gallery, 1988, Shelter Rock Gallery, 1989, Ridgefield Gallery Portrait Show, 1989-90, Ridgefield Artists' Guild, 1989, 93, Nardin Gallery, 1989, Hutchins Gallery L.I. U., 1991, Rose Gallery, Kent, Conn., 1991, 92, 94, Chelsea House Mus. Cultural Commn., 1991, Manhasset Gallery, 1990-91, Sacco, Ridgefield, 1991, Great Neck Libr. Gallery, 1991, Chase Manhattan Bank, Cross River, N.Y., 1992-94, 95, Tchrs. Art Yorktown Artists Club, 1994, Aldrich Mus., 1993-94, Ridgefield (Conn.) Art Guild Gallery, 1993, Hicksville (N.Y.) Art Gallery, 1993, Chase Manhattan Bank, N.Y., 1993, 94, 95, HBO, N.Y.C., 1995; choreographer contemporary ballet Crucifixion, 1960, Persephone, 1961, Cubes of Truth, 1962, Somewhere, 1965; appeared on radio show Coast to Coast on a Bus, 1939-47; Broadway prodn. Lady in the Dark, 1940-42; performed ballet in TV show Stars of Tomorrow, 1942, Sleeping Beauty, 1942. Dem. committeewoman, Glen Cove, N.Y., 1954-58. Recipient Del Rey Perpetual Race championship trophy, 1974, Little Sabot Perpetual Race trophy, 1972-74, So. Calif. Women's Sailing Conf. sabot championship, 1972-74, 1st Woman trophy Olympic Regatta, 1973. Mem. Dance Educators Am., Manhasset Art Assn., Women's Sailing Com. of U.S. Yacht Racing Union (fund raiser 1980-81), Am. Women's C. of C. L.A., Tri-County Artists Ridgefield Art Guild. Home and Office: 19 Autumn Ridge Rd South Salem NY 10590-1103

HOWARD, JOANNE FRANCES, marketing executive, funeral director, extended care coordinator, research analyst; b. St. Louis, Feb. 5, 1953; d. Frank Henry and Evelyn Julia (Haeckel) Spellazza; m. Claude Lorrain Howard, May 20, 1978; children: Amy Julia, Laura Ann. BA, U. Mo.-St. Louis, 1975; MS, Western Ill. U., 1976. Lic. funeral director. Analyst, Streett Industries, Inc., St. Louis, 1977-78; research analyst Gallup & Robinson Co., Princeton, N.J., 1978-80, Jack Eckerd Corp., Clearwater, Fla., 1980-82, sr. research analyst, 1982-88; mktg. cons. Howard Assocs., 1986—; cons. Anson Lee Rector Inc., Tarpon Springs, Fla., 1982-83, Med-Op Clinics, Tarpon Springs, Fla., 1983-88; funeral dir., extended care coord. Pugh Funeral Home, Golden City, Mo., 1992—; analyst, cons. H.L. Pugh Assocs. Consulting, Golden City, 1992—. Editor monthly newsletter Florida West Coast chpt. Am. Mktg. Assn., 1982-83. Mem. Pinebrook Homeowners Assn., Largo, Fla., 1983-84. Mem. Am. Mktg. Assn. (past sec.-treas.), Mo. Funeral Dirs. Assn., Nat. Funeral Dirs. Assn., Mo. Inst. Funeral Profls. Democrat. Home and Office: 708 SE 70th Ln Golden City MO 64748-8152

HOWARD, JULIA C., state legislator; b. Salisbury, N.C., Aug. 20, 1944; d. Allen Leary and Ruth Elizabeth (Snider) Craven; m. Abe N. Howard Jr., 1962; children: Amedia Paige, Abe N. III. Grad., Davie H.S., 1962. V.p. Davie Builders Inc.; pres. Howard Realty & Ins. Agy. Inc.; mem. N.C. Ho. of Reps.; chmn. bd. trustees Davie County Hosp., 1978-85. Commr. Town of Macksville, N.C., 1981-88; mem. youth coun. First United Meth. Ch., 1974-84, chmn. coun. of ministries, 1979-81. Mem. Realtors Assn. (pres. Davie County Bd. 1972, state dir. 1973-75), Sertoma Club. Home: 203 Magnolia Ave Mocksville NC 27028-2911 Office: NC Ho of Reps State Capitol Raleigh NC 27611

HOWARD, JULIET PEARL, lawyer, educator; b. N.Y., Aug. 8, 1964; d. Adolphus and Ruth Howard; life ptnr. Norma J. Jennings. BA, Barnard Coll., N.Y., 1986; JD, Bklyn. Law Sch., 1991. Bar: N.Y. 1993, N.J. 1992. Staff atty. civil divsn. Legal Aid Soc., Bklyn., 1991-95; staff atty., adj. legal instr. Elder Law Clinic Bklyn. Law Sch., 1995—. Mentor Legal Outreach, Inc., N.Y., 1993—. Mem. N.Y. State Bar Assn., N.Y. Assn. Black Women Attys., Assn. of the Bar of the City of N.Y. Democrat.

HOWARD, LESLIE SUE, lawyer; b. Englewood, N.J., Apr. 23, 1967. BBA cum laude, George Washington U., 1989; JD, Fordham U., 1992. Bar: N.J. 1992, N.Y. 1993. Ptnr. Anderson, Kill, Olick & Oshinsky, P.C., N.Y.C. Mem. ABA, Assn. of Bar of City of N.Y. Office: Anderson Kill Olick & Oshinsky PC 1251 Avnuee of the Americas New York NY 10020-1182*

HOWARD, LOU DEAN GRAHAM, elementary education educator; b. Conway, Ark., Aug. 11, 1935; d. Nathan Eldridge and Martha Regina (Sutherland) Graham; m. Robert Hunt Howard, June 4, 1961; 1 child, Kenneth Paul. BSE, U. Cen. Ark., 1957; MA, Vanderbilt U., 1960. Cert. sch. adminstr., prin./supr., curriculum specialist, mentor, grad. elem. Elem. tchr. Hughes (Ark.) Pub. Schs., 1957-59; supervisory tchr. Peabody Demonstration Sch., Nashville, 1959-61; elem. tchr. Orange County Pub. Schs., Orlando, Fla., 1965-68; elem. tchr., K-5 adminstr. Westchester Acad., High Point, N.C., 1968-77; tchr. alternative learning ctr.-mid. sch. Randolph County Pub. Schs., Archdale-Trinity, 1978; elem. tchr. Greensboro (N.C.) Pub. Schs., 1978-93, Guilford County Schs., High Point, N.C., 1993—; del. U.S./China Conf. on Women's Issues, 1995. Contbr. articles to newspapers and AAUW Bull. Active Stephen Ministry; citizen ambassador program of People to People Internat. del. to U.S./China Joint Conf. on Women's Issues, Beijing, 1995. Mem. ASCD, NEA (sch. rep., mem. instrnl. and profl. devel. com.), AAUW (pres. N.C. state 1982-84, Gift honoree Ednl. Found.), Assn. Childhood Edn. Internat. (past pres.), Ind. Schs. Assn., Peabody Coll. Elem. Coun. (sec.), N.C. Coun. Women's Orgns., Clan Graham Soc. (sec. 1983—, Disting. Svc. award), Internat. Platform Assn., Order of Golden Thistle (charter), Delta Kappa Gamma, Phi Delta Kappa. Methodist. Home: 1228 Kensington Dr High Point NC 27262-7316 Office: Allen Jay Elem Sch 1311 E Springfield Rd High Point NC 27263-2244

HOWARD, LYN JENNIFER, medical educator; b. Buxton, U.K., Jan. 19, 1938; came to U.S., 1965; naturalized, 1971; d. Peter and Bess (Donnelly) Marsh; m. Burtis Howard, Aug. 13, 1965 (div. 1988); children: Peter Howard, Thia Howard. BA, Oxford U., 1960, MA, BM, BCh, 1964. Diplomate Am. Bd. Internal Medicine. Intern London Hosp., 1964-65; intern Kans. City Med. Ctr., 1965-66, resident, 1966-70; fellow in clin. nutrition and gastroenterology Vanderbilt Hosp., 1971-73; dir. clin. nutrition program Albany (N.Y.) Med. Coll., 1973-80, asst. prof. medicine, pediat., 1973-76, assoc. prof. medicine, pediat., 1977-84, prof. medicine, 1984—, head divsn. clin. nutrition, 1986—; asst. dir. Clin. Studies Ctr., Albany Med. Ctr., 1973-78; attending physician Albany Med. Ctr. Hosp., 1973—; attending physician, cons. clin. nutrition Albany VA Hosp., 1973—; cons. pediat. gastroenterology St. Peter's Hosp., Albany, 1974—; med. dir. Albany Home Health Resources, 1991-92; mem. working group Nat. Commn. Digestive Diseases, 1977; mem. NIH Consensus Devel. Conf., 1978, nutrition rsch. directions, 1979, spl. study sect. clin. nutrition rsch. units, 1980, nutrition study sect., 1989-93; cons. AMA Drug Evaluations, 1982, Medicare, Blue Cross/Blue Shield S.C., 1987—; keynote spkr. Australian Soc. Parenteral and Enteral Nutrition, Perth, 1993, 1st Clin. Nutrition Symposium, Kuala Lumpor, Malaysia, 1994. Contbg. editor Nutrition Reviews, 1981-87, 89; mem. editl. bd. Jour. Drug-Nutrient Interactions, 1984, Contemporary Issues in Clin. Nutrition, 1985, Jour. Am. Soc. Parenteral and Enteral Nutrition, 1987-90; contbr. articles, abstracts to profl. jours., chpts. to books. Exec. dir. Oley Found. for Home Parenteral and Enteral Nutrition, 1983-87, pres., 1987-91, med. dir., 1991; pres. Camphill Found., Pa., 1994. Recipient Clifton C. Thorne Cmty. Svc. award, 1990, Physician of Yr. award Albany chpt. Crohn's Colitis Found. Am., 1991; elected 1st woman mem. Great Lakes Interurban Club, 1990; Major County scholar, 1956; grantee Nutrition Found., 1973-79, U.S. Dept. Agriculture, 1978-81, William F. Donner Found., 1983, Oley Found. for Home Parenteral and Enteral Nutrition Patients, 1983—, Home Health Care of Am., 1983-88, Hosp. for Incurables Found., 1987-88, 91, Schaeffer Found. for Faculty Devel., 1988. Fellow Royal Coll. Physicians, Am. Coll. Physicians, Am. Coll. Nutrition (dir. 1985-88); mem. Am. Bd. Nutrition (dir. 1980, pres. 1982-84), Brit. Med. Assn., Am. Soc. Parenteral and Enteral Nutrition (abstract selection com. 1980, nutrition support standards com. 1984, future directions com. 1991, OASIS working group 1991-92, award 1992), Am. Soc. Clin. Nutrition (rsch. com. 1978, edn. com. 1979, councilor 1982-85, chair post grad. clin. nutrition tng. com. 1983-88, clin. practice in health and disease 1991), Am. Inst. Nutrition, Am. Gastroent. Assn. (co-organizer post grad. tng. course 1987, tng. and edn. com. 1988-91, abstract selection com. 1989), N.Am. Soc. Pediat. Gastroenterology, Am. Fedn. Clin. Rsch. (abstract selection com. 1986), Alpha Omega Alpha. Office: Albany Med Coll Albany NY 12208

HOWARD, SALLY J., nurse, social worker; b. Grand Rapids, Mich., Apr. 7, 1925; d. John E. and Frances A. (Nyland) Yonkman; m. Frank W. Howard, Oct. 2, 1948 (dec. Mar. 1994); children: Susan, Nancy, Mark, David. AA, Lake Mich. Coll., 1977. RN, 1946. Head nurse Butterworth Hosp., Grand Rapids, Mich., 1948-52; dir. Safe Shelter, Inc., Benton Harbor, Mich., 1978-80. Mem. bd. Civic Benefit Berrien County, 1958; adv. coun. Area Agy. on Aging, St. Joseph, Mich., 1994—. Home: 302 Jakway Benton Harbor MI 49022

HOWARD, SANDRA ANITA, business educator; b. Washington, Oct. 26, 1945; d. Jennie Lee (Mozie) Smith; m. Robert Lee Howard, June 24, 1967; children: Robin L., Tamara A., Robert Lee, Troy A. BS, U. D.C., 1967; MS, N.C. A&T State U., 1979; EdD, U. N.C., Greensboro, 1993. Cert. tchr., D.C., Ill., Ohio, N.C. Pub. sch. tchr. local bds. edn., Washing, Chgo., Xenia, Ohio, 1967-77; grad. asst., instr. N.C. A&T State U., Greensboro, 1976-82; tchr. English and reading Prince Georges County Schs., Upper Marlbobo, Md., 1983-85; instr. Prince Georges C.C., Upper Marlbobo, 1984-85; tchr. social studies Greensboro Pub. Schs., 1985-86; instr. N.C. A&T State U., 1985-87, asst. prof., 1989—; cons. Greensboro Youth Task Force, 1992—; cof. judge Distributive Edn. Clubs Am., Greensboro, 1990, Future Bus. Leaders Am., Hillsboro, N.C., 1996. Co-author: The Freshman Year of Studies--A Guidebook, 1987, 2d edit., 1995. Block capt. Am. Heart Assn. and March of Dimes, Greensboro, 1991-94; mem. United Way Funds Allocation Panel, Greensboro, 1994-95; vol. pub. rels. com. YWCA, Greensboro, 1995. Recipient various grants and awards. Mem. AAUW, Nat. Bus. Edn. Assn., N.C. Bus. Edn. Assn, Assn. for Bus. Comm., Pi Omega Pi. Baptist. Office: NC A&T U 1601 E Market St Greensboro NC 27411

HOWARD, SHEILA ANN, insurance executive; b. Huntington, W.Va., June 28, 1956; d. George Richard and Mellie (Hager) Reed; m. William Homer Howard, June 28, 1977 (div. Mar. 1982); children: Melissa Danielle, Nathan William. Diploma, Cabell County Career Ctr., 1974, Marshall U., 1981. Acctg. clk. Branchland Pipe and Supply, Hungtington, 1981-83; adminstrv. asst. W.Va. Mid Valley Constrn., Hungtington, 1983-88; acct. R.E.X. Inc., Barboursville, W.Va., 1988-90, Silver Bear Coal Co., Huntington, 1990-95; pres. Rapid Electronic Claims Inc., Barboursville, 1995—. Author: How to Save Money, 1995; editor (newsletter) Rapid News, 1995. W.Va. scholar, 1974-78. Mem. Huntington C. of C., Linmont Estates Housing Assn. (sec. 1990-92). Office: Rapid Electronic Claims Inc 6472-B Farmdale Rd Barboursville WV 25504

HOWARD-PEEBLES, PATRICIA N., clinical cytogeneticist; b. Lawton, Okla., Nov. 24, 1941; d. J. Marion and R. Leona (prestidge) Howard; m. Thomas M. Peebles, Aug. 16, 1975. BSEd, U. Ctrl. Okla., 1963; student, Randolph-Macon Coll. Women, 1964; PhD in Zoology (Genetics), U Tex. at Austin, 1969. Diplomate Am. Bd. Med. Genetics; cert. clin. cytogeneticist, med. geneticist. Sci. and history tchr. Piedmont (Okla.) Pub. Schs., 1963-64; biochem. technician biochemistry sect. biology divsn. Oak Ridge (Tenn.) Nat. Lab., 1964-66; instr. rsch. pediatrics dept. pediatrics, instr. cytotech. U. Okla. Health Scis. Ctr., Oklahoma City, 1971-72; asst. prof., dir. Cytogenetics Lab. U. So. Miss., Hattiesburg, 1973-77, assoc. prof., dir. Cytogenetics Lab., 1977-80; assoc. prof. dept. pub. health, staff Lab. Med. Genetics U. Ala., Birmingham, 1980-81; assoc. prof., dir. Cytogenetics Lab. dept. pathology U. Tex. Health Sci. Ctr., Dallas, 1981-85, prof., dir. Cytogenetics Lab., 1985-87; prof. dept. human genetics Med. Coll. Va., Richmond, 1987—; clin. cytogeneticist, dir. Postnatal Lab. Genetics & IVF Inst., Fairfax, Va., 1987—; Am. Cancer Soc. postdoctoral fellow dept. human genetics U. Mich. Med. Sch., Ann Arbor, 1969-70, dept. human genetics and devel. Coll. Physicians and Surgeons, Columbia U., N.Y.C., 1970-71; genetic cons. Ellisville (Miss.) State Sch., 1973-80; attending staff dept. pathology Parkland Meml. Hosp., Dallas County Hosp. Dist., 1981-87; mem. sci. adv. com. Fragile X Found., 1985—; mem. Internat. Standing Com. on Human Cytogenetic Nomenclature, 1991-96. Contbr. articles to profl. jours., chpts. to books; reviewer Am. Jour. Human Genetics, Am. Jour. Med. Genetics, Clin. Genetics, Human Genetics. Fellow Am. Coll. Med. Genetics (founding mem.); mem. AAAS, Am. Soc. Human Genetics, Assn. Genetic Technologists, Tex. Genetics Soc. (chmn. planning com. ann. meeting 1984), Delta Kappa Gamma, Sigma Xi. Baptist. Office: Genetics & IVF Inst 3020 Javier Rd Fairfax VA 22031-4627

HOWATT, SISTER HELEN CLARE, human services director, former college library director; b. San Francisco, Apr. 5, 1927; d. Edward Bell and Helen Margaret (Kenney) H. BA, Holy Names Coll., 1949; MS in Libr. Sci., U. So. Calif., 1972; cert. advanced studies Our Lady of Lake U., 1966. Joined Order Sisters of the Holy Names, Roman Cath. Ch., 1945. Life teaching credential, life spl. svcs. credential, prin. St. Monica Sch., Santa Monica, Calif., 1957-60, St. Mary Sch., L.A., 1960-63; tchr. jr. high sch. St. Augustine Sch., Oakland, Calif., 1964-69; tchr. jr. high math St. Monica Sch., San Francisco, 1969-71, St. Cecilia Sch., San Francisco, 1971-77; libr. dir. Holy Names Coll., Oakland, Calif., 1977-94; activities dir. Collins Ctr. Sr. Svcs., 1994—. Contbr. math. curriculum San Francisco Unified Sch. Dist., Cum Notis Variorum, publ. Music Libr., U. Calif., Berkeley. Contbr. articles to profl. jours. NSF grantee, 1966, NDEA grantee, 1966. Mem. Cath. Libr. Assn. (chmn. No. Calif. elem. schs. 1971-72). Home and Office: 2550 18th Ave San Francisco CA 94116-3005

HOWE, BEVERLY JEANNE, nurse; b. Wichita, Kans., Nov. 2, 1939; d. Sherwood C. and Cora Avoleen (McCarter) Gregory; m. James Edward Howe, Jan. 5, 1963 (div. Feb. 1978). RN diploma, St. Francis Sch. Nursing, Wichita, 1962. Charge nurse emergency rm. St. Francis Hosp., Wichita, 1963-66; psychiat. staff nurse Somerset (Pa.) State Hosp., 1967-69; nurse mgr. emergency/outpatient svcs. St. Vincent Hosp., Indpls., 1969-71; staff nurse emergency rm. and surgery fl. Holy Family Hosp., Des Plaines, Ill., 1971; head nurse surg. fl. Meth. Med. Ctr., Dallas, 1971-79, staff nurse II, oper. rm. nurse, 1979—. spkr. in field. Vol. Meth. Med. Ctr. Health Fairs, Dallas, 1980-90, Med. Mission to Cotija, Mex., 1993-94. Mem. Assn. Oper. Rm. Nurses, Am. Soc. Plastic & Reconstructive Nurses. Home: PO Box 224243 Dallas TX 75222-4243 Office: Meth Med Ctr 1441 N Beckley Dallas TX 75208

HOWE, FLORENCE, English educator, writer, publisher; b. N.Y.C., Mar. 17, 1929; d. Samuel and Frances (Stilly) Rosenfeld. A.B., Hunter Coll., 1950; A.M., Smith Coll., 1951; postgrad., U. Wis., 1951-54; D.H.L. (hon.), New Eng. Coll., 1977, Skidmore Coll., 1979, DePauw U., 1987, SUNY Coll. Old Westbury, 1992. Teaching asst. U. Wis., 1951-54; prof. English City Coll. and the Grad. Sch. CUNY, 1954-57; lectr. English Queens Coll., 1956-57; asst. prof. English Goucher Coll., 1960-71; prof. humanities and Am. studies SUNY-Old Westbury, 1971-87; prof. English City. Coll. and Grad. Sch., CUNY, 1987—; pres., dir. The Feminist Press at CUNY, 1970—; vis. prof. U. Utah, 1973, 75, U. Wash., 1974, John F. Kennedy Inst. Am. Studies Free U. Berlin, 1978, Oberlin Coll., 1978, Denison U., 1979, MLA Summer Inst. U. Ala., 1979, Coll. Wooster, 1980, Grad. Sch. Dept. English CUNY, 1986-87. Author: The Conspiracy of the Young, 1970, Seven Years Later: Women's Studies Programs in 1976, 1977, Myths of Coeducation: Selected Essays, 1964-1984, 1984; editor: (with Ellen Bass) No More Masks! An Anthology of Poems by Women, 1973, Women and the Power to Change, 1975, (with Nancy Hoffman) Women Working: An Anthology of Stories and Poems, 1979, (with Suzanne Howard, Mary Jo Boehm Strauss) Wverywoman's Guide to Colleges and Universities, 1982, (with Marsha Saxton) With Wings: An Anthology of Literature by and About Disabled Women, 1987, An Anthology of 20th Century American Women Poets, (with John Mack Faragher) Women and Higher Education in American History, 1988, Tradition and the Talents of Women, 1991, No More Masks, 1993; mem. editl. bd. Women's Studies: An Interdisciplinary Jour., 1971—, SIGNS: Women in Culture and Society, 1974-80, Jour. Edn., 1976—, The Correspondence of Lydia Marie Child, 1977-81, Research in the Humanities, 1977—; contbr. essays to profl. jours. Recipient Mina Shaughnessy award Fund for Improvement of Post-Secondary Edn., 1982-83; NEH fellow, 1971-73; Ford Found. fellow, 1974-75; Fullbright fellow, India, 1977; Mellon fellow Wellesley Coll., 1979; U.S. Dept. State grantee, 1983, 93. Office: The Feminist Press at CUNY 311 E 94th St New York NY 10128-5603

HOWE, MAROLYN LOUISE, chemical engineer; b. Memphis, Jan. 17, 1957; d. William Chew and Lucretia Louise (Alldredge) H.; m. Gerald Francis Lenski, Feb. 16, 1985. BS in Chemistry, Christian Brothers Coll., Memphis, 1979; BS in Chem. Engring., Christian Brothers Coll., 1981. Registered profl. engr.-in-tng., Tex.; cert. asbestos inspectiro, mgmt. planner. Lectr. Christian Brothers Coll., Memphis, 1980-81, 93; petroleum engr. Texaco, USA, Midland, Tex., 1981-85; chem. engr. Hess Environ. Svcs., Inc., Hess Environ. Svcs., Inc., 1987-92; sr. environ. specialist Fisher & Arnold, Inc., Memphis, 1992—; chem. engr., project mgr. Crittenden County Emergency Response Planning Com., Marion, Ark., 1988—. Vol. Alzheimer Day Care Ctr., Memphis, 1987-90, Crittenden Meml. Hosp., West Memphis, Ark., 1972-73; vol. asst. for wastewater permitting City Atty. West Memphis, 1989; spl. adminstrv. asst. Mayor of Crawfordsville, 1990-93; mem. Collierville, Tenn. Design Rev. Commn. and Long Range Planning Steering Com. NSF rsch. fellow, 1974, 78. Mem. Soc. Petroleum Engrs., Nat. Assn. Corrosion Engrs. (cert. corrosion technologist), Am. Soc. Safety Engrs., Christian Bros. Chemistry Alumni (chmn.). Methodist. Office: Fisher & Arnold Inc 3205 Players Club Pkwy Memphis TN 38125

HOWE, NANCY, artist; b. Summit, N.J., Nov. 17, 1950; d. Herbert Benedict and Ruth Audrey (Guerard) H.; m. Richard Gray Kelley Jr., Jan. 7, 1973 (div. Dec. 1987); children: Ryan Travis Kelley, Tyler Gray Kelley; m. James Anthony Russell, May 20, 1989. AB in Art, Middlebury Coll., 1973. federal duck stamp artist U.S. Dept. Interior, 1991-92; sixth ann. conservation stamp and print Nat. Fish and Wildlife Found., 1993. Exhibited in groups exhibitions at Cin. Mus., 1996, Colo. History Mus./Denver Rotary Club, 1994-96, Washington State Hist. Soc., Bennington Ctr. for the Arts and Old Algonquin Mus., Ont., Can., 1993, 94, 95, 96, The Witte Mus., 1996, Nat. Park Acad. of the Arts Nat. Tour, 1987, 90, 92, 94, 95, Leigh Yawkey Woodson Art Mus., 1990, 90, 91, 93, 94, 95, 96, U.S. Embassy residence, 1990-92, Waterfowl Festival, 1990-93, Mich. Wildlife Art Festival, 1992, Vt. Inst. of Natural Sci., Stratton Arts Festival, 1994-96, others; permanent collections include R.W. Norton Art Gallery, Leigh Yawkey Woodson Art Mus., John and Alice Woodson Forester Miniature Collection, Ella Carothers Dunnegan Gallery of Art; illustrtor Working With Your Woodland, 1983, Country Jour., Rod and Reel. Mem. Soc. of Animal Artists (Wildlife Art News award 1993, Actitives Press Printers award 1993, Award of Excellence, 1995). Home: RR 1 Box 402 East Dorset VT 05253

HOWE, NORA SLAVIN, art educator; b. Balt., Aug. 2, 1949; d. Michael and Shirley Ann (Helyer) Slavin; m. Michael Dunn, July 31, 1971 (div. Sept. 1981); 1 child, Maureen E.; m. James A. Howe, Aug. 4, 1986. BS in Art Edn., U. Md., 1971; MS in Art Edn., No. Ill. U., 1986. Cert. tchr. art edn. K-12, Ill. Tchr. art East Aurora (Ill.) H.S., 1971-74; tchr. art, adult edn. Waubonsee Jr. Coll., Aurora, 1972-73; tchr. art Jefferson Jr. H.S., Naperville, Ill., 1974-77, 80—, exploratory dept. chmn. and head cross-country coach, 1989—; lectr. in field. Mem. Naperville Sisters City Commn., 1983-84; mem. Greenpeace, Chesapeake Bay Soc. Naperville Edn. Found. fine arts grantee, 1994. Mem. NEA, Ill. Art Edn. Assn. (conf. registration chmn. 1990, Art Educator of the Yr. 1990), Nat. Art Edn. Assn., Art Guild of Naperville (Mem. of the Yr. 1979, pres.), Naperville Unit Edn. Assn. (bldg. rep. 1992—). Democrat. Roman Catholic. Home: 948 Sylvan Cir Naperville IL 60540-5532 Office: Jefferson Jr High Sch 1525 N Loomis St Naperville IL 60563-1316

HOWE, SHERRY SUE, surgical nurse; b. Knox, Ind., Oct. 9, 1955; m. John Edward Howe, July 26, 1984; children: Ronald Bruce, Kirt Greggory, Denise, James, Janice. ADN, Monroe County C.C., Monroe, Mich., 1984; BAS, Sienna Heights Coll., 1992; postgrad., Ea. Mich. U., 1993—. RN, Mich., Ohio; cert. apprentice counselor on substance abuse, Mich. Staff nurse Mercy Meml. Hosp., Monroe, 1984; staff nurse CCU U. Mich. Hosp., Ann Arbor, 1985-89; staff nurse, nurse mgr. Substance Abuse Treatment Ctr., Bixby Hosp., Adrian, Mich., 1990; staff nurse operating rm., part-time nursing supr. Oakwood United Hosps.-Beyer Ctr., Ypsilanti, Mich., 1991—; cons. to hosps. on the impaired nurse, Mich. and Ohio, 1990—; founder support group Nurses Caring for Nurses, Ann Arbor, 1990—. Contbr. articles to profl. publs. mem. nursing del. to China citizens amb. program People to People Internat., 1993. Mem. ANA, Mich. Nurses Assn. (mem. impaired profl. com. 1990-93, testifier for nursing legis. 1990, presenter 1990-94). Home: 2371 Woodview Dr Ida MI 48140 Office: Oakwood United Hosps Beyer Ctr 135 S Prospect St Ypsilanti MI 48198-7914

HOWE, TINA, playwright; b. N.Y.C., Nov. 21, 1937; d. Quincy and Mary (Post) H.; m. Norman L. Levy, Aug. 31, 1961; children: Eben, Dara. BA, Sarah Lawrence Coll., Bronxville, N.Y., 1959; LittD (hon.), Bowdoin Coll., Brunswick, Maine, 1988. Adj. prof. playwriting NYU, 1983—; vis. prof. Hunter Coll., N.Y.C., 1990—. Author: (plays) The Nest, 1969, Museum, 1976, Birth and After Birth, 1977, The Art of Dining, 1979, Appearances, 1982, Painting Churches, 1983, Coastal Disturbances, 1986 (Tony award nomination for best play 1987), Approaching Zanzibar, 1989; publs. include Coastal Disturbances: Four Plays by Tina Howe, 1989, Approaching Zanzibar and other plays, 1995, One Shoe Off, 1993. Nat. Endowment of Arts fellow, 1985, 95, Guggenheim fellow, 1990; Rockefeller grantee, 1984; recipient Obie award, 1983, Outer Critic's Circle award, 1983, Acad. award in Lit. Am. Acad. Arts and Letters, 1993. Fellow PEN, Writers Guild Am.; mem. Dramatists Guild (coun. mem. 1990—). Address: care Flora Roberts Inc 157 W 57th St New York NY 10019-2210

HOWE, VIRGINIA HOFFMAN, nurse administrator; b. Buffalo, Apr. 14, 1940; d. George C. Jr. and Mabel (Parrish) Hoffman; m. Lawrence T. Howe, Apr. 11, 1970; children: Daniel George, Timothy Kelly. AAS, Trocaire, 1977; BS in Community Health Nursing, SUNY, Buffalo, 1986. RN, N.Y. Assoc. coord. oper. rm. Buffalo Gen. Hosp., head nurse oper. rm. gen. surgery, oper. rm. staff nurse, nurse clinician otolaryngology and ear, nose, throat dept., nurse clinician divsn. plastic and reconstructive surgery, nursing instr., educator, discharge planning nurse, cmty. health nurse. Mem. Assn. Operating Rm. Nurses.

HOWELL, CATHERINE JEANINE, visual arts educator; b. Benton, Ill., Apr. 15, 1935; d. Lloyd William Reed and Lena Pearl (Armstrong) Goodin; m. Charles Lindy Barnfield, Apr. 13, 1950 (div. Apr. 23, 1973); m. Charles E. Howell, June 28, 1975; children: Alan Reed, Robert, Timothy Michael Barnfield; stepchildren: Crystal Lee, Carla Sue. A in Technol., So. Ill. U., 1962, BA, 1968, MS in Edn., 1976, postgrad. specialist, 1986. Cert. educator and supr., Ill. Clk. Kroger, Benton, Ill., 1957-60; elem. tchr. Benton Elem. Sch. Dist. #47, 1968-70; secondary art tchr. Marion (Ill.) Cmty. Unit Sch. Dist. # 2, 1970-94, ret., 1994; art instr. John A. Logan Community Coll., Carterville, Ill., 1975-89, vocat.-edn. art instr., 1992; cons. in field. Prin. work includes Strings of Creation, 1988, Portrait Sketch of Brenda Edgar, 1991. Art judge DuQuoin (Ill.) State Fair, 1990-91; mem. Ill. State Bd. Edn. Leadership conf., 1989-96; co-founder Downstate Art Educator's Assn. Recipient Award of Excellence Ill. State Bd. Edn., 1988, Sch. Bell award Williamson Co. ESR, 1988-89, Outstanding Art Educator award Ill. Alliance for Arts Edn., 1988, Ill. Art Educator award, 1989, Nat. Ill. Art Educator award, 1990, Senate Resolution Senator James Rea, 1989, Proclamation Gov. James Thompson, 1990. Mem. AAUW, Ill. Art Edn. Assn. (sec. dir. 1990), So. Ill. U. Alumni Life, Downstate Art Edn. (life), Delta Kappa Gamma Tchr. Honor Soc., Phi Kappa Phi. Home: 3000 W Woodlawn Pl Marion IL 62959-5541

HOWELL, DOROTHY JULIA, environmental educator, writer; b. Washington, May 29, 1940; d. Clifford Warner Howell and Avice Williams (Kent) Kip. BA in Biol. Scis., Goucher Coll., 1962; MS in Botany, U. Conn., 1967; JD, John Marshall Law Sch., 1975. Microbiologist Chgo. Sanitary Dist., 1969-75; asst. atty. gen. Ill. Dept. Justice, Chgo., 1975-76; atty. Borg-Warner Corp., Chgo., 1976-85; environ. counsel Chem. Waste Mgmt., Oak Brook, Ill., 1985-87; postdoctoral rsch. fellow Boston U., 1987-88; prof. Vt. Law Sch., South Royalton, 1988—. Author: Intellectual Properties and the Protection of Fictional Characters, 1990, Scientific Literacy and Environmental Policy, 1992, Ecology for Environmental Professionals, 1994. Vol. sci. Sci.-By Mail, Boston. Mem. AAAS, ABA, Am. Sci. Affiliation, Nat. Assn. Environ. Profls. Office: ELC Vt Law Sch PO Box 96 Chelsea St South Royalton VT 05068

HOWELL, ELIZABETH ADELL, elementary education educator; b. Berkeley, Calif., Apr. 2, 1944; d. Edwin Anderson and Anna Adell (Carlton) Hunt; m. John Robert Howell, Nov. 1, 1968; children: Robert, Phillip. BA in History, Ariz. State U., 1966; MA in Phys. Edn., No. Ariz. U., 1971. Cert. tchr., Ariz. Tchr. 8th grade Holbrook, Ariz., 1966-68; tchr. phys. edn. Holbrook, Phoenix, 1968-71; tchr. English, reading Holbrook, 1980-84, tchr. 7th grade English, 1984-86, tchr. 6th grade, 1986-90, tchr. 6th/7th grade social studies and English, 1990-92, tchr. phys. edn., 1991-92, tchr. 7th grade English, 1992—. Den mother Cub Scouts, 1980-82; asst. mother advisor Internat. Order of Rainbow for Girls, Holbrook, 1994—. Mem. NEA, Lady Elks (bulletin editor 1993, Woman of Yr. 1980), Ariz. Ednl. Assn.

HOWELL, JANET D., state legislator; b. Washington, May 7, 1944; d. Edward Fulton and Elsie (Lightbown) Denison; m. A. Hunt Howell; children: Eric, Brian. BA, Oberlin Coll., 1966; MA, U. Pa., 1968. Tchr. Phila. Pub. Schs., 1968-69; legis. asst. Gen. Assembly, Va., 1989-91; senator Va. State Senate, 1992—. Chair Fairfax County (Va.) Social Svcs. Bd., 1979-82, State Bd. Social Svcs., Va., 1986-91, Reston (Va.) Transp. Com., 1986-91; pres. Reston Community Assn., 1982-85, Citizen of Yr., 1990. Named Restonian of Yr., Reston Times, 1984, Virginian of Yr., Va. Assn. Social Workers, 1991. Democrat. Mem. Unitarian Ch. *

HOWELL, JEANETTE DORIS RATHBURN, elementary education educator; b. Cazenovia, N.Y., July 10, 1936; d. Adelbert Wallace Rathburn and Erna Joan Matilda Reetz; m. Louis A. Howell, Sept. 16, 1963; children: William Henry, Joan Elizabeth Howell Loyd. AB Gen. Home Econs., Brenau Coll. U., 1960; BA in Edn., U. Ga., 1964. Tchr. fourth grade Hall County Bd. Edn., Gainesville, Ga., 1961-62, Oconee County Bd. Edn., Watkinsville, Ga., 1964-65; part-time tchr. Clarke County Bd. Edn., Athens, Ga., 1979—. Mem. Edn. Com. Athens, Ga., 1993-94; active Athens 1996 Olympic Com., 1994— Jeannette Rankin Found., Athens. Brenau Coll. scholar. Mem. AAUW (Am. Fellowship award 1993), LWV, Order Eastern Star (Outstanding Officer award 1993-94), Phi Delta Kappa. Republican. Lutheran. Home: 1710 Mars Hill Rd Watkinsville GA 30677-4840

HOWELL, JOYCE ANN, lawyer; b. Haddonfield, N.J., Dec. 15, 1955; d. Harry O. and Mary Ann (Beaudet) H. BS, Shippensburg U., 1977, MLS, 1980; MA, St. John's Coll., Annapolis, Md., 1983; JD, Rutgers U., 1986. Bar: N.J. 1986, Pa. 1986, D.C. 1988, U.S. Dist. Ct. N.J. 1986, U.S. Dist. Ct. Pa. 1993, U.S. Ct. Appeals (3d cir.) 1987, U.S. Mil. Ct. Appeals 1987. Law clk. to presiding judge N.J. Chancery Ct., Atlantic City, 1986-87; assoc. Riker, Danzig, Scherer, Hyland & Perretti, Morristown, N.J., 1987-92, Levin and Hluchan, Voorhees, N.J., 1992-93; atty. office regional counsel U.S. EPA Region 3, Phila., 1993—. Staff mem. Rutgers Law Jour., 1985-86. NEH fellow, 1981, Roothbert Found. fellow, 1982, 83; Rutgers Law Sch. Alumni grantee, 1985. Mem. N.J. Bar Assn., N.J. Women Lawyers Assn. (v.p. 1989-90, pres. 1990-93). Democrat. Mem. Soc. of Friends.

HOWELL, MARY L., diversified company executive; b. Springfield, Mass., July 10, 1952; d. Walter Edward and Mary Patricia (Landers) Lynch; m. John N. Howell, Oct. 27, 1980; 1 child, Patrick. B.A., U. Mass.; grad. advanced mgmt. program Harvard U. Dir. legis. affairs Health Industry Mfr.'s Assn., Washington; with Textron Inc., Washington, exec. v.p. govt. and int. rels. Office: Ste 400 1101 Pennsylvania Ave NW Washington DC 20004*

HOWELL, PAMELA ANN, federal agency professional; b. Pensacola, Fla., Mar. 12, 1957; d. Thomas Pugh and Edith Corinne (McGowan) H.; children: Corinne Elizabeth Howell Meadows. BS, Mississippi Coll., 1978. Benefit authorizer Social Security Adminstrn., Birmingham, Ala., 1979—. H.S. coach Tabernacle Christian Sch., Gardendale, Ala., 1993—. Mem. Am. Fedn. Govt. Employees (v.p.). Republican. Baptist. Home: 712 Cherrybrook Rd Kimberly AL 35091-9744

HOWELL, PAMELA MCKINLEY, secondary and gifted education educator; b. Decatur, Ill., May 28, 1949; d. Walter W. and Donna Jean (Black) McKinley; m. Richard Linn Howell, June 27, 1971; 1 child, Zachary. BA, Millikin U., 1971; postgrad., Ill. State U., St. Mary's, Eureka. Tchr. Warrensburg (Ill.) Latham Cmty. Unit Sch Dist. #11, 1971—, dist. gifted coord., 1988—. Grantee Ptnrs. in Edn., 1980, 85-91. Mem. Warrensburg Edn. Assn. (pres., v.p. 1993-95), Ill. Assn. Gifted, Pi Beta Phi. Office: Warrensburg Latham Cmty Unit Sch Dist #11 Box 379 Warrensburg IL 62573

HOWELL, SARALEE FISHER, pilot; b. Stillwater, Okla., Dec. 10, 1930; d. Earl E. and Ruth Carr (Cleverdon) Fisher; m. Jack Howell, Sept. 3, 1973 (dec. Jan. 1978). BS in Bus. Adminstrn., Okla. State U., 1953. Cert. airline transport pilot. Asst. editor The Shell Roar Shell Oil Co., Tulsa, 1953-55; exec. sec., office mgr. Dyer Drilling Co., Casper, Wyo., 1956-59; corp. pilot Read Pipe & Supply, Farmington, N.Mex., 1961-65; flight instr., charter pilot adminstr. VA flight records Clinton Aviation Co., Denver, 1966-70; corp. pilot Colo. Constructors, Inc., Denver, 1970-72; photogrammetric pilot Kucera & Assocs., Inc., Denver, 1972-74; co-owner, instr. pilot Howell Flight Proficiency, Denver, 1975-78; owner, pilot Avi-Graphics Aerial Photography, Denver, 1975-78; real estate broker assoc. L.C. Fulenwider, Inc., Denver, 1982-86; assoc. broker Sanibel & Marco Island Properties, Inc., Sanibel, Fla., 1987—. Treas. Barrier Island Group for the Arts, Sanibel, 1988. Mem. Ninety-Nines, Inc. (sec. Colo. chpt. 1969, chmn. 1970), Sanibel Captiva Power Squadron (editor the Soundings 1992-93), Kappa Kappa Gamma (ad sales/asst. editor Denver Alumnae directory 1982-85).

HOWELL, VICKY SUE, health researcher; b. Beaver, Okla., June 16, 1948; d. Alvin Henry and Alice Odessa (Redemer) H.; m. Ramiro Martinez, Aug. 20, 1971 (div. June 1977); 1 child, Micaela Martinez; m. Timothy Arthur Pierson, June 5, 1982 (div. July 1995). BA, U. Okla., 1971, MA, 1973, PhD, 1979. Lectr. U. Tex., El Paso, 1973-74, 77-78; tchg. asst. U. Okla., Norman, 1979; asst. prof. U. Miss., Oxford, 1980-81, Wichita (Kans.) State U., 1981-82; rsch. analyst II Mo. Dept. Health, Jefferson City, 1984-88, rsch. analyst III, 1988—. Contbr. articles to profl. jours. Mem. Friends for Peace, Jefferson City, 1993-94; vol. House of Clara, Jefferson City, 1992-95. Mem. Am. Polit. Sci. Assn., Am. Pub. Health Assn., Women's Caucus for Polit. Sci., NOW. Democrat. Roman Catholic. Office: State Ctr for Health Stats 1738 E Elm PO Box 570 Jefferson City MO 65101

HOWELL-DRAKE, MINDY ANNE, administrative assistant; b. Smithfield, N.C., Apr. 19, 1967; d. Larry Wayne and Patricia Anne (Whitley) Oliver; m. Bruce Michael Drake, June 22, 1996. BS in Bus. Adminstrn., N.C. Wesleyan Coll., 1994. Sec. Ctrl. YMCA, Raleigh, N.C., 1986-89, Ctrl. YMCA-Camp Sea Gull, Arapahoe, N.C., summer 1987, N.C. Dept. Human Resources, Raleigh, 1989-92; adminstrv. asst. N.C. State Edn. Assistance Authority, Chapel Hill, 1992-96. Asst. basketball coach Ctrl. YMCA, Raleigh, 1989-90; mentor Wake County Cmtys. in Schs., Raleigh, 1995-96. Mem. AAUW. Democrat. Baptist. Office: Corvel Corp Ste 202 3125 Poplarwood Ct/Aspen Bd Raleigh NC 27604

HOWELLS, MURIEL GURDON SEABURY (MRS. WILLIAM WHITE HOWELLS), volunteer; b. White Plains, N.Y., May 3, 1910; d. William Marston and Katharine Emerson (Hovey) Seabury; student Chapin Sch., 1928; m. William White Howells, June 15, 1929; children: Muriel Gurdon Howells Metz, William Dean. Founder Brit. War Relief Soc., Madison, Wis., 1941, pres., 1941-43; apptd. visitor, dept. decorative arts and sculpture Boston Mus. Fine Arts, 1955-72, dept. Am. decorative arts, 1972—; ladies com. Inst. Contemporary Art, Boston, 1955-68; bd. dirs. Boston br. English-Speaking Union, 1955-80; a founder, trustee Strawbery Banke, Inc., Portsmouth, N.H., 1958-75, overseer, 1975-81, hon. overseer, 1981—; a founder, mem. steering com. Guild, 1959-91; bd. dirs. Garden Club Am., 1959-62, nat. chmn. medal award com., 1962-65, judge flower arrangements; pres. Piscataqua Garden Club, 1952-54; mem. Harvard Solomon Islands Expdn., Malaita, 1968; 1st chmn. Boston chpt. Venice Com., Internat. Fund for Monuments (now Save Venice Inc.), 1970-71, vice chmn. Boston chpt., 1971-77, mem. exec. com., 1971-89, hon. chmn., 1989—. Awarded King's medal for Svc. in the Cause of Freedom (Britain), 1946; recipient Hist. Preservation award zone 1 Garden Club Am., 1976. Mem. Nat. Soc. Colonial Dames N.H., Soc. Preservation New England Antiquities (mem. Maine coun. 1976-78), Women's Travel Club (pres. 1967-69), Chilton Club (Boston), Colony Club (N.Y.C.). Address: 11 Lawrence Ln Kittery Point ME 03905

HOWES, SOPHIA DUBOSE, writer, editorial associate; b. Balt., Apr. 20, 1954; d. John Carleton and Marie Josephine (Meeth) Jones; m. Edward Phillip Howes, Jan. 26, 1996. Student, Barnard Coll., 1972-75; BFA with honors, NYU, 1982, MFA, 1994. Mktg. asst. Stewart Tabori & Chang/Welcome Enterprises, N.Y.C., 1982-83; supr. word processing Harcourt Brace Jovanovich, N.Y.C., 1983-84; legal asst. Skadden, Arps, Slate, Meagher & Flom, N.Y.C., 1984-93; script reader Haft Wassiter Co., N.Y.C., 1994; editorial assoc. Matthew Bender & Co. Inc., N.Y.C., 1994—. Author one act plays, including Better Dresses, Rosetta's Eyes, 1988, 1988, Adamov, 1992, two act play Harps in the Wind, 1994. Recipient Grad. award in playwriting, NYU-Tisch Sch. Arts, 1994, Seidman awrd for talent, 1982. Mem. The Dramatists Guild.

HOWETH, LYNDA CAROL, small business owner; b. Okemah, Okla., Sept. 19, 1949; d. Clyde Leon and Hattie Arlene (Hymer) Williamson; children: Amanda B. Knowles, Harold W., Jennifer M. Student, Okla. State Tech. U., 1969, South Okla. City C.C., 1974. Mgr. five stores European Flower Markets, Oklahoma City, 1972-76; dist. sales rep. Profl. Office Systems, Inc., Oklahoma City, 1976-81; exec., owner Bus. Med. Systems, Inc., Oklahoma City, 1981—. V.p. dist. 41 Sch. Bd. Western Heights, Oklahoma City, 1991-94, pres., 1994—; founding mem. steering com. Okla. Bus. Health Inst., 1994. Mem. Nat. Sch. Bd. Assn., Okla. State Sch. Bd. Assn., Vital Info. Profls. (v.p., treas. 1988-90), Med. Tips Club (v.p., treas. 1990-91). Democrat. Home: 3328 SW 47th St Oklahoma City OK 73119-4325 Office: Bus Med Systems Inc Bldg A-200 1601 SW 89th St Ste A-200 Oklahoma City OK 73159-6349

HOWL, JOANNE HEALEY, veterinarian; b. Mariemont, Ohio, Mar. 16, 1957; d. Joseph Daniel and Claire Helen (Baillargeon) H.; m. Arthur Wesley Howl, May 12, 1990. DVM, U. Tenn., 1987. Sr. lab. animal technician Lab Animal Facility, Knoxville, 1983-84; gnotobiology technician U. Tenn., Knoxville, 1984-86; assoc. vet. Mynatt Vet. Clinic, Knoxville, 1987-89; veterinary med. officer U.S. Dept. of Agr. Animal and Plant Health Inspection Svcs., Raleigh, N.C., 1989-90; owner Creature Comfort Veterinary Relief Svc., Laurel, Md., 1991-95; assoc.veterinarian Muddy Creek Animal Hosp., West River, Md., 1996—. Editor: The Vet Gazette, 1995—; contbr. articles to profl. jours. Sec. Vet. Med. Assistance Team-2. Mem. AVMA, Am. Animal Hosp. Assn., Am. Assn. Feline Practitioners, Md. Vet. Med. Assn. (chmn. pub. rels. com. 1995—). Roman Catholic. Home: 4304 Tenthouse Ct West River MD 20778 Office: 5518 Muddy Creek Rd West River MD 20778

HOWLAND, BETTE, writer; b. Chgo., Jan. 28, 1937; d. Sam and Jessie (Berger) Sotonoff; m. Howard C. Howland (div.); children—Frank, Jacob. B.A., U. Chgo., 1955. Assoc. prof. com. social thought U. Chgo., 1993—. Author: W-3, 1974, Blue in Chicago, 1978 (1st prize Friends of Am. Writers), Things to Come and Go, 1983. Fellow Rockefeller Found., 1969, Marsden Found., 1971, Guggenheim Found., 1978, Nat. Endowment for the Arts, 1981, MacArthur Found., 1984. Jewish. Address: PO Box 405 Union Pier MI 49129-0405

HOWLAND, CATHERINE REXFORD BRISTOL, environmental planner; b. Norwood, Mass., July 31, 1969; d. Edgar H. and Julia (Redhead) Bristol; m. Matthew J. Howland, June 27, 1992. BA in Environ. Studies, Brown U., 1992. Recycling/composting planner R.I. Solid Waste Mgmt., Johnston, 1993—; proprietor Second Thoughts, Norton, Mass., 1996—; com. mem. Solid Waste Adv. Com., Norton, 1993-95. Vol. Providence Animal Rescue League, 1994-96, Capron Park Zoo, Attleboro, Mass., 1993-95. Mem. AAUW.

HOWLAND, JOAN SIDNEY, law librarian, law educator; b. Eureka, Calif., Apr. 9, 1951; d. Robert Sidney and Ruth Mary Howland. BA, U. Calif., Davis, 1971; MA, U. Tex., 1973; MLS, Calif. State U., San Jose, 1975; JD, Santa Clara (Calif.) U., 1983. Assoc. librarian for pub. svcs. Stanford (Calif.) U. Law Library, 1975-83, Harvard U. Law Library, Cambridge, Mass., 1983-86; dep. dir. U. Calif. Law Library, Berkeley, 1986-92; dir. law libr., prof. law U. Minn. Sch. of Law, 1992—. Questions and answers column editor Law Libr. Jour., 1986-91; memt. column editor Trends in Law Libr. Mgmt. & Tech., 1987-94. Mem. ALA (chmn. cultural diversity com. 1995-97), Am. Assn. Law Librs. (chmn. edn. com. 1995-1997), Am. Assn. Law Librs. (chmn. edn. com. 1987-90), Am. Indian Libr. Assn. (treas. 1992—), Am. Law Inst. Office: U Minn Law Sch 229 19th Ave S Minneapolis MN 55455-0444

HOWLETT, PHYLLIS LOU, athletics conference administrator; b. Indianola, Iowa, Oct. 23, 1932; d. James Clarence and Mabel L. (Fisher) Hickman; m. Jerry H. Howlett, Jan. 2, 1955 (dec.); children: Timothy A., Jane A. Field; m. Ronlin Royer, Dec. 30, 1977. BA, Simpson Coll., 1954. Tchr. Oskaloosa (Iowa) High Sch., 1954-55; psychometrist Drake U., Des Moines, 1956-57, asst. to men's athletics dir., 1974-79; asst. dir. athletics U. Kans., Lawrence, 1979-82; asst. commr. Big Ten Conf., Park Ridge, Ill., 1982—; mem. football TV com. NCAA, 1980-87, chmn. NCAA com. on women's athletics, 1987-94, NCAA exec. com., 1990—, NCAA women's golf com., 1983-89, spl. com. NCAA women's basketball TV, 1989-90, chair NCAA com. for women's corp. mktg., 1990-94, NCAA Divsn. I championship com., 1990-95, chair NCAA task force on gender equity, 1992-94, NCAA exec. dir. search com., 1993, spl. NCAA com. divsn. I football playoff, NCAA adminstrv. com., 1995, NCAA joint policy bd., 1995—, NCAA sec., treas., 1995—. Chmn. Iowa Commn. Status of Women, 1976-79; pres. Vol. Bur. of Greater Des Moines, 1969-70; chair Arts and Recreation Coun. of Greater Des Moines, 1975; pres. Iowa Children's and Family Svcs., 1973; nat. pres. Assn. Vol. Burs., Inc., 1972-73, svc. award. Inducted into Simpson Coll. Hall of Fame. Mem. Nat. Assn. Dirs. of Collegiate Athletics (exec. com. 1986-90, NACDA award for adminstrv. excellence 1994), Nat. Assn. Women's Athletics Adminstrs., Simpson Coll. Alumni (Achievement award 1988). Republican. Office: 1309 Oak Hill Rd Barrington IL 60010

HOWLETT, STEPHANIE ANN, home care equipment sales representative, nurse; b. Kansas City, Kans., Dec. 23, 1957; d. Wayne Stewart and Anna Marie (Barancik) H. AA, Kansas City Community Coll., 1979; student, Colo. Ctr. for The Blind, 1995—. RN. Critical care nurse Providence-St. Margarets Health Ctr., Kansas City, Kans., 1979-82; primary pvt. duty nurse Quality Care In, Kansas City, Mo., 1980-81; dir. nursing Profl. Nursing Service, Kansas City, Mo., 1981-86; med. services cons. Crawford Health and Rehab. Services, Kansas City, Mo., 1986; sales rep. HOMEDCO, Lenexa, Kans., 1986-92, mem. presidents adv. coun., 1986-92; mem. adv. bd. Olsten Health Care Svcs., Kansas City, Mo., 1986-92, utilization rev. com., 1986-92, budget com., 1987. Mem. Jr. League, Wyandotte and Johnson County, 1991. Named one of Outstanding Young Women Am., 1987. Mem. NAFE, Nat. Rehab. Assn., Assn. Rehab. Nurses, Support Hospice Oncology Profls., Kansas City Met. Discharge Coords., Kansas City Regional Homecare Assn. (edn. com., infusion therapy com.), Kiwanis Club of Lenexa (bd. dirs.), Nat. Fedn. of the Blind. Republican. Home: 10507 College Ave Kansas City MO 64137-1763

HOWORTH, LUCY SOMERVILLE, lawyer; b. Greenville, Miss., July 1; d. Robert and Nellie (Nugent) Somerville; m. Joseph Marion Howorth, Feb. 16, 1928. A.B., Randolph-Macon Woman's Coll., 1916; postgrad., Columbia U., 1918; J.D. summa cum laude, U. Miss., 1922. Bar: Miss. 1922, U.S. Supreme Ct. 1934. Asst. in psychology Randolph-Macon Woman's Coll., 1916-17; gauge insp. Allied Bur. Air Prodn., N.Y.C., 1918; indsl. research nat. bd. YWCA, 1919-20; gen. practice law Howorth & Howorth, Cleveland, Greenville and Jackson, Miss., 1922-34; U.S. commr. So. Jud. Dist. Miss., 1927-31; assoc. mem. Bd. Vet. Appeals, Washington, 1934-43; legis. atty. VA, 1943-49; v.p., dir. VA Employees Credit Union, 1937-49; assoc. gen. counsel War Claims Commn., 1949-52, dep. gen. counsel, 1952-53, gen. counsel, 1953-54; ptnr. James Somerville & Assocs. (overseas trade and devel.), 1954-55; atty. Commn. on Govt. Security, 1956-57; pvt. practice law Cleveland, Miss., 1958—; mem. nat. bd. cons. Women's Archives, Radcliffe Coll.; mem. lay adv. com. study profl. nursing Carnegie Corp. N.Y., 1947-48; chmn. Miss. State Bd. Law Examiners, 1924-28; mem. Miss. State Legislature, 1932-36, chmn. com. pub. lands, 1932-36; treas. Com. for Econ. Survey Miss., 1928-30; mem. Research Commn. Miss., 1930-34. Editor: Fed. Bar Assn. News, 1944; assoc. editor: Fed. Bar Assn. Jour., 1943-44; editor: (with William M. Cash) My Dear Nellie-Civil War Letters (William L. Nugent), 1977; contbr. articles profl. jours. Keynote speaker White House Conf. on Women in Postwar Policy Making, 1944, at conf. on opening 81st Congress. Recipient Alumnai Achievment award Randolph-Macon Woman's Coll., 1981, Lifetime Achievmenet award Schlesinger Libr. of Radcliffe Coll., 1983; named for her outstanding lifetime achievments by Senate Concurrrent Resolution, adopted by Senate and Ho. of Reps., 1984; recipient Excellence medal Miss. U. for Women, 1989. Mem. AAUW (nat. dir., 2d v.p. 1951-55, mem. found. 1960-63), Nat. Fedn. Bus. and Profl. Women's Clubs (nat. dir.; rep. to internat. 1939, chmn. internat. conf. 1946), Nat. Assn. Women Lawyers, Miss. Library Assn. (life), Miss. Hist. Soc. (dir. 1982—, Merit award 1983), DAR, Daus. Am. Colonists, Am. Legion Aux. (past sec. Miss. dept.), Assembly Women's Orgns. for Nat. Security (chmn. 1951-52), Phi Beta Kappa, Pi Gamma Mu, Phi Alpha Delta, Alpha Omicron Pi (Wyman award 1985), Delta Kappa Gamma, Omicron Delta Kappa, Phi Kappa Phi (hon.). Democrat (del. nat. conv., 1932). Methodist. Club: Soroptimist (Washington). Address: 515 S Victoria Ave Cleveland MS 38732-3738

HOWSE, JENNIFER LOUISE, foundation administrator; b. Glendale, Calif., Jan. 31, 1945; d. Benjamin McCausland and Patricia Louise (Naylor) H. PhD in Linguistics, Fla. State U., 1973; LHD (hon.), SUNY, Bklyn., 1990. Rsch. asst., instr. Inst. Human Devel. Coll. Edn., Fla. State U., Tallahassee, 1967-69; dir. planning and evaluation Wakulla County (Fla.) Sch. System, 1969-72; dir. NARC/HEW Liaison Project Nat. Assn. for Retarded Citizens, Govtl. Affairs Office, Washington, 1972-73; dir. Developmental Disabilities Bur., dir. Bur. Tech. Assistance and Regulation Fla. Dept. Health and Rehab. Svcs., Tallahassee, 1973-75; exec. dir. Willowbrook Rev. Panel, N.Y.C., 1975-78; assoc. commr. N.Y. State Office Mental Retardation and Developmental Disabilities, N.Y.C., 1978-80; state commr. for mental retardation Dept. Pub. Welfare, Harrisburg, Pa., 1980-85; exec. dir. Greater N.Y. chpt. March of Dimes Birth Defects Found., N.Y.C., 1985-89; pres. March of Dimes Birth Defects Found., White Plains, N.Y., 1990—; advisor Ctr. for Family Life in Sunset Park, Bklyn., 1992—. Bd. dirs. Salk Inst., La Jolla, Calif., Nat. Health Coun., Washington, Barrier Island Trust, Tallahassee; mem. Kaiser Commn. on Future of Medicaid, Balt., 1992—. Office: March Dimes Birth Defects Found 1275 Mamaroneck Ave White Plains NY 10605-5201

HOXMEIER, MARLETTE MARIE, nurse manager; b. Anoka, Minn., May 14, 1953; d. Kenneth A. and Laurel (Edeburn) Nelson; m. Kenneth J. Hoxmeier, Apr. 16, 1977; children: Nicholas Nelson, Joseph Simon. Diploma, St. Cloud Sch. Nursing, 1974; BS in Health Arts, Coll. of St. Francis, Joliet, Ill., 1992, postgrad., 1995—. RN, Mn.; cert. in low risk neonatal nursing AAWONN. Staff nurse St. Paul Ramsey Hosp., 1974-79; nurse instr. Regional Kidney Disease Program, Mpls., 1979-83; staff nurse preceptor Mpls. Children's Med. Ctr., 1983-87; asst. head nurse St. Joseph's Hosp./Healtheast, St. Paul, 1987—; neonatal resuscitation instr. Am. Acad. Pediatrics, 1990—. Mem. Minn. Neonatal Nurses and Mgrs. (v.p. 1987-93). Democrat. Lutheran. Home: 4174 Oakcrest Dr Vadnais Hts MN 55127-7977 Office: St Joseph's Hosp 69 Exchange St W Saint Paul MN 55102-1004

HOY, KATHY PEI IN, artist; b. Hongzhou, Cejiang, China, Apr. 5, 1942; came to U.S., 1967; d. Ming Tsai and Hui Fen (Chu) Chen; m. Harold Henry Hoy, June 30, 1968; children: Cindy Mei, Raymond Sean. BA, Taiwan Normal U., 1966; MFA, U. Oreg., 1969. Instr. Maude Kerns Art Ctr., Eugene, Oreg., 1970-76, City of Eugene, Eugene, 1976-80, Lane C.C., Eugene, 1971—; assoc. and counselor E.F. Inst. for Cultural Exchange, Inc., Cambridge, Mass., 1992—. Art demonstrator: Oreg. Watercolor Soc., Portland, 1985, Roseburg (Oreg.) Art Soc., 1986, workshops Lane C.C., Florence, Oreg., 1987—; group shows include Spokane Art Mus., Wash., 1968, U. Oreg., Eugene, 1969, Maude Kerns Art Ctr., Eugene, 1972, 74, 82, 84, 86, Oreg. State U., Corvallis, 1982; one-woman shows include U. Oreg.

Art Mus., 1989, Eugene Pub. Libr., 1987, Opus 5 Gallery, 1988, Hult Ctr. Performing Art Ctr., Eugene, 1992. Recipient Hon. mention Salem (Oreg.) Fair Bd., 1982.

HOY, MARJORIE ANN, entomology educator; b. Kansas City, Kans., May 19, 1941; d. Dayton J. and Marjorie Jean (Acker) Wolf; m. James B. Hoy; 1 child, Benjamin Lee. AB, U. Kans., 1963; MS, U. Calif., Berkeley, 1966, PhD, 1972. Asst. entomologist Conn. Agrl. Expt. Sta., New Haven, 1973-75; rsch. entomologist U.S. Forest Svc., Hamden, Conn., 1975-76; asst. prof. entomology U. Calif., Berkeley, 1976-80, assoc. prof. entomology, 1980-82, prof. entomology, 1982-92, prof. emeritus, 1992—; Fischer, Davies and Eckes prof., dept. entomology and nematology U. Fla., Gainesville, 1992—; chairperson Calif. Gypsy Moth Sci. Adv. Panel, 1982—; mem. genetics resources adv. com. USDA, 1992—. Editor or co-editor: Genetics in Relation to Insect Managment, 1979, Recent Advances in Knowledge of the Photoseiidae, 1982, Biological Control of Pests by Mites, 1983, Biologica; Control in Agricultural IPM Systems, 1985, Insect Molecular Genetics, 1994, The Phytoseiidae as Biological Control Agents of Pest Mites and Insects: A Bibliography, 1996, Managing the Citrus Leafminer, 1996; mem. editorial bd. Exptl. and Applied Acarology, Biol. Control, Biocontrol Sci. and Tech., Internat. Jour. Acarology; contbr. numerous articles to profl. jours. Recipient citation for outstanding achievments in regulatory entomology Fla. Divsn. Plant Industry, 1995; NSF fellow U. Calif., Berkeley, 1963-64. Fellow AAAS, Royal Entomol. Soc. London, Entomol. Soc. Am. (mem. Pacific br. governing bd. 1985, Bussart award 1986, Founder's Meml. award 1992); mem. Am. Genetic Assn., Internat. Orgn. Biol. Control (v.p. 1984-85), Am. Inst. Biol. Scis. (adv. coun. 1996—), Acarological Soc. Am. (governing bd. 1980-84, pres. 1992), Soc. for Study of Evolution, Phi Beta Kappa, Sigma Xi (chpt. sec. 1979-81, Sr. Faculty Rsch. award 1996). Home: 4320 SW 83rd Way Gainesville FL 32608-4131 Office: U Fla Dept Entomology and Nematology Hull Rd # 970 Gainesville FL 32612

HOYER, MARY LOUISE, social worker, educator; b. Wausau, Wis., Dec. 4, 1925; d. Jacob and Julia (Anderson) Stuhlfauth; m. William Henriksen Hoyer, June 30, 1948; children: Mark Charles, Gail Maren. BS in Biochemistry, U. Minn., 1948; MSW, Cath. U., 1985, D of Clin. Social Work, 1994. Lic. cert. clin. social worker, Md. Rsch. biochemist NIH, Bethesda, Md., 1948-50; dir. Teller Tng. Ctr. Internat. Telephone and Telegraph, Washington, 1967-69; specialist employee devel. Civil Svc. Commn., Washington, 1969-75, supr. sys. sect., 1975-78; mgr. agy. assistance divsn. Office Pers. Mgmt., Washington, 1978-82; vol. counselor Comty. Crisis Ctr., Bethesda, 1980-82; classroom and field instr. Cath. U., Washington, 1986-91; clin. social worker St. Francis Ctr., Washington, 1985-88; pvt. practice as clin. social worker Bethesda, 1987—; dep. exec. dir. task force on exec. devel. in sr. exec. svc.: Policy Initiatives for Reform of Civil Svc., Office of Pers. Mgmt., Washington, 1978-79. Contbr. rsch. articles to profl. jours. Precinct chairperson Dem. Action Group, Bethesda, 1962-66; fin. cons. Sch. Bd., Hamilton, Mont., 1950-54; cons. Internat. Visitors Info. Svc., Washington, 1962-66; vol. Md. Fair Housing, Bethesda, 1962-66. Legis. fellow U.S. Congress, Washington, 1980. Mem. NASW, Greater Washington Soc. Clin. Social Workers. Democrat. Lutheran. Home and Office: 5901 Lone Oak Dr Bethesda MD 20814

HOYER, PHYLLIS SCARBOROUGH, elementary education educator; b. Salisbury, Md., Oct. 14, 1938; d. Paul Daniel and Norma (Luettinger) Scarborough; m. Lawrence Cogswell Hoyer, July 8, 1961; children: Brian Lawrence, Andrew Scarborough. BS, Hood Coll., 1960; MEd, Towson State U., 1986; post grad., Hood Coll., U. Md. Cert. early childhood edn., home econs., Md. Tchr. Anne Arundel County Bd. Edn., Annapolis, Md., 1960-61, Washington County Bd. Edn., Hagerstown, Md., 1961-64, Frederick County Bd. Edn., Md., 1972—; chairperson communication com., 1984-85; tchr. adv. com., 1977-80, 87-89; team leader, 1989-92; rep. kindergarten class, 1989-92. Instr. frederick County YMCA, 1976-79; participating mem. Earthwatch, Orca Survey, 1989, Fiji Coral Cmtys., 1990, Canary Island Sea Life, 1992, Sierra Wildlife, 1993; vol. ARC, 1993. Recipient Hon. Mention award Nat. Geographic Soc. Photography Contest, 1991. Mem. NEA, Md. State Tchrs. Assn., Frederick County Tchrs. Assn. (tchrs. rep. 1980-83, 94), Nature Conservancy. Republican. Home: 8398 Cub Hunt Ct Walkersville MD 21793-9325 Office: Waverley Elem Sch 201 Waverley Dr Frederick MD 21702

HOYSRADT, JEAN E., insurance company executive; b. N.Y.C., 1950. Grad., Duke U., 1972, Columbia U., 1974. Sr. v.p., investment N.Y. Life Ins. Co. Office: New York Life Ins Co 51 Madison Ave New York NY 10010*

HOYT, CHARLEE VAN CLEVE, management executive; b. Bluefield, W.Va., May 21, 1936; d. Charles Ives Van Cleve and Kathryn Margarete (Harden) Perrow; m. Ronald Reiner Hoyt, 1959 (div. 1983); children: Dean Christopher, Jason Allen. BA in Edn., U. Fla., 1959, MEd, 1962, postgrad., 1963-64. Cert. spl. edn. tchr. Tchr. Amherst County Schs., Elon, Va., 1958; tchr. spl. edn. Marion County Schs., Ocala, Fla., 1959-61; counselor Univ. Counseling Ctr., Gainesville, Fla., 1962-63, Sunland Tng. Ctr., Gainesville, 1963; mem. community faculty Minn. Met. State Coll., Mpls., 1972-83; mem. council City of Mpls., 1975-86; ptnr. Van Cleve Assocs., 1980-87, 91—; pres. Van Cleve, Doran & Bruno, Inc. 1987-91; corp. officer BAM Leasing Co., Inc., 1987—; dir. human resources Pascua Yagu Tribe, 1988-95; adj. faculty U. Phoenix, Tucson, 1995—; vis. tchr. Tucson Unified Sch. Dist., 1995—; pres. Van Cleve Assocs., 1991—; mem. faculty Govt. Tng. Service, St. Paul, 1978-86, Ariz. Govt. Tng. Services; pres. Minn. Women in City Govt., St. Paul, 1978-79; mem. Met. Land Use Adv. Bd., St. Paul, 1978-83; bd. dirs. Transp. Adv. Bd., St. Paul, 1979-81; mem. conf. faculty League of Minn. Cities, St. Paul, 1979-82; bd. dirs. Met. Council Criminal Justice Adv. Bd., St. Paul, 1979-82; pres. Women in Mcpl. Govt., Nat. League of Cities, Washington, 1980-81, founder minority caucus coalition, 1982, dir., 1982-84; curriculum cons. Nat. Women's Edn. Fund, Washington, trainer, 1982-86; officer JTPA Grantee Orgn. Region IX, 1994—; commr. Pima County/Tuscon Women's Commn. Presenter numerous workshops; contbr. articles to profl. jours. Mem. Women Helping Women YWCA, 1987—; various offices with Republican Party, Minn., 1970-86 ; pres. Burroughs Elem. Sch. PTA, Mpls., 1973-74; panelist White House Conf., 1981; chmn. Senator Durenburger's Task Force on Women's Issues, Mpls., 1981-84; bd. dirs. Nat. Conf. Rep. Mayors and Council Mems., 1984-85; mem. Senator Durenburger's Intergovtl. Relations Adv. Com., Mpls., 1984-86; bd. dirs. Twin Cities Internat. Program, Mpls., 1983-86; participant Women's Dialogue US/USSR, Moscow, 1985; trustee Council Internat. Programs, Cleve., 1985-90; bd. dirs. At the Foot of the Mountain Theater, Mpls., 1985-86, Tucson Ctrs. for Women and Children, 1988-92; bd. dirs. GOP Feminists, Hamline U. Ctr. for Women in Govt.; mem. Nat. Women's Polit. Caucus, Hennepin County Women's Polit. Caucus; mem. Tucson Support for Success Team, 1986-92, Tuscon YWCA Women Helping Women; bd. dirs. Tucson Ctrs. Women and Children. Mem. Am. Soc. Training and Devel., Minn. Women Elected Ofcls. (pres. 1983-85), Izaak Walton League, Tucson C. of C. Methodist. Club: Remington Investment (pres. 1968-70) (Mpls.). Avocations: lapidary, music, handwork, camping, science fiction. Home: 6932 E 2nd St Tucson AZ 85710-1222

HOYT, ELLEN, artist, educator; b. Bklyn., Nov. 8, 1933; d. Martin and Estelle (Rabinowitz) Reiss; m. Jack Hoyt, July 1, 1954; children: Elyse, Laurence. Student, N.Y. State Tech. Coll., 1951. Tchr. art Kingsway Acad., Bklyn., 1963-77, Studio Dragonette, Bklyn., 1977-84, El Art Studio, Bklyn., 1984—; art cons. Salute to Israel Parade, N.Y.C., 1973-78; art juror All Cmtys. Art, Bklyn., 1988-90; art demonstrator, lectr. and tchr. in field, 1985—. Exhibited in group shows Washington Square, N.Y.C., 1979—, Bklyn. Mus., 1981, 83, Met. Mus., N.Y.C., 1979, Stohr Mus., Nebr., 1985, Pa. State, 1986, Snug Harbor Cultural Ctr., 1989, Salmagundi Club, 1982-83, Henry Howells Gallery, 1992, Pan Am. Bldg., N.Y.C., 1991, Vista Hotel, N.Y.C., 1991, Nat. Arts Club, N.Y.C., others; solo exhibits include Ethical Culture, N.Y.C., 1985, N.Y.C. Librs., 1980, 85, 86, 91, Belanthi Gallery, N.Y.C., 1982, Nat. Arts Club, N.Y.C.; permanent collections include Health and Hosp. Corp., N.Y.C., FAB Steel Corp., L.A., Minigrip Ltd., N.Y.C., Gateway Nat. Park, N.Y.C., Grant Koo Cons. Group. Active Sierra Club, N.Y.C., 1980—. Recipient Best in Show award Bklyn. Mus., 1983; scholar Washington Square Outdoor Art Exhibit, 1979. Mem. Am. Watercolor Soc., Nat. Arts League, Nat. Artists Profl. League, Bklyn. Watercolor Soc. (demonstrator 1970—, sec., historian 1978-93, membership chairperson). Home and Studio: 1551 E 29th St Brooklyn NY 11229-1840

HOYT, ROSEMARY ELLEN, trust officer; b. Iowa City, Iowa, Apr. 12, 1949; d. Joseph Asa Hoyt and Mary Jane (Brobst) Vandermark; m. Louis O. Scott, Oct. 16, 1965 (div. Nov. 1968); children: Wayne L. Lawson, Jo Anna Jane Kollasch; m. David K. Duckworth, July 23, 1983 (div. Dec. 1994); 1 child, Mary Rose Duckworth. Cert. in applied banking/consumer credit, Am. Inst. Banking, 1988; cert. in trust adminstrn., Cannon Fin. Inst., 1989, cert. trust ops. specialist, 1991; BBA, So. Calif. U., 1992. Teller Community Bank of Fla., St. Petersburg, 1973-75; bookkeeper Chevron Svc. Sta., St. Petersburg, 1975-77, Landmark Bank, St. Petersburg, 1977-80; teller First Nat. Bank of Ely, Nev., 1981, Nev. Bank and Trust, Ely, 1982; asst. v.p. and trust officer First Nat. Bank Farmington, N.Mex., 1983—; pres., founder Day Camp Southside, St. Petersburg, 1976-77. Planning chmn. terr. 5 ann. meeting ARC, Farmington, 1990-91, babysitting instr., 1990—, basic aid tng. instr., 1992, Project Read instr., 1994. Recipient Appreciation award ARC, 1991. Mem. Fin. Women Internat. (by-laws com. 1990-91, treas. 1993-94), Nat. Assn. Trust Ops. Specialists (bd. dirs. 1992), Am. Bus. Women's Assn. (v.p. 1991, pres. 1992, Appreciation award 1989, Woman of Yr. 1995). Republican. Baptist. Home: 1302 Zuni Pl Farmington NM 87401 Office: First Nat Bank Farmington PO Box 4540 Farmington NM 87499-4540

HRANIOTIS, JUDITH BERINGER, artist; b. N.Y.C., Jan. 11, 1944; d. Richard Frederick and Barbara Ann (Blight) Beringer; children: Anthony J. Bellantoni, Robert John Bellantoni; m. Peter Hraniotis; stepchildren: Christine Hraniotis, Terry Hraniotis, Helen Finn. Student, Sch. Visual Arts, N.Y.C., 1962, NYU, 1994; studied with, John Hamburger. Exhibited in group, juried shows at Hudson Valley Art Assn., White Plains, N.Y., 1990, 91, Milford (Conn.) Arts Ctr. 1991-95, The Am. Artists Profl. League, N.Y.C., 1991, 95, Catharine Lorillard Wolfe Art Club, N.Y.C. 1991, 92, 95, 96, Kent (Conn.) Art Assn., 1991, 92, 93, 94, 95, Ridgewood (N.J.) Art. inst., 1992, Mt. St. Mary Coll., Newburgh, N.Y., 1993, 96, Arts. Coun., Orange County, Middletown, 1994, Mamaroneck Artist Guild at Westbeth Gallery, N.Y.C., 1994, Green County Coun. on the Arts, N.Y., 1996. Recipient 1st Pl. Graphics award Mt. St. Mary Coll., 1994, 96, Newburgh, 1990, 91, Grumbacher Silver medal Mt. St. Mary Coll., 1993, 1st Pl. Graphics award Ann. Open Art Exhibit, Arts Coun. of Orange County, 1994, Dutchess County Art Assn., 1995. Fellow Catharine Lorillard Wolfe Art Club; mem. Am. Artist Profl. League, Nat. Mus. of Women in the Arts, Kent Art Assn. (bd. dirs., rec. sec. 1993-95, 96, Cert. of Merit 1991), Woodstock Art Assn. Republican. Home: 245 Browns Rd Walden NY 12586-3027

HRDLICKA, ANITA MARIE, athletic trainer; b. San Antonio, Aug. 4, 1964; d. Alois J. and Georgia V. (Petrash) H. Student, Tex. Luth. Coll., 1982-85; BS in Health Edn., U. North Tex., 1988. Lic. athletic trainer, Tex. Dept. Health; cert. secondary sch. biology and health tchr., Tex. Edn. Agy. Exercise technician Orthopedic Inst. of Tex., Hurst, 1988-89; lic. athletic trainer S.W. Sports and Spine Ctr., Dallas, 1989-90, Associated Phys. Therapy, Plano, Tex., 1990-94, Tex. Back Inst., Plano, 1995—, Baylor Fitness Ctr. and Baylor Sportscare, Dallas, 1995—. Mem. Nat. Athletic Trainer's Assn., S.W. Athletic Trainer's Assn., Tex. Clin. Athletic Trainer's Assn. (v.p. 1994-95). Home: 2404 Evergreen Dr Plano TX 75075 Office: Baylor Fitness Ctr and Sports Care 411 N Washington Dallas TX 75246

HRIBAR, CELESTE REGINA, psychologist; b. Queens, N.Y., July 18, 1953; d. Peter Emmanuel and Grace Ella (Buono) Polito; m. James Matthew Hribar, Apr. 27, 1975; children: Matthew James, Kimberley Grace. BS in Social Work, St. Francis Coll., 1975; MA in Ednl. Psychology, Kean Coll. N.J., 1982, diploma in sch. psychology, 1986. Cert. sch. psychologist, N.J. Cons. psychologist Inst. Child Study Kean Coll. N.J., Union, 1986—; sch. psychologist Glenview Acad., South Orange, N.J., 1988-90, East Orange (N.J.) Pub. Sch., 1990-93, North Brunswick (N.J.) Pub. Sch., 1993—. Tchr. religious edn. St. Michael's Ch., Cranford, N.J., 1991-95. Mem. Nat. Assn. Sch. Psychologists, N.J. Assn. Sch. Psychologists. Roman Catholic. Home: 6 Oak Ln Cranford NJ 07016 Office: North Brunswick Pub Schs PO Box 6016 North Brunswick NJ 08902

HROVAT, CLAIRE ANN MARIE, elementary school educator; b. Lakewood, Ohio, Dec. 6, 1952; d. Frank R. and Clara (Dubnicka) H.; m. Harry James Stratton III, May 18, 1974 (div. May 16, 1995). BEd, Kent State U., 1973, MEd, 1983. Cert. elem. tchr., Ohio. Clk., bookkeeper Kmart, Maple Heights, Ohio, 1969-76; substitute tchr. various schs., Ohio, 1974-76; tchr. kindergarten Solon (Ohio) City Schs., 1976-78, tchr. 1st grade, 1978-79, tchr. 2d grade, 1979—; coop. tchr. Kent (Ohio) State U., 1987—. Jennings scholar Martha Holden Jennings Found., 1990-91. Mem. Solon Edn. Assn. (rep., sec., v.p. negotiations recorder), Ohio Coun. Tchrs. of Math. Roman Catholic. Office: Roxbury Sch 6795 Solon Blvd Solon OH 44139

HRUBETZ, JOAN, nursing educator; b. Collinsville, Ill., June 1, 1935; d. Frederick and Josephine (Nepute) H. RN, St. John's Hosp., St. Louis, 1956; BSN, St. Louis U., 1960, MA, 1970, PhD in Edn. and Counseling, 1975. Staff nurse St. John's Hosp., St. Louis, 1956-59; instr. med./surg. nursing St. Louis Mcpl. Sch. Nursing, 1960-63; asst. dir. nursing svc. Barnes Hosp., St. Louis, 1963-65; asst. dir. sch. nursing Barnes Hosp., 1965-68, ednl. cons., 1968-70, dir. sch. nursing, 1970-74; dir. undergrad. mprog. nursing St. Louis U., 1975-82, asst. to assoc. prof. nursing, 1975—, assoc. prof. pastoral health care, 1986—, dean Sch. Nursing, 1982—; lectr. in field. Contbr. articles to profl. jours. Bd. dirs. Paraquad, Inc., Ctr. Independent Living, 1985-87, hon. mem., 1987—; bd. dirs. Kenrick-Glennon Seminar, 1988, sec. bd., 1989-90; mem. adv. com. project on Clin. Edn. in Care of Elderly, 1989. Group Health Found. grantee, 1987-88, 88-89, St. Louise U. Hosps. grantee, 1980-83, others. Mem. Mo. Assn. Adminstrs. of Baccalaureate and Higher Deg. Progs. in Nursing, St. Louis Assn. Deans and Dirs. of Schs. Nursing, Am. Assn. Colls. of Nursing (adv. com. to baccalaureate data project), Am. Nurses Assn., Mo. Nurses Assn., 3rd Dist. Mo. Nurses Assn., Nat. League Nursing, Mo. League for Nursing, St. Louis Reg. League for Nursing, Midwest Alliance in Nursing (governing bd. 1985-87, chair 1986-87, resolutions com. 1987-89), Conf. Jesuit Schs. Nursing, St. Louis Met. Hosp. Assn. Office: St Louis U 3525 Caroline Blvd Saint Louis MO 63103*

HSIEH, HAZEL TSENG, elementary and secondary education educator; b. Beijing, Nov. 4, 1934; came to U.S., 1947; naturalized, 1968; d. Hung-tu and Man-lone (Huang) Tseng; m. Hsueh Ying Hsieh, July 1, 1961; children: Durwynne, Timothy. Student, Adelphi U., 1954-56; BS, Tufts U., 1958; postgrad., Harvard U., 1959, U. Hartford, 1962-64; MA, Columbia U., 1977. Cert. tchr., N.Y. Tchr., asst. dir. Parents Nursery Sch., Cambridge, Mass., 1957; tchr. Sch. for Young Children, St. Joseph Coll., West Hartford, Conn., 1958-63; dir. Ctr. Nursery Sch., Yorktown Heights, N.Y., 1967-68; tchr. Yorktown Ctrl. Schs., Yorktown Heights, 1968—; substitute Virginia Day Nursery, N.Y.C., summer 1953-57; co-chair adv. com. Lakeland-Yorktown BOCES Mass Comm. Project, Yorktown Heights, 1982-87; mem. Internat. Faculty, Challenger Ctr. Space Sci. Edn., Alexandria, Va., 1990—; mem. dist. task force Gifted/Talented Edn., 1995-96. Author: Living in Families, 1991; editor: Honor Society Competition Directory of Nominations, 1985-89. Past mem. Yorktown Schs. Dist. Mission State Com.; active Dist. Acad. Stds. Com., 1994—, Dist. Task Force on Gifted and Talented Edn., 1995—, Mohansic Shared Decision Making Coun., Yorktown Heights, 1992—, Mohansic Literacy Com. 1992-96, Tech. Sci. Coms., 1992—, Wee Deliver Com., 1993-94, Dem. Party; curriculum coord. Ch. Good Shepherd, Granite Springs, N.Y., 1967-69; organizer Parent Orgn. for Arlington Symphony Orch., 1982-84, Mohansic Space Day, 1993; tchr. rep. PTA, 1977-78; founder Internat. Young Astronaut chpt 27796, 1990, leader, 1990—; coord. project Marsville, Hudson Valley, 1992—. Recipient Kohl Internat. Teaching award, Wilmette, Ill., 1991; Challenger Seven fellow, 1990; Challenger Ctr. Internat. Faculty fellow, 1990—; grantee NASA, 1989, N.Y. State Electric and Gas Co., 1987, PTA, 1987, No. Westchester Tchr. Ctr., 1988, IBM, 1992, Readers Digest Found. and Westchester Edn. Coalition, 1995-97. Mem. Am. Fedn. Tchrs., Yorktown Congress Tchrs. (sr. bldg. rep. 1977-78), Sierra Club, Pi Lambda Theta (mem. curriculum innovation award com. 1985-93, chairperson Westchester area chpt. com, 1986-89, 1st v.p. 1989-91, 2d v.p. 1987-89, corr. sec. 1983-87, chairperson region I awards com. 1990-97, Region I sec. exec. bd., 1996—, pres. Westchester area chpt. 1991-95, advisor 1995-97, sec. 1996-98, Outstanding Chpt. 1991-92, grantee 1991). Home: 22 Mountain Pass Rd Hopewell Junction NY 12533-5331 Office: Mohansic Elem Sch 704 Locksley Rd Yorktown Heights NY 10598-3135

HSU, KATHARINE HAN KUANG, pediatrics educator; b. Foochow, Fukien, China, Feb. 12, 1914; came to U.S., 1948; d. Wen Chen and Shu Fong (Huang) H.; m. T.L. Hsu, Apr. 26, 1941 (dec. Apr. 1990). BS, Yenching U., Beijing, 1935; MD, Peking Union Med. Coll., 1939. Intern Peking Union Med. Coll., 1938-39, resident, 1939-41; asst. prof. Baylor Coll. Medicine, Houston, 1953-60, assoc. prof., 1960-69, prof. pediatrics, 1970-79, prof. emeritus, 1979-94; ret., 1994. Recipient Disting. Achievement award Am. Thoracic Soc., 1994. Home: 9427 Denbury Way Houston TX 77025-4036

HSU, MING CHEN, federal agency administrator; b. Beijing, China, Sept. 14, 1924; came to U.S., 1944; d. Chin-Men and Mary Sung Yung (Chu) Chen; 1 child, Victoria W. BA summa cum laude, George Washington U., 1949; LLD (hon.), Ramapo Coll., 1988, Kean Coll., 1989. Market rsch. analyst NBC Corp., N.Y.C., 1953-57; mg. market rsch. RCA Internat. Div., N.J., 1957-69; dir. internat. market RCA Corp., N.Y.C., 1969-78, staff v.p. for internat. trade, 1978-82; spl. trade rep. Gov. Tom Kean, Newark, 1982-90; dir. N.J. Div. Internat. Trade, Newark, 1982-90; commr. Fed. Maritime Commn., Washington, 1990—; speaker, lectr. on nat. and internat. affairs on numerous network and local TV programs. Author: American Arbitration Journal, 1956; editor: Suggested Amendments to the United Nations, 1960, Enabling Instruments of the United Nations, 1961; contbr. articles to jours. in field. At-large del to Rep. Nat. Conv., 1984, 88; mem. Def. Adv. Com. on Women in the Svcs., 1989, Nat. Commn. on Observance of Internat. Women's Yr., N.J. Adv. Coun. Channel Thirteen/WNET, U.S. Commn. on Civil Rights, U.S. Sec. Commerce's Adv. Com. on East-West Trade, Sec. Commerce's Export Now Adv. Com., Svc. Policy Adv. Com.; trustee Newark Mus.; bd. dirs. Com. of 100. Recipient Spl. award Women's Equity Action League, 1978, Alumni Achievement award George Washington U., 1983, Woman of Achievement award, N.J. Fedn. Bus. and Profl. Women, 1985, Achievement award Career Women's Achievement Network, 1986, Philbrook award Women's Polit. Caucus, 1989, N.J. Pride award for econ. devel., 1989, Paul L. Troast award, N.J. Bus.and Industry, 1989, Woman on the Move award, Bus. Jour. N.J., 1989; named Woman of Yr., Asian-Am. Profl. Women's Assn., 1983. Mem. Phi Beta Kappa. Office: FMC 800 N Capitol St NW Washington DC 20002-4244

HU, SUE KING, elementary and middle school educator; b. Prince Frederick, Md., Nov. 7, 1938; d. James Elliott and Anna Irene (Hutchins) King; m. Richard Chee Chung Hu, July 2, 1960; children: Stephen Tse Wen, Sharon Yen Mei. BS, Towson (Md.) State U., 1960; MA, Marymount U., Arlington, Va., 1987. Cert. tchr., Va. Elem. tchr. Arlington (Va.) County Pub. Schs., 1977-90, elem. sch. rep., 1986-90, tchr. sci. mid. sch., 1990-94; environ. edn. cons., instr. Phoebe Knipling Outdoor Edn. Lab., Broad Run, Va., 1994—; workshop presenter Nat. Wildlife Fedn., Vienna, Va., 1989, 90; ednl. cons. Greenhouse Crisis Found., Washington, 1989-91; adj. prof. George Mason U., 1991, 94-95, instr. in environ. sci. Audubon Naturalist Soc., Chevy Chase, Md., 1990—; presenter children's workshops Fairfax County Schs., 1990—. Writer children's newspaper Sci. Weekly, 1990-91. chair edn. com. Fairfax (Va.) Audubon Soc., 1987-92, bd. dirs., 1988-92, v.p. natural history and edn., 1990-92. Recipient cert. of accomplishment Arlington County Pub. Schs., 1989, svc. award Fairfax Aududon Soc., 1992; named Notable Woman of Arlington, Arlington Commn. on the Status of Women, 1993. Mem. ASCD, Nat. Assn. Biology Tchrs. (elem.-mid. sch. chair 1988-89, presenter conf. 1986-89), Nat. Sci. Tchrs. Assn. (presenter conf. 1988-89), Coun. Elem. Sci. Internat., , Va. Assn. Sci. Tchrs., Delta Epsilon Sigma, Kappa Delta Pi. Democrat. Methodist. Home: 2524 Leeds Rd Oakton VA 22124-1406

HUANG, THERESA C., librarian; b. Nanking, China; m. Theodore S. Huang, Dec. 25, 1959. B.A., Nat. Taiwan U., 1955; M.S. in L.S., Syracuse U., 1958. Cataloger, Harvard U., Cambridge, Mass., 1958-60; with Bklyn. Pub. Library, 1960-78, regional librarian, 1978— . Joint compiler bibliography: Asia: A Guide to Books for Children, 1966; Nuclear Awareness, 1983; The U.S.A. through Children's Books, 1986, 88. Mem. ALA, Assn. Library Service to Children, Pub. Library Assn., Chinese Am. Librarians Assn., Asia Pacific Am. Librarians Assn. Office: Bklyn Pub Libr 1743 86th St Brooklyn NY 11214-3714

HUBBARD, ELIZABETH, actress; b. N.Y.C.; d. Benjamin Alldritt and Elizabeth (Wright) H.; divorced; 1 son, Jeremy Danby Bennett. A.B. cum laude, Radcliffe Coll.; postgrad., Royal Acad. Dramatic Art, London. Leading role: CBS daytime TV serial As the World Turns, 1984— (7 consecutive Emmy nominations for Best Leading Actress), NBC daytime TV serial The Doctors; appeared on Broadway in Present Laughter, Joe Egg, Time for Singing, Look Back in Anger, I Remember Mama (musical), others; appeared in off-Broadway prodn. Boys from Syracuse, Threepenny Opera (musicals); movie appearances include I Never Sang for My Father, The Bell Jar, Ordinary People; frequent guest TV talk shows. Bd. dirs. Women's Commn. for Refugee Women and Children, Found. in Motion, Immigration and Refugee Svcs. of Am. Recipient Clarence Derwent award for The Physicists, 1965; Emmy award for best actress in The Doctors, 1974, Emmy award for best actress in First Ladies Diaries: Edith Bolling Wilson, 1976. Mem. Harvard Club.

HUBBARD, ELIZABETH LOUISE, lawyer; b. Springfield, Ill., Mar. 10, 1949; d. Glenn Wellington and Elizabeth (Frederick) H.; m. A. Jeffrey Seidman, Oct. 27, 1974 (div. May 1982). Student Millikin U., 1967-69; B.A., U. Ky., 1971; J.D. with honors, Ill. Inst. Tech.-Chgo. Kent Coll. Law, 1974. Bar: Ill. 1974, U.S. Dist. Ct. (no. dist.) Ill. 1974, U.S. Ct. Appeals (7th cir.) 1976, U.S. Supreme Ct. 1984. Atty. Wyatt Co., Chgo., 1974-75, Gertz & Giampietro, Chgo., 1975-76, Baum, Sigman, Gold, Chgo., 1976-81, Elizabeth Hubbard, Ltd., Chgo., 1981—; legal counsel NOW, Chgo., 1978—, sec., 1977. Editor Chgo. Kent Law Rev., 1970. Bd. dirs., mem. The Remains Theatre, 1985-94. Mem. Chgo. Bar Assn. (fed. civil procedure com.), Ill. State Bar Assn., Nat. Employment Lawyers Assn. (chair Ill. chpt. 1992-95). Democrat. Home: 420 West Grand Unit 4A Chicago IL 60610 Office: 55 E Monroe St Chicago IL 60603-5702

HUBBARD, SUSAN ELAINE, education consultant, state legislator; b. East Liverpool, Ohio, Aug. 4, 1943; d. Glen Wesley and Sara Margaret (Silliman) Horger; m. Frederick Robert Hubbard, Aug. 31, 1962; children: David, John. BA in Elem. Edn., Marshall U., 1970, MA in Reading Specialist, 1978. Cert. tch./reading specialist, W.Va. Dept. Edn. Elem. edn. tchr. W.Va.-Cabell County, Huntington, 1970-86; Uniserv cons. W.Va. Edn. Assn., Charleston, 1986—; state legislator W.Va. Ho. of Dels., Charleston, 1994—; past pres. Cabell County Edn. Assn., Huntington, 1976-80, 84-86. Mem. exec. com. Devel. Dis. Planning Coun., Charleston, 1995-96; legislator Pub. Voters, 1994-96; advisor Literacy Coun., 1994. Mem. NEA, LWV (membership chair 1992-93), W.Va. Edn. Assn. (vice-chair pr&r com. 1976-86, staff union rep.), Cabell County Dem. Women, Cabell County Dem. Women's Club (v.p., pres. 1993-94), Dem. Women's Club (parliamentarian 1992-94). Democrat. Methodist. Home: 6287 Division Rd Huntington WV 25705 Office: WVa Edn Assn 1558 Quarrier St Charleston WV 25311

HUBBARD, TINA LYNN, sales executive; b. Rochester, N.Y., July 30, 1967; d. George Roy and Martha Louise (McGee) H. BAin Internat. Bus., Adrian Coll., 1989; grad. student, U. Cin., 1996—. Resident asst. Adrian (Mich.) Coll., 1986-89; purchasing clk. asst. Eastman Kodak Co., Rochester, N.Y., 1987-89; indsl. internat. sales mgr. Fed.-Mogul, Southfield, Mich., 1989-90; territory mgr. nat. accts. NAPA Fed.-Mogul, Cin., 1990-93, heavy duty sales engr., 1993—. vol. Big Sisters/Big Brothers Gtr. Cin., 1994-95. Mem. Nat. Assn. Female Execs., Alpha Kappa Psi (pub. rels 1989—). Presbyterian. Home: 19 Stoneridge Ln Florence KY 41042 Office: Federal-Mogul 11875 Enterprise Dr Cincinnati OH 45241

HUBBELL, KATHERINE JEAN, marketing consultant; b. Norfolk, Va., Mar. 5, 1951; d. Lester Earle and Katherine Jean (Bush) H.; m. Daryl Paul Domning, July 10, 1987. BA in English, BS in Math., Clemson U., 1974; MBA in Mktg., Va. Polytech. Inst. & State U., 1991. Info. systems engr. MITRE Corp., McLean, Va., 1975-79; mem. tech. staff MITRE Corp., Bedford, Mass., 1980-81; design engr. GE, Wilmington, Mass., 1979-80;

budget assoc. nat. hdqs. ARC, Washington, 1982-92; mktg. cons. Dominion Group, Vienna, Va., 1993—; database mgr. Nat. Christian Life Cmtys. of U.S., 1993—. Recreation vol. ARC, Bethesda Naval Hosp., 1976-79; vol. Holy Cross Hospice, 1984-87; strategic planning com. Christian Life Cmtys. Mid-Atlantic Region, 1989-90; allocations com. United Way Nat. Captiol Area, 1989-91. Mem. Am. Mktg. Assn., Assn. Part-Time Profls., Soc. Competitive Intelligence Profls. Home: 9211 Wendell St Silver Spring MD 20901-3533 Office: The Dominion Group 8229 Boone Blvd Ste 710 Vienna VA 22182-2623

HUBBS, JOANNA, history educator; b. Warsaw, Poland, Nov. 17, 1939; m. Clayton A. Hubbs; children: Gregory, Victoria.; AA, Stephens Coll., 1959; BA, U. Mo., 1967; PhD, U. Wash., 1971. Prof. Russian history Hampshire Coll., Amherst, Mass., 1971—. Author: Mother Russia: The Feminine Myth in Russian Culture, 1988 (Heldt award AAASS 1989); mem. editl. bd. Mass. Rev., 1989-90, Metamorphosis: Translation Rev., 1992-95; contbr. articles to profl. jours., chpts. to books. Woodrow Wilson fellow U. Mo., 1966-67, NDEA fellow U. Wash., 1969-70. Mem. Am. Assn. for Advancement of Slavic Studies, Am. Assn. Tchrs. of Slavic and East European Langs., Phi Beta Kappa. Office: Hampshire Coll Amherst MA 01002

HUBER, SISTER ALBERTA, college president; b. Rock Island, Ill., Feb. 12, 1917; d. Albert and Lydia (Hofer) H. BA, Coll. St. Catherine, St. Paul, 1939; MA, U. Minn., 1945; PhD, U. Notre Dame, 1954. Mem. faculty Coll. St. Catherine, 1940—, prof. English, 1953—, chmn. dept., 1960-63, acad. dean, 1962-64, pres., 1964-79. Trustee Avila Coll., Kansas City, Mo., St. Joseph's Hosp., St. Paul, 1971-80; pres. UN Assn. Minn., 1980-81; bd. dirs. St. Paul YMCA, 1986-92. Decorated Chevalier, Ordre des Palmes Acad.; recipient Outstanding Achievement award U. Minn. Alumni Assn., 1981. Mem. Phi Beta Kappa, Pi Gamma Mu. Office: 2004 Randolph Ave Saint Paul MN 55105-1750

HUBER, JOAN ALTHAUS, sociology educator; b. Bluffton, Ohio, Oct. 17, 1925; d. Lawrence Lester and Hallie Moser (Althaus) H.; m. William Form, Feb. 5, 1971; children: Nancy Rytina, Steven Rytina. B.A., Pa. State U., 1945; M.A., Western Mich. U., 1963; Ph.D., Mich. State U., 1967. Asst. prof. sociology U. Notre Dame, Ind., 1967-71; asst. prof. sociology U. Ill., Urbana-Champaign, 1971-73; assoc. prof. U. Ill., 1973-78, prof., 1978-83, head dept., 1979-83; dean Coll. Social and Behavioral Sci., Ohio State U., Columbus, 1984-92; coordinating dean Coll. Arts and Sciences, Ohio State University, Columbus, 1987-92, provost, 1992-93; sr. v.p., provost emeritus prof. Sociology emeritus, 1994. Author: (with William Form) Income and Ideology, 1973, (with Glenna Spitze) Sex Stratification, 1983. Editor: Changing Women in a Changing Society, 1973, (with Paul Chalfant) The Sociology of Poverty, 1974, Macro-Micro Linkages in Sociology, 1991. NSF research awardee, 1978-81. Mem. Am. Sociol. Assn. (v.p. 1981-83, pres. 1987-90), Midwest Sociol. Soc. (pres. 1979-80). Home: 2880 N Star Rd Columbus OH 43221-2959 Office: Ohio State U Dept Sociology 300 Bricker Hall 190 N Oval Mall Columbus OH 43210-1321

HUBER, MARGARET ANN, college president; b. Rochester, Pa., July 27, 1949; d. Francis Xavier and Mary Ann (Socash) H. B.S. in Chemistry, Duquesne U., 1972; M.S.A., U. Notre Dame, 1975; Ph.D., U. Mich., 1979. Joined Sisters of Divine Providence of Pittsburgh, Pa., 1967-93; jr. high tchr. St. Martin Sch., Pitts., 1971-72; asst. to acad. dean LaRoche Coll., Pitts., 1972-75; research assoc. U. Mich., Ann Arbor, 1978; dir. planning LaRoche Coll., 1978-80, exec. v.p., 1980-81, pres., 1981-92; exec. dir. Archdiocese of Santa Fe Catholic Found., 1993-94; pres. Coll. Notre Dame, 1994—. Mem. Am. Assn. for Higher Edn. Democrat. Roman Catholic. Office: Coll of Notre Dame 1500 Ralston Ave Belmont CA 94002-1997*

HUBER, MARIANNE JEANNE, art dealer; b. Amboy, Ill., June 9, 1936; d. John Francis and Jeannette Marie (Wurth) Faivre; m. Robert L. Huber, Oct. 3, 1959; children: Michael Robert, Stephan Louis, Edward Francis. BA, Cardinal Stritch Coll., Milw., 1958. 6th grade tchr. St. Andrew's Sch., Rock Falls, Ill., 1958-59; jr. high tchr. Garside Sch., Mexico City, 1959-61; art dealer, cons. Huber Primitive Art, N.Y.C. and Dixon, Ill., 1963—; founder, pres. New World Art Svcs., N.Y.C. and Dixon, Ill., 1993—; lectr., cons. Primitive Art Soc., Chgo., 1987, Freeport (Ill.) Art Mus., 1993, Indpls. Mus. Art, 1994, Nprstk Mus., Prague, Czech Republic, 1995. Author: Echoes of a Distant Flute, 1984; co-prodr., author: (documentary films) The Cuna, 1980, Nebaj, Cotzal and Chajul, 1987; collector, organizer traveling exhbns. The Cuna, 1980—. Mem. AAUW, Internat. Platform Assn. (gov. 1993—), Am. Assn. Dealers in Ancient Oriental and Primitive Art, Ethnographic Art Soc. Indpls., Met. Mus. Art, Delta Epsilon Sigma. Democrat. Home and Office: 1012 Timber Trail Dixon IL 61021

HUBER, MELBA STEWART, dance educator, shop owner; b. Tex., Oct. 1, 1927; d. Carl E. and Melba (Holt) Stewart; m. William C. Kinsolving Jr.; children: William Carey, Keith Brian; m. James M. Huber (dec.); 1 child, Melba Laurin. AA, Lamar Coll., 1946. Establisher, owner Melba's, Inc., McAllen, Tex., 1958—; founder McAllen (Tex.) Dance Theatre Co., 1970; regional rep. Gus Giordano's Jazz Dance World Congress. Columnist Tap Talk, 1988—, Dance and the Arts mag., 1988—. Recipient Plaudit award Nat. Dance Assn. Am. Alliance for Health, Physical Edn. and Recreation, 1970, Flo-Bert award N.Y. Com. to Celebrate Nat. Tap Dance Day, 1996. Mem. Dance Masters Am., Tex. Assn. Tchrs. Dancing (pres. 1971-72), South Tex. Dance Masters Assn. (Mem. of Yr. 1989), U.S. Gymnastics Fedn., Gymnastic Assn. Tex., Profl. Dancers Soc., McAllen (Tex.) Music Club, McAllen Cmty. Concert Assn. Home: PO Box 3664 McAllen TX 78502

HUBER, RITA NORMA, civic worker; b. Cin., July 16, 1931; d. Andrew Elwood and Mary Gertrude (Hille) Stewart; student Cin. Coll. Conservatory Music, 1949-50, Berlitz Sch., Cin., 1951-52; m. Justin G. Huber, July 17, 1954; children: Monica Ann, Sarah Marie, Rachel Miriam. Tchr. Russian lang. for officers' wives Ft. Sill, Okla., 1955-56; bd. dirs. United Community Svcs., Cedar Rapids, Iowa, 1969; founder, chairperson Linn County Consumers League, 1969-70; founder, pub. rels. dir. Cedar Rapids Rape Crisis Svcs., 1974—; owner/operator Huber Janitorial Svcs., 1982-84; chairperson Linn County Dem. Womens Club, 1966-67, Linn County Com., Eugene McCarthy for Pres., 1967-68; campaign mgr. Delores Cortez for Iowa Legislature, 1968, Jan V. Johnson for Iowa Legislature, 1970, Stanley Ginsberg for county supr. Linn County, 1974, E.L. Colton for Cedar Rapids pub. safety commr., 1977; chairperson Linn County Dem. Cen. Com., 1976-77, 88-90; state coord. Jerry Brown for Pres., 1976; chairperson Pat Kane for Linn County Recorder, 1982; chmn. Linn County Bd. Health, 1982-85; supr. Linn County, 1990-95; chairperson Linn County bd. Suprs., 1992; instr. parliamentary procedures Cedar Rapids Women's Community Leadership Inst., 1975-77; lectr. local colls. and svc. orgns.; tchr. conversational Russian, Pierce Elementary Sch., Cedar Rapids, 1976; instr. Russian, Community Edn. div. Kirkwood Community Coll.; mem. care rev. com. Pineview Care Ctr., Cedar Rapids, 1987-90. Named to Iowa Dem. Party DVP Hall of Fame, 1986; recipient Woman of Yr. award Women's Equality Day Cedar Rapids Iowa, 1993. Mem. Am. Inst. Parliamentarians. Roman Catholic (extraordinary minister of Eucharist). Composer: She is Risen, 1973. Home: 2050 Glass Rd NE Cedar Rapids IA 52402-3451

HUBERT, SHELBY ANN, speech/language pathologist; b. Holbrook, Ariz., Jan. 5, 1962; d. Bradford Jay and Margaret Mary (Mense) Sweeney; m. David Eugene Hubert, July 15, 1983; children: Whitney, Lindsey, Hannah. B in Textile Mktg., Kans. State U., 1983; M in Speech-Lang. Pathology, Ft. Hays State U., 1992. Cert. clin. speech-lang. pathologist, Kans. Speech-lang. pathologist N.W. Kans. Ednl. Svc. Ctr., Oakley, 1992—; health adv. bd. dirs. Headstart, Oakley; mem. state com. Kans. Speech-Lang.-Hearing Pub. Rels.; mem. external adv. coun. Fort Hays State U. Speech-lang. scholar Ft. Hays State U., 1991. Mem. NEA, Am. Speech-Lang.-Hearing Assn., Kans. NEA, Kans. Speech-Lang.-Hearing Assn. (pub. rels. com. 1994—), Gamma Pi Alpha (sec., pres., v.p.). Roman Catholic. Home: 2608 County Rd 360 Monument KS 67747 Office: NW Kans Ednl Svc Ctr 703 W 2nd St Oakley KS 67748-1258

HUBKA, TERESA ANN, obstetrician and gynecologist, nutritionist; b. San Diego, Sept. 18, 1956; d. Verne Robert and Corinne Bernetta (Rens) H.; m. John Alexander Dunkas, Sept. 28, 1991. BS in Nutrition Sci. and Biochemistry, U. Calif., Davis, 1979; MS in Biochemistry, U. Bridgeport, Conn., 1981; DO, U. Osteo. Medicine Health Scis, Des Moines, 1989. Lic. physician, Ill.; registered dietitian. Intern in gen. medicine Atlantic City Med. Ctr., 1989-90; resident in ob/gyn. Mercy Hosp. and Med. Ctr., Chgo., 1990-94, mem. ob/gyn. staff, 1994—; owner Nutri Health Assocs., San Diego, 1981-85; dietitian San Diego Sports Medicine Ctr. 1979-85; lectr. in field, including ann. lectr. women's med. issues, Drake U., Iowa, 1985-87. Recipient CSCP Leadership award, 1986-89, Nat. Alumni Assn. Student Leadership and Svc. award, 1988-89, Stephen Bufton Meml. Edn. Fund award, 1988-89, Burroughs Wellcome Resident Leadership award, 1992—; Am. Bus. Women's Assn. scholar 1987-89, Merck Sharp & Dohme SOMA scholar for cmty. health svc., 1985-86; named Young Dietitian of Yr., Am. Dietetic Assn., 1984-85. Fellow ACOG (jr.), Am. Coll. Osteo. Ob-Gyn. (jr.); mem. Am. Assn. Osteo. Postgrad. Physicians (founding mem. 1990, regional chair 1991-92, v.p. 1992-93, pres. 1993-94), Am. Osteo. Assn. (ho. dels. student rep. 1985-89, com. on postgrad. tng. 1986—, Assn. Osteo. State Exec. Dirs. resident rep. 1993-94, Outstanding Svc. and Leadership award 1988-89), Assn. Am. Colls. of Osteo. Medicine Coun. Student Coun. Presidents (student coun. rep. 1985-87, exec. bd. mem. 1987-88, parliamentarian 1988-89), Am. Med. Women's Assn. (ho. del. student rep. 1986-88, nat. legis. com. 1987-89), Ill. Osteo. Physicians and Surgeons Assn. (resident rep. 1992—), Iowa Osteo. Med. Assn. (ho. dels. rep. and bd. dirs. student rep. 1986-87), N.J. Assn. Osteo. Physicians and Surgeons, Osteo. Physicians and Surgeons of Calif. Republican. Roman Catholic. Office: Mercy Med in Lincoln Park 990 W Fullerton Ave Ste 495 Chicago IL 60614

HUCKABEE, PHYLLIS, gas industry professional; b. Andrews, Tex., Aug. 11, 1963; d. Tommie Jack and Sylvia (Wingo) H. BBA in Fin., Tex. Tech U., 1984, MBA, 1986. Clk. loan escrow 1st Fed. Savs. Bank, Lubbock, Tex., 1984; mgmt. trainee El Paso (Tex.) Nat. Gas Co., 1986-87, analyst rate dept., 1987-88, specialist Calif. affairs, 1988-91, rep. Calif. affairs, 1991-92; asst. dir. Cambridge Energy Rsch. Assocs., Oakland, Calif., 1992-93; regulatory rels. mgr. Pacific Enterprises, San Francisco, 1994—; mem. adj. faculty No. Calif. campus U. Phoenix, San Francisco, 1994—. Bd. dirs. El Paso Community Concert Assn., 1988, bd. dirs. Performing Arts Workshop, 1991-92, mem. adv. bd., 1992—; vol. Bus. Vols. for Arts, San Francisco, 1989, East Bay Habitat for Humanity, 1993; tutor, fundraiser Project Read, San Francisco, 1990. Mem. Women Energy Assocs. (bd. dirs. 1990—), Leadership Calif. (Class of 1996), Pacific Coast Gas Assn. Methodist. Democrat. Home: 615 Mayfield Ave Stanford CA 94305-1225 Office: Pacific Enterprises 601 Van Ness Ave Ste 2014 San Francisco CA 94102-6310

HUCKEBA, KAREN KAYE, crafts designer, consultant; b. Decatur, Ind., Aug. 24, 1952; d. Donald Edward and Erma Louise (Morrison) Sliger; m. David Ardie Huckeba, Oct. 17, 1970; children: Scott Alan, Mark Andrew. Grad. high sch., Decatur. Cashier Lerner's Dress Shop, Ft. Wayne, Ind., 1970-71; head cashier Lerner's Dress Shop, Ft. Wayne and Newport News, Va., 1971-75; crafter various locations, 1976-89; pres. Karen's Kreations, Roswell, Ga., 1990—; cons. wearable art Fruit of the Loom, Bowling Green, Ky., 1993-94; demonstrator Tulip, Ga., 1994—. Designer (patriotic clothes line) Habitat, 1990—, (nautical clothes line) Designer Consignor, 1992-93; clothes displayed at Columbus (Ind.) Heritage Quilt Show, 1993; designer (catalogue) Fruit of the Loom 1995 Activewear Catalogue, 1994; contbr. articles to profl. jours. Pianist Huntingburg (Ind.) Bapt. Ch., 1975-78; children's worship leader Miles Rd. Bapt. Ch., Summerville, S.C., 1981-89; coaching asst. Summerville Soccer Club, 1981-87; co-tchr. singles and singles again Sunday sch. Wildwood Bapt. Ch., 1995-96. Mem. Hobby Industry Am., Soc. Craft Designers, Assn. Crafts and Creative Industries, Inc. Home and Office: Karen's Kreations 4611 Wickford Cir Roswell GA 30075-5733

HUCKSTEAD, CHARLOTTE VAN HORN, retired home economist, artist; b. Garwin, Iowa, Jan. 13, 1920; d. George Loren and Esther Olive (Carver) Van Horn; m. Lowell Raine Huckstead (dec.); children: Karen C., Roger H., Martha E., Paul R., Sarah S. BS, U. Wisc., 1942; BFA, Boise (Idaho) State U., 1989. Merchandising Montgomery Ward, Chgo. and Santa Monica, Calif., 1941-42; "Rosie the Riveter" WWII, Chgo. and Beloit, Wis., 1942-46; woman's editor Dairyland News, Milw., 1950-54; interior designer, cons., tchr. South Bend, Marshfield, Wis., Merced, Calif., 1952-69; extension home economist U. Minn., Rochester, 1973-78; dir. food svcs. Milton (Wisc.) Sch. Dist., 1978-85; artist, 1952—. Painting and sculpture. Bd. dirs. Rock County Hist. Soc., Janesville, Wis., 1979-84, Milton Hist. Soc., 1979-85; vol. Idaho Genealogy Libr., 1994-96; treas. Wis. Food Svc. Assn., 1980-85; leader/mem. Girl Scouts Am., 1934-78. Mem. AAUW, NOW, Idaho Hist. Soc. (vol. 1985-96), Idaho Centennial Art Group (sec. 1991, show chmn. 1992, historian 1993-95), Idaho Water Color Soc., Morrison Ctr. Aux. (vol. 1986-96, bd. dirs. 1992-93, Auxilian of Yr. 1995), Boise State Alumni Assn., Audubon Soc., Ch. Women United (editor 1985-86), Sierra Club, Boise Art Mus., Wis. Alumni Assn., Friends of Hist. Mus. Boise. Protestant. Home: 10507 Irving Ct Boise ID 83704-8054

HUCKSTEP, APRIL YVETTE, chemist; b. Aliquippa, Pa., May 12, 1961; d. Charles Jr. and Geraldine (Wilson) H. Cert., Parkway Tech. Coll., Oakdale, Pa., 1979; BS, Pa. State U., 1984; MS, U. Akron, 1991. Technician Arco Chem. Inc., Newton Square, Pa., 1979-81; technician DiversiTech, Akron, 1986; chemist Goodyear Tire and Rubber, Akron, 1986; intern Lord Corp., Erie, Pa., 1989; chemist, grad. asst. U. Akron, 1988—; chemist Delphi Chassis Gen. Motors, 1995—. U. Akron fellow. Mem. NAACP, Am. Chem. Soc., Soc. Women Engrs., Am. Inst. Chem. Engrs., Nat. Soc. Black Engineers. Home: 868 Monaca Rd Monaca PA 15061-2831 Office: U Akron Polymer Sci Dept Akron OH 44304

HUDAK, SHARON ANN., elementary education educator; b. Pitts., Mar. 22, 1942; d. Fred W. and Lillian M. (Huwalt) Kroll; m. Francis J. Hudak, Aug. 28, 1965; children: Leslie M., Nicole K., Kristen A. Hudak. BS in Art Edn., Edinboro (Pa.) State Coll., 1965; MEd in Art Edn., SUNY, Buffalo, 1969. Cert. elem., art edn. tchr., reading specialist, Pa. Jr. & sr. H.S. art tchr. Smethport (Pa.) Area Sch. Dist., 1965-68; art tchr. Beatty Jr. H.S., Warren, Pa., 1969; instr., supr. stds. tchr. Edinboro State Coll., 1969-70; art tchr., grades 5-8 Gen. McLane Sch. Dist., Edinboro, 1970-74; developmental reading tchr., grades 7, 8 Gen. McLane Sch. Dist., 1981-82; art tchr., grades 1-7 Escuela Campo Alegre, Caracas, Venezuela, 1982-84; TELLS reading tchr., chpt. I reading specialist N.W. Intermediate Unit #5, Edinboro, 1985, 86-87; reading specialist Penncrest Sch. Dist., Saegertown, Pa., 1985-86; TELLS reading tchr., chpt. I reading specialist Girard (Pa.) H.S., 1987, 87-91; art tchr., grades K-4 Elk Valley Elem. Sch., Girard Sch. Dist., Lake City, Pa., 1991—; mem. parent's adv. coun., Title I Edinboro Spl. Edn. Assn., 1985-86. Mem. Am. Fedn. Tchrs., Pa. Art Edn. Assn., Nat. Art Edn. Assn. Home: 207 Granada Dr Edinboro PA 16412-2363 Office: Elk Valley Elem Sch 2556 Maple Ave Lake City PA 16423-1515

HUDDLE, RITA KEGLEY, medical, surgical and home health nurse, administrator; b. Wythe County, Va., Dec. 26, 1955; d. Kenneth Leo and Neva Mae (Gallimore) Kegley; m. Jeb Stuart Earhart Huddle, Jan. 1, 1982; 1 child, Lauren Nichole. AA, Wytheville Community Coll., 1977. Cert. med.-surg. nurse ANCC. Staff nurse med.-surg. unit Norfolk (Va.) Gen. Hosp., 1980; charge nurse surg. unit Wythe County Community Hosp., Wytheville, Va., 1977-80, staff nurse ICU and CCU, 1980-85, house supr., 1985-87, dir. med. svcs., 1987-90, home health case mgr., 1990-93, home health clin. supr., 1993—. Home: RR 5 Box 108 Wytheville VA 24382-9509 Office: Circle Home Care Wythe County Cmty Hosp 600 W Ridge Rd Wytheville VA 24382

HUDDLESTON, ALICE KAYE, educational administrator; b. Greenville AFB, Miss., Aug. 31, 1957; d. Alfred and Betty K. Huddleston. BS, Jacksonville (Ala.) State U., 1979; MA, U. Ala., Tuscaloosa, 1980, 82, EdD, 1996. Tchr. Bynum (Ala.) Elem. Sch., 1979-82; tchr., asst. prin. Calhoun County Tng. Sch., Hobson City, Ala., 1982-83; prin. Lincoln (Ala.) Elem. Sch., 1983-87, Hill Elem. Sch., Munford, 1987—. Mem. Nat. Assn. Elem. Sch. Adminstrs., Ala. Assn. Elem. Sch. Adminstrs. (dist. V pres. 1989-90, rep. 1993-96). Baptist. Office: Hill Elem Sch 204 Hill School Cir Munford AL 36268

HUDDLESTON, MARILYN ANNE, international business financier, merchant banker, educator; b. Fayetteville, N.C., Jan. 28, 1953; d. Allen Paul and Julia Jewel (Hill) Miller; m. Roby Dwayne Huddleston, Sept. 13, 1946; children: Michelle, Christopher, Mathew Anthony, Danyel Paul, Michael David. D in Humanities Law (hon.), Central Tex. U., 1974; diploma Acad. of Coll. of Real Estate, 1977; postgrad. El Paso Community Coll. Owner, fin. cons. Cherokee Fin. Investments, Killeen, Tex., 1983-88; owner, broker All Am. Ins. Agy., Killeen, 1984-88; realtor, assoc. Exec. Fin., Austin, Tex., 1986-88; owner Geodesic Homes of Tex., Killeen, 1984-88; chmn., CFO Wall Street Internat., 1988-90, chmn. bd. dirs., 1988—; tchr. St. Joseph Catholic Sch., Killeen, 1991-92, tchr., adminstr., 1991-94; merchant banker Baytree Investors, Killeen, 1990—; grant writer, adminstrv. asst. to pres. and CEO Advantage Adult Day Care & Health Svcs., Harker Heights, Tex., 1994—. Author: Miracle Baby at Bracken Ridge Hospital, 1979; Financial Consulting Made Easy, 1983. Pres. Mil. Council of Catholic Women, Stuttgart, Fed. Republic Germany, 1980, Non-Commnd. Officers Wives, Stuttgart, 1980-82, Ciudad del Niño Orphanage Assn., Killeen, 1979—; instr. Christian Religion, Killeen, 1976-91, St. Joseph Cath. Sch., Killeen. Recipient Silver Poet award World of poetry Poets, 1989. Mem. Nat. Assn. Female Execs., Internat. Assn. Bus. and Fin. Cons. (hon.), Fort Hood Bd. Realtors, Nat. Assn. Realtors, Tex. Assn. Realtors Soc. Female Execs. (v.p. 1984-86), Internat. Soc. Financiers (cert.). Independent. Roman Catholic. Avocations: singing, writing, tennis, macrame.

HUDECHECK, ROSEMARY ANNE, music director, consultant; b. Phila., Nov. 5, 1949; d. Joseph James and Geraldine Marie (Rooney) H. MusB, Immaculata Coll., 1971; MusM, West Chester U. Pa., 1980; MA in Liturgical Studies, Cath. U. Am., 1989. Cert. music tchr., Pa. Music specialist Chester (Pa.)-Upland Sch. Dist., 1971-82; dir. Archdiocesan Boys Choir, Phila., 1975-87; assoc. dir. Cathedral Choir, Phila., 1975-82; music specialist Visitation Parish Cath. Sch., Norristown, Pa., 1984-87; dir. music and liturgy St. John the Baptist Cath. Community, Silver Spring, Md., 1987—, dir. children's choir, 1990—; music cons. Archdiocese Wilmington, Del., 1991; cantor Archdiocese Washington, 1987—. Vol. Shepherd's Table, Silver Spring, 1989—. Recipient Liturgy/Music award Pa. State Senate, 1985, Pa. Ho. of Reps., 1985. Mem. Nat. Assn. Pastoral Musicians, Dir. Music Ministries, Nat. Music Honor Soc., Pi Kappa Lambda. Democrat. Office: St John Bapt Cath Community 12319 New Hampshire Ave Silver Spring MD 20904-2957

HUDGENS, SANDRA LAWLER, retired state administrator; b. New Orleans, Feb. 15, 1944; d. Avril Lawler and Peggy V. (Crager) Kelly; m. Adolfo DiGennaro, Oct. 20, 1967 (div. 1970); 1 child, Daniel Darryn DiGennaro; m. Stanley Dalton Hudgens, Feb. 17, 1973; children: Stephanie Hudgens Cap, Richard Stanley, Michael Shane. Student, U. Nev., 1962-64, U. Grenoble, France, 1964-65, U. Aix-Marseille, Nice, France, 1965, U. Nev., Las Vegas, 1980—. Traffic ct. clk. III Clark County Juvenile Ct. Svcs., Las Vegas, 1965-71; planning commr. City of Las Vegas, 1988-92, chmn. planning commn., 1991-92; br. mgr. registration divsn. Dept. Motor Vehicles and Pub. Safety, State of Nev., Las Vegas, 1971-96; rep. Weststar FCU, Las Vegas, 1988—; advocate State of Nev. Employees Assn., Las Vegas, 1971—; coord. State of Nev. team City of Las Vegas Corp. Challenge, 1987-90. Past treas., sec. Las Vegas Civic Ballet Assn., Las Vegas, 1987-93; treas. Women's Dem. Club Clark County, Las Vegas, 1996; chmn., vice-chair United Blood Svcs. Adv. Coun., Las Vegas, 1993—; chmn. 1st Ann. Flood Awareness Week, mem. adv. coun. Clark County Regional Flood Dist., Las Vegas, 1987-88; treas., sec., badge and advancement counselor Boy Scouts Am., Las Vegas, 1976-90. Mem. Am. Bus. Women's Assn. (Centennial chpt. 1994-96). Democrat. Episcopalian. Home: 6532 Glen Martin Ct Las Vegas NV 89107

HUDGINS, CATHERINE HARDING, business executive; b. Raleigh, N.C., June 25, 1913; d. William Thomas and Mary Alice (Timberlake) Harding; m. Robert Scott Hudgins IV, Aug. 20, 1938; children: Catherine Harding Adams, Deborah Ghiselin, Robert Scott V. BS, N.C. State U., 1929-33; grad. tchr. N.C. Sch. for Deaf, 1933-34. Tchr. N.C. Sch. for Deaf, Morganton, 1934-36, N.J. Sch. for Deaf, Trenton, 1937-39; sec. Dr. A.S. Oliver, Raleigh, 1937, Robert S. Hudgins Co., Charlotte, N.C., 1949—, v.p., treas., 1960—, also bd. dirs. Mem. Jr. Svc. League, Easton, Pa., 1939; project chmn. ladies aux. Profl. Engrs. N.C., 1954-55, pres., 1956-57; pres. Christian High Sch. PTA, 1963; program chmn. Charlotte Opera Assn., 1959-61, sec., 1961-63; sec. bd. Hezekiah Alexander House restoration, 1949-52, Hezekiah Alexander House Aux., 1975—, treas., 1983-84, v.p., 1984-85, pres., 1985-89; sec. Hezekiah Alexander Found., 1986—; past chmn. home missions, annuities and relief Women of Presbyn. Ch., past pres. Sunday Sch. class; mem. Heritage Foun. Press. Club, 1995—, Empower Am., 1995—. Named Woman of Yr. Am. Biographical Soc., 1993. Mem. N.C. Hist. Assn., English Speaking Union, Internat. Platform Assn., Mint Mus. Drama Guild (pres. 1967-69), Internat. Biog. Ctr. Eng. (dep. dir. gen.), Heritage Found. (pres. club, 1994), Empower Am. (leadership coun. 1995), Daus. Am. Colonists (state chmn. nat. def. 1973-74, corr. sec. Virginia Dare chpt. 1978-79, 84-85, state insignia chmn. 1979-80), DAR (mem. nat. chmn.'s assn., rec. sec. nat. officers club 1990—, chpt. regent 1957-59, chpt. chaplain 1955-57 N.C. program chmn. 1961-63, state chmn. nat. def. 1973-76, state rec. sec. 1977-79, hon. state regent for life, chmn. N.C. Geneal. Register 1982, nat. vice chmn. S.E. region Am. Indians 1989—, rec. sec. Nat. Officers Club 1990-92, v.p. N.C. State Officer's Club 1991-92, pres. 1992-94), Children Am. Revolution (N.C. sr. pres. 1963-66, sr. nat. corr. sec., 1966-68, sr. nat. 1st v.p. 1968-70, sr. nat. pres. 1970-72, hon. sr. nat. pres. life 1972—, 2d v.p. Nat. Officers Club, 1st v.p. 1977-79, pres. 1979-81), Huguenot Soc. N.C., Carmel Country Club (Charlotte), Viewpoint 24 Club, (v.p. 1986, pres. 1987). Home: 1514 S Wendover Rd Charlotte NC 28211-1726 Office: Robert S Hudgins Co PO Box 17217 Charlotte NC 28270-0099

HUDSON, DEBORAH M., public relations practitioner; b. Elk River, Minn., Oct. 28, 1955; d. Thomas R. and Rosella A. (Libor) H.; m. Rick Scott Pallansch, Dec. 3, 1994. BA, U. Minn., 1980. Reporter, columnist St. Cloud (Minn.) Daily Times, 1982-87; asst. dir. pub. rels. & publs. St. Cloud State U., 1987-93; dir. univ. comms. Ball State U., Muncie, Ind., 1993-96; sr. dir. pub. rels. office of the chancellor Cmty. Colls. of Baltimore County, Towson, Md., 1996—; cons. media rels. Advantage Mktg. Group, St. Cloud, 1987—. Bd. dirs. Land of Lakes coun. Girl Scouts U.S., St. Cloud, 1989-93, chair nominating com., 1992; steering com. Muncie (Ind.) Children's Mus. Capital Campaign, 1995-96; bd. dirs. St. Cloud Area Arts Fund, 1987-92, Minn. Orch. at St. Benedict's, St. Cloud, 1989-93. Mem. Women in Communications, Nat. Assn. Women in Higher Edn., Phi Kappa Phi. Mem. United Ch. of Christ. Office: Cmty Colls Baltimore County 401 Washington Ave Ste 1010 Towson MD 21204

HUDSON, ELIZABETH MAE, elementary education educator; b. Evergreen Park, Ill., Aug. 27, 1949; d. Edward Henry and Virginia (Crask) Sumner; m. Daniel W. Hudson, Nov. 16, 1968; 1 child: Elizabeth V. BA in Edn., Aurora Coll., 1971; MS in Spl. Edn., No. Ill. U., 1979, MS in Edn. Adminstrn., 1989. Cert. elem. edn., spl. edn., learning disabilities, behavior disorders, social studies, lang. arts adminstrn. Tchr. Aurora (Ill.) Sch. Dist. 131, 1972—; tchr. 4th and 5th grades. Mem. Am. Fedn. Tchrs., PTA (treas.).

HUDSON, ELIZABETH PATRICIA, nurse; b. St. Charles, Ill., Jan. 14, 1962; d. Edward and Donna Marie (Huth) H. BSN, Elmhurst Coll., 1985. RN, Ill. Floor staff nurse Med. Ctr. Loyola U., Maywood, Ill., 1985-86, ICU staff nurse, 1986-88, outpatient staff nurse, 1988-90, neurosci. nurse, 1990—. Tutor Literacy Chgo., 1995—. Mem ANA (legis. com. 1994-96), Sigma Theta Tau.

HUDSON, JACQUELINE, artist; b. Cambridge, Mass.; d. Eric and Gertrude (Dunton) H.; student Columbia U., Art Students League, Sch. of the Nat. Acad. One-woman shows: Burr Gallery, N.Y.C., Rockport (Mass.) Art Assn., Present Day Club, Princeton, N.J., Maine Art Gallery, Wiscasset, Moulton Union, Bowdoin Coll., 1979; group shows: NAD, Pa. Acad. Fine Arts, Library of Congress, Cin. Mus., Riverside Mus., Portland (Maine) Mus. Art, Dayton Art Inst., Bixler Mus., Colby Coll., Maine Art Gallery, Wiscasset, Bowdoin Coll., Farnsworth Mus., Rockland, Maine, Vallombreuse Gallery, Palm Beach, Fla., Galerie Salammbo, Paris, many others; represented permanent collection Library of Congress, Farnsworth Mus.; pvt. collections. Recipient Pennell Purchase prize Library of Congress, 1951; Allen Kander Found. award Rockport Art Assn., 1957, Thelma Karr Graphic Prize, 1986; Edith Wengenroth Meml. prize, 1971, 75; Alice Standish Buell Meml. prize Nat. Assn. Women Artists, 1968, Helen Turner Graphic prize, 1974, Donna Miller Meml. prize, 1980; 3d graphic prize Butler Inst. Am. Art, 1983. Mem. Art Students League, Nat. Assn. Women

Artists (Elizabeth Erlanger Meml. award 1996), Rockport Art Assn. (Medal of Honor 1989, Excellence in Graphics prize 1992), Monhegan (Maine) Assn. (chmn. mus. com. 1963-67). Home: Monhegan Island ME 04852

HUDSON, JOY NUCKOLS, retired educator; b. Dumas, Ark., May 17, 1930; d. Walter Jennings and Katie Lee (Burrus) Nuckols; m. Charles Fred Hudson, Aug. 22, 1952; children: Donna Nelson, Hollis Gaston, Adrienne. AA, City Coll. San Francisco, 1950; BA, U. Ark., 1951. Cert. classroom tchr., Ark. Classroom tchr. Dumas Pub. Schs., 1952-55, 66-86; mem. Ark. Art Tchrs. Assn., Little Rock, 1975-82; treas. Ark. Assn. Spanish Tchrs., Little Rock, 1972-86. Mem., pres. PTA, Dumas, 1965-69, Hosp. Aux., Dumas, 1962-66; chair Desha County March of Dimes, 1960-66; bd. dirs., pres. Friends of the Libr., 1994—; mem. Meth. Choir, 1952—, U. Ark.-Little Rock Flute Ensemble, 1989-90; Sunday sch. tchr. United Meth. Ch.-Dumas, 1952-56. Named Woman of Yr., Dumas C. of C., 1994; named Choir Mem. of Yr., United Meth. Ch. Choir, 1995, Vol. of Yr., Trinity Village/Retirement Village, 1995; NDEA grantee. Mem. NEA, Ark. Edn. Assn., Dumas Edn. Assn., Am. Contract Bridge League (mem. unit 220, v.p. 1995—, Bronze Life Master), Hwy. Garden Club, Nat. Flute Assn. Methodist. Home: 410 Adams Dumas AR 71639

HUDSON, KATHERINE MARY, manufacturing company executive; b. Rochester, N.Y., Jan. 19, 1947; d. Edward Klock and Helen Mary (Rubacha) Nellis; m. Robert Orneal Hudson, Sept. 13, 1980; 1 child, Robert Klock. Student, Oberlin coll., 1964-66; BS in Mgmt., Ind. U., 1968; postgrad., Cornell U., 1968-69. Various postitions in fin., investor rels., communications, gen. mgr. instant photography Eastman Kodak Co., Rochester, 1970-87, chief info. officer, 1988-91, v.p., gen. mgr. printing and pub. imaging, 1991-93; pres., CEO W.H. Brady, Milw., 1994—; bd. dirs. Apple Computer. Mem. adv. coun. Ind. U. Sch. Bus., 1994—; trustee Alverno Coll., 1994—; bd. dirs. Med. Coll. Wis., 1995—. Recipient Chief of the Yr. award Info. Week Mag., 1990, Athena award Rochester C. of C., 1992; Lehman fellow N.Y. State, 1968. Republican. Roman Catholic. Office: W H Brady Co 6555 W Good Hope Rd P O Box 571 Milwaukee WI 53201-0571*

HUDSON, LEE (ARLENE HUDSON), environmental activist; b. Oakland, Calif., Apr. 17, 1936; d. Clyde Edward and Helen Therese McIrvin; m. James Joseph Coté, Mar. 28, 1958 (div. 1963); 1 child, Steven Michael. BA in Psychology, Calif. State U., Sacramento, 1976, postgrad., 1977-78. Exec. field dir. Dem. State Cen. Com., Sacramento, 1967-68; mem. staff Calif. Legis., Sacramento, 1967-72; founder, chmn., editor newsletter The Group for Alternatives to Spreading Poisons, Nevada City, Calif., 1983—; non-chem. advocate on adv. com. to Calif. Dept. Transp. Roadside Vegetation Mgmt. Com., 1993—. Vol. various state, fed. and local campaigns or initiatives, 1967—; founding mem. Toxics Coordinating Project, San Francisco, 1985-90; co-founder Calif. Coalition for Alternatives to Pesticides, Arcata and Eureka, 1983—, pres., chmn. bd. dirs., 1989—; mem. Com. for Sustainable Agriculture, 1986—, mem. mktg.-order subcom., 1986-89; bd. dirs. NW Coalition for Alternatives to Pesticides, Eugene, 1987-93; mem., chmn. tech. writing com. Nevada County Adv. Com. on Air Pollution, 1988-93; mem. Hazardous Waste Transfer Facility Siting Com. for Nevada County, 1989-90; mem. Nevada County Hazardous Waste Task Force, 1987-95, chair tech. sub-com., 1988-90; mem. Cen. Valley Hazardous Waste Minimization Com., 1990-91. Mem. Sierra Club (chmn. toxic subcom. Sierra Nevada group 1985-88), Amnesty Internat. Better World Soc., Cascade Holistic Econ. Cons., Coun. for Livable World, Nat. Peace Inst. Found., People's Med. Soc., Earth First, Nat. Resources Def. Coun., Nevada County C. of C., Greenpeace, Planning and Conservation League, Nevada County Greens Alliance, North Columbia Schoolhouse Cultural Ctr., South Yuba River Citizen's League, Siskiyou Mountains Resource Coun. (life), Rural Def. League, Beyond Pesticides, Environ. Protection Info. Ctr., Yuba Watershed Inst., Planet Drum. Mem. Universal Life Ch. Home and Office: Box 451 Nevada City CA 95959-8751

HUDSON, LINDA, health care executive; b. Tuscaloosa, Ala., Feb. 12, 1950; d. Elvin and Clara (Duke) Hudson; m. Charles Garrett Kimbrough, May 26, 1984. BS in Edn., U. Ala., 1971; MS in Psychology, U. So. Miss., 1984. Lic. profl. counselor. Recreational therapist West Ala. Rehab. Ctr., Tuscaloosa, 1971-72; flight attendant Delta Air Lines, Miami and New Orleans, 1972-80; pvt. practice psychotherapist Hattiesburg (Miss.) and Atlanta, 1984—; program dir. Eating Disorders Adventist Health System/Wedst, Atlanta, 1985-88, regional dir./cons., 1986-87, exec. dir. mental health svcs., 1988-89; owner Hudson Cons. Assocs., 1989—, nat. cons., 1986—. Contbr. articles to profl. jours. Mem. Covington Jr. Svc. League, La., 1981-83; co-chmn. St. Tammany Rep. Polit. Action Com., 1980-81; coord. United Way of St. Tammany Parish, 1979-80. Mem. Women Healthcare Execs., Ga. Mental Health Counselors Assn., Nat. Coun. Sexual Addiction and Compulsivity (bd. dirs., v.p.). Democrat. Office: Ste 238 1090 Northchase Pkwy Marietta GA 30067-6402

HUDSON, MARLENE MARY, speech and language pathologist; b. Detroit, Jan. 18, 1949; d. Jonathan Frederick and Albina Viola (Godzielski) Bishoff; m. Robert Andrew Hudson, Dec. 17, 1971; children: Jonathan Christian, Meredith Anne. BS, Wayne State U., 1971, MA, 1978. Cert. of clin. competence. Speech and lang. pathologist L'anse Creuse Pub. Schs., 1971-75; speech and lang. pathologist, supr. Saratoga Hosp., Detroit, 1977-79; speech and lang. pathologist St. John's Hosp., Bon SeCours Hosp., Cottage Hosp., Detroit and Grosse Pointe, Mich., 1977-79, Vis. Nurse Assn., Detroit, 1991—, Bon SeCours Hosp., Grosse Pointe, Mich., 1995—. Co-editor (conf. report) Guidance For Children in the 70's, 1970; speech pathologist (TV series) Family Concerns, 1994; narrator, creator: (cable TV program) Kids Everywhere Now Need You, 1986. Pres. K.E.N.N.Y. Kids Everywhere Now Need You, Mich., 1986-92, Richard Elem. PTO, Grosse Pointe, Mich., 1987-88; cub scout den leader, Grosse Pointe, 1986-88; exec. asst., pub. rels. chairperson Grosse Pointe Acad. Action Auction, 1990-92. Named Outstanding Vol., Grosse Point Pub. Schs., 1988, Employee of the Yr. Vis. Nurse Assn., 1994. Mem. Am. Speech-Lang.-Hearing Assn., The Garden Soc. (sec. 1990-91, 93-94), Sigma Gamma Assn. Roman Catholic. Home: 38 Lakecrest Ln Grosse Pointe Farms MI 48236

HUDSON, SHARON MARIE, credit and collections specialist; b. Chgo., Oct. 26, 1956; d. Lue James and Laura LaVerne (Mosby) H. AAS, Prairie State Coll., 1990; BA, Gov.'s State U., 1993, MA, 1995. Mental health specialist Elisabeth Ludeman Ctr., Park Forest, Ill., 1977-83; ins. agt. Met. Ins. Co., Chgo., 1983-84, Allstate Ins. Co., Park Forest, 1984-86; telemarketing rep. Progressive Mktg. Co., Hazel Crest, Ill., 1987-88; sales asst. AT&T, Chgo., 1988-89; customer sales rep. Ameritech, Chicago Heights, Ill., 1989-95, credit and collection specialist, 1995—; participant PhD project, 1995. Contbr. articles, mng. editor to univ. paper. Commr. Human Rels. Commn., Park Forest, 1992—; mentor Project Choice, Country Club Hills, Ill., 1995—; mem. Park Forest Youth Tax Force, 1994-95; vol. Pub. Action to Deliver Shelter, Chicago Heights, 1993, 95. With Ill. N.G., 1976-79; co-chair Regional Action Project 2000, 1995. U.S. Academic Achievement All-Am. scholar Gov.'s State U., 1993. Mem. LWV, NAFE, Nat. Coalition Bldg. Inst. (trainer 1995—), Women in Comms., Inc., Internat. Comms. Assn. Baptist.

HUDSON, SHEILA, track and field athlete; b. Wurzburg, Germany, June 30, 1967; m. Warren Strudwick. Grad., U. Calif., 1990. Long and triple jumper USA Track and Field Team. Office: USA Track and Field PO Box 120 Indianapolis IN 46206-0120

HUDSON, SUNCERRAY ANN, university analyst, research grants manager; b. San Francisco, Jan. 20, 1960; d. Charles Hudson and Nan Katherine (Coleman) Wagoner. BA, U. San Francisco, 1982; student, Southeast Community Coll., San Francisco, 1988. Stock transfer clk. The Bank of Calif., San Francisco, 1983-85; prin. clk. U. Calif., San Francisco, 1985-87, adminstrv. asst. II, 1987-88, adminstrv. asst. III, 1988-95, adminstrv. analyst, 1995—; ind. dealer Nat. Safety Assocs., Inc., San Francisco, 1990—; art cons. Artistic Impression, Inc., 1994—. Mem. NAFE, Gamma Phi Delta (Rho chpt. 1990-92, Zeta Nu chpt. 1992—). Office: U Calif Campus Box 0440 521 Parnassus Ave San Francisco CA 94122-2722

HUDSON, W. GAIL, social worker; b. Waxahachie, Tex., Apr. 15, 1953; d. Billy M. and Sarah W. (Bowen) H.; m. Garry H. Gillan, Sept. 7, 1991; 1 child, Logan Thomas Gillan. BS, S.W. Tex. State U., 1975, MA, 1976; PhD, So. Ill. U., 1979; MSW, U. Tex., Arlington, 1989. Lic. master social worker, advanced clin. practitioner. Asst., assoc. prof. Millikin U., Decatur, Ill., 1978-87; dept. chair communications Millikin U., Decatur, 1984-87; adj. faculty U. Tex., Arlington, 1987-89; social work fellow M.D. Anderson Hosp., Houston, 1988; social work intern U. Houston Counseling, 1989; social worker U. Houston Counseling & Testing, 1989-92, dir. employee assistance program, 1992—; rep. AIDS Consortium of Tex., 1991; tng. cons. Caterpillar Tractor Co., Decatur, 1979-81; planning com. Nat. Conf. Against Sexual Assault, 1994; cons. Profl. Devel. Program, Decatur, 1979-81; adj. grad. faculty dept. counseling psychology U. Houston, 1991—. Cons. Houston Area Planning Commn. for Substance Abuse Program, 1990-91; treas. ERA Decatur, 1978-82; vol. Coalition Against Domestic Violence, Decatur, 1979-81. Cons. Houston Area Planning Commn. for Substance Abuse Program, 1990-91; prin. investigator/dir. prevention of substance abuse, U. Houston and Higher Edn. Consortium, Houston/Galveston, 1991-94. Grantee U.S. Dept. Edn. Mem. NASW, NOW, Am. Coll. Personnel Assn. (bd. dirs. 1991, 94), Am. Assn. Counseling and Devel.. Home: 1123 Burning Tree Rd Humble TX 77339-3933 Office: U Houston Counseling 4800 Calhoun Rd Houston TX 77004-2610

HUDSON, WENDY JOY, software manager; b. New Brunswick, N.J., May 27, 1955; d. Herbert Roy and Dorothy Louise (Kaepernik) Hansen; m. William Howard Hudson, June 12, 1982. BA in Computer Sci., Rutgers U., 1977, MS in Computer Sci., 1979. Computer cons. Bell Labs., Holmdel, N.J., 1977-79; sr. mem. tech. staff Concurrent Computer, Tinton Falls, N.J., 1979-81; mgr. Concurrent Computer, Tinton Falls, 1981-83, sr. mgr., 1983-89, prin. mgr., 1989-91; mgr. Transarc, Pitts., 1991-92; group mgr. Ilex Sys., Shrewsbury, N.J., 1992-95; mgr. IBM, Piscataway, N.J., 1995—. Contbr. articles to profl. jours. Mem. Assn. Computing Machinery. Republican. Episcopalian. Home: 619 High Bridge Rd Colts Neck NJ 07722-1320 Office: IBM Corp 53 Knightsbridge Rd Piscataway NJ 08855

HUDSON-YOUNG, JANE SMITHER, real estate investor; b. Altavista, Va., July 5, 1937; d. Victor Nelson and Elois Reynolds Smither; A.A.S. summa cum laude in Mgmt., Central Va. Community Coll., 1978; m. J. Lee Hudson, May 15, 1954; 1 child, Michael Edward; m. Gordon M. Young, July 9, 1989. Adminstrv. asst. Altavista (Va.) High Sch., 1954-55; with Lane Co., Inc., Altavista, 1956-89, exec. sec. to chmn. bd., 1976-81, exec. sec. to chmn. exec. com., 1981-84, spl. asst. for pub. rels. communications, 1984-86, acct. exec. nat. accts, 1986, asst. sales mgr. contract div., 1986-87, mktg. adminstr., 1988-89; realtor R. B. Carr & Co., Altavista, 1980-87, assoc. broker, 1985-87; mem. adv. bd. Am. Fed. Savs. and Loan, 1985-89; pres. Hudson-Young Investments, 1989—. Corr. Lynchburg (Va.) News., 1966-72. Mem. town coun. Town of Altavista, 1980-86; sec. Altavista Community Improvement Coun., 1981-82; mem. bd. deacons First Bapt. Ch., Altavista, 1980-83. Home and Office: 1100 Heritage Plantation Dr Pawleys Island SC 29585

HUELSMAN, JOANNE B., state legislator; b. Mar. 21, 1938; married. JD, Marquette U., 1980. Attorney, realtor, businesswoman; former mem. Wis. Assembly from 31st dist.; mem. Wis. State Senate from 11th dist. Republican. Home: 235 W Broadway Ste 210 Waukesha WI 53186-2845 Office: Wis State Senate PO Box 7882 Madison WI 53707

HUENERGARDT, MYRNA LOUISE, college administrator, nurse practitioner; b. Medford, Oreg., Aug. 5, 1928; d. Henry and Matie Daisy (Vroman) H. BS, Columbia Union Coll., Takoma Park, Md., 1961; MA, Columbia U., 1963. RN, Calif.; cert. nurse practitioner. Charge nurse Glendale (Calif.) Adventist Hosp., 1954-57, 61-63; sch. nurse L.A. City Schs., 1957-60; instr. nursing Columbia Union Coll., Takoma Park, Md., 1964-68; dir. sch. nursing Branson Hosp. Sch. Nursing, Toronto, Ont., Can., 1968-71; chair paramed. dept. Southwestern C.C., Chula Vista, Calif., 1971-74; assoc. prof. nursing Loma Linda (Calif.) U., 1974-80; nurse rschr. U. So. Calif., L.A., 1981-83; nurse practitioner Community Health Projects, Covina, Calif., 1983-86; dir. student health svcs. Chaffey C.C., Rancho Cucamonga, Calif., 1986-94; med. edn. cons. Merck, Sharp & Dohme, West Point, Pa., 1991—; nurse practitioner New Horizon Care Corp., Loma Linda, 1987—; nurse cons., med. claims reviewer Aetna Ins., Loma Linda, 1994—. Bd. dirs. ARC, Inland Empire, Calif., 1986-91; cons. Master Plan Com., Substance Abuse, San Bernardino County, Calif., 1990—. Recipient Sameas award Outstanding Educators of Am., 1972, Disting. Leadership award Am. Biog. Inst., 1989; Fed. Govt. traineeship awards, 1961, 63, 64. Mem. Assn. of Calif. C.C. Adminstrs., Calif. Coalition of Nurse Practitioners, C.C. Health Svcs. Assn. of Calif. (pres. 1992-93), Sigma Theta Tau, Kappa Delta Pi. Republican. Home: 10636 Amapolas St Redlands CA 92373-8401

HUEY, CONSTANCE ANNE BERNER, mental health counselor; b. Tacoma, Wash., Jan. 20, 1938; d. Julian Boyd Berner and Beatta Kathryn (Day-Berner) Schoel; m. Donn R. Huey, July 26, 1961 (dec. June 1990); 1 child, Jennifer Anne. BA, U. Wash., 1959, MEd, 1976; cert. alcohol studies, Seattle U., 1980. Cert. mental health counselor, Wash. Speech, Eng. tchr. Pub. H.S., Seattle, 1959-68; tchr., supr., adminstr. U. Wash., Seattle, 1968-82; instr. in alcohol studies program Seattle U., Seattle, 1980-86; pvt. practice, 1980—; cons. in field; guest speaker Bastyr U.; presenter and trainer in numerous workshops and seminars. Contbg. author: We Did the Best We Could, 1993; guest on radio talk shows. Mem. Am. Counseling Assn., Seattle Counseling Assn., Women's Mental Health Assn., Nat. Assn. Alcoholism and Drug Abuse Counselors, Washington Assn. Alcoholism and Drug Abuse Counselors. Home: 1800 Taylor Ave N #10 Seattle WA 98109

HUF, CAROL ELINOR, tax service company executive; b. Milw., Apr. 21, 1940; d. William Weiss and Florence H. (Melcher) Weiss Lange; m. Walter Franklin Huf, Sept. 9, 1961; children: Mardell Leslie, Walter Albert III. Student Valparaiso U., 1958-60, Waukesha County Tech. Inst., 1968-69. Tax preparer H & R Block, Milw., 1967-84, instr. tax sch., 1969-83; job service interviewer State of Wis., Waukesha, 1984; pres. Personalized Tax Service, Inc., West Allis, Wis., 1984—, div. mgr. Primerica (formerly A.L. Williams), 1986. Vol. worker Girl Scouts US, Waukesha, 1970-80, Boy Scouts Am., Waukesha, 1975-92; swimming referee Wis. Interscholastic Athletic Assn., Milw., 1972-84. Recipient awards Boy Scouts Am. Mem. Nat. Soc. Pub. Accts., Wis. Womens Pub. Links Golf Assn. (past pres., 2d v.p. 1988—, state tournament chairperson 1987, 90, 94), United States Golf Assn. (regional affairs com. 1991—), Nat. Assn. Tax Practitioners (Wisc. bd. dirs. 1989—), Wis. Assn. Accts., Met. Swimming Ofcls., Edgewood Golf Club (pres. Big Bend, Wis. 1984-86). Lutheran. Home: 5508 Bauers Dr West Bend WI 53095-8782 Office: Personalized Tax Service Inc 10533 W National Ave Milwaukee WI 53227-2041

HUFF, CYNTHIA FAE, medical and orthopedic nurse; b. Albany, Ga., Jan. 3, 1950; d. Henry and Mary Catherine (Vannell) Piedmont; m. Michael Brian Shumaker, June 24, 1972 (div. 1979); 1 child, Brian Michael; m. Byron Lee Huff, Apr. 15, 1983. Diploma, Stuart Circle Hosp., Richmond, Va., 1970. RN, Va. Staff nurse St. Mary's Hosp., Richmond, 1970-71, asst. head nurse orthopedics, 1971, staff nurse emergency room, 1971-72, 73-74, head nurse orthopedics, 1972-73; office nurse Richmond, 1978-82; staff nurse Urology Ctr., Richmond, 1983-84; owner Sesroh Farm-Registered Quarterhorses, Powhatan, Va., 1984-89; nurse-technician for veterinarian for large and small animals, Midlothian, VA., 1986-90; staff nurse Amelia (Va.) Nursing Ctr., 1993—; nurse technician Edda C. Eliasson, D.V.M., Amelia, 1995—; bd. dirs. Amelia Patrons for Animal Welfare. Mem. Nat. Assn. Physicians' Nurses, Am. Heart Assn. (CPR instr.). Republican. Methodist. Home: 3009 Moyer Rd Powhatan VA 23139-7220

HUFF, GAYLE COMPTON, advertising agency executive; b. Washington, Nov. 28, 1956; d. Walter Dale and Jeanne (Parker) C.; m. Lanny Ross Huff, May 22, 1982. B in Gen. Studies, U. Mich., 1978. Mgr. br. merchandising CBS Records, Chgo., 1978; local promotion, mktg. mgr. CBS Records, Indpls., Boston, N.Y.C., 1978-81; spl. projects supr. Pickwick Internat. Musicland Group, Mpls., 1981-82; account exec. Campbell-Mithun Advt., Mpls., 1982-85; mktg. mgr., communications Universal Foods Corp., Milw., 1985-86; nat. advt. mgr. Thorobred Advt. Agy. (Jockey Internat., Inc.), Wis., 1986-88; dir. consumer and trade advt. Thorobred Advt. Agy. (Jockey Internat., Inc.), 1988-89, v.p. advt., 1990-92; dir. mktg./advt. Allen-Edmonds Shoe Co., Port Washington, Wis., 1993-95; v.p., dir. Fin. Mktg. Plus Direct Mktg. Group, Libertyville, Ill., 1995—; v.p., sec. Java Masters, Inc., 1992—. Mem. Traffic Audit Bur. for Media Measurement (bd. dirs. 1988-93), Assn. Nat. Advertisers (print adv. com., out of home advt. com. 1989-92). Office: Fin Mktg Plus Direct Mktg 1019 W Park Ave Libertyville IL 60048

HUFF, JOAN, retired physical education/dance educator; b. N.Y.C., May 10, 1929; d. Clarence R. and Marian W. (Waters) H. BS, Russell Sage Coll., 1950; MA, Mich. State U., 1958; EdD, U. Utah, 1967. Phys. edn., dance tchr. Hillsdale Dance Sch., Cin., 1950-52; phys. edn. tchr. Schoharie (N.Y.) Ctrl. Sch., 1952-57; prof. phys. edn., dance SUNY, Oswego, 1958-90. Bd. dirs. Oswego County Arts Coun., 1976-78; elder, trustee, bd. dirs., com. Presbyn. Ch./Faith United Ch., Oswego, 1971—. Grantee AAUW, 1994. Mem. AAUW (pres., v.p. program 1976—), Sacred Dance Guild (bd. dirs. 1974-77, dir. regions & chpts. 1988-96), Am. Dance Guild. Home: 49 Baylis St Oswego NY 13126

HUFF, LULA ELEANOR LUNSFORD, controller, accounting educator; b. Columbus, Ga., July 5, 1949; d. Walter Theophilus and Sally Marie (Bryant) Lunsford; m. Charles Efferidge Huff Jr., June 11, 1972; 1 child, Tamara Nicole. BA, Howard U., 1971; MBA, Atlanta U., 1973. CPA, Ga. Acct. Ernst and Young, Columbus, 1973-76; internal auditor First Consol. Gov., Columbus, 1976-84; instr., chair dept. acctg., dir. pers. mgmt. Troy State U., Phenix City, Ala., 1979-89; sr. fin./cost analyst Pratt and Whitney, Columbus, 1984-89; controller Pratt and Whitney, Southington, Conn., 1989-92, Columbus, 1992-95; contr. for precision components internat. Pratt and Whitney Joint Venture, Columbus, 1995-96; tchr. Troy State U., Phenix City. Mem. fin. bd. Diocese of Savannah; mem. Liberty Theater Hist. Preservation Bd., Columbus Housing Authority Bd., Columbus Hist. Found. Bd., Columbus Literate Comty. Program Inc. Bd., Columbus Beyond 2000, 1989-90; active Concharty coun. Girl Scouts, Inc., Women of Achievement, 1995. Recipient Disting. Black Citizen award Sta. WOKS, 1978, Black Excellence award Nat. Assn. Negro Bus. and Profl. Women's Clubs, Inc., 1977, Outstanding Svc. award St. Benedict Cath. Ch., 1971-76, cert. of merit Congressman Jack Brinkley, 1976, Achievement award Links Inc., 1976, Outstanding Achievement and Svcs. award 1st African Bapt. Ch., 1975, Ga. Jaycees Outstanding Young Woman award, 1989, Leadership Columbus award C. of C., 1983-84, Women on the Move award Spencer Owlettes, 1992; named Outstanding Woman of Yr., Ledger Enquirer Newspaper, 1976, Profl. Woman of Yr., Iota Phi Lambda, 1977, Bus. Woman of Yr., 1979, Columbus Ga. Outstanding Young Woman, Jaycees, 1980, Columbus Young Woman, 1980. Mem. NAACP, Am. Mgmt. Assn., Ga. Soc. CPAs, Howard U. Alumnae Assn., Urban League, Push, Toastmasters Am., Links, Inc. (Achievement award 1976), Delta Sigma Theta (auditor 1991). Roman Catholic. Home: PO Box 1742 Columbus GA 31902

HUFF, MARILYN L., federal judge; b. 1951. BA, Calvin Coll., Grand Rapids, Mich., 1972; JD, U. Mich., 1976. Assoc. Gray, Cary, Ames & Frye, 1976-83, ptnr., 1983-91; judge U.S. Dist. Ct. (so. dist.) Calif., San Diego, 1991—. Contbr. articles to profl. jours. Mem. adv. coun. Calif. LWV, 1987—, Am. Lung Assn.; bd. dirs. San Diego and Imperial Counties, 1989—; mem. LaJolla Presbyn. Ch. Named Legal Profl. of Yr. San Diego City Club and Jr. C. of C., 1990; recipient Superior Ct. Valuable Svc. award, 1982. Mem. ABA, San Diego Bar Found., San Diego Bar Assn. (bd. dirs. 1986-88, v.p. 1988, chmn. profl. edn. com. 1990, Svc. award to legal profession, 1989, Lawyer of Yr. 1990), Calif. State Bar Assn., Calif. Women Lawyers, Am. Bd. Trial Advs., Libel Def. Resource Ctr., Am. Inns of Ct. (master 1987—, exec. com. 1989—), Lawyers' Club San Diego (adv. bd. 1989-90, Belva Lockwood Svc. award 1987), Univ. Club, Aardvarks Lt. Office: US Dist Ct US Courthouse 940 Front St San Diego CA 92101-8994*

HUFF, SARA DAVIS, nurse; b. Moundville, Ala., May 16, 1935; d. George W. and Maggie A. (Callahan) Davis; m. Eugene H. Huff, May 21, 1956 (div. June 1992); children: John Davis Huff, Timothy Eugene Huff. RN, Druid City Hosp. Sch. Nursing, Tuscaloosa, Ala., 1956; BS, Oglethorpe U., 1980. CNOR. RN, oper. rm. Druid City Hosp., Tuscaloosa, 1956-58; asst. head nurse, thoracic cardiovascular St. Joseph's Hosp., Atlanta, 1958-60; charge nurse/open heart thoracic Emory U. Hosp., Atlanta, 1960-64; edn. coord. oper. room Emory U. Hosp., 1974-75; oper. rm. supr. H. Egleston Hosp. for Children, Atlanta, 1964-73; nurse cons. Cons. Surg. Svcs., Atlanta, 1986-92; dir. surg. svcs. Northside Hosp., Atlanta, 1975-86; staff nurse oper. rm. Northlake Hosp., Atlanta, 1990-92; dir. surg. svcs. Atlanta Hosp., 1989-90, Newton Gen. Hosp., Covington, Ga., 1992—; speaker in field. Mem. AORN (nat. bd. dirs. 1980-84, gen. AORN nat. congress 1980, other coms.), ANA, Assn. of Oper. Rm. Nurses of Atlanta (Nurse of Yr. 1975), Atlanta Area Oper. Rm. Suprs. (chmn. 1973-75). Home: 2534 Warwick Cir Atlanta GA 30345

HUFF, SHEILA MINOR, environmental scientist; b. Washington, Mar. 15, 1947; d. Lucien Harold Minor and Credella (Derricotte) Young; children: Jesse E. III, Kevin E. BS in Biology, Am. U., 1970; MS in Biology, George Mason U., 1979. Cert. wildlife biologist The Wildlife Soc., 1979. Biological technician U.S. Fish and Wildlife Svc. Dept Interior, Washington, 1970-72; biological rsch. asst. Smithsonian Inst. Environ. Rsch. Ctr., Edgewater, Md., 1972-75; wildlife biologist Fed. Energy Regulatory Commn. Environ. Analysis Br., Washington, 1975-77; instr. wildlife biology U. DC Sch. Natural Resources, Washington, 1977-79; spl. asst. to the asst. sec. for fish and wildlife and pks. U.S. Dept. Interior, Washington, 1977-80; regional environ. officer Office Environ. Affairs, Office of Sec. U.S. Dept. Interior, Chgo., 1980-94; environ. rev. officer, asst. sec. policy, budget & adminstrn. U.S. Dept. Interior, Washington, 1994—; teaching asst. taxidermy Smithsonian Inst. Assocs. Program, Washington, 1972; environ. edn. cons. YMCA CAmp Letts, Edgewater, 1973-74; vol. speaker Smithsonian Inst. Speakers Bur., Edgewater, 1972-75. Bd. trustees Howard Theater Found., Washington, 1978-79; bd. dirs. Friends of the Nat. Zoo, Washington, 1978-80; troop leader Troop 1278 Girl Scouts Am., Washington, 1978-90; mem. St. Monica's Guild, St. Edmund's Episcopal Ch., Chgo., 1988-94, St. Mary's Episcopal Ch., Washington, 1994—. Democrat. Mem. Ill. Assn. Environ. Profl. (bd. dirs., mem. chair 1987), Nat. Assn. Environ. Profl. Home: 6027 Curtier Dr Unit C Alexandria VA 22310-5128

HUFF, SHERRI LYNN, physical education educator; b. Owensboro, Ky., Sept. 29, 1963; d. John and Darleen Mae (Westphal) H. BS in Recreation, U. Ala., Birmingham, 1985; MA in Athletic Adminstrn., U. Ala., 1988, MA in Phys. Edn., 1990; EdS in Phys. Edn., U. Montevallo, 1994; cert. edn. adminstrn. K-12, Samford U., 1995. Cert. Rank AA tchr. phys. edn. K-12, rank 1 ednl. adminstr. grades K-12, Ala. Pre-sch. tchr. Jewish Comty. Ctr., Birmingham, Ala., 1985-88; phys. edn. tchr.'s aide, coach mid. sch. basketball Hewitt-Trussville Mid. Sch., Trussville, Ala., 1990-91; tchr. elem. phys. edn. K-5 Washington Elem. Sch., Birmingham, 1991-92; basketball coach Washington Mid. Sch., Birmingham, 1991-92; volleyball coach Tarrant (Ala.) H.S., 1993-94; basketball coach Tarrant Mid. Sch., 1992-95; tchr. elem. phys. edn. K-4 Tarrant Elem. Sch., 1992-96; golf coach Tarrant H.S., 1995-96, basketball coach, 1995-96; phys. edn. program specialist Birmingham City Schs., 1996—; summer activities instr. U. Ala., Birmingham, 1988-95; com. mem. bldg. leadership team Tarrant Elem. Sch., 1994-96; com. mem. sch. accreditation Fultondale (Ala.) Elem. Sch.-So. Assn. of Colls. and Schs., 1994. Coord. Jump Rope for Heart program Am. Heart Assn., Birmingham, 1992-96; coord. Jingle Bell Run for Arthritis Found., Birmingham, 1994-96. Named Faculty Mem. of Nat. Blue Ribbon Sch., U.S. Dept. Edn., 1994; inducted into Apollo H.S. Athletic Hall of Fame, 1996; Mervyn Goldstein Meml. scholar U. Ala., 1985-86; Adminstrn. Samford U. scholar, 1995—. Mem. ASCD, NEA, AAHPERD, Nat. Fedn. Interscholastic Coaches Assn., Ala. State Assn. for Health, Phys. Edn., Recreation and Dance (state bd. mem. dist. rep. 1993-95, v.p.-elect 1996—, presenter phys. edn. workshop 1993, coord. fall and spring conf. store), Ala. H.S. Athletic Dirs. and Coaches Assn., Magic City Phys. Educators and Coaches Assn. (pres. 1992-93). Republican. Presbyterian. Home: 153 Ashford Ln Alabaster AL 35007 Office: Rickwood Field Dept Ath Birmingham City Schs 1137 2d Ave W Birmingham AL 35204

HUFFINGTON, ANITA, sculptor; b. Balt., Dec. 25, 1934; d. Norris Jackson and Agnes (Hook) H.; m. Manuel Rubin Duque, Sept. 17, 1957 (div. Nov. 1964); 1 child, Lisa Huffington Duque; m. Henry Frederick Sutter, Dec. 4, 1964. BA, City Coll. N.Y., 1973, MFA, 1975. Resident La Napoule (France) Art Found., 1996. One- woman exhbns. include U. Ark.,

Fayetteville, 1982, Valley House Gallery, Dallas, 1986, Ark. Art Ctr., Little Rock, 1990, O'Hara Gallery, N.Y.C., 1994, 96; 2-person show Lisa Kurts Gallery, Memphis, 1995; 3-person shows Louis Stern Gallery, West Hollywood, Calif., 1996, Triangle Gallery, San Francisco, 1996; group exhbns. include Internatl Women's Art Festival, N.Y.C., 1976, U. Ark., Fayetteville, 1978, 92, Ark. Arts Ctr., Little Rock, 1979-81, Territorial Restoration Gallery, Little Rock, 1981, Harris Gallery, Houston, Tex., 1981-93, Sculptural Arts Mus., Altanta, 1982, Benton Gallery, Southampton, N.Y., 1988, 89, M.A. Doran Gallery, Tulsa, 1988-92, Kornbluth Gallery, Fair Lawn, N.J., 1989, 7th Regiment Armory Art Show, N.Y.C., 1989-95, Ft. Smith (Ark.) Art Ctr., 1990, Salon de Mars, Paris, 1992, U. Pa., Phila., 1992-95, ARTexas, Dallas, 1993-94, Art Fair Seattle, 1995-96, Art Miami (Fla.), 1996, Marisa del Re/O'Hara Gallery, Palm Beach, Fla.; featured in various profl. publs., mags., newspapers and videos. Visual arts fellow Ark. Arts Coun.

HUFFMAN, CAROL KOSTER, retired middle school educator; b. L.I., N.Y., Nov. 4, 1933; d. Harry C. Jr. and Mary M. (Wilchin) Koster; m. William Leslie Huffman. BS, Hofstra U., 1954, MS, 1967. Cert. elem., art, nursery and spl. edn. tchr., N.Y.; cert. advanced Irlen screener I and area coord. Dir. Child's World Sch., New Orleans; in-svc. instr. Half Hollow Hills Schs., Dix Hills, N.Y.; instr. in spl. edn. Hofstra U., Hempstead, N.Y.; resource, self-contained program, art and learning strategies tchr. Half Hollow Hills Schs., Dix Hills, N.Y.; cons. for curriculum, spl. edn. and reading; rschr. identification and ednl. accomodations for students with visual disabilities affecting schoolwork. Former editor: The Communicator. Former del. N.Y. State Retirement Sys. Mem. AFT (former del.), N.Y. State United Tchrs. (former del.), Half Hollow Hills Tchr. Assn. (exec. bd.), Kappa Pi, Kappa Delta Pi.

HUFFMAN, JANICE KAY, middle school educator, curriculum coordinator; b. Mt. Pleasant, Mich., Nov. 5, 1941; d. Charles Emerald and Norma Ilene (Gilmore) Brien; m. Charles William Huffman, Jan. 15, 1966; children: Victoria Lynn, Mary Kathleen, Jasmine Rae. BA, North Ctrl. Coll., 1963; student, U. Fla., 1966-67; MA, Ctrl. Mich. U., 1982. Cert. elem. tchr., Mich., Ill., Fla. Elem. tchr. Comm. Cons. Sch. Dist. 15, Palatine, Ill., 1963-65, Midland (Mich.) Pub. Schs., 1965; K-12 reading tchr. Alachua County Schs., Gainesville, Fla., 1966-67; 7-8 Title I Indian Culture tchr. Mt. Pleasant Pub. Schs., 1967-70, 7-8 reading tchr., 1967-72, 7-8 English, lang. arts tchr., 1972-95, K-12 curriculum coun. chmn., 1985-95; mem. edn. com. Sag. Chip Tribe, Mt. Pleasant, 1968-73; strategic planner Mt. Pleasant Pub. Schs., 1994-96. bd. dirs. Zion Luth. Nursery Sch., Mt. Pleasant, 1970-72; writing & pub. com. mem. Art Reach, Mt. Pleasant, 1989-94; edn. chmn. Countryside United Meth. Ch., 1975-95; mentor Coun. Exceptional Children, 1985. Mem. AAUW, ASCD (assoc.), Phi Delta Kappa, Delta Kappa Gamma (rsch. chair 198-85).

HUFFMAN, NONA GAY, financial consultant, retirement planning specialist; b. Albuquerque, June 22, 1942; d. William Abraham and Opal Irene (Leaton) Crisp; m. Donald Clyde Williams, Oct. 20, 1961; children: Debra Gaylene, James Donald. Student pub. schs. Lawndale, Calif. Lic. ins., securities dealer, N.Mex. Sec. City of L.A., 1960, L.A. City Schs. 1960-62, Aerospace Corp., El Segundo, Calif., 1962-64, Albuquerque Pub. Schs., 1972-73, Pub. Service Co. N.Mex., Albuquerque, 1973; rep., fin. planner Waddell & Reed, Inc., Albuquerque, 1979-84; broker Rauscher Pierce Refsnes, Inc., 1984-85; rep., investment and retirement specialist Fin. Network Investment Corp., 1985-89, John Hancock Fin. Svcs., 1989-90; account exec. Eppler, Guerin & Turner, Inc., 1990-91, Fin. Network Investment Corp., Albuquerque, 1991—; instr. on-site corp. training of fin. strategies for retirement Philips Semi Conductors, Honeywell & Motorola, instr. fin. strategies for successful retirement U. N.Mex. Continuing Edn., instr. employee retirement seminars BLM, Forest Svc., other govt. agys. Mem. Profl. Orgn. Women (co-chmn.), Women in Bus. (Albuquerque chpt.). Office: Fin Network Investment Corp 8500 Menaul Blvd NE # 195B Albuquerque NM 87112-2298

HUFFMAN, PATRICIA JOAN, retired accounting coordinator; b. Elmira, N.Y., Mar. 29, 1941; d. F. John and Alice E. (Patterson) Garbay; m. Edward L. Huffman, May 28, 1960; children: Debra L. Palmer, Thomas E., Matthew M. AA in Bus. Adminstrn., Corning C.C., 1984, AA in Data Processing, 1984; BS, Elmira Coll., 1991. Clk. typist Hardinge's Bros., Elmira, N.Y., 1959-62, Gen. Precision Labs., Pleasantville, N.Y., 1965 66; data entry clk. Reader's Digest, Pleasantville, 1966-68, Elmira Data Processing, 1968-69; acctg. clk. Am. LaFrance, Elmira, 1969-73, GE, Elmira, 1973-75, Elmira Star-Gazette, 1975-77; various temporary positions Manpower, Elmira, Corning, N.Y., 1980, 84-85; pers. clk. Atlantic & Pacific Tea Co., Horseheads, N.Y., 1980-82; sales tax clk. Corning, Inc., 1985-88; finished goods inventory clk. Corning, Inc., Big Flats, N.Y., 1988-89; credit & collection clk. Corning, Inc., 1989-94, acctg. coord., 1994-96; ret., 1996. Author: (poem) Those Black Nights/Where Dreams Begin, 1993 (Editor's Choice award, 1993), In Sorrow/Outstanding Poets of 1994 (Editor's Choice award, 1994), Remember the Good Times My Love/Dance on the Horizon, 1994, Lissa/Best Poems of 1995 (Editor's Choice award, 1995), Prairie Rattler/Best Poems of 1996, (Editor's Choice award, 1996). Sec. Ladies of Charity, Elmira, 1984-86, v.p., 1992-96, pres., 1996—; lector St. Mary Our Mother Ch., Horseheads, N.Y., 1986-90. Editors Choice Award, 1996, Prairie Rattler (Best Poems of 1996). Mem. Internat. Soc. Poets (adv. panel mem. 1993—, Internat. Poet of Merit award 1993-95), Inst. Mgmt. Accts. Home: 31 Wolcott Dr Horseheads NY 14845-1183

HUFFMAN, ROSEMARY ADAMS, lawyer, corporate executive; b. Orlando, Fla., Oct. 18, 1939; d. Elmer Victor and Esther (Weber) Adams; divorced; 1 child, Justin Adams Fruth. A.B. in Econs., Ind. U., 1959, J.D., 1962; LL.M., U. Chgo., 1967. Bar: Ind. 1962, Fla. 1963. Dep. prosecutor Marion County, Ind., 1963; ct. adminstr. Ind. Supreme Ct., 1967-68; pro-tem judge Marion County Mcpl. Ct., 1969-70; jud. coordinator Ind. Criminal Justice Planning Agy., 1969-70; dir. ctr. for Jud. Edn., Inc., 1970-73; pub. Jud. Xchange, 1972-73; instr. bus. law Purdue U., Indpls., 1962-63, Ind. U., Indpls., 1963-64; asst. Ind. Jud. Council, 1965; legis. intern Ford Found., 1965; sole practice, Indpls., 1962—; pres., owner Abacus, Inc., Indpls., 1980—. Mem. Ind. Bar Assn., Fla. Bar Assn., Indpls. Bar Assn. Home and Office: 6630 E 56th St Indianapolis IN 46226-1799

HUFFMAN, SHERRI DIANE, advertising and marketing consultant; b. Tulsa, June 14, 1962; children: Alexis Ann, Alexis Alan. Student, Colo. Inst. Art. Lic. series 7 securities SEC; lic. pvt. pilot FAA; lic. life ins., Colo. Fin. planner E.F. Hutton, Inc., Denver, 1983; securities broker Integrated Equities Realty Corp., Denver, 1983; fin. advisor Sears Fin. Network, Denver, 1984; owner Normad, Inc., Denver, 1994—; mktg. dir. I.L.S.A., Denver, 1995; nat. distbr. Nikken, Denver, 1995. Contbr. poetry to mags. Campaign vol. Crider Campaign, Denver, 1995, Bradley Campaign, Denver, 1996; mem. Libr. of Congress, Dem. Nat. Com. Mem. Nat. Assn. Underwater Instrn. (cert diving open I), Nat. Hist. Soc., N.Am. Hunting Club, Denver Press Club.

HUFHAM, BARBARA FRANCES, publishing executive, lawyer; b. Washington, Sept. 23, 1939; d. Ronald Lee and Barbara Adair (Brydon) H.; m. Richard Curtis Wells, Sept. 16, 1972. BA, Hood Coll., 1961; JD, NYU, 1968. Bar: N.Y. 1969. Writer Liberty Mut. Ins. Co., Boston, 1961-64; contracts asst. Macmillan Pub. Co., N.Y.C., 1964-65; mgr. rights and permissions div. Curtis Pub. Co., N.Y.C., 1965-68; asst. gen. counsel Harper & Row Pubs., N.Y.C., 1968-72, sec., asst. gen. counsel, 1972-85, assoc. gen. counsel, 1985-87, v.p., gen. counsel, 1987-89; sr. v.p. and gen. counsel Harper Collins Pubs. (formerly Harper & Row Pubs.), N.Y.C., 1989-94, sr. v.p. human resources, 1994—. Office: Harper Collins Pubs Inc 10 E 53rd St New York NY 10022-5244

HUFNAGEL, LINDA ANN, biology educator, researcher; b. Teaneck, N.J., Nov. 7, 1939; d. Ernest Albert and Frances Marie (Hrbek) H.; m. Dov Jaron, 1969; children: Shulamit, Tamara; m. Robert Van Zackroff, June 1984. BA, U. Vt., 1961, MS, 1963; PhD, U. Pa., 1967. Lectr. U. Pa., Phila., summer 1967; NSF postdoctoral fellow Yale U., New Haven, 1967-69; rsch. assoc. Columbia U., N.Y.C., 1970; asst. prof. Oakland Community Coll., Farmington, Mich., 1970; rsch. assoc. Wayne State U., Detroit, 1971-73; lectr. biology U. R.I., Kingston, 1973-75, asst. prof., 1975-79, assoc. prof., 1979-86, prof., 1986—, dir. cen. electron microscope facility, 1973-96. NSF rsch. grantee U. R.I., 1975, Am. Heart Assn. rsch. grantee, 1979; Steps fellow Marine Biol. Lab., Woods Hole, Mass., 1978, 79. Office: U RI Dept Biochem Microbio and Mol Gn Kingston RI 02881

HUFSTEDLER, SHIRLEY MOUNT (MRS. SETH M. HUFSTEDLER), lawyer, former federal judge; b. Denver, Aug. 24, 1925; d. Earl Stanley and Eva (Von Behren) Mount; m. Seth Martin Hufstedler, Aug. 16, 1949; 1 son, Steven Mark. BBA, U. N.Mex., 1945, LLD (hon.), 1972; LLB, Stanford U., 1949; LLD (hon.), U. Wyo., 1970, Gonzaga U., 1970, Occidental Coll., 1971, Tufts U., 1974, U. So. Calif., 1976, Georgetown U., 1976, U. Pa., 1976, Columbia U., 1977, U. Mich., 1979, Yale U., 1981, Rutgers U., 1981, Claremont U. Ctr., 1981, Smith Coll., 1982, Syracuse U., 1983, Mt. Holyoke Coll., 1985; PHH (hon.), Hood Coll., 1981, Hebrew Union Coll., 1986, Tulane U., 1988. Bar: Calif. 1950. Mem. firm Beardsley, Hufstedler & Kemble, L.A., 1951-61; practiced in L.A., 1961; judge Superior Ct., County L.A., 1961-66; justice Ct. Appeals 2d dist., 1966-68; circuit judge U.S. Ct. Appeals 9th cir., 1968-79; sec. U.S. Dept. Edn., 1979-81; ptnr. Hufstedler & Kaus, L.A., 1981-95; sr. of counsel Morrison & Foerster, L.A., 1995-96; ret., 1996; dir. Hewlett Packard Co., US West, Inc., Harman Industries Internat. Mem. staff Stanford Law Rev, 1947-49; articles and book rev. editor, 1948-49. Trustee Calif. Inst. Tech., Occidental Coll., 1972-89, Aspen Inst., Colonial Williamsburg Found., 1976-93, Constl. Rights Found., 1978-80, Nat. Resources Def. Coun., 1983-85, Carnegie Endowment for Internat. Peace, 1983-94; bd. dirs. John T. and Catherine MacArthur Found., 1983—. Named Woman of Yr. Ladies Home Jour., 1976; recipient UCLA medal, 1981. Fellow Am. Acad. Arts and Scis.; mem. ABA (medal 1995), L.A. Bar Assn., Town Hall, Am. Law Inst. (coun. 1974-84), Am. Bar Found., Women Lawyers Assn. (pres. 1957-58), Am. Judicature Soc., Assn. of the Bar of City of N.Y., Coun. on Fgn. Rels., Order of Coif. Office: Morrison & Foerster 555 W 5th St Ste 3500 Los Angeles CA 90013

HUGGINS, CHARLOTTE SUSAN HARRISON, secondary education educator, author, travel specialist; b. Rockford, Ill., May 13, 1933; d. Lyle Lux and Alta May (Bowers) H.; student Knox Coll., 1951-52; AB magna cum laude, Harvard U., 1958; MA, Northwestern U., 1960, postgrad., 1971-73; cert. in conversational French Berlitz Lang. Sch.; m. Rollin Charles Huggins, Apr. 26, 1952; children: Cynthia Charlotte Peters, Shirley Ann Cooper, John Charles. Asst. editor Hollister Publs., Inc., Wilmette, Ill., 1959-65; tchr. advanced placement English New Trier High Sch., Winnetka, Ill., 1965—; master tchr., 1979; leader tchr., 1988; Task Force Commn. on Grading, 1973-74; Sabbatical project 1 yr. world travel History-Lit. Prospectus; cons. Asian Studies New Trier, 1987-88; mem. New Trier Supts. Commn. on Censorship, 1991; instr. critiquing Northwestern U.; cons. McDougall-Littel's Young Writer's Manual, 1985-88; asst. sponsor Echoes, 1981, Trevia, 1982, 83; sponsor New Trier News, 1988—; pres. Harrison Farms, Inc., Lovington, Ill., 1976—; speaker North Suburban Geneal. Soc., 1990; presenter Asian lit. Ill. Humanities Coun., 1992, Nat. Scholastic Press Assn. Conv., 1993; speaker Ill. High Sch. Scholastic Press Assn., No. Ill. Sch. Press Assn., 1992, 93, 94; instr., travel expert New Trier Adult Edn. Keys to the World's Last Mysteries, 1986—. Author: A Sequential Course in Composition Grades 9-12, 1979, A History of New Trier High School, 1982, Passage to Anaheim: An Historical Biography of Pioneer Families, 1984, Cambodia: A Place in Time, 1987; (video tapes) The Glory That Was Greece, 1987, The World of Charles Dickens, 1987. Mem. women's bd. St. Leonard's House, Chgo., 1965-75; Central Sch. PTA Bd., Wilmette, 1960-64; mem. jr. bd. Northwestern U. Settlement, Chgo., 1965-75. Recipient DAR Citizenship award, 1953, Phi Beta Kappa award, 1957, Am. Legion award, 1959, cert. of merit Graphic Arts Competition Printing Industries of Am., 1983, Quill and Scroll George Gallup award, 1990, 1st pl. award Am. Scholastic Press Assn., 1990, cert. of merit Am. Newspaper Pubs. Assn., 1990. Mem. MLA, NEA, ASCD, Ill. Edn. Assn., New Trier Edn. Assn. (sec. 1992, pres.-elect 1994, pres. 1995—), Nat. Coun. Tchrs. English, Ill. Assn. Tchrs. English, Women Comm., Inc., Northwestern U. Alumni Assn., Jr. Aux. U. Chgo. Cancer Research Bd., Mary Crane League, Nat. Huguenot Soc., Ill. Huguenot Soc., Columbia Scholastic Press Assn. (del 1990, newspaper judge, medalist award), Ill. Journalism Edn. Assn. (awards chmn., bd. dirs. 1992—, sec. 1994-95), Quill and Scroll (George Gallup award 1990, bd. dirs. 1992-93), Nat. Scholastic Press Assn. (spring convention rep. 1991-92, 92-93, 93-94, 94-95, 95-96, newspaper judge, conv. del. 1991, All-Am. Newspaper award 1990-91, 91-92, Fall and Spring conv. presenter 1993-94, 94-95, 95-96), Women in Comm., Newberry Libr. (assoc.), Art Inst. Chgo. (life), Terra Mus. Chgo. (charter), Lyric Opera (assoc.), Women's Club Wilmette, Mich. Shores Club, Univ. Club Chgo., Knox Coll. Alumni Assn., Radcliffe Coll. Alumnae Assn., Harvard U. Alumni Assn., Pi Beta Phi (North Shore Chgo. alumnae bd., publicity chair). Home: 700 Greenwood Ave Wilmette IL 60091-1748 Office: 385 Winnetka Ave Winnetka IL 60093-4238

HUGGINS, ELAINE JACQUELINE, nurse, retired army officer; b. San Jose, Calif., Mar. 26, 1954; d. William Burt and Edith Gwendolyn (Schindler) Moreland; m. Bruce Carlton Allanach, Oct. 8, 1976, (div. Oct. 1989); stepchildren: Dawn Louise, Christopher Bruce, Jeffrey Scott, Sean Michael; m. Michael Henry Huggins, Dec. 8, 1991; children: Phoebe Marie, Chloe Anne; stepchildren: Abbey Rose, Jamin Michael. BS in Nursing, U.Md., 1976; MS in Nursing, Med. Coll. Ga., 1988; postgrad., Calif. Inst. Integral Studies. RN, Ga., Md., Calif. Commd. 2d lt. Nurse Corps, U.S. Army, 1972, advanced through grades to maj., 1986; staff nurse gen. medicine-oncology Walter Reed Army Med. Ctr., Washington, 1976-78, team leader gen. medicine-oncology, 1978-79, head nurse med. splty. ward, 1979-80; asst. head nurse gynecol. oncology unit Tripler Army Med. Ctr., Honolulu, 1980-81, head nurse med. splty. clinic, 1981-83; staff nurse orthopedics Eisenhower Army Med. Center, Ft. Gordon, Ga., 1983-84, patient edn. coord., 1984-85, head nurse recovery room, 1985-86; head nurse oncology/neurology unit Letterman Army Med. Ctr., Presidio of San Francisco, 1988-89, clin. nurse psychiat. unit, 1989-90, chief nursing adminstrn. E/N, Letterman Army Med. Ctr. Presidio of San Francisco, 1990-92, ret., 1992; casemanager Vis. Nurses Pomona, Claremont, Calif., 1993-94; nursing supr. Vis. Nurses Assn./Hospice of Pomona, San Bernadino, Calif., 1994-95, quality risk resource mgr., 1995—; mem. adj. faculty Sch. Nursing U. Phoenix-So. Calif. Campus, 1995-96; lectr. in field. Contbr. articles to nursing, mil., and med. publs. Mem. pub. edn. com. Am. Cancer Soc., Honolulu, 1982. Recipient Humanitarian Svc. medal, 1990. Mem. Am. Diabetes Assn., Am. Assn. Diabetic Educators, Grad. Student Nurses Assn. (sec. 1986-87), Am. Nurses Assn., Mensa, Sigma Theta Tau. Avocations: reading, walking, beach combing. Home: 7343 Stonebrook Pl Rancho Cucamonga CA 91730-7271 Office: Vis Nurses Assn Hospice of Pomona Claremont CA 91711

HUGHES, ANN, state legislator; b. Ogdensburg, N.Y., Sept. 28, 1943. BA in Biology, Wells Coll., 1965; student, McHenry County C.C., 1982. m. Earl Hughes; 3 children. Sec.-treas. Hughes Seed Farms; mem. Ill. Ho. of Reps., 1993—; chmn. com. on counties and twps., mem. insurance com., mem. health care and human svcs. com., mem. environ. and energy com., mem. global climate task force. Home: 407 N Dimmel Rd Woodstock IL 60098-9264 Office: Ill Ho of Reps State Capitol Springfield IL 62706 also: 2114-N Stratton Bldg Springfield IL 62706 also: 5400 W Elm St Ste 212 Mc Henry IL 60050-4049

HUGHES, ANN HANSZEN, physician; b. Dallas, Sept. 3, 1929; d. Eugene and Gilly May (Whitman) Hanszen; m. W. John Kinross-Wright, June 29, 1971 (div.); children: Robert H., Ann Louise. BA, So. Meth. U., 1955; MD, U. Tex. Southwestern Med., 1959. Diplomate Am. Bd. Psychiatry and Neurology. Asst. prof. U. Tex. Southwestern Med. Sch., Dallas, 1964-68; dep. commr. Tex. Dept. Mental Health, Austin, 1969-71; pres., med. dir. Discovery Land Hosp., Bryan, Tex., 1972-83; prof., chmn. psychiatry Tex. A&M Coll. of Medicine, College Station, Tex., 1978-79; clin. dir. Las Vegas (N.Mex.) Med. Ctr., 1986-90; med. dir. La Amistad Resdl. Treatment Ctr., Orlando, Fla., 1994-96; cons. Joint Commn. Accreditation of Health Orgns., Chgo., 1989-92, OCHAMPUS, Washington, 1992-95; examiner Am. Bd. Psychiatry and Neurology. Contbg. author: American Handbook of Child Psychiatry. Mem. Pres.'s Coun., U. Tex., Austin, 1994-96. Fellow APA.

HUGHES, ANN HIGHTOWER, economist, international trade consultant; b. Birmingham, Ala., Nov. 24, 1938; d. Brady Alexander and Juanita (Pope) H. B.A., George Washington U., 1963, M.A., 1969. Asst. U.S. trade rep. Exec. Office of Pres., Washington, 1978-81; dep. asst. sec. trade agreements Dept. Commerce, Washington, 1981-82, dep. asst. sec. Western Hemisphere, 1982-95; dir. C & M Internat., Washington, 1995—. Recipient meritorious exec. award Pres. of U.S., 1982, 88, disting. exec. award, 1993. Office: Ste 1275 1001 Pennsylvania Ave NW Washington DC 20004

HUGHES, ANN NOLEN, psychotherapist; b. Ft. Meade, Md.; d. George M. and Georgie T. Nolen; m. Edwin L. Hughes, Oct. 21, 1961; 1 child, Andrew G. BS in Psychology, Rollins Coll., 1985, MA in Counseling, 1986; student in pub. speaking and human rels., Dale Carnegie Inst., 1981; student, Duke U., 1950-52. Lic. mental health counselor; nat. cert. counselor; nat. cert. gerontol. counselor. Supr. top secret control, audio/visual small parts supply U.S. Army, Continental U.S. and Tokyo; adminstrv. sec. Sys. Devel. Corp., Rand Corp., Santa Monica, Calif.; adminstrv. asst., editor, exec. sec., adminstrv. sec. Aerospace Corp., El Segundo, Calif.; staff therapist Circles of Care, Melbourne, Fla.; developer program for leading divorce support groups for Brevard Women's Ctr. Various leadership positions PTA, Pittsford, N.Y., Brookfield, Wis., 1968-81; mem. Brevard Cmty. Chorus; docent Space Coast Sci. Ctr., 1991-92. Mem. ACA, Assn. for Adult Devel. and Aging, Space Coast PC User's Group, Nat. Geneal. Soc., Geneal. Soc. South Brevard, Suntree Country Club, Brevard County Alumnae Assn., Kappa Kappa Gamma, Kappa Kappa Gamma. Presbyterian. Home: 447 Pauma Valley Way Melbourne FL 32940-1918 Office: PO Box 410162 Melbourne FL 32941-0162

HUGHES, BARBARA ANN, dietitian, public health administrator, nutritionist; b. McMinn County, Tenn., July 22, 1938; d. Cecil Earl and Hannah Ruth (Moss) Farmer; BS cum laude in Home Econs. Carson Newman Coll., Jefferson City, Tenn., 1960; MS in Instl. Mgmt., Ohio State U., Columbus, 1963; MA (Adonarium Judson scholar), So. Bapt. Theol. Sem., 1968; MPH, U. N.C., Chapel Hill, 1972; postgrad. in nutrition U. Iowa, 1974, U. N.C., 1975-85, Case Western Res. U., 1979, Walden U.; PhD 1988; m. Carl Clifford Hughes, Oct. 13, 1962. Registered, lic. nutritionist, dietitian. Instr., clin. dietitian Riverside Meth. Hosp., Riverside Whitecross Sch. Nursing, Columbus, 1963-66; consulting dietitian Mount Holly Nursing Home, Ky. Dept. Mental Health, 1966-68, eastern region N.C. Bd. Health, Raleigh, 1968-73; dir. Nutrition and Dietary Services br., Div. Health Services, N.C. Dept. Human Resources, Raleigh, 1973-89, also dir. Women-Infants-Children Program; pres. B.A. Hughes and Assocs., 1990—; asst. to Rep. Karen Gottovi 14th Dist. N.C. Ho. of Reps., Gen. Assembly N.C., 1994; adj. instr. Case Western Res. U., Cleve., 1988-89; adj. asst. prof. dept. nutrition Sch. Public Health, U. N.C., Chapel Hill, 1975-89; mem. adv. bd. Hospitality Edn. program N.C. Dept. Community Colls., 1974-80, adv. com. Ret. Senior Vol. Program, Raleigh and Wake County, N.C., 1975-79, N.C. Network Coordinating Council for End-Stage Renal Disease, 1975, Nat. Adv. Council on Maternal, Infant, and Fetal Nutrition, Spl. Supplemental Food Program for Women, Infants, and Children, Dept. Agr., 1976-79, adv. com. Nutrition Edn. and Tng. program N.C. Dept. Pub. Instrn., 1978-80; mem.-at-large adv. leadership coun. N.C. Cooperative Ext. Svc., 1994—; advisor com. to Wake County N.C. Cooperative Ext. Svc., 1992—, chair. adv. coun., 1994-96; coord. undergrad. program in gen dietetics East Carolina U.; rep. Coll of Agrl. and Life Scis. N.C. State U. to Nat. Coun. for Agrl. Rsch. Extension and Tchg., 1996—; apptd. mem. Wake County Bd. Commrs. to New Wake County Human Svcs. Bd., 1996—; apptd. to adv. bd. Agromedicine Program East Carolina and N.C. State Univs., 1996—; adv. council N.C. Gov.'s Office Citizen Affairs; cons. dietitian Augusta Victoria Hosp. and Jerusalem (Israel) Crippled Childrens Center, 1968; witness U.S. congressional and Senate hearings in field. Active edn. programs Pullen Memorial Bapt. Church, Raleigh, deacon, 1976-80, 94—, area ministry capt., 1977-78, personnel com., 1978-80; bd. dirs. Community Outreach, 1989-92, futuring com., 1995—, coordinating coun. vice-chair, 1996—; dietitian/dir. food service archeol. expedition to Israel, 1968; bd. dirs. N.C. Literacy Assn. 1978-83, 93—, pres., 1981-83; v.p. Wake County Literacy Council, 1986-87; trustee Gardner-Webb Coll., Boiling Springs, N.C., 1979-82, chmn. curriculum com., 1981-82; chmn. Coalition Pub. Health Nutrition, 1983-85; del. various Democratic Convs., 1981-84, precinct sec.-treas., 1981-83, 1st vice chmn., 1983-85, 2nd vice chmn., 1993—, chair, 1985-87; chmn. adv. bd. dept. home econs. Carson-Newman Coll.; area coord. (N.C.) Pacific Intercultural Exch., 1990—; chair Wake County Affiliate food festival com., 1991-92, chair edn. and community program com., 1992—, Am. Heart Assn., bd. dirs., 1992-94; precinct coord. Ruth Cook for N.C. Senate, Dist. 14, 1994; chair chronic disease com. Wake County Bd. Health, 1995-96; pres. State N.C. Coun. Social Legislation, 1993—; dir. N.C. Bds. of Health, 1994—; del. Altrusa Internat., Inc. to 4th World Conf. on Women, Beijing, China, 1995; nutrition staff writer Sr. Source, Raleigh Extra, Durham Morning Herald. Named Woman of Yr., Wake County, 1975, N.C. Outstanding Dietitian of Yr., 1976, N.C. Outstanding Dietitian, Southeastern Hosp. Conf. for Dietitians, 1978; recipient Disting. Alumna award Carson-Newman Coll., 1983, Eleanor Roosevelt Humanitarian award Altrusa Internat., 1995. Fellow N.C. Inst. Polit. Leadership; mem. AAUW (life, pres. Raleigh br. 1971-75, 91-93, pres. N.C. div. 1978-80, coord. Wake Women Celebrate 1995, coord. partners for heart disease and stroke prevention 1995, nat. bd. dirs. 1980-82, area rep. 1980-82, nat. edn. found. bd. dirs. 1987-91, ednl. equity roundtable 1992), Am. Dietetic Assn. (del. 1971-74, 87-89, pres. N.C. state assn. 1976-77, N.C. network legis. coordinator 1978-81, 92—, nat. nominating com. 1979-80, nat. chmn. council on practice 1982-83, nat. chair legislation and pub. policy com. 1985-87, nat. area coord. Ho. of Dels. 1989-92, Commn. Dietetic Registration assessment devel. com. for credential of FELLOW program 1994, 95, nat. mem. bylaws com. 1989-90, 91-92, chair resolutions com. 1990-91), APHA (exec. com. So. br. 1977-87, sec.-treas. 1979-80, 1st v.p. 1980-81, Catherine Cowell award 1994, chair award com. food and nutrition sect. 1995-96), So. Health Assn. (pres. 1982-83, chair nominating com. 1985-86, 91-92, awards com. 1992-93, Spl. Meritorious award 1989), Assn. State and Territorial Pub. Health Nutrition Dirs. (pres. 1977-79, dir. 1981-89, liaison to Assn. Faculties Grad. Program in Pub. Health Nutrition, chair legis. and pub. policy com. 1984-89, Commendation award 1989), N.C. Assn. Bds. of Health, N.C. Council Foods and Nutrition (dir. 1976-78, chmn. membership 1975, nominating com. 1979). N.C. Council Women's Orgns. (mem. at large, bd. dirs. 1989-92, leadership com. 1991—, chair nutrition subcom., Wellness in State Employees adv. bd. 1989-91), Am. Acad. Health Adminstrn., Soc. Nutrition Edn., Nutrition Today Soc., N.C. Acad. Public Health, Ohio State U. Alumni Assn. (life), U. N.C. Gen. Alumni Assn. (life), U. N.C. Public Health Alumni Assn. (life), Altrusa Internat. (pres. Raleigh club 1973-74, 93-96, dir. 1976-78, 90—, 1st vice gov. 1978-79, chmn. nomination com. 1980-82, gov. dist. Three, 1979-80, internat. vocat. services chmn. 1977-79, 1st v.p. 1985-87, pres.-elect 1987-89, pres. 1989-91), Altrusa Internat. Found. (1st v.p. 1985-87, chmn.-elect 1990-92, chmn. 1992—, bd. dirs. 1993—), Greater Raleigh C. of C. (mem. west area bus. coun., chair legis. com., rep. leadership Raleigh 10 1994—, bd. dirs. leadership Raleigh Alumni Assn.), Women's Forum N.C. (young leadership award com. 1989-90, 92—, newsletter editor bd. dirs. 1992—, adminstr. 1995—), Kappa Omicron Nu. Achievements include olympic torchbearer. Co-author: Diet and Kidney Disease, Assn. for N.C. Regional Med. Program, 1969; contbr. numerous papers, articles to symposia, periodicals in field, vol. areas. Home: 4208 Galax Dr Raleigh NC 27612-3714

HUGHES, BARBARA BRADFORD, nurse; b. Bragg City, Mo., Jan. 21, 1941; d. Lawrence Hurl Bradford and Opal Jewel (Prater) Puttin; m. Robert Howard Hughes, Dec. 9, 1961; children: Kimberly Ann Hayden, Robert Howard II. ASN, St. Louis Community Coll., 1978; student, Webster U., 1980. RN, Mo. Med. surg. nurse Alexian Bros. Hosp., St. Louis, 1979-80; staff nurse Midwest Allergy Cons., St. Louis, 1980; nurse high altitude Aviation Nurse, Ltd., St. Louis, 1980-81; cardiac telemetry staff nurse Jefferson Meml. Hosp., Crystal City, Mo., 1992-94; pvt. practice real estate mgmt., 1962—. Vol. Luth. Hosp., St. Louis, 1967-70; mem. Mo. Bot. Garden, St. Louis, 1976—, Mo. Hist. Soc., 1993—, St. Louis Zoo Friends Assn., 1986-87, Nat. Trust for Hist. Preservation, 1990—; Channel 9-Ednl. TV, St. Louis; vol. blood drive ARC, St. Louis, 1980; vol. health tchr. Spartan Aluminum Products, Sparta, Ill., 1984. U. Mo. scholar, 1959. Mem. Mo. Pilots Assn., Women in Aviation Internat. (charter), U.S. Pilots Assn., Tyospaye Club. Republican. Home: 736 Windsor Harbor Rd Imperial MO 63052-2503

HUGHES, CAROL ANN, librarian, administrator; b. Galesburg, Ill., Aug. 25, 1950; d. Wayne Leroy and Hazel Kinney (Cole) Hughes; m. Robert Hudson Patterson (div. 1993). BA, U.Ill., 1972, MLS, 1973; MBA, UCLA, 1978; PhD, U. Mich., 1996. Dir. Tulsa Area Libr. Coop., 1981-84, Univ. Ctr. at Tulsa, 1985-87; asst. to dir. U. Mich. Librs., Ann Arbor, 1987-90; mem. svcs. officer Rsch. Librs. Group, Mountain View, Calif., 1993—. Co-author: Preferred Futures for Libraries I, 1991, II, 1993; contbr. articles to profl. jours. Office: Research Libraries Group 1200 Villa Mountain View CA 94041

HUGHES, DEBBIE KAYE, primary grade guidance counselor; b. Lebanon, Ky., Apr. 27, 1962; d. James Ronald and Iris June (Hagan) Medley; m. David G. Hughes, July 17, 1984; 1 child, Calla E. BS in Edn., Western Ky. U., 1984, MS in Edn., 1988, Rank I, 1992. Itinerant tchr. emotionally, mentally handicapped, learning behavioral disordered, Warren County Sch. Dist., Bowling Green, Ky., 1984-85; learning behavioral disordered resource tchr. Simpson County Bd. of Edn., Lincoln Elem. Sch., Franklin, Ky., 1985-93; elem. guidance counselor Simpson County Bd. of Edn., Franklin Elem. Sch., 1993—; adv. coun. mem. Simpson County Family Resource Ctr., Franklin, 1990—; scotopic sensitivity screener, Simpson County Schs., Franklin, 1991—; mem. Ky. Integrated Delivery System. Foster parent Bowling Green (Ky.) Cabinet for Human Resources, 1988—; mem. Holy Spirit Cath. Ch., Bowling Green, 1984—. Mem. NEA, Ky. Ednl. Assn., Simpson County Ednl. Assn. (sec. 1991-92, v.p. 1993-95), Ky. Sch. Counselors Assn. (named Outstanding Counselor, Emerging Leader in Counseling), Ky. Counseling Assn., S. Ctrl. Counseling Assn. Democrat. Home: 655 Morris Duff Rd Woodburn KY 42170-9703 Office: Franklin Elem Sch 211 S Main St Franklin KY 42134-2115

HUGHES, ELLEN RONEY, historian, museum exhibition curator; b. Washington, Jan. 11, 1943; d. Joseph A. and Elizabeth Marshall (Chamblin) Roney; m. Gary Hughes, Jan. 25, 1974. BA in History, Salve Regina U., 1965; MA in Am. Studies, U. Md., 1991, postgrad., 1991. Museum specialist in postal history Nat. Mus. Am. History, Smithsonian Instn., Washington, 1972-74, cultural historian for sport, leisure and popular culture collections, 1977—, project mgr., curatorial asst. A Nation of Nations Exhbn., 1974-91, curator Smithsonian's Am. Exhbn., 1991-94; exhbn. curator Sesame Street, 1969-1989, The First 20 Years, 1989, The Wizard of Oz and the Ruby Slippers, 1991, Television Comedy: Children's Television, 1992, numerous others; lectr. on mus.; presenter and organizer symposia; mem. adv. bd. history roundtable Smithsonian Instn., 1989—; mem. nominating com. for Women's Sports Hall of Fame, Women's Sports Found., 1975-85; v.p. Gary Hughes, Inc., Bethesda, Md., 1976—. AuthorP (with Bunch, Lubar and Brodie) Smithsonian's America: An Exhibition on American History and Culture, 1994; contbr. articles to profl. publs., chpts. to books; prodr. films, video, TV and radio prodns. Rsch. grantee Lemelson Ctr. for Study Invention and Innovation, 1996. Mem. Am. Studies Assn., Assn. Mus. Specialists and Technicians (co-founder, pres. 1975-76, 88-89), Hist. Soc. Washington, Material Culture Forum, N.Am. Soc. for Sport History, Soc. for History Tech. Democrat. Office: Smithsonian Instn Nat Mus Am History MRC 612 Rm 4101 Washington DC 20560

HUGHES, GRACE-FLORES, former federal agency administrator, management consulting executive; b. Taft, Tex., June 11, 1946; d. Adan Flores and Catalina San Miguel; m. Harley Arnold Hughes, May 25, 1980. BA, U. D.C., 1977; MPA, Harvard U., 1980. Sec. Dept. Air Force Kelly AFB, San Antonio, 1967-70, Pentagon-Office Sec. of Def., Washington, 1970-72; program asst., social sci. analyst HEW, Washington, 1972-78; social sci. analyst, acting dir. Office Hispanic Ams. HHS, Washington, 1978-81; vis. prof. Nebr. Wesleyan U., Lincoln, 1982-83, U. Nebr., Omaha, 1984; spl. asst. SBA, Washington, 1985-88, assoc. adminstr. for minority small bus., 1988; dir. community rels. Dept. Justice, Washington, 1988-92; pres. Grace, Inc., Alexandria, Va.; spl. asst. Reagan/Bush '84 Campaign, Nebr. and Washington, 1984, 50th Presdl. Inaugural, Washington, 1984-85, Office Pub. Liaison, The White House, 1985. Author: The Bureaucrat, Categorized Workforce, 1992; co-author: New Book of Knowledge, 1980; chair adv. bd. Harvard Jour. Hispanic Policy, 1989—; The Use and Abuse of Diversity Hispanic Mag., 1994. Adv. mem. U.S. Senate Rep. Task Force, Washington, 1988-91; alumni exec. bd. J.F. Kennedy Sch. Govt., Harvard U., Cambridge, Mass., 1989—; mem. Rep. Hispanic Assembly, 1984—; appointed by Gov. Allen of Va. to bd. for Profl. and Occupational Regulations, 1994-98. Recipient Excellence award Nev. Econ. Devel. Corp., 1988, Leadership award Am. GI Forum, Omaha, 1989; named one of 100 Most Influential Hispanics in U.S. Hispanic Bus. Mag., 1988. Mem. Assn. Pub. Adminstrs. (Outstanding Pub. Svc. award 1990), Exec. Women in Govt., Hispanic Bus. Roundtable, Hispanic Women's Network, Fedn. Republican Women, Mexican Am. Women's Nat. Assn., Univ. Club (Washington). Roman Catholic. Home and Office: 5208 Bedlington Ter Alexandria VA 22304-3551

HUGHES, J. DEBORAH, health care administrator; b. Pitts., Mar. 24, 1948; d. James Francis and Margaret Veronica (Wiullmier) H. Diploma, Columbia Sch. Nursing, Pitts., 1969; BSN, La Roche Coll., 1987; M of Pub. Mgmt., Carnegie-Mellon U., 1988. Cert. nursing adminstr., med. staff coord., profl. in healthcare quality. Staff nurse Forbes Health Sys., Pitts., 1969-78, head nurse recovery, 1978-79, supr. nursing, 1979-84, clin. asst. to med. dir., 1984-88, dir. med. staff svcs., 1988-90; quality tracking mgr. Humana Inc., Louisville, 1990-91; regional quality mgmt. dir. Galen Healthcare, Inc., Louisville, 1991-92; sr. cons. quality and resource mgmt. Metri Cor, Inc., Louisville, 1992-94; mgr. accreditation svcs. and performance improvement HCIA, 1994—. Mem. Am. Soc. for Quality Control, Nat. Assn. healthcare Quality, Ky. Assn. Quality Assurance Profls., Ky. Soc. Healthcare Risk Mgmt., Nat. Assn. Med. Staff Svcs., Internat. Soc., Quality Assurance, Sigma Theta Tau. Office: HCIA 462 S 4th Ave Ste 405 Louisville KY 40202-2941

HUGHES, JACQUELINE MICHELE, trainer; b. Omaha, Aug. 26, 1967; d. Kathleen Bridget Hughes. BS in Bus. Adminstrn., U. Nebr., Lincoln, 1990. Asst. account exec. Nat. Equity, Omaha, 1992-94; trainer First Data Corp., Omaha, 1994—. Active Make-A-Wish, Omaha, 1996. Mem. Assn. Tng. and Devel. Home: 3304 S 114 St Omaha NE 68144

HUGHES, JANET LOUISE, artist; b. Easton, Pa., June 10, 1927; d. William Stewart and Cecilia Louise (Fulmer) H.; divorced; 1 child, David Tod. Student, Baum Art Sch., Allentown, Pa., 1935-45, Moore Inst. Art, Phila., 1945-46, Fashion Acad., N.Y.C., 1946-47, Lehigh U., 1947-49. With Laros Lingerie Co., Bethlehem, Pa., 1950-54; artist R&D lab. Binney and Smith Inc., Easton, Pa., 1955-60; art instr. in field. One woman shows include Lafayette Coll., Pa., Womens Club of Easton, Pa., Little York Gallery, N.J., Walpack Art Gallery, N.J., Dover (N.J.) Art League, Easton Cmty. Art League, Nazareth (Pa.) Pub. Libr., Washington Libr., N.J., Easton Nat. Bank, Elkton County Bank and Trust, Md.; exhibited in group shows including Walpack Art Gallery; represented in permanent collections. Mem. Tri-State Profl. Artists, Easton Cmty. Art League, Sussex County Art Soc., Parkland Art League Allentown, Kittatinney Art Group, Allentown Art Mus., Nat. Mus. Women in the Arts.

HUGHES, JUDY LYNNE, political organization executive; b. San Antonio, Mar. 23, 1939; d. Timothy Endymion Gristy and Clovis Ruth (Mooring) Linville; m. Donald E. LaMora, Nov. 12, 1960 (div. Aug. 1980); children: Grant, Leigh, Eric; m. William J. Hughes, May 11, 1984 (div. 1990). Student, Tex. Tech. U., 1956-60. News reporter Colorado Springs (Colo.) Gazette Telegraph, 1960; vice chair pub. rels. Nat. Fedn. Rep. Women, Washington, 1974-76, mem.-at-large exec. com., 1976-78; 2d v.p. Nat. Fedn. Rep. Women, 1978-82, 1st v.p., 1982-86, pres., 1986-90; western rep. U.S. Dept. Interior, Golden, Colo., 1991-93; polit. edn. specialist Rep. Nat. Com., Washington, 1993-95, chief of staff to co-chmn., 1995—; ofcl. del. U.S. State Dept., El Salvador, 1989; mem. Dept. Interior's Representation on Denver Interagy. Coun. on Homeless, 1990-93; mem. Denver Fed. Exec. Bd. Pub. Rels. Coun., 1990-93. mem. RNC Com. Minority Participation, Washington, 1989; bd. dirs. Colo. Coun. on Econ. Edn., 1991-93. Named Rep. Woman of Yr., Shelby County Rep. Women's Club, 1988. Mem. Pikes Peak Rep. Women's Roundtable (Colorado Springs). Home: 501 Slaters Ln Apt 903 Alexandria VA 22314-1127 Office: Rep Nat Com 310 1st St SE Washington DC 20003-1801

HUGHES, KAREN SUE, geriatrics nurse; b. Wooster, Ohio, Oct. 16, 1955; d. Alvin S. and Pauline Katheryn (Troyer) Yutzy; m. Christopher Charles Marek, Sept. 3, 1977 (div. 1993); m. Raymond H. Hughes, July 20, 1993. LPN, Wayne County Vocat. Sch., 1974; BSN, Akron U., 1994. LPN, RN, Ohio. LPN, GPN, nurse aide Wooster Community Hosp., 1974-76; LPN Apple Creek (Ohio) Devel. Ctr., 1976-77, Smithville Western Care Ctr., Wooster, 1977-78, 78-80; supervisory LPN Gruter Found., Wooster, 1980-87; light indsl. worker Victor Temporary Svcs., Mansfield, Ohio, 1988-89; plant mgr. asst. Detroit Detroit Inc., Wayne, Mich., 1988-89; LPN charge nurse West View Manor, Wooster, 1989, Doylestown (Ohio) Health Care Ctr., 1989-93; charge nurse Manor Care Barberton, Ohio, 1993-94; RN supr., asst. dir. nursing Manor Care of Barberton, Ohio, 1994-95; RN Healthaven Nursing Home, Akron, Ohio, 1995—. Home: 985 Saxon Ave Akron OH 44314-2648

HUGHES, KATHARINE KOSTBADE, nurse consultant; b. Chgo., Sept. 6, 1956; d. Howard William and Christine Elizabeth Kostbade; m. Christopher Alan Hughes, Aug. 29, 1987. AB in Biol. Sci., Smith Coll., Northampton, Mass., 1978; BS in Nursing, Columbia U., 1980; MS in Nursing, U. Ill., Chgo., 1984, PhD in Nursing, 1988. Staff nurse Rush-Presbyn.-St. Lukes, Chgo., 1980-81; cons. Hinshaw, Culbertson, Chgo., 1981-83; staff nurse Northwestern Meml. Hosp., Chgo., 1982-84; clin. nurse U. Ill. Hosp., Chgo., 1983-84; infection control coord. U. Ill., Chgo., 1984-86, clin. asst. prof., 1989-91, asst. prof. nursing, 1991-94; dir. adminstrn. Nat. Coun. State Bds. Nursing, Chgo., 1987-90; coord. clin. integration Marian Health Ctr., 1995—; cons. ops. improvement task force to reduce overhead U. Ill. Hosp., Chgo., 1992—. Contbr. articles to profl. jours. Mem. Clarendon Hills (Ill.) Cmty. Caucus, 1980-91; mem. steering com. LaGrange (Ill.) Crisis Pregnancy Ctr., 1991-92; mem. Siouxland Humane Soc. Pub. Rels. Com.; city co-chair Woodbury Rep. Party. Mem. Sigma Theta Tau, Phi Kappa Phi. Republican.

HUGHES, LAUREL ELLEN, psychologist, educator, writer; b. Seattle, Oct. 30, 1952; d. Morrell Spencer and Eleanore Claire (Strong) Chamberlain; m. William Henry Hughes Jr., Jan. 27, 1973; children: Frank, Ben, Bridie. BA in Psychology, Portland State U., 1980, MS in Psychology, 1986; D in Clin. Psychology, Pacific U., 1988. Lic. psychologist, Oreg. Counselor Beaverton (Oreg.) Free Meth. Ch., 1982-85; psychotherapist Psychol. Svc. Ctr., Portland, Oreg., 1986, Psychol. Svc. Ctr. West, Hillsboro, Oreg., 1987-89; pvt. practice Beaverton, 1990—; adj. mem. faculty Portland C.C., 1990-91, U. Portland, 1992—, CU/Seattle, 1993-95; vis. asst. prof. U. Portland, 1991-92; psychol. cons. children's weight control group St. Vincent's Hosp., Portland, 1991. Author: How to Raise Good Children, 1988, How to Raise a Healty Achiever, 1991, Beginnings and Beyond, 1996; contbr. articles to profl. jours. Tchr. Sunday sch. Beaverton Free Meth. Ch., 1983-88; mother helper Walker Elem. Sch., Beaverton, 1988-90, 92-93; foster parent Washington County, Oreg., 1976-77, 79-80; vol. disaster mental health svcs. ARC, 1993—. Mem. APA, Oreg. Psychol. Assn. (bd. dirs. 1990-91, editor jour. 1990-91). Office: 4320 SW 110th Ave Beaverton OR 97005-3009

HUGHES, LIBBY, author; b. Pitts., Aug. 11, 1932; d. Lloyd Alfred and Vera Abby (Walker) Pockman; m. R. John Hughes, Aug. 20, 1955 (div. 1988); children: Wendy E., Mark E. BA, U. Ala., 1954; MFA, Boston U., 1955. Profl. actress Kenya, S. Africa, 1955-59; drama critic and feature writer Cape Cod Newspapers, 1977-86, assoc. pubr., 1977-81, pubr., 1981-85; pres. Desert Starfield Prodns., 1994. Author: Bali, 1969, Margaret Thatcher, 1989, Benazir Bhutto, 1990, Nelson Mandela, 1992, Good Manners for Children, 1992, H. Norman Schwarzkopf, 1992, West Point, 1992, Valley Forge, 1992, Colin Powell, 1996; editor: Ginger Rogers Autobiography, 1989, 91; author 20 plays. Bd. dirs. Wisdom Inst., 1984-86, Cape Cod Mus., 1984-86. Mem. Dramatists Guild, Authors Guild, Ala. Wildlife Rescue Svc. (pres. 1988-89), Nat. Soc. Arts and Letters (chpt. pres. 1984-86, protocol officer 1984-86). Home: PO Box 1000 Orleans MA 02653

HUGHES, LINDA J., newspaper publisher; b. Princeton, B.C., Can., Sept. 27, 1950; d. Edward Rees and Madge Preston (Bryan) H.; m. George Fredrick Ward, Dec. 16, 1978; children: Sean Ward, Kate Ward. BA, U. Victoria (B.C.), 1972. With Edmonton Jour., Alta., Can., 1976—, from reporter to asst. mng. editor, 1984-87, editor, 1987-92, pub., 1992—. Southam fellow U. Toronto, Ont., Can., 1977-78. Office: Edmonton Journal, 10006 101st St PO Box 2421, Edmonton, AB Canada T5J 2S6

HUGHES, LISA LYNN, lay church worker; b. Pinehurst, N.C., Apr. 16, 1964; d. Rollow Hershel and Annie Ruth (McIntosh) H. BA in Psychology, U. N.C., 1994. Youth leader Brownson Meml. Presbyn. Ch., Southern Pines, N.C., 1987-92, 94—, elder, 1988-91, Sunday sch. tchr., 1988-89, dir. Christian growth, youth dir., 1991; youth advisor Coastal Carolina Presbytery, Presbyn. Ch. (U.S.A.), 1989-91; dir. Moore County Day Reporting Ctr., 1995—; exec. dir. Drug-Free Moore County, Inc., Carthage, N.C., 1990-95, bd. dirs., 1996—. Vol. Bethesda Link, 1990-95; mem. Moore County Youth Svcs. Commn., 1990-91, Jr. Svc. League, 1993—, Moore for Tomorrow Lifestyle Task Force, 1993—, Moore Interagy. Coun., 1993-94, chmn., 1994-95; mem. Moore County Criminal Justice Partnership Adv. Bd., 1994-95; mem. C. of C. Drug Awareness Task Force, 1990—. Home: 1440 E Hedgelawn Way Southern Pines NC 28387-7429

HUGHES, MARGARET JANE, nurse; b. L.A., Sept. 13, 1950; d. John Lawarence and Etta May (Kenny) H. BSN, U. St. Thomas, Houston, 1984; ADN, Saddleback Coll., Mission Viejo, Calif., 1980; cert. in perfusion, Tex. Heart Inst., Houston, 1976. RN, Calif., Tex., Hawaii; CCRN; cert. BLS, ACLS, perfusionist. Nurse ICU Saddleback Hosp., Laguna Hills, Calif., 1974-76, 79-81; perfusionist Baylor Coll. Medicine, Houston, 1973-79, 81-86; nurse ICU VA Hosp., L.A., 1986-90; nurse, perfusionist Kay Med. Group, L.A., 1987-90; nurce ICU Hilo (Hawaii) Hosp., 1990-91; nurse recovery room King Khaled Eye Hosp., Riyadh, Saudi Arabia, 1992; clin. nurse specialist Kay Med. Group, L.A., 1992; nurse ICU and recovery room Kona (Hawaii) Hosp., 1992-94; clin. nurse specialist Sciemed Ltd., Cairo, 1994; nurse UCLA Dental Sch., 1994-95; nurse ICU, Whittier (Calif.) Hosp., 1995-96; missionary Anfoega, Ghana, 1996—. Vol. Am. Heart Assn., Kona, 1993, Diabetic Assn., Kona, 1993. Mem. AACN. Democrat. Roman Catholic. Home: 13496 Trumball St Whittier CA 90605-3331 Office: Anfoega Cath Hosp, PO Box 30, Anfoga Ghana

HUGHES, MARIJA MATICH, law librarian; b. Belgrade, Yugoslavia; came to U.S., 1960, naturalized, 1971; d. Zarija and Antonija (Hudowsky) Matich. BA in Music, Mokranjac, Belgrade; BA in English, U. Belgrade and Calif. State U.; MLS, U. Md.; student, McGeorge Sch. Law; MHA in Health Care Adminstrn., George Washington U., 1985, M. in Adminstrv. Scis., 1989. Counselor, gen. mgr. Career Counseling Service, Sacramento, Calif., 1962-64; sec. to mgr. Sacramento State Coll., 1965-66; student librarian High John program U. Md., Fairmont Heights, 1967; reference librarian Calif. State Law Library, Sacramento, 1968; head reference library-faculty liasion librarian Hastings Coll. Law U. Calif., San Francisco, 1969-72; head law librarian AT&T, Washington, 1972-73; chief law librarian Nat. Clearinghouse Library, U.S. Commn. on Civil Rights, Washington, 1973-86; tech. info. specialist U.S. Dept. Labor, OSHA, Tech. Date Ctr., 1988—; owner, pub. Hughes Press. Author, compiler: The Sexual Barrier, Legal and Econ. Aspects of Employment, 1970-73, The Sexual Barriers: Legal, Medical, Economic and Social Aspects of Sex Discrimination, 1977, Computer Health Hazards, 1990, 93, 96, (English translation) Sick from Computers, 1994; contbr. articles to profl. jours. Mem. Am. Assn. Law Librs., Assn. Internat. Law Librs., Washington Ind. Writers, Electromagnetic Radiation Alliance, Consumer Utilities Bd., Coalition of Citizens for Local Control. Home: 2400 Virginia Ave NW Apt C501 Washington DC 20037-2612

HUGHES, MARVALENE, academic administrator. Student, Tuskegee U., NYU, Columbia U.; PhD in Counseling and Adminstrn., Fla. State U.; postgrad., Harvard U., U. Calif., San Diego. Dir. counseling and career devel. Eckerd Coll., Fla.; dir. counseling svcs. and placement, prof. San Diego State U.; assoc. v.p. student affairs Ariz. State U.; v.p. student affairs, prof. counseling and human svcs. U. Toledo; v.p. student affairs, vice provost, prof. ednl. psychology U. Minn.; pres. Calif. State U., Stanislaus, 1994—; keynote spkr. Internat. Conf. on Women, Beijing; spkr. in field. Contbr. chpts. to books and articles to profl. jours. Mem. Am. Coll. Pers. Assn. (nat. pres.), Nat. Assn. for Counseling Svcs., Nat. Assn. Land Grant Univs. and Colls. (student affairs divsn.). Office: 801 W Monte Vista Turlock CA 95382

HUGHES, MARY KATHERINE, nurse; b. Phila., Nov. 3, 1945; d. James Simon and Mary Katherine (MacLellan) Kiening; m. Robert William Hughes June 11, 1967; children: William, Jonathan, Sarah. BS, Tex. Woman's U., 1968, MS, 1988. Staff nurse Planned Parenthood, Houston, 1968-70, Staff Builder's, Houston, 1979-81, Meml. Southwest Hosp., Houston, 1981-90; nurse psychotherapist Woman's Christian Home, Houston, 1989-90; clin. nurse specialist U. Tex. MD Anderson Cancer Ctr., Houston, 1990—, clin. instr., 1995—; mem. adj. faculty Tex. Woman's U., Houston, 1989-90; Mary Mazzwy lectr. Houston Oncology Nursing Soc., 1993. Facilitator Patient Group Am. Cancer Soc., 1993—, co-facilitator Grief Group, 1983—, Family Group, 1994—, bd. dirs. 1983-86, adv. bd., 1986-95. Recipient Sword of Hope award Am. Cancer Soc., 1986, Outstanding Nurse Oncologist Brown Found., 1993, Outstanding Vol. St. John's Presbyn. Ch., 1995. Presbyterian. Office: U Tex MD Anderson Cancer Ctr 1515 Holcombe Blvd Box 100 Houston TX 77030

HUGHES, MARY SORROWS, artist; b. Washington, Oct. 28, 1945; d. Howard Earl and Martha Jane (Summerville) Sorrows; m. Frank Broox Hughes, May 22, 1967; 1 child, Broox Bradley. BA in Art, Centenary Coll., 1967, BA in Edn., 1978. Draftsman for civil engring. dept. Texaco, New Orleans, 1967-70; owner, freelance artist Shreveport, La., 1979—. Illustrator Total Tales, 1984; included in The Best of Watercolor, 1995; represented in permanent collections Southwestern Electric Power Co., Shreveport. Bd. dirs. Child Care Svcs., Inc. of N.W. La., Shreveport, 1987-91, pres., 1991; Artport Airport Exhibit and Fundraiser for AIDS, Shreveport, 1991-96; worker Habitat for Humanity, Shreveport, 1992, 94; trustee St. Luke's Meth. Ch., Shreveport, 1993-95, chairperson for bldg. com., 1986. Recipient Gary, Field, Landry & Bradford award Seventh Exhbn. of La. Women Artists, Baton Rouge, 1994. Mem. Hoover Watercolor Soc. (pres. 1986, treas., publicity chair, others), Southwestern Watercolor Soc. (Signature Mem. award 1991, Edgar A. Whitney award 1992), Watercolor West (Yarka St. Petersberg Merchandise award 1995), La. Artists (pres. 1994), Med. Aux. Wive's Club, Shreveport Art Guild. Democrat. Home: 1045 Erie St Shreveport LA 71106 Studio: 1700 Creswell Shreveport LA 71101

HUGHES, MICHAELA KELLY, actress, dancer; b. Morristown, N.J., Mar. 31; d. Joseph Francis and Mary Elizabeth (Coughlin) H. Scholarship student, Houston Ballet Acad., 1970-73; part-time scholarship student, Sch. Am. Ballet, 1971. Founder, owner Classic Stocking Co., 1992—. Child actress with Alley Theatre, Houston, 1969, 71, mem. Houston Ballet, 1974, Eliot Feld Ballet, N.Y.C., 1975—, prin. dancer, 1974-79, mem., Am. Ballet Theatre, 1979-81; Broadway appearances include On Your Toes, 1982, as Gloria Upson in Mame, 1983, Raggedy Ann, 1986, as Cassie in A Chorus Line, 1987, Anything Goes, 1988; appeared as Fiona in Another World (serial), Loving, Saturday Night Live, numerous television commls. Mem. AFTRA, SAG, AEA, Am. Guild Mus. Artists.

HUGHES, MURIEL MILILANI, principal; b. Lahaina, Hawaii, May 31, 1949; d. Jacob Ah Nee and Risuko (Okimoto) Ah Sing; m. Donald Wayne Hughes, July 18, 1978; children: Cathy, Sunny, Jae Jin, Rebecca. AA, Maui C.C., Kahului, Hawaii, 1969; BEd, U. Hawaii, 1971; MEd, U. So. Miss., 1992. Cert. tchr. and adminstr., Hawaii. Tchr. English Jarrett Intermediate Sch., Honolulu, 1971-72, Kaiser H.S., Honolulu, 1972-75, Wakayam (Japan) Kita H.S., 1975-76, Kaiser High Sch., Honolulu, 1976-81; tchr. English, art, and health Mountain View (Hawaii) Internat. Sch., 1981-84; vice prin. Pahoa (Hawaii) Elem. and High Sch., 1984-86; prin. Hilo (Hawaii) High Sch., 1986-88, Mountain View Elem. Sch., 1988—. Mem. exec. bd. Mountain View PTA, 1988-94; steward Hawaii Govt. Employee Assn., Hilo, 1990-92; moderator Puna United Ch. of Christ, Kea'au, Hawaii, 1991-92. Mem. NEA, Phi Delta Kappa. Home: PO Box 647 Volcano HI 96785-0647

HUGHES, NORAH ANN O'BRIEN, bank securities executive; b. Taftville, Conn., Aug. 17, 1948; d. William James and Mabel (Gouin) O'Brien; m. Gary Lee Hughes, Sept. 27, 1975. BA, Cushing Coll., Brookline, Mass., 1970; MA, NYU, 1972. V.p. instnl. sales trading Pitfield, Mackay & Co., Inc., N.Y.C., 1972-83; v.p. U.S. Treasury Bond trading Carroll, McEntee & McGinley, N.Y.C., 1983-84; v.p., mgr. U.S. Treasury trading Swiss Bank Corp. Internat. Securities, N.Y.C., 1984-89; 1st v.p., mgr. U.S. Treasury trading and sales Swiss Bank Corp. Govt. Securities Inc., N.Y.C., 1989-91; pres. Sumitomo Bank Securities, Inc., N.Y.C., 1991—. Mem. Women's Fin. Assn., Women's Econ. Round Table, Corp. Bond Club N.Y., Women's Bond Club N.Y. Home: 1 Hickory Tree Ln Far Hills NJ 07931-2300 Office: Sumitomo Bank Securities Inc 277 Park Ave New York NY 10172-0099

HUGHES, PAULA T., accounting manager; b. Kansas City, Kans., Dec. 23, 1956; d. Frank P. and Monte L. (Moore) Moellers; m. Charles Michael Hughes, Mar. 10, 1978; children: C. David Hughes, Sara T. Hughes. BS in Acctg., Okla. State U., Stillwater, 1981. CPA, Okla. Property acct. Williams Pipe Line, Tulsa, 1981-83, supervisor treasury and fin. analysis, 1983-90, supervisor spl. projects, 1990-93; supervisor gen. acctg. Williams Energy Ventures, Tulsa, 1993-94; supervisor contract acctg. Williams Pipe Line, Tulsa, 1994, mgr. fin. reporting and property acctg., 1994—. Coach under 10 girls South Tulsa Soccer Club, 1995-96. Mem. Tulsa Chpt. CPAs, Inst. Mgmt. Accts. (dir. employment 1989-90), Williams Employees Credit Union (supervisory com. 1989-90). Republican. Roman Catholic. Office: Williams Pipe Line PO Box 3448 Tulsa OK 74101

HUGHES, SALLY PAGE, administrative secretary; b. Elizabeth, N.J.; d. Jeff and Irene (Miller) Page; m. July 31, 1954 (dec. Mar. 6, 1962); 1 child, Edward Joseph. Student, Kean Coll., Union, N.J., 1962-69, Upsala Coll., 1969-75. Sec., stenographer Vis. Nurse Assn., Plainfield, N.J., 1955-60, Kean Coll., Union, N.J., 1962-69; tchr. tng. program Upsala Coll., Urban Edn. Corps, East Orange, N.J., 1969-71; sec. to editor The Daily Jour., Elizabeth, N.J., 1971-75; prin. clk. Schering-Plough Corp., Union, 1976-80; unit sec. Elizabeth Multi-Svc. Ctr. Tng. Unit, Elizabeth, 1980-82; adminstrv. sec. Bd. of Edn., Elizabeth, 1982—. Author: (poetry) New Beginnings, 1991, Inspiration, 1993, Behold The Flowers, 1995; composer: (song) On the Winning Side, 1991; co-writer (song) Where Shall I Be, 1991; soloist/poetess Channel 12 and CTN-Gospel Hour Music, TV Nationwide and Internat. Recipient award of Merit, World of Poetry, 1991, Hon. Mention, Watermark Press, 1991, Editor's Choice award Outstanding Achievement in Poetry, Nat. Libr. Poetry, 1993; named Profl. Woman of Yr., Union County Club, Nat. Assn. Negro Bus. and Profl. Women's Club. Mem. NEA, Elizabeth Edn. Assn., N.J. Edn. Assn., Shiloh Bapt. Ch. Choir, Shiloh Bapt. Ch. Missionary Bd., Sun. Sch. Tchrs. Democrat. Baptist.

HUGHES, SHARON MARY, trade association executive; b. Chgo., July 28, 1952; d. George Ingersoll and Rose Myrtle (Reed) H. BA in Polit. Sci. and Communications cum laude, Am. U., 1980, MS in Bus., Govt. Rels., 1985. Cert. assn. exec. Freelance photographer N.Y.C., 1972-76; advt. account exec. R.L. Newport and Co., N.Y.C., 1976-78; direct mail advt. mgr. John Wanamaker's, Phila., 1981-83; legis. intern U.S. Congressman James Florio, Washington, 1985; asst. dir. legis. affairs Nat. Food Processors Assn., Washington, 1985-87; mgr. govt. affairs Synthetic Organic Chem. Mfrs. Assn., Washington, 1987-89; exec. v.p. Nat. Coun. Agrl. Employers, Washington, 1989—. Mem., sodalist Holy Rosary Ch. Sodality, Washington, 1989—. Mem. Women in Govt. Rels. (bd. dirs., co-chairperson environ. task force 1988-89, mem. agrl. task force 1989-90, co-chairperson congl. rels. com. 1992-93), Am. League Lobbyists, Am. Soc. Assn. Execs., Toastmasters. Democrat. Roman Catholic. Home: 3506 Halcyon Dr Alexandria VA 22305-1330 Office: Nat Coun Agrl Employers 1112 16th St NW Ste 920 Washington DC 20036-9999

HUGHES, SIMONE LANELL, nurse, educator; b. Shreveport, La., Jan. 8, 1953; d. Grady Lee and Sue LaNell (Von Hollen) H.; m. Craig H. Tadlock, July 22, 1995; children: Lisa Marie Kelpin Herzog, Devin, Seth, Brenna. Diploma in nursing, Mercy Hosp. Sch. Nursing, Des Moines, 1984; BSN, U. Iowa Coll. Nursing, 1989, MSN, 1994. RN. Staff nurse ob/gyn. Mercy Hosp., Des Moines, 1984-87; staff nurse cardio-thoracic unit U. Iowa Hosp. & Clinics, Iowa City, 1988-90; nursing clin. instr. Kirkwood C.C., Iowa City, 1990-92; staff nurse surgical intensive care, rsch. asst. U. Iowa Hosp. & Clinics, Iowa City, 1990-95; clin. nurse specialist, educator Good Samaritan Health Sys., Kearney, Nebr., 1995—. Author: Helping Children Cope with Intensive Care, 1994; contbr. article to profl. jour. Mem. HIV Consortium, Kearney, Nebr., 1995—; bd. dirs. Buffalo County chpt. Am. Cancer Soc., 1996—, youth edn. chair, 1996—. Mem. ANA, AACN (pres.-elect Mid-Nebr. chpt. 1996, InnoVision grantee 1994, 95), Every Woman Matters, Internat. Transplant Nurses Soc., Am. Soc. Healthcare Edn. and Tng., Midwest Alliance in Nursing, Nat. Assn. Clin. Nurse Specialists, Sigma Theta Tau. Baptist. Home: 3907 17th Ave Kearney NE 68847 Office: Good Samaritan Health Sys 10 E 31st St Kearney NE 68848

HUGHES, TERESA P., state legislator; b. N.Y.C., Oct. 3, 1932; m. Frank E. Staggers; children: Vincent, Deidre. BA, Hunter Coll.; MA, NYU; PhD, Claremont Grad. Sch. Prof. edn. Calif. State U., L.A.; social worker; mem. Calif. Senate, 1975—, former chair, mem. edn. com., mem. pub. employees and retirement com., mem. housing and cmty. devel. and local govt. coms.; bd. trustees L.A. County H.S. for Arts and Edn. Coun. Music Ctr., Calif.; active Mayor Bradley Edn. Com. Founder Aware Women. Mem. Nat. Coalition 100 Black Women, Calif. State Employees Assn., Calif. Tchrs. Assn., Coalition Labor Union Women. Democrat. Home: 1906 W 22nd St Los Angeles CA 90018-1644 Office: Calif Senate 4035 State Capitol Sacramento CA 95814 Office: 1 W Manchester Blvd Ste 401 Inglewood CA 90301-1750*

HUGHES, WAUNELL MCDONALD (MRS. DELBERT E. HUGHES), retired psychiatrist; b. Tyler, Tex., Feb. 6, 1928; d. Conrad Claiborne and Bernice Oletha (Smith) McDonald; B.A., U. Tex. at Austin, 1946; M.D., Baylor U., 1951; m. Delbert Eugene Hughes, Aug. 14, 1948; children—Lark, Mark, Lynn, Michael. Intern VA Hosp., Houston, 1951-52; resident Parkland Hosp., Dallas, 1964-67; practiced gen. medicine in Tyler, Tex., 1952-64; acting chief psychiatry service VA Hosp., Dallas, 1967-68, asst. chief, 1968-73, chief Mental Hygiene Clinic and Day Treatment Center, 1973-82, unit chief acute inpatient psychiatry Med. Center, 1982-88; clin. instr. psychiatry Southwestern Med. Sch., U. Tex. Health Sci. Center, Dallas, 1968-88; psychiat. cons. Dallas Family Guidance Clinics, 1990. Chmn. pre-sch. vision and hearing program Pilot Club, Tyler, 1960-64. Mem. Am. Med. Women's Assn. (pres. Dallas 1980-81), Am. Psychiat. Assn., Am. Group Psychotherapy Assn., (pres. Dallas chpt. 1984-86), North Tex. Soc. Psychiat. Physicians (co-chair Mental Health Mental Retardation pro bono clinic com. Dallas chpt. 1989-91, mem. patient advocacy com. 1992—), Dallas Area Women Psychiatrists (archivist 1985—), Alpha Epsilon Iota (pres. 1950-51). Home: 3428 University Blvd Dallas TX 75205-1834

HUGHES-FREELAND, TESSA JANE, filmmaker, writer; b. Amersham, Bucks, England, Dec. 6, 1957; Came to the U.S., 1981; m. Carlo Brian McCormick, Aug. 31, 1985. BA in History of Art, London U., 1980; MA in Cinema Studies, NYU, 1982. Foley asst. Last Temptation of Christ, N.Y., 1986; freelance writer Film Threat, L.A., 1988-92, Paper Mag., N.Y., 1988-96, British GQ, London, 1995-96, Filmaker Mag., N.Y., 1996; freelance stylist/costumer N.Y.C., L.A., Miami; founder, co-dir. N.Y. Film Festival Downtown, N.Y.C., 1984-90. Contbr. articles to profl. jours. Office: THF PO Box 20946 New York NY 10009

HUGHES-FULFORD, MILLIE, medical scientist, educator; b. Mineral Wells, Tex., Dec. 21, 1945; d. Charles and Lanore Hughes; m. George A. Fulford; children: Tori, Herzog. PhD in Radiation Chemistry, Tex. Woman's U., 1972. From asst. prof. to assoc. prof. U. Calif., San Francisco, 1973-92, prof., 1992—; med. scientist Dept. Vets. Affairs, San Francisco, 1973-94, adj. prof., 1994—; mem. com. on space biology NRC, Washington, 1987-90. Mem. editorial bd. UCSF mag., 1992—; contbr. articles to profl. jours. Trustee Embry-Riddle Aero. U., Fla., 1986-89; mem. admission com. Med. Sch., U. Calif., San Francisco, 1992—. Capt. U.S. Army, 1972-82. Recipient Presdl. award, 1984; NSF fellow, 1965, 68-72, AAUW, 1971-72. Mem. AAAS, Am. Soc. Cell Biology, Am. Physiol. Soc. Office: U Calif VAMC Code 151F 4150 Clement St San Francisco CA 94121-1545

HUGHS, MARY GERALDINE, accountant, social service specialist; b. Marshalltown, Iowa, Nov. 28, 1929; d. Don Harold, Sr., and Alice Dorothy (Keister) Shaw; A.A., Highline Community Coll., 1970; B.A., U. Wash., 1972; m. Charles G. Hughs, Jan. 31, 1949; children: Mark George, Deborah Kay, Juli Ann, Grant Wesley. Asst. controller Moduline Internat., Inc., Chehalis, Wash., 1972-73; controller Data Recall Corp., El Segundo, Calif., 1973-74; fin. adminstr., acct. Saturn Mfg. Corp., Torrance, Calif., 1974-77; sr. acct., adminstrv. asst. Van Camp Ins., San Pedro, Calif., 1977-78; asst. adminstr. Harbor Regional Ctr., Torrance, Calif., 1979-87; active bookkeeping svc., 1978—; instr. math. and acctg. South Bay Bus. Coll., 1976-77. Sec. Pacific N.W. Mycol. Soc., 1966-67; treas., bd. dirs. Harbor Employees Fed. Credit Union; mem. YMCA Club. Recipient award Am. Mgmt. Assn., 1979. Mem. Beta Alpha Psi. Republican. Methodist. Author: Iowa Auto Dealers Assn. Title System, 1955; Harbor Regional Center Affirmative Action Plan, 1980; Harbor Regional Center - Financial Format, 1978—; Provider Audit System, 1979; Handling Client Funds, 1983. Home and Office: 32724 Coastside Dr # 107 Rancho Palos Verdes CA 90275

HUGLEY, CAROLYN FLEMING, state legislator; m. Isaiah Hugley; children: Isaiah Jr., Kimberly. BA in Polit. Sci. summa cum laude, U. Ark., Pine Bluff, 1979; MPA, Miss. State U., 1980. Sr. analyst, joint com. on performance evaluation Miss. State Legis., mem. ins., edn., industry com., mem. legis. oversight com. for Ga. lottery, mem. Ga. legis. women's caucus, Ga. legis. Black caucus; planner Lower Chattahoochee Area Planning and Devel. Commn.; dir. planning and econ. devel. Lee County Coun. Govts.; ind. contractor, owner agt. State Farm Ins. Mem. choir and mission bd. dirs. Franchise Missionary Bapt. Ch.; mem. Gov.'s Task Force of Welfare Reform, 1992; chairperson Lower Chattahoochee Area Pvt. Industry Coun.; mem. Columbus Olympic Com., Columbus Conv. and Visitors Bur.; mem. local coord. coun. Peach Jobs Program. Mem. Columbus C. of C. (bd. dirs.) Alpha Kappa Alpha.

HUGUENARD, JOAN, writer; b. South Bend, Ind., Apr. 30, 1931; d. Peter Albert and Clementine (Dominski) Gadomski; children: Cathie, Jim, John, Tom, Bob, Frank, Charlie, Andy. BA in Theology, Marquette U., 1983. Advt. cons., sales mgr. Penny Saver, South Bend, Ind., 1973-76; records mgmt. cons. TAB Products Co., Palo Alto, Calif., 1976-84; chaplain in residence Frost Valley YMCA Camp, Oliveria, N.Y., 1984; ESL tchr. Univs. at Shenyang, Nanjing, Tianjin, China, 1986-89; recruiter World Teach, Harvard U., Cambridge, Mass., 1988-89; exec. dir. Office of Haitian Ministries, Norwich, Conn., 1990-91; cons. in office efficiency and assoc. dir. Washington Office on Haiti, Washington, 1992; small bus. owner, mgr. Clutterfly Corner, various locations, 1983—; freelance writer, 1989—. Contbr. articles to newspapers and mags. Founder, pres. S.T.A.R.T. Students Taking Action to Recycle Trash, South Bend, Ind., 1970-75; co-founder local chpt. Beginning Experience, South Bend, 1977-81. Roman Catholic. Home: PO Box 873 Kenwood CA 95452

HUHEEY, MARILYN JANE, ophthalmologist; b. Cin., Aug. 31, 1935; d. George Mercer and Mary Jane (Weaver) H.; B.S. in Math., Ohio U., Athens, 1958; M.S. in Physiology, U. Okla., 1966; M.D., U. Ky., 1970. Tchr. math. James Ford Rhodes High Sch., Cleve., 1956-58; biostatistician Nat. Jewish Hosp., Denver, 1958-60; life sci. engr. Stanley Aviation Corp., Denver, 1960-63, N.Am. Aviation Co., Los Angeles, 1963-67; intern U. Ky. Hosp., 1970-71; emergency room physician Jewish Hosp., Mercy Hosp., Bethesda Hosp. (all Cin.), 1971-72; ship's doctor, 1972; resident in ophthalmology Ohio State U. Hosp., Columbus, 1972-75; practice medicine specializing in ophthalmology, Columbus, 1975—; mem. staff Univ. Hosp., Grant Hosp., St. Anthony Hosp., 1975-79; clin. asst. prof. Ohio State U. Med. Sch., 1976-84, clin. assoc. prof., 1985—, dir. course ophthalmologic receptionist/aides, 1976; mem. Peer Rev. Systems Bd., 1986-92, exec. com., 1988-92; mem. Ohio Optical Dispensers Bd, 1986-91. Dem. candidate for Ohio Senate, 1982. Diplomate Am. Bd. Ophthalmology. Fellow Am. Acad. Ophthalmology; mem. AAUP, Am. Assn. Ophthalmologists, Ohio Ophthalmol. Soc. (bd. govs. 1984-89, del. to Ohio State Med. Assn. 1984-88), Franklin County Acad. Medicine (profl. rels. com. 1979-82, legis. com. 1981-89, edn. and program com. 1981-88, chmn. 1982-85, chmn. cmty. rels. com. 1987-90, chmn. resolution com. 1987-92, mem. fin. com. 1988-92), Ohio Soc. Prevent Blindness (chmn. med. adv. bd. 1978-80), Ohio State Med. Assn. (dr.-nurse liaison com. 1983-87), Columbus EENT Soc., Am. Coun. of the Blind (life, bd. dirs.), Life Care Alliance (pres. sustaining bd. 1987-88, United Way planning com. 1992-93), LWV, Columbus Council World Affairs, Columbus Bus. and Profl. Women's Club, Columbus C. of C., Grandview Area Bus. Assn., Federated Dem. Women of Ohio, Columbus Area Women's Polit. Caucus, Phi Mu. Clubs: Columbus Met. (forum com. 1982-85, fundraising com. 1983-84, chmn. 10th anniversary com. 1986), Mercedes Benz (dir. 1981-83), Zonta, (program com. 1984-86, chmn. internat. com. 1983), Herb Soc. Home: 2396 Northwest Blvd Columbus OH 43221-3829 Office: 1335 Dublin Rd Columbus OH 43215-1000

HUHN, DARLENE MARIE, county official, poet; b. Kearny, N.J., Feb. 13, 1967; d. Charles Joseph and Theresa Catherine (Foertsch) H. AAS, Essex County C.C., Newark, 1990. Sec. Hudson County Vo-Tech., North Bergen, N.J., 1983-84; law clk. Skoloff & Wolfe, Livingston, N.J., 1984-87; data entry clk. Robith, Lyndhurst, N.J., 1987-94; income maint. technician Hudson County Welfare, Jersey City, 1994—. Author: (poetry) Decisions, 1995, Have Faith, 1995 (Internat. Soc. Poetry Poet of Merit 1995, 96). Vice pres. Rosary Soc., East Newark, N.J., 1994—; mem. pastoral coun. Deanery 14 Archdiocese of Newark, 1990-96. Recipient Golden Poet award World of Poetry, 1987-90, Achievement award Cath. Youth Orgn., 1991, Editor's Choic award Nat. Libr. Poetry, 1996; named Best Poet of 1988, Am. Poetry Assn., 1988. Mem. Phi Theta Kappa. Democrat. Roman Catholic. Home: 330 N 2d St East Newark NJ 07029

HUHNDORF, SUSAN KOURA, advertising executive; b. Tokyo, Apr. 27, 1954; came to U.S., 1966; d. Tony and Alice (Yamane) Koura; m. Michael Stanley Huhndorf, Mar. 18, 1978; 1 child, Kimberly. BSc summa cum laude, UCLA, 1976. Account exec. Competitive Edge Advt., Costa Mesa, Calif., 1978-81, Harte Hanks Direct Mktg., Garden Grove, Calif., 1981-82; field account exec. Della Femina, Travisano & Ptnrs., L.A., 1982-84; v.p., mgmt. supr. Keye/Donna/Pearlstein, L.A., 1984-87, 88-91; account supr. Chiat/Day Advt., L.A., 1987-88; advt. mgr. Amati div. Mazda Motors Am., Irvine, Calif., 1991-92; prin. Huhndorf and Assocs., Tustin, Calif., 1992—. Publicity chair St. Paul's Episcopal Pre-Sch., 1996. Recipient Gold EFFIE award, 1989. Mem. L.A. Advt. Club (Belding Cert. 1987), Phi Beta Kappa. Republican. Office: Huhndorf and Assocs 2221 Bowman Ave Tustin CA 92782

HUI, DOREEN, financial executive; b. Hong Kong, Aug. 2, 1967; came to U.S., 1986; d. Hing Kee and Lun Sim (chan) H.; m. Lionel Etrillard, Nov. 23, 1996. B Acctg., U. Redlands, 1990; MBA, Pepperdine U., 1994. Staff cons. Arthur Andersen, Singapore, 1990-91; staff acct. Diamond Mission Import, Inc., L.A., 1991-92; accounts receivable mgr. Williams TV, Inc., L.A., 1993-94; fin. mgr. Matrix Ctr., Inc., L.A., 1994—. Home: 5918 Bixby Village Dr # 108 Long Beach CA 90803

HUIE, GEORGETTE LYNN, sales specialist; b. San Francisco, Apr. 22, 1951; d. George and Isabel (Chin) H. BS in Math., Calif. State U., Hayward, 1973, MS in Math., 1976. K-12 tchg. credential, Calif. Lectr. math. U. San Francisco, 1977-78, San Francisco State U., 1978-79; sys. engr. IBM, San Francisco, 1979-92, sales specialist, 1993—. Moderator Presbytery of San Francisco, Berkeley, Calif., 1990; mem. exec. com., bd. dirs. Nat. Coun. Chs., N.Y.C., 1992-95; sec., bd. dirs. San Francisco Food Bank, 1994—; vice chmn., chmn.-elect bd. dirs. Presbyn. Ch. (U.S.A.) Found., Jeffersonville, Ind., 1996—. Recipient cert. of recognition Calif. Senate, 1991. Democrat.

HUITINK, TERESA EVELYN, actress, model; b. Sioux City, Iowa, Apr. 15, 1951; d. Emil Nicholas and Joyce Marie (Beckman) Greuniesen; divorced; children: Benjamin Joseph Jacobs, Tosha Lyn Jacobs, Kara Huitink. Student, Morningside Coll., Sioux City, 1981. Ind. actress and model, 1975—; asst. dance instr. Sioux City Music & Dance, 1978-81; pubs. dir. Curtis Media, Sioux City, 1989-90; beauty cons. Mary Kay, Sioux City, 1989-92; owner, coord. Sears Model's Club, Sioux City, 1993-94; asst. instr. acting for camera The Acting Studio, Phoenix, 1995—. Video appearances include This is Sioux City, Historic Dell Rapids, Prelude to Design Vol. I, Vol. II, America Under Seige, 1996—; spokeswoman for several local businesses; appeared in nat. TV commercial for Century 21; performed several radio voice-overs. Bd. dirs. Spl. Troopers Adaptive Riding Sch., Sioux City, 1984-91, Women Aware, Sioux City, 1992-93; mem. com. Nativity Cath. Ch., Sioux City, 1981-91; ct. apptd. spl. adv. Woodbury County Courthouse, Sioux City, 1993; mem., team mem. ARISE, St. Tim's Cath. Cmty., Mesa. Roman Catholic. Office: 3522 W Barcelona Chandler AZ 85226

HULKA, BARBARA SORENSON, epidemiology educator; b. Mpls., Mar. 1, 1931; d. Herbert Fritchof and Mable (Alquist) Sorenson; m. Jaroslav Fabian Hulka, Nov. 13, 1954; children: Carol Ann, Gregory Fabian, Bryan Herbert. BS, Radcliffe Coll., 1952; MS, Juilliard Sch. Music, 1954; MD, Columbia U., 1959, MPH, 1961. Diplomate: Am. Bd. Preventive Medicine; Lic. physician, Pa., N.C. Research asst. prof. U. Pitts., 1966-67; asst. prof. U. N.C., Chapel Hill, 1967-71, assoc. prof., 1972-76, prof., 1977—, chmn. dept. epidemiology, 1983-93, Kenan prof., 1987—; adj. prof. medicine Duke U. Med. Ctr., Durham, N.C., 1982—; chmn. epidemiology and disease study sect. NIH, 1979-83, mem. Endpoint Rev. Safety Monitoring and Adv. Com., Breast Cancer Prevention Trial, Nat. Surg. Adjuvant Breast and Bowel Project, 1992—; bd. sci. counselors Nat. Cancer Inst., 1980—; mem. Inst. of Medicine com. toxic shock syndrome Nat. Acad. Sci., 1981-82; mem. Sci. Rev. and Evaluation Bd. subcom. VA, 1983—; mem. subcom. on long-term effects of short-term exposure to chem. agts. Nat. Acad. Scis., 1985—; mem. preventive medicine and pub. health test com. Nat. Bd. Med. Examiners, 1985—; mem. consensus conf. on smokeless tobacco Nat. Cancer Inst. Panel, 1986; chair WHO steering com. of Task Force on Safety and Efficacy of Fertility Regulating Methods, 1990—; counsellor Internat. Soc. for Environ. Epidemiology, 1990—; mem. Pres.' Cancer Panel Spl. Commn. on Breast Cancer, Nat. Cancer Inst., 1992-93; mem. bd. scientific counselors divsn. cancer etiology, Nat. Cancer Inst., NIH, 1992—; chair WHO steering com. of task force Epidemiologic rsch. in reproductive health, WHO, 1990—. Mem. editorial bd. Postgrad. Medicine, 1985—; assoc. editor Cancer Epidemiology, Biomarkers and Prevention, 1995; contbr. articles to profl. jours., chpts. to books. Bd. dirs. Am. Cancer Soc., 1993—. Recipient Disting. Achievement award Am. Soc. Preventive Oncology, 1991; Health Resources Adminstrn. grantee, 1975-77; tng. grantee in cancer epidemiology Nat. Cancer Inst., 1980—; prostate cancer grantee Nat. Cancer Inst., 1983-85; travel study fellow WHO, 1978. Fellow Royal Soc. Medicine; mem. APHA (governing coun. 1976-78, chmn. epidemiol. sect. 1976-77), NAS (Inst. Medicine 1988, mem. com. crossroads nuclear test 1994, mem. commn. antiprogestins 1992-93, mem. com. passive smoking 1985—), Am. Coll. Epidemiology (Abraham Lilienfield award 1994), Soc. Epidemiol. Rsch. (pres. 1975-76, exec. com. 1973-77), Am. Epidemiol. Soc., N.C. Pub. Health Assn. (award for excellence, stats. and epidemiology sect. 1975), Am. Coll. Preventive Medicine (bd. regents 1986), Delta Omega. Home: 2317 Honeysuckle Dr Chapel Hill NC 27514 Office: U NC Sch Pub Health McGavran-Greenburg Hall CB #7400 Chapel Hill NC 27599

HULL, ELIZABETH ANNE, English language educator; b. Upper Darby, Pa., Jan. 10, 1937; d. Frederick Bossart and Elizabeth (Schmik) H.; m. Dean Carlyle Beery, Feb. 5, 1955 (div. 1962); children: Catherine Doria Beery Pizarro, Barbara Phyllis Beery Wintczak; m. Frederik Pohl, July 1984. Student, Ill. State U., 1954-55; AA, Wilbur Wright Jr. Coll., Chgo., 1965; B in Philosophy, Northwestern U., 1968; MA, Loyola U., Chgo., 1970, PhD, 1975. Teaching asst. Loyola U., Chgo., 1968-71; prof. English, coord. honors program William Rainey Harper Coll., Palatine, Ill., 1971—; judge nat. writing competition Nat. Coun. Tchrs. of English, 1975—, John W. Campbell award, 1986—. Co-editor: (with F. Pohl) Tales from the Planet Earth; contbr. articles to profl. jours. Pres. Lexington Green Condominium Assn., Schaumburg, Ill., 1982-84; bd. dirs. Hunting Ridge Homeowner's Assn., Palatine, 1984-86, bd. dirs. Palatine LWV, 1992—;Candidate U.S. Rep. Ill. 8th Congrl. Dist., 1996. Recipient Northwestern U. Alumni award for Merit, 1995. Mem. MLA, Midwest MLA, Popular Culture Assn., Sci. Fiction Rsch. Assn. (editor 1981-84, sec. 1987-88, pres. 1989-90), Ill. Coll. English Assn. (pres. 1975-77), World Sci. Fiction Assn. (N.Am. sec. 1978—, pres. Honors coun. Ill. region 1992-93), Palatine Area LWV (bd. dirs. 1991—, v.p. 1995—), Am. Assn. for Women in C.C. (v.p. comm., bd. dirs. Harper Coll. chpt. 1993—). Democrat. Home: 855 Harvard Dr Palatine IL 60067-7026 Office: William Rainey Harper Coll 1200 W Algonquin Rd Palatine IL 60067-7373

HULL, GRETCHEN GAEBELEIN, lay worker, writer, lecturer; b. Bklyn., Feb. 5, 1930; d. Frank Ely and Dorothy Laura (Medd) Gaebelein; m. Philip Glasgow Hull, Oct. 24, 1952; children: Jeffrey R., Sanford D., Meredyth Hull Smith. BA magna cum laude, Bryn Mawr Coll., 1950; postgrad., Columbia U., 1950-52; DLitt (hon.), Houghton Coll., 1995. Major presenter Internat. Coun. on Bibl. Inerrancy, Chgo., 1986; guest lectr. London Inst. on Contemporary Christianity, 1988; lectr. at large Christians for Bibl. Equality, St. Paul, 1988—; major presenter Presbyn. Ch. (U.S.A.) Nat. Abortion Dialogue, Kansas City, Mo., 1989; disting. scholar lectr. Thomas F. Staley Found., Stony Brook, N.Y., 1991; elder Presbyn. Ch. (U.S.A.); mem. Madison Ave. Presbyn. Ch., N.Y.C.; vis. prof. Regent Coll., Vancouver, B.C., 1992. Author: Equal to Serve, 1987; (with others) Women, Authority and the Bible, 1986, Applying the Scriptures, 1987, Study Bible for Women (New Testament), 1996; editor: Priscilla Papers, 1989—; contbg. editor Perspectives, 1992—; mem. editl. bd. Prism, 1994—; contbr. articles to religious mags. Trustee Cold Spring Harbor Village Improvement Soc., 1966-69, Soc. of St. Johnland, Kings Park, N.Y., 1972-75. Mem. Woman's Union Missionary Soc. Am. (bd. dirs. 1954-71), Presbyns. United for Bibl. Concerns (bd. dirs. 1973-75), L.I. Presbytery (gen. coun. 1981-83), Christians for Bibl. Equality (bd. dirs. 1987-94), Latin Am. Mission (trustee 1989-95), Evangelicals for Social Action (bd. dirs. 1991—), Network Presbyn. Women in Leadership (steering com. 1994—), Presbyterians for Renewal (bd. dirs. 1994—). Home and Office: Oyster Bay Cove 1120 Cove Edge Rd Syosset NY 11791-9602

HULL, JANE DEE, state official, former state legislator; b. Kansas City, Mo., Aug. 8, 1935; d. Justin D. and Mildred (Swenson) Bowersock; m. Terrance Ward Hull, Feb. 12, 1954; children: Jeannette Shipley, Robin Hillebrand, Jeff, Mike. BS, U. Kans., 1957; postgrad., U. Ariz., 1972-78. Spkr. pro tem Ariz. Ho. of Reps., Phoenix, 1993, chmn. ethics com., chmn. econ. devel., 1993, mem. legis. coun., 1993, mem. gov.'s internat. trade and tourism adv. bd., 1993, mem. gov.'s strategic partnership for econ. devel., 1993, mem. gov.'s office of employement implementation task force, 1993, spkr. of house, 1989-93, house majority whip, 1987-88; now secretary of state State of Arizona, Phoenix. Bd. dirs. Morrison Inst. for Pub. Policy, Beatitudes D.O.A.R., 1992, Ariz. Town Hall, Ariz. Econs. Coun.; mem. dean's coun. Ariz. State U., 1989-92; assoc. mem. Heard Mus. Guild, Cactus Wren Rep. Women, ; mem. Maricopa Med. Aux., Ariz. State Med. Aux., Freedom Found., Valley Citizens League, Charter 100, North Phoenix Rep. Women, 1970, Trunk 'N Tusk Legis. Liaison Ariz. Rep. Party, 1993; Rep. candidate sec. of state, 1994. Recipient Econ. Devel. award Ariz. Innovation Network, 1993. Mem. Nat. Orgn. of Women Legislators, Am. Legis. Exch. Coun., Nat. Rep. Legislators Assn. (Nat. Legislator of Yr. award 1989), Soroptimists (hon.). Republican. Roman Catholic. Home: 10458 N 9th St Phoenix AZ 85020-1585*

HULL, JANE LAUREL LEEK, retired nurse, administrator; b. Ontario, Calif., July 4, 1923; d. William Abram and Susan Bianca (Pethick) Leek; R.N., Columbia Presbyn. Sch. Nursing, 1944; B.A., Redlands U., 1977; ; m. James B. Hull, Oct. 10, 1944 (dec.); children—James W., William P., Kenneth D. Supr. obstetrics Mid-Valley Hosp., Peckville, Pa., 1945-46; sch. and surg. nurse acute nursing Scranton (Pa.) State Hosp., 1947-52; nurse San Antonio Community Hosp., Upland, Calif., 1953-55; office nurse H.L. Archibald, Upland, 1965; vis. nurse Pomona West End Inc., continuity of care coordinator, Claremont, Calif., 1968-73, exec. dir., 1973-92 (named pres. 1991); tchr. ARC nursing course to high sch. students; cons. Livingston Meml. Vis. Nurse Assn. Ventura, Calif. Recipient Woman Achiever award, Pomona Valley, 1983, Excellence in Edn. award Nat. Assn. Home Care, 1988. Treas. PTA, Pomona, Calif.; vol. exec. dir. Inland Hospice Assn., 1979-80, accreditation commn., 1988-89. Nat. Found. for Hospice/Home Care, 1988. Mem. Am. Assn. Retired Persons (local coord.), Calif. Nurses Assn. (pres. dist. 53 1958), Calif. Assn. for Health Services at Home (dir.), Calif. League Nursing, Nat. Homecaring Council (dir.). Home Care Aide Assn. Am. (chmn.), bd. mem. Nat. Assn. of Home Care. Republican. Club: Zonta (Ontario, Upland, pres., 1976). Organizer Homemaker Dept. in Vis. Nurse Assn., 1972, pres., 1991; developer (with Don Baxter Corp.) plugs for in-dwelling Foley catheters, 1963. Home: 543 W F St Ontario CA 91762-3117

HULL, LOUISE KNOX, retired elementary educator, administrator; b. Springfield, Mo., May 24, 1912; d. William E. and Ruby Joe (Bradshaw) K.; m. Berrien J. Hull, Jan. 1, 1953. BS in Edn., S.W. Mo. State U., 1933; postgrad. Colo. U., 1939, Northwestern U., 1945; MA, NYU, 1952. Cert. elem. and secondary tchr., Mo. Elem. tchr. R12 Sch. Dist., Springfield, 1936-70, supr. tchr., 1956-70, mem. adv. com. to supt., 1955-57. Chmn. Christian edn. com. Westminster Presbyn. Ch., 1953-66, trustee, 1983-86, chmn. bd. trustees, 1986, circle chair, 1986-89, mem. women's adv. bd., 1987-89; pres. Women of Ch., 1970-73, 90-92, pres. bd. trustees, 1983-86; life mem. Wilson Creek Found., Springfield, 1954-67; sec. Greene County Hist. Soc., Springfield, 1960-96, life mem.; mem. Springfield Little Theater Guild, 1970—, Hist. Preservation Soc., Springfield, 1980—; docent Mus. Ozarks, Springfield, 1976-85; chmn. dist. Ill, John Calvin Presbyterial, 1974-76, sec., 1977-80. Mem. Springfield Ret. Tchrs. Assn. (life), Mo. Ret. Tchrs. Assn. (life), Ozarks Genealogy Soc (sec. 1985-87, pub. info. rep. 1987-89), DAR (Rachel Donelson chpt.), Mo. Fedn. Women's Clubs (chmn. home life com. 1986-89), Springfield City Fedn. Women's Clubs (pres. 1990-92), Sorosis Club (Springfield, pres. 1980-82, chmn. hobby dept. 1986-88, 94-96, chmn. fine arts dept. 1988-90, mem. perpetual endowment com. 1992-96, chmn. 1994), Alpha Delta Pi (treas. house corp. 1932-60), Alpha Delta Kappa (sec. 1965-67, corr. sec. Psi chpt. 1990-92).

HULL, MAGDALENE ELEANOR, obstetrician gynecologist; b. Bklyn., Sept. 22, 1953; d. Stanley F. and Genevieve (Tessman) H. BS in Biology, Fordham U., 1975; MD, N.Y. Med. Coll., 1979. Bd. cert. ob-gyn, 1986, reproductive endocrine and infertility, 1987 (recert. 1994). Resident Bronx Mcpl. Hosp., N.Y.C., 1979-83; fellow Wayne State U., Detroit, 1983-85, clin. instr., 1983-85; asst. prof. SUNY, Stonybrook, 1985-95; chief reproductive medicine Winthrop U. Hosp., Mincola, N.Y., 1995—. Fellow Am. Coll. Obstetricians and Gynecologists; mem. Am. Med. Women's Assn., Soc. Reproductive Surgeons, Soc. Reproductive Endocrinologists, Endocrine Soc. Home: 7 Kivy St Huntington Station NY 11746

HULL, MARGARET RUTH, artist, educator, consultant; b. Dallas, Mar. 27, 1921; d. William Haynes and Ora Carroll (Adams) Leatherwood; m. LeRos Ennis Hull, Mar. 29, 1941; children: LeRos Ennis, Jr., James Daniel. BA, So. Meth. U., Dallas, 1952, postgrad., 1960-61; MA, North Tex. State U., 1957, postgrad. R.I. Sch. Design, 1982. Art instr. W.W. Bushman Sch., Dallas Ind. Sch. Dist., 1952-57, Benjamin Franklin Jr. High Sch., Dallas, 1957-58; art instr. Hillcrest High Sch., Dallas, 1958-61, dean, pupil personnel counselor, 1961-70; tchr. children's painting Dallas Mus. Fine Art, 1956-70; designer, coordinator visual art careers cluster Skyline High Sch., Dallas, 1970-71, Skyline Career Devel. Ctr., Dallas, 1971-76, Booker T. Washington Arts Magnet High Sch., Dallas, 1976-82; developer curriculum devel./writing art, 1971-82; artist, ednl. cons., 1982—; mus. reprodns. asst. Dallas Mus. Art, 1984-93. Group shows include Dallas Mus. Fine Arts, 1958, Arts Magnet Faculty Shows, 1978-82, Arts Magnet High Sch., Dallas Art Edn. Assn. Show, 1981, D'Art Membership Show, Dallas, 1982-83; represented in pvt. collections. Trustee Dallas Mus. Art, 1978-84. Mem. Tex. Designer/Craftsmen, Craft Guild Dallas, Fiber Artists Dallas, Dallas Art Edn. Assn., Tex. Art Edn. Assn., Nat. Art Edn. Assn., Dallas Counselors Assn. (pres. 1968), Delta Delta Delta.

HULL, PATRICIA ANN, nursing administrator; b. Johnstown, Pa., May 26, 1942; d. Willard Earl and Florence Lucy (Grove) Merritt; m. Bruce Edward Dunn, July 31, 1965 (div. Aug. 1975); children: Rachel Dunn Bayush, Kelly Dunn Thomas, Heather Dunn Wyant; m. Harry Edwin Hull, May 21, 1988. Diploma in nursing, Conemaugh Hosp. Sch. Nursing, Johnstown, 1963. Cert. gerontol. nurse. Staff nurse Conemaugh Hosp., 1963-64; head nurse, supr. 1710 USAF Hosp., Savannah, Ga., 1964-66; part-time staff nurse Rochester (N.Y.) Gen. Hosp., 1966; part-time supr., clinic emergency rm. U. Miami (Fla.), 1967-68; staff supr. Arbutus Park Manor, Johnstown, 1979-92, dir. nursing, 1992—. Dist. rep., sec. Western Pa. Conf. United Meth. Bd. Health and Welfare, 1987-92; mem. Christ United Meth. Ch., Johnstown, health and welfare chmn., 1986-91, Stephens min., 1994—, trustee, adminstrv. bd., 1980-92; vol. ARC, Johnstown flood, 1977, blood drives; former Brownie, Girl Scout leader, Talus Rock Girl Scout Coun. 1st lt. USAF Nurse Corps, 1964-66. Recipient State of Pa. Gerontol. Nursing Study grant Indiana U. Pa., 1992. Mem. Pa. Assn. Dirs. Nursing Adminstrn/Long Term Care, Am. Soc. Long Term Care Nurses. Home: 1128 Boyd Ave Johnstown PA 15905-4413 Office: Arbutus Park Manor 207 Ottawa St Johnstown PA 15904-2337

HULL, RITA PRIZLER, accounting educator; b. Lone Tree, Iowa, Mar. 29, 1936; d. Ernest Ralph and Mildred Lennis (Huskins) Prizler; m. J.W. Hull, May 29, 1954 (div. 1963); children: Mark, Marshall; m. John O.

Everett, Sept. 1, 1976. BA in Acctg., Augustana Coll., Rock Island, Ill., 1967; MA in Acctg., Western Ill. U., 1973; PhD in Bus. Adminstrn., Okla. State U., 1978. CPA, Ill.; cert. internal auditor, Ill. Auditor Price Waterhouse & Co., Chgo., 1967-70; asst. prof. acctg. Bowling Green (Ohio) State U., 1976-78; assoc. prof. No. Ill. U., DeKalb, 1978-82; prof. Va. Commonwealth U., Richmond, 1982—. Contbr. articles, papers to profl. publs. Mem. AICPA, NOW (treas. Richmond chpt. 1987-88), Am. Soc. Women Accts. (treas. Richmond chpt. 1986-87, sec. 1987-88, pres. 1988-90, nat. bd. dirs. 1990-93, nat. sec. 1991-92, nat. v.p. 1992-93, Nat. Woman of Achievement award, 1994), Am. Acctg. Assn. (Trueblood seminars com. 1987-88, acctg. educator awards com. 1988-90, awards evaluation com. 1990-91, chmn.-elect gender issues in acctg. sect. 1991-92, chmn. 1992-93, coun. 1992-93), Inst. Internat. Auditors, Acad. Acctg. Historians. Democrat. Home: 810 Keats Rd Richmond VA 23229-6520 Office: Va Commonwealth U 1015 Floyd Ave Richmond VA 23284-4000

HULL, SUZANNE WHITE, author, retired administrator; b. Orange, N.J., Aug. 24, 1921; d. Gordon Stowe and Lillian (Siegling) White; m. George I. Hull, Feb. 20, 1943 (dec. Mar. 1990); children: George Gordon, James Rutledge, Anne Elizabeth. BA with honors, Swarthmore Coll., 1943; MSLS, U. So. Calif., 1967. Mem. staff Huntington Libr., Art Gallery and Bot. Gardens, San Marino, Calif., 1969-86, dir. adminstrn. and pub. svcs., 1972-86, also prin. officer; cons. Women Writers Project, Brown U., 1989—. Author: Chaste, Silent and Obedient, English Books for Women, 1475-1640, 1982, 88, Women According to Men: The World of Tudor-Stuart Women, 1996; editor: State of the Art in Women's Studies, 1986. Charter pres. Portola Jr. H.S. PTA, L.A., 1960-62; pres. Children's Svc. League, 1963-64, YWCA, L.A., 1967-69; mem. alumni coun. Swarthmore Coll., 1959-62, 83-86, mem.-at-large, 1986-89; mem. adv. bd. Hagley Mus. and Libr., Wilmington, Del., 1983-86, Betty Friedan Think Tank, U. So. Calif., 1985-93; hon. life mem. Calif. Congress Parents and Tchrs.; bd. dirs. Pasadena Planned Parenthood Assn., 1978-83, mem. adv. com., 1983—; founder-chmn. Swarthmore-L.A. Connection, 1984-85, bd. dirs., 1985-92; founder Huntington Women's Studies Seminar, 1984, mem. steering com., 1984-91, mem. adv. bd., 1991-96; bd. dirs. Pasadena Girls Club, 1988-91; mem. organizing com. Soc. for Study of Early Modern Women, 1993-94; adv. bd. the Early Modern Englishwoman: A Facsimile Libr. of Essential Works, 1995—. Mem. Monumental Brass Soc. (U.K.), Renaissance Soc., Brit. Studies Conf., Western Assn. Women Historians, Soc. Study of Early Modern Women, Authors Guild, Beta Phi Mu (chpt. dir. 1981-84). Home: 1465 El Mirador Dr Pasadena CA 91103-2727 Office: 1151 Oxford Rd San Marino CA 91108-1218

HULLOT-KENTOR, ODILE M., French language educator; b. Roubaix, France, Mar. 10, 1953; d. Bernard and Anne-Marie (Puppinck) Hullot; m. Robert S. Kentor, June 30, 1977. BA, Freiburg U., Germany, 1976, Sorbonne, Paris, 1977; MA, Sorbonne, Paris, 1978; PhD, U. Mass., 1988. Asst. prof. Wellesley (Mass.) Coll., 1988-89, Stanford (Calif.) U., 1989—. Contbr. articles to profl. jours. Office: Stanford U French Dept Stanford CA 94305-2010

HULME, DARLYS MAE, banker; b. Buckingham, Iowa, Apr. 2, 1937; d. Leland James and Dorothy Mae (Nation) Philp; m. Harlan Dale Hulme, Dec. 4, 1955 (div. Nov. 1971); children: Debra Jean Hulme Hanneman, Richard Dale. Student Iowa Sch. Banking, 1974, Sch. Bank Adminstrn. U. Wis.-Madison, 1982. Bookkeeper, Farmers Savs. Bank, Traer, Iowa, 1954-55, asst. cashier, 1962-72, v.p., 1973-83, sr. v.p., 1983-93, exec. v.p., 1993—, also bd. dirs.; acct. North Tama Housing, Inc., Traer, 1974-94; sec. to bd. Talen, Inc., Talen Aviation, Ltd., Traer; dir., vice chmn., exec. v.p., 1996—, cashier, 1988-96; sec. bd. dirs. Farmers Savs. Bank Trust, Vinton, Iowa, 1988—; dir., sec. to bd. Traer Nursing Care Ctr., Inc.; mem. Iowa State Banking Bd., 1985—. Mem. Nat. Assn. Bank Women (group treas. 1980-81, group v.p. 1981-82, group pres. 1982-83, state membership chair 1983-84, regional membership chair 1984-85), Iowa Bankers Assn. (mem. edn. com. 1985-86), Iowa Disting. Woman in Banking. Republican. Methodist. Club: PEO (Traer) (corr. sec. 1988, v.p. 1991). Avocations: gardening, traveling. Home: 108 Riverview Dr Vinton IA 52349 Office: Farmers Savs Bank 611 2nd St Traer IA 50675-1230

HULS, GLENNA L., sociology educator, photographer; b. Clinton, Okla., Mar. 18, 1944; d. Maurice McLain and Ruby Lue (Rittel) Huls. BS in Psychology, Okla. State U., 1966; MA in Sociology, U. Okla., 1971. Tchr. Dumas (Tex.) H.S., 1967-68; tchg. asst. dept. sociology U. Okla., Norman, Okla., 1968-71; faculty sociology Camden C.C., Blackwood, N.J., 1971-96, assoc. prof. sociology, 1985—, chairperson dept. sociology, 1975-80; tchg. asst. sociology U. Pa., Phila., 1974-76, chair dept. sociology, 1978, 79, 85, 86, 87; mem. gender equity taskforce Camden C.C., 1996, chair academic policies com. 1996. Mem. Faculty Assn. Camden C.C. (pres. 1979-83, chair grievance com. 1996), N.J. Edn. Assn. (mem. higher edn. com. 1980-95), Ea. Sociol. Assn. Office: Camden County C C P O Box 200 Blackwood NJ 08012

HULSEY, RUTH LENORA, state official; b. Athens, Ga., Nov. 28, 1927; d. Joseph Alonzo and Frances Rebecca (Bell) Johnson; student Pasadena Jr. Coll., 1938-40, San Bernardino Valley Coll., 1963-65; m. William A. Hulsey III, Mar. 28, 1958; children: William A., Stephen G., Alicia A. With State of Calif. Employment Devel. Office, 1960—, supr., San Bernardino Field Dept. Office, 1969-75, So. Region Office, Riverside, 1975-78, employment program mgr., asst. mgr. Ontario Field Office, 1979-80, employment program mgr., mgr. Fontana Field Office, 1980—; ret.; ret. dir. Calif. State Employees Credit Union, 1972-75, mem. employer adv. coun., 1978—. Mem. edn. com. Urban League, 1965, mem., 1965—; mem. Arrowhead Allied Arts Coun., 1966-72; mem. Social Lites, 1963—, pres., 1964-66, 80-81, bd. dirs., 1980—, rec. sec., 1981—. Mem. Internat. Assn. Personnel in Employment Security, Calif. State Employees Assn., Bloomington C. of C., Fontana C. of C., Rialto C. of C., San Bernardino C. of C. Democrat. Methodist. Home: 1246 Shamrock Dr San Bernardino CA 92410-1040 Office: State of Calif Employment Devel Dept Office 17590 Foothill Blvd Fontana CA 92335-3785

HULT, SUSAN FREDA, history educator; b. Roslyn, N.Y., Jan. 29, 1956; d. Thomas Joseph and Rosemary (Arthur) Freda; m. Allan Richard Hult, Nov. 18, 1978 (div. 1982). BA in Polit. Sci., Fla. So. Coll., 1977; MA in History, Clemson U., 1985; postgrad., Rice U., 1985-89, U. Houston, 1989—. Read-a-Thon coord. Multiple Sclerosis Soc., Tampa, Fla., 1977-78; divsnl. sales mgr., asst. buyer Ivey's Fla., Winter Park, 1978-81; pers. dir. Tampa Hilton Hotel, 1981-82; grad. asst. Clemson (S.C.) U., 1984-85; prof. history Ctrl. Coll., Houston, 1986—, head dept. history/geography, 1995—; vis. asst. prof. history U. Alaska Southeast, Sitka, 1993-94; adj. instr. Sheldon Jackson Coll., Sitka, 1994; archivist Liberty Life Ins. Co., Greenville, S.C., 1985; pres. faculty assn. coun. Houston C.C. Sys., 1995-96, pres.-elect, 1994-95, sec., 1992-93, treas., 1991-92, chair, 1992-93, chair salary com., 1992-94, chair fundraising com., 1991-92, chair governance com., 1990-91; presenter in field. Editl. asst. Papers of Jefferson Davis, Rice U., 1987-88, Jour. So. History, 1985-87. Mem., vol. Houston Grand Opera Guild, 1994—, Houston Ballet Guild, 1994—; mem. Houston Fedn. Profl. Women, 1995—; campaign worker various Dem. candidates, Houston, 1987— vol. Project Nicaragua, 1994, 95. NEH grantee, 1994-95, Houston C.C. Sys. grantee, 1991-95, Fulbright-Hays grantee, 1994; Illabelle Shanahan Morrisin fellow Alpha Chi Omega Found., 1985. Mem. Am. Assn. Women C.C.s, Orgn. Am. Historians, Tex. C.C. Tchrs. Assn., Tex. Assn. Women C.C.s, Assn. Women Adminstrs., Houston Fedn. Profl. Women, C.C. Humanities Assn., Phi Alpha Theta, Omicron Delta Kappa, Kappa Delta Pi, Phi Theta Kappa (Tex./N.Mex. adv. bd. 1996—, Horizon award 1996, seminar leader 1995-96). Home: 3601 Allen Pky 463 Houston TX 77019 Office: Ctrl Coll/Houston CC Sys 1300 Holman 1229 Houston TX 77004

HUMBACH, MIRIAM JANE, marketing and financial professional; b. N.Y.C., May 18, 1964; d. William Walter and Mildred (Wender) H. BA in Bus.-Econs./Psychology, SUNY, Oneonta, 1986; MBA, Adelphi U., 1996. Fin./acctg. staff The N.Y. Times Co., N.Y.C., 1987-92, media svcs. rsch. asst., 1992-93; circulation/staff asst. N.Y. Times Co., N.Y.C., 1993-95. Mem. NAFE. Home: 235 E 95th St Apt 12G New York NY 10128-4018

HUMBERD, DONNA SUE, social studies educator; b. Athens, Tenn., Apr. 7, 1949; d. Russell Hughes and Helen Jewell (Housley) H.; m. William P. Hemmings, Apr. 9, 1994; 1 stepchild, Julia Claire. BS, U. Tenn., 1971; MEd, Nicholls State U., 1980. Cert. secondary social studies tchr., adminstr. Tchr. McDonogh # 26 Jefferson Parish Schs., Gretna, La., 1971-76; tchr., dept. chair Worley Jr. H.S., Westwego, La., 1976-90; tchr. adult edn. Jefferson Parish Schs., Westwego, 1985-90; tchr., dept. chair J.Q. Adams Mid. Sch., Metairie, La., 1990—; mem. curriculum com. Sun King Exhbn., New Orleans, 1984; cons. Scott, Foresman and Co., 1985; reviewer Merrill Pub. Co., 1988, Instrnl. Design Assocs., Colo., 1988. Recipient Disting. Teaching award Advance Program for Young Scholars, Northwestern State U., 1994. Mem. Nat. Coun. for Social Studies. Office: J Q Adams Mid Sch 5525 Henican Pl Metairie LA 70003-1033

HUMBERT, CHERYL ANN, triage nursing administrator; b. Cin., Dec. 9, 1962; d. Thomas Anthony and Marilyn Rita (Schroot) H. BSN, U. Cin., 1990. RN, Ohio; cert. ACLS, TNCC. Staff nurse med. ICU Univ. Hosp., Cin., 1990-92, staff nurse emergency, 1992—; after house triage nurse coord. U. Cin. Med. Assocs. Family Practice, 1995—. Author: (poetry) On the Threshold of A Dream, 1989, The Witness, 1988. Mem. AACN, Ohio Nurses Assn. (media com. 1995—). Roman Catholic. Office: Univ Family Medicine Ctr 3306 Ruther Ave Cincinnati OH 45220

HUMBYRD, SHIRLEY J., educational consultant, therapist; b. Allentown, Pa., July 28, 1951; d. Frederick H. and Julia (Davis) Kinsey; m. Danny E. Humbyrd, Jan. 26, 1974 (div. Jan. 1996); children: Casey Jo, Matthew, Chelsea, Zachary. BS, Huntington (Ind.) Coll., 1973; MA, U. Mich., 1977; MS, U. R.I., 1996. Cert. by Am. Counseling Assn., Am. Assn. Marriage and Family Therapy; lifetime guidance counselor. Vice-chairperson bd. mgmt. Kent County YMCA, 1993-95; guidance counselor WBCA, N. Kingstown, R.I., 1986-92, tchr., 1985-91; pres., founder Ednl. Interventions, E. Greenwich, R.I., 1992—; family therapist South Shore Mental Health Agy., 1995—. Mem. Jr. League, E. Greenwich, 1984-87; bd. dirs. Kent County YMCA, Warwick, R.I., 1985-95; children and youth dir. Bapt. Ch., N. Kingstown, 1986-92, dir. day campt, 1987-92; chairperson United Way Task Force on Teens, Warwick, R.I., 1990-91. Mem. Ortho Psychiat. Assn. (assoc.). Home: 170 Adirondack Dr East Greenwich RI 02818

HUME, ELLEN HUNSBERGER, broadcast executive, media analyst, journalist; b. Chevy Chase, Md., Apr. 24, 1947; d. Warren Seabury and Ruth (Pedersen) H.; m. John Shattuck, Feb. 14, 1991; 1 child, Susannah; stepchildren: Jessica, Rebecca, Peter. BA, Harvard U., 1968; PhD (hon.), Daniel Webster Coll., 1990. Reporter Somerville (Mass.) Jour., 1968-69; feature writer Santa Barbara (Calif.) News Press, 1969-70; pub. service dir., copy writer KTMS Radio, Santa Barbara, 1970-72; edn. reporter Ypsilanti (Mich.) Press, 1972-73; bus. reporter Detroit Free Press, 1973-75; met. reporter L.A. Times, 1975-77; congl. reporter L.A. Times, Washington, 1977-83; White House corr., polit. writer Wall St. Jour., Washington, 1983-88; exec. dir. Shorenstein-Barone Ctr. on Press and Politics Harvard U., Cambridge, Mass., 1988-93; moderator The Editors TV program, Montreal, Que., 1990-93; adj. lectr. Kennedy Sch. Govt., 1991-93, Medill Sch. Journalism, 1993-94; commentator Washington Week in Rev. PBS-TV, 1973-88, CNN, 1993—; exec. dir. The Democracy Project, PBS, 1996—. Kennedy Inst. Politics fellow Harvard U., 1981, Annenberg Washington Program fellow, 1993-95. Mem. Coun. of Fgn. Rels., Fund for Free Expression, Nat. Press Club. Methodist. Office: Pub Broadcasting Svc 1320 Braddock Pl Alexandria VA 22314

HUMMEL, BRENDA ANDERSON, counselor; b. Portola, Calif., Jan. 25, 1951; d. Robert Ernest Broyles and Elberta Kofford; m. John Wesley Hardin, June 20, 1970 (div. July 1975); 1 child, Dustin Clay; m. Jeffrey Robert Hummel, Aug. 16, 1975; 1 child, Erin Vannessia. AA, San Diego City Coll., 1982; BA, U. North Fla., 1988, MEd, 1993. Nat. cert. counselor. Adolescent care therapist CareUnit Jacksonville, Jacksonville Beach, Fla., 1989-90; drug and alcohol counselor Sylvania (New South Wales) Cmty. Health, Australia, 1990-91; victim advocate U. North Fla., Jacksonville, 1992-93; women's counselor Quigley House, Orange Park, Fla., 1993-96; care team leader Clay County Behavioral Health Ctr., Inc., Middleburg, Fla., 1996—. Mem. ACA, Nat. Bd. for Cert. Counselors, Nat. Honor Soc. for Psychology, Phi Kappa Phi. Office: Clay County Behavioral Health Ctr Inc 3292 County Rd 220 Middleburg FL 23068

HUMMEL, DANA D. MALLETT, librarian; BA in Art History, Smith Coll., 1957; MA in Libr. and Info. Sci., Denver U., 1968; postgrad. Def. Lang. Inst., 1961, Instituto Mexicano-Norteamericano de Relationes Culturales, 1962, John F. Kennedy Ctr. for Spl. Warfare, 1974, Nat. War Coll., 1976, No. Va. Bus. Sch., 1978, Cath. U. Am., 1981. Head libr., adminstrn., Howard AFB Libr., C.Z., 1969-70; asst. libr. Holmes Intermediate Sch., 1970-71; tchr. Spanish and substitute tchr. J.E.B. Stuart High Sch., 1972-77; sec. Office of exec. dir.-Africa The World Bank, 1978-79; personal sec. to rector Falls Ch. (Va.), 1979-81; mgr. Info. Svcs. Ctr., BDM Internat. subs. Ford Aerospace Co., McLean, Va., 1981-88. Mem. vestry Falls Ch. Episcopal Ch., 1982; del. Republican State Conv., 1981, 86; pres. Ravenwood Civic Assn., 1979-80, 80-81, 81-82; rep. Mason Dist., Fedn. Civic Assns.; mem. ann. plan rev. task force Mason Dist., 1981-82; gov. trustee Fairfax County Pub. Libr. Bd., 1982-88; chmn. bd. trustees Fairfax County. Named Outstanding Woman of Yr., Fairfax County Bd. Suprs. and Com. of Women, 1982. Mem. AAUP, ALA, Am. Soc. for Info. Sci., Spl. Libr. Assn., Va. Libr. Assn., D.C. Libr. Assn., Women in Def., Villa D'Este Assn. (bd. dirs. 1995—), Jr. League Sarasota, Fla. Home: 7355 Villa D Este Dr Sarasota FL 34238-5649

HUMMEL, MARILYN MAE, elementary education educator; b. Cleve., June 20, 1931; d. John Winfield and Meta E. (Timm) H. BS, Ohio U., 1953. Cert. elem. educator. Elem. tchr. Lakewood (Ohio) Bd. of Edn., 1953-83. Mem. Centennial Planning Com., Lakewood, Ohio 1989; vol. United Way, Lakewood Hosp. Jennings scholar, 1969-70; named Tchr. of the Yr., Franklin Sch., 1983. Mem. Coll. Club West, Delta Kappa Gamma, Kiwanis Club. Republican. Presbyterian.

HUMMEL, MARLA JEAN, mental health therapist; b. Des Moines, Dec. 13, 1959; d. James Leo and Geraldine Patricia McDonald; m. Kevin Martin Hummel, Apr. 14, 1984. BS, U. Houston, 1982; MS, Drake U., 1987; postgrad., Iowa State U., 1995—. Lic. mental health counselor; cert. employee assistance profl. Counselor Employee/Student Assistance Program, Des Moines, 1988-94; mental health therapist IHS Assistance Ctr., Des Moines, 1994—. Mem. Am. Counseling Assn., Am. Mental Health Counselors Assn. Roman Catholic. Office: Assistance Ctr 6000 University # 200 West Des Moines IA 50266

HUMMEL-ROSSI, BARBARA, psychology educator; b. Buffalo, Sept. 11, 1942; s. Frederick Francis and Gertrude (Pecoroni) Hummel; m. Michael J. Rossi, Aug. 5, 1967; children: Brian, Andrea. BA, SUNY-Albany, 1964; PhD, SUNY-Buffalo, 1971. Cert. secondary tchr., N.Y. Tchr. math. Niskayuna pub. schs., Schenectady, N.Y., 1964-65; research asst. SUNY-Buffalo, 1965-68; research assoc. SUNY-Stony Brook, 1968-69; dir. research Skill Achievement Inst., N.Y.C., 1969-71; prof. applied psychology NYU, N.Y.C., 1971—; cons. in field. Contbr. articles to profl. publs. Vol. fundraising Huntington Hosp., N.Y., 1975-79; vol. Harborfields PTA, 1980—; chmn. citizen com. Harborfields Sch., Huntington, 1984; trustee Harborfields Pub. Libr. 1986—; bd. dirs. N.Y. Dance Theatre, Inc., 1989-92. Mem. AAUW, Am. Psychol. Assn., Eastern Psychol. Assn., Am. Ednl. Rsch. Assn., Nat. Council on Measurement in Edn., Eastern Ednl. Rsch. Assn., Multivariate Research Soc., Pi Lambda Theta. Clubs: Northport Tennis (N.Y.); Head of the Bay (Huntington). Home: 53 Cherry Ln Huntington NY 11743-2946 Office: NYU Dept Ednl Psychology 239 Greene St Rm 537A East Bldg New York NY 10003

HUMPHREY, CAMILLA MARIE, retired special education educator; b. Devils Lake, N.D., July 3, 1928; d. George O. and Annette Sophia (Monson) Loftness; m. Thomas Milton Humphrey, Dec. 26, 1950 (dec. Nov. 1992); children: Ana Oliva Johns, Marlena Marie Hensley. AA, Coll. Marin, 1948; attended, U. Calif., Berkeley, 1948-49; BA in Edn., Pacific Luth. U., 1950; grad., U. Oreg., 1951-53, U. Nev., 1968. Cert. spl. edn., Oreg., boating skills. Tchr. Albany (Oreg.) Elem. Sch., 1950-51; spl. edn. tchr. Children's Hosp. Sch., Eugene, Oreg., 1951-53, Eugene Jr. H.S., 1953-54, Clark County Sch. Dist., Las Vegas, 1968-71. Contbr. articles to profl. jours. Vol. English tchr. Luth. Mission, 1955-56; pres. Oil Wive's Club, Bogota, Colombia, 1956-57, Assistance League Las Vegas, 1980-81; nurse's aid Red Cross, Tripoli, Libya, 1958; fgn. rels. chmn. LVW, Carson City, Nev., 1963, fin. sec. Gen. Fedn. Women's Clubs, Las Vegas, 1983-84; adv. bd. mem. Salvation Army, Las Vegas, 1983-86; vol. R.S.V.P., 1993-95, Thrift Store and Food Bank, McKinleyville, Calif., Patricks Point State Park Bookstore, Trinidad, Calif.; adv. for world concerns, children's issues, preservation natural beauty; bd. dirs. Adult Day Health Care, Mckinleyville, Calif., 1994-95. Recipient 1st and 2d place photography award Gen. Fedn. Women's Clubs, 1982, Nev. short story award, 1984, vol. svc. plaque Help Ctr., Las Vegas, 1986; Silver Platter award Evang. Luth. Ch. in Am. Mission, Bogota, 1956. Mem. AAUW, DAV Aux., Nat. Assistance League (at-large), Pacific Luth. U. Alumni Assn. Lutheran. Home: 113 Maple Park SE Olympia WA 98501

HUMPHREY, LISA ANN, restaurant manager, writer; b. Excelsior Springs, Mo., Oct. 20, 1971; d. Stephen Francis Humphrey and Linda Lou (Osborn) Reddick. BS in Human Environ. Scis./Hotel & Restaurant Adminstrn., Okla. State U., 1994. Catering supr. Bob Burk Oil Co., Stillwater, Okla., 1990-93; intern, auditor Student Union Hotel/ Conf. Ctr., Stillwater, Okla., 1994; mgr. J.S. Ventures-Applebee's, Omaha, 1994—; mem. Long Ridge Writers Group, West Redding, Conn., 1994-96; mgr. safety com. All-Safety Com., Omaha, 1995-96. Poet. Senator Youth in Govt., Tallahassee, 1988; svc. project organizer Springtime Tallahasse, 1986, 88; freedom writer Amnesty Internat. With U.S. Army ROTC, 1989-90. Mem. NOW. Democrat. Office: JS Ventures-Applebee's 13208 W Maple Rd Omaha NE 68164

HUMPHREY, MARY FRANCES, historian, author, retired health care recruiter; b. Lowell, Mass., May 19, 1927; d. Frederick Vincent and Elizabeth Theresa Lynch; m. Keith Nelson Humphrey; children: Sharon Elizabeth Humphrey-Mason, Nancy Ellen Griffin, Janet Lynn Stephenson. Degree in Library Svcs., U. Maine, Presque Isle, 1977. Cert. librarian in charge. Payroll clerk Presque Isle AFB, 1944-46; sec. Maine Potato Growers, Inc., Presque Isle, 1946-52, U.S. Congressman Clifford G. McIntire, Washburn, 1954-58; librarian Washburn Meml. Library, 1970-73; librarian, sch. sec. Maine Sch. Adminstrn. Dist. # 45, Washburn, 1967-79; employment mgr.-recruiter The Aroostook Med. Ctr., Presque Isle, 1980-90; proofreader Echoes-No. Maine Jour., Caribou, 1992—; historian, author, 1990—; trustee Washburn Meml. Libr., 1973—, Washburn Regional Health Ctr., 1978-88; sec. Aroostook County Sch. Libr. Assn., Presque, 1968-79. Vol. Well Baby Clinic, Washburn, 1954-60; leader Little Sisters 4-H Club, Washburn, 1960-65; mem. chair P.I. Cmty. Concert Assn., Presque Isle, 1952-64; mem. & officer Washburn PTA, 1965-73, Washburn Women's Ext., 1952-80; officer and fundraiser Dollars For Scholars, Washburn, 1969-75; mem. Pool Study Com., Washburn, 1995—, 911E Study Com., Washburn, 1995—. Recipient Hon. Alumni award Washburn Dist. H.S. Alumni, 1970, Plaque Washburn Regional Health Ctr. Bd., 1988. Mem. Salmon Brook Hist. Soc. (officer 1980), Friends of Aroostook County Hist. Ctr. Home: PO Box 68 2 Thompson St Washburn ME 04786

HUMPHREY, PHYLLIS A., writer; b. Oak Park, Ill., July 22, 1929; d. Richard William and Antoinette (Chalupa) Ashworth; m. Herbert A. Pihl, Sept. 13, 1946 (div. 1957); children: Christine Pihl Gibson, Gary Fraizer Pihl; m. Curtis H. Humphrey, June 21, 1965; 1 child, Marc. AA, Coll. San Mateo, Calif., 1972; postgrad., Northwestern U., 1945-47. Ptnr. Criterion House, Oceanside, Calif., 1972—. Author: Wall Street on $20 a Month, 1986, Golden Fire, 1986, Sweet Folly, 1990, Flying High, 1995; author radio scripts Am. Radio Theatre, 1983-84; contbr. short stories and articles to popular mags. Mem. Mensa. Republican. Christian Sci. Ch. Office: Criterion House PO Box 586295 Oceanside CA 92058-6295

HUMPHREY, REBECCA ANN, artist; b. Reidsville, N.C., Aug. 12, 1944; d. Roy Lee and Frances Carolyn (Wilson) H. BFA in Studio Art, U. N.C., 1966, MFA in Painting, 1971; postgrad., Carnegie-Mellon U., 1978, Arrowmont Sch. Arts and Crafts, 1991. Art supr. Gastonia (N.C.) City Schs., 1966-68; art instr. Winston-Salem (N.C.) City Schs., 1968-69; prof. James Madison U., Harrisonburg, Va., 1972—. Exhibited in group shows including Taft Mus., Cin., 1980, Renwick Gallery, Washington, 1981, Tampa Mus. Art, 1986, Ga. World Congress Ctr., Atlanta, 1990. Recipient Achievement award Huntington Galleries, 1979, First prize, Assoc. Art Orgn. Western N.Y., 1980, Jurors award Towson State U., 1994. Office: James Madison Univ Sch Art and Art History Harrisonburg VA 22807

HUMPHREYS, ELENA, artist; b. Bklyn., Apr. 3, 1970; d. Robert and Helen (Cuce) H. BFA, Parsons Sch. Design, 1993; MFA, MC, SUNY, Stony Brook, 1996. Instr. SUNY, Stony Brook, 1993-96; asst. archivist, bookeeper Metro Pictures Gallery, N.Y.C., 1995-96; asst. Gavin Brown's Enterprise, N.Y.C., 1995—; founder, organizer RiotGrrrl, N.Y.C., 1992-94; summer student Skowhegan (Maine) Sch. Painting & Sculpture, 1996. Co-author: New Perspectives in Vernacular Music, 1996; editor Artcore, 1995—, Demizine, 1996—. Mem. Coll. Art Assn. Home and Studio: PO Box 188 Cooper Sta New York NY 10003

HUMPHREYS, KAREN M., judge; b. Ashland, Kans., Feb. 18, 1948; d. Frederick Mitchell and Carrie (Arnold) H. BA in History and Am. Studies, Univ. of Kans., 1970, JD, 1973. Bar: Kans. 1973, U.S. Dist. Ct. Kans. 1978, U.S. Supreme Ct. 1980. Estate and gift tax atty. IRS, Dept. of Treasury, 1973-75; staff atty. Legal Aid, 1975-76; founder, mng. atty. Senior Citizen Law Project, 1976-78; asst. U.S. atty. Topeka, Kans., 1978-83, Wichita, Kans., 1983-86; assoc. Redmond, Redmond & Nazar, 1986-87; staff atty. FDIC, 1987; dist. judge State of Kans., 18th Judicial Dist., 1987-93; magistrate judge U.S. Dist. Ct. Kans., Wichita, 1993—; bd. dirs. Women's Studies at Wichita State Univ., Kans. Health Inst. and Prairie View Inc.; advisory bd. Jr. League. Recipient Matrix award Women in Comm., 1989. Mem. Am. Bar Assn., Kans. Bar Assn., Wichita Bar Assn. (President's award for outstanding svc. 1988), Nat. Assn. of Women Judges, Wichita Women Attys. Assn. (Louise Mattox award 1994). Protestant. Office: US Courthouse 401 N Market St Rm 322 Wichita KS 67202-2000

HUMPHREYS, PEG DECHENE, fine arts educator; b. Oakland, Calif., Feb. 2, 1924; d. Ernest Raymond and Alviva Victoria (Johnson) DeChene; m. Walter Kenneth Humphreys (div. 1978); children: Pamela Joan Humphreys St. John, Sharon L. Humphreys Stoner, Craig Alan, Heidi Gwen. BS, U. Calif., Berkeley, 1947; postgrad., Diablo Valley Coll., 1970-76. Cert. art tchr., Calif. Art tchr. Pleasanton (Calif.) Sch. Dist., 1976-80, Pleasanton Recreation Dept., 1980—, Athenian Mid. Sch., Danville, Calif., 1984-87, San Ramon (Calif.) Schs., 1993-94; drawing and painting tchr. Acalanes Sch. Dist., Walnut Creek, Calif., 1976—, Lindsay Mus., Walnut Creek, 1993-94; juror Alamo-Danville Art Assn., 1991, Ctrl. Valley Art League, Modesto, Calif., 1992, Concord (Calif.) Art Assn., 1994. Pres. PTA, Lafayette, Calif., 1957; leader Girl Scouts U.S., Lafayette, 1957-69; vol. art tchr. Lafayette Schs., 1969-75. Recipient award traveling show Am. Water Color Soc., 1986. Mem. East Bay Water Color Soc. (pres. 1974-76, Grumbacher award 1992). Home and Office: 2701 Pine Knoll # 6 Walnut Creek CA 94595

HUMPHRIES, JOAN ROPES, psychologist, educator; b. Bklyn., Oct. 17, 1928; d. Lawrence Gardner and Adele Lydia (Zimmermann) Ropes; m. Charles C. Humphries, Apr. 4, 1957; children: Peggy Ann, Charlene Adele. BA, U. Miami, 1950; MS, Fla. State U., 1955; PhD, La. State U., 1963. Part-time instr. psychology dept. U. Miami, Coral Gables, Fla., 1964-66; prof. behavioral studies dept. Miami-Dade C.C., 1966—. Registered lobbyist State of Fla. Presenter in field. Prodr., prin. host (videos) Strategies in Global Modern Academia: Issues and Answers in Higher Education, 1993-94; prodr. and host (video) Strategies in Global Modern Academia: Issues and Answers in Higher Education, II, 1995. Mem. Biofeedback Delegation to the People's Republic of China and Hong Kong, 1995. Mem. AAUP (past v.p. and sec., pres. Miami-Dade C.C. chpt. 1986—, past v.p. Fla. conf., 1986-88, mem. exec. bd. Fla. conf. 1989-90, mem. Nat.), AAUW (life, former v.p. Tamiami branch 1983-88, Appreciation award 1977) Biofeedback Soc. of Am. (pres. 1989—), Biofeedback Assn. Fla. (pres. 1990—), Internat. Platform Assn. (gov. 1979—, Silver Bowl award 1993), APA, Am. Psychol. Soc. (charter), Fla. Psychol. Assn., Mexico Beach C. of C. (bus. 1991—), North Campus Speaker's Bur. (award for community lecture series), Physicians for Social Responsibility, Internat. Soc. for Study Subtle Energies and Energy Medicine (charter), Inst. Evaluation, Diagnosis and Treatment (past v.p. 1975-87, pres. 1987—, former bd. dirs.), Dade-Monroe Psychol. Assn., Assn. Applied Psychophysiology and Biofeedback, Noetic Scis., Colonial Dames 17th Century, N.Y. Acad. Scis. (life), Regines in Miami, Soc. Mayflower Descs. (elder William Brewster colony), Hereditary Order of Descendants of Colonial Govs., Phi Lambda (founder's plaque 1976, appreciation award 1987), Phi Lambda Pi. Democrat. Clubs: Country of Coral Gables (life), Jockey (life). Editorial staff, maj. author: The Application of Scientific Behaviorism to Humanistic Phenomena, 1975, rev. edit., 1979; researcher in biofeedback and human consciousness. Home: 1311 Alhambra Cir Coral Gables FL 33134-3521 Office: Miami Dade CC North Campus 11380 NW 27th Ave Miami FL 33167-3418

HUMPHRIES, LINDA JOINER, art educator; b. Somers Point, N.J., Oct. 8, 1949; d. Willie Clyde and Frieda Marie (Eble) Joiner; m. Raymond Franklin Humphries Jr., May 1, 1974; children: Raymond Franklin III, Brandon Joiner. BS in Edn., Auburn U., 1971; MEd, Francis Marion Coll., 1976. Tchr. Arnco-Sargent Elem. Sch., Newnan, Ga., 1971-72, Jonesboro (Ga.) High Sch., 1972-73, Jonesboro Jr. High Sch., 1973-74, Bleinheim (S.C.) Elem. Sch., 1974-75, Butler High Sch., Hartsville, S.C., 1975-77, Pate, Spring and St. John's Elem. Sch., Darlington, S.C., 1978-80, Hartsville Jr. High Sch., 1981-90, Brunson-Dargan Jr. High. Sch., Darlington, 1990-91, St. John's H.S., Mayo H.S. (now Darlington H.S.), Darlington, 1991—; tchr. Florence (S.C.) Darlington Tech. Sch., 1983. Mem. S.C. Art Edn. Assn., Nat. Art Edn. Assn., Palmette St. Tchrs. Assn. Home: 136 Oak St Darlington SC 29532-2627 Office: Darlington HS 525 Spring St Darlington SC 29532

HUMPHRIES, SUZANNE TESKE, elementary education educator; b. Birmingham, Ala., Dec. 1, 1968; d. Kenneth Howell and Eva Ann (Hice) Teske; m. Alvie Todd Humphries, Sept. 9, 1989; 1 child, Matthew Todd. BS in Elem. Edn., U. Ala., Birmingham, 1991. Cert. elem. tchr., Ala. Exceptional edn. tchr. Jefferson County Bd. Edn., Birmingham, 1993—; ednl. cons. pvt. practice, Birmingham, 1989—. Mem. NEA, Ala. Edn. Assn., Coun. for Exceptional Children (divsn. early childhood). Republican. Baptist. Home: 3119 Shera Ln Hueytown AL 35023

HUND, BARBARA MAURER, speech broadcasting and English educator; b. Wilkes-Barre, Pa., Dec. 11, 1930; d. Robert Henry and Nerline Maude (Smith) Maurer; m. Henry John Hund, June 10, 1961; children: Kirsten, John. BA in English and Edn., Hofstra U., 1952; cert. in devel. western civilization, U. Edinburgh, Scotland, 1952; cert. in English, art, lit. and music, U. London, 1955; MA in Speech and Broadcasting, U. Wis., 1957; cert. in conversational Chinese, Yale U., 1966; EdD in Higher Edn., Coll. William and Mary, 1987. Cert. elem. and secondary tchr., N.Y., Wis., N.J., Md., Va. Elem. tchr., Baldwin, N.Y., Madison, Wis., Montclair, N.J., 1952-58; elem. tchr., Norfolk (Va.) Acad., 1972-76; tchr. TV, Washington County Sch. Sys., Hagerstown, Md., 1958-61; ednl. TV prodr. WMHT-TV Mohawk-Hudson Pub. Broadcasting, Schenectady, 1961-64; TV prodr. Chinese Broadcasting Co., Taipei, Taiwan, 1969-70; tchr. English, Taipei Am. Sch., 1969-70; prof. speech, English and broadcasting Tidewater C.C., Portsmouth, Va., 1976—, chmn. coll. internat. task force-distance edn. task force, 1995—; tchr. Beijing Broadcasting Inst., 1988-89; China coord. exch. agreement between Tidewater C.C. and Beijing Broadcasting Inst., 1989—; instr. Fulbright-Hays Study Seminar in Czech and Slovak Republics, summer 1993; instrnl. TV writer, prodr., broadcaster elem. math., sci. and enrichments lessons Washington County TV Project, 1958-61. Organizer, prodr., co-host comml. TV show Spotlight on Hampton Roads, Norfolk, 1986-87. Edn. chmn. Luth. Ch., 1973-85, lay reader, lector, communion asst., 1985—; mem. cmty. adv. bd. WHRO Pub. Broadcasting, Hampton Roads, Va., 1980-84; leader leadership edn. and devel. for 12 Luth. chs., Hampton Roads area, 1981-83; speaker on China experiences to local civic group and local TV stas., 1989-91; participant 1st Sino-Am. Conf. on Women's Issues, China and Ednl. Exch., Beijing, summer 1990. Named Outstanding Faculty Mem., Va. C.C. Assn., 1994; scholar Hofstra U., 1948-52. Mem. AAUW, Am. Women in Radio and TV (charter, v.p., treas. Commonwealth chpt. 1962—). Office: Tidewater CC Humanities Divsn 7000 College Dr Portsmouth VA 23703

HUNDLEY, CAROL MARIE BECKQUIST, music educator; b. L.A., Oct. 19, 1936; d. Paul Albert and Virginia Mary (Noll) Beckquist; m. Norris Cecil Hundley, Jr., June 8, 1957; children: Wendy Michelle Hundley Harris, Jacqueline Marie Hundley Reid. Student, Mt. St. Mary's Coll., 1954-55; AA, Mt. San Antonio Coll., 1956; postgrad., Calif. State U., L.A., 1981-82, 85-86. Tchr. pvt. piano studio Arcadia, Calif., 1955-58, Pacific Palisades, Calif., 1965-95; vocal coach Corpus Christi Sch., Pacific Palisades, Calif., 1980-95, dir. instrumental music, 1980-95; vocal and instrumental accompanist Theater Palisades, Pacific Palisades, 1986-87, music arranger, 1970-95; accompanist in field. Author: (play) Bach to Broadway, 1986, The Spirit of America, 1987; arranger and choreographer in field. Piano recitals Tuesday Musicale Jrs., Pasadena, Calif., 1950-54; accompanist Arcadia (Calif.) Women's Club, 1953-54; choral music provider Optimist Club, Pacific Palisades, 1989-92. Recipient scholarship Tuesday Musical Srs., 1954, Mt. St. Mary's Coll., 1954. Mem. Music Tchrs. Assn. Calif. Democrat. Roman Catholic.

HUNGERFORD, KATE CLARK, manufacturing executive; b. Waterbury, Conn., May 22, 1955; d. Charles S. and Sally B. (Littlefield) H.; m. Daniel B. Fuessenich (div. Sept. 1987). Student, U. Denver, 1973-74; AA, Post Coll., 1980. Trader Rothschild Unterberg, Boston, 1977-80; asst. prodr. NBC Saturday Night Live, N.Y.C., 1980-82; v.p. Litchfield Internat., Torrington, Conn., 1985—. Home: 89 Old South Rd Litchfield CT 06759 Office: Litchfield Internat PO Box 1007 Torrington CT 06790

HUNING, DEBORAH GRAY, actress, dancer, audiologist, photographer/video producer-editor; b. Evanston, Ill., Aug. 23, 1950; d. Hans Karl Otto and Angenette Dudley (Willard) H.; divorced; 1 child, Bree Alyeska. BS, No. Ill. U., 1981, MA, 1983. Actress, soloist, dancer, dir. various univ. and community theater depts., Bklyn., Chgo. and Cranbrook, B.C., Can., 1967—; ski instr. Winter Park (Colo.) Recreation Assn., 1975-79; house photographer C Lazy U Ranch, Granby, Colo., 1979; audiologist, ednl. programming cons. East Kootenay Ministry of Health, Cranbrook, 1985-89; ind. video prodn./asst., 1991—; owner Maxaroma Espresso and Incredible Edibles, 1993-95; pres. Pan Prodns., 1989—; master of ceremonies East Kootenay Talent Showcase, EXPO '86, Vancouver B.C., Can., 1986; creator, workshop leader: A Hearing Impaired Child in the Classroom, 1986. Producer, writer, dir., editor (video) Down With Decibels, 1992; author: Living Well With Hearing Loss: A Guide for the Hearing-Impaired and Their Families, 1992. Sec., treas. Women for Wildlife, Cranbrook, 1985-86; assoc. mem. adv. bd. Grand County Community Coll., Winter Park, Colo., 1975-77; assoc. mem. bd. dirs. Boys and Girls Club of Can., Cranbrook, 1985. Mem. Internat. Marine Animal Trainers Assn.

HUNKER, EVELYN LOIS, artist; b. Pitts.; m. Walter Hunker; children: Susan L., Jeffrey A. Student, U. Colo., Denver, 1975-80, Mus. Sch. Art, Greenville, S.C., 1981-83; BA, U. Ala., Birmingham, 1987. Legal sec. Gulf Oil Corp., Denver and Pitts., 1971-80; artist Birmingham, Ala., 1987—. Author: Poems and Paintings by Evelyn Hunker, 1991; poem pub. in Where Dawn Lingers, 1996 (Editor's Choice award Nat. Libr. Poetry); exhibited in group shows at Agora Gallery, Soho, N.Y., 1990, 92, Allied Artists of Am., 1990, Soc. Watercolor Artists, 1992, Watercolor Soc. Ala., 1994, Ariz. Aqueous, Tubac, 1995; featured artist Art Alliance, Tutwiler Hotel, Birmingham, 1991, 94; paintings displayed at Shelby County Art Assn., 1994-96, Vestavia Art Assn., Vestavia Hills, Ala., 1996, Hoover (Ala.) Libr., 1996, numerous civic and mcpl. bldgs., Ala., S.C., Colo. and Pa. Charter mem. Nat. Mus. Women in Arts; mem. Birmingham Mus. Art; 1st v.p. Heritage Fine Arts Guild Arapahoe County, Englewood, Colo., 1978-79. Recipient Purchase award Magic City Art Connection, Birmingham, 1995, numerous others. Mem. Watercolor Soc. Ala. (historian 1994-96), Shelby County Art Assn. (charter), Mountain Brook Art Assn. (mem. show com. 1996), Vestavia Hills Art Assn. Home: 2405 Lullwater Rd Birmingham AL 35242

HUNNICUTT, VICTORIA ANNE WILSON, school system administrator; b. Tyler, Tex., July 23, 1944; d. Leroy G. and N. Joseline (Bobo) Wilson; m. John Walter Hubble, July 29, 1967 (div. Oct. 1972); m. Buford D. Hunnicutt, Aug. 1, 1982. BA, Emory and Henry Coll., 1966; MEd, Mercer U., 1970; Ed specialist, U. Ga., 1993. Tchr. Spanish/English Marion (Va.) Sr. H.S., 1966-67; tchr. Spanish Ballard Hudson Middle Sch., Macon, 1967-68; reading specialist Robins AFB Sch. System, Warner Robins, Ga., 1973-74, Spanish tchr., 1968-70, classroom tchr., 1970-86, computer/sci. specialist, 1986-90, prin. Robins Elem. Sch., 1991, curriculum coord., 1990—; adj. prof. Tift Coll., Forsyth, Ga., 1985-88, Ft. Valley State Coll., 1993—. Treas. Bibb County Dem. Women, Macon, Ga., 1986-88, membership chair 1989-93. Mem. AAUW, ASCD, NSTA, NAFE, Nat. Coun. Tchrs. of English, Ga. Coun. of Internat. Reading Assn., Internat. Reading Assn., HOPE Coun., Ga. coun. of Internat. Reading Assn. (pres. 1994-95), Nat. Audubon Soc., Ocmulgee Audubon Soc. (edn. chair 1986-93, v.p. 1991-92), Air Force Assn. (treas. chpt. 296 1989-91, v.p. for aerospace edn. chpt. 296 1991-93, v.p. chpt. 296 1993-94, v.p. for aerospace edn. Ga. State AFA, 1992—, Tchr. of Yr. 1995, Jane Shirley McGee award 1990, Medal of Merit 1990). Democrat. Methodist. Office: Robins AFB Sch System 1050 Education Way Robins AFB GA 31098-1043

HUNSBERGER, TINA LOUISE, special education educator; b. Providence, R.I., Nov. 29, 1958; d. William G. and Mary R. (Desjardin) H.; m. Patrick Richardson (dec. July, 1983). BS, R. I. Coll., 1992. Cert. tchr. R.I., N. Mex. Spl. edn. tchr. Artesia (N.Mex.) Pub. Schs., 1993—; co-coord. student mediation program Artesia Intermediate Sch., N.Mex. Co-coord. Slightly Older Students, R.I. Coll., 1991-92. Mem. Coun. for Exceptional Children, Kappa Delta. Office: Artesia Intermediate Sch 1100 Bullock Ave Artesia NM 88210

HUNSTEIN, CAROL, judge; b. Miami, Fla., Aug. 16, 1944. AA, Miami-Dade Jr. Coll., 1970; BS, Fla. Atlantic U., 1972; JD, Stetson U., 1976. Bar: Ga. 1976; U.S. Dist. Ct. 1978; U.S. Ct. Appeals 1978; U.S. Supreme Ct. 1989. Legal practice Atlanta, 1976-84; judge Superior Ct. of Ga. (Stone Mt. cir.), 1984-92; justice Supreme Ct. of Ga., Atlanta, 1992—; chair Ga. Commn. on Gender Bias in the Judicial System 1989—; pres.-elect Coun. of Superior Ct. Judges of Ga. 1990—. Recipient Clint Green Trial Advocacy award 1976, Women Who Made A Difference award Dekalb Women's Network 1986. Mem. Ga. Assn. of Women Lawyers, Nat. Assn. of Women Judges (dir. 1988-90), Bleckley Inn of Ct., State Bar Ga. Office: Supreme Ct Ga 244 Washington St Rm 572 Atlanta GA 30334

HUNT, EFFIE NEVA, former college dean, former English educator; b. Waverly, Ill., June 19, 1922; d. Abraham Luther and Fannie Ethel (Ritter) H. A.B., MacMurray Coll. for Women, 1944; M.A., U. Ill., 1945, Ph.D., 1950; postgrad., Columbia U., 1953, Univ. Coll., U. London, 1949-50. Keypunch operator U.S. Treasury, 1945; spl. librarian Harvard U., 1947, U. Pa., 1948; Instr. English U. Ill., 1950-51; librarian Library of Congress, Washington, 1951-52; asst. prof. English Mankato State Coll., 1952-59; prof. Radford Coll., 1959-63, chmn. dept. English, 1961-63; prof. Ind. State U., 1963-86; dean Ind. State U. (Coll. Arts and Scis.), 1974-86, dean and prof. emerita, 1987—. Author articles in field. Fulbright grantee, 1949-50. Mem. AAUP, MLA, Nat. Council Tchrs. English, Am. Assn. Higher Edn., Audubon Soc. Home: 3325 Wabash Ave Terre Haute IN 47803-1655 Office: Ind State U Root Hall Eng Dept Terre Haute IN 47809

HUNT, F. V. See VANCE-HUNT, FLORENCE

HUNT, HAZEL ANALUE STANFIELD, retired accountant; b. Butler, Mo., Apr. 4, 1921; d. Vernon Arthur and Myrrl Millicent (Henderson) Stanfield; m. Marvie Avanell Hunt, July 25, 1942; 1 child, Roger LeRoy. Grad., Sawyer Sch. Bus., L.A., 1939. Supr., bookkeeper, sec. Nethercutt Labs., Santa Monica, Calif., 1940-45; v.p., treas. Dwyer-Curlett, Inc., L.A., 1946-86; pres. Nat. Assn. Accts., West Los Angeles, 1970-96, other offices. Mem. DAR, Beta Sigma Phi (pres. 1942, other offices). Presbyterian. Home: 1540 Ontario Ave Pasadena CA 91103

HUNT, HELEN, actress; b. L.A., June 15, 1963; d. Gordon and Jane H. TV appearances include Amy Prentiss, The Swiss Family Robinson, The Fitzpatricks, It Takes Two, Having Babies, Land of Little Rain, Weekend, Mary Tyler Moore Show, Family, St. Elsewhere; TV movies include Pioneer Woman, All Together Now, Death Scream, The Spell, Transplant, Angel Dusted, Child Bride of Short Creek, The Miracle of Cathy Miller, Desperate Lives, Quarterback Princess, Bill: On His Own, Choices of the Heart, Sweet Revenge, Why Are You Here?, Murder In New Hampshire: The Pamela Smart Story, 1991, In the Comfort of Darkness, 1992; TV series Mad About You, 1992— (Emmy nomination, Lead Actress - Comedy, 1993, 94, Golden Globe award for Best Actress, musical or comedy, 1994, 95, Emmy award for Best Leading Actress in a Comedy series, 1996); films include Rollercoaster, 1977, Girls Just Want To Have Fun, 1985, Trancers, 1985, Empire, 1985, Peggy Sue Got Married, 1986, Project X, 1987, Miles From Home, 1988, Next Of Kin, 1989, The Waterdance, 1992, Only You, 1992, Bob Roberts, 1992, Mr. Saturday Night, 1992, Kiss of Death, 1995, Twister, 1996. Office: care Connie Tavel 9171 Wilshire Blvd Ste 436 Beverly Hills CA 90210-5516

HUNT, LINDA, actress; b. Morristown, N.J., Apr. 2, 1945. Student, Interlochen Arts Acad., Mich., Goodman Theatre and Sch. of Drama, Chgo. Stage appearances include Hamlet, 1972, 74, The Soldier's Tale, 1974, The Knight of the Burning Pestle, 1974, Down by the River Where Waterlilies are disfigured Every Day (off-Broadway debut) 1975, Ah, Wilderness (Broadway debut) 1975, The Rose Tattoo, 1977, Five Finger Excuse, 1975, The Recruiting Officer, 1978, Elizabeth Dead, 1980, A Metamorphis in Miniature (Obie award), 1983, Mother Courage and Her Children 1983, Top Girls (Obie award) 1983, Little Victories, 1983, End of the World, 1983, (Tony nomination 1984), Aunt Dan and Lemon, 1985, The Cherry Orchard, 1988; films include Popeye, 1980, The Year of Living Dangerously, 1982 (Acad. award Best supporting actress 1983), Dune, 1984, The Bostonians, 1984, Eleni, 1985, Silverado, 1985, Waiting for the Moon, 1987, She-Devil, 1989, Kindergarten Cop, 1990, If Looks Could Kill, 1991, Rain Without Thunder, 1993, Twenty Bucks, 1993, Younger and Younger, 1993, Ready to Wear (Prét-a-Portér), 1994, Pocahontas, 1995 (voice only); TV appearance in Ah, Wilderness, 1976, Fame (series) 1978, The Room, 1987, Chico Mendes: Voice of the Amazon, 1989, The Room Upstairs (T.V. movies) 1987, Distant Lives (host) 1989, Space Rangers (series), 1993. Office: care William Morris Agy 151 S El Camino Dr Beverly Hills CA 90212-2704*

HUNT, MARTHA, sales executive, researcher; b. N.Y.C., May 17, 1924; d. Paul Andrew and Monika (Dobberstein) Pankau; children: Philip Brian Hunt, Susan Monica Hunt. Student, Syracuse U., 1943-47. Asst. controller Commonwealth Fund, N.Y.C., 1947-50; sales tech. Caldwell & Bloor, Mansfield, Ohio, 1958-64; sales promotion mgr. Vita Craft Corp., Shawnee, Kans., 1964-91, cons., 1964—; mem. Meeting Planners Internat., Kans. City, 1982—. Author and editor: cookbooks, 1965-91. Pres. League Women Voters, Akron, Ohio, 1951-53; gov. Soroptimist Internat. of Am., 1978-80 (bd. dirs., Phila. 1978-80); pres. Soroptimist Internat. Kans. City, 1973-74; bd. dirs. Kans. City, Mo. cpt. Shepherd's Ctr., 1972—; nat. bd. dirs. Shepher's Ctrs. Am., 1990—; bd. dirs. Rose Brooks Ctr., 1979-86, v.p., 1984-85; bd. dirs., founder Safehome, Inc., 1979—; pres. Metro Citizens Crusade Against Crime, Kans. City., 1983. Recipient Meritorious Svc. award, Kans. City Police Dept., 1975, Disting. Govs. award, Soroptimist Internat. Am., Phila., 1978-79, 79-80, Woman of Distinction award Santa Fe Trl. Girl Scouts, 1993, Soroptimist Internat. Am., 1995. Mem. Kappa Kappa Gamma (pres. 1948-49), Alumnae Assn. (N.Y.C.). Republican. Presbyterian.

HUNT, MARY ALICE, humanities educator; b. Lima, Ohio, Apr. 14, 1928; d. Blair T. and Grace (Henry) H. BA, Fla. State U., Tallahassee, 1950, MA, 1953; PhD, Ind. U., Bloomington, 1973. Instr., librarian Fla. State U., Tallahassee, 1955-61, asst. prof., 1961-74, assoc. prof., 1974-82, prof., 1982-95, assoc. dean, 1986-95, prof. emerita, 1995—. Co-author: (book) Multimedia Indexes, Lists, etc., 1975; editor: (book) Multimedia Approach To Children's Literature, 1983, (periodical) FSU/SLIS Alumni Newsletter, 1966-95, Florida Libraries, 1961-67; assoc. editor: (book) Folders of Ideas for Library Excellence, 1991. Mem. ALA (councilor at large 1986-94), Southeastern Library Assn., Fla. Assn. Media in Edn., Delta Kappa Gamma, Pi Lambda Theta (life), Pi Kappa Phi, Beta Phi Mu. Home: 1603 Kolopakin Nene Tallahassee FL 32301

HUNT, MARY ELIZABETH, association executive; b. June 1, 1951. BA magna cum laude, Marquette U., Milw., 1972; M.Theol. Studies, Harvard Div. Sch., 1974; MDiv, Jesuit Sch. Theology, Berkeley, Calif., 1979; PhD, Grad. Theol. Union, Berkeley, Calif., 1980. Vis. prof. theology ISEDET, Frontier Internship in Mission, Buenos Aires, 1980-82; co-dir., co-founder Women's Alliance for Theology, Ethics and Ritual, Silver Spring, Md., 1983—; vis. asst. prof. religion Colgate U., Hamilton, N.Y., 1986-87; lectr., condr. workshops in field; bd. dirs. Caths. for a Free Choice, Inst. for Study of Christianity and Sexuality; adj. asst. prof. Women's Studies program Georgetown U., 1995—. Author: Fierce Tenderness: A Feminist Theology of Friendship, 1990; contbr. numerous articles to profl. jours.; editorial bd. Jour. Feminist Studies in Religion; women's adv. com. Concilium. Scholar, Marquette U., Harvard Div. U.; recipient Isaac Hecker award Paulist Ctr., Boston, Prophetic Figure award Women's Ordination Conf., prize Crossroad Women's Studies, 1990. Mem. Am. Acad. Religion, Phi Sigma Tau, Alpha Sigma Nu. Office: Women's Alliance Theology 8035 13th St # 5 Silver Spring MD 20910-4803

HUNT, MARY REILLY, organization executive; b. N.Y., Apr. 17, 1921; d. Philip R. and Mary C. (Harten) Reilly; m. Robert R. Hunt, Apr. 10, 1943,; children: Marianne Schram, Philip R., Robert R., Elise Paul. Student, CCNY, 1939. Tax investigator Ind. Dept. Revenue, 1970-80; pres. Ind. Right to Life, 1973-77; treas. Nat. Right to Life Com., Washington, 1974, 77, 78, mem. exec. com., 1974, 76-81, vice chmn., 1976, exec. dir., 1978, dir. devel., 1979-94, v.p. devel., 1994—, hon. bd. mem., 1983—; pres. Mary Reilly Hunt & Assoc., Inc., South Bend, Ind., 1985—. Bd. dirs., v.p. YWCA, 1968-73, bd. dirs. Mental Health Assn. St. Joseph Co., 1972-78; candidate for state legis., 1988; mem. St. Joseph County Rep. precinct com., South Bend, 1964-79, alt. del. to Nat. Rep. Conv., 1976, 84, 88, 92. Mem. NAFE, Women Bus. Owners, South Bend Symphony Women's Assn. Republican. Roman Catholic. Office: Nat Right to Life Com 1102 N Lafayette Blvd South Bend IN 46617-1136

HUNT, PATRICIA JACQUELINE, mathematician, system manager, graphics programmer; b. Pasadena, Calif., Feb. 20, 1961; d. Daniel Joseph and Jacqueline (Vautrain) Collins; m. Daniel Phillip Hunt, Oct. 10, 1987. BS in Applied Math., U. Calif., Santa Barbara, 1983; MS in Applied Math., Naval Postgrad. Sch., 1988. Mathematician Computer Ctr. Naval Postgrad. Sch., Monterey, Calif., 1983-87; computer analyst Metro Info. Svcs., Virginia Beach, Va., 1988-90; system mgr., computer analyst Lockheed Engring. and Sci. Corp., Hampton, Va., 1990—; instr. NASA Engr.'s Week, 1992. Mem. Math. Assn. Am., Assn. Computing Machinery (graphics spl. interest group). Home: 317 Willow Bend Ct Chesapeake VA 23323-1057 Office: Lockheed Engring and Sci Corp 144 Research Dr Hampton VA 23666-1339

HUNTE, BERYL ELEANOR, mathematics educator, consultant; b. N.Y.C.. BA, CUNY-Hunter Coll., 1947; MA, Columbia U., 1948; PhD, NYU, 1965. Instr. math. So. U., Baton Rouge, 1948-51; tchr. math. Bloomfield (N.J.) H.S., 1951-57; tchr. maths. Friends Sem., N.Y.C., 1957-62; asst. prof. maths. Rockland C.C., Suffern, N.Y., 1962-63; instr. maths., supr. tchr. trainees NYU, N.Y.C., 1964; chmn. dept. math. Borough of Manhattan C.C., N.Y.C., 1964-67, 70-73, prof. maths., 1970-95, prof. maths. emerita, 1996, acting dean students, 1985-87, acting dean acad. affairs, 1987-88; dean for spl. projects CUNY, 1988-89; assoc. U. Seminar on Higher Edn., Columbia U., N.Y.C., 1989-95. Author: (with others) (textbook) Mathematics Through Statistics, 1973. Mem. YWCA Greater N.Y. NSF fellow, summer 1960, 1963-64, Chancellor's Faculty fellow CUNY, 1980. Mem. N.Y. Acad. Scis., Am. Math. Soc., CUNY Acad. for Humanities and Scis. (bd. dirs. 1991—, first v.p. 1994—), UN Assn. N.Y.C. (bd. dirs., sec. 1980-86). Office: Borough Manhattan CC 199 Chambers St New York NY 10007-1079

HUNTER, ALYCE, school system administrator; b. Bayonne, N.J., Sept. 26, 1948; d. Theodore and Alyce (Matan) Psemeneki; m. Robert Howard Hunter, Dec. 19, 1970; children: Jay, Sean, Scott, Alyson, Jessica. AB, Douglass Coll., 1970; MEd, East Stroudsburg Univ., 1988; EdD, Lehigh Univ., 1996. Cert. tchr. English, elem. edn., supr., prin. Tchr. Dunellen (N.J.) High Sch., 1978-84, North Hunterdon Regional Sch. Dist., Annandale, N.J., 1986-89; instr. Hunterdon County Adult Edn., Flemington, N.J., 1989-90; tchr. Roxbury High Sch., Succsunna, N.J., 1990-91; dir., supr. Franklin Twp. Pub. Schs., Somerset, N.J., 1991-93; supr. West Windsor Plainsboro Mid. Sch., Plainsboro, N.J., 1993—; adj. instr. Raritan Valley Community Coll., Somerville, N.J., 1989-90; presenterworkshops N.J. Coun. Tchrs. of English, 1993, Nat. Assn. Secondary Sch. Prins., Va., 1994, Coun. on English leadership, Ill., 1994, adv. bd., 1992—;. Contbr. articles to profl. jours. Mem. Middlesex (N.J.) Bd. Edn., 1977-80; trustee Fanny B. Abbot Meml. Scholarship Fund, 1988—. Grantee N.J. Coun. for Humanities, 1991, N.J. Title IV-C/State, 1980. Mem. ASCD, N.J. Prin. and Suprs. Assn. (adv. bd. mid. level 1991—), Mensa, Delta Kappa Gamma. Office: West Windsor Plainsboro Mid Sch 55 Grovers Mill Rd Plainsboro NJ 08536-3105

HUNTER, BARBARA WAY, public relations executive; b. Westport, N.Y., July 14, 1927; d. Walter Denslow and Hilda (Greenawalt) Way; m. Austin F. Hunter, Jan. 24, 1953; children: Kimberley, Victoria. BA, Cornell U., 1949. Assoc. editor Topics Pub. Co., N.Y.C., 1949-51; publicist Nat. Dairy Product Corp., N.Y.C., 1951-53; account exec. Sally Dickson Assn., 1953-56; assoc. D-A-Y Pub. Relations (div. Ogilvy & Mather Co.), N.Y.C., 1964-70, exec. v.p., 1970-84, pres., 1984-89; pres. Hunter & Assocs., Inc., 1989—; bd. dirs. Mr. Steak Inc., Denver. Trustee Cornell U., Ithaca, N.Y., 1980-85; bd. dirs. Point O'Woods Assn., Fire Island, N.Y., 1980-87. Recipient Sparkplug award Internat. Foodservice Mfrs. Assn., 1970, Matrix award N.Y. Women in Communications Inc., 1980, Entreprenurial Woman award Women Bus. Owners, 1981, Nat. Headliner award Women in Communications Inc., 1984. Fellow Pub. Rels. Soc. Am. (pres. 1984, pres.-elect 1983, treas. 1982, pres. N.Y. chpt. 1986, Nat. Gold Anvil award 1993); mem. Internat. Pub. Rels. Assn., Found. Pub. Rels. Rsch. and Edn. (trustee 1982, 84), Women's Forum, Cornell Club of N.Y., The Club at Point O'Woods. Home: 137 E 38th St New York NY 10016-2650 Office: Hunter & Assocs 41 Madison Ave New York NY 10010-2202

HUNTER, BRINCA JO, education specialist; b. Athens, Ga., Feb. 24, 1940; d. Mattie Maude Patton; m. Levis Eugene Hunter, May 6, 1961 (dec. 1994); children: Daphne M. Inman, Jason L. BS in Spl. Edn., U. Akron, 1977, MS in Ednl. Supervision, 1992. Instr. Medina (Ohio) County Bd. Mental Retardation, 1969-88, edn. specialist, 1988—. Mem. Medina City Citizens Adv. Com., 1978-84; bd. dirs. YWCA, Medina, 1978-84; fin. sec. 2d Bapt. Ch., Medina, 1978-82. Mem. ASCD, AAUW, Am. Assn. Mental Retardation, Profl. Assn. Retardation (gen. bd. dirs. 1996—, adult svcs. bd. 1995—, scholar 1982). Democrat. Home: 226 N Harmony St Medina OH 44256 Office: Medina County Bd Mental Retardation 4691 Windfall Rd Medina OH 44256

HUNTER, DIANA LYNN, real estate consultant; b. Northampton, Mass., Aug. 28, 1963; d. Samuel Joseph and Ilda Cecile (Lindley) H. AB in Econs., Bryn Mawr Coll., 1985; MBA in Fin. and Real Estate, UCLA, 1991, MA in Urban Planning, 1991. Banking industry sr. analyst BEI Golembe Assocs., Washington, 1985-88; fin. analyst Heitman Fin. Svcs. Ltd., Beverly Hills, Calif., 1989; site location analyst First Interstate Bank, L.A., 1990-91; sr. cons. E & Y Kenneth Leventhal Real Estate Group, L.A., 1991-94, Arthur Andersen & Co. LLP, L.A., 1995-96; mgr. fin. analysis Newhall Land and Farming Co., Valencia, 1996—. Mem. Assn. Women in Comml. Real Estate, Urban Land Inst. Office: Newhall Land and Farming Co 23823 Valencia Blvd Valencia CA 91355

HUNTER, EDWINA EARLE, elementary education educator; b. Caswell County, N.C., Dec. 29, 1943; d. Edgar Earl and Bessie C. (Brown) Palmer; m. James W. Hunter, July 2, 1966; children: James W. Jr., Anika Z., Isaac Earl. BA, Spelman Coll., 1964; MA in Teaching, Smith Coll., 1966. Tchr. vocal music El Paso (Tex.) Schs., 1975-77, Prince George's County Schs., Laurel, Md., 1977—; instr. El Paso C.C., 1975-76; cons. Smithsonian Mus., Washington, 1978. Transcriber, performer rec. Children's Songs for Games from Africa, 1979. Named Outstanding Alumna, Nat. Assn. For Equal Opportunity in Higher Edn., 1989; grantee NEH, Vienna, Austria, 1990. Mem. Nat. Guild Piano Tchrs., Suzuki Assn. Am., Md. Music Educators, Nat. Alumnae Assn. Spelman Coll. (sec. Columbia chpt. 1985-87, pres. 1988-92, sec.-treas. N.E. region 1991-93). Democrat. Home: 10721 Graeloch Rd

Laurel MD 20723-1122 Office: James H Harrison Elem Sch 13200 Larchdale Rd Laurel MD 20707

HUNTER, GLORIA ELEANORE, middle school educator; b. Chgo., May 24, 1927; d. David Waldren and Eleanore Dorothy (Kline) H.; m. Thomas Alexander Hunter III; children: Thomas A. IV, William Craig, Eleanore Tracey. BA, U. Mich., 1949; MS, U. Bridgeport, 1972. Tchr. Fenger H.S., Chgo., 1949-50, U. Mich. H.S., 1950-55; reporter, columnist Westport News, 1965-68; program writer Action for Bridgeport Cmty., 1968-70; tchr. Fairfield Jr. H.S., 1970-72; tchr., dir. reading Weston Schs., 1972-91; cons. in field. Author cassette program READING/PLUS, Learning and Retention for Managers; contbr. articles to mags. and newspapers. Mem. Westport Bd. Edn., 1991-95; candidate Conn. Ho. of Reps., 1994. Mem. NEA (life), LWV. Democrat. Home: 33 High Point Rd Westport CT

HUNTER, HOLLY, actress; b. Atlanta, Mar. 20, 1958; d. Charles Edwin and Opal Marguerite (Catledge) H; m. Janusz Kaminski, May 20, 1995. BFA, Carnegie-Mellon U., 1980. Appeared in feature films Broadcast News, 1987 (Best Actress award N.Y. Film Critics Circle 1988, Best Actress award Berlin Film Festival 1988, Nat. Bd. Review award, Acad. award nominee best actress), Raising Arizona, 1987, Always, 1990, Miss Firecracker, 1989, Once Around, 1991, The Piano, 1993 (Best Actress award, Cannes Film Festival, 1993, Best Actress - Drama, Golden Globe, 1994, Acad. Award, Best Actress, 1993), The Firm, 1993 (Acad. award nominee, Best Supporting Actress, 1993), Home for the Holidays, 1995, Copycat, 1995, Crash, 1996; TV prodns. Roe vs. Wade (Best Actress Emmy award 1989); Broadway stage prodns. Crimes of the Heart, The Wake of Jamey Foster; regional stage prodns. Buried Child, A Doll's House, Artichoke; other stage prodns. include A Lie of the Mind, L.A., Battery, N.Y.C., Miss Firecracker Contest, The Person I Once Was, N.Y.C.; cable TV prodns. Crazy in Love, 1992 (Ace award nominee), The Positively True Adventures of the Alleged Texas Cheerleader Murdering Mom, 1993 (Best Actress award Am. TV Awards, Emmy award - Outstanding Lead Actress in a Miniseries or Special, Cable Ace award, Best Actress in a Movie or Miniseries). Bd. dirs. Calif. Abortion Rights Action League. *

HUNTER, KATHARINE MCPHAIL, publishing company executive; b. Welland, Ont., Can., Apr. 30, 1955; came to U.S., 1964; d. Alexander Charles McPhail and Diane Mary (Riddell) Church; m. David Horace Hunter, Feb. 15, 1981. BA, Reed Coll., 1978; MBA, Santa Clara U., 1990. Classified advt. mgr., prodn. mgr. Willamette Week newspaper, Portland, Oreg., 1979-84; with prodn. mgmt. staff San Jose Mercury News, 1985-92; project mgr. L.A. Times, 1992-95, advt. ops. mgr., 1995-96; pre-press mgr. Seattle Times, 1996—; cons. Portland Bus. Jour., 1984, Chico (Calif.) News and Rev., 1985. Democrat. Office: Seattle Times 1120 John St Seattle WA 98111

HUNTER, KIM (JANET COLE), actress; b. Detroit, Nov. 12, 1922; d. Donald and Grace Mabel (Lind) Cole; m. William A. Baldwin, Feb. 11, 1944 (div. 1946); 1 dau., Kathryn Emmett; m. Robert Emmett, Dec. 20, 1951; 1 son, Sean Emmett. Ed. pub. schs.; student acting with Charmine Lantaff Camine, 1938-40, Actors Studio. First stage appearance, 1939; played in stock, 1940-42; Broadway debut in A Streetcar Named Desire, 1947; appeared in (tour) Two Blind Mice, 1950, Darkness at Noon, N.Y.C., 1951, The Chase, 1952, N.Y.C., They Knew What They Wanted, N.Y.C., 1952, The Children's Hour, N.Y.C., 1952, The Tender Trap, N.Y.C., 1954, Write Me a Murder, N.Y.C., 1961, Weekend, N.Y.C., 1968, The Penny Wars, N.Y.C., 1969, (tour) And Miss Reardon Drinks a Little, 1971-72, The Glass Menagerie, Atlanta, 1973, The Women, N.Y.C., 1973, (tour) In Praise of Love, 1975, The Lion in Winter, N.J., 1975, The Cherry Orchard, N.Y.C., 1976, The Chalk Garden, Pa., 1976, Elizabeth the Queen, Buffalo, 1977, Semmelweiss, Buffalo, 1977, The Belle of Amherst, N.J., 1978, N.H., 1986, The Little Foxes, Mass., 1980, To Grandmother's House We Go, N.Y.C, 1980, Another Part of the Forest, Seattle, 1981, Ghosts, 1982, Territorial Rites, 1983, Death of a Salesman, 1983, Cat on a Hot Tin Roof, 1984, Life with Father, 1984, Sabrina Fair, 1984, Faulkner's Bicycle, 1985, Antique Pink, 1985, A Delicate Balance, 1986, Painting Churches, 1986, Jokers, 1986, Remembrance, 1987, Man and Superman, 1987-88, N.Y.C., The Gin Game, Lancaster, Pa., 1988, A Murder of Crows, N.Y.C., 1988, Watch on the Rhine, 1989, Suddenly Last Summer, 1991, A Smaller Place, 1991, Open Window, Houston, 1992, The Cocktail Hour, Pitts., 1992, The Belle of Amherst, Vero Beach., Fla., Palm Beach, Fla., Chester, Mass., 1992, Conn., 1993, The Eye of the Beholder, N.Y.C., 1993, Love Letters, Springfield, Mass., 1993, Worcester, Mass., 1993, Northhampton, Mass., 1994, Do Not Go Gentle, Bristol, Pa., 1994, The Gin Game, Chester, Mass., 1994—, tour, 1994-95, All the Way Home, Williamstown, Mass., 1995, The Children's Hour, Conn. Repertory Theatre, 1995; frequent appearences summer stock and repertory theater, 1940—; appeared Am. Shakespeare Festival, Stratford, Conn., 1961; film debut The Seventh Victim, 1943, films include Tender Comrade, 1943, When Strangers Marry (re-released as Betrayed), 1944, You Came Along, 1945, A Canterbury Tale, 1949, Stairway to Heaven, 1946 (re-released with original title A Matter of Life and Death, 1995), A Streetcar Named Desire (Oscar award best supporting actress), Anything Can Happen, 1952, Deadline U.S.A., 1952, Storm Center, 1956, Bermuda Affair, 1957, The Young Stranger, 1957, Money, Women, and Guns, 1958, Lilith, 1964, Planet of the Apes, 1968, The Swimmer, 1968, Beneath the Planet of the Apes, 1970, Escape from the Planet of the Apes, 1971, Dark August, 1975, The Kindred, 1987, Two Evil Eyes, 1991; TV debut Actors' Studio program, 1948; TV appearences include Requiem for a Heavyweight, 1956, The Comedian, 1957, Give Us Barabbas, 1961, 63, 68, 69, Love, American Style, Colombo, Cannon, Night Gallery, Mission Impossible, The Magician, 1972-73, Marcus Welby, Hec Ramsey, Griff, Police Story, Ironside, Medical Center, Bad Ronald, Born Innocent, 1974, Ellery Queen, 1975, Lucas Tanner, This Side of Innocence, Once an Eagle, Baretta, Gibbsville, Hunter, 1976, The Oregon Trail, 1977, Project UFO, Stubby Pringle's Christmas, 1978, Backstairs at the White House, 1979, Specter on the Bridge, 1979, Edge of Night, 1979-80, FDR's Last Year, 1980, Skokie, 1981, Scene of the Crime, 1984, Three Sovereigns for Sarah, 1985, Hot Pursuit, 1985, Private Sessions, 1985, Martin Luther King, Jr., The Dream and the Dream, 1986, Drop Out Mother, 1987, (mini-series) Cross of Fire, 1989, Murder, She Wrote, 1990, Vivien Leigh: Scarlett and Beyond, 1990, Bloodlines: Murder in the Family, 1993, Class of '96, 1993, All My Children, 1993, Hurricane Andrew, 1993, L.A. Law, 1994, Mad About You, 1994; recordings include From Morning 'Til Night (and a Bag Full of Poems), 1961, Come, Woo Me, 1964, The Velveteen Rabbit, 1989; author: Kim Hunter: Loose in the Kitchen, 1975. Recipient Donaldson award for best supporting actress in A Streetcar Named Desire, 1948, also on Variety N.Y. Critics Poll 1948, for film version 1952; winner AMPAS's Oscar, Look award, Hollywood Fgn. Corrs. Golden Globe award, Emmy nominations for Baretta, 1977, Edge of Night, 1980, Fla. Carbonell (for Big Mama in Cat on a Hot Tin Roof) award, 1984. Mem. Acad. Motion Picture Arts and Scis., ANTA, Actors Equity Assn. (council 1953-59), Screen Actors Guild, AFTRA.

HUNTER, MARGARET KING, architect; b. Balt., May 13, 1919; d. Talmage Damron and Margaret Julie (Greenough) King; m. Edgar Hayes Hunter, May 8, 1943 (dec. Mar. 1995); children: Christopher King, Margaret Greenough. A.B., Wheaton Coll., 1941; postgrad., Smith Coll. Sch. Architecture, 1941-42, Harvard Grad. Sch. Design, 1942-45. Draftsman H.V. Lawrence; landscape architect H.V. Lawrence, Mass., 1940, Antonin Raymond; architect Antonin Raymond, N.Y.C., 1942-43; designer Raymond Loewy, N.Y.C., 1943; partner E.H. & M.K. Hunter (architects-planners), Hanover, N.H., 1945-66, Raleigh, N.C., 1969—; owner Heritage Antiques, Raleigh, 1971—; writer Pencil Points, 1942-45; traveling exhibit of work, 1963-66; design instr. N.C. State U., 1968; lectr., writer architecture, conservation, 1945—. Author: Your Own Kitchen and Garden Survival Book, 1978, The Indoor Garden: Design, Construction, and Furnishing, 1978; Important works include Laconia (N.H.) State Sch. Dormitories, 1955, N.H. Toll Rd. Structures, 1955, Children's Study Home, N.H. State Hosp., 1954, apts. and classroom bldg., Dartmouth, 1960, House for Life mag., 1956, Colby Jr. Coll. Art Center and Sci. Bldg., New London, N.H., 1962; classroom bldg. Dormitories Bridgton Acad, Maine, 1964, Loon Mountain Ski Area, Lincoln, N.H., 1966; dormitory, Conn. Coll., New London, 1965, twenty year campus plan, N.C. Central U., Durham, 1971, Student Internat. Meditation Soc. Acad., Santa Barbara, Calif., Clearwater Office Park, 1972, N.C. Central U. Law Sch., 1974, Hunter's Creek Townhouses, 1983. Chmn. Dance Com., Hanover, 1964-66; v.p. Culture Arts for Students, Raleigh, 1970; N.H. del. 1st Internat. Conf. Women Engrs. and Scientists, 1964; mem. edn. com. N.C. Land Use Congress, 1971, chmn. soils com., 1974, dir., 1976-78. Recipient Progressive Architecture Mag. award, 1946, 47; award N.H. State Office Bldg. Competition, 1950. Mem. AIA (chmn. pub. relations N.H. chpt. 1953-54), Soc. Women Engrs., Soil Conservation Soc., Constrn. Specifications Inst. Presbyterian. Club: Women's (Raleigh). Home: 3808 Tall Tree Pl Raleigh NC 27612 Office: PO Box 30632 Raleigh NC 27622-0632

HUNTER, MARIE HOPE, library media generalist; b. Troy, N.Y., Nov. 21, 1950; d. Roger Walter Joseph and Cecilia Yvonne (Daudelin) Miller; m. Robert Hutchinson Hunter, June 3, 1972 (div. Sept. 1978); 1 child, Teal Miller. BA, Johnson (Vt.) State Coll., 1972; MS in Edn., Ind. U., 1978. Elem. tchr. Lo Nisky Elem. Sch., U.S. V.I., 1972-74; libr. Lockhart Elem. Sch., U.S. V.I., 1974-77; evening libr. Johnson State Coll., 1978-79; libr. Ticonderoga (N.Y.) Mid. Sch., 1980-85; libr. media generalist Richmond Mid. Sch., Hanover, N.H., 1985—; Author: (student workbooks) The Topic Paper Workbook: A Guided Process, 1993, The Thesis Paper Workbook: A Guided Process, 1994. Trustee Lebanon (N.H.) Pub. Libr. Named Tchr. of Yr., Richmond Mid. Sch./U. Vt., 1992. Mem. Vt. Ednl. Media Assn., N.H. Edn. Media Assn. Office: Richmond Mid Sch 39 Lebanon St Hanover NH 03755

HUNTER, ROBIN CATHLEEN, elementary education educator; b. Starke, Fla., Aug. 10, 1964; d. Charles S. and Carolyn J. (McLeod) Brewington; m. James Estee Hunter, Sept. 16, 1989; children: James Jacob, Zachary Ladd. BA with honors, U. Fla., 1988, MEd, 1989. Profl. teaching cert.; ESOL endorsement. Sec. John Wagner, Atty., High Springs, Fla., 1981-82; biol. lab. technician Insects Affecting Man and Animals Rsch. Lab.-USDA, Gainesville, Fla., 1982-89; tchr. 6th grade Bell (Fla.) Mid. Sch., 1992-94; tchr. 1st grade Bronson (Fla.) Elem. Sch., 1989-92, Bell Elem. Sch., 1994—; mem. sch. improvement team, 1995-96, chair, 1996—. Grad. scholar Santa Fe H.S., 1982. Baptist. Office: Bell Sch PO Box 639 Bell FL 32619

HUNTER, SARAH WALTON (SALLY HUNTER), elementary school educator; b. Houston, Dec. 9, 1957; d. Clifford James and Sarah Eugenia (Johnson) Richards; m. Michael David Hunter, June 27, 1981; children: David Hayes, Sarah Walton. BS in Edn., U. Tex., 1980; MEd in Ednl. Adminstrn., S.W. Tex. State U., 1983. Cert. tchr., Tex. 1st grade tchr. Askew Elem. Sch., Houston, 1980-81; kindergarten tchr. Hyde Park Bapt. Sch., Austin, 1981-82, tchr., social studies adviser, 1986-88; tchr., adminstrv. intern Pease Elem. Sch., Austin, 1982-86; 3d grade tchr. Highland Park Elem. Sch., Austin, 1988-95, grant writer, 1990—, social studies liaison, 1992—, 4th grade tchr., 1995—; mem. social studies rev. com. Tex. Edn. Agy., Austin, 1989-90; trainer, presenter Region XIII Edn. Svc. Ctr., Austin, 1985-91; curriculum developer, workshop presenter Murchison Chair of Free Enterprise, U. Tex., Austin, 1986-90; mem. state textbook com. social studies, 1996. Author: (children's book) Austin: A Workbook Tour of the Capital of Texas, 1986, (computer program) Hyde Park Tour, 1995; rschr., editor (computer program) On the Avenue: Archtl. Tour, 1992 (Jane Smoot award 1992). Trainer, project chair, ABC grants chair Jr. League of Austin, 1988—; mem. edn. com. Heritage Soc. Austin, 1981—; advocate, curriculum developer Hispanic Mother-Daugther Program, Austin, 1991-93. Recipient Profl. Best Tchr. Excellence award Learning '91 Mag., 1991. Mem. DAR, Nat. Coun. for the Social Studies, Assn. Tex. Profl. Educators, U. Tex. Alumni Assn. (bd. dirs. Travis County chpt., 1984-86), Laguna Gloria Mus. Art Guild, Zeta Tau Alpha (adv. bd. chair 1987-90, Honor Cup 1989). Office: Highland Park Elem Sch 4900 Fairview Dr Austin TX 78731-5422

HUNTER, SHARON JANET, secondary education educator; b. Akron, Ohio, May 17, 1952; d. Ross B. Emery and Jeanne (Anson) Hawkins; m. James R. Hunter, June 30, 1979; children: Erica, Stephanie. BS in Secondary Edn., Kent (Ohio) State U., 1975; MAT in French, Colgate U., 1983; postgrad., Empire State Coll., 1989. Cert. tchr. French, Spanish, Latin, N-12, Ohio, N.Y. Tchr. French and Spanish Tallmadge (Ohio) H.S., 1975-76, S.E. Local Sch., Ravenna, Ohio, 1977-79, VVS Middle/H.S., Vernon, N.Y., 1983-84, Clinton (N.Y.) Ctrl. Sch., 1981-83, 84—; mem., treas. policy bd. Center State Tchr. Ctr., New Hartford, N.Y.; N.Y. State fgn. lang. turnkey trainer Bur. Fgn. Langs., 1987-89. Mem. Clinton Tchrs. Assn. (pres. 1989-91, Svc. award 1990), N.Y. State Assn. Fgn. Lang. Tchrs., Fgn. Lang. Tchrs. Assn. Ctrl. N.Y., Alpha Delta Kappa. Home: PO Box 175 Deansboro NY 13328-0175 Office: Clinton Ctrl Sch Chenango Ave Clinton NY 13323

HUNTER, SUE PERSONS, former state official; b. Hico, Tex., Aug. 21, 1921; d. David Henry and Beulah (Boatwright) Persons m. Charles Force Hunter; children: Shelley Hunter Richardson, Kathy Hunter McCullough, Margaret Hunter Brown. BA, U. Tex., 1942. Air traffic controller CAA (now FAA), San Antonio and Houston, 1942-52; writer Bissonet Plaza News, 1969-72; coordinator Goals for La., 1971-74; adminstrv. dir. Jeff Publs. Inc., 1974; press sec. Jefferson Parish Dist. Atty., 1972-75, communications cons., 1975-78; adminstr. Child Support Enforcement Div., 1979-85; contbg. editor The Jeffersonian, 1975-76. Pres. United Ch. Women East Jefferson (La.), 1958-59, LWV Jefferson Parish, La., 1961-64, also bd. dirs., 1962-67, 93-96; mem. probation services com. Cmty. Svcs. Coun., Jefferson, 1966-73, v.p., 1970-72; mem. Library Devel. Com. La., 1967-71, Nat. Com. for Support of Pub. Schs., 1967-72; mem. Goals Found. Council Met. New Orleans, 1969-75, sec. 1970, 72; mem. Goals La. Task Force State and Local Govt., 1969-70; pres. MMM Investment Club, 1969-72; bd. dirs. New Orleans Area Health Planning Council, 1969-75, Friends of Westminster Tower, 1986, Coun. for Internat. Visitors, 1990—, pres. 1991-93, programmer, 1994—; bd. dirs. Jefferson Twenty Five, 1991—, v.p., 1995-96; mem. adv. coun. La. State Health Planning, 1971-76; title I adv. council La. State Dept. Edn., 1970-72; vice chmn. Jefferson Women's Polit. Caucus, 1977-78, chmn., 1979, treas., 1980; bd. dirs. New Orleans Area/Bayou-River Health Systems Agy., 1978-82, pres., 1980, 81; mem. Task force for La. Talent Bank of Women, 1980; exec. bd. La. Child Support Enforcement Assn., 1980-86, pres., 1982-84; bd. dirs., legis. chmn. Nat. Child Support Enforcement Assn., 1983-86; mem. Gov.'s Commn. on Child Support Enforcement, 1984-88; mem. La. Statewide Health Coordinating Coun., 1980-83, mgmt. com. edn. fund League of Women Voters La., 1988-89. Recipient Outstanding Citizens award Rotary Club, Metairie, La., 1962, River Ridge award, 1976. Mem. Am. Assn. Individual Investors (pres. New Orleans chpt. 1986-88), New Orleans Panhellenic (pres. 1956-57), Fgn. Rels. Assn. (bd. dirs. New Orleans chpt. 1992—, sec. 1996—), Les Pelicaneers (pres. 1988-90), Earn and Learn Investment Club (pres. 1992-94), Alpha Xi Delta. Presbyterian (elder). Home: 210 Stewart Ave New Orleans LA 70123-1457

HUNTER, TRUDY PEARL, surgical nurse; b. Beaver, Ky., Apr. 8, 1950; d. Charlie Hatler and Goldie Edith (Hall) Hamilton; m. James Norman Hunter; 1 child, James Randall. ADN, U. Ky., Prestonsburg, 1986. LPN 1979; RN, Ky.; cert. nurse oper. room Assn. Oper. Room Nurses; ACLS; CNOR, cert. in laser tng., arthroscopy, mgmt. and care of anesthetized patient, advance EKG interpretation. Scrub nurse Meth. Hosp. Ky., Pikeville, Ky., 1979-82; scrub nurse/circulator Pikeville Surg. Ctr., Pikeville, Ky., 1982-88; circulator/scrub nurse Meth. Hosp. Ky., Pikeville, Ky., 1988-94, oper. room charge nurse, 1995—. Home: 104 Lower Hollow Rd Betsy Layne KY 41605-7029 Office: Meth Hosp Ky 911 ByPass Rd Pikeville KY 41501

HUNTER-GAULT, CHARLAYNE, journalist; b. Due West, S.C., Feb. 27, 1942; d. Charles S.H. Jr. and Althea Hunter; m. Walter Storall (div.); 1 child, Susan; m. Ronald Gault, 1971; 1 child, Chuma. Attended, Wayne State U., Detroit; BA in Journalism, U. Ga., 1963. With The New Yorker, 1963-67; editor Trans-Action Mag., 1967; investigative reporter, anchorwoman local evening news WRC-TV; also with N.Y. Times; with MacNeil/Lehrer Report PBS, 1978—, became nat. correspondent, 1983, now chief nat. correspondent. Author: In My Place, 1992; contbr. various publs. Recipient NYT Publisher's award, 2 Emmys for national news and documentaries, the Nat. Urban Coalition for Dist. Urban Reporting, George Foster Peabody award for Excellence in broadcast Journalism. Office: Newshour w/Jim Lehrer 3620 S 27th St Arlington VA 22206*

HUNTLEY, DIANE E., dental hygiene educator; b. Concord, N.H., Oct. 1, 1946; d. George Williams and Esther A. (Gadwah) H. AS, Fones Sch. Dental Hygiene, Bridgeport, Conn., 1966; BA, U. Bridgeport, Conn., 1968; MA, SUNY, Buffalo, 1971; PhD, Kans. State U., 1985. Registered dental hygienist. Dental hygienist various gen. practice dentists Conn., Colo., 1966-76; clin. instr. Fones Sch. Dental Hygiene, 1971-74; asst. prof. U. Colo. Dental Sch., Denver, 1974-76; asst. prof. dental hygiene Wichita (Kans.) State U., 1976-82, assoc. prof., 1982—, vol. hygienist Good Samaritan Clinic, Wichita, 1989-90, 92—. Contbr. articles to profl. jours. Mem. dental adv. bd. United Meth. Urban Ministries, Wichita, 1990-92; mem. P.A.N.D.A. Coalition of Kans. Exec. Com., 1995—. Mem. AAUP (Wichita State U. chpt. sec.-treas. 1988-91), Am. Assn. Dental Schs., Wichita Dental Hygienists' Assn. (pres. 1982-83, treas. 1988-90, trustee 1990-91), Kans. Dental Hygienists' Assn. (del 1989-93), Am. Dental Hygienists' Assn. (editl. dir. 1983-85, historian 1993—), Phi Kappa Phi, Alpha Eta. Office: Wichita State U 1845 Fairmount St Wichita KS 67260-0144

HUNTLEY-WRIGHT, JOAN AUGUSTA (JOAN AUGUSTA HUNTLEY), musician; b. Tulsa, Aug. 17, 1934; d. John Augustus and Edna Ruby (Van Brunt) Murphy; m. Robert Walter Huntley, Sept. 6, 1955 (div. Feb. 14, 1981); children: Robert John, Gene Bush, Dawn Elise, Ben Patrick; m. Wilfred Cleveland Wright, Sept. 13, 1992. Student, New Eng. Conservatory, 1952-53, U. Tulsa, 1953-54, Boston U. & N.E. Conservatory, 1994-95, Roosevelt U., Chgo., 1970-72, Thronton C.C., 1970-72; B in Violin Performance, New Eng. Conservatory Music, 1981; M in Violin Performance, U. Mass., Lowell, 1990. Violinist Tulsa Philharm. Symphony, 1949-52, 53-54; first violinist Tassan Quartet, Chgo., 1962-64, Hucasa Trio, Chgo., 1964-72; concert mistress, leader of various orchestras and chamber ensembles, 1964—; artist in residence Thornton C.C., Harvey, Ill., 1968-72; first violinist Bowforte Ensemble, Boston, 1973-81; assoc. prof. Berklee Coll. of Music, Boston, 1985-91; designed, tchr. pre-sch. instrumental and ear tng. classes Raygor Day Sch., Matteson, Ill, 1963-65, Humpty-Dumpty and YMCA Nursery Schs., Beverly, Mass., 1976-78; organizer benefit concerts for tornado victims, Ill. Creator, performer radio program Music Personalities KAKC, 1953; mgr., music dir., founder LaFemme/LaFemme Women Composers Ensemble, 1990—; soloist Tulsa Philharm., 1952, Park Forest (Ill.) Symphony, 1958, 60, 62, Salem (Mass.) Philharm., 1981, 89. Mem. Ill. Constitutional Com.; active in Boy Scouts Am. and Girl Scouts; active in PTA. Recipient Profl. Devel. award Mass. Assn. Women in Edn., 1995. Mem. AAUW, North Shore Women in Bus., Boston Musician's Assn. Home: 116A Collins St Danvers MA 01923

HUNTOON, CAROLYN LEACH, physiologist; b. Leesville, La., Aug. 25, 1940; m. Harrison H. Huntoon; 1 child, Sally Ann. BS in Biology, Northwestern State Coll., Natchitoches, La., 1962; degree in med. technol., Ochsner Found. Hosp., New Orleans, 1962; MS in Physiology, Baylor U., 1966, PhD, 1968; D (hon.), Northwestern State U., 1994. Head endocrinology lab. NASA Johnson Space Ctr., Houston, 1968-74, head endocrine and biochemistry labs., 1974-76, spl. asst. to dir., 1976-77, chief space metabolism and biochemistry br., 1976-77, chief biomed. labs. br., 1977-84, assoc. dir., 1984-87, dir. space and life scis., 1987-94, dir., 1994—; mem. astronaut selection bd. NASA-Johnson Space Ctr., dep. chief for personnel devel. astronaut office. Contbr. articles to profl. jours. With USAF, 1985—. Recipient Arthus S. Fleming award, Career Achievement award Nat. Civil Svc. League, Paul Bert award, Hubertus Strughold award, Yuri Gagarin medal USSR Fedn. Cosmonautics, 1987, Presdl. Rank Meritorious Exec. award, 1991, Disting. Rank award, 1993; named Outstanding Alumna Northwestern State U., 1977, Outstanding Woman in Sci., Am. Women in Sci., Disting. profl. Woman of Yr., U. Tex. Health Sci. Ctr., 1985, Outstanding Scientist, State of Tex., 1991. Fellow Am. Astronautical Soc. (Lovelace award 1991, Space Flight award 1994), Aerospace Med. Assn. (Louis H. Bauer Founder's award); mem. AIAA, Assn. Bus. and Profl. Women, Am. Physiol. Soc., Endocrine Soc., Internat. Acad. Astronautics. Office: NASA Johnson Space Ctr # 1 2101 NASA Rd 1 Houston TX 77058-3607*

HUNTTING, CYNTHIA COX, artist; b. San Francisco, Sept. 2, 1936; d. E. Morris and Margaret (Storke) Cox; m. Edward Tyler Huntting Jr., Mar. 8, 1969 (div. 1974). BA, Smith Coll., 1958; San Francisco Art Inst., 1959. Artist Emporium White House, San Francisco, 1958-61; artist, staff Pace Program Stanford U., 1962-64; artist World Affairs Council No. Calif., San Francisco, 1964-67; artist pvt. practice San Francisco, 1968—; mem. Modern Art Council Bd. San Francisco Mus. Modern Art, 1970-78. Active Jr. League San Francisco, Inc. Republican. Episcopalian. Clubs: Town and Country, Metropolitan, Calif. Tennis. Home and Office: 2720 Lyon St San Francisco CA 94123-3815

HUOT, RACHEL IRENE, biomedical educator, research scientist; b. Manchester, N.H., Oct. 16, 1950; d. Omer Joseph and Irene Alice (Girard) H. BA in Biology cum laude, Rivier Coll., 1972; MS in Biology, Cath. U. Am., 1976, PhD in Biology, 1980. Sr. technician Microbiol. Assocs., Bethesda, Md., 1974-77; chemist Uniformed Svcs. Univ. of Health Scis., Bethesda, 1977-79; biologist Nat. Cancer Inst., Bethesda, 1979-82; postdoctoral fellow S.W. Found. for Biomed. Rsch., San Antonio, 1982-85, asst. scientist, 1985-87, staff scientist, 1987-88; instr. U. Tex. Health Sci. Ctr., San Antonio, 1988-89; asst. prof., dir. basic urologic rsch. La. State U., New Orleans, 1990-96; judge sr. div. Alamo Regional Sci. Fair, San Antonio, 1989-90. Contbr. articles to profl. jours. Vol. ARC; active Stephen Ministry. NSF grantee, 1972-74; recipient NIH Rsch. Svc. award, 1983-86, Searle Young Investigator award, 1994. Mem. AAAS, LWV, AAUW, AMA, Am. Soc. for Microbiology, Am. Assn. Cancer Rsch., Am. Soc. Cell Biology, Fedn. Am. Scientists, Sci. Club (pres. 1971-72), Soc. for In Vitro Biology, N.Y. Acad. Scis., St. Vincent De Paul Soc., Sierra Club, Fedn. Am. Soc. Experiment Biology, Sigma Xi, Iota Sigma Pi, Delta Epsilon Sigma. Democrat. Roman Catholic. Home: 701 Merrick St Shreveport LA 71104

HUPALO, MEREDITH TOPLIFF, artist, illustrator; b. Tarpon Springs, Fla., Apr. 28, 1917; d. Walter and Maurine (Martin) Topliff; cert. in design Pratt Inst., 1938; m. Nicholas Hupalo, July 13, 1940 (dec. Sept. 1977); children: Walter Topliff, John Nicholas. One-woman shows: Tarpon Springs Public Libr., 1945, Valley Stream (N.Y.) Mus., 1962, Contemporary Arts, Inc., N.Y.C., 1966, Jet Clubs Internat., N.Y.C., Henry Waldinger Libr., Valley Stream, N.Y., 1977, East River Savs. Bank, Valley Stream, 1978; two-person show: Art League of Daytona Beach, 1986; represented in permanent collection Valley Stream Pub. Libr., Tarpon Springs (Fla.) Pub. Libr., Eastern Airlines Exec. Offices, N.Y.C.; tchr. printmaking Nassau County (N.Y.) Home Extension Svc.; art adviser Valley Stream Mus., 1962-64; illustrator Eastern Airlines, 1964-68; artist Shell Oil Co., 1968-70; designer Continental Can Co., N.Y.C., 1970-73; art tchr. Astor (Fla.) Community Ctr., 1980-82. Active Mt. Dora Ctr. for the Arts of Lake County, 1991. Recipient spl. award oil painting 34th Nat. Spring Exhbn. Nat. Art League L.I., 1964, gold medal in oil painting 35th Membership Show, 1965; 1st pl. fine art Fla. Silver Springs Arts & Crafts Festival, 1980; 1st place award Umatilla Fall Festival (Fla.), 1983 merit award, 1985; merit award Tampa Realistic Artists, 1984; Best in Show award Nat. League Am. Pen Women, 1984; 1st pl. Fla. Extension Homemakers Cultural Arts; Award of Distinction, Pioneer Art Settlement, 1987, Honorable Mention Pioneer Art Settlement, 1991, 1st Pl. award Ann. Lake County Juried Art Show Mt. Dora Ctr. for Arts, 1992, Best in Show and 1st in Graphics awards Umatilla Fall Festival, 1993. Mem. Fla. Watercolor Soc. (assoc., participating artist II), Nat. Art League L.I. (treas. 1959-60), Art League of Daytona Beach (Lillian Gittner Meml. award 1988, 64th membership show Grumbacher gold award 1996), Nat. League Am. Pen Women (Fla. br. 1987, v.p. 1991, Grumacher silver medal 1995), Mus. Arts and Scis., DeLand Mus., Astor Area C. of C. (dir. 1981-82). Methodist. Works include Paintings With Markers, 1972. Home: 55809 Dale Cir Astor FL 32102-2628

HURD, GALE ANNE, film producer; b. L.A., Oct. 25, 1955; d. Frank E. and Lolita (Espiau) H. Degree in econs. and communications, Stanford U., 1977. Dir. mktg. and publicity, co-producer New World Pictures, L.A., 1977-82; pres., producer Pacific Western Prodns., L.A., 1982—. Producer: (films) The Terminator, 1984 (Grand Prix Avoiriaz Film Festival award), Aliens 1986 (nominated for 7 Acad. awards, recipient Best Sound Effects Editing award, Best Visual Effects award Acad. Picture Arts & Scis.), Alien Nation (Saturn award for best sci. fiction film), The Abyss, 1989 (nominated for 4 Acad. awards, Best Visual Effects award), The Waterdance, 1991 (2 IFP Spirit awards, 2 Sundance Film Festival awards), Cast a Deadly Spell, 1991 (Emmy award), Raising Cain, 1992, No Escape, 1994, Safe Passage (Beatrice Wood award for Creative Achievement), 1994, The Ghost and the Darkness, 1996, The Relic, 1996, Going West in America, 1996; exec. producer: (films) Tremors, 1990, Downtown, 1990, Terminator 2, 1991 (winner 3 Acad. awards), Witch Hunt, 1994, Sugartime, 1995; creative cons. (TV program) Alien Nation, 1989-90. Juror Focus Student Film Awards, 1989, 90, Nicholl Fellowship Acad. Motion Picture Arts & Scis., 1989—; mem. Show Coalition, 1988—; mem. Hollywood (Calif.) Women's Polit. Com., 1987—; mem. U.S. Film Festival Juror; bd. dirs. IFP/West, Artists Rights Found.; trustee Am. Film Inst.; bd. dirs. L.A. Internat. Film Festival, Coral Reef Rsch. Found., Ams. for a Safe Future; mentor Peter Stark Motion Picture Producing Program, Sch. of Cinema-TV, U. of So. Calif., Women in Film Mentor Program. Recipient Spl. Merit award Nat. Assn. Theater Owners, 1986, Stanford-La Entrepreneur of Yr. award Bus. Sch. Alumni L.A., 1990, Fla. Film Festival award, 1994. Mem. AMPAS (producer's br. exec. com. 1990—), Am. Film Inst. (trustee 1989—), Americans for a Safe Future (mem. bd dirs. 1993—), Women in Film (bd. dirs. 1989-90), Feminist Majority, Phi Beta Kappa. Office: Pacific Western Prodns 270 N Canon Dr # 1195 Beverly Hills CA 90210-5323

HURD, SUZANNE SHELDON, federal agency health science director; b. Elmira, N.Y., Dec. 17, 1939; d. Victor Sheldon H. BS, Bates Coll., 1961; MS, U. Wash., 1963, PhD, 1967. Post-doctoral fellow U. Calif., Berkeley, 1967-69; grants assoc. NIH, Bethesda, Md., 1969-70; health sci. adminstr. Nat. Heart, Lung and Blood Inst., Bethesda, 1970-78, dep. dir. div. lung diseases, 1979-84; dir. div. lung diseases Nat. Heart, Lung and Blood Inst., Bethesda, 1984—; acting dir. Nat. Inst. Nursing Rsch., Bethesda, 1994-95. Mem. Am. Thoracic Soc. Office: NIH/NHLBI/DLD/OD Two Rockledge Ctr Ste 10018 6701 Rockledge Dr MSC 7952 Bethesda MD 20892-7952

HURET, MARILYNN JOYCE, editor, puzzle constructor; b. N.Y.C., Dec. 5; d. Hyman and Clara (Weinberg) Moskowitz; m. Barry Saul Huret, Feb. 11, 1961; children: Abbey Beth, Eric Alan. BA in Math., Adelphi U., 1961. Tchr. math. Dist. 281, Robbinsdale, Minn., 1974-77; puzzle constructor Marvel Comics, N.Y.C., 1982-88, Great Puzzle Catalog, N.Y.C., 1982-83; adminstr. David Libr. of Am. Revolution, Washington Crossing, Pa., 1988-95; editor, online sysop Crossword Am. LYRIQ Internat., 1995—; mem. Bucks County Courier Times Readers Adv. Group, 1995—. puzzle constructor Soft Disk Electronic Pub.; writer biog. articles for crossword mag.; contbr. Crosswúrd Mag., 1995—; editor: Crossword Am. puzzle mag. online; crossword puzzle constructor N.Y. Times. Coop. weather observer Sta. WOR, N.Y.C., 1965-71; severe storm weather spotter NOAA, 1972-77, Mpls., 1977-79, Racine, Wis., 1980—, Phila.; commr. pub. safety City of Golden Valley, Minn., 1972-77; judge Delaware Valley Sci. Fairs, Phila., 1984—; dep. coord. emergency mgmt. Lower Makefield Twp., Pa., 1989—; bd. dirs. Delaware Valley Philharmonic Orch., mem. season planning com. Recipient Svc. Appreciation award Golden Valley City Coun., 1977. Mem. LWV, AAUW (editor Makefield Area Connections 1993—, Named Gift award 1994, Outstanding Woman of Yr. Makefield area 1995), Spl. Libr. Assn. (assoc.), Am. Cryptogram Assn., Nat. Puzzlers League, Bucks County Librs. Assn., Lower Bucks Computer Users Group, Adelphi U. Alumni Assn., Toastmasters. Home: 484 Kings Rd Yardley PA 19067-4652 Office: LYRIQ Internat 1701 Highland Ave Cheshire CT 06410

HURLBURT, ANNE WEDEWER, municipal official; b. Dubuque, Iowa, June 17, 1956; d. Walter Francis and Mildred Theresa (Meyer) Wedewer; m. Steve Arthur Hurlburt, Aug. 20, 1977. BS in Urban Planning, Iowa State U., 1978. Planner City of Cottage Grove (Minn.), 1979-82, dir. planning, 1982-88; mgr. comprehensive planning and local assistance Met. Coun. of the Twin Cities, St. Paul, Minn., 1988-93; cmty. devel. dir. City of Plymouth (Minn.), 1993—; bd. dirs. Sensible Land Use Coalition, Mpls., 1989—, v.p., 1995-96. Treas. Cottage Grove Jaycees, 1986, 87. Mem. Am. Inst. Cert. Planners, Am. Planning Assn. Office: City of Plymouth 3400 Plymouth Blvd Plymouth MN 55447-1448

HURLEY, ANNE IRÈNE, medical illustrator; b. Red Bank, N.J., Nov. 20, 1958; d. John Robert and Jo Adriènne (Mellina) H.; m. Edward McCabe, Sept. 10, 1989; 1 child, Lucas Hurley McCabe. BA in Biol. Scis., Rutgers U., 1981; MA in Med. Illustration, U. Tex., Dallas, 1983. Biomed. illustrator, sculptor Rutgers U., New Brunswick, N.J., 1978-81; pvt. practice Dallas, 1982-87, Plainfield, Lakewood, N.J., 1988—, Manalapan, N.J., 1988—. Illustrator: American Family Physician, 1982-83, A Woman's Decision, 1984, TMJ Internal Derangement and Arthrosis, 1985, Denny McKeown's Complete Guide to Midwest Gardening, 1985, Gardening in the South With Don Hastings, 1986-87, Orthopaedic Grand Rounds, 1987-88, A Teen Survival Guide, 1988, YMCA Healthy Back Book, 1994; author, illustrator: The Development and Production of a Sculptural Restoration of Edaphosaurus Boanerges: A Documentation, 1983; represented in permanent exhibit So. Meth. U. Recipient cert. of merit Soc. of Illustrators, 1986, award of excellence Am. Corp. Identity/10, 1994. Mem. Assn. Med. Illustrators (hon. mention 1982, 1st place award in exhbn. 1983, bd. cert. 1994, best of show 1994), Graphic Artists Guild. Libertarian. Studio: 16 Eliot Rd Manalapan NJ 07726

HURLEY, CHERYL JOYCE, book publishing executive; b. Pitts., Oct. 30, 1947; d. John and Violet Dernorsek; m. Kevin Hurley, July 27, 1974. Lang. and lit. cert., Université de Lyon, France, 1968; AB, Ohio U., 1969; MA, U. Mich., 1971. Research assoc. MLA, N.Y.C., 1972-74, dir. spl. programs, 1974-79; pub. The Library of America, N.Y.C., 1979—, pres., 1988—; cons. in field. Contbr. articles to profl. jours. Trustee French Inst./Alliance Francaise, 1992—, v.p., exec. com., 1994—; mem. libr. com. Hort. Alliance of Hamptons, 1989—; mem. benefit com. Hampton Libr., 1988—. Rackham fellow, 1969-70. Mem. Grolier Club, Century Assn., Am. Antiquarian Soc., Bridgehampton Club, Phi Beta Kappa. Home: 1172 Park Ave New York NY 10128 Office: Libr of Am 14 E 60th St New York NY 10022-1006

HURLEY, ELIZABETH ANN, health care administration, consultant; b. Norristown, Pa., Oct. 28, 1959; d. Kenneth C. and Ruth M. (Herr) Wilson; m. Jeffrey C. Bartlett, Mar. 22, 1986 (div. June 1989); 1 child, Meghan; m. Robert E. Hurley, Oct. 14, 1995. BS, Elizabethtown Coll., 1982; postgrad., Temple U., 1994, Immaculata Coll., 1995—. Adminstr. network mktg. and sales Contel, Inc., Hershey, Pa., 1982-87; v.p. The Bartlett Group, Harrisburg, Pa., 1987-88; dir. mktg. Milton S. Hershey Med. Ctr., Hershey, 1988-91; v.p. Alliance Comm., Harrisburg, 1991-92; dir. ob-gyn. adminstrn. Milton S. Hershey Med. Ctr., Hershey, 1992-95; dir. mktg. Tressler Lutman Svcs., Mechanicsburg, Pa., 1995—; cons. Chambersburg (Pa.) Hosp., 1991-92, Dbi Helathcare, Harrisburg, 1991-92, Nat. Minority Health Assn., Washington, 1991-92, Bonsall & Manfred, P.C., Carlisle, Pa., 1991—, IES, Inc., Harrisburg, 1995-96. Writer, designer newsletter Pa. State's Healthshare, 1989 (award Internat. Assn. Bus. Communicators 1989). Mem. fundraising com. children's Miracle Network, Hershey, 1990-95; mem. Pa. Gov.'s Coun. for Organ and Tissue Awareness, Harrisburg, 1990-91. Recipient outstanding cmty. edn. award Delaware Valley Transplant Program, 1991. Mem. Acad. Practice Assn. (spkr. 1992—, spkr.'s award 1994), Med. Group Mgmt. Assn. Republican. Home: 2456 Mercedes Ct Harrisburg PA 17112 Office: 500 Century Dr Mechanicsburg PA 17055

HURLEY, JANET LEE, university health facility administrator; b. Schenectady, N.Y., Sept. 8, 1948; d. Richard Kramer Fairley and Jean Bancroft Ashley; m. Douglas Edward Hurley, June 20, 1970; children: Scott Ashley, Jeffrey Douglas. BS, Miami U., Oxford, Ohio, 1970; MS, Kansas State U., 1980; PhD, U. Ky., 1993. Tchr. Lafayette Elem. Sch., Norfolk, Va., 1970-72, Roberts Pk. Elem. Sch., Norfolk, 1972-74, Westford (Vt.) Village Sch., 1974-76; coord. Univ. of Mid-Am. Kansas State U., Manhattan, 1978-80, coord. spl. projects, 1980-81, specialist continuing edn., 1981-85; assoc. dean continuing edn. U. Ky., Lexington, 1985-93, adminstr. univ. health svc., 1993—. Bd. dirs. YWCA, Lexington, 1995—, Coll. of the Finger Lakes, Corning, N.Y., 1991—, Tates Creek Band Boosters, Lexington, 1994, 95, 96. Mem. Am. Coll. Health Assn., Nat. Univ. Continuing Edn. Assn. (Program of Excellence award 1987, 92, Robertson Leadership award 1988, Advancing the Profession award 1992). Office: U Ky Univ Health Svc B-163 Ky Clinic Lexington KY 40536

HURLEY, STELLA HARLAN, artist, educator; b. West Point, Miss., July 20, 1924; d. Allen Dorset and Isabel Rosalie (Knaffl) Harlan; m. Rupert Bogle Hurley, June 16, 1951; children: Isabel Knaffl, Rupert Bogle, Dorset Harlan, William Dewey, Warner Hutson. BA, U. Ga., 1947; MA, U. N.C., 1949. Cert. tchr., Va. Stenographer Hartford A&I, Atlanta, 1942-44, Travellers Ins. Co., Atlanta, 1944-45; prof. Spanish Averett Coll., Danville, Va., 1949-51; assoc. prof. East Tenn. State U., Johnson City, Tenn., 1954-55; tchr. Williamsburg (Va.)-James City County Pub. Schs., 1969-80. Pres. Skipwith Garden Club, Williamsburg, 1963-64; v.p. Woman's Club of Williamsburg, 1967-68; advocate, founding pres. Williamsburg Area Alliance for Mentally Ill, 1987-90, 95—. Recipient Amos R.D. Rollins award Peninsula Mental Health Assn., 1989, Williamsburg Area Alliance for Mentally Ill., 1991. Mem. DAR (chmn. com. 1976-80), Nat. Mus. Women in Arts, Muscarelle Mus., Phi Beta Kappa, Phi Kappa Phi. Republican. Episcopalian. Home: 232 Tyler Brooks Dr Williamsburg VA 23185

HURST, CHRISTINA MARIE, respiratory therapist; b. San Diego, Jan. 29, 1955; d. Harvey Joseph Breighner and Doris Romaine March-Breighner; children: Heather Erin, Ian Richard. AAS, Del. Tech. Coll., 1989. Cert. and registered respiratory therapist Perinatal and Pediatric Registry. Respiratory therapist Med. Ctr. Del., Christiana, 1989—, Perinatal Pediat. Registry, Lenexa, Kans., 1995—; mem. Nat. Bd. Respiratory Care; instr. basic cardiopulmonary resuscitation, Wilmington, Del., 1989-90; spkr. Senate Labor Rels. Com., 1987. Vol. preschool asthma program Am. Lung Assn. Del., Wilmington, 1989, Del. Epilepsy Found. Wilmington, 1988-90; exec. coun. State Adv. Coun. for Svcs. to Handicapped, Dover, Del., 1989-90; charter mem. parent support group Children with Epilepsy, Wilmington, 1988-90. Mem. Am. Assn. for Respiratory Care, Epilepsy Found. Am., Phi Theta Kappa. Home: 518 Pheasant Run Bear DE 19701-2720 Office: Med Ctr Del Stanton Ogletown Rd Newark DE 19713

HURST, DEBORAH ANN STEFFENS, secondary education educator; b. Niles, Mich., Feb. 7, 1951; d. Homer Hubert Steffens and Margaret Eilene (Goldie) Osborne; m. Raymond Samuel Hurst Jr., Sept. 5, 1970; children: John Macon, Laura Ruth. BS in Social Studies Edn., Fla. State U., Tallahassee, 1973. Crt. tchr. secondary and mid. sch. social studies, Fla. Tchr. social studies Greenville (Fla.) H.S., 1978-80, Madison County H.S., Madison, Fla., 1980-83; tchr. Am. history Howard Mid. Sch., Monticello, Fla., 1983—. Vol. tour guide Knott House Mus., Tallahassee, 1992—. Mem. Nat. Coun. for Social Studies, Fla. Coun. for Social Studies (Jefferson County Social Studies Tchr. of Yr. 1993), Optimist Club of Tallahassee (comm. chair 1989—). Democrat. Presbyterian. Home: 2625 Stonegate Rd Tallahassee FL 32308-4021 Office: Howard Mid Sch 1145 2nd St Monticello FL 32344-2807

HURST, MARY JANE, English language educator; b. Hamilton, Ohio, Sept. 21, 1952; d. Nimrod and Leckie (Brumback) Gaines; m. Daniel L. Hurst, June 5, 1974; 1 child, Katherine Jane. BA summa cum laude, Miami U., 1974; MA, U. Md., 1980, PhD, 1986. Tchr. Groveport (Ohio) High Sch., 1974-77; teaching asst. U. Md., College Park, 1978-79, master tchr., 1979-82; asst. prof. Tex. Tech U., Lubbock, 1986-92, assoc. prof., 1992—; vis. scholar Stanford U., summer 1987; steering com. Nat. Cowboy Symposium, Lubbock, 1988-89. Author: The Voice of the Child in American Literature, 1990; tech. editor: HTLV-I and the Nervous System, 1989; mem. editl. bd. The Southwest Jour. of Linguistics, 1995—; contbr. articles to profl. jours. Mem. Lubbock Cultural Affairs Coun., 1986-92, All Saints Episcopal Sch. Parent's Orgn., Lubbock, 1986—, Lubbock Symphony Guild, 1992—; vol. Meals on Wheel, Lubbock, 1986—, Habitat for Humanity, Lubbock, 1986—. Mem. AAUW (alt. fellowships panel in linguistics 1988-90), AAUP (regional v.p. 1990-94), MLA, Linguistic Soc. Am., Am. Classical League, Linguistic Assn. S.W. (pres. 1996—), Coll. Tchrs. English Tex., South Ctrl. Modern Lang. Assn., Phi Beta Kappa, Phi Kappa Phi, Sigma Tau Delta, Alpha Lambda Delta. Office: Tex Tech U Dept English Lubbock TX 79409

HURST, SHARLEENE PAGE, state legislator; b. Northampton, Mass., Apr. 30, 1959; d. Benjamin William and Shirley Ann (Weiner) Dempsey; m. Lee E. Hurst III, Apr. 27, 1986. File processor Liberty Mus. Inst. Co., 1985-89, rater I, 1989-90, reconciliation asst. grad. 5, 1990-91; mem. N.H. Ho. of Reps., 1990—, mem. standing com. corrections and criminal justice, 1993—, constn. and statutory rev. com., 1991-94, mem. state and fed. rels. com., 1994—, clk., 1995—, mem. gender equity in sports study com., 1991-93, chmn. gender equity in sports study com., 1993, legis. task force on AIDS, 1993—; mem. state septic adv. com., 1994—; conf. attendee Maine Rep. State Com. Sch. of Campaign Mgmt., 1984, Young Rep. Nat. Leadership Conf., Washington, 1985, Norman Blackwell's Sch. Youth Campaign Mgmt., Nashua, N.H., 1986, N.H. Rep. State Com. Sch. of Campaign Mgmt., 1986, N.H. Sch. Bd. Assn., 1989, State Conv., 1989, New Eng. Rep. Day in Washington, 1989, N.H. State Conf. on Kids-at-Risk, 1990, Nat. Common Cause Conf. on State Leadership, Washington, 1991, Conf. on Substance Abuse in the Criminal System, Portsmouth, 1993. Mem. Hampton Sch. Bd., 1989-92, bd. rep. for transp. com., 1991-92, prin. search com., 1991, rep. to Hampton Mcpl. budget com., 1989, sch. dist. clk., 1987-89; mem. Hampton Mcpl. Budget Com., 1986-90, clk., 1995-96; mem. adv. bd. Rockland (Maine) Libr., 1982-84; co-chmn. Mayor's Adv. Com. on Alternative Energy, Northampton, 1980-81; mem. Hampshire County Energy Policy Congress, 1980; pres. Hampshire County (Mass.) Young Dems., 1980; assoc. mem. Northampton Energy Resource Commn., 1980-81; chmn. Maine Young Rep. State Conv., 1984; sec. Hampshire County Dem. Com., 1978-82, Rockland Rep. City Com., 1984, New Eng. Coun. Young Reps., 1985-87, New Eng. Young Rep. Conv., 1985; del. to Mass. Dem. State Conv., 1985; del. to Mass. Dem. State Conv., 1979, 81, Maine Rep. State Conv., 1984, Young Rep. Nat. Conv., N.H., 1985, N.H. State Conv., 1986, 90, 92; del-at-large Rep. Nat. Conv., 1984; Rep. nominee for Rockingham County Commr., 1984; active Maine Young Rep. State Fedn., 1982-84, Young Rep. Nat. Platform Com., 1984, N.H. Rep. Trust, 1989, Hampton Rep. Town Com., 1986—, New Eng. Rep. Coun., 1991—. Mem. Citizens for Term Limits, N.H. Tourism Caucus, Order of Women Legislators. Republican. Methodist. Home: PO Box 1572 38 Mill Rd Hampton NH 03842-2237 Office: NH Ho of Reps State House Concord NH 03301

HURTADO, TRACY ELLEN, accountant; b. Roseville, Calif., Aug. 4, 1968; d. Corydon Dicks and Nancy (Trott) H. BS in Acctg. cum laude, Calif. State U., Sacramento, 1991. CPA, Nev. Audit mgr. Deloitte & Touche LLP, Reno, Nev., 1991—. Mem. Nev. Soc. CPAs, Inst. Mgmt. Accts. (sec. 1994-96), Delta Sigma Pi (dist. dir. U. Nev.-Reno chpt. 1991-93). Office: Deloitte & Touche LLP 50 W Liberty St Ste 900 Reno NV 89501-1949

HURWITZ, ELLEN STISKIN, college president, historian; b. Stamford, Conn., May 4, 1942; d. D.O. Bernard and Marjorie (Kanter) Stiskin; children: Jason, Sarah. BA, Smith Coll., 1964; MA, Columbia U., 1965, PhD, 1972. Vis. asst. prof. Wesleyan U., Middletown, Conn., 1972-73; asst. prof. Lafayette Coll., Easton, Pa., 1974-80, assoc. prof., assoc. dean, 1980-88; dean acad. affairs Ill. Wesleyan U., Bloomington, 1988-89, provost, dean of faculty, 1989-92; pres. Albright Coll., Reading, Pa., 1992—; cons. Nat. Faculty Arts and Scis., Inst. for Ednl. Mgmt., Harvard U., 1990. Author: Andrej Bogoljubskij: Man and Myth, 1972. NEH fellow, 1973-74. Mem. AAAS, Am. Assn. Higher Edn., Phi Beta Kappa. Office: Albright Coll PO Box 15234 Reading PA 19612-5234

HURWITZ, JOHANNA (FRANK), author, librarian; b. N.Y.C., Oct. 9, 1937; d. Nelson and Tillie (Miller) Frank; m. Uri Hurwitz, Feb. 19, 1962; children: Nomi, Beni. BA, Queens Coll., 1958; MLS, Columbia U., 1959. Libr. children's sect. N.Y. Pub. Libr., 1959-64; lectr. in children's lit. Queen's Coll., N.Y.C., 1965-69; libr. Calhoun Sch., N.Y.C., 1968-75, New Hyde Park (N.Y.) Sch. Dist., 1975-77; libr. children's sect. Great Neck (N.Y.) Pub. Libr., 1978-92. Author: Busybody Nora, 1976, Nora and Mrs. Mind-Your-Own-Business, 1977, The Law of Gravity, 1978, Much Ado About Aldo, 1978, Aldo Applesauce, 1979, New Neighbours for Nora, 1979, Once I Was a Plum Tree, 1980, Superduper Teddy, 1980, Aldo Ice Cream, 1981, Baseball Fever, 1981, The Rabbi's Girls, 1982, Tough-Luck Karen, 1982, Rip-Roaring Russell, 1983, DeDe Takes Charge!, 1984, The Hot and Cold Summer, 1984, The Adventures of Ali Baba Bernstein, 1985, Russell Rides Again, 1985, Hurricane Elaine, 1986, Yellow Blue Jay, 1986, Class Clown, 1987, Russell Sprouts, 1987, The Cold and Hot Winter, 1988, Teacher's Pet, 1988, Anne Frank: Life in Hiding, 1988, Hurray for Ali Baba Bernstein, 1989, Russell and Elisa, 1989, Astrid Lindgren: Storyteller to the World, 1989, Class President, 1990, Aldo Peanut Butter, 1990, School's Out, 1991, E Is for Elisa, 1991, Roz and Ozzie, 1992, Ali Baba Bernstein, Lost and Found, 1992, The Up and Down Spring, 1993, Make Room for Elisa, 1993, Leonard Bernstein: A Passion for Music, 1993, New Shoes for Silvia, 1993, A Word to the Wise, 1994, School Spirit, 1994, A Llama in the Family, 1994, Ozzie on His Own, 1995, Birthday Surprises, 1995, Elisa in the Middle, 1995. Even Stephen, Down and Up Fall, 1996—. Recipient Bluebonnet award Tex. Libr. Assn., 1987, Sunshine State award Fla. Libr. Assn., 1990, Miss. Children's Book award Miss. Libr. Assn., 1990, S.C. Children's Book award, 1990, Garden State award N.J. Sch. Libr. Assn., 1991, 94, Weekly Reader Book Club award, 1993. Mem. PEN, Author's Guild, Soc. Children's Book Writers, Amnesty Internat. Address: 10 Spruce Pl Great Neck NY 11021-1904

HUSSELMAN, GRACE, innkeeper, educator; b. Paterson, N.J., July 24, 1923; d. Edward and Lydia (Kliphouse) Van Allen; B.A., William Paterson Coll.; m. Samuel Husselman, June 3, 1944; children—Samuel Glenn, Howard Lloyd. With personnel office Wright Aero. Corp., Fairlawn, Pub. 1942-45; library asst. Wyckoff (N.J.) Pub. Library, 1964-66; library dir. Allendale (N.J.) Pub. Library, 1967-81; elem. sch. tchr., assoc. ednl. media specialist, 1981-84; owner Ye Olde Buckmaster Inn, 1984—. Reading Merit Badge counselor Boy Scouts Am.; pioneer guide Pioneer Girls, nat. youth v.p., sec. friendship circle; sec. bookstore com. Christian Growth Ministries; sec. Ladies Aid Soc., Shrewsbury Community Ch.; bd. deacons Shrewsbury Community Ch.; bd. dirs. Shrewsbury Library, Vt. Mem. N.J., Bergen-Passaic library assns., Hist. Soc. of Shrewsbury (pres./sec.), Kappa Delta Pi. Club: Captains and Mates Yacht. Home: Lincoln Hill Rd Shrewsbury VT 05738

HUSSELS MAUMENEE, IRENE E., ophthalmology educator; b. Bad Pyrmont, Germany, Apr. 30, 1940. MD, U. Gottingen, 1964. Cert. Am. Bd. Ophthalmology, Am. Bd. Med. Genetics. Rsch. asst. U. Hawaii, 1968; vis. geneticist Population Genetics Lab., 1968-69; fellow dept. medicine Johns Hopkins U., 1969-71; ophthalmology preceptorship Wilmer Inst. Johns Hopkins Hosp., 1969-71, from asst. prof. to assoc. prof. Wilmer Ophthalmology Inst., 1972-87; prof. ophthalmology and pediatrics Wilmer Ophthalmology Inst., 1987—; dir. Johns Hopkins Ctr. Hereditary Eye Disease, Wilmer Inst., 1979—; cons. John F. Kennedy Inst. Visually & Mentally Handicapped Children, 1974—; dir. Low Vision Clinic, Wilmer Inst., 1977-88; vis. prof. French Ophthalmology Soc., Paris & French Acad. Medicine, 1988; advisor Nat. Eye Inst. Task Forces, 1976, 81. Mem. AMA, Am. Soc. Human Genetics, Am. Acad. Ophthalmology, Assn. Rsch. Vision & Ophthalmology, Internat. Soc. Genetic Eye Disease, Am. Ophthalmology Soc., Pan Am. Assn. Ophthalmology. Office: Johns Hopkins Hosp Ctr Hereditary Eye Diseases 600 N Wolfe St # 517 Baltimore MD 21205-2110

HUSTON, ANJELICA, actress; b. L.A., July 8, 1951; d. John and Enrica Huston; m. Robert Graham, 1992. Student, Loft Studio. Actress appearing in Hamlet, Roundhouse Theatre, London, Tamara, Il Vittorale Theatre, L.A.; appeared in films including A Walk with Love and Death, 1969, Hamlet, 1969, Sinful Davey, 1969, Swashbuckler, 1976, The Last Tycoon, 1976, The Postman Always Rings Twice, 1981, This is Spinal Tap, 1984, The Ice Pirates, 1984, Prizzi's Honor, 1985 (Academy award for best supporting actress 1985, N.Y.Film Critics award 1985, L.A. Film Critics award 1985), Captain Eo, 1986, Gardens of Stone, 1987, The Dead, 1987 (Best Actress award Ind. Filmakers 1987), Mr. North, 1988, A Handfull of Dust, 1988, Witches, 1989, Crimes and Misdemeanors, 1989, Enemies, A Love Story, 1989 (Acad. award nomination 1990), The Grifters, 1990 (Acad. award nomination 1991), The Addams Family, 1991, The Player, 1992, Addams Family Values, 1993, Manhattan Murder Mystery, 1993, The Crossing Guard, 1995, The Perez Family, 1995; TV films include the Cowboy and the Ballerina, 1984, Faerie Tale Theatre, A Rose for Miss Emily, Lonesome Dove, 1989, Family Pictures, 1993, And The Band Played On, 1993, Buffalo Girls, 1995. Office: Internat Creative Mgmt 8942 Wilshire Blvd Beverly Hills CA 90211-1934*

HUSTON, BEATRICE LOUISE, banker; b. Grantsburg, Wis., Dec. 26, 1932; d. Elvin and Fay Cynthia (Sybrant) H.; m. Gerald W. Huston, June 30, 1951 (dec.); 1 child, Linda Sandell. BA, Met. State U., Minn., 1992. With Northwest Bus. Service, Mpls., 1950-51, Progressive Machine Co., Huntington Park, Calif., 1951-52; v.p. and corp. sec. Apache Corp., Mpls., 1954-87; v.p. stock transfer Norwest Bank, Minn., 1987—. Mem. Am. Soc. Corp. Secs. Lutheran. Home: 8264 Xerxes Ave S Minneapolis MN 55431-1003 Office: Norwest Bank 6th and Marquette Minneapolis MN 55402

HUSTON, DEVERILLE ANNE, lawyer; b. Great Falls, Mont., Mar. 2, 1947; d. Orion Joseph and Beverly Rosemary (Mower) H. BA, U. Minn., 1969; JD, William Mitchell Coll. Law, 1975. Bar: Minn. 1975, Ill. 1976, U.S. Dist. Ct. (no. dist.) Ill. 1976). Assoc. Sidley & Austin, Chgo., 1977-83, ptnr., 1983—. Fellow Am. Bar Found.; mem. ABA, Ill. State Bar Assn., Chgo. Bar Assn., Chgo. Fin. Exch., Law Club. Office: Sidley & Austin 1 First National Plz Chicago IL 60603*

HUSTON, KATHLEEN MARIE, library administrator; b. Sparta, Wis., Jan. 7, 1944. BA, Edgewood Coll., 1966; MLS, U. Wis., Madison, 1969. Libr. Milw. Pub. Libr., 1969-90; city libr. Milw. Pub. Libr. System, 1991—. Office: Milwaukee Pub Libr 814 W Wisconsin Ave Milwaukee WI 53233-2309

HUSTON, MARGO, journalist; b. Waukesha, Wis., Feb. 12, 1943; d. James and Cecile (Timlin) Bremner; student U. Wis., 1961-63; AB in Journalism, Marquette U., 1965; m. James Huston, Dec. 9, 1967 (div.); 1 son, Sean Patrick. Editorial asst. Marquette U., Milw., 1965-66; feature editor, reporter Waukesha Freeman, 1966-67; feature reporter Milw. Jour., 1967-70; reporter Spectrum, women's and food sections, 1972-79, editl. writer, 1979-84, polit. reporter, 1984—, asst. picture editor, 1985-91, copy editor, 1992-95; reporter Milw. Jour. Sentinel (merger Milw. Jour. and The Sentinel), 1995—; instr. mass comm. U. Wis., Milw. Recipient Penney-Mo. award for consumer abortion series, 1975, Pulitzer Prize for investigation into plight of elderly, 1977, Clarion award, 1977, Knight of Golden Quill award, Milw. Press Club, 1977, Wis. AP writing award, 1977, special award Milw. Soc. Profl. Journalists, 1977, Penney-Mo. Paul Myhie award for excellence, 1978; By-Line award Marquette U. Coll. of Journalism, 1980; Wis. UPI best editorial award, 1982; Wis. Women's Network award for journalist achievement for women's issues, 1983, Dick Goldensohn Fund award, 1991; Wis. Arts Bd. Literary Arts grantee, 1992. Mem. Nat. News Coun. (dir.), Investigative Reporters and Editors, Nat. Conf. Editorial Writers, Sigma Delta Chi. Club: Milw. Press. Office: Milwaukee Journal Sentinel 333 W State St Milwaukee WI 53203-1305

HUTCHENS, KAREN D., communications executive; b. San Diego, Sept. 5, 1955. BA in Psychology, San Diego State U., 1972; BA in Bus. Adminstrn., Nat. U., 1980. Cmty. affairs mgr. San Diego Gas & Elec. Co., 1985-87, dir. govt. affairs, 1987-92; sr. v.p. Nelson Comms., San Diego, 1992-93, exec. v.p., 1993—. Office: Nelson Comms Group 501 W Broadway Ste 2020 San Diego CA 92101-3548*

HUTCHEON, WILDA VILENE BURTCHELL, artist; b. Ft. Fairfield, Maine, Sept. 9; d. Harvey George and Alanda Gallope (Hersey) Burtchell; m. Philip S. Hutcheon, Mar. 26, 1955 (dec. July 1992). Grad., Fed. design Sch., 1944; student seascape, Art Students League, 1963, student landscape painting, 1965, student portraiture, 1969; DFA (hon.), London Inst. Applied Rsch., 1990. Color cons., studio receptionist, 1954-56, art instr./lectr., 1960s; supr. art dept. Maine State Art Exhbn., Presque Isle, 1959-62; curator fine arts Nylander Mus., Caribou, Maine, 1958-63; art instr./judge Aroostook County, Maine, 1958-94; lectr./cons. in field. One woman shows include Woodfords Congregational Ch., Portland, Maine, 1967, Talent Tree Gallery, Augusta, Maine 1974, Maine State, Poland Springs, Restigouche Mus., New Brunswick, Can., 1978, Madison Ave., N.Y.C., 1978, Ogunquit Art Ctr., 1978, 16th Internat. Congress of Arts Group, Washington, 1989, Woods Edge Gallery, Perham, Maine, 1994; group shows include Talent Tree Gallery, Augusta, 1974, Laguna Beach, Calif., 1986-87; exhibited in permanent collections at Cary Meml. Hosp., Caribou, Maine, others, also in pvt. collections. Exec. coord. Beautification Arts and CRafts, Ft. Fairfield, 1986; art chmn. Maine Potato Blossom Festival, Ft. Fairfield, 1963; chmn. Aroostook County Cultural Ctr. Project, 1971. Recipient Internat. Art Gold medal Best of Show, IPA, Washington, Internat. Creative Achievement award New Orleans, Internat. Best of Show, New Eng., Internat. Disting. award for outstanding achievement and svc. in creative art with induction into Disting. Leadership Hall of Fame; commd. Ky. Col., Nat. Award for Svc., Provl. Photographers of A., 1962, Hastings Cup for Continued Excellence, P.P.A.N.E., 1964, Pres.'s Club for Outstanding Merit, M.P.P.A., 1969, numerous awards at art shows. Mem. Caribou C. of C., Cambridge World Found. of Successful Women, Nat. Mus. of Women in the Arts (charter), Caribou Garden Club (pres. 1968), Art Soc. Caribou (pres. 1964), Am. Portrait Soc., Nat. Trust for Hist. Preservation, The Portrait Inst., Profl. Photographers of Am., Beaverbrook Art Gallery (Can.), Maine Assn. of Women in Fine and Performing Arts, Farnsworth Mus., Bus. and Profl. Women's Club, Internat. Platform Assn. Republican. Ch. of Christ. Home and Studio: 51 Prospect St Caribou ME 04736-2473

HUTCHIN, NANCY LEE, consultant business process reengineering; b. Ft. Belvoir, Va., June 16, 1949; d. Walter James and Iyllis Elizabeth (Lee) H.; m. Stephen Lawrence Guiland Nov. 27, 1970 (div. 1983); children: Kai-Long Stephen Guiland, Petra Lee Guiland; m. John Edward Money, Jun. 7, 1986 (div. 1994). BA summa cum laude, U. Md., 1973, MA, 1976. Prin. sci. B-K Dynamics, Rockville, Md., 1978-86; sr. cons. James Martin Assoc., Reston, Va., 1986-88; cons. San Diego, 1989-95; cons. employee SAIC, San Diego, 1993-95; staff cons. Intergraph, Reston, 1995—; contbr. editor Enterprise Reengineering, 1994—; assoc. pub. Black Riders, 1994—; program com. Tools & Methods for Bus. Engrng. Conf., 1994; bd. dirs. Strategic Info. Mgmt. & Tech. Solutions, Inc., Ogden, Utah. Contbr. articles to profl. jours., various presentations. Mem. Women in Tech. DC chap., Soc. of Info. Mgmt. Office: Intergraph 2051 Mercator Dr Reston VA 22091

HUTCHINGS, LEANNE VON NEUMEYER, communications executive, research consultant, writer; b. L.A.; d. F. Louis and Greta Catherine (Clifford) von Neumeyer; children: Marc Lane, Kristin LeAnne, Michael Lane, Jamie Laird, Jeremy Leif, Breton Louis. Rschr., writer, owner Heritage Tree, Arcadia, Calif., 1970—; internat. bd. advisors, dir. protocol, mem. scholarship grant review com. Neeley Scholarship Found., 1988-89; dir. pub. communications Ch. of Jesus Christ of Latter-day Saints, Foothill and Glendale regions, Calif., 1975-92, dir. cmty. rels., 1984-92, asst. dir. area coun., 1984; adminstrv. asst. dir. grant propsal review com. Calif. Pub. Affairs Dept., L.A., 1990—; seminar coord. R.E.D.I., Inc., L.A., 1982-91, corp. rels. dir., 1984-91; design cons. H.M.J. Time & Eternity Collection, L.A., 1985-95; dir. Rexall Internat., 1995—; mem. nat. adv. coun. motion picture studio Brigham Young U., Provo, Utah, 1986-89; adminstrv. dir. Pasadena Geneal. Libr., Calif., 1977-82; writer, co-producer KBIG, Sideband Div. Radio, L.A., 1979-80; exec. assoc adminstr. Calif. Bicentennial Found. for the U.S. Constitution, 1987; regional cons. Latter-Day Sentinel Newspaper, L.A., 1985-89; mem. Scholarship Found., L.A., 1985-89, exec. dir., 1988-89; mem. Brigham Young U. Marriott Sch. Bus. Mgmt. Soc., L.A., 1990—; mem. com. on child pornography legis. chmn. pub. info. portfolio com., 1988-91, L.A. County Commn. on Obscenity & Pornography, 1988-91, artist. Author: Honored Heritage, 1975, Woman's Place of Honor, 1976, Prologue and Tapestry, 1976, Moments with the Prophets, 1977, Southern California: The Earthquake Threat, 1981, Quake!: Preparing Home, Family and Community, 1982, The Peregrine Papers, 1986; columnist HeritageTree Foothill Intercity News, Knight-Ridder Pub., 1977-79; contbg. writer Women's Exponent Southern Calif. edit.; Sentinel; journalism series, 1978-80; also articles, collected works, stage trilogy; art exhibits include Wilshire Alma Exhibit, 1985, The Grand Artists Hall, 1986-88. Pres. Daus. Utah Pioneers-Los Angeles County, 1983-85; dir. protocol L.A. County Law Enforcement Conf., 1990; dir. recept. protocol State of Calif. Law Enforcement Conf. of Child Pornography, 1990; chmn. So. Calif. Task Force on Pornography, 1989-92; instr. earthquake preparedness and survival Arcadia chpt. ARC, L.A., 1983-85; mem. Cmty. Coordinating Coun., Arcadia, 1983-86; mem. exec. bd. Calif. Utah Women, L.A., 1977-79, 85-86, chmn. L.A. County Commn. Pub. Rels. Portfolio, 1988; exec. dir. Neeley Scholarship Found., 1989-91; coord. planning com. California '96: One Hundred Fifty Years LDS Sequicentennial, 1994—; display coord. L.A. Temple Hill Visitors Ctr., 1994—; lineage rsch. dir. von Neumeyer-Burches & Assocs., 1992—. Recipient Best of Exhibit award Sculptor's West Workshop, 1982, cert. of recognition L.A. County, 1989, cert. appreciation L.A. County, 1990. Mem. Assn. Latter-Day Media Artists (assoc. editor Voice of ALMA 1978-83, exec. bd. 1977-81, chmn. spl. events, 1985-90, internat. bd. govs. fellow 1981-83), Am. Film Inst., LDS Bookseller's Assn., Deseret Bus. and Profl. Assn., Marriott Bus. Mgmt. Soc. (L.A. chpt.), Assn. L.D.S. Pub. Rels. Profls., Pub. Rels. Soc. Am. (L.A. chpt.), Nat. Mus. Women in the Arts (charter), Arcadia Tournament of Roses Assn., Arcadia C. of C. (chmn. industry commn. of women's div. 1983-85, mem. exec. bd. 1985-86), Internat. Platform Assn. Republican. Mem. Ch. of Jesus Christ of Latter-Day Saints. Avocations: sculpting, oil painting. Office: 1591 E Temple Way Los Angeles CA 90024-5801

HUTCHINS, CARLEEN MALEY, acoustical engineer, violin maker, consultant, writer, educator; b. Springfield, Mass., May 24, 1911; d. Thomas W. and Grace (Fletcher) Maley; m. Morton A. Hutchins, June 6, 1943; children: William Aldrich, Caroline. AB, Cornell U., 1933; MA, NYU, 1942; DEng (hon.), Stevens Inst. Tech., 1977; DFA (hon.), Hamilton Coll., 1984; DSc (hon.), St. Andrews Presbyn. Coll., 1988; LLD (hon.), Concordia U., Montreal, Que., Can., 1992. Tchr. sci. Woodward Sch., Bklyn., 1934-38, Brearley Sch., N.Y.C., 1938-49; asst. dir., asst. prin. All Day Neighborhood Schs., N.Y.C., 1943-45; sci. cons. Coward McCann, Inc., 1956-65, Girl Scouts Am., 1957-65, Nat. Recreation Assn., 1957-65; permanent sec. Catgut Acoustical Soc., Montclair, N.J., 1962—. Author: Life's Key, DNA, 1961, Moon Moth, 1965, Who Will Drown the Sound, 1972; author (with others): Science Through Recreation, 1964; Editor: (2 vols.) Musical Acoustics, Part I, Violin Family Components, 1975, Musical Acoustics, Part II, Violin Family Functions, 1976, The Physics of Music, 1978, Research Papers in Violin Acoustics 1973-1994, 1995; contbr. articles to profl. jours. in Sci. Am., Jour. of the Acoustical Soc. Am., Physics Today, Am. Viola Soc., Catgut Acoustical Soc. Martha Baird Rockefeller Fund for Music grantee, 1966, 68, 74; Guggenheim fellow, 1959, 61; recipient several spl. citations in music; grantee Nat. Sci. Found., 1971, 74. Fellow AAAS (electorate nominating com. 1974-76, Outstanding Performance in the Scis. award 1994), Audio Engrng. Soc. (life), Acoustical Soc. Am. (emeritus, membership com. 1980-86, exec. council 1984-87, medal and awards com. 1987-89, nominating com. 1987-88, Silver Acoustics Medal 1981, tech. com. music. acoustics 1964—, chmn. pres.'s ad hoc com. 1987-88, archives com. 1988—, mem. com. on women 1989—); mem. So. Calif. Violin Makers Assn. (hon.), Viola da Gambda Soc. Am. (hon.), Scandinavian Violin Makers Assn. (hon.), N.Y. Viola Soc., Guild Am. Luthiers, Am. Viola Soc., Violoncello Soc., Amateur Chamber Music Players Assn., Am. Philos. Soc. (award violin acoustics 1968, 81), Mich. Violin Makers Assn., Materials Rsch. Soc., Sigma Xi, Pi Lambda Theta, Alpha Xi Delta. Clubs: Three O'Clock, Dot & Circle, others. Home and Office: Catgut Acoustical Soc Inc 112 Essex Ave Montclair NJ 07042-4121

HUTCHINS, JOAN MORTHLAND, manufacturing executive, farmer; b. Pasadena, Calif., Aug. 8, 1940; d. Andrew and Constance Amelia (Gordon-Grant) Morthland; children: Andrew Bush, Georgia Bush, Alan Hutchins, Paul Hutchins. AB, Radcliffe Coll., 1961; hon. degree, Royal Coll. Music, London, 1979; AAS, SUNY, Farmingdale, 1985. Jr. mathematician Shell Devel. Co. (Shell Oil), Emeryville, Calif., 1961-63; mathematician Corp. for Econ. and Indsl. Rsch., London, 1964-65; mgmt. cons. McKinsey & Co., N.Y.C., 1965-67, investment mgr. family accounts, 1974-86; v.p. devel. Compotite Corp., L.A., 1985-87, pres., 1987-89, pres., CEO, 1989—; pres., CEO MBH Farms, Inc., Elizaville, N.Y., 1986—. Editor McKinsey & Co. Mgmt. Scis. News Bull., 1965-67; contbr. articles to profl. jours. Mem. bd. overseers Harvard U., Cambridge, Mass., 1994—, mem. overseers vis. com. Harvard athletic dept., 1986-91, mem. overseers vis. com. Arnold Arboretum, 1995—, mem. overseers vis. com. Harvard Grad. Sch. Edn., 1995—; bd. dirs., v.p. Royal Music Found., N.Y.C., 1978-90; trustee Bowdoin Coll. Summer Music Festival, Brunswick, Maine, 1978-88, L.I. Biol. Assn., Cold Spring Harbor, N.Y., 1986-88. Mem. Am. Nat. Stds. Inst. (nat. waterproofing stds. com. 1988—), Harvard U. Alumni Assn. (bd. dirs. 1990-93), Harvard-Radcliffe Club L.I. (pres. 1988-90). Home: 8 Seawanhaka Pl Oyster Bay NY 11771-1629 Office: Compotite Corp 355 Glendale Blvd Los Angeles CA 90026-5009

HUTCHINS, KAREN LESLIE, psychotherapist; b. Denver, Sept. 9, 1943; d. Kimball Frederick and Bonnie Illa (Small) H.; divorced; 1 child, Alec Klinghoffer. BA, U. Denver, 1965; MA, George Washington U., 1972. Lic. profl. counselor clin. hypnotherapist; cert. clin. hypnotherapist; cert. chem. dependency specialist; registered sex offender treatment provider. Tchr. Washington D.C. Sch., 1966-70; asst. housing adminstr. George Washington U., Washington, 1970-72; counselor/instr. No. Va. C.C., Annandale, Va., 1972-77, Austin (Tex.) C.C., 1977-80; co-owner Hearts Day Care, Austin, 1980-81; supr./therapist MaryLee Resdl. Treatment, Austin, 1981-82; child protective svc. worker Dept. Human Resources, Austin, 1982-84; probation officer Adult Probation Travis County, Austin, 1984-90; lead therapist Cottonwood Treatment Ctrs., Bastrop, Tex., 1990-91; psychotherapist Austin, 1991—. Author conf. presentation: Beyond Survival, 1990-92, Why Me? vs. Spirtuality, 1993, Integrating the Wounded Soul, 1994, Ritually Abused Children, 1994, Recognizing PTSD Symptoms in Children, 1996. Vol. trainer Hotline, Austin, 1993—. Mem. ACA, Internat. Soc. Trauma and Stress Studies, Tex. Assn. Alcoholism and Drug Abuse Counselors. Democrat. Jewish. Office: Cicada Recovery Svcs 3004 S 1st St Austin TX 78704-6373

HUTCHINSON, ANN, development director; b. East Stroudsburg, Pa., May 15, 1950; d. David Ellis and Susie (Ingalls) H.; m. Paul Harrison McAllister, Jan. 2, 1986. BS in Vocat. Edn., Fla. Internat. U., 1985; MBA, Pepperdine U., 1990. Cert. advanced vocat. tchr., Fla. Motorcycle technician Ft. Lauderdale, Fla., 1973-78, machinist, 1978-79; instr., motorcycle tech. Sheridan Vocat. Tech. Sch., Hollywood, Fla., 1979-85; adminstr., tng. program Am. Honda Motorcycle Div., Torrance, Calif., 1985-86, curriculum developer motorcycles svc. tech., 1986-90, coll. program coord., 1990-94; ednl. devel. dir. Clinton Tech. Inst., Phoenix, 1994-96; tng. officer Ariz. State Dept. Econ. Security, Phoenix, 1996—; chmn. high tech. acad. steering coms. Pasadena (Calif.) United Sch. Dist., 1991-94; ednl. cons. Ctr. for Occupation R&D Sch.-to-Work Awards, 1994—. Builder, supporter Fla. Sheriff's Youth Ranches, 1988—. Recipient State of Ky. Colonel award, 1990. Mem. Am. Motorcycle Assn., Am. Vocat. Assn., ASTD, Vocat. Indsl. Clubs Am. (co-chmn. motorcycle tech. com. 1988-90, 94—, automotive nat. tech. com. 1990-94, adv. Hollywood, Fla. 1979-85), Toastmasters Internat. Office: Ariz Dept Econ Security Office Tng and Orgnl Devel 1140 E Washington Rm 206 Phoenix AZ 85034

HUTCHINSON, BRENDA IRENE, sound artist, sound designer, audio engineer; b. Trenton, N.J., June 15, 1954; d. William Garwood Dean Hutchinson, Sr. and Mary Ann (McElhoes) Byrnes. BFA in Music, Carnegie-Mellon U., 1976; MA in Music, U. Calif., San Diego, 1979. Audio engr. Harvestworks, Studio Pass, N.Y.C., 1980—; exhibit builder, video prodr., artist in schs., sound perception co-dir. The Exploratorium, San Francisco, 1982-92; sr. sound designer Convivial Design, Inc., San Francisco, 1995—; co-curator homemade instruments Lincoln Ctr., N.Y.C., summer 1995; affiliate artist Headlands Ctr. for Arts, Sausalito, Calif., 1991-95; guest instr. Calif. Coll. Arts and Crafts, Oakland, Calif., 1993-94, Mission Sci. Workshop, San Francisco, 1992—. Composer (electro-acoustical works) A Grandmother's Song, 1979, (with Clive Smith) Liquid Sky, 1982, Apple Etudes, 1985, Interlude from Voices of Reason, 1985, Storytime, 1986, (with Gerald Lindahl) Slow Death on a Thorny Rose, 1986, Joy Chorus from Fly Away All, 1988, Sentences, 1989, EEEYAH!, 1988, Norris and American the Beautiful, 1990, Turaluralura Lament, 1990, Long Tube Solo, 1990, (with Constance De Jong) Vanishing Act, 1991, Voices of Reason, 1991, Delecate Lights, 1991, Long Tube Trio, 1993, Violet Flame, 1994, Another Long Tube, 1995, Every Dream Has Its Number, 1996, (with Laetitia Sonami and Beth Custer) Improvisation for Tube, Glove and Clarinets, 1996. Artist Ann Chamberlain Garden Project, San Francisco, 1995-96. Recipient Emergent Forms grant N.Y. Found. for Arts, 1985, 91, Media Arts grant Nat. Endowment for Arts, 1992, 94, grant Calif. Arts Coun., 1995-96, Meet the Composer Commn., 1995, Artist-in-residence Englehard Found., 1995. Mem. The Lab (bd. dirs. 1993—). Office: Exploratorium 3601 Lyon St San Francisco CA 94123

HUTCHINSON, ELAINE FRANCES, secondary education educator; b. Nanticoke, Pa., Jan. 9, 1938; d. William Henry and Frances Elizabeth (Redwood) H. BS, East Stroudsburg U., 1959; MEd, West Chester U., 1971. Sci., history and humanities classroom tchr. Phoenixville (Pa.) Area Sch. Dist., 1959—. Author ednl. activities, curriculum in field. Mem., sec. Booster Club, Phoenixville, 1992—; active Home and Sch. Assn., Phoenixville, 1992—. Named Outstanding Leader in Secondary Edn., 1976, Outstanding Sci. Tchr., Jaycettes, 1984. Mem. NEA, Nat. Sci. Tchrs. Assn., Nat. Coun. Social Studies, Pa. State Edn. Assn., Phoenixville Area Edn. Assn. (past pres.), Bus. & Profl. Women's Club (membership chmn. 1971-91, past pres.), Delta Kappa Gamma (rec. sec. 1994, past pres.). Baptist. Office: Phoenixville Area Sch Dist 1330 S Main St Phoenixville PA 19460-4452

HUTCHINSON, JANET LOIS, historical society administrator; b. Washington, May 2, 1917; d. Lewis Orrin and Gertrude Elizabeth Hutchinson; divorced; 1 child, Jefferson Troy Siebert. Grad., So. Sem. and Jr. Coll., Buena Vista, Va., 1936; student, N.Y. Sch. Expression, 1923-30, Christine Dobbins Sch. Dance; studied with, Maude Adams, Clare Tree Major, 1934-35. Owner Broadlawn Inn Art Gallery, Camden, Maine, 1955-64; dir. Old Merchants House Mus., N.Y.C., 1962-63, Hist. Soc. Martin County, Stuart, Fla., 1965-91, Elliott Mus., Stuart, 1965-91; dir. House of Refuge Mus., Stuart, 1965-91, dir. emeritus, 1991—; pres., editl. cons. Hutchinson/Paige, Stuart, 1991—. Author: Tiny Timid's Christmas Wish, 1953, The History of Martin County, 1975; host: (TV interview show) Chronicle. Active Nat. Hist. Preservation Soc., Nat. History Soc., Fla. History Soc.; bd. dirs. Pioneer Occupationa Ctr. for Handicapped, St. Michael's Pvt. Sch.; adv. bd. St. Joseph's Coll. and Fla. Inst. of Tech. Named Woman of Yr., AAUW, 1975. Mem. DAR (Halpatiokee chpt.), Antique Car Assn., Smithsonian Instn., Nat. Soc. Lit. and Arts, Nat. Pen Women (hon. mem.), Salmaqundi Club, Nat. Arts Club. Home: 1023 NW Spruce Ridge Dr Stuart FL 34994-9513

HUTCHISON, ELIZABETH MAY, nurse; b. Broomfield, Colo., Apr. 14, 1924; d. Percy William and Frances May (Cram) Marion; m. James Donald Hutchison, Dec. 9, 1945; children: John William, Daniel James, Janet May Morrell, Ronald Raymond. RN, U. Denver, 1945. Polio staff nurse Children's Hosp., Denver, 1945-53; home care staff nurse Weld County Health Dept., Greeley, Colo., 1970-73; community health coord. for adult health Boulder (Colo.) County Health Dept., 1973-87. Author: Adult Health Conference Protocol, 1985; editorial staff: Lafayette History Book, 1989. Mem., historian, co-dir. Lafayette Miners Mus., Lafayette Hist. Soc., 1978-95. Recipient Recognition award Boulder County, 1981, Appreciation award Boulder City-County Health Dept., 1976. Mem. DAR. Democrat. Methodist. Home: 778 Applewood Dr Lafayette CO 80026-8908 Office: Lafayette Miners' Mus 108 E Simpson St Lafayette CO 80026-2322

HUTCHISON, JANE CAMPBELL, art history educator, researcher; b. Washington (D.C.), July 20, 1932; d. James Paul and Leone Bailey (Warrick) H. BA fine arts, Western Maryland Coll., 1954; MA art history, Oberlin Coll., 1958; PhD art history, U. Wis., 1964. Tech. illustrator/ Dept. Model Basin U.S. Navy, Washington (D.C.), 1954-56; rsch libr. Toledo Mus. of Art, 1957-59; teaching asst. U. Wis., Madison, 1959-60,61-63; vis. asst. prof. Temple U., Phila., summer 1968; from instr. to assoc. prof. U. Wis., Madison, 1964—, prof., 1975—, dept. chmn., 1977-80, 92-93; cons. NEH, Washington (D.C.), 1972-77, Inst. Internat. Edn., N.Y.C., 1977,82,89, Nat. Gallery of Art, Washington, 1982-83, Rijksmuseum, Amsterdam, 1984, Cin. Art Mus., 1990—. Author: Master of the Housebook, 1972, Early German Artists, vol. I, 1980, vol. II, 1981, vol. III, 1991, German edit., 1994, Albrecht Dürer: A Biography, 1990. Pres. Madison chpt. AAUP, 1979-81, Midwest Art History Soc., 1983-85; sec.-treas. Historians of Netherlandish Art, 1995—; pres. St. Andrew's Soc. Madison, 1996—. Grad. fellow Oberlin Coll., 1955-57, fellow U. Wis., 1959-60, 61-63, Fulbright fellow Rijksuniversiteit Utrecht, Netherlands, 1960-61, rsch. grantee NEH, Germany, 1982, German Acad. Exch. Svc., Germany, summer 1989; Grant in aid Am. Coun. Learned Soc., Amsterdam, 1984; recipient Alumni award Western Md. Coll. Trustees, 1987. Mem. AAUP (pres. Madison chpt. 1979-81), Internat. Coun. Mus., Am. Assn. Mus., Medieval Acad. Am., Coll. Art Assn., Univ. Club U. Wis. (bd. dirs. 1976-80, pres. 1980), Wis. Assn. Scholars (v.p. Madison chpt. 1990—), Midwest Art History Soc. (pres. 1983-85), Historians of Netherlandish Art (sec.-treas. 1995—), Print Coun. Am. Home: 2261 Regent St Madison WI 53705-5321 Office: U Wis Dept Art History 800 University Ave Madison WI 53706-1414

HUTCHISON, KAY BAILEY, senator; b. Galveston, TX, July 22, 1943; d. Allan and Kathryn Bailey; m. Ray Hutchison. BA, U. Tex., 1992, LLB, 1967. Bar: Tex. 1967. TV news reporter Houston, 1969-71, pvt. practice law, 1969-74; press sec. to Anne Armstrong, 1971; vice chmn. Nat. Transp. Safety Bd., 1976-78; asst. prof. U. Tex., Dallas, 1978-79; sr. v.p., gen. counsel Republic of Tex. Corp., Dallas, 1979-81; of counsel Hutchison, Boyle, Brooks & Fisher, Dallas, 1981-91; mem. Tex. Ho. of Reps., 1972-76; elected treas. of Tex., 1990, U.S. senator from Tex., 1993—. Fellow Am. Bar Found., Tex. Bar Found.; mem. ABA, State Bar of Tex., Dallas Bar Assn., U. Tex. Law Alumni Assn. (pres. 1985-86). Republican.

HUTCHISON, PAT, nurse, administrator; b. Omaha, Mar. 4, 1943; d. Earl Edward and Sylvia Lorraine (Kronen) Moore; m. James M. Hutchison, June 23, 1963; children—Michael, Danny. Diploma in nursing, St. Joseph's Sch. Nursing, 1968; student Central Ariz. Coll., 1976-82; BS in Health Service Adminstrn., U. Phoenix, 1983; BS in Nursing, U. Phoenix, 1988. R.N.; cert. in advanced cardiac life support, Ariz. Nurse Armish Maag Hosp., Teheran, Iran, 1969-71; supr. Hoemako Hosp., Casa Grande, Ariz., 1973-84; asst. dir. nursing Casa Grande Regional Med. Ctr., 1984-86, nursing supr., 1986—. Nursing chmn. ARC, Casa Grande, 1986—, also bd. dirs., instr. disaster tng., 1982—; instr. cardiopulmonary resuscitation Am. Heart Assn., Casa Grande, 1978—. Recipient Care award Ariz. Hosp. Assn., 1984, Service and Appreciation award Bus. and Profl. Women's Assn., 1984. Mem. Ariz. Nurses in Mgmt., Emergency Nurses Assn. Democrat. Roman Catholic. Avocations: traveling; camping; boating; reading. Home: 1308 N Center Ave Casa Grande AZ 85222-3408 Office: Casa Grande Regional Med Ctr 1800 E Florence Blvd Casa Grande AZ 85222-5303

HUTCHISON, SHANDA LEE, secondary school educator; b. San Antonio, Dec. 19, 1960; d. Jerry and Janet C. (Gazay) Hines; m. Terry L. Hutchison, July 25, 1992; 1 child, Zachary Donovan. BS in Edn., S.W. Tex. State U., 1984; postgrad., U. Houston, 1987-88. Cert. secondary tchr., Tex. Journalism and English tchr. First Colony Mid. Sch., Sugar Land, Tex., 1988-92; writing, journalism and English tchr. Dilley (Tex.) H.S., 1992—. Republican. Office: Dilley HS 245 Hwy 117 Dilley TX 78017

HUTSON, KATHRYN MERLE, writer, corporate trainer; b. Yuba City, Calif., Apr. 28, 1945; d. George H. and Ruth G. (Gehrs) Flett; m. Michael W. Hutson, Apr. 6, 1968; children: David William, Andrew Michael. BA, Valparaiso U., 1967. Tchr. Royal Oak (Mich.) Schs., 1967-71; writer KMF Assocs., Troy, Mich., 1971-86; grammar trainer Grammar Group, Chgo., 1986-90; pres. The Write Co., Troy, 1991—; mem. Troy Coalition, 1993—. Author newspaper column, 1984—. Mem., vice chmn. Troy Schs. Found., 1988—; chmn. edn. Beautiful Savior Luth. Ch., Bloomfield Hills, Mich., 1994—. Mem. Village Club (newsletter writer). Office: The Write Co 292 Town Center Dr Troy MI 48084

HUTTENBRAUCK, JILL, college administrator, educator; b. Staten Island, N.Y., June 11, 1951; d. Frank Carl and Ruth Emma (Emden) Siegel; children: Jesse, Leigh. BS, Northwestern U., 1973; MA, U.S. Internat. U., 1978; postgrad., San Diego STate U., 1988-90. Lang., speech & hearing pathologist La Mesa (Calif.) - Spring Valley Sch. Dist., 1976-90, Grossmont-Union High Sch. Dist., La Mesa, 1990—; instr. Cuyamaca Coll., El Cajon, Calif., 1991—; cons. in field. Author: Sequential Activities and Materials Providing Listening Enhancement, 1974. Chmn. Sch. Site Coun., Lakeside, Calif., 1992; mem., tchr. rep. Sch. Governence Com., Lakeside, 1994; tchr. rep. PTSA, Lakeside, 1993—. Recipient Rose award LMSV Ednl. Found., 1988; Hon. Svc. award Calif. State PTA, 1987. Mem. Calif. Assn. Post Secondary Educators of Disabled (scholar com. 1992—), Am. Speech & Hearing Assn., Calif. Lang., Speech & Hearing Assn., San Diego Coun. Adminstrv. Women in Edn., Learning Disabilities Assn., Phi Delta Kappa. Home: 11755 Walnut Rd Lakeside CA 92040-5624 Office: El Capitan HS Grossmont Union HS Dist 10410 Ashwood St Lakeside CA 92040

HUTTNER, CONSTANCE S., lawyer; b. Youngstown, Ohio, 1958. BSc with honors, Ohio State U., 1977; JD magna cum laude, Boston Coll., 1980. Bar: N.Y. 1981. Ptnr. Skadden, Arps, Slate, Meagher & Flom, N.Y.C. Mem. Phi Beta Kappa. Office: Skadden Arps Slate Meagher & Flom 919 3rd Ave New York NY 10022*

HUTTON, DONNA MARIE, civilian military employee; b. Oak Ridge, Tenn., July 7, 1953; d. Gerald Lincoln and Virginia Hewitt H. BA in Psychology, Cath. U. Am., 1975, postgrad., 1978-80; MS in Contract and Acquisition Mgmt., Fla. Inst. Tech., 1993. Info. specialist U.S. Office Pers. Mgmt., Washington, 1981-85; contracting officer U.S. Army/Walter Reed Army Med. Ctr., Washington, 1985—, chief svcs. br., 1994—; trainer, tchr. in related bus. fields U.S. Army. Youth counselor, psychol. counselor Montgomery County Govt., 1970-85. Mem. Nat. Contract Mgmt. Assn., Psi Chi. Roman Catholic. Office: Directorate of Contracting Walter Reed Army Med Ctr Washington DC 20307

HUTTON, LAUREN (MARY LAURENCE HUTTON), actress, model; b. Charleston, S.C., 1944; d. Laurence Hutton. Student, U. Fla., Sophia Newcombe Coll. Fashion model, 1960—. Actress: (feature films) Paper Lion, 1968, Little Fauss and Big Halsey, 1970, Pieces of Dreams, 1970, The Gambler, 1974, Gator, 1976, Welcome to L.A., 1977, Viva Knievel!, 1977, A Wedding, 1978, American Gigolo, 1980, Zorro, the Gay Blade, 1981, Paternity, 1981, Lassiter, 1984, Once Bitten, 1985, A Certain Desire, 1986, Malone, 1987, Guilty As Charged, 1991, My Father, The Hero, 1994; (TV movies) Someone's Watching Me, 1978, Institute for Revenge, 1979, The Cradle Will Rock, 1983, Starflight: The Plane that Couldn't Land, 1983, Scandal Sheet, 1985, Timestalkers, 1987, Perfect People, 1988, Fear, 1990; (TV series) The Rhinemann Exchange, 1977, Central Park West, 1995—, (stage prodn.) Extremities. *

HUVER PLAMONDON, ARLENE E., small business owner; b. Traverse City, Mich., Nov. 27, 1953; d. George A. and Alice (Bodnar) Plamondon; m. Jacob John Huver; children: David, Anna. BBA, Nazareth Coll., Kalamazoo. Mgr. acctg. USPS, Kalamazoo, 1988-90, postmaster, 1990-92; postmaster USPS, Climax, Mich., 1992-95; propr. Bountiful Baskets & Crafts, Kalamazoo, 1994—, The Cake and Candy Shoppe, Kalamazoo, 1996—. Vol. Attitudinal Healing Ctrs., Kalamazoo, 1988-90. Mem. NAFE, NOW, Nat. Assn. Postmasters of U.S., League of Postmasters. Roman Catholic. Office: The Cake and Candy Shoppe Maple Hill Mall 5186 W Main Kalamazoo MI 49009

HUXLEY, CAROLE FRANCES CORCORAN, educational adminstrator; b. Evanston, Ill., 1938; d. Harold Francis and Angela Mary (Dawson) Corcoran; m. Michael Remsen Huxley; children: Samuel, Ian. BA, Mount Holyoke Coll., S. Hadley, Mass., 1960; MAT, Harvard U., 1961. Tchr. Woodbury (Conn.) H.S., 1961-62; staff to sr. adminstr. AFS/Internat., N.Y.C., 1962-71; program officer, State Programs to Div. Dir. Nat. Endowment for Humanities, Washington, 1971-82; deputy commr. for Cultural Edn. N.Y. State Edn. Dept., Albany, 1982—; bd. mem., vice chair N.Y. Coun. on Humanities, 1984-90; bd. mem. Commn. on Preservation and Access, Washington, 1987—; panel mem.,reviewer Nat. Endowment for Humanities, Washington, 1988, 90, 94; panel mem., chair, Arts as Basic Edn., Nat. Endowment for Arts, Washington, 1989-91; del. White House Conf. on Librs., Washington, 1989-91. Trustee, vice chair Mount Holyoke Coll., S. Hadley, Mass., 1982-87, 88—, vice chair 1994—; bd. mem. Albany Med. Ctr., 1984-90, Coun. on Women in govt., Albany, N.Y., 1991-93; planning com., bd. mem. Albany (N.Y.) Red Cross, 1992-94. Recipient Alumnae Medal of Honor Mount Holyoke Coll., S. Hadley, Mass., 1990, Leadership award Alliance for Arts Edn., N.Y. State, 1994. Mem. N.Y. State Mus. Assocs., Friends of New Netherlands, Nature Conservancy. Home: 355 Loudon Rd Loudonville NY 12211-1701 Office: New York State Edn Dept Rm 10A33 Cultural Edn Ctr Albany NY 12230

HUXLEY, LAURA ARCHERA, humanist, psychologist, writer; b. Turin, Italy, Nov. 2, 1914; came to U.S., 1937; d. Felice and Fede (Bellini) A.; m. Aldous Huxley, Mar. 19, 1956 (dec. Nov. 1963). Studies in violin and music, C. Flesh, Berlin, G. Enesco, Paris; diploma in Prof. of Music, Conservatory of St. Cecilia, Rome, 1929; student, Curtis Inst., Phila., 1938-40; D of Human Svcs. (hon.), Sierra U., 1981. Concert violinist Europe and U.S., 1927-39; violinist L.A. Philharm. Orch., 1944-47; free-lance assoc. producer documentary films U.S.; film editor RKO, L.A., 1948-51; pvt. practice psychotherapy L.A., 1952-70; lectr. Seminarist Human Potential Movement, 1964—; founder, dir. Our Ultimate Investment, L.A., 1978—, an orgn. for the nurturing of the possible human. Author: You Are Not the Target, 1963, This Timeless Moment, 1969, rev., 1991, Between Heaven and Earth,

1974, rev., 1991, One a Day Reason to be Happy, 1986, rev., 1991; (with Dr. Piero Ferrucci) The Child of Your Dreams, 1987, rev., 1992. Recipient Maharishi award World Govt. of the Age of Enlightenment, 1981; honoree UN, N.Y.C., 1978, World Health Fedn. for Devel. and Peace, 1990, Living Legacy award Women's Internat. Ctr., 1995. Mem. Authors Guild, Assn. for Humanistic Psychology, Assn. for Transpersonal Psychology, The Huxley Inst. Address: Our Ultimate Investment PO Box 1868 Los Angeles CA 90028

HUXTABLE, ADA LOUISE, architecture critic; b. N.Y.C.; d. Michael Louis and Leah (Rosenthal) Landman; m. L. Garth Huxtable. AB magna cum laude, Hunter Coll.; postgrad., Inst. Fine Arts, NYU; hon. degrees, Harvard U., Yale U., NYU, Washington U., U. Mass., Oberlin Coll., Miami U., R.I. Sch. Design, U. Pa., Radcliffe Coll., Oberlin Coll., Smith Coll., Skidmore Coll., Md. Inst., Mt. Holyoke Coll., Trinity Coll., LaSalle U., Pace Coll., Pratt Inst., Colgate U., Hamilton U., Williams Coll., Rutgers U., Finch Coll., Emerson Coll., C.W. Post Coll. at L.I. U., Cleve. State U., Bard Coll., Fordham U., Parsons Sch. Design, Mass. Coll. Art. Asst. curator architecture and design The Museum of Modern Art, N.Y.C., 1946-50; Fulbright fellow for advanced study in architecture and design Italy, 1950, 52; free-lance writer, contbg. editor to Progressive Architecture and Art in America, 1950-63; architecture critic N.Y. Times, N.Y.C., 1963-82; mem. editorial bd. N.Y. Times, 1973-82; Cook lectr. in Am. instns. U. Mich., 1977; Hitchcock lect. U. Calif.-Berkeley, 1982; corp. vis. com. Harvard U. Grad. Sch. Design, Sch. Visual and Environ. Arts; bd. dirs. N.Y. Landmarks Conservancy; mem. adv. bd. Am. Trust Brit. Libr.; bd. dirs. Ctr. Study Am. Architecture Columbia U.; archtl. cons. Nat. Gallery, London, J. Paul Getty Trust, L.A., San Francisco Pub. Libr., Mus. Contemporary Art, Chgo. Author: Pier Luigi Nervi, 1960, Classic New York, 1964, Will They Ever Finish Bruckner Boulevard?, 1970, Kicked a Building Lately?, 1976, The Tall Building Artistically Reconsidered: The Search for a Skyscraper Style, 1985, Goodbye History, Hello Hamburger 1986, Architecture Anyone? 1986. Recipient 1st Pulitzer prize for disting. criticism, 1970, Spl. award Nat. Trust for Historic Preservation, 1971, Archtl. Criticism medal AIA, 1969, medal for lit. Nat. Arts Club, 1971, Diamond Jubilee medallion City N.Y., 1973, Mayor's Cultural award, 1984, Woman of Yr. award AAUW, 1974, Sec.'s award for conservation U.S. Dept. Interior, 1976, Thomas Jefferson medal U. Va., 1977, Archtl. Criticism medal Acad. d' Architecture Française, 1988; Guggenheim fellow for studies in Am. architecture, 1958, MacArthur fellow, 1981-86, Henry Allen Moe prize Humanities Am. Philosophical Soc., 1992. Fellow Am. Acad. Arts and Scis., N.Y. Inst. Humanities, Royal Inst. Brit. Architects (hon.), AAAL; mem. AIA (hon.), Am. Acad. Arts and Letters, Am. Acad. Arts and Scis., Soc. Archtl. Home: 969 Park Ave New York NY 10028-0322

HUYCK, MARGARET HELLIE, psychology educator; b. Waterloo, Iowa, Apr. 14, 1939; d. Ole Ingeman and Mary Elizabeth (larsen) Hellie; m. William Thomas Huyck, June 24, 1961; children: Elizabeth, Karin. BA, Vassar Coll., 1961; MA, U. Chgo., 1963, PhD, 1970. Lic. psychologist, Ill. Asst. prof. Ill. Inst. Tech., Chgo., 1969-75, assoc. prof., 1975-89, prof. dept. psychology, 1990—; prof. dept. psychology; vis. lectr. U. Oslo, 1977-78; lectr. Provident Hosp. Sch. Nursing, Chgo., 1964-66, Am. Soc. Aging, 1989-91; cons. Northwestern U., Evanston, Ill., 1973-79, Elgin (Ill.) Mental Health Ctr., 1975-77, No. Trust Bank, Chgo., 1981-85, Evanston Hosp., 1992-93. Author: Growing Older, 1974; co-author: Adult Development, 1982. Bd. mem. S.E. Chgo. Commn. Recipient Rsch. award NIMH, 1982-86. Fellow Gertontol. Assn. Am., Gerontol. Soc. Am. (sec. 1991-94); mem. APA, Older Women's League Ill. (pres. 1994—). Unitarian-Universalist. Office: Ill Inst Tech Inst Psychology Chicago IL 60616-3732

HUYER, ADRIANA, oceanographer, educator; b. Giessendam, The Netherlands, May 19, 1945; arrived in Can., 1950; came to U.S., 1975; d. Jacob Catharinus and Sophia (Van Loon) H.; m. Robert Lloyd Smith. BS, U. Toronto, 1967; MS, Oreg. State U., 1971, PhD, 1974. Scientific officer Marine Scis. Branch, Ottawa, Can., 1967-73; rsch. scientist Marine Environ. Data Svc., Ottawa, Can., 1974-75; rsch. assoc. Oreg. State U., Corvallis, 1975-76, rsch. asst. prof., 1976-79, asst. prof., 1979-80, assoc. prof., 1980-85, prof., 1985—, vis. scientist Csiro Marine Labs, Hobart, Australia, 1988. Contbr. articles to profl. jours. Mem. AAAS, Am. Meterol. Soc., Am. Geophys. Union, Can. Meterol. and Oceanographic Soc., Am. Soc. Limnology and Oceanography. Office: Coll Oceanography Oreg State Univ Corvallis OR 97331

HUYSMAN, ARLENE WEISS, psychologist, educator; b. Phila.; d. Max and Anna (Pearlene) Weiss; BA, Shaw U., 1973; MA, Goddard Coll., 1974; Ph.D., Union Inst. Grad., 1980; m. Pedro Camacho; children: Pamela Claire, James David. Actress, dir. Dramatic Workshop, N.Y.C., 1956-68; music and drama critic and columnist Orlando (Fla.) Sentinel Star, 1966-68; psychodramatist Volusia County Guidance Center, Daytona Beach, Fla., 1966-68; free-lance journalist, 1968-70; psychodramatist Psychiat. Inst., Jackson Meml. Hosp., Miami, 1972-77, dir. Adult Day Treatment Center, 1974-77, dir. Lithium Clinic, 1976-77; psychodramatist South Fla. State Hosp., Hollywood, 1971-72; psychotherapy supr., Neurosci. program coord. Miami Heart Inst., 1984—, clin. dir. Family Workshop, 1985—, clin. dir. Adult Day Treatment Ctrs., 1987—; founder, dir. Geriatric Adult Day Treatment Ctrs.; adj. asst. prof. Med. Sch., U. Miami, 1976—; adj. prof., Union Inst., 1992—, Antioch U., 1995—; specialist in Bi Polar Disorders, U. Wis., 1980—; mem. adv. panel Fine Arts Council Fla., 1976-77; mem. Fla. Gov.'s Task Force on Marriage and the Family Unit, 1976, 89-90; vol. Rec. for Blind, 1974—. Recipient Best Dirs. award and Best Actress award Fla. Theatre Festival, 1967. Mem. Am. Psychol. Assn., Fla. Psychol. Assn., Dade County Psychol. Assn. (bd. dirs.), Mental Health Assn. Dade County, Internat. Assn. Group Psychotherapy, Union Inst. Grad. Alumni Assn. (bd. dirs., southeastern rep., pres.-elect), Am. Soc. Aging, Am. Assn. Group Psychotherapy and Psychodrama, Moreno Acad., Fedn. Partial Hospitalization Study Groups, World Fedn. Mental Health, Fla. Assn. Practicing Psychologists (bd. dirs., pres.). Office: Ctr Psychol Growth 3050 Biscayne Blvd Miami FL 33137-4143

HYATT, CAROLE S., writer, women's rights advocate; b. N.Y.C., Apr. 29, 1935; d. Arthur Edwin and Shirley (Unger) Schwartz; m. Gordon Hyatt, Oct. 25, 1966; 1 child, Ariel. BS in Theatre and Edn., Syracuse U., 1956; MA in Theatre Comm., U. Denver, 1959. Co-prodr., dir. Peppermint Players, N.Y.C. and elsewhere, 1960-66; prodr. CBS-TV, N.Y.C., 1961-66; instr., part-time faculty New Sch. for Social Rsch., N.Y.C., 1960-75; co-founder, CEO Child Rsch. Svc. Inc., N.Y.C., 1966-84; CEO, co-founder Hyatt/Esserman Assocs., Inc., N.Y.C., 1973-84; adv. bd. NAFE, N.Y.C., 1980-91, Avon/Women of Enterprise, N.Y.C., 1986—; bd. dirs. Women in Need, N.Y.C., 1986-92, Berkshire Botanical Gardens, 1994—, Stockbridge, Mass., 1994—, Edith Wharton Restoration, Lenox, Mass., 1989-94. Author (keynote seminars): The Woman's Selling Game, 1977, Woman and Work, 1980, When Smart People Fail, 1987, updated edit. 1993, Shifting Gears, 1991; creator videotape: Lifetime Employability, 1995; keynote spkr. and presenter of workshops in U.S., Asia, S.Am., Ctrl. Am., Europe, and Can., visiting over 60 cities annually. Mem. Internat. NOW (bd. dirs. Defense and Edn. Fund 1975-85), Women's Forum (program chair internat conv. 1995), N.Y. Women's Forum (bd. dirs. 1985-87, chair program com. 1987-90). Home and Office: 7 W 81st St New York NY 10024

HYATT, DIANE, psychotherapist; b. N.Y., Jan. 18, 1943; d. Phillip and Estelle H. BA in Psychology, Fordham U., N.Y., 1983; MSW, Fordham Grad. Sch. Social Svc., N.Y., 1985. ACSW, LCSW. Psychotherapist Stamford, Conn., Bridgeport, Conn.; tng., supr. and cons. in field. Fellow Am. Orthopsychiatry; mem. NASW. Home: 49 Coolidge Ave Stamford CT 06906 Office: 1653 Capitol Ave Bridgeport CT 06606

HYATT, SUSAN METZENBAUM, lawyer; b. Cleve., Mar. 8, 1950; d. Howard M. and Shirley (Turoff) Metzenbaum; m. Joel Z. Hyatt, Aug. 24, 1975; children: Jared, Zachary. Student, U. Ariz., 1968-69; BS, U. Cin., 1972; JD, Case Western Res. U., 1981. Bar: Mo. 1981, U.S. Dist. Ct. (we. dist.) Mo. 1981. Dir. legal personnel Hyatt Legal Svcs., Cleve., 1977-80, sr. ptnr., 1981—; dir. spl. projects HLS Mgmt. Co., Cleve., 1982—. Bd. dirs. Child Welfare League of Am., Washington, Career Paths, Boston; v.p. Women's Roundtable Greater Cleve.; chair Taskforce on Gender Equity in the Classroom, Pediat. AIDS Found. Cleve. Fundraiser, vis. com. Case Western Reserve Law Sch., mem. search com. for dean; bd. dirs. Ctr. for Prevention of Domestic Violence, chair nominating com.; adv. bd. U. Hosp. Women's McDonald Hosp.; past bd. dirs. Bellefaire/Jewish Children's Bur.; v.p. bd. dirs. Cleve. Anti-Defamation League; bd. dirs. Jewish Cmty. Fedn., cmty. rels. com.; mem. steering com. on reform of welfare sys. LWV of Cleve. Edn. Fund; mem. African/Am. Jewish Rels. Com. Leadership Forum; mem. planning com. Nat. Assembly on the Future of the Legal Profession in the 21st Century. Democrat. Office: Hyatt Legal Svcs Charter One Bank Bldg 1215 Superior Ave E Cleveland OH 44114-3249

HYDE, BONNIE PITTS, rehabilitation nurse; b. Jeffersonville, Ind., Mar. 16, 1957; d. Marvin Houston and Klyda Moretta (Nairon) Pitts; m. Lawrence Victor Kubiak, Dec. 21, 1985; m. William F. Hyde, Dec. 18, 1976 (div. June 1985); 1 child, Erick. ADN, Columbia State C.C., 1978. RN, CRRN, CCM. Staff nurse, charge nurse Williamson Med. Ctr., Franklin, Tenn., 1978-82; health occupations instr. Williamson County Bd. Edn., Franklin, 1982-83, dir. LPN program, 1983-85; rehab. nurse Liberty Mut. Ins. Co., Brentwood, Tenn., 1985-93; rehab. nurse mgr. Liberty Mut. Ins. Co., Brentwood, 1993—; mem. case mgmt. adv. bd. Baptist Hosp., Nashville, 1992—. Mem. Assn. Rehab. Nurses, Nashville Rehab. Assn. (chair 1989-90). Republican. Methodist. Office: Liberty Mutual Ins Co 155 Franklin Rd Brentwood TN 37027-4646

HYDE, GERALDINE VEOLA, retired secondary education educator; b. Berkeley, Calif., Nov. 26, 1926; d. William Benjamin and Veola (Walker) H.; m. Paul Hyde Graves, Jr., Nov. 12, 1949 (div. Dec. 1960); children: Christine M. Graves Klykken, Catherine A. Graves Hackney, Geraldine J. Graves Hansen. BA in English, U. Wash., 1948; BA in Edn., Ea. Wash. U., 1960, MA in Edn., 1962. Cert. tchr. K-16, Wash.; life cert. specialist in secondary edn., Calif. English educator Sprague (Wash.) Consol. Schs., 1960-62, Bremerton (Wash.) Sch. Dist., 1962-63, Federal Way (Wash.) Sch. Dist., 1963-66; English, journalism and Polynesian humanities educator Hayward (Calif.) Unified Sch. Dist., 1966-86. Charter mem. Hist. Hawai'i Found., Honolulu, 1977—; founding mem. The Cousteau Soc., Inc., Norfolk, Va., 1973—; life mem. Hawai'ian Hist. Soc., Honolulu, 1978—; mem. Moloka'i Mus. and Cultural Ctr., Kaunakaka'i, 1986—, Bishop Mus. Assn., Honolulu, 1973—, Mission House Mus., Honolulu, 1994, Bklyn. Hist. Assn., N.Y., 1994, Berkshire Family History Assn., Pittsfield, Mass., 1994, Richville (N.Y.) Hist. Assn., 1994, Wing Luke Asian Mus., Seattle, 1994. Mem. Libr. Congress Assocs. (charter), Nature Conservancy of Hawai'i, Smithsonian Inst. (contbg.), Nat. Geog. Soc., Nat. Trust Historic Preservation, USS Constitution Mus., Jr. League Spokane, U. Wash. Alumni Assn. (life), Ea. Wash. U. Alumni Assn. (life). Episcopalian. Home: 306 W Meadowbrook Dr Midland MI 48640-6006 also (winter): PO Box 1598 Kaunakaka'i Moloka'i HI 96748

HYDE, JEANETTE W., ambassador; b. Hamptonville, N.C., June 15, 1938; m. Wallace Nathaniel Hyde. Student, Wake Forest U., 1956-58; BA, Delta State U. English tchr. Greenville, Miss., 1962-63, Iraklion, Crete, 1964; social worker Fayetteville, N.C., 1965-67, court counselor, 1967-71, ptnr., operator women's retail bus., 1971-78; with N.C. Bd. Transportation, 1977-84; founder, bd. dir. Triangle Bank and Trust, Raleigh, N.C., 1987-93; amb. to Barbados, St. Vincent, St. Lucia and Dominica, 1993—; bd. dirs. N.C. Global Transpark. Bd. dirs. N.C. Child Advocacy Inst., Outward Bound of N.C., Capital City Club of Raleigh, Sch. of Social Work, U. N.C.; chair Women's Club of Raleigh. Recipient Outstanding Pub. Svc. award Cumberland County N.C. Mem. Kappa Delta Pi. Office: Barbados PO Box 302 FPO AA 34055 Office: Grenada Dept of State Washington DC 20521-3180

HYDER, BETTY JEAN, art educator; b. Elizabethton, Tenn., Oct. 19, 1940; d. Earl Bennick and Bonnie Thelma (Humphrey) Buck; m. Billy Joe Hyder, 1962 (div. 1990); 1 child, Billie Jean Hyder Wallace. BS, East Tenn. State U., 1962, MA, 1970, BA, 1971; postgrad. Tenn. Arts Acad., Belmont U., 1985-94. Visual art specialist grades K-5 Andrew Johnson Sch., Kingsport, Tenn., 1962—; visual art specialist Palmer Ctr. for Handicapped Students, Kingsport, 1976-80. Author: (art textbook) What's Cooking in Art?, 1987; works exhibited in one-woman show East Tenn. State U., 1979; interviewed and taught class for CNN Revolution in Edn., 1989; exhibited work at Renaissance Ctr., Kingsport, 1992, Arts and Crafts festival, Roan Mt., Tenn., 1990, Arts Acad. Capital Bldg., Nashville, 1991, Earth Day at Bays Mt., Kingsport, 1991-92; student art exhibited widely in Kingsport. Artist (booth art) Fun Fest, Kingsport, 1990; chairperson PTA cultural art com., Kingsport, 1989-94; chairperson Christian Fellowship for Singles, Kingsport, 1991-93; singer Christian Single Ensemble, Kingsport, 1991-94; presenter Tenn. Arts Acad., Nashville, 1993; host Pentel's Internat. Children's Exhibit from Japan, 1993; coord. Christine LaGuardia Phillips Cancer Ctr. exhibit, Kingsport, 1984-94; presenter East Tenn. Edn. Assn. art workshop, Knoxville, 1987, 90, 93; hospitality chair. Christian Fellowship for Singles; chair Kingsport Arts Assn., 1994; mem. Crackerjack Singers. Named Kingsport City Schs. Outstanding Educator of Yr., 1987. Mem. NEA, PTA, Tenn. Edn. Assn., Kingsport Edn. Assn. (publicity, pub. rels. chmn. 1962, chairperson edn. profl. stds. com. 1986-88), East Tenn. Art Edn. Assn., Nat. Art Edn. Assn., Delta Kappa Gamma (chairperson legis. com.), Madrigal Drama Players. Republican. Mem. Avoca Christian Ch. Home: 137 Walton Ct Kingsport TN 37663-2136 Office: Andrew Johnson Sch 1001 Ormond Dr Kingsport TN 37664-3235

HYMAN, MARY BLOOM, science education programs coordinator; m. Sigmund M. Hyman, 1947; children: Carol Ann Hyman Williams, Nancy Louise. BS, Goucher Coll., 1971; MS, Johns Hopkins U., 1977. Asst. dir. Edn. Md. Sci. Ctr., Balt., 1976-81, dir. edn., 1981-90; coord. sci. edn. programs Loyola Coll., Balt., 1990—, coord. Inst. for Child Care Edn., 1992—. Trustee Goucher Coll.; mem. Baltimore County Pub. Schs. Com. for Sch.-Based and Sch.-Linked Child Care; bd. dirs. Balt. Sch.-Age Child Care Alliance; mem. Gov.'s Task Force on Compensation of Child Care Providers, 1995-96. Recipient Disting. Women award Gov.'s Office, Annapolis, Md., 1981; Meritorious Svc. award Johns Hopkins U., 1983; Outstanding Svc. to Sci. Edn. award. Assn. Sci. Dept. Chairmen of Balt. County Pub. Schs., 1989. Mem. Md. Assn. Sci. Tchrs. (bd. dirs.), Md. Math. Coalition, Phi Beta Kappa, Phi Delta Kappa. Home: 10815 Longacre Ln Stevenson MD 21153

HYMAN, PAULA E(LLEN), history educator; b. Boston; d. Sydney Max and Ida Frances (Tatelman) H.; m. Stanley Harvey Rosenbaum, June 7, 1969; children: Judith Hyman Rosenbaum, Adina Hyman Rosenbaum. B.J.Ed., Hebrew Coll., Brookline, Mass., 1966; B.A., Radcliffe Coll., 1968; M.A., Columbia U., 1970, Ph.D., 1975. Asst. prof. Columbia U., N.Y.C., 1974-81; assoc. prof. history Jewish Theol. Sem., N.Y.C., 1981-86, dean Sem., Coll. Jewish Studies, 1981-86; Lady Davis. vis. assoc. prof. Hebrew U. of Jerusalem, 1986; Lucy Moses prof. history Yale U., New Haven, 1986—. Series editor Ind. U. Press. Bloomington, 1982—; contbg. editor Sh'ma Mag., N.Y.C., 1977—; author: From Dreyfus to Vichy, 1979, The Emancipation of the Jews of Alsace, 1991, Gender and Assimilation in Modern Jewish History, 1995; co-author: The Jewish Woman in America, 1976; co-editor: The Jewish Family; Myths and Reality, 1986; contbr. articles to pubs. Vice chmn. Zionist Acad. Coun., N.Y.C., 1982-83. NEH summer grantee, 1977;Am. Coun. Learned Socs. fellow, 1978; grantee N.Y. Council for Humanities, 1980, NEH fellow, 1986-87. Fellow Am. Acad. Jewish Rsch. (treas. 1995—); mem. Am. Hist. Assn. (com. 1983), Assn. for Jewish Studies (bd. dirs. 1978-81, 83-85, 86—, v.p. for mem., 1994—), Nat. Found. Jewish Culture (chairperson acad. adv. com. 1996—), Leo Baeck Inst. (bd. dirs. 1979—), Yivo Inst. for Jewish Rsch., Phi Beta Kappa. Jewish. Office: Yale U Dept History New Haven CT 06520

HYMAN-SPRUTE, BETTY HARPOLE, technical equipment consultant; b. Jasper, Tex., Nov. 20, 1938; d. Russell Charles and John Francis (Hilton) Harpole; m. Arthur Siegmar Hyman (dec.); children: Norma Sullivan, Eric, Jonathan, Lee Ann; m. Gerald J. Sprute. BA in Psychology, U. Tex., San Antonio, 1979. Spl. project coord. Tex. Stores, San Antonio, 1975-79; communications cons. Southwestern Bell Tel., Midland, Tex. and San Antonio, 1980-82; tech. cons. AT&T, San Antonio, 1983-85, 88—, Intelliserve Corp., Dallas, 1987-88; cons. IMS Group, San Antonio, 1985-87. Mem. devel. com. San Antonio Spl. Olympics, San Antonio Conservation Soc., 1975-96, San Antonio World Affairs Coun., 1985-92, 1994—; bd. dirs S.Tex. Chidren's Habilitation Ctr., San Antonio, 1985-87; mem. Riverfront task force in Asheville. Mem. Am. Bus. Women's Assn. (program com. 1987-88), Tex. Tennis Assn. (ranked player 1976-90), Prime Time Tennis Club (v.p. 1985-86), Blue Ridge Dance Club (pres. 1993-94). Republican. Episcopalian. Home: 3459 River Way San Antonio TX 78230-2518 Office: 107 W Nakoma St San Antonio TX 78216-2723

HYMES, NORMA, internist; b. N.Y.C., July 20, 1949; d. Richard and Ellen (Posner) H.; m. Vincent M. Esposito, Nov. 1978 (div.); 1 child, Richard Hymes-Esposito. BS, Oberlin Coll., 1971; MD, Mt. Sinai, 1975. Diplomate Bd. of Internal Medicine. Intern, resident Maimonides Med. Ctr., Bklyn., 1975-78; internist Manhattan Health Plan, N.Y.C., 1978-81, Manhattan Med Group, P.C., N.Y.C., 1981-92, N.Y. Med. Group, P.C., 1992—. Mgr. The Colonnade Condominium, N.Y.C., 1982-85; trustee N.Y. Soc. For Ethical Culture, N.Y.C., 1989-93, 96—. Mem. ACP, Am. Med. Women's Assn. Office: NY Med Group 172 Amsterdam Ave New York NY 10023-5034

HYNAN, LINDA SUSAN, psychology educator; b. Ft. Sill, Okla., Nov. 20, 1953; d. Christy J. and Barbara Jean (Camp) Genzel; m. Edward F. Hynan, Feb. 3, 1973; 1 child, Patrick Shane. MS, U. Ill., 1982, PhD, 1993. Tchg. asst., rsch. asst. dept. psychology U. Ill., Urbana, 1980-91; rsch. asst. dept. psychology Del. State Coll., Dover, 1983—; asst. prof. dept. psychology, neurosci., inst. grad. stats. Baylor U., Waco, Tex., 1991—; cons. Infosphere Devel. Systems, Waco, Tex., 1986—; reviewer Allyn & Bacon/Simon & Schuster, Needham Heights, Mass., 1992, 95, Harcourt Brace Coll. Publs., 1994, Worth Pubs., Inc., 1995. Contbr. chpt. to book Cognitive Bias, 1990, articles to profl. jours.; spl. reviewer jour. Behavior Rsch. Methods Instruments and Computers. Fellow U. Ill., 1988-89. Mem. APA, Am. Ednl. Rsch. Assn., Am. Psychol. Soc., Am. Statis. Assn., McLennan County Psychol. Assn., Midwestern Psychol. Assn., Psychometric Soc., Soc. for Judgement and Decision-Making, Soc. for Applied Multivariate Rsch., Soc. for Math. Psychology, Southwestern Psychol. Assn., Ctrl. Tex. Women's Alliance, Thyroid Found. Am., Inst. Math. Statistics, Am. Radio Relay League, Am. Numismatic Assn., Phi Kappa Phi. Home: 1312 Western Ridge Dr Waco TX 76712-8709 Office: Baylor Univ Psychology and Neurosci PO Box 97334 Waco TX 76798-7334

HYNDS, FRANCES JANE, communications management consultant; b. Martin, Tenn., Oct. 27, 1929; d. Loyd Orion and Hunter Elizabeth (Goad) H. BS in Journalism, McMurry Coll., 1951; MA in Telecommunications, U. So. Calif., 1961, PhD in Communications, 1984. Dir. pub. info., instr. journalism McMurry Coll., Abilene, Tex., 1951-53; dir. pub. rels. Oklahoma City U., 1953-55; acct. exec., corp. sec. Joe Leighton & Assocs. Inc., Hollywood, Calif., 1956-65; prin. Hynds Co., L.A., 1965—; pres., sole owner Matrix Works, Inc., L.A., 1987—; sr. lectr., adj. faculty, dir. pub. rels. program for mgmt. U. So. Calif. Sch. Journalism; lectr. Grad. Sch. Bus. U. So. Calif., 1981-84. Mem. Pub. Rels. Soc. Am. (dir. 1975-77, nat. assembly del., pub. rels. counselor), Women in Communications Inc. (dir. 1967-72; Far West region Woman of Achievement 1980, L.A. chpt. Freedom of Info. award, Nat. Founders award, 1982, pres. scholarship and edn. found. 1992-96). Recipient LULU award for the Best Corporate Pub. Rels. in the We. U.S., L.A. Advtg. Women, 1975. Author (with Norma L. Bowles): Psi Search, The New Investigation of Psychic Phenomena that Separates Fact from Speculation, 1978; transl. French, 1983; contbr. articles to profl. jours.

HYNES, FRANCES, artist, educator; b. N.Y.C., Feb. 20, 1945; d. William John and Frances (Nolen) H. BA, St. John's U., 1966; MA, NYU, 1968; Cert., Acad. of Fine Arts, Florence, Italy, 1969-70. Tchr. Internat. Nursery Sch., Jamaica, N.Y., 1970-75; art dir., tchr. Queen's Mus. of Art, N.Y.C., 1975-76; asst. prof. St. John's U., N.Y.C., 1975-81; lectr. La Guardia C.C., L.I.C., N.Y., 1981-82; asst. prof. L.I. U., Brookville, N.Y., 1991-92; vis. artist prof. Ill. State U., Normal, 1992; visual arts dir. Flushing (N.Y.) Arts Coun., 1985-95; vis. artist prof. Burren Coll. Art, County Clare, Ireland, 1995; artist-in-residence Ctrl. Mich. U., Mt. Pleasant, 1996; prof. painting dept. Savannah (Ga.) Coll. Art and Design, 1996—; visual arts cons. Queens Coun. on the Arts, Glendale, 1994-96; vis. artist/lectr. YM-YWHA of Mid-Westchester, N.Y., 1981, Women in the Arts, N.Y.C., 1981, Jamaica Arts Ctr., Jamaica, 1975, New Arts Program, Kutztown, Pa., 1988, U. R.I., Kingston, 1990, 91, Wittenberg Coll., Springfield, Ohio, 1993, Springfield Mus. Art, 1993; guest artist Printmaking Workshop, N.Y.C., 1984; resident Tyrone Guthrie Centre, Newbliss, County Monaghan, Ireland, 1995, Cill Rialaig Project, Ballinskelligs, Co. Kerry, Ireland. One-woman shows include Inst. for Contemporary Art, P.S. 1 Mus., L.I.C., 1980, Poindexter Gallery, N.Y.C., 1980, New Arts Program, Kutztown, Pa., 1988, June Kelly Gallery, N.Y.C., 1991, Terry Dintenfass Gallery, N.Y.C., 1981-93, Springfield (Ohio) Mus. Art, 1993, Wright Mus. Art, Beloit, Wis., 1994; group shows include Queens Mus. Art, Corona, N.Y., 1973, 75, 79, U.S. State Dept. Art in Embassies Program, 1973—, Poindexter Gallery, 1974, Bklyn. Mus., 1975, Bertha Urdang Gallery, N.Y.C., 1977, Nassau County Mus. Fine Arts, Roslyn, N.Y., 1977, Jamaica Art Ctr., 1978, 80, Queens Mus. Art, 1981, Francine Seders Gallery, Seattle, 1984, Forum Gallery, N.Y.C., 1984, Gallery Jazz, New Haven, 1985, Mus. Modern Art, N.Y.C., 1985, Nassau County Mus. Fine Arts, 1985, Ark. Art Ctr., Little Rock, 1985, Newark Mus., 1986, Bklyn. Mus., 1986, Bachelier-Cardonsky Gallery, Kent, Conn., 1988, Sewall Art Gallery, Houston, 1988, Terry Dintenfass Gallery, 1990, Heckscher Mus., Huntington, N.Y., 1990, Ogunquit (Maine) Mus. Am. Art, 1993, Springfield Art Mus., 1994, Queens Mus. Art, 1994, Anita Shapolsky Gallery, N.Y.C., 1995, Knoxville Mus. Art, 1995, Farnsworth Mus., Rockland, Maine, 1995, numerous others; works in permanent collections at Yellowstone Art Ctr., Valley Nat. Bank, Nassau Msu. Fine Arts, Newark Mus., Queens Mus. Art, Poindexter Family Collections, Godwin-Ternbach Mus. of Queens Coll., Farnsworth Mus., Bklyn. Mus., Bellevue Hosp., AT&T, others. Nat. Endowment for Arts Artist's fellow, 1980. Mem. Coll. Art Assn., Nat. Watercolor Soc., Maine Coast Artists. Home: 23-07 202 St Bayside NY 11360

HYNES, MARY ANN, publishing executive, lawyer; b. Chgo., Oct. 26, 1947; d. Ernest Mario and Emma Louise (Noto) Iantorno; m. James Thomas Hynes, Jan. 25, 1969; children: Christina, Nicholas. BS, Loyola U.; JD, John Marshall Law Sch., 1971, LLM in Taxation, 1975; MBA, Lake Forest Grad. Sch. Bus., 1993. Bar: Ill. 1971, U.S. Dist. Ct. (no. dist.) Ill. 1971. Exec. editor, law editor Commerce Clearing House, Inc., 1971-79, asst. sec, counsel, 1979-80; gen. counsel Commerce Clearing House, Inc., Chgo., now atty. rights and permissions. V.p., bd. dirs., exec. com. Chgo. Crime Commn.; mem. nat. strategy forum Midwest Coun. Nat. Security; adv. coun. Chgo. Symphony Orch. Chorus; deanery del. Chgo. Archdiocesan Pastoral Coun.; pres. local sch. bd., 1984-87; corp. coun. inst. planning com. Northwestern U. Sch. Law; mem. pres.' coun. Mus. Sci. and Industry, Chgo. Mem. ABA (coun., corp. law depts. com., litigation sect.), Ill. Bar Assn. (corp. law dept. sect. chair), Chgo. Bar Assn., Internat. Bar Assn., Women's Bar Assn., Ill. (former bd. dirs., found. adv. bd.), Internat. Fedn. Women Lawyers, Am. Corp. Counsel Assn., Am. Soc. Corp. Secs., Computer Law Assn., Justinian Soc. Lawyers, Law Club Chgo., Legal Club Chgo. (exec. com. 1987), Chgo. Club. Roman Catholic. Office: Commerce Clearing House Inc 2700 Lake Cook Rd Deerfield IL 60015-3867*

IACOBUCCI, JAMIE JO, elementary education educator; b. Cin., Nov. 15, 1965; d. Frank Anthony and Angela Jean (Ionna) I. BS in Edn., U. Cin., 1988. Cert. tchr., Ohio. Elem. sch. tchr. St. Teresa of Avila Sch., Cin., 1990—; faculty rep. Edn. Commn., 1991—; swim team coach Philipps Swim Club, Cin., summer 1993—, Three Rivers Dolphins, YMCA, Cin., winter 1994-95; dir. fundraising St. Teresa Sch. Bd., 1994—; devel. dir. publ rels. task force St. Teresa of Avila Sch., 1996—. Precinct exec. Cin. Bd. Elections, 1990-93; vol. St. Francis Hosp., Cin., 1980-81, Up/Downtowners, Cin., 1992. Mem. Nat. Audubon Soc., Greenpeace. Roman Catholic. Home: 5228 Relluk Dr Cincinnati OH 45238-3731

IACOBUCCI, SHARON GERARD, public relations professional; b. Akron, Ohio, Jan. 16, 1969; d. Dominic and Florence Jean (Damicone) I. BS in Journalism, Ohio U., 1991, MA in Orgnl. Comm., 1992. Pub. rels. asst. Ohio U. Coll. Osteopathic Medicine, Athens, 1989-92; mktg. dir. Ohio Renaissance Festival, Inc., Waynesville, 1992-95; pub. rels. specialist Robert Morris Coll., Coraopolis, Pa., 1995; dir. coll. comms. Chatham Coll., Pitts., 1995—. Literacy tutor Greater Pitts. Literacy Coun., Pitts., 1995—. Mem. Pub. Rels. Soc. Am., Women in Comms., Inc. (Pitts. chpt., pres.-elect 1995-96, pres. 1996-97). Democrat. Roman Catholic. Office: Chatham Coll Woodland Rd Pittsburgh PA 15232

IACOBUCCI-SHUSTER, LORI L., health and physical education educator; b. Little Falls, N.Y., Nov. 13, 1962; d. Primo B. and Wanda Mary (Masi) Iacobucci; m. Wayne Henry Shuster, July 4, 1989; children: Morgan Michele, Alexander James. Cert. phys./elem. edn. cum laude, SUNY, Cortland, 1985, M of Health Edn. with honors, 1990. Cert. health edn., N.Y. Phys. edn. tchr. K-6 Springfield Ctrl. (N.Y.) Sch., 1985-87; phys. edn. tchr. Cherry Valley (N.Y.) Springfield Ctrl. Sch., 1987-92, phys. edn. and health edn. tchr., 1992—; dist. health coord. Cherry Valley Springfield Ctrl. Sch., 1992—; chairperson shared decision making bldg. level team, 1994, 95; co-chair comprehensive health & wellness com., 1995—; presenter workshop N.Y. State Pub. Health Conf., 1994. Mem. AAHPERD, N.Y. State Fedn. of Profl. Health Educators. Home: 146 Crum Creek Rd Saint Johnsville NY 13452

IADAROLA, ANTOINETTE, college president. BA cum laude, Saint Joseph Coll., West Hartford, Conn., 1962; MA, Georgetown U., 1968; student, Oxford U., England, 1970; Fulbright Scholar, London Sch. Econs., 1971-73; PhD, Georgetown U., 1975; postgrad., Yale U., 1976-77. Asst. to grad. dean Georgetown U., Washington, 1968-71; dir. grants, asst. prof. history Saint Joseph College, 1974-78, dir. grants, chair dept. history, 1978-80, spl. asst. to pres. planning and ednl. affairs, chair dept. history, 1981-83; administrv. intern to pres. and provost Hood College, Frederick, Md, 1980-81; provost, dean of faculty College of Mount Saint Joseph, Cin., 1983-86, Colby-Sawyer Coll., New London, N.H., 1986-92; pres. Cabrini Coll., Radnor, Pa., 1992—; Mem. exec. com. Mercy Higher Edn. Colloquium, 1977-81; cons. Am. Coun. Edn., Ctr. Leadership Devel. and Acad. Adminstrn., 1980-92; bd. dirs. Am. Conf. Acad. Deans, 1987-90; chair Strategic Planning Com., Coll. Mt. St. Joseph, 1983-86, Com. Chief Acad. Officers, Greater Cin. Consortium colls. and Univs., 1985-86, Teaching/Learning Com. Coeducation Transition, Colby-Sawyer Coll., 1989-92. Contrb. articles to profl. jours. Cons. YWCA, Waterbury, 1974-80, Farmington C. of C. Teenage Scholarship Program, 1976-79; bd. dirs. Ursuline Acad., Cin., 1983-86, Private Industry Coun., Cin., 1983-86, N.H. Humanities Coun., 1987-92, vice chair 1989-90; mem. adv. com. civic literacy, Women's City Club, Cin., 1984-86, devel. com. Shakers Village, Enfield, N.H., 1989-92; chair Town/Gown Community Forum, New London, N.H., 1986-92; coord. ecumenical adult edn. program, Our Lady of Fatima ch., New London, 1987-92; trustee Girard Coll., Phila., 1995, academic affairs and investement coms. Valley Forge Mil. Acad., Radnor, Pa., 1994—. Fellow Georgetown U., 1968-71, Yale U., 1976-77, Danforth Assoc., 1979-86, Am. Coun. Edn. Fellowship in Acad. Adminstrn., 1980-81; grantee Inst. Internat. Edn. to Oxford U., 1970, NEH, 1979; Fulbright Scholar, 1971-73; recipient Dist. Alumna award Saint Joseph college, 1982, Purple Aster award Order of Sons of Italy, 1994. Mem. AAUP, Am. Assn. Higher Edn., Am. Hist. Assn., League of Women Voters. Office: Cabrini Coll 610 King Of Prussia Rd Radnor PA 19087-3698

IADAVAIA, ELIZABETH ANN, marketing professional; b. N.Y.C., June 28, 1960; d. Vincent Anthony and Sally (D'Angelo) I. BA in Econs., Georgetown U., 1982; postgrad., CUNY, 1996. Rsch. asst. Montefiore Hosp. Neurophysiology Labs., N.Y.C., 1979-80; in mktg. rsch. Sch. Bus. Adminstrn. Georgetown U., Washington, 1981-82; adminstrv. asst. Kolter Devel. Corp., N.Y.C., 1983-85; dir. ops. Merrill Lynch Realty, Stamford, Conn., 1985-88, Crown Group Real Estate Devel. & Fin., White Plains, N.Y., 1988-92; dir. mktg. Equitable, New Hyde Park, N.Y., 1992-94, N.Y.C., 1995—. Mem. St. Catherines Parish Coun., Bronxville. Winner 13th and 14th ann. Agy. Bull. contest Life Ins. Mktg. and Rsch. Assn. Mem. N.Y. State MBA Assn., Sch. of the Holy Child Alumni Assn. (bd. dirs., chmn. Rye, N.Y. chpt. 1983—), Georgetown U. Alumni Assn. (class chmn. 1986—), Women in Sales Assn. (v.p. 1993—), Nat. Second Mortgage Assn., VIP Young Adult Club (pres. 1985-87). Home: 17 Archer Dr Bronxville NY 10708-4601

IAROSSI, MARY AMELIA, photographer; b. Newark, Feb. 5, 1926; d. Pasquale and Marietta (Petinicchio) I. Student, NYU. Freelance photographer, 1947-77; founder, pres. Damiano Nittoli Assn., Hackettstown, N.J., 1961—. Treas. Order Sons of Italy, Newark; bd. dirs. Celtic Theatre Co., South Orange, N.J.; mem. Deborah Garfield (N.J.) Chpt., Paper Mill Womans Guild, Millburn, N.J., Am. Mus. Natural History, N.Y.C.; benefactor St. Rocco's Ch., Newark, St. Jude, Balt., St. Jude Hosp., Memphis, Salvation Army, Union, N.J., Father Flanagan Boys Town, Nebr., Seeing Eye, Morristown, N.J., World Wild Life, Washington, St. Anthony Guild, Paterson, N.J., Am. Lung Assn., Union, others. Named Woman of Yr., Italian Tribune News, 1994, Friend of the Theatre, Celtic Theatre, 1982. Mem. St. Joseph Rosary Soc. (East Orange, N.J.). Republican. Roman Catholic. Home: 60 Frederick St Belleville NJ 07109

IASIELLO, DOROTHY BARBARA, brokerage company executive; b. Bklyn., Oct. 6, 1949; d. Albert William and Josephine (Accardo) Rehorn; m. John Joseph Iasiello Jr., May 5, 1974. AAS in Mktg., N.Y.C. Community Coll., 1969; BS in Econs., Coll. Staten Island, 1978. With Lady Manhattan, N.Y.C., 1969-70; sec. Biscayne Fed. Savs. and Loan Assn., Miami, Fla., 1971, Morgan Guaranty Trust Co., N.Y.C., 1971-78; with mcpl. bond dept. J.P. Morgan Securities, N.Y.C., 1978-81, asst. treas. sales, 1981-84, asst. v.p. sales, 1984-88, v.p. sales adminstrn. mgmt., 1988-91, v.p. sales, 1991-95; v.p. sales Samuel A. Ramirez & Co., Inc., 1995—. Roman Catholic. Office: Samuel A Ramirez & Co Inc 61 Broadway New York NY 10006

IBACH, BARBARA ALICE, librarian; b. Mexico City, Feb. 23, 1945; (parents Am. citizens); d. Kenneth Lee and Evelyn (Griset) Pike; m. David Norman Ibach, June 3, 1968; children: Julie Ann, Benjamin David. BA, Spring Arbor Coll., 1968; MLS, U. Mich., 1984. Tchr. Whitko Cmty. Schs., Pierceton, Ind., 1968-70; head libr. Aquinas H.S., Southgate, Mich., 1985-86; libr. media specialist Northville (Mich.) H.S., 1986—. Active United Fund Speakers Bur., Detroit, 1978-89; chmn. Strong Scholarship Com., Dallas, 1990—; past pres. Silver Springs Elem. Sch. PTA, Northville, 1979-83. Presenter/instrnl. video grantee Project Gateway, Wayne County Regional Edn. Svc., 1994. Mem. Mich. Assn. for Media in Edn., Detroit Story League, Alpha Kappa Sigma. Presbyterian. Office: Northville H S 775 N Center St Northville MI 48167-2762

IBANEZ, JANE BOURQUARD, stress management consultant, lecturer; b. New Orleans, Oct. 11, 1947; d. Albert John and Josephine (Vachetta) Bourquard; m. Manuel Luis Ibanez, Oct. 16, 1970; children: Juana, Vincent, William, Marc. BS, U. New Orleans, 1970. Lab. researcher in organic chemistry U. New Orleans, 1967-68, genetics lab. instr., 1968-69, fitness instr., 1972-90, yoga and meditative instr., 1972-90, stress mgmt. instr., 1980-90; profl. lectr., stress mgmt. cons., 1972—; bd. examiners Tex. Supreme Ct., 1993—; guest lectr. U. New Orleans, Tex. A&M, Kingsville, ABWA Conv., South Tex. Banker's Assn., others. Author producer: (audiotapes) Childhood Stress, 1985, Yoga Workout, 1985, Jane's Way Mini Workout, 1986. Chmn. Tex. A&M U.-Kingsville Fund for Instnl. Advancement, Kingsville, 1989—, also presdl. asst.; pres. Am. Cancer Soc., Kingsville, 1992-94; mem. devel. bd. Spohn Kleberg Hosp., Kingsville, 1990—, trustee, vice chmn., 1991-93; chmn. devel. bd. Am. Heart Assn., Kingsville, 1990—; bd. dirs. Corpus Christi Women's Shelter, 1991-95; trustee South Tex. Ranching and Heritage Festival, 1992—. Mem. AAUW, Kingsville Garden Club, U. New Orleans Fitness Club (pres. 1975-89). Roman Catholic. Home: 905 N Armstrong Ave Kingsville TX 78363-3687 also: 2319 Prentiss Ave New Orleans LA 70122-5309

IBEABUCHI, CECILIA NKEIRU, nursing administrator; b. Jos, Nigeria, Apr. 5, 1959; came to U.S., 1982; d. Alfred Epundu and Rose Nneka (Amazu) Okoye; m. Stanley Chukwukelo Ibeabuchi, May 20, 1978; children: Chizoba, Chike, Nneka, Chibuzo, Chidozie. BS in Biology, Emmanuel Coll., 1985; LPN, Youville Hosp., 1987; MEd, Suffolk U., 1988; BSN, Simmons Coll., 1990. RN, Mass. Home health aide Quality Care, Boston, 1983-84, Staff Builders, Boston, 1985-86; nurse's aide St. John of God Hosp., Brighton, Mass., 1984-88, charge nurse, team leader, 1988-90, charge nurse, 1990; weekend supr. Park Marion Nursing Home, Brookline, Mass., 1991-92, Provident Nursing Home, Brighton, 1991-92; DON Hancock Manor Nursing Home, Dorchester, Mass., 1992-95, Boston Health Care for the Homeless Program, McInnis House, 1995—. Recipient Pauline Webble Triple award Simmons Coll., 1990. Home: 39 Bradlee St Hyde Park MA 02136-3205 Office: Boston Health Care/Homeless Barbara McInnis House 461 Walnut Ave Jamaica Plain MA 02130

IBY, WENDY RYDER, banker; b. Newton, Mass., Jan. 16, 1963; d. Walter Frederick and Cynthia Ellen (Baxter) R.; m. Robert Frederick Iby, Oct. 5, 1986; children: Alexander Payton, Nicholas Frederick. BSBA, U. Lowell, 1985. Cert. bank compliance officer Bank Adminstrn. Inst., 1994. Mgr. loan packaging and delivery, secondary market Boston Fed. Savings Bank, Burlington, Mass., 1985-89; compliance specialist Boston Fed. Savings Bank, Burlington, 1989-91, compliance officer, 1991—. Mem. Eastern Mass. Compliance Network. Office: Boston Fed Saving Bank 17 New England Executive Pk Burlington MA 01803

ICHINO, YOKO, ballet dancer; b. L.A.. Studies with Mia Slavenska, L.A. Mem. Joffrey II, N.Y.C., Joffrey Ballet, N.Y.C., Stuttgart Ballet, Fed. Republic Germany; tchr. ballet, 1976; soloist Am. Ballet Theatre, 1977-81; guest appearances, 1981-82; prin. Nat. Ballet Can., Toronto, Ont., 1982-90; tchr. Cullberg Ballet, Sweden, 1994—, Nat. Ballet Sch., 1994—, Ballet de Monte-Carlo, 1994—; various guest appearances including World Ballet Festival, Tokyo, 1979, 85, Tokyo Ballet, 1980, with Alexander Godunov and Stars, summer, 1982, Sydney Ballet, Australia, N.Z. Ballet, summer 1984, Ballet de Marseille, 1985-87, Deutsche Opera Ballet Berlin, 1985-90, Munich Opera Ballet, 1987-90, Australian Ballet, 1987, 89, Staatsoper Berlin, 1989, 90, Komische Opera, Berlin, 1991-93, David Nixon's Dance Theater, Berlin, 1990, 91, Birmingham Royal Ballet, 1990-93, Deutsche Opera Ballet, Berlin, 1994-95; tchr. Birmingham Royal Ballet, 1991, 93, Nat. Ballet of Can., 1993, Cullberg Ballet, Sweden, 1994, Nat. Ballet Sch., 1994, 95, Ballet de Monte-Carlo, 1994; tchr. numerous ballet workshops; dir. profl. program Ballet Met, 1995. First Am. women recipient medal Third Internat. Ballet Competition, Moscow, 1977.

IDEMOTO, BETTE KIYOKO, clinical nurse specialist; b. Cleve., Feb. 23, 1945; d. Shigeru and Helen R. (Matsuda) Furuki; m. Minoru Lester Idemoto, June 15, 1966; children: John, Cathy, David. BSN, Ohio State U., 1968; MSN, Med. Coll. Ohio, 1991. RN, Ohio; cert. med.-surg. clin. nurse specialist ANCC; cert. ACLS and BLS instr. and provider; CCRN. Step down nurse ICU Fairview Gen. Hosp., Cleve., 1968-75; staff nurse critical care S.W. Gen. Hosp., Middleburg Heights, Ohio, 1978-84, nurse clinician, dialysis coord., 1984-90; clin. nurse specialist, renal surg. ICU U. Hosps. Cleve., 1990-94, coord. cardiovasc. care, 1995—; mem. clin. faculty Case Western Res. U., Cleve., 1991—, clin. coord. acute care nurse practitioner program, 1992-94; chmn. strep throat health prevention program Berea (Ohio) Schs., 1979-90. Contbr. articles to profl. jours. Chair health panel subcom. United Way Svcs., Cleve., 1988—; 2d v.p. Lake Erie coun. Girl Scout U.S., Cleve., 1993-96, now pres.; pres. St. Paul Luth. Ch., Berea, Ohio, 1994. Recipient Thanks Badge Highest Adult award Lake Erie Girl Scout Coun., 1993, Honor Plaque, 1988. Mem. ANA, Ohio Nurses Assn. (health reform task force 1993—, sec. ethics com. 1992-94, minority issues assembly 1990—), Greater Cleve. Nurses Assn. (pres.-elect 1993-95, pres. 1995-97), Cuyahoga West Alumnae Assn., Sigma Theta Tau, Alpha Xi Delta (pres. 1993-95, Brinkman award 1991). Office: U Hosps of Cleve 11100 Euclid Ave Cleveland OH 44106

IGNAT, ANA, chemical engineer; b. Oradea, Romania, Aug. 27, 1959; came to U.S., 1991; d. Dumitru and Maria (Szodrai) Mihes; m. Adorian Nicolae Ignat, Aug. 21, 1982; 1 child, Andrei Dumitru. Chem. Engr., Politechnic Inst., Timisoara, Romania, 1983; Computer Programming, I.C.S., Pa., 1993. Registered profl. engr. Chem. engr., technologist Plastic Mfr., Jimbolia, Timis, Romania, 1983-87, sales mgr., 1987-91; clin. lab. technologist Bronx (N.Y.) Mcpl. Hosp. Ctr., 1992—; chemistry tchr. Plastic Mfr., Jimbolia, 1988-90. Mem. Am. Assn. Chem. Engrs. Home: 2965 E 196th #6S Bronx NY 10461

IGNATONIS, AUDRA CAROLE, paralegal; b. Huntsville, Ala., Sept. 10, 1971; d. Algis Jerome and Sandra Carole (Autry) I. BSA in Agrl. Economics, U. Ga., 1993. Cert. paralegal. Customer svc. rep. Ford New Holland Credit, Tucker, Ga., 1993-95; comml. paralegal Macey, Wilensky, Cohen, Wittner and Kessler LLP Law Firm, Atlanta, 1995—. Vol. Habitat for Humanity, Marietta, Ga., 1996. Mem. NAFE, Ga. Assn. Legal Assts., Ga. Agribus. Coun., Agrl. Alumni Assn. U. Ga. Republican. Roman Catholic. Home: 300 Somerset Ln Marietta GA 30067 Office: Macey Wilensky Cohen Wittner & Kessler 285 Peachtree Ctr Ave Atlanta GA 30303

IGNATONIS, SANDRA CAROLE AUTRY, special education educator; b. Dixon Mills, Ala., June 6, 1942; d. Charles Franklin Autry; m. Algis Jerome Ignatonis, June 15, 1968; children: Audra Carole, David Jerome. BA, Samford U., 1964; cert. in Gifted Edn., Kennesaw State U., 1989. Cert. tchr., Ga. Tchr. Jefferson County Bd. Edn., Birmingham, Ala., 1964, Huntsville (Ala.) Bd. Edn., 1964-71, Epiphany Cath. Sch., Miami, Fla., 1981, Cobb County Bd. Edn., Marietta, Ga., 1982, Bartow County Bd. Edn., Cartersville, Ga., 1990-92, Sequoria Group, Inc., Roswell, Ga., 1996; mem. Sch. Self-Governance Com., Emerson, Ga., 1990-91, Soccer Adv. Bd., Marietta, 1985-89; judge, mem. Social Sci. Fair Competitions, Huntsville, 1964-71. Team mom Metro N. Youth Soccer Assn., Marietta, 1991-92; block parent Somerset Subdivision, Marietta, 1982-86; polit. chmn. Student Nat. Edn. Assn., Samford U., Birmingham, Ala., 1963-64. Recipient grant Samford U. Faculty, 1963. Mem. Ga. Supporters of Gifted, Profl. Assn. Ga. Educators. Republican. Roman Catholic.

IGNATZ, AMY MARTIN, chemical engineer; b. Grove City, Pa., May 4, 1967; d. David Ferree and Patricia Jean (Swank) Martin; m. Thomas Stephen Ignatz, Jr., July 14, 1990; 1 child, Erica Jane. BS in Engring., U. Pitts., 1989. Chem. engr. U.S. Dept. Labor, Mine Safety & Health Adminstrn., Pitts., 1989—. Republican. Roman Catholic. Home: 202 3rd St Pittsburgh PA 15225-1337 Office: US Dept Labor Mine Safety & Health Adminstrn PO Box 18233 Pittsburgh PA 15236-0233

IHDE, MARY KATHERINE, mathematics educator; b. St. Louis, Jan. 19, 1942; d. Harold Orville and Katharine Marie (Bartsch) Nanninga; m. Daniel Carlyle Ihde, Dec. 22, 1968; children: Steven Carlyle, Douglas Harold. BA in Math., Northwestern U., 1964; MS in Math. Edn., Stanford U., 1968. Cert. tchr., N.Y., Calif., Md. Math. tchr. Shawnee Mission (Kans.) H.S. Dist., 1964-67; math. specialist Columbia Grammar and Prep. Sch., N.Y.C., 1969-72; math. tchr. Georgetown Visitation Prep. Sch., Washington, 1981-84; math. lectr. Mt. Vernon Coll., Washington, 1984-85; math. tchr. Nat. Cathedral Sch. for Girls, Washington, 1985-93, math. dept. chair, 1989-92; math. instr. Maryville U., St. Louis, 1994-95, Webster U., St. Louis, 1994-95; math. tchr., curriculum coord. Whitfield Sch., St. Louis, 1995-96; math curriculum cons., 1996—. Recipient 2nd pl. state level competition award Mathcounts, 1992, 4th pl., 1993; fellow Shell Oil Corp., 1967-68. Mem. Nat. Coun. Tchrs. Math., Math. Assn. Am., Pi Lambda Theta. Home and Office: 1686 Mason Knoll Ct Saint Louis MO 63131-1235

IKEDA, DONNA RIKA, state senator; b. Honolulu, Aug. 31, 1939; d. William G. and Lillian (Kim) Yoshida; div.; children: Rika, Aaron, Julie. BA in Speech, U. Hawaii. Substitute tchr., 1969-71; legis. rschr. Hawaii Rep. Rsch. Office, 1971-74; asst. v.p. Grand Pacific Life Ins. Ltd., Honolulu, 1989—; mem. Hawaii Ho. of Reps., 1974-86, Hawaii Senate, 1987—. Office: Hawaii Senate State Capitol Ste 210 Honolulu HI 96813

IKINS, RACHAEL ZACOV, writer, illustrator, photographer; b. Auburn, N.Y., July 5, 1954; d. Samuel Theodore and Phyllis Sylvia (Zacovitch) Killian; m. Phillip M. Ikins, Jan. 23, 1987. BS in Child and Family Studies, Syracuse (N.Y.) U., 1982. Pvt. practice sign lang. interpreter for the deaf Syracuse, 1980-81, Bd. of Coop. Ednl. Svcs., Syracuse, 1980-83; photographer, author greeting cards, Syracuse and Skaneateles, N.Y., 1985—, advertisements, West Columbia, S.C., 1985—. Columnist (poetry) Devon Rex Newsletter, 1995-96, Jour. Pot Bellied Pigs, 1994-96; author poetry. Recipient Honorable Mention, World of Poetry, 1991, New Eng. Writer's Conf., 1991. Jewish. Home and Office: 2636 E Genesee St Syracuse NY 13224-1521

IKLE, DORIS MARGRET, energy conservation company executive; b. Frankfort, Germany, May 28, 1928; came to U.S., 1937; d. Richard and Sonia (Pappenheimer) Eisemann; m. Fred Charles Ikle, Dec. 23, 1959; children—Judith, Miriam. B.A., NYU, 1949, M.A., 1953; postgrad. Columbia U., 1957. Economist, Nat. Bur. Econ. Research, N.Y.C., 1949-54, Am. Bankers Assn., 1954-56, Rand Corp., Santa Monica, Calif., 1957-60; Inst. Energy Analysis, Washington, 1976-77; cons. U.S. Dept. Commerce, Washington, 1975-76; founder, pres., CEO Conservation Mgmt. Corp., Bethesda, Md., 1977—; adv. council Am. for Energy Independence, 1985—. Author: The Complete Energy Audit Book, 1980, (software) Energy Audit Systems, 1984; contbr. articles to profl. jours. Home: 7010 Glenbrook Rd Bethesda MD 20814-1223 Office: Conservation Mgmt Corp 7300 Pearl St Bethesda MD 20814-3321

ILANIT, TAMAR, psychologist; b. Tel Aviv, May 5, 1929; d. Aharon and Ada (Berman) Pougatch; came to U.S., 1950, naturalized, 1970; grad. Levinski Tchr. Sem., 1949; Ph.D., U. So. Calif., 1959; m. Apr. 15, 1948; children—Rona, Gill. Research dir. United Cerebral Palsy Assn., Los Angeles, 1959-61; instr. Pepperdine U., Los Angeles, 1962-64; spl. cons. White Meml. Med. Center, Los Angeles; pvt. practice clin. psychology, Los Angeles, 1963—; mem. disability evaluation panel Social Security Adminstrn., 1961-85. Mem. Am. Psychol. Assn., Los Angeles County Psychol. Assn., Sigma Xi, Phi Beta Kappa, Phi Kappa Phi. Jewish. Contbr. articles to profl. jours. Office: 1964 Westwood Blvd Ste 430 Los Angeles CA 90025-4651

ILCHMAN, ALICE STONE, college president, former government official; b. Cin., Apr. 18, 1935; d. Donald Crawford and Alice Kathryn (Biermann) Stone; m. Warren Frederick Ilchman, June 11, 1960; children: Frederick Andrew Crawford, Alice Sarah. BA, Mt. Holyoke Coll., 1957; MPA, Maxwell Sch. Citizenship, Syracuse U., 1958; PhD, London Sch. Econs., 1965; LHD, Mt. Holyoke Coll., 1982, Franklin and Marshall Coll., 1983. Asst. to pres., mem. faculty Berkshire C.C., 1961-64; lectr. Ctr. for South and S.E. Asia Studies U. Calif., Berkeley, 1965-73; prof. econs. and edn., dean Wellesley (Mass.) Coll., 1973-78; asst. sec. ednl. and cultural affairs Dept. State, 1978; asso. dir. ednl. and cultural affairs Internat. Communication Agy., 1978-81; advisor to sec. Smithsonian Instn., 1981; pres. Sarah Lawrence Coll., Bronxville, N.Y., 1981—; intern, asst. to Sen. John F. Kennedy, 1957; dir. Peace Corps Tng. Program for India, 1965-66; chmn. com. on women's employment NAS. Author: The New Men of Knowledge and the New States, 1968, (with W.F. Ilchman) Education and Employment in India, The Policy Nexus, 1976. Trustee Mt. Holyoke Coll., 1970-80, Mass. Found. for Humanities and Pub. Policy, 1974-77, East-West Ctr., Honolulu, 1978-81, Expt. in Internat. Living, The Markle Found., The Rockefeller Found., chmn. bd. dirs.; trustee The U. of Cape Town, South Africa, Corp. Adv. Bd., Hotchkiss Sch.; mem. Smithsonian Coun., Yonkers Emergency Fin. Control Bd., 1982-88, Am. Ditchley Found. Program Com., Internat. Rsch. ans Exch. Bd., Com. for Econ. Devel.; bd. dirs. NYNEX, Seligman Group of Investment Cos. Mem. Nat. Acad. Pub. Adminstrn., NOW Legal Def. Edn. Fund, Coun. Fgn. Rels., Cosmpolitan Club (N.Y.C.), Century Assn. (N.Y.C.), Bronxville Field Club. Home: 935 Kimball Ave Bronxville NY 10708-5507 Office: Sarah Lawrence Coll Office of the President Bronxville NY 10708

ILDERTON, JANE WALLACE, small business owner; b. Gainesville, Ga., Mar. 10, 1936; d. William Lewis and Fay E. (Montgomery) Wallace; m. James Wilson Ilderton, June 12, 1954; children: James Wilson Jr., Mark Joseph, Andrew William. Grad. high sch., Gainesville. Owner, operator Designs by Jane, Charleston, S.C.; mfr., designer SGM Baby Bags Co., 1988—. Mem. Market Mchts. Assn., Charleston Trident C. of C., Smocking Arts Guild of Am., Longstreet Soc. (charter), United Daus. Confederacy (charter). Episcopalian. Office: Designs by Jane 188 Meeting St Charleston SC 29401-3155

ILES, EILEEN MARIE, bank executive, controller; b. Highland Park, Ill., Sept. 29, 1965; d. Dennis Jay and Ida Sigrid (Calderelli) Connolly; m. Kenneth Robert Iles, Dec. 14, 1985; 1 child, Kevin Andrew. Student, U. Ill., Chgo., 1983-85; BBA in Acctg. and Mktg. Mgmt., U. N.Mex., 1988, M in Acctg., 1992. Acct. Charter Bank for Savs., Albuquerque, 1989-90, bank acctg. supr., 1990-91, asst. contr., 1991—, asst. v.p., 1992—; instr. acctg. U. N.Mex., Albuquerque, 1994—; cons. in field. Mem. Inst. Mgmt. Accts.

ILI, ESTHER KAILI, educational administrator; b. Honolulu, Nov. 2, 1945; d. Mitchell Kala and Flora Nakilau (Gonsalves) Kamana; m. Taugata To'oto'o Ili, July 29, 1970; children: Jan Kaleolani, Jeff Kamana, Brett Kahililani. BS, Ch. Coll. Hawaii, 1968; MEd, U. Hawaii, 1981. Cert. tchr., Hawaii, Am. Samoa; cert. adminstrn., Am. Samoa. Tchr. history Hawaii Radford High Sch., Honolulu, 1969-75; tchr. English, head dept. Samoana High Sch., Pago Pago, Am. Samoa, 1975-83; tchr. English ch. edn. system LDS Ch., Pesega, Upolu, Western Samoa, 1984-85; tchr. English, head dept. Tafuna High Sch., Pago Pago, 1986-89, vice prin., 1989-92; vice prin., bd. dirs. Nu'uuli Vocat. Tech. High Sch., Pago Pago, 1992—; mem. English standing curriculum com. Am. Samoa Dept. Edn., 1995—, mem. Tchr. of the Yr. com., 1994—; team mem. Pacific Region Effective and Successful Schools. Tchr. LDS Ch., Pago Pago, 1975—, advisor to young women; mem. PTA; bd. dirs. C.D. 2000; active coop. dist. Pago Pago, Am. Samona, 1996—. Recipient nomination Internat. Citizen of Yr. for Hutt River, Australia, 1996; awarded hon. title Principality of Hutt River Province; named State Tchr. of Yr., Govt. Am. Samoa, 1982. Mem. ASCD, Am. Samoa Edn. Assn., Dept. Hawaiian Home Lands, Nat. Assn. Secondary Sch. Prins., Brigham Young U.-Hawaii Alumni Assn., Ch. Coll. Hawaii Alumni Assn., Am. Vocat. Assn., Pvt. Industry Coun., Mālama O Mānoa, Young Adult Relief Soc. (tchr. 1994—), Postal Commemorative Soc., Phi Alpha Theta. Home: PO Box 5094 Pago Pago AS 96799-5094 Office: Nu'uuli Vocat Tech High Sch D O E Pago Pago AS 96799

ILLK, SERENA PEARL, accountant; b. San Angelo, Tex., July 26, 1951; d. Paul Jacob and Goldie Alberta (Crippen) I.; m. Harry Daniel McCormack, June 20, 1984 (dec. Jan., 1990). BA in Acctg., Albertson's Coll. of Idaho, 1973. CPA, Alaska, Wash. From asst. supr. to supr. spl. funds. acctg. dept. Multnomah Sch. Dist., Portland, Oreg., 1974-75; payroll dept. acct. Alyeska pipeline Fluer Alaska, Inc., Valdez, Alaska, 1976-77; various temporary positions in acctg. Seattle, 1978-80; staff acct. Peasley, Tugby & Co., CPAs, Seattle, 1981-83; sr. acct. Boyle & Assocs., CPAs, Anchorage, Alaska, 1984-86; sr. acct. Minkemann & Assocs., CPAs, Anchorage, 1987-90, ptnr., 1991—. Vol. panel mem. KTVA Channel 11, Alaska TV answering tax questions for Alaskan taxpayers, Anchorage, 1991. Mem. AICPA, Alaska Soc. CPAs, Wash. Soc. CPAs. Office: Minkemann & Assocs CPAs 4300 B St Ste 308 Anchorage AK 99503-5926

ILLNER-CANIZARO, HANA, physician, oral surgeon, researcher; b. Prague, Czechoslovakia, Nov. 2, 1939; came to U.S., 1968; d. Evzen Pospisil and Emilie (Chrastna) Pospisilova; m. Pavel Illner, June 14, 1963 (div. 1981); children: Martin Illner, Anna Illner; m. Peter Corte Canizaro, Nov. 1, 1982. MD, Charles U., Prague, 1961. Diplomate State Bd. Oral Surgery, 1963. Resident in oral surgery Inst. of Health, Pribram, Czechoslovakia, 1961-63; attending physician Oral Surgery Clinic, Prague, 1963-68; rsch. assoc. dept. surgery U. Tex. Southwestern Med. Sch., Dallas, 1969-72, instr. surgery, 1972-74; instr. surgery U. Wash. Sch. Medicine, Seattle, 1974-77; asst. prof. surgery Cornell U. Med. Coll., N.Y.C., 1977-81, assoc. prof. surgery, 1981-83; assoc. prof. surgery Tex. Tech U. Health Scis. Ctr., Lubbock, 1984-88, prof. surgery, 1988—; site visitor NIGMS Postdoctoral Tng. Grant, Bethesda, Md., 1987. Mem. editorial bd. Circulatory Shock, N.Y.C., 1981—; manuscript reviewer Surgery, Gynecology and Obstetrics, Chgo., 1985—; contbr. chpts. to books, numerous articles to profl. jours. NIH grantee, 1979-83, 87-92; Tex. Tech U Health Scis. Ctr. grantee, 1985, 86; U.S. Dept. of Army grantee, 1988-90; Fogarty Sr. Internat. fellow, 1991-92. Mem. Shock Soc. Home: 4622 8th St Lubbock TX 79416-4722 Office: Tex Tech U Health Scis Ctr 3601 4th St Lubbock TX 79430-0001

ILLUZZI, JOANN M., computer programmer, computer analyst; b. Buffalo, N.Y., Oct. 2, 1962; d. Joseph and Mary (Sollami) I. Cert. in Computer Programming, SUNY, Buffalo, 1982, BA, 1984, MA, 1994. Microcomputer programmer SUNY, Buffalo, 1984-87, programmer, analyst, 1987-88, sr. programmer, analyst, 1988—; cons. Trocaire Coll., Buffalo, 1992; instr. HSC Syracuse, N.Y., 1995. Mem. IEEE, AAUW, ACM. Home: 452 Walck Rd North Tonawanda NY 14120 Office: Computing Ctr SUNY Buffalo NY 14260

IMBROGNO, CYNTHIA, judge. BA, Ind. Univ. of Pa., 1970; JD cum laude, Gonzaga Univ. Sch. of Law, 1979. Law clk. to Hon. Justin L.

Quackenbush U.S. Dist. Ct. (Wash. ea. dist.), 9th circuit, 1980-83; law clk. Wash. State Ct. of Appeals, 1984; civil rights staff atty. Ea. Dist. of Wash., 1984-85, complex litigation staff atty., 1986-88; with Preston, Thorgrimson, Shidler, Gates & Ellis, 1988-90, Perkins Coie, 1990-91; magistrate judge U.S. Dist. Ct. (Wash. ea. dist.), 9th circuit, Spokane, 1991—. Office: US Courthouse PO Box 263 920 Riverside Ave W 7th Fl Spokane WA 99210

IMES, SHARON KAY, labor arbitrator; b. Grand Island, Nebr., Mar. 31, 1943; d. George Stark and Julieanne Marie (Ayoub) McCormick; m. Roger Loren Imes, Sept. 4, 1962; children: Loren, Matthew. BA, U. Wis., 1969, MA, 1980. Instr. Western Wis. Tech. Inst., La Crosse, 1974-75; dir. Omni, Inc., La Crosse, 1975-76; dir. disaster housing assistance program State of Wis., La Crosse and Madison, 1978-80; labor arbitrator La Crosse, 1979—; instr. U. Wis., La Crosse, 1979-90, Chippewa Valley Tech. Coll., 1989; v.p. bd. dirs. La Crosse Luth. Hosp. Found., 1985-94, pres., 1993. Mem. Citizens Environ. Coun. State of Wis., Madison, 1975-78; mem. La Crosse City Coun., 1973-79; moderator First Congl. Ch., La Crosse, 1988, bd. dirs., 1986-88; bd. dirs. La Crosse Community Theatre, Inc., 1986-88. Recipient CAROL award Wis. Jaycettes, 1975; Bush fellow, Bush Found., 1976. Mem. LWV (Wis. bd. dirs. 1989-90, 3d v.p.), AAUW (pres. LaCrosse br. 1995), Nat. Acad. Arbitrators (bd. dirs. 1995—), Indsl. Rels. Rsch. Assn., La Crosse County LWV (pres., bd. dirs. 1984-88), Rotary Internat. (dist. gov. nominee 1996), Rotary Club of LaCrosse (treas. 1989, pres. 1992). Democrat. Home: 3465 Ebner Coulee Rd La Crosse WI 54601-4358

IMMERMAN, MIA FENDLER, artist; b. Antwerp, Belgium, 1935; arrived in U.S., 1948; d. Bernard and Berthe (Gangel) Fendler; m. Benjamin Joseph Immerman, Dec. 23, 1951 (div. Mar. 1967); children: Bruce, Bernard. 3-yr. cert., Pratt Inst., 1954; 1-yr. cert., Art Student's League, 1955; art student, League G. Grosz/A. Frasconi, New Sch. Social Rsch. Illustrator mags., colorist, stylist Cohn-Hall, Marx, N.Y.C., 1955-56; textile designer Studio-Art, Inc., N.Y.C., 1955-57; freelance designer N.Y. and N.J.; art lectr. Hecksher Mus., Huntington, N.Y., 1977, also pvt. collection, L.I., N.Y., Europe, 1980-96; lectr. on chess and art at museums and librs. One person shows Gallery 84, 1982 (Medal 1982), Va. Tech., 1992 (medal 1992); exhibited in group shows Brussels, Paris, Manhattan, Queens, North Shore, L.I., Antwerp, N.Y. Orgn. ADL/Hidden Children spkr. about the holocaust to schs., 1991-96. Recipient numerous awards for art, 1967-90; Art League scholar Pratt Inst., 1951-54. Mem. Queens Chess Club (trophies), USA Chess Fedn., Manhattan Chess Club (trophies), Marshall Chess Club (trophies), Queens Chess Club. Democrat. Jewish. Home: 75-40 Austin St Forest Hills NY 11375

IMPELLIZERI, MONICA, pension fund administrator, consultant; b. N.Y.C., June 7, 1920; d. Benjamin and Elizabeth (Priolo) LoPinto; m. Mario E. Impellizeri, June 8, 1941; children: MaryLou, LilaMonica. Student, NYU, 1952-55, 55-57. Asst. advt. mgr. Lily Tulip Cups, Inc., N.Y.C., 1940-45; asst. pub. sch. adminstr. N.Y.C. Bd. of Edn., 1950-68; cons. Imperllizeri Assocs., Inc., Ft. Lee, N.J., 1972—, v.p., 1985—. Author: Yesterday's Tomorrow, 1982; one woman shows include East End Arts Coun., Riverhead, N.Y., 1991; exhibited in Parrish Art Mus., Southampton, N.Y., 1974; artist in oils and water colors. Volunteer art instr. Westchester (N.Y.) Nursing Homes, 1965-71; bd. trustees Friends of Westhampton Free Libr., Westhampton Beach, N.Y., 1985—, Westhampton Free Libr., Westhampton Beach, 1990—. Recipient St. Gaudens medal, N.Y.C., 1936. Mem. Am. Contract Bridge League, Bus. and Profl. Lodge (bd. trustees Queens, N.Y. chpt. 1970—), Southampton Artists, Westhampton Artists.

IMPELLIZZERI, ANNE ELMENDORF, insurance company executive, social services executive; b. Chgo., Jan. 26, 1933; d. Armin and Laura (Gundlach) Elmendorf; m. Julius Simon Impellizzeri, Oct. 12, 1961 (dec.); children: Laura, Theodore (dec.). BA Smith Coll., 1955; MA, Yale U., 1957. CLU; chartered fin. cons. Tchr., Amity Regional H.S., Woodbridge, Conn., 1957-58; adminstrv. and editorial asst. East Europe Inst., N.Y.C., 1958-59; health educator Met. Life Ins. Co., N.Y.C., 1959-62, 71-76, adminstrv. asst. pub. affairs, 1976-78, asst. v.p., corp. social responsibility, 1978-80, v.p., 1980-85, v.p. group ins., 1985-88; v.p. N.Y.C. Partnership, 1988-90; pres., CEO Blanton-Peale/Inst. of Religion and Health, 1990—; dir. Nuveen Mcpl. Funds, 1994—; trustee Smith Coll., 1991-96; mem. Bus. Urban Issues Coun. of the Conf. Bd., 1981-85, chair, 1983-85. Pres. Am. Assn. Gifted Children, 1975-85, chair, 1985-90; bd. dirs. Nat. Safety Coun., 1974-80; trustee Lakeland Bd. Edn., Westchester County, N.Y., 1967-71, pres., 1970-71. Named to Acad. of Women Achievers, YWCA N.Y., 1978; Fulbright grantee, 1955-56. Mem. Assn. Yale Alumni (bd. govs. 1985-88), Phi Beta Kappa. Office: Blanton-Peale Inst 3 W 29th St New York NY 10001-4504

INCOCIATI, ESTELLE ANNE, real estate agent; b. Bklyn., Mar. 23, 1926; d. Louis Morris and Dorothy (Rosenthal) Biderman; m. Guido Incociati, Dec. 28, 1975 (div. Aug. 1996); children: Susan Rodin, Linda Hein. Grad., Andrew Jackson H.S., 1944. Exec. sec. Office of K. Luxenberg, M.D., North Miami Beach, Fla., 1968-75, Office of M. Shuster, M.D., Hollywood, Fla., 1975-78; realtor assoc. Dockside Properties, Key Largo, Fla., 1980—. Mem. Com. on Status of Women, Monroe County, Fla., 1996, Health and Human Svs. Adv. Coun., Monroe County, 1996; sec. New Dem. Club, Key Largo, 1996; precinct person Monroe County Dem. Exec. Com., Marathon, Fla., 1980—; vol. Victim Advocates, 1995-96; vol. Mariners Hosp. Aux., 1996; interfaith vol. worker St. Justin's Cath. Ch. and Keys Jewish Cmty. Ctr. Mem. NOW, LWV, Bus. and Profl. Women, Zonta (chair status of women 1996). Jewish. Home: PO Box 1967-974 Gibraltar Key Largo FL 33037

INDENBAUM, DOROTHY, musician, researcher; b. N.Y.C., Nov. 24; d. Abraham and Celia (Pine) Shapiro; m. Eli Indenbaum; children: Arthur, Esther. BA, Bklyn. Coll., 1942; BS, Queens Coll., 1962; PhD, NYU, 1993. Prof. Dalcroze Sch. Music, N.Y.C., 1957-93, chmn., 1995—; prof. Hunter Coll., N.Y.C., 1970-77; assoc. dir. Ariva Players, N.Y.C., 1977—. Performed various piano solos with chamber music ensembles. Chmn. Am. Jewish Congress, 1958-60, YIVO, 1980—, Bohemian Club, 1980—, 92nd St YMHA, 1985—. Mem. Am. Women Composers (bd. dirs. 1988-93), Internat. Alliance for Women in Music (bd. dirs. 1993—), Sonneck Soc., League for Yiddish, Musicians Club (bd. dirs. 1983—), Sigma Alpha Iota (program chmn.).

INDICK, JANET, sculptor, educational administrator; b. Bklyn., Mar. 3, 1932; d. Charles and Sarah (Goldsmith) Suslak; m. Benjamin Philip Indick, Aug. 23, 1953; children: Michael Korie, Karen Leigh Indick Maizel. B.S. in Art, Hunter Coll., 1953, postgrad., 1953; postgrad. New Sch., 1961-62. Tchr. kindergarten pub. schs., Elizabeth, N.J., 1953-54; dir. nursery sch. Teaneck Jewish Ctr., N.J., 1964-92. Commns. include sculpture for Netzach Yisroel, Teaneck Jewish Ctr., 1974, Etz Chaim 1981, Sanctuary Wall Menorah 1983, Temple Beth Rishon, Wyckoff, N.J., 1981, 83, Menorah, Franklin Lakes Pub. Sch., 1983, North Shore Synagogue, Syosset, N.Y., 1993, Temple Sharey Telfilo Israel, South Orange, N.J., 1993; one-woman shows include Discovery Art Gallery, Clifton, N.Y., 1976, Mari Art Gallery, Westchester, N.Y., 1983, Hebrew Tabernacle, N.Y.C., 1984, Chubb Corp., Basking Ridge, N.J., 1985, Edward Williams Gallery, Fairleigh Dickinson U., Hackensack, N.J., 1986, Vineyard Gallery, N.Y.C., 1986, Maurice M. Pine Gallery, Fairlawn (N.J.) Pub. Libr., 1990, Quietude Garden Gallery, East Brunswick, N.J., 1991-92, Bergen Mus. Art & Sci., Paramus, N.J., 1994; juried exhbns. include Morris (N.J.) Mus., 1979, 84, Newark Mus., 1982, Jersey City Mus., 1983, Hebrew Tabernacle, N.Y.C., 1984, Parsons Gallery, N.Y.C., 1984, Lillian Heidenberg Gallery, N.Y.C., 1984-96, Shering-Plough Corp., Madison, N.J., 1987, Kerygma Gallery, Ridgewood, N.J., 1989-96, Marabella Gallery, N.Y.C., 1989, So. Vt. Art Ctr., Manchester, 1990; Nat. Assn. Women Artists Traveling Exhbns., 1989-90, 96, Fgn. Traveling Exhbns., India, 1989-90, Columbus (Ohio) Mus. Fine Art, 1989-90, Balt. Mus. Art, 1989-90, Marunouchi Gallery, N.Y.C., 1994, Waterside Gallery, W. Stockbridge, Mass., 1995, L'Atelier Gallery, Piermont, N.Y., 1994-96, Polo Gallery, Edgewater, N.J., 1994-96; represented in collections Jane Voorhees Zimmerli Art Mus. Rutgers U., New Brunswick, N.J., Corp. Towers Perrin, N.Y.C., AMP Corp., Harrisburg, Pa., Myron Mfg. Corp., Maywood, N.J., Chiropractic Health Care, Bergenfield, N.J., Bergen Mus., Paramus, N.J., Weingroup Equities Corp., N.Y.C., Hubbards Cupboard Corp., Edison, N.J., Rosenthal Art Equities, N.Y.C., Franklin Lakes (N.J.) Pub. Schs., Temple Beth Rishon, Wykoff, N.J., North Shore Synagogue, Sysosset, N.Y., Temple Sharey Tefilo, South Orange, N.J., Teaneck (N.J.) Jewish Ctr.; mem. Teaneck Arts Adv. Bd., 198288. Recipient Sculpture awards Nat. Assn. Painters and Sculptors, 1978, 80, Sculpture award Art in the Park, Paterson, N.J., 1977, Merit award IFFRA/AIA Forum on Religion, Art and Architecture, 1984, H.W. Frismuth Bronze Sculpture award 1992, Corp. award 1995, Catherine Lorillard Wolfe Art Club, 1992-95, N.J. State Coun. Arts fellow, 1981. Mem. Nat. Assn. Women Artists (N.Y. chpt. v.p. 1995-96, Pauline Law sculpture prize 1974, Clara Shainess Meml. award 1994), N.Y. Soc. Women Artists (chmn. juror 1990-96). Democrat. Jewish. Home: 428 Sagamore Ave Teaneck NJ 07666-2626

INFANTE-OGBAC, DAISY INOCENTES, sales and real estate executive, marketing executive; b. Marbel, The Philippines, Aug. 3, 1946; came to U.S., 1968; d. Jesus and Josefina (Inocentes) I.; children: Desiree Josephine, Dante Fernancio, Darrell Enerico; m. Rosben Reyes Ogbac, Jan. 30, 1987. AA with highest honors, Notre Dame of Marbel, Philippines, 1963; AB in English magna cum laude, U. Santo Tomas, Manila, 1965, BS in Psychology, 1966; MA in Communications, Fairfield U., 1971. Columnist, writer Pinoy News mag., Chgo., 1975-76, Philippine News, Chgo., 1977-80; cons. EDP Cemco Systems, Inc., Oak Brook, Ill., 1980-81; pres. Daisener, Inc., Downers Grove, Ill., 1980-82; cons. EDP Robert J. Irmen Assocs., Hinsdale, Ill., 1981-82; pres. Data Info. Systems Corp., Downers Grove, Ill., 1982-84; broker, co. mgr. Gen. Devel. Corp., Chgo., 1984-86; columnist, writer Via Times, Chgo., 1984-86; owner, pres. Marbel Realty, Chgo., 1984-88; exec. v.p. Dior Enterprises, Inc., Chgo., 1986-88; real estate sales mgr. M.J. Cumber Co., Grand Cayman, Cayman Islands, 1988-89, Vet. Real Estate, Orlando, Fla., 1989-90; sales mgr. All Star Real Estate, Inc., Orlando, 1990-92; ruby network mktg. exec. Melaleuca, Inc., 1991—; pres. Dior Enterprises, Inc., Orlando, 1992—; bd. dirs. Network Mktg. Alliance, 1996—. Author: Poems of My Youth, 1982; (lyrics and music) My First Twenty Songs, 1981; featured contbr. poems; American Poetry Anthology, vol. VIII, no. 4, Best New Poets of 1987; inventor fryer-steamer. Sec. Movement for a Free Philippines, 1984. Mem. NAFE, Am. Soc. Profl. Exec. Women, Philippine C. of C. (sec. Chgo. chpt. 1985), Bayanihan Internat. Ladies Assn., Lions (twister Fil-Am. club 1978-79). Roman Catholic.

INFOSINO, IARA CIURRIA, management consultant; b. Campinas, Sao Paulo, Brazil, Aug. 24, 1952; came to U.S., 1982; d. Humberto and Mafalda (Pavan) C.; m. Konstantinos Stavropoulos, Feb. 2, 1980 (div.); m. Charles J. Infosino, Feb. 24, 1995; 1 child, Melissa Rose. BS in Math., São Paulo State U., São José do Rio Preto, Brazil, 1974; MS in Applied Math., UNICAMP, Campinas, Brazil, 1982; PhD in Ops. Rsch., Stanford U., 1989. H.S. tchr. Colegio Santo Andre, São Jose'do Rio Preto, Brazil, 1973-74; tchg. asst. UNESP, São Jose'do Rio Preto, Brazil, 1974; asst. prof. Bus. Sch., São Jose'do Rio Preto, Brazil, 1973-75, UNICAMP, Campinas, Brasil, 1978-82; sr. cons. Bender Mgmt. Cons., Arlington, Va., 1989—. Mem. INFORMS Inst. Office: Bender Mgmt Cons 1755 Jefferson Davis Hwy Ste 904 Arlington VA 22202

INGA, KANDRA JOYCE (KANDRA BAKER), actress, sales and marketing professional; b. Northridge, Calif., Dec. 18, 1959; d. Mel Frank and Joyce (Harrison) Baker; m. Joseph Vincent Inga, Sept. 14, 1985. BS summa cum laude, Calif. Luth. U., 1978. Nat. sales mgr. Tech Distributing, Canoga Park, Calif., 1979-81; v.p. sales and mktg. Morris Inc., Torrance, Calif., 1985—; dir. children's music Hope Chapel, Hermosa Beach, Calif., 1988—; dir. children's plays, 1989—; dance performer Norris Theatre, Palos Verdes, Calif., 1991, 92, 93. Appeared in film Eternity, 1990, Double O Kio, 1992, A Million to Juan, 1993, Better Harvest, 1993, Ava's Magical Adventure, 1994; (video) L.A. Bodyworks, 1990, Rock-A-Long with Bo Peep, 1992, (TV) Knots Landing, 1987, (theatre) The Outcasts of Poker Flat, 1983 (Best Actress 1983); co-prodr. (video) Computer Tng. Series, 1990, Learning DOS, 1990 (Am. Film award 1990). Mem. AFTRA, SAG, Women in Entertainment, Hope in Action, Media Focus (merchandising com. 1994). Republican. Home: 1746 Spreckels Ln Redondo Beach CA 90278-4734 Office: Morris Inc 2707 Plaza Del Amo Ste 601 Torrance CA 90503-7359

INGALLS, JEREMY, poet, educator; b. Gloucester, Mass., Apr. 2, 1911; d. Charles A. and May E. (Dodge) Ingalls. AB, Tufts Coll., 1932, AM, 1933; student, U. Chgo., 1938-39; LHD, Rockford Coll., 1960; LittD, Tufts U., 1965. Asst. prof. English Lit. Western Coll., Oxford, Ohio, 1941-43; resident poet, asst. prof. English lit. Rockford (Ill.) Coll., 1948-50, successively assoc. prof. English and Asian studies, prof., chmn. div. arts, chmn. English dept., 1950-60; Fulbright prof. Am. lit., Japan, 1957; Rockefeller Found. lectr. Kyoto Am. Studies seminar, 1958. Author: A Book of Legends, 1941, The Metaphysical Sword, 1941, Tahl, 1945, The Galilean Way, 1953, The Woman from the Island, 1958, These Islands Also, 1959, This Stubborn Quantum, 1983, Summer Liturgy, 1985, The Epic Tradition and Related Essays, 1989; translator (from Chinese) A Political History of China, 1840-1928 (Li Chien-Nung), 1956, The Malice of Empire (Yao Hsin-Nung), 1970, (from Japanese) Tenno Yugao (Nakagawa), 1975. Recipient Yale Series of Younger Poets prize, 1941, Shelley Meml. award, 1950, and other awards for poetry; apptd. hon. epic poet laureate United Poets Laureate Internat., 1965; Guggenheim fellow, 1943, Chinese classics rsch. fellow Republic of China, 1945, 46, Am. Acad. Arts and Letters grantee, 1944, Ford Found. fellow Asian studies, 1952, 53. Fellow Internat. Inst. Arts and Letters; mem. MLA (chmn. Oriental-western lit. rels. conf.), Assn. Asian Studies (life), Authors Guild, Poetry Soc. Am., New Eng. Poetry Soc., Dante Soc. Am. (life), Phi Beta Kappa, Chi Omega. Episcopalian. Home: 6269 E Rosewood St Tucson AZ 85711-1638

INGALLS, LEZA TAFT, artist, set designer; b. Cleve., June 18, 1957; d. Albert Stimpson Ingalls and Angela Marie (DiFrancesco) Sutherlin. AA, Santa Monica (Calif.) Coll., 1983; BFA, Otis Coll. of Art and Design, L.A., 1986; postgrad. in tching. credential program, Calif. State U., L.A., 1995—. Freelance scenic artist L.A., 1989—. Designer (furniture) and figurative painter; group shows include 50 Bucks Gallery, L.A., 1989, A B Gallery, L.A., 1994, 96, Downtown Arts Devel. Assn., L.A., 1994; exhibited in two-person show at Otis/Parson Gallery, L.A., 1986; one-person shows include Lhasa Club, Hollywood, Calif., 1986, Stockmarket Gallery, L.A., 1990. Democrat.

INGALLS, MARIE CECELIE, former state legislator, retail executive; b. Faith, S.D., Mar. 31, 1936; d. Jens P. and Ida B. (Hegre) Jensen; m. Dale D. Ingalls, June 20, 1955; children: Duane, Delane. BS, Black Hills State Coll., 1973, MS, 1978. Elem. tchr. Meade County Schs., Sturgis, S.D., 1957-72, Faith Sch. Dist. 46-2, 1973-76; elem. prin. Meade Sch. Dist. 46-1, Sturgis, 1976-81; owner, operator Ingalls, Sturgis, 1978—; mem., asst. majority whip S.D. House Reps., Pierre, 1986-92. Former sec. S.D. Rep. Orgn. Recipient Woman of Achievement award City of Sturgis, 1986. Mem. S.D. Cattlewomen, S.D. Stockgrowers (edn. chair), S.D. Farm Bur. (bd. dirs. dist. V), S.D. Retailers Assn. (bd. dirs., sec.-treas.), S.D. Ins. Commn., Faith C. of C. (pres. 1989), Sturgis C. of C. (past bd. dirs.), Optimists (bd. dirs.), Zonta. Republican. Lutheran. Home: PO Box 31 Mud Butte SD 57758 Office: Ingalls 1032 Main St Sturgis SD 57785-1523

INGBER, BARBARA, art gallery executive; b. N.Y.C., Apr. 18, 1932; d. Benjamin and Rose Adler; m. Miles R. Ingber, Oct. 26, 1958; children: Douglas, Madeline. Student NYU, 1953, New Sch. for Social Research, 1955. Br. merchandise distbr. Lord & Taylor, N.Y.C., 1955-65; dir. Ingber Art Gallery, 1972—. Office: Artists Mus 250 W 57th St Ste 1517 New York NY 10107

INGLETT, BETTY LEE, retired media services administrator; b. Augusta, Ga., Oct. 6, 1930; d. Wilfred Lee and Elizabeth Arelia (Crouch) I. BS in Edn., Ga. State Coll. for Women, 1953; MA in Library, Media and Edn. Adminstrn., Ga. So. U., 1980; EdD in Edn. Adminstrn., Nova U., 1988. Tchr. James L. Fleming Elem. Sch., Augusta, Ga., 1953-63, Murphey Jr. High Sch., Augusta, 1963-64, Sego Jr. High Sch., Augusta, 1964-68, Glenn Hills High Sch., Augusta, 1968-75; media specialist Nat. Hills Elem. Sch., Augusta, 1975-80; prin. Lake Forest Elem. Sch., Augusta, 1980-84, Joseph R. Lamar Elem. Sch., Augusta, 1984-86; dir. ednl. media services Richmond County Bd. Edn., Augusta, 1986—; owner, operator Betty Inglett Enterprises, Augusta. Contbr. articles to profl. jours. Bd. dirs. Am. Heart Fund, 1975-80, Am. Cancer Fund, 1986—; del. Dem. State Conv., 1982; council mem. PTA. (life), 1985. Named Adminstr. of Yr., 1988-89. Mem. Richmond County Edn. Assn. (sec. v.p. 1961-63, Adminstr. of Yr. 1989-90), AAUW (v.p. 1957-59), NEA, Ga. Assn. Edn., Ga. Assn. Ednl. Leaders, Ga. Library Media Dept., Ga. Library Assn., Ga. Assn. Instructional Tech., Ga. Assn. Curriculum Instructional Supr., Profl. Leadership Assn., Cen. Savannah River Area Library Assn., Alpha Delta Kappa, Phi Delta Pi, Phi Delta Kappa. Baptist.

INGMIRE, JENNIFER JOAN, aerospace engineer; b. Rochester, Mich., Feb. 7, 1969; d. Billy Raymond and Barbara Joan (Dorsch) Wheeler; m. Eric Alan Jackson (div. Dec. 1991); 1 child, Tia Marie Jackson; m. Gordon Duane Ingmire, Feb. 3, 1995; children: Toby Alexander, Taylor Shane. BS, U. Ariz., 1992, MS in Mech. Engring., 1995. Teaching asst. U. Ariz. Machine Shop, Tucson, 1991-93, NASA, U. Ariz., Tucson, 1993-95; aerospace engr. Naval Aviation Depot, Jacksonville, Fla., 1995—. Contbr. articles to profl. jours. Troop leader Girl Scouts Am., Tucson, 1994-95, Jacksonville, 1995—; Sunday sch. tchr. St. Catherine's Ch., Orange Park, Fla., 1995—. NASA grantee, 1994-95, others. Mem. AIAA (vice chair 1994-95). Roman Catholic. Home: 2601 Sandlewood Ct Orange Park FL 32065

INGOLD, CATHERINE WHITE, academic administrator; b. Columbia, S.C., Mar. 15, 1949; d. Hiram Hutchison and Annelle (Stover) White; m. Wesley Thomas Ingold, June 13, 1970; 1 child, Thomas Bradford Hutchison. Student, U. Paris-Sorbonne, 1969; BS in French with honors, Hollins Coll., 1970; MA in Romance Langs., U. Va., 1972, PhD in French, 1979; DHum honoris causa, Francis Marion U., Florence, S.C., 1992. Assoc. prof. romance langs. Gallaudet U., Washington, 1973-88, dir. hons. program, 1980-85, dean arts and scis., 1985-86, provost, v.p. acad. affairs, 1986-88; pres. Am. U. of Paris, 1988-92, Curry Coll., Milton, Mass., 1992—; pres. N.E. region Nat. Collegiate Honors Coun., 1983-84. Bd. dirs. Am. Sch. of Paris; vestry Christ Ch., Alexandria, Va., Milton Hosp. Corp. Recipient Prix Morot-Sir de Langue et Littérature françaises (Hollins). Mem. MLA, Nat. Collegiate Honors Coun., Lychnos Soc. (U.Va.), Phi Beta Kappa. Episcopalian. Home: 956 Brush Hill Rd Milton MA 02186-1227 Office: Curry Coll 1071 Blue Hill Ave Milton MA 02186-9984

INGRAM, JUDITH KEIG, university administrator, educator; b. Chgo., Dec. 7, 1932; d. Marshall and Gertrude (Woodruff) Keig; m. Gordon Lawrence Ingram, June 14, 1958; children: Elizabeth, Katherine Frank, Margaret, Michael. BA in History, Vassar Coll., 1954; MA in Edn. Adminstrn., No. Mich. U., 1977; PhD in Teaching and Learning Processes, Northwestern U., 1987. Cert. tchr. K-12, gen. adminstrn. with supts. endorsement, Ill. Dir. radio and tv Chgo. Coun. on Fgn. Rels., 1954-57; asst. dir. pub. rels. Chgo. Assn. Commerce and Industry, 1957-58; organizing prin. Marquette (Mich.) Alternative Sr. High., 1977-80; asst. to supt. Pub. Schs., Marquette, 1980-82; teaching asst., instr. Northwestern U., Evanston, Ill., 1983-87; chair dept. tchr. edn. Mundelein Coll., Chgo., 1989-91; chair dept. curriculum, instr., edn. psyc., assoc. prof. Loyola U. Sch. Edn., Chgo., 1991—; cons. in alternative edn. Mich. Pub. Schs., 1980-82; cons. edn. tech. Chgo. city and suburban schs., 1993-94; resource participant Mortimer Adler Seminar and Inst. for A Theol. Future Seminar, Aspen Inst. Humanistic Studies; bd. dirs. Mich. Assn. Ednl. Options. Contbr. articles to profl. jours. Elected mem. Bd. Edn. Dist. 2, Bensenville, Ill., 1973-75; ruling elder United Presbyn. Ch., 1975—; program developer Home Assistance Found., Bensenville, Ill., 1967-72; steering com. Econ. Devel. Corp., Marquette. Nominee Leadership for Learning award Nat. Assn. of Sch. Adminstrn. Nat. Convention, 1982. Mem. ASCD, Am. Assn. Coll. Tchrs. Edn., Am. Assn. Computers Edn., Ill. Assn. Coll. Tchrs. Edn., Internat. Soc. Tech. Edn., Phi Beta Kappa. Presbyterian. Home: 320 Washington Ave Wilmette IL 60091-1964 Office: CIEP Sch of Edn Loyola U Mallinckrodt Camp 1041 Ridge Rd Wilmette IL 60091-1560

INGRAM, MARCIA LYNNE, critical care nurse; b. Birmingham, Ala., June 23, 1956; d. Billy McCullough Ingram and Lillie Louise (Pope) Callahan; m. James Ronald Pierce, Sept. 22, 1979 (div. 1986); 1 child, Alana Nicole. AA, Tallahassee (Fla.) C. C., 1988; BSN, Fla. State U., 1991. Cert. RN, Ala., Emergency Nurse. Nurse tech. Tallahasse Meml. Reg. Med. Ctr., 1988-90, nursing asst., 1991, charge nurse, staff nurse, 1992; charge nurse U. Hosp. Birmingham, 1992—; chair emergency dept. Nurse Practice Coun., provider advanced cardiac life support, 1994—, advanced burn life support, 1995—, trauma nursing core course, 1993—. Contbr. Am. Cancer Soc. Mem. Emergency Nurses Assn. Republican. Baptist. Home: 3128 Midland Dr Birmingham AL 35223 Office: U Ala 619 S 19th St Birmingham AL 35233

INGRAM, MARGI, real estate broker; b. Central, Ala.; d. Jack and Dru (Graham) I. BS, U. Ala., 1969, postgrad., 1971-72. Tchr. pub. schs. Birmingham, Ala., 1970-78; broker Gilliland & Co., Birmingham, 1978-79; broker, pres. Ingram & Assocs., Birmingham, 1979—; mktg. cons. Collateral Mktg., Birmingham, 1982-84, Royal Homes, Inc., 1982—, Gibson-Anderson-Evins, 1983—, City Fed. Savs. & Loan Assn., 1983-85. Bd. dirs. Humane Soc. Birmingham, 1980, United Cerebral Palsy; trustee Hew Hours Mktg. Group Am. Named Bus. Exec. of Yr. Birmingham Bus. Jour., 1985. Mem. Nat. Assn. Realtors, Ala. Assn. Realtors, Birmingham Bd. Realtors, Fed. Land Inst., Sales Mktg. Execs. Internat., Birmingham C. of C. (trustee). Democrat. Episcopalian. Office: Ingram Hayes & Assocs 2336 20th Ave S Birmingham AL 35223-1006

INGRAM, PENNY ANN, bank executive; b. Nassau, Bahamas, Mar. 11, 1964; came to U.S., 1970; d. A. Stanley Cooper and Ann Lavendar (Wilson) Hopkins; m. William Roy Ingram, Mar. 10, 1990. A in Bus., Miami (Fla.) Dade C.C., 1985; B in Fin., Fla. Internat. U., 1988. Bank examiner U.S. Treasury-OTS, Maitland, Fla., 1989-93; v.p., compliance officer Unifirst Fed., Hollywood, Fla., 1993-95, First Security Bankshores, Inc., Hartwell, Ga., 1995—. Mem. Fin. Mgmt. Assn., Hartwell Rotary Club, Phi Kappa Phi. Democrat. Office: Bank of Hartwell 331 E Franklin St Hartwell GA 30643

INGRAM, SHIRLEY JEAN, social worker; b. Louisville, Oct. 22, 1946. BA in Social Sci., U. Hawaii, Pearl City, 1979; MSW, Fla. State U., 1982. Lic. clin. social worker, Fla.; bd. cert. diplomate social worker, qualified clin. social worker, Md.; cert. family mediator Fla. Supreme Ct., 1991. Case mgr. Geriatric Residential Treatment Ctr., Crestview, Fla., 1982-84; case mgmt. supr. Okaloosa Guidance Ctr., Fort Walton Beach, Fla., 1984-86; family counselor Harbor Oaks Hosp., Fort Walton Beach, 1986-87; pvt. practice Fort Walton Beach, 1987-95; social worker USAF Family Advocacy Office, Hurlburt Field, Fla., 1995—. Mem. Mental Health Assn. Okaloosa County (sec. bd. dirs. 1988—, mem. adv. bd. dirs. Area Agy. on Aging, chmn. adv. bd. dirs., Okaloosa County Area Agy. on Aging, pres.), NASW, Long Term Care Ombudsman Coun., AAUW, Sertoma. Home: 3 Palm Dr Shalimar FL 32579 Office: USAF Family Advocacy Office Hurlburt Field FL 32579

INGRAM, VALERIE K., college development administrator; b. Tucumcari, N.Mex., Feb. 24, 1967; d. Lawrence B. and Barbara T. (Martin) I.; m. Gregory O. Pringle, July 24, 1993. Cert. de la Langue Pratique, Univ. de Haute Bretague, Rennes, France, 1988; BA, Grinnell Coll., 1989. Registrar Mus. of N.Mex., Santa Fe, 1992-94; devel. officer Santa Fe C.C., 1994—. Active Santa Fe Pro Musica Guild, 1996. Mem. Santa Fe Downtown Kiwanis, Kiwanis Found. Bd. Office: Santa Fe CC PO Box 4187 Santa Fe NM 87502

INGRAM-TINSLEY, DOROTHY CATHERINE, library automation specialist, horse stables owner; b. Albemarle, N.C., Feb. 28, 1960; d. Daniel Hoyett and Lillian Ruth I.; m. Richard Edward Tinsley, July 1, 1989. B, Appalachian State U., 1981; ML, Cath. U. Am., 1982; student, J. Sargent Reynolds, 1983-93, Stanly County C.C., 1994—. Notary Pub., N.C. Tech. svc. libr. Telesec, Inc., Kinsington, Md., 1981-83; dir. data maintenance Va. State Libr., Richmond, Va., 1983-85, head serials dept. serials and automation, 1985-88; libr. specialist Fed. Res. Bank of Richmond, 1988-93; owner, mgr. Albemarle Stables, 1994—, New Horizons Equine Edn. Ctr., 1995—; rep. Innovative Enhancements Com., Berkeley, Calif., 1993. Active Richmond (Va.) Jaycees, 1985-86. Mem. ALA, N.C. Libr. Assn., Spl. Librs. Assn., Stanly Horse Coun., N.C. Horse Coun., N.C. Horse Coun., Am. Quarter Horse Assn. Avocations: hunting, camping, crafts, writing. Home: 32034 Valley Dr Albemarle NC 28001 Office: Albemarle Stables 32034 Valley Dr Albemarle NC 28001

INKELLIS, BARBARA G., lawyer; b. Rockville Ctr., N.Y., Apr. 8, 1949; d. Adolph J. and Edith (Zackowitz) Greenberg; m. Steven Alan Inkellis, May 19, 1979; children: Elizabeth, David. AB, Dickinson Coll., 1971; MEd., George Washington U., 1973, JD, 1978. Bar: D.C. 1978, U.S. Dist. Ct. D.C. 1979. Assoc. Bracewell & Patterson, Washington, 1978-79, Fried, Frank, Harris, Shriver & Jacobson, Washington, 1979-81; gen. counsel Cambridge Info. Group, Bethesda, Md., 1981—. Mem. ABA. Office: Cambridge Info Group 7200 Wisconsin Ave Bethesda MD 20814-4811

INMAN, ANA M. JIMENEZ, secondary education educator; b. Rio Piedras, P.R., Jan. 5, 1962; d. Antonio Jiménez del Toro and Ana E. Colon Fontan. BA, U. P.R., 1985, postgrad. Cert. secondary Spanish tchr., P.R., profl. edn. cert. continuing tchr. English 4-12, Spanish K-12, Wash., DSHS Med. and Social Svcs. interpreter/translator in Spanish, Wash., notary public, Wash.; cert. cmty. first aid and safety instr. ARC. Tutor La Mansion, Rio Piedras; tchr. Colegio Mater Salvatoris, Cupey, P.R., Colegio Nuestra Senora de Altagracia, Rio Piedras, Colegio San Jose, Rio Piedras; Am. Sch., Bayamón, P.R., Escuela Superior Católica de Bayamón; clk. I-II, interpreter Seafirst Bank-Trust Vault, Seattle; office mgr., adminstrv. asst. El Centro de la Raza, Seattle; adminstrv. team leader, mgr. Las Brisas housing program Consejo Counseling and Referral Svc., Seattle, vocat. rehab. program mgr.; instr. Spanish Rites Of Passage Experience program Ctrl. Area Motivation Program; pvt. tutor in Spanish and all subject matters; acad.-vocat. counselor/tchr. Sea Mar, Seattle. Vol., cert. instr. ARC. Mem. ASCD, Nat. Notary Assn., Wash. State Ct. Interpreters & Translators Soc., Phi Delta Kappa. Home: 21808-55th Ave W Mountlake Terrace WA 98043

INMAN, MARIANNE ELIZABETH, college administrator; b. Berwyn, Ill., Jan. 9, 1943; d. Miles V. and Bessee M. (Hejtmanek), Pizak; m. David P. Inman; Aug 1, 1964. BA, Purdue U., 1964; AM, Ind. U., 1967; PhD, U. Tex., 1978. Dir. Comml. Div. Worl Instruction and Translation, Inc., Arlington, Va., 1969-71; program staff mem. Ctr. for Applied Linguistics, Arlington, 1972-73; lectr. in French No. Va. Community Coll., Bailey's Crossroads, 1973; faculty mem., linguistic researcher Tehran (Iran) U., 1973-75; intern mgmt. edn. rsch. & devel. S.W Ednl. Devel. Lab., Austin, Tex., 1977-78; asst. prof., program dir. Southwestern U., Georgetown, Tex., 1978; dir. English lang. inst. Alaska Pacific U., Anchorage, 1980-87, chairperson all-U. requirements, 1984-88, assoc. dean acad. affairs, 1988-90; v.p. dean of coll. Northland Coll., Ashland, Wis., 1990-95; pres. Ctrl. Meth. Coll., Fayette, Mo., 1995—; contbr. Pres. Commn. Foreign Lang. and Internat. Studies, Washington, 1978-79; manuscript evaluator The Modern Lang. Jour., Columbus, Ohio, 1979-84; cons. Anchorage Sch. Dist., 1984-90; cons., evaluator N. Cen. Assn. Colls. and Schs., Chgo., 1990—; mem. dean's task force Coun. on Ind. Colls., 1993—. Co-author: English for Medical Students, 1976; co-author and editor: English for Science and Engineering Students, 1977; contbr. articles to profl. jours. Treas. Alaska Humanities Forum, Anchorage, 1982-87; mem. Anchorage Matanuska-Susitna Borough Pvt. Industry Coun., 1983-86; treas. Sister Cities Commn., Anchorage, 1984-90; mem. Multicultural Edn. Adv. Bd., Anchorage, 1987-90; active speakers bur. Wis. Humanities Com., 1992-95, Mcpl. Libr. Bd., 1993-95. Named Fellow of Grad. Sch., U. Tex. Austin, 1977-78, Nat. Teaching Fellow, Alaska Pacific U., Anchorage, 1980-81; recipient Pub. Svc. award Sister Cities Commn., Anchorage, 1987, Kellogg Found. Nat. fellowship, Battle Creek, Mich., 1988-91. Mem. League of Women Voters, Nat. Assn. Women in Edn., Am. Assn. for Higher Edn., Am. Coun on Teaching of Foreign Langs., Tchrs. of English to Speakers of Other Langs., Nat. Coun. Tchrs. of English, Sigma Kappa. Office: Ctrl Meth Coll 411 CMC Sq Fayette MO 65248-1198

INNIS, PAULINE, author, publishing company executive; b. Devon, Eng.; came to U.S., 1954; m. Walter Deane Innis, Aug. 1, 1959. Attended U. Manchester, U. London. Author: Hurricane Fighters, 1962; Ernestine or the Pig in the Potting Shed, 1963, paperback, 1992; The Wild Swans Fly, 1964; The Ice Bird, 1965; Wind of the Pampas, 1967; Fire from the Fountains, 1968; Astronumerology, 1971; Gold in the Blue Ridge, 1973, 2d edit., 1980; My Trails (transl. from French), 1975; (with Mary Jane McCaffery) Protocol, 1977; Prayer and Power in the Capital, 1982, The Secret Gardens of Watergate, 1987, Attention: A Quick Guide to the Armed Services, 1988, Desert Storm Diary, 1991, The Nursing Home Companion, 1993, Bridge Across the Seas, 1995. Bd. dirs. Washington Goodwill Industries Guild, 1962-66; membership chmn. Welcome to Washington Club, 1961-64; co-chmn. Internat. Workshop Capital Speakers' Club, 1961-64; pres. Children's Book Guild, 1967-68; dir. Ednl. Communications; bd. dirs. Internat. Conf. Women Writers and Journalists, Nat. Arboretum, 1992-95; mem. criminal justice com. D.C. Commn. on Status of Women; founder vol. program D.C. Women's Detention Center; chmn. women's com. Washington Opera, 1977-79; mem. Liaison Com. for Med. Edn., 1979-85; nat. trustee Med. Coll., Pa., 1980—; mem. Edn. Commn. for Fgn. Med. Grads., 1986—; bd. mem. Nat. Arboretum. Named Hoosier Woman of Yr., 1966. Mem. Soc. Woman Geographers, Authors League, Smithsonian Assocs. (women's bd.), English-Speaking Union, Spanish-Portuguese Group D.C. (pres. 1965-66), Brit. Inst. U.S., Am. Newspaper Women's Club (pres. 1971-73), Nat. Press. Club, Internat. Soc. Poets (disting.), Sulgrave Club, Venerable Order St. John of Jerusalem. Home: 2700 Virginia Ave NW Washington DC 20037-1908

INSARDI, NINA ELIZABETH, benefits administrator; b. Port Chester, N.Y., Dec. 8, 1960; d. Albert Charles and Dorothy Elizabeth (Adis) I. BA in English magna cum laude, U. Richmond, 1982. Exec. sec. CBS Inc., N.Y.C., 1984-85, adminstrv. asst., 1985-86, supr. insured plans, 1986-87, mgr. benefits adminstrn., 1987-89, mgr. benefits comm., 1989-96, assoc. dir. benefits comm., 1996—. Editor newsletter CBS Benefits Bull. Tutor Literacy Vols. of Am., Westchester, N.Y., 1989-94; fundraising vol. U. Richmond, N.Y. Alumni Chpt., 1993—; election dist. leader Rye (N.Y.) Dem. Com., 1992—. Mem. Phi Beta Kappa. Democrat. Presbyterian. Office: CBS Inc 51 W 52nd St New York NY 10019-6119

INSCHO, BARBARA PICKEL, mathematics educator; b. Bristol, Tenn., May 25, 1936; d. Robert Roger and Willa Etta (McCarter) Pickel; children: Sara Inscho Johnson, Paula Inscho Trentham. AA, BS, Tenn. Wesleyan Coll., 1957; MS, U. Tenn., Knoxville, 1977; postgrad., U. of the South, 1962-66. Cert. tchr., Tenn. Tchr. math. Sevier County H.S., Sevierville, Tenn., 1957-58, Cocoa (Fla.) H.S., 1958-62, Princeton (N.J.) H.S., 1963-65; assoc. prof. math. Hiwassee Coll., Madisonville, Tenn., 1966-69, 85-88; tchr. math. Madisonville H.S., 1972-83, Maryville (Tenn.) H.S., 1983-85, 88—; adj. prof. math. Tenn. Wesleyan Coll., Athens, 1983-85. Co-author: Basic Skills Practice Book, 1986. V.p. Monroe County Dem. Women, Madisonville, 1990-92; mem. Maryville Coll. Cmty. Choir, 1992-93, 94-95'; tchr. Sunday sch. 1st Bapt. Ch., Madisonville, 1990-92, ch. choir soloist Fairview United Meth. Ch., 1993—. Recipient Tandy Tech. Scholars award of excellence in math., sci. and computer sci. Tandy Found., 1994; NSF grantee, 1962-66; named Tchr. of Yr., Hiwassee Coll., 1986-87. Mem. NEA, Tenn. Edn. Assn., East Tenn. Edn. Assn. (pres. 1982-83, exec. com. 1976-84), Maryville Edn. Assn. (pres. 1991-92), Nat. Coun. Tchrs. Math., Tenn. Math Tchrs. Assn., Smoky Mountain Math. Edn. Assn. Methodist. Home: 1518 Raulston Rd Maryville TN 37803-2861 Office: Maryville H S Math Dept 825 Lawrence Ave Maryville TN 37803-4857

INSCHO, JEAN ANDERSON, social worker; b. Camden, N.J., Oct. 31, 1936; d. George Myrick and Alfrida Elizabeth (Anderson) Hewitt; m. James Ronald Inscho, June 4, 1955 (div. Mar. 1982); children: James Ronald Jr., Cynthia Ann, Michael Merrick. BA, Fla. Atlantic U., 1971; MA in Coll. Teaching, Auburn U., 1974. Lic. bachelor social worker. Instr. So. Union State Jr. Coll., Wadley, Ala., 1973-75; social worker Jefferson County Dept. Human Resources, Birmingham, Ala., 1976-77, Shelby County Dept. Human Resources, Columbiana, Ala., 1977-78, Houston County Dept. Human Resources, Dothan, Ala., 1978—; adj. instr. Troy State U., Dothan, 1982—. Bd. dirs., v.p. Adolescent Resource Ctr., 1992-93, sec., 1993-95; mem. Alzheimer's Assn., Dothan Area Bot. Gardens. EPDA fellow Auburn U., 1973, 74. Mem. Ala. State Employees Assn. (v.p. Wiregrass chpt. 1987-91, bd. dirs. 1996—), Dist. 7 State Employees Assn. (polit. action com. rep., 1994-96), Ala. Master Gardeners (bd. dirs.), Wiregrass Master Gardeners (pres. 1994-95), Am. Daffodil Soc., Ala. Gerontol. Soc. Episcopalian. Office: Houston County Dept Human Resources 1605 Ross Clark Cir Dothan AL 36301-5438

INSELBERG, RACHEL, retired educator, researcher; b. Manila, Jan. 2, 1934; came to U.S., 1955; d. Melecio and Rosalia (Medrano) Marzan; m. Edgar Inselberg, Aug. 12, 1956; 1 child, Louise Jesse. BS, Philippine Women's U., Manila, 1954; MS, U. Ill., 1956, PhD, Ohio State U., 1960. Tchr. nursery sch. Philippine Women's U., Manila, 1954-55; tchr. 3d grade Pleasant (Ohio) Sch., 1956-57; teaching asst. Ohio State U., Columbus, 1957-59; asst. prof. Carnegie Inst. Tech. Carnegie-Mellon U., Pitts., 1961-65; from asst. to assoc. prof. Western Mich. U., Kalamazoo, 1966-73, prof., 1973-95; ret., 1995. Contbr. articles to prof. jours. Active Dem. Campaign, Kalamazoo, 1984, 86, 88. Fulbright scholar, 1955; U. Ill. fellow, 1955; grantee U.S. Office Edn., 1963, Western Mich. U., 1972, 79, 87, Bronson Clin. Investigative Unit, 1987. Mem. Am. Ednl. Rsch. Assn., Nat. Assn. for the Edn. Young Children, Soc. for Rsch. Child Devel., Phi Kappa Phi. Jewish. Home: 3006 Winchell Ave Kalamazoo MI 49008-2176

INSELMAN, LAURA SUE, pediatrician; b. Bklyn., Nov. 2, 1944; d. Alexander M. and Rae (Bloom) Inselman. BA, Barnard Coll., 1966; MD, Med. Coll. Pa., 1970. Diplomate Am. Bd. Pediatrics, Am. Bd. Pediatric Pulmonology. Intern and resident St. Lukes Hosp. Ctr., N.Y.C., 1970-73; fellow in pediatric pulmonary disease Babies Hosp., N.Y.C., 1973-76; chief pediatric pulmonary div. Interfaith Med. Ctr., Bklyn., 1976-81; chief pediatric pulmonary div. North Shore Univ. Hosp., Manhasset, N.Y., 1981-86; clin. dir. pediatric pulmonary div. Newington Con. Children's Hosp., 1987-92; pulmunologist, med. dir. dept. respiratory care A.I. duPont Inst., Wilmington, Del., 1992—; asst. prof. pediatrics Cornell U. Med. Coll., N.Y.C., 1981-86; asst. clin. prof. pediatrics, Yale U. Sch. Medicine, New Haven, 1987-92; asst. prof. pediatrics, U. Conn. Health Ctr., Farmington, 1987-92; assoc. prof. pediatrics, Jefferson Med. Coll. Thomas Jefferson U. Hosp., Phila., 1992—; mem. staff Good Samaritan Hosp., West Islip, N.Y., 1982-87. Bd. dirs. Am. Lung Assn. Nassau-Suffolk, East Meadow, N.Y., 1983-86, Del., 1992—. Fellow Am. Acad. Pediatrics, Am. Coll. Chest Physicians; mem. Am. Thoracic Soc., Am. Fedn. Clin. Research, N.Y. Acad. Medicine, Harvey Soc., Soc. Pediatric Research. Office: AI DuPont Inst 1600 Rockland Rd Wilmington DE 19803-3607

INSKEEP, CAROLEE ROBERTS, writer, researcher; b. Walton, N.Y., Mar. 3, 1968; d. Rebecca Alice Dann; m. Steven Alan Inskeep, June 19, 1993. BS in Writing for TV, Radio and Film, Syracuse U., 1991; MA in Cinema Studies, NYU, 1993. Exec. sec. Roger Ailes Comm., Inc., N.Y.C., 1990-91; writer, rschr., N.Y.C., 1993—. Author: The New York Foundling Hospital, 1995, The Children's Aid Society, 1996. Methodist. Home: 121 Washington St Apt 4 Hoboken NJ 07030

INSPRUCKER, NANCY RHOADES, air force officer; b. Fort Campbell, Ky., June 16, 1959; d. Glen Lee and Mary Josephine (Lasell) Rhoades; m. John L. Inspruker III, July 20, 1991. BS in Astro Engring., U.S. Air Force Acad., 1981; MS in Aero. and Astronaut. Engring., Stanford U., 1985. Commd. 2d lt. U.S. Air Force, 1981, advanced through grades to maj., 1993; satellite test engr. space div. Los Angeles, 1981-84; instr. dept. astronautics USAF Acad., Colorado Springs, Colo., 1985-88; chief payload devel. and integration divsn. Office Sec. Air Force, L.A. AFB, 1988-90, chief mission processing divsn., 1990-92; chief sys. engr. Office Def. Landsat, Pentagon, Washington, 1992-94, chief sys. engr. divsn. Office of Space Sys. Office Asst. Sec. Air Force, 1994-95, dir. advanced spacecraft acquisition Office Space & Tech. Office Asst. Sec. Air Force, 1995—. Recipient Medal of Merit, Nat. Air Force Assn., 1985; named Colorado Springs Mil. Woman of Yr., Gazettte Telegraph newspaper, 1987. Mem. Air Force Assn., Am. Astronautical Soc., Soc. Women Engrs. Avocations: aerobics, long distance running, sewing. Home: 2202 Central Ave Vienna VA 22182-5193 Office: The Pentagon Washington DC 20050

INTILLI, SHARON MARIE, television director, small business owner; b. Amsterdam, N.Y., Aug. 11, 1950; d. Francisco Joseph Intilli and Virginia Eleanor (Tallman) Monaco. Cert., Paralegal Inst., 1973; BA in Psychology, Fordham U., 1995. Group assoc. editor Matthew Bender & Co., N.Y.C., 1974-77; prodn. sec. 20/20 program, ABC, N.Y.C., 1977-78, prodn. assoc., 1979-80, program prodn. asst., 1980-82; legal contract adminstr. ABC Sports, N.Y.C., 1978-79; assoc. dir. Capital Cities/ABC, N.Y.C., 1982—; dir., assoc. dir. freelance projects;owner GreenBeing, Inc. Contbg. editor Bender's Forms of Discovery, Vols. 15 & 16, 1975. Mem. Bd. Health, Hillsdale, N.J., 1989-95. Recipient Outstanding Individual Achievement cert. Nat. Acad. TV Arts & Scis., 1980-81. Mem. Dirs. Guild of Am.

INTRATER, CHERYL WATSON WAYLOR, risk management consultant; b. Montreal, Que., Can., Sept. 8, 1943; naturalized, 1978; d. Alan Douglas and Jean Mary (Hughes) Watson; m. Donald L. Intrater, Nov. 11, 1990. BBA, Ga. State U., 1980, postgrad. CPCU. Supr. div. Liberty Mut., Atlanta, 1969-76; instr. ins. DeKalb Coll., Clarkston, Ga., 1978-79; mgr. div. Kemper Group, 1979-85; owner Ins. Support Svcs., Inc., Overland Park, Kans., 1986-91; v.p., ins. cons. Fortune and Co. Risk Mgrs. Inc., 1987—; owner Career Trend, 1994—; adv. coun. Johnson County C.C. Ins. Inst., Overland Park; interim dir. profl. continuing edn. Johnson County C.C., 1994; lectr. in field. Vol. Girl Scouts U.S.A. Leadership Devel., 1987-95. Mem. Ins. Women of Greater Kansas City-Nat. Assn. Ins. Women (pres. 1989-90, named Region V Ins. Profl. of Yr. 1992, cert. profl. ins. woman, Outstanding Mem. of Yr. 1992), CPCU Soc. (Kansas City chpt.), Mission Area C. of C. (chmn. budget and fin. com. 1994, 95), Toastmasters Internat. (past dist. officer, parliamentarian 1991-96, named able toastmaster), Overland Park C. of C. Republican. Avocations: sky diving, fencing, fitness tng., reading, traveling. Office: 6800 College Blvd Ste 219 Overland Park KS 66211-1532

INTRILIGATOR, DEVRIE SHAPIRO, physicist; b. N.Y.C.; d. Carl and Lillian Shapiro; m. Michael Intriligator; children: Kenneth, James, William, Robert. BS in Physics, MIT, 1962, MS, 1964; PhD in Planetary and Space Physics, UCLA, 1967. NRC-NASA rsch. assoc. NASA, Ames, Calif., 1967-69; rsch. fellow in physics Calif. Inst. Tech., Pasadena, 1969-72, vis. assoc., 1972-73; asst. prof. U. So. Calif., 1972-80; mem. Space Scis. Ctr., 1978-83; sr. rsch. physicist Carmel Rsch. Ctr., Santa Monica, Calif., 1979—; dir. Space Plasma Lab., 1980—; cons. NASA, NOAA, Jet Propulsion Lab.; chmn. NAS-NRC com. on solar-terrestrial rsch., 1983-86, exec. com. bd. atmospheric sci. and climate, 1983-86, geophysics study com., 1983-86; U.S. nat. rep. Sci. Com. on Solar-Terrestrial Physics, 1983-86; mem. adv. com. NSF Divsn. Atmospheric Sci. Co-editor: Exploration of the Outer Solar System, 1976; contbr. articles to profl. jours. Recipient 3 Achievement awards NASA, Calif. Resolution of Commendation, 1982. Mem. AAAS, Am. Phys. Soc., Am. Geophys. Union, Cosmos Club. Home: 140 Foxtail Dr Santa Monica CA 90402-2048 Office: Carmel Rsch Ctr PO Box 1732 Santa Monica CA 90406-1732

INZANO, KAREN LEE, advertising agency executive; b. Cleve., July 27, 1946; d. William and Edith (Fisher) Phipps; children: Thomas, Laura, Sharon. Student, Litschert Sch. of Comml. Art, Cleve., 1970-72. Pres., founder AK Graphics Inc., Lakewood, Colo., 1973—; instr. advt. and small bus. Red Rocks C.C., 1983-90, mem. mktg. adv. bd., 1986-88. Chmn. Ch. Adminstrv. Bd., audio, visual adv. bd., 1995—, Red Rocks, C.C.; active caucus Colo. Rep. Com., 1980, Green Mountain Homeowners, Lakewood, 1980-84; sr. v.p. Lakewood on Parade, 1985-86; bd. dirs. Lakewood Sister Cities Internat., 1980-89, Lakewood Civic Found., 1986-94; vol. Children's Advocacy Ctr., 1994—; vol. tchr. Children's Ct. Sch., Jefferson County; mem. D.A.'s Adv. Bd., 1992-94. Named State Champion of Free Enterprise Salesman With A Purpose, 1985; recipient Disting. Svc. award Sister Cities Internat., 1984. Mem. Jefferson County C. of C. (bd. dirs. 1980-90, chmn. bd. 1988-89, Small Bus. Person of Yr. 1982), Denver Advt. Fedn. Typographers Internat. Assn., Mac User's Group # 2, Edn. 2000 # 3, Woman Bus. Owners. Home and Office: 778 S Alkire St Lakewood CO 80228-2508

IONE, AMY, artist, researcher; b. Phila., Sept. 3, 1949; d. Martin Kessler and Barbara Angert. BA, Pa. State U., 1967; MA, John F. Kennedy U., Orinda, Calif., 1995. Instr. John F. Kennedy U., Orinda, Calif., 1995; presenter in field. Exhbns. include u. Sch. Edn., Ann Arbor, Mich., 1974, ASUC Studio Gallery U. Calif., Berkeley, 1979, The Haggin Mus., Stockton, Calif., 1985, Nat. Artists Equity Assn., Washington, 1986, Walnut Creek (Calif.) Civic Arts Gallery, 1985, 88; included in pvt. and pub. permanent collections Mills Coll. Art Gallery; creator for logo Visual Art Access, 1995; illustrator (with J. Bass) Tjokjok, 1989, (poster, pub.) 40th Annual San Francisco Arts Commn. Festival, 1986, Campanus Houses, 1976; featured in Daily Californian. Home: PO Box 12742 Berkeley CA 94712

IONE, CAROLE, psychotherapist, writer; b. Washington, D.C., May 28, 1937; d. Hylan Garnet Lewis and Leighla (Whipper) Ford; m. Salvatore Bovoso (div.); children: Alessandro, Santiago, Antonio. Attended, Bennington (Vt.) Coll., 1959, NYU, New Sch. for Social Rsch.; practitioner, Helix Inst. for Psychotherapy and Healing, 1986-87, Chinese Healing Arts Ctr., 1995. Cert. qi gong therapist, hypnotherapist. Artistic dir. Renaissance House, N.Y.C., 1961, 62; founder, artistic dir., editor Letters (now Live Letters), N.Y.C., 1974—; editor of poetry choices Village Voice, N.Y.C., 1980-84; contbg. editor Essence, N.Y.C., 1981-83; co-artistic dir., v.p. Pauline Oliveros Found., Kingston, N.Y., 1985—; dir. Writers in Performance Manhattan Theatre Club, N.Y.C., 1985, 86; psychotherapist Kingston and N.Y.C., 1986—; poetry curator Unison Lng. Ctr., New Paltz, N.Y., 1990, 91. Mem. mayor's task force, Kingston, N.Y., 1996. Recipient S.C. Commn. for the Humanities award, 1983, Rockefeller Found. award, 1992, NEA award, 1992, N.Y. State Coun. for the Arts award, 1992, Charitable Trust award PEW, 1993, Dance Theater Workshop Suitcase Fund award, 1993. Fellow The Mac Dowell Colony, YADDO, Edward Albee Found., The Writer's Room; mem. Nat. Writers Union, Internat. Women's Writing Guild, The Author's Guild, Poets and Writers. Office: Pauline Oliveros Found PO Box 1956 Kingston NY 12401

IOVIENO-SUNAR, MARY SUSAN, secondary education educator; b. Worcester, Mass., May 21, 1951; m. Erdogan Sunar, Oct. 8, 1988. BA, Newton Coll. of Sacred Heart, 1973; MFA, Boston U., 1978; postgrad., U. Conn., 1975, Brockton Art Mus. Sch., 1983-88. Jr. H.S. art instr. Town of Winthrop Pub. Schs., 1974; art instr. West Jr. H.S., Town of Walpole Pub. Schs., 1975-81; art instr. Qualters Mid. Sch. Town of Mansfield (Mass.) Pub. Schs., 1981-83, visual arts instr., dept. chair Mansfield H.S., 1983—, dir. visual and performing arts, 1985—; adult edn. life drawing instr. Walpole Pub. Schs., 1983-85; guest lectr. Mass. Coll. Art, U. Mass., Dartmouth U.; presenter workshops in field. One woman shows include Boston City Hall, 1973, Cushing-Martin Libr., Stonehill Coll., Easton, Mass., 1985, Attleboro (Mass.) Mus., 1987; exhibited in group shows at Walpole Arts Coun., 1975-81, Brockton (Mass.) Art Mus., 1984—, Ames Estate, Borderlands State Park, Easton, Mass., 1984; prin. works include welded assemblage II at Digital Corp., Shrewsbury, Mass.; represented in permanent collection at Shrewsbury Pub. Libr., Starr Hair Stylists, Boston, also numerous pvt. collections; contbr. articles to profl. jours.; contbg. editor Mass. Dept. Edn. Arts Curriculum Frameworks, 1994-96; contbr. Discovery Art History, 3rd edit. Recipient Outstanding Arts Educator award State of Mass., 1988, Mass. Alliance Arts Edn. award, Outstanding Bus.-Edn. Collaboration Mass. award, 1990; Mass. State Arts Lottery Fund grantee, 1984. Mem. Southeastern Mass. Arts Collaborative (chair bd. dirs. 1989—, founding mem., steering com. curriculum writer 1986—), Mass. Dirs. Art Edn. (v.p. 1996—). Home: 10 Ray Rd Wrentham MA 02093-1818 Office: Mansfield Pub Schs care MHS 250 East St Mansfield MA 02048-2526

IOVINO, ANGELA MARIA, higher education administrator, educator; b. N.Y.C., July 29, 1952; d. Joseph Henry and Maria Laura (Mirabile) I. BA, Bklyn. Coll., 1974; MA, Ind. U., 1976, PhD, 1983; cert. knowledge, U. Stranieri, Perugia, Italy, 1971. Dir. Bilingual Italian Sch., San Francisco, 1979-83; asst. rschr. Italian Embassy, Washington, 1983-88; sr. program officer NEH, Washington, 1988-96; pres. Am. U. Rome, 1996—; vis. scholar Holy Names Coll., Oakland, Calif., 1979-83; cons. grants in humanities to maj. univs., 1995—; cons. to Chinese scholars Hangzhou (China) U., 1993—; lectr., China, 1992. Recipient Ind. Rsch. award NEH, 1993, Leadership in Fgn. Lang. Culture Studies award Nat. Early Lang. Assn., 1995. Mem. MLA (internat. bibliographer 1983-88), AAUP, Johns Hopkins China Forum. Home: 3526 S St NW Washington DC 20007 Office: The American Univ of Rome, Via Pietro Roselli 4, 00153 Rome Italy

IOVINO, DEBRA ANN, training coordinator; b. Bklyn., June 24, 1965; d. Frank Anthony Iovino and Bernadette Josephine (Buffolino) Iovino Stone. Student, CUNY. Police dispatcher II City of Sunrise, Fla., 1985-87; customer svc. rep. Bank of N.Y., N.Y.C., 1988-89; client svcs. rep. Dean Witter Reynolds, N.Y.C., 1989-90, client svcs. assoc., 1990-91, client svcs. supr., 1991-94; tng. coord. Dean Witter Trust, Jersey City, N.J., 1994—. Democrat. Roman Catholic. Home: 65 Bombay St Staten Island NY 10309 Office: Dean Witter Trust Pl 2 2d Fl Harborside Fin Ctr Jersey City NJ 07311

IPPOLITO, JANET ANNE, air freight company executive; b. Lawrence, Mass., Jan. 4, 1948; d. Joseph Vincent and Clara Rita (Artigiani) I.; m. Steven Richard Pruchansky, Feb. 16, 1967 (div. Sept. 1976); children: Lisa, Dina. Student, Boston U., 1965-67, Law Gen. Hosp. Sch. Nursing, Lawrence, Mass., 1972-73. V.p., contr. Ippolito's Furniture Showrooms, Lawrence, 1976-87; ins. mgr. Delta Leasing, Stamford, Conn., 1987-89; claims supr., claims mgr. ins. Air Express Internat., Darien, Conn., 1989—. Mem. Air Transport Assn. Roman Catholic. Home: 14 Platt St Unit # 5 East Norwalk CT 06855 Office: Air Express Internat Worldwide Hqrs 120 Tokeneke Rd Darien CT 06820

IRELAND, BARBARA HENNIG, newspaper editor; b. Batavia, N.Y., May 13, 1946; d. John Chester and Mae Electa (Schlagenhauf) Hennig; m. Allyn Lloyd Lamb, May 1, 1963 (div. 1979); children: Jeffrey Allyn, Celia Catherine; m. Corydon Boyd Ireland, May 25, 1985 (div. 1994). BA, Cornell U., 1969. English tchr. Homer (N.Y.) High Sch., 1969-70, Port Byron (N.Y.) High Sch., 1973; reporter Auburn (N.Y.) Citizen, 1973-77; copy editor Albany (N.Y.) Knickerbocker News, 1977; copy editor Buffalo News, 1977-80, editor Sunday mag., 1980-85, editorial writer, 1985-89, editor editorial page, 1989—; Pulitzer Prize juror, 1996. John S. Knight fellow Stanford U., 1988-89. Mem. Nat. Conf. Editorial Writers, Phi Beta Kappa. Office: Buffalo News PO Box 100 1 News Plaza Buffalo NY 14240

IRELAND, KATHY, actress; b. Santa Barbara, Calif., 1963; d. John and Barbara I.; m. Greg Olsen, 1988. Appearances in Sports Illustrated's Ann. Swimsuit Issues, 25th Anniversary Show Swimsuit Edit.; films include: Alien from L.A., 1988, Necessary Roughness, 1991, Mom and Dad Save the World, 1992, National Lampoon's Loaded Weapon I, 1993, The Player, Mr. Destiny, "Amore," "Backfire"; TV films include Beauty and the Bandit, 1994, Danger Island, 1994, Hello, She Lied, 1995, Gridlock, 1996; TV appearances include: Down the Shore, The Edge, Tales from the Crypt, Without a Clue, Grand, Charles in Charge, Perry Mason, Boy Meets World, Melrose Place, The Watcher, Deadly Games. Office: The Sterling and Winters Co 1900 Avenue Of The Stars Ste 1640 Los Angeles CA 90067-4407

IRELAND, LINDA ANN, naval officer, nurse; b. Cin., June 11, 1950; d. Robert and Helen Marie (Piepmeyer) Bohnstengel; m. Kent Lowell Ireland, April 4, 1970 (div. May 1975); children: Karen Lynn, Kerry Robert. ADN, Santa Rosa (Calif.) Jr. Coll., 1974; BSN, U. Fla., Gainesville, Fla., 1984; MS, U. Md., Balt., 1992. RN Fla., CCRN, cert. trauma nurse. Staff nurse Santa Rosa Meml. Hosp., 1972-75, St. Vincent's Med. Ctr., Jacksonville, Fla., 1975-84, Phila. Naval Hosp., 1984-87; staff nurse, divsn. officer U.S. Naval Hosp. Guantanamo, Guantanamo Bay, Cuba, 1987-90; staff nurse, evening supr. Nat. Naval Med. Ctr., Bethesda, Md., 1992-95; flight nurse, flight clin. coord. U.S. Transp. Commd., Global Patient Movement Requirements Ctr., Scott AFB, Ill., 1995—; adv. Jr. Military Nurses Orgn., Bethesda, 1993-95; affiliate faculty BCLS Am. Heart Assn., Guantanamo Bay, 1989-90. Manuscript reviewer: (jour.) Am. Jour. of Nursing, 1993-95. Vol. Vols. for the Visually Handicapped, Silver Spring, Md., 1994-95. Lt. Comdr. USN, 1984—. Recipient Achievement medal U.S. Navy, 1987, Achievement Gold Star, 1990, Commendation medal, 1995. Mem. AACN (cons. to military fed. spl. interest group 1992-93), Sigma Theta Tau.

IRELAND, PATRICIA, association executive; b. Oak Park, Ill., Oct. 19, 1945; d. James Ireland and Joan Filipek; m. James Humble, 1968. Grad., Univ. Miami Law Sch., 1975. Flight attendant Pan Am. World Airlines, 1967-75; ptnr. Stearns, Weaver, Miller, Weissler, Alhadeff and Sitterson, Miami; legal counsel Dade County and Fla. NOW; dir. Project Stand Up for Women NOW, initiator Global Feminist Conf.; NOW rep. European Parliament, Nat. Congress Brazilian Women, German-Am. Women's Confs., Cuban Women's Fedn., European Women's Solidarity Conf., England's Nat. Abortion Campaign; exec. v.p. NOW, from 1987, pres., 1991—. Contbr. law rev. Univ. Miami Law Sch. Office: NOW 1000 16th St NW Ste 700 Washington DC 20036-5705*

IRELAND, TRACY, human services program administrator, educator; b. Aurora, Ill., Sept. 14, 1961; d. Peg (Stewart) I. BA, U. Mass., Amherst, 1986, LSW, 1995—. Master addiction counselor; cert. criminal justice specialist. Tchr. Lawrence (Mass.) Sch. System, 1987-91; tchr., lead staff Baily South-Northeastern Family Inst., Danvers, Mass., 1991-93; resdl. coord. Seachanges-Northeaster Family Inst., Danvers, 1993—. Mem. NOW. Home: 158 S Common St Lynn MA 01905 Office: Northeastern Family Inst 1 Market St Lynn MA 01902

IRONBITER, SUZANNE, writer, religion educator; b. Milw., June 4, 1941; d. John Spoden and Willena Kalmbach; m. John Matthew Potter, Feb. 5, 1966 (wid. Apr. 1992); children: Sarah Potter Tyrrell, Anna Potter. BA, U. Mich., 1963; MA, Columbia U., 1966, PhD, 1972. Lectr. E. Mich. U., Ypsilanti, 1966-77; adj. asst. prof. NYU, 1968-80, Hunter Coll., N.Y.C., 1986—, SUNY, Purchase, 1992—. Author: Devi, 1987; editor, ghostwriter Cross Pond Editing Group, Katonah, N.Y., 1992—. Recipient Summer Seminar grant NEH, 1995. Mem. Am. Acad. Religion Poets and Writers.

IRONS, DIANE HAVELICK, small business owner; b. Lynn, Mass.; d. Peter and Frances (Roumeliotis) Havelick; m. David Eldon Irons, Oct. 3, 1971; children: Keith, Kirk. BA in English, Salem State Coll., 1971. Dir. pub. affairs Sta. WESX, Salem, Mass., 1972-80; editor Reporter, Lynnfield, Mass., 1981-85; dir. Barbizon Internat., Boston, 1986-88; pres. Fashion Assocs., Burlington, Mass., 1988-92, Internat. Image, Wakefield, Mass., 1992—; host Talk Am., 1993-95. Author: Real Secrets of Beauty, 1993, Secret Beauty, 1996. Mem. Assn. Image Cons. Internat., Internat. Assn. Talk Show Hosts, Nat. Speakers Assn. Office: Internat Image 196 Main St Wakefield MA 01880

IRONS, MARGE, paralegal, artist; b. Casper, Wyo., Nov. 5, 1956. AA in Actg., Coll. of Actg., Newport Beach, Calif., 1980; degree in Psychology, Red Rocks Cmty. Coll., Denver, 1991-93; paralegal, NCS Paralegal Coll., Scranton, Pa., 1992. Cert. paralegal, real estate agent. Paralegal Fed. Govt., Denver, Joseph H. Thibodeau, Denver, James J. Johnston, Denver; legal sec. The Law Offices, Denver; emergency dispatcher Cheyenne (Wyo.) Police Dept., Casper (Wyo.) Police Dept.; sec. Federally Employed Women, Denver, 1992-93 (scholarship 1991, 92). Author: (poetry) Creative Enterprises, 1987 (Bronze Quill award); artist: (woodburned clock) Ducks In Flight, 1994 (1st Place award 1995), (acrylic painting) A Day In September, 1995 (2d Place award 1995). Counselor Suicide Prevention, Denver, 1986-92, Compear, Denver, 1992-93. Recipient Liberty & Justice award Am. Police Hall of Fame, 1986, Patriotic Svc. award U.S. Savings Bonds, 1990, 91, 92. Mem. NAFE, Bus. & Profl. Women (Young Careerist award 1992).

IRVINE, PHYLLIS ELEANOR KUHNLE, nursing educator, administrator; b. Germantown, Ohio, July 14, 1940; d. Carl Franklin and Mildred Viola (Erisman) Kuhnle; m. Richard James Irvine, Feb. 15, 1964; children: Mark, Rick. BSN, Ohio State U., 1962, MSN, 1979, PhD, 1981; MS, Miami U., Oxford, Ohio, 1966. Staff nurse VA Ctr., Dayton, Ohio, 1962-66; mem. nursing faculty Miami Valley Hosp. Sch. Nursing, Dayton, 1968-78; teaching asst., lectr. Ohio State U., Columbus, 1979-82; assoc. prof. Ohio U., Athens, 1982-83; prof., dir. N.E. La. U., Monroe, 1984-88; prof., dir. sch. nursing Ball State U., Muncie, Ind., 1988—. Reviewer Health Edn. Jour., Reston, Va., 1987; contbr. articles to profl. jours. Mem. Mayor's Commn. on Needs of Women, La., 1984-88; 1st v.p., bd. dirs. United Way of Ouachita, La., 1986-88. Mem. ANA, Ind. Nurses Assn., Ind. Coun. Deans and Dirs. of Nursing Edn. (pres. 1992—), Internat. Coun. Women's Health Issues (bd. dirs. 1986-92), Assn. for the Advancement Health Edn., Sigma Theta Tau. Office: Ball State U Cn418 Nursing Muncie IN 47306

IRVINE, ROSE LORETTA ABERNETHY, retired communications educator, consultant; b. Kingston, N.Y., Nov. 14, 1924; d. William Francis and Julia (Flynn) A.; m. Robert Tate Irvine Jr., Dec. 18, 1965 (dec. June 1968). BA, Coll. St. Rose, 1945; MA, Columbia U., 1946; PhD, Northwestern U., 1964. Tchr. English Kingston High Sch., 1946-47; tchr. English and speech Croton-Harmon High Sch., Croton-on-Hudson, N.Y., 1947-49; instr. speech SUNY, New Paltz, 1949-53; asst. prof. SUNY, New Platz, 1953-57, assoc. prof., 1957-64, prof. speech communication, 1964-85, prof. emeritus, 1985—; guest prof. Yousoi U., Seoul, Republic Korea, 1970; U.S. del. U.S. Bi-Nat. Conf., Manila, 1976; adv. bd. Rondout Nat. Bank Norstar (now Fleet Bank), 1973-85; U. Chancellor's adv. bd. SUNY Senate, Albany, 1974-80; guest prof. Celtic lore Princess Grace Libr., Monaco, 1987; cons., rschr., writer, 1985—; presenter in field. Contbr. articles to Speech Teacher, Educational Forum, Readers Theatre, others. Mem. Nat. Jr. League, Kingston, 1958-90; dir. Puppet Theater for Srs., N.Y., 1982-83; mem. pres. adv. com. Ulster County C.C., 1986—. Honor Tuition scholar Coll. St. Rose, Albany, N.Y., 1941; named Outstanding Educator of Am., 1971. Mem. AAUW (liaison SUNY New Paltz 1966-85), Speech Comm. Assn. (mem. legis assembly 1967-68), N.Y. State Speech Assn. (emeritus), Zeta Phi Eta, Delta Kappa Gamma, Kappa Delta Pi, Pi Lambda Theta. Roman Catholic. Home: 105 Lounsbury Pl Kingston NY 12401-5231 Office: SUNY New Paltz NY 12561

IRVING, AMY, actress; b. Palo Alto, Calif., Sept. 10, 1953; m. Steven Spielberg, Nov. 27, 1985 (div.); 1 child, Max Samuel; m. Bruno Barreto, 1990; 1 child, Gabriel Davis Barreto. Student, Am. Conservatory Theatre, London Acad. Dramatic Art. Films include Carrie, 1976, The Fury, 1978, Voices, 1979, Honeysuckle Rose, 1980, The Competition, 1980, Yentl, 1983, Mickey and Maude, 1984, Crossing Delancey, 1988, (voice) Who Framed Roger Rabbit, 1988, A Show of Force, 1990, (voice) An American Tail: Fievel Goes West, 1991, Benefit of the Doubt, 1993, Kleptomania, 1995, Carried Away, 1996; TV appearances include: The Rookies, Policewoman, Happy Days; TV movies James Dean, 1975, James A. Michener's Dynasty, 1976, Panache, 1976, Anastasia: The Mystery of Anna, 1986, Heartbreak House, 1986, Rumpelstiltskin, 1986, The Turn of the Screw, 1989; miniseries Once an Eagle, 1976-77, The Far Pavilions, 1984, Twilight Zone, 1994; appeared as Juliet in Romeo and Juliet, Seattle Repertory Theatre, 1982-83; appeared on Broadway in Amadeus, 1981-82, Heartbreak House, 1983-84, Broken Glass, 1994, off Broadway The Road to Mecca, 1988, The Heidi Chronicles, 1990-91. *

IRVING, JOYCE ARLENE, social worker, consultant; b. LaGrange, Tex., Aug. 8, 1945; d. Major Lee and Cora (Williams) Brown; m. Daniel Lamar Irving, Dec. 4, 1966; children: Dana Lorraine, Jerren Alan. AA, Sacramento City Coll., 1971; BA, Calif. State U., Sacramento, 1975, MSW, 1978. Program and tng. asst. Social Scis. Tng. Div., Sacramento, 1965-73; investigator, interviewer Social Svcs. Fraud Unit, Sacramento, 1973-76; social worker Sacramento County Social Svcs., 1976-80; casework specialist Calif. State Dept. Youth Authority, 1980-86, background investigator, 1986-88, casework specialist, 1988—; historian, editor Jack & Jill of Am., Sacramento, 1986-89, program dir., 1990—; cons. Group Home Inc., Sacramento, 1989-90. Mem. Assn. Black Correctional Workers (treas., exec. bd. 1988-90, Pres.'s award 1985, 89), Black Child Inst., Calif. Correctional Peace Officers Assn. (exec. bd. Sacramento chpt. 1990—), Nat. Assn. Univ. Women, Delta Sigma Theta. Home: 9845 Florin Rd Sacramento CA 95829-9311 Office: Calif Dept Youth Authority 3001 Ramona Ave Sacramento CA 95826-3814

IRVING, JUDITH JANE, film producer and director, writer; b. Englewood, N.J., June 8, 1946; d. John Lancaster and Florence Templeton (James) I. BA, Conn. Coll., 1968; MA, Stanford U., 1973. Freelance writer and photographer for mags. and newspapers, Alaska, Calif., Can., 1968—; freelance filmmaker, San Francisco, 1972—; co-founder, exec. dir. IDG Films (Ind. Documentary Group), San Francisco, 1978—. Writer, prodr., dir. films Dark Circle, 1982, Treasures of the Greenbelt, 1986 (Emmy award 1987), Secrets of the Bay, 1990, Out of the Way Cafe, 1995 (award Uppsala Film Festival 1995); dir. play Trip Without A Ticket, 1989; dir. 3 films Quiet Revolution Series, 1995 (Earthwatch Film award 1996); co-prodr., dir. photog. exhbn. and film Nagasaki Journey, 1995 (Silver Apple award 1996); photographer: (book)) Rio Mazan Expedition, 1988; assoc. editor: (book) Nagasaki Journey, 1995. Recipient grand prize Sundance Film Festival, Park City, Utah, 1983, nat. Emmy award NATAS, 1990; film and writing fellow Breadloaf Writers' Conf., Middlebury, Vt., 1968, MacDowell Colony, Peterborough, N.H., 1983, Vcross Found., Clearmont, Wyo., 1988; Guggenheim fellow, 1983. Mem. Film Arts Found., South End Rowing Club, Phi Beta Kappa. Mem. Green Party. Office: IDG Films 394 Elizabeth St San Francisco CA 94114

IRWIN, ANNA MAE, English educator; b. Petrolia, Kans., Aug. 19; d. Clarence Newton and Elsie Mildred (Stump) Williams; m. Everett Irwin, Sept. 1, 1938; children: Stanley, Pamela, Steven. BS, Northeastern State U., 1940; postgrad., Denver U. and Colo. U., 1960-80. Bookkeeper, typist Fed. Bur. Pub. Rds., Denver, 1942-45; tchr. Denver Pub. Schs., 1945-46; typist State Dept. Employment, Denver, 1958-60; tchr. Aurora (Colo.) Pub. Schs., 1960-84; tutor ESL for refugees State Dept. Edn., Denver, 1988-91. Mem. adv. bd., bd. dirs. Unity Ch., Denver, 1986—; mem. and pres. aux. Goodwill Industries, Denver, 1996—, 2d v.p., 1st v.p. 1992-96, pres. 1993-96; state del., county del., congl. del., precinct com. woman Rep. Party, Denver, 1970-84. Recipient Mary Venable Svc. award for vol. work Goodwill Industries, 1996. Mem. Book Review Club (v.p., program chmn. 1990-93), Cherry Creek Womens Club. Home: 1131 Garfield St Denver CO 80206

IRWIN, G. STORMY, retired paper manufacturing professional; b. Melrose Park, Ill., Sept. 4, 1929; d. Charles W. and Mary E. (Worthley) I. With Zellerbach Paper Co. (div. Mead Co.), Sacramento, 1952-85, ret., 1985. Mng. editor, pub., owner Women in Softball mag. (Women in Sports 1957-72), 1957-78. Coach, mgr., participant Sacramento City Leagues. Recipient 1st place awards for continuous coverage of softball for non-daily pubsl. under 50,000 circulation Nat. Softball Broadcasters and Writers Assn., 1965-67, 69, 71-73; won 31 titles for volleyball, basketball, flag football and softball participation; named to Sacramento Softball Hall of Honor, 1980. Home: 1945 Piner Rd Space # 85 Santa Rosa CA 95403-6909

IRWIN, LINDA BELMORE, marketing consultant; b. Portland, Oreg., Apr. 29, 1950; d. Calvin C. and Dorothy B. (Belmore) Harper; m. Michael Hugh Irwin, June 24, 1989. Student Portland State U., 1968-72. With Hyatt Regency-New Orleans, 1975-78, catering Hyatt-Regency-Capitol Hill, Washington, 1978-80, dir. catering Hyatt-Anaheim, Calif., 1978-80; mgr. Dockside Yacht Sales, Annapolis, Md., 1981-85; dir. sales and mktg. Loew's Hotel, 1985-86; dir. mktg. Annapolis Marriot, 1986-88; ind. mktg. cons., Washington and Dallas, 1988—; ambassador State of Md., Annapolis, 1986-88; mktg. chair Tourism Council Annapolis and Anne Arundel County; curricula advisor Anne Arundel Community Coll.; mem. fund raising com. Ch. Circle Beautification Trust. Mem. Nat. Banquet Mgrs. Guild (founder Los Angeles chpt.), Nat. Assn. Female Execs. (area dir. 1985—), Annapolis C. of C. (ambassador 1985-88), Greater Washington Soc. of Assn. Execs., Anne Arundel Trade Council, Md. Tourism Council (adv. bd.), Internat. Platform Assn. Republican. Episcopalian. Avocations: sailing, travel, literature, calligraphy, ballet.

IRWIN, MARGARET LYNN, secondary education educator; b. Port Arthur, Tex., Jan. 10, 1962; d. Charles Weldon and Marjory (Barton) I. BA, U. Tex., 1984; MA, U. Tex., San Antonio, 1992; postgrad., St. Mary's U., 1985-86. Cert. tchr., Tex. Social studies tchr. Taft H.S., San Antonio, 1986—; adj. instr. history Palo Alto C.C., San Antonio, 1993—; advanced placement test grader College Bd., San Antonio, 1995; state secondary social studies com. Tex. Edn. Agy., Austin, 1994, evaluator grant application com., 1995. Advocate ATPE, 1989, 93, 95; mem. bond proposal com. Northside Ind. Sch. Dist., San Antonio, 1992. Recipient Leon Jaworski award for law related edn. Young Lawyers' Assn., 1993. Mem. AAUW, Assn. Tex. Profl. Educators (regional pres. 1991-93, dir. 1994-96), U. Tex. Ex-Students Assn., Phi Delta Kappa. Republican. Methodist. Office: Taft HS 11600 F M 471 West San Antonio TX 78253

IRWIN, MARY NORRINGTON, writer, artist; b. Toronto, Ont., Can., Apr. 9, 1922; came to U.S., 1930, naturalized, 1954; d. William Andrew and Roberta Mary (McLaughlin) I.; m. John Royston Coleman, Oct. 1, 1943 (div. Jan. 1967); children: John Michael Coleman, Nancy Jane Coleman, Patty Ann Coleman, Paul Richard Coleman, Stephen William Coleman; m. Irving Russell Murray, June 26, 1967 (div. Aug. 1988). Student, U. Chgo., 1939-40; BA, U. Toronto, 1944; postgrad., Art Inst. Chgo., 1946-48, Carnegie Mellon U., 1963-64; MA, Bowling Green State U., 1982, MFA, 1983. Freelance illustrator, graphic artist, 1945—; asst. art editor World Book Encyclopedia, Chgo., 1946-49; freelance painter, 1963—, freelance writer, 1983—; instr. Toledo (Ohio) Mus. Art, 1983-88, Pvt. Art Classes, Nassau County, N.Y., 1973-76, Bowling Green (Ohio) State U., 1985; judge numerous art exhbns., Ohio, Maine, 1984—. Author: On Our Own: Older Women After Marriage, 1991, The Full Price, 1994; columnist, art critic Dialogue, 1984-88. Mem., chpt. trustee League Women Voters, 1956-65, 77—; active Unitarian Universalist Ch., 1959-94; nat. sec. Unitarian Fellowship Social Justice, 1957-58. Mem. Maine Writers & Pubs. Alliance, Union Maine Visual Artists, Maine Coast Artists. Home: 2039 Gurnet Rd Brunswick ME 04011

IRWIN, MILDRED LORINE WARRICK, library consultant, civic worker; b. Kellerton, Iowa, June 21, 1917; d. Webie Arthur and Bonnie Lorine (Hyatt) DeVries; m. Carl Wesley Warrick, Feb. 11, 1937 (dec. June 1983); children: Carl Dwayne, Arthur Will; m. John B. Irwin, Feb. 1, 1994. BS in Edn., Drake U., 1959; M of Librarianship, Kans. State Tchrs. Coll., 1970. Cert. tchr., libr., Iowa. Elem. tchr. Monroe Ctr. Rural Sch., Kellerton, Iowa, 1935-37, Denham Rural Sch., Grand River, Iowa, 1945-48, Grand River Ind. Sch., 1948-52, Woodmansee Rural Sch., Decatur, Iowa, 1952-55, Centennial Rural Sch., Decatur, 1955-56; elem. tchr., acting libr. Cen. Decatur Sch., Leon, Iowa, 1956-71, media libr. jr. and sr. high sch., 1971-79; libr. Northminster Presbyn. Ch., Tucson, 1984-93, advisor, 1994—; media resource instr. Graceland Coll., Lamoni, Iowa, 1971-72; lit. dir. S.W. Iowa Assn. Classroom Tchrs., 1965-69. Editor (media packet) Mini History and Quilt Blocks, 1976, Grandma Lori's Nourishing Nuggets for Body and Soul, 1985, As I Recall (Loren Drake), 1989, Foland Family Supplement III, 1983; author: (with Quentin Oiler) Van Der Vlugt Family Record, 1976; compiler, editor Abigail Specials, 1991, Abigail Assemblage, 1996; compiler Tribute to Ferm Mills 1911-1992, 1992; co-editor: (with Dorothy Heitlinger) Milestones and Touchstones, 1993; contbr. articles to publs. Leader Grand River 4-H Club for Girls, 1954-58; sec. South Ctrl. Iowa Quarter Horse Assn., Chariton, 1967-68; chmn. Decatur County Dems., 1981-83, del., 1970-83; pianist Salvation Army Amphi League of Mercy Rhythm Noters, 1984-90; pianist, dir. Joymakers, 1990—; Sunday Sch. tchr. Decatur United Meth. Ch., 1945-54, 80-83, lay speaker, 1981-83, dir. vacation Bible sch., 1982, 83. Named Classroom Tchr. of Iowa Classroom Tchrs. Assn., 1962, Woman of Yr., Leon Bus. and Profl. Women, 1978, Northminster Presbyn. Ch. Women, 1990; named to Internat. Profl. and Bus. Women Hall of Fame for outstanding achievements in field of edn. and libr. sci., 1995; English and reading grantee Nat. Dept. Edn., 1966. Mem. NEA (life), AAUW (chmn. Tucson creative writing/cultural interests 1986-87, 89-93, historian, 1994—, Honoree award for edn. found. programs Tucson br., Svc. award 1991), Internat. Reading Assn. (pres. Clarke-Ringgold-Decatur chpts. 1967-68), Cen. Cmty. Tchrs. Assn. (pres. 1961-62), Pima County Ret. Tchrs. Assn. (pres. 1989-90), Decatur County Assn. (pres. 1961-63), Decatur County Ret. Tchrs. Assn. (historian 1980-83), Iowa Edn. Assn. (life), Presbyn. Women (hon. life 1990—), Luth. Ch. Libr. Assn. (historian Tucson area chpt. 1991-92, v.p. 1993-94, pres. 1994-95), Delta Kappa Gamma (pres. Iowa Beta XI chpt. 1974-76, sec. 1984-85, historian Ariz. Alpha Gamma chpt. 1986-89). Democrat. Presbyterian. Home: 2879 E Presidio Rd Tucson AZ 85716-1539

IRWIN, MIRIAM DIANNE OWEN, book publisher, writer; b. Columbus, Ohio, June 14, 1930; d. John Milton and Miriam Faith (Studebaker) Owen; m. Kenneth John Irwin, June 5, 1960; 1 child, Christopher Owen Irwin. BS in Home Econs., Ohio State U., 1952, postgrad. in bus. adminstrn., 1961-62. Editorial asst. Am. Home Mag., N.Y.C., 1953-56; salesman Owen Realty, Dayton, Ohio, 1957-58, Clevenger Realty, Phoenix, 1958-59; home economist Columbus and So. Ohio Electric Co., 1959-60; pub. Mosaic Press, Cin., 1977—; pub. distbr. D'Bridge Email Systems N.Am. (a Mosaic Press div.), 1991—; owner Bibelot Bindery, 1987—. Author: Lute and Lyre, 1977, Forty is Fine, 1977, Miriam Mouse's Survival Manual, 1977, Miriam Mouse's Costume Collection, 1977, Miriam Mouse's Marriage Contract, 1977, Miriam Mouse, Rock Hound, 1977, Silver Bindings, 1983; editor: Tribute to the Arts, 1984; contbg. author Publisher's Favorite, 1988; illustrator: Corals of Pennekamp, 1979. Daytime crew chief Wyoming Life Squad, Ohio, 1966-71. Mem. Miniature Book Soc. (past bd. dirs., chairperson 1987-89). Presbyterian. Avocation: book collecting. Home and Office: 358 Oliver Rd Cincinnati OH 45215-2615

ISAAC, BINA SUSAN, data processing executive; b. Nainital, India, Jan. 9, 1958; came to U.S. 1980; d. Rajan Kurian and Susan (Thomas) George; m. Mathew Isaac, July 14, 1980; children: Sonya Susan, Shawn George. BA, Sarah Tucker Coll., Tirunelvelli, India, 1978; MA, Madurai U., India, 1980; MEd, U. Toledo, 1981, MBA, 1984. Coord. computer svcs. and computer ctr. Lourdes Coll., Sylvania, Ohio, 1984-85; dir. computer svcs. and computer ctr. Lourdes Coll., Sylvania, 1985-95, dir. info. tech. dept. svcs., 1995—, dir. info. tech. dept./svcs., 1995—; instr. Continuing Edn. Dept., Sylvania, 1985—; dir. Instnl. Info. Tech., 1995—. Mem. Assn. Systems Mgmt., Ohio Assn. Ind. Rsch., SIG 3X Inc. (spl. interest group). Home: 7328 Gibley Park Rd Toledo OH 43617-2252 Office: Lourdes Coll 6832 Convent Blvd Sylvania OH 43560-2853

ISAACKS, VIOLET SIBLEY-HOWE, real estate investment executive; b. Little Rock, Aug. 13, 1924; d. Rife Wilson and Violet Keeton (Love) Sibley; m. Herbert Joseph Howe, Nov. 2, 1942 (dec. 1954); children: Patricia Howe Criner, H. Joseph Howe Jr., James M. Howe; m. Carl D. Burton, 1959 (dec. 1976); m. Stanley Allen Isaacks, June 23, 1983. Student, U. Ctrl. Ark., 1940-42; AS, Westark Coll., Ft. Smith, Ark., 1976-80. Cert. real estate broker. Theater owner Strand, Sunset Drive-in, 22 Drive In, Ark., 1945-76; owner, broker Strand Realty Co., Hot Springs, Ark., 1946-50; publicity writer S.W. Hotels, Hot Springs, Ark., 1952-53; owner Real Estate Devel., Ft. Smith, Ark., 1950—; genealogy instr. Westark Coll., Ft. Smith, Ark., 1974-78; owner, treas. F.P. Corp., Ft. Smith, Ark., 1980—. Author: Virginia Was Their Home; conducted genealogy workshops in three states, 1978-94; editor officers' wives newspaper, Marfa, Tex., 1943-45. Pres. Civic Improvement Assn., Hot Springs, 1951-53; co-chmn. steering com. Garland County Cmty. Coll., 1953-55; chmn. Ark. State Libr. bd., 1988—; life mem. White House Conf. on Libr. Sci. Tech. (award 1991); organizer, 1st pres. Jr. C. of C. Aux. DAR Ark., 1950; state regent (now hon. for life) DAR Ark.; pres. Nat. Cememtery Acquisition Com., Ft. Smith, 1991—; chmn. Civic Ctr. com., Ft. Smith, 1986—. Recipient Frontier Achievement award, Hist. Devel. Assn., Ft. Smith, 1988. Mem. Colonial Dames XVIIC (state pres.), Jamestown Soc. (mem. bd. 1994—). United Methodist. Home: 5000 Cliff Dr Fort Smith AR 72903

ISAAC NASH, EVA MAE, educator; b. Natchitoches Parish, La., July 24, 1936; d. Earfus Will Nash and Dollie Mae (Edward) Johnson; m. Will Isaac Jr., July 1, 1961 (dec. May 1970). BA, San Francisco State U., 1974, MS in Edn., 1979, MS in Counseling, 1979; PhD, Walden U., 1985; diploma (hon.), St. Labre Indian Sch., 1990. Nurse's aide Protestant Episcopal Home, San Francisco, 1957-61; desk clk. Fort Ord (Calif.) Post Exchange, 1961-63; practical nurse Monterey (Calif.) Hosp., 1963-64; tchr. San Francisco Unified Schs., 1974; counselor, instr. City Coll. San Francisco, 1978-79; tchr. Oakland (Calif.) Unified Sch. Dist., 1974—; pres. sch. adv. coun., Oakland, 1977-78, faculty adv. coun., 1992-93; advt. writer City Coll., San Francisco, 1978; instr. vocat. skill tng., Garfield Sch., Oakland, 1980-81; pub. speaker various ednl. insts. and chs., Oakland, San Francisco, 1982—; lectr. San Jose State U., 1993. Author video tape Hunger: An Assassin in the Classroom, 1993-94. Recipient Community Svc. award Black Caucus of Calif. Assn. Counseling and Devel., 1988, Cert. of Recognition, 1990; named Citizen of the Day, Sta. KABL, 1988. Mem. ASCD, Internat. Reading Assn., Nat. Assn. Female Execs., Am. Personnel and Guidance Assn., Calif. Personnel and Guidance Assn., Internat. Platform Assn. (Hall Fame 1989, Profl. Speaking cert. 1993), Phi Delta Kappa. Democrat. Office: Oakland Unified Sch Dist 1025 2nd Ave Oakland CA 94606-2212

ISAACS, AMY FAY, political organization executive; b. Phoenix, Nov. 11, 1946; d. Richard and Bessie (Wagner) Hamburger; m. John David Isaacs, Oct. 6, 1974; children: Rachel Elizabeth, Stanley Richard. Student, U. Cologne, Germany, 1967-68; BA, Am. U., 1969; MA, Sch. for Internat. Tng., Brattleboro, Vt., 1970. With AID, Washington, 1965-66; tchr. English, Turkish Am. Univs. Assn., Istanbul, 1969; direct mail and fundraising cons., Washington, 1986-87; sr. coord. communications Planned Parenthood Fedn. Am., Washington, 1987-89; various positions Ams. for Dem. Action, Washington, 1969-86, nat. dir., 1989—. Observer del. Liberal Internat., Stockholm, 1984; del. Am. Coun. on Germany, Berlin, Dallas, 1985-87; mem. fin. com. Dukasis for Pres., Washington, 1987-88; mem. quality of care com. Group Health Assn., Washington, 1987-93. Democrat. Jewish. Home: 2018 Pierce Mill Rd NW Washington DC 20010-1023 Office: Ams for Dem Action 1625 K St NW Ste 210 Washington DC 20006-1604

ISAACS, BARBARA SHIVITZ, painter; b. N.Y.C.. Student, Bennington (Vt.) Coll., 1955; BFA, Parsons Sch. Design, N.Y.C., 1990. One-person shows include Angeleski Gallery, N.Y.C., 1960, 61, exhibited in group shows at 11th Ann. New Eng. Exhbn., The Silvermine Guild of Artists, New Canaan, Conn., 1960, Parsons Sch. of Design, N.Y.C., 1989, 90; represented in permanent collections at Loeb Collection, NYU, Albright-Knox Gallery, Buffalo, Brewran Corp., Roslyn (N.Y.), Champion Internat. Corp., Stamford, Conn.; also pvt. collections; paintings exhibited at Edward Thorp Gallery, N.Y.C., 1996; writer, director, cinematographer Marie & Henry, The Knowledge Box, School of Design, 1964-67, Fifteen Women, 1968, Negative Earth, Revolution for Two, 1980-83, Town With the Jitters, 1985; contbr. articles to profl. jours. Recipient scholarship Parsons Sch. Design, 1987, Young Film Maker's grant USIA, Washington, 1968, fellowships Va. Ctr. for Creative Arts, Sweet Briar, 1994, 95. Home and Studio: 333 E 43rd St New York NY 10017

ISAACS, HELEN COOLIDGE ADAMS (MRS. KENNETH L. ISAACS), artist; b. N.Y.C., Jan. 17, 1917; d. Thomas Safford and Martha (Montgomery) Adams; student Miss Hewett's classes, N.Y.C., Miss Porter's Sch., Farmington, Conn., Fontainbleau (France) Sch. Art and Music, 1935, Art Students League, 1936; m. Kenneth L. Isaacs, Mar. 10, 1949; children: Kenneth Coolidge, Anne Isaacs Merwin. Represented by Child's Gallery, Boston. One-woman shows at Child's Gallery; group shows: 3 times at Allied Artists, N.Y., Boston Arts Festival; portraits of various prominent persons; murals in various pub. bldgs., Boston, Rochester, N.Y., Pittsfield, Mass., Daytona, Fla.; represented in painting and drawing collections Fogg Mus., Cambridge, Mass., Nat. Mus. Women in the Arts, Washington, Whaling Mus., New Bedford, Mass. Mem. Colonial Dames Am., Colony Club (N.Y.C.), Chilton Club (Boston). Home: 68 Beacon St Boston MA 02108-3422

ISAACSON, ARLINE LEVINE, food and beverage executive, hotel executive; b. Bklyn., Jan. 28, 1946; d. Harry and Sally (Fogelman) Levine; m. Leslie Robert Isaacson, Oct. 31, 1964 (div. July 1970); 1 child, Eric Michael. AAS in Hotel and Restaurant Mgmt., N.Y.C. Tech. Coll., 1983. Restaurant and lounge mgr. Holiday Inn, N.Y.C., 1982-83; mgr. Astors, St. Regis Hotel, N.Y.C., 1983-84; banquet and conf. mgr. Mariner 15 Conf. Ctr., N.Y.C., 1984-85; dir. banquets, confs. and sales Sardi's Restaurant Corp., N.Y.C., 1985-87; dir. catering sales Days Inn Hotel, N.Y.C., 1987-91; catering sales mgr. St. Moritz on the Park Hotel, N.Y.C., 1991-92; dir. catering Roosevelt Hotel, N.Y.C., 1992-93; catering sales mgr. Sheraton Park Ave., N.Y.C., 1993—. Dem. vol. Koch Relection Campaign, N.Y.C., 1985. Mem. Food and Beverage Mgrs. Assn. (sec. 1984-88, 91, exec. dir. 1995—), Roundtable for Women in Food Svc. (treas. 1986-87), Meeting Planners Internat., Soc. Incentive Travel, Hotel Sales and Mktg. Assn., Internat. Food Svc. Execs., N.Y.C. Tech. Coll. Alumni Assn. (bd. dirs. 1986—, v.p. 1986-87). Jewish. Avocations: dancing, travel, theatre, gourmet cooking. Home: 1836 E 18th St Brooklyn NY 11229-2965 Office: Sheraton Park Ave Hotel 45 Park Ave New York NY 10016-3406

ISAACSON, EDITH LIPSIG, civic leader; b. N.Y.C., Jan. 18, 1920; d. I.A. and Bertha (Evans) Lipsig; m. Selian Hebald; children: Anne Mandelbaum, Selian Jr.; m. William J. Isaacson. Student, Radcliffe Coll., 1936-39, 41; LLB, St. Lawrence U., 1943. Pres. Forest Knolls Corp., N.Y.C., 1960-95, Norman Homes Corp., N.Y.C., 1968-95; bd. govs. Medford Leas Residents Assn., 1990-92, v.p., 1991-92. Author biographies Am. artists; writer club handbooks. Fellow Pierpont Morgan Libr., N.Y.C.; mem. Carnegie Coun. Ethics Internat. Affairs, founders com. Am. Symphony Orch., N.Y., 1962; nat. sec. Women's Am. Orgn. Rehab. through Tng., 1950; trustee Allergy Found. Am.; bd. govs. Medford Leas Residents Assn., 1991; mem. Res. Fund Com., 1992—. Mem. Radcliffe Coll. Alumnae Assn. (chmn. clubs

1966). Clubs: Harvard (N.Y.C.), Cosmopolitan (N.Y.C.) (bd. govs. 1987—); Radcliffe (pres. Washington chpt. 1969) (pres. N.Y. chpt. 1959, 63, bd. sponsors 1974).

ISASI-DIAZ, ADA MARIA, ethics and theology educator; b. La Habana, Cuba, Mar. 22, 1943; came to U.S., 1960.; d. Domingo Isasi Batlle and Josefina Diaz Isasi. BA, Coll. New Rochelle, 1971; MA in medieval history, State U. at Brockport, 1977; MA in div., Union Theol. Sem., 1985, M in philosophy, 1989, PhD in ethics, 1990; JD (hon.), Lynchburg Coll., 1992. Parish min. St. Francis of Assisi Chpt., Rochester, 1977-78; office ministerial team Women's Ordination Conf., Rochester, 1978-81; assoc. gen. dir. Ch. Women United, N.Y.C., 1987-90; adj. prof. N.Y. Theol. Sem., 1990; assoc. prof. Drew U., Madison, N.J., 1991—; lectr. in field. Office: Drew U Theological Sch Madison NJ 07940

ISAY, JANE FRANZBLAU, publisher; b. Cin., Aug. 24, 1939; d. Abraham Norman and Rose (Nadler) Franzblau; children: David Avram, Joshua Daniel. AB, Bryn Mawr Coll., 1961. First reader Harcourt, Brace Co., 1963; asst. editor, then assoc. editor Yale U. Press, 1964-66, editor, then exec. editor, 1966-79; assoc. publisher Basic Books Inc., N.Y.C., 1979, co-pub., exec. v.p., 1979-83; v.p., dir. electronic and tech. pub. Harper & Row, 1983-84; v.p., pub. Touchstone Books, Simon & Schuster, N.Y.C., 1985-87; editorial dir. trade books Addison-Wesley Pub. Co., 1987-91, v.p., 1990-91; pub. Grosset Books G.P. Putnam's, N.Y.C., 1991—; bd. advisers pub. program NYU; mem. adv. bd. Wesleyan U. Press; bd. dirs. The New Press, 1994—. Bd. dirs. Ezra Acad., New Haven, 1964-79, Yale U. Friends of Hillel, 1965-68, Bd. Women's Media Group, 1994—; mem. vis. com. Harvard Grad. Sch. Edn. Fellow Timothy Dwight Coll., Yale U., 1969—. Mem. Assn. Am. Pubs. (chair freedom to read com. 1990-94), Jewish Publ. Soc. (bd. dirs. 1990-94). Office: Grosset Books 200 Madison Ave New York NY 10016-3903

ISELIN, SALLY CARY, writer; b. Nahant, Mass., June 16, 1915; d. Charles Pelham and Edith Goddard (Roelker) Curtis; m. Lewis Iselin, June 14, 1935 (dec.); children: Edith Byron, Sarah Iselin. Student, Harvard U., 1933. Editorial asst. sports and fgn. news depts. Newsweek mag., N.Y.C., 1942-45; soc. and non-fiction editor Town & Country Mag., N.Y.C., 1945-48; reporter, researcher Life Mag., N.Y.C., 1948-50; writer-contact CBS, N.Y.C., 1951; fashion editor Women's Home Companion, N.Y.C., 1956; freelance writer. Fund raiser Planned Parenthood, 1935—, Robert Kennedy for Senate, 1964. Mem. Colony Club, Fashion Group, Century Assn., Am. Club Paris. Democrat. Episcopalian. Home: 11 E 73rd St New York NY 10021-3501

ISENBARGER, ROSALIE ADAMS, retired educator; b. Bristol, Ind., June 12, 1934; d. G.W. and Ruth G. (Gregory) Adams; m. John Philip Raney, July 18, 1955 (div. July 1959); 1 child, Rosalie Kay Whited; m. Jerry Ross Isenbarger, Nov. 22, 1975; stepchildren: Tim S., Gary A., James L., also Russell K. Yoder (grandson). BS, Purdue U., 1956; MA in Tchg., Ind. U., 1962. Cert. secondary sch. tchr., Ind. English tchr. Middlebury (Ind.) Jr. H.S., 1957-58; English tchr. West Side Mid. Sch., Elkhart, Ind., 1958-60, 61-92, chair English dept., 1962-82, 89-92; chair jr. H.S. English dept. Elkhart Cmty. Schs., 1967-87; rep. Elkhart Cmty. Schs. in Japan; active numerous coms. in Elkhart Schs., including curriculum and advanced tng. approval coms., sponsored yearbook, newspaper, dance clubs, equestrian club, others; mem West Side Mid. Sch. Prin.'s Cabinet, Ind. Retired Tchrs. Assn. steering coms. Author: Youth Serving Organizations in Elkhart, Indiana, 1962. Chmn. bd. dirs. Christian Sci. Ch., Elkhart, 1994-95; chmn. usher com., mem. lectr. com. Christian Sci. Ch., Hudson, Fla., 1996—; mgr. Teen Turntable radio program for teens; V.p. Rice Sch. PTA, 1967-68; mem. Middlebury Schs. Bargaining Com.; sec. Elkhart Tchrs.' Assn.; past pres., v.p., numerous coms. AAUW; Brownie troop leader Girl Scouts U.S.; Y-teen leader YWCA; ednl. chmn. City of Elkhart Bicentennial Commn., 1976; mem. steering com. transition from jr. high to mid. sch., Elkhart, com. establishing gifted and talented Program. Elkhart Cmty. Schs. Tchrs.' Assn. scholar, 1952, Finnell Sys. Inc. scholar Purdue U., 1952-56; named to Outstanding Young Women of Am., 1967. Mem. NEA (life), Ind. Coun. Tchrs. English, Ind. Ret. Tchrs.' Assn., Delta Kappa Gamma (world fellowship chmn. 1996—, past pres., v.p., sec., numerous coms., parliamentarian, charter mem., Runner-Up Tchr. of Yr. City of Elkhart, Ind. 1968, State of Ind. 1970), Sigma Delta Pi (conductress, hostess). Home: 8741 Kipling Ave Hudson FL 34667

ISENBERG, SHEILA, freelance writer; b. N.Y.C., Mar. 19, 1943; d. Paul and Edith I.; m. July 4, 1981; 1 child. BA, Bklyn. Coll.; student, Hunter Coll. Investigative staff reporter The Daily Freeman, Kingston, N.Y., 1983-88; prin. media coord. N.Y. State Assembly Task Force on Women's Issues, 1988-92. Author: Women Who Love Men Who Kill, 1991, (with William M. Kunstler) My Life as a Radical Lawyer, 1994; contbr. articles to profl. jours. Mem. Nat. Writers Union. Democrat. Jewish. Office: Elizabeth Kaplan Ellen Levine Agency 15 E 26th St New York NY 10010*

ISENOR, LINDA DARLENE, grocery retailer, marketing professional; b. Calgary, Alta., Can., Oct. 3, 1955; d. Frank Carl and Mavis Ella (Jarnett) Kachmarski; m. Larry Douglas Isenor, Oct. 13, 1973. Diploma in mktg., So. Alta. Inst. Tech., Calgary, 1988. Cert. travel cons. Calgary Bd. Edn. Cashier to asst. mgr. G&S Restaurants Balmoral Ltd., Calgary, 1972-74; cashier, supr. Calgary Coop. Assn. Ltd., 1974-75, supr., 1975-78, head cashier, 1978-80, asst. grocery merchandiser, 1980-81, grocery merchandising specialist, 1981-82, grocery procurement specialist, 1982-83, grocery mktg. supr. for pricing and costing, 1983-93, grocery mktg. mgr., 1993-95, 96—, grocery & liquor mktg. mgr., 1995-96. Office: Calgary Coop Assn Ltd, 2735 39th Ave NE, Calgary, AB Canada T1Y 4T8

ISENSTEIN, LAURA, library director; b. Toledo. BA in History, U. Mich., 1971, MA in Libr. Sci., 1972. Libr. Baltimore County Pub. Libr., 1972-81, area branch mgr., 1981-85, coord. info. svcs., 1985-94; founder, prin. LIA Assocs., Tng. Consultancy, 1988—; dir. Pub. Libr. Des Moines, 1995—; mem. OCLC Adv. Coun. for Pub. Librs.; spkr. in field. Contbr. articles to profl. jours. Mem. gifted and talented adv. coun., cmty. edn. advt. coun. Des Moines Pub. Schs.; mem. Jewish Cmty. Rels. Coun. Des Moines. Mem. ALA, NFE, Pub. Libr. Assn. (chmn., mem. various coms.), Nat. Coalition for Networked Info., Urban Librs. Couns. (legis. adv. com.), Iowa Libr. Assn. Office: Pub Libr Des Moines 100 Locust St Des Moines IA 50309

ISHIKAWA-FULLMER, JANET SATOMI, psychologist, educator; b. Hilo, Hawaii, Oct. 17, 1925; d. Shinichi and Onao (Kurisu) Saito; m. Calvin Y. Ishikawa, Aug. 15, 1950; 1 child, James A.; m. Daniel W. Fullmer, June 11, 1980. BE, U. Hawaii, 1950, MEd, 1967; MEd, U. Hawaii, 1969, PhD, 1976. Diplomate Am. Acad. Pain Mgmt. Instr. Honolulu Bus. Coll., 1953-59; instr., counselor Kapiolani Community Coll., Honolulu, 1959-73; prof., dir. counseling Honolulu Community Coll., 1973-74, dean of students, 1974-77; psychologist, v.p., treas. Human Resources Devel. Ctr., Inc., Honolulu, 1977—; cons. United Specialties Co., Tokyo, 1979, Grambling (La.) State U., 1980, 81, Filipino Immigrants in Kalihi, Honolulu, 1979-84, Legis. Ref. Bur., Honolulu, 1984-85, Honolulu Police Dept., 1985; co-founder Waianae (Hawaii) Child and Family Ctr., 1979-92. Co-author: Family Therapy Dictionary, 1991, Manabu: The Diagnosis and Treatment of a Japanese Boy with a Visual Anomaly, 1991; contbr. articles to profl. jours. Commr. Bd. Psychology, Honolulu, 1979-85; co-founder Kilohana United Meth. Ch. and Family Ctr., 1993—. Mem. APA, ACA, Hawaii Psychol. Assn., Pi Lambda Theta (sec. 1967-68, v.p. 1968-69, pres. 1969-70), Delta Kappa Gamma (sec., v.p., scholarship 1975, Outstanding Educator award 1975, Thomas Jefferson award 1993, Francis E. Clark award 1993). Home: 154 Maono Pl Honolulu HI 96821-2529 Office: Human Resources Devel Ctr 1750 Kalakaua Ave Apt 809 Honolulu HI 96826-3725

ISKANDER, SYLVIA WIESE, English literature educator; b. Jamaica Plain, Mass., June 27, 1940; d. Herbert Edward and Mary Elizabeth (Cavin) Wiese; m. William H. Patterson Jr., June 2, 1962 (div. Apr. 1977); 1 child, Deborah Ann; m. Awad A. Iskander, May 22, 1982; 1 child, Alexandra Lucia. BS, La. State U., 1961; MA, U. Southwestern La., 1965; PhD, Fla. State U., 1969. From asst. to assoc. prof. English U. Southwestern La., Lafayette, 1969-82, prof. English, 1982—; lectr. English U. Houston, 1965-66; dir. writing ctr. U. Southwestern La., 1980-82, 83-86. Author: Rousseau's Emile and Early Children's Literature, 1971; contbr. articles to profl. jours.; editor (book) The Image of the Child, 1991. Founder Lafayette Greenbelt, 1975. Grantee AAUW, 1975. Mem. MLA, Children's Lit. Assn. (treas. 1994-96), Internat. Rsch. Soc. Children's Lit., Nat. Coun. Tchrs. English, Phi Kappa Phi. Office: Univ Southwestern La English Dept Lafayette LA 70504-4691

ISMAIL, FATHIMA MUNIRA, geographer, researcher; b. Colombo, Sri Lanka, Mar. 4, 1965; came to the U.S., 1990; d. Mohomed and Halima (Cader) I.; m. Dilshad Ahmed, Aug. 1, 1992. BS in Fin. and Geography, Slippery Rock U., 1992; MA in Geography, U. Calif., Davis, 1994. exec. com. mem. Gender and Global Issues Program, Davis, 1995-96. Rschr. Marga Inst., Colombo, 1988-89; tchg. asst. U. Calif., Davis, 1992—, Geog. Info. Sys. analyst/rschr., 1995—; Geog. Info. Sys. analyst Sierra Nevada Ecosystem Project, Davis, 1994-95. Scholar Slippery Rock U., 1990, 91, 92; fellow U. Calif., Davis, 1992, 93, A.M.M. Shahabdeen Found., Sri Lanka, 1994. Mem. AAUW, Assn. Am. Geographers, Assn. Pacific Coast Geographers, Gamma Theta Upsilon (treas. 1990-91). Home: 300 Solano Park Cir Davis CA 95616 Office: Univ Calif Davis Davis CA 95616

ISOBE, JEAN N., sales and marketing executive; b. Waipahu, Hawaii, Nov. 24, 1954; d. Harold Kenichi Isobe and Louise Yoshie Sato. BA in History, U. Calif., Berkeley, 1981. Sales cons. Prentice Hall Info. Network divsn. Gulf and Western, N.Y.C., 1986-87; account exec. Digital Equipment Corp., N.Y.C., 1987-90; sales cons. Jack Morton Prodsn. and AWED, N.Y.C., 1990-92; area sales and mktg. dir. Scholastic Inc., N.Y.C., 1992—. Assoc. pub.: (mag.) GIRL Mag., 1994. Mem. Women in Comms., Women in Cable and Telecomms., Am. Women in Radio and TV, Advt. Women of N.Y.

ISOM, HARRIET WINSAR, ambassador; b. Heppner, Oreg., Nov. 4, 1936; d. Blaine Eugene and Evelyn (Struve) I. BA, Mills Coll., 1958; MALD in Law and Diplomacy, Tufts U., 1960. Joined Fgn. Svc., U.S. Dept. State, Washington, 1961; various positions in Africa and Asia; dep. chief mission Am. Embassy, Bujumbura, Burundi, 1974-77; consul Am. Consulate, Medan, Sumatra, Indonesia, 1977-78; polit. counselor Am. Embassy, Jakarta, Indonesia, 1978-81; chargé d'affaires Am. Embassy, Vientiane, Laos, 1986-89; sr. assignments officer Bur. Pers. Dept. State, Washington, 1982-84, dir. Korean affairs Bur. East Asian and Pacific Affairs, 1984-86; amb. to Republic of Benin, Cotonou, 1989-92, Republic of Cameroon, Yaounde, 1993-96; ret., 1996.

ISOM, THERESA GILLESPIE, nursing administrator; b. Memphis, Mar. 3, 1953; d. Ernest Bernette and Emma Pearl (McClelland) Gillespie; m. Robert Earl Isom, June 6, 1987; 1 child, Antonio Harvey. ADN, Shelby State C.C., 1981; BS in Health Arts, Coll. St. Francis, 1990; MS in Adult Edn., U. Tenn., 1992; BSN, Union U., 1994. RN, Tenn. Staff nurse Meth. Hosp. Ctrl., Memphis, 1975-90, preceptor recovery rm., 1984-86; float charge nurse Trinity Nursing Agy., Memphis, 1983-91; clin. leader Meth. Ctrl., Memphis, 1989-90; nursing dir. Tenn. Tech. Ctr., Memphis, 1991—; mem. State Testing, Nashville, 1993—. Treas. Nat. Coalition 100 Black Women, Memphis, 1993—. Named Tchr. of Yr., 1992-93; Job Tng. Partnership Act grantee, 1993, 94. Mem. ANA, Tenn. Nurses Assn., Tenn. Orgn. Nurse Execs., Tenn. Hosp. Assn., Nat. Civil Rights Mus. Democrat. Baptist. Office: Tenn Tech Ctr Memphis 550 Alabama Ave Memphis TN 38105-3604

ISOM, VIRGINIA ANNETTE VEAZEY, nursing educator; b. Tallapoosa County, Ala., Nov. 19, 1936; d. Jimmy L. and Bessie (Pearson) Veazey; m. William G. Isom, May 1959; children: William Gary, Marleah, James Leland. BSN, Tuskegee Inst., 1959; MSN, Syracuse U., 1974; doctoral candidate, Howard U., 1984—, postgrad., 1994. Cert. in nursing adminstrn. Am. Nurses' Credentialing Ctr. Asst. prof. med. surg. nursing Howard U. Coll. Nursing, Washington, 1975-86; edn. and tng. quality assurance coord. Howard U., Washington, 1986-87; patient care coord. Howard U. Hosp., Washington, 1987-88, coord. for spl. projects, 1988-90; prof. nursing Prince George's C.C., Largo, Md., 1992—. Contbr. articles to profl. jours. Mem. ANA (cert. clin. specialist med. surg. nursing), D.C. Nurses' Assn., Sigma Theta Tau. Home: 534 Round Table Dr Fort Washington MD 20744-5638 Office: Prince George's C C Dept Nursing Largo MD 20772

ISRAEL, LESLEY LOWE, political consultant; b. Phila., July 21, 1938; d. Herman Albert and Florence (Segal) Lowe; m. Fred Israel, Dec. 18, 1960; children: Herman Allen, Sanford Lawrence. BA, Smith Coll., 1959. Dir. media advance Humphrey for Pres., Washington, 1967-68, dir. politic. intelligence, 1972; dir. scheduling Bayh for Pres., Washington, 1971; spl. asst. Jackson for Pres., Washington, 1975-76; coord. nat. labor Kennedy for Pres., Washington, 1979-80; sr. v.p. The Kamber Group, Washington, 1981-87; pres., CEO Politics, Inc., Washington, 1987-95; bd. dirs. The Kamber Group, Washington. Pres. Jewish Cmty. Ctr. of Greater Washington, Rockville, Md., 1981-83; bd. mgrs. Adas Israel Synagogue, 1981-83; mem. Dem. Charter Commn., 1982-83, Dem. Del. Selection Commn., 1983-84, Dem. Site Selection Com., 1989-90, 90—; mem. Nat. Dem. Club, 1986—; chmn. Washington regional bd. ADL, 1991-94, mem. nat. commn., 1991-94, mem. nat. exec. commn., 1994—, chmn. Washington affairs com.; chmn. Washington Bd. Friends of Tel Aviv U. Recipient Spl. Svc. award Jewish Cmty. Ctr., 1984; named one of 100 Most Powerful Women, Washingtonian mag., 1990. Jewish. Home: PO Box 69 Royal Oak MD 21662-0069

ISRAEL, LINDA CAROL, psychotherapist; b. Lineville, Ala., Dec. 9, 1948; d. Douglas Y. and Mildred Annelee (Bailey) Johnson; m. Don Philip Israel, Aug. 9, 1968 (div. Oct. 1989); m. James H. Hays, Apr. 15, 1995. BS, Jacksonville State U., 1971, MS in sec. edn. in counseling, 1991. Coord. cooperative edn. Jacksonville (Ala.) State Univ., 1990-91; coord. day C.E.D. Mental Health, Centre, Ala., 1991-92, dir. Mobile Com. Tx., 1992-94; therapist Marshall Jackson Mental Health, Scottsboro, Ala., 1994—; grad. student rep. Alac D, Ala. 1990-92. Co-author: Special Needs of Reentry State, 1991. Bd. mem. Hope Place, Huntsville, Ala, 1994—. Recipient Logan Walker grant Jacksonville State Univ., 1990-91. Mem. ACA, AMHCA, ALACD, AACW, Chi Sigma Iota. Protestant. Home: 500 7th Ave NE Jacksonville AL 36265 Office: Marshall Jackson Mental Health 508 Gregory St Scottsboro AL 35967

ISRAEL, MARGIE OLANOFF, psychotherapist; b. Atlantic City, Apr. 30, 1927; d. Herman and Mary (Salter) Olanoff; m. Allan Edward Israel, Sept. 20, 1953; 1 child, Janet. Student U. Miami, 1945-46, 50, Am. Acad. Dramatic Arts, 1946-47; BA in Psychology cum laude, Hunter Coll., 1970; MSW with honors in fieldwork, Hunter Sch. Social Work, 1972; psychoanalytic tng. N.Y. Soc. Freudian Psychologists, 1965-70, Manhattan Ctr. for Advanced Psychoanalytic Studies, 1972-74, 76. Bd. cert. diplomate in clin. social work Am. Bd. Examiners of Clin. Social Workers. Celebrity interviewer Lunchin' with Marge radio show Sta. WFPG, Atlantic City, 1947-48; co-host Steel Pier Midnight radio show, 1949; publicity writer Hy Gardner Astor Hotel, N.Y.C., 1948; writer theatrical interviews Miami (Fla.) Daily News, 1950-51; sec. to exec. dir. Hebrew Old Age Ctr., Atlantic City, 1951-55; sec. to dir. TV-films and radio Nat. Office, Am. Cancer Soc., N.Y.C., 1959-66, asst. to dir. TV-films and radio,1966-70; social worker Bellevue Hosp., N.Y.C., 1972-76; field instr. socialworkN.Y. U., 1975-76; pvt. practice psychotherapy, N.Y.C., 1973—, Providence, 1991—, Wilmington, N.C., 1996—. Fellow N.Y. State Soc. Clin. Social Work, Am. Orthopsychiat. Assn.; mem. NASW (diplomate), Nat. Fedn. Socs. Clin. Social Work (com. on psychoanalysis), Acad. Cert. Social Workers, N.Y. Acad. Scis., Psi Chi. Home and Office: 5711 Andover Rd Wilmington NC 28403

ISRAELOV, RHODA, financial planner, writer, entrepreneur; b. Pitts., May 20, 1940; d. Joseph and Fannie (Friedman) Kreinen; divorced; children: Jerome, Arthur, Russ. BS in Hebrew Edn. Herzlia Hebrew Tchr.'s Coll., N.Y.C., 1961; BA in English Language and Lit. U. Mo.-Kansas City, 1965; MS Coll. Fin. Planning, 1991. Cert. Fin. Planner, CLU. Tchr. Hebrew, various schs., 1961-79; ins. agt. Conn. Mut. Life, Indpls., 1979-81; fin. planner Smith Barney, Inc., Indpls., 1981—, v.p., 1986—; instr. for mut. fund licensing exams. Pathfinder Securities Sch., Indpls., 1983-87; cons. channel 6 News, 1984-85. Weekly fin. columnist Indpls. Bus. Jour., 1982—; bi-weekly fin. columnist Jewish Post & Opinion, 1982-86; regular guest WTUX Radio, 1990-94; monthly columnist, sr. Beacon, 1985-89. Recipient Gold Medal award Personal Selling Power, 1987; named Bus. Woman of Yr. Network of Women in Bus., 1986. Mem. Inst. Cert. Fin. Planners, Nat. Assn. Life Underwriters, Women's Life Underwriters' Conf. (treas. Ind. chpt. 1982, v.p. chpt. 1983), Internat. Assn. Fin. Planners (v.p. Ind. chpt. 1983-84, bd. dirs., sec.), Am. Soc. CLU, Women's Life Underwriters Conf., Nat. Coun. Jewish Women, Nat. Assn. Profl. Saleswomen , Nat. Speakers Assn. (pres. Ind. chpt. 1986-87, treas. 1984), Registry Fin. Planning Practitioners. Lodge: Toastmasters (chpt. ednl. v.p. 1985-86), Soroptimists (bd. dirs.). Avocations: piano, folk, square and ballroom dancing, theatre. Office: Smith Barney Bank One Center Tower 111 Monument Cir Ste 3100 Indianapolis IN 46204-5131

ISSEKS, EVELYN, retired educational administrator; b. N.Y.C., Feb. 9, 1925; d. David S. and Sadie (Jaffa) Sher; m. Jack Isseks, Dec. 22, 1946; children: Frederick Edward, Robert Nathan. BEd, SUNY, Oneonta, 1947; MS, SUNY, New Paltz, 1967, CAS, 1975. Tchr. Middletown (N.Y.) Sch. Dist., 1947-67; asst. prin. Monroe-Woodbury Sch. Dist., Central Valley, N.Y., 1967-69, prin., 1969-85; mem. Middletown Bd. of Edn., 1986-91, v.p., 1988-89. Membership co-chair Horton Hosp. Aux., Middletown, 1947-49; pres. Middletown Players Club, 1950s; chair ward drive Middletown Cancer Soc., 1950's; mem. exec. com. local PTA, 1967-85; life mem. Nat. PTA; mem. Childhood Services Cons. Com., 1983—; bd. dirs. Orange County Mental Health Bd, 1985-86. Recipient Nat. Disting. Service award PTA, 1983. Mem. Middletown Tchrs. Assn. (treas. 1965-67), Phi Delta Kappa (charter; membership com.). Democrat. Jewish. Club: Women's Univ. Home: 37 Watkins Ave Middletown NY 10940-4722

ITNYRE, JACQUELINE HARRIET, programmer; b. Camden, N.J., May 13, 1941; d. John Harold and Harriet Geraldine (Rankine) Bruynell; m. Thomas James Itnyre, Oct. 13, 1968 (dec. 1978); children: Beth Thierry, John. AS in Engring., Mercer County Coll., 1961; BA in Liberal Studies, San Jose State U., 1980, MLS, 1981. Media ctr. mgr. Milpitas (Calif.) Unified Sch. Dist., 1975-81; tech. libr. Lockheed Missiles and Space Co., Sunnyvale, Calif., 1981, programmer, 1982-83; with ground support dept. Challenger-Space Lab 2 Lockheed Missiles and Space Co., Palo Alto, Calif., 1984-85; systems mgr. gen. clin. rsch. ctr. Stanford (Calif.) U. Med. Sch., 1985-87, computing systems specialist divsn. epidemiology, 1988—; local network admiinstr. health resch. and policy. Edna B. Anthony scholar San Jose State U., 1981. Mem. Assn. for Computing Machinery, ALA, Nature Conservancy, Sierra Club. Home: 310 Santa Clara Ave Redwood City CA 94061

ITTNER, HELEN LOUISE, entrepreneur; b. Saginaw, Mich., June 12, 1935; d. David Harvey and Helen (Austin) Jones; m. Frederick E. Ittner; children: David (dec.), Philip. BA, St. Mary's Coll., 1981. Pres. H.L.I. Enterprises, Inc., Moraga, Calif., 1988—. Mem. Moraga Sch. Bd., 1981-85, pres., 1984-85; bd. dirs. Hospice of Contra Costa, 1990-94, Hearst Monument Found., 1992—; directress Altar Guild, St. Stephen's Episcopal Ch., 1993-95. Mem. AAUW (Disting. Woman award 1991). Republican. Episcopalian. Home: 1858 School St Moraga CA 94556-1729

IVANI, KRISTEN ANN, embryologist; b. San Francisco, Jan. 4, 1960; d. Roger Charles and Marguerite Diana (Rhodes) I.; m. Robert B. Addis, Sept. 25, 1993. BS, U. Calif., Davis, 1982; MS, U. Idaho, 1984; PhD, Colo. State U., 1990. Dir. Ctr. for Reproductive Medicine San Ramon (Calif.) Regional Med. Ctr., 1990—. Contbr. chpt. to book and articles to profl. jours. Recipient Young Investigator award Soc. for Study of Reproduction, 1984; named Outstanding Young Women of Am., 1983. Mem. AAUW (pres. 1995-96), No. Calif. Assn. Reproductive Biologists (pres. 1995—), Am. Soc. Reproductive Medicine, Internat. Embryo Transfer Soc., Gamma Sigma Delta, Phi Sigma, Sigma Xi. Office: San Ramon Reg Med Ctr 6001 Norris Canyon Rd San Ramon CA 94583

IVENS, MARY SUE, microbiologist, mycologist; b. Maryville, Tenn., Aug. 23, 1929; d. McPherson Joseph and Sarah Lillie (Hensley) I.; B.S., E. Tenn. State U., 1949; M.S. (NIH research trainee), Tulane U. Sch. Medicine, 1963; Ph.D., La. State U. Sch. Medicine, 1966; postgrad. Oak Ridge Inst. Nuclear Studies, Emory U. Sch. Medicine. Dir. microbiol. and mycol. labs. Lewis-Gale Hosp., Roanoke, Va., 1953-56; rsch. mycologist Ctrs. Disease Control, Atlanta, 1957-60; rsch. assoc. La. State U. Sch. Med., 1963-66, instr. medicine, 1966-72, instr. Microbiology, 1966-72, clin. prof., 1972—; dir. mycology lab, La. State U. Sch. Med., 1963-72; lectr. Sch. Dentistry, La. State U. Med. Ctr., 1968-70; assoc. prof. natural scis. Dillard U., New Orleans, 1972—; assoc. Marine Biol. Lab., Woods Hole, Mass., 1978— ; cons. in field. Commr. WHO conf. on ctr. for Mycotic sera 1969; chmn. Gold Medal Award Com. Sigma Xi, 1978; mem. La. assn. def. counsel expert witness bank, 1985—; bd. dirs. La. coun. Girl Scouts U.S., Community Relationships Greater New Orleans, Zoning Bd. River Ridge (La.); mem. exec. bd. River Ridge Civic Assn., 1982—, sec., 1982-84; chmn. pers. bd. Riverside Bapt. Ch., River Ridge; dir. Outreach First Baptist Ch., New Orleans, 1989—. Recipient Rosicrucian Humanitarian award, 1981; Macy fellow, MBL, Woods Hole, 1978-79; grantee NSF, NIH; diplomate Am. Bd. Microbiology. Mem. Internat. Soc. Human and Animal Mycology, Med. Mycological Soc. Am., Am. Soc. Microbiology (nat. com. on membership 1983-87), AAAS, Nat. Inst. Sci., Sigma Xi. Author articles in field. Home: 408 Berclair Ave New Orleans LA 70123-1504 Office: Dillard U Div Natural Sci New Orleans LA 70122

IVERSON, CAROL JEAN, retired library media specialist; b. Villisca, Iowa, July 2, 1937; d. Paul Gerald and Garnet Blanche (Dunn) Smith; m. Merlin Gerald Iverson, June 11, 1961; children: Robert Mark, Jean Marie Iverson Howe. BA, U. No. Iowa, 1960. Elem. tchr. Manning (Iowa) Community Schs., 1957-58, Mason City (Iowa) Sch. Dist., 1960-61, Manson (Iowa) Community Schs., 1961-63, Blooming Prairie (Minn.) Community Schs., 1963-64, 65-66; elem. tchr., K-12 librarian Rockwell (Iowa) Swaledale Community Schs., 1973-80; libr. media specialist Mason City Sch. Dist., 1980-96. County co-chair Cerro Gordo County Reps., Howard Baker campaign, 1979; campaign worker Dukakis for Pres., 1987. Mem. AAUW (v.p. 1989-91, pres. 1993-95), NEA (del. rep. assembly), Iowa State Edn. Assn. (del., resolutions com. 1975-78), Iowa Ednl. Media Assn. (legis. chair 1987-89), Delta Kappa Gamma (pres. 1986-88), Phi Delta Kappa. Democrat. Lutheran. Home: 429 20th Pl SW Mason City IA 50401-6428

IVES, ADRIENE DIANE, real estate executive; b. Washington, Oct. 6, 1951; d. Edwin Forrest and Carolyn Elizabeth (Wray) Warner; m. Perry Nelson Ives, May 12, 1972; children: Jesse Warner, James Robert. BS, U. Md., 1973. Tchr. Charles County (Md.) Bd. Edn., 1973-83, Broad Creek Day Sch., Ft. Washington, Md., 1983-85; sales counselor L.K. Farrall, Ltd., Camp Springs, Md., 1985-90; tchr. real estate Farrall Inst., Waldorf, Md., 1990—; assoc. broker Century 21, Donald & Assocs. Inc., Ft. Washington, 1990—; tchr. Christian Children's Ministry, Washington, 1982-83; v.p. The Warner Corp., Washington, 1982-83; bd. dirs. Nat. Plumbing Supply, Inc., Washington; devel. agt. Burgundy Farm Country Day Sch., Alexandria, Va., 1986-91; isntr. real estate edn. Farrall Inst., 1990. Author: Nat. City Christ Church, 1988, 89; contbr. articles to jours. Bd. dirs. Broad Creek County Day Sch., 1982-83; bd. deaconesses Nat. City Christian Ch., Washington, 1989-91. Recipient Citizenship award Prince Georges County Police, Forestville, Md., 1986. Mem. Prince Georges Assn. Realtors (Disting. Sales Assoc. of the Yr. 1995), Women's Coun. Realtors (pres. local chpt. 1994-95). Republican. Mem. Christian Ch. (Disciples of Christ). Office: Century 21 Donald and Assocs 10903 Indian Head Hwy Ste 307 Fort Washington MD 20744-4000

IVES, COLTA FELLER, museum curator, educator; b. San Diego, Apr. 5, 1943; m. E. Garrison Ives, June 14, 1966; 1 child, Lucy Barrett. BA, Mills Coll., 1964; MA, Columbia U., 1966. Staff Met. Mus. Art, N.Y.C., 1966-75, curator in charge prints and photographs, 1975—, curator dept. drawings and prints, 1993—; adj. prof. Columbia U., 1970-85. Author: The Great Wave, 1974, Art Libraries Assn. award, 1975, The Flight Into Egypt, 1972, (with others) The Painterly Print, 1980, R. Rauschenberg Photos In and Out City Limits: New York, 1981, French Prints in the Era of Impressionism and Symbolism, 1988; co-author: Pierre Bonnard: The Graphic Art, 1989, Daumier Drawings, 1992, Goya in the Metropolitan Museum of Art, 1995, Toulouse-Lautrec in the Metropolitan Museum of Art, 1996. Chmn. grants com. Met. Mus. Art, 1986-87. Mem. Print Council Am. (exec bd. 1975-77, 84-87, v.p. 1989-93). Club: Grolier (N.Y.C.). Office: Met Mus Art Fifth Ave New York NY 10028

IVESTER, VICKY JO, sales professional; b. Atlanta, July 27, 1951; d. Thomas Bryan and Duane (Neureuther) I. BBA, U. Ga., 1973; MBA, Ga. State U., 1982. Lic. real estate broker. Mgmt. trainee Citizens and So. Nat. Bank, Atlanta, 1973-75; sales merchandiser Chesebrough-Ponds, Inc., Atlanta, 1975; sales rep., key accounts Clairol, Inc., Macon and Atlanta, Ga., 1975-81; account mgr. Pepperidge Farm, Atlanta, 1982-84; dist. sales mgr., account mgr., mktg. mgr. Coca-Cola USA, Atlanta, Albuquerque, Dallas and, St. Louis, 1984-88; real estate broker CAMCO Realty, Albuquerque, 1989-91; registered sales asst. Prudential Securities, Inc., Albuquerque, 1991-92; area sales mgr. Nordic Track, Inc., Albuquerque, 1992-93; inside sales mgr. Kyser Co., Inc., Albuquerque, 1993-94; pres., owner Melon Rags, Inc., Albuquerque, 1994—. Pres. and founder Acad. Ridge East Neighborhood Assn., Albuquerque, 1989-91; founder U. Ga. Alumni Group, Albuquerque, 1989-92. Mem. Am. Mktg. Assn. (bd. dirs. 1983-84), NAFE. Presbyterian. Home: 10817 Malagueña Ln NE Albuquerque NM 87111 Office: Melon Rags Inc 5850 Eubank Blvd NE Ste B49 Albuquerque NM 87111-6118

IVEY, CHERYL LYNN, oncological nurse specialist; b. Omaha, Apr. 15, 1956; d. Robert Irwin and Patricia Marie (Barton) VandeBrake; m. John William Ivey, Jan. 6, 1979; children: Amanda, Matthew. ADN, Gulf Coast C.C., Panama City, Fla., 1982; BS, U. So. Miss., Long Beach, Miss., 1990; MSN, U. So. Ala., Mobile, 1992. Staff RN Brookwood Med. Ctr., Birmingham, 1982-83, Pvt. Duty Nursing, Picayne, Miss., 1983-84; staff RN Meml. Hosp. at Gulfport, Miss., 1984-89, inpatient oncology at Gulfport, 1989-90, radiation oncology at Gulfport, 1990-92, clin. nurse specialist oncology, 1992—; owner Oncology Solutions, Gulfport, Miss., 1992—; mem. Miss. Cancer Pain Initiative, Tupelo, Miss., 1993—; chairperson Nurses Edn. Subcommittee of Am. Cancer Soc., Jackson, Miss., 1993—. Contbr. chpts. to books, articles to profl. jours. Breast/prostate screening coord., Gulfport, Miss., 1990—; cancer survivor's day celebration coord., Gulfport, 1990—; govt. rels. corr. Oncology Nursing Soc., Gulfport, 1993—. Mem. ANA, Am. Assn. Clin. Nurse Specialists, Oncology Nursing Soc., Miss. Gulf Coast Oncology Nursing Soc. (nominated Oncology Nurse of Yr. 1993), Miss. Nurses Assn. (awards com., approver unit for So. Miss. 1996, mem. wellness task force 1996, v.p. dist. 5 1995, nominated Oncology Nurse of Yr. 1992-94), Advanced Practice Nurses Assn., Intravenous Nurses Assn., Sigma Theta Tau. Home: 11351 Oakleigh Blvd Gulfport MS 39503-3973 Office: Meml Hosp Gulfport 4500 13th St Gulfport MS 39501-2515

IVEY, JEAN EICHELBERGER, composer; b. Washington, July 3, 1923; d. Joseph S. and Elizabeth (Pfeffer) Eichelberger. AB magna cum laude, Trinity Coll., 1944; MusM in Piano, Peabody Conservatory, 1946; MusM in Composition, Eastman Sch. Music, U. Rochester, 1956; D of Music, U. Toronto, 1972. Founder electronic music studio, mem. composition faculty Peabody Conservatory, Johns Hopkins U., Balt., 1969—, dept. coord., 1982-86, 91—; music panelist Nat. Endowment for the Arts, 1989-91. Performer piano recitals, concert tours including own compositions, U.S., Mex., Europe; composer: for solo voice and orch. Tribute: Martin Luther King, 1969, Testament of Eve, 1976; for orch. Sea-Change, 1979, Voyager for Cello and Orchestra, 1987, Short Symphony, 1988, Sonata da Chiesa, 1993, Forms in Motion, 1994, My Heart is Like a Singing Bird, 1994, Flying Colors, 1994; opera The Birthmark, 1982, also choral and vocal chamber music, instrumental solos, ensembles, music for films and TV; subject TV documentary A Woman Is-A Composer; recorded Folkways, 1967, 73, Composers Records, Inc., 1974, 88, Grenadilla, 1987; contbr. to Electronic Music: A Listeners Guide, 1972; contbr. articles to mus. publs. Recipient residencies at MacDowell Colony and Yaddo, Disting. Alumni award Peabody Conservatory, 1975, Peabody Dir.'s Recognition award, 1988, Disting. Achievement citation Nat. League Am. Pen Women, 1988, Artists' Fellowship award N.Y. Found. for Arts, 1992; grantee Nat. Endowment Arts, 1978, 83, Martha Baird Rockefeller Fund, Am. Music Ctr.; Guggenheim fellow, 1986. Mem. ASCAP (ann. awards since 1972), Am. Soc. Univ. Composers (editor newsletter 1968-70), Phi Beta Kappa, Sigma Alpha Iota (composer-judge). Home: 320 W 90th St Apt 3A New York NY 10024-1622 Office: Johns Hopkins U Peabody Conservatory Baltimore MD 21202

IVEY, JUDITH, actress; b. El Paso, Tex., Sept. 4, 1951; d. Nathan Aldean and Dorothy Lee (Lewis) I.; m. Tim Braine, 1989; children: Maggie, Thomas Carter. BS, Ill. State U., 1973. Actress in stage plays: The Sea, 1974, The Philanthropist, Hay Fever, Romeo and Juliet, Two Gentlemen of Verona, Mourning Becomes Electra, 1975, Don Juan, Cactus Flower, As You Like It, Design for Living, 1976, The Goodbye People, The Moundbuilders, Oh, Coward, Much Ado About Nothing, 1977-78, Bedroom Farce, 1979, Dusa, Fish, Stas and VI, 1980, Piaf, 1980-81, The Dumping Ground, 1981, The Rimers of Eldritch, 1981, Pastorale, 1982, Two Small Bodies, 1982, Steaming, 1982-83 (Tony award 1983, Drama Desk award 1983), Second Lady, 1983, Hurlyburly, 1984 (Tony award 1985, Drama Desk award 1985), Precious Sons, 1986, Blithe Spirit, 1987, Mrs. Dally Has a Lover, 1988, Park Your Car in Harvard Yard, 1991, The Mooshot Tape, 1994 (Obie award 1994); films include: Harry and Son, 1984, The Lonely Guy, 1984, The Woman in Red, 1984, Compromising Positions, 1985, Brighton Beach Memoirs, 1986, Hello Again, 1987, Sister Sister, 1988, Miles from Home, 1988, Love Hurts, 1989, In Country, 1989, Alice, 1990, Everybody Wins, 1990, There Goes the Neighborhood, 1992; TV films include: The Shady Hill Kidnapping, 1980, Dixie Changing Habits, 1982, We Are The Children, 1986, The Long, Hot Summer, 1985, Jesse and the Bandit Queen, 1986, Decoration Day, 1990, The Betty Broderick Story, 1992, On Promised Land, 1994, Almost Golden, 1995; TV series: Down Home, 1990-91, Designing Women, 1992-93, The Five Mrs. Buchanans, 1994, Buddies, 1995. Office: care Bresler Kelly Kipperman 15760 Ventura Blvd Ste 1730 Van Nuys CA 91436-3002*

IVEY, LOUISE, community relations specialist, entrepreneur; b. Shaw, Miss., Aug. 28, 1926; d. James and Mary (Mitchell) Ray; m. Joe Ivey, Febr. 25, 1963 (div. Jan. 1965); children: Mary Dawson Holmes, Donald Thompson, Patricia Thompson, Lavern Thompson, Joyce Burgess. AS, Ind. U., Gary, 1979, BS, 1988. Notary public, Ind., 1978. Supervisor Joliet (Ill.) Ammunition Plant, 1960-68; entrepreneur Louise's Kitchen, Gary, 1968-70; mgr. Gary Hotel, 1970-73; dir. Gary Police Cmty. Rels., 1973-96; coord. telemktg. Gary (Ind.) Police Dept., 1989-90; conf. chair Nat. Baptist Congress, Gary, 1982, Nat. Police Assn., Chgo., 1976-82. Editor: (musical drama) Blacks Looking Back, 1973, The Message of the Cross, 1974, The Old Rugged Cross, 1975, (poetry) If All People Were Like Me, 1973. mem. neighborhood watch Gary Police Cmty. Rels., 1976, operation safe neighborhood, 1977, mem. jr. patrol, 1978, mem. sr. power and public safety, 1978. Mem. AAUW, Nat. Assn. Chief of Police, Am. Police Hall of Fame (patriot), Internat. Assn. Police Cmty. Relations Officers (region v.p., named Outstanding Region VI V.P.), Baptist Ministers of Gary. Democrat. Home: 2529 Van Buren Pl Gary IN 46407

IVINS, JENNIFER ANN, counselor; b. Camden, N.J., Mar. 17, 1971; d. Jesse Franklin III and Linda Louise (Buckley) I. B in Psychology, Trenton State Coll., 1993, M in Counseling, 1996. Resident asst. Trenton (N.J.) State Coll., 1992-93; med. assistance counselor The MARS Group, Camden, 1993—; counselor The Starting Point, Inc., Westmont, 1995—; presenter in field. Mem. Mcpl. Alliance Preventing Drug/Alcohol Abuse, Somerdale, N.J., 1995—. Mem. Am. Counseling Assn., Psi Chi Nat. Honor Soc. in Psychology. Home: 501 Stafford Ave Laurel Springs NJ 08021 Office: The Starting Point Inc 216 Haddon Ave Ste 608 Westmont NJ 08108

IVINS, MOLLY, columnist, writer; b. Texas, 1944; d. Jim and Margo I. BA, Smith Coll.; MA in Journalism, Columbia U.; postgrad., Inst. Polit. Sci., Paris. Former reporter The Houston Chronicle, The Mnpls. Star Tribune; reporter The Texas Observer, Austin, 1970-76, The New York Times, 1976-77; Rocky Mountain bur. chief The New York Times, Denver, Colo., 1977-80; former columnist The Dallas Times Herald; columnist Fort Worth Star-Telegram. Author: Molly Ivins Can't Say That, Can She?, 1991, Nothin' But Good Times Ahead, 1993; contbr. to periodicals including The Nation, N.Y. Times Book Rev., Mother Jones, Ms., Progressive, others. Office: Fort Worth Star-Telegram 1005 Congress Ave Rm 920 Austin TX 78711*

IVORY, GOLDIE LEE, social worker, educator; b. Chgo., Apr. 19, 1926; d. Percey Carr and Edna M. (Scott) Carr Williams; B.S., Ind. U., 1949; M.A., U. Notre Dame, 1956; M.S.W., Ind. U.-Purdue U., Indpls., 1977. Registered cert. clin. social worker Ind. m. Sam Ivory, Aug. 7, 1947; children: Kenneth L., Kevin D. Juvenile probation officer St. Joseph County Juvenile Probation Dept., South Bend, Ind., 1949-56, intake supr., 1956-59; chief probation officer South Bend City Ct., 1959; psychiat. social worker Beatty Meml. Hosp., Westville, Ind., 1960; instr. sociology Ind. U., South Bend, 1960-67; relocation rep. Urban Redevel. Commn., South Bend, 1960-62; social worker Elkhart (Ind.) Community Schs., 1962-66, supr. social services, 1966-69, dir. human relations, 1970-87; mem. faculty Goshen (Ind.) Coll., 1971—, asst. prof. social work, 1971-81, adj. prof. social work, 1981-91; assoc. prof. social work emeritus Goshen Coll., 1993—; pvt. practice social work, Ivory Caring Corner, 1981-87; family therapist Family Learning Ctr., South Bend, Ind., 1987-94, clinician emeritus, 1994—. workshop cons. human social services; instr. sociology and social work St. Mary's Coll., 1967-69, dir. Upward Bound program, 1970; guest lectr. dept. sociology U. Swaziland, 1983. Recipient Human Service award Acad. Human Services, 1974-75, Merit award Indpls. Public Schs. Dept. Social Work, 1977, Designation BCD award Am. Bd. Examiners in Clin. Soc., 1985; plaque for community services Mayor of Elkhart, 1981; Black Achiever award in edn. Ind. Black Expo, 1983; State chpt. Delta Kappa Gamma scholar, 1969-70. Registered clin. Social worker. Mem. Nat. Assn. Social Workers, Nat. Assn. Black Social Workers, Acad. Cert. Social Workers, The Links, Delta Kappa Gamma, Delta Sigma Theta, Alpha Delta Mu. Methodist. Club: Altrusa. Author articles in field. Home: 1309 Bissell St South Bend IN 46617-2108 Office: Family Learning Ctr 702 W Colfax St South Bend IN 46601

IVY, BERRYNELL BAKER, critical care nurse; b. Shreveport, La., June 24, 1954; d. Berry William and Zilphia Margaret (Nix) Baker; m. Kenneth James Ivy, Sr.,Apr. 17, 1988. ADN, Northwestern State U., 1981. RN, La., Tex.; cert. BLS, ACLS; cert. neurosci. RN; cert. CCRN. Charge nurse Doctors Hosp., Shreveport, La., 1982-85; staff nurse ICU Schumpert Med. Ctr., Shreveport, La., 1985-88; staff nurse ICU Bayshore Med. Ctr., Pasadena, Tex., 1988-89, asst. head nurse ICU, 1989-92; staff nurse/charge nurse ICU Bossier Med. Ctr., Bossier City, La., 1993—; co-chmn. profl. practice com. La. Organ Procurement Assn., Bossier City, 1988—. Mem. AACN, Nat. League Nurses, Am. Assn. Neurosci. Nurses. Home: PO Box 52 Haughton LA 71037-0052

IWASIW, SONYA ANNE, auditor; b. Rochester, N.Y., Oct. 5, 1970; d. William and Tatiana (Kartawets) I. BS, Geneseo State U., 1992; postgrad., Rochester Inst. Tech., 1997—. Cert. internal auditor. Staff auditor Fleet Investment Svcs., Rochester, 1992-94; internal analyst Brockport (N.Y.) State U., 1994-96. Mem. Inst. Internal Auditors (chair membership directory 1993-95, sec. 1993-94, bd. dirs. 1994-96). Home: 1079 Hrezent View Ln Webster NY 14580

IZADI, ELHAM, mathematics educator; b. Teheran, Iran, Feb. 27, 1965; d. Mansour and Ashrafalsadat (Araghian) I. Maitrise and licence, U. Paris VI, 1987; DEA math. pures, U. Paris XI, 1988, doctorat nouvelle these, 1993; PhD, U. Utah, 1991. Asst. prof. Harvard U., Cambridge, 1991-95; rsch. fellow MSRI, Berkeley, Calif., 1992-93; asst. prof. U. Ga., Athens, 1995—; referee Pacific Jour. of Math., L.A., 1995-96; reviewer math. revs. Contbr. articles to profl. jours. Grantee NSF, 1992-94. Fellow Math. Scis. Rsch. Inst.; mem. Am. Math. Soc. Office: Dept Math U Ga Boyd Grad Studies Rsch Ctr Athens GA 30602

IZZO, LUCILLE ANNE, sales representative; b. Rochester, N.Y., Apr. 1, 1954; d. Peter George and Dorothy June (Cusimano) I. B of Gen. Studies, U. Conn., 1995. Regional sales mgr. T.R. Miller Co., Inc., New Milford, Conn., 1986-87; program mgr. Jr. Achievement SW Conn., Stamford, 1987-88, adviser, cons., 1986-93; sec. Eastman Kodak Co., Rochester, 1972-84; consumer products sales rep. Eastman Kodak Co., Oklahoma City, 1984-86; copy products sales rep. Eastman Kodak Co., Stamford, 1988-91; office imaging sales rep. Eastman Kodak Co., Hartford, Conn., 1992—, major account rep., 1994-96; major account rep. Lexis-Nexis, Danbury, Conn., 1996—; grad. asst. Dale Carnegie Human Rels. Course, 1987, 88, 96. Bus. cons. Region One Jr. Achievement Conf., 1988, 90; guest speaker West Conn. Jr. Achievement Conf., 1990; adviser, recruiter Greater Rochester Jr. Achievement, 1980-83, Small Bus. Owner, Accessorize, 1994—. Mem. NAFE, Am. Mgmt. Assn. Home: 166 Old Brookfield Rd Bldg 2-5 Danbury CT 06811-4030

IZZO, MARY THERESA, nurse practitioner; b. Corning, N.Y., May 30, 1955; d. William John and Rita Marie (Reagan) McCaig; m. Robert Frank Izzo. RN, St. James Mercy Hosp., 1975; cert. nurse practitioner, Cmty. Gen. Hosp. Syracuse, 1987; B in Profl. Arts, St. Joseph's Coll., Windham, Maine, 1995. RN, N.Y., Fla.; registered nurse practitioner; cert. CPR instr. Nurse critical care Corning (N.Y.) Hosp., 1975-87; nurse practitioner Dr. Michael Cilip, Corning, 1987; mgr. Vicar's Landing Continuing Care Retirement Cmty., Ponte Vedra Beach, Fla., 1988-94, Steuben Med. Assoc., Corning, 1994—; mgr. health svcs. Suburban Hosp., Bethesda, Md., 1993, Bapt. Med. Ctr., Jacksonville, Fla., 1991; coord. resident care Manor Care, Silver Springs, Md., 1992; profl. privileges Three Rivers Health Care Facility, 1994—, Corning Hosp., 1996. Mem. Am. Acad. Nurse Practitioners, N.Y. State Coalition Nurse Practitioners. Republican. Roman Catholic. Home: 29 Federal Heights Dr Horseheads NY 14845 Office: Steuben Guthrie Med Assocs 123 Conhocton St Corning NY 14830

JABS, JENNIFER, financial planner; b. Bristol, Conn., Sept. 22; d. Arthur Gustav and Frances Mary (Demma) J. BA, U. Hartford, 1976; MA, Trinity Coll., 1993. Cert. history, consumer interviewer, real estate. Asst. mgr. Credit Bureau of Bristol, 1976-85; credit investigator, analyst Bristol Savings Bank, 1986-88; v.p. ops. and fins. Dr. William J. Lucey, Bristol, 1986—; organ procurer for dental rsch., U. Zurich, 1988—; presenter Trinity Coll. Lecture Series, Hartford, Conn., 1990. Organizer, author of article Plainville (Conn.) Pub. Schs., 1985; reviewer of religious edn. St. Joseph Ch., Bristol, 1987, com. mem. 1986—; vol. Bristol Civic Theater, 1990-92; participant NASA Town Meet, 1992. Mem. Am. Classical League, Classical Assn. New Eng. (cert. classical humanities 1991), Am. Inst. Archaeology, Am. Dental Assts. Assn., Conn. Dental Assts. Assn., Trinity Club. Democrat. Roman Catholic. Office: Dr William J Lucey 391 Main St Bristol CT 06010-5848

JACK, DANA CROWLEY, psychologist, educator; b. Houston, Mar. 19, 1945; d. John Thomas Crowley and Dorothy Jane (Mohr) Beach; m. Rand File Jack, Mar. 16, 1968; children: Darby, Kelsey. BA summa cum laude, Mt. Holyoke Coll., 1967; MSW, U. Wash., 1972; EdD, Harvard U., 1984. Counselor, therapist Western Wash. U., Bellingham, 1972-79, prof. Fairhaven Coll., 1986—. Author: Moral Vision and Professional Decisions, 1989, Silencing the Self: Women and Depression, 1991; contbr. articles to profl. jours., chpts. to books. Recipient Depression Rsch. grant Stone Ctr., Wellesley Coll., 1986, Rsch. grant Western Wash. U., 1993, 95. Mem. APA, Phi Beta Kappa. Office: Western Wash Univ Fairhaven Coll Bellingham WA 98225

JACK, ELAINE, religious organization administrator; m. Joseph E. Jack; 4 children. Student, U. Utah. 2d counselor Young Women Gen. Presidency, LDS Ch., Salt Lake City; gen. pres. Relief Soc., LDS Ch., Salt Lake City, 1990—. Mem. gen. bd. Relief Soc. LDS Ch., 1972-84; past counselor N.Y. State, Relief Soc. Presidency. Office: LDS Ch 50 E North Temple Salt Lake City UT 84150

JACK, JANIS GRAHAM, judge; b. 1946. RN, St. Thomas Sch. Nursing, 1969; BA, U. Balt., 1974; JD summa cum laude, South Tex. Coll., 1981. Pvt. practice Corpus Christi, Tex., 1981-94; judge U.S. Dist. Ct. (so. dist.) Tex., Corpus Christi, 1994—. Mem. ABA, Fed. Judges Assn., Fifth Cir. Dist. Judges Assn., Nat. Assn. Women Judges, Tex. Bar Found., State Bar Tex., Coll. State Bar Tex., Tex. Acad. Family Law Specialists, Corpus Christi Bar Assn., Corpus Christi Family Law Assn., Order of Lytae, Phi Alpha Delta. Office: US Dist Ct 521 Starr St Corpus Christi TX 78401-2349

JACK, MINTA SUE, hospital department head; b. Huntsville, Tex., Aug. 24, 1935; d. Clinton Orrin and Dorris Eugenia (Pierce) Bunn; m. Samuel Garred Jack, Jr., June 8, 1957 (div. 1984); children: Samuel Garred III, Paul Alan. BA with distinction, U. N.Mex., 1957. Cert. secondary educator. High sch. tchr. Albuquerque Pub. Schs., 1957-58; bd. dirs. Delta Delta Delta, Reno, 1962-63; com. chmn. Tustin (Calif.) Sch. Dist. PTO, 1965-70, Red Hill Luth. Sch., Tustin, 1970-74; bd. dirs. Assistance League of Tustin, 1972-83, Performing Arts Ctr. Guilds, Orange County, Calif., 1983-88; bd.d irs. Delta Delta Delta, Orange County, Calif., 1987-91; dir., vol. Western Med. Ctr., Santa Ana, Calif., 1986—. Vol. leader Boy Scouts/Little League, Tustin, 1966-72; vol. Olympic Organizing Com., L.A., 1984; assoc. Mexican Am. Nat. Women, Santa Ana, 1988-90; mem. Freedom Found./Valley Forge, Santa Ana, 1988-90. Recipient Writing award, 1989, Newsletter award, 1991, Community Svc. award Disneyland, 1981, Amelia Earhart award U. Calif., 1989, Ernestine Grigsby award Delta Delta Delta, 1989; named Woman of Yr. nominee Panhellenic Assn., 1989. Mem. AAUW, So. Calif. Assn. Dirs. of Vol. Svcs. (bd. dirs. 1987-91), Am. Soc. Dirs. Vol. Svcs. (membership com. 1989), Assistance League of Tustin (pres. 1980-81), Westmed Gold Club (membership com. 1986-92), Chapman Univ. Music Assocs. (bd. dirs. 1987-92), Mortar Bd., Delta Delta Delta (pres. 1988-89, bd. dirs. 1988-91), Dirs. Vols. in Agencies, Phi Kappa Phi, Phi Alpha Theta, Pi Lambda Theta. Episcopalian. Home: 7634 Appaloosa Trail Orange CA 92669 Office: Western Med Ctr 1001 N Tustin Ave Santa Ana CA 92705

JACK, NANCY RAYFORD, supplemental resource company executive, consultant; b. Hughes Springs, Tex., June 23, 1939; d. Vernon Lacy and Virginia Ernestine (Turner) Rayford; m. Kermit E. Hundley, Dec. 19, 1979; 1 child by previous marriage, James Bradford Jack, III. Cert. in bus. adminstrn., Keller Grad. Sch. Mgmt., 1980; cert. in acctg., Harper Coll., 1972, cert. in corp. law and tax law, paralegal, 1973. Sr. sec. Gould, Inc., Rolling Meadows, Ill., 1971-73; staff asst. Gould, Inc., 1973-74, asst. sec., 1974-77, corp. sec., 1977-89, v.p., 1985-89; pres. The Corp. Ofcl. Sec., Wheaton, Ill., 1989-92, Corp. Minutes and more, Wheaton, 1992—. Recipient cert. of leadership YWCA Met. Chgo., 1975. Mem. Fair Oaks Ranch Golf and Country Club, Beta Sigma Phi. Home and Office: 1040 Creekside Dr Wheaton IL 60187-6173

JACKLE, KAREN DEE, real estate executive; b. Santa Ana, Calif., June 26, 1945; d. Franklin Suits and Dorothy (Miller) Todd; m. Paul Herman Jackle, Oct. 12, 1968; children: Lara Irene, Julie Maureen. BA in History, Calif. State U., Long Beach, 1967. Elem. tchr. L.A. City Schs., 1967-68; social worker Los Angeles Dept. Pub. Social Svcs., 1968-70; with Seablue Pools, Salisbury, Rhodesia, 1970; co-owner, property mgr., appraiser Paul Jackle & Assocs., Inc., Huntington Beach, Calif., 1971—; property mgr., appraiser Paul Jackle & Assocs., Huntington Beach, Calif., 1973-86; property developer, mgr. Paul Jackle & Assocs., Huntington Beach, 1986—; pres. June Coast Corp., 1993—. Mem. Sister City Club, Huntington Beach, 1986—. Mem. AAUW (Huntington Beach chpt., chmn. edn. found. 1991-92, chmn. membership 1992-94, mem. mentoring program 1990-94, Mentor award 1991, pres. 1995—), Nat. Assn. Women in Constrn., H. Seacliff Homeowners Assn. (block rep.). Office: 18652 Florida St Ste 300 Huntington Beach CA 92648-6007

JACK-MOORE, PHYLLIS, corporate family strategist, educational consultant; b. Charlotte, N.C., Aug. 23, 1934; d. William Thomas and Connie LaVerne (Childers) Harris; children: Michael Harris, Julie Dawn Jack Rodgers. BA, U. N.C., 1965, MEd, 1969; postgrad., North Tex. State U., 1982-83. Cert. tchr., N.C., Tex. Elem. tchr. Chapel Hill (N.C.) Pub. Schs., 1965-68; staff devel. coordinator Learning Inst. N.C., Durham, 1969-72; child devel. specialist Tex. Dept. Human Resources, Ft. Worth, 1975-77; child care tng. coordinator North Tex. State Univ., Denton, 1978-81; dir., owner Resources for Children, Inc., Ft. Worth, 1984-88; pvt. practice Ft. Worth, 1988—; instr. Tarrant County Jr. Coll., Ft. Worth, North Tex. State U., 1982—; frequent guest speaker; appearances on TV; coord. for tng. in establishment of pub. sch. kindergarten program in State of N.C., 1972-73; cons. for family support svcs. State Dept. Pub. Instrn., Raleigh. Contbg. author: Room to Grow; mem. editorial rev. bd. Child Care Quar., Austin, 1984—. Trustee Tarrant County Youth Collaboration, 1982-86; bd. dris. Tarrant County Med. Aus., 1983-84; adv. bd. Ft. Worth's A Better Childhood Com., 1990—; coord. Tex. State Parent Action, 1989—; gov.'s task force mem. Head Start Collaboration, 1991—. Recipient Brous Outstanding Advocate award, 1984, All State Good Hands award, 1996. Mem. Nat. Assn. for the Edn. of Young Children (gov. bd. nominee 1988—, nat. field rep. 1983—), Tex. Assn. for the Edn. of Young Children (state pres. 1982-83, Adminstr. of the Yr. award 1993), Ft. Worth Assn. for the Edn. of Young Children (pres. 1976-78), So. Assn. for Children Under Six (com. chair 1978-80, conf. co-chair 1987), Rotary, Phi Beta Kappa, Phi Delta Kappa. Methodist. Club. Ft. Worth Woman's (v.p. and auditor 1983-86). Lodge: Rotary.

JACKSON, AGNES MORELAND, English educator; b. Pine Bluff, Ark., Dec. 2, 1930; d. Nathaniel Edmund Moreland and Rosa Lorenda Mae (Wood) Moreland Keaton; children: Barbara Ruth Arnwine, Lucretia Drane Peebles; m. Harold Andrew Jackson Jr., July 8, 1964. BA, U. Redlands, 1952; MA, U. Washington, 1953; PhD, Columbia U., 1960. Instr. English Spelman Coll., Atlanta, 1953-55; from instr. to asst. prof. Boston U. Coll. Basic Studies, 1959-63; from. asst. to assoc. prof. Calif. State U., L.A., 1963-69; prof. English, world lit. and black studies Claremont (Calif.) Coll., 1969—; vis. prof. theology and arts, Sclaremont Sch. Theology, spring, 1969; vis. prof. English U. Redlands, summer, 1963. Contbr. articles to profl. jours. Bd. dirs. Pomona Unified Sch. Dist., 1981-89, Soc. for Values in Higher Edn., 1985-88; nominating com., bd. dirs. Girl Scouts Am., Pomona, 1980-84, 86-88. NEH grant, 1980. Mem. MLA (del. 1993-95). Democrat. Mem. Ch. of Christ. Office: Pitzer Coll English World Lit Black 1050 N Mills Ave Claremont CA 91711

JACKSON, ALICE HUMBERT, retired psychologist and educator; b. Buffalo, Sept. 22, 1914; d. Herbert Earl and Eula (Brainard) Humbert; m. A. Leon Jackson, Nov. 1953 (div. 1964); 3 stepchildren. BA, U. Mich., 1936, MA, 1937; PhD, U. So. Calif., 1953. Cert. tchr., Mich.; standard designated svc. credential, life tchr., sch. psychologist, supr., cons., coord., prin., pupil pers., Calif. Tchr. pub. schs., Mich., Calif., 1937-43, 46, 49; psychometrist Calif. Test Bur., Hollywood, 1947-49; coord. sch. psychologists Los Angeles County Supt. Schs., L.A., 1950-55; prof. Ea. N.Mex. U., Portales, 1965-70, dir. Head Start regional tng., 1966-70; prof., dir. Kindergarten Insts. Tex. Woman's U., Denton, 1970-72; prof. head start supplementary tng. Redlands (Calif.) U., 1972-73; sch. psychologist Covina (Calif.) Valley Unified Sch. Dist., 1973-80. Author audio-visual curriculum activities in elem. reading and arithmetic, 1967-69; editor: Performance Based Activities for Kindergarten, 1971. Pres. Hosp. Auxs. Kans., 1964; mem. adv. bd. Head Start, Rogers, Ark., 1986-88; mem. Fed. Women's Club, Kans., N.Mex., 1954-66. With USN, 1944-46. Mem. AAUW, Pi Lambda Theta. Home: 5411 Rolling Green Rd Arlington TX 76017-6237

JACKSON, ANN WILLIAMS, publisher; b. Holland, Mich., Jan. 22, 1952; d. Byron Allen and Rozanne (Simon) Williams; m. Charles Miller Jackson, Oct. 18, 1980; children: Sam, Nicholas, Lucy. BA magna cum laude, Middlebury Coll., 1974; MBA, Columbia U., 1980. Fin. analyst Time Inc., N.Y.C., 1980-82; direct mail mgr. Time Life Books, London, 1982-85; bus. mgr. Money mag. Time Inc., N.Y.C., 1985-87, bus. mgr. Sports Illustrated mag., 1987-89, gen. mgr. Sports Illustrated mag., 1989-92, gen. mgr. People mag., 1992-94, pub. In Style mag., 1994—; bd. dirs. Nat. Parenting Assn., N.Y.C., Fashion Group Internat., N.Y.C., Cancer Rsch. Inst., N.Y.C. Mem. Advt. Women of N.Y., Women in Comms., Bronxville Field Club, Phi Beta Kappa. Office: In Style Time Inc 1271 6th Ave New York NY 10020

JACKSON, ANNE (ANNE JACKSON WALLACH), actress; b. Allegheny, Penn., Sept. 3, 1926; d. John Ivan and Stella Germaine (Murray) J.; m. Eli Wallach, Mar. 5, 1948; children: Peter, Roberta, Katherine. Studied with Sanford Meisner and Herbert Berghof at Neighborhood Playhouse, with Lee Strassberg at Actor's Studio. Profl. debut: Cherry Orchard; mem. Am. Repertory Co.; Broadway plays include: Summer and Smoke, Oh, Men! Oh, Women!, Middle of the Night, Major Barbara, Rhinoceros, Luv, Waltz of the Toreadors, Diary of Anne Frank, 1978, Twice Around the Park, 1982-83, Nest of the Woodgrouse, 1984, Café Crown, 1989, Love Letters, 1991-92, Lost in Yonkers, 1992, In Person, 1993, The Flowering Peach, 1994, off-Broadway plays: The Typists, The Tigers; film appearances include: So Young, So Bad, 1950, Secret Life of an American Wife, 1968, Dirty Dingus McGee, 1970, Lovers andOther Strangers, 1970, The Shining, 1980, Sam's Son, 1985, Funny About Love, 1992, Folks, 1992; TV appearances include: 84 Charing Cross Road, Private Battle, Everything's Relative, 1987; TV films: Family Man, Golda I and II, Out on a Limb, Baby M, 1988; author:

(autobiography) Early Stages, 1979. Recipient Obie award. Office: care Paradigm 200 W 57th St New York NY 10019-3211

JACKSON, BARBARA ANN, systems engineer; b. San Francisco, Feb. 15, 1955; d. Thomas John and Bertha Belle (Seeley) J. BS in Metall. Engring., Calif. Poly. State U., San Luis Obispo, 1979; MA in Marriage/Family/Child Counseling, Azusa Pacific U., 1985; MS in Sys. Mgmt., U. Denver, 1992. Registered counselor, Wash.; lic. massage therapist, Wash. Chief metallurgist Grove Valve and Regulator Co., Oakland, Calif., 1979; metallurgist, software sys. engr. Lockheed Missiles & Space Co., Sunnyvale, Calif., 1979-85; software test engr., project mgmt. engr. Hewlett Packard, Cupertino, Calif., 1985-87; aircraft safety engr. sys. integration Boeing Co., Seattle, 1987-93; sys. engr. Westinghouse Hanford Co., Richland, Wash., 1994—; pvt. practice family-centered massage Fully Alive Therapy, 1992—. Appeared in spotlight on infant massage KEPR-TV, 1995. Increasing human affectiveness instr. Nat. Mgmt. Assn., Sunnyvale, 1983, awards chair capital's Working Women's Seminar, 1984; elder Centerville Presbyn. Ch., Fremont, Calif., 1980, missionary to ch. in Tuxtepec, Mex., 1979, sr. high group leader, 1979; navigator, discipleship leader Fremont Neighborhood Ch., 1982-84; bone marrow transplant family vol. Fred Hutchinson Cancer Ctr., Seattle, 1987-88; crisis counselor Tri Cities Contact Helpline, Richland, 1994—; facilitator for survivors of sexualabuse group Eastside Foursquare Ch., Kirkland, Wash., 1993-94. Food Machinery Corp. scholar, 1978. Mem. Am. Assn. Marital and Family Therapy (assoc.), Am. Massage Therapy Assn., Internat. Coun. on Sys. Engring. Home: 1202 N Jefferson St Kennewick WA 99336 Office: Lockheed Martin Hanford 29550 George Washington Way M/S T3-01 Richland WA 99352

JACKSON, BARBARA W., school system administrator; b. Eudora, Ark., Feb. 13, 1929; d. John Leonard Sr. and Elise (Thompson) Wall; children: John David, Cheryl Lynn Jackson Woodberry, Charles Robert. BS, Ark. State Tchrs. Coll., 1949; MEd, U. Ga., 1968, EdS, 1973, EdD, 1983. Cert. counseling and sch. psychologist, Ga. Psychologist Clarke County Sch. Dist., Athens, Ga., counselor elem.; counselor elem.-title III Franklin County Sch. Dist., Royston, Ga.; coord. chpt. I and testing Clarke County Sch. Dist., Athens. Contbr. articles to profl. jours. Mem. APA, ASCD, Nat. Assn. Sch. Psychologists, Ga. Assn. Sch. Psychologists, Ga. ASCD, Ga. Ednl. Rsch. Assn., Profl. Assn. Ga. Educators, Alpha Chi, Kappa Delta Pi, Phi Kappa Phi, Delta Kappa Gamma.

JACKSON, BECKY L., physician; b. Toledo, Ohio, Nov. 2, 1958; d. James L. and Betty J. J. BS in Biology, U. Toledo, 1981; MD, Ohio State U., 1986. Diplomate Am. Bd. Internal Medicine. Resident in internal medicine Med. Coll. Pa., Pitts., 1986-89; attending physician Allegheny Gen. Hosp., Pitts., 1989-91; phys. Medica, Pitts., 1991-93, Forbes Health Sys., Pitts., 1993, Horizon Physicians Group, Knoxville, Tenn., 1994—; dir. AIDS Response, Knoxville, Tenn., 1995; mem. Quality Physicians Assurance Com., 1994—. Chmn. fund raising PERSAD, Pitts., 1992. Mem. Am. Coll. Physicians, Am. Physicians for Human Rights. Office: 220 Ft Saunders West Blvd #202 Knoxville TN 37922

JACKSON, BETTY L. DEASON, real estate developer; b. Wichita, Kans., Mar. 31, 1927; d. Orville John and Ida Mabel (Wolfe) Deason; m. James L. Jackson, July 2, 1966 (dec. Feb. 1983); children: Rebecca Lou, Jennifer Mae. AA, SW Baptist U., Bolivar, Mo., 1946; BA, Cen. Mo. State U., 1963; MA, U. Mo., 1964. Salesperson Sears, Kansas City, Mo., 1943-44; bookkeeping clk. Hallmark Cards, Kansas City, Mo., 1945-46; civil service Camp Pendleton, Oceanside, Calif., 1947; sec. Ford Motor Co., Kansas City, Mo., Jim Taylor Olds Co., Independence, Mo., 1952-54; tchr. Consol. Sch. Dist. #2, Mo., 1954-55; tchr. adminstr. Consol. Sch. Dist. #2, Raytown, Mo., 1963-78; owner mgr. B.J.'s Florist Car Wash Laundramat, Stockton, Mo., 1979-82; owner, ptnr. J and S Realty, Stockton, Mo., 1983—; officer J-S Corp., Stockton, 1986-94. Mem. Nat. Assn. Realtors, 5-County Bd. Realtors, Mo. Bd. Realtors, Mo. C. of C., AARP. Democrat. Baptist. Home: Lakeview Cir Owl Haven Estates Stockton MO 65785 Office: J-S Realty Sotckton Lake Pla PO Box 159 S Hwy 39 Ste 101 Stockton MO 65785

JACKSON, BEVERLEY JOY JACOBSON, columnist, lecturer; b. L.A., Nov. 20, 1928; d. Phillip and Dorothy Jacobson; student U. So. Calif., UCLA; m. Robert David Jackson (div. Aug. 1964); 1 child, Tracey Dee. Daily columnist Santa Barbara (Calif.) News Press, 1968-92, Santa Barbara Independent, 1992-94; nat. lectr. Santa Barbara History, History of China Recreated, Chinese Footbinding, Shoes for Bound Feet, China Today; free lance writer, fgn. corr. Bd. dirs. Santa Barbara br. Am. Cancer Soc., 1963—; mem. art mus. coun. L.A. Mus. Art, 1959—, mem. costume coun., 1983—; docent L.A. Mus. Art, 1962-64; mem. exec. bd. Channel City Club (formerly Channel City Women's Forum), 1969—; mem. adv. bd. Santa Barbara Mus. Natural History, Coun. of Christmas Cheer, Women's Shelter Bldg., Direct Relief Internat., Nat. Coun. Drug and Alcohol Abuse, Am. Oceans Campaign; mem adv. bd. Hospice of Santa Barbara, 1981—, Stop AIDS Coun., Arthritis Found.; bd. dirs. So. Calif. Com. for Shakespear's Globe Theatre; chmn. Santa Barbara Com. for Visit Queen Elizabeth II, 1982—; founder costume guild Santa Barbara Hist. Soc.; curator Chinese collections Santa Barbara Hist. Mus.; adv. bd. Santa Barbara Choral Soc.; hon. bd. Santa Barbara Salvation Army, Ensemble Theatre Santa Barbara; adv. bd. Storyteller Sch. Homeless Children. Author: Dolls and Doll Houses of Spain, 1970, (with others) I'm Just Wild About Harry, 1979, Spendid Slippers: The History of Chinese Footbinding and Lotus Shoes, 1997. Home: PO Box 5118 Santa Barbara CA 93150-5118

JACKSON, CAROL E., federal judge. BA, Wellesley Coll., 1973; JD, U. Mich., 1976. With Thompson & Mitchell, St. Louis, 1976-83; counsel Mallinckrodt, Inc., St. Louis, 1983-85; magistrate U.S. Dist. Ct., Ea. Dist. Mo., 1986-92, dist. judge, 1992—; adj. prof. law Washington U., St. Louis, 1989-92. Trustee St. Louis Art Mus., 1987-91; dir. bi-state chpt. ARC, 1989-91, Mo. Bot. Garden. Mem. Nat. Assn. Women Judges, Fed. Magistrate Judges Assn., Mo. Bar, St. Louis County Bar Assn., Bar Assn. Metro. St. Louis, Mound City Bar Assn., Lawyers Assn. St. Louis. Office: US Courthouse 1114 Market St Saint Louis MO 63101-2043

JACKSON, CINDY BURGETT, critical care nurse, emergency nurse, family nurse practitioner; b. Washington, July 11, 1956; d. Harry Carl and Betty (Gable) Sampson; m. James Jackson, Apr. 22, 1994; children: Justin, Jesse. BSN, George Mason U., 1991; MSN, Marymount U., 1995. RN, Va.; CCRN; cert. family nurse practitioner; cert. clin. nurse specialist in critical care; cert. prescriptive authority; cert. ACLS, CPR instr./trainer, EMT; cert. chemotherapy adminstr. Coord. ARC, Honesdale, Pa., 1985-88; instr. CPR Fair Oaks Hosp., Fairfax, Va., 1988—, extern critical care, 1990-91, trainer CPR instrn., 1991—; nurse critical care Washington Hosp. Ctr., 1991-94; flight nurse World Access Inc., 1993-94; emergency dept. nurse Mt. Vernon Hosp., Alexandria, Va., 1994—; emergency nurse practitioner Potomac Hosp., Woodbridge, Va., 1996—; lectr. in field; instr. sign lang. Fairfax County Schs., 1989-90; tissue and organ donation educator Nat. Student Nurses Assn., George Mason U., 1990-91, pres., 1990-91; 1st aid corps mem. ARC, Fairfax, 1988—. Active nat. disaster relief health svc. team for Hurricane Andrew, ARC, Homestead, Fla., 1992, Miss. River Flood, 1993, Hurricane Marilyn, St. Thomas, V.I., 1995, Tropical Storm Jerry, Bonita Springs, Fla., 1995. Named Nursing Student of Yr. Nursing Student Assn. Va., 1991, Student Leader of Yr. George Mason U., 1991. Mem. AACN (Essay award 1991), D.C. Nursing Assn., Va. Nurses Assn., Golden Key Honor Soc., Sigma Theta Tau (Leadership award Epsilon Zeta chpt. 1991), Alpha Chi, Delta Epsilon Sigma. Home: PO Box 1675 Lorton VA 22199-1675

JACKSON, CLORA ELLIS, counselor, psychologist; b. La., Apr. 7, 1934; d. Scott and Ethel J. (Peeler) Ellis; m. Harold Coyage Jackson, Jr., Aug. 26, 1951; children: Sheriel, Lauren (dec.), Adrienne, Duaine. AA in Secretarial Sci., U. So. Calif., 1971, BS in Psychology, 1975, MS in Higher Edn., 1977; MS in Psychology, Calif. State U., Long Beach, 1980, MS in Counseling, 1979. Bus. edn. instr. Orange Coast Coll., Costa Mesa, Calif., 1979-80; tchr., counselor L.A. Unified Sch. Dist., 1977-81, sch. psychologist, 1981-83; tchr. bus. edn./math. Long Beach Unified Sch. Dist., 1983-90, counselor, 1990—. Asst. chmn. Spiritual Assembly, Huntington Beach, Calif., 1995—; vol. Habitat for Humanity, 1990—. Mem. AAUW, Women in Arts, Pi Lambda Theta. Mem. Baha'i Faith.

JACKSON, CYNTHIA MARIE, elementary school educator; b. Phila., Dec. 18, 1941; d. Clarence and Dorothy (Booker) Cook; m. Howard C. Jackson, Nov. 14, 1964 (div. May 1983); 1 child, Michelle Yvette. BS in Edn., Cheyney (Pa.) U., 1964. Cert. tchr. elem. edn., Pa. Elem. tchr. Phila. Sch. Dist., 1964-67, Chester-Upland Sch. Dist., Chester, Pa., 1967—. Mem. ASCD, Nat. Coun. Tchrs. English. Democrat. Baptist. Home: 1927 Elston St Philadelphia PA 19138-2702 Office: Smedley Middle School 1701 Upland St Chester PA 19013-5734

JACKSON, DONNA BLUE, medical/surgical nurse; b. Durham, N.C., Dec. 8, 1956; d. David Lee and Frances Mae (Ferguson) Blue; m. Robert Finley Jackson, Mar. 26, 1976; children: Cory, Kimberly, Walton, Shaun. Student, Durham Tech. C.C., 1984. LPN. Charge nurse Hillcrest Convalescent Ctr., 1985—; med.-surg. staff nurse Durham Regional Hosp., 1986—; head nurse, trainer OSHA/clin. lab. Ctrl. Internal Medicine P.A., Durham, 1989—. Republican. Baptist. Home: 4508 Ryan St Durham NC 27704-1810

JACKSON, DOROTHY FAYE GREENE, nursing educator; b. Marlin, Tex., Mar. 18, 1947; d. Shellie Tom and Ruby Lee (O'Neal) Greene; m. David Lee Jackson, Jr., Dec. 20, 1967; children: David Lee III, Danese. AAS, Odessa Coll., 1967; BSN, West Tex. State U., 1977; MSN, U. Tex., Galveston, 1980. RN, Tex. Staff nurse Med. Ctr. Hosp., Odessa, Tex., 1967-68, charge nurse CCU, 1968-72, mgr. quality assurance and infection control, 1979-80, dir. nursing, critical care and edn., 1980-81, bd. mgrs. Med. Ctr. Hosp., 1988-89; instr. nursing Odessa Coll., 1972-79, 81-93, dept. chair, 1993; asst. prof. Sch. Nursing Tex. Tech. U. Health Scis. Ctr., Odessa, 1993—; advanced practice nurse Sch. Medicine Family Practice Ctr. Tex. Tech. Health Scis. Ctr., Odessa, 1994—; mem. adv. bd. Head Start, Odessa, 1981—; cons. to long term care facilities, Odessa, 1991-93, clin. specialist in gerontological nursing, 1994—; v.p. Seabury Nursing Home, 1985—; presenter Nat. Conf. on Gerontol. Nursing Edn., Norfolk, Va., 1992. Contbr. articles to jours. in field. Bd. dirs. Odessa Cultural Coun., 1989-93, Midland-Odessa Symphony and Chorale, 1991-94. Mem. ANA, Jr. League Odessa, Phi Delta Kappa, Sigma Theta Tau, Alpha Kappa Alpha. Episcopalian. Home: 410 E 42nd St Odessa TX 79762-6856 Office: Tex Tech U Univ Health Scis Ctr 800 W 4th St Odessa TX 79763

JACKSON, EVELYN ARDETH, nurse; b. Great Falls, Mont., Feb. 11, 1929; d. Henry and Esther Lillian (Morris) Bergdorf; m. Elmer Donald Jackson, May 16, 1952; children—Donita Jo, Jenice Evelyn. Student Gonzaga U., 1947-48; RN, St. Luke's Sch. Nursing, Spokane, Wash., 1950; postgrad. St. Joseph's Coll., Roanoke, Va., 1983-85. Cert. case mgr. 1992. Staff nurse in doctors' offices, Spokane, 1950-55, Houston, 1956-68; 76-78; supr. M.D. Anderson Hosp. and Cancer Inst., Houston, 1968-76; nursing supr. Austin Steel Co., Houston, 1978-80; charge nurse Reed Rock Bit Co., Houston, 1980—; safety instr. Reed Tool Co. Instr. ARC, 1980—; active Cancer Soc.. Mem. Am. Heart Assn., Houston Occupl. Health Nurses Assn. (documentation com. 1980-81, telephone com. 1981-82, nomination com. 1982-83, dir. 1982—, pres. 1993, 94), Am. Occupl. Health Assn., Tex. Occupl. Health Assn. (dir. 1986—), Nat. Mgmt. Assn., Profl. and Bus. Women, Am. Security Coun., U.S. Senatorial Club (presdl. task force 1985, Washington). Republican. Methodist. Home: 6510 Cedar St Katy TX 77493 Office: Reed Rock Bit PO Box 2119 Houston TX 77252-2119

JACKSON, GAYLE PENDLETON WHITE, venture capitalist, international energy specialist; b. Orange, N.J., June 22, 1946; d. Harold Dee and Marion Marvin (Harris) W.; m. Lothrop Brewster Jackson II, June 8, 1968 (div. 1986); m. Frederick T. Kraus, June 11, 1995; stepchildren: Grant, Madeleine, Caroline. BA cum laude, Smith Coll., 1967; MA in Polit. Sci., Washington U., 1969, PhD in Polit. Sci., 1972. Asst. prof. polit. sci. Washington U., St. Louis, 1972-73; market analyst Ralston Purina Co., St. Louis, 1973-74, adminstr. corp. energy dept., 1974-76; regional rep. to Sec. of Commerce U.S. Dept. of Commerce, Kansas City, Mo., 1976-78; dir. corp. planning Peabody Coal Co., St. Louis, 1978-81; v.p. bus. devel. Gateway Terminals, Peabody Holding Co., St. Louis, 1981-82; v.p. Premier Coal Sales Co., Peabody Holding Co., St. Louis, 1982-85; prs. Gayle P.W. Jackson, Inc., St. Louis, 1985—; chief of staff coal industry adv. bd. Internat. Energy Agy., Paris, 1985—. Chmn., pres. St. Louis County Local Devel. Co., 1979-84; bd. dirs. Webster U., St. Louis, 1983—, Ctr. for Internat. Pvt. Enterprise, 1993—, St. Louis Health Care Network, 1995—; bd. adjustment City of Clayton, St. Louis, 1985-91; sr. councillor Atlantic Coun., 1993. Recipient Spl. Leadership award St. Louis YWCA, 1984; fellow Woodrow Wilson, 1971-72, Fulbright-Hays, 1971-72. Mem. Women's Forum (pres. 1992), Internat. Women's Forum (bd. dirs. 1986-94, treas. 1991-93, v.p. 1993-95, leadership found. 1993—). Office: Gayle P W Jackson Inc 6445 Cecil Ave Saint Louis MO 63105-2224

JACKSON, GERALDINE, entrepreneur; b. Barnesville, Ga., Oct. 30, 1934; d. Charles Brown and Christine (Maddox) J.; 1 child, Prentiss Andrew. Nurses aide Grady Hosp., Atlanta; mail handler U.S. Post Office, Cicero, Ill.; sec., tour guide Walgreens Lab., Chgo.; credit clk. Sterling Jewelers, Atlanta; owner, broker Gerris Automobile Leasing Svc., Atlanta. Mem. Nat. Law Enforcement Officer Meml. Fund, Rep. Nat. Com.; active Sacred Heart League. Mem. AARP, DAV, NAACP, NAFE, Nat. Assn. Police Orgn. (assoc. mem. presdl. task force), Internat. Assn. Chief Police, Ga. Sheriff's Assn., Nat. Right to Life. Democrat. Home and Office: 1890 Myrtle Dr SW Apt 422 Atlanta GA 30311-4954

JACKSON, GINGER LEE, writer; b. Logan, W.Va., July 26, 1956; d. Daniel and Betty Jo J.; divorced; children: Daniel Luke, Britany Ann. AA, Arapahoe C.C., Littleton, Colo., 1988; BA, Met. State Coll., Denver, 1991. Reporter Sentinel Newspapers, Denver, 1985-87; gen. mgr., prodr. Auraria Cable, Denver, 1987-89; writer, TV prodr. Ken-Caryl Ranch (Sta. KCTV-33), Littleton, Colo., 1989-91; presentation mktg. specialist Harte-Hanks Comms., Brea, Calif., 1991-92; audio mgr. Vineyard Ministries, Anaheim, Calif., 1992-93; media buyer Kids Mart, Industry, Calif., 1994-95; writer MTech/Arbitron, Santa Monica, Calif., 1995—; Producer video documentary The Arts, 1996; contbr. articles to mags. Contbr. articles to mags. Asst. Victim Witness, Colo., 1983; bd. dirs. Nat. Repertory Theatre Found., 1996. Named for achievement Am. Bus. Women's Assn., 1990, 91. Mem. Women in Comm., Phi Theta Kappa, Sigma Tau Delta. Democrat. Office: MTech/Arbitron 100 Wilshire Blvd Ste # 800 Santa Monica CA 90401

JACKSON, GLENDA, actress; b. Birkenhead, Cheshire, Eng., May 9, 1936; d. Harry and Joan J.; m. Roy Hodges (div.); 1 son, Daniel. Ed., West Kirby County Grammar Sch. for Girls; DLitt (hon.), U. Liverpool, 1978; LLM (hon.), U. Nottingham, 1992. M.P. for Labor Party representing Hampstead and Highgate, Parliament, London, 1992—; Dir. United Brit. Artists, 1983—. Made stage debut as student in Separate Tables, Worthing, Eng., 1957; first appeared London (Eng.) stage as Ruby in All Kinds of Men, Arts Theatre, 1957; appeared in Hammersmith, 1962, The Idiot, 1963, Alfie, 1963; joined Royal Shakespeare Co. and appeared in exptl. Theatre of Cruelty season, L.A.M.D.A., 1964, Stratford season, 1965; played Princess of France in Love's Labour's Lost, Ophelia in Hamlet; reader in The Investigation, 1965; appeared as Charlotte Corday in Marat-Sade, 1965, and repeating performance in N.Y. debut at Martin Beck Theatre, 1965 (Variety award as most promising actress); appeared as Eva in Puntila at Aldwych Theatre, 1965, as Masha in Three Sisters at Royal Ct., 1967, as Tamara Fanghorn in Fanghorn at Fortune, 1967, as Katherine Winter in Collaborators, 1973, as Solange in The Maids, 1974, as Hedda Gabler, 1975, as Vittoria Corombona in The White Devil, 1976, Scenes from an Execution, 1990, Mother Courage, 1990; appeared on stage in Rose, N.Y.C., London, 1980-81, Phaedra, N.Y.C., 1984-85, Strange Interlude, 1985, Macbeth, 1988; appeared in numerous films, 1968— including Women in Love (Acad. award for Best Actress 1970), Sunday, Bloody Sunday, The Music Lovers, Marat-Sade, Negatives, Mary Queen of Scots, Triple Echo (being reissued as Soldier in Skirts), The Nelson Affair, A Touch of Class (Acad. award for Best Actress 1974), 1973, The Maids, The Romantic Englishwoman, The Incredible Sarah, Nasty Habits, House Calls, Lost and Found, 1979, Health, 1980, Hopscotch, 1980, Stevie, 1981, The Return of the Soldier, 1982, Giro City, Turtle Diary, 1986, Beyond Therapy, 1987, Salome's Last Dance, 1988, Business as Usual, 1988, The Rainbow, 1989, The Visit; also numerous TV appearances, 1960— including (series) Elizabeth R., The Patricia Neal Story, 1981, Sakharov, 1984, Strange Interlude, 1988, The House of Bernarda Alba, 1991. Office: Lionel Larner Ltd Ste 1412 119 W 57th St New York NY 10019-3325

JACKSON, GUIDA MYRL, writer, magazine editor; b. Clarendon, Tex., Aug. 30; d. James Hurley and Ina (Benson) Miller; m. Prentice Lamar Jackson (div. Jan. 1986); children: Jeffrey Allen, William Andrew, James Tucker, Annabeth Jackson; m. William Hervey Laufer, Feb. 14, 1986. BA, Tex. Tech U.; MA, Calif. State U., Dominguez Hills, 1986; PhD, Greenwich U., Hilo, Hawaii, 1990. Tchr. secondary sch. English, Houston Ind. Sch. Dist., 1951-53, Ft. Worth Ind. Sch. Dist., 1953-54; pvt. tchr. music, freelance writer, Houston, 1956-71; editor newsletter Tex. Soc. Anesthesiologists, Austin, 1972-80; editor-in-chief Tex. Country mag., Houston, 1976-78; mng. editor Touchstone, lit. mag., Houston, 1976—; contbg. editor Houston Town and Country mag., 1975-76; lectr. English, U. Houston, 1986—, book editor Arte Publico, 1987-88; freelance writer, Houston, The Woodlands, Tex., 1978—; instr. Montgomery Coll., 1996—. Author: (novel) Passing Through, 1979, (play) The Lamentable Affair of the Vicar's Wife, 1989, (biog. reference) Women Who Ruled, 1990 (best reference lists award Libr. Jour. and Sch. Libr. Jour. 1990), (nonfiction) Virginia Diaspora, 1992, (lit. reference) Encyclopedia of Traditional Epic, 1994 (best reference list award ALA), (lit. reference) Traditional Epics: A Literary Companion, 1995, Encyclopedia of Literary Epics, 1996; editor: (anthologies) Heart to Hearth, 1989, African Women Write, 1990, (nonfiction) Legacy of the Texas Plains, 1994, Through the Cumberland Gap, 1995. Mem. Women in Comm., PEN Ctr. West, Houston Writers Guild, Woodlands Writers Guild, Dramatists Guild, Montgomery Arts Coun. Office: Touchstone Lit Jour PO Box 8308 Spring TX 77387-8308

JACKSON, JANE W., interior designer; b. Asheville, N.C., Aug. 5, 1944; d. James and Willie Mae (Stoner) Harris; m. Bruce G. Jackson; children: Yvette, Scott. Student, Boston U., 1964; BA, Leslie Coll., 1967; postgrad., Artisan Sch. Interior Design, 1980-82. Tchr. Montessori, Brookline, Mass., 1969-72; interior designer, owner Nettle Creek Shop, Honolulu, 1980-88; owner Wellesley Interiors, Honolulu, 1988—. Active Mayor's Com. for Small Bus., Honolulu, 1984. Mem. Honolulu Club. Democrat. Office: Wellesley Interiors PO Box 1622 Kaneohe HI 96744

JACKSON, JANIS LYNN, biology educator; b. Houston, May 9, 1952; d. Harrell James and Patricia Ann (Vernon) Odom; m. James Arthur Jackson, May 18, 1974; 1 child, Megan Michelle. AA, San Jacinto Coll., 1972; BS, East Tex. State U., 1974, MS, 1976. Biology instr. McLennan C.C., Waco, Tex., 1975—; mem. chmn. instrn. subcom. McLennan C.C., Waco, 1980-81, chmn. faculty coun. rep., 1981-82, compensation com., 1990, co-chmn. instl. self study, 1990-91, profl. devel. com., 1992-93, mem. Tartan Scholars design com., 1995; judge paper presentations North Tex. Biol. Assn., Commerce, 1983, Tex. Acad. Sci., Nacodoches, 1990; vol. Assn. Locally Involved Vols. in Edn., Inc., Waco, 1979; rep. Gt. Tchrs. Workshop, Waco, 1989. Co-author: Basic Biological Concepts, 1983, rev. edit., 1984, 90, 95. Co-leader Camp Fire, Inc., Waco, 1993—; mem. Parents Assn.-St. Louis, Waco, 1991—. Recipient Nat. Inst. Staff and Orgn. Devel. Excellence award Internat. Conf. on Tchg. Excellence, 1991, 94. Mem. Tex. Jr. Coll. Tchrs. Assn., Instns. Master Plan Task Force (steering com. 1989). Republican. Presbyterian. Home: RR 5 Box 994 Waco TX 76705-9612 Office: McLennan C C 1400 College Dr Waco TX 76708

JACKSON, JEANNE M., paralegal; b. St. Paul, Oct. 24, 1957; d. Glen D. Sanft and Catherine F. (Eron) Mosley; m. Wayne A. Heim, Dec. 18, 1994; children: Christopher P. Jackson, Emily C. Jackson. BS in Edn., U. Wisc., Whitewater, 1977. Cert. legal asst. specialist in real estate. Dept. sec. mining engr. dept. W.Va. U., Morgantown, 1978-79; tchr. Steamboat Springs (Colo.) Jr. H.S., 1980-81; instr. Colo. Mountain Coll., Steamboat Springs, 1979-84; sec., treas. Irene Nelson Interiors, Inc., Steamboat Springs, Colo., 1982-84; pvt. practice, 1989-91; paralegal Moore & Myers, Jackson, Wyo., 1990—; sec., treas. Acme Painting Co., Inc., Moose, Wyo., 1994—. Mem. Nat. Assn. Legal Assts., Legal Assts. of Wyo. (regional dir. 1994-95, 96—), Jackson Hole Kiwanis, Phi Kappa Phi. Republican. Office: Moore & Myers PO Box 8498 Jackson WY 83002

JACKSON, JEWEL, retired state youth authority executive; b. Shreveport, La., June 3, 1942; d. Willie Burghardt and Bernice Jewel (Mayberry) Norton; children: Steven, June Kelly, Michael, Anthony. With Calif. Youth Authority, 1965—, group supr., San Andreas and Santa Rosa, 1965-67, youth counselor, Ventura, 1967-78, sr. youth counselor, Stockton, 1978-81, parole agt., 1986, treatment team supr., program mgr., Whittier and Ione, 1981-91; retired, 1991; pres. Valley Paralegal Svc., Stockton. Avocations: reading, horseback riding, interior design, fabric painting, stamp collecting. Home: 2416 Hall Ave Stockton CA 95205-8422

JACKSON, JO ANNE, speech pathologist; b. Lincoln, Nebr., Jan. 17, 1951; d. George B. and Evelyn Moore (Shirley) Scott; m. Joe Ellis Jackson, Dec. 18; children; Ty Joe, Clay Scott, Kyle Thomas, Jay Jordan. BA, N.Mex. State U., 1973, MA, 1992. Speech lang. pathologist Capitan (N.Mex.) Schs., 1987-88, High Plains Regional Ctr. Coop., Springer, N.Mex., 1988-95, Clayton Municiple Schs., 1995—. Advancement chair Boy Scouts Am., Springer, 1992-95. Mem. Am. Speech Lang. Hearing Assn. (cert.), Delta Kappa Gamma, N.Mex. Speech Lang. Hearing Assn.

JACKSON, KATHLEEN ANN, physical education educator; b. Auburn, N.Y., Mar. 5, 1950; d. William Joseph and Ruth Evelyn (O'Connell) McL.; m. Gary Kirk Jackson, June 30, 1973; m. Richard John Cooney, Dec. 30, 195; children: Casey, Ryan, Kellen. BS cum laude, SUNY, Buffalo, 1972, MALS, 1975. Dir. phys. edn. and athltetics Hauppauge (N.Y.) Unifed Sch. Dist., 1979—. Recipient Women's Sports awrd Hofstra U., 1994, Award N.Y. State Athletic Assn., 1993, Honor award N.Y. State Coaches Assn., 1987. Mem. Coun. of Adminstrn./Suprs., N.Y. State AHPER (Suffolk Zone Honor award 1990), Suffolk County Athletic Dir. Assn. (pres. 1984-85). Office: Hauppauge Unifed Sch Dist 500 Lincoln Blvd Hauppauge NY 11788

JACKSON, KATHRYN NELL, charitable organization executive; b. Sumter, S.C., Aug. 23, 1952; d. Francis Marion and Kathryn Grooms (Mitchell) Parrish; m. James Randall Jackson, Apr. 1, 1984. Student, Georgetown (S.C.) Edn. Ctr., 1970-74, Nat. Acad. Voluntarism, Alexandria, Va., 1982-83. With bookkeeping dept., then sec. S.C. Nat. Bank, Georgetown, 1968-71; program svc. dir. Trident United Way, Charleston, S.C., 1982-86, allocations dir., 1983, campaign dir., 1985-86; self-employed cons. Strickland's Wallpaper and Door Exch., 1986-88; exec. and adminstrv. dir. Georgetown County United Way, Georgetown, 1971-82, exec. dir., 1988—; condr. workshops and seminars in field; mem. exec. staff com. United Way S.C.; pres.-elect Interagy. Coun. Active numerous local, state and nat. polit. campaigns; mem. steering com. Georgetown County Devel. Commn., 1993; mem. tourism com. Future of Georgetown; chmn. Georgetown County program Fed. Exec. Mgmt. Agy.; vol. assistance coord. disaster recovery teams Georgetown County CD; spl. events vol. Front Street Mchts. Assn.; mem. pers. com. 1st Bapt. Ch., 1990, developer single adult ministry, 1982-86; mem. devel. project for young vols. in action Georgetown Career Ctr., 1988; mem. disaster svc. com. ARC, mem. long range planning com. Georgetown County, 1989; vol. Food Trust, Girl Scouts U.S.A., Sr. Citizens; active Greenskeeper program City of Georgetown; numerous others. Recipient cmty. svc. award Girl Scouts U.S.a., 1981; named Outstanding Woman of Georgetown County, Georgetown Times, 1992. Mem. Trident C. of C. (presenter Leadership Georgetown), Georgetown County Bus. and Profl. Women's Club (pres., Career Woman of Yr. award 1991), Girl Scout Alu mnae Assn. Home: PO Box 2171 147 Freeman Dr Georgetown SC 29442 Office: Georgetown Co United Way PO Box 1065 515 Front St Georgetown SC 29442

JACKSON, KRISTI LYNN, social worker; b. Dexter, Mo., Oct. 15, 1962; d. Edward Eugene Jackson and Shelba Dean (Lowery) Sifford. BSW cum laude, St. Louis U., 1985; MSW magna cum laude, Fla. State U., 1992. Lic. clin. social worker, Alaska. Youth specialist II W.E. Sears Youth Ctr., Poplar Bluff, Mo., 1985-89; enlisted airman 1st class USAF, 1989, advanced through grades to capt., 1994; family advocacy technician USAF, Keesler AFB, Miss., 1989-92; family advocacy officer USAF, Moody AFB, Ga., 1992-93, Eielson AFB, Alaska, 1993—. Mem. NASW, Am. Profl. Soc. on Abuse of Children, Nat. Mil. Family Assn., Co. Grade Officers' Assn. (pres.

1994-95), Phi Alpha. Democrat. Home: 5281 B Coman Eielson AFB AK 99702

JACKSON, LINDA ANN, book designer; b. Bklyn., Sept. 29, 1952; d. Frank Trifiletti and Louise Young; m. Eric David Jackson, June 14, 1975; children: Kamal, Aisha, Taheerah. Student, Boston U., 1970-72. Adminstrv. asst. Houghton Mifflin, Boston, 1972-73, new media assoc., 1973-76; production coord. Allyn & Bacon, Boston, 1977-81, Havard U. Press, Cambridge, Mass., 1982-85; production mgr. Little, Brown & Co., Boston, 1985-92, children's design and production mgr., 1992—. Office: Little Brown & Co 41 Mount Vernon St Boston MA 02108

JACKSON, LIZA DENISE, special education educator; b. Des Moines, Iowa, Feb. 20, 1950; d. Robert Mason and Lela Jean (Lustman) Wilkinson; m. Paul Edward Jackson, Aug. 21, 1971; children: Kevin Mason Jackson, Ryan Christopher Jackson. AA, Ottumwa Heights Jr. Coll., 1970; BS in Edn., Northeast Mo. State U., 1972; MS in Edn., Drake U., 1993. Cert. tchr., Mo., Iowa. Elem. tchr. Novinger (Mo.) Sch. Dist., 1972-73, Southeast Polk Sch. Dist., Runnells, Iowa, 1974-81; multicategorical tchr. Johnston, Iowa, 1991—; cons. Iowa Energy Resources, Des Moines, 1988-90. Den leader Cub Scout Troop 463, Altoona, Iowa, 1985-87, com. chair, 1988-90, com. mem. Boy Scout Troop 85, Des Moines, 1991-92; adult student amb. Drake U., 1991-93. Mem. Coun. for Exceptional Children. Republican.

JACKSON, LOLA HIRDLER, art educator; b. Faribault, Minn., Mar. 2, 1942; d. Earl Arthur and Marian Barbara (Pavek) Hirdler; children: Carilyn, Cherilyn, Marc. BS in Art Edn., Mankato State U., 1972, MA, 1975. Cert. tchr. Instr. art YWCA, Mankato, 1968-70; art instr. Mankato Area Vocat. Tech. Inst., 1971-72; pres., tchr., art dir. Jackson Studios, Mankato, 1969-78; art tchr. New Richland (Minn.) High Sch., Mankato (Minn.) State U., 1973-74; pres. Lola Ltd. Lt'ee Art Distbn., N.C., 1976—; tchr. art Lincoln Sch. Math. and Sci. Tech., Greensboro, N.C., 1988-90, chmn. dept., 1988, 89-90; tchr., chmn. art dept. Shallotte Mid. Sch., 1990—; instr. art Brunswick C.C., Supply, N.C., 1990—; staff artist The Reporter, 1970-73; pres., bd. dirs. Fine Arts Inc., Gallery 500, Mankato, 1972-75. Bd. mem. Mankato Area Found., 1976-83. Recipient award Busch Found. Minn. Arts Coun., Nat. Endowment Arts, 1974. Mem. Profl. Pictures Framers Assn., N.C. Assn. of Edn. Republican. Roman Catholic.

JACKSON, MAE BOGER, executive adminstrative assistant, secretary; b. Winston-Salem, N.C., May 19, 1963; d. Billy Charles and Leona (Heath) Key; m. John Talbert Jackson, June 13, 1987; 1 child, Thomas William. Student, U. N.C., Charlotte, 1981-83; BS, Johnson Bible Coll., 1986. Cert. profl. sec. Adminstrv. asst., exec. sec. The Shelton Cos., Winston-Salem, 1986-88; office automation specialist, personnel mgr. POPI Temp. Svcs., Winston-Salem, 1988-90; exec. asst. Inmar Enterprises, Inc., Winston-Salem, 1990-92, Chesapeake Display and Packaging co., Winston-Salem, 1992—. Mem. NAFE, Profls. Sec. Internat. (treas. 1990, v.p. 1991, pres.-elect 1992, pres. 1993-94, Winston-Salem Sec. of Yr. N.C. divsn. 1991, 96, Winston-Salem Outstanding mem. of Yr. award 1993), Assn. Info. Sys. Profls., Office Automation Soc. Internat. Mem. Christian Ch. (Ch. of Christ). Home: 310 Gatewood Dr Winston Salem NC 27104-2432 Office: Chesapeake Display & Packaging Co PO Box 12669 Winston Salem NC 27117-2669

JACKSON, MARY JANE MCHALE FLICKINGER, principal; b. Cleve., Feb. 23, 1938; d. Thomas William Flickinger and Margaret Julia (Lydon) Flickinger Nichols; m. robert Lowell Jackson, June 27, 1959; children: Julia Anna Jackson Sommers, Patricia L., Margaret Jacqueline Jackson Tyler. BS in Speech, St. Louis U., 1959; postgrad., U. Copenhagen, 1961-62; MS in Spl. Edn., Southern Ill. U., 1965; EdD, George Washington U., 1977. Cert. tcht. Md. 1972. Tchr. Ritenour Sch. Dist., Overland, Mo., 1959-60; tutor Spl. Sch. Dist. Handicapped, St. Louis, 1960-61; tchr. Rugaards Franske Skole, Copenhagen, Denmark, 1961-62; substitute tchr., primary tchr. St. Louis and Ladue, Mo., 1962-65; tchr. L.A. City Schs., 1966-67, Woodlin Elem. Sch., Silver Spring, Md., 1967-68; various teaching positions, 1968-71, 73-81; asst. prin. Ritchie Park Elem. Sch., Rockville, Md., 1971-73, various supr. positions, 1974-79; asst. prin. Stephen Knolls Sch., Kensington, Md., 1981-88, prin., 1988—; v.p. Concerned Citizens Exceptional Edn., Washington, 1968-70; surrogate parent Assn. Retarded Citizens, Washington. Bd. dirs. Archdiocesan of Washington, 1986-91; pres. Bd. Edn., Washington, 1990-91; bd. dirs. United Cerebral Palsy, Montgomery County, 1992—; presenter Young Adult Insts. Internat. Conf., 1994. Recipient Lisa Kane award, 1964. Mem. Wash. Hearing Soc. (bd. dirs. 1969-81), Coun. Exceptional Children (exec. bd., pres. Montgomery county chpt. 1992-93, polit. action coord. for Md. fedn. 1993, exec. com. divsn. of internat. spl. edn. and svcs. 1993), Alexander Graham Bell Assn. (pub. rels. com. 1979—), Rotary. Roman Catholic. Home: 9900 Georgia Ave # T-11 Silver Spring MD 20902-5244 Office: 10731 Saint Margarets Way Kensington MD 20895-2831

JACKSON, MARY L., health services executive; b. Phila., June 25, 1938; d. John Francis and Helen Catherine (Peranteau) Martin; m. Howard Clark Jackson III, Dec. 17, 1954; children: Michael, Mark, Brian. Student Bucks County Community Coll., 1977-83. Asst. mgr. retail div. Sears Roebuck & Co., Bensalem, Pa., 1972-77; educator, adminstr., dir. Trevose Behavior Modification Program, Pa., 1975—, leadership tng. workshops, 1979—; participant rsch. studies in field; salesman Makefield Real Estate, Morrisville, Pa., 1977-78; mortgage fin. cons. Tom Dunphy Real Estate, Feasterville, Pa., 1978-81; weight loss cons., Hulmeville, Pa., 1984—, also TV and radio appearances on behavior modification for weight loss and maintenance. Coauthor: The Official Calorie Book; pub., columnist monthly newsletter The Modifier, 1977—. Recipient Chapel of Four Chaplain award, 1977. Mem. Assn. Advancement of Behavior Therapy, Bucks County Bd. Realtors, Hulmeville Hist. Soc. (a founder, charter mem.). Democrat. Presbyterian. Avocations: reading, classical music, speed walking, knitting, fishing. Home: 218 Main St Langhorne PA 19047-5635

JACKSON, MARY TERESA, critical care nurse; b. Omaha, Oct. 1, 1950; d. Jacob Joseph and Bernice Louise (Hamann) Schumacher; m. William Howard Jackson Jr.; children: Jacob Kirby, Brian William. RN, Nebr. Meth. Nursing Sch., 1984; BA in Polit. Sci. and Journalism, Creighton U., 1992; MPA, U. Nebr., Omaha, 1994. RN, Nebr.; cert. ACLS. Sales supr. Marriott Corp., Omaha, 1985-90; ct. adv. Omaha (Nebr.) Police Divsn., 1990—; RN in critical care Bergan Mercy Med. Ctr., Omaha, 1990-92; RN in critical care and acute psychiatry Immanuel Med. Ctr., Omaha, 1992—. Mem. campaign staff presdl. campaign Senator Robert Kennedy, Omaha, 1968, Senator Robert Kerrey, Omaha, 1992, mem. campaign staff senate campaign, 1994; mem., del. Nebr. Dem. Ctrl. Com., Omaha, 1994—. Mem. ASPA. Roman Catholic. Office: Immanuel Med Ctr 6901 N 72nd St Omaha NE 68122-1709

JACKSON, MELANIE JOSEPHINE, psychotherapist; b. N.Y.C., Oct. 15, 1954; d. Joseph and Isabelle Jones; m. Aaron Lazarus Jackson (dec. 1981); 1 child, Mandi Rebeccah. AA, Suffolk County Cmty. Coll., 1974; BA, Fla. Atlantic U., 1976; MS, Nova U., 1985. Cert. counselor; diplomate Am. Acad. Forensic Counseling; lic. mental health counselor, Fla. Psychotherapist The Child Protection Team, Riviera Beach, Fla., 1984-88; child protective counselor Health and Rehab. Svcs., Riviera Beach, 1986-88; youth svcs. coord. Health Mothers/Healthy Babies, Mangonia Park, Fla., 1988-90; psycotherapist Western Palm Beach County Mental Health Clinic, Inc., Belle Glade, Fla., 1993-95; pvt. practice Psychotherapy and Cons., Wellington, 1993—; clin. dir. YWCA Domestic Assault Shelter, West Palm Beach, Fla., 1995—; adj. prof. psychology South Coll., West Palm Beach, 1992-94; mental health cons. East Coast Migrant Head Start Project, 1993—; sr. instr. U.S. Army Res., Coral Gables, 1977-92. Recipient Humanitarian Svc. medal U.S. Army, 1980, Vol. award East Coast Migrant Head Start, South Bay, Fla., 1995. Fellow Am. Bd. Med. Psychotherapists and Psychodiagnosticians; mem. ACA, Am. Acad. Forensic Counseling, Am. Mental Health Counselors Assn., Fla. Counseling Assn., Fla. Mental Health Counselors Assn. Roman Catholic. Office: Psychotherapy & Cons Wellington Profl Ctr 10111 W Forest Hill Blvd #202 Wellington FL 33414

JACKSON, MELISSA MARGARET, jewelry designer, marketing professional; b. Trenton, N.J., Jan. 26, 1962; d. William Tuttle and Shirley Marie (Sagi) J. BS in Mktg. and Spanish, Susquehanna U., 1984. Lic. real estate salesperson, N.J., residential real estate appraiser, N.J. Regional mktg. mgr. Cardell and Assocs., Inc., Morristown, N.J., 1984-87; asst. dir. mktg. and customer svc. Capital Adv. Group Inc., Parsippany, N.J., 1987-88; dir. ops. Zoch and Zoch Fin. Group, Inc., Fairfield, N.J., 1988-90; mortgage loan officer First Nat. Mortgage Co. N.J., Inc., Hamilton Square, 1990-93; v.p. mktg. United Evaluators, Inc., Whippany, N.J., 1993-95; pub. rels. dir. Peak Chiropractic Care, Princeton, N.J., 1995—; real estate sales assoc. Fox & Lazo Realtors, Hamilton, N.J., 1994—; pres. Pebble Beach Traders, Lawrenceville, N.J., 1994—; real estate sales assoc. Mem. NAFE, Mercer County Bd. Realtors, Sierra Club, Sigma Kappa (pres. Epsilon Delta chpt. 1981-82, treas. corp. bd. 1988-92). Republican. Presbyterian.

JACKSON, MILLIE, vocalist, songwriter, producer; b. Thompson, Ga., July 15, 1944; div.; children: Keisha, Jerrol. Sec., 1962-72; represented by Ichiban Records; performer Harlem's Crystal Ballroom, 1962; founder Keishval Enterprises, Inc., Atlanta; singer evenings and weekends, 1962-72; prodr., mgr. Recordings include Millie, 1973, Caught Up, 1974, Still Caught Up, 1975, Free and In Love, 1976, Lovingly Yours, 1976, Get It Out'cha System, 1978, A Moment's Pleasure, 1979, Royal Rappin', 1979, Live and Uncensored, 1979, I Had to Say It, 1980, For Men Only, 1980, Just a Little Bit Country, 1981, Live and Outrageous, 1982, Hard Times, 1982, ESP, 1984, An Imitation of Love, 1987, Back to the S--t, 1989, Young Man, Older Woman, 1992, The Very Best! of Millie Jackson, 1994, Rock N' Soul, 1994. Named Best Female Rhythm and Blues Vocalist, Cash Box, 1973. Office: Keishval Enterprises Inc 2095 High Point Tr SW Atlanta GA 30331 also: Ichiban Records PO Box 724677 Atlanta GA 31139-1677*

JACKSON, NICOLE RENEE, manufacturing engineer; b. Cleve., July 15; d. Eddie and Juliette Jackson. BS in Mech. Engring., N.C. State U. Engr.-in-tng., N.C. Follow up svcs. engr. Underwriters Labs., Research Triangle Park, N.C., 1989-90; sr. mfg. engr. in advanced mfg. tech. Delphi Chassis-GM, Dayton, Ohio, 1990—; former membership chair Nat. Soc. Black Engrs., Dayton, 1992-93. Contbr. articles to profl. jours. Mem. AAUW, NOW, NAFE. Office: 1435 Cincinnati St Dayton OH 45408

JACKSON, REBECCA R., lawyer; b. Ark., 1942. BA magna cum laude, St. Louis U., 1975, JD, 1978. Bar: Mo. 1978, Ill. 1979. Atty. Bryan Cave, St. Louis. Mem. ABA. Office: Bryan Cave One Met Sq 211 N Broadway Saint Louis MO 63102-2733*

JACKSON, REED MCSWAIN, educational administrator; b. Albemarle, N.C., Apr. 10, 1950; d. Wade Hampton and Louise Reed (Floyd) McSwain; m. William Austin Jackson, July 24, 1984. BA, Coker Coll., 1972; MEd, Francis Marion Coll., 1978; cert. Prin.'s Exec. Program, U. N.C., 1995. Lic. sch. adminstrn., sch. supervision, mentor, reading tchr. 2d grade tchr. Darlington (S.C.) County Schs., 1972-76; 4th grade tchr. Marlboro County Schs., Bennettsville, S.C., 1976-78; chpt. I reading tchr. Halifax (N.C.) County Schs., 1980-90, asst. prin. S.E. Halifax High Sch., 1990-91, dir. testing and secondary edn., 1991-95; accountability/instrnl. specialist Nash-Rocky Mount Schs., N.C., 1995—; mem. steering com. Roanoke Valley Tech Prep Consortium, Weldon, N.C., 1991—, chairperson mktg. com., 1991—; cons. So. Assn. Colls. and Schs.; chair Local Option Testing Svcs. governing bd.-N.C. state com. Mem., officer Tar River Embroiderers Guild, Rocky Mount, N.C., 1983-90; mem. Adv. Coun. for Coop. Extension Agy., Halifax, N.C., 1992. Named Halifax County Tchr. of Yr., 1984-85, Eastman Mid. Sch. Tchr. of Yr. 1984. Fellow N.C. Ednl. Policy Fellowship Program; mem. ASCD, Nat. Assn. Secondary Sch. Principals (named Leader 1-2-3 Coach), Phi Delta Kappa. Home: 4052 Ketch Point Dr Rocky Mount NC 27803-1418 Office: Nash/Rocky Mount Schs 800 Fairview Rd Rocky Mount NC 27801

JACKSON, RHONDA GAIL, secondary teacher; b. Albuquerque, Oct. 12, 1954; d. Jack Harold and Glenna Janelle (Welborn) Furr; m. Robert Evans Jackson, June 20, 1975; children: Richard Paul, Lindsey Beth. B in Social Work, Tex. Woman's U., 1977. English secondary edn. Adminstrv. asst. Tex. Women's U., 1977-84; secondary tchr. English and sociology Frisco H.S., Tex., 1990—. Mem. Nat. Coun. Tchrs. English. Home: 8704 Cameron Frisco TX 75034

JACKSON, RUTH MOORE, academic administrator; b. Potecasi, N.C., Sept. 27, 1938; d. Jesse Thomas and Ruth Estelle (Futrell) Moore; m. Roderick Earle Jackson, Aug. 14, 1965; 1 child, Eric Roderick. BS in Bus., Hampton Inst., 1960; MSLS, Atlanta U., 1965; PhD, Ind. U., 1976. Asst. edn. libr. Va. State U., Petersburg, Va., 1965-66, head reference dept., 1966-67, asst. prof., 1976-77, assoc. prof., program coord., 1977-84, interim dept. chair, 1978-79; teaching fellow Ind. U., Bloomington, Ind., 1968, vis. lectr., 1971-72; asst. dir. librs. U. N. Fla., Jacksonville, 1984-88; dean univ. librs. W.Va. U., Morgantown, W.Va., 1988—; pers. cons. Va. State U., 1980; archival cons. N.C. Ctrl. U., Durham, N.C., 1984-85; automation cons. W.Va. Acad. Libr. Consortium, 1991—. Editor: W.Va. U. Press, 1990—; contbr. to books. Active Big Brother/Big Sister of Am., Jacksonville, Fla., 1985-88; den leader Boy Scouts of Am., Petersburg, Va., 1976-78. U.S. Office Edn. fellow, 1968-71, Rsch. fellow So. Fellowships Found., 1973-74; recipient Outstanding Alumni award Hampton Inst., 1980, Non-Italian Woman of Yr. award, 1992, Disting. West Virginian award Gov. W.Va., 1992. Mem. NAFE, ALA, Southeastern Libr. Assn. (mem. standing com.), Assn. Coll. and Rsch. Librs. (mem. standing com., mem. Fla. chpt.), W.Va. Libr. Assn., Libr. Info. Tech. Assn., Coalition for Networking, Coun. of State Univ. Librs. (founding mem.), Alpha Kappa Alpha. Democrat. Roman Catholic. Home: 775 Springbranch Rd Morgantown WV 26505-3575 Office: W Va Univ Main Libr PO Box 6069 Morgantown WV 26506-6069

JACKSON, RUTH NAOMI, primary school music educator; b. Buffalo, Dec. 8, 1940; d. Frank Earl and Violet Arietta (Walker) Stevick; m. Ernest George Jackson, June 25, 1966 (div. Feb. 1980). AA, Pensacola Jr. Coll., 1975; BA, U. West Fla., 1977, MA, 1982. Music tchr. Dixon Primary Sch., Pace, Fla., 1977—, acting asst. to prin., 1994—, mem. sch. adv. coun., 1994-95; choral coord. Santa Rosa Sch. Bd., Milton, Fla., 1990—; asst. to minister of music Brownsville Assembly of God, Pensacola, 1991—; mem. sch. improvement team Dixon Elem. Sch., Pace, 1991-93. Sec.-treas. Pace Civic Assn., Inc., 1992—; mem. Choral Soc. of Pensacola, 1991—. Mini-grantee Jr. League of Pensacola, 1984-85, Santa Rosa Sch. Bd., 1993. Mem. NEA, Fla. Tchg. Profession, Santa Rose Profl. Educators, Music Educators Nat. Conf., Fla. Elem. Music Edn. Assn., Am. Orff-Schulwerk Assn., Delta Kappa Gamma. Republican. Home: 4372 W Avenida De Golf Pace FL 32571-3027 Office: Dixon Primary Sch 4585 SS Dixon St Pace FL 32571

JACKSON, SALLY DEE, public relations executive; b. Columbus, Ohio, Oct. 7, 1946; d. Jay Greene and Ann Elizabeth (Rodgers) J.; m. Paul Foley Nace, Dec. 31, 1993. Grad., The Masters Sch., Dobbs Ferry, N.Y., 1964; AA, Bradford Coll., 1966; BA, Columbia U., 1970. Asst. producer Boston Transcription Trust, 1970-71; registrar Berkshire Music Ctr., Boston Symphony Orch., 1970-71; editorial asst. Harvard U., Cambridge, Mass., 1972-73; script supr. Leonard Bernstein at Harvard U., Cambridge, 1973; dir. pub. relations ADS, Inc., Cambridge, 1974-75; account exec. Communique Inc., Boston, 1975-77, Arnold & Co., Boston, 1977-80; pres. Jackson & Co., Boston, 1980—. Contbr. articles to profl. jours. Mem. Gov.'s Com. on Small Bus., Boston, 1985-87; dir. Ford Hall Forum, Boston, 1986—; chmn. program com. State House Conf. on Small Bus., Boston, 1987; bd. dirs. Am. Inst. Wine & Food, Assocs. Boston Pub. Libr., Lionheart Found., WGBH Corp. Exec. Coun. Clubs: Advt. of Greater Boston; Annisquam Yacht. Office: Jackson & Co 29 Commonwealth Ave Boston MA 02116-2349

JACKSON, SHARON BROOME, elementary educator; b. Sarasota, Fla., Sept. 3, 1952; d. Stanley Frank and Aileen Rita (Murphy) Broome; m. Thomas Harold Jackson Jr., Nov. 22, 1975; children: Thomas Harold III, Stanley David. Student, Ga. So. Coll., 1970-71; BS in Edn., U. Ga., 1973, MS in Edn., 1976; postgrad., West Ga. Coll., 1976. Cert. tchr. Kindergarten-8th grades, Ga., supervising tchr. child abuse edn., drug/alcohol awareness tchr. Tchr. 7th and 8th grades Winder-Barrow Mid. Sch., Winder, Ga., 1973-75; tchr. 5th and 6th grades Dunson Elem. Sch., LaGrange, Ga., 1975-80; tchr. 4th grade Oconee County Schs., Watkinsville, Ga., 1980—; presenter, tchr. tng. Ga. Assn. Marine Sci. Educators, 1990; presenter tchr. stress mgmt. workshop, Watkinsville, 1990. Vol. local shelter for the homeless, local soup kitchen; mem. 1st United Meth. Ch., pres. United Meth. Women's Circle. Named Oconee County Tchr. of Yr., 1989-90; one of 20 tchrs. statewide chosen to participate in Marine Sci. Edn. program, 1989. Mem. Profl. Assn. Ga. Educators, Ga. Sci. Tchrs. Assn., Nat. Coun. Tchrs. Math. Home: 1021 Rossiter Ter Watkinsville GA 30677-5124 Office: Oconee County Intermediate Sch Colham Ferry Rd Watkinsville GA 30677

JACKSON, SHIRLEY ANN, federal agency administrator, physicist; b. Washington DC; d. George Hiter and Beatrice (Cosby) J.; m. Morris A. Washington; 1 son, Alan. B.S. in Physics, M.I.T., 1968, Ph.D., 1973; DSc (hon.) Bloomfield Coll., 1991, Fairleigh Dickinson U., 1993, hon. degree Dr Laws, Villanova, PA, 1996; Research asso. Fermi Nat. Accelerator Lab., Batavia, Ill., 1973-74, 75-76; vis. scientist European Orgn. for Nuclear Research, Geneva, 1974-75; mem. tech. staff AT&T Bell Labs., Murray Hill, N.J., 1976-91; visitor Stanford Linear Accelerator Center, 1976, Aspen Ctr. for Physics, 1976, 77; prof. physics Rutgers U., 1991-95; chairperson Nuclear Reg. Commn., 1995—; mem. com. edn. and employment women in sci. and engring. Nat. Rsch. Coun., 1980—; cons. NSF, 1977, Nat. Rsch. Coun., 1977—; dir. N.J. Resources Corp., Pub. Service Enterprise Group, PSE&G. Mem. ednl. council M.I.T., 1976-80, trustee, 1975-85, 1987—; trustee Lincoln U. (Pa.), 1980—, Rutgers U., 1986—; mem. N.J. Commn. on Sci. and Tech.; mem. Com. Status of Women in Physics, 1986-88. Recipient Candace award Nat. Coalition 100 Black Women, Salute to Policy Makers award Exec. Women of N.J., 1986, Black Achievers in Industry award Harlem YMCA, 1986, N.J. Gov.'s award, 1993; Martin Marietta Corp. scholar, 1964-68; Prince Hall Grand Masons scholar, 1964-68; NSF trainee, 1968-71; Ford Found. fellow, 1971-73; grantee, 1974-75; Martin Marietta Corp. grad. fellow, 1972-73; mem. Assn. for Advancement of Science, (com. on sci., freedom and responsibility), Fellow, Am. Phys. Soc. (mem. com. on status of women in physics 1986—); Fellow, Am. Acad. Arts & Sci, mem. N.Y. Acad. Scis., Nat. Inst. Sci., Nat. Soc. Black Physicists (pres. 1979—), MIT Alumni Assn. (v.p. 1986—), Sigma Xi, Delta Theta Sigma. Editorial adv. bd. Jour. Sci. Tech. and Human Values, 1982—; contbr. numerous articles to physics jours. Office: Nuclear Regulatory Comm USNRC Washington DC 20555

JACKSON, SUSANNE LEORA, creative placement firm executive; b. Rochester, N.Y., June 9, 1934; d. Daniel T. and Gertrude (Grantham) Sherriff; m. David K. Jackson, Mar. 12, 1954; children: Jonnie Sheehan, Jaynette Kettler. Student, Santa Fe Sch. Art, 1952-53, Midwestern U., 1953-55. Supr. ANR Prodn. Co., Houston, 1976-83; v.p. Robinhawk Drafting & Design, Houston, 1983-85; pres., CEO Houston Creative Connections, 1985—; advt. & mktg. dir. Geotech Assn., Houston, 1989-90; past pres. Am. Inst. Design & Drafting, 1984-86; CEO The Agy., 1996—, Full Svc. Advt. Agy., 1996—, Houston Tech. Connections, 1996—, Outsource and Tech. Placement, 1996—; bd. dirs. HyperDynamics. Design cons.: (mag.) Urbane, 1989-94. Mem. Mus. Fine Arts, Houston, 1988-95, Greater Houston Partnership, 1989-95; bd. dirs. Literacy Advance, 1993-94. Mem. NAFE, Houston Advt. Fedn. (Silver and Merit awards 1989, Merit award 1990, Bronze award 1991, 2 Bronze awards 1992, 2 Gold and 4 Merit awards 1992, Gold and Bronze awards 1995), Greater Heights C. of C. (bd. dirs. 1994, vice-chmn. 1996), Galleria C. of C., Rotary (treas. 1992, pres.-elect 1993, pres. 1994), U.S. C. of C. (Blue Chip Enterprise award 1993). Republican. Episcopalian. Office: Houston Creative Connection 701 N Post Oak Rd Ste 675 Houston TX 77024-3829

JACKSON, SUZANNE ELISE, health education coordinator; b. Webster, Mass., Mar. 1, 1942; d. John Edward and Marguerite Emmaline (Plante) Baczek; m. Dale Lynne Bagby, Sept. 28, 1968 (div. July 1975); m. Stephen Harvey Jackson, July 12, 1975; 1 child, Gabrielle Benette. Diploma, Henry Heywood Hosp., 1963; BA, U. Redlands, 1975. RN Calif. Clin. instr. surgery Henry Heywood Hosp., Gardner, Mass., 1963-64; asst. head nurse Los Gatos/Santa Clara County Valley Med. Ctr., San Jose, Calif., 1964-68; head nurse oper. rm. Good Samaritan Hosp., San Jose, Calif., 1970-76; corp. officer SHJ Corp., San Jose, Calif., 1976—; health edn. coord. Ac. Medicine Symposium, Monte Sereno, Calif., 1980—; design cons. Suzanne Jackson Designs, Monte Sereno, Calif., 1986—; pres. Calif. Med. Assn. Alliance, 1994-95, bd. dirs., 1986-96. Bd. dirs. Santa Clara County Med. Assn. Aux., San Jose, 1980—, pres. 1985-86; leader, sch. coord. Girl Scouts U.S., Los Gatos, 1983-89; fundraiser Hillbrook Sch., Los Gatos, 1983-90; bd. dirs. LWV, Los Gatos, 1986-90; mem. Monte Sereno City Coun., 1994—. Recipient Gilbert & Sullivan Soc. Gypsy Robe, 1984. Mem. Brandies U. Women, Capitol Club Silicon Valley. Republican. Office: 15984 Grandview Ave Monte Sereno CA 95030-3118

JACKSON, VALERIE PASCUZZI, radiologist, educator; b. Oakland, Calif., Aug. 25, 1952; d. Chris A. and Janice (Mayne) Pascuzzi; m. Price A. Jackson, Jr., July 24, 1976; children: Price Arthur III. AB, Ind. U., 1974, MD, 1978. Diplomate Am. Bd. Radiology. Intern, resident in diagnostic radiology Ind. U. Med. Ctr., 1978-82; from asst. prof. radiology to prof. radiology Ind. U. Sch. Medicine, Indpls., 1982-94, John A. Campbell prof. radiology, 1994—; dir. residency program radiology Ind. U. Sch. Medicine, 1994—. Contbr. over 50 articles to profl. jours., chpts. to books. Fellow Am. Coll. Radiology (chair 3 coms.), Soc. Breast Imaging (pres. 1990-92); mem. AMA, Am. Inst. Ultrasound in Medicine, Am. Roentgen Ray Soc., Radiol. Soc. N.Am., Alpha Omega Alpha. Office: Indiana U Sch Med Dept Rad 1001 W 10th St Indianapolis IN 46202-2859

JACKSON, VIVIAN MICHELE, school administrator; b. Yonkers, N.Y., Feb. 17, 1953; d. Evelyn Green Alexander-Booker; m. Harry R. Jackson, Jr., Dec. 25, 1976; children: Joni Michele, Elizabeth Rountree. BA in Edn., Wittenberg U., 1975; MA in Edn., Northeastern U., 1980; MA in Theology, Logos Bible Coll., Fla., 1986. Tchr. Cleve. Pub. Schs., 1975-77, Cin. Pub. Schs., 1977-78, Boston Pub. Schs., 1978-79; grad. asst. Northeastern U., Boston, 1979-80; pres. Word of Life Broadcast Christian Hope Ctr., Corning, N.Y., 1981-84, assoc. pastor, 1981-88; founder, dir. Hope Christian Acad., Corning, 1987-88; founder, dir. Hope Christian Acad., College Park, Md., 1989-96, dir. children's ministry, 1989-94, dir. children's ministry HCC, College Park, 1989-92; prof. Hope Bible Coll., 1994—; assoc. pastor Hope Christian Ch., 1994—; cons. Hope Christian Ch., 1988—. Named one of Outstanding Young Women of Am., 1981, 84. Office: Hope Christian Ch 5301 Edgewood Rd College Park MD 20740-4623

JACKSON, WENDY S LEWIS, social worker; b. Grand Rapids, Mich., May 9, 1965; d. Thomas James and Karen Susan (Kinard) L. BS, U. Mich., 1987, MSW, 1989. Investigator def. D.C. Pub. Defender Officer, Washington, 1985; program asst. Detroit Urban League, 1989; coord. housing Ann Arbor (Mich.) Housing Commn., 1989-90; sr. assoc. United Way, Grand Rapids, 1990-93; program coord. The Grand Rapids Found., 1993-94, program dir., 1994—; mgr. database Kent County Emergency Needs Task Force, Grand Rapids, 1990—, editor, 1990—; sec. Kent County Emergency Food Subcom., Grand Rapids, 1990—; mem. Kent County Domestic Violence Coordinating Com., Grand Rapids, 1990—; mem. pub. affairs com. Mich. League for Human Svcs., Lansing, 1990—; adj. prof. Grand Valley State U. Sch. of Social Work, 1994—. Contbr. articles to profl. jours. Vol. Blodgett Meml. Med. Ctr., Grand Rapids, 1982—; mem. task force Citizens League, Grand Rapids, 1990—; mem. pub. affairs task force United Way, Lansing, 1990—. Recipient Leadership award Kiwanis Club, 1983; Old Kent Bank and Trust scholar, 1983-87. Mem. NASW, Nat. Assn. Black Social Workers, U. Mich. Social Work Govs. (bd. mem. 1991—), U. Mich. Alumni Assn., Women's Leadership Coun., Urban League. Democrat. Episcopalian. Home: 16534 Huntington Rd Detroit MI 48219 Office: The Grand Rapids Found 209-C Waters Bldg 161 Ottawa Ave NW Grand Rapids MI 49503-2701

JACKSON LEE, SHEILA, congresswoman; b. Queens, N.Y., Jan. 12, 1950; m. Elwyn C. Lee; 2 children. BS, Yale U.; JD, U. Va. Sr. counsel select com. on assassinations U.S. Ho. of Reps., 1977; trial atty. Fulbright and Jaworski, 1978-80; sr. atty. United Energy Resources, Inc., 1980; assoc. judge Houston Mcpl. Ct., 1987-89; mem. Houston City Coun., 1990-94, 104th Congress from 18th Tex. dist., 1995—. Democrat. Office: US House Reps 1520 Longworth House Office Bldg Washington DC 20515*

JACKSON MADURO, MARTA, ballet educator, choreographer; b. Camaguey, Cuba, June 10, 1930; came to U.S., 1961; d. Manuel and Amelia (Leyra) Dante; m. Walter Edward Jackson, Aug. 13, 1949 (div. 1956); 1

child, Eddy (dec.); m. Bobby Maduro (dec. 1986). MA in Langs., U. Havana, Cuba, 1952; student, Havana Bus. U., 1953. ballet student of Alexandra Denisova, 1942-50, Anna Leontieva, 1943-44, George Balanchine, 1945-46, Fernando alberto and Alicia Alonso, 1942-57, Maestro Vincenzo Celli, 1945-56, Leon Fokine, 1954-55; dancer, Met. Opera, N.Y.C., 1947, Nat. Ballet of Cuba, 1951, 52; ballet tchr., Jacksonville, Fla., Miami, U. Miami; owner, tchr. Marta Jackson Sch. of Dance, Orange Park, Fla. Former dir. Nutcracker Suite Ballet, Jacksonville; organizer ballet co. The Clay Ballet Theatre, Jacksonville. Home: 7824 Loch Lomond Ct Jacksonville FL 32244 Studio: Marta Jackson Sch Dance Sts 1-3 769 Blanding Blvd Orange Park FL 32065

JACOB, DEIRDRE ANN BRADBURY, manufacturing executive, business educator, consultant; b. Providence, Mar. 7, 1952; d. John Joseph and Marion Damon (Shute) Bradbury; m. Thomas Keenan, Nov. 15, 1975 (div. Dec. 1980); 1 child, Victoria Irene; m. Robert A. Jacob, June 22, 1996. BA in Govt. and Law, Lafayette Coll., 1973. Supr. Procter & Gamble Mfg. Co., S.I., N.Y., 1973-76; mgr. warehouse dept. Procter & Gamble Mfg. Co., 1976-79, mgr. shortening and oils, 1979-81, fin. mgr. food plant, 1981-82, mgr. personnel, 1982-86, mgr. total quality and pub. affairs, 1986-91; ptnr. Avraham Y. Goldratt Inst., New Haven, Conn., 1991—; cons. Procter & Gamble, S.I., 1982—, Cin., 1989-91. Trustee Lafayette Coll., 1985-90. Mem. Lafayette Coll. Alumni Assn. (pres. 1992-94, Clifton P. Mayfield award), Maroon Club (Easton, Pa., pres. 1987-89). Roman Catholic. Office: Avraham Y Goldratt Inst 442 Orange St New Haven CT 06511-6201

JACOBI, KATHRYN, artist, illustrator; b. N.Y.C., Apr. 12, 1947; d. Ernst Albert and Lenore (Kunstler) J.; m. Robert H. Deutsch, Oct. 26, 1980 (dec.); 1 child, Arie Wolf; m. Richard A. Dysart, Sept. 5, 1987. BA, Calif. State U., Northridge, 1978, MA, 1980. Represented by Jan Baum Gallery, L.A., Harcourts Contemporary, San Francisco, Diane Farris Gallery, Vancouver, B.C., Can., Lizardi/Harp Gallery, L.A., Liasons Beaux Arts, Paris. Solo shows include Ankrum Gallery, L.A., 1986, 87, 88, Bannister Gallery, Providence, 1986, Gregory Ghent Gallery, San Francisco, 1987, Gallery 25, Fresno, Calif., 1989, Fresno Art Mus., 1989, 94, 96, Harcourts Contemporary, San Francisco, 1989, 92, John Szoke Gallery, N.Y.C., 1990, John Thomas Gallery, Santa Monica, Calif., 1991, Lizardi-Harp Gallery, Pasadena, Calif., 1991, Jan Baum Gallery, L.A., 1993, Diane Farris Gallery, Vancouver, 1993, 94, Blue Point Gallery, Berlin, 1993, Kunst pa Kalvo, Jutland, Denmark, 1994, Riverside (Calif.) Art Mus., 1995, Pierce Coll., Woodland Hills, Calif., 1996, Oreg. State U., Corvallis, 1996, Kirsten Kjaers Mus., Skagan, Denmark, 1996, McAllen (Tex.) Internat. Mus., 1996; group shows include Platt Gallery, L.A., 1988, Riverside Art Mus., 1989, 93, John Szoke Gallery, N.Y.C., 1989, 90, Brand Galleries, Glendale, Calif., 1989, Jose Drudid-Biada Art Gallery, L.A., 1990, Lillian Heidenberg Gallery, N.Y.C., 1991, Jan Baum Gallery, L.A., 1991, 95, Oakland (Calif.) Mus. Art, 1991, Gallery of Nat. Tech. Inst. Deaf, Rochester, N.Y., 1991, Faculdad de Bellas Artes de Madrid, Spain, 1992, Santa Barbara (Calif.) Contemporary Arts Forum, 1994, Lizardi/Harp Gallery, L.A., 1995, L.A. Mcpl. Gallery, Barnsdall Park, Calif., 1995, Forum Gallery, N.Y.C., 1995, Skirball Mus., L.A., 1996, and others; permanent collections include Adobe Krow Archives, Skirball Mus., Nat. Watercolor Soc., Brand Galleries, Fresno Art Mus., BC Hydro, Vancouver, others; subject of numerous articles and revs. Democrat. Jewish. Studio: 2938 Nebraska Ave Santa Monica CA 90404

JACOBI, KERRY LEE, planning and marketing professional; b. Smithtown, N.Y., Jan. 19, 1970; d. Patrick R. and Karen A. (Koch) J. BS in Acctg., Marymount Coll., 1991; MPA, Marist Coll., 1993. Asst. adminstr. Dutchess Radiology Assoc. P.C., Poughkeepsie, N.Y., 1992-94; planning, mktg. exec. Vassar Bros. Hosp., Poughkeepsie, N.Y., 1994—; adv. bd. neighborhood based alliance, Poughkeepsie, N.Y., 1994; mem. Ea. Dutchess County Rural Healthcare Network, Wassaic, N.Y. 1994—, Post-Natal subcom., 1995—. Mem. health adv. com. Dutchess Health 2000. Mem. AAUW, LWV, Nat. Orgn. for Women (pres. mid Hudson chpt. 1995—), Poughkeepsie Prog. Coalition, Dutchess County Human Rights Roundtable. Democrat. Home: 46-D Corlies Ave Poughkeepsie NY 12601 Office: Vassar Bros Hosp Reade Pl Poughkeepsie NY 12601

JACOBOWITZ, ELLEN SUE, museum and temple administrator; b. Detroit, Feb. 21, 1948; d. Theodore Mark and Lois Clairesse (Levy) J. BA, U. Mich., 1969, MA, 1970. Curator Phila. Mus. Art, 1972-90; adminstr. Cranbrook Inst. Sci., Bloomfield Hills, Mich., 1991-94; adminstr. Temple Emanu-El, Oak Park, Mich., 1995—. Author: The Prints of Lucas Van Leyden, 1983, American Graphics: 1860-1940, 1982. Past bd. dirs. Print Coun. Am., Balt., Netherlands Am. Amity Trust, Washington, 1982-84, Nat. Coun. Jewish Women, Detroit, 1990-91; treas. Sat. Luncheon Club, 1995-96; bd. Am. Jewish Com., 1996; active Leadership Oakland, Detroit Inst. Arts. Mem. Mich. Mus. Assn. (bd. dirs. 1993-95), Nat. Assn. Temple Adminstrs., Union Am. Hebrew Congs., Women's Econ. Club. Office: Temple Emanuel 14450 W 10 Mile Rd Oak Park MI 48237

JACOBOWITZ, RUTH SCHERR, writer, public relations consultant, lecturer; b. Pitts., Apr. 12, 1933; d. Irving and Claire (Chernoff) Scherr; m. B. Paul Jacobowitz, Jan. 19, 1952; children: Jan, Jody, Julie. Student, U. Pitts., 1951-53, Cuyahoga Community Coll., 1960-63, Ursuline Coll., Cleve., 1978. Free-lance writer Cleve. Plain Dealer, 1965-67, book reviewer, 1978-82; pub. rels. dir. Mt. Sinai Med. Ctr., Cleve., 1967-73, v.p. pub. affairs, 1973-84; pres. Ruth Jacobowitz Asscs., Cleve., 1984—; mem. pub. relations com. Univ. Circle, Cleve., 1976-84; regional chmn. Am. Assn. Med. Colls., Washington, 1978-79; mem. pub. affairs com. Ctr. for Health Affairs, Cleve., 1983-85; bd. dirs. Cleve. Breast Cancer Coalition, 1994—. Author: 150 Most Asked Questions About Menopause: What Women Really Want To Know, 1993, 150 Most Asked Questions About Osteoporosis, 1993, 150 Most Asked Questions About Midlife Sex, Love and Intimacy, 1995; co-author: Managing Your Menopause, 1990; columnist Eternelle, Your Health, Chagrin Valley Times, Women's Health Exch. Mem. Nat. Coun. on Women's Health. Mem. NOW, Pub. Rels. Soc. Am., Internat. Assn. Bus. Communicators (editor quar. mag. Caring, 1974-85), Authors Guild, Am. Assn. of Sex Educators, Therapists and Counselors, Am. Soc. Journalists and Authors, Sex Info. and Edn. Coun. U.S., Greater Cleve. Hosp. Assn. (chmn. pub. rels. com. 1980-82), Womenspace, N.Am. Menopause Soc. (founding mem.), Internat. Menopause Soc., Jacobs Inst. For Women's Health, Press Club.

JACOBS, BARBARA HEARN, psychologist; b. Jackson, Tenn.; d. William Nelson and Lerline (Houston) Hearn; m. John C. Jacobs, July 27, 1973; 1 child, Lesley Elizabeth. BA, Lambuth Coll.; MA in Psychology, Geo. Peabody Coll., 1972, PhD in Psychology, 1976. Lic. psychologist, Ala., Tenn. Clin. dir. Marshall Jackson Mental Health, Guntersville, Ala., 1976-79; psychologist pvt. practice, Scottsboro, Ala., 1980-95; adj. faculty mem. U. Ala. Med. Sch., Huntsville, Ala., 1985-87; cons. Three Springs, Inc., Huntsville, 1989-95, psychologist, 1995—; Mem. Ala. Bd. Examiners in Psychology, 1982-86. Mem. Scottsboro (Ala.) Women's League, 1980—, Jackson County Hist. Soc., Scottsboro, 1985—. Mem. AAUW (pres. Scottsboro 1984-85), Ala. Psychol. Assn. (exec. coun. 1996), N. Ala. Assn. Lic. Psychologists (past pres.), Friends of the Family Jackson County, Ala. Democrat. Episcopalian. Home: 413 Kyle St Scottsboro AL 35768 Office: Three Springs Inc 247 Chateau Dr Huntsville AL 35801

JACOBS, CHRISTINE, corporate executive; b. Columbus, Ohio, 1950. Grad., Rosary Hill Coll., 1972, Ga. State U., 1991. Pres., CEO Theragenics Corp., Norcross, Ga. Office: Theragenics Corp 5325 Oakbrook Pkwy Norcross GA 30093*

JACOBS, DELORES HAMM, secondary education educator; b. Tuscaloosa, Ala., Mar. 1, 1947; d. Howard Murphy and Nellie Mae (Booth) Hamm; m. Paul Thomas Jacobs, June 1, 1966; 1 child, Michael Paul. BS in Secondary Edn., U. Ala., 1971; BS in Middle Sch. Edn., Samford U., 1991; MA in Secondary Edn., U. Ala., Birmingham, 1974. English and Title I reading tchr. Locust Fork (Ala.) H.S., 1971-85; speech instr. Pizitz Middle Sch., Vestavia Hills, Ala., 1985-86, tchr. English, instr., 1986—, curriculum coord. English dept.; student-tchr. sponsor U. Ala., Birmingham, Samford U., Birmingham. Contbr. poetry to various poetry publs. and editorials to Tuscaloosa News, Vestavia Hills edn. newsletters, Am. Poetic Soc. poetic vols. Bd. dirs. First Ch. of the Nazarene Pre-Sch. and Daycare Sch., Vestavia Hills, 1987-93, ch. organist, 1976—; sch. rep. United Way; rep. Heart Fund, Jefferson County, Ala., vol. Olympic Games, 1996. Mem. NEA, Ala. Edn. Assn., So. Assn. of Schs. (accreditation com., visitation team), Nat. Coun. Tchrs. English, Ala. Reading Assn., Vestavia Hills Garden Club, Chi Delta Phi. Republican. Office: Pizitz Middle School 2020 Pizitz Dr Vestavia Hills AL 35216-3710

JACOBS, EDITH AMBLER, office manager; b. Phila., Sept. 22, 1938; d. Harry Conard and Edith (Rebmann) Ambler; m. Morrell LePage Jacobs, Aug. 27, 1960 (div. Feb. 1986); children: Wendi LePage Jacobs Thomas, Kimberle Mae, Morrell LePage III, Geoffrey Keith. AA, Greenbrier Jr. Coll. Gen. mgr. Monogram Products, Phila., 1979-92; sec. Amigaz, Warminster, Pa., 1992-94; office mgr. Geitz Machine Works, Telford, Pa., 1994—; part time sports photographer. Mem. Eastern Pa. Youth Soccer Assn., Phila. Oldtimers Soccer Assn. Republican. Episcopalian. Home: 422 Cloverly Ln Horsham PA 19044 Office: Geitz Machine Works 4422 Old Bethlehem Park Telford PA 18969

JACOBS, ELEANOR, art consultant, retired art administrator; b. N.Y.C., July 25, 1929; d. Samuel and Mary (Praw) Cohen; m. Raymond Jacobs, Dec. 29, 1955; children: Susan, Laura. BA, NYU, 1979. Co-founder, v.p. The Earth Shoe Co., N.Y.C., 1969-79; art adminstr. Print Dept., Sotheby's, N.Y.C., 1980-81; exec. asst. Care, N.Y.C., 1982-84; exec. adminstr. Hirschl & Adler Galleries, N.Y.C., 1984-93; art cons. Recipient Founders Day award NYU, N.Y.C., 1978. Mem. Nat. Arts Club (gov. 1989—, exhbns. com. 1984—, curatorial com. 1990—, founder, editor exhibiting artists newsletter 1987—, admissions com. 1995—).

JACOBS, ELEANOR ALICE, retired clinical psychologist, educator; b. Royal Oak, Mich., Dec. 25, 1923; d. Roy Dana and Alice Ann (Keaton) J. B.A., U. Buffalo, 1949, M.A., 1952, Ph.D., 1955. Clin. psychologist VA Hosp., Buffalo, 1954-83; EEO counelor VA Hosp., 1962-79, chief psychology service, 1979-83; clin. prof. SUNY, Buffalo, 1950-83; speaker on psychology to community orgns. and clubs, 1952—; Mem. adult devel. and aging com. NICHD, HEW, 1971-75. Researcher for publs. on hyperbaric medicine, hyperoxygenation effect on cognitive functions in aged. Recipient Outstanding Superior Performance award Buffalo VA Hosp., 1958, Spl. Recognition award SUNY, Buffalo, Spl. Recognition award SUNY, 1971; W.L. McKnight award Miami Heart Inst., 1972; Adminstrs. commendation VA, 1974; Dirs. commendation VA Med. Center, Buffalo, 1978; Disting. Alumni award SUNY, Buffalo, 1983; named Woman of Yr. Bus. and Profl. Women's Clubs, Buffalo, 1973. Mem. Am. Psychol. Assn., Eastern Psychol. Assn., N.Y. State Psychol. Assn., Am. Group Psychotherapy Assn., Am. Soc. Group Psychotherapy and Psychodrama, Psychol. Assn. Western N.Y. (Disting. Achievement award 1976), Group Psychotherapy Assn. Western N.Y., Undersea Med. Soc., Sigma Xi. Home: PO Box 432, Ridgeway, ON Canada L0S 1N0

JACOBS, JANE, author; b. Scranton, Pa., May 4, 1916; d. John Decker and Bess Mary (Robison) Butzner; m. Robert Hyde Jacobs, Jr., May 27, 1944; children—James Kedzie, Edward Decker, Mary Hyde. Author: Downtown Is For People in The Exploding Metropolis, 1959, The Death and Life of Great American Cities, 1961, The Economy of Cities, 1969, The Question of Separatism, 1980, Cities and the Wealth of Nations, 1984, (juvenile) The Girl on the Hat, 1989, Systems of Survival, 1992; editor, commentator: A Schoolteacher in Old Alaska: The Story of Hannah Breece, 1995. Address: care Random House 201 E 50th St New York NY 10022-7703

JACOBS, KAREN LOUISE, medical technologist; b. Kingston, N.Y., May 7, 1943; d. William Charles and Vera Elizabeth (Kelly) Jacobs; BS in Applied Tech., Empire State Coll., 1976; MS in Pub. Service Adminstrn., Russell Sage Coll., 1982. Sr. lab. technician, hosp. lab. supr. City of Kingston (N.Y.) Labs., 1962-68; sr. rsch. asst. Dudley Obs., Albany, N.Y., 1972-75; lab. adminstr. Albany Med. Coll., 1976—, mem. faculty, 1982—; mem. infection control com. and subcoms. on AIDS mgmt. and human immunodeficiency virus universal precautions Albany Med. Ctr. Infection Control, 1987—. Bd. dirs. chpt. Leukemia Soc. Am., 1983-87; judge sci. and tech. summer issue on excellence in Am. U.S. News and World Report; vol. asst. naturalist Five Rivers Environ. Ctr. Mem. Clin. Lab. Mgmt. Assn. (del. citizen amb. program to China 1989), Am. Soc. Clin. Pathologists, Sierra Club, Earthwatch, Nat. Speleological Soc., Helderburg-Hudson Grotto, Hudsonia (bd. dirs. 1995). Home: 11 Eastmount Dr Apt 202 Slingerlands NY 12159-2168 Office: Albany Med Coll Div Hematology and Oncolgy 47 New Scotland Ave Albany NY 12208-3412

JACOBS, LEAH ROSE, philosophy educator, business consultant; b. Paterson, N.J., Apr. 14, 1936; d. Samuel I. and Beatrice J. (Levine) J.; m. Robert L. Stern, Apr. 20, 1958 (div. 1974); 1 child, Aaron; m. Arnulf Zweig, Dec. 26, 1976; children: Rebecca, Jonathan. BA, Wellesley Coll., 1957; MA, U. Rochester, 1961, PhD, 1972; MBA, U. Oreg., 1982. Asst. prof. U. Conn., Storrs, 1962-64, Smith Coll., Northhampton, Mass., 1964-66, Westfield (Mass.) State Coll., 1970-76; prof. U. Oreg., Eugene, 1974-75, 77-80; owner, mgr. Wine & Co., Eugene, 1982-89; prof. Linfield Coll., McMinnville, Oreg., 1990—; cons. bus. ethics, 1989—; spkr. women entrepreneurs, 1984—. Contbr. articles to profl. jours. Com. mem. Eugene Citizens Involvement Com., 1994—; bd. dirs. Greenhill Humane Soc., Eugene, 1995—; bd. dirs., treas. Willamette Wildlife, Eugene, 1990-94, Soc. for Women in Philosophy, 1970-74; pres. Temple Beth Israel, Eugene, 1980-82. Postdoctoral fellow AAUW, 1972-73. Mem. NAFE, Am. Philos. Soc., Soc. Wine Educators. Jewish. Home: 331 Hunington Ave Eugene OR 97405 Office: Willamette U Philosophy Dept State St Salem OR 97301-3922

JACOBS, LINDA ROTROFF, elementary school educator; b. Peebles, Ohio, June 10, 1942; d. Joseph Harold Rotroff and Mary Lucille (Peterson) Nixon; m. Donald Eugene Jacobs, Nov. 29, 1968; 1 child, Donald Brett. BS in Edn., Ohio State U., 1963; MA in Edn., U. Cin., 1968; postgrad., U. Cin., Miami U., Xavier U., 1968—, Coll. Mt. St. Joseph, 1968—. Cert. tchr., Ohio. Tchr. kindergarten Forest Hills Bd. Edn., Cin., 1963-74, 77—, Chillicothe (Ohio) Bd. Edn., 1974-77; tchr. reading adult edn. Cin., 1975; tchr. kindergarten Mercer Elem. Forest Hills, Cin., 1977—; cooperating tchr. student tchrs. Ohio U., U. Cin., No. Ky. U., 1965—; tchr. summer sch. 4th, 5th, and 6th grades math./lang. arts, Cin., 1964-68, kindergarten and 1st grade Forest Hills, Cin., 1978-82; tchr. rep. Head Start, Chillicothe, 1975-77; kindergarten coord. Forest Hills and Hamilton County, Cin., 1965-70, 83-85; mem. supt.'s coun. Forest Hills, Cin., 1979, 82, 88; tchr. rep. PTA, Cin., 1967, 73, 82, 89; facilitator Forest Hills Summer Sch., 1993-96; master tchr./advisor entry tchrs. Forest Hills, 1993—; career mentor Ashford-McCarthy Resources, Inc., 1993-94; coord. early entrance screening Hamilton County, 1994, 95, faculty mem. Intervention Based Multifactored Evaluation Com., 1994, 95, mem. Collaboration Team for Inclusion of Spl. Children, 1994, 95; mem. responsive classroom team, 1996. Author: Getting Ready for Kindergarten, 1978, Parenting Tips, 1982, Intervention Assistance Team Handbook, 1992;. Cons. Women Helping Women, Cin., 1989. Recipient Ohio State U. Scarlet and Gray award, 1995; named Hamilton County Tchr. of Yr., 1965. Mem. NEA, Nat. PTA (rep.) Tchrs. Applying Whole Lang., Ohio Edn. Assn. (del. 1965), Southwestern Ohio Edn. Assn., Forest Hills Educators Assn. (sec. 1964-68, Martha Holden Jennings scholar 1976-77), DAR, Ohio State U. Alumni Club of Clermont County (sec. 1995-96), Alpha Kappa Delta (sec. 1975—). Mem. Ch. of Christ.

JACOBS, MARIAN, advertising agency owner; b. Stockton, Calif., Sept. 11, 1927; d. Paul (dec.) and Rose (Sallah) J. AA, Stockton Coll. With Bottarini Advt., Stockton, 1948-50; pvt. practice Stockton, 1950-64; with Olympius Advt., Stockton, 1964-78; pvt. practice Stockton, 1978—; pres. Stockton Advt. Club, 1954, Venture Club, Stockton, 1955; founder Stockton Advt. and Mktg. Club, 1981. Founder Stockton Arts Comms., 1976, Sunflower Entertainment for Institutionalized, 1976, Women Execs., Stockton, 1978; founding dir. Pixie Woods, Stockton; bd. dir. Goodwill Industries, St. Mary's Dining Room, Alan Short Gallery. Paul Harris fellow Rotary Club, 1994; recipient Woman of Achievement award San Joaquin County Women's Coun., Stockton, 1976, Achievement award San Joaquin Delta Coll., Stockton, 1978, Friend of Edn. award Calif. Tchrs. Assn., Stockton, 1988, Stanley McCaffrey Disting. Svc. award, U. of the Pacific, Stockton, 1988, Athena award for Businesswoman of Yr. Greater Stockton C. of C., 1989, Role Model award Tierra del Oro Girl Scouts U.S., 1989; named Stocktonian of the Yr. Stockton Bd. of Realtors, 1978, Outstanding Citizen Calif. State Senate & Assembly, 1978; the Marian Jacobs Writers & Poets Symposium was established in her honor. Republican. Roman Catholic. Home and Office: 4350 Mallard Creek Cir Stockton CA 95207-5205

JACOBS, MARILYN ARLENE POTOKER, gifted education educator, consultant, author; b. N.Y.C., Oct. 22, 1940; m. David Jacobs, Dec. 10, 1960. BA in Psychology, Hunter Coll. CUNY, 1961, MS in Edn., 1963; cert. in gifted edn., U. South Fla., 1977. Cert. elem. edn., gifted and early childhood edn., Fla. Tchr. Yonkers (N.Y.) Pub. Schs., 1961-63; dir., tchr. Creative Corners Pre-Sch., Pomona, N.Y., 1971-74; tchr. of gifted, tchr. trainer Pinellas County Schs., Clearwater, Fla., 1975—; pvt. practice computer edn. cons., 1987—; freelance grant writer, 1988—. Contbr. articles to profl. jours. Recipient numerous county, state and nat. Econs. Edn. Curriculum awards, 1982—. Mem. NEA, ASCD, Coun. for Exceptional Children (Educator of the Yr. 1985), Assn. for Gifted, Fla. Assn. Computer Educators, Phi Delta Kappa, Phi Beta Kappa, Kappa Delta Pi, Psi Chi. Office: Eisenhower Elem Sch 2800 Drew St Clearwater FL 34619-3010

JACOBS, MARISA FRANCES, lawyer; b. Phila., Aug. 13, 1957; d. Irving and Sylvia Sonia (Silver) J. BA, Dickinson Coll., 1978; JD, Columbia U., 1981. Bar: N.Y. 1982. Atty. Reavis & McGrath, N.Y.C., 1981-87; sr. v.p. Prism Assocs., N.Y.C., 1987-89; sec., assoc. gen. counsel Cooper Cos., Inc., Ft. Lee, N.J., 1989-96; dir. Johnnie D. Johnson & Co., Inc., N.Y.C., 1996—. Active Lenox Hill Hosp., N.Y.C., 1987-89; mem. bus. and profl. women's com. United Jewish Appeal, 1993—. Mem. ABA, Am. Soc. Corp. Secs., Bar Assn. City of N.Y. Office: Johnnie D Johnson & Co Inc 50 Broad St Ste 2000 New York NY 10004

JACOBS, NANCY CAROLYN BAKER, author; b. Milw., Dec. 9, 1944; d. Alvin Donald and Wilma Carolyn (Robertson) Moll; m. James Ross Baker, Aug. 28, 1965 (div. 1979); 1 child, Bradley; m. Jerome Martin Jacobs, June 20, 1981. BA, U. Minn., 1965, MA, 1973; MFA, U. So. Calif., 1977. Reporter St. Paul Dispatch, 1965-66; pub. rels. writer U. Minn., Mpls., 1966-67, Northwest Airlines, St. Paul, 1967-69; TV scriptwriter Control Data Corp., Mpls., 1971-73; dir. news and pub. Met. State U., St. Paul, 1973-75; author, free lance journalist, 1975—; pvt. investigator Spl. Reports, L.A., 1986-90; journalism lectr. Calif. State U., Northridge, 1977-92. Author: Deadly Companion, 1986, The Turquoise Tattoo, 1991, A Slash of Scarlet, 1992, See Mommy Run, 1992, The Silver Scalpel, 1993, Cradle and All, 1995, Daddy's Gone A-Hunting, 1995, Rocking the Cradle, 1996; (as Nancy C. Baker) Babyselling: The Scandal of Black Market Adoption, 1978, Act II: The Mid-Career Job Change and How to Make It, 1980, New Lives for Former Wives: Displaced Homemakers, 1980, Cashing in on Cooking, 1982, The Beauty Trap: Exploring Woman's Greatest Obsession, 1984, Relative Risk: Living with a Family History of Breast Cancer, 1991 (Am. Med. Writers Assn. Rose Kushner award). Mem. Mystery Writers Am., Pvt. Eye Writers Am., Authors Guild, Internat. Assn. Crime Writers, Sisters in Crime.

JACOBS, NORA C., public relations executive. BA, Kent State U., 1973; MA, John Carroll U., 1976. Advt., sales promotion, publicity staff mem. B.F. Goodrich Chem. Co., Akron, 1977-80, mgr. pub. rels., 1980-81, mgr. advt. svcs., 1981-83, mgr. advt. and pub. affairs, 1983-85; sr. account exec. Edward Howard & Co., Cleve., 1986-87, v.p., 1987-93, sr. v.p., 1993, sr. v.p. mgr., 1994—. Mem. Pub. Rels. Soc. Am., Press Club of Cleve., Am. Soc. for Health Care Mktg. and Pub. Rels., Health Acad. of Pub. Rels. Soc. Am. Office: Edward Howard & Co One Erieview Plz 7th Fl Cleveland OH 44114*

JACOBS, PATRICIA LOUISE, geriatrics nurse; b. Battle Creek, Iowa, Feb. 27, 1958; d. John Otto and Mary Ellen (Owens) J. Nurse aide cert., Western Iowa Tech., 1976. CNA. Nurse asst. Beverly Enterprises, Las Vegas, Nev., 1979-80, Hillhaven, West Des Moines, Iowa, 1983-86, Sunrise Manor, Sioux City, Iowa, 1988-89, Countryside Retirement Home, Sioux City, 1989-91, Julia's Valley Manor, Sioux City, 1991-93, Fellowship Village, Inwood, Iowa, 1993-96, Good Samaratin Home, Lennox, S.D., 1996—; nurse asst. Kimberly Nursing, West Des Moines, 1982-83, 86. Republican. Lutheran. Home: 209 S Maple St Inwood IA 51240

JACOBS, ROSETTA See LAURIE, PIPER

JACOBS, SHEILA JOAN, immunologist; b. N.Y.C., Oct. 10, 1939; d. Max and Rosalind (Goldstein) Lehrhaupt; m. Richard David Jacobs (div.); children: Marcy Jacobs Little, Sharon L. Jacobs; m. Robert Russell Carey, Apr. 21, 1985. BS, Carnegie Inst. Tech., 1961; MS, L.I. U., 1964; PhD, Columbia U., 1968. Instr. SUNY Downstate Med. Ctr., Bklyn., 1968-71; rsch. asst. CUNY Lehman Coll., Bronx, 1972-76; rsch. assoc. prof. N.Y. Med. Coll., Valhalla, 1976-81; assoc. prof. Wagner Coll., Staten Island, N.Y., 1981-82; sr. scientist Schering-Plough Corp., Bloomfield, N.J., 1982-84; prin. scientist Schering-Plough Corp., Bloomfield, 1984-85, sect. leader, 1985-87; sect. leader Schering-Plough Rsch. Inst., Kenilworth, N.J., 1987—. Mem. AAAS, Am. Chem. Soc., Internat. Soc. for Interferon and Cytokine Rsch., Phi Kappa Phi, Phi Sigma, Sigma Xi. Home: 52 Ivy Pl Wayne NJ 07470 Office: Schering-Plough Rsch Inst 2015 Galloping Hill Rd Kenilworth NJ 07033

JACOBSEN, JANICE A., pharmaceutical company executive; b. New London, Conn., June 18, 1954; d. Lawrence Randolph and Anne Elizabeth (Trail) J.; m. Ernest R. Messer, Apr. 14, 1995. Student, McGill U., Montreal, Can., 1972-74; BS, Duke U., 1976; MSc, U. N.H., 1977; MBA, Rensellaer Poly. Inst., 1985. Summer sch. tchr., substitute tchr. Groton (Conn.) Pub. Schs., 1976-78; tax preparer H&R Block, Groton, 1978-79; rsch. assoc. II Yale Med. Sch., New Haven, 1978-80; rsch. assoc. in biochemistry Pfizer Ctrl. Rsch., Groton, 1980-86, sr. clin. rsch. assoc., 1986-91, sr. coord. clin. ops., 1991-94, sr. devel. planner, 1995—. Bd. dirs. Big Bros., Big Sisters Orgn., New London, Conn., 1978-82. Mem. Off Soundings Club. Office: Pfizer Inc Ctrl Rsch Eastern Point Rd Groton CT 06340

JACOBSEN, JOSEPHINE, author; b. Coburg, Ont., Can., Aug. 19, 1908; d. Joseph Edward and Octavis (Winder) Boylan; m. Eric Jacobsen, Mar. 17, 1932; 1 son, Erlend Ericsen. Grad., Roland Park Country Sch., 1926; LHD (hon.), Coll. Notre Dame Md., 1974, Goucher Coll., 1974; MDiv. (hon.), St. Mary's Seminary & Coll., 1988; hon. degree, Johns Hopkins U., 1993. Critic; short story writer; lectr.; poetry cons. Library of Congress, 1971-73, hon. cons. in Am. letters, 1973-79; v.p. PSA, 1979-80. Author: The Human Climate, 1953, For the Unlost, 1948, The Animal Inside, 1966, (with William Mueller) The Testament of Samuel Beckett, 1968, Genet and Ionesco Playwrights of Silence, 1968, The Shade-Seller: New and Collected Poems, 1974, A Walk With Raschid and Other Stories, 1978 (Notable Books of 1978), The Chinese Insomniacs, New Poems, 1981, Adios Mr. Moxley, 1986, The Sisters: New and Selected Poems, 1987, Distances, 1992; writing also included O. Henry Awards Prize Stories, 1967, 71, 73, 76, 85, 93, Fifty Years of the American Short Story, 1970, On the Island: Stories, 1989, Best Poems, 1991, Pushcart Prizes, 1991. Mem. lit. panel Nat. Endowment for Arts, 1980-84. Recipient MacDowell Colony fellow; Yaddo fellow; Am. Acad. Poets fellow, 1987; recipient Shelly Meml. award for life work PSA, 1993. Mem. Am. Acad. Arts and Letters (Svc. to Lit. award 1982, Lenore Marshall award for best book of poetry pub. in U.S. in 1987, 1988), PEN (nominee Faulkner award for fiction 1990). Democrat. Roman Catholic. Home: 13801 York Rd Cockeysville MD 21030-1825

JACOBSEN, MAGDALENA GRETCHEN, mediator, federal agency executive; b. N.Y.C., July 26, 1940; d. Carl J. and Helen (Faber) J.; m. Bruce Donald Henricus, Dec. 20, 1986. Cert. labor studies, AFL-CIO, 1971; cert. labor studies, bargaining and arbitration, Harvard U., 1973; cert. indsl. rels., U. Calif., San Francisco, 1975; BS, U. San Francisco, 1987; MS, Golden Gate U., 1989. Sec. CBS TV, Hollywood, Calif., 1962-65; flight attendant Continental Airlines, L.A., 1965-69, mgr. labor rels., 1972-76; local union official, sec.-treas. steward and stewardess divsn. ALPA, Washington, 1966-72; commr. Fed. Mediation and Conciliation Svcs., San Francisco, 1976-89, Portland, Oreg., 1992-93; dir. employee rels. City and County of San Francisco, 1989-92; bd. Nat. Mediation Bd., Washington, 1993—. Mem. Indsl. Rels. Rsch. Assn. (mem. exec. bd. 1980—, pres. San Francisco chpt. 1985-87). Office: Nat Mediation Bd 1301 K St Ste 250 East Washington DC 20572

JACOBSEN-THEEL, HAZEL M., historian; b. Becker County, Minn., June 1, 1909; d. Julius and Helma Clara (Klug) Mielke; m. Albert Arthur Jacobsen, June 2, 1933 (dec. June 1984); children: Harry James, Karen Bel; m. Bruce Theel, Jan. 7, 1989 (dec. Dec. 1992). Student, U. Minn., 1926-27; BA in Science and Edn., U. N.D., 1930; postgrad., U. Minn., summers 32-33. Cert. tchr. N.D. and Minn.:. Dining room mgr. Lake Side Hotel, Detroit, 1922-30; tchr. N St. Paul (Minn.) Pub. Sch. system, 1930-33; with Gt. Northern Railway at Glacier Park Entrance Hotel, summer 1932; tchr. Dept. Interior Bur. Ind. Affairs, N.D., 1933-42; mem. aircraft assembly line Higgins Air Craft, La.; science tchr. St. Johns (N.D.) Pub. Sch. system, 1945-46; hardware mcht. Jacobsen Hardware Inc., Minn., 1946-73. Contbr. articles to profl. jours. Vol. tour guide of historic places, 1961; life mem., past officer Dakota County Hist. Soc.; charter mem. Dakota County Pioneer Village; tour leader Hastings Area, 1960-89; founder Hastings Vol. Group, 1976-77; established Albert A. and Hazel M. Jacobsen Meml. Find U. N.D., 1988, Archtl. Treasure Hunt, 1994; supporter Turtle Mountain Indian Mus., Belcourt, N.D., life mem., 1994—; charter mem. gov. apptd. Dakota County Bicentennial Commn. First woman to be selected Grand Marshall River Town Days and Minn. Aquatennial Miss. River Flotilla, 1992; established Bruce Theel High Sch. Vocat. scholarship meml. for Mt. Pleasant Pub. Sch. Dist. Found. Mem. AAUW, Women's Orgn. Minn. Hist. Soc. (charter mem., officer), Hastings Preservation Commn. (charter mem.), Minn. Territorial Pioneers (Outstanding award 1987), U. N.D. Alumni Assn. (Sioux award), U. Minn. Alumni Assn. (life), Am. Legion Aux. (life), Dakota County Hist. Soc. (rsch. assoc.), Fedn. Women N.D., OES (grand officer N.D.), 1006 Summit Ave. Soc. (life, charter). Home: 311 Mains St Rolla ND 58367 also: 313 Ramsey St Hastings MN 55033-1222

JACOBSON, ANNA SUE, finance company executive; b. Ft. Smith, Ark., Aug. 13, 1940; d. Ray Bradley and Joy Anna (Person) McAlister, (stepfather) Cleve J. McDonald, Sr.; m. Lyle Norman Jacobson, Nov. 23, 1958; children: Lyle Michael, Daniel Ray, Julie Anne, Eric Joseph. Cert. in Fin. Planning, Coll. for Fin. Planning, 1984. Certified fin. paraplanner. Office mgr. Twin Cities Lithographic Inst., St. Paul, 1963-66; sec., St. Paul, Mpls., 1971-78; asst. to pres., office mgr. Planners Fin. Svcs., Mpls., 1978-85, asst. corp. treas., 1987-88; fin. paraplanner McAlmont Investment Co., Mpls., 1985-96, office mgr., 1988-96; registered rep. USR Fin. Svc. Inc., 1996—; ind. fin. cons.; bd. dir. Planners Fin. Svcs.; mem. bd. advisors Coll. for Fin. Planning, Denver, 1982—; v.p., CFO J&J Specialty Co., 1993—; sr. v.p. AdPro Internat., Inc., Wayzata, Minn., 1996—; speaker various orgns. Co-creator Paraplanning Profession Advisor; mem. firm Fin. Alternatives of Mpls., Wayzata, Minn., 1996—, Mpls., 1985—. Del. Dem. Farmer Labor Com., St. Paul, 1980; campaign chmn. mayoral election, Roseville, Minn., 1983, county commr., city coun. election, Roseville, 1980, 84; local chmn. for passage of ERA, Minn.; mem. Am. Lung Assn., St. Paul, Ramsey Found. of Minn., Como conservatory Hist. Soc.; past. pres. PTA, Minn.; mem. exec. coun. Boy Scouts Am., 1977-81; mem. adv. bd. Sch. Dist. 623, Roseville, Minn., 1978-81; fund raising com. mem. Twin Cities Pub. TV Sta., 1975—; mem. ch. coun. deacons St. Michael's Luth. Ch., St. Paul, 1996—. Recipient Volunteerism award State of Minn., 1981, Cert. of Appreciation Minn. Bicentennial Com., 1976; named 1st Fin. Paraplanner in history of industry. Mem. Internat. Assn. Fin. Planning, Twin Cities Assn. Fin. Planners, Internat. Assn. Bus. and Profl. Women (bd. dirs. 1977-86, pres. 1980-82, Woman of Yr. 1982), Minn. Women's Consortium, Como Conservatory Hist. Soc., Concordia Acad. Booster Club, Beta Sigma Phi Nu Phi Mu Chpt. Democrat. Lutheran. Avocations: tennis, riding, reading, piano, harp. Home: 2171 Dellwood Ave Saint Paul MN 55113-4329 Office: Fin Alternatives of Mpls 1550 Twelve Oaks Ctr Wayzata MN 55391

JACOBSON, ANNETTE MOFF, chemical engineer; b. Latrobe, Pa., May 6, 1957; d. Charles James Jr. and Mary Agnes (Antinori) Moff; m. Donald Bruce Jacobson, Aug. 22, 1981; children: Jennifer Lynn, Amanda Rose. BSChE, Carnegie Mellon U., 1979, PhD in Chem. Engring., 1988. Chem. engr. PPG Inds., Inc., Pitts., 1979-81, Sr. rsch. engr., 1981-85; assoc. dir. colloids, polymers & surface program Carnegie Mellon U., Pitts., 1988-89, lectr. in chem. engring., 1988-95, sr. lectr. chem. engring., 1996—; workshop lectr. in field. Inventor in field. Amoco Found. fellow, 1986-88, Carnegie Mellon U. Women's Clan scholar, 1978-79, Dabcock & Wilcox scholar Carnegie Mellon U., 1977-79; recipient G.D. Parfitt award Chem. Engring. Student Group, 1987. Mem. AIChE, Am. Chem. Soc., Internat. Assn. Colloid and Interface Scientists, Sigma Xi (corr. sec. 1994—).

JACOBSON, AUDREY PLATT, artist; b. N.Y.C., Mar. 9, 1928; d. Joseph and Ann Faye (Eisenberg) Platt; m. Jerry H. Jacobson; children: John, Ben. BS, Skidmore Coll., 1949; diploma, Parson Sch. of Design, N.Y.C., 1951; postgrad., Potsdam Coll., 1971-73. Artist Osgood & Hezen, N.Y.C., 1951-53, Atlantic Adv., N.Y.C., 1953-54; dir. Pethe Galerie, Englewood, N.J., 1954-70; artist, 1973—; adj. prof. SUNY, Potsdam, 1994-95. One woman shows in N.Y. and N.Y.C. Mem. Albany Printmakers, Syracuse Printmakers, Boston Printmakers. Home: 412 Caroline St Ogdensburg NY 13669

JACOBSON, DOROTHY TROUP, English and education educator; b. Providence, Dec. 21, 1930; d. Charles Leon and Celia (Shulman) Troup; children: Deborah, Donald. BA, Boston U., 1952; MA, SUNY, Albany, 1962. Cert. permanent secondary edn. educator. Tchr. Enlarged City Sch. Dist., Troy, N.Y., 1965-95; tchr. trainer Am. Fedn. Tchrs.-Ind. Capital Dist., N.Y., 1980-96; adj. prof. SUNY, Albany, 1995—; Mem. exec. bd. N.Y. State United Tchrs.-Troy Tchrs. Assn., 1980-90; local site coord. Am. Fedn. Tchrs.-Ednl. Rsch. and Dissemination, Troy, 1990-92; chair edn. Berith Shalom, Troy, 1995—. Human rights commr., 1987-95; dir. GIVE-Learn and Serve Am., Troy, 1990-96; pres. Bethany Hospitality Ctr., Troy, 1991-96; trustee Joseph's House, Troy, 1991-96. Recipient Cert. of Merit, State Humanities Assn., N.Y., 1985; named Tchr. of Yr., Coalition of Tchr. Educators, 1987. Mem. N.Y. State Ret. Tchrs. Assn. Jewish. Home: 82 Troy Rd East Greenbush NY 12061

JACOBSON, HELEN GUGENHEIM (MRS. DAVID JACOBSON), civic worker; b. San Antonio; d. Jac Elton and Rosetta (Dreyfus) Gugenheim; m. David Jacobson, Nov. 6, 1938; children: Liz Helenchild, Dottie J. Miller. BA, Hollins Coll. With news and spl. events staff NBC, N.Y.C., 1933-38. 1st v.p. San Antonio, Bexar County coun. Girl Scouts U.S.A., 1957-63; Tex. State rep. UNICEF, 1964-69; bd. dirs. U.S. com. UNICEF, 1970-80, hon. bd. dirs., 1980—; bd. dirs. Nat. Fedn. Temple Sisterhoods, 1973-77, Temple Beth-El Sisterhood, Youth Alternatives, Inc.; bd. dirs. Child Guidance Ctr., chmn. bd., 1960-63; bd. dirs. Sunshine Cottage Sch. for Deaf Children, chmn. bd., 1952-54; pres. Cmty Welfare Coun., 1968-70; pres. bd. trustees San Antonio Pub. Libr., 1957-61; trustee Nat. Coun. Crime and Delinquency, 1964-70, San Antonio Mus. Assn., 1964-73; bd. dirs. Cancer Therapy and Rsch. Found. South Tex., 1977—, sec., 1977-83; pres. S.W. region Tex. Coalition for Juvenile Justice, 1977-79; chmn. Mayor's Commn. on Status of Women, 1972-74; del. White House Conf. on Children, 1970; mem. Commn. on Social Action of Reform Judaism, 1973-77; chmn. Foster Grandparent project Bexar County Hosp. Dist., 1968-69; sec. Nat. Assembly for Social Policy and Devel., 1969-74; pres. women's com. Ecumenical Ctr. for Religion and Health, 1975-77; chmn. criminal justice planning com. Alamo Area Coun. of Govts., chmn., 1975-77, 1987-88; mem. Tex. Internat. Women's Yr. Coordinating Com., 1977; co-chmn. San Antonio chpt. NCCJ, 1980-84; chmn. United Negro Coll. Fund Campaign, 1983, 84; sec. nat. bd. Avance, Inc., 1991-93; trustee Target 90/Goals for San Antonio, 1986-90; hon. mem. bd. dirs. Witte Mus., 1994—. Recipient Headliner award for civic work San Antonio chpt. Women in Communications, 1958, Nat. Humanitarian award B'nai B'rith, 1975, City of Peace award, 1991; named Vol. Woman of Yr. Express-News, 1959, Spl. Svc. award Tex. Soc. Psychiat. Physicians, 1994; honoree San Antonio chpt. NCCJ, 1970, Nat. Jewish Hosp., 1978; inductee San Antonio Women's Hall of Fame, 1986, others. Mem. Nat. Coun. Jewish Women (Hannah G. Solomon award 1979), Internat. Women's Forum, San Antonio 100, Argyle Club. Home: 207 Beechwood Ln San Antonio TX 78216-7345

JACOBSON, KAREN, elementary school educator; b. N.Y.C.; d. Lawrence and Doris (Case) J. BA in Elem. Edn., SUNY, Potsdam, 1966; MS in Elem. Edn., SUNY, Cortland, 1975. Cert. tchr., N.Y. Kindergarten tchr. Mohawk (N.Y.) Sch., summers 1966-72; primary grades tchr. Oriskany (N.Y.) Ctrl. Sch., 1966—, mem. various lang. arts, sci., report card coms., 1966—. Mem. Oriskany PTA. Mem. Oriskany Tchrs. Assn., N.Y. State United Tchrs. Home: Box 152 109 Ridge Rd Oriskany NY 13424 Office: NA Walbran Elem Sch PO Box 539 Oriskany NY 13424-0539

JACOBSON, KATHY LYNN, academic administrator; b. Muskegon, Mich., Mar. 21, 1952; d. Norman M. and Doris A. (Berntsen) J. BA, Ctrl. Mich. U., 1974, MA, 1976. Admissions advisor Baker Coll., Muskegon, 1981-88, asst. dir. admissions, 1988-90, dir. admissions, 1990-91, v.p., 1991—. Bd. dirs. Mich. Pines and Dunes chpt., Girls Scouts USA, 1986-92. Named one of Outstanding Young Women, Greater Muskegon Jaycees, 1988. Mem. Shoreline Area Counselors Assn. (sec. 1982-90), Zonta Internat. (sec. mgrs. and suprs. 1984-86, 2d v.p. 1986-88, 1st v.p. 1988-90, pres. 1990-92), Phi Kappa Phi. Office: Baker Coll 123 E Apple Ave Muskegon MI 49442-3404

JACOBSON, LESLIE SARI, biologist, educator; b. N.Y.C., May 22, 1933; d. William and Gussie (Mintz) Goldberg; m. Homer Jacobson, Aug. 18, 1957 (div. Dec. 1995); children: Guy Joseph, Ethan Samuel. BS, Bklyn. Coll., 1954, MA, 1955; postgrad., Columbia U., 1956; postgrad. (NIH fellow), Calif. Inst. Tech., 1960; Ph.D., NYU, 1962. Instr. dept. biology Bklyn. Coll., 1954-57, fellow dept. chemistry, 1961-63, prof. health sci., 1974—, dean Sch. Gen. Studies and Continuing Higher Edn., 1974-80, dean Grad. Studies and Continuing Higher Edn., 1980-82, dean Grad. Studies, 1980-88, dean Grad. Studies and Rsch., 1988-89, prof. dept. health and nutritions scis., 1989—, exec. dir. Applied Scis. Inst., 1994-95; awarded Koppelman Endowed Professorship, 1995-97; instr. dept. nursing L.I. Coll. Sch. Nursing, 1958; asst. prof. biology L.I. U., Bklyn., 1963, prof. biology, 1963-74, dean Grad. Sch., 1973-74, nat. program chmn. Assn. Continuing Higher Edn., 1978, nat. bd. dirs., 1978-81, pres.-elect, 1980-81, pres., 1981-82; bd. dirs. Center for Labor and Mgmt., N.Y.; dir. N.Y. Regional Cabinet Adult Continuing Edn., 1982—; mem. adv. com. on minorities Coun. Grad. Schs., 1987-90, svcs. com. Grad. Record Exam. Bd., 1990-93, chmn. Acad. policy com. all-univ. senate CUNY, 1992—; bd. dirs. Hyperion Capital Mgt.; invited speaker at nat. meetings Issues in Higher Edn. V.p. Alpha Sigma Lambda Found., 1983-88; v.p. Mapleton Midwood Cmty. Health Bd. Inc., 1990—; v.p. B'nai B'rith Hillel JACY Assn., 1986-93; exec. mem. Hillel of N.Y.; bd. dirs. Meth. Hosp., 1989—; v.p. Am. Lung Assn. of Bklyn. Recipient Founders Day award NYU, 1961, N.Y. Outstanding Adult Educator award, N.Y.C., 1978, Nat. Merit award, Assn. Continuing Higher Edn., 1984, Leadership award, 1986, Citation for svc. to community N.Y.C. Coun., 1987, Citation for excellence in edn. Bklyn. Boro Pres., 1987, Citation for outstanding svc. to community N.Y. State Assy., 1987, N.Y. State Senate, 1987. Mem. Sigma Xi, Alpha Sigma Lambda (nat. pres. 1978-80). Office: Bklyn Coll Dept Health and Nutrition Scis Bedford Ave # H Brooklyn NY 11210

JACOBSON, MINDY LEINER, art psychotherapist, educator; b. N.Y.C., July 25, 1954; d. Murray and Joan Lois (Rubenstein) Leiner; m. Christopher Harold Jacobson, Mar. 9, 1980 (div. 1984); 1 child, Stephanie Beth. Student, Union Coll., Schenectady, 1972-74; BA, SUNY, Stony Brook, 1975; MCAT in Creative Arts Therapies, Hahnemann U., 1978; cert. in adminstrn. social svcs., Temple U., 1985. Cert. open water diver. Sr. art psychotherapist Friends Hosp., Phila., 1978—; pvt. practice Phila., 1982—; asst. prof. Hahnemann U. Phila., 1979—, continuing edn. instr., 1990-91; clin. instr., supr. trenton (N.J.) State Coll., 1989; cons. U.S. Naval Regional Med. Ctr., Phila., 1978; faculty mem. Ea. Regional Conf. on Multiple Personality Disorders, 1988-94; articles reviewer Dissociation, 1989, 93, 96; presenter in field. Contbr. articles to profl. jours. Speaker on preventive child abuse Jewish Fedn. Phila., 1988, 89; asst. Brownie leader Girl Scouts U.S.A., Melrose Park, Pa., 1988-91; treas. Phila. Sea Horses, 1990-93. Mem. Am. Art Therapy Assn. (registered profl., editor film-video jour. 1994—), Internat. Soc. for Study Multiple Personality Disorders and Dissociative States (profl.), Delaware Valley Art Therapy Assn. (hon. life, profl., treas. 1979-82, newsletter com.). Democrat. Jewish. Office: Friends Hosp 4641 Roosevelt Blvd Philadelphia PA 19124-2343

JACOBSON, SUSAN BOGEN, psychotherapist; b. Far Rockaway, N.Y., June 19, 1957; d. Paul and Blanche (Itzkowitz) Bogen; m. Adam Hartley Jacobson. BS in Bus. Adminstrn., SUNY, Albany, 1977; MS in Mental Health Counseling, Nova U., Ft. Lauderdale, Fla., 1992. Nat. cert. counselor; lic. mental health counselor, Fla. Psychotherapist in pvt. practice Boca Raton, Fla., 1992—; psychotherapist Sandalfoot Mental Health Ctr., Boca Raton, Fla., 1996—; instr. CCM Partnerships, Inc., Delray Beach, 1995—; officer Coun. for Marriage Preservation and Divorce Resolution, Boca Raton, 1995; mem. 15th Judicial Cir. Ctl Arbitration Com. for Fla. Bar. Mem. APA, ACA. Office: 7300 W Camino Real Ste 230 Boca Raton FL 33433

JACOBSON-WOLF, JOAN ELIZABETH, minister; b. Flint, Mich., July 15, 1949; d. William and Helen Wolf; m. Don M. Jacobson, May 27, 1978; children: Lara Heather, Heidi Kirsten, Joan Noel, Jason Luke. AA, Concordia Coll., 1969; BA in Theology, Valparaiso U., 1972; postgrad., Luth. Sem., Mexico City, Phila. and Columbus, Ohio, 1974-76; M in Div., Luth. Sch. Theology, Chgo., 1978; D in Ministry, McCormick Theol. Seminary, 1986. Ordained minister Luth. Ch., 1979; cert. psychiatric chaplain. Community organizer Cleve. Hispanic Murals, Centro Juvenil de Puertoriqueña; deaconess, missionary Hispanic ministry Trinity Luth., Cleve., 1972-75; intern, asst. minister Berwyn (Ill.) United Luth. Ch., 1977-78, chaplain Tenn. Women's Prison, Nashville, 1978-79, Spencer Youth Ctr., Nashville, 1979-81; minister St. Paul's Luth. Ch., Nashville, 1979-81; chaplain Edison Park Home, Park Ridge, Ill., 1982; pvt. practice as pastoral psychotherapist Owosso, 1988-93; pastor Messiah Luth. Ch., Racine, Wis., 1993—. Author: When to Counsel, When to Refer, 1989; violinist Flint Summer Theater Orch., 1965-67, Ann Arbor (Mich.) Symphony, 1967-69, Valparaiso (Ind.) U. Orch., 1969-72, Cherokee String Quartet, Iowa, 1971, Cleve. Women's Symphony, 1973-75, Oak Park (Ill.) Symphony, 1977, Nashville Symphony, 1978-80. Home: 3727 Canada Goose Xing Racine WI 53403-4506 Office: Messiah Luth Ch 3015 Pritchard Dr Racine WI 53406-5401

JACOBUS, SARA WILSON, special education educator; b. Lynn, Mass., Sept. 19, 1943; d. William Broyles and Evelyn French (Scott) Wilson; m. Paul Bailey Francis, Mar. 18, 1964 (div. Feb. 1980); children: Gregory Scott Francis, William Paul Francis. BS in Zoology, Memphis State U., 1965; MEd in Spl. Edn., Ga. State U., 1976; EdS in Adminstrn. and Supervision, U. Tenn., 1989. Cert. career ladder III, Tenn. Med. rsch. technician med. unit U. Tenn., Memphis, 1965-66; gen. sci. tchr. Rochester (N.Y.) City Schs., 1967-68; tchr. Montessori Dean Meml. Learning Ctr., Dallas, 1972-74; tchr. spl. edn. DeKalb County Schs., Atlanta, 1977-83; edn. dir. Girls Club of Blount County, Maryville, Tenn., 1984; tchr. spl. edn. Maryville (Tenn.) City Schs., 1984-96, systemwide homebound tchr., assessment specialist, 1996—; counselor, co-leader Adventure Camp for At Risk Youth, Maryville City Schs., 1993, 94. Co-author: Learning Disabilities Handbook, 1980. Apptd. mem. Maryville Historic Zoning Commn., Maryville, 1993—. Mem. ASCD, Coun. Exceptional Children, Delta Kappa Gamma, Phi Kappa Phi, Phi Delta Kappa. Home: 224 Indiana Ave Maryville TN 37803-5938

JACOBY, BEVERLY SCHREIBER, art consultant; b. Cin., Mar. 25, 1950; d. Ben and Sylvia (Zukerman) Schreiber; m. John Eric Jacoby, Aug. 3, 1975; children: Elizabeth, Charles. BA magna cum laude, Barnard Coll., 1972; PhD in Fine Arts, Harvard U., 1983. Expert dept. old master drawings Sotheby's, N.Y.C., 1979-82; fine art cons. Nordstern Ins. Co. Am., N.Y.C., 1985-87; from head dept. old master drawings to sr. tech. expert Christie's, N.Y.C., 1989-92; pvt. practice N.Y.C., 1993—; lectr. in field. Contbr. articles to profl. jours. Chair arts & culture adv. com. 14th Congl. Dist., N.Y.C., 1992—; active Sec. Navys Adv. Subcom. on Naval History, Washington, 1995—. Guest scholar J. Paul Getty Art Mus., Malibu, 1986; Smithsonian fellow, 1978-79, Agnes Mongan Travelling fellow Harvard U., 1977. Fellow The Pierpont Morgan Libr.; mem. Am. Assn. Mus., Appraisers Assn. Am., N.Y. Hist. Soc. (search com. 1994, collections com., bd. trustees 1994—, co-chair cmty. adv. bd. 1994—, juror scholastic art & writing awards 1995), Soc. History Art France, Harvard Club N.Y., Tech. Adv. Svc. Attys.

JACOBY, JEANMARIE K., lawyer; b. Bklyn., Aug. 30, 1961; d. John Thomas and Marylou (Backus) J. BA, Ramapo Coll., 1983; JD, Western New Eng. Coll., 1986. With Weston Fin. Group, Wellesley, Mass., 1986-88; estate and bus. planning atty. Allmerica Fin., Worcester, Mass., 1989-91; dir. advanced sales Travelers, Hartford, Conn., 1991-94; dir. advanced sales and mktg. support Am. Gen. Life, Houston, 1994—; mem. advanced sales com. LIMBA, Hartford, 1991—. Mem. NAFE, Nat. Assn. Life Underwriters, Am. Soc. CLU and ChFC. Home: 802 Omar Ave Houston TX 77009 Office: Am Gen Life 2727-1 Allen Pkwy Houston TX 77019

JACOBY, PATRICIA JOHNSON, public relations executive; b. Pitts.; d. Rutherford Thompson and Orpha Marion (Emory) Johnsone; m. Harold Smith Johnson, 1950 (dec. Sept. 1963); children: Rutherford Scott Johnson, Julie Paige Johnson Lambdin; m. Alfred William JaCoby, 1970. AA, U. Calif., Berkeley; BJ, U. Mo., MA. Mem. news staff UPI, Dallas, Stockton (Calif.) Record, San Diego Union; editor, pub. Del Mar (Calif.) Surfcomber/ Rancho Santa Fe Times; pub. rels. adminstr. U. Calif., San Diego. Chair Del Mar Planning Commn., Design Rev. Bd., Del Mar; chair pub. rels. com. Planned Parenthood, San Diego, Balboa Theatre Found., San Diego; chair VCSP Cancer Ctr., San Diego. Mem. San Diego Mus. Art, San Diego Mus. Contemporary Art, Performing Arts League (pres. 1995—), LEAD, Sierra Club, Alpha Phi (v.p.). Home: 213 Ocean View Ave Del Mar CA 92014

JACOBY, TAMAR, journalist, author; b. N.Y.C., Nov. 28, 1954; d. Irving and Alberta (Smith) J. Grad., UN Internat. Sch., N.Y.C., 1972; BA, Yale U., 1976. Writer, editor Hudson Rsch. Europe, Paris, 1976-77; editorial staff N.Y. Rev. Books, 1977-81; dep. editor Op-Ed Page N.Y. Times, 1981-87; sr. writer Newsweek, N.Y.C., 1987-89, justice editor, 1988-89; self employed author, 1989—; lectr. Yale U., New Haven, Conn., 1986-90; instr. The New Sch. for Social Rsch., N.Y.C., 1991. Author articles for Fgn. Affairs, The New Republic, Times Lit. Commentary, Dissent, The Washington Monthly, others. Dir. N.Y. Civil Rights Coalition. Fellow Nat. Endowment for the Humanitites, 1992, Alicia Patterson journalism fellow, 1990. Mem. Coun. Fgn. Rels. Home: 78 Hawthorne Pl Montclair NJ 07042

JACOX, ADA KATHRYN, nurse, educator; b. Centreville, Mich.; d. Leo H. and Lilian (Gilbert) J. BS in Nursing Edn., Columbia U., 1959; MS in Child Psychiat. Nursing, Wayne State U., 1965; PhD in Sociology, Case Western Res. U., 1969. R.N. Dir. nursing Children's Hosp.-Northville State Hosp., Mich., 1961-63; assoc. prof., then prof. Coll. Nursing Univ. Iowa, Iowa City, 1969-76; prof., assoc. dean Sch. Nursing U. Colo., Denver, 1976-80; prof., dir. rsch. ctr. sch. nursing U. Md., Balt., 1980-90, dir. ctr. for health policy rsch., 1988-90; prof. sch. nursing, Independence Found. chair health policy Johns Hopkins U., Balt., 1990-95; assoc. dean for rsch. Wayne State U. Coll. Nursing, Detroit, 1996; co-chmn. panels to develop clin. guidelines for pain mgmt. U.S. Agy. for Health Care Policy and Rsch., 1990-94. Co-author: Organizing for Independent Nursing Practice, 1977 (named Book of Yr., Am. Jour. Nursing); A Process Measure for Primary Care: The Nurse Practitioner Rating Form, 1981 (named Book of Yr., Am. Jour. Nursing). Editor: Pain: A Sourcebook for Nurses, 1977 (named Book of Yr., Am. Jour. Nursing). Chair AIDS study sect. NIH, 1990-92. Recipient Disting. Achievement in Nursing Rsch. and Scholarship, Alumni Assn. Columbia U. Tchrs. Coll., 1975, Disting. Alumna award Ft. Wayne U. Coll. Nursing, 1994, award for spl. achievement Nat. Coalition for Cancer Survivorship, 1994; Carver fellow U. Iowa, 1972. Fellow Am. Acad. Nursing; mem. ANA (dir. 1978-82, 1st v.p. 1982-84), AMA (mem. health policy agenda work group 1983-86), Am. Nurses Found. (pres. 1982-85), Am. Acad. Nursing, Nat. Acad. Scis. (com. on nat. needs for biomed. and rsch. pers. 1984-87), Inst. of Medicine, Wayne State U. Alumni Assn. (Disting. Alumni award 1994). Office: Wayne State U Coll Nursing 5557 Cass Ave Detroit MI 48202

JACOX, MARILYN ESTHER, chemist; b. Utica, N.Y., Apr. 26, 1929; d. Grant Burlingame and Mary Elizabeth (Dunn) J. BA, Syracuse U., 1951; PhD, Cornell U., 1956; ScD (hon.), Syracuse U., 1993. Postdoctoral research assoc. U. N.C., Chapel Hill, 1956-58; fellow in fundamental research Mellon Inst., Pitts., 1958-62; rsch. chemist Nat. Bur. Stds., Washington, 1962—; fellow Nat. Bur. Stds. (now Nat. Inst. Stds. and Tech.), Gaithersburg, Md., 1986-95, sci. emeritus, 1996—. Mem. editorial bd. Revs. Chem. Intermediates, 1984-89, Jour. Chem. Physics, 1989-91; contbr. numerous articles to profl. jours. Recipient gold medal U.S. Dept. Commerce, 1970, Fed. Women's award, 1973, Lippincott award, 1989, Hillebrand prize Chem. Soc. Washington, 1990, WISE lifetime achievement award, 1991. Fellow AAAS, Am. Phys. Soc., Washington Acad. Scis. (Phys. Sci. award 1968); mem. Am. Chem. Soc., Exec. Women in Govt. (sec. 1981, vice-chmn. 1982), Inter-Am. Photochemical Soc. (exec. com. 1978-79), Sigma Xi (pres. elect NBS chpt. 1987-88, pres. 1988-89). Office: Nat Inst Standards & Tech Optical Technology Division Gaithersburg MD 20899

JAEGER, ELLEN LOUISE, small business owner; b. Spokane, Wash., Nov. 11, 1949; d. L. Walter and Patricia E. (Kelly) Matson; m. Jerald J. Jaeger, Mar. 24, 1948; children: Jennifer Ann, Jason Joseph. BS in Bus. Mgmt., Lewis-Clark State Coll., 1993; postgrad., U. Idaho, 1993—. Owner, operator, buyer Reflections Gift Shop, Coeur d'Alene, Idaho, 1986—; cons. Eagle Springs Gift Shop, Bonners Ferry, Idaho, 1987-90; appointee N.W. Retail Adv. Bd., Seattle, 1991-95. mem. bd., fundraiser Cancer Cmty. Charities, 1971-91, hon. mem. bd., 1991—; bd. mem. PTA-Lakes Jr. H.S., 1980-84, pres. bd., 1983-85; vol. office support staff Coeur d'Alene H.S., 1985-86; fundraiser United Way Kootenia County, 1988; bd. dirs. Kootenai Med. Ctr. Found., Coeur d'Alene, 1996, Coeur d'Alene Pub. Libr. Found., 1996. Mem. Rotary Internat. (chmn. group study exch. com. 1992—), Coeur d'Alene C. of C. (bd. mem.). Home: 1125 Stanley Hill Dr Coeur D Alene ID 83814

JAEGER, VIVIAN G., health facility administrator; b. Bronxville, N.Y., Aug. 17, 1956; d. Robert S. and Virginia (Lloyd) J. BSN, Skidmore Coll., 1978; MA, NYU, 1985. RN, N.Y. Instr. perioperative svcs. N.Y.H.-C.U.M.C., N.Y.C., coord. perioperative svcs., asst. dir. perioperative svcs.; dir. operating room svcs. Beth Israel Med. Ctr., N.Y.C., chair RWJ-PEW grant; dir. edn. and staff devel. Pascack Valley Hosp.; adj. prof. Dominican Coll. Reviewing editor Aspen Publ. Perioperative Nursing; contbr. articles to profl. publs. Former v.p. alumni programs Skidmore Coll., Saratoga, N.Y. Mem. ANA, Assn. Operating Rm. Nurses, Am. Assn. Critical Care Nurses, Am. Orgn. Nurse Execs.

JAEHNE, KAREN ELAINE, not-for-profit organization administrator; b. Reno, Nev., Sept. 2, 1948; m. Ernest H. Latham Jr., July 4, 1979 (div. May 1991); 1 child, Charlotte Latham. BA in Lit. and Philosophy, U. Nev., 1970; MA in Classics, U. Calif., Santa Barbara, 1972; postgrad. in Classics, Freie U., Berlin, 1973-77. Various staff assignments Berlin Internat. Film Festival, 1975-81; film programmer RAP Smithsonian Institution, Washington, 1982-86; acquisitions prodn. exec. Internat. Spectrafilm, N.Y.C., 1986-89; writer N.Y. Post, N.Y.C., 1989; exec. dir. St. Andrew's Soc. of N.Y., 1995—; bd. dirs. Cineaste Publ., N.Y., Hawk & Handsaw Shakespeare Co., Feminists for Free Expression, N.Y.; instr. Fgn. Svc. Inst., Roslyn, Va., 1983-86; film reviewer Film Scouts, Am. On Line. Editor Cineaste mag., 1986-92, Magill's Encyclopedia of Foreign Film, 1986, Almanac of Country Music, 1992, The Collected Works of Paddy Chayefsky, 1994, screenplays of William Goldman, 1995; film producer White Star, 1982, Jack & His Friends, Walls & Bridges, Chelsea Hotel, Vagablonde, 1992—; contbr. articles to mags.; film reviewer: Film Scouts, America on Line. Bd. dirs. Women Make Movies Dist., N.Y., 1986-89; speech and copy writer Com. to Elect Monika Braggs, Bronx, N.Y., 1993; exec. dir. St. Andrew's Soc. of the State of N.Y., 1995. Democrat.

JAFFE, ELAINE JUNE, creative fiberwork designer; b. Cleve., June 9, 1924; d. Benjamin and Beatrice (Rapkin) Michael; m. Leonard Jaffe, Oct. 23, 1949; children: Barbara (dec.), Ronald Howard, Norman David. tchr. fibrework for adults and children, 1975—. Originator (banner project) Threads of Jewish Life, 1986, (wall-hangings) Jerusalem 3000, 1996; exhibited fibre work in galleries, 1975—. Democrat. Jewish. Home: 418 Sisson Ct Silver Spring MD 20902

JAFFE, GWEN DANER, museum educator; b. N.Y.C., July 8, 1937; d. Izzy and Selma (Hess) Daner; m. Anthony R. Jaffe; children: Thomas, Elizabeth. BA in Art History, Skidmore Coll., 1957; cert. in elem. tchg., Hofstra U., 1960; postgrad., N.Y. Sch. Interior Design, 1964, Columbia U., 1973. Spl. edn. tchr. Payne Whitney Hosp., 1958-65, Bd. Coop. Ednl. Svcs., Westchester, N.Y., 1958-65; designer Jaffe-Halperin Design Firm, N.Y.C., 1965-86; tour guide Walker Art Ctr., Mpls., 1987-89; tchr. Art Express Sch.

mus. program Carnegie Mus. of Art, Pitts., 1989—; mem. staff Peace Arts Exch. program Pitts. Children's Mus., 1992-93; designer briefcases and handbags Gwynne Collection, 1993—. Mem. Fiber Arts Guild. Home: 5321 5th Ave Pittsburgh PA 15232-2142

JAFFE, LOUISE, English language educator, creative writer; b. Bronx, N.Y., May 17, 1936; d. Joseph and Anna (Movitz) Neuwirth; m. Steven Jaffe, Aug. 26, 1962 (div. 1975); 1 child, Aaron Lawrence; m. Leo Gerber, 1993. BA, Queens Coll., 1956; MA, Hunter Coll., 1959; PhD, U. Nebr., 1965; MFA, Brooklyn Coll., 1991. Instr. Kingsborough Community Coll., Bklyn, 1965-67, asst. prof., 1967-70, assoc. prof. English, 1970-88, prof., 1989-95, prof. emerita, 1995—. Author: Hyacinths and Biscuits, 1985, Wisdom Revisited, 1987, Light Breaks, 1995, also numerous poetry and fiction stories. Mem. editl. bd. Cmty. Review CUNY, 1984—. Recipient First prize N.Y. Poetry Forum, 1980, First prize, First honorable mention Shelley Soc. N.Y., 1983, 84, and others. Democrat. Jewish. Avocations: creative writing, scrabble, crossword puzzles, people-watching, attending and giving poetry readings. Home: 2411 E 3rd St Brooklyn NY 11223-5357 Office: Kingsborough Community Coll Oriental Blvd Brooklyn NY 11235-4906

JAFFE, RONA, author; b. N.Y.C., June 12, 1932; d. Samuel and Diana (Ginsberg) J. BA, Radcliffe Coll., 1951. Sec. N.Y.C., 1952; assoc. editor Fawcett Publs., N.Y.C., 1952-56. Author: The Best of Everything, 1958, Away From Home, 1960, The Last of the Wizards, 1961, Mr. Right Is Dead, 1965, The Cherry in the Martini, 1966, The Fame Game, 1969, The Other Woman, 1972, Family Secrets, 1974, The Last Chance, 1976, Class Reunion, 1979, Mazes and Monsters, 1981, After the Reunion, 1985, An American Love Story, 1990, The Cousins, 1995. Office: Janklow & Nesbit Assocs 598 Madison Ave New York NY 10022-1614

JAFFE, SUZANNE DENBO, investment banker, entrepreneur; b. Washington, Apr. 17, 1943; d. Milton Carl and Beatrice (Altman) Denbo; m. Howard M. Jaffe, Sept. 10, 1967 (div. 1973). BA, U. Pa., 1965; postgrad., NYU, 1965-67. Picture researcher Time, Inc., N.Y.C., 1967-68; analyst L.M. Rosenthal & Co., N.Y.C., 1968-69, Standard & Poor's Intercapital, Inc., N.Y.C., 1969-70; portfolio mgr., ptnr. Century Capital Assocs., N.Y.C., 1971-81; v.p. Highland Capital Corp., N.Y.C., 1982; exec. v.p. Lehman Mgmt. Co., Inc., N.Y.C., 1982-83; dep. compt. N.Y. State, N.Y.C., 1983-85; pres. S.D.J. Assocs., N.Y.C., 1985-89; mng. dir. Angelo, Gordon & Co., N.Y.C., 1990-93, Hamilton & Co., N.Y.C., 1994—; bd. dirs. Crossrods Capital LP, Hartford, Conn., Olin Corp., Nat. Postal Forum; bd. dirs., treas. Rsch. Corp.; trustee U.S. Social Security-Medicare, Washington, 1984-90; mem. adv. coun. Employees Retirement Income Security Act, U.S. Dept. Labor, Washignton, 1985-88. Bd. dirs. Fordham U., 1984—, mem. exec. com., 1992—, chmn. audit and fin. com., 1992—; assoc. trustee U. Pa., Phila., 1987—, treas. trustees coun. Penn women, 1991—; bd. dirs. Planned Parenthood, N.Y.C., 1976-83, Investor Responsibility Rsch. Ctr., 1984-85, Coun. Governing Bds. State Colls. and Univs.; mem. N.Y. women in bus. com. Overseas Edn. Fund Internat.; mem. adv. com. Children's Aid Soc. Mem. Internat. Women's Forum (bd. dirs., former sec., v.p. 1995—, v.p. leadership), Women's Forum (pres. 1992-95, bd. dirs., treas. 1987-89), Fin. Women's Assn. (treas. 1985-87), Columbia U. Grad. Sch. Bus. Adv. Bd., Harmonie Club (N.Y.C.), Econ. Club (N.Y.C.). Democrat. Jewish. Home: 784 Park Ave # 5A New York NY 10021-3553

JAGACINSKI, CAROLYN MARY, psychology educator; b. Orange, N.J., Apr. 12, 1949; d. Theodore Edward and Eleanor Constance (Thys) Jagacinski; m. Richard Justus Schweickert, Dec. 27, 1980; children: Patrick, Kenneth. AB with honors in psychology, Bucknell U., 1971; MA in Psychology, U. Mich., 1975, PhD in Psychology and Edn., 1978. Rsch. assoc. U. Mich., Ann Arbor, 1978-79; rsch. assoc. Purdue U., West Lafayette, Ind., 1979-80, vis. asst. prof., 1980-83, rsch. psychologist, 1983-86, vis. lectr., 1986-88, asst. dean, 1988-89, asst. prof. psychology, 1988-94, assoc. prof., 1994—. Contbr. articles to profl. jours. U. Mich. predoctoral fellow, 1977-78, dissertation grantee, 1977-78; Exxon Edn. Found. grantee, 1983-84. Mem. APA, Midwestern Psychol. Assn., Soc. for Judgment and Decision Making, Am. Ednl. Rsch. Assn., Psychonomic Soc., Sigma Xi, Psi Chi. Office: Purdue Univ Dept Psychol Scis West Lafayette IN 47907

JAGIELO, LINDA MARIE, early childhood teacher educator; b. Chgo., Nov. 22, 1949; d. Edward Stanley and Betty (Mokos) J. BS in Upper Elem. Edn., U. Wis., Oshkosh, 1972; BS in Early Childhood Edn., U. Wis., Stevens Point, 1974; MEPD in Early Childhood Adminstrn., U. Wis., Whitewater, 1983; postgrad., Kent State U., 1991—. Cert. tchr. PreK-8, gen. edn., PreK-9, music-all, Wis. Team tchr. Wee Know Nursery Sch., Hartland, Wis., 1976-77; program asst. U. Wis., Whitewater, 1978-81; dir./tchr. Adams Co. (Wis.) Child Devel. Ctr., 1983-84; tchr. Children's Learning & Care Ctr. U. Wis., Oshkosh, 1982-83; tchr./ctr. supervisor 3 County Head Start U. Wis., Neenah, 1984-89; acad. staff/instrnl. svc. U. Wis., Menomonie, 1989-90; mem. instrnl. acad. staff U. Wis., Oshkosh, 1990-91; tchg. fellow Kent (Ohio) State U., 1991-94, part-time instr., 1994-96; asst. prof. S.W. State U., Marshall, Minn., 1996. Contbr. chpt. to book; presenter in field. Mem. separated and divorced adv. com. Office of Marriage and Families, Catholic Diocese of Youngstown, Ohio, 1995-96. Recipient Univ. fellow Kent State U., 1994-95. Mem. AAUW, ASCD, NOW, Am. Ednl. Rsch. Assn. (mem. various spl. interest groups), Nat. Assn. for the Edn. of Young Children, Nat. Assn. Early Childhood Tchr. Educators, Nat Head Start Assn., Nat. Orgn. Child Devel. Lab. Schs., Ohio Assn. Study Coop. in Edn. (charter bd. dirs. 1993-96, chair resource and social policy com. 1993-96, corresponding sec., 1994-96, planning com. mem. 1993-96), Ohio Assn. Edn. Young Children (co-chair pub. policy com. 1994-96), Internat. Assn. for Study of Coop. in Edn. (planning com. 1996 internat. conf. 1994—), Educators for Social Reponsibility, Assn. for Children Edn. Internat., Orgn. Mondiale pour l'Edn. Prescolaire (OMEP-U.S. nat. com.), Phi Delta Kappa (co-v.p. mem. 1993-95, grad. student rep. 1995-96). Democrat. Roman Catholic. Office: SW State U Dept Edn 1501 State St Marshall MN 56258

JAGO, SANDRA LEE, physical education educator; b. Poughkeepsie, N.Y., Dec. 11, 1947; d. Howard B. and Shirley M. (Rymph) J. BS, SUNY, Cortland, 1970; MS, SUNY, Brockport, 1975. Cert. physical edn. tchr. Physical edn. instr. Fairport Ctrl. Schs, N.Y., 1970—; coach girls varsity basketball Fairport Ctrl. Schs, N.Y., 1971-77,; girls modified soccer coach Fairport Ctrl. Schs., 1979-90, girls modified basketball coach, 1978-86, girls modified volley ball coach, 1978—. Bldg. rep. Fairport Edn. Assn., 1974, 90, negotiating team, 1990. Fulbright Tchr. Exchange, 1987-88. Mem. AAHPERD (Ctrl. Western Zone N.Y. treas. 1989-93, pres. 1993-95, recipient Amazing Person award, 1991), Fairport Edn. Assn., N.Y. State United Tchr. Home: 610 Marsh Rd Pittsford NY 14534-3314 Office: Johanna Pernin Middle Sch 85 Potter Pl Fairport NY 14450-2444

JAGODZINSKI, RUTH CLARK, nursing administrator; b. N.Y.C., Feb. 24, 1938; d. John Kirkland and Ruth Fishwick Clark; m. Thomas John Jagodzinski, Nov. 1962 (div. 1974); children: Christine Ruth, James Clark. Diploma, Roosevelt Hosp. Sch. Nursing, 1959. Cert. substance abuse counselor and program adminstrn.; RN, Nev., N.Y. Head nurse drug/alcohol detox Sunrise Hosp., Las Vegas, Nev., 1973-75; program coord. careunit North Las Vegas (Nev.) Hosp., 1975-77; co-owner, adminstr. Sunrise Home Health, Las Vegas, 1983-89; dir. pers. PRN Home Health, Las Vegas, 1990-91; dir. home health svcs. Med. Pers. Pool, Las Vegas, 1990-92; dir. profl. svc. Olsten Kimberly Quality Care, Las Vegas, 1992-95; adminstr. Valley Home Health Valley Hosp., Las Vegas, 1995—; mem. Nev. State Cert. Bd. Substance Abuse Counselors and Program Adminstrs., 1976-86, 90—, pres., 1980-86. Mem. Nev. Gov.'s Adv. Bd. for Alcohol and Drugs; pres., bd. dirs. We Care Found., 1974—; trustee Community Referral Svcs., 1975-80; bd. dirs. Alcohol Program So. Nev., 1975-85; mem. In-Home Care Svcs. Clark County, 1978-83; bd. dirs. So. Nev. Girls Clubs, 1984-86; mem. adv. bd. Nathan Adelson Hospice, Las Vegas, 1977-89; chmn. nursing subcom. profl. ednn. div. So. Nev. chpt. Am. Cancer Soc., 1989-90, mem. Nev. Bd. Com. on Occupational Excellence, 1989-90. Recipient Community Svc. award Alcohol Program So. Nev., 1978, Svc. award We Care Found., 1989. Mem. Home Health Care Assns. Nev. (v.p. 1984-86, 94-95, pres. 1995—). Home: 4573 Royal Ridge Way Las Vegas NV 89103-5034 Office: Valley Home Health 620 Shadow Ln Ste G Las Vegas NV 89106

JAHNEL, AMY ELIZABETH, controller; b. Phila., Oct. 8, 1969; d. Roger Clinton and Judy Carol (Breckenridge) J. BSW, U. Tex., 1991; postgrad., U. Akron, 1992-94. Lic. social worker, Tex. Contr. Check Tech., Inc., Dallas, 1984—, asst. sec., 1995—. Mem. NOW, Rotary (cmty. svc. dir. 1996—), Tex. Ex-Students Assn., Mensa. Office: Check Tech Inc 10610 Metric Ste 100 Dallas TX 75243

JAILLET, TINA STEVENS, art association administrator; b. Boston, Mar. 16, 1962; d. Kevin J. and Shirley S. (Stevens) Kearney; m. Patrick Jaillet, July 11, 1987; children: Xavier, Clovis. BFA, Tufts U., 1987. Co-founder Artists' Coalition of Austin, 1992; exec. dir. Artists Coalition of Austin, 1992—; bd. dirs. Artists Coalition of Austin. Art exhibited in U.S., France, and Switzerland. Home: 706 Harris Ave Austin TX 78705 Office: Artists Coalition Austin 403 Baylor St Austin TX 78703

JAKAB, IRENE, psychiatrist; b. Oradea, Rumania; came to U.S., 1961, naturalized, 1966; d. Odon and Rosa A. (Riedl) J. MD, Ferencz József U., Kolozsvar, Hungary, 1944; lic. in psychology, pedagogy, philosophy cum laude, Hungarian U., Cluj, Rumania, 1947; PhD summa cum laude, Pazmany Peter U., Budapest, 1948; Dr honoris causa, U. Besançon, France, 1982. Diplomate Am. Bd. Psychiatry. Rotating intern Ferencz József U., 1943-44; resident in psychiatry Univ. Hosp., Kolozsvar, 1944-47, resident in neurology, 1947-50; resident internal medicine Univ. Hosp. for Internal Medicine, Pécs, Hungary, 1950-51; chief physician Univ. Hosp. for Neurology and Psychiatry, Pécs, 1951-59; staff neuropathol. rsch. lab. Neurol. Univ. Clinic, Zurich, 1959-61; sect. chief Kans. Neurol. Inst., Topeka, 1961-63; dir. rsch. and edn., 1966; resident psychiatry Topeka State Hosp., 1963-66; asst. psychiatrist McLean Hosp., Belmont, Mass., 1966-67; assoc. psychiatrist McLean Hosp., 1967-74; prof. psychiatry U. Pitts. Med. Sch., 1974-89, prof. emerita, 1989—, co-dir. med. student edn. in psychiatry, 1981-89; dir. John Merck Program, 1974-81; mem. faculty dept. psychiatry Med. Sch., Pecs, 1951-59; asst. Univ. Hosp. Neurology, Zurich, 1959-61; assoc. psychiatry Harvard U., Boston, 1966-69, asst. prof. psychiatry, 1969-74, program dir. grad course mental retardation, 1970-87; lectr. psychiatry, 1974—. Author: Dessins et Peintures des Aliénés, 1956, Zeichnungen und Gemälde der Geisteskranken, 1956; editor: Psychiatry and Art, 1968, Art Interpretation and Art Therapy, 1969, Conscious and Unconscious Expressive Art, 1971, Transcultural Aspects of Psychiatric Art, 1975; co-editor: Dynamische Psychiatrie, 1974; editorial bd.: Confinia Psychiatrica, 1975-81; contbr. articles to profl. jours. Recipient 1st prize Benjamin Rush Gold medal award for sci. exhibit, 1980, Bronze Chris plaque Columbus Film Festival, 1980, Leadership award Am. Assn. on Mental Deficiency, 1980; Menninger Sch. Psychiatry fellow, Topeka, 1963-66. Mem. AMA, Am. Psychol. Assn., Am. Psychiat. Assn., Société Medico Psychologique de Paris, Internat. Rorschach Soc., N.Y. Acad. Scis., Internat. Soc. Psychopathology of Expression (v.p. 1959—), Am. Soc. Psychopathology of Expression (chmn. 1965—, Ernst Kris Gold Medal award 1988), Royal Soc. of Medicine (overseas fellow), Internat. Soc. Child Psychiatry and Allied Professions, Internat. Assn. Knowledge Engrs. (v.p. for medicine 1988-95), Deutschsprachige Gesellschaft für Psychopathologie des Ausdruckes (hon. Prinzhorn prize 1967), Hungarian Psychiat. Assn. (hon. 1992). Home and Office: 74 Lawton St Brookline MA 02146-2501

JAKUB, PAULA SUE, association administrator; b. Omaha, Nov. 3, 1957; d. Arthur Coulter and Anne Edith (Kabbert) Roxlau; m. Michael Andrew Jakub; children: Neil, Elizabeth. Registered health underwriter. Customer svc. supr. Mut. of Omaha Ins. Co., Omaha, 1978-88; v.p. for ops. Am. Fgn. Svcs. Protective Assn., Washington, 1988—; bd. dirs. Nat. Assn. for Sr. Living Industries, Annapolis. Leader Girl Scouts USA, Washington, 1987-93; bd. dirs. PTO, Dale City, Va., 1991-93, Prince William Softball Assn., Dale City, 1991—. Mem. Nat. Assn. Health Underwriters. Home: 6385 Cherry Ridge Ct Manassas VA 22111-3859

JAKUCYN, NATALIE, secondary education educator; b. Chgo., Jan. 15, 1952; d. Joseph Frank and Irene Valerie (Rozak) J. BS in Math. with highest honors, DePaul U., 1974; MS in Tchg., U. Ill., Chgo., 1985. Cert. secondary edn. grades 7-12. Math. and sci. tchr., dept. chair The Willows Acad., Niles, Ill., 1975-85; math. tchr. Evanston (Ill.) Twp. H.S., 1985-86; mng. editor U. Chgo. (Ill.) Sch. Math. Project, 1986-88; dir. Metro Achievement Ctr., Chgo., 1988-89; nat. math. cons., product mgr. Scott Foresman, Glenview, Ill., 1989-94; math. tchr. Glenbrook South H.S., Glenview, 1994—; co-founder, adv. bd., vol. tchr. Metro Achievement Ctr., Chgo., 1985—. Co-author: UCSMP Advanced Algebra, 1990, 93, 96. Precinct capt., canvasser Ind. Precinct Orgn., Chgo., 1972-74; bd. dirs. St. Mary of the Angels Sch., Chgo.; lector, commentator St. Margaret Mary Ch., Chgo., 1989-93. State scholar Ill. State Scholarship Commn., 1970. Mem. Math. Assn. Am., Nat. Coun. Tchrs. Math., Ill. Coun. Tchrs. Math., Met. Math. Club Chgo. (bd. dirs., co-editor newsletter 1990-93, pres. 1996-97), Alpha Lambda Delta (historian 1972-73), Kappa Gamma Pi (Outstanding Regional Mem. 1990). Roman Catholic. Home: 3950 W Bryn Mawr Ave # 202 Chicago IL 60659 Office: Glenbrook South HS 4000 W Lake Ave Glenview IL 60025

JALALI, BEHNAZ, psychiatrist, educator; b. Mashad, Iran, Jan. 26, 1944; came to U.S., 1968; d. Badiolah and Bahieh (Shahidi) Samimy; m. Mehrdad Jalali, Sept. 18, 1968. MD, Tehran (Iran) U., 1968. Rotating intern Burlington County Meml. Hosp., Mt. Holly, N.J., 1968-69; resident in psychiatry U. Md. Hosp., Balt., 1970-73; asst. prof. psychiatry dept. psychiatry Sch. Medicine Rutgers U., Piscataway, N.J., 1973-76, Yale U., New Haven, Conn., 1976-81; assoc. clin. prof. psychiatry Yale U., New Haven, 1981-85; assoc. clin. prof. psychiatry dept. psychiatry UCLA, 1985-94, clin. prof. psychiatry dept. psychiatry Sch. Medicine, 1994—; dir. psychotherapy Sch. Medicine Rutgers U., Piscataway, 1973-76; dir. family therapy unit dept. psychiatry Yale U., New Haven, 1976-85; chief clin. svcs., mental health clin. coord., med. student educator West L.A. VA Hosp., 1987—. Author: (with others) Ethnicity and Family Therapy, 1982, Clinical Guidlines in Cross-Cultural Mental Health, 1988; contbr. articles to profl. jours. Fellow Am. Psychiatric Assn., Am. Orthopsychiatry Assn., Am. Assn. Social Psychiatry; mem. Am. Family Therapy Assn., So. Calif. Psychiatric Assn. (chair com. for women 1992), World Fedn. Mental Health. Home: 1203 Roberto Ln Los Angeles CA 90077-2304 Office: UCLA Dept Psychiatry West LA VA Med Ctr B116a12 Los Angeles CA 90073-1003

JAMATE, CAROLYN J., marketing professional; b. Bklyn., Sept. 3, 1969. BA in Journalism and Mass Comm., NYU, 1993. Comm. coord. KPMG Peat Marwick, N.Y.C., 1993-95; editl. and mktg. sr. assoc. Ernst & Young LLP, N.Y.C., 1995—. Campaign worker City Coun., S.I., 1994. Mem. NAFE. Roman Catholic. Office: Ernst & Young LLP 787 7th Ave New York NY 10019

JAMES, AMABEL BOYCE, freelance writer; b. Balt., Oct. 13, 1952; d. John Cowman George and Barbara Allen (Cobb) Boyce; m. Hamilton Evans James, Aug. 25, 1973; children: Meredith Evans, Rebecca Lee, Hamilton Boyce. AB, Wellesley Coll., 1974. Chartered fin. analyst, 1981. Systems analyst John Hancock Mut. Life Ins. Co., Boston, 1974-75; asst. buyer Lord & Taylor, N.Y.C., 1975; economist Lionel D. Edie, N.Y.C., 1977, E.F. Hutton & Co., N.Y.C., 1978-79, Schroder Capital Mgmt., N.Y.C., 1979-82; freelance writer N.Y.C., 1984—; cons. Keck & Co., N.Y.C., 1984. Editor, contbr. author numerous articles to popular mags., newsletters. Vol. Jr. League City of N.Y., 1975-93; bd. dirs. Friends Henry St. Settlement House, 1977-80; bd. dirs. Voluntary Assn. for Sr. Citizen Activities, 1984—, pres., 1994-96; cum laude speaker Garrison Forest Sch., 1993. Named Margaret Brand Smih lectr. So. Meth. U. Sch. Continuing Edn., 1980. Mem. N.Y. Soc. Security Analysts/Fin. Analyst Fedn., River Club of N.Y.C., Colony Cub, Tokeneke Club, Wee Burn Country Club, Little Harbor Club (Harbor Springs, Mich.). Republican. Episcopalian. Home and Office: 1001 Park Ave New York NY 10028-0935 Home: 50 Contentment Island Rd Darien CT 06820-6210 Also: PO Box 4223 Wequetonsing MI 49740

JAMES, BARBARA WOODWARD, small business owner, interior designer, antique appraiser, consultant; b. Owensboro, Ky., Feb. 14, 1936; d. J.T. and Thelma (Newman) Woodward; m. William E. James, Feb. 19, 1951 (div. June 1953); 1 child, Keith Douglas. Vice pres., Fla. Containers Inc., Sebring, 1978-81; v.p. Libra Ltd., 1980-88, Barda Svcs. Inc., Tampa, Fla., 1981-87; v.p., gen. mgr., owner BJ's Lounge of Tampa, Inc., 1981-86; founder, owner Flamingo Bar and Grill, Clearwater, Fla., 1986-89, BJ's Lounge, Tampa, 1989-94, The Clique, 1994—, Fanny's, Inc., Tampa, Fla., 1995—, The Oasis, Tampa, Fla., 1996—, Corsair Lounge, 1996—. Democrat. Roman Catholic.

JAMES, CHERYL, vocalist. Student, Queensborough C.C. Customer svc. rep. Sears Roebuck and Co.; vocalist Salt-N-Pepa, 1985—. Albums include Hot, Cool & Vicious (Platinum 1988), 1986, A Salt with a Deadly Pepa (Gold 1988), 1989, Blacks' Magic, 1990, A Blitz of Salt-N-Pepa, 1991, Juice, 1992; single releases include Push It (Gold 1988), Tramp; contbr. soundrack Colors. Contbr. For the Children: The Concert, 1993. Nominee Grammy award Nat. Acad. Recording Arts and Scis., 1989. Office: Next Plateau Records Salt-N-Pepa 1650 Broadway Rm 1103 New York NY 10019*

JAMES, CLARITY (CAROLYNE FAYE JAMES), mezzo-soprano; b. Wheatland, Wyo., Apr. 27, 1945; d. Ralph Everett and Gladys Charlotte (Johnson) J. Mus.B., U. Wyo., 1964; Mus.M., Ind. U., 1967. Cert. instr. Radiance Technique. Assoc. prof. voice Radford (Va.) U., 1990—; asst. prof. voice U. Iowa, Iowa City, 1968-72. Debut in opera as Madame Flora in: The Medium, St. Paul Opera, 1971; also sang role with Houston Grand Opera, 1972, Opera Theatre St. Louis, 1976, Augusta (Ga.) Opera Co., 1976; N.Y.C. Opera debut as Baroness in: The Young Lord, 1973; N.Y.C. Opera debut as Widow Begbick in Mahogonny, Opera Co. of Boston, 1973; created role Mother Rainey in: The Sweet Bye and Bye, 1973; Mrs. G. in: Captain Jinks, 1976; Mrs. Cratchit in A Christmas Carol (Musgrave), 1979; created Mrs. Doc in world premiere of A Quiet Place (Leonard Bernstein), Houston, 1983; debut Chgo. Lyric Opera, 1983, Vienna Staatsoper, 1986, National Symphony, 1986, Phila. Orch., 1986; numerous appearances with opera cos. throughout U.S. and fgn. countries including, Dallas Civic Opera, Cin. Opera Co., Netherlands Opera, Amsterdam, Florentine Opera. Rec. artist. Martha Baird Rockefeller grantee, Corbett Found. grantee, 1968; Met. Opera Assn. grantee; recipient Lillian Garabedian award Santa Fe Opera, 1967, Exemplary Alumni award U. Wyo., 1994; named Young Artist Nat. Fedn. Music Clubs, 1972. Office: Radford U Dept Music Radford VA 24142

JAMES, CLAUDIA ANN, business educator and trainer, motivational speaker; b. Kansas City, Mo., July 23, 1948; d. Claude Jr. and Edna Mae (Henderson) Hinton; m. Wavy L. James, Oct. 21, 1967 (dec. Apr. 1991); children: Edward Allan, Sheryl Evonne. AA, Maple Woods C.C., Kansas City, Mo., 1987; BSE cum laude, Mo. Western State Coll., St. Joseph, 1989. Fin. sec. EBC, Kansas City, Mo., 1977-87; instr. Capital City Bus. Coll., Kansas City, Mo., 1989-90, Career Point Bus. Sch., Kansas City, Mo., 1990-91; owner James Ednl. Mtgs./Seminars (JEMS), Kansas City, Mo., 1992—; instr. Am. Mgmt. Assn., 1993—, Mo. Western State Coll., St. Joseph, 1993—, Independence (Mo.) Sch. Dist., Park Hill Sch. Dist., Kansas City, Mo., North Kansas City Sch. Dist., 1993—, Maple Woods C.C., Kansas City, 1990—, Johnson County C.C., Overland Park, Kans., 1994—; guest spkr. on radio and TV. Mentor WNET-SBA, Kansas City, 1992—. Higgs Art scholar, 1987. Mem. Home Bus. Connection (v.p. 1994), Mo. Home BAsed Bus. Assn. (pres. 1994—), Clay County Women's Exch. (nteworking chair 1993—), Kansas City C. of C., Nat. Assn. Women Bus. Owners, Mo. We. State Coll. Alumni Assn., Kappa Delta Phi. Democrat. Baptist. Office: James Ednl Meetings/Seminar 1001 NE 86th St Kansas City MO 64155-2667

JAMES, ELIZABETH JOAN PLOGSTED, pediatrician, educator; b. Jefferson City, Mo., Jan. 15, 1939; d. Joseph Matthew Plogsted and Maxie Pearl (Manford) Plogsted Acuff; m. Ronald Carney James, Aug. 25, 1962; children: Susan Elizabeth, Jason Michael. BS in Chemistry, Lincoln U., 1960; MD, U. Mo., 1965. Diplomate Am. Bd. Pediatrics, Am. Bd. Neonatal-Perinatal Medicine. Resident physician pediatrics U. Mo. Hosps. & Clinics, Columbia, 1965-68, fellow in neonatology, 1968-69; dir. neonatal-perinatal medicine Children's Hosp. U. Mo. Hosps. & Clinics, 1971—; fellow in neonatal-perinatal medicine U. Colo. Hosps., Denver, 1969-71; from asst. to assoc. prof. pediatrics and obstetrics sch. medicine U. Mo., 1971-83, prof. child health and obstetrics, 1983—; dir. med. student edn. program dept. child health sch. medicine U. Mo., Columbia, 1989—. Mem. editl. bd. Mo. Medicine, 1983—; contbr. chpts. to books and articles to profl. jours. Fellow Am. Acad. Pediatrics (sect. neonatal-perinatal medicine); mem. Mo. State Med. Assn., Boone County Med. Soc., Alpha Omega Alpha. Roman Catholic. Office: U Mo Hosps & Clinics Childrens Hosp 1 Hospital Dr Columbia MO 65201-5276

JAMES, ESTELLE, economics educator; b. Bronx, N.Y., Dec. 1, 1935; d. Abraham and Lee (Zeichner) Dinerstein; m. Ralph James (div. 1971); children: Deborah, David; m. Harry Lazer, June 27, 1971 (wid. 1994). BS, Cornell U., 1956; PhD, MIT, 1961. Lectr., econs. dept. U. Calif., Berkeley, 1964-65; acting asst. prof. Stanford (Calif.) U., 1965-67; assoc. prof. SUNY, Stony Brook, 1967-72, prof., 1972-94, provost, div. Social and Behavioral Scis., 1975-79, chmn. dept., 1982-86; vis. scholar Yale U., Australian Nat. U., Tel Aviv U., Brookings Instn., others; cons. World Bank, Washington, 1986-91, sr. economist, 1991-94, lead economist, 1994—. Author: Hoffa and the Teamsters, 1964, The Nonprofit Sector in Market Economies, 1986, Public Policy and Private Education in Japan, 1988, The Nonprofit Sector in International Perspective, 1989, Averting the Old Age Crisis, 1994; contbr. numerous articles to profl. jours. Fellow Woodrow Wilson Internat. Ctr., Washington, 1981-82, Netherlands Inst. for Advanced Study, 1986-87, U.S. Dept. Edn., 1988, Sec. of Navy, 1990, AAUW, Soc. Sci. Rsch. Coun.; Rsch. grants Spencer Found, USAID, NEH, Exxon Edn. Found., NSF; recipient Fulbright award, 1979. Mem. Am. Econs. Assn. Office: World Bank 1818 H St NW Rm N 8023 Washington DC 20433

JAMES, ETTA, recording artist; b. L.A., Jan. 25, 1938; d. Dorothy Leatherwood Hawkins; m. Artis Dee Mills, May 20, 1969; children: Donto, Sametto. Blues singer Johnny Otis, L.A., 1954, Bihari Bros. Record Co., L.A., 1954, Leonard Chess Record Co., L.A., 1960, Warner Bros., L.A., 1978, Fantasy Record, L.A., 1985, Island Record, L.A., 1988. Record Albums include Come A Little Closer. The Essential Etta, 1993, Etta James Rocks the House, Etta, Red Hot'n Live, Her Greatest Sides, Vol. 1, Live, 1994, Mystery Lady: Songs of Billie Holliday, 1994 (Grammy award 1994), R&B Dynamite, 1987, reissue, 1991, The Right Time, 1992, Rocks the House, 1992, The Second Time Around, 1989, Seven Year Itch, 1988, Sticking to My Guns, 1990, The Sweetest Peaches, 1989, The Sweetest Peaches: Part One, 1989, The Sweetest Peaches: Part Two, 1989, Tell Mama, 1988, These Foolish Things: The Classic Balladry of Etta James, 1995, Time After Time, (with Eddie Cleanhead Vinson) Blues in the Night, Lane Supper Club, 1986, Blues in the Night, Vol. 2, 1987. Recipient Lifetime Achievement award Rigby & Blues Assn., 1989, Living Legends award KJLH, 1989, Image award NAACP, 1990 W.C. Handy award, 1989, Blue Soc. Hall of Fame award, 1991; 5th Handy Blues award, 1993, 94, Soul of Am. Music award, 1992; 8 Grammy nominations, Beyond War award, Best Song, 1984; inducted into Rock & Roll Hall of Fame, 1993; sang opening ceremony of 1984 Olympics. Office: Etta James Enterprises 642 W Athens Blvd Los Angeles CA 90044*

JAMES, GENEVA BEHRENS, secondary school educator; b. Marietta, Minn., Mar. 23, 1942; d. Siegfried and Dora (Schoenrock) Behrens; BS, Mankato State U., 1963; m. Howard James, Aug. 2, 1963; children: Scott, Dawn. Tchr. English high schs., Minn., 1964-65; instr. acctg., Adult Continuing Edn., Bellevue, Nebr., 1971-75, dir. Adult Basic Edn. Ctr., 1974-91, vol. coordinator, 1983-91, instr. secondary schs., 1980—, instr. computer literacy, 1984-91; Pilot Computer Program, 1987-88, seminar presenter Nebr. State Adult Edn. Assn., 1986, Commn. on Adult Basic Edn., 1987; mem. review bd. English Curriculum, 1996—, Bellevue (Nebr.) Pub. Schs. Computer Utilization Com., 1992—; mem. adv. bd. adult edn., 1993—; mem. student mgmt. team Bellevue West H.S., 1995, mem. disciplinary curriculum team, 1995; chmn. North Cen. Accreditation Team, 1996. Mem. exec. com. Boy Scouts Am., 1974-80; mem. metro cmty. PLUS task force, 1986-88. Recipient Indsl. Internship scholarship Careers 2000, 1996.Mem. AAUW, Nat. Assn. Public and Continuing Adult Edn., Adult and Continuing Edn. Assn. Nebr., NEA, Nat. Council Tchrs. English, WHAR Investment Club (pres.), Alpha Delta Kappa (chmn. scholarship com. 1985-86, 91—). Republican. Lutheran. Home: 1314 Hansen Ave Bellevue NE 68005-3016 Office: Bellevue West HS 1501 Thurston Ave Bellevue NE 68123-2498

JAMES, JEANNETTE ADELINE, state legislator, accountant; b. Maquoketa, Iowa, Nov. 19, 1929; d. Forest Claude and Winona Adeline

(Meyers) Nims; m. James Arthur James, Feb. 16, 1948; children: James Arthur Jr., Jeannette, Alice Marie. Student, Merritt Davis Sch. Commerce, Salem, Oreg., 1956-57. Payroll supr. Gen. Foods Corp., Woodburn, Oreg., 1956-66; cost acctg., inventory control clk. Pacific Fence & Wire Co., Portland, Oreg., 1966-67, office mgr., 1968-69; substitute rural carrier U.S. Post Office, Woodburn, 1967-68; owner, mgr., acct. and tax preparer James Bus. Svc., Goldendale, Wash., 1969-75, Anchorage, 1975-77, Fairbanks, Alaska, 1977-94; mem. Alaska Ho. of Reps., Juneau, 1993—; chmn. House State Affairs, 1995-96; vice chmn. Legis. Coun., 1995-96; workshop and seminar leader, 1989-91; instr. workshop Comm. Dynamics, 1988. Vice chmn. Klickitat County Dems., Goldendale, 1970-74; bd. dirs. Mus. and Art Inst., Anchorage, 1976-80; pres. Anchorage Internat. Art Inst., 1976-78; chmn. platting bd. Fairbanks North Star Borough, 1980-84, mem. Planning Commn., 1984-87; treas., vice chmn. 18th Dist. Reps., North Pole, Alaska, 1984-92; mem. City of North Pole Econ. Devel. Com., 1992-93. Mem. Internat. Tgn. in Comm. (winner speech contest 1981, 86), North Pole C. of C., Emblem Club, Rotary (treas. North Pole 1990), Eagles, Women of Moose. Presbyterian. Home: 3068 Badger Rd North Pole AK 99705-6117

JAMES, JUDY RAE, artist; b. Binghamton, N.Y., June 17, 1955; d. Fred Llewellyn and Thelma M. (Davis) J. BA with honors, SUNY, Binghamton, 1983, MBA in the Arts, 1990, MS in Acctg., 1993. Solo exhbns. include Roberson Mus. City Hall Gallery, Binghamton, N.Y., 1990, The Chalfonte Hotel, Cape May, N.J., 1990, SUNY at Binghamton Rosefsky Gallery, 1990, IBM Heritage Country Club, Endicott, N.Y., 1996; group exhbns. include Roberson Mus., 1994, SUNY at Binghamton, 1996; pvt. permanent collections include Catherine Rein, Anne French Thorington, Tom Kelley, Sol Polachek. N.Y. Found. for the Arts grantee, 1993. Home: 47 Albert St Johnson City NY 13790

JAMES, KAY LOUISE, management consultant, healthcare executive; b. Little Rock, Feb. 13, 1948; d. Charles Robert and Mary Virginia (Morgan) J. BA, Vanderbilt U., 1970; MBA, U. Chgo., 1986. Diplomate Am. Coll. Healthcare Execs.; CPA, Ill., Mo. Mgr. Wallace Community Mental Health Ctr., Nashville, 1973-78; sr. cons. Ernst & Whinney, Washington, 1978-79; sr. cons. Ernst & Whinney, Chgo., 1979-81, mgr., 1981-84; dir. Am. Hosp. Supply Corp., Evanston, Ill., 1984-85; mgr. Am. Hosp. Supply Fin. Corp., Evanston, 1985-86; sr. mgr. KPMG Peat Marwick, Kansas City, Mo., 1986-89, ptnr., 1989-92; ptnr. Katz, James & Assocs., Inc., Plymouth Meeting, Pa., 1992-93; pres. James Mgmt. Assocs., Inc., Nashville, 1994—; speaker healthcare topics various grad. programs and profl. assns.; mem. Women's Leadership Forum of Dem. Nat. Com. Reviewer The Coming Home Program, San Francisco, 1993. Mem. AICPA, Am. Hosp. Assn., Med. Group Mgmt. Assn., Healthcare Fin. Mgmt. Assn., The Healthcare Forum. Democrat. Office: James Mgmt Assocs 3200 W End Ave Ste 500 Nashville TN 37203-1322

JAMES, LINDA DIANE, special education educator; b. Dalhart, Tex., June 21, 1957; d. Lewis Daniel Wilcox and Claudene (Isaacs) Mayhan; m. Russell Dean James, Nov. 22, 1974; children: Steffanie, Ryan. BS, West Tex. A&M U., 1989, postgrad., 1991—. Cert. generic spl. edn. tchr., Tex.; cert. elem. sch. tchr., Tex. Tchr. spl. edn. reading and lang. Willow Vista Elem. Sch., River Road Ind. Sch. Dist., Amarillo, Tex., 1989-92, content mastery coord., 1993—, at-risk coord., 1994—; mem. strategic planning com. River Road Ind. Sch. Dist., 1992-93, mem. dist.-wide ednl. improvement coun., 1995-96; mem. Children's Emergency Home Com., 1995-96. Author pilot program Mastering Acad. Curriculum, Willow Vista Elem. Sch., 1993-95. Mem. com. mid. high youth group Lawndale Ch. of Christ, Amarillo, 1994-96; mem. com. Hi Plains Children's Home, Amarillo, 1995-96; mem. com. Boy Scouts Am., 1990-94, Explorer advisor, 1993-94; active Bonham Mid. Sch. PTA, 1993—; content mastery facilitator Region XVI, 1996; com. mem., treas. Boy Scouts Am., 1994-96. Named one of Outstanding Young Women of Am., 1988. Mem. Am. Tchrs. and Profl. Educators, Coun. for Exceptional Children (mem. divsn. for learning disabilities). Mem. Ch. of Christ. Office: Willow Vista Elem Sch 5703 W 48th Ave Amarillo TX 79109-5701

JAMES, LINDA GREEN, education specialist administrator, researcher; b. Memphis, Nov. 21, 1947; d. Frank Allen and Mary Elizabeth (Hankins) Green; m. John Newton Osborne, Feb. 7, 1975 (div. June 1979); 1 child, Suzanne; m. Phillip Harold James, Oct. 17, 1980; 1 child, Sarah Elizabeth. BA, U. Tenn., Martin, 1970; MA, Calif. State U., Long Beach, 1975; EdD in Higher Edn., U. Memphis, 1995. Instr. Memphis State U., 1979-85, dir. Wordsmith, 1984-85; asst. prof. Jackson (Tenn.) State C.C., 1985-90; adminstrv. intern State Tech. Inst. Memphis, 1990-91; asst. dir. Mid South Quality Productivity Ctr., Memphis, 1991-92; dir. acad. devel. State Tech. Inst. Memphis, 1992-93; edn. specialist Nat. Inst. Stds. and Tech., Gaithersburg, Md., 1993-94; systems mgmt. specialist U. Tenn., Martin, 1994-95; dir. assessment State Tech. Inst. Memphis, 1995—; bd. dirs., v.p. Greater Memphis Area Award for Quality; mem. adv. com. Nat. Govs. Conf. Edn., 1994; cons. City of Memphis Dept. Planning, 1993; mem. editl. bd. CQI Newsletter, 1994—; mem. adv. coun. Total Quality Learning Sys. Am. Soc. Quality Control, 1995—; trainer Koalaty Kids, 1996. Facilitator Leadership Memphis Diversity Program, 1993; vol. Girl Scouts, N.W. Tenn., 1986-89. Recipient grant Bell-South, 1991-93, fellow Tenn. Collaborative Acad., 1990-91. Mem. Am. Assn. Higher Edn., Am. Soc. Quality Control (assoc., Memphis sect. co-chair quality forum 1992-93), Tenn Assn. Devel. Educators, Phi Delta Kappa. Home: 51 Perkins Extd Memphis TN 38117 Office: State Tech Inst Memphis 5983 Macon Cove Memphis TN 38134

JAMES, LYNETTE A., public relations professional; b. Mountainview, Calif., May 10, 1966; d. Jimmy D. and Loralci A. (Funk) J. BA, East Tex. State U., 1988; MA, Tex. A&M U., 1996. Editor Living Ctrs. of Am., Houston, 1988-92; comm. specialist Tex. Agrl. Experiment Sta., College Station, 1992—. Mem. Agrl. Communicators in Edn. (Gold award 1995), Pub. Rels. Soc. Am. (Houston chpt., internship coord. 1991-92, Gold Excalibur and Silver Excalibur 1989—). Office: Tex Agrl Experiment Sta 229 Reed McDonald College Station TX 77843-2112

JAMES, MARIE MOODY, clergywoman, musician, vocal music educator; b. Chgo., Jan. 23, 1928; d. Frank and Mary (Portis) Moody; m. Johnnie James, May 25, 1968. B Music Edn., Chgo. Music Coll., 1949; postgrad., U. Ill., Champaign-Urbana, 1952, 72, Moody Bible Inst., Chgo., 1963-64; MusM, Roosevelt U., 1969, MA, 1976; DD, Internat. Bible Inst. and Sem., Plymouth, Fla., 1985; postgrad., Trinity Evang. Div. Sch., Deerfield, Ill., 1995; DRE, Logos Grad. Sch., 1995. exec. dir. House of Love DayCare, 1983, 99; Mary P. Moody Christian Acad., 1989, supt., 1989, founder, 1989; bd. dirs. Van Moody Sch. Music, Chgo.; dir. Handbell Choir for Srs. Maple Park United Meth. Ch., 1988-92. Key punch operator Dept. Treasury, Chgo., 1950-52; tchr. Posen-Robbins Bd. Edn., Robbins, Ill., 1952-59; tchr. vocal music Englewood High Sch., Chgo., 1964-84; music counselor Head Start, Chgo., 1965-66; exec. dir. House of Love DayCare, 1983, 88, Mary P. Moody Christian Acad., 1989, supt., 1989; dir. Handbell Choir for Srs. Maple Park United Meth. Ch., 1988-92. Composer, arranger choral music: Hide Me, 1963, Christmas Time, 1980, Come With Us, Our God Will Do Thee Good, 1986, The Indiana House, 1987, Behold, I Will Do a New Thing, 1989, Mary P. Moody Christian Academy School Song 1989, Glory and Honor, 1992. Organist Allen Temple A.M.E. Ch., 1941-45; asst. organist Choppin A.M.E. Ch., 1945-49; organist-dir. Progressive Ch. of God in Christ, Maywood, Ill., 1950-60; missionary Child Evangelism Fellowship, Chgo., 1955-63; unit leader YWCA, New Buffalo, Mich., 1956-58; min. of music God's House of All Nations, Chgo., 1960-80; pastor God's House of Love, Prayer and Deliverance, Robbins, 1982—; chmn. Frank and Mary Moody Scholarship Com., 1984—; dir. music Christian Women's Outreach Ministry, 1984-88; mem. Robbins Community Coun., 1987-88; camp counselor Abraham Lincoln Ctr., 1951-53. Coppin A.M.E. Ch. scholar, 1946; recipient Humanitarian award God's House of Love, Prayer and Deliverance, 1992, Disting. Leadership award Am. Biog. Inst., 1995. Mem. Music Educators Nat. Conf., Good News Club (tchr. 1987-90, Robbins, Ill.). Home: 8154 S Indiana Ave Chicago IL 60619-4712

JAMES, MARY SPENCER, nursing administrator; b. London, Ont., Can., July 10, 1949; d. Richard Spencer and Helen Frances (Winterbottom) James; m. Robert Peter Owler, Oct. 4, 1969 (div. June 25, 1975). AA, Norwich U., 1969; Nursing Diploma, Toronto (Ont.) Gen. Hosp., 1973; BA in Psychology, U. Vt., 1975. RN, Calif. Staff nurse Toronto Gen. Hosp., 1973-77, Stanford (Calif.) U. Hosp., 1977-81, B.C. Children's Hosp., Vancouver, 1981-83; sr. staff nurse King Abdul Aziz Mil. Hosp., Tabuk, Saudi Arabia, 1983-84, Charter Med. Ltd./Tawam Hosp., Al Ain, Abu Dhabi, UAE, 1984-87; nurse Dubai Petroleum Co., UAE, 1987-88; nursing dir. Ygia Polyclinic, Limassol, Cyprus, 1988-89; nurse Stat Travelers, Inc., L.A., 1990-91; staff nurse Lucile Salter Packard Children's Hosp. at Stanford, Palo Alto, Calif., 1991-92; case mgr. H.S.S.I. Home Care and Olsten Healthcare, Milbrae and San Francisco, 1992-93; nursing dir. CHS Home Health Agy., San Francisco, 1993-94; liaison nurse coord., pvt. duty supr. United Nursing Internat., San Francisco, 1994-95; nursing supr. Staff Builders Home Care Svcs., Santa Rosa, Calif., 1995; home health coord. Care Home Health Svcs., Sonoma, Calif., 1995—. Home: 340 Channing Way Apt 353 San Rafael CA 94903

JAMES, PHYLLIS, educator; b. Waterbury, Conn., May 6, 1944; d. Martin William and Phyllis (Gumpper) Connors; m. Svein Jensen, (dec.); 1 child, Margaretha Anne; m. Paul Makeig James, Apr. 30, 1990. AB, U. Miami, 1966; MLitt, U. London, 1990; diplomate of advanced study, So. Conn. State U., 1992. Cert. profl. tchr., English, history, art, and profl. adminstr., Conn. Rschr. U. Oslo (Norway) and Munch Mus., 1970-71; lectr. in art history U. Miami, Fla., 1971-73; rschr. Singapore, 1973-74; tchr. Waterbury Bd. of Edn., 1974—; mem. Fulbright scholar selection com. Conn. Fulbright Club, New Haven, 1991-93; advanced placement tchr. recognition award com. Coll. Bd., Waltham, Mass., 1996. Contbg. author: Learning Through Looking, 1994. Mem. arts/grants com. Waterbury (Conn.) Found., 1993—; friend Conn. Humanities Coun., 1993-96, Yale Art Gallery, 1993-96. Fellow Coun. for Basic Edn., Washington, 1994; Reader's Digest Tchr. Scholar, NEH, Washington, 1995. Mem. AAUW, MLA, Nat. Coun. Tchrs. English. Home: PO Box 386 Middlebury CT

JAMES, ROSE VICTORIA, sculptor, poet; b. East Amherst, N.Y., Feb. 11, 1922; d. Joseph and Mary (Plewniak) Glichowska; m. Clarence William James, Aug. 28, 1943 (dec. Dec. 1995); children: Robert, Sandra Lee, David, Mary, Kevin. Attended, Atlanta Coll. Art, 1960-64; B in Visual Arts in Sculpture, Ga. State U., 1973, postgrad., 1977-78. Legal sec. Law Office, Buffalo, 1941-42; sec. to comdr. Air Stas. Navy Dept., Washington, 1942-43; adminstr. pers. dept. NAS Alameda, Alameda, Calif., 1943-44; radio programmer, announcer ARC, Vets. Hosp., Buffalo, 1950-54, Atlanta, 1956-62; tchr., owner Studio 7 North Art Gallery, Roswell, Ga., 1974-76; freelance artist, studio art instr. regional adult programs, 1960-72; competitive exhibiting artist, 1976-95; chairperson 1st profl. women artist show Cushman Corp. Colony Sq., Atlanta, 1976; chairperson Atlanta Women in Arts Coop. Gallery, 1979-83; spkr. in field. Exhibited in group shows including Galleria Complex, Marietta, Ga., Colony Sq., Atlanta, Atlanta Hilton Ctr., Peachtree Ctr. Complex, Atlanta, Peachtree Summit, Atlanta, ACA Gallery, Woodruff Art Ctr., Atlanta, Bklyn. Coll. Student Ctr., N.Y.C., Alt. Space, N.Y.C., La Grange Coll., Ga., Ga. State U., Atlanta, Southeastern Colls. and Univs. 1-Yr. Traveling Exhibit, Auburn U., Ga. Inst. of Tech., Atlanta, DeKalb Coll., Atlanta, Hanson Gallery, New Orleans, AWIA Gallery, Atlanta, M. Baird Gallery, Atlanta, Handshake Gallery, Atlanta, Marietta Fine Arts Ctr., Ga., High Mus. of Art Regional Juried Art Shows, others. Visual arts panel Fulton County Commrs., Atlanta, 1980-81; panel moderator Ga. State U. So. Scholars on Women, 1981, Atlanta-Fulton County Libr., 1984. Grantee Bur. Cultural Affairs and Atlanta Arts Festival, 1978, Corp. Funding, 1980-81; recipient Mortar Bd. Honor Soc. Outstanding Leadership award, 1973. Mem. Internat. Sculpture Ctr., Cath. Artists Am., Cath. Fine Arts Soc. Republican. Roman Catholic. Home: 6240 Weatherly Dr NW Atlanta GA 30328 Studio: King Plow Arts Ctr 887 W Marietta St NW Atlanta GA 30318

JAMES, SHERYL TERESA, journalist; b. Detroit, MI, Oct. 7, 1951; d. Reese Louis and Dava Helen (Bryant) J.; m. Eric Torgeir Vigmostad, June 15, 1974; children: Teresa, Kelsey. BS in English, Ea. Mich. U., 1973. Staff writer, editor Lansing (Mich.) Mag., 1979-82; staff writer Greensboro (N.C.) News & Record, 1982-86, St. Petersburg (Fla.) Times, 1986-91, Detroit Free Press, 1991—; cons. Poynter Inst., St. Petersburg, 1989—; cons. to high sch. newspapers, St. Petersburg, 1989—. Recipient Penney Missouri Awd. U. Missouri/J.C. Penney, 1985, 1st Pl. Feature Writing Awd. Fla. Soc. Newspaper Editors, 1991, Pulitzer Prize, Feature Writing, 1991, finalist, 1992, Alumna Achievement Awd. Eastern Michigan U., 1992. Democrat. Roman Catholic. Office: Detroit Free Press Knight-Ridder Newspapers 321 W Lafayette Blvd Detroit MI 48226*

JAMES, VIRGINIA LYNN, contracts executive; b. March AFB, Calif., Feb. 6, 1952; d. John Edward and Azella Virginia (Morrill) Anderson; children: Raymond Edward, Jerry Glenn Jr. Student, Sinclair Community Coll., 1981-83, U. Tex., San Antonio, 1980, Redlands U., 1986, San Diego State U., 1994. With specialized contracting USAF, Wright-Patterson AFB, Ohio, 1973-77; with logistics contracting USAF, Kelly AFB, Tex., 1977-81; contract specialist USAF, Wright-Patterson AFB, Ohio, 1981-84; spl. asst. Peace Log, Tehran, Iran, 1977; acting chief of contracts cruise missile program Gen. Dynamics/Convair, San Diego, 1984-86; contracts mgr. VERAC, Inc., San Diego, 1986-90, Gen. Dynamics, San Diego, 1990-92; mgr. contracts Scientific-Atlanta, San Diego, 1992-93; dir. contracts GreyStone, San Diego, 1993—; cons. Gen. Dynamics, San Diego, 1985, Efratrom, 1986. Mem. Nat. Assn. Female Execs., Nat. Mgmt. Assn., Nat. Contract Mgmt. Assn. Republican. Office: GreyStone Tech 15010 Avenue Of Science Ste 200 San Diego CA 92128-3422

JAMES, VIRGINIA SCOTT, elementary school educator; b. Mobile, Ala., Feb. 5, 1955; d. Timothy Varian and Sarah (Watts) Scott; m. Jeffery Thomas Heathcock, June 7, 1980 (widowed, July 1988); m. Colvin Jerome James, Mar. 22, 1991. BS, Mobile Coll., 1978; grad. in pub. speaking, Dale Carnegie Sch., 1978. Cert. tchr. grades kindergarten through 8, Ala. Tchr. grades 1 and 2 Cypress Shores Christian Sch., Mobile, 1983-84; tchr. grade 2 Irvington Christian Sch., Mobile, 1984-85; early intervention tchr. reading and math. grades 1 through 8 Riggins Elem. Sch., Birmingham, Ala., 1985—, title one 3d grade tchr., 1995—. Sponsor various 3rd through 5th grade Just Say No Clubs, Riggins Elem. Sch., 1986—; choir Warrior United Meth. Ch. Mem. Ala. Edn. Assn., Birmingham Edn. Assn., Birmingham Area Reading Coun., Ala. Classroom Tchrs. (social dir. Birmingham chpt. 1991-92). Methodist. Home: 3680 Gobblers Knob Rd Warrior AL 35180-3118

JAMES, VIRGINIA STOWELL, retired elementary, secondary education educator; b. New Britain, Conn., July 9, 1926; d. Austin Leavitt and Doris Carolyn Stowell; m. William Hall James, June 24, 1950; 1 child, Hillery. BA, Middlebury Coll., 1947; MA, Yale U., 1955; PhD, U. Conn., 1988. Cert. tchr. Elem. tchr. Bd. Edn., Westport, Conn., 1950-58; art tchr. grades 6-9 Wallingford (Conn.) Bd. Edn., tchr. gifted/talented grades 4-5, kindergarten, 1958-91; ret., 1991. Contbr. articles to profl. jours. Mem. NEA, AAUW, ASCD, Nat. Art Edn. Assn., Nat. Assn. for Gifted Children, Conn. Assn. for the Gifted, Conn. Edn. Assn., Phi Delta Kappa, Pi Lambda Theta, Delta Kappa Gamma. Address: PO Box 234 Northford CT 06472-0234

JAMESON, DOROTHEA, sensory neuroscientist; b. Newton, Mass., Nov. 16, 1920; d. Robert and Josephine (Murray) Jameson; BA, Wellesley Coll., 1942; MA (hon.), U. Pa., 1973, DSc (hon.) SUNY, 1989; m. Leo M. Hurvich, Oct. 23, 1948. Rsch. asst. Harvard, 1941-47; research psychologist Eastman Kodak Co., Rochester, N.Y., 1947-57; rsch. scientist NYU, 1957-62; vis. scientist Venezuelan Inst. Sci. Rsch., 1965; research asso. to prof. Psychol. and Inst. Neurol. Scis., U. Pa., 1962-74, Univ. prof. U. Pa., 1975—; vis. prof. Center Visual Sci., U. Rochester, 1974, Columbia U., 1974-76, fall 1986; vis. com. of bd. overseers Harvard U., 1989—; cons. in field. Mem. Nat. Adv. Eye Council, NIH, 1985-89; corp. bd. Woods Hole Oceanographic Inst., 1978-84, 85-91, life mem., 1991—; U.S. Nat. Com. Internat. U. Psychol. Scis., 1985-91; Nat. Acad. Sci.-NCR Commn. on Human Resources, 1977-80, chmn. com. on vision, 1980-81; mem. rsch. & evaluation com. The Lighthouse, 1993—; participant Keystone Scientist to Scientist Coll., 1995. Recipient I.H. Godlove award Inter-Soc. Color Coun., 1973; Alumnae Achievement award Wellesley Coll., 1974; Deane B. Judd award Assn. Internationale 'de Couleur, 1985; Hermann von Helmholtz award Cognitive Neurosci. Inst., 1987; fellow Center for Advanced Study in the Behavioral Scis., 1981-82. Fellow AAAS, Soc. Exptl. Psychologists (Howard Crosby Warren medal 1971), Am. Psychol. Assn. (Disting. Sci. Contbn. award 1972), Am. Acad. Arts and Scis., Optical Soc. Am. (Tillyer medal 1982); mem. NAS (com. on human rights 1994—), Am. Psychol. Soc. (William James fellow 1989), Assn. Research in Vision and Ophthalmology, Internat. Brain Research Orgn., Internat. Research Group Color Vision Deficiencies, N.Y. Acad. Sci., Psychonomic Soc., Soc. Neurosci., Sigma Xi. Co-author: The Perception of Brightness and Darkness, 1966; co-author introduction and English translation: Outlines of a Theory of the Light Sense, 1964 (E. Hering); co-editor, author chpt.; Visual Psychophysics: Handbook of Sensory Physiology, Vol. VII/4, 1972; contbr. to History of Psychology in Autobiography, 1989; contbr. articles to profl. jours. Office: U Pa 3720 Walnut St Philadelphia PA 19104-3604

JAMESON, PATRICIA MARIAN, government agency administrator; b. Pitts., Mar. 17, 1945; d. Vernon L. and Dorothy Leam (Wilson) J.; B.A., Northwestern U., 1967; M.A., Ohio State U., 1969, with HUD, 1970—, project mgr., Detroit, 1976-77, acting dir. housing mgmt., 1978, dep. area mgr. Milw. Area Office, 1978-85, acting area mgr., 1979-80, 82, regional dir. adminstrn. Chgo. Regional Office, 1985-95, dir. adminstrv. svc. ctr., Denver, 1995—. Mem. Chgo. Council on Fgn. Relations. Recipient Quality Performance award HUD, 1973, 75, 80, Outstanding Performance award, 1980, 85, 87, 88, 90, 91, 92, 94, 96, Disting. Svc. award 1992; NDEA fellow, 1967-69. Mem. Nat. Assn. Female Execs., NOW, Fed. Execs. Inst. Alumni Assn., Phi Beta Kappa, Pi Sigma Alpha. Office: 633 17th St Denver CO 80202

JAMESON, PAULA ANN, lawyer; b. New Orleans, Feb. 19, 1945; d. Paul Henry and Virginia Lee (Powell) Bailey; children: Paul Andrew, Peter Carver. B.A., La. State U., 1966; J.D., U. Tex., 1969. Bar: Tex. 1969, D.C. 1970, Va., 1973, N.Y. 1978, U.S. Dist. Ct. D.C. 1970, U.S. Dist. Ct. (ea. dist.) Va. 1976, U.S. Ct. Appeals (D.C. cir.) 1972, U.S. Ct. Appeals (4th cir.) 1976, U.S. Ct. Appeals (5th cir.) 1978, U.S. Supreme Ct. 1973, U.S. Ct. Appeals (2d cir.) 1985. Asst. corp. counsel D.C. Corp. Counsel's Office, 1970-73; sr. asst. county atty. Fairfax County Atty.'s Office, Fairfax, Va., 1973-77; atty. Dow Jones & Co., Inc., Princeton, N.J., 1977-79, house counsel, 1979-81, asst. to chmn. bd., 1981-83, house counsel, dir. legal dept., 1983-86; sr. v.p., gen. counsel, corp. sec., PBS, Alexandria, Va., 1986—; bd. dirs. Advanced TV Tech. Ctr. Inc. Mem. ABA, Fed. Communications Bar Assn., D.C. Bar Assn., Assn. of Bar of City of N.Y., Am. Pub. TV Prodr. Assn. (chair), Copyright Soc. USA (former trustee). Democrat. Roman Catholic. Office: PBS 1320 Braddock Pl Alexandria VA 22314-1649

JAMES-STRAND, NANCY KAY LEABHARD, advertising executive; b. Oak Park, Ill., July 30, 1943; d. Arthur Ferdinand and Virginia Stella (Albertelli) Leabhard; m. Jack William Strand, July 1, 1971. Student, U. Madrid, 1963-64; BA in Teaching Spanish, U. Ill., 1965. With advt. sales Chgo. Tribune, 1968-69; asst. mgr. Nationwide Advt., Chgo., 1969-78, regional mgr., 1978—. Home: 140 S Grove Ave Oak Park IL 60302-2806 Office: Nationwide Advt 35 E Wacker Dr Chicago IL 60601

JAMIESON, SANDRA, English language educator, consultant; b. Haslemere, Eng., June 20, 1959; came to U.S., 1984; d. Frank Foster and Daphne Maud (Game) J. BA, U. East Anglia, Norwich, Norfolk, U.K., 1981; MA, SUNY, Binghamton, 1986, PhD, 1991. Tchg. asst. SUNY, Binghamton, 1984-89; asst. prof. Colgate U., Hamilton, N.Y., 1989-93; dir. composition Drew U., Madison, N.J., 1993—; adj. composition adv. bd. Regents Coll., Albany, N.Y., 1995—. Author: Bedford Guide to Teaching Writing in the Disciplines, 1994; bibliographer CCC Bibliography of Composition & Rhetoric, 1993, 94; contbr. chpts. to books. Mem. Nat. Coun. Tchrs. English (conf. Coll. Composition and Comm. 1986—, mem. coun. of writing program adminstrs. 1993—). Office: Drew U English Dept Madison NJ 07940

JAMISON, ELIZABETH ALEASE, drafting and design business owner; b. Rockwood, Tenn., July 8, 1954; d. Ross Leslie and Alice Elizabeth (Collier) J.; life ptnr., Terry; 1 child, Nicholas Alexandré Westervelt. Student, Roane State C.C., Harriman, Tenn., 1974-75, Tenn. Tech. U., 1980-83. Cert. Autocad Level I. Drafter ETE Consulting Engrs., Inc., Oak Ridge, Tenn., 1983-84, Edge Group, Nashville, 1984-88; sr. drafter Woodard & Curran, Inc., Portland, Maine, 1988-91; owner Casco Bay Drafting & Design, Portland, Maine, 1991—; tech. program coord. Portland Adult Edn., 1994—; adj. faculty mem. So. Maine Tech. Coll., South Portland, 1990—; instr. Women Unltd., Augusta, Maine, 1993—. Featured in film Women Working, 1994. Bd. officer Portland YWCA, 1992-94. Mem. NOW (1st v.p. Tenn. chpt. 1986-88, Tenn. state pres. 1988). Home and Office: Casco Bay Drafting & Design 82 Northwood Dr Portland ME 04103

JAMISON, JAYNE, magazine publisher. Group pub. Child mag., N.Y.C.; pub. Parents mag., N.Y.C. Office: Gruner & Jahr USA Publishing 685 Third Ave New York NY 10017*

JAMISON, JUDITH, dancer; b. Phila., May 10, 1943; d. John J. Student, Fisk U., Phila., Phila. Dance Acad. (now U. of Arts); studied with, Anthony Tudor, John Hines, Delores Brown, John Jones, Joan Kerr, Madame Swaboda. Dancer Alvin Alley's Am. Dance Theatre, N.Y.C., 1965-80; artistic dir. Alvin Ailey's Am. Dance Theatre, N.Y.C., 1990—; dancer, choreographer touring U.S., Europe, Asia, S.Am., Africa, 1980—; formerly with Maurice Hines Dance Sch., N.Y.C.; founder Jamison Project, 1988-91; vis. disting. prof. Univ. of Arts; guest assoc. artistic dir. 30th ann. tour Alvin Ailey's Am. Dance Theatre, 1990—; guest appearences with Harkness Ballet, Am. Ballet Theatre, San Francisco Ballet, Dallas Ballet. N.Y. dance debut in Agnes DeMille's "The Four Marys", 1965; starring role created for her in Joseph's Legend (John Neumeier), Vienna Opera, Le Spectre de la Rose (Maurice Bejart), Brussels, Paris, N.Y.C.; performed in Maskela Language, 1969, Cry, 1971, Choral Dance, 1971, Mary Lou's Mass, 1971, The Lark Ascending, 1972, The Mooche, 1975, Passage, 1978; star Broadway show Sophisticated Ladies, 1980; choreographer Divining Hymn for Alvin Ailey Am. Dance Theatre, works for Maurice Bejart, Dancers Unltd. Dallas, Washington Ballet, Jennifer Muller/The Works, Alvin Ailey Repertory Ensemble, Ballet Nuevo Mundo de Caracas, Riverside for Alvin Ailey Am. Dance Theatre, also for opera Boito's Mefistofele for Opera Co. Phila.; subject of PBS spl. The Dancemaker; subject of book Aspects of a Dancer; author: Dancing Spirit, 1993. Recipient Dance Mag. award, 1972, Key to the City of N.Y., 1976, Disting. Service award Mayor of N.Y.C., 1982, Disting. Service award Harvard U., 1982, Spirit of Achievement award Nat. Women's Divsn. Yeshiva U. Albert Einstein Coll. Medicine, 1992, Golden Plate award Am. Acad. Achievement, 1993. Address: Alvin Ailey Am Dance Theater 211 W 61st St Fl 3 New York NY 10023-7832

JAN, COLLEEN ROSE, secondary school educator; b. Toledo, Ohio, Sept. 1, 1953; d. Robert James and Irene Dolores (Bartnikowski) Kegerreis; children: Brett Robert Jan, Shawna Michele Jan. AA, Monroe County C.C., Mich., 1973; BS, U. Toledo, 1975, JD, 1978, MEd, 1992, postgrad., 1992—. Cert. in secondary edn., Mich. Sec. Family Planning, Monroe, 1971-73; paralegal Bedford Legal Bldg., Temperance, Mich., 1973-80; tchr. Bedford Pub. Schs., Lambertville, Mich., 1989-96, lang. arts chair, 1996, social studies chair, 1996—; mem. NCA Outcomes Visitation Team, Birney Middle Sch., Southfield, Mich., 1993—; mem. dist. assessment and profl. devel. com., 1995-96. Creater video: Winning at the MEAP, 1991. expository com. co-chair Sch. Improvement/Bedford, Temperance, 1991—, steering com., 1992—; social studies core curriculum mem. Intermediate Sch. Dist., Monroe, 1993-94, Bedford Pub. Schs., 1994—; co-chair NCA steering com., 1994—,; co-advisor Students United Against Drugs, Temperance, 1990—; designer The Cmty. Svc. Alternative, Temperance, 1993-94; facilitator Lion's Club Quest Program, Temperance, 1989-91; campaign mgr. Sch. Bd. Mem., 1987-88. Mem. AAUW, ASCD, Nat. Coun. for the Social Studies, Phi Delta Kappa, Phi Kappa Phi. Office: Bedford Jr High Sch 8405 Jackman Rd Temperance MI 48182-9459

JANAIRO, ALTHEA See CARRERE, TIA

JANCUK, KATHLEEN FRANCES, principal; b. Balt., Apr. 1, 1950; d. Joseph Frank and Dorothy Jane (Lowrey) J. BA in Elem. Edn., Notre Dame Coll., Balt., 1974; MEd in Reading, Towson State U., 1985; MEd in Adminstrn., Loyola Coll., Balt., 1992. Cert. tchr., reading specialist, adminstr. and supr., Md. Substitute tchr. St. Wenceslaus, Balt., 1970-72; tchr. 5th grade St. Boniface, Phila., 1972-77; tchr. 5th grade Cath. C.C., Balt., 1977-82, reading specialist K-5, 1982-88; reading specialist K-8 St. Mary's Elem. Sch., Annapolis, Md., 1988-91; prin. St. Clare Sch., Balt., 1991—. Non-voting mem. St. Clare Sch. Bd., Balt., 1991—; mem. Sch. Sisters of

Notre Dame, 1991; mem. area pastoral coun., 1993. Recipient Recognition of Svc. award Archdiocese of Balt., 1993. Mem. ASCD, Elem. Sch. Prins. Assn. (exec. bd. dirs. 1994—), Nat. Cath. Ednl. Assn., Mid. States Assn. Sch. Evaluation Teams. Democrat. Roman Catholic. Office: St Clare Sch 716 Myrth Ave Baltimore MD 21221-4824

JANECEK, LENORE ELAINE, insurance specialist, consultant; b. Chgo., May 2, 1944; d. Morris and Florence (Bear) Picker; M.A.J. in Speech Communications (talent scholar), Northeastern Ill. U., 1972; postgrad. (Ill. Assn. C. of C. Execs. scholar) Inst. for Organizational Mgmt., U. Notre Dame, 1979-80; M.B.A., Columbia Pacific U., 1982; cert. in C. of C. mgmt. U. Colo., 1982; m. John Janecek, Sept. 12, 1964; children: Frank, Michael. Adminstrv. asst., exec. dir. Ill. Mcpl. Retirement Fund, Chgo., 1963-65; personnel mgr. Profile Personnel, Chgo., 1965-68; personnel rep. Marsh Instrument Co., Skokie, Ill., 1971-73; restaurant mgt. Gold Mine Restaurant and What's Cooking Restaurant, Chgo., 1974-76; pres., owner Secretarial Office Services, Chgo., 1976-78; founder, pres. Lincolnwood (Ill.) C. of C. and Industry, 1978-85; pres. Lenore E. Janecek & Assocs., Lincolnwood, 1985—; rep. 10th dist. U.S. C. of C., 1978—; appointee Health Care Reform Task Force, 1992—; apptd. by Pres. Bill Clinton Selective Svc. Bd., 1993—; apptd. by Gov. Jim Edgar Ill. Health Care Cost Containment Coun., 1994—. Mem. mktg. bd. Niles Twp. Sheltered Workshop; pres. Lincolnwood Sch. Dist. 74 Sch. Bd. Caucus; bd. mem., officer, founder Ill. Fraternal Order Police Ladies Aux.; bd. dirs., officer Lincolnwood Girl's Softball League, PTA; bd. dirs. United Way, 1982-83; mem. sch. curriculum com. Lincolnwood Bd. Edn.; appointed by Pres. Reagan to the Selective Svc. Bd., 1983; pres. United Way, Skokie Valley, Ill., 1989; pres., founder Leadership Ill., 1992—, Twp. Coord. and Health Care advisor, Gov. Jim Edgar, Ill., 1990—. Named Disting. Grad. of Yr. Nat. Honor Soc., 1985; chosen one of Top 100 Women Leaders in Am., 1988; recipient Outstanding Woman in Healthcare Mgmt. award Women Health Exec. Network, 1994. Mem. NAFE, Am. Notary Soc., Hadassah. Jewish. Office: 4433 W Touhy Ave Ste 405 Lincolnwood IL 60646-1820

JANES, NANCY SEGAL, educational magazine publisher. BA, U. Vt., 1982; MEd, Lesley Coll., 1983; cert. advanced studies, Harvard U., 1989. Math tchr. Graland Country Day Sch., Denver, 1983-87, Belmont (Mass.) Day Sch., 1987-88; software developer Learningways, Cambridge, Mass., 1989-91; newsletter pub., editor Wonderful Ideas, Burlington, Vt., 1989—. Author: Problem Solving with Polyhedra Dice, 1994, Counter Logic, 1996. Mem. Nat. Coun. Tchrs. Math., Ednl. Press Assn. Am. Office: Wonderful Ideas PO Box 64691 Burlington VT 05406-4691

JANEWAY, ELIZABETH HALL, author; b. Bklyn., Oct. 7, 1913; d. Charles H. and Jeannette F. (Searle) Hall; m. Eliot Janeway (dec. 1993); children: Michael, William. Student, Swarthmore Coll.; A.B., Barnard Coll., 1935; Ph.D. in Lit. (hon.), Simpson Coll., Cedarcrest Coll., Villa Maria Coll.; D.H.L. (hon.), Russell Sage Coll., 1981, Florida Internat. U., 1988, Simmons Coll., 1989. Assoc. fellow Yale. Author: The Walsh Girls, 1943, Daisy Kenyon, 1945, The Question of Gregory, 1949, The Vikings, 1951, Leaving Home, 1953, Early Days of the Automobile, 1956, The Third Choice, 1959, Angry Kate, 1963, Accident, 1964, Ivanov Seven, 1967, Man's World, Woman's Place, 1971, Between Myth and Morning: Women Awakening, 1974, Powers of the Weak, 1980, Cross Sections: From a Decade of Change, 1982, Improper Behavior, 1987; contbr. to: Comprehensive Textbook of Psychiatry, 2d edit, 1980, Harvard Guide to Contemporary American Writing, 1979, also short stories and critical writing in periodicals and newspapers. Past chmn. N.Y. State Coun. Humanities; past bd. dirs. NOW Legal Def. and Edn. Fund, Fedn. State Humanities Coun.; bd. dirs. Nat. Cultural Alliance. Recipient educator's award Delta Kappa Gamma, 1972; named Disting. Alumna Barnard Coll., 1979; recipient Medal of Distinction, 1981. Mem. Authors Guild (council), Authors League Am. (council), PEN, Phi Beta Kappa (hon.). Home: 350 E 79th St New York NY 10021-9202

JANIAK, CATHY LYNN, sales consultant; b. Summit, N.J., Oct. 25, 1950; d. Anthony Tyrone and Jane (LaMaster) Cuva; m. Richard Walter Janiak, Sept. 10, 1968; children: Jacqueline, Jeffrey. BBA, Georgian Ct. Coll., 1986; M of Liberal Studies, Monmouth U., 1996. Teller Supreme Savs. and Loan, Irvington, N.J., 1972-73; with claims svcs. State Farm Ins., Summit, N.J., 1981-83; substitute tchr. Toms River (N.J.) Bd. Edn., 1986-87; sr. svc. analyst N.J. Bell, Toms River, 1982-84, sales cons., 1987—. Vol. Artist Guild, Island Heights, N.J., 1982; historian Welcome Wagon, Toms River, 1984-85. Recipient 1st pl. Latin category Star Dust Ball, Meadowlands, N.J., 1992. Home: 1119 Kells Ct Toms River NJ 08753-3162 Office: 79 Route 37 E Toms River NJ 08753-6672

JANICE, BARBARA, illustrator; b. Bklyn., Jan. 25, 1949; d. Irving and Blanche (Lass) Rothman; 1 child, Stacey-Alissa Mirsky. BS in Biology, L.I. U., 1971; studied with Frank Netter, MD. Staff illustrator Courier-Life Pubs., Bklyn., 1975-78, The Village Voice, N.Y.C., 1978-80; art dir., dept. anatomy SUNY Health Sci. Ctr., Bklyn., 1989-91; freelance illustrator Walt Disney Prodns., N.Y.C., 1990-95, Orlando, Fla., 1990-95; art dir. EuroDisney, Paris, 1990-95; illustrator EuroDisney, Orlando, N.Y.C., 1991-94; art dir. for Donald Duck character EuroDisney, Ft. Lauderdale, Fla., 1994—; human rels. analyst Microsoft Corp., 1995—; dir. Barbara Janice Graphics, N.Y.C. and Fla., 1980—; guest spkr. Pratt Sch. Art and Design, Bklyn., 1991; art dir. for character Donald Duck, EuroDisney, Paris, 1992—. Illustrator: Current Operative Urology, 6th edit., 1989, A Historical Profile of the Children's Medical Center, 1990, 2d rev. edit., 1992, The Day the Alphabet Was Born, 1991; represented in permanent collections SUNY Health Sci. Ctr., EuroDisney, Paris, Tokyo Disneyland. Vol. artist Coalition for the Homeless, N.Y.C., 1985, 91, AIDS Coalition, Ft. Lauderdale, N.Y.C., 1992—. Recipient 1st place N.Y. Art Critics award, 1984, 2d place award, 1992. Mem. Assn. Med. Illustrators, Soc. Illustrators (1st place 34th ann. exhbn. 1991, 2d place 33d ann. exhbn. 1990), Graphic Artists Guild (profl. rep.). Jewish. Home: 3881 NW 122nd Ter Sunrise FL 33323-3360 Office: Microsoft 899 W Cypress Creek Rd Fort Lauderdale FL 33309

JANIGA, MARY ANN, secondary school educator, artist; b. Lackawanna, N.Y., June 14, 1950; d. Jacob and Julia (Zatlukal) Mazurchuk; m. William B. Janiga, Nov. 23, 1972; children: Nicholas, Matthew. BS, State U. Coll., Buffalo, 1972, MS, 1974, cert. advanced study, 1995. Cert. in sch. adminstrn. and supervision. Tchr. art Buffalo Pub. Schs., 1972—; art facilitator Olmsted Sch., Buffalo, 1985—; supervising tchr. State Univ. Coll., Buffalo; liaison Albright-Knox Art Gallery, 1994—. Exhibited in group shows Cheektowaga (N.Y.) Art Guild, 1979, Erie County Parks Art Festival, 1979, Lockport Art Festival, 1980, Allentown Art Exhibit, Kennan Ctr. Recipient various awards for art; grantee Buffalo Tchr. Ctr., 1986-90, Olmstead Home Sch. Assn., 1991, 93, Allentown Village Soc., 1994. Mem. NEA, Olmsted Home Sch. Assn., SUNY-Buffalo Alumni Assn., PTA (life), Buffalo Tchrs. Fedn., Buffalo Fine Arts Acad., Buffalo Soc. Natural Scis., Zool. Soc. of Buffalo. Office: Olmsted Sch Amherst & Lincoln Pky Buffalo NY 14216

JANKLOW, LINDA LEROY, civic worker, volunteer; b. L.A., Apr. 17, 1938; d. Mervyn LeRoy and Doris (Warner) Vidor; m. Morton Lloyd Janklow, Nov. 27, 1960; children: Angela Janklow Harrington, Lucas Warner. BA, Smith Coll., 1959. Vice chmn., mem. exec. com., bd. dirs. Lincoln Ctr. Theater, N.Y.C., 1979-91, chmn., 1991—. V.p., treas. Vidor Found., N.Y.C., 1978—; chmn. ArtsConnection, N.Y.C., 1979—; founding trustee, mem. exec. com., chmn. collection com. Am. Mus. of Moving Image, N.Y.C., 1979—; mem. adv. coun. Tisch Sch. Arts, NYU, 1980-91; mem. adv. bd. Guggenheim Mus., N.Y.C., 1986-91; pres., chief exec. officer Janklow Found., N.Y.C., 1988—; trustee Nat. Coun. for Families and TV, L.A., 1989-92; bd. dirs. The New 42d St., N.Y.C., 1990—. *

JANNEY, JULIE, actress, singer, dancer; b. Anderson, Ind., Feb. 21, 1957; d. John William and Judith Ann (Binder) J. Tchr., choreographer Sacred Heart U., Fairfield, Conn., 1994. actress, singer: Health, 1979, Popeye, 1980; actress: Generation X, N.Y.C., 1994, Dominoes, Westport, Conn., 1995—; singer: Steinettes at the Gate, N.Y.C., 1983, Maureen Hamill Prodns., 1990—, Jerry's Girls, Fairfield, 1994; singer/choreographer: Consistancy Cole, Fairfield, 1995; co-author music and lyrics: Heath, 1979, Juno's Swans, 1985; choreographer Damn Yankess, Sister Us & Swing. Bd. dirs. Theatre Artists Workshop of Westport, 1994—. Mem. AFTRA, Screen Actor's Guild, Actor's Equity. Home: 75 Olmstead Ridgefield CT 06877-5507

JANOSOV, ROSE ANN, bankruptcy preparation service executive; b. Bridgeport, Conn., Aug. 15, 1944; d. Juraj and Annunziata Angelina (Fusco) Janosov; m. K. Daniel Washington, Jr., June 15, 1963 (div. Mar. 1978); children: Kirk Darren, Kenneth Dean, Sarah Reynolds. BA in Psychology, U. Colo., Denver, 1975, M of Urban Adminstrn., 1976; JD, U. Denver, 1979. Fair housing officer City of Norwalk, Conn., 1991-95; sole propr. Barniba's Bankruptcy Preparation Svc., Bridgeport, Conn., 1995—. Author bi-monthly article Fair Housing and You, 1992-94; designer pamphlet Fair Housing Opens Doors, 1993. Sec. Nat. Student Movement, Danbury, Conn., 1962-63; fair housing tester Greenwich (Conn.) Fair Housing Commn., 1963-64, Denver Fair Housing Commn., 1970; founder, bd. dirs. Citizens Against Inflation, Denver, 1972, Colo. Consumers Congress, Denver, 1973; Rocky Mountain regional dir. Nat. Consumers Congress, Washington, 1972-75; candidate Denver City Coun., 1975; bd. dirs. Malcolm X Ctr. for Mental Health,Denver, 1971-73; founder, bd. dirs. Lay Law Learning Ctr., Ojai, Calif., 1981-87. PEO Found. grantee, 1971; Colo. Scholars grantee, 1973; Pub. Adminstrn. scholar, Denver, 1976. Mem. Fair Housing Assn. Conn. (treas.), Vietnam Vets. of Ventura county Inc. (life). Office: Barnibas Bankruptcy Preparation Svc 2416 E Main St Bridgeport CT 06610

JANOW, LYDIA FRANCES, meeting planner; b. N.Y.C., Dec. 2, 1957; d. John and Angie (Bizzios) J. BA cum laude, CCNY, 1978; grad., CBS Div. Publ., 1984. Cert. meeting planner. Exec. sec. Family Weekly Mag., N.Y.C., 1978-81; asst. mdse. mgr. Family Weekly Mag., 1981-83; spl. events mgr. Family Weekly/USA Weekend, N.Y.C., 1983-86; mgr. meetings & events Mag. Pubs. Assn., N.Y.C., 1986-88; conv. svcs. mgr., sales & catering mgr. Sheraton Heights Hotel, Hasbrouck Heights, N.J., 1989-91; conf. mgr. Aviation Week Group McGraw Hill Inc., N.Y.C., 1991-93, dir. tradeshows and confs., 1993—. Editor: Newsletter Heights Hotel, 1991; contbr. articles to profl. jours. Camp counselor, Hellenic-Am. Neighborhood Action Com., N.Y.C., 1974-78; tchr., Sunday sch., St. Spyridon Ch., N.Y.C., 1974-80. Mem. Internat. Assn. Exhibit Mgrs., Internat. Soc. Meeting Planners, Meeting Planners Internat. Greek Orthodox. Home: 29 Levitt Ave Bergenfield NJ 07621-1904

JANSEN, DONNA MARIE, accountant; b. St. Paul, July 26, 1967; d. Joseph John and Donna Mae (Niles) Remackel; m. Joseph Charles Jansen, June 23, 1990. BA in Bus. Administrn., U. St. Thomas, 1989, MBA, 1995. CPA, Minn.; cert. mgmt. acct., Minn. Audit staff Larson, Allen, Weishair and Co., LLP, St. Paul, 1989-91, audit sr., 1991-94, audit mgr., 1994—. Mem. fin. com. The Godchild Project, St. Paul, 1994-95; mentor Metro East Devel. Partnership, St. Paul, 1994-95. Mem. AICPA, Inst. Mgmt. Accts., Minn. Soc. CPAs. Roman Catholic. Office: Larson Allen Weishair & Co 800 Minnesota World Trade C 30 E 7th St Saint Paul MN 55101

JANSON, BARBARA JEAN, publisher; b. Mason City, Iowa, Mar. 7, 1942; d. Harley Arnold and Helen Victoria (Henrickson) J.; m. W. John Shallenberger, Feb. 24, 1963 (div. Sept. 1980); children: Mona, Ann; m. John Batty Henderson, Sept. 8, 1984 (div. 1990). BS in Math., Iowa State U., 1965; MS in Math., Trinity Coll., 1970; MBA, U. R.I., 1982. Cert. math. tchr., Iowa, N.Y., Conn. Math. tchr. Pub. High Schs., Avon, Farmington, Bloomfield, Conn., 1966-68, Ulster Acad., Kingston, N.Y., 1971-73; math. instr. Ulster County Community Coll., Kingston, 1973; math. editor Houghton Mifflin Co., Boston, 1974-77; math. instr. Bristol County Community Coll., Fall River, Mass., 1977-78; asst. dir. editorial Am. Math. Soc., Providence, 1978-81, dir. of publ., 1982-85; pres. Janson Publs., Inc., Providence, 1985—; rep. sci. publ. com. Am. Heart Assn., 1986-90; mem. R.I. State Adv. Commn. on Librs.; mem. R.I. Legis. Commn. for Math. and Sci. Edn., 1991; mem. adv. com. R.I. State Systemic Initiative in Math. and Sci., 1993-94. Editor: Scholarly Publishing: Managing Today, Planning for Tomorrow, 1986. Bd. dirs. Planned Parenthood of R.I., Providence, 1986-87, First Parish Unitarian Ch., Beverly, Mass., 1975-76; mem. steering com. Am. Math. Project, Berkeley, Calif., 1986-92; mem. oversight com. Resources Math. Reform Ednl. Devel. Ctr., Newton, Mass.; adv. mem. R.I. State Coun. on Librs. Recipient Mortar Bd. award Iowa State U., 1965. Mem. AAAS, LWV, Soc. for Scholarly Publishing (bd. dirs. 1986-90, chair ann. meeting 1985), N.Y. Acad. Sci., Am. Math. Soc., Math. Assn. Am., Nat. Coun. Tchrs. Math., Assn. Am. Publishers (jours. com. 1982-85), Nat. Assn. Women Bus. Owners. Unitarian. Home: 8 Jackson Pond Dedham MA 02026-5524 Office: Janson Publs Inc 450 Washington St Ste 107 Dedham MA 02026-4449

JANSSEN, MARYBETH, airframe and powerplant mechanic; b. Tulsa, May 1, 1956; d. Henry Floyd and Bessie Viola (Barr) Kinyon; m. Lawrence Eric Janssen, Dec. 23, 1977 (div. Oct. 1987). Grad. H.S., Los Gatos, Calif. Cert. airframe and powerplant mechanic, FAA. Jet engine mechanic USAF, 1976-84; flight engr. USAFR McChord AFB, Tacoma, 1984-86; flight attendant Trans World Airlines, St. Louis, 1986-89, airframe and powerplant mechanic, 1989-90; airframe and powerplant mechanic Am. Airlines, Inc., Tulsa, 1990-92; tech. crew chief instr. Am. Airlines, Inc., Ft. Worth, 1992-94, airframe and powerplant mechanic, 1994—. Jet engine technician Mo. Air N.G., St. Louis, 1987-90, Okla. Air N.G., Tulsa, 1990-92, non-commd. officer-in-charge maintenance tng., 1992-94. With USAF, 1976-84. Decorated Air Force Achievement medal and Meritorious Svc. medal USAF, Robins AFB, Ga., 1983, Meritorious Svc. medals Mo. Air Nat. Guard, St. Louis, 1990, Okla. Air Nat. Guard, Tulsa, 1993. Mem. Transport Workers Union, Aircraft Mechanics Fraternal Assn., Am. Legion. Home: 7709 Briarcliff Ct Fort Worth TX 76180-3401

JANSSEN-PELLATZ, EUNICE CHARLENE, healthcare facility administrator; b. Urania, La., Mar. 23, 1948; d. Luther Clarence and Eunice Bobby (Pendarvis) Smith. BS in Nursing, Humboldt State U., 1970; MS in Nursing, Calif. State U., Fresno, 1980. Dir. nurses, asst. adminstr., coord. patient care svcs. Mad River Community Hosp., Arcata, Calif.; nursing supr. Fresno (Calif.) Community Hosp. Mem. Am. Soc. Healthcare Risk Mgmt., CANA (region 9 nurses interest group). Home: 824 Diamond Dr Arcata CA 95521

JANZEN, NORINE MADELYN QUINLAN, medical technologist; b. Fond du Lac, Wis., Feb. 9, 1943; d. Joseph Wesley and Norma Edith (Gustin) Quinlan. BS, Marian Coll., 1965; med. technologist St. Agnes Sch. Med. Tech., Fond du Lac, 1966; MA, Cen. Mich. U., 1980; m. Douglas Mac Arthur Janzen, July 18, 1970; 1 son, Justin James. Med. technologist Mayfair Med. Lab., Wauwatosa, Wis., 1966-69; supr. med. technologist Dr.'s Mason, Chamberlain, Franke, Klink & Kamper, Milw., 1969-76, Hartford-Parkview Clinic, Ltd., 1976-94, patient svc. ctrs. supr. Med. Sci. Labs., Wauwatosa, Wis., 1994—; coord. health in bus. Hartford Parkview Clinic, 1990-91, drug program coord., 1991-94; co-chair joint mtg. Clin. Lab. Mgrs. Assn. and Wis. Assn. for Clin. Lab. Scientists, 1993-94. Substitute poll worker Fond du Lac Dem. Com., 1964-65; mem. Dem. Nat. Com., 1973—. Mem. Am. Soc. for Clin. Lab. Scientists (people to people clin. lab. scientist del. to People's Republic of China 1989), Nat. Soc. Clin. Lab. Scientists (awards com. chair 1984-87, 88-91, chmn. 1986-88, nominations com. 1989-92), Wis. Assn. Clin. Lab. Scientists (exec. sec. 1991—, chmn. awards com. 1976-77, 84-85, 86-87, treas. 1977-81, pres.-elect 1981-82, pres. 1982-83, dir. 1977-84, 85-87, Mem. of Yr. award 1982, 95, numerous svc. awards, chair ann. meeting 1987-88), Clin. Lab. Mgmt. Assn. (co-chair joint meeting 1993-94), Milw. Soc. Clin. Lab. Scientists (pres. 1971-72, bd. dir. 1972-73), Communications of Wis. (originator, chmn. 1977-79), Southeastern Suprs. Group (co-chmn. 1976-77), LWV, Alpha Delta Theta (nat. dist. chmn. 1967-69, nat. alumnae dir. 1969-71), Alpha Mu Tau. Methodist. Home: N98w17298 Dotty Way Germantown WI 53022-4618 Office: Med Scis Labs 11020 W Plank Ct Ste 100 Wauwatosa WI 53226

JAPP, NYLA F., infection control services administrator; b. Sterling, Colo., Jan. 8, 1948; d. Leonard W. and Eleanor M. (Barnts) J. Assoc. in Nursing, Garden City Community Coll., 1980; diploma, Pikes Peak Inst. Med. Tech., 1970; BS in Human Resources Mgmt., Friends U., 1992. RN, Kans. With surg. unit St. Catherine Hosp., Garden City, Kans.; sanitarian Finney County Commrs., Garden City; mgr. sterile processing St. Catherine Hosp., Garden City, Kans., mgr. infection control. Mem. Am. Soc. Hosp. Ctrl. Svc. Pers. (regional bd. dirs., chmn. recognition com., mem. tech. cert. com., APIC liaison, AORN liaison, JCAHO liaison, educator of yr., Tom Samuels rsch. award), Great Plains Soc. Hosp. Ctrl. Svc. Pers. (chmn. program com., mem. newsletter com., chmn. nominating com., rsch. com., pres., bd. dirs.), Nat. Inst. for Cert. Healthcare Sterile Processing and Distbn. Pers. (bd. dirs.), Internat. Assn. Hosp. Ctrl. Svc. Mgmt., Assn. Practitioners in Infection Control. Home: 1712 E Fair St Garden City KS 67846-3558

JAQUES, KATHRYN MISBACH, tax consultant; b. Kansas City, Mo., June 23, 1936; d. Lorenz Edwin and Henrietta Louise (Satterlee) Misbach; m. Vernon P. Jaques, June 7, 1960; children: Barbara Louise, Valerie Kathryn. BA in Sociology magna cum laude, Oberlin Coll., 1959. Tax auditor Calif. Franchise Tax Bd., San Diego, 1975-82; tax mgr. Coopers and Lybrand LLP, San Diego, 1982-87; tax mgr. Arthur Andersen LLP, San Diego, 1987-92, tax prin., 1993—; cons. in field, San Diego, 1993; adj. instr. San Diego State U., 1981—; mem. adv. bd. U. Calif.-Davis State and Local Tax Inst., Davis, 1992—; spkr., conf. chair Calif. CPA Edn. Found., Redwood City, Calif., 1982—. Mem. editl. bd. Jour. Multistate Taxation, 1993—. Mem. fin. com. San Diego Automotive Mus., 1995-96. Tribute to Women in Industry honoree San Diego YWCA, 1986. Office: Arthur Andersen LLP Ste 1600 701 B St San Diego CA 92101

JARAMILLO, CHRISTINA M., banker; b. Belen, N. Mex., Dec. 13, 1966; d. Henry and Elsie Ida (Sanchez) J. BBA, N. Mex. State U., 1989; various banking courses, Am. Inst. Banking, Albuquerque Chpt., 1991-94; diploma, Western States Sch. Banking, 1993. Cert. real estate salesperson, N. Mex. Sec. State Farm Ins. Co., Los Lunas, N. Mex., 1984-87; telemarketer, teller trainee Ranchers State Bank, Belen, N. Mex., 1984, 87; mktg. dir., asst. cashier, customer acct. specialist Ranchers Banks (formerly Ranchers State Bank), Belen, 1990—; telemarketer Ideal Images Photography, Las Cruces, N. Mex., 1988; beauty cons. Mary Kay Cosmetics, Belen, 1989-95; bd. dirs. Am. Inst. Banking, 1992-96, instr. 1993—, rep. 1995. Bd. dirs. Boys and Girls Club of Valencia County, N. Mex., 1994—. Mem. Belen C. of C. (bd. dirs. 1993—), Belen Noon Optimist Club. Home: 202 Playa Verde Pl Belen NM 87002 Office: Ranchers Banks PO Box 545 Belen NM 87002

JARAMILLO, JUANA SEGARRA, dean; b. San Sebastian, P.R., Mar. 24, 1937; d. Joaquin M. and Carmen M. (Gerena) Segarra; m. Edgar J. Jaramillo, Apr. 13, 1957; children: Jeanette, Yila, Yvonne, Melissa, Edgar Jr. BA, Poly. Inst. P.R., San German, 1956; postgrad., U. Fla., 1956-57; MS, La. State U., 1963. Libr. dir. Inter-Am. U., Aguadilla (P.R.) Regional Coll., 1975-76, cons. libr. and accreditation, 1983—; libr. U.P.R.-Aguadilla Regional Coll., 1976-77, libr. dir., 1983-86, libr., 1986-89, chair steering com. for accreditation, mem. directive coun. honors program, 1989—, dir. instl. planning and rsch., 1989-90, libr. dir., 1990-94; acting assoc. acad. dean, 1994—, dean/dir., 1994—; libr. dir. EDP Coll. P.R., San Sebastian, 1979-83; acting assoc. acad. dean U. P.R., Aguadilla, 1994, dean, dir., 1994—; mem. steering com. nat. edn. program Am. Coun. Edn., P.R., 1982-86, adv. bd. Coun. Higher Edn., P.R., 1982—. Author: Manual bibliografico Electronica, 1987; co-author: El Desarrollo del Pensamiento Critico en Futuros Maestros, 1989; contbr. articles to profl. jours. Mem. Club Civico de Damas, Aguadilla, 1989—. With U.S. Army, 1963-66. Mem. ALA, Am. Assn. Higher Edn., Assn. Caribbean Univs., Rsch. and INstl. Librs., Sociedad de Bibliotecarios de P.R. (pres. continuing edn. 1984-90), Rotary-Anns (pres. 1974), Internat. Altrusan, Alpha Delta Kappa. Office: UPR Aguadilla PO Box 160 Ramey Aguadilla PR 00604

JARAMILLO, SANDRA JULIER, massage therapist; b. Queens, N.Y., Jan. 20, 1970; d. Leonel and Julier Jaramillo. Cert. chiropractic asst., Parker Coll., Dallas, 1992; cert. massage therapist, Austin Sch. Massage Therapy, Houston, 1993; student, Houston Bapt. U. Massage therapist Homeopathic Massage The Natural Approach, Houston, 1995—. Mem., I CARE, 1992. Mem. NAFE, Nat. Coalition of Hispanic Health and Human Svcs. Orgn., Ctr. Health Policy Devel. Home and Office: 7802 Vernwood Houston TX 77040

JARNAGIN, TERESA ELLIS, educator, nursing administrator; b. Jackson, Miss., Mar. 11, 1950; d. James Robert and Eloise (Cox) Ellis; m. Nathan O. Jarnagin, Dec. 19, 1970; children: Bethany, Nate. Diploma, RN, Gilfoy-Miss. Bapt. Hosp., Jackson, 1971; BSN, U. Miss., Jackson, 1993, MSN, 1995. RNC, CNA, ANCC; cert. med.-surg. nusring and nursing adminstrn. Staff nurse St. Dominic-Jackson (Miss.) Meml. Hosp., 1975-84, nurse mgr. urology/renal, 1984-93, DON behavioral health svcs., 1993-96; nursing instr. Miss. Coll., 1996—. Recipient first place non-fiction award Gulf Coast Writer's Assn. Contest, 1993. Mem. ANA, Miss. Nurse's Assn. (del. state conv. 1993, 94), Dist. Nurse's Assn. (publicity com. 1992, 93, 94), Am. Orgn. Nurse Execs., Am. Psychiat. Nurses Assn., Sigma Theta Tau, Phi Kappa Phi. Baptist. Home: 502 Merganser Trl Clinton MS 39056-6262 Office: Miss Coll North Campus Box 4225 Clinton MS 39058

JARNIGAN-WILLIAMS, ANGELA RENEE, elementary school educator; b. Savannah, Ga., Mar. 14, 1956; d. Walter Edwin and Marie Antoinette (Hardrick) Jarnigan; m. Walter Willis Williams, Apr. 2, 1985; children: Albert Clayton Smith II, Alisha Colette McKinnis. Student, S.C. State U., Orangeburg, 1974-77; BS, Armstrong State Coll., Savannah, 1989. Cert. tchr. elem. edn., Ga. Tchr. Young World, Greensboro, N.C., 1979-81, Parent and Child Day Care, Savannah, 1982-83; switchboard operator Hyatt Regency-Savannah, 1982, 83; para-profl. Chatham-Savannah Bd. Edn., 1984-88; tchr. 1st grade Windsor Forest Elem. Sch., Savannah, 1989—; camp tchr. Meml. Day Sch., Savannah, 1987; mentor Savannah-Chatham County Bd. Edn., 1994—. Mem. NEA, Ga. Assn. Educators, Chatham Assn. Educators. Roman Catholic. Home: 1705 Vassar St Savannah GA 31405-1739

JAROCHI, CATHERINE HANNAH, investment banker; b. Warsaw, Poland, Oct. 31, 1956; came to U.S., 1974; d. Piotr John and Victoria Mary (Kowieski) J. BS in Math., MIT, 1978; MBA, Harvard U., 1984. Rsch. assoc. Salomon Bros., N.Y.C., 1978-82; summer assoc. Bankers Trust, London, 1983; v.p. Goldman Sachs & Co., N.Y.C. and Tokyo, 1984-89; exec. v.p. Stolat Ptnrs., Dallas, 1990-94; pres., owner CHJ Capital, Duluth, Minn., 1994—; cons. N.Y.C. Women's Mensa Club, 1978-82. Co-patentee option pricing model. Bd. dirs. Polish Am. Soc., Washington, 1980-84; com. chmn. Dallas Symphony League, 1991-94; del. Tex. Dem. Conv., 1992; mem. Duluth Mayor's Inner Circle, 1995—. Sgt. Polish Army, 1972-74. Recipient Disting. Svc. award Polish Parliament, 1974. Mem. Minn. Fin. Planners Assn. (treas. 1995—). Roman Catholic.

JARRELL, IRIS BONDS, elementary educator, business executive; b. Winston-Salem, N.C., May 25, 1942; d. Ira and Annie Gertrude (Vandiver) Bonds; m. Tommy Dorsey Martin, Feb. 13, 1965; 1 child, Carlos Miguel; m. 2d, Clyde Rickey Jarrell, June 25, 1983; stepchildren—Tamara, Cris, Kimberly. Student U. N.C.-Greensboro, 1960-61, 68-69, 74-75, Salem Coll., 1976; B.S. in Edn., Winston-Salem State U., 1981; postgrad. Appalachian State U., 1983; M in Elem. Edn., Gardner-Webb Coll., 1992. Cert. tchr., N.C.Tchr. Rutledge Coll., Winston-Salem, 1982-84; owner, mgr. Rainbow's End Consignment Shop, Winston-Salem, 1983-85; tchr. elem. edn. Winston-Salem/Forsyth County Sch. System, 1985—. Contbr. poetry to mags. Mem. Assn. of Couples for Marriage Enrichment, Winston-Salem, 1984-86, Forsyth-Stokes Mental Health Assn., 1985-86; mem. Planned Parenthood. Mem. Internat. Reading Assn., N.C. Assn. Adult Edn., Forsyth Assn. Classroom Tchrs., Nat. Assn. Female Execs., NOW, Greenpeace, World Wildlife Fund, KlanWatch. Democrat. Baptist. Avocations: singing, writing, sewing, gardening, reading. Home: 101 Cheswyck Ln Winston Salem NC 27104-2905

JARRELL, PATRICIA LYNN, photojournalist; b. South Charleston, W.Va., Jan. 21, 1952; d. Ronald Eugene and Barbara Anne (Hill) J.; m. Timothy James Shortt, Mar. 10, 1990. Photographer PCA Internat., Tampa, Fla., 1974-77, Linwood/Gittings, Houston, 1977-78; sr. photographer Gittings/Neiman Marcus, Dallas, 1978-80; studio photographer PCA Internat., Dallas and Orlando, 1980-85; photographer, mgr. Charlton Studios, Altamonte Springs, Fla., 1985; photographer Fla. Today/Gannett, Melbourne, Fla., 1985—; mem. discussion panel covering tragedy Fla. Press Women, 1989. Works exhibited at So. Newspaper Pubs. Assn., 1989, Armory Art Ctr., West Palm Beach, Fla., 1994. Recipient Photojournalism/Spot News award Internat. Soc. Newspaper Design, 1986-87, award of excellence in photojournalism Soc. Newspaper Design, 1986-87, Best News Photography award Fla. Press Club, 1987, Clarion/News Photography award Women in Comms., 1988, 1st Pl./Spot News Fla. Soc. Newspaper Editors, 1988, 1st Pl. News Photography award Fla. Press Women, 1988, 1st Pl. Color Feature award Fla. Soc. Newspaper Editors, 1990. Mem. NOW, Nat. Press Photographers Assn. Democrat. Home: 1802 Crane Creek Blvd Melbourne

FL 32940-6788 Office: Fla Today Newspaper Gannett Plaza PO Box 419000 Melbourne FL 32941-9000

JARRELLE, AUDREY LEE, associate dean, educator; b. Washington, Oct. 31, 1943; d. Leslie Marshall and Helen Louise (Emmert) J. BS, Longwood Coll., 1966; MSHE, U. N.C., Greensboro, 1968, PhD, 1973. Instr. U. Conn., Storrs, 1967-73, asst. prof., 1973-78, assoc. prof., 1978—, assoc. dean, 1988—. Contbr. articles to profl. jours. Mem. Windham Textile and History Mus., Willimantic, Conn., 1990—. Mem. Internat. Textiles and Apparel Assn., Kappa Omicron Nu, Phi Kappa Phi (U. Conn. chpt. pres. 1993-94, v.p. 1992-93, sec. 1991-92). Office: Sch of Family Studies U Conn 348 Mansfield Rd U-58 Storrs Mansfield CT 06269-2058

JARRELL-EVENER, LINDA CAROL, psychologist; b. Miami, Mar. 26, 1942; d. Ross Henry Law and Vivian Estelle (Clay) Henninger; m. Harry H. Jarrell, Jan. 15, 1983 (div. 1990); m. Joseph Robert Evener, Apr. 24, 1992; children: Daria J. Evans, Mindie M. Knowles, Kamala Harrington. AA cum laude, Madison (Fla.) Jr. Coll., 1986; BA, Stetson U., 1988; Cert. Counselor, Cross Life Exch., Denver, 1990; MA, Cornerstone U., 1993. Ordained pastoral counselor, NCCA, Sarasota, Fla., 1994. Internship Deland Jr. H.S., 1988, Grace Fellowship, Denver, 1990; self-employed counselor Orange City, Fla., 1993-94. Guardian with Guardian Ad Litem, Daytona Beach, Fla., 1992-94; active seminars for youth Christian Missionary Alliance, Deland, Fla., 1989-93. Mem. Am. Bus. Women, Phi Theta Kappa. Baptist. Home: 225 W Fern Dr Orange City FL 32763

JARRETT, ALEXIS, insurance professional; b. Independence, Kans., July 2, 1948; d. Robert Patterson and Betty June (Johnson) J.; m. Victor K. O'Yek, Apr. 12, 1987. BS, U. Minn., Duluth, 1970; postgrad., U. Mo.; student, John Marshall Law Sch., 1996—. Lic. in Property and Casualty Ins., Ind., Life and Health Ins., Ind., Life Underwriting Tng. Coun. fellow; cert. coach, Minn. Tchr. Esko (Minn.) Pub. Schs.; pvt. practice Schererville, Ind.; asst. dir. athletics, head coach basketball, softball and track, U. Mo., Columbia; women's basketball and softball color analyst, Regional Radio Sports, N.W. Ind. Contbr. articles on sports to newspapers. Sponsor Lake County (Ind.) H.S. Girls Basketball Banquet; mem. adv. bd. indsl. rsch. liason program Ind. U., Bloomington; bd. dirs. Samaritan Counseling Ctr. N.W. Ind., pres. 1994; bd. dirs. VNA Found., sec.-treas., 1994; mem. mktg. and promotional subcom. Ind. U. N.W. Scholarship Fundraiser Com.; celebrity Am. Heart Assn. Celebrity Dinner; v.p. S.W. Lake divsn. Am. Heart Assn., 1992, 93, 94. Mem. Nat. Life Underwriters (bd. dirs. N.W. Ind. chpt. 1995), Lake County Med. Soc. Alliance (pres.), Am. Bus. Women's Assn. (pres. New Image chpt. 1983, Woman of Yr. 1993), Ind. State Med. Assn. Alliance (chair media rels. 1990-91, 93-94, treas. 1992-93). Address: 2330 Wicker Blvd Schererville IN 46375-2810

JARRETT, POLLY HAWKINS, secondary education educator, retired; b. Columbia, S.C., May 6, 1929; d. William Harold and Ann Beatrice (Carson) Hawkins; m. Nov. 21, 1953 (dec. Aug. 1984); children: William Guy Jr., Henry Carson. Student, Montreat Coll., 1947-49; BS in Secondary Edn., Longwood Coll., 1951. Tchr. 7th grade McDowell County Schs., Marion, N.C., 1951-52; tchr. 8th grade Marion City Schs., 1952-53, Burke County Schs., Morganton, N.C., 1954-56; tchr. 7th grade Wake County Schs., Raleigh, N.C., 1956-58, Durham (N.C.) County Schs., 1958-59; tchr. 7th and 8th grade Raleigh City and Wake County Schs., Raleigh, 1959-79; tchr. social studies Wake County Pub. Schs., Raleigh, 1979-90, ret., 1990; adv. bd. State Employees Credit Union, Raleigh, 1988-92, 94-96. Mem. United Daus. of the Confederacy (chpt. pres. 1978-81, 91-96, divsn. historian 1981-83, dist. VI dir. 1983-85, divsn. chaplain 1986-90, divns. parliamentarian 1994-96, chmn. bd. trustees 1990-91), Delta Kappa Gamma (chpt. pres. 1988-90, regional dir. 1990-92), Kappa Delta Pi, Pi Delta Epsilon, Pi Gamma Mu. Democrat. Methodist. Home: 3405 White Oak Rd Raleigh NC 27609-7620

JARVIS, ARLENE ELIZABETH, music educator; b. Valdosta, Ga., Feb. 20, 1955; d. Richard F. and Doris M. (LaBounty) J. B in Music Edn. cum laude, Morningside Coll., 1977; postgrad., Marywood Coll., 1986-96. Cert. tchr., Vt. Vocal music educator, church choral dir. Sts. Peter & Paul Sch., Omaha, Nebr., 1978-81; vocal music educator Assumption Sch., Omaha, 1978-80; soloist St. Cecelia's Cathedral, Omaha, 1978-81; mem. chorus Opera/Omaha, 1980; vocal music educator St. Albans (Vt.) City Sch.; dir. St. Albans Mid. Sch. Chorus performance at UN, 1995; mem. Three Penny Opera, Vt. Mozart Festival, 1995; mem. com. multicultural sch. event Africa Day, 1994, Asia Day, 1995; soloist Nebr. Chorals Arts Soc., 1978-81, Champlain Choris, 1981—, Burlington Oratorio Soc., 1981-94, solo recitals, 1981—; condr. Jr. High Dist. Music Festivals, St. Albans and Essex Jct., Vt., 1983, 85; chairperson Music Curriculum Com., St. Albans, 1987; co-founder, condr. Elem. Choral Festival, St. Albans, 1990-94. Mem. NEA, Vt. Edn. Assn., Vt. N.W. Dist. Music Educators Assn. (sec. 1994—). Home: 46 Bank St Saint Albans VT 05478-1635 Office: St Albans City Sch Bellows St Saint Albans VT 05478

JARVIS, DAPHNE ELOISE, laboratory administrator; b. Lithia, Fla., Feb. 18, 1945; d. Grady Edwin and Vera Eloise (Smith) Smith; m. Hubert E. Jarvis, Aug. 1, 1964; 1 child, Jessica Ellen. BS, Blue Mountain Coll., 1966; MA, Spalding U., 1972. Cert. med. technologist with specialist in blood bank. Med. technologist St. Anthony's Hosp., Louisville, 1968-69, Clark County Meml. Hosp., Jeffersonville, Ind., 1969-73; asst. to edn. coord. ARC, Washington, 1973-75; dir. Grace Bapt. Ch. Sch., Bryans Rd., Md., 1978-83; sect. chief blood bank Physicians Meml. Hosp., LaPlata, Md., 1975-76, 83-84; supr. donor blood labs. Southwest Fla. Blood Bank, Tampa, 1984-87, dir., 1987-89; asst. dir. tech. svcs. Ark. Region ARC, Little Rock, 1989-93, dir. tech. svcs./hosp. svcs. Ark. Regional Blood Svcs., 1993-95; mfg. team leader Lifeblood-Midsouth Regional Blood Ctr., Memphis, 1995—; lectr. UAMS Sch. Med. Tech., Little Rock, 1989-95. Children's leader Ingram Blvd Bapt. Ch., West Memphis, Ark., 1995—. Mem. Am. Assn. Blood Banks, South Ctr. Assn. Blood Banks (membership com. 1989-95). Office: Lifeblood Midsouth Reg Blood Ctr 1040 Madison Ave Memphis TN 38104-2106

JARVIS, TERESA LYNN, art educator, artist; b. Huntington, W.Va., May 10, 1956; d. Thomas Richard and Lovetta (Qualls) McComas; m. Roger Dale Jarvis, July 28, 1992; 1 child, Richard Allen. BA, Marshall U., 1979, MA, 1988. Cert. art and elem. tchr., W.Va. Tchr. St. Joseph Grade Sch., Huntington, 1979-88, Crum (W.Va.) Elem. and Mid. Schs., 1988—. Editl. cartoonist (newspaper) The Martin County-Tug Valley Mountain Citizen, 1991; executed mural Silver Creek United Bapt. Ch., Crum, 1995. Mem. ASCD, Nat. Art Educators Assn., Internat. Reading Assn., Am. Fedn. Tchrs., W.Va. Edn. Assn., Wayne County Reading Coun., Delta Kappa Gamma (Sigma chpt.). Democrat. Baptist. Home: PO Box 483 Kermit WV 25674-0483

JASICA, ANDREA LYNN, mortgage banking executive; b. Orlando, Fla., Aug. 21, 1945; d. Walter S. and Florence E. (Pasek) J. AA in Pre Bus. Adminstrn. cum laude, Orlando Jr. Coll., 1965; BS with honors, Rollins Coll., 1976. Sec. Am. Mortgage Co. Fla. Inc., Orlando, 1965-68; closing specialist Charter Mortgage Co., Orlando, 1968-70, Gen. Guaranty Mortgage Co. Inc., Winter Park, Fla., 1971; sr. loan processor C.E. Brooks Mortgage Co. Inc., Orlando, 1971-79; v.p. mktg. Twin Homes Ltd., Orlando, 1980-83; asst. v.p., mgr. region Atlantic Mortgage and Investment Corp. subs. Atlantic Nat. Bank, Orlando, 1984-86; v.p. Commerce Nat. Mortgage Co., Winter Park, 1987-88; supr. Bur. of Census, U.S. Dept. Commerce, Orlando, 1990; investor, 1990—; real estate assoc. Atlantic-to-Gulf Realty Inc., 1972-73, Medel Inc., Maitland, Fla., 1973-74; instr. Mortgage Personnel Svcs. Inc. Contbr. articles to profl. jours. Home: 1011 E Harwood St Orlando FL 32803-5706

JASINSKI-CALDWELL, MARY L., company executive; b. Chester, Pa., May 8, 1959; d. A. Robert and Helen M. Jasinski; m. William A. Caldwell, Aug. 4, 1990; children: Helaina M., Anna L. Student, Loyola Coll., Balt., 1980; BS, Goldey Beacom Coll., Wilmington, Del., 1983. Registered orthotic fitter, sr. pharmacy technician. Gen. mgr. pension plan City Pharmacy of Elkton (Md.), Inc., 1975-96, jr. ptnr., 1994, v.p., 1996—; disc jockey, promoter Garfield's Restaurant, Elkton; editl. writer local newspapers; pro-life columnist KC newsletter. Creator ednl. program PARTICIP.A.A.T.E. For Life. Bd. dirs. Cecil County chpt. ARC, 1996—, Mission Am., Inc., Md. Right to Life, 1993-94, co-chair Cecil County chpt.; adv. Cecil County Pro-life Coalition, Cecil County Bd. Edn. Textbook Adoption Policy Com., 1995; pro-life educator. Alpha Chi scholar, Lindback scholar; recipient J.W. Miller award, Outstanding Achievement in Excellence award K.C., 1994, named Family of Yr., 1995. Mem. NAFE, Am. Mgmt. Assn., Nat. Fedn. Ind. Bus., Nat. Right to Life Com., Am. Life League, Concerned Women Am., Internat. Platform Assn., Pro-Life Md., Christian Coalition, Cath. Alliance, Cecil County C. of C., Internat. Platform Assn., Am. Life League, Nat. Right to Life Com., Christian Coalition, Concerned Women for Am., Human Life Internat., Pharmacists for Life, Bd. Orthotic Cert., Goldey Beacom Coll. Alumni Assn., Alpha Chi. Republican. Roman Catholic. Office: City Pharmacy Inc 723 N Bridge St Elkton MD 21921-5309

JASITT, VICKY LYNN, accountant; b. Hanover, Pa., Aug. 8, 1967; d. Laverne and Kathryn Ardith (Brauen) Seibert; m. Douglas James Jasitt, May 8, 1994; 1 child, Jessica Lauren. BS, Messiah Coll., 1989. CPA, Pa. Staff acct. Miller & Co., York, Pa., 1989-91; acct. York County Solid Waste Authority, York, Pa., 1991—. Mem. Am. Inst. CPAs (award with high distinction 1989), Pa. Inst. CPAs (Outstanding Acctg. Student award 1989), Inst. Mgmt. Accts. Office: York County Solid Waste Authority 2700 Black Bridge Rd York PA 17402-7901

JASKOWIAK, CYNTHIA SHARE, educational administrator; b. Ft. Wayne, Ind., Sept. 7, 1951; d. Charles Edward and Rose Louise (Bender) Share; m. Dennis Jaskowiak, July 27, 1974; children: Derek, Emily, Allison. BS in Edn., U. Mo., Columbia, 1973; MA in Instructional Media Tech., U. Mo., St. Louis, 1979, Advanced Cert. in Adminstrn., 1983. Tchr. English Hazelwood Ctrl. H.S., St. Louis, 1973-78, Hazelwood West H.S., St. Louis, 1978-85; 11th grade prin. Lindbergh H.S., St. Louis, 1985-87, prin., 1987-91; dir. staff devel. Rockwood Sch. Dist., Eureka, Mo., 1991-92, asst. supt., 1992-94; area supt. Parkway Sch. Dist., St. Louis, 1994—; asst. dir./seminar leader I/D/E/A Fellows Program, Appleton, Wis., 1988-94. Fundraiser, Kilo Diabetic Found., St. Louis. Mem. ASCD, Am. Assn. Sch. Adminstrs., Am. Assn. Sch. Pers. Adminstrs., Nat. Staff Devel. Coun., St. Louis Suburban Prins. Assn. (v.p., pres. 1988-89), Phi Kappa Phi. Home: 1907 Dovercliff Ct Chesterfield MO 63017-8032 Office: Parkway Sch Dist 455 N Woods Mill Rd Chesterfield MO 63017

JASKULA, DIANE ELAINE MILLER, clinical therapist, managed care consultant; b. Chgo., Jan. 20, 1962; d. Russell George and Nancie Sara (Lewis) Miller; m. Michael Jaskula, June 7, 1992. BA in Liberal Arts, Drake U., Des Moines, 1984; MA in Counseling, Northeastern Ill. U., Chgo., 1990. Cert. self-employment tng., Ill.; lic. clin. profl. counselor, Ill.; cert. alcohol and drug counselor, Ill. Case mgr., intake coord., group therapist Ctr. for Addictive Problems, Inc., Chgo., 1988-91; addiction therapist Humana/Michael Reese HMO, Chgo., 1991-92; area counselor employee assistance program Human Effectiveness, Inc., Chgo., 1993-95, supervising counselor, 1993; case mgr. mental health Pvt. Healthcare Sys., Inc., Rosemont, Ill., 1991-93, supr. mental health, 1993-96; pres., clin. and consultation dir. Health Choice, P.C., Schaumburg, Ill., 1993—. Mem. ACA, Ill. Mental Health Counseling Assn. (mem. task force on managed care). Office: Health Choice PC # 112 830 E Higgins Rd Schaumburg IL 60172 Address: PO Box 412 Carpentersville IL 60110

JASON, ELAINE VIRGINIA, artist, educator; b. Glendale, Calif., Jan. 15, 1942; d. Williams Dallas Dean and Virginia Louise Smith; m. James L. Curry, May 10, 1971 (div. Apr. 1982); m. Darrell A. Jason, June 25, 1983; children: Wendy Jason Hedgcorth, Amanda Michelle Cowan, Courtney Heather Curry. BFA, Chouinard Art Inst., 1966. One-woman shows include Julie Dohan Gallery, L.A., 1971, Am. Hand Gallery, San Francisco, 1975, Deluxe Gallery, Reno, 1984, Lake Gallery, Tahoe City, Calif., 1985, LSX Gallery, Carson City, Nev., 1991, Mus. Neon Art, L.A., 1991, Sierra Arts Found. Gallery, Reno, 1992; group shows include: Chouinard Art Inst. Gallery, L.A., 1966, Spectrum Gallery, Berkeley, Calif., 1971, Museo Artes Moderno, Mexico City, 1980, Galeria San Miguel, 1982, Art Collector, San Diego, 1984, Valerie Millery Gallery, L.A., 1985, Nev. Biennials, 1988, 90, 94, 96, Matrix Gallery, Sacramento, 1989, Nev. Mus. Art, Reno, 1990, A.T. Galleries, Tahoe City, 1994, Sierra Nevada Coll., Incline Village, Nev., 1994, U. Nev., Reno, 1995; represented in pvt. collections; contbr. articles to profl. jours. Com. mem. City 2000 Arts Commn., Reno, 1991-93. Recipient Jurors award Sedona Sculpture Walk, 1994, Gov. Arts Commns. awards Nev. State Coun. Arts, 1995; grantee Salt Lake City Arts Ctr., 1986, Sierra Arts Found., 1995. Home: 3805 Wedekind Rd Sparks NV 89431

JASON, J. JULIE, money manager, author; b. Owensboro, Ky., May 14, 1949; d. Richard and Grazina Pauliukonis; m. Marius J. Jason, Dec. 19, 1970; children: Ilona, Leila. BA, Baldwin-Wallace Coll., 1971; JD, Cleve. State U., 1974; LLM, Columbia U., 1975. Bar: Ohio 1974, N.Y. 1976, U.S. Dist Ct. (so. dist.) N.Y. 1976, U.S. Ct. Appeals (2d cir.) 1976, U.S. Supreme Ct. 1978. Pvt. practice N.Y.C., 1974-78; asst. gen. counsel Paine Webber, N.Y.C., 1978-83; pres. P.W. Trust and Paine Webber Futures Mgmt. Co., N.Y.C., 1983-88; sr. fin. svcs. atty. Donovan, Leisure, Newton & Irvine, N.Y.C., 1988-89; co-founder, mng. dir. Jackson, Grant & Co., Stamford, Conn., 1989—; arbitrator NYSE. Author: You and Your 401(K), 1996. Mem. ABA, AAUW (chair scholarship com. 1992-93), Nat. Assn. Securities Dealers (cert., arbitrator), Am. Soc. Journalists & Authors, Investment Co. Inst. (sec. regulation com. 1978-83), The Corp. Bar, Columbia U. Alumni Club of Fairfield County (pres. 1993-94). Office: Jackson Grant & Co 1177 High Ridge Rd Stamford CT 06905-1211

JASTRZEMBSKI, SHEILA RAE, counselor, educator; b. La Porte, Ind., Oct. 24, 1942; d. Jesse Willard and Rachel Louisa (Gibbs) Simcox; m. Eugene Michael Feltman, Aug. 1, 1965 (div. Nov. 1978); children: Nathan Joseph Feltman, Lori Beth Feltman; m. Bernard Stanley Jastrzembski, Oct. 24, 1989. BS in Bus. Edn., Ind. U., Bloomington, 1965, MS in Secondary Edn., 1970; MS in Counseling/Human Svcs., Ind. U., South Bend, 1996. Tchr. bus. edn. Ben Davis H.S., Indpls., 1965-68, U.S. Army, Ft. Eustis, Va., 1969-70, Continuing Edn., Indpls., 1970-71; ct. reporter Chas. Olmsted & Assocs., South Bend, 1983; tchr. continuing edn. Bd. Continuing Edn., Rome, N.Y., 1985-86; tchr. bus. edn. Riley H.S., South Bend, 1986-87; tchr., adminstrv. support Elkhart (Ind.) Career Ctr., 1987-95, counselor, 1995—; mem. gender equity adv. bd., co-dir. gender equity grant Elkhart Career Ctr.; mem. vocat. edn. adv. bd. South Bend Schs., 1974-77; advisor Bus. Profls. Am., Cleve., 1986-95. Active Big Sister program Logan Ctr./Svc. Guild, South Bend, 1972—. Mem. NEA, ACA, Assn. for Assessment in Counseling, Questers Internat. Antique Club (sec., v.p., pres.), Delta Pi Epsilon. Republican. Methodist. Office: Elkhart Area Career Ctr 2424 California Rd Elkhart IN 46514

JASUTA, LISA MARIE, special education educator; b. North Wales, Pa., Apr. 7, 1968; d. Carl Thomas and Marjorie (Stanton) J. BA in Comm. Sci., U. Pitts., 1990; MEd in Spl. Edn., Beaver Coll., 1993. Cert. physically and mentally handicapped tchr. Confidential mail courier Univ. Internal Medicine, Pitts., 1988-90; clk./asst. mgr. Southland Corp., Montgomeryville, Pa., 1982-92; long-term instrnl. aide Upper Dublin Sch. Dist., Glenside, Pa., 1992; tchr. asst. The Quaker Sch. at Horsham, Pa., 1992-93, tchr., 1993—.

JAUDZEMIS, KATHLEEN A., judge; b. Omaha, Nebr., Jan. 18, 1949. BA, Univ. of Nebr., 1971, MA, 1976; JD, Univ. of Nebr. Law Coll., 1982. Bar: Nebr., U.S. Dist. Ct. Nebr., U.S. Ct. Appeals (8th cir.). Tchr. St. Paul pub. schs., Nebr., 1971-74, Lincoln pub. schs., Nebr., 1974-79; atty. Cline, Williams, Wright, Johnson & Oldfather, 1982-91; magistrate judge U.S. Dist. Ct. Nebr., 8th circuit, Omaha, 1992—. Mem. ABA, Nebr. Bar Assn., Fed. Magistrate Judges Assn. Office: Edward Zorinsky Fed Bldg PO Box 336 215 N 17th St Omaha NE 68101-4910

JAUQUET-KALINOSKI, BARBARA, library director; b. Crystal Falls, Mich., Mar. 12, 1948; d. Herbert Francis and Lenore Mary (Roell) Jauquet; m. Gregory Clem Kalinoski, Nov. 12, 1983; children: Stacia Amee, Sara Amee, Michael Thomas and Thomas Michael (twins.). BS, No. Mich. U., 1970; MLS, Western Mich. U., 1974. Adminstrv. asst. Mid-Peninsula Libr. System, Iron Mountain, Mich., 1970-74, asst. dir., 1975-79; periodical libr. U. Wis., Superior, 1980; dir. N.W. Regional Libr., Thief River Falls, Minn., 1981—; vice chmn. libr. devel. and svcs. adv. com. Minn. Dept. CFL, chmn. Clime com, LDS; chmn. planning, evaluation and reporting curriculum com. for sch. dist. Mem. Thief River Falls Acad. Boosters Club. Named Woman of Honor, AAUW, 1990. Mem. ALA, Minn. Libr. Assn. (pres.-elect, mem. of continuing edn. com.), Thief River Falls C. of C., Rotary (past pres.). Roman Catholic. Office: NW Regional Libr 101 1st St E Thief River Falls MN 56701-2041

JAX, CHRISTINE, educational administrator, writer; b. Detroit, Jan. 2, 1959; d. Donald P. and Merilyn E. (Baker) J.; m. Len F. Biernat, Apr. 1, 1989; children: Shelley, Marie, Ellen, Laura. BA in Child Psychology, U. Minn., 1991, postgrad. studes in Ednl. Policy, 1994—; MA in Pub. Adminstrn., Hamline U., 1994. Owner Christine's Child Care, Mpls., 1985-88; dir. Kinder Care Lng. Ctr., Shoreview, Mn., 1988-90, Working for Children, Mpls., 1989-92, Mayflower Nursery Sch., Mpls., 1991-92; exec. dir., founder Learning Ctr. for Homeless Families, Mpls., 1992-96; leader children's issues workshops various locations and orgns., 1985—; bd. dirs. Child Care Resource Ctr., Mpls., 1991-95, Minn. Coalition for the Homeless, 1992-95; exec. rels. coun. mem. Gillette Children's Hosp., Mpls.. 1994—. Author: Your Book: Ethics for Children, 1994; (thesis) Children without Choices: Educating School Age Homeless Childen in America, 1994; contbr. articles to law jours. Campaign mgr. various candidates, Mpls., 1989-96; mem. Early Edn. Com. Mpls. Schs., 1990-92, appointed mem. Mayor's Sch. Readiness Group, Mpls., 1991; resource person LWV's Valuing Children, 1993. Recipient Leadership in Child Care award Greater Mpls. Day Care Assn., 1989, Bush Leadership fellowship, Bush Found., St. Paul, 1996. Mem. AAUW, LWV, Citizens League, Pi Lambda Theta. Democrat. Home: 2246 Linclon St NE Minneapolis MN 55418

JAY, DELMA, social worker; b. Middletown, Ohio, Jan. 7, 1921; d. Earl Link and Lydia Theresa (Arkill) Coddington; m. William H. Jay, Apr. 22, 1944; children: Linda L. Farmer, Peggy Sue Pappas. BS in Social Adminstrn., Ohio State U., 1944. Field exec., camp dir. Girl Scouts Am., Columbus, Ohio, 1944-47; bus. mgr. Coddington Machine & Mfg., Inc., Middletown, Ohio, 1947-53; pub. rels. promo dir. Consolidated Bowling Corp., Memphis, 1962-65; social work dir. Pinellas Sch. Sys., St. Petersburg, Fla., 1964-65; aquatic dir. Women's Job Corp. Ctr., St. Petersburg, Fla., 1965-66; social svcs. dir. Shore Acres Nursing Home, St. Petersburg, Fla., 1966-67; program adminstr. youth svcs. Gulf Coast Lung Assn., St. Petersburg, Fla., 1967-68; resource developer Health & Rehab. Svcs., Clearwater, Fla., 1968-87; pres. Cmty. Camping Coun., St. Petersburg, 1978—; co-chair health com. Juvenile Welfare Bd., St. Petersburg, 1987-93; v.p., sec. Christmas Toy Shop, St. Petersburg, 1968—. Mem. edn. conf. com. Coalition for the Homeless, St. Petersburg, 1986—; mem. youth svcs. com. ARC, St. Petersburg, 1986-93. Recipient Va. Lazzara Svc. award YWCA Tampa Bay, 1992, Spotlight on Vols. award Pinellas Vol. Corp., 1992, Sr. Hall of Fame award City of St. Petersburg, 1992, Panhellenic Woman of Yr. award St. Petersburg chpt. Panhellenic, 1994, Cmty. Svc. award St. Petersburg Jr. League, 1996. Mem. Pub. Rels. Network (planner mem. expo com.), Women's C. of C. (chair spl. events 1993—), Phi Mu (mem. Queen of Hearts Ct.) Beta Women's Club (welfare chmn.). Democrat. Home: 2226 39th Ave N Saint Petersburg FL 33714 Office: Cmty Camping Coun 330 5th St N Saint Petersburg FL 33701

JAY, NORMA JOYCE, artist; b. Wichita, Kans., Nov. 11, 1925; d. Albert Hugh and Thelma Ree (Boyd) Braly; m. Laurence Eugene Jay, Sept. 2, 1949; children: Dana Denise, Allison Eden. Student Wichita State U., 1946-49, Art Inst. Chgo., 1955-56, Calif. State Coll., 1963. Illustrator Boeing Aircraft, Wichita, Kans., 1949-51; co-owner Back Door Gallery, Laguna Beach, Calif., 1973-88. One-woman shows include Milcir Gallery, Tiburon, Calif., 1978, Newport Beach City Gallery, 1981; group shows include Am. Soc. Marine Artists ann. exhbns., 1978-96, Peabody Mus., Salem, Mass., 1981, Mystic Seaport Mus. Gallery, Conn., 1982-95, Grand Cen. Galleries, N.Y., 1979-84, The Back Door Gallery, Laguna Beach, Calif., 1973-88, Mariners' Mus., Newport News, Va., 1985-86, Nat. Heritage Gallery of Fine Art, Beverly Hills, Calif., 1988—, Md. Hist. Mus., 1989, Kirsten Gallery, Seattle, 1991-93, R.J. Schaefer Gallery Mystic (Conn.) Seaport Mus., 1992, Vallejo Gallery, Newport Beach, Calif., 1992, Caswell Gallery, Troutdale, Oreg., 1994-95, Columbia River Maritime Mus., Astoria, Oreg., 1994, 95, Coos Art Mus., Coos Bay, Oreg., 1994-96, Arnold Art Gallery, Newport, Conn., 1994, Mystic Internat. Exhbn., Mystic, Conn., 1995, Lu Martin Galleries, Laguna Beach, Calif., 1996—; represented in permanent collections including James Irvine Found., Newport Beach, Niguel Art Assn., Laguna Niguel, Calif., Deloitte, Haskins & Sells, Costa Mesa, Calif., M.J. Brock & Sons Inc., North Hollywood, Calif., others. Recipient Best of Show award Ford Nat. Competition, 1961, First Pl. award Traditional Artists Exhbn., San Bernadino County Mus., 1976, Artist award Chriswood Gallery Invitational Exhbn., Rancho California, Calif., 1973, Dirs. Choice award, People's Choice award, Coos Art Mus. Marine Exhbn., 1996. Fellow Am. Soc. Marine Artists (charter); mem. Niguel Art Assn. (first pres. 1968, hon. life mem. 1978), Artists Equity, Am. Artists Profl. League. Democrat.

JAYNE, CYNTHIA ELIZABETH, psychologist; b. Pensacola, Fla., June 5, 1953; d. Gordon Howland and Joan (Rockwood) J. AB, Vassar Coll., 1974; MA, SUNY, Buffalo, 1978, PhD, 1983. Lic. psychologist, Pa. Instr. dept. psychiatry Temple U. Sch. Medicine, Phila., 1982-84, asst. prof., 1984-85, asst. dir. outpatient services, asst. dir. residency tng., 1982-85, clin. asst. prof., 1985—; pvt. practice psychology Phila., 1985—; adj. prof. Chestnut Hill Coll., 1994—. Contbr. articles to profl. jours. Soc. for Sci. Study Sex scholar, 1981; Sigma Xi grantee, 1981, Kinsey Inst. Dissertation award, 1983. Mem. APA, Ea. Psychol. Assn., Soc. for Sci. Study Sex (bd. dirs. 1984-86).

JAYNES, RUTH WATKINS, accountant, lawyer; b. Detroit, Nov. 13, 1952; d. Frederic Norman and Ruth Mary (Watkins) Pew; m. Gregory Albert Jaynes, Aug. 3, 1985. BBA, U. Mich., 1974, MBA, 1976; JD, Wayne State U., 1983. Bar: Mich. 1983; CPA, CMA. Tax sr. Arthur Andersen & Co., Detroit, 1976-80; investigator white collar crime Wayne County Prosecutor's Office, Detroit, summer 1981; mng. editor Wayne Law Rev., Detroit, 1982-83; legal assoc. Clark, Klein & Beaumont, Detroit, 1983-85; tax supr. Deloitte Haskins & Sells, Chgo., 1985-87; tax mgr. Friedman, Eisenstein, Raemer, Schwartz, Chgo., 1987-89; dir. tax practice Reinmund & Co., Ottumwa, Iowa, 1989-90; rsch. atty. Mich. Ct. Appeals, Grand Rapids, 1992-94; tax mgr. Deloitte & Touche LLP, Grand Rapids, 1994-95; self-employed cons. Plainwell, Mich., 1990—. Mem. Nat. Assn. Accts., Inst. Mgmt. Accts., Kalamazoo Downstreamers, Kalamazoo Gem and Mineral Soc. Home and Office: 1041 Fairlane Rd Plainwell MI 49080-9532

JAYSON, MELINDA GAYLE, lawyer; b. Dallas, Sept. 29, 1956; d. Robert and Louise Adelle (Jacobs) J. BA, U. Tex., 1977, JD, 1980. Bar: Tex. 1980, U.S. Dist. Ct. (no. dist.) Tex. 1980, U.S. Ct. Appeals (5th and 11th cirs.) 1981, U.S. Dist. Ct. (so. dist.) Tex. 1989, U.S. Ct. Appeals (8th cir.) 1990, U.S. Supreme Ct. 1991. Assoc. Akin, Gump, Strauss, Hauer & Feld, Dallas, 1980-86, ptnr., 1987—; mem. panel securities arbitrators, Dallas adv. coun. Am. Arbitration Assn. Mem. Am. Jewish Com., Dallas, 1982—. Named one of Outstanding Young Women Am., 1983. Mem. Nat. Assn. Securities Dealers (arbitrator), Tex. Bar Assn., Dallas Bar Assn. Office: Akin Gump Strauss Hauer & Feld LLP 1700 Pacific Ave Ste 4100 Dallas TX 75201-4624

JEANNETTE, JOAN MARIE, pediatrics nurse; b. Orlando, Fla., Sept. 16, 1961; d. Roy Benedict and Joan Theresa (Pleus) Laughlin; m. Ronald Clayton Jeannette, Apr. 25, 1987; 1 child, Patrick Laughlin. BSN, Vanderbilt U., 1983. Cert. pediatrics nurse, 1995. Staff nurse Vanderbilt Children's Hosp., Nashville, 1983-85, asst. nurse coord., 1985-87; office nurse Mid-South Pediat. Urology, Nashville, 1987-89; rehab. nurse pediats. Sea Pines Rehab., Palm Bay, Fla., 1989-90; nurse mgr. pediats. Polk Gen. Hosp., Bartow, Fla., 1990-93; nurse supr. Highlands Regional Med. Ctr., Sebring, Fla., 1993-94; head nurse pediatrics Highlands Regional Hosp., Sebring, Fla., 1994-95, dir. womens and children, 1995—. Recipient Polk County Outstanding Nursing award, 1992; grantee Jr. League of Lakeland, Fla., 1993.

JEANSONNE, ANGELA LYNNE, senior analyst; b. Honolulu, Oct. 3, 1961; d. Charles Preston and Beverly Jean (Ulstad) McKinney; m. William C. Jeansonne, June 11, 1988. BA, Am. U., 1984; MA, George Washington U., 1992. Legis. analyst Sch. Bd. Assn., Washington, 1983-84; edn. analyst Ind. Fed., Washington, 1984-86; analyst Xerox Corp., Arlington, Va., 1986-88; sr. analyst Student Loan Mktg. Assn., Washington, 1988-95. Recipient acad. scholars Am. Univ., Washington, 1982-84, Bryce Harlow scholarship,

1991. Mem. AAUW, Bus. and Profl. Women. Republican. Methodist. Address: PO Box 2787 Columbus MD 21045

JEBSEN, JOAN HELENE, medical records administrator; b. Bklyn., May 16, 1932; d. Henry William and Helene (Hastedt) Dannevig; m. Robert H. Jebsen, Mar. 25, 1951 (div. Jan. 1976); children: Eric Richard, James Mark, Brian William, Lawrence Bradford. BA, U. Cin., 1976. Statewide coord. Appalachian Coalition of Ohio, Cin., 1975-77; owner Women Assocs., Cin., 1977-79; adminstrv. sec. Highlands Hosp., Asheville, N.C., 1979-81; owner, cons. Mgmt. Sus., Radford, Va., 1981-83; sr. med. sec. U. Miss. Med. Ctr., Jackson, 1983—. Chaplain Unitarian Universalist Ch., Jackson; bd. dirs. Miss. Religious Leadership Conf., Jackson, 1987—; mem. Jackson Clergy Network, 1991—; chair Disaster Relief Mid-South Dist., 1990—; profl. storyteller Jackson Arts Alliance, 1984-91. Mem. LWV (pres. Miss. bd. dirs.). Unitarian.

JECKLIN, LOIS UNDERWOOD, art corporation executive, consultant; b. Manning, Iowa, Oct. 5, 1934; d. J.R. and Ruth O. (Austin) Underwood; m. Dirk C. Jecklin, June 24, 1955; children: Jennifer Anne, Ivan Peter. BA, State U. Iowa, 1992. Residency coord. Quad City Arts Coun., Rock Island, Ill., 1973-78; field rep. Affiliate Artists, Inc., N.Y.C., 1975-77; mgr., artist in residence Deere & Co., Moline, Ill., 1977-80; dir. Vis. Artist Series, Davenport, Iowa, 1978-81; pres. Vis. Artists, Inc., Davenport, 1981-88; pres., owner Jecklin Assocs., 1988—. asst. to exec. dir. Walter W. Naumburg Found., N.Y.C., 1990—; cons. writer's program St. Ambrose Coll., Davenport, 1981, 83, 85; mem. com. Iowa Arts Coun., Des Moines, 1983-84; panelist Chamber Music Am., N.Y.C., 1984, Pub. Art Conf., Cedar Rapids, Iowa, 1984; panelist, mem. com. Lt. Gov.'s Conf. on Iowa's Future, Des Moines, 1984; trustee Davenport Mus. Art, 1975—, Nature Conservancy Iowa, 1987-88; mem. steering com. Iowa Citizens for Arts, Des Moines, 1970-71; bd. dirs. Tri-City Symphony Orchestra Assn., Davenport, 1968-83; founding mem. Urban Design Council, HOME, City of Davenport Beautification Com., all Davenport, 1970-72; bd. gov. Am. Craft Mus., N.Y.C., 1995—. Recipient numerous awards Izaak Walton League, Davenport Art Gallery, Assn. for Retarded Citizens, Am. Heart Assn., Ill. Bur. Corrections, many others; LaVernes Noyes scholar, 1953-55. Mem. Nat. Assn. Performing Art's Mgrs. and Agents, Am. Symphony Orch. League, Crow Valley Golf Club, Outing Club, Rotary. Republican. Episcopalian. Home and Office: 2717 Nichols Ln Davenport IA 52803-3620

JEDJU, LINDA JO-ANNE, writer, poet, nurse; b. Lakehurst Naval Air Sta., N.J., Mar. 11, 1954; d. John Benedict and Joan Dolores (Kupper) Kalinowski; m. Joseph William Jedju, Sept. 20, 1986; children: Brian Richard, Shaun Michael. Diploma in nursing, St. Francis Med. Ctr., Trenton, N.J., 1974; BA in History and Social Sci., Thomas Edison State Coll., Trenton, 1993. RN, N.J.; cert. psychiat. and mental health nurse ANCC. Nurse Med. Ctr. at Princeton, N.J., 1974-76, Carrier Found., Belle Mead, N.J., 1977-78, 85-86; writer, 1986—. Contbr. poetry in Nursing Spectrum mag., Treasured Poems of Am.; contbr. articles to profl. jours. Mem. DAR, Colonial Dames 17th Century.

JEFF, GLORIA JEAN, federal government administrator; b. Detroit, Apr. 8, 1952; d. Doris Lee and Harriette Virginia (Davis) J. BSE in Civil Engring., U. Mich., 1974, MSE, 1976, M in Urban Planning, 1976; cert. program in Urban Transp., Carnegie Mellon U., 1979; cert. program sr. mgrs. in govt., Harvard U., 1994. Prin. planner, program analyst, equipment engr. Southeastern Mich. Transp. Authority, 1976-81; divsn. adminstr., multi-regional planning divsn. Mich. Dept. Transp., 1981-83, divsn. adminstr., urban transp. planning divsn., 1983-85, asst. dep. dir. Bur. of Transp. Planning, 1985-90, dep. dir. Bur. Transp. Planning, 1990-93; assoc. adminstr. for policy Fed. Hwy. Adminstrn., U.S. Dept. Transp., Washington, 1993—; adj. prof. Coll. Architecture and Urban Planing U. Mich., Ann Arbor, 1988—; chair standing com. on planning Mississippi Valley Conf. State Hwys. and Transp. Ofcls., 1987-89, vice chair strategic issues com., 1990-94; mem. Transp. Rsch. Bd., 1989—; adv. bd. U. Mich. Coll. Engring., 1995—, U. Calif., Davis, 1995—. Bd. dirs. Capitol chpt. Child and Family Svcs. of Mich. Inc., 1990-93, chair long-range planning com., 1991-93, sec. bd. dirs., 1993. Recipient Young Engr. of Yr. award Detroit chpt. Soc. Women Engrs., 1979, Young Engr. of Yr. award Detroit chpt. NSPE, 1979, Disting. Alumni award U. Mich., 1991, 92, Regional Amb. award S.E. Mich. Assn. Govts., 1993, others. Mem. Am. Assn. Hwy. and Transp. Ofcls. (mem. modal adv. tech. com. 1988-91, mem. econ. expansion and devel. com. 1990-91, vice chair intermodal issues com. 1990-93), Am. Planning Assn. (v.p. for programs Planning and the Black Cmty. divsn. 1990-92, mem. nat. membership com. 1990-92, chair transp. planning divsn. 1994—, pres. Mich. chpt. 1990-91), Am. Inst. Cert. Planners, U. Mich. Alumni Assn. (bd. dirs. 1985-90, v.p. 1995—), U. Mich. Coll. Architecture Alumni Soc., Delta Sigma Theta, others. Office: Dept Transp Policy Office 400 7th St SW Washington DC 20590-0001

JEFFERDS, MARY LEE, environmental education executive; b. Seattle, July 16, 1921; d. Amos Osgood and Vera Margaret (Percival) J.; AB, U. Calif. at Berkeley, 1943, gen. secondary teaching cert., 1951; MA, Columbia U., 1947; cert. Washington and Lee U., 1945. Sec. Fair Play Com. Am. Citizens Japanese Ancestry, 1943-44; adminstrv. asst. U.C. Alumni Assn. book Students at Berkeley, 1949; dir. Student Union Monterey Jr. Coll., 1949-50; mgr. Nat. Audubon Soc. Conservation Resource Ctr., Berkeley, 1951-66; dir. Nat. Audubon Soc. Bay Area Ednl. Svcs., 1966-71; curriculum cons. Project WEY, U. Calif. Demonstration Lab. Sch., Berkeley, 1972-83. Cons. Berkeley Sch. Dist., Alameda County Schs. Mem. land- use com. Environ. Edn. com. East Bay Mcpl. Utility Dist., 1968-87; mem. steering com. Nat. Sci. Guild, Oakland Mus., 1970-76; community adviser Jr. League of Oakland, 1972-76. Mem. Berkeley Women's Town Coun., 1970-91; mem. NAACP.; bd. dirs. East Bay Regional Park Dist., 1972-91, pres., 1978-80, 88-90; bd. dirs. Save San Francisco Bay Assn., 1969-91, People for Open Space, 1977-86, Calif. Natural Areas Coordinating Coun., 1968-90, Living History Ctr., 1982-85; mem. steering com. Bay Area Environ. Edn. Alliance, 1982-85, regional planning com. Assn. of Bay Area Govts., 1988-91, exec. com. Citizens for Eastshore State Park, 1985—; v.p. Friends of Bot. Garden, U. Calif., Berkeley, 1976-80, trustee, 1986—. With USAAF, 1944-46. Recipient Merit award Calif. Conservation Coun., 1953; Woman of Achievement award Camp Fire Girls, 1976; Merit award Am. Soc. Landscape Architects, 1979, Conservation award Golden Gate Audubon Soc., 1985, Benjamin I. Wheeler medal, 1991, Mary's Peak on Brooks Island named in her honor, 1996; mem. Am. Farmland Trust. Mem. AAUW (Calif. com. 1970-73), Prytanean Alumnae, Inc. (pres. 1969-71, chmn. adv. coun. 1971-73, adv. com. Urban Creeks Coun. 1986-91), Nature Conservancy (chmn. no. Calif. chpt. 1970-71), LWV, Regional Parks Assn. (citizens com. to complete the refuge), Nat. Women's Polit. Caucus, Golden Gate Audubon Soc., Sierra Club (environ. edn. com. No. Calif. chpt. 1973-77), U. Calif. Alumni Assn., Inst. Calif. Man in Nature, Calif. Assn. Recreation and Park Dists. (v.p. 1978-81, 1988-90, Oustanding Bd. Mem. award 1989, "Mary's Peak" named for her), Preserve Area Ridgelands, Calif. Native Plant Soc., Planning and Conservation League, Urban Ecology, Cousteau Soc., Soroptomists, Pi Lambda Theta, Mortar Board, Gavel (pres.). Democrat. Mem. adv. com. Natural History Guide Series U. Calif. Press, 1972-91. Home: 2932 Pine Ave Berkeley CA 94705-2349

JEFFERS, IDA PEARLE, management consultant, volunteer; b. Houston, Tex., Sept. 5, 1935; d. Stanford Wilbur and Ida Pearle (Kinkead) Oberg; m. Samuel Lee Jeffers, Aug. 29, 1956; children: John Laurence (dec.), Julie Elizabeth Flynn, Melinda Leigh. Student, U. Colo., 1953-56; BA in History, U. N.Mex., 1957. Asst. to mayor City of Albuquerque, 1978, dir. capital improvements, 1979-81; pres. Orgn. Plus, 1988—; guest lectr. U. N.Mex. Albuquerque Pub. Sch., 1968-71. Chmn. Comprehensive Plan Rev., Bond Issue, various coms., Albuquerque, 1968—; mem. Middle Rio Grand Coun. Govts., Albuquerque, 1972-74; mem. Environ. Planning Commn., Albuquerque, 1972-77, chmn. 1975-76; chmn. Citizen Adv. Group, Community Devel., Albuquerque, 1974-75; mem. Jr. League, Albuquerque, 1966—, bd. dirs. 1970-76; mem. N. Mex. Architect, Engrs. Joint Practice Bd. 1978-85, chmn. 1983-85; treas. St. Mark's Episcopal Ch., 1983-86; pres. Eldorado High Sch. Parents, Albuquerque, 1985-86; pres. Regional Conservation Land Trust, Albuquerque, 1987-91; trustee Found., Study and Care of Organic Brain Damage, Houston, 1972-82, pres. 1982-94; mem. Urban Transp. Planning Policy Bd., 1972-74; chmn. community advisors Albuquerque Youth Symphony, 1985-91; founder, chair Friends of Sandia (N.Mex.) Sch., 1965-68, chmn. devel. pre-sch. bd., 1974; mentor Leadership Albuquerque, 1987-91; bd. dirs. Good Govt. Group, Albuquerque, 1988-92, treas. 1988-92, mem., treas. Albuquerque Arts Alliance, 1988-91; mem. Albuquerque All Faiths, All Faith's Receiving Home Aux., 1964-68, sec. 1966, Jr. Women Club, 1963-66, Chaparral Coun. Girl Scouts leaders, 1971-73, selections chmn., 1973-74, Albuquerque Tutorial Coun., 1967-69; foundation bd. Albuquerque Youth Symphony, 1995—. Recipient Disting. Pub. Svc. award, State of N. Mex., 1975, Disting. Woman of N. Mex. award, N.Mex. Women's Polit. Caucus, 1976, Golden Talon award Eldorado High Sch., Albuquerque, 1985, Panhellenic Coun. Disting. Alumnae award 1979. Mem. Rotary, Delta Gamma (pres. 1963-67, chmn. collegiate adv. bd. 1968-71, Cable and Shield awards 1970, 77). Republican. Episcopalian.

JEFFERSON, BLANCHE WAUGAMAN, art educator; b. McKeesport, Pa., Apr. 30, 1909; d. George Timothy and Anna Mary (Scott) Waugaman; m. William Lynn Jefferson, June 16, 1954 (dec. June 1980); 1 child, Patricia. Student, Pa. State U., 1932, U. Colo., 1941; BS in Art Edn., Ind. (Pa.) U., 1945; MA, Columbia U., 1948, EdD, 1954. Cert. sch. administr., Pa. From elem. tchr. to art supr. Vandergrift Pa. Pub. Sch. Dist., 1929-49; assoc. prof. art edn. Ind. U., 1949-54; prof., head dept. art edn. U. Pitts., 1954-67; ret., 1967; lectr., demonstrator art edn. various sch. dists., Puerto Rico, 1965; state evaluator for pub. sch. and univ. art edn. programs State of Pa., 1948-67; com. on art edn. Mus. Modern Art, N.Y.C., 1952-66; workshop leader Nev. Art Tchrs. Legis., Las Vegas, 1960; sec. Westmoreland Coord. Com. for Pa. Tchrs., 1947-49; adminstrv. coun. U. Pitts., 1957-66; advisor Pitts. Head Start Program; participant Internat. Panel Educators, 1956. Author: Teaching Art to Children, 1957 (Internat Biennial award Delta Kappa Gamma 1958), My World of Art, 1960, So. Strong This Bond, 1995; prin. works include Ind. U. Mus. Sec. Internat. Soc. for Edn. Through Art, 1946-52; lectr., rschr. Ea. Arts Assn., 1945-66, Nat. Art Edn. Assn., Washington, 1945-66; Western Pa. com. sec. State of Pa., 1945-49. Mem. Nat. Art Edn. Assn., Naples Art Assn. Democrat. Home: 615 7th Ave N Naples FL 33940

JEFFERSON, DONNA REEDER, publisher; b. Annapolis, Md., July 19, 1954; d. Donald Reeder and Elwina Fletcher (Miller) McDonald; m. James Ray Jefferson, Jan. 7, 1977; children: Janet, Tyler. BS in Acctg., U. N.C., 1982. Jr. acct. Faw, Casson & Co., Annapolis, 1983-84; staff acct. Capital Gazette Comm., Annapolis, 1984-86, asst. contr., 1986-90; pub. Chesapeake Children News mag., Annapolis, 1990—. Contbr. articles to mags., 1990—. Mem. fin. com. YWCA, Annapolis, 1988-92, v.p. fin., 1992-93, pres., 1993-95, treas., 1995—; mem. Key Sch. Parent League, Annapolis, 1987—. Recipient Tribute to Women in Industry award YWCA, 1987. Mem. Parenting Publs. Am., Annapolis Striders. Democrat. Episcopalian. Office: Jefferson Comm 13 Southgate Ave Annapolis MD 21401

JEFFERSON, MARGO L., theater critic; b. Chgo., Oct. 17, 1947. BA in English and Am. Lit. cum laude, Brandeis U., 1968; MS, Columbia U., 1971. Editor Newsweek, 1973-78; asst. prof. dept. journalism NYU, 1979-83, 89-91; contbg. editor Vogue, 1984-89, 7 Days, 1984-89; lectr. Am. Lit., performing arts & criticism Columbia U., N.Y.C., 1991-93; critic culture desk The New York Times, 1993-95, Sunday theater critic, 1995—. Recipient Pulitzer Prize for criticism, 1995. Office: The New York Times 229 W 43rd St New York NY 10036-3913*

JEFFERSON, SANDRA TRAYLOR, choreographer, ballet coach; b. Tarboro, N.C., Feb. 28, 1942; d. Charles Labon and Doris Vivian (Parker) Traylor; m. Milton Franklin Jefferson, July 2, 1960; children: Mark Franklin, Todd Christopher. Student, Parks Sch. Dance, Petersburg, Va., 1947-58, Sch. of the Richmond (Va.) Ballet, 1958-60; diploma, Julia Mildred Harper Sch. Dance, Richmond, 1960; studied with Robert David Brown, Sterling, Va., 1978-80. Soloist Ballet Impromptu, Richmond, 1958-60; freelance dance instr. Chantilly, Va., 1968-70; ballet coach Artistic Skating Club of Sterling, 1980; founder, dir. Ballet for Skaters, Manassas, Va., 1980-89; artistic dir., cons. in choreography No. Va. Artistic Skating Club, Manassas, 1986-89; artistic dir. Skating Club of Manassas, 1989; founder, dir. Ballet for Skaters, Seabrook, Md., 1989-94; choreographer, ballet coach Nat. Capitol Dance and Figure Club, Seabrook and Washington, 1989-94; founder, dir. Ballet for Figure Skaters, Sterling, Va., 1993-94; students include nat. medalists in the U.S. and Can. and mems. Can. World Team, U.S. Olympic Sports Festival Team; freelance choreographer, ballet coach, Sterling, 1993—. Developer: Brosano Technique Vocabulary of Movement, 1986, Free Form Ballet, 1993; co-developer (artistic skating technique) Brosano Technique, 1981. Social dir. Jaycee-ettes, Winchester, Va., 1963-67. Recipient Achievement award Jaycee-ettes, 1963, 64, 65, 66, 67, U.S. S.E. Soc. Roller Skating Tchrs. Am. award, 1988, World Decoration of Excellence award Am. Biog. Inst., 1989. Mem. Profl. Dance Tchrs. Assn. Methodist. Home and Office: 507 S Maple Ct Sterling VA 20164-2710

JEFFORDS, MARY MARGARET, community activist; b. Huntington Station, N.Y., Mar. 20, 1956; d. Harry McClean and Margaret Marion (Gill) J. AA, Briarcliff Coll., 1977. Case worker County Govt., L.I., N.Y., 1980-89; journalist Metro Comm. News, Buffalo, 1989-91; freelance writer N.Y., 1989—; pub. rels. person-in-charge Injured Workers of N.Y., Syracuse, 1990—; pres. Western N.Y. Injured Workers of N.Y., Sanborn, N.Y., 1991—; cons. med. malpractice Alliance for Mentally Ill, Buffalo, 1991—. Author: Panic and Anxiety Disorders, 1992. Labor organizer Injured Workers of N.Y., Buffalo, 1991-93; organizer Reach to the Stars C. of C., Niagara Falls, 1990-94; coord. Niagara Falls Anxiety Group, 1990-96; exhibitor T-shirt project, Niagara Falls, 1992-96. Mem. N.Y. State Workers' Compensation Bd. (mem. practices and procedures com. 1995—), Soc. Profl. Journalists, Niagara Falls Assn. Profl. Women Writers, Coalition of Econ. Justice, Coalition on Safety and Health, Anxiety Disorders Assn. of Am. Methodist. Home: PO Box 252 Sanborn NY 14132

JEFFREY, NOELA MARY, publishing executive; b. Reading, Pa., Dec. 11, 1941; d. John Theodore and Mary M. (Linkowski) Slapikas; m. Alexander MacLean Jeffrey, June 22, 1968; children: Alexander Maclean Jr., Douglas Duart. BA, Seton Hill Coll., 1963. Corr. Harcourt, Barce, Javanovich, N.Y.C., 1963-65; editor Publs. of Most. Reverend Fulton J. Sheen, N.Y.C., 1965-68; editor, assoc. pub. Wells Pubs., Pasedena, Calif., 1985-91; principal Noel Jeffrey Editorial Svcs., 1991—. Editor Printing Jour., 1988, PINC Newsletter and Blueline, American Printer Mag., 1993—; contbr. articles to profl. jours. Bd. dirs. Graphic Arts Literacy Alliance, Pitts., 1990—; mem. adv. com. graphics comms. dept. Pasadena City Coll., 1988—; various bd. positions Pasadena Jr. Philharmonic Com., 1982-86, assoc. 1986—; cmty. svc. positions, Little League, PTA, 1972—. Named Pioneer of Yr. Printing Industries So. Calif., 1990. Mem. In Plant Mgmt. Assn., L.A. Phil. Affiliates. Democrat. Roman Catholic. Home: 330 Rosita Ln Pasadena CA 91105-1437

JEFFRIES, PAMELA DEPPERMAN, advertising company manager; b. Omaha, Aug. 1, 1965; d. Robert Edwin and Ruth Arlyn (Bock) Depperman; m. Cordell Ray Jeffries, Feb. 29, 1992. BS in Journalism, U. Mo., 1987. Asst. acct. exec. TBWA Chiat Day, St. Louis, 1988-90; acct. exec. Louis London, Inc., St. Louis, 1991-93, Randazzo & Blavins, Inc., San Francisco, 1993-95; acct. supr. Hodskins Simone & Searls, Inc., Palo Alto, Calif., 1995—. Project Bus. cons. Jr. Achievement, San Francisco, 1995; reading tutor/editor Literacy Coun., St. Louis, 1990-93; vol. Nat. Abortion Rights Action League, St. Louis, 1992-93. Mem. Omicron Delta Kappa.

JEGEN, SISTER CAROL FRANCES, religion educator; b. Chgo., Oct. 11, 1925; d. Julian Aloysius and Evelyn W. (Bostelmann) J. BS in History, St. Louis U., 1951; MA in Theology, Marquette U., 1958, PhD in Religious Studies, 1968; hon. degree, St. Mary of the Woods, Terra Haute, Ind., 1977. Elem. tchr. St. Francis Xavier Sch., St. Louis, 1947-51; secondary tchr. Holy Angels Sch., Milw., 1951-57; coll. tchr. Mundelein Coll., Chgo., 1957-91; prof. pastoral studies Loyola U., Chgo., 1991—; adv. coun. U.S. Cath. Bishops, Washington, 1969-74; trustees Cath. Theol. Union, Chgo., 1974-84. Author: Jesus the Peace Maker, 1986, Restoring Our Friendship with God, 1989; co-author: (with Byron Sherwin) Thank God, 1989; editor: Mary According to Women, 1985. Participant Nat. Farm Worker Ministry, Fresno, Calif., 1977—; mem. Pax Christi, U.S.A., 1979—, Jane Addams Conf., Chgo., 1989. Recipient Loyola Civic award Loyola U., Chgo., 1981; named one of 100 Women to Watch Today's Chgo. Woman, 1989. Mem. Cath. Theol. Soc. Am., Coll. Theology Soc., Cath.-Jewish Scholars Dialog, Liturgical Conf. Democrat. Roman Catholic. Home: Wright Hall 6364 N Sheridan Rd Chicago IL 60660-1700 Office: Loyola U Inst Pastoral Studies 6525 N Sheridan Rd Chicago IL 60626-5311

JELINEK, VERA, university program administrator; b. Kosice, Czechoslovakia, Dec. 16, 1935; d. Joseph and Margit (Lefkovits) Schnitzer; m. Joseph Jelinek, June 19, 1960; children: David, Paul. BA in History, Queens Coll., 1956; MA, Johns Hopkins U., 1958; PhD in Modern European History, NYU, 1977, diploma grad. sch. bus. adminstrn., 1981. Translator, analyst Rockefeller Bros. Fund, N.Y.C., 1958-59; exec. dir. U.S. Youth Coun., N.Y.C., 1959-63; asst. coord. Sch. Continuing Edn. NYU, N.Y.C., 1984-85, dir. internat. programs social & natural scis., 1985—; mem. adv. com. N.Y.C.-Budapest Sister City program, 1991-94; internat. ednl. travel coord. Sch. Continuing Edn., NYU, 1985—; program com. mem. Global Bus. Assn., N.Y.C., 1991-93. Author: The Hungarian Factor in Italian Foreign Policy, 1977; creator (audio cassette) Before You Go Tape Guides, 1984. Mem. internat. adv. com. Mus. Am. Folk Art, N.Y.C., 1992—. Recipient Franson award Nat. Univ. Continuing Edn. Assn., 1991; NYU curricular challenge fund grantee; Ford Found. Area tng. fellow, Johns Hopkins U. fellow. Mem. Am. Folk Art Soc. (conf. chair 1984), Global Bus. Assn., Carnegie Coun. Ethics & Internat. Affairs, Phi Beta Kappa. Democrat. Jewish. Office: NYU Sch Continuing Edn Internat Programs 50 W 4th St 331 Shimkin New York NY 10012

JELL-BAHLSEN, SABINE, anthropologist, filmmaker; b. Berlin, Jan. 11, 1950; came to U.S., 1975; d. Gehard Rolf and Manja (Wodowos) Bahlsen; m. Georg Sebastian Jell, Nov. 10, 1969; 1 child, Saskia. MA, Freie U., Berlin, 1974; PhD, The New Sch., N.Y.C., 1980. Pres. Ogbuide & Ogbuide Films, N.Y.C., 1983—; adj. faculty R.I. Sch. Design, Providence, 1990-96; lectr. dept. lang. and comm. Papua New Guinea U. Tech., 1996—. Dir. documentaries (with Georg Jell) Eze Nwata The Small King, 1983; dir. documentaries Mammy Water: In Search of The Water Spirits in Nigeria, 1989, Owu: Chidi Joins The Okoroshi, 1993, Tubali: Hausa Architecture of North Nigeria, 1994; contbr. articles to profl. jours. Mem. Am. Anthropol. Assn., African Studies Assn., Soc. Visual Anthropology, Assn. Ind. Film and Video Makers, N.Y. African Studies Assn. (exec. bd. dirs., sec. 1995-96).

JELLISON, KATHERINE KAY, historian, educator; b. Garden City, Kans., Jan. 5, 1960; d. Billy Dean and Margaret Ruth (Brown) Jellison; m. David John Winkelmann, Aug. 10, 1985. BA, Ft. Hays (Kans.) State U., 1982; MA, U. Nebr., 1984; PhD, U. Iowa, 1991. Asst. prof. Memphis State U., 1991-93; asst. prof. Ohio U., Athens, 1993-96, assoc. prof. history, 1996—. Author: Entitled to Power: Farm Women and Technology, 1913-1963, 1993. Named Outstanding Young Alumni Ft. Hays State U., 1994; recipient Excellence in Feminist Pedagogy award Ohio U., 1994; Smithsonian Instn. fellow, 1989. Mem. NOW, Am. Hist. Assn., Orgn. Am. Historians, Berkshire Conf. on History of Women, Social Sci. History Assn., Ohio Acad. History. Democrat. Methodist. Office: Ohio University Dept History Bentley Hall Athens OH 45701

JENKINS, ADRIENNE BETH, marketing research and planning consultant, artist; b. West Chester, Pa., Mar. 27, 1963; d. Norman Rodney and Kathleen Louise (Erb) J. BS in Mktg., Pa. State U., 1985; postgrad., Temple U., 1988-90. Market rsch. analyst Southeastern Mktg., Stuart, Fla., 1985; sales specialist GE, Pittsfield, Mass., 1986; rsch. assoc. Nat. Analysts-Booz Allen, Phila., 1987; market rsch. analyst Rorer Internat. Pharms., Ft. Washington, Pa., 1988-91; mgr. market rsch. Rorer Pharm. Corp. (USA), Ft. Washington; dir. devel. & pub. affairs Abington Art Ctr., Jenkintown, Pa., 1994-96; cons. Phila., 1996—. Cons., vol., bd. dirs. Abington (Pa.) Art Ctr., 1990—, Bus. Vols. for Arts, 1990—. Scholar Campbell Soup Co., 1981. Mem. Am. Mktg. Assn.

JENKINS, BARBARA ALEXANDER, pastor; b. Ft. Bragg, N.C., Oct. 13, 1942; d. Archie Herman Alexander and Hattie Elizabeth (Thigpen) Truitt; m. Warren Keith Jenkins, Aug. 22, 1964 (div. Sept. 1980); children: Pamela, Eric, Jason. BS, Ea. Mich. U., 1964, postgrad., 1964-66; postgrad., Duke U., 1978; DD (hon.), Ch. of Christ Bible Coll., Madras, India, 1988. Ordained to ministry, World Faith Clinic Inc., 1983, A.M.E. Zion Ch., 1982. Min. World Faith Clinic Inc., Fayetteville, N.C., 1981-83, A.M.E. Zion Ch., Fayetteville, 1982-84; pastor Noah's Ark Ministry, Fayetteville, 1985-86; founder, pastor Rainbow Tabernacle of Faith Ministries, Inc., Winston-Salem, N.C., 1984—; founder Rainbow Raleigh (N.C.) Outreach Ministries, 1986—, Rainbow Tabernacle of Faith, Charlotte, N.C., 1987—; dir. Spotlight on Truth Internat. Radio Ministries, Winston-Salem, 1985—, overseer hdqrs. Ogun State, Nigeria, 1992, others; founder Rainbow Internat. Crusade Ministry, Winston-Salem, 1986—; pres. Rainbow Bible Coll., Winston-Salem; dean Rainbow Inst. Commensurate Studies, Winston-Salem, 1985—; mem. Internat. Conv. Faith Ministries, Tulsa, 1989—. Author: Guidelines for Ministers, 1994; contbr. articles to religious jours. Concert vocalist N.C. Black Repertory Co., Winston-Salem, 1987, 88; youth coord. Jerry Lewis Muscular Dystrophy Telethon, Raleigh, 1987, 88; guest speaker Wake Forest U., Winston-Salem, 1991. Recipient Outstanding Svc. award Rainbow Tabernacle Faith, Inc., 1987; scholar March of Dimes-Easter Seals, 1960-64. Mem. NAFE, N.C. Women in Ministry (bd. dirs.), Am. Assn. Christian Counselors, Nat. Assn. Religious Profls., Delta Theta (project coord. 1979-80). Democrat. Office: Rainbow Tabernacle Faith Ministries Inc 4091 New Walkertown Rd Winston Salem NC 27105-9734 also: 1119 Cypress Cir Winston Salem NC 27106-3307

JENKINS, BILLIE BEASLEY, film company executive; b. Topeka, June 27, 1943; d. Arthur and Etta Mae (Price) Capelton; m. Rudolph Alan Jenkins, Nov. 1, 1935; 1 child, Tina Caprice. Student, Santa Monica City Coll., 1965-69. Exec. sec. to v.p. prodn. Screen Gems, L.A., 1969-72; exec. asst. Spelling/Goldberg Prodns., 1972-82; dir. adminstrn. The Leonard Co./Mandy Films, 1982-85, v.p., 1985-87; exec. asst. to pres. and chief oper. officer 20th Century Fox Film Corp., L.A., 1986-87, dir. adminstrn., 1987-90, dir. prodn. svcs. & resources Fox Motion Pictures div., 1990-92; program coord. Am. Film Inst. Gary Hendler Minority Filmmakers Program, 1990-93; pres., CEO Masala Prodns., Inc., 1991—. Asst. to exec. producer: (films) War Games, 1984, Spacecamp, 1986; (movies for TV) Something about Amelia, 1984, Alex, The Life of a Child, 1985; (series) Paper Dolls, 1985, Cavanaughs, 1987, Charlie's Angels, Rookies, others; exec. prodn. cons. (documentary) The Good, The Bad, The Beautiful, 1995. Commr. L.A. City Cultural Heritage Commn., 1992-93. Named 1991 Woman of Excellence, Boy Scouts Am. Mem. NAFE, Women in Film Assn. (pres. 1991, 92, advisor to exec. bd. 1993-95), Black Women's Network, Am. Film Inst., Ind. Feature Prodns./West, Motivating Our Students Through Experience (exec. bd. mem.), Top Ladies of Distinction (City of Angels chpt.- L.A.).

JENKINS, BRENDA GWENETTA, early childhood education specialist; b. Durham, N.C., Aug. 11, 1949; d. Brinton Alfred and Ophelia Arden (Eaton) Jenkins. BS, Howard U., 1971, MEd, 1972, Cert. Advanced Spl. Edn., 1975; postgrad. Trinity Coll., Am. U., U. D.C., Marymount Coll., 1976—. Cert. aerobics instr. Nat. Dance-Exercise Instr.'s Tng. Assn. Cheerleader coach Howard U., Washington, 1971-86; aerobics instr. D.C. Pub. Schs., 1982—, tchr., 1972—; v.p. Nerdlihc Corp., Washington, 1985—; co-owner Fantasia Early Learning Acad., 1985—; ptnr. Jenkins, Trapp-Dukes and Yates Partnership; aerobic instr. for handicapped Coun. for Exceptional Children, Washington, 1982, recreation svcs. City of Rockville, Md., 1986—; instr. Washington Tchrs.; instr. aerobics Langdon Park Recreation Ctr. Washington Dept. Recreation, 1988-93, You Fit, Inc. Nat. Children's Ctr., Washington, 1991-93, Anthony Bowen YMCA, Washington, 1992-93; instr. health and nutrition support, Rockville, Md., 1992; instr., coach Maryvale Pom Pom/cheerleaders, Montgomery County, Md., winter 1992—; early childhood tchr. collaborative program asst. chair, 1994-95; early learning years collaborative co-chair program com., 1995-96; fitness instr. Oxendine Performing Arts Acad., 1995-96; Goals 2000 English/Lang. Arts and History Curriculum Framework writer DCPS, 1995-96; bldg. rep. Washington Tchrs. Union AFT, AFL-CIO, 1987-89, 91-94, asst. bldg. rep., 1990-91, 94-95, bldg. rep., 1996—; elected. v.p. spl. edn. Washington Tchrs. Union Local # 6, 1994; developer, coord. My Spl. Friend program, 1984—; trainer AIDS in the Workplace, 1990; developer BJ's Thinking Cap, 1991, Learning Creations, 1994—; founder, developer Girlfriends, 1994; presenter numerous workshops, seminars; supr. foster grandparent program Sharpe Health Sch., 1988—; trainer Early Childhood Substance Abuse Project Tng., spring and summer, 1992-93; SAPE trainer, 1995; mental health trainer Metro. Foster

Grandparent Program, Washington, 1992-93; mem. presch. adv. bd. D.C. Pub. Schs., 1992-93, mem. coordinating curriculum coun., 1994-96; curriculum writer, trainer, summer 1993; master tchr. Coop. Tchr. Corp., 1993—; del. numerous confs. Recipient Conscientious Service award D.C. Pub. Schs., 1985; Outstanding Recognition award Howard U. Alumni Cheerleaders Assn., 1984 (award renamed The Brenda G. Jenkins Outstanding Cheerleader Award, 1987), Outstanding Service awards Kappa Delta Pi, 1978, 79, 81, 82, 84; citation Washington Tchrs. Union, 1985; Appreciation cert. D.C. Dept. Recreation, 1985, others; nominee Agnes Meyer Outstanding Tchr. award, 1988, Theodore R. Hogans Jr. Pub. Service award, 1988, Outstanding Svc. and Leadership award Howard U. Alumni Cheerleaders Assn., 1994, 95; Spl. Edn. grantee D.C. Pub. Sch. State Office, 1993, Citibank, 1994; named to Hall of Fame, Bison Found. Inc.-Howard U., 1995. Mem. Am. Fedn. Tchrs., D.C. Parents and Friends of Children with Spl. Needs (bd. dirs.), Theta Alpha chpt. Kappa Delta Pi (exec. com.), Howard U. Alumni Cheerleaders Assn. (co-founder 1977, pres. elect 1990-94). Democrat. Avocations: alumni cheerleading, fashion design, cooking, dancing, poetry writing.

JENKINS, CATHIE SUNDERLAND, middle school educator; b. Lewistown, Pa., Sept. 23, 1950; d. Ferman Miles and Joyce Arlene (Stewart) Sunderland; m. William Kenneth Jenkins, June 15, 1974; children: Andrew Graham, Rhett William. BA, wilson Coll., 1971. Cert. English, lang. arts, computer tchr., Pa. 7th grade English tchr. Lamberton Jr. H.S., Carlisle, Pa., 1971-79; 8th grade English tchr. Wilson Mid. Sch., Carlisle, 1979—, lead tchr., 1990—; head assessment planning team Carlisle Sch. Dist., 1995, supr. mid. sch. curriculum revision, 1995-96; presenter at workshops in field. Pres. Wilson Coll. Club, Carlisle, 1980-91; vol. Friends of Bosler Libr., Carlisle, 1984-95. Named Outstanding Educator, Shippensburg Sch. Study Coun., 1995-96. Mem. Nat. Coun. Tchrs. English. Home: 61 S College St Carlisle PA 17013

JENKINS, ELOISE, office manager, nurses aid; b. Castleberry, Ala., July 29, 1957; d. Robert Lee and Queen Anna (Armstrong) J.; m. Ronnie Thomas Lee; 1 child, Cheratta Renee. Grad., Bergen County Tech. Sch., Hackensack, N.J., 1994. Home health aide Hackensack, N.J., 1991; with Dept. Human Svcs., Hackensack, N.J., 1992, Gen. Edn. Devel. Program, Hackensack, N.J., 1992, CAP/TECH Partnership Bergen County Technical Sch. Integrated Office Sys., Hackensack, N.J., 1994; co-dir. Infant Toddler Teen Women, Hackensack, 1994-96. Active grad. Neighborhood Leadership Initiative, 1995. Recipient Cert. Achievement award METPATH, 1991. Home: 2 Tributary Plz Englewood NJ 07631 Office: Bergen County Cmty Action Program Inc 170 State St Hackensack NJ 07601

JENKINS, FRANCES OWENS, small business owner; b. Leonard, Tex., Nov. 12, 1924; d. R. Melrose and Maureen (Durrett) Owens; m. William O. Jenkins (div. 1961); children: Steven O., Tamara. Student theatre arts East Tex. State U., 1939-42, Ind. U., 1945-48, U. Tenn., 1954-56. Fashion model Rogers Modeling Agy., Boston, 1950-52, Rich's, Knoxville, Tenn., 1955-60; owner, instr. Arts Sch. of Self-Improvement and Modeling, Knoxville, 1959-69; owner, pres. Fran Jenkins Boutique, Knoxville, 1964-96; cons. Miss Am. Pageant, Knoxville, 1958-66. Actress Carousel Theatre, Knoxville, 1955-58. Home: 8833 Cove Point Ln Knoxville TN 37922-6402

JENKINS, JUDITH ALEXANDER, bank consultant; b. Fort Sill, Okla., Oct. 14, 1940; d. James Buchanan and Gerry Lee (Gibbs) Permenter; m. Robert Miles Turner, Oct. 28, 1962 (div. 1972); m. Clarence Withers Alexander, Dec. 19, 1975 (div. Jan. 1987); m. David Claude Jenkins, Apr. 23, 1994. Student, U. Okla., 1958-59; B.A. in English, U. Tulsa, 1962; M.B.A., U. Okla., 1969; postgrad., U. St. Thomas, 1975-78. Asst. cashier So. Nat. Bank of Houston, 1971-73, asst. contr., 1973-74, asst. v.p. and asst. contr., 1974, v.p., contr., 1974-77, sr. v.p., contr., 1977-79; cons., 1979—. Mem. NOW, Nat. Audubon Soc., Beta Gamma Sigma, Gamma Phi Beta. Office: 2211 Norfolk St Ste 612 Houston TX 77098-4044

JENKINS, KATHLEEN MARIA, webmaster; b. Evansville, Ind., Oct. 1, 1965; d. Ronald W. and Elizabeth G. (Gibbs) Butler; m. James H. Jenkins, Mar. 24, 1990. AA, Henderson C.C., 1985; BA, Western Ky. U., 1987. Anchor, reporter Sta. WVJS/WSTO-Channel 2, Owensboro, Ky., 1989-90; mktg. cons. Space Design Internat., Cin., 1990-92; product mgr. Cincom Systems Inc., Cin., 1992-96; internet editorial manager College View, 1996—; cons. in field. Home: 2479 Madison Rd # 24 Cincinnati OH 45208 Office: 10200 Alliance Rd Ste 100 Cincinnati OH 45242

JENKINS, LINDA DIANE, accountant; b. Detroit, Jan. 8, 1960; d. Robert A. Martinez and Marillyn June (Owens) Scheere; m. George Edwin Jenkins, Oct. 21, 1978 (div. May 1992); children: Stephanie Marie, Mark Richard. Student, RETS Electronics Sch., Detroit, 1978; AA in Bus. Adminstrn. with honors, St. Petersburg Jr. Coll., Tarpon Springs, Fla., 1987; BS in Acctg., U. South Fla., 1991. CPA, Fla. Acct. Carl Lawson & Assocs., Inc., New Port Richey, Fla., 1986-88, Garcia & Ortis PA CPA's-GOC Inc., St. Petersburg, Fla., 1992; treas. New Life Foursquare Gospel Ch., Bayonet Point, Fla., 1988-90; fin. adminstr. M.P. Spychala & Assocs., Inc., Safety Harbor, Fla., 1988-91; project acct., network adminstr. Harbour Assocs. Constrn. Co., Tampa, Fla., 1992-94; pvt. practice acctg. Clearwater, Fla., 1994—. Fla. Soc. CPAs. Home: 1701 Marion St Clearwater FL 34616-6200 Office: Linda D Jenkins CPA 1701 Marion St Clearwater FL 34616

JENKINS, LOUISE SHERMAN, nursing researcher; b. Normal, Ill., Jan. 19, 1943; d. Fred and Zylpha Louise (Garrett) Sherman; m. Gary L. Jenkins, Oct. 30, 1965 (div. July 1976). Diploma, Evanston Hosp. Sch. Nursing, 1963; BS, No. Ill. U., 1979; MS, U. Md., Balt., 1982, PhD, 1985. Asst. head nurse intensive care Community Meml. Hosp., LaGrange, Ill., 1963-65; head nurse coronary care Luth. Gen. Hosp., Park Ridge, Ill., 1965-69; nurse clinician hemodialysis unit Evanston Hosp., Evanston, Ill., 1969-74; head nurse Skokie Valley Community Hosp., Skokie, Ill., 1974-75; faculty dept. continuing edn. Northwest Community Hosp., Arlington Heights, Ill., 1975-80; Walter Schoeder chair nursing rsch. U. Wis. Milw. Sch. Nursing and St. Luke's Med. Ctr., Milw., 1987-96; faculty Sch. Nursing U. Md., Balt., 1996—. Mem. editl. rev. bd. Jour. Cardiopulmonary Rehab., Nursing Rsch.; mem. editl. bd. Cardiovasc. Nursing. chmn. Coun. Cardiovasc. Nursing, Dallas, 1995—, Am. Heart Assn., Milw., 1988-95, exec. bd. dirs. Wis. affiliate, 1995-96; fellow coun. on cardiovasc. nursing. Fellow, clin. nurse scholar Robert Wood Johnson Found., U. Calif., San Francisco, 1985-87. Mem. Am. Assn. Cardiovasc. and Pulmonary Rehab. (bd. dirs.-at-large 1993-95), Wis. Nurses Assn. (bd. dirs. 1988-90, Excellence in Nursing Rsch. award 1995), Midwest Nursing Rsch. Soc. (gov. bd. 1993-95), Coun. Nursing Rsch., Soc. Clin. Trials, Health Outcomes Inst., Soc. Behavioral Medicine, N.Am. Soc. Pacing and Electrophysiology, Sigma Xi, Sigma Theta Tau. Office: Sch Nursing U Md Ste 404 655 W Lombard St Baltimore MD 21201-1579

JENKINS, MARGARET BUNTING, human resources executive; b. Warsaw, Va., Aug. 3, 1935; d. John and Irma (Cookman) Bunting; children: Sydney, Jr., Terry L. Student, Coll. William and Mary, 1952; AA in Bus. Adminstrn., Christopher Newport U., 1973; BA in Human Resource Devel., St. Leo Coll., 1979; M in Human Resources, George Washington U., 1982; PhD in Human Rsch. Mgmt., Columbia Pacific U., 1986. Rehab. counselor, tchr. York County Schs., Yorktown, Va.; mgr. Waterfront Constrn. Co., Seafood Corp., Seaford, Va., 1960-72; labor rels. specialist Naval Weapons Sta., Yorktown, 1974-77; staffing specialist NWS, Yorktown, 1977-78; position classification specialist supr. shipbldg. repair Naval Weapons Sta., Newport News, Va., 1978-81; supr. personnel mgmt. specialist SupSHIP, Newport News, 1981-90; pers. mgmt. specialist Naval Weaptons Sta., Yorktown and Cheatham, Williamsburg, Va., 1990-95; bd. dirs. various health orgns.; owner Jenkins Consulting. Author: Organizational Impact on Human Behavior, 1996, (poetry) Heron Haven Reflections, 1996; poetry published in Mists of Enchantment, 1995, Treasured Poems of America, 1996, Poets of the 90's. Recipient Navy Meritorious Civilian Svc. award SUPSHIP, Newport News, 1990, 2 Navy commendations, others. Mem. Soc. for Human Resource Mgmt., Fedn. Women's Clubs, Sierra Club, Audubon Soc., Nature Conservancy, Classification and Compensation Soc. (pres. 1984), 4-Alumni Assn., Toastmasters Internat. (pres. 1985-87, various offices, award), Internat. Soc. of Poets (Disting. mem. 1996), Internat. Platform Assn. Methodist. Home and Office: PO Box 203 Seaford VA 23696-0203

JENKINS, MARIE HOOPER, manufacturing company executive, engineer; b. Alexandria, La., Apr. 22, 1929; d. Jesse Joseph and Katie B. Hooper; m. Charles Edward Jenkins, Jan. 28, 1950 (div. May 1990); children: Nancy Marie von Minden, Charles Edward Jr.. B.S. in Chem. Engring., U. Wash., 1956. Founder, prin. Decision Systems, Austin, Tex., 1975-76; chmn. bd., pres. NAPP Inc. and subsidiary LACE Engring., 1977—. Active Leadership Tex. program, Leadership Am., 1988, Tex. Found. for Women's Resources; bd. dirs. Com. Wild Basin Wilderness, 1993—. Mem. Am. Inst. Chem. Engrs. (chmn. Mojave Desert sect.), Calif. Soc. Profl. Engrs. (founding sec., treas. Desert Empire chpt.), Tex. Soc. Profl. Engrs., Nat. Soc. Profl. Engrs., Leadership Tex. Alumni Assn., Leadership Am. Alumnae Assn., Nat. Property Mgmt. Assn., Nat. Contract Mgmt. Assn., Greater Austin C. of C. (exec. com. North Cen. area coun.). Episcopalian. Home: 3710B Meredith St Austin TX 78703-2021 Office: NAPP Inc & LACE Engring 2104 Kramer Ln Austin TX 78758-4045

JENKINS, PAMELA RUTH, medical researcher; b. Denver, Aug. 26, 1949; d. Richard Parks and Geneva (Shaver) Carr; m. Larry William Jenkins, May 25, 1974; children: Michael, Tyler, Ryan. BSN, U. No. Colo., 1971; MSN, Va. Commonwealth U., 1981; postgrad., N.C. State U., 1993—. Commd. U.S. Army, 1969, advanced through grades to lt. col., 1990; staff nurse U.S. Army, U.S. and Germany, 1971-74, head nurse, 1974-79; critical care nurse U.S. Army, Germany, 1981-83; quality assurance nurse U.S. Army, Ft. Bragg, N.C., 1983-86, infection control officer, 1986-90; chief HIV sect. U.S. Govt., Ft. Bragg, N.C., 1990-91; sr. rsch. assoc. Henry M. Jackson Found., Ft. Bragg, N.C., 1991—; cons. Environ. Resource Ctr., Fayetteville, N.C., 1990-92. Chairperson Cumberland County HIV Task Force, Fayetteville, 1991-93, Dogwood AIDS Consortium, Fayetteville, 1992-93. Decorated Legion of Merit. Mem. Internat. AIDS Soc. Episcopalian. Home: Henry M Jackson Found Preventive Medicine Svc WAMC Fayetteville NC 28303 Office: Henry M Jackson Found WAMC Preventive Medicine Svc Fort Bragg NC 28307

JENKINS, PEGGY ANN, counselor; b. Utah, Aug. 16, 1946; d. George Woodrow and Mary Louise (O'Brien) McKellar; m. Charles John Jenkins, Feb. 6, 1965; children: Raymond Charles, Jannie Lynn, Jennifer Ann, Johnathan David. BS in Psychology with honors, U. Houston, 1984, MEd in Ednl. and Counseling Psychology, 1989. Lic. profl. counselor; cert. tchr.; cert. cognitive behavioral therapist. Co-owner, cons. Charles J. Jenkins & Assocs., Kemah, Tex., 1980—; presdl. asst. H.M.R. Cons., Houston, 1984-85; tchr. Houston Ind. Sch. Dist., 1985-89; inern Diagnostic Learning Ctr., U. Houston, 1988-89, Montrose Counseling Ctr., 1989; treatment psychologist adult forensic unit Mental Health and Mental Retardation Authority Harris County, Houston, 1989-92; psychol. evaluator Robbie Burnett and Assocs., Houston, 1993; pvt. practice Jenkins & Assocs., Houston and Clearlake, Tex., 1993—; adj. prof. Houston C.C., 1992—. Recipient McCarey Endowment scholarship U. Houston, 1984, Student rsch. grant U. Houston, 1984, Shell Oil grant Houston Ind. Sch. Dist., 1986, Impact II grant Houston Ind. Sch. Dist. 1988. Mem. Nat. Assn. Cognitive Behavioral Therapists, Assn. for Spiritual, Ethical and Religious Values in Counseling, Assn. Promotion of Profl. Women, Am. Assn. Counseling and Devel., Tex. Counseling Assn., Mortar Bd. Roman Catholic. Office: Jenkins & Assocs PO Box 575 Kemah TX 77565

JENKINS-ANDERSON, BARBARA JEANNE, pathologist, educator; b. Chgo.; d. Carlyle Fielding and Alyce Louise (Walker) Stewart; m. Sidney Bernard Jenkins, Sept. 22, 1951 (div. June 1970); children: Kevin Jenkins, Judy Kelly, Sharolyn Sanders, Marc Jenkins, Kayla French; m. Arthur Eugene Anderson, Sept. 30, 1972. BS, U. Mich., 1950; MD, Wayne State U., 1957. Diplomate Am. Bd. Pathology. Assoc. prof. pathology Wayne State U. Med. Sch., Detroit, 1973—; adminstrv. med. dir. DMC Univ. Labs., Detroit, 1988—; chief pathology DRH/UHC Hosp., Detroit, 1990—. Recipient Leonard Sain award U. Mich., 1980. Mem. Alpha Omega Alpha. Office: DMC Univ Labs 4201 Saint Antoine St Detroit MI 48201-2153

JENKINSON, JUDITH APSEY, librarian; b. Monroe, Mich., Apr. 9, 1943; d. Robert Henry Williams and Caroline (Pardee) Stephenson; m. Arnold Apsey, July 1, 1962 (div. 1977); 1 child, Amy Lou; m. Leif Jenkinson, May 21, 1977, 1 stepchild, Karl J. A.A., Alpena Community Coll., 1964; B.A., Mich. State U., 1966; Arts M.L.S., U. Mich., 1969. Elem. tchr., Lincoln, Mich., 1966-68, high sch. librarian, 1969-72; elem. librarian, Ketchikan, Alaska, 1972-75, 90—, high sch. librarian, 1975-90; mem. City Coun., Ketchikan City, Alaska, 1993—. Mem. Ketchikan Community Coll. Council, 1980-84, pres., 1984-85; del. Alaska Democratic Conv., 1982, 88, 92; dir., producer, actress, mem. stage crew First City Players, 1972—; mem. Ketchikan Greater Dem. Precinct's Com., 1988—, vice chair, 1992—; commr. Ketchikan Gateway Borough Planning Commn., 1989-93, vice-chair, 1992-93. Mem. ALA, NEA, AAUW, NOW, LWV, Ketchikan Edn. Assn., NEA-Alaska, Women's Internat. League for Peace and Freedom, Alaska Library Assn. VFW Aux., Swinging Kings Square Dancers (pres. 1985-86), Eagles, Women of the Moose, Delta Kappa Gama. Home: PO Box 5342 Ketchikan AK 99901-0342 Office: 1900 1st Ave Ketchikan AK 99901-6027

JENKS, JEANINE MARIE, writer; b. Portland, Oreg., Apr. 6, 1957; d. Thomas Barry and Kathryn Anne (Douthit) J. BA, U. Oreg., 1981. Editorial/prodn. asst. Ginn Press, 1982; prodn. editor Ginn & Co., Lexington, Mass., 1982-83, project coord. Silver Burdett Ginn, Lexington, 1983-85; copy editor Silver Burdett Ginn, Needham, Mass., 1985-90; devel. editor Ligature Creative Studios, Boston, 1991-94, sr. devel. editor, 1994-95; freelance writer, ednl. cons., 1995—. Author: (screenplays) How to Make a Very Disagreeable Odor, 1993, Le Chateau, 1994, Pig Fat, 1995. Instr. ESL ARC, Boston/Cambridge, 1987-89. Mem. Freelance Editl. Assn.

JENKS-DAVIES, KATHRYN RYBURN, retired daycare provider, civic worker; b. Lynchburg, Va., Oct. 9, 1916; d. Charles Arthur and Jessie Katherine (Moorman) Ryburn; m. Thomas Edgar Jenks Jr., Sept. 9, 1941 (dec. June 1975); children: Thomas Edgar III, Jessika, Timothy; m. Robert E. Davies, Dec. 27, 1986. BS, State Tchr. Coll., 1938; postgrad., Mary Washington Coll., 1947-48, U. Va., 1957-58, William and Mary Coll., 1967-68, Va. Commonwealth U., 1969-70. Elem. tchr. various schs., Grundy, Va., 1939-41; phys. therapist U.S. Army, Ft. Bragg, N.C., 1942; operator motor pool U.S. Army, Ft. Still, Okla., 1943-44; occupational therapist U.S. Army, Augusta, Ga., 1944-45; instr. phys. edn. King George (Va.) High Sch., 1947-48; instr. phys. edn. Stafford (Va.) High Sch., 1949-50, substitute tchr., 1950-53; owner, dir. Kay's Kindergarten, Fredericksburg, Va., 1959-82. Featured in Fredericksburg Times mag., The Free Lance-Star and Richmond Newspapers. Counselor Girl Scouts U.S.A., Grundy, Va., 1939-41; life mem. Kenmore Assn., 1949—; mem. Hist. Fredericksburg Found., Inc., 1953—, Mental Health Bd., 1978-84; founder Ford Franklin Found., 1968-78; mem. Fredericksburg Clean Cmty. Commn., 1987—; rep. United Way, Fredericksburg; instr. art ceramics Cmty. Ctr. Fredericksburg, 1950-80; bd. dirs. Miss Fredericksburg Fair Pageant, 1965-88; participant cmty. parades; coord. Fredericksburg Agrl. Fair 18th Century Craft People and Artisans, 1988-93, also others; bd. dirs. Antique Farm Implements, Gas and Steam Engines, 1989-93; active State Fair of Va., 1981—, Am. Heritage Showcase endl. reenactment Pioneer Farmstead, 1981—. Recipient Virginia Ellison Vol. Svc. award Fredericksburg Clean Community Commn., 1976-87, Recognition of Svc. award, 1983-84, 1st, 2nd. and 3rd pl. trophies cmty. parades, awards radio Stas. WFLS and WFVA, 1949-89; honored by Kiwanians for travelogue for fund raiser, 1995—. Mem. AAUW (advt. chmn. travelogue 1971-89, Donor Honoree award 1983, bd. dirs. 1971-79), Lioness Club (bd. dir. 1968-87, Lioness Tamer 1984, Tongue Wagger 1985), Soroptimist Internat. Fredericksburg (life mem., sec. 1971-73, pres. 1973-75, bd. dirs. 1971-78, co-chmn. Soroptimist Travelogue 1991-93, First Class Pub. Recognition Trophy 1986, Women Helping Women award 1982, named 1 of 5 who have made a difference in cmty. 1994), Order of Eastern Star, Nat. League of Fredericksburg (bd. dir., Svc. Recognition Trophies 1963, 69, 80), Izaac Walton League (bd. dir. Dog Mart parade 1965-72). Republican. Episcopalian. Home: 8 Blair Rd Fredericksburg VA 22405-3025

JENNESS, REBECCA ESTELLA, artist, educator; b. L.A., Aug. 16, 1946; d. Russell Albert and Estella Virginia (Guzman) J. Student, Cape Sch. Art, Provincetown, Mass., 1971; diploma, Vesper George Sch. of Art, 1972; BFA, Southeastern Mass. U., 1981. mem. panel R.I. State Coun. on the Arts, 1989-93; mem. adv. bd. Warwick Art Mus., R.I., 1990-94, New Eng. Found. on the Arts, Boston, 1990-94, Sarah Doyle Gallery, Brown U., 1991-95; mem. multicultural art literacy coun. State Coun. on the Arts, R.I., 1991-94. Exhibited in group shows at Soviet Hall of Art, Moscow, 1988, U. N.H., 1989, Fitchburg Art Mus., 1990, R.I. Sch. Design Mus. of Art, 1992-93, Lyman Allen Mus., Conn., 1994, Artists for Shelter, Providence, 1995. Art advocate New England Artists Trust, 1990-95, Perishable Theater, Providence, 1993, New Eng. Conf., Providence, 1993-94, Studio and Living Spaces for Artists, Providence, 1995-96; artists for food Amos House, Providence, 1993. Democrat. Home: PO Box 41395 Providence RI 02940 Studio: 220 Weybosset St Fl 4 Providence RI 02903-3712

JENNETT, SHIRLEY SHIMMICK, hospice executive, nurse; b. Jennings, Kans., May 1, 1937; d. William and Mabel C. (Mowry) Shimmick; m. Nelson K. Jennett, Aug. 20, 1960 (div. 1972); children: Jon W., Cheryl L.; m. Albert J. Kukral, Apr. 16, 1977 (div. 1990). Diploma, Rsch. Hosp. Sch. Nursing, Kansas City, Mo., 1958. RN, Mo., Colo., Tex., Ill. Staff nurse, head nurse Rsch. Hosp., 1958-60; head nurse Penrose Hosp., Colorado Springs, Colo., 1960-62, Hotel Dieu Hosp., El Paso, Tex., 1962-63; staff nurse Oak Park (Ill.) Hosp., 1963-64, NcNeal Hosp., Berwyn, Ill., 1964-65, St. Anthony Hosp., Denver, 1968-69; staff nurse, head nurse, nurse recruiter Luth. Hosp., Wheat Ridge, Colo., 1969-79; owner, mgr. Med. Placement Svcs., Lakewood, Colo., 1980-84; vol., primary care nurse, admissions coord., team mgr. Hospice of Metro Denver, 1984-88, dir. patient and family svcs., 1988, exec. dir., 1988-94; pres. Care Mgmt. & Resources, Inc., Denver, 1996—; mem. adv. com. Linkages Assn. for Older Adults, Denver, 1989-90. Community liaison person U. Phoenix, 1988-90. Mem. NAFE, Nat. Assn. Geriatric Care Mgrs., Nat. Women Bus. Owners Assn., Nat. Hospice Orgn. (bd. dirs. 1992-95), Colo. Hospice Orgn. (bd. dirs., pres. 1991-93), Denver Bus. Women's Network. Republican. Mem. Ch. of Religious Sci. Office: Care Mgmt & Resources Inc 820 S Monaco Pkwy # 250 Denver CO 80224

JENNINGS, CAROL, marketing executive; b. Marion, Ohio, Oct. 2, 1945; d. Richard P. and Mary (LeMaster) J.; m. John Putnam Merrill Jr., Jan. 3, 1981. BA, Miami U., Oxford, Ohio, 1967. News editor Penton Pub. Inc., Cleve., 1967-69; pub. rels. exec. Cen. Nat. Bank, Cleve., 1969-71; dir. pub. rels. New Eng. Conservatory of Music, Boston, 1971-74, Bklyn. Acad. Music, N.Y.C., 1974-75; account exec., supr. Hill and Knowlton, N.Y.C., 1975-81, from v.p. to mng. dir., 1981-87; sr. v.p., gen. mgr. Hill, Holliday, Connors, Cosmopolus, Boston, 1987, Hill and Knowlton, Boston, 1987-90; dir. corp. communications Bain and Co., Boston, 1991-93; dir. mktg. Heidrick and Stiuggles, Inc., Boston, 1995—. Office: Heidrick and Struggles Inc 1 Post Office Sq Boston MA 02109

JENNINGS, DEBRA VERA, lawyer; b. Meridian, Miss., Oct. 20, 1960; d. Rudolph and Fannie Mae (Cole) J. BA in Polit. Sci., U. Houston, 1981; JD, South Tex. Coll., 1986. Officer U.S. EEOC, Houston, 1986-89; loan adminstr. First City Nat. Bank, Houston, 1989-91; atty. Debra Jennings & Assocs., Houston, 1991—. Bd. dirs. Lawndale Art and Performance Ctr., Houston, 1993—, Milam House AIDS hospice, Houston, 1993. Kellogg scholar, 1981, scholar South Tex. Coll. Law Alumni Assn., 1985. Baptist. Home: 4915 Austin St Apt 3 Houston TX 77004-5715 Office: Debra Jennings & Assocs 3401 Louisiana St Ste 110 Houston TX 77002-9546

JENNINGS, GABRIELLE, artist; b. San Francisco, Dec. 23, 1966. Student, U. Paris, 1988; BFA, U. Calif.-San Diego, La Jolla, 1990; MFA, Art Ctr. Coll. Design, Pasadena, Calif., 1994. Artist-in-residence 200 Gertrude Street, Melbourne, Australia, 1996. Exhibited in group shows Rutgers U., New Brunswick, N.J., MFA Gallery, Art Ctr. Coll. Design, 1991, 94, Guggenheim Gallery, Chapman U., Orange, Calif., 1994, L.A. Ctr. for Photog. Studies, Hollywood, Calif., 1994, 95, Calif. State U., L.A., 1994, Mark Moore Gallery, Santa Monica, Calif., 1994, Bergamot Sta., Santa Monica, 1995, David Zwirner Gallery, N.Y.C., 1996, U. Chgo., 1996, also others; videography includes She Disappeared First, 1993, Agapanthus Lapsus, 1994, To Whom It May Concern, 1994, Momentary Suspension, 1995, The Kiss, 1996, (prelude) Eight Minutes, 1995. Fellow Art Matters Inc., 1996.

JENNINGS, LINDA LEE, volunteer; b. Norton, Va., July 16, 1952; d. Claude Clayborn and Beverly Jean (Pierson) Sturgill; m. Warner Craig Jennings, June 11, 1977; children: Warner Claybourne, William Cameron. BA in Elem. Edn., Va. Polytechnic Inst. and State U., 1974. Elem. tchr. Powhatan (Va.) County Sch. Dist., 1974-76, Alleghany County Sch. Dist., Covington, Va., 1976-77, Normandy Sch. Dist., St. Louis, 1977-79, Aurora (Colo.) Pub. Schs., 1979-82. Active United Meth. Women, pres., 1987, Republican Women, treas., 1988, Friends of Powder River Symphony, 1995—; trustee sch. bd. Converse County Sch. Dist., Douglas, Wyo., 1991-95; soccer coach Douglas Recreation, 1991-95. Named Disting. Sch. Bd. Mem., Wyo. Sch. Bd. Assn., 1995. Mem. AAUW, LWV, PEO. Home: 1100 Jason Ct Gillette WY 82718

JENNINGS, MARCELLA GRADY, rancher, investor; b. Springfield, Ill., Mar. 4, 1920; d. William Francis and Magdalene Mary (Spies) Grady; student pub. schs.; m. Leo J. Jennings, Dec. 16, 1950 (dec.). Pub. relations Econolite Corp., Los Angeles, 1958-61; v.p., asst. mgr. LJ Quarter Circle Ranch, Inc., Polson, Mont., 1961-73, pres., gen. mgr., owner, 1973—; dir. Giselle's Travel Inc., Sacramento; fin. advisor to Allentown, Inc., Charlo, Mont.; sales cons. to Amie's Jumpin' Jacks and Jills, Garland, Tex. Investor. Mem. Internat. Charolais Assn., Los Angeles County Apt. Assn. Republican. Roman Catholic. Home and Office: 509 Mount Holyoke Ave Pacific Palisades CA 90272-4328

JENNINGS, NADINE NELSON, English language educator; b. Troy, N.Y., Sept. 23, 1944; d. William LeRoy and Esther May (Coonley) Nelson; m. Robert Edgar Jennings, March 26, 1966; children: Robert Harvey, Cynthia Diana. BA, SUNY, Potsdam, 1979, MA, 1982. Asst. dir. Inst. Am. Studies SUNY, Potsdam, 1980-83; exec. dir. Inst. Am. studies SUNY, Potsdam, N.Y., 1983; adj. lectr. Mater Dei Coll, Ogdensburg, N.Y., 1983-86; assoc. prof. English Mater Dei Coll., Ogdensburg, N.Y., 1986—; adj. lect., Mater Dei Coll., Ogdensburg. N.Y., 1983-1986.s. Office: Mater Dei Coll 5428 State Hwy 37 Ogdensburg NY 13669-9699

JENNINGS, NANCY ANN, retired elementary education educator; b. Bristow, Okla., July 11, 1932; d. John Linard and Charlie Estelle (Hooper) Stucker; m. Jerald Leon Jennings, June 4, 1951; children: Jan, Catherine Jennings Hackman, Elizabeth Jennings Pineda. BS, U. Okla., 1956; MS, Washburn U., Topeka, Kans., 1974. Cert. elem. tchr., Kans. Tchr. Whitson Grade Sch. Dist. 501, Topeka, 1970-75, Delia Grade Sch Dist. 321, St. Marys, Kans., 1978-79, Silver Lake (Kans.) Grade Sch. Dist. 372, 1979-85, ret., 1985. Mem. Kans. Hist. Soc. Mem. NEA (life), AAUW (bd. dirs.), DAR (regent Topeka chpt. 1989-91, sec.-treas. N.E. dist. Kans. 1992-95, chmn. pres.-gen.'s project state com. 1992-95), Topeka Area Ret. Tchrs. Assn. (v.p. 1992-93), Internat. Reading Assn. (sec. 1983-84), Topeka Aux. Kans. Engring. Soc. (pres. 1987-88), Woman's Club (2d v.p. 1989-91), PEO Kans. (corr. sec. 1993—, guard 1994—, pres. 1995-97), Alpha Delta Kappa (pres. 1989-91), Kappa Delta Pi, Alpha Phi (2d v.p. 1989-90). Presbyterian. Home: 11340 NW 13th St Topeka KS 66615-9620

JENNINGS, SUSAN JANE, lawyer; b. Providence, June 23, 1952; d. John Edward and Betty Jean (Frost) Stedman; m. James Albert Jennings, Jan. 2, 1982; children: Olivia Arden, Caroline Alexis, Susan Alexandra. BA, Ind. U., 1973; JD, Tex. Tech U., 1978; LLM in Taxation, So. Meth. U., 1985. Bar: Tex. 1978, U.S. Dist. Ct. (no. dist.) Tex. 1979, U.S. Tax Ct. 1986. Advanced mktg. cons. Southwestern Life Ins., Dallas, 1978-81; asst. gen. counsel Res. Life Ins., Dallas, 1981-85; gen. counsel, corp. sec., v.p. Life Ins. Co. SW, Dallas, 1986—; of counsel Erhard, Ruebel and Jennings, Dallas, 1981—; bd. dirs. Tex. Legal Res. Ofcls. Assn., 1994-95. Contbr. articles to profl. jours. Mem. ABA (mem. editor's pub. bd., TIPS sect. 1993—), Dallas Bar ASsn. (v.p. corp. counsel sect. 1995—), Daus. of Penelope, Kappa Delta (pres. Dallas alumnae 1983-84), Phi Delta Phi. Republican. Presbyterian. Home: 4001 Miramar Ave Dallas TX 75205-3129 Office: Life Ins Co SW 1300 W Mockingbird PO Box 47421 Dallas TX 75247

JENNINGS, SISTER VIVIEN ANN, English language educator; b. Jersey City, May 18, 1934; d. Eugene O. and Alice (Smith) J. BA, Caldwell Coll., 1960; MA in English, Cath. U. Am., 1966; MS in Telecommunications, Syracuse U., 1980; PhD in English, Fordham U., 1972; EdD (hon.), Providence Coll.; LittD (hon.), Caldwell Coll.; postgrad., Oxford (Eng.) U., 1994. Assoc. prof. English Caldwell Coll., 1960-69; major supr. Domenican Sisters Caldwell, 1969-79; instr. broadcasting writing Syracuse U., 1979-80; with community affairs dept. Sta. WIXT TV, Syracuse, N.Y., 1980; dir. telecommunications Barry U., 1982-83; dir. pub. affairs Cath. Telecommunications Network Am., 1983-84; pres. Caldwell Coll., 1984-94; originator, designer campus TV studios Caldwell Coll., Barry U.; curriculum planner, coord. new grad.-level curriculum in telecommunications Barry U.; lectr. on ednl. and media issues. Producer: Centenary Journey, 1981, Advent Vesper Chorale, 1981, American Immigrant Church, 1982, Las Casas: Ministry of Presence, 1987; co-producer: The Boat People, 1980. Founder, dir. Children's TV Experience; founder Project Link Ednl. Ctr., Newark. Recipient Gov.'s Pride N.J. Albert Einstein award for edn., 1989. Mem. Assn. Cath. Colls. (coord. nat. teleconf.). Office: Caldwell Coll 9 Ryerson Ave Caldwell NJ 07006-6109

JENNIS, LISA ELLEN, lawyer; b. Newark, Mar. 28, 1967; d. Jay Martin and Thelma (Denburg) J. BA in Econs., Cornell U., 1989; JD, George Washington U., 1993. Atty. U.S. Dept. Justice, Washington, 1993—. Vol. atty. Washington Legal Clinic for the Homeless, 1993—; reporter Consumer Protection Reporting Svc., 1993. Mem. ABA, N.J. Bar Assn., Md. Bar Assn. Office: Dept Justice Ste 300 1331 Pennsylvania Ave NW Washington DC 20004

JENNY, BARBARA RITA, artist, educator; b. Newark, Sept. 3, 1966; d. Robert James and Marcelline Dolores (Acosta) J.; m. Matthew David Beebe; stepchildren: Elizabeth Katherine, Christopher Matthew. BA, Dartmouth Coll., 1988. Art instr. The Art Ctr., Exeter, N.H., 1992—, Phillips Exeter Acad., 1995—; bd. dirs. Exeter Ctr. Creative Arts; interim gallery dir. Lamont Gallery at Mayer Art Ctr. Phillips Exeter Acad., 1995—, instr. art, 1995—. Exhibited paintings and sculpture in numerous shows including Inaugural Exhbn. Women's Caucus for Arts N.H., 1996, Belknap Mill Gallery, Laconia, N.H., 1996, Prescott Park Arts Festival, Portsmouth, N.H., 1995, Back Room at the Brewery, Portsmouth, 1995, Artist Showcase Summer's Crossing, Rye, N.H., 1995, Outside at the Moses Kent House Mus., Exeter, 1995, Hera Gallery, Wakefield, R.I., 1995, New Eng. Woman Artists Levy Gallery, Portsmouth, 1995, First Winter show Kristal Gallery, Warren, Vt., 1995, many others; works represented in numerous collections including Hennepin County Med. Ctr., Mpls., Nature Conservancy of Maine, Dartmouth Coll. Adminstrn., Epsilon Kappa Dartmouth Coll., Orange (N.J.) Meml. Hosp., Jenny Engring. Corp., Springfield, N.J. Roster artist pub. art projects Very Spl. Arts/Arts for All, Concord, N.H., 1995—. Payson grantee Earthwatch, 1991; recipient Mayor's award City of Portsmouth, 1995. Mem. N.H. Art Assn., Women's Caucus for Art, N.H., Maine Arts Commn. Slide Registry, N.H. State Coun. on Arts Slide Registry, N.J. State Coun. on Arts Slide Registry. Office: Phillips Exeter Acad Art Dept Exeter NH 03833

JENNY, MARY, librarian; b. Vancouver, Wash., Nov. 1, 1940; d. Casper and Jennie (Pinster) J. BA, U. Kans., 1965; JD, U. Calif., 1972; MLIS, La. State U., 1988. Bar: Wash. 1972. VISTA atty. Alaska Legal Svcs., Bethel, 1972-73; rsch. assoc. U. Del., Newark, 1973-74; zoning adminstr. City of Seattle, 1975-76; pvt. practice law, 1976-79; dir. legal writing program La. State U., Baton Rouge, 1979-83; econ. devel., outreach libr. Oreg. State U., Corvallis, 1989-94; assoc. law libr., head pub. svcs. U. Wyo. Law Sch., Laramie, 1994—; cons. Shoreline Mgmt. Plan Sea Grant Program, Newark, 1974. Mem. Am. Assn. Law Librs., Wash. State Bar Assn. Office: U Wyo Law Sch PO Box 3035 Laramie WY 82071

JENS, ELIZABETH LEE SHAFER (MRS. ARTHUR M. JENS, JR.), civic worker; b. Monroe, Mich., Jan. 25, 1915; d. Frank Lee and Mary (Bogard) Shafer; m. Arthur M. Jens, Jr., Aug. 14, 1937; children: Timothy V., Christopher E., Jeffrey A. Student, Kalamazoo Coll., 1932-34, U. Wis., 1935, Northwestern U., 1934-36, BS, 1936; postgrad. Wheaton Coll., 1965; Lic. Practical Nurse, Triton Coll., 1968-69; Gray lady, Hines, (Ill.) Hosp., 1948-49, 51-53; vol. Elgin (Ill.) State Hosp., 1958-72; writer Newsletter Vol. Planning Coun., 1960-62; mem. Family Svc. Assn. Du Page County; vol. coord., chmn. bd. dirs., treas. Thursday Evening Club, social club for recovering mental patients Du Page County, 1966—; vol. FISH orgn., 1973-84. Bd. dirs. Du Page County Mental Health Soc., 1962-68, sec., 1963-64, 65-68, chmn. forgotten patient com., 1963-68, chmn. new projects, 1965-68; co-chmn. Glen Ellyn unit Cen. Du Page Hosp. Assn. Women's Aux., 1959-60; bd. dirs. chmn. com. on pesticides, Ill. Audubon Soc., 1963-73; mem. Ill. Pesticide Control Com., 1963-73, Citizens Com. Dutch Elm Disease, Glen Ellyn, 1960; bd. dirs. Natural Resources Coun. Ill., 1961-67, sec., 1961-64; bd. dirs. Du Page Art League, 1958-68, chmn. bd., 1961-63, Paint-out chairperson, 1968-84, 91—, chmn. new bldg. com., 1968-75, Best in Show award 1991; bd. dirs. mem. planning com., publicity chmn. Du Page Fine Arts Assn., 1965-67; bd. dirs. Friends Libr. Glen Ellyn, 1967-68; mem. adv. bd. Rachel Carson Trust for Living Environment 1971-74; bd. dirs. Mental Health Assn. of Du Page, 1973—, sec., 1973-75, pres., 1980-81, chmn. community liaison, 1981—, chmn. action group, 1976—; mem. Du Page Subarea adv. coun. Suburban Cook County-Du Page County Health Systems Agy., 1977-83; bd. dirs. Du Page County Comprehensive Health Planning Agy., 1976, DuPage County Bd. of Health, 1987-95; mem. DuPage County Mental Health Adv. Bd., 1977—; mem. com. on midlife and older women Ill. Commn. on Status of Women, 1978-85; bd. dirs., publicity chmn., DuPage County Coun. Vol. Coords., 1977-78; bd. dirs., membership chmn. Homemakers Equal Rights Assn. in DuPage County, 1979-84; publicity chmn., v.p. Homemakers Coalition for Equal Rights, 1984—, pres. 1986—; mem. ERA Ill. Bd., 1987—, v.p. 1994—; mem. DuPage County Health Planning Coun., 1984-94, chairperson task force on residences for mentally ill, 1990-93; mem. Community Care Coalition of DuPage County, 1988-93, NAACP; mem. pub. rels. com. Bethlehem Ctr. Food Bank of DuPage County, 1987-89; tour guide Stacy's Tavern-Glen Ellyn Hist. Mus., 1986—; chmn. Grass Roots Com. to Pass Ill. Marital Property Act, 1982—; mem. adv. bd. Older Adult Inst. Coll. DuPage, 1989-94; del. for Mental Health Assn. Du Page to DuPage County Consortium, 1989—, DuPage Consortium, Prevention and Intergenerational Task Force, 1991—; vol. Hospice of DuPage, 1990—; bd. dirs. Willowbrook Wildlife Found., 1992—, v.p., 1992-94; bd. dirs. Dupage area Older Women's League, chairperson publicity, 1992— (recipient Wonderful Older Woman ann. award. 1990); with clown ministry Fox Valley unity Ch., 1991—. Recipient Pathfinders award, 1965; hon. mention in Nat. Sonnet contest, 1967; Vol. of Yr. Ill. Mental Health Assn., 1975; Svc. award Ill. Rehab. Assn., 1980; named DuPage County Outstanding Woman Leader in Arts and Culture W. Suburban YWCA, 1984, Friend of the Mentally Ill, Alliance for the Mentally Ill of Dupage County Ann. award, 1988, Adade Wheeler award Coll. of DuPage, 1994, Mental Health Person of the Yr. Mental Health Assn. of Ill., 1995, Pub. Svc. award Ill. State Med. Soc., 1996. Mem. Mental Health Assn. DuPage, Wilderness Soc., Humane Soc. U.S., Nat. Trust for Hist. Preservation, Du Page County Hist. Soc. (life), Glen Ellyn Hist. Soc. (life), Nat. Audubon Soc., Nat. Writers Club (monthly meeting chmn. Midwest chpt. 1973-74, 4th award Ann. Mag. Con. test 1978), DuPage Art League (hon. life, Best of Show award 1991), Defenders of Wildlife, Theosophical Soc. Am. (Quest Study Group 1992—), Nature Conservancy Ill. (hon.), Chgo. Art Inst. (life), Ill. Assn. Mental Health (dir. 1966-68), Amnesty Internat., Pi Beta Phi. Writer column Mental Health and You for Press Publs., 1969-90, Life Newspapers, 1982-93, Pioneer Newspapers, 1984, Herald Newspapers, 1986-94; author: The Jewelled Flower: The True Account of a Courageous Young Man's Life and Death By His Own Hand, 1987. Home: 22W 210 Stanton Rd Glen Ellyn IL 60137-7111

JENSEN, ANNA BERNICE, retired special education educator and nurse; b. Wilkinsburg, Pa., Oct. 1, 1914; d. August Anderson and Anna Lovisa Jönsson; m. William F. Jensen, July 26, 1941 (dec. Oct. 1990); children: William Maehr (dec.), Robert Russell, Richard Bryan. RN, Bellevue Sch. Nursing, 1936; BA, Trenton State Coll., 1969, MA, 1972, supervisory cert., 1979. Charge nurse surgery Gouverneer Hosp., N.Y.C., 1936-39; indsl. nurse Todd Shipyard, Bklyn., 1939-41; substitute tchr. Hillsborough (N.J.) Sch. Sys., 1965-71; tchr. McNamara Sch. Presbyn. Ch., Flemington, N.J., 1972-73; title I tchr. Somerville (N.J.) Sch. Sys., 1973-75; dir. Hillsborough Leisure Time Learning Ctr., Jointure Adult Edn. Bd., Brook Hillsboro, others, 1979-83; tchr. creative writing Hunterdon Adult Edn., Flemington, 1976-79; dir. vols. Somerset County Chaplaincy to the Elderly, 1985-89; vol. Somerset Med. Ctr., 1981-92. Editor: (booklet) We Walk In Their Footsteps, 1976, 2d edit., 1977; rschr.: (book) Ladies At the Crossroads, 1978; contbr.: (books) Poems—Elder Hostel U. of Iowa, 1986, 87, 88, Memoirs—Elder Hostel U. of Iowa, 1991, 94. Coord. lit. program Older Wiser Program, Somerset County Libr., Bridgewater, N.J., 1986—, tchr. creative writing and memoirs, 1995—, mem. planning com., 1985—; mem. adv. com. RSVP Somerset County Office of Aging, Bridgewater, 1993-96; coord., founder Sixty Plussers, Good Shepherd Ch., Somerville, 1990—; statistician Women's Rsch. Ctr., Somerville, 1985—. Recipient award Adult Comty. Edn.—N.J., 1981. Mem. NEA, Am. Assn. Ret. Persons, Bellevue Alumnae Assn., Princeton Y. Lutheran.

JENSEN, ANNE TURNER, automobile service company executive; b. Upper Providence Twp., Pa., Sept. 15, 1926; d. Ellwood Jackson and Elizabeth Addis (Downing) Turner; student Hood Coll., 1944-45, Phila. Coll. Pharmacy and Sci., 1945-46, 47-48; m. Harry Frederick Jensen, Jr., Apr. 13, 1946; children—Frederick Howard, Richard Jordan, Peter Hielm. Legal sec. Robertson & Turner, Media, Pa., 1950-51; sec. Luncheon-is-Served, Media, 1951-53; asst. sec., treas. Delvale Realty Corp., Media, 1955-59; bookkeeper Turner Realty Co., 1960-64, William H. Turner, Atty., 1960-64, Media Auto Service, 1957-74; sec. Media Auto Service, Inc., 1957—. Capt. Heart Fund Dr., 1958-60. Republican. Presbyterian. Clubs: DAR (chpt. regent 1971-74, state corr. sec. 1977-80, nat. chmn. 1974-77), Daughters of Am. Colonists, Daughters of Colonial Wars (state treas. 1974-77, 80-83), Magna Carta Soc., Daus. of 1812, Navy League U.S. (N.Y. Coun.), Am. Legion.

JENSEN, ANNETTE M., mental health nurse, administrator; b. Albert Lea, Minn., Jan. 16, 1952; d. Oliver H. and Ardis R. (Nelson) J. BSN, Winona (Minn.) State U., 1974; postgrad., Calif. Coll. Health Scis. Staff nurse in adolescent psychiatry C.B. Wilson Ctr., Faribault, Minn., 1974-76, 79-80, Abbott Northwestern Hosp., Mpls., 1981-82; charge nurse in child psychiatry Med. Coll. Ga., Augusta, 1983-87; adminstr. child psychiat. program Charter Hosp. of Augusta, 1987-91; staff educator/quality mgmt. in psychiatry Ga. Regional Hosp. at Augusta, 1990-92; team leader child psychiatry Charter Peachford Hosp., Atlanta, 1992—. Mem. Girl Scouts of Am. Mem. NAFE, AAUW, ANA, Ga. Nurses Assn., Assn. Child/Adolescent Psychiat. Nurses, Am. Camping Assn. Presbyterian. Home: 725 Josh Ln Lawrenceville GA 30245-3157

JENSEN, BARBARA WOOD, interior design business owner; b. Salt Lake City, Apr. 30, 1927; d. John Howard and Loretta (Sparks) Wood; m. Lowell N. Jensen, June 26, 1947; children: Brent Lowell, Robyn Lynn, Todd Wood. Interior decorator paint and wall paper co., 1947-49; cons., interior designer, 1950-60; pres., treas. Barbara Jensen Interiors, Inc., Salt Lake City, 1960-79; interior designer, 1979—; owner Barbara Jensen Designs, St. George, Utah and Las Vegas; lectr. in field; dir. 1st Women's Bancorp, Utah. Chmn. Utah Legis. Rep. Ball, 1970, Utah Symphony Ball, 1979. Fellow Inst. Profl. Designers (London); mem. Assistance League, Com. Fgn. Affairs, Interior Design Soc. (assoc.), Ft. Douglas Country Club, Knife and Fork Club, Hi-Steppers Dance Club, Ladies Lit. Club, Pres.'s Club of Utah, Bloomington Country Club, Elks. Mormon.

JENSEN, BONNIE JEAN, secondary school educator; b. Rapid City, S.D., July 6, 1961; d. Dale Alfred and Dorothy Marie (Eisenbraun) Jensen; m. Ronald Brent Oyler, Apr. 26, 1980 (div. Dec. 1994); children: Jeremy Paul, Felicia Marie. A degree, U. Md., Heidelburg, Germany, 1992; BS in Elem. Edn./Spl. Edn. summa cum laude, S.W. Tex. State U., San Marcos, 1995; postgrad., Tex. Tech. State U. Home daycare provider San Antonio, 1984-86; parent vol. Northside Ind. Sch. Dist., San Antonio, 1986-88, spl. edn. tchr. asst., 1988-90; sales assoc. Garden Ridge Pottery, Schertz, Tex., 1992-95; spl. edn. tchr. Roosevelt H.S., San Antonio. Camp parent Children Achieving Maximum Potential (C.A.M.P.), San Antonio, 1984—; parent-tchr. asst. Spl. Olympics, San Antonio, 1988—; mem. PTA, San Antonio, 1986—; Sunday sch. helper Mt. Calvary Luth. Ch., San Antonio, 1983—. Recipient Empress Zedler scholarship S.W. Tex. U., 1994, Non-Traditional Students Orgn. scholarship, 1995, Aid Assn. for Lutherans scholarship, 1995. Mem. NAPVI, Tex. Assn. Health, Phys. Edn., Recreation and Dance, Coun. for Exceptional Children, Nontraditional Studies Orgn., Tourette Syndrome Assn., Golden Key Soc., Kappa Delta Pi. Republican. Home: 100 Shadow Tree St San Antonio TX 78233

JENSEN, DELORES (DEE JENSEN), physical education educator; b. Harvey, N.D., Apr. 20, 1944; m. Owen Jensen, Dec. 28, 1968. BS, Valley City State U., 1966; MA, No. Ariz. U., 1973. Master cert. official track and field, level 1 coaching cert. Bus., phys. edn. instr. Hatton (N.D.) Pub. Schs., 1966-72; phys. edn. instr. Midway Sch. Dist., Inkster, N.D., 1972-74; student svcs. asst., women's track coach N.D. State Coll. Sci., Wahpeton, 1974-77, bus. instr., women's track coach, 1974—; mem. exec. com. Nat. Athletic Ofcls. Com., 1984-94, U.S.A. Women's Track & Field, 1989—; co-mgr. Nat. Sports Festival, Baton Rouge, 1985; mem. Xth Pan Am. Games Ofcls. Selection Com., 1985-86, Olympic Trials Ofcls. Selection Com., 1988, Centennial Olympic Games Ofcls. Selection Com., 1993-96; mem. adminstrv. com. U.S. Olympic Sports Festival, 1987-95; bd. dirs. U.S.A. Track and Field, 1993—; mem. Nat. Track and Field Ofcls. Affirmative Devel. Com., 1993—. Mem. U.S.A. Track and Field Site Selection Com., 1992—, Budget and Fin. Com., 1995—; head mgr. Goodwill Games, 1990, U.S. Olympic Sports Festival, Norman, Okla., 1989, U.S.A. vs. Great Britain, 1993; ofcl. U.S. Olympic Trials, 1992, 96. Named Olympic ofcl. Track and Field, 1984, 96, Coach of Yr., Nat. Jr. Coll. Track Coaches Assn., 1986, Xth Pan Am. Games ofcl., 1987, Internat. Spl. Olympics ofcl., 1991, World Spl. Olympic Games, 1995; recipient Svc. award U.S. Women's Track Coaches Assn., 1989, Andy Bakjian award Nat. Track & Field Ofcls. Com., 1993, N.D. Girls Track Disting. Svc. award, 1991; grantee U.S. Olympic Acad., 1991. Mem. AAUW (treas. 1982-85), U.S. Women's Track and Field Coaches Assn. (exec. com. 1986-88), NJCAA Men's and Women's Track Coaches Assn. (v.p. 1991—), Kiwanis (bd. dirs. 1989-91, 1st v.p. 1996), Alpha Delta Kappa (chpt. pres. 1976-78, treas., exec. com. N.D. chpt. 1982-84). Home: 1621 5th St N Wahpeton ND 58075-3301 Office: ND State Coll Sci Old Main Wahpeton ND 58076

JENSEN, HANNE MARGRETE, pathology educator; b. Copenhagen, Dec. 9, 1935; came to U.S., 1957; d. Niels Peter Evald and Else Signe Agnete (Rasmussen) Damgaard; m. July 21, 1957 (div. Apr. 1987); children: Peter Albert, Dorte Marie, Gordon Kristian, Sabrina Elisabeth. Student, U. Copenhagen, 1954-57; MD, U. Wash., 1961. Resident and fellow in pathology U. Wash., Seattle, 1963-68; asst. prof. dept. pathology U. Calif. Sch. Medicine, Davis, 1969-79, assoc. prof., 1979—, dir. transfusion svc., 1973—; McFarlane prof. exptl. medicine U. Glasgow, Scotland, 1983. Mem. No. Calif. Soc. for Electron Microscopy, U.S. and Can. Acad. of Pathology, Am. Cancer Soc., Am. SOc. Clin. Pathologists, Am. Assn. for Advancement of Sci., Am. Assn. of Blood Banks, Calif. Blood Bank System, People to People Internat., Internat. Platform Assn; fellow Pacific Coast Obstetrician and Gynecol. Soc., Coll. of Am. Pathologists. Office: U Calif Sch Medicine Dept Pathology Davis CA 95616

JENSEN, JAKKI RENEE, retail company executive; b. Eugene, Oreg., Mar. 1, 1959; d. Philip William Jensen and Mary Katherine (Sommers) Henderson; m. Johnny Claiborne Hawthorne, May 7, 1983. Student, Oreg. State U., 1977-78; student (hon.), Portland State U., 1978-81. With Nordstrom Inc., Beaverton, Oreg., 1981—; mgr. cosmetics Nordstrom Inc., Beaverton, 1984; mgr. cosmetics Nordstrom Inc., Walnut Creek, Calif., 1984-86, buyer cosmetics, 1986-88; buyer cosmetics Nordstrom Inc., San Francisco, 1988-93; area mdse. mgr. Nordstrom Own Product, San Francisco, 1993—. Affiliate, vol. San Francisco Soc. for Prevention of Cruelty to Animals, 1990—. Mem. I/SPA, No. Calif. Cosmetic Assn., Exec. Women of Am. Republican. Home: 724 16th Ave # 4 San Francisco CA 94118 Office: 865 Market St San Francisco CA 94103-1900

JENSEN, KATHERINE KEMP, insurance company executive; b. Canandaigua, N.Y., July 22, 1955; d. Harry Frederick and Charlotte Ruth (Doebereiner) Kemp; m. Fred E. Jensen, Mar. 7, 1987; stepchildren: Brett, Stacey, Marceil. BA, Siena Coll., 1976. Cert. property and casualty ins. instr. Dir. local programs N.Y. State Assembly, Albany, 1976-77; assoc. realtor Grad. Realtor Inst. LaLonde Realty, Inc., Fairport, N.Y., 1978-81; ops. unit mgr. Allstate Ins. Co., Rochester, N.Y., 1981-84; adminstrv. svcs. mgr. Allstate Ins. Co., Rochester, 1984-88; market sales mgr. Allstate Ins. Co., Jamestown, 1988-92; agy. mgr. Allstate Ins. Co., Jamestown, N.Y., 1992—. Chmn. N.Y. State Teen Age Reps., 1973-74; mem. N.Y. State Rep. Platform Com., 1974; mem. Perinton Rep. Com., 1978-88, chmn., 1985-88; mem. Zoning Bd. Appeals, Perinton, N.Y., 1981-88, chmn., 1985-88; mem. Warren County Rep. Exec. Com., Pa. Recipient Mary Ann award N.Y. State Reps., 1974. Fellow Life Underwriting Tng. Coun. (cert.); mem. Am. Mgmt. Assn., Ind. Ins. Agts. Assn. N.Y., Inc., Western Pa. Paint Horse Club, Chatauqua Region Life Underwriters, Jamestown Area C. of C., Empire State Paint Horse Club (pres. 1986-87). Home: RR 1 Columbus PA 16405-9801 Office: Allstate Ins Co 560 W 3rd St Jamestown NY 14701-4733

JENSON, KATHY LAVON, marketing director; b. Bismarck, N.D., Oct. 24, 1943; d. Edward Michael and Clara Catherine (Ficker) Degen; m. Roy Kenneth Jenson, Oct. 22, 1977; children: Patricia, Elizabeth. BS in Math., N.D. State U., 1965; MBA in Mktg., U. St. Thomas, 1980. Sys. mgr. Control Data Corp., Bloomington, Minn., 1965-74, mgr. strategic planning, 1980-87; major account mgr. Digital Equipment Corp., Mpls., 1974-80; area applications sales mgr. Wang Labs., Mpls., 1987-89; nat. sales mgr. Faxbank Inc., St. Paul, 1990-91; dir. mktg. & sales Solutronix Corp., Eden Prairie, Minn., 1991-92; mktg. dir. NCS, Edina, Minn., 1992—; Baldridge quality examiner, 1996; guest spkr. in field. Vol. Bel Canto Voices, Mpls., 1990—, Regional Dance Competitions, Mpls., 1987—; pres. Edina H.S. Thespian Boosters. Mem. Am. Mktg. Assn., Sales and Mktg. Execs., Am. Soc. Quality Control, Minn. Quality Award Com. (Minn. Quality Award examiner 1994, sr. Minn. Quality Award examiner 1995).

JENSON, PAULINE MARIE, speech and hearing educator; b. Orange, N.J.; m. Bernard A. Jenson; 1 child, Mark J. BS, Trenton State Coll., 1948; MA, Columbia U., 1950, PhD, 1969. Lic. speech pathologist and audiologist, N.J. English, history tchr. Bordentown (N.J.) High Sch., 1948-49; teacher of the deaf Lexington Sch. for Deaf, N.Y.C., 1950-51, rsch. dept., 1969-70; teacher of the deaf N.J. Sch. for Deaf, West Trenton, 1951-56, 58-61, St. Mary's Sch. for Deaf, Buffalo, 1956-58; speech pathologist Hunterdon Med. Ctr., Flemington, N.J., 1959-60, dir. speech and hearing, 1960-62; asst. prof. Trenton (N.J.) State Coll., 1962-65; instr., lectr. Teacher's Coll., Columbia U., N.Y.C., 1966-69; prof. dept. speech pathology and audiology Trenton (N.J.) State Coll., 1970-95, dept. chairperson, 1991-94; prof. dept. lang. & comms. Coll. N.J. (formerly Trenton State Coll.), 1995—; cons. Universal Films & Visual Arts, N.Y.C., 1968-70, State Agys. & Schs. for Handicapped, N.J., N.Y., 1976—; evaluator Coun. on Edn. of Deaf, Washington, 1979-83. Author: (with others) Speech for the Deaf Child, 1971; inventor cueing system for deaf speakers, 1976; editor: (info. booklets) Topics, Princeton, N.J., 1980-86. Help line vol. N.J. Assn. for Children with Hearing Impairments, Princeton, 1973-95; co-author, cons. Senate Bills on Deafness, Trenton, 1979—; commr. Legislative Commn. to Study Svcs. for Hearing Impaired Children, Trenton, 1988-90. Recipient post masters scholarship U.S. Office Edn., Teacher's Coll., Columbia, U., 1965, Pauline Jenson award The Coll. of N.J., 1996—; grantee N.J. Dept. Edn., 1973, N.J. Dept. Human Svcs., 1992—. Mem. N.J. Assn. for Children with Hearing Impairment (founder, exec. dir. 1973-95, Pauline Jenson award at Trenton State Coll. named in her honor, 1996), N.J. Speech Lang. and Hearing Assn. (life mem., Disting. Svc. award 1985), Am. Speech Lang. and Hearing Assn. (cert.), Ctrl. Jersey Speech and Hearing Assn. Office: The Coll of NJ Hillwood Lakes Trenton NJ 08650-4700

JERACE, CHARLOTTE LOUISE, writer, consultant; b. Rockland, Maine, Nov. 17, 1942; d. Max and Ida (Shapiro) Gopan; m. Harvey Cohen, Aug. 22, 1964 (div. Oct. 1971): children: Scott, Melissa; m. Michael Crawley Jerace, July 12, 1986. MEd, Antioch U., 1981. pres. Coast-to-Coast Prodns., Truro, Mass., 1990—. Agt. Aetna Life Ins. Co., Boston, 1975-80; mng. editor Employee Comm. Svcs., Natick, Mass., 1980-85; sr. mgr. KPMG Peat Marwick, Boston, 1985-94; prin. Buck Consultants, Boston, 1994—. Author: A Survivor's Manual, 1978, Facing the Future, 1980, Secret Hiding Places, 1994; author short story. Chmn. Truro Beach Commn., 1993—; pres. Boston chpt. Eleanor Roosevelt group Hadassah, 1968-70, mem., 1966—. Recipient Telly award, 1990, 91, 92, Award of Excellence Bus. Ins. Mag., 1993. Mem. Internat. Assn. Bus. Communicators (Award of Excellence 1992), New. Eng. Employee Benefits Coun. Democrat. Jewish.

JERARD, CAROLYN EDITH, proofreader, writer; b. Burlington, Vt., Dec. 27, 1943; d. Albert Basil and Lucille Clara (Bristol) J.; life ptnr. John William Lillie (separated 1969); 1 child, Heather Liane Lillie Jerard Habich; m. Craig Michael Lawler, May 5, 1990; stepchildren: Scott Alan, Ryan Samuel. BA in Ancient Greek, U. Vt., 1965. Proofreader Am.-Stratford, Brattleboro, Vt., 1966-67; dept. supr. Baker's Bookstore, Brattleboro, 1969-70; computer programmer Holstein-Friesian Assn., Brattleboro, 1970-72; proofreader, copy editor Brattleboro (Vt.) Reformer, 1972-76; libr. technician Palm Beach Pub. Libr., West Palm Beach, Fla., 1976; proofreader Book Press, Brattleboro, 1978, Am.-Stratford Graphic Svcs., Inc., Brattleboro, 1979-85, N.K. Graphics, Inc., Keene, N.H., 1985—; vice chmn. Internat. Typographical Union, Brattleboro, 1980-81. Author booklet and monograph. Vol. Hotline, Brattleboro, 1973-76, Adult Tutorial Svc., Newport, N.H., 1989, Friends of the Libr., Acworth, N.H., 1991-92, Child & Family Svcs., Concord, N.H., 1995; bd. dirs. Southeastern Vt. Cmty. Action, Bellows Falls, Vt., 1974-75. Democrat. Congregationalist. Home: Cold Pond Rd Acworth NH 03601 Office: NK Graphics Inc 132 Washington St Keene NH 03431

JERGE, MARIE CHARLOTTE, minister; b. Mineola, N.Y., Dec. 26, 1952; d. Charles Louis and Helen Marie (Scheld) Scharfe; m. James Nelson Jerge, Aug. 27, 1977. AB, Smith Coll., 1974; MDiv, Luth. Theol. Sem. of Phila., 1978. Pastor St. Mark Evang. Luth. Ch., Mayville, N.Y., 1978-88; co-pastor Zion Evang. Luth. Ch., Silver Creek, N.Y., 1983-88; asst. to the bishop Upstate N.Y. Synod, Buffalo, 1988—; dir. Acad. of Preachers, Phila., 1995—, also bd. dirs.; bd. dirs. Acad. Preachers, Phila., 1982—. Chairperson Chautauqua County Commn. of Family Violence and Neglect, Mayville, 1981-82, bd. dirs., 1978-88. Named one of outstanding Young Women in Am., 1980. Home: 370 Borden Rd Buffalo NY 14224-1713 Office: Upstate NY Synod 49 Linwood Ave Buffalo NY 14209-2203

JERMINI, ELLEN, educational administrator, philosopher; b. Krefeld, Germany, Aug. 25, 1939; came to U.S., 1986.; d. Maximilian and Mathilde (Wachtberger) Wilms; m. Helios Jermini, 1961 (div. June 1989); children: Mariella Arnoldi, Diego Jermini. PhB, U. Healing, 1984, M in Healing Sci., 1985, PhD, 1986; PhB, U. Philosophy, 1992. Sec. Germany, Switzerland, 1962; pub. translator, 1984—; seminar organizer Europe, 1983—; dir. U. Philosophy/European Found., 1986—; pres. U. Healing, Campo, Calif., 1986—, U. Philosophy, Campo, 1986—; abbot Absolute Monastery, Campo, 1986—. Editor: (newsletter in Italian) Absolute, (newsletter in German) Absolute. Spkr. various univs. and orgns. in Calif. and N.Y., 1989-92, St. Petersburg, Moscow, 1991, Africa, 1994, Egypt, 1995, various seminars and workshops, Ghana, Nigeria. Mem. Toastmasters Internat. (Competent Toastmaster). Home and Office: Univ of Healing 1101 Far Valley Rd Campo CA 91906-3213

JERVIS, JANE LISE, college official, science historian; b. Newark, N.J., June 14, 1938; d. Ernest Robert and Helen Jenny (Roland) J.; m. Kenneth Albert Pruett, June 20, 1959 (div. 1974); children: Holly Jane Pruett, Cynthia Lorraine Pruett; m. Norman Joseph Chonacky, Dec. 26, 1981; children: Philip Joseph Chonacky, Joseph Norman Chonacky. AB, Radcliffe Coll., 1959; MA, Yale U., 1974, MPhil, 1975, PhD in History of Sci., 1978. Freelance sci. editor and writer, 1962-72; lectr. in history Rensselaer Poly. Inst., 1977-78; dean Davenport Coll., lectr. in history of sci. Yale U., 1978-82; dean students., assoc. prof. history Hamilton Coll., 1982-87; dean coll., lectr. in history Bowdoin Coll., 1988-92; pres. Evergreen State Coll., Olympia, Wash., 1992—. Author: Cometary Theory in 15th Century Europe; contbr. articles to profl. jours.; book reviewer; presenter in field. Trustee Maine Hist. Assn., 1991-92; chair Maine selection com. Rhodes Scholarship Trust, 1990-92, chair N.W. selection com., 1992-93; commr. N.W. Assn. Schs. and Colls. Commn. on Colls., 1994—. Office: Evergreen State Coll Office of President Olympia WA 98505

JESKE, JUDITH ZAVOSKI, accountant; b. Scranton, Pa., June 18, 1948; d. Stanley S. and Helen A. (Bentler) Zavuski; children: Karen L. Jeske, Richard Jeske, Renee Jeske. BS magna cum laude, U. Scranton, 1984. CPA, Pa. CPA Parente Randolph Orlando Carey & Assocs., Scranton, 1983—, ptnr., 1993—. Treas. Women's Resource Ctr., Scranton, 1994-96.

Mem. AICPA, Pa. Soc. CPAs. Home: 114 Jonslar Ln RR 2 Moscow PA 18444 Office: Parente Randolph Orlando Carey & Assocs 600 Linden St Scranton PA 18503

JESSE, SANDRA ELIZABETH, special education educator; b. Green Bay, Wis., Nov. 22, 1960; d. Albert Henry and Janice Elizabeth (Schroeder) J. BA in Edn., Ariz. State U., 1983; MA, No. Ariz. U., 1990. Cert. spl. edn. tchr., adminstr. Special edn. educator Peoria (Ariz.) Unifed Sch. Dist. # 11, 1983—. Religious edn. tchr. St. Helens Ch., Glendale, Ariz., 1989—, mem. religious edn. bd., 1994—. Mem. NEA, Am. Fedn. Tchrs., Learning Disabilities Assn. Roman Catholic. Office: Sky View Sch 8624 W Sweetwater Peoria AZ 85381

JESSEN, LINDA SUZAN, lawyer, legal administrator; b. Chgo.; d. Lyle Wayne and Mable Elizabeth (Brown) Ohlander; children: Robin, Heidi, John. BA, Lawrence U., 1960; JD, William Mitchell Coll. of Law, 1978. Bar: Minn. 1978, U.S. Dist. Ct. (no. dist.) Calif., U.S. Dist. Ct. Minn., U.S. Ct. Appeals (8th cir.), U.S. Dist. Ct. Appeals (D.C. cir.). Sr. editor Mason Pub. Co., St. Paul, 1976-81; dep. revisor Minn. Legislature, St. Paul, 1981-85; legis. counsel Nev. Legislature, Carson City, 1985-87; dir. divsn. statutory revision Fla. Legislature, Tallahassee, 1988—; commr. Nat. Conf. of Commrs. on Uniform State Laws, Chgo., 1986-87, 94—. Recipient award Fla. Assn. for Women Lawyers, 1995. Mem. Tallahassee Women Lawyers (treas., sec., dir. 1988—), Phi Beta Kappa. Office: Divsn Statutory Revision 111 W Madison St Ste 612 Tallahassee FL 32399

JESSUP, JAN AMIS, arts volunteer, writer; b. Chgo., Aug. 10, 1927; d. Herman Harvey and Anita (Lincoln) Sinako; m. Everett Orme Amis, Dec. 20, 1970 (dec. Nov. 1981); m. Joe Lee Jessup, Apr. 16, 1989. BA, U. Minn., 1948; postgrad., Rutgers U., 1969-70. bd. dirs., exec. com. Broward Ctr. for Performing Arts Pacers, Fort Lauderdale, Fla., 1985-88, pres., 1987-88; speaker U. Internat. Bus., Beijing, 1985. Active various not-for-profit orgns. including Girl Scouts U.S., Boy Scouts Am., Presbyn. Ch., others; mem. Beautification Com., Lighthouse Point, Fla., 1978-89, sec., 1988-91; rep. to Fla. Art Orgns., 1987-88; bd. dirs. Archways, Ft. Lauderdale, 1987-91; trustee Miami City Ballet, 1991-94; mem. adv. bd. Guild of the Palm Beaches, 1994-95; mem. bd. govs. Fla. Philharm. Orch., 1981—, v.p. representing all affiliates, 1985-87, 92, 94-96, mem. exec. com., 1989-93, v.p. individual giving, 1991-92, bd. dirs., 1994—, chmn. affiliate com., 1994-95, v.p. vols., 1995-96, chmns. adv. coun., 1996—; bd. dirs. Fla. Grand Opera, 1993—; bd. dirs. Concert Assn. Fla., Inc., 1996-97; mem. bus. com. for arts Palm Beach Cultural Coun., 1993—; advisor Friends of Philharmonic, 1996-97. Mem. Nat. Soc. Arts and Letters, Am. Symphony Orch. League (vice chmn. 1989-90, sec. vol. coun. 1986-87, v.p. 1987-88, pres. 1989-90, advisor 1990-91), assoc. Resource Devel. Inst. 1996—), The Opus Soc. (bd. dirs., mem. exec. com. 1981—, chmn. 1981-85), Ft. Lauderdale Philharm. Soc. (bd. dirs. 1986—), Opera Soc. (sec. 1986-87, v.p. pub. rels. 1987-88), Gold Coast Jazz Soc. (bd. dirs. 1992—, v.p. 1994—), Royal Dames of Cancer Rsch. (bd. trustees 1995—), Concert Assn. Fla., Inc (bd. dirs. 1996—), Boca Raton Resort and Club, Royal Palm Yacht Club, Royal Palm Country Club, Women's Club, Sea Grape Garden Club (past pres.). Republican. Home: 133 Coconut Palm Rd Boca Raton FL 33432-7975

JETER, KATHERINE LESLIE BRASH, lawyer; b. Gulfport, Miss., July 24, 1921; d. Ralph Edward and Rosa Meta (Jacobs) Brash; m. Robert McLean Jeter, Jr., May 11, 1946. BA, Newcomb Coll. of Tulane U., 1943; JD, Tulane U., 1945. Bar: La. 1945, U.S. Dist. Ct. (we. dist.) La. 1948, U.S. Tax Ct. 1965, U.S. Supreme Ct. 1971, U.S. Dist. Ct. (ea. dist.) La. 1975, U.S. Ct. Appeals (5th cir.) 1981, U.S. Dist. Ct. (mid. dist.) La. 1982. Assoc. Montgomery, Fenner & Brown, New Orleans, 1945-46, Tucker, Martin, Holder, Jeter & Jackson, Shreveport, 1947-49; ptnr. Tucker, Jeter, Jackson and Hickman and predecessors, Shreveport, 1980—; judge pro tem 1st Jud. Dist. Ct., Caddo Parish, La., 1982-83; mem. adv. com. to joint legis. subcom. on mgmt. of the community; pres. YWCA of Shreveport, 1963; hon. consul of France; Shreveport, 1982-91; pres. Little Theatre of Shreveport, 1966-67; pres. Shreveport Art Guild, 1974-75; mem. task force crim justice La. Priorities for the Future, 1978; pres. LWV of Shreveport, 1950-51. Recipient Disting. Grad. award Tulane U., 1983. Mem. Am. Law Inst., La. State Law Inst. (mem. coun. 1980—, adv. com. La. Civil Code 1973-77, temp. ad hoc. com. 1976-77, sr. officer 1993—), Am. Law Inst., Pub. Affairs Rsch. Coun. (bd. trustees 1976-81, 91—, exec. com. 1981-84, area exec. committeeman Shreveport area 1982), ABA, La. Bar Assn., Shreveport Bar Assn. (pres. 1986), Nat. Assn. Women Lawyers, Shreveport Assn. for Women Attys., C. of C. Shreveport (bd. dirs. 1975-77), Order of Coif, Phi Beta Kappa. Contbr. articles on law to profl. jours. Home: 3959 Maryland Ave Shreveport LA 71106-1021 Office: 401 Edwards St Ste 905 Shreveport LA 71101-3146

JEVNE, JOAN JONET, artist; b. Taipei, Taiwan, Feb. 10, 1946; came to U.S., 1967; d. Chi an dAu-thou (Lin) Chen; m. Terry Bryon Jevne, Feb. 9, 1966; children: Jonathan, Priscilla, Patricia. Artist, tchr. Minot AFB (N.D.) Arts & Crafts, 1984; tchr. art elem. sch. Lansford, N.D., 1994. Exhibited in shows at Minot Art Fest, Rough Rider Internat. Art Show, West Acre Art Show, Sheyenne Valley Art Fair, East Grand Fork Art Fair, numerous others. Recipient Best of Show N.D. State Fair Art Dept., Minot, 1983, People's Choice award Down Town St. Fair, Minot, 1984, Quick Draw Artist award Rough Rider Internat. Art Show, Williston, N.D., 1991. Mem. Sheyenne Valley Arts and Crafts, East Grand Forks Art Coun., Bismarck Art and Galleries Assn. Mem. Nazarene Ch. Home: Rt 1 Box 17A Lansford ND 58750

JEWELL, FLORENCE EVA, communications executive; b. Merigold, Miss., Sept. 5, 1955; d. Eugene and Willie Lou (Woodley) Holloway. BS, Am. U., BSGS; MPM, George Washington U., 1993; MBA, Georgetown U., 1996. Clerical stenographer FBI, Washington, 1974-75; rsch. asst. Booz, Allen & Hamilton, Washington, 1975-76; support & mktg. mgr. AT&T, Washington, 1976-83, quality assurance mgr., 1983-86, project mgr. Fed. Systems, 1986-88; program mgr. II AT&T, Silver Spring, Md., 1988-96, Lucent Techs., Silver Spring, Md., 1996—. Bd. dirs. Interages, Inc., Kensington, Md., 1995—; vol., patron John F. Kennedy Friends, Washington, 1992—. With U.S. Army Res., 1976—. Mem. Am. Univ. Alumni, Georgetown Alumni, Black MBA Assn., Project Mgmt. Inst., Alliance Black Telecomm. (co-chair), Golden Key Honor Soc. Democrat. Baptist.

JEWLER, SARAH, magazine editor; b. Washington, May 18, 1948; d. Samuel and Esther Jewler. BA, George Washington U., 1970. Prodn. mgr. Benwill Pub., Boston, 1975-79; asst. prodn. mgr. Rolling Stone, N.Y.C., 1980-81; editl. prodn. freelancer N.Y.C., 1981-83; art prodn. mgr. Cuisine Mag., N.Y.C., 1983-84; mng. editor Manhattan Inc., N.Y.C., 1984-89, The Village Voice, N.Y.C., 1989-94, New York Mag., N.Y.C., 1994—. Office: New York Magazine 755 2d Ave New York NY 10017

JEYNES, MARY KAY, college dean; b. Miami, Fla., Oct. 31, 1941; d. Nasrallah and Martha (Jabaly) Demetry; m. Paul Jeynes, Sept. 30, 1978. BS, Fla. State U., 1963. Program dir. Orange County YMCA, Orlando, Fla., 1964-69, Ea. Queens YMCA, Belrose, N.Y., 1970-73; regional coord. N.Y. State Park and Recreation Commn., N.Y.C., 1974-77; dir. health, fitness and recreation YWCA of N.Y.C., 1978-79; dean continuing edn. and adult programs Marymount Manhattan Coll., N.Y.C., 1980—. Mem. East Manhattan C. of C. (pres. 1996—). Office: Marymount Manhattan Coll 221 E 71st St New York NY 10021-4501

JHABVALA, RUTH PRAWER, author; b. Cologne, Germany, May 7, 1927; lived in India, 1951-75; came to U.S., 1975; d. Marcus and Eleonora (Cohn) Prawer; m. Cyrus S. H. Jhabvala, 1951; 3 children. MA, London U., 1951, DLitt (hon.), 1995, LHD (hon.), 1995, D Arts (hon.), 1996. Author: (novels) To Whom She Will, 1955, The Nature of Passion, 1956, Esmond in India, 1957, The Householder, 1960, Get Ready for Battle, 1962, A Backward Place, 1965, A New Dominion, 1972, Heat and Dust, 1975 (Booker award for fiction Nat. Book League 1975), In Search of Love and Beauty, 1983, Three Continents, 1987, Poet and Dancer, 1993, Shards of Memory, 1995; (short story collections) Like Birds, Like Fishes and Other Stories, 1964, A Stronger Climate: Nine Stories, 1968, An Experience of India, 1971, How I Became a Holy Mother and Other Stories, 1976, Out of India: Selected Stories, 1986; (film scripts) The Householder, 1963 (with James Ivory), Shakespeare Wallah, 1965 (with Ivory), The Guru, 1968, Bombay Talkie, 1970, Autobiography of a Princess, 1975, Roseland, 1977, Hullabaloo over Georgie and Bonnie's Pictures, 1978, The Europeans, 1979, Jane Austen in Manhattan, 1980, Quartet, 1981, Heat and Dust, 1983, The Bostonians, 1984, A Room With a View, 1986 (Writers Guild of Am. award for best adapted screeplay 1986, Acad. award for best adapted screenplay 1986), (with John Schlesinger) Madame Sousatzka, 1988, Mr. and Mrs. Bridge, 1990, Howards End, 1992 (Acad. award for best adapted screenplay 1992), Remains of the Day, 1993 (Acad. award nomination for best adapted screenplay 1993), Jefferson in Paris, 1995, Surviving Picasso, 1996. Guggenheim fellow, 1976; Neil Gunn. Internat. fellow, 1979; MacArthur Found. fellow, 1984-89. Home: 400 E 52nd St New York NY 10022-6404

JIMENEZ, BETTIE EILEEN, retired small business owner; b. LaCygne, Kans., June 8, 1932; d. William Albert and Ruby Faye (Cline) Montee; m. William R. Bradley, Aug. 21, 1947 (div. Sept. 1950); 1 child, Shirley; m. J.P. Jimenez, Feb. 20, 1951 (div. Nov. 1978); children: Pamela, Joe Jr., Robin Michelle. Student, Ft. Scott Jr. Coll., Paola, Kans., 1979-81. Reporter LaCygne Jour., 1943-45; union recorder I.L.G.W.U., Paola, 1956-57; mgr. Estes Metalcraft, Osawatomie, Kans., 1977-82; owner El Rey Tavern, Osawatomie, 1980-95; ret., 1995. Home: 516 Walnut Ave Osawatomie KS 66064-1254

JIMENEZ, JOSEPHINE SANTOS, portfolio manager; b. Lucena, Quezon, Philippines, June 6, 1954; came to U.S., 1972; d. Jose Hirang and Virginia Villapando (Santos) J. BS, NYU, 1979; MS, MIT, 1981. Securities analyst Mass. Mut. Life Ins. Co., Springfield, 1982-83; investment officer One Fed. Asset Mgmt., Boston, 1984-87; sr. analyst, portfolio mgr. Emerging Markets Investors Corp., Washington, 1988-91; mng. dir., portfolio mgr. Montgomery Asset Mgmt., San Francisco, 1991—; founding ptnr. Montgomery Emerging Markets Fund; Bd. trustees M.I.T. Corp. Trustee MIT Corp. Mem. Inst. Chartered Fin. Analysts. Office: Montgomery Asset Mgmt 101 California St San Francisco CA 94111-2702

JIMENEZ, KATHRYN FISHER, nurse, patient educator; b. Indiana, Pa., Nov. 23, 1948; d. Homer Leonard Fisher and Ruth Maxine (Foltz) Barclay; m. Adalberto Beltran Jimenez, Apr. 24, 1971; 1 child, Adalberto Jr. AAS in Nursing, Borough Manhattan C.C., 1982. RN, N.Y.; cert. BCLS Am. Heart Assn. Dietary cons. Indiana Hosp., 1966-68; LPN Brookdale Hosp. Med. Ctr., Bklyn., 1970-79, staff nurse, 1982—, asst. head nurse diabetes edn., 1990—; presenter workshops on diabetes mgmt.; presenter at profl. confs. Mem. Am. Assn. Diabetes Educators (cert.), Am. Diabetes Assn. Office: Brookdale Hosp Med Ctr 1 Brookdale Plz Brooklyn NY 11212-3139

JIRKANS, MARIBETH JOIE, school counselor; b. Cleve., May 3, 1945; d. Raymond Wenceslaus and Elsie Koryta J.; children: Annemarie Gurchik, Keith Robert Gurchik. Student, U. Vienna, Austria, 1965; BS in Edn., Coll. Mt. St. Joseph, 1967; MEd, Cleve. State U., 1984; postgrad., U. Akron, 1986-88, Kent State U., 1989—. Cert. elem., spl. edn. and adult edn. tchr., counselor. Tchr. North Olmstead (Ohio) City Schs., 1967-76; tchr. adult edn. Polaris Vocat. Sch., Middleburg Heights, Ohio, 1978; tchr. adult edn., ESL Lakewood (Ohio) City Schs., 1978-79; tchr. 2d grade Saint Rose Sch., Cleve., 1979-80; tchr. learning disabilities Cleve. Pub. Schs., 1980-85; tutor handicapped Cleve. Christian Home, 1982-84; elem. sch. counselor Cleve. Pub. Schs., 1985—; counselor West Side Community Mental Health Ctr., Cleve., 1983-84; sales mgr. Field Enterprises Inc., Cleve., 1977-82. Contbr. articles to newspapers. Vol. Fairview Gen. Hosp., Cleve., 1959-63, Cerebral Palsy Camp, 1959-63, Allen Halfway House for Children, Cin., 1963-67; cofounder Westshore Separated, Divorced and Remarried Caths., Cleve., 1975-85; chairwoman North Olmsted Jr. Women's Club; mem. parish coun. St. Brendan Ch., North Olmstead, 1975-87; mem. com. Cleve. Symphony, Cleve. Art Mus. Recipient Speaker's United Torch award United Way, Cleve., 1st Pl. prize in clothing design Stretch & Sew, 1975, 1st Pl. prize in needlepoint Framemakers Art, 1983. Mem. AACD, N.E. Ohio Counselor Assn., Coun. for Exceptional Children, Am. Sch. Counselor Assn., Internat. Assn. Marriage and Family Counselors, NOW, ASCD, Gestalt Inst., Audubon Soc., Eagle Valley Athletic Club, Greenpeace, Sierra Club, Cleve. Natural History Mus., North Coast Sailing Club, Holden Arboretum, Pi Lambda Theta. Democrat. Home: 727 Tollis Pky Cleveland OH 44147-1813

JISA, TANYA ELLEN, social worker; b. Mansfield, Ohio, Oct. 20, 1967; d. Burkley Warren and Mary Carol (McCarter) J. BS, Ohio U., 1990; MSW, Washington U., 1995. Lic. social worker Ga., master social worker. Childcare worker Athens County Children's Svcs., Ohio, 1987-89; coord. Franklin County Juvenile Detention Ctr., Columbus, Ohio, 1990-93; patient advocate Reproductive Health Svcs., St. Louis, 1993-95; case mgr. Grady Health Sys., Atlanta, 1995—. Bd. dirs. Boys and Girls Clubs Atlanta, 1996; vol. Dem. Party of Ga., 1995-96; supr. Youth Pride Helpline, Atlanta, 1996—. Mem. NASW, NOW, Nat. Assn. Women in Social Work, Bertha Cappen Reynolds Soc. Office: Grady Health Sys 100 Edgewood Ave Ste 810 Atlanta GA 30335

JIVIDEN, LORETTA ANN HARPER, secondary school educator; b. Charleston, W.Va., Jan. 30, 1939; d. Murry Deane and Marie Frances (Allison) Harper; m. Gay Melton Jividen, Jan. 30, 1959; children: Jon David, Ann Marie. BA in Sociology, N.C. State U., 1970, MEd in Curriculum and Instrn., 1979. Tchr. Our Lady of Lourdes, Raleigh, N.C., 1970-72; tchr. Wake County Pub. Sch. System, Raleigh, 1972-87, supr. Academically Gifted Program, 1987-90, tchr., 1990-92, math., computer specialist, 1992—; bd. dirs. Durant Rd. Elem. Sch. Found., Inc. Co-author: The EXCEL Program grant for Wake County Pub. Sch. System; past editor Special Edit., Parent Edit., Wake County Pub. Schs. Special Programs newsletters. Mem. NEA, Coun. for Exceptional Children, Assn. Classroom Tchrs., N.C. Edn. Assn., N.C. Assn. for the Gifted (pres. elect 1988-90, pres. 1991-93), N.C. Assn. Sch. Adminstrs., Parents for Advancement of Gifted Edn. (past v.p., past bd. dirs.), Nat. Assn. Gifted Children, Nat. Coun. Tchrs. Math., N.C. Assn. for the Gifted and Talented (Tchr. of Yr. award 1984), N.C. Edn. Assn., Delta Kappa Gamma Soc. Internat. (past pres., past coordinating coun. pres.). Home: 12501 Shallowford Dr Raleigh NC 27614-9664 Office: Durant Rd Elem Sch 9901 Durant Rd Raleigh NC 27614-9369

JOBE, MURIEL IDA, medical technologist, educator; b. St. Louis, Apr. 17, 1931; d. Ernest William and Mable Mary (Hefflinger) Meissner; m. James Joseph Jobe, Sr., May 17, 1952 (dec. 1984); children: James J. Jr., Timothy D. (dec. 1976), Jonathan J., Daniel D. BS, Wash. U., St. Louis, 1971; med. technologist tng., Mo. Bapt. Hosp., St. Louis, 1973-74; postgrad., Webster U., St. Louis, 1981-83. Cytogenetic tech. St. Luke's Hosp., St. Louis, 1963-65; med. technologist Mo. Bapt. Hosp., St. Louis, 1974-76, 82-84, sr. instr., 1976-82, lead technologist, 1985; mgr., clin. instr. St. Louis U. Hosp., 1985-96; retired, 1996; mem. student selection com. Mo. Bapt. Hosp. Med. Technologists, St. Louis, 1975-78; observer Nat. Com. Clin. Lab. Standards, Villanova, Pa., 1989-90, advisor, 1991-92, 93—. Co-author: Clinical Hematology: Principles, Procedures, Correlations, 1991, 2d edit., 1996, 8th Revision PER Handbook, A Review Manual for Clinical Laboratory Exams., 1992. Counselor La Leche League; participant Ecology Day; community rels. chmn. The Life Seekers, St. Louis. Mem. Am. Soc. Clin. Pathologists (staff asst. 1984, 86, 88, 89, 94, 95, dir. workshops 1990, 91, bd. dirs. 1990-92, state advisor 1992—, chmn. regional adv. com., adminstrv. bd. assoc. mem. sect., regional assoc. mem. award 1994), Am. Assn. Clin. Chemists, Am. Soc. Med. Tech. (dir. workshop 1984), Mo. Soc. Med. Tech. (pres. 1985-86), Clin. Lab. Mgrs. Assn. (chmn. devel. St. Louis chpt.). Mem. United Ch. of Christ. Office: St Louis U Hosp Hematology Lab 4 FDT 3635 Vista Ave Saint Louis MO 63110-2539

JOBLIN, MONIA, broadcast executive. V.p. original programming and internat. co-prodn. USA Networks, N.Y.C. Office: USA Networks 1230 Ave Americas New York NY 10020*

JOFEN, JEAN, foreign language educator. BA, Bklyn. Coll., 1943; MA, Brown U., 1945; PhD, Columbia U., 1960; MS, Yeshiva U., 1961. Cert. sch. psychologist, N.Y. Teaching fellow Brown U., 1943-44; lectr. adult edn. Bklyn. Coll., 1951-61; assoc. prof. Yeshiva U., N.Y.C., 1955-62; assoc. prof., chmn. dept. Germanic and Slavic langs. Bernard M. Baruch Coll., N.Y.C., 1962-77, prof., 1977—, chmn. dept. modern langs., 1977-83, chmn. dept. Germanic, Hebraic and Oriental langs., 1983—, bd. govs., 1973—; mem. adv. bd. Jewish Studies CUNY, 1986; lectr., speaker various sci., civic and religious orgns. and socs. in U.S. and Europe; scholar abroad, Vienna, Austria, 1991. Author: A Linguistic Atlas of Eastern European Yiddish, 1964, rev. edit., 1967, Das letzte Geheimnis (in German), 1972, The Jewish Mystic in Kafka, 1987, (textbooks) Yiddish for Beginners, 1963, Yiddish Literature for Beginners, 1972, (with Y. Kerstein) Hebrew for Beginners, 1975, (with E. Mok) Chinese for Beginners, 1980; editor Elizabethan Concordance series: The Concordance of The Works of Christopher Marlowe, 1979, A Concordance to The Shakespeare Apocrypha, 3 Vols., 1987; Nat. Endowment for Humanities; assoc. editor Jour. Evolutionary Psychology; contbr. numerous articles to profl. jours. Recipient Nat. Jewish Culture Found. award, 1963, Kohut Found. award, 1966, Bernard M. Baruch Coll. medal for 35 yrs. svc., AAUW award, 1968, 69, others; fellow Inst. for Yiddish Lexicological Rsch. CUNY, 1963—; grantee Ford Found., 1970, Population Coun. Rockefeller Inst., 1970-71, Rsch. Found. CUNY, 1985, Lucius N. Littauer Found., 1986, Austrian Fed. Ministry for Sci. and Rsch., 1991. Fellow Jewish Acad. Arts and Scis.; mem. Am. Assn. Tchrs. German, MLA, AAUP, Am. Assn. Profs. Yiddish (pres.), Am. Psychol. Assn., Marlowe Soc. Am. (founder 1975, pres. 1975-84, organizer 1st. Internat. Congress in Eng. 1983), Mich. Acad. Arts and Scis., Acad. Scis. and Humanities CUNY, Sigma Alpha. Address: 1684 52nd St Brooklyn NY 11204-1418

JOFFE, BARBARA LYNNE, computer project administrator; b. Bklyn., Apr. 12, 1951; d. Lester L. and Julia (Schuelke) J.; m. James K. Whitney, Aug. 25, 1990; 1 child, Nichole. BA, U. Oreg., 1975; MFA, U. Mont., 1982. Applications engr., software developer So. Pacific Transp., San Francisco, 1986-93; computer fine artist Barbara Joffe Assocs., San Francisco, Englewood, Colo., 1988—; instr. computer graphics Ohlone Coll., Fremont, Calif., 1990-91; adv. programmer, project mgr.-client/server Integrated Syss. Solutions Corp./IBM So. Pacific, Denver, 1994—. Artwork included in exhibits at Calif. Crafts XIII, Crocker Art Mus., Sacramento, 1983, Rara Avis Gallery, Sacramento, 1984, Redding (Calif.) Mus. and Art Ctr., 1985, Euphrat Gallery, Cupertino, Calif., 1988, Computer Mus., Boston, 1989, Siggraph Traveling Art Shown, Europe and Australia, 1990, 91, 7th Nat. Computer Art Invitational, Cheney, Wash., 1994, Visual Arts Mus., N.Y.C., 1994. Mem. Assn. Computing Machinery. Home: 7271 S Jersey Ct Englewood CO 80112-1512

JOHANSEN, KAREN LEE, sales executive; b. Sheldon, Iowa, Dec. 5, 1945; d. Alvin Anthony and Marjory Gertrude (Kuiper) Eich; m. Pete Brunsting, May 15, 1964 (div. Dec. 1983); children: Jeffrey Brunsting, Keri Wallenstein; m. Alan Brockberg, Oct. 30, 1988 (div. Apr. 1991); m. Alan Johansen, Aug. 21, 1993. Student, Sioux Valley Hosp. Sch. Nsg., 1963-65; grad., S.D. Police Acad., 1978; postgrad., Phoenix Paralegal Inst., 1981-82. Owner Redwood Steak House and Lounge, White, S.D., 1975-76; dep. sheriff Brookings (S.D.) County Sheriff's Office, 1978-79; clk. of ct. City of Gillette, Wyo., 1980-82; child support enforcement officer Campbell County, Gillette, 1982-84; jud. asst. Wyo. Dist. Ct., Sheridan, 1984-85; office mgr. Felt & Martin Law Firm, Billings, Mont., 1985-87; owner paralegal svcs. office, Pipestone, Minn., 1987-89; dist. agt. Prudential Ins. Co. Am., Pipestone, 1989-91; sales mgr. Prudential Ins. Co. Am., Austin, Minn., 1991-93; mgr. S.W. Minn. Prudential Ins. Co., Worthington, Minn., 1993-94; cons. Aanenson Agy., Inc., Fulda, Slayton, Minn., 1994—; estate planner, agt. Farm Bur. Ins. Co., Slayton, Minn., 1994-96, Prudential Ins., Slayton, Minn., 1996—. Asst. Campaign to Re-Elect Andy Steensma, Pipestone, 1990; mem. Ihlen (Minn.) City Coun., 1990; chair Brookings Summer Art Festival, 1976-79, chair, 1977-79, chair entertainment, 1976. Mem. Nat. Assn. Life Underwriters, Nat. Assn. Security Dealers, Farm Bur. Fedn. Democrat. Office: Prudential Ins 1491 150th Ave Slayton MN 56172

JOHNS, BEVERLEY ANNE HOLDEN, special education administrator; b. New Albany, Ind., Nov. 6, 1946; d. James Edward and Martha Edna (Scharf) Holden; m. Lonnie J. Johns, July 28, 1973. BS, Catherine Spalding Coll., Ky., 1968; MS, So. Ill. U., 1970; postgrad., Western Ill. U., 1973-74, 79-80, 82, U. Ill., 1984-85. Cert. adminstr., tchr. Ill. Demonstration tchr. So. Ill. U., Carbondale, 1970-72; instr. MacMurray Coll., Jacksonville, Ill., 1977-79, 90-93; intern Ill. State Bd. Edn., Springfield, 1981; program supr. Four Rivers Spl. Edn. Dist., Jacksonville, Ill., 1972—; chmn. Ill. Edn. of the Handicapped Coalition, 1982—; conf. coord. Ill. Alliance, Champaign, 1982-94; bd. dirs. Jacksonville Area Assn. Retarded Citizens, v.p., 1993-94, sec. 1996—; lectr. to profl. confs.; cons. in field. Author: Report on Behavior Analysis in Edn., 1972, (with V. Carr) Techniques for Managing Verbally and Physically Aggressive Students, 1995, (with V. Carr and C. Hoots) Reduction of School Violence: Alternatives to Suspension, 1995; editor: Position Papers of Ill. Council for Exceptional Children, 1981; contbr. articles to profl. jours. Govt. rels. chmn. Internat. Council Exceptional Children, 1984-87; fed. liason Ill. Adminstrs. Spl. Edn., 1985-86. So. Ill. U. fellow, 1968; resolution honoring Beverly H. Johns 60th Ann. Internat. Coun. for Exceptional Children Conv., 1982; cert. of recognition Ill. Atty. Gen., 1985. Recipient Lifetime Achievement award Ill. Coun. for Exceptional Children, 1989; named Jacksonville Woman of the Yr. Bus. and Profl. Women, 1988, First Lady Ill. Coun. Exceptional Children, 1993, Unsung Hero Jacksonville Jour.-Carrier, 1993. Mem. ASCD, Assn. Retarded Citizens (com. 1982—), Ill. Coun. for Children With Behavioral Disorders (founder, past pres., presdl. award 1985), pres. Ill. div. for learning disabilities 1991-92, Ill. Alliance for Exceptional Children (v.p 1982-94), Learning Disabilities Assn. (bd. dir.), Ill. Coun. Exceptional Children (past pres., chmn. govt. rels. com. 1982-95, governing bd. 1984-95, Presdl. award 1983), Internat. Coun. for Children With Behavioral Disorders (pres. elect 1996), West Cen. Assn. for Citizens with Learning Disabilities (founder, com. chair 197—), Internat. Pioneer Press (editor CEC pioneer divsn.), Internat. Divsn. Learning Disibilities (exec. bd.), Delta Kappa Gamma (chpt. pres. 1988-90, state exec. bd. 1991—), Phi Delta Kappa. Roman Catholic. Avocation: world travel. Home: PO Box 340 Jacksonville IL 62651-0340 Office: Four Rivers Spl Edn Dist 936 W Michigan Ave Jacksonville IL 62650-3113

JOHNS, CAROL JOHNSON, physician, educator; b. Balt., June 18, 1923; d. Ashmore Clark and Elsie Greacen (Carstens) Johnson; BA, Wellesley Coll., 1944; MD, Johns Hopkins U., 1950; DHL (hon.), Coll. Notre Dame of Md., 1981; m. Richard James Johns, June 27, 1953; children: James Ashmore, Richard Clark, Robert Shanard. Intern, Johns Hopkins Hosp., 1950-51, asst. resident in medicine, 1951-53, fellow, 1953-54, physician outpatient dept., 1953-64, dir. Sarcoid Clinic, 1962-93, active staff, 1964—, dir. med. clinic, 1967-76, dir. hosp. quality assurance, 1974-79, mem. hosp. med. bd., 1971-79; asst. in medicine Johns Hopkins U., 1951-58, instr., 1958-67, asst. prof., 1967-71, assoc. prof., 1971—, adv. bd. Applied Physics Lab., 1974-78; acting pres. Wellesley Coll., 1979-81, asst. dean, dir. continuing edn., 1981-93; chmn. bd. Balt. City PSRO, 1975-79; pres. Internat. Sarcoid Conf., 1984; mem. pulmonary allergy adv. com. FDA, 1973-75; faculty adv. editorial bd. Johns Hopkins U. Press, 1981-84. Contbr. articles to med. jours., chpts. in textbooks. Mem. vestry Ch. of Redeemer, 1967-70, sr. warden, 1976-79, layreader; bd. trustees Calvert Sch., 1968-72; trustee Wellesley Coll., 1971-90, exec. com., 1971-80, 84-90, chmn. nat. devel. fund, 1975-80, trustee fin. com., 1979-90, chmn. trustee faculty relations com., 1984-90, trustee emeritus, 1990—; trustee St. Paul's Sch. for Girls, 1973-75; bd. dirs. Stetler Rsch. Fund for Women, 1971-79, 84-93; mem. Armed Forces Epidemiol. Bd., 1985-90; bd. regents Uniformed Svcs. Univ. Health Scis., 1985—, vice-chair, 1988—. Named Med. Woman of Yr. Med. Coll. Pa., 1984. Fellow ACP; mem. Am. Clin. Climatol. Assn. (v.p. 1987, coun. 1994—, pres. 1994-95), Am. Thoracic Soc., Balt. City Med. Soc., Johns Hopkins Med. Surg. Assn. (sec.-treas. 1981-87, pres. 1987-89), Johns Hopkins Women's Med. Alumni Assn. (pres. 1957-59, dir.), Md. Med. Chirurg. Faculty (coun. 1978-79), Soc. Med. Coll. Dirs. Continuing Edn., Alliance for Continuing Med. Edn. (coun. 1987-93), Phi Beta Kappa, Sigma Xi, Alpha Omega Alpha (bd. dirs. 1978-87, v.p. 1985-86, pres. 1986-87), Johns Hopkins Club, Wellesley Coll. Club, Mt. Vernon Club, Cosmos Club. Episcopalian. Home: 203 E Highfield Rd Baltimore MD 21218-1105 Office: Johns Hopkins Sch Medicine 858 Ross Bldg 720 Rutland Ave Baltimore MD 21205-2196

JOHNS, CATHERINE, radio personality; b. Ft. Wayne, Ind., Nov. 3, 1952; d. Richard and Barbara Johns; married, Aug. 24, 1991. Student, Western Ill. U., Valparaiso U. Reporter WHBF-TV, Rock Island, Ill.; reporter, editor WRBC, Jackson, Miss.; morning drive anchor WQSA, Sarasota, Fla.; anchor, editor, reporter KEYH, Houston; midday co-anchor WERE, Cleve.; reporter WLS-AM, Chgo., 1979—, talk show host, 1990—. 'Fangette', NFG, 1969—. Office: WLS-AM 190 N State St Chicago IL 60601

JOHNS, CHRISTINE MICHELE, elementary school principal; b. Spangler, Pa., Nov. 11, 1965; d. George Warren and Walterine Johns. BS, U. Pitts., 1988; MS, Johns Hopkins U., Balt., 1992. Early childhood tchr. Salvation Army, Pitts., 1985-87; summer counselor YWCA, Pitts., summers 1987-88; tchr. sci. and math. Prince George's (Md.) County Pub. Schs., 1988-91, magnet sch. coord., 1991-92, instructional specialist, 1992-94; prin. Fort Foote Elem. Sch., Ft. Washington, Md., 1994—; tchr. trainer Lego Dacta Ednl. Sys., Enfield, Conn., 1988-92; tchr. adult edn. Prince Georges County Pub. Schs., 1993-94; sci. trek steering com. Prince George's C.C., 1988-92. Recipient Outstanding Adminstr.'s award Prince George's C. of C., 1996; grantee Nat. Found. for Improvement of Edn., 9191, 92, Mid-Atlantic Japan in the Schs., U. Md., 1989, Gov.'s Acad. for Math. and Sci., Md. Dept. Edn., 1992, Harvard U., 1996. Mem. ASCD, Md. Assn. Supervision and Curriculum Devel. Home: 13606 Lord Sterling Pl Upper Marlboro MD 20772-5918 Office: Prince Georges Co Pub Sch Fort Foote Elementary Sch 8300 Oxon Hill Rd Fort Washington MD 20744-4575

JOHNS, JENNI REBECCA, public relations and marketing coordinator; b. Alpena, Mich., May 27, 1960; d. Richard Joseph and Shirley Jean (Pierce) Ritzler; m. Roger Grant Johns, Sept. 7, 1988. AA, Alpena (Mich.) C.C., 1983; B of Applied Arts, Ctrl. Mich. U., 1985. Journalist Mich. Army Nat. Guard, Bay City, 1981-89; pub. rels. asst. Jervis B. Webb Co., Farmington Hills, Mich., 1986-88; pub. rels. and mktg. coord. Mercy/St. Charles Hosps., Toledo, 1988—; hosp. pub. rels. liaison Mercy Hosp. Aux., Toledo, 1988—. With U.S. Army, 1978-81, West Germany. Mem. Pub. Rels. Soc. of Am., Women in Comm., Inc., Am. Soc. for Health Care Mktg. and Pub. Rels., Ohio Soc. for Healthcare Pub. Rels., Phi Kappa Phi, Phi Theta Kappa. Democrat. Roman Catholic. Home: 2117 Talbot St Toledo OH 43613 Office: Mercy/St Charles Hospitals 2200 Jefferson Ave Toledo OH 43624

JOHNS, KAREN KAY, elementary education educator; b. Tecumseh, Nebr., Sept. 8, 1953; d. Victor John and Esta Katherine (Schweppe) Dierking; m. James Lee Johns, Apr. 1, 1972; children: Laura Xiao, Shawnee Phung. BEd., Peru (Nebr.) State Coll., 1975; MEd, U. Nebr., 1989. Cert. Elementary Edn., endorsement in early childhood curriculum and instrn., Nebr. Elem. tchr. Sch. Dist. #58, Syracuse, Nebr., 1975-76, 78-79, Sch. Dist. #19, Tecumseh, Nebr., 1979-87; libr. elem. art Johnson-Brock Schs., Johnson, Nebr., 1987-88; elem. tchr. Johnson-Brock Schs., Brock, Nebr., 1988—; mem. Dwight D. Eisenhower Adv. Coun., Auburn, Nebr., 1992—; presenter, cons. Activities Integrating Math and Sci., Fresno, Calif., 1991—. Compiler, editor: Johns Family History, 1986, Petersen Family History, 1985. Active Zion Lutheran Ch., 1974—; mem. Johnson County Chamber, Tecumseh, 1986—; pres., sec. Women Involved in Farm Econs., 1980—; mem. Nat. Farmer's Orgn., 1972-82. Named Outstanding Young Woman, Jaycee Women, Johnson, 1985; recipient Honorable Mention for Tchr. in Space, NASA, Nebr., 1985. Mem. Johnson-Brock Edn. Assn. (sec., negotiating sec.), Johnson County Edn. Assn. (pres., sec.), Internat. Reading Assn. (sec. 1989-91, pres. 1991-93), Phi Delta Kappa, Delta Kappa Gamma. Republican. Lutheran. Home: RR 3 Box 148 Tecumseh NE 68450-9561

JOHNS, KAREN LOUISE, nurse, psychotherapist; b. Chgo., Jan. 21, 1942; d. John Leonard and Virginia Selma (Kliner) J. Diploma in Nursing, St. Elizabeth Hosp., Chgo., 1962; BSN, Loyola U., Chgo., 1967; MSN, Calif. State U., L.A., 1972; MA in Psychology, Immaculate Heart Coll., L.A., 1978. RN, Calif.; registered marriage, family and child counselor; cert. clin. specialist in psychiat./mental health nursing; registered poetry therapist. Staff nurse Luth. Gen. Hosp., Park Ridge, Ill., 1962-63; staff nurse, insvc. edn. coord. Holy Family Hosp., Des Plaines, Ill., 1963-67; instr. St. Vincent's Coll. of Nursing, L.A., 1967-72; assoc. prof. L.A. Valley Coll., Van Nuys, Calif., 1972-76; nurse Brutman Med. Ctr., Culver City, Calif., 1976-77, St. John's Hosp., Santa Monica, Calif., 1977-78, VA Med. Ctr., L.A., 1982—; counselor Kedren Coll., L.A., 1980-81. Mem. Nat. Assn. Poetry Therapy (bd. dirs. 1989-91). Office: WLA VA Med Ctr 11301 Wilshire Blvd Los Angeles CA 90073

JOHNSEY, ANITA COLLEEN, special education educator; b. Birmingham, Ala., June 14, 1966; d. Judith Colleen (Bradberry) Steger. BS in Spl. Edn./Mental Retardation, Livingston (Ala.) U., 1988, MEd in Spl. Edn./Mental Retardation, 1990; EdS in Spl. Edn./Mental Retardation, U. Ala., 1994. Lic. tchr. spl. edn, area mental retardation. Tchr. multihandicapped Linden (Ala.) Elem. Sch., 1988-90; tchr. mentally retarded Jefferson County Schs., Hillview Elem. Sch., Birmingham, Ala., 1990-94, Jefferson County Schs., Pittman Mid. Sch., Birmingham, Ala., 1994—. Del. Citizens Ambassador Program, 1995. Mem. Coun. Exceptional Children (presenter Ala. conf. 1996, nat. conf. 1996), Ala. Edn. Assn., Phi Delta Kappa. Home: 1414 15th Ave S Birmingham AL 35205-5420

JOHNSON, ADDIE COLLINS, secondary education educator, former dietitian; b. Evansville, Ind., Feb. 28; d. Stewart and Willa (Shamell) Collins; m. John Q. Johnson, Sept. 6, 1958 (dec. Aug. 1991); 1 child, Parker. BS, Howard U., 1956; MEd, Framingham State Coll., Mass., 1967. Registered dietitian, Mass. Dietitian Boston Lying-In Hosp., 1957-61; dietitian Diet Heart Study, Harvard U. Sch. Pub. Health, Boston, 1962-63; tchr. Foxboro (Mass.) Pub. Sch., 1967—; dietitian Sch. Medicine Boston U., 1975-77, Westinghouse Health Systems, Boston; faculty Dept. Nursing Boston State Coll., 1979-82; nutrition cons. Head Start program Westinghouse Sch., Boston, 1979-82; instr. dept. nursing U. Mass., 1981—, Bridgewater (Mass.) State Coll., 1982—; mem. state adv. coun. Dept. Edn Bur. Nutrition Edn., 1981-83; participant NSF Project Seed, 1992. Bd. dirs. Norfolk-Bristol County Home Health Assn., Walpole, Mass., 1975-78; presenter Nat. Social Studies Assn., Boston, 1984-85; instr./trainer health svcs. edn. ARC, 1987-90. Mem. AAUW, NAACP (life), Am. Dietetic Assn., Am. Home Econs. Assn., Ea. Mass. Home Econs. Assn. (bd. dirs. 1978), Mass. Tchrs. Assn. (higher edn. com. 1984-87), Soc. Nutrition Edn., Delta Kappa Gamma (journalist Iota chpt. 1986-88, membership com. 1988-92, v.p. 1994), Delta Sigma Theta. Home: 92 Morse St Sharon MA 02067-2719 Office: Foxboro Pub Schs Mechanic St Foxboro MA 02035-2028

JOHNSON, ALEXANDRA, religious organization administrator. Pres. The Can. Coun. of Chs. Office: 40 Saint Clair Ave E Ste 201, Toronto, ON Canada M4T 1M9*

JOHNSON, ALICE BEATRICE, art educator, social worker; b. Asbury Park, N.J., Feb. 25, 1927; d. Robert Lee and Blanche Guess; m. William D. Johnson, Dec. 26, 1948 (dec. Nov. 1991); children: Deirdre, Diane, Linda. BFA, W.Va. State Coll., 1949; postgrad., N.Y. City Coll., 1966, Hofstra U., 1966-74, Adelphi U., 1973. Claims clk. Donut Corp. Am., N.Y.C., 1949-52; artist Timely Crafts, Bklyn., 1953-54; social worker Dept. Human Svcs., N.Y.C., 1955-64; freelance artist N.Y.C., 1955—; home econs. supr. O.E.D., Wyndanch, N.Y., 1964-65; art tchr. Andrew Jackson H.S., Queens, N.Y., 1966-67, Babylon (N.Y.) Schs., 1967-77, Amityville (N.Y.) Schs., 1967-77, Wyandanch Schs., 1977-82; art cons. Queens Coll. Parents & Child Ctr., 1964-65. Artist, writer The Stony Road, 1985; group shows include Bethune-Cookman Coll., African-Am. Mus. Art. Tchr. art classes for children NAACP, Wyandanch, 1965—; mem. Nassau Arts Decentralization Regrant Panel, Rosyln, N.Y., 1987—; art judge Tomoka Fla. Correctional, Volusia City, Fla., 1992, art presenter Suffolk County (N.Y.) Dept. Pks., Islip, N.Y. State Office Mental Health, 1969-80. Grantee Ludwig Vogelstein Found., 1983, N.Y. State Arts Coun., 1984. Mem. African Am. Cultural Soc. (bd. dirs. 1992—), African Am. Carribean Club, Palm Coast Art League, Delta Sigma Theta (recording sec. 1949—, corr. sec. 1996—, Spl. Art Recognition Nassau chpt. 1979). Methodist. Home: 9 Sherbury Ct Palm Coast FL 32137

JOHNSON, ANNE ELISABETH, executive assistant; b. Springfield, Mass., Nov. 3, 1955; d. Michael Francis Xavier and Miriam Rose (Coombs) Gigliotti. NSCC, Beverly, Mass., 1976. Cert. med. transcriptionist. Home health aide Sr. Home Care Svcs., Gloucester, Mass., 1974-76; lab asst., EKG technician, phlebotomist Addison Gilbert Hosp., Gloucester, Mass., 1976-80; exec. asst. MGA Inc., Gloucester, Mass., 1980-83, 85-94; med. asst. Cape Ann Med. Ctr., Gloucester, 1983-85; dance instr., 1973-80. Sec. Am. Cancer Soc., Gloucester, 1978-79; polit. asst. Dem. Party, Gloucester, 1974-85; active People for the Ethical Treatment of Animals. Mem. NAFE, Mass. Soc. for Prevention of Cruelty to Animals, Doris Day Animal League, Surfrider Found. Roman Catholic. Home: 27 Exchange St Gloucester MA 01930-3449 Office: Anne Elisas Profl Svcs Gloucester MA 01930

JOHNSON, ARLENE LYTLE, government agency official; b. Pitts., Jan. 20, 1937; d. Willis and Minnie Lee (Blackman) Neal; m. William Dalois Johnson, Aug. 27, 1971; children: Robin Gerome Lytle, Cheryl Rose Lytle Campbell. Student various profl. courses. Clk.-typist, Pa. Dept. Revenue, Harrisburg, 1955; office sec. Akron (Ohio) Jewish Center, 1956-57; clk.-stenographer Pa. Employment Service, Pitts., 1960-61; Dept. Treasury, Washington, 1961; sec.-stenographer HEW, Washington, 1961-70, exec. sec. to dir. Bur. Community Health Services, Health Services Adminstrn., Rockville, Md., 1970-81; staff asst. to dep. asst. sec. for children and families HHS, 1981-93, staff asst. to asst. sec. for children and families, 1993—. Recipient Spl. Recognition award USPHS, 1991, Superior Service award Health Services and Mental Health Adminstrn., 1973; Sustained Superior Service award HHS, 1984-90, 93, Spl. Recognition award Human Devel. Svcs. Adminstrn. for Children and Families, 1989, 91. Jehovah's Witness. Home: 5945 Addison Rd Capital Heights MD 20743-2166 Office: Aerospace Bldg Rm 610 370 Lenfant Promenade SW Washington DC 20447-0001

JOHNSON, AUDREY ANN, options trader, stockbroker; b. Chgo., June 7, 1954; d. Elmer and Diane Ann (Vassiv) J. Student, North Ctrl. Coll., 1972-75, U. Ill. Registered stockbroker, real estate salesperson, Ill. Real estate salesperson Century 21 Cahill Bros., Chgo., 1975-80; stockbroker Charles Schwab, Chgo., 1980-87; Chgo. Bd. Options Exch. floor trader Drexel Burnham, Chgo., 1987-90; pvt. practice specializing in futures, options, indexes and equities Chgo., 1990—; options broker, stockbroker Profl. Trader's Inst. Securities, Chgo., 1990—; real estate salesperson Coldwell Banker, Palos Heights, Ill., 1995; arbitrator Chgo. Bd. Options Exch., 1989-92; guest spkr. Chgo. TV Channel 26, 1993-94; participant in NAFTA. Mem. Nat. Assn. Securities Dealers, Ind. Floor Members Assn., Chgo. Bd. Options Exch., Palos Hills Horseman's Assn. Democrat. Roman Catholic. Home: 9174 South Rd Palos Hills IL 60465-2135

JOHNSON, BADRI NAHVI, sociology educator, real estate business owner; b. Tehran, Iran, Dec. 1, 1934; came to U.S., 1957; d. Ali Akbar and Monir Khazraii Nahvi; m. Floyd Milton Johnson, July 2, 1960; children: Robert, Rebecca, Nancy, Shahla. BS, U. Minn., 1967, MA, 1969; postgrad., 1994—. Stenographer Curtis 1000, Inc., St. Paul, 1958-62; lab. instr. U. Minn., Mpls., 1966-69, teaching asst., 1969-72; chief exec. officer Real Estate Investment and Mgmt. Enterprise, St. Paul, 1969—; instr. sociology Anoka-Ramsey Community Coll., Coon Rapids, Minn., 1973—; pub. speaker, bd. dirs., sponsor pub. radio KFAI, Mpls., 1989-93; established an endowed scholarship for women Anoka Ramsey C.C., 1991. Radio talk show host KCW, Brookline Parks, Minn., 1993. Organizer Iranian earthquake disaster relief, 1990. Recipient Earthquake Relief Orgn. citation Iranian Royal Household, 1968. Mem. NEA, Minn. Edn. Assn., Sociologists of Minn., U. Minn. Alumni Assn., Minn. Club. Home: 1726 Iowa Ave E Saint Paul MN 55106-1334 Office: Anoka-Ramsey Community Coll 11200 Mississippi Blvd NW Minneapolis MN 55433-3470

JOHNSON, BERNADETTE LEOLA, child care executive; b. Alexandria, Va., Feb. 9, 1954; d. Eugene Wadsworth and Dorothea Luvenia (King) J.; m. Donald Edward Green, Oct. 28, 1986 (div. 1995); children: Antoinette, Te'Lon, La'Rae. CEO Green Seed Learning Home, Alexandria, 1990—. Bd. dirs. Alexandria City Pub. Schs., 1994-97, vice chmn., 1994-95; mem. Charles Houston Parents Adv. Bd., Alexandria, 1993; mem. Neighborhood Leadership Devel. Inst., Washington, 1990—, Parent Policy Bd. Head Start, Alexandria, 1990—, Early Childhood Commn., 1995—. Mem. Nat. Assn. for Day Care. Democrat. Baptist. Home and Office: Green Seed Learning Home 317 Evans Ln Alexandria VA 22305-3003

JOHNSON, BESS ORR, retired librarian; b. Forest Hill, La., Feb. 12, 1917; d. Jesse Hiram and Kathryn (Jones) Orr; m. James Murphy Johnson, July 11, 1938; 1 child, Don. Student, La. State U., 1959, McNeese State U., 1961-62, La. Coll., 1968. Br. mgr. Oakdale (La.) Br. Libr., 1957-79; interim systems mgr. Allen Parish Libr., Oberlin, La., 1990; asst. in establishing Allen Parish Libr., Oberlin, 1947-57; bd. dirs., advisor Friends of Libr., Oakdale, 1989—. Author: History of Oakdale, 1980; artist collage, watercolor and acrylic painting. Leader Cub Scouts, 1946-49; active Little League Baseball, 1949-50; pres. Oakdale PTA, 1954-55; asst. in establishing Allen Parish Trade Sch., 1954-56; dramatizer of books and stories for children and adults, Oakdale, 1960—; vol. libr. First Bapt. Ch., Oakdale, 1970—, mem. ch. coun., 1991—; organizer, cataloger, bd. dirs. Leatherwood House Mus., Oakdale, 1988. Mem. Primetimers Adult Sr. Orgn. (pres. 1991-92). Democrat. Baptist. Home: 500 Oak St Oakdale LA 71463

JOHNSON, BETH EXUM, lawyer; b. Beaumont, Tex., July 4, 1952; d. James Powers Jr. and Betty Jean (Clement) Exum; m. Walter William Johnson, Apr. 25, 1981; 1 child, Stratton William. BA in Psychology, Tulane U., 1974; JD, Loyola U., New Orleans, 1985; LLM in Energy and Environ., Tulane U., 1989. Bar: La. 1985, Tex. 1993, U.S. Dist. Ct. (ea. dist.) La. 1985, U.S. Dist. Ct. (we. and mid. dists.) 1989. Paralegal McCloskey, Dennery, Page & Hennesy, New Orleans, 1975-80; oil and gas abstractor of title Frawley, Wogan, Miller & Co., New Orleans, 1980-82; assoc. trust counsel, asst. v.p. and trust officer Hibernia Nat. Bank, New Orleans, 1985-95; legal cons. New Orleans, 1995-96; assoc. Gelpi and Assocs., PLC, New Orleans, 1996—; faculty La. succession practice Tulane U., New Orleans, 1990-94, environ. law practice, 1991-94; mem. fundraising com. and atty. honor roll New Orleans Pro Bono Project. Mem. New Orleans Estate Planning Coun. Mem. ABA, La. Bar Assn., New Orleans Bar Assn., Friends City Park, Premier Athletic club, Rivercenter Tennis Club, Cavalier King Charles Spaniel Club, Phi Alpha Delta, Kappa Alpha Theta. Home: 959 Harrison Ave New Orleans LA 70124-3837 Office: 203 Carondelet St Ste 907 New Orleans LA 70130

JOHNSON, BETSEY LEE, fashion designer; b. Hartford, Conn., Aug. 10, 1942; d. John Herman and Lena Virginia J.; m. John Cale, Apr. 4, 1966; 1 child, Lulu; m. Jeffrey Olivier, Feb. 7, 1981. Student, Pratt Inst., N.Y.C., 1960-61; B.A., U. Syracuse, 1964. Editorial asst. Mademoiselle mag., 1964-65; ptnr., co-owner Betsey, Bunky & Nini, N.Y.C., from 1969; owner retail stores N.Y.C, L.A., San Francisco, Coconut Grove, Fla., Venice, Calif., Boston, Chgo., Seattle. Prin. designer: Paraphernalia (owned by Puritan Fashions, Inc.), 1965-69; designer, Alvin Duskin Co., San Francisco, 1970; head designer: Alley Cat by Betsey Johnson, div. LeDamor, Inc., 1970-74; freelance designer for, Jr. Womens div. Butterick Pattern Co., 1971, Betsey Johnson's Kids Children Wear for new div, Shutterbug, Inc., 1974-77, Betsey Johnson for, Jeanette Maternities, Inc., 1974-75; designer first line womens clothing for, Gant Shirtmakers, Inc., 1974-75; Tric-Trac by Betsey Johnson, Womens Knitwear, 1974-76; children's wear for Butterick's Home Sewing catalog, from 1975; head designer jr. sportswear co.: childrens wear for Star Ferry by Betsey Johnson and Michael Milea, 1975-77; owner, head designer, B.J., Inc., designer wholesale co., N.Y.C., 1978, pres., treas., B.J. Vines, N.Y.C., owner, Betsey Johnson store, N.Y.C., from 1979 (Recipient Mademoiselle mag. Merit award 1970, Coty award 1971, 2 Tommy Print awards 1971); owner 3 retail stores in N.Y.C., 3 in L.A., 1 San Francisco, 1 in Miami, 1 in Chgo., 1 in Seattle. Mem. Coun. Fashion Designers Am., Women's Forum. Office: Betsey Johnson Co 209 W 38th St New York NY 10018-4405 also: 110 E 9th St Ste A889 Los Angeles CA 90079-1885*

JOHNSON, BETTY ANNE, nurse; b. Centerville, Iowa, Sept. 14, 1924; d. Delazon Marion and Lucy Glen (Guernsey) Wilson; m. Vern William Johnson (dec. Oct. 1966); children: Richard Hugh, Russell William, John Allen. Grad., St. Joseph Sch. Nursing, Ottumwa, Iowa, 1946; BS in Health Arts, Coll. of St. Francis, Joliet, Ill., 1982. RN, Iowa. Tchr. Albany Sch., Bloomfield, Iowa, 1942-43; nurse Ottumwa Hosp., 1946-49, 78-83, Balboa Hosp., San Diego, 1949-50, Davis County Hosp., Bloomfield, Iowa, 1951-52, 74-78; nurse, pediatrics dept. St. Joseph Hosp., Ottumwa, 1967-73; nurse Glenwood (Iowa) State Hosp. for Retarded, 1973-74; substitute house parent Rainbow Acres, Ranch for Handicapped Adults, Camp Verde, Ariz., 1984-87; supr. Foothills Care Ctr., Cottonwoord, Ariz, 1985-87; with Kachine Point Health Ctr., Sedona, Ariz, 1987-89; nurse Easter Seals East Camp, Va., 1990, Good Samaritan Care Ctr., Ottumwa, Iowa, 1991; day substitute Child Care Ctr., Dallas; RN Vista Woods, Ottumwa, Iowa, 1994-95; residential care nurse Rescare, Bloomfield, Iowa, 1996—. Home: 425 S Willard St Ottumwa IA 52501-5032

JOHNSON, BETTY LOU, secondary education educator; b. Stockwell, Ind., Apr. 4, 1927; d. Paul Stanley Jones and Ethel Leona (Royer) J.; m. Kenneth Odell Johnson, Aug. 5, 1950; children: Cynthia Jo (Mrs. James P. Greaton), Gregory Alan. BS in Home Econs., Purdue U., 1948; postgrad., Northwood Inst. Culinary Arts, 1981, 83. Cert. home economist. Tchr. LaCrosse (Ind.) Jr.-Sr. High Sch., 1948-49, Wendell L. Willkie High Sch., Elwood, Ind., 1949-51, Thomas Carr Howe High Sch., Indpls., 1951-57; substitute tchr. Gt. Oaks Joint Vocat. Sch. Dist., Cin. Mem. AAUW, Am. Home Econs. Assn. (life), Ohio Home Econs. Assn. (life), John Purdue Club, Purdue U. Alumni Assn. (life), Gamma Sigma Delta. Home: Indian Hill Village 8360 Arapaho Ln Cincinnati OH 45243-2718

JOHNSON, BEVERLY PHILLIPS, bank officer; b. Richmond, Va., May 14, 1963; d. Harold Thomas and Betty Lucille (Trammell) Phillips; m. Robert Mark Johnson, Nov. 29, 1985; children: Margaret Elizabeth, Laura Ellen. BS, Lee Coll., Cleveland, Tenn., 1985. Comptroller Frank White Co., Cleveland, Tenn., 1983-86; credit analyst 1st Am. Nat. Bank, Chattanooga, 1986-88; mortgage banker 1st Am. Nat. Bank, Cleveland, Tenn., 1988-89; comml. real estate banker 1st Am. Nat. Bank, Chattanooga, 1989-92; comml. lender, v.p. SunTrust Bank, Cleveland, Tenn., 1992—. Divsn. campaign chairperson United Way, Bradley County, Cleveland, 1987-90, 93, 96; treas. Cleveland Cmty. Concert Assn., 1989—, pres., 1995—; mem. Leadership Cleveland, 1991-92; bd. dirs. Am. Heart Assn., blockwalkers capt., 1993; bd. dirs. Cleveland Family YMCA, 1993—, treas., 1995—; bd. dirs. 1st United Meth. Child Devel. Ctr., 1992; trustee First United Meth. Ch. Mem. Main St. Cleveland (treas. 1995—), Rotary (pres. Cleveland 1995—), Cleveland Country Club (assoc.), Civitan (bd. dirs. Cleveland chpt. 1984-91, 93—, Chattanooga chpt. 1991-92), United Way Pillars Club, Lee Coll. Pres. Cir., Cleveland/Bradley C. of C. (econ. devel. coun. 1992—). Republican. United Methodist. Home: 1220 Bramblewood Trl NW Cleveland TN 37311-4107 Office: Suntrust Bank PO Box 1149 Cleveland TN 37364-1149

JOHNSON, BONNIE JEAN, art educator; b. Keyser, W.Va., Jan. 8, 1947. BA, Berea (Ky.) Coll., 1968; MA in Teaching, Wesleyan U., Middletown, Conn., 1970, MA in Liberal Studies, 1981; supervisory cert., Ctrl. Conn. State U., New Britain, 1989. Cert. tchr. K-12, Conn., Mass. Chmn. art dept. Valley Regional H.S., Deep River, Conn., 1972-78, art instr., 1969-79; studio artist Farmington Valley Arts Ctr., Avon, Conn., 1980-88, program dir., 1981-83; art instr. Conn. pub./pvt. schs., 1987-91; adj. asst. prof. Iowa State U., Ames, 1991-95, coord. edn. Brunnier Mus. Artist abstract murals. Recipient Best in Show award 57th Ann. Art Exhbn., New Haven, 1986, Commn. of Artwork John Dempsey Hosp., West Hartford, Conn., 1988. Home: 42 Graham Rd Hartford CT 06118

JOHNSON, BRENDA LEE, elementary school principal, reading educator; b. Jamestown, N.Y., Oct. 5, 1950; d. Herbert Edwin and Betty Lou (Steck) J. Student, U. Buffalo, 1971; BA in Edn., SUNY, Fredonia, 1971, MEd in Reading, 1975, CAS, 1991. Cert. elem. and reading tchr., sch. dist. adminstr., sch. adminstr. and supr. Tchr. remedial reading Jamestown Pub. Schs., 1980-81; tchr. Panama (N.Y.) Cen. Sch., 1972-80, reading educator, 1981-91; elem. prin. Pine Valley Cen. Sch., 1991-95; prin. R.R. Rogers Elem. Sch., Jamestown, 1995—. Mem. NAESP, ASCD, AAUW, N.Y. State ASCD, Western N.Y. ASCD, Internat. Reading Assn., Nat. Coun. Tchrs. English, Sch. Adminstrs. Assn. N.Y. State, N.Y. State ACE, Women of Moose, Order Eastern Star, Delta Kappa Gamma, Phi Delta Kappa (corr. sec. 1993-96). Home: 240 Valleyview Ave Jamestown NY 14701-8417 Office: RR Rogers Elem Sch Jamestown NY 14701

JOHNSON, CAMILLE, media executive. Sr. v.p., media dir. Goldberg Moser O'Neill, San Francisco. Office: Goldberg Moser ONeill 77 Maiden Ln San Francisco CA 94108-5414*

JOHNSON, CANDICE ELAINE BROWN, pediatrics educator; b. Cin., Mar. 21, 1946; d. Paul Preston and Naomi Elizabeth (Lind) Brown; m. Thomas Raymond Johnson, June 30, 1973; children: Andrea Eleanor, Erik Albert. BS, U. Mich., 1968; PhD Microbiology, Case Western Reserve U., 1973, MD, 1976. Diplomate Am. Bd. Pediat. Intern, resident Rainbow Babies & Children's Hosp./Metro. Gen. Pediatrics, 1976-78; fellow in ambulatory pediatrics Metro. Gen. Hosp., Cleve., 1978-79; asst. prof. pediat. Case Western Reserve U., Cleve., 1980-90, assoc. prof. pediat., 1990—; mem. Lederle Spkr.'s Bur., 1992-94; mem. rev. panel NIH, Washington, 1993; faculty sen. Case We. Res. U., 1988-91. Contbr. articles profl. jours. Active 1st Unitarian Ch., Shaker Heights, Ohio, 1982-96. Mem. So. Utah Wilderness Alliance, Sierra Club, Am. Acad. Pediatrics, Amb. Ped. Assn., Soc. Pediatric Rsch. Mem. Green Party. Home: 3062 Huntington Rd Cleveland OH 44120-2474 Office: Dept Pediat Met Health Med Ctr 2500 Metrohealth Dr Cleveland OH 44109-1900

JOHNSON, CAROLINE REDER, advertising and marketing company executive; b. Pitts., July 15, 1949; d. Carl J. and Jimena B. (Williams) Reder; m. Neil K. Johnson, Aug. 8, 1970; children: Adam Randolph, Todd Arthur. BS in Bus. and Resource, Carnegie Mellon U., 1971. Exec. asst. to exec. dir. YMCA of Phila., 1971-74; exec. asst. to pres. Magnetic Metals Co., Camden, N.J., 1974-78; dir. comm. Mark Reed Furniture Restoration and Conservation, Bordentown, N.J., 1992-95; owner, creative dir. Imagine That! Advt. & Mktg., Cinnaminson, N.J., 1995—; lectr. bus. ethics Gloucester County Coll., Sewell, N.J., 1995. Mem. parent coun. Moorestown Friends Sch. Mem. AAUW. Office: Imagine That! Advt & Mktg New Albany Profl Bldg 2800 Rte 130 Ste 301 Cinnaminson NJ 08077

JOHNSON, CARYN See GOLDBERG, WHOOPI

JOHNSON, CECELIA DELPHINE, child therapist; b. Mobile, Ala., July 6, 1959; d. Willie James and Ruth Namid (Bell) J. BS, Troy State U., 1981; MS, U. South Ala., 1993. Cert. in hosp. prescreening, substance abuse and AIDS education. Houseparent Mobile Mental Health Ctr., Ala., 1982-84; clin. assoc. Northshore Psychiatric Hosp., Slidell, La., 1987-88; resident advisor Charter Acad., Mobile, Ala., 1988-94; child therapist Singing River Svcs., Lucedale, Miss., 1994—, also supr. Mem. Am. Counseling Assn., Am. Bus. Women Assn., Phi Kappa Phi. Roman Catholic. Office: Singing River Svcs 103 Industrial Park Rd Lucedale MS 39452

JOHNSON, CINDY COBLE, councilwoman, marketing executive; b. El Paso, Tex., Aug. 20, 1956; d. Walter Mylen and Dewyria Shirley (Hendrix) Coble; m. David Johnson, Feb. 8, 1974; children: David, Luke, Phillip. G-rad. high sch., Plattsmouth, Nebr. OB technician Clarkson Hosp., Omaha, 1975-76; pers. asst. Target, Lincoln, Nebr., 1985-86; loan adminstr. 1st Nat. Bank, Lincoln, 1987-91; past chair Lincoln City Coun., 1995-96, chair, 1995-96; pers. cons. Talent +, Lincoln, 1994-96; mktg. mgr. Signs Now, Inc., Lincoln, 1996—; mem. Joint Budget Com., Lincoln, 1993-94, Highlands Tech. Park Com., Lincoln, 1993-95. Pres. MADD, Lancaster County, 1985-91; past chair Traffic Safety Com., Lincoln, 1989-94; trustee Lighthouse-At Risk Youth, Lincoln, 1993-94; past bd. dirs. People's City Mission, Lincoln,, 1993-96; active MAD DADS; sec. Houses of Hope. Recipient Bradley Cuda Meml. award Lincoln Bd. Realtors, 1990, Svc. to Mankind award Sertoma, 1991, Pub. Svc. award U.S. Dept. Transp., 1991, Ptnrs. in Prevention award Lincoln Coun. on Alcoholism and Drugs, 1994, Free enterprise award LIBA, 1996. Mem. Lincoln Ind. Bus. Assn. (Free Enterprise award 1996), C. of C. Office: Signs Now Inc 525 N 48th St Lincoln NE 68504

JOHNSON, CLARA ELIZABETH, retired chemist, volunteer; b. Carlinville, Ill.; d. Elmer Killiam and Clara Henrietta (Kunart) J.; m. Eugene Roland McGrew, May 25, 1946 (div. Dec. 1975); 1 child, Gordon Neal McGrew. AA, Blackburn Coll., 1944; student, Bradley U., 1945-57. USDA classification. Chemist USDA, Peoria, Ill., 1944-82; office mgr. Ill. NOW; dir. feminist writers, cons. Des Plaines/Park Ridge (Ill.) NOW, 1989-95; vol. employee/ptnr. Prairie Moon Ltd. Feminist Book Store, Arlington Heights, Ill., 1994—; mem., chair EEEOC, USDA, Peoria, 1960s-70s; mem. Dextran prodn. and Alpha Amylase Teams, 1950s. Author feminist nonfiction; contbr. sci. papers to profl. jours. Officer, activist LWV, Peoria, 1940s-50s; officer, activist, writer Friends of Robert Ingersoll, Peoria, 1970s; mem. Feminist Majority, Planned Parenthood. Mem. NOW (officer, activist, writer 1970s—, pres., other offices), Nat. Abortion and Reproductive Rights Action League, Nat. Women's Polit. Caucus. Home: # 5 753 Busse Hwy Park Ridge IL 60068

JOHNSON, CLARICE P., materials procurement executive; b. Madison, N.C., Dec. 15, 1941; d. George Taylor and Betty Mae (Preston) Penn; m. William Howard Johnson, June 22, 1962; children: William Jr., Renata. BS in Biology, Upsala Coll., 1974, BSBA, 1983; MS, N.J. Inst. Tech., 1990. Mfg. biologist Organon, Inc., West Orange, N.J., 1975-80, prodn. supr., 1980-84, mfg. supr., 1982-84, sr. regulatory assoc., 1984-85, mgr. prodn. and inventory control, 1985-89, mgr. procurement and materials planning, 1989—; edn. counselor, Organon, Inc., 1988—; lectr., guest cons. Jersey City (N.J.) State Coll., 1990, Cenogenics, Old Bridge, N.J., 1989; mem. Organon Gender Focus Group, West Orange, 1993—. Author: Vendor Certification, 1990. Pres. College Park Neighborhood Assn., South Orange, N.J., 1983-87; mem. South Orange Community Rels. Bd., 1981-88; tutorer Essex County C.C., Newark, 1989. Mem. Am. Prodn. and Inventory Control Soc. (pres. No. N.J. chpt., exec. v.p. 1995-96, v.p. edn. 1994, v.p. membership 1994, Mem. of Yr. 1993, CPIM, company coord. 1992-93, Company of Month award 1992, pres. 1996-97), Nat. Assn. Purchasing Mgmt., Am. Soc. Quality Control, AAAS, Internat. Soc. Pharm. Engrs., People to People Internat., Delta Sigma Theta. Democrat. Home: 429 Wilden Pl South Orange NJ 07079-2518 Office: Organon Inc 375 Mount Pleasant Ave West Orange NJ 07052-2724

JOHNSON, CONSTANCE ANN TRILLICH, minister, internet service provider, small business owner, librarian, lawyer, writer, researcher, lecturer; b. Chgo., Apr. 16, 1949; d. Lee and Ruth (Goodhue) Trillich; m. Robert Dale Neal, Dec. 25, 1972 (div. 1988); 1 child, Adam Danforth; m. Lewis W. Johnson Jr., Feb. 14, 1990. BA in French, U. Tenn., 1971, cert. Sorbonne, 1970; MLn, Emory U., 1979; JD, Mercer Law Sch., 1982; PhD magna cum laude Internat. Sem., 1995. Bar: Ga. 1982. Reservationist AAA, Tampa, Fla., 1971-72; libr. tech. asst. I, Mercer U., Macon, Ga., 1973-74, libr. tech. asst. II, 1974-78; teaching asst. Mercer Law Sch., Macon, 1981; asst. prof. Mercer Med. Sch., Macon, 1980-82; pvt. practice, Macon, 1982-86; min. Ch. Tzaddi, 1986-89; writer/researcher ADC Project, 1988-89; min. Alliance of Divine Love, 1988—; co-owner Christians on the Net, 1995—; of counsel Read Found., Evansville, Ind., 1989; mgr. Lifestream Assocs., 1989; freelance editor Page Design Co., 1989; assoc. AA Computer Care, Winter Park, Fla., 1989; founder House of the Lord, 1989—; rsch. asst. Ctr. Constl. Studies, Macon, 1983; instr. bus. Wesleyan Coll., Macon, 1982; owner Christian Computer Care, Winter Park, Fla., 1990—; web designer Christians On The Net, 1995—. Mem. Ch. of Religious Rsch. Inc., 1992—. Author: (book) Treasures From Heaven, 1995; editor (periodical) Ray of Sunshine, 1989; assoc. prof. libr. sci., Internat. Sem., Plymouth Fla., 1991. Bd. dirs. Unity Ch., Middle, Ga., 1987, Sec., 1987. Bd. dirs. Macon Council World Affairs, 1981-82, Light of Creative Awareness, Northville, Mich., 1989; mem. Friends Emory Libraries, Atlanta, 1980-87; mem. Friends Eckerd Coll. Library, St. Petersburg, Fla., 1980-87. Mem. ABA, Am. Soc. Law and Medicine, Am. Judicature Soc., DAR (Kaskaskia chpt.), Mercer U. Women's Club (treas. 1974, pres. 1986, bd. dirs. 1987), Am. Assn. U. Women, Friends of the Libr., Mid. Ga. Gem and Mineral Soc., Macon Mus. Arts and Scis., La Leche League (sec. 1985), Phi Alpha Delta. Republican. Office: Christian Computer Care 1416 Pelican Bay Trl Winter Park FL 32792-6131

JOHNSON, CRYSTAL DUANE, psychologist; b. Houston, Mar. 2, 1954; d. Alton Floyd and Duane (Mullican) J.; m. Donald Beecher Hart, Mar. 21, 1989. BA, U. Tex., 1983, MS, 1985. Lic. profl. counselor, psychol. assoc., marriage and family therapist; cert. chem. dependency specialist. Student devel. specialist U. Tex., Tyler, 1985-86, intake counselor, 1986-88; staff psychologist Sabine Valley Ctr., Longview, Tex., 1987-88, Mental Health/Mental Retardation Ctr. of East Tex., Tyler, 1988-89; pvt. practice psychologist Tyler, 1989—; counselor Juvenile and Adult Probation Depts., 1988—, ICF/MR Residential Homes, 1991—; spl. edn. counselor, 1990—; counselor Child Protective Svcs., 1991—. Mem. Smith County Humane Soc., Tyler, 1985—, Humane Soc. of the U.S., Washington, 1987—, Am. Soc. Prevention Cruelty to Animals, 1987—, Nat. Wildlife Fedn., 1986—, World Wildlife Fedn., 1986—. Mem. Am. Psychol. Assn., Tex. Psychol. Assn., East Tex. Psychol. Assn.

JOHNSON, CYNDA A., physician, educator; b. Girard, Kans., July 16, 1951. MD, UCLA, 1977. Diplomate Am. Bd. Family Medicine (bd. dirs.). Tchg. fellow U. N.C., Chapel Hill, 1980-81; intern U. Kans. Med. Ctr., Kansas City, 1977-78, 1978-80, prof., dir. residency program, vice chmn. Mem. AMA, Am. Acad. Family Practice, Soc. Tchrs. Family Medicine, Kans. Assn. Family Physicians, Kans. Med. Soc. Office: U Kans Med Ctr 39th and Rainbow Sts Kansas City KS 66160*

JOHNSON, DEBORAH ANN COATS, accountant; b. Florence, Ala., Mar. 15, 1959; d. William and Margaret Kathleen (Horton) Coats; m. Samuel Keith Johnson, Aug. 30, 1980; children: William Matthew, Daniel Keith. BS in Acctg., U. North Ala., 1985. Bookkeeper Lanza, Inc., Florence, 1980-83, Shoals Pest Control, Sheffield, Ala., 1983; acct. Cantrell Body Works, Muscle Shoals, Ala., 1985-87, Gen. Hose and Power, Inc., Muscle Shoals, 1988-89, Don Bowlin, CPA, Florence, 1989-90, McKinney Group Cos., Muscle Shoals, 1990-93, Florence Housing Authority, 1993—. Mem. adminstrv. bd. St. James United Meth. Ch., Florence, 1990-93; mem. art com. Shoals C. of C., 1995-96; mem. Greenhill Dixie Youth, Florence, 1988-96. Mem. Inst. Mgmt. Accts. (bd. dirs. 1995-96), Bus. and Profl. Women (v.p. 1996-97, treas. 1995-96). Republican. Baptist. Home: PO Box 1167 322 Phillips Dr Killen AL 35645 Office: Florence Housing Authority 303 N Pine St Florence AL 35630

JOHNSON, D'ELAINE ANN HERARD, artist; b. Puyallup, Wash., Mar. 19, 1932; d. Thomas Napoleon and Rosella Edna (Berry) Herard; m. John Lafayette Johnson, Dec. 22, 1956. BFA, Ctrl. Wash. U., 1954; MFA, U. Wash., 1958, postgrad., 1975—; postgrad. U. London, 1975—. Instr. art Seattle Pub. Schs., 1954-78, instr. art workshops, 1960-70; instr. Mus. History and Industry, Seattle, 1954-56; art dir., instr. Martha Washington Sch. for Girls, Seattle, 1955-58; dir. Mt. Olympus Estate, Edmonds, Wash., 1971; cons. art groups, Wash. State, 1954—; lectr. Ctrl. Wash. State U., Seattle PTA, Creative Arts Assn., Everett, Everett C.C., Women's Caucus for Art, Seattle, Llubs Art Gallery d'Elaine, Edmonds, Wash., 1957-62, numerous others; pvt. art instr., Seattle, 1960-68; served as art juror for numerous shows. Founder Mt. Olympus Preserve for Arts, Edmonds, Wash., 1971, sponsor art events, 1971—; active Wash. Coalition Citizens with Disabilities; lectr. in field. Exhibited in group shows: Fry Art Mus., Seattle, 1964, Seattle Art Mus., 1959, Henry Art Gallery, Seattle, 1972, Vancouver Maritime Mus., B.C., Can., 1981, N.S. Art Mus., Can., 1971, Whatcom Mus., Bellingham, Wash., 1975, State Capitol Mus., Olympia, Wash., 1975, Corvallis State U., Oreg., 1982, Newport Mus., Oreg., Nat. Artist Equity, 1972, Bellvue Art Mus., Seattle, 1989, Rosicrusian Egyption Mus., San Jose, Calif., 1990, St. Mark's Cathedral, Seattkem 1991, Sidney Mus. and Arts Assn., Port Orchard, Wash., 1991, Bellvue Art Mus., 1992, Pacific Arts Ctr. Hauberg Gallery, Seattle, 1992, Bon Marche Gallery, Seattle, 1992, Northeast Trade and Exbn. Hall, 1993, Edmonds (Wash.) Art Mus., 1993, Ilwaco (Wash.) Heritage Mus., 1993, Robert Frey Gallery, Seattle, 1994, Northlight Gallery, Everett, 1995, Newmark Gallery, Seattle, 1995, Corvallis Art Ctr., Oreg., 1995, Maryhill Mus., Goldendale, Wash., 1996; 482 exhibits 1950—, over 1200 paintings through 1970; illustrator: The Bing Crosby Family Music Books for Children, 1961; TV art instr. TV-9 U. Wash., 1968. Elected to Wash. State Art Commn. Registry, Olympia, 1982; recipient numerous awards. Mem. Nat. Artist Equity, Internat. Soc. Artists, The Cousteau Soc., Am. Coun. for Arts, Nat. Women's Studies Assn., Assn. Am. Culture, Internat. Platform Assn., Nat. Pen Women Assn., Retired Tchrs.' Assn., Kappa Delta Pi, Kappa Pi. Avocations: scuba diving, camping, travel, violin, writing. Home and Office: 16122 72d St Ave W Edmonds WA 98206-4517

JOHNSON, DENISE REINKE, judge; b. Wyandotte, Mich., July 13, 1947. Student, Mich. State U., 1965-67; BA, Wayne State U., 1969; postgrad., Cath. U. of Am., 1971-72; JD with honors, U. Conn., 1974. Bar: Conn. 1974, U.S. Dist. Ct. Conn. 1974, Vt. 1980, U.S. Ct. Appeals (2d cir.) 1983, U.S. Dist. Ct. Vt. 1986. Atty. New Haven (Conn.) Legal Assistance Assn., 1974-78; instr. legal writing Vt. Law Sch., South Royalton, 1978-79; clerk Blodgett & McCarren, Burlington, Vt., 1979-80; chief civil rights divsn. Atty. Gen.'s Office, State of Vt., 1980-82; chief pub. protection divsn. Atty. Gen.'s Office, Montpelier, Vt., 1982-88; pvt. practice Shrewsbury, Vt., 1988-90; assoc. justice Vt. Supreme Ct., Montpelier, 1990—. Recipient Bd. Gov.'s scholarship U. Conn., Achievement awards St. Joseph and Castleton State Coll., 1991. Office: Vt Supreme Ct 109 State St Montpelier VT 05609-0001*

JOHNSON, DIANE LYNN, publishing consultant, management consultant; b. N.Y.C., Apr. 26, 1945; d. Lawrence Schlesinger and Rita (Gorman) Kingsley; m. Arnold Krull, Mar. 6, 1969 (div. Mar. 1973); m. Martin A. Johnson, Aug. 19, 1981. Student, New Sch. of Social Rsch., N.Y.C., 1967-69. Ops. mgr. Cambist Films, Inc., N.Y.C., 1963-69; pres. Fantasy Jewelry, Inc., N.Y.C., 1973-75; v.p., media Dynamic House/Tele House, Inc., N.Y.C., 1973-75; v.p., gen. mgr. Columbia Communications, Inc., N.Y.C., 1975-80; pres. Pub. Dynamics, Inc., Boca Raton, Fla., 1982—; cons. Key Pub., Inc., Katonah, N.Y., 1978-80, Milan Schuster, Inc., N.Y.C., 1980-81. Mem. Literacy Vols. Am., N.Y.C., 1973-75; big sister Big Sister Program, N.Y.C., 1973-75; tchrs. aide Jewish Community Ctr. Nursery Sch., Stamford, 1981-82; group leader Smokers Anonymous, Stamford, 1988-93. Mem. Landmark Club (Stamford, Conn.). Jewish. Home: 9037 Long Lake Palm Dr Boca Raton FL 33496 Office: Publishing Dynamics Inc Ste 6-227 5030 Champion Blvd Boca Raton FL 33496

JOHNSON, DOROTHY PHYLLIS, counselor, art therapist; b. Kansas City, Mo., Sept. 13, 1925; d. Chris C. and Mabel T. (Gillum) Green; BA in Art, Ft. Hays. State U., 1975, MS in Guidance and Counseling, 1976, MA in Art, 1979; m. Herbert E. Johnson, May 11, 1945; children: Michael E., Gregory K. Art therapist High Plains Comprehensive Mental Health Assn., Hays, Kans., 1975-76; art therapist, mental health counselor Sunflower Mental Health Assn., Concordia, Kans., 1976-78, Pawnee Mental Health Svcs., 1978-91, co-dir. Project Togetherness, 1976-77, coord. partial hospitalization, 1978-82, out-patient therapist, 1982-91; pvt. practice, 1991—; dir. Swedish Am. State Bank, Courtland, Kans., 1960—, sec., 1973-77. Mem. Kans., Am. art therapy assns., Am. Mental Health Counselors Assn., Am. Counseling Assn., Kans. Counseling Assn., Assn. for Humanistic Psychologists, Assn. Transpersonal Psychologists, Assn. Specialists in Group Work, Phi Delta Kappa, Phi Kappa Phi. Contbr. articles to profl. jours. Home: PO Box 200 Courtland KS 66939-0200 Office: 520 Washington St # B Concordia KS 66901-2117

JOHNSON, DOROTHY SUTHERLAND, school guidance counselor; b. Phila., Sept. 28, 1951; d. Robert Archibald and Lillian Mae (Armstrong) Sutherland; m. Maurice Hugo Johnson, Feb. 26, 1985. BS in Edn., Temple U., 1972; MA, Villanova U., 1976; postgrad., Pa. State U., 1995. Cert. elementary tchr and guidance counselor, elem. prin. Pa. Tchr. Sch. Dist. of Phila., 1972-85; guidance counselor Sch. dist. of Phila., 1985-91, Colonial Sch. Dist., New Castle, Del., 1991—. Recipient Ruth W. Hayre Community Svc. award Sch. Dist. of Phila., 1988, SuperStars! in Edn., Del. State C. of C., 1995. Mem. ASCD, ACA, Pa. Sch. Counselors Assn. (exec. bd. 1987-89), Del. Sch. Counselors Assn., Am. Sch. Counselors Assn., Phi Delta Kappa. Home: 119 Ridgewood Dr Landenberg PA 19350-9393 Office: Castle Hills Elem Sch Moores Ln New Castle DE 19720

JOHNSON, EDDIE BERNICE, congresswoman; b. Waco, Tex., Dec. 3, 1935; d. Lee Edward and Lillie Mae (White) J.; m. Lacy Kirk Johnson, July 5, 1956 (div. Oct. 1970); 1 child, Dawrence Kirk. Diploma in Nursing, St. Mary's Coll. of South Bend, 1955; BS in Nursing, Tex. Christian U., 1967; MPA, So. Meth. U., 1976; LLD (hon.), Bishop Coll., 1979, Jarvis Coll., 1979, Tex. Coll., 1989, Houston-Tillotson Coll., 1993, Paul Quinn Coll., 1993. Chief psychiat. nurse psychotherapist Vets. Hosp., Dallas, 1956-72; state rep. Tex. Ho. Reps. Dist. 33-0, Dallas, 1972-77; regional dir. HEW, Dallas, 1977-79; exec. asst. to adminstr. for primary health care policy HEW, Washington, 1979-81; v.p. Vis. Nurse Assn. of Tex., Dallas, 1981-87; mem. Tex. State Senate, dist. 23, 1986-93, 103rd Congress from 30th Tex. dist., Washington, D.C., 1993—; cons. div. urban affairs Zales Corp., Dallas, 1976-77; exec. asst. personnel div. Neiman-Marcus, Dallas, 1972-75; pres. Eddie Bernice Johnson & Assocs., Inc., Metroplex News, Dallas-Ft. Worth Airport. Bd. dirs. ARC. Recipient Citizenship award Nat. Conf. Christians and Jews, 1985; named an Outstanding Alumnus St. Mary's Coll. of Nursing, 1986. Mem. Alpha Kappa Alpha. Office: US Ho of Reps 1123 Longworth HOB Washington DC 20515

JOHNSON, EDNA RUTH, editor; b. Sturgeon Bay, Wis., Dec. 23, 1918; d. Charles Frederick and Georgina (Knutson) Johnson; m. Al Larson, 1955. BA, U. So. Fla., 1971. With The Churchman, 1950—; editor The Human Quest (formerly The Churchman), St. Petersburg, Fla., 1968—. Editor, Friendship News (USA-USSR), N.Y.C., 1975-88; mem. editorial bd. The Humaist, Amherst, N.Y., 1980—. Bd. Dirs. ACLU, Nat. Emergency Civil Liberties Com., N.Y.C.; instr. ballroom dancing Eckerd Coll., St. Petersburg, 1995-96. Named Fla. Humanist of Yr. Am. Humanist Assn. Fla., 1975, Pres. Soc. of Fine Arts Arts, Pinellas Park, Fla., 1970-90. Mem. Acad. Sr. Profls. at Eckerd Coll. Home and Office: 1074 23rd Ave N Saint Petersburg FL 33704-3228

JOHNSON, ELAINE BOWE, college dean, educational consultant; b. Seattle, May 22, 1940; d. Lyman Campbell Bowe and Elaine Ingeborg Larson; m. H. Thomas Johnson, July 17, 1971; 1 child, Thomas Christian. BA, Mills Coll., 1962; MA, Ind. U., 1964; PhD, U. Oreg., 1968. Instr. U. Oreg., Eugene, 1963-68; chair, asst. dean, assoc. prof. English Huron Coll., London, Ont., Can., 1968-78; instr. liberal studies dept. Western Washington U., Bellingham, 1979-82; chmn. English dept. Charles Wright Acad., Tacoma, 1982-88; lectr. Pacific Luth. U., Tacoma, 1982-88; assoc. dean English, fgn. langs., internat. studies, acting assoc. dean maths., chmn. curriculum com. Mt. Hood C.C., Gresham, Oreg., 1988—; cons. in applied acads. and ednl. reform, coord. internat. edn.; cons. in field. Author: American Literature for Life and Work, 1996, British Literature for Life and Work, 1996, Literature for Life and Work, Book 1, 1996, Literature for Life and Work, Book 2, 1996. Recipient Outstanding Tchr. award U. Chgo., 1987, Disting. Tchrs. award Charles Wright Acad., 1988; Woodrow Wilson fellow, 1962-63, Hon. fellow Huron Coll., 1982, Ind. Studies in the Humanities fellow Coun. for Basic Edn. and NEH, 1987; Peris H. Coleman scholar Mills Coll., 1962. Mem. MLA (pres. Oreg. writing and English adv. com. 1992-94), Assn. Oreg. C.C. Humanities Adminstrs., Am. Assn. Women in Jr. and C.C., NAt. Coun. Tchrs. English. Office: Mt Hood Community Coll 26000 SE Stark St Gresham OR 97030-3300

JOHNSON, ELAINE MCDOWELL, federal government administrator; b. Balt., June 28, 1942; d. McKinley and Lena (Blue) McDowell; m. Walter Johnson; children: Nathan H. Murphy, Michael W. Murphy. BA, Morgan State U., Balt., 1965; MSW, U. Md., 1971, PhD, 1988. Drug abuse adminstr., acting regional dir. State Md. Drug Abuse Adminstrn., Balt., 1971-72; social sci. analyst, pub. health advisor Nat. Inst. Drug Abuse, Rockville, MD, 1972-76, dep. dir., dir. div. community assistance, 1976-82, dep. assoc. dir. for policy devel., 1981-82, dir. div. prevention and communications, 1982-85; exec. asst. to adminstr. Alcohol, Drug Abuse & Mental Health Adminstrn., Rockville, Md., 1985; dep. dir. Nat. Inst. on Drug Abuse, Rockville, MD, 1985-88; dir. Office for Substance Abuse Prevention, 1988-94; acting adminstr. Alcohol, Drug Abuse and Mental Health Adminstrn., Rockville, Md., 1992; acting adminstr. Substance Abuse and Mental Health Svcs. Adminstrn., Rockville, Md., 1992-94, dir. Ctr. Substance Abuse Prevention, 1995—; expert cons. in substance abuse, treatment, and mental health fields. Active Presbyterian Ch., Balt., 1979—. Recipient Secretary's commendation HHS, 1989, Disting. Svc. award, 1990, Pride Bldg. Bridges award, 1991, Nat. Fedn. Parents Nat. Leadership award, 1991, Nat. Coun. on Alcoholism and Drug Dependence Ind., Pres. award for outstanding fed. leadership, 1991, Presdl. Meritorious Exec. Rank award, 1991, Presdl. Meritorious Disting. Rank award, 1993. Mem. NASW, ASPA, Sr. Execs. Assn., Fed. Exec. Inst. Alumni Assn. Office: Ctr for Substance Abuse Prevention Rockwell 2 Bldg 5600 Fishers Ln 9th Fl Rockville MD 20857

JOHNSON, ELEANOR MAE, education educator; b. St. Paul, Mar. 22, 1925; d. Emil H. and Leona W. (Warner) Busse; m. Edward Charles Johnson, May 13, 1950; 1 child, Mary Jo Johnson Tuckwell. BS, U. Wis.-Stout, 1946, MS, 1959, edn. specialist, 1981. Cert. home economist, tchr., Wis. Instr. home econs. various pub. schs., Wis., 1946-48, 56-64; home economist U. Wis. Extension, various locations, 1948-51, 52-56; tchr. educator U. Wis.-Stout, Menomonie, 1965-87; ret., 1987; summer session guest prof. U. Man., Winnipeg, Can., 1970, 71, S.D. State U., Brookings, 1978; dir. Native Am. curriculum for home econs. Fed. Vocat. Project, U. Wis.-Stout, 1978-80; cons. vocat. evaluation team U. Wis.-Stout, 1982-90; presenter at profl. confs.; team mem. interdisciplinary consumer edn. teaching materials Joint Coun. Econ. Edn., 1980-82. Editor teaching materials for Native Ams., 1978-80. Sr. statesman Wis. Coalition on Aging, 1990-91; adv., vol. Office of Aging, 1992-96. Mem. Am. Home Econs. Assn. (del. nat. and internat. confs., Inner City fellow 1970), Am. Vocat. Assn., Wis. Edn. Assn., U. Wis.-Stout Alumni, Assn. Tchr. Educators, Am. Assn. Ret. Persons. Home: 623 Elm Ave Barron WI 54812-1712

JOHNSON, ELISSA SARAH, speech pathologist, writer; b. Bklyn., Nov. 3, 1932; d. Frank Wilford and Doris Antonia (Licorish) Ward; m. Edward Paul Johnson, Dec. 31, 1957 (div. July 1962); 1 child, Paul. BA in Edn. Speech, Bklyn. Coll., 1954, MA in Speech Pathology, 1955; postgrad, Howard U., 1968-70. Speech tchr. therapist N.Y.C. Sch. Sys., Bklyn., 1954-67; speech pathologist Bklyn. Coll. Speech Clinic, 1955-57; instr. speech dept. Howard U., Washington, 1968-70; cons. Health Edn. Welfare, Washington, 1969-70; diagnostician speech pathology Tucson Unifed Sch. Dist., 1977-79, speech clinician spl. edn., 1979-86; writer poet Columbia, Md., 1970-77; freelance writer Tucson, 1986—; mem. Harlem Writer's Guild, Bklyn., 1962-68. Author: (book of poetry) Soul of Wit, 1978; contbr. poetry and articles to profl. publs. and mags. Pres. Bunche House, Bklyn. Coll., 1954; mem. steering com. Dem. Nat. Com., 1995—. Recipient Fire Prevention Theme medal Mayor's Office, 1942; scholar Bklyn. Coll., 1950-54. Mem. AAUW, NOW, NEA. Home: 500 S Placita Quince Tucson AZ 85748

JOHNSON, ELIZABETH DIANE LONG, lawyer; b. Pasadena, Calif., Nov. 16, 1945; d. Volney Earl and Sylvia Irene (Drury) Long; m. Lynn Douglas Johnson, Oct. 22, 1966; 1 child, Barbara Annette. BA, U. of Houston, 1967; JD, Rutgers U., 1980. Bar: N.J. 1980, U.S. Dist. Ct. N.J. 1980, Pa. 1984, U.S. Supreme Ct. 1986. Pvt. practice Riverside, N.J., 1980—; pub. defender Riverside Twp., 1988-91; speaker Comprehensive Justice Ctr. Burlington County, 1987-89. Del. Women in Law to Peoples Republic of China Citizen Amb. Program of People to People Internat., 1989; mem. Orchid Found., 1989—, rec. sec., 1991—; mem. Tenby Chase Civic Assn., Delran, N.J., 1972-87, treas., 1976, v.p., 1974; trustee Drenk Mental Health Ctr., 1988—, pres., 1991-94, chair bd. trustees, 1993-94, vice chair bd. trustees, 1995—. Mem. N.J. Women Lawyers Assn., Burlington County Bar Assn. (chmn. bench and bar com. 1989-91), Burlington County Bar Found. (trustee 1988-91, treas. 1988-90, v.p. 1990-91, pres. 1991-92), Soc. for Right to Die, Nat. Trust for Hist. Preservation, Mensa, Rotary (sec. Riverside 1991-92, v.p. 1992-93, pres.-elect 1993-94, pres. 1994-95, dir. 1995-96, area rep. 1995—), Delta Gamma. Methodist. Office: 23 Scott St Ste C PO Box 274 Riverside NJ 08075

JOHNSON, ELIZABETH ERICSON, retired educator; b. Rockford, Ill., Oct. 5, 1927; d. Gunnar Lawrence and Victoria Amelia (Carlson) Ericson; m. Barent Olaf Johnson, June 2, 1951; children: Ann E. Arellano, Susan M. Taber. BA, U. Ill., 1949; MSEd, No. Ill. U., 1969. Tchr. Sch. Dist. 205, Rockford, Ill., 1949-53, 65-92. Mem. Ct. Appointed Spl. Advocate, Rockford, 1992—. Mem. AAUW, LWV (bd. dirs. 1994-96, local bd.), Winnebago Ret. Tchrs. Assn. (various bds.), Phi Delta Kappa. Home: 1902 Valencia Dr Rockford IL 61108-6818

JOHNSON, ELIZABETH HILL, foundation administrator; b. Ft. Wayne, Ind., Aug. 21, 1913; d. Harry W. and Lydia (Buechner) Hill; m. Samuel Spencer Johnson, Oct. 7, 1944 (dec. 1984); children: Elizabeth Katharine, Patricia Caroline. BS summa cum laude, Miami U., Oxford, Ohio, 1935; MA in English Lit., Wellesley Coll., 1937; postgrad., U. Chgo., 1936. Cert. tchr., Ohio. Pres., co-founder S.S. Johnson Found., Calif. Corp., San Francisco, 1947—. Mem. Oreg. State Bd. Higher Edn., Eugene, 1962-75, Oreg. State Edn. Coord. Com., Salem, 1975-82, Assn. Governing Bds., Washington, 1970-80, chairperson, 1975-76; mem. Oreg. State Tchr. Standards and Practices Commn., Salem, 1982-89; bd. dirs. Lewis and Clark Coll., Portland, Oreg., 1985—, Pacific U., Forest Grove, Oreg., 1982—, Sunriver Prep. Sch., 1983-92, Oreg. Hist. Soc., Portland, 1985—, Cen. Oreg. Dist. Hosp., Redmond, 1982—, Oreg. High Desert Mus., 1984—, Bend, Oreg., Health Decisions, 1986-92, Ctrl. Oreg. Coun. Aging, 1991—. Lt. USNR, 1943-46. Named Honoree March of Dimes White Rose Luncheon, 1984; recipient Aubrey Watzek award Lewis and Clark Coll., 1984, Cen. Oreg. 1st Citizen award, Abrams award Emanuel Hosp., 1982, Pres. award Marylhurst Coll., 1991, Thomas Jefferson award Oregon Historical Soc., 1993. Mem. Am. Assn. Higher Edn., Am. Assn. Jr. Colls., ASCD, Soroptimists (hon.), Francisca Club, Town Club, Univ. Club, Waverley Club, Beta Sigma Phi, Phi Beta Kappa, Phi Delta Kappa, Delta Gamma. Republican. Lutheran. Home: 415 SW Canyon Dr Redmond OR 97756-2028 Office: S S Johnson Found 441 SW Canyon Dr Redmond OR 97756-2028

JOHNSON, ELIZABETH HUNTER, accounting educator; b. Philippi, W.Va., Jan. 23, 1956; d. Walter Clarke and Shirley Elizabeth (Doremus) Johnson. BS in Acctg., Alderson-Broaddus Coll., Philippi, 1977; MBA, W.Va. Wesleyan Coll., Buckhannon, 1994. CPA, W.Va. Tax examiner W.Va. State Tax Dept., Charleston, 1978-85, CPA liaison, 1985-87; county adminstr. Barbour County, Philippi, 1987-90; instr. in bus. Alderson-Broaddus Coll., Philippi, 1990—. Mem. bd. Barbour County Sr. Citizens, Philippi, 1987-88, Barbour County Emergency Svcs., 1987-90; elder Philippi Presbyn. Ch., 1987—. Mem. Inst. Cert. Mgmt. Accts. (cert.), W.Va. Soc. CPAs. Presbyterian. Home: 140 South Walnut St Philippi WV 26416 Office: Alderson-Broaddus College Box 1397 Philippi WV 26416

JOHNSON, ELLA GOODE, automobile company administrator; b. Hearne, Tex., Feb. 28; d. Harvey L. Goode and Everon F. (Polk) Goode-Robinson; m. Willie Earl Johnson, Sept. 26; children: Tobian, Jabari. BBA, U. North Tex., 1971; MS, Amber U., 1989. Adminstr. Chevrolet Motor Divsn., Dallas, 1973—. Co-prodr. (video tape) Legacy of Excellence: The History of Delta Sigma Theta, 1993. Bd. dirs. Jr. Black Acad. Arts and Letters, Dallas, 1992—; bd. sec. Celebrating Life Found., Dallas, 1995—. Recipient Maura award Women's Ctr., Dallas, 1995, African Am. Hero award ICKDA Radio, Dallas, 1995, Real Sister award Paul Quinn Coll., 1995. Mem. NAFE, AAUW, Women of Merit and Valor (award 1995), Delta Sigma Theta (numerous offices including chpt. pres. 1969—, Delta Diamond award 1988, Outstanding Tex. Delta 1995). Baptist. Home: 2531 Club Terrace Dr Dallas TX 75237

JOHNSON, EVELYN BRYAN, flying service executive; b. Corbin, Ky., Nov. 4, 1909; d. Edward William and Mayme Estelle (Fox) Stone; grad. Tenn. Wesleyan Jr. Coll., 1929; student U. Tenn., 1930-32; m. Wyatt J. Bryan, Mar. 21, 1931 (dec. 1963); m. 2d, Morgan N. Johnson, Feb. 25, 1965 (dec. 1977). With Morristown (Tenn.) Flying Service, Inc., 1947—, chief flight instr., 1949—, sec.-treas., 1949-62, pres., 1962-82; mgr. Moore Murrell Airport, 1962—. Gov.'s appointee Tenn. Aero. Commn., 1983-86, v. chmn., 1987-89, chmn., 1989, 94—. Recipient Carnegie Hero medal, 1958, Svc. to Mankind award Morristown Sertoma Club, 1981, Kitty Hawk award FAA, 1991, Friends of Aviation award Tenn. Aviation Assn., 1992, Stewart G. Potter Aviation Edn. award Aviation Distbrs. and Mfrs. Assn., 1992, Elder Statesman of Aviation award Nat. Aeronautics Assn., 1993; named Flight Instr. of Yr., Nashville dist., 1973, 79, So. region, 1979, Nat., 1979 (all FAA); Outstanding Alumnus, Tenn. Wesleyan Coll., 1981, Women in Aviation Pioneers Hall of Fame, 1994. Mem. Morristown Area C. of C., Nat. Assn. Flight Instrs. (dir., treas. 1987-89, award 1992), Ninety-Nines, Whirly Girls (plaque 1992), Aircraft Owners and Pilots Assn., CAP, Silver Wings (Woman of Yr. 1981, bd. dirs. 1987—, Carl Fromhagen award 1992, Ninety-Nines Award of Merit 1994). Holder record most flying time for women pilots, 1995, Guinness Book of Records, 1995-96. Republican. Baptist. Home: RR 1 Jefferson Cy TN 37760-9801 Office: PO Box 1013 Morristown TN 37816-1013

JOHNSON, GAYLE HARRISON, artistic director; b. Richmond, Va., Mar. 6, 1954; d. Mason Winfield and Adele Elizabeth (Kratz) J.; m. James Frederick Weaver, June 12, 1987; 1 child, Michael Justin. BA, Oberlin Coll., 1978; MusB, Oberlin Conservatory, 1978. Adminstrv. asst. Early Music Guild, Seattle, 1979-81; dir. Capriole, Seattle, 1979-87; artistic dir. Capriole, Williamsburg, Va., 1987—, Colonial Williamsburg Baroque Music Festival, 1995—; asst. choir dir. Williamsburg Presbyn. Ch., 1988—; mem. ensemble-in-residence Coll. of William and Mary, 1989-93, Old Dominion U., 1994—; adj. faculty Seattle Pacific U., 1979-85; pvt. tchr., 1979—; harpsichordist Colonial Williamsburg, 1987-88. Asst. choir dir. Williamsburg Presbyn. Ch., 1988—, Williamsburg Early Music Guild,1988-89, No. Rehab. Housing

Coop., 1983-85. Newberry Libr. fellow, Chgo., 1977. Mem. Early Music Am., Chamber Music Am. Office: Capriole PO Box 558 Williamsburg VA 23187-0558

JOHNSON, GENIFER JONES, women's health, critical care, and legal nurse consultant; b. Lafayette, La., Aug. 9, 1954; d. Walter L. and Janie Mayrie (Clark) Jones. Diploma, Mercy Sch. Nursing, Detroit, 1984; BSN, U. Phoenix, Honolulu, 1994. RN, Mich., Fla., Hawaii. Staff nurse VA Med. Ctr., Ann Arbor, Mich., 1984-86, Hutzel Hosp., Detroit, 1986-87; staff nurse II Catherine McAuley Health Ctr., Ann Arbor, 1987-90; staff nurse critical care Kaiser Found. Hosp., Honolulu, 1990-91; critical care staff nurse, rsch. ast. Queen's Med. Ctr., Honolulu, 1991-93; nurse case mgr. Med. Claims Mgmt. Svcs., Honolulu, 1993-94; legal nurse cons. Gary, Williams, Parenti, Finney, Lewis & McManus, Stuart, Fla., 1993—. Mem. AACN, Am. Assn. Legal Nurse Cons., Am. Bus. Women's Assn.

JOHNSON, GEORGIA C., humanities educator; b. Erie, Pa., Aug. 29, 1941; d. George P. Conway and Audrey J. (Steinfurth) Hamburger; m. Dec. 26, 1964; children: Ann Haibach and Mary K. Siegel. BA, Villa Maria Coll., Erie, 1963; MA, Gannon U., Erie, 1983. Cert. instrnl. II English and Latin, sec. prin. II. Tchr. English East H.S., Erie, 1963-66; substitute tchr. Erie, Iroquois and Millcreek, 1966-77; tchr. English Academy H.S., Erie, 1977-79; tchr. English Mercyhurst Prep., Erie, 1979-95, asst. prin., 1987-96; tchr. induction dir. Mercyhurst Prep., Erie, 1987-95; tchr. PLS courses, Erie, 1987-93; acad. dean MPS, Erie, 1987-96; adj. faculty Mercyhurst Coll., Erie, 1991-95; evaluator coll. tchr. prep. programs Pa. Dept. Edn., 1993-96. Editor: (newsletter of Sisters of Mercy) Mercy Echoes, 1989—, Middle States Reports, 1990-95, Blue Ribbon Schs. Application, 1992 (award 1993). Pres. VMC Alumni, Erie, 1980-86; mem. bd. dirs., nat. liaison NWPACoun. Tchrs. of English, 1980-89; mem. Leadership Erie Class of 1996. Recipient Best in Erie Tchr. award Erie Times-News, 1986; inducted into Gannon U. Edn. Hall of Fame, 1995. Mem. Nat. Coun. Tchrs. English, Sisters of Mercy (assoc.). Republican. Roman Catholic. Home: 514 Kahkwa Blvd Erie PA 16505 Office: Mercyhurst Prep 538 E Grandview Erie PA 16504

JOHNSON, GERALDINE ESCH, language specialist; b. Steger, Ill., Jan. 5, 1921; d. William John Rutkowski and Estella Anna (Mannel) Pietz; m. Richard William Esch, Oct. 12, 1940 (dec. 1971); children: Janet L. Sohngen, Daryl R., Gary Michael; m. Henry Bernard Johnson, Aug. 23, 1978 (dec. 1988). BSBA, U. Denver, 1955, MA in Edn., 1958, MA in Speech Pathology, 1963; vocat. credential, U. No. Colo., 1978, postgrad.; postgrad., Metropolitan State Coll., U. Colo., Colo. State U., Colo. Sch. of Mines, U. Hawaii. Cert. speech therapist, Colo.; cert. tchr., class A counselor, tchr. educationally handicapped, Colo. Tchr. music Judith St. John Sch. Music, Denver, 1946-52; tchr. West High Sch., Denver, 1955-61, chmn. bus. edn. dept., 1958-61, reading specialist, 1977-78; speech therapist, founder South Denver Speech Clinic, 1965-71; tchr. Educationally Handicapped Resource Rm., Denver, 1971-74, Diagnostic Ctr., The Belmont Sch., Denver, 1974-77; speech-lang. specialist elem. and jr. high schs., Denver, 1978-86; itinerant speech-lang. specialist various elem. and jr. high schs., Denver, 1978—; ret. Denver Pub. Sch. System, 1986; home lang tchr. Early Childhood Edn., Denver, 1975; mem. Ednl. TV Adv. com., Colo.; sec. Cen. Bus. Edn. Com., Colo; tchr. letter writing clinics, local bus., Denver, 1960—. Former judge Colo. State Speech Festivals; demonstrator, lectr. Speech-Lang. and Learning Disabilities area Colo. Edn. Assn., 1971-73; vol. communications and prereading skills tchr. YMCA. Recipient Spl. Edn. award Denver Pub. Schs., 1986. Mem. Speech-Lang.-Hearing Assn. (cert.), U. Denver Sch. Bus. Alumni Bd., Beta Gamma Sigma, Kappa Delta Pi, Delta Pi Epsilon. Home: 14050 E Linvale Pl Apt 502 Aurora CO 80014-3735

JOHNSON, GLORIA JEAN, counseling professional; b. St. Louis, Jan. 30, 1945; d. Willie Jr. and Ruby Bernice (Haynes) Stevens; m. Louis W. Johnson, Dec. 2, 1963; children: Anthony Kenneth, Marvin Louis, Andre Darnell. MS in Counseling, Evang. Sem., PhD in Marriage and Family Counseling, 1993. Dir. counseling dept. EC Bible Coll., St. Louis, 1987-88; cons. in field St. Louis, 1987-94; founder, exec. dir. Life Source Cons., Inc., St. Louis, 1994—. Vol. counselor CMC C-Star Program, St. Louis, 1992-93; mem. bd. dirs. Mo. Coalition Against Domestic Violence, Jefferson City, Mo., 1995—, Women: Elderly and Battered Task Force, St. Louis, 1995; chair African Am. Women Work Group Against Domestic Violence, St. Louis, 1996, Women of Color Task Force Against Domestic Violence State of Mo., 1996. Mem. ACA, Am. Assn. Christian Counselors, Nat. Black Women's Health Project, Internat. Assn. Marriage and Family Counselors. Office: Life Source Cons Inc PO Box 5752 Saint Louis MO 63121

JOHNSON, GWENAVERE ANELISA, artist; b. Newark, S.D., Oct. 16, 1909; d. Arthur E. and Susie Ellen (King) Nelson; m. John Wendell Johnson, Dec. 17, 1937; 1 child, John Forrest. Student, Mpsl. Sch. Art, 1930; BA, U. Minn., 1937; MA, San Jose State U., 1957. Cert. gen. elem., secondary, art tchr., Calif. Art tchr., supr. Austin (Minn.) Schs., 1937-38; art tchr. Hillbrook Sch., Los Gatos, Calif., 1947-52; art tchr., supr. Santa Clara (Calif.) Pub. Schs., 1952-55; art tchr., dept. chmn. San Jose (Calif.) Unified Schs., 1955-75; owner Tree Tops studio, San Jose, 1975—. Juried shows: Los Gatos Art Assn., 1976-79, 85-88, Artist of Yr., 1988 (1st and 2d awards), 83, 84 (Best of Show awards), Treeside gallery, 1991, Los Gatos, 1980, 81 (1st awards); Livermore Art Assn., 1977 (2d award), Los Gatos Art Mus., 1981 (1st award), 82 (2d award), 91 (best of show award), Rosicrucean Mus., 1983, Centre d'Art Contemporian, Paris, 1983; creator Overfelt portrait Alexian Bros. Hosp., San Jose, Calif., 1977; exhibited in group shows ann. Garden Art Show, 1981-95, Triton Art Mus., 1983-95. Recipient Golden Centaur award Acad. Italia, 1982, Golden Album of prize winning Artists, 1984, Golden Flame award Academia Italia, 1986, others. Mem. San Jose Art League, Santa Clara Art Assn., Los Gatos Art Assn. (Artist of Yr. 1988, 2d, 3d awards), Santa Clara Art Assn. (Artist of Yr. 1983, 3 First awards 1989, 2d award in spl. merit achiever's exhbn. 1992, 3 First awards in merit achiever's exhbn. 1993), Soc. Western Artists, Nat. League Am. Penwomen (corr. sec., Merit Achiever award), Los gatos Art Assn., Santa Clara Art Assn., San Jose Art League. Home and Office: 2054 Booksin Ave San Jose CA 95125-4909

JOHNSON, ISCEOLA ACQUILLA WINBUSH, educational program specialist; b. Baton Rouge, Feb. 10; d. William Ward and Clementine (Johnson) W.; m. Samuel M. Johnson, Dec. 24, 1943; 1 child, Colette Acquilla Johnson Norman. BS, Southern U., 1946, BA, 1948, MEd, 1961. Cert. tchr., Calif.; cert. tchr., adminstr., La. Tchr. Feliciana Parish Sch., St. Francisville, La., 1944-46; tchr. East Baton Rouge Parish, 1946-56, supervising tchr., 1956-85; supr., program specialist Ravenswood Sch. Dist., Palo Alto, Calif., 1985—; pvt. cons., Foster City, Calif., 1987—; cons. Dept. Edn., Baton Rouge, 1983-85. Author: Where the Mississippi Flows by Unnoticed, 1977, Combatting Teen-age Pregnancy, 1986, (handbook) Reaching for Distant Hills. V.p. Y.W.C.A., Baton Rouge, 1980-84; supr. 4-H Club, Baton Rouge, 1960-80; collector March of Dimes, ARC, Baton Rouge, 1960-84; leader Community Svcs./Homeless and Children, East Palo Alto, 1987—. Named Christian Woman of Yr., Allen Chapel, 1983, Outstanding Community worker Alpha Kappa Alpha Sorority, 1991, Outstanding educator East Baton Rouge Sch. System, 1982; recipient Recognition Svc. award Hammond, La. chpt. Delta Sigma Theta, 1980. Mem. NAFE, Les Professionals (founder, pres. 1980-85), Top Ladies of Distinction, Interfaith Ministers' Wives (v.p. 1993), Ministers' Wives (pres. 1990-93), Alpha Kappa Alpha, Delta Kappa Gamma Internat. (v.p. 1990). Home: 902 Beach Park Blvd Apt 136 Foster City CA 94404-3223

JOHNSON, JANE OLIVER, artist; b. Fresno, Calif., Jan. 3, 1929; d. Evan Donaca Oliver and Adaline Dorinda (Nelson) Edwards; m. Vernon Reddinger Allen, Aug. 11, 1946 (div. 1963); children: Lue Elizabeth, Mark Laroy, Stuart Vernon; m. Loren Theodore Johnson, Mar. 8, 1981. Student, Fresno City Coll., 1952-55, Fresno State, 1955-60, Hayward State Coll., 1965-70. Tech. artist Hughes, Northrup, Lockheed, Magnavox, L.A., 1972-84; artist Neighborhood Gallery, L.A., 1976-80. Works exhibited at Beyond Baroque, San Jose Mission, Tribal Treas., Calico Gallery. Mem. state ctrl. com. Calif. Dem. Party, 1993—; active 34th Assembly Dist. Exec. Bd., 1993—; elected San Bernardino County Dem. Ctrl. Com., 1994—. Mem. High Desert Cultural Arts, Bus. and Profl. Women (sec. 1980), Hesperia Dem. Club (mem. environ. women's caucus 1993—, pres. 1994), Mus. Contemporary Art (L.A.), Sierra Club. Home: PO Box 1323 Lucerne Valley CA 92356-1323

JOHNSON, JANE PENELOPE, freelance writer; b. Danville, Ky., July 1, 1940; d. Buford Lee Carr and Emma Irene (Coldiron) Sebastian; m. William Evan Johnson, July 15, 1958; children: William Evan Jr., Robert Anthony. Grad., Famous Writer's Sch. Fiction, Westport, Conn., 1967; grad. writer's div., Newspaper Inst. Am., N.Y.C., 1969; LittD (hon.), The London Inst. Applied Rsch., 1993. Freelance writer Lexington, Ky., 1969—. Contbr. poetry to Worldwide Poetry Anthologies; contbr. articles to mags. Patron Menninger. Ennobled by Prince John, The Duke of Avram, Tasmania, Australia; semifinalist N.Am. Poetry Open; recipient 2 Editor's Choice awards for poetry Nat. Libr. of Poetry, 1994. Mem. NAFE, Smithsonian Assocs., Peale Ctr. for Christian Living, Sweet Adelines, Internat. Soc. Poets (life, advisor), Internat. Platform Assn., Nat. Writer's Club. Democrat. Office: PO Box 8013 Gardenside Br Lexington KY 40504

JOHNSON, JANET DROKE, legal secretary; b. Bristol, Tenn., Feb. 26, 1961; d. Jimmie D. and Nancy Bell (Sluder) Droke; children: Leslie Ann, Laurie Elizabeth. AA, East Tenn. State U., 1980; student, Milligan Coll., Johnson City, Tenn., 1988-89. With Sullivan County Election Commn., Blountville, Tenn., 1978; legal sec. Boarman & Vaughn, Johnson City, 1980-84; legal asst. Bob McD. Green and Assocs., Johnson City, 1985-89; fed. judicial sec. to U.S. cir. judge U.S. ct. Appeals, 4th Cir., Abingdon, Va., 1989—; mem. adv. bd. Legal Assistant Program, Milligan Coll., Johnson City, 1988-89. Asst. ch. clk., newsletter editor Bluff City Bapt. Ch., 1994—. Mem. ABA (assoc.), Tenn. Paralegal Assn. (treas. 1989, pub. rels. dir. 1990—), Appalachian Paralegal Assn., Fed. Judicial Secs. Assn. Republican. Home: PO Box 727 Bluff City TN 37618-0727 Office: US Court of Appeals 4th Cir PO Box 868 Abingdon VA 24212-0868

JOHNSON, JANET HELEN, Egyptology educator; b. Everett, Wash., Dec. 24, 1944; d. Robert A. and Jane N. (Osborn) J.; m. Donald S. Whitcomb, Sept. 2, 1978; children: J.J., Felicia. BA, U. Chgo., 1967, PhD, 1972. Instr. Egyptology U. Chgo., 1971-72, asst. prof., 1972-79, assoc. prof., 1979-81, prof., 1981—; dir. Oriental Inst., 1983-89; research assoc. dept. anthropology Field Mus. of Natural History, 1980-84, 94—. Author: Demotic Verbal System, 1977, Thus Wrote Onchsheshonqy, 1986, 2d revised edit., 1991, (with Donald Whitcomb) Quseir al-Qadim, 1978, 80; editor: (with E.F. Wente) Studies in Honor of G.R. Hughes, 1977, Life in a Multi-Cultural Society, 1992. Smithsonian Instn. grantee, 1977-83; NEH grantee, 1978-81, 81-85; Nat. Geog. Soc. grantee, 1978, 80, 82. Mem. Am. Rsch. Ctr. in Egypt (bd. govs. 1979—, exec. com. 1984-87, 90—, v.p. 1990-93, pres. 1993-96). Office: U Chgo Oriental Inst 1155 E 58th St Chicago IL 60637-1540

JOHNSON, JANET LOU, real estate executive; b. Boston, Aug. 22, 1939; d. Donald Murdoch and Helen Margaret (Slauenwhite) Campbell; m. Walter R. Johnson, Mar. 31, 1962; children—Meryl Ann, Leah Kathryn, Christa Helen. Student, Gordon Coll., Hamilton, Mass., 1962-64. Adminstr., account exec. Fuller/Smith & Ross, Boston, 1958-63; adminstr. Walter R. Johnson, P.E., Gloucester, 1970-76; broker Realty World, Gloucester, 1976-77, Hunneman & Co., Gloucester, 1977-79; pres., owner Janet L. Johnson Real Estate, Gloucester, 1979—. Mem. Mass. Assn. Realtors (bd. dirs. 1985-87), Nat. Assn. Realtors, Cape Ann C. of C., Cape Ann Bd. Realtors (pres. 1984-85, state dir. 1985-86), Greater Salem Bd. Realtors. Home: 35 Norseman Ave Gloucester MA 01930-1026 Office: Janet L Johnson Real Estate 79 Rocky Neck Ave Gloucester MA 01930-4180

JOHNSON, JEAN ELAINE, nursing educator; b. Wilsey, Kans., Mar. 11, 1925; d. William H. and Rosa L. (Welty) Irwin. B.S., Kans. State U., 1948; M.S. in Nursing, Yale U., 1965; M.S., U. Wis., 1969, Ph.D., 1971. Instr. nursing Iowa, Kans. and Colo., 1948-58; staff nurse Swedish Hosp., Englewood, Colo., 1958-60; in-svc. edn. coord. Gen. Rose Hosp., Denver, 1960-63; rsch. asst. Yale U., New Haven, 1965-67; assoc. prof. nursing Wayne State U., Detroit, 1971-74, prof., 1974-79; dir. Ctr. for Health Rsch., 1974-79; assoc. dir. oncology nursing Cancer Ctr. U. Rochester, N.Y., 1979-93; prof. nursing U. Rochester, 1979-95, prof. emerita, 1995—; Rosenstadt prof. health rsch. Faculty Nursing U. Toronto, 1985; vis. prof. U. Utah Coll. Nursing, 1996. Contbg. author: Handbook of Psychology and Health, vol. 5, 1984; contbr. articles to profl. jours. Recipient Bd. Govs. Faculty Recognition award Wayne State U., 1975, award for disting. contbn. to nursing sci. Am. Nurses Found. and ANA Coun. for Nurse Rschrs., 1983, Grad. Teaching award U. Rochester, 1991, Disting. Rschr. award Oncology Nursing Soc., 1992, Outstanding Contbns. to Nursing and Psychology award divsn. of health psychology APA, 1993; NIH grantee, 1972-95. Fellow AAAS, APA (Outstanding Contbns. to Nursing and Psychology award 1993), Acad. for Behavioral Medicine Rsch., Am. Psychol. Soc.; mem. ANA (chmn. coun. for nurse rschrs. 1976-78, commn. for rsch. 1978-82), Inst. Medicine NAS (com. on patient injury compensation 1976-77, membership com. 1981-86, gov. coun. 1987-89), Sigma Xi, Omicron Nu, Phi Kappa Phi. Home: 1412 East Ave Rochester NY 14610-1619 Office: U Rochester Box 80N 601 Elmwood Ave Rochester NY 14642-0001

JOHNSON, JEANNE MARIE, nurse psychotherapist, clinical nurse specialist; b. N.Y.C.; d. Hector J. and Jean (Bershacht) Streyckmans; 1 child, Robert M. AAS, Queens Coll., 1963; BSN, Adelphi U., 1967, MSN, 1973; postgrad., Karen Horney Inst., N.Y.C., 1981-82. Cert. clin. nurse specialist, 1981. Pub. health nurse Nassau County Dept. Health, Mineola, N.Y., 1963-69; instr. cmty. nursing Molloy Coll., Rockville Centre, N.Y., 1977-78; cmty. mental health nurse, admiinstr., psychotherapist Cmty. Mental Health Ctr. Nassau County, Westchester County, N.Y., 1969-89; nurse psychotherapist Cen. Nassau Guidance and Counseling Svc., Inc., Hicksville, N.Y., 1990-91; geriatric psychotherapist New Hope Guild, 1989; pvt. practice as nurse/psychotherapist and cons., 1988—, clin. nurse specialist, 1981—; substitute sch. nurse Wantagh Sch. Dist., 1991-95, Bethpage Sch. Dist., 1995—; mem. disaster action team ARC, 1979—, Red Cross nurse, 1967—. Mem. ANA (congressional dist. coord.), N.Y. State Nurses Assn., Network of Clin. Nurse Specialists, Sigma Theta Tau. Home: 112 Hawthorn St Massapequa Park NY 11762-2001

JOHNSON, JENNIFER PARMAN, hypnotherapist; b. Sutton Cold Field, Eng., Sept. 16, 1944; came to U.S., 1946; d. George Eugene and Doris Elizabeth (Smith) Parman; m. James Ralph Johnson; children: Mark David, Amanda Elizabeth. BS in Edn., Ind. State U., 1966. Tchr. Bartholomew County Pub. Schs., Columbus, Ind., 1966-70; profl. recruiter JRW Tech. Svcs., Springfield, Va., 1986-93; pvt. practice Fairfax, Va., 1994—. Mem. NAFE, Am. Coun. Hypnotist Examiners, Assn. Traspersonal Psychology and Hypnotherapy, Nat. Assn. of Transpersonal Hypnothreapists, Nat. Bd. Hypnotherapy and Hypnoanaesthesiology, Soc. Advancement Past Life Rsch. and Therapy. Office: Clin Hypnotherapist 10505 Braddock Rd Ste D Fairfax VA 22032

JOHNSON, JENNIFER SUE, art educator, artist; b. Washington D.C., July 23, 1966; d. Roy Forrest Jr. and Sue Broumas Sansone. BA in Liberal Arts, U. Md., College Park, 1988, BA in Art Edn., 1993. Cert. in art edn. Md., Oreg. Merchandise supr. People For the Ethical Treatment of Animals (PETA), Rockville, Md., 1990-92; art educator Montgomery County Pub. Schs., Rockville, Md., 1994—; artist D&D Gallery, Washington D.C., 1995—. Mem. NEA, Nat. Art Edn. Assn., Montgomery County Edn. Assn., Montgomery County Art Edn. Assn. Home: 2735 Jennings Rd Kensington MD 20895

JOHNSON, JESSIE JONES, newspaper columnist, writer; b. Alleghany County, N.C., Mar. 24, 1924; d. Mack Astor and Lula Delta (Billings) Jones; m. Peter Dexter Johnson Sr., Oct. 3, 1943 (Sept. 1978); children: Peter Dexter Jr., Carol Osborne Johnson Haigh, William Todd. AB in English, U. N.C., 1949; postgrad., Cornell U., 1957, SUNY, Albany, 1959, Skidmore Coll., 1982, 84. Columnist Schenectady (N.Y.) Gazette, 1950-55; mag. feature writer Niskayuna (N.Y.) Bull., 1957-81; pub. rels. dir. Bellevue Women's Hosp., Niskayuna, 1967-75; med. scriptwriter Sta. WGY Radio, Niskayuna, 1970-77; newspaper columnist The Blue Ridge Sun, Sparta, N.C., 1990-93; corr. sec. Women's Press Club of N.Y. State, Albany, 1970-71; pres. Internat. Toastmistress, Schenectady, 1965; 3d v.p. AAUW, Schenectady, 1969. Author: History of Alleghany County, N.C., 1983, History of Grayson County, Va., 1996; editor: History of Niskayuna, N.Y., 1976; contbr. hist. and geneal. articles to Alleghany Hist. Soc., 1981—, Grayson County Hist. Soc., 1995—. Bicentennial chmn. Town of Niskayuna, 1974-80; mem. assoc. Nat. Trust for Hist. Preservation, Washington; mem. Met. Mus. Art, N.Y.C., N.C. Preservation Trust, Raleigh, N.C., Scott and Zelda Fitzgerald Mus., Montgomery, Ala., 1993—. Recipient 1st pl. award for feature story N.C. Roundtable, 1981, 82, 3d pl. award for short story, 1982. Mem. Women's Press Club. Home: 167 Westview Dr Sparta NC 28675

JOHNSON, JETSIE WHITE, nurse, consultant; b. Newport News, Va., Apr. 7, 1944; d. Breavoid Milton and Jetsie (Johnson) White; m. Henry Johnson Jr., Feb. 24, 1963; children: Cheryl Johnson Holmes, Henry Breavoid, Daryl Jay, Shamala Michelle. AAS magna cum laude, Thomas Nelson Community Coll., Hampton, Va., 1974; BS, Hampton U., 1985, MSN, 1987. RN, Va.; cert. family nurse practitioner, psychiat. clin. nurse specialist. Staff nurse Hampton Gen. Hosp., 1974-77; nurse practitioner Alvin Bryant, M.D., Hampton, 1978-80, VA Med. Ctr., Hampton, 1980-81; staff nurse VA Med. Ctr., Richmond, Va., 1983-84; nurse practitioner Naval Regional Med. Ctr., Norfolk, Va., 1981-82; nurse supr. Commonwealth Health Care, Hampton, 1982—; staff nurse Med. Coll. of Va., Richmond, 1988; nurse practitioner Ea. State Hosp., Williamsburg, Va., 1984-91; preceptor Old Dominion U., Norfolk, 1981-82, Hampton U., 1988-89; hon. instr. nurse practitioner program Med. Coll. of Va., 1979-80; cons. Alvin Bryant, M.D., 1981-91; mem. adv. coun. Hampton U. Nursing Ctr., 1989-90; pres. Minority Cancer Task Force, Hampton, 1989-92; corr. sec. Dept. Mental Health/Mental Retardation and Substance Abuse Svcs. Nurse Practitioner Practice Group, 1989-91. Co-leader Girl Scouts U.S., Hampton, 1985-86; v.p. La Progressive Ten, Hampton, 1982; pres. Young Profls. of Tidewater, Hampton, 1980-81. Recipient Cert. of Appreciation, Minority Cancer Task Force, 1985; NIMH Tng. grantee Dept. HHS, 1985, 86. Mem. Va. Coun. Nurse Practitioners, Phi Theta Kappa, Sigma Theta Tau. Democrat. Home: 66 Santa Barbara Dr Hampton VA 23666-1638

JOHNSON, JOAN BRAY, insurance company consultant; b. Kennett, Mo., Nov. 19, 1926; d. Ples Green and Mary Scott (Williams) Bray; m. Frank Johnson Jr., Nov. 6, 1955; 1 child, Victor Kent. Student, Drury Coll., 1949-51, Cen. Bible Inst. and Coll., 1946-49. Staff writer Gospel Pub. Co., Springfield, Mo., 1949-51; sec. Kennett Sch. Dist. Bd. Edn., 1951-58; spl. features corr. Memphis Press-Scimitar, 1959-60; sec. to v.p. Cotton Exchange Bank, Kennett, Mo., 1959-60; proposal analyst Aetna Life Ins. Co., El Paso, Tex., 1960-64, pension adminstr., 1964-71; office mgr. Brokerage div. Aetna Life Ins. Co., Denver, 1971-78; office adminstr. Life Consol. div. Aetna Life Ins. Co., Oakland, Calif., 1979-82; office adminstr. PFSD div. Aetna Life Ins. Co., Walnut Creek, Calif., 1983-86; office adminstr. PFSD-Health Mktg. div. Aetna Life Ins. Co., Sacramento, Calif., 1986-89; regional adminstr. Aetna Life Ins. Co., Hartford, Conn., 1989-91; cons. Aetna Life Ins. Co., Riverside, Calif., 1991—. Officer local PTA, 1964-71; prs. Wesley Svc. Guild, 1968-71; den mother Boy Scouts Am.; fin. sec. Green Valley United Meth. Ch., 1992—. Recipient Tex. Life Svc. award PTA, 1970. Fellow Life Office Mgmt. Assn. (instr. classes); mem. DAR (regent Silver State Nev. chpt. 1994-96, treas. 1996-98, bd. dirs. Nev. 1996-98), Assn. Bus. and Profl. Women, Life Underwriters Assn., Clark County Heritage Mus., Last Monday Club, Opti-Mrs., Allied Arts Club. Democrat. Home: 2415 La Estrella St Henderson NV 89014-3608 Office: 1677 N Main St Ste 250 Santa Ana CA 92701-2324

JOHNSON, JOANN, human resources specialist; b. Niagara Falls, N.Y., Aug. 25, 1943; d. Joseph A. and Olive I. (Savage) Malaney; m. Arthur William Johnson, Aug. 20, 1966; children: Joseph, Jillian. BS, Rosary Hill Coll., 1965; MS, Niagara U. Cert. tchr., N.Y. Tchr. North Wheatfield, Sanborn, N.Y., 1968-72; edn. coord. mid-city coord. com. Police Com. Svc., Niagara Falls, N.Y., 1972-74; dir. psychiat. halfway house Cmty. Missions, Niagara Falls; edn. dir. Niagara Ministries, Niagara Falls; tchr. St. Peters Sch., Lewiston, N.Y., 1983-87; dep. exec. dir. Rivershore, Inc., Lewiston, 1987—. Mem. NAFE, Pers. Mgmt. Assn., N.Y. State Cmty. Residence Assn., N.Y. State Cmty. Rehab., Devel. Disabilities Planning Coun. Home: 6707 Errick Rd North Tonawanda NY 14120 Office: Rivershore Inc 765 Cayuga St Lewiston NY 14092

JOHNSON, JOCELYN YVONNE, visual arts educator, artist; b. Atlanta, July 5, 1959; d. Fred and Margaret (Vaughn) J. AA, Atlanta Metro. Coll., 1980; B of Visual Arts, Ga. State U., 1983. Cert. elem. tchr., Ga. Salesperson Wolf Camera, Atlanta, 1983-85; telephone sales rep. Wachovia Bank, Atlanta, 1985-87; sales asst. mgr. Rich's Dept. Store, Atlanta, 1987-90; tchr., workshop dir. Atlanta Pub. Schs., 1992—. Photography included in So. Exposure, 1980, Atlanta Jour. Constn., 1983. Organizer Young Dems., Atlanta, 1992. Recipient Photography award Dancer's Collective Theater, 1983, Student Art award Chastain Art Gallery, 1992; African Art grantee Apple Corps, 1994. Mem. Nat. Assn. Educators, Nat. Coun. Negro Women (planner 1977-96, Cert. 1991), Assn. Art Educators (dir. 1990—), Ga. State U. Alumni Assn., Ga. State U. Black Alumni Assn. (organizer 1990—). Roman Catholic. Home: 1374 Woodland Ter SW Atlanta GA 30311 Office: Atlanta Pub Schs 210 Pryor St SW Atlanta GA 30322

JOHNSON, JOY ANN, diagnostic radiologist; b. New Richmond, Wis., Aug. 16, 1952; d. Howard James and Shirley Maxine (Eidem) J.; m. Donald G. Nieto, June 24, 1989. BA in Chemistry summa cum laude, U. No. Colo., 1974; D of Medicine, U. Colo., 1978. Diplomate Am. Bd. Radiology, Nat. Bd. Med. Examiners; cert. added qualification pediatric radiology. Resident in radiology U. Colo., 1978-81, fellow in radiology, 1981-82; asst. prof. diagnostic radiology and pediatrics, chief sect. pediatric radiology Clin. Radiology Found. U. Kans. Med. Ctr., Kansas City, 1982-87; radiologist Radiology Assocs. Ltd., Kansas City, Mo., 1987-92; mem. staff Bapt. Med. Ctr., Kansas City, Mo., 1987-92; radiologist Children's Mercy Hosp., Kansas City, 1992-95, Leavenworth-Kansas City Imaging, 1996—; assoc. prof. U. Mo., Kansas City, 1992—; speaker Radiol. Soc. Republic of China, 1985. Contbr. articles to med. jours. Nat. Cancer Inst. fellow, 1982. Mem. AMA, Am. Coll. Radiology, Radiol. Soc. N.Am., Am. Inst. Ultrasound in Medicine (mem. program com. Kansas City 1984), Soc. Pediatric Radiology, Am. Assn. Women in Radiology, Lambda Sigma Tau. Office: Leavenworth-Kansas City Imaging 9201 Parallel Pky Kansas City KS 66112

JOHNSON, JUANITA FAY SWAN, psychotherapist, storyteller; b. Oelwein, Iowa, Dec. 10, 1944; d. Richard E. and Eva Mae (McBride) Swan; m. Earl S. Johnson, June 9, 1965; children: Richard Earl, Jennifer Hope. AA, Stephens Coll., Columbia, Mo., 1965; BA, SUNY, Binghamton, 1990; MA, Norwich U., Montpelier, Vt., 1992. Cert. death educator, cert. grief therapist, cert. in thanatology. Founder, dir., therapist Good Mourning Ctr. for Life Transition and Loss, Norwich, N.Y., 1989—, Binghamton, N.Y., 1992—; instr. SUNY Morrisville Coll., Norwich, 1990-94; pub. spkr., storyteller, designer own workshops and talks Juanita Johnson Workshops, Norwich, N.Y., 1985—; cert. parent educator and trainer, 1985—; crisis cons., trainer schs., colls. and mental health profls. Author: Patterns on the Bedroom Wall, 1994, (study guide) Inner Views of Grief, 1995; author, pub.: Death and Dying Bibliography, 5th edit., 1996; prodr., dir. (video tape) Inner Views of Grief, 1995. Mem. AAUW, Nat. Assn. for the Perpetuation and Preservation of Storytelling, Assn. Death Educators/Counselors, Am. Assn. Mental Health Counselors. Home: 12 Locust St Norwich NY 13815 Office: Good Mourning Ctr for Life Transition & Loss The Eaton Ctr 15 Eaton Ave Norwich NY 13815 also: 19 Chenango St Ste 801 Binghamton NY 13901

JOHNSON, JUDITH HEAD, occupational therapist; b. Nashville, Nov. 21, 1944; d. Jack and Martha Nelson (Carlton) Head; m. John Evert Johnson, July 27, 1968 (div. 1981); children: Christopher Michael, David Sean. AA, Brevard Jr. Coll., Cocoa, Fla., 1964; BS in Occupl. Therapy, U. Fla., 1967; MA, U. South Fla., 1977. Occupl. therapist Tampa (Fla.) Gen. Hosp., 1967-71; chief occupl. therapist St. Josephs Hosp., Tampa, 1971-75; occupl. therapist cons. Meml. Hosp., Tampa, 1975-76; occupl. therapist Hills County Sch. Sys., Tampa, 1977-83; occupl. therapist, co-owner Tampa Hand Rehab. Ctr., Inc., 1983-95; occupl. therapist Rehab. Mgmt. Sys., Lakeland, Fla., 1994—. Mem. Am. Occupl. Therapy Assn. (Fla. rep. 1980-94, Recognition award 1994), Fla. Occupl. Therapy Assn. (Louise Samson Leadership award 1995), Occupl. Therapy Coun. Agy. for Health Care Adminstrn. (chair 1993—), Fla. Trail Assn. Roman Catholic. Home: 17548 Willow Pond Dr Lutz FL 33549

JOHNSON, JULIA F., bank executive. Sr. v.p. Banc One Corp, Columbus, Ohio. Office: Banc One Corp 100 E Broad St Columbus OH 43271*

JOHNSON, KARISA A., political activist; b. Stevens Point, Wis., Aug. 31, 1971; d. Fred H. Johnson and Lynn A. (Bierman) Gilles. BA in Polit. Sci., U. Wis., Madison, 1993. Various positions Wis. Sane/Freeze, Madison, 1990-92; asst. field dir. Clarenbach for Congress, Madison, 1992; finance asst. Feingold for U.S. Senate, Madison, 1992; legis. asst. State Sen. Alice Clausing, Madison, 1993; campaign coord. U.S. Sen. Russ Feingold, Middleton, Wis., 1993-94; legis. asst. State Sen. Chuck Chvala, Madison, 1994-95; state polit. dir. Dem. Ctrl. Com. Wis., Madison, 1995-96; campaign mgr. Jay Johnson for Congress, Green Bay, Wis., 1996—; mem. faculty Dem. Leadership Devel. Inst., Stevens Point, 1995-96. Vice chair elections, nominating chair Dem. Ctrl. Com. Dane County, Madison, 1992-94; orgnl. v.p. Young Dems. Wis., Madison, 1991-92. Mem. NOW, Wis. Citizen Action. Home: 101 Powers Ave Madison WI 53714

JOHNSON, KATHARYN PRICE (MRS. EDWARD F. JOHNSON), civic worker; b. Smyrna, Del., Mar. 24, 1897; d. Lewis M. and Jennie Cairl (Smithers) Price; grad. Centenary Coll., 1915; student Goucher Coll., 1915-18; m. Edward F. Johnson, Nov. 16, 1920; children—Edward A., Jane Cairl Johnson Kent. With Liberty Loan Com. for Md. and Liberty Loan Assn. of Balt., 1918-20; dir. Scarsdale Woman's Club, 1933-36; dir. White Plains Thrift Shop, 1930-43, pres, 1936-43; mem. exec. com. Scarsdale Community Fund, 1934-38; active Scarsdale council Girl Scouts, 1937-53, commr., 1939-41, now hon. mem. Scarsdale-Hartsdale council, 1953-69; mem. region 2 com. Girl Scouts U.S.A., 1942-56, mem. nat. bd., exec. com., 1947-55, chmn. orgn. and mgmt. dept., 1952-55, mem. nat. field com., 1943-55, mem. equipment service com. 1956-69, mem. internat. com., 1956-60, mem. meml. gifts com., 1974-81; mem. Bd. Edn., Scarsdale, N.Y., 1943-46; disaster chmn. Scarsdale chpt. ARC, 1942-45; mem. Commn. Human Rights, 1958-69, Commn. Status of Women, 1957-69; rep. World Assn. Girl Guides and Girl Scouts to UN, 1957-71, mem. NGO com. on UNICEF, 1965-72, sec., 1968-70; participant World Confs., World Assn. Girl Guides and Girl Scouts, Greece, 1960, Denmark, 1963, Japan, 1966, Finland, 1969, Can., 1972, Eng., 1975, Iran, 1978, World Conf., U.S., 1984. Recipient Juliette Low World Friendship medal Girl Scouts USA, 1984. Mem. Nat. Council Women U.S., Scarsdale Hist. Soc., Olave-Baden-Powell Soc. (founder), Pi Beta Phi. Republican. Presbyterian. Clubs: Scarsdale Woman's (life), Scarsdale Golf, Nat. Women's Republican; Shenorock Shore. Home: 165 Brewster Rd Scarsdale NY 10583-2021

JOHNSON, KATHERINE HOLTHAUS, health care marketing professional; b. Denver, Mar. 19, 1961; d. William Philip and Barbara Kristine (Nielsen) Holthaus; m. Robert Scott Johnson; children: Katie Maree, Brian David. B in Applied Math. Engring., U. Colo., 1983; MBA, U. Denver, 1992. Acctg. intern Cooper, Haugen & Co., CPAs, Englewood, Colo., 1982-84; market analyst mktg. dept. Porter Meml. Hosp., Denver, 1985-88; account exec. Tallant LaPointe & Ptnrs., Inc., Englewood, 1988-92; advt. mgr. Micromedex, Inc., Denver, 1992-93; mktg. cons. Highlands Ranch, Colo., 1993-96; planner Micromedex, Inc., Englewood, 1996—. Judge, vol. 4-H Clubs, Met. Denver, 1979—; supt. Sunday sch. Ascension Luth. Ch., Littleton, Colo., 1985-87. Recipient 2 Advantage awards Adventist Health System, 1987. Mem. Soc. for Healthcare Planning and Mktg., Am. Hosp. Assn., Acad. for Health Svcs. Mktg., Am. Mktg. Assn., Alpha Chi Omega. Republican.

JOHNSON, KAY ANN KING, librarian; b. Marysville, Mich., July 15, 1939; d. Kenneth S. and Grace D. (Reene) King; m. Darwin Lee Johnson, Sept. 10, 1960; children: Lisa, Joan, Carol. BA, Oakland U., 1973; AMLS, U. Mich., 1981. Cert. tchr., Mich. With Pontiac (Mich.) Libr., 1973-80, Waterford (Mich.) Schs., 1980-84. Bd. dirs., officer Waterford Jaycettes, 1965-75; dir., sec. and treas. Metro N. Fed. Credit Union, Waterford, 1992-94. Mem. AAUW, Tuesday Musicale of Pontiac (pres. 1988-90), Pontiac Oakland Town Hall (bd. dirs. pres.-elect 1982—), Beta Phi Mu. Home: 6512 White Lake Rd Clarkston MI 48346

JOHNSON, KAY DURBAHN, real estate manager, consultant; b. Crookston, Minn., Apr. 4, 1937; d. Wilbert John and Frieda (Johnson) Durbahn; m. Ray Arvin Johnson, May 14, 1960; children: Sherry Kay Johnson Johnston, Diane Rosalind Johnson Peterson, Laura Faye Johnson. BA, U. Minn., 1959. Reference analyst Indsl. Rels. Ctr. U. Minn., Mpls., 1959-61; real estate mgr. Minnetonka, Minn., 1976—; ptnr. Broadmoor Plantation Investors, Fargo, N.D., 1976—; v.p. D&T Property, Inc., Minnetonka, 1990—, also bd. dirs.; tax reduction cons. R.A. Johnson & Assocs., Minnetonka, 1985—. City of Minnetonka Planning Commn., 1972-74, vice chair, 1973-74; mem. Land Use Task Force, 1972-74; liaison Ridgedale Devel., 1972-74; chair Evangelism Bd. Minnetonka Luth. Ch., 1974-76, 85-87, chair Stewardship Bd., 1992-94, mem. choir; mem. GMC Motorcoach Assn. Mem. Mpls. Inst. Arts. Republican.

JOHNSON, KIRSTEN DENISE, elementary education educator; b. L.A., Sept. 21, 1968; d. Daniel Webster Johnson and Marinella Venesia (Ishem) Johnson Miller; 1 child, Khari Malik Manning-Johnson. BBA in Ins., Howard U., 1990; student, Southwestern Sch. Law, L.A., 1991-92, Calif. State U., Dominguez Hills, 1993—. Asst. Ctr. for Ins. Edn. Howard U., Washington, 1988-89; intern Cigna Ins. Co., L.A., 1989; agt. asst. McLaughlin Co., Washington, 1989-90; legal sec. Harris & Baird, L.A., 1990-92; legal asst. Hamrick & Garrotto, L.A., 1992-94; tchr. 5th grade L.A. Unified Sch. Dist., 1993—; free-lance writer Calif. Mus. Sci., L.A., 1994—; workshop presenter in field. All Am. scholar, 1989, John Schumacher scholar, 1991. Mem. UTLA, CTA. Democrat.

JOHNSON, LADY BIRD (MRS. LYNDON BAINES JOHNSON), widow of former President of U.S.; b. Karnack, Tex., Dec. 22, 1912; d. Thomas Jefferson Taylor; B.A., U. Tex., 1933, B.Journalism, 1934, D.Letters, 1964; LL.D., Tex. Woman's U., 1964; D.Letters, Middlebury Coll., 1967; L.H.D., Williams Coll., 1967, U. Ala., 1975; H.H.D., Southwestern U., 1967; m. Lyndon Baines Johnson (36th Pres. U.S.), Nov. 17, 1934 (died Jan. 22, 1973); children: Lynda Bird Johnson Robb, Luci Baines. Mgr. husband's congl. office, Washington, 1941-42; owner, operator radio-TV sta. KTBC, Austin, Tex., 1942-63, cattle ranches, Tex., 1943—. Hon. chmn. Nat. Headstart Program, 1963-68, Town Lake Beautification Project; also cotton and timberlands, Ala. Mem. Advisory council Nat. Parks, Historic Sites, Bldgs. and Monuments; bd. regents U. Tex., 1971-77, mem. internat. conf. steering com., 1969; trustee Jackson Hole Preserve, Am. Conservation Assn., Nat. Geog. Soc.; founder Nat. Wildflower Research Ctr., Austin, 1982. Recipient Togetherness award Marge Champion, 1958; Humanitarian award B'nai B'rith, 1961; Businesswoman's award Bus. and Profl. Women's Club, 1961; Theta Sigma Phi citation, 1962; Disting. Achievement award Washington Heart Assn., 1962; Industry citation Am. Women in Radio and Television, 1963; Humanitarian citation Vols. of Am., 1963; Peabody award for White House TV visit, 1966; Eleanor Roosevelt Golden Candlestick award Women's Nat. Press Club; Damon Woods Meml. award Indsl. Designers Soc. Am., 1972; Conservation Service award Dept. Interior, 1974; Disting. award Am. Legion, 1975; Woman of Year award Ladies Home Jour., 1975; Medal of Freedom, 1977; Nat. Achievement award Am. Hort. Soc., 1984. Life mem. U. Tex. Ex-Students Assn. Episcopalian. Author: A White House Diary, 1970. Address: LBJ Libr 2313 Red River St Austin TX 78705-5702*

JOHNSON, LAURA STARK, secondary school educator, administrator; b. Unityville, S.D., Jan. 9, 1913; d. Fred Hartman and Catherine (Culver) Stark; m. Falk Simmons Johnson, June 11, 1940; children: Mark, Bruce, Martha, Craig (dec.). BA, Dakota Wesleyan U., 1937; MA, Northwestern U., 1966; MS in Edn., No. Ill. U., 1982. Tchr. pub. schs., Unityville, 1932-36, McIntosh (S.D.) H.S., 1937-38; tchr. Washington Sch., Wauwatosa, Wis., 1938-40, Mark Twain Sch., Des Plaines, Ill., 1964-65, Maine S. H.S., 1965-69, Evanston (Ill.) H.S., 1969-96; tchr., reading cons., 1969-76; tchr. Adult Continuing Edn., 1972-85; adult edn. dept. coord. ABE/GED/Literacy, 1985-96; adj. faculty mem. Northeastern Ill., 1974-76, Loyola U., Chgo., 1974-75, Oakton C.C., 1977-79, Triton C.C., 1981-86; spkr. World Congress Reading, Singapore, 1976, Gold Coast, Australia, 1988, Stockholm, 1990. Chost writer Ency. Britannica Films, Sci. Rsch. Assn., 1958-60; author, cons. Coronet Instrnl. Media, 1974-79; editor Reading and Adult Learner, 1980, Internat. Reading Assn., Alaska Jour. Collection, 1981, Curriculum Guide for ABE Language Arts, 1988, Curriculum Pub. Clearing House, Reading in the Content Areas, New Readers Press, 1990-92; mem. adv. bd. Jour. Reading, 1972-76; contbr. articles to profl. jours. Mem. Internat. Reading Assn. (pub. com. 1976-79), Internat. Reading Assn., Ill. Reading Assn. (officer 1969-72), Suburban Reading League, Ill. Adult Continuing Edn. Assn. Home: 7624 Maple St Morton Grove IL 60053

JOHNSON, LEAYN HUTCHINSON, nursing educator, mental health nurse; b. Elizabeth, Pa., June 3, 1936; d. Ernest Eba and Edna (Caley) Hutchinson; m. Donald E. Johnson, Mar. 10, 1959; children: Donna Lynn, Donald E. Diploma, McKeesport Hosp. Sch. Nursing, 1957; BSN cum laude, Wright State U., 1975; MS, Ohio State U., 1977; PhD in Psychology, U.S. Internat. U., 1987. RN, Calif. From lectr. to asst. prof. U. Hawaii, Honolulu; prin. Ourself Counseling Ctr., Newport Beach, Calif.; asst. prof. Calif. State U., Long Beach; assoc. prof. Mem. ANA, Calif. Nurses Assn., Sigma Theta Tau. Home: 16932 Edgewater Ln Huntington Beach CA 92649-4206 Office: 1400 Quail St Ste 235 Newport Beach CA 92660

JOHNSON, LILLIAN BEATRICE, sociologist, educator, counselor; b. Wilmington, N.C., Nov. 8, 1922; d. James Archie and Mary Gaston (Atkins) J. AA, Peace Coll., 1940; BRE, Presbyterian Sch. Christian Edn., 1942; MS, N.C. State U., 1965, PhD, 1972. Dir. Christian edn. First Presbyn. Ch., Pensacola, Fla., 1945-47, Greenwood, S.C., 1947-48, Durham, N.C., 1948-51; club dir. Army Spl. Svcs., No. Command, Japan, 1951-53; teenage dir. YWCA, Washington, 1953-56, assoc. exec. Honolulu, 1956-59, exec. dir. Tulsa, 1959-62; instr. N.C. State U., 1962-72; asst. prof. Greensboro Coll., 1972-75; mem. faculty sociology dept. Livingston U., 1975-89, emerita prof., 1989—; pvt. practice family counselor, Fayetteville, N.C., 1989—. Ct. counselor, mediator Cumberland County Dispute Resolution Ctr. Mem. DAR (treas. Robert Rowan chpt.). Home: 405A Tradewinds Dr Fayetteville NC 28314-2449 Office: 155 Gillespie St Fayetteville NC 28301-5670

JOHNSON, LINDA ARLENE, petroleum transporter; b. Sparta, Wis., Mar. 6, 1946; d. Clarence Julius and Arlene Mae (Yahnke) Jessie; children: Darrick, Larissa. With Union Nat. Bank & Trust Co., Sparta, 1964-69, Hill, Christensen & Co., CPA's, Tomah, Wis., 1969-75; owner Johnson of Wis. Oil Co., Inc., Tomah, 1969-95; with Larry's Express, Inc., Tomah, 1975-78; owner Johnson Rentals, 1979—, Johnson of Wis. Transport Co., Inc., Tomah, 1982—. Mem. St. Paul's Luth. Ch., Tomah. Mem. Petroleum Marketers Assn. Am., Nat. Assn. Convenience Stores, Nat. Fedn. Ind. Bus., Am. Trucking Assn., Wis. Assn. Convenience Stores, Petroleum Marketers Assn. Wis., Wis. Ind. Businessmen, Inc., Tomah Area C. of C., Tomah Area Credit Union (bd. dirs. 1993—, sec. 1993-94), Rotary Club Tomah. Home and Office: RR 1 Box 428 Tomah WI 54660-9602

JOHNSON, LINDA KAYE, art educator; b. Port Lyautey, Morocco, Feb. 6, 1956; d. Arthur Joseph and Iona Belle (Marshall) J. BFA, Radford U., 1980; MS in Art Edn., Fla. State U., 1994. Art instr. dept. psychology Fla. State U., Tallahassee, summers 1985,86; art instr. Western Psychiat. Inst. and Clinic, Pitts., summers 1987-89, Blacksburg (Va.) Mid. Sch., 1981; jeweler Tallahassee, 1981-85; art instr. Fla. Pub. Schs., Fla., 1985—; participant Nat. Assessment of Edn. Progress, Fla. Team, 1994; chmn. Winter Festival Youth Art Show, Tallahassee, 1992, 93, 95; participating artist Very Spl. Arts Festival, Tallahassee, 1986-90; field test coord. Fla. Inst. for Art Edn.-CHAT, Tallahassee, 1992, 93; co-chair Arts for a Complete Edn. Coalition, 1993-96. Grantee Leon County Tchr.'s Assn., Tallahassee, 1992, Gadsden (Fla.) Edn. Found., 1986, 87. Mem. NEA, Profl. Art Instrs. Near Talla (pres. 1991-93), Fla. Art Educators Assn. (Fla. Mid. Sch. Art Educator of Yr. 1993), Nat. Art Educators Assn., Fla. Teaching Profession.

JOHNSON, LINDA LUCILLE, special reading teacher; b. Joliet, Ill., July 11, 1945; d. William Marion and Ada Lucille (Bates) Caldwell; m. Michael Lee Johnson, June 9, 1972; 1 child, Ryan Michael. BS in Edn., No. Ill. U., 1967. Cert. K-12 lang. arts specialist, elem. and high sch. tchr. Grades 9 and 11 English tchr. Joliet Twp. High Sch., 1967-73; grade 7 reading tchr. Stevens Middle Sch., Wilmington, Ill., 1973-75; chpt. I reading tchr. grades 1-5 Booth Cen. Elem. Sch., Wilmington, 1975—; trainer Reading Styles at numerous schs., Ill., 1985-87; mem. Reading-Writing Cadre/Ednl. Svc. Ctr. 10, Channahon, Ill., 1986-89; edn. mem. K-W Coop., Peotone, Ill., 1975-83; accreditation process dir. Wilmington Sch. Dist. 209-U, 1994-95. Adult study group leader First Christian Ch., Wilmington, 1978—. Mem. Internat. Reading Assn. Protestant. Home: 830 Joann Dr Wilmington IL 60481 Office: Booth Cen Sch 201 Kankakee St Wilmington IL 60481

JOHNSON, LINDA SUSAN SHOPE, secondary education educator; b. Kokomo, Ind., Apr. 1, 1950; d. Junior Lavone and Charlene Maggie (Cowan) Shope; children: Jennifer Anne, Christopher Allyn. BA in English, U. Miss., 1983; MA in Secondary Edn., U. North Ala., 1995. Cert. secondary tchr., Ala., Miss. Tchr.'s aide Booneville (Miss.) H.S., 1970; med. transcription, ins. sec. Bapt. Hosp., Jackson, Miss., 1971-72, The Med. Clinic, Jackson, 1972-74; adminstrv. asst., office mgr., bookkeeper Dwight Johnson, M.D., Booneville, 1976-84; adminstrv. asst., mktg. asst. Heritage Cablevision, Inc., Booneville, 1984-91; tchr. English New Site (Miss.) H.S., 1991—. Past tchr. 1st grade Sunday sch. 1st Bapt. Ch., Booneville, past dir. mission friends, past tchr. vacation bible sch., past dir. vacation bible sch., 1981, 82, 84; mem. Booneville Intercivic Coun., 1986-87, 95-96; mem. Prentiss County bd. dirs. Am Cancer Soc., 1980-87, residential chmn., 1980, chmn. Prentiss County Crusade, 1981, pres. bd. dirs., 1982-83, chmn. pub. info., 1984-87; tutor adult literacy Prentiss County Literacy Coun., Booneville, 1989. Recipient Cert. of Appreciation Am. Cancer Soc. Prentiss County, 1984-85. Mem. Nat. Coun. Tchrs. of English, Miss. Profl. Educators, Bus. and Profl. Women's Club (pres. Booneville chpt. 1986-87, 95-96, chmn. Miss. State Expansion Task Force 1987-88, chmn. Fall bd. dirs. meeting 1995, chair Lena Brock Scholarship com. 1996, Woman of Achievement 1986-87), Tupelo Kennel Club, Kappa Kappa Iota, Phi Kappa Phi, Kappa Delta Pi, Sigma Tau Delta, Pi Delta Phi (life). Baptist. Home: 300 Wickwood Booneville MS 38829

JOHNSON, LINDA THELMA, information specialist; b. New Britain, Conn., May 18, 1954; d. Oren and Lois Elizabeth (Armstrong) J.; 1 child, Portia Lauren. BS in Econs., Va. State U., 1978; cert. in computer programming, Morse Sch. Bus., 1978; cert. in legal assisting, Morse Sch. Bus., Hartford, Conn., 1994. Programmer analyst Vitro Automation Industries, Silver Spring, Md., 1980-83; sr. analyst Sci. Mgmt. Corp., Lanham, Md., 1984-86; sr. programmer analyst Applied Mgmt. Scis. Inc., Silver Spring, 1986; programmer analyst Computer Data Systems Inc., Rockville, Md., 1986-88; project leader systems cert. dept. Arbitron Co., Laurel, Md., 1988-90; systems analyst Engring. and Econ. Rsch., Inc., Vienna, Va., 1990; computer cons. Comsys Tech. Svcs. Inc., Rockville, 1990, CPU Inc., Fairfax, Va., 1991; quality assurance cons. Cigna Corp., Bloomfield, Conn., 1992; info. systems specialist The Travelers Ins. Group, Hartford, Conn., 1994—; mem. rsch. bd. advisors The Am. Biographical Inst., Inc. Mem. NAFE, NAACP, Am. Bus. Women's Assn. Democrat. Baptist. Home: 386 Park Ave Bloomfield CT 06002-3106

JOHNSON, LISA, marketing professional; b. Providence, Dec. 14, 1963; d. Richard Leonard and Kathryn Ann (Gutowski) Johnson; m. Harry James Ogrinc, Oct. 17, 1992. BA in Econs., Fairfield U. Supr. online svcs. CVC Internat., Stamford, Conn., 1985-88; account exec. Modem Media Advt., Westport, Conn., 1988-91; pres. Dunhill Mgmt., Stamford, 1991-93; sr. analyst LINK Resources Corp., N.Y.C., 1993-94; dir. interactive comms. group Wunderman Cato Johnson, N.Y.C., 1994—. Vol. Women's Crisis Ctr., Norwalk, 1990—, N.Y. Cares, N.Y.C., 1996; mentor Fairfield (Conn.) U., 1996, soup kitchen vol., 1994—. Mem. N.Y. New Media Assn. (charter), Interactive Svcs. Assn., Women in New Media. Roman Catholic. Office: Wunderman Cato Johnson 675 Ave of Americas New York NY 10010

JOHNSON, LISA ANN, mental health counselor; b. Denver, May 9, 1968; d. Freddie Lee and Elaine Roberta (Tovik) J.; m. Kent Andrew Cheeseboro, June 1, 1995. BA, Met. State Coll. Denver, 1992; MS, CCAS-Miami Inst. Psychology, 1995. Shift mgr. Round the Corner Restaurant, Denver, 1985-91; elderly care therapist Temenos House, Wheatridge, Colo., 1991-93; intern in psychology Denver City Jail, 1992; intern in psychology South Fla. Evaluation and Treatment Ctr Dept. of Health and Rehab. Svcs., Miami, Fla., 1994-95; unit treatment rehab. specialist SFETC-HRS, Miami, Fla., 1995-96; counselor supr. children & families State of Fla. Dept. Health & Rehab. Svcs., Miami, 1996—. Mem. ACA, Internat. Assn. of the Addictions and Offender Counselors. Democrat. Office: 2200 NW 7th Ave Miami FL 33127

JOHNSON, LIZABETH LETTIE, insurance agent; b. Dallas, Aug. 24, 1957; d. Winfred Herschel Johnson and Mary Francis (Flowers) Goff; children: Brandi, Elissa. Student, Georgetown (Ky.) Coll., 1975-76, U. Ky., 1976-78. Staff analyst Met. Ins. Co., Lexington, 1979-81, ins. agt., 1981-82; sr. account agt. Allstate Ins. Co., Lexington, 1982—. Vol. Big Bros./Big Sisters, 1979-84, Life Adventure Camp, 1989-92; hotline counselor Lexington Rape Crisis Ctr., 1984-92, bd. dirs., 1988-91; vol. Christians in Comty. Svc., 1986-93; mem. Bluegrass Adoptive Parent Support Group, 1985-92. Fellow Life Underwriting Tng. Council; mem. NAACP, Nat. Assn. Life Underwriters, Progressive Execs. Democrat. Baptist. Office: Allstate Ins Co 694 New Circle Rd NE Rm 3 Lexington KY 40505-4513

JOHNSON, LOLA NORINE, advertising and public relations executive, educator; b. Austin, Minn., Dec. 28, 1942; d. Alton E. and Evelyn M. (Quast) Milbrath; m. Dennis D. Johnson, June 15, 1963 (div. July 1973); children: Brenda J., Erik B. Attended, Coll. of St. Thomas. Pub. rels. account rep. Kerker & Assocs. Advt. and Pub. Rels., Bloomington, Minn., 1973-78; comm. mgr. Norwest Bank Mpls., 1978-83; dir. media rels., account supr. Edwin Neuger & Assocs. Pub. Rels., Mpls., 1983-85; v.p., mng. dir. The Richards Group, Mpls., 1985-86; owner, pres. PR Plus, Edina, Minn., 1986—; mem. cmty. faculty, instr., counselor Met. State U., Mpls., St. Paul, 1980-93. Cons. comm. United Way, Mpls., 1982. Recipient Gold award United Way Mpls., 1982. Home and Office: PR Plus 6400 Barrie Rd Apt 1402 Minneapolis MN 55435-2317

JOHNSON, LUAN, speech education educator; b. Provo, Utah, Apr. 27, 1956; d. Jack R. and Colleen (Kesler) J. BA, Brigham Young U., 1981, MA, 1984; PhD, U. Wash., 1994. Dir. Teaching Resource Ctr., Provo, 1980-84; teaching asst. communications dept. Brigham Young U., Provo, 1982-83; counselor Master Acad., Salt Lake City, 1985; ednl. designer, program mgr. City of Sunnyvale, 1986-90; teaching asst., rsch. asst., speech communications dept. U. Wash., Seattle, 1991-93; program mgr. City of Seattle, 1993—. Pres. Youth Assn. Retarded Children, Brigham City, 1976-77. Mem. Phi Kappa Phi. Mormon. Avocation: collecting and flying kites. Home: 21329 76th Ave W # 11 Edmonds WA 98026-7502 Office: SPAN 9792 Edmonds Way # 112 Edmonds WA 98020-5940

JOHNSON, LYNN MARIE, educational administrator; b. Phila., Oct. 22, 1961; d. Norman Lynnewood and Marie Sophia (Butler) J. Degree in journalism, Pa. State U., 1981; degree in comms., Temple U., 1984. Writer, prodr. Sta. KVW-TV, Phila., 1984-88; pub. rels. exec. Paolin & Sweeney, Cherry Hill, N.J., 1988-89; pub. rels. dir. Chiara Assocs., Phila., 1989; spl. asst. to pres. Cheyney (Pa.) U., 1989-92; exec. dir. NAACP, Phila., 1992-94; regional dir. of devel. Pa. State U., Abington, 1994—; cons. Pa. Ho. of Reps., Phila., 1994, Coalition for Police Acct., Phila., 1993-94; mgr. Sta. KVW-TV/Westinghouse, Phila., 1986-88. Mem. Urban League, Phila., 1991-94, NAACP, 1992-94. Named Miss Black Pa., 1984. Mem. AAUW, NAACP, Nat. Soc. Fundraising Execs., Urban League. Democrat. Roman Catholic. Home: 7519 Boyer St Philadelphia PA 19119-1604 Office: Pa State U 1600 Woodland Rd Abington PA 19001-3918

JOHNSON, LYNNE RENEE, secondary education educator; b. Des Plaines, Ill., Mar. 8, 1956; d. Richard Bruce and Laraine Celeste (Rupinski) J. BFA, U. Tex., 1978. Interior designer various firms, Austin, Tex., 1978-88; art tchr. Westwood H.S., Austin, 1988-92, McNeil H.S., Austin, 1992—; sponsor Nat. Portfolio Day Assn., Austin, 1993—. Mem. Nat. Art Educators Assn., Austin Visual Arts Assn., Williamson County Art Guild. Home: HCO 3 Box 60 Spicewood TX 78669 Office: McNeil H S 5720 Mcneil Dr Austin TX 78729-6901

JOHNSON, MADELINE MITCHELL, retired administrative assistant; b. Cleve., Oct. 24, 1930; d. Maidlon and Katherine (Reynolds) Mitchell; m. Elvyn Frank Johnson, Dec. 4, 1954. BS, Case Western Res. U., 1976. Adminstrv. asst. Fed. Res. Bank Cleve., 1950-92, tng. coord. data svcs., 1988-92, ombudsman rep., 1989-92; ret., 1992; mem. tng. task force bd. govs. FRS, Washington, 1987-92. Chair bd. trustees Affinity Bapt. Ch. Mem. Am. Bus. Women's Assn. (pres. 1986-88, Women of Yr. Cleve. chpt. 1987), Nat. Coun. Negro Women, Top Ladies of Distinction (nominee Woman of Yr. Cleve. chpt. 1993-94, pres. 1995—). Home: 33705 Wellingford Ct Solon OH 44139

JOHNSON, MARGARET ANN, library administrator; b. Atlanta, Aug. 11, 1948; d. Odell H. and Virginia (Mathiasen) J.; m. Lee J. English, Mar. 4, 1978; children: Carson J., Amelia J. BA, St. Olaf Coll., 1970; MA, U. Chgo., 1972; MBA, Met. State U., 1990. Music cataloger U. Iowa Librs., Iowa City, 1972-73; analyst Control Data Corp., Bloomington, Minn., 1973-75; br. libr. St. Paul (Minn.) Pub. Librs., 1975-77; head tech. svcs. St. Paul (Minn.) Campus Librs., U. Minn., 1977-86; collection devel. office U. Librs., U. Minn., Mpls., 1987-90; asst. dir. St. Paul (Minn.) Campus Librs., U. Minn., 1987-95; planning officer U. Librs. U. Minn., Mpls., 1993—; libr. cons. Mekerere U., Kampala, Uganda, 1990, U. Nat. Rwanda, 1990, Inst. Agriculture and Vet. Hassan II, Rabat, Morocco, 1992—. Author: Automation and Organizational Change in Libraries, 1991, The Searchable Internet, 1996; (bimonthly column) Technicalities Jour.; editor Guide to Tech. Svcs. Resources, 1994, Recruiting, Educating and Tng. Librarians for Collection Devel., 1994, Collection Mgmt. and Devel., 1994; contbr. articles to profl. jours. Recipient Samuel Lazerow Rsch. fellowship Assn. Coll. and Rsch. Librs., Inst. for Sci. Info., 1987. Mem. ALA, Minn. Libr. Assn., Internat. Assn. Agrl. Librs. and Documentalists, Assn. for Internat. Agrl. and Extension Edn., U.S. Agrl. Info. Network, Women in Devel. Office: U of Minn Librs 499 Wilson Libr 309 19th Ave South Minneapolis MN 55455

JOHNSON, MARGARET ANNE, sociologist; b. Ypsilanti, Mich., Oct. 23, 1964; d. John Daniel and Clarie Elaine (Campbell) J.; m. Murat Cil. BA in Sociology with honors, Tex. A&M U., 1987; MA in Sociology, U. Tex., 1990, PhD in Sociology, 1993. Teaching asst. in introductory sociology U. Tex., Austin, 1987-88, 91, teaching asst. liberal arts computer lab., 1988-89; rsch. asst., 1989-93; rsch. assoc. Population Studies Ctr. Urban Inst., 1990; lectr. social stats. and population problems U. Tex., Austin, 1993-94; asst. prof. sociology Okla. State U., Stillwater, 1994—. Contbr. articles to profl. publs. Bd. dirs. Payne County Habitat for Humanity. Dan Russell Sociology scholar, 1986; fellow Ctr. on Philanthropy, Ind., 1992-93. Mem. AAUW (v.p. membership Stillwater chpt.), Am. Sociol. Assn., Assn. Rsch. on Nonprofit Orgns. and Voluntary Action, Southwestern Social Sci. Assn., Sociologists for Women in Soc., Alpha Phi Omega. Office: Okla State U Dept Sociology 006CLB Stillwater OK 74078

JOHNSON, MARGARET H, welding company executive, author; b. Chgo., June 3, 1933; d. Harold W. and Clara J. (Pape) Glavin; m. Odean Jack Johnson, Nov. 18, 1950; children: Karen Ann, Dean Harold. Student Moody Bible Inst., 1976-78. V.p., sec. Seamline Welding, Inc., Grayslake, 1956—, dir.; trustee SWCEPS, Grayslake, 1963—. Author: Living Faith, 1973, 80, Lord's Ladder of Love, 1976, God's Rainbow, 1982; contbr. articles to religion mags. Life mem. Rep. Presdl. Task Force, 1982—, trustee, 1986-88; charter founder Ronald Reagan Rep. Ctr., 1987; mem. Lake View Neighborhood Group, Chgo., Small Group Ch. Community; active Mary, Seat of Wisdom Cath. Women's Club, 1970-90, renew facilitator 1986-88, co-chairperson 1986-88; Sunday sch. tchr., 1985; mem. St. Gilbert's Parish, 1990—. Mem. ASCAP, Fedn. Ind. Small Bus., Internat. Platform Assn., Women's Aglow Fellowship Internat., Grayslake C. of C.. Exch. Club Grayslake, Grayslake Devel. Corp. Home: 20 Hawley Ct Grayslake IL 60030-1517

JOHNSON, MARGARET HILL, retired educational administrator; b. Dundee, Scotland, June 26, 1923; came to U.S., 1946, naturalized, 1957; d. John Barnet and Isabella Rae (Watson) Hill; children: Ann Hill Doughty, James Appleton Doughty (dec.), Joanna Elizabeth Doughty Going. Student Inverness (Scotland) Royal Acad., 1940, Edinburgh (Scotland) Royal Coll. Art, 1940-43; Doctor in Edn., U. Mass., Amherst, 1985. Latin and remedial English tutor Harvey Sch., N.Y.C., 1947-52; tchr. athletics Pingree Sch. for Girls, Hamilton, Mass., 1959-61, Shore Country Day Sch., Beverly, Mass., 1952-59; asso. dir. Theodore S. Jones & Co., design mgmt. cons., Milton, Mass., 1961-72; dir. career planning and placement Mass. Coll. Art, 1972-96, v.p.; ind. art cons.; design cons. Theodore S. Jones & Co.; Fulbright advisor Mass. Coll. Art, 1974—; speaker Lesley Coll., 1977, Cambridge (Mass.) Community Schs., 1977—, MIT, Harvard U., R.I. Sch. Design, Hofstra U.

Served with Brit. Women's Royal Naval Service, 1943-46. Mem. Am. Craft Coun., Am. Assn. Mus., Boston Soc. Architects, Coll. Placement Coun., Am. Assn. Higher Edn., Coll. Art Assn. Am., Internat. Educators Network. Author: (with others) Your Future in Art and Design, 1977. Home: PO Box 75 Marshfield Hills MA 02051-0075

JOHNSON, MARGARET KATHLEEN, business educator; b. Baylor County, Tex., Oct. 30, 1920; d. George W. and Julia Rivers (Turner) Higgins; m. Herman Clyde Johnson, Jr., July 27, 1949 (dec.); 1 child, Carolyn Kay. B.S., Hardin-Simmons U., 1940; M.Bus. Edn., North Tex. State U., 1957, Ed.D., 1962. Clk. Farmers Nat. Bank, Seymour, Tex., 1940-41; adminstrv. sec. U.S. Navy, Corpus Christi, Tex., 1941-46; adminstrv. asst. Hdqrs. 8th Army, Yokohama, Japan, 1946-49; instr. Coll. Bus. Adminstrn., U. Ark., 1957-60; teaching fellow Sch. Bus. Adminstrn., North Tex. State U., 1960-62, instr., 1962-63; asst. prof. bus., tchr. edn. and secondary edn. Tchrs. Coll., U. Nebr., Lincoln, 1963-65; asso. prof. Tchrs. Coll., U. Nebr., 1966-70, prof., 1970—; guest lectr. U. N.Mex., 1967, Curriculum Devel. in Bus. Edn., N.S. Dept. Edn., 1969, North Tex. State U., 1970, East Tex. State U., 1972; in Policies Commn. for Bus. and Econ. Edn., 1979-83. Author: Standardized Production Typewriting Tests series, 1964-65, National Structure for Research in Vocational Education, 1966; co-author: Introduction to Word Processing, 1980, 2d edit., 1985, Introduction to Business Communication, 1981, 2d edit., 1988, Business Communication Principles and Applications, 1996; editor: Nat. Bus. Edn. Assn. Yearbook, 1980. Recipient United Bus. Edn. Assn. award as outstanding grad. student in bus. edn. North Tex. State U., 1957; award for outstanding service Nebr. Future Bus. Leaders Am., 1968; Mountain-Plains Bus. Edn. Leadership award, 1977; merit award Nebr. Bus. Assn., 1979. Mem. Nat. Bus. Edn. Assn. (exec. bd. 1975, 76-78), Mountain-Plains Bus. Edn. Assn. (exec. sec. 1970-73, pres. 1975), Nebr. Bus. Edn. Assn. (pres. 1966-67), Nebr. Council on Occupational Tchr. Edn., Delta Pi Epsilon. Office: U Nebr 529 Nebraska Hall Lincoln NE 68588

JOHNSON, MARIAN ILENE, education educator; b. Hawarden, Iowa, Oct. 3, 1929; d. Henry Richard and Wilhelmina Anna (Schmidt) Stoltenberg; m. Paul Irving Jones, June 14, 1958 (dec. Feb. 1985); m. William Andrew Johnson, Oct. 3, 1991. BA, U. La Verne, 1959; MA, Claremont Grad. Sch., 1962; PhD, Ariz. State U., 1971. Cert. tchr., Iowa, Calif. Elem. tchr. Cherokee (Iowa) Sch. Dist., 1949-52, Sioux City (Iowa) Sch. Dist., 1952-56, Ontario (Calif.) Pub. Schs., 1956-61, Reed Union Sch. Dist., Belvedere-Tiburon, Calif., 1962-65, Columbia (Calif.) Union Sch. Dist., 1965-68; prof. edn. Calif. State U., Chico, 1972-91. Home: 26437 S Lakewood Dr Sun Lakes AZ 85248-7246

JOHNSON, MARIANNE THERESE, assistant principal, elementary school educator; b. Waukegan, Ill., May 30, 1951; d. Frank Anthony and Mildred Therese (Norton) Belmont; m. Edward Jay Johnson, Aug. 16, 1974 (div. Aug. 1995); children: Brian, Anne. B of Elem. Edn., Dominican Coll., 1973. Tchr. St. Louis Sch., Caledonia, Wis., 1973-74; owner Baskin-Robbins Ice Cream, Waukegan, Ill., 1974-88; tchr. St. Anastrasia Sch., Waukegan, Ill., 1988—, asst. prin., 1994—; prin. search bd. St. Anastasia, 1994, mem. fin. sch. bd., 1981-87, mem. PTO bd., 1983-89, mem. long range planning bd., 1981-93. Roman Catholic. Office: St Anastasia Sch 629 W Glen Flora Ave Waukegan IL 60085-1835

JOHNSON, MARJORIE R., special education educator; b. Boston, Jan. 3, 1929; d. Irving Benjamin and Florence Emma (Alling) Akerson; m. Richard Johnson, May 19, 1951; children: William Benjamin, Gerald Dennis, Peter Charles. BS in Occupational Therapy, Columbia U., N.Y.C., 1951. Cert. tchr. spl. edn., primary edn. and occupational therapy, Pa. Occupational therapist ABC Children's Clinic, Reading, Pa., 1951-52; clerk Kaiser Metal Co., Bristol, Pa., 1952-54; spl. edn. tchr. Chester Co. Intermediate Unit, Coatesville, Pa., 1964-91; ret., 1991; union v.p. CCIU branch PSEA, 1964, pres. 1965. Active in establishing group homes ARC, Chester County, 1973. Mem. Soc. Pa. Archaeology (sec. 1984-86, v.p. 1996—). Home: 40 Forest Rd Honey Brook PA 19344

JOHNSON, MARLENE M., furniture company executive; b. Braham, Minn., Jan. 11, 1946; d. Beauford and Helen (Nelson) J.; m. Peter Frankel. BA, Macalester Coll., 1968. Founder, pres. Split Infinitive, Inc., St. Paul, 1970-82; pres., bd. dirs. Face to Face Health and Counseling Clinic, 1977-78; with Working Opportunities for Women, 1977-82; lt. gov. State of Minn., St. Paul, 1983-91; sr. fellow Family Support Project, Ctr. for Policy Alternative, 1991-93; assoc. adminstr. for adminstrn. GSA, Washington, 1994-95; v.p. for people and strategy Rowe Furniture Corp., McLean, Va., 1995—; founder, past chmn. Nat. Leadership Conf. Women Execs. in State Govt.; mem. exec. com., midwestern chair Nat. Conf. Lt. Govs.; bd. dirs. AFS-USA, Inc.; mem. adv. bd. Ctr. for Children in Poverty, Columbus U. Chmn. Minn. Women's Polit. Caucus, 1973-76, Dem.-Farmer-Labor Small Bus. Task Force, 1978, Child Care Task Force, 1987; dir. membership sect. Nat. Women's Polit. Caucus, 1975-77; vice chmn. Minn. Del. to White House Conf. on Small Bus., 1980; co-founder Minn. Women's Campaign Fund, 1982; bd. dirs. Nat. Child Care Action Campaign; chair Children's 2000 Commn., 1990; candidate for Mayor St. Paul, 1993. Recipient Outstanding Achievement award St. Paul YWCA, 1980, Disting. Svc. award St. Paul Jaycees, 1980, Disting. Citizen citation Macalester Coll., 1982, Disting. Contbns. to Families award Minn. Coun. on Family Rels., 1986, Minn. Sportfishing Congress award, 1986, Royal Order of Polar Star Govt. Sweden, 1988, Children's Champion award Def. Fund, 1989, Jane Preston award Minn. State Coun. on Vocat. Tech. Edn., 1989, Legis. Leadership award Am. Fedn. Tchrs., 1991; named One of Ten Outstanding Young Minnesotans, Minn. Jaycees, 1980; Swedish Bicentennial Commn. grantee, 1987. Mem. Nat. Assn. Women Bus. Owners (past pres.).

JOHNSON, MARY ALICE, magazine editor; b. Rochester, Ind., Apr. 16, 1942; d. Nolan Lee and Alice Lavida (Ruede) Lewis; m. Manford Warren Johnson, May 28, 1960; children: Nola (dec.), John Jay, June Jeannette Johnson Brady. Grad. high sch., Hillsboro, Oreg., 1960. Owner, baker, decorator Mary's Custom Cakes and Cake Parts, St. Helens, Oreg., 1980-87; creator Sweet Tooth Confections Candy, 1981—; founder, mng. editor Sugar Art Sharing Confectionary Ideas mag., 1986-88; chmn. Sugar Art Ltd. Partnership, McMinnville, Oreg., 1986-93; owner Double Rainbow Enterprises, McMinnville, 1993—; creator products for hobbyist and handicapped decorators, 1989—; tchr. cake decorating, candy and gingerbread houses, 1981—; cons., presenter cake decorating and sugar art demonstrations, various youth clubs and area high schs. Author: ABC Bible, 1967, I Can See God In Everything, 1975, The Wedding Book, 1983, Friends Feasts & Fellowship, 1992, God and Money, 1992, Looseleaf Pattern Library, 1992, Mary's Cook Book, 1993, It's Time to Oil the Lamps, 1994, (videotape) Gingerbread Mansions, 1996. Leader, Country Kids and Friends 4-H, St. Helens, 1979-85; organizer rural fire dept., Rainier, Oreg.; Sunday sch. tchr. Luth. Ch., 1956-74, officer women's groups, 1960-77; sec. Tualitan Vallye Rabbit Breeders Assn., 1964-67, fair dinner booth chmn., 1965-66; ballot clk. Columbia County Election Bd., 1972-80; decorated cake supt. Columbia County Fair, 1983-85; decorations chmn. Christian Women's Club, McMinnville, 1989-90; founder youth hobby club Pettis Fours Club, 1989. Winner awards for entries in numerous county and state fairs, cake shows. Mem. Women Entrepreneurs Oreg., Internat. Cake Exploration Soc. Republican. Lutheran. Office: Double Rainbow Enterprises 1301 NE Highway 99W # 298 McMinnville OR 97128-2722

JOHNSON, MARY ANN, computer training vocational school owner; b. Joliet, Ill., June 26, 1956; d. Truly and Pearlie Mae (Bell) J.; m. Russell Alan Jackson, May 18, 1976 (div. 1983); children: Pamela Ann, Russell Alan Jr. AA, Joliet (Ill.) Jr. Coll., 1990; student mgmt. info. systems, Governor State U. Student intern Argonne (Ill.) Nat. Lab., 1972-79, sec. II, 1979-82; word processor specialist SunGard Corp., Hinsdale, Ill., 1982-86; desktop designer, adminstrn. Amoco Chem. Corp., Naperville, Ill., 1988-89; desktop designer Travelers Corp., Naperville, 1989-90; adminstrv. sec., computer operator Metromail Donnelly, Lombard, Ill., 1990-91; owner, mgr. Tech. Soft Svcs., Joliet, 1991—; lectr., condr. seminars on running small bus. Author: Running a Small Business, 1996. Mem. Women Bus. Devel., Joliet Region C. of C. Office: Tech Soft Svcs 323 Springfield Ave Joliet IL 60435-6501

JOHNSON, MARY ELIZABETH, retired speech educator; b. Powhatan Pt., Ohio, Mar. 10, 1905; d. John McFadden and Nancy Ramsay (Shannon) J. BA, Muskingum Coll., New Concord, Ohio, 1926; MA, U. Mich., 1933; postgrad., Northwestern U., 1956, 60, Ohio State U., 1946, 68. Cert. in edn., speech correction, Ohio, 1960. Tchr. Moundsville (W.Va.) High Sch., 1926-37, dean of girls, 1935-37; chmn. English dept. Martins Ferry (Ohio) High Sch., 1937-44, instr. speech, 1944-48; asst. prof. Muskingum Coll., 1948-52, assoc. prof. speech, 1952-72, emeritus assoc. prof., 1972—; chmn. drama and poetry reading conf. Muskingum Coll., 1946-68, communications area, 1950-53, acting chmn. dept. speech, 1965-66, adviser Nat. Collegiate Players, 1957-65; author Ohio dist. state scholarship tests in English for secondary schs., 1941, 43, 46. V.p. Women's Forum, New Concord, 1966-67; mem. First Community Village Coun., Columbus, Ohio, 1984, 85; chmn. Children's Hosp. Twig #15, Columbus, 1987, 88. Mem. AAUW, Am. Assn. Retired Persons, Am. Speech and Hearing Assn., Ohio Speech and Hearing Assn., Comparative Edn. Soc. (seminar and field study in Europe 1967), Ohio Ret. Tchrs. Assn., Heritage Club, Parchment Club (pres. New Concord 1968, 78), Delta Kappa Gamma Internat. (pres. Psi chpt., Alpha Delta State 1941-43, pres. Alpha Psi chpt. 1951, state recording sec. 1965-67). Presbyterian.

JOHNSON, MARY ELIZABETH, elementary education educator; b. St. Louis, Sept. 17, 1943; d. Richard William Blayney and Alice Bonjean (Taylor) Blayney Needham; m. Clyde Robert Johnson, Aug. 31, 1963; children: Brian (dec. 1991), Elizabeth Johnson Meyer, David. BS cum laude, U. Ill., 1966; MA, Maryville U., 1990; postgrad., So. Ill. U., 1990. Cert. elem. tchr., Ill., Mo. Tchr. Hazelwood Sch. Dist., Florissant, Mo., 1971-93, positive intervention tchr., 1989-91; Author play: Say No to Drugs, 1991. Author: Secret Study Skills for Third Graders, 1990. Mem. Hazelwood Schs. Music Boosters, 1980-88; mem. coms. Townsend PTA, Florissant, 1976—; contbr. Schlarship Run-Walk, 1982—; mem. Children's United Rsch. Effort in Cancer, 1986—; vol. Spl. Love, Inc., camp for children with cancer, 1986—; active The Children's Inn, Bethesda, Md., 1990—, Bailey Scholarship Fund, U. Ill., 1994—. Fred S. Bailey scholar, 1962-66, Edmund J. James scholar, 1964-65; named Townsend Tchr. of Yr., 1989-90. Mem. NEA, Internat. Platform Assn., Kappa Delta Pi, Alpha Lambda Delta, Phi Kappa Phi. Baptist. Home: 12 Shamblin Dr Florissant MO 63034-1354

JOHNSON, MARY KATHRYN, legal assistant; b. Oak Park, Ill., Sept. 5, 1942; d. Herbert Gold and Vera Lillian (Engel) Oldham; m. James Arnold Johnson, Feb. 17, 1968 (div. 1970); 1 child, Stephanie Louise. BA in German, U. Ill., 1966. Cert. legal assistantship; cert. tchg. ESL; lic. tax preparer, Calif. Editl. asst. U. Chgo., 1968; legal asst. Harry W. Brelsford, Atty., Santa Barbara, Calif., 1974-83; pvt. legal asst. Santa Barbara, 1984—; instr. H&R Block, Santa Barbara, 1992, Santa Barbara City Coll., 1992-93; tax preparer, Santa Barbara, 1992—. Mem. Legal Assts. Assn. Santa Barbara (life, pres. 1987-89). Home and Office: PO Box 2280 Santa Barbara CA 93120-2280

JOHNSON, MARY LOU, lay worker; b. Moline, Ill., July 15, 1923; d. Percy and Hope (Aulgur) Sipes; m. Blaine Eugene Johnson, May 30, 1941; children: Vivian A. Johnson Sweedy, Michael D. (dec.), Amelia Johnson Harms Thomas, James Michael (dec.). Grad. high sch., Moline. Chmn. Christian edn. 1st Christian Ch., Moline, 1971-73, 77-79, 84-86, elder, 1973-76, 77-80, chmn. official bd., 1979-81, dir. Christian edn., 1988-93, ret., 1993; Sunday sch. tchr. 1st Christian Ch, Moline, 1958-84; cluster del. Christian Chs. Ill. and Wisc., Moline, 1988-89. Author: (poem) What Is A Mother?, 1965. Officer various positions PTA, Moline, 1972-75, hon. life mem. State of Ill., 1972; leader, dist. dir. Girl Scouts U.S., Moline, 1955-65; skywatcher USAF Ground Observer Corps, Moline, 1955-57; vol. telethon coord. Muscular Dystrophy Assn., Moline, 1971-94; del. lt. gov.'s Commn. on Aging, Springfield, Ill., 1990. Recipient numerous appreciation awards Muscular Dystrophy Assn., 1964-94. Republican. Home: 2014 9th St Moline IL 61265-4779

JOHNSON, MARY MURPHY, social services director, writer; b. N.Y.C., Mar. 5, 1940; d. Richard and Nora (Greene) Murphy; m. Noel James Johnson, Oct. 8, 1961; children: Valerie Johnson Powell, Donna Homan, Noreen Marie Pettitt, Richard. BA in English/History magna cum laude, Jacksonville State U., 1983, BS in Sociology magna cum laude, 1983, MA in History, 1984, B in Social Work magna cum laude, 1988. Cert. gerontology specialist. Asst. activities dir. Jacksonville (Ala.) Nursing Home, 1985-86; social services dir. Beckwood Manor, Anniston, Ala., 1987—; Cons. in field. Editor: Vladivostak Diary, 1987. Mem. AAU, Ala. Archaeol. Soc., Coosa Valley Archaeol. Soc. (sec. 1982-87), Soc. Ala. Archivists, Human Svcs. Coun., Vietnam Vets. Am., Soc. for Creative Anachronism (Reeve, Canton of the Peregrine), Phi Eta Sigma, Phi Alpha Theta, Sigma Tau Delta, Omicron Delta Kappa. Russian Orthodox.

JOHNSON, MARY SUSAN, transportation company professional; b. Bloomingdale, Ind., Nov. 19, 1937; d. William Blaine Shade and Goldina VandaVeer (Newlin) Brown; children: Roger, Tisa, Julia, Angela, Robert, William. Grad. high sch., Rockville, Ind. Sec., treas. Tri-State Transport, Inc., 1968-73; road driver Roadway Express, Chicago Heights, Ill., 1977—, safety team capt., 1991-92, 94; completed Passport Tour (Abate), 1990, 94; mem. Roadway Express Dist. Road Team Dist. 12, 1995. Mem newsletter com. focus group Roadway Express; mem. focus group Kenworth Driver's Bd., 1992-94. Recipient rodeo awards. Mem. Am. Motorcycle Assn., Am. Bikers Aim Toward Edn., Am. Radio Relay League, Am. Radio Emergency Svc. (Lake County), Internat. Platform Assn., Stars Radio Club, Harley Owners Group (newsletter editor Calumet region, Hammond, Ind., asst. dir. 1996), Ladies of Harley, Kankakee Valley Harley Owners Group, Dunelands Chpt. Harley Owners Group. Home and Office: PO Box 316 Griffith IN 46319-0316

JOHNSON, MARY ZELINDA, artist; b. Hopkinton, Mass., June 3, 1914; d. Pietro and Ida (Sora) Sabettini; m. Paul Y. Johnson; 1 child, Paula Johnson Cooper. Student, AIC, Springfield, Mass., 1945-46, Sarah Whitney Olds, Patchogue, N.Y., 1947-49, Edna Ross, Patchogue, N.Y., 1949-51, Emile Gruppe, Gloucester, Mass., 1948, Pratt Inst., Bklyn., 1952-54, L'Acad. Julien, Paris, 1957-58, U. Fine Arts, Bangkok, 1960-62, Khiem Yemsiri/Royal Sculptor a, Sch. Fine Arts, Bangkok, 1961-62. Dir. Swinburne Sch., Newport, R.I., 1970-73. Art exhbns. include: Brookhaven, N.Y., 1948, Patchogue, L.I., 1949, Stoney Brook Mus., 1951, Athens, Greece, 1955, Casablanca, Morocco, 1958, Arts Club/Washington, 1959, 22nd Met. Exhibit at Smithsonian, Washington, 1959, Nat. Mus. of Bangkok, 1961, Bangkok Art Ctr., 1961, Tourist Orgn. of Thailand, 1961, Panamanian N.A. Assn., Panama City, 1963, Naval Officer's Club, Newport, 1972, Wharf Gallery, Newport, 1972, Swinburne Sch., 1972, Springfield Coll. Hastings Gallery, 1986, Westfield Atheneum Jasper Rand Gallery, 1990, Biltmore Studio, Washington, 1984, Nat. Greek Art Exhbns., Springifled, 1990, Washington Arts Club, 1993, others; internal. artist and sculptor/multi-media and woodcuts. Vol. USO, Portland, Maine, 1942-43, Ft. Hancock, N.J., 1941-42; driver Red Cross Motorcorps, Charleston, S.C., 1943-45, Springfield, 1945-46, others. Recipient 1st prize in State Dept. Bridge Tournament, worldwide, 1964. Mem. Arts Club/Washington, Young Artists Group/Bangkok, Am. Fgn. Svc. Assn., Washington Arts Club, Siam Soc./Bangkok, Naval Officers Wives Club/Washington, USIA Alumni Assn. Republican. Roman Catholic. Home: Vinson Hall # 105 6251 Old Dominion Dr Mc Lean VA 22101

JOHNSON, MARYANNA MORSE, business owner; b. Oxford, Miss., Dec. 21, 1936; d. Hugh McDonald and Anna Sullivan (Virden) Morse; children: Julianna, Hunter, Cynthia, Capp. Student, Miss. U. for Women, 1957; BSN cum laude, Tex. Woman's U., 1986. RN, Tex. Owner MJM & Assocs., Boulder, Colo., 1968—; health promotion cons., 1986—. Mem. Sigma Theta Tau. Home: 3102 Bell Dr Boulder CO 80301-2277

JOHNSON, MARYL RAE, cardiologist; b. Fort Dodge, Iowa, Apr. 15, 1951; d. Marvin George and Beryl Evelyn (White) J. BS, Iowa State U., 1973; MD, U. Iowa, 1977. Diplomate Am. Bd. Internal Medicine; diplomate of Subspeciality of Cardiovascular Diseases. Intern, U. Iowa Hosps., Iowa City, 1977-78, resident 1978-81, fellow, 1979-82; assoc. in cardiology U. Iowa Hosps. and Clinics, Iowa City, 1982-86, asst. prof. medicine cardiovascular div., 1986-88; asst. prof. medicine Med. Ctr. Loyola U., 1988-92, assoc. prof. 1992-94; assoc. prof. Rush U., 1994—; med. dir. cardiac transplantation U. Iowa Hosp., 1986-88, assoc. med. dir. cardiac transplantation Loyola U., 1988-94; assoc. med. dir. Rush Heart Failure and Cardiac Transplant Program, 1994—. Mem. Nat. Heart Lung and Blood Adv. Council, Bethesda, Md., 1979-83, biomed. rsch. tech. rev. com NIH, 1990-93 (chairperson 1992-93). Assoc. editor: Jour. Heart and Lung Transplantation, 1995—. Barry Freeman scholar, 1974; recipient Jane Leinfelder Meml. award U. Iowa Coll. Medicine, 1977, Clin. Investigator award NIH, 1981, New Investigator Research award, NIH, 1986. Mem. AMA, AAAS, ACP, Internat. Soc. Heart and Lung Transplantation, Am. Heart Assn., Am. Fedn. Clin. Rsch., Am. Coll. Cardiology, Am. Soc. Transplant Physicians, Ill. State Med. Soc., Chgo. Med. Soc., Order of the Rose, Alpha Lambda Delta, Phi Kappa Phi, Iota Sigma Pi, Alpha Omega Alpha.

JOHNSON, MAXINE FRAHM, bank executive; b. Mason City, Iowa, Dec. 18, 1939; d. Peter Jr. and Emily Marian (Bistline) Frahm; m. Robert W. Johnson, June 3, 1962; children: Brenda Lynn, Janine Suzanne. BA, Grinnell Coll., 1961; MBA, U. Pitts., 1976. Cert. fin. planner; cert. trust and fin. advisor. Contract writer Bankers Life Co., Des Moines, 1961-62; music tchr. Haworth (N.J.) Pub. Sch., 1962-63; pvt. practice Setauket, N.Y., 1963-65, Joliet, Ill., 1965-70, Glenshaw, Pa., 1970-76; trust officer Pitts. Nat. Bank, 1976-82; sr. trust officer Bank of New England, N.A., Boston, 1982-84, v.p., 1984-90, head personal trust adminstrn., 1990-91; v.p. R.I. Hosp. Trust Nat. Bank, 1991-95, trust mgr., 1995-96, 1st v.p., trust mgr., 1996—; mem. faculty New Eng. Banking Inst., 1984—; adj. faculty Northeastern U., Dedham, Mass., 1989-95. Author: Implications of the Generation Skipping Transfer Tax for Trust Administrators, 1980. Sec. bd. dirs. Children's Mus. R.I. Mem. AAUW (treas.), Inst. Cert. Fin. Planners, Boston Estate Planning Coun., R.I. Estate Planning Coun., Amateur Chamber Music Players Inc., Chaminade Club, Pi Kappa Lambda, Delta Gamma Sigma. Office: RI Hosp Trust Nat Bank One Hosp Trust Pla T 03 03 Providence RI 02903-2449

JOHNSON, MILDRED GRACE MASH, investment company executive; b. Castle Rock, Wash., Mar. 3, 1922; d. Percival and Hilda C. (Nyberg) M.; widowed, 1988; children: John, Joy, Judy, Chris, Steven. Student, U. Wash. V.p. Johnson Constrn. Co., Seattle, 1950-58, pres., 1988-91; v.p. Johnson Investment Co., Seattle, 1950-58, pres., 1988—. Deacon U. Presbyn. Ch., Seattle, 1981—. Mem. Am. Bus. Women's Assn. (v.p. 1979-89, Woman of Yr. 1981), Apt. Assn., Master Builders, Daus. Nile, Order of Ea. Star. Republican. Home: 3812 E Mcgilvra St Seattle WA 98112-2427

JOHNSON, MYRNA ELLEN, government relations executive; b. Wagner, S.D., Jan. 17, 1960; d. Wesley Eugene and Erma Harriet (Stephenson) J. BA magna cum laude, Wartburg Coll., 1982. Organizer Clean Water Action/Md. League Conservation Voters, Balt., 1982-83; membership recruiter Cope Energy Svcs., Balt., 1983-84, co-dir., 1984-85; govt. rels. asst. Bicycle USA, Balt., 1985-86, dir. govt. rels., 1986-87; govt. rels. assoc. Nat. Pub. Radio, Washington, 1987-95; dir. govt. affairs Outdoor Recreation Coalition of Am., Boulder, Colo., 1995—; mem. Outward Bound Land Mgmt. Adv. Coun., Golden, Colo., 1996. Bd. mem., newsletter editor Greater Balt. Environ. Ctr., 1984-89; bd. mem. Balt. Clergy and Laity Concerned, 1985-86, Gwynn Oak Improvement Assn., Balt., 1989-90; mem. nat. steering com., chair long range planning com. Luth. Vol. Corps, Washington, 1990-94; mem. Cmty. Leadership Coun., Balt., 1990-94; founding mem. Watershed Alliance, Balt., 1990; vol. McGuire for Congress, Sioux City, Iowa, 1994, Indian Peaks Working Group, 1996; participant Colo. Outdoor Recreation Resource Project, 1995-96; gardener Boulder Cmty. Garden, 1996. State of Iowa scholar, 1978; Regents scholar Wartburg Bd. Regents, 1978, Vera B. Will scholar Wartburg Coll., 1981. Democrat. Office: Outdoor Recreation Coalition Am 2475 Broadway Boulder CO 80304

JOHNSON, NANCY LEE, congresswoman; b. Chicago, Ill., Jan. 5, 1935; d. Noble Wishard and Gertrude Reid (Smith) Lee; m. Theodore H. Johnson, July 16, 1958; children—Lindsey Lee, Althea Anne, Caroline Reid. B.A., Radcliffe Coll., 1957; postgrad., U. London, 1957-58. Vice chmn. Charter Commn. New Britain, Conn., 1976-77; mem. Conn. Senate from 6th dist., 1977-82, 98th-104th Congresses from 6th Conn. dist., Washington, 1983—; mem. ways and means com., subcom. health, chair oversight com. Pres. Friends of Libr., New Britain Pub. Libr., 1973-76, Radcliffe Club Northern Conn., 1973-75; bd. dirs., pres. Sheldon Cmty. Guidance Clinic, 1974-75; dir. religious edn. Unitarian Universalist Soc. New Britain, 1967-72; bd. dirs. United Way New Britain, 1976.79. Recipient Outstanding Vol. award United Way, 1976; English Speaking Union grantee, 1958-59. Republican. Home: 141 S Mountain St New Britain CT 06052-1511 Office: Ho of Reps 343 Cannon Bldg Washington DC 20515-0003*

JOHNSON, NELLIE BURKE, educator, college counselor; b. Phila., Nov. 10, 1939; d. Dennis and Claudia Bell (Spivey) B.; m. Walter W. Johnson, Aug. 29, 1964; chidren: Harvey W., Deidre E. BS, Temple U., 1962; MS, Phila. Coll. Textiles & Scis., 1994. Cert. instructional technologist. Elem. sch. tchr. Phila. Sch. Dist., 1962-76, math. resource tchr., 1976—; minority counselor Rosemont (Pa.) Coll., 1989—; liaison tchr. PATHS/Prism Partnership for Edn., Phila., 1980-84; workshop leader Nat. Coun. Tchrs. of Math., 1983-89; mem. K-12 Ctrl. Math. Com., Phila., 1984-88; asst. dir. Youth Summer Program, Greater Fedn. of Phila., 1986-88; mem. Divsn. Ednl. Testing and Evaluation, Pa. Dept. Edn., 1987. Vol. fundraiser United Negro Coll. Fund, Phila., 1990-93, Easter Seals, Phila., 1995; bd. dirs. altar guild Grace Episcopal Ch., Mt. Airy, Pa., 1990-92. Recipient Hon. membership Chapel of Four Chaplains, Pa., 1970, I.T.E.C., Commonwealth of Pa. PHEAA, 1991. Mem. ASCD, Jack and Jill of Am., Inc. (pres. local chpt. 1988-90, Nat. Mother of Yr. 1990), Phila. Kappa Silhouettes (pres. 1970-71), Alpha Kappa Alpha (mem.-at-large 1993-94). Office: Charles R Drew Sch 3800 Powelton Ave Philadelphia PA 19104

JOHNSON, NORMA HOLLOWAY, federal judge; b. Lake Charles, La.; d. H. Lee and Beatrice (Williams) Holloway; m. Julius A. Johnson, June 18, 1964. B.S., D.C. Tchrs. Coll., 1955; J.D., Georgetown U., 1962. Bar: D.C. 1962, U.S. Supreme Ct. 1967. Pvt. practice law Washington, 1963; atty. civil divsn. Dept. Justice, Washington, 1963-67; asst. corp. counsel Office of Corp. Counsel, Washington, 1967-70; judge D.C. Superior Ct., 1970-80, U.S. Dist. Ct. (D.C. dist.), Washington, 1980—. Bd. dirs. Judiciary Leadership Devel. Coun. Fellow Am. Bar Found.; mem. Nat. Bar Assn., Fed. Judges Assn., Am. Judicature Soc., Supreme Ct. Hist. Soc., Am. Inns of Ct. (William Bryant inn). Office: US Dist Ct US Courthouse 3rd & Constitution Ave NW Washington DC 20001

JOHNSON, NORMA J., specialty wool grower; b. Dover, Ohio, Aug. 30, 1925; d. Jasper Crile and Mildred Catherine (Russell) J.; m. Robert Blake Covey, Oct. 7, 1951 (div. 1960); 1 child, Susan Kay. Student Heidelberg Coll., 1943; cert. drafting techniques Case Sch. Applied Sci., 1944; student Western Res. U., 1945-47, Ohio State U., 1951, Muskingum Coll., 1965; AA, Kent State U., 1979, Buckeye Joint Vocat. Sch., 1979-84. Instr. arts and crafts Univ. Settlement House, Cleve., 1944; mech. draftswoman Nat. Assn. Civil Aeros., Cleve., 1944-46; mfrs. rep. Nat. Spice House, 1947-49; tchr. econs., home econs., English, math, history, high sch., Tuscarawas County Sch. System, New Philadelphia, Ohio, 1962-69; owner, mgr., operator Sunny Slopes Farm, producer of specialty wools and grains, Dover, Ohio, 1969—. Tchr., Meth. Sunday Sch., 1956-61; chaplain Winfield PTA, 1960; program dir. Brandywine Grange, 1960-62; troop leader Girl Scouts U.S.A., 1961-70; mem. assoc. bd. Norma Johnson Conservation Ctr. Recipient cert. of merit Tuscarawas County Schs., 1965, Ohio Wildlife Conservation award Tuscarawas County, 1972, 1st and 3d premiums for handspinning fleece, Ohio State Fair, 1984, 8th and 10th premiums, Mich. Stat Fair, 1985, proclamation of appreciation Bd. Commrs. Tuscarawas County, 1990, Zeisberger-Heckewelder medal Ohio State Ho. Reps. presented by Tuscarawas County Hist. Soc., 1992., State of Ohio Senate honor for commitment to conservaiton edn., 1992, Community Svc. award VFW, 1992. Mem. Mid States Wool Growers, Am. Angus Assn., Am. Tree Farm System, Nat. Arbor Day Found., Nat. Wildlife Fedn., Ohio Nut Growers Assn., Midwest Weavers Assn., Canton Weavers and Spinners, Ohio Hist. Soc., Ohio Arts and Crafts Guild, Tuscarawas County Geneal. Soc., Inc., Tuscarawas County Hist. Soc. Bldg. designed and constructed interior facilities for the Scheuer-Haus. Home and Office: 4033 State Route 39 NW Dover OH 44622-9742

JOHNSON, PAM, newspaper editor. Mng. editor Ariz. Republic, Phoenix. Office: Ariz Republic PO Box 1950 Phoenix AZ 85001*

JOHNSON, PAMELA DEA, curriculum coordinator; b. Moline, Ill., Nov. 13, 1943; d. Peter Dale and Doryse Maxine (Beckwith) J.; m. V. James Tansey, Dec. 21, 1963 (div. Aug. 1986); children: Melissa Ann Tansey Peña, James Roger Tansey. BA, U. Iowa, 1965; MA, U. No. Iowa, 1979; PhD, Iowa State U., 1995. Cert. elem. edn., adminstrn. Tchr. Waterloo (Iowa) Schs., 1975-87, program coord., 1982-87; dir. curriculum West Des Moines (Iowa) Schs., 1987-90, curriculum coord., 1990-95; bd. mem. Iowa Acad. Decathlon, 1989—. Mem. chancel choir Plymouth Ch., Des Moines, 1987—; vol. Rep. Party, Des Moines, 1988—; alumna Greater Des Moines Leadership Inst., 1991—; bd. dirs. Friends Found.-West Des Moines Libr., 1992—, v.p., 1995-96, pres., 1996—. Mem. ASCD, Iowa ASCD (bd. dirs. 1993—), Iowa Talented and Gifted (bd. dirs. 1982—, pres. 1996—), Sch. Adminstrs. Iowa, Nat. Assn. for Gifted Children, Phi Kappa Phi. Congregationalist. Home: 1103 Woodland Park Dr West Des Moines IA 50266-4951 Office: West Des Moines Schs 3550 George M Mills Civic Pkwy West Des Moines IA 50265

JOHNSON, PATRICIA BEA, medical, surgical nurse, mental health nurse; b. Memphis, Feb. 27, 1934; d. Walter Jones and Georgia Taylor; m. Clarence Johnson, July 23, 1961; 1 child, Pamela Suzanne Johnson Taylor. Diploma, Homer G. Phillips Sch. Nurses, St. Louis; diploma in nursing, L.A. City Coll.; diploma, Oakwood Coll.; postgrad., San Antonio Coll. CPR instr., BLS. Staff RN Homer G. Phillips Hosp., St. Louis, Barnes Hosp., St. Louis, Milw. City Hosp.; charge RN Brooke Army Med. Ctr./Fort Sam Houston, San Antonio. Contbr. to videos on nursing, skill books in field. Mem. Iota Phi Lamba.

JOHNSON, PATRICIA DIANE, psychotherapist, consultant; b. L.A., June 16, 1958; d. Frederick Alexander and Mary Jane (Andel) J.; m. John Joseph Casey, June 22, 1995. BA in Psychology, Calif. State U., Domiguez Hills, 1981; MA in Clin. Psychology, Antioch U., Marina del Rey, Calif., 1990. Psychotherapist, marriage and family therapist, cons., L.A., 1991—; head spl. treatment track for HIV clients Matrix Inst. on Addictions, Beverly Hills, Calif., 1991-93; project dir., case mgr. L.A. C.C. dist. L.A. Trade Tech. Coll., 1992—, instr. psychology, 1995; instr. psychology East L.A. Coll., Monterey Park, Calif., 1996—; cons. Motown Records, L.A., 1994; appearances as profl. expert on biracial people include Oprah Winfrey Show, Montel Williams Show, Marilyn Kagan Show; condr. workshops and class on interracial and biracial issues; mem. gender equity planning com. Calif. Chancellor's Office, Sacramento, 1995-96; staff writer, cons. Biracial Child and Interrace mags.; cons. on conflict resolution and orgnl. mgmt. to pub. and pvt. sector cos.; presenter in field. Contbr. articles to mags. Bd. dirs. for Women In Non-Traditional Employment Roles (WINTER), Long Beach, Calif., 1996; mem. Dem. Nat. Com., Washington, 1995—. Mem. APA (assoc.), NOW, Am. Assn. Marriage and Family Therapists (clin.), Calif. Psychol. Assn. (assoc.), Calif. Assn. Marriage and Family Therapists (clin.). Home: PO Box 291567 Los Angeles CA 90029 Office: 6345 Balboa Blvd Ste 218 Encino CA 91316

JOHNSON, PATRICIA DUREN, health insurance company executive; b. Columbus, Ohio, Oct. 22, 1943; d. James and Rosetta J. Duren; m. Harold H. Johnson, Jr., Dec. 25, 1965; 1 child, Jill. BS in Edn., Ohio State U., 1965. Tchr. various locations, 1966-72; sales rep. ITT Hartford, Portland, Oreg., 1972-73; sr. v.p. Blue Cross of Calif., 1975-92; v.p. nat. mktg. officer Wellpoint Health Networks, Calabasas, Calif., 1996—. Mem. editorial adv. bd. RN Times. Mem. cmty. adv. bd. KCET, L.A.; bd. dirs. Am. Cancer Soc., 1988-92; bd. trustees Calif. Hosp. Found. Mem. Am. Hosp. Assn., Women in Health Adminstrn., Delta Sigma Theta. Office: Wellpoint Health Networks Check Up Ctrs Am 26565 Agara Rd Calabasas CA 91302

JOHNSON, PATRICIA GAYLE, public relations executive, writer; b. Conway, Ark., Oct. 23, 1947; d. Rudolph and Frances Modene (Hayes) J. Student U. Calif., Irvine, 1965-68. Advance rep. Disney on Parade, Los Angeles, 1971-75; mktg. dir., dir. field ops. Am. Freedom Train, 1975-77; publ. rels. mgr. Six Flags, Inc., Los Angeles, 1977-81; mgr. corp. communications Playboy Enterprises, Inc., Los Angeles, 1981-82; external rels. mgr. Kal Kan Foods, Inc., Los Angeles, 1982-86; v.p. Daniel J. Edelman, Inc., 1986-88; sr. v.p. Amies Advt. and Pub. Rels., Irvine, 1988-89, dir. pub. rels. World Vision, Monrovia, Calif., 1989-92; v.p. The Bohle Co., L.A., 1992-95; dir. pub. rels. D.A.R.E. Am., L.A., 1995—; lectr. U. So. Calif., UCLA, Calif. State U., Northridge, Calif. State U., Dominguez Hills. Mem. Pub. Rels. Soc. Am. (past officer), Pub. Affairs Council, Delta Soc. (advisor). Mem. Foursquare Gospel Ch. Collaborator TV scripts; contbr. articles to various consumer and profl. mags. Office: The Bohle Co 1999 Avenue Of The Stars Los Angeles CA 90067-6022

JOHNSON, PATRICIA MARY, publisher; b. Evanston, Ill., Mar. 14, 1937; d. Harold W. and Florence M. (Miller) J.; children: William, Nancy, Richard. Degree in Interior Design LaSalle U., Chgo., 1972; student Art Inst., Chgo., 1970-73. Interior design communicator, producer/host weekly syndicated cable TV program on interior design, 1980-86; owner Design Communications, Rosenhayn, N.J., 1976; exec. dir., founder Corp. for Disabled/Handicapped, 1985—, A Positive Approach, Inc. Author: Eliminating Barriers From Your LIfestyle, 1988, Guide to Securing Housing for People with Developmental Disabilities, 1993; pub. (mags.) A Positive Approach, 1985-96, An Approach to Barrier Free Design, 1992; prodr. A Guide to Securing Independent Housing for Individuals with Disabilities, 1994. Recipient award N.J. Gov., 1985, Practitioner of Yr. award N.J. Rehab. Assn., 1987, Humanitarian Service award United Cerebral Palsy, 1987, Jefferson award NBC, 1988, Healing Community United Nations Pub. award, 1989, Community Svc. award Pres. George Bush, 1991.

JOHNSON, PAULA BOUCHARD, preschool administrator, educator, consultant; b. St. Albans, Vt., Dec. 9, 1954; d. Leo Paul and Irene Mary (Goldsbury) B.; m. John Howard Johnson, July 1, 1978; children: Mathieu, Meredith, Marc. BA in French and Drama, Marymount Coll., Tarrytown, N.Y., 1977; cert., Cath. Inst., Paris, 1975; EdM in Bilingual Edn., Boston U., 1981. Cert. 7-12 French tchr., N.Y.; cert. profl. std. 7-12 French tchr., K-12 bilingual and bicultural tchr., prin. lic. grades K-12, Vt. Bilingual specialist Enosburg (Vt.) Elem. Sch., 1977-78; adminstrv. asst. Bilingual Resource and Tng. Ctr., Boston, 1979-80; dir. Title VII Elem. & Secondary Edn. Act bilingual program Franklin N.E. Supervisory Union, Richford, Vt., 1980-82; tchr. French, Enosburg Falls (Vt.) H.S., 1983-84; instr. French, C.C. of Vt., St. Albans, 1985-92; co-owner, tr. Kinderhaüs Pre-Sch., St. Albans, 1990-95; mem. adj. faculty Johnson State Coll., 1981-82; French cons. Berkshire (Vt.) Elem. Sch., 1984-86; coord. A Bilingual Curriculum Guide for the Classroom, Tchr. Vols. I, II and III, 1982. Mem. St. Albans City Elem. Sch. Bd., 1988—, vice chmn., 1994-95, chair, 1995—; justice of peace Bd. Civil Authority, St. Albans, 1994—. mem. ASCD, Vt. Fgn. Lang. Assn. (bd. dirs. 1991-93), Vt. Assn. for Edn. Young Children. Home: 54 High St Saint Albans VT 05478-1651

JOHNSON, PAULINE BENGE, nurse, anesthetist; b. London, Ky., May 10, 1932; d. Chester G. and Bertha M. (Hale) Benge; m. Scottie W. Johnson, Apr. 29, 1950 (dec. 1976); children: Rita Johnson, Nita Johnson Yaw, Gina Johnson Carlson. AA, U. Ky., 1968; diploma, U. Cin. Sch. Nurse Anesthesia, 1971; BS summa cum laude, U. Cin., 1974, M., 1977, D., 1981. RN, Ohio, Ky., Tenn., Ind., W.Va., Fla., Tex.; cert. lic. RN anesthetist; cert. RN anesthetist. Staff anesthetist Jewish Hosp., Cin., 1971-72, Mercy North Hosp., Hamilton, Ohio, 1972-86, Ft. Hamilton Hosp., Hamilton, 1972-86, McCullough-Hyde Hosp., Oxford, Ohio, 1986-88; freelance anesthetist multiple hosps. Ohio, Ky., 1982-88; staff anesthetist, ind. contractor Shriner Burn Inst., Cin., 1989; pres., staff anesthetist, ind. contractor multiple hosps. Pauline B. Johnson Co., Inc., Ohio, Ky., Tenn., Ind., W. Va., Fla., Tex., 1989—; provider hosp. anethesia relief svcs. to under-serviced rural hosp. oper. rms., 1990—. Ch. clk. Lindenwald Bapt. Ch., Hamilton, 1955-72, mem. 1955-85, instr., 1955-76; mem. 1st Bapt. Ch., Hamilton, 1985—, NOW, 1978—, nominating com. major polit. party, Hamilton, 1986-89; mem., med. com. Planned Parenthood, Hamilton, 1987—. Scholar U. Cin., 1969-71, 77-81; recipient Spl. Recognition Higher Edn., Laurel County Homecoming, London, Ky., 1988. Mem. Am. Assn. Nurse Anesthetists (speaker nat. conv. 1982, speaker rsch. forum nat. meeting 1989, mem. nominating com. 1978), Ohio State Assn. Nurse Anesthetists (state bd. dirs. 1989-92, 88-90, 79-80, chair bylaws com. 1991-92, 92-93, nominating com. 1993-94, chair edn. com. 1990-91, pres. 1982-84, state editor Highlights 1974-82, co-chair state meeting 1982, pres. dist. 5 Cin. 1978, govt. rels. chpt. Greater Cin. chpt. 1976-87, speaker meetings), Kappa Delta Pi. Home: 128 S F St Hamilton OH 45013-4710

JOHNSON, PENELOPE B., librarian; b. Lewiston, Maine, Nov. 26, 1946; d. Wesley I and Bertha (Leavitt) J.; m. Milton F. Bornstein, July 12, 1969. BA, U. Maine, 1969; MS, Simmons Coll., 1970; CAGS, Boston U., 1978. Cert. profl. librarian. Children's libr. Wilmington Mem'l Libr., Wilmington, Mass., 1970-71, Worcester Pub. Libr., Worcester, Mass., 1971-79; children's cons. Ctrl. Mass. Regional Libr. System, Worcester, Mass., 1979-80; divsn. head Worcester Pub. Libr., Worcester, Mass., 1980-87, assoc. libr., 1987-91, head libr., 1991—. Pres. YMCA of Ctrl. Mass., 1989-91, bd. dirs., 1979-96; mem. exec. com. City Adminstrv. Affairs Assn., 1993-96. Mem. ALA, New England Libr. Assn., Mass. Libr. Assn., Simmons Coll. Alumni Assn. (pres. grad. sch. libr. and info. 1990-91). Office: Worcester Pub Libr 3 Salem Sq Worcester MA 01608-2015

JOHNSON, RAYMONDA THEODORA GREENE, humanities educator; b. Chgo., Jan. 12, 1939; d. Theodore T. and Eileen (Atherley) Greene; m. Hulon Johnson, June 27, 1964; children: David Atherley, Theodore Cassell, Alexander Ward. BA in English, DePaul U., 1960; MA in English, Loyola U., Chgo., 1965. Cert. high sch. English tchr., Ill. Tchr. high sch. English, Chgo. Pub. Schs., 1960-65; instr. English, Harold Washington Coll. (formerly Loop Coll.), City Coll., Chgo., 1965-66, asst. prof., 1966-91, assoc. prof., 1991-96, faculty advisor coll. newspaper, 1989-92, 96—, pres. faculty coun., 1990-92, chairperson English and Speech Dept., 1992—, coord. coll. assessment plan com., 1995—, prof., 1996—; mem. faculty coun., 1992-94. Middle sch. v.p. parents coun. Latin Sch., Chgo., 1974-76, trustee, 1987-93; mem. adv. bd. high jump program Latin Sch. Chgo., 1989—; cubmaster, leader cub scouts Boys Scouts Am., Chgo., 1974-81; active black creativity adv. com. Mus. Sci. and Industry, Chgo., 1984—. Recipient svc. award religious edn. program St. Thomas the Apostle Ch., Chgo., 1984. Mem. Twigs Mothers Club (pres. 1982-84), Alpha Kappa Alpha. Democrat. Roman Catholic. Home: 6747 S Bennett Ave Chicago IL 60649-1031 Office: Harold Washington Coll Rm 602A 30 E Lake St Chicago IL 60601-2420

JOHNSON, ROMANZA LAMOYNE, home economist; b. Scottsville, Ky., Dec. 1, 1939; d. John Coyner and Virginia Hall (Sledge) Oliphant; m. Ralph Eugene Johnson, June 22, 1961. BS in Home Econs., Western Ky. U., 1960, MA, 1968; postgrad., U. Tenn. Tchr. home econs. Scottsville High Sch., Ky., 1960-65, Western Ky. U., 1965-70; home economist Bowling Green (Ky.) Mcpl. Utilities, 1970-93. Contbr. articles to profl. jours. Hostess Eastwood Bapt. Ch., 1975—, chmn. pulpit flowers; bd. dirs. Ky. Heart Assn. (pres. 1984-85), 1978-88, chmn. pub. rels., 1980-81, 81-82, Ky. vice chmn. pub. rels., 1983-84, Ky. chmn. bd., 1984-86; mem. health com. Barren River Area Devel. Dist., 1979; mem. adv. coun. Home-Health Agy. City-County Hosp., 1974-94, v.p. and sec.; mem. Vols. in Action, 1981—, Bowling Green Interagy.; mem. adv. coun. Head Start of Bowling Green. Recipient Farm-City Activities award Warren County, 1972, 73, 74, Nat. Alma award, 1973, Honor award Warren County Soil Conservation Dist., 1974, Girls Club award, 1978-82, Vol. award Ky. Heart Assn., 1983; named Outstanding Citizen Bowling Green, 1976, Citizen of Yr. Optimist Club, 1984, recipient Hertiage award Landmark Assn., 1988. Mem. Am. Home Econs. Assn. (mem. nat. program com., pub. relations com.), Ky. Home Econs. Assn., Ky. Home Econs. in Bus. (nominating chmn. 1977-78, mem. com. 1978-79, nat. edn. and personal devel. com. 1977-78, 78-79, others), Bluegrass Elec. Womens Roundtable Assn. (pres. 1975-76, co-chmn. nat. meeting 1976, other positions), Ky. Nutrition Council (bd. dirs. 1977-80, treas. 1978-79, vice chmn. 1979-80, 80-81, pres. 1981-82, counselor 1981-82, Bowling Green area Nutrition Council chmn. 1984-85), Bowling Green-Warren County Home County Home Econmist (pres. 1968), Bowling Green Dist. Home Econs. Tchrs. (pres. 1963). Home: 3341 Cemetery Rd Bowling Green KY 42103-9063

JOHNSON, RONDA JANICE, fundraising consultant; b. Muleshoe, Tex., Sept. 28, 1943; d. Randolph Revere and Betty Jo (Pool) J. BS in Edn., U. Tex., Austin, 1966; MBA, Houston Bapt. U., 1980. Cert. fund raising exec. Tchr. Galena Park Ind. Sch. Dist./Houston Ind. Sch. Dist., 1966-68; adminstrv. asst. Houston-Galveston Area Coun., 1968-69, Johns Hopkins U. Applied Physics Lab., Columbia, Md., 1969-73; dir. adminstrn. Edmondson Coll. Bus., Chattanooga, 1973-76; dir. Branell Women's Coll., Atlanta, 1976-78; dir. devel. U. Tex. Health Sci. Ctr., Houston, 1978-84, Houston Symphony Orch., 1984-85, Houston Child Guidance Ctr., 1985-87; pres. ctrl. divsn. Douglas M. Lawson Assocs., Inc., Houston, 1987-96; instr. Vol. Support Ctr., Houston, 1992, continuing edn. div. Rice U., Houston, 1992-95. Adv. bd. Houston Achievement Pl., 1992; bd. dirs. Escape Ctr., Houston, 1992-94. Named Woman of the Yr. by S.W. Houston News, 1994. Mem. Nat. Soc. Fundraising Execs. (bd. dirs. 1989-96, pres. 1994-95), Planned Giving Coun., Houstonian Network. Republican. Home: 5612 Saint Moritz St Bellaire TX 77401-2617 Office: Cargill Assocs 4701 Altamesa Blvd Fort Worth TX 76163-0339

JOHNSON, ROSEMARY WRUCKE, personnel management specialist; b. Leith, N.D., Sept. 21, 1924; d. Rudolph Aaron and Metta Tomina (Andersen) Wrucke; m. Robert Johnson Jr., Sept. 28, 1945 (div. 1964). Student, George Washington U., 1944-45, 47, Nat. Art Sch., Washington, 1943-45. Supr. Displaced Persons Commn., Frankfurt, Germany, 1950-52, FBI, Washington, 1952-81; cons. position mgmt. orgn. design Arlington, Va., 1981—. Mem. NAFE, Classification and Compensation Soc., Soc. FBI Alumni (membership chmn. 1985-91), Internat. Platform Assn. Lutheran. Home and Office: 2525 10th St N Apt 820 Arlington VA 22201-1968

JOHNSON, RUBY LAVERNE, retail executive; b. Ada, Okla., Oct. 31, 1917; d. James Lee and Minta Estelle (Speights) Eppler; m. Albert Howard Johnson, Dec. 22, 1938; children: Phyllis, Richard, Jim, Bruce. With So. Bell Telephone, Ada, 1936-38; founder, owner, buyer Johnson's Furniture, Bossier City, La., 1963—. Mem. La. Home Furniture Assn., Bossier City C. of C., Univ. Club Shreveport. Home: 3376 Jon Rd Shreveport LA 71119-2236 Office: Johnsons Furniture 921 Westgate Ln Bossier City LA 71112-3525

JOHNSON, RUTH FLOYD, university educator, consultant; b. Plateau, Ala., Apr. 19, 1935; d. Nathan Daniel and Ora Anna (Ellis) Floyd; children: Anthony, Walter, Camille. Student, Tuskegee Inst., 1951-53; BS in History, Bowie (Md.) State U., 1970; MEd in Counseling, U. Md., 1977; PhD in Human Svcs. Adminstrn., Univ. for Humanistic Studies, San Diego, 1982. Cert. tchr., counselor. Radio personality Sta. WMOZ, 1953-56; owner, dir. Azalea Sch. Dance, 1954-56; numerous posts for fed. govt., 1957-69; tchr., adminstr. Pub. Schs. of Prince George's County, Md., 1970-78; tchr.-counselor Dunbar S.T.A.Y. Sch., Washington, 1974-75; instr. child and youth study divsn. U. Md., 1977-78; CEO Diametron Corp., 1979-81; tchr. L.A. Unified Sch. Dist., 1980-82, Pasadena (Calif.) Unified Sch. Dist., 1982-83, Rialto (Calif.) Unified Sch. Dist., 1984—; profl. devel. coord. Calif. State Polytech. U., 1995—. Author: Remediating Mass Poverty: Development of a Model Program, 1982, Pep Squad handbook, 1991, (with others: Government/Contemporary Issues: A Curriculum Guide, 1976. Active PTAs; mem. organizing com. Peppermill Village Civic Assn., 1966; vol. Boy Scouts Am., 1968-72, Sr. Citizens of Prince George's County, 1974-76; bd. dirs.Mill Point Improvement Assn., 1975-78, Combined Communities in Action, 1976-78; mem. Prince George's County Hosp. Commn., 1978; mem. Altadena Town Coun., 1983; founder Rialto Freedom and Cultural Soc., 1988; mem. Calif. 36th Dist. Bicentennial Adv. Com., 1989; mem. exec. com. Rialto Police/Community Rels. Team, 1993. Recipient Outstanding Svc. to Children and Yourh award Md. Congress PTA, 1969, Services to Boy Scouts Am. award, 1969, Svcs. to Sr. Citizens award, 1975, Community Svc. award Rialto Freedom and Cultural Soc., 1993, others. Mem. NEA, NAACP, Nat. Assn. Univ. Women, Nat. Coun. Negro Women, Zeta Phi Beta, Gamma Phi Delta. Home: PO Box 1946 Rialto CA 92377-1946

JOHNSON, SANDRA LYNN, civilian military employee; b. Chgo.; d. Albert Kenneth and Alice Pauline Johnson. BA, Miami U., Oxford, Ohio, 1971; M in Pub. Policy, U. Mich., 1974; diploma in nat. security mgmt., Nat. Def. U., 1989. Staff asst. Alaska Office on Aging, Juneau, 1973; mgmt. analyst Navy Fin. Ctr., Cleve., 1977-79, ops. rsch. analyst, 1979-86, data adminstr., 1986-91; data adminstr. Def. Fin. & Acctg. Svc.- Cleve. Ctr., 1991—; mem. Navy Data Adminstrn. Coun., Washington, 1987—, Cleve. Data Adminstrn./Subject Area Interest Group, 1991-94, Def. Fin. & Acctg. Svc. Data Adminstrn. Coun., Washington, 1991—. Mem. Am. Soc. Mil. Comptrs., VASA Order of Am., Data Adminstrn. Mgmt. Assn. Internat., Swedish Cultural Soc. Am., Ohio Watercolor Soc. (assoc.), East Light Yacht Club, Clev. Hiking Club, Phi Beta Kappa, Pi Sigma Alpha. Lutheran. Office: Def Fin & Acctg Svc-Cleve Ctr 1240 E 9th St Cleveland OH 44199

JOHNSON, SHANNON JOY, child advocate; b. Gretna, La., Sept. 16, 1967; d. Wayne Thomas Sr. and Suzanne Margaret (Vinyard) J. BA, Loyola U., New Orleans, 1990. Rsch. asst. Inst. Human Rels., New Orleans, 1989-90; outreach/ops. coord. Agenda For Children, New Orleans, 1990-93; cons. State of La., Baton Rouge, 1996—; kids count coord. Agenda For Children, New Orleans, 1993—; co-convenor Child Watch Coalition, New Orleans, 1995; mem. bd. dirs. Women's Resource Ctr., New Orleans, 1993—, La. Health Care Campaign, Baton Rouge, 1996—. Co-author, editor (data book) Kids Count Data Book on La. Children, 1993—. Vol. Project SHIELD/Agenda For Children, New Orleans, 1989-90, Women Elect 2000, New Orleans, 1992; gala vol. La. State U. Eye Ctr., New Orleans, 1991-96. Democrat. Home: 1707 Second St New Orleans LA 70113 Office: Agenda For Children 1326 Josephine St New Orleans LA 70130

JOHNSON, SHARON DENISE, office administrator, treasurer; b. Kans. City, Mo., Nov. 18, 1947; d. Leland Earl and Leona (Gover) Dailey; m. Herbert Johnson, Oct. 27, 1973. AA in Studio Art, Met. C.C., Kans. City, Mo., 1967; BA in Studio Art, U. Mo., Kans. City, 1969, MPA, 1976. Draftsman, stat. analysis JBM & Assoc., Kans. City, 1969-73; office mgr., adminstr. Felix Camera & Video, Overland Park, Kans., 1976-93; contr., treas. Hedlund & Assoc., Mission, Kans., 1993—. Chair fin. com. Luth. Ch. of Resurrection, Prairie Village, Kans., 1992-95, chair computer com., 1993—, mem. coun., 1991-95. Mem. Inst. Mgmt. Accts., William Jewell Fine Arts Guild, Phi Kappa Phi. Republican. Home: 8404 Meadow Ln Leawood KS 66206-1422 Office: Hedlund & Assoc 5909 Martway St Mission KS 66202-3338

JOHNSON, SHIRLEY ELAINE, management consultant; b. Terre Haute, Ind., Sept. 15, 1946; d. Mervil Ray and Sarah Kathryn (Tucker) W.; children: Richard Alan, Gary Michael. BA, DePaul U., 1991. Sec. to v.p. fin. Cenco Inc., Oak Brook, Ill., 1972-74, exec. asst. to group pres., 1974-75, asst. to chmn., 1975-77, corp. personnel/office mgr., 1977-80; corp. sec. Acadia Petroleum Corp., Denver, 1980-82; mgr. office Chapman, Klein & Weinberg, PC, Denver, 1982-84; asst. to chmn. The Heidrick Ptnrs., Inc., Chgo., 1984-92, v.p., 1992—. Mem. NAFE, Am. Mgmt. Assn., Exec. Women Internat., The River Club, Rsch. Roundtable. Home: 820 McKenzie Sta Dr Lisle IL 60532 Office: The Heidrick Ptnrs Inc 20 N Wacker Dr Ste 2850 Chicago IL 60606-3101

JOHNSON, SHIRLEY Z., lawyer; b. Burlington, Iowa, Mar. 6, 1940; d. Arthur Frank and Helen Martha (Nelson) Zaiss; m. Charles Rumph, Jan. 19, 1979. BA summa cum laude, U. Iowa, 1962; JD with honors, U. Mich., 1965. Bar: Calif. 1966, D.C. 1976, U.S. Supreme Ct. 1979. Trial atty. antitrust divsn. U.S. Dept. Justice, San Francisco, 1965-72; counsel antitrust subcom. U.S. Senate Jud. Com., Washington, 1973-75; ptnr. Baker & Hostetler, Washington, 1976-85; pvt. practice Washington, 1985—; mediator U.S. Dist. Ct., Washington, 1990—. Contbr. articles to profl. jours. Trustee The Textile Mus., Washington, 1991—, v.p. bd. trustees, 1994—. Mem. ABA, Women's Bar Assn. (bd. dirs. 1989-91), Am. Law Inst., Order of Coif, Phi Beta Kappa. Democrat. Office: 1250 Connecticut Ave NW Washington DC 20036

JOHNSON, STACI SHARP, lawyer; b. Dallas, July 3, 1960; d. William Wheeler and Rublyin (Slaughter) S.; m. Byron Wade Johnson, Jan. 8, 1984; 1 child, Mollie Beatrice. BA in Dance, U. Tex., 1983, BA in Govt., 1983; JD, Tex. Tech. U., 1987. Bar: Tex. 1987, U.S. Dist. Ct. (ea. dist.) Tex. 1989, U.S. Dist. Ct. (no. dist.) Tex. 1990, U.S. Supreme Ct. 1991. Law clk. Dist. Atty.'s Office, Lubbock, Tex., 1987; rsch. asst. law libr. Tex. Tech. U., Lubbock, 1985-87; assoc. Henderson Bryant & Wolfe, Sherman, Tex., 1987-93, Law Offices of Richard F. Harrison, 1993-95; asst. atty. gen. Child Support divsn. Office of the Atty. Gen. of Tex., 1995—. Vol. Lubbock Crisis Ctr., 1985-87; mem. outreach com. Grace United Meth. Ch., Sherman, 1992; judge law and psychology Jan. term session Austin Coll., Sherman, Tex., 1992; Sunday sch. tchr. Stonebridge United Meth. Ch., 1995-96. Recipient Pro Bono Svc. award Legal Svcs. North Tex., 1991; named one of Outstanding Young Women of Am., 1987. Mem. Tex. Bar Assn., Tex. Young Lawyers Assn., Tex. Assn. Def. Counsel (co-author workers' compensation newsletter 1988), Grayson County Bar Assn. (mem. county law libr. com. 1989—, chair 1989-90, pres. 1990-91, sec. 1988-89, pres.-elect 1989-90, chair successful nomination of Judge R.C. Vaughan for Tex. Bar Found.'s Outstanding Jurist award 1990, chair minimum continuing legal edn. video presentations 1990-93, chair Law Day program 1992), Coll. of State Bar Tex., Phi Delta Phi. Methodist. Home: 707 Long Hill Ct Mc Kinney TX 75070-3230 Office: Office of the Atty Gen 201 S Jupiter Allen TX 75002

JOHNSON, STEPHANIE KAY, school counselor; b. Water Vliet, Mich., Oct. 18, 1951; d. Dexter F. and Shirley L. (Fogelsanger) Beary; m. Loyd Edwin Johnson; 1 child, James Edwin. BA, Southwestern Adventist Coll., 1973; MA, Rollins Coll., 1991. Choir dir. Jefferson (Tex.) Acad., 1973-74; piano tchr., choir dir. Houston Jr. Acad., 1974-77; from English tchr., music tchr. to chaplain Mt. Pisqah Acad., Candler, N.C., 1977-88; sch. counselor Forest Lake Acad., Apopka, Fla., 1988—; student esteem program dir., trainer Walker Meml. Jr. Acad., Mt. Pisqh Acad., Forest Lake Acad., 1990-95. Mem. Am. Sch. Counseling Assn., Nat. Peer Helper Assn., Am. Assn. Christian Counselors. Adventist. Home and Office: Forest Lake Acad 3909 E Semoran Blvd Apopka FL 32703

JOHNSON, STEPHANIE L., financial analyst; b. Mpls., May 31, 1964; d. David Thomas and Vivian Lorraine (Weekley) J. BA, Oberlin Coll., 1986; MBA, NYU, 1992. Fin. analyst Am. Brands, Inc., Old Greenwich, Conn., 1988-92; mgr. corp. devel. Gen. Signal, Stamford, Conn., 1992-95, mgr. fin. analysis, 1996—. Mem. Phi Beta Kappa, Beta Gamma Sigma. Office: Gen Signal 1 High Ridge Park Stamford CT 06904

JOHNSON, SUE RENEE, art educator, artist; b. San Francisco, Mar. 13, 1957; d. Robert William and Helene (Crow) J. BFA, Syracuse U., 1979; MFA, Columbia U., 1981. Gallery dir. Lincoln Ctr. for Performing Arts Gallery, N.Y.C., 1982-83; instr. art Parsons Sch. Design, N.Y.C., 1987-89; workshop coord. Trangle Artists' Workshop, N.Y.C., 1989-93; asst. prof. art St. Mary's Coll. of Md., St. Mary's City, Md., 1993—; vis. asst. prof. Herron Sch. Art, Indpls., 1983-85. One-woman shows Syracuse U., 1982, Pa. State U., 1983, Alverno Coll., 1985, Dance Theatre Workshop, N.Y.C., 1995, Va. Ctr. for Creative Arts, 1995; group shows include Stiebel Modern, White Columns, Drawing Ctr., others. Fellow N.J. State Arts Coun., 1983-84, Mid-Atlantic Arts Found./NEA, 1994; recipient Sally and Milton Avery Outstanding Visual Arts Work award MacDowell Colony, 1991, Visual Art award Md. State Arts Coun., 1995. Mem. Coll. Art Assn. Office: St Marys Coll of Md Art Dept Saint Marys City MD 20686

JOHNSON, SUSAN L. B., human resource administrator; b. Granite City, Ill.; d. Richard C. and Helen N. (Newhart) Buenger; m. Brian K. Johnson, Apr. 25, 1987. BS, So. Ill. U., 1986; MS, Nat. Coll. of Edn., 1990. Office mgr. Soccer for Fun, Granite City, Ill., 1981-85; adminstrn. St. Louis U. Hosp., 1985-91, Barnes Hosp., St. Louis, Mo., 1991—. Office: Barnes Hosp 1 Barnes Plz Saint Louis MO 63110

JOHNSON, SUSIE M., city and regional planner, educator; b. Washington, Oct. 15, 1950. BA in Polit. Sci., Gettysburg Coll., 1972; MCP in City and Regional Planning, U. Calif., Berkeley, 1974. Regional task force staff analyst Office of the Gov. State of Calif.; legis. analyst Calif. State Legislature; econ. devel. planning analyst Port Authority N.Y. and N.J.; fin. and planning analyst corp. real estate divsn. Am. Express Co., N.Y.C.; bus. and fin. planning analyst Pitney Bowes, Stamford, Conn.; mgr. bus. devel. Mayor's Office Econ. Devel., N.Y.C.; mgr. mktg. and devel. Women's World Banking, N.Y.C.; interim exec. dir., dep. dir. East Harlem Block Cmty. Devel. Orgn., Inc., N.Y.C.; program officer econ. devel. program MS. Found. for Women, Inc., N.Y.C., 1991-94; dir. small minority and women's bus. devel. Office of the Bronx Borough Presedent/Bronx Overall Econ. Devel. Corp., 1995—; adj. prof. small bus. mgmt. SUNY, 1987—; bd. mem.

Take Charge!, Women's Empowerment Devel. Group Enterprise; guest lectr Urban Econ. Devel. Hunter Coll. Grad. Sch. City Planning & Urban Affairs. Author: Business Planning Basics: How to Write a Winning Business Plan, Guide to Contemporary American Craft Art Galleries; editor Social Venture Network Minority Vendor Directory. Appointed mem. Mayor's Small Bus. Adv. Bd., 1996—; mem. Democratic County Com., Manhattan County, 1993-95. Mem. Assn. for Enterprise Opportunity (former bd. mem., chmn. resource devel. and fin. com., appreciation award 1993, 94), Assn. Balck Found. Execs., Nat. Congress for Cmty. Econ. Devel. (co-chmn. 1996 ann. conf.), Urban Affairs Assn., Internat. Coalition on Women and Credit, Three Parks Democratic Club, Phi Lambda Sigma. Baptist.

JOHNSON, SUZANNE CURTIS, advertising and public relations executive; b. Anna, Ill.; d. Edward Earl Jr. and Juanita Curtis; m. Don Edwin Johnson, Aug. 23, 1959; children: Jennifer, Marc Wade. BS in English, Millikin U., 1960; MS in Journalism and Pub. Relations, So. Ill. U., 1985. Admissions counselor Millikin U., Decatur, Ill., 1980-88; devel. cons. John A. Logan Coll., Carterville, Ill., 1987; owner Suz-and Co., Pinckneyville, IL, 1990—, "Duffies" by Suz-, Pinckneyville, IL, 1990—. Co-author U.S.A. Parents' College Survival Handbook, 1986-87; staff writer (mag.) Accent on Southern Illinois, 1982-84; contbr. articles to mags. and newspapers. Trustee U. of the Ozarks, Clarksville, Ark., 1979-85; pres. Millikin U. Parents Assn., Decatur, Ill., 1980-84; county organizer Girl Scouts U.S.A.; founder Jr. Women's Club, Pinckneyville, Ill.; publicity chmn. ARC, Rep. Women, Perry County, Ill.; Ill. del. White House Conf. on Children and Youth. Named to Outstanding Young Women of Am., AAUW. Mem. Pub. Relations Soc. Am., Nat. Council for Resource Devel., AAUW (past pres. county and state coms.), Kappa Tau Alpha, Phi Kappa Phi, Pi Kappa Delta, Pi Beta Phi. Presbyterian. Home and Office: PO Box 467 605 W South St Pinckneyville IL 62274-1236

JOHNSON, SYLVIA SUE, university administrator, educator; b. Abiline, Tex., Aug. 10, 1940; d. SE Boyd and Margaret MacGillivray (Withington) Smith; m. William Ruel Johnson; children: Margaret Ruth, Laura Jane, Catherine Withington. BA, U. Calif., Riverside, 1962; postgrad., U. Hawaii, 1963. Elem. edn. credential, 1962. Mem. bd. regents U. Calif.; mem. steering com. Citizens Univ. Com., chmn., 1978-79; bd. dirs., charter mem. U. Calif.-Riverside Found., chmn. nominating com., 1983—; pres., bd. dirs. Friends of the Mission Inn, 1969-72, 73-76, Mission Inn Found., 1977—, Calif. Bapt. Coll. Citiznes Com., 1980—; bd. dirs. Riverside Comty. Hosp., 1980—, Riverside Jr. League, 1976-77, Nat. Charity League, 1984-85; mem. chancellors blue ribbon com., devel. com. Calif. Mus. Photography. Named Woman of Yr., State of Calif. Legislature, 1989, 91, Citizen of Yr., C. of C., 1989. Mem. U. Calif.-Riverside Alumni Assn. (bd. dirs. 1966-68, v.p. 1968-70).

JOHNSON, TERESA LAVERNE, mathematics educator; b. Valdosta, Ga., Feb. 19, 1945; d. Clyde H. and Nora Blanche (Smith) Blanton; 1 child, David W. BS in Math., Valdosta State U., 1967, MEd in Secondary Math., 1972. Cert. tchr., Ga., Fla. Math. tchr. Valdosta City Sch. Sys., 1967-72, Lowndes County Sch. Sys., Valdosta, 1972-75, Lanier County H.S., Lakeland, Ga., 1982-85, Meigs Jr. H.S., Fort Walton Beach, Fla., 1985-87, Camden County H.S., Kingsland, Ga., 1987—; math. instr. Ga. Mil. Coll., Kings Bay Submarine Base, Ga., 1987—, Troy State U., Kings Bay Submarine Base, Ga., 1996—. Den mother Cub Scouts/Boy Scouts Am., 1974-75; sec. Lanier County chpt. ARC, 1976-79; youth leader, adult dept. leader, mem. adult choir, mem. prayer group, Sunday sch. tchr., pianist, vacation Bible sch. tchr., Lakeland (Ga.) First Bapt. Ch., 1963-85; speaker Life-Cancer fundraiser, 1994. Mem. Profl. Assn. of Ga. Educators. Home: PO Box 38 Kingsland GA 31548 Office: Camden County HS 1585 Colerain Rd E PO Box 1549 Kingsland GA 31548

JOHNSON, VICKI LEE, elementary education educator; b. Coshocton, Ohio, Sept. 19, 1950; d. Willian Howard and Virginia Katherine (Blackson) Bush; m. James Prescott Johnson, July 31, 1968; children: James, Andrea. BS, Ohio State U., Newark, 1988; MA, Muskingum Coll., New Concord, Ohio, 1994; postgrad., Ashland U., Columbus, Ohio, 1994-95. Elem. tchr. River View Sch. Dist., Coshocton County, Ohio, 1988-95; elem. prin. Union Elem. Sch., Warsaw, Ohio, 1995—. Home: 46523 Township Road 479 Coshocton OH 43812-9573

JOHNSON, VICKI R., insurance company executive; b. Glens Falls, N.Y., June 19, 1952; d. Leonard H. and Rose (Petrosky) J. AB, Franklin and Marshall Coll., 1974; postgrad. U. Portland, 1979-80; MBA, UCLA, 1986. ChFC, CLU. Group mgr. The Prudential, San Diego, 1974—; mem. Oreg. Accident and Health Claim Assn., 1976-81. Pres., Ridgeview Condominium Assn., 1978-81; mem. Los Angeles Olympic Organizing Com., 1984; active San Diego Employee Benefit Coun. Fellow Life Mgmt. Inst.; mem. AAUW (Del Mar-Levcadia br.), Nat. Health Underwriters, UCLA Alumni Bd. (dir. at large, exec. MBA). Presbyterian. Home: 1691 Neptune Ave Encinitas CA 92024-1051 Office: 9171 Towne Centre Dr Ste 380 San Diego CA 92122-1237

JOHNSON, VICTORIA KAPRIELIAN, medical educator; b. The Bronx, N.Y., June 30, 1959; d. Walter V. and Julia (Hachigian) K. BA, Brown U., 1981; MD, UCLA, 1985. Diplomate Am. Bd. Family Practice. Resident Duke-Watts Family Practice, Durham, N.C., 1985-88; fellow UCLA Family Medicine, L.A., 1988-89; asst. clin. prof. Duke U. Med. Ctr., Durham, N.C., 1989—; chief, divsn. predoctoral edn. and faculty devel., dept cmty and family medicine Duke U., Durham, N.C., 1994—, fellowship dir., dept. cmty. and family medicine, 1994—; dir. inpatient svc. divsn. cmty. medicine Duke U., 1989-90, dir. sports medicine, 1989-94, dir. arts medicine, 1989-95, dir. predoctoral edn., 1990—. Mem. Am. Acad. Family Physicians (pub. com. 1985, mental health com. 1986-88), N.C. Acad. Family Physicians (edn. com. 1989-90, med. sch. affairs 1990—, chair of com. 1991—), Soc. Tchrs. Family Medicine (steering com., predoc. dir. working group 1995—). Office: Duke U Div Family Medicine PO Box 3886 Durham NC 27710-0001

JOHNSON, WILLIE SPOON, hospital administrator; b. Burlington, N.C., Apr. 14, 1943; d. William Luther and Ruth Viola (Baldwin) Spoon; m. Mark C. Johnson, Feb. 25, 1967; 1 child, Christy. Diploma in nursing, Watts Hosp. Sch. Nursing, Durham, N.C., 1964; BS, Pheiffer Coll., Misenheimer, N.C., 1971; MPH, U. N.C., 1983. RN, N.C., S.C., Calif.; cert. profl.in healthcare quality. Staff nurse med.-surg. Wesley Long Hosp., Greensboro, N.C., 1964-66; pub. health nurse Guilford County Health Dept., Greensboro, 1966-68; staff nurse ARC, L.A., 1967-68; pub. health nurse Health Dept., Sanford and Albemarle, N.C., 1968-72; dir. practical nurse edn. Sandhills C.C., Carthage, N.C., 1971-77; quality assurance/DRG coord. Humana Hosp. Greensboro, 1977-88; dir. quality mgmt. Women's Hosp. Greensboro, 1988—; mem. utilization rev. bd. Upjohn Health Care, Greensboro, 1980-92; cons. Quality Mgmt. Resources, Duluth, Ga., 1993—. Bd. mem. Health System Agy., 1976-77. Mem. Nat. Assn. Healthcare Quality (N.C. del. 1991, 93), Am. Soc. Healthcare Risk Mgmt., Healthcare Quality Certification Bd. (bd. mem. region III rep. 1993-96, sec.-treas. 1995-96), N.C. Assn. Healthcare Quality (bd. mem. 1989-94, co-chair edn. com. 1990-93). Lutheran. Home: 4532 Peeples Rd Oak Ridge NC 27310-9763 Office: Womens Hosp Greensboro 801 Green Valley Rd Greensboro NC 27408-7097

JOHNSON, WILMA DAVIS, business administration educator; b. Rock Hill, S.C., Nov. 26, 1931; d. Bratton Cecil and Wilma Marie (King) Davis; m. Horace Andral Johnson, Feb. 27, 1959; children: Andral, David, Gina, Karen, Kathryn. BS, Winthrop U., Rock Hill, 1955; MAT, Winthrop U., 1975; EdD, Tenn. State U., Nashville, 1991. Tchr. Coll. of Commerce, Rock Hill, 1954-59; dir. Jefferson Sch. Commerce, Chester, S.C., 1960-61; tchr. Aragon (Ga.) Elem. Sch., 1968-69, Crest Jr. H.S., Boiling Springs, N.C., 1975-76; instr. Cleve. C.C., Shelby, N.C., 1976-79; prof. bus. adminstrn. Trevecca Nazarene U., Nashville, 1979—; historian Delta Pi Epsilon, Nashville, 1986-89. Canvasser, Mothers March Against Birth Defects, Nashville, 1986-90, Heart Fund, Nashville. Recipient Disting. Svc. award Grace Nazarene Ch., Nashville, 1989. Mem. Nat. Bus. Edn. Assn., Phi Beta Lambda, Phi Kappa Phi. Republican. Nazarene. Home: 3045 Runabout Dr Nashville TN 37217-4308 Office: Trevecca Nazarene Coll 333 Murfreesboro Rd Nashville TN 37210-2834

JOHNSON, YVONNE AMALIA, elementary education educator, science consultant; b. DeKalb, Ill., July 1, 1930; d. Albert O. and Virginia O. (Nelson) J. BS in Edn., No. Ill. State Tchrs. Coll., 1951; MS in Edn., No. Ill. U., 1960. Tchr. Love Rural Sch., DeKalb, 1951-53, West Elem. Sch., Sycamore, Ill., 1953—; Bd. dirs. Sycamore Pub. Libr., 1974-84, pres. bd. dirs., 1984—, major donor chmn. capitol fund drive for addition to existing bldg. Contbr. articles to profl. publs. Bd. dirs. Sycamore Pub. Libr., 1974-84, pres. bd. dirs., 1984—, chmn. maj. fund drive for addition to libr., 1994—. Named DeKalb County Conservation Tchr., 1971, Gov.'s Master Tchr., State of Ill., 1984, Outstanding Agrl. Tchr. in the Classroom Dekalb County Farm Bur., 1993; grantee NSF, 1961, 62, 85, 86, 87; Sci. Lit. grantee State of Ill., 1992-94. Mem. NEA, ASCD, NSTA (cert. in elem. sci.), Ill. Sci. Tchrs. Assn., Ill. Edn. Assn., Sycamore Edn. Assn., Coun. for Elem. Sci. Internat. Office: West Elem Sch 240 Fair St Sycamore IL 60178-1641

JOHNSON-BROWN, HAZEL WINFRED, nurse, retired army officer; b. West Chester, Pa., Oct. 10, 1927; d. Clarence Lemont and Garnett (Henley) J.; RN diploma Harlem Hosp., N.Y.C., 1950; BS in Nursing, Villanova U., 1959; MS in Nursing, Tchr.'s Coll., Columbia U., 1963; PhD in Ednl. Adminstrn., Cath. U. Am., 1978. 1st lt. U.S. Army Nurse Corps, 1955, advanced through grades to brig. gen., 1979; mem. staff U.S. Army Med. Research and Devel. Command, Washington, 1967-73; dir. Walter Reed Army Inst. Nursing, Washington, 1976-78; asst. for nursing Office of Surgeon, Med. Command, Korea, 1978-79; chief Army Nurse Corps, Office Surgeon Gen., Dept of the Army, Washington, 1979-83; cons. edn. com. Operating Room Nurses Assn. Decorated Disting. Svc. medal, Legion of Merit, Meritorious Svc. medal, Army Commendation medal; recipient Evangeline G. Bovard Army Nurse of Yr. award Letterman Army Med. Center, San Francisco, 1964, Dr. Anita Newcomb McGee award DAR, Washington, 1971. Mem. Assn. Black Nursing Faculty, Black Women United for Action, Assn. U.S. Army, Nat. Assn. Military Family, Am. Nurses Assn., Nat. League Nursing, Sigma Theta Tau.

JOHNSON-CHAMP, DEBRA SUE, lawyer, educator, writer; b. Emporia, Kans., Nov. 8, 1955; d. Bert John and S. Christine (Brigman) Johnson; m. Michael W. Champ, Nov. 23, 1979; children: Natalie, John. BA, U. Denver, 1977; JD, Pepperdine U., 1980; postgrad. in library sci. U. So. Calif., 1983—. Bar: Calif. 1981. Sole practice, Long Beach, Calif., 1981-82, L.A., 1981-87, Woodland Hills, Calif., 1993—; legal reference librarian, instr. Southwestern U. Sch. Law, L.A., 1982-88; adj. prof. law, 1987-88; atty. Contos & Bunch, Woodland Hills, 1988-93. Editor-in-chief: Southern Calif. Assn. Law Libraries Newsletter, 1984-85. Contbr. articles to profl. journs. Mem. law rev. Pepperdine U., 1978-80. West Pub. Co. scholar, 1983; trustee United Meth. Ch., Tujunga, Calif., 1986-88. Recipient H. Wayne Gillis Moot Ct. award, 1980, Vincent S. Dalsimer Best Brief award, 1979. Mem. ABA, So. Calif. Assn. Law Libraries, Am. Assn. Law Libraries, Calif. Bar Assn., Southwestern Affiliates, Friends of the Library Los Angeles. Democrat. Home and Office: 5740 Valerie Ave Woodland Hills CA 91367-3967

JOHNSON-COUSIN, DANIELLE, French literature educator; b. Geneva, Nov. 7, 1943; d. Edouard Henri and Suzanne Louise (Maurer) Cousin; m. Harry Morton Johnson, Jan. 25, 1970; 1 child, Eliza Suzanne. Cert. de Maturite cum laude Coll. of Geneva, 1962; BA, U. Alaska, 1966; MA, Purdue U., 1968; PhD, U. Ill., 1977; postgrad. Oxford U., summer 1968, Northwestern U., 1968-69, Maximilian U., Munich, 1970, Lozanov Workshop, Tenn. State U., 1985, Mellon Regional Seminar Lit. Crit., Vanderbilt U., 1987. Vis. lectr. U. Ill.-Urbana-Champaign, 1976-77; asst. prof. French Amherst Coll., 1979-82; asst. prof. French, Andrew W. Mellon fellow Vanderbilt U., Nashville, 1982-88; dir. Vanderbilt-in-France program, Aix-en-Pce, 1984-85; assoc. prof. French Fla. Internat. U., 1988—; cons. Princeton Ednl. Testing Svcs., 1993—. Contbr. articles to profl. jours. and papers to profl. meetings and conferences. U. Mass. Oxford scholar, 1968; U. Ill. summer fellow, 1971, fellow, 1972-73, Inst. Advanced Studies in Humanities vis. hon. fellow U. Edinburgh (Scotland), summer 1979; and numerous others. Mem. MLA, S. Atlantic MLA, Am. Assn. Univ. Women, Am. Assn. Tchrs. of French, Am. Soc. 18th-Century Studies, ACLA, Assoc. of Literary Scholars & Critics, Soc. des Etudes Staëliennes (Paris), Friends of George Sand, Assn. Mme de Charrière (Neuchâtel), Soc. Benjamin Constant (Lausanne), Soc. des Professeurs Francais et Francophones en Am., Soc. Diderot (Langres), Centre de Recherches Révolutionnaires Et Romantiques (Clermont-Ferrand), Soc. des Amis du C.R.R.R., Assn. J.J. Rousseau (Neuchâtel), Soc. Vaudoise d'Histoire et d'Archéologie (Lausanne), Fondation C.F. Ramuz (Lausanne), Internat. Soc. for Study of European Ideas, Internat. Parliament of Writers (Strasbourg), Internat. Dir. of 18th Century Studies, Oxford, Assn. Literary Scholars and Critics, Pi Delta Phi. Home: 9805 SW 115th Ct Miami FL 33176-2582 Office: Fla Internat U Dept Modern Langs Univ Park DM 493 C Miami FL 33199

JOHNSON-DENNIS, MARGARET FRANCIS, accountant, educator; b. Keokuk, Iowa, Nov. 27, 1941; d. Luther R. and Flora Margaret (Gould) J.; m. J. Ned Casady, Aug. 11, 1961 (div. Jan. 1985); children: William W., Debra Roskamp, Paul; m. Jim E. Dennis, June 24, 1989. BS in Math., Parsons Coll., 1962; M of Acctg., We. Ill. U., 1988. CPA Ill., CMA. Faculty asst. Parsons Coll., Fairfield, Iowa, 1962-63; tchr. math Warsaw (Ill.) High Sch., 1965-68; mgr. fin. mgmt. Casady Farm, Warsaw, 1972—; teller, computer operator Hill Dodge Bank, Warsaw, 1980-86; tax preparer Tax Preparation Svc., Keokuk, Iowa, 1986; instr. acctg. Spoon River Coll., Canton, Ill., 1988-89; asst. prof. acctg. Quincy (Ill.) U., 1989-96; instr. Quincy CPA Rev., 1995—; vol. tchr. English as 2d lang. Warsaw Sch. Dist., 1979-80; vis. asst. prof. acctg. Monmouth Coll., Ill., 1996—; presenter in field. Chair bd. trustees Presbyn. Ch., Warsaw, clk. of session; vol. Fulton County Women's Crisis Intervention, Canton, 1988-89. Mem. AICPA, Am. Acctg. Assn., Ill. CPA Soc., Inst. Mgmt. Accts. (sec. 1989-93, CMA dir. 1993-96), Beta Alpha Psi, Chi Beta Phi, Phi Kappa Phi. Home: 705 N County Rd 400 Warsaw IL 62379

JOHNSON-LEESON, CHARLEEN ANN, former elementary school educator, insurance agent, insurance consultant; b. Battle Creek, Mich., June 10, 1949; d. Kenneth Andrews Leeson and Ila Mae (Weed/Lesson) McCutcheon; m. Lynn Boyd Johnson, Aug. 8, 1970; children: Eric Andrew, Andrea Marie. BA, Spring Arbor Coll., 1971; MS, Reading Specialist, Western Ill. U., 1990. Cert. elem. and secondary tchr., Mich., elem. tchr., Ill., reading K-9, Ill. Tchr. Hanover (Mich.) Horton Schs., 1972-73, Virden (Ill.) Elem. Sch., 1984-90; ins. agt. State Farm Ins., Virden, Ill., 1990—; collegiate and jr. high sch. cheerleading advisor in field; course leader Agt. Schs. 1, 2, and 3. Music dir., pianist Zion Luth. Ch., Farmersville, Ill., 1979-88, organist, pianist Olvie St. Friends, Battle Creek, 1961-67. Recipient Honor the Educator award World Book, 1988, 89, Soaring Eagle award, 1991; Wilson Stone scholar, 1990, Mich. State scholar, 1967. Mem. AUA, Internat. Reading Assn., Ill. Assn. Life Underwriters, Sangamon Valley Estate Planners, Wise Buys Investment Club, Millionaire Club (v.p. 1992), Multi Illini Club, Alpha Upsilon Alpha. Home: 2512 W Lake Dr Springfield IL 62707 Office: State Farm Agy Field Office 3001 Spring Mill Dr Springfield IL 62704

JOHNSON-LIBKIND, JEAN SUE See LIBKIND, JEAN SUE JOHNSON

JOHNSON-MCKEWAN, KAREN GABRIELLE, lawyer; b. San Francisco, Sept. 7, 1959; d. Douglas Eric and Rose Marie (Hoch) Johnson; m. Thomas Richard McKewan, Aug. 29, 1981; children: Caitlin Rose McKewan, Caroline June McKewan. BA in Internat. Rels. and Econs., U. Calif., Davis, 1981, JD, 1985. Bar: Calif. 1985. Reporter various newspapers and wire svcs. Davis and Sacramento, Calif., 1978-82; assoc. LeBoeuf, Lamb, Leiby and MacRae, San Francisco, 1985-86; assoc. Brobeck, Phleger and Harrison, San Francisco, 1987-92, ptnr., 1992—. Mem. Women in Comms., Inc. (treas. 1996-97). Democrat. Roman Catholic. Office: Brobeck Phleger & Harrison One Macker Spear St Tower San Francisco CA 94105

JOHNSTON, DARCIE LANG, campaign consultant; b. Montpelier, Vt., Dec. 30, 1966; d. James Arthur and Linda (Ortiz) J. BA in History, Randolph-Macon Woman's Coll., 1989. Systems adminstr. U.S. Senator James Jeffords, Washington, 1989-94; fin. dir. U.S. Senator James Jeffords, Montpelier, 1994-95; dir. major donors Rep. Senate-House Dinner, Washington, 1995; dir. of dels. Pete Wilson for Pres., Sacramento, Calif., 1995; campaign mgr. Sweetser for Congress, Montpelier, 1995—; fundraising cons. Vt. Rep. Party, Montpelier, 1995. Roman Catholic. Home: 604 S 23rd St Arlington VA 22202

JOHNSTON, DIANE MILLER, librarian; b. Attleboro, Mass., Nov. 30, 1947; d. Gordon William and Rena Mae (Miller) J. BA, Wheaton Coll., 1969; MA in Classics, NYU, 1970; MLS, Columbia U., 1981. Libr. N.Y. Pub. Libr., N.Y.C., 1970—; selection officer for classics, women's studies, Romanian and Albanian, N.Y. Pub. Libr., N.Y.C., 1981—. Office: NY Pub Libr Fifth Ave and 42d St New York NY 10018

JOHNSTON, GESSICA T., emergency physician; b. New Haven, May 11, 1940; d. George Leonard and Sadie (Grabel) Trager; m. Melvin M. Johnston, Mar. 8, 1989. BA, Cornell U., 1961; PhD, U. Calif., Berkeley, 1965; MD, U. Calif., L.A., 1971. Diplomate Am. Bd. Emergency Medicine. Dir. emergency medicine Yuma (Ariz.) Regional Med. Ctr., 1994—. Patent Yin Yang Clasp, 1993. Recipient Jewerly Gold Medal award INPEX, 1994. Office: 2400 Avenue A Yuma AZ 85364

JOHNSTON, GWINAVERE ADAMS, public relations consultant; b. Casper, Wyo., Jan. 6, 1943; d. Donald Milton Adams and Gwinavere Marie (Newell) Quillen; m. H.R. Johnston, Sept. 26, 1963 (div. 1973); children: Gwinavere G., Gabrielle Suzanne; m. Donald Charles Cannalte, Apr. 4, 1981. BS in Journalism, U. Wyo., 1966; postgrad., Denver U., 1968-69. Editor, reporter Laramie (Wyo.) Daily Boomerang, 1965-66; account exec. William Kostka Assocs., Denver, 1966-71, v.p., 1969-71; exec. v.p. Slottow, McKinlay & Johnston, Denver, 1971-74; pres. The Johnston Group, Denver, 1974-92; chair, CEO The Johnston-Wells Group, Denver, 1992—; adj. faculty U. Colo. Sch. Journalism, 1988-90. Bd. dirs. Leadership Denver Assn., 1975-77, 83-86, Mile High United Way, 1989-95, Colo. Jud. Inst., 1991—, Denver's 2% Club. Fellow Am. Pub. Rels. Soc. (pres. Colo. chpt. 1978-79, bd. dirs. 1975-80, 83-86, nat. exec. com. Counselor's Acad. 1988-93, sec.-treas. 1994, pres.-elect 1995, profl. award Disting. Svc. award 1992); mem. Colo. Women's Forum, Rocky Mountain Pub. Rels. Group (founder), Denver Athletic Club, Denver Press Club. Republican. Home: 717 Monaco Pky Denver CO 80220-6040 Office: The Johnston Wells Group 1512 Larimer St Ste 720 Denver CO 80202-1622

JOHNSTON, JOSEPHINE ROSE, chemist; b. Cranston, R.I., Aug. 9, 1926; d. Robert and Rose (Varca) Forte; m. Howard Robert Johnston, Mar. 7, 1949; 1 child, Kevin Howard. Student, Carnegie Inst., 1945-47; BS, Mich. State U., 1972, MA, 1973; postgrad., MIT, 1973—. Med. technologist South Nassau Community Hosp., Rockville Centre, N.Y., 1947-50; med. technologist Mich. State U., East Lansing, 1950-53, faculty specialist, 1966-76; dept. pathology Albany (N.Y.) Med. Ctr., 1953-54; med. lab. supr. Bulova Watch Co., Jackson Heights, N.Y., 1954-57; sr. chemistry technologist Mid Island Hosp., Bethpage, N.Y., 1958-66; sr. rsch. assoc. Uniformed Svcs. Univ., Bethesda, Md., 1976-78; asst. to chmn. dept. physiology Uniformed Svcs. Univ., Bethesda, 1978-82, assoc. to chmn., 1982—. Author: Patriarch: The Life of T.J. Haddy, 1994; contbr. articles to profl. jours. Danzinger Found., Lauderdale, Fla. Mem. Analytical Chem. Soc., Data and Electronic Soc., Internat. Platform Assn. Lutheran. Office: 6813 Woodville Rd Mount Airy MD 21771-7611

JOHNSTON, KATHLEEN SUSANNE, publications executive; b. Salt Lake City, May 30, 1951; d. Richard Sterling and Joan Ora (Simon) J.; m. Toby James McIntosh, June 6, 1982; children: Jamail, Marya. BA cum laude, Stephens Coll., 1973; MS, Columbia U., 1974. Domestic news mgr. McGraw Hill, N.Y.C., 1974-75; reporter McGraw Hill, Washington, 1975-80; writer AAAS and CBS Radio, Washington, 1980-82; editor Sci. Books and Films AAAS, Washington, 1982-89; dir. publs. Nat. Sci. Resources Ctr., Smithsonian Inst., 1989-94; cons. nat. sci. edn. stds. Nat. Acad. of Scis., Washington, 1993—; mem. benefits com. chair Smithsonian Women's Coun., Washington, 1992-94. Author: (with others) Vital Connections. Mem., pres. Lee Gardens Corp., 1982—; mem. Arlington (Va.) Housing Corp., 1987-92; sec., mem. Arlington Outdoor Edn. Assn., 1982-83. Mem. Women's Nat. Book Assn. (pres. 1987-89), Ednl. Press, Washington Book Publishers. Home and Office: 917 N Irving St Arlington VA 22201

JOHNSTON, KELLY A., customer service adminstrator; b. Syracuse, N.Y., June 19, 1962; d. Dean H. Abbott and Patricia (Blye) Tucci; m. Jay L. Johnston, Dec. 24, 1986; 1 child, Nicole. BA, Le Moyne Coll., Syracuse, 1983. Claims processor Mutual of Omaha, Addison, Tex., 1988-91; customer svc. rep. N. Tex. Healthcare Network, Irving, Tex., 1991-93; customer svc. supervisor Pvt. Healthcare Systems, Irving, 1993-96; claims info. mgr. All-state, Irving, 1996—. Mem. Internat. Customer Svc. Assn., Call Ctr. Network Group. Home: 3438 Sunyview Ln Flower Mound TX 75028

JOHNSTON, LINDA LOUISE HANNA, public health analyst. Student, Mt. Mercy Coll., 1961; BS, Slippery Rock State U., 1964; MEd, Pa. State U., 1966; postgrad., San Diego State U., 1979, Johns Hopkins U., 1986, U. Md., 1988. Educator various sch. sys. and colls., 1967-82; prof. health edn. Howard C.C., Columbia, Md., 1982-92; analyst office of planning and evaluation Health Resources and Svcs. Adminstrn., Rockville, Md., 1992-93; pub. health analyst, equal employment officer Maternal and Child Health Bur., Rockville, Md., 1993—; presenter in field. Contbr. articles to profl. jours. Mem. Nat. Consensus Bldg. Conf., Washington, 1994; elected mem. Howard County (Md.) Bd. Edn., 1992—; mem. Planning Com. for Annual Sch. Health Confs., Atlanta, 1992-95; mem. Md. Higher Edn. Wellness Team for State Wellness Conf., 1991; mem. Howard County AIDS Task Force, 1991-92; v.p. Health for Ea. Dist. Assn. Am. Alliance, 1991-93; pres. Howard C.C. Faculty, 1986-88; bd. dirs. Howard County Sexual Assault Ctr., 1984-86; mem. Subarea Health Coun., Howard County, 1983-86; bd. dirs. ARC, 1982-84. Recipient Creative Writing award Inst. Creative Rsch., 1993, Internat. C.C. Teaching Excellence award, Austin, Tex., 1989. Mem. Md. Assn. Health, Phys. Edn., Recreation and Dance (pres. 1987-88). Office: Maternal & Child Health Bur Health Resources & Svcs Parklawn Bldg Rm 11A-22 Rockville MD 20857

JOHNSTON, MARGUERITE, journalist, author; b. Birmingham, Ala., Aug. 7, 1917; d. Robert C. and Marguerite (Spradling) J.; m. Charles Wynn Barnes, Aug. 31, 1946; children: Susan, Patricia, Steven, Polly. A.B., Birmingham-So. Coll., 1938. Reporter Birmingham News, 1939-44; Washington corr. Birmingham News, Birmingham Age-Herald, London Daily Mirror, 1945-46; columnist Houston Post, 1947-69, fgn. news editor, mem. editorial bd., 1969-85, assoc. editor editorial page, 1972-77, asst. editor editorial page, 1977-85; lectr. in field, 1947—; instr. creative writing U. Houston, 1946-47, lectr. feature writing, 1965-66; lectr. Baker Coll., Rice U., 1977-78; del. Asian Am. Women Journalists Conf., Honolulu, 1965, 1st World Conf. Women Journalists, Mexico City, 1969. Author: Public Manners, 1957, A Happy Worldly Abode, 1964, Houston: The Unknown City, 1836-1946, (Winedale Historical Ctr. Ima Hogg award, Otis Lock award East Tex. Historical Assn.), 1991. Bd. dirs. Tex. Bill of Rights Found., 1962-64; bd. dirs. Planned Parenthood, 1953-55, Population Inst., 1985—; mem. Mcpl. Art Commn., 1971-76, Houston Com. Fgn. Relations. Recipient Theta Sigma Phi Headliner award, 1954, 1st ann. award of merit Houston Com. Alcoholism, 1956, cert. of merit Gulf Coast chpt. Am. Soc. Safety Engrs., 1960, Agnese Carter Nelms award Planned Parenthood, 1968, Sch. Bell award Tex. State Tchrs. Assn., 1974, 75, Gold Key award Nat. Council Alcoholism, 1975, Global award Population Inst., 1981. Mem. Tex. Soc. Architects (hon.), Philos. Soc. Tex., Phi Beta Kappa, Pi Beta Phi. Home: 5319 Cherokee St Houston TX 77005-1701

JOHNSTON, MARILYN FRANCES-MEYERS, physician, medical educator; b. Buffalo, Mar. 30, 1937; B.S., Dameon Coll., 1966; Ph.D., St. Louis U., 1970, M.D., 1975. Diplomate Am. Bd. Pathology, Diplomate Nat. Bd. Med. Examiners. Fellow in immunology Washington U., St. Louis, 1970-72; resident in pathology Washington U. Hosp., St. Louis, 1975-77, St. John's Mercy Med. Ctr., St. Louis, 1977-79; research fellow hematology St. Louis U. Sch. Medicine, 1979-80; instr. biochemistry St. Louis U., 1972-75, asst. prof. pathology, 1980-87, assoc. prof. 1987-92, prof., 1992—, dir. transfusion service, 1980—; med. dir. Mo./Ill. Regional Red Cross, 1983-88; area chmn. for inspection and accreditation Am. Assn. Blood Banks, Arlington, Va., 1984. Author: Transfusion Therapy, 1985. Recipient Transfusion Medicine Acad. award Nat. Heart, Blood and Lung Inst., 1984; Goldberger fellow AMA, 1979. Mem. Am. Assn. Blood Banks, Am. Assn. Immunologists,

Internat. Soc. Blood Transfusion, Am. Soc. Clin. Pathologists, Sigma Xi. Office: St Louis U Hosp 3635 Vista at Grand Saint Louis MO 63110

JOHNSTON, MARY ELIZABETH, library director; b. Boston, Apr. 12, 1959; d. Thomas William Johnston and Edna May Storer; m. Stephen Paul Capoccia, Oct. 3, 1982. BS, Suffolk U., 1982; MS, Simmons Coll., 1987. Cert. libr. Dir. Sherborn (Mass.) Libr., 1988—; chair sml. librs. con., Wa. MAss. Regional Libr. System, Boston, 1992, subregional rep. planning and budget com., 1993; mem. Mass. Bd. Libr. Commrs. Tech. Task Force, 1993-94. Mem. ALA, Mass. Libr. Assn., Beta Phi Mu. Office: Sherborn Library 4 Sanger St Sherborn MA 01770-1439

JOHNSTON, NANCY DAHL, data processing specialist, paralegal; b. Waco, Tex., Sept. 18, 1954; d. Howard Edward and Gladys Marie (Haynes) Dahl; children: Russell Edward, Dennis Aaron. Student, Tex. Woman's U., Denton, Victor Valley Coll., Victorville, Calif.; cert., Nat. Acad. Paralegal Studies, 1991. Data processing coord. Denton County, 1986-89; customer svc. mgr. Jet-Line Svc., Inc., Portland, Maine, 1989-92; exec. sec. to state court adminstr. State of Maine, Portland, Maine, 1993-95; billing specialist UNUM Corp., Portland, Maine, 1996—. Vol. Maine Audubon Soc., Global Response, Com. for Responsible Transp. Mem. NAFE, Maine Assn. Paralegals, Mcpl. Software Users Group (sec. 1988-89), Greenpeace. Home: PO Box 185 Standish ME 04084-0185

JOHNSTON, PAMELA MCEVOY, clinical psychologist; b. Forest Hills, N.Y., Mar. 8, 1937; d. Renny T. and Pamela (Sweeny) McE.; m. Percy H. Johnston, Jr. (dec.); children: Michael B. Anderson, Jeffery A. Thomas, Candy L. Watts, Kenneth L. Anderson. BA, U. La Verne, 1978, MS, 1980; PhD, U.S. Internat. U., 1982. Instr. psychology-sociology Allan Hancock Coll., Santa Maria, 1977-78; mental health asst. Santa Barbara City Alcoholism Dept., 1977-78; gen. mgr. Profl. Suites, San Diego, 1978-81; therapist Chula Vista (Calif.) Community Counseling Ctr., San Diego, 1978-85; research asst. U.S. Internat. U., 1979-82; rsch. coordinator Mil. Family research Ctr., San Diego, 1981-82; assoc. dir. Acad. Assoc. Psychotherapists, 1982-86; pvt. practice, San Diego, 1982—; pres. Borrego Springs Med. Clinic, 1987-90, 91—, Family Custody Santa Maria Superior Ct., 1994-95, Santa Barbara County Mental Health Assn., Santa Maria, Calif., 1995—; bd. dirs. Women's Internat. Ctr., 1984-86. Bd. dirs. San Diego County Mental Health Assn., 1978-84, Civic Fedn., 1993-95. State fellow, 1979, 80, 81, 82, Calif. State scholar, 1976-77. Mem. Am. Psychol. Assn., Calif. State Psychol. Assn., Rotary Internat. Republican. Roman Catholic. Home: PO Box 1198 Borrego Springs CA 92004-1198

JOHNSTON, VICKIE J., special education education consultant; b. Mt. Clemens, Mich., June 4, 1962; d. Thomas E. and Madelyn M. (Pearl) Proctor; m. Paul S. Johnston, Apr. 6, 1985; 1 child, Devon Elisabeth. B Music Edn., Drury Coll., 1984, MEd, 1987. Cert. spl. edn. and music tchr., Mo.; cert. K-12 mildly handicapped and seriously emotionally disturbed edn. tchr., spl. edn. adminstr., Ark.; cert. trainer Behavior Autism and Communication Assocs.; Project RIDE trainer, Level II COMP trainer. Elem. tchr. music, high sch. tchr. learning disabled Cabool (Mo.) Pub. Schs., 1984-85; tchr. seriously emotionally disturbed-behavior disordered Mansfield (Mo.) Pub. Schs., 1985-87; elem. resource behavior disordered tchr. Van Buren (Ark.) Pub. Schs., 1987-90, indirect svc. coord., 1990-91; regional cons. for serious emotional disturbance and autism Western Ark. Edn. Svc. Coop., Branch, 1991—; level II trainer Classroom Orgn. and Mgmt. Program, Nashville, 1993—. Mem. ASCD, Coun. for Exceptional Children, Coun. for Children with Behavioral Disorders (charter, state sec. 1992-93, pres.-elect 1994-95, pres. 1995—), Western Ark. Regional Children and Adolescent Svc. System Program (team mem.). Democrat. Lutheran. Office: Western Ark Edn Svc Coop RR 1 Box 104 Branch AR 72928-9715

JOHNSTON, VIRGINIA EVELYN, editor; b. Spokane, Wash., Apr. 26, 1933; d. Edwin and Emma Lucile (Munroe) Rowe; student Portland C.C., 1964, Portland State U., 1966, 78-79; m. Alan Paul Beckley, Dec. 26, 1974; children: Chris, Denise, Rex. Proofreader, The Oregonian, Portland, 1960-62, teletypesetter operator, 1962-66, operator Photon 200, 1966-68, copy editor, asst. women's editor, 1968-80; spl. sects. editor (UPDATE), 1981-83, 88-95, editor FOODday, 1982—; pres. Matrix Assos., Inc., Portland, 1975—, chmn. bd., 1979—; pres. Bone & Brew Inc.; bd. dir. Computer Tools Inc. Cons. Dem. Party Oreg., 1969, Portland Sch. Dist. No. 1, 1978. Mem. Eating and Drinking Soc. Oreg. (past pres.), We. Culinary Inst. (mem. adv. bd.), Portland Culinary Alliance (mem. adv. bd.), Internat. Food Media Conf. (mem. adv. bd.). Democrat. Editor Principles of Computer Systems for Newspaper Mgmt., 1975-76. Home: 4140 NE 137th Ave Portland OR 97230-2624 Office: Oregonian Pub Co 1320 SW Broadway Portland OR 97201-3469

JOHNSTONE, JEAN (JEAN JOHNSTONE RAY), health services company executive; b. Kansas City, Mo., Jan. 23, 1921; d. Paul Nugent and Cecelia Alta (Taylor) Johnstone; m. William Dean Ray, June 29, 1943 (dec. June 1973); children: William Johnstone Ray, Bradley Taylor Ray. Assoc. degree, Stephens Coll., 1940; AB, BS, U. Mo., 1943; MEd, Nebr. U., 1964; M of Med. Record, Emory U., 1970. Cert. registered record adminstr. Founder, pres. Mediquest, Inc., Palm Beach, Fla., 1972-85, AR/Mediquest, Inc., Lansing, Mich., 1982—; founder, dir. RX Med., Ft. Lauderdale, Fla., 1989-93; co-chair bd. Churchill, Delray, Fla., 1993-95; chmn. bd. Heart Labs. of Am., Boca Raton, Fla., 1995—. Editor: (book of poetry) Golden Trove, 1995; contbr. poetry to anthologies; patentee in field; sculptor. Mem. AAUW, DAR, Am. Health Info. Mgmt. Assn., Zonta. Office: AR/Mediquest Inc Ste 104 6105 W St Joseph Lansing MI 48917

JOHNSTONE, PAULA SUE, medical technologist; b. Springfield, Mo., July 5, 1947; d. Nathan Paul and Ima Louise (Glenn) Johnstone. BS, S.W. Mo. State U., 1969. Cert. med. technologist Am. Soc. Clin. Pathologists. Vol., Cox Med. Ctr., Springfield, 1964-68; lab., office aide Springfield Med. Lab., 1964-68; chief technologist Springfield Gen. Osteo. Hosp., 1969-73; staff technologist St. John's Regional Health Ctr., Springfield, 1973-75, evening supr., 1975-76, asst. adminstrv. dir., 1976-86, clin. lab. coord., 1986-89, lab. computer coord., 1989-96, hosp. LIS coord., 1996—. Dir., Glidewell Bapt. Ch. Tng., Springfield, 1984-85, chmn. budget and fin. com. 1986-87; pres. MER class Broadway Bapt. Ch., 1993-94, 95-96. Mem. NAFE, Am. Soc. for Clin. Lab. Sci., Mo. Soc. Med. Technologists (pres. 1976-77, columnist newsletter 1976-77), S.W. Mo. State U. Alumni Assn. Baptist. Clubs: Nat. Travel, Frommer's Dollarwise Travel Club. Avocations: International. travel, reading, knitting, house plants. Home: 1384-A E Arlington Springfield MO 65803-9622 Office: St Johns Regional Health Ctr 1235 E Cherokee St Springfield MO 65804-2203

JOHNSTONE, SALLY MAC, educational association administrator, psychology educator; b. Macon, Ga., Dec. 8, 1949; d. Ralph E. and Maxine A. J.; m. Stephen R. Tilson, 1977; 1 child, Emma. BS, Va. Poly. Inst., 1974, MS, 1976; PhD, U. N.C., 1982. Lectr. European div. U. Md., Heidelberg, Fed. Republic of Germany, 1982-84; instr. psychology U. Md., College Park, 1984-89, asst. dean, 1984-86, dir. Ctr. for Instructional Telecom., 1986-89; dir. Western Coop. for Ednl. Telecom., Boulder, Colo., 1989—; cons. Nowthwest Legis. Leadership Forum, Seattle, 1990, Pacific Northwest Econ. Region, Whistler, B.C., 1991, Calif. State U. System, 1993; invited panelist U.S. Dept. Edn., Washington, 1990, Aspen Inst., Washington, 1990, Pacific Northwest Econ. Region, 1991-92; presenter Pacific Rim Pub. U. Pres. Conf. Asia Found., Bangkok, Thailand, 1990, Workshops Pacific Telecom Coun., Honolulu, 1991; keynote spkr. Mountain States C.C. Assn., Farmington, N.Mex., 1991; spkr. EDUCOM, San Diego, 1991, edn. commn. states' Legislator's Workshop, Cin., 1992; mem. higher edn. conf. NEA, New Orleans, 1993, meeting Nat. Assn. State Univs. & Land Grant Colls. Distance Edn. & Telecomm. Working Group; witness U.S. Senate Subcom. Edn., Humanities and Arts, Washington, 1991; study advisor Corp. Pub. Broadcasting, 1993; panelist ann. meeting Am. Assn. Colls., 1994, Pacific Mountain Network, 1994, keynote regional meeting Am. Assn. Continuing Edn., 1994; bd. dirs. Okla. State U. Inst. Telecomm. Co-author: (with Witherspoon and Wasem) Rural TeleHealth: Telemedicine, Distance Education and Informatics, 1996; co-editor: (with Markwood) New Pathways to a Degree: Technology Opens the College, 1994. Judge sci. fair U. Hills Elem. Sch., Md., 1986-89. Grantee Annenberg/CPB Project, 1988, 91-96, Fund for Improvement of Postsecondary Edn., 1993, Dept. Commerce Nat. Telecomms. and Info. Adminstrn., 1994, U.S. Dept. Edn., 1991; recipient Disting. Rsch. award Nat. U. Continuing Edn. Assn., 1989. Mem. Am. Psychology Assn., Internat. Teleconferencing Assn. Office: Western Coop Ednl Telecoms 1540 30th St Boulder CO 80303-1012

JOLLY, BARBARA LEE, home healthcare professional; b. Central City, Nebr., Dec. 23, 1952; d. Louis Carl and Elizabeth (Mesner) Lindahl; m. William C. Zimmerman, June 2, 1973 (div. Aug. 1986); m. Daniel Ehs Jolly, May 7, 1988 (div. Mar. 1996). BS in Pharmacy, U. Mo., Kansas City, 1976, MPA, 1984. Registered pharmacist. Pharmacy supr. Truman Med. Ctr., Kansas City, Mo., 1976-87; dispensing dept. mgr. Nursing Ctr. Svcs., Hilliard, Ohio, 1988-90; v.p. Pharmacy Systems, Inc., Dublin, Ohio, 1990-96; chief pharmacist Integrity Healthcare Svcs., Inc., Columbus, Ohio, 1996—; trustee Ohio Cancer Pain Initiative, Columbus, 1987—. Bd. dirs. Open Ch., Inc., Columbus, 1991—; mem. social svcs. bd. Salvation Army, Kansas City, 1986-88; co-dir. Siouxland Hotline, Inc., Sioux City, Iowa, 1972-73; med. missionary, Honduras, 1992-96; del. to state conv. Easter Seals of Ohio, Columbus, 1989-91. Recipient Outstanding Vol. award Salvation Army, Kansas City, 1987. Mem. Am. Soc. Hosp. Pharmacists, Ohio Soc. Hosp. Pharmacists, Ohio Pharmacists Assn., Ky. Soc. Hosp. Pharmacists, Midwest Pain Soc., Pi Alpha Alpha (pres. 1983-84). Mem. United Ch. of Christ. Home: 6337 Tamworth Ct Dublin OH 43017

JOLLY, PENNY HOWELL, art history educator; b. N.Y.C., Feb. 3, 1947; d. William Richard and Mildred (Cerutti) Howell; m. George A. Jolly, Dec. 28, 1968 (div. Dec. 1990); children: Jennifer Ann, Joseph Howell; m. Jay Rogoff, June 16, 1994. BA, Oberlin Coll., 1969; MA, U. Pa., 1970, PhD, 1976. Prof. art history Skidmore Coll., Saratoga Springs, N.Y., 1976—. Contbr. articles to profl. publs. NDEA Title IV fellow, 1969-73. Office: Skidmore Coll Dept Art and Art History Saratoga Springs NY 12866

JONAKAIT, GENE MILLER, developmental neurobiologist; b. Evanston, Ill., May 15, 1946; d. William Cleveland and Mary Gene (Herren) Knopf; m. Randolph N. Jonakait, Mar. 21, 1970; 1 child, Amelia. AB, Wellesley (Mass.) Coll., 1968; MA, U. Chgo., 1969; PhD, Cornell U., 1978. Postdoctoral fellow Cornell U. Med. Coll., N.Y.C., 1978-81, asst. prof., 1981-85; asst. prof. Rutgers U., Newark, N.J., 1985-90, assoc. prof., 1990-94, prof., 1994—, chmn. dept. biol. scis., 1994-96, assoc. dean, 1996—; chmn. conf. com. N.Y. Acad. Scis., N.Y.C., 1991-92; chmn. summer conf. neuroimmunology Fedn. Am. Socs. Exptl. Biology, Bethesda, Md., 1994, 96. Author: (with others) Handbook of Experimental Pharmacology: Catecholamines II, 1989, Neuropeptides and Immunopeptides, Messengers in a Neuroimmune Axis, 1990, Substance P and Related Peptides, Cellular and Molecular Physiology, 1991; editor NeuroImmunoModulation; contbr. articles to profl. jours. including Neuron, Jour. Neurosci. Rsch., Jour. Neuroimmunology, Trends in Neurosci., Devel. Biology, Adv. Pharmacol., others. AAAS fellow Rutgers U. Bd. Trustees, 1990; Wellesley scholar, 1968; grantee NIH, 1982-84, 86-89, 93-96, BRSG, 1986-90, Rutgers U. Busch grantee, 1990—, grantee Johnson & Johnson, 1987-89, NIMH, 1990-93, Office Naval Rsch., 1990-93, NSF, 1993—, Merck Rsch. Labs., 1994-95. Fellow AAAS; mem. Soc. Neurosci. Office: Rutgers U 101 Warren St Newark NJ 07102

JONAS, ALICE MIRIAM, psychiatric nurse, program director; b. N.Y.C., Oct. 3, 1946; d. Jess and Lillian (Reinschreiber) Spitzer; m. Alan Jonas, May 23, 1971 (div. Dec. 1978); 1 child, Louisa; m. Philip Koch, May 8, 1982; 1 stepchild, Susan Koch. BSN, Boston U., 1968; MSN, CUNY, 1970. Cert. profl. counseler. Instr. Sch. Nursing Hunter Coll., N.Y.C., 1970-72; program dir. N. Charles Gen. Hosp., Balt., 1978-85, Homewood Hosp. Johns Hopkins Health Sys., Balt., 1985-91, Union Meml. Hosp., Balt., 1991—; cons. Helix Health Sys., Balt., 1991—; contact Adv. Bd. Co., Washington, 1993—; faculty assoc. Grad. Sch. Nursing U. Md., Balt., 1987—; bd. dirs. Transitional Living Coun., Balt., 1993—. Sr. nurse officer USPHS, 1972-74. Grantee NIMH, 1967-70. Mem. ANA, Am. Assn. Partial Hospitalization (presenter conf. 1988), Md Assn. Partial Hospitalization (pres. 1993—, v.p. 1987-92, bd. dirs. 1984-87), Sigma Theta Tau. Home: 71 Penny Lane Baltimore MD 21209 Office: 3300 N Calvert St Baltimore MD 21218-2820

JONAS, KATHLEEN RISTINEN, artist; b. Menahga, Minn., Mar. 30, 1936; d. Arno Feodor and Katherine (Koski) Ristinen; m. Abner Jonas, Sept. 9, 1956; children: Matthew, Arnold. BA, Concordia Coll., 1957; MA, U. Iowa, 1964; PhD, Ohio U., 1994. Exhbns. include Works on Paper, Western Ill. U., Macomb, 1974, Artifacts Gallery, Athens, Ohio, 1977, Potsdam (N.Y.) Prints, 1980, Plains Art Mus., Moorhead, Minn., 1982, Boston Printmakers, 1986, 89, Rourke Gallery, Moorhead, 1987, Morehead State U., 1988, Gov.'s Residence Art Collection, Columbus, Ohio, 1988-89, Davidson Print Exhbn., Elon, N.C., 1996, So. Graphics Coun. Traveling Exhbn., 1996—, others. Home: 2 N Shannon Athens OH 45701

JONAS, MARY, mental health counselor; b. Waterbury, Conn., May 23, 1961; d. Joseph Peter and Barbara Anne (Stolfi) Szczepanski; m. Marc Charles Jonas, Feb. 6, 1988. BA, U. Miami, 1982; MS, St. Thomas U., 1990. lic. mental health counselor. Dir., counselor YMCA, Miami, Fla., 1983-84; domestic violence, lead victim, witness counselor Office of the State's Atty., Miami, 1984-89; pvt. practioner Inst. for Family Therapy, 1992—; mem., cons. Adult Protection Team Spl. Task Force, 1987-90, Dade/Monroe Coalition on Aging, 1987-90, Developmentally Disabled Adults Task Force, 1988-89, Domestic Violence Task Force, 1987-89. Facilitator Parents of Murdered Children, 1986—. Recipient Polish Nat. Alliance scholarship, 1979, Cert. of Appreciation MADD, 1986. Mem. AACD, AAMFT.

JONAS, RUTH HABER, psychologist; b. Tel Aviv, Aug. 24, 1935; d. Fred S. and Dorothy Judith (Bernstein) Haber; m. Saran Jonas, Sept. 16, 1956; children: Elizabeth, Frederick. AB, Barnard Coll., 1957; MA, New Sch. for Social Rsch., 1977, PhD, 1987. Lic. psychologist, N.Y. 1st and 2d yr. intern clin. psychology NYU Med. Ctr.-Bellevue Hosp., N.Y.C., 1985-87; postdoctoral rsch. fellow NYU Med. Ctr., N.Y.C., 1987-88; clin. instr. psychiatry NYU Sch. Medicine, N.Y.C., 1987, clin. asst. prof. psychiatry, 1991; sr. psychologist forensic svc. Bellevue Hosp., N.Y.C., 1988—; pvt. practice psychology N.Y.C., 1988—. Fellow Am. Orthopsychiat. Assn.; mem. APA, N.Y. State Psychol. Soc., Manhattan Psychol. Assn., Am. Heart Assn. (fellow stroke coun.). Office: 200 E 33rd St Apt 10B New York NY 10016-4827

JONASSON, OLGA, surgeon, educator; b. Peoria, Ill., Aug. 12, 1934; d. Olav and Swea C. (Johnson) J. MD, U Ill., Chgo., 1958; DSc, Newberry (S.C.) Coll., 1982. Diplomate Am. Bd. Surgery (bd. dirs. 1988-94). Intern and resident U. Ill. Rsch. & Ednl. Hosps., 1959-64; prof. surgery U. Ill., 1975-87; chief of surgery Cook County Hosp., Chgo., 1977-86; chmn., prof. dept. surgery Ohio State U., Columbus, 1987-93; mem. staff U. Ill. Hosps., Chgo., 1993—. Markle scholar John & Mary Markle Found., 1969. Fellow ACS; mem. Am. Surg. Assn. Office: Am Coll Surgeons Surg Svcs Dept 55 E Erie St Chicago IL 60611-2731

JONDAHL, TERRI ELISE, importing and distribution company executive; b. Ukiah, Calif., May 6, 1959; d. Thomas William and Rebecca (Stewart) J. AA in Bus. Adminstrn., Mendocino Coll., 1981; BA in Adminstrn. and Mgmt., Columbia Pacific U., 1993. Sec. to planning commn. County of Mendocino, Ukiah, Calif., 1977-80; office systems analyst County of Mendocino, Ukiah, 1980-83; micro systems analyst Computerland of Annapolis, Md., 1983-84; controller Continental Mfg. Inc., Nacogdoches, Tex., 1984-87; mktg. mgr. Continental Mfg. Inc., Nacogdoches, 1987-89, dir. sales and mktg., 1989-95, sec., treas., 1985-95; ptnr. CAB Inc., Norcross, Ga., 1995—; Mem. JSEC Com. Tex. Employment Commn., 1990-93. Co-author: National Federation of Business & Professional Women Local Organization Revitalization Plan, 1989. Mem. NAFE, Tex. Fedn. Bus. and Profl. Women (state pres. 1994-95), Nacogdoches Bus. and Profl. Women (pres. 1987-88), Ukiah Bus. and Profl. Women (pres. 1981-82), Nacogdoches County C. of C. (small bus. adv. com. 1990). Home: 1587 Martin Nash Rd Lilburn GA 30247 Office: CAB Inc 5964 G Peachtree Corners E Norcross GA 30071

JONDLE, MARNITA LEA, journalist, desktop publisher; b. Shenandoah, Iowa, Mar. 13, 1962; d. Virgil Wayne and Helen Margaret (Larabee) Hein; m. Brian Joseph Jondle, Dec. 29, 1984. BS in Journalism, N.W. Mo. State U., 1984; postgrad., Laramie County C.C., 1987. Registered massage therapist, 1996. Mng. editor Corydon (Iowa) Times-Rep., 1984; advt. coord. Wyo. Stockman-Farmer, Cheyenne, 1985; classified line advt. rep. Wyo. Tribune-Eagle, Cheyenne, 1986; edn., gen. assn. reporter Wyo. State Tribune, Cheyenne, 1986-87, news editor, edn. reporter, 1987-91; city editor Wyo. Tribune-Eagle, Cheyenne, 1991; pub. rels. coord. Laramie County Sch. Dist. # 1, Cheyenne, 1991-93; temporary agrl. editor/county reporter Medina Valley Times/Castroville (Tex.) & La Coste New Bull., 1993; mktg. svcs. adminstr. Colin Med. Instruments Corp., San Antonio, Tex., 1993—; editor, designer, co-owner Jondle Pub., Cheyenne and San Antonio, Tex., 1990—. Mentor Laramie County Sch. Dist. # 1, Cheyenne, 1993; edn. adv. bd. dirs. Head Start, Cheyenne, 1993. Mem. Am. Med. Writers Assn., Am. Mktg. Assn., Soc. Profl. Journalists, Associated Bodyworks & Massage Profls., Cheyenne C. of C. (tourism com. 1990, edn. com. 1990). Home: 2838 Bear Springs Dr San Antonio TX 78245-2570

JONES, ALICE JANE, soil scientist, educator, federal agency administrator; b. Michigan City, Ind., Apr. 9, 1953; d. Harry William and Helen Zell (Moore) J.; m. Lloyd Norman Mielke, Oct. 22, 1988; children: Janet, Steve. BS Biology, Ecology, Mich. Tech. U., 1975; MS Soil Fertility, Mont. State U., 1978; PhD Soil, Physics Engring., Utah State U., 1982; Bus. Mgmt. cert., U. Nebr. Lincoln, 1992. Grad. rsch. asst. plant and soil sci. dept. Mont. State U., 1976-78; rsch. asst. agronomy dept. Wash. State U., 1978-79; grad. rsch. asst. soil sci. and biometeorology dept. Utah State U., 1979-80; instr. plant and soil sci. dept. Mont. State U., 1980-81, asst. prof. western triangle agrl. rsch. ctr., 1983-85; asst. prof. biology dept. Mont. Coll. Mineral Sci. and Tech., 1981-83; asst. prof., extension specialist agronomy dept. U. Nebr. Lincoln, 1985-88, assoc. prof., extension specialist agronomy dept., 1988—, vice chair agronomy dept., 1991-92, asst. dean, adminstrv. intern agrl. rsch. divsn., 1991-92; program mgr. natural resources food and social scis. divsn. USDA Cooperative State Rsch. Svc., Washington, 1992-93; dir. sustainable agriculture USDA, Washington, 1993-94; cons. and presenter in field. Contbr. numerous articles to profl. and popular jours., abstracts, author video prodns., computer software. Recipient Soil and Water Conservation Steward award State of Nebr., 1987, Outstanding Ednl. Aids Blue Ribbon award Am. Soc. Agrl. Engrs., 1987-91; numerous grants in field. Mem. Soil Sci. Soc. Am. (chair divsn. S6 1993-94), Soil and Water Conservation Soc. (fellow, mem. numerous coms., state commendation award 1987, pres'. citation award 1987, 88, internat. commendation award 1988, pres. Lincoln NE chpt., bd. dirs. 1989-92, vice pres. 1991-92), Internat. Soil Tillage Rsch. Orgn., Am. Soc. Agronomy (pub. rels. com. 1991—, fellow award com. 1992—), Nebr. Coop. Extension Assn. (outstanding new specialist award 1988), Sigma Xi, Gamma Sigma Delta (award com., Phi Sigma, Epsilon Sigma Phi. Office: Univ of Nebraska Lincoln 279 Plant Sci Lincoln NE 68588

JONES, AMY HOLDEN, film director, writer; b. Phila., Sept. 17, 1953; m. Michael Chapman. BA, Wellesley Coll., 1974. Editor: (movies) Hollywood Boulevard, 1976, American Boy, Corvette Summer, Second Hand Hearts; dir. Slumber Party Massacre, Love Letters, Mystic Pizza, Maid to Order, It Had to Be Steve; writer Beethoven, Indecent Proposal, The Getaway; writer (TV pilot) Jack's Place. Recipient Washington Nat. Student Film Festival 1st prize, 1973. Office: United Talent Agy 9560 Wilshire Blvd 5th Fl Beverly Hills CA 90212*

JONES, ANITA KATHERINE, computer scientist, educator; b. Ft. Worth, Mar. 10, 1942; d. Park Joel and Helene Louise (Voigt) J.; m. William A. Wulf, July 1, 1977; children: Karin, Ellen. AB in Math., Rice U., 1964; MA in English, U. Tex., 1966; PhD in Computer Sci., Carnegie Mellon U., 1973. Programmer IBM, Boston, Washington, 1966-69; assoc. prof. computer sci. Carnegie-Mellon U., Pitts., 1973-81; founder, v.p. Tartan Labs. Inc., Pitts., 1981-87; free-lance cons. Pitts., 1987-88; prof., head computer sci. dept. U. Va., Charlottesville, 1988-93; dir. def. rsch. and engring. Dept. Def., Washington, 1993—; mem. Def. Sci. Bd., Dept. Def., 1985-93, USAF Sci. Adv. Bd., 1980-85; bd. dirs. Sci. Applicatins Internat. Corp.; trustee Mitre Corp., 1989-93. Editor: Perspectives on Computer Science, 1977, Foundations of Secure Computation, 1971. Recipient Air Force Meritorious Civilian Svc award, 1985. Fellow ACM (editor-in-chief Transactions on Computer Sys. 1983-91); mem. IEEE, Nat. Acad. Engring., Sigma Xi.

JONES, ARDELLE HENRIETTA, retired home economist, educator; b. Ft. Payne, Ala.; d. Earl Augustus and Dessie Ellen (Skaggs) Thompson; m. Clyde Wilson Carroll, Sept. 12, 1947 (dec.); m. James Howard Jones, Nov. 25, 1959 (dec.); 1 child, Marvin Earl Jones (dec.). BS, Auburn U., 1945; MS, U. North Ala., 1966, Ednl. Specialist, 1977. Dietitian ECM Hosp., Florence, Ala., 1945-47; home econs. tchr. DeKalb County H.S., Ft. Payne, 1947-48; sci. tchr., 7th grade tchr., home econs. tchr. Lauderdale County Schs., Florence, Ala., 1948-69, county supr. food svc., 1969-89; cons. Architect for Kitchens, Florence, 1987-89. Cub scout leader Boy Scouts Am., Florence, 1967-68; pres. Lauderdale County Tchrs. Assn., Florence, 1966-67. Recipient Dist. award of merit Boy Scouts am., 1996. Mem. AAUW (mem. coms. 1989-96), Ret. Tchrs. Assn. (local v.p., pres.-elect 1996—), Pilot Club Internat. (local pres. 1987-88, mem. coms. 1976—). Democrat. Methodist. Home: 431 Cypress Mill Rd Florence AL 35630

JONES, BARBARA CHRISTINE, educator, linguist, creative arts designer; b. Augsburg, Swabia, Bavaria, Fed. Republic Germany, Nov. 14, 1942; came to U.S., 1964, naturalized, 1971; d. Martin Walter and Margarete Katharina (Roth-Rommel) Schulz von Hammer-Parstein; m. Robert Edward Dickey, 1967 (div. 1980); m. Raymond Lee Jones, 1981. Student U. Munich, 1961, Philomatique de Bordeaux, France, 1962; BA in German, French, Speech, Calif. State U., Chico, 1969, MA in Comparative Internat. Edn., 1974. Cert. secondary tchr., community coll. instr., Calif. Fgn. lang. tchr. Gridley Union High Sch., Calif., 1970-80, home econs., decorative arts instr., cons., 1970-80, English study skills instr., 1974-80, ESL coordinator, instr. Punjabi, Mex. Ams., 1970-72, curriculum com. chmn., 1970-80; program devel. adviser Program Devel. Ctr. Supt. Schs. Butte County, Oroville, Calif., 1975-77; opportunity tchr. Esperanza High Sch., Gridley, 1980-81, Liberty High Sch., Lodi, Calif., 1981-82, resource specialist coordinator, 1981-82; Title I coordinator Bear Creek Ranch Sch., Lodi, 1981-82, instr., counselor, 1981-82; substitute tchr. Elk Grove (Calif.) Unified, 1982-84; freelance decorative arts and textiles designer, 1982-85; internat. heritage and foods advisor AAUW, Chico, Calif., 1973-75; lectr. German, Schreiner Coll., Kerrville, Tex., 1993. Workshop dir. Creative Arts Ctr., Chico, 1972-73; workshop dir., advisor Bus. Profl. Women's Club of Gridley, 1972-74; v.p. Golden State Mobile Home League, Sacramento, 1980-82; mem. publicity Habitat for Humanity, Kerrville br., 1992-94. Designer weavings-wallhangings (1st place 10 categories, Silver Dollar Fair, Chico, 1970). Mem. AAUW (publicity dir. cultural activities Kerrville br. 1991-92), Am. Cancer Soc. (publicity 1992-95), United European Am. Club, Am. Assn. German Tchrs., U.S. Army Res. Non-Commd. Officer's Assn. (ednl. adv. 1984-86), German Texan Heritage Soc., Turtle Creek Social Cir. (pioneer 1992—), Kerrville Garden Club (publicity 1993—), Kappa Delta Pi. Avocations: weaving, fiber designs, swimming, skiing, internat. travel and culture. Home: 2894 Lower Turtle Creek Rd Kerrville TX 78028-9743

JONES, BEVERLY ANN MILLER, nursing administrator, patient services executive; b. Bklyn., July 14, 1927; d. Hayman Edward and Eleanor Virginia (Doyle) Miller. BSN, Adelphi U., 1949; m. Kenneth Lonzo Jones, Sept. 5, 1953; children: Steven Kenneth, Lonnie Cord. Chief nurse regional blood program ARC, N.Y.C., 1951-54; asst. dir., acting dir. nursing M.D. Anderson Hosp. and Tumor Inst., Houston, 1954-55; asst. dir. nursing Sibley Meml. Hosp., Washington, 1959-61; assoc. dir. nursing svc. Anne Arundel Gen. Hosp., Annapolis, Md., 1966-70; asst. adminstr. nursing Alexandria (Va.) Hosp., 1972-73; v.p. patient care svcs., Longmont (Colo.) United Hosp., 1977-93; pvt. cons., 1993—; instr. ARC, 1953-57; mem. adv. bd. Boulder Valley Vo.-Tech Health Occupations Program, 1977-80; chmn. nurse enrollment com. D.C. chpt. ARC, 1959-61; del. nursing adminstrs. good will trip to Poland, Hungary, Sweden and Eng., 1980. Contbr. articles to profl. jours. Bd. dirs. Meals on Wheels, Longmont, Colo., 1978-80, Longmont Coalition for Women in Crisis, Applewood Living Ctr., Longmont; mem. Colo. Hosp. Assn. Task Force on Nat. Commn. on Nursing, 1982; mem. utilization com. Boulder (Colo.) Hospice, 1979-83; vol. Longmont Police Bur., Colo.; mem. coun. labor rels. Colo. Hosp. Assn., 1982-87; mem.-at-large exec. com. nursing svc. adminstrs. Sect. Md. Nurses' Assn., 1966-69; mem. U. Colorado Task Force on Nursing, 1990; vol. Champs program St. Vrain Valley Sch. Dist.; vol. Longmont Police Dept.

Mem. Am. Orgn. Nurse Execs. (chmn. com. membership svcs. and promotions, nominee recognition of excellence in nursing adminstrn.), Colo. Soc. Nurse Execs. (dir. 1978-80, 84-86, pres 1980-81, mem. com. on nominations 1985-86). Home: 853 Wade Rd Longmont CO 80503-7017

JONES, BLANCHE, nursing administrator, orthopaedic and gerontology consultant; b. Edgecombe, N.C., Nov. 11, 1935; d. Cosevelt Ewuell and Evelyn (Jones) Harrison. Diploma, CUNY Hunter Coll., 1971; AAS, CUNY Medgar Evers Coll., 1986; BS in Cmty. Health, Gerontology and Med. Surg. Sci., St. Joseph's Coll., 1990. RN, N.Y.; RN in med.-surg., ANCC. Nurse aide Bellevue Hosp., N.Y.C., 1958-61, lic. practical nurse, 1961-71, staff nurse, 1971-72, head nurse, 1972-77; head nurse Coney Island Hosp., Bklyn., 1978-90, clin. supr., 1990—. Contbr. articles to profl. jours. Bd. dirs. Baisley Park Neighbors Inc., Jamaica, N.Y., 1968—. Mem. Orthopaedic Nurses Assn., N.Y. Nurses Assn. (del. 1972), Bowling League, Fishing Club, Target Pistol Club. Democrat. Baptist. Home: 15026 119th Ave Jamaica NY 11434-2009 Office: Coney Island Hosp 2601 Ocean Pky Brooklyn NY 11235-7791

JONES, BRENDA GAIL, school district administrator; b. Winnipeg, Man., Can., Nov. 5, 1949; d. Glen Allen and Joyce Catherine (Peckham) McGregor. BA, San Francisco State U., 1972; MA, U. San Francisco, 1983. Cert. tchr., sch. adminstr., Calif. Tchr. Lakeport (Calif.) Unified Sch. Dist., 1973-82, asst. prin., 1982-88, dir. ednl. svcs. and spl. projects, 1988—; instr. English Mendocino Coll., Ukiah, Calif., 1977-82. Mem. Assn. Calif. Sch. Adminstrs. (past pres. 1987, Lake County charter), Order Ea. Star (past matron Clear Lake chpt. 1995). Democrat. Episcopalian. Home: 1315 20th St Lakeport CA 95453-3051 Office: Lakeport Unified Sch Dist 100 Lange St Lakeport CA 95453-3297

JONES, BRENDA KAYE, public relations executive; b. Oklahoma City, Jan. 4, 1958; d. Bobby Lee and Betty Ruth (Hillburn) J. Student, Okla. Bapt. U., 1976-77; BA in Journalism, U. Okla., 1980. Polit. reporter, copy editor The Okla. Daily, Norman, 1978-80; field dir. of Coll. Reps. Rep. Nat. Com., Washington, 1979; office mgr. "Reagan for Pres. in 80" Fundraising Com., Washington, 1980; pers. rsch. asst. The White House and Office of Pres.-Elect, Washington, 1980-81; pub. liaison officer U.S. Info. Agy., Washington, 1982-85; office of presdl. pers. sr. writer The White House, Washington, 1985-88; sr. asst., prin. advisor to ambassador Am. Embassy, Bern, Switzerland, 1988-89; mktg. cons. The People's Pl., Washington, 1990-91; spl. asst. to chmn., dir. The Pres.'s Commn. on Mgmt. of A.I.D. Program, Washington, 1992—; dir. pub. rels Feed The Children, Oklahoma City, 1993-95; v.p. pub. rels. Ackerman McQueen Agy., Oklahoma City, 1995—. Vol. Don Nickles for U.S. Senate campaign and Ron Shotts for Gov., 1978; v.p. Okla. Coll. Reps., 1979-80, U. Okla. Washington Chpt., 1986-88. Selected as one of Outstanding Young Women in Am., 1979. Mem. Women in Comm. Inc., Pub. Rels. Soc. Am., Jr. League, Reagan Alumni Assn. Republican. Office: Ackerman McQueen 1601 NW Expressway Ste 1100 Oklahoma City OK 73118

JONES, CAROLINE ROBINSON, advertising executive; b. Benton Harbor, Mich.; d. Ernest and Mattie Robinson; 1 child, Anthony R. BA, U. Mich., 1963. Copywriter J. Walter Thompson, N.Y., 1963-68, v.p., co-creative dir. Zebra Assocs., Inc., N.Y., 1968-71; copywriter Kenyon & Eckhardt, N.Y., 1971-74; ptnr., creative dir. Black Creative Group, N.Y., 1974-77; v.p., creative group head Batten, Barton, Durstine & Osborn, Inc., N.Y., 1977; exec. v.p., creative dir. Mingo-Jones Advt., N.Y., 1978-86; pres. Caroline Jones Advt. Inc., N.Y.C., 1986-95, Caroline Jones, Inc., N.Y.C., 1995-95, pres. 1995—. Bd. dirs. Advt. Council, L.I.U., Smithsonian Ctr. Advt. History. Recipient creative advt. awards Clio, One Show, ANNY, NYMRAD, Art Dirs., CEBA, Ad Woman of Yr., 1990, and others, Matrix award Women in Comm.; mem. Com. of 200. Mem. N.Y.C. Partnership, N.Y. Mem. N.Y. Women's Forum. Home: 200 E 66th St New York NY 10021-6603 Office: Caroline Jones Inc 641 Lexington Ave Fl 21 New York NY 10022-4503

JONES, CAROLYN ELLIS, publisher, retired employment agency and business service company executive; b. Marigold, Miss., Feb. 21, 1928; d. Joseph Lawrence and Willie Decelle (Forrest) Peeples; m. David Wright Ellis, May 30, 1945 (div. 1966); children—David, Lyn, Debbie, Dawn; m. Frank Willis Jones, Jan. 1, 1980. Student La. State U., 1949. Owner, mgr. Personnel and Bus. Service, Inc., Greenwood, Miss., 1962-88, now v.p.; owner Honor Pub. Co., Greenwood, 1988—. Author: The Lottie Moon Storybook, 1985; Editor: An Old Soldier's Career, 1974. Contbr. articles to religious and gen. interest publs. Mem. adv. bd. career edn. Greenwood Pub. Schs., 1975-76, mem. adv. bd. vocat.-tech. dept., 1975-88; conf. leader Miss. Bapt. Convention Singles Retreat, 1980; Mission Service Corps del. Home Mission Bd., So. Bapt. Conv., Hawaii, 1979. Mem. Greenwood C. of C. (edn. com. 1980—, guest speaker career day program local high sch.), Mothers Against Drunk Drivers, Altrusa Internat., Nat. Fedn. Ind. Bus., Miss Delta Rose Soc., Miss. Native Plant Soc., Gideon Aux. (pres. 1986-88). Avocations: writing, rose exhibitions. Office: Honor Pub 802 W President Ave Greenwood MS 38930-3326

JONES, CAROLYN EVANS, small business owner; b. Middleboro, Mass., Sept. 5, 1931; d. King Israel and Kleo Estelle (Hodges) Evans; m. John Homer Jones, Sept. 9, 1966 (dec. July 1986); 1 child, David Everett. BA in English, Tift Coll., 1952; M of Religious Edn., Carver Sch. Missions and Social Work (now So. Bapt. Theol. Sem.), 1958; BA in Art, Mercer U., 1982. Cert. secondary tchr., Ga. Tchr. McDuffie County Bd. Edn., Thomson, Ga., 1952-53, Colquitt County Bd. Edn., Norman Park, Ga., 1953-55; missionary Home Mission Bd. SBC, New Orleans and Macon, 1958-66; spl. edn. tchr. Bibb County Bd. Edn., Macon, 1968-70, 75-79; owner, operator Laney Co. Imprinted Specialties, Macon, 1986—. Contbr. numerous articles and poems to profl. jours. Bible tchr. YWCA, Macon, 1980-85; deacon 1st Bapt. Ch., Macon. Mem. Macon-Bibb County C. of C., Internat. Tng. in Comm., Alumnae Assn. Tift Coll. (exec. com.), Greater Macon Women Bus. Owners Club. Democrat. Office: Laney Co Imprinted Specialties 2451 Kingsley Dr Macon GA 31204-1718

JONES, CATHERINE ANN, library administrator; b. Conneaut, Ohio, Apr. 30, 1936; d. Leo Joseph and Mary Louise (McGinty) Delanty; m. Thomas Michael Jones, May 18, 1957; 1 child, Michael S. BA in English, U. Ala., 1965; MLS, Cath. U. Am., 1969; MA in Govt., George Washington U., 1980. Chief reference libr. Exec. Office of Pres. Office of Mgmt. and Budget, Washington, 1968-72; assoc. dir. Washington office ALA, 1972-73; asst. univ. libr. George Washington U., Washington, 1973-78; chief congl. reference div. Congl. Rsch. Svc., Libr. of Congress, Washington, 1978—; adj. prof. Cath. U. Am., Washington, 1983—. Fellow Spl. Librs. Assn. (pres. Washington chpt. 1980-82, nat. treas. 1988-91, profl. devel. com. 1992—, Pres. award 1987, editor jour. issues summer 1988); mem. D.C. Libr. Assn. (pres. 1977-78), Cath. U. Alumni Assn. (pres. 1977-78, Alumni Achievement award 1994). Roman Catholic. Office: Libr Congress Congl Reference Div CRS Independence Ave & 1st St SE Washington DC 20540-7420

JONES, CHERRY, actress; b. Paris, TN, Nov. 21, 1956. Founder Amer. Rep. Theatre, Cambridge, Mass., 1980—; guest artist Arena Stage, Washington, D.C., 1983-84. stage appearances include: (with Amer. Rep. Theatre) King Lear, Twelfth Night, Major Barbara, Caucasian Chalk Circle, The Serpent Woman, Platonov, Life Is a Dream, The School for Scandal, The Three Sisters, As You Like It, Baby with the Bathwater, A Midsummer Night's Dream, Journey of the Fifth Horse, (Off Broadway) Desdemona, Goodnight Desdemona, Baltimore Waltz (Obie award), And Baby Makes Seven, Light Shining in Buckinghamshire, Big Time, Ballad of Soapy Smith, I Am a Camera, The Philanthropist, The Importance of Being Earnest, (Broadway) Angels in America, Our Country's Good, Macbeth, Stepping Out, The Heiress (Tony award Best Actress 1995), The Night of the Iguana, 1996; television appearances include: (movies) Alex: The Life of a Child, 1986; film appearances include: The Big Town, 1987, Light of Day, 1987, Housesitter, 1992. Office: Gersh Agy care Rhonda Price 130 W 42d St Fl 24 New York NY 10036*

JONES, CHRISTINE ELIZABETH, set designer; b. Summit, N.J., Oct. 6, 1966; d. Donald Edmund and Linda Gray (Greason) J. BA, Concordia U., Montreal, Que., Can., 1989; MFA, NYU, 1992. design tchr. Concordia U., 1994. Designer for plays at N.Y. Shakespeare Festival, Hartford Stage Co., Glimmerglass Opera, Oreg. Shakespeare Festival, Williamstown Theatre Festival, Am. Repertory Theatre, Theatre for a New Audience, Phila. Theatre Co., The Manhattan Class Co., Seven Stages, The N.J. Shakespeare Festival. Named Tyro Talent, Theatre Crafts Internat., 1993; FCAR grantee Govt. of Que., 1990-96. Office: Christine Jones Prince St Sta PO Box 44 New York NY 10012

JONES, CHRISTINE MASSEY, furniture company executive; b. Columbus, Ga., Nov. 7, 1929; d. Lewis Everett and Donia (Spivey) Massey; divorced; children—James Raymond, Jr., James David. Student, Ga. Southwestern Coll., 1947-48. With Muscogee Mfg. Co., Columbus, Ga., 1948-56; sec. to pres. Muscogee Mfg. Co., 1956; sec. to pres. and treas., corp. sec. Haverty Furniture Cos., Inc., Atlanta, 1956-59, sec. to pres. and treas., 1959-63, sec. to pres., 1963-72, sec. to pres., adminstrv. asst., 1972-74, sec. to pres., admintrv. asst., asst. corp. sec., 1974-78, corp. sec., 1978-86, corp. sec., asst. v.p., 1986-93; v.p. stockholder rels., sec. Haverty Furniture Cos., Atlanta, 1993—. Mem. Am. Soc. Corp. Secs. (securities industry com.). Home: 5245 Chemin De Vie NE Atlanta GA 30342-2547 Office: 866 W Peachtree St NW Atlanta GA 30308-1123

JONES, CONSTANCE PATTEN, colon hydrotherapist; b. Parris Island, S.C., Apr. 18, 1949; d. Joseph Kempton and Eunice (Patten) J. BA in Am. Studies with honors, U. N.C., 1971. Cert. Level I & II instr. colon hydrotherapy. Stock analyst, adminstr. Rudman Assocs., N.Y.C., 1973-78; colon hydrotherapist Boston, 1980—; pres. Northeast Assn. Colon Hygienist, Boston, 1990-93. Mem. Internat. Assn. Colon Hydrotherapy (bd. dirs. 1996-98). Home: 314A Webster St Needham MA 02194

JONES, CYNTHIA TERESA CLARKE, artist; b. Bklyn., Aug. 12, 1938; d. Arthur Ottio and Emma (Gibbs) Clarke; m. Robert H. Jones. Apr. 21, 1968 (div. Sept. 1977); 1 child, Kim Marie. Student, Bklyn. Mus., 1954-57, Art Career Sch., 1958, Hunter Coll., N.Y.C., 1963-65. One woman shows include Queens Borough Pub. Libr., Jamaica, N.Y., 1986, Baruch Coll., 1972; exhibited in group shows Queens Coun. on Arts Exhibit at Gertz Dept. Store, 1972, Queens Coll. Arts Festival, 1972, Dist. Coun. 37, First Art Exhbn., 1972, Artist Equity Group Shows Union Carbide, 1975, 77, Queensborough Community Coll. Invitational Show at Holocaust Resource Ctr., 1985, Pen and Brush, 1990, AQA Gallery, 1990, AQA at Chung Cheng Gallery at St. Johns U., 1987-90, Lowenstein Libr. Gallery Fordham U., 1989, Arlington Arts Ctr., 1991, Pursuit of Peace Ceres Gallery, 1991; designer cover Rsch. Papers Stats. Dept. Bernard M. Baruch Coll., 1973; works reprinted in Locally Speaking Local 384 newsletter. Donator work to MUSE Gallery, 1990, to Hale House Ctr., Inc.; active Women's Caucus for Art. Recipient Joseph Grumbacher Co. award, 1958, Scholastic Art award and key, 1957, Fine Arts award Queensboro Soc., 1973, Outstanding Painting award, 1973, France Lieber Meml. award Nat. Assn. Women Artists, Inc., 1992, two certs. of merit Latham Found., 1956-58; scholar Latham Found., 1958. Mem. Artists Equity Assn., Inc. N.Y., Alliance of Queens Artists, Coll. Art Assn., Queens Coun. on Arts, Ind. Arts Assn., Arlington Arts Ctr. Va., Queensboro Coll. Art Gallery (assoc.), Nat. Assn. Women Artists (The Kreindler Meml. award 1995), Print Club, Guild Am. Papercutters. Office: 11332 Mayville St Jamaica NY 11412-2410

JONES, DONNA MARIE, public administrator, lawyer, consultant; b. Chgo., Mar. 2, 1950; d. Nathaniel Beck Jr. and Merle Rowe; children: André Jamal, Aerle Taree. BA, U. Wis., 1972, JD, 1978; MPA, CUNY, 1984. Bar: Wis. 1979, U.S. Dist. Ct. (we. dist.) Wis. 1979. Recruitment-selection specialist U. Wis. System, Madison, 1973-75; pers. analyst City of Madison, 1975, asst. to city atty., 1976, contract compliance officer, 1979-82, 83-85, asst. to mayor, 1988-89; exec. asst. to dir. Maricopa County Human Resources Dept., Phoenix, 1982-83; dir. Office of Disadvantaged Bus. Devel. Milwaukee County, Milw., 1985-88; interim pers. mgr. Supreme Ct. of Wis., Madison, 1989; dir. Office of Affirmative Action and Compliance U. Wis., Madison, 1989-94, sr. adminstrv. program specialist, 1994-95; cons. in affirmative action/equal employment opportunites, human resource mgmt., diversity and sexual harassment, 1996—; bd. govs. State Bar Wis., Madison, 1990-92, program. co-chair com. for participation of women in the bar, 1990, 92; mem. nat. steering com. Nat. Conf. on Women and the Law, San Antonio, 1978-79. Author articles, book revs. and poetry. Bd. dirs. Child Devel., Inc., Madison, 1976; Wis. del. Nat. Observance of Internat. Women's Yr., Houston, 1977-78; bd. dirs. South Madison Neighborhood Ctr., 1981-82, Ko-Thi Dance Co., Inc., 1985-88, Dane County Cultural Affairs Commn., Madison, 1991-94; vol. The Atlanta Project, 1996. Named Woman of Distinction, Madison YWCA, 1982, one of Am.'s top bus. and profl. women Dollas and Sense Mag., 1992; Nat. Urban fellow, 1982. Mem. Madison NAACP, Legal Assn. for Women, Am. Assn. for Affirmative Action, Urban League of Greater Madison, Wis. Minority Women's Network, Wis. Women's Network.

JONES, DONNA MARILYN, real estate broker, legislator; b. Brush, Colo., Jan. 14, 1939; d. Virgil Dale and Margaret Elizabeth (McDaniel) Wolfe; m. Donald Eugene Jones, June 9, 1956; children: Dawn Richter, Lisa Shira, Stuart. Student, Treasure Valley Community Coll., 1981-82; grad., Realtors Inst. Cert. residential specialist. Co-owner Parts, Inc., Payette, Idaho, 1967-79; dept. mgr., buyer Lloyd's Dept. Store, Payette, Idaho, 1979-80; sales assoc. Idaho-Oreg. Realty, Payette, Idaho, 1981-82; mem. dist. 13 Idaho Ho. of Reps., Boise, 1987-90, mem. dist. 10, 1990—; assoc. broker Classic Properties Inc., Payette, 1983-91; owner, broker ERA Preferred Properties Inc., 1991—. Co-chmn. Apple Blossom Parade, 1982; mem. Payette Civic League, 1968-84, pres. 1972; mem. Payette County Planning and Zoning Commn., 1985-88, vice-chmn. 1987; field coordinator Idaho Rep. Party Second Congl. Dist., 1986; mem. Payette County Rep. Cen. Com. 1978—; precinct II com. person, 1978-79, state committeewoman, 1980-84, chmn. 1984-87; outstanding county chmn. region III Idaho Rep. Party Regional Hall of Fame, 1985-86; mem. Payette County Rep. Women's Fedn., 1988—, bd. dirs., 1990-92; mem. Idaho Hispanic Commn., 1989-92, Idaho State Permanent Bldg. Adv. Coun., 1990—; bd. dirs. Payette Edn. Found., 1993—, Western Treasure Valley Cultural Ctr., 1993—; nat. bd. dirs. Am. Legis. Exchange Coun., 1993—; mem. legis. adv. coun. Idaho Housing Agy., 1992—; committeeperson Payette County Cen.; chmn. Ways and Means Idaho House of Reps., 1993—; Idaho chmn. Am. Legis. Exchange Coun., 1991—. Recipient White Rose award Idaho March of Dimes, 1988; named Payette/Washington County Realtor of Yr., 1987. Mem. Idaho Assn. Realtors (legis. com. 1984-87, chmn. 1986, realtors active in politics com. 1982—, polit. action com. 1986, polit. affairs com. 1986-88, chmn. 1987, bd. dirs. 1984-88), Payette/Washington County Bd. Realtors (v.p. 1981, state dir. 1984-88, bd. dirs 1983-88, sec. 1983), Bus. and Profl. Women (Woman of Progress award 1988, 90, treas. 1988), Payette C. of C., Fruitland C. of C., Wiesr C. of C.. Republican. Home: 1911 1st Ave S Payette ID 83661-3003 Office: ERA Preferred Properties 1610 6th Ave S Payette ID 83661-3348

JONES, DOROTHY CLEMENT, accountant; b. Greensboro, N.C., July 6, 1963; d. Robert Ellsworth and Dorothy (Young) Clement; m. Benjamin Patrick Jones. BA in Acctg., N.C. State U., 1986, BA in Bus. Mgmt., 1987. Order processor Fin. Svcs. Corp., Atlanta, 1986; systems mgr. Continental Benefit Adminstrs., Atlanta, 1987-88; fin. analyst Systems Energy & Automation, Atlanta, 1988-90; bus. planning analyst Atlanta, 1990, sr. fin. analyst, 1991, project leader, 1992, bus. unit controller, 1993-94; controller Scripps Howard Cable TV, Atlanta, 1994—. Mem. Inst. Mgmt. Accts., Soc. Cable and Telecommunications Engrs., Women in Cable and Telecommunications. Office: 3425 Malone Dr Chamblee GA 30341-2707

JONES, EDITH HOLLAN, judge; b. Phila., Apr. 7, 1949; BA, Cornell U., 1971; JD with honors, U. Tex., 1974. Bar: Tex. 1974, U.S. Supreme Ct. 1979, U.S. Ct. Appeals (5th and 11th cirs.), U.S. Dist. Ct. (so. and no. dists.) Tex. Assoc. Andrews & Kurth, Houston, 1974-82, ptnr., 1982-85; judge U.S. Ct. Appeals (5th cir.), Houston, 1985—. Gen. counsel Rep. Party of Tex., 1981-83. Mem. ABA, State Bar Tex. Presbyterian. Office: US Ct Appeals 12505 US Courthouse 1515 Rusk Ave Houston TX 77002

JONES, EDITH IRBY, physician; b. Conway, Ark., Dec. 23, 1927; d. Robert and Mattie (Buice) Irby; m. James Beauregard Jones, Apr. 16, 1960 (dec. Oct. 1989); children: Gary, Myra, Keith. BS, Knoxville Coll., 1948; MD, U. Ark., 1952. Intern Univ. Hosp., Little Rock, Ark., 1952-53; gen. practice medicine Hot Springs, Ark., 1953-59; resident in internal medicine Baylor Coll. Medicine, Houston, 1959-62; practice medicine specializing in internal medicine Houston, 1962—; mem. staff Meth. Hosp., Houston, Hermann Hosp., Houston, Riverside Gen. Hosp., Houston, St. Elizabeth Hosp., Houston, St. Anthony Ctr., Houston, St. Joseph Hosp., Houston, Thomas Care Ctr., Houston; mem. staff Town Park, Houston, chief of staff; clin. asst. prof. medicine Baylor Coll. Medicine, U. Tex. Sch. Medicine, Houston; dir. Prospect Med. Lab.; bd. dirs., sec. Mercy Hosp. Comprehensive Health Care Group; ptnr. Jones, Coleman and Whitfield; grand med. examiner Ct. Calanthe Jurisdiction, Tex.; cons. Social Security Agy., Tex. Pub. Welfare Dept., Vocat. Rehab. Assn., Tex. Rehab. Commn.; bd. dirs. Standard Savs. Assn., Houston; numerous others. Contbr. articles to profl. jours. Bd. dirs. Houston Internat. U., Drug Addiction Rehab. Enterprise, March of Dimes, Houston, Odessey House, Houston; mem. adv. bd. Houston Council on Alcoholism; mem. com. for revising justice code, Harris County, Tex.; chmn. bd. trustees Knoxville Coll.; impartial hearing officer Houston Ind. Sch. Dist.; trustee Mut. Assn. for Profl. Service; mem. Community Welfare Planning Assn., Friends of Youth, Human Services Adv. Council, Houston; mem. bd. visitors U. Houston; numerous others. First black to receive BS and MD degrees from U. Ark; Dr. Edith Irby Jones Day proclaimed by State of Ark., 1985, City of Little Rock, 1985, City of N.Y.C., 1986; named One of 30 Most Influential Black Women Houston, 1984; inducted into Tex. Black Women's Hall of Fame, 1986; commended by Calif. Senate, 1969; proclaimation by city council, Houston, 1985, Mayor of Houston, 1986; recipient cert. of citation Ho. of Reps. State of Tex., 1986; portrait placed in entrance hall U. Ark. for Med. Scis., 1985; numerous others. Mem. AMA, Am. Med. Women's Assn. (v.p. Houston chpt.), Nat. Med. Assn. (past pres.), Lone Star Med. Assn., Harris County Med. Assn., Houston Med. Forum, Tex. Assn. Disability Examiners, Bus. and Profl. Women, Nat. Council of Negro Women, Inc. (v.p. Dorothy Height chpt.), NAACP, PTA, YMCA, Alpha Kappa Mu, Delta Sigma Theta, Eta Phi Beta. Democrat. Clubs: Links, Inc., Top Ladies of Distinction, Girl Friends, Inc., Women of Achievement, Inc. (Hall of Fame 1985). Lodge: Order Eastern Star. Home: PO Box 14207 Houston TX 77221-4207 Office: 2601 Prospect St Houston TX 77004-7737

JONES, ELAINE HANCOCK, humanities educator; b. Niagara Falls, N.Y., Feb. 17, 1946; d. Roy Elmer and June Edna (Clark) Hancock; m. Ralph Jones III, Oct. 9, 1971 (div. June 1981). AAS in Comml. Design, U. Buffalo, 1962; BFA, SUNY, Buffalo, 1971, MFA in Painting, 1975; postgrad., Fla. State U., 1993—. Med. illustrator Roswell Park Meml. Inst., Buffalo, 1967-70; designer, animator Acad. McLarty Film Prodns., Buffalo, 1970-73; publs. designer Buffalo/Erie County Hist. Soc., 1974-78; dir. publs. Daemen Coll., Amherst, N.Y., 1978-80; owner, art dir. Plop Art Prodns., Melbourne, Fla., 1981-86; instr. humanities Brevard C.C., Melbourne, 1986—; prof. humanities Brevard campus Rollins Coll., Melbourne, 1995—. One-woman shows include SUNY, Buffalo, 1974, Upton Gallery, N.Y., 1975, Gallery Wilde, Buffalo, 1978; exhibited in group shows at Fredonia Coll., N.Y., 1975, Upton Gallery, 1975, Brevard Art Mus., Melbourne, Fla., 1987. Mem. docent program Art Mus./Sci. Ctr., Melbourne, 1983-84, mem. edn. com., 1995—; officer Platinum Coast chpt. Sweet Adelines Internat., 1984-90. Nat. Merit scholar, 1971-75; recipient cert. of merit Curtis Paper Co., 1977; N.Y. State Coun. on Arts grantee, 1975. Republican. Home: 2240 Sea Ave Indialantic FL 32903-2524 Office: Brevard CC Liberal Arts Dept 3865 N Wickham Rd Melbourne FL 32935-2310

JONES, ELAINE R., civil rights advocate; b. Norfolk, Va., Mar. 2, 1944. AB, Howard U., 1965; LLB, U. Va., 1970. Dir.-counsel, atty. NAACP Legal Def. and Ednl. Fund, Washington; mem. panel arbitration Am. Stock Exch. Recipient Recognition award Black Am. Law Student Assn, 1974, Spl. Achievement award Nat. Assn. Black Women Attys., 1975. Mem. Nat. Bar Assn., Internat. Fedn. Women Lawyers, Old Dominion Bar Assn., Va. trial Lawyers Assn., Delta Sigma Theta. Office: NAACP Legal Defense & Ednl Fund 99 Hudson St Fl 16 New York NY 10013-2815*

JONES, ELIZABETH WINIFRED, biology educator; b. Seattle, Mar. 8, 1939; d. Kenneth Clifford Harris and Dorothea (Dowty) J. BS, U. Wash., 1960, PhD, 1964. Postdoctoral fellow MIT, Cambridge, 1964-67, instr. in biology, 1967-69; asst. prof. Case Western Res. U., Cleve., 1969-74; assoc. prof. Carnegie Mellon U., Pitts., 1974-82, prof., 1982—; vis. scientist Sch. Medicine Wash. U., 1981-82; adj. prof. in psychiatry U. Pitts., 1985—; mem. genetics tng. com. NIH, Bethesda, Md., 1972-73, mem. genetics study sect., 1976-80, 84-86, chair, 1990-93. Editor: Molecular Biology of the Yeast Saccaromyces, 2 vols., 1981, 82, Molecular and Cellular Biology of the Yeast Saccaromyces, 2 vols., 1991, 92; editor Genetics, 1980-96, editor-in-chief 1997—, Yeast, 1984—, Molecular Biology of the Cell, 1992—; assoc. editor Ann. Rev. of Genetics, 1990—. Recipient Rsch. Career Devel. award NIH, 1971-74, 75-77. Fellow AAAS; mem. Am. Soc. Microbiology, Am. Soc. Cell Biology (coun. 1992-95), Genetics Soc. Am. (pres. 1987), Am. Soc. Human Genetics. Office: Carnegie Mellon U 4400 5th Ave Pittsburgh PA 15213-2617

JONES, ELLEN ELIZABETH, public relations professional; b. Flint, Mich., Jan. 7, 1953; d. Ralph Eugene and Mary Louise (Crank) J. BS, U. Mich., 1975. Reporter, anchor WEYI TV, Flint, 1975-77; press aide U.S. Congress, Washington, 1977; legis. aide Mich. State Senate, Lansing, 1977-79; reporter, documentary producer WNEM TV, Saginaw, Mich., 1979-83; dep. press sec. Gov. James Blanchard, Lansing, 1983-85; dir. pub. info. Mich. Dept. Mgmt. and Budget, Lansing, 1985-90; media rels. mgr., on-line content developer, web mgr. Mich. Dept. Agriculture, Lansing, 1990—; co-mgr. Mich. Recycles Alcoholism, Lansing, 1994—. Gov.'s advance team Gov. James Blanchard, 1983-90. Recipient Alice award Nat. Commn. on Working Women, 1980. Mem. Pub. Rels. Soc. Am. (Silver Anvil award 1996), Women in Comms. Office: Mich Dept Agriculture 611 W Ottawa Lansing MI 48933

JONES, ERIKA ZIEBARTH, lawyer; b. Washington, June 10, 1955; d. Thomas Arthur and Ruth (Helm) Ziebarth; m. Gregory Monroe Jones, June 7, 1978; 1 child, Katherine Anne. AB, Georgetown U., 1976, JD, 1980. Bar: D.C. 1980, U.S. Ct. Appeals (D.C. cir.) 1987, U.S. Supreme Ct. 1987. Atty., regulatory analyst U.S. Office Mgmt. and Budget, Washington, 1980-81; spl. counsel Nat. Hwy. Traffic Safety Adminstrn., Washington, 1981-85, chief counsel, 1985-89; of counsel Mayer, Brown and Platt, Washington, 1989-90, ptnr., 1991—. Bd. dirs. Immaculata Coll. High Sch., 1985-88. Mem. ABA, Fed. Bar Assn., Women's Bar Assn. D.C., D.C. Bar Assn., Phi Beta Kappa. Republican. Roman Catholic. Home: 6612 31st Pl NW Washington DC 20015-2302 Office: 2000 Pennsylvania Ave NW Washington DC 20006-1812

JONES, EVE SHEILA, sales executive; b. Lynchburg, Va., June 21, 1944; d. William and Virginia Elizabeth (Brown) Tapley; m. Adam S. Jones; children: Christopher, Adam Lamont. BS in Nursing Edn., Hampton (Va.) U., 1966. Head nurse VA Hosp., Mpls., 1966-69; staff nurse Mt. Sinai Hosp., Mpls., 1970-73; sr. sales dir. MK Cosmetics, Dallas, 1978—. Baptist. Home: 324 Evergreen Ct Schaumburg IL 60193

JONES, FLORENCE M., music educator; b. West Columbia, Tex., Apr. 11, 1939; d. Isaiah and Lu Ethel (Baldridge) McNeil; m. Waldo D. Jones, May 29, 1965; children: Ricky, Wanda, Erna. BS, Prairie View A&M U., 1961, MEd, 1968; postgrad., Rice U., 1988, U. Houston, 1980. Cert. tchr. elem. edn., math. Tchr. English and typing Lincoln High Sch., Port Arthur, Tex., 1961-62; tchr. grades three and four Houston Ind. Sch. Dist., 1963-90, tchr. gifted and talented, 1990-94; tchr. piano Windsor Village Liberal Arts Acad., Houston, 1994—; dist. tchr. trainer Houston Ind. Sch. Dist., 1985-90; shared decision mem. Sch. decision Making Team, 1993-94; coord. gifted/talented program, Petersen Elem. Sch., Houston, 1990-94; participant piano Recital Hartzog Studio, 1985-88; film previewer Houston Media Ctr. Curriculum writer Modules to Improve Science Teaching, 1985; author sci. pop-up book, 1980, gifted/talented program, 1994; contbr. poems to lit. jours. Youth camp counselor numerous non-denominational ch. camps, U.S., 1961-89; active restoration of Statue of Liberty, Ellis Island Found., N.Y.C., 1983-85; lay minister Ch. of God, 1961-94. Recipient Letter of Recognition for Outstanding Progress in Edn., Pres. Bill Clinton, 1994, Congresswoman Sheilia Jackson Lee, Tex. Gov. George Bush, State Rep. Harold V. Sutton Jr., Houston Mayor Bob Lanier, Tex. Gov. Ann Richards; Gold Cup/Highest Music award Hartzog Music Studio, 1987, Diamond Key award Nat. Women of Achievement, 1995, Editors Choice award Nat. Library Poetry, 1995, others. Mem. NEA, Houston Assn. Childhood Edn. (v.p.

1985-88), Assn. for Childhood Edn. (bd. dirs. 1979-91), Houston Zool. Soc., World Wildllife Fund, Nat. Storytelling Assn., Tejas Storytelling Assn. (life), Soc. Children's Book Writers and Illustrators, Nat. Audubon Soc., Am. Mus. Natural History, Tex. Ret. Tchrs. Assn. (life), Internat. Soc. Poets (disting. life mem.), others. Democrat. Home: 3310 Dalmatian Dr Houston TX 77045-6520

JONES, GAIL KATHLEEN, educational administrator; b. Oklahoma City, June 28, 1935; d. Lloyd Clifton Jones and Cleo Kathleen (Shackelford) Ahlstedt; m. Jerry Lynn Jones, Aug. 8, 1954; children: Kathleen DeVaughan, Jerry Clifton, Gregory Taylor. BA in English, Cen. Wash. U., 1971. Coordinator outreach program Ellensburg City Library, Wash., 1971-77; dir. alumni affairs and community rels. Cen. Wash. U., Ellensburg, 1977-95, ret., 1995, now disting. emeriti adminstr.; Pub. newsletter Central Today, 1977—. Mem. Wash. Gov.'s com. for Handicapped, 1978-83; officer United Way Bd., Ellensburg, 1982-86; mem. Beautification Commn., Ellensburg, 1980-83, Distributive Edn. Adv. Council, Ellensburg, 1978-82, chair, Ctrl. Wash. U. Centennial, 1990-92. Mem. Council Advancement and Support Edn., AAUW, LWV, Ellensburg C. of C. Presbyterian. Lodge: Soroptimists (charter pres. Kittitas County (Wash.) club 1986-88, dist. dir. 1990-92). Home: 405 N Anderson St Ellensburg WA 98926-3145

JONES, GWENDOLYN, business management educator; b. Sawyerville, Ala., Jan. 27, 1950; d. William Jr. and Emmo O'Neal (Hayes) Hudson; m. Herbert L. Jones, Dec. 24, 1970; children: Vincent (dec.), Erica L. BA, Notre Dame Coll., Euclid, Ohio, 1981; MBA, Baldwin Wallace Coll., 1983; PhD, U. Akron, 1989. Prodn. contr. Bendix Warner & Swasey, Cleve., 1976-78, supr. stenography, 1978-82; program mgr., instr. Cuyahoga C.C., Cleve., 1983-85, program coord., instr., 1985-88; vis. prof. bus. mgmt. tech. U. Akron, Ohio, 1988-89; asst. prof. bus. mgmt. tech. U. Akron, 1989-93, assoc. prof. bus. mgmt. tech., 1994—; vocat. counselor cmty. edn. svcs. dept. Cuyahoga C.C., Cleve., 1985-86, program mgr. cmty. edn. svcs. dept., 1986-87; mentor for minority students dept. minority affairs U. Akron, Ohio, 1989-90, instr. pre-algebra pre-coll. programs, 1989-92, presenter freshman orientation pre-coll. programs, 1992, orientation spkr. upward bound program, spring 1993, supr. tech. edn. program dept. secondary edn., spring 1994, supr. higher edn. program internship, summer 1994, supr. tech. edn. student tchr., summer 1994; faculty advisor U. Arkron's Chpt. Bus. Profls. Am. State and Nat. Recognition in Competitive Events, 1994—; mem. various coms. U. Akron's Cmty. and Tech. Coll.; presenter U. Akron, Ohio, spring 1991, guest spkr., fall 1992; keynote spkr. Greensboro (Ala.) H.S., summer 1992; ind. contractor, dir. fin. Office of Mayor, Village Oakwood, Ohio, 1992-93; cons. in field; spkr. and presenter in field. Textbook reviewer: Practical Business Math Procedures, 3d edit., summer 1991, Business Mathematics, fall 1993, Practical Business Math Procedures, 4th edit., fall 1994. mem. adv. com., adult edn. and devel. programs Akron (Ohio) Pub. Schs., 1991-92; mem. Adv. Com. for the Bedford Bd. Edn. Adult Edn., 1991-93; program facilitator Project HOPE-HUD Programs for Residents of Oakwood, Oakwood Village, 1992-93; bd. trustee Project Reading Enrichment for Adult Devel., Cleve., 1993—, co-chair pub. rels., 1993—; adv. bd. mem. vital vol. program Bedford (Ohio) City Schs., spring 1994; advisor bd. tech-prep. asst. chair Medina (Ohio) Career Ctr., Medina (Ohio) Pub. Sch. Sys., fall 1994. Recipient Cert. leadership Nat. Inst. for Leadership Devel., Phoenix, 1992; Faculty grantee Ednl. Rsch. and Devel. Ctr., U. Akron, Ohio, 1994. Mem. Am. Ednl. Rsch. Assn., Ohio Assn. Two-Yr. Coll. Baptist. Office: Univ Akron Polsky Bldg M186F Akron OH 44235

JONES, HETTIE COHEN, writer, educator; b. Bklyn.; d. Oscar and Lottie (Lewis) Cohen; m. LeRoi Jones, Oct. 13, 1958 (div. 1965). BA in Drama cum laude, U. Va., 1955; postgrad., Columbia U., 1956. Freelance editl. svcs. N.Y.C., 1965—; adj. prof. Parsons Sch. Liberal Studies, 1992—; faculty writing 92nd St Y, N.Y.C., 1992—, New Sch., 1991, SUNY Purchase, NYU, CUNY, Mercy Coll., U. Wyo, 1993-94; asst. to the editors Partisan Rev., 1957-61; staff writer Mobilization for Youth, 1966-68; editl. cons. Curriculum Concepts, Inc., 1984, Visual Edn. Corp., 1983; lectr. in field. Contbr. numerous articles to profl. jours.; contbr. poetry to publs.; author: (How I Became Hettie Jones, 1990, paperbacks, 1991, 97, The Trees Stand Shining, 1971, 2d edit. 1993, Big Star Fallin' Mama, 1974, 2d edit. 1995 (selected as one of 20 best new books for young adults N.Y. Pub. Libr.); co-editor: Yugen mag., 1958-61. Chmn. bd. dirs. Ch. of All Nations, 1972-76; cons. Grace Ch. Opportunity Project, Day Care Coun. of Greater N.Y., 1968-72, 85; co-chair PEN Prison Writing Com.; condr. writing workshop N.Y. State Correctional Facility for Women, Bedford Hills, 1989—; grant recommender Lower Manhattan Cultural Coun., 1994—; mem. lit. panel N.Y. State Coun. on the Arts.

JONES, HUDA, association president. Pres National Federation of Republican Women, Washington DC. Office: National Federation of Reb Women 310 1st St SE Washington DC 20003-1801*

JONES, JAMIE DENISE See WATFORD, JAMIE DENISE

JONES, JAN LAVERTY, mayor. Grad. Stanford Univ. Mayor, City of Las Vegas. Office: Office of Mayor City Hall 10th Fl 400 Stewart Ave Las Vegas NV 89101-2942

JONES, JANET DULIN, writer, film producer; b. Hollywood, Calif., Sept. 6, 1957; d. John Dulin and Helen Mae (Weaver) J. BA, Calif. State U., Long Beach, 1980. Developer mini-series and TV series Embassy Communications, Los Angeles, 1981-84; assoc. to producer Hotel Aaron Spelling Prodns., Los Angeles, 1984-85; writing intern Sundance Film Inst., Los Angeles, 1985; feature film story analyst Carson Prodns., Los Angeles, 1985-86; freelance screenplay and play writer Los Angeles and N.Y.C., 1986—. Author (screenplays) Fad Away, 1986, Alone in the Crowd, 1987, Story of the Century, 1988, The Long Way Home, 1989 (play) Cousin Judy, 1989, The Set-up, 1990, Roommates, 1991, Local Girl, 1991, Dickens and Crime, 1992, (books) Little Bear Books, Vols. 1-5, A Weighty, Waity Matter-My Adventures with India (screenplays), 1992, Coming and Going, 1993, Watching the Detectives, 1994, The Ambassadors, 1994, Words of Love, 1995, Map of the World, 1995, Katherine, 1996. Bd. dirs. Sterling Cir. of Aviva Ctr. for Girls, 1990; bd. dirs., recording sec., steering com. The Creative Coalition, 1991-92. Mem. ACLU, WOmen in Film, Earth Communication Office (TV and film coms.), Writers Guild Am., Ind. Feature Project, Am. Film Inst., Sundance Film Inst. (pre-selection com. 1985-87), People for Am. Way, Habitat for Humanity, Anmesty Internat., Delta Gamma.

JONES, JEAN CORREY, organization administrator; b. Denver, Jan. 12, 1942; d. Robert Magnie and Elizabeth Marie (Harpel) Evans; m. Stewart Hoyt Jones, Aug. 3, 1963; children: Andrew and Correy. BS in History, Social Studies and Secondary Edn., Northwestern U., 1963. Cert. non-profit mgr. History tchr. Glenbrook South H.S., Glenview, Ill., 1963-65; advocacy rsch. dir. Episc. Diocese of Denver, 1977-80; pub. affairs adminstr. United Bank of Denver, 1980-82; exec. dir. Mile Hi coun. Girl Scouts U.S., Denver, 1982—; substitute tchr. Denver Pub. Schs., 1965-80. Active Minoru Yasui Cmty. Vol. Award com., 1979-96, Women's Forum of Colo., 1989-96, Leadership Denver (Member of Yr., 1988), 1988—; pres. Jr. League, Denver, 1979-80, Rotary, Denver, 1995-96, pres., 1995-96, commr., chair Colo. Civil Rights commn., Denver, 1987-96, vice chair Health One, Denver, 1996; bd. dirs. Hist. Denver, Inc., 1994-96, Samaritan Inst., Denver, 1996; trustee Colo. Trust, 1996. Named Profl. Woman of Achievement Colo. Women's Leadership Coalition and Colo. Easter Seal Soc., 1995. Mem. Denver Metro C. of C., Univ. Club. Republican. Episcopalian. Office: Girl Scouts - Mile Hi Coun 400 S Broadway PO Box 9407 Denver CO 80209-0407

JONES, JEANNE PITTS, director early childhood school; b. Richmond, Va., Oct. 19, 1938; d. Howard Taliaferro and Anne Elizabeth (Warburton) Pitts; m. Jack Hunter Jones, Nov. 17, 1962; children: Jack Hunter, Jr., Judith Anne, James Howard, Jon Martain. BA, Marshall U., 1961, post-grad. studies, 1962 summer; postgrad. studies, Presbyn. Sch. Christian Edn., Richmond, 1974, 94, Va. Commonwealth U., 1987-88, 95-96. Cert. tchr. Va. Tchr. Richmond (Va.) Pub. Schs., 1961-65; founder Bon View Sch. for Early Childhood Edn., Richmond, 1971, teacher, 1971-91, dir., 1971—; validator Nat. Assn. for Edn. of Young Children, 1993—, mentor children, 1994—; acad. affairs chmn. Good Shepherd Episcopal Sch. Bd., Richmond, 1985-88; mentor Ecumenical Child Care Network Nat. Coun. Chs., Washington, 1990-92. Chmn. room parents Crestwood Sch. PTA Bd., Richmond, 1974-80; publicity chmn. Va. Swimming, Richmond, 1978-88, children's coord. Bon Air United Meth. Ch., Richmond, 1985-93, v.p. Bon Air United Meth. Women, 1991-94; dir. Camp Friendship, Bon Air UMC, Richmond, 1992—; Va. Children's Action Network, Va. Conf. of United Meth. Ch., rep., 1993-95; Va. Conf. United Meth. Ch., weekday com. 1992-94. Recipient Spl. Mission recognition Bon Air United Meth. Women, Richmond, 1987. Mem. Richmond Early Childhood Assn. (mem.-at-large 1994-96, rec. sec. 1996—), Presch. Assn. Ch. Ednl. Dirs. (pres. 1993-95), Chesterfield Coalition Early Childhood Educators (bd. dirs. 1993—). Republican. Home: 9103 Whitaker Cir Richmond VA 23235 Office: Bon View Sch Early Childhood Edn 1645 Buford Rd Richmond VA 23235

JONES, JEN, actress, educator; b. Salt Lake City, Mar. 23, 1927; d. John William and Jean (Winder) J.; m. Robert Louis Bauder, Sept. 14, 1950 (div. 1960); children: Leslie Jean Bauder Caputo, Catherine Golda Bauder Donadio; m. Earl Clarence Theroux. Lic. acting tchr. Tchr. Am. Acad. Dramatic Arts, N.Y.C., 1962-64, 75-95. Actress (broadway) The Octette Bridge Club, The Music Man, The Eccentricities of a Nightingale, But Seriously, Dr. Good's Garden; (off broadway) Three Sisters, Uncle Vanya, Hen House, The Ecnetricities of a Nightingale, Catsplay; (off off broadway) The Glass Menagerie, Spacewalk, Oh Dad, Poor Dad, Romeo and Juliet, Surviving the Barbed Wire Cradle, The Coroner's Plot; TV Law and Order, The Ultimate in Long Distance, A Very Remarkable Man, One Life to Live; (reigonal theater) Three Tall Women, The Sweet Bye n Bye, Eleemosynary, The Jeremiah, Romeo & Juliet, Steel Magnolias, November, Children of Lesser God, Conflict of Interest, Shorts 82, Christmas Carol & Murder at the Vicarage, The Eccentricities of a Nightingale. Mem. AFTRA, SAG, Equity. Home: 178 W Houston St New York NY 10014-4821

JONES, JOAN MEGAN, anthropologist; b. Laramie, Wyo., Sept. 7, 1933; d. Thomas Owen and Lucille Lenoir (Magill) J. BA, U. Wash., 1956, MA, 1968, PhD, 1976. Mus. educator Burke Mus. U. Wash., Seattle, 1969-72; anthropologist Quinault Indian Nation, Taholah, Wash., 1976-77; researcher, corp. officer Profl. Anthropology Consulting Team/Social Analysts, Seattle, 1977-79; research assoc. dept. anthropology U. Wash., Seattle, 1982-91; research investigator Dept. Social and Health Services State of Wash., Seattle, 1977; vis. lectr. Dept. Anthropology U. B.C., Vancouver, 1978; research specialist Artsplan Arts Alliance Wash. State, Seattle, 1978; vis. instr. Dept. Anthropology Western Wash. U., Bellingham, 1981; cons. in field. Author: Northwest Coast Basketry and Culture Change, 1968, Basketry of Quinault, 1977, Native Basketry of Western North America, 1978, Art and Style of Western Indian Basketry, 1982, Northwest Coast Indian Basketry Styles. Wenner-Gren Found. Anthrop. Research fellow, 1967-68; Ford Found. fellow, 1972-73; Nat. Mus.'s. Can. grantee, 1973-74. Fellow Am. Anthrop. Assn., Soc. Applied Anthropology; mem. Nat. Assn. Practicing Anthropologists, Assn. Women in Sci., Skagit Valley Weavers Guild (v.p. Skagit County chpt. 1985-86, 89-90, corr. sec. 1988-89), Whidbey Weavers.

JONES, JULIA PEARL, elementary school educator; b. Kesler, W.Va., Nov. 22, 1942; d. Wallace Leon and Wilda Thelma (Doss) Frazier; m. James Victor Jones, Jr., Nov. 26, 1961; children: Julie Lorraine Lynch, Jamie Lynn Dunston Smith. BS in Elem. Edn. cum laude, Memphis State U., 1979; MEd cum laude, U. Va., 1986. Cert. elem./mid. sch. prin., supr., K-7th grade tchr., art tchr. Tchr. 4th grade Spotsylvania County (Va.) Schs., 1979-91, reading resource specialist, 1991—. Mem. ASCD, Nat. Tchrs. Assn., Va. Edn. Assn., Spotsylvania Edn. Assn., Nat. Congress of Parents and Tchrs., Internat. Reading Assn., Va. Reading Assn. Rappahannock Reading Coun. (past pres., Reading Tchr. of Yr. 1993-94), Internat. Platform Assn., Order Ea. Star, Kappa Delta Pi, Phi Delta Kappa. Methodist. Home: 5414 Jamie Ct Fredericksburg VA 22407-1618

JONES, KATHLEEN ANN, nuclear medicine technologist; b. Allentown, Pa., July 15, 1964; d. Edward Thomas and Catherine Marie (Steve) Jones. BS in Nuclear Med. Tech. magna cum laude, Cedar Crest Coll., Allentown, Pa., 1986. Cert. in nuclear med. tech. Staff nuclear med. technologist Lehigh Valley Hosp., Allentown, 1986—, clin. coordinator, 1988—. Editor ednl. programs Greater N.Y. chpt. Jour. Nuclear Med. Tech., 1990-93. Mem. Soc. Nuclear Medicine (technologist sect. bylaws chmn. 1990-91, area councilor 1991-92, technologist sect. treas. Greater N.Y. chpt. 1988-90, pres.-elect 1992-93, pres. 1993-94, awards chmn. 1995), Lehigh Valley Soc. Nuclear Med. Technologists (sec. 1987-88, pres. 1989-90, nominating chmn. 1990-91, bylaws com. 1991—), Del. Valley Soc. Nuclear Medicine Technologists. Democrat. Roman Catholic. Home: 1234 California Ave Whitehall PA 18052-4634 Office: Lehigh Valley Hosp 1200 S Cedar Crest Blvd Allentown PA 18103-6202

JONES, KATHRYN ANN, writer, artist; b. L.A., Oct. 12, 1956; d. Samuel Andrew and Wanda Faye (Smith) J.; m. Dan F. Malone, June 27, 1981. BA in English and Journalism, Trinity U., San Antonio, 1979. Staff writer Corpus Christi (Tex.) Caller-Times, 1979-81, Harts-Hanks Comm., Austin, Tex., 1981, Dallas Times Herald, 1984-86, Dallas Morning News, 1986-91; bur. chief MIS Week, Fairchild Pubs., Dallas, 1982-84; freelance writer Time, Life, D Mag., N.Y.C. and Dallas, 1991-93; contbg. writer N.Y. Times, 1993—. Co-author: How to Be Happily Employed in Dallas-Fort Worth, 1990, Fort Worth, 1990; exhibited in group shows Dallas Women's Caucus for Art, 1991, 94, 96. Recipient award of excellence Dallas Press Club, 1988. Mem. Assn. Women Journalists (bd. dirs. 1993), Dallas Women's Caucus for Art (bd. dirs. 1996), Southwestern Watercolor Soc. Home: 5140 Malinda Ln N Fort Worth TX 76112-3832

JONES, KATHRYN CHERIE, pastor; b. Breckenridge, Tex., Nov. 26, 1955; d. Austin Thomas and Margaret May (Mohr) J. BA, Calif. U., San Diego, 1977; MDiv, Fuller Theol. Sem., 1982. Assoc. pastor La Jolla (Calif.) United Meth. Ch., 1982-84; pastor in charge Dominguez United Meth. Ch., Long Beach, Calif., 1984-88, San Marcos (Calif.) United Meth. Ch., 1988-90; dir. The Walk to Emmaus Program, The Upper Room, Nashville, 1990—; coord. chaplains Pacific Hosp., Long Beach, 1986-88. Bd. dirs. So. Calif. Walk to Emmaus Cmty., L.A., 1987-88, San Diego chpt., 1988-90. Mem. Christian Assn. Psychol. Studies, Evangs. for Social Action. Democrat. Office: The Upper Room 1908 Grand Ave PO Box 189 Nashville TN 37202-0189

JONES, KATHY, motion picture company executive; b. Aug. 27, 1949. Acct. exec. Stan Levinson Assocs., Dallas; sr. publicist field mktg. Paramount Pictures, exec. dir. field mktg., v.p. domestic publicity & promotion, 1981-84, sr. v.p. motion picture group, 1984-87; v.p. domestic mktg. Time-Life Films; cons., 1987—; exec. v.p. mktg. Columbia Pictures, 1989-91, Tri-Star Pictures, 1991—. *

JONES, LACINDA, assistant principal; b. Baton Rouge, Mar. 1, 1962; d. Carl Lester and Joan (Alford) J. BS, La. State U., 1984; MEd in Guidance/Counseling, Southeastern La. U., 1990; postgrad., Southern U., Baton Rouge, 1990-92. Cert. tchr., elem. sch. prin., adminstr., supr., guidance counselor, resource devel., leadership, supervision of student tchrs. Tchr. grades 1-4 Livingston Parish (La.) Sch. Bd., 1985-89; tchr. grade 5 East Baton Rouge Sch. Bd., 1989-90, guidance counselor, 1990-95, adminstrv. intern, 1993-94, asst. prin., 1995—; lectr. in field; condr. workshops for tchrs./adminstrs., and parents; asst. in implementing Reading Recovery program for at-risk students; assisted other sch. dists. in implementating their guidance programs; helped implemented La. Bd. Elem. and Secondary Edn./La. Quality Ednl. Support Fund Grant, 1993-94. Featured on WFMF Radio Pub. Affairs program; featured in articles in Baton Rouge Advocate, Ctrl. News newspapers, other pubs.; pub. handbook: Parent-Student Handbook, 1993. Tutor underprivileged children, Baton Rouge, 1986-90; libr. vol. Goodwood Libr., Baton Rouge, 1990; Sunday sch. tchr. Deerford United Meth. Ch., Baton Rouge, 1980-84; vol. fundraiser Acad. Distinction, Baton Rouge, 1990-94; vol. Vols. in P ub. Schs. (VIP), Baton Rouge, 1993. Grantee Exxon Chem. Edn. Involvement Fund, 1996, South Ctrl. Bell, La., 1989, Nat. 4-H Found., 1991, Acad. Distinction Fund, Baton Rouge, 1991, 93. Mem. Am. Sch. Counselor Assn. (membership chair 1990), La. Sch. Counselor Assn. (elem. v.p. 1993-94), East Baton Rouge Counselor Assn. (elem. v.p. 1992-93), Assoc. Prof. Educators (La. membership rep. 1992), East Baton Rouge Counselor Assn. (pres.-elect 1995—), Delta Kappa Gamma (historian 1994). Democrat. Home: 17157 Wax Rd Apt D Greenwell Springs LA 70739-5042 Office: Northeast Elem Sch PO Box C Pride LA 70770

JONES, LAURA V., lawyer; b. N.Y.C., Apr. 10, 1949. AB, Vassar Coll., 1970; JD, Columbia U., 1975. Bar: N.Y. 1976. Ptnr. Anderson, Kill, Olick & Oshinsky, P.C., N.Y.C. Mem. Columbia Law Rev., 1974-75. Mem. Assn. of Bar of City of N.Y. Office: Anderson Kill Olick & Oshinsky PC 1251 Avenue of the Americas New York NY 10020-1182*

JONES, LAURIE LYNN, magazine editor; b. Kerrville, Tex., Sept. 2, 1947; d. Charles Clinton and Jean Laurie (Davidson) J.; m. C. Frederick Childs, June 26, 1976; children: Charles Newell (Clancy), Cyrus Trevor; 1 stepchild, Ariel Childs. B.A., U. Tex., 1969. Asst. to dir. coll. admissions Columbia U., N.Y.C., 1969-70; asst. to dir. Office Alumni-Columbia U., N.Y.C., 1970-71; asst. advt. mgr. Book World, 1971-72, Washington Post-Chgo. Tribune, 1971-72; editorial asst. N.Y. Mag., N.Y.C., 1972-74, asst. editor, 1974, sr. editor, 1974-76, mng. editor, 1976-92; mng. editor Vogue Mag., N.Y.C., 1992—. Mem. Am. Soc. Mag. Editors, Women in Coummunication, Advt. Women N.Y. Republican. Methodist. Home: 40 Great Jones St New York NY 10012-1115 Also: 62 Giles Hill Rd Redding Ridge CT 06876 Office: Vogue Magazine 350 Madison Ave New York NY 10017-3704

JONES, LEONADE DIANE, newspaper publishing company executive; b. Bethesda, Md., Nov. 27, 1947; d. Leon Adger and Landonia Randolph (Madden) J. BA with distinction, Simmons Coll., 1969; JD, Stanford U., 1973, MBA, 1973. Bar: Calif. 1973, D.C. 1979. Summer assoc. Davis Polk & Wardwell, N.Y.C., summer 1972; securities analyst Capital Rsch. Co., L.A., 1973-75; asst. treas. Washington Post Co., 1975-79, 86-87, treas., 1987—; dir. fin. services Post-Newsweek Stas., Inc., Washington, 1979-84, v.p. bus. affairs, 1984-86; bd. dirs. Am. Balanced Fund, Inc., Income Fund Am., Inc., Growth Fund Am., Inc., The New Economy Fund, Smallcap World Fund, Inc.; mem. investment mgmt. subcom. of benefit plans com. Am. Stores Co., 1992—. Treas., bd. dirs. Big Sisters Washington Met. Area, 1984-85; bd. dirs. D.C. Contemporary Dance Theatre, 1987-89, Washington Performing Arts Soc., 1990-94, treas., 1992-94; mem. adv. coun. Charlin Jazz Soc., 1988-92; mem. adv. bd. Sta. WHMM-TV, 1989-93; asst. chmn. budget and audit D.C. chpt. Met. Washington, Edges Group, Inc., 1989-93; mem. adv. coun. Bus. Sch., Stanford U., 1991—, bd. visitors Law Sch., 1982-84, 93—; trustee Am. Inst. Mng. Diversity, Inc., 1991—; mem. corp. Simmons Coll., 1992—. Recipient Candace award for bus., 1992, Serwa award, 1993; named to D.C. Women's Hall of Fame, 1992. Mem. ABA, Calif. Bar Assn., D.C. Bar Assn., Stanford U. Bus. Sch. Alumni Assn. (bd. dirs. 1986-88, pres. Washington-Balt. chpts. 1984-85), Nat. Assn. Corp. Treas. Office: Washington Post Co 1150 15th St NW Washington DC 20071-0001

JONES, LINDA KAREN, speech, language pathologist; b. Lindsay, Okla., July 5, 1949; d. Howard Curtis and Berniece (Farrow) Swindell; m. Wayne Ardrey, Aug. 29, 1968 (div. Oct. 1973); children: Misty, Brian; m. David Ray Jones, Nov. 6, 1980; children: Robbie, Noah. BS, Okla. State U., 1984, MA, 1987. Lic. speech/lang. pathologist, Okla. Speech/lang. pathologist Winfield (Kans.) State Hosp. and Tng. Ctr., 1987-88, Pauls Valley (Okla.) State Sch., 1988-90, Developmental Disabilities Svcs. Divsn., Pauls Valley, 1990-92, J.D. McCarty Ctr. for Children with Developmental Disability, Norman, Okla., 1992—; cons. Dept. Human Svcs., Pauls Valley, 1992—, Saber Mgmt., Ardmore, 1994—. Vol. Spl. Olympics, Stillwater, Okla., 1986-88, Health Fair, Stillwater, 1985-88. Mem. Am. Speech/Lang./Hearing Assn. (cert., award 1994), Okla. Soc. for Augmentative and Alternative Comm., Golden Key, Phi Kappa Phi. Office: JD McCarty Ctr Children DD 1125 E Alameda St Norman OK 73071-5254

JONES, LINDA R. WOLF, organization executive; b. Jersey City, Sept. 4, 1943; d. Eugene Leon and Lottie (Pinkowitz) Rubin; m. Frank Paul Jones, Oct. 21, 1973 (div. Nov. 1987); 1 child, Elisabeth Noel. AB, Bryn Mawr Coll., 1964; MA, Yale U., 1968; DSW, Yeshiva U., N.Y.C., 1985. Dir. planning and tng. N.Y.C. Dept. Employment, 1971-77; dir. legislation N.Y.C. Community Devel. Agy., 1977-78, supervisory legis. analyst N.Y.C. Human Resources Adminstrn., 1978; sr. policy analyst Community Svc. Soc. N.Y., 1978-85; dir. pub. policy YMCA Greater N.Y., 1985-89; dir. spl. projects Phoenix House, N.Y.C., 1990-92; dir. income security policy Community Svc. Soc., N.Y.C., 1992-94; exec. dir. Therapeutic Communities Am., Washington, 1994—; mem. adj. extension faculty Cornell U./N.Y. State Sch. Indsl. and Labor Rels., N.Y.C., 1975-80; dir. Nonprofit Coordinating Com. N.Y., N.Y.C., 1986-94, Govt. Affairs Profls., N.Y.C., 1989-94. Author (book) Eveline M. Burns and the American Social Security System 1935-60, 1991; mem. editorial bd. New Eng. Jour. Human Svcs., 1981—; contbr. articles to profl. jours. Mem. Civic Affairs Forum, N.Y.C., 1985-94; mem. legis. task force N.Y. State Gov.'s Office Vol. Svc., N.Y.C., 1987-90. Mem. Women in Govt. Rels., Am. Pub. Welfare Assn. (dir. 1982), Bryn Mawr Club Westchester (bd. dirs., past pres. 1974-94), Bryn Mawr Club Washington. Home: 6621 7th Pl NW Washington DC 20012-2607 Office: Therapeutic Communities Am Ste 4-B 1611 Connecticut Ave NW Washington DC 20009

JONES, LISA MARIE, banker; b. Middletown, Conn., May 22, 1961; d. Bobby Louis and Sadie Mae J. AS, Middlesex C.C., 1989. Author: An Autobiography of His Creation, 1993. Voter Dem. Town Com., Durham, Conn., 1990-96; chmn. Rep. Legion Merit, Washington, 1992-96. With U.S. Army, 1986-95. Pell grantee, 1986-89. Baptist. Home: 437 Main St Durham CT 06422-1314

JONES, LOIS NEWBERRY, English educator; b. Bridgeton, N.J., May 7, 1943; d. Donald Henry and Lois Leora (Peterson) Newberry; m. L. Curtis Jones, Feb. 23, 1970 (div. Feb. 1975); 1 child, Jason Wardwell. BA, Houghton Coll., 1965; MA, Glassboro State U., 1979, postgrad. Cert. English tchr., N.J. Tchr. So. Freehold H.S., Farmingdale, N.J., 1965-67; pers. dir. Wilmington Dry Goods, Vineland, N.J., 1973-75; tchr., adminstrv. asst. Leesburg (N.J.) State Prison, 1975-78; tchr. Cumberland Regional H.S., Seabrook, N.J., 1979—. Capt. USAF, 1968-72. Mem. Concerned Women for Am., Christian Coalition. Republican. Home: 336 Broad St Elmer NJ 08318

JONES, MALLORY See DANAHER, MALLORY MILLETT

JONES, MARCIA A., legislative staff member, lawyer; b. Austin, Tex., Jan. 11, 1961; d. Paul Byron and Sheila (Gallagher) J. BA in Econs., Georgetown U., 1984; JD, George Washington U., 1990. Staff mem. to Rep. Don Young, Washington, 1981-85, Senator Frank H. Murkowski, Washington, 1985-87; with Jellinek, Schwartz, Connolly & Freshman, Washington, 1987-88; legis. dir. and tax counsel to Senator John B. Breaux, Washington, 1988—. Mem. ABA, Tax Coalition. Roman Catholic. Office: Sen John Breaux D-La 516 Hart Senate Office Bldg Washington DC 20510

JONES, MARGARET LOUISE, supervisory production analyst; b. Roswell, N.Mex., Aug. 12, 1944; d. William Presley and Ida Margaret (Wright) Bratcher; m. Jeffrey Dean Holman, Dec. 19, 1970; 1 child, Sean Eric; m. Don Jones, Dec. 22, 1982. Student, Ea. N.Mex. U., 1962, Red Rocks C.C., Golden, Colo., 1984. Clk. U.S. Geol. Survey, Roswell, N.Mex., 1962-66; resource clk. U.S. Forest Svc., Tallahassee, Fla., 1966-68; apt. mgr. Brinkley Bros., Tallahassee, 1968-69; sec. State of Fla., Tallahassee, 1969-70, 1st Nat. Bank, Roswell, 1970, Bur. Land Mgmt./Soil Conservation Svc./U.S. Geol. Survey, Roswell, 1970-81; supr. clk. BLM, Roswell, 1981-82; fgn. activities asst. Bur. Reclamation, Lakewood, Colo., 1982-84; lead prodn. technician Minerals Mgmt. Svc., Lakewood, Colo., 1984-85, prodn. analyst, 1985-88, staff prodn. analyst, 1988-92, supervisory prodn. analyst, 1992—. Named Outstanding Young Woman of Am., 1980. Mem. Southampton Townhome Assn. (bd. dirs. 1983-85, v.p. 1985-90, pres. 1990—). Democrat. Baptist.

JONES, MARGUERITE JACKSON, English language educator; b. Greenwood, Miss., Aug. 12, 1949; d. James and Mary G. (Reedy) Jackson; m. Algee Jones, Apr. 4, 1971; 1 child, Stephanie Nerissa. BS, Miss. Valley State U., 1969; MEd, Miss. State U., 1974; EdS, Ark. State U., 1983; postgrad. U. Ark., 1982. Tchr. English Henderson High Sch., Starkville, Miss., 1969-70, creative writing Miami (Fla.) Coral Park, 1970-71, English, head dept. Marion (Ark.) Sr. High Sch., 1971-78, East Ark. Community Coll., Forrest City, 1978-79; migrant edn. supr. Marion (Ark.) Sch. Dist.,

1979-83; mem. faculty Draughons Coll., Memphis, 1978-83; assoc. prof. State Tech., 1984—; cons. writing projects; condr. workshops for ednl., bus., civic groups. Bd. dirs. Bountiful Blessings Christian Acad., Memphis; dir. Leadership Tng. Inst. for 4th Eccles. Jurisdiction, Tenn.; Christian edn. dir. Temple Deliverance-The Cathedral Bountiful Blessings, Memphis. Mem. ASCD, Nat. Coun. Tchrs. English, Ark. Assn. Profl. Educators, Memphis Assn. Young Children, Tenn. Assn. Young Children, Nat. Assn. Young Children, Phi Delta Kappa. Home: 1239 Meadowlark Ln Memphis TN 38116-7801 Office: State Tech Inst 5983 Macon Cove Memphis TN 38134-7642

JONES, MARIA AZUCENA, school superintendent; b. Robstown, Tex., Dec. 22, 1938; d. Ben and Delphine (Salinas) Garza; m. Servando Wilson Laurel, Aug. 10, 1958 (div. Mar. 1070); children: Robert Charles, Hector Omar; m. William B. Jones, Aug. 4, 1972. BS, Tex. A&I U., 1961, MS, 1964; Specialist in Adminstrv. Edn., Miss. State U., 1981. Cert. tchr., supr., adminstr., supt., Miss. Tchr./supr. Corpus Christi (Tex.) Ind. Sch. Dist., 1961-73; tchr./supr. Madison County (Miss.) Schs., 1973-80, asst. prin., fed. programs coord., 1980-91, elem. prin., 1991-95; supt. schs. Madison County (Miss.) Schs., Canton, 1995—. Adv. bd. Belhaven Coll., Jackson, Miss., 1992—, Holmes Jr. C.C., Goodman, Miss., 1996—; chmn. edn. com. Madison County Rep. Women, 1995—; mem. Miss. rep. Women, Jackson, 1995—, Miss. Rep. Party, 1980—; pres. Flora (Miss.) Women's Club, 1984-87. Mem. ASCD, AAUW, Nat. Sch. Adminstrs. Assn., Nat. Sch. Bd. Assn., Internat. Reading Assn., Madison County C. of C. (adv. bd. Leadership Madison County 1992-95), Madison City C. of C. (adv. bd. 1995-96), Madison-Ridgeland C. of C., Rotary (amb. of edn. 1994). Baptist. Home: 376 First St Flora MS 39071

JONES, MARSHA REGINA, public relations specialist, journalist; b. Bklyn., Jan. 26, 1962; d. Eudolphin and Iona Louisa (Williams) J.; m. Donald Collins, May 24, 1996. BJ, Purdue U., 1984. Mgr. mktg. comms. SUNY, Brockport, 1989-93; coord. pub. rels. Hillside Children's Ctr., Rochester, N.Y., 1993-95; dir. comm. Camp Good Days and Spl. Times, Mendon, N.Y., 1995—. Contbg. author: Visions and Viewpoints: Voices of the Genesee Valley, 1993, 94; editor: Shadows of Dreams, 1996; columnist, editor, Rochester-Metro Challenger, 1990. Co-chmn. Boys and Girls Club Rochester, 1994—. Scholar Urban League Rochester, 1980. Mem. Rochester Assn. Black Communicators (pres. 1992-94, editor Communicator 1992-93).

JONES, MARY ANN, geriatrics nurse; b. Suffern, N.Y., July 15, 1943; d. Ralph and Hilva (Kelly) Osborne; m. Richard D. Jones, Aug. 31, 1985. AAS, Rockland C.C., Suffern, 1963; BS, St. Thomas Aquinas Coll., Sparkill, N.Y., 1983. Cert. dir. nursing adminstrn./long term care. Supr. to asst. DON Ramapo Manor Nursing Ctr., Suffern, 1964-87; coord. to DON Carnegie Gardens Nursing Ctr., Melbourne, Fla., 1987—. Mem. Nat. Assn. Dirs. Nursing Adminstrn. in Long Term Care, Fla. Assn. Dirs. Nursing Adminstrn. in Long Term Care (1st v.p. local chpt., cert. Dir. Nursing Adminstrn. in Long Term Care 1995), Gericulture Soc. Home: 426 Lackland St SW Palm Bay FL 32908-7111

JONES, MARY ANN, nurse, educator; b. Bklyn., Jan. 20, 1946; d. Anthony and Angela (Tapogna) Morelli; m. John W. Jones, May 31, 1981. BSN, Hunter Coll., 1967; MA in Edn., NYU, 1976. RN. Staff nurse ICU Maimonedes Hosp., Bklyn., 1967-68, staff nurse emergency rm., 1969-70; office nurse Rome, 1968-69; staff nurse ICU Pacific Presbyn. Med. Ctr., San Francisco, 1970-71; instr. physician asst. program USPHS Hosp., S.I., N.Y., 1971-72; in-svc. edn. instr. St. Vincent Hosp., N.Y.C., 1972-74; staff nurse cardiovascular ICU NYU Med. Ctr., 1974-75; asst. DON, dir. insvc. edn. Saphardic Home for the Aged, Bklyn., 1976-78; sr. risk mgmt. cons. Ebasco Risk Mgmt. Cons., N.Y.C., 1978-81; v.p. sales, dir. tng. Telerx Mktg. Inc., Springhouse, Pa., 1981-88; pub., editor J&T Pub., Montvale, N.J., 1988-93; pres. Imaj Tng. and Comm., Palm Coast, Fla., 1988—; chmn. editl. bd. Med. Econs. Pub., Montvale, 1993—, Office Nurse Mag. Editor, author risk mgmt. manuals. Grantee Merck Sharp Dohme, 1988, 89, Marion Merrill Dow, 1992. Mem. AAUW, Am. Bus. Womens Assn., Am. Holistic Nurses Assn., Am. Assn. Office Nurses (founder, 1st pres., dir.), Sigma Theta Tau. Home: 11 Collington Ct Palm Coast FL 32137 Office: PO Box 352597 Palm Coast FL 32135

JONES, MARY ELLEN, biochemist; b. La Grange, Ill., Dec. 25, 1922; d. Elmer E. and Laura A. (Klein) J.; children: Ethan Vincent Munson, Catherine Laura Munson. BS, U. Chgo., 1944; PhD, Yale U., 1951. AEC fellow, Am. Cancer Soc. fellow, assoc. biochemist Mass. Gen. Hosp., Boston, 1951-57; asst. prof. grad. dept. biochemistry Brandeis U., Waltham, Mass., 1957-60, assoc. prof., 1960-66; assoc. prof. dept. biochemistry Sch. Medicine, U. N.C., Chapel Hill, 1966-68, prof. depts. biochemistry and zoology, 1968-71; prof. dept. biochemistry Sch. Medicine, U. So. Calif., 1971-78; prof., chmn. dept. biochemistry Sch. Medicine, U. N.C., Chapel Hill, 1978-89, Kenan prof. biochemistry, 1980-95, prof. emeritus biochemistry, 1995—; mem. study sect. Am. Cancer Soc., 1971-73, mem. com. biochemistry and endocrinology, 1991-94, NIH, 1971-75; mem. sci. adv. bd. Nat. Heart, Lung and Blood Inst., 1980-84; mem. metabolic biology study sect. NSF, 1978-81; mem. VA Merit rev. bd., 1975-78; mem. life sci. com. NASA, 1976-78; pres. Chairs of Assn. Med. Sch. Depts. Biochemistry, 1985; mem. Nat. Adv. Gen. Med. Scis. Council, 1988-91. Am. Cancer Soc. scholar, 1957-62; NIH grantee, 1957-94; NSF grantee, 1957-90. Mem. NAS, AAAS, Am. Acad. Arts and Scis., Am. Chem. Soc. (councilor 1975-79, nominating com. 1971-72, chair biochem. divsn. 1973-74), Am. Soc. Biol. Chemists (councilor 1975-78, 81-84, pres. 1986), Am. Philos. Soc., Inst. Medicine of Nat. Acad. Scis. (councilor 1984-87), Assn. Women in Sci., N.Y. Acad. Sci., Sigma Xi. Democrat. Unitarian. Clubs: Appalachian Mountain, Sierra. Contbr. numerous articles on biochem. research to sci. publs.; editorial bd. Jour. Biol. Chemistry, 1975-80, 82-87, Cancer Research, 1982-86; assoc. editor Can. Jour. Biochemistry, 1969-74. Office: U NC Dept Biochemistry and Biophysics Chapel Hill NC 27599-7260

JONES, MARY FRANCES, sales executive; b. St. Louis, Feb. 24, 1958; d. Millard Robert and Mary Frances (Lark) J. BA, Dallas Bapt. U., 1992. Exec. asst. Southwestern Bell, Dallas, 1976-81; acccount exec. AT&T, Dallas, 1982-89, mktg. mgr., 1990-95, nat. sales mgr., 1996—. Mem. Salesmanship Club (vol./com. chair 1989—). Roman Catholic. Office: AT&T 2020 K St NW Rm 7102 Washington DC 20006

JONES, MARY PAUMIER, librarian; b. Rome, N.Y., Oct. 29, 1941; d. Charles Joseph and Jeannette Rose (Durr) Paumier; m. James E. Jones, Mar. 18, 1967; children: Morgan Charles, Tyler Mac. BA, Seattle U., 1963; MLS, SUNY, Buffalo, 1995. Cert. profl. pub. libr., N.Y. Tchr. Montessori Schs., Inc., Pasadena, Calif., 1965-68, Univ. Parents' Nursery Sch., L.A., 1970-72; bookseller, asst. mgr. Waldenbooks, Rochester, N.Y., 1979-86; writer Rochester, 1986—; libr. Rochester Pub. Libr., 1995—. Co-editor: In Short: A Collection of Brief Creative Nonfiction, 1996; author essays Ga. Rev., 1994, 96, Creative Non-Fiction, 1993. Mem. ALA, N.Y. Libr. Assn., Colo.. Libr. Assn. Democrat. Home: 100 Crosman Terr Rochester NY 14620 Office: Rochester Pub Library Science Divsn 115 South Ave Rochester NY 14604

JONES, MAXINE, vocalist; b. Patterson, N.J., 1966. Vocalist En Vogue, Atco/Eastwest Records, N.Y.C., 1988—. Albums include Born to Sing (Platinum 1990), Funky Divas, Remis to Sing, Runaway Love. Recipient Soul Train Music award, 1991; nominated Grammy award, 1990. Office: care En Vogue Atco/Eastwest Records 75 Rockefeller Plz New York NY 10019-6908*

JONES, MEREDITH J., federal government official; b. Hartford, Conn., Mar. 24, 1948; d. Cyril Johnstone and Rose Victoria (Randolph) Jones. BA, Swarthmore Coll., 1968; JD, Yale U., 1974. Bar: N.Y. 1975, Calif. 1983, D.C. 1994. Assoc. Cleary, Gottlieb, Steen & Hamilton, N.Y.C., 1974-83; ptnr. Chickering & Gregory, San Francisco, 1983-86; sr. counsel Bechtel Financing Svcs., Inc., San Francisco, 1986-93; gen. counsel Nat. Oceanic & Atmospheric Adminstrn., Washington, 1993-94; chief cable svcs. bur. FCC, Washington, 1994—. Mem. Bar Assn. City of N.Y. Democrat. Office: Cable Svcs Bur FCC FCC 1919 M St NW Washington DC 20036-3505

JONES, NANCY GALE, retired biology educator; b. Gaffney, S.C., Nov. 12, 1940; d. Louransey Dowell and Sarah Louise (Pettit) J. BA, Winthrop Coll., 1962; MA, Oberlin Coll., 1964; postgrad., Duke U. Marine Biology Lab., 1963, Marine Biol. Lab., Woods Hole, Mass., 1964, N.C. State U., 1965, Ohio State U., 1966, Ariz. State U., 1970. Lectr. biology Oberlin (Ohio) Coll., 1964-66; from instr. to asst. prof. zoology Ohio U., Zanesville, 1966-73; media specialist Muskingum Area Vocat. Sch., Zanesville, 1973-74; salesperson Village Bookstore, Worthington, Ohio, 1975. Vol. hortitherapist for mentally disabled adults Habilitation Svcs., Inc. Gaffney, S.C., 1977-80; vol. dir. emergency assistance to needy PEACHcenter Ministries, Gaffney, 1991-94; mem. planned giving adv. coun. Winthrop U. Recipient Winthrop U. Alumni Disting. Svc. award, 1996. Mem. Ohio Retired Tchrs. Assn., Sigma Xi (assoc.). Baptist. Home: 1643 W Rutledge Ave Gaffney SC 29341-1023

JONES, NANCY LANGDON, financial planning practitioner; b. Chgo., Mar. 24, 1939; d. Lewis Valentine and Margaret (Seese) Russell; m. Lawrence Elmer Langdon, June 30, 1962 (div. 1970); children: Laura Kimberley, Elizabeth Ann; m. Claude Earl Jones, Jan. 1, 1973. BA, U. Redlands, Calif., 1962; MS, Coll. for Fin. Planning, 1991. CFP; registered investment advisor; accredited tax advisor. Bookkeeper Russell Sales Co., Santa Fe Springs, Calif., 1962-70; office mgr. Reardon, McCallum & Co., Upland, Calif., 1970-77; broker, assoc. ERA Property Ctr., Upland, 1977-84; registered rep. Fin. Network Investment Corp., Pasadena, Calif., 1984-92; pvt. practice fin. planning Upland, 1984—; ptnr. Jones, Graham & Assocs., Registered Investment Advisors, Upland, Calif., 1994; mem. adj. faculty Coll. Fin. Planning, Denver, 1986-94; mem. nat. comprehensive exam. question writing com. CFP Bd. Stds., 1994—; del. U.S. fin. and investment leaders study mission to China and Hong Kong, 1993. Leader Spanish Trails coun. Girl Scouts U.S., 1974-81; mem. exec. com. Corp. 2000 Coun., San Antonio Cmty. Hosp. Recipient Hon. Svc. award Valencia Elem. Sch., 1978. Mem. SAG, Inland Soc. Tax Cons., Internat. Assn. Fin. Planners (pres. San Gabriel Valley chpt. 1987-88, mem. exec. bd. So. Calif. conf. 1992—, chmn. So. Calif. Conf., 1996—), Am. Bus. Women's Assn. (pres. Upland chpt. 1989-90, gen. chmn. 1995, Pacific Spring Conf. Woman of Yr. award 1988), Inst. CFP San Gabriel Valley Soc. (pres. 1992-93, chmn. 1993-94, bd. dirs. 1990—), Inst. CFPs (nat. practice mgmt. & tech. com. 1996), Nat. Coun. Exchangers (sec. 1986-87), Estate Planning Coun. Pomona Valley (bd. dirs. 1995—), Women's Bus. Network (pres. 1987-88), Registry Fin. Planning Practitioners, Inland Valley Profl. Aux. (charter, bd. dirs. 1991-92), Assistance League Upland, Upland C. of C. Home and Office: 2485 Mesa Ter Upland CA 91784-1078

JONES, NORMA LOUISE, librarian, educator; b. Poplar, Wis.; d. George Elmer and Hilma June (Wiberg) J. BE, U. Wis.; MA, U. Minn., 1952; postgrad, U. Ill., 1957; PhD, U. Mich., 1965; postgrad., NARS, 1978, 79, 80, Nova U., 1983-96. Librarian Grand Rapids (Mich.) Public Schs., 1947-62; with Grand Rapids Public Library, 1948-49; instr. Central Mich. U., Mt. Pleasant, 1954, 55; lectr. U. Mich., Ann Arbor, 1954, 55, 61, 63-65, asst. prof., 1966-68; librarian Benton Harbor (Mich.) Public Schs., 1962-63; asst. prof. library sci. U. Wis., Oshkosh, 1968-70; assoc. prof. U. Wis., 1970-75, prof., 1975—, chmn. dept. library sci., 1980-84, exec. dir. librs. and learning resources, 1987-93; dir. Adult Ctr., 1993-95. Recipient Disting. Teaching award U. Wis.-Oshkosh, 1977. Mem. ALA (chmn. reference cons. 1975), Wis. Libr. Assn., Assn. Libr. and Info. Sci. Educators, Spl. Libr. Assn., Wis. Spl. Libr. Assn., Soc. Am. Archivists, Wis. Assn. Acad. Librs., Phi Beta Kappa, Phi Kappa Phi, Pi Lambda Theta, Beta Phi Mu, Sigma Pi Epsilon. Home: 1220 Maricopa Dr Oshkosh WI 54904-8121

JONES, ORA MCCONNER, foundation administrator; b. Augusta, Ga., Jan. 2, 1929; d. Landirs and Mamie (Elderidge) Williams; m. Walter R. McConner, June 27, 1953 (div.); 1 child, Susan L.; m. Courtney P. Jones, Feb. 14, 1991. BA, Paine Coll., Augusta, 1949; MA, Boston U., 1951; EdD, Nova U., Ft. Lauderdale, Fla., 1982. Instr. Paine Coll., Augusta, 1951-55; tchr. Chgo. Pub. Schs., 1956-66, adminstr., 1966-79, asst. supt., 1979-89, supt. dist. 6, 1989-91; exec. dir. Branch County Cmty. Found., Coldwater, Mich., 1991—. Pres., bd. trustees Paine Coll., 1996; mem. Profl. Women's Aux. Provident Hosp. Danforth study grantee, 1955; recipient Image award League of Black Women, 1974, Silver Beaver award Boy Scouts Am., 1985; named Educator of Yr. Chgo. Black Sch. Educators, 1984; recipient Outstanding Educator's award Beatrice Coffee's, 1989. Mem. Am. Assn. Sch. Adminstrs., Nat. Alliance of Black Sch. Educators, Coun. for Exceptional Children, Altrusa Club, Beta Sigma Phi, Phi Delta Kappa, Alpha Gamma Psi. Episcopalian. Home: 10591 Simco Dr Coldwater MI 49036-9582 Office: Branch County Cmty Found 116 N Clay St Coldwater MI 49036-1330

JONES, PATRICIA LOUISE, elementary counselor; b. Moorhead, Minn., Aug. 20, 1942; d. Harry Wilfred and Myrtle Louise Rosenfeldt; m. Edward L. Marks (div.); m. Curtis C. Jones, July 16, 1973; children: Michon, Andrea, Nathan, Kirsten, Leah. BS, Moorhead State U., 1965; MS, Mankato State U., 1990. Cert. K-12 sch. counselor, Minn. Tchr. Anoka (Minn.) Hennepin Schs., 1966-68; pvt. practice Youth Ctr., Truman, Minn., 1969-72; bookkeeper Fairmont (Minn.) Glass & Sign, 1973, Truman Farmers Elevator, 1973-87; libr. Martin County Libr., Truman, 1988-89; sch. counselor St. James (Minn.) Schs., 1989—; coord. Internat. Fun Fest, St. James, 1992, 96; originator, advisor Armstrong After Sch. Hispanic Club, St. James, 1991—. Coord. Truman Days Parade, 1991, 92, 94, 95, 96; mem. adv. bd. Watonwan County Big Buddy Program, 1993—. Mem. Am. Counseling Assn., Am. Sch. Counselors Assn., Minn. Sch. Counselors Assn., S.W. Minn. Counselors Assn. (Elem. Counselor of Yr. 1993). Office: Saint James Sch Dist 1273 10th Ave N Saint James MN 56081-2029

JONES, RENEE KAUERAUF, health care administrator; b. Duncan, Okla., Nov. 3, 1949; d. Delbert Owen and Betty Jean (Marsh) Kauerauf; m. Dan Elkins Jones, Aug. 3, 1972. BS, Okla. State U., 1972, MS, 1975; PhD, Okla. U., 1989. Diplomate Am. Bd. Sleep Medicine. Statis. analyst Okla. State Dept. Mental Health, Okla. City, 1978-80, divisional chief, 1980-83, adminstr., 1983-84; assoc. dir. HCA Presbyn. Hosp., Okla. City, 1984—; adj. instr. Okla. U. Health Sci. Ctr., 1979—; assoc. staff scientist Okla. Ctr. for Alcohol and Drug-Related Studies, Okla. City, 1979—; cons. in field. Assoc. editor Alcohol Tech. Reports jour., 1979-84; contbr. articles to profl. jours. Mem. assoc. bd. Hist. Preservation, Inc., treas. 1994. Mem. APHA, Assn. Health Svcs. Rsch., Alcohol and Drug Problems Assn. N.Am., Am. Sleep Disorders Assn., N.Y. Acad. Scis., So. Sleep Soc. (sec.-treas. 1989-91), Phi Kappa Phi. Democrat. Methodist. Home: 401 NW 19th St Oklahoma City OK 73103-1911 Office: HCA Presbyn Hosp NE 13th at Lincoln Blvd Oklahoma City OK 73104

JONES, ROSALIE MAY, dancer, dance educator, choreographer; b. Browning, Mont., Nov. 1, 1941; d. William Owen and Amy Rosalie (Jackson) J. BFA, Ft. Wright Coll., Spokane, Wash., 1964; MS, U. Utah, 1968; postgrad., Juilliard Sch., 1969. Lectr. dnce Inst. Am. Indian Arts, Santa Fe, N.M., 1966-68, prof., 1989-95, chmn., 1989-92; dir. dance project Ctr. for Arts Indian Am., Washington, D.C., 1969-70; instr. dnce Wis. Mime Co., Spring Green, 1974-75, Mt. Senario Coll., Ladysmith, Wis., 1975-78; founder, artistic dir., choreographer, tour dir. Daystar Dance Co., Wisconsin Dells, Wis., 1980-89, Great Falls, Mont., 82-89, Santa Fe, N.M., 1989—; artist-in-residence state arts couns., Mont., S.D., Ariz., 1984-89; guest instr. dance Am. U. in Bulgaria, Blagovegrad, 1996. Contbg. author: Native American Dance, 1992, Smithsonian Institution; choreographer dance-dramas Sacred Woman, Sacred Earth, 1990, Mythic Cycles, 1996; choreographer, performer numerous solo and ensemble works, 1980—. Choreographer's Fellow Nat. Endowment for Arts, 1995-97. Mem. Congress on Rsch. in Dance, World Dance Alliance, Smithsonian Instn., Mus. Women in Arts. Office: Daystar Dance Co 2471 Camino Capitan Santa Fe NM 87505

JONES, ROSEMARIE FRIEDA, service executive; b. Heidelberg, Germany, May 15, 1950; came to U.S., 1952; d. Duane W. Blodgett and Imargard P. (Reinmuth) Boczanski; m. Curtis B. Jones, June 3, 1989; children: Spencer E. Jones, Steven T. Kratzer. BS in Bus. Edn., U. Nebr., 1972, MEd, 1980. Instr. Columbus (Ga.) Vo-Tech., 1975-76; adminstrv. asst. to commdr. 1st Inf. Divsn., Goeppingen, Germany, 1976-79; grad. asst. U. Nebr., Lincoln, 1979-80; instr. bus. occupations S.E. Community Coll., Lincoln, 1980-84; br. mgr. Imprimis Legal Staffing, Dallas, 1985—; adv. bd. Dallas County Community Coll., Brookhaven Coll., curriculum writer Eastfield Community Coll., Dallas; speaker in field; instr. bus. comms. Brookhaven Coll., Dallas. Recipient Victor Trophy Sales and Mktg. Execs. Dallas, 1991. Mem. Am. Mgmt. Soc., Assn. Information Systems Profls. (pres. 1984). Home: 1615 Auburn Dr Richardson TX 75081-3046 Office: Imprimis Legal Staffing 1717 Main St Ste 3390 Dallas TX 75201-7348

JONES, ROSEMARY, education director; b. Washington, Pa., Aug. 15, 1951; d. Roy F. and Grace Vivian (Beton) J. BA in Sociology, Ohio State U., 1974, MA in Pub. Adminstrn., 1977. Mgmt. analyst office planning studies Ohio State U., Columbus, 1974-76; staff assoc., edn. rev. com. Ohio Gen. Assembly, Columbus, 1977-78; from adminstr. to asst. dir. info. systems and rsch. Ohio Bd. Regents, Columbus, 1978-90; from project dir. instl. rsch. to dir. rsch. planning Lakeland C.C., Mentor, Ohio, 1990-93; dist. dir. instl. planning evaluation Cuyahoga C.C., Cleve., 1994—; mem. com. on info. sys. design Ohio Bd. Regents, 1995—, subsidy cons. com., 1996; mem. com. on student outcomes measures Nat. Post Secondary Edn. Coop., 1996; mem. NPECSS planning com. Dept. Edn., 1994-96, NPEC student outcomes data working group, 1996, NCES coop. sys. fellows program, 1996; mem. com. on revising info. sys. for higher edn. Ohio Bd. Regents, Columbus, 1994-96, mem. subsidy consultation com., 1996, cons., 1990-91. Consumr adv. bd. United Health Plan, Columbus, 1978-82, chair, 1980-82; vol. Ronald McDonald House, Columbus, 1989, operating bd. mem., 1989; bd. dirs. Netcare Found., Columbus, 1988; state and regional conf. chair ASPA, Columbus, 1981, 83-84; steering com. Ctrl. Ohio Salute to Pub. Employees, Columbus, 1983. Mem. Assn. Instl. Rsch., Ohio Conf. for Coll. and Univ. Planning, Ohio Assn. Instl. Rsch. (two-yr. campus coun. rep. 1994-96), Cleve. Planning Forum, Soc. for Coll. and Univ. Planning, Cleve. Commn. on Higher Edn. Strategic Planning Com. (temp. chair 1991). Office: Cuyahoga CC 700 Carnegie Ave Cleveland OH 44115-2833

JONES, SALLY DAVIESS PICKRELL, writer; b. St. Louis, June 4, 1923; d. Claude Dildine and Marie Daviess (Pittman) Pickrell; m. Charles William Jones, Sept. 2, 1943; 1 son, Matthew Charles (dec.). Student, Mills Coll., Oakland, Calif., 1941-43, U. Calif.-Berkeley, 1944, Columbia, 1955-58. Author: (novel) The Lights Burn Blue, 1947. Mem. UN Women's Guild, Fgn. Policy Assn., Nat. Coun. Women, Asia Soc., English-Speaking Union, Met. Mus. Art, Internat. Platform Assn., Women's Internat. Forum. Episcopalian. Address: 311 E 58th St New York NY 10022-2003

JONES, SANDRA LAVERN, day care administrator, small business owner; b. Washington, Jan. 2, 1948; d. Julius Ellis and Evelyn Augusta (Best) Moon; m. Ronald Edwin Jones, Dec. 14, 1985; 1 child, Daniel. BA, Fed. City Coll., 1975; MS, U. D.C., 1978, MA in Adminstrn. and Supervision, 1992. Adminstrv. specialist Immigration and Naturalization Svc., Washington, 1975-79; archivist Nat. Archives and Record Svc., Washington, 1980-82; libr. D.C. Pub. Schs., 1983-93; adminstr. parks/coop. play program Langston Pre-Sch., Washington, 1993-94; owner, dir. Evelyn-Ron Day Care, Clinton, Md., 1994—; cons. D.C. Transp. Pub. Space Project, 1982-83. Vol. libr. Lorton (Va.) Reformatory Youth Ctr., 1979-80; co-founder Neighborhood Watch Program, Washington, 1981, cmty. coord., 1987—; v.p. 6th Dist. Adv. Coun., 1982-83; historian East Washington Park Citizens Assn., 1982-84, editor, 1982-83; bd. dirs. U. D.C., 1994—. Recipient Grass Roots award D.C. Fedn. Civic Assns., 1983. Mem. ALA, D.C. Libr. Assn. (program coord. 1986), Prince George's County Day Care Assn., Prince George's Child Care Resource Ctr., NAFE. Democrat. Methodist. Office: Evelyn-Ron Day Care 6201 Edward Dr Clinton MD 20735-4134

JONES, SANDRA LEE, internship program director; b. Chgo., May 21, 1950; d. Clifford Robert and Dorothy Lucille (Rutzen) Harry; m. Martin Dexter Jones, Sept. 5, 1970; 1 child, Matthew Shawn Jones. BA in English, Columbus Coll., 1972, MEd in English Edn., 1977; EdD in Vocat. and Adult Edn., Auburn U., 1991. Classroom English tchr. Don C. Faith Jr. H.S., Ft. Benning, Ga., 1972-73, McIntosh Jr. H.S., Albany, Ga., 1977-80; lang. arts supr. Dougherty County Schs., Albany, 1980-82; classroom English tchr. Carroll H.S., Ozark, Ala., 1982-83; adj. instr. English Troy State U. at Dothan, Ala., 1983-84, instr. of English, 1984-93; asst. prof. edn. Troy State U. at Dolthan, Ala., 1993-94; dir. profl. internship program, certification officer Troy State U. at Dothan, Ala., 1994—; mem. adv. bd. Troy State U., Dothan, 1992—, advisor Student Ala. Edn. Assn., 1995—. Mem. ASCD, NEA, Nat. Coun. Tchrs. of English, Mensa, TSUD Ala. Edn. Assn. (sec., treas. 1990-94), Sigma Tau Delta (advisor 1996—), Kappa Delta Pi. Office: Troy State U at Dothan 501 University Dr Dothan AL 36303

JONES, SHEILA MCLENDON, construction company executive; b. Bennettsville, S.C., July 11, 1965; d. Charlie Garrett and Ruby (Hatcher) McLendon; m. James Robert Jones, July 24, 1987; children: Robert Shane, Ashley Sunny. Student, Chesterfield/Marlboro Tech., 1981. Nurse asst. Marlboro Park Hosp., Bennettsville, S.C., 1983-84; inspectopr INA Bearing Co., Inc., Cheraw, S.C., 1985; with Big Apple Fashions, Cheraw, S.C., 1985; inspector ADS Co., Inc., Star, N.C., 1985-86; machine operator Legg's Hosery, Rockingham, N.C., 1986-87; masonry cons. Robert Jones Masonry, Morven, N.C., 1987—. Active Cmty. Choir of Morven, 1996—. Democrat. Baptist. Home and Office: 128 N Church St Morven NC 28119-8705

JONES, SHIRLEY, actress, singer; b. Smithton, Pa., July 31, 1934; d. Paul and Marjorie (Williams) J.; m. Jack Cassidy, Aug. 5, 1956 (div. 1975); children: Shaun, Patrick, Ryan; m. Marty Ingels, 1977. Grad. high sch., 1952; student, Pitts. Playhouse. Appeared with chorus South Pacific, 1953, in Broadway prodn. Me and Juliet, 1954; other state appearences include The Beggar's Opera, 1957, The Red Mill, 1958, Maggie Flynn, 1968, On a Clear Day, 1975, Show Boat, 1976, Bitter Suite, 1983; films include role of Laurey in Oklahoma, 1954, later stage tour Paris and Rome, sponsorship U.S. Dept. State, Carousel, 1956, April Love, 1957, Never Steal Anything Small, 1959, Bobbikins, 1959, Elmer Gantry, 1960 (Acad. Best Supporting Actress award 1961), Pepe, 1960, The Two Rode Together, 1961, The Music Man, 1962, The Courtship of Eddie's Father, 1963, A Ticklish Affair, 1963, Bedtime Story, 1964, The Secret of My Success, 1965, Fluffy, 1965, The Happy Ending, 1969, The Cheyenne Social Club, 1970, Beyond the Poseidon Adventure, 1979, Tank, 1984, There Were Times, Dear, 1985; night club tour with husband, 1958, later TV and summer stock; star TV series The Partridge Family, 1970-74, Shirley, 1979; guest star: TV series McMillan, 1976; TV films include: Silent Night, Lonely Night, 1969, But I Don't Want To Get Married!, 1970, The Girls of Huntington House, 1973, The Family Nobody Wanted, 1975, The Lives of Jenny Dolan, 1975, Winner Take All, 1975, Yesterday's Child, 1977, Evening in Byzantium, 1978, Who'll Save Our Children, 1978, A Last Cry for Help, 1979, The Children Of An Lac, 1980, Inmates: A Love Story, 1981, There Were Times Dear, 1987; one-woman concert: TV series Shirley Jones' America 1981; author: Shirley and Marty: An Unlikely Love Story, 1990. Nat. chairwoman Leukemia Found. Named Mother of Yr. by Women's Found., 1978.

JONES, SONIA JOSEPHINE, advertising agency executive; b. Belize, Brit. Honduras, Nov. 9, 1945; came to U.S., 1962, naturalized, 1986; d. Frederick Francis and Elsie Adelia (Gomez) Alcoser; m. John Marvin Jones, Mar. 21, 1970; children: Christopher William Edward, Joshua Joseph Paul. Student, Lamar U., 1964-66. With Foley's Federated Dept. Store, Houston, 1965-67; media buyer Vance Advt., Houston, 1967-68; media buyer, planner O'Neill & Assocs., Houston, 1968-75; media supr. Ketchum Houston, 1975-76; v.p., media dir. Rives Smith Bladwin Carlberg/Y & R, Houston, 1976-86; sr. v.p. media dir. Black Gillock & Langberg, Houston, 1986-89; pres. JMM Group, Inc., Houston, 1989—; lectr. U. Houston, 1983—. Vol. Women in Yellow, Houston, 1966; mem. St. Thomas High Sch. Mothers Club, 1992—; translator vol. St. Cecilia Clinic, 1993—; mem. sch. bd. St. Cecilia Cath. Sch., St. Thomas High Sch. Women's Club, fundraising vol., 1992—. Mem. Houston Advt. Fedn. Republican. Office: JMM Group Inc 2500 City West Blvd Ste 300 Houston TX 77042

JONES, SUSAN EMILY, fashion educator, administrator, educator; b. N.Y.C., Sept. 9, 1948; d. David and Emily Helen (Welke) J.; m. Henry J. Titone, Jr., Oct. 21, 1974 (div. 1980); m. Douglas S. Robbins, Aug. 21, 1985. B.F.A., Pratt Inst., Bklyn., 1970. Designer Sue Brett, N.Y.C., 1970-74; prof. fashion Pratt Inst., Bklyn., 1972-80, prof., 1980—, chairperson fashion dept., 1981-83, chairperson merchandising and design programs fashion dept., 1983—; computer software cons., 1988-89; internat. observer Jeunes Createurs de Mode, Paris, 1987, judge, 1988; U.S. rep. SAGA International. Design Ctr., Copenhagen, 1992. Recipient Young Am. Designer award Internat. Ladies Garment Workers Union, 1970. Mem. Fashion Group (regional com. 1983-87, mem. com. 1990-93, ednl. com. 1995-96, co-chair ednl. com. 1996—), Nat. Retail Fedn., Under Fashion Assn. Home: 220 Willoughby Ave Brooklyn NY 11205-3805 Office: Pratt Inst Dept of Fashion Design 200 Willoughby Ave Brooklyn NY 11205-3817

JONES, SUSAN RENEE, counselor, mental health services professional; b. Lynchburg, Va., Jan. 20, 1965; d. Lloyd Hundley Jones and Jane (Conner) Hopton. Student, Ctrl. Va. C. C., Lynchburg, 1983-86; BA, Randolph-Macon Women's Coll., 1988; MA with honors, St. Mary's U., 1991. Lic. profl. counselor. Counselor Bridge Emergency Youth Shelter, Fort Worth, 1989; grad. asst. St. Mary's U., San Antonio, 1989-90; counseling intern Incarnate Word Coll., San Antonio, 1991; counseling intern Charter Real Hosp., San Antonio, 1991, program asst., 1991-92; psychotherapist Life Resource, Beaumont, Tex., 1992-93; mental health counselor Teen Health Ctr., Galveston, Tex., 1993-94; cons. Galveston (Tex.) Ind. Sch. Dist., 1994; youth counselor Texans War on Drugs Youth Camp, San Antonio, 1994. Mentor Cmties. in Schs. Burger King Acad., San Antonio, 1991; vol. Camp Meadowlark, Lynchburg, Va., 1978, Lynchburg Social Svcs., 1983-88. Summer fellow Universal Energy Syss., 1990. Mem. ACA, Psi Chi. Home: 328 11th St Altavista VA 24517

JONES, TAMIA NICOLE, elementary education educator; b. Lynwood, Calif., Apr. 16, 1969; d. Joel Morris and Cathy Elaine (Bartlett) J. AA, El Camino Jr. Coll., Torrance, Calif., 1991; BA, Calif. State Northridge, 1992; MPA, Calif. State Long Beach, 1996. Litigation asst. Donfeld, Kelley & Rollman, L.A., 1993-94; customer svc. assoc. Circuit City, Torrance, 1988—; sub. tchr., coll. aid Long Beach Unified Sch. Dist., 1994—, elem. tchr., 1996—; cons. tng. & employement divsn. City of Long Beach, 1996—. Vol. Kathleen Brown for Gov., L.A., 1994, Dem. Nat. Com. to elect Clinton/Gore; organizer African Am. Community Adv. Assn., Long Beach, 1996. Mem. Western Polit. Sci. Assn., Am. Polit. Sci. Assn., Internat. City/Cty. Mgmt. Assn., Mcpl. Mgmt. Assts. of So. Calif., AAUW, African Am. Community Adv. Assn. (corr. sec. 1995-96), World Wildlife Fedn., Nature Conservancy, Sierra Club. Democrat.

JONES, TINA CHARLENE, music educator, genealogy and law researcher; b. Washington, May 27, 1961; d. Charles Timothy Jones and Tiney Ruth (Marion) Haynie; James H. Haynie (stepfather). Paralegal degree, George Washington U., Washington, 1986. Music educator Creative Music Melodies Co., Silver Spring, Md., 1984—; freelance geneal. and legal rschr., Silver Spring, 1986. Contbr. articles on geneal. rsch. to The Afro-American Newspaper, 1994-95. Recipient grants Delta Sigma Theta, 1979, Nat. Christian Choir, 1986. Mem. Am. Coll. Musicians, Nat. Piano Found., Music Educators Nat. Conf., Internat. Ctr. Rsch. in Music Edn. Home: 6611 Gude Ave Silver Spring MD 20912 Office: Creative Music Melodies Co 8209 Fenton St Ste 1 Silver Spring MD 20910

JONES, VALERIE KAYE, insurance company executive; b. Cleve., Oct. 26, 1956; d. Daniel Edward and Katherine (Donaldson) J. BS with high honors, Ohio U., 1978; postgrad., Cleve. State U. Lic. ins. agt. Asst. personnel dir. The Higbee Co., Cleve., 1977-78; tchr. learning disabilities and behavior disorders Cleve. Heights-Univ. Heights (Ohio) Sch., 1978-83; mem. ins. specialist CUNA Mut. Ins. Group, Madison, Wis., 1983-84, rep. group coverages, 1984-87, field communications adminstr. cen. dist., 1987-88, sr. field comms. adminstr., 1988-93; sr. dist. account cons., 1993-94; mktg. support mgr. east ctrl. mktg. divsn. CUNA Mut. Ins. Group, Madison, Wis., 1994—; bd. sec. Liberty Hill Credit Union, Cleve., 1978-83. Asst. to dir. directory project Cuyahoga Spl. Edn. Service Ctr., 1974; mem. 21st Dist. Congl. Caucus, Cleve., 1984. Mem. Nat. Assn. Female Execs., Delta Sigma Theta. Democrat. Home: 14840 Greenview Rd Detroit MI 48223-2329 Office: CUNA Mut Ins Group 20800 Civic Center Dr Southfield MI 48076-4117

JONES, VIVIAN M., secondary and elementary education educator; b. Etowah, Tenn., Oct. 19, 1941; d. James Washington and Bessie Mae (Miller) Givens; m. James H. Hines, Aug. 25, 1963; 1 child, Deanna Marie; m. Thomas B. Jones, Jr., Oct. 22, 1977. BS, Tenn. Tech., 1963, MA, 1974. Cert. elem./secondary edn. tchr., Tenn. Tchr. fifth grade McMinn County Bd. Edn., Athens, Tenn., 1966-67, tchr. reading and English, 1967-69, kindergarten tchr., 1969-88; tchr. English McMinn Cen. High, 1990—; state evaluator, career ladder Tenn. State Dept. of Edn., Nashville, 1988-90; tchr. English, adult edn., McMinn County Bd. Edn., Athens, 1973-88, homebound tchr., 1987—. Mem. Nat. Coun. Tchrs. of English, East Tenn. Tchrs. of English, NEA, Tenn. Edn. Assn., McMinn County Edn. Assn. (faculty rep. 1966—). Republican. Baptist. Office: McMinn Ctrl HS 145 County Road 461 Englewood TN 37329-5237

JONES, WINONA NIGELS, retired library media specialist; b. St. Petersburg, Fla., Feb. 24, 1928; d. Eugene Arthur and Bertha Lillian (Dixon) Nigels; m. Charles Albert Jones, Nov. 26, 1944; children: Charles Eugene, Sharon Ann Jones Allworth, Caroline Winona Jones Pandorf. AA, St. Petersburg Jr. Coll., 1965; BS, U. South Fla., 1967, MS, 1968; Advanced MS, Fla. State U., 1980. Libr. media specialist Dunedin (Fla.) Comprehensive H.S., 1967-76; libr. media specialist, chmn. dept. Fitzgerald Middle Sch., Largo, Fla., 1976-87; dir. Media Svcs. East Lake H.S., Tarpon Springs, Fla., 1987-93, ret., 1993. Active Palm Harbor and Pinellas County Hist. Soc.; del. White House Conf. for Libr. and Info. Svcs. Named Educator of Yr. Pinellas County Sch. Bd. and Suncoast C. of C., 1983, 88, Palm Harbor Woman of Yr. Palm Harbor Jr. Women's Club, 1989. Mem. ALA (coun. 1988-92), NEA, AAUW, ASCD, Fla. Assn. Media in Edn. (pres.), U. So. Fla. Alumni Assn., Assn. Ednl. Comm. and Tech. (divsn. sch. media specialist, coms.), Am. Assn. Sch. Librs. (com., pres.-elect 1989, pres. 1990-91, past pres., exec. bd. 1991-92), Southeastern Libr. Assn., Fla. Libr. Assn., Fla. State Libr. Sci. Alumni, U. South Fla. Libr. Sci. Alumni Assn. (pres. 1991-92, 92-93), Phi Theta Kappa, Phi Rho Pi, Beta Phi Mu, Kappa Delta Pi, Delta Kappa Gamma (parliamentarian 1989-90, legis. chmn. 1990, sec. 1994—), Inner Wheel Club, Pilot Club, Civic Club, Order of Eastern Star (Palm Harbor, past worthy matron). Democrat. Home: 911 Manning Rd Palm Harbor FL 34683-6344

JONES-ATKINS, DEBORAH KAYE, state official; b. Bradenton, Fla., July 2, 1958; d. Ralph and Jewelle Vanessa (Gayle) Jones; m. Larry Bobby Atkins, July 30, 1983; 1 child, Omari Gayle Jones-Atkins. AS with distinction, Monroe Community Coll., Rochester, N.Y., 1986, cert. in human svcs, 1986; BIS, Va. State U., Petersburg, 1996. Credit investigator Sears Roebuck & Co., Rochester, N.Y., 1980; customer svc. rep. B. Forman Co., Rochester, 1980-81; youth counselor Brighton Youth Agy., Rochester, 1976-81; staff asst. Makro Inc., Capitol Hts., Md., 1981-82; customer svc. rep. MetroVision Inc., Capitol Hts., 1983-84; teen parent counselor Urban League of Rochester, 1985; job developer YWCA of Rochester, 1985-87; program coord. Urban League of Rochester, 1988; prog. support technician, sr. Dept. Med. Assistance Svcs., Commonwealth of Va., Richmond, 1989—; alt. health care supr. Commonwealth of Va. Med. Assist. Svcs., 1989-96. Mem. Women's Resource Ctr., Richmond, 1989—; heir link The Links Inc., Rochester, 1982—; vol. United Negro Coll. Fund Telethon, Rochester, 1988, N.Y. State Dept. Labor Career Edn. Expo, 1989, WXXI Auction 21, Rochester, 1989, YMCA Greater Rochester, 1989, Arts Coun., Richmond, Richmond Children's Festival, 1989, Sci. Mus. Va., Richmond, 1989, Arts Coun. Richmond 15th Ann. June Jubilee, 1990, Children's Book Festival, 1990, Maymont Found. Flower Garden Show, 1990, 91, Va. Spl. Olympics, 1990—, Jr. League Richmond 45th Book and Author Dinner, 1990, dinner asst. ticket chairperson 46th Book and Author Dinner, 1991, hostee 45th Dinner, Children's Book Festival Arts Coun. Richmond; mem. agy. svc. com. Friends Assn. for Children, 1990—, student adv. com. Va. Commonwealth U. Health Svcs., 1991, Friends of Art Richmond Mus. Fine Arts, 1991, membership com., audience devel. com., Richmond Profl. Women's Network; placement counselor Placement Com. Jr. League Richmond, 1991, mem. tng. com., 1991, adv. com. Children's Mus. Richmond; mem. exec. bd. YWCA of Richmond, 1992-95, fin. com., 1996—; mem. policy bd. Jr. League Richmond, 1992-93; mem. bd. dirs. Urban League of Richmond, 1996—. Mem. NAFE, Nat. Coun. Negro Women, Jr. League of Rochester, Nat. Trust Hist. Preservation, Richmond Profl. Women's Network (rec. sec., exec. bd. 1992—), Richmond Jaycees. Democrat. Home: 243 Elmwood Terr Rochester NY 14620

JONES BLASE, CONNIE J., insurance/investment counselor, consultant; b. Paul, Idaho, June 11, 1936; d. Coy Conley and Evelyn Marie (Craven) McK.; m. Marlin Charles Jones, Sept. 7, 1956 (div. Sept. 1985); children: Marla Nixon, Troy C. Jones, Debra Dee Cammann, Brian Scott Jones; m. August Robert Blase, Sept. 4, 1987. Attended, Idaho State Coll.; secretarial diploma, Twin Falls (Idaho) Bus. Coll., 1955. Lic. insurance agent, real estate agent. Sec. Dept. of Agr. State of Idaho, Rupert, 1955-56; sec. State of Idaho, Moscow, 1956-58, GE, Louisville, Ky., 1958-59; owner Golden Fawn Art Gallery, Ontario, Oreg., 1976-81, Everybody Unlimited, Ontario, 1978-85, Hair Unlimited I & II, Ontario, 1976-81; owner Everybody Unlimited, Ontario, 1978-85, Moses Lake, Wash., 1978-80; sales cons. Prudential Ins. Invest, Ontario, 1985-91; owner Carmel Kandy Shope, Ontario, 1986-93; cons. Sun Valley Potatoes, Paul, Idaho, 1987—; owner C. Stained Glass Design, Rupert, 1990—. Apptd. mem. Security Exch. Commn.; mem. county planning commn. Master Plan State, Vale, Oreg., 1978-80; city dir. County Hosp., Ontario, 1981-82; city coord. recreation dept. City of Ontario, 1968-84; mem. city libr. bd. Malhenr County Libr., Ontario, 1978-80; mem. city drug coun. Ontario, Oreg. TaskForce, 1981-84; elected mem. city coun. Mcpl. Govt., Ontario, 1976-84; mem. budget com. City of Ontario, 1972-84; active Aid to Aged, 1972-80, Help Them to Hope Holiday for Unfortunate, Ontario, 1970-88; mem. hosp. aux. Holy Rosary, Ontario, 1970-84; advisor Occupl. Health, Rupert, 1995—. Republican. Episcopalian. Home: 413 S Valverde Rupert ID 83350

JONESCO, JANE RIGGS, lawyer, development officer; b. Delaware, Ohio, Feb. 7, 1949; d. Edgar Gray and Bettie Pauline (Lowther) Riggs; m. John Michael Jonesco, Aug. 8, 1970; children: Amy Jane, John Michael III, Michael Andrew, Katherine Elizabeth. BA, Ohio Wesleyan U., 1971; JD, DePaul U., 1980. Bar: Ohio 1980. Atty. in pvt. practice Oberlin, Ohio, 1981-91; dir. planned giving Oberlin Coll., 1991—; mem. adminstrn. and profl. coun. Oberlin Coll., 1992-93; chair, mem. Oberlin City Income Tax Bd. of Rev., 1995. Mem. Oberlin Bd. Edn., 1987-93, v.p., 1988-89, pres., 1990-93; founder, mem. Oberlin Interagy. Coun., 1990-93; mem. Oberlin Community Svcs. Coun., 1986-90; mem. Oberlin Bicentennial Commn., 1985-86; pres., mem. Oberlin Baseball Softball Fedn., 1981-86; mem. Nat. Planned Giving Coun., No. Ohio Planned Giving Coun.; mem. Jr. League of Columbus, 1979-80, Oberlin Schs. Endowment Bd., 1996. Episcopalian. Home: 440 E College St Oberlin OH 44074-1305 Office: Oberlin Coll 208 Bosworth Hall Oberlin OH 44074

JONES GREGORY, PATRICIA, secondary art educator; b. La Grange, Ga., Apr. 15, 1944; d. Eddie Burrel Jones (dec.), Samuel Lee (stepfather) and Mildred Jones (Johnson) Turrentine; m. Bernard Gregory, Oct. 12, 1985. BFA in Art Edn., Pratt Inst., 1966; MS in Photography, Ill. Inst. Tech., 1970; postgrad. in African Studies and Rsch., Howard U., 1970-74; EdD in Ednl. Adminstrn. and Supervision, Seton Hall U., 1994. Cert. prin./supr., supr., ednl. adminstrn. and supervision, art tchr. grades K-12. Art tchr. Westfield (N.J.) Sch. Dist., 1966-68; art instr. Howard U., Washington, 1970-71; art tchr. Newark (N.J.) Sch. Dist., 1974-79, Irvington (N.J.) Sch. Dist., 1979-80, South Orange (N.J.)-Maplewood (N.J.) Sch. Dist., 1980-81, Montclair (N.J.) Sch. Dist., 1981-82; art instr., docent Newark (N.J.) Mus., 1982-84; art tchr. Weequahic H.S., Newark, 1983—; Com. mem. textbook evaluation curriculum svcs. Bd. Edn., Newark, 1983—; art dir. Ergo-Weequahic H.S., Newark, 1984-93, founder, advisor Kuumba Art Club, 1989-94, PB Graphics Design. Author: Many Moods of the Afro-American Woman, 1971, (catalog) Multicultural Arts Exhibition Catalog, 1992; co-author: (brochure) Multiethnic/Multicultural Women's Initiation Seminar, 1992, Secondary Art Curriculum Guide, 1994, (brochure) Young Women's Seminar Program Brochure, 1996. Rschr. Goldman and Kennedy The New York Urban Athlete, Simon and Schuster, N.Y., 1983. Grace B. Monroe grantee Pratt Inst., Bklyn., 1964; Grad. scholar Ill. Inst. Tech., Chgo., 1968-70; Rsch. fellow Howard U., Washington, 1972-73; recipient Cert. of Recognition, Gov.'s Tchr. Recognition Program, N.J., 1993. Mem. ASCD, Nat. Assn. for Multicultural Edn., Nat. Assn. Art Educators, Newark Mus., Newark Art Coun., Studio Mus. in Harlem, Kappa Delta Pi. Home: 78 Woodland Ave East Orange NJ 07017-2006

JONES-JOHNSON, GLORIA, sociologist, educator, consultant; b. Donaldsonville, Ga., Feb. 4, 1956; d. Willie James Jones and Annie Lois (Backey) Facen; m. Willie Roy Johnson, Aug. 14, 1982; children: Kyle Jamary Johnson, Nia Kiara Johnson. BA, Talladega Coll., 1978; MA, Bowling Green State U., 1980; PhD, U. Mich., 1986. Teaching asst. Bowling Green (Ohio) State U., 1978-80; rsch. asst. U. Mich., Ann Arbor, 1980-84, teaching asst., 1984-85; lectr. Wayne State U., Detroit, 1986; asst. prof. Iowa State U., Ames, 1986-92, assoc. prof., 1992—; vis. scholar U. Ga., Athens, 1996—; cons. United Rubber Workers, Des Moines, Iowa, 1988—, Tenn. Valley Authority, Nashville, 1987—. Grant reviewer NSF, 1988—, U.S. Dept. Edn., 1991—; contbr. articles to Jour. Social Psychology, Jour. Applied Social Psychology, Am. Sociologist, and others. Mem. Am. Sociological Assn., Midwest Sociological Soc. (state dir. Iowa 1991—), Assn. Black Sociologists, Rural Sociological Soc. (assoc. editor 1990—), Indsl. Rels. Rsch. Assn., Alpha Chi, Sigma Xi. Democrat. African Methodist. Home: 418 Wellons Dr Ames IA 50014-7624

JONES-LUKÁCS, ELIZABETH LUCILLE, physician, air force officer; b. Norfolk, Va.; d. Oliver C. and Gertrude (Layden) Jones; B.S., Oglethorpe U., 1955; m. Michel J. Lukacs (dec.); children—Amanda, Laurel, Angelique, Klara. Intern Beth Israel Hosp., N.Y.C., 1964-65; family practice medicine, Goshen, N.Y., 1965-73, Buckingham, Va., 1973-78; commd. maj. U.S. Air Force, 1978; flight surgeon, Andrews AFB, Md., 1978-85, chief exec. med. program, 1991—; unit charge physician Student Health Ctr., U. Md., College Park, 1985-91. Col. USAFR, commd. 459th USAF Clinic. Diplomate, fellow Am. Bd. Family Practice. Mem. Am. Med. Womens Assn. (pres. Br. I), Md. Thoroughbred Breeders. Episcopalian. Author: The Curies Radium & Radioactivity, 1962; The Golden Stamp Book of Flying Animals, 1963. Home: 4310 Woodberry St Hyattsville MD 20782-1173 Office: Malcolm Grow Med Ctr Dept Family Practice Andrews AFB Washington DC 20331

JONES-MORTON, PAMELA, human resources specialist; b. Balt., Aug. 21, 1947; d. Robert Alfred and Lois Enola (Skilliter) Jones; m. Wayne Daniel Morton, Sept. 7, 1968 (div. Aug. 1990). BS, Frostburg State U., 1970; MA, Mich. State U., 1976; PhD, Ohio State U., 1989. Tchr. Alleghaney High Sch., Cumberland, Md., 1970-72; tchr. Am. Sch. in Japan, Tokyo, 1972-74, dept. head, 1974-77; tchr. The Tatnall Sch., Wilmington, Del., 1977-78; dept. head, athletic dir. Internat. Sch. Dusseldorf, West Germany, 1979-82; athletic dir. Escola Americana De Rio de Janeiro, 1982-85, Am. Cmty. Sch., London, 1985-86; grad. asst. Ohio State U., Columbus, 1986-89; univ. prof. W.Va. U., Morgantown, 1989-91; mgr. human and bus. devel. Honda of Am. Mfg., Inc., Columbus, 1991-95, mgr. expatriate adminstrn. dept., 1995—; pres. Kanto Plains Athletic Assn., Tokyo, 1973-77; mem accreditation team European Coun., London, 1982; spkr., mem. acad. adv. com. Tolles Tech. Sch., Plain City, Ohio. Contbr. articles to profl. jours. Active Dolphin Rsch. Ctr., Marathon Shores, Fla., 1992—, Marine Conservation, 1994—. Mem. ASTD (benchmarking forum 1991-95, spkr. 1993, 94, 95), AAHPED, Phi Delta Kappa. Democrat. Office: Honda of Am Mfg Inc 24000 Honda Pky Marysville OH 43040

JONES-RUSSELL, HOLLY LEIGH, mental health counselor; b. Gatesville, Tex., Sept. 11, 1970; d. Stanley David and Ruth (Gilbreath) Jones; m. Ronald Thomas Russell, May 28, 1994; children: Amanda, James, Whitney. BA, Baylor U., 1991; MA, U. Mary Hardin-Baylor, 1993. Lic. profl. counselor, Tex. Min. of youth Lorena (Tex.) Meth. Ch., 1990-91; substitute tchr. Gatesville Ind. Sch. Dist., 1990-92; unit dir. Ctrl. Counties Mental Health and Mental Retardation, Temple, Tex., 1992-93; instr., lectr. Ctrl. Tex. Coll., Gatesville, 1993—; counselor Heart of Tex. Mental Health and Mental Retardation, Waco, Tex., 1993—; cons. DePaul Ctr. Psychiat. Hosp., Waco, 1993—, Austin (Tex.) State Hosp., 1993—, Family Practice Clinic, Waco, 1993—. Com. mem. Gatesville Mus. Soc., 1991-93. Mem. ASCD, Tex. Counseling Assn. (counseling advocacy com. 1994—), Tex. Assn. for Assessment in Counseling, Gatesville Collector's CClub (com. 1990-92). Democrat. Methodist. Office: Heart of Tex MH-MR PO Box 890 110 S 12th St Waco TX 76703-0890

JONG, ERICA MANN, writer, poet; b. N.Y.C., Mar. 26, 1942; d. Seymour and Eda (Mirsky) Mann; m. Michael Werthman, 1963 (div. 1965); m. Allan Jong (div. Sept. 1975); m. Jonathan Fast, Dec. 1977 (div. Jan. 1983); 1 child, Molly; m. Kenneth David Burrows, Aug. 5, 1989. B.A., Barnard Coll., 1963; M.A., Columbia U., 1965. Faculty, English dept. CUNY, 1964-65, 69-70, overseas div. U. Md., 1967-69; mem. lit. panel N.Y. State Council on Arts, 1972-74; faculty Breadloaf Writers Conf. Middlebury, Vt., 1982; mem. faculty Saltzburg Seminar, Saltzburg, Austria, 1993. Author: (poems) Fruits and Vegetables, 1971, Half Lives, 1973, Loveroot, 1975, At the Edge of the Body, 1979, Ordinary Miracles, 1983, Becoming Light: Poems New and Selected, 1992; (novels) Fear of Flying, 1973, How to Save Your Own Life, 1977, Fanny: Being the True History of the Adventures of Fanny Hackabout-Jones, 1980, Parachutes and Kisses, 1984, Serenissima, 1987 (reissued as Shylock's Daughter, 1995), Any Woman's Blues, 1990, (poetry and non-fiction) Witches, 1981, (juvenile) Megan's Book of Divorce, 1984 (reissued as Megan's Two Houses, 1995), (memoir) The Devil at Large, 1993, (autobiography) Fear of Fifty, 1994; composer lyrics: Zipless: Songs of Abandon from the Erotic Poetry of Erica Jong, 1995. Woodrow Wilson fellow; recipient Bess Hokin prize Poetry mag., 1971; named Mother of Yr., 1982; Nat. Endowment Arts grantee, 1973. Mem. PEN, Authors Guild U.S.A. (coun. 1975—, pres. 1991-93), Poets and Writers Bd., Writers Guild Am.-West, Poetry Soc. Am. (Alice Faye di Castagnola award 1972), Phi Beta Kappa. Office: Erica Jong Prodns 205 E 68th St New York NY 10021

JONG, THERESA ANN, human resource executive; b. Chgo., Aug. 27, 1965; d. Ronald Walter and Marilyn Ruth (Krase) W. BS, San Diego State U., 1989. Dir. personnel and facilities Guild Mortgage Co., San Diego, 1988. Vol. Easter Seals Soc. San Diego, 1988—, Am. Heart Assn., 1989—, Zool. Soc. San Diego, 1986—; coord. (ETC) mgmt. employee transp. San Diego Traffic Demand, 1989—. Mem. Pers. Mgmt. Assn. Roman Catholic. Office: Guild Mortgage Co 9160 Gramercy Dr San Diego CA 92123-4020

JONIENTZ, ROSEMARY, public relations executive, adult education educator; b. Fulton, N.Y.. BA in Political Science, State U. Coll., Buffalo, 1979; Certificate in Pub. Rels., SUNY, Buffalo, 1989. Cert. OSHA instr., trainer. Mental health specialist Dept. Spl. Svcs., Baker Hall, Our Lady of Victory Homes of Charity, Lackawanna, N.Y., 1979-81, supr., cottage mgr., 1981-83; acct. exec. The Copeland Cos., Orchard Park, N.Y., 1985-89; cmty. rels. specialist Housing Opportunities Made Equal, Inc. (HOME), Buffalo, 1990-91; program coord. The Central N.Y. Coun. on Occupational Safety & Health, Syracuse, 1991—; pub. rels. chair, mem. bd. dirs. Women For Downtown, Buffalo, 1990-91; matrix chair, mem. bd. dirs. Women in Comms., Inc., Syracuse, N.Y., 1995-96; radio mktg. cons. WECK Radio, Buffalo; program coord. The Buffalo News/Print Pluss. Mem. APHA, Women in Comms., Inc. (bd. dirs. 1995), Alumni Assn. Buffalo State Coll. Democrat. Roman Catholic. Home: 123 Plaxdale Rd Liverpool NY 13088

JONKOUSKI, JILL ELLEN, materials scientist, ceramic engineer, educator; b. Chgo.; d. Joseph and Ruth Jonkouski. BS in Ceramic Engring., U. Ill., MS in Ceramic Engring. Former researcher Battelle Meml. Inst., Columbus, Ohio; former ceramic engr. Austenal Dental, Inc., Chgo.; former rsch. scientist BIRL Indsl. Rsch. Lab. Northwestern U., Evanston, Ill.; ceramics mfg. engr., program mgr. rsch. and engring. Environ. Programs Group divsn. U.S. Dept. Energy, Argonne, Ill., 1991—; past adj. faculty Triton Coll., River Grove, Ill.; presenter Nat. Thermal Spray Conf., 1991, 92, Pacific Coast regional meeting Am. Ceramic Soc., 1994, Coal-Fired Sys. 94, 1994, Ceramic Industry Mfg. Conf. & Exposition, 1995. Mem. Am. Ceramic Soc. (spkr., tech. presenter 1983, 84, 95, 96, chair Chgo.-Milw. sect. 1993-94), U.S. Figure Skating Assn., U. Ill. Alumni Assn. Office: US Dept Energy Environ Programs Group 9800 S Cass Ave Argonne IL 60439-4899

JONSON, BERNADETTE J., judge. Former civil ct. judge La. Dist. Ct., New Orleans; assoc. justice Supreme Ct. La., New Orleans, 1994—. Office: 301 Loyola Ave New Orleans LA 70112*

JOO, PILJU KIM, agronomist; b. Korea, Sept. 9, 1937; came to U.S., 1962; d. Myung Ryun and Ockjin (Chu) Kim; m. Young Don Joo, Nov. 27, 1963; children: Michael Wuchung, Thomas Wuil, Eungie. BS in Agronomy, Seoul Nat. U., Suwon, Korea, 1960; MS in Agronomy, Seed Tech., Miss. State U., Starkville, 1964; PhD in Agronomy, field Crops, Cornell U., 1970. Ext. specialist Rural Adminstrn. Office, Suwon, 1960-62; grad. rsch. asst. Miss. State U., Korea, 1962-64; rsch. asst. Miss. State U., State College, 1964-65; grad. rsch. asst. Cornell U., Ithaca, N.Y., 1965-67, rsch. asst., assoc., 1969-75; rsch. asst. Pa. State U., University Park, 1967-69; mgr. and dir. seed sci. rsch. Northrup King Co., Mpls., 1975-84; dir. seed sci. rsch. Stauffer Chem. Corp., Richmond, Calif., 1984-85; tech. svcs. dir. Pioneer Hi-Bred Internat., 1986-92; v.p. Agglobe Technologies, Mpls., 1992—; chmn. ad hoc com., editor Seed Vigor Handbook, AOSA-SCST, 1980-82; chmn. corn rsch. working groups Internat. Seed Testing Assn., 1983-86, 89-92; hon. scientist Rural Adminstrn. Office, Suwon, 1992—; lectr. in field; adj. prof. U. Minn., 1995—. Contbr. articles to profl. jours. Mem. AAAS, Am. Soc. Agronomy, Crop Sci. Soc. Am., Soc. Comml. Seed Technologist, Am. Forage and Grassland Coun., Am. Seed Trade Assn., Minn. Forage and Grassland Coun., Korean Am. Scientists and Engrs. Assn., Korean Soc. for Hort. Sci. Presbyterian. Office: Agglobe Technologies 3530 E 28th St Minneapolis MN 55406-1765

JOONDEPH, MARCIA, diplomat; b. N.Y.C., Mar. 3, 1930; d. Isadore Horowitz and Bess Benenson Starfield; m. Norman H. Joondeph, July 17, 1920; children: Wendy, Michael. BA, Columbia U., 1952. Office mgr. dr.'s office Stamford, Conn., 1974-84; sculptor Pietra Santa, Italy, 1991; UN del. Promoting Enduring Peace, Milford, Conn., 1991—; bd. dirs., chmn. exec. bd. dirs., v.p., v.p. fin. com. Promoting Enduring Peace, Milford, 1991—. Exhibited in several juried shows, 1991—. Bd. dirs. Peace Action Internat., Geneva, 1992—; del. 4th World Conf. on Women in Beijing, China. Home: 44 Caprice Dr Stamford CT 06902

JOOS, OLGA MARTÍN-BALLESTERO DE, Spanish language educator; b. Zaragoza, Spain, May 2, 1944; came to U.S., 1973; d. Luis and Olga Helena (Hernandez) Martin-Ballestero; m. William Joseph Joos, Oct. 9, 1973; children: Catalina, Louis, Olga, William. Grad., U. Zaragoza, Spain, 1969; postgrad., UNF. Substitute lang. tchr. Assumption Sch., 1989-91, Bolles Sch., 1991-93; h.s. Spanish tchr. Douglas Anderson Sch. of Arts, Jacksonville, Fla., 1994—. Home: 2641 River Rd Jacksonville FL 32207-4020

JORAJURIA, ELSIE JEAN, elementary education educator; b. Flagstaff, Ariz., June 28, 1946; d. Frank Y. and Elsie (Barreres) Auza; m. Ramon Jorajuria, June 23, 1973; children: Tonya, Nina. BS in Edn., No. Ariz. U., 1971, MA in Elem. Edn., 1975. Cert. elem. edn., Ariz. First grade tchr. Kinsey Sch., Flagstaff, Ariz., 1971-73; third grade tchr. Mohawk Valley Sch., Roll, Ariz., 1973-77, migrant edn. coord., 1980-83, second lang. English Kindergarten tchr., 1983-84, first grade tchr., 1984—; tchr. ESL Ariz. Wester Coll., Yuma, Ariz., 1987. Cheerleader sponsor, Roll, Ariz., 1984-97; vol. 4-H, Roll, 1986-97, project leader, 1990-97, cmty. leader, 1994-97, sponsor Student Coun., Roll, 1994-95. Named Tchr. of Yr., Mohawk Valley Sch., 1987-88, 88-89, 95-96, Woman of the Yr., Bus. Profl. Woman, 1994. Mem. NEA, Ariz. Edn. Assn., Mohawk Valley Tchr. Assn. (pres. 1992-94), Ariz. Wool Growers Assn. Democrat. Roman Catholic. Home: PO Box 485 40154 Colorado Ave Tacna AZ 85352 Office: Mohawk Valley Sch PO Box 67 Tacna AZ 85352-0067

JORCZAK, NANCY, history educator; b. Trenton, N.J., May 4, 1948; d. Joseph Stanley and Phyllis (Grotkowski) J. BA, Colby Coll., Waterville, Maine, 1970; MA in Teaching, Trenton (N.J.) State Coll., 1973. Cert. secondary tchr., Pa., N.J. Tchr. Okayama (Japan) Cultural Ctr., 1971-72, Coun. Rock H.S., Newtown, Pa., 1973—. Fulbright scholar, 1981. Mem. Huntingdon Valley Kennel Club (pres. 1995), Pharaoh Hound Club Am. (pres. 1995—). Republican. Home: PO Box 745 Washington Crossing PA 18977-0745 Office: Coun Rock H S 62 Swamp Rd Newtown PA 18940

JORDAHL, KATHLEEN PATRICIA (KATE JORDAHL), photographer, educator; b. Summit, N.J., Aug. 23, 1959; d. Martin Patrick and Marie Pauline (Quinn) O'Grady; m. Geir Arild Jordahl, Sept. 24, 1983. BA in Art & Art History magna cum laude with distinction, U. Del., 1980; MFA in Photography, Ohio U., 1982. Lifetime credential in art and design, Calif. Teaching assoc. Sch. Art Ohio U., Athens, 1980-82; adminstrv. asst. A.D. Coleman, S.I., N.Y., 1981; placement asst. career planning & placement U. Calif., Berkeley, 1983; instr. Coll. for Kids, Hayward, Calif., 1987-88; supr.

student/alumni employment office Chabot Coll., Hayward, 1983-87, tchr. photography, 1987—; workshop coord. Friends of Photography, San Francisco, 1990; instr., workshop leader, coord. PhotoCen. Photography Programs, Hayward, 1983—; mem., co-coord., publ. evaluation accreditation com. Chabot Coll., Hayward, 1984, instrnl. skills workshop facilitator, 1994, speaker opening day, 1986, coord. ann. classified staff devel. workshop, 1985; workshop leader Ansel Adams Gallery, Yosemite, Calif., 1991, 92, artist-in-residence Yosemite Nat. Park Mus., 1993; ind. curator numerous exhbns., 1984—; coord., curator Women's Photography Workshop & Exhbn., 1993—. Exhibited in group shows Parts Gallery, Minn., 1992, The Alameda Arts Commn. Gallery, Oakland, 1992, Panoramic Invitational, Tampere, Finland, 1992, Photo Forum, Pitts., 1992, Photo Metro Gallery, San Francisco, 1993, Ansel Adams Gallery, Yosemite, 1994, Yosemite Mus., 1994, Vision Gallery, San Francisco, 1994, 95, San Francisco Mus. Modern Art Rental Gallery, 1994; represented in permanent collections Muse Gallery, Phila., 1982, Ohio U. Libr. Rare Books Collection, Athens, 1982, Yosemite Mus., 1994, Bibliotheque Nationale de France, Paris; contbr. photos and articles to photography mags. and publs. Recipient Innovative New Program award Calif. Parks and Recreation Soc., 1990; Sons of Norway scholar U. Oslo, summer 1996. Mem. Internat. Assn. Panoramic Photographers, Soc. Photographic Edn., Friends of Photography, Sun Gallery, Phi Beta Kappa. Democrat. Address: PO Box 3998 Hayward CA 94540-3998

JORDAN, ANNE ELIZABETH D., journalist; b. Golden Valley, Minn., Mar. 30, 1964; d. Allen L. and Marcia G. (Landeen) Dollerschell; m. James Lawrence Jordan, Aug. 16, 1986; children: Davyd C., Scott A. Attended, Rochester (Minn.) C.C., 1982-83, U. Warwick, Coventry, England, 1984-85; BA in History and Political Science, U. Wis., Madison, 1986. Editl. asst. Governing Mag., Washington, D.C., 1987-88, rsch. dir., 1989-92, asst. mng. editor, 1993—. Mem. Phi Beta Kappa, Phi Kappa Phi, Phi Theta Kappa. Presbyn. Office: Governing Mag Ste 760 2300 N St NW Washington DC 20037

JORDAN, BERNICE BELL, elementary education educator; b. Calvert, Tex.; d. Ocie Wade and Nannie B. (Westbrook) Bell; m. William B. Jordan, Sept. 28, 1956; children: Beverly, Terrence, Keith Jordan. BA, San Jose State Coll., 1959, MA, 1985; student, Prairie View A and M, Tex. Western Coll. Cert. elem. edn., fine arts, multi-cultural. Writer curriculum guide, fine arts Alum Rock Union Elem. Sch. Dist., San Jose, Calif.; writer sch. plan Goss Elem.; tchr. 3rd grade Alum Rock Union Elem. Sch. Dist., San Jose; adv. com., tchr.-cons. San Jose Area Writing Project, San Jose U., 1992—. Mem. Assn. for Supervision and Curriculum Devel., Alum Rock Edn. Assn., Calif. Tchrs. Assn., Calif. Reading Assn., Calif. Elem. Edn. Assn., Santa Clara County Reading Coun., NEA, Alpha Delta Kappa. Home: 3282 Fronda Dr San Jose CA 95148-2015

JORDAN, BETTY SUE, retired special education educator; b. Lafayette, Tenn., Sept. 4, 1920; d. Aubrey Lee and Geneva (Freeman) West; m. Bill Jordan, Oct. 22, 1950; 1 child, L. Nicha. Student, David Lipscomb Coll., 1939-41; BS, U. Tenn., 1943; registered dietitian Duke U. Hosp., 1945; MEd, Clemson U., 1973. Dietitian U. Ala., Tuscaloosa, 1945-46, Duke U., Durham, N.C., 1946-48, Stetson U., DeLand, Fla., 1948-50, Furman U., Greenville, S.C., 1950-52; elem. tchr. Greenville County Schs., S.C., 1952-66, tchr. orthopedically handicapped, 1966-85; with Shriners Hosp. for Crippled Children Sch.; pres. Robert Morris S.S. class U. Meth. Ch., 1992. Mem. NEA, Assn. Childhood Edn. (treas. 1980-85), United Daus. Confederacy (pres. Greenville chpt. 1978—), Greenville Woman's Club (exec. bd. 1991-94), Lake Forest Garden Club (pres. 1970-71, 77-79, 80-81, historian 1981-87, 1st v.p., 1991-92, Woman of Yr. awards 1991, 92, Rachel McKaughan Horticulture award 1992, 94, 95, Lois Russel Arrangement award 1993-95), Greater Greenville Rose Soc. (pres. 1983-84), Am. Rose Soc. (accredited rose judge 1986, rose arrangement judge, cons., Rosarian), Clarice Wilson Garden Club (pres. 1987-89, Woman of Yr. 1991, Award for Arrangements), Delta Kappa Gamma (pres. Tau chpt. 1976-78, state chmn. communications 1979-81, state chmn. rsch. 1983-85, leadership/mgmt. seminar Austin, Tex. 1989), Kappa Kappa Iota (state pres. 1972-73, conclave pres. 1983-85), Democrat. Methodist. Avocations: collecting antiques, growing roses, flower arranging. Home: 21 Lisa Dr Greenville SC 29615-1350

JORDAN, DEBBIE CONLEY, accountant; b. Mount Holly, N.J., Dec. 11, 1955; d. Norman Stewart and Helen Gertrude (Dorsey) Conley; m. Patrick Scott Jordan, Mar. 17, 1994; 1 child, Kathryn Rose Jordan. BA, Cook Coll., Rutgers U., New Brunswick, N.J., 1978; MBA, Johnson Grad. Sch. Mgmt., Cornell U., Ithaca, N.Y., 1981. CPA, Md., N.Y. Tax cons. Price Waterhouse LLP, Washington, D.C., 1981-84, sr. tax cons., 1984-87; mgr. Ciaschi Dietershagen Little & Mickelson LLP, Ithaca, N.Y., 1987-90, ptnr., 1990—; mem. bd. dirs. Estate Planning Coun. of Tompkins County, Ithaca, N.Y., 1989-92, Tompkins County C. of C., 1992-96. Pres., treas., v.p. Ithaca Bus. & Profl. Women, 1989-92; mem. bd. dirs. The Sciencenter, Ithaca, 1991-94. Named Outstanding Com. Chair Tompkins C. of C., 1993. Mem. AICPA, N.Y.S. Soc. CPA's, Ithaca Bus. & Profl. Women (treas. 1989-90, v.p. 1990-91, pres. 1991-92), Estate Planning Coun. of Tompkins County, Downtown Bus. Women. Democrat. Office: Ciaschi Dietershagen Little & Mickelson LLP 118 Prospect St Ste 103 Ithaca NY 14850

JORDAN, GABRIELLA, lawyer; b. Phila., July 26, 1958. BA magna cum laude, U. Pa., 1980; JD, Columbia U., 1984. Bar: N.Y. 1985, U.S. Dist. Ct. (so. and ea. dists.) N.Y. 1985, U.S. Ct. Appeals (6th cir.) 1985, U.S. Dist. Ct. (we. dist.) N.Y. 1990, U.S. Ct. Appeals (2d cir.) 1991. Ptnr. Anderson Kill Olick & Oshinsky, P.C., N.Y.C. Contbr. articles to profl. jours. Harlan Fiske Stone scholar. Mem. ABA, Assn. of Bar of City of N.Y. Office: Anderson Kill Olick & Oshinsky PC 1251 Ave of the Americas New York NY 10020-1182*

JORDAN, JENNIFER B., lawyer. Ptnr Cadwalader, Wickersham & Taft, N.Y.C. Office: Cadwalader Wickersham & Taft 100 Maiden Ln New York NY 10006*

JORDAN, JUDITH VICTORIA, clinical psychologist, educator; b. Milw., July 28, 1943; d. Claus and Charlotte (Backus) J.; m. William M. Redpath, Aug. 11, 1973. AB, Brown U., 1965; MA, Harvard U., 1968, PhD, 1973. Diplomate Am. Bd. Profl. Psychology. Psychologist Human Relations Service, Wellesley, Mass., 1971-73; assoc. psychologist McLean Hosp., Belmont, Mass., 1978-93, psychologist, 1993—, dir. women's studies program, 1988—, dir. tng. in psychology, 1991, dir. Women's Treatment Network, 1992—; vis. scholar Stone Ctr. Wellesley Coll., 1985—; asst. prof. psychiatry Harvard Med. Sch., 1988—; cons. in field. Author: Empathy and Self Boundries, 1984, Women's Growth in Connection, 1991, (with others) The Self in Relation, 1986; editor, author: Relational Self in Women. Mem. Am. Psychol. Assn., Mass. Psychol. Assn. (bd. dirs. 1983-85), Phi Beta Kappa. Office: McLean Hosp 115 Mill St Belmont MA 02178-1041

JORDAN, JULIA CRAWFORD, secondary education educator; b. Memphis, Oct. 17, 1934; d. Elijah Cornelius and Zeffa Louise (Simms) Crawford; divorced; 1 child, Cheryl Lynn. BA, Harris Stowe State Coll., 1967; MA, Wash. U., St. Louis, 1973. Cert. tchr., Mo. Tchr., dept. head social studies dept. St. Louis (Mo.) Bd. Edn.; chmn. No. Ctrl. Vis. Com. Rosary H.S., St. Louis, 1977; mem. tchr. work group on acad. stds. Dept. of Elem. and Secondary Edn., State of Mo., 1993—, Regional Commerce and Growth Assn. Mem. Persona Players, rec. sec., pres. 1985-89; vol. Brean Homeless Ctr., St. Louis, 1990—. Recipient Cert. Exemplary Citizen Participation Citizen Edn. Clearing House, Letter of Appreciation Nat. Kidney Found., 1984-93. Mem. ASCD, Top Ladies of Distinction, Nat. Coun. of Negro Women (life), Annie Malone Children's Home,. Democrat. Baptist. Home: 8406 January Ave Saint Louis MO 63134-1414 Office: Vashon HS St Louis Bd Edn 3405 Bell Ave Saint Louis MO 63106-1604

JORDAN, KAREN LEIGH, newspaper travel editor; b. Freeport, Tex., Nov. 20, 1954; d. Matt Culum and Laura Louise (English) Arrington; m. William David Jordan, May 8, 1982; 1 child, Lauren Kathryn. BA in Journalism magna cum laude, Tex. A&M U., 1976. Intern Wall St. Jour., Dallas, summer 1976; asst. news editor Abilene (Tex.) Reporter-News, 1976-77; sports copy editor Dallas Morning News, 1977-79, asst. travel editor, 1979-81, travel editor, 1981—; judge journalism competition Univ. Interscholastic League, Tex., 1976. Contbg. writer (guidebook) Fodor's Tex., 1983—; writer (guidebook) Fodor's Dallas-Fort Worth, 1983—; copy editor Dallas-Ft. Worth Metroplex Football mag., 1978-80. Teaching asst. Garden Ridge Ch. of Christ, Lewisville, Tex., 1988—. ecipient state headline writing award AP Mng. Editors, 1977. Mem. Soc. Am. Travel Writers (writing, editing and photography awards 1981—), Phi Kappa Phi, Sigma Delta Chi, Alpha Lambda Delta. Office: Dallas Morning News Comm Ctr PO Box 655237 Dallas TX 75265-5237

JORDAN, LOIS WENGER, university official; b. Madison, Wis., Dec. 28, 1943; d. Alfred and Phyllis Mae (Schaeffer) Wenger; m. William Malcolm Jordan, Dec. 28, 1963; children: William Andre, Christopher Allan. BS, Millersville (Pa.) U., 1969. Tchr. Hempfield Sch. Dist., Lancaster, Pa., 1969-70, Lancaster Sch. Dist., 1975-80; dir. Upward Bound, Millersville U., 1980-82; dir. devel. St. Joseph Hosp., Lancaster, 1982-87; assoc. dir. devel. Pa. State U. Coll. Medicine, Hershey, 1987—. Author: (children's book) What's a Hospital Like?, 1972. Mem. Lancaster Jr. League, 1975—; trustee St. Joseph Hosp., 1979-82, James Buchanan Found., Lancaster, 1982-94, Highland Presbyn. Ch., Lancaster, 1982-85. Recipient Cheston M. Berlin svc. award Pa. State U. Alumni Assn., 1995, Outstanding Cmty. Svc. award Jr. League Assn., 1995. Mem. Assn. Healthcare Philanthropy (bd. dirs. 1990-92), Assn. Am. Med. Colls. Republican. Home: 1734 Colonial Manor Dr Lancaster PA 17603 Office: Pa State U Coll Medicine PO Box 852 Hershey PA 17033-0852

JORDAN, LORNA, news director; b. Washington, D.C., Nov. 3, 1958; d. Edwin C. and Mary (Kahle) J.; m. John A. Romano, Aug. 30, 1986. PhB, Miami U., 1981. News reporter Sta. WING-AM, Dayton, Ohio, 1981-84, Sta. WHIO-AM, Dayton, Ohio, 1984-85, Sta. WKRC-AM, Cin., 1985-87; from news reporter to news dir. Sta. WVXU-FM, Cin., news dir., 1988—; stringer Nat. Pub. Radio, Washington, 1987—, CBS News, N.Y., 1987-88; instr. Xavier U., 1991—. Bd. dirs. YWCA, Kettering, Ohio, 1985-87; bd. dirs. statehouse com. Ohio Ednl. Broadcasting. Mem. Soc. for Profl. Journalists, Kappa Delta. Office: WVXU FM Radio Station 3800 Victory Pky Cincinnati OH 45207-1035

JORDAN, MARIANNE WALLACE, nursing administrator, educator; b. Abington, Pa., July 10, 1950; d. Ambrose Culver and Gertrude Kimber (Clark) M. Diploma in Nursing, Madison (Wis.) Gen. Hosp., 1974; BS, UCLA, 1984. Cert. emergency nurse, flight RN, basic life support instr., ACLS instr., pediatric advanced life support instr., advanced trauma life support, flight nurse advanced trauma. Staff nurse Brotman Hosp., Culver City, Calif., 1975-78, Torrance (Calif.) Meml. Hosp., 1978-79; rsch. assoc. UCLA, 1983-85; rsch. technician U. So. Calif., L.A., 1987-88; critical care transport nurse Schaeffer Ambulance, L.A., 1986-88; staff murse Emergency Med. Ctr., UCLA, 1979-88; med. crew coord. Sierra Med-Evac, Mammoth Lakes, Calif., 1992-93; chief flight nurse Sierra Life Flight, Bishop, Calif., 1993-94; supr./instr. Centinela Mammoth Hosp., Mammoth Lakes, 1988-96; ACLS instr.-cons. Centinela Mammoth Hosp., 1989-96; EMT instr., cons. Lake Tahoe (Calif.) C.C., 1992—; flight nurse Golden Empire Air Rescue, Bakersfield, Calif., 1995-96, Valley Children's Hosp., Fresno, Calif., 1996—. Author: ACLS Study Guide, 1992, 94; reviewer Air Medical jour. Chmn. Task Force on Pre-Hosp. Care, Mono County, Calif., 1994. Mem. Emergency Nurses Assn., Nat. Flight Nurses Assn., Aircraft Owners and Pilots Assn., Assn. of Air Med. Svcs., Post Anesthesia Nurse Assn. of Calif., Alpha Lambda Delta. Home and Office: 385 W Shaw # 138 Fresno CA 93704

JORDAN, MARY LEE, retired elementary education educator; b. Cin., Oct. 22, 1931; m. T. Paul Jordan, July 29, 1975 (dec. 1988); children: Aaron, Marc, Carrie. BS in Edn., U. Cin., 1965, AA, 1984. First grade tchr. St. Louis County, Mo., 1963-65; first grade, kindergarten tchr. Cin., 1965-80; sec. personnel dept. Longview State Hosp., 1983; word processor Nat. Inst. Occupational Safety & Health, 1984; bookkeeper L. Levine & Co., Inc., 1985-88; Bd. dirs., membership chmn., newsletter co-producer Cin. Alliance for the Mentally Ill, 1983-86; park ranger U.S. Nat. Park Svc., Cin., 1993—. Author: History of Camp Dennison, Ohio, 1956. Pres. Cin. chpt. Zero Population Growth, 1976. Mem. AAUW (v.p. Cin. br. 1994—, bd. dirs. 1970-71), LWV (pres. N.C. br. 1994—, program coord. 1970-71), Am. Horse Show Assn., Ohioana Libr. Assn., DAR (vice-regent, mus. trustee Mariemont, Ohio chpt. 1988-89, regent 1990-91). Home: 27 Sherry Rd Cincinnati OH 45215-4225

JORDAN, MARY LUCILLE, commisioner; m. Ben C. Elliott, Aug. 24, 1980; children: Elizabeth Elliott, Armando Elliott, C. Daniel Elliott. Student, Hull U., 1969-70; BA cum laude, Bonaventure U., 1971; JD, Antioch Coll., 1976. Bar: N.Y., 1977, D.C., 1978. Atty. Office of Fed. Register Nat. Archives & Records Adminstrn., Washington, 1976-77; sr. staff atty. United Mine Workers Am., Washington, 1977-94; chmn. Fed. Mine Safety and Health Rev. Commn., Washington, 1994—. Office: Fed Mine Safety & Health Rev Commn 1730 K St NW 6th Fl Washington DC 20006

JORDAN, MICHELLE DENISE, lawyer; b. Chgo., Oct. 29, 1954; d. John A. and Margaret (O'Dood) J. BA in Polit. Sci., Loyola U, Chgo., 1974; JD, U. Mich., 1977. Bar. Ill. 1977, U.S. Dist. Ct. (no. dist.) Ill. 1978. Asst. state's atty. State's Attys. Office, Chgo., 1977-82; pvt. practice Chgo., 1983-84; with Ill. Atty. Gen.'s Office, Chgo., 1984-90, chief environ. control div., 1988-90; ptnr. Hopkins & Sutter, Chgo., 1991-93; apptd. dep. regional adminstr. region 5 U.S. EPA, Chgo., 1994—. Active Operation Push, Chgo., 1971—. Recipient Kizzy Image Achievement and Svc. award, 1990; named in Am.'s Top 100 Bus. and Profl. Women, Dollars and SenseMag., Chgo., 1988. Mem. Ill. Bar Assn., Chgo. Bar Assn. (bd. mgrs., chmn. criminal law com. 1987-88, mem. hearing divsn., jud. evaluation com. 1987-88, exec. coun. 1987-88), Cook County Bar Assn., Nat. Bar Assn., Alpha Sigma Nu. Democrat. Baptist. Office: US EPA 19th Fl 77 W Jackson Chicago IL 60604

JORDAN, MICHELLE HENRIETTA, public relations company executive; b. Sussex, Eng., Sept. 19, 1948; came to U.S., 1975; d. Raymond Cameron and Liliane (Ambar) J.; m. Billy Owens, 1994. Student, Sorbonne, 1966-67. With Coordinated Mktg. Services Ltd., London, 1967-71; dir. Spectrum Public Relations, London, 1971-74; with Rowland Co., N.Y.C., 1975-87, exec. v.p.; sr. v.p., mng. dir. mktg. svcs. div. Hill and Knowlton, N.Y.C., 1987-91; prin. The Dilenschneider Group, N.Y.C., 1991-94; v.p. Digital Pictures, San Mateo, Calif., 1994-96; exec. v.p. The GCI Group, L.A., 1996—. Mem. Mayor N.Y.C. Commn. Status Women, 1980-86; bd. dirs. New Dramatists, Religion in Am. Life, 1992-94. Recipient Matrix award N.Y. Women in Communications, 1990. Mem. Players Club, N.Y. Road Runners. Office: GCI Group 6100 Wilshire Blvd Los Angeles CA 90048

JORDAN, PAULINE ROSE, financial consultant, educator, retirement planner; b. Jacksonville, Ill., May 31, 1934; d. Edward Isidore and Gertrude Frances (McAnarney) J. BA, Coll. St. Francis, 1957; MA, Loyola U., 1969; PhD, U. Ill., 1973. Chartered fin. cons. Tchr. St. Francis Acad., Joliet, Ill., 1963-71, Melbourne (Fla.) H.S., 1969-71; computer edn. specialist U. Ill., Urbana, 1973-76; prin. specialist Control Data, Washington, 1976-78; staff spl. planning GE Aerospace, Valley Forge, Pa., 1978-95; cons. Wayne, Pa., 1995—. Mem. So. Poverty Law Ctr., Montgomery, 1985—. Mem. Valley Forge (Pa.) Hist. Soc., Internat P.E.O. Sisterhood, Phi Kappa Phi, Phi Delta Kappa. Roman Catholic. Home: 30 Treaty Dr Wayne PA 19087

JORDAN, RUTH ANN, physician; b. Richmond, Ind., Oct. 12, 1928; d. Willard and Esther (Fouts) J.; children: Diane M., Linda J. AB, Ind. U., 1950; MD, Columbia U., 1957. Intern, St. Luke's Hosp., N.Y.C., 1957-58, asst. resident in medicine, 1958-59; physician clinic Met. Life Ins. Co., N.Y.C., 1960-62, Standard Oil Col. of N.J., N.Y.C., 1962; physician in med. dept. MIT, Cambridge, 1963-71; physician clinic New Eng. Mut. Life Ins. Co., Boston, 1963-66, asst. med. dir., 1971-74; fellow internal medicine Mass. Gen. Hosp., Boston, 1974-75; physician Simmons Coll., Boston, 1975-78, Northeastern U., Boston, 1976-78; therapeutic dietitian Meth. Hosp., Indpls., 1951-53, Presbyn. Hosp., N.Y.C., part-time 1954-57; assoc. med. dir. New Eng. Telephone Co., 1978, med. dir. clin. svcs., 1978-86; dir. occupl. medicine Gen. Med. Assn., 1986-91; assoc. med. dir. Allmerica, 1991—; nat. coord. com. on cholesterol, 1986—, Mass. Adv. Coun. for Workers Compensation, 1986-89. Fellow Am. Coll. Occupl. and Environ. Medicine (membership com. 1985-88, health edn. com. 1984—, bd. dirs. 1986-92); mem. AMA, DAR, Norfolk County Med. Soc., New Eng. Occupational Med. Assn. (bd. dirs. 1980-89, pres. 1981-84), Mass. Med. Soc. (mem. council 1984—, chmn. environ. and occupational health com. 1985-88), Columbia U. Club of New Eng. (v.p. 1981-84, pres. 1989-91), Roxbury Clin. Records Club, The Country Club, Alpha Chi Omega. Home: 105 Rockwood St Brookline MA 02146-7408

JORDAN, SANDRA, public relations professional; b. Pasadena, Tex., Oct. 10, 1952; d. Royal Wilson and Kathryn Ann (Speck) J.; m. William Anderson Mintz, Aug. 10, 1974 (div. 1980). B of Journalism, U. Tex., 1974. Reporter Austin (Tex.) American Statesman, 1974-76; news dir. KTAE Radio, Taylor, Tex., 1974-76; dir. of news and info. Inst. of Texan Cultures, San Antonio, 1976-82; pub. rels. dir. San Antonio Mus. Assn., 1982-83; dir. news/info. Univ. Tex., San Antonio, 1983-86; sr. publicist Rogers & Cowan, Inc., Washington, 1986-87; communications dir. NARAL, Washington, 1987-88; assoc. Parker, Vogelsingers & Assocs., Washington, 1988-90; pub. rels. and mktg. dir. Girl Scout Coun., Washington, 1990—; pub. rels. cons. YWCA, Washington; judge, ad contest, Women in Communications, Iowa, 1992; workshop organizer Washington Ind. Writers, 1990; mem. publicity com. CASE Conf., San Antonio, 1986, Smithsonian Nat. Assoc. Prog., San Antonio, 1980. Contbg. author: Folk Art in Texas, 1985. Prog. cons. KLRN-TV (pub. TV) San Antonio, 1981, 82; del. Dem. Nat. Conv., Taylor, 1976; docent Kennedy Ctr., Washington, 1989. Recipient Apex '91, '92, '93 and '95 awards, Communications Concepts, 1991, Design honors, Tex. Assn. of Mus., 1993, IABC Silver Inkwell award, 1995, Silver Anvil award ABC, 1996. Mem. Women in Communications (D.C. chpt., mem. literacy project 1992, mentoring program), Women in Advt. and Mktg., Am. Soc. Assn. Execs., The Writers Ctr. Home: 6305 E Halbert Rd Bethesda MD 20817-5409 Office: Girl Scout Council of Nation's Capitol 2233 Wisconsin Ave NW Washington DC 20007-4104

JORDAN, SANDRA DICKERSON, law educator; b. Phila., Dec. 3, 1951; m. Byron Neal Jordan, July 21, 1973; children: Nedra Catherine, Byron Neal II. BS in Edn., Wilberforce U., 1973; JD, U. Pitts., 1979. Bar: Pa. 1979, U.S. Dist. Ct. (we. dist.) Pa. 1979, U.S. Ct. Appeals (3d cir.) 1979. Asst. U.S. atty. U.S. Dept. Justice, Pitts., 1979-88; assoc. ind. counsel Ind. Counsel-Iran/Contra, Washington, 1988-91; prof. U. Pitts. Sch. Law, 1988—, assoc. dean, 1993—; jud. ct. bd. Commonwealth of Pa., 1995—; hearing com. disciplinary bd. Pa. Supreme Ct., PItts., 1989-95; lectr. U.S. Dept. Justice, Pa. Trial Judges Assn., Acad. Trial Lawyers, Pa. Bar Inst. Author tng. video in field, 1982; contbr. articles to profl. jours. Vice pres. Health and Welfare Planning Commn., Pitts., 1986-89; mem. Program to Aid Citizen Enterprise, Pitts., 1983—. Mem. ABA (mem. white collar crimes com. 1988—), Homer S. Brown Law Assn., Allegheny County Bar Assn., Nat. Bar Assn., Urban League (v.p. Pitts. chpt. 1988-90), Alpha Kappa Mu, Alpha Kappa Alpha. Office: U Pitts Law Sch 3900 Forbes Ave Pittsburgh PA 15213

JORDAN, SHARIE CECILIA, industrial artist; b. Grand Rapids, Mich., Sept. 12, 1961; d. Erwin Francis and Ardis Jean (Gilbert) Schmuker; m. Thomas William Jordan, Dec. 4, 1982. Registered well drilling contractor, Mich., 1996. Fashion cons. Mullberry Bush, Houghton Lake, Mich., 1982-84; freelance artist Houghton Lake, Mich., 1984-90; owner Jordan Illustration and Design, Houghton Lake, Mich., 1991—; co-owner Jordan Well Drilling, Houghton Lake, Mich., 1994—; cons. Buyers Guide Weekly, Houghton, 1988-90. Founding chmn. Annual Meml. Day Parade, Houghton Lake, 1992—. Recipient Emily Hilton-Janice Reeney Art award, 1979. Mem. Eagle Aux. (chaplain 1991-92, activity chmn. 1991-92, trustee 1992-94, v.p. 1992-94, Mrs. Eagle award 1991-92, Outstanding Vol. Work and Svc. award 1991-92).

JORDEN, ELEANOR HARZ, linguist, educator; b. N.Y.C.; d. William George and Eleanor (Funk) Harz; m. William J. Jorden, Mar. 3, 1944 (div.); children: William Temple, Eleanor Harz, Marion Telva. A.B., Bryn Mawr Coll., 1942; M.A., Yale U., 1943, Ph.D., 1950; D.Litt. (hon.), Williams Coll., 1982; D.H.L. (hon.), Knox Coll., 1985; D. Langs. (hon.), Middlebury Coll., 1991; D. Univ. (hon.), U. Stirling, Scotland, 1993. Instr. Japanese Yale U., 1943-46, 47-48; dir. Japanese lang. program and Fgn. Service Inst. Lang. Sch., Am. Embassy, Tokyo, 1950-55; sci. linguist Fgn. Service Inst., Dept. State, Washington, 1959-69; acting head Far East langs., 1961-64, chmn., 1964-67, 69, chmn. Vietnamese lang. div., 1967-69; vis. prof. linguistics Cornell U., 1969-70, prof., 1970-87, Mary Donlon Alger prof. linguistics, 1974-87, prof. emeritus, 1987—; Bernhard disting. vis. prof. Williams Coll., 1985-86; vis. prof. Williams Coll., 1986-87, adj. prof., 1987-92; dir. Japanese FALCON program, 1972-87; Univ. prof., Disting. fellow Nat. Fgn. Lang. Ctr. Sch. Advanced Internat. Studies Johns Hopkins U., 1987-91; acad. dir. Exchange: Japan's Tchr. Tng. Inst., 1988—, for high sch. tchrs., 1993—; sr. cons. prep. framework Japanese lang. curriculum and Japanese coll. bd. exam, 1991-93; dir. SPENG Program, 1980—; co-dir. Survey on Japanese Lang. Study, 1988-92; guest scholar Wilson Ctr. Smithsonian Instn., 1982; cons., permanent mem. exec. com. Nat. Assn. Self-Instructional Lang. Programs, pres., 1977-78, 84-85; mem. Fulbright-Hays Com. on Internat. Exchange Scholars, 1972-75; mem. area adv. com. for East Asia, 1972-76; chmn. Social Sci. Research Council Task Force on Japanese Lang. Tng., 1976-78; mem. adv. com. Japan Found., 1979-81; mem. Lang. Attrition Project, 1981-87; advisor Centre for Japanese Studies, Stirling U., Scotland, 1988-92; mem. Yale U. Coun. com. Langs. and Lit., 1990—. Author: (with Bernard Bloch) Spoken Japanese, 1945, Syntax of Modern Colloquial Japanese, 1955, Gateway to Russian, 1961, Beginning Japanese, Part 1, 1962, Part 2, 1963, (with Sheehan, Quang and others) Basic Vietnamese, vols. I, II, 1965, (with Quang) Vietnamese Familiarization Course, 1969, (with Hamako Chaplin) Reading Japanese, 1976, (with Mari Noda) Japanese: The Spoken Language, part 1, 1987, part 2, 1988, part 3, 1990, (with Richard Lambert) Japanese Language Instruction in the U.S.: Resources, Practice and Investment Strategic, 1992. Decorated Order of Precious Crown Emperor of Japan, 1985; recipient Superior Svc. award Dept. State, 1965, Japan Found. and Social Sci. Rsch. Coun. sr. fellow, 1976, Toyota award Twentieth Anniversary Fund grantee, 1978; Japan Found. prize, 1985, Papalia award for Excellence Tchr. Tng., 1993, N.E. Conf. award Disting. Svc. and Leadership in Profession, 1994; honoree Eleanor Harz Jorden Festival, Portland State U., 1995. Mem. Assn. Asian Studies (v.p. 1979-80, pres. 1980-81), Linguistic Soc. Am., Am. Coun. Tchrs. Fgn. Langs., Nat. Assn. Self-Instrnl. Lang. Programs (pres. 1978, 85, premanent disting. dir. 1991—), Assn. Tchrs. Japanese (exec. com., pres. 1978-84), Japan Soc. N.Y. (bd. dirs. 1982-88). Office: 3300 Darby Rd Apt 1302 Haverford PA 19041-1067

JORGENSEN, ANN, farmer; b. Cedar Rapids, Iowa, Sept. 16, 1940; d. Kenneth Edward and Velma Ann (Baumhoefener) Fry; m. Marlyn L. Jorgensen, Feb. 27, 1961; children: Christopher, Peter, Timothy, Jennifer. BA, U. Iowa, 1962. Lic. commodity broker. Tax acct. Bill Burrell Tax Svc., Urbana, Iowa, 1968-70, Hansen Acctg., Vinton, Iowa, 1970-75; commodity broker First Mid. Am., Cedar Rapids, 1975-85; owner Lakeview Enterprises, Osage Beach, Mo., 1975-85; v.p., treas. Timberlane Hogs, Ltd., Garrison, Iowa, 1971—; mng. ptnr., owner Jorg-Anna Farms, Garrison, 1963—; pres., founder Farm Home Offices, Vinton, 1981—; bd. dirs. Farm Bur. Mut. Funds, Des Moines; commr. Interstate Agrl. Grain Commn. Midwest Compact, 1986-88; mem. Agriculture Products Adv. Bd., Des Moines, 1990—, bd. dirs.; spkr. in field; mem. environ. com. Nat. Pork Producers Coun., 1996—; chair info. tech. com. Am. Farm Bur. Fedn., 1996—. Author: Put PaperWork in its Place, 1982; contbr. articles to profl. jours. Mem., chair Iowa Arts Coun., 1973-79; regent Iowa Bd. Regents, 1979-85; dir., pres. Iowa Alcoholic Beverages Commr., Des Moines, 1985-88; nat. chair Tauke for U.S. Senate, Iowa, 1987-88; bd. dirs. Iowa Dept. Econ. Devel., 1988—; chair bd. Iowa Rural Devel. Coun., 1991-95; mem. Iowa Supreme Ct. Study Com., 1995-96. Named to Iowa Vol. Hall of Fame, 1989. Mem. AACC (bd. dirs. 1995—), Vinton Am. Assn. U. Women (various offices 1980—), Iowa Pub. TV Found. (sec. 1987-95). Home: 1965 64th St Garrison IA 52229-9647 Office: Farm Home Offices PO Box 840 Vinton IA 52349-0840

JORGENSEN, JUDITH ANN, psychiatrist; b. Parris Island, S.C.; d. George Emil and Margaret Georgia Jorgensen; BA, Stanford U., 1963; MD, U. Calif., 1968; m. Ronald Francis Crown, July 11, 1970. Intern, Meml. Hosp., Long Beach, 1969-70; resident County Mental Health Services, San Diego, 1970-73; staff psychiatrist Children and Adolescent Services, San Diego, 1973-78; practice medicine specializing in psychiatry, La Jolla, Calif., 1973—; staff psychiatrist County Mental Health Services of San Diego, 1973-78, San

Diego State U. Health Services, 1985-87; psychiat. cons. San Diego City Coll., 1973-78, 85-86; asst. prof. dept. psychiatry U. Calif., 1978-91, assoc. prof. dept. psychiatry, 1991-96; chmn. med. quality rev. com. Dist. XIV, State of Calif., 1982-83. Mem. Am. Psychiat. Assn., San Diego Soc. Psychiat. Physicians (chmn. membership com. 1976-78, v.p. 1978-80, fed. legis. rep. 1985-87, fellowship com. 1989), Am. Soc. Adolescent Psychiatry, San Diego Soc. Adolescent Psychiatry (pres. 1981-82), Calif. Med. Assn. (former alternate del.), Soc. Sci. Study of Sex, San Diego Soc. Sex Therapy and Edn. (cert. sex therapist), San Diego County Med. Soc. (credentials com. 1982-84). Club: Rowing. Office: 470 Nautilus St Ste 211 La Jolla CA 92037-5970

JORGENSEN, JUDITH STRONG, public relations executive; b. Los Angeles, May 9, 1959; d. James Knox and Mary Elizabeth (Leonard) Strong; m. Gregory Arnold Jorgensen, Apr. 25, 1987. AB in Comparative Lit., Occidental Coll., 1981; MS in Journalism, Northwestern U., 1982. With Harcourt Brace Jovanovich, N.Y.C., 1983-84, Esquire Mag. Group Inc., N.Y.C., 1984-87; mgr. pub. rels. Esquire Mag., N.Y.C., 1987; group mgr. pub. relations Hearst Mags., N.Y.C., 1987-88; mgr. publicity Condé Nast Publs. Inc., N.Y.C., 1988-89; dir. comm. Mag. Pubs. of Am., N.Y.C., 1989-93, v.p. comm., 1994—. Mem. Pub. Rels. Soc. Am., N.Y. Women in Communications, N.Y. Jr. League. Office: Mag Pubs of Am 919 Third Ave New York NY 10022

JORGENSEN-HUNT, JANICE LYNN, educator; b. Fairfield, Ill., Sept. 1, 1952; d. William Allen and Evelyn (Newby) Hunt; m. Glen Jorgensen-Hunt, Sept. 21, 1986. AA, Olney Ctrl. Coll., 1972; BA, So. Ill. U., 1974, MS in Edn., 1978; PhD, Southeastern U., 1982. Lic. optician, Fla. Computer panel operator So. Ill. U., Carbondale, 1975-79; dir. women's programs Kankakee (Ill.) C.C., 1980-81; counselor Family Shelter Svcs., Glen Ellyn, Ill., 1981-82; dir. partial hosp. program Green River Comp. Care Ctr., Henderson, Ky., 1982-84; exec. dir. Harbor House Shelter Svc., Kankakee, 1983-84; therapist Northside Mental Health Ctr., Tampa, Fla., 1985-89; owner-optician Internat. Optics, Tampa, 1990-93; instr. Baywinds, Tampa, 1993—; mem. adv. bd. Tolentime Ctr. Grief Resolution, Olympia Fields, Ill., 1982, Ill. State Bd. Shelters, Springfield, 1983-84, St. Anthony's Hospice, Henderson, 1983, Henderson County Coun. on Human Svcs., 1983; presenter in field. Children's support group leader MacDill AFB, Tampa, 1980-81; fundraiser YWCA, St. Petersburg, Fla., 1994, Tampa AIDS Network, 1996; spiritum assembly mem. Baha'i Faith, 1985-96. Recipient Vol. of Yr. award Constance Morris Family Crisis Ctr., 1982; Chgo. Refugee Found. grantee, 1984. Mem. NOW (newsletter editor 1995-96), AAUW, People for the Am. Way, U.S. Golf Assn. Home: 4201 Ohio Ave Tampa FL 33616 Office: Baywinds PO Box 82188 Tampa FL 33682

JOSELL, JESSICA (JESSICA WECHSLER), public relations executive; b. Balt., June 17, 1943; d. Maury J. and Rose E. (Lodin) Snyder; m. Neil B. Josell, Apr. 30, 1965 (dec. Nov. 1967); m. Steven James Wechsler, Jan. 12, 1980. BA, U. Fla., 1965. V.p., gen. mgr. Morton Dennis Wax & Assocs., N.Y.C., 1976-81; v.p. The Raleigh Group, Ltd., N.Y.C., 1981-87; pres. Josell Communications, Inc., N.Y.C., 1981—; exec. officer, bd. dirs. The Bridge, Inc., N.Y.C. Mem. N.Y. Women in Film and TV, Internat. Teleproduction Soc. Office: Josell Communications Inc 185 W End Ave Apt 22C New York NY 10023-5549

JOSEPH, EDITH HOFFMAN, retired editor; b. Syracuse, N.Y., Jan. 4, 1928; d. Max and Ida (Hodis) Finkelstein; m. Irving Hoffman, Sept. 4, 1949 (dec. Dec. 1965); children: Kenneth R., Maxine E. Neuhauser; m. William Jacob Joseph, May 19, 1968; stepchildren: David E., Harlan L., Saul J., Gail C. BS in Journalism/Bus. Adminstrn., Rider Coll., 1949. Copywriter advt. Swern's-Lit Bros., Trenton, N.J., 1949-51; pub. info. asst. N.J. Div. Pensions, Trenton, 1967-69; pub. rels. asst. N.J. Dept. Labor & Industry, Trenton, 1969-70; mng. editor newsletter N.J. Dept. Environ. Protection, Trenton, 1971-74; environ. news editor N.J. Dept. Environ. Protection-N.J. Outdoors Mag., 1974-84; editor newsletter N.J. Dept. Environ. Protection-Environ. News, 1985-90; editor environ. news sect. N.J. Dept. Environ. Protection-N.J. Outdoors Mag., 1991. Contbr. articles to profl. jours. Home: 8 Llanfair Ln Trenton NJ 08618-1012

JOSEPH, ELEANOR ANN, hospital association administrator; b. Cleve., Mar. 6, 1944; d. Emil and Eleanor (Leelais) Dienes; m. Abraham Albert Joseph, Oct. 28, 1984. BS in Math. cum laude, Cleve. State U., 1978, MPA in Health Care Adminstrn., 1991. Cert. profl. for healthcare quality, coding specialist, procedural coder, accredited records technician, 1967. Asst. dir. med. records Suburban Hosp., Warrensville Heights, Ohio, 1963-77; coder Shaker Med. Ctr., Shaker Heights, Ohio, 1965, Huron Rd. Hosp., Cleve., 1965; instr. Cuyahoga C.C., Cleve., 1970-72; dir. med. records Hillcrest Hosp., Mayfield Heights, Ohio, 1977-84; med. records technician Vis. Nurse Assn., Cleve., 1985; coord. med. record svcs. Ctr. for Health Affairs Greater Cleve. Hosp. Assn., 1985-88, dir. coding svcs. Ctr. Health Affairs, 1988-89; dir. health record svcs. Ctr. for Health Affairs/Greater Cleve. Hosp. Assn., 1989—; cons. in field, Cleve., 1976—; mem. speakers' bur. Hillcrest Hosp., Mayfield Heights, 1978-84; mem. adv. com. Cuyahoga C.C., 1973-80, 94—; cons. Suburban Pavilion Manor Care Nursing Homes, Luth. Home, Cleve., 1976-88; condr. seminars in field. Co-author: (manual) Quality Assurance Program for Medical Records Department, 1981, Dollars and Sense: A Reference Guide to Coding and Prospective Payment System Reimbursement Issues, 1988; co-editor: Care and Management of Health Care Records, 1988, 92. Active Holden Arboretum, Kirtland, Ohio, 1975—, Ohio Hist. Soc., Columbus, 1975—, mem. adv. task force Cert. program in Med. Office mgmt., Lakeland C.C., 1992—. Mem. Am. Acad. Procedural Coders (treas. local chpt. 1994), Am. Med. Record Assn. (mem. long term care sect., cons. roster 1976, charter mem. assembly on edn. 1989), Am. Health Info. Mgmt. Assn. (quality assurance sect., long term care sect., ambulatory records sec. 1992—), Am. Guild Patient Accounts Mgrs., Nat. Assn. for Healthcare Quality, East Ohio Med. Record Assn., N.E. Ohio Med. Record Assn. (mem. audit com., membership com., bylaws com., pub. rels. com., counselor 1983, ednl. com. 1984, 87, chmn. nominating com. 1986, treas. 1979, v.p. 1980, pres. elect 1981-82, pres. 1982-83, mem. cons. com. 1987-91), Ohio Med. Record Assn. (mem. legis. com. 1989-90, bylaws com. 1983-84, nominating com. 1982-83, med. record coun. 1985-92, alt. del. 1982, del. for state assn. mems. at nat. ann. mtg. Am. Med. Record Assn. 1989, 90), Am. Coll. Healthcare Execs., Ohio Assn. Healthcare Quality, Ohio Health Info. Mgmt. Assn. (co-chair data quality and reimbursement coun. 1996-97, project leader-alliances 1992-94, data quality and reimbursement coun. 1992—, liaison to ambulatory sect. of Am. Health Info. Mgmt. Assn. 1994—), Northeast Ohio Health Info. Mgmt. Assn. (chair coding roundtable 1993—), Soc. Clin. Coders, Cleve. City Club. Lutheran. Office: Greater Cleve Hosp Assn Ctr for Health Affairs 1226 Huron Rd Cleveland OH 44115-1702

JOSEPH, GERI MACK (GERALDINE JOSEPH), former ambassador, educator; b. St. Paul, June 19, 1923. B.S., U. Minn., 1946; LL.D. (hon.), Bates Coll., 1982. Staff writer Mpls. Tribune, 1946-53, contbg. editor, 1972-78; amb. to The Netherlands The Hague, 1978-81; sr. fellow internat. programs Hubert H. Humphrey Inst. Pub. Affairs, U. Minn., 1984-94; dir. Mondale Policy Forum, 1990-94; bd. dirs. Nat. Dem. Inst. for Internat. Affairs, George A. Hormel Co.; mem. U.S. President's Commn. on Mental Health, Minn. Supreme Ct. Commn. on Mentally Disabled and the Cts.; mem. com. on Mid. East, Brookings Instn., 1987; mem., bd. dirs. German Marshall Fund, 1987—. Vice chmn. Gov.'s Commn. on Taxation, 1983-84; trustee Carleton Coll., 1975-94; mem. Democratic Nat. Com., 1960-72, vice chmn., 1968-72; co-chairperson Minn. Women's Campaign Fund, 1982-84; co-chmn. Atty. Gen.'s Com. on Child Abuse within the Family, 1986. Office: U Minn Humphrey Ctr 301 19th Ave S Minneapolis MN 55455-0429

JOSEPH, HARRIET, English literature educator; b. Montreal, Mar. 14, 1919; came to U.S., 1944; d. Samuel and Hanna Mai (Brown) Bloomfield; m. Edward D. Joseph, Aug. 16, 1942; children: Leila Muriel, Alan Pinto, Brian Daniel. BA, McGill U., Montreal, Que., 1941; MA, Bryn Mawr Coll., 1942. Instr. to assoc. prof. English lit. Pace U., Pleasantville, N.Y., 1966-81; prof. Pace U., Pleasantville, 1981—. Author: Shakespeare's Son-in-Law: Man & Physician, 1964; contbr. articles on Eng. litr. to jours. Active LWV, Scarsdale, N.Y. Mem. MLA, Internat. Shakespeare Assn., Shakespeare Assn. Am., Am. Jewish Congress, Women's Am. Orgn. for Rehab. Through Tng., Author's League, AAUW. Home: 9 Putnam Rd Scarsdale NY 10583-2009 Office: Pace U Bedford Rd Pleasantville NY 10570-1002

JOSEPH, JEAN, artist; b. New Rochelle, N.Y., Jan. 28, 1914; d. Barnet and Alimeta Edna (Calder) J.; m. Paul Heinz Mertens, Oct. 19, 1941 (dec. Oct. 1979); children: Bruce, Mark, Gail. Student, Art Students League, 1930-34, U. Miami, 1935. Freelance artist. One woman shows at Manhasset Libr., 1974, Unitarian Soc., 1984; exhibited in group shows at Wildenstein Galleries, N.Y., 1952, 53-55 tour (Internat. Hallmark awards, 1952, 53-55), Nat. Acad. Design, 1953 (Allied Artists of Am. award 1953), Fire House Gallery, 1973, Port Washington Libr., 1977, Unitarian Universalists Soc., Plandome, N.Y., 1977, Lincoln House, 1980 (sculpture prize), Port Washington Libr., 1981 (hon. mention), Nassau County Mus. Fine Art, 1983, Heckscher Mus., 1986 (Top of the Eighties award 1986), Nassau County Mus. Art, 1986 (Silver award 1986), 88 (hon. mention), Discovery Gallery, N.Y., (Jurors Merit award, 1993), 1992. Vol. 1000 hours St. Francis Hosp., Roslyn, N.Y., 1970-75. Recipient Hon. Mention award Cannon Photo Contest, 1986. Home and Studio: 11 Chanticlare Dr Manhasset NY 11030-1206

JOSEPH, LYNNE CATHIE, art educator; b. Manchester, N.H., Aug. 14, 1965; d. George and Jane Helen (Nita) J. BA, Notre Dame Coll., 1987; MEd, Lesley Coll., 1995. Cert. tchr., N.H. Art tchr. Manchester Schs., 1987-88, East Derry (N.H.) Meml. Schs., 1989-93, Hood Middle Sch., Derry, 1993-94, West Running Brook Mid. Sch., Derry, 1995—; asst. dir., spl. events dir. Camp Mataponi, Naples, Maine, 1989-94, dir. Camp Runels, Pelham, N.H, 1995; site coord., mem. adv. bd. Scholastic Art Awards, Boston, 1985-93. Mem. Nat. Art Edn. Assn., Manchester Artists Assn., N.H. Art Edn. Assn. Home: 50 Harrington Ave Manchester NH 03103-6561

JOSEPH, MARILYN SUSAN, gynecologist; b. Bklyn., Aug. 18, 1946; d. S. Seymour and Maxine Laura (Stern) J.; m. Warren Erwin Regelmann, Dec. 20, 1969; children: Adam Gustave, David Joseph. BA, Smith Coll., 1968; MD cum laude, SUNY Downstate Med. Ctr., Bklyn., 1972. Diplomate Am. Bd. Ob-Gyn, Nat. Bd. Med. Examiners. Intern U. Minn. Hosps., 1972-73, resident in ob-gyn, 1972-76; med. fellow specialist U. Minn., 1972-76, asst. prof. ob-gyn, 1976—, dir. women's clinic, 1984—; med. dir. Boynton Health Svc., 1993—. Author: Differential Diagnosis Obstetrics, 1978. Fellow Am. Coll. Ob-Gyn (best paper dist. VI meeting 1981); mem. Am. Assn. Gynecol. Laparoscopy, Hennepin County Med. Soc., Minn. State Med. Assn., Mpls. Council Ob-Gyn, Minn. State Ob-Gyn Soc. Jewish. Office: Boynton Health Svc 410 Church St SE Minneapolis MN 55455-0346

JOSEPH, ROBERTA B., psychologist; b. Long Beach, Calif., May 29, 1950; d. Terrence and Hazel (Ritger) Conner; m. James Joseph, Aug. 26, 1972. BA, Pomona Coll., 1971; MA, Stanford U., 1972, PhD, 1976. Asst. prof. dept. psychology U. Va., Charlottesville, 1976-81, assoc. prof., 1981-90; pvt. practice Grand Rapids, Mich., 1990—. Contbr. numerous articles to profl. jours. Grantee NSF, 1972, Soc. for Psychol. Studies, 1973. Fellow APA; mem. AAUW, Am. Psychol. Soc. Office: Werik Towers 800 Lafayette Ave NE Ste 100 Grand Rapids MI 49503-1631

JOSEPH, ROSALINE RESNICK, hematologist and oncologist; b. N.Y.C., Aug. 21, 1929; d. Joseph and Malca (Rosenbeg) Resnick; m. Robert J. Joseph, Jan. 2, 1954; children: Joy S., Nina B. AB, Cornell U., 1949; MD, Women's Med. Coll. Pa., Phila., 1953; MS, Temple U., 1958. Intern Kings County Hosp., Bklyn., 1953-54; resident Phila. Gen. Hosp., 1954-55, Temple U. Hosp., 1955-57; instr. dept. medicine Temple U. Med. Ctr., Phila., 1957-60; assoc. in medicine Temple U. Med. Ctr., 1960-63, asst. prof. medicine, 1963-69, assoc. prof. medicine, 1969-77; course co-coordinator Sys. Oncology Interdisciplinary Course, 1968-73; prof. medicine, dir. Med. Coll. Pa., Phila., 1977; course coordinator Med. Coll. Pa., 1978, dir. hematology/oncology, to date; pres. med. staff Med. Coll. Pa., 1990—. Contbr. articles to profl. jours. Del. dir. Am. Cancer Soc., 1989—. Recipient Lindback award for disting. teaching, Christian & Mary Lindback Found., 1982, Am. Cancer Soc. Div. Disting. Svc. award, 1987. Fellow ACP; mem. Am. Soc. Hematology, Am. Soc. Clin. Oncology, Alumni Assn. Med. Coll. Pa. (pres. 1988-90). Office: Med Coll of Pa 3300 Henry Ave Philadelphia PA 19129-1121

JOSEPH, SHIRLEY TROYAN, retired executive; b. Buffalo, N.Y., Dec. 13, 1925; d. Louis and Betty (Eisman) Troyan; m. Norman Clifford Joseph, Oct. 20, 1946; children: Todd Michael, Marc Dana, Jonathan L. BA in Polit. Sci., U. Mich., 1947; postgrad., Vanderbilt U., 1973. Instr. SUNY, Buffalo, 1977; area rep. Am. Jewish Com., Buffalo, 1980-82; pub. policy coord. Jewish Fedn., Buffalo, 1984-87; first exec. dir. Erie County Commn. on Status of Women, 1988-92; accredited non-govtl. rep. UN World Confs. on Women, Copenhagen, Nairobi, Beijing, 1980, 85, 95; mem. Hilary Clinton's Beijing Conf. Circle; mem. steering com. Food for All, Buffalo Area Met. ministries, 1984-88; cmty. adv. bd. Sch. Health Demonstration Project, Buffalo, 1989-92; cmty. advisor Jr. League, Buffalo, 1989—; founding pres. Women's Taking Action in Politics Fund, Western N.Y. State, 1992—. Vice chair U.S. Nat. Commn. for UNESCO, 1973-77, Nat. Jewish Cmty. Rels. Adv. Coun., 1989-93; v.p. Jewish Fedn. Greater Buffalo, 1975-80; del. U.S. Nat. Women's Conf., Houston, 1977; bd. Erie County Mental Health Svcs.-Corp. 2, 1979-80; pres. Jewish Fedn. Housing, Buffalo, 1980-82. Mem. Nat. Coun. Jewish Women (nat. v.p. 1975-83, hon. nat. v.p. 1985—, Buffalo sect. Hannah Solomon Woman of Yr. award 1978), Nat. Women's Conf. Com. (various chairs 1979—). Democrat.

JOSEPH, SUSAN B., lawyer; b. N.Y.C., June 1, 1958; d. Alfred A. and Bella (Muniches) J. BS in Econ. and Bus. Mgmt., Ramapo Coll. of N.J., 1981; JD cum laude, Seton Hall U., 1985. Bar: N.J. 1985, U.S. Dist. Ct. N.J. 1985, N.Y. 1988, U.S. Dist. Ct. (so. and ea. dist.) N.Y. 1991. Legal asst. Prudential Ins. Co. Am., Newark, 1982-85; assoc. Fox & Fox, Newark, 1985-86, Elkes, Maybruch & Weiss, P.A., Freehold, N.J., 1986-87; asst. counsel N.Am. Reins. Corp., N.Y.C., 1987-90; assoc. Mark D. Lefkowitz, Esq., 1991; mgr. GRE Ins. Group, Princeton, N.J., 1991; atty. GRE Ins. Group, N.Y.C., 1992—. Vol. campaign Bill Bradley for Senate, 1984, 90; vol. Starlight Found., N.Y.C., 1988—, mem. exec. com. Friends of the Maplewood (N.J.) Lib., 1995—. Mem. ABA, N.J. State Bar Assn. (sect. on entertainment and arts law, newsletter editor 1992-93, bd. dirs. 1993—; ins. law com. 1993—), N.Y. State Bar Assn. (sect. on entertainment, arts and sports law). Democrat. Jewish. Home: 747 Valley St Apt 3K Maplewood NJ 07040-2663

JOSEPHS, BABETTE, legislator; b. N.Y.C., Aug. 4, 1940; d. Eugene and Myra A. Josephs; children: Lee Aaron Newberg, Elizabeth Newberg. BA, Queens Coll., 1962; JD, Rutgers U., 1976. Sole practice Phila., 1976-78; exec. dir. Nat. Abortion Rights Action League of Pa., Phila., 1978-80, Citizens Coalition for Energy Efficiency, Phila., 1980-81; pvt. practice cons., fundraiser Phila., 1981-84; mem. Pa. Ho. of Reps., Phila., 1984—. Bd. dirs. ACLU. Mem. Phila. Bar Assn. Democrat. Jewish. Office: Pa Ho of Reps State Capitol Harrisburg PA 17120

JOSEPHS, EILEEN SHERLE, mediator, financial consultant; b. Johnstown, Pa.; d. David and Freda (Beerman) Venetsky; m. Gerald Lisowitz, June 27, 1953 (div. 1968); children: Mara Lisowitz, Carlyn Lisowitz Walker; m. Marvin Josephs, May 25, 1969 (div. 1988); m. Michael N. Berger, Aug. 28, 1993. BS cum laude, U. Pitts., 1956, MA, 1969. Cert. mediator. Tchr. Pitts. Pub. Schs., 1958-59; tchr. mil. Ft. Lee, Va., 1960; docent edn. staff Carnegie Inst., Pitts., 1971-77; real estate developer, sales rep. Equity Real Estate, Pitts., 1977-79; women's div. buyer and retail cons. Coach House Stores, Pitts., 1980; ptnr., mediator Divorce and Separation Ctr., 1980—; ptnr. Mediation Masters, Pitts., 1992—; guest lectr. U. Pitts., 1982-88, Duquesne U., 1995-96, C.C. Pitts., 1988-91; co-owner Michael Berger Gallery, 1995—. Author: Landmark Mediations-Long Term Marriage, 1992, Divorce Agreements and Landmark Adoption Mediation Resulting in Shared Parenting, 1993, Expanding Non-Adversarial Dispute Resolution in Business Practice, 1993, Advance Mediation in Profl. Practices; contbr. articles to profl. jours. Pub. co-chair Three Rivers Arts Festival, Pitts., 1965; found. bd. dirs. Group Against Smog & Pollution, Pitts., 1967-70; bd. dirs. nat. Coun. Jewish Women, Pitts., 1979; vol. Pitts. Mediation Ctr., 1988—; mem. Family Mediation Coun. Bd. Senatorial scholar U. Pitts., Marshall scholar, 1954. Mem. Pitts. Plan Art, Acad. Family Mediators (cons. 1985—, presentor workshops 1988, 89, 90, 92), Family Mediation Coun. Western Pa. (charter, bd. dirs. 1992—), Greater Pitts. Bd. Realtors. Office: Mediation Masters 7514 Kensington St Pittsburgh PA 15221-3224

JOSEPHSON, DIANA HAYWARD, government agency official; b. London, Oct. 17, 1936; came to U.S., 1959; d. Robert Hayward and Barbara (Clark) Bailey. BA with honors, Oxford U., Eng., 1958, MA, 1962; M in Comparative Law, George Washington U., 1962. Bar: Eng. and Wales 1959, D.C. 1963. Assoc. Covington & Burling, Washington, 1959-68; asst. dir. Office of the Mayor, Washington, 1968-74; exec. dir. Nat. Capital Area ACLU, Washington, 1975-78; dep. asst. adminstr. policy and planning, satellites NOAA, U.S. Dept. Commerce, Washington, 1978-82; pres. Am. Sci. and Tech. Corp., Bethesda, Md., 1982-83, Space Am., Bethesda, 1983-85; v.p. mktg. Arianespace, Inc., Washington, 1985-87; v.p. Martin Marietta Comml. Titan Inc., Washington, 1987-89; dir. bus. devel. Martin Marietta Advanced Launch Systems, Denver, 1989-90, Martin Marietta Civil Space and Communications Co., Denver, 1990-93; dep. under sec. of commerce for oceans and atmosphere NOAA, U.S. Dept. Commerce, Washington, 1993—; mem. Space Applications Bd., NRC, 1988-89, Comml. Space Transp. Adv. Commn., U.S. Dept. Transp., Washington, 1984-85; adv. bd. Washington Space Bus. Roundtable, 1985-87. Mem. D.C. Law Revision Commn., Washington, 1975-78, D.C. Internat. Women's Yr. State Coordinating Com., 1977. Recipient Gold medal for Disting. Svc., U.S. Dept. Commerce, 1981. Mem. Am. Astronautical Soc. (bd. dirs. 1985-88), Nat. Space Club (bd. govs.), Women in Aerospace, Washington Space Bus. Roundtable (adv. bd. 1985-87). Office: Dept of Commerce Nat Oceanic & Atmospheric Admin 14th & Constitution Ave NW Washington DC 20230

JOSEY, DONNA PEARSON, art gallery director; b. Lynchburg, Va., Nov. 21, 1942; d. Gordon Trout and Eloise Virginia (Seabolt) Pearson; m. Joseph Oscar Neuhoff, May 1, 1965 (div. Mar. 1990); children: Laurel Neuhoff Page, Donna Ann, Emily Pearson, Joseph Oscar III, Virginiaa Folsom; m. Jack Smyth Josey, Jan. 16, 1992. Cert. in letters, U. Paris, 1963; BA, Sweet Briar Coll., 1964; postgrad., Rice U. Tchr. French, St. Mark's Sch., Dallas, 1964-65, Jesuit Coll. Prep. Sch., Dallas, 1981-83; pres. Neuhoff Galleries, Dallas, 1983—, Houston; aesthetic advisor The Crescent Devel., Dallas, 1984-85; art curator Josey Oil Co., Houston, 1992-96; pvt. art dealer, 1994—. Bd. dirs. Cath. Charities, Dallas, 1980—, Nat. Wildflower Found., Austin, Tex., 1995—, Am. Hosp. Paris, 1994—; mem. arts adv. bd. U. Tex., Austin, 1995—, Sweet Briar (Va.) Coll., 1995—. Mem. Met. Club (N.Y.C.), Crescent Club (Dallas), James River Country Club (Va.). Roman Catholic. Home: 1537 Kirby Dr Houston TX 77019 Office: Neuhoff Galleries 504 Waugh Dr Houston TX 77019

JOSHI-PETERS, KARUNA LAXMIPRASAD, psychologist; b. Patan, Gujerat, India, July 18, 1944; came to U.S., 1971; d. Laxmiprasad Chunilal and Leelvati Laxmiprasad (Shukla) Joshi; m. Ramashanker Misra, May 10, 1965 (div. July 1977); m. Michael Wood Peters, Sept. 8, 1977; children: Adrian Manoj Rohit, Julian Vikram Suhas. BA in English Lit. with honors, Banaras Hindu U., Varanasi, India, 1960, MA in Philosophy, 1962; MA in Psychology, U. Hawaii, 1990, PhD in Psychology, 1992. Lic. clin. psychologist, Hawaii. Jr. rsch. fellow Banaras Hindu U., 1962-64, lectr., 1963; lectr. Patna (India) U., 1964-65; sr. rsch. asst. Indian Inst. Tech., Kanpur, India, 1965-71; teaching asst. dept. philosophy U. Hawaii, Honolulu, 1975-76; psychol. intern Oreg. Health Scis. U., Portland, 1991-92; psychol. examiner spl. svcs. State of Hawaii Dept. Edn., Honolulu, 1992; psychologist State of Hawaii Dept. Health, Kaneohe, 1993; pvt. practice psychology Kaneohe, 1993—; organizer Hawaii Neuropsychology Group, Kaneohe, 1990—. Author rsch. papers in field. East West Ctr. grantee, 1971-75; jr. rsch. fellow Univ. Grants Commn., New Delhi, India, 1962-64. Mem. APA, Hawaii Psychol. Assn., Nat. Acad. Neuropsychology, Internat Neuropsychol. Soc. Democrat. Office: 46-001 Kamehameha Hwy Ste 419B Kaneohe HI 96744-3735

JOSKOW, RENEE W., dentist, educator; b. N.Y.C., Mar. 15, 1960; d. Melvin Lawrence and Eunice Lila (Levine) J. BA, SUNY, Binghamton, 1981; MPH, Columbia U., 1985, DDS, 1985. Cert. Shiatsu practitioner, Am. Oriental Bodywork Therapy Assn. Gen. practice resident Hackensack (N.J.) Med. Ctr., 1985-86; pvt. faculty practice, gen. practitioner Sch. of Dental and Oral Surgery, Columbia U., N.Y.C., 1986-90; asst. prof., dentistry Columbia U., N.Y.C., 1986—, dir. freshman dental courses, 1987—; pvt. practice gen. dentistry N.Y.C., 1990—; cons. alternative delivery sys. Sch. Dental and Oral Surgery, Columbia U., 1985-86, workshop leader, 1993, mem. curriculum com. Ctr. for Alt. and Complementary Medicine; cons. on quality assurance Prudential Ins. Co., 1994—; clin. program coord. health of pub. grant Columbia Sch. Pub. Health, 1987-88; workshop leader Columbia-Presbyn. Med. Ctr., 1993; guest lectr. Inst. for Child Devel.-Cmty. Outreach lectr. oral health Hackensack Med. Ctr., 1986. Mem. Julliard Evening Divsn. Chorale. Recipient L.I. Acad. of Odontology award, N.Y., 1985, Ella Marie Ewell award for Meritorious Svc., Columbia Univ., 1985, Alumni award for Excellence in Preventive Dentistry, Columbia U., 1985. Fellow N.Y. Acad. Dentistry, Acad. Gen. Dentistry; mem. ADA, Am. Assn. Women Dentists (faculty advisor 1986—), 1st Dist. Dental Soc., Columbia U. Alumni Assn. (com. chmn. 1989—), Nat. Assn. Women Bus. Owners, Omicron Kappa Upsilon. Office: 29 W 57th St New York NY 10019-3406

JOSLIN, LINDA JOY HARBER, elementary education educator; b. Abilene, Tex., Dec. 16, 1946; d. William E. and Frances Rowena (Robinson) Harber; m. Fred Leon Joslin, May 29, 1970; 1 child, Jeremy Lee. BS in Elem. Edn., Sul Ross State U., 1968; cert. educable emotionally mentally handicapped, Hardin Simmons U., 1972, MS in Reading, 1983. Cert. tchr., Tex. 2d and 4th grade tchr. Lamesa (Tex.) Ind. Schs., 1968-72; educable emotionally mentally handicapped tchr. Tri-County Edn. Co-op, Anson, Tex., 1972-73, Taylor/Calahan County Edn. Co-op, Merkel, Tex., 1973-75; 3d grade tchr., jr. high educable emotionally mentally handicapped Snyder (Tex.) Ind. Schs., 1975-77; 11-12 yr. olds educable emotionally mentally handicapped tchr. Midland (Tex.) Ind. Schs., 1977-78; 1st grade tchr. Deltac-7 Pub. Schs., Deering, Mo., 1978-95; tchr. grade 1 Malden Pub. Sch., 1995—; mem. profl. devel. com. County and Sch. Dist. Delta C-7 and Pemiscot County, 1992—, tchr. Caruthersville Summer Sch. Acad., 1994-95 (del. 1993-95), presenter Mo. State Tchrs. Convention Workshop, Kansas City, 1994. Contbr. articles in profl. jours. Summer food program monitor Pemiscot Health Ctr., Hayti, Mo., 1990-93. Mem. Mo. State Tchrs. Assn. (del. 1993-94), Delta C-7 Classroom Tchrs. Assn. (pres., v.p., recording sec. 1978—), Beta Sigma Phi (Girl of Yr. 1980-82), Delta Kappa Gamma. Baptist. Home: 906 Alberta Malden MO 63863-9443

JOURDAIN, ALICE MARIE, philosopher, retired educator; b. Brussels, Mar. 11, 1923; came to U.S., 1940, naturalized, 1948; d. Henri and Marthe (van de Vorst) J.; m. Dietrich von Hildebrand, July 16, 1959. Student, Manhattanville Coll., 1942-44; PhD, Fordham U., 1949; D honoris causa, U. Steubenville, Ohio, 1987. Mem. faculty dept. philosophy Hunter Coll., CUNY, 1947—, prof., 1971-84; vis. prof. U. de los Andes, Bogotá, Colombia, summer 1955, Thomas More Inst., Rome, Spring 1985, Catechetical Inst., Yonkers, N.Y., 1985, Notre Dame Catechetical Inst., Arlington, Va., summer 1986, 87, 88; lectr. Internat. Congress on Family, Caracas, Venezuela, 1985; lectr. various instns., The Netherlands, Germany, Austria, Mex., Can., Colombia, Liechtenstein, Eng., U.S. Author: Greek Culture: The Adventure of the Human Spirit, 1966, Introduction to a Philosophy of Religion, 1971, By Love Refined, 1988, By Grief Refined, 1994; (with D. von Hildebrand) Graven Images, 1957, Art of Living, 1965, Situation Ethics, 1966. Recipient William O'Brien award Newman Club, 1963. Roman Catholic.

JOW, PAT See KAGEMOTO, PATRICIA JOW

JOY, CARLA MARIE, history educator; b. Denver, Sept. 5, 1945; d. Carl P. and Theresa M. (Lotito) J. AB cum laude, Loretto Heights Coll., 1967; MA, U. Denver, 1969, postgrad., 1984—. Instr. history Community Coll. Denver; prof. history Red Rocks Community Coll., Lakewood, Colo., 1970—; cons. for innovative ednl. programs; reviewer fed. grants, 1983-89; mem. adv. panel Colo. Endowment for Humanities, 1985-89. Contbr. articles to profl. publs. Instr. vocat. edn. Mile High United Way, Jefferson County, 1975; participant Jefferson County Sch. System R-1 Dist., 1983-88; active Red Rocks Community Coll. Speakers Bur., 1972-89, strategic planning com., 1992—; chair history discipline Colo. Gen. Edn. Core Transfer Consortium, 1986—; mem. history, geography, civics stds. and geography frameworks adv. com. Colo. Dept. Edn., 1995—; steering com. Ctr. Teaching Excellence, 1996—. Cert. in vocat. edn. Colo. State Bd. Community Colls. and Occupational Edn., 1975; mem. evaluation team for Colo. Awards, edn.

and civic achievement for Widefield Sch. Dist. #3, 1989; mem. Red Rocks Community Coll.-Clear Creek Sch. System Articulation Team, 1990-91. Ford Found. fellow, 1969; recipient cert. of appreciation Kiwanis Club, 1981, Cert. of Appreciation Telecommunication Coop. for Colo's. Community Colls., 1990-92; Master Tchr. award U. Tex. at Austin, 1982. Mem. Am. Hist. Assn., Am. Assn. Higher Edn., Nat. Council for Social Studies, Nat. Geog. Soc., Inst. Early Am. History and Culture, Nat. Edn. Assn., Colo. Edn. Assn., Colo. Council for Social Studies, The Smithsonian Nat. Assocs., Denver Art Mus., Denver Mus. of Nat. Hist., Community Coll. Humanities Assn., Orgn. Am. Historians, The Colo. Hist. Soc., Colo. Endowment for the Humanities, Colo. Geographic Alliance, Soc. History Edn., Phi Alpha Theta. Home: 1849 S Lee St Apt D Lakewood CO 80232-6252 Office: Red Rocks Community Coll 13300 W 6th Ave Golden CO 80401-5398

JOYCE, ANN IANNUZZO, art educator; b. Scranton, Pa., May 23, 1953; d. Albert Joseph and Lucy (Giumento) Iannuzzo; m. Patrick Francis Joyce, July 23, 1977; children: Ryan Patrick, Shawn Patrick. BFA, Maryland Inst., Balt., 1975; MS, U. Scranton, 1988; postgrad., Pa. State U., 1990—. Mech. artist Internat. Corr. Schs., Scranton, Pa., 1975-77; layout artist Lynn Orgn., Wilkes-Barre, Pa., 1977-78; prodn. coord. Jewelcor Merchandising, Wilkes-Barre, 1978-82; adj. lectr. Kings Coll., Wilkes-Barre, 1981-89; art dir. WVIA-TV Pub. Broadcasting, Pittston, Pa., 1985-86; publs. dir. U. Scranton, 1986-89; asst. prof. King's Coll., Wilkes-Barre, 1989—; exec. bd. v.p. Northeastern Pa. Writing Coun., Wilkes-Barre, 1993—; edn. co-chair Northeast Pa. Ad Club, 1994—. Contbg. author: Handbook of Classroom Assessment: Learning, Achievement, and Adjustment, 1996. Cub Scout leader Boy Scouts Am., Moosic, Pa., 1992-95. Mem. ASCD, Nat. Art Edn. Assn., Am. Inst. Graphic Arts (Phila. chpt.), Calligraphers Guild, Artists for Art, Pa. Art Edn. Assn., Nat. Assn. Desktop Pubs., Seminar for Rsch. in Art Edn., Caucus for Social Theory in Art Edn. Democrat. Roman Catholic. Home: 812 Grace Ln Moosic PA 18507-1610 Office: King's Coll 133 N River St Wilkes Barre PA 18711-0851

JOYCE, BERNITA ANNE, federal government agency administrator; d. Albert A. and Margaret C. Joyce. BA, Duchesne Coll.; MBA, U. Santa Clara, 1968, PhD, 1974; m. Kenneth B. Lucas, Aug. 2, 1975. With Wolfe & Co., CPA's, Washington, 1971-72; fin. dir. Nat. Forest Products Assn., Washington, 1972-74; budget and fiscal officer ICC, Washington, 1974-77, Office Mgmt. and Budget, 1977-80; asst. dir. mgmt. svcs. Bur. Mines, Dept. Interior, 1980-85, asst. dir. Office Policy Analysis Dept. Interior, 1985-96, asst. spl. trustee for Am. Indian., 1996—. Author: Financial Viability of Private Elementary Schools. Mem. AICPA, Sr. Execs. Assn., Exec. Women in Govt., Assn. Govt. Accts., Beta Gamma Sigma. Home: 6001 Bradley Blvd Bethesda MD 20817-3807

JOYCE, CAROL BERTANI, social studies educator; b. N.Y.C., Apr. 9, 1943; d. Joseph and Ethel Marie (Bracchi) Bertani; m. William Leonard Joyce, Aug. 13, 1967; children: Susan A., Michael J. BA, Coll. New Rochelle, 1964; MA, St. John's U., 1966; postgrad., U. Mich., 1970-71. Cert. tchr., N.J., N.Y., Mass., Mich. Tchr. Christ the King High Sch., Middle Village, N.Y., 1966-67, Willow Run High Sch., Ypsilanti, Mich., 1967-68, Notre Dame Acad., Worcester, Mass., 1974-81, Salesian High Sch., New Rochelle, N.Y., 1981-82, Ursuline Sch., New Rochelle, 1982-88, Burlington Twp. (N.J.) Schs., 1988-89; edn. planner N.J. Dept. Edn., Trenton, 1989-91; tchr. Princeton (N.J.) Regional Schs., 1991—; participant Tri-States Global Workshop, Boylston, Mass., 1980, NEH summer seminar fellowship U. Mass., Dartmouth, North Dartmouth, 1993, Tchrs. Inst. in History, Princeton U., summer 1994, Seminar in African-Am. Studies for Secondary Sch. Tchrs. Princeton U., 1995-96; tchr., counselor European tour Am. Leadership Study Group, 1987; master tchr. DeWitt-Wallace World History Tchrs. Summer Inst., Woodrow Wilson Nat. Scholarship Found., Princeton, 1992. Tchr. religious edn. various parishes in Mass., N.Y., 1974-83; chair edn. com. LWV, Pelham, N.Y., 1983-84; vol. Profl. Roster, Princeton, 1989, Profl. Svc. Group, New Brunswick, N.J., 1991; panelist N.J. Bar Found. High Sch. Curriculum Panel on Law-Related Edn., 1993—. Grantee Women's Ctr. U. Mich., 1970-71. Mem. Nat. Coun. for Social Studies (participant social studies coun. meeting N.E. regional conf. 1981), Nat. Coun. for History Edn. Home: 99 Mccosh Cir Princeton NJ 08540-5626 Office: Princeton High Sch 151 Moore St Princeton NJ 08540-3312

JOYCE, KRISTINA ANN, artist, educator; b. Carthage, Mo., May 28, 1945; d. Robert Monroe and Harriet Annabel (McBride) Campbell; m. William Robert Joyce; children: Keir Robert, Tara Kirstin. BA in French, Hood Coll., 1967; MS in Art Edn., Mass. Coll. Art, 1981. Cert. K-12 art tchr., Mass. Office asst. Investors Loan Co., Virginia Beach, Va., 1968-69; trilingual asst. Millipore Corp., Bedford, Mass., 1969-72; registrar, tchr. Cambridge Sch., Weston, Mass., 1973-81; artist Orchard House, Concord, Mass., 1981—; pvt. tchr. art, Concord, 1981—; instr. calligraphy Bentley Coll., Waltham, Mass., 1983-85, Bunsai Gakuen, Lincoln, Mass., 1991; freelance graphic artist and illustrator, 1981—. Calligrapher: (books) Lay of a Golden Goose, 1987, Alcott Wit and Wisdom, 1991; exhibited in group shows Francesca Anderson Gallery, Boston, 1982, Thoreau Lyceum, Concord, 1983, Grove Street Gallery, Worcester, Mass., 1984, DeCordova Mus., Lincoln, 1984, Cannon Rotunda, U.S. Ho. of Reps., Washington, 1985, Prudential Tower, Boston, 1986, Walters Gallery, Regis Coll., Weston, Mass., 1987, Bentley Coll. Gallery, 1988, Concord Art Assn., 1990, Samponis Gallery, Burlington, Mass., 1991, Cape Cod Mus. Natural History, Brewster, Mass., 1991, 96, Sakharov Congress, Moscow, 1991, North Mus., Lancaster, Pa., 1992; commns. Mass. gov.'s inauguration, Boston, 1983, include St. Mandé, France, 1989. Mem. LWV, Thoreau Soc. (life), Guild Natural Sci. Illustrators, Conchologists Am., Concord Art Assn., Boston Malacological Club. Roman Catholic. Home and Studio: 646 Main St Concord MA 01742

JOYCE, MARY ANN, principal; b. Bklyn., May 29, 1935; d. Alfred and Antoinette (Polito) Lo Sasso; m. Michael J. Joyce, Jr., Mar. 2, 1957 (dec. 1982); children: Michael, Debra Grammer, Patricia Sommers. BA in Elem. Edn., Social Scis., Mount St. Mary Coll., 1972; MS in Elem. Edn., Reading, SUNY, New Paltz, 1975, CAS in Ednl. Adminstrn., 1983. Cert. tchr. N-6, N.Y., reading tchr., K-12, N.Y., sch. dist. administr., N.Y., sch. administr./supr., N.Y. Tchr. grades 3 and 4 Temple Hill Sch., Newburgh, N.Y., 1972-74, tchr. reading, 1974-83, tchr. gifted and talented, 1976-83, asst. prin., 1983-85; prin. Horizons-on-the-Hudson Magnet Sch., Newburgh, 1985—; tchr. summer sch. Newburgh (N.Y.) Free Acad., 1976-81; adj. prof. SUNY, New Paltz, 1989-91; nat. review panelist Blue Ribbon Sch. Competition, 1991, 92, FIRST family-sch. partnership program, 1992; speaker numerous confs., seminars. Recipient Elem. Sch. Recognition award U.S. Dept. Edn., 1989-90, 93-94, Excellence in Adminstrn. award Mid-Hudson Sch. Study Coun., 1993, award for Outstanding Leadership, Achievements and Contributions Toward Making the Edn. of our Nation's Youth a Safe and Productive Experience, 1991. Mem. ASCD, Am. Assn. Female Execs., Nat. Assn. Elem. Sch. Prins. (Excellence in Edn. award 1990, 94), State Adminstrs. Assn. N.Y. State (Elem. Schs. Excellence award 1990, 94), Newburgh Suprs. and Adminstrs. Assn., United Univ. Profs., Delta Kappa Gamma. Office: Horizons-on-the-Hudson Magnet Sch 137 Montgomery St Newburgh NY 12550-3636

JOYCE, VICKI MARIE, special education educator; b. Chgo., Sept. 8, 1936; d. Walter and Victoria Juckins; m. Robert Daniel Joyce, Aug., 1956 (div. 1974); children: Jennifer Brining, David. BA, Calif. State U., L.A., 1962; MA, Calif. State U., San Bernadino, 1992. Home econs. tchr. L.A. City Sch. Dist., 1962-65; real estate broker Homes Unltd., Orange County, Calif., 1970-82; tchr. Riverside and San Bernadino County (Calif.) Sch. Dists., 1982-95; resource specialist San Bernadino Unified Sch. Dist., 1995—. Author: A Theoretical Meta-Analysis and Review of Kinesis For Special Education Teachers and Resource Specialists, 1993. Named Outstanding Tchr. Orton Dyslexia Soc., 1993. Mem. Calif. Tchrs. Assn., San Bernadino Tchrs. Assn., Nat. Tchrs. Assn., Nat. Assn. Resource Specialists. Home: 1965 Coulston Unit # 37 Loma Linda CA 92354 Office: San Bernardino HS 1850 North E St San Bernardino CA

JOYCE-HAYES, DEE L., lawyer; b. Lexington, Va., Aug. 29, 1946; d. Robert Newton and Dorothy Lucille (Markham) Joyce; m. Lester Stephen Vossmeyer, Dec. 28, 1971 (div. Apr. 1984); 1 child, Robert Stephen; m. Gary Lee Hayes, Aug. 29, 1986; 1 child, Elena. BA in Govt., Coll. William and Mary, 1968; JD, St. Louis U., 1980. Bar: Mo. 1980. Spl. asst. to dep. under sec. U.S. Dept. Transp., Washington, 1970-72; rsch. analyst Lee Creative Rsch., St. Louis, 1972-74; bank officer Mark Twain Banks, St. Louis, 1974-77; asst. cir. atty. Cir. Atty.'s Office St. Louis, 1981-92; cir. atty. Office of Cir. Atty., St. Louis, 1993—; v.p. bd. dirs. Children's Advocacy Ctr., St. Louis, 1990-96; gubernatorial appointee Mo. Sentencing Advs. Commn., 1995—; co-chmn. Operation Weed and Seed, St. Louis, 1994—; mem. disciplinary com. 22d Cir. Bar Com., St. Louis, 1992—. Pres. of bd. The Backstoppers, St. Louis, 1996-97; mem. steering com. United Way Comty. Action to Prevent Violence Initiative, Mo. and western Ill., 1994-96; mem. nat. and St. Louis chpt. Women's Polit. Caucus; mem. com. on missions and social concerns Grace United Meth. Ch., St. Louis, 1988—. Mem. ACLU, Nat. Dist. Atty. Assn., Mo. Assn. Prosecuting Atty. (treas. 1996-97), Met. St. Louis Bar Assn., Mound City Bar Assn., Kappa Alpha Theta. Democrat. Office: St Louis Cir Atty Rm 330 1320 Market St Saint Louis MO 63103

JOYE, AFRIE SONGCO, minister; b. Guagua, Pampanga, Philippines, Aug. 8, 1942; d. Emilio Lelay and Elmerita (Atienza) Laus Songco; m. Charles James Joye, Aug. 28, 1971. BA in Christian Edn., Harris Meml. Coll., Manila, 1963; MA in Christian Edn., Scarritt Grad. Sch., Nashville, 1970; PhD in Theology and Religious Edn., Sch. Theology at Claremont, Calif., 1990. Dir. Christian edn. First United Meth. Ch., Naga, Philippines, 1963-66; dist. Christian Edn. coord. Bicol-Palawan Region of United Meth. Ch., 1963-66; dir. Christian Edn. Cen. United Meth. Ch., Manila, 1966-68; dir. youth ministry and student ctr. Cen. United Meth. Ch., 1970-71; instr. psychology and Christian edn. Philippin Christian Coll./Harris Meml. Coll., Manila, 1970-71; dir Christian Edn. Aldersgate United Meth. Ch./John Wesley United Meth. Ch., Charleston, S.C., 1971-74; instr. Palmer Coll., Charleston, S.C., 1972-74; nat. dir. Christian edn. in Asian and Native Am. chs. Gen. Bd. Discipleship, Nashville, 1976-79, nat. dir. Christian edn. in small membership chs., 1979-83; cons.-trainer in Christian edn., 1983-87; minister Christian edn. Community United Meth. Ch., Huntington Beach, Calif., 1987-90; assoc. minister Laguna Hills (Calif.) United Meth. Ch., 1990-92; co-pastor Hollywood (Calif.) First United Meth. Ch., 1992-94; sr. pastor St. Paul's United Meth. Ch., Tarzana, Calif., 1994—. Editor: Program Ideas and Training Designs for Pacific and Asian American Church Schools, 1981; contbr. articles to profl. jours. Nat. mem. Bread for the World, Fellowship of Reconciliation, Amnesty Internat. Coolidge Colloquium fellow, Assn. for Religion and Intellectual Life, 1989. Mem. AAUW (life), Nat. Christian Educators Fellowship, Am. Acad. Religion, Assn. of Profs. and Researchers of Religious Education, Nat. Fedn. Asian Am. United Meth., Religious Edn. Assn.

JOYNER, JANICE IRENE, accountant; b. Reform, Ala., Dec. 1, 1969; d. Floyd Harold and Ruby Ann (Gore) J. ASBA, Brewer State Jr. Coll., Fayette, Ala., 1990; BS in Acctg., U. Ala., 1992. CPA. Staff acct. Pickens County Med. Ctr., Carrollton, Ala., 1992-93, asst. comptr., 1993—. Charter mem. Leadership Pickens, Pickens County, Ala., 1993-94. Mem. Inst. Mgmt. Accts., Ala. Soc. CPAs. Office: Pickens County Medical Ctr PO Box 478 Carrollton AL 35447

JOYNER, JO ANN, geriatrics nurse; b. Glenwood, Ga., Mar. 9, 1947; d. Roy and Lucille (Mercer) Powell; m. Henry Gene Lamb, Dec. 3, 1965 (div. 1984); children: Henry G. Lamb, Jr., Roy, Melinda, Jody; m. Robert Eugene Joyner, June 14, 1991. Diploma, Swainsboro Vocat./Tech., 1979; student, Ga. So. Coll., 1980. LPN, Ga. Staff nurse Meadows Meml. Hosp., Vidalia, Ga., 1980-82; staff nurse in ICU and critical care unit Toombs Alcohol and Drug Abuse Ctr., Vidalia, 1982-84; charge nurse Conners Nursing Home, Glenwood, Ga., 1984-85; supr. Bethany Nursing Ctr., Vidalia, 1990-92, charge nurse, 1985-92; nurse Claxton (Ga.) Nursing Home, Toombs Nursing and Intermediate Care Home, Lyons, Ga., 1992-93; staff nurse Laurens Convalescent Ctr., Dublin, Ga., 1994, 1994; staff nurse Meadow Brook Manor, 1994—, Dublin, 1994-95; relief house supervisor Dulinair Healthcare & Rehab. Ctr., Dublin, Ga., 1995-96; mem. ind. nursing registry, Claxton; nurse Meml. Med. Ctr., Savannah, Ga.; office nurse Montgomery County Correctional Inst., Mt. Vernon, Ga., Laurens Convalescent Ctr., 1994-95, Meadowbrook Manor, 1994—; 3-11 relief house supr., supr. medicare spl. unit, 1995-96. Democrat. Apostolic. Home: 315 Clover St Dublin GA 31021-7719

JOYNER-CLINARD, PAULA ELLEN, secondary education educator, choral director; b. Jacksonville, Fla., Aug. 15, 1951; d. Paul and Dorothy June (McGukin) Hennis; m. Richard William Joyner, July 31, 1971 (div. Sept. 1981); 1 child, Richard Paul; m. Robert Kenneth Clinard, June 13, 1987; 1 child, Matthew Evan Clinard. B of Music Edn., Cen. Mich. U., 1972; postgrad., Mich. State U., 1969-71, 74-75, Wayne State U., 1981-87. Cert. tchr. 7-12 secondary music edn., K-6 music edn., Mich. Tchr., choral dir. Livonia (Mich.) Pub. Schs., 1973, Farmington (Mich.) Pub. Schs., 1973-78, Novi (Mich.) Comty. Schs., 1978—; dept. chmn. Novi H.S., 1992—, chair restructuring com., 1995—; alto sect. leader, mem. Detroit Symphony Chorale, 1987-93; mem. Vocal Point Jazz Ensemble, Detroit, 1985-91; mem. long range planning com. Novi Comty. Schs., 1994—. Pres. Novi Arts Coun., 1991-94; mgr. nat. program Project Concern U.S. Jaycettes, San Diego, 1979-80; precinct del. Mich. Dem. Party, Livonia, 1974; v.p. Mich. Jaycettes, 1977-78; pres. Livonia Jaycettes, 1976-77; nat. v.p. U.S. Jaycettes, Tulsa, 1979-80; mem. Livonia Ecology Commn., 1975. Named Congresswoman, U.S. Jaycettes, 1989, Young Careerist Livonia Bus. Profl. Women's Club, Outstanding Young Woman of Am., 1980, 95, Ky. Col., 1980. Mem. Am. Choral Dirs. Assn. of Mich. (newsletter editor, sec., repertoire & standards chair 1985—), Mich. Sch. Vocal Music Assn. (exec. bd. dirs., dist. mgr. 1973—, Regional Honors Choral Dir. 1993), Libr. of Congress Assocs., Smithsonian Instn. Assocs., Detroit Inst. of Arts Founders Soc., Novi Arts Coun. Democrat. Office: Novi H S 24062 Taft Novi MI 48375

JOYNER KERSEE, JACQUELINE, track and field athlete; b. East St. Louis, Ill., Mar. 3, 1962; d. Alfred Sr. and Mary Joyner; m. Bob Kersee, Jan. 11, 1986. BA in History, UCLA, 1985. Winner 4 consecutive Nat. Jr. Pentathlon Championships; winner heptathlon Goodwill Games, Moscow, 1986, U.S. Olympic Festival, 1986; winner USA/Mobil Outdoor Track and Field Championship, 1987; winner, long jump and heptathlon World Track and Field Championships, 1987; winner Grand Prix Indoor Championships, winner indoor world record 55m hurdlers 7:37 seconds, 1989; winner heptathlon Goodwill Games, St. Petersburg, Russia, 1994; pres., founder JJK & Assocs., Inc. Founder JJK Cmty. Found. Recipient Silver medal for heptathlon L.A. Summer Olympic Games, 1984, Sullivan award, 1986, Jesse Owens award, Am. Black Achievement award Ebony mag., 1987, Gold medal for long jump at 24 ft. 3 1/2 in. and heptathlon Seoul Summer Olympic Games, 1988, 1st Female Athlete of Yr. award Sporting News, 1988, Gold medal for heptathlon Barcelona Summer Olympic Games, 1992, Bronze medal for long jump Barcelona Summer Olympic Games, 1992, Gold medal for heptathlon World Track and Field Championships, 1993, Jim Thorpe award, 1993, Jackie Robinson "Robie" award, 1994, Grand Prix Outdoor Champion, 1994; named Athlete of Yr., Track & Field News, 1986, Female Athlete of Yr., AP, 1987, Female of Yr. IAAF, 1994, St. Louis Ambassadors Sportswoman of Yr. Office: JJK & Assocs 3466 Bridgeland Dr Ste 105 Bridgeton MO 63044-2606*

JUBINSKA-CHRISTIANSEN, PATRICIA ANN, ballet instructor, choreographer; b. Norfolk, Va., Nov. 10, 1949; d. Joseph John and Lucy (Babey) Topping; m. Paul Christiansen, June 5, 1971; children: Vanessa Meredith, Courtney Hilary. Student, Md. State Ballet Sch., 1959-60, Sch. Am. Ballet, N.Y.C., 1960-67; BA, R.I. Coll., 1976; MA, Wesleyan U., 1995. Mem. N.Y.C. Ballet, 1968-72; freelance artist Chamber Ballet of L.A., San Antonio Ballet, Md. State Ballet, 1972-81, 92-95; artistic dir. Blackstone Valley Ballet, Harrisville, R.I., 1983-84, Am. Ballet, Pascoag, R.I., 1984-92; asst. artistic dir. Odessa Ukrainian Dancers, Woonsocket, R.I., 1991-92; freelance guest artist, 1992—; mem. Mandrivka Dancers of Boston, 1993—. Home: 1264 Round Top Rd Harrisville RI 02830-1013

JUCHNICKI, JANE ELLEN, secondary education educator; b. Greenfield, Mass., Jan. 18, 1949; d. Francis W. and Helen (Helstowski) J. BS in Secondary History Edn., U. Vt., 1970; MS in Colonial U.S. History, Ctrl. Conn. State U., 1976; MA in Archeology, U. Conn., 1979. Tchr. social studies, history Gideon Wells Jr. High Sch., Glastonbury, Conn., 1970-72, Glastonbury Adult Edn., 1976-86, Glastonbury High Sch., 1972—; mem. Pub. Archeology Survey Team, Storrs, Conn., 1978-79, Secondary Social Studies Curriculum Devel. Com., 1989—. Author: (booklet) Career/Resume Prep Unemployment, 1979. Active Fulbright Assn., Washington, 1990—; vol. Smithsonian Excavation, Tell Jemmeh, Israel, 1976. Fellow U.S. Dept. Edn., Egypt, 1987; Fulbright-Hayes Found. tchr. exch., London, 1987-89 tchr. rsch. fellow U. London, 1992. Mem. NEA, Conn. Edn. Assn., Glastonbury Edn. Assn. Democrat. Office: Glastonbury HS 330 Hubbard St Glastonbury CT 06033-3047

JUDD, JACQUELINE DEE (JACKIE JUDD), journalist, reporter; b. Johnstown, Pa., Nov. 29, 1952; d. Myer and Lillian J.; m. Michael James Shulman, Oct. 6, 1985; 2 children. BA in Journalism and Polit. Sci., Am. U., 1973. Reporter WKXL Radio, Concord, N.H., 1974-75, WBAL Radio, Balt., 1975-76; reporter, anchor All Things Considered, Morning Edit., Nat. Pub. Radio, Washington, 1976-82; news anchor, reporter, anchor CBS Radio, N.Y.C., 1982-87; reporter ABC TV, Washington, 1987—. Recipient Overseas Press Club citation Overseas Press Club, N.Y.C., 1989, Emmy award Am. Acad. Arts and Scis., N.Y.C., 1990, Lodestar award Am. U., 1993, Dupont award, 1994. Mem. Radio TV Corr. Assocs. of Capital Hill (exec. com. 1993-96), Am. Fedn. Radio and TV Artists. Office: ABC News Washington Bur 1717 Desales St NW Washington DC 20036-4401

JUDD, WYNONNA, vocalist, musician; b. 1964; d. Naomi Judd; 1 child, Elijah. Mem. country and western mus. duo The Judds; now pursuing solo career; songs include Had a Dream, 1983, Mama, He's Crazy, 1984, Why Not Me, 1984, Love Is Alive, 1985, Have Mercy, 1985, Rockin' with the Rhythm, 1985, Grandpa, 1986; albums include The Judds, Why Not Me?, Rockin' with the Rhythm, Christmas Time with the Judds, Heartland, 1987, River of Time, 1989, Love Can Build a Bridge, 1990, Wynonna, 1992, Tell Me Wy, 1993, Revelations, 1996, Greatest Hits Vols. I and II; co-author: (with Naomi Judd) Love Can Build a Bridge, 1993. Recipient Grammy award, 1985, 86, 87, 89, duet award (with Naomi Judd), Acad. Country Music award, 1985-91, Vocal Duo award (with Naomi Judd), Country Music Assn. award, 1984-91, 2 Grammy nominations, Acad. Country Music award for Top Female Artist, 1994.

JUDELL, CYNTHIA KOLBURNE, craft company executive; b. N.Y.C., Mar. 23, 1924; d. Luma L. and Stella E. (Robins) Kolburne; m. Samuel Judell, Oct. 30, 1949; children: Joy C., Neil H.K. BSEE, Antioch Coll., Yellow Springs, Ohio, 1945; MA, Columbia U., 1948. Cert. secondary tchr. Engr., Jet Propulsion Lab., Pasadena, Calif., 1946-47; tchr. math., sci. Leonard Sch. for Girls, N.Y.C., 1948-49; substitute tchr. Bd. Edn., Ridgefield, Conn., 1964-67; part-time tchr. Bd. Edn., Brookfield, Conn., 1967-73; owner T W M Enterprises, Wilton, Conn., 1976—. Dep. registrar of voters Town of Wilton, 1977-93; elected mem. Bd. of Tax Rev., Wilton, 1980-87; treas. Town Assn., Inc., Wilton, 1980-84. Recipient Intergroup scholar Columbia U., 1948. Mem. LWV (budget chair, treas. Conn. chpt. 1978-86, treas. Wilton chpt. 1986-88), Conn. Soc. Women Engrs. (treas. 1971-72). Office: T W M Enterprises PO Box 266 Wilton CT 06897-0266

JUDGE, BERYL JUNE BRANDMILL, family education specialist; b. Elma, Iowa, Sept. 23, 1936; d. Dinsmore and Ruth Marcella (Bailard) Brandmill; m. Thomas E. Judge, Sept. 5, 1957 (div. 1977); children: Steven, John, David, Katherine, Michael. BS, Iowa State U., 1957, postgrad., 1979; MEd, Notre Dame Coll., Belmont, Calif., 1978. Tchr. Montessori Children's House, Palo Alto, Calif., 1974-79; tchr. learning disabilities/behavior disorders Hampton, Iowa, 1980-91; family edn. specialist Nat. Alliance Mentally Ill, 1991—; dir. Compeer North Iowa, Inc.; freelance lectr. mental illness and the family. Contbr. articles about mental illness to newspapers and newsletters. Democrat. Home: 1023 Pepper Dr Iowa City IA 52240

JUDGE, DOLORES BARBARA, real estate broker; b. Plymouth, Pa.; m. Richard James Judge; children: Susan, Nancy, Richard Jr. Student, North Harris County Coll., 1984-85, U. Tex., 1985, Houston Community Coll., 1988-89. Real estate agt. comml. real estate cos. in area, 1981-84; owner D-J Investment Properties, Conroe, Tex., 1984—; pres. Judge Real Estate, 1996—; pres., ptnr. J&M Mgmt. Co., 1996—; mem. first adv. bd. First Nat. Title Co., Conroe, 1989-90. Chmn. North Houston Econ. Devel. Showcase, 1990; bd. dirs. Montgomery County Crime Stoppers, Inc., 1993—. Mem. Comml. Real Estate Assn. Montgomery County (pres. 1986, 87, bd. dirs. 1988), Conroe C. of C. Office: D-J Investment Properties 180 Tara Park Conroe TX 77302

JUDGE, ROSEMARY ANN, oil company executive; b. Jersey City; d. Frank T. and Frances M. (O'Brien) J. A.B., Seton Hall U. Exec. sec. Socony Vacuum, N.Y.C., 1944-56; sec., confidential asst. to v.p. and dir. Socony Mobil, N.Y.C., 1956-59; sec., confidential asst. to pres. Mobil Oil Co. Div., N.Y.C., 1959-61; sec., adminstrv. asst. to pres. Mobil Oil Corp., N.Y.C., 1961-69; adminstrv. asst. to chmn. Mobil Oil Corp., 1969-71, asst. to chmn., sec. exec com., 1971-84, corp. sec., 1975-76; asst. to chmn., sec. bd. and exec. com. Mobil Corp., 1976-84; pres. Mobil Found., N.Y.C., 1973-85. Mem. bd. regents Seton Hall U., 1982-88. Club: Women's Econ. Round Table.

JUDY, MARILYN BARRETT, elementary school educator; b. Frankfort, Ky., Mar. 9, 1946; d. Charles Frederick and Iris (Reed) Barrett; m. Michael Lee Judy, June 1, 1968; children: Michelle Day Judy Harnsberger, Michael David. BA, Georgetown (Ky.) Coll., 1968, MA, 1976. Cert. elem. tchr. (life) accredited k. and gifted, Ky. Tchr. Deep Springs Elem. Sch., Lexington, Ky., 1968-69, Bondurant Middle Sch., Frankfort, 1979-85, Collins Ln. Elem. Sch., Frankfort, Ky., 1970-78, 85—; sponsor student coun., cheerleading, Ky. youth assembly, Bondurant Middle Sch., Frankfort, 1979-85, academic team Collins Ln. Elem. Sch., Frankfort, 1989-94; accreditation evaluator Edn. Dept. State of Ky., 1980-84; coach tennis, Western Hills H.S., Frankfort, 1985—. Del. Young Democrats, Frankfort, 1971-81; sec., treas., pres. Jaycettes, Frankfort, 1976-81; mem. PTA, Frankfort, 1969—. Mem. NEA (sch. rep. 1970—), ASCD (sch. rep. 1980-86) Ky. Edn. Assn. (sch. rep. 1970—), Franklin County Edn. Assn. (sch. rep. 1970—), Middle Sch. Assn. (sch. rep. 1979-85), YMCA, Western Hills Basketball Boosters Club (sec.-treas 1982-87, pres. 1992-94), Alpha Delta Kappa (altruistic chmn. 1984-88, sec. 1990-92). Democrat. Baptist. Home: 311 Leawood Dr Frankfort KY 40601-4449

JUE, SUSAN LYNNE, interior designer; b. Berkeley, Calif., July 7, 1956; d. Howard Lynn and Rosie (Fong) J. AA with honors, Cabrillo Coll., 1977; BA, Calif. Coll. Arts and Crafts, 1979. Interior designer Lucasfilm Ltd., San Anselmo, Calif., 1980-81, Whisler-Patri Architects and Planners, San Francisco, 1982, Barry Reischmann Design Studio, San Francisco, 1983, Kaplan, McLaughlin, Diaz Architects and Planners, San Francisco, 1984-85, Gensler & Assocs., Architects San Francisco, 1985, Hirano Assocs., San Francisco, 1987-88, Clocktower Design, San Ramon, Calif., 1988-89, Reel/Grobman & Assocs., San Francisco, 1989-90; interior designer Primo Angeli Inc., San Francisco, 1990-92, Guillermo Rossello, Architect, Berkeley, Calif., 1992—, Jean Coblentz & Assocs., San Francisco, 1995—. Recipient No. Calif. Home & Garden Design Achievement award 1992. Mem. Internat. Interior Design Assn. (newsletter editor No. Calif. chpt. 1987-88, resource index com. 1987-88, chmn. graphic com. 1987-88, Ronald McDonald House com. 1988-89, chmn. Salvation Army project com. 1990-91, chmn. Bread and Roses project com. 1991, chmn. Ctr. for AIDS, 1991-92, chmn. Maitri AIDS Hospice, 1995-96, chmn. ARIS, 1995-96, bd. dirs. 1991—, Cert. of Appreciation 1989, 91, 92, Cmty. Svc. Program award 1993), Designers Lighting Forum. Home: 241 Stanford Ave Kensington CA 94708-1103

JUHLIN, DORIS ARLENE, French language educator; b. Atlanta, Dec. 1, 1942; d. Lawrence Alfred and Doris (South) J. BA, Greenville (Ill.) Coll., 1964; MA, Baldwin-Wallace Coll., 1979. Cert. elem. and secondary French and reading tchr., Ohio. Tchr. French Cleve. Bd. Edn., 1965—; chmn. bldg. activities Cleve. Pub. Schs., 1983-93, writer French curriculum, 1980, Acad. Challenge, Cleve., 1995; workshop presenter Ohio Modern Lang. Tchrs. Assn., Columbus, Ohio, 1978; fgn. lang. cons. WV12-TV (PBS), Cleveland, Ohio, 198 0; contbr. CP's Fgn. Lang. Exploratory Program, 1995-96. Cons. and tchr.: Exploring Languages video series, Cleve. Pub. Schs., 1994-95. Dir. jump for heart sch. program Am. Heart Assn., 1986-90; v.p. Womens Ministries Internat.; speaker, editor ann. program resource books Free Meth. Ch., Indpls., 1985-95; sec. Free Meth. Ohio Conf. Bd. Camping Dirs., Mansfield, Ohio, 1990-94; organist, Sunday Sch. tchr. Free Meth. Ch., Westlake, Ohio, 1964—; vol. Nat. Welsh Home for Aged, Rocky River, Ohio, 1970—;

mem. task force Edn. 2000, 1992-93. Jennings scholar Martha Holden Jennings Found., 1980. Mem. Ohio Fgn. Lang. Assn., Cleve. Tchrs. Union, Nat. Audubon Soc., MENSA (gifted child coord. 1985-94, columnist Graffiti 1986-94. Democrat. Home: 3745 W 213th St Cleveland OH 44126-1216 Office: Wilbur Wright Mid Sch 11005 Parkhurst Dr Cleveland OH 44111-3601

JUISTER, BARBARA JOYCE, retired mathematics educator; b. Ottawa, Ill., Sept. 4, 1939; d. Ralph Edward and Imogene (Wilson) Weber; m. Robert Milton Gibson, Sept. 9, 1959 (dec. May 1961); 1 child, Robert Milton Jr.; m. Charles Harry Juister, Apr. 2, 1966 (div. Dec. 30, 1991); children: Charles Edward, Leslie Elizabeth. BS in Math. Edn., Ill. State U., 1961; MA in Math. Teaching, Purdue U., 1965. Tchr. math. Lew Wallace High Sch., Gary, Ind., 1961-63, Paxton (Ill.) High Sch., 1963-64; prof. math. Elgin (Ill.) C.C., 1964-95; ret., 1995; reviewer textbooks for numerous pubs., 1977—; article reviewer Math. Tchr. mag., 1983—; reviewer modules Univ. Math. Applications Project, 1978—. Author: (book) The Development of the Illinois Mathematics Association of Community Colleges Through 1994. Treas. Sybaquay coun. Girl Scouts U.S.A., 1985-92; del. Nat. Coun. Girl Scouts, 1993-96: elder 1st Presbyn. Ch., Elgin, 1986-92. Recipient Faculty Mem. of Yr. award Ill. C.C. Trustees Assn., 1992, Ctrl. region Outstanding Faculty Mem. award Assn. C.C. Trustees, 1993, Excellence in Tng. award Nat. Inst. Staff and Organizational Devel., 1993, Leader award for Edn. Elgin YWCA, 1994. Mem. Math. Assn. Am. (vis. lectr. 1981-92, bd. dirs. Ill. sect. 1985-94, chmn. 1992-93, Ill. Sect. Disting. Svc. award 1995), Am. Math. Assn. 2-yr. Colls. (libr. subcom. edn. com. 1990-91, Ill. del. to Del. Assembly 1992-96), Ill. Math. Assn. C.C. (sec. 1978-83, pres. 1984-85, Disting. Svc. award 1992), Nat. Coun. Tchrs. Math. (speaker nat. meeting 1988), Ill. Coun. Tchrs. Math. (program com. 1988-89, spkr.), No. Ill. Assn. Tchrs. Math. (bd. dirs. 1994-96), Consortium for Math. and Its Applications, Altrusa Internat. Svc. Club (treas. Elgin chpt. 1995—). Presbyterian.

JULANDER, PAULA FOIL, professional society administrator; b. Charlotte, N.C., Jan. 21, 1939; d. Paul Baxter and Esther Irene (Earnhardt) Foil; m. Roydon Odell Julander, Dec. 21, 1985; 1 child, Julie McMahan Shipman. Diploma, Presbyn. Hosp. Sch. Nursing, Charlotte, N.C., 1960; BS magna cum laude, U. Utah, 1984; MS in Nursing Adminstrn., Brigham Young U., 1990. RN, Utah. Nurse various positions Fla. and S.C., 1960-66; co-founder, office mgr. Am. Laser Corp., 1970-79; gen. staff nurseoper. rm. Salt Lake Surg. Ctr., Salt Lake City, 1976-79; self employed Salt Lake City; teaching asst. U. Utah, Salt Lake City; rep. Utah State Legislature Coms., 1989-92; demo. nominee lt. gov., 1992; adj. faculty Brigham Young U. Coll. Nursing, 1987—, clin. asst. prof. of nursing, 1996—; bd. dirs. Block Fin. Svcs.; mem. Utah state exec. bd. U.S. West Comm., 1993-96; bd. regents Calif. Luth. U., 1994. Pres. Utah Nurses Found., 1986-88; mem. Statewide Task Force on Child Sexual Abuse, 1989-90, Utah Nursing Resource Study, 1985-96, State Feasibility Task Force for Nurses, 1985-96, Women's Polit. Caucus, Statewide Abortion Task Force, 1990; bd. dirs. Community Nursing Svc. Home Health Plus, 1992-94; trustee Westminster Coll., 1994—, HCA-St. Mark's Hosp., 1994-95. Mem. ANA (del. conv. 1986-90), LWV, Utah Nurses Assn. (legis. rep. 1987-88, pres.), Nat. Orgn. Women Legislators, Sigma Theta Tau, Phi Kappa Phi (Susan Young Gates award 1991). Home: 1467 Penrose Dr Salt Lake City UT 84103-4466 Office: Utah Nurses Assn 455 E 400 S Ste 402 Salt Lake City UT 84111-3008

JULIBER, LOIS, manufacturing executive; b. 1949; m. John Adams. BA, Wellesley Coll.; MBA, Harvard U. Former v.p. Gen. Foods Corp.; from gen. mgr. to pres. Far East/Can. divsn. Colgate-Palmolive Co., N.Y.C., 1988-92, chief tech. officer, 1992-94, pres. Colgate—N.Am. divsn., 1994—; bd. dirs. DuPont Corp. Trustee Brookdale Found., Wellesley Coll. Mem. Harvard Bus. Sch. Club N.Y. (bd. dirs.). Office: Colgate Palmolive Co 300 Park Ave New York NY 10022-7402

JULIEN, GAIL LESLIE, model, public relations professional; b. L.I., N.Y., Apr. 13, 1940; d. David William Syme and Virginia Martha (Burth) Miller; m. Michael Louis Woodman, Sept. 12, 1958 (div.); children: Jho'meyr Renei, Sabrina Michelle; m. Francis Dana Julien, Dec. 24, 1977. Diploma in modeling, Coronet of Calif., 1960; grad., Am. Beauty Finishing Sch., 1961. Playboy bunny Playboy Club, Kansas City, Mo., 1970-72; Gremlin girl AMC, Kansas City, 1972; Dodge girl Dodge, Kansas City, 1972-73; owner, pres. Gail Woodman Enterprises Inc., Overland Park, Kans., 1972-76; sales rep. Kansas City Brit. Motors, Lenexa, Kans., 1976-78; dir. pub. rels., mktg. Downtown Air Ctr., Kansas City, 1978-80; dir. pub. rels., media rels. Bretney Corp., Kansas City, 1980-82; v.p. Nuwalters Co., Overland Park, 1983-84; regional mgr. aviation Multi Svc. Corp., Overland Park, 1984—; rep. Nat. Bus. Aircraft Assn., 1984—, Can. Bus. Aircraft Assn., 1984—, Nat. Aircraft Transp. Assn., 1984—, Abbotsford Internat. Airshow, 1991, 93, 05, Schedulars & Dispatchers Conv., 1994-96. Author: Physician's Nutritional Guide, 1984; author numerous poems, self improvement and modeling course. Vol. Live On Stage '88 (AIDS), Santa Ana, Calif., 1988, St. Joseph Hosp., Kansas City, 1986-88; v.p. Young Dems., Midland, Mich., 1960; active Northshore Animal League, Christian Children's Fund, City of Hope, L.A., 1991; bd. dirs., fundraiser Make A Wish of Tri Counties. Recipient Outstanding Sales Achievement award Brit. Leyland, 1976-77. Mem. Am. Bus. Women's Assn. Home: 28129 Peacock Ridge Dr Apt 312 Palos Verdes Peninsula CA 90275-7121 Office: Multi Svc Corp 8650 College Blvd Shawnee Mission KS 66210-1886

JULIFS, SANDRA JEAN, community action agency executive; b. Jersey City, July 12, 1939; d. Roy Howard and Irma Margrete (Barkhausen) Walters; m. Harold William Julifs, July 22, 1961; children: David Howard, Steven William. BA, U. Va., 1961; postgrad., U. Minn., 1962-63, Mankato State Coll., 1963. Cert. comty. action profl. Tchr. St. James (Minn.) Pub. Schs., 1961-62; substitute tchr. Sleepy Eye (Minn.) Pub. Schs., 1963-67, home bound tutor, 1967; lay reader, rater U. Wis., Stevens Point, 1968; co-founder Family Planning Service Portage County, Stevens Point, 1970-72; family planning dir. Tri-County Opportunities Coun., Rock Falls, Ill., 1971-77; energy programs coord. Tri-County Opportunities Coun., Rock Falls, 1977-78, planner, EEO officer, 1978-83, pres., chief exec. officer, 1983—; sec. Ill. Ventures for Comty. Action Springfield, 1983-91, bd. dirs. 1991-94, 96—. Mem. Nat. Cmty. Action Found., Washington, 1987—; bd. dirs. Twin Cities Homeless Coalition, 1989—; mem. adv. coun. Sauk Valley Coll. Human Svcs., 1990—; mem. Whiteside County Overall Econ. Devel. Coun., 1990—; mem. adv. coun. Inst. for Social and Econ. Devel., 1992-95; cons. com. No. Ill. Synod Evang. Luth. Ch. Am., 1993—, churchwide assembly del., 1995; mem. Statewide Rural Poverty Conf. Com., 1996. Recipient Appreciation award Western Ill. Agy. on Aging, 1980, 81, Spl. Recognition award Ill. Head Start and Day Care Assn., Recognition award Ill. Community Action Fund, 1984, Recognition award Ill. Ventures for Cmty. Action, 1996. Mem. AAUW, NAFE, Am. Soc. Pub. Adminstrn., Whiteside County Welfare Assn., Lee County Welfare Assn. (sec.-treas. 1983-84), Nat. Cmty. Action Assn., Ill. Cmty. Action Assn. (com. chair 1985-88, dir. exec. com. 1986-95, treas. 1988, 89, sec. 1989, 90, v.p. 1991-93, pres. 1993-95, Recognition award 1985-95). Lutheran. Office: Tri-County Opportunities Coun 405 Emmons Ave PO Box 610 Rock Falls IL 61071

JUNCK, MARY, newspaper publishing executive. Pub., pres. St. Paul Pioneer Press, St. Paul, until 1993; pub., CEO The Baltimore Sun, 1993—. Office: Baltimore Sun 501 N Calvert St Baltimore MD 21278

JUNCKER, JUDITH DIANNE, psychotherapist; b. Montgomery, Ala., Nov. 18, 1942; d. Walter E. and Mary Juette (Singleton) Graddy; m. Phillip Richard Bailey (wid. 1964); m. Rodney K. Juncker, Aug. 31, 1968; children: Phillip Richard, Jeffrey K. BA, San Francisco State U., 1968; MA, Am. Acad., Scotts Valley, Calif., 1981. Cert. clin. hypnotherapist; lic. marriage and family counselor. Psychotherapist San Jose, Calif., 1981—. Visual art exhibited pvt. collections. Vol. Aris Chiv Relief Orgn. Office: 1190 So Bascom # 216 San Jose CA 95128

JUNE, CATHY J., nurse administrator, educator; b. Detroit, May 22, 1960; d. William H. and Dolores J. (Nagel) Woodcock; m. Michael S. June, Apr. 16, 1988. BSN, Mercy Coll., 1982; postgrad., Wayne State U., 1990—. RN, Mich.; CEN; cert. in staff devel. ANCC. Clin. coord. Olsten Health Care, Southfield, Mich., 1980-95; nurse ICU, Harper Hosp., Detroit, 1988-89, preceptor emergency room, 1989-90, educator, 1990-94; critical care educator Grace Hosp., Detroit, 1994-95; mgr. catherization lab. Sinai Hosp., Detroit, 1995—; mem. affiliate faculty Mich. Heart Assn., 1995-96; mem. nominating com. Mich. League for Nursing, 1993-95, co-chair nursing scholarship fashion show, 1995; presentor, co-author rsch. presentation Grace Hosp. Rsch. Day, 1995; manuscript reviewer Mosby, 1994, 95, Sigma Theta Tau-Image, 1995; presenter in field. Team mem. Detroit Grand Prix Med. Team, 1990-96; mem. Warren Ave. Comty. Orgn., 1992-96; coord. First Aid, Mich. Heart Assn. Heartide, 1994, 95. Scholar am. Legion Voiture, Detroit, 1979, 80, 81. Mem. AACN (staff devel. cert.), Nat. Nursing Staff Devel. Orgn., Mich. League for Nursing Edn. Counsel, Detroit Emergency Nurses Assn. (pres. 1990-91), Sigma Theta Tau. Office: Sinai Hosp 6767 W Outer Dr Detroit MI 48235

JUNG, BETTY CHIN, epidemiologist, educator; b. Bklyn., Nov. 28, 1948; d. Han You and Bo Ngan (Moy) C.; m. Lee Jung, Oct. 1, 1972; children: Daniel, Stephanie. AA, Kings Coll., 1968; BS, Columbia U., 1971; MPH, So. Conn. State U., 1993. RN, Conn., Miss., N.Y.; cert. health edn. specialist. Adminstrv. asst. Columbia U., N.Y.C., 1968-69; practical nurse Babies Hosp., N.Y.C., 1969-70, charge nurse, 1974-76; staff nurse Columbia-Presbyn. Hosp., N.Y.C., 1971-73; sch. nurse Nassau County Sch. System, Long Island, N.Y., 1984-85; grad. asst. So. Conn. State U., New Haven, 1991-92; coop. edn. intern Conn. Dept. Health Svcs., Hartford, 1991-92; intern North Ctrl. Dist. Health Dept., Enfield, Conn., 1992; epidemiologist Conn. Dept. Pub. Health, Hartford, Conn., 1992—; health promotion cons. So. Conn. State U. Dept. Pub. Health, New Haven, 1991, tchg. asst. So. Conn. State U., New Haven, 1992, curriculum developer, 1992, vol. rsch. analyst, 1993, founder grad. alumni mentor program, 1993-94; instr. Albertus Magnus Coll., 1995—; health columnist Baldwin (N.Y.) Newcomers Club, 1977-78; coord. Dept. Pub. Health and Svcs./Conn. EPI Info. Network, Hartford, 1994—. Mem. editl. bd. Data Quality, 1994—; mem. manuscript rev. bd. Jour. Clin. Outcomes Mgmt., 1995—; contbr. articles to profl. jours. Vol. nurse health educator, coord. Chinatowns First Ann. Health Fair, 1971-72; treas. Tenant Assn., Bronx, N.Y., 1976-77; pre-confirmation tchr. Bethlehem Luth. Ch., Baldwin, N.Y., 1981-85. Merit scholar Kings Coll., 1968, Columbia U. scholar, 1968-69, Bessie Lee Gambrill scholar So. Alumni Assn., 1992; grantee USPHS, 1992—. Fellow Soc. for Pub. Health Edn.; mem. APHA (health care reform activist network, peer assistance the model stds. project), Am. Med. Writers Assn., Am. Statis. Assn., Coun. State and Territorial Epidemiologists (alternate cons. environ. health 1996—, cons. HIV/AIDS and surveillance 1996—), Conn. Pub. Health Assn., So. Conn. State U. Alumni Assn. (founder pub. health chpt. 1994, interim pres. 1994, pres. 1994—, chair exec. com. 1994—, chair MPH accreditation com. 1994—, chair svc. com. 1994, svc. com. survey rschr. 1994—, coord. pub. health alumni mentor program 1994—, editor MPH Alumni Record 1995—, database cons. 1994—, data mgr. 1994—, rsch. analyst 1994—), Conn. Women in Healthcare Mgmt., Inc., Columbia U. Sch. Nursing Alumni Assn. (survey cons. 1994—). Home: 25 Driftwood Ln Guilford CT 06437-1929 Office: Conn Dept Pub Health PO Box 340308 Hartford CT 06138-0308

JUNG, DORIS, dramatic soprano; b. Centralia, Ill., Jan. 5, 1924; d. John Jay and May (Middleton) Crittenden; m. Felix Popper, Nov. 3, 1951; 1 son, Richard Dorian. Ed., U. Ill., Mannes Coll. Music, Vienna Acad. Performing Arts; student of, Julius Cohen, Emma Zador, Luise Helletsgruber, Winifred Cecil. Debut as Vitellia in: Clemenza di Tito, Zurich (Switzerland) Opera, 1955, other appearances with, Hamburg State Opera, Munich State Opera, Vienna State Opera, Royal Opera Copenhagen, Royal Opera Stockholm, Marseille and Strasbourg, France, Naples (Italy) Opera Co., Catania (Italy) Opera Co., N.Y.C. Opera, Met. Opera, also in Mpls., Portland, Oreg., Washington and Aspen, Colo.; soloist: Wagner concert conducted by Leopold Stokowski, 1971; with, Syracuse (N.Y.) Symphony, 1981, voice tchr., N.Y.C., 1970—. Home: 40 W 84th St New York NY 10024-4749

JUNG, HILDA ZIIFLE, physicist; b. Gretna, La.; d. William Christian and Leonora Margaret (Giboney) Ziifle; m. Julius Robert Jung Jr., Nov. 2, 1968. BS, Tulane U., 1943. Engring. release clk. Higgins Aircraft Co., Michoud, La., 1943-44; rsch. physicist So. Regional Rsch. Ctr., USDA, New Orleans, 1944-79; retired, 1979. Contbr. articles to profl. jours.; patentee chem. process. Named Woman of Yr. New Orleans Fed. Exec. Bd., 1978. Mem. AAAS, AARP (program dir. Terrytown chpt. 1991-95, chmn. social com. 1989), Am. Chem. Soc. (sec. La. sect. 1977), Orgn. Profl. Employees Dept. Agrl. (life, pres. 1978, Profl. of Yr. 1979), Am. Legion Aux., Post 64 Chaplain, 1995, 96, Nat. Assn. Ret. Fed. Employees (life, 1st v.p., legis. chmn. 1980, pres. 1981, 92, pub. rels. officer 1984, 89-91, newsletter editor 1993, program chair 1995, program chmn. 1996), Sigma Xi. Lutheran.

JUNG, MAUREEN ANN, consulting company owner, writer; b. Ashland, Wis., Apr. 23, 1949; d. Raymond Joel and Marjorie Elaine (Jack) Bloomquist; m. Henry Charles Jung, Aug. 7, 1967 (div. 1971); 1 child, Dionne Marie; m. Gregory Charles Schiller, Apr. 24, 1991. BA, Colo. State U., 1979; MA, U. Calif., Santa Barbara, 1983, PhD, 1989. Various positions sociology dept. U. Calif., Santa Barbara, 1980-87; intern Calif. State Archives, Sacramento, 1988; exec. dir. Wilson Riles Edn. Archives, Sacramento, 1989-91; owner WordSpring Writing Cons., Sacramento, 1992—; mktg. dir. Calif. Bus. Women's Expo, Sacramento, 1995; co-chair Sacramento Bus. Women's Expo, 1994; dir. Sacramento Heritage Festival, Inc., 1994-95, mem. adv. bd., 1996—; contbg. writer Living Blues, Ctr. for Study of So. Culture, U. Miss., University, 1994—. Contbr. articles to profl. jours. and mags. Fellow South Coast Writing Project; mem. NAFE, Women Inc., Ctrl. Valley Rock, Sand & Gravel Assn. Office: WordSpring Writing Cons # 7 1021 H St Sacramento CA 95814-2824

JUNGBLUTH, CONNIE CARLSON, senior tax compliance specialist; b. Cheyenne, Wyo., June 20, 1955; d. Charles Marion and Janice Yvonne (Keldsen) Carlson; m. Kirk E. Jungbluth, Feb. 5, 1977; children: Tyler, Ryan. BS, Colo. State U., 1976. CPA, Colo. Sr. acct. Rhode Scripter & Assoc., Boulder, Colo., 1977-81; mng. acct. Arthur Young, Denver, 1981-85; asst. v.p. Dain Bosworth, Denver, 1985-87; v.p. George K. Baum & Co., Denver, 1987-91; acct. Ariz. Luth. Acad., 1994-95; sr. tax acct. Ernst & Young, LLP, Phoenix, 1995—. Active Denver Estate Planning Coun., 1981-85; organizer Little People Am., Rocky Mountain Med. Clinic and Symposium, Denver, 1986; adv. bd. Children's Home Health, Denver, 1986-89; fin. adv. bd. Gail Shoettler for State Treas., Denver, 1986; campaign chmn. Kathi Williams for Colo. State Legislature, 1986; mem. Sch. dist. 12 Colo. Edn. Found. Bd., 1991, Napa Sch. Dist. Elem. Site Com., 1992-94. Named one of 50 to watch, Denver mag., 1988. Mem. AICPA, Colo. Soc. CPAs (strategic planning com. 1987-89, instr. bank 1983, trustee 1984-87, pres. bd. trustees 1986-87, bd. dirs. 1987-89, chmn. career edn. com. 1982-83, pub. svc. award 1985-87), Colo. Mcpl. Bond Dealers, Am. Herb Assn., Ariz. Herb Assn., Little People of Am., Metro North C. of C. (bd. dirs. 1987-90), Denver City Club (bd. dirs. 1987-88), Phi Beta Phi. Office: Ernst & Young LLP Ste 900 40 N Central Phoenix AZ 85004

JUNGER, PATRICIA CAROL, nurse; b. Buffalo, Mar. 16, 1943; d. James John and Rose (Menno) Colello; m. Edward Michael Junger, Sept. 19, 1964 (div. 1990); children: Kevin, Steven and Paul (twins). AAS, Erie C.C., 1976. RN, N.Y. Staff nurse med. tchg. fl. Buffalo Gen. Hosp., 1977—. Mem. Comm. Workers of Am. Democrat. Roman Catholic.

JUNKER, SANDRA JEAN, state official, retired army enlisted woman; b. Binghamton, N.Y., Dec. 18, 1947; d. Frank Cameron Wayman Sr. and Louise Lucille (DeLarco) Wayman; m. Melvin Rudolph Junker, April 11, 1970. Student, U. Alaska, 1973-76, Liberty U., 1989-92. Enlisted U.S. Army, 1969, advanced through grades to sgt. 1st class, 1983; radiol. technician USA MEDDAC Sandia Base, Albuquerque, 1969-71, Kimbrough Army Hosp., Ft. Meade, Md., 1971-73, Ft. Richardson, Anchorage, 1973-77, Walter Reed Army Med. Ctr., Washington, 1977-79; field recruiter Richmond RBN, Petersburg, Va., 1979-83, nurse recruiter, 1983-85; sta. comdr. Charlotte RBN, Lenoir, N.C., 1985-87, Hickory, N.C., 1987-88; recruiter trainer Charlotte RBN, Asheville, N.C., 1988-89; quality control non-commd. officer mil. entrance processing sta. Charlotte (N.C.) RBN, 1989; sta. comdr. Houston RBN, Beaumont, Tex., 1989—; sta. comdr. Houston RBN, Orange, Tex., 1990, ret., 1990; mem. disabled veterans outreach program N.Y. State Dept. Labor, Binghamton, 1991—. Leader Girl Scouts, U.S.A.; bd. dirs. SHARE, Binghamton, Food Bank Central N.Y.C. Mem. NOW, LWV (dir. voter svc.), Am. Legion (chair Broome County oratorical contest), Disabled Vets. Am. Avocations: cross stitching, crochet, reading, sewing. Home: 27 Frederick Dr Apalachin NY 13732 Office: NY State Dept Labor 30 Wall St Binghamton NY 13901-2718

JURA, DEBRA DOWELL, bilingual educator; b. Modesto, Calif., Feb. 20, 1952; d. Charles Hubert and Peggy Sue (Hittle) Dowell; divorced; children: Aaron Vincent, Amanda Lael. Cert. tchr., Calif. State U., Fresno, 1986, BS, 1994; M Lang. Devel., Pacific Coll., 1995. Cert. lang. devel. specialist, Calif., cert. reading recovery tchr. Bilingual tchr. Selma (Calif.) Unified Sch. Dist., 1986—, mentor tchr. drug prevention edn., 1989-93, mentor tchr. health edn., 1993—, mentor tchr. lang. devel. and early literacy, 1996—; project D.A.T.E. coord. Selma Unified Sch. Dist., 1989—, chair Healthy Kids Healty Calif. task force, 1990—, parent educator, 1992—; mem. adv. bd. Gang Task Force, Selma, 1993—; mem. English Lang. Arts Curriculum Com., 1990—, Health Curriculum Com., 1993—. Author: Mostly Magnets, 1990, Supplemental Guide to HLAY 200, 1995, other curriculum materials; co-author: Gang Curriculum 1993. Mem. El Concilio, Fresno, 1993-94, Fresno Zool. Soc., 1980—. Grantee Selma Unified Sch. Dist., 1987, Selma Pub. Edn. Found., 1994. Mem. NEA, Calif. Tchrs. Assn., Nat. Coun. Tchrs. Edn., C.U.E. Democrat. Methodist. Home: 2051 Oak St Selma CA 93662

JURCZYK, JOANNE MONICA, price analyst; b. Orange, Calif., Dec. 27, 1958; d. Edward Joseph and Helen Imogene (Shelly) J. BSBA in Econs., Chapman U., 1981. Guest rsch. specialist Disneyland-Walt Disney Co., Anaheim, Calif., 1985-88, guest rsch. coord., 1988-89, guest rsch. survey ops. supr., 1989-91, indsl. engring. tech. analyst, 1991-92; pricing coord. Kirk Paper Corp., Downey, Calif., 1995-96; price analyst Coors Distributing Co., Anaheim, Calif., 1996—; active Work Exposure Day, Disneyland/U. Disneyland, Anaheim, 1990. Assoc. Met. Mus. Art, 1991—; active youth motivation task force Orange County Unified Sch. Dist., 1992; mem. Orange County chpt. Habitat for Humanity. Mem. Am. Film Inst. Democrat. Roman Catholic. Office: Coors Distributing Co 1625 S Lewis St Anaheim CA 92805

JURGENSEN, MONSERRATE, clinical nurse, consultant; b. Guyanailla, P.R., Oct. 25, 1945; d. Francisco and Felicita (Feliciano) Muniz; m. Timothy J. Jurgensen, Dec. 1, 1978; children: Timothy J. Jr., Jeremy J. Diploma, Presbyn. Hosp. Sch. Nursing, San Juan, P.R., 1967; BSN, Barry U., 1990; postgrad., Webster U., 1992—. RN, Fla. Surg. unit and surg. ICU staff nurse U. Hosp., P.R., 1967-69; commd. 2d lt. USAF, 1969, advanced through grades to maj., 1986; pediat. unit staff nurse USAF Hosp., Sheppard AFB, Tex., 1969-70; orthopedic and psychiat. unit staff nurse USAF Hosp., Cam Ranh Bay, Vietnam, 1970-71; staff nurse obstetrics unit USAF Hosp., Torrejon AFB, Spain, 1971-74; obstetrics head nurse USAF Hosp., K.I. Sawyer AFB, Mich., 1974-78; staff nurse obstetrics unit, head nurse pediatric clinic USAF Hosp., Langley AFB, Va., 1978-81; med.-surg. nurse USAFR, Langley AFB, Va., 1984-86; staff nurse Primary Care Clinics USAFR, Norfolk, Va., 1985-86; staff nurse Cigna HMO, Miami, Fla., 1986-87; staff nurse long-term care unit VA Hosp., Miami, 1988-90, med.-surg. nurse psychiat. unit, 1990-91; quality control nurse, infection control Immunization Clinic, Duke Field, Fla., 1989-91; evening-night supr., mgr. med.-surg. unit same day surgery Army Hosp., Ft. Jackson, S.C., 1991-94; mgr. same day surgery med.-surg. unit Reynolds Army Cmty. Hosp., Ft. Sill, Okla., 1994—. Mem. Soc. Presbyn. Hosp. Sch. Nursing. Republican. Office: US Army Ft Sill Lawton OK 73503

JURKA, EDITH MILA, psychiatrist, researcher; b. N.Y.C., Dec. 4, 1915; d. Charles Anton and Edith Dorothy (Schevcik) J. BA, Smith Coll., 1936; postgrad., Charles U., Prague, Czechoslovakia, 1936-38; MD, Yale U., 1944. Diplomate Am. Bd. Psychiatry and Neurology. Intern in children's med. svc. Bellevue Hosp., N.Y.C., 1944-45, asst. alienist, 1947-49; rotating intern Gallinger Hosp., Washington, 1945-46; intern N.Y. State Psychiat. Inst., N.Y.C., 1946-47; asst. psychiatrist Mt. Sinai Hosp., N.Y.C., 1949-51; pvt. practice N.Y.C., 1949—; asst. psychiatrist Roosevelt Hosp., N.Y.C., 1954-57; chief psychiatrist Pleasantville (N.Y.) Cottage Sch., 1961-74; bd. dirs. intuition network Inst. Noetic Scis.; dir. Wind Song Programs. Fellow Am. Orthopsychiat. Assn.; mem. Am. Psychiat. Assn., N.Y. Coun. Child and Adolescent Psychiatry, N.Y. County Med. Soc., N.Y. State Med. Soc., Westchester Psychiat. Soc. Home: 16 Apple Bee Farm Ln Croton On Hudson NY 10520 Office: 116 E 66th St New York NY 10021-6547

JURMAN, ELISABETH ANTONIE, economist; b. Gnadenfeld, Germany, Aug. 3, 1938; came to U.S. 1961, naturalized, 1979; d. Alois and Margarete Koschella; MBA in Econs. with honors, U. Bridgeport, 1979; PhD, Fordham U., 1996; m. Stanley Jurman, Apr. 7, 1960; children: Derek, Tina, Sonja. Market rsch. analyst Richardson-Merrell, Wilton, Conn., 1977-79; bus. analyst Am. Chain & Cable Co., Trumbull, Conn., 1979-81; planner Emery Air Freight, Wilton, 1981-82; corp. economist So. Conn. Gas Co., Bridgeport, 1982-94; sr. economist Am. Soc. Composers, Authors & Pubs., N.Y.C., 1994—; grad. research asst. U. Bridgeport, 1978; staff economist, energy rev. team State of Conn., spring 1978. Mem. Blue Ribbon Commn. on Revaluation for City of Bridgeport, 1983-84; mem. adv. com. Advanced Workshop in Regulation and Pub. Utility Econs., Rutgers U., 1985—. Recipient Disting. Alumni award U. Bridgeport, 1986; mem. economists' forum Adv. Group to the Commr. Dept. of Econ. Devel. for the State Conn., 1989—. Mem. Am. Econ. Assn., Nat. Assn. Bus. Economists (bd. dirs., past pres., mem. exec. com. Conn. Chpt.), M.B.A. Assn. U. Bridgeport, Beta Gamma Sigma, Phi Kappa Phi. Asst. editor Thrust, The Jour. for Employment and Tng. Profls., 1978. Home: 20 Arrowhead Ln Fairfield CT 06430-7201 Office: 1 Lincoln Plz New York NY 10023

JURVETSON, KARLA T., physician; b. New Haven, Conn.; d. Jared R. and Mae (VanderWeard), Tinklenberg; m. Steve T. Jurvetson, Sept. 23, 1990. B in Human Biology, Stanford U., 1988; MD, U. Calif., Davis, 1993. Diplomate Am. Bd. Medicine. Rsch. asst. Vets. Hosp., Palo Alto, Calif., summers 1981/84, U. Calif., San Francisco, summer 1983; clk. Same Day Surgery Ward Stanford (Calif.) Hosp., summer 1986; rsch. intern Scios Nova/Calif. Biotechnology, Mountain View, 1987-88; intern San Mateo (Calif.) County Gen. Hosp., 1993-94; resident Stanford Hosp., 1994—. Contbr. articles to profl. jours. Vol. pub. health worker Amigos de las Americas, Micheacan, Mexico, summer 1985; precinct capt. Congl. Race/Palo Alto, 1988, Gov. Race, Redwood City, Calif., 1994; vol. U.S. Senate Race, Walnut Creek, Calif., 1992. Mem. APA, Calif. psychiatric Assn., Calif. Med. Assn. (com. on women in medicine). Democrat. Office: Stanford Psychiatry Residency Office 401 Quarry Rd Stanford CA 94305

JUSKO, ANNMARIE, court stenographer; b. Buffalo, Jan. 25, 1968; d. Thomas Stanley and Frances Katherine Jusko. A in Occupl. Studies Ct. Reporting, Cen. City Bus. Inst., Syracuse, N.Y., 1988. Receptionist Cen. City Bus. Inst., Syracuse, 1986-88; freelance ct. reporter Edith Forbes Reporting, Batavia, N.Y., 1988; ofcl. ct. reporter Potter County, P.A., Coudersport, Pa., 1988—; sec. Borough Zoning Bd., Coudersport, Pa., 1995—; student career spkr. Coudersport (Pa.) Elem. Sch., 1993-94. Tchr. St. Eulalia Cath. Ch., Coudersport, 1993—; vol. Charles Cole Meml. Hosp., Coudersport, 1995, Coudersport Libr. Fall Festival, 1994-95. Mem. Nat. Shorthand Reporter's Assn., Cath. Daus. of Ams. (Youngest Active Mem. 1995). Roman Catholic. Office: State of Pa Potter Cty Cths Courthouse Rm 30 Coudersport PA 16915

JUST, DONNA, advertising executive. Sr. v.p. mgmt. supr. GHB & M. Office: 100 Ave of the Americas New York NY 10013*

JUST, GEMMA RIVOLI, retired advertising executive; b. N.Y.C., Nov. 29, 1921; d. Philip and Brigida (Consolo) Rivoli; B.A., Hunter Coll., N.Y.C., 1943; m. Victor Just, Jan. 29, 1955. Copy group head McCann Erickson, N.Y.C., 1958-62; copy. supr. Morse Internat., N.Y.C., 1962-67; v.p., dir. creative svcs. Deltakos div. J. Walter Thompson, N.Y.C., 1967-75; v.p., copy dir. Sudler & Hennessey, div. Young & Rubicam, N.Y.C., 1980-87; sr. v.p., assoc. creative dir. copy, 1987-88, ret., 1989. Mem. Episcopal Ch. Women of Incarnation, N.Y.C., also ch. altar guild and acolyte. Named Best Writer, Art Dirs. Club N.Y., 1979, Best Writer Young & Rubicam, 1981; recipient Aesulapius awards Modern Medicine mag., 1980-88. Mem. Coun. Communications Socs., Pharm. Advt. Coun., Am. Med. Writers Assn. (exec. com. 1973). Home: 155 E 38th St Apt 5D New York NY 10016-2663

JUSTUS, CAROL FAITH, linguistics educator; b. Lodi, Ohio, Mar. 21, 1940; d. Ernest and Esther Mary (Cockrell) J.; m. Rahim Raman; div. 1976. BA in French, King Coll., 1960; MA in Linguistics, U. Minn., 1966; PhD in Linguistics, U. Tex., 1973. Assoc. prof., asst. prof., linguistics coord. SUNY, Oswego, 1973-77; asst. prof. U. Calif., Berkeley, 1977-82; rsch. assoc. U. Tex., Austin, 1982-84; tech. staff Microelectronics & Computer Tech. Corp., Austin, 1984-88; rsch. fellow U. Tex., 1988-89; assoc. prof. San Jose (Calif.) State U., 1989-94; rsch. fellow U. Tex., 1994—; adj. assoc. prof. Ctr. for Mid. Eastern Studies and Classics, 1995—. Review editor Diachronica, 1988-91; contbr. articles to profl. jours. NEH grantee, 1976. Mem. MLA (div. chair 1979, 81, 84, 87, del. 1991-93), Linguistic Soc. Am. (Inst. dir. 1976), Am. Oriental Soc., Societe de Linguistique de Paris. Home: 3517 Peregrine Falcon Austin TX 78746-7436

JUTRAS, CINDY MICHELE, marketing professional; b. Middleton, Mass., Aug. 23, 1953; d. Michael and Villa Tolman (Walker) Lavorgna; m. B. Glenn Jutras, Oct. 9, 1977. BA, Merrimack Coll., 1975; MS, Boston U., 1978. Mgr. data processing Barry Controls, Watertown, Mass., 1975-77; project analyst Arthur D. Little Sys., Burlington, Mass., 1977-78; product mgr. Interactive Mgmt. Sys., Belmont, Mass., 1978-83; mfg. cons. mgr. Ask Computer Sys., Burlington, 1984-94; dir. product mktg. Computer Assocs., Andover, Mass., 1994—. Office: Computer Assocs 1 Tech Dr Andover MA 01810

KABACK, ELAINE, career counselor, consultant; b. Phila., Feb. 22, 1939; d. Sol and Evelyn Zitman; children: Douglas, Stepen, Michelle. Student Pa. State U., 1956-58; B.A., Temple U., 1960; M.S., Calif. State U., 1977. Cert. career counselor. Tchr. English Sayre Jr. High Sch., Phila. Public Schs., 1960-62; tchr. English and history Beth Tfiloh Pvt. Day Sch., Balt., 1968-72; mgmt. cons., trainer SWA, Palos Verdes, Calif., 1975-85; counselor Career Planning Ctr. and Mid-Life Ctr., Long Beach City Coll., 1977-78; dir. program devel. Univance Career Ctrs., Inc., Los Angeles, 1978-80; pvt. practice career counseling, 1980—, outplacement cons. Exec. Horizons, Inc., Newport Beach, Calif., 1985—; coord. career transition program, trainer, instr. UCLA Extension, 1980—; cons. in career systems, outplacement and orgnl. devel. Pres. Palos Verdes chpt. NOW, 1974-76; treas. S.W. chpt. Nat. Women's Polit. Caucus, 1973, 78; bd. dirs. STEP Adult Edn. Programs, Palos Verdes, 1974—, cert. community coll. life counselor, Calif.; cert. tchr., Pa. Mem. Calif. Counseling and Devel., Am. Counseling Assn., Orgn. Devel. Network, Phi Kappa Phi. Office: 11340 W Olympic Blvd Ste 255 Los Angeles CA 90064-1612

KABAT, SYRTILLER DÉLORES MCCOLLUM, marriage, family, and child counselor; b. Tampa, June 18, 1937; d. Theodore and Katie (McCoy) McCollum; m. Lucien Kabat, July 16, 1965; children: Luke, Michael (adopted), Soon Yun Kwon (adopted), Debi Estell (adopted). BA, Montclair State Coll., 1960; MA in Psychol., Wright Inst., 1972, PhD, 1975. Cert. tchr., N.J., Calif.; lic. profl. counselor, Calif., Mo.; cert. Nat. Bd. Cert. Counselors, Am. Bd. Med. Psychotherapists; cert. marriage, family and child counselor. Asst. prof. counseling San Jose (Calif.) St. U., 1972-79; prof. John F. Kennedy U., Orinda, Calif., 1974-83; instr. U. Mo., Kansas City, 1984-86; pvt. practice marriage, family, child counselor Kansas City and Lee's Summit, Mo., 1984—. Contbr. articles to profl. jours. Bd. dirs. Ravenswood Sch. Dist., Palo Alto, Calif., 1967-75; pres. Lee's Summit Housing Commn., 1987—, Adolescent Resource Com., Kansas City, 1987, Shekinah Found., 1987—. Mem. Am. Assn. Marriage and Family Therapists, Mo. Assn. Marriage and Family Therapists, Calif. Assn. Marriage and Family Therapists. Home: 410 SE Independence Ave Lees Summit MO 64063-2854 Office: 120 SE Second St Lees Summit MO 64063

KABRIEL, MARCIA GAIL, psychotherapist; b. El Reno, Okla., Jan. 8, 1938; d. Gail Frederick and Katherine (Marsh) Slaughter; m. J. Ronald Kabriel, May 25, 1957 (div. Sept. 1985); children: Joseph Charles, Jeffrey Gail, Jae B. BA, U. Okla., 1965, MSW, 1968; postgrad. Am. U. Psychiat. social worker Dept. Mental Hygiene, N.Y.C., 1968-69; psychiat. social worker Washington Hosp. Ctr., 1970-72, assoc. mem. dept. psychiatry, 1972-75, sr. psychotherapist Counseling Ctr., 1972-75; psychotherapist Md. Inst. Pastoral Counseling, Annapolis, Md., 1972—; chief dept. social svcs. Washington Hosp. Ctr., 1979-82, cons. spl. projects, 1974-82; supr. continuing protective svcs. State Md., 1983-91; supr. rsch. project on child sexual abuse for AACO, 1991-93; forensic social worker Anne Arundel Cir. Ct., 1991—; exec. v.p. Kent Island Transport, Inc., 1985—; field instr. Cath. U., Washington, 1973-75, U. Md., 1976-91; adjunct prof. U. Md. 1992-94. Mem. Nat. Assn. Social Workers, Acad. Cert. Social Workers (bd. cert. diplomate). Democrat. Presbyterian. Home: 1416 Regent St Annapolis MD 21403-1247 Office: 104 Forbes St Suite F Annapolis MD 21404

KACHELE, KRISTINA ELISE, book designer, photographer; b. Astoria, N.Y., Apr. 28, 1962; d. Howard Christopher and Terri Antonia (Scicluna) K.; m. Larry Durwood Ball, Jr., Sep. 17, 1994. BA magna cum laude, Princeton U., 1984; MA, U. N. Mex., 1989, MFA, 1989—. Prodn. asst. Farrar, Straus & Giroux, N.Y.C., 1985-87; freelance graphic designer U. N. Mex. Press., Albuquerque, 1988-90, graphic designer, 1990-92, art dir., 1992—; freelance book design; profl. devel. com. Assn. of Am. U. Presses, N.Y.C., 1995. Recipient Design award Maine Photog. Workshops, 1993. Mem. Women in Scholarly Publishing, Soc. for Photographic Edn., Albuquerque United Artists, Phi Beta Kappa. Democrat. Home: 110 Arno SE St #B Albuquerque NM 87102 Office: U N Mex Press 1720 Lomas Blvd NE Albuquerque NM 87131

KACHUR, BETTY RAE, elementary education educator; b. Lorain, Ohio, June 12, 1930; d. John and Elizabeth (Stanko) K. BS in Edn., Kent State U., 1963; MEd, U. Ariz., 1971. Cert. tchr.; cert. in reading. Tchr. Lorain City Schs., 1961-94. Mem. AAUW (social com.), Internat. Reading Assn. (by-laws com. Ohio Coun.), Daniel T. Gardner Reading Assn. (pres. 1978-79, treas. 1988-94). Mem. United Ch. of Christ.

KACIR, BARBARA BRATTIN, lawyer; b. Buffalo, Ohio, July 19, 1941; d. William James and Jean (Harrington) Brattin; m. Charles Stephen Kacir, June 3, 1973 (div. Aug. 1977). BA, Wellesley Coll., 1963; JD, U. Mich., 1967. Bar: Ohio 1967, D.C. 1980. Assoc. Arter & Hadden, Cleve., 1967-74, ptnr., 1974-79; ptnr. Jones, Day, Reavis & Pogue, Washington, 1980-83, Cleve., 1983-95; dep. gen. counsel-litigation Textron Inc., Providence, 1995—; instr. trial tactics Case-Western Res. U., Cleve., 1976-79. Mem. nat. com. visitors, nat. fund raising com. U. Mich. Mem. ABA, Ohio Bar Assn., D.C. Bar Assn., Cleve. Bar Assn. (trustee 1973-76, treas. 1978-79), Am. Law Inst., Def. Rsch. Inst. Republican. Office: Textron Inc 40 Westminster St Providence RI 02903

KACZOR, ELIZABETH MARY, human resources specialist; b. Elmhurst, Ill., Oct. 25, 1965; d. William Carl and Mildred Louise (Lingenfelder) Rakow; m. Thomas Michael Kaczor, June 20, 1987. BA, Adrian Coll., 1987; postgrad., Western Mich. U., 1988. Admissions dir. Health Care and Retirement Corp., Kalamazoo, Mich., 1988-90; social svc./activities dir. Health Care and Retirement Corp., Grand Rapids, Mich., 1990-91; corp. recruiter Health Care and Retirement Corp., Toledo, 1991-92, employee rels. specialist, 1992-93, employee rels. mgr., 1993-94, area human resources mgr., 1994—. Republican. Lutheran. Home: 5595 FryerAve Toledo OH 43615

KADAR, KARIN PATRICIA, librarian; b. Oil City, Pa., May 30, 1951; d. Michael Joseph and Bette Lee (Painter) Kadar; divorced; 1 child, Michael K. BS, Clarion U., 1973; MLS, U. Pitts., 1975. Lic. instrnl. II in libr. sci. and elem. edn. Substitute tchr. McKeesport (Pa.) Area Schs., 1973, elem. sch. libr., 1973-75, 3d grade tchr., 1975-78, elem. sch. libr., 1978-81; adj. prof. Pa. State U., McKeesport, 1988; periodicals libr. Seton Hill Coll., Greensburg, Pa., 1986-89; dir. Penn Twp. Pub. Libr., Level Green, Pa., 1989-90; grade sch. libr. substitute St. Agnes Sch., North Huntington, Pa., 1992; mid. sch. libr. substitute Belle Vernon (Pa.) Area Sch. Dist., 1993-95; dir. West Newton (Pa.) Pub. Libr., 1993-95, Highland Cmty. Libr., Richland, Pa., 1996; libr. Ridgeland (S.C.) Elem. Sch., 1996—; mem. consumer appeals bd. Ford Motor Co., 1989-92. Author: (booklet) Sammy the Smokeless Dragon, 1976; mem. adv. panel Pa. Mag., 1992-94. Panelist Scan Trak Shoppers, 1984—, Nat. Family Opinion, 1984—; vol. Am. Cancer Soc., 1969-94, pub. edn. chmn., 1974-80, cancer prevention study II chmn., 1982-88, pub. affairs chmn., 1984-86, residential area crusade chmn., 1984-85. Named Vol. of Yr. Am. Cancer Soc. Mon Youch Unit, 1983-84; recipient Crusade award Am. Cancer Soc., Mon Yough unit, 1985-86. Mem. ALA, Pa. Libr. Assn., Parent-Tchr. Guild, Pa. State Edn. Assn., Westmoreland County Hist. Soc., McKeesport Coll. Club. Office: Highland Cmty Libr Schoolhouse Rd Richland PA 15904

KADEN, BARBARA ANN, retired principal; b. Milw., May 2, 1934; d. David Charles and Esther Elizabeth (Schroth) Schilke; m. Harold R. Kaden, July 21, 1956; children—Kristin Sue, Laurie Ann. B.S., Concordia Tchrs. Coll., 1955; M.A., U. San Francisco, 1975; postgrad. Calif. State U.-Sacramento, 1964-70. Tchr., Immanuel Luth. Sch., Albuquerque, 1955-56, St. Paulus Luth. Sch., San Francisco, 1956-57, Town and Country Luth. Sch., Sacramento, 1958-71, Legette Sch., Fair Oaks, Calif., 1972-82, Sch. for Gifted Children, Orangevale, Calif., 1982-85, Mary A. Deterding Elem. Sch., Carmichael, Calif., 1985-91; elem. sch. prin. Town and Country Luth. Sch., Sacramento, 1991-93, St. Peter Luth. Sch., Lodi, Calif., 1995-96; ret., 1996. Pres., pub. relations dir. Luth. Women's Missionary League, 1974-80; pres. Theatre Ballet Assn., 1981-82. Mem. Calif. Assn. Gifted, Sacramento Area Gifted Assn. Lutheran. Club: River City Chorale. Author: Opening Wider Doors: An Approach to Gifted Education, 1975; contbg. author: Integrating the Faith, 1996. Home: 2740 Tioga Way Sacramento CA 95821-3442

KADEN, ELLEN ORAN, lawyer, broadcasting corporation executive. AB, Cornell U., 1972; MA, U. Chgo., 1973; JD, Columbia U., 1977. Bar: N.Y., 1978. Law clerk U.S. Dist. Ct. (so. dist.) N.Y., 1977-78; asst. prof. Columbia U. Sch. Law, 1978-82, assoc. prof., 1982-84; now exec. v.p., gen. counsel, sec. CBS Inc., N.Y.C., 1991—; reporter jud. coun. 2nd Cir. Adv. Comm. on Planning for Dist. Cts., 1979-81. Office: CBS Inc 51 W 52nd St 36th Fl New York NY 10019-6119

KADER, NANCY STOWE, nurse, consultant; b. Ogden, Utah, May 29, 1945; d. William Hessel and Mildred (Madsen) Stowe; m. Omar Kader, Jan. 25, 1967; children: Tarik, Gabriel, Aron, Jacob. BSN, Brigham Young U., 1967; postgrad., U. Md. RNICU Glendale (Calif.) Adventist Hosp., 1970-75; RN ICU Utah Valley Hosp., Provo, 1975-83; campaign coord. Matheson for Gov., Salt Lake City, 1976-85, Wilson for Senate, Salt Lake City, 1980; RN cons. MESA Corp., Reston, Va., 1984-85; mgr. cost containment Health Mgmt. Strategies, Washington, 1985-88; nurse cons. Birch & Davis, Washington, 1988-90; cons. Inst. of Medicine, Washington, 1990-92, Pal-Tech Inc., Reston, Va., 1992—; vice chmn. Utah State Bd. Nursing, Salt Lake City, 1977-83. Dem. county chmn., Utah, 1977-79; del. Dem. Nat. Conv., 1980; del. Va. State Dem. Conv., 1984-95; vice chmn. Gov.'s Commn. on Status of Women, Salt Lake City, 1975-78. Democrat. Home: 11401 Tanbark Dr Reston VA 22091-4121

KADISH, ANNA STEIN, pathologist, educator, researcher; b. Mexico City, Feb. 27, 1942; came to U.S., 1942; d. Emanuel and Rose (Herzig) Stein; m. Lawrence J. Kadish, July 1, 1965; children: Deborah, Rachel, Sam. BA, Barnard Coll., 1963; MD, Harvard U., 1967. Diplomate Am. Bd. Pathology. Resident in pathology Alber Einstein Coll. Medicine, Bronx, N.Y., 1967-69, 71-72, Roosevelt Hosp., N.Y.C., 1970-71; from asst. to assoc. prof. pathology Albert Einstein Coll. Medicine, 1972-84, prof., 1984—, vice chmn., 1993—, dir. residency tng., 1993—; attending pathologist Bronx Mcpl. Hosp., 1972—. Contbr. articles to profl. jours. Chmn. bd. edn. Solomon Schechter Sch., White Plains, N.Y., 1986-92. Grantee NIH, Am. Cancer Soc. Office: Albert Einstein Coll Medicine 1300 Morris Park Ave # U421 Bronx NY 10461-1926

KADISH, RACHEL SUSAN, writer; b. Bronx, N.Y., Aug. 12, 1969; d. Lawrence Jerome and Anna (Stein) K. AB summa cum laude in English and Women's Studies, Princeton U., 1991; MA in English and Creative Writing, NYU, 1994. Book reviewer Lilith Mag., N.Y.C., 1990—; editor newsletter Israel Women's Network, Jerusalem, 1991; creative writing instr. Goldwater Hosp., N.Y.C., 1993, NYU, N.Y.C., 1993; fiction fellow Bunting Inst./Radcliffe Coll., Cambridge, Mass., 1994-95; literary editor The Radio Play/Pub. Media Found., Boston, 1995—. Author of short stories, articles and book revs. Recipient Barbara Deming award in fiction Deming Found., 1993, grant for emerging writers Rona Jaffe Found., N.Y.C., 1994, grant for writers of exceptional promise Whiting Found., N.Y.C., 1994. Jewish.

KADOHIRO, JANE KAY, diabetes nurse educator, consultant; b. Lima, Ohio, July 20, 1947; d. Howard M. and Betty J. (Johoske) Keller; m. Howard M. Kadohiro, Dec. 27, 1969; children: Christopher, Jennifer. BA in Sociology and Edn., U. Hawaii, 1969; BS in Nursing, U. Hawaii, Honolulu, 1977, MPH, 1990; MS, U. Hawaii, 1994, DrPHC, 1996, postgrad., 1994—. Staff nurse Children's Hosp., Honolulu, 1977-78; staff pub. health nurse Hawaii State Dept. Health, Honolulu, 1978-80, coord. hypertension and diabetes, 1980-85, projects adminstr., 1985-89, chief chronic diseases, 1989-91; office mgr. Hanalei Trends, Honolulu, 1985-89; clin. nurse specialist Queen's Med. Ctr., Honolulu, 1991-94; cons. Aiea, Hawaii, 1991—; nurse investigator Honolulu Heart Program, 1991-95; instr. U. Hawaii at Manoa, Honolulu, 1991—; mem. diabetes project Office Hawaiian Affairs, Honolulu, 1993-95. Leader, advisor, life mem. Girl Scouts U.S., Honolulu, 1978-90; mem. nat. programs com. Nat. Youth Congress, 1993-96; steering com. Internat. Diabetes Camping Program, 1989—. Named Disting. Alumni U. Hawaii Sch. Nursing, 1987; one of Hawaii's Unsung Heroes, Honolulu Star Bull., 1993; recipient Outstanding Contbns. to Diabetes and Camping award, 1994. Mem. ANA (polit. action com. 1994—), APHA, Hawaii Nurses Assn. (Excellence in Clin. Practice award 1995), Am. Diabetes Assn. (vol., founding bd. dirs. 1978—, cano nurse and camp dir. 1982—, past pres. 1986, outstanding contbns. to diabetes and camping award 1994), Hawaii Diabetes Assn., Hawaii Pub. Health Assn., Am. Assn. Diabetes Educators, Hawaii Assn. Diabetes Educators (founding mem., bd. dirs. 1989—, pres. 1996—, state legis. coord. 1996—, treas. 1994-95, pub. affairs chair 1996—, diabetes camp edn. award 1995), Internat. Diabetes Fedn., Internat. Soc. Pediat. and Adolescent Diabetes, Am. Heart Assn. (mem. cardiovascular nursing coun. 1985—), Sigma Theta Tau (founding mem., chair nominating com. 1995—Gamma Psi chpt.). Home: 98 1773 Kaahumanu St # C Aiea HI 96701 Office: Univ Hawaii at Manoa 2528 The Mall/Webster Honolulu HI 96822

KADRAGIC, ALMA, public relations and marketing executive; b. Budapest, Hungary, June 17, 1953; d. Al M. and Catherine S. (Schaffer) K. BA, CUNY, MA, PhD, 1973. Lectr. Herbert H. Lehman Coll., 1972-74; from writer to prodr. ABC News, N.Y.C., 1974-82; coord. prodr. ABC News, London, 1982-83; bur. chief ABC News, Warsaw, Poland, 1983-90; v.p., sec. Alcat Prodn., Huntington, N.Y., 1990—; mng. ptnr. Alcat Comm., Warsaw, 1991—; mem. exec. bd. World Press Freedom Com., Va., 1976—; pres. N.Y.C. chpt. Am. Women in Radio and TV, 1977-78. Contbr. chpt. in book Ency. of Polish Industry 1993, 1994, 95, 96, Hollis Guide to PR Agys., 1992, 1996. Mem. Polish Pub. Rels. Assn. (pres. 1994-97), Am. C. of C. in Poland (bd. dirs.). Republican. Home and Office: Alcat Prodns Ltd 139 Carley Ave Huntington NY 11743

KAE, SHERYL JEAN, business educator; b. Gibson City, Ill., Sept. 11, 1953; d. Erwin Louis and Dorothy Mae (Nordine) Suntken; divorced; 1 child, Jamie Michelle Gudenrath Stonebraker. BS in Edn. summa cum laude, Ill. State U., 1982, MBA, 1990; PhD, U. Ky., 1994. Cert. secondary sch. tchr., Ill. Master tng. instr. USAF, 1983-88; grad. asst. Ill. State U., Normal, 1989-90, U. Ky., Lexington, 1990-93; asst. prof. Morehead (Ky.) State U., 1993—; dir. mentoring program, 1994-96, MBA coord., 1996—. Author: Women in Business Resource Directory, 1995-96; contbr. articles to profl. publs. Mem. Acad. Mgmt., Am. Collegiate Retailing, So. Mgmt. Assn., Alpha Omega, Kappa Omicron Phi, Sigma Iota Epsilon. Methodist. Office: Morehead State U Coll Bus Morehead KY 40351

KAEHELE, BETTIE LOUISE, accountant; b. Sherwood, Tenn., Oct. 29, 1950; d. James Henry and Ruby Katherin (Clark) Shetters; divorced; children: Josiah Dean, Dana Marie. AAS, Albuquerque Tech. Vocat. Inst., 1980; BSBA, Nat. Coll., Albuquerque, 1991. Acctg. clk. Am. Auto Assn., Albuquerque, 1980-81, Ryder Truck Rental, Inc., Albuquerque, 1981-82; bookkeeper, sec. Grants Steel Sash & Hardware, Albuquerque, 1986-87; owner Sherwood Svcs., 1982-86; acctg. specialist Burton & Co., Albuquerque, 1987, Neff & Co., Albuquerque, 1987-91; acctg. tech. U. N.Mex. Found., Albuquerque, 1991-92, acct., 1992—; acct. biology dept. U. N.Mex., Albuquerque, 1992—. Mem. Evang. Christian Ctr. Choir. Cpl. U.S. Army, 1974-76, Germany. Mem. Inst. Mgmt. Accts., NAFE, Nat. Soc. Tax Profls., N.Mex. Soc. CPAs. Republican. Baptist. Home: Apt F4 4033 Montgomery Bldg NE Albuquerque NM 87109

KAEL, PAULINE, film critic, author; b. Petaluma, Calif., June 19, 1919; d. Isaac Paul and Judith (Friedman) K.; 1 child, Gina James. Student, U. Calif., Berkeley, 1936-40; LLD (hon.), Georgetown U., 1972; D. Arts and Letters (hon.), Columbia Coll., Chgo., 1972; LittD (hon.), Smith Coll., 1973, Allegheny Coll., 1979; LHD (hon.), Kalamazoo Coll., 1973, Reed Coll., 1975, Haverford Coll., 1975; DFA (hon.), Sch. Visual Arts, N.Y.C., 1980. Movie critic New Yorker mag., 1968-91. Author: I Lost it at the Movies, 1965, Kiss Kiss Bang Bang, 1968, Going Steady, 1970, Deeper into Movies, 1973 (Nat. Book award 1974), Reeling, 1976, When the Lights Go Down, 1980, 5001 Nights at the Movies, 1982, enlarged edit., 1991, Taking It All In, 1984, State of the Art, 1985, Hooked, 1989, Movie Love, 1991, For Keeps, 1994; contbg. author: The Citizen Kane Book, 1971; contbr. to numerous other mags. Recipient George Polk Meml. award, 1970, Front Page award Newswomen's Club N.Y., 1974, 83; Guggenheim fellow, 1964. Mem. Phi Beta Kappa (hon.). Office: New Yorker Mag 20 W 43rd St New York NY 10036-7400

KAGAN, CHERYL C., state legislator; b. Washington, July 2, 1961. AB, Vassar Coll., 1983; postgrad., U. Md., 1991—. Polit. cons.; lobbyist Handgun Control Inc.; chief of staff U.S. Congress; exec. dir. Ind. Action; dir. devel. Nat. Women's Polit. Caucus; state legislator Md. Ho. of Dels., Rockville, 1995—. Mem. Md. State Arts Coun., 1995—. Named one of Top 10 Rising Stars Balt. Sun, 1996. Democrat. Office: 726 College Pkwy Rockville MD 20850

KAGAN, CONSTANCE HENDERSON, psychotherapist, consultant; b. Houston, Sept. 16, 1940; d. Bessie Earle (Henderson) Davis; m. Morris Kagan, May 27, 1967. BA, Baylor U., 1962; MSSW, U. Tex. Austin, 1966; PhD, U. Okla., 1979. Lic. social worker, Va., Tex.; diplomate. Cons., 1966—, pvt. practice, 1969—; congl. fellow, 1981-82. Mem. NASW, Am. Philos. Assn. Home: 9804 Orchid Circle Great Falls VA 22066

KAGAN, GLORIA JEAN, secondary education educator; b. Kansas City, Mo., Oct. 6, 1946; d. Charles A. and Betty Lou (Mour) Glass; m. Stuart Michael Kagan, Aug. 1, 1971; children: Jennifer Anne, Abigail Elizabeth. BA, U. Mo., 1968; MEd, U. Ariz., 1970. Cert. secondary edn. tchr. Tchr. Ctr. Sch. Dist., Kansas City, Mo., 1970-73, N. Chgo. Sch. Dist., 1974-75, Hyman Brand Hebrew Acad., Overland Park, Kans., 1988—; mem. edn. com. Hyman Brand Hebrew Acad., 1993—. Author poetry. Mem. B'Nai Brith Women, Kansas City, 197—, Hadassah, Kansas City, 1971—, LWV, Kansas City, 1976—. Nominated for Outstanding Tchr. of the Yr., Kansas City C. of C., 1991, High Sch. Tchr. Recognition award U. Kans., 1994. Mem. Nat. Coun. Tchrs. of English. Home: 12005 Overbrook Rd Leawood KS 66209-1149 Office: Hyman Brand Hebrew Acad 5801 W 115th St Overland Park KS 66211-1824

KAGAN, JULIA LEE, magazine editor; b. Nurnberg, Fed. Republic Germany, Nov. 25, 1948; d. Saul and Elizabeth J. (Koblenzer) K. A.B., Bryn Mawr Coll., 1970. Researcher Look Mag., N.Y.C., 1970-71; editorial asst., asst. editor McCall's Mag., N.Y.C., 1971-74, assoc. editor, 1974-78, sr. editor, 1978-79; articles editor Working Woman mag., N.Y.C., 1979-85, exec. editor, 1985-88; editor Psychology Today, 1988-90; sr. editor McCalls, 1990-91; contbg. editor Working Woman, 1991-93; editor-in-chief Lamaze Parents' Mag., 1992-93, Lamaze Baby Mag., 1993; spl. projects dir. Child Mag., 1993-94; sr. v.p. EDK Assocs., N.Y.C., 1994; psychology/health dir. Fitness Mag., N.Y.C., 1995-96; dep. editor Consumer Reports, Yonkers, N.Y., 1996—; vis. J. Stewart Riley prof. journalism Ind. U., 1991-93. Co-author: Manworks: A Guide to Style, 1980; contbg. author: The Working Woman Success Book, 1981, The Working Woman Report, 1984. Pres. Appleby Found., N.Y.C., 1982-84. Recipient 2d Ann. Advt. Journalism award Compton Advt., 1983. Mem. Am. Soc. Mag. Editors, Am. Soc. Pub. Opinion Researchers, Womens Media Group (bd. dirs.), Journalism and Women Symposium (treas. 1993-94). Club: Princeton (N.Y.C.). Home: 523 W 121st St Apt 42 New York NY 10027-5901

KAGEMOTO, PATRICIA JOW (PAT JOW), artist, printmaker; b. N.Y.C., Feb. 20, 1952; d. Tong Fook and Toy Kuen (Lee) Jow; m. Haro Kagemoto, Sept. 21, 1991. BFA, SUNY, New Paltz, 1975. Printmaking workshop asst. SUNY, New Paltz, 1974-75, print shop asst., 1975; printmaking cons. Comm. Village, Ltd., Kingston, N.Y., 1975-84; arts and crafts tchr. Neighborhood Svc. Orgn., Poughkeepsie, N.Y., 1976; printmaking instr., adminstrv. asst. Comm. Village, Ltd., Kingston, 1977-79; exhbn. auditor N.Y. State Coun. on Arts, N.Y.C., 1984-87; gallery asst. Watermark/Cargo Gallery, Kingston, 1988-91; vis. artist N.Y. State Summer Sch. of Visual Arts, Fredonia, 1978, SUNY, New Paltz, 1983-84; cons. printer Printmaking Workshop, N.Y.C., 1984; children's printmaking workshop dir. Woodstock (N.Y.) Libr., 1989. One-woman shows Woodstock Libr., 1989, Watermark/Cargo Gallery, 1991, also others; 2-person shows Catherine Street Gallery, N.Y.C., 1983, 84, Cinque Gallery, N.Y.C., 1984, Watermark/Cargo Gallery, 1989; exhibited in numerous group shows, including Schenectady Mus., 1977, Albany (N.Y.) Inst. History and Art, 1978, Aaron Faber Gallery, N.Y.C., 1984, Printmaking Workshop, N.Y.C., 1984, Woodstock Artists' Assn., 1985, 91, Watermark/Cargo Gallery, 1989. Recipient grant Am. the Beautiful Fund, 1976, Ulster County Decentralization grant N.Y. State Coun. on Arts, 1989. Studio: 2806 Truman Ave Oakland CA 94605-4847

KAGGEN, LOIS SHEILA, non-profit organization executive; b. N.Y.C., Jan. 2, 1944; d. Elias and Sylvia (Muntner) K.; m. Harold Jay Burns, June 29, 1969 (dec. June 1975); 1 child, David Henry (dec.); m. Michael Francis McCann, Sept. 26, 1984. BS in Fine Arts, Skidmore Coll., 1964; postgrad., Cooper Union, 1967-70; MA in Art Edn., CCNY, 1973; postgrad., NYU, 1987—. Founder, pres. Resources for Artists With Disabilities, N.Y.C., 1987—; tchr. fine arts grades 7-9 Jr. H.S. 149, Bronx, N.Y., 1967-74; mem. adv. com. Art in Edn. Project Ctr. for Safety in Arts, N.Y.C., 1987; cons. Ea. Paralyzed Vets. Assn., Guggenheim Mus. Art, N.Y.C., 1990; mem. bd. advisors Ind. Arts Gallery, Queens Ind. Living Ctr., Jamaica, N.Y., 1987—; mem. steering com. Ann. Disability Inc. Day March, 1992-95, mem. Media Outreach, 1992; provider written and oral testimony in field to orgns. including N.Y. City Coun., 1992, 93, Nat. Coun. on Disability, N.Y.C., 1994, Washington, 1995, N.Y. State Assembly mems. and N.Y. State senators, 1994, N.Y. State Standing Com., 1996, others; mem. Media Outreach, 1992; art presenter in field. Photography exhbns. include 80 Washington Sq. East Galleries, N.Y.C., 1977, Soho Photo Gallery, N.Y.C., 1978, 4th St. Photo Gallery, N.Y.C., 1979, Leslie-Lohman Gallery, N.Y.C., 1980, 81, Window Gallery, Met. Savs. Bank, N.Y.C., 1980, Cathedral St. John-the-Devine Gallery, N.Y.C., 1980, Donnell Libr. Gallery, 1981; originator, organizer various exhbns. African-Am. Artists with Disabilities, Artists with Phys. Disabilities; contbr. articles, photographs to profl. jours. Mem. disability rights steering com. 504 Dem. Club for Persons with Disabilities, 1987-88, mem. exec. com., 1991-95; active Disabled in Action of Greater N.Y., 1989—, Manhattan Borough Pres. Adv. Com. on Disabled, 1988—, Mayor's Adv. Com. on People with Disabilities, N.Y.C., 1991-93, Citywide Coalition on Disability, N.Y.C., 1994-95, Nat. Inst. on Disability and Rehab. Rsch., Office Spl. Edn. and Rehab. Svcs., U.S. Dept. Edn., Washington, mem. peer rev. registry, 1995—; mem. New York County Dem. Com., 1995—. Grantee, Whitney Mus. Am. Art, summer 1967, summer film inst. Stanford U., 1968; Cooper Union scholar, 1967-70; recipient Chancellor's Svc. award NYU, 1987, Appreciation cert. Manhattan Borough Pres., 1991. Mem. Coll. Art Assn. (com. mems. with disabilities for accessible programs and places 1990—). Office: Resources Artists with Disabilities 77 7th Ave Ph H New York NY 10011-6644

KAGIWADA, HARRIET HATSUNE NATSUYAMA, mathematician; b. Honolulu, Sept. 2, 1937; d. Kenjiro and Yakue Natsuyama; children: Julia, Conan. BA, U. Hawaii, 1959, MS, 1960; PhD, Kyoto U., 1965. Math. Rand Corp., Santa Monica, Calif., 1961-68, cons., 1968-77; adj. assoc. prof. U. So. Calif., L.A., 1974-79; sr. scientist Hughes Aircraft Co., El Segundo, 1979-87; chief engr. Infotec Devel. Inc., Camarillo, 1987-89; prof. systems engrng. Calif. State U., Fullerton, 1990—. Author: Invariant Imbedding and Time-Dependent Transport Processes, 1963, System Identification: Methods and Applications, 1974, Integral Equations via Imbedding Methods, 1974, Multiple Scattering Processes: Inverse and Direct, 1975,

Numerical Derivatives and Nonlinear Analysis, 1986. Mem. IEEE, AAAS, Am. Math. Soc., Inst. Advanced Engring., Grad. Women in Sci. (pres. 1990-91), Phi Beta Kappa, Phi Kappa Phi. Office: Calif State U Fullerton CA 92634

KAHAN, ROCHELLE LIEBLING, lawyer; b. Chgo., Sept. 5, 1939; d. Arnold Leo and Helly (Ichilson) Liebling; m. Barry D. Kahan, Sept. 22, 1962; 1 child, Kara. BA, Northwestern U., 1960, JD, 1963. Bar: Ill. 1963, Tex. 1977. Atty. Treasury Dept., Chgo., 1964-65, Boston, 1965-66, 68-72, Washington, 1966-67; atty. pvt. practice, Chgo. and Houston, 1972—. Mem. ABA, Tex. Bar Assn. Houston Bar Assn., Tuesday Musical Club (program chmn.), Treble Clef Club (treas.), Kappa Beta Pi (past pres.), Mu Phi Epsilon.

KAHANA, EVA FROST, sociology educator; b. Budapest, Hungary, Mar. 21, 1941; came to U.S., 1957; d. Jacob and Sari (Mayer) Frost; m. Boaz Kahana, Apr. 15, 1962; children: Jeffrey, Michael. BA, Stern Coll., Yeshiva U., 1962; MA, CCNY, CUNY, 1965; PhD, U. Chgo., 1968; HLD (hon.), Yeshiva U., 1991. Nat. Inst. on Aging predoctoral fellow U. Chgo. Com. on Human Devel., 1963-66; postdoctoral fellow Midwest Council Social Research, 1968; with dept. sociology Washington U., St. Louis, 1967-71, successively research asst., research assoc., asst. prof.; with dept. sociology Wayne State U., Detroit, 1971-84, from assoc. prof. to prof., dir. Elderly Care Research Ctr., 1971-84; prof. Case Western Res. U., Cleve., 1984—, Armington Prof., 1989-90, chmn. dept. sociology, 1985—, dir. Elderly Care Research Ctr., 1984—, Pierce and Elizabeth Robson prof. humanities, 1990—; cons. Nat. Inst. on Aging, Washington, 1976-80, NIMH, Washington, 1971-75. Author: (with E. Midlarsky) Altruism in Later Life, 1994; editor: (with others) Family Caregiving Across the Lifespan, 1994; mem. editl. bd. Gerontologist, 1975-79, Psychology of Aging, 1984-90, Jour. Gerontology, 1990-94, Applied Behavioral Sci. Rev., 1992—; contbr. articles to profl. jours., chpts. to books (recipient Pub.'s prize 1969). Bd. dirs. com. on aging Jewish Community Fedn., Cleve.; vol. cons. Alzheimer's Disease and Related Disorders Assn., Cleve. NIMH Career Devel. grantee, 1974-79, Nat. Inst. Aging Merit award grantee, 1989—; Mary E. Switzer Disting. fellow Nat. Inst. Rehab., 1992-93; recipient Arnold Heller award excellence in geriatrics and gerontology Menorah Park Ctr. for Aged, 1992; named Disting. Geontological Rschr. in Ohio, 1993. Fellow Gerontol. Soc. Am. (chair behavioral social sci. com. 1984-85, Disting. Mentorship award 1987); mem. Am. Sociol. Assn. (coun. sect. on aging 1985-87), Am. Psychol. Assn., Soc. for Traumatic Stress, Wayne State U. Acad. Scholars (life), Sigma Xi.

KAHL, MARY L(OUISE), communication educator; b. Cheboygan, Mich., Apr. 17, 1954; d. Harris Allan and Mollie Grace (Riordan) K. BA, U. Mich., 1976; MA, Ind. U., 1979, PhD, 1994. Lectr. U. Calif., Davis, 1982-86; asst. prof. Stonehill Coll., North Easton, Mass., 1986-90, SUNY, New Paltz, 1990—. Contbr. articles to profl. jours. Vol. Dukakis Presdl. Campaign, Boston, 1988; mem. local Dem. com., Newburgh, N.Y., 1992—. Rsch. grantee Ind. U., Bloomington, 1980; recipient Term Faculty Devel. award United Univ. Professions, SUNY, New Paltz, 1994. Mem. Speech Comm. Assn., Ea. Comm. Assn. (rhetoric divsn. chair 1988-89, exec. coun. 1989-92, polit. comm. divsn. chair 1995-96). Office: SUNY New Paltz 75 S Manheim Blvd New Paltz NY 12561

KAHLER, ELIZABETH SARTOR (MRS. ERVIN NEWTON CHAPMAN), physician; b. Washington, Oct. 20, 1911; d. Armin Adolphus and Lenore Elome (Sartor) K.; m. Dr. Ervin Newton Chapman, Feb. 24, 1942 (dec. Apr. 1987). B.S., George Washington U., 1933, M.A., 1935, M.D. with distinction, 1940. Intern Gallinger Municipal Hosp. (now D.C. Gen. Hosp.), Washington, 1940-41; resident Children's Hosp., Washington, 1941-42; practice medicine Washington, 1942-78; assoc. univ. physician George Washington U., 1942-50; examining physician YWCA, 1942-45; courtesy staff Washington Hosp. Center, until 1978, George Washington U. Hosp., until 1978; physician for health services br. resources div. Bur. Social Services and Resources Social Services Adminstrn. D.C. Dept. Human Services, 1953-75; sch. physician D.C. pub. schs., 1959-89; mem. cons. com. for practical nursing program D.C. Pub. Schs., 1962-70. Everitt-Pomery trustee Wilson Coll., 1993—; vol. Widowed Persons Svc., 1993—; mem. exec. com. Nat. Voluntary Orgns. for Ind. Living for Aging, 1978-82, liaison from Am. Med. Women's Assn., 1975-82; mem. nat. program com. Camp Fire Girls Inc.; treas. Women's Assn. of Nat. Presbyn. Ch., 1981-83, fin. chmn., 1983-85, 87-89, asst. treas., 1989-91, chmn. memls., 1985-87, 91-93, cir. leader, 1994-96, nat. pres. ch. memls. com., 1986—, mem. libr. com. 1991—, Stephen min., 1993—. Mem. AMA, Women's Med. Assn. (pres. 1957-58, treas. Past Presidents Coun. 1976-78), Med. Soc. D.C. (life, chmn. com. on medicine and religion 1967-72, aging com. 1985-86, 88, mem. pub. info. and edn. com. 1986), D.C. Assn. Mental Health, Am. Heart Assn., Columbia Women of George Washington U. (life). Republican. Presbyterian. Office: 3601 Davis St NW Washington DC 20007-1428

KAHLER, KATHRYN SCHILLER, communications executive; b. Denton, Tex., Aug. 18, 1953; d. James Harlan and Martha Pearla (Speer) K. BA in Sociology, Tulane U., 1975; MA in Mass Comm., U. Minn., 1977. Writer, editor U. Minn. News Svc., Mpls., 1976-77; freelance health writer Twin Cities Reader, Mpls., 1977; health/scis. reporter The Jour.-News, Nyack, N.Y., 1977-83; nat. corr. Newhouse Newspapers, Washington, 1983-93; comm. dir. U.S. Dept. Edn., Washington, 1993—; chmn. bd. dirs. Nat. Press Bldg. Corp., 1991-93; adviser WHO, Commn. on Health and Environ., 1990; freelance writer The Boston Globe, Regardie's, Southern Mag., Dallas Morning News Mag., Am. Way, Spl. Report: Personalities. Editorial advisor to editorial bd. Tulane U. pubs. Panelist Washington Week in Rev., Washington Waypoints; hon. chmn. fundraiser for Youth Comm.; bd. dirs. USA Vote; judge Robert F. Kennedy awards, John Hancock awards, Nat. Press Club consumer awards, numerous other journalism contests; spkr. various press, edn., cmty. events. Vis. fellow Woodrow Wilson nat. fellow, 1992—; recipient Pub. Svc. award AP Mng. Editors Assn., 1982, Cert. of Merit, ABA, 1992. Mem. Nat. Press Club (chmn. bd. govs. 1989-90, 92-93, pres. 1991), USA Vote (bd. dirs.), Nat. Press Bldg. Corp. (bd. dirs.). Democrat. Methodist. Home: 3020 Tilden St NW Apt 304 Washington DC 20008-3080 Office: US Dept Edn 600 Independence Ave SW Washington DC 20202-0004

KAHLOW, BARBARA FENVESSY, statistician; b. Chgo., June 26, 1946; d. Stanley John and Doris (Goodman) Fenvessy; m. Lloyd Fitch Reese, Dec. 6, 1969 (div. 1977); m. Allan Howard Young, Mar. 31, 1979 (div. 1982); m. Ronald Arthur Kahlow, Sept. 28, 1985 (div. 1990). BA, Vassar Coll., 1968. Statistician U.S. Govt./Dept. HEW, Nat. Ctr. Health Statistics, 1968-70, Nat. Ctr. for Ednl. Statistics, 1970-72, Exec. Office of Pres. Office Mgmt. and Budget, Washington, 1972—. Author: Motor Vehicle Accident Deaths in the U.S.: 1950-69, 1970; contbr. articles to profl. jours. N.Y. State Regents scholar, 1964-68. Mem. Am. Statis. Assn., Foggy Bottom Assn., League of Rep. Women of D.C., Friends of the Kennedy Ctr., Friends of the Corcoran, Smithsonian Assocs., Washington Vassar Club, Univ. Club Washington. Republican. Episcopalian. Home: #404 2555 Pennsylvania Ave NW Washington DC 20037-1640 Office: Office Mgmt and Budget 6025 New Exec Office Bldg Washington DC 20503

KAHN, ARLENE JUDY MILLER, nurse, educator; b. Chgo., Dec. 16, 1940; d. Fred and Sophie (Schelbe) Miller; RN, AB, U. Ill., Chgo., 1963, MSN, 1970; EdD, U. San Francisco, 1986; m. Roy M. Kahn, Oct. 25, 1968; 1 child, Jennifer M. Head nurse psychiat. unit Grant Hosp., Chgo., 1966; supervising nurse Ill. Psychiat. Inst., Chgo., 1967; instr. psychiat. nursing Calif. State U., San Francisco, 1968-70; mem. faculty Calif. State U., Hayward, 1974—, assoc. prof. nursing, 1980-86, prof., 1986—, chair dept. nursing and health scis. Sch. Sci., 1992—; cons. in field. Research grantee Calif. State U., Hayward, 1980-81. Fellow Am. Assn. Psychiat. Nursing; mem. United Profs. Calif., Calif. Assn. Colls. of Nursing (treas. 1996—), Calif. Nursing Assn., Bay Area Nursing Diagnosis Assn. (officer 1986—), Sigma Theta Tau. Author articles in field. Home: 95 Sonia St Oakland CA 94618-2548 Office: Hayward State U School of Science Hayward CA 94542

KAHN, FAITH-HOPE, nurse, administrator, writer; b. N.Y.C., Apr. 25, 1921; d. Leon and Hazel (Cook) Green; RN, Beth Israel Med. Center, N.Y.C., 1942; student N.Y. U., 1943; m. Edward Kahn, May 29, 1942; children: Ellen Leora, Faith Hope II, Paula Amy. First scrub nurse operating room Beth Israel Hosp., N.Y.C., 1942; supr., operating room Hunts Point Gen. Hosp., 1942; gynecol. reconstrn. procedures researcher Phoenixville (Pa.) Gen. Hosp., 1943, Sydenham Hosp., N.Y.C., 1945; supr. ARC Disaster Field Hosp., Queens, N.Y., 1950-51; adminstr., mgr. team coordinator Dr. Edward Kahn, FACOG, Queens Village, N.Y., 1945—. Inventor, publicity chmn. Girl Scouts U.S.A., 1953; exec. dir. publicity Woodhull Schs., 1956-60, pres., 1961-62; exec. dir. publicity N.Y. Dept. Parks Figure Skating, 1956-70; exec. dir. publicity and applied arts St. John's Hosp., Smithtown, N.Y., 1965-66; state advisor N.Y., U.S. Congressional Adv. Bd., Washington, 1981—; nat. adv. bd. Am. Security Council, 1978—; founder Am. Security Found.; bd. trustees, Am. Police Hall of Fame and Mus., 1983—; mem. Republican Presdl. Task Force, 1986, Statue of Liberty and Ellis Island Centennial Commn., N.Y., 1986—. Recipient citation ARC, 1951, Am. Law Enforcement Officers Assn., Bronze medal Am. Security Council Ednl. Found., 1978, spl. recognition award Center Internat. Security Studies, 1979, Meml. Plate, Patriots of Am. Bicentennial, 1976, Great Seal of U.S.A. Plate, cert. Am. Sons Liberty, 1987, Good Smaritan award, 1987, Justice award Cross of Knights, 1987 Knights of Justice award, 1987; named Knight Chevalier Venerable Order of Michael the Archangel, 1987. Fellow, World Lit. Acad. (life), Acad. Nat. Law Enforcement (hon.); mem. Am. Acad. Ambulatory Nursing Adminstrn., Nurses Assn., Nat. League Nursing, Am. Coll. Obstetricians and Gynecologists, Nat. Assn. Physicians' Nurses, Nat. Critical Care Inst., Assn. Operating Room Nurses, AAAS, Nat. Assn. Female Execs., N.Y. Acad. Scis., Am. Police Acad. (cert. appreciation 1979, 83), Am. Fedn. Police, The Retired Officers Assn., Internat. Platform Assn., Security and Intelligence Found. (cert. appreciation 1986), Internat. Intelligence and Orgnd. Crime Investigators Assn., Smithtown Hist. Soc., Nat. Audubon Soc., NRA. Clubs: Tiyospaye, Paul Revere, Sterlingshire Woman's. Author, editor: The Easy Driving Way for Automatic and the Standard Shift, 1954; (with Edward Kahn) The Pelvic Examination, Outline and Guide for Residents, Internes and Students, 1954; (with Edward Kahn) Traction Hysterosalpingography for Uterine Lesions, 1949; contbr. articles profl. and lay jours. Home and Office: 213-16 85th Ave Jamaica NY 11427

KAHN, LINDA MCCLURE, maritime industry executive; b. Jacksonville, Fla.; d. George Calvin and Myrtice Louise (Boggs) McClure; m. Paul Markham Kahn, May 20, 1968. BS with high honors, U. Fla.; MS, U. Mich., 1964. Actuarial trainee N.Y. Life Ins. Co., N.Y.C., 1964-66, actuarial asst., 1966-69, asst. actuary, 1969-71; v.p., actuary US Life Ins., Pasadena, Calif., 1972-74; mgr. Coopers & Lybrand, Los Angeles, 1974-76, sr. cons., San Francisco, 1976-82; dir. program mgmt. Pacific Maritime Assn., San Francisco, 1982—. Bd. dirs. Pacific Heights Residents Assn., sec.-treas., 1981; trustee ILWU-PMA Welfare Plan, SIU-PD-PMA Pension and Supplemental Benefits Plans, 1982-90, Seafarers Med. Ctr., 1982-90, others. Fellow Soc. Actuaries (chmn. com. on minority recruiting 1988-91, chmn. actuary of future sect. 1993-95), Conf. consulting Actuaries (enrolled); mem. Internat. Actuarial Assn., Internat. Assn. Cons. Actuaries, Actuarial Studies Non-Life Ins., Am. Acad. Actuaries, Western Pension and Benefits Conf. (newsletter editor 1983-85, sec. 1985-88, treas. 1989-90), Actuarial Club Pacific States, San Francisco Actuarial Club (pres. 1981), Met. Club, Commonwealth Club, Soroptimists Club (v.p. 1973-74). Home: 2430 Pacific Ave San Francisco CA 94115-1238 Office: Pacific Maritime Assn Sacramento St Tower 550 California St San Francisco CA 94104-1006

KAHN, MADELINE GAIL, actress; b. Boston; d. Bernard B. Wolfson and Paula Kahn. BA, Hofstra U.; trained as opera singer; ArtsD (hon.), Boston Conservatory. Appeared in: satirical revue Upstairs at the Downstairs, N.Y.C., 1966-67, New Faces of 1968, New Faces, Booth Theatre, N.Y.C., Candide, Philharmonic Hall, 1968, Two by Two, Imperial Theatre, N.Y.C., 1970-71, Broadway mus. Two by Two; motion picture appearances include What's Up Doc?, 1972, Paper Moon, 1973 (Academy award nomination 1973, Golden Globe award nomination), From the Mixed-up Files of Mrs. Basil E. Frankweiler, 1973, Blazing Saddles, 1974 (Academy award nomination 1974, First Ann. Acad. of Humor award 1975), Young Frankenstein, 1974 (Golden Globe award nomination), At Long Last Love, 1975, The Adventure of Sherlock Holmes' Smarter Brother, 1975, Won-Ton-Ton, the Dog Who Saved Hollywood, 1976, High Anxiety, 1977, The Cheap Detective, 1978, The Muppet Movie, 1979, Simon, 1980, Happy Birthday Gemini, 1980, Wholly Moses!, 1980, First Family, 1980, History of the World, Part I, 1981, Yellowbeard, 1983, Slapstick of Another Kind, 1984, City Heat, 1984, Clue, 1985, (voice) My Little Pony, 1986, (voice) An American Tail, 1986, Betsy's Wedding, 1990, Shadows and Fog, 1992, Mixed Nuts, 1994, Nixon, 1995; stage appearances in Boom Boom Room, Vivian Beaumont Theater, 1973 (Tony nominee, Drama Desk award), Broadway prodn. On the 20th Century, 1978 (Tony nominee), Born Yesterday, 1989 (Tony nominee), Broadway prodn. The Sisters Rosensweig (Tony Award Best Actress in a Play), 1992-93; in ABC-TV afterschool special, 1986-87 (Emmy award); star TV series Oh, Madeline, ABC, from 1983 (People's Choice award), Mr. President, FOX-TV, 1987; appeared as Madame Arcati in Blithe Spirit, Santa Fe Festival Theater, 1983. Recipient Disting. Service award Hofstra Alumni Assn., 1975. *

KAHN, MARILYN ZELDIN, artist, art educator; b. N.Y.C., Nov. 21, 1928; d. Jacob and Sarah Zeldin; m. Ernest Joseph Kahn, June 4, 1950; children: David Lawton, Richard Barry. Cert., Traphagen Sch., N.Y.C., 1948, Art Students League, N.Y.C., 1950; attended, Bklyn. Mus. Sch., 1949. Art tchr. studio classes Sharon, Mass., 1960—; juror Mansfield Art Festival, 1985, Easton Art Festival, 1987, Stoughton Art Assn. Show, 1988, 94. One-woman show Audubon Gallery at Moosehill Sanctuary, Sharon, Mass., 1992, Stonehill Coll., Easton, Mass., 1987; group shows include Caccivio & Sons Gallery, 1990-92, Cambridge Art Assn. Gallery, 1968—, Wenninger's Gallery, Rockport, Mass., 1970-89, Attleboro (Mass.) Mus., 1972, Easton Art Festival, 1989, Fuller Art Mus., Brockton, Mass., 1994, 95, Ogunquit Art Ctr., 1995, 96. Pres. Sharon (Mass.) League of Women Voters, 1975-76; chairperson Sharon (Mass.) Planning Bd., 1980, 85, active, 1976-86. Recipient numerous 1st Prizes, and other honorable mentions. Mem. Nat. Mus. Women in Arts, New Eng. Watercolor Soc. (assoc.), Cambridge Art Assn., Sharon Creative Arts Assn. (program co-chair 1993-95, past pres. 1972, 73), Fuller Art Mus. Home: 114 Ames St Sharon MA 02067-2118

KAHN, NANCY VALERIE, publishing company executive, consultant; b. N.Y.C., Dec. 15, 1952; d. Alfred Joseph and Miriam (Kadin) K. BA magna cum laude, Princeton U., 1974. Dir. prodn. and devel. Bus. Rsch. Publs., Inc.-MacRAE's Directories, N.Y.C., 1984-86; assoc. pub., exec. editor Monitor Pub. Co., N.Y.C., 1987-88; dir. new product devel. Gale Rsch. Inc., N.Y.C., 1988-89; pub., editorial dir. directories and info. devel. Adweek/BPI Comms., N.Y.C., 1989-93; v.p. Everlink Corp., N.Y.C., 1993-94; prin. Info. Enterprises, N.Y.C., 1994—. Univ. scholar Princeton U., 1974. Mem. Info. Industry Assn., Directory Pubs. Forum N.Am., Manhattan Assn. Cabarets, Princeton Club. Office: Info Enterprises PO Box 826 New York NY 10021-0008

KAHN, SANDRA S., psychotherapist; b. Chgo., June 24, 1942; d. Chester and Ruth Sutker; m. Jack Murry Kahn, June 1, 1965; children: Erick, Jennifer. BA, U. Miami, 1964; MA, Roosevelt U., 1976. Tchr. Chgo. Pub. Schs., 1965-67; pvt. practice psychotherapy, Northbrook, Ill., 1976—. Host Shared Feelings, Sta. WEEF-AM, Highland Park, Ill., 1983—; author: The Kahn Report on Sexual Preferences, 1981, The Ex Wife Syndrome Cutting The Cord and Breaking Free After The Marriage Is Over, 1990; columnist Single Again mag. Mem. Ill. Psychol. Assn., Chgo. Psychol. Assn. (past pres. 1990). Jewish. Office: 2970 Maria Dr Northbrook IL 60062-2017

KAHN, SUSAN BETH, artist; b. N.Y.C., Aug. 26, 1924; d. Jesse B. and Jenny Carol (Peshkin) Cohen; m. Joseph Kahn, Sept. 15, 1946 (dec.); m. Richard Rosenkranz, Feb. 1, 1981. Grad., Parsons Sch. Design, 1945; pupil, Moses Soyer, 1950-57. Subject of: book Susan Kahn, with an essay by Lincoln Rothschild, 1980; One-man shows Sagittarius Gallery, 1960, A.C.A., Galleries, 1964, 68, 71, 76, 80, Charles B. Goddard Art Center, Ardmore, Okla., 1973, Albrecht Gallery Mus. Art, St. Joseph, Mo., 1974, N.Y. Cultural Center, N.Y.C., 1974, St. Peter's Coll., Jersey City, 1978, Heidi Neuhoff Gallery, N.Y.C., 1989, Sindin Galleries, 1996; exhibited in group shows Audubon Artists, N.Y.C., Nat. Acad., N.Y.C., Springfield (Mass.) Mus., City Center, N.Y.C., A.C.A., Galleries, N.Y.C., Nat. Arts Club, N.Y.C., Butler Inst., Youngstown, Ohio, Islip Art Mus., East Islip. N.Y., 1989, Fine Arts Mus. of S., Mobile, Ala., 1989, Chatanooga Regional History Mus, 1989, Longview (Tex.) Mus. Art, 1990; represented in permanent collections, Tyler (Tex.) Mus., St. Lawrence U. Mus., Canton, N.Y., Fairleigh Dickinson U. Mus., Rutherford, N.J., Syracuse U. Mus., Sheldon Swope Gallery, Terre Haute, Ind., Montclair (N.J.) Mus. Fine Arts, Butler Inst. Am. Art, Youngstown, Ohio, Reading (Pa.) Mus., Albrecht Gallery Mus. Art, St. Joseph(Mo.), Cedar Rapids (Iowa) Art Center, N.Y. Cultural Center, N.Y.C., Edwin A. Ulrich Mus., Wichita, Kans., Wichita State U., Johns Hopkins Sch. Advanced Internat. Studies, Washington, Joslyn Mus., Omaha, U. Wyo., Laramie. Recipient Knickerbocker prize for best religious painting, 1956; Edith Lehman award Nat. Assn. Women Artists, 1958; Simmons award, 1961; Knickerbocker Artists award, 1961; Nat. Arts Club award, 1967; Knickerbocker Medal of Honor, 1964; Famous Artists Sch. award, 1967. Mem. Nat. Assn. Women Artists (Anne Barnett Meml. prize 1981, Solveig Stromsoe Palmer Meml. award 1987, Dorothy Schweitzer award 1990), Artists Equity, Met. Mus., Mus. Modern Art, Nat. Assn. Women Artists (meml. award 1987). Office: Sindin Galleries 956 Madison Ave New York NY 10021

KAIDO, BONNELL DOLORES, medical education administrator; b. Cooperstown, N.Y., Dec. 5, 1951; d. Samuel Wellington and Bernadette Elizabeth (Rafferty) K. AAS in Bus., SUNY, 1972; BS in Bus., Coll. of St. Rose, 1974; MS in Edn., U. Albany, 1978. Bus. educator Sharon Springs Cen. Sch., 1975-80; supr. The Mary Imogene Bassett Hosp., Cooperstown, 1980-82, coord. med. edn., 1982-86, asst. dir. med. edn., 1986—; mem. com. Assn. for Hosp. Med. Edn., 1989—, vice chair mem. com., 1991—, nominating com., 1993-95; dir. Med. Alumni Assn. MIBH, Cooperstown, 1988—; spkr. Alliance for Continuing Med. Edn., 1991, Assn. Hosp. Med. Edn. Spring Inst., 1988-91, 94, N.J. Assn. Med. Edn. New Directions in Med. Edn., 1988, N.J. Med. Soc., Coun. Adminstrn. Direct in Med. Edn. Workshop, 1986, 89, chmn.-elect, 1988-91, chair, 1992-94, immediate past chair, 1994-96; instr. emergency med. svcs. Otsego County Emergency Svcs.; mem. regional EMS faculty N.Y. State Dept. Health, 1995—. Mem. Otsego EMS Coun., 1990—, chair, 1996—; CPR instr. Am. Heart Assn.; capt. Cooperstown Fire Dept. Emergency Squad, 1992-96; mem. Adirondack-Appalachian Regional Emergency Med. Svcs. Coun., 1990—, LWV. Mem. LWC, Delta Kappa Gamma, Delta Pi Epsilon. Democrat. Roman Catholic. Office: The Mary Imogene Bassett Hosp One Atwell Rd Cooperstown NY 13326

KAIGE, ALICE TUBB, retired librarian; b. Obion, Tenn., Jan. 27, 1922; d. George Easley and Lucile (Merryman) Tubb; m. Richard H. Kaige, Aug. 1952; children: Robert H., Richard C. (dec.), John S. (dec.). BA, Vanderbilt U., 1944; BS in Libr. Sci., Geo. Peabody Coll., 1947. Libr. Martin (Tenn.) High Sch., 1946-47, Demonstration Sch. Geo. Peabody Coll. Joint U. Librs., Nashville, Tenn., 1947-52; acquisitions libr. Lincoln Libr., Springfield, Ill., 1967-70; office coord. Springfield (Ill.) Chpt. ACLU, 1974; staff rep. Am. Fed. State, County & Mcpl. Employees, Springfield, 1975; libr. Ill. Dept. of Commerce and Community Affairs, Springfield, 1976-89. Vice chmn. Women's Internat. League for Peace and Freedom, 1969-70, various coms., 1970—; treas. Cen. Ill. Women's Lobby, 1971-72; com. on local govt. League of Women Voters, 1973-76; career day com. Urban League Guild, 1970-71; mem. NAACP,steering com. Springfield chpt. ACLU, 1974-75; co-founder West Side Neighborhood Assn., Springfield, 1977. Recipient Elizabeth Cady Stanton award, Springfield Women's Political Caucus, 1982. Mem. Sangamon County Hist. Soc., NOW, Women's Internat. League for Peace and Freedom, War Resisters League, LWV, Springfield Women's Polit. Caucus. Home: 701 S State St Springfield IL 62704-2445

KAIN, HANNAH, marketing professional; b. Odense, Denmark, Nov. 14, 1956; d. Herbert Herman and Birthe Ragnhild Kain; m. Jakob Nielsen, Feb. 18, 1984. BS in Polit. Sci., Odense U., 1979; MS in Comm., Aarhus (Denmark) U., 1982; HD in Mktg., South Jutland Bus. Sch., 1986. Asst. European Parliament, Luxembourg, 1979, 80; mgr. global comm. Alfa-Laval Flow Equipment, Kolding, Denmark, 1983-85, advt. mgr., 1986; mktg. project mgr. Baltica Fin., Copenhagen, Denmark, 1986-88, asst. v.p. mktg., 1988-90; dir. mktg. Citibag, Inc., Newark, N.J., 1990-94; dir. sales and mktg. Grimes Co., Sacramento, Calif., 1996, COO Turnkey Tech. Divsn., 1996—; cons. Ernst & Young, Copenhagen, 1987-90; lectr. Copenhagen Bus. Sch., 1987-90; mem. Nat. Coun. for Rsch., Copenhagen, 1983-87. Author: Market Analyse, 4th edit., 1989; editor: Dansk Studiehaandbog, 1978. Pres. STS Nat. U. Students, Copenhagen, 1977-78, GLO Nat. H.S. Student Assn., 1976-77; candidate for parliament Venstre, Denmark, 1978-83. Recipient Award Kosan, 1985. Mem. NAFE, Women in Computing, Silicon Valley Am. Mktg. Assn. (pres.-elect 1995—, bd. dirs.). Home: 38 Walnut Ave Atherton CA 94027 Office: Grimes Co 2050 Ringwood Ave San Jose CA 95131

KAIN, JANET LYNN, marriage and family therapist; b. Perth Amboy, N.J., Apr. 27, 1964; d. Philip Granville and Renee Viola (Wood) Riddle; m. Charles Lawrence Kain, Mar. 20, 1994. BS, Ind. State U., 1986, MS, 1988. Therapist Family Svc. Assn., Terre Haute, Ind., 1988-89; therapist Charter Hosp., Terre Haute, 1989-90, presenter, cons., 1990; therapist partial hospitalization dept. Geisinger Med. Ctr., Danville, Pa., 1990-94, presenter, cons., 1991; supr. seriously mentally ill Cummins Mental Health Ctr., Avon, Ind., 1994-95; marriage and family therapist Charter Hosp., Indpls., 1995-96; presenter, cons. Pa. Assn. for Partial Hospitalization, Danville, 1992. Abuse and neglect assessor Child Protective Svcs., Terre Haute, 1986-88. Mem. ACA, Am. Assn. for Marriage and Family Therapists.

KAISER, JEAN MORGAN, real estate broker; b. Johnson City, Tenn., June 28, 1932; d. Samuel Harold and Mabel Loretta (Burleson) Morgan; m. Edward Latham Kaiser, June 21, 1957; children: Gary Charles, Janet Lynne. Grad., Realtors Inst., 1978. Cert. real estate broker. Copywriter, announcer Sta. WGRV, Greeneville, 1952-58; exec. dir. Washington County United Fund, Abingdon, Va., 1961; personnel sec. Hubbard Aluminum Products Co., Abingdon, 1962-63; exec. sec. Roy Heyse and Assocs., Prairie Village, Kans., 1969-72; realtor assoc. Claiborne Co., Bartlesville, Okla., 1973-77; sec., treas. Blasting Svcs. Inc., Bartlesville, 1985—, Elko Inc., Bartlesville, 1987—; pres. Kaiser Realty/Better Homes and Gardens, Bartlesville, 1977—; Okla. Real Estate Commr., Oklahoma City, 1984-88; mem. rsch. bd. advisors Am. Biog. Inst., Inc. Mem. Women's Council Realtors, Real Estate Educators Assn., Bartlesville Bd. Realtors (bd. dirs. 1981-83), Okla. Assn. Realtors (bd. dirs. 1987—), N.E. Okla. Bd. Realtors (bd. dirs.), Nat. Assn. Real Estate Lic. Law Ofcls. (legis. and interstate coop. coms. 1986-87), Okla. Cert. Residential Specialists (forum com. 1986-87). Democrat.

KAISER, LINDA SUSAN, state commissioner, lawyer; b. Alexandria, Va., Apr. 7, 1956; d. Thomas Raymond Kaiser and Joanne May (Wilber) Raynolds. BA, Pa. State U., 1978; JD, U. Pitts., 1981. Asst. counsel Pa. Ins. Dept., Harrisburg, 1981-85; sr. counsel Cigna Corp., Phila., 1985-92; asst. gen. counsel Reliance Ins. Co., Phila., 1992-95; ins. commr. Commonwealth of Pa., Harrisburg, 1995—; mem. property casualty steering com. Ins. Fedn. Pa., Phila., 1992-95; alternate Pa. Workers Compensation Gov. Bd., 1993-95. Pres. Huntington's Disease Soc. of Am., Delaware Valley, Phila., 1993—. Mem. ABA, Soc. CPCU, Soc. Nat. Assn. Ins. Commrs. (sec. N.E. zone 1996—), Order of Coif, Barristers. Office: 1326 Strawberry Sq Harrisburg PA 17120

KAISER, MARTHA WINNIFRED, elementary school educator; b. Boston, Sept. 9, 1948; d. William Burrows and Jane Phillips (Thompson) Mercaldi; m. Christopher Barina Kaiser, June 27, 1970; children: Justin, Matthew, Patrick. AB in Edn., Smith Coll., 1970; MA in Reading, Western Mich. U., 1989, postgrad., 1992-93. Cert. reading and reading recovery tchr., Mich. 6th grade tchr. Centerville Sch., Beverly, Mass., 1970-71; 3d and 4th grade tchr. George Watsons' Boys Coll., Edinburgh, Scotland, 1971-74; presch. tchr. Presbyn. Coop., Holland, Mich., 1977-78; 2d grade tchr. Zeeland (Mich.) Pub. Schs., 1988-91, 1st grade tchr., 1991-92, reading recovery tchr., 1992—. Classroom tchr. mini-grantee State of Mich., 1989. Mem. NEA, Mich. Edn. Assn., Zeeland Edn. Assn., Internat. Reading Assn., Mich. Reading Assn., Reading Recovery Coun. of NAm. Office: Zeeland Pub Schs Roosevelt Sch 175 W Roosevelt Ave Zeeland MI 49464-1127

KAISER-BOTSAI, SHARON KAY, early chilhood educator; b. Waterloo, Iowa, Aug. 9, 1941; d. Peter A. Ley and Lorraine (Worthington) Burton; m. Hugh W. Kaiser, Aug. 28, 1968 (div. 1981); 1 child, Kiana; m. Elmer E. Botsai, Dec. 5, 1981; children: Kiana, Don, Kurt. BSBA, U. Ariz., 1963; MEd, U. Hawaii, Honolulu, 1970; postgrad., Hawaii Loa Coll., 1971, U. Hawaii, 1972-88. Cert. elem. edn. tchr., Hawaii. Sec. Donald M. Drake, San

Francisco, 1964-66; tchr. St. Mark's Kindergarten, Honolulu, 1966-73; head tchr. Cen. Union Preschool, Honolulu, 1967-77; tchr. Waiokeola Preschool, Honolulu, 1974-76, 77-88; tchr. staff instruction Honolulu Dist. Dept. of Edn., 1989-90; tchr. students of ltd. English proficiency Kaahumanu Sch., Honolulu, 1990-94; tchr. kindergarten Palolo Sch., Honolulu, 1991—; pvt. instr. in Hawaiian dance, 1977-79; workshop leader marine sea crafts Sea Grant Inst. for Marine Educators, 1977, HAEYC Conf., 1979, 82, 84, 85, 86, chair workshops in music and creative drama, 1977, drama workshop, 1994; speaker Celebration of Life Sta. KHON-TV, 1979; workshop leader MECAP Conf., 1985; mem. com. Improvement Symphony Performance for Preschoolers, 1977; art advisor, coord. Sunday sch. program Waiokeola Ch., 1973, speaker creative communication, 1984; validator accreditation program Nat. Acad. for Edn. of Young Children, 1986—; asst. to co-chair conf. Hawaii Assn. for Edn. Young Children, 1987-88; Hawaii State Tchrs. Assn. rep. Palolo Sch., 1993. Author: Creative Dramatics, 1990; co-author: Preschool Activities, 1990. Actress Presido Playhouse, San Francisco, 1962, Little Theatre, Honolulu Zoo, 1976; instr. spl. edn. students Kaneohe YWCA, 1967; troop co-leader Girl Scouts U.S.A., 1981-84; bd. dirs. Zoo Hui, 1984-86; trustee, stewardship chmn. Waiokeola Ch., 1986-88. Mem. Hawaii Assn. for Edn. of Young Children (First recipient Phyllis Loveless Excellence in Teaching award 1979), Delta Delta Delta. Lutheran. Home: 321 Wailupe Cir Honolulu HI 96821-1524

KAISERLIAN, PENELOPE JANE, publishing company executive; b. Paisley, Scotland, Oct. 19, 1943; came to U.S., 1956; d. W. Norman and Magdalene Jeanette (Houlder) Hewson; m. Arthur Kaiserlian, June 29, 1968; 1 child, Christian. B.A., U. Exeter, Eng., 1965. Copywriter, sales rep. Pergamon Press, Elmsford, N.Y., 1965-68; exhibits mgr. Plenum Pub., N.Y.C., 1968-69; asst. mktg. mgr. U. Chgo. Press, 1969-76, mktg. mgr., 1976-83, assoc. dir., 1983—. Mem. Soc. for Scholarly Pub., Am. Geog. Assn., Quadrangle Club. Office: U Chgo Press 5801 S Ellis Ave Chicago IL 60637-1404

KAJI, HIDEKO KATAYAMA, pharmacology educator; b. Tokyo, Jan. 1, 1932; came to U.S., 1954; d. Sakae and Tsuneko (Matsuda) Katayama; m. Akira Kaji, Aug. 23, 1958; children: Kenneth, Eugene, Naomi, Amy. BS, Tokyo Coll. Pharmacy, 1954; MS, U. Nebr., 1956; PhD, Purdue U., 1958. Vis. scientist Oak Ridge (Tenn.) Nat. Lab., 1962-63; assoc. U. Pa., Phila., 1963-64; rsch. assoc. The Inst. Cancer Rsch., Phila., 1965-66, asst. mem., 1966-76; vis. mem. Max Planck Inst. Molek. Gen., Berlin, 1972-73, Nat. Inst. Med. Rsch., London, 1973; assoc. prof. Jefferson Med. Coll., Phila., 1976-82; vis. prof. Wistar Inst., Phila., 1984-85; prof. pharmacology and structural biology Jefferson Med. Coll., Phila., 1983—; cons. Nippon Paint Co., Ltd., Tokyo, 1990—, Coatesville (Pa.) VA Hosp., 1982-84. Contbr. articles to profl. jours. Fellow NIH (bd. dirs. 1986-89); mem. Am. Soc. Biochemistry and Molecular Biology, Am. Soc. Pharmacol. and Exptl. Therapeutics, Am. Soc. Microbiology, Sigma Xi. Home: 334 Fillmore St Jenkintown PA 19046-4328 Office: Jefferson Med Coll 1020 Locust St Philadelphia PA 19107-6731

KALANGE, JUNE BURTON, secondary school educator; b. Winston Salem, N.C., Mar. 16, 1951; d. Hilary J. and Myrtle (Miller) Burton; m. Christopher D. Kalange, Aug. 26, 1972; children: David Christopher, Jason Michael. BS in Biology, U. Ala., 1973. Tchr. sci. dept. Huntsville (Ala.) H.S., 1988, Grissom H.S., Huntsville, 1989—. Mem. Huntsville Edn. Assn., Ala. Edn. Assn., Huntsville Coun. of Sci. Tchrs., Nat. Assn. of Biology Tchrs., Sigma Xi (Tchr. of Yr. 1992), Delta Kappa Gamma. Office: Grissom HS 7901 Bailey Cove Rd Huntsville AL 35802

KALAYJIAN, ANIE SANENTZ, psychotherapist, nurse, educator, consultant; b. Aleppo, Syria; came to U.S., 1971; d. Kevork and Zabelle (Mardikian) K.; m. Shahé Navasart Sanentz, Dec. 16, 1984. BS L.I. U., 1979; MEd, Columbia U., 1981, EdD, 1985, profl. nurses tng. course, 1984; cert. photography, Pratt Inst., 1979. R.N., N.Y., N.J., Conn.; cert. psychiat. mental health specialist; Dutch diplomate in logotherapy; advanced cert. in Eye Movement Desensitization and Reprocessing, advanced cert. in disaster mgmt. ARC. Psychiat. nurse Met. Hosp., N.Y.C., 1979-84; staff psychiat. mental health nurse Manhattan Bowery Project, N.Y.C., 1978-86; instr. Hunter Coll., N.Y.C., 1980-82; prof. Bloomfield Coll., N.J., 1984-85; lectr. Jersey City Coll., 1985; prof. Seton Hall U., South Orange, N.J., 1985-87; assoc. prof. grad. program St. Joseph Coll., 1987-91; prof. John Jay Coll. Criminal Justice Fairleigh Dickinson U., 1991-92, vis. prof., 1991-92, Pace U., N.Y.C., 1994-95; adj. prof. Coll. Mt. St. Vincent, Riverdale, N.Y., 1995—, disting. lectr., Columbia U., N.Y.C., 1995; spkr. in field; keynote spkr. Mid Am. Logotherapy Inst., 1995, Coll. Mt. St. Vincent, 1995, Hollins Coll., Va., 1995, UN. Active com. for presdl. task force on nursing curriculum Soc. for Traumatic Stress Studies; co-founder, East coast coord. Mental Health Outreach to Earthquake Survivors in Armenia; dir. Julia Richman-Pace Univ.-N.Y. State Bd. Edn.-Visiting Nurse Svc.-Partnership program, 1991-92; UN rep. World Fedn. For Mental Health, mem. mental health/ human rights com. 1996—. Author: Disaster and Mass Trauma: Global Perspectives on Post Disaster Mental Health Management, 1995; contbr. articles to profl. jours, chpts. to books; reviewer: Readings: A Journal of Reviews and Commentary in Mental Health, 1995. Recipient Clark Found. scholarship award, 1985, Outstanding Rsch. award Columbia U., 1993, Disting. Svc. award N.Y. Counties RN Assn., 1994, ABSA Outstanding Achievement award APA, 1995; rsch. grantee Pace U., 1992; Endowed Nursing Edn., Columbia U., scholar, 1984; Armenian Relief Soc. scholar, 1976-77, Armenian Students Assn. Am. scholar, 1976-78, Columbia U. Tchrs. Coll., Outstanding Rsch. award, 1993. Fellow Am. Orthopsychiat. Assn., N.Y. State Nursing Assn. (planning com. nursing edn.); mem. APA (outstanding achievement award 1995), Coun. on Continuing Edn., Psychiat. and Mental Health Nursing, Am. Psychol. Soc., Am. Psychiat. Nurses Assn., Am. Acad. Experts in Traumatic Stress, Internat. Coun. Psychologists, Internat. Trauma Counselors, Inst. for Psychodynamics and Origins of Mind, Armenian Students Assn. (treas. 1980-81, pres. 1981-83, scholarship chairperson 1983-85, v.p. Cen. Exec. Com. 1987-88, pres. 1988-89, elected nat. pres. 1988-90), Armenian Info. Profls. (corr. sec., 1992—), Armenian-Am. Soc. for Studies on Stress and Genocide (founder, pres. 1988—), N.Y. Registered Nurses' Assn. (chairperson edn. com., 1989—), World Fedn. for Mental Health (UN rep. 1994—, treas., sec., UN com. on human rights, 1994—, co-chair human rights com. 1996—), Univ. for Peace (cooresponding sec. UN com.), Internat. Soc. Tramatic Stress Studies (v.p. N.Y. chpt. 1993-95, pres. 1995—), N.Y. State Nurses Assn. (coun. Human Rights, 1996—), N.Y. Counties RN Assn. (Jane Delano Disting. Svc. award 1994), N.Y. State Nurses Assn. (coun. on human rights 1995—), Kappa Delta Pi (advisor 1989-90), Sigma Theta Tau (Alpha Zeta chpt. 1981—). Avocations: aerobics, photography, acting. Office: 130 W 79th St New York NY 10024-6477

KALER, REBECCA, curator, educator; b. Mansfield, Ohio, May 30, 1942; d. Peter Nicolaus and Frances Rose (Siwek) K.; children: Joseph D. Langley, Jessica D. Langley. Diploma, Cleve. Inst. Art, 1964; student, U. Okla., 1964; BA in Journalism, U. No. Colo., 1980; MEd, Colo. State U., 1984. Vol. Peace Corps, Bolivia, 1964-66; promotional writer Mansfield News Jour., 1967; cartoonist, gag writer Varsity House, Inc., Columbus, Ohio, 1968-69; wallcovering designer Columbus Coated Fabrics and Can. Wallpaper, 1969-72, 1973-78; ind. designer Mountain Mama Designs, 1973-79; staff artist Ripley's Believe It Or Not! Mus., 1973; instr. Aims C.C., Greeley, Colo., 1983-87; adminstr. A Woman's Place, Greeley, Colo.; instr. Mansfield Art Ctr., 1989-91; curator Pearl Conard Gallery/Ohio State U., Mansfield, 1991—; adv. bd. mem. Pioneer Joint Vocat. Sch., Shelby, Ohio; steering com. mem. Ohio Indsl. Tng. Program, Mansfield; juror various art orgns. Author, illustrator: Blueberry Bear, 1994; art shows include Mansfield Playhouse, 1960, Cleve. Mus., 1964, Poudre Valley Regional Exhibit, 1983, Lazarus Gallery, 1991, Mansfield Art Ctr., 1989, 91, 94-95, others; also pvt. collections; contbr. articles to newspapers & mags. Bd. dirs. Domestic Violence Shelter. Grad. fellow Colo. State U., 1983-84; Working scholar Cleve. Inst. Art, 1963-64. Mem. Mansfield Art Ctr., Phi Kappa Phi. Home: 282 Ruth Ave Mansfield OH 44907 Office: Ohio State U 1680 University Dr Mansfield OH 44906

KALICK, LAURA JOY, lawyer, tax specialist; b. N.Y.C., Mar. 1, 1949; d. Murray Gordon and Selma B. (Suekoff) Lowenthal; m. Theodore Kent Kalick, Oct. 22, 1972; children: Sara, Daniel, Lila. BA, U. Mich., 1970; JD, George Washington U., 1973; LLM in Taxation, Georgetown U., 1977. Bar: Pa. 1973, D.C. 1976. Tax law specialist Internal Review Svc., Washington, 1973-77; tax legis. counsel U.S. Senator Haskell, Washington, 1977-79; tax mgr. Laventhol & Horwath, Washington, 1979-85; tax dir. Coopers & Lybrand, Washington, 1985—; adv. bd. Exempt Orgn. Tax Rev., Washington, 1990—. Primary author: Hospital Tax Management, 1983, NACUBO Guide to IRS Audits: A Manual for Colleges and Universities, 1994. Incorporator, treas., Bethesda-Chevy Chase Ednl. H.S. Found., 1995—; subcom. chair of compensation and benefits, ABA exempt orgn. com. Chgo., 1995—. Mem. ABA, Nat. Health Lawyers Assn., Am. Acad. Hospital Attys., Healthcare Fin. Mgmt. Assn. Democrat. Jewish. Office: Coopers & Lybrand LLP 1800 M St NW Washington DC 20036

KALIKOW, THEODORA JUNE, university president; b. Lynn, Mass., June 6, 1941; d. Irving and Rose Kalikow. AB, Wellesley Coll., 1962; ScM, MIT, 1970; PhD, Boston U., 1974. From instr. to prof. Southeastern Mass. U., North Dartmouth, 1968-84; dean Coll. Arts and Scis., U. No. Colo., Greeley, 1984-87; dean of the coll. Plymouth (N.H.) State Coll., 1987-94, interim pres., 1992-93; pres. U. Maine, Farmington, 1994—. Contbr. articles to profl. jours., 1975—. NSF grantee, 1978; Am. Council on Edn. fellow Brown U., Providence, 1983-84. Mem. Am. Philos. Assn., Soc. Values in Higher Edn. (bd. dirs. 1991-94), Assn. Gen. and Liberal Studies (exec. coun. 1990-93). Office: Office of the Pres Univ Maine Farmington Farmington ME 04938

KALIN, D(OROTHY) JEAN, artist, educator; b. Kansas City, Mo., Feb. 11, 1932; d. William Warner and Esther Dorothy (Peterson) Johnson; m. John Baptist Kalin, Jr., Jan. 5, 1952; children: Jean Loraine, Debra Ann, Diana Yvonne. AA, St. Joseph (Mo.) Jr. Coll., 1951. Artist Hallmark Cards, Inc., Kansas City, Mo., 1952-53, 73-93; freelance artist Kansas City, 1953-72; owner Portraits of Life, Kansas City, 1986—, art tchr., 1988—. Illustrator article for Directory of Am. Portrait Artists, 1985. Kansas City Art Inst. scholar, 1951-52. Mem. Nat. Oil and Acrylic Painters Soc. (signature mem.), Nat. Acrylic Painters Assn., Kans. Watercolor Soc. (signature mem.), Am. Watercolor Soc. (assoc.), Nat. Watercolor Soc. (assoc.), Midwest Watercolor Soc. (assoc.), Nat. Mus. Women in the Arts (charter mem.), Internat. Platform Assn.

KALIN, KARIN BEA, secondary school educator, consultant; b. N.Y.C., June 22, 1943; d. Lawrence Leon and Celia (Siskind) Elkind; children: Laura, Howard. BS, SUNY, Oswego, 1965; MS, CUNY, 1967. Cert. social studies tchr., N.Y. Tchr. Benjamin Franklin High Sch., N.Y.C., 1965-66, Grover Cleveland High Sch., Ridgewood, N.Y., 1967-73; tchr. Aviation High Sch., Long Island City, N.Y., 1979—, sex equity coord., 1982-90, local equal opportunity coord., 1983-91, sch. recruiter, 1985-91; curriculum developer OEO, N.Y.C. Bd. Edn., fall 1985; panelist Aerospace Edn. Workshop for Elem. Tchrs., Career Exploration Seminar, Aerospace Edn. Conf., 1990, East Meadow (N.Y.) Sch. Dist., 1989—; cons. Coll. Aeros., N.Y., 1986; cons. Profl. and Clerical Employees of Internat. Ladies Garment Workers Union, N.Y.C., 1989; with L.I. Coun. for Equal Edn. and Employment, 1990. Mem. Women on Job, Port Washington, N.Y., 1986-91; mem. com. Nassau Dem. Com., Westbury, N.Y., 1988—; mem. L.I. Coun. Equal Edn. and Employment, 1990—, Coalition To Advocate for Women of Color in Edn. William Robertson Coe fellow, 1992; grantee Columbia U., 1967, 69, N.Y.C. Bd. Edn., 1983, Nat. Coun. for Humanities, 1985, Project Voice/Move, 1984-85. Mem. AAUW (roundtable on gender equity in classroom 1992), NAFE, NOW (chair women and employment com. 1987-90, chair consciousness raising com. 1982), LWV, AFL-CIO, United Fedn. Tchrs., Assn. Tchrs. of Social Studies, N.Y. State Alliance for Women and Girls in Tech., Nat. Women's Polit. Caucus (bd. dirs., chair polit. action com.), Bachelor and Bachelorettes for Square Dancing (founder, pres. L.I. chpt.). Jewish. Home: 700 Barkley Ave East Meadow NY 11554-4501 Office: Aviation High Sch 36th St Queens Blvd Long Island City NY 11101

KALIPOLITES, JUNE E. TURNER, rehabilitation professional; b. Grasmere, N.H., Aug. 10, 1932; d. Louis O. and Edith Mae (Allen) Turner; m. Nicholas G. Kalipolites, Feb. 12, 1955; children: George, Stephanie, Athena. AA, Hesser Coll., Manchester, N.H., 1977; B of Gen. Studies, U. N.H., 1980; MS in Rehab. Adminstrn. and Svcs., So. Ill. U., Carbondale, 1982; EdD in Ednl. Adminstrn., Vanderbilt U., 1992. Cert. rehab. counselor. Office mgr. Harris Upham and Co., Inc., Manchester; mgr. Amoskeag Bank & Trust Co.; rehab. counselor Div. Vocat. Rehab., Nashua, N.H.; rehab. cons. N.H. Divsn. Vocat. Rehab., Concord, 1986—, tng. coord., 1993-94; rehab. cons. spl. svcs. N.H. Divsn. Adult Learning and Rehab., Concord, 1995—. Author: Profile of Women in Rehabilitation Administration: A Common Theme, 1992, Projects with Industry: A Unique Concept for Providing Rehabilitation Services to Persons with Severe Disabilities, 1982. LaVerne Noyes scholar. Mem. ACA, Am. Rehab. Counseling Assn., Nat. Rehab. Assn. (nat. bd. dirs. 1994—), Nat. Rehab. Counseling Assn. (bd. dirs. 1986-87), Nat. Rehab. Adminstrn. Assn. (nat. bd. dirs. 1983-87, 92-94), N.E. Rehab. Counseling Assn. (pres. 1987, bd. dirs. 1986-88), N.H. Rehab. Assn. (bd. dirs. 1977—, treas. 1978, 89-92, sec. 1977-78), Nat. Assn. Ind. Living, Rho Sigma Chi, Chi Sigma Iota. Republican. Greek Orthodox. Home: 668 Lake Ave Manchester NH 03103-3538 Office: NH Divsn Adult Learning and Rehab 78 Regional Dr Concord NH 03301-8508

KALISCH, BEATRICE JEAN, nursing educator, consultant; b. Tellahoma, Tenn., Oct. 15, 1943; d. Peter and Margaret Ruth Petersen; m. Philip A. Kalisch, Apr. 17, 1965; children—Philip P., Melanie J. BS, U. Nebr., 1965; MS, U. Md., 1967, PhD, 1970. Pediatric staff nurse Centre County Hosp., Bellefonte, Pa., 1965-66; instr. nursing Philipsburg (Pa.) Gen. Hosp. Sch. Nursing, 1966; pediatric staff nurse Greater Balt. Med. Center, Towson, Md., 1967; asst. prof. maternal-child nursing Am. U., 1967-68; clin. nurse specialist N.W. Tex. Hosp., Amarillo, 1970; assoc. prof. maternal-child nursing, curriculum coordinator nursing Amarillo Coll., 1970-71; chmn. baccalaureate nursing program, asso. prof. nursing U. So. Miss., 1971-74; prof. nursing, chmn. dept. parent-child nursing U. Mich. Sch. Nursing, Ann Arbor, 1974-86; Shirley C. Titus Disting. prof. U. Mich. Sch. Nursing, 1977—, Titus Disting. prof. nursing mgmt., 1989—; prin., dir. nursing consultation svcs. Ernst & Young, Detroit, 1986-89; prin. investigator USPH grant to study image of nurses in mass media and the informational quality nursing news, U. Mich., 1977-86, prin. investigator to study intrahosp. transport of critically ill patients, 1991—; prin. investigator to study use of HIA nurse in N.Y.C. labor market, U. Mich.; prin. investigator to study the impact of managed care on critical care, U. Mich.; vis. disting. prof. U. Ala., 1979, U. Tex., 1981, Tex. Christian U., 1983. Author: Child Abuse and Neglect: An Annotated Bibliography, 1978; co-author: Nursing Involvement in Health Planning, 1978, Politics of Nursing, 1982, Images of Nurses on Television, 1983, The Advance of American Nursing, 1986, revised, 1994, The Changing Image of the Nurse, 1987; co-editor: Studies in Nursing Mgmt.; contbr. articles to profl. jours. Recipient Joseph L. Andrews Bibliog. award Am. Assn. Law Libraries, 1979; Book of Yr. award Am. Jour. Nursing, 1978, 83, 86, 87, Outstanding Achievement award U. Md., 1987, Distinguished Alumni award U. Nebr., 1985, Shaw medal Boston Coll., 1986; USPHS fellow. Fellow Am. Acad. Nursing; mem. Am. Coll. Healthcare Execs., ANA, APHA, Am. Orgn. Nurse Execs., Sigma Theta Tau, Phi Kappa Phi. Presbyterian. Home: 27675 Chatsworth St Farmington MI 48334-1821 Office: U Mich Sch Nursing 400 N Ingalls St Ann Arbor MI 48109-2003

KALISH, ROSANN BROWN, elementary school educator; b. N.Y.C., Mar. 8, 1943; d. Joseph A. and Fannie R. (Taubman) Brown; m. Jay S. Kalish (div.); children: Amy Robyn, Jennifer Beth. BA, Hunter Coll., N.Y.C., 1964; MS, Marywood Coll., Scranton, Pa., 1982; MA, Kean Coll., Union, N.J., 1995. Cert. tchr. early childhood, elem. edn., supr., adminstr. Kindergarten tchr. Pub. Schs. 19, Bronx, 1964-67; Head Start tchr. N.Y. Schs., summers 1964-68; kindergarden tchr. Washington Hts. Sch., Middletown, N.Y., 1967-68; tchr. 2d grade Montague Twp. (N.J.) Elem. Sch., 1977-93, tchr. gifted/talented and computer literacy, 1993—. Pres. Sisterhood, Temple Beth El, Port Jervis, N.Y., 1981, mem., 1967—; mem. Hadassah, Port Jervis, 1967—, Friends, a charitable orgn., Milford, Pa., 1994—. Named Tchr. of the Yr., Montague Twp. Bd. Edn., 1989. Mem. NEA, N.J. Edn. Assn., Phi Kappa Phi, Delta Kappa Gamma. Home: 534 Keystone Park Milford PA 18337 Office: Montague Twp Elem Sch 475 Rte 206 Montague NJ 07827-9527

KALLEM, CHERYL MARCIA, diversified financial services company executive; b. N.Y.C.. BA, Colgate U., 1976; MBA, Rutgers U., 1977. CPA, N.Y. Prin. Arthur Young, N.Y.C., 1977-88; corp. v.p. Drexel Burnham, N.Y.C., 1988-90; CFO J.J. Kenny, N.Y.C., 1990-92; mng. dir. Kidder Peabody, N.Y.C., 1992-95, Bear Stearns, Bklyn., 1995—; chair Pub. Securities Assn. capital com., 1995—. Mem. AICPA, Fin. Women's Assn. N.Y., Securities Industry Assn. (fin. mgmt. divsn., capital com. 1995—), N.Y. State Soc. CPAs. Office: Bear Stearns 1 Metrotech Ctr North Brooklyn NY 11201

KALLEN, JACKIE, professional boxing manager; b. Detroit, 1946; d. Phil Kaplan and Marge Mahoney; m. Mike Kallen; children: Brad, Brian. Entertainment columnist Oakland (Mich.) Press, 1970-88; publicist Kronk Boxing Club, Detroit, 1978-88; mgr. profl. boxers, 1988—. *

KALLET, HARRIET FELDMAN, real estate broker, sales associate; b. Jersey City, N.J., Aug. 4, 1941; d. Emanuel and Clara (Holstein) Feldman; m. Stephen M. Kallet, Aug. 15, 1965; children: Jill, Beth. BA, Elmira Coll., 1962; postgrad., Bank St. Coll. Edn., 1963-64. Cert. elem. sch. tchr., N.J., N.Y. Tchr. grade 4 Teaneck (N.J.) Bd. Edn., 1962-68; tchr. jr. high sch. Barnstable Acad., Glen Rock, N.J., 1979-84, 1984-87; real estate salesperson Murphy Realty, Montvale, N.J., 1986-93, ReMax Real Estate Assocs., Woodcliff Lake, N.J., 1994—. Mem. Sisterhood Temple Emanuel. Mem. Nat. Assn. Realtors, Prk Ridge Rotary Club, West Bergen (N.J.) Assn. Realtors (com. chairperson 1995-96), N.J. Assn. Realtors (Million Dollar Sales Club 1988-95), Pascack Valley BD. Realtors-N.W. Bergen Bd. Realtors (com. chairperson 1992-95, bd. dirs. 1993-95). Home: 326 Spring St Saddle River NJ 07458 Office: ReMax Real Estate Assocs 188 Broadway Westwood NJ 07675

KALLGREN, JOYCE KISLITZIN, political science educator; b. San Francisco, Apr. 17, 1930; d. Alexander and Dorothea (Willett) K.; m. Edward E. Kallgren, Feb. 8, 1953; children: Virginia, Charles. BA, U. Calif., Berkeley, 1953, MA, 1955; PhD, Harvard U., 1968. Jr. researcher to asst. researcher Ctr. Chinese Studies U. Calif., Berkeley, 1961-65, research assoc., 1965—, chair, 1983-88; assoc. dir. Inst. of East Asian Studies, Berkeley, 1987-95; from lectr. to prof. polit. sci. emeritus U. Calif., Davis, 1965—; cons. in field. Contbg. editor: Asean and China: An Evolving Relationship, 1988, Academic Exchanges: Essays on the Sino-American Experience, 1987, Developing a Nation State: China After Forty Years, 1990; editor: Jour. Asian Studies, 1980-83, Asian Survey, 1991—; contbr. articles to profl. jours. and chpts. to books. Ford Found. awardee, 1978-79. Mem. Am. Polit. Sci. Assn., Assn. Asian Studies, Nat. Com. U.S./China Rels., U.S. Com. on Security and Coop. in Asia Pacific. Home: 28 Hillcrest Rd Berkeley CA 94705-2807 Office: U Calif Inst East Asian Studies Berkeley CA 94720

KALLMAN, KATHLEEN BARBARA, marketing and business development professional; b. Aurora, Ill., Mar. 23, 1952; d. Kenneth Wesley and Germaine Barbara (May) Eby. Legal sec. Sidley & Austin, Chgo., 1973-76, Winston & Strawn, Chgo., 1976-78; exec. sec. Beatrice Cos., Inc., Chgo., 1978-81, adminstrv. asst., 1981-83, asst. to chmn. bd. dirs., 1983-84, asst. v.p., 1984-85; pres., mng. dir. Stratxx Ltd., Charlotte, N.C., 1985—. Mem. Chgo. Coun. on Fgn. Rels., 1986—. Mem. Am. Soc. Profl. and Exec. Women, Nat. Assn. Women Bus. Owners, Charlotte Women Bus. Owners Assn., Charlotte Assn. Profl. Saleswomen. Office: Stratxx Ltd PO Box 470008 Charlotte NC 28247-0008

KALLOWAY, LOIS JANE, telecommunications executive, writer; b. Chgo., July 30, 1954; d. Harry Anthony and Helen Frances (Kudlaty) K. BA in History, Northwestern U., 1976; cert. in Polish, Copernicus U., Poland, 1976, Yale U., 1979; MA in History, U. Mich., 1979; ABD, U. Pitts., 1989. Broker various telecomms. firms, 1991—; pres. Kalloway Comms., McKeesport, Pa., 1993—; founder Pitts. Telecomm. Consortium, 1994. Editor: Music: An Understanding and Enjoyment, 1995. Nominated Network Visionary Communication Week, 1993. Office: Kalloway Comm 514 Chanucey Cir Mc Keesport PA 15132-5101

KALMUS, ELLIN, art historian, educator; b. N.Y.C.; d. Victor and Mata (Heineman) Roudin; m. Murray L. Silberstein, Oct. 6, 1949 (dec. 1968); children: James, Barbara Silberstein Keezell, John; m. Allan H. Kalmus, May 16, 1969. BA cum laude, Vassar Coll., 1946. Asst. dept. publs. and exhbns. Mus. Modern Art, N.Y.C., 1946-49; asst. tchr. Mus. Modern Art, 1950; lectr. Riverdale Country Sch., N.Y.C., 1970-90, Dalton, Trinity, Columbia Grammar, Birch Wathen Schs., N.Y.C., 1971-83, Fifth Ave. Presbyn. Ch., St. James Episcopal Ch., N.Y.C., 1982-83; lectr. pvt. groups N.Y.C., 1975—; mem. vis. com. photograph and slide libr. Met. Mus. Art, N.Y.C., 1978—, lectr., 1986, 87; mem. tchg. staff Ethical Culture Sch. for Adult Edn., New Sch. for Social Rsch., 1980-81; Paris lectr. Friends of Vieilles Maisons Françaises, 1988; series lectr. Darien Cmty. Assn., 1988—; London lectr. Arts Club of London, 1990; lectr. Albert Einstein Coll. Medicine, 1993-95, Christie's, London, 1994, Old Westbury Gardens, 1994-95, Cosmopolitan Club, 1988. Trustee, head edn. com. Riverdale Country Sch., N.Y.C., 1978-84. Pierpont Morgan Libr. fellow, 1986, Frick Collection fellow, 1992. Mem. Phi Beta Kappa, Cosmopolitan Club, Sunningdale Club (Scarsdale, N.Y.). Home: 125 E 72nd St New York NY 10021-4250

KALNAY, EUGENIA, government official, meteorologist; b. Buenos Aires, Oct. 1, 1942; came to U.S., 1971; d. Jorge and Susana (Zwicky) K.; m. Alberto Mario Rivas, July 24, 1965 (div. 1981); 1 child, Jorge Rodrigo; m. Malise Cooper Dick, July 13, 1981. Lic. in meteorology, U. Buenos Aires, 1965; PhD in Meteorology, MIT, 1971. Asst. prof. U. Uruguay, Montevideo, 1971-73; rsch. assoc. MIT, Cambridge, 1973-75, asst. prof. meteorology, 1975-76, assoc. prof., 1977-78; sect. head NASA Goddard Space Flight Ctr., Greenbelt, Md., 1979-82, br. head, 1983-86; chief devel. div. Nat. Weather Svc., NOAA Nat. Meteorology Ctr., Washington, 1987—; mem. several coms. NRC, NAS, Washington; prin. investigator NASA, 1973—; adj. prof. meteorology U. Md., 1980-83. Editor several jours.; contbr. over 100 articles to sci. jours. Recipient gold medal for exceptional sci. achievement NASA, 1981, silver medal Dept. Commerce, 1990, Gold medal Dept. Commerce, 1993. Mem. NAE, Am. Meteorl. Soc. (Charney award 1995). Home: 8103 Sligo Creek Pky Takoma Park MD 20912-6205 Office: Eugenia Kane NCEP W NP 2 WWB Rm 207 Washington DC 20233

KALOTRA, INDIRA KAUR, educational administrator, consultant; b. Calcutta, India, Aug. 24, 1968; came to U.S., 1984; d. Jayant Singh and Amrit Kaur (Jaspal) K. BS in Psychology, George Mason U., 1990; MA in Internat. Rels., U. Chgo., 1991. Program officer Internat. Bus. & Technical Cons., Inc., Ashburn, Va., 1991-95; pres. The Kaur Group, Vienna, Va., 1995—. Contbr. articles to profl. jours. Office: The Kaur Group 8614 Westwood Ctr Dr Ste 400 Vienna VA 22182

KALSOW, KATHRYN ELLEN, library clerk; b. Stevens Point, Wis., Dec. 31, 1938; d. Wilbert Otto and Vivian Frances (Peterson) K. BA, Luther Coll., 1961. Libr. clk. Luther Coll. Libr., Decorah, Iowa, 1961—. Del. county conv. Rep. com., Decorah, Iowa, 1970-84, state conv., Des Moines, 1970-84; del. Nat. Fedn. Rep. Women, Washington, 1971. Mem. AAUW (treas. 1966-68, 79-81, internat. rels. area rep. 1975-77, 85-87, 90-92, named Gift Honoree, 1982), UN Assn. of USA, Iowa Libr. Assn. Lutheran. Home: Luther Coll Instrnl Media 700 College Dr Decorah IA 52101

KALVEN, JANET, educator, writer, consultant; b. Chgo., May 21, 1913. BS, U. Chgo., 1934; MEd, Boston U., 1971. Instr. Great Books program U. Chgo., 1937-42; lectr., adminstr. ednl. program for women U.S. Grail Movement, Libertyville, Ill., 1942-43, Loveland, Ohio, 1944-64; coord. internat. meetings Internat. Grail Movement, Paris, 1964-67; coord. academic program Grailville Conf. Ctr., Loveland, Ohio, 1967-78, conf. coord., lectr., 1978—; assoc. dir. self directed learning program U. Dayton (Ohio), 1972-86; founder, trainer Women Into Tomorrow, Cin., 1971-76. Co-author, editor: Your Daughters Shall Prophesy, 1980, Value Development, 1982, Women's Spirit Bonding, 1984, With Both Eyes Open, 1988; contbr. article to profl. jour. Mem. nat. commn. Ch. Women United, N.Y., 1970-71; bd. dirs. Women Ch. Convergence, Balt., 1984—, Metro. Area Religious Coalition, Cin., 1969-72, Cin. Indsl. Mission, 1971-74; founder, bd. dirs. Womens Inst. for Religion and Soc., Cin., 1985-93; co-founder, bd. dirs. Womens Rsch. Devel. Ctr., Cin., 1988—. Elected to Ohio Women's Hall of Fame, 1990. Mem. NOW, Nat. Women's Studies Assn., Women's Ordination Conf. (program com.), Phi Beta Kappa. Home: 932 O'Bannonville Rd Loveland OH 45140-9740 Office: Grailville 932 O'Bannonville Rd Loveland OH 45140

KAMALI, NORMA, fashion designer; b. N.Y.C., June 27, 1945; d. Sam and Estelle (Mariategui) Arraez. Grad., Fashion Inst. of Tech., 1965. Established Kamali Ltd., N.Y.C., 1967-78; owner, designer On My Own Norma Kamali, N.Y.C., 1978—. Designer costumes for Emerald City in The Wiz, 1977; for Twyla Tharp dance In the Upper Room, 1986; Parachute Designs displayed Met. Mus. of Art, N.Y.C., 1977; prodr., dir. (video) Fall Fantasy; dir. (video) Fashion Aid, 1985. Recipient CFDA award for Outstanding Women's Fashion, 1982, Cotay Return award, 1982, Coty Hall of Fam award, 1983, Ernie awards Earnshaw Rev., 1983, Fashion Inst. Design and Merchandising award, 1984, Salute to Women award N.Y. Fashion Group, 1986, Disting. Arch. award N.Y. chpt. AIA, 1986, Outstanding Grad. award Pub. Edn. Assn. N.Y., 1988, Award of Merit, Internat. Video Culture Competition, 1988, Am. Success award Fashion Inst. Tech., 1989. Office: 11 W 56th St New York NY 10019-3902*

KAMASKI, MONICA LYNN, accountant; b. Michigan City, Ind., Aug. 10, 1955; d. Frank John and Mary Frances (Ray) K. BS in Bus., Ind. U. N.W., Gary, 1991, MBA, 1994. Cons. Hair Master, Chesterton, Ind., 1977-94; acct. SB Assocs., Valparaiso, Ind., 1994—. Precinct com. person Porter County, Ind., 1989-91; fin. chmn. St. Patricks Festival, Chesterton, 1993, 94; vol. Spring Valley Homeless Shelter, Valparaiso, 1993—. Mem. Inst. Mgmt. Accts. Republican. Roman Catholic. Home: 1120 Beam St Porter IN 46304

KAMATOY, LOURDES AGUAS, artist; b. San Fernando, Pampanga, Philippines, June 29, 1945; came to U.S., 1966; d. Juan Gutierrez and Segunda Mercado (De La Cruz) Aguas; m. Ernesto Gabriel Kamatoy, Apr. 28, 1973; 1 child, Lisette Marie. BA in English, U. Santo Tomas, Manila, Philippines, 1964; MA in Ednl. Theatre, NYU, 1972; overseas cert. theatre, Rose Bruford Coll. Speech, Kent, Eng., 1966. Supr. Arthur Andersen & Co., N.Y.C., 1966-73; instr. theatre U. So. Ind., Evansville, 1973-75; pres. Bodega, Evansville, 1975-79; artist rep. Lulu Represents, Chgo., 1986-92; ptnr. MK Videostar, Chgo., 1989-92; account exec. Kamatoy Creative, Encino, Calif., 1992—. Pres. Evansville Arts and Edn. Coun., 1983; v.p. U. Evansville Theatre Soc., 1984; panelist Ind. Arts Commn., Indpls., 1985; bd. dirs. Arts Insight, Indpls., 1985, USI Soc. Arts and Humanities, Evansville, 1988, Valley Cultural Ctr., Woodland Hills, Calif., 1996. Roman Catholic. Office: 4630 Woodley Ave Apt 105 Encino CA 91436-2701

KAMERMAN, SHEILA BRODY, social worker, educator; b. Jan. 7, 1928; d. S. Lawrence and Helen (Golding) Brody; m. Morton Kamerman, Sept. 11, 1947; children: Nathan Brody, Elliot Herbert, Laura Kamerman-Katz. BA, NYU, 1946; MSW, Hunter Coll., 1966; D. Social Welfare, Columbia U., 1973. Social worker N.Y.C. Dept. Social Svcs., 1966-68; social work supr. Bellevue Psychiat. Hosp., 1968-69; assoc. prof. social work Hunter Coll., 1977-79; from rsch. assoc. to sr. rsch. assoc. Columbia U. Sch. Social Work, 1971-79, assoc. prof. social policy and planning, 1979-81; prof. Sch. Social Work Columbia U., 1981—; chmn. NAS-NRC panel on work, family and community, 1980-82; mem. Com. Child Devel. Rsch. and Pub. Policy, 1983-88; mem. com. on prenatal care Inst. Medicine, 1986-88; cons. in field; mem. numerous social welfare coms. and adv. bds.; mem. Gov. Cuomo's Task Force on Poverty and Welfare Reform, 1986-87, adv. com. on Work and Family, 1987-88, UN Expert groups on social welfare and family policies. Author: (with Alfred J. Kahn) Not for the Poor Alone, 1975, Social Services in the United States, 1976, Social Services in International Perspective, 1977, Family Policy: Government and Families in Fourteen Countries, 1978, Child Care, Family Benefits and Working Parents, 1981, Parenting in an Unresponsive Society, 1980, Maternity and Parental Benefits and Leaves, 1980, Helping America's Families, 1982, Maternity Policies and Working Women, 1983, Income Transfers for Families with Children, 1983, Child Care: Facing the Hard Choices, 1987, The Responsive Work Place, 1987, Child Support: From Debt Collection to Social Policy, 1988, Mothers Alone: Strategies for a Time of Change, 1988, Privatization and the Welfare State, 1989, Social Services for Children, Youth and Families in the United States, 1990, Child Care, Parental Leave, and the Under 3's, 1991, A Welcome for Every Child, 1994, Starting Right: How America Neglects Its Youngest Children and What We Can Do About It, 1995; contbr. numerous articles to profl. jours. Recipient Hexter award Hunter Coll. Sch. Social Work, 1977, Nat. Leadership award in Social Policy, Heller Sch. Brandeis U., 1989; named to Hunter Coll. Hall of Fame, 1981; fellow Ctr. Advanced Study in Behavioral Scis., 1983-84. Mem. NASW, Am. Pub. Welfare Assn., Assn. Policy Analysis and Mgmt., Phi Beta Kappa. Home: 1125 Park Ave New York NY 10128-1243 Office: Columbia U Sch Social Work 622 W 113th St New York NY 10025-7982

KAMIL, ELAINE SCHEINER, physician, educator; b. Cleve., Jan. 26, 1947; d. James Frank and Maud Lily (Severn) Scheiner; m. Ivan Jeffery Kamil, Aug. 29, 1970; children: Jeremy, Adam, Megan. BS magna cum laude, U. Pitts., 1969, MD, 1973. Diplomate Am. Bd. Pediats., Am. Be. Pediat. Nephrology. Intern in pediats. Children's Hosp. Pitts., 1973-74, resident in pediats., 1974-76; clin. fellow in pediat. nephrology Sch. Medicine, UCLA, 1976-79, acting asst. prof. pediats., 1979-80; rsch. fellow in nephrology Harbor-UCLA Med. Ctr., Torrance, Calif., 1980-82; med. dir. The Children's Clinic of Long Beach, Calif., 1984-87; med. dir. pediat. nurse practitioner program Calif. State U., Long Beach, 1984-87; asst. clin. prof. pediats. Sch. Medicine, UCLA, 1988-90, assoc. clin. prof. pediats., 1991—; assoc. dir. pediat. nephrology and transplant immunology Cedars-Sinai Med. Ctr., L.A., 1990—; adj. asst. prof. pediats. Harbor-UCLA, Torrance, Calif., 1983-87, UCLA, 1987-88; cons. in pediat. nephrology Hawthorne (Calif.) Cmty. Med. Group, 1981—. Author chpts. to books; contbr. articles to profl. jours. Mem. AAUW, Am. Soc. Nephrology, Am. Soc. Pediat. Nephrology, Am. Fedn. Clin. Rsch., Internat. Soc. Nephrology, Internat. Soc. Pediat. Nephrology, Internat. Soc. Peritoneal Dialysis, Renal Pathology Soc., Nat. Kidney Found. So. Calif. (mem. med. adv. bd. 1987—, rsch. com. 1987-90, chmn. pub. info. med. adv. bd. 1988-92, mem. handbook com. 1988, co-chair med. adv. bd. cmty. svcs. com. 1992-93, chair-elect patience svcs. and cmty. edn. com. 1993-94, chair patients svcs. and cmty. edn. com. 1994-95, kidney camp summer vol. physician 1988-91, 93, 94, Arthur Gordon award 1991, Exceptional Svc. award 1992, Exceptional Leadership and Support award 1995, bd. dirs. 1995-96), Alpha Omega Alpha, Phi Beta Kappa. Office: Cedars-Sinai Med Ctr 8700 Beverly Blvd Los Angeles CA 90048-1804

KAMINSKY, ALICE RICHKIN, English language educator; b. N.Y.C.; d. Morris and Ida (Spivak) Richkin; m. Jack Kaminsky; 1 son, Eric (dec.). B.A., NYU, 1946, M.A., 1947, Ph.D., 1952. Mem. faculty dept. English NYU, 1947-49, Hunter Coll., 1952-53, Cornell U., 1954-57, Broome Community Coll., 1958-59, Cornell U., 1959-63; mem. faculty dept. English SUNY, Cortland, 1963—, prof., 1968-91, prof. emeritus, 1991—, faculty exchange scholar. Author: George Henry Lewes as Critic, 1968, Logic: A Philosophical Introduction, 1974; editor: Literary Criticism of George Henry Lewes, 1964, Chaucer's Troilus and Criseyde and the Critics, 1980, The Victim's Song, 1985; contbr. articles and revs. to numerous jours. Mem. MLA, Chaucer Soc. Office: SUNY Coll Dept English Cortland NY 13045

KAMLER, SUSAN MARIE, psychotherapist; b. York, Nebr., Jan. 19, 1954; d. Linus Joseph and Frances Madalen (Zieren) K. AA, Coll. St. Mary, Omaha, 1974; BA, Creighton U., 1980; MA, Lesley Coll., 1994; cert. in pastoral Ministry, St. Thomas Sem., Denver, 1994. Staff educator New Covenant Justice & Peace Ctr., Omaha, 1981-83; comm. dir. Sisters of Mercy, Omaha, 1983-88; mental health worker Mercy Hosp., Denver, 1988-90, Columbine Psychiat. Hosp., Denver, 1990-92; asst. resident coord. Mercy Housing, Denver, 1992-93; psychotherapist Maria Droste Svcs., Denver, 1994—. Mem. Am. Counseling Assn., Colo. Counseling Assn., Eating Disorder Profls. Colo. Democrat. Roman Catholic. Office: Maria Droste Svcs Colo 1355 S Colorado Blvd #C-100 Denver CO 80222

KAMMER, MARY EILEEN, social services specialist; b. Cin., Mar. 22, 1960; d. Joseph C. and Shirley A. (Huber) K. BS in Home Econs. and Consumer Sci., Miami U., Oxford, Ohio, 1982; postgrad., U. Cin., 1988. Food supr. Colonnade Cafeteria, Cin., 1982-83; restaurant mgr. L.S. Ayres, Cin., 1983-85; dining rm. mgr. Maple Knoll Village, Cin., 1985-88, activities coord., 1988-95, vol. resources coord., 1995—. Recipient plaque for dedication Southwestern Ohio Srs.' Svcs., Inc., 1995. Roman Catholic. Home: 2061 Waycross Rd Apt 12 Cincinnati OH 45240 Office: Maple Knoll Village 11100 Springfield Pike Springdale OH 45246

KAMMERDEINER, NANCY ALYCE, city official; b. Natrona Heights, Pa., Jan. 25, 1946; d. Ivan M. and Sylvia E. (Klingensmith) K.; m. F. Gerald Callan, Oct. 17, 1987. BA in Polit. Sci., Allegheny Coll., 1967; MPA, Syracuse U., 1969. Program asst. informational devel. br. AID, New Delhi, 1968; adminstrv. analyst Office of Mng. Dir., City of Phila., 1969-72, mgmt. analyst Office of Mayor, 1972-80, fin. svcs. adminstr. Office Dir. of Fin., 1980-86, mgr. human resources info. ctr., 1986-88, asst. to dir. fin., 1988-95, revenue commr., 1995—; treas. Southeastern Regional Coun. for Intergovtl. Personnel Act, Phila., 1972-80. Mem., chmn. rev. com. United Way Southeastern Pa., Phila., 1982-89; bd. dirs. Big Sisters Phila., 1989—, pres., 1993—; mem. self evaluation com. Greater Phila. coun. Girl Scouts U.S.A., 1989. Mem. Am. Soc. for Pub. Adminstrn. (coun. 1971-89, pres. 1973-74, 93-95), Leadership Inc. Office: City of Phila 630 Mcpl Svcs Bldg 1401 John F Kennedy Blvd Philadelphia PA 19102

KAMMEYER, SONIA MARGARETHA, real estate agent; b. Stockholm, June 21, 1942; came to U.S., 1964; d. Bengt Henrik and Margot Elsa M. (Hodin) Sjoberg; m. Whitman Ridgway, June 13, 1964 (div. 1978); children: Sean, Siobhan; m. Kenneth C.W. Kammeyer, Dec. 28, 1982. Student, Fleisher's Art Meml. Sch., Phila., 1966-69. With Ben Bell Real Estate, Lanham, Md., 1972-73, Robert L. Gruen Real Estate, Silver Spring, Md., 1973-81, Panarama Real Estate, Silver Spring, 1981-82, Long & Foster Real Estate, Inc., Silver Spring, 1982—. Named to Montgomery County Bd. Realtors Hall of Fame, 1994. Mem. Montgomery County Bd. Realtors (life), Howard County Bd. Realtors, Washington D.C. Bd. Realtors, Swedish Profl. Women. Home: 14600 Triadelphia Mill Rd Dayton MD 21036-1217 Office: Long & Foster Real Estate 3901 National Dr Burtonsville MD 20866-1105

KAMPE, CAROLYN JEAN, special education educator, elementary school educator; b. Chicago Heights, Ill., July 8, 1943; d. Fred H. and Harriet (Bobrowski) K. Student, Mt. St. Clare Jr. Coll., Clinton, Iowa, 1966-68; BA in Art, St. Ambrose U., 1970; MA in Cultural Studies, Gov. State U., 1974; EdD in Art Edn., Ill. State U., 1990. Cert. art tchr.; cert. spl. edn.; cert. K-12 specialist. Art supr., coord., and elem. art tchr. Dist. 170, Chicago Heights, 1970-87; grad. asst. art dept. Ill. State U., Normal, 1987-90; spl. edn. tchr. Hugh Jr. H.S., Matteson, Ill., 1990-91, Burr Oak and Calumet Park, Ill., 1991-92; homebound tchr. Dist. 162, Matteson, 1991-94; art edn. for spl. edn. Dist. 170, Chicago Heights, 1992—; art tchr. Field Sch. Dist. 152, Harvey, Ill., 1994-96; vis. faculty and adaptive art specialist St. Norbert Coll., DePere, Wis., 1990-92; active in Put Your Heart Illinois Youth Art Month, 1985-86 and 1993-94, spl. edn. "Earth Day" Art Exhbn. (200 works on display); homebound tchr. Dist. 162 and 227, 1991-96; bd. dirs. Very Spl. Arts, Ill. State U., Normal, 1992-96. Group exhbns. include Chicago Heights Libr., Chicago Heights Mcpl. Bldg., 1993-94, Wash. Jr. H.S., Chicago Heights, 1994; contbr. articles to profl. jours. Bd. dirs. Very Spl. Arts Ill., Ill. State U., Normal, 1992-94; Ill. Coalition for Disabilities, Normal, 1985-86; pres. Self Help for Hard of Hearing, Ill., 1984-86; mem. White House Exhbn. Com., Chgo., 1992-93; vol. Chgo. Pub. Libr., 1993; mem. Put Your Heart in Month, Ill. Youth Art Month, 1985-86; art judge Girl Scout Art Contest, 1982, Chicago Heights Jaycees, 1982-83. Named One of 5 Best and Brightest Outstanding Disabled Coll. Grads., 1990, Mainstream Mag. and Am. Bus. Women's Assn.; recipient Kohl Internat. Tchg. award 1993. Mem. Nat. Assn. Art Edn., Ill. Art Edn. Assn. (Best Art Tchr. award 1984). Roman Catholic.

KAMPITS, EVA, accrediting association administrator, educator; b. Budapest, Hungary, Feb. 22, 1946; came to U.S., 1951; d. Ernest Michael and Ilona (Gondi) K.; m. Dan Catalin Stefanescu, Aug. 4, 1979; children: Andreea N., Cristina F. Cert., U. Innsbruck, Austria, 1963; BA, Harvard U., 1968; MA, Boston Coll., 1971, PhD, 1977. Instr. freshman seminars MIT, Cambridge, 1973-80, freshman advisor, 1975-80, sophomore advisor, 1976-80, adminstrv. officer Artificial Intelligence Lab., 1967-78, asst. to dir. Lab. for Computer Sci., 1987-88, rsch. affiliate Media Lab., 1987-88; acad. dean Pine Manor Coll., Chestnut Hill, Mass., 1980-94, dir. sponsored programs, grad. sch. dean, 1994; dir. sch./coll. rels. New Eng. Assn. Schs. & Colls., Inc., Bedford, Mass., 1994—; mem. NEARnet, 1989-94, Gov.'s Ednl. Tech. Adv. Coun., 1990-93; mem. steering com. Mass. Telecomputing Coalition, 1991—, New Eng. Network Acad. Alliances in Fgn. Langs. and Lits., 1995 , Eisenhower Regional Alliance for Math. and Sci. Reform, 1996—; trustee Boston Archtl. Ctr., 1996—. Founding mem. bd. editors NERComp Jour. Founding mem. bd. visitors Brimmer and May Sch., Chestnut Hill, Mass., 1992—; trustee Boston Archl. Ctr., 1996—. Mem. Assn. for Computing Machinery, Coll. Bd., Am. Assn. Higher Edn., Tchg. and Learning Exploratorium (exec. bd. dirs.). Republican. Roman Catholic. Office: New Eng Assn Schs & Colls Inc 209 Burlington Rd Bedford MA 01730-1406

KAN, DIANA ARTEMIS MANN SHU, artist; b. Hong Kong, Mar. 3, 1926; came to U.S., 1949, naturalized, 1964; d. Kam Shek and Sing-Ying (Hong) K.; m. Paul Schwartz, May 24, 1952; 1 son, Kan Martin Meyer Sing-Si. Student, Art Students League, 1949-51, Beaux Arts, Paris, 1951-52, Grande Chaumiere, Paris, 1951-52. Fgn. corr., city editor Cosmorama Pictorial Mag., Hong Kong, 1968; art reviewer Villager, N.Y.C., 1960-69; lectr. Birmingham So. U., N.Y. U., Mills Coll., St. Joseph's Coll., Phila. Mus., Smithsonian Instn. Author: White Cloud, 1938, The How and Why of Chinese Painting, 1974; One-man shows, London, 1949, 63, 64, Paris, 1949, Hong Kong, 1937, 39, 41, 47, 48, 52, Shanghai, 1935, 37, 39, Nanking, 1936, 38, Macao, 1947, 48, Bankok, 1947, Casablanca, 1951, 52, San Francisco, 1950, 67, N.Y.C., 1950, 54, 59, 67, 71, 72, 74, 78, Naples, 1971, Elliot Mus., Stuart, Fla., 1967, 73, Bruce Mus., Greenwich, Conn., 1969, Nat. Hist. Mus., Taipei, Taiwan, 1971, N.Y. Cultural Center Mus., 1972, Galerie Barbarella, Palm Beach, Fla., 1972, Hobe Sound (Fla.) Galleries, 1976, 81, Nat. Arts Club, 1979, Dyansen Galleries, 1987-90 others; exhibited in group shows Allied Artists of Am., 1957-90, Royal Acad. Fine Arts, London, 1963-64, Royal Soc. Painters, London, 1964, Nat. Arts Club, N.Y.C., 1964-90, Am. Water Color Soc., N.Y.C., 1966-90, Nat. Acad., N.Y.C., 1967-90, Charles and Emma Frye Mus., Seattle, 1968, Willamette U., Salem, Oreg., 1968, Columbia (S.C.) Mus. Art, 1969, Audubon Artist, 1974-90, Evansville (Ind.) Mus., 1991, Dyansen Gallery, Boston, 1991; represented permanent collections, Met. Mus. Art, Phila. Mus. Art, Nelson Gallery, Elliot Mus., Fla., Bruce Mus., Dalhousie U., Atkin Mus., Kansas City, Nat. Hist. Mus., Taipei; subject of film Eastern Spirit, Western World—A Profile of Diana Kan. Recipient Summer Festival award N.Y.C., 1959, 1st Prize Nat. Art Club, 1982; named most Outstanding Profl. Woman of the Yr., Washington Sq. chpt. N.Y. League Bus. and Profl. Women's Club, 1971, 79, Gold medal of honor Knickerbocker Artists, 1990, Gold medal of honor Audubon Artists, 1991; Diana Kan Appreciation Day proclaimed by Mayor of Boston, 1991; offl. citation proclaimed by Pres. Senate of Mass., 1991. Fellow Royal Soc. Arts; mem. Pen and Brush Club (dir. 1968, Brush Fund award 1968, Alice S. Buell Meml. award 1969, Margaret Sussman award 1991), Nat. Acad. Design (assoc., John Pike Meml. award 1987, cert. of merit 1991), Am. Watercolor Soc. (traveling award 1968, Marthe T. McKinnon award 1978, dir. 1975-77), Art Students League, Nat. League Pen Women, Audubon Artists (v.p. 1983), Allied Artists Am. (Barbara Vassilieff Meml. award 1969, Ralph Fabri Meml. award 1975, corr. sec. 1975-78), Catharine Lorillard Wolf Art Club (Anna Hyatt Huntington bronze medal 1970, 74, Gold medal of honor 1982). Clubs: Overseas Press Am., Lotos, The Nat. Arts (N.Y.C.). Home: 15 Gramercy Park S New York NY 10003-1705

KANE, CAROL, actress; b. Cleve., June 18, 1952. Stage debut in The Prime of Miss Jean Brodie, 1966; other N.Y.C. theatre appearances include Ring 'Round the Bath Tub, 1972, The Tempest, 1974, 80, The Effect of Gamma Ray on Man-in-the-Moon Marigolds, 1978, Are You Now or Have You Ever Been?, 1978, Benefit of a Doubt, 1978, Tales from Vienna Woods, 1979, Sunday Runners in the Rain, 1980, Macbeth, 1980, The Fairy Garden, 1984, The Debutante Ball, 1988, Frankie and Johnny in the Clair de Lune, 1988; film appearances include Carnal Knowledge, 1971, Desperate Characters, 1971, Wedding in White, 1972, The Last Detail, 1974, Dog Day Afternoon, 1975, Hester Street, 1975 (Acad. award nomination for Best Actress), Harry and Walter Go to New York, 1976, Annie Hall, 1977, Valentino, 1977, The World's Greatest Lover, 1977, The Mafu Cage, 1978, When a Stranger Calls, 1979, The Muppet Movie, 1979, The Sabiana, 1979, Les Jeux, 1980, Pandemonium, 1982, Norman Loves Rose, 1982, Can She Bake A Cherry Pie?, 1983, Over the Brooklyn Bridge, 1984, Racing With the Moon, 1984, The Secret Diary of Sigmund Freud, 1984, Transylmania 6-5000, 1985, Jumpin' Jack Flash, 1986, The Princess Bride, 1987, Ishtar, 1987, License to Drive, 1988, Scrooged, 1988, Sticky Fingers, 1988, Flashback, 1990, Joe Versus the Volcano, 1990, The Lemon Sisters, 1990, My Blue Heaven, 1990, Ted and Venus, 1991, In the Soup, 1992, Adams Family Values, 1993, When a Stranger Calls Back, 1993, Even Cowgirls Get the Blues, 1993, Baby on Board, 1993; TV series Taxi, 1981-83, All is Forgiven, 1986, American Dreamer, 1990, (voice) Alladin, 1994; TV films An Invasion of Privacy, 1983, Burning Rage, 1984, All is Forgiven, 1986, Drop Out Mother, 1988, Dad, the Angel & Me, 1995; TV spls. Shelly Duvall's Tall Tales and Legends: Case at the Bat, 1985, Bob Goldthwait—Don't Watch This Show, 1986, Paul Reiser: Out on a Whim, 1987, Rap Master Ronnie-A Report Card, 1988, Tales from the Crypt, 1992. Recipient Emmy award for outstanding supporting actress in a comedy series, 1981. Office: Krost/Chapin Artists Talent Agy 9911 W Pico Blvd Ph I Los Angeles CA 90035-2718*

KANE, CHERYL CHASE, education program developer; b. Great Barrington, Mass., Dec. 26, 1947; d. Alexander and Mildred (Tatsapaugh) Shmulsky. BA, U. Mass., 1969; MA, U. Colo., 1979; PhD, Fla. State U., 1988. Project dir. Colo. State Dept. Edn., Denver, 1977-79; rsch. assoc. Nat. Inst. Edn., Washington, 1979-81; pvt. practice cons. Washington, 1981-88; assoc. exec. dir. Nat. Found. for the Improvement of Edn., Washington, 1988-92; dir. rsch. Nat. Edn. Commn. on Time and Learning, Washington, 1992-94; dir. strategy New Am. Schs. Devel. Corp., Arlington, Va., 1994—; cons. U.S. Dept. Edn., Washington, 1981-88, World Bank, Washington, 1981-88, Acad. for Edn. Devel., Washington, 1981-88. Author: Prisoners of Time: What We Know and What We Need to Know, 1994; contbr. chpt. to book. Sec. Logan Circle Cmty. Assn., Washington, 1993. Mem. Am. Edn. Rsch. Assn., Phi Delta Kappa. Home: 1325 13th St NW # 36 Washington DC 20005 Office: Ste 2710 1000 Wilson Blvd Arlington VA 22209

KANE, GRACE MCNELLY, maternal, women's health and pediatrics nurse; b. Auburn, Ill., Mar. 31, 1939; d. Irving Benjamin and Ruby Louise (Stinnett) McNelly; m. Robert John Kane, July 23, 1960 (dec. 1994); children: Scott Robert, Timothy Phillip, Pamela Collette, Glenn Randall, Andrew Keith, Bruce Ryan. Diploma, Mem. Hosp. Sch. Nursing, Springfield, Ill., 1960; BS in Profl. Arts, St. Joseph's Coll., North Windham, Maine, 1985. RN, Ill.; cert. in occupational hearing conservation, fetal monitoring I and II; cert. ACLS. Staff nurse nursery-newborn units Walther Meml. Hosp., Chgo., 1962-67; staff nurse rooming-in nursery Luth. Gen. Hosp., Park Ridge, Ill., 1977-85; staff nurse med.-surg. unit Swedish Covenant Hosp., Chgo., 1989; staff nurse occupational clinic Rush-Presbyn-St. Luke's, Elk Grove Village, Ill., 1988; staff replacement nurse Nursefinders, Arlington Heights, Ill., 1989-90; staff nurse newborn nursery Alexian Bros. Med. Ctr., Elk Grove Village, 1990-91; nurse Kingsley Med. Ctr., Arlington Heights, Ill., 1991-92; Turner Family Practice, Elk Grove Village, Ill., 1993. Home: 675D Versailles Cir Elk Grove Village IL 60007

KANE, KAREN ANN, speech language pathologist; b. Lakewood, Ohio, Apr. 29, 1966; d. John Joseph and Roberta Clare (Quigley) Kelley; m. Christopher Joseph Kane, June 24, 1989; children: Christopher Joseph Jr., Megan Clare. BS, Marquette U., Milw., 1988; MA, Cleve. State U., 1996. Cert. clin. competence speech-lang. pathology. Speech lang. pathologist PSI Affiliates, Twinsburg, Ohio, 1992-94, Lakewood (Ohio) Bd. Edn., 1994-95; Fairview Park (Ohio) Bd. Edn., 1995-96; pvt. practice speech and language pathology, 1996—. Mem. Am. Speech and Hearing Assn., Ohio Speech and Hearing Assn., Nat. Stutterers Assn., Irish Heritage Club. Roman Catholic. Home: 1366 Hall Ave Lakewood OH 44107-2326

KANE, KAREN MARIE, public affairs consultant; b. Colorado Springs, Colo., Mar. 7, 1947; d. Bernard Francis and Adeline Marie (Logan) K. Student, Mills Coll., Oakland, Calif., 1965-66; BA, U. Wash., 1970, MA, 1973, PhC, 1977, postgrad. Pub. affairs cons., housing subcom. Seattle Ret. Tchrs. Assn., 1981-84; pub. affairs cons. 1st U.S. Women's Olympic Marathon Trials, 1982-83, Seattle, 1985—. Contbr. articles to newsletters and mags. Vol. various polit. campaigns, Seattle; bd. dirs. Showboat Theatre Found./Bravo (formerly Showboat Theatre Found.), 1984—; hist. preservation chmn. LWV, Seattle, 1989—; trustee Allied Arts of Seattle, 1987—. past chmn. hist. preservation com., sec. bd. trustees, mem. exec. com., 1987=96; mem. Mayor's Landmark Theatre Adv. Group, 1991-93; mayoral appointee as commr. on Pike Pl. Market Hist. Commn., Seattle, 1992—. Recipient Award of Honor Wash. Trust for Hist. Preservation, 1990, Recognition award Found. for Hist. Preservation and Adaptive Reuse, Seattle, 1991; Am. Found. grantee, 1989, 91. Mem. Am. Assn. Univ. Women, Mills Coll. Alumnae Assn., U. Wash. Alumni Assn., Nat. Trust for Hist. Preservation, Hist. Hawai'i Found., Found. for San Francisco's Archtl. Heritage, Internat. Platform Assn., Wash. Trust for Hist. Preservation. Office: Allied Arts of Seattle 105 S Main St Seattle WA 98104-2535

KANE, LUCILE MARIE, archivist, historian; b. Maiden Rock, Wis., Mar. 17, 1920; d. Emery John and Ruth (Coty) Kane. BS, River Falls State Tchrs. Coll., 1942; MA, U. Minn., 1946. Tchr. Osceola (Wis.) High Sch., 1942-44; asst. publicity dept. U. Minn. Press, Mpls., 1945-46; rsch. fellow, editor Forest Products History Found., St. Paul, 1946-48; curator manuscripts Minn. Hist. Soc., St. Paul, 1948-75; sr. rsch. fellow Minn. Hist. Soc., 1979-85, sr. rsch. assoc. emeritus, 1985—, mem. hon. counc., 1988—; state archivist, 1975-79. Author, compiler: A Guide to the Care and Administration of Manuscripts, 2d edit., 1966, (with Kathryn A. Johnson) Manuscripts Collections of the Minnesota Historical Society, Guide No.2, 1955, The Waterfall That Built a City, 1966 (updated edit. pub. as The Falls of St. Anthony, 1987), Guide to the Public Affairs Collection Minn. Historical Society, (with Alan Ominsky) Twin Cities: A Pictorial History of Saint Paul and Minneapolis, 1983; transl., editor, Military Life in Dakota, The Jour. of Philippe Regis de Trobriand, 1951; editor: (with others) The Northern Expeditions of Major Stephen H. Long, 1978; contbr. articles to profl. jours. Recipient Award of Merit Western History Assn., 1982, Disting. Svc. award Minn. Humanities Commn., 1983, Award of Distinction Am. Assn. State and Local History, 1987. Fellow Soc. Am. Archivists, 1958. Home: 1298 Fairmount Ave Saint Paul MN 55105-2703 Office: 345 Kellogg Blvd W Saint Paul MN 55102-1903

KANE, MARGARET BRASSLER, sculptor; b. East Orange, N.J., May 25, 1909; d. Hans and Mathilde (Trumpler) Brassler; m. Arthur Ferris Kane, June 11, 1930; children: Jay Brassler, Gregory Ferris. Student, Packer Collegiate Inst., 1920-26, Syracuse U., 1927, Art Students League, 1927-29, N.Y. Coll. Music, 1928-29, John Hovannes Studio, 1932-34; PhD (hon.), Colo. State Christian Coll., 1973. head craftsman sculpture, arts and skills unit ARC, Halloran Gen. Hosp., N.Y., 1942-43; jury mem. Bklyn. Mus., 1948, Am. Machine & Foundry Co., 1957; com. mem. An Am. Group, Inc. Work exhibited at Jacques Seligmann Gallery, N.Y., Whitney Ann. Exhbns., all Sculptors Guild Mus. and Outdoor Shows, Nat. Sculpture Soc. Ann. Bas-Relief Exhbn., 1938, Whitney Mus. Sculpture Festival, 1940, Bklyn. Mus. Sculptors Guild, 1938, Bklyn. Soc. Artists, 1942, Lawrence (Mass.) Art Mus., 1938, N.Y. World's Fair, 1939, Sculptors Guild World's Fair Exhbn., 1940, Robinson Gallery, N.Y., 1939, Traveling Mus. and Instns., 1938, Lyman Allyn Mus., 1939, Met. Mus., Internat. Exhbns., 1940, 1949, Roosevelt Field Art Ctr., N.Y.C., 1957, Phila. Mus., N.Y. Archtl. League, Nat. Acad., Penn. Acad., Chgo. Art Inst., Am. Fedn. Arts, Riverside Mus., Montclair Mus., Grand Cen. Art Galleries, Lever House, N.Y.C., 1959-81, Rye (N.Y.) Library, 1962, Lever House Sculptors Guild Ann. Exhbn., 1973-81, N.Y. Bot. Garden, 1981, Sculptors Guild 50th Anniversary Exhbn., Lever House, 1987-90, 1st Bi-Coastal exhibits San Francisco, Collection Donald Trump, 1988, Collection Rene Anselmo, 1991, Shidoni Galleries, Santa Fe, N.Mex., 1989, Am. Sculpture, Hofstra Mus., 1990, Stamford Mus. and Nature Ctr., 1996; permanent collections Zimmerli Art Mus., Rutgers U., N.J., 1992, Nat. Mus. Am. Art, Smithsonian Instn., Washington, 1993, (CD-ROM) Nat. Mus. Am. Art, Smithsonian Instn., Washington, 1995; nat. tour. Am. sculpture by EducArt Projects Inc., 1992; also exhbns. of nat. scope, 1938—; solo sculpture exhbn., Friends Greenwich (Conn.) Library, 1962; executed plaque for Burro Monument, Fairplay, Colo.; exhibited N.Y. Bank for Savs., 1968, Mattatuck Mus., Con., 1967, Lamont Gallery, N.H., 1967, Phila. Art Alliance Exhibition Sculpture of the American Scene, 1987, Am. References (Artists) Chicago, 1989—; executed: 18 foot carving in limewood depicting History of Man; reprodns. in Contemporary Stone Sculpture, 1970, Contemporary American Sculptures, Am. References, Chgo., 1989—; contbr. articles to mags.; feature article in Greenwich (Conn.) Time, 1990, 93. Recipient Anna Hyatt Huntington award, 1942; Am. Artists Profl. League and Montclair Art Assn. Awards, 1943; 1st Henry O. Avery Prize, 1944; Sculpture Prize Bklyn. Soc. Artists, Bklyn. Mus., 1946; John Rogers Award, 1951; Lawrence Hyder Prize, 1952, 54; David H. Zell

Meml. Award, 1954, 63; hon. mention U.S. Maritime Commn., 1941 and; A.C.A. Gallery Competition, 1944; Med. of honor for sculpture Nat. Assn. Women Artists, 1951, Med. of honor for sculpture Nat. Acad. Galleries, N.Y.; prize for carved sculpture, 1955; animal sculpture, 1956; 1st award for sculpture Greenwich Art Soc., 1958, 60; 1st award for sculpture Annual New Eng. Exhbns., Silvermine, Conn. Fellow Internat. Inst. Arts and Letters (life); mem. Nat. Assn. Women Artists (2nd v.p. 1943-44), Nat. League Am. Pen Women, Inc. (OWL award for the Arts 1991), The Pen and Brush (emeritus 1992), Artists Coun. U.S.A., Bklyn. Soc. Artists, Greenwich Soc. Artists (mem. coun.), Internat. Sculpture Ctr., Internat. Soc. Artists (charter), Sculptors Guild, Inc. (lifetime mem., 1993—, sec. to exec. bd. 1942-45, chmn. exhbn. com. 1942, 44), Silvermine Guild Artists, Nat. Trust for Hist. Preservation. Home and Studio: 30 Strickland Rd Cos Cob CT 06807-2729

KANE, MARILYN ELIZABETH, small business owner; b. Butler, Pa., May 7, 1941; d. James and Anna (Supko) Holot; m. Paul D. Kane Sr., May 6, 1961; children: Kristina Marie, Paul D. Jr., Marilyn E. Grad. high sch., Butler, Earl Wheeler Modeling, Pitts., 1960; student, Palmer Talent Agy., N.Y.C., 1983—, UCLA, 1988. Cert. to teach modeling through World Modeling Assn. Exec. dir. Kane Finishing and Modeling Sch., Butler, 1970—; former instr. personal devel. Butler County Community Coll.; exec. dir. Kane Model and Talent Mgmt., Butler, 1970—. Fashion photographer Kane Sch. and Mgmt., 1980—; pageant dir. Miss Butler County USA, Cameo Model USA, Butler, 1977—; pageant judge various local, state, nat. levels competitions, 1970—. Mem. NAFE, World Modeling Assn. (life, Dir. of Yr. award 1978, 79, 85, Jr. Internat. Fashion Model award 1979, 80, 81, 83). Democrat. Byzantine Catholic. Home: 203 Reiber Ave Butler PA 16001-3126 Office: Kane Finishing & Modeling Sch 1022 N Main St Butler PA 16001-1956

KANE, NANCY JO, dancer, choreographer; b. Sayre, Pa., Oct. 22, 1964; d. Albert Henry and Dorothy (Connor) Daw; m. Robert Thomas Kane, June 1, 1991. BFA, U. Colo., 1986; MA, U. London, 1988; PhD, NYU, 1996. Soloist Theatre de la Danse Golovine, Avignon, France, 1987-88; guest artist, instr. Sch. Dance Arts, Elmira, Corning, N.Y., 1988-89; dance specialist Elmira City Sch. Dist., 1989-91; tchg. fellow NYU, 1991-94; grants mgr. Dance Theater Workshop, N.Y.C., 1994-95; co. adminstr. Creach/Koester Dance, N.Y.C., 1995-96; choreographer, dancer SAI Dance, N.Y.C., 1995-96. Mem. AAHPERD, Nat. Dance Assn. (com. on aging and adult devel. 1985-96, higher edn. com. 1992-95), Soc. Dance History Scholars, Congress on Rsch. in Dance, Phi Beta Kappa. Democrat. Office: Catawba Coll Shuford Sch Performing Arts Salisbury NC 28144-2488

KANE, NANCY JUNE, psychotherapist; b. Milw., Aug. 6, 1953; d. Elbert Edwin and Gloria (Bixby) Allison; m. Raymond Allen Kane, Aug. 6, 1977; children: Eric, Krista. BS, U. Wis., 1975; MS in Counselor Edn., No. Ill. U., 1980; postgrad., Gestalt Inst., Chgo., 1981. Assoc. dean of students Trinity Coll., Deerfield, Ill., 1980-82; psychotherapist, pvt. practice Grace Family Counseling, Northbrook, Ill., 1982—; asst. prof. Moody Bible Inst., Chgo., 1992—; conf. and workshop speaker, various women's groups and churches in Chicago suburbs, 1984—. Cmty. outreach chair PTA, Arlington Heights, Ill., 1993. Named to Outstanding Young Women of Am., 1987. Mem. Am. Counseling Assn., Ill. Mental Health Counselors Assn., Ill. Counseling Assn. Office: Grace Family Counseling 1501 Shermer Rd Northbrook IL 60062-5313

KANE, PATRICIA LANEGRAN, language professional, educator; b. St. Paul, June 23, 1926; d. Walter B. and Lita E. (Wilson) Lanegran; m. Donald Patrick Kane, Apr. 1, 1947; children: Laura Kane Gustafson, Maura L. B.A. cum laude, Macalester Coll., St. Paul, 1947; M.A., U. Minn., 1950, Ph.D., 1961. Mem. faculty Macalester Coll., 1950-91, prof. English, 1971-91, DeWitt Wallace prof., 1978-91, prof. emeritus, 1992—, chmn. dept., 1977-86, faculty assoc., office of v.p. acad. affairs, 1979-83; mem. Minn. planning com. nat. identification project advancement women in acad. adminstrn. Nat. Council Edn., 1979-81. Co-author: A St. Paul Omnibus, 1979; Contbr. articles to profl. jours. Recipient Jefferson prize for teaching excellence, 1980, Disting. Alumni citation Macalester Coll., 1992; Danforth grantee, 1957-58. Mem. MLA, Soc. Study So. Lit.

KANE, RUTH ANNE, principal; b. Beaumont, Tex., Jan. 20, 1948; d. Lewis Barclay "Red" III and Lois Virginia (Metzke) Herring; m. Gabriel Christopher Kane, Apr. 27, 1974 (div. Sept. 24, 1980); children: David Kane, Elijah Kane. BS, U. Tex. at Austin, 1981; MEd, 1982, PhD, 1991. Cert. secondary English, Spanish, spl. edn., adminstrn. Tchr. Adventure Bound Sch., Charlottesville, Va., 1978-79, Austin State Sch., Tex., 1979-80, Clear Lake H.S., Houston, 1982-84, McCallum H.S., Austin, Tex., 1984-88; adminstrv. intern Fulmore Middle Sch., Austin, Tex., 1988; tchr. Travis H.S., Austin, Tex., 1988-89; asst. prin. Martin Jr. H.S., Austin, Tex., 1989-90, Reagan H.S., Austin, Tex., 1990-93; prin. Lanier H.S., Austin, Tex., 1993—; cons. Ednl. Svc. Ctr. Region XIII, Austin, Tex., 1989—; instr. ExCet Reviews, Austin, 1991—; test adminstr. Nat. Evaluation Sys., Mass., 1991-93. Co-author: Futurism in Education, 1988, Special Education ExCet Review Guide, 1993. Vol. AIDS Svcs. of Austin, Tex., 1993-94; mem. City of Austin Joint Truancy Task Force, Austin, 1993—, Leadership Austin, Tex., 1994-95. Recipient Career Advancement scholarship Bus. and Profl. Woman's Assn., 1980, Am. Bus. Women's Assn. scholarship Austin-Lake Travis chpt., Austin, Tex., 1980, 81, Jesse H. Jones scholarship Kappa Delta Pi Internat., 1990, Univ. fellowship U. Tex. at Austin, 1981. Mem. ASCD, Austin Assn. Secondary Sch. Adminstrn., Nat. Assn. Secondary Sch. Prin/. Tex/ Assn. Secondary Sch. Prin., Phi Delta Kappa, Delta Kappa Gamma. Home: 2704 Thrushwood Dr Austin TX 78757-6947 Office: Lanier H S 1201 Payton Gin Rd Austin TX 78758-6616

KANE, STEPHANIE C., social anthropologist, educator; b. N.Y.C., Jan. 24, 1951; d. Bernard David and Gerry (Sirota) K. BA in Biology, Cornell U., 1972; MA in Zoology, U. Tex., 1981, PhD in Social Anthropology, 1986. Tchg. asst. Biology and Physiology Labs, Dept. Zoology, U. Tex., Austin, 1981, Dept. Anthropology, U. Tex., Austin, 1985-86; resident faculty Sch. for Field Studies, Virgin Islands, 1987; adj. asst. prof. Dept. Anthropology, Ind. U., 1992—; asst. prof. Dept. Criminal Justice, Ind. U., 1992—. Author: The Phantom Gringo Boat, 1994; contbr. to profl. papers and jours. Recipient rsch. grant Inst. Latin Am. Studies U. Tex., Austin, 1979-80, 84-85, Fulbright rsch. grant Coun. for Internat. Exch. of Scholars, 1989-90, rsch. grant Rural Ctr. for Study and Promotion of HIV/STD Prevention, Ind., 1995, rsch. grant Wenner-Gren Found. for Anthropol. Rsch., 1995-96; scholarship U. Tex., Austin, 1979-83; Lang. and Area Studies fellowship Inst. Latin Am. Studies, U. Tex., Austin, 1982-83, Tng. fellowship Orgn. Am. States, 1984-85, Rockefeller Humanities fellowship rsch. grant SUNY, Buffalo, 1991-92, Coll. Arts and Scis. Summer Faculty fellowship Ind. U., Bloomington, 1994. Mem. NOW, AAUW, Am. Anthropol. Assn. (mem. task force on AIDS, 1991-93), Am. Soc. Criminology, Acad. Criminal Justice Scis., Law and Soc. Assn., Am. Jail Assn., Midwestern Criminal Justice Assn., Amnesty Internat. Office: U Ind Dept Criminal Justice 302 Sycamore Hall Bloomington IN 47405

KANE, YVETTE, state official, lawyer; b. Donaldsonville, La., Oct. 11, 1953; d. Thomas R. Pregeant and Julia Tucker; m. Michael Kane; children: Kathleen, Madeline. BA, Nicholls State U., Thibodeaux, La., 1973; JD, Tulane U., 1976. Bar: Pa. Dep. atty. gen. rev. and advice sect. Pa. Office Atty. Gen., 1986-91; chief counsel Pa. Ind. Regulatory Rev. Commn., 1991-92; sr. assoc. Wolf, Block, Schorr & Solis-Cohen, Harrisburg, Pa., 1993-95; sec. state Commonwealth of Pa., 1995—. Mem. Parents Anonymous of Ctrl. Pa. Office: Office Sec of State North Office Bldg Rm 302 Harrisburg PA 17120*

KANEKO-ADAMS, NAOKO, business executive; b. Kobe, Hyogo, Japan, Aug. 2, 1943; d. Mikiya and Kazuko Kaneko; m. Albert Adams, Nov. 28, 1976. Cert. in ESL, St. Michael's Sch., Cambridge, Eng., 1962; AA, Lehigh County C.C., Schnecksville, Pa., 1980; BS, Cedar Crest Coll., 1985. Coord. Blue Cross and Blue Shield, Balt., 1977-78, Air Products and Chems., Allentown, Pa., 1980-86; adminstr. Odani Rsch. Co., Inc., Larchmont, N.Y., 1986-87; sr. rsch. analyst, rsch. mgr. Sunstar Inc., N.Y.C., 1987—; info. broker Kaneko-Adams Joho Ctr., Mamaroneck, N.Y., 1995—. Interpreter area TV program, Toronto, Ont., Can., 1975. Mem. Am. Mktg. Assn., Soc. Competitor Intelligence Profls., Cosmetic Exec. Women. Home: 490 Bleeker Ave Mamaroneck NY 10543 Office: Kaneko-Adams 490 Bleeker Ave Mamaroneck NY 10543

KANE-VANNI, PATRICIA RUTH, lawyer, consultant; b. Phila., Jan. 12, 1954; d. Joseph James and Ruth Marina (Rameriz) Kane; m. Francis William Vanni, Feb. 14, 1980; 1 child, Christian Michael. AB, Chestnut Hill Coll., 1975; JD, Temple U., 1985. Bar: Pa. 1985, U.S. Ct. Appeals (3d cir.) 1988. Freelance art illustrator Phila., 1972-80; secondary edn. instr. Archdiocese of Phila., 1980-83; contract analyst CIGNA Corp., Phila., 1983-84; jud. aide Phila. Ct. of Common Pleas, 1984; assoc. atty. Anderson and Dougherty, Wayne, Pa., 1985-86; atty. cons. Bell Telephone Co. of Pa., 1986-87; sr. assoc. corp. counsel Independence Blue Cross, Phila., 1987-96; cons. Coll. Consortium on Drug and Alcohol Abuse, Chester, Pa., 1986-89; speaker in field. Contbr. articles and illustrations to profl. mags. Judge Del. Valley Sci. Fairs, Phila., 1986, 87; Dem. committeewomen, Lower Merion, Pa., 1983-87; ch. cantor, soloist, mem. choir Roman Cath. Ch.; mem. Phila. Assn. Ch. Musicians, also bd. dirs. Recipient Legion of Honor award Chapel of the Four Chaplins, 1983. Mem. ABA, Pa. Bar Assn., Phila. Bar Assn. (Theatre Wing), Phila. Assn. Def. Counsel, Phila. Vol. Lawyers for Arts (bd. dirs.), Nat. Health Lawyers Assn. (spkr. 1994 annual conv.), Hispanic Bar Assn. Democrat. Home: 119 Bryn Mawr Ave Bala Cynwyd PA 19004-3012

KANG, BANN C., immunologist; b. Kyungnam, Korea, Mar. 4, 1939; d. Daeryong and Buni (Chung) K.; came to U.S., 1964, naturalized, 1976; A.B., Kyungpook Nat. U., 1959, M.D., 1963; m. U. Yun Ryo, Mar. 30, 1963. Intern, L.I. Jewish Hosp.-Queens Hosp. Center, Jamaica, N.Y., 1964-65, resident in medicine, 1965-67; teaching assoc. Kyungpook U. Hosp., Taegu, Korea, 1967-70; fellow in allergy and chest Creighton U., Omaha, 1970-71; fellow in allergy Henry Ford Hosp., Detroit, 1971-72; clin. instr. medicine U. Mich. Hosp., Ann Arbor, 1972-73; asst. prof. Chgo. Med. Sch., 1973-74; chief allergy-immunology Mt. Sinai Hosp., Chgo., 1975—; asst. prof. Rush Med. Sch., Chgo. 1975-84, assoc. prof., 1984-86; assoc. prof. U. Ky. Coll. Medicine, 1987-92, prof., 1992—; cons., 1976—, Nat. Heart, Lung, Blood Inst., 1979—; mem. Exptl. Transplantation Adv. Bd., Ill., 1985-86, Diagnostic and Therapeutic Tech. Assessment (AMA), 1987—, Gen. Clin. Rsch. Com. (NIH), 1989-93; adv. com. Ctr. for Biologics and Rsch., FDA, 1993-96; counselor Chgo. Med. Soc., 1984-86, mem. policy com., adv. com. to health dept. Chgo. and Cook County, 1984-86. Recipient NIH award U. Mich., 1972-73. Diplomate Am. Bd. Internal Medicine, Am. Bd. Allergy-Immunology. Fellow ACP, Am. Acad. Allergy; mem. Am. Fedn. Clin. Research, AMA, Inter-Asthma Assn. Contbr. over 50 articles to profl. jours. Home: 2716 Martinique Ln Lexington KY 40509-9509 Office: U Ky Coll Medicine K528 Albert B Chandler Med Ctr 800 Rose St Lexington KY 40536

KANG, JULIANA HAENG-CHA, anesthesiologist; b. Mokpo, Cheonnam, People's Republic of Korea, July 1, 1941; came to U.S., 1965; d. Johan and E-E-Suk (Lee) Kang; m. Chang-Song Choi; children: Mee-Kyung, Mee-Ae, Han-Bae. MD, Yonsei U., Seoul, People's Republic of Korea, 1965. Diplomate Am. Bd. Anesthesiology. Intern Pittsfield (Mass.) Gen. Hosp., 1965-66; asst. prof. biology Yonsei U., 1965; resident in anesthesiology D.C. Gen. Hosp., 1966-67, Yale-New Haven (Conn.) Hosp., 1967-69; asst. prof. anesthesiology U. Conn., Farmington, 1970-75, 82-85; vice chairperson anesthesia dept. Conn. Surgery Ctr., Hartford, Conn., 1985-86; med. dir., chairperson anesthesia dept. Conn. Surgery Ctr., Hartford, 1986—. Fellow Am. Coll. Anesthesiologists; mem. Am. Med. Women's Assn., Am. Soc. Ambulatory Surgery Anesthesia, Am. Soc. Anesthesiologists, Conn. Soc. Anesthesiology, Nat. Abortion Rights Action League, Naral Polit. Arm of Pro-Choice. Office: Conn Surgery Ctr 81 Gillett St Hartford CT 06105-2630

KANICK, VIRGINIA, radiologist; b. Coaldale, Pa., Nov. 10, 1925; d. Martin and Anna (Pisklak) K. BA, Barnard Coll., 1947; MD, Columbia U., 1951. Diplomate Am. Bd. Radiology. Intern Western Reserve U. Hosps., Cleve., 1951-52; resident in radiology St. Luke's Hosp., N.Y.C., 1952-55, attending radiologist, 1955-74; acting dir. radiology St. Luke's Roosevelt Hosp., N.Y.C., 1981-84, dep. dir. of radiology, 1984-89; ptnr. West Side Radiology, N.Y.C., 1989—; clin. prof. radiology Coll. Physicians and Surgeons Columbia U., N.Y.C., 1975—; pres. Med. Bd. St. Luke's Roosevelt Hosp., 1980-82. Contbr. articles to profl. jours. Bd. dirs. Health System Agy. of N.Y.C., 1978-81. Fellow Am. Cancer Soc., 1955. Fellow Am. Coll. Radiology; mem. Am. Roentgen Ray Soc., Radiol. Soc. N.Am., N.Y. County Med. Soc. (sec., dir. 1978—), N.Y. State Radiol. Soc. (bd. dirs. 1975—). Republican. Roman Catholic. Home: 560 Riverside Dr Apt 17B New York NY 10027-3215 Office: West Side Radiology 1090 Amsterdam Ave New York NY 10025-8107

KANIN, FAY, screenwriter; b. N.Y.C.; d. David and Bessie Mitchell; m. Michael Kanin (dec.); children: Joel (dec.), Josh. Student, Elmira Coll., L.H.D. (hon.), 1981; B.A., U. So. Calif. mem. western regional exec. bd., judge Am. Coll. Theatre Festival, 1975-76; appointed v.p. Marstar Prodns., L.A. Writer: (with Michael Kanin) screenplays including The Opposite Sex, Teacher's Pet; Broadway plays including His and Hers, Rashomon, Grind (Tony nomination 1985); writer, co-producer TV spls. including Friendly Fire, ABC-TV (Emmy award for best TV film, San Francisco Film Festival award, Peabody award), Hustling (Writers Guild award for best original drama), Tell Me Where It Hurts (Emmy award, Christopher award); Heartsounds (Peabody award). Mem. Writers Guild Am. West (pres. screen br. 1971-73, Val Davies award 1975), Am. Film Inst. (trustee), Acad. Motion Picture Arts and Sci. Found. (past pres., v.p.), Nat. Ctr. Film and Video Preservation (co-chmn.).

KANNADY, GRACE BELLE, education coordinator, instructor; b. Kansas City, Mo., May 1, 1951; d. Roscoe Jewel and Margaret Grace (Welter) Sebring; m. Howard Dale Kannady, May 28, 1971; 1 child, Joseph Dale Kannady. BS in Psychology, Ctrl. Mo. State U., 1973, MS in Clin. Psychology, 1977; EdS in Counseling, U. Mo., Kansas City, 1987; PhD in Adult & Continuing Edn., Kans. State U., 1992. Diplomate in logotherapy; registered master level psychologist, Kans. Therapist Cmty. Mental Health Ctr., South Lee's Summit, Mo., 1977-78, Marillac Ctr. for Children, Kansas City, Mo., 1979-80; contract counselor Cath. Social Svcs., Kansas City, Kans., 1989; adj. instr. Avila Coll., Johnson County C.C., St. Mary Coll., 1980-90; grad. teaching asst., adult and continuing edn. Kansas State U., Manhattan, 1990-92; adj. faculty, grad. counseling program Webster U., Kansas City, Mo., 1993—; instr., edn. coord. Kansas City (Kans.) C.C., 1993—; dir. edn. MidAm. Inst. Logotherapy, Kansas City, Mo., 1992-93; trainer, stress reduction in police families, Kansas City (Mo.) Police Dept., Avila Coll., 1989-90; cons. Learning Exch. Resource Network, Manhattan, Kans., 1995—. Contbr. articles to profl. jours.; also pub. in poetry jours. Vol. Johnson County Coalition for the Prevention of Child Abuse., Mission, Kans., 1980-86 (Disting. Vol. Svc. award, 1986). Recipient Cert. of Award for Outstanding Achievment and Accomplishment in Logotherapy Viktor Frankl Inst. Logotherapy, Kansas City, Mo., 1989. Mem. Am. Assn. Adult and Continuing Edn., MidAm. Inst. Logotherapy, Phi Kappa Phi, Phi Delta Kappa. Office: Kansas City Kansas C C 7250 State Ave Kansas City KS 66112-2816

KANNE, ELIZABETH ANN ARNOLD, secondary school educator; b. Atlanta, Sept. 16, 1945; d. Robert Earl and Elizabeth Ann (Jetton) A.; m. Robert Edward Lee, Jr., Aug. 20, 1967 (div. Oct. 1977); children: Robert Edward III, Edward Andrew; m. William Rudolph Kanne, Jr., June 4, 1979; 1 child, William Edward. BA, Furman U., 1967; MA, U. S.C., 1978. Cert. elem., early childhood, mid. sch. tchr., S.C. 1st grade tchr. Aiken (S.C.) County Schs., 1967-70, 4th and 5th grade tchr., 1978-90, guidance counselor, 1990-92, 6th grade math. tchr., 1992—; mem. S.C. Curriculum Congess, Columbia, 1991—, Dist. Screening Team, Aiken, 1991—, Sch. Improvement Coun., Aiken, 1992—. S.C. Ednl. Improvement Act grantee State Dept. Edn., 1991-92, 93-94. Mem. NEA, S.C. Edn. Assn., S.C. Mid. Sch. Assn., Aiken County Edn. Assn. Office: Schofield Mid Sch 220 Sumter St NE Aiken SC 29801-4471

KANNENSTINE, MARGARET LAMPE, artist; b. St. Louis, Apr. 1, 1938; d. John Avery and Elizabeth (Phillips) Lampe; m. Louis Fabian Kannenstine, Oct. 3, 1959; children: David Edward, Emily Ann. BFA, Washington U. St. Louis, 1959. bd. trustees Pentangle Coun. Arts, 1982-88, 93-96, chair, 1984-87, 94, 95; bd. trustees Vt. Studio Ctr., 1989-94, chair, 1990, 91, 92, 93, tchr. Fleming Mus., Burlington, 1991, Kimball Union Acad. Enfield, N.H., 1993; bd. trustees Vt. Coun. Arts, 1994—, chair, 1994-96. One-woman shows include Vt. Artisans, Strafford, 1976, Gallery Two, Woodstock, Vt., 1974, 77, 85, Red Mill Gallery, Johnson, Vt., 1990, Green Mountain Power Corp., South Burlington, Vt., 1991, Vt. Coun. on Arts, Montpelier, Vt., 1991, Woodstock Gallery Art, 1991, 94, Beside Myself Gallery, Arlington, Vt., 1992, Taylor Gallery, Meriden, N.H., 1993, Dartmouth Coll., Hanover, N.H., 1993, Kent (Conn.) Sch., 1993, Chittenden Bank, Burlington, 1994, Windy Bush Gallery, New Hope, Pa., 1995, N.H. Coll., Manchester, 1996, The Flynn Theater Gallery, Burlington, 1996, Nat. Wildlife Fedn. Gallery, Vienna, Va., 1996; group shows include Gallery Two, 1973-88, Carl Battaglia Gallery, N.Y.C., 1979-80, The Gallery, Williamstown, Mass., 1981-84, Vt. Coun. Arts, 1988, AVA Gallery, Hanover, 1989, 90, Woodstock Gallery Art, 1989, Beside Myself Gallery, 1990, Fleming Mus., U. Vt., Burlington, 1991, Arts Festival for AIDS, Bennington Coll., 1992, Windy Bush Gallery, 1994, VCA, Woodstock, 1994, Riverfest, White River Junction, Vt., 1995, Firehouse Gallery, Burlington, 1995, McGowan Fine Art, Concord, N.H., 1995; represented in permanent collections at The Hood Mus., Hanover, Robert Hull Fleming Mus., Burlington, Vt. Employees Credit Union, Montpelier, Union Mut. Ins. Co., Montpelier, Vt. Law Sch., South Royalton, others. Trustee New Eng. Found. for the Arts, 1996—. Washington U. scholar, 1955. Mem. Nat. Women's Caucus Art, Cosmopolitan Club.

KANSAS, HELENE VIVIAN, retired secondary education educator; b. N.Y.C., Mar. 25, 1926; d. Louis and Birdie (Kleinberg) Felner; m. Robert Kansas, May 28, 1949; children: Susan, Geoffrey, Tina. BA, CUNY, 1947; postgrad., Columbia U., 1979. Tchr. fgn. langs. N.Y.C. Bd. Edn., 1947-49, Brevard County (Fla.) Bd. Edn., 1968-88; ret., 1988; project dir. Fla. Latin Forum, 1975-85. Mem. Dem. Exec. Com. Brevard County, Satellite Beach, Fla., 1965—, treas., 1992—; chmn. Charter Commn., Satellite Beach City Coun., 1985-86. White Rose honoree March of Dimes, 1995. Mem. Classical Assn. Fla. (exec. sec. 1993—), Fla. Fgn. Lang. Assn. (Latin Tchr. of Yr. award 1986), Classical Assn. Midwest and South, ACLU, Sierra Club, Environ. Def. Fund. Home: 725 Robin Way S Satellite Beach FL 32937

KANT, GLORIA JEAN, neuroscientist, researcher; b. Chgo., June 6, 1944; d. Hans Georg and Jo Sefa (Pick) K.; m. Philip Herbert Balcom, July 1, 1967 (div. 1976). BS in Chemistry, Mich. State U., 1965; PhD in Physiol. Chemistry, U. Wis., 1969. Chemist dept. psychiatry Walter Reed Army Inst. Rsch., Washington, 1970-71, neurochemist dept. microwave rsch., 1971-77, neurochemist dept. med. neuroscis., 1977-87, chief dept. med. neuroscis., 1987-95, dir. divsn. neuroscis., 1995—. Mem. editl. bd. Pharmacology, Biochemistry and Behavior, 1991—; contbr. over 80 articles to sci. jours. Mem. AAAS, Soc. for Neurosci., Internat. Behavioral Neurosci. Soc., Women in Neurosci., Pavlovian Soc. Home: 1124 Dennis Ave Silver Spring MD 20901-2171 Office: Walter Reed Army Inst Rsch Divsn Neurosciences Washington DC 20307

KANTER, ROSABETH MOSS, management educator, consultant, writer; b. Cleve., Mar. 15, 1943; d. Nelson Nathan and Helen (Smolen) Moss; m. Stuart Alan Kanter, June 20, 1963 (dec. Mar. 1969); m. Barry Alan Stein, July 2, 1972; 1 child, Matthew Moss Kanter Stein. BA in Sociology magna cum laude, Bryn Mawr Coll., 1964; MA, U. Mich., 1965, PhD, 1967; postgrad., Harvard U. Law Sh., 1975-76; MA (hon.), Yale U., 1978, Harvard U., 1986; DSc (hon.), Bucknell U., 1980, Babson Coll., 1984, Bryant Coll., 1986, Bentley Coll., 1990, U. Mass., Boston, 1996; LHD (hon.), Antioch U., Westminster Coll., 1984, Suffolk U., N. Adams State Coll., 1987, Colby-Sawyer Coll., 1988, U. New Haven, 1989; DCL (hon.), Union Coll., 1987; LLD (hon.), Regis Coll., 1987; DSS (hon.), Fla. Internat. U., 1990; DHL (hon.), SUNY Inst. Tech., 1991, Dowling Coll., 1991, Claremont Coll., 1992, Monmouth Coll., 1994. Vis. prof. mgmt. Harvard U., 1973-74, MIT, 1979-80; from assoc. to asst. prof. Brandeis U., 1967-77; prof. Yale U., 1977-86; Class of 1960 prof. mgmt. Harvard U. Bus. Sch., 1986—; chmn. bd. Goodmeasure, Inc., 1977—; trustee Coll. Retirement Equities Fund, N.Y., 1985-89, Am. Leadership Forum, Houston, 1982-86; mem. work group on entrepreneurship Pres.'s Commn. Indsl. Competitiveness, 1984; Govs.'s innovation adv. com. Commonwealth of Mass. chair subcom., 1986; mem. Spl. Commn. on Employee Involvement and Ownership, Mass., 1986-87; mem. Gov.'s Commn. Rev. Anti-Takeover Laws, Mass. 1988; mem. Gov.'s Counc. Econ. Growth, Mass., 1994—, co-chair internat. trade task force, 1995—; Katz-Newcomb lectr. in social psychology U. Mich., 1986; Disting. speaker Orgn., Theory, Careers and Women in Mgmt. divs. Nat. Acad. Mgmt., 1987, Eastern Acad. Mgmt., 1993; Centenniel lectr. APA, 1992; Lilly Found. Disting. lectr. Nat. Assn. Community Leadership Orgns., 1985; Leavey Disting. lectr. U. Santa Clara, 1984; vis. scholar Newberry Libr. Program in Humanities, Chgo., 1973, Norwegian Rsch. Coun. on Sci., and Humanities, Oslo, 1980; Kellogg Found. 50th Anniv. lectr. Am. Assn. Higher Edn., 1979, Blazer lectr. U. Ky., 1974, Davidson lectr. U. N.H., 1975; Sigma Chi scholar-in-residence Miami U., Oxford, Ohio, 1978; bd. dirs. Am. Productivity and Quality Ctr., Houston. Author: Work and Family in the U.S., 1977, Men and Women of the Corporation, 1977 (C. Wright Mills award 1977), 93, The Change Masters, 1983, (with M.S. Dukakis) Creating The Future: The Massachussetts Comeback and Its Promise for America, 1988, When Giants Learn to Dance, 1989 (Johnson Smith Knisely Exec. Leadership award 1990), (with B.A. Stein and T.F. Jick) The Challenge of Organizational Change: How Companies Experience It and Leaders Guide It, 1992, World Class: Thriving Locally in the Global Economy, 1995; 5 other books, also monographs; mem. editorial bd. Human Resource Mgmt. jour., 1982-89, Orgn. Dynamics jour., 1983-85, 89, Jour. Bus. Venturing, 1985-89, Jour. Contemporary Bus., 2987-89, others; adv. bd. Society jour., 1987-89; editor Harvard Bus. Rev., 1989-92; contbr. over 150 articles to profl. jours., books, mags. (articles Harvard Bus. Rev. McKinsey award). Bd. dirs. Alliance for the Commonwealth, 1995—, City Yr., 1995—, NOW Legal Def. and Edn. Fund, N.Y.C., 1979-86, 93-95, Ctr. New Democracy, Washington, 1985-88, Am. Prodn. and Quality Ctr., Houston, 1989—, Econ. Policy Inst., 1994—; incorporator Babson Coll., 1984-87, Boston Children's Mus., 1984—, Mt. Auburn Hosp., 1991—; bd. overseers Malcolm Baldridge Nat. Quality Award U.S. Dept. Commerce, 1994—. Guggenheim fellow; numerous rsch. grants; named Woman of Yr. New Eng. Women's Bus. Owners, 1981, Internat. Assn. Personnel Women, 1981, MS Mag., 1985; named to Cleve. Heights H.S. Hall of Fame, 1986, Working Woman Hall of Fame AT&T/Working Women Mag., 1986, Ohio Women's Hall of Fame, 1990; recipient Athena award Intercollegiate Assn. Women Students, 1980, Gold medal award Big Sister Assn. Greater Boston, 1985, Women Who Make a Difference award Internat. Women's Forum, 1988, Richard M. Cyert award Profl. Excellence Carnegie-Mellon U. Grad. Sch. Indsl. Adminstrn., 1989 Project Equality award, 1990, Crohn's and Colitis Found. award, 1993, 1994, McFeely award YMCA, 1995, Leadership award New Eng. Coun., 1995. Fellow Acad. Mgmt. (Disting. speaker mgmt. cons. divsn. 1985, women in mgmt. divsn. 1987, orgn. mgmt. theory divsn. 1994, Disting. Scholar award OMT divsn. 1994), Am. Soc. Quality & Participation, World Productivity Cong. (Ams. divsn.), World Econ. Forum; mem. Am. Sociol. Assn. (exec. coun. 1982-85), Eastern Sociol. Soc. (exec. com. 1975-78, Gellman award 1978), Soc. for Advancement of Socio-Econs., Com. of 200 (founder), Internat. Women's Forum, Coun. on Fgn. Rels. Office: Harvard U Grad Sch Bus Adminstrn Soldiers Field Boston MA 02163

KANTER, STACY J., lawyer; b. N.Y.C., 1958. BS magna cum laude, SUNY, Albany, 1979; JD, Bklyn. Law Sch., 1985. Bar: N.Y. 1985. Ptnr. Skadden, Arps, Slate, Meagher & Flom, N.Y.C. Mng. editor Bklyn. Law Rev., 1983-84. Office: Skadden Arps Slate Meagher & Flom 919 3rd Ave New York NY 10022*

KANTROWITZ, SUSAN LEE, lawyer; b. Queens, N.Y., Jan. 15, 1955; d. Theodore and Dinah (Kotick) Kantrowitz; m. Mark R. Halperin; 1 child, Jacob Josef Kantrowitz-Sirotkin. BS summa cum laude, Boston U., 1977; JD, Boston Coll., 1980. Bar: Mass. 1982. Assoc. producer Sta. KOCE-TV, Huntington Beach, Calif., 1980-81; account exec. Bozell & Jacobs, Newport Beach, Calif., 1981; atty. WGBH Ednl. Found., Boston, 1981-84, dir. legal affairs, 1984-86, gen. counsel, dir. legal affairs, 1986—; v.p., gen. counsel, 1993. Co-Author: Legal and Business Aspects of the Entertainment, Publishing and Sports Industries, 1984. Mem. ABA, Mass. Bar Assn., Boston Bar Assn.

KANY, JUDY C(ASPERSON), health policy analyst, former state senator; b. June 29, 1937; d. Helmer C. and Florence P. Casperson; m. Robert Kany,

Aug. 16, 1958; children: Kristin, Geoffrey, Daniel. BBA, U. Mich., 1959; MPA, U. Maine-Orono, 1976. Mem. Maine Ho. Reps., 1975-82, Maine Senate, 1982-92; project dir. for health professions regulation Med. Care Devel., Augusta, Maine, 1993—; mem. Pew Health Professions Commn. task force on health workforce regulation, 1994—; chmn. Maine's Adv. Commn. on Radioactive Waste, 1981-87, Joint Standing Com. Legal Affairs, 1987-88, Joint Standing Com. on State Govt., 1979-82, Joint Standing Com. Energy and Natural Resources, 1983-84, 89-90, Joint Standing Com. Banking and Ins., 1991-92, com. Maine Lakes, 1990-92, adv. com. on accountability to the Maine Health Care Reform Commn., 1994-95; mem. Commn. on Maine's Future, 1976, 87-89; mayor Waterville, Maine, 1988-89; mem. issues and policy adv. com. Citizens Advocacy Ctr., Washington, 1994—. Democrat. Home: PO Box 508 Belgrade Lakes ME 04918-0508 Office: Med Care Devel 11 Parkwood Dr Augusta ME 04330-6252

KANYUK, JOYCE STERN, secondary art educator; b. Irvington, N.J., June 29, 1951; d. Paul Stern and Jean Hannah (Oberdofer) Dubin; m. Peter Kanyuk, June 10, 1973; 1 child, Paul. BFA in Art Edn., Syracuse (N.Y.) U., 1973; MA, Coll. of New Rochelle, 1977. Art tchr. Felix Festa Jr. H.S., West Nyack, 1973—. Exhibited in group shows at Orangeburg Town Hall, 1991, Nanuet Libr., 1992, 93, 94, 95, Suffern Libr., 1992, 93, Allendale Borough Hall, 1992, N.E. Watercolor Soc., 1991, 94, Audubon Artists Ann. Exhbn., 1994-96, Cmty. Arts Assn. Tri-State Open Juried Show, 1990, 91, 92, 96, South Nyack Fine Arts Festival, 1989-95, Ringwood Manor Assn. of the Arts Open Juried Show, 1990, 92, 1992 Morris County ARt Assn. Tri-State Juried Exhbn., Mari Galleries Nat. Fine Arts Exhbn., 1992, 93, 94, Exhibit of Mixed Media, Nabisco Gallery, 1993. Recipient Best of Show award Milburn-Short Hills Art Fair, 1994, Second Pl. award Mari Galleries, 1994, Honorable Mention Morris Count Art Assn., 1992, South Shore Watercolor Artists award East Islip Arts Coun., 1994, 95. Mem. Arts Coun. of Rockland, Cmty. Arts Assn. (membership chmn.), Ringwood Manor Art Assn., Audubon Artists, North East Watercolor Soc., N.Y. State Art Tchrs. Assn. Home: 29 John St New City NY 10956 Office: Felix Festa Jr High Sch 30 Parrott Rd West Nyack NY 10994

KANZLER, KATHLEEN PATRICIA, kennel owner; b. Detroit, Apr. 13, 1934; d. Vincent William and Helen Elizabeth (Murtagh) McGivney; m. Norbert Alvin Kanzler, Dec. 21, 1954; children: Patricia, John, Sheila. Assocs. in Animal Scis., Mich. State U., 1954. Owner Innisfree Kennel, Chateaugay, N.Y., 1948—; instr. Ecology Ferguson Found., Accokeek, Md., 1974-80; judge Am. Kennel Club, 1970—; chairperson Morris Animal Found., Englewood, Colo., 1986—; cons. for episode on arctic dogs (T.V. show) Northern Exposure, (mag. article) Nat. Geographic, 1986; hon. judge Japan Kennel Club, 1990—; internat. lectr. and judge on kennel mgmt. Author (mag. column) AKC Gazette, 1992—, (book chpt.) The Complete Siberian Husky, 1978, Medical & Genetic Aspects of Purebred Dogs; contbr. articles to jours. in field. Docent Nat. Zoo, 1970-73. Recipient Best in Show award Westminster Kennel Club, 1989, Asian Internat. Dog Show, 1996, Number One Siberian Husky Show Dog, 1992, 93, Best in Show award Asian Internat. Dog Show, 1996; named Breeder of Yr., Mexican Kennel Club, 1984. Mem. Siberian Husky Club (v.p. 1961—, Top Breeder award 1985, 88, 91, 92, 93, 94). Home and Office: Innisfree 94 Ryan Rd Chateaugay NY 12920

KAO, YASUKO WATANABE, retired library administrator; b. Tokyo, Mar. 30, 1930; came to U.S., 1957; d. Kichiji and Sato (Tanaka) Watanabe; m. Shih-Kung Kao, Apr. 1, 1959; children: John Sterling, Stephanie Margaret. B.A., Tsuda Coll., 1950; B.A. in Lit., Waseda U., 1955; M.S.L.S., U. So. Calif., 1960. Instr., Takinogawa High Sch., Tokyo, 1950-57; catalog librarian U. Utah Library, 1960-67, Marriott Library, 1975-77, head catalog div., 1978-90; dir. libr. Teikyo Loretto Heights U., 1991-95. Contbr. articles to profl. jours. Vol., Utah Chinese Am. Community Sch., 1974-80, Asian Assn. Utah, 1981-90. Waseda U. fellow, 1958-59. Mem. ALA, Asian Pacific Librs. Assn., Assn. Coll. and Research Libraries, ALA Library and Info. Tech. Assn., Colo. Library Assn., Utah Coll. Libr. Coun., Beta Phi Mu. Home: 2625 Yuba Ave El Cerrito CA 94530

KAPITAN, MARY L., retired nursing administrator, educator; b. Lawrence, Mass., July 9, 1920; d. Vincent and Concetta (Tomaselli) Zazzo; m. John A. Kapitan, Sept. 6, 1947. Diploma, Somerville (Mass.) Hosp., 1944; BS in Nursing Edn., DePaul U., Chgo., 1960, MS in Nursing Adminstrn., 1962. RN; lic. health facility adminstr., Ind. Occupational health nurse E. I. duPont de Nemours & Co., Lincolnwood, Ill., Senco Corp., Newtown, Ohio; asst. prof. psychiat. and med. nursing No. Ky. U., Highland Heights; nursing coord. VA Hosp., Butler, Pa.; instr. psychiat. nursing Ohio Valley Community Hosp., McKees Rocks, Pa.; dir. nursing svc. Presbyn. Home, Evanston, Ill., Edgewater Hosp., Chgo., Franklin Blvd Hosp., Chgo. 1st lt. U.S. Army Nurse Corps, 1944-47. Mem. ANA, Am. Assn. Occupational Health Nurses, Am. Coll. Health Facility Adminstrs., Ohio Nurses Assn., Ill. Nurses Assn., Ind. Nurses Assn., Mass. Nurses Assn., Southwestern Ohio Assn. Occupational Health Nurses (chmn. legislation and edn. com.), Women in Mil. Svc. for Am., Women's Meml. Found.

KAPLAN, BARBARA JANE, city planner; b. N.Y.C., Sept. 8, 1943; d. Richard S. and Fannie I. (Schutz) Benson; m. Jerry Martin Kaplan, May 29, 1966. BA, Barnard Coll., 1965; MS, U. Southern Calif., 1969. Asst. planner L.A. Regional Planning Commn., 1968-69; from asst. planner to assoc. planner San Diego Comprehensive Planning Orgn., 1969-71; asst. dir. of regional planning North Ctrl. Tex. Coun. of Govts., Arlington, 1971-73; dir. Pennsport Civic Assn., Phila., 1974; city planner III Phila. City Planning Commn., 1974-76, city planner V, 1976-80, dep. exec. dir., 1980-83, exec. dir., 1983—. Trustee U. of the Arts, Phila., 1987—; pres. Ctr. for Literacy, Phila., 1991—; bd. dirs. Neighborhood Gardens Assn., Phila., 1987—, Pa. Horticultural Soc., 1993—. Mem. Am. Planning Assn., Nat. Trust for Hist. Preservation. Home: 2421 Fairmount Ave Philadelphia PA 19130 Office: Phila City Planning Commn 1515 Market St Philadelphia PA 19102

KAPLAN, CAROLE, interior designer; b. N.Y.C., Aug. 22, 1940; d. Dwight W. and Helen Marie (Cifelli) Schrock; m. Franklin Lewis Kaplan, Apr. 11, 1965; children: Elizabeth Ann, Jeremy David. BA, Miami U., 1963. Pres. Two By Two Interior Design, Inc., Andover, Mass., 1985-96. Mem. Am. Soc. of Interior Designers (pres. 1990-92). Democrat. Office: Two By Two Interior Design Ltd 34 School St Andover MA 01810

KAPLAN, CATHY M., lawyer; b. N.Y.C., Jan. 22, 1953. BA, Yale U., 1974; JD, Columbia U., 1977. Bar: N.Y. 1978. Ptnr. Brown & Wood, N.Y.C. Office: Brown & Wood 1 World Trade Ctr New York NY 10048-0202*

KAPLAN, DORIS WEILER, social worker; b. Phila., Mar. 28, 1945; d. Edgar E. and Marianne S. (Gunzenhauser) Weiler; m. Daniel I. Kaplan, Apr. 15, 1967; children: Tammy G., Bradley E. BA in Sociology, U. Pitts., 1966; MA in Counseling, Social Work, Montclair State Coll., 1980. Social worker N.J. Div. Youth & Family Svcs., 1967-71, Union (N.J.) Twp. Bd. Edn., 1982—; cons. Head Start Social Svc., Union, 1982—. Treas. Livingston (N.J.) Coun. Girl Scouts U.S., 1977—, outstanding vol. Essex County Coun. 1993; editor Livingston High Sch. PTA, 1985-89. Mem. Nat. Coun. Jewish Women, N.J. Assn. Sch. Social Workers (treas., bd. dirs. 1990—), Crestmont Country Club. Office: Union Twp Schs Morris Ave Union NJ 07083

KAPLAN, ERICA LYNN, typing and word processing service company executive, pianist; b. Jamaica, N.Y., Aug. 6, 1955; d. George William and Raylia (Eagle) Kaplan; m. James Laurence Kellermann, Feb. 26, 1982. B in Mus., Manhattan Sch. Music, N.Y.C., 1976, M in Mus., 1979. Clk. dept. edn. 92d St. Y, N.Y.C., 1972-76, assoc. dept. pub. rels., 1977-78, catalogue coord., sec. to exec. dir., 1978, assoc. dept. performing arts, 1978-79, assoc. dir. dept. pubs., 1979-80; pres. Erica Kaplan Typing/Word Processing/Music Svcs., N.Y.C., 1980—; piano soloist Huntington (N.Y.) Philharmonia, 1975; rehearsal pianist, performance accompanist The Mikado, Playwrights Horizons, N.Y.C., 1975, Fiona in Swan Song, N.Y.C., 1986; mus. dir., accompanist A Salute to Vaudeville/A Tribute to Fred Astaire, N.Y.C., 1980—; mus. dir., pianist Portrait of a Man, Hyde Pk. (N.Y.) Festival Theatre, 1981, Am. Renaissance Theater, N.Y.C., 1982, 86, The Fantasticks, Dalton Sch., N.Y.C., 1983; performance accompanist Okla., Theatreworks, Bklyn., 1984; resident pianist Am. Renaissance Theater, N.Y.C., 1981—; audition accompanist Interboro Repertory Theater, N.Y.C., 1986—; accompanist, vocal lessons class Stuyvesant Adult Ctr., N.Y.C., 1988—, The Singing Experience, 1990-91; mus. dir. Gift of the Magi, 1991. Translator and annotator with additional mus. examples: L'Anacrouse dans la Musique Moderne, 1978; composer (songs) Four by Feiffer, 1978, Hey Boys, 1984, Unborn Child, 1988, Neighbor, 1991; arranger Postcards from the Apple, 1993. Mem. New Eng. Anti-Vivisection Soc., Boston, 1982—, Nat. Anti-Vivisection Soc., 1988—, Common Cause, Washington, 1983—, SANE/FREEZE, 1988—. Mem. Am. Fedn. Musicians, NAFE, Union Concerned Scientists, Mensa. Democrat. Jewish. Avocations: theater, travel.

KAPLAN, HELENE LOIS, lawyer; b. N.Y.C., June 19, 1933; d. Jack and Shirley (Jacobs) Finkelstein; m. Mark N. Kaplan, Sept. 7, 1952; children: Marjorie Ellen, Sue Anne. AB cum laude, Barnard Coll., 1953; JD, NYU, 1967; LLD (hon.), Columbia U., 1990. Bar: N.Y. 1967. Pvt. practice law N.Y.C., 1967-78; ptnr. Webster & Sheffield, N.Y.C., 1978-86, counsel, 1986-90; of counsel Skadden, Arps, Slate, Meagher & Flom, N.Y.C., 1990—; bd. dirs. The May Dept. Stores Co., Met. Life Ins. Co., The Chase Manhattan Corp., Mobil Corp., Nynex, Coun. Fgn. Rels. Trustee N.Y. Coun. for Humanities, 1976-82, chmn., 1978-82; trustee Barnard Coll., 1973—, chmn. bd. trustees, 1984-94; trustee Columbia U. Press, 1977-80, MITRE Corp., 1978-95, N.Y. Found., 1976-86, John Simon Guggenheim Meml. Found., 1981—, NYU Law Ctr. Found., 1985-87, Inst. for Advanced Study, 1986—, Neuroscis. Rsch. Found., 1986-92, Am. Mus. Natural History, 1989—, Am. Trust for Brit. Libr., 1991-93, Com. for Econ. Devel., 1993—, Commonwealth Fund, 1990—, J. Paul Getty Trust, 1990—, Olive Free Libr.; trustee Carnegie Corp. N.Y., 1979—, vice chmn. bd. trustees, 1981-84, chmn. bd. trustees, 1984-91; trustee Mt. Sinai Hosp. Med. Ctr. and Med. Sch., 1977—, vice chmn. bd. trustees, 1993—; trustee N.Y.C. Pub. Devel. Corp., 1978-83, vice chmn. bd. trustees, 1978-82; mem. adv. com. on South Africa, U.S. Sec. of State, 1986-88; mem. N.Y. State Gov.'s Task Force on Life and the Law, 1985-90, Women's Forum, Inc., 1982—, Rockefeller U. Coun., 1984-94, Bretton Woods Com., 1985—, Carnegie Coun. on Adolescent Devel., 1986-96; chairperson task force on sci. and tech. and jud. decision making Carnegie Commn. on Sci., Tech. and Govt., 1988-93; ptnr. N.Y.C. Partnership, 1987-92; bd. dirs. Am. Arbitration Assn., 1978-82. Mem. ABA, AAAS, Am. Philos. Soc., N.Y. State Bar Assn., N.Y.C. Bar Assn. (treas. 1991-93, mem. com. on philanthropic orgns. 1975-81, mem. com. on recruitment of lawyers 1978-82, mem. com. on profl. responsibility 1980-83), Century Assn., Cosmopolitan Club. Home: 146 Central Park W New York NY 10023-2005 Office: Skadden Arps Slate Meagher & Flom 919 3rd Ave Fl 29 New York NY 10022

KAPLAN, HUETTE MYRA, business educator, training consultant; b. Chgo., July 11, 1933; d. Max and Jeannette (Smith) Lazan; m. Jerrold M. Kaplan, Feb. 14, 1954; children: Lawrence, Jeffrey. BS in Bus. Edn., DePaul U., 1971. Instr. Pub. Svc. Careers Program State of Ill., Chgo., 1971-72; instr., dir. Patricia Stevens Bus. Sch., Chgo., 1972; relocation mgr., tng. specialist, dir. tng. and devel. Zurich-Am. Ins. Cos., Chgo. and Schaumburg, Ill., 1972-80; pres., tng. cons. H.K. & Assocs., Lansing, Ill., 1980—; tng. dir. Calumet Area Lit. Coun., Hammond, Inc., 1985—; trainer Chgo. Literacy Coordinating Ctr., 1988-93; instr. Purdue U.-Calumet, Hammond, 1976—. Bd. dirs. Temple Beth El, Hammond, 1986-88, Calumet Area Literacy Coun., 1990-92, 94-95, pres. 1995—; mem. task force Chgo. Coalition for Edn. and Tng. for Employment, 1984-86; literacy vol. tutor. Mem. ASTD, Nat. Bus. Edn. Assn., Kappa Gamma Pi. Jewish. Home and Office: HK & Assocs 2843 192nd St Lansing IL 60438-3717

KAPLAN, JANET ANN, art historian, educator; b. Chgo., May 14, 1945; d. Morris and Dorothy (Weiss) K.; m. Warren O. Angle, June 17, 1984; 1 child, Dana Kaplan-Angle. BA, Brandeis U., 1966; PhD, Columbia U., 1982. Arts faculty U. Wis., River Falls, 1975-76; arts faculty chair Franconia (N.H.) Coll., 1976-78; arts faculty U. N.H., Plymouth, 1978-79; prof., chair liberal arts Moore Coll. Art and Design, Phila., 1980—; grad. faculty Vt. Coll., Montpelier, 1991—; exec. editor Art Jour., N.Y.C., 1996—; adv. bd. Voices of Dissent Conf., Phila., 1987-89; cons. U.S. Holocaust Meml. Mus., Washington, 1990-92; reviewer NEH, Washington, 1990; co-orgn. of alternative sites exhbns. Internat. Sculpture Conf., Phila., 1992. Author: Unexpected Journeys: the Art and Life of Remedios Varo, 1988, 94, in Spanish 1988, 94, in Japanese, 1992; editor: A Woman's Thesaurus, 1988; contbr. articles to profl. jours. Organizer Art Squad-Polit. Activists, Phila., 1980-83. Summer Inst. fellow NEH, Stanford, Calif., 1979, Geneva, N.Y., 1987, fellow NEH, 1984-85, Program for Cultural Cooperation Between Spain's Ministry of Culture and U.S. Univs., 1990; scholar-in-residence Rockefeller Found., Bellagio, Italy, 1985. Mem. Coll. Art Assn., Assn. Internat. des Critiques D'Art. Home: 250 Grape St Philadelphia PA 19128 Office: Moore Coll Art & Design 20th and The Pkwy Philadelphia PA 19103

KAPLAN, (NORMA) JEAN GAITHER, retired teacher, reading specialist; b. Cumberland, Md., Dec. 14, 1927; d. Frank Preston and Elizabeth (Mcneil) Gaither; m. Robert Lewis Kaplan, Dec. 4, 1959; 1 child, Benjamin Leigh. AB in Edn., Madison Coll., Harrisonburg, Va., 1950; MA in Edn., U. Va., 1956; postgrad., U. Va., William and Mary, 1958-61; reading specialist degree, U. Va., 1976. Tchr. Frederick County Sch. System, Winchester, Va., 1950-51, Washington County Sch. System, Hagerstown, Md., 1951-55, Charlottesville (Va.) Sch. System, 1955-60, York County (Va.) Sch. System, 1962, Newport News Sch. System, Denbigh, Va., 1963, Internat. Sch. Bangkok, 1965-67; tutor Reston Reading Ctr., Fairfax County, Va., 1972-74; tutor homebound, substitute tchr. Fairfax County Sch. Systems, 1974-78, pvt. practice pvt. tutor McLean/Middleburg, Va., 1978-89; pres. Tutorial Svcs., Inc., McLean, 1985-87; sec. The Rumson Corp., Middleburg, 1981—. Mem. No. Va. Conservation Coun., Fairfax County, 1976-81; bd. dirs. Nat. Environ. Leadership Coun.; active Piedmont Environ. Coun. Mem. AAUW, LWV, Bangkok Am. Wives Assn., Tuesday Afternoon Club (pres. 1974-75, treas. 1995—), Ayr Hill Garden Club, Soc. John Gaither Descs. Inc., Kappa Delta Pi, Alpha Sigma Tau. Home and Office: PO Box 1943 Middleburg VA 22118-1943

KAPLAN, JOCELYN RAE, financial planning firm executive; b. Lynbrook, N.Y., Apr. 23, 1952; d. Eugene S. and Adeline (Dembo) K. B.S., Northwestern U., 1975. Cert. fin. planner. Ins. agt. Fidelity Union Life Ins. Co., College Park, Md., 1976-77, Bankers Life Ins. Co., Rockville, Md., 1977-80; fin. planner Reutemann & Wagner, McLean, Va., 1980-82; fin. planning casewriter McLean Fin. Group, 1982-83; dir. fin. planning DeSanto Naftal Co., Vienna, Va., 1983-85; pres. Advisors Fin., Inc., Falls Church, Va., 1985—. Founding mem., treas. Congregation Bet Mishpachah, Washington, 1981, v.p., 1982, pres., 1983. Recipient Nat. Quality award Nat. Assn. Life Underwriters, 1978; Agt. of Yr. award Gen. Agt. and Mgrs. Assn., 1978. Mem. Internat. Assn. Fin. Planners, Inst. Cert. Fin. Planners, Registry of Fin. Planning Practitioners. Home: 1029 N Stuart St # 308 Arlington VA 22201 Office: Advisors Fin Inc 131 Great Falls St # 300 Falls Church VA 22046-3402

KAPLAN, JUDITH HELENE, corporate professional; b. N.Y.C., July 20, 1938; d. Abraham and Ruth (Kiffel) Letich; m. Warren Kaplan, Dec. 31, 1958; children: Ronald Scott, Elissa Aynn. BA, Hunter Coll., 1955; postgrad., New Sch. for Social Rsch., 1955-56. Registered rep. Herzfeld & Stern, N.Y.C., 1963; agt. New York Life Ins. Co., N.Y.C., 1964-69; registered rep. Scheinman, Hochstin & Trotta, 1969-70; v.p. Alpha Capital Corp., N.Y.C., 1970-74; pres. Tipex, Inc., N.Y.C., 1966-84; v.p. Alpha Pub. Relations, N.Y.C., 1970-73; pres. Utopia Recreations Corp., 1971-73, Howard Beach Recreation Corp., 1972-73; chmn. bd. Alpha Exec. Planning Corp., 1970-72; field underwriter N.Y. Life Ins. Co., 1974-75; pres. Action Products Internat. Inc., 1978-87, chairperson, 1980—, Ronel Industries, Inc., 1982-84; pres. Orlando Orange, Inc., 1995; participant White House Conf. on Small Bus., 1979; founder Women's History Mus., Judith Kaplan & Warren Kaplan's Women's History Collection Cen. Fla. C.C., Ocala, 1991; advisor Kaplan Women's History Collection CFCC Found., Ocala, Fla. Author: Woman Suffrage, 1977; co-author: Space Patches-from Mercury to the Space Shuttle, 1986; contbg. editor: Stamp Show News, M & H Philatelic Report; creator, producer Women's History series of First Day Covers, 1976-81; contbr. articles to profl. jours. Active Wyo. adv. on woman suffrage; trustee Found. for Innovative Lifelong Edn. Inc., 1986-88; owner Orlando Orange, Inc. Profl. Baseball Team, 1995-96; bd. dirs. Ctrl. Fla. Regional Libr., 1996—. Named Outstanding Young Citizen Manhattan Jaycees, Small Bus. Person of Yr. State of Fla, 1986. Mem. NOW (ins. coord. nat. task force on taxes, v.p. N.Y. chpt., co-founder Ocala/Marion County chpt. 1982, bd. women's adv. coun. Ocala and Marion Counties 1986-88), Nat. Women's Polit. Caucus, Women Leaders Round Table, Nat. Assn. Life Underwriters, Assn. Stamp Dealers Am., Am. First Day Cover Soc. (life), Am. Philatelic Soc. (life), Bus. and Profl. Women, AAUW. Home: 2901 SW 41st St Apt 3508 Ocala FL 34474-7424 Office: 344 Cypress Rd Ocala FL 34472-3102

KAPLAN, LAURA GARCIA, emergency and disaster preparedness consultant; b. Hollywood, Fla., Mar. 11, 1957; d. Thomas Tubens and Felicia (Acebal) Garcia; 1 child, Kristin. BSEE, U. Miami, 1979. Utilities exec. Fla. Power and Light Co., Miami, 1980-93, ops. mgr. Dade County, 1991-93; pres. L.G.K. Assocs., Inc., Ft. Lauderdale, Fla., 1993—. Author: Disaster Can Happen Anywhere in the World. . .Are You Prepared?, 1994, Emergency and Disaster Planning Manual, 1996. Counselor Soc. Abused Children, Kendall, Fla., 1985-86; instr. Jr. Achievement, Miami, 1986-87, Adult Illiteracy Program, 1987; bd. dirs. YWCA, 1988-92, Convenant House, 1995-96. Early admission scholar U. Miami, 1975; recipient Hurricane Andrew Hero award Dade County Rebuilding Program. Mem. Leadership Miami Assn., Greater Miami C. of C. Republican. Roman Catholic. Club: Hurricane. Office: LGK Assocs Inc 3100 SW 133 Ter Davie FL 33330

KAPLAN, LESLIE SCHENKMAN, school system administrator; b. N.Y.C., Nov. 23, 1946; d. Colman Maurice and Terry (Nemlich) Schenkman; m. Michael Lewis Kaplan, June 15, 1969; 1 child, Reid Colman. BA, Rutgers U., 1968; MA, Columbia U., 1969; MS, U. Nebr., Omaha, 1974; EdD, The Coll. of William & Mary, 1978. Lic. profl. counselor; nat. bd. cert. counselor; cert. profl. tchr. English with endorsement in sch. adminstrn., sch. guidance and counseling. Tchr. English jr. high sch. Schenectady (N.Y.) Pub. Schs., 1969-70, tchr. English high sch., 1970-71; grad. asst., fellow U. Nebr., Omaha, 1973-74, The Coll. of William and Mary, Williamsburg, Va., 1976-77; h.s. counselor Newport News (Va.) Pub. Sch., 1977-85, middle sch. counselor, 1985-86; dir. program devel. York County Pub. Schs., Yorktown, Va., 1986-92, asst. prin., 1992-96; asst. prin. Newport News (Va.) Pub. Schs., 1996—. Author: Coping with Stepfamilies, 3d edit., 1993, Coping with Peer Pressure, 4th edit., 1994; mem. editl. bd. The Sch. Counselor, 1985-94, The Virginia Counselor's Jour., 1985—, Jour. of Counseling and Development, 1995—; contbr. chpts. to books, articles to profl. adminstr. and counseling jours. Bd. dirs. Youth Svcs. of Newport News, 1980-84; sch. divsn. coord. United Way of Va., 1992. Recipient Gov.'s award for anti-drug efforts Gov. Douglas Wilder, 1992. Mem. ASCD, Va. Counselors Assn. Found., Va. Counselors Assn. (treas. 1986-88, Counslor of Yr. 1988, pres. 1993-94), York County Mgmt. Assn. (pres. 1991-93), Am. Counseling Assn., Nat. Assn. for Secondary Sch. Prins., Nat. Assn. for Supervision and Curriculum Devel. Office: Denbigh HS 259 Denbigh Blvd Newport News VA 23602

KAPLAN, MADELINE, legal administrator; b. N.Y.C., June 20, 1944; d. Leo and Ethel (Finkelstein) Kahn; m. Theodore Norman Kaplan, Nov. 14, 1982. AS, Fashion Inst. Tech., N.Y.C., 1964; BA in English Lit. summa cum laude, CUNY, 1982; MBA, Baruch Coll., 1990. Free-lance fashion illustrator N.Y.C., 1965-73; legal asst. Krause Hirsch & Gross, Esquires, N.Y.C., 1973-80; mgr. communications Stroock & Stroock & Lavan Esquires, N.Y.C., 1980-86; dir. adminstrn. Cooper Cohen Singer & Ecker Esquires, N.Y.C., 1986-87, Donovan Leisure Newton & Irvine Esquires, N.Y.C., 1987-93, Proskauer Rose Goetz & Mendelsohn, N.Y.C., 1993-95, Kaye, Scholer, Fierman, Hays & Hadler, LLP, N.Y.C., 1995, Kaye, Scholer, Fierman, Hays & Handler, LLP, N.Y.C., 1995—. Contbr. articles to profl. jours. Founder, pres. Knolls chpt. of Women's Am. Orgn. Rehab. Through Tng., Riverdale, N.Y., 1979-82, v.p. edn., Manhattan region, 1982-83. Mem. ASTD, Assn. Legal Adminstrs. (program com.), Career Planning Com., Soc. Human Resources Mgmt., Exec. MBA Alumni Assn. (bd. dirs.), Sigma Iota Epsilon (life). Office: 1583 Broadway New York NY 10036

KAPLAN, MARY, clinical social worker, educator; b. Phila., Aug. 4, 1945; d. Alfred Roosevelt Henderson and Mary Alice (Heath) O'Donnell; m. H. Roy Kaplan, June 26, 1966; 2 children: Eric, Ian. BSW, SUNY, Buffalo, 1974; MSW, Cath. U., 1978. Lic. clin. social worker, Fla. Caseworker Erie County Office for Aging, Buffalo, 1974-76; dir. social work dept. Sheghan Meml. Hosp., Buffalo, 1978-79, Indian River Meml. Hosp., Vero Beach, Fla., 1980-86; instr. nursing program Indian River C.C., Ft. Pierce, Fla., 1981-82; clin. social work practice Gerontol. Svcs., Tampa, Fla., 1986-89; fellowship coord. U. South Fla., Tampa, 1988-89, clin. social worker Psychiat. Ctr., 1989-90; adj. faculty health scis. SUNY, Buffalo, 1979-80; adj. faculty health arts Coll. St. Francis, Tampa, 1988—; supr. social work dept. St. Joseph's Hosp., Tampa, 1990-92; edn. coord. Alzheimer's Assn., Tampa, 1992-93; dir. dementia program Menorah Manor, St. Petersburg, Fla., 1993-95; faculty gerontology U. South Fla., Tampa, 1995—. Author: Clinical Practice with Caregivers of Dementia Patients, 1996; editor: Special Care Programs for People with Dementia, 1996; contbr. articles to profl. jours. Mem. adv. bd. Ret. Sr. Vol. Program, Vero Beach, 1985-86, Vis. Nurses Assn., Indian River County, Fla., 1981-86; pres., bd. dirs. Spouse Abuse of Indian River County, Vero Beach, 1983-86. Tng. grantee Pinella County Juvenile Welfare, 1994-95, Unicare Found., 1993. Mem. NASW (mem. Fla. com. on aging 1979—, Social Worker of Yr. 1985), Acad. Cert. Social Workers, Gerontology Soc. Am. Office: U South Fla Gerontology Dept Tampa FL 33620

KAPLAN, MURIEL SHEERR, sculptor; b. Phila., Aug. 15, 1924; d. Maurice J. and Lillian J. (Jamison) Sheerr; BA, Cornell U., 1946; postgrad. Sarah Lawrence Coll., 1958-60, U. Calif. at Oxford (Eng.), summer 1971, U. Florence (Italy), summer 1973, Art Students League, N.Y.C., summers 1975-89, New Sch., N.Y.C., 1974-78, m. Murray S. Kaplan, June 3, 1946 (dec.); children: Janet Belsky, James S., S. Jerrold, Amy Sheerr Eckman. Exhbns. at Women's Clubs in Westchester, 1954-60, Allied Artists Am., 1958-73, Nat. Assn. Women Artists, 1966-89, Bklyn. Mus., 1968, Sculptors Guild, 1972, Bergen County (N.J.) Mus., 1974; 2-person shows: Camino Real Gallery, Boca Raton, Fla., 1980; represented in group shows at Norton Art Gallery, Palm Beach, Fla., 1980, Govt. Ctr., West Palm Beach, Fla., 1984, Northwood U. Gallery, 1993; represented in permanent collections Israel, Columbia U., Brandeis U., U. Tex., Harvard Law Sch., 1990; executed twin 30 foot cor-ten steel sculptures, Tarrytown, N.Y., 1972, 2 large rotating steel sculptures Art Park, Trans-Lux Corp., 1978; art cons., interior designer, 1971-89; sec. commn. to establish art mus. in Westchester, 1956; chmn. Westchester Creative Arts Festival, 1956. Bd. dirs. Fedn. Jewish Philanthropies, 1956; chmn. 1st Sta. WNET, Channel 13 Art Auction; mem. com. art in pub. places, Palm Beach County, Fla., 1984; mem. art adv. com. Boca Raton Mus. Art, 1987-93; bd. dirs. Palm Beach County Cultural Coun. of Arts, 1992-94; tchr. sculpture Armory Arts Ctr., Palm Beach, 1987-92, bd. dirs., 1992—. Recipient prizes Nat. Assn. Women Artists, 1966, Westchester Women's Club, 1955, 56, Allied Artists Am., 1969, Artists Guild, Palm Beach, 1987, 88, 90, 91, 92, 93, 94, 96. Mem. NAD, Art Students League N.Y. Nat. Assn. Women Artists, Allied Artists Am., Nat. Sculpture Soc., Internat. Sculpture Ctr., Portraits Inc. N.Y. Address: 339 Garden Rd Palm Beach FL 33480-3221

KAPLAN, NADIA, writer; b. Chgo., Feb. 28, 1921; d. Peter and Aniela (Buchynska) Charydchak; m. Norman Kaplan, July 25, 1942 (dec. July 1989); children: Fawn Marie Stom, Norma Jean Martinez. BEd, Pestalozzi Froebel Tchrs. Coll, Chgo., 1948; postgrad., UCLA, 1947, L.A. City Coll., U. Hawaii, Pepperdine U., 1970, Santa Monica Coll., 1981-87. Cert. tchr., Calif. Photographer, mgr. Great Lakes (Ill.) Naval Tng. Sta., 1942-45; primary/kindergarten tchr. L.A. Unified Sch. Dist., 1946-81. Contbr. articles to profl. jours.; creator puzzles various mags. Vol. recreational tchr. Found. for Jr. Blind, L.A., 1956-75, vol. camp counselor Camp Bloomfield, Calif., camp dir., 1956-61, leader cross-country study tour for blind teenagers, 1962; mem. dem. Nat. Com., 1985—. Pestalozzi Froebel Tchrs. Coll. scholar, 1938-41. Mem. AAUW, Women Writers West (membership chair 1982-84), United Tchrs. L.A., Calif. Ret. Tchrs. Assn., Assn. Ret. Tchrs. Ukrainian Orthodox. Home: 1827 Fanning St Los Angeles CA 90026

KAPLAN, PHYLLIS, computer artist; b. Bklyn., July 4, 1950; d. Abraham and Ida (Heller) K. BFA, Cooper Union, 1972; postgrad., Domus Acad., Milan, Italy, 1985. Designer Precision Industries, N.Y.C., 1972; design trainee Dell Pub. Co., N.Y.C., 1972-73; asst. art dir. ThermaSol, N.Y.C., 1973; illustrator Bronx (N.Y.) C.C., 1974-76; graphic artist ABC TV, N.Y.C., 1977, Dept. City Planning, N.Y.C., 1977-84; assoc. graphic artist

HRA, N.Y.C., 1984-92; computer artist N.Y.C. Transit, 1992—; curator art exhibit Orgn. Ind. Artists, N.Y.C., 1995-96; lectr., presenter in field. Contbr. paintings to various publs. including Kings Courier, 1974, The Villager, N.Y.C., 1994, CPM News, 1994, World Jour., N.Y.C., 1996, Sing Tao Daily, 1996, Bklyn. Graphic, 1996. Vol. Art Initiatives, N.Y.C., 1995. Recipient award for patriotism U.S. Savs. Bond Dr., 1987, hon. mention award Internat. Female Artist's Art Biennial, Stockholm, 1994. Mem. Orgn. Ind. Artists (contbr. to ann. calendar), Nat. Mus. Women in the Arts, Greene County Coun. on Arts. Home: 98 Park Ter East New York NY 10034

KAPLAN, ROSALIND PERLOW, ophthalmologist; b. Bklyn., Oct. 23, 1939; d. Jack and Sylvie (Novick) Perlow; m. Barry Kaplan, June 24, 1962; children: Andrew, Scott. BS magna cum laude, CUNY, 1960; postgrad., Yeshiva U., 1960-62; MD, U. Md., Balt., 1964. Diplomate Am. Bd. Ophthalmology. Intern Washington Hosp. Ctr., 1964-65; resident in ophthalmology Bronx (N.Y.) Eye Imfirmary, 1965-69; pvt. practice, N.Y.C., 1969-91; fellow in neuro-ophthalmology Columbia-Presbyn. Hosp., N.Y.C., 1992-93, assoc. attending in neuro-ophthalmology, 1993-95. Fellow Am. Acad. Ophthalmology; mem. Am. Med. Women's Assn. (exec. bd. Westchester br., past chpt. pres.), New York County Med. Soc., Phi Beta Kappa. Home: 199 Weaver St Scarsdale NY 10583

KAPLAN, SANDRA LEE, artist; b. Cin., May 23, 1943; d. Howard and Helen (Katz) K.; m. Stanley Joseph Dragul, 1964 (div. 1974); 1 child, Sacha; m. Robert Lawrence Denerstein, 1986. Student, Art Acad. Cin., 1960-61; BFA with honors, Pratt Inst., Bklyn., 1965; student, CUNY, 1968-70. Illustrator Christian Sci. Monitor, Boston, 1991-94; drawing instr. Denver C.C., 1991-92; antique dealer Wazee Deco, Denver, 1992—; com. mem. Arvada Ctr. for the Arts, 1994-96. Sole exhibits in various galleries including Dubins Gallery, L.A., 1988, Ventana Gallery, Santa Fe, 1985-90, Land-Escapes in Aruada Ctr. for the Arts, Arvada, Colo., 1991, Human and or Nature in Nicolaysen Mus., Casper, Wyo., 1992, Rule Modern & Contemporary, Denver, 1993, Land-Escape in Wave Hill, Riverdale, N.Y., 1995; commd. works Hong Kong Marriott Hotel, 1988, Gt. West Life Assurance Co., 1991, Arvada City Hall, 1993, Sch. Pharmacy U. Colo., 1994. Yaddo Corp. fellow, 1985; Ludwig Vogelstein grantee, 1986, Covisions grantee Colo. Coun. of Arts, 1992. Mem. Arapahoe Acres Design Rev. Democrat. Jewish. Home: 2939 S Lafayette Dr Englewood CO 80110 Office: 235 S Sherman St Denver CO 80209

KAPLAN, SUSAN, lawyer; b. Worcester, Mass., July 27, 1958; d. Alvin H. and Elaine (Levy) K.; m. Matthew T. Gerson, Nov. 1, 1987; 1 child. BA, Bowdoin Coll., 1980; JD, Georgetown U., 1983. Chief minority counsel/counsel Constitiution subcom. U.S. Senate Judiciary Com., Washington, 1987—. Office: US Senate Judiciary Com 524 DirksenSt Washington DC 20510

KAPLAN, SYDNEY JANET, English educator; b. L.A., Dec. 28, 1939; d. Leo and Frieda (Kaufman) Zendell; divorced; 1 child, Frederick Nathan Kaplan. BA, UCLA, 1961, MA, 1966, PhD, 1971. Tchr. Manual Arts High Sch., L.A., 1963-64; asst. prof. U. Wash., Seattle, 1971-77, assoc. prof., 1978-91, dir. women's studies, 1982-92, prof., 1992—. Author: Feminine Consciousness in the Modern British Novel, 1975, Katherine Mansfield and the Origins of Modernist Fiction, 1991; contbr. articles to profl. jours; assoc. editor Signs: Jour. of Women in Culture and Soc., 1995—; mem. editorial bd. Tulsa Studies in Women's Literature, 1981. Travel grantee U. Wash., 1978. Mem. Modern Lang. Assn., Virginia Woolf Soc., Wash. Trails Assn., Sierra Club. Democrat. Office: U Wash Dept English Box 354330 Seattle WA 98195

KAPP, ELEANOR JEANNE, impressionistic artist, writer, researcher; b. Hagerstown, Md., Oct. 16, 1933; d. James Norman and Nellie Belle (Welty) Weagley; m. Alan Howard Kapp, Sept. 25, 1972. Cert., L.A. Interior Design, 1969; student, U. Utah, 1976-82. Artist Farmers Ins. Group, L.A., 1960-63; interior designer W&J Sloane, Beverly Hills, Calif., 1965-70; ski resort exec. Snowpine Lodge, Alta, Utah, 1970-84; dir. mktg. and pub. rels. Alta Resort Assn., 1979-84; free-lance photographer Alta, 1979—; bus. owner Creative Art Enterprises, Sandy, Utah, 1984-85; artist-resident Collector's Corner Art Gallery, San Ramon, Calif., 1991—; owner Art of Jeanne Kapp, Lafayette, Calif., 1985—; artist-resident St. Germain Gallery, Tiburon, Calif., 1993—, Regional Art Ctr. Gift Store, Walnut Creek, Calif., 1994—, Valley Art Ctr., Walnut Creek, 1995—. Author, pub.: The American Connection, 1985, 91; author, prodr. (documentary) A Look at China Today, 1981; photographer: Best of the West, 1983. Promotion liaison Alta Town Coun., 1980-84; floral decorator Coun. State Govts., Snowbird, Utah, 1976; photographer Utah Dems., Salt Lake City, 1981; exhibit curator Salt Lake County Libr. System, 1982, founder Alta Br. Libr., 1982; fundraiser Friends of Libr., Alta, 1982; mem. Alta Town-Libr. Adv. Bd., 1983. Recipient Cert. of Appreciation, Salt Lake County Libr. System, 1981, Cert. of Recognition, Gov. Cal Rampton, Salt Lake City, 1972-74, Calendar Cover award Utah Travel Coun., 1981, Internat. Invitational Art Exhibit, Centre Internat. D'Art Contemporain, Paris, 1983. Mem. Internat. Platform Assn., Diablo Art Assn. (pub. rels. chmn. 1987, Hon. Mention award 1989), Concord Art Assn. (qst pl. award 1991), Alamo and Danville Artist's Soc. (cir. leader 1990—, hon. Mention award 1991, chmn. art exhbn. 1993, chmn. art program 1994), Las Junas Artist Assn. (juror's asst. 1992, 2d pl. award 1992, curator art exhbn. 1995—, Ann. 1st pl. award 1995). Home: 411 Donegal Way Lafayette CA 94549-1707

KAPPA, MARGARET MCCAFFREY, resort hotel consultant; b. Wabasha, Minn., May 14, 1921; d. Joseph Hugh and Verna Mae (Anderson) McCaffrey; B.S. in Hotel Mgmt., Cornell U., 1944; grad. Dale Carnegie course, 1978; cert. hospitality housekeeping exec.; m. Nicholas Francis Kappa, Sept. 15, 1956; children—Nicholas Joseph, Christopher Francis. Asst. exec. housekeeper Kahler Hotel, Rochester, Minn., 1944; exec. housekeeper St. Paul Hotel, 1944-47, Plaza Hotel, N.Y.C., 1947-51; exec. housekeeper, personnel dir. Athearn Hotel, Oshkosh, Wis., 1952-58; dir. housekeeping The Greenbrier, White Sulphur Springs, W.Va., 1958-84; cons., 1984—; tchr. housekeeping U.S. and fgn. countries; cons.; vis. lectr. Cornell U. Author: (with others) Managing Housekeeping Operations, 1989. Pres. St. Charles Borromeo Parish Assn., White Sulphur Springs, 1962, v.p., 1980, 82; tech. adv., host 2 ednl. videos Am. Hotel and Motel Assn., 1986; host Kappa on Kleaning for video Spectra Vision AHMA Ednl. Inst, 1994. Recipient diploma of honor Société Culinaire Philanthropique, 1961, Lamp of Knowledge award for promotion of professionalism Am. Hotel and Motel Assn., 1995. Mem. AARP, Cornell Soc. Hotelmen (pres. 1980-81, exec. com. 1981-82), Nat. Exec. Housekeepers Assn. (pres. N.Y. chpt. 1950), N.Y.U. Hotel and Restaurant Soc. (hon. life), Nat. Woman's Quota (charter mem. Greenbrier County), St. Charles Parish Assn., White Sulphur Springs Busy Bees, AARP, Senior Friends. Republican. Roman Catholic. Home and Office: 207 Azalea Trl White Sulphur Springs WV 24986-2001

KAPTUR, MARCIA CAROLYN, congresswoman; b. Toledo, Ohio, June 17, 1946. B.A., U. Wis., 1968; M. Urban Planning, U. Mich., 1974; postgrad., U. Manchester, (Eng.), 1974, MIT; LLD (hon.), U. Toledo. Urban planner; asst. dir. urban affairs domestic policy staff White House, 1977-79; mem. 98th-103rd Congresses from 9th Ohio dist., Washington, D.C., 1983—; mem. Appropriations com., subcom. Agrl., D.C., Veterans, HUD, indep. agys. Bd. dirs. Nat. Ctr. Urban Ethnic Affairs; adv. com. Gund Found.; exec. com. Lucas County Democratic Com.; mem. Dem. Women's Campaign Assn. Mem. Am. Planning Assn., Am. Inst. Cert. Planners, NAACP, Urban League, Polish Mus., U. Mich. Urban Planning Alumni Assn. (bd. dirs.), Polish Am. Hist. Assn. Roman Catholic. Clubs: Lucas County Dem. Bus. and Profl. Women's, Fulton County Dem. Women's. Office: US House of Reps 2104 Rayburn Bldg Washington DC 20515-0005*

KARABATSOS, ELIZABETH ANN, aerospace industry executive; b. Geneva, Nebr., Oct. 25, 1932; d. Karl Christian and Margaret Maurine (Emrich) Brinkman; m. Kimon Tom Karabatsos, Apr. 21, 1957 (div. Feb. 1981); children: Tom Kimon, Maurine Elizabeth, Karl Kimon. BS, U. Nebr., 1954; postgrad., Ariz. State U., 1980; Cert. contemporary exec. devel., George Washington U., 1985; M Orgnl. Mgmt., U. Phoenix, 1994. Instr. bus. Fairbury (Nebr.) High Sch., 1954-55; staff asst. U.S. Congress, Washington, 1955-60; with Karabatsos & Co. Pub. Relations, Washington, 1960-73; conf. asst. to asst. adminstr. and dep. adminstr. Gen. Services Adminstrn., Washington, 1973-76; dir. corr. Office Pres.-Elect, Washington, 1980; assoc. dir. adminstrv. services Pres. Personnel-White House, Washington, 1981; dept. asst.to Sec. and Dep. Sec. Def., Washington, 1981-86, asst. to, 1987-89; dir. govt. and civic affairs McDonnell Douglas Helicopter Co., Mesa, Ariz., 1989-90, gen. mgr. gen. svcs., 1990-92, co. ombudsman, community rels. exec., 1992-95; cons., counselor dispute resolution Ariz., 1995—; exec. asst. to dir. adminstrn. State of Ariz., 1995—. Mem. Nat. Mus. Women in Art, Washington; bd. dirs. U.S. C. of C. Com. on Labor & Tng.; mem. Gov.'s Sci. and Tech. Com.; mem. Ariz. Com. Employer Support the Guard and Res., 1991; active Gov. Com. for Ariz. Clean and Beautiful, World Affairs Coun. Ariz. Mem. AAUW, Women in Def., Am. Arbitration Assn., Nat. Inst. Dispute Resolution, Ariz. Dispute Resolution Assn., Order Eastern Star, Pi Omega Pi, Pi Beta Phi. Episcopalian. Home: 7818 E Montebello Ave Scottsdale AZ 85250-6173

KARAIM, BETTY JUNE, librarian; b. Devils Lake, N.D., May 27, 1936; d. Erick Henry and Anna Caroline (Steen) Keck; m. William James Karaim, Dec. 7, 1955 (dec. 1983); children: Reed, Lisa, Ryan, Lynn, Rachel, Lee, Lara. BS in Edn., Mayville (N.D.) State U., 1958; postgrad., U. N.D., summer 1961; MLS, U. Okla., 1972; postgrad., No. Mont. Coll., 1979, 81. Libr. Cando (N.D.) High Sch., 1960-62; asst. libr., tchr. Mayville State Coll., 1962-79; libr. Havre (Mont.) Pub. Schs., 1979-82; libr. dir. Mayville State U., 1982—. Recipient Orville Johnson Meritorious Svc. award, 1992. Mem. ALA, NEA, Assn. of Coll. and Rsch. Librs. (nat. adv. coun. 1990-94), Mountain Plains Libr. Assn., N.D. Libr. Assn. (chair acad. sect. 1987-88), N.D. Edn. Assn. (chpt. pres. 1985-89), N.D. Pub. Employees Assn. Democrat. Home: 320 1st St NW Mayville ND 58257-1107 Office: Mayville State U 330 3rd St NE Mayville ND 58257-1217

KARALEKAS, ANNE, publishing executive; b. Boston, Nov. 6, 1946; d. Christus and Helen (Vogiantzis) K. AB, Wheaton Coll., Norton, Mass., 1968; AM, Harvard U., 1969, PhD, 1974. Chief project mgr. def. and arms control project Commn. on Orgn. of Govt. for Conduct of Fgn. Policy, Washington, 1974-75; sr. staff mem. Senate Select Com. on Intelligence, Washington, 1975-78; sr. assoc. McKinsey & Co., Washington, 1978-85; mktg. mgr. The Washington Post, 1985-87, dir. mktg., 1987-89; pub. Washington Post Mag., 1989—, dir. specialty products group, 1993—. Author: History of the CIA, 1976; contbr. articles and book revs. to profl. publs. Advisor fgn. policy Mondale-Ferraro Presdl. Campaign, Washington, 1984; trustee Wheaton Coll., Norton, 1985-88. Mem. Council on Fgn. Relations, Phi Beta Kappa. Greek Orthodox. Office: The Washington Post 1150 15th St NW Washington DC 20071-0001

KARAN, DONNA (DONNA FASKE), fashion designer; b. Forest Hills, N.Y., Oct. 2, 1948; m. Mark Karan; 1 child, Gabrielle. BFA, Parsons Sch. Design, 1987. With Addenda Co., to 1968; with Anne Klein & Co., N.Y.C., 1968-84; co-designer Anne Klein & Co., 1971-74, designer, 1974-84; owner, designer, ptnr., CEO Donna Karan Co., N.Y.C., 1984—. Showed first complete collection for Anne Klein & Co. in 1974; collaborator on Anne Klein collections with Louis dell'Olion. Recipient Coty award, 1977, Awards Coun. of Fashion Designers of Am., 1985, 86, 92, Frontrunner award Sara Lee Corp., 1992; co-recipient (with Louis dell'Olio) Coty Return award, 1981, Coty Hall of Fame citation, 1982, Coty award, 1984. Office: Donna Karan Co 550 7th Ave New York NY 10018-3203*

KARDON, JANET, museum director, curator; b. Phila.; d. Robert and Shirley (Drasin) Stolker; m. Robert Kardon, Nov. 19, 1955; children: Ross, Nina, Roy. BS in Edn., Temple U.; MA in Art History, U. Pa. Lectr. Phila. Coll. Art, 1968-75, dir. exhbns., 1975-78; dir. Inst. Contemporary Art, Phila., 1978-89, Am. Craft Mus., N.Y.C., 1989-95; ind. curator, 1996—; cons., panel mem. Nat. Endowment for Arts, 1975—; mus. panel mem. Pa. Coun. on Arts, Phila., 1988—; U.S. commr. Venice Biennale, Venice, 1980. Curated and created essays for 30 exhbns., including Labyrinths, Time, Artists Sets and Costumes, Laurie Anderson, Robert Mapplethorpe, David Salle, Gertrude and Otto Natzler; editor: Twentieth Century American Craft: A Centenary Project, 1900-1920, Revivals/Diverse Traditions, 1920-45, Craft in the Machine Age, 1920-45. Grantee Nat. Endowment for Arts, 1978. Home and Office: 203 E 72d St 25B New York NY 10021

KAREN, LINDA TRICARICO, fashion designer; b. Bklyn., June 8, 1961; d. John William and Phyllis Jean (D'Addario) T. Student, Bucks County Community Coll., 1978-79; AAS, Fashion Inst. Tech., 1992. Retail mgr. Canadians, Brooks, Casual Corner, 1980-83; coord. sales and design Sure Snap Corp., N.Y.C., 1983-84; asst. designer E.S. Sutton Inc., N.Y.C., 1984-86; designer Good 'N Plenty Inc., N.Y.C., 1986-90; designer, merchandiser Leonard A. Feinberg, Inc., N.Y.C., 1991—; free-lance illustrator, designer. Contbr. fashion trend reports, Milan, Italy, 1984, Rome, 1985, Milan and Florence, Italy, 1986, London and Paris, 1987, Montreal, 1988, 94, 95, L.A., 1993, 95, 96. Mem. Fashion Soc., NAFE. Republican. Roman Catholic. Home: 316 Berry Rd Monroe NY 10950

KARIG, RITA REICHMAN, educator; b. Bklyn., Oct. 1, 1936; d. Sol and Ethel (Potash) Reichman; 1 child, Stephen Chul Karig. BA, CCNY, 1960; MS, Herbert H. Lehman Coll., 1972. Tchr., coord. reading programs N.Y.C. Bd. Edn., Bronx, N.Y., 1966—. Dist. leader Dem. Party, Bronx, 1964-66, del. Dem. Nat. Conv., Chgo., 1968. Recipient Outstanding Achievement award Behavioral Rsch. Labs., 1972, award N.Y.State Coun. on Humanities, 1995, NEH, 1996; Arts Partnership grantee Bronx Coun. on Arts, 1996. Mem. Audubon Soc., Co-op Am., CCNY Alumni Assn., Bronx Coun. on Arts. Office: NYC Bd Edn 99 Terrace View Ave Bronx NY 10463

KARL, HELEN WEIST, pediatric anesthesia educator, researcher; b. N.Y.C., Oct. 28, 1948; d. Edward C. and Louise (Stursberg) Weist; m. Stephen R. Karl, June 1, 1974 (div. 1990); children: Katherine L., Thomas R., John W. BA in Philosophy, Smith Coll., 1970; MD, U. Va., 1976. Diplomate Am. Bd. Anesthesiology, Nat. Bd. Med. Examiners. Intern in surgery Hartford (Conn.) Hosp., 1976-77, resident in anesthesia, 1977-79; fellow in pediatric anesthesiology Children's Hosp. of Phila., 1979-81; staff anesthesiologist St. Christopher's Hosp. for Children, Phila., 1981; asst. prof. anesthesiology and pediatrics Pa. State U., Hershey, 1981-90; asst. prof. anesthesiology U. Washington, 1990—; Parker B. Francis fellow in pulmonary rsch. Pa. State U., Hershey, 1986-88. Contbr. articles to profl. jours. Grantee Am. Lung Assn. of Pa., 1986-88. Fellow Am. Acad. Pediatrics (sec. on anesthesiology com. on drugs 1989—); mem. Am. Soc. Anesthesiologists (task force for preparation self-evaluation exam. 1982-83), Am. Med. Women's Assn., Internat. Anesthesia Rsch. Soc., Wash. Soc. Anesthesiologists, Anesthesia Patient Safety Found. Office: Children's Hosp & Med Ctr 4800 Sand Point Way NE Seattle WA 98105-3901

KARLE, ISABELLA L., chemist; b. Detroit, Dec. 2, 1921; d. Zygmunt Apolonaris and Elizabeth (Graczyk) Lugoski; m. Jerome Karle, June 4, 1942; children: Louise Hanson, Jean Marianne, Madeleine Tawney. BS in Chemistry, U. Mich., 1941, MS in Chemistry, 1942, PhD, 1944; DSc (hon.), U. Mich., 1976, Wayne State U., 1979, U. Md., 1986; LHD (hon.), Georgetown U., 1984. Assoc. chemist U. Chgo., 1944; instr. chemistry U. Mich., Ann Arbor, 1944-46; physicist Naval Rsch. Lab., Washington, 1946—; Paul Ehrlich lectr. NIH, 1991; mem. exec. com. Am. Peptide Symposium, 1975-81, adv. bd. Chem. and Engring. News, 1986-89. Mem. editorial bd. Biopolymers Jour., 1975—, Internat. Jour. Peptide Protein Rsch., 1981—; contbr. articles to profl. jours. Recipient Superior Civilian Service award USN, 1965, Fed. Women's award U.S. Govt., 1973, Annual Achievement award Soc. Women Engrs., 1968, Annual Achievement award U. Mich., 1987, Dexter Conrad award Office Naval Rsch., 1980, WISE Lifetime Achievement award Women in Sci. and Engring., 1986, award for disting. achievement in sci. Sec. of Navy, 1987, Gregori Aminoff prize Swedish Royal Acad. Scis., 1988, Adm. Parsons award Navy League U.S., 1988, Ann. Achievement award CCNY, 1989; Bijvoet medal U. Utrecht, The Netherlands, 1990, Vincent du Vigneaud award Gordon Conf. (Peptides), 1992, Bower Sci. award Franklin Inst., 1993, Nat. medal of Sci. Pres. of the U.S., 1995; named to Michigan Women's Hall of Fame, 1989, Chem. Scis. award Nat. Acad. Scis., 1995, Nat. Medal of Sci., 1995. Fellow Am. Acad. Arts Scis., Am. Inst. Chemists. (Chem. Pioneer award 1984); mem. NAS (Chem. Scis. award, 1995), Am. Crystallographic Assn. (pres. 1976), Am. Chem. Soc. (Garvan award 1976, Hillebrand award 1970), Am. Phys. Soc., Am. Philos. Soc., Biophys. Soc. Home: 6304 Lakeview Dr Falls Church VA 22041-1309 Office: Naval Rsch Lab Code 6030 Washington DC 20375-5341

KARLIN, LISA MARIE, academic administrator; b. Hays, Kans., June 21, 1968; d. Gary Paul and Mary Louise (Weigel) Dinkel; m. Craig Eugene Karlin. BBA, Ft. Hays State U., 1990. Bank examiner Fed. Deposit Ins. Corp., Hays, Kans., 1990-92; asst. alumni dir. Ft. Hays State U. Alumni Assn., 1992—; sponsor Student Alumni Assn., Ft. Hays State U., 1992—. Mem. Coun. Advancement & Support Edn., Mortar Bd. Sr. Honor Soc., Alpha Kappa Psi (bus. fraternity sec. 1989-90). Independent. Roman Catholic. Home: 108 W 38th St Hays KS 67601 Office: Ft Hays State U Alumni Assn 600 Park St Hays KS 67601

KARLINS, MIRIAM, mental health and volunteer services consultant; b. Cleve., Aug. 23, 1918; widow; children: Annette Weinberg, Sandra, Marvin. Dir. vol. svcs. Minn. Dept. Pub. Welfare, St. Paul, 1951-74, dir. edn. and tng. mental health divsn., 1960-74; mental health cons., 1974—; cons. NIMH, Washington, 1974-80, Minn. Gov.'s Coun. on Devel. Disabilities, 1986-94; former guest lectr., cons. on devel. and expansion vol. svcs. to hosps., London; former mem. adj. faculty dept. hosp. adminstrn. U. Minn., Mpls.; lectr., condr. tng. sessions for numerous pvt. and pub. agys.; condr. tng. for surveyors mental facilities Health Care Fin. Adminstrn., Social Security Adminstrn. Contbr. articles to rofl. publs.; prodr. films, TV and radio prodns., including For Whose Good?, Dehumanization and Total Institution, World of the Right Size, How Are You?. Life hon. mem. bd. dirs., advisor Opportunity Workshop. Recipient numerous awards Nental Health Assn., Assn. for Retarded Citizens, Minn. Dept. Human Svcs.; Miriam Karlins scholarship named in her honor Minn. Assn. Vol. Adminstrn.; Karlins Ctr. named in her honor Opportunity Workshop, 1996. Fellow Assn. Vol. Adminstrs. (hon. life, organizer, 1st pres., awards). Home: 6450 York Ave S Minneapolis MN 55435

KARLL, JO ANN, state agency administrator, lawyer; b. St. Louis, Nov. 16, 1948; d. Joseph H. and Dorothy Olga (Pyle) K.; m. William Austin Hernlund, Sept. 9, 1990. Bar: Mo. 1993. Ins. claims adjuster, 1967-88; state rep. Mo. Gen. Assembly dist. 104, 1991-92; mem. from dist. 105 Mo. Gen. Assembly, 1992-93; dir. Mo. State Divsn. Worker's Compensation, Jefferson City, 1993—. Mem. exec. bd. Jefferson County Dem. Club, 1988-92; committeewoman Jefferson County Ctrl. Dem. Com., Rock Twp., 1988-91; bd. dirs. Mid-East Area Agy. on Aging, 1991-93. Mem. NOW, Nat. Women's Polit. Caucus, Bus. and Profl. Women's Clubs (treas. 1987-89). Office: Mo St Divsn Worker's Compensation 3515 W Truman Blvd Jefferson City MO 65109-5715

KARLSTADT, ROBYN GAIL, physician, pharmaceutical researcher; b. N.Y.C., Aug. 21, 1949; d. Bernard David and Esther Dorothy (Glickman) K.; m. Stephen Henry Meyeroff, Dec. 7, 1980; children: Joshua Hamilton, Elizabeth Faith. AB, MD, Boston U., 1974. Intern Beth Israel Med. Ctr., N.Y.C., 1974-75, resident, 1975-77, surg. endoscopy fellow, 1979-80; gastroenterology fellow SUNY Downstate Med. Ctr., Bklyn., 1977-79; pvt. practice N.Y.C., 1980-82; med. rsch. physician Roche, Nutley, N.J., 1982-83; asst. dir. Ayerst, N.Y.C., 1984-87; assoc. dir. Smithkline French, Phila., 1987; dir. Smithkline Beecham, Phila., 1988—. Contbr. articles to profl. jours. Leader Daisies and Brownies Camden County Girl Scouts, Cherry Hill, N.J., 1990-94. Mem. Soc. Advancement Women's Health Rsch. (chair med. health adv. bd. 1994-95, mem. strategic planning com. 1995—), Am. Coll. Gastroenterology (chair women's com. 1990-92, gastroenterology women's coalition 1993-94). Office: Smithkline Beecham 1 Franklin Plz Philadelphia PA 19101

KARLUK, LORI JEAN, craft designer, copy editor; b. Scranton, Pa., Aug. 29, 1958; d. Edward Julius and Josephine Anne (Cuozzo) K. Grad., high sch., 1976. Consignor, designer various shops, Pa., 1982-85; owner mail order bus. Loveables, 1983-85; staff designer Tradition Today, Roselle, Ill., 1985-86; designer All Occasion Crafts, Sparks, Nev., 1986-88; copy editor McCalls, N.Y.C., 1987-90; copy editor, product designer Herrschners, Inc., Schaumburg, Ill., 1988-92; designer Banar Designs, Fallbrook, Calif., 1991-92, Yarn Kits, Inc., N.Y.C., 1992-94; freelance designer, 1984—, teddy bear artist, 1994—. Author: Safari Friends, 1987, Bear-E-Tale Bears, 1991. Sec. MADD, Lackawanna County, 1991. Recipient numerous spl. awards for designs. Mem. NOW, Soc. Craft Designers, People for the Ethical Treatment of Animals, United Friends of the Children, Internat. Soc. for Animal Rights, Teddy Bear Artists Assn., Good Bears of the World. Home and Office: 849 Goodman St Throop PA 18512-1156

KARMEL, ROBERTA SEGAL, lawyer, educator; b. Chgo., May 4, 1937; d. J. Herzl and Eva E. (Elin) Segal; m. Paul R. Karmel, June 9, 1957 (dec. Aug. 1994); m. Philip, Solomon, Jonathon, Miriam; m. S. David Harrison, Oct. 29, 1995. BA, Radcliffe Coll.; LLB, NYU, 1962. Bar: N.Y. 1962, U.S. Dist. Ct. (so. and ea. dists.) N.Y. 1964, U.S. Ct. Appeals (2d cir.) 1968, U.S. Supreme Ct. 1968, U.S. Ct. Appeals (3d cir.) 1987. With SEC, 1962-69, 77-80, asst. regional adminstr., until 1969; commr. SEC, Washington, 1977-80; assoc. firm Willkie Farr & Gallagher, N.Y.C., 1969-72; ptnr. firm Rogers & Wells, N.Y.C., 1972-77, of counsel, 1980-85; ptnr. firm Kelley Drye & Warren, N.Y.C., 1987-94, of counsel, 1995—; adj. prof. law Bklyn. Law Sch., 1973-77, 82-85, prof., 1985—, co-dir. Ctr. for Study of Internat. Bus. Law; bd. dirs. Mallinckrodt Group, Inc., Kemper Nat. Ins. Cos.; trustee Practicing Law Inst. Author: Regulation by Prosecution, 1982; contbr. articles to legal publs. Fellow Am. Bar Found.; mem. ABA, Assn. Bar City N.Y., Am. Law Inst., Fin. Women's Assn. Home: 66 Summit Dr Hastings on Hudson NY 10706-2310 Office: Bklyn Law Sch 250 Joralemon St Brooklyn NY 11201

KARNATH, LORIE MARY LORRAINE, bank officer, consultant; b. Chgo.; d. Albert Welch and Carole Margaret (Bohrer) K. m. Robert Emil Roethenmund, Jan. 8, 1994. BA, Fordham U., 1981; MBA, Inst. Superior des Etudes Adminstrv., Fontainebleau, France, 1990. Loan officer Chem. Bank, N.Y.C., 1981-84; team leader Credit Suisse, N.Y.C., 1984-86; assoc. Kidder, Peabody, N.Y.C. and Madrid, 1986-91; cons. E.M.C. Group, Hamburg, Germany, 1991-95; v.p. licensing, strategic planning, mergers and acquisitions The Stride Rite Corp., Lexington, Mass., 1995—. Contbg. author: Adventure Challenge, 1988; contbg. editor Next Mag., 1984-85. Mem. N.Y. Acad. Scis., Explorers Club (internat.), Royal Geog. Soc. (com.). Home: 6 Passage Chesnard, 27750 La Couture Boussey France

KARNAUSKAS, LESLIE ANN, accountant; b. Berlin, Wis., Sept. 9, 1949; d. Marvin Thomas Dugenske and Joyce Della (Yablonsky) Harris. BSBA in Fin., U. Minn., 1980; MBA in Acctg., U. Colo., Denver, 1986. Acct. Western Devel. and Investment, Denver, 1983-84; asst. contr. Guerdon Industries, Denver, 1984-88; supr. gen. acctg. Ohmeda divsn. BOC Group, Englewood, Colo., 1988; mgr. fin. planning, cost planning Ohmeda divsn. BOC Group, Englewood, 1988-89; mgr. fin. planning Ohmeda divsn. BOC Group, Louisville, Colo., 1989-92; contr. Ohmeda divsn. BOC Group, Louisville, 1992—. bd. dirs., pres. Worldwide Children's Connection, Denver, 1996; mem. fin. com. ARC Mile High chpt., Denver, 1992—; chpt. pres., state treas., state pres.-elect Bus. and Profl. Women, Denver, 1988—. Mem. Inst. Mgmt. Accts. (cert. mgmt. acct., chpt. pres., nat. dir.). Office: Ohmeda 1315 W Century Dr Louisville CO 80027

KARNES, LUCIA ROONEY, psychologist; b. Moncton, N.B., Can., Mar. 9, 1921; d. Charles William and Jean Waring (Robson) Rooney; m. Thomas Campbell Karnes, June 7, 1946; children: Eleanore, Campbell, Timothy, Charles. BS, Ga. State Coll., 1942; MA, Emory U., 1946; PhD, U. N.C., 1967. Tchr. Decatur Girls High, Decatur, Ga., 1942-46; tchr. Summit Sch., Winston-Salem, N.C., 1947; prof. Salem Coll., Winston-Salem, 1949-54, 60-77; lang. therapist Bowman Grey Sch. Medicine, Winston-Salem, 1950-57, Orton Reading Ctr., Winston-Salem, 1957-72; dir. Ctr. for Spl. Edn., Salem Coll., Winston-Salem, 1972-77; pvt. practice psychology Winston-Salem, 1977—; dyslexic cons. Jefferson Acad., Winston-Salem, 1980—, Greenfield Sch., Wilson, 1986—, Wingate (N.C.) Coll., 1988—. Creator Using Computers in Psychology courses, 1972; author (video) Teaching Dyslexics, 1975. Founder, pres. state bd. LWV, Winston-Salem, 1953; pres. state bd. AAUW, Winston-Salem, 1950-54; bd. dirs. YWCA, Winston-Salem, 1950-54; v.p. bd. dirs. Arts Coun., Winston-Salem, 1954-60. Named Outstanding Reading Tchr., Reading Assn., Winston-Salem, 1982; fellow Orton-Gillingham Acad. Mem. APA, Orton Dyslexia Soc. (v.p. bd. dirs. 1960-77), N.C. Psychol. Assn., Assn. for Children with Learning Disabilities (v.p. bd. dirs. 1972—, Orton-Gillingham Acad. fellow), Sorosis Club, Delta Kappa

Gamma. Democrat. Presbyterian. Home: 200 Lamplighter Cir Winston Salem NC 27104-3419

KARNOWSKY, DEBORAH A., advertising agency executive. V.p., sr. v.p. W.B. Doner & Co., Southfield, Mich., until 1989; exec. v.p., creative dir. Campbell-Ewald Advt., Warren, Mich., 1989—. Recipient numerous creative awards; named Midwest Creative All-Star, AdWeek MAg., 1991. Office: Campbell-Ewald Advt 30400 Van Dyke Ave Warren MI 48093-2316

KAROL, MERYL HELENE, immunotoxicology educator; b. N.Y.C., Aug. 10, 1940; m. Paul Jason; children: Darcie, Deverin, Meredith. BS, Cornell U., 1961; PhD, Columbia U., 1967. NIH fellow SUNY-Stony Brook, 1967-68; research assoc. U. Pitts., 1974-76, research asst. prof., 1976-79, assoc. prof., 1979-85, prof. environ. and indsl. health, 1985—; advisor numerous govt. health adv. bds., agys.; lectr. in field. Assoc. editor Jour. Chem. Rsch. in Toxicological Environ. Health, Toxicology and Ecotoxicology News; mem. editl. bd. Methods in Toxicology; contbr. articles to profl. jours. Recipient Women in Sci. award U. Mich., 1986, Rachel Carson award, 1993. Mem. AAAS, Am. Chem. Soc., Am. Thoracic Soc., Am. Conf. Govt. Indsl. Hygienists, Soc. Toxicology (v.p. 1993, pres. 1994, Frank R. Blood award), N.Y. Acad. Scis., Am. Assn. Immunologists. Avocations: sports, decorating, design, travel. Office: U Pitts Dept Environ Occupational Health 260 Kappa Dr Pittsburgh PA 15238-2818

KAROLYI, MARGARET S., educational psychology educator; b. N.Y.C., Mar. 16, 1940; d. Joseph Sziracky and Mary (Francovsky-Sziracky) Quinn; m. Alexander F. Karolyi, Oct. 24, 1959; children: Elizabeth, Susan, Anne. BS in Home Econs., Marywood Coll., 1975, MS C.C. Edn., 1978, MA in Psychology, 1986; PhD in Higher Edn. Adminstr., Kent State U., 1993. First lectr. Luzerne County C.C., Nanticoke, Pa., 1978-81; lectr. Marywood Coll., Scranton, Pa., 1981-83, Walsh Coll., North Canton, Ohio, 1986; mem. adj. faculty U. Akron, Ohio, 1987-96, Kent State U., 1986-96; mem. adj. faculty Wayne Coll., Orrville, Ohio, fall 1992, Cleve. (Ohio) State U., spring 1993, John Carroll U., Cleve., 1993-94. Judge Ohio Acad. Sci. Dist. 13, Canton (Ohio) Country Day Sch., 1991-96. Mem. APA, Am. Ednl. Rsch. Assn. Home: 374 Amy Way Wadsworth OH 44281-9205

KARP, JUDITH ESTHER, oncologist, science administrator; b. San Diego, July 15, 1946; d. Louis Moses and Bella Sarah (Perlman) K.; m. Stanley Howard Freedman, Sept. 21, 1975. BA in Chemistry, Mills Coll., Oakland, Calif., 1966; MD, Stanford U., 1971. Diplomate Am. Bd. Internal Medicine. Intern in medicine, jr. resident in medicine Stanford Hosps., 1971-72; asst. resident in medicine Johns Hopkins Hosp., 1972-73; clin. and rsch. fellow oncology Johns Hopkins Med. Sch., 1973-75, instr. oncology and medicine, 1975-78, asst. prof., 1978-85, assoc. prof., 1985-92; spl. asst. to dir. Nat. Cancer Inst., NIH, 1990-94, asst. dir. applied sci., 1995-96; prof. medicine U. Md. Cancer Ctr. Dept. Medicine, U. Md. Sch. Medicine, 1996—; mem. consensus com. Immuno-compromised Host Soc., 1987-88. Mem. med. adn sci. affairs com. Leukemia Soc. Am., 1995—. Am. Cancer Soc. Jr. clin. faculty fellow, 1976-79; San Diego Heart Assn. grantee, 1965-67; recipient Aurelia Henry Reinhardt prize Mills Coll., 1966, Cancer Rsch. award Washington chpt. Awards for Rsch. Coll. Scientists, 1975, Resolution of Commendation award State of Md., 1982, Recognition award City of Balt., 1984, NIH Dirs. award, 1995. Mem. Am. Soc. Hematology, Am. Soc. Clin. Oncology, Cell Kinetics Soc. (clin. counsellor governing council 1985-87), Am. Soc. Microbiology, Immunocompromised Host Soc., Internat. Soc. Exptl. Hematology, Leukemia Soc. Am. (mem. med. and sci. affairs com. 1995—), Nat. Bd. Med. Examiners, Phi Beta Kappa. Democrat. Jewish. Home: 3422 Manor Hill Rd Baltimore MD 21208-1824 Office: U Md Cancer Ctr 22 S Greene St Rm S9D15 Baltimore MD 21201

KARP, NATALIE LYNN, financial executive; b. N.Y.C., July 6, 1962; d. Samuel Bernard and Arelene (Nass) Nekrutman; m. Jason Bruce Karp, June 11, 1989; children: Samantha, Reid. BA, SUNY, Binghamton, 1984; MBA, Fordham U., 1995. Rsch. analyst Morgan Olmstead Kennedy & Gardner, N.Y.C., 1985-87; dir. health and sci. group Cameron Assocs., N.Y.C., 1987-89; mgr. investor rels. Thermo Electron, N.Y.C., 1989—. Mem. Nat. Investor Rels. Inst., Fin. Women's Assn. of N.Y. Office: 545 Madison Ave 10th fl New York NY 10022-4219

KARP, ROBERTA S., retail services executive; married; 2 children. BA, SUNY, Binghampton; JD, Hofstra U. Atty. Kramer, Levin et al., N.Y.C.; from legal counsel to v.p. corp. affairs Liz Claiborne, Inc., N.Y.C., 1986—. Office: Liz Claiborne Inc 1 Claiborne Ave North Bergen NJ 07047

KARP, VICKIE ANN, writer; b. N.Y.C., May 3, 1953; d. Henry Karp and Helen Lee Kaplan; m. Tsvi Dym, July 11, 1976. BA, CUNY, 1974, MA, 1976. Mem. editl. staff New Yorker Mag., N.Y.C., 1974-90; sr. writer, editor Thirteen/WNET, N.Y.C., 1991—; adj. lectr. The New Sch. for Social Rsch., N.Y.C., 1990-93, Wesleyan U., Middletown, Conn., 1989-90; playwright Symphony Space Theater, N.Y.C., 1987-88; scriptwriter Good Morning Am./WABC, N.Y.C., 1980-81, N.Y. Ctr. for Visual History, N.Y.C., 1986-87, Robert Yuhas Prodns., L.A., 1994—. Author: (play) Driving to the Interior, 1988, (film documentaries) Marianne Moore: In Her Own Image, 1987, Would You Kindly Direct Me to Hell: The Infamous Dorothy Parker, 1995; contbr. poetry to popular mags. and anthologies including The Best Poetry of 1991, The Best Poetry of 1993, The New Yorker, The N.Y. Rev. of Books, Yale Rev.; contbr. articles to popular mags. Nat. Endowment Arts fellow, 1994; grantee CAPS, 1981. Mem. Poets House, Poets and Writers. Office: Thirteen/WNET 356 W 58th St New York NY 10019

KARPATKIN, RHODA HENDRICK, consumer information organization executive, lawyer; b. N.Y.C., June 7, 1930; d. Charles and Augusta (Arkin) Hendrick; m. Marvin Karpatkin, June 16, 1951 (dec.); children: Deborah Hendrick, Herbert Isaac, Jeremy Charles. BA, Bklyn. Coll., 1951; LLB, Yale U., 1953. Bar: N.Y. 1954. Pvt. practice law, 1954-74; ptnr. Karpatkin & Karpatkin, 1958-61, Karpatkin, Ohrenstein & Karpatkin, N.Y.C., 1961-74; pres. Consumers Union of U.S. Inc., Yonkers, N.Y., 1974—; pres. Internat. Orgn. Consumers Unions, 1984-91, v.p., 1991—; exec dir Consumers Union U.S., N.Y.C.; Spl. counsel for decentralization N.Y.C. Bd. Edn., 1969-70; adj. prof. dept. urban studies Queens Coll., 1972-74; commr. Nat. Commn. on New Tech. Uses of Copyrighted Works, 1975-78; mem. Pres.'s Com. Trade Policy and Negotiation, 1993—. Contbg. author: Current School Problems, 1971, Consumer Education in the Human Services; contbr. articles to profl. publs. Mem. Local Sch. Bd. 5, N.Y.C., 1966-70, chmn., 1967-69; mem. Community Sch. Bd. 3, N.Y.C., 1970-71; mem. com. acad. freedom ACLU, 1973-84; mem. Pres.'s Commn. for Nat. Agenda for the Eighties., 1979-80; trustee Pub. Edn. Assn., 1972-85. Mem. ABA (commn. on law and the economy 1976-79, commn. to reduce costs and delay 1978-84, commn. access to justice 2000 1993—), Assn. of Bar of City of N.Y. (com. consumer affairs 1969-80, chmn. 1974-79, com. on internat. human rights 1980-83, audit com. 1982-83, com. Ea. European affairs), Nat. Inst. for Dispute Resolution (bd. dirs. 1982-89), Assn. Yale Alumni (rep.-at-large 1982-85). Office: Consumers Union US Inc 101 Truman Ave Yonkers NY 10703-1044

KARPEL, FRANCESCA JORDAN, business educator; b. Boston, May 25, 1953; d. Frank Wysong and Virginia (Leahy) Jordan; m. Ron Aaron Karpel, Sept. 8, 1984; children: Ethan David and Daphne Lee. AB, Smith Coll., 1975; MM, Northwestern U., 1977. Asst. v.p. Wells Fargo Bank, N.A., San Francisco, 1977-85; asst. prof. Coll. San Mateo, Calif., 1987-92; cons. accelerated schs. project Stanford (Calif.) U., 1994-95; with Edn. Ptnrs., San Francisco, 1995—; cons. Karpel & Assoc., 1989—. Mem. gov. bd. trustees Belmont (Calif.) Elem. Sch. Dist., 1993—; del. assembly mem. govtl. rels. chair Calif. Sch. Bds. Assn., Sacramento, 1994—, legis. com., 1996—; legis. com. chair San Mateo County Sch. Bds. Assn., 1995; mem. hist. preservation task force, Belmont, 1995; chair, spokesperson San Mateo County Citizens Against Prop 174, Burlingame, 1993. Office: Edn Ptnrs Ste 100 2601 Mariposa St San Francisco CA 94110

KARPF, JUANITA, music educator, cellist; b. Rochester, N.Y., Oct. 31, 1951; d. John Andrew and Carol Jean (Boyce) K. BM, State U. Coll., Potsdam, N.Y., 1973; MM, U. Ga., 1986, DMA, 1992. Music tchr. Auburn (N.Y.) City Schs., 1973-75; music tchr. Fayetteville-Manlius Schs., Manlius, N.Y., 1976-77, Altamont Sch., Birmingham, Ala., 1977-79, Bibb County Schs., Macon, Ga., 1979-84; instr. music Mercer U., Macon, 1981-84, U. Ga., Athens, 1984-91; mem. faculty Middlebury (Vt.) Coll., 1991-92; asst. prof. music and women's studies U. Ga., Athens, 1992—; music dir. Macon Symphony Youth Orch., 1982-84. Performer recital Weill Recital Hall, N.Y.C., 1989, (album) Indigo Girls-Strange Fire, 1987, (CD) The Voice and the Virtuoso, 1993; contbr. articles to Notable Black Am. Women, 1992, African Am. Women; reviewer High Performance Rev. Mem. Am. Musicological Soc., Am. String Tchrs. Assn., Coll. Music Soc., Ga. Cello Soc., AAUW (Athenian scholar 1988), Nat. Women's Studies Assn., Sonneck Soc., Phi Kappa Phi, Pi Kappa Lambda. Office: U Ga Sch Music 250 River Rd Athens GA 30602-3153

KARPINSKI, HUBERTA ELAINE, library trustee; b. Cato, N.Y., Jan. 4, 1925; d. Alfred Raymond and Lena Margaret (Fuller) Tuxill; m. Edward Karpinski, Nov. 17, 1956; children: Susan Tanielian, Rebecca Hitch, Amy Jaward. Student, U. Mich., 1943-45, Wayne U., 1949-50; grad., N.Y. Art Acad. Design, 1972. Operator to svc. observer supr. Mich. Bell Telephone Co., Detroit, 1946-57; tchr. art Birmingham (Mich.) Pub. Sch., 1977-87; libr. trustee Redford (Mich.) Twp. Dist. Libr., 1971—. Chmn. Lola Valley Civic Assn., Redford, 1960-70; vice chmn. Redford Twp. Coun. Civic Assn., 1967-71; bd. dirs. 17th Dist. Mich. Dem. Party, Redford, 1968-71. Mem. Nat. Mus. Women in arts (charter), Mich. Porcelain Artists, Internat. Porcelain Art Tchrs. Home: 17418 MacArthur Redford MI 48240-2241

KARPMAN, LAURA ANNE, composer; b. L.A., Mar. 1, 1959; d. Harold Lew and Rodelle (Grisor) K. MusB in Composition magna cum laude, U. Mich., 1980; MusM, Juilliard Sch., 1983, MusD in Composition, 1985. Instr. Manhattan Sch. Music, N.Y.C., 1985-87, New Sch. for Social Rsch. Eugene Lang Coll., N.Y.C., 1986-87; assoc. dir. Ken Boxley Inst., Rutgers U., New Brunswick, 1987-88; tchg. artist Lincoln Ctr. Inst., 1985-87; vis. asst. prof. Whittier Coll., 1989-90; assoc. editor Holt, Rinehart and Winston, 1986; vis. theorist Ariz. State U., 1989; lectr. in field. Composer music for feature films Lovers Knot, Johnny 99, Dogfight, for cable films Dancing into the Dream, Blacktide, for mini-series A Woman of Independent Means, Sex, Censorship and the Silver Screen, A Century of Women, movies of week A Promise to Carolyn, Journey Home, If Someone Had Known, Shameful Secrets, Doing Time on Maple Drive, The Broken Chord, A Child Lost Forever, Abandoned and Deceived, A Mother's Revenge, Based on an Untrue Story, The Sitter, My Brother's Wife, Moment of Truth: A Mother's Deception, Moment of Truth: Broken Pledges, Moment of Truth, To Walk Again, TV pilots and series Mondo Bizarro, Beauty, WIOU, The Los Angeles History Project, Between Two Worlds, Hollywood Strike, documentaries and spl. projects ABC World of Discovery, Earthquakes: The Terrifying Truth, What Really Happened to Adolph Hitler, The Power of Russian Psychics, Walt Disney-40 Years of Television Magic, Voice of Disney Introductions, Indian Jones and the Temple of the Forbidden Eye; commns. include Bibliotheque, U. Mich. Dance Ensemble, 1979, Six Forms for Five Brass, Detroit Civic Brass Quintet, 1979, Duets, Trios, Quintets, Am. Composers Orch., 1986, Greetings, Gina Gallery, Tokyo, 1989, Switching Stations, Concordia Chamber Symphony, 1990, Caprices for string trio Ensemble Capriccio, 1990; work broadcast on numerous radio stas., including San Diego, N.Y.C., Boston, San Francisco, Mpls.; contbr. articles to profl. publs. Grantee ASCAP Found., 1981, 83; Charles Ives scholar AAAL, 1984, also others. Office: care Cathy Schleussner 15622 Royal Oak Rd Encino CA 91436

KARR, KATHLEEN, writer; b. Allentown, Pa., Apr. 21, 1946; d. Stephen and Elizabeth (Szoka) Csere; m. Lawrence F. Karr, July 13, 1968; children: Suzanne, Daniel. BA, Cath. U. of Am., 1968; MA, Providence Coll., 1971; postgrad, Corcoran Sch. Art, 1972. Tchr. English and speech Barrington (R.I.) H.S., 1968-69; curator R.I. Hist. Soc. Film Archives, 1970-71; archives asst. Am. Film Inst., Washington, 1971-72; mem. catalog staff Am. Film Inst., 1972; gen. mgr. Washington Circle Theatre Corp., Washington, 1973-78; advt. dir. Circle/Showcase Theatres, Washington, 1979-83; dir. pub. rels. Circle/Showcase Theatres, 1984-88; mem. pub. rels. staff Circle Mgmt. Co./Circle Releasing, Washington, 1988-93; asst. prof. George Washington U., 1979, 80-81; lectr., instr. in film and comms. at various instns.; lectr. at film and writing confs.; juror Am. Film Fest., 1971, Rosebud Awards, 1991; mem. adv. bd. Children's Literature, 1994—. Author: It Ain't Always Easy, 1990 (finalist, outstandin emerging artist, Washington Mayor's Arts awards, 1986; "100 Books for Reading and Sharing" citation N.Y. Public Libr., 1990), Oh, Those Harper Girls!; or, Young and Dangerous, 1992 (Parents' Choice Story Book citation, 1992), Gideon and the Mummy Professor, 1993, The Cave, 1994, In the Kaiser's Clutch, 1995, Light of My Heart, 1984, From This Day Forward, 1985 (Golden Medallion award for best inspirational novel Romance Writers of Am., 1986), Chessie's King, 1986, Destiny's Dreamers Book I: Gone West, 1993, Destiny's Dreamers Book II: The Promised Land, 1993; editor: The American Film Heritage: Views from the American Film Insitute Collection, 1972; author of various short films; contbr. to numerous jours. Mem. Washington Romance Writers (bd. dirs. 1985-86, pres. 1986-87). Office: care Renee Cho McIntosh & Otis 310 Madison Ave Ste 607 New York NY 10017*

KARSEN, SONJA PETRA, retired Spanish educator; b. Berlin, Apr. 11, 1919; came to U.S., 1938, naturalized, 1945; d. Fritz and Erna (Heidermann) K. Titulo de Bachiller, 1937; BA, Carleton Coll., 1939; MA (scholar in French), Bryn Mawr Coll., 1941; PhD, Columbia U., 1950. Instr. Spanish Lake Erie Coll., Painesville, Ohio, 1943-45; instr. modern langs. U. P.R., 1945-46; instr. Spanish Syracuse U., 1947-50, Bklyn. Coll., 1950-51; asst. to dep. dir. gen. UNESCO, 1951-52, Latin Am. Desk, tech. assistance dept., 1952-53, mem. tech. assistance mission Costa Rica, 1954; asst. prof. Spanish Sweet Briar Coll., Va., 1955-57; assoc. prof., chmn. dept. Romance langs. Skidmore Coll., Saratoga Springs, N.Y., 1957-61, chmn. dept. modern langs. and lits., 1961-79, prof. Spanish, 1961-87, prof. emerita, 1987; cons. Hudson-Mohawk Assn. Colls. and Univs., 1990; faculty rsch. lectr. Skidmore Coll., 1963; mem. adv. and nominating com. Books Abroad, 1965-67; lectr. U. Gesamthochschule, Paderborn, Germany, June 1995. Author: Guillermo Valencia, Colombian Poet, 1951, Educational Development in Costa Rica with UNESCO's Technical Assistance, 1951-54, 1954, Jaime Torres Bodet: A Poet in a Changing World, 1963, Selected Poems of Jaime Torres Bodet, 1964, Versos y prosas de Jaime Torres Bodet, 1966, Jaime Torres Bodet, 1971, Ensayos de Literatura E Historia Iberoamericana/Essays on Iberoamerican Literature and History, 1988, Papers on Foreign Languages, Literature and Culture, 1982-87, 88, Bericht Uber Den Vater: Fritz Karsen 1885-1951, 1993; translator: The Role of the Americas in History (Leopoldo Zea), 1992; editor Lang. Assn. Bull., 1980-83; mem. editorial adv. bd. Modern Lang. Studies; contbr. articles to profl. jours. Decorated chevalier dans l'Ordre des Palmes Académiques, 1964; recipient Leadership award N.Y. State Assn. Fgn. Lang. Tchrs., 1973, 76, 78, Nat. Disting. Leadership award, 1979, Disting. Service award, 1983, 86, Capital Dist. Fgn. Language Disting. Service award, 1987; recipient Spanish Heritage award, 1981, Alumni Achievement award Carleton Coll., 1982; exchange student auspices Inst. Internat. Ednl. at Carleton Coll., 1938-39; Buenos Aires Conv. grantee for research in Colombia, 1946-47; faculty research grantee Skidmore Coll., summer 1959, 61, 63, 64, 67, 69, 70, 73, ad hoc faculty grantee, 71, 78, 85. Mem. Am. Assn. Tchrs. Spanish and Portuguese, Nat. Assn. Self-Instructional Lang. Programs (v.p. 1981-82,pres. 1982-83), AAUW, AAUP, MLA (del. assembly 1976-78, Mildenberger medal selection com 1984-86), El Ateneo Doctor Jaime Torres Bodet (founding mem.), Nat. Geog. Soc., Asociación Internacional de Hispanistas, UN Assn. U.S.A., Am. Soc. French Acad. Palms, Fulbright Alumni, Phi Sigma Iota, Sigma Delta Pi. Home: 1755 York Ave Apt 37A New York NY 10128-6875

KARSON, CATHERINE JUNE, computer programmer, consultant; b. Salt Lake City, Jan. 26, 1956; d. Gary George and Sylvia June (Naylor) Anderson; m. Mitchell Reed Karson, June 14, 1987; 1 child, Rhonda. A in Gen. Studies, Pima C.C., Tucson, 1989, AAS in Computer Sci., 1990. Night supr. F.G. Ferre & Son, Inc., Salt Lake City, 1973-76, exec. sec., 1977-79; operating room technician Cottonwood Hosp., Salt Lake City, 1976-77; customer svc. rep., System One rep. Ea. Airlines, Inc., Salt Lake City and Tucson, 1979-88; edn. specialist Radio Shack Computer Ctr., Tucson, 1988-89; programmer/analyst Pinal County DPIS, Florence, Ariz., 1989-90; systems analyst Carondelet Health Svcs., Tucson, 1990; programmer/analyst Sunquest Info. Sys., Tucson, 1990-94, sr. tech. proposal specialist, 1994-95; software developer, 1995—; cons. Pinal County Pub. Fiduciary, Florence, 1990, UBET, Barbados, W.I., 1990—, numerous clients, Tucson, 1990-93. Mem. bus. adv. coun. Portable Practical Ednl. Preparation, Inc., Tucson, 1990-91. Mem. Nat. Sys. Programmer Assn. Republican. Jewish. Home: 6066 N Serendipity Ln Tucson AZ 85704-5322

KARSTETTER, EMILY ANNE, lawyer; b. Bellefont, Pa., Dec. 8, 1962; d. Allan Boyd and Anne Louise (Nelson) K. BA, Wellesley (Mass.) Coll., 1984; JD, New England Sch. of Law, 1991. Bar: Mass. 1991. Ops. mgr. Carney, Sandoe & Assocs., Boston, 1983-86; agy. auditor Ticor Title Ins. Co., Boston, 1986-87, computer specialist, 1987-90, asst. agy. mgr., 1990-91; assoc. Bellotti & Barretto, Cambridge, Mass., 1991—; coach mock trial team New England Sch. of Law, Boston, 1991—. Mem. Boston Bar Assn., Mass. Bar Assn., Middlesex County Bar Assn. (v.p. young lawyers divsn. 1992-93), Assn. of Trial Lawyers of Am. Democrat. Office: Bellotti & Barretto 25 Thorndike St Cambridge MA 02141

KARTERMAN-STORCK, SUZANNE, art educator, artist; b. Pottsville, Pa., Nov. 14, 1940; d. Kenneth Robert and Wilhelmina Carlene (Bausch) Karterman; m. Walter John Whitehouse, Sept. 12, 1961 (div. 1984); children: Michele Lyn, Amy Sue; m. Allen Lee Storck, Nov. 11, 1988. BS in Art Edn., Kutztown U., 1974, MEd, 1981. Substitute art tchr. Berks County Schs., Reading and others, Pa., 1974-75; elem. art tchr. Twperhocken Area Sch. Dist., Rehrersburg, Pa., 1974-81; adj. instr. Reading Area C.C., 1981-91, instr., 1991-94, asst. prof., 1995; painting instr. Wyomissing (Pa.) Inst. Fine Arts, 1988-89, Adult Workshops, Chester County, Pa., 1989-94. Artist: works accepted in juried shows: Art Assn. of Harrisburg, Pa., Allentown (Pa.) Art Mus., Reading Pub. Mus. and Art Gallery, Lebanon Valley Coll. (Pa.) Arts Festival, York (Pa.) Art Assn. 16th Juried Show, Allied Artists of Schuylkill County 25th Annual Show, Kent Art Assn. Pres. Show, Canton Gallery on the Green. Purchase award Gilbert Assocs., Reading, Pa. State U. (Berks County); Graphic award Canton Artists' Guild, Conn. Mem. Berks Art Alliance (pres. 1981-82, past treas., chmn. of juried show 1982). Office: Reading Area CC 10 S Second St Reading PA 19603-1706

KARU, GILDA M(ALL), lawyer, government official; b. Oceanport, N.J., Dec. 1, 1951; d. Harold and Ilvy (Meriloo) K.; m. Frederick F. Foy, May 23, 1981. AB, Vassar Coll., 1974; JD, Ill. Inst. Tech., 1987. Bar: Ill. 1987, U.S. Dist. Ct. (no. dist.) Ill. 1987. Quality control reviewer Food and Nutrition Svc. USDA, Robbinsville, N.J., 1974-77, team leader, 1977-78, supr., 1978-81; sect. chief Food and Consumer Svc. USDA, Chgo., 1991—; employer adviser Ctr. for Rehab. and Tng. Disabled Persons, Chgo., 1986-93; chief mgmt. negotiator for collective bargaining agreement Nat. Treasury Employees Union, 1990. Bd. dirs., legal counsel, regional dir. North Ctrl. Estonian Am. Nat. Coun., N.Y.C.; v.p. 1st Estonian Evang. Luth. Ch., Chgo., treas., 1994—; mem. Chgo. Vol. Legal Svcs., Friends of Arlington Heights Meml. Libr.; vol. dep. voter registration officer Cook County, Ill.; pres. Arlington Heights-Mt. Prospect-Buffalo Grove area LWV. Recipient cert. of recognition William A. Jump Meml. Found., 1987, Arthur S. Flemming award Washington Downtown Jaycees, 1987, Ill. Dem. Ethnic Heritage award, 1989, cert. of appreciation Assn. for Persons with Disabilities in Agr., 1992, Group Honor award for work on 1993 Miss. River Flood Disaster Relief, Sec. of USDA, 1994. Mem. ABA, NAFE, LWV (bd. dirs. 1992—), Ill. Bar Assn., Chgo. Bar Assn., Baltic Bar Assn., United Coun. on Welfare Fraud, Internat. Platform Assn., Nat. Audubon Soc., Mensa, Vassar Club (chpt. treas. 1988-90, v.p. 1990-91, coord. pub. rels. 1991—). Office: USDA Food and Consumer Svc 20th Fl 77 W Jackson Blvd Chicago IL 60604-3504

KARWEICK, BETTY JANE, law educator, librarian; b. Green Bay, Wis., Jan. 21, 1948; d. Claude Albert and Genevieve Doris (Arndt) K.; life ptnr. Robert Arnold Schnur. BSc, Carroll Coll., 1970; M in Libr. Sci., U. Wis., Milw., 1976; JD, U. Wis., Madison, 1985. Bar: Wis. 1985, Minn. 1985. Elem. sch. tchr. Elem. Sch., Appleton, Wis., 1969-70, Franklin Sch., Madison, Wis., 1970-71, Lake Bluff Sch., Shorewood, Wis., 1972-75; law libr. Michael Best & Friedrich, Milw., 1976-82; assoc. Dorsey & Whitney, Mpls., 1985-87, Quarles and Brady, Milw., 1987-88; law lectr., libr. Duke U. Sch. of Law, Durham, N.C., 1988-90, Wm. Mitchell Coll. Law, St. Paul, Minn., 1990-94, Univ. Wis., Madison, 1995—. Named fellow libr. sch. U. Wis., Milw., 1975-76. Mem. Wis. Bar Assn., Minn. Bar Assn., Wis. Law Librs. Assn., Minn. Assn. Law Librs. (mem. at large 1995), Am. Assn. Law Librs. (nat. edn. com. 1988-90). Office: U Wis Law Sch 975 Bascom Hall Madison WI 53706

KASAKOVE, SUSAN, interior designer; b. Newark, N.J., Nov. 11, 1938. BFA, U. Buffalo, 1958, Hunter Coll., 1960; postgrad., N.Y. Sch. of Interior Design, 1960-64, New Sch. for Social Rsch., 1967-68, Pratt Inst., 1968-69. Asst. interior designer Rodgers Assocs., N.Y.C., 1964-66; interior designer Walter Dorwin Teague Assocs., N.Y.C., 1966-70; sr. interior designer N.Y. State Facilities Devel. Corp., N.Y.C., 1970-95; Dormitory Authority for the State of N.Y., 1995—. Reading tutor Vols. for Children's Svcs., N.Y.C., 1976-82; chair Friends of White Plains (N.Y.) Symphony, 1981-83; vol. dept. Asian Dept. Work Endod, 1995, vol. guide edn. dept., 1978—; Rep. treas. 11th Ward, Yonkers, N.Y., 1979-81. Recipient Outstanding Svc. to Sch. award Rockland County (N.Y.) Lions Club, 1955. Mem. Environ. Design Rsch. Assn. Home: 793 Palmer Rd Apt 3F Bronxville NY 10708-3337 Office: 1 Penn Plaza 52nd Fl New York NY 10119-0118

KASAKS, SALLY FRAME, apparel executive; b. 1944. With Lord & Taylor, Garfinckels, Saks Fifth Avenue, N.Y.C., 1966-83; pres., CEO AnnTaylor, Inc., N.Y.C., 1983-85; chmn., CEO Talbots, Inc., Hingham, Mass., 1985-88; pres. Abercrombie & Fitch (divsn. The Limited, Inc.), Columbus, Ohio, 1989-92; chmn., CEO AnnTaylor Stores Corp. and AnnTaylor, Inc., N.Y.C., 1992—. Office: Ann Taylor Stores Corp 142 W 57th St New York NY 10019*

KASCUS, MARIE ANNETTE, librarian; b. Boston, June 2, 1943; d. Anthony Joseph and Mildred (Lochiatto) Martucci; m. Joseph Edward Kascus, July 3, 1966. BA, Northeastern U., Boston, 1966; MSLS, U. Ill., 1969. Libr. asst. Boston Pub. Libr. Br., East Boston, Mass., 1961-66; rsch. asst. Hanscom AFB/Decision Scis. Lab., Bedford, Mass., 1964-66; asst. binding libr. Univ. Ill., Champaign-Urbana, 1970-72; head serials dept. Cen. Conn. State Univ., New Britain, 1972—, collection mgmt. coord., 1984-86; abstracter ABC-CLIO, Santa Barbara, Calif., 1979—; indexer Productivity, Inc., Stamford, Conn., Cambridge, Mass., 1981-86; mem. editl. bd. Cataloging and Classification Quar., 1984—; cons. Post Coll., Waterbury, Conn., 1986, State of Conn. Pers. Divsn., Harford, Conn., 1987-88, Choice Mag., Middletown, Conn., 1990—; mem. program adv. bd. Sixth Off-Campus Libr. Svcs. Conf., 1992-93; mem. ASIS Thesaurus of Info. Sci. and Librarianship Adv. Bd., 1993. Referee and contbr. articles to profl. jours.; presenter at profl. confs.; co-author: Library Services for Off-Campus and Distance Education: The Second Annotated Bibliography, 1996. Cons. New Eng. Assn. Schs. and Colls., Newton, Mass., 1990, 92, CCSU Found./George R. Muirhead Scholarship Fund, New Britain, Conn., 1991, Harriet Kiser Opera Fund, Hartford, 1991—. Recipient Sears B. Condit award for excellent scholarship Sears Roebuck, Inc., Boston, 1966, Alumni award for profl. promise Northeastern U., Boston, 1966; AAUP Faculty Rsch. grantee Cen. Conn. State U., New Britain, 1991; Higher Edn. Act fellow U.S. Govt. U. Ill., Champaign, 1969-70. Mem. AAUP, ALA, Assn. Coll. and Rsch. Librs. (Extended Campus Libr. Svcs. sect., chmn. rsch. com., nominations com., del. at large), Assn. Coll. and Rsch. Librs. (K.G. Saur award com. 1995-96), Am. Soc. Indexers (Conn. chpt. pres. 1988—, organizer, voting rep. Nat. Info. Stds. Orgn. 1995-98), Phi Delta Kappa, Phi Kappa Phi, Pi Sigma Alpha, Beta Phi Mu. Office: Ctrl Conn St U 1615 Stanley St New Britain CT 06053-2439

KASE-POLISINI, JUDITH BAKER, theatre educator, playwright; b. Wilmington, Del., Dec. 13, 1932; d. Charles Robert and Elizabeth Edna (Baker) Kase; stepchildren: James, Elizabeth, John, Katherine, Ann. BA, U. Del., 1955; MA, Case Western Res. U., 1956. Tchr., dir. children's theatre Agnes Scott Coll., 1956, U. Tenn., 1957, U. Md., Germany, 1958-60, Denver Civic Theatre, Denver U., Kent Sch., 1960-61; dir. children's theatre U. N.H., Durham, 1962-69; dir. theatre resources for youth, Somersworth, N.H., 1966-69; assoc. prof. theatre U. South Fla., Tampa, 1969-74, assoc. prof. edn., 1975-83, prof., 1984-95, artistic dir. ednl. theatre, 1976—; project dir. Hillsborough County Artists-in-Schs. Evaluation and Inservice Project, 1980-82; dir. Internat. Ctr. for Studies in Theatre Edn. Bd. dirs. Fla. Alliance for Arts Edn., sec., 1976-77, vice-chmn., 1979-82, chmn. 1982-84;

chmn. Wingspread Conf on Theatre Edn., 1977; drama adjudicator Nat. Arts Festival, Ministry of Edn., Bahamas, 1975, 76, 79, 80; regional chmn. Alliance for Arts Edn., chmn. nat. adv. council, mem. edn. adv. com., 1986—; trustee Children's Theatre Found.; bd. dirs. Coll. Fellows Am. Theatre of J.F. Kennedy Ctr. for Performing Arts, 1991-93, Fla. Assoc. Theatre Ed. (exec. dir. 1995—). Coll. Bus., 1993— cons. Southeast Ctr. for Edn. in Theatre, (1995), Fla. Dept Edn., (1994-96); cons. theatre edn. and prodn.; steering com. Arts for a Complete Edn., 1991-95; mem. curriculum writing com. Fla. Dept. Edn., 1994-96. Recipient Disting. Book of Yr. award, 1989. Mem. Children's Theatre Assn. Am. (pres.-elect 1975-77, pres. 1977-79, chmn. symposia 1981-85, spl. recognition citation 1984), Am. Theatre Assn. (chief div. pres.'s coordinating council 1977-78 commn. on theatre edn. 1982—, elected), Am. Alliance for Theatre and Edn. (dir. & project dir. theatre literacy collaborative study Internat. Ctr. for Studies in Theatre Edn., Presdl. award 1992), Speech Communication Assn. (membership dir. 1961), Southeastern Theatre Confs. (Sara Spencer award 1980), Fla. Theatre Confs. (Disting. Career award), Nat. Theatre Conf., Internat. Assn. Theatres for Children and Youth, Internat. Amateur Theatre Assn. (N.Am. bd. dirs.), Fla. Assn. for Theater Edn. (theatre edn. of yr. award 1986), Tampa Mus. Democrat. Episcopalian. Club: Carrollwood Village. Author: The Creative Drama Book: Three Approaches, other books; editor: Creative Drama in a Developmental Context; Children's Theatre, Creative Drama and Learning, Drama as a Meaning Maker, Introduction to Drama Teacher Resource Guide, The Arts: Interconnecting Pathways to Human Experience; contbr. articles to profl. jours.; pub. (plays) Snow White and The Seven Dwarfs, 1960, The Emperor's New Clothes, 1966, Southern Fried Cracker Tales, 1995. Home: 5321 Taylor Rd Lutz FL 33549-4823 Office: U South Fla Dept Secondary Edn Tampa FL 33620

KASHDAN, JOANNE GRAY, English language educator, author; b. L.A., June 14, 1935; d. Ben and Anne Katherine (Nagy) Gray; m. Laurence Kashdan, 1969 (div. 1973). BA, U. So. Calif., 1959; MA, Calif. State U., L.A., 1962; PhD, Occidental Coll., 1972. Instr. Colo. State U., Ft. Collins, 1962-63; instr. Calif. State U., L.A., 1963-66, East L.A. Coll., 1967-68, Occidental Coll., 1967-68; adj. prof. Calif. State U., Long Beach, 1968, 73-77, Fullerton, 1974-75; adj. prof. Coastline C.C., Costa Mesa, Calif., 1976-77; prof. English Golden West Coll., Huntington Beach, Calif., 1975—; coord. English dept. assessment Golden West Coll., 1988—, editor accreditation report, 1986. Author: (textbook) Preparing for Police Report Writing, 1988, 2d edit., 1995; contbr. articles to profl. jour., reference books. Vol. advisor Cancer Survivor's Group, Orange County, Calif., 1993—. Recipient Intercollegiate Program of Grad. Studies fellowship Occidental Coll., 1964-66. Mem. MLA, Nat. Coun. Tchrs. of English, Coll. Conf. on Composition and Communication, Medieval Acad. Am., Am. Comparative Lit. Assn., Am. Fedn. Tchrs. Democrat. Office: English Dept Golden West Coll 15744 Golden West St Huntington Beach CA 92647

KASHDIN, GLADYS SHAFRAN, painter, educator; b. Pitts., Dec. 15, 1921; d. Edward M. and Miriam P. Shafran; m. Manville E. Kashdin, Oct. 11, 1942 (dec.). BA magna cum laude, U. Miami, 1960; MA, Fla. State U., 1962, PhD, 1965. Photographer, N.Y.C. and Fla., 1938-60; tchr. art, Fla. and Ga., 1956-63; asst. prof. humanities U. South Fla., Tampa, 1965-70, assoc. prof., 1970-74, prof., 1974-87, prof. emerita, 1987—; works exhibited in 58 one-woman shows, 38 group exhbns.; maj. touring exhibits include: The Everglades, 1972-75, Aspects of the River, 1975-80, Processes of Time, 1981-91, Retrospective 1941-96, Tampa Mus. Art, 1996; represented in permanent collections: Taiwan, Peoples Republic of China, Columbus Mus. Arts, LeMoyne Art Found., Tampa Internat. Airport, Tampa Mus. Art, Kresge Art Mus., U. So. Fla., Tampa Mus. of Art, 1996—; lectr.; adv. bd. Hillsborough County Mus., 1975-83. Mem. U. S. Fla. Status of Women Com., 1971-76, chmn., 1975-76. Recipient Women Helping Women in Art award Soroptimist Internat., 1979, Citizens Hon. award Hillsborough Bd. County Commrs., 1984, Mortar Bd. award for teaching excellence, 1986. Mem. AAUW (1st v.p. Tampa br. 1971-72), Phi Kappa Phi (chpt.-pres. 1981-83, artist/scholar award 1987). Home: 441 Biltmore Ave Temple Terrace FL 33617

KASHIAN, BARBARA JOY, photographer, artist; b. Evanston, Ill., Nov. 18, 1942; d. Puzant and Florence (Megerdichian) K.; m. John L. Gubbins, Dec. 14, 1968 (div. Oct. 1991); children: James Kashian Gubbins, Alexander Kashian Gubbins; m. Joel A. Snow, Feb. 7, 1992. Student, Sch. of Mus. of Fine Arts, Boston, 1961-63, Sorbonne, Paris, 1965; BA in English, Barat Coll., 1968; MA in English, U. Chgo., 1975. Assoc. editor Columbia Reports Columbia U., N.Y.C., 1972-74; dir. Friends of Channel 11 WTTW/Channel 11, Chgo., 1974-77; dir. Office of Comms. Dept. Employment Security, Chgo., 1977; dir. pub. rels. The Goodman Theatre, Chgo., 1975; mgr. spl. events Argonne (Ill.) Nat. Lab., 1989-91; personal photographer to Sen. Carol Moseley Braun Chgo., 1992; freelance photographer polit. figures, 1993-95; pres., CEO Barbara Kashian Creative, Ames, Iowa, 1995—; photo editor Iowa State Daily, Ames, 1994. Photographs published in Newsweek/Emerge, 1992, Ency. Brittanica's Book of Yr., 1992, Iowa Sesquicentennial book, 1995; photographs exhibited Columbia U. Loew Meml. Libr., 1972, U. Chgo. Lab. Schs., 1990, U. Chgo., 1996, Iowa State U. Women's Ctr., 1995. Recipient Pollie award for nation's best statewide direct mail piece Am. Assn. Polit. Cons., 1992. Mem. AAUW, Nat. Press Photographers Assn., Nikon Profl. Photographers Assn. Home and Office: 2237 Ironwood Ct Ames IA 50014

KASI, LEELA PESHKAR, pharmaceutical chemist; b. Bombay, July 15, 1939; came to U.S., 1971; d. Subbaraman and Lakshmi (Shastri) Peshkar; m. Kalli R. Kasi, June 10, 1971. BS, U. Bombay, India, 1958; PhD, U. Marburg, W. Germany, 1968. Jr. chemist Khandelwal Labs., Bombay, India, 1958-59; trainee Farbwerke Hoechst, Frankfurt, W. Germany, 1960; teaching asst. U. of Marburg, W. Germany, 1967-68; sr. chemist Boehringer-Knoll Ltd., Bombay, India, 1969-71; mgr. quality control Health Care Ind., Michigan City, Ind., 1972-77; mgr. quality control U. Tex.-M.D. Anderson Cancer Ctr., Houston, 1979-95, assoc. prof. nuclear medicine, faculty mem., 1990-95, dir. Exptl. Nuclear Medicine Lab., 1987-95; cons. Radiopharms. Devel., Houston, 1995—; mem. grad. faculty U. Tex., 1984-90. Asst. editor Jour. Nuclear Medicine, 1984-89. Mem. AAAS, Am. Assn. Cancer Rsch., Soc. of Nuclear Medicine. Home and Office: 4710 Mcdermed Dr Houston TX 77035-3706

KASINDORF, BLANCHE ROBINS, educational administrator; b. N.Y.C., May 18, 1925; d. Samuel David and Anna (Block) Robins; B.A., Hunter Coll., 1944; M.A., N.Y.U., 1948; postgrad. Cornell U., 1946-50; m. David Kasindorf, July 1, 1960. Tchr. pub. schs., Bklyn., 1945-56; instr. Bklyn. Coll., 1956-57; asst. in research for Puerto Rican Study Ford Found. and N.Y.C. Bd. Edn., 1956-57; asst. prin. N.Y.C. Pub. Schs., 1957-59; research assoc. ednl. program rsch. and stats. N.Y.C. Bd. Edn., 1959-63, coordinator spl. edn. liaison div. child welfare for Bur. Curriculum Research, 1963-64; jr. prin., integration coordinator Bklyn. Sch. Dist. 44, 1964-65; prin. Pub. Sch. 7-8, Bklyn., 1965-87; cons. to numerous social agys. Mem. NEA, Council Exceptional Children, N.Y.C. Elementary Sch. Prins., Council Supervisory Assns. Contbr. to profl. publs.; also editor instructional materials. Home: 1655 Flatbush Ave Brooklyn NY 11210-3262

KASKINEN, BARBARA KAY, author, composer, songwriter, musician, music educator; b. Manistee, Mich., June 26, 1952; d. Norman Ferdinand and Martha Agnes (Harju) Kaskinen; m. David H. Riesberg, Feb. 14, 1985 (div.). AA, Broward C.C., Coconut Creek, Fla., 1978; BA with honors, Fla. Atlantic U., 1981, MA, 1995; postgrad., Nova U., 1989. Instr. adult piano Atlantic H.S., Delray Beach, Fla., 1981-82; organist, combo dir. Affirmation Luth. Ch., Boca Raton, Fla., 1981-86; studio musician, composer/arranger Electric Rize Prodns., Margate, Fla., 1982-94; ind. instr. piano, electronic keyboard and guitar, Margate, 1979—; bass and keyboard player Electric Rize Band, Margate, 1982—; in-house composer and arranger Hansen House, Miami Beach, Fla., 1987-88; co-founder Oasis Coffee House, Boca Raton, 1990—; co-owner Electric Rize Pub., 1991—; grad. tchg. asst. Fla. Atlantic U., 1994-96, mem. adj. faculty, 1995—; asst. dir. T.O.P.S. Piano Camp, 1994—; mem. adj. faculty Broward C.C., 1996—. Author: Barbara Riesberg's Adult Electronic Keyboard Course Book I, 1988, Books II and III, 1989. Reporter Coalition to Stop Food Irradiation, Broward, Fla., 1989. Mem. NOW, ASCAP, Fla. Atlantic U. Alumni Assn., Nat. Guild Piano Tchrs., Broward County Music Tchr.'s Assn. (treas.), Fla. State Music Tchr.'s Assn., Music Guild of Boca Raton. Home: 6601 NW 22nd St Pompano Beach FL 33063-2117

KASLEY, HELEN MARY, corporate secretary, legal counsel; b. Chgo., May 9, 1951; d. John F. and Michaeline J. (Wesolowski) Czachorski; m. William L. Kasley, Aug. 18, 1973; children: Joseph Anthony, Gabrielle Alexandra. BA, Bradley U., 1973, MA, 1978; MEd, U. Ill., Champaign, 1974; JD, U. Chgo., 1986. Bar: Calif. 1986, U.S. Dist. Ct. (no. dist.) Calif. 1986, U.S. Ct. Appeals (9th cir.) 1986; cert. sch. psychologist, Ill., cert. tchr. social and emotional disorders, Ill., cert. tchr. early childhood spl. edn., Ill. Disseminator Precise Early Edn. of Children with Handicaps outreach inst. child behavior & devel. U. Ill., 1975-76; head tchr. ctr. study early childhood devel. Bradley U., Peoria, Ill., 1976-77, rsch. and teaching asst. psychology dept., 1976-78; sch. psychologist Tazewell-Mason Counties Spl. Edn. Assn., Pekin, Ill., 1978-82, Cath. Social Svc., Peoria, 1983; assoc. atty. McCutchen, Doyle, Brown & Enersen, San Francisco, 1986-90; sec., legal counsel Calif. Water Svc. Co., San Jose, 1990—. Mem. mng. bd. U. Chgo. Legal Forum, 1984-85. Mem. Am. Corp. Counsel Assn., Am. Soc. Corp. Secs., Inc., Bar Assn. Calif. Home: 340 Valdez Ave Half Moon Bay CA 94019-1895 Office: Calif Water Svc Co 1720 N 1st St San Jose CA 95112-4508

KASMIR, GAIL ALICE, insurance company official, accountant; b. N.Y.C., Aug. 19, 1958; d. Fred and Evelyn Silvie (Mailman) K. BSBA summa cum laude, U. Cen. Fla., 1979. CPA, Fla. Acct. Ernst and Young, Orlando, Fla., 1979-83; fin. mgr. Harcourt Brace Jovanovich (Harvest Life Ins. Co.), Orlando, Fla., 1983-85; sr. v.p., treas., sec., cons. to bd. dirs., mem. investment com. LifeCo Investment Group, Inc. and subs. Nat. Heritage Life Ins. Co., Maitland, Fla., 1985-89, exec. v.p., 1991-94; CFO Nat. Heritage Life Ins. Co. in Rehab., Orlando, Fla., 1994-95, Nat. Heritage Life Ins. Co., 1995—; bd. dirs., exec. v.p., sec.-treas., CFO Nat. Heritage Life Ins. Co., LifeCo Investment Group, Inc., LifeCo Mktg. Svcs. Vol. Am. Cancer Soc., 1987-94, Am. Soc. for Cancer Rsch., 1987—. Fellow Life Office Mgmt. Assn.; mem. AICPAs, Fla. Inst. CPAs, Ins. Acctg. and Systems Assn., Beta Alpha Psi, Beta Gamma Sigma. Republican. Jewish. Home: 1351 Richmond Rd Winter Park FL 32789-5060 Office: Nat Heritage Life Ins Co 950 S Winter Park Dr Casselberry FL 32773

KASPAR, VICTORIA ANN, educator English; b. Omaha, Jan. 6, 1952; d. Rudolph Hans and Rose Marie (Kettle) Boysen; m. Ronald Michael Kaspar Sr., Apr. 28, 1948; children: Ron Jr., John, Jim. BS in Secondary Edn., U. Nebr., Omaha, 1974, MS in Secondary Adminstrn., 1995. Tchr. English Bellevue (Nebr.) Pub. Schs., 1974-75; dir. daycare pvt. practice, Omaha, 1978-88; tchr. English Millard South High Sch., Omaha, 1988—; chairperson Dept. English, 1995—. Author of poems. Mem. NEA, Nat. Coun. Tchrs. English, Nebr. Edn. Assn., Nebr. Lang. Arts Coun. (sec. 1993-95), Millard Edn. Assn., Phi Delta Kappa. Home: 14071 Drexel Cir Omaha NE 68137

KASPER, DIANA LINDA, education administrator; b. Chgo., Mar. 9, 1942; d. Jerome Albert and Clara (Dyner) Greenblau; m. Duane Charles Kasper, Feb. 20, 1965; children: Brian Peter, Debra Ann. BS, St. Cloud State Coll., 1970, MS, 1976, EdS, 1988. Cert. dir. cmty. edn., supr. schs., Minn. Outreach doord. St. Cloud (Minn.) State U., 1974-78; dir. cmty. edn. Dist. 742, St. Cloud, 1978—. Pres. Minn. Cmty. Edn. Assn., 1992-93. Named Cmty. Edn. Dir. Yr. Minn. Cmty. Edn. Assn., 1981; exec. fellow Bush Found., 1991-92. Mem. AAUW, LWV, Delta Kappa Gamma (pres., scholar), Phi Delta Kappa, Phi Kappa Phi. Office: Dist 742 628 Roosevelt Rd Saint Cloud MN 56301

KASPERBAUER, ISABEL GILES, art educator; b. Huancayo, Peru, Jan. 26, 1940; came to the U.S., 1960; d. Andres Humberto and Sofia Catalina (Saez) Giles; m. Michael John Kasperbauer, June 3, 1962; children: Maria Isabel, John Michael, Paul Andrew, Sandra Anne. BS, Iowa State U., 1962; BA, U. Ky., 1980. Cert. tchr., Ky. Art and Spanish tchr. Newman Ctr. U. Ky., Lexington, 1975-77; art tchr. Living Arts and Sci. Ctr., Lexington, 1980-82; after sch. art tchr. So. Elem. Sch., Lexington, 1980-82; art and Spanish tchr. Lexington Sch., 1982-85, art tchr., 1985—; del. Internat. Woman's Yr. Conf., Houston, 1977; co-chair dept. fine arts Lexington Sch., 1993—. V.p. Lexington Assn. for Parent Edn., 1967; treas. Lexington Talent Edn. Assn., 1971; co-pres. PTA James Lane Allen Sch., Lexington, 1978. Recipient Martha V. Shipman award Kappa Delta Pi, 1980. Mem. Ky. Art Edn. Assn. (sec. 1981-82, Art Educator of Yr. 1993), Am. Art Edn. Assn. Office: The Lexington Sch 1050 Lane Allen Rd Lexington KY 40504

KASPERSON, JEANNE XANTHAKOS, librarian, editor, educator; b. Southbridge, Mass., Feb. 3, 1938; d. James and Mary (Mitsakos) Xanthakos; m. Roger Eugene Kasperson, Sept. 6, 1959; children: Demetri Alexander, Kyra Eleni. BA with honors in English, Clark U., 1959; postgrad. in L.S., U. Chgo., 1959-60, MA in English, 1962; MS in L.S., Simmons Coll., 1967. Asst. librarian circulation and reference Edn. Library, U. Chgo., 1959-60; asst. acquisitions librarian Wilbur Cross Library, U. Conn., Storrs, 1964-66; asst. to chief bibliographer Mich. State U. Library, East Lansing, 1966-67; research librarian Hazard Assessment Group, Clark U., Worcester, Mass., 1977-78, Center Tech., Environ., and Devel., 1979-90, George Perkins Marsh Inst., Marsh Libr., 1991—; rsch. assoc. prof. Clark U., 1993—; sr. rsch. assoc. World Hunger Program, Brown U., 1986—; editor Aquarius Project, 1972-73; dir. publs. CENTED, 1983—. Co-editor: Water Re-use and the Cities (best sci. book award 1977), 1977; Risk in the Technological Society, 1982; co-author, co-editor: Natural Hazards Observer, 1984; Perilous Progress: Managing the Hazards of Technology, 1985 (Choice Outstanding Acad. Books 1987); Nuclear Risk Analysis in Comparative Perspective, 1986, Corporate Management of Health and Safety Hazards, 1988, Global Environmental Change: The Contributions of Risk Analysis and Management, 1990, Managing Nuclear Accidents: A Model Emergency Plan for Power Plants and Communities, 1992, Preparing for Nuclear Power Plant Accidents, 1995, Regions at Risk: Comparisons of Threatened Environments, 1995; contbg. editor Environment 1987-92; bd. editors Risk Abstracts, 1988—, book rev. editor, 1990—; contbr. articles to profl. jours. Exec. bd. Woodstock Library Assn., 1974-75, v.p., 1975-77, pres., 1978-80, book selection com., 1980-85; pres. N. Woodstock Library Assn., 1977-82. Mem. ALA, N.Y. Acad. Sci., Soc. Risk Analysis, Union of Concerned Scientists, Research Com. Disasters, Risk Assessment and Policy Assn., Internat. Disaster Inst., Internat. Assn. Impact Analysis, Spl. Librs. Assn., Am. Soc. Environ. History, Soc. Internat. Devel., U.S. Agrl. Info. Network, Assn. Population Family Planning Librs. Info. Ctrs. Internat., Nat. Hazards Soc. Democrat. Greek Orthodox. Office: Brown Univ World Hunger Program PO Box 1831 Providence RI 02912-1831

KASPIN, SUSAN JANE, child care specialist; b. Bklyn., May 28, 1950; d. Stanley Engel and Thelma Rosenblum; m. Jeffrey Marc Kaspin, Apr. 17, 1977; children: Jodi-Anne, Stacey, Melanie. BA, Bklyn. Coll., 1972. Cert. tchr. N.J. Adminstrv. asst. Stone & Webster Mgmt. Cons., N.Y.C., 1972-74, Am. Electric Power Co. (formerly in N.Y.C.), Columbus, Ohio, 1974-78; program dir. Office for Youth/Sch. Age Child Care Twp. of E. Brunswick, N.J., 1989—; staff liaison E. Brunswick Alliance for the Prevention of Alcoholism and Drug Abuse, 1990—. Mem. twp. ad-hoc com., N.J. tpk. expansion, E. Brunswick, 1985-90. Mem. N.J. Sch. Age Child Care Coalition, Middlesex County Sch. Age Child Care Coalition, Assn. for Children of N.J. (John Alexander Outstanding Project award 1992), N.J. Recreation and Parks Assn., Middlesex County Mcpl. Alliance Network.

KASREL, DENI, freelance writer; b. Phila., May 21, 1958; d. Jerry Jerome and Phyllis Anne (Maneloveg) K. BA in Polit. Sci. and Pub. Policy, U. Pa., 1979. Advt. mgr. Fenway Machine, Phila., 1979-81; freelance graphic prodn. Phila., 1982-88; graphic art prodn. Bus. Pub. Svcs., Phila., 1988-92; contbg. writer, freelancer Art Matters, Phila., 1988—, Welcomat, Phila., 1989-95, Weekly Press, Phila., 1989—, Phila. Bus. Jour., 1989—, Jazztimes, Silver Spring, Md., 1991—, Phila. Inquirer, 1993—, Jazz Phila., 1993—, Phila. City Paper, 1995—. Contbg. author Revolutionary Laughter: The World of Women Comics, 1995; contbr. Images in the Dark, 1995. Mem. Jazz Journalists Assn., Dance Critics Assn. Home and Office: PO Box 13299 Philadelphia PA 19101

KASSAS, JOY ALLEGRA, medical technologist; b. Kinston, N.C., May 18, 1956; d. Wiley Washington and Hazel (Rodwell) Jones; m. Michele Kassas, Aug. 29, 1984 (div. May 1987). BS in Biology, St. Andrews Presbyn. Coll., 1978; cert. med. tech., Presbyn. Hosp., Charlotte, N.C., 1979; MBA, East Carolina U., 1992. Med. technologist Duke U. Med. Ctr., Durham, N.C., 1979-80, VA Med. Ctr., Durham, 1980-83, Whitaker Life Scis. Corp., Khamis Mushayt, Saudi Arabia, 1983-84; civilian tech. advisor, supr. Langley AFB, Hampton, Va., 1985-87; med. technologist U. Med. Ctr. Ea. N.C., Greenville, 1987-95; chief technologist Wayne Meml. Hosp., Goldsboro, N.C., 1995—; advisor Allied Health Scis. Coastal C.C., Jacksonville, N.C., 1995-96, Beaufort C.C., Washington, N.C., 1995-96, Wayne C.C., Goldsboro, 1995-96. Active N.C. Zool. Soc., Asheboro, 1992—, Pillar Club United Way, Wayne County, N.C., 1995—. Mem. AAUW, NAFE, Am. Soc. Clin. Pathologists (assoc.), The Nature Conservancy, Ronald McDonald House Greenville, Mu Kappa Tau. Baptist. Office: Wayne Meml Hosp 2700 Wayne Memorial Dr Goldsboro NC

KASSEBAUM, NANCY LANDON, senator; b. Topeka, July 29, 1932; d. Alfred M. and Theo Landon; children: John Philip, Linda Josephine, Richard Landon, William Alfred. BA in Polit. Sci, U. Kans., 1954; MA in Diplomatic History, U. Mich., 1956. Mem. Maize (Kans.) Sch. Bd., 1972-75; mem. Washington staff Sen. James B. Pearson of Kans., 1975-76; mem. U.S. Senate from Kans., 1979—, mem. fgn. relations com., labor and human resources com., Indian Affairs com.; mem. com. fgn. rels., subcom. African affairs, 1980—, mem. subcom. arts, edn. Arts & Humanities, mem. com. banking, housing & urban affairs, subcom. internat. fin. & monetary policy. Mem. Kans. Press Women's Assn., Women's Assn. Instnl. Logopedics. Republican. Episcopalian. Office: US Senate 302 Russell Senate Bldg Washington DC 20510*

KASSELL, NANCY, scholar, poet; b. Albany, N.Y., Oct. 24, 1936; d. Mortimer and Marion (Harris) K.; m. Scott Zumwalt, Apr. 24, 1955 (div. 1974); children: Lise, Batia. BA summa cum laude, U. Calif., 1958, MA in Latin, 1960, PhD in Classics, 1970. Faculty classics U. Pa., Phila., 1971-76, Boston U., 1977-79, Tufts U., 1980, U. Mass., Boston, 1980-88; copy editor SUNY Press, 1980-83; staff editor U. Mass. Office of Grad. Studies, Boston, 1987-88. Editl. bd. The Independent Scholar, 1986-88; contbr. articles to profl. jours and poems to profl. publs. Exec. dir. Alliance of Ind. Scholars, 1986-88, bd. dirs., 1983-88. Mem. The Writers Rm. of Boston, Inc. (v.p., bd. dirs.). Home: 17 Short St #5 Brookline MA 02146

KASSELL, PAULA SALLY, editor, publisher; b. N.Y.C., Dec. 5, 1917; d. Daniel Herman and Bertha Blanche (Jaret) K.; m. Gerson Gustav Friedman, Aug. 16, 1941 (dec.); children: Daniel, Claire Florence Friedman. BA, Barnard Coll., 1939. Tech. editor Bell Labs., Whippany, N.J., 1955-65; methods analyst Bell Labs., Murray Hill, N.J., 1965-70; founder, editor, pub. New Directions for Women, Dover, N.J., 1971-77; assoc. editor New Directions for Women, Englewood, N.J., 1977-87; sr. editor New Directions for Women, Englewood, 1987-93; index editor New Directions for Women, Dover, 1993—; v.p., UN rep. Women's Inst. for Freedom of Press, Washington, 1990—; convenor, mem. media task force Com. on Status of Women, UN, 1990—. Co-convenor Lakeland chpt. NOW, Dover, 1970; v.p. Dover (N.J.) Child Care Ctr., 1979-91; Bd. dirs. Nat. Woman's Party, Washington, 1991—; mem. media com. Forum 95, UN, N.Y.C., 1994-95; mem. adv. bd. Vet. Feminists Am., Lafayette, La., 1995—; mem. TV task force Morris County NOW, Morristown, N.J., 1995—. Recipient First Feminist Action award NOW N.J., 1985, Women Making Herstory award, 1995, Elizabeth Cady Stanton award Women's Rights Info. Ctr., 1993, Woman of Achievement award Douglass Coll., 1994. Mem. Am. Journalism Historians Assn., Internat. Women's Media Found., Journalism & Women Symposium. Home: 25 W Fairview Ave Dover NJ 07801

KASSEWITZ, RUTH EILEEN BLOWER, retired hospital executive; b. Columbus, Ohio, May 15, 1928; d. E. Wallett and Helen (Daub) Blower; BS in Journalism-Mgmt., Ohio State U., Columbus, 1951; m. Jack Kassewitz, July 28, 1962 (dec.); 1 stepchild, Jack. Copywriter, Ohio Fuel Gas Co., Columbus, 1951-55, Merritt Owens Advt. Agy., Kansas City, Kans., 1955-56; account exec. Grant Advt., Inc., Miami, Fla., 1956-59; account supr. Venn/Cole & Assocs., Miami, 1959-67; dir. communications Ferendino/Grafton/Candela/Spillis Architects & Engrs., Miami, 1967-69; dir. communications Dade County Dept. Housing and Urban Devel., Miami, 1969-72; dir. communications Met. Dade County Govt., 1972-78; adminstr. pub. rels. U. Miami/Jackson Meml. Med. Ctr., 1978-90, ret., 1990. Pres., U. Miami Women's Guild, 1973-74; bd. dirs. Girls Scouts Tropical Fla., 1974-76, 81-83, Lung Assn. Dade-Monroe Counties, 1976-87, Met. YMCA, 1996—; mem. exec. com. Miami-Dade C.C. Found., 1984—; pres. Mental Health Assn. Dade County, 1982; mem. Miami Ecol. and Beautification Com., 1978—, also vice-chmn.; bd. govs. Barry U., Miami, 1981-83; trustee Nat. Humanities Faculty, 1981-83; trustee emeritus United Protestant Appeal, 1984-92; treas., past chmn. Health, Edn., Promotion Council, Inc.; adv. bd. Miami's for Me, 1987-88; mem. Coral Gables Cable TV Bd., 1983-86; ch. moderator Plymouth Congl. Ch., 1986-88 (trust. 1995—); community adv. bd. Jr. League Greater Miami, Inc., 1989-92; founding mem. Nat. Honor Roll Women in Pub. Rels., No. Ill. U., 1993. Recipient Disting. Service award Plymouth Congl. Ch., Miami, 1979; Ann Stover award, 1983, Golden Image award Fla. Pub. Rels.Assn, 1987; named Woman of Yr., Plymouth Congl. Ch., U. Miami Med. Sch., 1991. Fellow Public Relations Soc. Am. (pres. South Fla. chpt. 1969-70, nat. chmn. govt. sect. 1973-74, nat. dir. 1974-78; continuing edn. council 1981-83; Silver Anvil award 1973, Assembly del. 1970-73, 86-89, Paul M. Lund Pub. Svc. award 1993, Miami chpt. Lifetime Achievement award, 1995); mem. Women in Comm. (pres. Greater Miami chpt. 1962-63; Clarion award 1973, 75, Community Headliner 1985), Miami Internat. Press Club (bd. dirs. 1986-87, treas. 1992), Greater Miami C. of C. (gov. 1983-86), Rotary Club of Miami (bd. dirs., 1988—, pres. 1993-94). Home: 1136 Aduana Ave Miami FL 33146-3206

KASSOY, HORTENSE (HONEY KASSOY), artist; b. N.Y.C., Feb. 14, 1917; d. Adolph and Mary (Apfel) Blumenkranz; m. Bernard Kassoy, June 30, 1946; children: Meredith, Sheila. Diploma, Pratt Inst., 1936; BS, Columbia U., 1938, MA, 1939; student, Parsons Sch. Design, Paris, U. Colo., 1966, NYU, 1966-67; studied with Sahl Swarz, Chaim Gross and Oronzio Maldarelli. Solo exhbns. include Caravan House Gallery, 1974, Women in the Arts Gallery, 1978, Ward-Nasse Gallery, 1986, Pioneer Gallery, Cooperstown, N.Y., 1987, 91; group exhbns. include Bronx (N.Y.) Mus., 1971, 75, 85-86, Toledo Mus. Art, Toronto Mus. Art, Hudson River Mus., Bklyn. Mus., New Age Gallery, Lever House, Bklyn. Coll., Fordham U., Lehman Coll., Cork Gallery, Nat. Acad. Design; permanent collections include Slater Meml. Mus. Co-chair visual arts Bronx (N.Y.) Coun. on Arts, 1973-76. Fellow Va. Ctr. for Creative Arts, 1986, 88, 89, 92, 95; recipient 1st prize in watercolor Painters Day at N.Y. World's Fair, 1940. Mem. Am. Soc. Contemporary Artists (v.p. 1989-94, awards in sculpture 1979, 80, 83, 90, 92), N.Y. Artists Equity Assn. (v.p., bd. dirs. 1971-83), Internation Assn. Art (corr. sec. 1979-93, del. to 10th Congress 1983), Contemporary Arts Guild (rec. sec.). Home: 130 Gale Pl Apt 6B Bronx NY 10463-2853 Also: Butternut Hill RR 1 Box 74 Burlington Flats NY 13315-9728

KASTEN, BETTY LOU, state legislator; b. Sharon, Pa., Apr. 6, 1938; d. Louis and Betty Todut; m. David Kasten; children: Tod Louis, Elaine Katherine. BA, U. Denver, MS. Rancher, farmer; mem. Mont. Ho. of Reps., 1989—; past bd. trustees Mid River Telephone; past mem. Mont. Health Sys. Agy., Ea. Sub-Area Coun. Kellogg fellow Mont. State U. Mem. Mont. Farm Bur., Mont. Stockgrowers, Mont. Woolgrowers, Mont. Grain Growers, McCone County Cowbelles, Brockway Homemakers. Republican. Home: HC 77 Box A-14 Brockway MT 59214-9701 Office: Mont Ho of Reps State Capitol Helena MT 59620-0001

KASTENS, BEVERLY ANN, special and elementary education educator; b. Wichita, Kans., June 22, 1941; d. Ray Francis and Ava Marie (Lambert) Poole; children: Kelly, Cyndi; m. Gary Michael Kastens, Apr. 22, 1978. BA in Elem. Edn. magna cum laude, Wichita State U., 1973; MS in Edn., Kans. State U., 1980. Cert. tchr., Kans. Math. lab. instr. Goddard (Kans.) Sch. Dist., Unified Sch. Dist. #265, 1973-74, reading lab. instr., 1975-76, 8th grade remedial reading tchr., 1976, 6th grade tchr., 1977-78, 5th grade tchr., 1979-91, tchr. gifted grades K-9, 1992—; faculty advisor Intermediate Learning Ctr., Goddard, 1979, 81, 83, gifted screening com., 1980-83, dept. head, 1984-91; curriculum com. Unified Sch. Dist. #265, Goddard, 1987-88. Author: (teaching curriculum) Christmas Traditions, 1979, (poetry) Memoirs of Grandma, 1979, Memoirs of Student, 1982. Facilitator Wichita (Kans.) Park Bd., 1988-89; cast Voices of Ctrl. Community, Wichita, 1990—, Majesty of Christmas-Easter, Wichita, 1990—. Named Master Tchr., Intermediate Learning Ctr., Goddard, 1985, 87, 89; recipient grant in literature Kans. State Dept. Edn., Topeka, 1987. Mem. Nat. Assn. for Gifted Children, Nat. Rsch. Ctr. on the Gifted and Talented, Kans. Nat. Edn. Assn. (negotiator 1973-91, faculty rep.-negotiation team NEA, Goddard 1985-88). Republican. Mem. Church of God. Home: 547 Pamela St Wichita KS 67212-3733 Office: Clark Davidson Sch 333 S Walnut Goddard KS 67052

KASTER, LAURA A., lawyer; b. N.Y.C., May 24, 1948. BA, Tufts U., 1970; JD magna cum laude, Boston U., 1973. Bar: Mass. 1973, Ill. 1975. Law clk. to Hon. Frank M. Coffin U.S. Ct. Appeals (1st cir.), 1973-75; ptnr. Jenner & Block, Chgo. Co-author: Sanctions in Federal Litigation, 1991; co-editor: The Attorneys' Guide to the Seventh Circuit Court of Appeals, 1987; note editor Law Rev. Boston U., 1973-72; contbr. articles to profl. jours. Fellow Am. Bar Found.; mem. ABA, Ill. State Bar Assn., 7th Cir. Bar Assn.

KASTNER, CHRISTINE KRIHA, newspaper correspondent; b. Cleve., Aug. 27, 1951; d. Joseph Calvin and Grace (Weber) Kriha; m. Donald William Kastner, June 30, 1979; 1 child, Paul Donald. Assoc., Lakeland C.C., 1976; BA in Comms., Cleve. State U., 1983. Asst. editor, comms. specialist TRW, Inc., Cleve., 1978-85; editor Kaiser Permanente, Cleve., 1985-87; dir. pub. rels. Northeastern Ohio chpt. Arthritis Found., Cleve., 1991-92; newspaper corr. The Plain Dealer, Cleve., 1992—. Contbg. author: Encyclopedia of Cleveland History, 1988. Recipient Gold Addy award Am. Advt. Fedn., 1986, Award of Excellence Women in Comms., Inc., 1987, Bronze Quill award Internat. Assn. Bus. Communicators, 1987. Mem. Soc. Profl. Journalists. Roman Catholic. Home: 1383 Gordon Rd Lyndhurst OH 44124-1349

KASTNER, CYNTHIA, lawyer; b. Woonsocket, R.I., July 22, 1948; d. Everett Lathrop and Edith Stark; m. Robert W. Kastner, June 26, 1971. BA, Rutgers U., Newark, 1970; postgrad., Cornell U., 1970-71; JD, Seton Hall U., 1973. Bar: N.J. 1973, U.S. Dist. Ct. N.J. 1973, U.S. Supreme Ct. 1984. Assoc. Wharton, Stewart & Davis, Somerville, N.J., 1973-76; v.p., gen. counsel AT&T Consumer Products, Parsippany, N.J., 1992-96; gen. counsel Lucent Techs.-Global Real Estate & Procurement, 1996—. Mem. adminstrv. coun., pres. Women's Circle, Sunday sch. tchr. New Providence (N.J.) Meth. Ch. Mem. ABA, N.J. Bar Assn., N.J. Assn. Corp. Counsel. Home: 70 Lacey Ave Gillette NJ 07933-1407 Office: Lucent Techs Inc 222 Mt Airy Rd Basking Ridge NJ 07960

KATHAN, JOYCE C., social worker, administrator; b. Middletown, Conn., Oct. 28, 1931; d. Herbert G. and Mabel Elizabeth (Lee) Clark; m. Boardman W. Kathan, Aug. 17, 1952; children: Nancy Lee, David Wardell, Robert Boardman. B of Social Work magna cum laude, Southern Conn. State U., 1976. Dir. sr. citizen programs Town Woodbury (Conn.); dist. dir. Coun. Greater Boston Camp Fire Girls; participant Global Assembly of Women and Environ., 1991; mem. adv. bd. VNA health Care, 1985-95. Co-author: Youth Where the Action Is, 1970, (with others) Management of Hazardous Agents, Vol. 2: Social and Political Aspects, 1992. Bd. dirs. Waterbury YWCA, 1977-83, rec. sec.; mem. Prospect Commn. on Aging, Prospect, Conn., 1979-89, chair 1979-87; apptd. mem. Congl. Dist. 5 adv. coun. Conn. Permanent Commnon Status of Women, 1996—. Recipient Outstanding Conn. Women award, 1987. Mem. NASW, AAUW (Conn. chpt., pub. policy chair 1996-98, com. mem. Assn. Pub. Policy Com. 1985-89, mem. local and state coms. 1978-96, Award for Outstanding Cmty. Svc. Conn. chpt. 1994), LWV (pres. Cheshire chpt. 1989-93), Conn. LWV (pub. policy com. 1988—), Conn. Assn. Sr. Ctr. Pers. (charter mem., rec. sec. 1995-97, Svc. award 1986), Wetern Conn. Area Agy. Aging (bd. dirs. 1986-92, pres. 1990-92), Conn. Soc. Gerontology.

KATO, PAMELA KIYOMI, lawyer; b. Mountain View, Calif., Oct. 24, 1964; d. George Mas and Satsuki May Kato. BA, U. Calif., Santa Barbara, 1987; JD, Santa Clara U., 1990. Bar: U.S. Dist. Ct. (no. dist.) Calif., 1991, U.S. Ct. Appeals 1991. Asst. dist. atty. Santa Cruz County, Santa Cruz, Calif., 1991—. Office: 701 Ocean St Santa Cruz CA 95060-4027

KATONA, ANNE HELENE, travel agency owner; b. Shamokin, Pa., Apr. 15, 1966; d. Joseph Anthony and Elizabeth Caroline (Marcinek) K. BA in Pre-Phys. Therapy, San Francisco State U., 1990. Cert. athletic trainer Nat. Athletic Trainer's Assn. Rsch. asst. Stanford Weight Control Project, Palo Alto, Calif., 1987-89; athletic trainer Functional Rehab. and Sports Therapy Clinic/Sacred Heart, Palo Alto, 1989-93, Sports and Orthopedic Rehab. Svcs./Tampa Prep., Palm Harbor and Tampa, Fla., 1994-95; counselor devel. disabled Comty. Support and Treatment, Tampa, 1995—; owner Aries Travel and Tours, Tampa, 1994—. Mem. AAUW, NAFE. Democrat. Roman Catholic. Home: # 1308 4711 S Himes Ave Tampa FL 33611

KATSEKAS, BETTE SUSAN, counseling education educator; b. Goffstown, N.H., May 8, 1951; d. Charles J. and Angelina (Chagrasuis) K. BA, U. N.H., 1973, MEd, 1976, CAGS, 1979; EdD, U. Maine, 1979. Lic. clin. profl. counselor, Maine; lic. substance abuse counselor, Maine. Counselor, cons. Human Devel. Cons., Portland, Maine, 1979—; asst. prof. of counselor edn. U. So. Maine, Portland, 1992—; mental health adv. bd. U. So. Maine, Gorham, 1993-95, coord., counseling edn. program, 1993-95, trained mediator, 1994-95. Mem. Maine Clin. Counselors Assn. (chair profl. devel. com. 1992-94). Office: Univ of So Maine 400 Bailey Hall Gorham ME 04038

KATSER, DONNA DURHAM, critical care nurse, educator; b. Detroit, Aug. 19, 1952; d. Harry Richard and Mary Lou (Purcell) Durham; m. Arther Normon Katser, Sept. 10, 1978. Nursing diploma, Grace Hosp. Sch. Nursing, 1973; BS in Nursing, Wayne State U., 1980, MS in Nursing, 1994. CCRN, ACLS provider, instr., BLS instr. trainer. Staff nurse Grace Hosp., Detroit, 1973-74; staff nurse intensive care William Beaumont Hosp., Royal Oak, Mich., 1974-76, staff nurse hemodialysis, 1976-77; staff nurse intensive care Hutzel Hosp., Detroit, 1977-79, critical care educator, 1979-82, staff nurse, 1983-85; critical care educator, asst. dir. nursing Detroit Osteopathic Hosp., 1985-87; critical care educator Harper Hosp., Detroit, 1987—; cons. Radius Nursing Svc., Southfield, Mich., 1982-83; presenter in field. Mem. Interfaith Roundtable, 1988—. Mem. Am. Assn. Critical Care Nurses, Am. Heart Assn., Nat. Staff Devel. Orgn., Mich. Abortion Rights Action League, Southeast Mich. Assn. Critical Care Nurses (program planning com. 1995-96, pres.-elect 1981-82, pres. 1982-83, Outstanding Mem. 1981), Southeast Mich. Staff Devel. Orgn., Detroit Zool. Soc., Sigma Theta Tau. Home: 26066 YorkSt Huntington Woods MI 48070

KATSON, ROBERTA MARINA, economist; b. Albuquerque, Oct. 5, 1947; d. Robert V. and Penelope (Papafrangos) Katson; student Emory U., 1966-67, Ga. State U., 1967-69; m. Cyrus Butner, 1980; children: Justin Cyrus, Renee Alexis. BA, U. N.Mex., 1974, MA, 1977. Gen. mgr. Window Rock (Ariz.) Motor Inn, Navajo Reservation, 1972-73; research asst. dept. econs. U. N.Mex., Albuquerque, 1974-75, research asso. Resource Econ. Group, 1975-77; economist program analysis Econ. Devel. Adminstrn., Dept. Commerce, Washington, 1977-79; economist Dept. Energy, Washington, 1979-84; cons. Calligraphic Design, Fairfax, Va., 1986-88, owner, 1989-91; economist Office of Fin. Mgmt., Adminstrn. for Children and Families, Dept. of HHS, Washington, 1991—. Mem. Phi Kappa Phi, Omicron Delta Epsilon. Democrat. Contbr. articles to profl. jours. Home: 10722 Midsummer Dr Reston VA 20191-5115 Office: HHS/ACF/OFM 370 Lenfant Plz SW Washington DC 20447-0001

KATZ, ANNE ROSALIND, arts administrator; b. N.Y.C., Mar. 26, 1958; d. Sanford Herbert and Phyllis (Abramson) Katz; m. David L. Wallner, Sept. 20, 1987. BA in Theatre Arts, Brandeis U., 1980; student, Marymount Coll., London, 1978-79. Dir. devel. Madison (Wis.) Repertory Theatre, 1984-86; arts coord. City of Madison, 1986-88; cultural planning cons. Opinion Rsch. Assocs., Madison, 1989-92; dir. of devel. and outreach Madison (Wis.) Civic Ctr., 1990-95; executive dir. Wis. Assembly of Local Arts Agy., Madison, Wis., 1995—; pub. rels. dir. Nat. Playwrights Conf. O'Neill Theatre Ctr., Waterford, Conn., 1987. Vol. programmer Madison Festival of Lakes, 1985—. Arts adminstrn. fellow Nat. Endowment for Arts, 1988. Mem. Nat. Assembly Local Arts Agys. Democrat. Jewish. Home: 419 Jean St Madison WI 53703-1615 Office: Wis Assembly Local Arts Agy PO Box 1054 Madison WI 53701

KATZ, FERN SALLY, retired educator; b. Detroit, Mar. 14, 1928; d. Harry and Yetta (Katz) Metz; m. Joseph S. Katz, Dec. 19, 1948; 3 children. BS, Wayne State U., 1950, MEd, 1963. Tchr. math. dept. chair Oak Park (Mich.) Schs., 1963-92, ret., 1992; tchr. math. Birmingham (Mich.) Schs., 1966-68. Bd. dirs. Nat. Coun. Jewish Women, Metro Detroit, 1994-96, co-chair ct. appointed spl. advocate, 1994-96, del. 4th world conf. on women, N.Y.C., 1995; chair Will Lobby Corps Women Legislators Lobby, Metro Detroit, 1995-96; co-chair Women's Action for New Directions, 1995-96; sponsor Nat. Honor Soc. Oak Park Schs., 1986-92. Mem. AFT, MFT, Oak Park Fedn. Tchrs. (pres. 1987-92, bull. editor 1987-92). Home: 27065 Fairfax Rd Southfield MI 48076-3600

KATZ, HEATHER ALICIA, education professional; b. Somerville, N.J., Aug. 5, 1967; d. Carolyn Eva Kwasny Katz. BS Environ. Sci., Howard U., 1992, MEd Spl. Edn., 1993; postgrad., U. N.Mex., 1994-95, U. Tex., 1995—. Engr. intern Fed. Hwy. Adminstrn., Sterling, Va., 1989-90, Fed. Emergency Mgmt. Agy., Washington, 1989; water safety instr. ARC, Washington, 1985-94; asst. rsch. asst. Howard U. Rsch. and Tng. Ctr., Washington, 1991-92; rsch. asst. Ctr. for Disability and Socio-Econ. Policy Studies/Howard U., Washington, 1992-93; spl. educator Price George's County Pub. Schs., Upper Marlboro, Md., 1993-94; adminstrv. asst. libr. tech. dept. U. N.Mex., Albuquerque, 1994-95; instrnl. designer and trainer Philips Semiconductor, Albuquerque, 1995; instrnl. technologist cons., 1995; computer analyst U. Tex., Austin, 1996; grad. rsch. asst., Web page developer Tex. Edn. Network, Austin, 1996—; HIV/AIDS workplace tng., Albuquerque, 1995; presenter Office of Spl. Edn. and Rehab. Svcs., Washington, 1992, NIDRR/Dole Found. Conf., Washington, 1992. Co-author: School of Education Guide to Outreach and Collaborative Services, 1993, Center Source Book for Access to Federal Programs, 1993; author/designer: (tng. manual) Designing and Implementing on HIV & AIDS Workplace Program, 1994. Vol. ARC, Washington, 1985-94. Young Scholars fellow Howard U./Robert Dole Found., 1991-92, Grad. fellow, 1992; recipient Grad. Opportunity Program fellowship U Tex., 1996—. Mem. ASTD, Nat. Soc. Planning and Instrn., Kappa Delta Pi, Phi Delta Kappa.

KATZ, HILDA, artist, poet; b. June 2, 1909; d. Max and Lina (Schwartz) K. Student, Nat. Acad. Design; student (3 awards; New Sch. Social Research scholarship), 1940-41. Author: (under pen name Hulda Weber) poems including numerous anthologies, spl. ltd. edit., 1987-88, Library of Congress D.C. Poetry, author's limited edit., 1991-92, Arlington National Cemetery & Memorial, D.C. Poetry, author's limited edit., 1993, Author's Limited Edition Original Manuscript-36 Poems, 1994; anthologies include The Bloom, 1984-85, 87, Perfume and Fragrance, 1988, 89, Lightning & Rainbows, 1989, 90; contbr.: numerous poems, short stories to books and mags. including Humpty Dumpty's Mag. (publ. for children); contbr. commemorative poetry to mus. and govt. including Pres. Ronald W. Reagan, 1985, Pres. Chaim Herzog of Israel, 1987, series of poems in N.Y. State Mus. of Albany, 1987, 89, Yad Vashem Meml. Archives, Jerusalem, 1987, Mus. of Jewish Heritage, 1988, 89, Jewish Theol. Sem. of Am., 1989, Ft. Lewis Coll. Found., 1990, Jewish Nat. and Univ. Libr., Jerusalem, 1990, The Simon Wiesenthal Ctr., U.S.A., 1990, U.S. Holocaust Meml., Washington, 1991, Libr. Congress, Washington, 1991, 92; one-woman exhbns. include Bowdoin Coll. Art Mus., 1951, Calif. State Libr., 1953, Print Club Albany, N.Y., 1955, U. Maine, 1955, 58, Jewish Mus., 1956, Pa. State Tchrs. Coll., 1956, Massillon Mus., 1957, Ball State Tchrs. Coll., 1957, Springfield (Mass.) Art Mus., 1957, Miami Beach (Fla.) Art Ctr., Richmond (Ind.) Art Assn., 1959, Old State Capitol Mus. La., other exhbns. include: Corcoran Bienniale Libr. of Congress, Am. in the War Exhbn, N.Y. State Mus. of Albany, 1989, Jewish Theol. Sem. of Am., 1989, 26 mus., Am. Drawing anns. at: Albany Inst., Nat. Acad. Design, Conn. Acad. Fine Arts, Bklyn. Mus., Delgado Mus., Art-U.S.A., 1959, Congress for Jewish Culture, Met. Mus. Art., Springfield (Mo.) Art Mus., Children's Mus. Hartford, Conn., Miniature Printers, Peoria (Ill.) Art Ctr., Pa. Acad. Fine Arts, Originale Contemporate Graphic Internat., France, Bezalel Nat. Mus., Israel, Venice (Italy) Bienniale, Royal Etchers and Painters Exchange Exhibit, Eng., Bat Yam Mus., Israel, Paris, France, 1958, 59, Am.-Italian Print Exchange, numerous libraries, artists socs., invitational exhbns. include, Rome, Turin, Venice, Florence, Naples (all Italy), Nat. Academe Muse, France, Israel, USIA exhbns. in, Europe, S. Am., Asia, Africa; also represented in spl. permanent collections U.S. Nat. Mus., U. Maine Art Mus., Libr. of Congress, Met. Mus. Art, Nat. Coll. Fine Arts, D.C., Nat. Gallery Art, D.C., Nat. Air and Space Mus., D.C., N.Y. Pub. Libr., Nat. Mus. History and Tech., Bklyn. Mus. Art, New Britain Mus. Am. Art, Mus. of City of N.Y., Jewish Mus. of N.Y., N.Y. State Mus. of Albany, Israel Mus., Jerusalem, Boston Pub. Libr., Ft. Lewis Coll. Art Mus., Colo., Balt. Mus. Art, Franklin D. Roosevelt, Fogg Mus., Harvard, Santa Barbara (Calif.) Art Mus., Syracuse U., Colorado Springs Fine Arts Ctr., Pennell Collection, Am. Artists Group Prize at Samuel Golden Coll., U. Minn., Calif. State Library, Pa. State Library, Bezalel Nat. Mus., Smithsonian Archives Am. Art (art and poetry), 1979-93, Washington, Archives and State Mus. Albany, N.Y. (120 works), Newark Pub. Library, Addison Gallery Am. Art, Bat Yam Municipal Mus., Safed Mus., Israel, Pa. State Tchrs. Coll., Richmond Art Assn., Peoria (Ill.) Art Ctr., St. Margaret Mary Sch. Art, Musee Nat. d'Art Modern, Yad Vashem Meml. Archives, Jerusalem (poetry), 1987, N.Y. State Mus. and Archives, Columbia U. Librs., SUNY Albany, Simon Wiesenthal Ctr., U.S. Holocaust Meml. Mus., Mus. Jewish Heritage, Jewish Theol. Sem. of Am., Jewish Nat. & U. Libr., Arlington Nat. Cemetary & Meml., Washington. Represented as artist and poet: Miss. Art Assn. Internat. Water Color Club award 1947, 51, New Haven Paint and Clay Club, purchase award Peoria Art Ctr. 1950, Print Club Albany 1962, also Library of Congress, U. Minn., Calif. State Library, Met. Mus. Art, Pa. State Tchrs. Coll., Art Assn. Richmond, Ind., N.Y. Pub. Libr., Newark Pub. Libr., St. Margaret Mary Sch. Art Coll., landscape award Soc. Miniature Painters, Gravers and Sculpture, James Joyce award Poetry Soc. Am. 1975; presented spl. commemoration to Yad Vashem Meml. Hist. Site, Jerusalem, 1987; named to Exec. and Profl. Hall of Fame (plaque of honor 1966); all art works, paintings, drawings, prints, print blocks acquired by 19 nat. or internat. mus., librs., archives, spl. permanent collections; original manuscripts, including spl. author's limited editions acquired by 14 nat. or internat. mus., librs., archives, spl. permanent collections under pen name Hulda Weber, including Archives Am. Art, Washington; paintings and artwork in permanent spl. collections include U.S. Nat. Mus., 1965, U. Maine Art Mus., 1965, Library of Congress, 1965, 71, Metropolitan Mus. Art, 1965, 80, Nat. Coll. Fine Arts, 1966, 70, 71, Nat. Gallery of Art, 1966, Nat. Air & Space Mus., 1966, N.Y. Pub. Library, 1971, 78, Nat. Mus. History/Technology, 1971, Bklyn. Mus. Art, 1970, New Britian Mus. Am. Art, 1978-79, Mus. City of N.Y., 1978, Jewish Mus. of N.Y., 1979, N.Y. State Mus. of Albany, 1979-80, Hyatt Mayor Art Coll., 1980, Israel Mus., Jerusalem, 1980, Boston Pub. Library, 1980, Ft. Lewis Coll. Art Mus., 1980, Ft. Lewis Coll. Found., 1980; poetry in spl. collections include Yad Vashem Meml. Mus., 1987, Pres. Chaim Herzog, 1987, N.Y. State Mus. Albany, 1987, 89, Ft. Lewis Coll. Art Mus., 1990, The Simon Wiesenthal Ctr., Calif., 1990, U.S. Holocaust Meml. Mus., 1991, Library of Congress, D.C., 1991, Mus. Jewish Heritage, 1989, The Jewish Theological Seminary of Am., 1989, The Jewish Nat. & Univ. Library, Jerusalem, 1989, Arlington Nat. Cemetery & Meml., D.C., 1993, others. Named to World Order of Narrative Poets; recognized as founder for ednl. and cultural support Mus. and Librs., U. Art Mus., U. Librs. of SUNY, Albany, 1994; named Membro Honoris Causa dell'Accademia di Scienze, Letteri, Arti Classe Accademica "Nobel", Milan, 1974, 75, Classe Storia Letteratura Americana "Nobel", Milan, 1978, Exec. and Profl. Hall of Fame-Life, 1966, A Dau. of Mark Twain, 1970. Fellow Internat. Acad. Poets (founder 1977), Met. Mus. Art; mem. Soc. Am. Graphic Artists (group prize 1950), Print Club Albany (N.Y.), Boston Printmakers (award 1955), Washington Printmakers (exhbns.), Conn. Acad. Fine Arts, Am. Color Print Soc., Audubon Artists (group exhbns., award 1944), Phila. Watercolor Club (life, group exhbns.), Nat. Assn. Women Artists (hon. life, award 1945, 47), Print Council Am., Hunterdon Art Center, Internat. Platform Assn., Poetry Soc. Am., Artists Equity N.Y., Authors Guild, Inc., Accademia Di Scienze, Lettere, Arti-Milano, Italy (Consigliere, named hon. mem. as artist 1974, author/poet 1975, Nobel designate 1978); Academia Di Scienze. Lettere, Arti, Classe, Daughter of Mark Twain (hon. life). Office: 915 W End Ave Apt 5D New York NY 10025-3503

KATZ, ILLANA PAULETTE, writer; b. N.Y.C., May 30, 1946; d. Emanuel and Alice (Reich) Schear; m. David Arthur Katz, July 31, 1966; children: Heather, Todd, Ethan, Seth. BA in Anthropology summa cum laude, Calif. State U., 1977, postgrad. Pres., pub. Real Life Storybooks, West Hills, Calif., 1992—; mini-course instr. L.A. Unified Sch. Dist., 1985, 93; lectr. State Autism Conv., 1994, Nat. Autism Conv., 1994. Author: Joey and Sam, 1993 (award 1994), Show Me Where It Hurts, 1993, Uncle Jimmy, 1994, Sarah, 1994, Hungry Mind-Hungry Body, 1995; (audio-cassette) Was Einstein Autistic?, 1994. Head of Israeli affairs United Synagogue, Beverly Hills, 1988; aliyah councelor Jewish Fedn., L.A., 1991—. Mem. Authors and Celebrities Forum (award of excellence 1994), Soc. of Children's Book Writers, Book Publicists Assn., Pub. Mktg. Assn. Home and Office: 8370 Kentland Ave West Hills CA 91304-3329

KATZ, JANE, swimming educator; b. Sharon, Pa., Apr. 16, 1943; d. Leon and Dorothea (Oberkewitz) Katz; B.S. in Edn., CCNY, 1963; M.A., NYU, 1966; M.Ed., Columbia Tchrs. Coll., 1972, Ed.D., 1978. Mem. faculty Bronx C.C., CUNY, 1964—, prof. phys. edn., 1972—; mem. U.S. Round-the-World Synchronized Swim Team, 1964; synchronized swimming solo tour of Eng., 1969; founding co-organizer, coach 1st Internat. Israeli Youth Festival Games, 1970; mem. winning U.S. Maccabiah Swim Team, 1957; vice chmn. Metro Master AAU Swim Team, 1974—; mem. AAU Nat. Masters All-Am. Swimming Team, 1974—, synchronized swimming solo champion, 1975; speaker, judge in field. Trainee Fed. Adminstrn. Aging, 1971-72; mem. Internat. Hall. of Fame, Ft. Lauderdale, Fla. Named Healthy Am. Fitness Leader U.S. Jaycees and the Pres's. Coun. on Phys. Fitness, 1987, Outstanding Masters Synchroured Swimming, 1987; winner CCNY Towsend Harris Acad. medal, 1989. Mem. AAHPER, U.S. Com. Sports for Israel (dir., co-chmn. women's swimming com. 1970—), Nat. Jewish Welfare Bd., Internat. Aquatics. Author: Swimming for Total Fitness, A Progressive Aerobic Program, 1981, rev. ed. 1993, Swimming Through Your Pregnancy, 1983, W.E.T. Workouts: Water Exercises and Techniques to Help You and Tone Up Aerobically, 1985, Fitness Works: Blueprint for Lifelong Fitness, 1988, Swim 30 Laps in 30 Days, 1991, The Workstation Workout, 1994, Aquatic Handbook for Lifetime Fitness, 1996; author: (video) The W.E.T. Workout, 1994, The All-American Aquatic Handbook: Your Passport to Lifetime Fitness, 1996, The New W.E.T. Workout, 1996; papers in field. Address: 400 2nd Ave Apt 23B New York NY 10010-4052

KATZ, JOETTE, judge; b. Bklyn., Feb. 3, 1953. BA, Brandeis U., 1974; JD, U. Conn., 1977. Bar: Conn. 1977. Pvt. practice, 1977-78; asst. pub. defender Office Chief Pub. Defender, 1978-83; chief legal svcs. Pub. Defender Svcs., 1983-89; judge Superior Ct., 1989-92; assoc. judge Conn. Supreme Ct., Hartford, 1992—; instr. U. Conn. Sch. law, 1981-84. Office: Conn Supreme Ct Drawer N Sta A 231 Capitol Ave Hartford CT 06106-1537*

KATZ, LILIAN GONSHAW, education educator; b. London, Eng., June 7, 1932; came to the U.S., 1947; d. Joseph and Eva (Freidine) Gonshaw; m. Boris Isaac Katz, Nov. 8, 1962; children: Daniel, Stephen, Miriam. BA cum laude, San Francisco State U., 1964; PhD, Stanford U., 1968; DLitt (hon.), Whittier Coll., 1993. From asst. to full prof. U. Ill., 1968—. Author: Engaging Children's Minds, 1989, Talk With Teachers of Young Children, 1995. Recipient Fulbright award, New Zealand, 1992; Fulbright lectr., India, 1983. MEm. Nat. Assn. for Edn. Young Children (pres. 1992-94). Office: Univ Ill 805 W Pennsylvania Ave Urbana IL 61801-4822

KATZ, LOIS ANNE, internist, nephrologist; b. Rockville Centre, N.Y., Dec. 1, 1941; d. Irvin Martin and Frances (Berenstein) Fradkin; m. Arthur A. Katz, Aug. 18, 1962; children: David, Brian. BA, Wellesley Coll., 1962; MD, NYU, 1966. Diplomate Am. Bd. Internal Medicine, Am. Bd. Nephrology. Intern medicine Bellevue Hosp., NYU, N.Y.C., 1966-67, resident medicine, 1967-68; sr. resident medicine N.Y. Hosp., N.Y.C., 1968-69; chief resident medicine N.Y. VA Med. Ctr., N.Y.C., 1969-70, fellow nephrology, 1970-71, staff physician, 1970-74, assoc. chief nephrology, 1974—, assoc. chief of staff ambulatory care, 1980—; asst. prof. clin. medicine NYU Sch. Medicine, N.Y.C., 1974-79, assoc. prof., 1979-94, prof. clin. medicine, 1994—. Alumna admission rep. Wellesley-in-Westchester, N.Y.; bd. mem. Women's Med. Assn., N.Y.C., 1986—. Fellow ACP; mem. Am. Soc. Nephrology, Am. Med. Women's Assn., Soc. Gen. Internal Medicine, Women in Nephrology (treas. 1985-89), Am. Soc. Hypertension, Sigma Xi, Alpha Omega Alpha. Jewish. Office: Dept Vets Affairs Med Ctr 423 E 23rd St New York NY 10010-5050

KATZ, MARTHA LESSMAN, lawyer; b. Chgo., Oct. 28, 1952; d. Julius Abraham and Ida (Oiring) Lessman; m. Richard M. Katz, June 27, 1976; children: Julia Erin, Meredith Evin. AB, Washington U., St. Louis, 1974; JD, Loyola U., Chgo., 1977. Bar: Ill. 1977, U.S. Dist. Ct. (no. dist.) Ill. 1977, Calif. 1981, U.S. Dist. Ct. (so. dist.) Calif. 1981, U.S. Dist. Ct. (no. dist.) Calif. 1982, Md. 1993, U.S. Supreme Ct. 1993, D.C. 1994. Assoc. Fein & Hanfling, Chgo., 1977-80, Rudick, Platt & Victor, San Diego, 1981-82, 84-91; asst. sec., counsel Itel Corp., San Francisco, 1982-84; ptnr. Katz & Mann, Attys. at Law, 1991-94; sole practitioner, 1995—. Active Friends of Mayor's Commn. on Women. Mem. Calif. State Bar Assn., Md. Bar Assn., Ill. State Bar Assn., San Diego County Bar Assn., Lawyers Club San Diego, Bar Assn. Balt. City, Bar Assn. D.C., Phi Beta Kappa. Jewish.

KATZ, PHYLLIS POLLAK, magazine publisher and editor; b. N.Y.C., Dec. 29, 1939; d. Henry Abraham and Rose (Chaiken) P.; m. Edward Katz, Sept. 12, 1971; children: Charles Daniel, Jacob Evan. B.A., Cornell U., 1961; postgrad., U. Pa., 1961-68, Am. Sch. Classical Studies, Athens, 1964-66. Dept. asst. Univ. Mus., U. Pa.; lectr. NYU, 1970-71; asst. editor Archaeology mag., N.Y.C., 1968-72; editor Archaeology mag., 1972-87, pub., 1978—. Mem. archaeol. excavations, Gordion, Turkey, 1965, Porto Cheli, Greece, 1965, Samothrace, Greece, 1966, Torre del Mordillo, Italy, 1967. Heinemann fellow, 1964-66. Mem. Archaeol. Inst. Am. Jewish. Office: Archaeology 135 William St New York NY 10038-3805*

KATZ, SHERI LYNN, learning disabilities specialist, tutor; b. Balt., June 10, 1953; d. Irving and Sybil (Breskin) K.; m. Asher Samuel Kahn; children: Zachary Aaron, Alexandra Katz. BA, New Coll. USF, 1976; MS, Bank St. Coll. of Edn., 1978. Cert. early childhood and spl. edn. Tchr., therapist Infant Care Ctr. of JBFCS, N.Y.C., 1978-81; learning disabilities specialist Fieldston Lower Sch., Riverdale, N.Y., 1982—; pvt. tutor, Riverdale, N.Y., 1979—, East Hampton, N.Y., 1991—. Contbr. articles to profl. jours. Recipient grants Ethical Culture/Fieldston Schs., 1988-95. Mem. NOW, Planned Parenthood, Orton Dyslexia Soc., Wave Hill, Wildlife Conservation Soc., Am. Mus. Natural History. Democrat. Jewish. Home: 4525 Henry Hudson Pkwy Riverdale NY 10471 Office: Fieldston Lower Sch Fieldston Rd Riverdale NY 10471

KATZ, TONNIE, newspaper editor. BA, Barnard Coll., 1966; MSc, Columbia U., 1967. Editor, reporter newspapers including The Quincy Patriot Ledger, Boston Herald Am., Boston Globe; Sunday/projects editor Newsday; mng. editor Balt. News Am., 1983-86, The Sun, San Bernardino, Calif., 1986-88; asst. mng. editor for news The Orange County Register, Santa Ana, Calif., 1988-89, mng. editor, 1989-92, editor, v.p., 1992—. Office: Freedom Newspapers Inc Orange County Register 625 N Grand Ave Santa Ana CA 92701-4347*

KATZ, VERA, mayor, former college administrator, state legislator; b. Dusseldorf, Germany, Aug. 3, 1933; came to U.S., 1940; d. Lazar Pistrak and Raissa Goodman; m. Mel Katz (div. 1985); 1 child, Jesse. BA, Bklyn. Coll., 1955, postgrad., 1955-57. Market research analyst TIMEX, B.T. Babbitt, N.Y.C., 1957-62; mem. Oreg. Ho. of Reps., Salem; former dir. devel. Portland Community Coll., from 1982; mayor City of Portland, Oreg., 1993—; mem. Gov.'s Council on Alcohol and Drug Abuse Programs, Oreg. Legis., Salem, 1985—; mem. adv. com. Gov.'s Council on Health, Fitness and Sports, Oreg. Legis., 1985—; mem. Gov.'s Commn. on Sch. Funding Reform; mem. Carnegie task Force on Teaching as Profession, Washington, 1985-87; vice-chair assembly Nat. Conf. State Legis., Denver, 1986—. Recipient Abigail Scott Duniway award Women in Communications, Inc., Portland, 1985, Jeanette Rankin First Woman award Oreg. Women's Polit. Caucus, Portland, 1985, Leadership award The Neighborhood newspaper Portland, 1985, Woman of Achievement award Commn. for Women, 1985, Outstanding Legis. Advocacy award Oreg. Primary Care Assn., 1985, Service to Portland Pub. Sch. Children award Portland Pub. Schs., 1985. Fellow Am. Leadership Forum (founder Oreg. chpt.); mem. Dem. Legis. Leaders Assn., Nat. Bd. for Profl. Teaching Standards. Democrat. Jewish. Office: Office of the Mayor City Hall Rm 303 1220 SW 5th Ave Portland OR 97204-1995*

KATZ, VICTORIA MANUELA, public relations executive, educator, consultant; b. N.Y.C., Mar. 12, 1941; d. Isaac William and Sylvia (Katz) Penner; m. Ronald Mark Katz, Sept. 8, 1974. BA in Journalism, Hofstra Coll., 1962. Sr. editor real estate, fin. Long Island (N.Y.) Comml. Review, 1962-72; freelance writer, publicist N.Y., 1972-74; managing editor North Shore News Group, Smithtown, N.Y., 1974-88; dir. u. news svcs. SUNY, Stony Brook, 1988—; dir. Long Island Bus. Inc., Ronkonkoma, N.Y., 1965—; adj. journalism prof. C.W. Post, Greenvale, N.Y., 1986-88, Hofstra Coll., Hempstead, N.Y., 1987. Author: (study) Smithtown Minorities, 1983. Trustee Harbor County Day Sch., St. James, N.Y., 1977-93, mktg. and pub. rels. com. mem. United Way, L.I., 1988—; program com. mem. Mus. at Stony Brook, 1990-93. Recipient Media award for govtl. reporting Press Club L.I., 1987, 88. Mem. AAUW (past v.p.), Pub. Rels. Soc. Am., Soc. Profl. Journalists (nat. com. mem., co-chair chpt. health and welfare com., regional dir. 1994—), Press Club L.I. Chpt. Soc. Profl. Journalists (pres. 1974, treas. 1985-93, Deadline Club bd. 1994, program co-chair 1993, v.p. 1995-96). Home: 19 Millbrook Dr Stony Brook NY 11790-2930 Office: SUNY at Stony Brook Adminstrn Bldg 144 Stony Brook NY 11794

KATZEN, SALLY, lawyer; b. Pitts., Nov. 22, 1942; d. Nathan and Hilda (Schwartz) K.; m. Timothy B. Dyk, Oct. 31, 1981; 1 child, Abraham Benjamin. BA magna cum laude, Smith Coll., 1964; JD magna cum laude, U. Mich., 1967. Bar: D.C. 1968, U.S. Supreme Ct. 1971. Congl. intern Sente Subcom. on Constl. Rights, Washington, 1963; legal rsch. asst. civil rights div. Dept. Justice, Washington, 1965; law clk. to Judge J. Skelly Wright U.S. Ct. Appeals (D.C. cir.), 1967-68; assoc. Wilmer, Cutler & Pickering, Washington, 1968-75, ptnr., 1975-79, 81-93; gen. counsel Coun. on Wage and Price Stability, 1979-80; dep. dir. for policy, 1980-81; adminstr. Office of Info. and Regulatory Affairs, Office of Mgmt. and Budget, Washington, 1993—; pub. mem. Adminstrv. Conf. U.S., 1988-93, govt. mem. and vice chair, 1993-95; mem. exec. com. Prettyman-Leventhal Inn of Ct., 1988-90, counselor, 1990-91; mem. Jud. Conf. for D.C. Cir., 1972-91; adj. prof. Georgetown U. Law Ctr., 1988, 90-92. Editor-in-chief U. Mich. Law Rev., 1966-67. Mem. com. visitors U. Mich. Law Sch., 1972—. Fellow ABA (ho. of dels. 1978-80, 89-91, coun. adminstrv. law sect. 1979-82, chmn. adminstrv. law and regulatory practice sect. 1988-89, governing com. forum com. communications law 1979-82, chmn. standing com. Nat. Conf. Groups 1989-92); mem. D.C. Bar Assn., Women's Bar Assn., FCC Bar Assn. (exec. com. 1984-87, pres. 1990-91), Women's Legal Def. Fund (pres. 1977, v.p. 1978), Order of Coif. Home: 4638 30th St NW Washington DC 20008-2127 Office: Info & Regulatory Affairs Office Mgmt & Budget Old Exec Office Bldg Rm 350 Washington DC 20503

KATZENSTEIN, THEA, retail executive, jewelry designer; b. N.Y.C., Mar. 30, 1927; d. Carl E. and Lillian (Rosenblatt) Schustak; m. William Katzenstein, Sept. 10, 1950; children: Leo, Ranee. Student, Sarah Lawrence Coll., 1948-50; BS, Columbia U., 1962, MA, 1967. Pres. Gallery A., N.Y.C., 1967-71, Melita, N.Y.C., 1972-77, TK Studio, Miami Beach, Fla., 1977—; adj. prof. of jewelry Fla. Internat. U., 1989-90; enamelling instr. U. Miami, 1991. Author: Early Chinese Art and The Pacific Basin, 1967; painting, graphics and jewelry represented in numerous pvt. collections. Trustee Miami Metro Zoo, 1994—. Mem. Soc. N.Am. Goldsmiths, Enamel Guild South, Nat. Enamelist Guild, Fla. Soc. Goldsmiths (pres. S.E. chpt.), Fla. Craftsmen, Zonta (sec. Coral Gables chpt. 1989-90). Democrat. Jewish. Home: Apt 1501 9 Island Ave Miami Beach FL 33139-1360

KATZOWITZ, LAUREN, philanthropic manager and foundation consultant; m. Marc Shenfield. BS in Comparative Lit. with honors, Brandeis U., 1970; MS with honors, Columbia U., 1971. With, Newsweek mag., then Phila. Bull.; free-lance writer, editor, cons., until 1975; cons. Ford Found., 1972-75; mgr. PBS programs Exxon Corp., 1978-81, Great Performances, Live From Lincoln Ctr., Dance in America, NOVA, The MacNeil/Lehrer Report; communications mgr. Exxon Rsch. and Engring. Co., 1981-84; regional liaison Europe and Africa, Exxon Corp., 1984-86; exec. dir. Found. Svc., 1986—; pres. LK Consulting, Croton on Hudson, N.Y., 1986—. Named one of 12 Women to Watch in the Eighties, Ladies' Home Jour., 1979. Regional Finalist Pres.'s Commn. on White House fellow, 1984. Office: LK Consulting 4 Hamilton Ave Croton On Hudson NY 10520-2521

KAUFFMAN, B. SUZANNE, investment company professional; b. Macomb, Ill., June 14, 1930; d. Kenneth Dill and Louise (Zimmerli) Murrell; m. Thomas Lindenfelser (div. 1953); children: Charles Thomas II, Donald Mark. BA, U. Fla., 1982. Registered Nat. Assn. Security Dealers. Field archaeologist Yorktown (Va.) Hist. Ctr., 1985-86; dist. mgr. First Investors Corp., N.Y.C., 1986—. Mem. Nature Conservancy, Libr. Congress (charter assoc.), Nat. Wildlife Assn., Whale Adoption/Friends of the Forest, Lawrenceburg Art League (recorder 1996).

KAUFFMAN, DAGMAR ELISABETH, writer, researcher; b. Hamburg, Fed. Republic of Germany, Feb. 24, 1961; came to U.S., 1983; d. Gustav Ewald and Margot Hildegard (Holz) Franke; m. Bruce Alan Kauffman, July 25, 1986; children: Philip Uwe, Patrick Axel. BA, U. Hamburg, 1984; MA, U. Md., 1987, postgrad., 1987-90. Rschr., teaching asst. U. Hamburg, 1982-83; editorial/mktg. asst. Ednl. Svcs. USA Today, Arlington, Va., 1983-84; adminstrv. asst. U. Md., College Park, 1985-86; rschr., info. program assoc. Am. Assn. Colls. for Tchr. Edn., Washington, 1986-89; freelance rschr., edn. writer Columbia, Md., 1989—; editl. cons. Morgan Fin. Group, Balt., 1993-95. Author, rschr.: A Practical Guide to Recruiting Minority Teachers, 1989, Comprehensive Services Guide, 1995; editor: Minority Teacher Recruitment and Retention: A Public Policy Issue, 1987; contbr. articles to profl. jours. German Acad. Exch. Svc. scholar, 1983-84. Mem. AAUW, Am. Studies Assn. (regional Chesapeake chpt.), Formerly Employed Mothers at Leading Edge, Balt. Coun. on Fgn. Affairs. Democrat. Lutheran.

KAUFFMAN, KAETHE COVENTON, art educator, artist, author; b. Washington, Aug. 12, 1948; d. Richard G. and Kathleen B. (Coventon) K.; m. James William Hite, Oct. 23, 1983; children: James Haydn, Kauffman Hite. BA, U. Wash., 1970, U. Nev., 1975; MFA, U. Calif., Irvine, 1978; PhD, Union Inst. Cin., 1989. Art dept. faculty U. Nev., Las Vegas, Mount St. Mary's Coll., L.A.; chmn. art dept. Sierra Nevada Coll., Incline Village, 1989-91, assoc. prof., 1991—; mem. faculty dept. art U. Calif., Irvine; mem. editorial adv. bd. Collegiate Press. Author: Sex and the Avant-Garde: A Gender Revolution in the Visual Arts 1830-1993, Female Forms of Originality and the New, Women Artists in the Avant-Garde, How Art Professors Teach Avant-Garde Values, Women Artists Deconstruct the Male Avant-Garde, A Modern Renaissance of the Arts; columnist: Lake Tahoe World newspapers; art exhibited at Utrecht, Holland, 1977, Inst. Modern Art, Brisbane, Australia, 1978, George Patton Gallery U. Melbourne, Australia, 1979, Newport Harbor Art Mus., Calif., 1980, Fiberworks Gallery, Berkeley, Calif., 1981, Galerie Triangle, Washington, 1982, Nev. Mus., Reno, 1983, Schoharie Nat., Cobleskill, N.Y., 1984, Pinnacle Gallery, N.Y., 1986, Space Gallery, Las Vegas, Nev., 1988, Manville Gallery, U. Nev., Reno, 1989, Galerie Art-Jeunesse, Montreal, Que., 1990, Kleinert Gallery, N.Y., 1991, West Gallery, Claremont Grad. Sch., 1992, Sierra Nev. Coll. Art Gallery, Lake Tahoe, Nev., 1995, Exhbn. Hall U. Prague, Czech Republic, CERES Gallery, N.Y., 4th Women's UN Conf., Beijing, Nat. Mus. Women in Arts, Washington, Gallery of the Pali, Honolulu, Czech Mus. of Fine Arts, Prague; represented in permanent collections Women's Studio Workshop, N.Y.C., Calif. Mus. Photography, L.A., Fluor Corp., L.A., Harris Found., Las Vegas, Nev., Computer Scis. Corp., L.A., Sheraton Plaza Inn, L.A., Glendale Fed. Bank, L.A. Juror 3d biennial Nev. Craft Show. Recipient Max H. Block award for Humanism, Juror's award Am. Pen Women Bienniale; Laguna Beach Festival of the Arts fellow; TOSCO Corp. grantee; Artists grantee Sierra Arts Found. Mem. Nat. Mus. Women in Arts, Women's Caucus for Art, Nat. Assn. for Women Artists (medal of honor for works on paper, Elizabeth Morse Genius Found. award), Ceres Gallery, Am. Pen Women (3 awards for non-fiction writing nat. competition), Arts and Letters.

KAUFFMAN, SANDRA DALEY, state legislator; b. Osceola, Nebr., Jan. 26, 1933; d. James Richard and Erma Grace (Heald) Daley; m. Larry Allen Kauffman, Sept. 4, 1955; children: Claudia Kauffman Boosman, Matthew Allen. BA, U. Nebr., 1954; postgrad., U. Kansas City, summer 1957. Tchr. Falls City (Nebr.) High Sch., 1954-55, Westport High Sch., Kansas City, Mo., 1955-59; sales rep. Manson Industries, Topeka, Kans., 1974-75; dir. pub. affairs Bishop Hogan High Sch., Kansas City, 1985-86; mem. Mo. Ho. of Reps., Jefferson City, 1987—. Mem. Kansas City Citizens Assn., 1981—, Kansas City Consensus, 1985—; mem. women's coun. U. Mo., Kansas City, 1986—; mem. rsch. mental health bd., bd. govs. Carondelet Aging Svcs., 1992—. Recipient Friend of Edn. award Ctr. Edn. Assn., 1986, Disting. Legislator award Mo. C.C. Assn.; named Mem. of Yr., Mo. Congress Parents and Tchrs., 1979. Mem. Am. Legis. Exch. Coun., Nat. Conf. State Legislatures, Network Bd., Nat. PTA (hon. life), Nat. Order Women Legislators, Mo. PTA (hon. life), South Kansas City C. of C., Grandview C. of C., Women C. of C., Mo. Women's Coun., Women Legislators Mo. (pres.). Republican. Methodist. Home: 620 E 90th Ter Kansas City MO 64131-2918 Office: Mo Ho of Reps State Capitol Building Jefferson City MO 65101-1556

KAUFMAN, CHARLOTTE KING, artist, retired educational administrator; b. Balt., Dec. 5, 1920; d. Ben and Belle (Turow) King; A.B., Goucher Coll., 1969; M.P.H., Johns Hopkins U., 1972, M.Ed., 1976; m. Albert Kaufman, July 22, 1945; children—Matthew King, Ezra King. Dir. public relations Balt. Jewish Community Center, 1962-67; research and editor Johns Hopkins U. Sch. Hygiene and Public Health, Balt., 1969-72, admissions officer, 1972-74, dir. admissions and registrar, 1974-86, dir. study cons. program undergraduates, 1986-89, pub. health acad. adviser, 1989-95. Mem. Am. Pub. Health Assn., Am. Assn. for Higher Edn., Am. Assn. Collegiate Registrars and Admissions Officers, Artists Equity Assn. (v.p. Md. chpt. 1988-90), Md. Printmakers (exec. bd. 1989-94), Delta Omega. Democrat. Jewish. Home: Monterey Country Club 159 Las Lomas Palm Desert CA 92260

KAUFMAN, DENISE NORMA, psychologist, addictions counselor, educator; b. Trenton, N.J., Feb. 7, 1954; d. Charles Edwin and Luella (Barcroft) Farr; m. Peter Alan Kaufman, May 15, 1986 (div. Nov. 1989). BS, Trenton State Coll., 1976, MEd, 1977; EdD, Temple U., 1983. Cert. tchr. health, driver edn., spl. edn., N.J., cert. sch. psychologist, cert. addictions counselor, cert. in student pers. svcs., N.J. Health edn. tchr., dept. dir. Haddon Heights (N.J.) Pub. Schs., 1976-81; tchr. educationally handicapped adolescents Haddon Twp. (N.J.) High Sch., 1984-85; tchr. educationally handicapped adolescents, psychologist Archway Programs, Atco, N.J., 1984-90; tchr., psychologist Ferris Sch. for Boys, Dept. Children, Youth and Families, Wilmington, Del., 1991-92; tchr., cons. psychologist Willingboro (N.J.) Twp. Pub. Schs., 1991-92; pvt. practice psychology, addictions counselor Haddon Heights, 1979—; psychologist Atlantic County Spl. Svcs. Sch. Dist., Mays Landing, N.J., 1992-93; prof., supr. student interns Rowan Coll. of N.J., Glassboro, 1993-95; adj. prof. psychology Camden County Coll., Blackwood, N.J., 1993—; psychologist, coord. mental health Little Neighborhood Ctrs., Phila., 1995-96; behavior specialist United Health and Human Svcs., North Wales, Pa., 1996—; mem. Gov. Brendan Byrne's Smoking and Health Com., 1978-80; assoc. prof. health edn. Mercer County Community Coll., Trenton, 1981; program dir. Phila. (Pa.) Health Mgmt. Corp., 1982; cons. Clearview Regional High Sch., Jr. High Sch. Pub. Sch. Dist., 1986—, Lower Camden County Regional Sch. Dist., 1986—; lectr. Assn. Schs. and Agys. for the Handicapped, 1986—; cons., lectr. Charter Fairmont Inst., Phila., 1991—. Instr. Camden chpt. ARC, S.E. Pa. chpt. Am. Heart Assn.; lectr., cons. Haddon Heights (N.J.) Rotary, 1988—. Mem. APA, ACA, NJCA, Eta Sigma Gamma, Kappa Delta Pi. Home: 1604 Chestnut Ave Haddon Heights NJ 08035-1506 Office: United Health and Human Svcs 1201 Bethlehem Pike Ste 210 North Wales PA 19454

KAUFMAN, ELAINE SUE SOMMERS, special education educator; b. Bklyn., Dec. 25, 1933; d. Samuel and Lily Vivian (Schiller) Sommers; m. Harold Alexander Kaufman, June 24, 1956; children: Michele Beth, Roy Sommers. BA, Bklyn. Coll., 1955; MEd, U. Pitts., 1959. Cert. elem., spl. edn., reading tchr., reading specialist, N.Y., Pa., N.J. Elem. tchr. East Meadow (N.Y.) Pub. Schs., 1955-56, Pitts. Pub. Schs., 1956-61; elem. tchr. Piscataway (N.J.) Bd. Edn., 1961-63, supplemental tchr., 1972-80, learning strategist, 1980-82, tchr. handicapped, 1982—; cons. Piscataway Adult Edn. Adv. Coun., 1975—. Editor: (booklet) Multi-Ethnic Traditional Cooking for the Microwave, 1991; contbg. food editor (newsletter) In Common, 1992; contbr. articles to local newspaper. Counselor Piscataway Helpline, 1971-73; pres. Women's Am. ORT, Piscataway, 1970-73, North Cen. N.J. regional v.p., 1973-75; v.p. Pitt Dames, U. Pitts., 1957-58; trustee Anshe Emeth, 1977-78, v.p., pres. Couples Club, 1977-79; active Planned Parenthood. Frick Commn. scholar, 1958; Piscataway Bd. Edn. grantee, 1990-91, grantee Innovative Ideas in Teaching. Mem. NEA, NOW, AAUW, N.J. Edn. Assn., Piscataway Tchrs. Assn., Middlesex Reading Coun. (membership chmn. 1987-88, parliamentarian 1988-90, news reporter 1992, Outstanding Contbr. award 1987), Brandeis Women's Assn. (life Middlesex chpt.), Phi Kappa Delta. Home: 142 Fountain Ave Piscataway NJ 08854-4607 Office: Schor Mid Sch N Randolphville Rd Piscataway NJ 08854

KAUFMAN, JANICE HORNER, foreign language educator; b. Mattoon, Ill., Apr. 30, 1949; d. Daniel Ogden and Julia Betty (McDermid) Horner; m. Richard Boucher Kaufman, June 24, 1972; children: Julia Ogden, Richard Pearse. AB, Duke U., 1971; MA in Liberal Studies, Hollins Coll., 1979; postgrad., NYU, 1986; doctoral candidate in French, U. Va., Charlottesville, 1994—. Tchr. Roanoke (Va.) City Pub. Schs., 1971-72, North Cross Sch., Roanoke, Va., 1974-82; instr. in French Va. Poly. Inst. and State U., Blacksburg, 1984-86, 88, 90, 94, asst. dir fgn. lang. camps, 1984-85, administrv. dir., 1986; French, English interpreter, translator Coll. Architecture and Urban Studies, Blacksburg, 1988; instr. ESL U. Community Internat. Coun., Cranwell Internat. Ctr., Blacksburg, 1987-89; instr. French Hollins Coll., Roanoke, Va., 1989-90, Radford (Va.) U., 1989, 90; grad. teaching asst. U. Va., Charlottesville, 1992; student counselor Am. Inst. Fgn. Study, Greenwich, Conn., 1977; session leader Russell County Pub. Schs., Lebanon, Va., 1985, Va. Assn. Ind. Schs., Richmond, 1986; reader Mountain Interstate Fgn. Lgn. Conf., Radford U., 1990, East Carolina U., Greenville, N.C., 1991, Va. Poly. Inst. and State U., Blacksburg, 1992, Clemson (S.C.) U., 1993, Va. Fgn. Lang. Conf., Richmond, 1993, African Lit. Assn. Conf., Guadeloupe, 1993; asst. tchr. Am. Coun. for Internat. Studies "Toujours en France", 1995; faculty cons. advanced placement exam in French, Ednl. Testing Svc., Trenton State Coll., 1991, 92, 93, 94, 95; presenter South Atlantic MLA, 1994. Mem. Jr. League of Roanoke Valley, Inc., 1975-95, Jr. League of No. Va., 1995—; treas. Women of Christ Ch., 1984-86; Sunday sch. tchr. Christ Episc. Ch., Blackburg, 1987-89; co-coord. jr. high youth group St. Timothy's Episc. Ch., Herndon, Va., 1994-96, mem. Christian edn. com., 1995—. Mem. MLA, Am. Assn. Tchrs. French, African Lit. Assn., Jr. League of No. Va., Pi Delta Phi. Home: 900 Barker Hill Rd Herndon VA 20170-3014

KAUFMAN, MARY SUSAN, elementary education educator; b. Ellwood City, Pa., Sept. 8, 1946; d. Richard Francis and Harriet Augusta (Stillwagon) Oswald; m. Lawrence William Kaufman, Nov. 21, 1970; children: Steven, Kristina, Amy. BS in Elem. Edn., Clarion State U., 1968; Master Equivalency, Slippery Rock U., 1992. Cert. elem. edn. Reading tchr. Aliquippa (Pa.) Area Sch. Dist., 1968; tchr. grades 1 and 2 Blackhawk Sch. Dist., Beaver Falls, Pa., 1969-79; tchr. grades 4 and 6 Pittsburgh Diocese, Beaver Falls, 1985-87; tchr. grade 6 Beaver (Pa.) Area Sch. Dist., 1987—; mem. steering com. Regional Math Sci. Collaborative, Pitts., 1994—. Rschr., author: Twentieth Century History of Beaver County, 1989. Mem., past pres. New Brighton (Pa.) Area PTA, 1980-85; trustee, rec. sec. Beaver County Hist. and Landmarks Found., Beaver, 1987-91. Recipient Scholarship award West Mayfield PTA, Beaver Falls, 1974, Beaver County Times Cmty. Svc. award Beaver County Times, Beaver, 1985; named Environ. Educator of Yr., Beaver County Conservation Dist., 1996. Mem. Pa. Sci. Tchrs. Assn., Leotta Hawthorne Reading Coun. Democrat. Roman Catholic. Home: 1058 6th St Beaver PA 15009-1824 Office: Beaver Area Sch Dist College Square Sch 375 College Ave Beaver PA 15009-2238

KAUFMAN, MERILEE DALE, public relations executive; b. N.Y.C., June 24, 1943; d. Louis and Sylvia (Schnall) Sisapel; m. Herbert H. Kaufman, Sept. 10, 1972. BA, NYU, 1965, MA, 1970. Adminstrv. asst. The Shubert Orgn., N.Y.C., 1965-72; exec. v.p. Bernie Ilson Inc., N.Y.C., 1972-75; pres. Merilee Kaufman Pub. Rels., Oceanside, N.Y., 1995—; pub. rels. advt. dir. Theatre Guild of Oceanside, N.Y., 1978-84; pub. rels. cons. Poetry Soc. Am., N.Y.C., 1992-93; condr. workshops in field. Poetry pub. in Confrontation, Nassau Rev., Long Pond Rev., Sarah's Daughter's Sing, A Sampler of Poems by Jewish Women, The Best Metroplitan Diary, Live Poets Anthologies. Info. officer health fair Am. Diabetes Assn., Hempstead, N.Y., 1980, support group leader, Rockville Center, N.Y., 1985. Recipient Cert. of Achievement Fresh Meadows Poets Ann. Poetry Competition, 1993; named in A Directory of Am. Poets and Writers. Mem. Nat. Assn. Women Bus. Owners, Am. Women for Econ. Devel., Poetry Soc. Am., Poets House.

KAUFMAN, MICHELE BETH, clinical pharmacist, educator; b. Perth Amboy, N.J., May 13, 1963; d. Harold Alexander and Elaine Sue (Sommers) K. BS in Pharmacy, U. R.I., 1986; PharmD, Mass. Coll. Pharmacy, 1991. RPh, Mass., N.J., N.Y. Staff pharmacist Robert Wood Johnson U. Hosp., New Brunswick, N.J., 1986-91; product devel. pharmacist Reed & Carnrick Pharm. Co., Piscataway, N.J., 1987-89; poison info. specialist Mass. Poison Control System Children's Hosp., Boston, 1990-92; drug info. specialist U. R.I. Drug Info. Ctr., Providence, 1991-92; asst. clin. prof. pharmacy St. John's U., Jamaica, N.Y., 1992-96; clin. pharmacist coord. Health Ins. Plan Greater N.Y., N.Y.C., 1996—; clin. coord. internal medicine, drug info. specialist L.I. Jewish Med. Ctr., New Hyde Park, N.Y., 1992-96; clin. pharmacist coord. HIP of Greater N.Y.C., 1996—; reviewer Micromedex Info. Systems. Contbr. articles and revs. to profl. jours.; patent pending for pineapple colon electrolyte lavage solution. Active St. John's Univ. Jazz Ensemble, 1992—. Fellow Drug Info., 1992; recipient Indsl. Pharm. Tech. award Am. Pharm. Assn., 1986. Mem. Am. Soc. Health Systems Pharmacists, New Eng. Coun. Health Systems Pharmacists, Am. Soc. Pharmacy Law, Am. Inst. History Pharmacy, N.Y. State Coun. Health-Systems Pharmacists, Lambda Kappa Sigma (pres. Xi chpt. 1985-86, v.p. 1984-85, fundraiser 1983-84), Rho Chi. Home: 97 Preusser Rd Craryville NY 12521 Address: 212-72 73d Ave #3G Bayside NY 11364

KAUFMAN, MICHELLE STARK, lawyer; b. N.Y.C., June 11, 1954; d. Maurice E. and Mary (Murray) Stark; m. Daniel M. Kaufman, Oct. 6, 1984; children: Jane Stark, David Stark, Carolyn Stark. BA, Iowa State U., Ames, 1976; JD, U. Mo., Kansas City, 1983. Bar: Mo. 1983, U.S. Dist. Ct. (we. dist.) Mo. 1983. Graphic artist Douglas Stone & Assocs., Newport Beach, Calif., 1976-78; chief news bur. Midwest Records, Kansas City, Mo., 1978-80; ptnr. Stinson, Mag and Fizzell, P.C., Kansas City, 1983-95, Sonnenschein Nath & Rosenthal, Kansas City, 1995—; lectr. in law U. Mo. Sch. Law, Kansas City, 1984-85; trustee U. Mo.-Kansas City Law Sch. Found., 1992—. Bd. dirs. Heart of Am. Family Svcs., Kansas City, 1989—, vice-chmn., 1991-93, chmn., 1994-95; bd. dirs., sec. Countryside Homes Assn., Kansas City, 1985; mem. Kansas City Tomorrow Alumni Assn., 1992—, bd. dirs., 1995—. Mem. ABA (forum on franchising), Am. Acad. Healthcare Attys., Nat. Health Lawyers Assn., Mo. Bar Assn., Greater Kansas City C. of C. (chmn. club 1990—, vice chmn. 1991-92, chmn. 1992-93, Mo. state affairs com. 1995—), U. Mo. Kansas City Law Alumni Assn. (bd. dirs. 1992—, pres. 1994-95), Delta Delta Delta (exec. bd. 1979). Office: Sonnenschein Nath & Rosenthal 4520 Main St Ste 1100 Kansas City MO 64111

KAUFMAN, PAULA T., librarian; b. Perth Amboy, N.J., July 26, 1946; d. Harry and Clara (Katz) K.; m. L. Ratner, 1989. AB, Smith Coll., 1968; MS, Columbia U., 1969; MBA, U. New Haven, 1979. Reference librarian Columbia U., N.Y.C., 1969-70, bus. librarian, 1979-82, dir. library services, 1982-86, dir. acad. info. services, 1986-87, acting v.p., univ. librarian, 1987-88; dean of librs. U. Tenn., Knoxville, 1988—; reference coord. McKinsey & Co., N.Y.C., 1970-73; founder, ptnr. Info. for Bus., N.Y.C., 1973-76; prin. reference libr. Yale U., New Haven, 1976-79; bd. dirs., chair Ctr. Rsch. Librs.; bd. dirs. CAUSE, 1996—. Contbr. articles to mags., 1983—. Bd. dirs. Cmty. Shares, Knoxville, 1993—. Mem. ALA, Soc. for Scholarly Pub., Solinet (bd. dirs., chmn. 1992-93).

KAUFMANN, RACHEL NORSWORTHY, administrative assistant; b. L.A., Feb. 12, 1964; d. Ralph Henry and Audely (Gutierrez) N.; m. Karl Alexander Kaufmann, May 28, 1988. BA, Scripps Coll., 1988. Pharmacy tech. Torrance (Calif.) Meml. Hosp., 1982-88, St. Mary Med. Ctr., Long Beach, Calif., 1987-88; asst. area mgr. AutoFuel Co., Abilene, Tex., 1989-90; adminstrv. asst. McMurry U., Abilene, 1990-92; 911 tech. asst. West Cen. Tex. Coun. of Govts., Abilene, 1992-94; adminstrv. asst. Piedmont Natural Gas, Greenville, S.C., 1995—. Auction com. Am. Cancer Soc., Abilene, 1994; bd. dirs. West Tex. Girl Scout Coun., Abilene, 1992-94. Mem. AAUW (bd. dirs. 1989-94). Presbyterian. Home: 316 Halifax Ln Greenville SC 29615

KAUFMANN, SYLVIA NADEAU, office equipment sales company executive; b. Eagle Lake, Maine, Dec. 1, 1940; d. Edwin Joseph Nadeau and Emily (Beaulieu) Gadbois; m. Max Daniel Kaufmann, Sept. 21, 1958 (div. 1985); children: Mark A., Laura A., Max D. Jr. Grad. high sch., East Hartford, Conn., 1958. Registered arbitrator Am. Registry Arbitrators. Bookkeeper United Bank and Trust, Hartford, Conn., 1959-66; real estate agt. Barcombe Agy., South Windsor, Conn., 1967-74; sales rep. Duplicating Methods Co., East Windsor, Conn., 1974-80; gen. mgr., officer Duplicating Methods Co., East Windsor, 1980—; bd. dirs. Enfield (Conn.) Community Fed. Credit Union. Commr. ethics commn. Town of Enfield, Conn. Mem. Nat. Office Machine Dealers Assn., North Cen. Conn. C. of C., Bus. Profl. Women Greater Hartford, Exec. Females Inc. Democrat. Roman Catholic. Home: 6 Hoover Ln Enfield CT 06082-5314 Office: Duplicating Methods Co 170 North Rd East Windsor CT 06088-9678

KAUFMANN, VICKI MARIE M., social services administrator; b. Lansing, Mich., Nov. 7, 1946; d. Frank Richard and Sophia Mary (Scieszka) Marczynski; m. Felix Kaufmann, May 28, 1988. BA, Carlow Coll., Pitts., 1970; MS in Pastoral Studies, St. Paul U., Ottawa, Ontario, Can., 1976, MA, 1977. Tchr. Mt. Nazareth Acad., Pitts., 1969-71; family services dir. Mt. Nazareth Ctr., Pitts., 1971-75, 77-78; parish outreach worker St. Casimir Ch., Lansing, 1978-81; parish outreach cons. Diocese of Lansing, 1980-83; family life educator Cath. Social Services, Lansing, 1981-84; agy. dir. Cath. Social Services, Brighton, Mich., 1985-93, Broward Cath. Comm. Svc., Wilton Manors, Fla., 1994—; chmn. Consortium on Aging, Howell, Mich., 1988-89; cons. Lansing chpt. Nat. Stepfamily Assn., 1982-84; facilitator Cath. Coun. on Aging, Livingston County, Mich., 1986-89. Author: (with others) Welcoming the Seasons, 1977, Parish Social Ministry, 1985. Co-chmn. Livingston County Emergency Shelter, Howell, 1988—; bd. dirs. Livingston County United Way, Howell, 1988-89, Mich. Coun. of Family Rels., 1990-93; exec. sec. Coun. of Chs. Bd., Lansing, 1982-84; agy. rep. Energy Bank Coalition, Lansing, 1982-84; vice chmn. Livingston County Emergency Shelter, Howell, 1990. Mem. NAFE, Nat. Coun. Family Rels., Cath. Charities USA, Mich. Coun. Family Rels. (bd. dirs. 1990-93), NSFRE. Roman Catholic. Office: Cath Comm Svc 1505 NE 26th St Wilton Manors FL 33065

KAUGER, YVONNE, state supreme court justice; b. Cordell, Okla., Aug. 3, 1937; d. John and Alice (Bottom) K.; m. Ned Bastow, May 8, 1982; 1 child, Jonna Kauger Kirschner. BS magna cum laude, Southwestern State U., Weatherford, Okla., 1958; cert. med. technologist, St. Anthony's Hosp., 1959; J.D., Oklahoma City U., 1969, LLD (hon.), 1992. Med. technologist Med. Arts Lab., 1959-68; assoc. Rogers, Travis & Jordan, 1970-72; jud. asst. Okla. Supreme Ct., Oklahoma City, 1972-84, justice, 1984-94; vice chief justice Okla. Supreme Ct., 1994—; mem. appellate div. Ct. on Judiciary; mem. State Capitol Preservation Commn., 1983-84; mem. dean's adv. com. Oklahoma City U. Sch. Law; lectr. William O. Douglas Lecture Series Gonzaga U., 1990. Founder Gallery of Plains Indian, Colony, Okla., Red Earth (Down Towner award 1990), 1987; active Jud. Day, Girl's State, 1976-80; keynote speaker Girl's State Hall of Fame Banquet, 1984; bd. dirs. Lyric Theatre, Inc., 1966—, pres. bd. dirs., 1981; past mem. bd. dirs. Civic Music Soc., Okla. Theatre Ctr., Canterbury Choral Soc.; mem. First Lady of Okla.'s Artisans' Alliance Com. Named Panhellenic Woman of Yr., 1990, Woman of Yr. Red Lands Coun. Girl Scouts, 1990, Washita County Hall of Fame, 1992. Mem. ABA (law sch. accreditation com.), Okla. Bar Assn. (law schs. com. 1977—), Washita County Bar Assn., Washita County Hist. Soc. (life), St. Paul's Music Soc., Iota Tau Tau, Delta Zeta (Disting. Alumna award 1988, State Delta Zeta of Yr. 1988, Nat. Woman of Yr. 1988). Episcopalian.

KAULA, JUDITH MUDD, diplomat, foreign service officer; b. Louisville, June 5, 1946; d. William Frederick and Mary Julia (Harris) M.; divorced; 1 child, Rekha. BA, Morgan State U., 1968; MA, Am. U., 1974. Joined Fgn. Svc., 1975; with USIA, Washington, 1975—. Fulbright grantee, 1968; recipient Martin Luther King Jr. award NATO Support Activity, Brussels, 1992. Mem. NAFE.

KAULKIN, DONNA BROOKMAN, editor, writer; b. Phila., May 2, 1943; d. Philip and Minnie (Markovitz) Brookman; m. Marvin Kaulkin, Jan. 20, 1963 (div. 1981); children: Andrew Jon, Michael. BA, Georgetown U., 1977. Mng. editor U.S. Pharmacopeia, Rockville, Md., 1978-83; editorial dir. World Aviation Directory, Washington, 1984—, China Buyer's Guide, 1987—, Internat. Air Show Directories, 1987-92, Milestones in Aviation, 1990, Asia/Pacific Aviation, 1991, Airport Business Opportunities, 1991, 92, 93, Overhaul & Maintenance, 1993—, Aviation in Ireland, 1991, Regional Report: Russia and the Newly Independent States, 1993, Regional Report: China, 1994; playwright: Woman at the Washington Zoo, 1980; contbr. many poems, stories, articles to profl. jours. and newsletters. Founder Women's Ctr. Montgomery County, Md., 1975; crisis counselor Crisis Ctr. Montgomery County, 1983-84; speaker, 1983-84. Mem. Internat. Avation Women's Assn., Aviation Space Writers Assn., Aero Club Washington (bd. dirs.), Internat. Aviation Club, UNIFEM, Am. News Women's Club (bd. dirs.). Democrat. Jewish. Avocations: acting, directing, playwriting, travel, theater, music. Home: 4200 Cathedral Ave NW Apt 711 Washington DC 20016-4934 Office: McGraw-Hill World Aviation Directory 1200 G St NW Washington DC 20005-3814

KAUPPI, ELIZABETH AILEEN, civic volunteer; b. Minot, N.D., July 30, 1917; d. Arthur Russell and Ida (Wilson) Trace; m. Clifford Gust Kauppi, June 5, 1941; children: Sharon Elizabeth Kauppi Pleimling, Charles G., Roberta Louise Kauppi Erickson. BS in English and Music, Moorhead State U., 1939. Tchr. h.s. music and English Williams, Minn., 1939-40; tchr, music pub. schs., Coleraine, Minn., 1968-80; dir., organizer spl. performing groups in elem. sch. choirs. Dir. Presbyn. Ch. Choirs, Grand Rapids, Minn., 1947-70; organizer/dir. Arion Male Chorus, Grand Rapids, 1953-70, Melodies Women's Chorus, Grand Rapids, 1958-60, Sweet Adelines, Grand Rapids, 1971-72; organizer Grand Rapids Choristers, 1947; bd. dirs. Pub. Access TV, Grand Rapids; organizer, dir. Second Wind Harmonica Band, Grand Rapids, 1981—. Recipient Success Over Sixty award Options North, 1988. Home: 815 SW 5th Ave Grand Rapids MN 55744

KAUTZMAN, JEAN L. PFLIGER, nurse educator; b. Hazen, N.D., Oct. 4, 1942; d. Lawrence Raymond and Louise A.M. (Hagerott) Pfliger; m. Raymond L. Kautzman, Aug. 1, 1969; children: Jerry, Linda, Timothy, Terry, Marty, Tracy. Diploma, Bismarck Hosp. Sch. Nursing, 1963; BSN, Mary Coll., 1969; MS, S.D. State U., 1984; postgrad., U. N.D., N.D. State U., U. Mary. RN, N.D. Head nurse pediatrics Bismarck (N.D.) Hosp.; faculty mem. Bismarck Hosp./Medcenter One; dir. alumni affairs Medcenter One, Bismarck; acting dir. sch. nursing Medcenter One Coll. Nursing, Bismarck, assoc. prof., home healthcare nurse; state ANA advisor Nursing Student Assn. N.D. Editor The Alumni Connection. Dist. dir. Center Pub. Sch. Recipient Medcenter One Coll. Nursing Svc. award, You're Number One Medcenter One award; grantee Helene Fuld Health Trust, Oliver County Ambulance Assn. Mem. Bismarck C. of C. (higher edn. com.), N.D. Bd. Nursing (mem. entry into practice com.), N.D. Childhood Immunization Program, ANA (cert. nursing adminstr.), Nat. League Nursing, Lewis & Clark Dist. Nurses Assn., Bismarck Hosp./Medcenter One Nursing Alumni Assn. (1st v.p.), N.D. Nurses Assn. (dir. at large). Home: RR 1 Box 14A Center ND 58530-9717

KAVADAS-PAPPAS, IPHIGENIA KATHERINE, preschool administrator, teacher, consultant; b. Manchester, N.H., Oct. 24, 1958; d. Demetrios Stefanos and Rodothea (Palaiologou) K.; m. Constantine George Pappas, July 29, 1979; children: George Demetrios, Rodothea Constance. BA, U. Detroit, 1980; MAT summa cum laude, Oakland U., 1985. Cert. tchr., Mich. Pre-sch. tchr. Assumption Nursery Sch., St. Clair Shores, Mich., 1977-80, interim dir., 1984, bd. dirs., 1980—; Sunday sch. tchr. Assumption Greek Orthodox Ch., St. Clair Shores, 1985—; chairperson pre-sch. curriculum com. Greek Orthodox Archdiocese Dept. Religious Edn., Brookline, Mass., 1987—; cons. Assumption Nursery Sch., 1985—; validator preschs. program for cert. Co-author: Pre-School Curriculum Manual for Greek Orthodox Archdiocese, 1990, Pre-School Curriculum for National Use, 1991. Mem. Assumption Greek Orthodox Ch. Philoptochos Soc., 1978-87; trustee Assumption Nursery Sch., 1979—, Sunday sch. presch. tchr., 1985—; vol. svcs. Bemis Elem. Sch., Boulan Park Mid. Sch., 1991-96. Recipient Vol. Svc. award Angus Elem. Sch., 1989. Mem. Nat. Assn. for the Edn. Young Children (validator presch. programs for accreditation). Office: Assumption Greek Orthodox 21800 Marter Rd Saint Clair Shores MI 48080-2464

KAVALER-ALDER, SUSAN, clinical psychologist; b. N.Y.C., Jan. 31, 1950; d. Solomon and Alice (Zelikow) Weiss; m. Thomas Kavaler, July 12, 1970 (div. 1975); m. Saul Michael Adler, Aug. 14, 1983. PhD in Clin. Psychology, Adelphi U., 1974. Psychologist Beth Israel Hosp., N.Y.C., 1974-76, Manhattan Psychiat. Children's Ctr., N.Y.C., 1977-80; pvt. practice psychotherapy-psychoanalysis, N.Y.C., 1976—, condr. writing and mourning groups; founding dir., supr. faculty, tng. analyst Object Rels. Inst. for Psychotherapy and Psychoanalysis, 1991—; mem. faculty Postgrad. Ctr. Mental Health, N.Y.C., 1984-86, 90—; mem. faculty, supr. Nat. Inst. Pychotherapies, N.Y.C., 1985-91; bd. dirs., supr. Bklyn. Inst. Psychotherapy and Psychoanalysis, 1985-91, mem. psychoanalytic inst. faculty; bd. dirs. Women and Psychoanalysis; adj. prof. Fordham U.; founding exec. dir. Object Rels. Inst. Psychotherpy and Psychoanalysis; pvt. practice in psychotherapy, psychoanalysis; spkr. pvt. seminars, writing groups. Office: 115 E 9th St New York NY 10003-5414

KAVNER, JULIE, actress; b. Sept. 7, 1951. Grad., San Diego U. Actress: (TV series) Rhoda, 1974-78 (Emmy award 1978), The Tracey Ullman Show, 1987-90, The Simpsons, (voice only) 1990— (TV movies) Katherine, 1975, No Other Love, 1979, Revenge of the Stepford Wives, 1980, Dont' Drink the Water, 1994, (TV spl.) The Girl Who Couldn't Lose, 1975, (feature films) National Lampoon Goes to the Movies, 1981, Bad Medicine, 1985, Hannah and her Sisters, 1985, Radio Days, 1987, Surrender, 1987, New York Stories, 1989, Awakenings, 1990, This Is My Life, 1992, Shadows and Fog, 1992, I'll Do Anything, 1994, Forget Paris, 1995, (stage prodn.) Particular Friendships, 1981. *

KAWAZOE, ROBIN INADA, federal official; b. Wilkinsburg, Pa., Jan. 13, 1959; d. George and Hanako (Nishio) Inada; m. Howard Eugene Kawazoe, Oct. 23, 1982; children: Amy, Steven. BA, U. Md., 1982. Program analyst Alcohol, Drug Abuse & Mental Health Adminstrn., Rockville, Md., 1981-85, 85-87, com. mgmt. officer, 1985, extramural programs officer, 1987-88; spl. asst. Nat. Inst. on Drug Abuse, Rockville, 1988-91, dep. dir. Office Sci. Policy and Comm., 1991-94, acting dir. Office Sci. Policy and Comm., 1995—. Recipient Recognition award Pub. Health Svc., 1992, NIH Dir.'s award, 1994. Office: NIH/Nat Inst on Drug Abuse 5600 Fishers Ln Rm 10A-55 Rockville MD 20857-0001

KAWCZYNSKI, DIANE MARIE, elementary and middle school educator, composer; b. Milw., Jan. 22, 1959; d. Adalbert Lawrence and Joan (Zernia) K. BMus, Lawrence U., 1981; MMus, U. Wis., 1985. Cert. music tchr., Va. Suzuki violin instr., string methods instr. Brandon (Manitoba, Can.) Univ. Sch. Music, 1982-83; violin/viola instr., univ. prep program U. Wis. Sch. of Music, Madison, 1983-85; elem. and middle sch. string instr. Albuquerque Pub. Schs., 1985-86; middle sch. string and chorus instr. Ft. Morgan (Colo.) Pub. Schs., 1986-87; elem. string instr., middle sch. orchestra instr. Norfolk Pub. Schs., 1987—. Mem. NEA, Am. String Tchr. Assn., Music Educators Nat. Conf. Home: 860 Gaslight Ln Virginia Beach VA 23462-1232

KAWECKI, JEAN MARY, sculptor; b. June 24, 1926; came to U.S., 1951; d. Donald McRae and Doris (Hankey) Cameron; m. Wladyslaw Kawecki, May 16, 1951; 1 child, Tim Stefan. Student, Lowther Coll., North Wales, 1937-41, Liverpool (Eng.) Coll. Art, 1941-44. Freelance artist London, 1946-51, N.Y.C. and N.J., 1951-68; sculptor, 1970—; founder, dir. Doubletree Gallery Fine Art, Montclair, N.J., 1975-85. Prin. works include wall sculpture First Montclair Housing Corp., 1982, Acquisitional Frenzy (Audubon Artists award 1978), Three Robed Figures in Motion (Carrier Found. award 1993), series of 8 sculptures for Ctr. for Women Policy Studies. Mem. Women Artists Montclair, Montclair Art Mus., World Wildlife Fund. Home: 28 Mountainside Park Ter Upper Montclair NJ 07043-1209

KAY, GAIL GARRETT (STORM KAY), food broker, communications company owner; b. Oct. 10, 1969; d. David and Aliza (Kirshtein) Kashi. BS, N.Y. Inst. Tech., 1992, MBA, 1994. Asst. Hyakugo Bank Ltd., N.Y.C., 1992-93; coord. Oppenheimer Mgmt. Corp., N.Y.C., 1994; pres., owner G.V.C., Great Neck, N.Y., 1994—. Author: (bus. jours.) Mgmt. Quar., 1994-95, Jour. Mgmt. Devel., 1995. Recipient Nat. award ALA, 1987. Office: G V C PO Box 222173 Great Neck NY 11022

KAY, HERMA HILL, law educator; b. Orangeburg, S.C., Aug. 18, 1934; d. Charles Esdorn and Herma Lee (Crawford) Hill. BA, So. Meth. U., 1956; JD, U. Chgo., 1959. Bar: Calif. 1960, U.S. Supreme Ct. 1978. Law clk. to Justice Roger Traynor, Calif. Supreme Ct., 1959-60; asst. prof. law U. Calif., Berkeley, 1960-62; assoc. prof. U. Calif., 1962, prof., 1963, dir. family law project, 1964-67, Jennings prof., 1987—, dean, 1992—; co-reporter uniform marriage and div. act Nat. Conf. Commrs. on Uniform State Laws, 1968-70; vis. prof. U. Manchester, Eng., 1972, Harvard U., 1976; mem. Gov.'s Commn. on Family, 1966. Author: (with Martha S. West) Text Cases and Materials on Sex-based Discrimination, 4th edit., 1996, (with R. Cramton, D. Currie and L. Kramer) Conflict of Laws: Cases, Comments, Questions, 5th edit., 1993; contbr. articles to profl. jours. Trustee Russell Sage Found., N.Y., 1972-87, chmn. bd., 1980-84; trustee , bd. dirs. Equal Rights Advs. Calif., 1976—, chmn., 1976-83; pres. bd. dirs. Rosenberg Found., Calif., 1987-88, bd. dirs. 1978—. Recipient rsch. award Am. Bar Found., 1990, award ABA Commn. Women in Profession, 1992, Marshall-Wythe medal, 1995; fellow Ctr. Advanced Study in Behavioral Sci., Palo Alto, Calif., 1963. Mem. Calif. Bar Assn., Bar U.S. Supreme Ct., Calif. Women Lawyers (bd. govs. 1975-77), Am. Law Inst. (mem. coun. 1985-), Assn. Am. Law Schs. (exec. com. 1986-87, pres.-elect 1988, pres. 1989, past pres. 1990), Am. Acad. Arts and Scis., Order of Coif (nat. pres. 1983-85). Democrat. Office: U Calif Law Sch Boalt Hall Berkeley CA 94720

KAY, KAREN ANN, athletics coach; b. Marlborough, Mass., Feb. 23, 1963; d. Robert Theodore and Elaine Margaret (Hamilton) K. BA in Psychology, Providence (R.I.) Coll., 1985, BS in Bus., 1985. Cert. athletic trainer, master's level coach. Vet. asst. Sudbury (Mass.) Animal Hosp., 1977-81; coach, counselor Babson Coll., Wellesley, Mass., 1981-85; athletic trainer Framingham (Mass.) State Coll., 1985-86, Hardy Physical Therapy, Northboro, Mass., 1986-88; med. sales rep. Medtronic, Inc., Mpls., 1988-92; head coach, ice hockey U. New Hampshire, Durham, N.H., 1992—; head coach U.S. Nat. Hockey Team, Colorado Springs, Colo., 1992-95; head coach, program dir. RinkSport Hockey Camps, Rockville, Md., 1994—. Recipient Silver medal Internat. Ice Hockey Fedn., 1990, 94, Bob Johnson Medallion award USA Hockey, 1994, Budget Coach of the Yr. award Women's Sports Found., 1995. Mem. Am. Women's Coaches Assn., Am. Coll. Hockey Coaches Assn., Women's Sports Found. Democrat. Roman Catholic. Office: U New Hampshire Field House Durham NH 03824

KAY, KELLY W., lawyer; b. Houston, June 14, 1954; d. Rayford G. and Patsy A. (Crow) K. BA, Southwestern U., 1975; MFA, U. Tex., 1978; JD, Columbia U., 1982. Bar: Calif. 1983, U.S. Dist. Ct. (cen. dist.) Calif. 1983, U.S. Ct. Appeals (9th cir.) 1987. Assoc. Stutman, Treister & Glatt, L.A., 1982-85, Rosenfeld, Meyer & Susman, Beverly Hills, Calif., 1985-90; sr. counsel Sony Pictures Entertainment, Burbank, Calif., 1990—; bd. dirs. L.A. Internat. Gay & Lesbian Film & Video Festival, v.p., 1994-95, pres. 1995—. Bd. trustees Life AIDS Lobby, Sacramento, 1987—. Mem. L.A. County Bar Assn. (vice chair individual rights sect. 1985-91, trustee 1988-90, chmn. 1991—), L.A. Lawyers for Human Rights (bd. govs., pres. 1988). Office: Sony Pictures 10202 Washington Blvd Culver City CA 90232-3119

KAY, LOIS JEANNE, writer, educator, publisher; b. Phila., June 13, 1928; d. Maurice Lantz and Lena Barbara (Hoover) Umble; m. William David Kay, Sept. 10, 1949; children: Barbara Ellen, William David. AS cum laude, Dickinson Jr. Coll., Williamsport, Pa., 1948; BA magna cum laude, Syracuse U., 1968; BA, Empire State U., 1984; MA, Goddard Coll., 1986. Tchr. pub. schs., 1965-70; real estate salesperson Utica, N.Y., 1970-74; owner/mgr. Bird-in-Hand Store, Clinton, N.Y., 1974-79; assoc. prof. SUNY, Utica, 1986—; owner/condr. lit. workshops, pub. Greenwood Press, Clinton, 1985—; lectr. in field. Author: A Sounding Inland, 1986, Some Certainties, 1987, Adirondack Diner, 1988, Letters From Sagamore, 1994, White Garden Night, 1996; contbr. numerous articles to profl. jours. Recipient Award for Writing Fiction, Regioart; Ctrl. N.Y. Art grantee, 1994, 95. Home: 54 Kirkland Ave Clinton NY 13323-1414

KAY, PATRICIA KREMER, business owner; b. Arlington, Va., July 10, 1957; d. George Andrew and Eileen Lois (Ludwig) Kremer; m. Jimmy Lamar Kay, Dec. 4, 1989; children: Sabrina Lea, Kelly Marie. Dir. admissions Sawyer Coll., Dayton, Ohio, 1985-89; mgr. shipping/receiving Stolle R & D, Cin., 1989-90; materials mgmt. customer svc. rep. Medisorb Techs. Internat. L.P. a Stolle/Dupont Co., Cin., 1990-91; customer svc. adminstr. Medisorb Techs., Cin., 1991-93; adminstr. shipping/receiving Medisorb Techs., Wilmington, Ohio, 1993-94, purchasing agt., 1994—; svc., mktg. purchasing mgr. Medison Technologies Internat. Office: JP Resources Inc 4576 Yankee Rd Middletown OH 45044

KAYE, CELIA ILENE, pediatrics educator; b. July 12, 1943; m. Tod B. Sloan. BS, Wayne State U., 1965, MS, 1968, MD, 1969, PhD, 1975. Diplomate Am. Bd. Pediatrics, Am. Bd. Med. Genetics; lic. physician, Mich., Ill., Tex. Resident in pediatrics Bronx (N.Y.) Mcpl. Hosp. Ctr., 1969-71, U. Ill. Hosp., Chgo., 1971-72; fellow in biochem. genetics Children's Meml. Hosp., Chgo., 1972-75; instr. pediatrics Northwestern U. Coll. Medicine, Chgo., 1974-75; from asst. prof. to assoc. prof. pediatrics U. Ill. Coll. Medicine, Chgo., 1975-89; chmn. divsn. genetics dept. pediatrics Cook County Hosp., Chgo., 1975-80, attending physician divsn. genetics, dept. pediatrics, 1980-89; dir. sect. genetics and genetics lab., divsn. pediatrics Luth. Gen. Hosp., Park Ridge, Ill., 1980-89, co-med. dir. Perinatal Ctr., 1986-89; dep. chmn. Santa Rosa Children's Hosp. Activities, co-dir. clin. cytogenics lab. U. Tex. Health Sci. Ctr., San Antonio, 1990—, prof. depts. pediatrics and cellular and structural biology, 1990—, chief sect. of metabolism, 1990—, vice chmn. dept. pediatrics, 1993—, co-dir. cytogenetics lab., 1990—; mem. quality assurance com. cytogenetics lab. dept. cellular and structural biology U. Tex. Health Sci. Ctr., 1991—, chair clin. faculty promotions com. dept. pediats., 1991—, chair com. for devel. plan for selection, evaluation and promotion of clin. faculty dept. pediats., 1990-91, med. perinatal mktg. com. dept. pediats., 1990-91, mem. residency adv. com. dept. pediats., 1990—, mem. faculty tenure and promotions com., 1995—, mem. search com., chmn. dept. pathology, 1995-96, mem. dual degree program com., 1995—, vice-chmn. bd. dirs. univ. physicians group, 1995—, mem. contract rev. com. 1995—; mem. clin. coord. com., 1990—, ad hoc clin. care com., 1990—, MSRDP adv. bd., 1991-93, search com. chmn. dept. medicine, 1992-93; chmn. program comm. sect. on genetics and birth defects Am. academy of pediat., 1995—; dir. sect. genetics, Ctr. Craniofacial Anomalies, U. Ill. Coll. Medicine, Chgo., 1975-85; mem. med. adv. bd. Santa Rosa Children's Hosp., 1990-91, mem. exec. com. sect. on genetics and birth defects, Am. Acad of pediat., 1995—; dir. med. edn., 1991—, exec. com., 1992—, medicine policy com., 1992—, chair med. edn. com., 199—; assoc. med. dir. cytogenetics lab. Santa Rosa Med. Ctr., San Antonio, 1991—; vis. assoc. prof. pediats. Rush-Presbyn.-St. Luke's Med. Ctr., Chgo., 1979-89; mem. Genetics Task Force Ill., 1981-89, sec., 1981-83, pres., 1983-85; mem. genetics svc. com. Tex. Genetics Network, 1989—, chmn. steering com., 1992—; chmn. sci. adv. com. on birth defects Tex. Dept. Health, 1995—; del. Nat. Coun. Regional Genetics Networks, 1992—, mem. exec. com., 1993—; mem. Ill. Genetic and Metabolic Diseases Adv. Bd., 1984-89, chmn. lab. subcom., 1985-89; mem. sci. adv. com. Tex. Dept. Health, 1992—; mem. steering com. Children's Regional Health Care Network, San Antonio, 1992-93; mem. mgmt. com. Children's Regional Health Care Sys., San Antonio, 1993—; mem. instl. rev. bd. Cook County Hosp., Chgo., 1975-80, Luth. Gen. Health Care Sys., Park Ridge, Ill., 1988-89; chmn. pediat. edn. com. Luth. Gen. Hosp., Park Ridge, Ill., 1981-86, chmn. pediat. bioethics com., mem. faculty adv. com., 1986-89; mem. fac. com. tenure and promotion com., 1995, mem. serea com. chmn. dept. pathology, 1995-96, mem. cons. Med. Ctr. Hosp. Ward and Nursery, Bapt. Hosp. Sys., Santa Rosa Children's Hosp., Meth. Hosp., Humana Women's Hosp.; mem. by laws com. Santa Rosa Healthcare, San Antonio, 1995—. Mem. adv. bd. Am. Jour. Med. Genetics; reviewer Am. Jour. Human Genetics, Pediatric Dermatology; contbr. articles to profl. jours., chpts. to books. Mem. program planning com. March of Dimes Defects Found., Chgo., 1985-89, mem. health profl. adv. com., 1983-89, chmn., 1981-83; mem. health profl. adv. com. South Ctrl. Tex. chpt., 1989-90; bd. dirs., mem. exec. com. Harkness House for Children, Winnetka, Ill., 1988-89; mem. Ill. Spina Bifida Assn., 1983-89; mem. exec. bd. El Valor Corp. for Handicapped Children, Chgo., 1980-81; mem. med. adv. com. Tex. Sickle Cell Assn., 1990-91. Fellow Am. Coll. Med. Genetics (founding, edn. com. 1993—, moderator pub. health and delivery of svcs. sect. ann. meeting 1994); mem. AMA, Am. Soc. Human Genetics (info. and edn. com. 1990—), Am. Acad. Pediats. (genetics sect., judge sci. awards uniformed svcs. sect. 1992-93, chair program com. sect. on genetics and birth defects 1995—, mem. exec. com. sect. on genetics and birth defects 1995—), Soc. for Pediat. Rsch., Teratology Soc., Soc. for Inherited Metabolic Diseases, So. Soc. for Pediat. Rsch. (moderator genetics sect. ann. meeting 1993—), Tex. Med. Soc., Tex. Genetics Soc., Tex. Pediat. Soc., Bexar County Med. Soc., San Antonio Pediat. Soc. Office: U Tex Health Sci Ctr Genetics Dept 7703 Floyd Curl Dr San Antonio TX 78284-6200

KAYE, GAIL LESLIE, healthcare consultant; b. Upland, Pa., Aug. 6, 1955; d. Ronald E. and Doris T. (Welfley) K. BS, W.Va. Welseyan Coll., 1977; MS, Ohio State U., 1982, PhD, 1989. Lic. profl. clin. counselor; registered dietitian. Asst. dir. food svc., chief clin. dietitian Albert Einstein Med. Ctr., Phila., 1983; asst. prof. Ind. State U., Terre Haute, 1983-85; nutrition cons. Ohio State U. Hosp. Clinics, Columbus, 1986-88, grad. rsch. asst., 1986-89; legis. rep. Ohio Assocs. Counseling and Devel., Columbus, 1988-89; rsch. cons. State Dept. Edn., Columbus, 1988-89; lectr. counselor edn. Ohio State U., Columbus, 1989—; program devel. and clin. rschr. Ross Labs., Columbus, 1990-94; pres. Kaye Consultation Svcs., Inc., 1994—. Inventor in field; contbr. articles to profl. jours. Recipient Pres. award Ohio Mental Health Counselors Assn., 1990. Mem. ACA, Am. Mental Health Counselors Assn., Am. Dietetics Assn., Ohio Dietetics Assn. Home and Office: 365 Helmbright Dr Gahanna OH 43230-3290

KAYE, JANET MIRIAM, psychologist; b. New Haven, Mar. 2, 1937; d. Al and Rose (Marcus) Sovitsky; m. Donald Kaye, June 26, 1955; children: Kenneth, Karen, Kendra, Keith. BS, NYU, 1958, MA, 1960; PhD, Med. Coll. of Pa., 1980. Clin. instr. Med Coll. of Pa., Phila., 1980-82, asst. prof., 1982-86, assoc. prof., 1986-96; prof. Med. Coll. Pa., Phila., 1996—; prof. Allegheny U. of the Health Scis. MCP Hahnemann Sch. of Medicine, East Falls, 1996—. Contbr. articles to profl. jours. Mem. APA, Am. Assn. Cancer Edn., Am. Soc. Clin. Hypnosis, Soc. Health and Human Values, Gerontol. Soc. Am., Am. Soc. Psychiat. Oncology, Coll. Physicians Pa., Internat. Soc. Exptl. Hypnosis. Office: Allegheny Univ of the Health Scis 3300 Henry Ave East Falls PA 19129

KAYE, JENNIFER LYNN, healthcare executive; b. Vallejo, Calif., Oct. 15, 1964; d. Edward Humphrey and Susan Kathy (Album) Bogart. BA in Psychology, U. Va., 1987. Programmer analyst U. Va. Med. Ctr., Charlottesville, 1987-88; personal computer cons. Northwestern U., Chgo., 1988-90; rsch. analyst Blue Cross Blue Shield Minn., St. Paul, 1990-93; mgr. nat. sales Pharmacy Gold, Inc., St. Paul, 1993-94; sr. dir. mktg. and ops. Group Health Cooperative of Eau Claire, Altoona, Wis., 1994—; instr. Grad. Mgmt. Admissions Test preparatory course, Bar Bri, Mpls., 1990-92. Vol. adult self-sufficiency program Project for Pride in Living, Mpls., 1991; vol. mission control officer 1st flight launch action group (1st flag) Minn. Air N.G. Mus., Mpls., 1994—; vol. instr. gen. acad. and study skills St. Thomas U., St. Paul, Minn., 1995—. Mem. Am. Coll. Healthcare Execs.

KAYE, JUDITH SMITH, judge; b. Monticello, N.Y., Aug. 4, 1938; d. Benjamin and Lena (Cohen) Smith; m. Stephen Rackow Kaye, Feb. 11, 1964; children: Luisa Marian, Jonathan Mackey, Gordon Bernard. BA, Barnard Coll., 1958; LLB cum laude, NYU, 1962; LLD (hon.), St. Lawrence U., 1985, Union U., 1985, Pace U., 1985, Syracuse U., 1988, L.I. U., 1989. Assoc. Sullivan & Cromwell, N.Y.C., 1962-64; staff atty. IBM, Armonk, N.Y., 1964-65, asst. to dean Sch. Law NYU, 1965-68; ptnr. Olwine Connelly Chase O'Donnell & Weyher, N.Y.C., 1969-83; judge N.Y. State Ct. Appeals, N.Y.C., 1983—, now chief justice; bd. dir. Sterling Nat. Bank. Contbr. articles to profl. jours. Former bd. dirs. Legal Aid Soc. Recipient Vanderbilt medal NYU Sch. of Law, 1983, Medal of Distinction, Barnard Coll. 1987. Fellow Am. Bar Found.; mem. Am. Law Inst., Am. Coll. Trial Lawyers, Am. Judicature Soc. (bd. dirs. 1980-83). Democrat. Home: 101 Central Park W New York NY 10023-4204 Office: NY Ct Appeals Hall 20 Eagle St Albany NY 12207-1004*

KAYE, YVONNE FRANCES, motivational consultant, thanatologist; b. London, Sept. 15, 1933; came to U.S., 1969; d. Colin Eyre and Cecelia (Simmons) Silverman; m. Samuel Bernard Kaye, Jan. 1, 1956 (div. 1980); children: Rosanne Holt, Michelle Falbo, Colin Kaye, Daniel Kaye. BA, Antioch U., 1974; MS, Marywood Coll., 1976; PhD, Columbia Pacific U., 1982. Cert. compulsive gambling counselor, 1990. Apprentice Probation Dept., London, 1952-54; cons. Pa. Sch. Dists., Harrisburg, Pa., 1970-80, Creative Edn., Inc., 1970-76; faculty Marywood Coll, Scranton, Pa., 1976-82, Pa. State U., 1995—; prin. Dr. Y. Kaye Consulting, Willow Grove, Pa., 1970—; radio talk show host WWDB Radio, Bala Cynwyd, Pa., 1982—; keynoter, presenter UN, 1986, Health Comm., Deerfield Beach, Fla., 1988-92, Compassionate Friends, Eng., 1994—; keynoter, trainer Great Lakes Conf. Inc., Indpls., 1986—, Vietnam Vets. Health Initiative, 1996. Author: The Child That Never Was, 1990, Credit, Cash & Codependency, 1991, 366 Encouragements to Prosperity, 1993. Vol. trainer Pa. Prisons, 1970-80. Recipient Humanitarian award Maharishi, Jenkintown, Pa., 1977, Mental Health Inc., Phila., 1990, Media award Tough Love Inc., Phila., 1984. Mem AAUW, ADEC, Holocaust Soc., Assn. of Death Edn. and Counseling. Office: 22 N York Rd Willow Grove PA 19090

KAYE/KANTROWITZ, MELANIE, writer, educator; b. Bklyn., Sept. 9, 1945; d. Milton E. Kantrowitz and Violette E. (Wolfgang) Kaye. BA, CUNY, 1966; MA, U. Calif., Berkeley, 1968, PhD, 1975. Instr. comparative lit. U. Calif., Berkeley, 1971-72; asst. prof. Univ. Scholars Portland (Oreg.) State U., 1972-76, instr. women's studies, 1977-79; counsellor Rape Relief Hotline, Portland, 1977-78; adj. faculty Goddard Coll., Plainfield, Vt., 1978-81; adj. faculty Vt. Coll., Montpelier, 1981-85, asst. then assoc. prof., 1985-92; exec. dir. Jews for Racial and Econ. Justice, N.Y.C., 1992-95; Jane Watson Irwin prof. Hamilton Coll., Clinton, N.Y., 1995—. Co-editor: The Tribe of Dina, 1986; editor, pub. (jour.) Sinister Wisdom, 1983-87; author: (poetry) We Speak in Code, 1980, (fiction) My Jewish Face, 1990, (essays) The Issue is Power, 1992. Mem. Phi Beta Kappa. Jewish. Home: Stony Clove Ln Chichester NY 12416

KAYE JOHNSON, SUSAN, educational consultant; b. N.Y.C., Jan. 23, 1932; d. Albert and Goldie (Feldman) Sroge; m. Carroll F. Johnson, Jan. 16, 1990; children from previous marriage: Richard M. Kaye, Gillian Kaye Karran. BA in History, Bklyn. Coll., 1953, MS in Counseling, 1958; MEd in Adminstrn., Columbia U., 1976, EdD in Adminstrn., 1978. Cert. adminstr., supr. N.Y., N.J., guidance counselor, history tchr., N.Y. Tchr. 3d grade Ollie Perry Storm Sch., San Antonio, 1954-55; tchr. social studies Jr. High Sch. 214, Bklyn., 1955-57; guidance counselor Jr. High Schs. 214 and 510, Bklyn., 1957-59; evaluation asst., coord. career devel. Great Neck (N.Y.) Pub. Sch., 1966-71, dir. chpt. I, 1971-79; dir. pupil svcs. Bellmore-Merrick High Sch. Dist., Long Island, N.Y., 1979-83; asst. supt. schs. Longwood Sch. Dist., Middle Island, N.Y., 1983-89; supt. schs. Florham Park (N.J.) Pub. Schs., 1989-92; ednl. cons. Longboat Key, Fla., 1992—; chair women's caucus Am. Assn. Sch. Adminstrs., 1980-82. Co-author: An Analysis of Problems in a School District, 1980, Managing Schools in Hard Times, 1981. Assoc. trustee Dowling Coll., Long Island, 1983-87; trustee Women Svcs. Divsn., Brookhaven, N.Y., 1986, Brookhaven Twp. Youth Bd., 1987, Adult Sch., Florham Park, 1989-92. Mem. AAUW, NOW, Archael. Inst. Am., Phi Delta Kappa. Home and Office: 2077 Gulf Of Mexico Dr Longboat Key FL 34228-3202

KAYS, AMY LYNN, art educator; b. Sussex, N.J., July 17, 1970; d. Roger Lee Kays and Donna Lynn Paiva. BA in Fine Arts, William Paterson Coll., 1993. Cert. tchr. art K-12. Art specialist Jersey City (N.J.) Bd. Edn., 1993—; conductor workshop comml. art Jersey City Bd. Edn., 1994. Mem. Nat. Art Educators Assn., Jersey City Edn. Assn., Alpha Phi Omega (Leadership award). Home: 20 Victoria Ave Lake Hiawatha NJ 07034

KAYS, LINDA JEAN, sculptor; b. Bklyn., N.Y., Mar. 8, 1952; d. Ronald J. and Rosa Isabel (Paralitici) Brown; m. Ronald W. Kays, Oct. 24, 1969 (div. Apr. 1975); children: Jeremy Ronald, Jennifer Lyn, Jacki Lyn. Grad. h.s., Newton, N.J. Farmer N.Y., 1976-88; ins. rater N.Y. Cen. Mut., Edmeston,

N.Y., 1981-86; owner, artist Lil Bit of Country Craft & Fabric Store, Morris, N.Y., 1988-93; weight sta. operator Norwich (N.Y.)-Chenango County, 1992-94; sculptor Norwich, 1994—; tchr. sculpting Norwich Art Guild, 1993-95, BOCES Adult Edn., Norwich, 1996. Sculptor: Bus Stop (Judge's Choice award 1993), Bag Lady (1st prize 1991), Wizard (1st prize 1994), Homecoming Desert Storm (1st prize 1992). Donator of sculptures Suffolk Burn Ctr., Stony Brook Coll., N.Y., 1994, 95, Hospice, Seattle, 1995, Cystic Fibrosis Found., Dallas, 1996. Mem. Chenango County Coun. Arts, Chenango County C. of C. Republican. Roman Catholic. Home and Office: Gnomebodies & Somebodies 42 Mitchell St Norwich NY 13815

KAZENAS, SUSAN JEAN, consultant; b. Oregon, Ill., Dec. 29, 1956; d. Charles Leroy and Vera Jean (Groenhagen) K. BS, Northwestern U., 1982. CPA, Ill., 1985. Acctg. analyst Allstate Ins. Co., Northbrook, Ill., 1977-80; asst. dir. Steel Tank Inst., Deerfield, Ill., 1980-85; owner, acct. Decker Drug, Oregon, 1981-84; acct., auditor Crone, Kipp & Blomgren, Rockford, Ill., 1984-87; acct., internal auditor Woodward Gov. Co., Rockford, 1987-88; acct., sr. cons. McGladrey & Pullen, Rockford, 1988-90; cons. mgr. BDO Seidman, Rockford, 1990-92, Chgo., 1992-93; acctg. mgr. Danfoss Electronic Drives, Rockford, Ill., 1993-96; prin. cons. Oracle Corp., Chgo., 1996—. Bd. dirs. pub. info. Am. Cancer Soc., Winnebago County, Ill., 1988-92. Mem. AICPA, Ill. CPA Soc. (No. chpt. sec. 1988-89, pres. 1989-90, state bd. dirs. 1993-95), Inst. Mgmt. Accts. Home: 154 Millers Crossing Itasca IL 60143-2834 Office: Oracle Corp 203 N LaSalle St Ste 2000 Chicago IL 60601

KAZMAREK, LINDA ADAMS, secondary education educator; b. Crisfield, Md., Jan. 18, 1945; d. Gordon I. Sr. and Annie Ruby (Sommers) Adams; m. Stephen Kazmarek, Jr., Aug. 2, 1981. B of Music Edn., Peabody Conservatory of Music, 1967; postgrad., Morgan U., Towson U. Cert. advanced profl. tchr., K-12, Md.; nat. cert. tchr. Mayron Cole piano method. Organist, choir dir. Halethorpe United Meth. Ch., Balt., min. music, 1978-92, 93—; organist, choir dir. Olive Branch United Meth. Ch., 1973-77;, 1978-92, 93—; piano tchr. Modal Cities Program, Balt., Balt. Community Schs; tchr. vocal music Balt. City Schs., 1967—; min. music Halethorpe Meth. Ch., 1993—; pvt. tchr. piano and organ.; mem. music faculty, McKendree Sch. of Religion, 1996. Composer: A Family of Care (award, 1991, Praise Song, 1992, Thy Way, Lord, 1993, I Asked the Lord, 1993, Peace and Rest, 1994, Sing Praise to Jesus, 1994, Trilogy for piano solo, 1994, Shine Your Light, 1994, Resurrection, 1995, 1-800-Heaven, 1995, God Has A Plan for You, 1995. Concert performer for Meth. Bd. Child Care, 1989, Balt. S.W. Emergency Svcs., 1991, Halethorpe Meth. Ch., 1994; guest performer Balt. City Tchrs. Appreciation Banquet, 1991. Recipient vol. award for music enrichment summer program, 1973, award for voluntarism Fund. for Ednl. Excellence, 1985; Fund for Ednl. Excellence grantee, 1988. Mem. NEA, Md. State Tchrs. Assn., Balt. City Tchrs. Assn., Md. Music Educators Assn., Music Educators Nat. Conf., Md. State Music Tchrs. Assn., Nat. Music Tchrs. Assn., Washington Songwriters Assn., Gospel Music Assn., Washington Area Music Assn., Peabody Alumni Assn.

KEAGY, DOROTHY (DOTTI KEAGY), copy director; b. Waltham, Mass., March 3, 1945; d. Albert Stanley and Bertha (Bluestein) Rouffa; m. Neil Woolf, 1996; children: Meredith, Brian. Student U. Ill., 1963-65, Pratt Inst., N.Y.C., 1965-66. Mgr. depts. Neiman-Marcus, Lou Lattimore, Tex., 1970-75; writer, editor Dallas Morning News, Fashion Showcase, 1975-78; bur. chief, regional editor Women's Wear Daily, Dallas, 1978-84; dir. mktg. communications Dallas Apparel Mart, Trammel Crow Co., 1984-85; sr. editor Women's Wear Daily, N.Y.C., 1985-88; editor fitness N.Y. Times Mag. Group, 1988-90; writer, publicist, 1990-95; copy dir., promotion & design Rowland Co., 1995—. Mem. Tacassociates, Dallas, 1982-83. Recipient Editorial award Dallas Apparel Mart, Dallas Fashion awards, 1980. Mem. Fashion Group Internat., Sigma Delta Phi. Contbr. mag. articles to publs. Home: 420 E 64th St Apt 11D New York NY 10021 Office: The Rowland Co 1675 Broadway New York NY 10019

KEANE, KEELY GENE, gifted and talented educator; b. Washington, Pa., Sept. 17, 1961; d. Curtis Eugene and Patricia Louise (Amos) Havener; m. Martin Edwin Keane, June 18, 1988; children: Ashlee Alexa, Tighe Bradean. BA in Elem. Edn., Point Park Coll., Pitts., 1983; MA in Curriculum Leadership, U. Redlands, Calif., 1995. Cert. tchr. gifted and talented, Calif. Tchr. Upper St. Clair (Pa.) Sch. Dist., 1983-85, McGuffey Sch. Dist., West Alexander, Pa., 1985-88; tchr. gifted and talented Redlands Unified Sch. Dist., 1988—, gifted and talented testing coord., 1990—; gifted and talented coord. Crafton Elem. Sch., Redlands, 1989—. Recipient Reading Tchr. of Yr. award Arrowhead Reading Coun., 1989; Redlands Ednl. Partnership Tech. grantee, 1994. Mem. ASCD, Calif. Tchrs. Assn., Redlands Tchrs. Assn. Republican. Baptist. Home: 144 N Plymouth Way San Bernardino CA 92408-4128 Office: Crafton Elementary School 311 N Wabash Ave Redlands CA 92374-4261

KEANE, MARIE JEANETTE (MARIA KEANE), educator, artist; b. N.Y.C., Mar. 31, 1931; d. Nicholas Joseph and Mary Christine (Passaretti) Santora; m. Thomas Roger Keane; children: Roger, Kathleen, Elisabeth, Mary, Julia. BA, Hunter Coll., N.Y.C., 1953; MA, U. Del., 1994. Cert. tchr., N.Y. Tchr. Niagara Falls (N.Y.) Pub. Sch. Sys., 1953-56; instr. watercolor DuPont Country Club, Wilmington, Del., 1975-78; tchr. Mt. Pleasant Sch. Dist., Wilmington, 1975-78; artist in residence Archmere Acad., Claymont, Del., 1979-83; sr. docent Del. Art Mus., Wilmington, 1987-88; artist in residence Del. Divsn. of Arts, Wilmington, 1983-93; asst. prof. fine arts and art history Wilmington Coll., 1986—; lectr. U. Del., Wilmington, 1981—; docent Historic Howard Pyle Studio, Wilmington, 1990—; lectr. arts in edn. Del. Divsn. Arts, 1982—; participant master workshop in art L.I. U., 1991; participant master workshop in monoprint Bennington (Vt.) Coll., 1993; printmaker Benning Coll., 1992, 95; juror Internat. Art Exhibit, Hercules; vol. Classes for Christian Formation of Spl. Populations, 1970-80; art chair Christ in Christmas Com., 1979-88; exec. bd. for physically challenged Cath. Diocese of Wilmington, 1980-87; exec. bd., com. Very Spl. Arts Festival, 1984-90; docent Del. Art Mus., 1987-88; juror Del. Camera Club Regional Exhbn., 1992; exhbn. chair Christ in Christmas Retrospect, 1992; juror Reflections Del. Scholastic State-wide Exhbn., 1993-94; lectr. excellence in tech., art history U. Del., 1993; scholarship chair Studio Group, Inc., 1992—; docent Smithsonian Tour, Howard Pyle Studio, Wilmington, pres., 1980-82; lectr. various colls., orgns. and confs. Illustrator: Touch of Spring, 1976; author, illustrator: Watercolor Wings, 1976; author: Heroines and Housewives, 1994; one-person shows at Luther Towers Gallery, Wilmington, Friends Sch., Wilmington, Du Pont Country Club, Wilmington, Wilmington Drama League, 1995, 909 Gallery, Wilmington, Immaculata Coll., Exton-Paoli, Pa., Del. State Arts Coun., 1989, Goldey Beacom Coll., 1992, Wilmington Drama League, 1995; exhibited in group shows at Atrium Gallery, Wilmington, 1988, Wilmington Coll., 1988, 89, 90, 94, 96, Del. Nature Soc., 1990, Del. Mus. Natural History, 1990, L.I. U., 1991, U. Del., 1992, 93, Howard Pyle Studio, 1993, Chester County Art Assn., 1993, Wilmington Coll., 1994, Gov. of Del., 1995, others; represented in permanent collections Wilmington Coll., Newcastle, Del., U. Del., Newark, Zimmerli Mus., Rutgers State U., New Brunswick, Archmere Acad., Claymont, Del., Wilmington Divsn. Librs., So. Va. Coll. for Women, Buena Vista, Va., Del. Divsn. Arts, Wilmington, Mary Mother of Hope House, Wilmington, Del. Art Mus. Circulating Gallery, Studio Group Inc. Barnes Found. scholar, Merion, Pa., 1978-80; recipient Jill Jones Nauta award Chester County Art Assn., 1988, J. Lanier Jordan Meml. award, 1989, awards Chester County Art Assn., 1992, 93, 95, award Ctr. for Creative Arts, 1992, 94, award Howard Pyle Studio Regional Exhbn., 1994, Mary Derrickson McCurdy award Rehoboth Art League, 1994, awrds Rehoboth Art League, 1995, profl. fellowship Del. Divsn. Arts and Nat. Endowment Arts, 1996-97. Mem. Coun. Del. Artists (publicity and exhbn. curator, Svc. award), Studio Group, Inc., Nat. League Am. Pen Women (prizes 1985, 87, 89, 91, 93, 95), Chester County Art Assn., Am. Watercolor Soc. (assoc.), Phila. Watercolor (assoc.), Phi Kappa Phi. Democrat. Roman Catholic. Home: 332 Spalding Rd Wilmington DE 19803 Office: Wilmington Coll 320 N DuPont Hwy New Castle DE 19720

KEANE, REGINA MARIE, elementary school educator; b. Boston, Nov. 22, 1955; d. James Francis and Dorothy (Carr) K. BA, Stonehill Coll., 1977. 1st grade tchr. Blessed Sacrament Sch., Walpole, Mass., 1977—. Mem. Dem. City Com., Brockton, Mass., 1992-94. Roman Catholic. Home: 290 W Elm St Brockton MA 02401-4240 Office: Blessed Sacrament Sch 808 East St Walpole MA 02081-3621

KEARNEY, ANNA ROSE, history educator; b. Mount Pleasant, Pa., Mar. 1, 1940; d. John Joseph and Marguerite Costello (Gettings) K. BA, St. Mary's Coll., Notre Dame, Ind., 1962; MA, U. Notre Dame, 1967, PhD, 1975; MS in Libr. Sci., Ind. U., 1983. Cert. tchr., Pa. Tchr. Hempfield Area Schs., Greensburg, Pa., 1962-66, Mishawaka (Ind.) Sch. Dist., 1967-68; teaching asst. U. Notre Dame, 1968-70, libr. clk., 1974-76, libr. assoc., 1976-86; divsn. chair gen. edn. Ind. Vo-Tech. Coll., South Bend, 1970-72; asst. to univ. libr. U. Louisville, 1986-89; assoc. prof. Am. history Jefferson C.C./U. Ky., Louisville, 1989—; faculty cons. Ednl. Testing Svc., San Antonio, 1993, 96. Contbr. articles to profl. jours. Judge Nat. History Day, Louisville and Indpls., 1990-94; exec. on loan United Way of St. Joseph County, South Bend, 1982; food coord. Ethnic Festival, South Bend, 1974; lector Our Lady of Lourdes Ch., Louisville, 1987—. Grantee U. Louisville, 1987, U. Notre Dame, 1988, Ky. Libr. Assn., 1988, NEH, 1990-92, 95. Mem. Assn. of Coll. and Rsch. Librs. (exec. com. for 5th nat. conf. 1987-89), Orgn. Am. Historians, So. Hist. Assn., Cath. Hist. Assn., Ky. Assn. Tchrs. History, Nat. Coun. of Women's Studies Assn., St. Mary's Coll. South Bend Alumnae Assn. (pres. 1984-85), Phi Alpha Theta. Democrat. Roman Catholic. Home: 3316 Cawein Way Louisville KY 40220-1908 Office: Jefferson Cmty Coll/U Ky 109 E Broadway Louisville KY 40202-2005

KEARNEY, MARY ELIZABETH, investment company executive; b. New Bedford, Mass., Dec. 18, 1950; d. James Michael and Mary Elizabeth (McGrath) K.; m. Robert Joseph Ciolek, Oct. 14, 1974. BA, Emmanuel Coll., 1972; MBA, Harvard U., 1981. From credit analyst to sr. credit analyst New Eng. Merchant's Nat., Boston, 1972-75, asst. loan officer, 1975-76, loan officer, 1976-77, asst. v.p., 1977-79; assoc. McKinsey & Co., Cleve., 1981-83; ptnr. Monitor & Co., Boston, 1983-86; sr. engagement mgr. McKinsey & Co., Boston, 1986-87; sr. mgr. Price Waterhouse, Boston, 1987-89, ptnr., 1989-95; mng. dir. Putnam Investments, Boston, 1995—. George F. Baker scholar Harvard Bus. Sch., 1981; John L. Loeb fellow, 1981. Office: Putnam Investments One Post Office Square Boston MA 02109

KEARNEY, PATRICIA ANN, university administrator; b. Wilkes-Barre, Pa., May 15, 1943; d. William F. and Helen L. (Hartz) K. BA, Mich. State U., 1965; MSEd, Ind. U., 1966. Head resident advisor Western Ill. U., Macomb, 1966-68; asst. v.p. SUNY, Buffalo, 1968-70; asst. dean student life Lock Haven (Pa.) State Coll., 1970-72; dir. residential life U. Calif., Davis, 1974-83, bus. mgr., 1983-85, dir. housing and food services, 1985-90, asst. vice chancellor student affairs, 1990-95, exec. dir. housing and fin. aid, 1995—; speaker nat. and state convs. Contbr. articles to profl. jours. Mem. Am. Coll. Personnel Assn. (pres.), Assn. Coll. and U. Housing Officers Internat., Sierra Club. Home: 714 Borchard Ct Woodland CA 95695-5002 Office: U Calif 127 Student Housing Davis CA 95616

KEARNEY NUNNERY, ROSE, nursing administrator, educator, consultant; b. Glen Falls, N.Y., July 8, 1951; d. James J. and Helen F. (Oprandy) K.; m. Jimmie E. Nunnery. BS with honors, Keuka Coll., 1973; M of Nursing, U. Fla., 1976, PhD, 1987. Asst. prof. La. State U. Med. Ctr., New Orleans, 1976-87, U. of South Fla., Tampa, 1987-88; project coord. indigent health care U. Fla., Gainesville, 1984-85; dir. nursing programs SUNY, New Paltz, N.Y., 1988-94; project dir. MS in gerontol. nursing advanced nursing edn. grant U.S. Health Resources and Svcs. Adminstrn. Div. Nursing, 1992-94; head nursing dept. Tech. Coll. of the Lowcountry, Beaufort, S.C., 1995—. Bd. dirs. Ulster County unit Am. Cancer Soc., 1991-94, mem. nursing edn. com., 1990-92; bd. dirs. Mid-Hudson Consortium for Advancement Edn. for Health Profls., 1988-94, mem. nursing edn. com., 1988-92, mem. scholarship com., 1989-93, com. chmn., 1990-93, treas., 1992-94; mem. prof. devel. program SUNY, Albany, 1989-92; mem. adv. coun. Ulster C.C., 1989-94; mem. adv. regional planning group for early intervention svcs. United Cerebral Palsy Ulster County Inc., Children's Rehab. Ctr., 1989-91; mem. Ulster County adv. com. Office for Aging, 1991-94; state del. S.C. Conf. on Aging, 1995; bd. dirs. Beaufort County Coun. on Aging, 1995; mem. cmty. adv. bd. Hilton Head Hosp., 1996—, Hilton Head Med. Ctr. and Clinics, 1996—. Mem. ANA, Sigma Theta Tau. Roman Catholic. Home: 41 S Shore Ct Hilton Head Island SC 29928-7656

KEARNS, JANET CATHERINE, corporate secretary; b. Chgo., Oct. 29, 1940; d. Casimir J. and Eleanor (Galus) Kubik; m. Edward P. Kearns, May 4, 1975. Grad., Madonna High Sch., 1958. Legal sec. Seyfarth, Shaw, Fairweather & Geraldson, Chgo., 1960-66; sec. to pres. Bowey's, Inc., Chgo., 1966-69, Sealy, Inc., Chgo., 1969—; corp. sec. Sealy, Inc., 1977-89; adminstrv. sec. RHR Internat. Co., Wood Dale, Ill., 1989—. Asst. dir. religious edn. St. Matthew Parish, Glendale Heights, Ill., 1988-89. Office: RHR Internat Co 220 Gerry Dr Wood Dale IL 60191-1139

KEARNS, MERLE GRACE, state senator; b. Bellefonte, Pa., May 19, 1938; d. Robert John and Mary Catharine (Fitzgerald) Grace; m. Thomas Raymond Kearns, June 27, 1959; children: Thomas, Michael, Timothy, Matthew. B.S., Ohio State U., 1960. Tchr. St. Raphael Elem. Sch., Springfield, Ohio, 1960-62; substitute tchr. Mad River Green dist., Springfield, 1972-78; instr. Clark Tech. Coll., Springfield, 1978-80; commr. Clark County, Ohio, 1981-91; mem. Ohio State Senate from 10th dist., 1991—; chair Senate human svcs. and aging com.; mem. edn. com., health com.; vice chair Senate agrl. com.; co-chair Supreme Ct. domestic violence com.; mem. Joint Com. Agy. Rule Review; pres. bd. county commrs., 1982, 83, 86, 87, 90, v.p., 1985, 88, 89. Bd. dirs. Springfield Symphony, 1980-86, Arts Council, 1980-85, County Commrs. Assn. of Ohio, sec., 1988, 2d v.p., 1989-90, 1st v.p., 1990; mem. exec. com. Springfield Republicans, 1984—; bd. pres. Ohio Children's Trust Fund, 1995-96. Ohio State U., scholar, 1957-59; named Woman of Yr. Springfield Pilot Club, 1981, Wittenberg Woman of Accomplishment, 1991, Watchdog of Treasury, 1991. Mem. LWV (bd. dirs. 1964-78, pres. 1975-78), Ohio Nurses Assn. (Legislator of the Yr. 1995). Rotary, Omicron Nu. Roman Catholic. Avocations: reading, golf. Office: Ohio Senate Senate Bldg Rm 041 Columbus OH 43215

KEARSE, AMALYA LYLE, federal judge; b. Vauxhall, N.J., June 11, 1937; d. Robert Freeman and Myra Lyle (Smith) K. B.A., Wellesley Coll., 1959; J.D. cum laude, U. Mich., 1962. Bar: N.Y. 1963, U.S. Supreme Ct. 1967. Assoc. Hughes, Hubbard & Reed, N.Y.C., 1962-69; ptnr. Hughes, Hubbard & Reed, 1969-79; judge U.S. Ct. Appeals (2d cir.), 1979—; lectr. evidence N.Y. U. Law Sch., 1968-69. Author: Bridge Conventions Complete, 1975, 3d edit., 1990, Bridge at Your Fingertips, 1980; translator, editor: Bridge Analysis, 1979; editor: Ofcl. Ency. of Bridge, 3d edit, 1976; mem. editorial bd. Charles Goren, 1974—. Bd. dirs. NAACP Legal Def. and Endl. Fund, 1977-79; bd. dirs. Nat. Urban League, 1978-79; trustee N.Y.C. YWCA, 1976-79, Am. Contract Bridge League Nat. Laws Commn., 1975—; mem. Pres.'s Com. on Selection of Fed. Jud. Officers, 1977-78. Named Women's Pairs Bridge Champion Nat. div., 1971, 72, World div., 1986, Nat. Women's Teams Bridge Champion, 1987, 9o, 91. Mem. ABA, Assn. of Bar of City of N.Y., Am. Law Inst., Lawyers Com. for Civil Rights Under Law (mem. exec. com. 1970-79). Office: US Ct Appeals US Courthouse Foley Sq New York NY 10007-1501

KEATH, KATHLEEN CLAIRE, auditor; b. Wilmington, Del., Aug. 1, 1966; d. John Joseph and margaret Ann (Mitchell) K. BS in Acctg., U. Del., 1990. CPA; cert. mgmt. acct., cert. internal auditor. Bookkeeper Godwin Enterprises, Inc., Newark, Del., 1984-86; acct./bookkeeper White Oak, Inc., Newark, 1986-88; staff acct. Whisman & Assocs., CPA, Wilmington, 1988-89; paraprofl. McBride, Shopa & Co., CPA, Greenville, Del., 1989-90; income tax preparer H&R Block, Inc., Wilmington, 1990; staff acct. Daney, Cannon, Truitt & Sarnecki, Wilmington, 1991-92; sr. staff auditor Artisans' Savs. Bank, Wilmington, 1992-93, dir. internal audit, 1993-96; pvt. practice in tax and audits Newark, 1992—; lic. acct. Montell Polyolefins, Elkton, Md., 1996—; treas. Rutledge Maintenance Corp.; external auditor Kiwans of Wilmington, 1992—. Spkr. Mil. Order World Wrs, 1993. Mem. AICPAs, Del. Soc. CPAs (industry com. mem. 1993—), Inst. Internal Auditors, Inst. Mgmt. Accts. Roman Catholic.

KEATING, KAREN GREENBLATT, association executive; b. Sacramento, May 23, 1957; d. Owen Lee and Barbara Ann (Trost) Greenblatt; m. Philip Comfort Tyson, Oct. 26, 1996. BA, Va. Poly Inst. & State U., 1979. Comm. specialist Show Off Internat., McLean, Va., 1979-80; asst. dir. advt., prodn. and promotion, copywriter Sta. WEEL, Fairfax, Va., 1980-82; production and traffic asst. Abramson Assocs., Washington, 1982, asst. traffic mgr., 1982-83; production dir. Sta. WGAY-FM / Sta. WWRC, Silver Spring, Md., 1983-85; assoc. editor Nat. Assn. Life Underwriters, Washington, 1985-89; dir. comm. and meetings Assn. Advanced Life Underwriting, Washington, 1989—. Producer and editor of quar. newsletters (Am. Soc. Assn. Execs. Gold Cir. award 1993, APEY award 1994). Active Junior League Washington, 1992-94. Mem. Ins. Co. Planners Internat., Am. Soc. Assn. Execs. (comm. sect. coun. 1996—, Gold Cir. award 1993, APEX award 1994), Profl. Conv. Mgmt. Assn.

KEATING, MARGARET MARY, entrepreneur, business consultant; b. Chgo., Feb. 18, 1950; d. Jeremiah Joseph and Margaret Mary (Donnelly) K. Student, Harvard U., 1986-87; cert. in law, U. Mass., 1993; postgrad., Emmanuel Coll., 1994; MBA, Simmons Coll., 1996. Sr. merchandiser J.C. Penney Co., Chgo., 1971-73, dist. mgr. fashions, 1973-75, regional mgr., 1976-78; gen. mgr. merchandise J.C. Penney Co., Aurora, Ill., 1978-82; co-founder, exec. v.p., dir. mktg. The Pres. Mgmt. Group, Inc., Hingham, Mass., 1984-88; pres., dir. Keating Konsult, Inc., Accord, Mass., 1988—; v.p., co-founder Video Tours, Inc., Hartford, Conn., 1986-87. Founder Advocates for Moral and Ethical Treatment by Divorce Attys., Accord, Mass., 1991—. Mem. NAFE, LWV, Nat. Assn. for Women in Careers, Nat. Womens Polit. Caucus, Am. Mgmt. Assn., Ctr. for Entrepreneurial Mgmt. Democrat. Office: Keating Konsult Inc PO Box 171 Accord MA 02018-0171

KEATING, NORMA STORRS, professional genealogist, small business owner; b. Newburyport, Mass., June 16, 1943; d. Ernest Nels and Annie Thomas (Brooks) Storrs; m. John Joseph Keating, July 27, 1968; 1 child, Anne Marie. BSN, Ind. U., 1965; cert. profl. genealogist, Salt Lake Inst. Genealogy, 1996. RN, N.J., Calif. Staff nurse Morristown (N.J.) Meml. Hosp., 1965-67; clin. rsch. assoc. Ortho Pharms., Raritan, N.J., 1967-73; owner, CEO, Stained Glass Creations, Yorba Linda, Calif., 1978-88, Your Family Connection, Yorba Linda, 1996—; presenter, leader workshops in genealogy field. Author: (with Nancy Carlberg) Beginning Danish Research, 1992. Bd. dirs., editor newsletter Friends Yorba Linda Pub. Libr., also past pres.; past sec. Friends of Libr. Found.; chmn. Indian Christmas svc. project Orange County coun. Girl Scouts U.S.A., 1990—, publicity chmn., 1987-94, Brownie leader, 1981-82, jr. leader, 1982-85; past pres. Yorba Linda Woman's Club, 2d v.p. membership, 1996—. Recipient Woman of Distinction awad Soroptimists, Placentia-Yorba Linda, 1992, Appreciation pin Orange County coun. Girl Scouts U.S.A., 1992, appreciation plaque Yorba Linda Pub. Libr. Commn., 1993, also others. Mem. DAR (registrar Mojave chpt. 1996—), Assn. Profl. Genealogists (cert.), Nat. Genealogy Soc. (cert.), Orange County Geneal. Soc. (pres. 1980-85), New Eng. Hist. and Geneal. Soc., N.C. Geneal. Soc. Home and Office: 4653 Avenida Rio Del Oro Yorba Linda CA 92886-3013

KEATON, DIANE, actress; b. Santa Ana, Calif., Jan. 5, 1946. Student, Neighborhood Playhouse, N.Y.C., 1968. Appeared on N.Y. stage in Hair, 1968, Play It Again Sam, 1969, The Primary English Class, 1976; appeared in numerous films including Lovers and Other Strangers, 1970, Play It Again Sam, 1972, The Godfather, 1972, Sleeper, 1973, The Godfather Part II, 1974, Love and Death, 1975, I Will, I Will...For Now, 1975, Harry and Walter Go To New York, 1976, Annie Hall, 1977 (Best Actress Acad. award 1978, Brit. Acad. Best Actress award 1978, N.Y. Film Critics Circle award 1978, Nat. Soc. Film Critics award 1978), Looking for Mr. Goodbar, 1977, Interiors, 1978, Manhattan, 1979, Reds, 1981 (Acad. award nominee), Shoot the Moon, 1982, Little Drummer Girl, 1984, Mrs. Soffel, 1984, Crimes of the Heart, 1986, Radio Days, 1987, Baby Boom, 1987, The Good Mother, 1988, The Lemon Sisters, 1990, The Godfather Part III, 1990, Father of the Bride, 1991, Manhattan Murder Mystery, 1993, Look Who's Talking Now, 1993 (voice), Father of the Bride 2, 1995, Marvin's Room, 1996, First Wives Club, 1996; (TV movie) Running Mates, 1992, Amelia Earhart, 1994; dir. film: Heaven, 1987, Wildflower, 1991, Unstrung Heroes, 1995; accomplished artist and singer; author book of photographs: Reservations, 1980; editor: (with Marvin Heiferman) Still Life, 1983, Mr. Salesman, 1994. Recipient Golden Globe award, 1978. Office: John Burnham William Morris Agy 151 S El Camino Dr Beverly Hills CA 90212-2704*

KEATON, FRANCES MARLENE, sales representative; b. Redfield, Ark., July 1, 1944; d. John Thomas and Pauline (Hilliard) Wells; m. Larry Ronald Keaton, Sept. 17, 1946. Cert. in acctg., Draughon's Sch. Bus., 1972. Lic. ins. agt. Acctg. supr. Home Ins. Co., Little Rock, 1962-70; auditor St. Paul Ins. Co., Little Rock, 1970-74; spl. agt. Continental Ins. Co., Little Rock, 1974—. Vol. Ark. Sch. for the Blind, Little Rock, 1968. Mem. Little Rock Field Club, Casualty Roundtable, Auditor's Assn., Ins. Women, Underwriters Roundtable, The Executive Female, Ind. Ins. Agts. Assn., Profl. Ins. Assn. Democrat. Methodist. Home and Office: 111 Red River Dr Sherwood AR 72120-5851

KECK, JEANNE GENTRY, artist. Student, Coll. William and Mary, Dayton Art Inst. Artist in resident Berkshire Sch. Contemporary Art, North Adams, Mass., 1991; participating artist Vermont Studio Ctr., Johnson, 1992, Assisi, Italy, 1993; residency fellowship Vt. Studio Ctr., 1995. Pvt. and pub. exhibits include C. Grimaldis Gallery, Balt., 1989, Virginia Lynch Gallery, Tiverton, R.I., 1993, Reynolds Gallery, Richmond, Va., Ruby Blakeney Gallery, Annapolis, Md., 1991, Brenda Taylor Gallery, Boston, 1994, Brenda Taylor Gallery, N.Y.C., 1995, 96. Home: 1117 Kalmia Ct Crownsville MD 21032-2126 Studio: 801 Chase St Annapolis MD 21401

KECKLEY, BONNIE SUE, medical facility administrative coordinator, clinical hypnotherapist; b. Winchester, Va., Apr. 25, 1953; d. Robert William and Ruby (Barham) K.; divorced; children: Robert Stephen Rodeffer II, Mark Stephen Rodeffer. LPN, Dowell J. Howard Vocat. Sch., 1972; ADN, Shenandoah U., 1976; BS in Psychology, Liberty U., 1993, PhD in Theocentric Counseling, 1995. Cert. ACLS, BCLS, lay counselor, emergency nurse, Va.; cert. clin. hypnotherapist. Practical nurse critical care unit Winchester Med. Ctr., 1972-76, charge nurse critical care unit, 1976-79, asst. head nurse emergency dept., 1980-86, clin. nurse II PACU, 1986-89, adminstrv. coord., 1989—; dir. nursing Hillcrest Nursing Home, Winchester, 1979-80; cons. InterAct, Winchester, 1993—; faculty speaker Lake Area Health Edn. Ctr., Erie, Pa., 1993—; presenter workshop in field. Pub. Successful Singles Network monthly digest, 1994. Facilitator Parent-to-Parent, Winchester, 1990-93; mem. MADD, Winchester, 1988—; active Nat. Red Ribbon Campaign for Substance Awareness, Winchester, 1990. With Va. Def. Force, 1986-87; ordained minister World Ch. Orgn., 1996. Mem. Am. Holistic Nurses Assn., Am. Assn. Christian Counselors, Assn. Radiol. Nurses (sec.), Nat. Bd. Hypnotherapists, Bus. and Profl. Women's Club. Mem. Brethren Ch. Home: 304 Tudor Dr Winchester VA 22604 Office: Successful Singles Network PO Box 339 Stephenson VA 22656-0339

KEDDERIS, PAMELA JEAN, insurance company executive; b. Waterbury, Conn., May 15, 1956; d. Leo George and Evelyn Helen (Fenske) K. Student, U. Nice, 1976-77; BA, Assumption Coll., 1978; MBA, U. New Haven, 1981. Credit analyst, Citytrust Bank, Bridgeport, Conn., 1980-81, sr. credit analyst, 1981-82, fin. analyst, 1982-83, seminar instr., 1981-83; planning analyst Continental Ins. Co., N.Y.C., 1983-84, sr. planning analyst, 1984-85, dir. planning, 1985-87, asst. v.p. 1987-92, v.p., 1992-95, v.p., controller Marine Office of Am., Cranbury, N.J., 1995—; mem. Planning Forum. Mem. Soc. Ins. Fin. Mgmt., North Shore Animal League. Democrat. Lutheran. Avocations: music, traveling. Home: 1166 Schmidt Ln North Brunswick NJ 08902-1363

KEEBLER, LOIS MARIE, elementary school educator; b. Jasper, Ala., Nov. 24, 1955; d. Roosevelt T. and Marie (Smiley) K. Student, Cen. State U., Wilberforce, Ohio; cert., North Ala. Regional Hosps., 1981. Cert. tchr., Ala. Tchr. Mamani Vallied Children Devel. Ctr., Dayton, Ohio. Vol. pub. schs. Democrat. Baptist.

KEECH, ELOWYN ANN, interior designer; b. Berrien County, Mich., Oct. 5, 1937; d. Earl Docker and Elizabeth Hall (Paullin) Stephenson; 1 child, Robert Earl Stephenson. Cert. contract interior designer. Print designer, copywriter newspaper accounts, dept. stores, resorts, svc. orgns., industry, 1957-75; freelance interior designer, photoset and video set designer, St. Joseph, Mich., 1975—; owner Fog Horn Records & Tapes. Bd. dirs. Blossomland United Way, 1981-86; bd. dirs., mem. steering and long-range planning coms. United Way Mich., 1980-87. Designer interiors 1st Fed. Savs. & Loan Assn., Three Oaks, Mich., 1975, Holland (Mich.) Cen. Trade

Credit Union, 1978, 1st. Fed. Savs. & Loan Assn., Holland, 1978, Yonker Realty, Co., Holland, 1979, People's Bank of Holland, 1979, exec. offices Whirlpool Corp., 1980—, human resources St. Joe div., 1985, Claeys Residence, 1984, Calley Dental Office, 1985, Sarett Nature Ctr., 1985, Imperial Printing, 1986, Miller Residence, 1986, Schraders Super Market, 1986, Dave's Garage, 1987, Merritt Residence, 1987-88, Smith Residence, 1988, Emergency Shelter Svcs. 1991, Butzbach Residence, 1992, Merritt Residence, Del Mar, Calif., 1993-94, Fister Better Homes & Gardens Conf. Room, 1994, Vanderboegh Residence, 1994-96, S.W. Mich. Regional Airport, 1994—, Berrien Hills Country Club, 1995-96, Butzbach Offices, 1995, Molhoek Residence, 1996, Merritt Residence, Houston, 1996, Mich. Maritime Mus., 1996, St. Paul Episcopal Church, 1996, Bacchiocchi residence, 1996, other contract and residential projects. Trustee Mich. Martime Mus., 1994—. Mem. AIA (profl. affiliate S.W. Mich. chpt.), Nature Conservancy, Nat. Trust Hist. Preservation Forum, Assn. Great Lakes Maritime History, Econ. Club of S.W. Mich., Am. Rottweiler Club, Internat. Interior Design Assn., Rotary. Espiscopalian, 1996 Home and Office: 375 Ridgeway St Saint Joseph MI 49085-1062

KEEFE, CAROLYN JOAN, tax accountant; b. Huntington Park, Oct. 11, 1926; d. Paul Dewey and Mary Jane (Parmater) K. AA, Pasadena (Calif.) City Coll., 1947; BA, U. So. Calif., 1950. Tax acct. Shell Oil Co., L.A., 1950-71; tax acct. Shell Oil Co., Houston, 1971-91, ret., 1991. Advisor Midwest Mus. of Am. Art, 1993—; vol. Houston Mus. of Fine Arts, 1991—; vol. docent Houston Mus. of Natural Sci., 1991—, Theatre Under the Stars, 1991—, Houston Pub. TV Channel 8, Houston, 1989—; donor 2 ann. coll. scholarships in memory of Paul Dewey and Mary Jane Keefe. Mem. LWV, Inst. Mgmt. Accts. (emeritus life mem.), Desk and Derrick Club (bd. dirs. 1994-95), Houston Alumni Club of Alpha Gamma Delta, USC Houston Alumni Club. Christian Scientist. Home: 1814 Auburn Trails Sugar Land TX 77479

KEEFER, BETSY ANN, association executive; b. Sharon, Pa., July 31, 1945; d. Dale and Edna (Spangler) K. BA, Hiram (Ohio) Coll., 1967; MEd, Kent State U., 1973. Various positions Western Res. Coun. Girl Scouts USA, Akron, Ohio, 1967-74; dir. outdoor program and facilities Girl Scouts of Greater Phila., 1974-76; exec. dir. Pioneer Valley Coun. Girl Scouts USA, Springfield, Mass., 1976-79; exec. dir. Hemlock Coun. Girl Scouts USA, Harrisburg, Pa., 1979-88; cluster dir. Girl Scouts USA, N.Y.C., 1989-90, nat. dir. coun. svc., 1990-93; exec. dir. Girl Scouts USA, Wilton, 1994—. Bd. dirs. Pinewood Co-op Assn., Hartsdale, N.Y., 1995.

KEEGAN, JANE ANN, insurance executive, consultant; b. Watertown, N.Y., Sept. 1, 1950; d. Richard Isidor and Kathleen (McKinley) K. BA cum laude, SUNY-Potsdam, 1972; MBA in Risk Mgmt., Golden Gate U., 1986. CPCU. Comml. lines mgr. Lithgow & Rayhill, San Francisco, 1977-80; risk mgmt. account coordinator Dinner Levison Co., San Francisco, 1980-83; ins. cons., San Francisco, 1983-84; account mgr. Rollins Burdick Hunter, San Francisco, 1984-85; account exec. Jardine Ins. Brokers, San Francisco, 1985-86; ins. cons., San Francisco, 1986-87, ins. adminstr. Port of Oakland, 1987—, risk mgr., 1989—, accts. payable mgr., 1996—. Vol. San Francisco Ballet vol. orgn., 1981-96, Bay Area Bus., Govt. ARC disaster conf. steering com., 1987-88, 89, 90, 91-92; mem. Nob Hill Neighbors Assn., 1982—. Mem. Nat. Safety Mgmt. Soc., CPCU Soc. (spl. events chairperson 1982-84, continuing profl. devel. program award 1985, 88, chair loss prevention), Calif. Assn. of Port Authorities (ins. chair 1995), Risk and Ins. Mgr. Soc. (dep., sec. 1990—, dir. legis. 1993, dir. conf.). Democrat. Roman Catholic. Home: 1065 Las Gallinas Ave San Rafael CA 94903-2464

KEEGAN, MARY BARDEN, volunteer; b. Yonkers, N.Y., Nov. 18, 1921; d. James J. and Mary Agnes (Linehan) Barden; m. James Magner Keegan, June 12, 1948; children: James, Patrick, Colleen, Kathleen, Michael. BS in Edn., Columbia U., 1943, MA in Pers. Adminstrn., 1944. Mem. World Svc. Coun. YWCA of U.S.A, N.Y.C., 1962—; first pres., founder Women's Pub. Rels. Coun., St. Joseph's Hosp., Houston, 1963-66; bd. dirs., v.p. YWCA, Houston, 1965-71, Houston Area Urban League, 1981-86; Houston chair 1st Nat. Women's Conf., Houston, 1977; pres. U.S. del. Friendship Among Women, St. Paul, 1979—; co-chair Women in Devel. Adv. Com. Voluntary Fgn. Aid, Dept. State, Washington, 1983-93; founder, CEO, chmn. bd. End Hunger Network, Houston, 1985-95, chair emeritus 1995; bd. dirs. Citizens Network for Fgn. Affairs, Washington, 1987-94; U.S. dep. observer to Ireland Internat. Fund for Ireland, Washington, 1990-92; bd. dirs. St. Joseph Hosp. Found., Houston, 1984—, 1st v.p. exec. com., 1994, pres., 1995; bd. dirs., mem. exec. com., chmn. pub. affairs com. U. St. Thomas, Houston, 1994—; mem. adv. com. Houston Food Bank, St. Joseph Hosp. Benefit "For Our Children's Future", Fox TV; mem. internat. adv. com. Counterpart; trustee, advisor Care; gov. bd. St. Joseph Hosp. Recipient Brotherhood award NCCJ, 1981, Spl. Fundraiser award YWCA, Houston, 1981, Outstanding Woman award YWCA, 1986, Whitney M. Young Vol. Yr., Houston Area Urban League, 1987, U.S. Presdl. Hunger award Pres. U.S., 1987, Martin Luther King Jr. Life and Legacy award, 1989, Galleria C. of C. Commerce Cmty. Culture award, 1995; named Houston's Pioneer Houston Woman's Club, 1975. Mem. Fedn. Profl. Women, Houston Forum. Home: 121 N Post Oak Ln Apt 2304 Houston TX 77024-7717

KEEGAN, PATRICIA ANN, art educator, visual arts consultant; b. Waterbury, Conn., Sept. 25, 1945; m. Edward D. Keegan, Aug. 16, 1968; 1 child, Sean Patrick Keegan. BS in Art Edn., So. Conn. State U., New Haven, 1967, MS in Art Edn., 1975, EdS, 1996. Art tchr. Milford (Conn.) H.S., 1967-68, Newtown (Conn.) H.S., 1968-73, Shepaug Valley Sch., Washington, Conn., 1975—; visual arts cons. The Edison Project, N.Y.C., 1993—; adv. bd. Celebration of Excellence Hamden, Conn., 1991—; visual arts com. mem. Conn. dept. Edn., Hartford, 1993—; arts/social studies integrated com. mem. Conn. Dept. Edn., Hartford, Conn., 1993—; cons. interdisciplinary and art based curriculum devel., Conn. Author: K-12 Resource Guide: Immersion in Living History, 1996; co-author: Transformational Geometry and Art in the Real World, 1993; contbr. to Visions, 1994. Dem. Town com. Bethlehem (Conn.) Hist. Soc., 1988—; active Bethlem Fair Soc., 1979—. Recipient Celebration of Excellence award Conn. State Dept. Edn., Hartford, 1991, Hilda-Maehling award Nat. Found. for Improvement Edn., Washington, 1993; named Runner-up Conn. Tchr. of Yr. State of Conn., 1993, Art Educator of Yr. Conn. Art Edn. Assn., 1992. Mem. ASCD, Nat. Art Edn. Assn., Conn. Art Edn. Assn., IMPACT II Nat. Tchrs. Network, Internat. Soc. for Edn. Through Art. Home: PO Box 82 Bethlehem CT 06751-0082 Office: Shepaug Valley School South St Washington CT 06793

KEELER, LYNNE LIVINGSTON MILLS, psychologist, educator, consultant; b. Detroit, Sept. 18, 1934; d. Robert Livingston Mills Staples and Lyda Charlotte (Diehr) Staples; m. Lee Edward Burmeister, July 16, 1955 (div. 1982); children: Benjamin Lee, Lynne Ann; m. Robert Gordon Keeler, Oct. 26, 1986. BS, Ctrl. Mich. U., 1957; MA, U. Mich., 1965; student, Marygrove Coll., Cen. Mich. U., 1971-74. Ltd. lic. psychologist, sch. psychologist; cert. social worker, elem. permanent cons. and tchr. for mentally handicapped. First grade tchr. Shepherd (Mich) Schs., 1957-59; tchr. Kingston (Mich.) Schs., 1959-65; tchr. educationally handicapped Rialto (Calif.) Unified Sch. Dist., 1965-66; tchr., cons. Tuscola Int. Sch. Dist., Caro, Mich., 1966-71; sch. psychologist Huron Int. Sch. Dist., Bad Axe, Mich., 1971-74, Tuscola Int. Sch. Dist., Caro, 1974-89; instr. Delta Coll., University Center, Mich., 1976-88; tchr. spl. day classes Victorville (Calif.) High Sch., 1989; sch. psychologist Bedford (Ind.) Schs., 1990-91; clin. psychologist ACT team and outpatient therapy Sanilac County Mental Health Svcs., Sandusky, Mich., 1991—; cons. sch. psychologist Marlette (Mich.) Schs., 1982-86, Bartholomew Pub. Schs., Columbus, Ind., 1989, Johnson County Schs., Franklin, Ind., 1990; clin. psychologist Thumb Family Counseling, Caro, 1985-88; personnel com. Team One Credit Union, 1993. Conf. presenter in field. Del. NEA-Mich. Edn. Assn. Rep. Assemblies, 1970-89; pres., auction chmn. Altrusa Club, Marlett, 1982-88; style show chmn. Marlette Band Boosters, 1983; mem. exec. bd. Lawrence County Tchrs. Assn., Bedford, 1991; mem. Sanilac Symphonic Band, 1993-94; bd. dirs. Team One Credit Union, 1994—. Fed. govt. grantee Wayne State U., 1968. Mem. Am. Federated State and Mcpl. Employees (chairperson #219 1993, chairperson #15 chpt. 1993-96), Ind. State Tchrs. Assn. (rep. assembly del. 1991), Ind. Assn. Sch. Psychologists (pub. rels. bd. 1990-91), Lions (bd. dirs. 1996—). Democrat. Methodist. Home: 6726 Clothier Rd Clifford MI 48727-9501 Office: Sanilac County Cmty Mental Health 190 N Delaware St Sandusky MI 48471-1009

KEELEY, IRENE PATRICIA MURPHY, federal judge; b. 1944. BA, Coll. Notre Dame, 1965; MA, W.Va. U., 1977, JD, 1980. Bar: Va. Atty. Steptoe & Johnson, Clarksburg, W.Va., 1980-92; dist. judge U.S. Dist. Ct. (no. dist.), W. Va., 1992—; adj. prof. law coll. law W.Va. U., 1990-91; mem. bd. dirs. W.Va. U. Alumni Assn. Bd. dirs. United Way; mem. vis. com. Coll. Law W.Va. U., 1987-91, 94—; mem. bd. advisors W.Va. U. Mem. ABA (judicial adminstrn. divsn. ct. tech. com.), W.Va. State Bar, W.Va. Law Inst., W.Va. Bar Assn., Harrison County Bar Assn., Clarksburg Country Club, Oral Lake Fishing Club, Immaculate Conception Roman Cath. Ch. Office: US Courthouse PO Box 2808 500 W Pike St Rm 202 Clarksburg WV 26302-2808

KEELEY, MARY DIANE, guidance counselor; b. Chgo., Nov. 3, 1934; d. James E. and Helen Marie (McCarthy) K. BS, Ind. U., 1957, MS, 1965; MA, St. Mary's U., San Antonio, 1979. Cert. tchr., Ind., Ill., Fla. Assoc. dir. USO, Okinawa, 1962-64; tchr. Ill., Ind., Fla., 1965-75; lang. instr. Def. Lang. Inst., Lackland AFB, Tex., 1975-80; guidance counselor Edn. Svcs. USAF, Kelly AFB, Tex., 1980; guidance counselor Edn. Svcs. USAF, Europe, 1996—, edn. svcs. officer, 1987-92; curriculum developer Sch. Allied Health, Fort Sam Houston, Tex., 1980-84; test writer, editor Extension Course Inst., Gunter AFB, Ala., 1984-85; dir. measurement Def. EEO Mgmt. Inst., Patrick AFB, Fla., 1985-87; edn./tng. specialist Hines (Ill.) VA Hosp., 1992-96; ESL cons., program developer Chgo., 1970-75; literacy, workplace educator VA Hosps., Chgo., 1992-95. ESL tchr., program developer, Korea, 1960-62, Okinawa, 1962-64; vol. guidance counseling Dept. Def. Schs., Germany, 1989-92. Mem. TESOL, Nat. U. Continuing Edn. Assn. Democrat. Roman Catholic. Office: 52 MSS/DPE APO AE 09126-5000

KEEN, MARIA ELIZABETH, retired educator; b. Chgo., Aug. 19, 1918; d. Harold Fremont and Mary Eileen Honore (Dillon) K. AB, U. Chgo., 1941; postgrad., U. Wyo., summer 1943; MA, U. Ill., 1949; postgrad., U. Mich., 1957. Tchr. high sch. Wyo., 1942-43, Mich., 1943-44; tchr. Am. Coll. for Women, Istanbul, Turkey, 1944-47; mem. faculty U. Ill., Urbana, 1947-88, prof. emerita, 1988—. Mem. Champaign Community Devel. Com. Mem. AAUW, AAUP (past treas.), AASL, LWV, Animal Protection Inst., Defenders of Wildlife, Am. Inst. Biol. Scis., Nat. Coun. Tchr. Educators, U. Ill. Athletic Assn. (sec., bd. dirs.), Ont. Geneal. Soc., Orton Dyslexia Soc., Art Inst. Chgo., Women's Philharm. (charter), Women in Arts (charter), Women's Humane Soc., Illini Union (faculty staff social com.), Nat. Humane Soc., Phi Kappa Epsilon (hon.). Baptist. Home: 608 S Edwin St Champaign IL 61821-3834

KEENA, DOLORES MAY, retired elementary education educator; b. Delta, Colo., Aug. 1, 1935; d. Cleve Shannon and Myrtle May (Cross) Buckmaster; m. Earl E. Keena, Aug. 21, 1960; children: James, Dennis, Melody, Carol. BA in Elem. Edn., Pasadena (Calif.) Coll., 1961. Cert. elem. tchr. Telephone operator Mountain States Bell Telephone, Delta, 1953-58; tchr. Garvey Sch. Dist., South San Gabriel, Calif., 1962-64, Thermalito Sch. Dist., Oroville, Calif., 1968-96; sec. Poplar Ave. Sch. Site Coun., Oroville, 1990-96. Mem. Arbor Day Found., 1990; mem. Rep. Nat. Com., Washington, 1989. Pres. scholarship Pasadena Coll., 1958, PTA scholarship, 1959. Mem. Thermalito Tchrs. Assn. (former sec. 1968—), Calif. Tchrs. Assn. Home: 2160 D St Oroville CA 95966-6672

KEENAN, BARBARA MILANO, judge. Former judge U.S. Cir. Ct. (19th cir.) Va., U.S. Ct. Appeals of Va.; judge Supreme Ct. Va., McLean; assoc. justice Supreme Ct. Va., Richmond, 1991—. Office: Va Supreme Ct 100 N 9th St Richmond VA 23219*

KEENAN, MARY JOSEPHINE, administrative assistant; b. Grand Island, NB, Can., Mar. 14, 1954; d. Joseph Lyle and Mary Elizabeth (Brand) K. Student, Spoon River Coll., 1984. Bookkeeper, receptionist Rush Motor Co., Boulder, Colo., 1972-74, Royal Pontiac Buick GMC, Macomb, Ill., 1974-80; acctg. clk. III We. Ill. U., Macomb, Ill., 1980-83; office mgr. Kelly Pontiac/Kelly Equipment, Macomb, Ill., 1981 87; bookkeeper, acct., sec. bd. Pro-Class Gym Syss., Macomb, Ill., 1987—; office mgr. Intercontinental Mktg. LTD, Macomb, Ill., 1987-88; stenographer McDonough County Rehab. Ctr., Macomb, Ill., 1988-89; officer mgr. Lamberson Chrysler-Plymouth-Dodge, Macomb, Ill., 1989-91; exec. asst. to pres. Kelly Co. World Group, Inc., Carthage, Ill., 1991 ; Fundraiser Radio Info. Svcs., Macomb, Ill., 1981. Mem. Bushnell (Ill.) Presbyn. Bell Choir, 1987—. Mem. Philanthropic Edn. Orgn. (guard), Nat. Notary Assn. Republican. Roman Catholic. Office: Kelly Co World Group Inc 96 South Madison Carthage IL 62321

KEENAN, RETHA ELLEN VORNHOLT, nurse, educator; b. Solon, Iowa, Aug. 15, 1934; d. Charles Elias and Helen Maurine (Konicek) Vornholt; BSN, State U. Iowa, 1955; MSN, Calif. State U., Long Beach, 1978; m. David James Iverson, June 17, 1956; children: Scott, Craig ; m. Roy Vincent Keenan, Jan. 5, 1980. Publ. health nurse City of Long Beach, 1970-73, 94—, Hosp. Home Care, Torrance, Calif., 1973-75; patient care coord. Hillhaven, L.A., 1975-76; mental health cons. InterCity Home Health, L.A., 1978-79; instr. Community Coll. Dist., L.A., 1979-87; instr. nursing El Camino Coll., Torrance, 1981-86; instr. nursing Chapman Coll., Orange, Calif., 1982, Mt. Saint Mary's Coll., 1986 87; cons., pvt. practice, Rancho Palos Verdes, Calif., 1987-89. Contbg. author: American Journal of Nursing Question and Answer Book for Nursing Boards Review, 1984, Nursing Care Planning Guides for Psychiatric and Mental Health Care, 1987-88, Nursing Care Planning Guides for Children, 1987, Nursing Care Planning Guides for Adults, 1988, Nursing Care Planning Guides for Critically Ill Adults, 1988. Cert. nurse practitioner adult and mental health, 1979; mem. Assistance League of San Pedro, Palos Verdes, Calif. NIMH grantee, 1977-78. Mem. Sigma Theta Tau, Phi Kappa Phi, Delta Zeta. Republican. Lutheran. Avocations: travel, writing, reading. Home: 27849 Longhill Dr Rancho Palos Verdes CA 90275 Office: 2525 Grand Ave Long Beach CA 90815

KEENAN-ABILAY, GEORGIA ANN, service representative; b. Denver, Oct. 3, 1936; d. Lawrence Edward and Helen Kathleen (Gray) K.; m. Charles Henry Dupree, May 31, 1958 (div. Nov. 1977); children: Phoenix, Therese, Mark, John; m. Joseph D. Abilay, Nov. 26, 1988. BA, Regis Coll., 1968; MA, St. Thomas U., 1978. With reservations United Airlines, Denver, 1956-57; stewardess Trans World Airlines, Chgo., 1957-58; in elem. edn. Notre Dame Sch., Denver, 1969-72; dir. religious edn. Notre Dame Parish, Denver, 1972-77, Archdiocese Denver, 1977-80; v.p., treas. Kilfinane and Cook, Denver, 1980-82; dir. human resources Cosmopolitan Hotel, Denver, 1982-83, Kaanapali Beach Hotel, Lahaina, Hawaii, 1983-85, Royal Lahaina Resort, Hawaii, 1985-90; corp. dir. human resources Hawaiian Hotels and Resorts, Lahaina, 1988; dir. human resources Rock Resorts Lanai Resorts Ptnrs., Island of Lanai, 1990-94; ptnr. Blue Ginger Cafe, Lanai, 1995—; trainer Amfac Hotels and Resorts, Hawaii, 1984-86; vice chmn. Maui Hotel Assn., 1987; bd. dirs. Project 714, Lahaina, 1987. Bd. dirs. Archdiocesan Women's Bd., Denver, 1981-83, Passages, Denver, 1980-83, Maui Econ. Devel. Bd., Kahalui, 1984; chairperson Charity Walk, 1984-86. Named Handicapped Employer of Yr., State of Hawaii, 1987. Mem. Council Hawaii Hotels, Am. Soc. Personnel Assn. Club: Distributive Edn. of Am. (Hawaii) (bd. dirs. 1984—). Home: PO Box 721 Lanai City HI 96763-0721 Office: Blue Ginger Cafe PO Box 1090 Lanai HI 96763-1090

KEENE-BURGESS, RUTH FRANCES, army official; b. South Bend, Ind., Oct. 7, 1948; d. Seymour and Sally (Morris) K.; m. Leslie U. Burgess, Jr., Oct. 1, 1983; children: Michael Leslie, David William, Elizabeth Sue, Rachael Lee. BS, Ariz. State U., 1970; MS, Fairleigh Dickinson U., 1978; grad., U.S. Army Command and Gen. Staff Coll., 1986. Inventory mgmt. specialist U.S. Army Electronics Command, Phila., 1970-74, U.S. Army Communications-Electronics Material Readiness Command, Fort Monmouth, N.J., 1974-79; chief inventory mgmt. div. Crane (Ind.) Army Ammunition Activity, 1979-80; supply systems analyst Hdqrs. 60th Ordnance Group, Zweibruecken, Fed. Republic Germany, 1980-83; chief inventory mgmt. div. Crane (Ind.) Army Ammunition Activity, 1983-85, chief control div., 1985; inventory mgmt. specialist 200th Theater Army Material Mgmt. Ctr., Zweibruecken, 1985-88; analyst supply systems U.S. Armament, Munitions and Chem. Command, Rock Island, Ill., 1988-89; specialist logistics mgt. U.S. Army Info. Systems Command, Ft. Huachuca, Ariz., 1989—. Mem. Federally Employed Women (chpt. pres. 1979-80), NAFE, Soc. Logistics Engrs., Assn. Computing Machinery, Am. Soc. Public Adminstrn., Soc. Profl. and Exec. Women, Assn. Info. Systems Profls., AAAS, NOW. Democrat.

KEENER, MARY LOU, lawyer; b. Flint, Mich., Aug. 9, 1944; d. Robert Sherman Keener and Rosemary (Kowalski) Brady. BSN, Cath. U. Am., 1966; MN, Emory U., 1972; JD, Cath. U. Am., 1982. Bar: Ga. 1983, Md. 1983, Supreme Ct. Ga. 1992. Congl. caseworker Congressman D. W. Riegle, Jr., Washington, 1969-71; asst. prof. dept. nursing Ga. State U., Atlanta, 1972-76; exec. dir. Ga. Nurses Assn., Atlanta, 1976-79; atty. Arfken, Caldwell, Steckel & Mack, Atlanta, 1982-84, Lavigno & Dawkins, Conyers, Ga., 1985, Butler & McDonald, Atlanta, 1986-88, Law Offices Mary Lou Keener, Atlanta, 1989-93; gen. counsel Dept. Vet. Affairs, Washington, 1993—. Bd. dirs. Ga. Vietnam Vets. Leadership Program, 1983-93, chmn., 1984-86, Atlanta Vietnam Vets. Bus. Assn., 1989-93; mem. adv. bd. Agent Orange Class Assistance Program, 1989-93. Lt. USN, 1966-69, Vietnam. Recipient Nat. Svc. Def. medal, Vietnam Svc. medal, Republic of Vietnam Campaign medal, Air Force Commendation medal; named Winner Nat. Moot Ct. Competition, 1980. Mem. ABA, ANA (bylaws com. 1978-82), Am. Trial Lawyers Assn., Ga. Trial Lawyers Assn. (LAWPAC 1992-93, legis. com. 1992-93), Ga. Underwriting Assn. (bd. dirs. 1991-93), Atlanta Bar Assn., Atlanta Vietnam Vets. Bus. Assn. (bd. dirs. 1989-93). Office: Dept Vets Affairs 810 Vermont Ave NW Washington DC 20420-0001

KEENER, POLLY LEONARD, illustrator; b. Akron, Ohio, July 14, 1946; d. George Holman and Alice June (Bolinger) Leonard; m. Robert Lee Keener, Dec. 29, 1967; children: Robert Edward Alan, June Whitney. Student, Kent State U., 1967, Princeton U., 1968, 73; BA, Conn. Coll., 1968. Cert. tchr., Ohio. Illustrator Akron, 1969—; instr. cartooning Northeastern Ohio Univs. Coll. Medicine, 1992-94; instr. cartooning U. Akron, 1979—, instr. soft sculpture, 1979-84; cartoon text writer Prentice Hall Pubs., Englewood Cliffs, N.J., 1985—; pres. Keener Corp., Akron, 1977—; judge arts and crafts competition, Akron, 1982—. Author: Cartooning, 1992; illustrator: Eat Dessert First, 1987, It's Our Serve, 1989, 80+ Great Ideas For Making Money At Home, 1992; contbr. articles to profl. jours. Trustee Stan Hywet Hall Found., Akron, 1972—; trustee and v.p. Women's History Project, Akron, 1993-96; v.p. Jr. League, Akron, 1988-89, Western Res. Acad. Women's Bd., Hudson, Ohio, 1987-88; active Women's Bd. Blossom Music Ctr., Penninsula, Ohio, 1969—. Named Woman of Yr. Women's History Project Ohio, 1989; recipient Unsung Hero award Jr. League Akron, 1988. Mem. AAUP, DAR (trustee, vice-regent Cuyahoga-Portage chpt. 1992—), Nat. Cartoonists Soc. (chmn. Ohio/Mich. chpt. 1996—), Soc. Illustrators, Coll. Art Assn., Portage Country Club. Episcopalian. Home: 400 W Fairlawn Blvd Akron OH 44313-4510

KEENEY, REGINA MARKEY, lawyer; b. Sumter, S.C., Aug. 20, 1955; d. John Patrick and Margaret Mary (Rogers) Markey; m. Terence J. Keeney, Aug. 16, 1980; children: Teresa Marie, Anne Mairead. BS, Georgetown U., 1977; JD, Harvard U., 1980. Bar: D.C. Assoc. Hamel, Park, McCabe & Saunders, Washington, 1980-83; atty., advisor FCC, Washington, 1983-85, bur. chief Wireless Telecom. Bur., 1994—; sr. counsel comm. Senate Commerce Com., Washington, 1985-94. Roman Catholic. Office: FCC Wireless Telecomm Bur Pvt Radio Bur 2025 M St Washington DC 20554

KEENON, NANCY JEAN, golf course owner; b. Gladwin, Mich., Dec. 25, 1944; d. Francis William and Ardis Katherine (Hales) Bowers; m. Michael Nels Keenon, June 19, 1965 (div. June 1974); children: Michael, Trisha, Tracie. Diploma, Clare (Mich.) H.S., 1962. Accts. payable clerk Dow Chemical, Midland, Mich., 1965-67; credit mgr. Fuelgas, Clare, 1970-74; office mgr. Beaverton Plastics, Clare, 1974-79; adminstrv. aide II CMU, Mt. Pleasant, Mich., 1979-95. Mem. Clare C. of C. Office: Firefly Golf Links 7795 S Clare Ave Clare MI 48617

KEEP, JUDITH N., federal judge; b. Omaha, Mar. 24, 1944. B.A., Scripps Coll., 1966; J.D., U. San Diego, 1970. Bar: Calif. 1971. Atty. Defenders Inc., San Diego, 1971-73; pvt. practice law, 1973-76; asst. U.S. atty. U.S. Dept. Justice, 1976; judge Mcpl. Ct., San Diego, 1976-80; judge U.S. Dist. Ct. (so. dist.) Calif., San Diego, 1980—, chief judge, 1991—. Office: US Dist Ct 940 Front St Rm 6 San Diego CA 92101-8916*

KEESEE, PATRICIA HARTFORD, volunteer; b. Nashville, Apr. 29, 1928; d. William Donald and Mary Carolyn (Gwyn) Hartford; m. Thomas Woodfin Keesee Jr., June 26, 1953; children: Thomas Woodfin III, Anne Hartford Keesee Niemann; 1 stepson: Allen P.K. Keesee. BA in English, Radcliff Coll., 1950; BA in Environ. Scis., SUNY, Purchase, 1977. Lab. asst. Rockefeller U. (formerly Rockefeller Inst. Med. Rsch.), N.Y.C., 1951-54. Chmn. Byram com. Nature Conservancy, Bedford, N.Y., 1978-81; mem. Conservation Bd. Town of Bedford, 1978-88, Westchester County Environ. Mgmt. Commn., 1979-88, Coun. of N.Y. Bot. Garden, Bronx, N.Y., 1982—, Wetlands Commn., Bedford, 1988—; trustee Lower Hudson chpt. Nature Conservancy, Katonah, N.Y., 1980-90, 91—, chmn., 1983-86, vice chmn., 1995—; pres. Fed. Conservationists of Westchester County, Purchase, 1985-87; trustee N.Y. State Bd. Nature Conservancy, Albany, 1983-91, vice-chmn., 1986-88. Mem. N.Y. Acad. Scis., Garden Club Am. (conservation com. 1983-85, 95—, vice chmn. conservation com. 1985-87, bd. dirs. 1989-91, vice chmn. scholarship com. 1991-94). Episcopalian. Home: 140 Sarles St Rd # 3 Mount Kisco NY 10549-2812

KEESHEN, KATHLEEN KEARNEY, public relations consultant; b. N.Y.C., Dec. 4, 1937; d. James William and Hannah Pauline (Mansfield) Kearney; 1 child (by previous marriage), John Christopher Day; m. Walt Keeshen Jr.; stepchildren: Michael Patrick, Walt John III, Kathleen Marie, William Thomas, Ralph Timothy. BA in English, U. Md., 1959, MA in Journalism, 1973, PhD in Am. Studies, 1983; MLA, Stanford U., 1995. Cert. profl. sec. Congl., legal, med., acad., corp. sec. various orgns., East and Midwest, 1954-63; staff and mgmt. positions IBM, Washington, Md., 1963-73; lab. comm. mgr. Systems Comm. Div. IBM, Manassas, Va., 1974-76; comm. staff corp. hdqrs. IBM, Armonk, N.Y., 1977-83; comm. and community rels. mgr. Almaden Rsch. Ctr. IBM, San Jose, Calif., 1983-92; prin. Keeshen Comm., Coyote (Calif.) Press., 1992—. Contbr. articles to profl. jours.; lectr. in field. Mem. adv. bd. Friends of San Jose Pub. Libr., 1987—, Silicon Valley Info. Ctr., 1986-92, Media Report to Women; mem. corp. task force Stanford U. Inst. for Rsch. on Women and Gender, 1990—, affiliated scholar, 1992-94, assocs. bd., 1994—; affiliated scholar Beatrice M. Bain Rsch. Group on Gender, U. Calif., Berkeley, 1994-95. Mem. Am. Journalism Historians Assn., Assn. for Edn. in Journalism and Mass Comm., Women in Comm., Am. Studies Assn., Dean's First Edition Club, Coll. of Journalism U. Md., San Jose Rotary Club, San. José Profl. Womens Literary Assn., Calif. Writers Club, Sigma Delta Chi, Alpha Xi Delta. Office: Keeshen Comm Coyote Press PO Box 13154 Coyote CA 95013-3154

KEESLING, KAREN RUTH, lawyer; b. Wichita, Kans., July 9, 1946; d. Paul W. and Ruth (Sharp) K. BA, Ariz. State U., 1968, MA, 1970; JD, Georgetown U., 1981. Bar: Va. 1981, Fla. 1981. Asst. dean of women U. Kans., Lawrence, 1970-72; exec. sec. , sec.'s adv. com. on rights and responsibilities of women HEW, Washington, 1972-74; dir. White House Office of Women's Programs, Washington, 1974-77; head civil rights and equal opportunity sect., Gov. Div., Congl. Rsch. Svc. Libr. Congress, Washington, 1977-80; legis. aide Sen. Nancy Kassebaum, Washington, 1979-81; mem. pers. office staff Office of Pres.-elect, Washington, Jan. 1981; pvt. practice Falls Church, Va., 1981-88, 90-96; dept. for equal opportunity dept. Dept. Air Force, Washington, 1981-82, dep. asst. sec. manpower res. affairs and installations, 1982-83; prin. dep. asst. sec. manpower res. affairs Dept. Air Force, 1983-87; prin. dep. asst. sec. readiness support dept. Dept. Air Force, Washington, 1987-88, prin. dep. asst. sec. manpower and res. affairs, 1988, asst. sec. manpower and res. affairs, 1988-89; acting wage and hour adminstr. U.S. Dept. Labor, Washington, 1992-93; counsel Baskin, Jackson and Hansbarger, P.C., Falls Church, 1996—; bd. advisers Outstanding Young Women Am., 1983-90. Mem. Nat. Fedn. Republican Women's Club, Washington, 1975, Nat. Women's Polit. Caucus, Washington, 1980. Named one of Ten Outstanding Young Women of Am., 1975; recipient Ariz. State U. Alumni Achievement award, 1976, Elizabeth Boyer award Women's Equity Action League, 1986, Meritorious Civilian award USAF, 1987, Woman of Distinction award Nat. Conf. Coll. Women, Student Leaders and Women of Distinction, 1988, Exeptional Civilian Svc. award USAF, 1988. Mem. Va. Bar Assn., Fla. Bar Assn., Va. Fedn. Bus. and Profl. Women's Clubs (2d v.p. 1987-88, 1st v.p. 1988-89, pres.-elect 1989-90, pres. 1990-91), No. Va.

Women Atty.'s Assn. (steering com. 1990-95), Va. Bus. and Profl. Women's Found. (trustee 1985-93), The Women's Inst. Inc. (adv. coun. 1985—), U.S. Com. for the UNIFEM (gen. counsel 1983—), P.E.O. (Wichita), Pi Beta Phi. Home: 10213 Manzanita Dr Sun City AZ 85373 Office: 301 Park Ave Falls Church VA 22046-4500

KEETH, BETTY LOUISE, geriatrics nursing director; b. Hayward, Okla., Nov. 15, 1931; d. Harley Enoch and Violent Verona (Space) George; m. Melvin L. Gillham, May 4, 1951 (div. July 1979); children: Melvin L., Dennis Ray, Debra Lynne Gillham. ADN, Carl Albert Jr. Coll., 1984. LPN, Ark. DON MENA Manor, Mena, Ark., 1987-89, Living Ctrs. of Am., Oklahoma City, 1989-90, Westlake Sq. Ctr., Oklahoma City, 1990-91, Bethany Village, 1991-94, East Moore Nursing, Moore, Okla., 1994-95; dir. Ctrl. Okla. Christian Home, Oklahoma City, 1995—; cons. Precision Home Health, Oklahoma City. Registrar Lefiore County, Poteau, Okla., 1989; sec. Dem. Women, 1984-90. Home: 2908 Pinto Trl Edmond OK 73003-6667 Office: Ctrl Okla Christian Home 6312 N Portland Oklahoma City OK 73112

KEEVER, REBECCA REGAN, copy editor; b. Richmond, Va., July 4, 1955; d. William Whitfield and Peggy Elizabeth (Gibson) Regan; m. Joseph Jefferson Keever, Aug. 21, 1982; children: Virginia Grace, Andrew Whitfield Keever. BA, Mary Baldwin Coll., 1977; MS, Old Dominion U., 1991. Paralegal McGuire, Woods & Battle, Richmond, 1977-79, Kaufman & Canoles, Norfolk, Va., 1979-87; rsch. asst. Med. Coll. Hampton Roads, Norfolk, 1988-90; job analyst Canon Va., Inc., Newport News, 1990; pers. asst. Norshipco, Norfolk, 1990; administrv. analyst Dept. Social Svcs., Virginia Beach, Va., 1991-92; proofreader, copy editor of psychol. rsch. articles, books, 1994—. Editor newsletter Royster Meml. Presbyn. Ch., Norfolk, 1994—, elder, 1994—. Mem. Am. Soc. Tng. and Devel. (S.E. chpt.), Alliance Française, Phi Kappa Phi. Home: 409 Sinclair St Norfolk VA 23505-4359

KEGLEY, JACQUELYN ANN, philosophy educator; b. Conneaut, Ohio, July 18, 1938; d. Steven Paul and Gertrude Evelyn (Frank) Kovacevic; m. Charles William Kegley, June 12, 1964; children: Jacquelyn Ann, Stephen Lincoln Luther. BA cum laude, Allegheny Coll., 1960; MA summa cum laude, Rice U., 1964; PhD, Columbia U., 1971. Asst. prof. philosophy Calif. State U., Bakersfield, 1973-77, assoc. prof., 1977-81, prof., 1981—; vis. prof. U. Philippines, Quezon City, 1966-68; grant project dir. Calif. Council Humanities, 1977, project dir. 1980, 82; mem. work group on ethics Am. Colls. of Nursing, Washington, 1984-86; mem. Am. Bd. Forensic Examiners. Author: Introduction to Logic, 1978, Genuine Individuals and Genuine Communities, 1996; editor: Humanistic Delivery of Services to Families, 1982, Education for the Handicaped, 1982; mem. editl. bd. Jour. Philosophy in Lit., 1979-84; contbr. articles to profl. jours. Bd. dirs. Bakersfield Mental Health Assn., 1982-84, Citizens for Betterment of Community. Recipinet Outstanding Prof. award Calif. State U., 1989-90, Golden Roadrunner award Bakersfield Community, 1991. Mem. Philosophy of Sci. Assn., Soc. Advancement Am. Phil. soc. (chmn. Pacific div. 1979-83, nat. exec. com. 1974-79), Philosophy Soc., Soc. Interdisciplinary Study of Mind, Am. Philosophical Assn., Dorian Soc., Phi Beta Kappa. Democrat. Lutheran. Home: 7312 Kroll Way Bakersfield CA 93309-2320 Office: Calif State U Dept Philosophy & Religious Studies Bakersfield CA 93311

KEHELA, KAREN, film company executive. Pres. prodn. Imagine Entertainment, L.A. Office: Imagine Entertainment 1925 Century Park E 23rd Fl Los Angeles CA 90067*

KEHLER, JUDYTH LYNN, municipal official; b. Lansing, Mich., Mar. 28, 1965; d. Richard Ray and Mamie Judith (Riggins) Creagh; m. Eric James Kehler, June 25, 1988. BA, U. Mich., 1988. Acct., gen. mgr. Christy Assocs., Lansing, 1988; sr. acct. State of Mich., Lansing, 1988-93; city treas., income tax adminstr. City of Lansing, 1994—. Bd. dirs. Met. YMCA, Lansing, 1996; vice chair funding panel Capitol Area United Way, Lansing, 1996; com. mem. March of Dimes Walkamerica, Lansing, 1995, 96; campaign chair, rep. United Way, Lansing, 1995. Mem. Fed. Tax Adminstrs., Mich. Tax Adminstrs. (sec. 1994-96), Mich. Treas. Assn., Mcpl. Treas. Assn. Home: 2117 Northwest Lansing MI 48906

KEHOE, SUSAN, quality project manager; b. Cleve., Dec. 5, 1947; d. John William and Mary Margaret Kehoe; m. Gerald Nicholas, May 15, 1970 (div.); children: Patricia, Mark; m. George Vivier, Sept. 19, 1992. BA, U. Detroit, 1970; MA, Oakland U., 1980, PhD, 1983. Cert. secondary tchr., Mich. Trainer ESL Utica Community Schs., Mich., 1974-78; coord. program Oakland Univ., Rochester, Mich., 1980-83; adj. prof. mktg. Wayne State Univ., Detroit, 1983-85, U. Mich., Ann Arbor, 1984-85; pres., owner The Kehoe Group, Birmingham, Mich., 1983-89; trainer, program designer Gen. Motors, Detroit, 1984-89; trainer, cons. Nat. Steel, Ecorse, Mich., 1984-89; tng. specialist electronics div. Ford Motor Co., Dearborn, Mich., 1990-92, program dir. quality oper. systems, 1991-92; project mgr. Ford Motor Co. Powertrain, 1992-95; mgr. quality tng. and edn. strategy, 1995—. Presenter Nat. Reading Conf., 1981, 83, Internat. Reading Assn., 1982, Am. Edn. Rsch. Assn., 1982, Conf. on Coll. Composition, 1984. Mem. Am. Soc. For Tng. and Devel., Nat. Soc. Performance in Instrn. Avocations: art, travel, music. Home: 2477 Hickory Glen Dr Bloomfield Hills MI 48304-2207 Office: Ford Automotive Operations 17101 Rotunda Dr Dearborn MI 48121

KEHRET, PEG, writer; b. LaCrosse, Wis., Nov. 11, 1936; d. Arthur Robert and Elizabeth (Showers) Schulze; m. Carl Edward Kehret, July 2, 1955; children: Bob. C., Anne M. Kehret Konen. Student, U. Minn., 1954-55. trustee Pacific Northwest Writers Conf., Seattle, 1983-86. Author: Vows of Love and Marriage, 1979, Refinishing and Restoring Your Piano, 1985, Winning Monologs for Young Actors, 1986, Deadly Stranger, 1987 (Children's Choice award 1988), The Winner, 1988, ENCORE!-More Winning Monologs for Young Actors, 1988, Nightmare Mountain, 1989 (Young Hoosier Book award 1992, Golden Sower award Nebr. Libr. Assn. 1993, Iowa Children's Choice award 1994, Maud Hart Lovelace award 1995), Wedding Vows, 1989, Sisters, Long Ago, 1990, Cages, 1991 (Maud Hart Lovelace award 1996), Acting Natural, 1992, Terror at the Zoo, 1992 (Pacific N.W. Young Reader's Choice award 1995, N.Mex. Land of Enchantment award 1995, Iowa Children's Choice award 1996), Horror at the Haunted House, 1992 (Sequoyah Children's Book award 1995, Young Hoosier award 1995), Night of Fear, 1994, Richest Kids in Town, 1994, Cat Burglar on the Prowl, 1995, Danger at the Fair, 1995, Bone Breath and the Vandals, 1995, Don't Go Near Mrs. Tallie, 1995, Desert Danger, 1995, The Ghost Followed Us Home, 1996, Earthquake Terror, 1996, Race to Disaster, 1996, Screaming Eagles, 1996, Backstage Fright, 1996, Smaller Steps: The Year I Got Polio, 1996, (plays) Cemeteries are a Grave Matter, 1977, Let Him Sleep 'Till It's Time for His Funeral, 1978, Spirit!, 1979 (Forest Roberts Playwriting award No. Mich. U. 1979, Best New Play award Pioneer Drama Svc. 1980), Dracula, Darling, 1980, Charming Billy, 1981, (musical) Bicycles Built for Two, 1985; contbr. 300 articles and short stories to mags. Vol. Humane Soc., SPCA, Bellevue, Wash., 1975—; bd. dirs. Bellevue Playbarn, 1975-78, Alzheimer's Assn., Bellevue, 1982. Recipient Achievement award Pacific N.W. Writers, Celebrate Lit. award N.W. Reading Coun. of Internat. Reading Assn., 1993. Mem. Author's Guild, Soc. Children's Book Writers, Seattle Freelancers. Office: Curtis Brown Ltd Ten Astor Pl New York NY 10003

KEIGLEY, JUDY CLARK, elementary education educator, consultant; b. Crowley, La., Dec. 10, 1943; d. Stephen G. and Eunice L. (Marx) Clark. BA in Elem. Edn., McNeese State U., Lake Charles, La., 1965. Cert. in elem. edn., La. Tchr. 1st grade South Crowley Elem. Sch., Crowley, La., 1965-66; tchr. 5th grade Estherwood (la.) Elem. Sch., 1966-67; tchr. 3d grade South Rayne Elem. Sch., Rayne, La., 1967-71, Richard (La.) Elem. Sch., 1971-80; tchr. 2d grade Ross Elem. Sch., Crowley, 1980—; ednl. instrnl. specialist IBM/EduQuest, La., 1991—; cons., mem. adv. panel La. Tchr. Assessment Local Personal Evaluation Program, 1992-94. AAUW Edn. Found. Named Endowment grantee, 1987; named Tchr. of Yr. Acadia Parish, 1995. Mem. La. Assn. Computer Using Educators, Assoc. Profl. Educators of La. (pres. 1992-94), Delta Kappa Gamma (pres. 1992-94), Alpha Delta Kappa (pres. 1983-84). Democrat.

KEIL, MARILYN MARTIN, artist; b. Balt., Nov. 6, 1932; d. Francis and Mary Blanche (Murphy) Martin; m. Herbert Bruce Keil, Dec. 18, 1954; children: Braden, Mary-Beth, Sue-Ann, Nancy, Bryant. Student, Corcoran Sch. Art, Washington, 1991-94, U. Md., 1995. active art in embassies program U.S. Dept. State; juried Washington area printmakers calendar Balt. Mus. fine Arts, 1995—. One-woman show Ralls Collection, Washington, 1993; exhibited in group shows at Rockville Art League (watercolor award), 1991, Corcoran Sch. Art, 1994, Nat. Cathedral, Washington, 1994, U. Md. Sch. Arts and Sociology, 1995, West Gallery, 1995, Md. Fedn. Art, 1996,; represented in permenant collections at Corcoran Gallery Art, Washington, 1996, Nat. Mus. Women in the Arts, 1996. Bd. dirs. Potomac Glen Civic Assn., Potomac, Md., 1988-94. Mem. Rockville Art League, Nat. Mus. Women in the Arts (charter), Washington Area Printmakers, Alpha Lambda. Home: 11540 S Glen Rd Potomac MD 20854-1852

KEILLOR, SHARON ANN, computer company executive; b. St. Thomas, Ont., Can., July 10, 1945; d. Mary Keillor; m. Russel C. Jones; children: Kimberly Nicole, Tamara Melissa. BSChemE, U. Western Ont., 1968; diploma mech. engring., Imperial Coll. Sci. and Tech., London, 1972; PhDME, U. London, 1972; MBA in Bus. Mktg./Fin., Ohio State U., 1976. Asst. prof., faculty engring. and applied sci. Meml. U. Nfld., St. John's, Can., 1972-76; assoc. dir. div. continuing edn., budget planning and fin. U. Mass., Amherst, 1977-78, spl. asst. to provost, 1978-80; corp. mgr. software svcs. tng. Digital Equipment Corp., Stow, Mass., 1980-83, corp. mgr. digital mgmt. edn. and office automation, 1982-83, corp. mgr. software svcs., software engring., 1983-91, v.p. computer spl. systems, 1989-91; v.p. bus. and mktg. mgmt. The Software Group, Stow, Mass., 1991-93, v.p. shared engring. svcs., 1993-95; exec. v.p. CTA Inco., Rockville, Md., 1995—; vis. asst. prof. faculty engring. sci. U. Western Ont., London, Can., 1973, 75. Athlone fellow; Nat. Rsch. Coun. Can. scholar. Mem. IEEE, NAFE, AIAA, Soc. Women Engrs., Am. Soc. Engring. Edn. Home: 2001 Mayfair McLean Ct Falls Church VA 22043 Office: 6116 Executive Blvd Ste 800 Rockville MD 20852

KEIM, BETTY ADELE T., mayor; b. California, Pa., Nov. 14, 1935; d. Glenn L. and F. Edith (Carson) Tinley; m. Richard P. Keim, Mar. 2, 1957 (dec. Sept. 1987); children: Susan Keim Rohrer, Sheila Marie (dec.), Karen Keim Smoot, R. Paul Jr., David C., Katherine A. Grad. nursing, Allegheny Gen. Hosp., Pitts., 1956; student, U. Pitts., 1957-58; BS in Nursing Edn., U. Kans., 1965. RN, Kans., Pa. Nurse biochemistry and nutrition rsch. dept. U. Pitts., St. Margaret's Hosp., 1956-57; pres. Jr. League, Wyandotte, Johnson County, Kans., 1975-76; founding pres. Kans. Action for Children, Topeka, 1978-80; founding mem. Kans. Children's Endowment Fund, Topeka, 1981; pres. Aux. to Kans. Dental Assn., Topeka, 1983-84, United Community Svcs., Johnson County, 1985-87; adv. mem. bd. trustees Bethany Med. Ctr., Kansas City, Kans., 1986-89; dir. Bethany Med. Ctr. Found., Kansas City, Kans., 1989—; pres. Johnson County C.C. Found., 1990-92. Author resource documents. Bd. mem. Community Blood Ctr., Kansas City, Mo., 1988—; mem. Leadership Kans., Topeka, 1991; mem. bd. govs. Am. Royal, Kansas City, Mo., 1990—; precinct committeewoman, Mission Hills, Kans., 1988-96; active City Coun., Mission Hills, 1989—, pres., 1991-93, mayor, 1993—; mem. bd. zoning appeals, Mission Hills, 1987-89. Recipient Ann. Child Advocacy award Kans. Action for Children, 1981, Child Abuse Prevention award Kans. Com. for Prevention Child Abuse, 1979, Community Svc. award Jr. League, 1978; named Milton E. Erickson Citizen of Yr. United Community Svcs., Johnson County, 1988, Woman of Yr. Aux. Kans. Dental Assn., 1986. Mem. Allegheny Gen. Hosp. Nurse Alumni Assn., ANA, Kans. State Nurses Assn., Kans. U. Med. Ctr. Nurse Alumni Assn., Jr. League Wyandotte and Johnson Counties Kans., Rep. Elephant Club, Sigma Theta Tau. Presbyterian.

KEIPER, MARILYN MORRISON, elementary education educator; b. South Gate, Calif., June 12, 1930; d. David Cline and Matilda Ruth (Pearce) M.; m. Edward E. Keiper, June 18, 1962; children: Becky S. Swickard, Edward M. BA, Calif. State U., L.A., 1954; postgrad., UCLA, 1968. Elem. tchr. Rosemead (Calif.) Sch. Dist., 1954—; recreation leader L.A. County, 1951-62, 2d reader 1st Ch. Christ Scientist, Arcadia, Calif., 1991-94; mem. cons. Janson Adv. Group, Rosemead, 1985—; bd. dirs. Janson PTA, Rosemead, 1985—; participant Sta. KNBC Spirit of Edn., 1990-92. 2d leader 1st Ch. Christ Scientist, Arcadia, Calif., 1991-94; mem. cons. Janson Adv. Group, Rosemead, 1985—; bd. dirs. Janson PTA, Rosemead, 1985—; participant Sta. KNBC Spirit of Edn., 1990-92. Named Tchr. of the Yr., L.A. County, 1983-84. Fellow Rosemead Tchrs. Assn., Delta Kappa Gamma.

KEIR, LISA STEFANON, legislative aide; b. Bellefonte, Pa., Dec. 10, 1946; d. Severino and Dorothy Mae (Albright) Stefanon; m. Duncan Wray Keir, Dec. 22, 1968; children: Scott, Andrew. BA, Gettysburg Coll., 1968; MLA, Johns Hopkins U., 1973; postgrad., Western Md. Coll., 1976. Tchr. English various pub. schs. S.C., Pa., Md., 1968-76; sch. libr. Carroll County Pub. Schs., Westminster, Md., 1976-80; freelance writer, editor various newspapers and mags. Balt., 1980-85; exec. dir. Valleys Planning Coun., Towson, Md., 1985-89; planner II Balt. County Office of Planning, Towson, 1989-90; sr. legis. aide Balt. County Coun., Towson, 1990—; sec., bd. dirs. Towson Partnership, Inc., 1992—; mem. nominating com. Valleys Planning Coun., Towson, 1992—. Columnist: Balt. Chronicle, 1980-95; contbr. articles to popular publs. Pres., sec. Chestnut Ridge Improvement Assn., Owings Mills, Md., 1980-85; pres. Interarts, Owings Mills, 1990-93; publicity chmn. Naked Feet, Balt., 1988; bd. dirs. St. Thomas Coop. Sch., Owings Mills, 1983-84. Republican. Episcopalian. Office: Coun of Balt County 400 Washington Ave Towson MD 21204

KEISER, ARLENE PHYLLIS, special education educator; b. Pitts., Oct. 7, 1951; d. David Aaron and Lois Jean (Doeblin) Carey; m. Robert Allan Keiser, June 9, 1973; children: Celia, Robert Allan Jr. BS in Elem. Edn., U. Dayton, 1973. Cert. tchr. Ohio, Mich., N.Y. Tchr. spl. edn. Dayton (Ohio) Pub. Schs., 1973-75; tchr. Reading R.R. Tutoring, Ann Arbor, Mich., 1977-80; dir. ABC Day Care Ctr., Ann Arbor, 1980-86; tchr. spl. edn. Nyack (N.Y.) Pub. Schs., 1989—; educator children with extended illness, susbtance addictions, and emotional problems prohibiting sch. attendance. Editor newsletter La Maze, Ann Arbor, 1976-78. Mem. bd. Nyack PTA, 1987-94, mem. exec. bd., 1992-93, 94-95, co-pres., 1995-96; mem. choir, floutist Reformed Ch., Nyack, 1992-96. Democrat. Home: 144 Castle Heights Ave Upper Nyack NY 10960-1503 Office: Nyack Pub Schs Adminstrv Offices Dickinson Ave Nyack NY 10960

KEISLING, KRISTA LOUISE, legal assistant; b. Harrisburg, Pa., Apr. 8, 1965; d. Paul Noah and LaRue Ann (Lesher) Welker; m. Kevin Burton Williard, Dec. 4, 1981 (div. Mar. 1984); 1 child, Ashlee Louise; m. David Wesley Keisling, Oct. 13, 1990; 1 child, Margaret Marie. Cert. paralegal, Harrisburg (Pa.) Area C.C., 1985. Legal asst. Legis. Budget and Fin. Com., Harrisburg, 1986—. Mem. Trinity United Ch. of Christ. Mem. Ctrl. Pa. Paralegal Assn. Republican. Office: Legis Budget and Fin Com PO Box 8737 Harrisburg PA 17105

KEIST, SANDRA LOUISE HOHENSTEIN, library director; b. Muckegon, Mich., July 13, 1938; d. Ronald Henry and Frances Louise (Grimm) Hohenstein; m. Richard T. Keist, Aug. 23, 1958; children: Michelle Louise, Richard Ronald Christopher Jon, Jay Scot. BA, Mich. State U., 1958; MLS, U. Wis., Milw., 1985. Asst. libr. Lakeland Coll., Sheboygan, Wis., 1982-85; serials libr. Ark. Tech. U., Russellville, 1985-86; media dir. high sch. Cobre Sch. Dist., Bayard, N.Mex., 1986-88; libr./dir. Kans. Wesleyan U., Salina, 1988—; founder, dir. Coop. Pre-Sch., 1973. book reviewer in field. Bd. dirs. Friends of Pub. Libr., Salina, 1991—. Fellow AAUW, 1979. Mem. LWV (bd. dirs.), ALA, Kans. Godart (sec., treas. 1991—), Mountain Plains Libr. Assn. (com. chair), Assn. Coll. and Rsch. Libraries, Pvt. Acad. Librs. (officer), Toastmasters (archivist), Girls Club (bd. dirs. 1973-76). Office: Kans Wesleyan U 100 E Claflin Ave Salina KS 67401-6146

KEISTER, JEAN CLARE, lawyer; b. Warren, Ohio, Aug. 28, 1931; d. John R. Keister and Anna Helen Brennan. JD, Southwesten, 1966. Bar: Calif. 1967, U.S. Supreme Ct. 1972, U.S. Dist. Ct. (so. dist.) Calif. 1988. Legal writer Gilbert Law Summaries, L.A., 1967; instr. Glendale (Calif.) Coll. Law, 1968; pvt. practice Glendale, 1967-70. Mem. Themis Soc., 1989-93. Recipient Golden Poet award World of Poetry. Mem. Burbank Bar Assn. (sec. 1993), Antelope Valley Bar Assn.

KEISTLER, BETTY LOU, accountant, tax consultant; b. St. Louis, Jan. 2, 1935; d. John William and Gertrude Marie (Lewis) Chancellor; m. George E. Keistler, Aug. 3, 1957 (div. Mar. 1981); children: Kathryn M. Morrissey, Deborah J. Birsinger. AS, St. Louis U., 1956; BBA, U. Mo., 1986. Asst. treas. A.G. Edwards & Sons, St. Louis, 1956-57; owner, mgr. B.L. Keistler & Assoc., St. Louis, 1969-82; contr. Family Resource Ctr., Inc., St. Louis, 1982-87; registered rep. Equitable Fin. Svcs., Mo., 1987-88; bus. mgr. Mo. Bapt. Coll., St. Louis, 1987-88, Barnes Hosp. Sch. of Nursing, St. Louis, 1989-91, U. South Fla., St. Petersburg, 1991—; cons. in field, 1982-91; cert. two star sales assoc. Youngevity, Inc., 1995, area assoc. trainer; registered rep. Equitable Fin. Svcs., 1987-88; adminstrv. and profl. coun. mem. U. South Fla., 1994. Treas. Pky. Townhouses at Village Green, Chesterfield, Mo., 1985-87; exec. core United Way Greater St. Louis, 1984-91; mem. Gulfport Hist. Soc., 1996—; mem. bldg. and grounds com. Pasadena Bapt. Ch., Sunday sch. gen. sec., 1994-95, trustee. Scholar Phillip Morris Corp., St. Louis, 1982-84. Mem. Am. Bus. Womens Assn. (v.p. 1978-79, pres. Lewis & Clark chpt. 1979-80, treas. nat. conv. 1981, pres. ADITI chpt. 1988-90, Sand & Sea chpt. 1992—, Woman of Yr. 1979-80, 94-95), U. South Fla. Women's Club, Am. Soc. Women Accts., Ind. Accts. Mo. (sec. 1978-79, v.p. 1980-81, state sec. 1978-79), St. Louis Women's Commerce Assn., 1904 World's Fair Soc., Internat. Platform Assn., Gulfport Hist. Soc., Am. Biog. Inst. (hon. advisor, rsch. bd. advisors nat. divsn. 1991), NAFE, Gulfort Hist. Soc., Alpha Sigma Lambda (life, treas. 1985-87). Republican. Home: 6060 Shore Blvd S #103 Gulfport FL 33707

KEITH, CAMILLE TIGERT, airline marketing executive; b. Ft. Worth, Feb. 27, 1945; d. Marvin and Catherine Frances (Tuscany) K. Student, Tex. Tech U.; BA in Broadcasting and Journalism, Tex. Christian U., 1967. Pub. relations, publicity mgr. Sta. WFAA-TV, Dallas; media relations dir. Read-Poland Pub. Relations Co., Dallas; pub. relations dir. Southwest Airlines Co., Dallas, 1972-76, asst. v.p. pub. relations, 1976-78, v.p. pub. relations, 1978-84, v.p. spl. mktg., 1984—; chair Tex. Travel Summit, 1992, 93; mem. adv. bd. bus. leaders coun. City of Dallas Mktg. and Promotions. Com. Bd. dirs. Dallas Repertory Theatre, Communities in Schs., Vis. Nurses of Dallas, Vis. Nurses Tex., United Cerebral Palsy Dallas, Press Club, Dallas Found., Shared Housing, Project Independence for Older Ams., Jr. Achievement Dallas, exec. com., 1991—; mem. adv. bd. sch. journalism com. Tex. Christian U.; mem. advt. com. Tex. Tech. U., Women's Ctr. of Dallas, adv. bd.; deacon, past chmn. dept. ch. growth Ctrl. Christian Ch., pres. women's fellowship, mem. adv. bd. nat. task force on comm.; sr. nat. v.p. Children Am. Revolution Women's Resource Ctr. YWCA, Dallas; bd. dirs. Dallas/Ft. Worth Area Tourism Coun., Dallas Heart Assn.; bd. advs. nat. Coun. on Aging; Gov.'s adv. bd. tourism, com. of 60 Tex. Dept. Commerce; v.p. pub. rels. Freedom Found., Dallas, 1989-94; pres. bus. womens group, Ctrl. Christian Ch., Christian Women's Fellowship; mem. adv. bd. Girl Scouts Am., Dallas, Sr. Citizens Greater Dallas, Ret. Sr. Vol. Program, Okla. Bus. and Leadership Coun., Okla. Dept. Aging, Tex. Dept. Aging; lay rep. nat. Eldercare Inst. on Elder Abuse and State Long Term Care Ombudsman Svc., SR. Tex. Newspaper, Dallas Ind. Sch. Dist., Tex. Dept. Health; active adminstrn. on aging project eldercare strategy task force Region VI Dept. Health and Human Svcs. Named Rising Star, Tex. Bus. Mag., 1984; named to Hall of Fame, Tex. Tech. Sch. Mass Comm.; recipient Women Helping Women Maura award Women's Ctr., Dallas, Nat. Heatlines award Women in Comms., 1994. Mem. Discover Tex. Assn. (bd. dirs.), Tex. Pub. Rels. Assn., Tex. Travel Industry Assn. (exec. com. 1990—, chair), Women in Comm., Inc. (Excellence in Comm. award), 500, Inc., Women Entrepreneurs of Tex. (adv. bd.), Tex. Children of the Am. Revolution (past nat. chaplain, regional v.p.), Tex. Women's Alliance, Exec. Women Dallas (bd. dirs. 1991-92, v.p. programs 1992-93, pres.-elect 1994-95, pres.), Dallas C. of C. (pub. svc. com.), Children of the Am. Revolution (sr. nat. v.p. 1988-90, sr. nat. chaplain 1990-92, hon. v.p.), Press Club Dallas (pres. 1988-89), Dallas Advt. League (pres. 1980-81, Bill Kerrs Cmty. Svc. award), Leadership Tex. Alumni Assn., Exec. Women of Dallas (pres. 1994-95), Tex. Travel Industry Assn. (chair 1995-97). Office: Southwest Airlines Co PO Box 36611 Dallas TX 75235-1611

KEITH, CAROLYN AUSTIN, secondary school counselor; b. Mobile, Ala., July 15, 1949; d. Lloyd James Jr. and Aletia Delores (Taylor) Austin; m. Carlos Lamar Keith Sr., Aug. 14, 1971; children: Carlos Lamar Jr., Carolyn Bernadette Austin Keith. BA in English and History, Mercer U., 1971; cert. in gifted edn., Valdosta State Coll., 1979, MEd in Counseling, 1982, postgrad., 1987. Tchr. English Crisp County High Sch., Cordele, Ga., 1971-77; tchr. gifted Tift County Jr. High Sch., Tifton, Ga., 1977-81, Dooly County Sch. System, Vienna, Ga., 1981-82; counselor Worth County High Sch., Sylvester, Ga., 1982-86, Monroe Comprehensive High Sch., Albany, Ga., 1986-91, Dougherty Alternative Sch., Albany, 1991—; cons. Ga. State U., Atlanta, 1986-89, Dept. Family and Children Svcs., Albany, 1993, 94. Mem. West Point Parent's Club, U.S. Mil. Acad., 1992—, Dougherty County Commn. on Children/Youth, Albany, 1991-95; mem. adv. bd. Southwest Ga. Prevention Resource Ctr. Named Vol. of Yr., Dougherty County Coun. on Child Abuse, 1993, Student Assistance Program Counselor of Yr. for State of Ga., 1994. Mem. Am. Counseling Assn., Ga. Sch. Counselors Assn. (sec. 2d dist. 1985-91, Counselor of Yr. 1993), Am. Sch. Counselors Assn., Nat. Bd. Cert. Counselors, Ga. Lic. Profl. Counselors, South Ga. Regional Assn. Lic. Profl. Counselors. Democrat. Roman Catholic. Office: Dougherty County Altern Sch 600 S Madison St Albany GA 31701-3140

KEITH, JENNIE, anthropology educator and administrator, writer; b. Carmel, Calif., Nov. 15, 1942; d. Paul K. and Romayne Louise (Fuller) Hill; m. Marc Howard Ross, Aug. 25, 1968 (div. 1978); 1 child, Aaron Elliot Keith Ross; m. Roy Gerald Fitzgerald, June 21, 1980; 1 child, Kate Romayne Keith-Fitzgerald. BA, Pomona Coll., 1964; MA, Northwestern U., 1966, PhD, 1968. NIMH fellow Paris, 1968-70; asst. prof. anthropology Swarthmore Coll., 1970-76, assoc. prof., 1976-82, prof., 1982—, Centennial prof. anthropology, 1990—, chmn. sociology and anthropology, 1987-92, provost, 1992—; mem. rsch. edn. rev. com. NIMH, Washington, 1979-82; co-dir. workshop on age and anthropology Nat. Inst. Aging, Washington, 1980-81, task group leader nat. rsch. plan on aging, 1981; mem. human devel. rev. bd. NIH, 1985-89; mem. adv. coun. Brookdale Found., 1990-93. Author: Old People, New Lives, 1977, 2d paperback edit., 1982 (Am. Jour. Nursing Book of Yr. 1978), Old People as People, 1982; co-author: The Aging Experience, 1994; co-editor: New Methods for Old-Age Research, 1980, 2d edit., 1986, Age in Anthropological Theory, 1984; mem. editorial bd. Gerontologist, 1981-89, Jour. Gerontology, 1987-91, Jour. Aging Studies, 1989—; assoc. editor Rsch. on Aging, 1981-88. Bd. dirs. Cmty. Svcs., Folsom, Pa., 1980-82, Inst. Outdoor Awareness, Swarthmore, 1980—; bd. dirs. Kendal-Crosslands, 1987-92, chmn., 1989-92, Kendal Corp., 1992-95. Conf. grantee Nat. Inst. Aging, 1980, rsch. grantee, 1982-90. Fellow Am. Anthrop. Assn., Gerontol. Soc. Am. (exec. bd. behavioral and social scis. sect. 1985-87, program chmn. 1989, chair 1989-90, publs. com. 1993—); mem. Assn. Anthropology and Gerontology (founder, sec. 1980-81). Office: Swarthmore Coll Office of the Provost Swarthmore PA 19081

KEITH, PAULINE MARY, artist, illustrator, writer; b. Fairfield, Nebr., July 21, 1924; d. Siebelt Ralph and Pauline Alethia (Garrison) Goldenstein; m. Everett B. Keith, Feb. 14, 1957; 1 child, Nathan Ralph. Student, George Fox Coll., 1947-48, Oreg. State U., 1955. Illustrator Merlin Press, San Jose, Calif., 1980-81; artist, illustrator, watercolorist Corvallis, Oreg., 1980—. Author 5 chapbooks, 1980-85; editor: Four Generations of Verse, 1979; contbr. poems to anthologies and mags. and articles to mags.; one-woman shows include Roger's Meml. Libr., Forest Grove, Oreg., 1959, Corvallis Art Ctr., 1960, Human Resources Bldg., Corvallis, 1959-61, Chintimini Sr. Ctr., 1994—, Corvallis Parteral Counseling Ctr., 1992-94, 96, Hall Gallery, Sr. Ctr., 1993, 94, Consumer Power, Philomath, Oreg., 1994, Art, Etc., Newburg, Oreg., 1995, 96; exhibited in group shows at Hewlett-Packard Co., 1984-85, Corvallis Art Ctr., 1992, Chintimini Sr. Ctr., 1992, Hall Gallery, Corvallis, 1995, 96, Art Etc., Newberg, 1995-96. Co-elder First Christian Ch. (Disciples of Christ), Corvallis, 1988-89, co-deacon, 1980-83, elder, 1991-93; sec. Hostess Club of Chintimini Sr. Ctr., Corvallis, 1987, pres., 1988-89, v.p., 1992-94. Recipient Watercolor 1st price Benton County Fair, 1982, 83, 88, 89, 91, 2d prize, 1987, 91, 3d prize, 1984, 90, 92. Mem. Oreg. Assn. Christian Writers, Internat. Assn. Women Mins., Am. Legion Aux. (elected poet post II Corvallis chpt. 1989-90, elected sec. 1991-92, chaplain 1992-93, 94-95, v.p. 1994-95), Chintimine Artists, Corvallis Art Guild. Republican. Office: 304 S College Newberg OR 97132

KEITH, SUSAN WHATLEY, physical education educator; b. Birmingham, Ala., Sept. 1, 1961; d. James Bertis and Elizabeth Sue (Wilhite) Whatley; m. Jerry Wayne Keith, Nov. 16, 1991; 1 child, Michael. BS, Campbellsville Coll., 1983; M HPERDS, Mid. Tenn. State U., 1984. Tchr., coach Briarwood Christian H.S., Birmingham, 1984-87; dir. youth and activities Woodlawn Bapt. Ch., Birmingham, 1987-88; tchr., coach Altamont Sch., Birmingham, 1988—, athletic dir., 1989-92; coord. Jump Rope for Heart, Altamont Sch., 1988—, State Tennis Tournament, Birmingham, 1992—; cert. CPR tchr., ARC, Birmingham, 1989—. Sunday sch. tchr. Liberty Park Bapt. Ch., Birmingham, 1987—, mem. bldg. com., 1993—. Mem. AAHPERD, Ala. Health, Phys. Edn., Recreation Assn. Home: 361 Stonebridge Rd Birmingham AL 35210-4118 Office: Altamont Sch PO Box 131429 Birmingham AL 35213-6429

KEITH, SUZANNE GREGORY, court administrator; b. Grand Rapids, Mich., Sept. 20, 1946; d. Joseph Eldridge and Yvonne LeBone (Belmont) Gregory; m. Thomas Alexander Harvey, May 31, 1964 (div. 1968); 1 child, William Alexander; m. W. Steven Keith, May 31, 1969; children: Martin Gregory, Nathan Edan. Student, Murray State U., 1964-66; MusB, Western Ky. U., 1969; JD, Nashville Sch. of Law, 1981. Bar: Tenn. 1983; cert. tchr. Tenn., Ky. Music band and vocal tchr. Fayette County Schs., Lexington, Ky., 1969-73; pub.'s asst. Freeman-Harr Pub. Co., Nashville, 1974-75; customer svc. rep. Baird Ward Printing Co., Nashville, 1977-80; asst. to pres. W.F. Holt Constrn. Co., Brentwood, Tenn., 1981-83; cheif jud. planner Tenn. Supreme Ct.- Adminstrn. Office, Nashville, 1984-92, dep. state ct. adminstr., 1992—; jud. edn. consortium mem. State Justice Inst., Washington, 1990-93. Author: Presiding Judge Handbook; editor: Court Clerk Manual. Vol. St. Patrick's Shelter for the Homeless, Nashville, 1988-94, St. Thomas Hosp., Nashville, 1995—. Mem. Nat. Assn. Ct. Mgmt., Nat. Assn. State Jud. Educators (jud. edn. and ct. mgmt. cons. 1990—, chair nominating com. 1992-94, 95—). Presbyterian. Home: 3510 Richland Ave Nashville TN 37205 Office: Tenn Supreme Ct Adminstrn Office 600 City Ctr Nashville TN 37243-0609

KEIZER, SUSAN JANE, artist; b. Montreal, Que., Can., Sept. 26, 1940; d. Roy Laver and Eulalia Frances (Shively) Swank; m. Joel Edward Keizer, Dec. 8, 1964; children: Sidney Jacob, Sarah Rebecca. BA, Reed Coll., 1964; postgrad., U. Calif. Davis, 1973-77, Md. Inst., 1978-79; MA, Calif. State U. Sacramento, 1981. Sci. illustrator Oreg. Health Scis. U., Portland, 1964, Santa Cruz, Davis, Calif., 1967-87; instr. drawing Davis Art Ctr., 1976-78; guest instr. art Calif. State U., Sacramento, 1983; vis. lectr. U. Calif. Davis, 1989; artist Davis, 1976—; guest artist San Jose (Calif.) Mus. Sch., 1986; coord. West Coast Women's Conf., Heceta Head, Oreg., 1983; assoc. dir. Lester Gallery, Inverness, Calif., 1981-82. Exhibited in numerous one-woman and group shows, 1976—; represented in numerous corp. and pvt. collections. Exec. bd. mem. Nelson ARTfriends U. Calif., Davis, 1992-96. MacDowell Colony fellow, Peterborough, N.H., 1986. Mem. Women's Caucus for Art, Atists Equity. Home and Office: 2513 Madrid Ct Davis CA 95616

KELEHEAR, CAROLE MARCHBANKS SPANN, administrative assistant; b. Morehead City, N.C., Oct. 2, 1945; d. William Blythe and Gladys Ophelia (Wilson) Marchbanks; m. Henry M. Spann, June 5, 1966 (div. 1978); children: Lisa Carole, Elaine Mabry; m. Zachariah Lockwood Kelehear, Sept. 15, 1985. Student Winthrop Coll., 1963-64; grad. Draughon's Bus. Coll., 1965; cert. in med. terminology Greenville Tech. Edn. Coll., 1972; grad. Millie Lewis Modeling Sch. Office mgr. S.C. Appalachian Adv. Commn., Greenville, 1965-68, Wood-Bergheer & Co., Newport Beach and Palm Springs, Calif., 1970-72; asst. to Dr. J. Ernest Lathem, Lathem & McCoy, P.A., Greenville, 1972-75, Gov. Robert E. McNair, McNair, Konduros, Corley, Singletary and Dibble Law Firm, Columbia, S.C., 1975-77; office mgr. Dr. James B. Knowles, Greenville, 1977-78; office mgr. Constagny, Brooks & Smith, Columbia, 1978-83; legal asst. to sr. ptnr. William L. Bethea Jr., Bethea, Jordan & Griffin, P.A., Hilton Head Island, S.C., 1983-88; adminstrv. asst./paralegal to Dr. Rajko D. Medenica, Hilton Head Island, 1988-95; office mgr. Dibble Law Offices, Columbia, S.C., 1995—; notary pub.; vol. Ladies aux. Greenville Gen. Hosp., 1966-72, South Coast Hosp., Laguna Beach, Calif., 1973, St. Francis Hosp, Greenville, 1974-76, Hilton Head Hosp., 1983-92. Mem. Hilton Head Hosp. Aux., Profl. Women's Assn. Hilton Head Island, Am. Bus. Women's Assn., Nat. Assn. Female Execs., Am. Soc. Notaries, Beta Sigma Phi. Home: PO Box 337 Lexington SC 29071-0337

KELLAIGH, KATHLEEN, conservatory artistic director; b. N.Y.C., June 28, 1955; d. Joseph Anderson and Alice Rendell (French) Kelly; m. Joel Wayne Robertson, Oct. 1, 1988; children: Christopher, Sarah. BFA summa cum laude, U. Ill., 1976. Performer United Stage, Mich., 1977-78, Hartman Stage, Conn., 1978-79, Guiding Light-CBS TV, N.Y.C., 1979-81; dir. Center Stage Bravo, 1981-82; performer Nassau Rep., N.Y., 1983-84, Sail-Away Prodns., World Cruises, 1983-86; producer (transferred from City of London Festival) Narnia, Adonai Arts Found., N.Y.C., 1986; performer All My Children, N.Y.C., 1987, America's Most Wanted, Fox TV, N.Y.C., 1988; producer, assoc. producer Adonai Arts Found., N.Y.C., 1988-90; founder, artistic dir. Action Theatre Conservatory, Clifton, N.J., 1990—; dir. Waldwick, N.Y.C., 1992, An Evening of Ed Dixon One-Acts, N.Y.C., 1994, The Fourth Chair, N.Y.C., 1995; make-up artist Sarah Caldwell's Bicentennial Prodn., Pa., 1976; make-up artist, instr. Nat. Acad. Dance, 1974-77; playwright-in-residence Little Theatre/Genesis Guild, Ill., N.Y., 1971-72, 81-90; artistic dir. Art for God's Sake, Montclair, N.J., 1992, 94. Author: (plays) The Separate World, 1971, Chapter 33, 1981, Alternatives, 1993, Bridges, 1993, The Music's Not So Beautiful Anymore, 1994; lyricist for musical Beauty and the Beast, 1989. Chmn. Episcopal Peace Fellowship, N.Y.C., 1982-86; mem. Diocesan Task Force on World Peace, N.Y., 1982-88. Phi Kappa Phi Acad. scholar, 1975-76. Mem. Am. Fedn. TV and Radio Artists, Screen Actors Guild, Actors Equity Assn., Actors Fund, Episcopal Actors Guild, Genesius Guild (sec. 1987-88), Phi Kappa Phi.

KELLAM, NORMA DAWN, medical, surgical nurse; b. Benton Harbor, Mich., June 13, 1938; d. Edgar Arnold and Bernice (Cronk) K. AA, San Bernardino Valley Coll., 1958; student, Calif. State Coll., Long Beach, 1961-1964, 1965, 1966, 1967; BS, San Diego State Coll., 1961; MS, Calif. State U., Fresno, 1972. Nursing instr. Porterville (Calif.) State Hosp., 1968-69; staff nurse Northside Psychiat. Hosp., Fresno, 1969-72; nursing instr. Pasadena (Calif.) City Coll., 1972-73; night shift lead Fairview Devel. Ctr., Costa Mesa, Calif., 1973-96; freelance writer, 1996—. Contbr. articles to newspapers. Vol. Spanish translator for Interstitial Cystitis Assn. Recipient Cert. of Appreciation for vol. work Interstitial Cystitis Assn. Mem. Calif. Nurses Assn., Soc. Urologic Nurses and Assocs., Inc., Phi Kappa Phi.

KELLEHER, ELISABETH SHERRILL, fraternal organization administrator; b. Brussels, Oct. 21, 1966; (parents Am. citizens); d. Henry Hunt Jr. and Carol Ann (Davis) Sherrill; m. Christopher Robert Kelleher, Apr. 22, 1967. BA in Comms., Bowling Green State U., 1989; MS in Edn., Ind. U., 1992. Leadership cons. Alpha Chi Omega Fraternity, Inc., Indpls., 1989-90; career counselor Ind. U., Bloomington, 1990-92; asst. dir. ann. giving Vanderbilt U., Nashville, 1992-94; dir. Greek life Fla. So. Coll., Lakeland, 1995—; province collegiate chmn. Alpha Chi Omega, Indpls., fraternity rep. Lakeland Alumnae Panhellenic Coun., 1995-96. Com. mem. United Way, Lakeland, 1995-96, Polk Art Mus. Contemporaries, Lakeland, 1995-96; United Way liaison Jr. League Lakeland, 1996. Named Outstanding Mem., Nashville Alumnae Panhellenic, 1994. Mem. Assn. Fraternity Advisors (com. mem. 1995—). Home: 4955 Stonecrest Dr Lakeland FL 33813 Office: Fla So Coll 111 Lake Hollingsworth Dr Lakeland FL 33801-5698

KELLER, BARBARA LYNN, special education educator, reading teacher; b. Great Falls, Mont., July 18, 1941; d. Edward Jerome and Alvina Elizabeth (Kampsnider) Daly; m. Ray B. Keller, Dec. 28, 1961; 1 child, Forest Ry. Student, Ea. Mont. Coll., 1967-69; BA, U. Mont., 1976; postgrad., Mont. State U., 1976-79, No. Mont. Coll., 1989-91; MEd, Mont. State U., 1996. Tchr. grades 1-4 Pub. Schs. Birch Creek Hutterite Colony, Dupuyer, Mont., 1962-63; tchr. grade 2 Pub. Sch. Blackfeet Indian Reservation, Heart Butte, Mont., 1963-64; tchr. reading remediation Pub. Sch., Fort Benton, Mont., 1967-68; tchr. emotionally disturbed Manzanita Ranch Residential Sch., Hyompom, Calif., 1968-69; tchr. reading remediation Pub. Schs., Bigfork, Mont., 1975-78; tchr. ESL Flathead C.C., Kalispell, Mont., 1978-82; pvt. practice tchr. reading, ESL, emotionally disturbed Bigfork, 1982-85; tchr. spl. edn. Pub. Schs. Blackfeet Indian Reservation, Browning, Mont., 1985-94; tchr. study skills and reading Browning (Mont.) H.S., 1994—; pres. Eagle's View Publs., Bigfork, 1989—; author-in-residence Am. Edn. Inst., 1994—; cons. adult edn. Author: Reading Pals—A Handbook for Volunteers, 1990, Reading Pals—A Teacher's Manual, 1990, The Parents' Guide—Studying Made Easy, 1991, Gifts of Love and Literacy—A Parent's Guide to Raising Children Who Love to Read, 1993, Read With Your Child—Make a Difference, 1994; (ednl. program) Studying Made Easy—The Complete Program, 1992, The Students' Guide—Studying Made Easy, 1996, Teachers Manual Studying Made Easy. Reading cons. Personal Vol. Svc., Bigfork, 1970—, Browning, Mont., 1985—. Recipient Author of Yr. award Am. Edn. Inst., 1993. Mem. ASCD, Internat. Reading Assn., Am. Fedn. Tchrs., Literacy Vols. Am., Mont. Counseling Assn., Learning Disabilities Assn., SPAN (Small Publs. Assn. No. Am.). Home: PO Box 1814 Browning MT 59417-1814 Office: Eagle's View Publs 750 Cascade Ave Bigfork MT 59911-3625

KELLER, CHARLENE LUCILLE, financial educator; b. San Antonio, Sept. 22, 1949; d. Charles Bernard and Zodia Lucille (Corder) Wingert; m. Gerald Andrew Keller, Aug. 7, 1971. BA, St. Mary's U., San Antonio, 1971; MA, U. Tex., San Antonio, 1981; PhD, U. Tex., Austin, 1985. Tchr. Winston Churchill H.S., San Antonio, 1971-73; tng. specialist U. Tex. Health Sci. Ctr., San Antonio, 1973-76, dir. employee devel. and tng., 1976-82; exec. dir. enrollment svcs. U. Dallas, Irving, 1985-90; investment broker A.G. Edwards and Sons, Inc., Dallas, 1991-93; owner Fin. Edn. Dynamics, Dallas, 1995—; chmn. tng. and devel. coun. Coll. and Univ. Pers. Assn., Washington, 1980-82. Author: Getting Ahead: Personal Finance for a Changing Age, 1995. Bd. dirs. Pond at Briarwyck Assn., Carrollton, 1993—. Named Woman of the Yr., N.W. Bus. and Profl. Women's Club, San Antonio, 1981. Mem. AAUW (Farmers Br.-Carrollton, pres. elect 1996—), Area Bus. Womens Exch. of the Metrocrest (v.p. 1996). Home and Office: Fin Edn Dynamics 2524 Lake Bend Terr Carrollton TX 75006

KELLER, DOROTHY MARGARET MILLER, elementary education educator; b. Crafton, Pa., June 2, 1910; d. George Walter and Edna Lida (Daum) Miller; m. Frank Rugh Keller, Sept. 7, 1935; children: Marjorie Ann Hottel, Nancy Louise Wilson, David Frank. BS in Edn., U. Pitts., 1934. Cert. tchr. kindergarten through high sch. With H. C. Frick Sch. for Pitts. Tchrs., 1928-31; tchr. Shady Side Jr. Acad., Pitts., 1931-34; arts and crafts tchr. Pitts. (Pa.) Pub. Sch. Humboldt Sch., 1934-35; tchr. in ch. sch. classes and depts. Coraopolis United Meth. Ch., 1935-48, Ravenna, Ohio, 1948-53, dept. supt., 1955-70. Editor: Historic Calendar, 1988, Original Pen and Ink Drawings Historic Landmarks 200th Ann. book of Moon Twp., Pa. Pres. Corapolis United Meth. Women's Soc., 1964-65; bd. dirs., sec. Moon Twp. Pks. and Recreation Bd., Coraopolis, 1963-70; organizer property given to Moon Twp., Robin Hill Pk. nature preserve and cultural ctr., 1971-79, West Area Conservation Coun., Pa., 1970; active PTA, Coraopolis and Ravenna, pres. 1949-51, 55-57, 61-63; mem. adminstrv. bd. United Meth. Ch., Coraopolis. Named Woman of Yr., Moon Twp. Jaycees, 1968, Western Br. Pitts. YWCA, 1965, Garden Club Dist. of Western Pa., Pitts., 1966-71, Woman of Yr. for Community Activities, 1971, Woman of Yr., Coraopolis-Sewickley AAUW, 1994; recipient conservation award DAR, 1991. Mem. AAUW, We. Area Art League (Moon Twp., Coraopolis), Old Moon Twp. Hist. Soc. (co-editor Bicentennial History Book 1988), Am. Assn. Ret. Persons, United Meth. Women. Republican. Methodist. Home: Asbury Methodist Village 407 Russell Ave Gaithersburg MD 20877

KELLER, KIM FRANCES, speech/language pathologist; b. N.Y.C., May 16, 1966; d. John Paul and Joan M. (Fogarty) K. BS in Speech Pathology/Audiology, SUNY, Geneseo, 1988; MS in Speech Pathology, Towson State U., 1992. Lic. speech pathologist, Md.; cert. tchr. N-12. Speech therapist St. Charles & North Country Learning Ctrs. Bd. Coop. Ednl. Svcs., Pt. Jefferson, N.Y., 1988-90; tchr. spl. edn. Balt. City Pub. Schs., 1990-91; speech/lang. pathologist Frederick (Md.) County Pub. Schs., 1992—; cons. in field, Frederick, 1993—; mem. comprehensive planning com. presch. level Frederick County Pub. Schs., 1993—, workshop presenter for speech pathology, 1994—, sch. rep. for task force on edn. that is multicultural bylaws, 1994—. Vol. Pets on Wheels, Montgomery County Mental Health and Hygiene, Rockville, Md., 1993—; mem., workshop presenter PTA, Myersville, Md., 1992—. Inclusion project grantee Frederick County Pub. Schs.-Med. Assistance Funds, 1994. Mem. Am. Speech/Lang. and Hearing Assn. (cert., spl. task force for pub. schs. 1993—), Spl. Interest Pub. Schs. Group (mem. task force 1993—), Choral Arts Soc. Frederick. Democrat. Unitarian. Home: 13 Sunny Ct Thurmont MD 21788 Office: Frederick County Pub Schs Hayward Rd Complex Frederick MD 21701

KELLER, MARTHA ANN, artist, painter; b. N.Y.C., Dec. 8, 1948; d. Charles and Judith (Herman) K.; m. Bradford H. Ensminger, July 12, 1989. Student, Overseas Sch. of Rome, 1961-64, St. Stephen's Sch., Rome, 1964-66, Temple U., 1968, Boston U., 1966-69; BFA, Md. Inst., 1971; postgrad., George Washington U., 1972-73. vis. artist Whitaker Found., Palermo, Italy, 1982, U. Calif., Santa Barbara, 1987, Sch. of the Art Inst. of Chgo., 1990, R.I. Sch. of Design, Providence, 1993, Sarah Lawrence Coll., Bronxville, N.Y., 1991; instr. multi-level painting Sch. of Art Inst. Chgo., 1991, 95; lectr. in visual arts Princeton U., 1991-92; instr. N.Y. Studio Sch. of Painting, 1992; adj. instr. Kingsborough Cmty. Coll., Bklyn., 1993, 94; guest lectr. Temple U., Tyler Sch. of Art, Rome, 1994, Parsons Sch. of Art, 1995. One woman shows include Albuquerque Arts Ctr., U. N.Mex., 1978, Whitaker Found. Mus., Palermo, 1982, Stephen Rosenberg Gallery, N.Y., 1986, 87, 89, Conlon Gallery, Santa Fe, N.Mex., 1990, Galleria Plurima, Udine, Italy, 1991, Halsey Gallery, Coll. of Charleston, 1994, Turchetto Gallery, Milan, 1994; exhibited in group shows at Stephen Rosenberg Gallery, 1986, 89, 90, 91, McNay Art Mus., San Antonio, 1986, Gallery 53 Cooperstown, N.Y., 1986, Carlo Lamagna Gallery, N.Y., 1988, Genovese Gallery, Boston, 1988, Dart Gallery, Chgo., 1988, Ill. Ctr. Gallery, Chgo., 1989, 55 Mercer Gallery, N.Y., 1990, Galleria Plurima, Udine and Milan, 1992, Edwin A. Ulrich Mus. of Art, Wichita, 1992, Cummings Art Ctr., Conn. Coll., 1992, 55 Ferris St, Bklyn., 1993, Jessica Berwind Gallery, Phila., 1993, Krasdale Foods Gallery and Lehman Coll., Westchester, N.Y., 1993, Lilian Heidenberg Gallery, N.Y., 1993, Werner Kramarsky, N.Y., 1993, Art in Embassies Program, Vienna, Austria, 1994, Noyes Mus., Oceanville, N.J., 1994, Art Initiatives and Bill Bace, 1995, Rosenberg & Kaufman Fine Art, N.Y., 1995; represented in permanent collection Met. Mus. Art, N.Y.C., 1996. Recipient fellowships The Mac Dowell Colony, 1990, Nat. Endowment for the Arts, 1989-90, The Mac Dowell Colony, 1989-90; grantee Ludwig Vogelstein Found., 1987, CETA grantee for costume design Albuquerque Dance Theatre, 1978. Home: 39 Walker St New York NY 10013

KELLER, MARTHA DUDLEY, fundraiser; b. Balt., Feb. 12, 1952; d. Albert Henry and Emily Jane (Belding) Dudley; m. John N. Keller, Aug. 2, 1975; children: Alexis Dudley, John Belding. BA in French Lit., Duke U., 1974; cert. paralegal, Georgetown U., 1974. Asst. dir. admissions Western Md. Coll., Westminster, 1978-80, asst. dir. devel., 1980-81; asst. dir. devel. Gettysburg (Pa.) Coll., 1981-82, acting dir. ann. giving, 1993-94; cons. Waynesboro, Pa., 1982-93; cons. Renfrew Mus. and Park, Waynesboro. Cochair gala auction Am. Cancer Soc., 1983, active auction com., 1984—; active capital campaign com. Waynesboro YMCA, 1985; pres. bd. dirs. Renfrew Inst. Cultural and Environ. Studies, Waynesboro, 1990-93, co-chair membership com., 1994—; bd. dirs. Waynesboro Hosp., 1992—; active ann. fund leadership gifts com. Duke U., Durham, N.C., 1993—, coun. women's studies, 1995—; active Pa. Humanities Coun., Phila., 1994—; mem. Waynesboro adv. com. Cumberland Valley Sch. of Music, 1995—. Republican. Methodist. Home: 110 Myrtle Ave Waynesboro PA 17268

KELLER, PATRICIA JANE, curator American decorative arts; b. Norristown, Pa., May 30, 1955; d. P. Kenneth and Esther B. (Oberholtzer) K.; m. Warren C. Conner, Oct. 5, 1983 (div. Dec. 1991); m. Kory R. Berrett, Oct. 17, 1992. BA in History, Temple U., 1978; MA in Early Am. Culture, U. Del., 1984, PhD, 1995, cert. Mus. Studies, 1996. Dir. Lancaster (Pa.) County Quilt Harvest, 1988-93; dir., curator Heritage Ctr. Mus., Lancaster, 1984-93; curator, cons. Berrett Conservation Studio, Oxford, Pa., 1993—; cons. Hershey Mus., James-Lorah Meml. Home, Reading Mus.; adv. bd. Alliance for Am. Quilts, Louisville, 1994—. Contbr. articles to profl. jours. Competitive fellow U. Del., 1995-96, Stewart fellow, 1993-94, Sullivan Rsch. fellow Mus. Am. Textile Hist., 1994, Winterthur fellow Winterthur Mus., 1981-83; Charles Price Sch. scholar, 1979; Barra dissertation fellow Phila Ctr. for Early Am. Studies U. Pa., Phila., 1996-97. Mem. Pa. German Soc., Soc. Winterthur Fellows, Am. Quilt Study Group, Can. Quilt Study Group. Office: Berrett Conservation Studio 3054 Reisler Rd Oxford PA 19363

KELLER, POLLY NIELSEN, cosmetics entrepreneur, consultant; b. Hastings, Nebr., Aug. 2, 1935; d. Juul Christian and Cora Virginia (Wyatt) Nielsen; m. Walter Leroy Keller, Dec. 18, 1975; children: Charles M. Kelly Jr., Shaun N. Kelly. BA in Philosophy, U. Miami, 1959. Pres. mental health assn. Dina, Collier Co., Naples, Fla., 1970—; cosmetic rep. Mary Kay Cosmetics; cons. Mental Health Fedn., Naples, 1990-93. Pres., founder David Lawrence Found., Naples, 1976, David Lawrence Aux., Naples, 1980; cons., fundraiser David Lawrence Ctr., 1976-96; exec. bd. mem. Civic Assn., Naples, 1979-86; chmn. cmty. improvement program Naples Women's Club, 1978-94; lobbyist Mental Health Assn., Tallahasse, Fla., 1973; fund raiser United Way. Naples, 1971. Recipient Edward D. Jones Heart of Gold award Edward D. Jones & Co., 1992, Outstanding Citizen award Naples Daily News, Jaycees, 1987. Mem. Women's Network. Republican. Home: 3901 Gordon Dr Naples FL 33940

KELLER, SHIRLEY INEZ, accountant; b. Ferguson, Iowa, Sept. 15, 1930; d. Adelbert Leslie and Inez Marie (Abbey) Hilsabeck; m. Earl Wilson Keller, Feb. 2, 1957 (dec. 1987); children: Earl William, Cynthia Marie, Eric Walter, Kenneth Paul. Student, U. Iowa, 1949-51; AS, Cameron U., 1971, BS, 1973; postgrad., Arapahoe Community Coll., 1986. High speed radio operator U.S. Army Signal Corps, N.Y.C., Japan, 1951-57; auditor U.S. Dept. Justice, Washington, 1973-76, U.S. Dept. Energy, Oklahoma City, 1976-83, U.S. Dept. Interior, Albuquerque, 1983-86; acct. U.S. Dept. Interior, Denver, 1986-95, ret., 1995; seminar instr. U.S. Dept. Interior, Denver, other cities, 1989-94. Author: Oil and Gas Payor Handbook, 1993. Scorekeeper Boy's Baseball, Lawton, Okla., 1964-72; den mother Boy Scouts Am., Lawton, 1965-66. Sgt. U.S. Army, 1951-57. Decorated Merit Unit Commendation, U.N. Commendation, Korean Svc. medal. Mem. Toastmasters Internat. (sec. Buffalo chpt. 1991, sgt.-at-arms Buffalo chpt. 1992, Competent Toastmaster 1993). Democrat. Roman Catholic. Home: PO Box 280535 Lakewood CO 80228-0535

KELLER, SUSAN AGNES, insurance officer; b. Moline, Ill., July 12, 1952; d. Kenneth Francis and Ethel Louise (Odendahl) Hulsbrink. Grad. in Pub. Relations, Patricia Stevens Career Coll., 1971; grad. in Gen. Ins., Ins. Inst. Am., 1986. CPCU; lic. ins. and real estate agt.; notary public. Comml. lines rater Bitiminous Casualty Corp., Rock Island, Ill., 1973-78; with Roadway Express, Inc., Rock Island, 1978-81; front line supr. Yellow Freight System, Inc., Denver, 1982-83; supr. plumbing and sheet metal prodn. Bell Plumbing and Heating, Denver, 1983-84; v.p. underwriting farm/ranch dept. Golden Eagle Ins. Co., San Diego, 1985—; cons. real estate foreclosure County Records Svc., San Diego, 1986-89; tchr. Ins. Inst. of Am., 1991. Vol. DAV, San Diego, 1985—; tchr. IEA and CPCU courses. Mem. Soc. CPCU (pres., bd. dirs.), Profl. Women in Ins., NAFE. Roman Catholic. Home: 1771 Jamacha Rd El Cajon CA 92019 Office: Golden Eagle Ins Co 7175 Navajo Rd PO Box 85826 San Diego CA 92119-1642

KELLER, TONI L., elementary education educator; b. Cin., Sept. 19, 1945; d. Umberto Giacomo and Dora (Casagrande) Colussi; m. Thomas L. Keller, Aug. 21, 1971; children: Sara, Karen, Ann. BA, Thomas More Coll., Ft. Mitchell, Ky., 1971; MA in Edn., Coll. Mount St. Joseph, Cin., 1985. Cert. reading specialist. Elem. tchr. Detroit Parochial Schs., 1966-68, Sycamore Cmty. Sch., Cin., 1969-77, Our Lady of Visition Sch., Cin., 1983-85, St. Teresa of Avila Sch., Cin., 1986—; adjunct instr. Coll. Mount St. Joseph, Cin., 1990—; edn. adv. bd. Coll. Mount St. Joseph, Cin., 1992—; sci. adv. com. St. Teresa of Avila Sch., Cin., 1994—; curriculum devel. Sci., Archdiocese of Cin., 1993-94. Mem. Nat. Cath. Edn. Assn., Ohio Cath. Edn. Assn., St. Teresa Parent Tchr. Group, Internat. Reading Assn., St. Teresa Edn. Commn., Nat. Sci. Tchrs. Assn. Office: St Teresa of Avila School 1194 Rulison Ave Cincinnati OH 45238-4425

KELLERMAN, FAYE MARDER, novelist, dentist; b. St. Louis, July 31, 1952; d. Oscar and Anne (Steinberg) Marder; m. Jonathan Seth Kellerman, July 23, 1972; children: Jesse Oren, Rachel Diana, Ilana Judith, Aliza Celeste. AB in Math, UCLA, 1974, DDS, 1978. Author: The Ritual Bath, 1986 (Macavity award best 1st novel 1986), Sacred and Profane, 1987, The Quality of Mercy, 1989, Milk and Honey, 1990, Day of Atonement, 1991, False Prophet, 1992, Grievous Sin, 1993, Sanctuary, 1994, Justice, 1995, Prayers for the Dead, 1996; contbr. short stories to Sisters in Crime vols. 1 and 3, Ellery Queen Mag., A Woman's Eye, Women of Mystery, the year's 2d finest crime: mystery stories, The Year's 25 Finest Mystery and Crime Stories, A Modern Treasury of Great Detective and Murder Mysteries, Mothers, Murder for Love. UCLA rsch. fellow, 1978. Mem. Mystery Writers of Am. (So. Calif. bd. dirs.), Womens' Israeli Polit. Action Com., Sisters in Crime. Jewish.

KELLERMAN, SALLY CLAIRE, actress; b. Long Beach, Calif., June 2, 1937; d. John Helm and Edith Baine (Vaughn) K.; m. Richard Edelstein, Dec. 19, 1970; 4 step-daughters; m. Jonathan Krane, 1980. Student, Los Angeles City Coll., Actor's Studio, N.Y.C. Stage appearances include Singular Man, N.Y.C., Breakfast at Tiffany's; films include Reform School Girl, 1959, The Third Day, 1965, The Boston Strangler, 1968, The April Fools, 1969, M*A*S*H, 1970 (Acad. award nominee 1970, Golden Globe award 1970), Brewster McCloud, 1970, Last of the Red-Hot Lovers, 1972, Slither, 1973, Reflection of Fear, 1973, Lost Horizon, 1973, Rafferty and the Gold Dust Twins, 1975, The Big Bus, 1976, Welcome to L.A., 1977, The Mouse and His Child, 1977 (voice), Magee and the Lady, 1978, It Rained All Night The Day I Left, 1978, A Little Romance, 1979, Foxes, 1980, Loving Couples, 1980, Serial, 1980, Head On, 1980, September Gun, 1983, Moving Violations, 1985, Lethal, 1985, Back to School, 1986, That's Life, 1986, Meatballs III, 1987, Three for the Road, 1987, Someone to Love, 1987, Paramedics (voice), 1988, You Can't Hurry Love, 1988, All's Fair, 1989, Limit Up, 1989, The Secret of the Ice Cave, 1990, Happily Ever After, 1990 (voice), The Player, 1992, Younger and Younger, 1993, Mirror, Mirror 2: Raven Dance, 1994, Ready to Wear (Prêt-à-Porter), 1994; also TV roles Chrysler Theatre, Mannix, It Takes a Thief; TV films Verna: USO Girl, 1978, For Lovers Only, 1982, Dempsey, 1983, Secret Weapons, 1985, Elena, 1985, Boris and Natasha, 1992; miniseries Centennial, 1978-79. Recipient nominations Acad. and Golden Globe awards for MASH. Mem. Actor's Equity, AFTRA. Office: Innovative Artists 1999 Ave of the Stars Ste 2850 Los Angeles CA 90067*

KELLEY, BETH MAUREEN, vocational consultant; b. Lafayette, Ind., Sept. 30, 1949; d. Winston Roy and Junis Mary (Jensen) K.; m. David Alfred Williams, July 3, 1971 (div. Apr. 1979); children: Marcus Todd, Kira Michelle. BS in Edn., Valparaiso U., 1971; MA, U. Mich., 1979. Diplomate Am. Bd. Vocat. Experts; cert. rehab. counselor, ins. rehab. specialist, counselor, case mgr. Rehab. counselor Mich. Rehab. Svcs., Pontiac, Mich., 1980-82; rehab. counselor Rehab. and Placement, Inc., Troy, Mich., 1982-83, clin. coord., 1983-84; mgr. Action Rehab. Svcs., Phila., 1984-85; pres. Kelley Cons. Group, Phila., 1985—; sec. Commn. on Rehab. Counselor Certification, Rolling Meadows, Ill., 1988-90, vice chair, 1990-91. Mem. ACA, Nat. Rehab. Assn., Nat. Rehab. Counseling Assn., Am. Rehab. Counseling Assn., Nat. Assn. Rehab. Profls. in the Pvt. Sector (bd. dirs. 1983-84, 86-88). Office: Kelley Cons Group 842 S 2nd St Ste 5 Philadelphia PA 19147-3430

KELLEY, BETTY MARIE, restaurant owner, cook; b. Oil City, Pa., Feb. 23, 1955; d. Robert Charles Miles and Ethel Eleanor (Kelley) Miles. Grad. high sch., high sch., Titusville, Pa. lectr. Cambridge Grange, 1990—. Owner Betty's Restaurant, Cambridge Springs, Pa., 1980—. Mem. Cambridge Pride: Coming Alive, 1992-93; chair Cambridge Springs Cmty. Picnic, 1992—; mem. Cambridge Springs Discover Days Com., 1994—, co-chair baby photo contest, cookie contest; mem. Prison Runathon com. State Correctional Inst., Cambridge Springs, 1993—, other civic activities; assoc. mem. Cambridge Area Vol. Ambulance Svc. Mem. U.S. C. of C., Cambridge Grange (chaplain 1987-90, lectr. 1990—). Republican. Baptist. Office: 164 Venango Ave Cambridge Springs PA 16403-1038

KELLEY, DELORES GOODWIN, state legislator; b. Norfolk, Va., May 1, 1936; d. Stephen Cornelius and Helen Elizabeth (Jefferson) Goodwin; m. Russell Victor Kelley, Jr., Dec. 26, 1956; children: Norma Kelley Johnson, Russell III, Brian. BA, Va. State Coll., 1956; MA, NYU, 1958, Purdue U.,

1972; PhD, U. Md., 1977. Dir. religious edn. N.Y.C. Protestant Coun., Bronx, 1959-60; tchr. N.Y.C. Pub. Schs., Bklyn., 1962-64, Ctrl. Sch. Dist., Plainview, N.Y., 1965-66; asst. prof. Morgan State U., Balt., 1966-70; prof. speech comms. and English Coppin State Coll., Balt., 1973—; legislator Md. Ho. of Dels., Annapolis, 1991-94, state senator, 1995—; chmn. Joint Com. on Fed. Rels./Md. State Senate; panelist, reviewer NEH, Washington, 1978-82; mem. editorial bd. Md. English Jour., Salisbury, 1980-88; dean Coppin State Coll., Balt., 1979-82; fellow Am. Coun. on Edn., Washington, 1982-83; vice chair bd. dirs. Harbor Bank Md., 1982—; mem. jud. proceedings com. Md. State Senate, chair joint com. fed. rels., legis. com., women legislators of Md., 1st v.p., 1995-96; mem. Gov.'s Commn. on Adoption, 1995, Atty. Gen's. and Lt. Gov's. task force on family violence, 1996—, Md. Commn. on Criminal Sentencing Policy, 1996—. Editor (monograph) Concepts of Race, 1981; moderator (TV series) Teaching Writing: Process Approach, 1982. Sec. Md. Dem. Party, Annapolis, 1986-90; bd. dirs. Balt. Urban League, 1986-89; pres. Black Jewish Forum, Balt., 1990-92; commr. Md. Commn. on Values, Annapolis, 1980-85; bd. dirs. Balt. Mental Health Systems, 1991-95; host Internat. Visitors Ctr., 1976—; commn. mem. Md. Commn. Hereditary and Congenital Disorders, Balt., 1992-95. Fellow Purdue U., 1970-72; grantee Md. Com. for Humanities, Balt., 1977-78, NEH, Washington, 1988-89; recipient Racial Justice award Warfields Bus. Record, 1995; named to Mds. Top 100 Women, 1995. Mem. Inst. for Govtl. Svcs. (bd. dirs. 1993-94), Nat. Polit. Congress Black Women (bd. dirs., Balt. chair 1993-95). Baptist. Office: 209 Senate Office Bldg Annapolis MD 21401 also: 6660 Security Blvd Ste 10 Baltimore MD 21207-4012

KELLEY, SISTER HELEN, hospital executive; b. Niagara Falls, N.Y., July 25, 1922; d. Robert Vincent Jr. and Helen Gertrude (O'Neil) K. BSN, Cath. U., 1953; MHA, St. Louis U., 1957; postgrad., Cath. U., Seton Hall, Wayne U., St. Louis U. RN, D.C., N.Y., Mass., Mo. Tchr. elem. and jr. high sch. Endicott, N.Y., 1942-50; faculty divsn. nursing St. Joseph Coll., Emmitsburg, Md., 1953-55; adminstr., pres. bd. dirs. St. Agnes Hosp., Balt., 1958-62; asst. adminstr. Sisters of Charity Hosp., Buffalo, N.Y., 1962-64; adminstr., pres. bd. dirs. Carney Hosp., Boston, 1964-69; provincial councilor Daughters of Charity, Northeast Province, 1969-71; internat. work with Vincentian priests Mex., Rep. Panama, 1971-73; adminstr., pres. Our Lady of Lourdes Hosp., Binghamton, N.Y., 1973-76; pres. Nat. Cath. Health Assn., St. Louis, 1976-78; exec. dir. Laboure Ctr., 1979-82; adminstr. St. Louise House, Albany, N.Y., 1982-83; dir. mktg., plannig Carney Hosp., 1983-85; assoc. dir. Intercounty Home Health Care Agy. Diocese of Albany, 1985-86; dir., coord. health and social svcs. Cath. Worker of Niagara Falls, 1986-88; dir./coord. clin. svcs. Cath. Charities' Programs Adult Mentally Retarded Developmental Disabilities, Bklyn. and Queens, N.Y., 1988-91; v.p. mission svcs. Sisters of Charity Hosp., Buffalo, 1991—; dir. activities St. Louise Retirement Residence and Infirmary, Albany; mem. bd. Filmore Leroy Residents Assn., FLARE, Inc., Buffalo; bd. dirs. St. Mary's Hosp., Rochester; trustee Good Samaritan Hosp., Pottsville, Pa.; participant internat. Commns. Daus. of Charity, 1968; pres. bd. trustees Carney Hosp., Our Lady of Lourdes Hosp., St. Agnes Hosp.; chair, participant profl. religous cmty. studies; cons., spkr. Mercy Hosp., Pitts., St. Mary's Hosp., Amsterdam, N.Y.; mem. couns., coms. nursing, pers., profl. practice, other groups. Recipient Community Svc. award Cedar Grove Civic Assn., Boston, Ladies of Charity, Binghamton, CHA Pres., St. Louis. Fellow Am. Coll. Healthcare Execs.; mem. Am. Acad. Cath. Leadership. Home: 1305 Sausse Ave Troy NY 12180-1613 Office: DePaul Provincial House 96 Menands Rd Albany NY 12204-1499

KELLEY, JANE, special education educator; b. Waterloo, Iowa, May 13, 1951; d. Jerry and Elizabeth (Maas) Molendorp; m. Dale Wayne Kelley, May 26, 1973; children: Joshua Wayne, Jennifer Elizabeth. AA, Ellsworth Jr. Coll., Iowa Falls, Iowa, 1971; BS in Edn., N.E. Mo. State U., 1973, MA, 1975. Tchr. K-8 educable mentally retarded Lincoln County RIII Sch. Dist., Troy, Mo., 1973—. Youth leader 1st Christian Ch., Troy. Mem. Mo. Tchrs. Assn. (past pres., bd. dirs. Found. 1995—, Leader of Yr. award 1994), Greater St. Louis Tchrs. Assn. (various offices 1990—), Troy Cmty. Tchrs. ssn. (various offices 1973—).

KELLEY, JANE ELIZABETH, marketing consultant; b. Alexandria, La., Mar. 12, 1954; d. James Joseph and Nell Yow (Russell) K.; m. Henry John Fieselman, Jan. 9, 1993. BA in Speech/Psychology, U. N.C., 1975. Asst. mgr. Kelley's Photo, Myrtle Beach, S.C., 1975-77; media buyer NW Ayer, San Francisco, 1977-79; media dir. Morris White & Assocs., Charlotte, N.C., 1980-81; dir. broadcast Ivey's, Charlotte, 1982-84; broadcast mgr. Rich's Dept. Stores, Atlanta, 1984-88; pres. KO Mktg., Atlanta, 1988-90; v.p. The Mktg. Consortium, Charlotte, 1990-92; dir. mkt. devel. Sta. WSMV-TV, Nashville, 1992-94; pres. Alliance Internet Mktg., Nashville, 1994—. Mem. Sales and Mktg. Execs., Nashville Advt. Fedn., Nashville Area C. of C. (new mem. amb.). Office: Alliance Internet Mktg 4219 Hillsboro Rd # 338 Nashville TN 37215

KELLEY, LINDA ANNE, golf course manager; b. Drexill Hill, Pa., Apr. 11, 1958; d. Victor Francis and Patricia Anne Kelley. Student, U. Maine, 1976-77, Boston U., 1977-78; cert. turfgrass mgr., U. Mass., Amherst, 1989. Asst. supt. Penobscot Valley Country Club, Orono, Maine, 1978-85, supt., 1985-86; asst. supt. Sable Oaks Golf Club, South Portland, Maine, 1988-90; supt., turfgrass mgr. Bedrock Golf Club, Rutland, Mass., 1991—. Mem. Golf Course Supt. Assn. Am., Golf Course Supts. Assn. New Eng. Office: Bedrock Golf Club 87 Barre-Paxton Rd Rutland MA 01543

KELLEY, LYN SCHRAFF, insurance broker; b. Cleve., Mar. 30, 1956; d. Albert Gerald Schraff and Mary Patricia (McCarty) Urban; m. Kevin E. Kelley, Feb. 28, 1949. BBA, Cleve. State U., 1982, MBA, 1990. Mem. nat. task force for quality mgmt. Johnson & Higgins, Cleve., 1977—, client mgr., 1996—; bd. dirs. Ct. Community Svc. Agy. Mem. leadership devel. program United Way, 1991, also mem. allocations panel. Mem. Exec. Women's Roundtable. Roman Catholic. Home: 27631 Whitehill Cir Cleveland OH 44145-1217 Office: Johnson & Higgins 1301 E 9th St Ste 1900 Cleveland OH 44114-1800

KELLEY, MARY ELIZABETH (LAGRONE), computer specialist; b. Temple, Tex., Feb. 12, 1947; d. Harry John and Mary Erma (Windham) LaGrone; m. Roy Earl Kelley, May 10, 1968; children: Roy John, James Lewis, Joanna Marylu. BS, U. Mary Hardin-Baylor, 1968. Cert. tchr., Tex. Math tchr. Killeen (Tex.) High Sch., 1977-78; clk. typist Readiness Region VIII, Aurora, Colo., 1979; statis. clk. Fitzsimons Army Med. Ctr., Aurora, 1980-81, mgmt. asst., 1981-83; clk. typist Corpus Christi (Tex.) Army Depot, 1984; mgmt. asst. Health Care Studies and Clin. Investigation Act, Fort Sam Houston, Tex., 1984-85; computer programmer/analyst Health Care Systems Support Act, Fort Sam Houston, 1985-88, computer systems analyst, 1988-92, computer specialist, 1992-94, data base adminstr., 1994-95, lotus notes sys. adminstr., 1995—; tchr. Fitzsimons Army Med. Ctr., 1978-79, cons., 1978-79. Author: (databases) Health Care Management System, 1988-94. Vol. Heidi Search Ctr., San Antonio, 1990, Friends of Safe House, Denver, 1980-83, Parents Encouraging Parents, Denver, 1979-83. Recipient achievement medal for civilian svc. Dept. Army, 1991. Mem. DAR, Daus. of Republic of Tex., United Daus. of Confederacy, Tex. Soc. of Mayflower Descs., Alpha Chi, Delta Psi Theta, Sigma Tau Delta. Roman Catholic.

KELLEY, MICHAELANN, art educator; b. Cin., June 18, 1963; d. William Donald and Bettylu (Powell) K. BA in Graphic Design, Coll. Mount St. Joseph, Cin., 1985, M of Art in Edn., 1992. Cert. art tchr. Ohio, Tex. Advtg. coord. A.C.G.I.H., Inc., Cin., 1984-92; tchr. ceramics/art Eisenhower H.S., Houston, 1992—; mem. tchr. of the yr. com. Eisenhower H.S., Houston, 1992-94, mem. tchr's. adv. com., 1993-95; mem. vertical com. on math Aldine I.S.D., Houston, 1995. Presenter numerous confs. in field. Sunday sch. tchr. All Saints Ch., Houston, 1994. Recipient Outstanding Alumna award Coll. Mount St. Joseph, 1995. Mem. Nat. Art Edn. Assn., Am. Craft Coun., Tex. Art Edn. Assn., Tex. Fedn. of Tchrs., Houston Art Edn. Assn., Mus. Fine Arts Houston. Roman Catholic. Office: Eisenhower HS 7922 Antoine Dr Houston TX 77088

KELLEY, PATRICIA HAGELIN, geology educator; b. Cleve., Dec. 8, 1953; d. Daniel Warn and Virginia Louise (Morgan) Hagelin; m. Jonathan Robert Kelley, June 18, 1977; children: Timothy Daniel, Katherine Louise. BA, Coll. of Wooster, 1975; AM, Harvard U., 1977, PhD, 1979. Instr. New Eng. Coll., Henniker, N.H., 1979; asst. prof. U. Miss., University, 1979-85, assoc. prof., 1985-89, acting assoc. vice chancellor acad. affairs, 1988, prof., 1989-92, assoc. dean, 1989-92; program dir. NSF, Washington, 1990-92; prof., chmn. dept. geology U. N.D., Grand Forks, 1992—. Contbr. articles to profl. jours. Deacon Bethel Presbyn. Ch., Olive Branch, Miss., 1985-90. Rsch. grantee NSF, 1986-89, 90—; NSF fellow, 1976-79. Fellow Geol. Soc. Am.; mem. AAAS, Paleontol. Soc. (coun. 1984-85, 95—, chair S.E. sect. 1984-85, chair N.C. sect. 1995), Paleontol. Rsch. Inst., Soc. Econ. Paleontologists and Mineralogists, Sigma Xi, Phi Beta Kappa. Presbyterian. Office: U ND Dept Geology & Geol Engring PO Box 8358 Grand Forks ND 58202-8358

KELLEY, SANDRA KAY, school system administrator; b. Terre Haute, Ind., Sept. 30, 1946; d. Norman David and Mary Ann (Gaiter) Neiswinger; m. Paul Joseph Kelley II, June 17, 1967; children: Karen, Paul III, David. BA, Ind. State U., 1968, MS, 1979; PhD, Ind. U., 1989. Tchr. Vigo County Sch. Corp., Terre Haute, 1979-87; asst. prin. Sarah Scott Middle Sch., Terre Haute, 1987-93, prin., 1993—; cons. Ind. Assn. Secondary Sch. Adminstrs., Indpls., 1985-93, Ind. Dept. Pub. Welfare, Terre Haute, 1988-92, U. N.C., Chapel Hill, 1991-93; adj. faculty Ind. State U., Terre Haute, 1991. Rsch. assoc. North Cen. Assn. Coll. and Schs., Bloomington, Ind., 1982-83; past pres. Coun. for Children and Youth, Wabash Valley, Ind.; exec. com. Family Svc. Assn., Wabash Valley; cmty. rep. Ind. Coalition of Caring Communities, Indpls.; bd. dirs. Minority Health Coalition, Intervention Ctr., Y-Me, Wabash Valley. Grantee Ind. Dept. Edn., Lilly Endowment. Fellow Middle Grades Network Adminstrs.; mem. Ind. Assn. Sch. Prin., Vigo County Edn. Found. (pres. 1991-92), Middle Grades Network-Ind. (exec. com. 1993—), Phi Delta Kappa (pres. 1987-88). Office: Sarah Scott Middle Sch 2000 S 9th St Terre Haute IN 47802

KELLEY, SHARON LEE, physical education educator; b. Utica, N.Y., Dec. 4, 1941; d. Lee G. and Vera M. (Byrns) K. BA, State Univ. Coll. at Cortland, N.Y., 1963; MA, U. Iowa, 1969. Phys. edn. tchr. and coach Pine Plains (N.Y.) Ctrl. Sch., 1963-66; grad. asst. U. Iowa, Iowa City, 1966-68, tchr. phys. edn., 1968-69; phys. edn. tchr. Luther Coll., Decorah, Iowa, 1969-70, Glens Falls (N.Y.) Elem. and Jr. H.S., 1970-71, Fowler Elem. Sch., Gouverneur, N.Y., 1971—. Author and presenter in field. Recipient Outstanding Leadership in Swimming and Aquatics award ARC, 1965, others; grantee in field. Mem. AAHPERD (life), N.Y. State Assn. for Health, Phys. Edn. and Recreation, Gouverneur Tchrs. Assn./United Tchrs., Girls and Women's Sports. Home: PO Box 49 Gouverneur NY 13642-0049 Office: Fowler Elem Sch RR 3 Box 332 Gouverneur NY 13642-9567

KELLEY, SHEILA SEYMOUR, public relations executive, crisis consultant; b. Bronxville, N.Y.; d. William Joseph and Jane (Seymour) K.; m. Robert Max Kaufman, 1959. BA magna cum laude, Syracuse U., 1949. Reporter Yonkers Herald Statesman, N.Y.C., 1950; reporter, editor Close Up column Herald Tribune, N.Y.C., 1950-53; writer, producer Sta. WNBC-TV, N.Y.C., 1953-54; media cons. to Senator Jacobs K. Javits, N.Y.C., 1956-74; press sec. Senator Jacobs K. Javits, Washington, 1958-61; account supr., v.p. Harshe Rotman Druck, N.Y.C., 1961-76; founder, pres. VOTES, Inc., N.Y.C., 1973-75; v.p. Doremus Pub. Rels., N.Y.C., 1976-86, sr. v.p., 1987-90, mng. dir., exec. v.p., 1990; exec. v.p. Gavin Anderson & Co., N.Y.C., 1990-96, sr. counselor, 1996—. Mem. Pub. Rels. Soc. Am. (accredited), Women Execs. Pub. Rels. (pres. 1987-88), Phi Beta Kappa. Republican. Office: Gavin Anderson & Co 1633 Broadway New York NY 10019-6708

KELLEY, SYLVIA JOHNSON, financial services firm executive; b. Butte, Mont., Dec. 29, 1929; d. John O. and Hilja W. (Koski) J.; m. Dan H. Kelley, June 1, 1950 (div. Jan. 1973); children: David D., Bruce J., Sheila K. Miller, Mona K. Nance; m. Richard T. Marshall, June 10, 1979. CLU; charger fin. cons.; cert. fin. planner; registered fin. cons. Legal sec. various law firms, L.A., 1959-69; registered rep. Met. Life, N.Y.C., 1969-75, SMA Equities, Inc., Worcester, Mass., 1975-89, Multi-Fin. Securities Corp., Denver, Colo., 1989—; pres., chief exec. officer Advance Funding, Inc., El Paso, Tex., 1981—. Contbr. articles to profl. jours. Bd. dirs., chmn. bus. adv. com. Marina Del Rey C. of C., 1974-75; bd. dirs., pub. rels. chmn. Am. Heart Assn., El Paso, 1972-74; charter pres. El Paso Exec. Women's Coun., 1972-73; mem. fin. adv. com. El Paso C.C., 1992—; bd. dirs. El Paso Estate Planning Coun., 1993—. Mem. Am. Soc. CLUs and ChFC (past pres. El Paso chpt., bd. dirs. 1981-85), Registry of CFP Practitioners. Office: Advance Funding Inc 6070 Gateway Blvd E Ste 104 El Paso TX 79905-2027

KELLIHER, JUSTINE OREN, retired nurse, educator; b. Boston, Oct. 22, 1920; d. Ralph Sidney and Margaret Elizabeth (Smith) Woollett; m. Giles Clement Kelliher, Apr. 10, 1948; children: Giles Jr., Ralph, Margaret Anne, Justina, Julia, David. BA, Manhattanville Coll., 1942; MA, Brown U., 1943; MN, Yale U., 1946; MS, Boston U., 1970. Staff nurse Boston Lying-In Hosp., 1946-47, Boston Vis. Nurse Assn., 1947-48; instr. childbirth educator Boston Assn. Childbirth Edn., 1953-78; parent educator St. Elizabeth's Hosp., Boston, 1967; staff nurse Beth Israel Hosp., Boston, 1968, Newton-Wellesley Hosp., Newton, Mass., 1970-71, Chetwynde Nursing Home, Newton, 1972-77; staff nurse Bapt. Nursing Home, Newton, 1980-82, ret., 1982. Mem. Boston Assn. Childbirth Edn. (founder, instr., cons. 1953-96). Home: 25 Chestnut Terr Newton MA 02159

KELLISON, DONNA LOUISE GEORGE, accountant, educator; b. Hugoton, Kans., Oct. 16, 1950; d. Donald Richard and Zepha Louise (Lowry) George. BA in Elem. Edn. with honors, Anderson (Ind.) U., 1972; MS in Elem. Edn., Ind. U., 1981. CPA, Ind.; lic. tchr., Ind. Tchr. elem. Maconaquah Sch. Corp., Bunker Hill, Ind., 1972-73; office mgr. Eskew & Gresham, CPA's, Louisville, Ky., 1973-78; para-profl. Blue & Co., Indpls., 1979-83, tax compliance specialist, 1983-84, tax sr., 1984-86, tax supr., 1986-87, tax mgr., 1987-90, tax prin., 1990-92, tax sr. mgr., 1992-94, dir., 1995—. Vol. Children's Clinic, Indpls., 1985—; chairperson Most Wanted campaign Am. Cancer Soc., 1995; bd. dirs. Indpls. Estate Planning Coun., 1995-96, sec., 1996—. Mem. AICPA, Ind. CPA Soc. (tax inst. com. 1989-93, govt. rels. com. 1994—), Ind. Tax Inst. (chairperson 1993). Presbyterian. Home: 9318 Embers Way Indianapolis IN 46250-3419 Office: Blue & Co PO Box 80069 Indianapolis IN 46280-0069

KELLOGG, ANN MARIE, publishing executive, consultant; b. Pitts., Oct. 2, 1939; m. Eugene Krasnoff (div.); children: Peter Lawrence, Stephanie Ann; m. Jack L. Kellogg, Nov. 10, 1979. BS, U. Wis., 1961. Prodn. and bus. mgr. Collective Advt., Inc., Princeton, N.J., 1973-83; dir. pubs. Community Pride, Inc., Princeton, 1983-87, Exclusive Publs., Ltd./Relocation Guides, Boca Raton, Fla., 1987-94. Chair Abortion Law Reform Com. of N.J., Princeton, 1967-71. Mem. Soroptimist Internat. (pres. Pompano Beach chpt. 1991-92). Home and Office: 4 Clarendon Ct Williamsburg VA 23188

KELLOGG, JOAN BARRETT, grief therapist, counseling astrologer, educator, author; b. Evanston, Ill., Aug. 3, 1947; d. Arthur Merritt Jr. and Ruth Eleanor (Hammond) Barrett; children: Christine Elizabeth, Caroline Elizabeth. AA in Bus. Real Estate, William R. Harper Coll., 1982, AS in Engring. and Math., 1982; BA in Psychology with honors, Roosevelt U., 1985, MA in Thanatology, 1988; postgrad., Ill. Sch. Profl. Psychology, 1995—. Cert. transpersonal therapist, profl. cert. in astrology. Hotel/real estate mgr. Ambassador Hotels, Chgo., 1974-76, Deer Path Inn, Lake Forest, Ill., 1976-77, Am. Invsco, Chgo., 1977-78; ptnr. The Concord Group, Barrington, Ill., 1979-88; pvt. practice as counseling astrologer Barrington, Ill., 1979—, pvt. practice as grief therapist, 1988—; coord. Cmty. Bereavement Support Groups Hospice Northeastern Ill., Barrington, 1987-89, Rainbows for all Children, Barrington, 1988-90; developer The Goddess Network, 1990—; cons. Compassionate friends, Arlington Heights, Ill., 1995, 96. Author: The Yod: It's Esoteric Meaning, 1989; contbr. articles to profl. jours. Mem. HIV Coalition, Arlington Heights, 1995—; mem. Ct. Appointed Spl. Advocate (CASA), Lake County, Ill., chmn. Friends of CASA, 1995—; forum dir. Sacred Psychology, Microsoft New Age Network. Mem. APA, ACA, Nat. Assn. Grief Therapists, Nat. Coun. for Geocosmic Rsch., Am. Fedn. Astrologers, Inc. (dir. 1992-94), Porfl. Astrologers, Inc. (honors in lectures 1992), Internat. Soc. for Astrol. Rsch., Lake County Counselors Assn. (pres. 1996—). Episcopalian. Office: 135 Park Ave Barrington IL 60010-4354

KELL-SMITH, CARLA SUE, federal agency administrator; b. Highland Park, Mich., Sept. 15, 1952; d. Carl William and Margie May (Cannon) Bodner; m. Joseph Mark Kell, Oct. 10, 1971 (div. Dec. 1980); m. Richard Charles Smith, Jan. 28, 1989; Student, Anderson Coll., 1970-71, Glendale Coll., 1976-77, Ariz. State U., 1978-79, Mesa Coll., 1979-80. Private tutor English, Fed. Republic of Germany, 1971-74; office mgr. Bell & Schore, Rochester, Mich., 1974-75, COL Press, Phoenix, 1978-80; publicity mgr. O'Sullivan Woodside & Col, Phoenix, 1980-81, gen. mgr., 1982-84; pub. relations/promotion cons. GPI Publs., Cupertino, Calif., 1985; pub. cons., 1985-88; project adminstr. FAA, 1986—; account coord. Bernard Hodes Advt., Tempe, Ariz., 1981; cons. freelance mktg., Phoenix, 1983. Vol., Fiesta Bowl Parade Com., Phoenix, 1983, FAA Airport Improvement Project. Office: 1200 Bayhill Dr Ste 224 San Bruno CA 94066

KELLUM, CARMEN KAYE, apparel company executive; b. Greensburg, Pa., Oct. 15, 1952; d. Bruce Lowell and Mildred Louise (Montgomery) Taylor; m. John Douglas Kellum, Aug. 2, 1975 (div. May 1987). Student, MacMurray Coll., 1971-72, Elgin Community Coll.; AA, Coll. DuPage, 1975; BA with honors, Nat. Coll. Edn., 1978. Cert. tchr. Aide occupational therapy Mercy Ctr., Aurora, Ill., 1972-76; tchr. behavior disorders Lake Park High Sch., Roselle, Ill., 1978-80, Salk Pioneer Sch., Roselle, 1980-81; mgr. So-Fro Fabrics Stores, Lombard, Joliet & Chgo., Ill., 1981-84; offshore coord. Florsheim Shoe Co., Chgo., 1984-90; mgr. Linens N Things, Rolling Meadows, Ill., 1990-91; mgr. House of Fabrics, Aurora, Ill., 1992-94, Glen Ellyn, Ill., 1994; ops. mgr. T.J. Maxx, Naperville, Ill., 1994—. Mem. Orton Dyslexia Soc., Nat. Assn. Female Exec., Kappa Delta Pi. Lutheran. Home: 30 W 156 Wood Ct and Hwy 59 PO Box 8137 Bartlett IL 60103 Office: T J Maxx 540 S Rt 59 Naperville IL 60540

KELLY, ANGELA MARY, photographer, educator; b. Belfast, No. Ireland, Oct. 25, 1950; arrived in U.S., 1980; d. Patrick Joseph and Mary Frances (Somerville) K.; m. Bernard Joseph Hasken, Sept. 25, 1982; 1 child, Emma. Diploma in edn., Mary Ward Coll., Nottingham, Eng., 1972; diploma in photography, Trent Poly., Nottingham, 1975; MA, Columbia Coll., Chgo., 1989. Lectr. I Nelson (Eng.) & Colne Coll., 1975-78; lectr. II Manchester (Eng.) Met. U., 1978-80; vis. artist Sch. Art Inst. Chgo., 1980-94, assoc. prof., 1992-94; instr. Columbia Coll., Chgo., 1985-89; assoc. prof., coord. MFA program Rochester (N.Y.) Inst. Tech., 1994—; co-chair Randolph St. Gallery exhibns., Chgo., 1990-94; coord. women's caucus program Soc. Photographic Edn., 1993-94, MFA photo program Rochester Inst. Tech., 1995—; juror nat. grad. seminar NYU, 1995. Participant, exhibitor: Spaces for the Self: The Symbolic Imagery of Place, 1995, Visions of Hope and Despair, 1995; participant: (photo history book) A History of Women Photographers, 1995; curator, exhibn. organizer: (multi-media art exhibit) When Push Comes To Shove, 1993. Vol. photographer Rainbow House Shelter, Chgo., 1993-94. NEA Artists fellow, 1987, Ill. Arts Coun. Artists fellow, 1989; recipient Focus Infinity Fund commn., 1992. Fellow Inst. of Incorporated Photographers; mem. Soc. Photographic Edn. (mem. womens caucus conf. program coord. 1993). Office: Rochester Inst Tech 70 Lomb Memorial Dr Rochester NY 14625

KELLY, ANN ELISE, small business owner, public relations consultant; b. Grand Rapids, Mich., Feb. 19, 1963; d. Robert Floyd and Elise Williams (Beckwith) Cole; m. Mamadou Danfa, Oct. 29, 1987 (div. Mar. 1995); 1 child, Marieme Elise; m. David Michael Kelly, June 8, 1996. BA in Internat. Mktg., Ea. Mich. U., 198. Cert. in practical comml. French, Paris C. of C. Mktg. asst. Computrol, Inc., Belleville, Mich., 1984-85; internat. journeyman fgn. mission bd. So. Bapt. Conv., Dakar, Senegal, 1986-88; sr. sales counselor RKL Cemetery Mgmt., Midland, Mich., 1988-89; mktg. specialist Jackson (Mich.)-Hillsdale Cmty. Mental Health, 1989-94; owner, office mgr. Superior Finish Floors, Inc., Jackson, 1993-95; owner, cons. Verve Comm., Jackson, 1994—; instr. comm. Jackson Bus. Inst., 1995; instr. pub. rels. Jackson C.C., 1996; vol. Transport, Educate, Activate, Motivate Coun. for People with Disabilities Jackson, 1993, Home of My Own Com., Jackson, 1996. Vol. spkr.'s bur. United Way, Jackson, 1990-94; spkr. Mich. Assn. Rehab. Facilities, Detroit, 1992; instr. CPR, ARC, Jackson, 1993—. Mem. Jackson Bus. and Profl. Women (corr. sec. 1991-92, chmn. individual devel. 1992-93, state individual devel. spkr. award 1991), Christian Bus. Women's Club. Office: Verve Comm 701 S West Ave Jackson MI 49203

KELLY, ANNE CATHERINE, retired city official; b. Buffalo, Mar. 6, 1916; d. John Patrick and Elizabeth Marie (Edwards) Donohue; m. Thomas Edward Kelly, Apr. 19, 1941 (dec. 1993); children: Maureen Anne Kelly, Michael Thomas, Edward John, Kevin Joseph, Theresa Elizabeth Callahan. Student SUNY-Buffalo. Tchr., St. Teresa Sch., Buffalo, 1956-64; clk. City of Buffalo, 1964, sec. to comptroller, 1967-70, coun. clk., 1970-76, sr. coun. clk., 1976-81. Com. woman N.Y. Democratic Com., 1970-87, mem. exec. bd., 1970-87; vice chmn. Erie County Dem. Com., 1985-87; past pres. Mercy League of Buffalo Mercy Hosp., Nash Ladies Guild, South Side Dem. Club; mem. Women for Downtown Buffalo. Roman Catholic. Clubs: Daus. of Erin, Nash Ladies. Lodge: KC (past pres. Nash guild). Home: 9 Haig Pl Apt 404 Dunedin FL 34698-8547

KELLY, BARBARA JEANA, physical education educator; b. Dover, Del., Sept. 24, 1933; d. Edward and Viola H. (Chase) K. BS, Bridgewater Coll., 1955; MA, U. Md., 1961; PhD, U. Del., 1972. Tchr., coach Caesar Rodney H.S., Camden, Del., 1955-60, Claymont (Del.) H.S., 1961-62; mem. faculty dept. phys. edn. U. Del., Newark, 1992—; vis. lectr. All China Sports Fedn., Beijing, Xian and Shanghai, 1992. Author: Issues in Physical Education Studies, 1993; contbg. author: The 20th Century: Great Athletes, 1992, 94, Wellness A Way of Life, 1992. Recipient Pathfinder award Nat. Assn. for Girls and Women's Sports, 1994. Mem. AAHPERD, Ea. Assn. Phys. Edn. for College women (v.p. 1990-92), Internat. Assn. for Phys. Edn. aand Sports for Girls and Women (U.S. rep. 1994-97, internat. v.p. 1996—), Del. Nature Soc., Del. Hist. Soc., Phi Kappa Phi (honoree), Psi Delta Kappa (honoree). Office: U Del Carpenter Sports Bldg Newark DE 19716

KELLY, CAROL WHITE, company executive; b. Shreveport, La., Dec. 23, 1946; d. Verlin Ralph and Mary Louise (Humphries) White; m. James Patrick Kelly, June 6, 1968; children: Mary Louise, Christopher John. BA, Centenary Coll. La., Shreveport, 1968. Corp. sec., treas. Kelly Law Firm P.C., Atlanta, 1986—. Mem. NAFE, Ga. Baptist Med. Guild (life), Atlanta Hist. Soc., Atlanta Ballet Guild (life), Internat. Platform Assn., High Mus. Art, Episcopal Ch. Women (sec.-treas. 1976-80), Chi Omega Alumnae Assn. (pres. 1979-80). Office: Kelly Law Firm PC Ste 1510 200 Galleria Pky NW Atlanta GA 30339-5946

KELLY, CHRISTINE ANN, small business owner, educator; b. Bklyn., May 11, 1952; d. William John and Joan Ellen (Sullivan) K. AAS in Acctg., Kingsborough Community Coll., 1973; BS in Phys. Edn., Bklyn. Coll., 1976. Cert. physical edn. tchr., N.Y. Head softball coach C.W. Post Coll., Greenvale, N.Y., 1979-84; sales mgr. Karnival Sports Ctr., Bklyn., 1984-88; owner, founder Shortstop Silkscreening, S.I., N.Y., 1988—; tchr. St. Edmund High Sch., Bklyn., 1979-81; adj. lectr. Kingsborough Community Coll., Bklyn., 1984—; head coach softball Empire State Games, N.Y., 1987-89. Bd. dir. holiday basketball tournament Tournament of Champions, N.Y., 1986—. Mem. Screen Printing Assn. Internat., N.Y. Bd. Ofcls. for Women Sports. Democrat. Roman Catholic. Office: Shortstop Silkscreening 1255 Bay St Staten Island NY 10305-3111

KELLY, CHRISTINE MARIE, curriculum director; b. Chgo., Sept. 22, 1941; d. Stanley Anthony and Irene Maarie (Kantorowski) Wasielewski; m. Bernard James Kelly, Aug. 21, 1965; children: Robert James, Margaret Ann, Timothy James. BA in Math., De Paul U., 1963; MEd, Nat. Coll. Edn., 1980; EdD, Nat. Lewis U., 1993. Tchr. math. Resurrection H.S., Chgo., 1963-67, 80-94; substitute tchr. H.S. Dist. 214, Arlington Heights, Ill., 1970-80; coord. ACT rev. series High Sch. Dist. 214, Arlington Heights, Ill., 1985-93; cons. study skills Elk Grove High Sch., Elk Gorve Village, Ill., 1991; curriculum dir. Resurrection High Sch., 1994—. Tchr. religion St. Zachary Ch., Des Plaines, Ill., 1984, 93, dir. youth ministry, 1972-80, adult religious edn., 1993—. Mem. AAUW, ASCD, Ill. ASCD, Nat. Cath. Edn. Assn., Nat. Coun. Tchrs. Math., Ill. Coun. Tchrs. Math., No. Ill. Math. Educators, Kappa Delta Pi. Roman Catholic. Home: 480 Florian Dr Des Plaines IL 60016-5716 Office: Resurrection High Sch 7500 W Talcott Ave Chicago IL 60631-3705

KELLY, EILEEN PATRICIA, management educator; b. Steubenville, Ohio, Oct. 24, 1955; d. Edward Joseph and Mary Bernice (Cassidy) K. BS, Coll. Steubenville, 1978; MA, U. Cin., 1979, PhD, 1982. LPA, Ohio; sr. profl. in human resources. Lectr. U. Cin., 1981-82; asst. prof. bus. Creighton U., Omaha, 1982-87, chmn. mgmt., mktg. and systems dept., 1986-88, assoc. prof., 1987-88, coordinator project Minerva, 1987-88; assoc. prof. La. State U., Shreveport, 1988-93, chmn. dept. mgmt. and mktg., 1988-93; assoc. prof. Ithaca (N.Y.) Coll., 1993—, chmn. mgmt. dept., 1993-95; comml. arbitrator, 1988—. Contbr. articles to profl. jours. and acad. presentations. Mem. Acad. Mgmt., Acad. Legal Studies in Bus., Soc. Human Resource Mgmt., Soc. for Bus. Ethics, Soc. for History in the Fed. Govt., Beta Gamma Sigma (faculty adviser 1985-88, 92-93). Roman Catholic. Office: Ithaca Coll Sch Bus Ithaca NY 14850

KELLY, EILEEN PATRICIA, computer programmer and analyst; b. Abington, Pa., Jan. 3, 1965; d. William Joseph and Phyllis (Boutcher) K. BS, Beaver Coll., 1986. Designer Automated Sys. Inc., Blue Bell, Pa., 1986-88; programmer Analysis & Tech., Mt. Laurel, N.J., 1988, Drug Scan, Inc., Warminster, Pa., 1991-93; programmer, analyst Profl. Press, Willow Grove, Pa., 1988-90, Nat. Sch. Bds. Assn., Alexandria, Va., 1993—. Office: Nat Sch Bds Assn 1680 Duke St Alexandria VA 22314

KELLY, GAY ANNE, social worker, educator; b. Peoria, Ill., Nov. 13, 1951; d. Walter Reuel and Ada Frances (Dixon) Wright; children: James, N. Jason, Justin; m. Kevin J. Kelly, May 14, 1994. AA, Lincoln Land C.C., 1975; BA in Child Family Comty. Svc., U. Ill. Sangamon campus, 1978; MEd, U. Ill., 1990. Cert. child protective investigator, child devel. specialist II, Ill. Case coord. Jacksonville (Ill.) Area Assn. Retarded Citizens, 1975-76; surrogate parent/ednl. advocate Ill. State Bd. Edn., Vermillion County, 1977-79; child care specialist Parents Anonymous, Champaign, Ill., 1990-91, parent facilitator, 1991-93; child devel. specialist Devel. Svcs. Ctr., Champaign, 1990-94; child protective investigator Ill. Dept. Children and Family Svcs., Urbana, 1994—; parent group facilitator, sponsor Parents Anonymous, Champaign, Ill., 1990-92; vol. EMT Midleford Vol. Ambulance, Potomac, Ill., 1986-89; surrogate parent/ednl. advocate Ill. State Bd. Edn., Vermillion County, 1986-89; grad. rsch. asst. dept. spl. edn. U. Ill., Champaign, 1987-90; v.p., rep. dept. spl. edn. Coun. Grad. Students in Edn., U. Ill., Champaign, 1987-90. Sec. Middlefork Twp. Vol. Ambulance, Potomac, Ill., 1987-89. Grantee Kappa Delta Pi, U. Ill., Champaign, 1990; Hilton-Perkins scholar, 1993. Mem. Coun. Exceptional Children (div. phys. handicaps, div. mental retardation, div. early childhood), Ill. Div. Early Childhood, Kappa Delta Pi. Republican. Mem. LDS Ch. Home: 1706 Nancy BethSt Champaign IL 61821 Office: Ill Dept Children and Fam Svcs 508 S RaceSt Champaign IL 61821-2099

KELLY, JANICE HELEN, elementary school educator; b. Akron, Ohio, Nov. 28, 1951; d. Joe Ralph and Barbara Ann (Goins) Long; m. W. Gary Kelly, May 10, 1973; children: Benjamin, Chad. BS in Elem. Edn., Akron U., 1984; M in Edn., Kent (Ohio) State U., 1994. Tchr. Suffield United C.C. Coop., Suffield, Ohio, 1984-86, Mogadore (Ohio) Local Schs., 1986—; cadre mem. Summit County Tech. Acad., Cuyahoga Falls, Ohio, 1994; participant Nat. Bd. Profl. Tech. Stds., 1996. Mem., tchr. Randolph (Ohio) United Meth. Ch., 1973—. Recipient Outstanding Educator award Somers Elem. PTA, Mogadore, 1989; Eisenhower grantee Kent State U., 1990-92, Tech., Industry, Environ. Edn. grantee Gen Corp, 1993. Mem. ASCD, Ohio Edn. Assn., Mogadore Edn. Assn. (sec. 1990-92, v.p. 1995—), Sci. Edn. Coun. Ohio. Home: 534 Hartville Rd Atwater OH 44201-9785 Office: Somers Elementary School 3600 Herbert St Mogadore OH 44260-1125

KELLY, JUDITH JOHANNA COVA, elementary language arts consultant; b. Detroit, Jan. 27, 1947; d. Vasile and Margaret Ilene (Gehrke) Cova; m. Daniel Ward Golds, Mar. 19, 1966 (div.); 1 child, Jeffrey Alan; m. Michael Thomas Kelly, Jan. 3, 1981. BS, Wayne State U., 1972; MA in Reading, Ea. Mich. U., 1977. From pre-sch. tchr. to chpt. I reading tchr. Monroe (Mich.) Pub. Schs., 1972-91, elem. lang. arts cons., 1991—; founder, facilitator Monroe County Tchrs. Exploring Lang. & Lit., 1990—; co-facilitator Mich. English Lang. Arts Framework project Monroe Pub. Schs., 1994-96. Coord. African-Am. Read-In, Monroe, 1994-96. Fellow Ea. Mich. Writing Project, 1993, 94. Mem. Internat. Reading Assn. (conf. presenter 1990), Nat. Coun. Tchrs. English, Whole Lang. Umbrella (conf. co-chair 1995), Mich. Coun. Tchrs. English (conf. presenter 1994), Mich. Reading Assn. (conf. presenter 1990, workshop presenter Monroe County Reading Coun. 1993-94). Office: Monroe Pub Schs 908 E 2nd St Monroe MI 48161-1950

KELLY, JULIA B., psychotherapist, counselor; b. Calhoun, Ga., May 30, 1950; d. Herman R. and Inez I. (Pruitt) Bennett; m. Andrew J. Kelly; 1 child: Michelle. PhD, Logos Grad. Sch., 1994. Adminstr. asst. Mount Paran Ch. of God, Atlanta, 1980-90; owner Daystar Found. Counseling Ctr., Marietta, Ga., 1990—. Rschr., editor: Post Traumatic Stress, 1992; editor: Protocol for Counselors, 1993, Clinical Treatment Protocol, 1992. Mem. Am. Assn. Christian Counselors, Ga. Christian Counselors Assn., Ga. Bd. Examiners for Christian Counselors and Therapists (exec. dir. 1992), Cobb City C. of C. Home: 1018 Powder Springs Dr Marietta GA 30064-3936 Office: Day Star Found 302 Old Clay St Marietta GA 30060

KELLY, KATE, writer, book packager, editor; b. Baraboo, Wis., Jan. 11, 1958; d. John Michael and Berneice Emily (Schlemmer) K.; m. Carleton Cato Ealy, Mar. 22, 1986; 1 child, Kendra Leigh. Student, Sch. for Irish Studies, Dublin, Ireland, 1978-79; BA, Yale U., 1980. Editl. asst. William Morrow & Co., N.Y.C., 1980-82; editor, sr. editor, exec. editor Facts On File, Inc., N.Y.C., 1983-89; exec. editor Prentice Hall Gen. Reference, N.Y.C., 1989-91; co-founder, prin. Irving Place, Inc., N.Y.C., 1991—; cons. Swanston Pub., London, 1992-94, Kid Stuff Multimedia, Trumbull, Conn., 1994-96. Author: (book series) Scholastic Homework Reference Series, 1992-96, Primary School Basics, 1995; editor: (reference books) Encyclopedia Mysteriosa, 1994 (Edgar award 1995), To the ends of the Earth, 1986 (Geo Soc. Chgo. award. 1986). Mentor Tashua Sch., Trumbull, 1992—, mem. PTA, 1991—; organizer Tashua-Princeton (N.J.) Study Group, Trumbull and Princeton, 1994-95; tchr. Christian edn. Grace Episcopal Ch., Trumbull, 1992—. Mem. Women in Publishing, Women in New Media, Yale Club N.Y. Episcopalian. Home: 129 Beechwood Ave Trumbull CT 06611 Office: Irving Place Inc 632 Broadway New York NY 10003

KELLY, KATHLEEN S(UE), educator; b. Duluth, Minn., Aug. 6, 1943; d. Russell J. and Idun N. Mehrman; m. George F. Kelly, Apr. 29, 1961; children: Jodie A., Jennifer L. AA, Moorpark (Calif.) Coll., 1971; BS in Journalism, U. Md., College Park, 1973, MA in Pub. Rels., 1979, PhD in Pub. Communication, 1989. Accredited pub. rels.; cert. fundraising exec. Dir. pub. info. Bowie (Md.) State U., 1974-77; asst. to dean, instr. Coll. Journalism U. Md., College Park, 1977-79, assoc. dir. devel., 1979-82; v.p. Mt. Vernon Coll., Washington, 1982-83; dir. devel. U. Md., College Park, 1983-85, assoc. dean, lectr. Coll. Journalism, 1985-88, asst. dean Coll. Bus. and Mgmt., 1988-90; prof. U. S.W. La., 1991—; cons. NASA, NIH, Mt. St. Marys Coll., 1986—; lectr. CASE, Pub. Rels. Soc. Am., 1987—. Author: Fund Raising and Public Relations: A Critical Analysis, 1991, Building Fund-Raising Theory, 1994. Named PRIDE Book award winner Speech Comm. Assn., 1991, article award winner 1994, John Grenzebach award winner for rsch. on philanthropy CASE and Am. Assn. Fund-Raising Coun., 1991, PRIG award winner for outstanding dissertation Internat. Comm. Assn., 1990, winner 1995 Pathfinder award Inst. for Pub. Rels. Rsch. and Edn. Fellow Pub. Rels. Soc. (chmn. ednl. and cultural orgn. sect. 1989, pres. Md. chpt. 1986-87, Pres.' Cup 1981, nat. bd. dirs. 1994-96); mem. Nat. Soc. Fund Raising Execs. (mem. rsch. coun.), Coun. Advancement and Support of Edn. (women's forum 1983), Phi Kappa Phi. Democrat. Home: 1033 Rue Bois De Chene Breaux Bridge LA 70517-6735 Office: U SW La Dept Comm PO Box 43650 Lafayette LA 70504-3650

KELLY, KATHLEEN SUZANNE, marketing professional; b. Inglewood, Calif., Dec. 20, 1966; d. Robert Duane and Anne Margaret (Halpin) K. BS, U. So. Calif., L.A., 1989. Asst. media buyer Kelly, Scott & Madison, Chgo., 1989-90; pub. rels. rep. In-N-Out Burger, Baldwin Park, Calif., 1990-91, interim mktg. dir., 1991-92, advt. and pub. rels. adminstr., 1992-93; project mgr. L.A. Unified Sch. Dist., 1993—; cons. in field. Pres. bd. dirs. Haven House, 1995-97. Mem. NAFE, AAUW, Pub. Rels. Soc. Am., Am. Mgmt. Assn., Trojan Jr. Aux., San Gabriel Valley Trojan Club (bd. dirs.), U. So. Calif. Trojan Club-SGV. Republican. Roman Catholic. Home: 1111 Cresthaven Dr Los Angeles CA 90042-1431 Office: Sch Vol Program 450 N Grand Ave Bldg G-253 Los Angeles CA 90012-2100

KELLY, KRISTINE JOAN, telecommunications industry executive; b. Easton, Pa., Mar. 24, 1951; d. Edward and Edith M. (Vosper) Falco; m. Eric V. Ottervik, Dec. 3, 1976 (div. Jan. 1987); m. Gerard J. Kelly, Aug. 22, 1992. AA, Northampton Coll., 1981, AAS, 1980; BA summa cum laude, Lehigh U., 1984. Mgr. telecommunications dept. Lehigh U., Bethlehem, Pa., 1972-80, dir. telecommunications dept., 1984-86; sr. cons. Flack & Kurtz Cons. Engrs., N.Y.C., 1986-88; asst. v.p. worldwide telecommunications Chem. Bank, N.Y.C., 1988-89, v.p. telecom. svcs., 1989-94; v.p. global tech. J.P. Morgan, N.Y.C., 1994—. Recipient Achievement award Women's Inner Circle; Williams scholar Lehigh U., 1982-84. Mem. IEEE (assoc.), NAFE, Phi Beta Kappa. Home: 6 Glenmere Dr Chatham NJ 07928-1308 Office: JP Morgan 60 Wall St New York NY 10260-0060

KELLY, LOIS, technical company executive. BA, U. N.H.; grad. bus. degree, Harvard U. With AT&T; v.p. Creamer Dickson Basford, 1982-90; pres. Potter Hazelhurst Pub. Rels., 1990-93; sr. v.p. high tech. divsn. Weber Group, Inc., Cambridge, Mass., 1993—. Office: The Weber Group Inc 101 Main St Cambridge MA 02142*

KELLY, LUCIE STIRM YOUNG, nursing educator; b. Stuttgart, Germany, May 2, 1925; came to U.S., 1929; d. Hugo Karl and Emilie Rosa (Engel) Stirm; m. J. Austin Young, Aug. 30, 1946 (div. Feb. 1971); m. Thomas Martin Kelly, 1972; 1 child by previous marriage, Gay Aleta (Mrs. Donald Meyer). BS, U. Pitts., 1947, MLitt, 1957, PhD (HEW fellow), 1965; D in Nursing Edn. (hon.), U. R.I., 1977; LHD (hon.), Georgetown U., 1983; DSc (hon.), Widener U., 1984, U. Mass., 1989; D of Pub. Svc. (hon.), Am. U., 1985; DHL (hon.), SUNY, 1996. Instr. nursing McKeesport (Pa.) Hosp., 1953-57, asst. adminstr. nursing, 1966-69; asst. prof. nursing U. Pitts., 1957-64, asst. dean, 1965; prof., chmn. nursing dept. Calif. State U., Los Angeles, 1969-72; co-project dir. curriculum research Nat. League for Nursing, 1973-74; project dir. patient edn., office consumer health edn., also adj. asso. prof. community medicine Coll. Medicine and Dentistry N.J.-Rutgers Med. Sch., 1974-75; prof. pub. health and nursing Sch. Pub. Health and Sch. Nursing Columbia U., N.Y.C., 1975-90, prof. emeritus Sch Pub. Health, Sch. Nursing, 1990—, assoc. dean acad. affairs Sch. Pub. Health, 1988-90, hon. prof. nursing edn. Tchrs. Coll., 1977-93, acting head div. health adminstrn. Sch. Pub. Health, 1980-81, 86-88; on leave as exec. dir. Mid-Atlantic Regional Nursing Assn., 1981-82; cons. U. Nev., Las Vegas, 1970-72, Ball State U., Ind., 1971, Long Beach (Calif.) Naval Hosp., 1971-72, Travis AFB, Calif., 1972, Brentwood VA Hosp., L.A., 1971-72, Ctrl. Nursing Office VA, Washington, 1971-94, N.J. Dept. Higher Edn., 1974-78, John Wiley Pub., 1974-76, Sch. Nursing Am. U. Beirut; mem. spl. med. adv. group VA Dept. Medicine and Surgery, Washington, 1980-84; cons. nursing com. AMA, 1971-74, Citizen's Com. for Children, N.Y.C.; v.p. Pa. Health Coun., 1968-69; mem. adv. com. physicians assts. Calif. Bd. Med. Examiners, adv. com. Cancer Soc. L.A., 1970-72, com. nursing VA, Washington, 1971-74, regional med. programs, Pa., 1967-69, Calif. 1970-72; mem. spl. adv. coun. on med. licensure and profl. conduct N.Y. State Assembly, 1977-79, mem. nat. adv. com. Encore (nat. YWCA post-mastectomy group rehab. project), 1977-83; assoc. mem. N.Y. Acad. Medicine, 1988-90; mem. ethics com. Palisades Gen. Med. Ctr., 1993—, bd. govs., 1995—; lectr., cons., guest Beijing Med. Coll., China, 1982, Aga Khan U., Pakistan, 1990; bd. visitors U. Pitts. Sch. Nursing, 1986-93; mem. editl. adv. bd. Am. Jour. Pub. Heallth, 1992, chair, 1993—; nat. and internat. lectr. in field; chair adv. com. grad. program in pub. health U. Medicine and Dentistry of N.J., 1995—. Author: Dimensions of Profl. Nursing, 7th edit., 1995, The Nursing Experience: Trends, Challenges, Transitions, 3d edit., 1996; contbg. editor Jour. Nursing Adminstrn., 1975-82; mem. editl. bd. Nurse Practitioner, 1976-82; columnist Nursing Outlook, editor-in-chief, 1982-91; mem. bd. advisors Nurses Almanac, 1978, Nurse Manager's Handbook, 1979, Nursing Administration Handbook, 1992; mem. editl. adv. bd. Am. Health, 1981-91, Nursing and Health Care, 1991-95; contbr. articles to prof. jours. Bd. dirs. ARC, Los Angeles, 1971-72, Vis. Nurse Service N.Y., 1980—, mem. exec. com., chmn. human resources, 1989—; bd. dirs. Concern for Dying, 1983-89; trustee Calif. State Coll. Los Angeles Found., 1971-72, U. Pitts, 1984-90, mem. exec. com. 1988-90; chair bd. visitors U. Pitts. Sch. Pub. Health, 1988; bd. visitors U. Miami Sch. Nursing, 1986—; mem. health services com. Children's Aid Soc., N.Y., 1978-84; v.p. Am. Nurses Found., 1980-82; mem. nat. adv. council on nurse tng. HRA, 1981-85. Named Outstanding Alumna U. Pitts. Sch. Nursing, 1966, Pa. Nurse of Yr., 1967, to Roll of Honor N.J. State Nurses Assn., 1990; recipient Disting. Alumna award U. Pitts. Sch. Edn., 1981, Shaw medal Boston Coll., 1985, Bicentennial Medallion of Distinction, U. Pitts., 1987, R. Louise McManus Medallion for Disting. Svc. to Nursing, Tchrs. Coll. Columbia U., 1987, Dean's Disting. Svc. award Columbia Sch. Pub. Health, 1995, Second Century award in health care Columbia U. Sch. Nursing, 1996. Fellow Am. Acad. Nursing; mem. ANA (dir. 1978-82, Hon. Recognition award 1992), APHA (Ruth Freeman Pub. Health Nursing award 1993), Pa. Nurses Assn. (pres. 1966-69), Nat. League Nursing (bd. govs. 1991-95), Nurses Ednl. Funds Bd., U . Pitts. Sch. Nursing Alumni (pres. 1959), Am. Hosp. Assn. (com. chmn. 1967-68), Assn. Grad. Faculty Cmty. Health/Pub. Health Nursing (v.p. 1980-81), Sigma Theta Tau (sr. editor Image 1978-81, pres.-elect 1981-83, pres. 1983-85, nat. campaign chair Ctr. for Nursing Scholarship 1987-89, chair devel. com. 1989-95, Mentor award 1985, 93), Pi Lambda Theta, Alpha Tau Delta (Cert. of Merit). Home: 6040 Boulevard E Apt 11G West New York NJ 07093-3809

KELLY, MARGARET BLAKE, accountant, state official; b. Crystal City, Mo., Sept. 17, 1935; d. Emory and Florine (Stovesand) Blake; m. William Clark Kelly; children: Kevin, Tom, John. BSBA, U. Mo., 1957; MBA, S.W. Mo. State U., 1975; D in Bus. Administrn. (hon.), S.W. Bapt. U., 1986. CPA, Mo.; cert. govt. fin. mgr. Acct. Williams-Keepers, Columbia and Jefferson City, Mo., McNabb, Westermann, Mitchell & Branstetter, Springfield, Mo., Fox & Co., Springfield; county auditor Cole County, Mo., 1982-84; state auditor State of Mo., Jefferson City, 1984—. Rep. nom. for lt. gov., 1992; Rep. candidate for U.S. House Governor Mo., 1996. Recipient Faculty-Alumni Gold Medal award U. Mo., 1985. Mem. AICPA, Assn. Govt. Accts., Nat. State Auditors Assn. (past pres.), Nat. Assn. State Auditors, Comptrs., and Treas. (first v.p.), Am. Soc. Women Accts., Am. Women Soc. CPAs, Mo. Soc. Cert. Pub. Accts., Women Execs. in State Govt., Govt. Fin. Officers Assn., Delta Gamma. Republican. Baptist. Office: Friends of Margaret Kelly PO Box 104613 Jefferson City MO 65110

KELLY, MARGUERITE STEHLI, fashion executive, consultant; b. N.Y.C., June 9, 1931; d. Henry E. and Grace (Hays) Stehli; m. Charles J. Kelly, Jr., Dec. 23, 1962; children: Marguerite Grace, Lisa Stehli. BA, Bryn Mawr Coll., 1953. Exec. trainee Macy's, N.Y.C., 1953-54, asst. buyer, 1954-57; buyer Bloomingdale's, N.Y.C., 1957-63; pres. Maggie, Inc., Wayzata, Minn., 1964-86; also brs. Maggie, Inc., Georgetown, D.C., 1964-70, Locust Valley, N.Y., 1970-75; ret., 1986; founder Workshop for Learning, 1987—. Mem. com. for spl. fund Foxcroft Sch., Middleburg, Va., 1974-76, trustee, 1978-87; mem. alumnae coun. Brearley Sch., N.Y.C., 1973-75; trustee Abbott Northwestern Hosp., Mpls., 1984-86; co-founder Citizens for Colin Powell Presdl. Draft Movement, 1994—. Episcopalian. Home: 3018 N St NW Washington DC 20007-3404

KELLY, MAXINE ANN, retired property developer; b. Ft. Wayne, Ind., Aug. 14, 1931; d. Victor J. and Marguerite E. (Biebesheimer) Cramer; m. James Herbert Kelly, Oct. 4, 1968 (dec. Apr. 74). BA, Northwestern U., 1956. Sec., Parry & Barns Law Offices, Ft. Wayne, 1951-52; trust sec. Lincoln Nat. Bank & Trust Co., 1956-58; sr. clk. stenographer div. Mental Health, Alaska Dept. Health, Anchorage, 1958-60; office mgr. Langdon Psychiat. Clinic, 1960-70; propr. A-1 Bookkeeping Svc., 1974-75; ptnr. Gonder-Kelly Enterprises & A-is-A Constrn., Wasilla, Alaska, 1965-92; sales assoc. Yukon Realty/Gallery of Homes, Wasilla, 1989; sec. Rogers Realty, Inc., Wasilla, 1989, MMC Constrn., Inc., 1992-96. Dir. Alaska Mental Health Assn., Anchorage, 1960-61; pres., treas. Libertarian Party Anchorage, 1968-69, Alaska Libertarian Party, 1969-70. Mem. AAUW (life), Anchorage C. of C., Whittier Boat Owners Assn. (treas. 1980-84). Home: 8651 Augusta Cir Anchorage AK 99504-4202

KELLY, MOIRA, actress; b. 1969. Student, Marymount Coll. Appeared in films The Boy Who Cried Bitch, Billy Bathgate, The Cutting Edge, Twin Peaks: Fire Walk With Me, Chaplin, With Honors, Little Odessa, The Tie That Binds, (voice) The Lion King; television appearances include (movies) Love Lies and Murder, Daybreak. Office: care Gersh Agy 232 N Canon Dr Beverly Hills CA 90210*

KELLY, NANCY FOLDEN, theatre director; b. Fredericksburg, Va., Oct. 28, 1951; d. Virgil Alvis Jr. and Frances Virginia (DeShazo) Folden; m. Frank R. Kelly, Aug. 11, 1973; 1 child, Katherine Elizabeth Kelly. BA in Theatre Arts, Va. Poly. Inst. and State U., 1973; MFA in Theatre Directing, So. Meth. U., 1975. Coord. student programs Lincoln Ctr. Inst., N.Y.C., 1976-79; dir. N.Y.C. Opera Nat. Co. and edn. dept. Lincoln Ctr., 1979-93, mem. coun. on ednl. programs, 1979-93; mng. dir. Broadway Arts Theatre for Young Audiences, 1994—.

KELLY, NANCY FRIEDA WOLICKI, lawyer; b. Chgo., Sept. 8, 1953; d. Samuel and Ingrid (Rappel) W.; B.A. in Journalism and Sociology, U. Ariz., 1974, J.D., 1977. Bar: Ariz., 1977; law clk. Ariz. Ct. Appeals, 1977-78; legis. asst. fgn. policy and armed svcs. health, staff atty. Billy Carter investigation to U.S. Sen. Dennis DeConcini, 1979-81; staff dir. Senate Subcom. on Alcoholism and Drug Abuse, Washington, 1981-84; mem. staff Senator Gordon J. Humphrey, Washington, 1984-87; coord. adv. com. Voluntary Fgn. U.S. Aid, 1987; sr. analyst legal and drug related issues President's Commn. on the HIV Epidemic, 1987-88; sr. policy analyst Commn. Exec. Legis. Jud. Salaries, 1988-89; counselor Sec. Energy, 1989-93; sr. cons. Kelly, Anderson, Pethick & Assocs., Washington, 1993—. Recipient William Spaid Meml. award U. Ariz. Coll. Law, 1977, Senate commendation for Billy Carter investigation, 1980. Mem. Ariz. Bar Assn., Phi Kappa Phi. Jewish. Office: 1020 19th St NW Ste 800 Washington DC 20036-6101

KELLY, NANNETTE FABRE, art and humanities educator; b. Omaha, Nebr.; d. John Kenneth and Rachel Ann (Fabre) K. BA, Calif. State U., 1980; MA, Claremont Sch. of Theology, 1983; postgrad., Union Inst., 1995—. Art history instr. Calif. State U., Fullerton, 1986-88, Saddleback Coll., Mission Viejo, Calif., 1987, UCLA Extension, 1988, Watterson Coll., West Coving, Calif., 1988; asst. prof. art history, humanities Imperial (Calif.) Valley Coll., 1988—; mgr. Shelby Fine Arts Gallery, San Diego, 1986-88, display designer Pacesetter Pavilion, Costa Mesa, Calif., 1987-89, dir. Imperial Valley Art Gallery, 1988-92, freelance writer, 1992—. Author: Two Irish Women Who Might Also Be French, 1994, Writing Dream Worlds, 1995; solo exhbn. State U. Art Gallery San Diego. Fundraising Chair Imperial Valley Coll. Art Gallery, 1988-92, sen., treas. Acad. Sen., Imperial, 1991-94, co-coord. Humanities Action Comm., 1994-95, co-founder, chair Imperial Valley Literary Soc., 1993—. Recpient 1st prize Art Historical Writing UNC, 1984, 2d prize for Painting Calif. Midwinter Fair, Profl. Divsn., 1989. Mem. Coll. Art Assn., Calif. C. C. Humanities Assn., Imperial Valley Arts Assn. Office: Imperial Valley Coll PO Box 158 Imperial CA 92251

KELLY, PATRICIA ANNE, marketing director, graphic artist; b. Wakefield, Mass., Apr. 28, 1964; d. Edward Joseph and Bernice Audrey (Bennett) K. BA, Flagler Coll., 1986; MBA in Mktg., U. North Fla., 1994. Radio announcer, personality Sta. WMKM-FM, St. Augustine, Fla., 1984, Sta. WAOC-AM, St. Augustine, 1985-86; mktg. cons. Shull Broadcasting, St. Augustine, 1984-85, Sta. WSOS-FM, St. Augustine, 1987, St. Augustine Record, 1989-92; motorsports mktg. dir. St. Augustine Speedway, 1992-94, #12 Nascar Winston Cup-Straight Arrow, St. Augustine, 1994, #31 Nascar Winston Cup, Charlottesville, Va., 1995—; marketing specialist NASCAR, 1996—; cons. in field. Apptd. cons. St. John's County Sports Mktg. Com., St. Augustine, 1994-95; vol. organizer St. Augustine C. of C., 1990-95. Office: Corporate Sports Marketing Lakeside Park Mooresville NC 28115

KELLY, PATRICIA ELLEN, financial analyst; b. Massena, N.Y., Apr. 16, 1958; d. John James and Edith Ellyn (Veitch) K. BS, SUNY, 1979; MS, Western Ill. U., 1980; BS, SUNY, 1986. Dir. athletic programs D'Youville Coll., Buffalo, 1981-83; project mgr. Buffalo & Erie County Pub. Libr., 1983-84, computer operator IBM, Kingston, 1986-87; computer ops. supervisor GTech Corp., Saugerties, N.Y., 1987-88; from computer programmer to adv. fin. analyst IBM, Poughkeepsie, N.Y., 1988—; recreation leader Mohonk Mtn. House, New Paltz, N.Y., 1984—; athletic adv. coun. SUNY Coll., Cortland, 1975-76. Bd. dirs. Massena (N.Y.) Girls Softball League, 1974-76, 81; site selection chair ULster County Habitat for Humanity, Kingston, 1993-95; registration com. Crop Walkathon for Hunger, New Paltz, N.Y., 1994; kids activities com. Taste of New Paltz, 1994; grounds team leader Christmas in April project, Poughkeepsie, 1995. Mem. NAFE, NOW, Cortland State Athletic Club. Democrat. Roman Catholic. Home: 748 Springtown Rd Tillson NY 12486

KELLY, RACHEL CATHERINE BUBAR, association executive; b. Blaine, Maine; d. Benjamin C and Rachel Bubar; m. Henry Kelly; children: Henry Jr., Nicci Kelly Kobritz, David, Lani Star Kelly Swartzentruber. Sudent, Colby Coll.; grad., U. Maine. From tchr. to prin. Pub. Sch. Dist., Brewer, Maine; pres. WCTU Maine, Portland, 1982-88, WCTU U.S., Evanston, Ill., 1988—. Mem. Rep. Bus. and Profl. Women's Club. Mem. NEA, Maine Tchrs. Assn., Pro Life Edn. Assn. (bd. dirs.), Internat. Toastmasters, Alpha Delta Kappa (pres. Portland chpt.). Home: 1732 Chicago Ave Evanston IL 60201 Office: Nat Woman's Christian Temperance Union 1730 Chicago Ave Evanston IL 60201-4502

KELLY, RITA MAE, academic administrator, researcher; b. Waseca, Minn., Dec. 10, 1939; d. John Francis and Agnes Mary (Lorentz) Cawley; m. Vincent Peter Kelly, June 2, 1962; children: Patrick, Kathleen. BA, U. Minn., 1961; MA, U. So. Calif., L.A., 1966, Ind. U., 1964; PhD, Ind. U., 1967. Rsch. scientist Ctr. for Rsch. in Social Systems, 1968-70; sr. rsch. scientist Am. Inst. for Rsch., Inc., Kensington, Md., 1970-72; cons. OEO, 1972-73; pres. Rita Mae Kelly & Assocs., 1973-75; tenured prof. Rutgers U., 1977-79, prof., 1979-82; from tenured to full prof. Sch. Justice Studies Ariz. State U., Tempe, 1982-87, tenured prof. justice studies, pub. affairs, polit. sci. and women's study, 1987-96, chair, dir. Sch. Justice Studies, 1990-95; dean social scis. U. Tex., Dallas, 1996—; mem. credentials com. U.S. Dem. Party, Atlanta, 1988; mem. state com. Ariz. Dem. party, Phoenix, 1988; dist. committeeman Tempe Dist. 27 Dem. Party, 1988; charter mem., hon. bd. dirs. Ariz. Women's Inst., 1988; founding mem. Inst. for Women's Policy Rsch., Washington, 1988, Ariz. Found. for Women, Inc., 1995—; bd. dirs. Ariz. Leadership 2000 Alumni Assn., 1993—; co-dir. Ariz. Leadership 2000 and Beyond, 1993—; co-chair Arizonians for a Healthy Future, 1994-95. Author: (with others) The Making of Political Women: A Study of Socialization and Role Conflict, 1978, Promoting Productivity in the Public Sector: Problems, Strategies, Prospects, 1988, Comparable Worth, Pay Equity, and Public Policy, 1988, (with Mary M. Hale) Gender, Bureaucracy, and Democracy: Careers and Equal Opportunity in the Public Sector, 1989, The Gendered Economy, 1991, Advances in Policy Studies Since 1950, 1992, Gender Power, Leadership and Governance, 1995; editor: book series Women in Politics Series, 1981-88, (with Dennis J. Palumbo) Sage Series in Public Policy, 1989-94, Women & Politics Jour. Dep. gov. Am. Biog. Inst., 1995—; co-chair Airz. Women's Vote Project, 1996—. Internat. Soroptomists of Phoenix, Inc. grantee, 1987, GTE Found. Rsch. grantee, 1988, Ind. U. Rsch. grantee, 1964-65; Ford Found. fellow, 1962-63; recipient Rutgers U. Outstanding Faculty merit award, 1979, All-Am. Women's award, 1985, YWCA Camden County award, 1980; Fulbright award to Brazil, 1991; recipient Aaron Wildovsky award for best book pub. policy, 1992, 93, Outstanding Mentor award Women's Caucus for Polit. Sci., 1991, Miriam Mills award, 1995; U.S. Dept. Labor Step Out grantee, 1993-95. Mem. Am. Polit. Sci. Assn. (chair roundtable 1985, chair B. William Anderson award com. 1983-84, reviewer 1977-78, 83-84, head policy sect. 1989), APA Soc. for Psychol. Study of Social Issues (chair nat. task force on productivity in the pub. sector 1975-80), Am. Soc. for Pub. Adminstrn. (exec. coun. sect. on mgmt. sci. and policy analysis 1986-89, vice chair planning and evaluation com. 1985-86, Achievement award 1981, Disting. Rsch. award for rsch. on women 1991), Internat. Polit. Sci. Assn. (chair com. on status of women 1986-88), Western Polit. Sci. Assn. (pres. 1988-89), Policy Studies Orgn. (pres. 1988-89, Merriam Mills award 1995). Office: U Tex Box 830688 Richardson TX 75083

KELLY, SUE W., congresswoman; b. Lima, Ohio, Sept. 26, 1936; m. Edward; 4 children. BA, Denison U., 1958; MA in Health Advocacy, Sarah Lawrence Coll., 1985. Researcher New England Inst. Med. Rsch., 1958; tchr. John Jay Jr. H.S., 1962-63, Harvey Sch.; real estate rehabilitator, 1963—; campaign coord. Rep. Hamilton Fish, N.Y., 1971-72; intern Ruth Taylor Home, 1973-74; florist, owner Somerstown Flower Shop, 1978-79; patient advocate St. Luke's Hosp., 1984-87; adj. prof. of health advocacy Sarah Lawrence Coll., 1987-92; mem. 104th Congress from 19th N.Y. dist.

U.S. Ho. of Reps., 1995—; mem. Banking & Financial Services subcoms. on capital mrkts., secuities & gov't sponsored enterprises; domestic & international monetary policy; Small Business subcoms. on gov't. programs; regulators & paperwork; Transportation & Infrastructure subcoms. on aviation; railroads. Office: US House Reps 1037 Longworth House Office Bldg Washington DC 20515

KELM, BONNIE G., art museum director, educator; b. Bklyn., Mar. 29, 1947; d. Julius and Anita (Baron) Steiman; m. William G. Malis; 1 child, Michael Darren. BS in Art Edn., Buffalo State U., 1968; MA in Art History, Bowling Green (Ohio) State U., 1975; PhD in Arts Adminstrn., Ohio State U., 1987. Art tchr. Toledo Pub. Schs., 1968-71; ednl. cons. Columbus (Ohio) Mus. Art, 1976-81; prof. art Franklin U., Columbus, 1976-88; legis. coord. Ohio House of Reps., Columbus, 1977; pres. bd. trustees Columbus Inst. for Contemporary Art, 1977-81; tech. asst. cons. Ohio Arts Coun., Columbus, 1984-88; dir. Bunte Gallery Franklin U., Columbus, 1978-88; dir. art mus. Miami U., Oxford, Ohio, 1988-96; assoc. prof. Miami U., 1988-96; dir. Muscarelle Mus. of Art Coll. of William & Mary, 1996—; assoc. prof. art & art history Coll. of WIlliam & Mary, 1996—; grant panelist Ohio Arts Coun., Columbus, 1985-87, 91—; art book reviewer William C. Brown Pub., Madison, Wis., 1985-92; mem. acquisitions adv. bd. Martin Luther King Ctr., Columbus, 1987-88; field reviewer Inst. Mus. Svcs., Washington, 1990—; chairperson grant panel Art in Pub. Places, 1992-95; trustee Ohio Mus. Assn., 1993-96; state apptd. mem. adv. com. Ohio Percent for Art, 1994-96. Author, editor (mus. catalogues) Connections, 1985, Into the Mainstream: Contemporary Folk Art, 1991, Testimony of Images: PreColumbian Art, 1992, Collecting by Design: The Allen Collection, 1994, Photographs by Barbara Hershey: A Retrospective, 1995; contbr. chpt. to book, articles to profl. jours. Founding mem., mem. adv. coun. Columbus Cultural Arts Ctr., 1977-81; coord., curator Cultural Exch. Program, Honolulu-Columbus, 1980; mem. acad. women achievers YWCA, 1991; guest speaker 1991 Scholastic Arts Award, Cin., 1991; keynote speaker Ohio Mus. Assn., ann. meeting, 1992; speaker Internat. Coun. Mus. Triennial Conf., Quebec City, 1992; session chair Midwest Mus. Assn. ann. meeting, St. Louis, 1993. Recipient Marantz Disting. Scholar award Ohio State U., 1995, Gelpe award YWCA, 1987, Cultural Advancement of City of Columbus award, The Columbus Dispatch, 1984, Disting. Svc. award, Columbus Art League, 1984, Critic's Choice award Found. for Cmty. of Artists, N.Y., 1981; Fulbright scholar USIA, 1988 (The Netherlands); NEH fellow East-West Ctr., Honolulu, 1991. Mem. Am. Assn. Mus. (advocacy task force), Assn. of Coll. and Univ. Mus. and Galleries, Midwest Mus. Assn., Fulbright Assn., Coll. Arts Assn., Internat. Coun. Mus., Ohio Mus. Assn. (bd. dirs. 1993-96). Office: Muscarelle Mus of Art Coll William & Mary PO Box 8795 Williamsburg VA 23187-8795

KELM, LINDA, opera singer; b. Salt Lake City, Dec. 11, 1944; d. Robert Gordon and Hettie Frances Kelm. Studies with Elizabeth Hayes Simpson, Salt Lake City, 1963-75; studies with Jennie Tourel, Aspen, Colo., 1968; studies with Judith Oas, N.Y.C., 1975-84, L.A., 1994—. Profl. debut in Der Ring des Nibelungen, 1977; performed in Die Walküre and Götterdämmerung, 1977-83; sang title role in Turandot, 1979, Salome, 1984, Fidelio, 1987, Elektra, 1990, Tristan und Isolde, 1991; performed with: Rai Radio Orch. (Rome), Residentie Orkest of Holland, Minn. Orch., Utah Symphony, Opera Orch. N.Y., Chgo. Symphony, San Francisco Symphony, St. Louis Symphony, Pitts. Symphony, Balt. Symphony, Denver Symphony, Detroit Symphony, Seattle Symphony, N.J. Symphony, L.I. Philharm., San Antonio Symphony, Houston Grand Opera, N.Y.C. Opera, San Francisco Opera, Deutsche Oper/Berlin, Associaciones Bilbania de Amigos de Opera-Bilbao, Spain, Hamburgische Staatsoper, Mexico City Opera, Ky. Opera, Utah Opera, Portland Opera, Greater Miami Opera, L.A. Philharm., City of Birmingham Symphony Orch., Tokyo Symphony Orch., Orchestre de Bordeaux-Aquitaine, Cin. Orch., Phoenix Symphony Orch., Bklyn. Philharm. Orch., Symphony of the New World, Philippine Youth Symphony Orch., Spokane Opera; sang role of Brünnhilde, Seattle Wagner Festival, 1986, 87; appeared in maj. opera houses throughout the world; Met. Opera debut Brünnhilde in Siegfried, 1988; Avery Fisher Hall debut, 1987; Carnegie Hall debut, 1988, Concertgebouw debut, 1983, Royal Festival Hall debut, 1989, May Festival debut, 1986; rec. debut Helmwige in Deutsche Gramophon, Die Walküre Met. Opera, 1988 (Grammy award). Nat. Fedn. of Women's Club scholar, 1968; grantee PEO Sisterhood, 1979, Nat. Inst. of Music Theatre grantee, 1979, 80. Mem. Am. Guild of Musical Artists, Internat. Order of Job's Daughters (past Bethel guardian, majority mem.). Methodist. Home: 2744 Grandview Cir Salt Lake City UT 84106 Office: Herbert Barret Mgmt 1776 Broadway Ste 1610 New York NY 10019

KELMAN, LORRAINE MACELLARO, biology educator; m. Zvi Kelman, May 18, 1996. AB in Biochemistry, Mt. Holyoke Coll., 1982; MS in Biology, St. John's U., Jamaica, N.Y., 1984; PhD in Molecular Biology, Cornell U., 1994. Lab. technician The Rockefeller U., 1984-86; rsch. asst. Sloan-Kettering Inst., 1986—; asst. prof. biology Iona Coll., New Rochelle, N.Y., 1991-96; assoc. prof. biology Iona Coll., 1996—; numerous coms. with Iona Coll., including women's studies com., com. on art of tchg., chmn. health professions recommendations com., 1994, task force on acad. quality, 1993, elected mem. acad. senate, 1994, others. Contbr. articles to profl. jours. Recipient First Place award Am. Soc. for Microbiology, 1989; Frank L. Horsfall fellow Sloan-Kettering Inst., 1990. Mem. AAAS, AAUW (chmn. gender issues in edn. group 1993), N.Y. Acad. Scis. (chmn. sect. biol. scis. 1995), Genetics Soc. Am., Met. Area Coll. and Univ. Biologists, Am. Women in Sci. Office: Iona Coll Dept Biology 715 North Ave New Rochelle NY 10801

KELSEY, FRANCES OLDHAM (MRS. FREMONT ELLIS KELSEY), government official; b. Cobble Hill, Vancouver Island, Can., July 24, 1914; came to U.S., 1936, naturalized, 1956; d. Frank Trevor and Katherine (Stuart) Oldham; m. Fremont Ellis Kelsey, Dec. 6, 1943; children—Susan Elizabeth, Christine Ann. B.Sc., McGill U., 1934; M.Sc., 1935; Ph.D., U. Chgo., 1938, M.D., 1950. Instr., asst. prof. pharmacology U. Chgo., 1938-50; editorial assoc. AMA, Chgo., 1950-52; assoc. prof. pharmacology U. S.D., 1954-57; med. officer FDA, Washington, 1960—; dir. divsn. sci. investigations Office of Compliance, FDA, Rockville, Md., 1967-95, dep. dir. for sci. and medicine Office of Compliance, 1995—. Author: (with F.E. Kelsey, E.M.K. Geiling) Essentials of Pharmacology, 1960. Recipient Pres.'s award for Distinguished Fed. Civilian Service (refusal to approve coml. distbn. thalidomide in U.S.), 1962. Mem. Am. Soc. Pharmacology and Exptl. Therapeutics, Soc. Exptl. Biology and Medicine, Am. Med. Writers Assn., Teratology Soc., Sigma Xi, Sigma Delta Epsilon. Home: 5811 Brookside Dr Bethesda MD 20815-6669 Office: FDA Office of Compliance 7520 Standish Pl Rockville MD 20855-2737

KELSEY, LINDA JEAN, radiology educator, mental health counselor; b. Charleston, W.Va., Feb. 9, 1948; d. John Arliss and Frances Lorraine (Smith) Peters; m. George Daniel Kelsey, Apr. 29, 1977; 1 child, Ruth Ann. AA, St. Petersburg Jr. Coll., 1981; BA in Bus. Mgmt., Eckerd Coll., 1986; MA in Christian Counseling, Christian Internatl., 1991; MA in Counseling, Liberty U., 1995. Staff technologist Montefiore Hosp., Pitts., 1968-70, St. Margaret Meml. Hosp., Pitts., 1970-73; evening supr. Presbyn. Hosp., Pitts., 1973-77; staff technologist Palms of Pasadena Hosp., St. Petersburg, Fla., 1977-78; supr. Computerized Tomography scanning Suncoast Hosp., Clearwater, Fla., 1978; control supr. Morton Plant Hosp., Clearwater, Fla., 1978-86, staff technologist, 1988-95; clin. instr. radiology program St. Petersburg Jr. Coll., Pinellas Park, Fla., 1995—. Mem. Am. Registry of Radiologic Technologists, Office of Radiation Control, Am. Counseling Assn., Am. Assn. Christian Counselors. Home: 1994 Hastings Dr Clearwater FL 34623

KELSH, JANICE EILEEN, club executive; b. Hagerstown, Md., May 5, 1947; d. Robert Henry and Mary Ellen (Slaughter) K. Student, U. D.C., 1971-77. Exec. dir. Miniature Piano Enthusiast Club, Hagerstown, 1990—; conv. coord. Miniature Piano Enthusiast Club, 1992, Rochester, N.Y., 1993, Akron, Ohio, 1994, Las Vegas, Nev., 1995, Cedar Rapids, Iowa, 1996. Editor: (newsletter) Musically Yours, 1991—. Baptist. Home: 633 Pennsylvania Ave Hagerstown MD 21740

KELSO, APRIL D., auditor; b. Great Falls, Mont., Apr. 30, 1948; d. Jack Charles and June Marie (Peterson) Gallagher; m. Thomas W. Kelso Jr., Oct. 14, 1972; children: Jennifer Aileen, Sean Thomas. BFA, U. Mont., 1971. Asst. ops. officer 1st Nat. Bank Whitefish (Mont.), 1981-93; internal auditor Glacier Bancorp, Kalispell, Mont., 1993—. Treas. United Meth. Ch., Whitefish, 1994—. Republican. Office: GBCI 220 Main Kalispell MT 59901

KELSO, GWENDOLYN LEE, silver appraiser, consultant; b. Washington, Jan. 5, 1935; d. Leon Hugh and Katherine Estelle (Henderson) K. Mgr. Shaw & Brown Co., Washington, 1967-71, Chas. Schwartz & Son, Washington, 1972-76; silver appraiser, Washington, 1976—; ptnr. The Silver Lion, Washington, 1983-85; owner, mgr. The Rampant Lion, Washington, 1985—; cons. FBI and law enforcement agys. and ctrs., 1982—; cataloguer, conservator his. silver belonging to USN and U.S. Naval Acad., 1987—; appraiser presentation silver aboard U.S. Naval vessels and at installations, 1986-88; cataloguer, conservator silver Forbes mag. collection, N.Y.C., 1989; mem. USS Alexandria Commissioning Com., 1990, USS Maryland Commissioning Com., 1993; conservator State of Md. for preservation battleship USS Maryland presentation silver, 1990; instr. USN pers. for care and maintenance preservation silver. Author: United States Navy Presentation Silver- a History and a Manual for its Care and Preservation, 1989, Silver Reflections an American Naval History, 1991. Mem. NAFE, Internat. Soc. Appraisers (scholar 1989), Am. Soc. Appraisers (sr.), Appraisers Assn. Am., N.Y. Silver Soc., Silver Soc. (London), U.S. Naval Inst., Navy League U.S., Newcomen Soc. U.S. Republican. Episcopalian. Home: 3731 39th St NW Washington DC 20016-5522 Office: The Rampant Lion PO Box 5887 Washington DC 20016-1487

KEMMERER, SHARON JEAN, computer systems analyst; b. Sellersville, Pa., Apr. 11, 1956; d. John Musselman and Esther Jone (Landis) K. BS, Shippensburg U., 1978; MBA, Marymount U., 1982. Mgmt. analyst Navy Internat. Logistics, Phila., 1978-81; computer systems analyst Navy Supply Sys. Commn., Crystal City, Va., 1981-86, Nat. Inst. Stds. and Tech., Gaithersburg, Md., 1986—; bd. dirs. ComSci, Derwood Sta., 1994—; adult tutor, 1991-95. Contbr. articles, poetry to newspapers; author publs. Moderator Lung Assn., Fairfax, Va., 1986; vol. Project Heart, Washington, 1986-87, Montgomery County Health Buddy, 1988—, Stepping Stones Shelter for Homeless, 1989-91, Pets of Wheels, 1994-96; deacon Alexandria (Va.) Ch., 1985-86, v.p. coun., 1985, chair stewardship com., 1995—. Lutheran. Office: NIST/CSL Gaithersburg MD 20899

KEMNA, MARGARITA ELISABETH, medical technologist; b. Wiesbaden, Germany, Dec. 21, 1947; d. Robert. I. and Elli E. (Mahler) K. BS in Med. Technology, Hartwick Coll., 1969; cert., United Hosp. Sch. Med. Tech., Pt. Chester, N.Y., 1969. Technologist lab. VA Med. Ctr., Iowa City, 1969-71, Bklyn. Jewish Hosp., 1971-77; sr. instr. microbiology Sch. Med. Tech. Albany (N.Y.) Med. Ctr. Hosp., 1977-82; supr. mycology lab. Wadsworth Ctr. for Labs. and Rsch. N.Y. State Dept. Health, Albany, 1982-93; mgr. mycology reference lab. dept. dermatology Case Western Res. U., Cleve., 1993—, instr. sch. medicine, 1994—; Com. mem., chmn. public employees fedn. health and safety com. Dept. Health, Albany, 1990-93; mem. adv. com. med. tech. program Hudson Valley C.C., Troy, N.Y., 1991-93. Contbr. rsch. articles to sci. jours. and procs. Named one of Outstanding Young Women of Am., 1979. Mem. Internat. Soc. Human and Animal Mycology, Mycology Soc. of the Ams., Am. Soc. Clin. Pathologists (registered med. technologist), Am. Soc. Microbiology, Med. Mycology Soc. of the Ams., Med. Mycol. Soc. N.Y., Omicron Sigma.

KEMP, BETTY RUTH, librarian; b. Tishomingo, Okla., May 5, 1930; d. Raymond Herrell and Mamie Melvina (Hughes) K.; BA in Libr. Sci., U. Okla., 1952; MS, Fla. State U., 1965. Extramural loan libr. U. Tex., Austin, 1952-55; libr. lit. and history dept. Dallas Pub. Libr., 1955-56, head Oaklawn Br., 1956-60, head Walnut Hill Br., 1960-64; dir. Cherokee Regional Libr., LaFayette, Ga., 1965-74; dir. Lee County Libr., hdqrs. Lee-Itawamba Libr. System, Tupelo, Miss., 1975-92; bd. libr. commrs. State of Miss., 1979-83, chmn., 1979-80. Chmn. Chickasaw Hist. Soc., 1994—; active Native Am. Chickasaw Nation, United Meth. Women. Mem. AAUW, ALA, Nat. Soc. Daus.Am. Colonists, Nat. Soc. U.S. Daus. of 1812, United Daus. of the Confedercy, Nat. Soc. Dames of Ct. of Honor, Am. Indian Cultural Soc. (Norman Okla.), First Families Twin Ters., Beta Phi Mu. Democrat. Home: 3313 Winchester Cir Norman OK 73072-2937 Office: Kemp Rsch & Cons Svc PO Box 720531 Norman OK 73070

KEMP, GINA CHRISTINE, human services provider; b. New Orleans, June 5, 1968; d. Donald Rue and July Carol (Sallee) K.; m. Patrick E. Hutto, May 15, 1994; 1 stepchild, Patrick B. BA in Psychology, So. Coll., Collegedale, Tenn., 1989; MA in Edn., U. Ga., 1991. Cert. nat. counselor; master addiction counselor; criminal justice specialist. Sociology tchr. So. Coll., 1989; counselor offender rehab., GED examiner IW Davis Detention Ctr., Jefferson, Ga., 1991; counselor offender rehab. drug specialist Alcovy Diversion Ctr., Monroe, Ga., 1991-96; v.p. H&M Sales, Loganville, Ga., 1994—; human svc. provider Rockdale Mental Health, Conyers, Ga., 1996—; boot camp officer Ga. Dept. Corrections. Mem. ACA, Internat. Assn. Addictions and Offender Counseling, Chi Sigma Iota, Psi Chi. Republican. Adventist. Home: 2823 Claude Brewer Rd Loganville GA 30249-4203 Office: Rockdale Mental Health 1429 Business Center Dr Conyers GA 30207

KEMP, JEANNE FRANCES, office manager; b. L.A., Dec. 8, 1942; d. Damian Thomas and Helen Catherine (Bohin) Hanife; m. Don H. Kemp, Dec. 16, 1966 (div. 1972). AB, San Francisco State U., 1965. Food svc. technician United Air Lines, San Francisco, 1961-65; clk. N.Y. Life Ins., San Francisco, 1965-66; inventory clk. Ingersoll-Rand, San Francisco, 1966; advt./order clk. Patrick's Stationers, San Francisco, 1966-67; sec. Dartmouth Travel, Hanover, N.H., 1967-68, Olsten Temp. Svcs., N.Y.C., 1968-70; office mgr. Brown U. Devel., N.Y.C., 1970-73; asst. dir. Cen. Opera Svc., N.Y.C., 1974-85; office mgr., sec. Payne, Thompson & Walker, San Francisco, 1986-95; office mgr. Weatherfore & Taaffe LLP, San Francisco, 1996—. Editor: Career Guide...Singers, 1985, Operas...for Children, 1985; asst. editor COS Bull., 1976-85; editorial asst.: Who's Who in Opera, 1975. Democrat. Roman Catholic. Office: Weatherford & Taaffe LLP Steuart Tower 16th Fl One Market Plz San Francisco CA 94105

KEMP, JULIEANN CATHERINE, home health care nurse; b. Clinton, Iowa, Dec. 30, 1948; d. Robert William and June Ruth (Sawyer) Phillips; m. David Joseph Bebensee, Oct. 3, 1969 (div. Feb. 1987); children: Sara Lynn Bebensee, Michael Jon Bebensee; m. Gary Lee Kemp, July 11, 1988. Diploma, Moline Pub. Sch. of Nursing, Ill., 1970. RN, Ill., Iowa, Nebr.; cert. ACLS instr. Staff nurse in critical care St. Joseph's Mercy Hosp., Clinton, 1970-71; staff nurse Prairie View Nursing Home, Sanborn, Iowa, 1971-72; staff nurse CCU Bergan Mercy Hosp., Omaha, 1972-81, CCU mgr., 1981-84, critical care supr., 1984-86; head nurse ICU/CCU Davenport (Iowa) Med. Ctr., 1986-89; staff nurse Amicare Home Health Care, Mt. Carroll, Ill., 1989-91; assessment nurse Amicare Home Health Care, Clinton and Mt. Carroll, 1991-94; hospice nurse Samaritan Hospice, Clinton, Iowa, 1994—, clin. supr., 1995—. Author pamphlet on stress reduction. Participant in Health Fairs, various hosps., 1981-89. Mem. Women of the Moose (publicity chair 1988). Roman Catholic. Home: 511 10th Ave Fulton IL 61252-1522 Office: Samaritan Hospice 638 S Bluff Blvd Clinton IA 52732

KEMP, MAE WUNDER, real estate broker, consultant; b. Balt.; d. Edward J. and Helen (Robel) Wunder; m. George C. Segerman, May 17, 1941 (div. 1959); children: Barbara, George C.; m. Robert B. Kemp, July 23, 1960 (dec. 1989). BA, Notre Dame Coll., 1941. Pres. Realty Sales corp., Balt., 1958-60; records mgmt. cons. Boeing Co., Seattle, 1960-65; v.p., real estate broker Satellite Realty, Mercer Island, Wash., 1973-76; real estate broker Washington Properties Real Estate, Seattle, 1970-76; assoc. broker John L. Scott Real Estate, Seattle, 1976-92; tech. adviser of real estate North Seattle C.C., 1973-80. Mem. Seattle Women's Commn., 1973; precinct committeewoman Seattle Rep. Com., 1973; v.p. Freedoms Found., Valley Forge, Pa., 1974; past pres., pres. emeritus Hawthorne Hills Community Club, Inc., Seattle, 1974-90; chmn. Seattle's First Citizen Award. Recipient 5 State Regional Chmn. award, Woman of Yr., Omega Tau Rho medal Nat. Assn. Realtors, Seattle, Sales Assoc. of Yr. award Seattle Real Estate Bd., Outstanding Woman in Real Estate award Past Pres. Club, Woman of Day award Sta. KIXI, CBS. Mem. Wash. Assn. Realtors, Seattle-King County Bd. Realtors (bd. dirs.), Nat. Assn. Real Estate Brokers, Women's Assn. Hilton Head Island, Wash. Athletic Club, Country Club Hilton Head (mem. com., house com.), Navy League of U.S., Hilton Head Island Coun. Republican. Roman Catholic. Home: The Cypress 99 Bird Song Way D-401 Hilton Head Island SC 29926

KEMP, SUZANNE LEPPART, educator, clubwoman; b. N.Y.C., Dec. 28, 1929; d. John Culver and Eleanor (Buxton) Leppart; m. Ralph Clinton Kemp, Apr. 4, 1953; children—Valerie Gale, Sandra Lynn, John Maynard, Renee Alison. Grad. Ogontz Jr. Coll., 1949; B.S., U. Md., 1952. Elem. sch. tchr. Mem. Nat. Soc. Women Descs. of Ancient and Hon. Arty. Co., Nat. Soc. Daus. of Founders and Patriots of Am. (corr. sec.), Nat. Soc. Sons and Daus. of Pilgrims, Nat. Soc. U.S. Daus. of 1812 (chpt. organizing Md. state pres. 1977-79, chpt. v.p. 1979—), Nat. Soc. New Eng. Women (colony pres. 1978-80, Nat. Soc. Colonial Dames XVII Century (state chmn. heraldry and coats of arms 1977-79), Nat. Soc. D.A.R. (chpt. regent 1970-73, chpt. v.p., Md. soc. chmn. transp. 1976-79), Md. State Officers Club, Md. Hist. Soc., Friends of Animals, Defenders of Animal Rights Inc., U. Md. Alumni, English Speaking Union, Star Spangled Banner Flag House Assn., Potter-Balt. Clayworks, Balt. Mus. Art, Walters Art Gallery, Dames of the Court of Honor, Kappa Delta Alumni. Clubs: Baltimore Country; Lago Mar (Ft. Lauderdale, Fla.); Roland Park Women's; Woodbrook-Murray Hill Garden Club, Federation Garden Clubs. Editor; The Spinning Wheel, 1973-76. Home: 7 Ruxton Green Ct Baltimore MD 21204-3548

KEMPER, DORLA DEAN (DORLA DEAN EATON), real estate broker; b. Calhoun, Mo., Sept. 10, 1929; d. Paul McVey and Jesse Lee (McCombs) Eaton; student, William Woods Coll., 1947-48; B.S. in Edn., Cen. Mo. State U., 1952; m. Charles K. Kemper, Mar. 1, 1951; children: Kevin Keil, Kara Lee. Tchr. pub. schs., Twin Falls, Idaho, 1950-51, Mission, Kans., 1952-53, Burbank, Calif., 1953-57; real estate saleswoman, Minn., 1967-68, Calif., 1971-73; Deanie Kemper, Realtor (name changed to Deanie Kemper, Inc. Real Estate Brokerage 1976), Loomis, Calif., 1974-76, pres., 1976-91; sr. couns. Capital Holding Corp., Louisville, 1991-93, dir. Pres., Battle Creek Park Elem. Sch. PTA, St. Paul, 1966-67; mem. Placer County (Calif.) Bicentennial Comm., 1976; mem. Sierra Coll. Adv. Com., 1981—; active Placer County Hist. Soc. Named to Million Dollar Club (lifetime) Sacramento and Placer County bds. realtors, 1978-94; designated Grad. Realtors Inst., Cert. Residential Specialist. Mem. Nat. Assn. Realtor, Calif. Assn. Realtors, Nat. Assn. Real Estate Appraisers, Placer County (mem. profl. standards com.) bds. realtors, DAR (chpt. regent 1971-73, organizing chpt. regent 1977—, dist. dir. 1978-80, state registrar Calif. 1980-82, state vice regent 1982-84, state regent 1984-86, nat. resolutions com., nat. recording sec. gen., 1986-89, nat. chmn. units overseas 1983-86, nat. pres. gen. 1995—), Nat. Gavel Soc., Daus. Am. Colonists, Colonial Dames Am., Dames Ct. of Honor, Internat. Platform Assn. Republican. Mem. Christian Ch. Clubs: Hidden Valley Women's (pres. Loomis club 1970-71), Auburn Travel Study (pres. 1979). Home: 8165 Morningside Dr Loomis CA 95650-9185

KEMPER LITTMAN, MARLYN, information scientist, educator; b. Balt., Mar. 26, 1943; d. Louis and Augusta Louise (Jacobs) Janofsky; m. Bennett I. Kemper, Aug. 1, 1965 (dec. June 1987); children: Alex Randall, Gari Hament, Jason Myles; m. Lewis Littman, Apr. 22, 1990. BA, Finch Coll., 1964; MA in Anthropology, Temple U., Phila., 1970; MA in Library Sci., U. S. Fla., 1983; PhD in Info. Sci., Nova Southeastern U., 1986. Dir., Hist. Broward County Preservation Bd., Hollywood, Fla., 1979-87; automated systems librarian Broward County Main Library, Ft. Lauderdale, Fla., 1983-86; assoc. prof., 1987-94, dir. info. sci. doctoral program Nova U., Ft. Lauderdale, 1987-94; prof. Nova Southeastern U., 1995—. Pub. info. officer Broward County Hist. Commn., 1975-79. Vice chmn. Broward County Library Adv. Bd., 1987-92. Bd. dirs. Ctrl. Agy. Jewish Edn., 1992-94. Recipient Judge L. Clayton Nance award, 1977; Broward County Hist. Commn. award, 1979. Mem. ALA, IEEE, Assn. for Ednl. Comms. and Tech., Internat. Soc. for Tech. in Edn., Assn. Computing Machinery, Beta Phi Mu, Phi Kappa Phi. Author: A Comprehensive Documented History of the City of Pompano Beach, 1982 A Comprehensive History of Dania 1983, Hallandale, 1984, Deerfield Beach, 1985, Plantation, 1986, Davie, 1987, Networking: Choosing A Lan Path to Interconnection, 1987, (with others) Mosaics of Meaning, New Ways of Learning, 1996; author weekly columns Ft. Lauderdale News, 1975-79; author chpts. to books; contbr. articles to Microcomputer Environment: Management Issues, and articles to profl. jours. and procs. Home: 2845 NE 35th St Fort Lauderdale FL 33306-2007 Office: Nova U Sch Computer & Info Sci 3100 SW 9th Ave Fort Lauderdale FL 33315-3025

KEMPF, JANE ELMIRA, marketing executive; b. Phila., Sept. 28, 1927; d. Albert Thomas and Alice (Gaston) Mullen; m. Peter Kempf, Sept. 4, 1948 (dec. Mar. 1985); children: Peter Albert, Jan Michael, Richard Allen, Jeffery Val. Grad. high sch., Yeadon, Pa. News dir. Sta. WIFF, Auburn, Ind., 1968-69; city editor The Evening Star, Auburn, 1969-76, columnist, 1969—; paralegal Warren Sunday Atty., Auburn, 1977-85; mktg. mgr. City Nat. Bank, Auburn, 1986-89; with communications mktg. Lincoln Fin. Corp., Ft. Wayne, Ind., 1989-90; prin. JK Communications Bus. Svcs., Auburn, Ind., 1990—; bd. dirs. Tri-County Power Wash, Inc. Contbr. articles to profl. jours. Mem. Auburn Network Enterprising Women, Ladies Literary Club, PEO Sisterhood (past pres.), Auburn C. of C. (past sec., bd. dirs.). Presbyterian. Home: 1117 Packard Pl Auburn IN 46706-1340 Office: JK Communicatons Bus Svcs PO Box 430 Auburn IN 46706-0430

KEMPF, MARTINE, voice control device manufacturing company executive; b. Strasbourg, France, Dec. 9, 1958; came to U.S., 1985; d. Jean-Pierre and Brigitte Marguerite (Klockenbring) K. Student in Astronomy, Friedrich Wilhelm U., Bonn, Fed. Republic of Germany, 1981-83. Owner, mgr. Kempf, Sunnyvale, Calif., 1985—. Inventor Comeldir Multiplex Handicapped Driving Systems (Goldenes Lenkrad Axel Springer Verlag 1981), Katalavox speech recognition control system (Oscar, World Almanac Inventions 1984, Prix Grand Siecle, Comite Couronne Francaise 1985). Recipient Medal for Service to Humanity Spinal Cord Soc., 1986; street named in honor in Dossenheim-Kochersberg, Alsace, France, 1987; named Citizen of Honor City of Dossenheim-Kochersberg, 1985, Outstanding Businessperson of Yr. City of Sunnyvale, 1990. Office: 1080 E Duane Ave Ste E Sunnyvale CA 94086-2628

KEMPLEY, RITA A., film critic, editor; b. Frankfort, Ky., Sept. 12, 1945; d. Noah and Musaetta (Lathrem) Abrams; m. William Holcomb Kempley, June 31, 1968 (div. 1978); m. Edward Ronald Schneider, Aug. 11, 1986. BJ, U. Mo., 1967. Reporter Copley News Svc., La Jolla, Calif., 1967-68; assoc. editor John F. Holman & Co., Washington, 1968-71; reporter Graphic Arts Mag., Washington, 1972-75; freelance editor-writer Washington, 1975-76; mng. editor Washington Dossier, 1977-79; editor/critic Washington Post, 1979—; commentator Sta. WETA, 1989-96. Mem. Newspaper Guild, Kappa Tau Alpha. Office: The Washington Post 1150 15th St NW Washington DC 20071-0001

KENAS, JANE HAMILTON, musician; b. Fond du Lac, Wis., June 17, 1951; d. Vern Aaron and Marilyn Jane (Bluemke) K. MusB, U. Wis., Stevens Point, 1975; MA, Northeastern Ill. U., 1987. Staff accompanist dept. music Northeastern Ill. U., Chgo., 1982—; music dir. USO Tour to Europe, Germany, 1973; cantorial soloist Temple Beth El, Northbrook, Ill.; music dir., composer Harlequin Players Theatre Co., Palatine, Ill.; accompanist Maine Twp. Chorale, Park Ridge, Ill. Composer: (mus. play) The Adventures of Goldilocks, 1990; (one-act opera) Romance Novel, 1993. Office: Northeastern Ill U 5500 N Saint Louis Ave Chicago IL 60625-4625

KENDALL, DIANE STONE, educational editor; b. Rochester, N.Y., Feb. 12, 1952; d. Ben Ervin and Doris Julie (MacRae) Stone; m. Donald R. Kendall, Jr., June 10, 1976; children: Corinne, Lincoln. BA, Skidmore Coll., 1973; MS, Nazareth Coll., Rochester, N.Y., 1976. Cert. social studies tchr. Tchr. Ben Franklin H.S., Rochester, 1973-76; rsch. asst. Global Perspectives in Edn., N.Y.C., 1976-79; editor Holt, Rinehart & Winston, N.Y.C., 1979-81; instr./cons. Tchr. Coll., Columbia U., N.Y.C., 1981-93; editor Children's Software Press, Houston, 1992—. Author: Computers in the Social Studies, 1986, Kids, Computers and Homework, 1995; editor Children's Software newsletter. Trustee Berkeley Carroll Sch., Bklyn., 1992-93. Mem. Nat. Coun. for the Social Studies. Home and Office: 720 Kuhlman Rd Houston TX 77024-5502

KENDALL, DOLORES DIANE PISAPIA, artist, author, marketing executive; b. Newark, N.J., June 1, 1946; d. Dominick Pisapia and Ann Fanfone Pisapia Kendall. Grad. Berkeley Bus. Coll., East Orange, N.J., 1965; postgrad. Middlesex County Coll., Edison, N.J., 1966-67, Rutgers U., 1967-69, Todd Butler Art Workshop, Edison, 1964-74, Art Inst. Boston, 1976, Graham Art Studio, Boston, 1975-77, Sch. Visual Arts, N.Y.C., 1978, NYU, 1977, Advt. Club N.Y., 1978. Proofreader, supr. N.J. State Diagnostic Ctr., Menlo Park, N.J., 1965-75; apprentice, instr. Graham Art Studio, Boston, 1975-77; dir. direct mktg. Boardroom Reports Inc., N.Y.C., 1977-82; pres., chief operating officer Roman Managed Lists, N.Y.C., 1982; dir. direct mktg. Mal Dunn Assocs., N.Y.C., 1983; dir. lists and card deck mgmt. Warren, Gorham & Lamont Inc., N.Y.C., 1984-86, direct mktg. cons., 1986-87; v.p., Marketry, Inc., N.Y.C. and Bellevue, Wash., 1987-93; cons. direct mktg., N.Y.C., 1993—. Exhibited in group art shows: N.Y.C., Boston, Middlesex County, N.J., Somerset County, N.J., Morris County, N.J., 1965-74, Greenwich Village Art Show, N.Y.C., 1972, Graham Art Studio, Boston, 1975-77; represented in numerous pvt. art collections throughout the U.S. Author: My Eyes Are Windows, 1972, Feelings and Thoughts (poetry), 1979, The Direct Marketing Handbook, 2d edit., 1992; contbr. articles to profl. jours. Recipient Desi award Direct Mail Mktg. Promotion Package, 1980, Poetry award One Mag., 1972, Internat. Cert. of Recognition for List Day, 1982. Mem. NAFE, Direct Mktg. Assn. (Echo awards bd. judges 1982-85, List Day lectr., N.Y.C.), Can. Direct Mktg. Assn., Internat. Poetry Assn. (Clover Collection of Verse VI 1973, Danae in Clover 1973—), Direct Mktg. Creative Guild, Nat. Mail Order Assn. (adv. bd. 1979-80), NOW, Direct Mktg. Club N.Y.C., Internat. Platform Assn., Nat. Bus. Circulation Assn. Home: 530 2nd Ave 5H New York NY 10016-8207

KENDALL, DOROTHY HELEN, retired art historian; b. Bayonne, N.J., May 27, 1912; d. Frank and Mary Elizabeth (Hart) Hovell; m. Henry John Steinbomer, Dec. 26, 1933 (dec. July 11, 1964); children: Shirley Ann, Richard Henry, Robert Alan; m. James Irving Kendall, Aug. 29, 1972. BA, Our Lady of the Lake U., San Antonio, 1933; MLS, Our Lady of the Lake U., 1968; MFA in Latin Am. Arts, U. Americas, Puebla, Mexico, 1972. Cert. secondary tchr., Tex. Tchr. Covington Park Sch., San Antonio, 1933-34; tchr. St. Mary's Hall H.S., San Antonio, 1941-42; fine arts libr. San Antonio Pub. Libr., 1959-68; dir. Religious Expression in the Arts Hemis-Fair '68, 1967-69; fine arts libr. St. Mary's U., 1968-72; founder, 1st chmn. Urban Studies Dept., St. Mary's U., 1970. Author: Gentilz, Artist of the Old Southwest, 1974; designed stained glass windows for 3 San Antonio chs., 1953-56; developed type of fused glass for decorative use in ch., office, 1956; organizer of exhibit Am. Fedn. Arts, Houston-San Antonio, 1961. Pres. San Antonio Art League, 1958-60 (initiated Artists in Action program, 1958-59); appointed to Fine Arts Adv. Coun., U. Tex., 1959-65; organized Faith into Form nat. exhbn. for Stained Glass Assn. Am., Dallas, 1963; mem. Area Policy Coun., San Antonio, 1969-72. Recipient hon. membership San Antonio Craft Guild, 1962-63; invited with group of artists to visit Mexico's artists by Mexico's Pres. Diaz Ordaz, 1965. Democrat. Episcopalian. Home: #205 4401 Spicewood Springs Rd Austin TX 78759

KENDALL, ELIZABETH BEMIS, writer, journalist, educator; b. St. Louis, Apr. 7, 1947; d. Henry Cochran and Elizabeth Thompson (Conant) K. BA cum laude, Harvard U., 1969, MAT in Lang. and Lit., 1971. Lectr. Princeton U., 1993; guest lectr. Rimsky Korsakov Counservatory of Music, St. Petersburg, Russia, 1992; lectr., Bard Ctr. fellow Bard Coll., 1988, 89; guest lectr., panel mem. various univs.; cons. WNET Channel Thirteen's Dancing, Whitney Mus., TBS Prodns.' A Century of Women, Image and Popular Culture; cons. in dance Ford Found., Office of the Arts; speaker in field. Author: Where Se Danced, 1979, 84, The Runaway Bride: Hollywood Romantic Comedy of the 1930's, 1990; author monographs; scriptwriter Trailbrazers of Modern Dance, 1977, Philobolus: New Directions in Dance, 1977; dance critic Ballet News, 1977-82, Vogue, 1982-87, Elle, 1987-91, Harper's Bazaar, 1991—; contbr. articles to Mirabella, Elle Decor, French Vogue, N.Y. Times, Newsday, Dance Inc., New Republic, Dance Mag., Ballet Rev., Dance Connection, L.A. Times, others. Rockefeller Found. fellow in Am. history, 1976, Ford Found. writer's fellow, 1980, John Simon Guggenheim Found. fellow, 1982. Home: 400 W 43d St # 2L New York NY 10036

KENDALL, KAY LYNN, interior designer; b. Cadillac, Mich., Aug. 20, 1950; d. Robert Llewellyn and Betty Louise (Powers) K.; 1 child, Anna Renee Easter. BFA, U. Mich., 1973. Draftsman, interior designer store planning dept. Jacobson Stores, Inc., Jackson, Mich., 1974-79; sr. interior designer store planning dept. Jacobson Stores, Inc., Jackson, 1981—; prin. Kay Kendall Designs, Jackson, 1979—; cons. in field. Big sister Big Bros./Big Sisters Jackson County. Mem. Am. Soc. Interior Designers (profl. mem., assoc. Cen. Mich. chpt.). Home: 701 Church St Grass Lake MI 49240 Office: Jacobson Stores Inc 3333 Sargent Rd Jackson MI 49201-8847

KENDALL, LAUREL ANN, geotechnical engineer; b. Detroit, Dec. 4, 1956; d. James McNair and Dorothy Mildred (Frost) K. BSE in Environ. Sci., U. Mich., 1979, MSCE, 1983. Registered profl. engr., Mich., Ill., Ohio. Geotech. egnr. Bechtel Assocs., Ann Arbor, Mich., 1979-84; with Bechtel Assocs. P.C., 1979-84, NTH Cons., 1984-90; gen. mgr. solid waste ops. Wayne Disposal, Inc., 1990—; instr. Lawrence Inst. Tech., Southfield, Mich., 1985-91, Wayne State U., 1991-95. Mem. ASCE (past pres. southeastern br., officer Mich. sect. 1990—), Mich. Soc. Profl. Engrs. (officer 1990—), Engring. Soc. Detroit. Congregationalist. Office: Wayne Disposal-Canton Inc 5011 S Lilley Canton MI 48188

KENDALL, SCIPIARUTH, programmer, analyst; b. Boston, May 29, 1955; d. Scipio Hoover and Connie Lee (Lester) K. BS in Computer Info Systems, Calif. Polytech. U., Pomona, 1986; MA in Orgnl. Mgmt., U. Phoenix, 1995. Noncommd. lab. tech. USAF-George AFB, Victorville, Calif., 1977-81; lab. asst. Covina (Calif.) Reference Lab., 1981-85; credit processor Informative Rsch., Inc., Anaheim, Calif., 1985; inventory specialist Washington Inventory Inc., Riverside, Calif., 1985; tax asst. Borsch Tax Svc., Fullerton, Calif., 1986; phlebotomist Meth. Hosp., Arcadia, Calif., 1986; eligibility worker County of L.A., El Monte, Calif., 1986-87; programmer analyst L.A. County, Downey, Calif., 1987-92, Riverside Dist. Atty., 1992—; enlisted lab. technician USAFR, March AFB, Calif., 1981-89, commd. Med. Svc. Corps, 1990—. Canvasser U.S. Savs. Bond of L.A. County, Downey, 1988; fundraiser Brotherhood Crusade and United Way, Downey, 1988; walker March of Dimes L.A. County, Downey, 1989, 90. With USAF, 1977-81, USAFR, 1981—. Recipient Community Support award L.A. County Data Processing Dept., 1990. Mem. NAFE, Orange County Women Networkers, Data Processing Mgmt. Assn., Assn. Med. Surgeons U.S., Res. Officers Assn., Computer Security Inst., IEEE, Toastmasters Internat., Soc. Air Force Res. Med. Svc. Corp., Air Force Assn., Assn. Legal Adminstrs., Project Mgmt. Inst. Office: Riverside Dist Atty Criminal Divsn 4075 N Main St Riverside CA 92501-3707

KENIS, SUZANN KEYES, special education educator; b. Oceanside, N.Y., June 16, 1966; d. William J. and Carol M. (Devine) Keyes; m. Michael Neil Kenis, June 16, 1990. BA in Edn., U. Fla., 1988, MEd, 1989. Cert. spl. edn. Tchr. spl. edn. Homosassa (Fla.) Elem. Sch., 1989, Deltona (Fla.) Mid. Sch., 1990—. Mem. Coun. for Exceptional Children (Tchr. of Yr. Volusia County 1994). Home: 426 N Pine Meadow Dr Debary FL 32713-2306 Office: Deltona Mid Sch 250 Enterprise Rd Deltona FL 32725

KENLEY, ELIZABETH SUE, commerce and transportation executive; b. Kansas City, Mo., Oct. 4, 1945; d. Ralph Raymond and Josephine Allen (Wells) Cummins. BS, Kans. U., 1968, MPA, 1972. Asst. city mgr. Winfield (Kans.), 1968-70; adminstrv. asst. Kansas City (Mo.) Police Dept., 1970; cons., 1973; with E.I. DuPont Co., Kingwood, Tex., 1974—, regional tech. buyer, 1977-79, cons., plant start up, 1979, regional tech. buyer, 1980-82; internat. project buyer Aramco, Houston, 1982-86, quality assurance liaison, supr. refinery no. area projects unit, 1986-89, owner, pres. Internat., Inc. , Houston, 1988—. Mem. Houston C. of C., Am. Mgmt. Assn. Home: 9632 Briar Forest Dr Houston TX 77063-1007 Office: 2230 Harbor St Houston TX 77020-7506

KENNAN, ELIZABETH TOPHAM, university executive; b. Phila., Feb. 25, 1938. AB summa cum laude, Mt. Holyoke Coll., 1960; MA, Oxford (Eng.) U., 1962; PhD, U. Wash., 1966; LHD (hon.), Trinity Coll., 1978, Amherst Coll., 1980, St. Mary's Coll., 1982, Oberlin Coll., 1983; LLD (hon.), Smith Coll., 1984; LittD (hon.), Cath. U. of Am., 1985, U. Mass., Amherst, 1988. Asst. prof. history Cath. U., Washington, 1966-70, assoc. prof. history, dir. medieval and Byzantine studies, 1970-78, dir. program in early Christian humanism, 1970-78; pres. Five Colls. Inc., 1985-94; pres., prof. history Mt. Holyoke Coll., South Hadley, Mass., 1978-95; bd. dirs. Coun. on Libr. Resources; mem. com. Folger Shakespeare Libr., 1994—; mem. Com. on Econ. Devel., 1991—; bd. selectors Jefferson Awards, Am. Inst. for Pub. Svc., 1991—; bd. trustees U. Notre Dame, 1985-94, Miss Porter's Sch., 1980-85; mem. higher edn. program com. Dana Found., 1986-90; mem. Indo-U.S. Subcommn. on Edn. and Culture, 1986-91; vice chair 1000 Friends of Mass., 1989-91; mem. Gov.'s Nominating Coun., 1990-91; chair audit com. NYNEX Corp., White Plains, N.Y., 1984—; chair compensation and bd. affairs com. N.E. Utilities, Hartford, Conn., 1980—, chair audit com.; bd. dirs. Ky. Home Life Ins. Co., Louisville, Ky. Home Mut. Life Ins. Co., The Putnam Funds, Boston, Talbots, Hingham, Mass. Contbr. articles to profl. jours. including Georgetown Univ. Press, Univ. of Wash. Press, Cath. Univ. of Am., Cath. Univ. Press, Cistercian Publs., Marshall scholar, 1960; Woodrow Wilson fellow (hon.), 1960. Mem. Coun. Fgn. Rels. Office: Home and Office Spring Hill Farm South Woodstock VT 05071

KENNARD, DENISE E., nurse; b. Lyons, N.Y., Oct. 28, 1965; d. Byron C. Jr. and Lorraine J. (Pierson) K. Diploma, Crouse-Irving Hosp., Syracuse, N.Y., 1988. RN, N.Y. LPN Blossom View Nursing Home, Sodus, N.Y., 1986-88; RN Newark Wayne Community Hosp., Newark, 1988-90; nurse Newark Devel. Ctr., 1990-92, Seneca Nursing Home, Waterloo, N.Y., 1992-94; nursing supr. Huntington-Taylor Brown Nursing Home, Waterloo, 1994—. Mem. Wayne County Humane Soc. Methodist.

KENNARD, JOYCE L., judge. Former judge L.A. Mcpl. Ct., Superior Ct., Ct. Appeal, Calif.; assoc. justice Calif. Supreme Ct., San Francisco, 1989—. Office: Calif Supreme Ct South Tower 303 2nd St San Francisco CA 94107-1366

KENNARD, MARGARET ANNE, middle school educator; b. Dayton, Ohio, Nov. 28, 1944; d. Dwight Clinton and Martha Ellen (Risser) K. BA, Asbury Coll., Wilmore, Ky., 1967; MA, Eastern Mich. U., 1972; EdD, Western Mich. U., 1983; postgrad., Wayne State U., 1984-85. Cert. tchr., Mich. Tchr. L'Anse Creuse Schs., Harrison Twp., Mich., 1967—; adj. prof. Oakland U., Rochester, Mich., 1989; twp. trustee Harrison Twp., Mich., 1984-92; participant Tchr. in Space program NASA, Washington, 1985-86; chair visitation team Mich. Accreditation Program, Lansing, 1990-95; accreditation facilitator North Ctrl. Accreditation Assn., Ann Arbor, Mich., 1986-90. Author: (poetry) On Turning Fifty, 1995. Mem. State of Mich. Hazardous Waste Commn., 1992-96; sec., mem. Zoning Bd. Appeals, Harrison Twp., 1983-88; sec., trustee Econ. Devel. Corp., Harrison Twp., 1982-92; mem. Selective Svc. Bd., Mt. Clemens, Mich., 1993-96; mem. bd. advisors Lake St. Clair Task Force, 1994-96; co-chair Clean Water Com., 1996, Harrison Twp. Hist. Commn., 1992-96; vol. Detroit Inst. Arts, Gt. Lakes Maritime Inst. Recipient Famous Women of Macomb County, Girl Scouts, 1995. Mem. Kiwanis Internat. (trustee 1995-96). Democrat. Home: 34720 E Lake Dr Harrison Township MI 48045 Office: L'Anse Creuse Schs 38000 Reimold St Harrison Township MI 48045

KENNEDY, ADRIENNE LITA, playwright; b. Pitts., Sept. 13, 1931; d. Cornell Wallace and Etta (Haugabook) Hawkins; m. Joseph C. Kennedy, May 15, 1953 (div. 1966); children: Joseph C., Adam. BS, Ohio State U., 1953; student creative writing, Columbia U., 1954-56; student playwrighting, New Sch. Social Research, Am. Theatre Wing, Circle in the Sq. Theatre Sch., 1957-58, 62. Mem. playwriting unit Actors Studio, N.Y.C., 1962-65; lectr. Yale U., New Haven, 1972-74; CBS fellow Sch. Drama, N.Y.C., 1973; lectr. Princeton (N.J.) U., 1977; vis. assoc. prof. Brown U., 1979-80; rep. to conf. Internat. Theatre Inst., Budapest, 1978; vis. lectr. Harvard U., 1990, 91. Author: (plays) Funnyhouse of a Negro, 1964, Cities in Bezique, 1965, A Rat's Mass, 1966, A Lesson in Dead Language, 1966, The Lennon Plays, 1968, Sun, Cities of Bezique, 1969; A Movie Star Has To Star in Black and White, 1976, Ohio State Murders, She Talks to Beethoven, 1990, (with Adam Kennedy) Sleep Deprivation Chamber, 1995; (memoirs) People Who Led to My Plays, 1987 (Manhattan Borough Pres.'s award 1988), Letter to My Students, Lancashire Lad; commd. by Empire State Youth Inst., 1979, Onestes, Electra, Juilliard Sch. Music, 1980, Black Children's Day, Rites and Reason, Brown U., 1980; represented in numerous anthologies Norton Anthology of Am. Lit. Recipient Obie award, 1964, 96, Pierre Lecomte du Novy award Lincoln Ctr., 1994, award Am. Acad. Arts and Letters, 1994; fellow Guggenheim Found., 1968, Rockefeller Found., 1967-68, NEA, 1993, Lila Wallace Readers Digest, 1994, Yale U., 1974-75; grantee Nat. Endowment Arts, 1973, Rockefeller Found., 1974, Creative Artists Pub. Svc., 1974; Disting. lectr. U. Calif., Berkeley, 1980, 86. Mem. PEN (bd. dirs. 1976-77).

KENNEDY, BARBARA ELLEN PERRY, art therapist; b. Columbus, Ohio, Apr. 22, 1937; d. Donald Earl Perry and Elsie Irene (Strait) Modglin; m. Marvin Roosevelt Kennedy, July 1, 1955 (div. Sept. 1969); children: Sherry Lynn Kennedy Anderson, Michelle Reneé Kennedy Byrd. AS in Mental Health Technology cum laude, Purdue U., 1975, BA in Psychology, 1976; MA in Art Therapy, Wright State U., 1990. Registered art therapist; cert. social worker; cert. marriage and family therapist. Probation officer intern Allen County Juvenile Probation Dept., Ind., 1975; prodn. supr. asst. Allen County Assn. for Retarded, Ft. Wayne, Ind., 1975, relief supr. semi-ind. living, 1975-76; occupational therapist asst. Logansport (Ind.) State Hosp., 1977; rehab. therapist Richmond (Ind.) State Hosp., 1977—, recreation therapy dir. acute intensive treatment unit, 1983-85, dir. art therapy dept., 1986—; pvt. counselor, 1986—; counselor Mental Health Assn., Richmond, 1986; art therapy counselor Battered Women's Shelter, Richmond, 1986; counselor Dayton (Ohio) Pub. Schs., Family Svc. Assn., 1989-90, expressive therapy counselor with Mentally Ill Chemically Addicted population, 1993—; lectr. in field of mental health and art therapy. Author, editor: Mental Stimulation Activities, 1992. Mem. com. LWV, Richmond, 1977-80; publicity officer USCG Aux., Richmond, 1985; chairperson legis. group AAUW, Richmond, 1982-84; bd. dirs. Community Coun. on Disabilities Awareness, Richmond, 1985-86; vol. ARC, Muncie, Ind. and Ft. Wayne, 1969-73; vol. tutor Adult Literacy Resource Ctr., 1991—; pres. Richmond Art Club, 1996-97. Recipient Merit scholarship Purdue U., 1971-76, Gov.'s Showcase award State of Ind., 1990. Mem. Am. Art Therapy Assn., Buckeye Art Therapy Assn., Ind. Art Therapy Assn. (v.p. 1992-95), Mensa. Reorganized Ch. of Jesus Christ of Latter-day Saints. Office: Richmond State Hosp 498 NW 18th St Richmond IN 47374-2851

KENNEDY, BEVERLY (KLEBAN) B., financial consultant, radio talk show host; b. Pitts., Sept. 23, 1943; d. Jack and Ida (Davis) Kleban; m. Thomas E. Burris, Dec. 31, 1967 (div.); 1 child, Laura Danielle Burris; m. Ed A. Kennedy, Jan 14, 1984; stepchildren: Kathleen, Patricia, Thomas. BS, Pa. State U., 1964; postgrad., Va. Commonwealth U., 1967. Founder, exec. dir. Broward Art Colony, Inc., Broward County, Fla., 1978-80; dir. sales Holiday Inn, Plantation, Fla., 1980-81; agent, registered rep. Equitable Life Assurance Soc., Ft. Lauderdale, Fla., 1982—; pres. Fin. Planning Svcs. Assn., Inc., Ft. Lauderdale, Fla., 1984-86; owner, fin. cons. Beverly B. Kennedy & Assocs., Ft. Lauderdale, Fla., 1982—; adv. bd. Transflorida Bank, 1983-88; bd. arbitration Nat. Assn. Securities Dealers, Inc., 1992-96. Talk show host Sta. WWNN, 1992-93. Bd. dirs. Community Appearance Bd., 1988-89, Riverwalk, Ft. Lauderdale, 1988-89; trustee Police and Fireman Fund of Fort Lauderdale, 1990-91; appointed by gov. to Fla. State Bd. Profl. Engrs., 1988-91; cons. Com. on Fin. for Nat. Coun. examiners for Engring and Surveying, 1990-91; Rep. nominee for U.S. Congress 20th dist. Fla., 1992, 94. Named Woman of the Year (Bus. for Profit), Women in Communications, Broward County, 1986, Bus. & Profl. Women, 1988-89, oustanding alumni, Pa. State Univ. Coll . Edn., 1988-89. Mem. Internat. Assn. Fin. Planning, Nat. Assn. Life Underwriters, East Broward Fed. Women's Rep. Club (pres. 1992-93).

KENNEDY, CHERYL LYNN, museum director; b. Pekin, Ill., Nov. 25, 1946; d. Paul Louis and Ann Marie (Bingham) Wieburg; children: Kurt Alan, Kimberly Ann. Grad. high sch., Pekin, Ill. Prin., and profl. quilter Mahomet, Ill., 1976-81; program coord. Early Am. Mus., Mahomet, 1981-85; dir. Early Am. Mus. Champaign County Forest Preserve, Mahomet, 1986—; chmn. Ill. quilt documentation project Early Am. Mus. and Land of Lincoln Quilt Assn., 1986—. Historian Meth. Local History Com., Mahomet, 1984-86; chair The Attractions Coun., Champaign-Urbana Conv. and Visitors Bur. Mem. Midwest Mus. Coun., Am. Assn. Mus., Am. Assn. State and Local History Mus., Ill. Assn. Mus. (past pres., Heritage Awareness chair), Ill. Heritage Assn., Ill. State Hist. Soc., Champaign County Hist. Soc., Nat. Quilt Assn., Am. Quilt Soc., Antique Quilt Study Group, Quilt Conservancy, Nat. Soc. Fundraising Execs., Rural Ptnrs. (bd. dirs.). Home: 219A S Lake Of The Woods Rd Mahomet IL 61853-9201 Office: Early Am Mus PO Box 1040 Mahomet IL 61853-1040

KENNEDY, CORNELIA GROEFSEMA, federal judge; b. Detroit, Mich., Aug. 4, 1923; d. Elmer H. and Mary Blanche (Gibbons) Groefsema; m. Charles S. Kennedy, Jr. (dec.); 1 son, Charles S. III. B.A., U. Mich., 1945, J.D. with distinction, 1947; LL.D. (hon.), No. Mich. U., 1971, Eastern Mich. U., 1971, Western Mich. U., 1973, Detroit Coll. Law, 1980, U. Detroit, 1987. Bar: Mich. bar 1947. Law clk. to Chief Judge Harold M. Stephens, U.S. Ct. of Appeals, Washington, 1947-48; assoc. Elmer H. Groefsema, Detroit, 1948-52; partner Markle & Markle, Detroit, 1952-66; judge 3d Judicial Circuit Mich., 1967-70; dist. judge U.S. Dist. Ct., Eastern Dist. Mich., Detroit, 1970-79; chief judge U.S. Dist. Ct., Eastern Dist. Mich., 1977-79; circuit judge U.S. Ct. Appeals, (6th cir.), 1979—. Mem. Commn. on the Bicentennial of the U.S. Constitution (presdl. appointment). Recipient Sesquicentennial award U. Mich. Fellow Am. Bar Found.; mem. ABA, Mich. Bar Assn. (past chmn. negligence law sect.), Detroit Bar Assn. (past dir.), Fed. Bar Assn., Am. Judicature Soc., Nat. Assn. Women Lawyers, Am. Trial Lawyers Assn., Nat. Conf. Fed. Trial Judges (past chmn.), Fed. Jud. Fellows Commn. (bd. dirs.), Fed. Jud. Ctr. (bd. dirs.), Phi Beta Kappa. Office: US Ct of Appeals 744 US Courthouse 231 W Lafayette Blvd Detroit MI 48226-2719*

KENNEDY, DEBRA JOYCE, marketing professional; b. Covina, Calif., July 9, 1955; d. John Nathan and Drea Hannah (Lancaster) Ward; m. John William Kennedy, Sept. 3, 1977 (div.); children: Drea, Noelle. BS in Communications, Calif. State Poly. U., 1977. Pub. rels. coord. Whittier (Calif.) Hosp., 1978-79, pub. relations mgr., 1980; pub. rels. dir. San Clemente (Calif.) Hosp., 1979-80; dir. pub. rels. Garfield Med. Ctr., Monterey Park, Calif., 1980-82; dir. mktg. and community rels. Charter Oak Hosp., Covina, 1983-85; mktg. dir. CPC Horizon Hosp., Pomona, 1985-89; dir. mktg. Sierra Royale Hosp., Azusa, 1989-90; mktg. rep. PacifiCare, Cypress, 1990-92; regional medicare mgr. Health Net, Woodland Hills, Calif., 1992-95; dist. sales mgr. Kaiser Permante Health Plan, Pasadena, Calif., 1995—. Mem. Am. Soc. Hosp. Pub. Rels., Healthcare Mktg. Assn., Healthcare Pub. Rels. and Mktg. Assn., Covina and Covina West C. of C., West Covina Jaycees. Republican. Methodist. Club: Soroptimists. Contbr. articles to profl. jours.

KENNEDY, DIANE, religious organization adminstrator. V.p. Aquinas Trust of Theology. Office: 10 Summit Park Dr Pittsburgh PA 15275-1103*

KENNEDY, ELIZABETH LEVINE, retail buyer; b. N.Y.C., Sept. 16, 1963; arrived in Australia, 1987.; d. Stephen Maxwell and Rhea Joy (Cotler) Levine; m. Robert William Kennedy, Aug. 30, 1987; 1 child, Zoe Isabella. BA, Smith Coll., 1985; BS, U. New South Wales, 1986; MBA, Fordham U., 1996. Dep. mgr. Macy's, N.Y.C., 1988-89; mgr. Saks 5th Avenue, N.Y.C., 1989-90; buyer, merchandise mgr. Galeries Lafayette, N.Y.C., 1992-94. V.p. Fordham U. Mktg. Club, N.Y.C., 1995-96. Mem. Am. Mktg. Assn., Shipley Sch. Alumni Assn., Smith Coll. Alumni Assn.

KENNEDY, EVELYN SIEFERT, foundation executive, textile restoration specialist; b. Pitts., Nov. 11, 1927; d. Carmine and Assunta (Iacobucci) Rocci; BS magna cum laude, U. R.I., 1969, MS in Textiles and Clothing, 1970; cert. appraiser of personal property; m. George J. Siefert, May 30, 1953 (div. 1974); children: Paul Kenneth, Carl Joseph, Ann Marie; m. Lyle H. Kennedy, II, Oct. 12, 1974 (div. Feb. 1986). With Pitts. Pub. Schs., 1945-50; with Goodyear Aircraft Corp., Akron, Ohio, 1950-54; clothing instr. Groton (Conn.) Dept. Adult Edn., 1958-68; pres. Sewtique, Groton, 1970, Sewtique II, New London, Conn., 1986; v.p. Kennedy Capital Advisors, Groton, 1973-85, Kennedy Mgmt. Corp., Groton, 1974-85, Kennedy InterVest, Inc., Groton, 1975-85; pres., exec. dir. P.R.I.D.E. Found., Inc., Groton, 1978—; clothing cons. Coop. Extension Service, Dept. Agr.; internat. lectr. on clothing for disabled and elderly; adj. faculty U. Conn., Eastern Conn. State Coll., St. Joseph Coll.; hon. prof. U. R.I., assoc. prof., 1987—; fed. expert witness Care Label Law, FTC, 1976; mem. Major Appliance Consumer Action Panel, 1983-89. Regional adv. coun. SBA active corps Execs., Hartford, 1985—; bd. dirs. Small Bus. Devel. Ctr., 1989—, Easter Seal Rehab. Ctr. Southeastern Conn.; bus. adv. council U. R.I., 1979—, trustee, 1985—; active LWV; mem. Groton Vocat. Edn. Adv. Council. Recipient award of distinction U. R.I., 1969, Adv. of Yr. SBA. 1984, Outstanding Svc. in Community, 1991; named Woman of Yr. Bus. and Profl. Women's Club, 1977, Conn. Home Economist of Yr., 1987. Mem. Internat. Sleep Council (consumer affairs rep., Small Bus. Adminstrn. award 1991), Internat. Soc. Appraisers (cert. appraiser personal property, panelist FMHA roster, farmer's credit mediator 1989—), Nat. Assn. Bedding Mfrs., Conn. Home Economists in Bus. (founder 1977, Women of Yr. 1987), Nat. Home Economists in Bus. (chmn. internat. relations, nat. fin. chmn. 1986), Am. Home Econs. Assn., Coll. and Univ. Bus. Instrs. of Conn., Am. Occupational Therapy Assn. (resource cons. 1986—), Web-Re-Stor Assn. (wedding restoration specialist 1993—), Southeastern Women's Network, Fashion Group, Omicron Nu, Phi Kappa Phi. Democrat. Roman Catholic. Clubs: New London Zonta, Bus. and Profl. Women's (Outstanding Women of Year 1977). Author: Dressing With Pride, 1980, Clothing Accessibility: A Lesson Plan to Aid the Disabled and Elderly, 1983. Office: 391 Long Hill Rd Groton CT 06340-3812

KENNEDY, FRANCES THERESE CIRILLO, financial consultant; b. Darby, Pa., Oct. 3, 1950; d. Joseph Anthony and Anna Irene (Calise) Cirillo; m. William George Kennedy, June 10, 1972; children: Robert, Julie. BA cum laude, Trinity Coll., 1971. Chief info. processing WAOB/UDSA, Washington, 1979-83; dir. info processing divsn. Farm Credit Adminstrn., McLean, Va., 1983-86; v.p. Systems & Solutions, Ltd., Fairfax, Va., 1986-92; computer cons. Fairfax, Va., 1992-95, fin. cons., 1995—; cons. Comptroller Currency, Washington, 1986-87. Vol. Hanley for Chmn., Falls Church, Va., 1995; treas. Canterbury Woods PTA, Annandale, Va., 1990-91, Thomas Jefferson H.S. PTSA, Alexandria, Va., 1992-94, TJ Crew Boosters, Alexandria, 1994-96; coach, age group dir. BRYC, 1981-90. Mem. Soc. Univ. Women, Phi Beta Kappa. Roman Catholic. Home: 9812 Ceralene Dr Fairfax VA 22032

KENNEDY, JERRIE ANN PRESTON, public relations executive; b. Quanah, Tex.; children: Brandon, Cameron. Student, Sunset Sch. Preaching, Lubbock, Tex., 1975-78, Jo-Susan Modeling Sch., Nashville, 1984, Film Actors Lab., 1986. Co-prodr. Vincent Cirrincione & Assocs., N.Y., 1986; freelance internat. mktg. and public rels. exec. U.S., and Papua, New Guinea, 1988—; military del. NATO Allies for The French Liaison, Ft. Hood, Tex., 1992. Author screenplay, also fed. and comty. pub. spl. events prodn. Recipient 1st and 3d pl. awards Modeling Assn. Am., N.Y.C., 1985.

KENNEDY, JOAN CANFIELD, volunteer; b. Washington, Mar. 24, 1931; d. Austin Francis and Gertrude Rita (MacBride) Canfield; m. Keith Furnival Kennedy, Feb. 11, 1956; children: Joseph Keith, Austin Robert, Thomas Canfield, Richard Furnival. BA, Coll. New Rochelle, 1953. Trustee Ctr. Preventive Psychiatry, White Plains, N.Y., 1973-85, Catawba Lands Conservancy, 1992-95; bd. dirs. Scarsdale chpt. LWV, 1974-85, Charlotte-Mecklenburg (N.C.) chpt., 1985-89, pres. 1989-93, bd. dirs. N.C., 1993-96); bd. dirs. Coll. New Rochelle Alumnae Assn., 1977-81, 89-92; chmn. Coun. Human Rels., Scarsdale, N.Y., 1983-85; bd. dirs. New Neighbors League, 1986-87, Shalom Homes, 1987-88, Kids Voting N.C., 1993-97. Recipient Ursulas Laurus Citation, 1968, Angela Merici award, 1988; named New Neighbor of Yr. New Neighbors League, 1987. Mem. Niantic Bay Yacht Club, Larchmont (N.Y.) Yacht Club. Roman Catholic. Home: 1441 Carmel Rd Charlotte NC 28226-5011

KENNEDY, KATHLEEN, film producer. Student, San Diego State U. With KCST, San Diego; pres. Amblin Entertainment, Universal City, Calif. Assoc. prodr.: (films) Poltergeist, 1982, Twilight Zone-The Movie, 1983, Indiana Jones and the Temple of Doom, 1984; prodr.: (films) Twister, 1996; (with Steven Spielberg) E.T. The Extra-Terrestrial, 1982 (Academy award nomination for best picture 1982); (with Quincy Jones, Frank Marshall, and Spielberg) The Color Purple, 1985 (Academy award nomination for best picture 1983), (with Marshall and Art Levinson) The Money Pit, 1986 (with Marshall and Spielberg) Empire of the Sun, 1987, Always, 1989; (with Richard Vane) Arachnophobia, 1990; (with Marshall and Gerald R. Molen) Hook, 1991; (with Robert Watts) Alive, 1993; (with Molen) Jurassic Park, 1993, (with Marshall) Milk Money, 1994; (with Clint Eastwood) The Bridges of Madison County, 1995; exec. prodr.: (films) A Dangerous Woman, 1993, Schindler's List, 1993 (Academy award for best picture 1993), Congo, 1995, The Indian in the Cupboard, 1995; (with Marshall and Spielberg) Gremlins, 1984, The Goonies, 1985, Back to the Future, 1985, Young Sherlock Holmes, 1985, *batteries not included, 1987, Dad, 1989, Back to the Future Part II, 1990, Gremlins 2: The New Batch, 1990, Back to the Future Part III, 1990, Joe Versus the Volcano, 1990, Cape Fear, 1991, We're Back! A Dinosaur's Story, 1993, Balto, 1995; (with Marshall) Fandango, 1985; (with Marshall, Spielberg, and David Kirschner) An American Tail, 1986; (with Marshall, Spielberg, Peter Guber, and Jon Peters) Innerspace, 1987; (with Spielberg) Who Framed Roger Rabbit, 1988; (with Marshall, Spielberg, and George Lucas) The Land Before Time, 1988; (with Marshall and Lucas) Indiana Jones and the Last Crusade, 1989; (with Marshall and Kirschner) An American Tail: Fievel Goes West, 1991; (with Peter Bogdanovich) Noises Off, 1992; (with Marshall and Molen) A Far Off Place, 1993; (with Molen, Kirschner, William Hanna, and Joseph Barbera) The Flintstones, 1994. Office: 650 Bronson Los Angeles CA 90004*

KENNEDY, KIMBERLY KAYE, history educator, bookkeeper; b. Naples, Fla., Nov. 2, 1961; d. George Eugene and Viola (Passmore) K. BA, Valdosta Coll., 1989, MA, 1990. Mgr. asst. Avon Products, Valdosta, 1983-88; bookkeeper Kennedy Rentals, Valdosta, 1983—; history educator Ga. Mil. Coll., Valdosta, 1993—; owner Kennedy Rentals, Valdosta, 1994—. Author: What Rainbow Means, 1976 (Internat. Order of Rainbow 1st pl. award 1986), (with others) Reflections, 1978. Recipient Grand Cross of Color Internat. Order of Rainbow, 1977. Mem. Order Ea. Star (worthy matron 1982-83). Democrat. Methodist. Home: 3647 Guest Rd Valdosta GA 31605-4833 Office: Ga Mil Coll 3010 Robinson Rd Moody AFB GA 31699

KENNEDY, LOUISE AVERY, newspaper editor, writer; b. Dayton, Ohio, Feb. 6, 1959; d. Grafton Sherwood and Gertrude Avery (Harder) K.; m. George Langdon Gibson, May 13, 1989 (div. May 1994). BA, Yale U., 1980. Reporter, asst. editor, mng. editor New Haven Advocate, 1980-83; asst. Living editor, asst. mng. editor/Living New Haven Register and Jour. Courier, 1984-86; copy editor, Living copy desk chief Boston Globe, 1988-93, asst. book editor, 1993-95, asst. Living editor, 1995, asst. Mag. editor, 1995—; freelance theatre, book and mag. critic Boston Globe, 1988—. Named Disting. Alumna, Phillips Acad., Andover, Mass., 1994. Mem. PEN New Eng., Soc. Profl. Journalists. Office: Boston Globe PO Box 2378 135 Morrissey Blvd Boston MA 02107

KENNEDY, MARY VIRGINIA, diplomat; b. Pocatello, Idaho, Sept. 5, 1946; d. Charles Millard and Martha Lorissa (Evans) K. BA, U. Denver, 1968, MA, 1969; MAT, U. Idaho, 1971. Tchr. cert. Idaho. Recreation aide ARC, South Vietnam, 1969-70; ops. officer State Dept. Ops. Ctr., Washington, 1977-78; spl. asst. amb. Philip Habib, Washington, 1979-80, Sec. State, Washington, 1980-81; econ. officer U.S. Embassy, Cairo, Egypt, 1981-84; consul Am. Consulate, Adana, Turkey, 1985-88; Pearson fellow Office Cong. Bereuter Ho. Reps., 1988-89; exec. asst. Dept. Sec. State, Washington, 1989-91; dep. chief mission Dept. State U.S. Embassy, Kuwait, 1991-93; consul gen. Am. Consulate, Karachi, Pakistan, 1994-96; dean Sch. Profl. Area Studies, Fgn. Svc. Inst., 1996—. Mem. Am. Fgn. Svc. Protective Assn. (bd. dirs. 1988-91), Phi Beta Kappa, Mortar Bd. Home: 905 Bashford Ln Alexandria VA 22314

KENNEDY, MAUREEN, government administrator; b. Gulfport, Miss., Nov. 15, 1957; m. Konrad S. Alt. BA, Mt. Holyoke Coll., 1979; MPA, Harvard U., 1988. Lobbyist Rapoza Assocs., Washington, 1988-89; dir. rural policy The Aspen Inst., Washington, 1989-93; dep. asst. sec. for policy U.S. Dept. HUD, Washington, 1993-95; adminstr. USDA/Rural Housing Svc., Washington, 1995; cons. The Ford Found., 1992—. Author: Searching for The Way That Works, 1988; editor: Electronic Byways, 1990. Bd. dirs. Alaska chpt. ACLU, Anchorage, 1984-85. Mem. Women in Housing and Fin. Democrat. Office: USDA Rm 5014 So Bldg Washington DC

KENNEDY, MAUREEN AGNES, market researcher; b. Washington, Feb. 15, 1946; d. Daniel Bernard and Ann Aurelia (Caldwell) Kennedy; m. James H. Mangan, Sept. 10, 1977 (div. Oct. 1987); 1 child, James Daniel; m. David R. Bartlow, June 8, 1996. BA, U. Md., 1970. Dir. rsch. Daniel J. Edelman, Washington, 1976-80; v.p., rsch. dir. N.Am. Mktg., Richmond, Va., 1980-83; pres. Mangan & Smith Rsch., Richmond, 1983-84; dir. mktg. Comms. Resource Group, Richmond, 1984-85; dir. rsch. The Bomstein Agy., Washington, 1985-94, DeLima Assocs., McLean, Va., 1995—; adj. faculty Va. Commonwealth U., Richmond, 1980-83. Recipient Golden Candlestick award Am. Mktg. Assn., 1985. Roman Catholic. Home: 4446 1st Pl S Arlington VA 22204-1317 Office: DeLima Assocs 6723 Whittier Ave Ste L-6 Mc Lean VA 22101

KENNEDY, NANCY LOUISE, retired draftsman; b. Mar. 14, 1925; d. William Richardson and Mary Enroughty (Youmans) Humphrey; m. William Dwyer Kennedy, Sept. 3, 1952 (dec. May 1953); 1 child, Kathleen Dwyer. Student, Gulf Park Coll., 1943; B of Interior Design, Washington U., 1948. Land draftsman Carter Oil Co., Ft. Smith, Ark., 1954-60, Sinclair Oil and Gas, Oklahoma City, 1960-69, Atlantic Richfield Oil and Gas Co., Tulsa, 1969-82. Mem. Altar guild Trinity Episcopal Ch., Tulsa. Mem. Kappa Alpha Theta. Republican. Home: 6362 S 80th East Ave Apt D Tulsa OK 74133-3825

KENNEDY, PATRICIA BERRY, music educator; b. Alexandria, La., May 8, 1944; d. Gerald Adair and Zennia Juanita (Francis) Berry. B of Music Edn., Va. Commonwealth U., 1968, MEd, 1974. Cert. music tchr., gen., choral and instrumental, adminstrn. and supervision, Va. Tchr. choral music Colonial Hgts. (Va.) Pub. Schs., 1968-71; tchr. choral, instrumental and gen. music King William (Va.) Pub. Schs., 1972—; coun. chair Dominion UniServ Unit, Richmond, Va., 1987-90, 91-93; bd. dirs. Va. Edn. Assn., 1987-90, 91-93, 96-98. Va. Wing CAP, Civil Air Patrol, Chesterfield, Va., 1971—. Named Sr. Mem. of Yr., Civil Air Patrol Va. Wing, 1984, PTA Mem. of Yr., Hamilton-Holmes PTA, 1985, Tchr. of Yr., Acquinton Elem. Sch., 1990, King William County Schs., 1990-91, Exceptional Mem. of Yr., Acquinton PTA, 1993-94. Mem. NEA, Music Educators Nat. Conf., Va. Elem. Music Edn. Assn. (pres. 1994-96), Va. Music Educators Assn., King William Edn. Assn. (faculty rep., sec. 1992-93, pres. 1994-97). Republican. Baptist. Home: RR 1 Box 285 King William VA 23086-9719 Office: Acquinton Elem Sch RR 1 Box 97 King William VA 23086-9755

KENNEDY, STEPHENIE KAY, mental health services professional; b. Clarksburg, W. Va, Nov. 13, 1965; d. W. Gene and Cinda Kay (Swiger) K. BS, Wheeling Jesuit Coll., 1988; MA, W. Va. U., 1992. Nat. cert. counselor; lic. profl. counselor, master addictions counselor. Pers. dir. Apples Supermarket, Morgantown, W. Va., 1990-91; residence hall dir. W. Va. U., Morgantown, 1991-92; therapist Pressley Ridge Sch., Clarksburg, 1992-94; family devel. ctr. coord. Pressley Ridge Sch., 1994—. Mem. ACA, Internat. Assn. Marriage and Family Therapists. Democrat. Roman Catholic. Office: Pressley Ridge Sch Route 5 Box 697 Clarksburg WV 26301

KENNEDY-SHIELDS, KATHLEEN ANN, health care administrator, consultant; b. Bklyn., Sept. 9, 1951; d. Vincent B. and Ann M. (Dunlap) Kennedy; m. Paul J. Shields, May 6, 1977; 1 child, Christopher Ryan. BA, U. South Fla., 1973; MS magna cum laude, St. Johns U., 1977. Child care worker Mission of Immaculate Virgin, S.I., 1973-74, caseworker, 1974-76; caseworker N.Y. State Office Mental Retardation and Devel. Disabilities, S.I., 1976-77; team leader S.I. Devel. Ctr., 1977-78, placement specialist, 1978-80, program planning specialist, 1980-83, community service adminstr., 1983-86; dir. S.I. Planning and Devel., 1986-93; dir. devel. Ind. Living Assn., Bklyn., 1993-95; bd. trustees, chmn. Life Skills Resource Ctr., 1994—; pres. Kennedy Shields and Assocs., S.I., N.Y., 1995—; project cons. to numerous orgns. including Northfield Cmty. Local Devel. Corp., S.I., Cmty. Resources for the Developmentally Disabled, Ind. Living Assn., Bklyn., and many others; dir. planning Willowbrook Closure Exec. Task Force, 1986-87; presenter N.Y.C. Rent Stabilization Bd., 1994. Mem. Commr.'s Task Force for Redesign of N.Y.C. Service Delivery System 1989, N.Y. State Task Force of Needs and Assessment and Evaluation, 1988-92, Commr.'s Task Force on Strategic Planning in N.Y.C., 1988-92, S.I. Interagy. Coun. on Aging, co-chair social activities com., 1993—; panelist Commr.'s Forum Planning for the Future, 1988; den mother Boy Scouts Am., S.I., 1988-89; mem. info. exch. com. S.I. Regional Retardation and Devel. Disabilities, N.J. Assn. of Cmty Providers, 1995—, Parents Assn., St. Peters Boys H.S., 1993—. Named Woman of Yr. on Your Mark, Inc., 1989; recipient Commendation Mission of Immaculate Virgin, 1989, Commendation Ind. Living Assocs., 1990. Mem. Am. Mgmt. Assn., Am. Women in Econ. Devel., Mid Island Kiwanis (chair priority one children birth to 5, pres. 1996—). Roman Catholic. Home and Office: 650 Victory Blvd Apt 4B Staten Island NY 10301-3545

KENNEDY SPARACIO, JULIANNA, advertising and public relations executive; b. Coral Gables, Fla., Sept. 12, 1963; d. Allan Ball and Angeline (Garibay) Kennedy; m. Kevin John Sparacio, June 25, 1994. BA in Comm. and Journalism, Loyola U., Chgo., 1991. Acct. coord. Leibson, Lightle & Assoc., Chgo., 1986-88; asst. acct. exec. Haddon Advt., Inc., Chgo., 1988-89; acct. exec. Unti, Joyce & Siegel, Inc., Chgo., 1989-90; mktg. coord. Miglin-Beitler Mgmt. Corp., Chgo., 1990-92; sr. acct. exec. Bev Kennedy & Co., Highland Park, Ill., 1992-94; dir. pub. rels. Welch & Nehlen, Inc., Garden City, N.Y., 1994-95; pub. rels. cons. Okeanos Ocean Rsch. Found., Riverhead, N.Y., 1995—. Dir. mktg. comm. United Way of L.I., 1996—. Mem. Women in Comm. Inc., Photographic Mktg. Assn., Long Ridge Writers Group. Republican. Roman Catholic. Home: 130 Skyline Dr Coram NY 11727

KENNELLY, BARBARA B., congresswoman; b. Hartford, Conn., July 10, 1936; d. John Moran and Barbara (Leary) Bailey; m. James J. Kennelly, Sept. 26, 1959 (dec. 1995); children: Eleanor Bride, Barbara Leary, Louise Moran, John Bailey. BA in Econs, Trinity Coll., Washington, 1958; grad., Harvard-Radcliffe Sch. Bus. Adminstrn., 1959; M.A. in Govt, Trinity Coll., Hartford, 1971. Mem. Hartford Ct. of Common Council, 1975-79; sec. of state State of Conn., Hartford, 1979-83; mem. 98th-103rd Congresses from 1st Dist. Conn., Hartford, 1982—; mem. ways and means com. Trustee Trinity Coll., Hartford, Conn.; previously active in numerous civic, polit., and govt. orgns. in Greater Hartford, Conn. Democrat. Roman Catholic. Office: 201 Cannon HOB Washington DC 20515

KENNELLY, SISTER KAREN MARGARET, college administrator; b. Graceville, Minn., Aug. 4, 1933; d. Walter John Kennelly and Clara Stella Eastman. BA, Coll. St. Catherine, St. Paul, 1956; MA, Cath. U. Am., 1958; PhD, U. Calif., Berkeley, 1962. Joined Sisters of St. Joseph of Carondelet, Roman Cath. Ch., 1954. Prof. history Coll. St. Catherine, 1962-71, acad. dean, 1971-79; exec. dir. Nat. Fedn. Carondelet Colls., U.S., 1979-82; province dir. Sisters of St. Joseph of Carondelet, St. Paul, 1982-88; pres. Mt. St. Mary's Coll., L.A., 1989—; cons. N. Cen. Accreditation Assn., Chgo., 1974-84, Ohio Bd. Regents, Columbus, 1983-89; trustee colls., hosps., Minn., Wis., Calif., 1972—; chmn. Sisters St. Joseph Coll. Consortium, 1989-93. Editor, co author: American Catholic Women, 1989; author: (with others) Women of Minnesota, 1977. Fulbright fellow, 1964, Am. Coun. Learned Socs. fellow, 1964-65. Mem. Am. Hist. Soc., Am. Cath. Hist. Soc., Medieval Acad., Am. Assn. Rsch. Historians on Medieval Spain. Roman Catholic. Home and Office: Mt St Marys Coll 12001 Chalon Rd Los Angeles CA 90049-1597

KENNER, MARILYN SFERRA, civil engineer; b. Youngstown, Ohio, Oct. 16, 1959; d. Joseph James and Mary (Conti) Sferra; m. Walter Sherden Kenner, July 7, 1984. B in Engring., Youngstown State U., 1982. Registered profl. engr., Ohio. Design and constrn. engr. Mahoning County Engr.'s Office, Youngstown, 1982-89, chief dep. engr., 1989—; mem. engring. dean search com. Youngstown State U. Mem. Mahoning Valley Soc. Profl. Engrs. (pres., v.p. 1990-93, treas. 1987-90). Democrat. Roman Catholic. Home: 6941 Lockwood Blvd Youngstown OH 44512 Office: Mahoning County Engr Office 940 Bears Den Rd Youngstown OH 44511-1218

KENNETTE, JENNIE LAURA FAKES, medical and surgical nurse; b. Hanston, Kans., Jan. 16, 1935; d. Jack Delmont and Bertha Mabel (Law) Fakes; m. Leslie Cleland Koontz, Dec. 4 1958 (dec.); children: Kim, Lynn, Gay, Jan, Jay, Lee; m. Robert Ray Hamill, Oct. 21, 1979 (div.); m. Russell T. Kennette Jr., Nov. 17, 1990. ADN, Barton County Community Coll., 1971; BSN, U. Wyo., 1988. RN; cert. med.-surg. nurse, gerontol. nurse. Staff nurse clin. level III Laramie County Hosp., Cheyenne, Wyo.; asst. head nurse DePaul Hosp., Cheyenne; charge nurse St. Catherine's Hosp., Garden City, Kans.; DON Spearville (Kans.) Dist. Hosp.; charge nurse Meml. Hosp. Laramie County, Laramie County Hosp., Cheyenne, Wyo.; supr. Wyo. Retirement Ctr. Mem. ANA, Barton County C.C. Alumni Assn. Home: PO Box 841 Basin WY 82410-0841

KENNEY, DONNA DENISE, accountant; b. Bklyn., Oct. 4, 1960; d. Donald and Sherry Sheila (Nedol) Yules; m. Eugene L. Kenney, Jr., May 31, 1981; children: Kyle Asher, Graham Stewart. BBA in Bus. Mgmt., Adelphi U., 1981, MBA with distinction, 1989. CPA, N.Y. Grad. asst. dept. acctg. and law Adelphi U., Garden City, N.Y., 1984-89; sr. acct. Kreitzman Barragato and Kreitzman, CPAs, Smithtown, N.Y., 1989-91, Kreitzman and Kreitzman, CPAs, Smithtown, 1992-94, Susnick and Harris, CPAs, Cedarhurst, N.Y., 1994—. Mem. N.Y. State Soc. CPAs (com. mem. acctg. and auditing Suffolk chpt. 1991-92, award of honor 1989), Delta Mu Delta, Eta Chi Alpha. Office: Susnick and Harris 357 Central Ave Cedarhurst NY 11516

KENNEY, PATTI MARLENE, sales executive; b. St. Louis, Nov. 6, 1952; d. Herbert Martin and Marlene Marguerite (Short) Foerster; m. Thomas Francis Kenney, June 1, 1968 (div. Aug. 1995); children: Paulette Marlene Potter, Brian Patrick, Thomas Michael. Student, Comty. Coll., 1982-83. Cert. advt. specialist, master advt. specialist. Customer svc. rep. Hazel, Hazel, So. Calif., 1983; customer svc./salesperson Cubegraphics, Sunnyvale, No. Calif., 1984-86, Mission Laser Works, El Monte, Calif., 1986-88; customer svc. mgr. Penn Corp., St. Louis, 1988-89; nat. sales mgr. Ocean Specialty, So. Calif., 1989-94; nat. sales dir. The Newport Connection, Orange County, Calif., 1994-95; regional sales mgr. Vantage Custom Classics, Orange County, 1995—; bd. dirs. Specialty Advt. Assn., editor, 1992-94, sec.-treas., 1993-94, v.p., 1994-95, pres., 1995-96. Lutheran. Home: 101 Murica Isle Irvine CA 92714 Office: Vantage Custom Classics 3111 S Shannon Santa Ana CA 92704

KENNEY, SISTER EUGENIE MARY, education educator; b. Phila., May 13, 1950; d. Charles Joseph and Florence Joan (Woyner) K. BA, Immaculata Coll., 1975; MA, Glassboro State U., 1987; post grad., Temple U., 1988-93; MA, Immaculata Coll., 1996. Cert. tchr. Pa. elem. edn., secondary (social studies), reading specialist, elem. prin., reading supr., early childhood edn. 1st grade tchr. Various parochial elem. schs. in Pa., 1971-1986; 4th grade tchr. St. Matthew Sch., Phila., 1986-89; 7th and 8th grades tchr. Holy Saviour Sch., Norristown, Pa., 1989-91, St. Philip and James Sch., Exton, Pa., 1991-92; 8th grade tchr. Incarnation Sch., Phila., 1992-93; asst. prof. Immaculata (Pa.) Coll., 1993—; mem. continuous progress com. Archdiocese of Phila., 1976-80, art curriculum com., 1987—, reading curriculum com., 1992-93. Mem. Servants of the Immaculate Heart of Mary, 1968—. Mem. ASCD, Nat. Assn. for Edn. Young Children, Internat. Reading Assn., Nat. Cath. Edn. Assn., Pa. Assn. for Colls. and Tchr. Edn. Home and Office: Immaculata Coll Education Dept Immaculata PA 19345-0684

KENNON, GLORIA OLIVER, guidance counselor; b. Birmingham, Ala., Nov. 6, 1942; d. Leavy Winston Oliver and Lida Moore White; m. Rozmond Herron Kennon, Oct. 10, 1985. BS, St. Augustine's Coll., 1966; MS, Ala. A&M U., 1975. Lic. guidance counselor. Tchr. A. H. Parker Sch., Biringham, Ala., 1966-68, Morse Elem. Sch., Tarrytown, N.Y., 1968-70; cons. VII Human Rels. Desegregation U. S. Ala., Mobile, 1970; counselor Opportunities Indstrialization Ctr., Washington, 1971-73; teacher, counselor Sch. Comty Anti Narcotic Progam, N.Y.C., 1973-75; guidance counselor Birmingham Pub. Schs., 1975-8%, Mpls. Pub. Schs., 1985—. Pres. Mpls Counselor's Forum, 1989-90. Mem. Minn. Sch. Counselors' Assn. (bd. dirs. 1989-90), Minn. Counseling and Devel. Assn., Am. Counseling Assn., Delta Sigma Theta. Home: 6135 Forestview Ln Plymouth MN 55442 Office: Kennon Middle Sch 1501 Aldridge Ave Mpls. MN 55411

KENNY, MAUREEN EMILY, psychology educator; b. Providence, June 21, 1949; d. Elinor Miriam (Chantler) K.; m. Michael Kurgansky, Jan. 25, 1981; 1 child, Katherine Emily. BA, Brown U., 1971; MEd, Columbia U., 1975; PhD, U. Pa., 1985. Lic. psychologist/health svc. provider, Mass. Vocat. counselor Devereux Found., Devon, Pa., 1975-81; psychologist Benchmark Sch., Media, Pa., 1983-85; lectr. U. Pa., Phila., 1985-88; asst. prof. Boston Coll., Chestnut Hill, Mass., 1988-93, assoc. prof., 1993—; dir. tng. Doctoral Program in Counseling Psychology, Boston Coll., Chestnut Hill, 1993—. Co-author: Adolescent Psychology, 1994; mem. editl. bd. Jour. Counseling Psychology, 1994—; contbr. articles to profl. jours. Faculty fellow Boston Coll., 1992; Small grantee The Spencer Found., 1993-94. Mem. APA (divsn. 17), Eastern Psychol. Assn., Soc. Rsch. in Adolescence. Home: 85 Tremont St Mansfield MA 02048 Office: Boston Coll Campion 305D Chestnut Hill MA 02167

KENNY, SHIRLEY STRUM, university administrator; b. Tyler, Tex., Aug. 28, 1934; d. Marcus Leon and Florence (Golenternek) S.; m. Robert Wayne Kenny July 22, 1956; children: David Jack, Joel Strum, Daniel Clark, Jonathan Matthew, Sarah Elizabeth. BA, BJ, U. Tex., 1955; MA, U. Minn., 1957; PhD, U. Chgo., 1964; LHD (hon.), U. Rochester, 1988. Chair English dept. U. Md., College Park, 1973-79, provost Arts and Humanities, 1979-85; pres. CUNY Queens Coll., Flushing, 1985-94, SUNY, Stony Brook, 1994—; bd. dirs. Toys 'R' Us, Computer Assocs., Chem. Bank Regional Adv. Bd. Author: The Conscious Lovers, 1968, The Plays of Richard Steele, 1971, The Performers and Their Plays, 1982, The Works of George Farquhar, 2 vols., 1988; editor: British Theatre and the Other Arts, 1984; contbr. numerous articles to profl. jours. Bd. dirs. Carnegie Found. for the Advancement of Teaching, Assn. Am. Colls. and Univs., Citizens Com. for N.Y.C., Goodwill of Greater N.Y., Long Island Assn. Recipient Disting. Alumnus award U. Chgo. Club Washington, 1980, Svc. and Leadership award N.Y. Urban League, 1988; named Outstanding Woman, U. Md., 1983, Outstanding Alumnus, U. Tex. Coll. Communication, 1989. Mem. Am. Handel Soc., Am. Soc. for 18th Century Studies, Bibliog. Soc. Va., Sigma Alpha Iota. Office: SUNY PO Box 0701 Stony Brook NY 11790-0701

KENOFER, DORIS DILLON See DILLON, DORIS

KENT, BEVERLY HOPE, business educator; b. Petersburg, Va., Feb. 8, 1964; d. Gene Wesley and Zeanetter (Roberts) Williams; m. Daniel James Kent, Apr. 27, 1991. BA in Arts Mgmt., Mary Baldwin Coll.; MS in Bus. Edn. magna cum laude, N.H. Coll., 1992. Tchr. GED and bus. Barclay Career Inst., Washington, 1992; tchr. bus. Fairfax County Pub. Schs., Alexandria, Va., 1992—; advisor FBLA, Fairfax County, 1992-93; rep. for West Potomac supts. adv. coun. RCPS, 1993-95. Mem. ASCD, Nat. Bus. Edn. Assn., Bus. Edn. Tchrs. Assn. (historian 1992-95), Va. Bus. Edn. Assn. Republican. Methodist. Home: 6932 Vanderbilt Dr Alexandria VA 22307 Office: Fairfax County Pub Schs West Potomac HS 6500 Quander Rd Alexandria VA 22307

KENT, JEANNE YVONNE, artist; b. Lawrence, Mass., Feb. 6, 1947; d. Gerard George and Cecile Fecteau Galarneau; m. Martin Joseph Kent, Dec. 4, 1971; 1 child, Nicole Michelle. Student, Lowell State Tchr.'s Coll., 1966-68, Northea. U., 1970-73; BFA, Mass. Coll. Art, 1989. Resident asst., slide lectr. Elderhostel Mass. Coll. Art, Boston, 1988; slide lectr. Weymouth North H.S., East Weymouth, Mass., 1990, 93; instr. art Lee Wards Arts and Crafts Store, Quincy, Mass., 1990. One-woman shows include Brookline Pub. Libr., Brookline Art Soc., 1995, West Roxbury (Mass.) Pub. Libr., 1995; exhibited in group shows at Mass. Coll. Art, Boston, 1988-89, 95, Rubin O'Barry's Coffee Shop, Jamaica Plain, Mass., 1989, Arts in the Pks., Boston, 1989, Brookline (Mass.) Art Soc., 1989-96, Boston Visual Artist's Union, 1990, Arnold Arboretum of Harvard U., Jamaica Plain, 1992; contbr. poems to various publs. Recipient Silver medal World of Poetry, 1989, Intergenerational Poetry hon. mention award West Roxbury Pub. Libr., 1989, 4th Pl. painting award Dedham (Mass.) Arts and Crafts Fair, 1990, Calendar Illustration painting award 1st ann. Dedham Cmty. Art Competition, Dedham Cmty. Ho. Gallery, 1993; poems named Best Poems of the '90s, Nat. Libr. Poetry. Mem. West Roxbury Art Assn., Greater Roslindale Arts Assn., Brookline Art Soc. Home: 5 Eastland Rd Jamaica Plain MA 02130-4616

KENT, JILL ELSPETH, academic healthcare administrator, lawyer, former government official; b. Detroit, June 1, 1948; d. Seymour and Grace (Edelman) K.; m. Mark Elliott Solomons, Aug. 20, 1978. BA, U. Mich., 1970; JD, George Washington U., 1975, LLM, 1979. Bar: D.C. 1975. Mgmt. intern U.S. Dept. Transp., Washington, 1971-73; staff analyst Office Mgmt. and Budget, Exec. Office of Pres., Washington, 1974-76; legis. counsel U.S. Treasury Dept., Washington, 1976-78; dir. legis. reference div. Health Care Financing Adminstrn., Washington, 1978-80; sr. budget examiner Office Mgmt. and Budget, Exec. Office Pres., Washington, 1980-84; chief Treasury, Gen. Services, OMB, 1984-85; dep. asst. sec. for departmental fin. and planning U.S. Dept. Treasury, 1985-86; dep. asst. sec. for dept. fin. and mgmt., 1986-88; asst. sec. of treasury, 1988-89, CFO, U.S. Dept. State, 1989-93, acting under sec. of state for mgmt., 1991; exec. devel. program Office Mgmt. and Budget, 1984; CFO George Washington U. Med. Ctr., Washington, 1993—; prin. Coun. Excellence in Govt., 1993—; gen. mgr. The Fragge Co., 1995—; adj. prof. pub. policy U. Md., 1993—; bd. dirs. Mobile Med. Care Inc., 1987-91. Trustee Newport Sch., 1988-91; bd. trustees Washington Civic Symphony, 1994-95. Recipient Adminstrs. award Health Care Financing Adminstrn., 1980; named one of Top 40 Performers, Management mag., 1987, Disting. Svc. award Dept. Treasury, 1989, Am. Assn. Govt. Accts. award, 1992, Disting. Svc. award Dept. State, 1993. Mem. ABA, D.C. Bar Assn., Pres's. Council on Mgmt. Improvement, CFO Roundtable Healthcare Forum, Fin. Execs. Inst., Exec. Women in Govt. (treas. 1991-92, pres. 1992-93), Va. Assn. of Female Exec. (adv. coun. 1990). Republican. Home: 2419 California St NW Washington DC 20008-1615 Office: George Washington Med Ctr Washington DC 20037

KENT, JULIE, ballet dancer, actress, model; b. Bethesda, Md., July 11, 1969; d. Charles Lindbergh and Jennifer Elsie (Machirus) Cox. Grad. high sch., Potomac, Md. Apprentice Am. Ballet Theatre, N.Y.C., 1985-86, mem. corps de ballet, 1986-1990, soloist, 1990-93, prin. dancer, 1993—. Starring role (film) Dancers, 1986; performed as a guest artist nationally and internationally. Recipient Prix de Lausanne Internat. Ballet competition, 1986, 1st prize at Erik Bruhn Competition in Toronto, 1993; named one of 50 Most Beautiful People, People Mag., 1993. Office: Am Ballet Theatre 890 Broadway Fl 3 New York NY 10003-1211

KENT, LINDA GAIL, dancer; b. Buffalo, Sept. 21, 1946; d. Jerol Edward and Dorismae (Kohler) K. BS, Juilliard Sch., 1968. Dancer Alvin Ailey Am. Dance Theater, 1968-74, then prin. dancer, 1970-74; prin. dancer Paul Taylor Dance Co., N.Y.C., 1975-89; faculty Juilliard Sch., 1984—; artist-in-residence Union Theological Seminary, N.Y. Mem. Am. Guild Mus. Artists, Actors Equity. Democrat. Unitarian. Home: 175 W 92nd St New York NY 10025-7501 Office: 552 Broadway New York NY 10012-3922

KENT, M. ELIZABETH, lawyer; b. N.Y.C., Nov. 17, 1943; d. Francis J. and Hannah (Bergman) K. AB, Vassar Coll. magna cum laude, 1964; AM, Harvard U., 1965, PhD, 1974; JD, Georgetown U., 1978. Bar: D.C. 1978, U.S. Dist. Ct. D.C. 1978, U.S. Ct. Appeals (D.C. cir.) 1978, U.S. Supreme Ct. 1983, U.S. Dist. Ct. Md. 1985. From lectr. to asst. prof. history U. Ala., Birmingham, 1972-74; assoc. Santarelli and Gimer, Washington, 1978; sole practice Washington, 1978—. Mem. Ripon Soc., Cambridge and Washington, 1968-93; rsch. dir. Howard M. Miller for Congress, Boston, 1972; vol. campaigns John V. Lindsay for Mayor, 1969, John V. Lindsay for Pres., 1972, John B. Anderson for Pres., 1980. Woodrow Wilson fellow 1964-65; Harvard U. fellow 1968-69. Mem. ABA, ACLU, D.C. Bar Assn., Women's Bar Assn., Women's Legal Def. Fund, D.C. Assn. Criminal Def. Lawyers, Superior Ct. Trial Lawyers Assn., Nat. Women's Polit. Caucus, Phi Beta Kappa. Republican. Home: 35 E St NW Apt 810 Washington DC 20001-1520 Office: 601 Indiana Ave NW Ste 605 Washington DC 20004-2907

KENT, ROBERTA B., literary consultant; b. N.Y.C., Sept. 7, 1945; d. Robert B. and Rose (Linker) K. BA magna cum laude, NYU, 1967, MA, 1969; postgrad., Princeton U., 1967-68. Asst. to head literary dept. Creative Mgmt. Assocs., N.Y.C., 1969-70; asst. to pres. Curtis Brown Ltd., N.Y.C., 1970-72, literary agt., v.p. dept. motion pictures, 1978-79; ptnr., literary agt.

W.B. Agy., N.Y.C., 1972-78; literary agt., v.p. dept. motion pictures Kohner-Levy Agy., Los Angeles, 1979-81; literary agt. The Ufland Agy., Beverly Hills, Calif., 1981-83; literary agt., v.p. literary dept. S.T.E. Representation, Ltd., Beverly Hills, 1983-91; ind. cons. Cowling, Heysell, Plouse, Ingalls & Moore, Medford, Oreg., 1991-96, Black, Chapman, Webber & Stevens, Medford, Oreg., 1996—. Mem. Phi Beta Kappa. Democrat. Office: Black Chapman Webber & Stevens 930 W 8th St Medford OR 97501

KENT, SUSAN GOLDBERG, library director, consultant; b. N.Y.C., Mar. 18, 1944; d. Elias and Minnie (Barnett) Solomon; m. Eric Goldberg, Mar. 27, 1966 (div. Mar. 1991); children: Evan, Jessica, Joanna; m. Rolly Kent, Dec. 20, 1991. BA in English Lit. with honors, SUNY, 1965; MS, Columbia U., 1966. Libr., sr. libr. N.Y. Pub. Libr., 1965-67, br. mgr. Donnell Art Libr., 1967-68; reference libr. Paedergaat br. Bklyn. Pub. Libr., 1971-72; reference libr. Finkelstein Meml. Libr., Spring Valley, N.Y., 1974-76; coord. adult and young adult svcs. Tucson Pub. Libr., 1977-80, acting libr. dir., 1982, dep. libr. dir., 1980-87; mng. dir. Ariz. Theatre Co., Tucson and Phoenix, 1987-89; dir. Mpls. Pub. Libr. and Info. Ctr., 1990-95; city libr. L.A. Pub. Libr., 1995—; tchr. Pima C.C., Tucson, 1978, grad. libr. sch. U. Ariz., Tucson, 1978, 79; panelist Ariz. Commn. Arts, 1981-85; reviewer pub. programs NEH, 1985, 89, panelist challenge grants, 1986-89, panelist state programs, 1988; cons. to librs. and nonprofit instns., 1989-90, 92—; mem. bd. devel. and fundraising Child's Play, Phoenix, 1983; bd. dirs., mem. organizing devel. and fundraising com. Flagstaff (Ariz.) Symphony Orch., 1988; cons., presenter workshops Young Adult Svcs. divsn. ALA, 1986-88; presenter in field. Contbr. articles to profl. jours. Chair arts and culture com. Tucson Tomorrow, 1981-85; bd. dirs., v.p. Ariz. Dance Theatre, 1984-86; bd. dirs. women's studies adv. coun. U. Ariz., 1985-90, Arizonans for Cultural Devel., 1987-89, YWCA Mpls., 1991-92; commr. Ariz. Commn. on Arts, 1983-87; participant Leadership Mpls., 1990-91. Fellow Sch. Libr. Sci., Columbia U., 1965-66. Mem. ALA (membership com. S.W. regional chair 1983-86, com. on appts. 1986-87, planning and budget assembly del. 1991-93, gov. coun. 1990—), Pub. Libr. Assn. (nominating com. 1980-82, v.p. 1986-87, pres. 1987-88, chair publs. assembly 1988-89, chair nat. conf. 1994, chair legis. com. 1994-95), Calif. Libr. Assn., Urban Librs. Coun. (exec. bd. 1994—, treas. 1996—), Libr. Adminstrn. and Mgmt. Assn. (John Cotton Dana Award com. 1994-95). Office: LA Pub Libr 630 W 5th St Los Angeles CA 90071-2097

KENTY, JANET ROGERS, nursing educator; b. Washington, Jan. 25, 1945; d. Howard Lewis and Alice Elizabeth (Smith) Rogers; m. Richard Donald McHugh, June 10, 1967 (div. Aug. 1978); 1 child, Kerry; m. Jay William Kenty, Aug. 5, 1978; children: Howard, Elizabeth. BSN, U. Mass. Amherst, 1967; MSN, Boston U., 1979; PhD, U. Conn., 1995. Instr. Cooley Dickinson Hosp., North Hampton, Mass., 1967-68; staff nurse Beverly (Mass.) Hosp., 1975-76; instr. Lynn (Mass.) Hosp. Sch. Nursing, 1976-78; asst. prof. Salve Regina U., Newport, R.I., 1978-85; coord. perinatal outreach edn. Women and Infants Hosp., Providence, 1985-87; vis. lectr. U. Mass., Dartmouth, 1987-95, asst. prof., 1996—. Author: (with Doenges and Moorhouse) Maternal-Newborn Care Plans, 1988. Mem. ANA, Nat. League for Nursing, R.I. Nurses Assn. (sec. dist. I 1993-95), Sigma Theta Tau, Phi Lambda Theta. Home: 222 Brookhaven Rd North Kingstown RI 02852-1976

KENYON, DAPHNE ANNE, economics educator; b. Augusta, Ga., Aug. 14, 1952; d. Lawrence Austin and Shirley (Knaus) Kenyon; m. Peter George Kachavos, Oct. 22, 1988. BA, Mich. State U., 1974; MA in Econs., U. Mich., 1976, PhD in Econs., 1980. Asst. prof. Dartmouth Coll., Hanover, N.H., 1979-83; sr. analyst U.S. Adv. Commn. on Intergovt. Relations, Washington, 1983-85; fin. economist U.S. Treasury Dept., Washington, 1985-87; sr. research assoc. Urban Inst., Washington, 1987-88; Lincoln fellow Lincoln Inst. of Land Policy, Cambridge, Mass., 1988-89; asst. prof. econs. Simmons Coll., Boston, 1989-90, assoc. prof. econs., 1991—, chair dept. econs., 1996—; cons. U.S. IRS Adv. Panel, Washington, 1987—; appt. to Mass. Dept. of Revenue Adv. Group, 1991; bd. dirs. New Eng. Econ. Project. Assoc. editor Urban Studies, 1988-93, mem. U.S. editl. adv. com., 1993—; co-editor: Coping with Mandates, 1990, Competition Among States and Local Governments, 1991; N.H. corres. State Tax Notes, 1990; contbr. articles to profl. jours. Mem. N.H. Gov.'s Revenue Adv. Com., Concord, 1982. NSF grad. fellow, 1974. Mem. Am. Econ. Assn. (mem. com. on the status of women in econs. profession 1995—), Nat. Tax Assn. (chair intergovernmental fiscal rels. com. 1996—), Nat. Tax Jour. (referee). Episcopalian.

KENYON, ELINOR ANN, social worker; b. Otto, Tex., July 8, 1936; d. William Karl and Anna Malinda (Achelpohl) Hannusch; m. Curtis E. Kenyon; children: John Kyle, Joel Leonard. L.A., St. John's Coll., 1956; BA, Valparaiso U., 1958; MSW, U. Kans., 1961. Adoption worker/dir. Kansas City Area Office Luth. Social Svc., 1958-71; area rep. Luth. Immigration and Refugee Svc., Met. Luth. Ministry, Kansas City, Mo., 1979-83; domestic adoption worker Family and Children Svcs. of Kansas City, 1983-85; pvt. practice social worker Kansas City, 1985-87; coord. refugee family stress edn. program Cmty. Svc. Ctr., Kansas City, Kans., 1987-88; sch. social worker Turner Unified Sch. Dist., Kansas City, Kans., 1988—. Co-author: Resources for Refugee Resettlement, 1981. Mem. NASW, Kans. NEA, Coun. Exceptional Children, Kans. Assn. Sch. Social Workers, Valparaiso U. Guild. Lutheran. Office: Turner Unified Sch Dist 202 Spl Svcs Dept 800 S 55thSt Kansas City KS 66106

KENYON, GERALDINE MONA, psychologist, consultant; b. Niagara Falls, N.Y., Nov. 26, 1929; d. John Warner and Mona Vivian (Slone) K.; m. Stanley Paul Gluck, Aug. 4, 1953 (div. Aug. 1966); children: Ethan, Jenny, Shayna, Jody. BS, Purdue U., 1956; MS, Trinity U., 1962; postgrad., Syracuse U., 1970-73. Lic. ednl. psychologist, Calif; registered behavior analyst; cert. sch. psychologist, Calif., N.Y. Adj. faculty Onondaga C.C., Syracuse, N.Y., 1968-73; counseling asst. Syracuse U., 1971, staff psychologist Reading Clinic,, 72; sch. psychologist Syracuse City Sch. Dist., 1966-73; asst. prof. Mich. Technol. U., Houghton, 1973-76; adj. prof. Calif. Luth. Coll., Thousand Oaks, 1981-83; sch. psychologist L.A. Unified Sch. Dist., 1978—. Pres. Topanga (Calif.) Dem. Club, 1993-94. Mem. NEA (del. 1993—), APA, Calif. Fedn. Tchrs. (del. 1993-96), Calif. Assn. for Behavioral Analysis, United Tchrs. L.A. (dir. health and human svcs., bd. dirs.), Calif. Tchrs. Assn. (state coun.), Nat. Assn. Sch. Psychologists, Calif. Assn. Sch. Psychologists. Jewish. Office: Univ High Sch 11800 Texas Ave Los Angeles CA 90025

KEOGH, HEIDI HELEN DAKE, publishing executive; b. Saratoga, N.Y., July 12, 1950; d. Charles Starks and Phyllis Sylvia (Edmunds) Dake; m. Randall Frank Keogh, Nov. 3, 1973; children: Tyler Cameron, Kelly Dake. Student, U. Colo., 1972. Reception, promotions Sta. KLAK, KJAE, Lakewood, Colo., 1972-73; account exec. Mixed Media Advt. Agy., Denver, 1973-75; writer, mktg. Jr. League Cookbook Devel., Denver, 1986-88; chmn., coordinator Colorado Cache & Creme de Colorado Cookbooks, 1988-90; speakers bur. Mile High Transplant Bank, Denver, 1983-84, Writer's Inst., U. Denver, 1988; bd. dirs. Stewart's Ice Cream Co., Inc., Jr. League, Denver. Contbr. 6 articles to profl. jours. Fiscal officer, bd. dirs. Mile High Transplant Bank; blockworker Heart Fund and Am. Cancer Soc., Littleton, Colo., 1978—, Littleton Rep. Com., 1980-84; fundraising vol. Littleton Pub. Schs., 1980—; vol. Gathering Place, bd. dirs., 1996—, chmn. Brown Bag benefit, 1996; vol. Hearts for Life, 1991—, Oneday, 1992, Denver Ballet Guild, 1992—, Denver Ctr. Alliance, 1993—, Newborn Hope, 1980—. Mem. Jr. League Denver (pub. rels. bd., v.p. ways and means 1989-90, planning coun./ad hoc 1990-92, sustainer spl. events 1993-94), Community Emergency Fund (chair 1991-92), Jon D. Williams Cotillion at Columbine (chmn. 1991-93), Columbine Country Club, Gamma Alpha Chi, Pi Beta Phi Alumnae Club (pres. Denver chpt. 1984-85, 93-94). Episcopalian. Home: 63 Fairway Ln Littleton CO 80123-6648

KEOGH, MARY CUDAHY, artist; b. Milw., Nov. 11, 1920; d. John and Katherine (Reed) Cudahy; m. Frank Stephen Keogh, Jan. 17, 1947 (dec. 1980); children: Mary K., Anne C., Patricia, Margaret E.; m. Warren Stringer, July 5, 1985. Student, Smith Coll., 1939-42; BFA, Milw. Downer Coll., 1944; post grad., Parsons Sch. of Design, 1945. Artist, 1969—; lectr. Woman's Club of Wis., 1977, workshops, Omaha, 1978-80, demo. Cape Coral (Fla.) Art League, 1991. One and two person shows include Lee County Alliance for the Arts, 1988, 90, 96, Barbara Mann Hall, Ft. Myers, 1992, Phillips Gallery, Sanibel, Fla., 1993, Uihlein-Peters Gallery, Milw., 1994; exhibited in group shows Sarasota Visual Arts Ctr., 1995, Fla. Artists' Group, Winter Haven, 1996; represented in permanent collections U. Utah, Cedar City, Northwestern Bell, Omaha, Health Park, Ft. Myers, others. Named Best of Show, Nebr. Wesleyan Coll., Lincoln, 1981; recipient 3d place Sarasota Visual Arts Ctr., 1995, Big Arts, Sanibel, 1995. Mem. Nat. Women's Caucus for Art, Nat. Mus. Women in the Arts (charter), Fla. Artists Group. Roman Catholic. Home and Office: 9439 Coventry Ct Sanibel FL 33957

KEOHANE, NANNERL OVERHOLSER, university president, political scientist; b. Blytheville, Ark., Sept. 18, 1940; d. James Arthur and Grace (McSpadden) Overholser; m. Patrick Henry III, Sept. 16, 1962 (div. May 1969); 1 child, Stephan; m. Robert Owen Keohane, Dec. 18, 1970; children: Sarah, Jonathan, Nathaniel. BA, Wellesley Coll., 1961, Oxford U., Eng., 1963; PhD, Yale U., 1967. Faculty Swarthmore Coll., Pa., 1967-73, Stanford U., Calif., 1973-81; fellow Ctr. for Advanced Study in the Behavioral Scis. Stanford U., 1978-79, 87-88; pres., prof. polit. sci. Wellesley (Mass.) Coll., 1981-93, Duke U., Durham, N.C., 1993—; bd. dirs. IBM. Author: Philosophy and the State in France: The Renaissance to the Enlightenment, 1980; co-editor: Feminist Theory: A Critique of Ideology, 1982. Trustee Colonial Williamsburg Found., 1988—, Ctr. for Advanced Study Behavioral Scis., 1991—; mem. MIT Corp., 1992—. Marshall scholar, 1961-63; AAUW dissertation fellow; inducted, National Women's Hall of Fame, 1995. Fellow Am. Acad. Arts and Scis., Am. Philos. Soc.; mem. Coun. on Fgn. Rels., Saturday Club (Boston), Watauga Club (N.C.), Phi Beta Kappa. Democrat. Episcopalian. Office: Duke Univ 207 Allen Bldg Durham NC 27708-0001

KEPNER, RITA MARIE, sculptor, writer, editor, educator, public affairs officer, marketing and communications professional; b. Binghamton, N.Y., Nov. 15, 1944; d. Peter Walter and Helena Theresa (Piotrowski) Kramnicz; m. John C. Matthiesen; 1 child, Stewart. Student, Elmira Coll., 1962-63; BA, SUNY, 1966; postgrad., Okla. U., 1988, Seattle Pacific U., 1991, Western Wash. U., 1991, 92, City U., Seattle; diplome of merit (hon.), Acad. Bedriacense, Calvatore, Italy, 1984. Instr. exptl. coll. U. Wash., 1972-74; instr. sculpture internship program Evergreen Coll., Olympia, Wash., 1974-78; informal visual arts amb. between U.S. and Poland, 1976-81; pres. fed. women's program coun. Seattle dist., 1985-86; fed. women's program mgr., Schweinfurt, Fed. Republic Germany, 1986-87, Wiesbaden, Fed. Republic Germany, 1988; artist-in-residence City of Seattle, 1975, 77-78; del. Internat. Sculptors Conf., Toronto, Ont., Can., 1978; writer, editor, pub. affairs specialist Seattle dist. U.S. Army C.E.; pub. affairs officer Wiesbaden Milcom Hdqrs., 1987-88, editor, Schweinfurt, 1986-87; instr. writing & editing for mgrs. Dept. of Navy, Bremerton, Wash., 1991-93; apptd. disaster assistance spokesperson and pub. affairs officer Hdqs., pub. info. officer, Fed. Emergency Mgmt. Agy., Washington, mid-western U.S., 1993, So. Calif., 1993, Northridge, Calif., 1994, States of Ga., Oreg., Wash. and Alaska, 1994, No. Calif. floods, 1995, Wash. State floods, 1996, N.Y. State snowstorms and floods, 1996, Pa. and W.Va. floods, 1996, Hurricane Fran, N.C., 1996. One-woman shows include Willoughby Wallace Meml. Gallery, Branford, Conn., 1967, Penryn Gallery, Seattle, 1970, 73, 76, Haines Gallery, Seattle, 1975, Zoliborz Gallery, Warsaw, Poland, 1981, Yorkshire 510, Norman, Okla., 1988, Women's Ctr., Port Townsend, Wash., 1995; group shows include SUNY, Binghamton, 1966, Manawata Art Gallery, Palmerston North, N.Z., 1976, Modern Art Mus., Seattle, 1976, Portland (Oreg.) Art Mus., 1976, Hajnowka (Poland) Gallery, 1977, Die Roemer Gallery, Wiesbaden, Fed. Republic Germany, 1988, Blue Heron Gallery, Port Hadlock, Wash., 1991-92, Quimper Arts, Bruskin Gallery, Port Townsend, Wash., 1993, 94; major works include Peace Pipe, Zalaegerszeg, Hungary, Human Forms in Balance, City of Seattle, 1975, Unity, City of Znin, Poland, 1976, Rough to Smooth, Seattle Pub. Libr., 1978, The Surveyor, Savannah, Ga., 1995; sculpture commn. U.S. Army Corps of Engrs., 1995; contbr. articles to N.W. Arts, Seattle Post-Intelligencer, Leonardo mag., Polska Panorama, Poland mag. Founder Bainbridge Island Arts Coun., 1984; VISTA vol., 1982-84; bd. dirs. Aradia Med. Clinic, Seattle, 1972-74; founder Chimacum (Wash.) Sch. Dist. Learning Boosters, 1989; loaned exec. to govt. campaigns United Way, 1989; trainer for campaign coords. and key workers, 1989; 1st aid trainer Medic I, Seattle, 1989-91; elected chair Marrowstone Island Groundwater Com., 1989-94; mem. adv. com. Seawater Intrusion Team Dept. of Ecology, Wash. State; pres. Marrowstone Island Community Assn., 1993-94. Recipient merit award for superior journalistic achievement U.S. Army CE, 1984, 85, 2d place news category competition award, 1985, 86; suggestion award Dept. Army, 1984, ofcl. commendation Dept. of Army, 1985, 86, 87, 90, Dept. of Navy, Puget Sound Naval Shipyard, 1990, 91, Achievement cert. Washington Assn. Educators of the Talented and Gifted, 1990, Specialist Achievement award, 1991, Recognition cert. FEMA, 1993 (3), 1994, 95; named Citizen of Yr., City of Marrowstone Island, Wash., 1994; Kosciuszko Found. grantee, 1975, 76, 79, 81; pres.'s scholarship City U., Bellevue, Wash. Mem. Internat. Artists Cooperation (Edewecht, Fed. Republic Germany), N.W. Multihull Assn. (commodore 1974), Marrowstone Island Community Assn. (pres. 1993). Holder USCG capt. lic. for passenger carrying aux. sailing vessels up to 50 tons, 1980—. Home: 8643 Flagler Rd Nordland WA 98358-9600

KEPPLE, CYNTHIA BOYD, military officer; b. Cheyenne, Wyo., Feb. 3, 1956; d. Thomas Edward Sr. and Anna (Blakeney) Boyd; m. Steven Lewis Kepple Sr., Mar. 4, 1984; children: Steven L. Jr., Annamarie Boyd. AA, Gulf Coast C.C., 1978, C.C. of the Air Force, 1987; BBA, Fla. Atlantic U., 1981. Commd. officer Calif. Air N.G., 1987; field maintenance officer 129 MXS/MAF Calif. N.G., Moffett Fed. Airfield, Calif., 1987-90, info. mgmt. officer 129 MXS/MAE, 1990-95, chief social actions 129 RQW/SL, 1995—. Treas., bd. dirs. Pro-Choice Coalition Santa Clara County, Calif., 1992—; field rep. Women in Mil. Svc. for America Meml. Found., 1988—; Brownie leader Girl Scouts of Am., 1995. Mem. NOW, Air Force Assn. (life), Nat. Abortion Rights Action League. Democrat. Lutheran. Home: 2221 Walnut Grove Ave San Jose CA 95128-1241 Office: Calif Air NG 129 RQW/SL Moffett Field CA 94035

KER, LORA KAY, elementary music educator; b. Denver, Apr. 4, 1947; d. Delbert Scott and Betty Laura (Allen) Van Reeth; m. Bruce Campbell Ker, Aug. 2, 1969; children: Kara, Kristen, Kevin. BFA, Ohio U., 1969. Choral/gen. music tchr. Wilson Jr. H.S., Newark, Ohio, 1969-73; children's choir dir. St. Paul United Meth. Ch., Newark, 1970-77, Fields United Meth. Ch., North Ridgeville, Ohio, 1977-79; dir. youth ministries St. Paul United Meth. Ch., Woodbridge, Va., 1980-87; elem. music tchr. Prince William County Pub. Schs., Woodbridge, 1987—; music instr. Ctr. for Arts, Manassas, Va., 1994-95. Mission chair, music leader, youth usher coord., mem. choir St. Paul United Meth. Ch., Woodbridge, 1987—, chair edn. work area, 1996. Mem. NEA, Va. Edn. Assn., Am. Orff Schulwerk Assn. (cert.), Sigma Alpha Iota. Republican. Home: 13008 Amesbury St Woodbridge VA 22192-3702 Office: Westridge Elem Sch 12400 Knightsbridge Dr Woodbridge VA 22192-5190

KERBER, LINDA KAUFMAN, historian, educator; b. N.Y.C., Jan. 23, 1940; d. Harry Hagman and Dorothy (Haber) Kaufman; m. Richard Kerber, June 5, 1960; children: Ross Jeremy, Justin Seth. AB cum laude, Barnard Coll., 1960; MA, NYU, 1961; PhD, Columbia U., 1968; DHL, Grinnell Coll., 1992. Instr., asst. prof. history Stern Coll., Yeshiva U., N.Y.C., 1963-68; asst. prof. history San Jose State Coll., (Calif.), 1969-70; vis. asst. prof. history Stanford U., (Calif.), 1970-71; asst. prof. history U. Iowa, Iowa City, 1971-75, prof., 1975-85; May Brodbeck prof. U. Iowa, 1985—; vis. prof. U. Chgo., 1991-92. Author: Federalists in Dissent: Imagery and Ideology in Jeffersonian America, 1970, paperback edit., 1980, Women of the Republic: Intellect and Ideology in Revolutionary America, 1980, paperback edit., 1986; co-editor: Women's America: Refocusing the Past, 1982, 4th edit., 1995; co-editor: U.S. History As Women's History, 1995; mem. editl. bd. Signs: Jour. Women in Culture and Society, Law and History Rev.; contbr. articles and book revs. to profl. jours. Fellow Danforth Found., Barnard Coll., NEH, 1976, 83-84, 94, Am. Coun. Learned Socs., 1975, Nat. Humanities Ctr., 1990-91, Guggenheim Found., 1990-91. Mem. Orgn. Am. Historians (pres. 1996—), Am. Hist. Assn., Am. Studies Assn. (pres. 1988), Am. Soc. for Legal History, Berkshire Conf. Women Historians. Jewish. Office: U Iowa Dept History Iowa City IA 52242

KERBIS, GERTRUDE LEMPP, architect; m. Walter Peterhans (dec.); m. Donald Kerbis (div. 1972); children: Julian, Lisa, Kim. BS, U. Ill.; MA, Ill. Inst. Tech.; postgrad., Grad. Sch. Design, Harvard U., 1949-50. Archtl. designer Skidmore, Owings & Merrill, Chgo., 1954-59, C.F. Murphy Assocs., Chgo., 1959-62, 65-67; pvt. practice architecture Lempp Kerbis Assocs., Chgo., 1967—; lectr. U. Ill., 1969; prof. William Rainey Harper Coll., 1970—, Washington U., St. Louis, 1977, 82, Ill. Inst. Tech., 1989-91; archtl. cons. Dept. Urban Renewal, City of Chgo.; mem. Northeastern Ill. Planning Commn., Open Land Project, Mid-North Community Orgn., Chgo. Met. Housing and Planning Council, Chgo. Mayor's Commn. for Preservation Chgo.'s Hist. Architecture; bd. dirs. Chgo. Sch. Architecture Found., 1972-76; trustee Chgo. Archtl. Assistance Ctr., Glessner House Found., Inland Architect Mag.; lectr. Art Inst. Chgo., U. N.Mex., Ill. Inst. Tech., Washington U., St. Louis, Ball State U., Muncie, Ind., U. Utah, Salt Lake City. Prin. archtl. works include U.S. Air Force Acad. dining hall, Colo., 1957, Skokie (Ill.) Pub. Library, 1959, Meadows Club, Lake Meadows, Chgo., 1959, O'Hare Internat. Airport 7 Continents Bldg, 1963; prin. developer and architect: Tennis Club, Highland Park, Ill., 1968, Watervliet, Mich. Tennis Ranch, 1970, Greenhouse Condominium, Chgo., 1976, Webster-Clark Townhouses, Chgo., 1986, Chappell Sch., 1993; exhibited at Chgo. Hist. Soc., 1984, Chgo. Mus. Sci. and Industry, 1985, Paris Exhbn. Chgo. Architects, 1985, Spertus Mus.; represented in permanent archtl. drawings collection Art Inst. Chgo. Active Art Inst. Chgo.. Recipient award for outstanding achievement in professions YWCA Met. Chgo., 1984. Fellow AIA (bd. dirs. Chgo. chpt. 1971-75, chpt. pres. 1980, nat. com. architecture, arts and recreation 1972-75, com. on design 1975-80, head subcom. inst. honors nomination); mem. Chgo. Women in Architecture (founder), Chgo. Network, Internat. Women's Forum, Arts Club Chgo., Cliff Dwellers (bd. dirs. 1987-88, pres. 1988, 89), Lambda Alpha. Office: Lempp Kerbis Assocs 172 W Burton Pl Chicago IL 60610-1310

KERCHER, MARY HELEN, computer educator; b. LeMars, Iowa, Oct. 11, 1943; d. Golden Orville and Helen Elizabeth (Wendel) Thompson; m. Barry Lee Kercher, Dec. 20, 1964; children: Steven Lee, Richard Paul. BA in English, SUNY, 1967; MA in Computers in Edn. & Tng., Trinity Coll., 1986. Ednl. asst. Corkran United Meth. Ch., Temple Hills, Md., 1972-75; tchr. English Crossland High Sch., Temple Hills, Md., 1978-85, G. Gardner Shugart Mid. Sch., Hillcrest Heights, Md., 1986-87; tchr. computer tng. Prince Georges County Schs., Upper Marlboro, Md., 1987-93; tchr. computer tech. Buck Lodge Mid. Sch., Adelphi, Md., 1993—; team leader Johns Hopkins Applied Physics Lab., Laurel, Md., 1988-92; grad. workshop instr. U. Md., College Park, 1990-93; cons. Nat. Cristina Found., San Jose, Costa Rica, 1992. Mem. NEA, Internat. Soc. Tech. in Edn., Md. Internat. Computer Coords. Assn., Md. State Tchrs. Assn., Prince Georges County Educators Assn., Assembly for Computers in English. Home: 10101 White Ave Clinton MD 20735-3752 Office: Buck Lodge Mid Sch 2611 Buck Lodge Rd Adelphi MD 20783-1519

KERCKHOVE, LINDA ANN, career consultant; b. Cornell, Wis., Apr. 3, 1942; d. Carl and Delilah M. (Richards) Heyder; m. Donald E. Kerckhove, June 8, 1963 (div. Jan. 1979); 1 child, Jeffrey Scott. BS in Liberal Arts, U. Wis.-Superior, 1987; MS in Edn., U. Wis.-Stout, Menomonie, 1993. Program asst. U. Wis.-Eau Claire, 1978-83; mgr. devel. Luther Hosp., Eau Claire, 1983-88; customer svc. mgr. Delta Tech., Internat., Eau Claire, 1988-90; admission counselor U. Wis.-Stout, 1993; coord. Career Ctr. North, Rhinelander, Wis., 1994—; bd. dirs. Wis. Career Info. Sys., Madison; sec. Literacy Coun. Am., Rhinelander, 1995—; mem. Nat. Assn. Hosp. Devel., Eau Claire, 1983-88, Chippewa Valley Pers. Assn., Eau Claire, 1988-91. Mem. LWV, Eau Claire, 1989; bd. dirs. Northwoods Concert Assn., Rhinelander, 1995. Mem. LWV, Eau Claire, 1983-88, Chippewa Valley Pers. Assn., Eau Claire, 1988-91, Edn. for Employment, 1995—; bd. dirs. Northwoods Concert Assn., Rhinelander, 1995.

KERIKAS, SHARON MAREL, special education educator; b. South Bend, Ind., Jan. 14, 1943; d. Edward John and Mary Agnes (Babinski) Nawrocki; m. Emanuel John Kerikas, July 11, 1970. BS, Ball State U., Muncie, Ind., 1963; MA, Northwestern U., 1964. Cert. in elem. edn., secondary edn., spl. edn. Educator Gallaudet U., Washington, 1964-65; tchr. Utah Sch. for the Deaf, Salt Lake City, 1965—, mentor tchr., 1990—. Named Tchr. of Yr., Utah Sch. for the Deaf, 1991. Mem. Utah Edn. Assn., Internat. Reading Assn., Alexander Graham Bell Assn. Home: 1428 Ambassador Way E Salt Lake City UT 84108-2859 Office: Utah Sch for the Deaf 2870 Connor St Salt Lake City UT 84109-1932

KERKEL, LYNN, middle school educator; b. Baton Rouge, Nov. 14, 1942; d. Peter Phillip and Rosa Emaline (Dunnam) K.; m. James O. Skidmore, Dec. 23, 1972 (div. Jan. 6, 1978). AA, Mt. San Antonio Jr. Coll., 1962; BE, Kent State U., 1965, MEd in Reading, 1973. Cert. elem. educator, reading specialist, Ariz., Mich. Elem. educator Willoughby (Ohio) Eastlake Bd. Edn., 1965-84, mid. sch. educator, 1984—; inservice instr. Willoughby-Eastlake Bd. Edn. Recipient Jennings grant Martha Holden Jennings Found., 1992; Named to South High Sch. Hall of Fame Willoughby-Eastlake Bd. Edn., 1989; Jennings grantee Martha Holden Jennings Found., 1992, scholar, 1978-79. Mem. NEA (rep. 1979—), AAUW, Willoughby Eastlake Tchr. Assn. (past pres. 1981-86, grievance co-chair 1965—), Galilee Shrine #41 Order of the White Shrine of Jerusalem, Am. Profl. Partnership for Lithuanian Edn., Ohio Edn. Assn. (rep. 1970—), Northeastern Ohio Edn. Assn., Internat. Reading Assn., Delta Kappa Gamma Soc. Internat. Democrat. Methodist. Home: 5457D Millwood Ln Willoughby OH 44094-3263

KERKLO, NORMA JEAN, publications executive; b. McKeesport, Pa., Dec. 6, 1947; d. John and Edythe (Steiner) Moore; m. John M. Kerklo, Sept. 8, 1964 (div. 1989); children: Mark, Michelle. AA in Journalism, Riverside City Coll.; BA in Tech. Writing, U. Colo. Comm. coord. U. Tex., El Paso; journalist Norco (Calif.) Pony Express; pub. info. asst. State Bd. for C.C. and Occupational Edn., Denver, 1984-85; from assoc. tech. writer to sr. tech. writer McData Corp., Broomfield, Colo., 1986-92; trainer, tech. writer Micro Decisionware, Inc., Boulder, Colo., 1992-94; tech. publ. mgr. EMASS, Englewood, Colo., 1995—. Mem. Soc. for Tech. Comm. (sr. mem., competition mgr. 1990, awards mgr. 1992-94, Achievement award 1991, Excellence award 1994), Soc. for Computing and Informational Processing. Home: Unit C 19692 E Mann Creek Dr Parker CO 80134 Office: EMASS 10949 E Peakview Ave Englewood CO 80111

KERKOVIUS, RUTH, artist; b. Berlin, June 9, 1921; raised in Riga, Latvia; came to U.S., 1949; m. Jay L. Johnson. Student, U. Munich, 1946-48, Pratt Graphic Art, 1958-62, Art Students League, 1951-53, 86-88; hon. degree in textile engring., Ga. Tech., 1955. Head mill designer Wamsutta Mills, New Bedford, Mass., 1949-52; car upholstery designer Chicopee Mills, Johnson & Johnson, N.Y. & Ga., 1953-58; printmaker etcher Assoc. Am. Artist, Weyhe, Main Galleries, N.Y., Ariz. and Chgo., 1962-85; painter, sculptor, 1988—. Represented in collections at IBM Gallery, Bell Telephone, Mobil, Exxon, Mayo Clinic, Mus. Fine Arts, Boston, Pa. Acad. Fine Arts, Phila., Mus. Western Art, Ft. Worth, U. Chgo., Cin. Art Mus., Pepsi-Cola, De Pauw U., Greencastle, Ind., also numerous pvt. collections. Home: 145 E 16th St New York NY 10003-3405 Studio: 426 E 91st St New York NY 10128-6802

KERLEY, JANICE JOHNSON, personnel executive; b. Coral Gables, Fla., Nov. 28, 1938; d. Howard Love and Lois Dean (Austin) Johnson; m. Bobby Joe Kerley, May 16, 1959; children: Janice Elisabeth Kerley Smothers, Meredith Ann Kerley Tucker. AA, Stephens Coll., 1958; B in Music Edn., U. Miami, Fla., 1960. Tchr. Dade County Pub. Schs., Miami, 1960-69; asst. to v.p. engr. Racal-Milgo, Inc., Miami, 1972-80; dir. sales and mktg. B. Joe Kerley, Realtor, Miami, 1980-83; dir. customer service, ops. mgr. Modern-Age Furniture Co., Miami, 1983-85; chief exec. officer Adia Pers. Svcs., Greensboro, Winston-Salem, N.C., 1985—; CEO Jan-Ker, Inc., dba ADIA Pers. Svcs., Greensboro, Winston-Salem and ADIA Tech. Ctr., Greensboro, N.C. Named Small Bus. Person of Greensboro, Greensboro C. of C., 1988, Remarkable Woman of Greensboro, Greensboro Coll. Honor Soc., 1991. Mem. Am. Bus. Women's Assn. (nat. bd. dirs. 1978-79, trustee nat. scholarship fund 1978-79, named one of top ten businesswomen, 1988). Office: Adi Tech Ctr 7031 Albert Pick Rd Ste 100 Greensboro NC 27409 also: 4500 Indiana Ave Ste 35 Winston Salem NC 27106 also: ADIA Tech Ctr Ste 202 7031 Albert Pick Rd Greensboro NC 27409

KERLEY, JORDANA DOWELL, elementary education educator; b. Poteau, Okla., Oct. 2, 1962; m. Michael Auston Kerley, May 21, 1985;

children: Arista, Blayne, Graham. BS in Edn., Southwestern Okla. State U., 1987, MEd, 1989. Elem. tchr. Weatherford (Okla.) Pub. Schs., 1987-88, El Reno (Okla.) Pub. Schs., 1989—. Mem. ASCD. Home: 1008 S Hadden Ave El Reno OK 73036-5353 Office: Webster Elem Sch 100 N L Ave El Reno OK 73036-3130

KERMANI, ANNE ELISE, artistic director; b. Michigan City, Mich., Dec. 23, 1960; d. Norbert John Schaaf and Mary Elise Dudine; m. Sirus Asky Kermani; 1 child, Natasha. BA in Music Composition, DePauw U., 1983; MA in Inter Arts, Columbia Coll., 1985. Artistic dir. Mishinnah Prodns., Bklyn., 1985—. Curator, prodr.: (CD rec.) DICE compilation of women composers, I, 1993, II, 1996. Puffin Found. grantee, 1995, electronic arts grantee, 1996. Office: Mishinnah Prodns PO Box 97 Gracie Sta New York NY 10028

KERMIS, MARY ANNE, school adminstrator, principal; b. Rochester, N.Y., Oct. 14, 1946; d. George F. and Doris Marian (Reeves) K.; m. Allan B. Collins III, Aug. 28, 1987; 1 child, Elizabeth Collins. BS in Chemistry, Daemen Coll., 1968; MS in Chemistry, Canisius Coll., 1970, MS in Edn. Adminstrn., 1986. Cert. edn. adminstrn.; cert. tchr. chemistry, biology, math., gen. sci. K-6. Chemistry tchr. Mount St. Joseph Acad., Buffalo, 1970-72; chemistry, biology tchr. North Tonawanda (N.Y.) H.S., 1972-78; math. tchr. East Aurora (N.Y.) Middle Sch. and H.S., 1978-86; asst. prin. Kenmore (N.Y.) -Town of Tonawanda Unified Sch. Dist., 1986-91, prin., 1991—; chair Erie County Middle Sch. Prins., Buffalo, 1994—; treas. Women in Adminstrn., Buffalo, 1986-89; chair Erie County Asst. Prins., Buffalo, 1988-91. Mem. Women in Adminstrn., Nat. Elem. Sch. Prins., Nat. Secondary Sch. Prins., Nat. Middle Sch. Assn., Phi Delta Kappa. Office: Benjamin Franklin Mid Sch 540 Parkhurst Blvd Kenmore NY 14223-2102

KERN, ANGELINE FRAZIER, educational administrator; b. Jackson, Tenn., Apr. 27, 1939; d. William Raymond and Sarah Louise (Harris) Frazier; divorced; children: Tiffany Louise, Kevin James. BA, Lambuth Coll., Jackson, 1961; MA, Memphis State U., 1962; postgrad., U. Tenn., 1963. Cert. assessor trainer, Nat. Assn. Secondary Sch. Prins. Tchr. phys. edn. Jackson City Schs., 1960-62; tchr. English, guidance counselor Georgian Hills Jr. High Sch., Memphis, 1962-65; guidance counselor Colonial Jr. High Sch., Memphis, 1965-70; adminstrv. asst. Kingsbury High Sch., Memphis, 1970-72; prin. Avon Elem. Sch., Memphis, 1972-77, Balmoral Elem. Sch., Memphis, 1977-93, Cordova Sch., 1993—. Mem. adv. bd. East Memphis YMCA, 1984-87; mem. Memphis City Beautiful Commn., 1985-89; pres. St. John's Creek Home and Garden Club, Memphis, 1968-70. Recipient Youth Svc. award YMCA, Memphis, 1983, Vol. Recognition award, 1986; finalist Rotary Club Prin. of Yr. award, 1989. Mem. NEA, Nat. Assn. Elem. Sch. Prins., Assn. for Sch. Curriculum Devel., Tenn. Assn. Elem. Sch. Prins. (fall conf. planning com. 1985), Memphis Pub. Sch. Prins. Assn. (auditing com. 1983-85), Memphis State U. Rebounders, Educators Bridge Club, Phi Delta Kappa, Delta Kappa Gamma (fin. chmn. Epsilon chpt. 1976-84, corr. sect. 1990-92). Republican. Roman Catholic. Office: Cordova Sch 900 N Sanga Rd Cordova TN 38018-6552

KERN, CAROL RAE, special education educator; b. Ladysmith, Wis., Dec. 20, 1957; d. Clarence Everett and Mary Anita (Kroll) K.; m. Randy Ystad, May 9, 1996; stepchildren: Brent, Tyler, Jared. AS in Gen. Studies, U. Wis., 1978; MS in Spl. Edn., U. Wis., Eau Claire, 1991; BA, Cardinal Stritch Coll., 1980. Clerical aide U. Wis., Rice Lake, 1976-78; nurses' aide Northland Care Ctr., Rice Lake, 1978, 82, 83; clerical aide Cardinal Stritch Coll., Milw., 1978-80; 1st and 2d grade tchr. St. Mary's Sch., Greenwood, Wis., 1980-84; evening recreation coord. Adult Devel. Svc., Greenwood, 1984-85; tchr. aide for cognitively delayed Sch. Dist. Greenwood, 1985-86, long-term substitute tchr., 1986-87, exceptional edn. needs tchr., chpt. I presch. tchr., 1990—; exceptional edn. needs tchr. Sch. Dist. Loyal, Wis., 1987-90; grad. asst. dept. spl. edn. U. Wis., Eau Claire, 1989, 90; evaluator spl. edn. component Head Start, Greenwood, 1991, 92, 93, 94; mem., leader wellness com. Sch. Dist. Greenwood, 1993-94. Emergency med. tech. Greenwood Area Ambulance, 1994—; leader Greenwood Girl Scouts, 1986-87; religious educator St. Mary's Parish, Greenwood, 1982-84, 86-87, Holy Family Parish, Willard, Wis., 1984-85, 94-95. Mem. Jaycees, Delta Epsilon Sigma, Kappa Gamma Pi, Phi Kappa Phi. Roman Catholic. Home: N 10637 Madison Ave Greenwood WI 54437 Office: Sch Dist Greenwood 708 E Division St Greenwood WI 54437-9330

KERN, CONSTANCE ELIZABETH, retired real estate broker; b. Cleve., Dec. 18, 1937; d. Walter Anthony and Irene (Davies) Matthews; divorced; children: James, David, Douglas, Kathleen. Student, John Carroll U., 1957, Case Western Res. U., 1958; BA in Speech and English, Marietta (Ohio) Coll., 1959; postgrad., Sul Ross State U., Midland, Tex., 1967-68, Comml. Coll. Real Estate, Ft. Worth, 1984, 86. Cert. tchr., Ohio, Tex.; lic. real estate broker, Tex. Tchr. South Euclid and Lyndhurst (Ohio) Schs., 1959-60; sec. Pan Am. Petroleum, Midland, 1960-61; tchr. St. Ann's Sch., Midland, 1967-69; real estate agt. McAfee & Assocs., Arlington, Tex., 1985-86; real estate broker Constance Kern Real Estate, Arlington, 1986-94, property mgr., 1986-94; ret. Constance Kern Real Estate, 1994; oil operator, investor, Midland and Arlington, 1975-92. Vol. Pink Ladies Midland Meml. Hosp., 1970-73; troop leader Brownies Girl Scouts Am., Midland, 1971; vol. speech therapist Children's Service League Cerebral Palsy Ctr., Midland, 1975-76. Mem. Pi Kappa Delta. Republican. Roman Catholic.

KERNAN, BARBARA DESIND, senior government executive; b. N.Y.C., Jan. 11, 1939; d. Philip and Anne (Feuer) Desind; m. Joseph E. Kernan, Feb. 14, 1973. BA cum laude, Smith Coll., 1960; postgrad. Oxford U., 1963; MA, Harvard U., 1963; postgrad. in edn. policy George Washington U., 1980. Editor Harvard Law Sch., 1960-62; tchr. English, Newton High Sch. (Mass.), 1962-63; editor Allyn & Bacon Pubs., Boston, 1963-64; edn. assoc. Upward Bound, Edn. Assocs., Inc., Washington, 1965-68; edn. program specialist Title I, Elem. and Secondary Edn. Act, U.S. Office Edn., 1969-73; fellow Am. Polit. Sci. Assn., Senator William Proxmire and Congressman Alphonzo Bell, 1973-74; spl. asst. to dep. commr. for elem. and secondary edn. and dir. dissemination, sch. finance and analysis, U.S. Office Edn., 1975-77, chief program analysis br. div. edn. for disadvantaged, 1977-79; chief grant program coordination staff Office Dep. Commr. for Ednl. Resources, 1979-80; chief priority concerns staff Office Asst. Sec. Mgmt., U.S. Dept. Edn., Washington, 1980-81; dir. div. orgnl. devel. and analysis Office of Dep. Undersec. for Mgmt., 1981-86; Sr. Exec. Svc. candidate on spl. project to improve status of women Sec. Transp., Washington, 1983-84; inducted Sr. Exec. Svc., 1986; assoc. adminstr. for adminstrn. Nat. Hwy. Traffic Safety Adminstrn., U.S. Dept. Transp., 1986—, career devel. leader to presdl. mgmt. interns, 1989-91. Recipient awards U.S. Office Edn., 1969, 71, 77, U.S. Dept. Edn., 1981-86, U.S. Dept. Transp., 1991, 94, Small Agy. Coun., 1990; scholarships U. Mich., 1956-58, Smith Coll., 1958-60, Harvard U., 1962-63; Am. Polit. Sci. Assn. fellow, 1973-74; Sr. Exec. fellow John F. Kennedy Sch. Govt. Harvard U., 1983.

KERN-FOXWORTH, MARILYN LOUISE, journalism educator; b. Kosciusko, Miss., Mar. 4, 1954; d. Jimmie and Manella (Dickens) Kern; m. Gregory Lamar Foxworth, July 3, 1984; 1 child, Gregory Lamar II. BS, Jackson State U., 1974; MS, Fla. State U., 1976; PhD, U. Wis., 1982. Pub. rels. asst. Sta. WJTV, Jackson, Miss., 1974; communications specialist Fla. State U., Tallahassee, 1974; advt. coordinator City of Tallahassee, 1975-76; coll. rels. rep. GTE Automatic Electric, Northlake, Ill., 1977; AM traffic mgr. Sta. WWQM Radio, Madison, Wis., 1978-79; prodn. mgr. Sta. WHA-AM, Madison, 1979-80; columnist, reporter Mid-West Observer, Madison, 1979-80; asst. prof. U. Tenn., Knoxville, 1980-87; prof. Tex. A&M U., College Station, 1987—. Assoc. editor Nashville Banner, 1983; contbr. chpt. to Dictionary Lit. Biography, 1985; contbr. articles to mags. including Black Collegian (Unity award 1985). Co-chair advisory Phyllis Wheatley YWCA, Knoxville, 1983-85. Recipient Kizzy award Black Women's Hall of Fame, Chgo., 1980, Pathfinder award Pub. Rels. Inst., 1988, PRSSA Adviser of Yr. award Kreighbaum Under-40 award Assn. for Men Educators in Journalism and Men in Comm., 1993, Best and Brightest Bus. and Profl. award Dollars and Sense Mag., 1995; named Woman of Achievment, U. Tenn., 1983; 1st Black person in U.S. to receive PhD in Advt. and Pub. Rels.; Tex. State Senate Proclamation, 1993; Amon Carter Evans scholar U. Tenn., 1983; Agnes Harris ffellow AAUW, 1991-92, Am. Press Inst. fellow, 1988, Poynter Inst. fellow, 1988. Me. Pub. Rels. Soc. Am. (accredited; Recognition of Excellence 1985), Assn. for Ednl. Journalism (nat. com., Rsch. award 1980), Nat. Communication Assn. (planning com.), Black Media Assn., Alpha Kappa Alpha. Home: 3710 Stillmeadow Dr Bryan TX 77802-3913 Office: Tex A&M U Dept Journalism 230 Reed McDonald College Station TX 77843-4111

KERNS, HEIDI FABER, accountant; b. Huntington, N.Y., Sept. 25, 1963; d. Charles Frederick and Joan Ernestine (Villa) Faber; m. William Thomas Kerns, Jr., Dec. 6, 1986 (div. Feb. 1996); 1 child, Allison Pearson. BA magna cum laude, Wofford Coll., 1985; MBA, U. S.C., 1991. CMA. Acct. Pulliam Investment Co., Inc., Spartanburg, S.C., 1985-88, Menzel, Inc., Spartanburg, S.C., 1988-90, Spartanburg County Sch. Dist. 7, Spartanburg, S.C., 1990-92; dir. bus. svcs. Spartanburg County Sch. Dist. 2, Spartanburg, S.C., 1992—. Co. chmn. Blood Bank, 1986-88; team capt. March of Dimes Team Walk, Spartanburg, 1987-88; spl. project coord. Liz Patterson for Congress, Spartanburg, 1988; v.p. Cannon's Bapt. Ch. BYW, Spartanburg, 1990. Mem. Inst. Mgmt. Accts. (past pres., mem. nominating com. Carolina's coun. del. 1995-96, officer 1989-95, dir. 1986-89), S.C. Assn. Sch. Bus. Officials (mem. conf. com. 1992), Spartanburg C. of C. (mem. small bus. coun. 1988, com. mem. Bus. Expo 1988), Blue Key Honor Soc., Phi Beta Kappa. Office: Spartanburg County Sch Dist 2 3655A Boiling Springs Rd Spartanburg SC 29303

KERNS, MARY PORTER, insurance agent; b. Charleston, W.Va., July 29, 1960; d. William L.G. and Sue Camden (Cook) Porter; m. Daniel William Kerns, June 10, 1989; children: Christopher, David. BA, Wake Forest U., 1983. V.p. Ramsey Ins. Agy., Charleston, W.Va., 1983—. Mem. Profl. Ind. Ins. Agts. Assn. (young agts. com.). Episcopalian. Office: Ramsey Ins Agy Inc 4301 MacCorkle Ave SE Charleston WV 25304

KERNS, PEGGY SHOUP, state legislator; b. Columbus, Ohio, Mar. 17, 1941; d. Ronald Traxler and Marie (Strausbaugh) Shoup; m. Pat L.J. Kerns, Nov. 9, 1963; children: Jerry, Deborah. BA, Duquesne U., 1963. Editor co. newspaper Samsonite Corp., Denver, 1978-83; mgr. customer svc. dept. Mt. Med. Equipment, Littleton, Colo., 1983-88; mem. State Ho. of Reps., Colo., 1989—; mem. bd. trustees Aurora (Colo.) Regional Med. Ctr., 1984—. Mem. coun. City of Aurora, 1983-89, mayor pro tem., asst. minority leader, 1993-94, minority leader, 1994—. Named Bus. and Profl. Women's Woman of Yr., 1991, Legislator of Yr. Colo. Assn. Commerce and Industry, 1993, Colo. Sch. Nurses Assn., Colo. Children's Campaign, 5th Most Effective Legislator by Colo. Bus. Mag., 1994, Legislator of Yr. by AP, 1994. Mem. AAUW, LWV, Aurora C. of C. (Woman of Yr. 1989), BPW. Democrat. Roman Catholic. Home: 1124 S Oakland St Aurora CO 80012-4260 Office: State Ho Reps State Capitol Denver CO 80201

KERPER, MEIKE, family violence, sex abuse and addictions educator, consultant; b. Powell, Wyo., Aug. 13, 1929; d. Wesley George and Hazel (Bowman) K.; m. R.R. Milodragovich, Dec. 25, 1963 (div. 1973); children: Dan, John, Teren, Tina, Stana. BS, U. Mont., 1973; MS, U. Ariz., 1975; postgrad. Ariz. State U., 1976-78, Columbia Pacific U., 1990—. Lic. marriage & family therapist, Oreg.; cert. domestic violence counselor, alcoholism and drug abuse counselor, mental health profl. and investigator. Family therapist Cottonwood Hill, Arvada, Colo., 1981; family program developer Turquoise Lodge, Albuquerque, 1982; co-developer abusers program Albuquerque Shelter Domestic Violence, 1984; family therapist Citizens Coun. Alcoholism and Drug Abuse, Albuquerque, 1984-86; pvt. practice cons. and trainer family violence and treatment, Albuquerque, 1987—; developer sex offender program Union County, Oreg. Co-author: Court Diversion Program, 1985; author Family Treatment, 1982. Lobbyist CCOPE, Santa Fe, 1983-86; bd. dirs. Union County Task Force on Domestic Violence, 1989-91; developer Choices program treatment of sex offenders and victims Union, Wallowa and Baker Counties, Oreg.; mem. Child Abuse Prevention Team, Union County, Baker County and Wallowa County, Oreg. Recipient commendation Albuquerque Shelter Domestic Violence, 1984. Mem. Assn. for the Treatment Sexual Abusers, Nat. Assn. Marriage and Family Therapists, Nat. Assn. Alcoholism Counselors, Delta Delta Delta. Republican. Episcopalian. Club: PEO. Avocations: Art history; reading; Indian culture; swimming; public speaking. Home: 61002 Love Rd Cove OR 97824-8211

KERR, DARLENE DIXON, electric power company executive; b. Syracuse, N.Y., Nov. 26, 1951; d. James and Mary Dixon; children: E. Kaye, J. Craig. BA, SUNY, Potsdam, 1973; MBA, Syracuse U., 1984. V.p. sys. electric ops. Niagara Mohawk Power Corp., Syracuse, 1988-91, v.p. gas mktg. and rates, 1991-93, v.p. electric customer svc., 1993-94, sr. v.p. electric customer svc., 1994-95, sr. v.p. energy distbn., 1995—, past mem. steering com. and past chmn. polit. action com.; mem. adv. bd. Rural Metro; mem. policy coun. Success by 6. Trustee Onondaga C.C.; bd. dirs. Cmty.-Gen. Hosp.; mem. Syracuse U. Thursday Morning Roundtable and Corinthian Found.; mem. task force Bus. Alliance for a New N.Y.; past pres. and bd. dirs. Onondaga Citizens League; past v.p. bd. dirs. Regional Learning Svc., Inc.; past mem. policy and planning com. Leadership Grater Syracuse; former mem. Downtown Improvement Task Force; former committeewoman and vice chmn. Onondaga Rep. Com.; former mem. numerous campaign ad. coms. and Onondaga County Rep. task forces; mem. chmn.'s coun. and fin. com. Onondaga County Rep. Com. Named Mover and Shaker for bus. Syracuse Herald Am., 1990, Woman of Achievement for career Post-Std., 1991, Alumni of Distinction, SUNY, 1993; recipient Spirit Am. Women award Girls Inc. Ctrl. N.W., 1993. Mem. Edison Elec. Inst. (com.), N.Y. State Women in Comm. and Energy (pres.), Mfrs. Assn. Ctrl. N.Y. (bd. dirs.), Greater Syracuse C. of C. (bd. dirs.). Office: Niagara Mohawk Power Corp 401 S Salina St Syracuse NY 13202

KERR, JEAN, writer; b. Scranton, Pa., July 10, 1923; d. Thomas J. and Kitty (O'Neill) Collins; m. Walter Kerr, Aug. 16, 1943; children: Christopher, John and Colin (twins), Gilbert, Gregory, Katharine. B.A., Marywood Coll., 1943; M.F.A., Cath. U. Am., 1945; L.H.D., Northwestern U., 1962, Fordham U., 1965. Author: (plays) Jenny Kissed Me, 1948, (with Walter Kerr) Thank You, Just Looking, 1949 (produced on Broadway as Touch and Go, 1949), (with Eleanor Brooke) King of Hearts, 1954, (with Kerr) Goldilocks, 1958, Mary, Mary, 1961, Poor Richard, 1965, Finishing Touches, 1973, Lunch Hour, 1980; (essays) Please Don't Eat the Daisies, 1957, The Snake Has All the Lines, 1960, Penny Candy, 1970, How I Got to Be Perfect, 1978; adapter: (plays) (with Kerr) The Song of Bernadette, 1944, Our Hearts Were Young and Gay, 1946, The Big Help, 1947, The Good Fairy, 1955. Recipient Campion award, 1971, Laetare medal Univ. Notre Dame, 1971. Mem. Nat. Inst. Social Scis. Democrat. Roman Catholic. Home: 1 Beach Ave Larchmont NY 10538-4004*

KERR, JUDITH P., lay professional ministry; b. Milroy, Pa., July 5, 1939; d. Ralph Lee Sr. and Mettie Pauline (Gardiner) K.; m. Walter Scott Sizer, July 9, 1977. BA, Western Md. Coll., 1961; B in Sacred Theology, Boston U., 1966. Cert. deaconess/diaconal min. United Meth. Ch. Dir. Christian edn. United Meth. Ch., Cochituate, Mass., 1963-68; social worker N.H. Dept. Welfare, Berlin, 1968-70; outreach worker Social Svc. Ctr., Springfield, Mass., 1970-72; dir. nutrition program for the elderly Home Care Corp., Springfield, 1972-77; part-time campus min. Wesley Found.-So. Ill. U., Carbondale, 1978-80; social planner Planning Divsn.-City Hall, Carbondale, 1978-80; program coord. Faith United Meth. Ch., Fargo, N.D., 1980-84; retreat leader Koinonia Ecumenical Spirituality Ctr., Grand Forks, N.D., 1989-91; rsch., editor Charis Ecumenical Ctr., Moorhead, Minn., 1994—; spiritual retreat leader various orgns., 1986-96. Rschr., author: Comprehensive Human Service Plan for Carbondale Illinoise, 1979; rschr., co-author: Ecumenical Shared Ministry and The United Methodist Church, 1995. Active Bread for the World, 1974—, NOW, 1977—, LWV, 1977-80, Amnesty Internat., 1980-84. Mem. Nat. Assn. Deaconesses and Home Missionaries (regional pres. 1976-77). Democrat. Home: 3207 12 St S Moorhead MN 56560 Office: Charis Ecumenical Ctr Concordia Coll Moorhead MN 56560

KERR, NANCY HELEN, psychology educator; b. L.A., June 27, 1947; d. Edmund James and Sally (Byrd) K.; m. David Foulkes, Apr. 19, 1978. BA, Stanford U., 1969; PhD, Cornell U., 1974. Asst. prof. psychology U. Wyo., Laramie, 1974-78; vis. asst. prof. psychology Emory U., Atlanta, 1978-79, vis. asst. prof. psychiatry, 1979-82; vis. asst. prof. psychology Mercer U., Macon, Ga., 1982-83; asst. prof. to prof. psychology Oglethorpe U., Atlanta, 1983—, chair div. behavioral scis., 1989—, interim acad. dean, 1996—. Contbr. articles to profl. jours. Recipient James McKeen Cattell award, 1990. Mem. Am. Psychol. Soc., Psychonomic Soc., Southeastern Psychol. Assn. Office: Oglethorpe U 4484 Peachtree Rd NE Atlanta GA 30319-2737

KERR, NANCY KAROLYN, pastor, mental health consultant; b. Ottumwa, Iowa, July 10, 1934; d. Owen W. and Iris Irene (Israel) K. Student Boston U., 1953; AA, U. Bridgeport, 1966; BA, Hofstra U., 1967; postgrad. in clin. psychology Adelphi U. Inst. Advanced Psychol. Studies, 1968-73; MDiv Associated Mennonite Bibl. Sems., 1986; m. Richard Clayton Williams, June 28, 1953 (div.); children: Richard Charles, Donna Louise. Ordained pastor Mennonite Ch., 1987; inducted pastor Presbyn. Ch., Can., 1992. Pastoral counselor Nat. Council Chs., Jackson, Miss., 1964; dir. teen program Waterbury (Conn.) YWCA, 1966-67; intern in psychology N.Y. Med. Coll., 1971-72; rsch. cons., 1972-73; coord. home svcs., psychologist City and County of Denver, 1972-75; cons. Mennonite Mental Health Svcs., Denver, 1975-78; asst. prof. psychology Messiah Coll., 1978-79; mental health cons., 1979-81; called to ministry Mennonite Ch., 1981, pastor Cin. Mennonite Fellowship, 1981-83, coord. campus peace evangelism, 1981-83, mem. Gen. Conf. Peace and Justice Reference Council, 1983-85; instr. Associated Mennonite Bibl. Sems., 1985; teaching elder Assembly Mennonite Ch., 1985-86; pastor Pulaski Mennonite Ch., 1986-89; v.p. Davis County Mins.' Assn., 1988-89; exec. dir., pastoral counselor Bethesda Counseling Svcs., Prince George B.C., 1989—; bd. dirs. Tri-County Counselling Clinic, Memphis, Mo., 1980-81; spl. ch. curriculum Nat. Council Chs., 1981; mem. Cen. Dist. Conf. Peace and Justice Com., 1981-89; mem. exec. bd. People for Peace, 1981-83. Mem. Waterbury Planned Parenthood Bd., 1964-67; mem. MW Children's Home Bd., 1974-75; bd. dirs. Boulder (Colo.) ARC, 1977-78, PLURA, B.C. Synod, 1995; elder St. Giles Presbyn. Ch., 1996; mem. Mennonite Disabilities Respite Care Bd., 1981-86; active Kamloops Presbytery Presbyn. Ch. Can., 1992—; P.G. Children's Svcs. com., 1992-94; bd. dirs. Prince George Neighborlink, 1995—; adv. com. Prince George Planning, 1995—. Mem. APA (assoc.), Can. Psychol. Assn., Soc. Psychologists for Study of Social Issues, Christian Assn. Psychol. Studies, Davis County Mins. Assn. (v.p. 1988-89), Prince George Ministerial Assn. (chmn. edn. and Airport chapel coms. 1990-92), Soc. Bib. Lit. & Exegesis. Office: 575 Quebec St, Prince George, BC Canada V2L IW6

KERR, PATRICIA CASEY, counselor, psychologist; b. McMinnville, Tenn., Sept. 28, 1948; d. Billy James and Mary Sue (Cecil) Casey; m. James Marvin McCormack, July 30, 1974 (div. Sept. 1993); 1 child, Allison Casey; m. Douglas Moseley Kerr, Aug. 11, 1994. BS, Middle Tenn. State U., 1970, MA, 1971; postgrad., Tenn. State U. Lic. psychol. examiner; lic. profl. counselor; cert. hypnotherapist; lic. sch. psychologist. Instr. Columbia (Tenn.) State Coll., 1971-76; psychol. examiner Lawrence County Schs., Lawrenceburg, Tenn., 1978-83; sch. psychologist Metro Schs., Nashville, 1984—; pvt. practice counseling Brentwood, Tenn., 1988—; adj. prof. Trevecca Coll., Nashville, 1990—, Middle Tenn. State U., Murfreesboro, 1992—; spkr. in field. Mem. ACA, Am. Soc. for Clin. Hypnosis, Tenn. Assn. Sch. Psychologists. Home: PO Box 4 8666 Valley View Rd Lascassas TN 37085 Office: Coolsprings Exec Ctr Ste 345 1749 Mallory Ln Brentwood TN 37027

KERR, SYLVIA JOANN, educator; b. Detroit, June 19, 1941; d. Frederic Dilmus and Maud (Dirst) Pfeffer; widowed; children: David, Kathleen. BA, Carleton Coll., 1963; MS, U. Minn., 1966, PhD, 1968. Asst. prof. Augsburg Coll., Mpls., 1968-71; instr. Anoka Ramsey Community Coll., Coon Rapids, Minn., 1973-74; from asst. prof. to full prof. Hamline U., St. Paul, 1974—. Contbr. numerous articles to profl. jours. NIH fellow U. Minn., 1972, 74-75. Office: Hamline U Dept Biology 1536 Hewitt Av Saint Paul MN 55104-1205

KERSHAW, CAROL JEAN, psychologist; b. New Orleans, Apr. 11, 1947; d. Neal Howard and Gloria Jackson (Moss) Perkins; m. John William Wade, Aug. 20, 1983; stepchildren: Chris Wade, Stephen Wade, Tiffany Wade. BS in Secondary Edn., U. Tex., 1969; MS in Speech Communication, North Tex. State U., 1971, MEd in Counseling, 1976; EdD in Counseling, East Tex. State U., 1979. Lic. psychologist, Tex. Assoc. prof. DeVry Inst., Dallas, 1971-73; instr., counseling psychologist East Tex. State U., Commerce, 1976-78; counselor, instr. Tarrant County Jr. Coll., Hurst, Tex., 1971-74; dir. spl. svcs. Goodwill Industries, Dallas, 1974-76; marriage and family therapist, cons. mental health clinic Tex. Dept. Mental Health and Retardation, Greenville, 1977-79; asst. prof., dir. grad. program in marriage & family therapy Tex. Woman's U., Denton, 1980-83; coord. child devel. dept. Tex. Woman's U., Houston, 1983-88; pvt. practice Inst. for Family Psychology, Houston, 1986—; co-dir. Milton H. Erickson Inst. Houston, 1986—; bd. dirs. Milton H. Erickson Inst. Tex., Houston, 1986—; internat. presenter in field. Author: Therapeutic Metaphor in the Treatment of Childhood Asthma: A Systemic Approach, Ericksonian Monographs, Vol. 2, 1986, The Couple's Hypnotic Dance, 1992, The Healing Power of the Story, Ericksonian Monographs, Vol. 9, 1994, audio Mind/Body Healing and Hypnosis, 1996; co-author: Learning to Think for an Organ, Bridges of the Bodymind, 1980, Psychotherapeutic Techniques in School Psychology, 1984, Restorying the Mind: Using Therapeutic Narrative in Psychotherapy in Ericksonian Methods, 1994. Sec. Tex. Assn. for Marriage and Family Therapy, 1978-80. Recipient Visionary award, Meritorious Svc. award Tex. Assn. for Marriage & Family Therapy, 1980. Mem. Am. Psychol. Assn, Am. Assn. for Marriage and Family Therapy (clin., approved supr.), Soc. for Exptl. & Clin. Hypnosis, Am. Soc. for Clin. Hypnosis (cons., appointed to ethics com., 1996), Internat. Soc. for Clin. & Exptl. Hypnosis, Psi Chi. Democrat. Methodist. Office: Inst for Family Psychology 2012 Bissonnet St Houston TX 77005-1647

KERSHNER, PAMELA LYNN, physician; b. San Jose, Calif., May 24, 1957; d. Richard Dudley and Marian (Lumpkin) K. BA, Univ. Calif., 1979; MA, Univ. Iowa, 1981; MD, Medical Coll. Wis., 1987. Diplomate Am. Bd. Internal Medicine, Am. Bd. Diabetes, Endocrinology and Metabolism. Faculty lectr. Univ. Wis., River Falls, Wis., 1981-83; intern, resident in internal medicine Kaiser Found. Hosp., San Francisco, 1987-90; internist ECS Family Health Svcs./Sharp Rees-Stealy, San Diego, 1990-91; endocrinology fellow Scripps Clinic, La Jolla, Calif., 1991-93; internist/endocrinologist Kaiser Permanente Medical Group, Walnut Creek, Calif., 1993—. Contbr. articles to profl. jours. Fellow ACP; mem. Am. Diabetes Assn., Am. Assn. Clinical Endocrinologists, Sierra Club. Office: Kaiser Permanente 1425 S Main St Walnut Creek CA 94596

KERZ, LOUISE, historian; b. N.Y.C., Sept. 16, 1936; d. Louis and Catharine (Sohn) Tittmann; m. Leo Kerz, Apr., 1965 (dec. 1976); children: Jonathan, Antony. Student, Queens Coll., 1954-56, Marymount Coll., 1972-74. Theatre producer Leo Kerz Prodns., N.Y.C., 1960-74; theatrical curator N.Y. Cultural Ctr., N.Y.C., 1974, Theatre of Max Reinhardt, 1974, N.Y. Pub. Libr. Lincoln Ctr., N.Y.C., 1984, Calif. Mus. Sci. and Industry, L.A., 1985, The Demille Dynasty, 1984; rsch. cons. CBS: On the Air, 1978, Smith-Hemion TV Prodns., L.A., 1987—, The Phantom of the Opera, 1995; dir. rsch. Greengage Prodns., Julie Andrews/Greengage Prodns., L.A., 1988, Tony Awards telecast 50th Annivrsary show 1947-96; rsch. cons. TV Acad. Hall of Fame and Tony Awards telecasts, 1993-96; dir. rights and permissions The Line King (The Al Hirschfeld Story), N.Y. Times, TV documentary. Prodr. (Broadway) Rhinoceros, 1961; contbg. editor N.Y.C. Access, 1983; picture editor: The DeMilles: An American Family, 1988; curator, dir. Exhibit Broadway, 1995. Vol. Persian Gulf war Am. Jewish Congress, Israel, 1991. Mem. Theatre Libr. Assn. Democrat. Home: 333 E 69th St New York NY 10021-5549

KESCHL, CONSTANCE FRANCES, home economics educator; b. Elizabeth, N.J., Mar. 31, 1949; d. Michael Peter and Helen Ann (Pazahanich) Lokuta; m. Dennis Lee Keschl, Sept. 5, 1970; children: Dennis Kurt, Thomas Michael. BS in Home Econs., Mansfield State Coll., 1971. Cert. home econs. tchr., N.J., Maine. Instr., curriculum developer child care Perth Amboy (N.J.) Adult Sch., 1975-76, educator family life/consumer edn., coord. home econs. dept., 1976, supr. sch. cafeteria, 1976, project dir., 1976-78; home econs. educator Livermore Falls (Maine) High Sch., 1979-87; home econs. educator, dept. chairperson Gardiner (Maine) Area High Sch., 1987-93; health/nutrition coord. Head Start No. Kennebec and Somerset Counties, Waterville, Maine, 1993-95; home econs. educator Georges Valley (Maine) H.S., 1995—; substitute tchr. Manville (N.J.) Pub. Schs., Middlesex (N.J.) Pub. Schs., Union County Tech. Inst. and Vocat. Ctr., Scotch Plains, N.J., 1978-79; cooperating tchr. U. Maine, Farmington, 1980—. Grantee

Carl D. Perkins, 1987. Mem. NEA, Maine Tchrs. Assn., Maine Home Econs. Assn., Pine Tree Quilters Guild Inc., Backroad Quilters, Cabin Fever Quilters. Roman Catholic. Home: 316 Wings Mls Rd Belgrade ME 04917 Office: Georges Valley High Sch PO Box 192 Thomaston ME 04861-0192

KESS, LYDIA E., lawyer; b. Bklyn., Sept. 17, 1935. BBA, Pace U., 1957; MBA, CUNY, 1958; LLB, Bklyn. Law Sch., 1962. Bar: N.Y. 1963. Ptnr. Davis Polk & Wardell, N.Y.C. Mem. ABA, N.Y. State Bar Assn., Assn. of the Bar of the City of N.Y. Office: Davis Polk & Wardwell 450 Lexington Ave New York NY 10017-3911*

KESSEL, BRINA, ornithologist, educator; b. Ithaca, N.Y., Nov. 20, 1925; d. Marcel and Quinta (Cattell) K.; m. Raymond B. Roof, June 19, 1957 (dec. 1968). BS (Albert R. Brand Bird Song Found. scholar), Cornell U., 1947, PhD, 1951; MS (Wis. Alumni Research Found. fellow), U. Wis.-Madison, 1949. Student asst. Patuxent Research Refuge, 1946; student teaching asst. Cornell U., 1945-47, grad. asst., 1947-48, 49-51; instr. biol. sci. U. Alaska, summer 1951, asst. prof. biol. sci., 1951-54, assoc. prof. zoology, 1954-59, prof. zoology, 1959—, head dept. biol. scis., 1957-66; dean U. Alaska (Coll. Biol. Scis. and Renewable Resources), 1961-72, curator terrestrial vertebrate mus. collections, 1972-90, curator ornithology collection, 1990-95, adminstrv. assoc. for acad. programs, grad. and undergrad., dir. acad. advising, office of chancellor, 1973-80; project dir. U. Alaska ecol. investigation for AEC Project Chariot, 1959-63; ornithol. investigations NW Alaska pipeline, 1976-81, Susitna Hydroelectric Project, 1980-83. Author books, monographs; contbr. articles to profl. jours. Fellow AAAS, Am. Ornithologists' Union (v.p. 1977, pres.-elect 1990-92, pres. 1992-94), Arctic Inst. N.Am.; mem. Wilson, Cooper ornith. socs., Soc. for Northwestern Vertebrate Biology, Pacific Seabird Group, Assn. Field Ornithologists, Sigma Xi (pres. U. Alaska 1957), Phi Kappa Phi, Sigma Delta Epsilon. Office: U Alaska Mus PO Box 80211 Fairbanks AK 99708-0211

KESSINGER, MARGARET ANNE, medical educator; b. Beckley, W.Va., June 4, 1941; d. Clisby Theodore and Margaret Anne (Ellison) K.; m. Loyd Ernst Wegner, Nov. 27, 1971. MA, W.Va. U., 1963, MD, 1967. Diplomate Am. Bd. Internal Medicine and Med. Oncology. Internal medicine house officer U. Nebr. Med. Ctr., Omaha, 1967-70, fellow med. oncology, 1970-72, asst. prof. internal medicine, 1972-77, assoc. prof., 1977-90, prof., 1990—, assoc. chief oncology/hematology sect., 1988-91, chief oncology/hematology sect., 1991—. Contbr. articles to profl. publs. Fellow ACP; mem. Am. Assn. Cancer Edn., Am. Soc. Clin. Oncology, Am. Assn. Cancer Rsch., Internat. Soc. Exptl. Hematology, Am. Soc. Hematology, Sigma Xi, Alpha Omega Alpha. Republican. Methodist. Office: U Nebr Med Ctr 600 S 42nd St Omaha NE 68198-3330

KESSLER, GLADYS, federal judge; b. 1938. BA, Cornell U., 1959; LLB, Harvard U., 1962. Staff atty. enforcement divsn. Nat. Labor Rels. Bd., 1962-64; legis. asst. Sen. Harrison A. Willians, N.J., 1964-66, Rep. Jonathan B. Bingham, 1966-68; staff atty. office labor rels N.Y.C. Bd. Edn., 1968-69; ptnr. Berlin, Roisman and Kessler (and successor firms), 1969-77; assoc. judge D.C. Superior Ct., 1977-94; judge U.S. Dist. Ct. D.C., Washington, 1994—; asst. lectr. law sch. George Washington U., 1971-73; del. to judicial adminstrn. divsn. D.C. Superior Ct., 1985-90; mem. adv. bd. Ctr. for Dispute Settlement Inst. for Judicial Adminstrn., State Justice Inst., mem. adv. com. nat. judicial edn. project on domestic violence; mem BNA adv. bd. Alternative Dispute Resolution Report, 1987-90; mem. family law cirriculum planning com. Georgetown U.; lead judge permanency planning project Nat. Coun. Juvenile and Family Ct. Judges; chair Nat. Conf. on Bioethics, Family and the Law, D.C., 1991; mem. faculty Nat. Inst. Trial Advocacy. Contbr. articles to legal jours. Recipient Women Lawyer of Yr. award Women's Bar Assn., 1983, Svc. award D.C. Coalition Against Domestic Violence, 1987, Judicial Excellence award Trial Lawyers Assn. Washington, 1987. Fellow Am. Bar Found.; mem. ABA (judicial adminstrn. divsn., com. on bioethics and AIDS, adv. com. on youth, alcohol and drug problems, nat. adv. bd. on child support and criminal justice, individual rights and responsibilities sect.), Am. Judicature Soc. (bd. dirs. 1985-89), NOW Legal Def. and Edn. Fund, Inc., Nat. Assn. Women Judges (v.p. 1979-81, pres. 1981-82), Nat. Ctr. for State Cts. (bd. dirs. 1984-87), Women's Legal Def. Fund (founding pres. 1971), Women Judges' Fund. for Justice (bd. dirs. 1980—), Found. for Women Judges (pres. 1980-82), Pres.'s Coun. Cornell Women, Thurgood Marshall Am. Inn. Ct. Office: US Courthouse Rm 6333 3rd & Constitution Ave NW Washington DC 20001-2802*

KESSLER, JOAN F., lawyer; b. June 25, 1943; m. Frederick P. Kessler, Sept. 1967; 2 children. BA, U. Kans., 1961-65; postgrad., U. Wis., 1965-66; JD cum laude, Marquette U., 1968. Law clk. Hon. John W. Reynolds U.S. Dist. Ct. (ea. dist.) Wis., Milw., 1968-69; assoc. Warschafsky, Rotter & Tarnoff, Milw., 1969-71; pvt. practice Milw., 1971-74; assoc. Cook & Franke, S.C., Milw., 1974-78; U.S. atty. Eastern Dist. Wis., Milw., 1978-81; ptnr. Foley & Lardner, Milw., 1981—; lectr. profl. responsibility U. Wis. Law Sch., Marquette U. Law Sch., Milw.; mem. bd. govs. State Bar of Wis., 1985-89, 90-92, 93-95, chair, 1993, bd. dirs. family law sect., 1991-94; mem. Jud. Coun. Wis., Madison, 1989-92; mem. Milw. Bd. Attys. Profl. Responsibility, 1979-85. Bd. dirs. Legal Aid Soc., 1974-78, v.p., 1978, Urban League, 1980-82, Women's Bus. Initiative Corp., 1989-91, Girl Scouts U.S., Milw., 1994-96; bd. dirs., pres. Voters for Choice in Wis., 1989-93. Fellow Am. Matrimonial Lawyers (bd. govs. 1990-96), Am. Law Inst., Am. Bar Found.; mem. ACLU. Office: Foley & Lardner 777 E Wisconsin Ave Milwaukee WI 53202-5302

KESSLER, KENDALL SEAY FERIOZI, artist; b. Washington, Nov. 4, 1954; d. Dan John and Anne Fletcher (Trotter) Feriozi; m. Clyde Thomas Kessler, June 25, 1977; 1 child, Alan. BA in Art Edn., Va. Polytech. Inst. & State U., 1976; MFA in Painting & Printmaking, Redford U., 1983. Tchr. art, Spanish Cherrydale Christian Sch., Arlington, Va., 1976-77; tchr. community arts sch. Radford (Va.) U., 1980-82, adminstr., 1982-83; tchr. art Fine Arts Ctr., Pulaski, Va., 1984; instr. art Radford U., 1985-87, 88-93, interim gallery dir., 1987-88; freelance profl. artist, tchr. Radford, 1993—. Illustrator (poetry books) Shooting Creek, 1982, Dancing at Big Vein, 1987, Preservations, 1989; book jacket illustrator: The Rosewood Casket by Sharon McCrumb, 1996; exhibited in group shows Agora Gallery, Soho, N.Y., 1994, 95. Officer PEO Sisterhood, Radford, 1992-94, mem., 1989—; mem. Lamplighters, Radford Pub. Libr., 1991—, Valley-Wide Newcomers, Radford, 1993—. Recipient Am. Artist award Soc. West Coast 4th Nat. Exehibit, Scramento, Calif, first place Oils, Paris (Tex.) Art Fair, 1991. Mem. Nat. Mus. Women in the Arts, Internat. Platform Assn., Blacksburg Regional Art Assn., Lynwood Artists, Piedmont Arts Assn, Am. Artist award, Pastel soc. of the West Coast 4th Nat. Exhibit, juror, Daniel Greene, firts placeOils, Paris Art Fair, 1991. Home: PO Box 3612 Radford VA 24143-3612

KESSLER, LEONA HANOVER, interior designer; b. Phila., Sept. 15, 1925; d. Herman and Ida (Gleaner) Hanover; B.S. in Textile Engring. (Sara Tyler Wister scholar), Phila. Coll. Textiles and Sci., 1948; m. Sydney Kessler, Aug. 28, 1948; children—Andrew Louis, Todd Hanover. Pvt. practice interior design and cons. Lee Kessler Interiors, Phila., 1957—; textile designer, stylist, color cons.; mem. faculty Moore Coll. Art, 1970-72, Art Inst. Phila., 1973-78, Phila. Coll. Textiles and Sci., 1972-81; juror textile design and interior design; works exhibited designer showcases, local house tours, faculty shows. Named Alumnus of Month, Textile Engr., 1971. Mem. Am. Soc. Interior Designers (dir. Pa. East chpt. 1967-78, chpt. recognition awards 1974, 80). Author: That Which Was Once a Warp, 1971; contbr. articles and photographs to mags. and newspapers. Address: 101 Hawthorne Ct Wyomissing PA 19610-1028

KESSLER, LUCINDA LOAY, visual arts educator; b. Gallipolis, Ohio, Jan. 28, 1950; d. Lucius H. Kessler and J. Fredelene (Farley) Wagoner. BFA in Art Edn. summa cum laude, Ohio U., 1976, MA in Art Edn., 1993. Clk. Wellston (Ohio) Sundry Store, 1968-79; substitute tchr. Jackson (Ohio) City Schs., 1976-77, Wellston City Schs., 1976-77; visual arts instr. K-12 Ea. Local Schs., Beaver, Ohio, 1977—; arts and crafts counselor Camp Opportunity, Jackson County, 1982-85. Group shows include Foothills Arts Festival, Ohio State Fair; represented in pvt. collections. Guitarist, soloist, organist Sts. Peter & Paul Ch., Wellston, 1976—; mem., solist Jackson County Ecumenical Choir, 1980-90; mem., trustee, tchr. Jackson County Arts Coun., 1976—, So. Hills Arts Coun., 1976—; co-dir., soloist Jackson County Cmty. Chorus, 1990—. Recipient Martha Holden Jennings Found. scholar, 1983, Golden Apple Tchr. Achievement award Ashland Oil, 1993. Mem. The Ohioana Libr. Assn. Roman Catholic. Home: 1602 S Maine Ave Wellston OH 45692 Office: Ea Local Schs 1170 Tile Mill Rd Beaver OH 45613

KESSLER, PAULA GAIL, controller; b. Chgo., Nov. 21, 1952; d. Herbert C. and Shirley R. (Rubin) Redman; m. Donald R. Kessler, July 9, 1978; children: Bryan, Samantha. BS in Math., Purdue U., 1974; M Acctg. Sci., U. Ill., 1976. CPA, Ill. Devel. assoc. to planning analyst Esmark, Inc., Chgo., 1976-78; fin. analyst, dir. planning, v.p. fin. and adminstrn. Estech Inc. subs. of Esmark, Inc., Chgo., 1978-86; contr. E-II Consumer Products, Inc., Chgo., 1986-88, MasterBrand Industries, Inc., Deerfield, Ill., 1988—. Mem. AICPA, Ill. Soc. CPAs, Sigma Iota Epsilon. Office: MasterBrand Industries Inc 510 Lake Cook Rd Ste 150 Deerfield IL 60015-4916

KESSLER-HODGSON, LEE GWENDOLYN, actress, corporate executive; b. Wellsville, N.Y., Jan. 16, 1947; d. James Hewitt and Reba Gwendolyn (Adsit) Kessler; m. Bruce Gridley, June 22, 1969 (div. Dec. 1979); m. Jeffrey Craig Hodgson, Oct. 31, 1987. BA, Grove City Coll., 1968; MA, U. Wis., 1969. Prof. Sangamon State U., Springfield, Ill., 1969-70; pers. exec. Bullock's, L.A., 1971-74; owner Brunnen Enterprises, L.A., 1982—. Author: A Child of Arthur, 1981; producer, writer play including Anais Nin: The Paris Years, 1986; actress appearing in TV movies, mini-series including Roots, 1978, Backstairs at The White House, 1979, Blind Ambition, 1980, Hill Street Blues, 1984-87, Murder By Reason of Insanity, 1985, Hoover, 1986, Creator, 1987, Our House, 1988, Favorite Son, 1988, Lou Grant 1983, 84, Barney Miller, 1979, L.A. Law, 1990, Hunter, 1991, (screenplay) Settlers Way, 1988; recurring role TV series Matlock, L.A. Law, numerous others. Knapp Prize fellow U. Wis., 1969. Mem. AFTRA, SAG, Actors Equity Assn. Republican. Mem. Ch. Scientology. Home: 1650 Oaken Gate Dr Glendale CA 91207

KESTENBAUM, ELISE ANN, critical care nurse; b. Stamford, Conn., Feb. 12, 1966; d. Sidney Emmanuel and Sandra A. (Hayes) K. BS, Boston U., 1987. RN, Mass., Fla.; cert. med.-surg. nurse, ACLS, neonatal advanced life support. Staff/primary RN Beth Israel Hosp., Boston, 1987-91; staff RN ICU stepdown St. Mary's Hosp., West Palm Beach, Fla., 1992-94, staff/primary RN NICU, 1994—. Mem. NLN, Sigma Theta Tau. Home: 109 Mainsail Cir Jupiter FL 33477-1401

KESTON, JOAN BALBOUL, government agency administrator; b. N.Y.C., Feb. 6, 1937; d. Sol and Adele (Gredinger) Balboul; (div. Mar. 1986); children: Lisa, Vicky, Sol. BA, N.Y.U., 1958; postgrad., Rutgers U., 1959; MPA, U. So. Calif., 1981, D in Pub. Adminstrn., 1991. Br. mgr. Social Security Adminstrn., Rockville, Md., 1978-86; exec. dir. Pub. Employees Roundtable, Washington, 1984-94, pres., 1994—; exec. asst. to dir. adminstrn. and mgmt. Office of Sec. of Def., Arlington, Va., 1994-96; sr. policy advisor Def. Info. Sch. Am. Forces Info. Svcs., Office of Sec. of Def., Ft. Meade, Md., 1996—. Editor: (books) Hagadah, 1972, Building Bridges with the Community, 1995, (newsletter) Unsung Heroes, 1986-94; co-author: (booklet) How to Celebrate Public Service Recognition Week, annually, 1986-94; contbr. articles to profl. publs. Recipient Office of Sec. of Defense Outstanding Performance award, 1991, PRes. Coun. Mgmt. Improvement Cert. Mgmt. Excellence, 1988. Mem. ASPA (nat. coun., Pres. award 1990), Federally Employed Women, Drs. Pub. Adminstrn. Assn. of U. So. Calif., Am. Consortium Pub. Arminstrn., Sr. Exec. Assn., World Affairs Coun., Inter Policy Inst. Jewish. Home: 330 Lynn Manor Dr Rockville MD 20850-4429

KESWANI, SATTY GILL, reproductive endocrinologist; b. Punjab, India, Jan. 4, 1932; came to U.S., 1958; d. Ujagar Singh and Mohindar (Kaur) Gill; m. Moti Sugnomal Keswani, Aug. 4, 1962; children: Raj Moti, Sonia. AA, U. Santo Tomas, Manila, 1950; Med. Diploma, Lady Hardinge Med. Coll., New Delhi, 1955. Intern in ob.-gyn. and surgery Lady Hardinge Med. Coll. Women, New Delhi, 1956-57, with ob-gyn and surgery, 1957-63; resident in ob.-gyn. St. Luke's Hosp., N.Y.C., 1959-60, Meth. Episcopal/Jefferson Med. Coll., Phila., 1960-61, Margaret Hague Maternity Hosp., Jersey City, N.J., 1961-63; with obstet. anesthesia Margaret Hague Maternity Hosp., Jersey City, 1963-65; rsch. fellow infertility & gynecology-endocrinology N.Y. Med. Ctr., 1965-72; pvt. practice Livingston (N.J.) Fertility, 1972—. Author: (with others) The Women's Complete Health Book, 1994. Named Woman of Yr., John Greco Found., 1986. Fellow Am. Coll. Obstetrics and Gynecology, Internat. Coll. Surgeons, Royal Soc. Health; mem. Am. Fertility Soc., Am. Med. Women Assn. (v.p. fin. 1994), N.Y. Acad. Scis., N.J. Am. Med. Women Assn. (pres. 1972-74), Med. Women Internat. Assn. (nongovtl. orgn. rep. to UN 1993-94). Home and Office: Livingston Fertility 176 W Mount Pleasant Ave Livingston NJ 07039-2751

KETCHMAN, NIKI, artist, sculptor; b. N.Y.C., May 24, 1942; d. Morton A. and Marjorie (Gropper) Shapiro; m. Jeffrey Ketchman, Dec. 27, 1962; children: Linda, Karen. BA in Fine Arts cum laude, Fairleigh Dickinson U., 1971; MA in Fine Arts, Montclair U., 1976. Tchr. painting, drawing Quinnipiac Coll., Hamden, Conn., 1977-79; tchr. painting, drawing, art history Sacred Heart U., Bridgeport, Conn., 1978-81; docent New Mus. Contemporary Art, N.Y.C., 1992 93. One woman shows include Bell Gallery, Greenwich, Conn., 1981, Pindar Gallery, N.Y.C., 1981, 83, 84, Mona Berman Gallery, New Haven, Conn., 1983, 84, Aetna Gallery Inst., Hartford, Conn., 1987, Alena Adlung Gallery, N.Y.C., 1989, Cortland Jessup Gallery, Provincetown, Mass., 1990, 91, 92, 94, Humphrey Gallery, N.Y.C., 1991, Kouros Gallery, N.Y.C., 1993, 96, Stamford Mus. and Nature Ctr.; group shows include Fairleigh Dickinson U., Madison, N.J., 1971, Montclair State Coll., Upper Montclair, N.J., 1976, Hansen Gallery, N.Y.C., 1978, 79, Aldrich Mus. Contemporary Art, Conn., 1978, Bell Gallery, Greenwich, 1980, Fairfield U. Gallery, Conn., 1981, Mona Berman Gallery, 1982, The GE Gallery, 1983, Heckscher Mus., N.Y., 1984, Bronx Mus. Arts, N.Y., 1987, John Szoke Gallery, N.Y.C., 1988, 89, Kouros Gallery, 1990, 91, 92, Stamford Mus., Conn., 1990, Bruce Mus., Conn., 1991, Philippe Staib Gallery, N.Y.C., 1992, Kyoto Gallery, Japan, 1993, Lyman Allyn Mus., Conn., 1993, 94, 95, Boise Art Mus., Idaho, 1994, DeCordova Mus., Mass., 1994, 95, 96, Gallery Contemporary Art, Fairfield, 1995, John Slade Ely House, New Haven, 1996, Grounds for Sculpture, N.J., 1995, 96, others; represented in permanent collections Nat. Mus. Women in the Arts, Washington, Housatonic Mus. Art, Bridgeport, Conn., CUNY, S.I., N.Y., Westport Pub. Sch. Sys., Royal Caribbean Cruise Lines, Song of Norway, So. New Eng. Tel., Conn., Pepsico, Purchase, N.Y., Cigna, Brookfield, Conn., Champion Paper, Stamford, Conn., GE Corp. Hdqrs., Fairfield & Washington, Rax Restaurants, Columbus, Ohio, Westport Libr., N.Y. Twist Drill, Huntington, N.Y., others; work reviewed in N.Y. Times, Art News, Art New Eng., Arts mag., Artspeak. Home: 14 Caccamo Ln Westport CT 06880 Office: 180 Varick St New York NY 10014

KETCHUM, LINDA ELLEN, science and medical writer; b. Rochester, N.Y., Oct. 4, 1956; d. Roy J. and Katsuko (Kuwahara) K. BA in Biology, U. Rochester, 1978; MS in Sci. Comm., Boston U., 1980. Mng. editor newsline Jour. Nuclear Medicine, N.Y.C., 1984-87; sr. writer, editor ProClinica Inc., N.Y.C., 1987-89; freelance writer N.Y.C., 1989—. Coauthor: Living with Radiation: The Risk, the Promise, 1989. Dep. campaign mgr. N.Y. State Presdl. Primary Campaign for Paul Tsongas, N.Y.C., 1992; del. Dem. Nat. Conv., N.Y.C., 1992. Mem. Soc. Nuclear Medicine. Democrat. Episcopalian. Home: 945 Second Ave #3 New York NY 10022-7744

KETTLE, SALLY ANNE, consulting company executive, educator; b. Omaha, Feb. 2, 1938; d. Elaine Josephine (Winston) Smiley; m. William Frederick Kettle, July 20, 1968 (div. 1973); children: Christopher, Winston. BEd, U. Nebr., 1960, postgrad. Cert. tchr., S.C., Nebr. Tchr. Omaha Pub. Schs., Omaha, 1966-72; owner, mgr. The Rick Rack, Ltd., Lakewood, Colo., 1974-75; coord. merchandising communications 3M, St. Paul, 1978-80, sr. coord. internat. corp. comm., 1981-83; corp. dir. communications Intran Corp., St. Paul, 1984; pres. Sally Kettle & Co., Bloomington, Minn., 1985—; mem. cmty. faculty Met. State U., Mpls., 1983-90, St. Olaf Coll., Northfield, Minn., 1992—; mem. adj. faculty U. Minn. Sch. Journalism and Mass Comm., Mpls., St. Thomas U., 1994-95. TV hostess City of Bloomington Cable TV, 1984-86. Co-founder Women's Resource Ctr., bd. dirs., mem. adv. bd., 1978-88; chair 13th Precinct, Bloomington, 1978-83; bd. dirs. 41st Sen. Dist., Bloomington, 1982-83; cable TV commr. Bloomington City Coun., 1984-85; pub. rels. com. U.S. Olympic Festival, 1989-90; bd. dirs. Minn. Prayer Breakfast Bd., 1984—; mem. Better Bus. Bur.; founder Ad Rev. Coun.; v.p. Christian Mgmt. Assn., Minn.; internat. com. bd. Carlson Grad. Sch. Mgmt., U. Minn.; mem. state ctrl. com. and platform commn. DFL, 1988-90; bd. dirs. Fellowship of Christian Athletes, 1988-89; pub. rels. com. '96 Billy Graham Minn. Crusade, 1996; bd. commrs. Shoreland Zoning Commn. Dakota County, Minn., 1996—. Named one of Outstanding Young Women of Am., 1965. Mem. Am. Advt. Fedn. (conf. com. 1985-87, pub. svc. com. 1986-88), Pub. Rels. Soc. Am., Advt. Fedn. Minn. (bd. dirs. 1982-86), Women's Econ. Roundtable, Internat. Platform Assn., Nat. Grad. Women's Honor Soc., Minn. Press Club (co-chair newsmaker com., bd. dirs. 1989-92), Phi Delta Gamma, Kappa Alpha Theta. Home: 13390 Gunflint Path Apple Valley MN 55124-7376

KETTREN, CYNTHIA SEXTON, mathematics educator, health association administrator; b. Pitts., Sept. 26, 1949; d. Robert M. and Agnes M. (Murray) Sexton; m. Leroy Paul Kettren, Mar. 16, 1974 (div. Sept. 1981); 1 child, Jennifer Lynn. AB, Grove City Coll., 1971; MS in Hygiene, U. Pitts., 1972; postgrad., U. S.C., 1987-89. Cert. tchr., Pa. Instr. Georgetown (S.C.)-Horry Tec, 1984-88; tchr. Williamsburg County Schs., Kingstree, S.C., 1984-89; prof. Coll. Charleston, S.C., 1989-90; instr. Westmoreland County C.C., Youngwood, Pa., 1993—; co-dir. Mental Health Assn., Greensburg, Pa., 1994—; pvt. tutor, Greensburg, 1995—. Mem. Nat. Steering Com. to Re-elect the Pres., Washington, 1995, Nat. Dem. Party, Washington, 1995. Pub. Health fellowship U.S. Pub. Health, 1971. Mem. Nat. Soc. DAR (mus. officer 1994-95), Smithsonian Inst., Kappa Mu Epsilon. Episcopalian. Home: 103 Monica Dr Apt 11-A Greensburg PA 15601

KETZNER, AMY H., accountant, controller; b. Ferdinand, Ind., Nov. 14, 1970; d. Joseph F. and Theresa V. (Hayes) K. BS in Acctg., U. So. Ind., 1995. Acct. MAI, Mt. Vernon, Ind., 1990-96; contr. Jack Frost, Inc., Evansville, Ind., 1996—. Mem. Inst. Mgmt. Accts. Home: 1127 Lincoln Ave Apt 643 Evansville IN 47714 Office: Jack Frost Inc 5701 Old Boonville Hwy Evansville IN 47715

KEULEGAN, EMMA PAULINE, special education educator; b. Washington, Jan. 21, 1930; d. Garbis H. and Nellie Virginia (Moore) K. BA, Dumbarton Coll. of Holy Cross, 1954. Cert. tchr. elem. and spl. edn. Tchr. St. Dominic's Elem. Sch., Washington, 1954-56, Sacred Heart Acad., Washington, 1956-59, Our Lady of Victory, Washington, 1959-63, St. Francis Acad., Vicksburg, Miss., 1963-78; tchr. Culkin Acad., Vicksburg, 1978-91, substitute tchr. spl. edn., 1991—. Treas. PTA, Vicksburg, 1980. Mem. Internat. Reading Assn. (pres. Warren County chpt.), Colonial Dames 17th Century (state v.p. 1987-89, state pres. 1989, hon. state pres. 1991—), Daus. Am. Colonists (state pres. 1992-94, hon. state pres. 1994—, chaplain 1985-89), DAR (chpt. regent 1967-69, sec. 1994, chpt. chaplain 1996). Republican. Roman Catholic. Home: 215 Buena Vista Dr Vicksburg MS 39180-5612 Office: Cedars Elem School 235 Cedars School Cir Vicksburg MS 39180

KEWLEY, SHARON LYNN, systems analyst, consultant; b. Geneseo, Ill., Sept. 23, 1958; d. James Leslie and Geraldine (Myers) K. BBA with honors, U. Miami (Fla.), 1988. Gen. agent Varvaris & Assocs., Cedar Rapids, Iowa, 1981-84; programmer, analyst U. Miami, Coral Gables, Fla., 1984-88; systems analyst Metro Dade County, Miami, 1988-91, Nat. Coun. on Compensation Ins., Boca Raton, Fla., 1991-93; owner Boca Byte, Boca Raton, Fla., 1993—; owner Boca Byte, Boca Baton, Fla. Mem. NAFE, Kendall Jaycees, Nat. Gold Key Honor Soc., PADI Divemaster. Republican. Lutheran. Office: Boca Byte PO Box 7072 Boca Raton FL 33431-0072

KEY, HELEN ELAINE, accountant, consulting company executive, educator; b. Cleve., Jan. 16, 1946; d. Maud and Helen (Key) Vance. B.S., W.Va. State Coll., 1968; M.Ed., Cleve. State U., 1977. Asst. prin. Cleve. Bd. Edn., 1968—; instr. Cuyahoga Community Coll., Cleve., part-time, 1969-78, Dyke Coll., Cleve., part-time, 1979—; pres. H.E. Key & Assos., Cleve., 1983—; treas. BK4W Inc., Cleve., 1981; sec. Progressive Pioneers, Inc. Mem. Am. Assn. Notary Pubs., Women Bus. Owners Assn., AAUW, NAACP, Cleve. Area Bus. Tchrs., NEA, Pi Lambda Theta, Alpha Kappa Alpha. Democrat. Baptist. Club: Toastmistress (sec. 1978) (Cleve.). Home: 564 Wilkes Ln Cleveland OH 44143-2622

KEY, MARY RITCHIE (MRS. AUDLEY E. PATTON), linguist, author, educator; b. San Diego, Mar. 19, 1924; d. George Lawrence and Iris (Lyons) Ritchie; children: Mary Helen Key Ellis, Harold Hayden Key (dec.), Thomas George Key. Student, U. Chgo., summer 1954, U. Mich., 1959; M.A., U. Tex., 1960, Ph.D., 1963; postgrad., UCLA, 1966. Asst. prof. linguistics Chapman Coll., Orange, Calif., 1963-66; asst. prof. linguistics U. Calif., Irvine, 1966-71; assoc. prof. U. Calif., 1971-78, prof., 1978—, chmn. program linguistics, 1969-71, 75-77, 87—; cons. Am. Indian langs., Spanish, in Mexico, 1946-55, S.Am., 1955-62, English dialects, 1968-74, Easter Island, 1975, Calif. Dept. Edn., 1966, 70-75, Center Applied Linguistics, Washington, 1967, 69; lectr. in field. Author: Comparative Tacanan Phonology, 1968, Male/Female Language, 1975, Paralanguage and Kinesics, 1975, Nonverbal Communication, 1977, The Grouping of South American Indian Languages, 1979, The Relationship of Verbal and Nonverbal Communication, 1980, Catherine the Great's Linguistic Contribution, 1980, Polynesian and American Linguistic Connections, 1984, Comparative Linguistics of South American Indian Languages, 1987, General and Amerindian Ethnolinguistics, 1989, Language Change in South American Indian Languages, 1991; founder, editor: newsletter Nonverbal Components of Communication, 1972-76; mem. editoral bd. Forum Linguisticum, 1976—, Lang. Scis., 1978—, La Linguistique, 1979—, Multilingua, 1987—; contbr. articles to profl. jours. Recipient Friends of Libr. Book award, 1976, hon. mention, Rolex awards for Enterprise, project Computerizing the Languages of the World, 1990; U. Calif. Regent's grantee, 1974, Fulbright-Hays grantee, 1975; faculty rsch. fellow, 1984-85. Mem. Linguistic Soc. Am., Am. Dialect Soc. (exec. council; regional sec. 1974-83), Internat. Reading Assn. (dir. 1968-72), Delta Kappa Gamma (local pres. 1974-76). Office: U Calif-Irvine Dept Of Linguistics Irvine CA 92717

KEY, SABRINA LYNN, elementary education educator; b. Galax, Va., Aug. 18, 1968; d. John Howard Jr. and Shirley Ann (Smith) K. Bachelor, Radford U., 1991. Cert. elem. tchr., Va. 2d grade tchr. Galax Elem., 1993—. Home: Rt 1 Box 458 Galax VA 24333 Office: Galax Elem Sch 225 Academy Dr Galax VA 24333

KEYES, JOAN ROSS RAFTER, education educator, author; b. Bklyn., Aug. 12, 1924; d. Joseph W. and Hermia (Ross) Rafter; m. William Ambrose, Apr. 26, 1947 (dec.); children: William, Peter, Dion, Alexandrea. BA, Adelphi U., Garden City, N.Y., 1945; MS, Long Island U., Greenvale, N.Y., 1973. Prodn. asst. CBS Radio, N.Y., 1943-44; cub news reporter Bklyn. Daily Eagle, 1945-46; advt. copywriter Gimbel's Dept. Store, N.Y., 1946-47; adj. prof. L.I. U., Greenvale, N.Y., 1984—; tchr. Port Wash. Pub. Schs., N.Y., 1970-94; lectr., cons. pub. sch. dists. nationwide, 1978—; workshop leader Tchrs. English to Speakers Other Langs. convs., 198l—. Author: Beats, Conversations in Rhythm, 1983, (video program) Now You're Talking, 1987, (computer program) Quick Talk, 1990; contbr. articles to ednl. mags. Lectr., catechist Our Lady of Fatima Ch., Port Washington, 1987—; vol. Earthwatch, Mallorca, 1988. Australia/New Zealand ednl. grantee Port Washington Pub. Schs., 1992. Mem. Tchrs. of English to Speakers of Other Languages, Am. Fedn. of Tchrs., N.Y. State United Tchrs., Port Wash. Tchrs. Assn. Republican. Roman Catholic. Office: Port Washington Pub Schs Campus Dr Port Washington NY 11050-3719

KEYSER, LYNDA JEANNE, physical education educator, coach; b. South Bend, Ind., Sept. 28, 1949; d. William Clemet and Mary Louise (Merritt) Roberts; m. Steven Thomas Keyser, Nov. 26, 1977; children: Jayme Rhem, Brett Thomas. Student, Fullerton (Calif.) City Coll., 1967-69; BA, San Diego State U., 1971; MA, Mich. State U., 1979; postgrad., We. Mich. U. Cert. tchr., Mich., Calif. Tchr. phys. edn., coach Niles (Mich.) Cmty. Schs., 1973—; del. People-to-People Russia and Hungary Fitness Del., 1992. Bd. dirs. Nile Assn. Exceptional Citizens, 1973-85; troop leader Girl Scouts of Singing Sands, Granger, Ind., 1986—. Mem. AAHPERD (life), People-to-People. Home: 55939 Riverdale Dr Elkhart IN 46514-1153 Office: Niles Cmty Schs 111 Spruce St Niles MI 49120-2963

KEYSTON, STEPHANI ANN, small business owner; b. Daytown, Tex., Aug. 6, 1955; d. Herbert Howard and Janice Faye (Stowe) Cruickshank; m. George Keyston III, Oct. 8, 1983; children: Jeremy George, Kristopher Samuel. AA with honors, Merced Coll., Merced, Calif., 1975; BA in Journalism with distinction, San Jose State U., 1976. Reporter, Fresno (Calif.) Bee, 1974-75; reporter, photographer Merced (Calif.) Sun-Star, 1974-77; pub. info. officer Fresno City Coll. (Calif.), 1977-80; dir. comms. Aerojet Tactical Sys. Co., Sacramento, 1980-83; co-owner, v.p. Keyco Landscape Contractor Inc., Loomis, Calif., 1984—. Co-coord. Aerojet United Way Campaign, 1981; Aerojet Tactical Sys. Co. coord. West Coast Nat. Derby Rallies, 1981-83; co-founder, pres. Calif. Lion Awareness. Mem. Internat. Assn. Bus. Communicators (dir. Sacramento chpt. 1983), Citrus Heights C. of C. (v.p. 1983). Republican. Home: 13399 Lakeview Pl Auburn CA 95602-8920 Office: Keyco Landscape Contractor Inc 3350 Swetzer Rd Loomis CA 95650

KEZLARIAN, NANCY KAY, social services administrator; b. Royal Oak, Mich., Aug. 26, 1948; d. Barkev A. and Nancy (Israelian) K.; m. Robert S. Vinetz, Aug. 1995. Student, U. Vienna, Austria, 1969; BA, Albion Coll., 1970; MA in Theatre and TV, U. Mich., 1971; MA in Clin. Psychology, Pepperdine U., 1992. Cert. secondary tchr., Mich., Calif. Tchr. West Bloomfield Hills (Mich.) High Sch., 1971-76; tchr. ESL, L.A. Pub. Schs., 1976-80; personnel dir. Samuel Goldwyn Co., L.A., 1985-86; dir. adminstrn. and human resources (Norman Lear) Act III Communications, L.A., 1986-90; dir. programs Salvation Army Booth Meml. Ctr., L.A., 1993-94; asst. exec. dir. Florence Crittenton Ctr., L.A., 1994-96, exec. dir., 1996—; owner, mgr. KAZ, hand painted clothing co., L.A., 1980-85. Writer, actress My Seventeenth Summer, The Big Blue Marble, 1979 (Emmy award for childen's TV programming). Named Tchr. of Yr., West Bloomfield Hills High Sch., 1976. Mem. SAG, Pers. and Indsl. Rels. Assn. (legis. rep. dist. 5 1989, 90), Calif. Assn. of Marriage and Family Therapists, L.A. Group psychtherapy Soc., Psi Chi.

KHAN, ARFA, radiologist, educator; b. Srinagar, Kashmir, India, Dec. 4, 1943; came to U.S., 1966; d. Ghulam Rasool and Ruqia Hayat; m. Faroque A. Khan, Apr. 16, 1966; children: Arif O., Shireen. B of Medicine, B of Surgery, Govt. Med. Coll., Kashmir, 1964. Diplomate Am. Bd. Radiology. Intern Barberton (Ohio) Citizen Hosp., 1966-67; resident in radiology L.I. Jewish Med. Ctr., New Hyde Park, N.Y., 1967-70, from instr. to assoc. prof. radiology, 1970-93, prof., 1993—, assoc. chmn. radiology, 1994—; program dir., 1995. Contbr. 50 articles to radiology jours. Mem. Am. Coll. Radiology, Am. Soc. Neuroradiology, Am. Soc. Head & Neck Radiology, Am. Soc. Thoracic Radiology, Radiol. Soc. N.Am. Democrat. Muslim.

KHARASCH, VIRGINIA SISON, pediatric pulmonologist; b. Manila, Aug. 14, 1956; came to U.S., 1983; d. Gregorio Beljano and Luz (Mendoza) Sison; m. Sigmund Joseph Kharasch, Dec. 29, 1956. BS in Zoology, U. of Philippines, 1977, MD, 1981. Diplomate Am. Bd. Pediatrics. Resident in pediatrics Phoenix Hosp., 1983-84, Michael Reese Hosp./U. Chgo., 1984-86; mem. pediatric staff Michael Reese Health Plan and Hosp., Chgo., 1986-87; pediatric pulmonology specialist Harvard U./Children's Hosp., Boston, 1987-89; pediatrician Children's Hosp., Boston, 1990—, clin. dir. pulmonary divsn., 1992-96; mem. faculty med. sch. Harvard U., Boston, 1990—; asst. prof. Boston U., 1992—; basic sci. researcher Harvard U. Sch. Pub. Health, 1987-90; cons. Cystic Fibrosis Ctr., Boston, 1987-90. Contbr. articles to med. jours. Rsch. fellow Nat. Rsch. Coun. of The Philippines, 1982. Fellow Am. Acad. Pediatrics; mem. AMA, Am. Coll. Chest Physicians, Pi Gamma Mu, Phi Kappa Phi, Phi Sigma. Office: Childrens Hosp 300 Longwood Ave Boston MA 02115-5724

KHASDAY, ALYCE FIELD, literary and film agent, psychic consultant, business owner; b. Bklyn., May 2, 1943; children: Jamie, Cortnie. Student, NYU, 1961-63; grad., La Varenne Culinary Inst. Sales mgr. Malom Lingerie, N.Y.C., 1962-66; sales coord. Sherman Underwear, N.Y.C., 1966-71; pub. rels. cons. Espon, Can., Can., 1977; organizer press confs. preventive medicine, 1977—; pres., fin. planner Greenbelt Equities, Inc., N.Y.C., 1982-84; archtl. planner, developer, pres. Kasday Design, N.Y.C., 1977-87; pres., syndicator, developer real estate, mgr. M & M Mgmt. Corp., Fla., 1984—; beverage company founder, pres., CEO Kombucha Magic Mushroom Farms, Inc., Cherokee Station, N.Y.; asst. chef to Isabelle Marique, N.Y.C., Albert Jorant, Paris; founder Psychic Life Counselling, Fla., 1990—; psychic cons. various orgns. including Am. Women in Radio and T.V. Office: 500 E 77th St Apt 520 New York NY 10021 also: Magic Mushroom Farms Inc PO Box 20717 New York NY 10021-0074

KIBLER, VIRGINIA MARY, economist; b. Meadville, Pa., July 30, 1960; d. Richard Dale and Jean Katherine (Brunner) K. BS in Biology, Clarion (Pa.) U., 1982, BA in Econs., 1983; MS in Natural Resource Econs., Pa. State U., 1986. Rsch. asst. Pa. Dept. Agrl. Econs., University Park, 1984-85; office mgr. League of Conservation Voters, Washington, 1986; pvt. practice econ. cons. Washington, 1986-88; economist Office of Pesticide Program EPA, Washington, 1988-91, team leader, program analyst Office of Comptroller, 1991-94, economist Office of Water, 1994—; spl. asst. U.S. Senate, Washington, 1990. Contbr. articles to profl. jours. Vol. cook So Others May Eat/Homeless Shelter, Washington, 1988—; tutor Cmty. Club, Washington, 1989-92; sec., treas. Timberwood on the Park Homeowners Assn., Wheaton, Md., 1991-93. Named one of Outstanding Young Women of Am., 1986. Mem. EPA Breakfast Club (charter chpt. 8428), Toastmasters. Office: EPA Office of Water 401 M St SW # 4102 Washington DC 20460-0001

KIBRICK, ANNE, nursing educator, university dean; b. Palmer, Mass., June 1, 1919; d. Martin and Christine (Grigas) Karlon; m. Sidney Kibrick, June 16, 1949; children: Joan, John. RN, Worcester (Mass.) Hahnemann Hosp., 1941; BS, Boston U., 1945; MA, Columbia Tchrs. Coll., 1948; EdD, Harvard U., 1958; LHD (hon.), St. Joseph's Coll., Windham, Maine, 1973. Asst. edn. dir. Cushing VA Hosp., Framingham, Mass., 1948-49; asst. prof. nursing Simmons Coll., Boston, 1949-55; dir. grad. div. Boston U. Sch. Nursing, 1958-63, dean, 1963-68, prof., 1968-70; chmn. dept. nursing Boston Coll. Grad. Sch. Arts and Sci., 1970-74; chmn. sch. nursing Boston State Coll., 1974-82; dean Sch. Nursing U. Mass., Boston, 1974-88, prof., 1988-93, prof. emeritus, 1993—; cons. div. nursing USPHS, 1964-68; cons. Nat. Student Nurses Assn., 1985-88; mem. nat. adv. council nurse tng. USPHS, NIH, 1968-73; cons. Hebrew U.-Hadassah Med. Orgn., Jerusalem, 1971—; mem. Inst. Medicine of Nat. Acad. Scis., 1972—, mem. steering com. costs of edn. of health professions, 1972-74; mem. Nat. Med. Audiovisual Tng. Center, 1972-76, Gov.'s Com. and Area Bd. Mental Health and Mental Retardation, Nat. Commn. for Study Nursing and Nursing Edn., 1970-73; mem. faculty com., regent's external degree program in nursing SUNY, 1974-82; mem. hosp. mgmt. bd. U. Hosp., U. Mass., 1976-81; dir. Medic Alert, Am. Jour. Nursing Co.; cons. Cumberland Coll. Health Scis., New South Wales, Australia, 1986, Menoufia U., Shibin El Kom, Egypt, 1987. Mem. editorial bd. Mass. Jour. Community Health. Bd. dirs. Brookline Mental Health Assn., Met. chpt. ARC, Children's Ctr. Brookline and Greater boston, Inc., 1984-89, Boston Health Care for Homeless, 1988-90; bd. dirs. Landy-Kaplan Nurses Coun., 1992—, treas., 1994—; mem. Brookline Town Meeting, 1995—; mem. nat. adv. com. Hadassah Nurses Coun., 1996—. Fellow Am. Acad. Nursing; mem. Nat. Mass. Leagues Nursing (pres. 1971-73), Am. Nurses Assn., Mass. Nurses Assn. (dir. 1982-86), AIDS Internat. Info. Found. (founding mem. 1985), Mass. Nurses Found. (v.p. 1983-86), Nat. Acads. of Practice, Mass. Med. Soc. (bd. dirs. postgrad. med. inst. 1983—, exec. com. 1989—), Mass. Blueprint 2000, Sigma Theta Tau, Pi Lambda Theta. Home: 381 Clinton Rd Brookline MA 02146-4146

KICKERT, JULIANA ARLENE, private investor; b. Blue Island, Ill., Sept. 1, 1943; d. Robert J. and Delia (Vander Giessen) K.; m. Durwood Perry Long, July 14, 1973 (div. Oct. 1974). AA, U. Fla., 1963, BS, 1965; MS, Ind. U., 1971. Registered real estate sales, Ill., Chgo. Instr. Chgo. Bd. Edn., 1965-71; dir. legal office program Sauk Area Career Ctr., Crestwood, Ill., 1973-76; real estate sales Kahn Kaplan Realty, Inc., Chgo., 1977-86; pvt. investor Sedona, Ariz. Apptd. Yavapai County Mounted Posse Search and Rescue Team, 1994—. Recipient Life Time Coop. Sales award North Side Real Estate Bd., Chgo., 1984, Top 20 Residential Salesperson award Condex Info. Svcs., 1984, 86; named Ariz. Horsewoman of Yr. Bridle & Bit Newspaper, 1990. Mem. Verde Valley Horsemen's Coun., Sedona Saddle Club (founding mem., pres. 1990-92, bd. dirs. 1993-94). Republican. Home and office: PO Box 1047 Sedona AZ 86339

KICKISH, MARGARET ELIZABETH, elementary education educator; b. Atlantic City, N.J., Nov. 30, 1949; d. James Bernard and Margaret Elizabeth (Egan) Parlett; m. Robert Anthony Kickish, June 30, 1973; children: Eileen, Kathleen, Robert Jr. BS, Franciscan U., 1971; MEd, Trenton State Coll., 1977. Cert. elem. educator, learning disabilities tchr. cons. Tchr. Our Lady Star of the Sea Sch., Atlantic City, N.J., 1971-75, Weymouth Twp. Elem. Sch., Dorothy, N.J., 1975-89; curriculum coord. Port Republic (N.J.) Sch., 1990-91; tchr. Brigantine (N.J.) Bd. Edn., 1991-94, supr. curriculum and instrn., 1995—; cognetics coach St. Joseph Sch., Somers Point, N.J., 1989—. Treas. PTA, Somers Point, 1987-89, pres., 1989-90; asst. coach Somers Point Softball Assn., 1991—; mem. St. Joseph Ch. Choir, Somers Point, 1985—. Mem. AAUW, NEA, ASCD, N.J. Edn. Assn. (treas. 1977-86), Prins. and Suprs. Assn., Coun. Exceptional Children, Assn. Learning Cons., Seashore Mother of Twins Club (pres. 1994—), South Jersey Irish Cultural Soc., Kappa Delta Pi, Delta Zeta, Phi Delta Kappa. Democrat. Roman Catholic. Home: 526 9th St Somers Point NJ 08244-1458 Office: Brigantine Bd of Edn 301 E Evans Blvd Brigantine NJ 08203-3424

KICKLIGHTER, TARA MICHELLE, elementary education educator; b. Maysville, Ky., Jan. 6, 1957; d. Gayle Blair and Barbara Alice (Foxworthy) Bowen; m. James Kicklighter, Aug. 19, 1982 (div. 1985); 1 child, Ali. BS in Edn., Ea. Ky. U., 1979. Cert. elem., early childhood tchr., Fla. Tennis profl. Deland (Fla.) Parks & Recreation, 1979-83; title I tchr. Bunnell (Fla.) Elem. Sch., 1979—. Creative tchr. grantee Flaglas County Edn. Found., 1995; named Tchr. of Yr., Flagler County, 1988. Mem. Phi Delta Kappa. Methodist. Home: 2701 Saratoga Pl Deland FL 32720 Office: Bunnell Elem Sch Box 937 Bunnell FL 32110

KIDD, BEVERLY ANN, home health care provider; b. Cin., Feb. 4, 1952; d. Matthew James Christopher and Martha Gaye (Underwood) S.; m. James Chatman Johnson (div. Oct. 1977); children: Douglas, Jamaica S. Caine, La'Shonda r.; m. Lawrence Wayne Kidd, Apr. 5, 1985. AA, So. Ohio Coll., 1988; Degree (hon.) Inst. for Comm. Capacity, Xavier U., 1996. Cert. tax preparer. Candy striper Christ Hosp., Cin., 1969; nurse asst. LeBrauns Nursing Home, Cin., 1969-71, Kenwood Nursing ctr., Cin., 1973-74; early childhood educator Cin. Pub. Schs., 1977; comms. Tate's Towing Svcs., Cin., 1978-79; home health care provider Mental Health Svcs. West, Cin., 1985—; songwriter Five Star Music Masters, Dedham, Mass., 1995—, Talent & Assocs., Quincy, Mass., 1986-87. Writer poetry. Active Leadership Devel. Workshop, Neighborhood Housing and Conservation, Millvale/Cin., 1985; corr. sec. millvale Comm. Coun., 1996; comm. cons. Hamilton County Partnership, 1995; bd. dirs. Millvale Primary Elem., Cin., 1995—. Fellow Nat. Trust for Hist. Preservation, Libr. of Congress Assocs.

KIDD, DEBRA JEAN, communications executive; b. Chgo., May 13, 1956; d. Fred A. and Jean (Pezzopane) Winchar; m. Kim Joseph Kidd, July 22, 1978; children: Jennifer Marie, Michele Jean. AA in Bus. with high honors, Wright Jr. Coll., 1977. Legal sec. Sidley & Austin, Chgo., 1977-80; investment adminstr. Golder, Thoma & Co., Chgo., 1980-81, exec. asst., 1981-84; sales rep. Dataspeed, Inc., Chgo., 1984, midwestern regional mgr. Dataspeed, Inc., Chgo., 1985; comm. cons. Chgo. Comm., Inc., Chgo., 1986-88; owner, founder Captain Kidd's Video, Niles, 1981-84. Vol. Am. Lung Assn., Chgo., 1979; vol. tchr. religious edn. Our Lady Mother of Ch., Norridge, Ill., 1981-83, St. Raymonds, Mt. Prospect, 1993-94; vol. Parents Who Care, 1988-94, pres., 1991-93; vol. PTA Lion's Park Sch., 1993-95, bd. dirs., 1993-94; editor Lion's Roar, 1993-95; founder Young Journalist Club, 1994-95; leader Girl Scouts, 1992—, cons., 1994-95, del., registrar, organizer, 1994—. Mem. NAFE, Nat. Assn. Bus. Women, Nat. Assn. Profl. Saleswomen, Phi Theta Kappa. Roman Catholic. Avocations: camping, skiing, snorkeling, sailing, reading, needlepoint.

KIDD, JULIE KELLY, elementary education educator; b. Washington, Sept. 20, 1958; d. John Francis and Eldora Jean (Ostby) Kelly; m. John Shawler Kidd, Aug. 16, 1980; 1 child, Christopher. BA, U. Richmond, 1980; MEd, James MAdison U., 1984; EdD, Va. Tech. U., 1992. Tchr. 6th & 7th grades Page County Pub. Schs., Luray & Shenandoah, Va., 1980-84; reading specialist Alexandria (Va.) City Pub. Schs., 1984-87, 87-92, lead tchr., 1992-94, tchr. 4th grade, 1994-96, reading specialist, 1996—; tchr., cons. No. Va. Writing Project, Fairfax, 1988—. Recipient Excellence in Edn. award; Washington Post grantee, 1987. Mem. ASCD, Nat. Coun. Tchrs. English, Nat. Coun. Tchrs. Math., Internat. REading Assn. Office: George Mason Elem Sch Cameron Mills Rd Alexandria VA 22314-2702

KIDD, KATHRYN ISABELLA, elementary education educator; b. Phila., Aug. 4, 1961; d. James Gurwood Jr. and Mary Therese (Graham) K. (dec.). BA in Journalism, Temple U., 1983; MEd, Holy Family Coll., 1995. Cert. elem. tchr., Pa. Pub. rels. asst. Sisters of the Most Blessed Trinity, Phila., 1981-82; prodn. asst. WHYY-FM, Phila., 1982-84; promotions/mktg. asst. Walnut St. Theatre, Phila., 1984-85; typist, receptionist Dover Group, Phila., 1985-87; asst. editor Orthopedics Today and Radiology Today Slack Inc., Thorofare, N.J., 1987-88, asst. editor jour. divsn., 1988-89; 5th grade tchr. St. Joachim Sch., Phila., 1989-94; 6th grade tchr. St. Hugh of Cluny Sch., Phila., 1994—; guide Phila. Coun. for Internat. Visitors, 1983-85. Copy editor: Research Traditions in Occupational Therapy, 1988; contbr. articles to profl. jours. Mem. ASCD, Nat. Coun. Tchrs. English, Nat. Coun. Social Studies, Nat. Cath. Educators Assn., Kappa Delta Pi. Roman Catholic. Office: St Hugh of Cluny Sch Mascher and Tioga Streets Philadelphia PA 19140

KIDD, RITA CAROLYN, government process redesign consultant; b. Merced, Calif., Feb. 27, 1943; d. Vivian Grace (Reyburn) Broddrick-Hagan; m. James Tony Kidd, Feb. 24, 1962; 1 child, Alexandra Grace. Sec. Merced Planning Dept., 1960-61, Svc. Bur. Corp., San Jose, Calif., 1961-62, Mountain View (Calif.) Planning Dept., 1962-64; adminstrv. asst.. Syntex Labs., Palo Alto, Calif., 1965-69; stockbroker Harrison Fin. and Emmett Larkin, Sacramento, 1971-77; cons. on EEO law, affirmative action, pers. mgmt. Sacramento, Merced, 1974-80; asst. dir. project planning and devel. group Merced County Human Svcs. Agy., Merced, 1980-93; instr. Merced Coll., 1970-71, 77-79; cons. to govt. and industry in process redesign & govt. reengring., 1993—. Columnist, freelance writer govt. tech. mag. Mem., chmn. Merced Downtown Improvement Dist., 1977-79. Recipient recognition award Nat. Assn. Counties, 1987, 88, project award Urban and Regional Info. Systems Assn., 1991; named AMS/Carnegie Mellon finalist, Fifth awards for achievement in mng. info. tech. Mem. Internat. Platform Assn. Democrat.

KIDDER, MARGOT, actress; b. Yellowknife, Can., Oct. 17, 1948; m. Tom McGuane, 1975 (div.); 1 dau., Maggie; m. John Heard. Student, U. B.C. Began career in Can. theater and TV; film debut in Gaily, Gaily, 1969; other films include Quackser Fortune Has a Cousin in the Bronx, 1970, Sisters, 1973, Black Christmas, 1974, A Quiet Day in Belfast, 1974, Gravy Train, 1974, Black Christmas, 1974, The Great Waldo Pepper, 1975, The Reincarnation of Peter Proud, 1975, 92 in the Shade, 1975, Superman, 1978, The Amityville Horror, 1979, Mr. Mike's Mondo Video, 1979, Miss Right, 1980, Superman II, 1980, Willie and Phil, 1980, Shoot the Sun Down, 1981, Heartaches, 1981, Some Kind of Hero, 1981, Trenchcoat, 1983, Superman III, 1983, Little Treasure, 1985, Speaking Our Peace, 1985, Little Treasure, 1985, The Canadian Conspiracy, 1986, Gobots: Battle of the Rock Lords (voice), 1986, Keeping Track, 1987, Superman IV: The Quest for Peace, 1987, Mob Story, 1990, The White Room, 1990, Crime and Punishment, 1992, Maverick, 1994, Henry & Verlin, 1994, Windrunner, 1995, Blodknot, 1995, Never Met Picasso, 1996; dir., screenwriter And Again, 1975; starred in TV series Nichols, 1971-72, Shell Game, 1987, The Pornographer, 1993, Phantom 2040, 1994 (voice); guest appearance: Boston Commons, 1995; TV movies Suddenly Single, 1971, The Bounty Man, 1972, Honky Tonk, 1974, Louisiana, 1984, The Glitter Dome, 1984, Such Dust as Dreams are Made Of, 1984, Picking Up the Pieces, 1985, Vanishing Act, 1986, Body of Evidence, 1987, Curiosity Killed, 1992, To Catch a Killer, 1992, One Woman's Courage, 1992, Young Ivanhoe, 1995; other TV appearances include Mod Squad. *

KIDMAN, NICOLE, actress; b. Hawaii, 1967; m. Tom Cruise, 1990; children: Isabella Jane Kidman, Connor Antony Kidman. Film appearences include BMX Bandits, 1983, Bush Christmas, 1983, Wills and Burke-The Untold Story, 1985, Windrider, 1986, The Bit Part, 1987, Emerald City, 1989, Dead Calm, 1989, Days of Thunder, 1990, Flirting, 1991, Billy Bathgate, 1991 (Golden Globe Award nomination 1992), Far and Away, 1992, Malice, 1993, My Life, 1993, Batman Forever, 1995, Portrait of a Lady, 1995, To Die For, 1995, The Aventers, 1996; TV appearences include Bangkok Hilton, 1990 (Australian Film Inst. Best Actress in Miniseries), Vietnam (Australian Film Inst. Best Actress in Miniseries). Office: care Catherine Olin PMK Pub Rels 955 Carrillo Dr Ste 200 Los Angeles CA 90048-5400*

KIDWELL, MARY F., accountant; b. Seymour, Ind., Dec. 29, 1953; d. Rudolph Franz and Frances C. (Haag) Schlatterer; m. Richard L. Kidwell, May 26, 1979; children: Melinda, Ann, Frances, Christopher. BS in Fin., Ind. State U., 1975. Cert. mgmt. acct. Ind. Acctg. mgr. Cummins Engine Co., Columbus, Ind., 1981-82, fin. systems leader, 1982-85, invoicing mgr., 1985-88, gen. acctg. mgr., 1988-91, inventory mgr., 1991-92, material fin. dir., 1992-96. Mem. Inst. Mgmt. Accts. (dir. manuscripts south ctrl. Ind. chpt. 1993-94). Office: Cummins Engine Co 500 Jackson Columbus IN 47201

KIEFER, RENATA GERTRUD, pediatrician, economist, international health consultant; b. Lorrach, Baden, Germany, July 4, 1946; came to U.S., 1970; d. Friedrich W. and Gertrud Anna (Keller) K.; m. James C. Bridgman. BA, Stanford U., 1963; MA, U. Calif., Berkeley, 1967; MD, U. Geneva, Switzerland, 1982; MPH, U. Calif., Berkeley, 1990. Diplomate Am. Bd. Pediatrics; cert. in environ. health, Germany. Asst. instr. dissection lab. dept. morphology U. Geneva Sch. of Medicine, Switzerland, 1979-80; interim resident dept. diagnostic radiology Univ. Hosp., Geneva, 1980, intern physician, 1982-83; clin. fellow in pediatrics Harvard Med. Sch., Boston, 1983-85; resident physician Mass. Gen. Hosp., Boston, 1983-85; sr. resident dept. pediatrics U. Calif., San Francisco, 1985-86; attending physician emergency dept. Children's Hosp. Med. Ctr., Oakland, Calif., 1986-94; fellow dept. epidemiology and internat. health U. Calif., San Francisco, 1988-90; German tech. cooperation expert tropical medicine & internat. health Inst. for Health Sci. Rsch., Asuncion, Paraguay, 1990-94, vis. prof. epidemiol. and preventive medicine, 1992—; sci. methods advisor Nat. U. Asuncion, 1994—; chief adv. Health Strategies Internat.; rep. of IICS/Internat. Orgns., cons. and presenter in field. Contbr. numerous articles to profl. jours. Recipient Pub. Health Svc. Nat. Rsch. Svc. award, 1989-90; co-winner Nat. Sci. prize Paraguay Parliament, 1994; ASSU scholar Stanford U., 1962-63, Fulbright scholar, 1962-64, Internat. scholar Swedish Inst., 1968, Internat. Health scholar U. Calif., 1990; AAUW fellow, 1968. Address: 6 Locksley Ave San Francisco CA 94122-3839

KIEHNE, ANNA MARIE, consultant; b. Preston, Minn., Dec. 15, 1947; d. Alvin H. and Anna M. Kiehne; m. Lyman F. Loveland, June 15, 1991; children: Aaron, Amy. BA in Bus. Adminstrn., Winona State U., 1969; cert. in sys. analysis, UCLA, 1984; M in Internat. Bus. Adminstrn., West Coast U., 1992. Analyst Home Savs. of Am., L.A., 1983-87, Cray Rsch., Mpls., 1988-89; v.p. Bowest Corp., La Jolla, Calif., 1989-90; cons. Tigard, Oreg., 1990—. Organizer recycling program for condominium assn., 1991. Mem. Inst. Mgmt. Accts., Am. Mgmt. Assn. Democrat. Lutheran. Home and Office: 15085 SW Chardonnay Ave Tigard OR 97224

KIEL, CATHERINE ANN, public relations executive; b. Phila., Aug. 8, 1961; d. Seymour and Alice (Wolf) K. BA, BS, Miami U., Oxford, Ohio, 1983. Asst. to dir. spl. events Penn's Landing Corp. Phila. Tri-Centennial, 1982; account exec. Jessica Dee Communications, N.Y.C., 1983-85; v.p. Grossich & Ptnrs., Inc., N.Y.C., 1985-89; exec. v.p. G.S. Schwartz & Co. Inc., N.Y.C., 1989—; with Laws Hall & Assocs., Miami U., Oxford, 1983; pub. rels. cons. N.Y.C. Opera Guild, 1989-90. Mem. exec. com. John Ravitz Campaign, N.Y.C., 1988; exec. v.p. Eastside Young Reps. Club, N.Y.C., 1987-90. Recipient Ptnrship. in Edn. award N.Y.C. Bd. Edn., 1983, 88, Silver Anvil, Pub. Rels. Soc. Am., 1992, Big Apple, N.Y. chpt. Pub. Rels. Soc. Am., 1992, Creativity in Pub. Rels. award, 1994. Mem. Women Execs. Pub. Rels., Miami U. Alumni Club (pres. N.Y.C. chpt. 1988-94), Miami U. Alumni Assn. (bd. dirs. 1992—), N.Y. Jr. League. Home: 245 E 83rd St New York NY 10028-2803 Office: GS Schwartz & Co Inc 470 Park Ave S New York NY 10016-6819

KIELY, KATHY, advertising executive. Sr. v.p., creative dir. Arnold Fortuna Lawner & Cabot, Boston. Office: Arnold Fortuna Lawner & Cab 101 Arch St Boston MA 02110*

KIENHOLZ, LYN SHEARER, international arts projects coordinator; b. Chgo.; d. Mitchell W. and Lucille M. (Hock) Shearer; student Sullins Coll., Md. Coll. Women. Assoc. producer Kurt Simon Prodns., Beverly Hills, Calif., 1963-65; owner, mgr. Vuokko Boutique, Beverly Hills, 1969-75; bd. dirs. L.A. Inst. Contemporary Art, 1976-79, Fellows of Contemporary Art, 1977-79, Internat. Network for Arts, 1979-89, L.A. Contemporary Exhbns., 1980-82; exec. sec., bd. dirs. Beaubourg Found. (now George Pompidou Art and Culture Found.), 1977-81; visual arts adv. Performing Arts Coun., L.A. Music Ctr., 1980-89; bd. govs. Calif. Inst. Tech. Baxter Art Gallery, 1980-85; adv. bd. dirs. Fine Arts Communications, pub. Images & Issues mag., 1981-85; founder, chmn. bd. Calif./Internat. Arts Found., 1981—; bd. dirs., western chmn. ArtTable 1983-89; bd. dirs. Galef Inst., 1992—; exec. bd. Sovereign Fund, 1981-93; exec. bd. dirs. Scandinavia Today, 1982-83, Art L.A., 1987, 88, 89; mem. adv. bd. Otis/Parsons Sch. Design, 1983-85, U. So. Calif. dept. fine arts, 1983-85; bd. dirs. UK/LA Festival of Britain, 1986-88, 92-94; hon. bd. dirs. L'Ensemble des Deux Mondes, Paris, 1986-91; mem. Comité Internat. pour les Musées d'Art Moderne, 1985—, bd. dirs., 1991—; Bd. dirs. Arts, Inc., 1987-89. Co-host nat. pub. radio program ARTS/L.A., 1987-91; contbg. editor Calif. mag., 1984-89. Address: 2737 Outpost Dr Los Angeles CA 90068-2061

KIES, COSETTE NELL, library science educator; b. Platteville, Wis., Sept. 2, 1936; d. Guerdon Francis and Gertrude Caroline (Pitts) K. B.S., U. Wis.-Platteville, 1957; M.A. in Art History, U. Wis.-Madison, 1961, M.A. in Library Sci., 1962; D.L.S., Columbia U., 1977. Art tchr. Grafton Pub. Schs., Wis., 1957-59; children's librarian Fond du Lac Pub. Library, Wis., 1962-63; sr. asst. librarian, asst. prof. U. Nebr., Lincoln, 1963-67; profl. asst. ALA, Chgo., 1968-69; library career cons. Ill. State Library, Springfield, 1969-71; asst. dir., personnel and pub. relations Ferguson Library, Stamford, Conn., 1971-74; asst. prof. Sch. Library Sci., Goerge Peabody Coll. for Tchrs., Nashville, 1975-78; assoc. prof. Sch. Library Sci., Goerge Peabody Coll. for Tchrs., 1978-83; vis. assoc. prof. Sch. Library Sci., Simmons Coll., Boston, 1978; sr. lectr. Fulbright-Hays Program, Escola de Biblioteconomia, U. Fed. de Minas Gerais, Brazil, 1979-80; vis. prof. Escola de Biblioteconomia, U. Fed. de Paraiba, Joao Pessoa, Brazil, 1980; chmn., prof. dept. library and info. studies No. Ill. U., De Kalb, 1983-94, prof. dept. leadership and ednl. policy studies, 1994—; mem. planning com. Children's Lit. Inst., 1983—; speaker various orgns., radio and TV. Author: Problems in Library Public Relations, 1974, Projecting a Positive Image Through Public Relations, 1979, Occult Books in the Western World, 1986, Marketing and Public Relations for Libraries, 1987, Supernatural Fiction for Teens, 1987, 92, Horror Fiction for Young Adults, 1991, Presenting Lois Duncan, 1994; editor: The Literary Allusions Cookbook, 1982. Recipient George Virgil Fuller award Columbia U., 1976. Mem. ALA (life, adv. com. Office for Libr. Pers. 1979-83, chair nat. libr. week com. 1985-87, editor Recruitment Newsletter 1968-69, editor Fin. Assistance for Libr. Edn. 1970-73, H.W. Wilson Recruitment award 1970), Assn. Libr. Svcs. for Children (Newbery-Caldecott com. 1976), Libr. Edn. Divsn. (chmn. fin. assistance for libr. edn. com. 1969-73, Beta Phi Mu award com. 1976), Assn. Libr. and Info. Sci. Edn. (comm. com. 1978-80, coord. joint libr. sch. reunion 1984-85), Women's Nat. Book Assn. (dir. pub. affairs, spl. asst. to pres. 1980-82, pres. Nashville chpt. 1981-83, newsletter editor 1980-82), Ill. Libr. Assn., Ill. Coalition Libr. Advocates (bd. dirs. 1984-86), Children's Internat. Edn. Ctr. (chmn. pub. rels. com. 1981-83). Home: 607 Normal Rd De Kalb IL 60115-2204 Office: No Ill U Dept Leadership/Ednl Policy De Kalb IL 60115

KIESEL, BEVERLY JEAN, administrative assistant; b. St. Louis, Mar. 12, 1953; d. Paul Harvey and Miriam Joyce (Butler) McMinn; m. James Rodney Pagel, June 25, 1982 (div. June 1991); children: Michael Edward, Brian James; m. Donald Wayne Kiesel, Dec. 16, 1995; stepchildren: Kelly Lee Kiesel Ryan, David Mark. Student, Mo. Bapt. Coll., 1971-72, Okla. Bapt. U., 1972-75; BS in Bus. Mgmt., LeTourneau U., 1995. Libr. aide clk. McCluer Sr. High Sch., Florissant, Mo., 1970-72; music aide Okla. Bapt. U., Shawnee, 1972-74; clk. Revco Drug Store, Shawnee, 1975-76; receptionist

Snelling & Snelling Pers., Ft. Worth, 1976-77; unit stock control clk. Montgomery Ward, Ft. Worth, 1977-79; exec. sec. Westpark Communications, Arlington, Tex., 1979-80; payroll and customer svc. Stone Container Corp., Grand Prairie, Tex., 1980-87; fin. mgr. Dobbs Internat. Svcs., Unit 800, Dallas-Ft. Worth Airport, 1987-93; adminstrv. asst. IBM Corp., Roanoke, Tex., 1993—. Ch. pianist Mission Ch. of 1st Baptist, Shawnee, 1974-75; children's choir dir. 1st Bapt. Ch., Shawnee, 1975-76; Sunday sch. pianist Fielder Rd. Baptist Ch., Arlington, Tex., 1982-84, Hurst (Tex.) Bapt. Ch., 1994-95; vol. Goodfellows, Ft. Worth, 1988, Animal Rescue League of Denton County, 1993—; mem. recycling com. PTA, 1991-95. Mem. Sigma Alpha Iota. Republican. Home: 201 E Round Grove Rd Apt 2032 Lewisville TX 75067-8335 Office: IBM Corp 5 W Kirkwood Blvd (02-03-30) Roanoke TX 76299

KIESEL, MARILYN J., realtor; b. Flint, Mich., Apr. 29, 1937; d. Leonard and Muriel Grace (Andrews) Clark; m. Charles A. Kiesel, May 2, 1964 (div. Sept. 1979); children: Charles A., Cheryl E. BSN, U. Mich., 1959; postgrad., Mich. State U. RN, Mich., 1959; GRI: Realtors, 1986; CRP: Employee Relocation Coun., 1992. Head nurse U. Mich. Adolescent Psychiatry, Ann Arbor, 1959-61; asst. supr. nursing U. Mich. Children's Psychiatric Hosp., Ann Arbor, 1962-64; instr. Flint (Mich.) Cmty. Jr. Coll., 1964-67; sales assoc. Phipps Realty, East Greenwich, R.I., 1979-86; broker assoc. Re/Max Profls., East Greenwich, R.I., 1986—. East Greenwich Town Coun. Mem., 1994—, Town Com. Mem. 1992—. Named Realtor of Yr. Kent County Bd. Realtors, 1993, Re/Maxer of Yr. R.I. Brokers Owners, 1992, East Greenwich Rep. Town Com., 1982—. Mem. Nat. Assn. Realtors (fed. coord. 1986—), R.I. Assn. Realtors (dir., com. chairs 1995—), Kent Washington Bd. Realtors (pres. 1995-96). Republican. Home: 178 Overfield Rd East Greenwich RI 02818

KIEST, HEATHER LENORE, secondary school educator; b. Seattle, Sept. 18, 1959; d. Morgan O. Griffin and Carol M. (Eserman) Marshall; m. David S. Brownell, Aug. 10, 1985 (div. 1993); children: Anna K. Brownell, Robert J. Brownell; m. Alan S. Kiest, Feb. 12, 1995; 1 child, Jennifer S. BA in Math. Edn., Seattle Pacific U., 1980. Cert. K-12 tchr. Tchr. Marysville (Wash.) Sch. Dist. #25, 1980-96, K-12 health adoption coord., 1993-95, instructional materials curriculum com. mem., 1993-96, staff devel. coordinating coun. mem., 1995-96, mem. site-based curriculum adoption com., 1994-95, math assessment devel. implementation com., 1995-96, head dept. math, 1996 . Mem. ASCD, Wash. Edn. Assn. Democrat. Lutheran. Home: 18810 26th Ave NE Lake Forest Park WA 98155 Office: Cedarcrest Sch 6400 88th St NE Marysville WA 98270

KIHLSTEDT, MAJA (ANNA MARIA KIHLSTEDT), artist; b. Stockholm, Sweden, Jan. 26, 1952; came to U.S., 1977; d. Olof Kihlstedt and Ingegerd Kihlstedt Carlsten. BA, Royal Danish Art Acad., Copenhagen, 1977; student, N.Y. Studio Sch., 1977-79, Yale U., 1979. Exhbns. include Den Frie Mus., Copenhagen, 1978, N.Y. Studio Sch., N.Y.C., 1979, Yale Sch. Arts, Norfolk, Conn., 1983, Lucky Strike Gallery, N.Y.C., 1987, 55 Mercer St. Gallery, N.Y.C., 1989, Kenkeleba Gallery, N.Y.C., 1989, Art Now Gallery, Gothenburg, Sweden, 1992, Jan Eric Lowenadler Gallery, Sweden, 1992, Blondies Contemporary Art, N.Y.C., 1995, The Painting Ctr., N.Y.C., 1995, Fletcher Gallery, Woodstock, N.Y., 1996, Dosttl Ctr. Contemporary Art, Harrisburg, Pa., 1996; represented in collections at Va. Ctr. for the Arts, also pvt. collections. Change Inc. grantee, 1984; Art Coun. Sweden fellow, 1983-87; Yaddo fellow, 1981, Battel-Stoeckel Found. scholar, 1979, MacDowell Colony fellow, 1981, others. Mem. Art Initiative, The Art Group (founder). Studio: 6 W 28th St New York NY 10001

KIHLSTROM, APRIL LYNN, writer; b. Buffalo, Sept. 13, 1951; d. Ernest H. and Victorine (Salvage) K.; m. Joseph L. Gerver, Aug. 24, 1974; children: Daniel Gerver, Rachel Gerver. BS in Math. with honors, Purdue U., 1974; MS in Ops. Rsch., Cornell U., 1975. Author: Paris Summer, 1977, Trondelaine Castle, 1979, My Love Betrayed, 1980, A Choice of Cousins, 1982, A Scandalous Bequest, 1982, An Improper Companion, 1983, The Wary Spinster, 1983, The Mysterious Governess, 1984, Twice Betrothed, 1984, The Charming Impostor, 1985, The Counterfeit Betrothal, 1986, Captain Rogue, 1986, Miss Redmond's Folly, 1986, The Nabob's Widow, 1987, The Scholar's Daughter, 1989, The Reckless Wager, 1991, Dangerous Masquerade, 1992, The Wicked Groom, 1996, The Widowed Bride, 1996. Mem. NOW, Romance Writers Am., Phi Beta Kappa. Home and Office: 107 Woodland Ave Cherry Hill NJ 08002-4417

KIJANKA, DOROTHY M., library administrator; b. Mt. Olive, Ill.; d. Michael and Catherine (Zupsich) Kaganich; m. Stanley J. Kijanka, Jr., Nov. 20, 1970 (dec. 1981). AB in History with honors, U. Ill.; MLS, Rutgers U. Reference librarian Greenwich Pub. Library, Conn., 1966-68; reference librarian Fairfield U., Conn., 1968-74, assoc. librarian, 1974-84; dir. Sacred Heart U. Library, Fairfield, 1984—; bd. dirs. Bibliomation, 1990—; chair Conn. Acad. Libr. Dirs., 1993—; panelist Off-Campus Libr. Svcs. Conf., 1993. Contbr. articles to profl. jours. Mem. ALA, Library Group of Southwestern Conn. (pres. 1977-78), Southwestern Conn. Library Council (trustee 1977-78), Fairfield County Library Adminstrs. Group (pres. 1986-87), New Eng. Library Assn., Conn. Library Assn. (chmn. reference sect. 1975), Assn. Coll. and Rsch. Librs. (planning com. 1987-89, mem. internat. rels. com. 1991), Libr. Adminstrn and Mgmt. Assn. (orgn. com. 1987, risk mgmt. and ins. com. 1987-89, mem. fund raising com. 1990, mentor 1990-92). Office: Sacred Heart Univ Library 5151 Park Ave Fairfield CT 06432-1023

KILBANE, CATHERINE M., lawyer; b. Cleve., Apr. 10, 1963. BA cum laude, Case Western Res. U., 1984, JD cum laude, 1987. Bar: Ohio 1987. Ptnr. Baker & Hostetler, Cleve. Mem. Delta Theta Phi. Office: Baker & Hostetler 3200 Nat City Ctr 1900 E 9th St Cleveland OH 44114-3985*

KILBOURNE, BARBARA JEAN, health and human services consultant; b. Milw., Mar. 21, 1941; d. Burton Conwell and Marjorie Janet (Tufts) K.; m. Kenneth Keith Kauffman, Feb. 10, 1962 (div. 1983). BA, U. Minn., 1972; MBA, Coll. St. Thomas, St. Paul, 1980. Adminstr. Ebenezer Soc., Mpls., 1974-85; v.p., dir. housing Walker Residence and Health Svcs., Inc., Mpls., 1985-88; exec. v.p. Oblate Ministries Health and Aging, West St. Paul, Minn., 1988-94; cons., 1995—; pres. Barbara J. Kilbourne, Ltd., 1996—; bd. dirs. Westminster Resident Svcs. Corp., St. Paul, chmn., 1996—, River Region Health Svcs., Red Wing, Minn., chmn. seminary plaza, 1995—, St. Olaf Residence; mem. commn. on aging Cath. Charities USA, Washington, 1989—; presenter, cons. and spkr. in field. Author: Family Councils in Nursing Homes, 1981. Chmn. bd. dirs. Dakota Inc., Eagan, Minn., 1985-96, Minn. Assn. Homes for Aging, 1991-92, Sem. Plz., Red Wing, 1995; project chair Dialog 2000, Dakota County, Minn., 1988-91. Episcopalian. Home: 1021 Sibley Memorial Hwy Lilydale MN 55118-6100

KILBOURNE, CLAIRE ANNE, gifted and talented education educator; b. Pt. Jervis, N.Y., Aug. 3, 1939; d. Eston Arthur and Elizabeth Anna (Coss) Garrison; m. Charles Warren Kilbourne, June 17, 1961; children: Caroline Kilbourne Stahle, Kevin Charles. BA, Trenton State Coll., 1961; postgrad., Rider U., 1980. Cert. tchr. secondary edn., N.J. Tchr. English Hopewell, N.J., 1961-62; supplemental instr. Hamilton Twp., 1974-77; tchr. gifted edn. Grice Mid. Sch., Hamilton, N.J., 1977-89, Crockett Mid. Sch., Hamilton, 1989—; workshop presenter Hamilton Sch. Dist., 1977-96; cons. gifted edn., N.J., 1977-95. Author: (anthologies) Best Poems of 1996, Best Loved Contemporary Poems, 1979, Our World's Favorite Poems, Our World's Favorite Gold and Silver Poems, 1991; contbr. poetry to audiotapes: Sounds of Poetry, 1996, Expressions. Mem., donor Lakota Indians, 1985-95; writing mentor, 1977-95; dep. gov. Am. Biog. Inst. Bd. Govs. Recipient plaque N.J. Assn. for Supervision and Curriculum Devel.; named Golden Poet of World, 1989-92, Most Admired Woman of Decade, 1994; grantee Kodak Cameras in the Curriculum, Hamilton Twp. Dist. Mem. NEA, Internat. Platform Assn., Archaeol. Inst. Am., Planetary Soc., Internat. Soc. Poets, Hamilton Twp. Edn. Assn. (life). Home: 200 Carlisle Ave Yardville NJ 08620-1212 Office: Crockett Mid Sch 2631 Kuser Rd Trenton NJ 08691

KILBOURNE, KRYSTAL HEWETT, rail transportation executive; b. Sandersville, Ga., Apr. 7, 1940; d. John Ray and Kathleen (Perkins) Hewett; m. Alan Arden Kilbourne, July 1, 1961 (div. May 1972); children: Arden Alan, Keith Ray. A, U. Ga., 1960. Tchr. Massey Bus. Coll., Jacksonville, Fla., 1968-72, editor, reporter, photographer, 1968-72; asst. to pres. Luter Advt. Agy., Jacksonville, Fla., 1973-74; asst. to dir. Leukemia Soc., Jacksonville, Fla., 1975-76; asst. to pres. TeleCheck Corp., Jacksonville, Fla., 1979; mgr. customer svc. railroad ops. CSX Transp., Jacksonville, Fla., 1980—. Tuition scholar U. Ga., 1958; recipient Transp. Workers Leadership award, 1995. Mem. Nat. Assn. Railway Bus. Women, Am. Coun. Railroad Women (chair equal employment opportunity coun. 1992-94). Democrat. Presbyn. Home: 4856 Deermoss Way South Jacksonville FL 32217-9306 Office: CSX Transportation 6737 Southpoint Dr South Jacksonville FL 32216

KILDE, SANDRA JEAN, nurse anesthetist, educator, consultant; b. Eau Claire, Wis., June 25, 1938; d. Harry Meylan and Beverly June (Johnson) K. Diploma Luther Hosp. Sch. Nursing, Eau Claire, 1959; grad. anesthesia course Mpls. Sch. Anesthesia, 1967; BA, Met. State U., St. Paul, 1976; MA, U. St. Thomas, 1981; EdD, Nova Southeastern U., 1987. RN, Wis., Minn. Operating room nurse Luther Hosp., Eau Claire, 1959-61, head nurse operating room, 1961-63; supr. operating room Midway Hosp., St. Paul, 1963-66; staff anesthetist North Meml. Med. Ctr., Robbinsdale, Minn., 1967-68, St. Joseph's Hosp., St. Paul, 1992—; program dir. Mpls. Sch. Anesthesia, St. Louis Park, Minn., 1968-96; adj. assoc. prof. St. Mary's U., Winona, Minn., 1982-96, adj. prof., 1996—, program dir. Masters Degree Program, 1984-96, nurse anesthesia cons., 1996—; ednl. cons. accreditation visitor Coun. on Accreditation of Nurse Anesthesia Ednl. Programs, Park Ridge, Ill., 1983-92, elected to coun., 1992—, vice chmn., 1994—; presentations in field. Recipient Good Neighbor award Sta. WCCO, Mpls., 1980, Disting. Alumni Achievement award Nova Southeastern U., 1993. Mem. Am. Assn. Nurse Anesthetists (pres. 1981-82, pres. and bd. dirs. Edn. and Rsch. Found. 1981-83, cert. profl. excellence 1976, Program Dir. of Yr. award 1992), Minn. Assn. Nurse Anesthetists (pres. 1975-76). Lutheran. Avocations: gardening, fishing, photography, choir directing, playing guitar and piano. Home and Office: PO Box 80 Palisade MN 56469-0080

KILDUFF, BONNIE ELIZABETH, director of expositions; b. Washington, Sept. 25, 1959; d. Macolm McGreggor and Betty (Alvino) K. Adminstr. Aircraft Owners & Pilot Assn., Bethesda, Md., 1977-79; mktg. pub. rels., meeting planning, exec. asst. Dairy and Food Inds. Supply Assn., Rockville, Md., 1979-89; dir. expns. Packaging Machinery Mfrs. Inst., Washington, 1989—; secmem. Trade Show Adv. Coun., Denver, 1992-94. Mem. Maj. Trade Show Organizers (chmn. 1996—), Internat. Assn. Expn. Mgrs. (cert expn. mgr., sec. found. com. 1994, mem. mktg. com. 1993—, chmn. internat. com. 1996—), Trade Show Cur., Women in Packaging, Confedn. Organizers Packaging Expns. Office: Packaging Machinery Mfrs Inst 4350 Fairfax Dr Ste 600 Arlington VA 22203-1620

KILE, CAROL ANN, lawyer; b. Cleve., Dec. 26, 1946; d. Walter John and Leona Eleanor (Koeppen) Ripich; m. William Simons Kile, Aug. 12, 1972; children: Evan William, Warren Ripich. BA cum laude, Wittenberg U., 1968; MA, U. Ariz., 1970; JD cum laude, Cleve. State U., 1991. Bar: Ohio, 1991. Tchr. Cleve. Pub. Schs., 1969-74; children's libr. Cuyahoga County Pub. Libr., Cleve., 1976-92; clerk externship Ohio 8th Dist. Ct. Appeals, Cleve., 1991; staff atty. Legal Aid Soc. Lorain County Inc., Elyria, Ohio, 1992—; lectr. on Islamic law and constitutional history, Cleve., 1987—. Contbr. articles to profl. jours. Com. woman Rocky River (Ohio) United Meth. Ch., 1980—. Recipient award for excellence in constl. law Fed. Bar Assn., 1989, Am. Jurisprudence award in constl. law, 1989. Mem. ABA, AAUW, LWV, Ohio Bar Assn., Phi Alpha Theta.

KILGORE, JANICE KAY, musician, educator; b. Dallas, July 6, 1955; d. Jean Kendall and Dorothy Helen (King) K. Student, Oral Roberts U., 1973-76; AA, Mountain View Coll., 1979; MusB, U. North Tex., 1983, M in Mus. Edn., 1990, doctoral studies in music performance. Cert. music tchr., Tex. Tchr. aide ESL Dallas Pub. Schs., 1979, substitute tchr., 1979-83, class piano tchr., 1983-84, choir dir./class piano instr., 1988-90, orch. tchr., 1992—; owner TNET Telecomm. Network Engring. Technologies LLC, 1995—; asst. dir. Jazz Singers, Oral Roberts U., Tulsa, 1975-76; music dir., vocalist, keyboardist, booking agent, violist Janal, High Soc., Dallas Woodwind Ensemble Imperial String Quartet, Imperial Brass Ensemble, 1978—; music instr. Project Upward Bound, Denton, Tex., 1981; tech. Waxahachie (Tex.) Ind. Sch. Dist., 1990-92, choir dir., coord. dept. voice, orch. tchr., 1992-96; class keyboard instr. Baldwin Family Music, Dallas, 1987-89; music instr. North Lake Coll., Irving, Tex., 1990—; creator, dir. numerous outdoor concerts; owners Southwest Music Enterprises. Author: British English to American English Dictionary, 1994; composer (symphonic poem) Scottish Suite, 1977, (choral work) The Wisemen, 1990; contbr. articles to mags. dir. Urbandale Christian Ch., Dallas, 1977-79, Centenary United Meth. Ch., Dallas, 1984-85, First United Meth. Ch., Midlothian, Tex., 1985-87, St. Luke United Meth. Ch., Dallas, 1989-90, First United Meth. Ch., Waxahachie, 1990-93, Trinity United Meth. Ch., Duncanville, Tex., 1993-94, Tyler St. United Meth. Ch., Dallas. Recipient Missionary Svc. award United Meth. Women, 1986. Mem. Tex. Music Educators Assn. (presenter 1994), Tex. Choral Dir. Assn., Tex. Orch. Dirs. Assn., Dallas Music Educators Assn., Denton B. Soc., Wichita Falls Symphony Orchestra, Kappa Delta Pi, Pi Kappa Lambda. Republican. Home: 317 Oak Meadow Ln Cedar Hill TX 75104-3283

KILHEFNER, TESS ANN, kitchen designer; b. Ephrata, Pa., Nov. 7, 1951; d. Russell Burdett Kurtz and Phyllis Shealer) m. Rodney R. Kilhefner, Jan. 2, 1971 (dev. Feb. 1977); 1 child, Heather Joy. Student, Phila. Career Modeling Sch., Nat. Kitchen and Bath Sch. Model Boscov's, Reading, Pa., 1970-72; mem. staff Pine Crest Distributing, Denver, Pa., 1978-84, Jenson Cabinetry, Ephrata, Pa., 1984-86, R&K Kitchens, Mohnton, Pa., 1986-88, Design Plus, York, Pa., 1988-92, Home Werks, New Holland, Pa., 1992-94; specification rep., kitchen designer Pioneer Plastics, Auburn, Maine, 1994—. Campaign organizer Dem. Club, Lancaster, Pa., 1991; mem. re-election com. Nat. Dem. Club, Washington, 1993. Mem. Nat. Kitchen and Bath Assn., Builders Industry Assn., Arch. Industry Assn., Associated Soc. Interior Designers, Shreiners Rajah Temple Ladies Aux. Roman Catholic. Home and Office: 130 Main St Denver PA 17517

KILIAN, PAMELA REEVES, journalist, author; b. Chgo., July 27, 1946; d. Roy Hester and Marguerite (Shaw) R.; m. Michael D. Kilian, Oct. 17, 1970; children: Eric Shaw Kilian, Colin David Reeves Kilian. B in Journalism, U. Mo., 1969. From reporter to editor United Press Internat., Chgo., Washington, 1970-84; news editor Scripps Howard News Svc., Washington, 1984—. Author: (children's book) What Was Watergate?, 1990 (Hon. Mention Va. Coll. Stores Assn. 1991); (nonfiction) Ellis Island, 1991; (biography) Barbara Bush, 1992. Home: 1003 Heather Hill Ct McLean VA 22101 Office: Scripps Howard New Svc 1090 Vermont Ave NW Washington DC 20005

KILKELLY, MARJORIE LEE, state legislator; b. Hartford, Conn., Dec. 1, 1954; d. Bruce Hamilton and Corlys Lucille (Lux) Brewer; children: Jeffrey Jr. (dec.), Robert, Sarah A.E. BS in Human Services, N.H. Coll., 1986, MS in Community Econ. Devel., 1986. Asst. to dir. Lincoln County Summer Youth Employment Program, Wiscasset, Maine, 1978; coordinator Community Food & Nutrition Program Coastal Enterprises, Inc., Wiscasset, 1978-79, Coastal Econ. Devel. Corp., Wiscasset, 1979-80; dir. Head Start Program Coastal Econ. Devel. Corp., Bath, Maine, 1980-84; asst. instr. N.H. Coll., Manchester, 1985-86; dir. Jr. Tots Wiscasset Recreation Program, 1985-88; dir. food services Boothbay Sch. Dept., Boothbay Harbor, Maine, 1985-88; owner Hurricane Hill Catering Co., Wiscasset, 1989—; mem. Maine Ho. of Reps., Augusta, 1988—; house chair com. on agr., forestry and conservation, 1995-96; co-chmn. coastal caucus Maine Ho. of Reps., Augusta, candidate for speaker of house, 1992, candidate for house majority whip, 1994, chair agriculture, forestry and conservation com., 1995—; candidate Maine Senate, 1996; treas. Coastal Enterprises, Inc., Rundlet Block, Wis., 1981—; rep. to Internat. Conf. on Econ. Devel., New Delhi, 1983—; 3d Selectman Town of Wiscasset, 1993—. Mem. planning com. Blaine House Conf. on Families, 1979-80; active Maine Human Svcs. Coun. Sta. 23, Augusta, 1980-88; Sunday sch. tchr., lectr. St. Philips Episcopal Ch., Wiscasset, 1984-85, chmn. coord. com. food bank, 1986-88, sr. warden, 1995-96; chmn. Wis. Dem. Com., 1986; nat. chmn. Schs. S.O.S. Nat. Hunger Awareness Program, Denver, 1986; mem. exec. com. Maine Rural Devel. Coun., 1995—; spkr. pro tempere 117th Legislature, 1996; candidate Main State Senate Dist. 16, 1996. New England Rural fellow, Coun. State Govts. Toll fellow; grantee Maine Welfare Edn. Employment Tng. Program, 1983. Mem. Bus. and Profl. Women (Maine Young Career Woman award 1989), Huntoon Hill Grange Club, Lincoln County Pomona Grange Club, Sportsmans Alliance Club of Maine, Am. Coun. Young Polit. Leaders. Democrat. Episcopalian. Clubs: B.P.W. (Damariscotta, Maine); CONA (Newcastle, Maine). Home: PO Box 180 W Alna Rd Wiscasset ME 04578-0180 Office: Maine Ho Reps State Capitol Augusta ME 04333

KILLA, LEANN KATHLEEN, accountant; b. Colorado Springs, Colo., Feb. 22, 1971; d. Harry William and Jane Ellen (Dadds) K. BS in Acctg., DeVry Inst. Tech., 1992. Account specialist Sears Roebuck and Co., Phoenix, Ariz., 1989-92; acct. Sierra Sci. Inc., Phoenix, 1992-94; billing supr. Integra Hospice/WilCare, Phoenix, 1994—. Half-tuition competitive acad. scholar DeVry Inst. Tech., 1989. Mem. Inst. Mgmt. Accts.

KILLEA, LUCY LYTLE, state legislator; b. San Antonio, July 31, 1922; d. Nelson and Zelime (Pettus) Lytle; B.A., Incarnate Word Coll., San Antonio, 1943; M.A. in History, U. San Diego, 1966; Ph.D. in History, U. Calif., San Diego, 1975; m. John F. Killea, May 11, 1946; children: Paul, Jay. Research analyst for Western Europe, Army Intelligence, Spl. Br., Washington, 1944-48; adminstrv. asst. Dept. State, London, 1946; econ. officer Econ. Coop. Adminstrn., The Hague, Netherlands, 1949; research analyst CIA, Washington, 1948-56; part time book reviewer USIS, 1956-60; teaching and research asst. U. Calif., San Diego, 1967-72; exec. dir., exec. v.p. Fronteras de las Californias, San Diego, 1974-78; mem. City Council, San Diego, 1978-82, dep. mayor, 1982, mem. planning commn., 1978; mem. Calif. State Assembly, 1982-89; mem. Calif. State Senate, 1989—; lectr. socioeconomics of Baja, Calif. and Mex., Southwestern Coll., Chula-Vista, 1976; lectr. dept. history San Diego State U., 1976-77; participant, organizer, panelist, moderator confs. in field, U.S., Mex.; mem. Palm City Sanitation Dist., 1978-82, Met. Transit Devel. Bd., 1978-82. Regional Employment and Tng. Consortium Bd., 1978-80, City-County Reinvestment Task Force, 1978-80. Bd. trustees San Diego Zool. Soc., 1976-78; mem. San Diego County Cultural Heritage Com., 1971-78, vice chmn., 1973-75; mem. Hist. Site Bd., City San Diego, 1968-75, vice chmn., 1971-75; bd. dirs. San Diego Hist. Soc., 1971-77; chmn. Internat. Com. Conv. and Visitors Bur., 1978, host com., 1976-77; adv. bd. Sharp Hosp.; bd. dirs., com. mem. Friends of Library, U. Calif., San Diego; founding mem. Caridad Internacional; mem. James S. Copley Library Adv. Council, U. San Diego, 1981—; active community orgns. including LWV, Fine Arts Soc. San Diego, YWCA, San Diego Mus. Art, San Diego Chpt. ARC, Dimensions, Aardvarks Ltd., Pacific Beach Hist. Soc., San Diego Symphonic Assn. Research grantee, Justice Found., 1965, U. Calif., San Diego, 1971; recipient awards, Conf. Calif. Hist. Socs., 1966, Inst. for Protection of Children, City of Tijuana and Tijuana Com., 1966, Alice Paul Award, Nat. Women's Polit. Caucus, 1982; named one of 12 Women of Valor, Beth Israel Sisterhood of Temple Beth Israel, San Diego, 1966, Woman of Accomplishment, Bus. and Profl. Clubs. San Diego, 1979, Woman of Yr., San Diego Irish Congress, 1981; honored Leukemia Soc., 1980; named alumna of distinction Incarnate Word Coll., San Antonio, 1981. Mem. Nat. Women's Polit. Caucus, Calif., Women in Bus., Mus. Photog. Arts, San Diego Arts Center, Nat. Trust Historic Preservation, San Diego Hist. Soc. (life), San Diego County Congress of History, Travelers Aid Soc., Navy League, Vietnam Vets. Assn. Mid City C. of C., San Diego C. of C., Nat. Assn. State Legislatures, NCCJ, World Affairs Council, Am. Fgn. Service Assn., Incarnate Word Alumnae Assn., U. San Diego Alumni Assn., U. Calif. San Diego Alumni and Friends, Calif. Elected Women's Assn. for Edn. and Research (bd. 1980-85, sec., treas., 1980-81, v.p. 1982-85). Roman Catholic. Clubs: Catfish, Army-Navy (Arlington, Va.). Contbr. writings to publs. in field. Office: State Capitol Rm 4062 Sacramento CA 95814-4906

KILLEBREW, ELLEN JANE (MRS. EDWARD S. GRAVES), cardiologist; b. Tiffin, Ohio, Oct. 8, 1937; d. Joseph Arthur and Stephanie (Beriont) K.; BS in Biology, Bucknell U., 1959; MD, N.J. Coll. Medicine, 1965; m. Edward S. Graves, Sept. 12, 1970. Intern, U. Colo., 1965-66, resident 1966-68; cardiology fellow Pacific Med. Center, San Francisco, 1968-70; dir. coronary care, Permanent Med. Group, Richmond, Calif., 1970-83; asst. prof. U. Calif. Med. Center, San Francisco, 1970-83, assoc. prof., 1983-93, clin. prof. medicine, Univ. Calif., San Francisco, 1992—. Contbr. chpt. to book. Robert C. Kirkwood Meml. scholar in cardiology, 1970; recipient Physician's Recognition award continuing med. edn., Lowell Beal award excellence in teaching, Permante Med. Group/House Staff Assn., 1992. Diplomate in cardiovascular disease Am. Bd. Internal Medicine. Fellow ACP, Am. Coll. Cardiology: mem. Fedn. Clin. Rsch., Am. Heart Assn. (rsch. chmn. Contra Costa chpt. 1975—, v.p. 1980, pres. chpt. 1981-82, chm. CPR com. Alameda chpt. 1984, pres. Oakland Piedmont br. 1995—). Home: 30 Redding Ct Belvedere Tiburon CA 94920-1318 Office: 280 W Macarthur Blvd Oakland CA 94611-5642

KILLEBREW, JANA ROSS, aerospace engineer; b. Clarksville, Tenn., Nov. 7, 1958; d. Fred Parker and Amanda Jane (Ross) Killebrew; m. Steven Robert Noneman, Aug. 13, 1983 (div. Jan. 1993); children: Craig James, Robert Paul. BA in Math., U. Tenn., 1980. Software programmer/analyst R.R. Donnelly & Sons, Gallatin, Tenn., 1980-81, Boeing Computer Support Svcs., Huntsville, Ala., 1981-82; European Space Agy. payload ops. engr. Christian Rovsing Internat., Copenhagen, 1982-84; NASA payload cadre team (Essex)/Payload Sys., Inc., Wesley, Mass., 1984; simulation engr. spacelab Essex Corp., Huntsville, 1984-89; payload ops. engr., mgr. Teledyne Brown Engrng., Huntsville, 1989—. Mem. peace and justice com. St. John the Bapt. Cath. Ch., 1996; vol. Big Springs Jam, Civic Arts Festival, Huntsville, 1993-95; supporter Habitat for Humanity/St. Bonaventure and St. Joseph Indian Schs. Mem. NAFE, AIAA, AAUW, Women in Aerospace, Songwriters Guild of Am., Phi Beta Kappa. Democrat. Roman Catholic. Office: Teledyne Brown Engring 300 Sparkman Dr MS172 Huntsville AL 35807-7007

KILLEEN, BARBARA JEANNINE, journalist; b. L.A., Oct. 30, 1957; d. Martin Hoffman and Bella Ruth (Goldstein) Hoffman-Hayashi; m. Scott Killeen, Apr. 14, 1994. AA in English, Santa Monica Coll., 1978; BA in English, UCLA, 1980. Entertainment editor Teen Mag., L.A., 1984-86; road test editor Motor Trend Mag., L.A., 1986-95; journalist, owner Motor Mouth Prodns., Sherman Oaks, Calif., 1995—. Mem. NAFE, Motor Press Guild. Home and Office: Am Women Motorscene 13950 Valleyheart Dr Sherman Oaks CA 91423

KILLGALLON, CHRISTINE BEHRENS, healthcare administrator; b. Portsmouth, Ohio, June 29, 1958; d. Carl William Behrens and Karin Rita (Roeder) Behrens-Ellis; m. William Casley Killgallon, June 21, 1989. AS in Sci., Brunswick Coll., 1979, AS in Nursing, 1981; BA in Econs., George Mason U., 1987; M in Healthcare Adminstrn., Xavier U., 1989. CCRN. Staff nurse Bath County Community Hosp., Hot Springs, Va., 1981-82; critical care nurse U. Va. Med. Ctr., Charlottesville, Va., 1982-85; med. paralegal Donahue, Ehrmantraut, Montedonico, Washington, 1986; adminstrv. intern U. Va. Med. Ctr., Charlottesville, 1987; adminstrv. resident Alleghany Regional Hosp., Lowmoor, Va., 1989-95; exec.v.p. Odin Co., 1995—; bd. dirs. Odin Co.; v.p. comms. Odin Sys. Internat. Mem. aux. Safe Harbor, St. Simons, Ga., 1991; active Med. Assistance Program, Brunswick, 1990, Rep. Women's Orgn., St. Simons, 1990; mem. found. bd. S.E. Ga. Regional Med. Ctr. mem. AACCN, Am. Hosp. Assn., Am. Coll. Healthcare Execs., Golden Isles Investment Club St. Simons (pres. 1994), Omicron Delta Epsilon Theta. Presbyterian. Home: 1335 Hilltop Rd Charlottesville VA 22903-1224

KILLGORE, LE, journalist, political columnist; b. Poughkeepsie, N.Y., Mar. 16, 1926; m. James A. Killgore, July 24, 1948; children: Lynne, Robert, Andrew. BA in Romance Langs., Skidmore Coll., 1948; postgrad., Auburn U., 1961-62. Classroom tchr. music Stare Baldwin Sch., Dallas, 1949-50, The Little Sch., Dallas, 1950-51; substitute tchr. DOD Sch., Clark AB, Philippines, 1964-65, Dayton Ohio Schs., 1966-67, Jeb Stuart High Sch., Fairfax County, Va., 1967-68; staff writer Standard-Times, San Angelo, Tex., 1972-79, sr. staff writer, 1979-83, political affairs editor, 1983-92; polit. cons. San Angelo, Tex., 1992—; co-host radio/TV pub. affairs show. Staff writer, editor Officers Wives Club mags., Clark AB, Philippines, 1964, McClellan AFB, Calif., 1966, Panama Canal Zone, 1969-71. Recipient Overall Excellence in News Gathering award Headliners Club, 1973, Outstanding Continuous Coverage of Edn. award Tex. State Tchrs. Assn., 1977, Excellence in Health-related Reporting Tex. Med. Assn., 1977. Mem. Soc. Profl. Journalists (pres. San Angelo chpt. 1984, bd. dirs. 1986, 87, 89).

KILLION, CINDY L., photojournalist, educator; b. Coffeyville, Kans., Sept. 8, 1955; d. Wayne Melvin and Julia Amanda (Maxwell) K. AA, Coffeyville Comty. Jr. Coll., 1975; BJ, U. Mo., 1980; MA, U. Okla., 1992. Photographer Coffeyville Jour., 1980, Jefferson City (Mo.) Tribune, 1980-81; reporter, photographer The Daily Ardmoreite, Ardmore, Okla., 1981-82; mng. editor Lone Grove (Okla.) Ledger, 1982-84; sports editor Wagoner (Okla.) Newspapers Inc., 1984-86; reporter Bartlesville (Okla.) Examiner-Enterprise, 1986-87, photo editor, 1987-89, news editor, 1989-92; asst. prof. Winona (Minn.) State U., 1992—; advisor Native Am. Heritage Awareness Club, Winona State U., 1992—, Gay and Lesbians Alliance for Dignity, 1995-96; tchg. fellow The Poynter Inst., 1994. Newsletter editor Leaping LaCrosse News, 1996; contbr. articles to jours. Bd. dirs. Women's Resource Ctr., Winona, 1992-94, Women and Children in Crisis, Bartlesville, Okla., 1987-92; chair Sexual Assault Safety Ctr., Bartlesville, 1987-92; founder, organizer Out Front Rural Inst., Mpls., 1996, Traditional Intertribal Pow Wow, Winona, 1995-96. Named Single Divsn. II Handicapped Champion, Winona Women's Bowling Assn., 1996, Advocate of Yr., Sexual Assault Safety Ctr., 1991. Mem. Assn. for Edn. of Journalism and Mass Comms. (tchg. fellow Freedom Forum 1994). Democrat. Home: PO Box 371 222 S Main Fountain City WI 54629 Office: Winona State U Phelps 116A Winona MN 55987

KILLMAN, KATHLEEN MAE, clinical nurse practitioner educator; b. Chgo., Sept. 24, 1948; d. Howard Stewart and Lorraine Evelyn (Prescott) Boardman; m. Charles L. Killman, Jr., July 22, 1984; 1 child, Wade Charles. BSN, U. Mich., 1970; MS in Psychiat. Nursing, U. Ill., Chgo., 1985. RN, Ill.; cert in nursing continuing edn. and staff devel. Staff, charge nurse psychiatry U. Mich., Ann Arbor, 1970-73; instr. in nursing North Park Coll., Chgo., 1973-76; staff, charge nurse psychiatry Ravenswood Hosp. Med. Ctr., Chgo., 1976-82; instr. nursing Ill. Masonic Med. Ctr., Chgo., 1982-87, psychiat. clin. specialist, 1987-89; clin. practitioner educator Evanston (Ill.) Hosp., 1989—; cons., tutor RN Tutoring Project, Chgo., 1987—; psychiat. consultation liaison nurse Evanston Hosp., 1989—. Mem. Nat. Nursing Staff Devel. Orgn., N.Am. Nursing Diagnosis Assn. Office: Evanston Hosp Nursing Edn and Devel 2650 Ridge Ave Evanston IL 60201-1718

KILLORAN, CYNTHIA LOCKHART, retired educator; b. Collinsville, Ill., June 19, 1918; d. Hugh McLelland and Estelle (Jones) Lockhart; m. Timothy Thomas Killoran, Feb. 9, 1944 (dec. Mar. 1991); children: Margaret, Kathleen, Timothy P., Cynthia, Mary. BS, U. Ill., 1940, postgrad. Home econs. tchr. LaMoille (Ill.) H.S., 1940-41; home supr. Farm Security, Dept. Agr., Pittsfield, Ill., 1941-42; civilian instr. radio operating procedure USAAC, Sioux Falls, S.D., 1942-44, Batavia, Ill., 1944-69; kindergarten tchr. Batavia Sch. Dist. # 101, 1969-93; ret., 1993. Methodist.

KILMER, PAULETTE DIANE, reporter, writer, educator; b. Mauston, Wis., May 10, 1949; d. Donald Jay and Meredith Marie (Clausius) K. BA in Journalism/History, U. Wis., 1971, MA in Journalism, 1973; MA in Speech/Theater, U. Kans., 1980; PhD in Media Studies, U. Ill., 1992. Instr. comm. arts U. Wis. Ctr. Sys. Campus, Medford, 1980-81; instr. speech U. Wis., Platteville, 1982-83; tchr. English, history, geography Pittsville (Wis.) H.S., 1984-85; instr. journalism dept. So. Ill. U., Carbondale, 1985-86; instr. speech U. Ill., Urbana, 1987-88; instr. reporting Ill. State U., Normal, 1988-89; instr., guest scholar Sch. Journalism Columbia U. of Mo., 1989-90; asst. prof. No. Mich. U., Marquette, 1990-93; instr., asst. prof. bus. comms. and journalism Marion Coll., Fond du Lac, Wis., 1994-96; reporter, writer The Reporter, Fond du Lac, 1995—. Author: The Fear of Sinking: The Success Formula in the Gilded Age, 1996; author children's plays. Prodr., dir. Children's Theater, Kenosha and Medford, Wis., 1974-83. Recipient Best Feature award in Midwest and L.A. Group by Thomson Chain, 1996, 3d pl. Feature award Wis. Newspaper Editors Assn., 1995; fellow U. Wis., 1971. Mem. AAUW (com. mem.), Am. Journalism Historians Assn. (chair edn. com. 1992-93), Assn. for Edn. in Journalism and Mass Comms., Kappa Tau Alpha. Democrat. Mem. United Ch. of Christ. Home: 94 E 12th # 2 Fond Du Lac WI 54935

KILPATRICK, CAROLYN CHEEKS, state legislator, educator; b. Detroit, June 25, 1945; d. Marvell and Willa Mae (Henry) Cheeks; divorced; children: Kwame, Ayanna. AS, Ferris State Coll., Big Rapids, Mich., 1965; BS, Western Mich. U., 1972; MS in Edn., U. Mich., 1977. Tchr. Murray Wright High Sch., Detroit, 1972-78; mem. Mich. Ho. of Reps., Lansing, 1978—; Dem. whip, mem. appropriations com.; del. Dem. Convs., 1980, 84, 88. Rep. Detroit Substance Abuse Adv. Coun.; participant Mich. African Trade Mission, 1984, UN Internat. Women's Conf., 1986; del. participant Mich. Dept. Agr. to Nairobi (Kenya) Internat. Agr. Show, 1986. Recipient Anthony Wayne award Wayne State U., Disting. Legislator award U. Mich., Disting. Alumni award Ferris State U., Woman of Yr. award Gentlemen of Wall St., Inc., Burton-Abercrombie award 15th Dem. Congrl. dist. Mem. Nat. Orgn. 100 Black Women, Nat. Black Caucus of State Legislators (chairperson Mich. legis. session 1983-84), Nat. Order Women Legislators, Nat. Orgn. Black Elected Legis. Women (treas.). Mem. Pan African Orthodox Christian Ch. Office: House Reps State Capitol Lansing MI 48909

KILSON, MARION, academic administrator; b. New Haven, Conn., May 8, 1936; d. J.G. and Emily L. (Greene) Dusser de Barenne; m. Martin L. Kilson, Aug. 8, 1959; children: Jennifer Kilson-Page, Peter, Hannah Kilson Kuchtic. BA, Radcliffe Coll., 1958; MA, Stanford U., 1959; PhD, Harvard U., 1967. Instr., asst. prof. U. Mass., Boston, 1966-68; fellow Radcliffe Inst., 1968-70; assoc. prof. Simmons Coll., Boston, 1969-73; prof. sociology Newton (Mass.) Coll., 1973-75; dir. rsch. and dir. Bunting Inst., Cambridge, Mass., 1975-80; dean Emmanuel Coll., Boston, 1980-86; rsch. fellow Harvard Divinity Sch., Cambridge, 1986; assoc. editor Simon & Schuster, Newton, Mass., 1987-89; dean arts & scis., grad sch. Salem State Coll., Salem, Mass., 1989—; adv. bd. Bunting Inst., 1992—; chair New Eng. Bapt. Hosp. Sch. Nursing, Boston, 1992—. Author: Kpele LaLa, 1971, African Urban Kinsmen, 1974, Royal Antelope & Spider, 1976, Mother of the Japan Mission, 1991. Bd. dirs. AAUW Edn. Found., 1993—, program v.p., 1996—; mem., co-chair Fair Housing Human Rels., Lexington, Mass., 1993-95. Recipient rsch. grants NIMH, 1965-66, NEH, 1968, 72, 74, Soc. Sci. Rsch. Coun., 1968; Mary Lyon award Mass. AAUW, 1994. Fellow Am. Anthropol. Assn.; mem. Am. Assn. of Higher Edn., Mass. Women in Pub. Higher Edn. (pres. 1995-96). Home: 4 Eliot Rd Lexington MA 02173-5610 Office: Salem State Coll Salem MA 01970

KILSTON, VERA MARESH, systems engineer; b. Balt., Jan. 11, 1939; d. Jaroslav and Frantiska Anna (Stoll) Maresh; m. Peter Norman Dobson, Nov. 25, 1957 (div.); children: David, Laurel, Heather; m. Steven David Kilston, July 30, 1976; children: Lyra, Rigel. BS in Physics, U. Hawaii, 1970. Sci. tchr. L.A. Unified Sch. Dist., 1972-80; engr. Hughes Aircraft Co., El Segundo, Calif., 1980-87; systems engr. Lockheed Martin Missiles & Space Co., Sunnyvale, Calif., 1987—. Co-host sci. news radio program No Appointment Necessary, KPFK-L.A., 1975-85. Bd. dirs. Ragazzi (Boy's Chorus), San Mateo, Calif., 1988-94; dir. women's activities Sokol (phys. culture orgn.), San Mateo, 1991-94. Mem. Nature Conservancy, Calif. League of Conservation Voters. Democrat. Home: 651 Tennyson Ave Palo Alto CA 94301

KIM, CHARLOTTE CHUNG-SOOK, librarian, administrator; b. Seoul, Korea, Apr. 15, 1940; came to U.S., 1963; d. Soon Kyung and Un Yun (Kim) Hong; m. Samuel C. Kang, Dec. 19, 1964 (div. Aug. 1976); Ben H. Kim, Nov. 17, 1985; children: Patricia Lan, Claudia Suk-Jin. BA, Yonsei U., 1962; MEd, Duquesne U., 1967; MLS, U. Pitts., 1968. Children's libr. Whitehall (Pa.) Pub. Libr., 1965-67; children's libr. Carnegie Libr. Pitts., 1969-71, br. head, 1971-76, divsn. head, 1976-85; br. head Chgo. Pub. Libr., 1986-88, chief N.W. dist., 1989-90, asst. commr., 1990—; bd. trustees North Cen. Coll., Naperville, Ill., 1995—. Bd. dirs. YWCA Met. Chgo., 1996—, Korean Am. Scholarship Found., Chgo., 1992—, Chgo. Libr. Sys., 1991-96; v.p. Korean Am. Sr. Ctr., Chgo., 1994—, Korean Am. Comty. Svcs., Chgo., 1990-93; del. White House Conf. on Libr. and Info. Svcs., 1991; trustee North Ctrl. Coll., 1995—. Recipient Outstanding Pub. Svc. award Friends of Chgo. Pub. Libr, 1987, Disting. Pub. Svc. award Asian Human Svcs. of Chgo., 1992, Outstanding Comty. Svc. award Korean Am. Assn. Chgo., 1995; named Man of Yr., Korea Cen. Daily of Chgo., 1988. Mem. ALA (councilor 1993—), ALA/Ethnic Materials and Info. Exch. Round Table (bd. dirs. 1994-96), Pub. Libr. Assn. (internat. rels. com. 1992—), Ill. Libr. Assn., Asian/Pacific Am. Librs. Assn. (past pres. 1991-92). Democrat. Methodist. Home: 6245 N Kirkwood Ave Chicago IL 60646 Office: Chgo Pub Libr 400 S State St Chicago IL 60605

KIM, CHRISTINE S., physician; b. Seoul, Korea, Nov. 11, 1942. MD, Ewha Womens U., 1967. Pvt. practice Atlanta, 1973-80, Danbury, Conn., 1988—; asst. prof. U. Conn. Med. Sch., Farmington, 1980-88. Home: 5 Apple Hill Ct South Salem NY 10590-1401

KIM, SANGDUK, biochemistry educator, researcher; b. Seoul, Korea, June 15, 1930; came to U.S., 1954; d. Tak Won and chungHee (Kil) K.; m. Woon Ki Paik, June 15, 1959; children: Margaret, Dean, David. MD, Korea U., Seoul, 1953; PhD, U. Wis., 1960. Intern Evang. Deaconess Hosp., Milw., 1954-55; rsch. assoc. U. Wis., Madison, 1959-61, U. Ottawa, Ont., Can., 1961-66; rsch. assoc. Fels Inst. Temple U., Phila., 1966-73, sr. investigator Fels Inst., 1973-78, assoc. prof. biochemistry Fels Inst., 1978-90, prof. biochemistry, 1990—. Author: (monograph) Protein Methylation, 1980; editor: Protein Methylation, 1990. NIH Rsch. grantee, 1973-81, NSF Rsch. grantee, 1979-85, Nat. Multiple Sclerosis Rsch. grantee, 1985—. Mem. Am. Soc. Biol. Chemists, Am. Assn. for Cancer Rsch., N.Y. Acad. Sci., Am. Chem. Soc., Am. Soc. for Neurochemistry. Home: 7818 Oak Lane Rd Cheltenham PA 19012-1015 Office: Temple U Fels Inst 3420 N Broad St Philadelphia PA 19140-5104

KIM, TONG RIM, art foundation administrator; b. Seoul, Korea, Jan. 20, 1916; came to U.S., 1964; d. Kuk Sun and Yoo Dang; m. Whanki Kim, May 1, 1944 (dec. July 1974); 1 child, Wha Young. Student, Ewha U., Seoul, 1934-36, U. Sorbonne, Paris, 1955-56, Ecole du Louvre, Paris, 1956-58. Dir. Whanki Found. Fine Arts for Young Artists, N.Y.C., 1979—. Author: Life & Work, 1992, also essays. Founder Whanki Mus., Seoul. Home: 160 W 73d St New York NY 10023-3012

KIM, WILLA, costume designer; b. L.A.; d. Shoon Kwan and Nora Kim; m. William Pene Du Bois. Costume designer New Theatre for Now, Mark Taper Forum, L.A., 1969-70, Goodman Theatre, Chgo., 1978-79; set and costume designer Feld Ballet, Joffrey Ballet, Am. Ballet Theatre, San Francisco Ballet. Costume designer: (theatre) Red Eye of Love, 1961, Fortuna, 1962, The Saving Grace, 1963, Have I Got a Girl for You!, 1963, Funnyhouse of a Negro, 1964, Dynamite Tonight, 1964, A Midsummer Night's Dream, 1964, The Old Glory, 1964 (Obie award 1964-65), Helen, 1964, The Day the Whores Came out To Play Tennis, 1965, Sing to Me Through Open Windows, 1965, The Star King, 1965, Malcolm, 1966, The Office, 1966, Chu Chem, 1966, Hail Scrawdyke!, 1966, Scuba Duba, 1967, The Ceremony of Innocence, 1967, Promenade, 1969 (Drama Desk award 1969-70), Papp, 1969, Operation Sidewinder, 1970 (Drama Desk award 1969-70), Sunday Dinner, 1970, The Screens, 1971 (Maharam award 1971-72, Drama Desk award 1971-72, Variety N.Y. Drama Critics Poll award 1971-72), Sleep, 1972, Lysistrata, 1972, The Chickencoop Chinaman, 1972, Jumpers, 1974, Goodtime Charley, 1975 (Tony award nomination best costume design 1975), The Old Glory: a trilogy, 1976, Dancin', 1978 (Tony award nomination best costume design 1978), The Grinding Machine, 1978, Bosoms and Neglect, 1979, Sophisticated Ladies, 1981 (Tony award best costume design 1981), Family Devotions, 1981, Lydie Breeze, 1982, Chaplin, 1983, Elizabeth and Essex, 1984, Song and Dance, 1985 (Tony award nomination best costume design 1986), Long Day's Journey Into Night, 1986, The Front Page, 1986, Legs Diamond, 1989 (Tony award nomination best costume design 1989), The Will Rodgers Follies, 1991 (Tony award best costume design 1991), Four Baboons Adoring the Sun, 1992, Tommy Tune Tonight!, 1993, Grease, 1994, Victor/Victoria, 1995; (ballets) Birds of Sorrow, 1962, Gamelan, 1963, Game of Noah, 1965, Daphins et Chloe, Papillon, Scenes for the Theatre, A Song for Dead Warriors, Shinju, Rodin, Dream Dances; (TV) The Tempest, 1981 (Emmy award 1981), Le Rossignol; (film) Gardens of Stone, 1987; (operas) The Magic Flute, Le Rossignol, Help, Help, the Gobolinks. Recipient Asian Woman of Achievement award Asian Am. Profl. Women, 1983. Democrat. Home: 250 W 82nd St New York NY 10024-5421*

KIMBER, CAROLYN KASS, human resources professional; b. Eau Claire, Wis., Jan. 22, 1969; d. Warren Albert and Sandra (Haase) K.; m. Scott R. Kimber. BA, Mo. U., 1991; MSEd, Kans. U., 1993. Personnel dir. Boone Clinic, Columbia, 1993—; grad. rsch. asst., 1993—; group leader Kans. U., Lawrence, 1993. Mem. Human Resource Assn., Job Security Employment Com., Resident Spouse Assn., Mo. U. Alumni Assn., Alpha Delta Pi (chpt. adv.), Psi Chi. Republican. Lutheran. Home: 211 Nikki Way Columbia MO 65203 Office: Boone Clinic 401 Keene St Columbia MO 65203

KIMBRIEL-EGUIA, SUSAN, engineering planner; b. San Francisco, July 22, 1949; d. Scott Slaughter and Kathleen (Edens) Smith; m. Floyd Thomas Kimbriel; 1 child, John Thomas; m. Candelario Eguia, Feb. 14, 1991; 1 child, Daniel. Engrng. planner, sys. adminstr. various mainframe and PC based sys. Northrop Aircraft, Hawthorne, Calif., 1982-91; PC cons. Moselle Ins. Corp., North Hollywood, Calif., 1989-96, Northrop Aircraft, 1991-96.

KIMBROUGH, JENNIFER LACIVITA, artist, columnist; b. Chgo., Dec. 23, 1965; d. Nicholas Joseph and Michaeleen Loretta (Fabianski) LaCivita; m. Brian Mitchell Kimbrough, Sept. 2, 1989; children: Emily Rose, Eric. BA in Art and English, St. Mary of the Woods Coll., Terre Haute, Ind., 1988. Artist S. Mark Graphics, Chgo., 1988; corr. Commerce Clearing House, Chgo., 1988-89; dir. devel./recruitment/pub. rels. Good Counsel H .S., Chgo., 1989-92; wedding cons. Photo By Robert, Chgo., 1991-92; weekly columnist Lerner Comm., Chgo., 1992—; freelance artist, writer Chgo., 1992—; bd. dirs. Woman Made Gallery, Chgo., 1995—. Mem. Chgo. Artists' Coalition, St. Mary of the Woods Coll. Alumnae Club (pres. 1992—). Home: 5304 W Belle Plaine Ave Chicago IL 60641

KIMES, BEVERLY RAE, editor, writer; b. Aurora, Ill., Aug. 17, 1939, d. Raymond Lionel and Grace Florence (Perrin) K.; m. James H. Cox, July 6, 1984. BS, U. Ill., 1961; MA in Journalism, Pa. State U., 1963. Dir. publicity Mateer Playhouse, Neff's Mills, Pa., 1962, Pavillion Theatre, University Park, Pa., 1963; asst. editor Automobile Quar. Publs., N.Y.C., Princeton, N.J., 1963-64, assoc. editor, 1965-66, mng. editor, 1967-74, editor, 1975-81; editor The Classic Car, 1981—. bd. corporators Mus. Transp., Brookline, Mass.; bd. trustees Nat. Automotive History Collection, Detroit Pub. Libr. Recipient Thomas McKean trophy, 1983, 85, 86, Moto award Nat. Assn. Automotive Journalists, 1984, 85, 86, Benz award, 1994, Disting. Svc. Citation Automotive Hall of Fame, 1993. Mem. Internat. Motor Press Assn., Milestone Car Soc. (bd. dirs.), Soc. Automotive Historians (pres. 1987-89, Cugnot award 1978-79, 83, 85-86, Friend of Automotive History award 1985). Author: The Classic Tradition of the Lincoln Motor Car, 1968; (with R.M. Langworth) Oldsmobile: The First Seventy-Five Years, 1972; The Cars That Henry Ford Built, 1978; (with Rene Dreyfus) My Two Lives, 1983; (with Robert C. Ackerson) Chevrolet: A History from 1911, 1984; The Standard Catalog of American Cars 1805-1942, 1985; The Star and the Laurel: The Centennial History of Daimler, Mercedes and Benz, 1986; editor: Great Cars and Grand Marques, 1976; Packard: History of the Motor Car and the Company, 1979; Automobile Quarterly's Handbook of Automotive Hobbies, 1981, The Classic Car: The Ultimate Book About the World's Grandest Automobiles, 1990.

KIMMEL, ELLEN BISHOP, psychologist, educator; b. Knoxville, Tenn., Sept. 16, 1939; d. Archer W. and Mary Ellen (Baker) Bishop; BA summa cum laude, U. Tenn., 1961; MA, U. Fla., 1962, PhD, 1965; div.; children: Elinor, Ann, Jean, Tracy. Asst. prof., rsch. assoc. Ohio U., 1965-68; asst. prof. U. South Fla., Tampa, 1968-72, assoc. prof., dean Univ. Studies Coll., 1972-73, prof. psychology and ednl. psychology, 1975-95, chair, 1992-94, disting. svc. prof., 1996—; disting. vis. prof. psychology Simon Fraser U., Vancouver, B.C., Can., 1980-81; cons. numerous sch. systems, bus. and govt. Mem. Fla. Blue Ribbon Task Force on Juvenile Delinquency, 1976-77; mem. Fla. Gov.'s Commn. on Women, 1979-83; mem. adv. bd. Stop Rape, Good Govt., Inc.; bd. dirs. NCCJ. Recipient Outstanding Svc. award State of Fla., 1975, Outstanding Teaching award U. South Fla., 1978; Career Achievement award U. Tenn., 1983; 16 research grants. Fellow APA (governing council 1982-85, pres. div. 1986-88, Disting. Leadership award 1993), Am. Psychol. Soc. (charter fellow, conf. chair 1990), Am. Assn. Applied and Preventive Psychol. (bd. dirs. 1994—,charter fellow, program chair 1991, Disting. Edn. award 1994); mem. Women in Psychology, Southeastern Psychol. Assn. (pres. 1978-79), Athena Soc., Sigma Xi, Delta Kappa Gamma, Omicron Delta Kappa. Democrat. Contbr. articles to jours., chpts. to books. Office: U South Fla FAO 268 Tampa FL 33620

KIMURA, KIMI TAKEUCHI, social worker, educator; b. Kyoto, Japan, Apr. 13, 1926; came to U.S., 1954; d. Kinzo Fujiwara and Miyo Takeuchi; divorced; 1 child, Fumi Kimura Inouye. BA, Doshisha Women's Coll., Kyoto, 1938; postgrad., Columbia U., 1955-56; MFA, Boston U., 1957. Cert. secondary English tchr., interpreter, Japan. Rsch. assco. South Manchurian RR Rsch., Toyko, 1936-41; travel cons. SITA Internat. Travel, N.Y.C., 1957-58; vis. prof. Howard U., Washington, 1958-59; overseas adv. Japan Pubs. Assn., Tokyo, 1959-68; asst. cultural attache Embassy of Japan, Washington, 1962-66; sr. rsch. assoc. Columbia U., N.Y.C., 1973-76; case worker Lenox Hill Neighborhood Assn., N.Y.C., 1977-78; ret., 1978; trade negotiator, various bus. firms, Tokyo, N.Y.C., 1945—; dir. social work Japan/Am. Assn., N.Y.C., 1983-84; cons. Nat. Theatre of Japan, Tokyo, 1966-73; fundraiser The Vol. Coun. of Philharmonic- Symphony Soc. N.Y. Inc., 1986—, N.Y.C. Opera Guild (vol. 1994—). Contbr. numerous features articles to jours.; producer various plays, 1957. Campaign worker Dem. Party, n.Y.C., 1976-78; vol. Lincoln Ctr. Performing Arts, Inc.; fundraiser Consol. Corp. Fund, 1992—. Recipient Translation award, Nat. Sci. Found., Washington, 1973-76, Older Am. Act, Title III, Washington, 1977—. Mem. Am. Ednl. Theatre (officer 1972-73, Citation 1973), N.Y. Philharmonic (assoc. mem., Citation 1989). Home: 350 65th St Apt 12A Brooklyn NY 11220-4942

KINARD, AGNES DODDS, historian, author, retired lawyer; b. Pitts.; d. Robert James and Agnes Julia Raw; m. Morton Frank, June 4, 1944 (div. 1958); children: Allan Dodds, Michael Robert, Marilyn Morton; m. James Pinckney Kinard, Dec. 27, 1961 (dec. Mar. 1994). BA in History cum laude, U. Pitts., 1936, LLB, 1939, JD, 1961; postgrad., Chatham Coll., 1980. Bar: Pa. 1940. Law researcher Reed, Smith, Shaw & McClay, Pitts., 1940-41; Lynne A. Warren, N.Y.C., 1940-41; exec. sec. Allegheny County War Price and Ration Bd., Pitts., 1941-44; British Colonies section chief, asst. to the deputy adminstr. Lend-Lease Adminstrn., Washington, 1944-46; women's editor, columnist Canton (Ohio) Economist, 1946-58; assoc. broker, sales Kelly Wood Real Estate, Pitts., 1959-72; broker, pres., co-owner Mountain Real Estate Co., Inc., Confluence, Pa., 1973-83. Author: Historical Survey of the Landscape Design Society of Western Pennsylvania, 1962-83, 1983, Celebration of Carnegie in Pittsburgh, 1981, The Jane Holmes Residence—A Century of Caring, 1982, Seasons of the Heart, 1988-89, Fanfare for Fifty Years, 1989, History of the Pittsburgh Symphony Association, 1939-1989, 1989, Celebrating the First 100 Years of The Carnegie in Pittsburgh, 1995; commd. symphony by Nikolai Lopatnikoff for Pitts. Symphony Orch., 1972, works of John Lennon for Youth Symphony Orch., 1989. Bd. dirs. Pitts. Plan for Art, Sch. Vol. Assn., Pitts. Youth Symphony Orch. Assn., Pitts. Symphony Assn.; founder, mem. Rachel Carson Homestead Assn.; founder, pres. Pioneer Crafts Coun. (now Touchstone Crafts Ctr.); mem. women's com. Carnegie Mus. Art. Recipient Award of Merit Pitts. History and Landmark Found., Three Rivers Environ. award, 1993; named No. 60 of the First 100 Women Lawyers in Allegany County, Pa., 1992. Mem. Pitts. Civic Garden Ctr. (life), Nat. Coun. State Garden Clubs (life), Nat. Soc. Arts and Letters (life, landscape design critic), Landscape Design Soc. Western Pa. (founding bd. dirs., past pres., Helen S. Hull plaque for lit. hort. interest 1986), Kappa Kappa Gamma.

KINCAID, CAROLYN WADE, special education educator; b. Cynthiana, Ky., Aug. 22, 1948; d. Joseph Daniel and Norma Vivian Martin; m. Wilburn R. Kincaid, June 5, 1966; children: Wil, Jennie, Richard. BA in Sociology and History, Ea. Ky. U., 1985, MA in Spl. Edn., 1991. Cert. secondary tchr., tchr. of exceptional children. Rank I spl. edn. tchr. Pulaski County Bd. Edn., Somerset, Ky., 1987—. Info. giver Spl. Olympics, Somerset, 1987-94. Mem. NEA, Ky. Edn. Assn., Pulaski County Edn. Assn., Kappa Delta Pi. Home: 210 Linwood Dr Somerset KY 42501-1121

KINCAID, JAMAICA, writer; b. St. John's, Antigua and Barbuda, May 25, 1949; came to U.S., 1966; d. Annie Richardson; m. Allen Shawn; 1 child. Student pub. schs., St. John's; hon. degree, Williams Coll., 1991, L.I. Coll., 1991. Author: At the Bottom of the River, 1983 (Morton Dauwen Zabel award Am. Acad. and Inst. of Arts and Letters 1984), Annie John, 1985, A Small Place, 1988, Annie Gwen Lilly Pam and Tulip, 1989, Lucy, 1990, Autobiography of My Mother, 1996.

KINCAID, JUDITH WELLS, electronics company executive; b. Tampa, Fla., July 1, 1944; d. George Redfield and Louise Wells (Brodt) K.; B.A., Stanford U., 1966, M.S. in Indsl. Engring., 1978; 1 dau., Jennifer Wells Maben. Scientific programmer med. research Stanford (Calif.) U., 1972-77; info. systems mgr. Hewlett Packard Corp., Palo Alto, Calif., 1978-84, mgr. strategic systems, 1985-91; direct mktg. mgr., 1991—, worldwide customer info. mgr., 1995—. Mem. Inst. Indsl. Engrs., Dir. Mktg. Assn. Office: Hewlett Packard Corp 3495 Deer Creek Rd Palo Alto CA 94304

KINCAID, MARILYN COBURN, medical educator; b. Bennington, Vt., July 14, 1947; d. E. Robert and Jean A. (Flagg) Coburn; m. William Louis Kincaid, Dec. 21, 1970. AB, Mt. Holyoke Coll., 1969; MD, St. Louis U., 1975. Cert. Am. Bd. Ophthalmology, Am. Bd. Pathology. Asst. prof. ophthalmology & pathology U. Tex., San Antonio, 1982-86; assoc. prof. ophthalmology & pathology U. Mich. Med. Sch., Ann Arbor, 1986-87; assoc. prof. ophthalmology & pathology St. Louis U. Sch. Medicine, 1989-94, prof., 1994—; bd. dirs. Singular Vision Outreach, St. Louis. Author (book) Intraocular Lenses, 1989; contbr. articles to profl. jours. Fellow Am. Acad. Ophthalmology (Honor award 1990), Coll. Am. Pathologists; mem. Am. Assn. Ophthalmic Pathologists (sec.-treas. 1983-86). Office: St Louis U The Eye Inst 1755 S Grand Blvd Saint Louis MO 63104-1540

KINCAID, TINA, entertainer, producer; b. Lenoir, N.C., Dec. 24, 1959; d. Joseph George and Betty Gail (Prestwood) K.; m. Stephen Kim Cretella, June 11, 1988 (div. May 1994). Student, Am. Theater Arts, 1979-81. Entertainer, 1979—; TV producer, actor Video Record Albums of Am., Pasadena, Calif., 1980-83; v.p. sales, mktg. prodns. Amity Sales Inc., Hudson, N.C., 1980—; co-founder, producer, singer T'NT Entertainments, Inc., Pasadena, 1981-83; founder, pres. ProductVision, Inc., L.A., 1984-86; co-founder, v.p. prodns. Kincaid Enterprises, Morganton, N.C., 1988-89; founder, owner VAT Pub., Hudson, 1989—; cons. Mary Kay Cosmetics, Hudson, 1989—; co-founder, v.p., performer Rappin' Grandmas, Inc!, Hickory, N.C., 1991—; founder, owner Gingerbread Treasures, Hudson, 1992—; owner Charmingly Yours, Hudson, 1995—; entertainer, singer The Troy Cory China Goodwill Concert Tour, 1991. Actor, author TV spl. Catching Christmas, 1981; singer, author album Isn't A Shame, 1990, The Real Country, 1990; co-songwriter album/CD: Dancing Across the Finish Line, 1995; author, editor: The Wedding Book, 1990, Recipes for Love, 1991. Mem. SAG. Republican. Mem. Christian Ch. Home: 4491 Magnolia Ln Hudson NC 28638-8708

KINCH, JANET CAROLYN, English and German language/literature educator; b. Cleve., Mar. 6, 1954; d. H. Joseph Brozic and Eleanor Ruth Peters; m. Timothy Lee Kinch, July 30, 1983. AB in English, Kenyon Coll., 1976; MA in English, Bowling Green State U., 1981, MA in German, 1982, PhD in English, 1986. Counselor Am. Inst. Fgn. Study, Salzburg, Austria, 1975, 76; acting dean Am. Inst. Fgn. Study, Vienna, Austria, 1977; Fulbright tchg. asst. Austrian Fulbright Commn., St. Johann, Austria, 1977-79; tchg. fellow Bowling Green (Ohio) State U., 1981-86, instr. English and theatre arts, 1986-87, asst. prof., 1987-88; asst. prof. Edinboro U. of Pa., 1988—; founder, coord. AIDS Awareness, Edinboro U. of Pa., 1993—; rep. State Sys. Com. for Can. Studies, Harrisburg, Pa., 1993—. Author: Mark Twain's German Critical Reception, 1989; contbr.: Mark Twain Encyclopedia, 1993. Mem. Erie (Pa.) AIDS Network, 1993—; mem. Univ. Senate, sec., 1995-96, mem. exec. com., 1995-96. Univ. fellow Bowling Green State U., 1984-85. Mem. Mark Twain Cir. Office: Edinboro U of Pa English Dept Meadville St Edinboro PA 16444

KIND, ANNE WILSON, engineer; b. Carmel, Calif., Dec. 1, 1958; d. Patrick Wayne and Mary Elaine (Bryan) Wilson; m. David Lee Kind, June 5, 1992; 1 child, Vivian Elaine Wilson. AAS in Music, Everett C.C., 1981; BSME, Calif. State U., Long Beach, 1987. Lic. pilot, FAA. Engr. Rockwell-Aircraft Divsn., El Segundo, Calif., 1983-86, Rockwell-Satellite Divsn., Seal Beach, Calif., 1986-89; Engr. Rockwell-Space Divsn., Downey,

Calif., 1989, Northrop B-2 Divsn., Pico Rivera, Calif., 1989-91, McDonnell Douglas-Space Sta., Huntington Beach, Calif., 1991-94. Pianist Ridgecrest Christian Ch., Albuquerque, 1982-83. Mem. Soaring Soc. Am. (Symons Wave meml. award 1993), Orange County Soaring Assn. (editor 1991-95, v.p. 1993, pres. 1994-95), Pres. award 1993), United Radio Amateur Club. Republican. Home and Office: PO Box 1347 529 Holmes Ln Sugarloaf CA 92386-1347

KINDBERG, SHIRLEY JANE, pediatrician; b. Newark, Feb. 4, 1936; d. John Bertil and Mabel Jacoba (deJonge) K.; m. Charles Dale Coln, May 12, 1962; children: Sara, Eric, Lois, Ruth, Mary. BS, Wheaton Coll., 1957; MD, Baylor U., 1961. Intern Tex. Children's Hosp., Houston, 1961-62; resident Children's Med. Ctr., Dallas, 1962-63; fellow in pediat. pulmonary disease U. Tex. S.W. Med. Sch., Dallas, 1963-64, fellow in pediat. infectious disease, 1965-67; pvt. practice gen. pediat. Dallas, 1969-81, pvt. practice newborns, 1981—. Active Northwest Bible Ch., 1972—. Fellow Am. Acad. Pediatrics; mem. Tex. Pediatric Assn., Dallas Symphony Assn., The Dallas Opera. Republican. Office: 3600 Gaston Ave Ste 406 Dallas TX 75246-1804

KINDZRED, DIANA, communications company executive; b. Chgo., Apr. 13, 1946; d. Bernell and Katherine L. (Gee) K. Student, Northwestern U., 1970-73. Owner, pres. Kindzred & Co. Comm., Chgo., 1978—. Contbr. articles to profl. jours.; author numerous poems. Co-founder mid-west div. Am. Sephardi Fedn., Evanston, Ill., 1990; coord. Amnesty Internat., Evanston, 1991. With U.S. Army, 1964-67. Democrat. Jewish. Home: 7333 N Ridge Blvd Apt 101 Chicago IL 60645-2070 Office: Kindzred & Co Comm 1440 S Indiana Ave Apt 1004 Chicago IL 60605-2841

KINEE-KROHN, PATRICIA, special education educator; b. Phila.; d. William J. and Lillian L. (Long) K.; m. Eugene J. Krohn, July 21, 1995. BS, Westchester State Coll., 1982; AB, Immaculata Coll., 1988; MEd, St. Joseph's U., 1992. Cert. spl. edn. tchr., elem. edn. tchr., reading specialist. Spl. edn. tchr. Holly Hills Elem., Mt. Holly, N.J., 1982-84; elem. edn. tchr. St. James Elem. Sch., Falls Church, Va., 1987-88, Most Blessed Sacrament, Phila., 1988-90; spl. edn. tchr. Kingsway Learning Ctr., Haddonfield, N.J., 1991—; instr. Immaculata (Pa.) Coll., 1994—, Chestnut Hill Coll., 1996—; in-svc. devel. Gesu Sch., Phila., 1994—, reading cons., 1992—; tutor Progressive Edn. Svcs., Sewel, N.J., 1993-95. Vol. Trinity Hospice, Runnemede, N.J., 1993—; CCD instr. Annunciation Cath. Ch., Bellmawr, N.J., 1994-95. Mem. Internat. Reading Assn., So. Jersey Reading Assn., Alpha Zeta (v.p. 1993-95). Home: 542 S 4th St Colwyn PA 19023 Office: Kingsway Learning Ctr 144 Kingway Haddonfield NJ 08033

KING, ADELE COCKSHOOT, French language educator; b. Omaha, July 28, 1932; d. Ralph Waldo and Thera Cecil (Brown) Cockshoot; m. Bruce Alvin King, Dec. 28, 1955; 1 child, Nicole Michelle. BA, U. Iowa, 1954; MA, U. Leeds, England, 1960; Doctorate in French Lit., U. Paris, 1970. Lectr. in French U. Ibadan, Nigeria, 1963-65, U. Lagos, Nigeria, 1967-70; reader in French Ahmadu Bello U., Zaria, Nigeria, 1973-76; prof. French Ball State U., Muncie, Ind., 1986—, chmn. dept. fgn. langs., 1991-94; vis. assoc. prof. U. Mo., Columbia, 1976-77. Author: (critical studies) Camus, 1964, 3d edit., 1968, Proust, 1968, Paul Nizan: écrivain, 1976, The Writings of Camara Laye, 1980, French Women Novelists: Defining a Female Style, 1989; (study guides) L'Enfant Noir, L'Etranger, Farewell to Arms, The Power and the Glory, Ghosts, 1980-82; editor: Camus's L'Etranger Fifty Years On, 1992; co-editor Modern Dramatists, 1982—, Women Writers, 1987—; contbr. articles to profl. jours. Summer Rsch. grantee Ball State U., 1987, 90, 95; postdoctoral fellow AAUW, 1977-78. Mem. MLA, Assn. Drs. of Univs. of France (v.p. 1991—), Am. Comparative Lit. Assn., Soc. des Etudes Camusiennes, Am. Assn. Tchrs. French, Marguerite Yourcenar Soc., Women in French (sec. 1988-92, v.p. 1996 , editor Women in French Studies 1996—). Office: Ball State Univ Dept Modern Langs Muncie IN 47306

KING, ALMA JEAN, former health and physical education educator; b. Hamilton, Ohio, Feb. 28, 1939; d. William Lawrence and Esther Mary (Smith) K. BS in Edn., Miami U., Oxford, Ohio, 1961; MEd, Bowling Green State U., 1963; postgrad., Fla. Atlantic U., 1969, '92, Nova U., Ft. Lauderdale, Fla., 1979. Cert. elem. and secondry tchr., Ohio, all levels incl. coll., Fla. Tchr. health, physical edn. Rogers Middle Sch., Broward County Bd. Pub. Instrn., 1963-64; assoc. prof. health, phys edn., recreation, dance Broward C.C., Fort Lauderdale, Fla., 1964-94; ret., 1994; dir. Intramurals and Extramurals Boward C.C., Fort Lauderdale, Fla., 1964-67, chair person Women's Affairs, 1978, health and safety com., 1975, faculty evaluation com. 1980-85, mem. faculty ins. benefits com. 1993-94. Sponsor Broward County Fire Fighters, Police; active mem. Police Benevolent Assn.; Historical Soc. Grantee Broward C.C. Staff Devel. Fund, 1988. Mem. AAHPERD, NEA, Fla. Edn. Assn., Fla. Assn for Health, Physical Edn., Recreation and Dance, Am. Assn. for Advancement of Health Edn., United Faculty of Fla., Fla. Assn. of C.C., Order of the Eastern Star (past Worthy Matron), Order of Shrine. Home: 4310 Buchanan St Hollywood FL 33021

KING, BETSY, professional golfer. Winner U.S. Open-Women, 1989, 1990, LPGA, 1992; 3d ranked woman LPGA Tour, 1992; LPGA tour victories include: Orlando Classic, 1984, Columbia Savings Classic, 1984, Henredon Classic, 1986, Rail Charity Classic, 1986, 88, Tucson Open, 1987, Dinah Shore Invitational, 1987, McDonald's Classic, 1987, Atlantic City Classic, 1987, Kemper Open, 1988, Cellular One-Ping Championship, 1988, Jamaica Classic, 1989, Nabisco Dinah Shore, 1990, U.S. Women's Open, 1989, 1990, Corning Classic, 1991, Mazda Championship, 1992, ShopRite Classic, 1995. Inductee LPGA Hall of Fame, 1995. Office: LPGA Ste B 2570 W International Speedway Blvd Daytona Beach FL 32114-1118*

KING, BILLIE JEAN MOFFITT, former professional tennis player; b. Long Beach, Calif., Nov. 22, 1943; d. Willard J. Moffitt; m. Larry King, Sept. 17, 1965. Student, Calif. State U. at Los Angeles, 1961-64. Amateur tennis player, 1958-67, profl., 1968—; mem. Tennis Challenge Series, 1977, 78; dir., ofcl. spokesperson World TeamTennis, Chgo., 1985—; Singles champion tournaments Wimbledon, 1966-68, 72, 73, 75, U.S. Open, 1967, 71, 72, 74, U.S. Hardcourt, 1966, Italian Open, 1970, West German Open, 1971, Australian Open, 1968, South African Open, 1966, 67, 69, U.S. Indoor, 1966-68, 71, U.S. Clay Court, 1971, French Open, 1972, Avon, 1980; doubles champion Wimbledon, 1961, 62, 65, 67, 68, 70-73, U.S. Open, 1965, 67, 74, 80, French, 1972, Italian, 1970, South African, 1967-70, Bridgestone, 1976, Virginia Slims, 1974, 76; mixed doubles champion Wimbledon, 1967, 71, 73, U.S. Open, 1967, 71, 73, French, 1967, 70, South African, 1967, Australian, 1968; winner 29 Virginia Slims singles titles, 1970-77, 4 Colgate titles, 1977, Fedn. Cup, 1963-67, 76-79, Wightman Cup, 1961-67, 70, 77, 78; World Tennis Team All-Star, 3 times; host Colgate women's sports TV spl. The Lady is a Champ, 1975; co-founder, dir. Kingdom, Inc., San Mateo, Calif.; sports commentator ABC-TV, 1975-78; co-founder, pub. WomenSports mag., 1974—; founder Women's Tennis Assn., 1973; first woman commr. (Team Tennis League) profl. sports history, 1984; TV commentator HBO-Sports Wimbledon coverage; capt. Fed. Cup for USA, 1995; cons. Virginia Slims World Championship Series; bd. dirs. Challenger Ctr.; amb. Adventures in Movement Charity; nat. spokesperson Literary Vols. Am.; tennis tchr. to profls. Author: Tennis to Win, 1970, (with Kim Chapin) Billie Jean, 1974, (with Cynthia Starr) We Have Come a Long Way, The Story of Women's Tennis, 1988. Named Sportsperson of Yr., Sports Illustrated, 1972; Woman Athlete of Yr., A.P., 1967, 73, Top Woman Athlete of Yr., 1972; Woman of Yr., Time mag., 1976, One of 10 Most Powerful Women in Am., Harper's Bazaar, 1977, One of 25 Most Influential Women in Am., World Almanac, 1977, One of 100 Most Important Ams. of 20th Century, Life mag., 1990; named to Internat. Tennis Hall of Fame, 1987, Nat. Women's Hall of Fame, 1990; Lifetime Achievement award, March of Dimes, 1994. Office: World TeamTennis 445 N Wells St Ste 404 Chicago IL 60610-4534

KING, CAROL ANN, critical care nurse; b. Valentine, Nebr., Oct. 8, 1956; d. Jerome R. and Beryle A. (Sell) Dvorak; m. Thomas R. King, Oct. 23, 1976; children: Jessica, Timmi. Assoc. Sci. in Nursing with honors, Presentation Coll., 1981. CCRN; cert. ACLS instr., BLS. Staff nurse St. Francis Med. Ctr., Grand Island, Nebr., 1981-94; staff nurse Critical Care Unit-ICU Mary Lanning Hosp., Hastings, Nebr., 1994-95, patient care coord. Critical Care Unit-ICU, 1995—; co-lectr., instr. hemodynamic monitoring for coronary care classes St. Francis Med. Ctr., Grand Island, 1992, 93, preceptor, 1991-94. Co-author: Preceptor's Tool, 1992, Yecch! and Other Comments About: Invasive Techniques for Hemodynamic Measurements, 1993, Preceptor's Guide to 12-Leap EKG's, 1994, Basic Homodynamic Monitoring, A Reference Guide, 1995. Mem. PTA, Grand Island, 1983—. Mem. AACN. Democrat. Roman Catholic.

KING, CAROLYN DINEEN, federal judge; b. Syracuse, N.Y., Jan. 30, 1938; d. Robert E. and Carolyn E. (Bareham) Dineen; children: James Randall, Philip Randall, Stephen Randall; m. John L. King, Jan. 1, 1988. A.B. summa cum laude, Smith Coll., 1959; LL.B., Yale U., 1962. Bar: D.C. 1962, Tex. 1963. Assoc. Fulbright & Jaworski, Houston, 1962-72; ptnr. Childs, Fortenbach, Beck & Guyton, Houston, 1972-78, Sullivan, Bailey, King, Randall & Sabon, Houston, 1978-79; circuit judge U.S. Ct. Appeals (5th cir.), Houston, 1979—; mem. coun. Am. Law Inst., 1991—. Trustee, mem. exec. com., treas. Houston Ballet Found., 1967-70; trustee, mem. exec. com., chmn. bd. trustees U. St. Thomas, 1988—; mem. Houston dist. adv. coun. SBA, 1972-76; mem. Dallas regional panel Pres.'s Commn. White House Fellowships, 1972-76, mem. commn., 1977; bd. dirs. Houston chpt. Am. Heart Assn., 1978-79; nat. trustee Palmer Drug Abuse Program, 1978-79; trustee, sec., treas., chmn. audit com., fin. com., mem. mgmt. com. United Way Tex. Gulf Coast, 1979-85. Mem. ABA, Fed. Bar Assn., State Bar Tex., Houston Bar Assn. Roman Catholic. Office: US Ct Appeals 11020 US Courthouse 515 Rusk St Houston TX 77002*

KING, CATHLEEN (CATHIE KING), rehabilitation nurse; b. Wright Patterson AFB, Ohio, Dec. 3, 1959; d. Richard Earl Sr. and Virginia R. (Levendoski) Winland; m. Henry Grady King IV, Feb. 14, 1984; children: Andrew, Deanna, Philip, Thomas. BSN, Tex. Woman's U., 1983. RN, Tex.; cert. rehab. RN, BCLS. Charge nurse, staff pool, supr. Dallas Rehab. Inst., 1983-88; agy. nurse, 1988-91; rehab. nurse Baylor Inst. for Rehab., Dallas, 1991-93; case mgr. Dallas VA Med. Ctr., 1996—, clin. nurse mgr. Spinal Cord Injury Ctr., 1993-95. Basic nursing grantee, scholar; recipient ANA/DFW Great 100 Nurse award. Mem. Am. Assn. Spinal Cord Injury Nurses (mem. program com.), Assn. Rehab. Nurses.

KING, CLAUDIA LOUAN, film producer, lecturer; b. Merced, Calif., May 1, 1940; d. Alvin Cecil and Thelma May (Matthew) K.; m. Douglas McLean, July 10, 1965 (div. 1975); children: Kia Gabrielle, Kendra Sue. BA, U. Calif., 1963; MA, Ind. U., 1969. Lectr. U. Fla., Gainesville, 1969-70; asst. prof. U. Nev., Las Vegas, 1973-79; producer Source 17 Prodns., Santa Monica, Calif., 1979-85; freelance producer Chico, Calif., 1985—. Author: Life Mastery: A Self-Esteem Handbook for Adults and Children, 1994, (screenplays) The Garden of Eden, 1983, My Sister's Keeper, 1986, (documentary) The Evolution of Women, 1988, 92 (short stories) In the Realm of the Invisible, 1991; prodr.: Rape is Everybody's Concern, 1978, Los Angeles Personally Yours, 1986; pub. Light Paths Communications, 1994—. Mem. Chico Annie's Com. for Dramatic Arts, 1996. Carnegie grantee, 1969; Nev. Endowment for Humanities grantee, 1978. Mem. Women in Film, Coll. Art Assn. Democrat. Home: PO Box 3576 Chico CA 95927-3576

KING, CORETTA SCOTT (MRS. MARTIN LUTHER KING, JR.), educational association administrator, lecturer, writer, concert singer; b. Marion, Ala., Apr. 27, 1927; d. Obidiah and Bernice (McMurray) Scott; m. Martin Luther King, Jr., June 18, 1953 (dec. Apr. 1968); children: Yolanda Denise, Martin Luther III, Dexter Scott, Bernice Albertine. A.B., Antioch Coll., 1951; Mus.B., New Eng. Conservatory Music, 1954, Mus.D., 1971; L.H.D., Boston U., 1969, Marymount-Manhattan Coll., 1969, Morehouse Coll., 1970; H.H.D., Brandeis U., 1969, Wilberforce U., 1970, Bethune-Cookman Coll., 1970, Princeton U., 1970; LL.D., Bates Coll., 1971. Voice instr. Morris Brown Coll., Atlanta, 1962; commentator CNN, Atlanta, 1980—; lectr., writer; founding pres., chief exec. officer Martin Luther King Jr. Ctr. for Nonviolent Social Change Inc. Author: My Life With Martin Luther King, Jr., 1969; contbr. articles to mags.; syndicated newspaper columnist N.Y. Times Syndication Sales Corp., 1986-90, United Features Syndicate, 1990-94; concert debut, Springfield, Ohio, 1948; numerous concerts throughout U.S., concerts, India, 1959, performances, Freedom Concert. Del. to White House Conf. Children and Youth, 1960; sponsor Com. for Sane Nuclear Policy, Com. on Responsibility, Moblzn. to End War in Viet Nam, 1966, 67, Margaret Sanger Meml. Found.; mem. So. Rural Action Project, Inc.; pres. Martin Luther King, Jr. Found.; chmn. Commn. on Econ. Justice for Women; mem. exec. com. Nat. Com. Inquiry; co-chmn. Clergy and Laymen Concerned about Vietnam, Nat. Com. for Full Employment, 1974; pres. Martin Luther King Jr. Center for Nonviolent Social Change; co-chairperson Nat. Com. Full Employment; mem. exec. bd. Nat. Health Ins. Com.; active YWCA; bd. dirs. So. Christian Leadership Conf., Martin Luther King, Jr. Found. Gt. Britain; trustee Robert F. Kennedy Meml. Found., Ebenezer Bapt. Ch. Recipient Outstanding Citizenship award Montgomery (Ala.) Improvement Assn., 1959, Merit award St. Louis Argus, 1960, Distinguished Achievement award Nat. Orgn. Colored Women's Clubs, 1962, Louise Waterman Wise award Am. Jewish Congress Women's Aux., 1963, Myrtle Wreath award Cleve. Hadassah, 1965, award for excellence in field human relations Soc. Family of May, 1968, Universal Love award Premio San Valentine Com., 1968, Wateler Peace prize, 1968, Dag Hammarskjold award, 1969, Pacem in Terris award Internat. Overseas Service Found., 1969, Leadership for Freedom award Roosevelt U., 1971, Martin Luther King Meml. medal Coll. City N.Y., 1971, Internat. Viareggio award, 1971, numerous others; named Woman of Year Utility Club N.Y.C., 1962, Woman of Year Nat. Assn. Radio and TV Announcers, 1968, UAW Social Justice award, 1980. Mem. Nat. Council Negro Women (Ann. Brotherhood award 1957), Women Strike for Peace (del. disarmament conf. Geneva, Switzerland 1962, citation for work in peace and freedom 1963), Women's Internat. League for Peace and Freedom, NAACP, United Ch. Women (bd. mgrs.), Alpha Kappa Alpha (hon.). Baptist (mem. choir, guild adviser). Club: Links (Human Dignity and Human Rights award Norfolk chpt. 1964). Address: Martin Luther King Jr Ctr 449 Auburn Ave NE Atlanta GA 30312-1503*

KING, DIANE MARIE, creative services national manager; b. Winchester, Mass., Jan. 7, 1960; d. Frank Anthony Cushenette and Etta Priscilla (Gentile) Nadeau; m. Brian Thomas King, May 12, 1990. BS, Fitchburg (Mass.) State Coll., 1983. Mktg. dir. Lustre Diamonds, Boston, 1983-85; mgr. Living Well Fitness Ctr., Cambridge, Mass., 1985-87; Desktop Pub. trainer Gemini Cons., Cambridge, 1987-89; assoc. systems engr. EDS, Bloomfield Hills, Mich., 1989-90; prodn. mgr. Gemini Cons., Cambridge, 1990-92; prodn. mgr. Coopers & Lybrand, Boston, 1992-95, creative svcs. nat. mgr., 1995—; v.p. Mktg. Mgmt. Assistance Program, Fitchburg, 1981-83. Roman Catholic. Home: 3-B Carnation Cir Reading MA 01867-2774 Office: Coopers & Lybrand One Post Office Sq Boston MA 02109

KING, ELAINE A., curator, art historian, critic; b. Oak Park, Ill., Apr. 12, 1947; d. Casimir Stanley and Catherine Mary (Chemle) Czerwien. BS, No. Ill. U., 1968, MA, 1974; PhD, Northwestern U., 1986. Intern George Eastman House, Rochester, N.Y., 1977; lctr. history of photography Northwestern U., Evanston, Ill., 1977-81; curator Dittmar Meml. Gallery, Evanston, 1978-81; dir. Artemesia Gallery, Chgo., 1976-77; dir. Carnegie-Mellon Art Gallery, Pitts., 1985-91; assoc. prof. critical theory and history of art, Carnegie Mellon U., Pitts., 1981—; bd. dirs. Mountain Lake Criticism Conf., Blacksburg, Va., 1982-91; ind. curator, 1991—; exbhn. rev. panel Pa. Coun. on Arts, 1991; exec. dir., chief curator Contemporary Art Ctr., Cin., Ohio, 1993-95; guest curator Pitts. Cultural Trust, 1992, 93, 95, 96; adj. prof. U. Cin., 1994; art critic-in-residence U. Ariz., Tucson; organizing com. Hungarian Bienale Exhibition II, Györ, 1993, curator Bienale III, 1995; panelist NEA Visual Arts, 1993; grant reviewer Inst. Mus. Sci., Washington, 1994, Ohio Arts Council fellowship and grant evaluator, 1994-95; mem. organizing com. Midwest Mus. Con., 1994-95; Am. rep. Inter Arts Spring 1996 Budapest (Hungary) Festival, Chain Coll. Arts Assoc. Com. distinguished exibition award, AICA conference central European cross-roads, 1996. Active Dem. Party, Evanston, Ill., award judge, 1977-78, precinct capt. 1977. Curator and author: The Figure As Fiction, 1993, Alfred DeCredico: Drawings, 1985-93, Emily Cheng: Monoprints, 1994, (exhibition catalogues) Barry LeVa: 1966-88, Mel Bochner: 1973-85, Elizabeth Murray: Drawings: 1980-86, Michael Gitlin: Sculpture & Drawings, 1990, New Generations: Chgo., 1990, New Generations: N.Y., 1991, Magdalena Jétalova, 1991, Martin Puryear: Sculpture & Drawings, 1987, Abstraction/Abstraction, Tishan Hsu, Paintings, Drawings & Sculpture, 1987, N.Y. Painting Today, Michel Gerand: Drawings and Site Works, 1989, Drawings and Sculpture, 1990, Art in the Age of Information, 1993, Five Artists at the Airport: Insights into Public Art, 1992, Martha Rosler: IN Place of the Public, 1994, Lyzabeth Sallan: 2 Installations Light Into Art: From Video to Virtual Reality (also booklet), David Humphrey: Paintings and Drawings 1987-95 (also catalogue), others; author: The Misunderstood Patron, The National Endowment for the Arts; free lance art critic, Arts, Tema Celeste, & Sculpture, Cin. Enquirer; art critic in residence Delaware Contemporary Center for the arts, 1992, Mid-Atlantic Arts Fellow, 1991; editor Diaglogue, Columbus, Ohio, 1984-89; contbr. articles to profl. jours. Recipient Hunt Art award, 1977; Art Critics fellow Pa. Coun. on Arts, 1985, 89, 95; faculty research grantee, 1985, 87, 89-90,(1996—), Grant Trust for Mutral understanding , Rockefeller Found., 1994, Thendora Found. 1995, Mem. Coll. Art Assn., Am. Assn. Mus., Assn. Historians of Am. Art, Internat. Assn. Art Critics (Am. sect.). Avocations: cooking, gardening, tennis, swimming, sailing. Office: Carnegie Mellon U Coll Fine Arts Pittsburgh PA 15213

KING, FRANCES, education educator; b. Dallas, Nov. 14, 1929; d. Grover W. and Clara (Blailock) Beckham; m. Erwin C. King, Jr., Jan. 27, 1951; children: Carol, Melody. BA, Austin Coll., 1951; Writer's Cert., Children's Inst. of Lit., Redding Ridge, Conn., 1987. Cert. tchr. of mentally retarded, early childhood, learning disabilities, Tex. Tchr., fourth grade O'Brien (Tex.) Consolidated Ind. Sch. Dist., 1958-62; tchr., first grade, early childhood/spl. edn. tchr. Knox City (Tex.) Consolidated Ind. Sch. dist., 1961-71; spl. edn. tchr. mid. sch. Knox City-O'Brien Consolidated Ind. Sch. Dist., 1971-76, 76-89; spl. edn./adult edn. tchr. Knox City-O'Brien and Sweetwater Dist., Knox City, 1989-95; subs. tchr. Knox City-O'Brien Dist., 1995—; spl. edn. spelling coach Knox City H.S. Co-author: Guide Program for Special Education. Named Tchr. of the Yr. in Spl. Edn., Region IVX. Mem. Tex. State Tchrs. Assn. (local pres.), ATPE (local pres.).

KING, GLYNDA B., state legislator; b. Chattanooga, July 5, 1946; d. William Cass and Johnnie Olivan (Griffin) Bowman; m. Thomas Wayland King, Jan. 12, 1963; children: Denise Schon, Kelly Todd. Grad. high sch., Tyner, Tenn. Mem. Clayton County (Ga.) Drug Adv. Com., 1976—, Ga. Arts Caucus, Atlanta, 1991—, Clayton County Disabilities Early Intervention for Families and Children; bd. dirs. Clayton County Bd. Edn., 1983-89, Gov.'s Commn. on Mental Health, Mental Retardation and Substance Abuse, Atlanta, 1992—, Leadership Clayton; state rep. Ga. Gen. Assembly, Atlanta, 1991-92; mem. success by six coun. United Way, Atlanta, 1992—; hon. life mem. E.J. Swint Elem. Sch. PTA, 1979—. Recipient Founders award 16th Dist. Ga. PTA, 1985, Pub. Policy-Lay Advocacy award Mental Health Assn. of Ga., 1993. Mem. Mental Health Assn. Met. Atlanta (pres. 1992-93), Clayton County C. of C., Southlake Kiwanis. Democrat. Baptist. Home: PO Box 961032 Riverdale GA 30296-7032

KING, GWENDOLYN BAIR, former White House staff member, public speaker; b. Hartsville, S.C., Oct. 27, 1915; d. William Parlor and Mary Margaret (Scurry) Bair; m. LaBruce Ward King, Dec. 26, 1937; children: John LaBruce King, Margaret Gwendolyn King Farrow. AB, Coker Coll., 1936. With asst. pers. office Libr. Congress, Washington, 1937-39; sec., dir. Libr. Congress, Union Catalog, Washington, 1939-43; asst. to appointments sec. for the President The White House, Washington, 1953-69, dir. correspondence for Pat Nixon, 1969-74; pub. speaker on White House career Calif., 1977—. Contbr. to Presidential Records, The Nat. Archives, Washington, 1988. Dir. Speakers' Bur., Home Hospice, Santa Rosa, Calif., 1985, cert. caregiver, 1982-84; mem. Oakmont Archtl. Com., Santa Rosa Symphony League. Named Paul Harris Fellow, Rotary Internat., 1983, Citizen of the Day, KABL, San Francisco, 1983. Mem. AAUW, Newcomers Club (pres. Santa Rosa chpt. 1977-78), Oakmont Book Club (chmn. 1981-82), Oakmont Golf Club (sec. 1986), Saturday Afternoon Club. Republican. Home: 451 Pythian Rd Santa Rosa CA 95409-6346

KING, GWENDOLYN S., utility company executive, former federal official; b. East Orange, N.J.; d. Frank M. and Henryne (Walker) Stewart; m. Colbert I. King. BA cum laude, Howard U., 1962; postgrad., George Washington U.; hon. doctorate, U. Md., 1990, U. New Haven, 1992. With HEW, 1971-76; dir. div. consumer complaints HUD, Washington, 1976-78; legis. asst. to Sen. John Heinz Washington, 1978-79; dir. Commonwealth of Pa. Office, Washington, 1979-86; dep. asst. to the pres. and dir. Office Intergovtl. Affairs The White House, Washington, 1986-88; commr. Adv. Commn. on Intergovtl. Rels.; mem. Interagency Com. Women's Bus. Enterprise; dir. The White House Task Force on P.R.; exec. v.p. Gogol & Assocs., 1988-89; commr. Social Security Adminstrn., Balt., 1989-92; sr. v.p. corp. & pub. affairs PECO Energy Corp., Phila., 1993—; bd. dirs. Lockheed Martin, Monsanto Co. Bd. dirs. Phila. Conv. and Vis. Bur. Recipient Drum Major for Justice award So. Christian Leadership Conf., 1990, Alumni award Howard U., 1991, Black Achievement Bus. and Fin. award Ebony Mag., 1992. Mem. Forum Exec. Women, Internat. Women's Forum. Office: PECO Engery Co 2301 Market St Philadelphia PA 19103-1338

KING, HELEN LOUISE, art gallery director; b. N.Y.C., July 24, 1938; d. Herbert Lincoln and Helen Vivian (Perez) K. AAS, No. Va. C.C., 1985; BA in Comms., Western Conn. State U., 1987; MA in Comms., Fordham U., 1988. Cert. Am. Registry Radiologic Technologists. Adminstr. dept. radiology Arlington (Va.) Hosp., 1963-83; ptnr., dir. Gingerbread Gallery and Framing Studio, Hawley, Pa., 1991—. Mem. AAUW, Profl. Picture Framers Assn., Hawley Merchants Assn., Hawley-Lake Wallenpanpack C. of C., Wayne County C. of C., Fordham U. alumni Fedn. Office: Gingerbread Gallery PO Box 405 309 Main Ave Hawley PA 18428

KING, IMOGENE M., nurse, educator; b. West Point, Iowa, Jan. 30, 1923. Diploma, St. John's Hosp., 1945; B.S. in Nursing, St. Louis U., 1948; M.S. in Nursing, 1957; Ed.D., Columbia U., 1961; Ph.D. (hon.), So. Ill. U., 1980. Instr. med.-surg. nursing, asst. DON St. John's Hosp., St. Louis, 1947-58; asst. prof. nursing, then assoc. prof. Loyola U, Chgo., 1961-66; prof., dir. grad. program in nursing Loyola U, 1972-80; prof. U. South Fla., Tampa, 1980-90, prof. emeritus, 1990—; asst. chief rsch. grants br. div. nursing HEW, Washington, 1966-68; prof., dean sch. nursing Ohio State U., Columbus, 1968-72; mem. def. adv. com. on women in svcs. Dept. Def., 1972-75; adj. prof. U. Miami Sch. Nursing, 1986-89; cons. VA Hosp., health care agencies. Author: Toward a Theory for Nursing, 1971, transl. to Japanese, 1975, A Theory for Nursing: Systems, Concepts, Process, 1981, transl. to Japanese, 1983, transl. to Spanish, 1985, Curriculum and Instruction in Nursing, 1986; contbr. articles in nursing to profl. jours., chpts. to books. Alderman, chmn. fin. com. Ward 2, Wood Dale, Ill., 1975-79; bd. dirs. operation PAR Inc., Pinellas County, Fla., 1990-92. Recipient Founders award St. Louis U., 1969, Recognition of Contbns. to Nursing Edn. award Columbia U. Tchrs. Coll., 1983, Disting. Scholar award U. So. Fla., 1988-89. Fellow Am. Acad. Nursing (hon.); mem. ANA (Jessie M. Scott award 1996, conv. lectr. 1996), Ill. Nurses Assn. (highest recognition award 1975, award 19th dist. 1975), Fla. Nurses Assn. (del. to ANA conv. 1982—, dir. region 2 1981-83, 2d v.p. 1983-85, Nurse of Yr. 1984, Nursing Rsch. award 1985), Dist. IV Fla. Nurses Assn. (del. to Fla. Nurses Assn. 1981-96, pres.-elect 1982-83, pres. 1983-84), Fla. Nurses Found. (sec. 1986-88, pres. 1988-91), Sigma Theta Tau (counselor Delta Beta chpt. 1981-83, pres.-elect 1986-87, pres. 1987-89, disting. lectr. 1990-91, co-chmn. biennial conv. 1991, nominating com. 1993-95, Founders award for excellence in nursing edn. 1989, life, Virginia Henderson fellow 1993), Phi Kappa Phi (scholar award 1988).

KING, JANE CUDLIP COBLENTZ, volunteer educator; b. Iron Mountain, Mich., May 4, 1922; d. William Stacey and Mary Elva (Martin) Cudlip; m. George Samuel Coblentz, June 8, 1942 (dec. June 1989); children: Bruce Harper, Keith George, Nancy Allison Coblentz Patch; m. James E. King, August 23, 1991 (dec. Jan. 1994). BA, Mills Coll., 1942. Mem. Sch. Resource and Career Guidance Vols., Inc., Atherton, Calif., 1965-69, pres., CEO, 1969—; part-time exec. asst. to dean of admissions Mills Coll., 1994—. Proofreader, contbr., campus liaison Mills Coll. Quarterly mag. Life gov. Royal Children's Hosp., Melbourne, Australia, 1963—; pres. United Menlo Park (Calif.) Homeowner's Assn., 1994—; nat. pres. Mills Coll. Alumnae Assn., 1969-73, bd. trustees, 1975-83. Named Vol. of Yr., Sequoia Union High Sch. Dist., 1988, Golden Acorn award for outstanding svc. Menlo Park C. of C., 1991. Mem. AAUW (Menlo-Atherton branch pres. 1994-96, v.p. programs 1996—), Atherlons, Palo Alto (Calif.) Area Mills Coll. Club (pres. 1986), Phi Beta Kappa. Episcopalian. Home: 1109 Valparaiso Ave Menlo

Park CA 94025-4412 Office: Menlo-Atherton HS Resource-Career Guid Vols 555 Middlefield Rd Atherton CA 94027

KING, JANET FELLAND, family nurse practitioner; b. Ann Arbor, Mich., May 5, 1947; d. Robert Marcy and Marjorie Marie (Sherman) Felland; m. William Curtis Runyon, May 20, 1967 (div. May 8, 1972); m. Robert Allen King, Oct. 26, 1974; 1 child, Stephen Tremain King. Student, U. Mich., 1965-67, Earlham Coll., 1968-69; BSN, Ball State U., 1971; MNSc, U. Ark., 1976. RN, Idaho. Med. surg. nurse Meml. Hosp., Oxford, Ohio, 1971-72; migrant health nurse Colo. Dept. Health, Lamar, 1972-74; pub. health nurse City Health Dept., Little Rock, 1974-75; family nurse practitioner Idaho Migrant Coun., Burley, 1976-81; pub. health nurse South Ctrl. Dist. Health, Burley, 1981-82; family nurse practitioner Family Health Svcs., Burley, 1982—; treas. Mini Cassia Child Protection Team, Burley, 1982—; mem. Idaho Health Profl. Loan Repayment Bd., Pocatello, 1992—. Vol., nurse and deacon Diocese of Honduras, Roatan, 1990; archdeacon Diocese of Idaho, 1990—; trustee Episcopal Camp & Conf. Bd., 1991—. Named Woman of Progress, Bus. and Profl. Women, 1981-82; recipient Outstanding Clinician Achievement award N.W. Primary Care Assn., 1984-92. Mem. Idaho Nurses Assn. (regional rep. 1982-84), Sigma Theta Tau. Episcopalian. Home: 678 E 400 N Rupert ID 83350-9414 Office: Family Health Svcs 2311 Park # 11 Burley ID 83318-1530

KING, KATHRYN FRENCH, artist, horse breeder; b. Amarillo, Tex., Jan. 17, 1957; d. Richard Wilson French and Dorothy Alice (Gilliland) Farquhar; m. James Leonard Yarborough, Mar. 3, 1981 (div. 1994); children: Sarah Elizabeth, Katrina Alicia, James Kleberg. Student, Midland Coll., 1978-79. Cert. equine appraiser, Tex. Polo groom Midland (Tex.) Polo Club, 1974-83; geolog. draftsman Pennzoil, Midland, Tex., 1980-81; hunting guide King Ranch, Inc., Kingsville, Tex., 1981-93; horseback guide, wrangler Turquiose Trailrides, Terlingua, Tex., 1991-95; owner, pres., artist, equine appraiser Running K, Inc., Alpine, Tex., 1995—; mem. bd. dirs., exec. v.p., sec. Big Bend Transp., Inc., 1995; trust and estate planning advisor Beneficial Fin. Svcs., 1996—; art coord. asst. Permian Basin Petroleum Mus., 1974. Pub. Jehovah's Witnesses, Floresville and Alpine, Tex., 1977-94. student amb. P.R. People to People, 1974; Miss Midland rep. Miss. America Pageants. Recipient 8 Goal U.S. Pres. Cup awards Polo Tournament, 1981, various awards and ribbons in English & Western Horsebackriding, 1970-93. Mem. Am. Quarter Horse Assn., Nat. Found. Quarter Horse Assn., Tri-County Horseman's Assn. (bd. dirs. 1992-93). Home: #13 Sierra Vista Dr Alpine TX 79830 Office: Running K Inc PO Box 26 Alpine TX 79831

KING, KAY SUE, investment company executive; b. Indpls., Sept. 14, 1948; d. George W. and Nadine M. K.; 1 child, Christopher G. Student, U. Ariz., 1966-70; BS in Edn., Ind. U., 1971; MA in Speech Communication, U. Hawaii, 1974. Tchr. Indpls. High Schs., 1971-1973; sec., treas. G. W. King Co., Indpls., 1974—; domestic sales mgr. Regal Travel, Indpls., 1975-90; pres., bd. dirs. K.S. King, Inc., Indpls., 1977—; mng. ptnr. K.S. King Co., Indpls., 1982—. Mem. pub. rels. com. Indpls. Zoolog. Xoc., 1976-85; vol. Indpls Humane Soc., 1966—, Indpls. Aid to Zoo Horse Show, 1974-78, Save the Ducks campaign, Indpls., 1978, Pan Am. Games Olympic Sports Com., Indpls., 1981-82; tchr. Sunday sch. Meridian St. Methodist Ch., Indpls., 1988-90. Elected Festival Princess 500 Festival Assn., Indpls., 1968. Mem. Internat. Assn. Bus. Communicators, Internat. Wildlife Fedn., Indpls. Zool. Soc. (charter), Indpls. Pub. Libr., Indpls. Children's Mus., Indpls. Ski Club, U. Ariz. Alumni Assn., Ind. Univ. Alumni Assn., Channel 20, Riviera Club, Lilly Pool, Meridian Hills Country Club, Delta Delta Delta. Home: 702 Holliday Ln Indianapolis IN 46260-3589 Office: King Co 5665 N Meridian St Indianapolis IN 46208-1502

KING, KAY WANDER, design educator, fashion designer, consultant; b. Houston, Oct. 16, 1937; d. Aretas Robert and Verna Elizabeth (Klann) Wander; m. George Ronald King, Feb. 21, 1960; 1 child, Collin Wander. BA, U. North Tex., 1959; M of Liberal Arts, Houston Bapt. U., 1991. Fashion designer Kabro Houston, Inc., 1959-66, Joe Frank, Inc., Houston, 1966-68; fashion dir. Foley's, Houston, 1968-70; prin. Kay King Designer/Cons., Houston, 1970—; chair fashion dept. Houston C.C., 1981—; mem. adv. bd. Spring (Tex.) Ind. Sch. Dist. Tech. Edn., 1990—; bd. dirs. Make it Yourself with Wool, Tex.; site evaluator Tex. Coord. Bd. for Higher Edn., 1994. Designer Mrs. Am., 1966, Houston Oilers Cheerleaders, 1968-92, Astroworld and The Astrodome, 1968-69, Brian Boru Opera, 1991, Design Industries Found. Fighting AIDS, 1994-96. Chair Gulf Coast area United Cerebral Palsy Telethon, 1981; chair Whiteley Endowment Scholarship Awards, Houston, 1990-93, Sickle Cell Found., Houston, 1995-96; adminstr. Bedichek Faculty Devel. Grants, 1995-96; pres. Spring Br. Ind. Sch. Dist. Coun., PTAs, Houston, 1987-88; bd. dirs. Houston C.C. Found., 1988-93, Mus. Fine Arts Costume Inst., Houston, 1991—, acquisitions com., 1993—. Recipient Yellow Rose of Tex., Gov. Tex., 1982, Nat. Inst. for Staff and Orgnl. Devel. Tchg. Excellence award U. Tex., 1993, Award of Excellence, Houston C.C. Faculty Assn. Coun., 1995, Fin. Advisors' Excellence in Cmty. Leadership award Am. Express, 1996, Innovation award Houston C.C., 1996, Tony Chee Teaching Excellence award, 1996; named Woman to Watch, Houston Woman mag., 1991, Woman of Excellence, Fedn. Houston Profl. Women, 1992; Bedichek Faculty Devel. grantee, 1986, 89, 90, 93, 94. Mem. Nat. PTA (life, hon., coun. pres. 1987-88), Costume Soc. Am. (awards chair 1992-93, exec. bd. dirs., sec. 1993—), Tex. Jr. Coll. Tchrs. Assn. (sect. chair 1990-92), Fashion Group Internat. (bd. dirs. 1969—, cultural exch. chair 1965-71, regional dir. 1969-70, program dir., chair career conf. 1994, retail chair 1995), Houston C.C. Women Adminstrs. Assn. (bd. dirs. 1993-95, v.p. 1994-95, Star award 1989, Keynote address 1996), Houston Fashion Designers Assn. (charter, publicicty chair 1989-93, v.p. bd. dirs. 1993—), Fedn. Houston Profl. Women (bd. dirs., program dir. 1993, adminstrv. sec. 1994, pres.-elect 1995, pres. 1996, charter mem. Classy Clown Corps 1994—), Zeta Tau Alpha (charity showhouse chair 1985, Nat. Cert. of Merit 1986). Office: Houston CC System 1300 Holman St # 319A Houston TX 77004-3898

KING, KIMBERLY N., construction executive, lawyer. Assoc. counsel, corp. sec. Kaufmann and Broad Home Corp., L.A. Office: Kaufman and Broad Home Corp 10990 Wilshire Blvd Los Angeles CA 90024*

KING, LAURA JANE, librarian, genealogist; b. Pemberville, Ohio, Jan. 19, 1947; d. Richard D. and Jessie Florence (Brown) Zepernick; m. Bruce William King, June 17, 1972; 1 child, Christian Andrew. BA, Bowling Green (Ohio) State U., 1969, MEd, 1976; MLS Kent State U., 1995. Cert. geneal. lectr. County extension agt. home econs. Ohio Coop. Extension Svc., Paulding County, 1970-77; asst. dir., historian Pemberville Pub. Libr.; mem. PRIDE com., vocat. home econs. dept. Paulding Exempted Village, 1975—; instr. genealogy Continuing Edn. Bowling Green State U., Eastwood Sch. Dist. Cmty. Edn. Mem. Paulding County Bicentennial Commn., 1975-77; organist 1st Presbyn. Ch., Pemberville, ruling elder, ch. historian; state chmn. Friends of Libr., 1992-95; advisor 4-H. Recipient Tenure award Coop. Extension Svc., 1975; mem. Wood County Citizen's Com. for Bicentennial of U.S. Constn. and NW Ordinance; mem. Pemberville Sch. Adv. Com.; sr. state historian Children of Am. Revolution; pres. Eastwood Local Schs. Band Boosters. Mem. ALA, Mary Sherman Hayes Soc. (sr. pres.), Flag of the U.S. of Am. (sr. state chmn., sr. state registrar 1994—), Libr. Adminstrn. and Mgmt. Assn., Children of the Am. Revolution, Ohio Geneal. Soc. (pres. Wood County chpt. 1978-80, chmn. pub. rels. chmn. 1982-83, chmn. First Families of Wood County com., state program chmn. ann. conf. 1991, 95, state chmn. History Writing Contest 1993, trustee 1995—), Berks County Geneal. Soc., Palatines to Am., DAR (vice regent chpt. 1975-77, regent chpt. 1979-83, registrar chpt. 1985—, state vice chmn. pages 1978-80, state chmn. lineage rsch. 1980-87, state and divsn. outstanding jr. mem. 1980, state chmn. membership commn. 1983-87, state recording sec. 1987-89, state corr. sec. 1989-92, area spkr.'s staff, state chmn. Friends of the Libr. 1992-95), U.S. Daus. of 1812 (chmn. state insignia), First Families Ohio, Daus. Union Vets., Nat. Soc. Magna Charta Dames, Colonial Dames 17th Century, Daus. Am. Colonists (chpt. regent 1986—, state chmn. pub. rels., 1987, chmn. mideast region pub. rels.), Bus. and Profl. Women's Club (pres. Paulding 1975-76, v.p. 1974-75), Ohio Libr. Assn., Coun. Ohio Genealogists (v.p. 1992—), Colonial Order Crown of Charlemagne, SAR (medal of Appreciation). Club: Order Eastern Star. Corr. docent DAR Mus., Washington. Home: 14553 N River Rd Pemberville OH 43450-9797

KING, LEA ANN, community volunteer and leader; b. Elkhart, Ind., July 26, 1941; d. Lloyd Emerson and Mildred Salome (Hostetler) Hartzler; children: Thomas Ellsworth III, Alden Elizabeth. BA in History, DePauw U., 1963. participant in Intensive Workshop in Intercultural Comm. U. Calif., Irvine, 1993, Study Tour of Ethnic Minorites of China, UCLA Extension, 1990; audited The Ethics of War and Peace, Ethikon Inst., Jerusalem, 1993; attended Three Intercultural Colloquia of Family Life, Cultural Diversity and Human Values, Ethikon Inst., 1989. Producer, hostess Pub. Access cable TV programs; travel writer, photographer. Bd. dirs., chair The Ethikon Inst. for Study of Ethical Diversity and Intercultural Rels.; pres. Vol. Ctr. S. Bay-Harbor-Long Beach, 1993-95; v.p. Comty. Assn. of the Peninsula, chair multicultural com., chair PV 2000; sec. Planned Parenthood L.A., 1991—; past pres. Jr. League L.A.; past chair San Pedro Peninsula Hosp. Found.; founding chair Forward-Looking Strategies for Women Coalition, 1985; co-chair United Way System Wide Admissions Com.; mem. Nordstrom's Com. for Salute to Cultural Diversity, L.A., 1993-95, diversity com. Planned Parenthood Fedn. We. Region, 1996. Named Woman of Yr. Nat. Women's Polit. Caucus, San Fernando Valley, 1986, South Bay YWCA; recipient John Anson Ford award L.A. County Commn. on Human Rels., 1992, Spirit of Volunteerism award Jr. League L.A., 1991, Founders award Vol. Ctrs. Calif., 1996, commendations from L.A. Mayor Tom Bradley, L.A. County Bd. Suprs., Calif. State Sen. Robert Beverly, Congressmen Dana Rohrabcher and Howard Berman; apptd. to L.A. County Commn. on Human Rels. by Supr. Deane Dana, 1993, 96. Home and Office: 49 Strawberry Ln Rolling Hills Estates CA 90274

KING, LINDA ORR, museum director; b. Washington, June 21, 1948; d. William Baxter and Jayne (Reiser) Orr; children: David, Adam, Lindsay. BA, La. State U., 1970, MA in Fine Arts, 1971. Fine arts history asst. La. State U., Baton Rouge, 1967-70, grad. asst., 1970-71; assoc. curator La. State Mus., New Orleans, 1971-74; curator Coastal Ga. Hist. Soc./Mus. Coastal History, St. Simons Island, 1984-87; dir. Coastal Ga. Hist. Soc., St. Simons Island, 1987—. Co-editor: (photograph essay) George Francois Mugnier, 1975. Pres. Glynn County Soc. of St. Vincent de Paul, 1990-94; mem. adv. coun. on hist. preservation Coastal Regional Devel. Commn., 1987—, chmn., 1994-96; mem. Glynn County Courthouse Renovation Com., 1989—; Ga. state dir. S.E. Mus. Conf., 1990-94, also membership chair; mem. adv. coun. Brunswick Downtown Devel. Authority; mem. Leadership Glynn, 1992; mem. Commn. on Preservation of Ga. State Capitol. Recipient Kellogg Career Enhancement award Kellogg Found., 1989, Leadership award Southeastern Mus. Conf., 1995; Internat. Partnership Among Museums fellow to Sierra Leone, 1992. Mem. Ga. Assn. Mus. and Galleries (treas. 1987-89, Mus. Profl. of Yr. 1993), Coastal Mus. Assn. (treas. 1987-89), Am. Assn. Mus., Low Country Mus. Network (treas. 1993—). Roman Catholic. Office: Mus of Coastal History PO Box 21136 Saint Simons Island GA 31522

KING, LIS SONDER, public relations executive, writer; b. Roskilde, Denmark; came to U.S., 1956, naturalized, 1961; d. Carl Otto and Gerda Vohnsen (Sonder) Petersen; m. Robert King (div. 1972); 1 dau., Dorte; m. Theodore Allin Pace, 1972; grad. Roskilde Katedralskole, arts degree Sch. Fine Arts, Copenhagen, 1952. Feature writer Berlingske Tidende, Copenhagen, 1956-58; reporter, editor Moreau Pub. Co., Bloomfield, N.J., 1957-59; reporter, editor St. Thomas (V.I.) Daily News, Island Times, San Juan, P.R., 1962-63; editor The Advance, Dover, N.J., 1961-63; pub. relations dir. Fluid Chem. Co., Newark, 1963-64, Keyes, Martin & Co., Springfield, N.J., 1964-69; pres. Lis King Pub. Relations, Mahwah, N.J., 1969—; columnist Harris Pubs., N.Y.C., 1981—, Suburban News, Paramus, N.J., 1986—. Author, editor: St. Thomas Directory, 1962; author: Furniture: Make-Do, Make-Over, Make Your Own, 1977; contbr. articles to various nat. pubs. Mem. Nat. Home Fashions League, Taxpayers Assn. Mahwah. Avocations: travel, gardening, reading, breeding Great Danes. Home and Office: 30 Dundee Ct PO Box 725 Mahwah NJ 07430-0725

KING, LUCY JANE, psychiatrist, health facility administrator; b. Vandalia, Ill., Dec. 23, 1932; d. Ira and Lucy Jane (Harris) K. AB, Washington U., St. Louis, 1954, MD, 1958. Diplomate Am. Bd. Psychiatry and Neurology, subspecialty Addiction Psychiatry. From instr. to assoc. prof. psychiatry dept. Washington U., 1963-74; prof. dept. psychiatry Med. Coll. of Va., Richmond, 1974-79; clin. prof. dept. psychiatry George Washington U., Washington, 1981-84, Ind. U. Med. Sch., 1994—; mem. editorial bd. Annals of Clin. Psychiatry, 1989—. Author: (with others) Psychiatry in Primary Care, 1983; contbr. articles to profl. jours. Fellow Am. Psychiat. Assn.; mem. Am. Acad. Clin. Psychiatrists, Am. Med. Women's Assn., Am. Acad. Addiction Psychiatry, Am. Soc. Addiction Medicine (cert., dual diagnosis com. 1990—). Office: Midtown CMHC 1001 W 10th St Indianapolis IN 46202

KING, MARCIA, management consultant; b. Lewiston, Maine, Aug. 4, 1940; d. Daniel Alden and Clarice Evelyn (Curtis) Barrell; m. Howard P. Lowell, Feb. 15, 1969 (div. 1980); m. Richard G. King Jr., Aug., 1980. BS, U. Maine, 1965; MSLS, Simmons Coll., 1967. Reference, field advisory and bookmobile libr. Maine State Libr., Augusta, 1965-69; dir. Lithgow Pub. Libr., Augusta, 1969-72; exec. sec. Maine Libr. Adv. Com., Maine State Libr., 1972-73; dir. Wayland (Mass.) Free Pub. Libr., 1973-76; state libr. State of Oreg., Salem, 1976-82; dir. Tucson Pub. Libr., 1982-91; mgmt. cons. King Assocs., Tucson, 1991—. Past chmn. bd. dirs. Tucson United Way; past chmn. adv. bd. com. Sta. KUAT (PBS-TV and Radio); mem. adv. bd. Resources for Women, Inc.; bd. dirs., past chmn. Salvation Army. Mem. ALA, Nat. Ctr. for Non-Profit Bds. Unitarian. Office: King Assocs 7130 N Camino Caballos Tucson AZ 85743

KING, MARCIA JONES, potter, physicist, photographer; b. Oak Park, Ill., May 17, 1934; d. Walter Leland Jones and Florence W. (Dull) Anderson; m. James Craig King, Nov., 1953 (div. 1966); 1 child, James Craig King, Jr. BS, Johns Hopkins U., 1960, PhD, 1969. Elec. engr. Electronic Communications, Inc., Timonium, Md., 1959-63; research assoc. theoretical particle physics Syracuse (N.Y.) U., 1969-72; asst. editor The Physical Rev. Brookhaven Nat. Lab., Upton, N.Y., 1972-74; physicist Argonne (Ill.) Nat. Lab., 1974-78; pvt. practice potter and physicist Syracuse, N.Y., 1978—. Contbr. articles to profl. jours.; exhibitor pots throughout cen. N.Y.; one-woman photography shows in Ctrl. N.Y. and So. Calif.; author: Nature's Telling: Anza-Borrego Desert, 1996. Mem. AAAS, Am. Physical Soc., Syracuse Ceramic Guild (pres. 1982-84), Phi Beta Kappa, Sigma Xi. Democrat. Home and Office: 228 Buckingham Ave Syracuse NY 13210-3024

KING, MARGARET ANN, communications educator; b. Marion, Ind., Feb. 27, 1936; d. Paul Milton and Janet Mary (Broderick) Burke; m. Charles Claude King, Aug. 25, 1956; children: C. Kevin, Elizabeth Ann, Paul S., Margaret C. Student, Ohio Dominican, 1953-56, U. Kans., 1980-81; BA in Communication, Purdue U., 1986, MA in Pub. Communication, 1990. Regional rep. Indpls. Juv. Justice Task Force, 1984-85; vis. instr. dept. communication Purdue U., West Lafayette, Ind., 1992; lectr. dept. communication, 1992—; bd. mem. Vis. Nurse Home Health Svcs. Grad. mem. Leadership Lafayette, 1983. Purdue U. fellow, 1986-87. Mem. AAUW, Speech Comm. Assn. Am., Ctrl. States Comm. Assn. (conf. presenter 1989), Golden Key, Phi Kappa Phi. Republican. Roman Catholic. Home: 1613 Redwood Ln Lafayette IN 47905-3939 Office: Purdue U Dept Communication West Lafayette IN 47907

KING, MARY LOU, artist, medical technologist; b. Vernon, Tex., Apr. 11, 1927; d. H. Raymond and Alma Vivian (Davenport) Hudson; m. Jack E. King, June 3, 1948; children: Paul Hudson, Karen Anne, Julie Louise. BS in Biology and Med. Tech., N. Tex. State U., 1948, Med. Technician, 1948; AS in Art, Midland (Tex.) Coll., 1987. Cert. med. technologist Am. Soc. Clin. Pathologists. Dept. head Santa Rosa Hosp., San Antonio, Tex., 1948-49; lab. dir. Drs. Offices, San Antonio, 1949-50; artist pvt. practice, Midland, 1986—. Painter landscapes in water colors; shown in 70 national and regional exhibitions, with 3 gallery representations. Bd. dirs. First United Meth. Ch., Midland, 1963-85, adult class leader and lay speaker, 1970—; Troop leader Girl Scouts U.S.A., Midland, 1958-75, officer, dir. coun., trainer, coord., 1968-80. Mem. Tex. Water Color Soc. (signature mem. 1987, regional del. 1995, mem. Purple Sage Soc. 1995), West Tex. Watercolor Soc. (signature mem. 1995), So. Watercolor Soc. (signature mem. 1993, regional del. 1988-89), Midland Arts Assn. (bd. dirs., officer 1983—), Arts Assembly of Midland (chmn. visual arts, mem. planning coun. 1983-86), Watercolor USA Hon. Soc. Home: 4513 Cardinal Ln Midland TX 79707

KING, MARY-CLAIRE, geneticist, educator; b. Evanston, Ill., Feb. 27, 1946; m. 1973; 1 child, Emily King Colwell. BA in Math., Carleton Coll., 1966; PhD in Genetics, U. Calif., Berkeley, 1973. Prof. Am. Cancer Soc., U. Wash., Seattle; mem. bd. sci. counselors Nat. Cancer Inst.; cons. Com. for Investigation of Disappearance of Persons, Govt. Argentina, Buenos Aires, 1984—. Contbr. more than 140 articles to profl. jours. Recipient Alumni Achievement award Carleton Coll. Mem. AAAS, Am. Soc. Human Genetics, Soc. Epidemiologic Research, Phi Beta Kappa, Sigma Xi. Office: U Wash Depts Medicine & Genetics Seattle WA 98101

KING, MONIQUE ANNE, librarian; b. San Francisco, July 5, 1965; d. Antoine and Maria Anna (Janssen) le Conge; m. Jon Benjamin King, June 11, 1988; children: Joshua Douglas, Marissa Rose, Gregory Alexander. BS in Design, U. Calif., Davis, 1987; MLIS, U. Calif., Berkeley, 1988. Librarian Solano County Lib., Fairfield, Calif., 1989-91; children's librarian Solano County Lib., Vallejo, Calif., 1991-94; young adult librarian Benicia (Calif.) Pub. Lib., 1994-95, youth svcs. librarian, 1995—; lib. cons. Benicia (Calif.) H.S., 1989. Editor, reviewer: (profl. review jour.) BayViews, 1992—. Mem. AAUW, ALA, Assn. Libr. Svc. Children (mem. com. Randolph Caldecott medal, Andrew Carnegie medal), Calif. Libr. Assn., Young Adult Libr. Svc. Assn. (com. YALSA trainer), Pub. Libr. Assn., Assn. Children's Librs. No. Calif. (pres. 1995-96), Bay Area Young Adult Reviewers. Republican. Roman Catholic. Office: Benicia Pub Lib 150 E L St Benicia CA 94510

KING, NANCY, communications educator; b. Blytheville, Ark., May 10, 1945; d. Willie Lee and Janie (Jones) Garrett; m. Perry King, June 17, 1967; children: Perry Jr., Tiffany, Christopher. BA in Speech Communication, Calif. State U., L.A., 1974, MA in Speech Communication, 1981. Asst. supr. Pacific Telegraph & Telephone, 1968-70; computer operator West Coast Community Exch. Fenton & Lavine, L.A., 1970-71; computer operator So. Gas Co., L.A., 1972-81, communication cons., 1982—; devel. lang. specialist Charles Drew Headstart Program, L.A.; assoc. prof. speech dept. Marymount Coll., Rancho Palos Verdes, Calif., 1986—; speechwriter various regional ofcls.; instr. Calif. State U., L.A., 1979-86; mem. Calif. Libr. Svcs. Bd., 1984-94, pres., 1988-89, 90-91; mem. Calif. Libr. Networking Task Force, 1985—, Calif. Librs. Adv. Bd., 1984-94, Orange County Friends of Libr. Found., 1988-94, Calif. Alliance for Literacy Task Force, 1988, 89. Contbr. articles to profl. jours. Co-chmn. black coun. Orange County Hist. and Cultural Found., pres. bd., 1992; campaign mgr. Fran Williams for Santa Ana City Coun. Mem. NEA, Nat. Speech Communication Assn., Western Speech Communication Assn., Am. Fedn. Tchrs., AAUW, L.A. Southcentral Planning Coun. (bd. dirs.). Republican. Roman Catholic. Office: Marymount Coll 30800 Palos Verdes Dr W Palos Verdes Peninsula CA 90274

KING, NAOMI MINNIE, artist, educator; b. L.A., June 5, 1913; d. Leander Leroy and Minnie M. (Dodge) Breard; m. Francis Hartford; 1 child, Margaret Mary Hartford Weintraub; m. John M. Riley; 1 child, John Martin Riley; m. J. Deane King. Fashion designer Milw., Dallas, L.A., 1945-62; owner Piccolinos, Glendale, Calif., 1962-73; curator pub. art Descanso Gardens, La Canada, Calif., 1979-81; artist, tchr. continuing edn. Santa Barbara (Calif.) City Coll., 1990-96. One woman shows include Descanso Hospitality House, 1981, Faulkner Gallery East, Santa Barbara, 1984, The Astra Gallery, 1985, 86, Downey Mus. Art, 1991, Alley Gallery, 1994; exhibited in group shows at Cabrillo Art Ctr., 1980, Reynolds Gallery, Santa Barbara, 1993, others; works included in archives of Nat. Mus. Women in the Arts, 1993.

KING, NINA DAVIS, journalist; b. Coco Solo, Panama, May 7, 1941; d. James White and Ruth (Steele) Davis. B.A. in French, U. N.C., 1963, M.A. in Comparative Lit. (Chancellors fellow), 1967; Ph.D. in English, Wayne State U., 1973. Lectr. Queens Coll., 1970-73; copy editor Newsday, L.I., N.Y., 1973-76; asst. news editor Newsday, 1976-77, asst. book rev. editor, 1977-79, book rev. editor, 1979-88; book editor The Washington Post, 1988—. Mem. Nat. Book Critics Circle, Phi Beta Kappa. Office: The Washington Post 1150 15th St NW Washington DC 20071-0001

KING, NORAH MCCANN, federal judge; b. Steubenville, Ohio, Aug. 13, 1949; d. Charles Bernard and Frances Marcella (Krumm) McCann; m. Tunney Lee King, Mar. 22, 1975; children: Catherine, Colin, Hilary, Adrienne. BA cum laude, Rosary Coll., 1971; JD summa cum laude, Ohio State U., 1975. Bar: Ohio 1975, So. Dist. of Ohio 1980. Law clerk U.S. Dist. Ct., Columbus, Ohio, 1975-79; counsel Frost, King, Freytag & Carpenter, Columbus, Ohio, 1979-82; asst. prof. Ohio State U., Columbus, Ohio, 1980-82; U.S. magistrate judge U.S. Dist. Ct., Columbus, Ohio, 1982—. Recipient award of merit Columbus Bar Assn., 1990. Mem. Coun. U.S. Magistrate Judges, Fed. Bar Assn. Office: US Dist Ct 85 Marconi Blvd Ste 351 Columbus OH 43215-2823

KING, SHARON L., lawyer; b. Ft. Wayne, Ind., Jan. 12, 1932. AB, Mt. Holyoke Coll., 1954; JD with distinction, Valparaiso U., 1957; LLM in Taxation, Georgetown U., 1961. Bar: Ind. 1957, D.C. 1958, Ill. 1962. Trial atty. tax divsn. U.S. Dept. Justice, 1958-62; ptnr. Sidley & Austin, Chgo. Fellow Am. Coll. Tax Counsel; mem. ABA (chmn. com. closely-held corps. taxation sect. 1979-81, regulated pub. utilities com. taxation sect. 1982-83, coun. dir. taxation sect. 1983-86), Chgo. Bar Assn. (bd. mgrs. 1973-75, chmn. fed. tax com. 1983-84), Ill. State Bar Assn. (counsel dir. sect. fed. taxation 1989-91), Women's Bar Assn. Ill. (bd. dirs. Found., v.p. Found., dir. scholarship). Office: Sidley & Austin 1 First National Plz Chicago IL 60603

KING, SHERI LYNN, counselor; b. Crawfordsville, Ind., Mar. 4, 1966; d. James Hubert Thomas and Karen Ann (Vance) Loden; m. Brian G. King, June 3, 1989; children: Jessica Marie, Jennifer Lynn. BA, Purdue U., 1988; MEd, U. N.C., Greensboro, 1994. Nat. cert. counselor. Exec. dir. Birghright Winston Salem, N.C., 1993—. Office: Birthright of Winston-Salem 129 Fayette St Winston Salem NC 27101

KING, SHERYL JAYNE, secondary education educator, counselor; b. East Grand Rapids, Mich., Oct. 29, 1945; d. Thomas Benton III and Bettyann Louise (Mains) K. BS in Family Living, Sociology, Secondary Edn., Cen. Mich. U., 1968, M in Counseling, 1971. Educator Newaygo (Mich.) Pub. Schs., 1968-72; interior decorator Sue King Interiors, Grand Rapids, Mich., 1972-73; dir. girl's unit Dillon Family and Youth Svcs., Tulsa, 1973-74; mgr. Fellowship Press, Grand Rapids, Minn., 1974-76; educator, counselor Itasca Community Coll., Grand Rapids, 1977-81; dept. head Dist. 318, Grand Rapids, 1977-81, 85-87; bd. dirs., chairperson program com. Marriage and Family Devel. Ctr., Grand Rapids, 1985-89. Treas. Cove Whole Foods Coop., 1978-80; chmn. bd. Christian Community Sch., 1977-78; jr. high softball coach, 1983-86; mem. issues com. No. Minn. Citizens League, Grand Rapids, 1984—, Blandin Found. Study, 1985-86; chairperson Itasca County Women's Consortium, Grand Rapids, 1983-87; Women's Day Conf., Grand Rapids, 1983-87; bd. dir. audio tech. Fellowship of Believers, Grand Rapids, 1974-87, 90—, deaconess, 1974—; bd. dir. audio tech Camp Dominion, Cass Lake, Minn., 1976-80; mem. fitness com., chmn. aquatic com., YMCA, Grand Rapids, 1974-87. Recipient 6 Outstanding Svc. awards Fellowship of Believers, 1974-79. Mem. Alpha Delta Kappa. Republican. Home: 1914 McKinney Lake Rd Grand Rapids MN 55744-4330

KING, SIDSEL ELIZABETH TAYLOR (BETH KING), hotel catering-hospitality professional; b. Edmonton, Alta., Can., July 27, 1932; d. Claude L. and Sadie (Hommy) Taylor; m. Otis A. King, Mar. 21, 1953; children: Ronald R., Lori Beth. AAS in Hotel Mgmt. and Food Svc Industry, U. Alaska, 1989. Sec. Sheriff's Office Courthouse, Edmonton, 1950-51; new accounts clk. First Nat. Bank Anchorage, 1952-53; sec., receptionist rate clk. Alaska Freight Lines, Anchorage, 1954-59; co-owner King's Rentals, Anchorage, 1953—; sec. State of Alaska Dept. Fish and Game, Anchorage, 1959-64, Anchorage Sch. Dist., West High, Wendler and East High, Anchorage, 1964—; exec. sec. Anchorage Daily News, 1969-70; with freight svc. Anchorage Slnd., 1970-71; caterer Clarion Hotel, Anchorage, 1989—; ambassador Clarion Hotel, Anchorage, 1991, Red Cross person, 1990-91. Preservation charter mem. Nat. Soc. Hist. Preservation, 1980's, Nat. Women in the Arts, Washington, 1980's, Nat. Secs. Assn. Anchorage, 1959—. Mem. Alaska Watercolor Soc., U. Alaska-Anchorage Alumni. Home: PO Box 244304 Anchorage AK 99524-4304 Office: Regal Alaskan Hotel 4800 Spenard Rd Anchorage AK 99517-3236

KING, SUSAN BENNETT, retired glass company executive; b. Sioux City, Iowa, Apr. 29, 1940; d. Francis Moffatt Bennett and Marjorie (Rittenhouse) Sillin; divorced. AB, Duke U., 1962. Legis. asst. U.S. Senate, Washington, 1963-66; dir. Nat. Com. for Effective Congress, Washington, 1967-71, Ctr. Pub. Financing of Election, Washington, 1972-75; exec. asst. to chmn. Fed. Election Commn., Washington, 1975-77; chmn. U.S. Consumer Product Safety Commn., Washington, 1978-81; dir. consumer affairs Corning (N.Y.) Glass Works, 1982, v.p. corp. communications, 1983-86; pres. Steuben Glass, N.Y.C., 1987-92; sr. v.p. corp. affairs Corning Inc., 1992-94; consumer affairs del. OECD, Paris, 1980-81; bd. dirs. Coca-Cola Corp., Guidant Corp., Health Effects Inst. Trustee Duke U., Durham, N.C., 1987—, Eurasia Found., Washington, Nat. Pub. Radio Found. Fellow Inst. Politics, Harvard U., 1981, Sanford Inst. Pub. Policy, Duke U., 1995-97. Mem. Nat. Consumers League (pres. 1984-85), Am. Alliance Rights and Responsibilities.

KING CALKINS, CAROL COLEMAN, health science association administrator; b. L.A., May 31, 1949; d. Harold S. and Gladys (Blumenthal) Coleman; 1 child, Katrina Elizabeth King; m. Michael Steven Calkins, Oct. 10, 1987. BA in Psychology, U. Colo., 1972; MBA, U. No. Colo., 1982. Dir. group living Nat. Jewish Ctr. Immunology and Respiratory Medicine, Denver, 1980-82; dir. clin. support svcs. Nat. Jewish Ctr. Immunology and Respiratory Medicine, 1982-83, dir. spl. projects, 1983-84, asst. dir. adminstrv. svcs., 1984, dir. adminstrv. svcs., 1984-95; dir. facilities svcs. U. Colo. Health Scis. Ctr., Denver, 1995—; chair purchasing and contract subcom. Denver Health and Hosps. New Authority, 1994-96; speaker in field. Recorder improvement process coun. Jefferson County (Colo.) Schs., 1989. Mem. Colo. Hosp. Assn. Risk Mgrs., Am. Coll. Healthcare Execs., Assn. Commuter Transp. (v.p. Rocky Mountain chpt. 1992). Office: 1400 Jackson St Denver CO 80206-2761

KING-COOPER, JENNIFER LAINE, educator; b. Pitts., Sept. 6, 1950; d. Donald Frederick and Nancy Elaine (Clark) King; m. Timothy Dean Cooper, Dec. 27, 1986. BA, Allegheny Coll., 1972; MA, Bowling Green State U., 1973; PhD, U. Pitts., 1986, The Union Inst., 1995. Residence hall dir. Bowling Green State U., Bowling Green, Ohio, 1973-77; asst. dir. student life svcs. Wilmington (Ohio) Coll., 1977-78; dir. residence life Allegheny Coll., Meadville, Pa., 1978-82; asst. to dean for student affairs U. Cin. Clermont Coll., Batavia, Ohio, 1983-86; lectr. psychology U. Cin., Batavia, Ohio, 1985-86; admissions coord. The Union Inst., Cin., 1987-94, adj. instr., 1987—; co-facilitator Domestic Safety Program, Marathon, Fla., 1995-96. Author: Explorations in Voice: Women's Psychosocial Development, 1995. Vol. mem. Clermont 2001 Health Care Subcom., Clermont County, Ohio, 1989-90; disaster vol. Am. Red Cross, Greater Miami, Fla., 1995. Mem. NOW (sec. Fla. Keys chpt. 1995-96), Nat. Womens Studies Assn., Nat. Assn. for Women in Edn. Home and Office: care Mapes 586 Randolph St Wilmington OH 45177

KINGDON, MARY ONEIDA GRACE, elementary education educator; b. Canton, Ohio, Aug. 11, 1934; d. Virgil Ezra and Donnie Mabel (Rowe) Sell; m. Harold Ivor Edwin Kingdon, Feb. 22, 1957; children: Sheryl Lynn, Harold Ivor Edwin Jr., Jill Renée, James Todd Ezra. BA in History and Social Sci., Houghton Coll., 1956; postgrad., U. Ky., 1963-67, SUNY, Geneseo, 1969-71; MS in Edn., Alfred U., 1983. Cert. permanent N-6 elem. tchr., reading tchr., N.Y. Tchr. English, Cherry Street City Sch., Canton, 1956-57; tchr. English Mercer County Pub. Sch., Harrodsburg, Ky., 1963-64, Cardinal Valley Fayette County Sch., Lexington, Ky., 1965-67; intermediate tchr. Friendship (N.Y.) Cen. Sch., 1967—; primary tchr. Bearss Acad., Jackson, Miss., 1983-84. Mem. N.Y. State Tchrs. Retirement Assn. (Allegany and Cattaraugus counties del. 1985—), N.Y. State Union Tchrs., Friendship Cen. Sch. Tchrs. Assn. (sec. 1970-72, pres. 1982-83, 92-93). Republican. Mem. Wesleyan Ch. Home: RR 1 Box 14K Houghton NY 14744-9711 Office: Friendship Cen Sch Friendship NY 14735

KINGDON-LABAY, ALICE MARIE, computer lab aide; b. Vermillion, S.D., June 14, 1951; d. Frederick William and Lorraine Ellen (Brady) Kingdon; m. Gerald Adam Labay, Nov. 19, 1971; children: Adam Scott, Alan Frank. BS, Calif. State U., San Francisco, 1971; AA, L.A. City Coll., 1982. Gen. mgr. Advance Music Co., San Francisco, 1972-75; microbiologist Cutter Labs., Berkeley, Calif., 1975-79; microcomputer tech. Computerama, Burbank, Calif., 1980-82; field svc. engr. Digital Equipment Corp., Oakland, Calif., 1982-84; computer lab. aide Robert Semple Sch., Benicia, Calif., 1995—; mem. tech. com. Robert Semple Sch., 1993-95. Sem. Robert Semple Sch. Site Coun., 1992-94; mem. La Leche League, 1984—. NSF scholar, 1968, Clarinet scholar U. Nev., Reno, 1969-71. Mem. LWV, NOW, AAUW. Home: 475 Rinconada Ct Benicia CA 94510 Office: Robert Semple Elem Sch 2015 E 3d St Benicia CA 94510

KING-JOHNSON, SONIA ELISE, academic director; b. Lead Vale Christ Church, Barbados, Jan. 1, 1967; came to U.S., 1985; d. Selwyn George Powlett and Miriam Matilda (King) Taylor; m. Douglas L. Johnson, Jr., June 30, 1991. BS in Mktg., S.C. State U., 1988, MS in Agribus., 1990. Rsch. specialist S.C. State U., Orangeburg, 1991-93; dir. planned giving Claflin Coll., Orangeburg, 1993—; mem. S.C. Planned Giving Coun., Columbia, 1993—; chair Heritage Coun., Orangeburg, 1993—; mem. CASE Dist. III, Atlanta, 1993—. Mem. Nat. Planned Giving Coun., Delta Sigma Theta. Home: 1258 Lake Cir Orangeburg SC 29115 Office: Claflin Coll 700 College Ave Orangeburg SC 29115

KINGORE, EDITH LOUISE, retired geriatrics and rehabilitation nurse; b. Parsons, Kans., Nov. 18, 1922; d. George Richard and Josephine (Martin) K. Diploma, Mo. Meth. Hosp., St. Joseph, 1955. RN. Staff nurse El Cerrito Hosp., Long Beach, Calif., 1966-69; nurse Alamitos-Belmont Convalescent Hosp., Long Beach, 1973-75; staff nurse Freeman Hosp., Joplin, Mo., 1975-76, Oak Hill Osteo. Hosp., Joplin, 1976-77; surg. care and rehab. nurse St. Francis Med. Ctr., Cape Guiardo, Mo., 1977-78; psychiat. nurse Western Mo. Mental Health Ctr., Kansas City, Mo., 1978; pvt. duty nurse, 1978-83. Historian South Coast Ecumenical Coun., 1993-94. Home: 3333 Pacific Pl Apt 108 Long Beach CA 90806-1261

KINGRY, BETH, social worker; b. Dothan, Ala., June 23, 1946; d. Jack and Ella Mae (Jenkins) Kingry; children: Brian M. Williams and Wade K. Williams. BS in Psychology, Huntingdon Coll., 1968. lic. social worker, Ala. Social worker Dept. Human Resources, Ozark, Ala., 1968-69, child welfare worker, 1969-70; chpt. I tchr. Dothan City Schs., 1987-90; social worker Dept. Human Resources, Abbeville, Ala., 1990-92, svc. supr., 1992—; bd. dirs. S.E. Ala. Child Advocacy Ctr., Dothan, 1991—; mem. health coun. Henry County Nursing Home, Abbeville, 1992—; multi-needs team chmn. Dept. Human Resources, Abbeville, 1994—; adv. bd. Settlement, Midland City, Ala., 1994—.

KINGSLEY, AMY COMSTOCK, financial analyst; b. Gloversville, N.Y., Aug. 23, 1966; d. John Alonzo and Arlene (Thomas) Comstock; m. John David Kingsley, Oct. 3, 1992. BA in Math., Cornell U., 1987. Fin. analyst Equitable Life Assurance Soc., N.Y.C., 1987-90, Fed. Res. Bank Boston, 1990—. Mem. Phi Beta Kappa, Phi Kappa Phi.

KINGSLEY, EMILY PERL, writer; b. N.Y.C., Feb. 28, 1940; d. Alan F. and Florence (Schneider) Perl; m. Edwin H. Kaplin, July 15, 1963 (div. Feb. 1970); m. Charles R. Kingsley, June 25, 1972; 1 child, Jason. BA, Queens Coll., 1960. Book prodn. staff Harper, Harcourt Brace and Random House, N.Y.C., 1960-63; prodn. asst. Talent Assocs., N.Y.C., 1963-66; assoc. producer Everybody's Talking ABC-TV, L.A., 1966-67; researcher Dick Cavett Show ABC-TV, N.Y.C., 1967; talent coord. Emmy Awards Show CBS-TV, N.Y.C., 1970; writer Sesame Street Children's TV Workshop, N.Y.C., 1970—. Author teleplay Kids Like These, 1987 (Christopher award 1988, 1st prize Rehab. Internat. Film Festival, Arc of Excellence award Nat. Assn. for Retarded Citizens of U.S., Nat. Easter Seals award). Co-chair Parent Assistance Com. on Downs Syndrome, White Plains, N.Y., 1976—; bd. dirs. Nat. Downs Syndrome Congress, chair adoption com., 1979-88. Recipient 11 Emmy awards, 6 Emmy award nominations NATAS, Exceptional Svc. award Nat. Down Syndrome Congress, 1985, Media award MCCJ/ARC; named Humanitarian of the Yr., Girl Scouts U.S., 1988, Joseph P. Kennedy award, 1991. Home and Office: 226 S Greeley Ave Chappaqua NY 10514-3333

KINGSOLVER, BARBARA ELLEN, writer; b. Annapolis, Md., Apr. 8, 1955; d. Wendell and Virginia (Henry) K.; m. Joseph John Hoffmann, Apr. 15, 1985 (div.); 1 child, Camille. BA, DePauw U., 1977; MS, U. Ariz., 1981; LittD (hon.), DePauw U., 1994. Sci. writer U. Ariz., Tucson, 1981-85; free-lance journalist Tucson, 1985-87, novelist, 1987—; book reviewer N.Y. Times, 1988—, L.A. Times, 1989—. Author: The Bean Trees, 1988 (Enoch Pratt Libr. Youth-to-Youth award 1988, ALA award 1988), Homeland and Other Stories, 1969 (ALA award 1990), Holding the Line: Women in the Great Arizona Mine Strike of 1983, 89, Animal Dreams, 1990 (PEN West Fiction award 1991, Edward Abbey Ecofiction award 1991), Another America, 1992, Pigs in Heaven, 1993 (L.A. Times Fiction prize 1993, Mountains and Plains Fiction award 1993, Western Heritage award 1993, ABBY Honor Book 1994), Essays, High Tide in Tucson, 1995. Recipient Feature-writing award Ariz. Press Club, 1986; citation of accomplishment UN Nat. Coun. of Women, 1989; Woodrow Wilson Found./Lila Wallace fellow, 1992-93. Mem. PEN Ctr. USA West, Nat. Authors Guild, Nat. Writers Union, Phi Beta Kappa. Home and Office: PO Box 31870 Tucson AZ 85751*

KINGSTON, MAXINE HONG, author; b. Stockton, Calif., Oct. 27, 1940; d. Tom and Ying Lan (Chew) Hong; m. Earll Kingston, Nov. 23, 1962; 1 child, Joseph Lawrence. B.A., U. Calif., Berkeley, 1962; hon. doctoral degrees, Ea. Mich. U., 1988, Colby Coll., 1990, Brandeis U., 1991, U. Mass., 1991, Starr King Sch. for the Ministry, 1992. Tchr. English, Sunset High Sch., Hayward, Calif., 1965-66, Kahuku (Hawaii) High Sch., 1967, Kahaluu (Hawaii) Drop-In Sch., 1968, Kailua (Hawaii) High Sch., 1969, Honolulu Bus. Coll., 1969, Mid-Pacific Inst., Honolulu, 1970-77; prof. English, vis. writer U. Hawaii, Honolulu, 1977; Thelma McCandless Disting. Prof. Eastern Mich. U., Ypsilanti, 1986, Chancellor's Disting. Prof. U. Calif., Berkeley, 1990—. Author: The Woman Warrior: Memoirs of a Girlhood Among Ghosts, 1976 (Nat. Book Critics Cir. award for non-fiction; cited by Time mag., N.Y. Times Book Rev. and Asian Mail as one of best books of yr. and decade), China Men, 1981 (Nat. Book award; runner-up for Pulitzer prize, Nat. Book Critics Cir. award nominee 1988), Hawai' One Summer, 1987 (Western Books Exhbn. Book award, Book Builders West Book award), Tripmaster Monkey-His Fake Book, 1989 (PEN West award in Fiction), Through the Black Curtain, 1988; contbr. short stories, articles and poems to mags. and jours., including Iowa Rev., The New Yorker, Am. Heritage Redbook, Mother Jones, Caliban, Mich. Quarterly, Ms., The Hungry Mind Rev., N.Y. Times, L.A. Times, Zyzzyva; prodr. The Woman Warrior, Berkeley Repertory Co., 1994, The Huntington Theater, Boston, 1994, The Mark Taper Forum, L.A., 1995. Guggenheim fellow, 1981; recipient Nat. Endowment for the Arts Writers award, 1980, 82, Mademoiselle mag. award, 1977, Anisfield Wolf Book award, 1978, Calif. Arts Commn. award, 1981, Hawaii award for lit., 1982, Calif. Gov.'s award art, 1989, Major Book Collection award Brandeis U. Nat. Women's Com., 1990, award lit. Am. Acad. & Inst. Arts & Letters, 1990, Lila Wallace Reader's Digest Writing award, 1992, 93-95, Spl. Achievement Oakland Bus. Arts award, 1994; named Living Treasure Hawaii, 1980, Woman of Yr. Asian Pacific Women's Network, 1981, Cyril Magnin award for Outstanding Achievment in the Arts, 1996, Disting. Artists award The Music Ctr. of L.A. County, 1996. Office: Univ Calif Dept English 322 Wheeler Hall Berkeley CA 94720

KINION, MICHELLE, graphic designer, training specialist; b. Oct. 10, 1972; d. Stephen Ray and Carol Lee (Collins) K. Assoc. Degree, Okla. State U., Okmulgee, 1995. Stocker Six Star, Colorado Springs, Colo., 1990; restaurant worker Peter Piper's Pizza, Colorado Springs, 1990, Bogey's Hamburgers, Broken Arrow, Okla., 1990-91; muralist Woodland Park Home, Tulsa, 1991-92; habilitation tng. specialist Developmental Svcs. Tulsa, 1992-96, ResCare of Okla., Tulsa, 1995—; developer 1 WilTel Internat Svcs., 1996. Mem. Phi Theta Kappa.

KINKADE, JILL ANNETTE, writer, artist, educator; b. Evansville, Ind., Nov. 5, 1961; d. Jack Neal and Carolyn A. (Hess) Kroeger; m. C. Lynn Kinkade, Oct. 10, 1987. BA summa cum laude, Hunter Coll., 1995; MA, U. Louisville, 1995—. Owner Lady Day Cafe, Evansville, Ind., 1984-86; bookkeeper Alpha Lumber, Astoria, N.Y., 1987-89; mgr. gift shop Cabrini Med. Ctr., N.Y.C., 1989-93; info. and referral specialist United Cerebral Palsy of N.J., Trenton, 1994; mktg. resources rep. Atlantic City C.C., 1995; English composition instr. U. Louisville, 1995—. Author: The Olivetree Rev., 1994. Mem. Phi Beta Kappa. Home: 1206 Parrett St Evansville IN 47713

KINLAW, HILDA HESTER, primary education educator; b. Elizabethtown, N.C., June 21, 1938; d. Joseph Woodrow and Mildred Lucille (Butler) Hester; m. William Robert Kinlaw, Aug. 2, 1957; children: Richard William, Gary Lynn, Lisa Faye. Grad. in cosmetology, Fayetteville Beauty Acad., 1957; BS, Pembroke (N.C.) State U., 1976, K-12 reading cert., MEd, 1979. Cosmetologist, Dublin, N.C., 1957-59, 60-76; sec. Edwards Store, Charleston, S.C., 1959-60; K-6 tchr. reading Bladen County Schs., Elizabethtown, 1960-76, tchr., 1983-90, 91—. Adv. bd. Bladen County Nursing Homes, 1990-93, Bladen County Hosp., 1990—; fund chmn. Dublin (N.C.) Area Heart Fund, 1985; area chmn. bike-a-thon St. Jude Hosp. Recipient NCAE human rels. commn. dist. 13 award Bladen County, 1983. Mem. ASCD, N.C. Assn. Educators, Homemakers Club. Home: PO Box 237 Dublin NC 28332-0237 Office: P O Box 27347 Raleigh NC 27611

KINNEY, JANIS MARIE, librarian, consultant, storyteller; b. Cresson, Pa., Dec. 26, 1935; d. Cecil and Ruth Ellen (Moyer) Powell; m. James Leroy Kinney; 1 child, Janis Cecilia. BS in Libr. Sci., Clarion U., 1957; MEd in Curriculum and Instrn., Pa. State U., 1987. Librarian N. Huntingdon Sch. Dist., Irwin, Pa., 1957-58, Greater Gallitzin (Pa.) Schs., 1959-61, Hollidaysburg (Pa.) Area Sch. Dist., 1961-90; storyteller Altoona, Pa., 1990—; chair Allegheny Storytellers of Pa., 1991—; rostered artist Pa. Coun. on the Arts in Edn. Program; cons. various sch. dists. Author/producer audio cassettes; featured teller Corn Island Storytelling Festivals, Louisville; contbr. articles to profl. jours. Active Blair County Arts Found., Altoona, 1991—, Blair County Tourist & Conv. Bur., 1992—, Blair County Hist. Soc., 1994—; Railroaders Meml. Mus., 1993—, Pa. Rural Arts Alliance, 1992—. Mem. Internat. Order E.A.R.S., Nat. Storytelling Assn., Allegheny Storytellers Pa. Home and Office: 1900 16th Ave Altoona PA 16601-2502

KINNEY, LISA FRANCES, lawyer; b. Laramie, Wyo., Mar. 13, 1951; d. Irvin Wayne and Phyllis (Poe) K.; m. Rodney Philip Lang, Feb. 5, 1971; children: Cambria Helen, Shelby Robert, Eli Wayne. BA, U. Wyo., 1973, JD, 1986; MLS, U. Oreg., 1975. Reference libr. U. Wyo. Sci. Libr., Laramie, 1975-76; outreach dir. Albany County Libr., Laramie, 1975-76, dir., 1977-83; mem. Wyo. State Senate, Laramie, 1984-94, minority leader, 1992-94, with documentation office Am. Heritage Ctr. U. Wyo., 1991-94; assoc. Corthell & King, Laramie, 1994-96; ptnr. Corthell & King, 1996—; owner Summit Bar Rev., 1987—. Author: (with Rodney Lang) Civil Rights of the Developmentally Disabled, 1986; (with Rodney Lang and Phyllis Kinney) Manual For Families with Emotionally Disturbed and Mentally Ill Relatives, 1988, rev. 1991; Lobby For Your Library; Know What Works, 1992; contbr. articles to profl. jours; editor, compiler pub. relations directory for ALA, 1982. Bd. dirs. Big Bros./Big Sisters, Laramie, 1980-83, Am. Heritage Ctr., Children's Mus., Laramie Area C. of C., 1996—. Recipient Beginning Young Profl. award Mt. Plains Libr. Assn., 1980; named Outstanding Wyo. Libr. Wyo. Libr. Assn., 1977, Outstanding Young Woman State of Wyo., 1980. Mem. ABA, Nat. Confs. of State Legislatures (various coms. 1985-90). Democrat. Avocations: photography, dance, reading, traveling, languages. Home: 2358 Jefferson St Laramie WY 82070-6420 Office: Corthell & King 221 S 2nd St Laramie WY 82070-3610

KINNEY, MARJORIE SHARON, marketing executive, artist; b. Gary, Ind., Jan. 11, 1940; d. David H. and Florence C. Dunning; student El Camino Coll., 1957, 58; LHD (hon.), West Coast U., 1982, Coll. San Mateo, 1987-88; MBA, Pepperdine U., 1989; m. Daniel D. Kinney, Dec. 31, 1958 (div. 1973); children: Steven Daniel, Michael Alan, Gregory Lincoln, Bradford David; m. Bradley Thomas Jr., Nov. 9, 1985 (div. Apr. 1987). Ptnr., Kinney Advt. Inc., Inglewood, Calif., 1958-68; pres. Greeters of Am., 1967-69; chmn. Person to Person Inc., Cleve., 1969-72; pres. Kinney Mktg. Corp., Encino, Calif., 1972-80; sr. v.p. Beverly Hills (Calif.) Savs. & Loan Assn., 1980-84; chmn., pres. Kinney & Assocs., Dana Point, Calif., 1985—; dir. Safeway Stores, Inc., Chubb/Pacific Indemnity Co.; freelance artist; motivational spkr. Neurosurg. Soc. Am., Buick, Anheuser Busch, YPO, Lawyers Title; lectr. Contbr. lic. artwork to maj. corps. including Ritz Carlton. Bd. dirs. ARC, 1976-81, United Way, 1979-81; trustee West Coast U.; v.p., trustee Capistrano Valley Symphony, 1989—; adv. bd. U.S. Human Resources, Womens Legal Edn. Fund; briefing del. to Pentagon Fed. Res. Dept. and White House, 1986; pres. Santa Fe Rep. Women, 1987; co-chair Childcare Action Day, 1986; participant Women of Faith and Courage, program for homeless girls, 1987—; chair Caps for Calypso, clothing project for homeless, 1988, Artist's Benefit Tour for Laura's House, 1995; v.p. Laguna Beach Art-A-Fair, 1992-94. Presbyterian. Office: 357 Baywood Dr Newport Beach CA 92660

KINNEY, MARTHA ELIZABETH, data management executive, consultant; b. Greeneville, Tenn., Aug. 25, 1963; d. James William and Lois Marie (Bouknight) K. BA with hons., Converse Coll., 1984; postgrad., Calif. State U., Hayward, 1995—. Data mgr. Littler, Mendelson et al, San Francisco, 1988-91; data coord. Levine & Fricke, Emeryville, Calif., 1991-94; pres. CEO Kinney Resources, Hayward, Calif., 1994—. Lt. U.S. Army, 1984-88; capt. USAR, 1988-96, maj. 1996—. Mem. NAFE, AAUW, Am. Hist. Assn., Mortar Bd. Republican. Roman Catholic.

KINNEY, MARY MAY, secondary education educator; b. Lebanon, Mo., Apr. 11, 1954; d, Oscar Junior and Rilda May (Moss) Kelso; m. Richard L. Kinney, Oct. 11, 1986; children: Jesse Ryan, Kyle Thomas. BS in Social Sci. Edn. and English, S.W. Bapt. Coll., Bolivar, Mo., 1977. Cert. social sci. and English tchr. 7-12, Mo. Tchr. English and history Macks Creek (Mo.) Sch., 1977—. Mem. Nat. Coun. Social Studies, Mo. Coun. Social Studies, Mo. State Tchrs. Assn., Macks Creek Cmty. Tchrs. Assn., PTA. Republican. Mem. Assembly of God Ch. Office: Macks Creek Sch Box 38 N Rd Macks Creek MO 65786

KINNEY, SHIRLEY STRUM, academic administrator. Pres. Sch. Medicine SUNY, Stony Brook. Office: SUNY Health Scis Ctr Stony Brook NY 11794-8430*

KINO, MARY MAYUMI, psychometrician; b. Tokyo, Oct. 27, 1962; came to U.S., 1969; d. George Yoichi and Mitzie Michiko (Uemoto) K. BA, U. Chgo., 1985, BS, 1985; MA, Mich. State U., 1987, PhD, 1993. Cons. Mich. Dept. Edn., Lansing, 1987-90; rsch. assoc. SMSO-Third Internat. Math. and Sci. Study, East Lansing, Mich., 1990-93; project dir. Psychol. Corp., San Antonio, 1993-96; mgr. data analysis Advanced Systems in Measurement and Evaluation Inc., Dover, N.H., 1996—. Contbr. chpts. to books Meta-Analysis for Explanation: A Casebook, 1990, NATD 1990 Symposium: Issues in Large Scale Assessment Programs, 1990. Mem. Zonta Internat., San Antonio, 1993-96, bd. dirs. San Antonio chpt., 1994-96. William W. Turnbull Disting. fellow Ednl. Testing Svc., Princeton, N.J., 1989, ETS Summer predoctoral fellow, 1989. Mem. Am. Ednl. Rsch. Assn., Nat. Coun. on Measurement in Edn., Spl. Interest Group Rasch Measurement. Home: 10 Sunrise Dr Rochester NH 03867 Office: Advanced Sys in Measurement Evaluation Inc 171 Watson Rd Dover NH 03820

KINOSIAN, JANET MARIE, journalist; b. Los Angeles, June 20, 1957; d. Kasper John and Carol Grace (Boghosian) K. BA in Psychology, UCLA, 1980; MA in Psychology, Loyola Marymount, 1987. Intern L.A. Mag., 1980-81; staff writer Orange County Media Group, Costa Mesa, Calif., 1982-84; contbg. editor Orange Coast Mag., Costa Mesa, Calif., 1984-91, Palm Springs Life mag., 1984—; pres. JMK & Co., Brentwood, Calif., 1991—. Contbr. numerous articles to regional and nat. mags. and newspapers; extensive reporting, writing L.A. Times; internationally syndicated by N.Am. Syndicate, Times of London, N.Y. Times Syndicate, L.A. Times Syndicate. Co-founder Campus Coalition for Peace, 1978, Internat. Women's Coalition, 1979; mem. Amnesty Internat., 1980-94, Child Help USA, 1985-94, Free Arts for Abused Children, 1991-94. Mem. APA, L.A. Press Club, Hollywood Women's Press Club, Calif. Assn. Ind. Writers, Am. Soc. Journalists, Pi Beta Phi.. Democrat. Presbyterian. Home and Office: 18001 Leafwood Ln Santa Ana CA 92705-2005

KINSER, CYNTHIA D., judge; b. Pennington Gap, Dec. 20, 1951; d. Morris and Velda (Myers) Fannon; m. H. Allen Kinser, Jr., March 17, 1974; children: Charles Adam, Terah Diane. Student, Univ. of Ga., 1970-71; BA, Univ. of Tenn., 1974; JD, Univ. of Va., 1977. Bar: Va. 1977, U.S. Dist. Ct. (we. dist.) Va. 1977, U.S. Ct. Appeals (4th cir.) 1977, U.S. Supreme Ct. 1988. Law clk. to Judge Glen M. Williams U.S. Dist. Ct., 1977-78; pvt. law practice, 1978-90; commonwealth's atty. Lee County, Va., 1980-83; magistrate judge U.S. Dist. Ct. (we. dist.) Va., Abingdon, 1990—; trustee Chapter 7 Panel, U.S. Bankruptcy Ct., 1979-90. Mem. Va. Bar Assn., Va. Trial Lawyers Assn., Am. Bar Assn. Methodist. Office: US District Court PO Box 846 Abingdon VA 24212*

KINSEY, JULIA CATHERINE, medical records coding specialist; b. Midland, Tex., Jan. 12, 1957; d. Hershel H. and Julia Blackford (Jette) K.; m. Bryce Douglas Welch, Apr. 3, 1993. Student Plan II honors Program, U. Tex., 1975-77. Cert. coding specialist. Instr. English conversation Lang. House, Inc., Takamatsu, Japan, 1978; med. transcriptionist Brackenridge Hosp., Austin, Tex., 1979-82, St. David's Hosp., Austin, 1982-84; coding technician St. David's Health Care Sys., Austin, 1984-94, Health Info. Assocs. LLC, Richardson, Tex., 1995—. Mem. Am. Assn. Med. Transcription (organizer, 1st pres. local chpt. 1983-84), Am. Health Info. Mgmt. Assn., Soc. Clin. Coding, Tex. Health Info. Mgmt. Assn., Am. Acad. Procedural Coders, Am. Hosp. Assn., Soto Zen. Soto Zen. Office: Austin Coding Coop PO Box 4540 Lago Vista TX 78645

KINSLOW, MARGIE ANN, volunteer worker; b. Salt Lake City, Dec. 7, 1931; d. Diamond and Sarah (Chipman) Wendelboe; m. James Ferol Kinslow, Apr. 6, 1954 (dec. July 1982). Student, U. Utah, 1949-53. Jr. vol. chmn. various hosps., Okla., Mont., Colo., 1967-81; pres. Ch. Woman's Orgn., Bartlesville, Okla., 1968; fin. advisor, v.p., vol. chmn. Swedish Med. Ctr., Englewood, 1971-92; pres. Delta Gamma Alumnae, Denver, 1975-76; jr. vol. chair Colo. Assn. Hosp. Aux., Denver, 1977-82, 2d v.p., 1982-84; transp. chair, master class chmn. Rocky Mountain Regional Auditions, Met. Opera, Denver, 1986—. Office vol. Rep. Office, Billings, Mont., 1969-70, Colo. Senator, Denver, 1974-76; vol. various polit. candidates, Denver, 1974-90; various offices Newcomers, Okla., Mont. and Colo., 1967-75. Mem. PEO, Gen. Fedn. of Women's Clubs (bd. dirs. 1994-96), Colo. Fedn. of Women's Clubs (pres. 1994-96, various offices 1986-94), Denver Lyric Opera Guild, Cherry Creek Woman's Club (pres. 1985), Littleton Rep. Women's Club, Delta Gamma Alumnae (pres. 1975-76, Stellar award 1979, Cable award 1991). Episcopalian.

KINSMAN, SARAH MARKHAM, investment company executive; b. L.A., Oct. 1, 1951; d. Robert Starr and Barbara Ann (Yates) K.; m. Kevin H. Olsen, Oct. 15, 1984 (div.); 1 child, Robert Kinsman. AB, UCLA, 1973; MBA, Harvard U., Boston, 1976. Account officer Citibank's World Corp. Group, N.Y.C., 1976-79; fin. mgr. Union Pacific Corp., N.Y.C., 1980-86; v.p./sr. transactor Citibank, N.A., N.Y.C., 1986-88; v.p. Bank N.Y., N.Y.C., 1988-92; sr. v.p. GE Capital, N.Y.C., 1992—. Com. chmn. Jr. League, N.Y.C., 1988—; mem. women's com. Am. Cancer Soc., N.Y.C., 1988-90; Cub Scout den leader Boy Scouts Am. Mem. Assn. for Corp. Growth, Women's Harvard Bus. Sch. Club N.Y.C., Harvard Bus. Sch. Club N.Y.C., Harvard Bus. Sch. Club N.J., Phi Beta Kappa. Home: 2 Rowlands Rd Flemington NJ 08822-7020 Office: GE Capital 335 Madison Ave New York NY 10017-4605

KINZELL, LA MOYNE B., school health services administrator, educator; b. Melstone, Mont., May 4, 1930; d. William Edward and Iro Millicent (Keeton) Berger; m. Les Kieth Kinzell, Sept. 18, 1954; children: Yvette Li Goins, Anitra Elise Chew, Antony Mikhail Kinzell. BS, Mont. State U., 1954; MA, Calif. State U., 1982. RN, Calif. Instr. surg. nursing Mont. Deaconess Hosp., Great Falls, 1954-55; instr. nursing arts St. Patrick's Hosp., Missoula, Mont., 1957-59; instr. sci. Palmdale (Calif.) Sch. Dist., 1966-86, dir. health svcs., 1986—; adv. bd. facilitator Palmdale Healthy

Start, 1992—; com. mem. Am. Cancer Soc., 1986—, United Way, 1991—. Mem. Citizen Amb. Sch. Nursing Del. to Europe, 1994; treas. campaign sch. bd. mem., Palmdale, 1989, 93. Recipient Tchr. of Yr. award Palmdale, 1985-86, La. County Sheriffs Dept. award, 1985, Nat. Every Child by Two, Immunization Ptnrs. award, 1995; grantee Drug, Alcohol and Tobacco Edn., 1987, Healthy Start Planning, 1994, 95, Healthy Start Operational award, 1996. Mem. Am. Lung Assn. (chair edn. 1988-94), Calif. Sch. Nurse Orgn. (sec. 1992-95), Phi Kappa Phi, Alpha Tau Delta, Sigma Theta Tau, Delta Kappa Gamma (chair legislature 1993-95, area IX dir. 1995-97). Democrat. Episcopalian. Home: 38817 2nd St E Palmdale CA 93550-3201 Office: Palmdale Sch Dist 39139-49 10th St E Palmdale CA 93550

KINZIE, JEANNIE JONES, radiation oncologist; b. Great Falls, Mont., Mar. 14, 1940; d. James Wayne and Lillian Alice (Young) Jones; m. Joseph Lee Kinzie, Mar. 26, 1965 (div. Sept. 1982); 1 child, Daniel Joseph; m. Johnson Wachira, Oct. 7, 1991. Student, Oreg. State U., 1960; BS, Mont. State U., 1961; MD, Washington U., 1965; postgrad., U. Phoenix, 1995—. Diplomate Am. Bd. Radiology. Intern. in surgery U. N.C., Chapel Hill, 1965-66; resident in therapeutic radiology Washington U., St. Louis, 1968-71, instr. in radiology, 1971-73; asst. prof. in radiology Med. Coll. of Wis., Milw., 1973-75; asst. prof. in radiology U. Chgo., 1975-78, assoc. prof. in radiology, 1978-80; assoc. prof. of radiation oncology Wayne State U., Detroit, 1980-85; prof. radiology U. Colo., Denver, 1985-95; dir. radiation oncology U. Hosp., Denver, 1985-91; cons. Denver Vets. Hosp., Denver Gen. Hosp., Rose Med. Ctr., FDA Ctr. for Devices and Radiologic Health, Denver; sci. adv. bd. Cancer League Colo., 1985-88; examiner Am. Bd. Radiology, 1985-88; adv. physician Colo. Med. Found., 1988—; chmn. faculty promotion com. U. Colo. Health Scis. Ctr., 1988-89. Assoc. editor Internat. Jour. Radiation Oncology Biology and Physics, 1985-95; contbr. articles to profl. jours.; chpts. to books. NIH grantee, 1973-75; Am. Coll. Radiology fellow, 1984; fellow nuclear medicine U. Colo., 1996—. Mem. AMA, Colo. Med. Soc., Denver Med. Soc. (del. to Colo. Med. Soc. Ho. of Dels. 1989—), Am. Coll. Radiology, Colo. Radiol. Soc., Rocky Mountain Oncology Soc. (bd. dirs. 1989-93, pres. 1991-93), Soc. Head and Neck Surgeons, Am. Radium Soc., Am. Soc. Therapeutic Radiologists, Am. Cancer Soc. (bd. dirs. Denver unit 1986-87), Am. Soc. Clin. Oncology, Wilderness Med. Soc., Xeriscape Colo. Republican. Lutheran. Home: PO Box 2767 Evergreen CO 80437-2767 Office: Nuclear Medicine Box A034 4200 E 9th Ave Denver CO 80262

KIPPER, BARBARA LEVY, corporate executive; b. Chgo., July 16, 1942; d. Charles and Ruth (Doctoroff) Levy; m. David A. Kipper, Sept. 9, 1974; children: Talia Rose, Tamar Judith. BA, U. Mich., 1964. Reporter Chgo. Sun-Times, 1964-67; photo editor Cosmopolitan Mag., N.Y.C., 1969-71; vice chmn. Chas Levy Co., Chgo., 1984-86, chmn., 1986—; pres. Charles and Ruth Levy Found.; life dir. The Joffrey Ballet of Chgo. Mem. exec. com. Spertus Inst. Jewish Studies, Golden Apple Found.; life dir. The Joffrey Ballet of Chgo.; trustee Chgo. Hist. Soc. Recipient Deborah award Com. Women's Equality, Am. Jewish Congress, 1992, Shap Shapiro Human Rels. award The Anti-Defamation League of B'nai B'rith, 1993, WSFRE's Chgo. chpt. Disting. Philanthropist award, 1995. Mem. Nat. Found. Fund Raising Execs. (disting. philanthropist 1995), Com. of 200, Coun. on Founds., Chgo. Women in Philanthropy, Econ. Club of Chgo., Chgo. Found. for Women, Chgo. Network, Women's Issues Network, The Standard Club. Jewish. Office: Chas Levy Co 1200 N North Branch St Chicago IL 60622-2410

KIRBY, DIANA CHERNE, nurse, retired military officer; b. Guttenberg, Iowa, Jan. 22, 1951; d. Albert Edward and Bernadette Lucretia (Berns) Cherne; BS in Nursing, U. Iowa, 1973; MS in Edn., U. So. Calif., 1977; MS in Nursing, U. Md., 1987; lic. pilot; m. Fred W. Kirby, Nov. 24, 1981. Mem. nursing staff Mercy Med. Ctr., Dubuque, Iowa, 1973-74; commd. 1st lt. Nurse Corps, U.S. Army, 1974, advanced through grades to lt. col., 1991; service in W. Ger.; community health nurse William Beaumont Army Med. Center, 1978-80, Ft. Leonard Wood, Mo., 1980-82, Ft. Meade, Md., 1987; chief community nursing Dewitt Army Community Hosp., Ft. Belvoir, Va., 1987-92, Korea, 1992-93; community health nurse Walter Reed Army Med. Ctr., Washington, 1993-95; pub. health nurse Fairfax County (Va.) Health Dept., 1995—; cons. community health nursing. Mem. APHA, Am. Nurses Assn., Va. Nurses Assn., Nat. Trust for Hist. Preservation, Am. Philatelic Soc., Sigma Theta Tau. Roman Catholic. Address: 6833 Silver Ann Dr Lorton VA 22079-1311

KIRBY, KATE PAGE, physicist; b. Washington, Dec. 5, 1945; d. Vance Nathaniel and Harriet (Geary) K.; m. Arch William Horst, May 21, 1977; children: Andrew, Elizabeth, Carolyn, Jonathan. AB, Radcliffe Coll., 1967; MS, U. Chgo., 1968, PhD, 1972. Postdoctoral fellow Harvard U. Observatory, Cambridge, Mass., 1972-73; rsch. physicist Smithsonian Astrophys. Observatory, Cambridge, 1973—; lectr. dept. astronomy Harvard U., Cambridge, 1973-83, 84-86; assoc. dir. Harvard-Smithsonian Ctr. for Astrophysics, Cambridge, 1988—. Contbr. articles to profl. jours. Fellow Am. Phys. Soc. (sec.-treas. div. atomic, molecular and optical physics 1984-87, chmn. membership com. 1989-90). Office: Harvard-Smithsonian Ctr Astrophy 60 Garden St Cambridge MA 02138-1596

KIRBY, KATHERINE LEIGH, marketing/sales incentives executive; b. Dearborn, Mich., Aug. 12, 1965; d. Douglas T. and Rebecca A. (Hartley) Heinrichs; m. John J. Kirby IV, Mar. 4, 1995. BA in English, So. Ill. U., 1988, MS in Speech Comm., 1990. Asst. to v.p. The NutraSweet Co., Deerfield, Ill., 1992-94; sr. sales coord. The NutraSweet Co., Deerfield, 1994-95; project dir. Maritz Performance Improvement Co., Fenton, Mo., 1995—. Office: Maritz Perform Improvt Co Mktg Support Svcs Divsn Tng Divsn Fenton MO 63026

KIRBY, MARY WEEKS, elementary education educator, reading specialist; b. Cheverly, Md., Nov. 23, 1947; d. Isaac Ralph and Dorothea (Huppert) Weeks; m. William Charlie Kirby, Feb. 14, 1976; children: Joie, Fatimah, Tariq. B in Music Edn., James Madison U., 1969; MEd, Va. Commonwealth U., 1976; cert. Writers' Digest Sch., 1988. Cert. tchr. of music, reading and elem., Va. Music instr. Charles City County Schs., Providence Forge, Va., 1969-70, Hanover Learning Ctr., Va., 1970-72; sales cons. Boykins's Music Shop, Richmond, Va., 1972-74; elem. tchr. New Kent Pub. Schs., Va., 1974—, writing cons., 1980—; owner/operator Wacky Timepieces; presenter ednl. and reading workshops, 1980-82, 95. Sponsor Young Authors' Workshop, New Kent, 1985—; co-chmn., presentor Parents Anonymous of Va., 1984-88; trustee Islamic Ctr. of Va., 1985-88, sec., 1981-85, prin. Islamic Sch., 1995—; active Boy Scouts Am., Girl Scouts U.S., U.S. Naval Sea Cadet Corps. Mem. NEA, New Kent Edn. Assn. (officer 1977-81, 90-92, 94-95), Va. Edn. Assn., Internat. Reading Assn., Va. State Reading Assn., Richmond Area Reading Council (sec. 1982-83, bd. dirs. 1992—), Sigma Alpha Iota (life). Avocations: needlework, reading, swimming. Home: 1309 Bull Run Dr Richmond VA 23231-5103 Office: New Kent Pub Schs New Kent VA 23124

KIRBY, PAULETTE LINDENBERG, special education educator, English language educator; b. Fredericksburg, Tex., Oct. 22, 1946; d. Paul August and Irene Christine (Dreyer) Lindenberg; m. Andrew Harrison Kirby II, Sept. 22, 1967; children: Andrew Harrison III, Paul Chad. BA, Sam Houston State U., Huntsville, Tex., 1992. Cert. tchr., Tex. Mem. Coun. for Exceptional Children, Alpha Chi, Kappa Delta Pi, Sigma Delta Tau. Lutheran. Home: 3407 Willow Run Montgomery TX 77356

KIRBY, RENEÉ MARIE SARTIN, disability services administrator; b. Milw., Oct. 15, 1959; d. Obbie B. and Ethelen Mary (McClain) Sartin; m. Lawrence Lee Kirby, June 30, 1979; children: Lawrence II, Charisse. BS in Exceptional Edn. magna cum laude, U. Wis., Milw., 1984; MA in Edn., Viterbo Coll., 1992; postgrad., U. Wis., Milw., 1993—. Cert. learning disabilities educator, K-8. Dental asst. Dr. F.V. Campbell, Sr., Milw., 1976-78; learning disabilities tchr. grades 4-6 Milw. Pub. Schs., 1984; learning disabilities tchr. grades 7-8 Racine (Wis.) Unified Sch. Dist., 1984-89; exec. trainer BPI, Inc., Atlanta, 1989-91; coord. disability svcs. U. Wis.-Parkside, Kenosha, 1991—; mem. program rev. Racine Literacy Coun., 1993. Mem. State Rehab. Planning and Adv. Coun., 1996—. Mem. ASCD, NAACP, Nat. Assn. of the Deaf, Nat. Alliance for Mentally Ill, Assn. on Higher Edn. and Disability. Baptist. Home: 5014 Indian Hills Dr Racine WI 53406-2330 Office: U of Wis-Parkside Box 2000 900 Wood Rd Kenosha WI 53141

KIRBY, SARAH ANN VAN DEVENTER, aerospace engineer; b. Champaign, Ill., Mar. 10, 1961; d. David Bruce Kirby and Florence May Van Deventer. BS in Aerospace Engrng., U. Mich., 1983; MEd, U. Houston, Clear Lake, 1989. Space systems ops. engr. NASA/JSC-MOD, Houston, 1983—. Contbr. articles to profl. jours. Bd. dirs. Hidden Cove Homeowners Assn., Friendswood, Tex., 1991—. Mem. AIAA (sr.). Home: 45 Hideaway Dr Friendswood TX 77546-4868 Office: NASA JSC Mail Code DF83 Houston TX 77058

KIRCHER, ANNE CATHERINE, communications consultant; b. Portland, Oreg., Dec. 27, 1962; d. John Lawrence and Helen (Morris) K. Student, U. N.Mex., 1981-83. Planning and rsch. clk. Albuquerque Pub. Schs., 1985-89, desktop publisher, designer, 1989-90; pub. info. and comm. cons. Presbyn. Healthcare Svcs., Albuquerque, 1990—. Mem. N.Mex. Soc. Healthcare Mktg. and Pub. Rels. (sec. 1994-95, v.p. 1995). Home: 1405 San Carlos Dr SW # 2 Albuquerque NM 87104-1060 Office: Presbyn Healthcare Svcs 5901 Harper Dr NE Albuquerque NM 87109-3587

KIRCHNER, TERESA ANN, pharmacist; b. Belleville, Ill., Mar. 13, 1961; d. John P. and Joan L. (Osterhaut) K. Student, Hudson Valley C.C., Troy, N.Y., 1978-80; AAS in Animal Husbandry, SUNY, Cobleskill, 1981; BS in Animal Sci., U. Mass., Amherst, 1983; BS in Pharmacy, Albany Coll. Pharmacy, 1989. Registered pharmacist, N.Y. Lab. technician rsch. Albany Med. Coll., 1983-84; teller Cohoes (N.Y.) Savs. Bank, 1984-87; pharmacy intern Meml. Hosp., Albany, 1987-89; animal technician Shaker Vet. Hosp., Latham, N.Y., 1987-90; pharmacist Mary McClellan Hosp., Cambridge, N.Y., 1990, Samaritan (N.Y.) Hosp., 1990—. Mem. N.Y. Soc. Health Profls. Home: 142 North Rd Averill Park NY 12018 Office: Samaritan Hosp 2215 Burdett Ave Troy NY 12180

KIRDANI, ESTHER MAY, school counselor; b. Nunda, N.Y., Aug. 27, 1936; d. Herbert Stewart and Sarah Edith (Veley) Stewart Kernahan; m. Rashad Y. Kirdani, Aug. 16, 1958; children: Lavinia Helen, Leila Andrea. BS in Home Econs. Edn., SUNY Coll., Buffalo, 1958; MEd in Secondary Guidance, U. Buffalo, 1972. Permanent cert. home econs. edn. and secondary sch. guidance. Tchr. home econs. Royalton-Hartland (N.Y.) Cen. Sch., 1958-60; tchr. math. Grafton (Mass.) Jr. H.S., 1962-65, Clarence (N.Y.) Jr. H.S., 1967-68; sch. counselor West Seneca (N.Y.) Sch. Dist., 1973—. Mem. ACA, Am. Sch. Counselor Assn., Western N.Y. Guidance Dirs. and Chairpersons (coord. 1987-94). Home: 44 Buttonwood Ln East Amherst NY 14051

KIRK, CAROL, state official, lawyer; b. Henry, Ill., Dec. 23, 1937; d. Howard P. and Mildred Root McQuilkin; m. Robert James Kirk, Aug. 20, 1961; children: Kathleen, Nancy, Sally. BS in Music Edn., U. Ill., 1960; JD, Ind. U., Indpls., 1989. Bar: Ind. 1989. Pvt. piano tchr., 1957-85, pub. sch. music tchr., 1960-62; dir. Ind. State Ethics Commn., Indpls., 1989—; pres. Coun. on Govtl. Ethics Laws, (Internat.), 1993-94. Exec. editor Articles & Prodn. Ind. Law Rev., 1988-89. Mem. Met. Devel. Commn., Indpls., 1982-87; chairperson Pub. Radio Adv. Bd., Indpls., 1983-84, treas. Cmty. Svc. Coun., Indpls., 1988-91. Invitee to Nat. 4H Congress, Chgo., 1956; named 4H Family of Yr., Washington Twp., 4-H, Indpls., 1980, Vol. of Week, Voluntary Action Ctr., Indpls., 1980. Mem. LWV (pres. Indpls. 1979-83), Ind, Bar Assn., Indpls. Bar Assn., Phi Alpha Delta, Mu Phi Epsilon. Office: State Ethics Commn 402 W Washington Rm W189 Indianapolis IN 46204

KIRK, FLORA KAY STUDE, artist, accountant, insurance company official; b. San Diego, Feb. 16, 1944; d. Lawrence Wilbur Stude and Lois Eileen (Johnson) Plunkett; m. Bobby Gene Kirkpatrick, Feb. 16, 1960 (div. 1974); children: Jeffery Lane, Ladina B.J. Kirkpatrick Wingfield; m. Charles Robert Kirk, June 11, 1977 (div.); 1 child, Robert Marcel. Student, Western Tex. Coll., 1973-74, Ft. Hays (Kans.) State Coll., 1974-75, U. Nebr., Kearney, 1988; AA, Mid-Plains C.C., North Platte, Nebr., 1987. Decorator, Snyder, Tex., 1960-73; bookkeeper, office mgr. Tri-State Constrn., Snyder, 1973-75; acct. Aid Feed Yard, Syracuse, Kans., 1975-77; agt., broker Woodmen Accident & Life Ins. Co., Lincoln, Nebr., 1977—; owner, mgr., artist Kirk's Pottery and Painting Studio, North Platte, 1984—; acct., corp. sec.-treas. Profl. Ag Products, Inc., North Platte, 1988-93; chmn. bd. Artists Coop. Art & Gift Gallery, North Platte, 1987—; ceramics & painting instr. Mid Plains C.C., 1992—; mem. artist Artists in Embassies Program, Washington, 1991, 92; artist Carolyn Nelson Galleries, Pasadena, Calif., 1992, Robert Henri Mus., Conad, Nebr., 1996. One-woman show Art & Gift Gallery, 1987-96, Morin-Miller Galleries, N.Y.C., 1989, Gt. Plains Regional Med. Ctr., 1989-96, Bismark State Coll., Arroyo Theatre Gallery, L.A., 1993, 94, Pen & Brush Club, 1995, Broom St. Gallery, N.Y.C., 1995, U.S. Senate, 1995, Vanderbilt Mus., 1995, Noyes Gallery, Lincoln, Nebr., 1995-96, Robert Henri Mus., Crozad, Nebr., 1996; exhibited in group shows Fiske Planetarium, Boulder (recipient 1st place award 1992-94, 1st pl. in 1993-94), Nat. Arts Club, N.Y.C., 1987, ARiel Gallery, N.Y.C., 1988, Univ. Place Gallery, Lincoln, 1990-93, Gallery 525, Loveland, Colo., 1990, 91, C.W. Post Coll., L.I. U., 1990, U. Colo., 1990, Jacob Javits Fed. Bldg. Gallery, N.Y.C., 1991-92, U.S. Ho. Reps., Washington, 1992, 94, 95, Antiquarium Gallery, Omaha, Artel Gallery, White Crane Gallery, Omaha, 1993, Cork Gallery, Lincoln Ctr. Performing Arts, N.Y.C., Arroyo Theatre Gallery, L.A., 1993, 94; represented in permanent collections Mus. Cultural Exch., Cairo, Prarie Peace Park, Lincoln, Bismark State Coll. Chmn. North Platte Arts and Humanities Coun., 1991-92; vol. Kerry for Pres. Campaign, North Platte, 1992. Mem. Soc. Exptl. Artists, Nat. Soc. Painters in Casein and Acrylic (assoc.), Nat. Watercolor Soc. (assoc.), Visual Individual United (1st place award 1992), The Artel (merit award 1991), North Platte Art Guild, Platter Painters Art Club (pres. 1987-88, 1st place award 1987-91), Assn. Nebr. Art Clubs, Phi Theta Kappa. Democrat. Home: 1021 W 4th St North Platte NE 69101-3715

KIRK, JANET BROWN, artist, educator, art gallery owner; b. Cisco, Tex., Oct. 3, 1929; d. Olen Benjamin Brown and Evelyn (White) Pitman; m. Glenn L. Kirk, Aug. 5, 1949; children: David Patrick, Dennis Paul, Steven Lloyd, Lisa Evelyn Nave. Student, U. Colo., 1973, 74, 76, Metro State Coll., 1978, 80, Rocky Mountain Sch. Art., 1982. instr. art classes and workshops, Wyo., Colo., 1982—; gallery affiliations Cornerstone Gallery, Longmont, 1970-92, Wild Basin Gallery, Allenspark, Colo., 1988-91, Eastin Gallery, Allenspark, 1992—, Profl. Galleries, St. Cloud, Minn., 1989—, J. Michaels Gallery, Edina, Minn., 1989—, San Juan Art Ctr., Ridgeway, Colo., 1992, Gwendolyn's Art Gallery Ltd., Lake City, Colo., 1993—. Exhibited in one person shows Niwot (Colo.) Art Gallery, 1982, Santa Fe Gallery, Odessa, Tex., 1984, Cornerstone Gallery, Longmont, Colo., 1988; exhibited in group shows The COORS Show, Golden, Colo., 1988, Colo. Artists ABS Shows, Loveland, 1988, 89, Denver, 1991, Colo. Watercolor Soc. Show, Botanical Gardens, Denver, 1992-96, Colo. Artists Guild State Hist. Mus. Show, Denver, 1992, New England Art Inst. State of the Arts 1993, Boston, 1993, Colo. Watercolor Soc. State Show, 1996; represented in permanent collections Citi-Corp., USA, Energy Div., Denver, John Cox Drilling Co., Midland, others. Bd. mem. Longmont (Colo.) Coun. for the Arts, 1990-91; speaker and demonstrator in field. Recipient Purchase award Glenwood Springs (Colo.) Art Show, 1992. Mem. Am. Watercolor Soc. (assoc.), Nat. Watercolor Soc. (assoc.), Southwest Watercolor Soc. (assoc.), Colo. Watercolor Soc. (qualified signature membership 1995), Western Colo. Watercolor Soc., Colo. Art Guild, Coun. on Arts and Humanities (bd. mem. 1990-92), Colo. Artists Assn. (regional rep. 1982-86, exec. bd. mem. 1986—, Juror's Choice award State Conv. 1991, Spl. Merit award State Conv. 1992). Home: 719 3rd Ave Longmont CO 80501-5926

KIRK, JENNIFER JOY, employee benefits specialist; b. Valencia, Pa., Apr. 14, 1955; d. Maxwell Harry and Hazel Mae (Leisie) Burford; m. Stewart A. Kirk, Sept. 19, 1981; children: Nathan S., Rachel N. AAS, Butler County C.C., 1975; BS in Bus. Adminstrn., Robert Morris Coll., 1979, MBA, 1992. Cert. employee benefits specialist, compensation profl. Libr. aide Butler County C.C., Butler, Pa., 1973-75; accounts receivable and cost acctg. clk. John R. Ellison & Sons, Inc., Butler, 1975-78; tax acct. Silvermen's Menswear,Inc., Warrendale, Pa., 1978; cost acct. Halstead Industries, Inc., Zelienople, Pa., 1978-83, payroll and benefits supr., 1983-86, supr. employee benefits, 1986-89; benefits mgr. Mine Safety Appliances Co., Pitts., 1989—; instr. part-time Robert Morris Coll. Fellow Internat. Soc. Cert. Employee Benefit Specialists; mem. Inst. Mgmt. Accts., Pitts. Person. Assn., Pitts. Internat. Soc. Cert. Employee Benefit Specialists, Am. Compensation Assn. (instr.). Republican. Mem. Christian Missionary Alliance Ch. Home: 127 Burford Ln Valencia PA 16059-8820 Office: Mine Safety Appliances Co RIDC Indsl Park 121 Gamma Dr Pittsburgh PA 15238-2919

KIRK, LYNDA POUNDS, biofeedback therapist, neurotherapist; b. Corpus Christi, Tex., Dec. 17, 1946; d. James Arthur and Elizabeth Pauline (Sanders) Pounds; m. Edward C. Randolph Kirk, June 10, 1967; children: Leslie Jennifer, Edward Christopher. BA, U. Tex., Austin, 1977; MA, St. Edwards U., 1996. Therapist Austin (Tex.) State Hosp., 1977-80; dir. stress mgmt. The Hills Med./Sports Complex, Austin, 1980-82; founder, owner Austin Biofeedback Ctr., 1982—, Health Mastery Concepts, Austin, 1982—; cons. State of Tex., Austin, 1983—, City of Austin, 1985—, Lower Colo. River Authority, Austin, 1984—. Author: (book/cassette series) Regenerative Relaxation, 1981; Urological Applications of Biofeedback, Stress Mastery and Peak Performance, 1986. Bd. dirs. South Austin Polit. Action Coalition, 1986-87, South Austin Civic Club, 1983—, pres., 1987; bd. dirs., treas. Texans for the Preservation of Hist. Structures, 1990—; bd. dirs. Austin Ctr. for Attitudinal Healing, 1992—. Mem. Assn. Applied Psychophysiology and Biofeedback, Internat. Soc. for Study of Subtle Energies and Energy Medicine, Biofeedback Soc. Tex. (pres. 1995—, mem. exec. bd., citation award 1989), Behavioral Medicine Soc. Am., Am. Holistic Med. Assn., Biofeedback Cert. Inst. Am., Assn. Cert. QEEG Technologists, Soc. for Study of Neuronal Regulation, Acad. Cert. Neurotherapists, Phi Beta Kappa. Episcopalian. Home: 420 Brady Ln Austin TX 78746-5502 Office: Austin Biofeedback Ctr 3624 N Hills Dr Ste B205 Austin TX 78731

KIRK, REA HELENE (REA HELENE GLAZER), special education educator; b. N.Y.C., Nov. 17, 1944; d. Benjamin and Lillian (Kellis) Glazer; 3 stepdaughters. BA, UCLA, 1966; MA, Eastern Mont. Coll., 1981; EdD U. So. Calif., 1995. Life cert. spl. edn. tchr., Calif., Mont. Spl. edn. tchr., L.A., 1966-73; clin. sec. speech and lang. clinic, Missoula, Mont., 1973-75; spl. edn. tchr., Missoula and Gt. Falls, Mont., 1975-82; br. mgr. YWCA of L.A., Beverly Hills, Calif., 1989-91; sch. adminstrn., ednl. coord. Adv. Schs. of Calif., 1991-94; dir. Woman's Resource Ctr., Gt. Falls, Mont., 1981-82; dir. Battered Woman's Shelter, Rock Springs, Wyo., 1982-84; dir. Battered Victims Program Sweetwater County, Wyo., 1984-88, Battered Woman's Program, San Gabriel Valley, Calif., 1988, Spl. Edn., Pasadena, 1994-96, prin., 1995; instr. U. Wis., 1996—; mem. Wyo. Commn. on Aging, Rock Springs; mem. Community Action Bd. City of L.A. Pres., bd. dirs. battered woman's shelter, Gt. Falls, Woman's Resource Ctr., Gt. Falls; founder, advisor Rape Action Line, Gt. Falls; founder Jewish religious svcs., Missoula; 4-H leader; hostess Friendship Force; Friendship Force ambassador, Wyo., Fed. Republic Germany, Italy; mem. YWCA Mont. and Wyo. Recipient Gladys Byron scholar U. So. Calif., 1993, Dept. Edn. scholar U. So. Calif., 1994, honors Missoula 4-H; recognized as significant Wyo. woman as social justice reformer and peace activist Sweetwater County, Wyo.; nominated Wyo. Woman of the Yr., 1981, 82; honored by L.A. Mayor Bradley for Anti-Poverty work. Mem. Council for Exceptional Children (v.p. Gt. Falls 1981-82), Assn. for Children with Learning Disabilities (Named Oustanding Mem. 1982), Phi Delta Kappa, Delta Kappa Gamma, Psi Chi, Pi Lamda Theta. Democrat. Jewish.

KIRK-DUGGAN, CHERYL ANN, religious studies educator; b. Lake Charles, La., July 24, 1951; d. Rudolph Valentino and Naomi Ruth (Mosely) Kirk; m. Michael Allan Duggan, Jan. 1, 1983. BA, U. S.W. La., 1973; MS, U. Tex., 1977; MDiv, Austin Presbyn. Theol. Sem., 1987; PhD, Baylor U., 1992. Ordained minister Christian Meth. Episcopal Ch., 1984. Instr. Prairie View (Tex.) A&M U., 1977-78; pvt. music instr. N.Y.C., Austin, Tex., 1979-85; asst. prof. Meredith Coll., Raleigh, N.C., 1993-97; organist, music dir. Russell Meml. Christian Meth. Episcopal Ch., Durham, N.C., 1979—, assoc. pastor, 1993—. Author: African American Special Days: 15 Complete Worship Services, 1996, It's In the Blood: A Trilogy of Poetry Harvested from a Family Tree, 1996; mem. editorial bd. Contagion: Jour. Violence, Mimeses and Culture, 1994—. Coolidge scholar Assn. for Religion and Intellectual Life rsch. colloquium Yale, 1996; Lily scholar, 1994-96. Mem. Am. Soc. Aesthetics, Am. Acad. Religion, Soc. Christian Ethics, Ctr. Black Music Rsch., Soc. Biblical Lit., Colloquium on Violence & Religion, Soc. Study Black Religion, Golden Key Honor Soc. (W.T. and Ethel L. Burton Scholarship), Sigma Alpha Iota. Office: Grad Theol Union Ctr for Women and Religion 2400 Ridge Rd Berkeley CA 94709

KIRKHAM, M. B., plant physiologist, educator; b. Cedar Rapids, Iowa; d. Don and Mary Elizabeth (Erwin) K. BA with honors, Wellesley Coll.; MS, U. Wis., PhD. Cert. profl. agronomist. Plant physiologist U.S. EPA, Cin., 1973-74; asst. prof. U. Mass., Amherst, 1974-76, Okla. State U., Stillwater, 1976-80; from assoc. prof. to prof. Kans. State U., Manhattan, 1980—; guest lectr. Inst. Water Conservancy and Hydroelectric Power Rsch., Inst. Farm Irrigation Rsch., China, 1985, Inst. Exptl. Agronomy, Italy, 1989, Agrl. U. Wageningen, Inst. for Soil Fertility, Haren, The Netherlands, 1991, Massey U., New Zealand, 1991; William A. Albrecht seminar spkr. U. Mo., 1994; vis. scholar Biol. Labs., Harvard U., 1990; vis. scientist environ. physics sect. dept. sci. and indsl. rsch., Palmerston North, New Zealand, 1991; participant Internat. Grassland Congress, New Zealand, 15th Internat. Congress of Soil Sci., Apaculco, Mex., 13th Internat. Soil Tillage Rsch. Orgn. Conf., Aalborg, Denmark; spkr. Internat. Symposium on Plant Growth and Environ., Seoul, 1993; peer rev. panel mem. USDA/Nat. Rsch. Initiative, Washington, 1994. Cons. editor Plant and Soil Jour., 1979—; mem. editl. bd. Field Crops Rsch. Jour., 1983-91; mem. editl. adv. bd. Trends in Agrl. Scis.-Agronomy, 1992—; contbr. over 160 articles and papers to sci. jours. NSF postdoctoral fellow U. Wis., 1971-73, Nat. Def. Edn. Art fellowship, E.I. du Pont de Nemours and Co. summer faculty fellow, 1976, grantee NSF, USDA, Office Water Rsch. and Tech., U.S. Dept. Energy, Dept. Sic. and INdsl. Rsch., New Zealand; invited paper Internat. Grasslands Congress, New Zealand. Fellow AAAS, Am. Soc. Agronomy (editorial bd. 1985-90), Soil Sci. Soc. Am. (travel grantee to internat. congress Japan 1990), Royal Meteorol. Soc., Crop Sci. Soc. Am. (editorial bd. 1980-84); mem. Am. Soc. Plant Physiology (editorial bd. 1982-87), Am. Soc. Horticultural Sci., Internat. Soil Tillage Rsch. Organ., Internat. Soil Sci. Soc. (elected 1st vice chmn. commn. soil physics 1994—), Bot. Soc. Am., Am. Meteorol. Soc., Société Française de Physiologie Végétale, Japanese Soc. Plant Physiology, Scandinavian Soc. Plant Physiology, N.Y. Acad. Sci., Soc. for Exptl. Biology (London), Growth Regulator Soc. Am., Water Environment Fedn., Phi Kappa Phi, Gamma Sigma Delta, Sigma Xi. Home: 1420 Mccain Ln Apt 244 Manhattan KS 66502-4680 Office: Kans State U Dept Agronomy Throckmorton Hall Manhattan KS 66505-5501

KIRKIEN-RZESZOTARSKI, ALICIA MARIA, academic administrator, researcher, educator; b. Lodz, Poland; came to U.S., 1965; d. Leszek Tadeusz and Francesca Irene (Mortkowicz) Kirkien. MS in Chem. Engring., Polish U. Coll., London, 1951; PhD, U. London, 1955. Asst. prof. chemistry U. W.I., Jamaica, 1956-59, assoc. prof., 1959-61; assoc. prof. U. W.I., Trinidad, 1961-65; assoc. prof. Trinity Coll., Washington, 1966-68, prof. chemistry, 1968-92, chair chemistry dept., 1969-91, prof. emeritus, 1992—; sr. rsch. assoc. George Washington U. Med. Ctr., Washington, 1984. One person show at Trinity Coll., Washington, 1994; watercolors and oils exhibited in show at Sorrento, Italy, 1994, 96, Karistos, Greece, 1993; contbr. numerous articles to profl. publs. Sec., treas. Polish Vets. ASSC, Washington, 1981-83. Named one of Outstanding Educators of Am., 1973, 75; Univ. Coll. Sr. Rsch. fellow, 1965-66, 71, UCSB, 1967. Fellow Royal Inst. Chem. (Gt. Britain); mem. Md. Fedn. Art (Critics Choice award for pottery 1992), Am. Chem. Soc. (adv. bd. Chem. and Engring. News 1978-81), Chem. Soc. Gt. Britain, Polish Inst. Arts and Scis. of N.Y., Phi Beta Kappa. Republican. Roman Catholic. Home: 407 Buckspur Ct Millersville MD 21108-1764 Office: Trinity Coll 125 Michigan Ave NW Washington DC 20010-2916

KIRKLAND, BERTHA THERESA, project engineer; b. San Francisco; d. Lawrence and Theresa (Kanzler) Schmelzer; m. Thornton C. Kirkland, Jr., Dec. 27, 1937 (dec. July 1971); children: Kathryn Elizabeth, Francis Charles. Ed. pub. schs., Calif. Supr. hosp. ops. Am. Potash & Chem. Corp., Trona, Calif., 1953-54; office mgr., estimator T.C. Kirkland, elect. contractor, San Bernardino, Calif., 1954-58, estimator, sec./treas., bd. dir., 1958-74; estimator design-installation engr. Add-M Electric, Inc., San Bernardino, 1972-82, v.p., 1974-82; estimator, engr. Corona (Calif.) Indsl. Electric, Inc., 1982-83; project engr. Fiscbach & Moore, Inc., L.A., 1984-91; project engr. cons. Fischbach & Moor, Inc., L.A., 1993-94. Mem. Arrowhead Country Club. Episcopalian. Home: 526 Sonora Dr San Bernardino CA 92404-1762

KIRKLAND, GELSEY, dancer; b. Bethlehem, Pa., 1953; m. Greg Lawrence. Student, Sch. Am. Ballet. With N.Y.C. Ballet, 1968-74, soloist, 1969-72, prin. dancer, 1972-74; ballerina Am. Ballet Theatre, 1974-81, 82-84; free-lance ballet teacher; guest artist Royal Ballet, London, 1980, 86, Stuttgart Ballet, 1980; teacher, coach Am. Ballet Theatre, 1992—. Created roles in ballets including: Firebird, 1970, The Goldberg Variations, Scherzo fantastique, An Evening's Waltzes, The Leaves are Fading, Hamlet, The Tiller in the Field, Four Bagatelles, Stravinsky Symphony in C, Song of the Nightingale Connotations, others; guest dancer Royal Ballet, London, 1980, 81, 86, Stuttgart Ballet, 1980; appeared in TV show The Nutcracker, 1977; author: (with Greg Lawrence) Dancing on My Grave, 1986, The Shape of Love: Footnotes on My Life, 1990, (with Greg Lawrence) The Little Ballerina and Her Dancing Horse, 1993. Office: care Dubé Zakin Mgmt Inc 67 Riverside Dr Apt 3B New York NY 10024-6165*

KIRKLAND, NANCY CHILDS, secondary education educator, consultant; b. Ideal, Ga., July 20, 1937; d. Millard Geddings and Bessie Vioda (Forbes) C.; m. Allard Corley French, Jr., Apr. 22, 1961 (div. Dec. 7, 1978); children: Vianne Elizabeth French Ouzts, Nancy Alysia French Joyce; m. Clarence Nathaniel Kirkland, Jr., Dec. 12, 1987. AB in Speech and Religious Edn., LaGrange Coll., 1959; MS, Troy State U., 1977; EdD in Child and Youth Studies, Nova U., 1993. Cert. tchr. English, Religion; cert. instr. Profl. Refinements in Developing Effectiveness, Tchr. Effectiveness and Classroom Handling. Dir. Christian edn. First Meth. Ch., Thomson, Ga., 1959-61; tchr. English Flanagan (Ill.) Jr.-Sr. H.S., 1962-63; tchr. English and social studies Woodland Jr. H.S., Streater, Ill., 1963-64; tchr. 5th grade Sheridan Elem. Sch., Bloominton, Ill., 1964-65; tchr. English Samson (Ala.) H.S., 1965, Choctawhatchee H.S., Fort Walton Beach, Fla., 1966-68, Marianna (Fla.) H.S., 1972-77; dir. devel. reading lab. Chiefland (Fla.) H.S., 1979-82; tchr. English Buchholz H.S., Gainesville, 1982—; co-founder, cons. KPS Leadership Specialists, Jonesboro, Ga., 1993—; chairperson Buchholz facilitis com., Gainesville, Fla., 1993—; instr. English Santa Fe C. C., Gainesville, Fla., 1982-87, 96; asst. chairperson Buchholz English Dept., Gainesville, Fla., 1989-92. Contbr. articles to profl. jours. Sec., co-chmn., mem. Buchholz sch. adv. coun., Gainesville, 1994-95; tchr., dir., tchr. trainer Sunday sch., vacation sch., Fla.; actress, dir. Little Theaters, ch. groups, Ill., Ga., Ala.; coord. Gainesville Sister Cities Youth Correspondence Program, 1991-93. Mem. AAUW, ASCD, Alachua Multicultural Coun. (grantee 1992), Nat. Coun. Tchrs. English, Fla. Coun. Tchrs. English, Alachua Coun. Tchrs. English (v.p. 1991-92, pres. 1992-93), Gainesville C. of C. Methodist. Home: 1728 N W 94th St Gainesville FL 32606 Office: Buchholz H S 5510 NW 27th Ave Gainesville FL 32606-6499

KIRKLEY, D. CHRISTINE (D. CHRISTINE KIRKLEY), non-profit organization administrator; b. Horton, Ala., Aug. 28, 1932; d. Vester Boyd and Josephine Prumrytle (Parrish) K.; m. Jack Stanley I, July 4, 1952; 1 child, Jack Stanley II. Student, U. Ala., 1951-52, Samford U., 1963-65, Cathedral Coll., 1982. Svr. rep. South Ctrl. Bell, Birmingham, Ala., 1984—; dir. Helpline Christian Outreach Ministries Inc, Birmingham, 1991—. Area mgr. Operating Blessing, Birmingham, 1989—; mem. Christian Helplines Internat., 1990—, sec. exec. com., 1994—. Mem. Telephone Pioneers Am. (fund raiser 1976-78, pres. 1979, cmty. edn. coord. 1982-83, drug abuse chairperson 1982-83), Internat. Platform Assn., Kiwanis. Mem. Assemby of God Ch. Office: Helpline Christian Outreach Ministries Inc 8 Roebuck Dr Birmingham AL 35215-8046

KIRKMAN, KAREN REBECCA, retail executive; b. Cin., Sept. 30, 1963; d. Charles Gordon Kirkman Jr. and Irene Sophronia Feltner. BA in English, Colby Coll., 1985. Cook Schooner Heritage, Rockland, Maine, 1985, O'Neill's Restaurant, Camden, Maine, 1985-87; reservation sales assoc. AutoEurope, Camden, 1987; store mgr. Puffin's of Ireland, Camden, 1987-90; store clk. Tuttle's Shoe Barn, Rockland, 1990-92; dept. mgr. Wal-Mart, Rockland, 1992-94; corp. pres. Adobe Boutique, Taos, N.Mex., 1994—. Home and Office: Adobe Boutique 102 Teresina Ln Taos NM 87571

KIRKPATRICK, ANNE SAUNDERS, systems analyst; b. Birmingham, Mich., July 4, 1938; d. Stanley Rathbun and Esther (Casteel) Saunders; children: Elizabeth, Martha, Robert, Sarah. Student, Wellesley Coll., 1956-57, Laval U., Quebec City, Can., 1958, U. Ariz., 1958-59; BA in Philosophy, U. Mich., 1961. Systems engr. IBM, Chgo., 1962-64; sr. analyst Commonwealth Edison Co., Chgo., 1981—. Treas. Taproot Reps., DuPage County (Ill.), 1977-80; pres. Hinsdale (Ill.) Women's Rep. Club, 1978-81. Club: Wellesley of Chgo. (bd. dirs. 1972-73). Home: 222 E Chestnut St #8B Chicago IL 60611 Office: Commonwealth Edison Co 72 W Adams St Ste 1450 Chicago IL 60603-5108

KIRKPATRICK, ELEANOR BLAKE, civic worker; b. Mangum, Okla., Mar. 10, 1909; d. Mack Barkley and Kathryn (Talbott) Blake; m. John Elson Kirkpatrick, June 20, 1932; 1 child, Joan Elson. B.A. in French, Smith Coll., 1931; D.Humanities (hon.), Oklahoma City U., 1968. 1st v.p. Kirkpatrick Found., Oklahoma City, Kirkpatrick Family Fund. Named to Okla. Hall of Fame, Okla. Heritage Assn., Oklahoma City, 1975, Woman of Yr., Redlands Coun. Girl Scouts, 1991; recipient Outstanding Woman Okla. Soroptimist Club, 1966, Evergreen Disting. Service award Nat. Assn. Mature People, Okla., 1982, Bd. Trustees award Omniplex Sic. Mus., Oklahoma City, 1984, Wall of Fame award Oklahoma City Pub. Sch. Found., 1990, Humanitarian award Nat. Conf. Christians and Jews, 1990, Humanitarian award Nat. Arthritis Found., Okla. chpt., 1993, Ptnrs. award World Neighbors, 1991, Pathmaker award Oklahoma County Hist. Soc., 1992, Outstanding Philanthropist award Civic Music Assn. Co-founder, hon. pres. Alliance Française, Oklahoma City; bd. dirs. Okla. City Art Mus.; mem. Oklahoma City Univ. Socs. Avocations: backgammon. Office: Kirkpatrick Oil Co PO Box 268822 Oklahoma City OK 73126-8822

KIRKPATRICK, JEANE DUANE JORDAN, political scientist, government official; b. Duncan, Okla., Nov. 19, 1926; d. Welcher F. and Leona (Kile) Jordan; m. Evron M. Kirkpatrick, Feb. 20, 1955; children: Douglas Jordan, John Evron, Stuart Alan. AA, Stephens Coll., 1946; AB, Barnard Coll., 1948; MA, Columbia U., 1950, PhD, 1968; postgrad. (French govt. fellow), Inst. Polit. Sci., U. Paris, 1952-53; LHD (hon.), Georgetown U., 1981, U. Pitts., 1981, U. Charleston, 1982, Hebrew U., 1982, Colo. Sch. Mines, 1983, St. John's U., 1983, Universidad Francisco Marroquin, Guatemala, 1985, Coll. of William and Mary, 1986, U. Mich., 1988, Syracuse U., 1994; hon. degree, Loyola U., Chgo., 1996. Asst. prof. polit. sci. Trinity Coll., 1962-67; assoc. prof. polit. sci. Georgetown U., Washington, 1967-73, prof., 1973—, Leavey prof., 1978—; sr. fellow Am. Enterprise Inst. for Pub. Policy Rsch., 1977—; mem. cabinet U.S. permanent rep. to UN, 1981-85. Author: Elections USA, 1956, Perspectives, 1962, The Strategy of Deception: A Study in World-Wide Communist Tactics, 1963, Mass Behavior in Battle and Captivity, 1968, Leader and Vanguard in Mass Society; The Peronist Movement in Argentina, 1971, Political Woman, 1974, The New Presidential Elite, 1976, Dismantling the Parties: Reflections on Party Reform and Party Decomposition, 1978, The Reagan Phenomenon, 1983, Dictatorships and Double Standards, 1982, Legitimacy and Force (2 vols.), 1988, The Withering Away of the Totalitarian State, 1990; syndicated columnist, 1985—; contbr. articles to profl. jours.; editor, contbr. various pubs. Trustee Helen Dwight Reid Ednl. Found., 1972—, pres., 1990—. Recipient Disting. Alumna award Stephens Coll., 1978, B'nai B'rith Humanitarian award, 1982, Award of the Commonwealth Fund, 1983, Gold medal VFW, 1984, French Prix Politique, 1984, Dept. Def. Disting. Pub. Svc. medal, 1985, Bronze Palm, 1992, Disting. Svc. medal Mayor of N.Y.C., 1985, Presdl. Medal of Freedom, 1985, Jamestown Freedom award, 1990, Centennial medal Nat. Soc. DAR, 1991, Disting. Svc. award USO, 1994. Mem. Internat. Polit. Sci. Assn. (exec. coun.), Am. Polit. Sci. Assn. (Hubert Humphrey award 1988), So. Polit. Sci. Assn. Office: Am Enterprise Inst 1150 17th St NW Washington DC 20036-4603

KIRKPATRICK, V. HELEN LENOX, counselor, educator; b. Albuquerque, N. Mex., Aug. 17, 1931; d. Louis and Christine Elizabeth (Leftwich) Lenox; m. William Noble Kirkpatrick, Nov. 30, 1961; children: Timothy Lenox, Matthew Claude. BA, U. N. Mex., 1971, MA, 1973. Lic. LPCC, NBCCC, NBCC, N.Mex. Dir. career, life devel. U. Albuquerque, 1979-81, dir. heights branch, 1979-81; asst. prof. Chapman U., Albuquerque, 1985—; adj. prof. U. N. Mex., Albuquerque, 1987—, career cons., 1986—; voc. expert SSI Count Hearings and Appears, 1986-94; mem. advisory bd. Chapman U., N. Mex., 1995—. Mem. ACA, Inst. of Noetic Scis., N.Mex. Career Devel. Assn. (pres.). Democrat. Office: U N Mex 220 Student Services Ctr Albuquerque NM 87131-2096

KIRKSEY, LAURA ELIZABETH, medical, surgical nurse; b. San Antonio, May 11, 1943; d. Robert Taylor and Laura Hulda (Fischer) Autry; m. Frank Lynn Hays, May 27, 1961 (div. Oct. 1968); children: Frank Lynn, Michael Devin, Michele Dyanne; m. Franklin James Kirksey, Sept. 1, 1969; 1 child, James Che. AD in Edn., Garland County C.C., 1985, ADN, 1991; BSN, Henderstate State U., 1995; postgrad., U. Ark. RN, Ark. Claims clk. H. L. Davis Ins. Co., San Antonio, 1966-69; policy typist U.S.A.A. Ins. Co., San Antonio, 1969; key punch operator 1st Nat. Bank, St. Louis, 1972, Sigma Chem. Corp., St. Louis, 1972-74; data entry operator Hager Hinge Corp., St. Louis, 1974-78; office mgr. Chiropractic Ctr., Hot Springs, Ark., 1991-92; staff nurse Bapt. Meml. Hosp., Little Rock, 1991-92, St. Joseph Hosp., Hot Springs, Ark., 1992—; assoc. clin. instr. Henderson State U., 1995. Pres. South Hot Springs Lioness, 1985, sec., 1986. Mem. Student Nurses Assn. Home: 1605 Central Ave Hot Springs National Park AR 71901-6117 Office: St Joseph Hosp 300 Werner St Hot Springs National Park AR 71913-6406

KIRKWOOD, SANDRA CLOSE, physical therapist; b. Neenah, Wis., Jan. 13, 1965; d. James Donald and Joan Louise (Coffin) Close; m. Michael Wayne, Sept. 28, 1991; 1 child, Lauren Elizabeth. BS in Biology, Ind. U., 1987, postgrad.; MS in Phys. Therapy, Columbia U., 1989. Cert. phys. therapist, Ind. Physical therapist Riley Hosp. for Children, Indpls., 1989-92; dir. rehab. Caremark Therapeutic Svcs., Redlands, Calif., 1992—; bd. dirs. Children's Limb Found., Indpls.; cons. Ind. Resdl. Living, Greenfield, Ind., 1989—; vice-chmn. Nat. Hemophilia Found., N.Y.C., 1992-95. Co-author: (manual) Improving Outcomes Through Physical Therapy, 1992, Pulmonary Rehabilitation for Alpha -1 Antitrypsin, 1994; co-author: (video) Improving Outcomes Through Physical Therapy. Recipient Mary E. Callahan award Columbia U., N.Y.C., 1989; fellow Ind. U., Indpls., 1995. Mem. Am. Phys. Therapy Assn., World Fedn. of Hemophilia.

KIRMSE, SISTER ANNE-MARIE ROSE, nun, educator, researcher; b. Bklyn., Sept. 23, 1941; d. Frank Joseph Sr. and Anna (Keck) K. BA in English cum laude, St. Francis Coll., 1972; MA in Theology with honors, Providence Coll., 1975; PhD in Theology, Fordham U., 1989. Joined Sisters of St. Dominic, Roman Cath. Ch., 1960; cert. elem. tchr., N.Y. Tchr. elem. sch. Diocese Bklyn., 1962-73; instr. adult edn. Diocese Rockville Centre, N.Y., 1974—; dir. religious edn. St. Anthony Padua Parish, East Northport, N.Y., 1975-83; dir. spiritual programs Diocese of Rockville Centre, 1979—; demonstration tchr. Paulist Press, N.Y.C., 1968-70; cons. Elem. Sch. Catechetical Assocs., Bklyn., 1971-73; mem. adj. faculty grad. program Sem. Immaculate Conception, Huntington, N.Y., 1979-80; adj. instr. Molloy Coll., Rockville Centre, 1985, St. Joseph's Coll., Patchogue, N.Y., 1990-91; adj. asst. prof. Ignatius Coll., Bronx, N.Y., 1996—; asst. to Rev. Avery Dulles, Fordham U., Bronx, 1988—, rsch. assoc. Laurence J. McGinley chair in religion and society, 1989—. Recipient Kerygma award Diocese of Rockville Centre, 1980; Dominican scholar Providence Coll., 1973, Presdl. scholar Fordham U., 1988; McGinley fellow Fordham U., 1988. Mem. Cath. Theol. Soc. Am., Amnesty Internat. Democrat. Roman Catholic. Office: Fordham U Keating Hall 322 Bronx NY 10458

KIRNOS, DINA, technology support professional; b. Dushanbe, Russia, Oct. 6, 1953; came to the U.S., 1979; d. Sholom and Klara (Blitshteyn) Kirnos; children: Semyon Shnayderman, Mallory McCoy. BA, U. Dushanbe, 1974. Programmer Royal Ins. Co., N.Y.C., 1979-82; systems analyst Chem. Bank, N.Y.C., 1982-84, Securities Industry Automation Corp., N.Y.C., 1984-89; sr. systems analyst N.Y. Stock Exch., 1989-94, dir. support, 1994—; mgr. customer svcs. N.Y. Stock Exch., Inc., 1994—. Mem. Assn. Info. Techs., Help Desk Inst. Republican. Jewish. Office: NY Stock Exch Inc 20 Broad St New York NY 10005

KIRSCH, MARY ANNE G., elementary education educator; b. Chgo., July 9, 1951; d. Steven R. and Helen S. (Krawczyk) Wilczynski; m. Robert Romano (div.); 1 child, Jeff Romano; m. Ronald I. Kirsch, July 21, 1973; 1 child, Justin. BA with high honors, Elmhurst Coll., 1991; MEd, Nat. Louis U., 1995. Cert. elem. tchr., Ill. Tchr. St. Isidore Sch., Bloomingdale, Ill., 1991-92, Elmwood Sch. Dist. #401, Elmwood Park, Ill., 1992—. Mem. West Suburban Reading Coun., Phi Kappa Phi.

KIRSCH, ROSLYN RUTH, art educator, painter, printmaker; b. N.Y.C., Dec. 30, 1928; d. Harry Morris and Lillian (Zemachson) Friedenberg; m. Louis Kirsch, Dec. 26, 1948; children: Libby Ann, Andrew Lawrence. Student, Queens Coll., 1946-48; BA, Hunter Coll., 1950. Art dir. Ladies' Ready-to-Wear Buying Office, N.Y.C., 1948-50; profl. artist, self employed, 1965—; art educator Armory Art Ctr., West Palm Beach, Fla., 1987—, Boca Raton (Fla.) Mus. Art, 1990—. One-person shows include Peter Drew Galleries, Fla., Joel Kessler Gallery, Fla., Indigo Gallery, Fla., Palm Beach Internat. Airport; exhibited in group shows Ann. Hortt Exhbn., Mus. Fine Art, Ft. Lauderdale, 1994 (award), Nat. Assn. Women Artists, West Palm Beach, 1995 (award). Recipient Honorable Mention award Mus. Art, Ft. Lauderdale, 1994, others. Mem. Nat. Assn. Women Artists, Profl. Artists Guild, Norton Artists Guild, others.

KIRSCHENBAUM, LISA L., portfolio manager, financial advisor; b. N.Y.C., May 7, 1971; d. J. Michael and Paulenne Lydia (Roeske) K. BA, Brandeis U., 1994. Lic. portfolio mgr. Pres., CEO Financier's Internat. Inc., Mendham, N.J., 1992-95; account exec. T.R. Winston, Inc., Bedminster, N.J., 1994-95; quantum portfolio mgr., fin. advisor Prudential Securities, N.Y.C., 1995—. Mem. Women's Rep. Com. Somerset County, 1994—. Mem. Internat. Platform Assn., N.Y. Health & Racquet Club, Park Ave Dining Club, Mendham Raquet Club. Republican. Jewish. Home: 80 Chapin Rd Bernardsville NJ 07924 Office: Prudential Securities Inc 1 Liberty Plz 46th Fl New York NY 10006-1486

KIRSCHNER, BARBARA J., community health and women's health nurse; b. Patch Grove, Wis., Jan. 19, 1925; d. Charles D. and LaVona S. (Moore) Cook; m. Leonard B. Kirschner, Dec. 18, 1950 (div. Nov. 1978); children: Richard D., Frances B. McCormack, Dan S., Heidi. Diploma, Immanuel Hosp., Omaha, 1950; student, UCLA, 1973. RN; cert. women's health nurse; cert. nurse practitioner. Staff nurse U. Wis. Hosp., Madison, 1950-51, Meml. Hosp., Pullman, Wash., 1953-64; exec. dir. Family Planning Ctr., Pullman, 1970-77, clinician, 1973-76; clinician, epidemiologist North Ctrl. Dist. Health Dept., Lewiston, Idaho, 1977-93; county planner Whitman County Retardation Bd., Colfax, Wash., 1967-68, pres. bd. dirs. 1967-68; clinician, outreach worker Whitman County Coun. on Aging, Colfax, 1977; rsch. assoc., acting dir. nursing Wash. State U., Pullman, 1972; adv. bd. United Way of Pullman, 1974-75, Whitman Co. March of Dimes bd., 1976-78; cons. AIDS adv. com. Lewis and Clark State Coll., Lewiston, 1990-92; mem. AIDS adv. com. Asotin County Health Dept., Clarkston, Wash., 1989-91. Author booklet and pamphlets. Trustee, chair profl. com. Meml. Hosp., Pullman, 1975-78; mem. Uniontown Parks and Recreation Commn., 1995; bd. dirs. Lewiston Civic Theatre, 1996. Mem. ANA, Idaho Nurses Assn., WSNA (bd. dirs. 1970-76, 2nd v.p. 1976-80). Home: PO Box 22 So 115 Washington Uniontown WA 99179

KIRSCHNER, BARBARA STARRELS, pediatric gastroenterologist; b. Phila., Mar. 23, 1941; m. Robert H. Kirschner. M.D., Woman's Med. Coll. of Pa., 1967. Diplomate Am. Bd. Pediatrics; cert. in pediatric gastroenterology and nutrition. Intern, U. Chgo., 1967-68, resident, 1968-70; Wyler Children's Hosp., U. Chgo., 1984—, assoc. prof. pediatrics, 1984-88; prof. pediatrics and medicine, 1988—, mem. com. on nutrition and nutritional biology. Contbr. articles to profl. jours. Recipient Davidson award in pediatric gastroenterology Acad. Pediatrics, 1993. Mem. Am. Gastroenterologic Assn., N.Am. Soc. Pediatric Gastroenterology, Soc. Pediatric Rsch., Alpha Omega Alpha. Office: U Chgo Med Ctr 5825 S Maryland Ave # 4065 Chicago IL 60637-1463

KIRSCHNER, RUTH BRIN, elementary education educator; b. Mpls., Mar. 12, 1924; d. Sigman and Leah (Chazankin) Brin; m. Norman Bernard Kirschner, June 19, 1949; children: Sally Jo Kirschner Minsberg, William Arthur. BS cum laude, U. Minn., 1946. Primary tchr. Robert Fulton Sch., Mpls., 1946-52; elem. tchr. St. Louis Park (Minn.) Schs., 1962—; tchr. religious sch. Adath Jeshurun Synagogue, Mpls., 1946-83, Bnai Emet Synagoguue, St. Louis Park, 1989—; primary tchr. Latch Key, Mpls., 1986-88; nursery sch. tchr. Westwood Luth. Ch., St. Louis Park, 1989—; customer svc. rep. Am. Automobile Assn., St. Louis Park, 1985—. Sec. 4th Dist. Dem. Com., St. Louis Park, 1986-90; state del. St. Louis Park Dem. Com., 1986, 88, 90; mem. Cmty. Rels. coun. St. Louis Park, 1986-88; mem. St. Louis Park Charter Commn., 1993—; pres. Friends of St. Louis Park Libr., 1987-88, sec., 1990—; pres. St. Louis Park Friends, 1991-92, 93-94; del. to 44th Dist. Dem. Farmer Labor Exec. Bd.; alt. to 5th Dist. Dem. Farmer Labor ctrl. com.; apptd. mem. charter commn. St. Louis Park, 1993—; mem. Visions, 1994; bd. dirs. Suburban Alliance, 1994. Mem. AAUW (sec.-treas. 1970-72, parliamentarian 1974-76), Lioness (pres. Lyn-Lake 1995—, v.p. 1993-95), Alpha Delta Kappa (state scholarship chmn. 1988-90, sec. Gamma chpt. 1990—). Jewish. Home: 3135 Colorado Ave S Minneapolis MN 55416-2050

KIRSCHSTEIN, RUTH LILLIAN, physician; b. Bklyn., Oct. 12, 1926; d. Julius and Elizabeth (Berm) K.; m. Alan S. Rabson, June 11, 1950; 1 child, Arnold. B.A. magna cum laude, L.I. U., 1947; M.D., Tulane U., 1951; D.Sc. (hon.), Mt. Sinai Sch. Medicine, 1984; LL.D. (hon.), Atlanta U., 1985; DSc (hon.), Med. Coll. Ohio, 1986; LHD (hon.), L.I. U., 1991. Intern Kings County Hosp., Bklyn., 1951-52; resident pathology VA Hosp., Atlanta, Providence Hosp., Detroit, Clin. Ctr., NIH, Bethesda, Md., 1952-57; fellow Nat. Heart Inst. Tulane U., 1953-54; asst. dir. div. biologics standards NIH, 1971-72; dep. dir. Bur. Biologics, FDA, 1972-73, dep. assoc. commr. sci., 1973-74; dir. Nat. Inst. Gen. Med. Scis., 1974-93;; acting assoc. dir. woman's health NIH, Bethesda, 1974-93; acting dir. NIH, 1993, dep. dir., 1993—; mem. Found. Advanced Edn. Scis.; chmn. grants peer rev. study team NIH; mem. Inst. Medicine, NAS, 1982—; co-chair, sec. Spl. Emphasis Oversight Com. on Sci. and Tech., 1989—; co-chair PHS Coordinating Com. on Women's Health Issues, 1990—; mem. Office of Tech. Assessment Adv. Com. on Basic Rsch., 1989—. Recipient Superior Svc. award, 1980, Presdl. Disting. Exec. Rank award, 1985, 95, Pub. Svc. award Fedn. Am. Socs. for Exptl. Biology, 1993, Nat. Pub. Svc. award Am. Soc. Pub. Adminstrn./Nat. Acad. Pub. Adminstrn., 1994, Roger W. Jones award for exec. leadership Am. U., 1994, Georgeanna Seegar Jones Women's Health Lifetime Achievement award, 1995. Mem. AMA (Dr. Nathan Davis award 1990), NAS-IOM, Am. Assn. Immunologists, Am. Assn. Pathologists, Am. Soc. Microbiology, Am. Acad. Arts and Scis., Inst. Medicine. Home: 6 West Dr Bethesda MD 20814-1510 Office: NIH Shannon Bldg 1 Rm 126 1 Center Dr MSC 0148 Bethesda MD 20892-0148

KIRTLEY, HATTIE MAE, realtor; b. Ludlow, Okla., July 9, 1934; d. Adam Marion and Hattie Ethel (Buttler) Williams; m. Albert David Kirtley, Aug. 21, 1954; children: Sharon Ann, Gary Dean. BS in Secondary Edn., Northwest Mo. State U., 1970; postgrad., Mo. Western, 1972. Cert. Mo. realestate salesperson. Waitress Greyhound Bus Depot, Wichita, Kans., 1951; telephone operator S.W. Bell Telephone Co., Wichita, 1952; key punch operator Cudahy Packing Co., Wichita, 1954, Kans. Gas & Electric Co., Wichita, 1955, Kans. State Income Tax Bur., Topeka, 1956, M.F.A. Dairy Breeders, Springfield, Mo., 1957; tchr. vocat. home econs. South Holt High Sch., Oregon, Mo., 1969-70; tchr. various schs., Cosby, Denton, Mo., Kans., 1971-72, 72-74; real estate salesperson St. Joseph, Mo., 1980-82, 82-84, Savannah, Mo., 1984—. Charter mem. Riverview Bapt. Ch., Wichita, Kans., 1951, Sharon Bapt. Ch., 1952, Kings Hwy. Bapt. Ch., 1953. Baptist.

KIRTLEY, JANE ELIZABETH, professional society administrator, lawyer; b. Indpls., Nov. 7, 1953; d. William Raymond and Faye Marie (Price) K.; m. Stephen Jon Cribari, May 8, 1985. BJ, Northwestern U., 1975, MS in Journalism, 1976; JD, Vanderbilt U., 1979. Bar: N.Y. 1980, U.S. Dist. Ct. (we. dist.) N.Y. 1980, D.C. 1982, U.S. Dist. Ct. D.C. 1982, U.S. Ct. Appeals (4th cir.) 1982, U.S. Ct. Claims 1982, U.S. Ct. Appeals (D.C. cir.) 1985, U.S. Supreme Ct. 1985, Va. 1995. Assoc. Nixon, Hargrave, Devans & Doyle, Rochester, N.Y., 1979-81, Washington, 1981-84; exec. dir. Reporters Com. for Freedom of Press, Washington, 1985—; adj. faculty Am. U. Sch. Communication, 1988—. Exec. articles editor Vanderbilt U. Jour. Internat. Law, 1978-79; editor: The News Media and the Law, 1985—, The First Amendment Handbook, 1987, 4th edit., 1995, Agents of Discovery, 1991, 93, 95; columnist NEPA Bull., 1988—, Virginia's Press, 1991—, Am. Journalism Rev., 1995—; mem. editorial bd. Govt. Info. Quar., Comm. Law and Policy, Comm. Law and Policy. Bd. dirs. 1st Amendment Congress, Denver, Student Press Law Ctr., Arlington, Va.; mem. steering com. Libel Def. Resource Ctr., N.Y.C.; adv. bd. Pa. Ctr. for the 1st Amendment, University Park, Freedom Forum 1st Amendment Ctr., Nashville. Mem. ABA, N.Y. State Bar Assn., D.C. Bar Assn., Va. State Bar Assn., Sigma Delta Chi. Home: 724 Franklin St Alexandria VA 22314-4104 Office: Reporters Com Freedom of Press 1101 Wilson Blvd Ste 1910 Arlington VA 22209-2248

KIRWAN, KATHARYN GRACE (MRS. GERALD BOURKE KIRWAN, JR.), retail executive; b. Monroe, Wash., Dec. 1, 1913; d. Walter Samuel and Bertha Ella (Shrum) Camp; m. Gerald Bourke Kirwan Jr., Jan. 13, 1945. Student, U. Puget Sound, 1933-34; BA, BS, Tex. Woman's U., 1937; postgrad., U. Wash., 1941. Libr. Brady (Tex.) Sr. High Sch., 1937-38, McCamey (Tex.) Sr. High Sch., 1938-43; mgr. Milady's Frock Shop, Monroe, 1946-62, owner, mgr., 1962-93. Meml. chmn. Monroe chpt. Am. Cancer Soc., 1961—; mem. Snohomish County Police Svcs. Action Coun., 1971; mem. Monroe Pub. Libr. Bd., 1950-65, pres. bd., 1964-65; mem. Monroe City Coun., 1969-73; mayor City of Monroe, 1974-81; commr. Snohomish County Hosp. dist. 1, 1970-90, chmn. bd. commrs., 1980-90; mem. East Snohomish County Health Planning Com., 1979—; mem. Snohomish County Law and Justice Planning Com., 1974-78, Snohomish County Econ. Devel. Coun., 1975-81, Snohomish County Pub. Utility Dist. Citizens Adv. Task Force, 1983; sr. warden Ch. of Our Saviour, Monroe, 1976-77, 89, sr. warden, 1976-77, 89-90; mem. Monroe Breast Cancer Screening Project community planning group Fred Hutchinson Cancer Rsch. Ctrs., 1991-93. With USNR, 1943-46. Mem. AAUW, U.S. Naval Inst., Ret. Officers Assn., Naval Res. Assn., Bus. and Profl. Women's Club (2d v.p. 1980-82, pres. 1983-84), Washington Gens., Snohomish County Pharm. Aux., C. of C. (pres. 1972), Valley Gen. Hosp. Guild (pres. 1994, 95, 96), Valley Gen. Hosp. Found. (sec. 1993—). Episcopalian. Home: 538 S Blakely St Monroe WA 98272-2402

KISCADEN, SHEILA M., state legislator; b. St. Paul, Apr. 21, 1946; d. Harvey Richard and Bea Mae (Conway) Martineau; m. Richard Craig Kiscaden, Sept. 12, 1970; children: Michael, Karen. BS in Edn., U. Minn., 1969; MS in Pub. Adminstrn., U. So. Calif., L.A., 1986. Tchr. So. St. Paul Secondary Schs., Minn., 1969-70, Jobs 70, Rochester, Minn., 1970-71; regional coord. Planned Parenthood, Rochester, Minn., 1971-76; vol. svc. coord. Olmsted County, Rochester, Minn., 1977-80, human svc. planner, 1980-82, legis. liaison, 1982-85; prin. Cons. Collaborator, Rochester, Minn., 1987—; senator Minn. State Senate, St. Paul, 1992—. Bd. dirs. Ability Bldg. Ctr. Found. Bd., Rochester, Minn., 1989-94, Dyslexia Inst. Minn., Rochester, Minn., 1989-94; team leader Global Vols., 1989—. Fulbright scholar, 1970. Mem. Phi Beta Kappa. Republican. Home: 724 11th St SW Rochester MN 55902-6339 Office: Minn State Senate State Office Bldg 143 Saint Paul MN 55155-1201*

KISER, ANITA HOPE, planner, technical writer; b. Charlotte, N.C., June 24, 1955; d. Robert Phillip Sr. and Mary Faith (Hansil) K. AA, Ctrl. Piedmont C.C., 1976; BA, Queens Coll., 1982; MS in Info. Sci., U. N.C., 1988; MBA, Meredith Coll., 1996. Coord. sch. media Cabarrus County Schs., Concord, N.C., 1982-87; writer, project team leader IBM, Research Triangle Park, N.C., 1989—; computer cons. N.C. Dept. Pub. Instruction, Raleigh, 1985-88. Author: Using Appleworks in the School Media Center, 1988. Mem. NAFE, NOW. Home: 3520 Donna Rd Raleigh NC 27604-4270

KISER, NAGIKO SATO, retired librarian; b. Taipei, Republic of China, Aug. 7, 1923; came to U.S., 1950; d. Takeichi and Kinue (Sōma) Sato; m. Virgil Kiser, Dec. 4, 1979 (dec. Mar. 1981). Secondary teaching credential, Tsuda Coll., Tokyo, 1945; BA in Journalism, Trinity U., 1953; BFA, Ohio State U., 1956, MA in Art History, 1959; MLS, cert. in library media, SUNY, Albany, 1974. Cert. community coll. librarian, Calif., cert. jr. coll. tchr., Calif., cert. secondary edn. tchr., Calif., cert. tchr. library media specialist and art, N.Y. Pub. rels. reporter The Mainichi Newspapers, Osaka, Japan, 1945-50; contract interpreter U.S. Dept. State, Washington, 1956-58, 66-67; resource specialist Richmond (Calif.) Unified Sch. Dist.,

1968-69; editing supr. CTB/McGraw-Hill, Monterey, Calif., 1969-71; multimedia specialist Monterey Peninsula Unified Sch. Dist., 1975-77; librarian Nishimachi Internat. Sch., Tokyo, 1979-80, Sacramento City Unified Sch. Dist., 1977-79, 81-85; sr. librarian Camarillo (Calif.) State Hosp. and Devel. Ctr., 1985-93. Editor: Short Form Test of Academic Aptitude, 1970, Prescriptive Mathematics Inventory, 1970, Tests of Basic Experience, 1970. Mem. Calif. State Supt.'s Regional Coun. on Asian Pacific Affairs, Sacramento, 1984-91. Library Media Specialist Tng. Program scholar U.S. Office Edn., 1974. Fellow Internat. Biog. Assn. (life); mem. ALA, Am. Biog. Inst. (life, dep. gov. 1988—), Claif. Libr. Assn., Med. Libr. Assn., Asunaro Shogai Kyoiku Kondankai (Lifetime Edn. Promoting Assn., Japan), The Mus. Soc., Internat. House of Japan, Matsuyama Sacramento Sister City Corp., Japanese Am. Citizens League, UN Assn. U.S., Ikenobo Ikebana Soc. Am., L.A. Hototogisu Haiku Assn., Ventura County Archeol. Soc., Internat. Platform Assn., Internat. Soc. Poets. Mem. Christian Science Ch. Office: Camarillo State Hosp & Devel Ctr Profl Libr PO Box 6022 Camarillo CA 93011-6022

KISH, CAROL RUTH, principal, realtor; b. Trenton, N.J., Dec. 22, 1941; d. Karl and Ruth E. (Thompson) K. BA, Trenton State Coll., 1959; MEd, Boston U., 1972. Cert. chief sch. adminstr., prin., supr., tchr., realtor, N.J. Tchr. Ewing (N.J.) Pub. Schs., 1963-66, Saddle River (N.J.) Pub. Schs., 1966-67, Hartford (Conn.) Pub. Schs., 1967-68; demonstration tchr. Ewing Pub. Schs./Trenton State Coll., 1969-71; instr. California State Coll., Uniontown, Pa., 1972; curriculum supr. Marlboro (N.J.) Twp. Pub. Schs., 1972-77; supr. state & fed. programs Hamilton (N.J.) Twp. Pub. Schs., 1977-90, prin., 1990—; mgmt. cons., Iselin, N.J., 1976-77. Mem. Mercer County Commn. States of Women, Trenton, 1988—, Boheme Opera Guild, Trenton, 1995—, PTA. Recipient Literacy award PTA, 1992. Mem. ASCD, N.J. Prins. & Suprs. Assn., Delta Kappa Gamma, Phi Delta Kappa. Office: Hamilton Twp Bd Edn 90 Park Ave Hamilton NJ 08619

KISH, ELISSA ANNE, educational administrator; b. Bklyn., Sept. 29, 1934; d. Robert Joseph and Yolanda Filomina (Romano) Lucadamo; m. Joseph Laurence Kish Jr., Oct. 16, 1955; children: Grace Edna Kish, Joseph Robert, Frances Caroline Kish Burrell. BA, CUNY, 1956; EdM, Rutgers U., 1965. Elem. tchr. N.Y. City Pub. Schs., Bklyn., 1956-57, U.S. Army Dependent Schs., Hanau, West Germany, 1958, Piscataway (N.J.) Pub. Schs., 1961-62, New Brunswick (N.J.) Pub. Schs., 1965, 71-76; vice prin. Hopatcong (N.J.) Pub. Schs., 1977-78; asst. supt. Dunellen (N.J.) Pub. Schs., 1978-80; supr. K-12 instrn. Elmwood Park (N.J.) Pub. Schs., 1980-90; interim high sch. adminstr. Dunellen Pub. Schs., 1991-92; adminstr. ctrl. office Elmwood Park Pub. Schs., 1992—; cons. Newark Pub. Schs., 1976-77; evaluator Middle States Assn., Navesink, N.J., 1988; cons. State U. N.Y., Garden City, 1992, Mt. Vernon Pub. Schs., N.Y., 1992. Author: Nutrition Program For Schools, 1979; contbng. author: Curriculum & Values: An Inquiry, 1976. Strategic planning team Town of Elmwood Park, 1993-95; officer, mem. Westfield Coll. Women's Club, Westfield, N.J., 1969-92; founder, 1st pres. Vocational Adv. Coun., Elmwood Park, 1980-90; rep. Friends of Animals, N.Y.C., 1967-71; trustee Christopher Montessori Acad., Westfield, 1968-72. Recipient numerous grants for rsch. and curriculum devel., 1979—. Mem. ASCD, NEA, Elmwood Park Prins. and Suprs. Assn. (pres. 1989-90), Elmwood Park Adminstrs. Assn. (pres. 1986-89), Nat. Geographic Soc., Smithsonian Assocs., Kappa Delta Pi, Alpha Epsilon Phi. Home: 619 Mountain Ave Bound Brook NJ 08805

KISLING, FANNY, counselor, educator; b. Preble County, Ohio, Jan. 14, 1931; d. William Benjamin and Anna Viola (Wing) Banis; m. Donald Robert Kisling, May 14, 1950 (dec. 1991); children: Emily Margaret, Rebecca Jane, Karen Lea, Suzanne Michele, Orval William, David Guy. BS, Miami U., Oxford, Ohio, 1973, MEd, 1974, PhD, 1986. Lic. profl. counselor; cert. tchr. Commuter advisor Miami U., 1975-76, program cons., 1976-78; prof., counselor Sinclair C.C., 1978—; lectr. Kent (Ohio) State U., 1990; presenter in field. Mayor Eaton, Ohio, 1995; mem. Eaton City Coun., 1993-95; mem., bd. dirs. Miami Valley Regional Planning, Dayton, Ohio, 1993; elder First Presbyn. Ch., Eaton, 1993. Mem. AAUW, Am. Counseling Assn., Am. Coll. Pers. Assn., Ohio Coll. Pers. Assn., Phi Kappa Phi, Kappa Delta Pi, Phi Delta Kappa. Republican. Home: 305 East Ave Eaton OH 45320-2005 Office: Sinclair CC 444 W Third St Dayton OH 45402

KISMARIC, CAROLE LEE, editor, writer, book packaging company executive; b. Orange, N.J., Apr. 28, 1942; d. John Joseph and Alice Felicia (Gruskos) K.; m. Charles Vincent Mikolaycak, Oct. 1, 1970. B.A. in Psychology, Pa. State U., 1964. Reporter, writer Parkersburg News, W. Va., summers 1960, 61; reporter, writer UPI, Columbus, Ohio, summer 1962; writer Conde Nast Publs., N.Y.C., 1964; picture editor, assoc. editor Time Life Book Div., N.Y.C., 1965-75; editorial dir. Aperture, Inc., N.Y.C., 1976-85; freelance pub. cons., editor, writer N.Y.C., 1985—; co-founder, co-owner book packaging co. Lookout Books, N.Y.C., 1990—; founder Lookout with Marvin Heiferman, comms. co.; mem. visual arts and policy panels NEA, Washington, 1977-81, 93; tchr. grad. sch. photography program Sch. Visual Arts, N.Y.C., 1990—. Author: Duel of the Ironclads, 1969, The Boy Who Tried to Cheat Death, 1971, The Rumor of Pavel and Paali, 1988, A Gift From Saint Nicholas, 1988, Forced Out: The Agony of the Refugee in Our Time, 1989, I'm So Happy, 1990, My Day, 1993, Talking Pictures, 1994, Growing Up With Dick and Jane: Living and Learning and American Dream, 1996, Love is Blind, 1996; author, editor: The Photography Catalogue, 1976; contbr. numerous articles to profl. jours.; assoc. curator From the Picture Press, Mus. Modern Art, 1973; co-curator traveling exhbns. L.A. Mcpl. Art Gallery: Forced Out in Time, 1989-93, Internat. Ctr. of Photography, Talking Pictures, 1994—. Recipient award Communications Graphics Assn., 1971, 72; Book of Yr. award Am. Inst. Graphic Arts, 1974, 75, 91. Home: 64 E 91st St New York NY 10128-1359 Office: Lookout Books 1024 6th Ave New York NY 10018-5415

KISS, MARY CATHERINE CLEMENT, writer; b. Johnson City, Tenn., July 28, 1928; d. Hugh Wilfred and Ruby Pearl (Sammons) Clement; m. Alvin Ferencz Josef Kiss, Feb. 27, 1954; children: Tony, Stephen, Mary Margaret. Student, St. Mary-of-the-Woods Coll., Terre Haute, Ind., 1946-47; BA in Journalism, U. Mich., 1950. Staff writer Kingsport (Tenn.) Times News, 1950-90; video co-producer, script writer, cons. Get The Picture, Kingsport, 1990—; owner Mary Kiss Media Svcs., Kingsport, 1990—; staff writer The Independent, Bluff City, Tenn., 1994-95; freelance writer, 1996—. Recipient 1st Pl. award Best Local Feature Tenn. Press. Assn., 1970, 1st Pl. award Pub. Svc. Features, 1978. Mem. Investigative Reporters and Editors. Home and Office: Mary Kiss Media Svcs 100 Edmond Cir Kingsport TN 37663-2612

KISSER, CYNTHIA S., social services administrator. MA in Am. Studies. Exec. dir. Cult Awareness Network, Chgo.; lectr. in field. Author: Touchstones: Reconnecting After a Cult Experience. Office: Cult Awareness Network Ste 1173 2421 W Pratt Blvd Chicago IL 60645

KISTIAKOWSKY, VERA, physics researcher, educator; b. Princeton, N.J., Sept. 9, 1928; d. George Bogdan and Hildegard (Moebius) K.; m. Gerhard Emil Fischer, June 16, 1951 (div. 1970); children: Marc Laurenz Fischer, Karen Marie Fischer. A.B., Mt. Holyoke Coll., 1948, Sc.D. (hon.), 1978; Ph.D., U. Calif.-Berkeley, 1952. Staff scientist U.S. Naval Rsch. Def. Lab., San Francisco, 1952-53; fellow U. Calif.-Berkeley, 1953-54; rsch. assoc. Columbia U., N.Y.C., 1954-57, instr., 1957-59; asst. prof. Brandeis U., Waltham, Mass., 1959-62, adj. assoc. prof., 1962-63; staff mem. MIT, Cambridge, 1963-69, sr. rsch. scientist, 1969-72; prof. physics, 1972-94; prof. emerita, 1994—. Author: Atomic Energy, 1959; One Way Is Down, 1967; contbr. articles on nuclear and elem. particle physics and astrophysics to profl. jours. Dir. Coun. for a Liveable World, Boston, 1983—. Recipient Centennial award Mt. Holyoke Coll., 1972. Fellow AAAS, Am. Phys. Soc. (councilor 1974-77); mem. Assn. for Women in Sci. (pres. 1982-83), Phi Beta Kappa (vis. scholar 1983-84, senator 1988-96), Sigma Xi (lectr. 1990-92). Office: MIT 77 Massachusetts Ave # 6-108 Cambridge MA 02139-4301

KISTLER, DARCI ANNA, ballet dancer; b. Riverside, Calif., June 4, 1964; d. Jack B. and Alicia (Kinner) K.; m. Peter Martins, 1992. Student, Profl. Children's Sch., N.Y.C., Sch. Am. Ballet, N.Y.C. With N.Y.C. Ballet, 1980—, soloist, 1981-82, prin. dancer, 1982—; tchr. Sch. of Am. Ballet, 1994—. Performed roles in Andantino, Gershwin Concerto, Valse-Scherzo, Piano-Rag Music, Pastorale, Suite for Histoire du Soldat, N.Y.C. Ballet's Balanchine Celebration, 1993, Symphonic Dances, 1994, Apollo, 1994; performed in Film George Balanchine's The Nutcracker, 1993; danced with the Kirov, St. Petersberg, Russia; made appearence in PBS-TV Dance in America; author: Ballerina: My Story, 1993. Recipient Capezio Dance award, 1991, Dance Mag. award, 1992. Office: NYC Ballet NY State Theater 20 Lincoln Center Plz New York NY 10023-6913*

KISVARSANYI, EVA BOGNAR, retired geologist; b. Budapest, Hungary, Dec. 18, 1935; came to U.S., 1957; d. Kalman and Ilona (Simon) Bognar; m. Geza Kisvarsanyi, July 3, 1956; 1 child, Erika G. Student, Eotvos Lorand U., Budapest, 1954-56; BS in Geology, U. Mo., Rolla, 1958, MS, 1960. Geologist Mo. Geol. Survey, Rolla, 1959-68; from rsch. geologist to sect. chief Mo. Dept. Natural Resources/Geol. Survey Program, Rolla, 1968-90; asst. dir. MODNR/Geol. Survey Program, Rolla, 1990-93; cons. Sarasota, Fla., 1993—. Editor geological guidebooks, 1976—; contbr. articles to profl. jours. Fellow Geol. Soc. Am. (mem. rep. 1985-93), Soc. Econ. Geologists (rsch. com. 1989-92); mem Sigma Xi (pres. Rolla chpt. 1990-91).

KITAGAWA, AUDREY EMIKO, lawyer; b. Honolulu, Mar. 31, 1951; s. Yonoichi and Yoshiko (Nagaishi) K. B.A. cum laude, U. So. Calif., 1973; J.D., Boston Coll., 1976. Bar: Hawaii, 1977, U.S. Dist. Ct. Hawaii, 1977. Assoc., Rice, Lee & Wong, Honolulu, 1977-80; sole practice, Honolulu, 1980—. Exec. editor Internat. Law Jour., 1976. Mem. Historic Hawaii Found., 1984. Mem. Hawaii Bar Assn., ABA, Assn. Trial Lawyers Am., Japan-Hawaii Lawyers Assn. (v.p. 1982—), Law Office Mgmt. Discussion Group, Hawaii Lawyers Care, Phi Alpha Delta. Republican. Club: Honolulu. Office: 820 Mililani St Ste 615 Honolulu HI 96813-2936

KITT, EARTHA MAE, actress, singer; b. North, S.C., Jan. 26, 1928; d. John and Anna K.; m. William McDonald, June 1960 (div.); 1 child, Kitt Shapiro. Grad. high sch. Soloist with Katherine Dunham Dance Group, 1948; night club singer, 1949—, appearing in France, Turkey, Greece, Egypt, N.Y.C., Hollywood, Las Vegas, London, Stockholm; actress: (plays) Dr. Faustus, Paris, 1951, New Faces of 1952, N.Y.C., Mrs. Patterson, N.Y.C., 1954, Shinbone Alley, N.Y.C., 1957, Timbuktu, 1978, Blues in the Night, 1985, (films) including New Faces, 1953, Accused, 1957, Anna Lucasta, 1958, Mark of the Hawk, 1958, St. Louis Blues, 1957, Saint of Devil's Island, 1961, Synanon, 1965, Up The Chastity Belt, 1971, Dragonard, Ernest Scared Stupid, 1991, Boomerang, 1992, Fatal Instinct, 1993, also 2 French films, also numerous TV appearances including Cat Woman role in Batman series; star: (documentary film) All By Myself, 1982; albums include In Person at the Plaza, 1987, My Way: A Musical Tribute to Rev. Dr. Martin Luther King Jr., 1987; author: Thursday's Child, 1956, A Tart Is Not a Sweet, Alone With Me, 1976, I'm Still Here, 1990, Confessions of a Sex Kitten, 1991. Named Woman of Yr. Nat. Assn. Negro Musicians, 1968; nominated 2 Grammys, 2 Tony awards, 1 Emmy. Office: care Eartha Kitt Prodns 888 7th Ave Fl 37 New York NY 10106-3799

KITT, OLGA, artist; b. N.Y.C., July 29, 1929; d. Elias and Mary (Opiela) K.; m. Nicholas Rawluk, Aug. 6, 1955 (div. 1960); 1 child, Wade. BA, Queens Coll., 1951; MA, State U. Iowa, 1952; studied with Meyer Schapiro, N.Y.C., 1954; studied with Hans Hofmann, N.Y.C., Provincetown, 1954-55; postgrad., Inst. Fine Arts, NYU, 1955, NYU, 1960-62; studied with Robert Beverly Hale, N.Y.C., 1979. Gallery asst. Chappellier Gallery, N.Y.C., 1952-53; asst. to Walter Pach N.Y., 1953-56; teaching asst. CCNY, 1953-58; tchr. art N.Y., 1962-80. One-person shows include CCNY, 1957, Manhattan Coll., Riverdale, N.Y., 1980; exhibited in group shows at Whitney Mus., N.Y.C., 1954, Mus. Bronx History, 1978, Mus. Modern Art, N.Y.C., 1978, Art Students League, N.Y.C., 1979, Bronx Mus. Arts, 1979; represented in permanent collections including Bronx Arts Ensemble, Riverdale Press, Riverdale YM-YWHA, U. Iowa, Iowa City, Fordham U., Fordham Prep. Sch., Hostos Coll., N.Y.C., Harris Sch. of Art, Tenn.; represented in pvt. collections. Home: 5610 Netherland Ave Bronx NY 10471 Studio: 495 S Broadway Yonkers NY 10705

KITTLITZ, LINDA GALE, small business owner; b. Waco, Tex., Jan. 22, 1949; d. Rudolf Gottlieb and Lena Hulda (Landgraf) K. BA in Art, Tex. Tech. U., 1971. Sales rep. Taylor Pub. Co., San Francisco and Dallas, 1972-73, Internat. Playtex Corp., San Francisco, 1974-76, Faberge Inc., San Francisco, 1976-78, Soflens div. Bausch and Lomb Co., San Francisco, 1978-81, Ben Rickert Inc., San Francisco, 1981-86; mfr.'s sales rep. Dearing Sales, San Francisco, 1986-87; sales rep. Golden West Envelope Co., San Francisco, 1987-89; sales assoc. R.G. Creations, Inc., San Francisco, 1989-90; owner, mgr. Linda Kittlitz & Assocs. (Custom Packaging and Printing Solutions), San Francisco, 1990—. Mem. NAFE. Democrat. Baptist.

KITZINGER, CHARLENE ANN, fund raising executive; b. Pitts., July 20, 1963; d. John C. and Charlotte L. (Fronczak) K.; divorced; 1 child, Erica L. Zamulevic. A of Bus., C.C. Allegheny County, 1989; BS in Mktg. magna cum laude, Robert Morris Coll., 1995. Adminstrv. asst. SMA Fin. Svcs., Pitts., 1983-91; asst. dir. devel. United Cerebral Palsy of Pitts., 1991-93; v.p. devel. Arthritis Found. Western Pa., Pitts., 1993—. Mem. Phi Theta Kappa. Republican. Home: 54 Barry St Pittsburgh PA 15203

KIVEL, MICKIE KESSLER (MAXINE KIVEL), public health advisor; b. Sebewaing, Mich., Aug. 8, 1934; d. Morris Bernard Kessler and Irene Nass; m. Joseph Kivel, June 16, 1956 (div. 1982); children: Karen Sue, Patricia Lynn. BA, U. Mich., 1956. Tech. writer, editor Atlantic Rsch. Corp., Alexandria, Va., 1965-68, Bell Tel. Labs., Whippany, N.J., 1968-69, U.S. FDA, Rockville, Md., 1970—. Editor: (tech. newsletter) Radiol. Health Bull., 1975-93, Med. Devices Bull., 1992-93, Mammography Matters, 1993—. Represented U.S. in World Bridge Olympiad, 1978, 86, 90. Recipient N.Am. Bridge Championship (Women's Pairs), 1986. Mem. Am. Contract Bridge League (life).

KIVELL, VICKIE WILLIAMS, superintendent of schools; b. Shreveport, La., Dec. 25, 1949; d. Vardaman Jr. and Hilda Rose (Dennard) Williams; m. Robert Lloyd Kivell, Aug. 29, 1969; 1 child, Lance Robert. BS, U. Tex., 1975; MS, East Tex. State U., 1987, EdD, 1991. Cert. supt., S.C., Tex., Ky., Miss. Tchr. Burleson (Tex.) Ind. Sch. Dist., 1975-79, Hobbs (N.Mex.) Mcpl. Schs., 1979-84; tchr. Community Ind. Sch. Dist., Nevada, Tex., 1984-86, adminstrv. asst., 1986-87; asst. prin. for instrn. Allen (Tex.) Ind. Sch. Dist., 1987-89, prin.-elect, 1989-90, prin., 1990-92; supt. schs. Farmersville (Tex.) Ind. Sch. Dist., 1992-95, Laurens County Sch. Dist. 56, Clinton, S.C., 1995—. Fellow Meadows Found., 1986-87, Scottish Rite, 1988-91. Mem. ASCD, Nat. Staff Devel. Coun., Am. Soc. Quality Control, Am. Assn. Sch. Adminstrs., S.C. Assn. Sch. Adminstrs., Phi Delta Kappa (v.p. rsch. Dallas Metro North chpt. 1992-94). Office: Laurens County Sch Dist 56 600 E Florida Clinton SC 29325

KIVELSON, MARGARET GALLAND, physicist; b. N.Y.C., Oct. 21, 1928; d. Walter Isaac and Madeleine (Wiener) Galland; m. Daniel Kivelson, Aug. 15, 1949; children: Steven Allan, Valerie Ann. AB, Radcliffe Coll., 1950, AM, 1951, PhD, 1957. Cons. Rand Corp., Santa Monica, Calif., 1956-69; asst. to geophysicist UCLA, 1967-83, prof., 1983—, also chmn. dept. earth and space scis., 1984-87; prin. investigator of magnetometer, Galileo Mission, Jet Propulsion Lab., Pasadena, Calif., 1977—; overseer Harvard Coll., 1977-83; mem. adv. coun. NASA, 1987-93; chair atmospheric adv. com. NSF, 1986-89, Com. Solar and Space Physics, 1977-86, com. planetary exploration, 1986-87, com. solar terrestial phys., 1989-92; mem. adv. com. geoscis. NSF. Editor: The Solar System: Observations and Interpretations, 1986; co-editor: Introduction to Space Physics, 1995; contbr. articels to profl. jours. Named Woman of Yr., L.A. Mus. Sci. and Industry, 1979, Woman of Sci., UCLA, 1984; recipient Grad. Soc. medal Radcliffe Coll., 1983, 350th Anniversary Alumni medal Harvard U. Fellow AAAS, Am. Geophysics Union; mem. Am. Phys. Soc., Am. Astron. Soc., Internat. Inst. Astronautics (corr. mem.). Office: UCLA Dept Earth & Space Scis 6843 Slichter Los Angeles CA 90095-1567

KIZER, CAROLYN ASHLEY, poet, educator; b. Spokane, Wash., Dec. 10, 1925; d. Benjamin Hamilton and M. (Ashley) K.; m. Stimson Bullitt, Jan., 1948 (div.); children: Ashley Ann, Scott, Jill Hamilton; m. John Marshall Woodbridge, Apr. 11, 1975. BA, Sarah Lawrence Coll., 1945; postgrad. (Chinese govt. fellow in comparative lit.), Columbia U., 1946-47; studied poetry with Theodore Roethke, U. Wash., 1953-54; LittD (hon.), Whitman Coll., 1986, St. Andrew's Coll., 1989, Mills Coll., 1990, Wash. State U., 1991. Specialist in lit. U.S. Dept. State, Pakistan, 1964-65; first dir. lit. programs Nat. Endowment for Arts, 1966-70; poet-in-residence U. N.C. at Chapel Hill, 1970-74; Hurst Prof. Lit. Washington U., St. Louis, 1971; lectr. Spring Lecture Series Barnard Coll., 1972; acting dir. grad. writing program Columbia, 1972; poet-in-residence Ohio U., 1974; vis. poet Iowa Writer's Workshop, 1975; prof. U. Md., 1976-77; poet-in-residence, disting. vis. lectr. Centre Coll., Ky., 1979; disting. vis. poet East Wash. U., 1980; Elliston prof. poetry U. Cin., 1981; Bingham disting. prof. U. Louisville, Ky., 1982; disting. vis. poet Bucknell U., Pa., 1982; vis. poet SUNY, Albany, 1982; prof. Columbia U. Sch. Arts, 1982; prof. poetry Stanford U., 1986; sr. fellow in humanities Princeton U., 1986; vis. prof. writing U. Ariz., 1989, 90, U. Calif., Davis, 1991; Coal Royalty chair U. Ala., 1995; participant Internat. Poetry Festivals, London, 1960, 70, Yugoslavia, 1969, 70, Pakistan, 1969, Rotterdam, Netherlands, 1970, Knokke-le-Zut, Belgium, 1970, Bordeanx, 1992, Dublin, 1993, Glasgow, 1994; sr. fellow humanities council Princeton U., 1986. Author: Poems, 1959, The Ungrateful Garden, 1961, Knock Upon Silence, 1965, Midnight Was My Cry, 1971, Mermaids in the Basement: Poems for Women, 1984 (Gov.'s award State of Wash. 1985, San Francisco Arts Commn. award 1986), Yin: New Poems, 1984 (Pulitzer prize in poetry 1985), The Nearness of You, 1987 (Theodore Roethke prize, 1988); Proses: On Poems & Poets, 1994, Picking & Choosing: Prose on Prose, 1995, Harping On: Poems 1985-1995, 1996, Picking and Choosing: Essays on Prose, 1996; editor: Woman Poet: The West, 1980, Leaving Taos, 1981, The Essential Clare, 1993, 100 Great Poems by Women, 1995; translator Carrying Over, 1988; founder, editor: Poetry N.W., 1959-65; contbr. poems, articles to Am. and Brit. jours. Recipient award Am. Acad. and Inst. Arts and Letters, 1985, Pres.'s medal Ea. Washington U., 1988. Mem. PEN, Amnesty Internat., Poetry Soc. Am. (Masefield prize 1983, Frost medal 1988), Acad. Am. Poets (chancellor 1995—). Episcopalian. Address: 19772 8th St E Sonoma CA 95476-3803

KJELLBERG, ANN C., editor; b. Boston, Jan. 11, 1962; d. Raymond N. and Judith (Priestley) K. BA, Yale U., 1984. Asst. to exec. editor Farrar, Strauss & Giroux, N.Y.C., 1986-87, asst. editor, 1987; asst. to the editor N.Y. Rev. of Books, N.Y.C., 1988-93; Am. editor Artes, Stockholm, Sweden, 1993-95; asst. editor N.Y. Rev. of Books, 1993—. Mem. comms. com. Am. Friends Svc. Com., Phila., 1991—; lit. exec. Estate of Joseph Brodsky. Office: NY Rev of Books 250 W 57th St New York NY 10014

KJELSTRUP, CHERYL ANN, librarian; b. Madison, Wis., Sept. 23, 1947; d. Robert A. and Katherine E. (Benish) Heiman; m. Glen W. Wildenberg, Apr. 6, 1968 (div. June 1984); 1 child, William G. Wildenberg; m. Rod R. Kjelstrup, Jan. 3, 1987; children: Christopher M., Andrew J. BA in Social Scis., Kans. State U., 1970; student, U. Wis., Oshkosh, 1983, U. Wis., Milw., 1993—. Cert. K-12 libr. and computer instr., Wis. Libr. aide Two Rivers (Wis.) Pub. Schs., 1976-88; libr. Wrightstown (Wis.) Cmty. Schs., 1988-90; libr., computer coord. Brillion (Wis.) Schs., 1990—. Bd. dirs. Cmty. Concerts Assn., Manitowoc, Wis., 1980-88; mem. long-rang planning com. Brillion Pub. Libr., 1993-94. Recipient State scholarship Delta Kappa Gamma Sigma 1994, 95. Mem. Wis. Ednl. Media Assn. (mem. info. literacy com. 1992-93), Brillion Fedn. Tchrs. (pres. local 1994-96), Delta Kappa Gamma (pres. 1992-94). Home: 14415 Jambo Creek Rd Mishicot WI 54228-9734 Office: Brillion Pub Schs 315 S Main St Brillion WI 54110-1207

KJOS, VICTORIA ANN, lawyer; b. Fargo, N.D., Sept. 17, 1953; d. Orville I. and Annie J. (Tanberg) K. BA, Minot State U., 1974; JD, U. N.D., 1977. Bar: Ariz. 1978. Assoc. Jack E. Evans, Ltd., Phoenix, 1977-78, pension and ins. cons., 1978-79; dep. state treas. State of N.D., Bismarck, 1979-80; freelance cons. Phoenix, 1980-81, Anchorage, 1981-82; asst. v.p., v.p., mgr. trust dept. Great Western Bank, Phoenix, 1982-84; assoc. Robert A. Jensen P.C., Phoenix, 1984-86; ptnr. Jensen & Kjos, P.C., Phoenix, 1986-89; assoc. Allen, Kimerer & LaVelle, Phoenix, 1989-90, ptnr., 1990-91; dir. The Yoga and Fitness Inst., Phoenix, 1994—; lectr. in domestic relations. Contbr. articles to profl. jours. Bd. dirs. Arthritis Found., Phoenix, 1986-89, v.p. for chpt. devel., 1988-89; bd. dirs. Ariz. Yoga Assn., 1993-95, v.p., 1993-95. Mem. ABA, ATLA, Ariz. Bar Assn. (exec. coun. family law sect. 1988-91), Maricopa Bar Assn. (sec. family law com. 1988-89, pres. family law com. 1989-90, judge pro tem 1989-91), Ariz. Trial Lawyers Assn.

KLADZYK, PAMELA ZIEMBA, artist, history educator; b. Bad Axe, Mich., Mar. 5, 1949; d. Franklin James and Marie Josephine (Ziemba) K. BFA in Painting, U. Mich., 1971; MFA in Painting, Eastern Mich. U., 1975; PhD in Art History, Cath. U. Lublin, Poland, 1987. Artist in residence Wards Island Psychiat. Hosp., N.Y.C., 1979, N.Y. Found. Arts., N.Y.C., 1986-87; painting & drawing instr. Adult Hispanic Psychiat. Outpatient Clinic Columbia Presbyn. Hosp., N.Y.C., 1986-87; painting & drawing instr., exhbn. coord. Washington Heights Cmty. Ctr., N.Y.C., 1988-89; adj. assoc. prof. fine arts dept. Dowling Coll., Oakdale, N.Y.; adj. asst. prof. dept. fgn. langs & fine arts St. Francis Coll., Bklyn., 1991; mem. faculty arch. & environ. design Parsons Sch. Design, N.Y.C., 1991—; faculty mem. Bard Grad. Ctr. Studies Decorative Arts, N.Y.C., 1994—; proprietor Kladzyk Tribeca Studio, N.Y.C., 1993—; vis. prof. dept. art & art history Oakland U., Rochester, Mich., 1990; chmn. membership com. Polish Inst. Arts & Scis. Am., 1994—. Group exhbns. include Air Gallery, N.Y.C., 1984, Boricua Coll., 1985, Parsons Sch. Design, 1995. Anti-war activist, pacifist Students Democratic Soc., 1967-68. Grantee Kosciuszko Found., 1989, Jagiellonian U., 1989, Woodrow Wilson Internat. Ctr. Scholars & Am. Coun. Learned Socs., 1990, Parsons Sch. Design, 1995. Mem. Am. Assn. Advancement Slavic Studies, Nat. Mus. Am. Indian (charter), Coll. Art Assn., Czechoslovak Soc. Arts & Scis. Am., Kosciuszko Found. Home: 60 Lispenard St New York NY 10013 Office: Parsons Sch Desin Arch & Environ Design Dept 66 Fifth Ave New York NY 10013

KLAICH, DOLORES, health educator; b. Cleve., Aug. 9, 1936; d. Jacob and Caroline (Stampar) K. BA, Case Western Res U., 1958; postgrad., SUNY Stony Brook, 1994—. Reporter Life mag., N.Y.C., 1962-67; freelance writer, editor, lectr., 1967—; edn. coord. L.I. Assn. for AIDS Care, Huntington, N.Y., 1987-89; lectr. SUNY Sch. Health, Tech. and Mgmt., 1989—; judge Ferro-Grumley Lit. Awards, N.Y.C., 1989, 90. Author: Woman Plus Woman: Attitudes toward Lesbianism, 1974, Heavy Gilt, 1988. Co-chmn. East End Lesbian and Gay Orgn., Southampton, N.Y., 1977-85; del. Nat. Women's Conf., Houston, 1977. Mem. Suffolk County Women and AIDS Coalition. Democrat. Home: 407 W Main St Huntington NY 11743 Office: SUNY R07551 L-2 075 AIDS Resource Ctr Stony Brook NY 11794

KLAINBERG, MARILYN BLAU, community health educator; b. N.Y.C., Jan. 6, 1942; d. George Blau and Etta (Nagel) Konrad; m. Bernard Klainberg, June 3, 1961; children: Dennis, Danielle, Gregory, Joshua. BS, Adelphi Coll., 1963; MS, Adelphi U., 1977; EdD, Columbia U., 1994. RN, N.Y. Mem. adj. faculty Adelphi U., Garden City, N.Y., 1977-86, mem. vis. faculty, 1986-87, mem. adj. faculty, 1987-89; asst. prof., dir. continuing edn. SUNY Health Sci. Ctr., Bklyn., 1989—, faculty officer, 1992-93, dir. continuing edn., asst. prof. Coll. Nursing, 1995—; summer program nurse, dir. Manhasset (N.Y.) Pub. Schs., 1974-88, cons. health promotion programs, 1991-92, chmn. substance abuse com., 1991; edn. dir. Friends of Hospice, Manhasset, 1990—, chmn. rsch. grant com.; cons. on drugs and alcohol Manhasset Youth Coun.; presenter in field. Newspaper columnist Manhasset Press, 1980-84; co-author: A Guidebook for the Prevention of Substance Abuse, 1990; mem. editl. bd. NACLI. Mem. Manhasset Student Com., 1989—; mem. exec. bd. Manhasset Student Aid Assn., 1990-95, Manhasset Schs. Parent Coun.; chmn. Safe Homes, 1988; edn. chair exec. bd. Friends of Hospice, 1993—, rsch. grant chairperson, 1994-95. Recipient Ruth W. Harper Disting. Svc. award Nurses Assn. of Counties of L.I., 1995; New Faculty rsch. grantee SUNY, 1991. Mem. ANA, Am. Assn. Higher Edn., Assn. Counties of L.I. (membership com., exec. bd. 1992-93), Kappa Delta Pi, Sigma Theta Tau (exec. bd. by-laws com. 1990-93, chmn. fundraising com. 1989, nominating com. 1994, dist 14 editl. bd. 1993-94, co-chmn. spring conf. and 1995 25th anniversary celebration, co-chmn. by-laws com., pres. Alpha Omega chpt. 1996—). Home: 14 Short Dr Manhasset NY 11030-3421 Office: SUNY Health Sci Ctr 450 Clarkson Ave Brooklyn NY 11203-2012

KLAJBOR, DOROTHEA M., lawyer, consultant; b. Dunkirk, N.Y., Dec. 2, 1915; d. Joseph M., Sr., and Susan R. (Schrantz) K.; student George Washington U., 1949-52; JD, Am. U., Washington, 1956. Bar: D.C., 1957. From legal asst., legis. atty., atty., 2d asst. to Chief U.S. Marshal, civil rights compliance officer Dept. of Justice, Washington, 1938-70; supr. Town of Dunkirk, N.Y., 1973-76; mem. N.Y. State Liquor Authority, Buffalo, 1976-80. Bd. dirs. Center for Women Govt., Albany, N.Y., 1978-82, Dunkirk Sr. Citizens Ctr., 1983; mem. Chautauqua County Task Force on Aging, 1972-73, Town of Dunkirk Indsl. Devel. Agy., 1972-76, Chautauqua County Planning Bd., 1973-76, No. Chautauqua County Intermcpl. Planning Bd., 1974-76, Chautauqua County Overall Econ. Devel. Planning Bd., 1974-76, Literacy Vols., 1972-76, West Dunkirk Vol. Fire Dept., 1973—; adv. bd. Dunkirk Sr. Citizens, 1974-76; mem. women's divsn. N.Y. State Democratic Com. Mem. Am. Bar Assn. (life), Fed. Bar Assn., D.C. Bar, Women's Bar Assn. D.C. (life), AAUW, Nat. Lawyers Club, Cath. Daus. Am., No. Chautauqua Club Assocs. (life), Dunkirk Hist. Soc. (life), Friends of Rockefeller Art Ctr. SUNY Fredonia, Brooks Meml. Hosp. Aux., Chautauqua County Home Aux., Kappa Beta Pi. Roman Catholic. Clubs: Chautauqua County Dem. Women's (treas. 1974-76), Zonta Internat. (chmn. com. on status of women; Industry Person of Yr. award 1980, Calista Jones award for advancement rights of women 1984), Fredonia Dem. Home: 91 Forest Pl Fredonia NY 14063-1701

KLAMEN, DEBRA LEE, psychiatrist, medical educator; b. Dixon, Ill., Apr. 25, 1959; d. Samuel and Bonnie Lee (Freeberg) K.; m. Leonard Gerard Servedio, May 11, 1986 (div. Sept. 1992); m. Philip Dean Pan, Oct. 27, 1996. BS, U. Ill., 1981; MD, U. Chgo., 1985. Intern in psychiatry U. Ill., Chgo., 1985-86, resident in psychiatry, 1986-89, med. dir. inpatient unit, 1989-91, med. dir. peri-hosp., 1991-94, dir. undergrad. med. edn., 1994—; cons. for stress mgmt., 1986—; spkr. in field. Contbr. articles to profl. jours., chpts. to books. Recipient COMCOR grant U. Ill., 1990; recipient Award Harvard Macy Inst., 1996. Mem. AMA (mem. physician health com. 1995—), Am. Psychiatric Assn., Assn. for Acad. Psychiatry (mem. program planning com. 1994—), Assn. Dirs. Med. Student Edn. in Psychiatry, Ill. Psychiatric Soc. (mem. pub. affairs com. 1993—, chair program com. 1995—). Office: U Ill Dept Psychiatry 912 S Wood M C 913 Chicago IL 60612

KLAMERUS, KAREN JEAN, pharmacist, researcher; b. Chgo., Aug. 10, 1957; d. Robert Edward and Jane Mary (Nawoj) K.; m. Frederick P. Zeller. BS in Pharmacy, U. Ill., 1980; PharmD, U. Ky., 1981. Registered pharmacist Ky., Ill., Pa. Staff pharmacist Haggin Meml. Hosp., Harrodsburg, Ky., 1980-81, Regional Med. Ctr., Madisonville, Ky., 1982; critical care liasion Regional Med. Ctr., Madisonville, 1982; clin. pharmacist resident U. Nebr., Omaha, 1983; clin. pharmacist cardiothoracic surgery U. Ill., Chgo., 1983-88, clin asst. prof. dept. pharmacy practice, 1983-86, asst. prof., 1986-88, departmental affiliate dept. pharmaceutics, 1986-88; sr. pharmacokineticist Wyeth-Ayerst Rsch., Phila., 1988-91, asst. dir. clin. pharmacology, 1991-95, assoc. dir. clin. pharmacology, 1995—; cons. Dimensional Mktg. Inst., Chgo., 1983-88, Channing Weinbergs' Co., Inc., N.Y.C., 1983-88. Fellow Am. Coll. Clin. Pharmacy (mem. indsl. rels. com. 1995); mem. Am. Soc. Clin. Pharmacol. and Therapeutics, Mid-Atlantic Coll. Clin. Pharmacy (sec. 1991, pres. 1992-94). Office: Wyeth-Ayerst Rsch PO Box 8299 Philadelphia PA 19101-0082

KLARIN, DONNA LITA, elementary education educator; b. L.A., May 7, 1947; d. Sol and Estelle Klarin; 1 child, Todd. BA, Calif. State U., Northridge, 1971; MS, Coll. for Ctr. of Early Edn., 1981; MA in Bus., Nat. U., 1989. Classroom tchr. Coachella Valley Unified Sch. Dist., Thermal, Calif., 1983-89; founder, dir. Children's Mus. of the Desert, Rancho Mirage, Calif., 1988-93; art cons. Desert Sands Unified Sch. Dist., 1990-92; art instr. Calif. State U., San Bernardino, 1990-93; ednl. cons. Desert Ctr. Unified Sch. Dist., 1996—. Pub. Coachella Valley Family News, Rancho Mirage, 1993—. Mem. cultural commn. City of Rancho Mirage, 1994-95; treas. Adopt a Class, 1994—; sec. Palm Desert H.S. Found., 1993—. Mem. Calif. Assn. Gifted, Computer User Educators. Office: PO Box 191 Rancho Mirage CA 92270-0191

KLASING, SUSAN ALLEN, environmental toxicologist, consultant; b. San Antonio, Sept. 10, 1957; d. Jesse Milton and Thelma Ida (Tucker) Allen; m. Kirk Charles Klasing, Mar. 3, 1984; children: Samantha Nicole, Jillian Paige. BS, U. Ill., 1979, MS, 1981, PhD, 1984. Staff scientist Life Scis. Rsch. Office, Fedn. Am. Socs. Exptl. Biology, Bethesda, Md., 1984-85; assoc. dir. Alliance for Food and Fiber, Sacramento, 1986; postgrad. rschr. U. Calif., Davis, 1986-87, 94-96; project dir. Health Officers Assn. Calif., Sacramento, 1987-89; cons. Klasing and Assocs., Davis, Calif., 1989—; mem. expert com. for substances-of-concern San Joaquin Valley Drainage Program, Sacramento, 1987, follow-up task force, 1990-91, drainage oversight com., 1992-94. Author: (chpt.) Consideration of the Public Health Impacts of Agricultural Drainage Water Contamination, 1991. Mem. AAAS. Office: Klasing and Assocs 515 Flicker Ave Davis CA 95616-0178

KLAUSNER, AMY HOFFMAN, lawyer; b. N.Y.C., Apr. 8, 1963; d. Peter Lawrence Klausner and Carol Miller Hoffman; m. Everardo Aniceto Rodriguez, Feb. 27, 1993; 1 child, Caroline Adele Rodriguez. BA, U. Vt., Burlington, 1985; JD, Cornell U., 1989. Bar: N.Y. 1990, D.C. 1991, Fla. 1992. Assoc. Kelley, Drye & Warren, Kelley, Drye & Warren, 1989-91, Weintraub & Rosen, Miami, Fla., 1992-93. Vol. Planned Parenthood, Miami, 1991-93, Monroe County Dem. Party, Rochester, N.Y., 1993—. Mem. Greater Rochester Assn. Women Attys. Home: 7926 E Main Rd Lima NY 14485

KLAUSNER, HILARY WEINBERG, lawyer; b. Skokie, Ill., Aug. 25, 1969; d. Henry and Estelle (Cutler) Weinberg; m. Andrew Russell Klausner, Aug. 6, 1994. BA, Ariz. State U., 1991; JD, Calif. Western Sch. Law, San Diego, 1993. Law clk. Pima County Superior Ct., Tucson, 1994-95; legal intern City Prosecutor's Office, Tucson, 1995—; mock trial coach Amphitheatre H.S., Tucson, 1994—; tutor Lawyers for Literacy, Tucson, 1994—. Vol. Hermitage Cat Shelter, Tucson, 1995—. Mem. ABA, ATLA, Phi Alpha Delta. Republican. Jewish. Office: City Prosecutor's Office 103 E Alameda #501 Tucson AZ 85701

KLAVITER, HELEN LOTHROP, magazine editor; b. Lima, Ohio, Mar. 5, 1944; d. Eugene H. and Jean (Walters) Lothrop; m. Douglas B. Klaviter, June 7, 1969 (div. 1982); 1 child, Elizabeth. B.A., Cornell Coll., Mt. Vernon, Iowa, 1966. Communication specialist Coop. Extension Service, Urbana, Ill., 1969-71; mng. editor Poetry Mag., Chgo., 1973—; editorial cons. Harper & Row, N.Y.C., 1983-87. Bd. dirs. Ill. Theatre Ctr., 1989-95, St. Clement's Open Pantry, 1990—, Episc. Diocese of Chgo. Hunger Commn., 1992—, Comms. Commn., 1993—. Episcopalian. Home: 395 Dogwood St Park Forest IL 60466-1863 Office: Poetry Mag Modern Poetry Assn 60 W Walton St Chicago IL 60610-3305

KLAW, BARBARA VAN DOREN, author, editor; b. N.Y.C., Sept. 17, 1920; d. Carl and Irita (Bradford) Van Doren; m. Spencer Klaw, July 5, 1941; children: Joanna Klaw Schultz, Susan Klaw (Del Tredici), Rebecca Klaw (Feldman), Margaret Klaw (Metcalfe). B.A., Vassar Coll., 1941. Writer-researcher OWI, Washington, 1942-43; reporter N.Y. Post, 1943-45; free-lance editor, writer, 1945-63; editor Am. Heritage mag., N.Y.C., 1963-88. Author: One Summer, 1936, One Winter, 1938, A Pony Named Nubbin, 1939, Joan and Michael, 1941, all under pseudonym Martin Gale; under pseudonym Eleanor Benton: The Complete Book of Etiquette, 1956; Camp Follower, 1944; editor folklore anthology, 1960. Home: 280 Cream Hill Rd West Cornwall CT 06796-1207

KLEER, NORMA VESTA, critical care nurse; b. London, Apr. 23, 1933; d. Harold N. and Julia Bonanova (Ball-Dale) Wragg; divorced; children: Valerie Mainguy, David. Diploma, Torbay (South Devon, Eng.) Hosp., 1954, St. Francis Hosp., Trenton, N.J., 1964. Critical care nursing mgr. Bayfront Med. Ctr., St. Petersburg, Fla.; dir. nursing PRN Inc., St. Petersburg, Am. Healthcare Mgmt., St. Petersburg; nursing coord. Care Plus Inc. Hi-Tech. Home Infusion Co., Fla.; case mgr., DON Bayada Nurses Home Care Specialists, St. Petersburg, Fla.; dir. nurses Nurses PRN, Tampa Bay, Fla.; pioneer in devel. of EMS Sys., Pinellas Co. Mem. Fla. Emergency Nurses Assn. (founder, 1st pres.).

KLEES, JUNE MARIE, speech language pathologist; b. Milw., Sept. 4, 1965; d. Robert Alois and Karen Ann (Leonard) Jasniewski; m. Eugene Kenneth Klees Jr., June 7, 1987; children: Theresa Marie, Stephanie Jean, Victoria Rose. BS in Communication Disorders, U. Wis., Stevens Point, 1987; MS in Speech Lang. Pathology, Marquette U., 1988. Speech lang. pathologist New Medico Rehab. Ctr., Waterford, Wis., 1988-90, Racine County Spl. Edn., Union Grove, Wis., 1990-93; area supr., regional clin. dir. Med. Rehab., Mequon, Wis., 1993; speech lang. pathologist Med. Rehab., Milw., 1993-96; presenter Regional In-Svc. Spl. Edn., Racine, 1993. Mem. Am. Speech and Hearing Assn., Wis. Speech Lang. Hearing Assn. (presenter conf. 1995). Home: 4090 Edelweiss Ln West Bend WI 53095-8605 Office: St Joseph's Hosp 551 Silverbrook West Bend WI 53095

KLEIMAN, VIVIAN ABBE, filmmaker; b. Phila., Oct. 11, 1950; d. Philip and Hilda (Kramer) K. BA, U. Calif., 1974. Filmmaker; lectr. Grad. Program in Documentary Film Prodn. Stanford U., 1995, 96; bd. dirs. Cultural Rsch. and Comm., Berkeley, Calif., The Living Room Festival, San Francisco, Catticus Corp., Berkeley; founding dir. Jewish Film Festival, Berkeley, 1981-85, Frameline, San Francisco, 1985—; pres., exec. dir. Signifyin' Works, Berkeley, 1991—; v.p. Film Arts Found., San Francisco, 1983-93; lectr. Stanford (Calif.) U., 1992, 95, 96, U. Calif., Berkeley, 1990, 91, 92, 93; cinematographer Tongues Untied, 1989. Producer, dir. films including Judy Chicago: The Birth Project, 1985, Ein Stehaufmannchen, 1991, My Body's My Business, 1992; producer films including Routes of Exile: A Moroccan Jewish Odyssey, 1982, California Gold, 1984, Color Adjustment, 1992, Roam Sweet Home, 1996; assoc. producer The Disney Channel, 1982-83; rschr. for various films including A Woman Named Golda, 1982. Recipient George Foster Peabody award Sundance Film Festival, Outstanding Achievement award Internat. Documentary Assn., Nat. Emmy award nominee, The Eric Barnouw awards Orgn. Am. Historians, Red ribbon Am. Film and Video Festival, Best of Festival award Black Maria Festival, Black Internat. Cinema Berlin, Gold Plaque, Social/Polit. Documentary Chgo. Internat. Film Festival, N.C. Silver Juror's prize. Mem. Bay Area Video Coalition, Film Arts Found., Internat. Documentary Assn. Office: 2600 10th St Berkeley CA 94710-2522

KLEIN, ANNE SCEIA, public relations executive; b. Phila., Apr. 25, 1942; d. Charles B. and Kathryn L. (Lucas) Sceia; m. Gerhart L. Klein, June 19, 1976. BS in Econs., U. Pa., 1964, MA in Communications, 1965. Promotion asst. S.E. Pa. Transit Authority, Phila., 1965; pub. rels. dir. Pa. Lung Assn., Phila., 1965-68; info. dir. H2L2 Architects, Phila., 1968; pub. rels. officer Girard Bank, Phila., 1969-76; acct. exec. Aitkin-Kynett Co., Inc., Phila., 1977; mgr. media rels. Sun Co., Radnor, Pa., 1978-80; mgr. exec. communications Sun Co., Radnor, 1980-82; pres. Anne Klein & Assocs., Inc., Mt. Laurel, N.J., 1982—. Mem. Ethics Com., Mt. Laurel, 1988-92; mem. Citizens Adv. Com., Mt. Laurel, 1988-92; mem. water quality com. Old Taunton Colony Club, Medford, N.J., 1995—. Recipient Super Communicator of 80's award Women in Comm., 1987, Tribute to Women in Industry award YMCA, 1990, Hale's Legacy award Women in Comm., 1996; named Small Bus. Person of Yr. So. N.J. C. of C., 1991. Fellow Pub. Rels. Soc. Am. (accredited, pres. Phila. chpt. 1979, mid-Atlantic chmn. 1984, assembly del. 1980-82, 88—, exec. com. Counselors Acad. 1990-91, Pepperpot awards, Coll. of Fellows 1991), Pub. Rels. Profls. So. N.J. (chmn. 1987—, pres. 1985-87), Forum Exec. Women (sec. bd. dis. 1981-83), Phila. Pub. Rels. Assn., Harbor League Club, U. Pa. Faculty Club, Kappa Delta. Office: Anne Klein & Assocs Ste 200 3 Greentree Ctr Marlton NJ 08053

KLEIN, CAROL J., communications executive; b. Schenectady, N.Y., Mar. 7, 1951; d. Leonard A. and Jean E. (Carlton) K. BA in English, Hartwick Coll., 1974. Comm. asst. Planning Rsch. Corp., Washington, 1978-79; mgr. corp. comm. Household Internat., Prospect Heights, Ill., 1979-86; external cons. Henley Group, Inc., La Jolla, Calif., 1986-89; v.p. corp. affairs Dole Food Co., Westlake Village, Calif., 1989-93; v.p. comm. NovaCare Inc., King of Prussia, Pa., 1993-95, Gen. Instrument, Hatboro, Pa., 1995-96; sr. v.p. comm. Red Roof Inns, Inc., Hilliard, Ohio, 1996—. Home: 5001 Brittany Ln Bryn Mawr PA 19010-2079

KLEIN, CHARLOTTE CONRAD, public relations executive; b. Detroit, June 20, 1923; d. Joseph and Bessie (Brown) K. BA, UCLA, 1945. Corr. UPI, Los Angeles, 1945-46; staff writer CBS, Los Angeles, 1946-47; publicist David O. Selznick Studios, Culver City, Calif., 1947-49, Foladare and Assocs., Los Angeles, 1949-51; publicist to v.p. Edward Gottlieb & Assocs., N.Y.C., 1951-62; v.p. to sr. v.p. Harshe Rotman & Druck, N.Y.C., 1962-78; dir. press/govt. affairs Sta. WNET-TV, N.Y.C., 1978-79; pres. Charlotte C. Klein Assocs., N.Y.C., 1979-84; sr. v.p., group supr. Porter Novelli, N.Y.C., 1984-89; prin. Charlotte Klein Assocs., N.Y.C., 1989—; adj. prof. pub. rels. NYU. Contbr. articles to profl. jours. Bd. dirs. Manhattan chpt. Am. Cancer Soc., 1988-92. Recipient Cine Golden Eagle, 1977, Matrix award Women in Communications, 1975. Mem. Pub. Rels. Soc. Am. (accredited; pres. N.Y. chpt. 1985-86, Silver Anvil award 1978, John Hill award 1988), Women's Forum (bd. dirs. N.Y. chpt. 1986-87, 96—), Internat. Women's Forum (leadership com. chair dialogue for democracy 1993—), Women Exes. in Pub. Rels. (pres. 1965).

KLEIN, DYANN LESLIE, theater properties company executive; b. Clifton, N.J.; d. Alfred L. and Florence (Slaff) K.; divorced. BA, Ohio State U., 1973; postgrad., Rutgers U., 1976, Sch. Visual Arts, 1983-86. Art therapist Jackson Meml. Hosp., Miami, Fla., 1973-74; prodn. asst. Dom Albi Assocs., N.Y.C., 1974-75; freelance prodn. asst. N.Y.C., 1975-76, freelance designer and stylist, 1976-80; pres. Props For Today, Inc., N.Y.C, 1980—; guest speaker Fashion Inst. of Tech., N.Y.C., 1987, mem. faculty; bd. dirs. Tipps Directory, N.Y.C. Mem. NAFE, Internat. Home Furnishings Assn., N.Y. Women in Film and TV, Pro New York. Jewish. Office: Props For Today Inc 330 W 34th St New York NY 10024

KLEIN, EDITH MILLER, lawyer, former state senator; b. Wallace, Idaho, Aug. 4, 1915; d. Fred L.B. and Edith (Gallup) Miller; m. Sandor S. Klein (dec. 1970). BS in Bus., U. Idaho, 1935; teaching fellowship, Wash. State U., 1936; JD, George Washington U., 1946, LLM, 1954. Bar: D.C. 1946, Idaho 1947, N.Y. 1955, U.S. Supreme Ct. 1954. Pers. spec. Labor and War Depts., Wash., 1942-46; practice law Boise, Idaho, 1947—; judge Mcpl. Ct., Boise, 1947-49; mem. Idaho Ho. Reps., 1948-50, 64-68, Idaho Senate, 1968-82; atty. FCC Wash., 1953-54; FHA N.Y.C., 1955-56. Chmn. Idaho Gov.'s Commn. Status Women, 1964-72, mem., 1965-79, 82-92; mem. Idaho Gov.'s Coun. Comprehensive Health Planning, 1969-76, Idaho Law Enforcement Planning Commn., 1972-82, Nat. Adv. Commn. Regional Med. Programs, 1974-76, Idaho Endowment Investment Bd., 1979-82; trustee Boise State U. Found., Ind., 1973-95; pres. Boise Music Week, 1991-94; bd. dirs. Harry W. Morison Found. Ind., 1978—, St. Alphonsus Regional Med. Ctr. Found., 1982—; past pres. bd. dirs. Boise Philharm. Assn., Boise Opera. Named Woman of Yr. Boise Altrusa Club, 1966, Boise C. of C., 1970, Disting. Citizen, Idaho Statesman 1970, Woman of Progress, Idaho Bus. Prof. Women, 1978; recipient Women Helping Women award Soroptimist Club, 1980, Stein Meml. award Y.M.C.A., 1983, Silver and Gold award for Outstanding Svc., U. Idaho, 1985, March of Dimes award to Honor Outstanding Women, 1987, Cert. of Appreciation by Boise Br., AAUW, 1990, Morrison Ctr. Hall of Fame award, 1990, Disting. Cmty. Svc. award Boise Area C. of C., 1995. Mem. DAR (regent Pioneer chpt. 1991-93). Republican. Congregationalist. Home: 1588 Lenz Lane PO Box 475 Boise ID 83701 Office: 1400 West One Plaza PO Box 2527 Boise ID 83701

KLEIN, ELAINE, advertising executive; b. Bklyn., Mar. 12, 1929; d. Sidney and Bertha (Smith) Laks; m. Melvin Klein, Dec. 23, 1951; children: Cyd Robin Klein Tomack, Amy Susan Klein Len. Exec. sec. to pres. Muzak Corp., N.Y.C., 1949-55; expeditor The Van Ard Co., Forest Mills, N.Y., 1968-70; advt. sales mgr., West Coast advt. dir. Playbill mag., N.Y.C., 1970—. Mem. Nat. Assn. Exec. Women, The New Dramatists, Friars Club, Mus. of Natural History, Advt. Club of L.A. Democrat. Jewish. Office: Playbill Mag 6531 W 6th St Los Angeles CA 90048

KLEIN, ESTHER MOYERMAN (MRS. PHILIP KLEIN), author, retired publisher; b. Phila., Nov. 3, 1907; d. Louis and Rebecca (Feldman) Moyerman; BS, Temple U., 1929; student U. London, 1954; m. Philip Klein, Apr. 26, 1930; children: Arthur, Karen Louise Klein Mannes. Reporter, Phila. Jewish Times, 1925, Atlantic City Times, 1927; feature writer Pub. Ledger Syndicate, 1928-29, Pub. Ledger, Evening Bull., Phila. Record, 1929-32; pub. rels. counselor, editor Art Alliance Bull., 1945-49; commentator Sta. WPEN, 1949-53; pub. Phila. Jewish Times, 1953-74; author, hist. researcher, 1974—; lectr. women's clubs, 1951—; del. Internat. Conf. Residential Adult Edn., Holland, 1957, Germany, 1959; participant in first workshop Residential Adult Edn. for Adult Edn. Assn. U.S., 1954. Mem. Gov.'s Commn. on Charitable Orgns., 1969—; chmn. Rittenhouse Sq. Women's com. for Phila. Orch., 1957; organizer bicentennial women's com. Walnut St. Theatre; adv. com. Friends Nat. Independence Hist. Park; chmn. bicentennial program Beth Zion - Beth Israel Congregation; bd. dirs. Rittenhouse Found., Phila. Jewish Times Inst., also dir. ann. cooking festivals; exec. com. Long Beach Island Found. Arts and Scis., N.J.; bd. dirs. University City Sci. Ctr. Named Distinguished Dau. Pa.; recipient Gimbel Phila. award, 1975; awards Alumnae Girls High Sch., Phila. Art Alliance, Temple U., City Coun. Phila., Colonial Hist. Soc.; Klein Recital Hall at Temple U. named in her honor, Esther M. Klein Art Gallery named in her honor University City Sci. Ctr. Mem. Pa. Newspaper Pubs. Assn., Temple U. Alumni (honored at 80th anniversary, 1964), Phila. High Sch. for Girls Alumnae, Hannah Penn House, Emergency Aid of Pa., Chgo. Art Mus., Mus. Modern Art N.Y., Pan Am. Assn., Print Club. Author: A Guidebook to Jewish Philadelphia, 1965; International House Celebrity Cookbook, 1965; History and Guidebook of Fairmount Park, 1974. Address: 135 S 18th St Philadelphia PA 19103-5228

KLEIN, FAY MAGID, health administrator; b. Chgo., Jan. 12, 1929; d. Victor and Rose (Begun) Magid; m. Jerome G. Klein, June 27, 1948 (div. 1970); children: Leslie Susan Janik, Debra Lynne Maslov; m. Manuel Chait, Aug. 28, 1994. BA in English, UCLA, 1961; MA in Pub. Adminstrn., U. So. Calif., 1971. Cert. health adminstrn. Supr. social workers L.A. County, 1961-65; program specialist Econ. and Youth Opportunity Agy., L.A., 1965-69; sr. health planner Model Cities, L.A., 1971-72; dir. prepaid health plan Westland Health Svcs., L.A., 1972-74; exec. dir. Coastal Region Health Consortium, L.A., 1974-76; grants and legis. cons. Jewish Fed. Council of L.A., 1976-79; planning council Jewish Fed. Councils of So. Fla., Palm Beach to Miami, 1979-82; adminstrv. dir. program in kidney diseases Dept. Medicine UCLA, 1982-84; exec. dir. west coast Israel Cancer Rsch. Fund, L.A., 1984-94; cons. to non-profit orgns. Santa Monica, 1994—; cons. Arthritis Found., Los Angeles, 1984, Bus. Action Ctr., Los Angeles, 1982, Vis. Nurses Assn., Los Angeles, 1982. Charter mem. Los Angeles County Mus. of Art, Mus. of Contemporary Art, Los Angeles; cons. Los Angeles Mcpl. Art Gallery, 1979; mem. Art Council Wight Gallery, UCLA. Fellow U.S. Pub. Health, U. So. Calif., 1970-71. Mem. Am. Pub. Health, UCLA Alumni Assn. (life), U. So. Calif. Alumni Assn. (life).

KLEIN, FLORENCE WEBER, elementary school principal, computer coordinator; b. N.Y.C., Jan. 15, 1930; d. Arthur and Malvina (Herman) Weber; m. Philip Morton Klein (dec. Dec., 1993); children: Robert Mitchell, Melissa Beth Klein Morrissey. BS in Edn., CCNY, 1951, MA, 1954; postgrad. studies, Temple U., 1956, Teachers Coll., N.Y.C., 1959-60. Cert. tchr., prin., supt. N.Y. State and City. Tchr. Fallsburg (N.Y.) Ctrl. Sch., 1951-52; tchr. N.Y.C. Bd. Edn., 1952-56, 57-59, asst. prin., 1959-75, prin., 1975-85, computer coord. and tchr., 1985—; tchr. Phila. Bd. Edn., 1956-57. Vol. dispatcher Little Neck (N.Y.) Ambulance Corps, 1994-95; clown Schneider Children's Hosp., Long Island Jewish Hosp., Queens, N.Y., 1995—. Mem. AAUW (computer tchr. North Shore br. 1994-95), Retired Suprs. and Sch. Adminstrs. (chmn. social and cultural com. 1994-95). Home: 249-10 Cullman Ave Little Neck NY 11362

KLEIN, FREDA, retired state agency administrator; b. Seattle, May 17, 1920; d. Joseph and Julia (Caplan) Vinikow; m. Jerry Jerome Klein, Oct. 20, 1946; children: Jan Susan Klein Waples, Kerry Joseph, Robin Jo Klein. BA, U. Wash., 1942; MS, U. Nev., Las Vega, 1969, EdD, 1978. Owner, mgr. Smart Shop, Provo, Utah, 1958-60, Small Fry Shop, Las Vegas, 1961-66; vocat. counselor, test adminstr. Nev. Employment Security Dept., Las Vegas, 1966-77, local office mgr., 1978-95; ret., 1995. Contbr. articles to profl. jours. Exec. bd. Pvt. Industry Coun., Las Vegas, 1988—, Interstate Conf. on Employment Security Agys., Nev., 1988-90, Area Coordinating Com. for Econ. Devel., Las Vegas, 1988—. Recipient Achievement award Nev. Bus. Svc., 1990, Cert. of Spl. Congl. Recognition, 1992; named Outstanding Woman, Goodwill Industries sci. and rsch. divsn., 1977. Mem. AAUW, Internat. Assn. Pers. in Employment Security, U. Nev. Las Vegas Alumni Assn., Henderson C. of C. (exec. bd. 1986—), Soroptimist Internat. (pres. 1987-88), Phi Kappa Phi (scholastic hon.). Home: 2830 Phoenix St Las Vegas NV 89121-1312

KLEIN, GABRIELLA SONJA, communications executive; b. Chgo., Apr. 11, 1938; d. Frank E. Vosicky and Sonja (Kosner) Becvar; m. Donald J. Klein. BA in Comm. and Bus. Mgmt., Alverno Coll., 1983. Editor, owner Fox Lake (Wis.) Rep., 1962-65, McFarland (Wis.) Community Life and Monona Community Herald, 1966-69; bur. reporter Waukesha (Wis.) Daily Freeman, 1969-71; community rels. staff Waukesha County Tech. Coll., Pewaukee, Wis., 1971-73; pub. rels. specialist JI Case Co., Racine, Wis., 1973-75, corp. publs. editor, 1975-80; v.p., bd. dirs. publs. Image Mgmt., Valley View Ctr., Milw., 1980-82; pres. Communication Concepts, Unltd., Racine, 1983—; mem. cmty. com. Racine Unified Sch. Bd. Past pres. Big Bros./Big Sisters Racine County, v.p. devel. Girl Scouts Racine County; bd. dirs. Racine Cmty. Found.; mem. steering com. Racine Cmty. Coalition for Youth. Recipient awards Wis. Press Assn., Nat. Fedn. Press Women; named Wis. Woman Entrepreneur of Yr., 1985, Vol. of the Yr. Racine Area United Way, 1995, Woman of Distinction Bus. Racine YWCA, 1995. Mem. Internat. Assn. Bus. Communicators (accredited mem.; bd. dirs. 1982-85, various awards), Ad Club of Racine. Home: 3045 Chatham St Racine WI 53402-4001 Office: 927 S Main St Racine WI 53403-1524

KLEIN, GAIL BETH MARANTZ, freelance writer, dog breeder; b. Bklyn., Dec. 1, 1946; d. Herbert and Florence (Dresner) Marantz; m. Harvey Leon Klein, Mar. 17, 1979. AB cum laude, U. Miami, Coral Gables, Fla., 1968, MEd, 1969, MBA, 1977. Cert. residential contractor, Fla. Asst. dir. student activities Miami-Dade Community Coll., 1969-79, instr. photography for mentally retarded adults, 1974, acting dir. student activities, 1976, acting advisor student publs., 1978-79, asst. prof. bus. adminstrn., 1979; dog breeder Vizcaya Shepherds, Palm Beach Gardens, Fla., 1979—; trainer Dog Obedience and Conformation Show Handling, West Palm Beach, 1980—; owner, CEO Word Master Profl. Comm.; freelance writer WordMaster Profl. Comms.; mgr. proposal devel., specialist Profl. Food-Svc. Mgmt., Inc.; cons., speaker in field; appeared on various radio talk shows. Editor (booklet) 1978 Consumers Guide to Banking, 1978, (newsletter) Newsletter of German Shepherd Dog Club Ft. Lauderdale, Inc., 1980-83, Sunshine State Shepherd, 1988-89; contbr. articles to newspapers and mags. Chair spl. events com. Third Century U.S.A., Dade County, Fla., 1976; mem. adv. com., mktg. cons. YWCA of Greater Miami, 1976-79; mem. comty. rels. com. Greater Miami Jewish Fedn., 1976-79; mem. Met. Miami Art Ctr., 1977-79; vice chair, chair appeals bd. Palm Beach County Animal Care and Control, 1989—, mem. pet overpopulation com., 1991-93; co-developer, co-admintr. OFA Verifications for German Shepherd Dogs, 1985—; pub. info. coord. Am. Kennel Club, Palm Beach County, 1991-94. Recipient Job Training Partnership Act Employee of Yr. award State of Fla., 1994. Mem. Assn. Proposal Mgmt. Profls., Nat. Assn. Dog Obedience Instrs., Conformation Judges Assn. Fla., Inc., Palm Beach Users Group, Am. Sewing Guild, German Shepherd Dog Club Am., Inc. (hip dysplasia/orthopedic com. 1987-89), German Shepherd Dog Club of Can., Inc., German Shepherd Dog Club of Greater Miami (bd. dirs. 1981-82, 89—, rec. sec. 1977-78, corr. sec. 1978-80, life), Jupiter-Tequesta Dog Club, Inc. (pres. 1984-85, bd. dirs., various other offices, Gaines Sportsmanship award 1993), Obedience Tng. Club Palm Beach County, Inc. (AKC Cmty. Achievement Merit award 1994), Wolf Song of Alaska (grant/proposal writer), Hadassah (life), Alpha Lambda Delta, Epsilon Tau Lambda, Phi Kappa Phi, Mortar Board. Republican. Jewish. Home: 12956 Mallard Creek Dr Palm Beach Gardens FL 33418

KLEIN, IRMA MOLLIGAN, career development educator, consultant; b. New Orleans, Jan. 5, 1936; d. Harry Joseph and Gesina Frances (Bauer) Molligan; m. John Vincent Chelena (dec. 1963); 1 child, Joseph William; m. Chris George Klein, Aug. 14, 1965. BS in Bus. Augustine Coll., postgrad. Mktg. Inst., Chgo., Loyola U., Chgo., Realtors Inst., Baton Rouge. Mgr. Stan Weber & Assocs., Metairie, La., 1971-75; tng. dir., 1975-81; cons. Coldwell Banker Comml. Co., New Orleans, 1981; dir. career devel. Coldwell Banker Residential Co., New Orleans, 1982-85; pres. Irma Klein Career Devel., Inc., Les Quarante Ecolieres, 1994-95; pres. Klein Enterprises, Inc., 1994—; instr. U. New Orleans, Bonnabel H.S., Realtors Inst., La. Real Estate Commn. Author: Career Development, 1982; Training Manual, 1978,

Obtaining Listings, 1986, Participative Marketing, 1986, Marketing & Servicing Listings, 1987, Designing Training Curriculum, 1987, Participative Management. Active Friends of Longue Vue Gardens, La. Hist. Assn. Meml. Hall Found. Mem. La. Realtors Assn. (bd. dirs. 1973-74, grad. Realtors Inst. 1976), Jefferson Bd. Realtors (v.p. 1984), Edn. and Resources (cert., pres. La. chpt.), Rsch. Club of New Orleans (pres. 1984-85), Realtors Nat. Mktg. Inst. (amb. Tex. and La. 1985—, Outstanding Achievement award 1985, cert. broker 1980, residential specialist 1977), Nat. Assn. Realtors (nat. conv. speaker 1986), CRB (pres. La. chpt. 1982-83, chmn. edn.), CRS (pres. La. chpt. 1988-90), Forty Scholars Soc., Am. Dental Assts. Assn., Les Quarante Ecolieres. Republican. Roman Catholic. Clubs: Antique Study Group, Confederate Lit. (New Orleans) (pres.), Rsch. (New Orleans), Metairie Woman's. Avocation: antiques.

KLEIN, JANICE ELLEN, counselor, educator; b. Chicopee Falls, Mass., Mar. 4, 1953; d. Raymond Arno and Margaret Helen (Stokell) Hager; m. Martin Gerrard Klein, July 16, 1979; children: Adam C., Geoffrey M. BS, Tex. Tech. U., 1976; MA, Webster U., 1985; postgrad., St. Louis U., 1992—. Cert. substance abuse counselor, U. Mo.; cert. pastoral counselor Eden Seminary, St. Louis; lic. profl. counselor. Counselor Ctrs. for Psychol. Growth, St. Charles, Mo., 1988—; in-patient psychiat. counselor Barnes-St. Peters (Mo.) Hosp., 1990-92; dir. counseling svcs. Parks Coll. of St. Louis U., Cahokia, Ill., 1992-95; adj. prof. Webster U., St. Louis, 1995—; staff counselor Ch. of The Sheperd, St. Charles, 1988. Capt. USAF, 1976-90. Mem. ACA, AAUW, Am. Assn. Marriage and Family Therapy (clin. mem.), Employee Assistance Program Assn. Home: 3 Shadowood Ct Saint Peters MO 63376

KLEIN, JOAN DEMPSEY, judge; b. San Jose, Calif., Aug. 18, 1924; d. Edward Joseph and Estelle (Kottinger) Dempsey; m. Donrad Lee Klein, Mar. 16, 1963; children: Marc Dempsey Gross, Brad Hunter Gross; stepchildren: Karen Beth , Susan Linda. BA, San Diego State Coll., 1948; LLB, UCLA, 1955. Bar: Calif. 1955, U.S. Supreme Ct. 1964. Dep. atty gen., trial lawyer State of Calif., 1955-63; judge L.A. Mcpl. Ct., 1963-75, presiding judge, 1974; mem. L.A. Superior Ct., 1974-78; presiding justice Calif. Ct. Appeals, L.A., 1978—; prof. jud. adminstrn. U. So. Calif. 1974-75; mem. Calif. Coun. on Criminal Justice, 1970-74, Jud. Criminal Justice Planning Com., 1974-76; del. Nat. Adv. Commn. Criminal Justice Standards and Goals, Washington, 1973; chmn. adv. com. Calif. Hwy. Patrol, 1976; participant S. Am. Lecture Tour Internat. Communication Agy. Mem. adv. bd. Girls Week L.A. City Schs., Gifted Children's Assn., San Fernando Valley, Vol. League San Fernando Valley. Named Alumna of Yr. Law Sch. UCLA, 1963, Angel of Distinction L.A. Cen. City Assn., 1969, Woman of Achievement Calif. Fedn. Bus. and Profl. Women's Club, 1973, Mcpl. Ct. Judge of Yr. Calif. Trial Lawyers, 1973, Woman of Yr. L.A. Times, 1975; recipient Profl. Achievement award UCLA Alumni Assn., 1975, Myrtle Wreath award Hadassah, 1977, Community Woman of Achievement award Big Sisters L.A., 1979, cert. merit from Gov. Brown, 1979, Portrait in Excellence award B'nai Brith Women, Woman of the Yr. award Met. News, 1992, Woman of Vision award Valley Presbyn. Hosp., 1991. Mem. Internat. Fedn. Women Lawyers, Nat. Assn. Women Judges (founding and current pres.), Calif. Women Lawyers (pres. 1975), Calif. Judges Assn., L.A. County Bar Assn., Women Lawyers Assn., Bus. and Profl. Women's Club. (L.A. chpt.), Legion Lex. U. Soc. Calif., UCLA Law Sch. Alumni Assn. (past pres.). Democrat. Office: Ct Appeals 300 S Spring St Los Angeles CA 90013-1230

KLEIN, JULIA MEREDITH, newspaper reporter; b. Phila., Dec. 11, 1955; d. Abraham and Murielle (Pollack) K. BA magna cum laude, Harvard U., 1977. Copy editor J.B. Lippincott, Phila., 1977; features reporter The Oakland Press, Pontiac, Mich., 1978; freelance writer, researcher, editorial cons., 1978—; reporter The Phila. Inquirer, 1983—. Nat. Arts journalism fellow, 1996-97. Mem. Soc. Profl. Journalists, Phi Beta Kappa. Home: 307 Monroe St Philadelphia PA 19147-3211 Office: Phila Inquirer 400 N Broad St PO Box 8263 Philadelphia PA 19101

KLEIN, RUTH B., civic worker, packaging company executive, poet, author; b. Cin., Jan. 31, 1908; d. Samuel and Minnie (Schunke) Becker; student U. Calif. at Los Angeles, 1926-28, San Jose State Coll., 1928-29; m. Charles Henle Klein, Sept. 23, 1938; children: Betsy Klein Schwartz, Charles Henle, Carla Klein Fee III. Sec., Novelart Mfg. Co., Cin., 1960—, dir., 1960—. Vol. Aid to Visually Handicapped program Cin. sect. Nat. Council of Jewish Women, 1951-82, sec., 1954-56, 63-64, bd. dirs., 1952-70; bd. dirs. Civic Garden Center of Greater Cin., 1956-63, chmn. spl. services for aid to visually handicapped, 1952-82. Mem. Nat. Braille Assn., Greater Cin. Writers League, Verse Writers' Guild Ohio. Club: Contemporary Literary. Author: Latitude of Love; Longitude of Lust, 1979; contbr. poems to various anthologies. Home: 6754 Fair Oaks Dr Cincinnati OH 45237-3606

KLEIN, SAMI WEINER, librarian; b. Worcester, Mass., July 6, 1939; d. Phillip and Barbara Rose (Ginsberg) Weiner; m. Eugene Robert Klein, Oct. 22, 1961; children: Pamela, Jeffrey, Elizabeth. BS, Simmons Coll., 1961; MLS, U. Md., 1973; postgrad., Johns Hopkins U., 1976-78. Chemist Hercules, Wilmington, Del., 1961-62, FDA, Washington, 1965-66; libr. NSWC, White Oak, Md., 1973-78; chief Hdqs. Libr. EPA, Washington, 1978-82; chief rsch. info. svcs. Rsch. Info. Ctr. Nat. Inst. Stds. and Tech., Gaithersburg, Md., 1982—; cons. in field; mem. librs. exec. coun. Met. Washington Coun. of Govts., 1981-82; elected mem. com. Fed. Libr. Info. Ctr., 1993-95, chair fin. working group, 1994—. Editor OIS Sci.-Tech Info; mem. editorial bd. Assn. Ofcly. Analyt. Chemists, 1985-92. Fed. govt. rep. Inst. for Sci. Info. Internat. Users Group, 1985-86; mem. edn. com. Fed. Libr. and Info. Ctr. Com., 1987-91. Recipient Gold medal Am. Soc. Chemists, 1961. Mem. ALA (sec.-treas. Fed. Librs. Round Table 1983-84, rep. to NTIS 1984-90, bd. dirs. 1986-89, v.p. 1991, pres. 1991-92, nominations chair 1992-93, scholar 1994—, chair privatization com. 1995—, 1st FLRT Disting. Svc. award 1995), Spl. Librs. Assn. (treas. info.-tech. group 1986-87, student loan com. 1984-85), D.C. Law Librs. Soc. (NIST v.p. standards com. for women 1988, pres. 1989, bd. dirs. Constar Credit Union 1994—), Fed. Libr. and Info. Network (exec. adv. com. 1989-91, sec. 1989, vice chair 1990-91), Beta Phi Mu. Democrat. Jewish. Home: 11041 Woodelves Way Columbia MD 21044-1002 Office: Nat Inst Standards and Tech Route 270 Gaithersburg MD 20899

KLEIN, SUSAN ELAINE, librarian; b. Cedar Falls, Iowa, Aug. 5, 1952; d. Elmo Calvin and Mabel Audrey (Taylor) Boone; m. Richard Joseph Klein II, Oct. 16, 1982; children: Michael Joseph, Christopher James. BA, U. No. Iowa, 1974. Reporter The No. Iowan, Cedar Falls, summer 1972; res. desk clk. U. No. Iowa Libr., Cedar Falls, summer 1974; paralegal for migrant action program VISTA, Muscatine, Iowa, 1975-76; office asst. Cedar Falls Pub. Libr., 1976-77, libr. asst., 1977-78, cataloger, 1978-86, young adult libr., 1988—. Mem. Iowa Libr. Assn. (cert.). Democrat.

KLEIN, SUSAN LYNNE, organization development consultant, educator; b. Prarie Village, Kans., Aug. 9, 1954; d. Andrew Michael and LaVonne Madeline (Holzmeister) K. BA, Macalester Coll., St. Paul, 1976; MS, U. Mont., Missoula, 1981. Cert. sec. edn. Sec. tchr. Chaska (Minn.) Pub. Schs., 1976-79; teaching asst. U. Mont., Missoula, 1979-80; policy analyst Solar Energy Rsch. Inst., Golden, Colo., 1980-83; pvt. cons. Denver, 1983-85; tng. program mgr. Colo. Alliance of Bus., Denver, 1985-89; systems change coord. Edn. Commn. of the States, Denver, 1989-93; orgn. devel. cons. Klein & Assocs., Denver, 1993—; cons. Alaska State Dept. Edn., Sysytems Change Initiative, 1995—. Recipient Pres'. Citation award for pvt. sector initiative, 1988. Office: Klein & Assocs Ste # 312 157 7150 Leetsdale Dr Denver CO 80224

KLEINBERG, JUDITH G., lawyer, children's advocate; b. Hartford, Conn., Jan. 28, 1946; d. Burleigh B. and Ruth (Leven) Greenberg; m. James Paul Kleinberg, Aug. 30, 1970; children: Alexander, Lauren. BA cum laude, U. Mich., 1968; JD, U. Calif., Berkeley, 1971. Atty. pvt. practice, San Francisco, 1971-74; legal affairs reporter comml. and pub. TV, San Francisco, 1974-76; prof. law Mills Coll., Oakland, Calif., 1977-84; chief of staff The Global Fund for Women, Los Altos, Calif., 1987-88; pub. interest atty., non-profit corp. law/orgn. specialist alternative dispute resolution Palo Alto, Calif., 1988-94; exec. dir. Kids in Common: A Children & Families Collaborative, San Jose, Calif., 1994—; arbitrator/mediator, legal adv. for abortion rights, women and children's rights and environ. groups, Santa Clara County and Calif., 1980—; speaker in field. Mem. bd. editors Calif. Law Rev., 1969-71. Mem. steering com. lawyers coun. No. Calif. sect. ACLU, bd. dirs., 1990-92; founder, chairperson No. Calif. Friends of Pediat. AIDS Found.; past pres. Com. for Green Foothills; mem. legis. and steering coms. Calif. Coalition for Childhood Immunization, 1995—; mem. Calif. Children's Advs. Roundtable, 1995—; bd. dirs. Palo Alto SAFE, Support Network for Battered Women, 1990-92, Palo Alto Coun. PTAs, Leadership Midpeninsula, 1994-96; pres. Palo Alto Stanford divsn. Am. Heart Assn., 1994-95; v.p. Assn. for Sr. Day Health, 1994-95; founder Safer Summer Project; pres., legal counsel Calif. Abortion and Reproduction Rights Action League, 1980-86. Recipient Calif. Pks. and Recreation Soc. Merit award, 1995, World of People award Girl Scouts Am., Santa Clara County, 1996. Mem. Am. Arbitration Assn. (mem. atty. panel), Nat. Assn. Child Advocates, Calif. Women Lawyers (v.p. 1986-88).

KLEINER, HEATHER SMITH, academic administrator; b. N.Y.C., Mar. 31, 1940; d. Henry Lee Smith and Marie (Ballou) Edwards; m. Scott Alter Kleiner, Mar. 20, 1961; children: Greta, Catherine. BA in Sociology, Smith Coll., 1961; MAT in Edn., Lynchburg Coll., 1969; postgrad., U. Ga., 1974-82. Rsch. analyst Edward Weiss Advt., Chgo., 1963-65; acad. advisor U. Ga. Coll. Arts and Scis., Athens, 1982-88; asst. dir. womens studies program U. Ga., Athens, 1988-90, assoc. dir. womens studies program, 1990—. Co-founder, 1st pres. Jeannette Rankin Found., Athens, 1976-77, hon. dir., chair capital fund drive, 1995; sec. Friends of Oconee County Libr., 1995—; co-organizer Parents-Friends of Lesbians and Gays, Athens, 1995—. Mem. Nat. Womens Studies Assn., South Ea. Womans Studies Assn. Office: Univ Ga Womens Studies Program Main Libr Athens GA 30602

KLEINLEIN, KATHY LYNN, training and development executive; b. S.I., N.Y., May 2, 1950; d. Thomas and Helen Mary (O'Reilly) Perricone; m. Kenneth Robert Kleinlein, Oct. 30, 1983. BA, Wagner Coll., 1971, MA, 1974; MBA, Rutgers U., 1984. Cert. secondary tchr., N.Y., N.J., Fla. Tchr. English, N.Y.C. Bd. Edn., S.I., 1971-74, Matawan (N.J.) Bd. Edn., 1974-79; instr. English, Middlesex County Coll., Edison, N.J., 1978-81; med. sales rep. Pfizer/Roerig, Bklyn., 1979-81, mgr. tng. ops., N.Y.C., 1981-87; dir. sales tng. Winthrop Pharms. div. Sterling Drug, N.Y.C., 1987-88; dir. tng. Reuters Info. Systems, N.Y.C., 1988—; pres., dir. tng., Women in Transition, career counseling firm; pres. Kleinlein Cons.; pers. mgmt. officer U.S. Army Res., N.J., 1981-86; cons. Concepts & Producers, N.Y.C., 1981-85. Trainer United Way, 1982-83, mem. polit. action com., 1982—; mem. Rep. Presdl. Task Force, Washington, 1983—; mem. Sarasota Library Adv. Bd.; sec. Intracoastal Civic Assn.; elected com. mem. Epiphany Parish Coun.; exec. bd. Selby Found. Edn. Capt. U.S. Army, 1974-78. First woman in N.Y. N.G., 1974; first woman instr. Empire State Mil. Acad., Peekskill, N.Y., 1976. Mem. Rep. Women's Club, Alpha Omicron Pi. Republican. Roman Catholic. Home: 1840 Hudson St Englewood FL 34223-6433 Office: Kleinlein Cons 1840 Hudson St Englewood FL 34223-6433

KLEINMAN, ROBERTA SANDRA, financial services executive. BA in Polit. Sci., San Francisco State U., 1974; JD, Ill. Inst. Tech., 1977. Bar: Ill. 1977. Project mgr. Computer Info. Svc. Inc., Chgo., 1977-81; programming dir. Commodity Exch. Inc., N.Y.C., 1981-85; project mgr. Thomson McKinnon Securities, N.Y.C., 1985-86; v.p. Comex Clearing Assn., N.Y.C., 1986-94; sr. dir., staff atty. Chgo. Mercantile Exch., 1994—. Mem. Futures Industry Assn. (Chgo. divsn.). Office: Chgo Mercantile Exch 30 S Wacker Dr Chicago IL 60606-4541

KLEINSCHNITZ, BARBARA JOY, oil company executive, consultant; b. Granite Falls, Minn., Aug. 25, 1944; d. Arthur William and Joy Ardys (Roe) Green; m. Charles Lewis Kleinschnitz, Dec. 28, 1963 (div.); 1 child, Katheryn JoAnn Kleinschnitz Hartsock. BBA, U. Denver, 1983; student, Colo. Women's Coll. Leadman Schlumberger Well Services, Denver, 1968-76; supr., log processing Scientific Software-Intercomp, Denver, 1976-82; tech. cons. Tech. Log Analysis, Inc., Lakewood, Colo., 1982-83; customer support mgr. Energy Systems Tech., Inc., Englewood, Colo., 1983-86; cons. technical Littleton, Colo., 1986-87; documentation specialist Q.C. Data, Inc., 1987-91; tng. specialist Advanced Data Concepts, Ft. Collins, Colo., 1991-93; tech. writer Computer Data Sys., Inc., Ft. Collins, 1993—; cons. Tech. Log Analysis, Inc., Denver, 1983-89, Energy Systems Tech., 1986-93. Vol. Denver Police Reserve, 1973-75. Mem. NOW, NAFE, Assn. Women Geoscientists, Soc. Profl. Well Log Analysts (bd. dirs. 1989-90, v.p. 1990-91), Denver Well Log Soc. (bd. dirs. 1986-87, v.p. 1987-88, pres. 1988-89). Democrat. Roman Catholic. Home: 1130 Muirfield Way Fort Collins CO 80525-9144 Office: Ste 150 2625 Redwing Rd Fort Collins CO 80526-2878

KLEKODA-BAKER, ANTONIA MARIE, forensic handwriting specialist, consultant; b. Grand Rapids, Mich., June 30, 1939; d. Anthony Joseph and Adele Elizabeth (Fifelski) Zoppa; m. Raymond Syl Klekoda, Aug. 31, 1957 (div. 1977); children: Cecilia (dec.), Vanessa, Rhonda, Darla, Norman, Yvette, Patrice; m. Frederick John Baker, Dec. 31, 1986. Student, Davenport Coll., Grand Rapids, Mich., 1956, Aquinas Coll., Grand Rapids, Mich., 1957-58, 77. Cert. document examiner. Organist, choir dir. Basilica of St. Adalbert, Grand Rapids, Mich., 1957-62; music instr. Mich. Acad. of Music, Northern Mich., 1962-63; owner Handwriting Analysis Service, Grand Rapids, 1963-87; editor Garfield Park Assn., Grand Rapids, Mich., 1974-76; feature columnist Grand Rapids Press., 1966-76; staff Diocesan Pubs., Grand Rapids, 1977-85; musician, Convs., community theater, Western Mich. Author: A Guide for Document Examiners in Preparing Your Curriculum Vitae, 1991; contbr. over 4000 articles to profl. jours. and mags.; delivered over 3500 lectrs. Resource authority Grand Rapids Pub. Library, 1976—; organizer City Neighborhood Assn., Garfield Park, Grand Rapids, 1973, mem. Greater Grand Rapids Convention Bur., 1984-85. Recipient Safety Engrs. award W. Mich. Chpt. Soc. Safety Engrs., 1985, Holland Rotarian award, Holland, Mich. Rotary Club, 1985, Sparta Rotary award, Sparta, Mich. Rotary Club, 1986. Mem. Nat. Assn. Pastoral Musicians, Nat. Assn. of Document Examiners (edn. chmn. 1991, v.p. nominee 1992, pres. nominee 1992), Alliance Women Entrepreneurs, Grand Rapids Fedn. Musicians, Mich. Graphol. Resources (chairperson, Woman of Yr. 1986-87), Data Personnel Mgmt. Assn. Roman Catholic. Home and Office: 325 Aurora St SE Grand Rapids MI 49507-3123

KLEMP, NANCY J., secondary school educator; b. Leavenworth, Kans., Aug. 29, 1943; d. Michael L. and Clara I. (Kochanowski) Buselt; m. Louis A. Klemp; children: Louis III, Jeffrey C., Jennifer R. BA, St. Mary Coll., Leavenworth, 1965. Cert. secondary sch. tchr., Kans. Biology tchr. Unified Sch. Dist. 453, Leavenworth, 1988—; sec., treas. Storage Box, Inc., Leavenworth, 1976—. Mem. St. John's Hosp. Guild. Mem. LNEA, Ladies' C. of C. Republican. Roman Catholic. Home: 1816 Pine Ridge Dr Leavenworth KS 66048 Office: Storage Box Inc 1314 Eisenhower Rd Leavenworth KS 66048

KLEPPEL, NANCY B., architect; b. Bklyn., June 12, 1964; d. Noel Harvey Kleppel and Harriet Freida (Kershaw) Burack. BA, Brown U., 1986; MArch, Harvard U., 1995. Asst. to project architects C.E. Maguire Architects/Engrs., Providence, 1985-86; asst. to project architects William Rawn Assocs., Boston, 1986-87; freelance design cons. Stewart/Ferguson Design, Santa Fe, N.M., 1990; designer Michael F. Bauer Assocs., Santa Fe, 1990; free lance archtl. designer Bklyn., 1994—. Democrat. Jewish. Home and Office: 314 Garfield Pl #6 Brooklyn NY 11215

KLEPPER, CAROL JEAN, mental health therapist; b. Wagner, S.D., July 17, 1933; d. Forrest Glenwood and Augusta Wilhamina (Mills) Herdman; m. Albert Raymond Klepper, May 14, 1955; children: James David, Leesa Lynn, Krista Patrice. BS in Psychology cum laude, S. Oreg. State Coll., 1987; MS in Counseling, Oreg. State U., 1989. Nat. cert. counselor, lic. profl. counselor. Dir. counseling Klamath Hospice, Klamath Falls, Oreg., 1990-91; staff therapist Klamath Mental Health Ctr., 1991-94; in-house counselor Wednesday's Child, 1995—, title 19 adminstr., 1996—; data rschr. Rich Pickett and Co., Klamath Falls, 1986-90; pre-commitment investigator Klamath Mental Health Ctr., 1991-94; EPSDT coord. County of Klamath, 1991-94. Mem. youth svcs. team local mid-schs., Klamath Falls, 1992-94; juv. fire-setters network Klamath Falls Fire Dist. # 1, 1992—; head start health bd., Klamath Falls, 1991—, RAPP Team Mem., 1995—. Mem. Psi Chi. Home: 8926 Highway 66 Klamath Falls OR 97601-9538 Office: 8926 Hwy 66 Klamath Falls OR 97601-9638

KLEPPER, ELIZABETH LEE, physiologist; b. Memphis, Mar. 8, 1936; d. George Madden and Margaret Elizabeth (Lee) K. BA, Vanderbilt U., 1958; MA, Duke U., 1963, PhD, 1966. Research scientist Commonwealth Sci. and Indsl. Research Orgn., Griffith, Australia, 1966-68, Battelle Northwest Lab., Richland, Wash., 1972-76; asst. prof. Auburn (Ala.) U., 1968-72; Plant physiologist USDA Agrl. Research Service, Pendleton, Oreg., 1976-85, research leader, 1985—. Assoc. editor Crop Sci., 1977-80, 88-90, tech. editor, 1990-92, editor, 1992—; mem. editorial bd. Plant Physiology, 1977-92; mem. editorial adv. bd. Field Crops Rsch., 1983-91; mem. editorial bd. Irrigation Sci., 1987-92; contbr. articles to profl. jours., chpts. to books. Marshall scholar British Govt., 1958-59; NSF fellow, 1964-66. Fellow AAAS, Crop Sci. Soc. Am. (fellows com. 1989-91, pres.-elect 1995-96), Soil Sci. Soc. Am. (fellows com. 1986-88), Am. Soc. Agronomy (monograph com. 1983-90); mem. Sigma Xi. Home: 1454 SW 45th Pendleton OR 98701 Office: USDA Argl Rsch Svc PO Box 370 Pendleton OR 98701

KLEY, CAROLYN ANDREA, fundraiser; b. Ann Arbor, Mich., Mar. 3, 1964; d. Robert Raymond and Eleanor K. BBA, U. Mich., 1986, MBA, 1991. CPA. Sys. cons. Golodetz Fin. Co., Fribourg, Switzerland, 1985; sr. staff acct. Ernst & Whinney, Chgo., Boston, 1986-89; cons. Mich. Bus. Assistance Corps., Krakow, Poland, 1990; from assoc. dir. planned giving to dir. western devel. Hillsdale (Mich.) Coll., San Diego, 1991—. Active La Jolla (Calif.) Rep. Women, 1996—. Mem. AICPAs, Mich. Assn. CPAs, Calif. Soc. CPAs, State Bar Calif., Rotary. Roman Catholic. Office: Hillsdale Coll 3d Fl 4350 La Jolla Village Dr San Diego CA 92122

KLICKA, MARY V., dietitian, consultant; b. Winnepeg, Manitoba, Canada, Apr. 30, 1921; Came to the U.S., 1923; d. William Henry and Clara Myrtle (Ferguson) Richardson; m. William John Klicka, Sept. 20, 1946 (div. Oct. 1953); 1 child, William John Klicka. Reg. dietitian. Intern Michael Reese Hosp., Chgo., 1945; dietitian Rsch. & Ednl. Hosp. U. Ill., Chgo., 1945-47; dietitian Quality Control Group Western Electric Co., Cicero, 1947-51; cons. dietitian Shriners Children's Hosp., Chgo., 1950-51; nutritionist Quartermaster Food & Container Inst., Chgo., 1951-63; nutritionist U.S. Army Rsch., Devel. & Engring. Ctr., Natick, Mass., 1963-75, chief ration design & evaluation branch, 1975-86; sr. scientist Geo-Centers, Inc., Newton Centre, Mass., 1990-94; panelist biomass processing tech. panel Am. Inst. Biol. Scis., Washington, D.C., 1987-88; cons. dietitian Compu-Cad, Inc., Taunton, Mass., 1988-89; NSCORT site visit team panel mem. Am. Inst. Biol. Scis., Washington, D.C., 1995. Contbr. articles to profl. jours. Mem. Am. Dietetic Assn., Mass. Dietetic Assn., Inst. Food Technologists. Home: 168 Oak Crest Dr Framingham MA 01701

KLIEBHAN, SISTER M(ARY) CAMILLE, academic administrator; b. Milw., Apr. 4, 1923; d. Alfred Sebastian and Mae Eileen (McNamara) K. Student, Cardinal Stritch Coll., Milw., 1945-48; B.A., Cath. Sisters Coll., Washington, 1949; M.A., Cath. U. Am., 1951, Ph.D., 1955. Joined Sisters of St. Francis of Assisi, Roman Catholic Ch., 1945; legal sec. Spence and Hanley (attys.), Milw., 1941-45; instr. edn. Cardinal Stritch Coll., 1955-62, assoc. prof., 1962-68, prof., 1968—, head dept. edn., 1962-67, dean students, 1962-64, chmn. grad. div., 1964-69, v.p. for acad. and student affairs, 1969-74, pres., also bd. dirs., 1974-91, chancellor, 1991—. Bd. dirs. Goals for Milw. 2000, 1980-83; treas. Wis. Found. Ind. Colls., 1974-79, 87-90, v.p., 1979-81, pres., 1981-83; bd. dirs. DePaul Hosp., 1982-91, Sacred Heart Sch. Theology, Viterbo Coll., Milw. Cath. Home, St. Ann Adult Day Care, Wis. Psychoanalytic Found., St. Coletta's of Mass., Internat. Inst. Wis., 1984-94, Friends of Internat. Inst. Wis., Mental Health Assn. Milwaukee County, 1983-87, Pub. Policy Forum, 1987-90, Better Bus. Bur. of Wis. Inc., St. Camillus Campus, mem. adv. bd., 1989-96; mem. TEMPO, 1982—, bd. dirs., 1986-89; bd. govts. Wis. Policy Rsch. Inst., 1987—. Mem. Am. Psychol. Assn., Rotary Club of Milw. (v.p., pres. elect 1992-93, pres. 1993-94), Phi Delta Kappa, Delta Epsilon Sigma, Psi Chi, Delta Kappa Gamma, Kappa Delta Pi.

KLIGER, HANNAH, humanities educator; b. Tel Aviv, Nov. 26, 1953; d. Roman and Frieda (Lorberbaum) K.; m. Rakhmiel Peltz, Mar. 2, 1977; children: Eliezer, Bina. BJL, Jewish Tchrs. Sem., N.Y.C., 1975; BA, Barnard Coll., 1975; MA, U. Pa., 1977, PhD, 1985. Prof. comm. U. Mass., Amherst, 1985—. Author: Jewish Hometown Associations and Family Circles in New York, 1992. Grantee in field. Office: U Mass Machmer Hall Amherst MA 01003

KLIMA, MARTHA SCANLAN, state legislator; b. Balt., Dec. 3, 1938; d. Thomas Moore and Catherine A. (Stafford) Scanlan; m. James Patrick Klima Jr., Apr. 8, 1961; children: Jennifer, J. Patrick III, Andrew. AA, Villa Julie Coll., 1958. Med. stenographer U. Md. Med. Sch., Balt., 1958-63; mem. appropriations com. Md. Ho. of Dels., Annapolis, 1982—; sec. Cen. Md. Health Systems Agy., 1981-83; commr. State Planning Commn., State of Md., 1983—. Del. Rep. Nat. Conv. Dallas, 1984; bd. dirs. Greater Balt. Med. Ctr., Towson, 1986-91, Md. Spl. Olympics, 1987—. Named Freshman of Yr., Ho. of Dels., 1984, Woman of Yr. Towsontowne Bus. and Profl. Women's Club; recipient Gov.'s Citation for Outstanding Svc. to Citizens of Md., 1988, Pub. Svc. award for Outstanding Support to Balt. Assn. Retarded Citizens, Inc., 1994, Legis. award Balt. County Commn. on Disabilities, 1994. Mem. Am. Legis. Exchange Coun. (state chmn. 1987—, Outstanding State Legislator award 1994), Women Legis. Md., Congress of PTA's (hon. life), Balt. County C. of C. (Merit award 1981). Republican. Roman Catholic. Home: 1403 Newport Pl Lutherville Timonium MD 21093-5920 Office: Ho Reps State Capital Annapolis MD 21401

KLINCK, CYNTHIA ANNE, library director; b. Salamanaca, N.Y., Nov. 1, 1948; d. William James and Marjorie Irene (Woodruff) K.; m. Andrew Clavert Humphries, Nov. 26, 1983. BS, Ball State U., 1970; MLS, U. Ky., 1976. Reference/ young adult libr. Bartholomew County Libr., Columbus, Ind., 1970-74; dir. Paul Sawyier Pub. Libr., Frankfort, Ky., 1974-78, Washington-Centerville Pub. Libr., Dayton, Ohio, 1978—; libr. cons.; mem. OPLIN Task Force. Contbr. articles to profl. mags. Bd. dirs. Bluegrass Comty. Action Agy., Frankfort, Ky., 1971-73; founder, bd. dirs. FACTS, Inc. (info. & referral), Frankfort, 1972-74; co-founder, bd. dirs. Seniors, Inc., Dayton, Ohio, 1980-81, 91—; trustee, officer South Comty., Inc. Mental Health Ctr., Dayton, 1980-89; pres. Miami Valley Librs. Mem. ALA, Am. Soc. for Info. Sci., Am. Soc. for Pers. Adminstrn., Ohio Libr. Assn. (chmn. legis. com.), South Metro C. of C. (bd. dirs.), Rotary Internat. Office: Washington-Centerville Pub Libr 111 W Spring Valley Pike Dayton OH 45458-3761

KLINCK, PATRICIA EWASCO, state official; b. Albany, N.Y., May 13, 1940; d. Albert C. and Mary Ann (Sopko) Ewasco; m. C. Hoagland Klinck, Jr., Sept. 12, 1970; 1 dau., Natalie Childs. B.A. in History, Smith Coll., 1961; M.S. in L.S, Simmons Coll., Boston, 1963; postgrad. in edn., SUNY, Albany, 1964-67; student sr. exec. program, Harvard U., 1989. Young adult worker Boston Pub. Libr., 1961-63; libr. dir. Colonie Central High Sch., Albany, 1963-67; libr. Libr./U.S.A., U.S. Pavilion, N.Y. World's Fair, summer 1965; libr. dir. Simon's Rock Coll., Gt. Barrington, Mass., 1967-70; regional dir. N.W. Regional Libr. Vt. Dept. Librs., Montpelier, 1970-72; dir. extension svcs. div. Vt. Dept. Librs., 1972-73, 73-74, acting asst. state libr., 1973, asst. state libr., 1974-77, state libr., 1977—; chmn. New Eng. Libr. Bd., 1979-81; vice chmn. Chief Officer State Libr. Agys., 1978-80, chmn., 1981-82; mem. White House Conf. Preliminary Design Commn., 1985-86, Gov.'s Telecomms. Tech. Coun. Vt., 1994—, Info. Resources Mgmt. Adv. Coun., 1993—. Bd. dirs. Vt. Hist. Soc., 1977—; mem. Vt. Bicentennial Commn., 1986-72; mem. Vt. Coun. on Humanities, 1987-91; incorporator Vt. Ctr. of the Book, 1993; mem. gov's Telecommunications Tech. Council Vt., 1994—. Mem. ALA (legis. com. 1966-68), Assn. State Libr. Agys. (bd. dirs. with ALA 1986-88), New England Libr. Assn., Vt. Libr. Assn. Office: Vt State Dept of Librs 109 State St Montpelier VT 05609-0001

KLINE, BUNNY, artist, poet; b. N.Y.C., Oct. 11, 1924; d. Ernest Herman and Sophye (Goodman) Schneider; m. Jeremiah Harding Kline, Apr. 10, 1949; children: Andrea Jane Kline Donnelly, Robert David. AS, Bradford Jr. Coll., Haverhill, Mass., 1944; BA, U. Mich., 1946; postgrad., Cuttermill Sch. Art, Gt. Neck, N.Y., 1950-62. Founding mem. Cuttermill Group Coop, Gt. Neck, 1972-84; mem. Gallery 84 Coop, N.Y.C., 1982-84; represented by Robley Gallery, Roslyn, N.Y., 1960-87, Hodgell Gallery, Sarasota, Fla., 1987—, Gallery I, Naples, Fla., 1990-96, Ambassador Gallery, N.Y.C., 1995—. One-woman shows include Manhasset (N.Y.) Pub. Libr., 1979,

Bryant Libr., Roslyn, N.Y., 1980, Hodgell Gallery, Sarasota, Fla., 1992, 94, 95; group exhbns. include Longboat Key (Fla.) Art Assn., 1987, 88, 89, 90, Sarasota Art Assn., 1987, 88, 89, 90, Arts Ctr. of St. Petersburg, 1990, 95, Veridian Gallery, N.Y.C., 1991, Lee County Alliance of Arts, Sanibel, 1991, Barrier Island Group, Sanibel, 1992, Raleigh Gallery, Dania, Fla., 1992, Gallery I, Naples, Fla., 1993, 94, 95, Albertson/Peterson Gallery, Winter Park, Fla., 1994, Boca Mus., Boca Raton, Fla., 1994, Art League of Manatee County, Bradenton, Fla., 1994, Sarasota Arts Coun., 1995, others; represented in permanent collections Cowen & Co., N.Y.C., Defotanghe Spril., Antwerp, Belgium, Marcus & Co., Copenhagen, Denmark, Nierenberg, Zieff & Weinberg, N.Y.C., Ouro Fino Ltd., Rio de Janiero, Marco Island (Fla.) Country Club; contbr. poetry to anthologies. Active Nat. Assn. Jewish Women, Roslyn Heights, N.Y., 1953-65; troop leader Girl Scouts U.S.A., Roslyn Heights, 1958-64; vol. art therapist VA Hosp., Centrl Islip, N.Y., 1970-72. Recipient Best in Show award North Shore Child Guidance Assn., 1972, 2d prize Artists of Fla., 1980, 3d prize Sarasota Art Assn., 1988. Home and Studio: 3156 Lake Park Ln Sarasota FL 34231

KLINE, HARRIET DENNIS, psychologist, school psychologist; b. Sheridan, Wyo., Oct. 4, 1943; d. Thomas Gordon and Anna Townsend (Pyle) Dennis; m. Alan Herbert Kline, June 15, 1964 (div. Dec. 1976); children: Rebecca, David, Benjamin. BA, NYU, 1969; MS, SUNY, Potsdam, 1977; PhD, Temple U., 1988; cert. in sch. psychology, Bryn Mawr Coll., 1986; postgrad., Family Inst. Philadelphia, 1992-95. Lic. psychologist, Pa.; cert. tchr., N.Y., N.J., Pa. Reading tchr. Lake Placid (N.Y.) Sch. Dist., 1974-81; tchg. assoc. Temple U., Philadelphia, 1981-84; dir. Ednl. Records Bur., Philadelphia, 1985-90, Main Line Ednl. Svc., Rosemont, Pa., 1990—; sch. psychologist Chester (Pa.) Uplands Sch. Dist., 1990-91, Gladwyne (Pa.) Montessori Sch., 1991-94, Upper Moreland Sch. Dist., Willow Grove, Pa., 1994-95; vis. lectr. Rutgers U., Immaculata Coll. Contbr. articles to profl. jours. Founder Hunterdon Recycling Ctr., Flemington, N.J., 1969-71; founding mem. Literacy Vols., Laranac Lake, N.Y., 1979-81. Mem. APA, NASP, Pa. Psychol. Assn., Orton Soc., Temple U. Sch. Edn. Alumni Assn. (bd. dirs. 1988—). Office: Main Line Ednl Svcs 1062 Lancaster Ave Rosemont PA 19010

KLINE, JO ANN, medical/surgical nurse, educator; b. Muskingum County, Ohio, May 5, 1945; d. Ralph Howard and Ruth (Horner) Wright; m. C. Edward Kline, Aug. 14, 1966. Diploma, Good Samaritan Sch. Nursing, 1966; BSN, Ohio U., 1980; MEd, Ashland U., 1988; postgrad., Otterbein U., 1993—. Staff nurse surg. fl. Mercy Hosp., Mt. Vernon, Ohio, 1966-67; office nurse Drs. Robert Sooy & Clinton Trott, Mt. Vernon, 1967-70; staff nurse ICU, critical care unit, pediats. and med. fl. B.W. Martin Meml. Hosp., Mt. Vernon, 1970-72, head nurse ICU, critical care, pediats. and med. fl., 1972-74, head nurse coronary care unit and ICU, 1974-78; relief supr. ICU and recovery rm. staff nurse Knox Comty. Hosp. (merged Mercy and B.W. Martin Meml. Hosp.), Mt. Vernon, 1978-79; on-call staff nurse med.-surg. unit Knox Comty. Hosp., Mt. Vernon, 1979—; instr. theory/practice Knox County Career Ctr. Sch. Practical Nursing, Mt. Vernon, 1979—; mem. steering com., bd. dirs., v.p., pres. Hospice of Knox County, Mt. Vernon, 1980-92, dir. emeritus, 1990. Bd. dirs. Knox County Heart Assn., Mt. Vernon, 1970-80; mem.-at-large adminstrv. coun. Mulberry St. United Meth. Ch., Mt. Vernon, 1990-95. Named one of Outstanding Young Women of Am., 1979. Mem. ANA (cert., del. to convs. 1970s), Ohio Nurses Assn. (del. to convs. 1970s, bd. dirs 1970s), Ohio Orgn. Practical Nurse Educators (treas. 1980-95, Tchr. of Yr. 1989), Ohio Edn. Assn., Knox Comty. Hosp. Found. (bd. dirs. 1991-95), Knox-Licking Dist. Nurses Assn. (pres. 1980-83, treas. 1980—, Heart of Nursing award 1995), Phi Kappa Phi, Sigma Theta Tau. Democrat. Home: 201 Quarry Chapel Rd Gambier OH 43022 Office: Knox County Career Ctr 306 Martinsburg Rd Mount Vernon OH 43050-4225

KLINE, LINDA, employment consultant; b. Boston, Aug. 8, 1940; d. George and Eva (Weiner) Kline; B.A. in Biology, Boston U., 1962. Pers. dir. Block Engring. Inc., Cambridge, Mass., 1964-66; brokerage mgr. Eastern Life Ins. Co. N.Y., Boston, 1966-68; mgr. direct placement Lendman Assos., N.Y.C., 1968-72; dir. women-in-mgmt. div. Roberts-Lund, Ltd., N.Y.C., 1972-77; pres. Kline-McKay, Inc., (name changed to Kline Cons., Inc. 1991), 1978-93, pres., mng. dir. Ptnrs. in Human Resources Internat., Inc. (formerly The Arbor Group, Inc.), N.Y.C., 1994—; exec. dir. Majority Money, women's network, 1976-79; tchr. fin. planning for women Marymount-Manhattan Coll., 1977; lectr. and/or cons. women's programs at several colls. and univs. and corps. Co-author: Career Changing: The Worry-Free Guide, 1982. Bd. dirs. Women Bus. Owners Edn. Fund, 1982-86, Mom's Amazing, 1985-88; community bd. dirs. Mt. Sinai Med. Ctr., 1984—; adv. counselor U.S. Small Bus. Adminstrn. WNET Program. Mem. Internat. Assn. Outplacement Profls., Women Bus. Owners N.Y. (bd. dirs. 1978-84), Nat. Coalition Women's Enterprise (adv. bd. 1988-89). Office: Ptnrs in Human Resources Internat Inc 9 E 37th St New York NY 10016-2822

KLINE, MABLE CORNELIA PAGE, retired secondary school educator; b. Memphis, Aug. 20, 1928; d. George M. and Lillie (Davidson) Brown; 1 dau., Gail Angela Page. Student LeMoyne Coll.; BSEd, Wayne State U., 1948, postgrad. Tchr., Flint, Mich., 1950-51, Pontiac, Mich., 1953-62; tchr. 12th grade English, Cass Tech H.S., Detroit, 1962-95, coord. Study Skills Program; ret., 1995; mem. English Book Selection com., 1986—. Life mem. YWCA, NAACP. Detroit Pub. Edn. Fund grantee, 1989. Mem. NEA (life), ASCD, Am. Fedn. Tchrs., Nat. Council Tchrs. English, Wayne State U. Alumni Assn., Delta Sigma Theta. Episcopalian. Home: 555 Brush St Apt 1512 Detroit MI 48226-4332 Office: Cass Tech High Sch English Dept 2421 2nd Ave Detroit MI 48201-2601

KLINE, NANCY M., foundation administrator, writer; b. Clovis, N.Mex., May 1, 1946; d. Max Irby and Edelweiss (Corbin) Meadors; m. Peter Lee Kline, June 27, 1972 (div. 1986); m. Christopher Alexander Spence, June 9, 1990. BA in Literature, Scripps Coll., Claremont, Calif., 1968. Tchr. Sandy Spring (Md.) Friends Sch., 1968-70, Madeira Sch., Greenway, Va., 1970-72; founding dir. Thornton Friends Sch., Silver Spring, Md., 1973-84, The Leadership Inst., Sandy Spring, 1984-92; pres. The Leadership Found. (formerly The Leadership Inst.), Oxfordshire, Eng., 1992—, Leadership 2020, London, 1995—. Author: Physical Movement for the Theater, 1969, Enjoying the Arts: Dance, 1973, Women and Power: How Far Can We Go?, 1993; author BBC-TV program Breaking Glass: Women and Men in Leadership, 1995. Mem. P.E.O. Women, Nat. Assn. Independent Schs., Sandy Spring Civic Assn. (housing spkr. 1979-83). Democrat. Quaker. Home: 63 Preston Crowmarsh, Wallingford Oxfordshire OX10 6SL, England Office: The Leadership Found Box 305 Sandy Spring MD 20860

KLINE, SUSAN ANDERSON, medical school administrator, internist; b. Dallas, June 4, 1937; d. Kenneth Kirby and Frances Annette (Demorest) Anderson; m. Edward Mahon Kline, Dec. 26, 1964 (dec. July 1990). BA, Ohio U., 1959; MD, Northwestern U., 1963. Diplomate Am. Bd. Internal Medicine, Nat. Bd. Med. Examiners (bd. dirs. 1977-81). Dir. cardiac catheterization lab. The New York Hosp., 1971-80; assoc. dean student affairs Cornell Med. Sch., Ithaca, N.Y., 1974-78, assoc. dean admissions and student affairs, 1978-80; mgr. occupl. med. programs GE Co., 1980-84; sr. assoc. dean student affairs N.Y. Med. Coll., Valhalla, 1984-94, interim dean, v.p. med. affairs, 1994—, exec. vice dean acad. affairs, vice provost student svcs., 1996—; bd. dirs. Nat. Residency Matching Program, 1996—. Bd. visitors Coll. of Arts, Ohio U., Athens, 1981-91; mem. test com. ECFMG, Phila., 1985-92, USMLE tests accommodations com. NBMZ, Phila., 1992—. Recipient Leaders of the Future award Nat. Coun. Women, N.Y.C., 1978, Cert. of Appreciation, Ohio U., 1978. Fellow Am. Coll. Cardiology, Coun. on Clin. Cardiology of Am. Heart Assn., N.Y. Cardiologists Soc.; mem. AAMC (N.E. group on student affairs vice chair, chair 1989-93), Cruising Club of Am., Alpha Omega Alpha (Roache award 1963). Home: 561 Pequot Ave Southport CT 06490 Office: New York Medical College Sunshine Cottage Valhalla NY 10595

KLINE, SYRIL LEVIN, writer, educational consultant; b. Washington, Oct. 19, 1953; d. Irvin and Blanche (Hewitt) Levin; m. Raymond B. Lessans (div.); children: Seth Adam, Jonathan Rafael; m. Peter Lee Kline, Dec. 28, 1989. BS, U. Md., 1975. Cert. integrative learning master facilitator, 1990. Tchr. Hebrew Washington Hebrew Congregation, 1974-80; sec., realtor Coldspitt-Carruthers Inc., Montgomery County, Md., 1974-80; adminstrv. asst. Bd. Jewish Edn., Silver Spring, Md., 1980-81; tchr. presch. and kindergarten Children's Learning Ctr., Rockville, Md., 1982-89; curriculum designer, dir. integrative learning Nat. Acad. Integrative Learning, Rochester, N.Y., 1990-92; ednl. cons. Integra Learning Systems, South Bend, Ind., 1992—; free-lance radio and print writer South Bend, 1992—; ednl. cons. Integrative Learning Systems, Damascus, Md., 1988-89; ind. cons., course designer Prince George's County (Md.) Libr., 1989, North Syracuse (N.Y.) Schs., 1989-92, Oswego (N.Y.) Cmty. Schs., 1989-92, Xerox, Rochester, N.Y., 1990-92, Eastman Kodak, Rochester, 1990-92, Penn Yann (N.Y.) Schs., 1991, Utica (N.Y.) Schs., 1991, City of Rochester Schs., 1991, Bellcore, Elizabeth, N.J., 1991, Alliant Tech Sys., St. Paul, 1991, Paramus (N.J.) Cmty. Schs., 1992, Govt. Can., 1992, Project Read, San Francisco, 1992, Sandia Labs, Santa Fe, 1992, City of Elkhart, Ind., 1992-94, Trinity Corp., Joliet, Ill., 1995, Scottsdale Mall, South Bend, 1995, Pathfinders, Plymouth, Ind., 1996; assessment designer Integra Learning Systems, 1995. Author: Isaiah, 1996; featured commentator WVPE radio, 1995-96; contbr. articles to newspapers. Spkr., presenter Little Bear Child Abuse Prevention Program, Madison Ctr. Hosp., South Bend, 1993-95; vol. fundraiser Jewish Fedn. St. Joseph Valley, South Bend, 1995-96; mem. com., writer, presenter Holocaust Commemoration; actress, dir. Osceola Players, South Bend Civic Theatre; soloist, guest performer Temple Beth El, South Bend, 1995, poet, 1996. Mem. Hadassah (life, corres. sec. 1994-95), Omicron Nu. Democrat. Home: 19109 Johnson Rd South Bend IN 46614-5461

KLINEFELTER, DONNA JEAN, secondary education educator; b. Sparta, Wis., Feb. 21, 1943; d. Donald Dean and Clara Lydia (Zietlow) Williams; m. Gerald Raymond Klinefelter, Aug. 29, 1964; children: Ann Katherine, Lisa Marie. BS with honors, U. Wis., Madison, 1965; MA, Cen. Mich. U., 1968. Bilingual cert. in Spanish, social studies. Tchr. Spanish, Janesville (Wis.) H.S., 1966-67, Midland (Mich.) Pub. Schs., 1967—; adj. instr. Spanish, Delta Coll., University Center, Mich., 1991—; presentor Cen. States Conf. on Tchg. of Fgn. Langs., 1992; mem. sch. improvement com. NE Intermediate, Midland H.S., strategic planning decision-making action team, 1991-92. Past pres., activity dir. People to People Internat., Midland, 1968—; homeowner's rep. on ad-hoc com. on storm water retention, Midland; vol. Com. to Elect Karen Sherwood, 1994, Creativity Ctr., Northwood U., Alden Dow Archtl. Tours. Recipient Gerstacker award for Excellence in Tchg., Midland, 1992. Mem. AAUW, Am. Assn. Tchrs. of Spanish and Portuguese, NEA, Mich. Edn. Assn., Midland City Edn. Assn. (bd. dirs., mem. profl. stds. com. 1967—); Mich. Fgn. Lang. Assn., Wis. Alumni Assn. Democrat. Methodist. Home: 1208 Crescent Dr Midland MI 48640

KLINEFELTER, HYLDA CATHARINE, obstetrician and gynecologist; b. Gettysburg, Pa., Sept. 28, 1929; d. Roscoe Emanuel and Sara Catherine (Wagner) K.; m. Edward Ralph Kohnstam, June 18, 1955; children: Charles, Kathryn. Student, Gettysburg Coll., 1947-48; AB, U. Pa., 1951; MD, Med. Coll. Pa., 1955. Diplomate Am. Bd. Ob-Gyn. Rotating intern Phila. Gen. Hosp., 1955-56; resident in ob.-gyn. Presbyn. U. Pa. Med. Ctr., Phila., 1956-59; mem. teaching staff Med. Coll. Pa., Phila., 1959-62; pvt. practice, solo practice, 1959-9; rsch. asst. maternal and child health Pa. Hosp., Phila., 1964-66; co-supr. family planning clinic Presbyn. Hosp./U. Pa. Med. Ctr., 1967-68; ptnr. Media (Pa.) Clinic, 1969-81; pvt. practice, 1981-86; ptnr. Granite Run Ob.-Gyn. Assocs., Media, 1986—; mem. staff Riddle Meml. Hosp., vice chmn. ob-gyn., 1989-93, chmn. ob-gyn., 1993—. Contbr. articles to med. jours. Fellow ACOG; mem. AMA, Am. Med. Womens Assn. (past treas. dist. 25), Reproductive Medicine Assn., Am. Assn. Gyn. Laparoscopists, Internat. Soc. Gynecology Endoscopy, Delaware County Med. Soc., Pa. Med. Soc., Fox Valley Civic Assn., Soroptimist, Alpha Xi Delta. Republican. Lutheran. Home: 264 South Ivy Ln Glen Mills PA 19342-1322 Office: Granite Run Ob Gyn Assn 10881W Baltimore Pike Ste 2303 Media PA 19063-5104

KLINEFELTER, SARAH STEPHENS, division dean, radio station manager; b. Des Moines, Jan. 30, 1938; d. Edward John and Mary Ethel (Adams) Stephens; m. Neil Klinefelter. BA, Drake U., 1958; MA, U. Iowa, Iowa City, 1968; postgrad., Harvard U., July, 1984, U. Wis., Sept., 1987, Vanderbilt U., 1991-92. Chmn. humanities dept. High Sch. Dist. 230, Orland Pk., Ill., 1958-68; chmn. communications and humanities div. Kirkwood Community Coll., Cedar Rapids, Iowa, 1968-78; prof. English Sch. of the Ozarks, Point Lookout, Mo., 1978-86; gen. mgr. Sta. KSOZ-FM, Point Lookout, 1986-90; dean div. of performing and profl. arts Coll. of the Ozarks, Point Lookout, 1989—. Commr. Skaggs Community Hosp., Branson, Mo., 1986—; chmn. Branson Planning and Zoning Commn., 1983; project dir. Mo. Humanities Bd.; commr., examiner North Cen. Assn. Higher Edn., 1978-85; commr. Iowa Humanities Bd., 1971-78; mem. Taney County Planning and Zoning Commn., 1989—. Democrat. Presbyterian. Home: PO Box 828 Point Lookout MO 65726-0828 Office: Coll of the Ozarks Point Lookout MO 65726

KLING, LOIS ANN, banker; b. Jersey City, Mar. 16, 1959; d. Robert Vincent and Mary Elizabeth (Osborne) K. BS, U. Ctrl. Fla., 1982; MS, Ctrl. Mich. U., 1989. Loan officer McGuire Fed. Credit Union, Wrightstown, N.J., 1985-89; credit analyst, supr. Security Pacific, Cherry Hill, N.J., 1989-90; asst. v.p. of lending South Jersey Savs. & Loan, Turnersville, N.J., 1990—. Mem. AAUW (v.p. programs 1992-96, treas. 1996—). Roman Catholic.

KLING, PHRADIE (PHRADIE KLING GOLD), small business owner; b. N.Y.C., July 2, 1933; d. Samuel A. and Mary Leah (Cohen) K.; m. Lee M. Gold, Sept. 5, 1955 (div. 1976); children: Judith Eileen, Laura Susan, Stephen Samuel, James David. BA, Cornell U., 1955; MA in Human Genetics, Sarah Lawrence Coll., 1971. Genetic counselor assoc. Coll. Medicine and Dentistry N.J., Newark, 1970-73; assoc. genetic counselor Sarah Lawrence Coll., Bronxville, N.Y., 1970-73; genetic counselor N.Y. Fertility Rsch. Found., N.Y.C., 1971-73; staff assoc., genetic counselor depts. pediatrics, ob-gyn and neurology Columbia U. Coll. Physicians and Surgeons, N.Y.C., 1973-78; asst. in genetics St. Luke's Hosp. Ctr., N.Y.C., 1977-79; health program assoc. Conn. Dept. Health Svcs., Hartford, 1978-84; edn. cons. Conn. Traumatic Brain Injury Assn., Rocky Hill, 1984-85; office mgr. Anderson Turf Irrigation Inc., Plainville, Conn., 1986-92; owner, mgr. KlingWorks, contract adminstrn., Avon, Conn., 1992—; speaker, instr. on health and health ethics issues, Conn., N.Y., N.J., 1971-85; dir. confs. on genetics and traumatic brain injury, 1980-85; project dir. edn. field testing Biol. Scis. Curriculum Study, 1981-83; scientist AAAS Sci.-by-Mail, 1991—. Mem. Farmington River Watershed Assn., Simsbury, Conn., 1988—; docent Sci. Mus. Conn., West Hartford, 1989-90. Recipient citation for dedicated svc. Conn. Safety Belt Coalition, 1985. Mem. Am. Human Genetics Soc., Bus. and Profl. Microcomputer Users Group (bd. dirs.), Conn. Assn. for Jungian Psychology (bd. dirs.), Hastings Ctr., Am. Mensa (chpt. coord. gifted children 1985—). Home and Office: 33 Hunter Rd Avon CT 06001-3618

KLINGELE, JANINE MARIE, nursing administrator; b. St. Paul, Apr. 4, 1947; d. Robert Claire and Janet Mae (Kelly) Emerson; m. Lawrence Thomas Klingele, Aug. 8, 1969; children: Maria, Brenda, Paul, David, John. BSN, Coll. of St. Catherine, 1969. Cert. ACLS, BLS. Charge nurse, relief supr. Southview Acres Nursing Home, South Saint Paul, Minn., 1974-76; charge nurse ICU Ransom Meml. Hosp., Ottawa, Kans., 1980-86, relief supr., 1982-86, orientation dir., 1984-86, head nurse med.-surg., 1984-86, co-instr. for health careers secondary edn., 1986-88, asst. dir. nursing, 1986-92, chmn. nursing quality assurance, 1986-90; dir. patient svcs. Ransom Meml. Hosp., Ottawa, 1992—; presenter of continuing edn. Kans. Fedn. of LPN, Topeka, 1991; co-presenter Am. Soc. Hosp. Pharmacists, Washington, 1992. Mem. Sacred Heart Choir, Ottawa, 1990—; presenter Continuing Edn. on Health Care and Ethical Issues, 1994, Continuing Edn. Kans. Assoc. of Risk and Quality Mgrs., 1995, Continuing Edn. for Nurisng on Spirit-ful Care: Ethical Issues, 1996. Mem. ANA, Kans. State Nurses Assn. (appointed mem. coun. on edn. 1992-96), Kans. Orgn. Nursing Execs., Sigma Theta Tau. Roman Catholic. Home: 3930 Iowa Ln Ottawa KS 66067-8028 Office: Ransom Meml Hosp 13 & Main Sts Ottawa KS 66067

KLINGENBURG, ANNE LOUISE, graphic design artist; b. Williamsport, Pa., June 30, 1935; d. George Milard and Frances Mary (Roberts) Williams; m. Neil A. Klingenburg, June 21, 1976 (div. July 1989); 1 child, Laura. Cert. advt. design, Ringling Sch. Art, 1956; student, Newark Sch. Fine-Indsl. Art, 1953-55, N.Y. Sch. Visual Art, 1991—. With Julian Burg Advt. Agy., Miami, Fla., 1957-59; separation artist Am. Greeting Card Co., Miami, 1959-62; promotion artist Miami News, Miami, 1962-64; with Lafond Advt. Agy., N.Y.C., 1965-66, Rodgers Studio, N.Y.C., 1966-68, Lasky Printing Co., Millburn, N.J., 1968-77; pvt. practice graphic design artist New Providence, N.J.; computer graphic artist Logical Design Solutions, Inc., Morristown, N.J. Commd. painting Footprints on the Moon, Print N.J., 1988 (in Air and Space Mus., OH).

KLINGER, DEBORAH LEIGH, psychotherapist; b. San Francisco, Mar. 6, 1956; d. William Ralph and Irene Susan (Ames) K.; m. Glenn Adam Mehrbach, July 22, 1992; children: Lennon Jeremy Klinger-Mehrbach. BA in Theater Arts, UCLA, 1978; MA in Marriage, Family and Child Therapy, Phillips Grad. Inst., Encino, Calif., 1990. Cert. marriage, family and child counselor, Calif.; lic. marriage and family therapist, N.C. Staff therapist Beverly Hills (Calif.) Med. Ctr., 1990-92; marriage, family, child counseling intern Century Counseling Ctr., L.A., 1990-94; continuing care coord. The Rader Inst., North Hollywood, Calif., 1992-94; pvt. practice as psychotherapist L.A., 1994-96; staff therapist Structure House, Durham, N.C., 1996—; cons. Profl. Advancement Success Sys., Sherman Oaks, Calif., 1995. Contbr. articles to popular publs. Foster parent tng. instr. Optimist Foster Family Agy., L.A., 1994—. Mem. Internat. Assn. Eating Disorders Profls. (cert. eating disorders specialist), Am. Assn. Marriage and Family Therapists (clin. mem.), Calif. Assn. Marriage and Family Therapists (clin. mem.). Democrat.

KLINGER, JUDITH ANN, elementary education educator; b. Phila., Apr. 3, 1943; d. Ralph Paul and Margaret Elizabeth (Griffiths) Tarbutton; divorced; 1 child, Gayle Michele Grove. BS in Edn., Shippensburg State Coll., 1964, MEd, 1966; postgrad., Pa. State U., Millersville U., Shippensburg U., 1967-92. Cert. elem. tchr., Pa. Elem. educator Red Lion (Pa.) Area Sch. Dist., 1964-66, 70—, elem. libr. sci. educator, 1966-69; mem. lang. arts com. Red Lion Area Sch. Dist., 1988-92, mem. whole lang. com., 1990-95, assessment com., 1992. Mem. Friends of Kaltreider Meml. Libr., Red Lion, 1989-94; chmn. edn. com. St. Paul's United Meth. Ch., 1982-87, Sunday sch. supt., 1984-87, chmn. coun. on ministries, 1988-90; Republican committeewoman, 1996—. Mem. Order of Eastern Star (worthy matron 1974-75). Home: 706 S Main St Red Lion PA 17356-2605 Office: Mazie C Gable Elem Sch Cedar St Red Lion PA 17356-1199

KLINGERMAN, KAREN NINA, elementary school educator, teacher consultant, course coordinator; b. Rahway, N.J., Sept. 12, 1952; d. Nelson Randolph and Alma Margaret (Magnani) Terry; m. William Robert Klingerman, May 25, 1975; children: Bryan William, Brad Nelson. BS in Secondary Edn., Bloomsburg (Pa.) U., 1974; MEd, Trenton State Coll., 1977; Elem. Edn. Cert., Holy Family Coll., Phila., 1992. Cert. secondary edn. educator, elem. edn. educator, Pa. Tchr. Bensalem (Pa.) Sch. Dist., 1974—; tchr. cons., course coord. Pa. Writing Project West Chester (Pa.) U., 1988—. Contbr. articles to Pa. Writing Project Newsletter. Educators adv. bd. Mercer Mus./Bucks County Hist. Soc., Doylestown, Pa., 1993—. Recipient Bucks County IU # 22 grant, 1986, Award for Innovative Teaching, Pa. State Educators Assn., 1988. Fellow Pa. Writing Project; mem. NEA, Nat. Coun. Tchrs. English, Pa. State Edn. Assn. Home: 49 Sharon Dr Richboro PA 18954-1049 Office: Bensalem Sch Dist 3000 Donallen Dr Bensalem PA 19020-1829

KLINGHOFFER, JUNE FLORENCE, physician, educator; b. Phila., Feb. 12, 1921; d. Harry and Esther (Uram) K.; m. Sidney U. Wenger, June 24, 1947; 1 child, Robert Klinghoffer Wenger. BA, U. Pa., 1941; MD, Woman's Med. Coll. Pa., Phila., 1945. Diplomate Am. Bd. Internal Medicine, Am. Bd. Rheumatology. Intern , then resident Albert Einstein Med. Ctr., Phila., 1945-47; fellow in pathology Woman's Med. Coll. Pa., 1947-48; prof. medicine Med. Coll. Pa., Phila., 1969—, Ethel Russell Morris prof. medicine, 1987—. Contbr. articles to med. jours. Recipient Lindback award for disting. teaching, 1965, Alumnae Achievement award Med. Coll. Pa., 1978. Fellow ACP, Phila. Coll. Physicians; mem. AMA, AAUP, Am. Med. Women's Assn., Assn. Am. Med. Colls., Am. Coll. Rheumatology, Alpha Omega Alpha. Home: 356 Meadow Ln Merion Station PA 19066-1331 Office: Med Coll Pa 3300 Henry Ave Philadelphia PA 19129-1121

KLINKER, SHEILA ANN J., state legislator, middle school educator; m. Victor Klinker; children: Kerri, Kevin, Kelly. BS in Edn., Purdue U., MS in Elem. Edn., MS in Adminstrn. and Supervision. Tchr. Tecumseh Mid. Sch., 1982—; state rep Ind. Ho. of Reps., Indpls., 1982—. Mem. St. Mary's Cathedral Parish; 1st woman appointee Tippecanoe Area Plan Commn.; bd. dirs. Lafayette Symphony, Opera de Lafayette, Tippecanoe County Chid Care, Purdue Musical Orgn.; past chairwoman pub. svc. divsn. United Way. Recipient Outstanding Svc. award Ind. Advocates for Children, Legis. award Assn. of RAAUW's Outstanding Woman in Politics, Woman of Distinction award Sycamore Girl Scout Coun., Salute to Women in Politics award, Outstanding Svc. for Pub. Interest award Ind. Optometric Assn., Pres.'s Spl. Svc. award Ind. Soc. Profl. Land Surveyors, Spl. Recognition award Ind. Chpt. NASW, Legis. Efforts Recognition award Ind. Residential Facilities Assn., Ind. Assn. for Counseling and Devel. Mem. Bus. and Profl. Women's Assn., Lafayette C. of C. (edn. com.), Delta Kappa Gamma, Phi Delta Kappa, Kappa Alpha Theta (mem. adv. bd.). Democrat. Home: 633 Kossuth St Lafayette IN 47905-1444 Office: Ind Ho of Reps State House Third Fl Indianapolis IN 46204*

KLINMAN, JUDITH POLLOCK, biochemist, educator; b. Phila., Apr. 17, 1941; d. Edward and Sylvia (Fitterman) Pollock; m. Norman R. Klinman, July 3, 1963 (div. 1978); children: Andrew, Douglas. AB, U. Pa., 1962, PhD, 1966. Postdoctoral fellow Weizmann Inst. Sci., Rehovoth, Israel, 1966-67; postdoctoral assoc. Inst. for Cancer Research, Phila., 1968-70, research assoc., 1970-72, asst. mem., 1972-77, assoc. mem., 1977-78; asst. prof. biophysics U. Pa., Phila., 1974-78; assoc. prof. chemistry U. Calif., Berkeley, 1978-82, prof., 1982—; mem. ad hoc biochemistry and phys. biochemistry study sects. NIH, 1977-84, phys. biochemistry study sect., 1984-88. Mem. editl. bd. Jour. Biol. Chemistry, 1979-84, Biofactors, 1991—, European Jour. Biochemistry, 1991-95, Biochemistry, 1993—; contbr. numerous articles to profl. jours. Fellow NSF, 1964, NIH, 1964-66; Guggenheim fellow 1988-89. Mem. NAS, Am. Chem. Soc. (exec. coun. biol. div. 1982-85, chmn. nominating com. 1987-88, program chair 1991-92, Repligen award 1994), Am. Acad. Arts and Scis., Am. Soc. Biochemistry and Molecular Biology (membership com. 1984-86, pub. affairs com. 1987-94, program com. 1995), Sigma Xi. Office: U Calif Dept Chemistry Berkeley CA 94720

KLOC, EMILY ALVINA, retired elementary school principal; b. Chgo., Apr. 8, 1933; d. Francis Joseph and Emily Mary (Gucwa) K. BMus, Mundelein Coll., Chgo., 1954; MEd, Loyola U., Chgo., 1960. Grade 2 tchr. Our Lady Help of Christians, Chgo., 1954-58; grades 5, 6, 7, 8 tchr. St. Mary of the Angels, Chgo., 1958-87, prin., 1987-95; ret., 1995. Mem. Near N.W. Orgn., Chgo., 1988—. Summer grantee U. Ill. NDEA Inst., Chgo., 1968; recipient Excellence in Mgmt. award Office Cath. Edn., Chgo., 1991, Tchr. Achievement award St. Mary of Angels Sch., Big Shoulders Fund, Chgo., 1992. Mem. ASCD, Nat. Cath. Educators Assn., Archdiocesan Prins. Assn. (chmn. coun. III-5A 1991—). Roman Catholic. Home: 1721 N Wood St Chicago IL 60622-1357 Office: St Mary of the Angels 1810 N Hermitage Ave Chicago IL 60622-1101

KLOEPFER, SHARON ANN, special education educator; b. Long Beach, Calif., July 16, 1960; d. Germain Leo and Clerina Cecile Lamarche; m. Robert Alan Kloepfer, Sept. 16, 1989; children: Nathan, Sarah, Erin. BA in English, Calif. State U., San Bernardino, 1992; M in Spl. Edn. summa cum laude, Nat. U., 1995. English tchr. Calif. Pace Schs., Yucaipa; sci./English R.S.D. tchr. Redlands Unified Sch. Dist. H.S. Parent rep. Arrowhead Christian Acad., Redlands, 1994. Scholarship Mel S. Walters Found., 1990. Mem. Nat. Tchr.'s Assn., English Jour., Nat. Coun. Tchrs. of English, Gentlemen's Club (pres., founder). Republican. Home: 35960 Vineyard St Yucaipa CA 92399-4967 Office: Redlands HS 840 E Citrus Ave Redlands CA 92374-5325

KLOKER, MARJORIE MARIE, internal auditor; b. Saxonburg, Pa., Dec. 25, 1953; d. Dallas George and Sarah Catherine (Faith) Silvis; m. Robert L. Fisher Jr., May 26, 1973 (div. May. 1982); m. Nelson G. Kloker, Oct. 13, 1990; 1 child, Shawn Fisher; 1 stepchild, Jennifer. BS in Acctg. summa cum laude, LaRoche Coll., 1989. CMA, Pa. Bookkeeper Auto Club Butler County, Butler, Pa., 1973-74; acctg. clk. Servistar Corp., Butler, 1974-85, internal auditor, 1985-93, internal audit supr., 1993—. Mem. Inst. Mgmt.

Accts. (dir. pub. rels. 1994, treas. 1995—). Office: Servistar Corp PO Box 1510 Butler PA 16003

KLOPFLEISCH, STEPHANIE SQUANCE, social services agency administrator; b. Rupert, Idaho, Dec. 21, 1940; d. William Jaynes and Elizabeth (Cunningham) Squance; B.A., Pomona Coll., 1962; M.S.W., UCLA, 1966; m. Randall Klopfleisch, June 27, 1970; children—Elizabeth, Jennifer, Matthew. Social worker, Los Angeles County, 1963-67; program dir. day care, vol. services Los Angeles County, 1968-71; div. chief children's services Dept. Public Social Services, Los Angeles County, 1971-73, dir. bur. of social services, 1973-79; chief dep. dir. Dept. Community Services, Los Angeles County, 1979—;with Area 10 Devel. Disabilities, 1981-82; bd. dirs. Los Angeles Fed. Emergency Mgmt. Act, 1985-91, pres., 1987; bd. dirs. Los Angeles Shelter Partnership, Pomona Coll. Assocs., 1988—. Mem. Calif. Commn. on Family Planning, 1976-79; mem. Los Angeles Commn. Children's Instns., 1977-78; bd. dirs. United Way Info., 1978-79; chmn. Los Angeles County Internat. Yr. of Child Commn., 1978-79; bd. govs. Sch. Social Welfare, UCLA, 1981-84. Mem. Nat. Assn. Social Workers, Am. Soc. Pub. Adminstrn., L.A. Philhamonic Affiliates, 1995, Soroptimist Internat. (bd. dirs. 1989—, pres. L.A. chpt. 1993).

KLOSINSKI, DEANNA DUPREE, medical laboratory sciences educator; b. Goshen, Ind., Dec. 28, 1941; d. George C. and Gertrude (Todd) Dupree (dec.); m. Michael A. Klosinski, Jan. 30, 1965; children: Elizabeth, John, Robert, Lara. BS, Ind. State U., 1964; MS, Purdue U., 1972; PhD, Wayne State U., 1990. Diplomate in lab. mgmt. Am. Soc. Clin. Pathologists; cert. med. technologist. Med. technologist South Bend (Ind.) Med. Found., 1959-68; lab. specialist Home Hosp., Lafayette, Ind., 1968-74; program dir. Ind. Vocat. Tech. Coll., Lafayette, 1968-75; clin. asst. prof. Oakland U., Rochester, Mich., 1985—; adj. asst. prof. Wayne State U., Detroit, 1991—, Mich. State U., Lansing, 1991—, chair adv. com. Schs. Allied Health; program dir., asst. adminstr. William Beaumont Hosp., Royal Oak, Mich., 1979—. Author: (videotape, monograph) Blood Collection: The Difficult Draw, 1992; co-author: (videotape, monograph) Blood Collection: The Routine Venipuncture, 1989 (chpt.) Molecular Biology and Pathology, 1993. Mem. pastoral coun. St. Hugo Cath. Ch., Bloomfield Hills, Mich., 1991-94. Named Outstanding Bus. Person Mich. Coun. on Vocat., 1992, Mich. Clin. Lab. Scientist, 1993; rsch. grantee William Beaumont Hosp., 1989-90. Mem. Am. Soc. Clin. Pathologists (chmn. Tech. Sample 1984-93, mem. editl. bd. Lab. Medicine 1993-96, editor Profl. Perspectives 1993-95, Technologist of Yr. 1994), Am. Assn. for Clin. Chemistry (mem. continuing edn. com. 1995-97), Am. Soc. for Clin. Lab. Sci. (mem. edn. sci. assembly, co-chairperson clin. lab. edn. conf. 1991, bd. dirs. edn. and rsch. fund 1996—), Internat. Fed. Clin. Chemistry (edn. & mgmt. divsn. com. programmes & courses 1996—), Assn. Women in Sci., Mich. Soc. for Clin. Lab. Sci. (treas. 1984-86, 88-92, pres. 1995-96, past pres., ann. meeting gen. chair 1996—), Internat. Fedn. Clin. Chemistry (mem. edn. and mgmt. divsn. com. on programmes and courses 1996—), Sigma Xi (sec. Oakland U. chpt. 1994-96), Alpha Mu Tau (Scholarship award 1985, 87, 90), Delta Gamma Alumnae (treas. 1978-81, v.p. 1991-93, pres. 1993-95). Home: 90 Devon Rd Bloomfield Hills MI 48302-1119 Office: William Beaumont Hosp 3601 W Thirteen Mile Rd Royal Oak MI 48073-6769

KLOSOWSKI-GOROMBEI, DEBORAH ANN, nursing manager; b. Chgo.; d. Timothy Joseph Sr. and Rose J. 9Garbel) Klosowski; m. James Thomas Gorombei, Apr. 3, 1993. BSN with honors, Loyola U., Chgo.; MS, Purdue U. Calumet, 1995. RN, Ill., Ind.; cert. BLS, ACLS, ATLS. Staff nurse ER St. Margaret Mercy Hosp., Hammond, Ind., 1989-96; staff nurse SICU U. Chgo., 1990-92; supr. St. Francis Hosp., Blue Island, Ill., 1993; renal nurse clinician WSKC, Blue Island, 1993-94; chief flight nurse, 1995; asst. mgr. clin. ops. Med. ICU at Christ Hosp., Oak Lawn, Ill., 1995—; nurse educator/cons., bd. dirs. Allied Health Care Resources, Olympia Fields, Ill.; speaker in field. Co-investigator for publs. in field. Nurse ARC, Lamont, Ill., 1991; campaign asst. for politician, Chgo., 1988; vol. Camp Quality children with cancer, 1995—. Recipient Washington Square Health Found., 1988-90, Pres.'s Medallion for Nursing, 1990, Donald S. Powers Nursing Talent award, 1994-95. Mem. Emergency Nurses Assn., U.S. Parachuting Assn., Nat. Flight Nurses Assn., Alpha Sigma Nu, Sigma Theta Tau. Roman Catholic. Home: Advocate Christ Hosp and Med Ctr 4440 W 95th St 4th Fl MICU Oak Lawn IL 60453

KLOSTER, AMY LAWSON, researcher; b. Oneonta, N.Y., Dec. 8, 1966; d. James Brooks and Dorothy Ann (Rydelek) L.; m. Brent M. Kloster, Nov. 14, 1992. BS in Biology, William Smith Coll., 1989. Rsch. asst. N.Y. State Agrl. Experiment Sta., USDA, Geneva, 1988-89, Cornell U. Med. Sch., N.Y.C., 1989-90; rsch. asst. II Harvard Med. Sch., Boston, 1990-91; rsch. asst. III James A. Baker Inst. for Animal Health, Cornell U., Ithaca, N.Y., 1992—. Mem. AAUW, LWV, SPCA. Home: 117 Roat St Ithaca NY 14850-2735 Office: JA Baker Inst Animal Health NY State Coll Vet Medicine Cornell U Ithaca NY 14853

KLOTZ, FLORENCE, costume designer; b. N.Y.C.; d. Philip K. and Hannah Kraus. Student, Parsons Sch. Design, 1941. Designer: Broadway shows Take Her She's Mine, 1960, Never Too Late, 1962, Nobody Loves An Albatross, 1963, On An Open Roof, 1963, Owl and the Pussycat, 1964, One by One, 1964, Mating Dance, 1965, The Best Laid Plans, 1966, Superman, 1966, Paris Is Out, 1970, Norman Is That You, 1970, Legends, Follies, 1971 (Drama Desk award, Tony award), A Little Night Music, 1973 (Drama Desk award, Tony award), Side By Side Sondheim, 1975, Pacific Overtures, 1976 (Drama Desk award, Tony award, Los Angeles Critic Circle award), On the 20th Century, 1978 (Drama Desk award), Broadway Broadway, Dancin' In The Streets, 1982, Grind, 1984 (Tony award), Jerry's Girls, 1985; (ballet-jazz opus) Antique Epagraph, N.Y.C.; Broadway musicals Rags, 1986, Roza, 1987; Ctr. prodns. Carousel, 1956, Oklahoma, 1956, Annie Get Your Gun, 1956, 4 Baggatelle; movies Something for Everyone, 1969, A Little Night Music, 1976 (Oscar nomination, Los Angeles Critic Circle award); ice shows John Curry's Ice Dancing, 1979; Broadway musical A Doll's Life; ballet 8 Lines, 1986, I'm Old Fashioned (Jerome Robbins), Ives Songs (Jerome Robbins), City of Angels, 1989 (Tony award nomince, Outer Critics Circle award), Kiss of the Spider Woman, 1989 (Tony award 1989, Drama Desk award 1989), Show Boat, Toronto, Can., 1993, Broadway, 1994-95 (N.Y. Outer Critics Cirlce award 1995, Drama Desk award 1995, Tony award nominee 1995). Recipient Life Achievement award Theatre Crafts Internat., 1994. Democrat. Home: 1050 Park Ave New York NY 10028-1031

KLOZE, IDA IRIS, lawyer; d. Max and Bertha (Samet) K. A.A., George Washington U., 1944, AB, 1947; LLB, U. Md., 1926; JD, 1967. Bar: Md. 1927, U.S. Supreme Ct. 1949. Sole practice, Balt., 1927-34; dep. collector IRS, Balt., 1934-39; with GAO, 1943-45, War Assets Adminstrn., 1945-49, Labor Dept., 1950-53, FTC Antitrust Divsn., 1956-71; vol. atty. Pro Bono Law Litigation Divsn. Pub. Citizen, Washington, 1972-76; ret. Mem. Mrs. Rosalyn Carter's Com. Mental Health; exec. sec. Commn. for Prevention Infantile Paralysis, Balt., 1940-42; lobbyist Md. Legis., U.S. Congress for Equal Rights Amendment Constitution; rep. Indsl. Coun. Nat. Womens Party, Balt., 1940-42; sec. Citizen's Commn. Md., Balt., 1935-39. Mem. ABA, Women's Bar Assn. (v.p. Balt. 1928-32), Profl. Women's Coun. (pres. 1928-33), Nat. Women's Party (lobbyist, co-chmn. campaign com. Md. for re-election FDR for 4th term, legal asst. life mem. 1951—), Fed. Bar Assn. (rec. sec., mem. nat. coun., sec. com. gen. counsels 1951-52).

KLUCK, SHARON A., accountant; b. Columbus, Nebr., June 10, 1950; d. Ralph A. and Eva V. (Sheridan) Braun; m. Jan. 1977; children: Annette S., Allen D. BA, Mt. Marty Coll., 1972; M in Acctg., U. Nebr., 1980. Loan positions USDA, Bloomfield, Nebr., 1972-78; acct. AT&T, Omaha, 1979-88; acctg. mgr. Abitibi-Price, Hiawatha, Kans., 1988-92; cost acctg. mgr. Alcan Pipe, York, Nebr., 1992-94; sales coord. Kroy Industries, York, 1995—. Mem. Inst. Mgmt. Accts. (bd. dirs. 1995). Republican. Home: 6800 Rexford Dr Lincoln NE 68506 Office: Kroy Industries 522 W 26th St York NE 68506

KLUCKHOHN, LUCY WALES, biology educator; b. Cambridge, Mass., Oct. 1, 1937; d. Guilbert Quincy and Lucy Clabaugh (Douglas) Wales; m. Richard Paul Rockwood Klckhohn, Sept. 8, 1962 (dec. July, 1973); children: Bruce Maben; Guilbert Rockwood; m. Donald Lloyd Jones, Feb. 21, 1992; stepchildren: Susan Turpin, Lucile M., Christopher Jones. AB in Anthropology, Bryn Mawr Coll., 1959; MS in Biology, Calif. State U., Northridge, 1986. Cert. animal health technician, Calif. Editor, rschr. U. Calif. Press, L.A., 1970-85; grad. student, teaching asst. Calif. State U., Northridge, 1980-86; assoc. prof. life sci. Santa Monica (Calif.) Coll., 1986—. Co-author: (book) Navaho Material Culture, 1971; reviser: (books) The Navaho, 1962, Indians of the United States, 1966. Mem. AAAS, Am. Soc. for Microbiology, Calif. Vet. Med. Assn. Office: Santa Monica Coll 1900 Pico Blvd Santa Monica CA 90405

KLUCZYNSKI, JANET, computer company marketing executive; b. Chgo., Aug. 5, 1955; d. Thomas Edward and Melanie Irene (Lakoma) K. BA in English cum laude, Dartmouth Coll., 1977; M in Mgmt., Kellogg Grad. Sch. Mgmt., 1980. Asst. product dir. McNeil Consumer Products Co. div. Johnson & Johnson, Ft. Washington, Pa., 1980-83; mktg. rep. IBM, Boston, 1984-87; assoc. cons. corp. competitive analysis Digital Equipment Corp., Concord, Mass., 1987-88; mktg. programs mgr. Stratus Computer, Inc., Marlboro, Mass., 1988—. Alumnae admissions interviewer Dartmouth Coll., class officer, 1992-97; mem. Jr. League Boston, 1984-89; English tutor, fundraiser, mem. bus. leaders bd. One with One, Brighton, Mass., 1986—. Mem. Kellogg Alumni Club of Boston (bd. dirs. 1991—). Democrat. Roman Catholic. Home: 15 Westminster Ave Lexington MA 02173

KLUGER, RUTH, German language educator, editor; b. Vienna, Austria, Oct. 30, 1931; came to U.S., 1947, naturalized, 1952; d. Viktor and Alma (Gredinger) Kluger Hirschel; m. Werner T. Angress, Mar. 1952 (div. 1962); children: Percy, Dan. B.A., Hunter Coll., N.Y.C., 1950; M.A., U. Calif.-Berkeley, 1952, Ph.D., 1967. Asst. prof. German lang. and lit. Case Western Res. U., 1966-70; assoc. prof. U. Kans., Lawrence, 1970-73; assoc. prof. U. Va., Charlottesville, 1973-75, prof., 1975-76; prof. U. Calif.-Irvine, 1976-80, 86-88, dir. Göttingen Study Ctr., Edn. Abroad Program, 1988-90; prof. Princeton U., 1980-86; editor German Quar., 1977-84. Author: The Early German Epigram: A Study in Baroque Poetry, 1971, Weider Leben Ein Jugend, 1992, Katastrophen, Uber Deutsche Literatur, 1994; corr. editor Simon Wiesenthal Ctr. Ann., 1987; contbr. articles to profl. jours. Recipient Rauriser Literaturpreis, 1993, Grimmelshausen-Preis, 1993, Niedersachsen Preis, 1993, Marie-Louise-Kaschnitz preis, 1994; ACLS fellow, 1978. Mem. MLA (exec. coun. 1978-82), Am. Assn. Tchrs. German (exec. coun. 1976-81), Am. Assn. Tchrs. German (exec. coun. 1976-81), Deutsche Akademie für Sprache und Dichtung, Lessing Soc. (pres. 1977-79), PEN Club. Democrat. Jewish. Home: 62 Whitman Ct Irvine CA 92715-4066 Office: U Calif Dept German Irvine CA 92717

KLUKA, DARLENE ANN, human performance educator, researcher; b. Berwyn, Ill., Oct. 6, 1950; d. Aloysius Louis and Lillian (Malkovsky) K. BA, Ill. State U., 1972, MA, 1976; PhD, Tex. Woman's U., 1985. Educator, coach Fenton High Sch., Bensenville, Ill., 1972-73, New Trier East High Sch., Winnetka, Ill., 1973-80; coach Bradley Univ., Peoria, Ill., 1980-82; grad. teaching asst. Tex. Woman's Univ., Denton, 1982-85; prof. Newberry (S.C.) Coll., 1985-86; prof., rschr., dir. Human Performance Ctr., Grambling (La.) State U., 1986-90; asst. prof. human studies and sport adminstrn. U. Ala., Birmingham, 1990-94, rschr., dir. Motor Behavior and Sports Vision Lab., 1990-94; dir. human performance lab motor behavior, grad. program dir. U. Ctrl. Okla., Edmond, 1994—; head of del. Internat. Olympic Acad., U.S. Olympic Com., Olympia Greece, 1990; adv. bd. Women's Sports Found., 1992—; U.S.A. Volleyball Sports Medicine and Performance Commn., 1994-2000; bd. dirs. U.S.A. Volleyball. Author: Visual Skill Enhancement for Sport Exercises, 1989, Volleyball, 1989, 3d edit., 1996, Volleyball Drills, 1990; founding co-editor Internat. Jour. Sports Vision, 1991—; mem. editl. bd. Am. Volleyball Coaches Assn., 1988—; contbr. articles to profl. jours. Pres. USA Volleyball, 1996—, bd. dirs., 1993—. Recipient Rsch. award So. Assn. Phys. Edn. Coll. Women, 1994. Mem. AAHPERD (rsch. fellow, Taylor Dodson Young Profl. award so. dist. 1991, bd. govs. 1993-96, deputy del. 1996—), Nat. Assn. for Girls and Women in Sport (bd. dirs., exec. com. 1989-92, 93-96, pres. 1990-91, Honor award 1996), Internat. Acad. Sports Vision (adv. bd. 1989—, v.p. 1993—), Am. Optometric Assn. (assoc., sports vision sect.), Internat. Coun. for Health, Phys. Edn. and Recreation Sport and Dance (Disting. Scholar in Sport award 1995), Women's Sports Found. (internat. com. 1993—, Pres.'s award 1996), Internat. Assn. Phys. Edn. and Sports for Girls and Women. Roman Catholic.

KLUNDER, JANICE MARIE, medicinal chemist; b. Corvallis, Oreg., Mar. 3, 1958; d. Bruce W. Klunder and Joanne Klunder (Lehman) Hardy; m. Kollol Pal, June 23, 1984; children: Shonali Marie Pal, Anjali Joanne Pal. BA, Swarthmore Coll., 1980; PhD, MIT, 1987. Scientist Bristol Labs., Syracuse, N.Y., 1980-82; NIH postdoctoral fellow Johns Hopkins U., Balt., 1987-89; sr. scientist Boehringer Ingelheim, Ridgefield, Conn., 1989-93, prin. scientist, 1993-94; assoc. dir. chemistry, dir. patent affairs Pro Script, Inc., Cambridge, Mass., 1994—; expert analyst Chem Tracts: Organic Chemistry, 1992—. Co-author: Comprehensive Organic Synthesis, 1991; patentee in field; contbr. articles to profl. jours. Nat. Merit scholar, 1976. Mem. Am. Chem. Soc., Phi Beta Kappa. Office: Pro Script Inc 38 Sidney St Cambridge MA 02139

KMAN, SHARON LOUISE, rehabilitation services professional; b. Chgo., Mar. 21, 1945; m. Norman Kman, July 20, 1968. AB with highest honors, U. Calif., Berkeley, 1976; MS, San Francisco State U., 1986. Cert. rehab. counselor; lic. marriage, family and child counselor. Cons. pulmonary dept. Alta Bates Hosp., Berkeley, Calif., 1986-95, U. Calif., San Francisco, 1990-95; clin. supr. Baker Pls., San Francisco, 1983-88; lectr., rehab. counseling dept. San Francisco State U., 1988-93; clin. supr. Crisis Intervention and Suicide Prevention Ctr. of San Mateo, Calif., 1992—; coord. family/child abuse prevention program Project Focys, San Mateo, Calif., 1989-90; pvt. practice psychotherapist San Francisco/San Mateo, 1988—. Mem. Calif. Assn. for Marriage and Family Therapy, Am. Rehab. Counseling Assn., Am. Assn. for Marriage and Family Therapy, Internat. Soc. for Study of Multiple Personality and Dissociation, Chi Sigma Iota. Office: 4154 24th St San Francisco CA 94114

KMET, REBECCA EUGENIA PATTERSON, pharmacist; b. Ellisville, Miss., June 17, 1948; d. Eugene Roberts and Ruth Winn (Pettis) Patterson; m. Joseph Paul Kmet, Mar. 29, 1969. BS in Pharmacy, U. Ariz., 1971; MBA, Nat. U., 1981. Pharmacist Santa Monica (Calif.) Bldg. Profl. Pharmacy, 1972-73, Vets. Hosp., West Los Angeles, Calif., 1973-74, Kaiser Med. Ctr., San Diego, Calif., 1979-82, Farmersville Drug Store, Farmersville, Calif., 1991-95. Community svc. vol. Lt. USN, 1975-78. Recipient Presdl. Achievement award Rep. Party Nat. Congl. com. Mem. Navy League, Naval Hist. Found., Marine Corps Hist. Found., U.S. English, Am. Immigration Control Fedn., Rho Chi, Kappa Epsilon, NSDAR. Independent. Episcopalian. Home: 2912 N Wilson Ave Tucson AZ 85719

KNABENSHUE, CATHERINE SUE, special education educator; b. South Bend, Ind., Oct. 19, 1953; d. Joseph Francis and Marjorie Ann (Steenbergen) Goepfrich; m. Kerry Lee Knabenshue, Oct. 4, 1975; children: Tara, Christopher, Rebecca. BS, Ind. U., 1976, MS, 1983. Tchr. Holy Family Sch., South Bend, 1977-79; preschool tchr. Sunshine Corner Nursery Sch., South Bend, 1982-84; tchr. Holy Cross, South Bend, 1984-86; first grade tchr. St. Mary of the Assumption, South Bend, 1986-87; jr. high tchr. St. Bavo, Mishawaka, Ind., 1987-89; second grade tchr. St. Matthew, South Bend, 1987-94, resource tchr. spl. svcs., 1994—; computer curriculum Ft. Wayne/South Bend Diocese, 1991-94; pub. rels. dir. St. Matthew Sch., 1993—; presenter in field, mem. various textbook coms.; team leader Intervention Team, St. Matthew, 1993—; mem. com. to develop sch. year, 1992-93. Vol. Right to Life, South Bend; CCD instr. Holy Family, 1977-79, St. Matthew, 1975-78. Recipient Cert. of Completion Profl. Edn. Resources, 1994. Mem. CHADD, Nat. Assn. Catholic. Sch. Tchrs. Roman Catholic.

KNAFO, DANIELLE SYLVIA, clinical psychologist; b. Morocco, Mar. 18, 1953; d. Maurice and Rosine (Cohen) Knafo. BA magna cum laude, Tel Aviv U., Israel, 1977, MA magna cum laude, 1979; PhD, CUNY, 1987; cert. in psychoanalysis, NYU, 1992; postgrad., Inst. Psychoanalytic Tng., 1994. Clin. psychology intern Bronx (N.Y.) Psychiatric Ctr., 1984-85; dir. psychol. svcs. St. Barnabas Hosp., Bronx, 1986-88; pvt. practice N.Y.C., 1987—; psychodiagnostician Holliswood (N.Y.) Hosp., 1988-89; supervising psychologist Bronx-Lebanon Hosp. Ctr., 1988-90; adj. lectr. CCNY, Bklyn. Coll., 1982-83, New Sch. Social Rsch., 1983-84; mem. faculty Eugene Lang Coll., 1989—, Tel-Aviv U., 1995—; clin. supr. grad. psychology program Pace U., 1988—; program content cons. telecourse on abnormal psychology, PBS; clin. adj. CUNY PhD Clin. Psych. Program, 1996. Author: Egon Schiele: A Self in Creation, 1993; reviewer jours. Hosp. and Cmty. Psychiatry, 1988—, Psychoanalytic Books, Contemporary Psychology. Counselor St. Vincent's Hosp. Rape Crisis Program, 1981-84; dir. Suicide Prevention Program, Bronx, 1986-88. Fellow NIMH, 1981, BRA Found. fellow, 1987, Faculty Devel. Fund fellow, 1991. Mem. Am. Psychol. Assn., Internat. Psychoanalytic Assn., N.Y. Acad. Scis., World Fed. for Mental Health, Internat. Psychohistory Assn. (rsch. assoc.), Israel Psychol. Assn., Women Psychoanalysts (study group). Office: 2166 Broadway Apt 14F New York NY 10024-6671

KNAPP, BARBARA ALLISON, financial services, oncological nurse consultant; b. Boston, May 30, 1936; d. Henry Philip and Mary Veronica (Norton) Frank; m. John Northcott Knapp, July 27, 1963 (dec. June 12, 1994); children: Linda, David, Diana. BSN, Hood Coll., 1959; MA, U. Iowa Sch. of Nursing, 1981. Instr. Mass.Gen. Hosp. Sch. of Nursing, Boston, 1959-63; acting dir. Aga Khan Hosp., Nairobi, Kenya, East Africa, 1963-65; dir. dept. of pt. edn. Mercy Hosp., Cedar Rapids, Iowa, 1975-78; clin. nurse specialist dept. otolaryngology U. Iowa Hosp. and Clinics, Iowa City, 1981-84; clin. nurse specialist in oncology U. Iowa Hosp. and Clinics, Iowa City, 1992-94; clin. nurse specialist in surgical nursing U. Chgo. Med. Ctr., 1984-92; nursing cons., chmn. CEO SCI Fin. Group Inc., Cedar Rapids, 1994—; mem. bd. accreditation Nat. League for Nursing N.Y.C., 1993—; mem. adv. bd. Mercy Hosp. Women's Health Ctr., 1994—. Dir., editor: (instructive films) Preoperative Teaching Film, 1976 (Am. Hosp. Assn. Film of the Yr. 1976), Learning About Diabetes, 1978, Head and Neck Postoperative Care, 1984, Psychosocial Effects of Head and Neck Cancer, 1984. Bd. dirs. United Way, Cedar Rapids, 1994—, Cedar Rapids Symphony Orch., 1994—, YMCA, Cedar Rapids, Meth-Wick Retirement Cmty., Jr. Achievement, 1996—; trustee Mt. Mercy Coll., YMCA, 1996—. Mem. Am. Cancer Soc., Oncology Nursing Soc., Cedar Rapids C. of C. (dir. 1996—), Rotary Internat., Sigma Theta Tau. Roman Catholic. Home: 307 Crescent St SE Cedar Rapids IA 52403-1731

KNAPP, CANDACE LOUISE, sculptor; b. Benton Harbor, Mich., Feb. 28, 1948; d. Claire Warren and Frances Mary (Collins) K.; m. Björn Andrén, Mar. 3, 1988. BFA, Cleve. Inst. Art, 1971; MFA, U. Ill., 1974. Sculptures exhibited in numerous galleries and colls. including Northwood Inst. Collection, West Palm Beach, Fla.; represented in permanent collections at Malone & Hyde, Memphis, Mobil Oil Co., Stockholm, HageGården Music Ctr., Edane, Sweden, others; included in book Contemporary American Women Sculptures; numerous commns. including St. Vincent de Paul Cath. Ch., Arlington, Tex., Padre Pio Found., Cromwell, Conn., Temple Emanuel, Dallas, West Haven, Conn., Tampa (Fla.) Gen. Hosp., Pub. Art Commn. City of St. Petersburg, Fla. Helen Greene Perry traveling scholar, 1971. Mem. Assn. Fla. Liturgical Artists (co-founder).

KNAPP, JANIS ANN, elementary school educator; b. Coffeyville, Kans., Nov. 15, 1949; d. Harry Clarence and Dorothy (Lehr) Herman; m. Stephen Foxall Knapp, Feb. 12, 1972; children: Marysa Monica, Stephen Weslee, Alexandria Annastasia, Janna Jacqualan. BE, U. Kans., 1971; MEd, Pittsburg State U., 1983, EdS, 1986. Cert. elem. tchr., Fla. Tchr. Overland Park (Kans.) Elem. Sch., 1971-72, Alamo Heights (Tex.) Jr. High Sch., 1972-73, Hoover Elem. Sch., Bartlesville, Okla., 1974, 79-80, Limestone Elem. Sch., Bartlesville, 1975-76, Whittier Elem. Sch., Coffeyville, 1980-83, Edgewood Elem. Sch., Coffeyville, 1983-85, J.C. Mitchell Community Sch., Boca Raton, Fla., 1985-88; math. specialist Palm Beach County Schs., Riviera Beach, Fla., 1988-90; tchr. Meadow Park Elem. Sch., Palm Beach, Fla., 1990-91, Conniston Mid. Sch., Palm Beach, 1991-93, Pine Grove Elem. Sch., Delray Beach, Fla., 1993—. Vol. high sch. debate judge, Delray Beach, Fla., 1990; Heart Fund vol., Ft. Lauderdale, 1985-91; assoc. mem. Rep. Club, Boca Raton, 1990-91. Mem. ASCD, AAUW, Nat. Coun. Tchrs. of Math., Nat. Coun. Suprs. Math., South Fla. Ctr. for Exec. Educators, Fla. Coun. Tchrs. Math., Fla. Assn. Math. Suprs., Fla. ASCD, Palm Beach County Classroom Tchrs. Assn., Math. Assn. Am., Phi Delta Kappa, Alpha Phi (pres. alumni assn.). Roman Catholic. Home: 18755 Cape Sable Dr Boca Raton FL 33498-6377 Office: Pine Grove Elem Sch 400 SW 10th St Delray Beach FL 33444-2214

KNAPP, LUCY CLARA, medical technologist; b. Vancouver, Wash., June 20, 1953; d. Samuel Boyd and Nellie Bridwell (Wallace) K.; m. Tom Elwood Furseth, Aug. 21, 1976 (div. July 1993); children: Kristen Anne, Brian James. AS in Chemistry, Olympic Coll., Bremerton, Wash., 1973; BS in Med. Tech., U. Wash., 1976. Med. technologist Whitman Cmty. Hosp., Colfax, Wash., 1976, Moscow (Idaho) Clinic, 1976-77; clin. technologist dept. vet. microbiology and pathology Wash. State U., Pullman, 1977-79; med. technologist, supr. night shift S.W. Wash. Med. Ctr., Vancouver, 1979—, also chief immunochemistry technologist. Mem. Am. Soc. Clin. Pathologists. Home: 610 NE 3d Ave Battle Ground WA 98604 Office: SW Wash Med Ctr 600 NW 92d Ave Vancouver WA 98664

KNAPP, MADONNA FAYE, property manager, administrator; b. Greenup, Ill., Nov. 13, 1933; d. Rella James Packer and Ruth Evelyn (Mills) Lam; m. Carl E. Helmick, Feb. 8, 1953 (div.); children: Carl E. Jr., Cheryl A. Helmick Pease, Madonna J. Helmick Zelazny, Timothy J.; m. Glenn E. Knapp, Sept. 24, 1984. Grad. high sch., Champaign, Ill. Notary pub., Ind. Justice of peace, Ill., 1957-61; owner, mgr. Feathercrafts, Champaign, Ill., 1961-64; hostess Town and Country Steak House, Champaign/Urbana, Ill., 1966-68; leasing agt. Pinehurse Village Apts., Indpls., 1976-78, Shortridge Mobile Home Park, Indpls., 1978-79; adminstr. Kingston Square Homes, Inc., Indpls., 1981—. Precinct committeewoman Champaign Dem. Com., 1966-67; mem. Indpls. Dem. Com., 1970, 91-92. Recipient letter of accomodation State's Atty. Piatt County, 1961, others. Mem. Internat. Platform Assn., Midwest Assn. HUD Mng. Agts., Fraternal Order Police. Democrat. Methodist. Home: 7168 Twin Oaks Dr Indianapolis IN 46226-5720 Office: Kingston Square Homes Inc 7171 Twin Oaks Dr Indianapolis IN 46226-5719

KNAPP, MILDRED FLORENCE, social worker; b. Detroit, Apr. 15, 1932; d. Edwin Frederick and Florence Josephine (Antaya) K.; BBA, U. Mich., 1954, MA in Cmty. and Adult Edn. (Mott Found. fellow 1964), 1964, MSW (HEW grantee 1966), 1967. Dist. dir. Girl Scouts Met. Detroit, 1954-63; planning asst. Coun. Social Agys. Flint and Genessee County, 1965; sch. social worker Detroit public schs., 1967—; field instr. grad. social workers. Mem. alumnae bd. govs. U. Mich., 1972-75, scholarship chmn., 1969-70, 76-80, chmn. spl. com. women's athletics, 1972-75, class agt. fund raising Sch. Bus. Adminstrn., 1978-79; mem. Founders Soc. Detroit Inst. Art, 1969—, Friends Children's Mus. Detroit, 1978—, Women's Assn., Detroit Symphony Orch., 1982-89, Mich. Humane Soc., 1991—; vol. Coun. Detroit Symphony Orch., 1990—; trustee, fin. chmn. Children's Mus. Recipient various certs. appreciation. Mem. Nat. Assn. Social Workers, Acad. Cert. Social Workers, Nat. Cmty. Edn. Assn. (charter), Sch. Social Work Assn. Am. (charter), Outdoor Edn. and Camping Coun. (charter), Mich. Sch. Social Workers Assn. (pres. 1980-81), Detroit Sch. Social Workers Assn. (past pres.), Detroit Assn. U. Mich. Women (pres. 1980-82), Detroit Fedn. Tchrs. Methodist. Home: 702 Lakepointe St Grosse Pointe MI 48230-1706 Office: Longfellow Annex Rm 247 13141 Rosa Parks Blvd Detroit MI 48238

KNAPP, NANCY HAY, mental health administrator; b. Cleve., June 2, 1922; d. Henry Homer and Aurore Louise (LaCroix) Hay; m. Richard Dominick Knapp, Sept. 11, 1955; 1 child, Pamela Hay. BA, Hunter Coll., 1957; MSEd in Counseling Psychology, U. Pa., 1971, EdD in Counseling Psychology, 1987. Nat. cert. counselor; clin. assoc. Am. Bd. Med. Psychotherapists. Career and edn. counselor Johnson O'Connor Rsch. Found., N.Y.C., 1950-53; counselor, report writer The Pers. Lab., N.Y.C., 1953-63; cons. Chapel Hill, N.C., 1963-65; cons., Phila., 1965-69; counseling dir. Resources for Women U. Pa., Phila., 1972-78; dir. profl. svcs. Crossroads Career Planning Corp., Phila., 1978-80; dir. consultation and edn. Crozer-Chester Med. Ctr., Upland, Pa., 1980-90, chmn. staff tng. com., 1985-90; pvt. practice counseling, couples and family therapy, 1971—; mem. faculty Main Line Sch. Night, Ardmore, Pa., 1978-80; trainer Pa. Dept. Health, Harrisburg, 1982-85. Author: (tng. manuals) Prevention: Drug Misuse, 1983, Growing, Together, 1985. Bd. dirs. Resources for Women, U. Pa., Phila., 1976-80; mem. steering com. Coalition for Edn./Placement of Women, Phila., 1976-78, coord., 1978-80; mem. Chester (Pa.) Vocat./Ednl.

Outreach, 1980-82, dir., 1982-84. Recipient Community Devel. award Pa. Cons. Edn. Coun., 1981; grantee Pa. Dept. Health, 1981, 83. Mem. Am. Counseling Assn., APA (assoc.), Cons. Assn. Greater Phila., Phi Delta Kappa. Home: 326 Sprague Rd Narberth PA 19072-1124

KNAPP, ROSALIND ANN, lawyer; b. Washington, Aug. 15, 1945; d. Joseph Burke and Hilary (Eaves) K.; B.A., Stanford U., 1967, J.D., 1973. Admitted to Calif. bar, 1973, D.C. bar, 1980; with Dept. Transp., Washington, 1973—, asst. gen. counsel legislation, 1979-81, dep. gen. counsel, 1981—. Mem. D.C. Bar Assn., Calif. Bar Assn. Office: Dept Transp Office of the General Counsel 400 7th St SW Washington DC 20590-0001

KNAPPMAN, ELIZABETH FROST See **FROST-KNAPPMAN, (LINDA) ELIZABETH**

KNAUER, VELMA STANFORD, retired savings and loan executive; b. Pottstown, Pa., July 4, 1918; d. Chester Miller and Pearl Fretz (Miller) Stanford. Student pub. schs.; m. Joseph Daniel Knauer, Feb. 17, 1940; children: Joseph Daniel, Susan Velma Knauer Metz. With U.S. Axle Co., Inc., Pottstown, 1936-45; with First Fed. Savs. & Loan Assn., Pottstown, 1953-88, contr., 1953-88, asst. treas., 1953-62, asst. sec., 1962-75, treas., 1976-89, ret., 1989. Mem. Am. Soc. Profl. and Exec. Women. Home: 970 Feist Ave Pottstown PA 19464-3955

KNAUST, CLARA DOSS, retired elementary school educator; b. Freistatt, Mo., Feb. 18, 1922; d. John Fredrick and Hedwig Louise (Brockschmidt) Doss; m. Donald Knaust, July 7, 1946 (dec.); children: Karen Louise, Ramona Elizabeth, Heidi Marie. BS in Edn., S.W. Mo. State U., 1969. Elem. tchr. Trinity Luth. Sch., Freistatt, 1942-46; tchr. kindergarten Trinity Luth Ch., Springfield, Mo., 1961-65, Redeemer Luth Ch., Springfield, 1962-63, 66-69; tchr. kindergarten Springfield R-12 Sch. System, 1969-70, 73-84, elem. tchr., 1970-73; elem. and kindergarten tchr. Springfield Luth. Sch., 1984-88; mem. planning bd. Early Childhood Conf., U. Mo., Columbia, 1977-80. Pres. Springfield Gen. Hosp. Guild, 1969-71; local and zone pres. Luth. Women's Missionary League, Springfield, 1986-94; historian Trinity Luth. Ch., 1985-94; chair bd. edn. Grace Luth. Ch., Tulsa. Mem. Assn. for Childhood Edn. Internat. (br. state pres. 1980-84, president's coun. 1983-85, Hall of Fame plaque 1988, state pres. 1989-93), Springfield Edn. Assn. (life), Springfield Luth. Sch. Assn. (pres. 1992-94), S.W. Dist. Kindergarten Assn. (pres. 1978-79), Alpha Delta Kappa. Home: Univ Club 1722 S Carson Apt 1710 Tulsa OK 74119-4641

KNECHT, VICTORIA L., guidance counselor; b. Mpls., Nov. 17, 1955; d. Raymond and Lila C. (Dumdie) Bachman; m. Roger L. Simon (div.); children: Melanie Marie, Carrie Catherine; m. Duane D. Knecht, June 6, 1979; children: Sandra Susan, Erin Emily. BS in Secondary Edn. summa cum laude, No. State U., 1986, MS Edn., 1993. Bookkeeper/tax preparer, 1974-83; tchr. geography, govt., Spanish, English Bowdle (S.D.) Dist. # 22-1, 1989—, guidance counselor, 1994—; presenter workshops in field; coach H.S. Quiz Bowl Team, 1991-94; yearbook advisor, others; com. mem., writer S.D. Content Standards for Geography Adopted by the State, 1995; rep. Internat. Leadership Inst., summer 1995. Mem. Ed. County Reps., Ipswich, S.D., 1975—. Mem. Am. Legion Aux., Internat. Reading Assn., Am. Counselors Assn., Bowdle Edn. Assn., S.D. Geographic Alliance, Kappa Delta Phi. Lutheran. Office: Bowdle Sch Dist 22-1 PO Box 563 Bowdle SD 57428-0563

KNECHTGES, MARY KAY, coach; b. Elyria, Ohio, Jan. 4, 1945; d. Edwin Jospeh and Geneva Mae (Swan) K. BS, Bowling Green State U., 1967; postgrad., Wayne State U., 1968-70. Educator L'Anse Creuse H.S., Harrison Twp., Mich., 1968—, cheerleading coach, 1968-76, basketball coach, 1968-80, softball coach, 1976-78, basketball coach, 1990—; basketball coach Bishop Gallagher H.S., Harper Woods, Mich., 1981-83; asst. basketball coach U. Mich., Dearborn, 1985-87. Contbr. articles to profl. jours. Mem. Clinton Twp. (Mich.) Youth Svc. Com., 1973-75. Named Coach of Yr., Macomb County Coaches, 1977, 78, 79, Mich. Coach of Yr., Detroit Free Press, 1978, Dist. 4 Coach of Yr., Nat. H.S. Coaches, 1981; nominated Sportswoman of Yr., United Found., 1981. Mem. NEA, Nat. H.S. Athletic Assn. (state rep. 1980-83), Mich. High Sch. Athletic Assn. (ofcls. com. 1979, summer basketball com. 1981, volleyball ofcl. 1981-82, women in sports leadership com. 1994—), Mich. H.S. Basketball Coaches (regional chairperson 1980-82), Mich. H.S. Coaches Assn. (dist. rep. 1980-83), Mich. Edn. Assn., L'Anse Creuse Edn. Assn. Roman Catholic.

KNEE, RUTH IRELAN (MRS. JUNIOR K. KNEE), social worker, health care consultant; b. Sapulpa, Okla., Mar. 21, 1920; d. Oren M. and Daisy (Daubin) Irelan; m. Junior K. Knee, May 29, 1943 (dec. Oct. 21, 1981). BA, U. Okla., 1941, cert. social work, 1942; MASSA, U. Chgo., 1945. Psychiat. social worker, asst. supr. Ill. Psychiat. Inst., U. Ill. at Chgo., 1943-44; psychiat. social worker USPHS Employee Health Unit, Washington, 1944-46, chief psychiat. social worker, 1946-49; psychiat. social work assoc. Army Med. Ctr., Walter Reed Army Hosp., Washington, 1949-54; psychiat. social work cons. HEW, Region III, Washington, 1955-56; with NIMH, Chevy Chase, Md., 1956-72; chief mental health care adminstrn. br. USPHS, 1967-72, assoc. dep. adminstr. Health Svcs. and Mental Health Adminstrn., 1972-73, dep. dir. Office of Nursing Home Affairs, 1973-74; long-term mental health care cons.; mem. com. on mental health and illness of elderly HEW, 1976-77; mem. panel on legal and ethical issues Pres.'s Commn. on Mental Health, 1977-78; liaison mem. Nat. Adv. Mental Health Coun., 1977-81. Mem. editorial bd. Health and Social Work, 1979-81. Bd. dirs. Hillhaven Found., 1975-86, governing bd. Cathedral Coll. of the Laity, Washington Nat. Cathedral, 1988-94. Fellow Am. Pub. Health Assn. (sec. mental health sect. 1968-70, chmn. 1971-72), Am. Orthopsychiat. Assn. (life), Gerontol. Soc. Am., Am. Assn. Psychiat. Social Workers (pres. 1951-53); mem. Nat. Conf. Social Welfare (nat. bd. 1968-71, 2d v.p. 1973-74), Inst. Medicine/Nat. Acad. Sci. (com. study future of pub. health 1986-87), Coun. on Social Work Edn., Nat. Assn. Social Workers (sec. 1955-56, nat. dir. 1956-57, 84-86, chmn. competence study com., practice and knowledge com. 1963-71), Acad. Cert. Social Workers (social work pioneer 1993), Am. Pub. Welfare Assn., DAR, U. Okla. Assocs., Woman's Nat. Dem. Club (mem. gov. bd. 1992-95, ednl. found. bd. 1992-96), Cosmos Club (Washington), Phi Beta Kappa (assoc. 1985—), Psi Chi. Address: 8809 Arlington Blvd Fairfax VA 22031-2705

KNELL, DORA MARIE, publishing executive; b. Sonoma, Calif., Nov. 30, 1924; d. Viggo Riis Sorensen and Inez Frances Bonvecchio; m. Frederick Gerald Knell, June 22, 1947 (dec. June 1986); children: Gregory L., Catherine L., Theodora C., Valerie P., Vivian M., Geoffrey F., Derek P. AA, Santa Rosa Jr. Coll., 1944; AB in Journalism, U. Calif., Berkeley, 1954; credential in Spanish, Univ. Iberoam., Mexico City, 1970; credential in graphic arts, Indian Valley Coll., 1978. CEO Graphic Arts Mgmt. Co., San Rafael, Calif., 1978—. Editor: Manifestations of Thought, 1980, Sahar, 1981, California Controversies, 1986, (newspaper) The Active Democrat, 1988-92; prodr.: (TV show) The Square Table, 1995—. Chmn. bd. dirs. HOPE, Inc., Chgo., 1969-72, housing com. FACSAC, Marin County, San Rafael, 1972-76; bd. dirs. LWV, Marin County, 1974-76, Nat. Women's Polit. Caucus, Marin County, 1994-96; elected mem. Dem. Cen. Com., Marin County, 1974-92; deacon St. Luke Presbyn. Ch., San Rafael, 1989-92; co-owner R-Ranch, R-Wild Horse Ranch. Recipient Cert. of Appreciation, AAUW, 1976, Nat. Women's Polit. Caucus, 1991, Cert. of Recognition, Santa Rosa Jr. Coll., 1987. Mem. San Rafael C. of C. Democrat. Presbyterian. Home: 11 Peacock Ln San Rafael CA 94901 Office: Graphic Arts Mgmt Co 3140 Kerner Blvd Ste B San Rafael CA 94901

KNEPP, VIRGINIA LEE HAHN, legal assistant; b. South Bend, Ind., Nov. 1, 1946; d. Charles William and Mary Louise (Hunter) Hahn; m. James Patrick Knepp, Apr. 20, 1968; children: Meredith Leigh, Melanie Leigh. BS in Bus., Ind. U., 1971. Legal asst. Hahn, Walz, Knepp & Dvorak, South Bend, Ind., 1983—; mem. Ind. allocation com. for Social Svc. Block Grants. Founder YWCA Women's Shelter, South Bend, 1978; founder, facilitator Women's Support Group, South Bend, 1979-90; vol. coord. Olympic Town Internat./Spl. Olympics, 1984-87, Kids Kingdom, South Bend, 1991, Children's Dispensary, South Bend, 1981-93, adv. coun., 1994, St. Joseph County Scholarship Found., 1990, Am. Cancer Soc., St. Joseph County, 1988-89; bd. dirs. Corvilla Inc., South Bend, 1989-96; treas. Dvorak for State Rep., 1986—, Very Spl. Arts Ind., 1980—, pres., 1995-97, South Bend Heritage Found., 19990-95; active Gov. Bayh Commn., 1991—; chmn. Domestic Violence Prevention and Treatment Coun., Michiana Arts and Sci. Coun.'s Carnival for the Arts; bd. dirs. South Bend Heritage Found., 1991-95. Mem. AAUW, Hoosier Art Patrons, Thalia Sorority (pres. 1988), Ind. Lawyers Aux. Home: 17725 Juday Lake Dr South Bend IN 46635-1758 Office: Hahn Walz Knepp & Dvorak 509 W Washington St South Bend IN 46601-1527

KNES, STACEY LYN, elementary education educator; b. St. Louis, Mo., May 18, 1970; d. Dave Charles and Barbara Jean K. BS in Elem. and Early Childhood Edn., U. Mo., St. Louis, 1993; MS in Elem. and Early Childhood Edn., Lindenwood Coll., 1995. Cert. elem. and early childhood tchr., Mo. 3d grade tchr. Fort Zumwalt Sch. Dist., O'Fallon, Mo., 1993—; mem. respect com. Fort Zumwalt Sch. Dist., O'Fallon, Mo., 1994-95. Access control mgr. Olympic Festival, St. Peter's (Mo.) Police, 1994. Mem. NEA, Internat. Reading Assn. Office: Fort Zumwalt Sch Dist 110 Virgil St O'Fallon MO 63336

KNEWSTEP, NANCY GAY, language educator; b. Hampton, Va., Aug. 22, 1943; d. William Edward and Dorothy Marie (Hunt) K.; m. Kenneth J. Stavisky, Sept. 6, 1975 (div. 1996); 1 child, C. Alexandra Stavisky. BA, Longwood Coll., 1965; MA, Regent U., 1994. Cert. libr. sci. Tchr. Hampton (Va.) City Schs., 1965-77; libr. Gloria Dei Luth. Sch., Hampton, 1984-91; tchr. English Hampton City Schs., 1991—; adj. instr., adj. faculty Old Dominion U., 1995—. Exec. bd. mem. Longwood Coll. Found. Bd., Farmville, Va., 1990-96. Mem. ASCD, Nat. Coun. Tchrs. English, Va. Assn. Tchrs. English. Presbyterian. Home: 220 Creekview Ln Hampton VA 23669-1088 Office: Hampton Sch Bd Nickerson Blvd Hampton VA 23669

KNEZO, GENEVIEVE JOHANNA, science and technology policy researcher; b. Elizabeth, N.J., Aug. 8, 1942; d. John and Genevieve (Sadowski) K.; 1 child, Alexandra M. AB in Polit. Sci., Douglass Coll., Rutgers U., 1964; MA in Sci., Tech. and Pub. Policy, George Washington U., 1981; grad., Nat. Def. U., 1989. With Congl. Rsch. Svc., Libr. of Congress, Washington, 1967—, specialist in sci. and tech., 1979—, head sci., rsch. and tech. sect., 1986-88, sr. level specialist in sci. and tech. policy, 1991—. Author profl. publs. Mem. Phi Beta Kappa, Pi Sigma Alpha. Avocations: whitewater canoeing, hiking, gymnastics, classical music, community volunteer activities. Home: 606 Oakley Pl Alexandria VA 22302-3611 Office: Libr of Congress Congl Rsch Svc Sci Policy Rsch Divsn Washington DC 20540

KNIERIEM, BEULAH WHITE, retired educator, clergyman; b. Appomattox, Va., Oct. 31, 1930; d. George Harrison and Virgie Ade (Kestner) White; m. Robert William Knieriem, July 11, 1953; children: Shawn, Roxanne, Roberta. AA, Mars Hill (N.C.) Coll., 1950; BA, Lynchburg (Va.) Coll., 1952; student, Baldwin-Wallace Coll., 1964-69, Ashland Sem., 1992-93. Lic. elem. tchr., Ohio; lic. to ministry, 1995. Tchr. Bd. Edn., Cleve., 1966-79; min. United Ch. of Christ, Cleve., 1990—; min. nursing homes, Cleve., 1990—; chaplain Ky. Cols., 1990—. Democrat. Home: 7324 Grant Blvd Cleveland OH 44130

KNIGHT, ALICE DOROTHY TIRRELL, state legislator; b. Manchester, N.H., July 14, 1903; d. Nathan Arthur and Clara (Stiles) Tirrell; m. Norman Knight, Nov. 15, 1952. B.A., U. N.H., 1925, postgrad., 1933; postgrad. Boston U., 1941-42. Tchr. Newton Falls (N.Y.) High Sch., 1925-26; prin. Oswegatchie (N.Y.) Union Sch., 1926-27, Bartlett Sch., Goffstown, N.H., 1932-35; home lighting specialist Pub. Svc. Co. N.H., Manchester, 1935-39; tchr. merchandising Mt. Ida Jr. Coll., Newton Centre, Mass., 1939-45; home svc. dir. Boyd Corp., Portland, Maine, 1945-47; dist. home economist Frigidaire Sales Corp., Boston, 1948-64; mem. N.H. Ho. of Reps., 1967-74, 76-78, 80-90; rep to N.H. Gen. Ct., 1967-91; mem. joint legis. com. on elderly affairs, 1983-87; pres. Greater Manchester Community Concert Assn., 1985 87; co-chmn. Goffstown Bicentennial Com. of the Constn., 1986—. Mem. budget com. Town of Goffstown, 1966-72; mem. Gov.'s Adv. Com. Alcoholism, 1972-73, 74-78, Statewide Health Coordinating Coun., 1977-78, N.H. Hist. Soc.; past pres. bd. dirs. Hillsborough County North Cancer Soc.; bd. dirs. N.H. Cancer Soc. Recipient award N.H. Program on Alcohol and Drug Abuse, 1971, 75, Gov.'s Recognition award Hillsborough County, 1986, Pub. Svc.award Union Pomona Grange, 1987. Mem. Nat. Home Fashions League (pres. 1957-58), Nat. Order State Legislators, Vis. Nurses Assn. (bd. dirs. Greater Manchester chpt. 1981-87), N.H. Coun. World Affairs, Nat. Grange (life), DAR (regent 1974-76), Nat. Order Women Legislators (treas. 1968-71), Manchester Bus. and Profl. Women (pres. 1972-74), Nat. Soc. New Eng. Women, Order Eastern Star (life), Soroptimist (life, Boston), Goffstown Unity Club, Goffstown Garden Club (pres. 1976-78), Goffstown Shirley Club (pres. 1977-78), Goffstown Hist. Soc. (life). Republican.

KNIGHT, ATHELIA WILHELMENINA, journalist; b. Portsmouth, Va., Oct. 15, 1950; d. Daniel Dennis and Adell Virginia (Savage) K. B.A. with honors in English, Norfolk State Coll., 1973; M.A. with honors in Journalism, Ohio State U., 1974. Cert. tchr., Va. Aide D.C. Coop. Extension Service, 1969-72; sub. tchr. Portsmouth Pub. Schs., 1973; reporter Virginian Pilot, Norfolk, 1973, Chgo. Tribune, 1974; met. desk reporter Washington Post, 1975-81, investigative reporter, 1981-94, sports writer, 1994—; lectr. high schs., colls. Recipient Mark Twain award, 1982, 87, Front Page award Washington-Balt. Newspaper Guild, 1982, Nat. award for edn. Edn. Writers Assn., 1987, Pub. Svc. award Md.-Del.-D.C. Press Assn., 1990, 93; Ohio State U. fellow, 1974, Nieman fellow Harvard U., 1985-86. Mem. Women in Comm., Nat. Assn. Black Journalists, Washington-Balt. Newspaper Guild, Investigative Reporters and Editors. Baptist. Home: 1435 4th St SW Apt B507 Washington DC 20024-2213 Office: Washington Post 1150 15th St NW Washington DC 20071-0001

KNIGHT, BRENDA LEE, quality engineer; b. Oil City, Pa., Aug. 22, 1958; d. Clarence Benjamin and Donna Jean (Grosteffon) K. BS in Indsl. and Ops. Engring., U. Mich., 1980; MBA, So. Ill. U., 1992. Cert. quality engr.; cert. quality auditor. Quality engr. Continental Gen. Tire, Inc., Mt. Vernon, Ill., 1981—. Mem. Am. Soc. for Quality Control, Am. Inst. Indsl. Engrs., Am. Mgmt. Assn., Beta Gamma Sigma. Home: 4411 Woodglen Ln Mount Vernon IL 62864-2171 Office: Continental Gen Tire Inc PO Box 1029 Mount Vernon IL 62864-1029

KNIGHT, IDA BROWN, retired elementary educator; b. Macon, Ga., Aug. 8, 1918; d. Morgan Cornelius and Ida (Moore) Brown; m. Dempsey Lewis Knight, Apr. 11, 1942; children: Lavera Knight Hughes, Eugene Charles. BS, Spelman Coll., 1940; MS, SUNY, Fredonia, 1958; postgrad., SUNY, 1974, U. Manchester, Eng., 1974. Cert. tchr. home econs. Clothing tchr. Bibb County Vocat. Sch., Macon, 1940-42; tchr. home econs. Ballard Normal Sch., Macon, 1943-45; elem. tchr. Jamestown (N.Y.) Pub. Schs., 1955-77. Bd. dirs. Jamestown Girls Club, 1970-78, Jamestown Cmty. Schs., 1989—; ch. organist, 1974-82; jr. bd. mem. Elizabeth Marvin Cmty. House, 1994—. Mem. AAUW, Chautauqua County Ret. Tchrs. Assn., N.Y. State Congress Parents and Tchrs. (hon. life), Links, Inc. (past pres. Jamestown chpt.), Delta Kappa Gamma (corr. sec. 1963-64). Home: 140 Federal Pl Jamestown NY 14701-2010

KNIGHT, JANET ANN, elementary education educator; b. Covina, Calif., July 22, 1937; d. Arnold M. and Thelma (Lyle) Ostrum; m. Ronald L. Knight, Sept. 14, 1957; children: Barbara Lynne, Susan Kaye. BA in Edn., Cen. Wash. U., 1979; MA in Edn., Heritage Coll., 1992. Cert. elem, secondary tchr., Wash. 2nd grade tchr. Kennewick (Wash.) Pub. Schs., 1980-81, 1st grade tchr., 1981-85, 3rd grade tchr., 1985-93, 4th grade tchr., 1993—; lang. arts dist. com. Kennewick Sch. Dist., 1985-89, curriculum, instrn. com., 1989-92, dist. curriculum and instruction renewal cycle for learning excellence, 1992-94, dist. assessment com., 1992-95. Mem. Richland (Wash.) Light Opera Co., 1963-75. Mem. NEA, ASCD, Wash. Edn. Assn., Kennewick Edn. Assn., Wash. Orgn. Reading Devel., Benton County Coun. of Internat. Reading Assn., Order of Rainbow for Girls, Sigma Tau Alpha. Episcopalian. Home: 120 Heather Ln Richland WA 99352-9155 Office: Westgate Elem Sch 2514 W 4th Ave Kennewick WA 99336-3115

KNIGHT, JANNA MARGARET, accountant; b. Alabaster, Ala., May 2, 1968; d. Dan Peck and Jo Anne (Chandler) K. BS in Acctg., Centenary Coll. La., 1990, BA in English, 1990; MSC in Internat. Acctg. and Fin., London Sch. of Econ., 1991. CPA, Ark., La. Staff acct. Ernst & Young, Little Rock, 1992-1993; acct. ALLTEL Svc. Corp., Little Rock, 1993-96; sr. investment adminstr. Myers Loveless Brandsgaard Inc., Little Rock, 1996—. Scholar Rotary Internat. Found., 1990-91. Mem. AICPA, Ark. Assn. Cert. Pub. Accts., Am. Bus. Women's Assn. (treas. Razorback chpt. 1993-94, v.p. 1994-95, pres. 1995-96, Woman of Yr. 1996—). Methodist. Home: 2400 Riverfront Dr Apt 432 Little Rock AR 72202

KNIGHT, JOAN ALDRICH, educator; b. Providence, Apr. 28, 1948; d. William Remington and Edna (Higginbottom) Aldrich; m. Philip Marshall, Nov. 18, 1967; children: Jennifer Aldrich, Jason Remington. BS, U. Vermont, 1970; MEd, Stetson U., 1981. Elementary tchr. Burlington, Vt., 1970-71; early childhood tchr Brooksville, Fla., 1971-77, early childhood tchr., dir., owner, 1977-82; early childhood tchr., dir. Casper, Wyo.; kindergarten tchr. Chpt. 1 Reading Recovery tchr. Callaghan Meml. Sch., St. Albans, Vt., 1985—; ednl. cons. Early Prevention of Sch. Failure, Peotone, Ill., 1986—, nat. cons. Whole Lang., 1989—; instr. C.C. of Vt., St. Albans, 1987—, Coll. of St. Joseph's, Rutland, Vt., 1987—, Champlain Coll., 1995—. Author: It Happened by Chants, 1989, Knight Lights, 1991, Reading Recovery Training, 1993, Literacy Links, 1996; co-author ednl. video Reading-Writing Connection, 1988. Mem. Reading Recovery Coun. Named Outstanding Young Educator, Vt. Jaycees, 1987, Tchr. of Yr., U. Vt., 1991. Republican. Congregationalist. Home and Office: 159 High St PO Box 1271 Saint Albans VT 05478

KNIGHT, KAREN ANNE MCGEE, artist; b. Florence, Ala., July 5, 1956; d. Glenn Houston and Juanita May (Fowler) McGee; m. Charles Ronald Knight, June 3, 1980; 1 child, Lara-Elizabeth. AA, Fla. Coll., 1976; BS, U. N. Ala., 1978, MA in Edn., 1994. Cert. tchr., Tenn., Ala. Title I reading aide Florence City Schs., 1978-79, 1st grade tchr., 1980-83; pre-kindergarten tchr. Belmont Weekday Sch., Nashville, 1984-85; kindergarten tchr. Metro-Davidson County Schs., Nashville, 1985-87; freelance watercolorist Shoals Artist's Guild, Florence, 1992—; chair Shoals Artists Guild, 1993—, v.p., 1996. Sunday sch. tchr. Exhibited in shows at N. Ala. State Fair, 1993 (1st place landscape award, 2d place still life award). Mem. Nat. Mus. Women in Arts, Watercolor Soc. Ala. (N.W. Ala. area rep. 1996), Tenn. Valley Art Assn., So. Watercolor Soc., Tenn. Valley Art Assn. Guild. Home: Rt 13 Box 25 Florence AL 35630

KNIGHT, LOUISE OSBORN, lawyer; b. Evanston, Ill., June 17, 1944; d. Newell Sloss and Helen (Willis) K. AB, Wellesley Coll., 1966; JD, George Washington U., 1969. Bar: Mo. 1969, D.C. 1970, Pa. 1972, U.S. Dist Ct. D.C. 1970, U.S. Dist. Ct. (mid. dist.) Pa. 1972, U.S. Ct. Appeals (D.C. cir.) 1976, U.S. Ct. Appeals (5th cir.) 1971, U.S. Ct. Appeals (3d cir.) 1976. Staff atty. Nat. Assn. Broadcasters, 1969-70, asst. gen. counsel, 1970-72; assoc. Kury & Kury, Sunbury, Pa., 1972-74; ptnr. Clement & Knight, Lewisburg, Pa., 1974—; adj. assoc. prof. Bucknell U., 1975—; chairperson Hearing Com. 3.04, Disciplinary Bd. Pa. Supreme Ct., Contbr. articles to profl jours. Solicitor Lewisburg Area Sch. Dist., 1975—, Lewisburg Bur. Zoning Hearing Bd., 1985—. Mem. Mo. Bar Assn., D.C. Bar Assn., Pa. Bar Assn., Pa. Sch. Bd. Solicitors Assn. (pres. 1986). Republican. Episcopalian. Home: RR3 Box 316 Mifflinburg PA 17844 Office: Clement & Knight 25 S 4th St Lewisburg PA 17837-1801

KNIGHT, LOUISE WILBY, writer; b. Evanston, Ill., May 2, 1949; d. Augustus, Jr. and Frances (Berna) K.; BA, Wesleyan U., Middletown, Conn., 1972, MA in Tchg., 1972. Rsch. asst. Learning Mag., Palo Alto, Calif., 1973; mktg. editor Addison-Wesley Co., Menlo Park, Calif., 1973-74; editor, ann. report Fund for the Improvement of Postsecondary Edn., Washington, 1974-75; editor Edn. Funding Rsch. Coun., Washington, 1975-78; coord. Office of Rsch. Support Duke U., Durham, N.C., 1978-86; dir. Found. and Corp. Relations Wheaton Coll., Norton, Mass., 1986-91; dir. devel. United South End Settlements, Boston, 1991-92; trainer, cons. The Grantsmanship Ctr., L.A., 1993-96; workshop leader, Coun. for Advancement and Aupport of Edn., Washington, 1989-91; cons. for nonprofits, 1992—; adj. faculty Spertus Coll., 1994—, Sch. Art Inst., 1996—; rsch. assoc. Five Coll. Women's Studies Ctr. Mt. Holyoke Coll., 1996. Author essays; contbr. articles to profl. jours., publs. Co-founder Durham Dispute Settlement, 1981-85; bd. dirs. Wesleyan U., Middletown, 1979-82, Boston Women's Fund, Boston, 1988-89; rsch. assoc. Five Coll. Women's Studies Rsch. Ctr., Mt. Holyoke Coll., 1996. Grantee Ind. U. Ctr. on Phil., 1993, NEH, 1992, Ludwig Vogelstein Found., 1989, Spencer Found., 1996. Office: PO Box 7038 Evanston IL 60201

KNIGHT, MARGARET ELIZABETH, music educator; b. Biddulph, Staffordshire, Eng., July 3, 1938; came to U.S., 1972; d. William Bateman and Amy Elizabeth (Willshaw) Whitehurst; m. Richard Alan Scudder, Apr. 5, 1972 (div. Mar. 1979); m. Arthur James Knight, May 26, 1979. Grad., No. Sch. of Music, Manchester, Eng., 1959; Assoc. in Piano Teaching, Royal Coll. Music. Lic. in voice culture, aural tng., sch. music and psychology. Asst. to head dept. music Thistley Hough Sch., Stoke, Eng., 1959-65; head dept. music Macclesfield (Eng.) High Sch., 1966-72; pvt. piano tchr. Shamong, N.J., 1972—; adj. mem. faculty dept. music Crewe (Eng.) Tchrs. Coll., 1963-72; dir. student activities South Jersey Music Tchrs. Assn., 1986-88; N.J. state rep. for Assoc. Bd. Royal Schs. Music, London, 1993—, developmental cons., 1994—. sec. Conservative Party, Congleton, Eng., 1968-71; active Town Coun., Congleton, 1971-72. County Music scholar Cheshire County Coun., Chester, Eng., 1955. Mem. Music Tchrs. Nat. Assn., Nat. Guild Piano Tchrs. (judge 1987—), N.J. Music Tchrs. Assn. (dir. student activities 1988-92, pres. 1992-94). Episcopalian. Home: 3 Blueberry Rd Shamong NJ 08088-8627

KNIGHT, PATRICIA MARIE, optics researcher; b. Schnectady, N.Y., Jan. 25, 1952; d. Donald Orlin and Mary Ann (Rooney) K. BS in Engring. Sci., Ariz. State U., 1974, MS in Chem. Engring., 1976; PhD in Biomed. Engring., U. Utah, 1983. Teaching and rsch. asst. Ariz. State U., Tempe, 1974-76; product devel. engr. Am. Med. Optics, Irvine, Calif., 1976-79, mgr. materials rsch., 1983-87; rsch. asst. U. Utah, Salt Lake City, 1979-83; dir. materials rsch. Allergan Med. Optics, Irvine, 1987-88, dir. rsch., 1988-91, v.p. rsch., devel. and engring., 1991—; Contbr. articles to profl. jours. Mem. Soc. Biomaterials, Am. Chem. Soc., Soc. Women Engrs., Assn. Rsch. in Vision and Opthalmology, Biomed. Engring. Soc. Office: Allergan Inc. 2525 Dupont Dr VK 1B Irvine CA 92713-9534

KNIGHT, SALLY ANN, school library director; b. Buffalo, Nov. 7, 1932; d. Frederick Jacob and Gertrude (Boily) Tellner; divorced; children: Eric Dean, Kurt Christopher. BA magna cum laude, St. Bonaventure U., 1976; MLS, SUNY, Buffalo, 1978. Cert. sch. media specialist N.Y. St.; prof. pub. libr. Libr. media specialist Cattarauqus (N.Y.) Ctrl. Sch., 1979-80, Franklinville (N.Y.) Ctrl. Sch., 1980-85; from dir. sch. libr. sys. to mgr. media/tech. librs. Cattarauque-Allegany BOCES, Olean, N.Y., 1985-96, ret., 1996; bd. dirs. Western N.Y. Libr. Resources Coun., Buffalo, 1993—; mem. Tech. Com., Olean, ABC Consortium, N.Y., 1985—. Trustee Blount Libr., Franklinville; bd. dirs. Indsl. Mgmt., Olean, 1986-94, Friends of Libr., Olean, 1990-94, Coun. Arts, Cattaraqus County, 1986-88, Mental Health Assn., Olean, 1986-94. Mem. Sch. Librs. Assn. N.Y., N.Y. Libr. Assn., Phi Delta Kappa (sec.), Delta Kappa Gamma. Home: 11 Pine St Franklinville NY 14738

KNIGHT, SARA CHAMBERS, sales executive; b. Memphis, June 17, 1948; d. Macie Marion and Sarah (Hendrix) Chambers; m. Robert Dewey Knight, Aug. 17, 1969 (div. July 1981); children: Macy Marian, Robert Miles. BBA in Banking and Fin. cum laude, U. Miss., 1970; grad., Inst. of Banking, 1972. Mgmt. trainee Deposit Guaranty Nat. Bank, Jackson, Miss., 1970-72; asst. tng. mgr. Deposit Guaranty Nat. Bank, Jackson, 1971-72; office mgr. Holiday Inn, Columbus, Miss., 1972-77, Old South Coors, Inc., Columbus, 1981-82; sales rep. J.L. Teel Co., Inc., Columbus, 1982-85; mgr. sales Teel Bus. Sys., Columbus, Miss., 1985-90, br. mgr., 1990—. Mem. Columbus Jr. Aux., 1978—. Mem. Am. Bus. Women's Assn., U. Miss. Alumni Assn., Krewe of Bacchus, Presidents Club, Woodland Garden Club (Columbus), Old Waverly Golf Club (West Point, Miss.), Phi Kappa Phi, Beta Gamma Sigma, Delta Gamma Alumni Assn. (pres. N.E. Miss. chpt. 1980-81). Republican. Episcopalian. Home: 220 Huckleberry Hills Columbus MS 39705-8113 Office: Teel Bus Sys Hwy 45 N Columbus MS 39701

KNIGHT, SHARON A., lawyer; b. Jacksonville, Fla., Feb. 24, 1955. BS in Bus. Adminstrn., U. Fla., 1977, JD, 1981. Bar: Fla. 1981, N.Y. 1987. Ptnr. Brown & Wood, N.Y.C. Office: Brown & Wood One World Trade Ctr New York NY 10048-0557*

KNIGHT, VALERIE, psychotherapist; b. N.Y.C., Nov. 3, 1932; d. Merit and Ethel K. BA, CUNY, 1991; MA, Norwich U., 1993; postgrad., Union Inst., 1994—. Adminstr. N.Y. St. Theatre Caravan, N.Y.C., 1975-89; analyst arts in edn. N.Y. State Coun. on the Arts, N.Y.C., 1989-91; cons. Educators for Social Responsibility, N.Y.C., 1992-94; pvt. practice psychotherapy N.Y.C., 1993—; psychotherapist, cons. Women At Risk, N.Y.C., 1994—; drama therapist, cons. Satellite Acad. H.S., N.Y.C., 1992-94; drama therapist Changing Scenes/Theatre for Forgotten, N.Y.C., 1993-94; staff trainee Elizabeth Kubler Ross Ctr., Headwaters, Va., 1993-95. Actor, dir., writer, adminstr. various profl. theatres, including N.Y. St. Theatre Caravan, 1977 (Obie award for sustained theatre excellence 1977). Recipient Artists of Social Concern award The Yuletiders, 1986. Mem. ACA, Nat. Assn. Drama Therapy. Office: Maria Droste Svcs 386 Park Ave S Ste 903 New York NY 10128

KNIGHT-MCCONNELL, KATHY, small business owner, writer; b. Oakland, Calif., June 22, 1950; d. William Pell Bruns and Doris Diana (Koofman) Burrell; m. Paul C. LoCascio, Apr. 29, 1967 (div. Jan. 1979); m. John B. McConnell, Sept. 24, 1995. Student, Radio Electronic Tech. Sch., 1965-67, Albert Merrill Computer Sch., 1988—. Owner, dispatcher At Your Service Limousine, N.Y.C., 1979-87; v.p., art dir. Golden Sphinx Records, N.Y.C., 1980-92; financier Recording Project- UFO, N.Y.C., 1980; pres., owner Knight Mfg., N.Y.C., 1987; mgmt. asst. Curtis Knight Mgmt. & Prodn. Co., N.Y.C., 1976-92; assoc. producer Cosmic Prodns., N.Y.C., 1987-88; adminstrv. credit asst. St. Martin's Press, N.Y.C., 1988-94; gen. asst. to pres. PPX Enterprises, Inc., N.Y.C., 1994-96; founder Knight-McConnell Tracing and Office Svcs., Bronx, N.Y., 1996—; cons. Documentary Jimi Hendrix. Author: (poetry) 9 anthologies; artist for various album covers and posters. Vol. Am. Heart Assn.; mem. Rep. Nat. Com., 1987. Recipient Internat. Poet of Merit award, 1995. Mem. NAFE, Am. Mus. Natural History, Nat. Audubon Soc., Nat. Arbor Day Found., Nat. Author's Registry, Am. Film Inst. Mayan Order, Christian Children's Fund, Internat. Soc. Poets. Mem. Worldwide Ch. God. Office: PPX Enterprises Inc Ste 2R 300 W 55th St New York NY 10019-5141

KNIGHTS, PHYLLIS LOUISE, tax preparer, accountant; b. Hartford, Conn., Jan. 6, 1943; d. Harold Daniel and Louise Edith (Hart) Hall; m. Richard Lowe, Sept. 2, 1960 (div. Sept. 1995); children: Richard, James, Daniel, Charles, Debbie Sue, Penny Candy; m. Weldon G. Knights, Sept. 17, 1983; stepchildren: Lynn, Peter, Terry. BSA, Plymouth State Coll., 1984, MBA, 1986. Cert. accreditation Coun. Acctg. Owner H & R Block Satellite, Bellows Falls, Vt., 1970-74, Littleton, N.H., 1975-80; owner Knights Tax Svc., Monroe, N.H., 1983—. Contbr. articles to newsletters. Bd. dirs. Littleton Self-Help Clinic, 1979-86; town chair Reps. for Wayne King, Monroe, 1988. Mem. VT-Woodsville (sec., Presdl. citation 1994), Rotary (past pres. Woodsville-Wells River Club, 1st woman to be admitted, 1st woman to hold office). Home: 131 Harley View Dr Monroe NH 03771 Office: Knights Tax Svc 131 Harley View Dr Monroe NH 03771

KNISELY BONK, HELEN, corporate customs broker; b. Cleve., Apr. 12, 1950; d. Angelo and Laura (Kelepouris) Pappis; m. Robert B. Knisely Sr., July 5, 1969 (div. Dec. 1986); children: Robert Jr., Laura; divorced; 1 child, Alexandra. Degree in computer, AG Computer Tng., Cleve., 1984-93; student, Columbia Pacific U., 1989; B in Internat. Bus./Law, World Trade Inst., 1991; cert. NAFTA specialist, U.S. Customs, 1994; cert. customs audits and investigations specialist, World Trade Inst., 1995. Lic. customs broker; cert. internat. law. Corp. customs broker Am. Greetings, others cos., worldwide locations, 1983—; pres., instr., seminar leader, cons. Internat. Trade Cons., Cleve., 1989—; fgn. buyer Am. Greetings Corp., Cleve., 1990—. Author: (trade book) Foreign Trade Zones and Subzones, 1993; contbr. articles to profl. jours. Named Woman of Yr., Orgn. Women in Internat. Trade, 1992-93. Mem. NAFE, Internat. Freight Assn. (hon.), Women in Internat. Trade, C. of C. (student sponsor 1993—). Republican. Greek Orthodox. Home: 3209 Bay Landing Dr Westlake OH 44145-4437 Office: Am Greetings Corp One American Rd Cleveland OH 44144

KNISLEY, ELSILYNN, music educator; b. Chattanooga, Tenn., June 18, 1957; d. David Paul and Bettye Jeane (Longley) K. MusB, Carson-Newman Coll., 1979; postgrad., Kodaly Ctr. Am., Boston, 1980-82, Kecksemet, Hungary, 1989; MusM, Ithaca Coll., 1987. Cert. elem. tchr., Tenn. Tchr. music Hamilton County Schs., Chattanooga, 1979—; organ study tour, Western Europe, 1990. Mem. NEA, Music Educators Nat. Conf., Am. Guild of Organists, Orgn. of Am. Kodaly Educators. Baptist. Home: 4366 Prospect Church Rd Ooltewah TN 37363-8532 Office: Ooltewah Elem Sch 9232 Lee Hwy Ooltewah TN 37363

KNITTEL, DIANE LYNNE, insurance marketing executive; b. Warsaw, N.Y., Feb. 24, 1961; d. George Willard and Betty Jean (Wheeler) Sonricker; m. Philip James Knittel, June 3, 1989. BS in Microbiology, Pa. State U., 1983; Assoc. in Risk Mgmt., Ins. Inst. Am., 1993. Cert. profl. ins. woman. Agt. State Farm, Olean, N.Y., 1985; comml. marketer The Bowersox Ins. Agy., St. Louis, 1986-92, account exec., 1994—; comml. mktg. mgr. The Warren Group, Chesterfield, Mo., 1992-94; tchr. Met. St. Louis (Mo.) Ins. Assn., 1992—. Mem. Met. St. Louis Ins. Assn. (bd. dirs. 1993—, v.p. 1994-95, pres.-elect 1995, pres. 1996), Nat. Assn. Ins. Women.

KNIZESKI, JUSTINE ESTELLE, insurance company executive; b. Glen Cove, N.Y., June 4, 1954; d. John Martin and Elsie Beatrice (Gozelski) Knizeski. B.A., Conn. Coll., 1976; M. Mgmt., Northwestern U., 1981. Customer service supr. Brunswick Savs., Freeport, Maine, 1977-79; investment analyst Bankers Life and Casualty Co., Chgo., 1980-83, dir. corp. planning and analysis, 1983-87; dir. budgets, cost acctg. Blue Cross/Blue Shield of Ill., 1987—. Chmn. bd. dirs. Alternatives, Inc., Chgo., 1984-87, vice chmn., 1987-91, sec., 1991-92, bd. dirs., 1983-84; mem. Chgo. Council Fgn. Relations, 1984-85. Mem. Planning Forum. Avocations: sailing; bicycling; traveling; painting.

KNOEBEL, SUZANNE BUCKNER, cardiologist, medical educator; b. Ft. Wayne, Ind., Dec. 13, 1926; d. Doster and Marie (Lewis) Buckner. A.B., Goucher Coll., 1948; M.D., Ind. U.-Indpls., 1960. Diplomate: Am. Bd. Internal Medicine. Asst. prof. medicine Ind. U., Indpls., 1966-69, assoc. prof., 1969-72, prof., 1972-77, Krannert prof., 1977—; asst. dean rsch. Ind. U., Indpls., 1975-85; assoc. dir. Krannert Inst. Cardiology, Indpls., 1974-90; asst. chief cardiology sect. Richard L. Roudebush VA Med. Ctr., Indpls., 1982-90; editor-in-chief ACC Current Jour. Rev., 1992—. Fellow Am. Coll. Cardiology (v.p. 1980-81, pres. 1982-83); mem. Am. Fedn. Clin. Research, Assn. Univ. Cardiologists. Office: Ind U Sch Medicine 1111 W 10th St Indianapolis IN 46202-4800

KNOELL, NANCY JEANNE, kindergarten educator; b. Boone, Iowa, Dec. 12, 1941; d. Wallace Knute and Dorothy Althea (Walker) Johnson; m. Gerald Dwain Brown, June 21, 1970 (div. Dec. 1987); children: Renae Jeanne, Arlan Gerald; m. Lawrence Hubert Knoell, Oct. 19, 1991. BS, Gustavus Adolphus Coll., 1963; postgrad., Hamlin U., U. Minn., Coll. St. Thomas. Cert. tchr. elem. K-6, Minn. Tchr. kindergarten Rochester (Minn.) Pub. Schs., 1963-66, Robbinsdale Area Ind. Sch. Dist. 281, New Hope, Minn., 1966—; mem. sci. design team Robbinsdale Area Ind. Sch. Dist. 281, New Hope; mentor to 1st year tchr., 1995-96. Mem. Am. Fedn. Tchrs., Assn. Childhood Edn. Internat. (bldg. rep., sec., pres. Robbinsdale br.), Delta Kappa Gamma. Lutheran. Home: 8209 Toledo Ave N Brooklyn Park MN 55443-2228 Office: Neill Elem Sch 6600 27th Ave N Crystal MN 55427

KNOFF, LISA ANN, pharmacist; b. Slayton, Minn., Sept. 25, 1968; d. Robert Lucian and Elaine Mary (Bulawski) K. BS, U. Minn., 1992, Pharm D, 1993. Lic. Minn. Intern Hennepin County Med. Ctr., Mpls., 1991-93, staff pharmacist, 1993-96; clin. pharmacy resident U. Minn. Health Sys., Mpls., 1993-94, clin. pharmacist, 1994-96; pharmacist Appleton (Wis.) Med. Ctr., 1996—; instr. U. Minn. Coll. of Pharm. Mem. Am. Soc. of Health Sys. Pharmacists, Minn. Soc. of Health Sys. Pharmacists, Am. Coll. of Clin. Pharmacists, Minn. Coll. of Clin. Pharmacists. Office: Appleton Med Ctr Dept of Pharmacy 1818 N Meade St Appleton WI 54911

KNOLL, FLORENCE SCHUST, architect, designer; b. Saginaw, Mich., May 24, 1917; d. Frederick E. and M. Haisting Schust; m. Hans G. Knoll, July 1, 1946 (dec. 1955); m. Harry Hood Bassett, June 22, 1958 (dec. 1991). Student, Cranbrook Art Acad., Bloomfield Hills, Mich., 1935-37, Archtl. Assn., London, 1938-39; B.Arch., Ill. Inst. Tech., Chgo., 1941; D.F.A. (hon.), Parsons Sch. Design, 1979. Archtl. draftsman, designer Gropius & Breuer, Boston, 1941; design dir. Knoll Planning Unit, 1942-55; pres. Knoll Internat., N.Y.C., 1955-65; pvt. practice architecture and designer Coconut Grove, Fla., 1965—. Recipient Ill. Inst. Tech. Hall of Fame award, 1982; recipient Athena award R.I. Sch. Design, 1982, others. Mem. AIA (recipient Gold medal for indsl. arts 1961), Indsl. Designers Am. (hon.).

KNOPMAN, DEBRA S., hydrologist, federal agency administrator; b. Phila., Aug. 13, 1953; d. Harold L. and Minnette (Smulyan) Knopman; m. Donald Weightman, Sept. 29, 1985; children: Leah Alana, David Atwood. BA, Wellesley Coll., 1975; MSCE, MIT, 1978; PhD, Johns Hopkins U., 1986. Various positions as sci. writer and editor Washington, 1975-78; legis. asst. Daniel P. Moynihan, Washington, 1979-80; prof. staff mem. U.S. Senate Com. on Environ. and Pub. Works, Washington, 1980-83; student asst., office of groundwater U.S. Geol. Survey, Reston, Va., 1984-85, rsch. hydrologist, nat. rsch. program, 1985-86, hydrologist, br. of systems analysis, 1987-91, chief, br. or systems analysis, 1991-93; dep. asst. sec. water and sci. Dept. Interior, 1993-95; dir. Progressive Found. Ctr. for Innovation and Environ., 1995—. Editor: Scientific Research in Israel, 1976; editor Geophysics News, 1990-92; contbr. articles to profl. jours. Henry R. Luce Found. scholar, Taiwan, 1978-79. Mem. Am. Geophys. Union (chair pub. info. com. 1990-92). Democrat. Jewish. Office: Progressive Found Ctr for Innovation and Environ 518 C St NE Washington DC 20002*

KNOWLAND, BEVERLY ANN LYNCH, art director; b. Austin, Tex., June 1, 1960; d. Raymond Augustus Lynch, Jr. and Virginia Ann (Keehn) Leber; m. William Fife Knowland II, July 17, 1983; 1 child, Forrest Beall. BA in Indsl. Arts magna cum laude, San Francisco State U., 1986. Graphic designer AS Performing Arts, San Francisco, 1983-84, AS Graphics, San Francisco, 1985; syss. mgr. Greystone Mgmt., San Francisco, 1986-92; art dir. Direct Images, San Leandro, Calif., 1993—. Office: Direct Images 14020 Outrigger Dr San Leandro CA 94577

KNOWLES, AMANDA GAY-LORD, artist; b. Wilmington, Del., Mar. 30, 1971; d. John Appleton and Barbara Anne (Bang) K. Student, Parsons Sch. Design, 1988, Cleve. Art Inst., Florence, Italy, 1992; BA, U. Pa., 1993. Gallery asst., printer The Fabric Workshop, Phila., 1989; gallery asst. The Print Club, Phila., 1991; artist asst. Eleanor Hubbard, Phila., 1992-93; auctioneers asst. Satoris Fine Art & Antiques Auctioneer & Appraisers, Seattle, 1993-94; photo archivist, cataloger dept. arch. U. Washington, Seattle, 1993-94; photo archivist Tony Stone Images, Seattle, 1994—. One-woman shows include Philomathean Soc., Phila., 1993; exhibited in group show at Palazzo Strozzi, Florence, Italy, 1992. Recipient Etching award Studio Art Ctrs. Internat., Florence, Italy, 1992. Democrat.

KNOWLES, BARBARA WAGONER, publisher; b. Greensboro, N.C., May 29, 1928; d. Vaden W. and Florence Edna (Dumas) Wagoner; children: Carolyn A., Robert Vaden, William David. BA, Woman's Coll U. N.C., 1950. Changes not made are inappropriate to house style. Art tchr. Arlington County, Va., 1950-51; cartographic tch. U.S. Geol. Survey, Washington, 1951-53, 55-58; chief cartographer, plant mgr. Marshall Penn-York, Inc., Syracuse, N.Y., 1973-79; map pub. Candlewood Publs., Fayetteville, N.Y., 1979-96. Literacy tutor R.E.A.C.H., Syracuse, 1995-96; staff Camillus Erie Canal Restoration, 1980-96; vol. Citizens Advocacy, Syracuse, 1994-96. Mem. Am. Congress on Surveying & Mapping, Am. Cartographic Assn., Manlius C. of C. Office: Candlewood Publs Box 111 De Witt NY 13214

KNOWLES, ELIZABETH PRINGLE, art museum director; b. Decatur, Ill., Jan. 9, 1943; d. William Bull and Elizabeth E. (Pillsbury) P.; m. Joseph E. Knowles; 1 child, Elizabeth Bakewell. BA in Humanities with honors, Stanford, 1964; MA in Art History, U. Calif., Santa Barbara, 1968; grad., Mus. Mgmt. Inst., 1984. Cert. jr. coll. tchr., Calif. Instr. art history Murray State U., Murray, Ky., 1967-68; instr. art history Santa Barbara Art Inst., 1969, Santa Barbar City Coll., 1969-70, 76-78; staff coord. docents Santa Barbara Mus. Art, 1974-78; instr. continuing edn. Santa Barbara City Coll., 1973-86; curator edn. Santa Barbara Mus. Art, 1978-86; assoc. dir. Meml. Art Gallery, Rochester, N.Y., 1986-88; instr. mus. studies Calif. State U., Long Beach, 1989; exec. dir. Lyman Allyn Art Mus., New London, Conn., 1989-95; pres. Conn. Spl. Interest Tours, Chester, 1995—. Contbr. essays to art catalogues. Board dirs., chmn. Met. Transit Dist., Santa Barbara, 1978-80; founding pres. Santa Barbara Contemporary Arts Forum, Santa Barbara, 1976-78; commr. Santa Barbara City Planning Commn., 1975-77. Kellogg Found. fellow Smithsonian Inst., 1985. Mem. Am. Assn. Mus. (treas. edn. com. 1986-88), Coll. Art Assn., New Eng. Mus. Assn. (v.p. 1993-95).

KNOWLES, MARIE L., transportation executive. Sr. v.p., pres. Arco Transp. Co., Long Beach, Calif. Office: Arco Transp Co 300 Oceangate Long Beach CA 90802*

KNOWLES, MARJORIE FINE, lawyer, educator, dean; b. Bklyn., July 4, 1939; d. Jesse J. and Roslyn (Leff) Fine; m. Ralph I. Knowles, Jr., June 3, 1972. BA, Smith Coll., 1960; LLB, Harvard U., 1965. Bar: Ala., N.Y., D.C. Teaching fellow Harvard U., 1963-64; law clk. to judge U.S. Dist. Ct. (so. dist.), N.Y., 1965-66; asst. U.S. atty. U.S. Atty.'s Office, N.Y.C., 1966-67; asst. dist. atty. N.Y. County Dist. Atty., N.Y.C., 1967-70; exec. dir. Joint Found. Support, Inc., N.Y.C., 1970-72; asst. gen. counsel HEW, Washington, 1978-79; insp. gen. U.S. Dept. Labor, Washington, 1979-80; assoc. prof. U. Ala. Sch. Law, Tuscaloosa, 1972-75, prof., 1975-86, assoc. dean, 1982-84; law prof., dean Ga. State U. Coll. Law, Atlanta, 1986-91, law prof., 1986—; cons. Ford Found., N.Y.C., 1973—, trustee Coll. Retirement Equities Fund, N.Y.C., 1983—; mem. exec. com. Conf. on Women and the Constn., 1986-88; mem. com. on continuing profl. edn. Am. Law Inst.-ABA, 1987-93. Contbr. articles to profl. jours. Am. Council Edn. fellow, 1976-77, Aspen Inst. fellow, Rockefeller Found., 1976. Mem. ABA (chmn. new deans workshop 1988), Ala. State Bar Assn., N.Y. State Bar Assn., D.C. Bar Assn., Am. Law Inst. Office: Ga State U Coll Law University Plz Atlanta GA 30303

KNOWLTON, DEBORAH ANN, school system administrator, researcher; b. Long Beach, Calif., Mar. 8, 1949; d. John Albert and Patricia Ann (MacDonald) K. BA, U. Calif., Davis, 1971; MA, Calif. State U., 1981; postgrad., U. Calif., Riverside, 1991—. Cert. elem. and secondary tchr., bilingual cross-cultural specialist, administrator; lic. real estate salesperson. Tchr. Garden Grove (Calif.) Unified Sch. Dist., 1972-85, curriculum specialist, 1985-88, asst. prin. intermediate sch., 1988—; intermediate sch. rep. Garden Grove Adminstrs. Assn., 1994—. Mem. AAUW (pres., program chair, legis. rep. 1989-92. Eleanor Roosevelt grantee 1990), Assn. Calif. Sch. Adminstrs., Seal Beach Yacht Club, Phi Delta Kappa, Pi Lamda Theta, Phi Kappa Phi. Office: Garden Grove Unified Sch Dist 10331 Stanford Ave Garden Grove CA 92640

KNOWLTON, GRACE FARRAR, sculptor, photographer; b. Buffalo, Mar. 15, 1932; d. Frank Neff and Esther Sargeant (Norton) Farrar; m. Winthrop Knowlton, July 8, 1960 (div. 80); children: Eliza, Samantha. B.A., Smith Coll., 1954; M.A., Columbia U., 1981. Asst. to curator of graphic arts Nat. Gallery of Art, Washington, 1955-57; tchr. art Arlington Pub. Schs., Va., 1957-60; sculptor and photographer, 1960—. Exhbns. include Hirschl & Adler Modern, N.Y.C., 1995. Avocations: reading, bird-watching. Home and Studio: 67 Ludlow Ln Palisades NY 10964-1606

KNOWLTON, KATHRYN LEE, special education and elementary educator; b. Emporia, Kans., Aug. 29, 1952; d. Thomas Hamlin and Ramona Kathryn (Seltzer) Turner; m. John Paul Knowlton III; 1 child, Janelle Elizabeth. BS in Edn., Emporia State U., 1973; MS in Edn., U. Kans., 1978. Cert. tchr. elem., spl. edn., supr, prin. Tchr. Spl. Edn. Coop. Unified Sch. Dist. # 434, Overbrook, Kans., 1973-75; tchr. Spl. Edn. Presch. U. Kans., Lawrence, 1976-78; tchr. spl. edn. Mesa (Ariz.) Pub. Schs., 1978-87, tchr. kindergarten, 1987-90, tchr. spl. edn., 1990-95, 4th grade tchr., 1995—. Publ. cons. Kans. Dept. Edn., Topeka, summer 1976; statis. cons. Kans. Neurol. Inst., Topeka, summer 1977; writing cons. Ednl. Materials Support, Scottsdale, Ariz., summer 1994, Pierian Spring Software, Portland, Oreg., 1994-95. Residential monitor Ariz. Assn. Retarded Citizens, Phoenix, 1986-90. Recipient Emma Jean West award Mesa Assn. Retarded Citizens, 1982. Mem. Coun. Exceptional Children (pres. Ariz. Fedn. 1989, pres. chpt. 86 1983, treas. 1986), Phi Delta Kappa. Home: 118 E Geneva Dr Tempe AZ 85282-3639

KNOWLTON, NANCY, biologist; b. Evanston, Ill., May 30, 1949; d. Archa Osborn and Aline (Mahnken) K.; m. Jeremy Bradford Cook Jackson; 1 child, Rebecca Knowlton. AB, Harvard U., 1971; PhD, U. Calif., Berkeley, 1978. Asst. prof. biology Yale U., New Haven, 1979-84, assoc. prof., 1984; biologist Smithsonian Tropical Rsch. Inst., Panama, Republic of Panama, 1985—; panelist animal learning and behavior NSF, Washington, 1989-92; vis. scholar Wolfson Coll., Oxford (Eng.) U., 1990-91. Editor Am. Scientist, 1981-90, Evolution, 1995—. NATO postdoctoral fellow NSF, Liverpool, Cambridge, Eng., 1978-79. Mem. AAAS (coun. del. sect. on biol. scis.), Ecol. Soc. Am., Soc. Study Evolution. Office: Smithsonian Tropical Rsch Institute Unit 0948 APO AA 34002-0948

KNOX, ELIZABETH ANN, painter; b. Miami, Fla., June 13, 1944. Studies in art, Parsons Sch. of Design, New Sch. for Social Rsch., Art Students League. Instr. painting & drawing Round Top Ctr. for the Arts, Damariscotta, Maine, 1991—; adj. instr. painting & drawing Unity (Maine) Coll., 1992—; guest lectr. Bowdoin Coll., Brunswick, Maine, 1995; guest panelist Maine Coast Artists, Rockport, Maine, 1995. One-woman shows include The Great Indoors, Brunswick, Maine, 1980, Vision, Wiscasset, Maine, 1981, Round Top Ctr. for the Arts, Damariscotta, 1991, Gleason Fine Art, Portland, Maine, 1993; other exhbns. include Whitney Mus., N.Y.C., 1975, Salmagundi Club, N.Y.C., 1975, 76, Bennington (Vt.) Coll., 1976, Water Street Gallery, Damariscotta, 1977, Maine Art Gallery, Wiscasset, 1978, 79, U. Maine, Augusta, 1980, Maine Coast Artists, Rockport, 1981, Payson Gallery Art, Westbrook Coll., Portland, 1982, L.A. Arts, Lewiston, Maine, 1994, Maine Coast Artists, Rockport, 1994, Barn Gallery, Ogunquit, Maine, 1994, Gleason Fine Art Boothbay Harbor, Maine, 1994, Fitzpatrick Gallery, Portland, Maine, 1994, J.S. Ames Gallery, Belfast, Maine, 1994, O'Farrell Gallery, Brunswick, Maine, 1995, Maine Coast Artisits, Rockport, 1995, Atrium Gallery, Lewiston, 1996, Round Top Ctr. Arts, 1996. Residency fellow Vt. Studio Ctr., 1995. Address: 601 Spring St Brunswick ME 04011-2331

KNOX, ELIZABETH LOUISE, community volunteer, travel consultant; b. Forest Hills, N.Y.; d. Frederick Conrad and Emma M. Wissel; m. Rudolph T. Haas Jr., Feb. 1944 (div. June 1955); 1 child, Rudolph T. III; m. James Henry Knox, Aug. 22, 1956 (dec. Feb. 1987),; children: Julie Frances, Alice Carrie. Student, Hunter Coll. Ret. co-owner Del Mar (Calif.) Travel Bur. Mem. bd. trustees Salk Inst., La Jolla, 1994—; co-chair Salk Inst. Coun., 1995—; v.p. women's assn., 1969-70, pres., 1970-72, trustee, 1981-82, chmn. Andy Williams golf tournament benefit, 1969-70, chmn. 30th anniversary com., 1990-92; co-chmn. fashion show benefit Bishop's Sch., La Jolla, 1967, chmn., 1968, trustee, devel. chmn., 1971—, v.p., 1980-82, pres., 1982-86, headmaster's adv. coun., 1986—; bd. dirs. women's aux. Scripps Meml. Hosp., La Jolla, 1963-64, co-chmn. candlelight ball, 1963; charter mem. La Jolla unit Children's Hosp., San Diego, 1956, chmn. ways and means La Jolla unit, 1956-59, chmn. 10th annual fair benefit, 1963, pres. La Jolla unit, 1965, bd. dirs. women's auxiliary, 1962-64, chmn. San Diego stadium premiere benefit, 1967; bd. regents Calif. Luth. Univ., 1994—. Recipient Nat. Lane Bryant award, 1966, Woman of Valor award Temple Beth Israel, 1967, Jonas Salk award of Congress Salk Inst., 1972, Pres.'s award Women's Assn./Salk Inst., 1978, Woman of Dedication award San Diego Door of Hope Aux./Salvation Army, 1986. Mem. La Jolla Beach and Tennis Club, Del Mar Turf Club. Home: 2688 Hidden Valley Rd La Jolla CA 92037-4025

KNOX, GLENDA JANE, retired health and safety specialist, educator; b. Abernathy, Tex., Mar. 8, 1939; d. Raymond Arnold and Viola Jane (Melton) Boykin; m. William Gene Bright, Mar. 2, 1954 (dec. July 1974); children: Rocky Dwain, Jeannie Ann, Mary Jane, Tommy Lynn; m. Arthur Richard Knox, May 1, 1978; step-sons: Ricky Lynn Stinson, Tony Ray Knox; foster son, Roy David Haney. Grad., Comml. Coll., Baton Rouge, 1985; student, Odessa Coll., 1986-89. Cert. water safety instrn. trainer, health and safety specialist, infant, presch. and parent swimming instr. specialist. Sales clk. Flying B Western Wear, Odessa, Tex., 1975-76; mgr. Redondo Western Wear, Odessa, Tex., 1976-78, Andy's Western Wear, Odessa, Tex., 1978-79; owner Classy Original's Western Wear, Odessa, Tex., 1979-81; water safety instr. Odessa Family YMCA, 1979-82; water safety instr. Odessa Coll., 1981-83, water safety coord., 1983-96, health and safety instr., 1987-96, aquatics coord. continuing edn., 1983-92; ret., 1996; instr. Arthritis Found. YMCA Aquatics Program, Odessa, 1990—, Aquatic Exercise Assn., Odessa, 1987—; instr. specialist ARC Adapted Aquatics, Midland, Tex., 1986—; lifeguard instr. trainer ARC, Odessa, 1979—, CPR instr. trainer, 1981—, 1st aid instr. trainer, 1981—, canoeing instr., 1988-91; water safety specialist Boy Scouts and Girl Scouts Am., Odessa, 1980—; 1st aid instr. Medic First Aid, Odessa, 1990—. Author, editor, artist: Water Aerobics, 1986; author, editor: Food Safety Svc., 1992; designer logo and pin West Tex. Ter. Am. Red Cross, 1988. Vol. Salvation Army, Odessa, 1979-83; mem. exec. bd. ARC, Odessa, 1992, nat. awards chmn., 1992-95, health and safety chmn. region III, terr. 3, 1987-95. Recipient Outstanding Vol. Svc. award Commodore Longfellow Soc., 1994, 95, ARC, 1994, others. Mem. NAFE, Commodore Longfellow Soc. (Outstanding Svc. award 1990, 94), Smithsonian Inst., Nat. Trust for Hist. Preservation, Northshore Animal League (Benefactor award 1988, 89). Baptist. Home: 10177 W 26th St Odessa TX 79763-6333

KNOX, HAVOLYN CROCKER, financial consultant; b. Charlotte, N.C., Oct. 20, 1937; d. Earl Reid and Etta Lorain (Wylie) Crocker; m. Charles Eugene Knox, July 20, 1963 (div. 1981); children: Charles Eugene Jr., Sandra Leigh. Cert. Stenography, U. N.C., Greensboro, 1956. ChFC, CLU. Exec. sec. Stellings-Gossett Theatres, Inc., Charlotte, 1956-57; legal sec. McDougle, Ervin, Horack & Snepp, Charlotte, 1957, Pierce, Wardlow, Knox & Caudle, Charlotte, 1957-63; adminstrv. asst. Charlotte-Mecklenburg Planning Commn., 1980; exec. asst. Conn. Mut. Life Ins. Co., Charlotte, 1981-86; assoc. The Hinrichs Fin. Group, Charlotte, 1986-91, Lyn Knox & Assocs., Charlotte, 1991—. Ops. dir. Eddie Knox for Mayor campaign, Charlotte; campaign mgr. Herb Spaugh for City Coun., Charlotte, 1981, 83, 85; registration chmn. Kemper Open Golf Tournament, Charlotte, 1976-79; pres. The Legal Aux., Charlotte, 1972-73; bd. dirs. Oratorio Singers of Charlotte, 1986-93. Recipient William Danforth Found. award, 1955. Mem. Am. Soc. CLU and ChFC (bd. dirs. Charlotte chpt. 1994-95), Nat. Assn. Life Underwriters, Charlotte Assn. Life Underwriters, Charlotte Estate Planning Coun., Charlotte Civitan Club. Republican. Presbyterian. Home: 2331 Carmel Rd Charlotte NC 28226-6322 Office: Lyn Knox & Assocs PO Box 4115 Charlotte NC 28226-0099

KNUCKLES, BARBARA MILLER, academic administrator; b. Hinsdale, Ill., Jan. 11, 1948; d. John Gillis and Anne Agatha (Albert) Miller; m. Jeffry J. Knuckles, June 7, 1969; 1 child, James Albert. BA, U. Ill., 1970, MS, 1971. Editor ctr. for advanced computation U. Ill., Urbana, 1972-73; v.p., dir. rsch. Marsteller Inc., Chgo., 1973-78; corp. v.p. mktg. rsch. Beatrice, Chgo., 1978-86; v.p., gen. mgr. The Wirthlin Group, Chgo., 1986-88; pres. NNI, Inc., Naperville, Ill., 1988-95; dir. corp. and external rels. North Ctrl. Coll., Naperville, 1992—; bd. dirs. J.R. Short Milling Co., Chgo., Harris Bank, Naperville, Dollar Gen. Corp.; owner Naperville Nannies, Inc., 1985-95. Trustee Edward Hosp., Naperville, 1986—; elder Knox Presbyn. Ch., Naperville, 1995—; vol. Avery Coonley Sch., Downers Grove, Ill., 1988—. Named outstanding alumni U. Ill., 1986, outstanding vol. Second Harvest Food Bank, Chgo., 1986, Ill. 4-H Found., Urbana, 1988. Mem. Econ. Club Chgo., Woman's Athletic Club Chgo. (bd. dirs., com. chair), Rotary Club (Naperville). Presbyn. Office: North Cen Coll 30 N Brainard Naperville IL 60540

KNULL, YOLANDA CHAVEZ, lawyer; b. Pasadena, Calif., June 20, 1949; d. Raul A. and Doris J. (Fields) Chavez; m. William H. Knull III, June 2, 1970; children: Anna, Warren. BA, Vassar Coll., 1970; postgrad., U. Va., 1976-77; JD, NYU, 1979. Bar: N.Y. 1980, Tex. 1986. Trust and estate adminstrn. atty. Morgan Guaranty, N.Y.C., 1979-81; atty. Shearman & Sterling, N.Y.C., 1981-86; assoc. Vinson & Elkins, Houston, 1986-91, ptnr., 1991—. Fellow Houston Bar Found.; mem. ABA (tax sect., real estate, probate & trust law sect.), Tex. Inst. Arts in Edn. (dir., gen. coun.). Office:

Vinson & Elkins LLP 3300 1st City Tower 1001 Fannin St Houston TX 77002

KOART, NELLIE HART, real estate investor and executive; b. San Luis Obispo, Calif., Jan. 3, 1930; d. Will Carleton and Nellie Malchen (Cash) Hart; m. William Harold Koart, Jr., June 16, 1951 (dec. 1976); children: Kristen Marie Kittle, Matthew William. Student Whittier Coll., 1947-49; BA, U. Calif.-Santa Barbara, 1952; MA, Los Angeles State Coll., 1957. Life diploma elem. edn., Calif. Farm worker Hart Farms, Montebello, Calif., 1940-48; play leader Los Angeles County Parks and Recreation, East Los Angeles, Rosemead, Calif., 1948-51; elem. tchr. Potrero Heights Sch. Dist., South San Gabriel, Calif., 1951-55, vice prin., 1955-57; real estate salesman William Koart Real Estate, Goleta, Calif., 1963-76, real estate investor KO-ART Enterprises, Goleta, 1976—, pres. Wm. Koart Constrn. Co., Inc., Goleta, 1975-91; real estate sales person Joseph McGeever Realty Co., Goleta, 1976-91; adv. bd. Bank of Montecito, Santa Barbara, Calif., 1983—. Editor: Reflections, 1972. Charter mem. Calif. Regents program Calif. Fedn. Republican Women, 1989; treas. Santa Barbara County Fedn. Republican Women, Alamar-Hope Ranch, 1981-82, treas. County Bd., 1983-84, auditor, 1996; treas. Com. to Recall Hone, Maschke and Shewczyk, Goleta, 1984; treas. Santa Barbara County Lincoln Club, 1983-87, bd. dirs., 1983-93; assoc. mem. state central com. Calif. Republican Party, 1985-87. Mem. Santa Barbara Apartment Assn., Antique Automobile Club of Am. (sec. treas. Santa Barbara 1980-84), Serena Cove Owners Assn. (sec.-treas, bd. dirs 1990—), Goleta Bus. Roundtable Advisory Group. Club: Santa Barbara County Lincoln Club. Avocations: swimming, numismatics, geneology, college and professional football. Office: KO-ART Enterprises PO Box 310 Goleta CA 93116-0310

KOBAYASHI, GRACE RICAKO, artist, architect; b. West Lafayette, Ind., Mar. 27, 1959; d. Toshio and Tatsuko (Toyama) K. B Architecture, Cornell U., 1982; M Architecture, Harvard U., 1986; postgrad., Hunter Coll., 1995—. Registered architect, N.Y. Urban designer, architect James Stirling/Michael Wilford Architects, London, 1982-83; architect Fred Koetter & Assoc., Boston, 1984, Benjamin Thompson & Assocs., Cambridge, Mass., 1984, Richard Meier & Ptnrs., N.Y.C., 1986-89; arch. I.M. Pei, Arch., N.Y.C., 1991; adj. asst. prof. architecture CCNY, N.Y.C., 1991, Columbia U., N.Y.C., 1991-92, Parsons Sch. Design, N.Y.C., 1992, N.J. Inst. Tech., Newark, 1993; vis. lectr. N.Y. Inst. Tech., N.Y.C. and Rome, 1992-94, U. Va., Charlottesville, 1993; vis. assoc. prof., Pratt Inst., Bklyn., 1994, U. Fla., Gainesville, 1994. Group shows include: Venice Biennale, Italy, 1985, Am. Acad., Rome, Italy, 1990, City Coll. N.Y., 1991, Parsons Sch. Design, N.Y.C., Gallery 91, N.Y.C., 1992, Gallery 128, N.Y.C., 1993, Orgn. of Independent Artists, N.Y.C., 1994. Recipient Third prize award ASCA Nat. Design and Energy Competition, 1980, AIA/ASCA Washington Monument Vis. Ctr. Competition, 1980, First Cert. and Medal, AIA, 1982, Clifton Beckwith Brown Meml. medal Cornell U., 1982, Letter of Commendation, Harvard U., 1986; Beinecke Meml. scholar, 1981; Skidmore, Owings & Merrill Traveling fellow, 1982, Prix de Rome fellow Am. Acad. Rome, 1989-90; Graham Found. Traveling grantee, 1989.

KOBE, LAN, medical physicist; b. Semarang, Indonesia; naturalized; d. O.G. and L.N. (The) Kobe. BS in Physics, IKIP U., Bandung, Indonesia, 1964, MS in Physics, 1967; MS in Med. Physics and Biophysics, U. Calif.-Berkeley, 1975. Physics instr. Sch. Engring., Tarumanegara U., Jakarta, Indonesia, 1968-72; research fellow dept. radiation oncology U. Calif.-San Francisco, 1975-77; clin. physicist in residence dept. radiation oncology UCLA, 1977-78, asst. hosp. radiation physicist, 1978-80, hosp. radiation physicist, 1980—; instr. radiation oncology physics to resident physicians and med. physics graduate students. Contbr. sci. papers to profl. publs. Newhouse grantee U. Calif.-Berkeley, 1974-75, grantee dean grad. div. U. Calif.-Berkeley, 1975; recipient Pres. Work Study award U. Calif., Berkeley, 1974-75, Employee of Month award UCLA, 1983, Outstanding Service award, 1986, devel. Achievement award, 1988, Ptnrs. in Excellence award, 1996. Mem. Am. Soc. for Therapeutic Radiology and Oncology, Am. Assn. Physicists in Medicine (nat. and So. Calif. chpts.), Am. Bd. Radiology (cert.), Am. Assn. Individual Investors (life). Office: UCLA Dept Radiation Oncology 200 UCLA Medical Plz Ste B265 Los Angeles CA 90095-6951

KOBER, ARLETTA REFSHAUGE (MRS. KAY L. KOBER), educational administrator; b. Cedar Falls, Iowa, Oct. 31, 1919; d. Edward and Mary (Jensen) Refshauge; BA, State Coll. Iowa, 1940; MA, U. No. Iowa; m. Kay Leonard Kober, Feb. 14, 1944; children: Kay Mary, Karilyn Eve. Tchr. high schs., Soldier, Iowa, 1940-41, Montezuma, Iowa, 1941-43, Waterloo, Iowa, 1943-50, 65-67, co-ordinator Office Edn. Waterloo Cmty. Schs., Waterloo, Iowa, 1967-84; head dept. co-op. career edn. West H.S., Waterloo, 1974-84. Mem. Waterloo Sch. Health Council; nominating com. YWCA, Waterloo; Black Hawk County chmn. Tb Christmas Seals; ward chmn. ARC, Waterloo; co-chmn. Citizen's Com. for Sch. Bond Issue; pres. Waterloo PTA Council, Waterloo Vis. Nursing Assn., 1956-62, 82—; pres. Kingsley Sch. PTA, 1959-60; v.p. Waterloo Women's Club, 1962-63, pres., 1963-64, trustee bd. clubhouse dirs., 1957-58; mem. Gen. Fedn. Women's Clubs, Nat. Congress Parents and Tchrs.; Presbyterial world svc. chmn. Presbyn. Women's Assn.; bd. dirs. Black Hawk County Republican Women, 1952-53, United Svcs. Black Hawk County, Broadway Theatre League, St. Francis Hosp. Found.; deacon Westminister Presbyn. Ch., 1995—. Mem. AAUW (v.p. Cedar Falls 1946-47), NEA, Internat. Platform Assn., LWV (dir. Waterloo 1951-52), Black Hawk County Hist. Soc. (charter), Delta Pi Epsilon (v.p. 1966-67), Delta Kappa Gamma. Club: Town (dir.) (Waterloo), P.E.O. Home: 3436 Augusta Cir Waterloo IA 50701-4608 Office: 503 W 4th St Waterloo IA 50701-1554

KOBER, JANE, lawyer; b. Shamokin, Pa., May 17, 1943; d. Jeno Daniel and Angela Agnes (Kogut) DiRienzo; m. Arthur Kober, June 20, 1970 (div. 1975). AB, Pa. State U., 1965; MA, U. Chgo., 1966; JD, Case Western Res. U., 1974. Bar: Ohio, N.Y. Lectr. U. Baghdad, Iraq, 1966-67; editor, cons. Ernst & Young, Washington, 1968-70; law clk. to Hon. William K. Thomas, U.S. Dist. Ct. for No. Dist. Ohio, Cleve., 1974-75; atty., ptnr. Squire, Sanders & Dempsey, Cleve. and N.Y.C., 1975-87; ptnr. Shea & Gould, N.Y.C., 1987-89, LeBoeuf, Lamb, Greene & MacRae, L.L.P., N.Y.C., 1989—. Mem. Union Club Cleve. Office: LeBoeuf Lamb Greene MacRae 125 W 55th St New York NY 10019-5369

KOBES, JANIE SIEGLITZ, financial planner; b. San Fernando Valley, Calif., Apr. 22, 1942; d. Robert A. Sr. and E. Jane Guthmann Sieglitz; m. Richard G. Kobes, Aug. 14, 1965; children: Glenn R., Jeffrey W. BS in Chemistry, U. N.Mex., 1965; postgrad., Tex. A&M U., 1965-67; CFP, Coll. for Fin. Planning, 1983. Cert. fin. planner. Workshop leader and developer, 1972-88; owner Kobes Fin. Planning Svcs., Conroe, Tex., 1981—; agt. Tex. Bd. Ins., 1987—; registered investment advisor U.S. SEC, 1984—, Tex. SEC, 1984—; apptd. by gov. to Tex. Appraiser Licensing Cert. Bd., 1991-94; adv. mem. Asset Mgmt. Com. of Tex. State Treasury, Austin, 1983—; mem. area edn. commn. Houston-Galveston Area Coun., 1978-84. Fin. officer bd. mgrs. Conroe YMCA, 1983-85. Named Woman of Yr., Montgomery County YWCA, 1982, Notable Woman of Tex., Awards and Honor Soc. Am., 1984-85, Vol. of Yr, Conroe Br. Greater Houston Area YMCA, 1984; recipient Cert. Disting. Svc, State Treas. of Tex., 1983. Mem. Inst. CFP (nat. mem. svcs. com. 1996—), Houston Soc. Inst. CFP (pres. 1994-95, chair bd. dirs. 1995-96), Nat. Assn. Securities Dealers (registered rep., prin. 1983—). Office: Kobes Fin Planning Svcs Conroe Tower Ste 505 300 W Davis Conroe TX 77301

KOBLIK, CAROLE ANN, jewelry designer; b. Sacramento, June 10, 1944; d. William and Meriam Bertrice (Welfield) K.; m. Donald Clark Garrett, Dec. 1974 (div. June 1977); 1 child, Gillian Kay Garrett. BA in Art and Art History, U. Calif., Davis. Cert. tchr., Calif. 6th grade tchr. Folsom/Cordova Unified Sch. Dist., Calif., 1971-75; owner Arareity Jewelers, Sacramento, 1974—. Mem. Camp Sacramento Bd., 1984-86. Mem. Soroptomists. Office: A Rareity Jewelers 1021 R St Sacramento CA 95814

KOBS, ANN ELIZABETH JANE, nursing administrator, consultant; b. Clinton, Iowa, Feb. 13, 1944; d. Francis Hubert and Leora Elizabeth (Sodeman) Boeker; m. Dennis Raymond Kobs, Oct. 15, 1966 (div. 1989); children: Michael, Peter, Amy. Diploma, Mercy Hosp. Sch. Nursing, 1965; BS in Nursing, Marycrest Coll., 1978; MS in Nursing Adminstrn., No. Ill. U., 1981. Staff charge nurse Mercy Hosp., Davenport, Iowa, 1965-66; clin. instr. Marycrest Coll., Davenport, 1967; health care cons., Chgo., 1973—; pre-reviewer for continuing edn. and career counselor in residence Ill. Nurses Assn., Chgo., 1978-80; career devel. cons. Ill. Hosp. Assn., Oak Brook, 1980-81, staff specialist nursing, 1981-83, dir. nursing, Naperville, 1983-84; dir. nursing surg./maternal-child health Alexian Bros. Med. Ctr., Elk Grove Village, Ill., 1984-87; dir. nursing svcs. Rochelle (Ill.) Community Hosp., 1987-89; cons. Medicus Systems Corp., 1989-91; assoc. dir. dept. of stds. Joint Commn. on Accreditation of Healthcare Orgns., 1991—, interpretation function leader, 1996—; lectr. No. Ill. U., 1981-87, St. Xavier Coll., 1987; mem. faculty Aurora U., 1988-91; clin. teaching asst. U. Iowa, 1988—; expert witness for med. malpractice cases, 1987—. Contbr. numerous articles on materials mgmt., infection control, nursing and quality improvement, 1991—. Mem. City Beautification Commn. Rock Island, 1972-76, also sec., vice-chmn.; mem. com. perinatal health March of Dimes, 1991—. Mem. Am. Orgn. Nurse Execs. (cons., legis. and regulation com. 1987-89, commn. environment and practice 1994—), Ill. Orgn. Nurse Execs. (mem. exec. com., chmn. Task Force on Sunset Ill. Nursing Act 1984-87, pres. 1988-89, bd. dirs. 1984-92, archivist 1992-93, mem. nursing adminstrn. conf. group 1996—), Sigma Theta Tau. Roman Catholic. Editor: Ill. Nurses Assn. Directory of Baccalaureate Degree Completion Programs for RNs in Ill., 1979; adv. bd. Cross Country Staffing, Boca Raton, Fla., 1996—; writer, producer, dir.: Nursing: Opportunities Unlimited, 1980.

KOCH, EDNA MAE, lawyer, nurse; b. Terre Haute, Ind., Oct. 12, 1951; d. Leo K. and Lucille E. (Smith) K.; m. Mark D. Orton. BS in Nursing, Ind. State U., 1977; JD, Ind. U., 1980. Bar: Ind. 1980, U.S. Dist. Ct. (so. dist.) Ind. 1980. Assoc. Dillon & Cohen, Indpls., 1980-85; ptnr. Tipton, Cohen & Koch, Indpls., 1985-93, LaCava, Zeigler & Carter, Indpls., 1993-94, Zeigler Carter Cohen & Koch, Indpls., 1994—; leader seminars for nurses, Ind. U. Med. Ctr., Ball State U., Muncie, Ind., St. Vincent Hosp., Indpls., Deaconess Hosp., Evansville, Ind., others; lectr. on med. malpractice Cen. Ind. chpt. AACCN, Indpls. "500" Postgrad. Course in Emergency Medicine, Ind. Assn. Osteo. Physicians and Surgeons State Conv., numerous others. Mem. ABA, ANA, Ind. State Bar Assn., Indpls. Bar Assn., Am. Soc. Law and Medicine, Ind. State Nurses Assn. Republican. Office: Zeigler Carter Cohen & Koch 8500 Keystone Xing Ste 510 Indianapolis IN 46240-2461

KOCH, KATHERINE DELORES, educational association administrator; b. Raymond, Minn., July 24, 1944; d. Glen Eugene and Mary Rosamond (Hardebeck) Walrath; m. Roland Stanley Hultberg (dec. 1984); 1 child, Scot; m. Richard Joseph Koch, Sept. 7, 1990; children: Wade, Angela, Chad. BS in English and Journalism, Bemidji State U., 1966; MA in Media, St. Cloud State U., 1981. Cert. tchr. English, journalism, speech tchr. Ind. Sch. Dist., Mora, Minn., 1966-81, tchr., media dir., 1981-88, tchr. Mora Alt. Program, 1988-95; bus. agent Minn. Fedn. Tchrs., St. Paul, 1995—. Sec. Dem.-Farmer Labor Party, Kanabec County, 1982-88, dir., Dist. 14, 1982-88. Mem. Minn. Fedn. Tchrs. (1st v.p. 1982-95, v.p. 1978-95). Democrat. Office: Minn Fedn Tchrs Copper Corte II Ste 114 4180 Thielman Ln Saint Cloud MN 56301

KOCH, KATHERINE ROSE, communications executive; b. Pitts., Apr. 21, 1949; d. Irving Samuel Stapsy and Betty Ruth (Sachs) Blake; m. Stanley Christopher Brown, July 26, 1986; 1 child, Matthew. BFA, Rochester Inst. Tech., 1973. Instr. Ivy Sch. Profl. Art, Pitts., 1973-74; advt. dir. Buhl Optical Co., Pitts., 1974-77; pres., creative dir. Ambit Mktg. Comm., Ft. Lauderdale, Fla., 1977—; instr. Point Park Coll., Pitts., 1977-78. Mktg. dir. United Way Broward, Ft. Lauderdale, 1994, mem. exec. com., 1994 ; mem. women's adv. bd. Columbia Plantation Gen. Hosp., 1993—; bd. dirs., comm. chair Broward Econ. Devel. Coun., 1994—. Mem. Greater Ft. Lauderdale Mktg. Alliance (chair 1993-94), Womens Exec. Club (pres. 1995-96, co-chair Tower Forum 1995-96). Office: Ambit Mktg Comm 888 E Las Olas Blvd Ste 520 Fort Lauderdale FL 33301-2239

KOCH, KATHLEEN DAY, lawyer; b. St. Louis, Nov. 27, 1948; d. Edward J. and Margaret (Beckmeier) D.; children: Stefan, Martha, Rebecca. Student, Concordia Coll., River Forest, Ill., 1966-69; BS in Edn., U. Mo., 1971; JD, U. Chgo., 1977. Bar: Ill. 1977, D.C. 1978. Atty. HUD, Washington, 1977-79, U.S. Merit Sys. Protection Bd., Washington, 1979-84; sr. atty. U.S. Dept. Commerce, Washington, 1984-87; assoc. counsel to pres. White House, Washington, 1987-88; gen. counsel Fed. Labor Rels. Authority, Washington, 1988-91; spl. counsel Office Spl. Counsel, Washington, 1991—. Recipient Disting. Alumni award U. Mo.-St. Louis, 1990. Office: U S Office Spl Counsel 1730 M St NW Ste 300 Washington DC 20036-4505

KOCH, KIMBERLY ANN, marketing professional; b. Fort Knox, Ky., Oct. 29, 1965; d. George P. and Maureen R. (Burke) K. BBA in Fin., Loyola Marymount U., Calif., 1987; MBA in Mktg., Pepperdine U., 1995. Sales, fin. mgr. Campbell Automotive Group, Santa Ana, Calif., 1987-92; owner, cons. Alternative Concepts, Inc., Newport Beach, Calif., 1992-93; mktg. mgr. Cartel Mktg., L.A., 1993—. Ministres Our Lady Queen of Angels, Newport Beach, Calif., 1994. Mem. Nat. Assn. Female Execs., Loyola Marymount U. Pride of Lions (exec. bd. mem.). Republican. Roman Catholic. Office: Cartel Mktg Inc 9841 Airport Blvd Ste 1424 Los Angeles CA 90045-5428

KOCH, LINDA, artist, art educator; b. San Francisco, Apr. 28, 1942; d. Frederick Charles and Winifred Marie (Holmes) Koch; m. Leonard Bronce Robertson, July 1, 1967; children: Chad Michael Robertson, Brandt Richard Robertson; m. Stephen Joseph Saude, Jan. 28, 1990; stepchildren: India Saude, Steve Saude. BA, San Jose State U., 1965; M Art Edn., R.I. Sch. Design, Providence, 1990. Tchr. Campbell (Calif.) Sch. Dist., 1966-67, Orcutt (Calif.) Union Sch Dist., 1967-72; art tchr. Hancock C.C., Santa Monica, Calif., 1974-78; art specialist Sierra Unified Sch. Dist., Prather, Calif., 1979—; mentor tchr. Sierra Unified Sch. Dist., Auberry, 1992—. Artist (painting series): Human Imagery and Beyond, 1991, Hats Happen, 1993-94, Education With Out Art, 1991—, Plants in Isolation, 1995—. Recipient Bank of Am. art award, San Rafael, Calif., 1960. Fellow Calif. Arts Project; mem. Nat. Art Educators Assn. (Marie Walsch Art Found. award 1993), Soc. Childrens' Book Writers and Illustrators, Calif. Art Educators Assn. (Douc Langur award 1987), Fig Tree Gallery.

KOCH, NANCY JOY, music educator, choral director, vocal coach; b. Wellsboro, Pa., May 15, 1940; d. Alvan Robert and Irene Mildred (Howells) K. BS in Music Edn., Mansfield State Coll., 1962; postgrad., Mich. U., 1963; MA in Voice, Trenton State Coll., 1972; Fellowship, Oberlin Conservatory, 1967; pvt. vocal study with Emile Renan, Manhattan Sch. Music, N.Y.C., 1968-81; postgrad., Pa. State U., 1989. Cert. music educator, Pa. Tchr. vocal music, choral dir. East Strousburg (Pa.) Jr. Sr. H.S. Area, 1962-68, McDonald Elem. Sch., Warminster, Pa., 1968-72; tchr. vocal music, choral dir. Log Coll. Jr. High, Warminster, Pa., 1972-89, dept. chairperson, 1976-80; tchr. vocal music Log Coll. Middle Sch., Warminster, Pa., 1989—; choir dir. Warminster Presbyn. Ch., Warminster, 1987-92; dept. chmn. Log Coll. Jr. H.S., Warminster, 1976-80; founder, dir. New Beginning Youth Cmty. Choral Group, 1976-86. Soprano soloist (Bach cantata) Oberlin-Robert Fountain Dir., 1967, Verdi Requiem, Trenton State Coll., 1972, Schubert Mass in G, Nativity Cath. Ch., 1996. Recipient Rockefeller Found. grant Oberlin Conservatory, 1967, 1st Place award-Log Coll. Vocal Ensemble, Music In The Pks., 1980-95, Cmty. Svc. award Hatboro YMCA, 1981, Overall Outstanding Trophy, Music In the Pks., 1989, 91-94, Centennial/S.D. Tchr. of Yr. Achievement award, 1992. Mem. NEA, Pa. State Edn. Assn., Penn State Music Educators, Nat. Music Educators Assn., Pa. State Edn. Assn., Bucks County Music Educators, Bucks County Music Educators (treas. 1978-88). Lutheran. Home: 1524 Mulberry Cir Warminster PA 18974-1871

KOCHER, JUANITA FAY, retired auditor; b. Falmouth, Ky., Aug. 9, 1933; d. William Birgest and Lula (Gillespie) Vickroy; m. Donald Edward Kocher, Nov. 18, 1953. Grad. high sch., Bright, Ind. Cert. internal auditor and compliance officer. Bookkeeper Mchts. Bank and Trust Co., West Harrison, Ind., 1952-56, teller, asst. cashier, 1962-87, br. mgr., 1979-87, internal auditor, 1987-96, ret., 1996; bookkeeper Progressive Bank, New Orleans, 1956-58; with proof dept. 1st Nat. Bank, Cin., Ohio, 1958-59; teller 1st Nat. Bank, Harrison, Ohio, 1959-62; bookkeeper Donald E. Kocher Constrn., Harrison, 1981—. Mem. Am. Bankers Assn., Ind. Bankers Assn. Home: 11277 Biddinger Rd Harrison OH 45030

KOCHEVAR, KATHLEEN MARY, adult education educator; b. Pueblo, Colo., Oct. 9, 1949; d. Edward John and Katherine Ann (Mikatich) K. BA summa cum laude, Coll. Mt. St. Joseph, Cin., 1971; MA with honors, Middlebury (Vt.) Coll., 1975. Cert. secondary tchr., Colo., Ariz.; cert. c.c. tchr.; cert. tchr. Jr. Gt. Books Program; vocat. credential in applied comms. Tchr. lang. arts Central H.S., Sch. Dist. 60, Pueblo, Colo., 1971-73; tchr. lang. arts, French, theology St. Scholastica Acad., Canon City, Colo., 1973-75; chair dept. lang. arts Gerard Cath. H.S., Phoenix, 1975-86; corr. tchr. Phoenix Spl. Programs, Phoenix, 1986-90; chair dept. English Xavier Coll. Prep., Phoenix, 1988-90; tchr. lang. arts, lead tchr., bldg. chair Keating Edn. Ctr., Sch. Dist. 60, Pueblo, 1990—; adj. faculty Pueblo (Colo.) C.C., 1990-92; rep. Site-Based Shared Decision-Making Com., Pueblo, 1992-95. Contbg. reporter The Pueblo Chieftain; contbr. poetry: Hungry Eye anthology, Nat. Libr. of Poetry, 1996. NEH grantee, Tucson, 1993, London, 1994. Mem. Nat. Coun. Tchrs. English, Colo. Lang. Arts Soc., Kappa Gamma Pi. Home: 1221 Berwind Ave Pueblo CO 81006-1001 Office: Keating Edn Ctr 215 E Orman Ave Pueblo CO 81004-2143

KOCHTA, RUTH MARTHA, art gallery owner; b. N.Y.C., Jan. 5, 1924; d. Harry Joseph and Anna (Braun) Evers; m. Albert Emil Kochta, Nov. 7, 1948; children: Alan, Carol. Student, CUNY, Queens, 1965-68, Art Students League, 1970-75. Artist Queens, N.Y. and Lenox, Mass., 1965—; dir. Imperial Gallery, N.Y.C., 1981; owner, dir. Clark Whitney Gallery, Lenox, 1983—. Work exhibited at Nat. Acad., N.Y.C. 1969, Audubon Artists, N.Y.C. 1971, Heckscher Mus., Huntington, N.Y., 1972, Elizabet Ney Mus., Austin, Tex., 1972, Wadsworth Atheneum, Hartford, Conn., 1975, Philathea Mus., Ont., Can., 1976, New Britain (Conn.) Mus., 1978, Guild Gallery, N.Y.C. 1979, other exhibits. Recipient over 50 awards in various competitions.

KOCKA, ANNETTE CYKALO, nurse; b. Cleve., Apr. 19, 1962; d. Walter and Nancy (Wolynczuk) Cykalo; m. Russell James Kocka, Sept. 5, 1981; 1 child, Alexander Walter. Diploma, Lorain C.C., 1986. Staff nurse Aristocrat Berea (Ohio), 1986-90; agy. nurse Glenbeigh Hosp., Cleve., 1988; staff nurse Southwest Gen. Hosp., Middleburg Heights, Ohio, 1990-91; instr. Aristocrat South, Parma Heights, Ohio, 1991-94; staff nurse Mt. Royal Villa, North Royalton, Ohio, 1994-95. Nurse hearing and visual assessment for pre-kindergarten enrollment St. John Bosco Sch., Parma Heights, 1991-94. Republican. Home: 3343 Concord Dr Brunswick OH 44212-3131

KOCO, LINDA GALE, writer; b. Chgo., Ohio, Sept. 3, 1945; d. Peter Robert and Laura Sylvia (Albert) Young; m. Gary Paul Kocolowski, Dec. 20, 1968 (div. 1987); 1 child, Charles Adam. BA with honors, Lake Forest (Ill.) Coll., 1967. Cert. secondary sch. educator, Ill. English and writing tchr. Lake Forest High Sch., 1967-68; writer, copywriter Allstate Ins. Co., Northbrook, Ill., 1969-70; staff writer Nat. Underwriter Co., Cin., 1970-73, asst. editor, 1974-78; assoc. editor Nat. Underwriter Co., Lakewood, Ohio, 1988-92, sr. editor, 1992—; pvt. practice Lakewood, 1970—; founder, co-leader Cin. Poets' Workshop, 1973-78; founder, moderator Lakewood Poets Workshop, 1979-83; speaker numerous writing and bus. orgns., 1980—. Contbr. articles to numerous publs. Active Lakewood Congrl. Ch., 1984-92, chair diaconate, 1988-91; active Pilgrim Congrl. Ch., 1992—; learning ctr. vol. Madison Sch., Lakewood, 1984-88; parent mem. young author's com. Lakewood Bd. Edn., 1987-92. Mem. Poets League Greater Cleve., NAFE, Habitat for Humanity, Phi Beta Kappa. Office: PO Box 771037 Lakewood OH 44107-0045

KODIS, MARY CAROLINE, marketing consultant; b. Chgo., Dec. 17, 1927; d. Anthony John and Callis Ferebee (Old) K.; student San Diego State Coll., 1945-47, Latin Am. Inst., 1948. Controller, div. adminstrv. mgr. Fed. Mart Stores, 1957-65; controller, adminstrv. mgr. Gulf Mart Stores, 1965-67; budget dir., adminstrv. mgr. Diana Stores, 1967-68; founder, treas., controller Handy Dan Stores, 1968-72; founder, v.p., treas. Handy City Stores, 1972-76; sr. v.p., treas. Handy City div. W.R. Grace & Co., Atlanta, 1976-79; founder, pres. Hal's Hardware and Lumber Stores, 1982-84; retail and restaurant cons., 1979 . Treas., bd. dirs. YWCA Watsonville, 1981-84, 85-87; mem. Santa Cruz County Grand Jury, 1984-85. Recipient 1st Tribute to Women in Internat. Industry, 1978; named Woman of the Yr., 1986. Mem. Ducks Unltd. (treas. Watsonville chpt. 1981-89). Republican. Home and Office: 2705 Robin Dr Virginia Beach VA 23454-1813

KODISH, ARLINE BETTY, principal; b. Alliance, Ohio, Sept. 20, 1934; d. Edward J. and Frances Harris; m. Phillip Kodish, June 13, 1954; children: Douglas, Lori D. M in Ednl. Adminstrn., U. Akron, 1979. Cert. prin., tchr., Ohio. Owner Shatto Acad., Akron, 1973—. Mem. Nat. Assn. Elem. Sch. Prins., Ohio Assn. Elem. Sch. Adminstrs., Nat. Assn. for Early Childhood Edn., Assn. for Childhood Edn. Internat. Office: Shatto Acad 707 Schocalog Rd Akron OH 44320-1035

KOEBEL, SISTER CELESTIA, health care system executive; b. Chillicothe, Ohio, Jan. 12, 1928. BS, Coll. of Mount St. Joseph, 1958; MHA, St. Louis U., 1964; D. U. Albuquerque, 1976. Asst. dir. nursing svcs. Good Samaritan Hosp. & Health Ctr., Dayton, Ohio, 1961-62; adminstrv. resident Providence Med. Ctr., Seattle, 1963-64; pres. St. Joseph Healthcare Corp., Albuquerque, 1964-85, Sisters of Charity Health Care Systems, Cin., 1985—. Mem. Am. Hosp. Assn. (adv. coun., 1987-88), N.Mex. Hosp. Assn. (treas. 1968-69, v.p. 1970, pres. 1972). Office: Sisters Charity Health Care System Inc 345 Neeb Rd Cincinnati OH 45233-5102

KOEHL, CAMILLE JOAN, accountant; b. Chgo., Nov. 9, 1943; d. Alfonse James and Genevieve V. (Riche) Daurio; children: David A., Laura L., Robert M., Karen M. BS in Acctg., De Paul U., 1976; postgrad., Roosevelt U., 1987—. CPA, Ill.; cert. fin. planner. Treas. Meritex Corp., Carpentersville, Ill., 1966-68; controller Di Com Corp., Glenview, Ill., 1968-73; v.p., treas. Ridge Road Co., Northbrook, Ill., 1982-87, Decker Gardens, Inc., Northbrook, 1979-87, S&L Engring. Co., Northbrook, 1973-87; ptnr. HJS Constrn. Co., Barrington Hills, Ill., 1979—; pres. Lé Tan Ltd., Palatine, Ill., 1984—, CJIC Enterprises Ltd., Barrington Hills, 1985—; owner Camille J. Koehl & Assoc., Barrington Hills, 1978—; pres. Koehl Constrn. and Devel. Corp., Barrington Hills, 1990—, Pressing Matters Ltd., McHenry, Ill., 1990—. Mem. Internat. Bd. Cert. Fin. Planners, Ill. CPAs. Home and Office: 7 Bow Ln Barrington IL 60010-9618

KOEHLER, BOBBI J., bank executive. Sr. v.p. spl. assets Calif. Fed. Bank, L.A. Office: Calif Fed Bank 5700 Wilshire Blvd Los Angeles CA 90036*

KOEHN, CONNIE LEE, secondary education educator, coach; b. Houston, Sept. 8, 1968; d. Douglas Herbert and Nancy Lee (Morrison) K. BS, Houston Bapt. U., 1991. Mgr. Cinemark Theatres, Houston, 1986-91; tchr., coach Alief Ind. Sch. Dist., Houston, 1993—. Mem. Tex. State Tchrs. Assn., Tex. Girls Coaches Assn. Home: 4110 Laguna Circle Missouri City TX 77459 Office: Elsik HS PO Box 68 Houston TX 77411

KOELKER, GAIL, family nurse practitioner; b. Wichita, Feb. 5, 1956; d. John Howard and Jean (McWilliams) K. BSN summa cum laude, Ariz. State U., 1986; MS in Nursing, U. Tex., Arlington, 1993. RN Tex.; cert. family nurse practitioner. Staff nurse El Dorado Hosp. & Med. Ctr., Tucson, 1986-88; traveling nurse Travcorp, Inc., Walden, Mass., 1988-90; nurse home health Health Corp., Inc., Dallas, 1990-94; family nurse practitioner Good Sheperd Med. Ctr., Longview, Tex., 1994—; facilitator chronic pain/chronic disease support group Hughes Springs, Tex., 1995—; clin. preceptor nurse practitioner program U. Tex. Sch. Nursing, Arlington, 1993—; lectr. in field. Mem. Am. Acad. Nurse Practitioners, Am. Coll. Nurse Practitioners, Tex. Nurse Practitioners, Sigma Theta Tau, Phi Kappa Phi. Home: RR 1 Box 344 Avinger TX 75630-9641 Office: Good Shepherd Med Clinic Hwy 11 E PO Box 1440 Hughes Springs TX 75656

KOELLIKER, MARILYNN LEE, social worker; b. St. Joseph, Mo., Apr. 19, 1948; d. Harold Edward and Rosalie Marlin (Taylor) Koelliker; m. Charles R. Ricklefs, Aug. 30, 1969 (div. 1985); children: Tonya Ricklefs Wells, Rachael. AA, Highland C.C., 1968; BA in Sociology, Kans. State U., 1970; MSW, U. Kans., 1985. Lic. specialist in clin. social work, Kans. Paraprofl. Atchison-Jefferson Edn. Coop., Oskaloosa, Kans., 1982-83; transitional home counselor Breakthrough Satellite Program, Topeka, 1984;

house mgr. Breakthrough Group Home, Topeka, 1984-85; social worker II Topeka-Shawnee County Health Dept., 1985-93; counselor Washburn U. Topeka, 1993—; mem. TV panel Baby Your Baby Topeka/Shawnee County Health Dept., 1993; practicum instr. U. Kans., Lawrence, 1987-88, 89-90; mem. panel Children & AIDS U. Kans. Social Work Day, 1989. Allocations com. mem. United Way, Topeka, 1987, 88, 89; vol. Topeka AIDS Project, 1988-91, AIDS Quilt Display, Topeka, 1993; mem. city coun. Nickerson, Kans., 1976. Named Vol. of Yr. Topeka AIDS Project, 1989, one of Outstanding Young Women Am., 1984. Mem. NASW, Kans. Chpt. Assn. Social Workers, ACA. Democrat. Office: Washburn U Topeka 1700 College Topeka KS 66621

KOELMEL, LORNA LEE, data processing executive; b. Denver, May 15, 1936; d. George Bannister and Gladys Lee (Henshall) Steuart; m. Herbert Howard Nelson, Sept. 9, 1956 (div. Mar. 1967); children: Karen Dianne, Phillip Dean, Lois Lynn; m. Robert Darrel Koelmel, May 12, 1981; stepchildren: Kim, Cheryl, Dawn, Debbie. BA in English, U. Colo., 1967. Cert. secondary English tchr. Substitute English tchr. Jefferson County Schs., Lakewood, Colo., 1967-68; sec. specialist IBM Corp., Denver, 1968-75, pers. administr., 1975-82, asst. ctr. coord., 1982-85, office systems specialist, 1985-87, backup computer operator, 1987—; computer instr. Barnes Bus. Coll., Denver, 1987-92; owner, mgr. Lorna's Precision Word Processing and Desktop Pub., Denver, 1987-89; computer cons. Denver, 1990—. Editor newsletter Colo. Nat. Campers and Hikers Assn., 1992-94. Organist Christian Sci. Soc., Buena Vista, Colo., 1963-66, 1st Ch. Christ Scientists Thornton-Westminster, Thornton, Colo., 1994—; chmn. bd. dirs., 1979-80. Mem. NAFE, Nat. Secs. Assn. (retirement ctr. chair 1977-78, newsletter chair 1979-80, v.p. 1980-81), Am. Guild Organists, U. Colo. Alumni Assn., Alpha Chi Omega (publicity com. 1986-88). Republican. Club: Nat. Writers. Lodge: Job's Daus. (recorder 1953-54).

KOENIG, ELIZABETH BARBARA, sculptor; b. N.Y.C., Apr. 20, 1937; d. Hayward and Selma E. (Rosen) Ulman; m. Carl Stuart Koenig, Sept. 10, 1961; children: Katherine Lee, Kenneth Douglas. BA, Wellesley Coll., 1958; MD, Yale U., 1962; postgrad., Art Students League N.Y., 1963-64, Corcoran Sch. Art, 1964-67. Exhibited one-woman shows including St. John's Coll., Annapolis, Md., 1974, also solo retrospectives Lyman Allyn Mus., New London, Conn., 1978, Rotunda of Pan-Am. Health Orgn., Washington, 1978; group shows include Internat. Dedication Nat. Bur. Standards, Gaithersburg, Md., 1966, No. Va. Mus., Alexandria, 1975, Textile Mus., Washington, 1974-75, Meridian House Internat., Washington, 1980; commd. works include: Free Spirit marble carving Washington Hebrew Congregation, 1978, Monumental Torso bronze for grounds George Meany Ctr. for Labor Studies, 1982; represented in many pvt. collections, U.S. and Europe, 1965—. Recipient 1st prize sculpture Tri-State Regional Exhbn., Md., 1970, 2d and 3d prize sculpture, 1971. Mem. Artists Equity Assn. (v.p. Washington 1977-83), Art Students League N.Y. (life), Internat. Sculpture Ctr., New Arts Ctr. Avocations: reading, gardening. Home: 9014 Charred Oak Dr Bethesda MD 20817-1924

KOENIG, GINA LEE, microbiologist; b. Scranton, Pa., July 3, 1962; d. Leon Henry Koenig and Carmela Ann (Romolo) Koenigsberg; m. John Henry Carter III, Feb. 11, 1989 (div. 1995). BS, Pa. State U., 1984; MA with honors, San Francisco State U., 1993. Rsch. asst. Ctr. for Air Environ. Studies, State College, Pa., 1983-84; fisheries biologist Nat. Marine Fisheries Svc., Seattle, 1984-85; rsch. asst. Monterey Mushrooms, Watsonville, Calif., 1985-87; microbiologist Genencor, Internat., South San Francisco, 1987-92; rsch. scientist, curator culture collection dept. Roche Molecular Sys., Alameda, Calif., 1992-96, mem. instnl. biol. safety com., 1992—, sr. scientist, 1996—. Contbr. articles to profl. jours. Recipient 1st pl. award Calif. State U. Biology Student Rsch. Competition, 1992. Mem. Am. Soc. Microbiology (com. for culture collections 1994—), Soc. for Cryobiology, U.S. Fedn. Culture Collections (program com. 1992, chmn. publicity com. 1992-94, exec. bd. dirs.-at-large 1993-96, v.p. 1996—), World Fedn. Culture Collections (program com. 1996), Toastmasters Internat. (v.p. edn. 1996, Competent Toastmaster 1996), Mycological Soc. Am., Mycological Soc. San Francisco, Pa. State U. Alumni Assn., Soc. for Indsl. Microbiology. Democrat. Mem. Christian Ch. Office: Roche Molecular Systems Inc 1145 Atlantic Ave Alameda CA 94501-1145

KOENIG, HEIDI MARGARET, medical educator; b. Newman Grove, Nebr., Apr. 8, 1958; d. Paul Fritz and Barbara Ann (Kaempf) K.; m. William Walter Holt, May 21, 1993; 1 child, William Paul Holt. BS, Wayne State Coll., Wayne, Nebr., 1980; MD, U. Nebr. Med. Ctr., Omaha, 1985. Intern Southwest Mich. Area Health Edn. Ctr., Kalamazoo, 1985-86; surg. resident Michael Reese Hosp., Chgo., 1986-89; anesthesiology resident U. Ill., Chgo., 1989-92, neuroanesthesiology fellow, 1992-93; Asst. prof. anesthesiology U. Ill. Chgo., Michael Reese Hosp., Chgo., 1993—. Co-author: (chpt. in book) International Anesthesiology Clinics, 1996; contbr. articles to profl. jours. Recipient FY94 grant Michael Reese Hosp., 1994-95, nat. grant Am. Heart Assn., 1996—. Mem. Am. Soc. Anesthesiology, Internat. Anesthesia Rsch. Soc., Ill. Soc. Anesthesiology, Chgo. Soc. Anesthesiology, Soc. Neuroanesthesia and Critical Care. Office: U Ill at Chgo Dept Anesthesiology 1740 W Taylor Ste 3200 West Chicago IL 60612

KOENIG, JUDITH ELLEN, broadcasting company executive; b. Morehead City, N.C., Apr. 3, 1954; d. Charlie Perry and Dorothy Ellen (Hardesty) Dyess; m. Dominic John Pardio Jr., Sept. 12, 1970 (div. 1974); children: Charles Perry, Regina Antonette; m. Danny Carl Koenig, May 23, 1975 (div. 1992). Office mgr. S.E. State Broadcasting Corp., Havelock, N.C., 1977-78, Musicradio of N.C., Inc., Havelock, N.C., 1978-80; credit/traffic mgr. Holiday Radio Inc., Salem, Oreg., 1980-81; prog./ops. mgr. Greater Willamette Vision Ltd., Salem, Oreg., 1981-85, Emerald City Broadcasting Inc., Salem, Oreg., 1985-87; prog. mgr. Silver King Broadcasting of Oreg., Inc., Salem, Oreg., 1987-88; prog. mgr. Blackstar Communications of Oreg., Inc., Salem, Oreg., 1988-89, gen. mgr., 1989—. Mem. Oreg. Assn. Broadcasters, Nat. Assn. Broadcasters, Salem C. of C., Salem Conv. and Visitors Assn., West Salem Rotary. Office: KBSP TV22 4923 Indian School Rd NE Salem OR 97305-1128

KOENIG, MARIE HARRIET KING, public relations director, fund raising executive; b. New Orleans, Feb. 19, 1919; d. Harold Paul and Sadie Louise (Bole) King; m. Walter William Koenig, June 24, 1956; children: Margaret Marie, Susan Patricia. Major in Voice, La. State U., 1937-39; Pre-law, Loyola U., 1942-43; BS in History, U. LaVerne, 1986. Adminstrv. asst. to atty. gen. State of La., New Orleans, 1940-44; contract writer MGM Studios, Culver City, Calif., 1944-46; asst. sec., treas. Found. for Ind., L.A., 1950-56, Found. for Social Rsch., L.A., 1950-56; dir. communications Incentive Rsch. Corp., L.A., 1969-78; rsch. supr., devel. dept. Calif. Inst. Technology, Pasadena, Calif., 1969; dir. funding devel. Rep. Party of L.A. County, South Pasadena, 1989-92. Author: Does the National Council of Churches Speak for You?, 1978; delivered lecture series on U.S. fgn. policy. Named Hon. Citizen Colonial Williamsburg Found., 1987; active Nat. Trust for Historic Preservation, 1986, Autry Western Heritage Mus., 1986, Friends of the Huntington Libr., 1986, Town Hall of L.A., 1986—, Pasadena City Women's Club, 1982-84, The Masquers Club; mem. Coun. Women's Clubs; charter mem. Nat. Mus. of Women in Arts; bd. mem. Pasadena Opera Guild; contbg. mem. L.A. World Affairs Coun., 1990, L.A. County Mus. Art, 1990; pres., pub. chmn., Pasadene Rep. Women Federated; charter mem. Freedoms Found. at Valley Forge L.A. County Chpt. Recipient Pres.'s award So. Calif. Motion Picture Coun., 1996, Cert. Recognition Calif. State Assembly, 1989, 95, Recognition of Excellence, Achievement and Commitment U.S. Ho. Reps., 1989, Cert. Merit Rep. Presdl. Task Force, 1986, Cert. Appreciation U.S. Def. Com., 1984, Hon. Freedom Fighter award U.S. Def. Com., 1985, Cert. Appreciation Am. Conservative Union, 1983, Cert. Commendation Rep. Cen. Com. L.A. County, 1972, Cert. Appreciation Eisenhower-Nixon So. Calif. Com., 1952. Mem. Greater L.A. Press Club. Republican. Home: 205 Madeline Dr Pasadena CA 91105-3311

KOENIGSBERG, JUDITH Z. NULMAN, clinical psychologist; b. Bklyn., Apr. 21, 1951; d. Macy and Sarah (Rosenberg) Nulman; m. David I. Koenigsberg, June 18, 1972; children: Benjamin, Rachel. Grad. summa cum laude, Yeshiva U. Tchrs. Inst., New York City, 1971; BA with honors, Bklyn. Coll., 1972; MA, Northeastern Ill. U., 1980; postgrad., U. Chgo., 1980-82; MEd, Loyola U., Chgo., 1985; PhD in Psychology, Northwestern U., 1990. Lic. and reg. clin. psychologist, Ill.; Nat. Register of Health Service Providers in Psychology. Clin. specialist Charter Barclay Hosp., Chgo., 1985-86; psychology extern Luth. Gen. Hosp., Park Ridge, Ill., 1987-88; psychol. testing extern Evanston (Ill.) Hosp., 1988-89, psychology intern, 1989-90; psychology postdoctoral resident Loyola U. Chgo., 1991-92; clin. psychologist U. Chgo., 1993-94; cons. Tutors Unltd., Inc., 1995—; co-investigator rsch. project U. Chgo., 1995—. Contbr. articles to profl. jours. Recipient Outstanding Achievement award Nat. Culture Coun., 1972; scholarship award dept. modern langs. Bklyn. Coll., 1972, Kappa Delta Pi, 1972. Fellow Prescribing Psychologists' Register (cand.); mem. APA, Ill. Psychol. Assn., Northwestern U. Alumni Assn. Sch. Edn. and Social Policy (dir. bd. 1993-94), Early Career Preventionists Network (steering com. 1995). Office: 708 Church St Ste 243 Evanston IL 60201 also: 166 E Superior St Ste 311 Chicago IL 60611-2920 also: Tutors Unltd Inc 7366 N Lincoln Ave Ste 404 Lincolnwood IL 60646

KOENIGSMARK, JOYCE ELYN SLADEK, geriatrics nurse; b. Chgo., Sept. 29, 1938; d. John E. and Elsie (Volman) Sladek; m. Jerry Koenigsmark, Sept. 12, 1959; children: Jeffrey, Joy, Jocelyn, Joletta, Janine. Diploma in nursing, Presbyn. Sch Nursing, Chgo., 1959. RN, Ill.; cert. low risk nursery nurse. Co-owner Hawthorne Pharmacy and Gift Shop, Wheaton, Ill., 1967-78; staff nurse Parkway Terrace Nursing Home, Wheaton, Ill., 1977-78; staff nurse med./surg. Cen. DuPage Hosp., Winfield, Ill., 1978-80, staff and charge nurse well baby nursery, 1980-85; staff and charge nurse, advanced clinician well baby nursery, mother-baby care, spl. care nursery Edward Hosp., Naperville, Ill., 1985-94; prin. Joyce Koenigsmark, Document Examiner, 1978-84; staff nurse Alpha Christian Registry, 1995-96; prin. Joyce Koenigsmark, Master Graphoanalyst, 1978-86; staff nurse Alpha Christian Registry, Glen Ellyn, 1995-96, Franciscan Sisters, Our Lady of Angels Convent Health Ctr., Wheaton, 1996—. Mem. AWHONN, Internat. Graphoanalysis Soc. (life, sec. Ill. chpt. 1980, v.p. 1981, pres. 1982, cert. graphoanalyst, Master graphoanalyst, cert. document examiner, Ill. Graphoanalyst of Yr. 1983, Pres.'s citation of merit 1983). Home: 1510 Center Ave Wheaton IL 60187-6102

KOENKER, DIANE P., history educator; b. Chgo., July 29, 1947; m. Roger Koenker; 1 child. AB in History, Grinnell Coll., 1969; AM in Comparative Studies in History, U. Mich., 1971, PhD in History, 1976. From asst. prof. to assoc. prof. in history Temple U., Phila., 1976-83; asst. prof. history U. Ill., Urbana-Champaign, 1983-86, assoc. prof., 1986-88, prof. history, 1988—, dir. Russian and East European Ctr., 1990-96, editor Slavic Rev., 1996—; vis. lectr. history U. Ill., Urbana-Champaign, 1975; vis. fellow Australian Nat. U., 1989; Fulbright-Hays Faculty Rsch. Abroad, 1993; active Study Group on Russian Revolution, Study Group on Internat. Labor and Working-Class History; lectr. in field. Author: Moscow Workers and the 1917 Revolution, 1981, paperback edit., 1986, (with William G. Rosenberg) Strikes and Revolution in Russia 1917, 1989, editor: Tret'ya Vserossiiskaya Konferentsiya Professional'nykh Soyuzov 1917, 1982, (with William G. Rosenberg and Ronald Grigor Suny) Party, State and Society in the Russian Civil War: Explorations in Social History, 1989; editor, translator: (with S.A. Smith) Notes of a Red Guard, 1993; mem. editl. bd. Cambridge Soviet Paperbacks; mem. adv. bd. Soviet Studies in History, 1986-89; book reviewer to numerous jours.; contbr. articles to profl. jours. Rsch. fellow Temple U., 1977, 82, Sr. fellow Russian Inst.-Columbia U., 1977-78, Individual fellow NEH, 1983-84, Rsch. fellow NEH, 1984-85, 94-95, MUCIA Exch. fellow Moscow State U., 1991; grantee Am. Coun. Learned Socs.-Social Sci. Rsch. Coun., 1977-78, Temple U., 1979-81, 82-83, William and Flora Hewlett Internat. Rsch. grantee, 1986, Nat. Coun. for Soviet and East European Rsch. grantee, 1989, IREX Travel grantee, 1993; recipient Fulbright-Hays Faculty Rsch. award for USSR, 1989, Arnold O. Beckman Rsch. Bd. award, 1990-91. Mem. Am. Hist. Assn. (mem. George Louis Beer Prize com. 1993-95), Am. Assn. Advancement Slavic Studies, Midwest Workshop of Russian and Soviet Historians, Assn. Women in Slavic Studies. Office: U Ill Slavic Rev 104 Internat Studies Bldg 57 E Armory Champaign IL 61820 also: U Ill Dept History 309 Gregory Hall 810 S Wright St Urbana IL 61801-3611

KOENNECKE, DEBORAH A., banker; b. Ft. Worth, Tex., July 23, 1956; d. John T. and Florence M. (Prewitt) Sutton; m. Michael E. Koennecke, July 15, 1978. Adminstrv. asst. Northwest Bank, Ft. Worth, 1974-83; exec. v.p., cashier Trinity Nat. Bank, Ft. Worth, 1983-90; sr. v.p., cashier Woodhaven Nat. Bank, Ft. Worth, 1990—. Mem. Am. Inst. Banking (bd. dirs. 1993—), Breakfast Optimist Club East Ft. Worth (pres.-elect 1995-96), Ind. Bankers Assn. Roman Catholic. Office: Woodhaven Nat Bank 6750 Bridge St Fort Worth TX 76112

KOEPP, DONNA PAULINE PETERSEN, librarian; b. Clinton, Iowa, Oct. 8, 1941; d. Leo August and Pauline Sena (Outzen) Petersen; m. David Ward Koepp, June 5, 1960 (div. June 1984). BS in Edn., U. Colo., 1967; MA in Libr., U. Denver, 1974; postgrad., U. Colo., 1984-85. Subject specialist govt. publs., map dept. Denver Pub. Libr., 1967-85; head govt. documents, map libr. U. Kans., Lawrence, 1985—. Prodn. mgr. Meridian Jour., 1988-93, 96—; editor: Index and Carto-Bibliography of Maps, 1789-1969, 1995. Mem. Map & Geography Round Table of Am. Libr. Assn. (chmn. 1986-87, Outstanding Contbn. to Map Librarianship 1991), Govt. Documents Round Table of Am. Libr. Assn., Western Assn. Map Librs. (sec. 1983-84). Office: Univ Kans Librs 6001 Malott Hall Lawrence KS 66045

KOEPPE, PATSY PODUSKA, internist, educator; b. Memphis, Nov. 18, 1932; d. Ben F. and Lily Mae (Reid) Poduska; m. Douglas F. Koeppe Sr., Sept. 8, 1967; 1 child, Douglas F. Jr. BA, Tex. Woman's U., 1954; MD, U. Tenn., 1957. Intern Roanoke (Va.) Meml. Hosp., 1960-61; resident in internal medicine VA Teaching Group Hosp., Memphis, 1961-62, Lahey Clinic, Boston, 1962-63; fellow in endocrinology and metabolism U. Tex. Med. Br., Galveston, 1963-65; pvt. practice Kingsville, Tex., 1972-73; dir. Women's Health Care Ctr., College Park, Md., 1974-77; instr. internal medicine and endocrinology U. Tex., Galveston, 1965-69; asst. prof. endocrinology Med. Br., U. Tex., Galveston, 1969-72, asst. prof. internal medicine, 1969-72, 78-87; assoc. prof. U. Tex., Galveston, 1987-93, prof., 1994—; mem. grad. faculty biomed. sci. Med. Br., U. Tex., Galveston, 1983—, acting dir. div. geriatrics, 1991-92. Mem. Am. Geriatric Soc., Tex. Med. Assn., Tex. Med. Found., Galveston County Med. Soc. Presbyterian. Home: 323 Brookdale Dr League City TX 77573-1668 Office: Univ Tex Med Br 30325 Jennie Sealy Hosp D60 Galveston TX 77555-0460

KOEPPEL, MARY SUE, communications educator, editor; b. Phlox, Wis., Dec. 12, 1939; d. Alphonse and Emma Petronella (Marx) K.; B.A., Alverno Coll., 1962; M.A., Loyola U., Chgo., 1968; postgrad. U. Wis., St. Louis U., U. N.H., U. Calif., U. Fla., U. Minn. Tchr., St. Joseph High Sch, Milw., 1962-68, Pius XI High Sch., Milw., 1968-72; instr., head dept. communications, dir. learning center Waukesha County Tech. Inst., Pewaukee, Wis., 1972-80; pres., exec. bd. West Suburban Council Teaching Profession, 1976-80; adv. Waukesha chpt. Parents Without Partners, 1975-80; cons. Learning Centers, 1976—, also coll. and univ. faculties; instr. communications Fla. Community Coll., Jacksonville, 1980—; instr. Inst. for Tchrs. of Writing, Westbrook Coll., Portland, Maine, summers 1980-84, instr. nat. master tchr. seminar, summers 1982—; editor in chief Kalliope Jour. of Women's Art, 1988—; instr. Nat. Inst. For Tchrs. of Writing, Greenfield, Mass., 1987-94; contbg. editor State Street Rev., 1992—. Mem. Sherman Park Community Center, 1975-80; co-founder, bd. dirs. Instructional Network for Coll. Faculty, 1981-85. NDEA grantee, 1968, Art Ventures grantee, 1992. Mem. Nat. Council Tchrs. of English. Editor Instructional Network Notes, 1982-85; author: Writing Resources for Conferencing and Collaboration, 1989, Writing Strategies Plus Collaboration, 1996; editor in chief Lollipops, Lizards and Lit., 1994; contbr. articles to profl. jours. Home: 3879 Oldfield Trail Jacksonville FL 32223 Office: Kalliope 3939 Roosevelt Blvd Jacksonville FL 32205

KOERBER, MARILYNN ELEANOR, gerontology nursing educator, consultant, nurse; b. Covington, Ky., Feb. 1, 1942; d. Harold Clyde and Vivian Eleanor (Conrad) Hilge; m. James Paul Koerber, May 29, 1971. Diploma, Christ Hosp. Sch. Nursing, Cin., 1964; BSN, U. Ky., 1967; MPH, U. Mich., 1970. RN, Ohio, S.C.; cert. gerontologist. Staff nurse premature and newborn nursery Cin. Gen. Hosp., 1964-65; staff nurse, hosp. discharge planner Vis. Nurse Assn., Cin., 1967-69; asst. dir. Vis. Nurse Assn., Atlanta, 1976-78; instr. Coll. Nursing, U. Ky., Lexington, 1970-71; supr. Montgomery County Health Dept., Rockville, Md., 1971-74; asst. prof. Coll. Nursing, U. S.C., Columbia, 1979-86, instr., 1987-89; alzheimer's project coord. S.C. Commn. on Aging, Columbia, 1988-90; dir. edn. and tng. Luth. Homes S.C., White Rock, 1988-91; grad. asst. U. S.C. Sch. of Pub. Health, 1991-94; trainer for homemakers home health aides S.C. Divsn. on Aging, 1991—; coord. to train homemakers home aides nursing assts. State Pilot Program, DSS and Divsn. on Aging, 1993—; mem. utilization rev. bd. Palmetto Health Dist., Lexington, 1984—; test item writer, nurse aide cert. Psychol. Corp., San Antonio, 1989, 91, 92; bd. examiners Nursing Home Adminstrn. and Community Residential Care Facility Adminstr., chmn. of edn. com., Columbia, S.C., 1990-93; presenter gerontol. workshops and residential care facilities adminstrn. Contbg. editor: (handbook) Promoting Caregiver Groups, 1984; reviewer gerontology textbooks, 1983-91; contbr. tng. video and manuals on Alzheimers, 1988 (hon. mention Retirement Rsch. Found. 1989). Del. S.C. Gov. White House Conf. on Aging, Columbia, 1981; chmn. ann. mtg. S.C. Fedn. for Older Ams., Columbia, 1989-91. USPHS trainee, 1965-67, Adm. on Aging trainee, 1969-70. Mem. ANA (recert. gerontol. nurse 1988, 92, community health nurse 1989, 93), S.C. Nurses Assn., Am. Pub. Health Assn., So. Gerontol. Soc., Gerontol. Soc. Am., S.C. Gerontol. Soc. (treas. 1989-91, Rosamond R. Boyd award 1986, Pres. award Mid State Alzheimers Chpt., 1993), Soc. for Pub. Health Edn., Am. Soc. on Aging, Alzheimers Assn. (bd. dirs. Columbia chpt. 1988-93, sec. 1992, chmn. nominating com. 1991-92; bd. dirs. S.C. combined health appeal 1991-93), Nat. Coun. on Aging, Nat. Gerontol. Nursing Assn. Democrat. Unitarian Universalist.

KOERING, MARILYN JEAN, anatomy educator, researcher; b. Brainerd, Minn., Jan. 7, 1938; d. Clement J. and Vi K. (Holtkamp) K. B.A., Coll. St. Scholastica, Duluth, 1960; M.S., U. Wis.-Madison, 1963, Ph.D., 1967, post-grad., 1968. Instr. dept. anatomy U. Wis., 1963-64; asst. prof. George Washington U., Washington, 1969-73, assoc. prof., 1973-79, prof. anatomy, 1979—, dir. neurosci. program, 1990-94; vis. assoc. div. biology Calif. Inst. Tech., 1976; affiliate scientist Wis. Primate Research Ctr., Madison, 1975-78; guest worker Pregnancy Research br. Nat. Inst. Child Health and Devel., 1977-84; vis. prof. Jones Inst. for Reproductive Medicine, Eastern Va. Med. Sch., 1985-92. Mem. editorial bd. Biology of Reproduction, 1974-78; contbr. articles to profl. jours. Recipient Alumni award Coll. of St. Scholastica, 1989; NIH fellow, 1967-68; NIH grantee, 1969—. Mem. AAAS, Am. Assn. Anatomists, Soc. Study Reproduction. Office: George Washington U Med Ctr Dept Anatomy 2300 I St NW Washington DC 20037-2337

KOESTER, DIANE KAY, academic administrator, language educator; b. Warrensburg, Mo., May 25, 1948; d. Cornelius J. and Elda Ruth (Albers) K.; m. Kenneth E. Larson, Sept. 4, 1977; children: Benjamin, Miriam. BA, Valparaiso U., 1970; MA, Johns Hopkins U., 1972, PhD, 1982. Asst. prof. German Wells Coll., Aurora, N.Y., 1983-89, assoc. prof. German, 1989—, dir. acad. advising, 1989-93, assoc. dean for acad. affairs, 1993-94, interim dean coll., 1994-95, assoc. dean coll., dir. acad. advising, 1995—. Parent rep. com. on spl. edn. So. Cayuga Ctrl. Schs., Aurora, 1990—. Mem. MLA, Am. Assn. Tchrs. of German, Women in German, Leasing Soc., Goethe Soc. of N.Am., Nat. Acad. Advising Assn. Democrat. Office: Wells Coll Po Box 500 Aurora NY 13025-0500

KOETTER, LEILA LYNETTE, college administrator; b. McCook, Nebr., June 12, 1963; d. Larry Wayne and Leanna Lois (Leibrandt) Hoyt; m. Darin Koetter, May 29, 1993; children: Michaela Nichole, Logan Walter. BS in Elem. Edn., U. Nebr., 1985, BS in Early Childhood, 1985; postgrad. in early childhood, U. Nebr. Lincoln at Kearney, 1987—. Asst. volleyball coach McCook (Nebr.) Community Coll., 1985-88; dir. nature camp YMCA, McCook, 1985-89; dir. nature camp child devel. ctr. McCook Community Coll., 1985-94, master tchr. child devel. ctr., 1985-90, faculty, instr., 1985—, adminstr. child devel. ctr., 1985—; adv. bd. head child devel. ctr. McCook Community Coll., 1985—; advisor, instr. Coun. for Early Childhood Profl. Recognition, Washington, 1990—; founder, coord. Cmty. Children's Fair (instr. Cmty. Discovery Week for Elementary Sch. children 1995—) 1995—. Coord. Week of Young Child, McCook; youth coach YMCA, McCook, 1987—; program coord. Sidewalk Culture Fair and Children's Fair, 1996. Mem. ASCD, Nat. Assn. Edn. Young Children, Nat. Coalition for Campus Childcare, Nebr. Assn. Edn. Young Children, Nebr. Edn. Assn. Home: Rt 3 Box 84 Mc Cook NE 69001-3639 Office: McCook Community Coll 1205 E 3rd St Mc Cook NE 69001-2631

KOFFINKE, CAROL, writer; b. Titusville, Pa., Sept. 21, 1949; d. Harry and Shirley (LePenotiere) Graves; m. Steve Jordan, Aug. 15, 1973 (div. Aug. 1978; 1 child, Julie Jordan; m. Richard Koffinke, Jr., Mar. 23, 1979; 1 child, Richard III. BS, Western Md. Coll., 1971; MEd, Boston U., 1975. COO New Beginnings at Hidden Brook, Bel Air, Md., 1988—; lectr. on addictions, codependency, and parenting; cons. Office of Edn. and Tng. of Addiction Svcs. for Md.; adv. bd. mem. Essex C.C., Harford Coun. of Cmty. Svcs. Author: I'll Never Do That to My Kids, 1991, (with daughter, Julie Jordan) Mom, You Don't Understand, 1993, (with others) Treating the Chemically Dependent and Their Families, 1989. Recipient cert. of appreciation Coun. on Child Abuse and Neglect, 1992. Mem. Nat. Assn. of Alcohol and Drug Abuse Counselors, Nat. Coun. on Alcohol and Drug Dependence. Home: 203 Briarcliff Ln Bel Air MD 21014 Office: PO Box 1607 Bel Air MD 21014-7607*

KOH, CHRISTA M., technical translator, realtor, physical therapist; b. Berlin, Germany, Apr. 18, 1941; came to U.S., 1965; d. Hans Wolfgang and Maria Theresia Heinrich; m. Kwan S. Koh, July 1, 1972; children: Kimberly Kristen, Alexis Korene, Karsten Kwan. Cert., Phys. Therapy Sch., Berlin, 1961; lic. in phys. therapy, Chgo., 1969. Lic. realtor, Fla.; lic. phys. therapist, Ill., Germany. Intern in phys. therapy Evang. Hosp., Saarbruecken, Germany, 1962-63; staff phys. therapist Walton Hosp., Liverpool, Eng., 1963-64, St. Joseph Hosp., Guelph, Ont., Can., 1964-65, Schwab Rehab. Hosp., Chgo., 1965-68, Kostner Manor Nursing Home, Chgo., 1968-69; dir. phys. therapy St. Elizabeth's Hosp., Chgo., 1969-81, Bethesda Hosp., Chgo., 1981-85; realtor Century 21, Country Hills, Pitts., 1986-88; systems analyst Columbia Healthcare Corp., Ft. Myers, Fla., 1991-92; realtor Coldwell Banker McFadden & Sprowls, 1993-95, Guaranteed Real Estate Svcs., Inc., 1995—; technical translator Fischer Internat. Systems Corp., Naples, Fla., 1994—. Symphony usher, vol. S.W. Fla. Symphony Soc., 1993—; mem. Ft. Myers Women's Network, 1993-94, Chicagoland Phys. Therapy Dirs. Forum, 1975-85; vol. usher Barbara M. Mann Hall, 1994—. Mem. Am. Phys. Therapy Assn. (Fla. chpt.).

KOHL, JEANNE ELIZABETH, state senator, sociologist, educator; b. Madison, Wis., Oct. 19, 1942; d. Lloyd Jr. and Elizabeth Anne (Sinness) K.; m. Kenneth D. Jenkins, Apr. 15, 1973; children: Randall Hill, Brennan Hill, Terra Jenkins, Kyle Jenkins, Devon Jenkins; m. Alexander Sumner Welles, Nov. 10, 1985. BA, Calif. State U., Northridge, 1965, MA, 1970; MA, UCLA, 1973, PhD, 1974. Tchr. L.A. Sch. Dist., 1965-68; lectr. Calif. State U., Long Beach, 1973-85; vis. asst. prof. U. Calif., Irvine, 1974-77; So. Calif. mgr. Project Equity/U.S. Dept. Edn., 1978-84; asst. dean, coord. women's programs U. Calif., Irvine, 1979-82; lectr. Calif. State U., Fullerton, 1982-85, U. Wash., Seattle, 1985—; asst. prof. Pacific Luth. U., Tacoma, Wash., 1986-88; state legislator from 36th dist. Wash. Ho. of Reps., Olympia, 1992-94, majority whip, 1993-94; mem. Wash. Senate, Olympia, 1994—. Author: Explorations in Social Research, 1993, Student Study Guide-Marriage and the Family, 1993; contbr. articles to profl. jours. Bd. dirs. Com. for Children, Seattle, 1986-91, Queen Anne Cmty. Coun., Seattle, 1988-93, Stop Youth Violence, Wash., 1993—, Queen Anne Helpline, Seattle, 1992-94; mem. Wash. State Sentencing Guidelines Commn., 1995—, Wash. State Child Care Coord. Com., 1995—; mem. Gov.'s Task Force on Higher Edn. Grantee U.S. Dept. Edn., 1988-89, 90-91. Home: 301 W Kinnear Pl Seattle WA 98119-3732 Office: Wash State Senate PO Box 40436 Olympia WA 98504-0436

KOHLHORST, GAIL LEWIS, librarian; b. Phila., Dec. 5, 1946; d. Richard Elliott and Lucille (Lampkin) Lewis; m. Allyn Leon Kohlhorst, Feb. 14, 1974; 1 child, Jennifer Marion. B.A. in Govt, Otterbein Coll., Westerville, Ohio, 1969; M.S. in L.S, Cath. U. Am., 1977. Info. classifier U.S. Ho. of Reps. Commn. on Internal Security, Washington, 1969-70; adminstrv. asst. Office of Gen. Counsel, GSA, Washington, 1971-76; chief tech. services sect. GSA Libr., Washington, 1976-79; chief GSA libr., 1979-88; acting chief, div. info. and libr. svcs. U.S. Dept. Interior, Washington, 1988-89; chief libr. svcs. br. GSA, Washington, 1989-96; chief mgmt. analysis FDA, Rockville, Md.,

1996; dir. (Act) mgmt. sys. and policy FDA, Rockville, 1996—. Author: Art and Architecture: An Annotated Bibliography, 1986, Total Quality Management: An Annotated Bibliography, 1990, 91, 93, Federal Librarians Round Table, ALA, Yearbook, 1989, Federal Librarian, 1991-94; contbr. Calendar Commn. on the Bicentennial for the U.S. Constn. Recipient Outstanding Performance awards, 1973, 75, 76, 79, 81-86, 88-89, 91-96, Spl. Achievement awards, 1982-84, Commendable Svc. award, 1984, Nat. Capital Performance award, 1985, Meritorious Svc. award, 1992, Disting. Svc. award, 1995. Mem. ALA (Fed. Libr.'s Achievement award 1995), Fed. Librs. Round Table (pres. 1990-91, membership chair 1994-96), Fed. Libr. and Info. Ctr. (observer 1984-96, exec. bd. 1992-94, chair 1994, membership and governance com.), Fed. Pre-Conf. on the White House Conf. on Librs. and Scis. (del. 1990), Fedlink Adv. Coun. (chair exec. adv. coun. 1990), Pub. Employees Roundtable (bd. dirs. 1994-96), D.C. Libr. Assn., United Meth. Women (mem. Dulin outreach com. 1994-96, pres. Joshua's Way 1995—), Beta Phi Mu. Methodist. Home: 1721 Linwood Pl Mc Lean VA 22101-5121 Office: FDA 5100 Fishers Ln Rockville MD 20857

KOHLSTEDT, SALLY GREGORY, history educator; b. Ypsilanti, Mich., Jan. 30, 1943. BA, Valparaiso U., 1965; MA, Mich. State U., 1966; PhD, U. Ill., Urbana, 1972. Asst. prof. Simmons Coll., Boston, 1971-75; assoc. prof. to prof. Syracuse (N.Y.) U., 1975-89; prof. history of sci. U. Minn., Mpls., 1989—; vis. prof. history of sci. Cornell U., 1989; lect. univs. in U.S. and abroad; mem. nat. panels. Author: The Formation of the American Scientific Community: AAAS, 1848-1860, 1976; editor: (with Margaret Rossiter) Historical Writing on American Science, Osiris, 2d Series, 1, 1985, (with R.W. Home) International Science and National Scientific Identity: Australia between Britain and America, 1991, The Origins of Natural Science in the United States: The Essays of George Brown Goode, 1991; contbr. articles to profl. jours.; mem. editl. bd. Signs, 1980-88, 90-93, Sci., 1980-81, News and Views: History of Am. Sci. Newsletter, 1980-86, Sci., Tech. and Human Values, 1983-90, Syracuse Scholar, 1985-88, chair, 1988; assoc. editor Am. Nat. Biography, 2d edit., 1988—, consulting edit., 1993—; reviewer books, articles, proposals for NSDF, NEH, U. Chgo. Press, numerous other pub. cos. NSF grantee, 1969, 78-79, 84, 93-95, Smithsonian Instn. predoctoral fellow, 1970-71, Danforth Assoc., 1975-82, Syracuse U. grantee, 1976, 82, Am. Philos. Soc. rsch. grantee, 1977, Haven fellow Am. Antiquarian Soc., 1982, Fulbright Sr. fellow U. Melbourne, Austaalia, 1983, Woodrow Wilson Ctr. fellow, 1986, Smithsonian Instn. Sr. fellow, 1987. Fellow AAAS (nominating com. 1980-83, 96—, sect. chair 1986), Am. Hist. Assn. (profl. com. 1974-76, rep. U.S. Nat. Archives Adv. Coun. 1974-76), Berkshire Conf. Women Historians (program com. 1974), Forum on the History Sci. in Am. (coord. com. 1980-86, chair 1985, 86), History of Sci. Soc. (sec. 1978-81, coun. 1982-84, 89-91, 94-96, com. on publs. 1982-87, chair nominating com. 1985, women's com. 1972-74, vis. lectr. 1988-89, chair edn. com. 1989, pres. 1992, 93), Internat. Congress for History of Sci. (U.S. del. 1977, 81, vice chair 1985) Orgn. Am. Historians (chair com. on status of women 1983-85, endowment fund drive, auction subcom. 1990-91). Lutheran. Home: 4140 Edmund Blvd Minneapolis MN 55406-3646

KOHN, JEAN GATEWOOD, medical facility administrator, physician; b. Chgo., July 8, 1926; d. Gatewood and Esther Lydia (Harper) Gatewood; m. Martin M. Kohn, Feb. 10, 1951; children: Helen, Joel, Michael, David. BS, U. Chgo., 1948, MD, 1950; MPH, U. Calif., Berkeley, 1973. Diplomate Am. Bd. Pediatrics. Physician Permanente Med. Group, San Leandro, Calif., 1953-60; pediatric cons. Calif. Children Svcs., 1961-72; lectr. maternal and child health U. Calif., 1973-91; med. advisor rehab. engring. ctr. Packard Children's Hosp. at Stanford, Calif., 1976—, med. dir. child prosthetic clinic, 1977—; asst. neurologic diagnostic ctr. U. Calif., San Francisco, 1960-72; pediatric cons. Project HOPE, Nicaragua, 1966, Peru, 1962; pediatric cons. sch. pub. health U. Hawaii, Okinawa, 1975. Contbr. chpts. to books and articles to profl. jours. Mem. adv. panel State of Calif. Dept. Spl. Edn., Calif. Children Svcs.; bd. dirs. Mental Health Assn., United Cerebral Palsy Assn., Head Start, San Mateo County, 1993—. Recipient Lyda M. Smiley award Calif. Sch. Nurses Orgn., 1987. Fellow Am. Acad. Pediats., Am. Acad. Cerebral Palsy and Devel. Medicine; mem. Assn. Child Prosthetic and Orthotic Clinics (bd. dirs. 1993-96), Project HOPE Alumni Assn. (pres. 1988-92). Home: 1 Baldwin Ave Apt 616 San Mateo CA 94401-3850 Office: Packard Children's Hosp at Stanford Rehab Engring Ctr 725 Welch Rd Palo Alto CA 94304-1601

KOHN, JULIEANNE, travel agent; b. Detroit, Apr. 15, 1946; d. Ralph Merwin and Jane Tacke (Meyers) K.; BA, Heidelberg Coll., Tiffin, Ohio, 1968; postgrad. Eastern Mich. U., 1969-70; diploma Inst. Cert. Travel Agts., 1979. Travel agt. Am. Express Co., Detroit, 1970-73, Thomas Cook Inc., Detroit, 1973-75; mgr. Island Traveller, Grosse Ile, Mich., 1975-76; pres., owner Flying Suitcase, Inc., Grosse Ile, 1976—; owner Tri-Kohn Investments, Grosse Ile, Mich., 1983—; ptnr. Gifts of the World, Grosse Ile, Mich., 1993—. Mem. Trenton Soroptomists Club, Am. Soc. Travel Agts., Inst. Cert. Travel Agts. (life). Episcopalian. Club: Grosse Ile Golf and Country, Grosse Ile Exchange Club. Home: 9781 Hawthorne Glen Dr Grosse Ile MI 48138-1687 Office: JK Enterprises 8117 Macomb St Grosse Ile MI 48138-1565

KOHN, KAREN JOSEPHINE, graphic and exhibition designer; b. Muskegon, Mich., Jan. 8, 1951; d. Herbert George and Catherine Elizabeth (Johnson) K.; m. Robert Joseph Duffy Jr. , July 10, 1982; children: Megan Kathleen, Sarah Evelyn. BFA, cum laude, U. Mich., 1973; MFA, Sch. Art Inst. Chgo., 1975. Free-lance designer, Chgo., 1976-77; designer Stevens Exhibits, Chgo., 1977-78; artist-in-residence Chgo. Council on Fine Arts, 1978-79; designer Chgo. Hist. Soc., 1979-81, dir. design, 81-84; prin. Karen Kohn & Assocs. Ltd., Chgo., 1985—. Work appeared in Mus. News, Kraft Gen. Foods hdqrs. Recipient Superior Achievement award for temporary exhbn. Congress of Ill. Hist. Socs. and Mus., 1985, Superior Achievement award for permanent exhbn., 1989, Cert. Excellence Strathmore Graphics Gallery, 1990, award of Merit Ill. Assn. Bus. Comm., 1993, Motorola Pinnacle award, 1994. Mem. Am. Assn. Mus. (Distinctive Merit awards 1982, 84, 85, Highest Honor awards 1982, 83, 84, 92), Nat. Assn. Mus. Exhibitors (Midwest regional rep. 1983-84), Am. Ctr. Design, Chgo. Women in Pub. (Individual Excellence in Design First prize 1995).

KOHN, LISA SALKOVITZ, lawyer; b. Washington, May 16, 1951; d. Edward Isaac and Suzanne (Feld) Salkovitz. AB, Harvard U., 1972; JD, U. Calif., Berkeley, 1975. Bar: Ill. 1970, U.S. Dist. Ct. (no. dist.) Ill. 1976, U.S. Ct. Appeals (7th cir.) 1976, U.S. Supreme Ct. 1979. Assoc. Jenner & Block, Chgo., 1975-78; assoc., then ptnr. Borovsky, Ehrlich & Kronenberg, Chgo., 1978-83; sr. labor atty. GTE Communication Systems Corp., Northlake, Ill., 1984; sr. atty. GTE Svc. Corp., Northlake, Ill., 1985-89; ptnr. Sonnenschein, Nath & Rosenthal, Chgo., 1989-91; labor arbitrator and mediator Chgo., Ill., 1991—; hearing officer, conciliator City of Chgo. Commn. on Human Rights, 1993—, Cook County Commn. on Human Rels., 1994—. Former bd. dirs. young leadership div., past chmn. profl. women's div. Jewish Fedn. Met. Chgo.; bd. dirs. Hyde Park Jewish Community Ctr. Mem. ABA, Ill. Bar Assn., Chgo. Bar Assn. Office: Ste 433 1525 E 53rd St Chicago IL 60615

KOHN, MARY LOUISE BEATRICE, nurse; b. Yellow Springs, Ohio, Jan. 13, 1920; d. Theophilus John and Mary Katharine (Schmitkons) Gaehr; m. Howard D. Kohn, 1944; children: Marcia R., Marcia K. Epstein. AB, Coll. Wooster, 1940; M.Nursing, Case Western Res. U., 1943. Nurse, 1943-44, Atlantic City Hosp., 1944, Thomas M. England Gen. Hosp., U.S. Army, Atlantic City, 1945-46, Peter Bent Brigham Hosp., Boston, 1947, Univ. Hosps., Cleve., 1946-48; mem. faculty Frances Payne Bolton Sch. Nursing Case Western Res. U., 1948-52; vol. nurse Blood Svc., ARC, 1952-55; office nurse, Cleve., part time 1955-94; free-lance writer. Author: (with Atkinson) Berry and Kohn's Operating Room Technique, 5th edit., 1978, 6th edit., 1986, 7th edit., 1992; asst. editor Cleve Physician Acad. Medicine, 1966-71. Bd. dirs. Aux. Acad. Medicine Cleve., 1970-72, officer, 1976; mem. Cleve. Health Mus. Aux., Am. Cancer Soc. vol.; mem. women's com. Cleve. Orch., 1970; mem. women's coun. WVIZ-TV. Mem. ANA, Ohio, Greater Cleve. Nurses Assn., alumni assns. Wooster Coll., Frances P. Bolton Sch. Nursing (pres. 1974-75), Assn. Oper. Rm. Nurses, Assn. Oper. Rm. Nurses of Greater Cleve., Antique Automobile Assn. Am., Western Res. Hist. Soc., Am. Heart Assn., Cleve. Playhouse, Internat. Fund for Animal Welfare, Cleve. Animal Protective League, U.S. Humane Soc., Friends of Cleve. Ballet, Smithsonian Instn., Council World Affairs, Orange Cmty. Arts Coun., Cleve. Art Mus., Cleve. Children's Mus., Cleve. Zool. Soc., Cleve. Racquet Club, Women's City Club (Jewel award 1992). Home: 28099 Belcourt Rd Cleveland OH 44124-5615

KOKORAS, VICTORIA, retired elementary school educator; b. Peabody, Mass., Aug. 13, 1927; d. Nicholas and Theodora (Triantafillou) K.; m. Francis Edward Quinn (div.). BA cum laude, Boston U., 1955; MA, NYU, 1968. Exec. sec. Com. for the Study of Mankind, Chgo., 1956-59; elem. sch. tchr. N.Y.C. Pub. Schs., 1966-67, Peabody Schs., 1968-92. Founder, chair Peabody Coalition for Nuclear Freeze, 1982-86; mem. Ralph Nader Pub. Citizens, 1992—, People for the Am. Way, 1987—, So. Poverty Law Ctr., Montgomery, Ala., 1994-95. Mem. AAUW, Nat. Women's History Project, Nat. Sci. Tchrs. Assn. Democrat. Home: 20 Greenwood Rd Peabody MA 01960-6316

KOLAR, JEANNE KAY, educator; b. Belfast, Maine, Feb. 1, 1944; d. Laurent Glen and Willena Caro (Howard) Larrabee; m. Bruce Gordon Hutchins, 1967 (div. 1972); m. Edward David Kolar, May 14, 1972; 1 child, Michael Hutchins. BS, Willimantic State Coll., 1966; MS, Eastern Conn. State U., 1976. Tchr. elem. sch. Regional Dist. #4, Chester, Conn., 1966-67; tchr. elem. sch. Groton (Conn.) Pub. Schs., 1968-82, tchr. reading, 1982—. Grantee Sci. Learning Ctrs., Groton, 1987. Mem. NEA, ASCE, Conn. Edn. Assn. Groton Edn. Assn., Nat. Audubon Soc., Nature Conservancy, Nat. Parks and Conservation Assn., World Wildlife Fund, Natural Resources Defense Coun., Environ. Defense Fund. Home: 149 Buddington Rd Groton CT 06340 Office: Claude Chester Sch 130 Ft Hill Rd Groton CT 06340

KOLAR, MARY JANE, professional society administrator; b. Benton, Ill., Aug. 9, 1941; d. Thomas Haskell and Mary Jane (Sanders) Burnett; m. Otto Michael Kolar, Aug. 13, 1966; children: Robin Lynn, Deon Michael. B.A. with high honors, So. Ill. U., 1963, M.A. with highest honors, 1964. Tchr. pub. schs. Benton and Zeigler, Ill., 1960-63; grad. asst. and grad. fellow So. Ill. U., Carbondale, 1963-64; instr. Ridgewood High Sch., Norridge, Ill., 1964-67, Maine Twp. High Sch., Des Plaines, Ill., 1967-70; freelance writer Chgo., 1970-71; cons. Contractor Promotions, Chgo., 1970-71; ednl. coord. Am. Dietetic Assn., Chgo., 1971-72; dir. profl. devel. Am. Dental Hygienists Assn., Chgo., 1972-78; dir. Learning Ctr. div. Am. Coll. Cardiology, Bethesda, Md., 1978-80; dir. edn. Nat. Moving and Storage Assn., Alexandria, Va., 1980-82; exec. dir. Women in Communications, Inc., Austin, Tex., 1982-84, Altrusa Internat., Chgo., 1984-87, Assn. Govt. Accts., Alexandria, 1987-90, Bus./Profl. Advt. Assn., Alexandria, 1991-92, Am. Assn. Family and Consumer Scis., Alexandria, 1992-96; pres., CEO The Alexandria Group, Inc., 1996—; cons. spkr. various profl. assn., ednl. instns. and fed. ays.; dir. project taking charge, adolescent pregnancy prevention program, 1993-95. Contbr. articles to profl. jours., chpts. to books. Mem. adv. council Accrediting Commn. Assn. of Ind. Colls. and Schs., 1980-88; treas. Pub. Employees Roundtable, 1988-90, Hollin Hills Civic Assn., 1989-90. Fellow Am. Soc. Allied Health Professions (dir. 1978-79), Am. Soc. Assn. Execs. (cert., mem. Key Profl. Assn. coun. 1994-96, rsch. com. 1996—, strategic leadership forum com. 1996, awards com. 1992-93, univ. affairs commn. 1986-92, chair 1990-91, found. bd. 1987-91, chmn. edn. sect. 1982-83, bd. dirs. 1983-86, chair higher edn. task force 1990-91, chair fellows 1987, Educator of Yr. award 1978, Key award 1990), Greater Washington Soc. Assn. Execs. (edn. com. 1979-82, CEO com. 1990-92, vice chair 1995-96, mem. strategic planning com. 1994-95, exec. search task force 1996—); mem. Future Home Makers Am. (bd. dirs. 1992-96), Alexandria C. of C. (assn. coun. 1990—, steering com. 1993—), Women in Comm. (newsletter editor, legis. and career re-entry chmn., chair ERA task force, dir. Washington profl. chpt. 1981-83, program com. Chgo. chpt. 1984-86), So. Ill. U. Alumni Assn. (bd. dirs. 1984-89, v.p. 1986-89, presdl. search com. 1986-87). Office: 526 King St Ste 423 Alexandria VA 22314

KOLASA, KATHRYN MARIANNE, food and nutrition educator, consultant; b. Detroit, July 26, 1949; d. Marion J. and Blanche Ann (Gasiorowski) K.; m. Patrick Noud Kelly, Jan. 3, 1983. BS, Mich. State U., 1970; PhD, U. Tenn., 1974. Test kitchen home economist Kellogg Co., 1971; instr. dept. food sci. and food systems adminstrn. U. Tenn.-Knoxville, 1973-74; asst. prof. dept. food sci. and human nutrition Mich. State U., East Lansing, 1974-76, assoc. prof., 1976-82; prof., chmn. food, nutrition and instn. mgmt. Sch. Home Econs., East Carolina U., Greenville, N.C., 1982-86, prof., head nutrition edn. and svcs. sect. Dept. Family Medicine, Sch. Medicine, 1986—, sect. head resident edn., 1995—; mem. subcom. food and nutrition bd. NAS on Uses of the RDA, 1981-83; cons. food and nutrition; vice chmn. edn. subcom. Am. Heart Assn. Consumer Nutrition, 1992-93. Recipient grants in nutrition and food service and med. nutrition edn., 1974—; Kellogg nat. fellow, 1985-88. Mem. Soc. Nutrition Edn. (pres. 1984, Career Achievement award 1995), Am. Instn. Nutrition, Inst. Food Technologists, Am. Dietetic Assn., Soc. Tchrs. Family Medicine. Roman Catholic. Author: (with Ann Bass and Lou Wakefield) Community Nutrition and Individual Food Behavior, 1978, (interactive video disc, with Ann Jobe) Cardiovascular Health: Focus on Nutrition, Fitness and Smoking Cessation, CD-ROM: Images of Cancer Prevention, The Nutrition-Cancer Link.

KOLB, BERTHA MAE (BERTHA MAE RAGSDALE), travel agency administrator; b. Dumas, Ark., Nov. 3, 1925; d. Harold Dewey and Hallie Eugenia (Muskelley) Ragsdale; m. Charles Rudolph Kolb, Oct. 9, 1951 (dec. 1982); 1 child, Charles Harold. Student, La. State U., 1959-61. Sec. Le Tourneau Co., Vicksburg, U.S. Govt. Waterways Experiment Sta.; travel agt. Am. Internat. Travel, Inc., 1983-. Pres. Vicksburg Coun. of Garden Clubs, 1972; bd. dirs. Garden Clubs of Miss., 1977-89; active numerous Vicksburg civic svc. clubs, 1953-. Mem. Vicksburg Country Club (pres. ladies orgn. 1969-70), Town and Country Garden Club (pres. Vicksburg chpt. 1973-75). Episcopalian.

KOLB, DOROTHY GONG, elementary education educator; b. San Jose, Calif.; d. Jack and Lucille (Chinn) Gong; m. William Harris Kolb, Mar. 22, 1970. BA (with highest honors), San Jose State U., 1964; postgrad., U. Hawaii, Calif. State U., L.A.; MA in Edni. Tech., Pepperdine U., 1992. Cert. life elem. educator, mentally retarded educator K-12, learning handicapped pre-sch., K-12, adult classes. Tchr. Cambrian Sch. Dist., San Jose, Calif., 1964-66, Cen. Oahu (Hawaii) Sch. Dist., Wahiawa, 1966-68, Montebello (Calif.) Unified Sch. Dist., 1968—. Named to Pi Lambda Theta, Kappa Delta Pi, Pi Tau Sigma, Tau Beta Pi; recipient Walter Bachrodt Meml. scholar.

KOLB, KATHLEEN, artist; b. Cleve., June 19, 1954; d. Edwin Richard and Nancy (Cooney) K.; m. Timothy Wilcox Fisher, Dec. 28, 1976 (div. May 1991); children: Anna Merriam Fisher, Nathaniel Kolb Fisher. BFA, RISD, 1976; student, Vt. Sudio Ctr., 1991, 92, 94, 95, 96. Sign painter Melbourne, Fla., 1975; art tchr. Greensboro (Vt.) Elem. Sch., 1978-79, C. C. of Vt., Hardwick, 1978, Woodbury (Vt.) Elem. Sch., 1979; faculty, resident artist Gov.'s Inst. of the Arts, Vt., 1990—; instr. watercolor, Greensboro, Vt., 1978-81, T.W. Wood Gallery, Montpelier, 1993-94. One woman exhbns. include Granite Hills Gallery, Hardwick, Vt., 1982, Cardigan Mountain Sch., Canaan, N.H., 1983, Fern Gallery, E. Hardwick, Vt., 1981, 82, 83, 84, North Country Hosp., Newport, Vt., 1985-86, Catamount Art Ctr., St. Johnsbury, Vt., 1985, 86, 90, Passepartout Gallery, Winooski, Vt., 1985, 87, 90, 92, Clarke Galleries, Stowe, Vt., 1993, 96, Furchgott/Sourdiffe Gallery, Shelburne, Vt., 1994, Wood Art Gallery, Montpelier, 1995, Sheldon Mus., Middlebury, 1996, Lewiston Auburn Coll., Maine, 1996; group exhbns. include Gallery 2, Woodstock, Vt., 1981, 86, No. Vt. Art Assn., 1981, Helen Day Art Ctr., Stowe, Vt., 1987-89, 91, Stratton (Vt.) Arts Festival, 1987-89, Francesca Anderson Fine Art, Lexington, Mass., 1988-89, 91-96, Passepartout Gallery, Winooski, Vt., 1991, Wood Art Gallery Vt. Coll., Montpelier, 1991, 92, Webb and Parsons Gallery, Burlington, Vt., 1991, Frog Hollow State Craft Ctr., Middlebury, Vt., 1991, Woods-Gerry Gallery RISD, 1993, 96, Furchgott/Sourdiffe Gallery, Shelburne, Vt., 1993, 94, Sherry French, N.Y.C., 1996; represented in permanent collections Howard Bank, Merchants Bank, Med. Ctr. Hosp. Vt., Otis Elevator Co., others; illustrator: (Timothy Fisher) Huts, Hovels and Houses, 1977, (Timothy Fisher) Hammocks, Hassocks and Hideaways, 1980, (Lewis Hill) Cold Climate Gardening, 1981, (Janet Lind) Bird at Bear Mountain, 1988, (Alan Pastorius) Cutting Hill, 1990, (Deidre McNamer) (cover) Rima in the Weeds, 1991, (Sara Jane Von Trapp) The Landscape Doctor, 1994; illustrator, co-author: Efficient Vegetable Gardening, 1993; featured in Family Fun mag., Harrowsmith/Country Life mag., Vermont Life mag., Vermont mag., New England Living, others. Auditor Town of Greensboro, Vt., 1981, 82; gov.'s adv. coun. on spl. edn. State Dept. Edn., Montpelier, 1995—. Touring exhbn. grantee Vt. Coun. Arts, 1986, 95, Arts Endowment grantee Vt. Cmty. Found., 1994, 95, grantee Haymarket People's Fund, 1995. Home: RD 4 Box 677 Middlebury VT 05753

KOLB, STEPHANIE VICTORIA INEZ, electrical engineer; b. Seattle, Mar. 21, 1955; d. Howard James K. and Dorothy Irene (Lombard) Todd; m. Pat A. Bailey Kolb (div. Dec. 1990); 1 child, Jon Allen. BSEE, Cogswell Coll., 1985; MBA in High Tech. Mgmt., City U., 1992. Sr. technician Tel-Tone, Kirkland, Wash., 1976-78; tech. aide Boeing Comml. Airplanes, Everett, Wash., 1978-84, Boeing Customer Svc., Everett, Wash., 1984-86; sr. engr. Boeing Comml. Airplanes, 1986—; v.p. Career Resource Ctr., Seattle, 1994—. WIth USCG, 1972-76. Mem. Seattle Profl. Engr. Employees Assn. (coun./union rep. 1990—, women's adv. com. 1994—). Democrat. Home: 21011 Damson Rd Lynnwood WA 98036

KOLB, VERA M., chemistry educator; b. Belgrade, Yugoslavia, Feb. 5, 1948; came to U.S., 1973; d. Martin A. and Dobrila (Lopicic) K.; m. Cal Y. Meyers, 1976 (div. 1986). BS, Belgrade U., 1971, MS, 1973; PhD, So. Ill. U., 1976. Postdoctoral fellow So. Ill. U., Carbondale, 1977-78, mem. faculty, 1978-85; assoc. prof. chemistry U. Wis., Parkside, 1985-90, prof. chemistry, 1990—, dept. chair, 1995—; vis. scientist The Salk Inst. for Biol. Studies, U. Calif.-San Diego, 1992-94. Editor: Teratogens, Chemicals Which Cause Birth Defects, 1988, 2d edit., 1993; contbr. articles to sci. publs.; patentee in field. Violinist Racine (Wis.) Symphony Orch., Civic Orch. Milw.; assoc. dir. higher edn. Wis. Space Grant Consortium, 1995—. Fulbright grantee, 1973-76, grantee NIH, 1984-87, Am. Soc. Biochemistry and Molecular Biology, 1988; NASA fellow, 1992-94. Mem. Am. Chem. Soc. (task force on occupational safety and health 1980-94). Office: Univ Wis Parkside Dept Chemistry PO Box 2000 Kenosha WI 53141-2000

KOLBE, JANE BOEGLER, state librarian; b. Olivet, S.D., Mar. 17, 1944; d. Stanley and Grace (Schoepke) Boegler; m. Robert E. Kolbe, June 24, 1967. BA in Math., Westmar Coll., 1966; MLS, U. Minn., 1968; postgrad. bus. adminstrn., Sioux Falls Coll., 1974-76; EdD in Adult and Higher Edn., U. S.D., Vermillion, 1986. Catalog librarian I.D. Weeks Library, U. S.D., Vermillion, 1967-68, circulation librarian, 1968-69; library dir., assoc. prof. Norman B. Mears Library, Sioux Falls (S.D.) Coll., 1969-86; state librarian State of S.D., Pierre, 1986—; trustee Sioux Falls Pub. Library, 1973-79, chmn. bd., 1978-79; mem. S.D. State Library Commn., 1973-80, pres. 1977-78; faculty mem. Sioux Falls Coll. Bd. Trustees, 1979-81, 84-86; bd. trustees N. Cen. Univ. Ctr., Sioux Falls, 1982-84; adv. bd. Bibliog. Ctr. for Research, Denver, 1977-79, trustee, 82-84. NIH fellow U. Minn., 1966-67. Mem. ALA, PLA, S.D. Libr Assn. (chair acad. sect. 1971-72, 84-85), Mountain Plains Libr. Assn. (v.p. 1979-80, pres. 1980-82, Disting. Svc. award 1981), Western Coun. State Librs. (sec. 1989-90, pres. 1991-92), Chief Officers of State Libr. Agys. (sec. 1992-94, exec. bd. 1994—), Bus. and Profl. Women's Club (Pierre treas. 1988-90, pres. 1990-91), Zonta (pres. Sioux Falls 1972-74). Democrat. Methodist. Office: SD State Libr 800 Governors Dr Pierre SD 57501-2291

KOLBE-MIMS, MARGIE LORETTA, safety and health engineer; b. New London, Wis., Feb. 6, 1949; d. Albert Emil and Loretta (Rohloff) Kolbe; m. Albert Mims, Apr. 12, 1985. B, U. Wis., Green Bay, 1992; MS, U. Wis., Whitewater, 1994. Cert. safety exec., cert. safety mgr., cert. safety specialist. Supr. plastics mfg. Presto Products Co., Appleton, Wis., 1967-94; v.p., sec.-treas. A. Mims Assocs., Inc., Madison, Wis., 1985-94, pres., sec.-treas., 1994—; adj. prof. U. Wis., Whitewater; constrn. outreach program trainer OSHA, 1995, gen. industry outreach program trainer, 1996. Editor World Safety Jour., 1986-88. Mgr., player Presto Products Softball League, Appleton, Wis., 1976-77; co-organizer, player Golf League Presto Products Co., Appleton, 1988—; Heart Fund neighborhood solicitor Appleton Heart Fund, 1988—; active Neighborhood Watch Team, 1995. Mem. NAFE, Am. Soc. Safety Engrs., World Safety Orgn. Republican. Lutheran. Home: 31 Apache Ct Appleton WI 54911-1012 Office: A Mims Assocs Inc PO Box 2102 Appleton WI 54913-2102

KOLBESON, MARILYN HOPF, organization and management consultant, educator, artist, retired advertising executive; b. Cin., June 9, 1930; d. Henry Dilg and Carolyn Josephine (Brown) Hopf; children: Michael Llen, Kenneth Ray, Patrick James, Pamela Sue Kolbeson Lang, James Allan. Student U. Cin., 1947, 48, 50. Sales and mktg. mgr. Cox Patrick United Van Lines, 1977-80; sales mktg. mgr. Creative Incentives, Houston, 1980-81; pres. Ad Sense, Inc., Houston, 1981-87, M.H. Kolbeson & Assocs., Houston, 1987, Seattle, 1987—, The Phoenix Books, Seattle, 1987-90; cons. N.L.P. Communications; lectr., cons. in field. Mem. adv. bd. Alief Ind. Sch. Dist., 1981-87, pres., 1983-84; bd. dirs. Santa Maria Hostel, 1983-86, v.p., 1983-84; founder, pres. Mind Force, Houston, 1978-87 and Seattle, 1987-95; founder META Group, Seattle, 1991—. Pub.: You Make the Difference in the Nat. Lit. Poetry Anthonology, Morning Song, 1996. Mem. citizen's adv. bd. Arcola (Ill.) Sch. Bd., 1966-67; mem. Greater Houston Conv. and Visitors Coun., loaned exec., 1986-87; mem. adv. bd. Am. Inst. Achievement, 1986-87; vol. Seattle Pub. Schs., 1992 ; charter mem. Rep. Task Force. Mem. Internat. Platform Assn., Houston Advt. Splty. Assn. (bd. dirs. 1984-87, treas. 1985, v.p. 1986-87), Inst. Noetic Scis. (charter), Galleria Area C. of C. (bd. dirs. 1986-87), Toastmasters (area gov. 1978), Grand Club (v.p. 1986), Lakewood Seward Park Community Club (bd. dirs. 1992—), Fair and Tender Ladies Book Group. Republican. Christian Scientist. Office: 5247 S Brandon St Seattle WA 98118-2522

KOLBYE, MELANIE DAWN BOWMAN, physical education educator; b. Paris, Tex., Feb. 20, 1961; d. Thomas Boyd and Juanita (Powers) Bowman. BS, East Tex. State U., 1983, MEd, 1990. Cert. tchr., Tex. Tchr. phys. edn. Garland (Tex.) Ind. Sch. Dist., 1984-87, 91, tchr. adapted phys. edn., 1991-96; tchr. adapted phys. edn. Plano (Tex.) Ind. Sch. Dist., 1996—; coach Spl. Olympics, Garland, 1991. Mem. Tex. APHERD, PTA, Phi Beta Kappa. Republican. Baptist.

KOLE, JANET STEPHANIE, lawyer, writer, photographer; b. Washington, Dec. 20, 1946; d. Martin J. and Ruth G. (Goldberg) K. AB, Bryn Mawr Coll., 1968; MA, NYU, 1970; JD, Temple U., 1980. Bar: Pa. 1980. Assoc. editor trade books Simon & Schuster, N.Y.C., 1968-70; publicity dir. Am. Arbitration Assn., N.Y.C., 1970-73; freelance photojournalist, N.Y.C., 1973-76; law clk. Morgan Lewis & Bockius, Phila., 1977-80; assoc. Schnader, Harrison, Segal & Lewis, Phila., 1980-85; ptnr. Cohen, Shapiro, Polisher, Shiekman & Cohen, Phila., 1985-95; ptnr., chmn. environ. practice group Klehr, Harrison, Harvey, Branzburg & Ellers, 1995—. Author: Post Mortem, 1974; editor Environmental Litigation, 1991; contbr. numerous articles to gen. interest publs., profl. jours.; past mem. bd. editors New Am. Rev. Mem. Mayor's Task Force on Rape, N.Y.C., 1972-77; adv. Support Ctr. Child Advs., Phila., 1980—; mem. Phila. Vol. Lawyers for the Arts; steering com. Lawyers for Reproductive Rights. Fellow Acad. Advocacy; mem. ABA (dir. publs., former coun. mem. sect. litigation, dir. publs., former co-div. dir. substantive areas of litigation, former editor litigation news, former chmn. com. on monographs and unpublished papers, com. spl. pubs.), ATLA. Democrat. Office: Klehr Harrison Harvey Branzburg & Ellers 1401 Walnut St Philadelphia PA 19102

KOLENIAK ROLD, BARBARA DONNA, nurse; b. N.Y.C., Feb. 20, 1950; d. William Zazula and Catherine Sheridan (Quigley) Koleniak; m. James Lee Rold, Dec. 29, 1974 (div. June 1991); children: Christopher, William, Cara. Nursing Diploma, St. Vincent's Sch. Nursing, Richmond, 1971; BA, Marymount Manhattan Coll., N.Y.C., 1973. RN; cert. HIV/AIDS testing and counseling. Staff nurse N.Y. Med. Coll., N.Y.C., 1971-72; pvt. duty nurse N.Y. Nurse Registry, N.Y.C., 1972-73; staff nurse U. Nebr. Med. Ctr., Omaha, 1973-74, Children's Hosp., Omaha, 1975, ENCOR Med. Support Unit, Omaha, 1987-89; nurse mgr. St. Clare's Home A.R.F., Neptune, N.J., 1990; clin. nurse pediat. HIV/AIDS program Jersey Shore Med. Ctr., Neptune, 1990—; pub. speaker on pediat. HIV/AIDS. Reviewer curriculum manual The Best Parent I Can Be, 1989. Recipient Starfish award Starfish Soc. N.J., 1992. Democrat. Roman Catholic. Office: Jersey Shore Med Ctr 1945 State Route 33 Neptune NJ 07753-4859

KOLFLAT, GAIL L., artist; b. Evanston, Ill., Apr. 5, 1956; d. Tor Dagfin Kolflat and Luetta Coumbe (Robertson) Johnston; m. William Stephen Warrenburg, Oct. 12, 1986; children: Lindsay Alison, Terrill Elizabeth Amelia. BFA with honors, Parsons Sch. Design, 1979. lectr. in field. Exhibited paintings in numerous shows in N.Y.C, Chgo., N.J., New Eng. and Hawaii, 1981—; painting At the Shore portrayed on front and back cover CALYX Jour., summer 1995; columnist Monmouth County Arts Coun. State of the Art newspaper, 1995—. Home: 34 Laurel Dr Little Silver NJ 07739

KOLINER, FRANCES ELOISE, special education educator; b. L.A., June 6, 1949; d. Julius and Elizabeth (Pasternak) K.; m. Robert McNeil Crawford, Oct. 16, 1972; children: Rose Gabrielle, Ian McNeil Joseph. BA, Humboldt State U., 1972; learning handicapped credential, Sonoma State U., 1985. Cert. resource specialist, Calif. Ind. study tchr. Willits (Calif.) Unified Sch. Dist., 1973—, mem. adv. cabinet, 1993—; mem. Calif. Arts Project, 1990—, Telementer, 1995—; mem. inst. staff drama team Redwood Arts Project, Arcata, Calif., 1992, 94. Named State Tchr. of Yr. for Small Schs., 1994; fellow Calif. Arts Project, 1990, 92. Mem. ASCD, Willits Tchrs. Assn. (officer negotiation com. 1993—), Consortium Ind. Studies, Computer Using Educators. Home: PO Box 1063 Willits CA 95490-1063

KOLKER, SONDRA G., fund raising/special events executive; b. N.Y.C., Nov. 30, 1943; d. Morris Henry and Alice (Cohen) Budow; m. Justin William Kolker, Aug. 23, 1963 (div.); children: Lawrence Paul, David Brett. Student, Hofstra U. Dir. N.Y.C. Office N.Y. State Dem. Com., 1977-79; v.p., exec. dir. Fund for Higher Edn., N.Y.C., 1980-88; pres. Sondra Kolker & Assocs., Halesite, N.Y., 1988-96, Miami, Fla., 1996—; spl. cons. Internat. Devel. Svcs. subs NMP of Am., Inc., 1989-90; dist. rep. Congressman Robert J. Mrazek, 1990-93. Speechwriter for numerous speakers at corp. banquets, 1980-88. Bd. dirs. Huntington (N.Y.) Townwide Fund, 1978-96; active Huntington Hosp. Aux., 1965-96, Great Gatsby Soc. for Multiple Sclerosis, 1988-96, Marble Hills Civic Assn., Halesite, 1958-96; committeewoman Huntington Dem. Com., 1974-82; fundraiser/dist. rep. Congressman Robert J. Mrazek, L.I., N.Y., 1991-93. Recipient Meritorious Svc. award Huntington Twp. C. of C., 1974, 76, 77, 78, Bicentennial Citation Town of Huntington, 1977. Mem. NAFE, MOMA, Met. Mus. Art, Nat. Mus. Women in the Arts, L.I. Crafts Guild, Huntington Twp. C. of C., Women's Econ. Round Table, Huntington Bus. and Profl. Women. Jewish. Home and Office: Sondra Kolker & Assoc 9385 SW 77th Ave #3033 Miami FL 33156

KOLKEY, GILDA P., artist; b. Chgo.; d. David and Evelyn (Jacobson) Cowan; widowed; children: Daniel, Sandor, Eric. BA in Painting, U. Ill., Champaign; postgrad., Art Inst. Chgo., 1978-79. art tchr. Highland Park (Ill.) Recreational Ctr., 1976. Group exhbns. include Art Inst., Chgo., 1949, 50, 56; contbr. paintings to Rainbow House for Battered Women, Traveler's Aid, Art Resources in Tchg., Art Encounter. Recipient award of Excellence, North Shore Art League, 1965-66, painting awards New Horizons in Painting, 1959, Scan Members Show, 1992, hon. mention Women's Club of Evanston, 1972. Mem. Arts Club Chgo., Mid.-Am. Club, Chgo. Soc. Artists. Republican. Home: 1100 N Lake Shore Dr Apt 21B Chicago IL 60611-1027

KOLLMANN, HILDA HANNA, banker; b. Tinley Park, Ill., Dec. 12, 1913; d. Ernest A. and Rosalie (Blume) K. Ed., Bryant and Stratton Bus. Coll. Asst. cashier State Bank of Blue Island (became County Bank & Trust Co. 1962), Ill., 1945-53; cashier State Bank of Blue Island (became County Bank & Trust Co. 1962), 1953-60, asst. sec., 1953-54, sec., 1954-55, v.p., 1955-70, dir., 1956-95, trust officer, 1959-66; v.p. Pullman Bank & Trust Co., Chgo., 1969-70, Standard Bank & Trust Co., Chgo., 1969-70, First Nat. Bank of Lockport, 1969-70, Heritage Bancorp., 1970-94; bd. dirs. Heritage Fin. Svcs. Sec.-treas. Blue Island Pub. Welfare Assn., 1956-60, pres., 1961-63; chmn. indsl. and expansion com. Blue Island Planning Commn. Mem. Nat. Assn. Bank Women (pres. 1961-62), Assn. Chgo. Bank Women (pres. 1956-57). Club: Blue Island Woman's (pres. 1985-87). Home: 4051 Sandy Ct Santa Maria CA 93455 Office: 12015 Western Ave Blue Island IL 60406-1118

KOLLSTEDT, PAULA LUBKE, communications executive, writer; b. Cin., Aug. 27, 1946; d. Elmer George and Mary Margaret (Kelly) Lubke; m. Stephen Leonard Kollstedt, Jan. 21, 1968; children: Kelly, Lance, Stacey, Jonathan. BA, Xavier U., 1968, MEd, 1982. Cert. secondary tchr., Ohio. Editor, writer Shillito's Dept. Store, Cin., 1966-69; freelance writer, Cin., 1969-74; pub. info. coord. Prince William County Parks and Recreation Com. (Va.), 1974-75; communications coord. City of Cin. Recreation Com., 1975-78; cons. Warner Amex Cable Television, Cin., 1982-84, Moellers Assocs., Cin., 1982-84; writer Cin. Enquirer, 1982-83; executive communication specialist Gen. Electric Aircraft Engines, 1984-87, employee communication specialist 1987-90, mgr. communication 1990—; speaker Cin. Preschool Coops., 1981, Cin. Women's Conf., 1984, lectr., presenter workshops on self-esteem for parents, 1975-86; lectr. bus. communications, 1992—. Author: Surviving the Crisis of Motherhood, 1982; contbr. articles to newspapers; writer, producer multi-media presentation Communication Cincinnati, (Unique Program award Ohio Parks and Recreation), 1978. Mem. Women in Communications (v.p. programs 1981-82; Gt. Lakes regional 1st pl. award 1984, 86, 87, 88, 95, recipient Nat. Clarion award, 1990, Gem award, 1992). Recipient Prism award Pub. Rels. Soc. Am., 1983, 85, 86, 87, 88, 92, 94, 95, 96, Bronze Quill award Internat. Assn. Bus. Communicators, 1986, 87, 88, 90, 92, 95, 96, Pres.'s award 1995, Silver Quill award Internat. Assn. Bus. Communicators, 1989. Roman Catholic. Home: 5391 Haft Rd Cincinnati OH 45247-7419 Office: GE Aircraft Engines 1 Neumann Way # J4 Cincinnati OH 45215-1915

KOLODZIEJ, MONIKA EWA, psychology trainee; b. Gdynia, Poland, May 15, 1968. Diploma in Collegial Studies, Vanier Coll., Montreal, 1987; BS with distinction, Concordia U., Montreal, 1990; MS, Syracuse U., 1993, postgrad., 1993—. Tchg. asst. dept. psychology Syracuse (N.Y.) U., 1990-91, clin. asst. Psychol. Svcs. Ctr., 1991-92, clin. asst. Counseling Ctr., 1992-93, 94-95; psychology trainee St. Joseph's Hosp., Syracuse, 1993-94; intern South Shore Mental Health, Quincy, Mass., 1996—; presenter in field. Contbr. articles to profl. jours. Mem. health issues com. Allston Brighton Healthy Boston Coalition, 1995-96; vol. Douglas Psychiat. Ctr., Montreal, 1989. Recipient Tuition scholarship Syracuse U., 1990-95, Rsch. award Grad. Sch. Syracuse U., 1991. Mem. AAUW (ednl. found. chair Syracuse br. 1993-95), APA (student mem.), Soc. Behavioral Medicine (student mem.), Internat. Scholar Honor Soc. (student rep. Syracuse br. 1991-92). Office: Syracuse Univ Dept Psychology 430 Huntington Hall Syracuse NY 13244

KOLPAKOVA, IRINA, dancer, educator, coach; b. Leningrad, USSR, May 22, 1933; m. Vladilen Semenov. Student, Leningrad Choreographic Sch.; studies with Agrippina Vaganova. Mem. Leningrad-Kirov Ballet; ballet mistress, instr., coach Am. Ballet Theatre, N.Y.C., 1990—. Leading roles include Cinderella, 1955, Coast of Hope, 1959, Ala and Lolly, 1969, Creation of the World, 1971; repertoire with the Leningrad-Kirov Ballet includes Chopiniana (Les Sylphides), The Creation of the World, Giselle, The Fountain of Bakhchiserai, The Nutcracker, Othello, Pushkin, Romeo and Juliet, The Sleeping Beauty, Raymonda; created roles include Katerina in The Stone Flower, 1957, Shyrin in The Legend of Love, 1961. Named Merited Artist R.S.F.S.R., 1957, People's Artist, 1960, First prize Gold Etoile Internat. Dance Festival, 1965. Office: Am Ballet Theatre 890 Broadway New York NY 10003-1211

KOMANDO, KIMBERLY ANN, computer company executive, radio and television host; b. Union, N.J.. BS in Computer Info. Systems, Ariz. State U., 1985. Mktg. rep. IBM, Phoenix, 1984-85; major account rep. AT&T, Phoenix, 1985-87; pres. The Komando Corp., Ariz./Fla., 1991—; mgr. UNISYS, Phoenix, 1987-91; domestic and internat. mktg. cons.; speaker in field. Author: 401 Great Letters, 1993, 1,001 Komputer Answers, 1995, CyberBucks, 1996; talkshow and weekly radio show host; internationally syndicated radio talk show host; internationally weekly syndicated columnist; contbr. articles to profl. jours. Office: The Komando Corp 4332 N Wells Fargo Ave Ste 200 Scottsdale AZ 85251-3408

KOMP, BARBARA ANN, technical publications executive; b. La Porte, Ind., Nov. 3, 1954; d. Gerald Lee and Betty Mae (Schelin) K. BA in Elem. Edn., Ball State U., 1977. Cert. in lang. arts & reading competencies, 1977. Quality control insp. Foreman Mfg. Co., Rolling Prairie, Ind., 1978-80; quality control insp. Weil-McLain Co., Michigan City, Ind., 1980-81, jr. quality control engr., 1981-84, tech. writer, 1984-88. Advisor Jr. Achievement, Michigan City, 1982-84; mem. bd. dirs. Mich. City YMCA, 1992-93, Christman-in-April, Michigan City, chair in-kind donations com., 1993-95, bd. sec., 1994-95. Mem. Soc. for Tech. Communication (Tech. Manual Achievement award 1986, Tech. Manual Merit award 1990, 92, 93, 96, Tech. Manual Excellence award 1996), Women in Mgmt. Avocations: jazz aerobics, photography, volleyball. Office: Weil-McLain A Marley Co 500 Blaine St Michigan City IN 46360-2387

KONDYLIS, BARBARA RANDALL, county official; b. Seymour, Ind., July 8, 1943; d. Edward M. and Nathalie R. (Smith) Fox; m. Gabriel A. Kondylis, Mar. 26, 1968; children: Nathalie R., Alexandros G. BPA, U. San Francisco, 1982; MPA, Calif. State U., 1993. Mem. city coun. City of Vallejo, Calif., 1979-88; mem. bd. suprs. Solano County, Calif., 1993—; commr. Bay Conservation Devel. Commnn., San Francisco, 1979-88, 93—; trustee Vallejo Sanitation & Flood Control Dist., 1993-95; bd. dirs. Solano County Water Authority, Vacaville, Calif. Democrat. Home: 41 B St Vallejo CA 94590 Office: Solano County Bd Suprs 321 Tuolumne St Vallejo CA 94590

KONECKY, EDITH, writer; b. N.Y.C., Aug. 1, 1922; d. Harry and Elizabeth (Smith) Rubin; m. Murray Leon Konecky, May 14, 1942 (div. 1963); children: Michael, Joshua. Student, NYU, 1938-41. Author: Allegra Maud Goldman, 1976, reprinted 1978, 87, 90, 93, A Place at the Table, 1989, reprinted 1990; contbr. short stories to various mags. and anthologies, including Best American Short Stories of 1964; contbr. poetry to various mags. and anthologies, and chpt. to The Writer's Handbook, 1991; work discussed in Her Testimony, 1995 and Jewish-American Women Writers. 1994. N.Y. Found. for the Arts fellow 1992, 1962-88; MacDowell Colony fellow, 1971-95; Helene Wurlitzer Found. fellow, 1973; VCCA fellow, 1981, Djerassi Found. fellow, 1987; Blue Mountain Ctr. fellow, 1983-88; Leighton Artist Colony at the Banff Ctr. for Fine Arts fellow, 1990; recipient Mabel Louise Robinson prize for best short story of yr., Columbia U., 1961; recipient Quill award for best fiction, 1963, Mass. Rev.; recipient citations ALA, 1976, Sch. Libr. Jour., 1977 (Best Young Adult books). Mem. Authors' Guild, PEN, Poets and Writers.

KONER, PAULINE, dancer, choreographer, author; b. N.Y.C., June 26, 1912; d. Samuel and Ida (Ginsberg) K.; m. Fritz Mahler, May 23, 1939 (dec. 1973). Student, Columbia U., 1928-30; studies with Michel Fokine, studies with Michio Ito, studies with Angel Cansino; DFA (hon.), R.I. Coll., 1985. Faculty dance div. Juilliard Sch., 1986—; mem. faculty Sch. Performing Arts, N.Y.C., N.C. Sch. Arts, Winston-Salem; adj. prof. Bklyn. Coll., 1975-79; guest tchr. modern dance Internat. Ballet Seminar, Dopenhagen, 1971, 72, Am. Dance Ctr., N.Y.C., 1972; lectr. and guest artist many leading univs. in U.S.; performed under auspices State Dept. in Mex., S.Am., Europe; artist-in-residence N.C. Sch. Arts, Winston-Salem, 1965-76; tchr. choreographer workshop Cultural Ctr. of Philippines, 1973; nat. adjudicator Am. Coll. Dance Festival, Kennedy Ctr., 1981; guest lectr. U. Arts, Phila., 1991, 92, 93; staged farewell for dancer Margie Gillis, 1995. Performed at White House, 1967; conducted choreography workshops Nat. Assn. Regional Ballets, 1968; staged ballet Dayton (Ohio) Civic Ballet, 1969, Alvin Ailey Repertory Co., 1969, Atlanta Ballet Co., 1969; filmed TV broadcasts of numerous performances; premiere: The Farewell, 1962, Solitary Songs, Am. Dance Festival, 1975, Pauline Koner Dance Consort, 1976-82, A Time of Crickets, Am. Dance Festival, 1976, Mosaic, Dance Umbrella Series, 1977, Cantigas, Am. Dance Festival, 1978, Flight Riverside Festival, 1980; resident dancer Riverside Dance Festival, 1979-81; solo concerts in N.Y.C., 1930—, Near East, 1932, Russia, 1935, Riverside Co., 1980-82; guest artist Jose Limon Co., 1945-60; guest artist, tchr. Jacob's Pillow Dance Festival, intermittently 1945-70; dir. Pauline Koner Dance Co., 1947-64; guest choreographer Nat. Sch. Dance, Rome, 1960-63, Nat. Ballet Chile, 1961; performer, tchr. Conn. Coll. Sch. Dance, 1948-60; pioneer TV dance CBS, 1946; artist-in-residence: U. Ill., 1984, Alvin Ailey Repertory Co., 1984; choreographer: Solitary Songs at Alvin Ailey Repertory Co., 1984; author: (autobiography) Solitary Song, 1989, Elements of Performance, 1993; contbr. articles to books and mags.; State Dept. tour of India, Singapore and Korea, 1967; restaged Poéme for N.C. Sch. Art, 1991, Concertino for Dance-Fusion, Phila., 1991; spl. coaching Jacobs Pillow, 1991; solo performance The Farewell for Margie Gillis, 1995. Recipient Dance Mag. award, 1963, Citation award De La Torre Bueno Awards Com., 1990; Nat. Endowment of Arts grantee, 1969, 75, 77-78, 79.

KONIGSBURG, ELAINE LOBL, author; b. N.Y.C., Feb. 10, 1930; d. Adolph and Beulah (Klein) Lobl; m. David Konigsburg, July 6, 1952; children—Paul, Laurie, Ross. B.S., Carnegie Mellon U., 1952; grad. student chemistry, U. Pitts., 1952-54. Author: juveniles Jennifer, Hecate, Macbeth, William McKinley and Me, Elizabeth, 1967 (Newbery Honor Book), From The Mixed-Up Files of Mrs. Basil E. Frankweiler, 1967 (Newbery medal 1968), About the B'nai Bagels, 1969, (George), 1970, Altogether, One at a Time, 1971, A Proud Taste for Scarlet and Miniver, 1973 (Nat. Book award nominee), The Dragon in the Ghetto Caper, 1974, The Second Mrs. Giaconda, 1975, Father's Arcane Daughter, 1976, Throwing Shadows, 1979 (Am. Book award nominee), Journey to an 800 Number, 1981, Up From Jericho Tel, 1986, Samuel Todd's Book of Great Colors, 1990, Samuel Todd's Book of Great Inventions, 1991, Amy Elizabeth Explores Bloomingdale's, 1992, T-backs, T-shirts, COAT and Suit, 1993, TalkTalk, 1995, The View From Saturday, 1996.

KONIGSMARK, JOCELYN ANN, antiquarian bookseller; b. Ames, Iowa, Nov. 21, 1932; d. Burch Hart and Violet Genoveve Marie (Siemers) Schneider; m. Bruce William Konigsmark, Aug. 25, 1968 (dec. 1973); 1 child, David. BA, Washington State U., 1955; MDiv, Princeton Theol. Sem., 1967; MLS, U. Md., Beltsville, 1972. Tchr. Wenatchee (Wash.) Pub. Schs., 1955-58, Seattle Pub. Schs., 1958-63, Woodstock Sch., Musoorie, India, 1964; cataloger St. Mary's Sem. & U., Balt., 1968-71; proprietor, antiquarian bookseller Koniqsmark Books, Wayne, Pa., 1980—; mem. Philobiblon, Phila., 1983—. Bd. dirs. Radnor Libr., Wayne, 1981-91, CareLink, Broomall, Pa., 1992—, Planned Lifetime Assn. Network, 1991—, Alliance for Mentally Ill, 1989—; com. mem. Dem. Com., Radnor, 1976-80; active Haverford Coll. Libr., U. Pa. Libr., Rosenbach Libr., Bryn Mawr Coll. Libr. Mem. Phi Kappa Phi. Democrat. Presbyterian. Home and Office: 309 Midland Ave Wayne PA 19087

KONIOR, JEANNETTE MARY, elementary school educator; b. Bronx, N.Y., Jan. 7, 1947; d. Stephen Louis and Frieda Anna (Schmautz) Sirko.; m. Richard Henry Drago, Nov. 13, 1971 (div. Mar., 1989); 1 child, Christina Angelina; m. John Anthony Konior, Feb. 20, 1993; stepchildren: John Adalbert, Joseph Anthony. AA in Social Sci., Orange County C.C., Middletown, N.Y., 1983; BS in Elementary Edn., SUNY, New Paltz, 1985, MS in Elementary Edn., Secondary English, 1993. Cert. tchr. elementary, secondary English, N.Y. Sec. M.W. Kellogg Co., N.Y.C., 1964-69; legal sec. Kaye, Scholar et al., N.Y.C., 1969-72; records coord. Orange & Rockland Utilities, Pearl River, N.Y., 1975-76; personal sec. Hercules, Inc., Middletown, N.Y., 1976-82; substitute tchr. various dists., Orange County, N.Y., 1986-87; tchr. Archdiocese of N.Y. Most Precious Blood Sch., Walden, N.Y., 1987—; student tchr. advisor Most Precious Blood Sch., Walden, N.Y., 1992—, editor-in-chief Yearbook, 1988—, dir. Christmas Play, 1987, coord. various classroom plays, 1987—. Vol. religious edn. tchr. St. Matthew's Ch., Bklyn., 1969-70, Mt. Carmel Ch., Middletown, 1973-83, St. Mary's Ch., Montgomery, N.Y., 1992-93, St. John's Ch., Woodstock, N.Y., 1994—; chair mem. com. Village on Green I Homeowners' Assn., Middletown, 1980-81, v.p., sec., 1981-82, pres., 1982-84; mem. Parents without Ptnrs., 1990-91. Home: 97 Jockey Hill Rd Kingston NY 12401-7433 Office: Most Precious Blood Sch 180 Ulster Ave Walden NY 12586-1060

KONLANDE, HEATHER LEIGH, marketing professional; b. Odessa, Tex., July 28, 1965; d. Charles Ernest and Margaret Eva (Townsend) McIntyre; m. Edward Paul Konlande, Feb. 16, 1985; children: Alex Paul, Kelsey Erin. BA in History summa cum laude, U. Tex., Odessa, 1995. Teller Univ. Savs., Houston, 1984-87, head savs. counselor, 1987, sec. to v.p., 1987-89; fin. svcs. rep. Nations Bank, Houston, 1989-91; teller Tex. Commerce Bank, Odessa, 1991; mktg. asst. Merit Behavioral Care, Houston, 1995—; team leader annuity sales Univ. Savs., Houston, 1985-86; trainer new employees Nations Bank and Univ. Savs., Houston, 1985-91; mem. CARES com. Merit Behavioral Care, Houston, 1995—. Editor Eagle News, St. Johns Episc. Sch., Odessa, 1995. Mem. NOW, Houston, 1995—, Planned Parenthood, Houston, 1995—. Mem. Phi Alpha Theta. Democrat. Episcopalian.

KONNER, JOAN WEINER, university administrator, educator, broadcasting executive, television producer; b. Paterson, N.J., Feb. 24, 1931; d. Martin and Tillie (Frankel) Weiner; children: Rosemary, Catherine; m. Alvin H. Perlmutter. Student, Vassar Coll., 1948-49; BA, Sarah Lawrence Coll., 1951; MS, Columbia U., 1961. Editorial writer, columnist, reporter Hackensack (N.J.) Record, 1961-63; producer, reporter WNDT Ednl. Broadcasting Corp., N.Y.C., 1963-65; producer, writer, reporter NBC News, N.Y.C., 1965-77; exec. producer nat. pub. affairs programs WNET Ednl. Broadcasting Corp., N.Y.C., 1977-78, v.p. programming WNET, 1981-84, exec. producer, 1984-86; exec. producer Bill Moyers' Jour., 1978-81; pres. Pub. Affairs TV, Inc.; exec. producer Bill Moyers' series for PBS, 1986-88; prof. broadcast and journalism, dean Grad. Sch. Journalism Columbia U., N.Y.C., 1988—, pub. Columbia Journalism Rev. Past trustee Columbia U. Rockland Ctr. for Arts, Sarah Lawrence Coll. Recipient 12 Emmy awards NATAS, Columbia-du Pont award, Peabody award, Gavel award ABA, Edward R. Murrow award, others. Mem. Dirs. Guild, Writers Guild, Soc. Profl. Journalists, Pulitzer Prize Bd., Newspaper Women's Club of N.Y.C., Century Assn., Cosmopolitan Club. Office: Columbia U Grad Sch Journalism Journalism Bldg New York NY 10027

KONON, NEENA NICHOLAI, corporate interior designer; b. Chgo., Dec. 4, 1951; d. Nicholas Alexander and Marie G. (Korotkoff) K. BFA cum laude, Ohio U., 1973. Interior designer Architectonics, Inc., Chgo., 1973-75, sr. interior designer, 1978-82; interior designer Space Mgmt. Assoc., Inc., Chgo., 1975-78; design prin. Borkon & Konon Assoc., Inc., Chgo., 1982-84; dir. interiors Perkins & Will, Chgo., 1984-91; pres. Nicholai Ltd., Chgo., 1991—; assoc. Woman Bus. Enterprise (WBE), Chgo., 1984-91, interiors cons., 1991—. Founding mem. Orthodox Christian Synergy, 1988—. Mem. Chgo. Real Estate Exec. Women. Republican.

KONRAD, AGNES CROSSMAN, retired real estate agent, retired educator; b. Rutland, Vt., Nov. 26, 1921; d. Warren Julius and Susan Anna (Cain) Crossman; children: Suzanne Martha, Dianna Marie; m. Henry Konrad, Nov. 27, 1954. Assoc. degree in Edn., Castelton Coll., 1943; BS in Edn., Castelton State Coll., 1952; postgrad., SUNY, New Paltz, 1969-70, Fla. Atlantic U., 1973; Graduate, Realtors Inst. Fla., 1981. Cert. realtor-assoc.; grad. Realtors Inst. Tchr. Pittsford (Vt.) Pub. Schs., 1943-44, tchr. 1st grade, 1950-52; tchr. 3d grade Hyde Park (N.Y.) Elem. Schs., 1952-73; realtor assoc. Four Star Realty of Boca Raton (Fla.), 1974-93; ret., 1993; tchr. 3d grade Violet Ave. Sch., Hyde Park (N.Y.) Sch. System, 1969-73. Mem. AAUW, Nat. Assn. Realtors, N.Y. State Ret. Tchrs. Assn. (life), Castleton Vt. State Coll. Alumni., Fla. Realtors Assn., State Fla. Realtors Assn. Home: 1229 SW 13th St Boca Raton FL 33486-5307

KONRAD, CATHY JANE, nursing educator; b. Des Moines, Dec. 27, 1948; d. Howard Carl and Marjorie Ruth (Cambron) Tipton; m. Herbert James Konrad, June 13, 1970; children: Jeffrey, Aaron. Diploma, Iowa Meth. Hosp. Sch. Nursing, 1970; BSN, Marycrest Coll., 1975; MA, U. Iowa, 1980. RN, Ill.; cert. maternal-newborn nurse; cert. PALS, neonatal resuscitation procedure. Staff nurse Iowa Meth. Hosp., Des Moines, 1970-74; coll. health nurse Marycrest Coll., Davenport, Iowa, 1975; staff nurse Mercy Hosp., Davenport, 1976; instr. nursing Black Hawk Coll., Moline, Ill., 1976-78, Moline (Ill.) Pub. Hosp. Sch. Nursing, 1976, 78; NCLEX rev. instr. Ednl. Resources, Inc., Shawnee Mission, Kans., 1988—; assoc. prof. nursing Trinity Coll. Nursing (formerly Sch. Nursing), Moline, 1980—. Pres. Holy Trinity Cath. Sch., Davenport, 1984-86. Named Outstanding Young Woman of Am., 1984. Mem. Assn. Women's Health, Obstetric and Neonatal Nurses, Nat. Co-Alliance for Teaching Excellence (hon., Recognition award 1993), Sigma Tau Theta (Gamma chpt.). Roman Catholic. Home: 18219 241st Ave Bettendorf IA 52722-6375 Office: Trinity Coll Nursing 501 10th Ave Moline IL 61265-1217

KONWINSKI, MAUREEN KAVANAUGH, secondary school educator; b. Columbus, Nebr., Mar. 5, 1948; d. Daniel Sebastian and Pauline Mary (Carson) Kavanaugh; m. Gene Thomas Konwinski, Dec. 27, 1969; children: Todd Allen, Kelly Ann, Erin Renee. BA, Creighton U., 1970; M degree, U. Nebr., Omaha, 1986. Cert. tchr., Nebr. Tchr. Sts. Peter & Paul Jr. H.S., Omaha, 1971-77, Millard South H.S., Omaha, 1978; tchr. Millard North H.S., Omaha, 1979—, sponsor History Club, 1994—. City councilwoman Ralston (Nebr.) City, 1993—; bd. dirs. Ralston Soccer Club, 1992—, sec., 1992—; participant Gov.'s Conf. on Youth Violence, Omaha, 1993—. Recipient Econ. Labor scholarship Teamster's, 1986. Mem. Nat. Coun. for Social Studies, Nebr. Coun. Econ. Edn. Roman Catholic. Office: Millard North HS 1010 S 144th St Omaha NE 68154-2801

KOOLOIAN, ELIZABETH, construction company executive; b. Providence, Dec. 24, 1931; d. Anthony Antranig and Noyemzar (Mardigian) Krikorian; m. Azarig Kooloian Sr., Apr. 25, 1954; children: Julie Ann, Elizabeth Marguerite, Nina Lori, Kim Elaine, Azarig Jr. Grad., Armenian Lang. Sch., 1945; cont. edn. student, Providence Coll., 1982. Registered apt. mgr. Exec. sec. State of R.I., Providence, 1950-55; v.p. A. Kooloian Constrn. Co., Inc., North Providence, R.I., 1956—, Kooloian Realty, North Providence, R.I., 1978—; partner Bay Tower Nursing Ctr., Providence, 1984—. Mem. Norton Art Gallery, Palm Beach, Fla.; founder, co-chair Friends Armenian Chorale R.I., 1995. Mem. NAFE, Armenian Students Assn. Am. (donar), Armenian Gen. Benevolent Union (pres. club, donar), Met. Mus. Art (assoc.), Women in the Arts (charter). Armenian Apostolic Ch.

KOONS, ELEANOR (PEGGY KOONS), clinical social worker; b. Sarasota, Fla., July 26, 1927; d. James Lee and Odessa (Dobbs) Swafford; m. Nelson A. Koons, Dec. 27, 1945. BA in Human Resources, Eckerd Coll., 1986; MSW, U. So. Fla., 1988. Lic. clin. social worker. Indsl. nurse Electro-Mech. Rsch. Co., Sarasota, Fla., 1963-65; office mgr. Koons Constrn. Co., Sarasota, 1970-80; day treatment counselor Manatee Community Mental Health Ctr., Bradenton, Fla., 1980-81, day treatment counselor geriat. residential treatment sys., 1981-82, community liaison, counselor, 1982-83; office mgr. Koons Constrn. Co., 1983-88; hospice intern Hospice S.W. Fla., 1987-88, sr. social svc. counselor, 1988-92; pvt. practice Sarasota, 1992—; presenter Nat. Hospice Assn. Conf., Detroit, Fla. Hospice Symposium, Ocala, Fla. Assn. Pediatric Tumor Programs, State Conf., Clearwater, others. Mem. spl. adv. bd. Storytelling World; contbr. articles to Bereavement Mag. Recipient Retired Social Worker of Yr. award Tampa Bay (Fla.) Unit; Grad. record fellow U. So. Fla. Mem. NASW (co-chairperson 1993-94), ACA. Home: Rt 67 Box 219 Cullowhee NC 28723

KOONTZ, EVA ISABELLE, medical technologist; b. Jetmore, Kans., Feb. 3, 1935; d. Vernon Ward and Lillian Mae (Bell) K. BS in Natural Scis., Sterling (Kans.) Coll., 1957; cert. in med. tech., U. Kans. Med. Ctr., 1958. Office technologist Group Practice, Mission, Kans., 1958-60; chemistry supr. Bethany Hosp., Kansas City, Kans., 1960-64; rsch. asst. pediatric hematology and metabolic rsch. U. Kans. Med. Ctr., Kansas City, Kans., 1964-72, R&D Tech., Providence-St. Margaret's Health Care Ctr., Kansas City, Kans., 1972-74; staff technologist St. Lukes Hosp., Kansas City, Mo., 1974-79; clin. lab. mgr. and supr. Quincy Rsch. Ctr., Kansas City, Mo., 1979-80; staff technologist Lakeside Hosp., Kansas City, Mo., 1980-82; med. technologist supr. Midwest Rsch. Inst., Kansas City, Mo., 1982-88; cert. toxicology scientist Clin. Reference Labs., Inc., Lenexa, Kans., 1988—. Mem. Am. Soc. for Med. Tech., Am. Assn. for Clin. Chemistry, Mo. Soc. Med. Technologists. Republican. Presbyterian. Home: 10251 Cedarbrooke Ln Kansas City MO 64131-4209 Office: Clin Reference Labs Inc 8433 Quivira Rd Lenexa KS 66215

KOOPMANN, RETA COLLENE, sales executive; b. Oklahoma City, Feb. 27, 1944; d. Henry William and Hazel (Rollins) Singleton; children: Rebecca Dawn, Christiana Collene. BS, Calif. Coast U., 1987, postgrad. in bus. adminstrn., 1987—. Front end mgr. Kroger Co., Cleve., 1969-72; with acctg. dept. Johns Manville, Denison, Tex., 1972-74; bakery/deli merchandiser Kroger Co., Columbia, S.C., 1974-83; v.p. bakery, deli ops. Kash n' Karry div. Lucky's Inc., Tampa, Fla., 1983-88, Kash n' Karry Food Stores Inc., Tampa, 1988-90; LBO, corp. dir. bakery/deli/sea food ops. United Supermarkets, Inc., Lubbock, Tex., 1990-91; mgr. regional supermarket accounts Tenneco-Packaging, Deerfield, Ill., 1991—. Author tng. manuals, 1984, 86, 87. Bd. trustees Jim Borck Ednl. Found., Inc., 1988—, pres. elect, 1993, chairperson of bd., 1994, 95, 96, chair com. for deli skills tng. program; vol. Spl. Olympics, Tampa, 1986, 87, 88; bd. govs. Am. Biog. Inst. Rsch. Assn., 1989—. Mem. NAFE, Internat. Deli/Bakery Assn. (exec. bd. 1986-89), Internat. Platform Assn., Retail Bakers Assn. (bd. dirs. 1989—, chmn. deli com., deli dir.), Eagles. Republican. Methodist. Home: 3010 Ridge Run Dr Hiram GA 30141-3337 Office: Packaging Corp Am 3010 Ridge Run Dr Hiram GA 30141-3337

KOÓS, ANNA, film maker, writer, typesetter; b. Budapest, Jan. 12, 1948; came to US, 1977; d. Bela K. and Vera Sós; m. Peter Halasz, 1968 (div. 1977); m. Eric Daillie, Feb. 17, 1978 (div. May 1984); children: Galus Halasz, Simon Daillie; m. Theo Cremona, 1985. MA Tchr. Diploma in Hungarian and English Lang. and Lit., U. Lorand Eótvós, Budapest, 1973. Literary translator Europa Publishers, Budapest, 1969-76; translator film subtitle Hunnia Film Studio, Budapest, 1971-76; typesetter Record Press, Inc., N.Y.C., 1986-96; Co-author: Squat Theatre, 1996; dir., producer essay film Three Degrees of Knowledge, 1995. Co-founder, actress, co-author Squat Theatre in Budapest, 1969-76, in N.Y.C. 1977-85; (theatre) Pig, Child, Fire!, 1977, Andy Warhol's Last Love, 1978 (Obie 1978), (film theatre) Mr. Dead & Mrs. Free, 1981 (Obie 1982), (film) Tongue in a Bottle, 1987 (named Best US short 1988). Pres. Budapest-N.Y. Theater Art Found., N.Y.C., 1977-85. N.Y. Found. Arts fellow, 1989-90. Mem. Assn. Ind. Film and Videomakers. Home: 146 Stanton St New York NY 10002

KOPACK, PAMELA LEE (PAMELA LEE MACMINN), business services executive; b. Portland, Maine, July 25, 1951; d. Everett John Foye and Lois Florence (Loveland) MacMinn; student Sears, Roebuck Extension Inst., 1969-73, Newspaper Inst. Am., 1979-85; m. Charles Thomas Kopack, Apr. 2, 1971. Sales staff Sears Roebuck & Co., Cleve., 1966-69, credit collector, 1972-75; exec. sec., asst., Cole Nat. Corp., Cleve., 1976-79; pres. Kopack Svc. Bur., Cleve., 1979—. Author poetry pub. in Poetry-People, 1975, Recollections of Yesterday, 1996, other publs., 1974—, lyrics for songs recorded on single records and albums, 1974-79; author greeting cards, articles, short stories. Recipient poetry award for Facets of a Housewife, 1977. Mem. NAFE, Career Guild (New Feature award 1982), Secs. Workshop, P.S. for Profl. Secs. (Bur. Bus. Practice, article award 1979), Internat. Platform Assn., Ohio Women Bus. Leaders. Clubs: Women's Opportunity Workshop. Office: PO Box 81573 Cleveland OH 44181-0573

KOPENHAVER, PATRICIA ELLSWORTH, podiatrist. Student, Columbia U., 1950-53; BA, George Washington U., 1954; MA, Columbia U., 1956; Dr. Podiatric Medicine, N.Y. Coll. of Podiatric Medicine, 1963; postgrad., N.Y. Coll. Podiatric Medicine, 1980. Diplomate Nat. Bd. Podiatry Examiners. Pvt. practice podiatry Greenwich, Conn., 1964—; mem. staff Laurelton Convalescent Hosp., Greenwich. Bd. dirs. Monmouth Opera Guild, 1965; trustee Monmouth Opera Festival, 1966, v.p., 1964; mem. Greenwich Arts Coun.; program chmn. Greenwich Women's Rep. Club, 1983-84, 4th dist. rep., 1984-85, 87—. Recipient Hosp. Fund award for med. research translations ARC. Mem. AAUW (v.p. 1991, pres. Greenwich br. 1992-94, bd. dirs. 1996), NOW, Conn. Podiatric Med. Assn., Hist. Soc., Asian Soc., Fairfield Podiatry Assn., Am. Assn. Women Podiatrists (charter pres. 1969-78), Acad. Podiatry, Am. Podiatry Coun., UN Assn. U.S.A., Acad. Podiatric Medicine (chmn. nominating com. 1981, 1st v.p. 1983-84, chmn. fundraising 1984-85, chmn. women's issues 1985, chmn. cmty. edn. 1989), Am. Acad. Sports Medicine, Am. Acad. Podiatric Sports Medicine (assoc. 1989), George Washington U. Alumni Assn., Columbia Alumni Assn., Fairfield County Alumni Assn. Columbia U., Nat. Fedn. Rep. Women, Bruce Mus., Nature Conservancy, Federated Garden Clubs Conn., St. Mary Ladies Guild, Greenwich Gardeners, Womans' Club (ways and means com. 1989, pres.), English Speaking Union, Soroptimists Internat. Am. (pres. Greenwich br. 1990—, bd. dirs. 1995-96), Inc. (vice chmn. program com. 1985—, regional med. scholarship chmn. 1987, med. scholarship chmn. N.E. region 1988, program dir. 1988—, pres. Greenwich br. 1990-92), Toastmasters, Travel Club (program com. 1984—), Pi Epsilon Chi. Home: 2 Sutton Pl S New York NY 10022-3070 Office: 8 Dearfield Dr Greenwich CT 06831-5348

KOPLEY, CATHERINE S., investment company executive; b. Passaic, N.J., Sept. 15, 1948; d. Alex W. and Rita M. Sudol; m. James M. Kopley, May 27, 1970; children: Anne, Michael. BS, St. Peter's Coll., 1970; JD, Seton Hall U., 1974. Bar: N.J. 1974, Pa. 1976. Pres. Pruco Securities, Prudential Ins. Co., Newark, N.J., 1974-96; v.p. alliance svcs. Prudential Ins. Co., Newark, N.J., 1995—. Office: Prudential Ins Co 213 Washington St 15th Fl Newark NJ 07101

KOPLOVITZ, KAY, communication network executive; b. Milw., Apr. 11, 1945; d. William E. and Jane T. Smith; m. William C. Koplovitz Jr., Apr. 17, 1971. BS, U. Wis., 1967; MA in Communications, Mich. State U., 1968. Radio and TV producer, dir. Sta. WTMJ-TV, Milw., 1967; editor Communications Satellite Corp., Washington, 1968-72; dir. community services UA Columbia Cablevision, Oakland, N.J., 1973-75; v.p., exec. dir. UA Columbia Satellite Services Inc., Oakland, 1977-80; founder, chmn., ceo USA Network and Sci-Fi Channel, N.Y.C., 1980—. Mem. bd. overseers NYU Grad. Sch. Bus., 1984-87; bd. dirs. Nat. Jr. Achievement, 1986—. Recipient Outstanding Alumnus award Mich. State U. Grad. Sch. Bus., 1985, Outstanding Corp. Social Responsibility CUNY, 1986, Women Who Run the World award Sara Lee Corp., 1987, Muse award N.Y. Women in Film and TV, 1992, Ellis Island medal of honor, 1993, Crystal award Women in Film, 1993; named to Broadcasting Mag. Hall of Fame, 1992. Mem. Nat. Cable TV Assn. (bd. dirs. 1984—), Advt. Coun. Inc. (chmn. 1992-93, bd. dirs. 1985—), Internat. Coun., Nat. Acad. TV Arts and Scis. (chmn. 1994-95, bd. dirs. 1984-93), Women in Cable (founding bd. dirs., membership chmn. 1979-80, v.p. 1981-82, pres. 1982-83), Cable Advt. Bur. (bd. dirs., exec. com., treas. 1981-87, Chmn.'s award for leadership 1987), Nat. Acad. Cable Programming (bd. dirs. 1984-87), Com. of 200, Womens Forum, N.Y.C. Partnership (bd. dirs. 1987—). Office: USA Networks 1230 Avenue Of The Americas fl 20 New York NY 10020-1513*

KOPP, NANCY KORNBLITH, state legislator; b. Coral Gables, Fla., Dec. 7, 1943; d. Lester and Barbara M. (Levy) Kornblith; m. Robert E. Kopp, May 3, 1969; children: Emily, Robert E. III. BA with honors, Wellesley Coll., 1965; MA, U. Chgo., 1968; LittD (hon.) Hood Coll., 1988. Instr. polit. sci. U. Ill., 1968-69; staff spl. subcom. on edn. U.S. Ho. of Reps., Washington, 1970-71; legis. staff Md. Gen. Assembly, Annapolis, 1971-74; mem. Md. Ho. of Dels., 1974—, speaker Pro Tem, 1991-93, chmn. appropriations subcom. on edn. and human resources, 1981-91; mem. exec. com. Nat. Conf. State Legislators; exec. com. So. Reg. Edn. Bd. Mem. LWV, AAUW, Common Cause. Democrat. Jewish. Office: Md Ho of Reps State Capitol Annapolis MD 21401*

KOPPELMAN, DOROTHY MYERS, artist, consultant; b. N.Y.C., June 13, 1920; d. Harry Walter and May (Chalmers) M.; m. Chaim Koppelman, Feb. 13, 1943; 1 child, Ann. Student Bklyn. Coll., 1938-42, Am. Artists Sch., 1940-42, Art Students League, 1942; student of Aesthetic Realism with Eli Siegel, 1942-78, Ellen Reiss, 1978—. Instr. Art Bklyn. Coll., 1952-75; dir. Terrain Gallery, N.Y.C., 1955-83; dir. Visual Arts Gallery, Sch. Visual Arts, 1961-62; pres. Aesthetic Realism Found., 1973-85, cons., 1973—; instr. Nat. Acad. Sch. of Design, 1988-89, 96. One woman shows include Terrain Gallery, 1961, Rina Gallery, Jersey City, 1963; exhibited in group shows at Mus. Modern Art, N.Y.C., 1962, Balt. Mus., 1962, Bklyn. Mus., 1962, N.J. State Mus., Jersey City, Butler Art Inst., Youngstown, Ohio, San Francisco Art Inst., 1961-62, 65, Nat. Acad. Ann., 1986, 90; group shows incl. Swiss Inst., N.Y.C., Susan Teller Gallery, N.Y.C., 1993, 95, Drawing Ctr., N.Y.C., Audubon Soc. ann., N.Y.C., 1995, 96, Chuck Levitan Gallery, N.Y.C., 1996, Washington Square East Gallery, N.Y.C., 1992, 96; represented in permanent collections Hampton Inst. Author: (with others) Aesthetic Realism: We Have Been There - Six Artists, 1969. Illustrator Children's Guide to Parents (by Eli Siegel), 1971. Tiffany grantee for painting, 1965. Home: 498 Broome St New York NY 10013-2213 Office: Aesthetic Realism Found Inc 141 Greene St New York NY 10012-3201

KOPROWSKA, IRENA, cytopathologist, cancer researcher; b. Warsaw, Poland, May 12, 1917; came to U.S., 1944; d. Henryk and Eugenia Grasberg; m. Hilary Koprowski, July 14, 1938; children: Claude, Christopher. BA, Popielewska/Roszkowska, Warsaw, 1934; MD, Warsaw U., 1939. Cert. Am. Bd. Pathology, Internat. Bd. Cytology. Intern in medicine Villejuif Lunatic Asylum, Seine, France, 1940; asst. pathologist Rio De Janeiro City Hosp., Miguel Couto, Brazil, 1942-44; rsch. fellow dept. pathology Cornell U. Med. Coll., N.Y.C., 1945-46, rsch. asst. dept. pharmacology, 1949-50, rsch. fellow dept. of anatomy, 1949-54; rsch. fellow applied immunology Pub. Health Rsch. Inst. of The City of N.Y., 1946-47; asst. pathologist N.Y. Infirmary for Women and Children, N.Y.C., 1947-49; asst. prof. dept. pathology SUNY Downstate Med. Ctr., N.Y.C., 1954-57; assoc. prof. pathology, dir. cytology lab./Sch. Cytotech. Hahnemann Med. Coll., Phila., 1957-64, prof. pathology dir. cytology lab., sch. cytotechnology, 1964-70; prof. pathology, dir. cytology lab. Temple U. Sch. Med., Phila., 1970-87, prof. emerita, 1987—; cons. WHO, Switzerland, Egypt, Iran, Latin Am., India, 1960-85, Armed Forces Inst. Pathology, Air Force Cytology Rescreen Project, 1979-80. Author: Woman Wanders Through Life and Science, 1996; contbr. articles on cancer rsch. to profl. and sci. jours. Named Woman Physician of Yr., Polish Am. Med. Assn., 1977; grantee USPHS-Nat. Cancer Insts., 1954-75, rsch. grantee Bender Co., Vienna, Austria, 1983-89. Fellow Am. Soc. Clin. Pathologists (emeritus), Coll. Am. Pathologists (emeritus), Coll. Physicians of Phila., Internat. Acad. Cytology (hon.), Internat. Acad. Pathology (emeritus); mem. Am. Assn. for Cancer Rsch. Inc. (emeritus), Am. Assn. Pathologists Inc. (emeritus), Am. Med. Women's Assn., Am. Soc. Cytology (life, Papanicolaou award 1985), Am. Soc. Exptl. Pathology, Argentinian Soc. Cytology (hon.), Path. Soc. Phila. Home: 334 Fairhill Rd Wynnewood PA 19096-1804

KORALWESKI, MARY ADELE, clinical psychologist; b. Denver, Jan. 4, 1963; d. Robert Andrew and Shirley Larene (Pankonin) K. BS, Tex. A&M U., 1985; MS, Purdue U., 1988, PhD, 1992. Lic. clin. psychologist, Tex. Tchr./rsch. asst. Purdue U., West Lafayette, Ind., 1985-91; psychology intern VA Med. Ctr., Houston, 1991-92; staff psychologist Wetcher Clinic, Houston, 1992-93; adj. prof. U. Houston, 1992—; clin. psychologist Devereux Hosp., League City, Tex., 1993—. Editor: Sexual Coercion: A Sourcebook on its Nature, Causes and Prevention, 1991; contbr. articles to profl. jours. Clin. vol., defender Planned Parenthood, Houston, 1991—. Mem. NOW, APA, Houston Psychol. Assn. Office: Devereux Hosp 1150 Devereux Dr League City TX 77573

KORAN, JANA L., chemical engineer; b. Hradec Kralove, Czech Republic, May 26, 1946; d. Jan Losos and Wanda (Lubienska) Lososova; m. George Francis Koran (div.); 1 child, Martin. MS, Czech Tech. U., Pardubice, Czech Republic, 1970; MBA, Sch. of Mgmt. and Econs., Pardubice, 1977. Mem. tech. staff Fotochema, Hradec Kralove, 1970-74, asst. to company's pres. on tech. issues, 1974-80; analytical chemist Redken, Woodland Hills, Calif., 1981-82; engr., specialist Litton GCS, Woodland Hills, 1982—. Vol. Czech Red Cross, Hradec Kralove, 1958-80; nurse Civil Def., Hradec Kralove, 1970-80; youth organizer/vol. Czech Youth Orgn., 1964-80; troop leader Boy Scouts Am., Calif., 1985-92. Recipient Women of Achievements award Litton GCS, Woodland Hills, 1995. Mem. AAUW, Am. Chem. Soc., Sierra Club. Republican. Roman Catholic. Office: Litton GCS 5500 Canoga Ave Woodland Hills CA 91367

KORB, ELIZABETH GRACE, nurse midwife; b. Wilmington, N.C., Mar. 1, 1951; d. Carl Wilhelm Bissenger Korb and Betty Jane Stroup; m. Joel Vincent LeFebvre, May 19, 1973 (div. June 1976); m. James Clinton Queen, June 22, 1984; 1 child, James Michael Andrew Queen. BSN, U. N.C., Greensboro, 1973; MSN, U. Utah, 1980. Cert. nurse midwife. Staff nurse, instr. New Hanover Meml. Hosp., Wilmington, N.C., 1973-76; staff nurse Meml. Mission Hosp., Asheville, N.C., 1976-78, LDS Hosp., Salt Lake City, 1978-79; practising nurse midwife Dr. Michael Watson, Bamberg, S.C., 1980, Fletcher (N.C.) Ob-Gyn Assocs., 1981-83, Nurse-Midwifery Assocs., Fletcher, 1983-85, Asheville (N.C.) Women's Med. Ctr., 1985-86, 88; practising nurse midwife, clin. coord. Regional Perinatal Assocs., Asheville, 1986-88; perinatal clin. coord., practicing nurse midwife Mountain Area Health Edn. Ctr., Asheville, 1988—; clin. preceptor Cmty.-Based Nurse-Midwifery Edn. Program, 1993—, East Carolina U. Nurse-Midwifery Edn. Program, 1993—; mem. mgmt. team Mountain Area Perinatal Substance Abuse Program, 1993—; bd. dirs. Mary Benson House, Asheville; mem. adv. panel Emory U., Nurse Midwifery in Pub. Sector, Atlanta, 1988—. Named to Outstanding Young Women of Am., 1982; recipient Profl. award March of Dimes, Asheville, 1993. Mem. ANA, Nat. Perinatal Assn., N.C. Perinatal Assn. (bd. dirs. 1988-93), N.C. Nurses Assn., Am. Coll. Nurse Midwives (N.C. del. legis. conf. 1993, 94, nominating com. 1981-82), Internat. Childbirth Edn. Assn., Phi Kappa phi, Sigma Theta Tau. Democrat. Lutheran. Office: Mountain Area Health Edn Ctr Ob-Gyn 60 Livingston St Ste 100 Asheville NC 28801

KORB, MIRIAM MEYERS, computer analyst; b. Latrobe, Pa., Dec. 5, 1942; d. Roy Craver and Anne Meriam (Loughran) Meyers; m. Otto Joseph Korb, Sept. 23, 1967 (div. Feb. 1983); children: Andrew Otto, Brian Joseph. BS in Edn., U. Pitts., 1964. Programmer AT&T, N.Y.C., 1964-65; sr. programmer U.S. Trust Co., N.Y.C., 1965-66; sr. programmer analyst Programming Methods, Inc., N.Y.C., 1966-71; computer analyst Chase Manhattan Bank, New Hyde Park, N.Y., 1977; sys. analyst St. Regis Paper Corp., West Nyack, N.Y., 1977-82, Nestle Foods, White Plains, N.Y., 1982-88; project leader United Parcel Svc., Mahwah, N.J., 1988—. Bd. mem., sec.-treas. YMCA-Rockland County, Nyack, 1981-90; vol. Hist. Soc. Rockland, New City, N.Y., 1988—, Am. Cancer Soc., Suffern, N.Y., 1993—. Recipient Vol. award Town of Ramapo, Suffern, N.Y., 1995. Mem. AAUW (chmn. Rockland County Edn. Found. 1981—, pres., treas. Rockland County chpt. 1990-93). Home: 81 Country Club Ln Pomona NY 10970 Office: United Parcel Svc 340 MacArthur Blvd Mahwah NJ 07430

KORBER, LOUISE ANN, artist; b. Wilmington, Del., Oct. 23, 1934; d. Stanley Kasmir and Margaret Helen (Kelly) Czajkowski; m. Ernest Andrew Korber, Oct. 28, 1961; children: Edward Andrew, Jonathan Paul, Ann Louise. BA, U. Del., 1956, MA, 1962; postgrad., U. Pa., 1959, 60, Pa. Acad. Fine Arts, 1960-61, 62-63. Elem. art instr. Oak Grove Sch., Elsmere, Del., 1956-57; elem. and middle sch. art instr. Wilmington Friends Sch., 1957-60; recipient Winsor Newton '89 Award. Exhibited in juried shows Pa. Watercolor Soc., Harrisburg, 1982, Galerie Triangle, 1982, 96, and Martin Luther-King Meml. Libr., Washington, 1983, Ctr. for the Creative Arts, Hockessin, Del., 1985, Sketch Club, Phila., 1993, 95, Chester County Art Assn., West Chester, Pa., 1987, 88, 89, 90, 91, 94, 95, 96, West Chester U., 1987, Balt. Watercolor Soc., 1987, 88, 89, 96, Mayflower Hotel, Washington, 1988, J. Low Art Gallery, 1989; represented in permanent collections Univ. Del., Del. Trust Co., Prudential Savs. Bank, Hotel duPont, Wilmington Trust Co., Hempt Bros., Inc., Chem. Bank, Skadden, Arps, Slate, Meagher & Flom, Texaco, AmeriHealth Inc., others. Mem. Studio Group, Balt. Watercolor Soc., Phila. Watercolor Club, Pa. Watercolor Soc. Roman Catholic. Home: 212 Unami Trail Newark DE 19711-7509

KORCZYNSKI, PATRICE, accountant; b. Butler, Pa., Feb. 10, 1967; d. Karl and Elizabeth Rosalie (Pohrer) K. BA, Waynesburg College, 1991. Acct. Korco Mfg. Inc., Ellwood City, Pa., 1990—. Vol. St. Fierdinand Youth Ministry, Diocese of Pitts., 1992—, Forbes Regional Hospice, Pitts, 1993. Fellow NAFE, Pitts. Penguins Booster Club, Nat. Cath. Young Adult Ministry Assn.; mem. Nat. Right to Life, Am. Hiking Soc., N.Am. Vegetarian Soc., Pa. Pro-Life Fedn., Cath. Action League, Cath. Alumni Club of Pitts., Pitts. Ceili Club, Alpha Sigma Tau. Roman Catholic. Home: PO Box 63 Zelienople PA 16063

KOREMAN, DOROTHY GOLDSTEIN, physician, dermatologist; b. Bklyn., Nov. 1, 1940; d. Benjamin and Ida (Krenick) Goldstein; m. Neil M. Koreman, Aug. 16, 1964; children: Elizabeth Koreman Landau, Robert Stephen. BA, Bklyn. Coll., 1961; MD, SUNY, Bklyn., 1965. Diplomate Am. Bd. Dermatology. Intern pediatrics Kings County Hosp. Ctr., Bklyn., 1965-66; resident dept. dermatology Wayne State U. Sch. Medicine, Detroit, 1966-69; clin. instr. dermatology Sch. Medicine Wayne State U., Detroit, 1969-71; asst. clin. prof. dermatology U. Miami, 1971-75, assoc. clin. prof. dermatology, 1975-82, clin. prof. dermatology and cutaneous surgery, 1982—; chief of staff Ami Palmetto Gen. Hosp., Hialeah, 1990-91. Mem. North Dade bd. dirs. Greater Miami Jewish Fedn., 1975—. Mem. Miami Dermatol. Soc. (pres. 1978-79). Office: 7100 W 20th Ave Ste 107 Hialeah FL 33016-1813

KORFF, PHYLLIS G., lawyer; b. N.Y.C., 1943. BA, Bklyn. Coll., 1964; EdM, Boston U., 1967; JD, NYU, 1981. Bar: N.Y. 1982. Ptnr. Skaden, Arps, Slate, Meagher & Flom, N.Y.C. Office: Skadden Arps Slate Meagher & Flom 919 3rd Ave New York NY 10022*

KORN, IRENE ELIZABETH, elementary education educator, consultant; b. Wellston, Mo., May 28, 1937; d. Nicholas Anthony and Myrtle Marie (Knowles) Kuntz; m. Dale Stanley Korn, Sept. 12, 1959; children: Kurt Lawrence, Kenneth Dale, Nancy Ann. BS in Edn., U. Mo., St. Louis, 1969, MS in Edn., 1972, MS in Spl. Edn., 1985. Cert. K-12 reading, social studies tchr., learning disabilities, behavior disorders, Mo. Elem. tchr. N.W. R-1 Sch. Dist., House Springs, Mo., 1969—; tchr. cons. geography program adv. coun. U. Mo., 1989—, Advanced Summer Inst., summer 1990; writer test items Mo. Mastery Achievement Test, fall 1990; mem. social studies work group to write state stds. edn. Mo. Dept. Elem. and Sec. Edn., 1994-95; mem. task force to restructure cert. stds. for U. Mo., Coll. of Edn., 1994. Named Woman of Yr., George Khoury Baseball Leagues, St. Louis, 1987. Mem. ASCD, Nat. Coun. Social Studies, Nat. Coun. for Geographic Edn., Am. Geographical Soc., Mo. State Tchrs. Assn. (professorial rights and responsibilities com. 1987-91, pres. N.W. 1984-86), Mo. Coun. Social Studies, Jefferson County Dist. Edn. Assn. (pres.-elect 1988-89, 91-92), Mo. Geog. Alliance (steering com. 1991—, chmn. elem. curriculum materials 1991-92, tchr. cons. Columbia 1988—, Advanced Inst. P.R. 1992), Phi Delta Kappa. Home: 37 Black Oak Ln Fenton MO 63026-3409

KORN, THERESA MARIE, former electrical engineer, consulting firm co-owner, technical writer; b. St. Louis, Nov. 5, 1926; d. William John McLaughlin and Mary Rose Heinz; m. Granino Arthur Korn, Sept. 3, 1948; children: Anna M. and John M. BSEE, Carnegie Inst. Tech., 1947; MSEE, UCLA, 1954. Lic. comml. radio transmission engr., 1942. Elec. engr. Curtiss-Wright Aircraft Co, Columbus, Ohio, 1947-49, Boeing Airplane Co., Seattle, 1949-50; tech. writer, co-owner G.A. & T.M. Korn Indsl. Cons., Tucson, 1952-92, Chelan, Wash., 1992—; expert witness Ariz. Corp. commn., Tucson, 1971; mem. gov.'s adv. commn. on environ. State of Ariz., 1974-76; mem. Master Tech. com. City of Tucson, 1975-76. Co-author (with E.P. Korn) Trailblazer to Television, 1950; (with G.A. Korn) Electronic Analog Computers, 1952, 2d edit., 1956, Electronic Analog and Hybrid Computers, 1964, 2d. edit., 1974, Mathematical Handbook for Scientists and Engineers, 1961, 2d edit., 1968, Manual of Mathematics, 1968. Active, vol. engr. Tucson Consumer's coun., 1970-76; active Ariz. Consumer's coun., 1970-76, Profl. Women's coalition, Tucson, 1988-91, Nat. Women's Polit. Caucus; citizen's adv. bd. Tucson E. Cmty. Mental Health Ctr., 1974-76; bd. dirs., treas., risk mgr. Planned Parenthood of So. Ariz., Tucson, 1983-89; mem. ad hoc com. Establishing Tucson Women's Commn., 1975-76. Warrant officer Pa. Wing USNG Civil Air Patrol, 1941-43. Named Woamn on the Move YWCA, 1976. Mem. Soc. Women Engrs. (co-founder Tucson chpt., former v.p.), AAUW, Quarter Century Wireless Assn., Quarter Century Wireless Women, Young Ladies' Radio League. Home: RR 1 Box 96C Chelan WA 98816 Office: Korn Indsl Cons 7750 S Shore Dr # 15 Chelan WA 98816

KORNBLEET, LYNDA MAE, insulation, fireproofing and acoustical contractor; b. Kansas City, Kans., June 15, 1951; d. Seymore Gerald Kornbleet and Jacqueline F. (Hurst) Kornbleet Malka. BA, U. St. Thomas, Houston, 1979. Lic. real estate salesperson. Temporary counselor Lyman's Personnel, Houston, 1974-75; real estate salesperson Coldwell Banker, Houston, 1975-77; sales, office mgr. Acme Insulation, Dallas, also Houston, 1977-79; owner, pres. Payless Insulation, Houston, 1979—; contractor City of Houston, 1985—. Bd. dirs. Disadvantaged Bus. Cert. State of Tex., 1989—; vender Houston Bus. Coun. Named Contractor of the Yr., Sears Home Improvement, 1988; active Houston Ind. Sch. Dist., 1989—. Awarded and completed acoustical treatment of Astrodome for Rep. Nat. Conv. 1992; recipient award Internat. Cellulose 1,000,000 sq. ft., 1995-96. Mem. Houston Air Conditioning Coun. (bd. dirs. 1982-83), Cellulose Insulation Contractors (chmn. Houston 1981-82), Houston Bus. Coun., 1987—, Insulation Contractors Assn. Greater Houston (pres. 1991—). Democrat. Jewish. Avocations: bridge, golf. Office: Payless Insulation 207 Reinerman St Houston TX 77007-7228

KORNEL, ESTHER, psychologist; b. Basel-Stadt, Switzerland, Dec. 16, 1928; came to U.S., 1958; d. Salomon and Perla (Muller) Muhlrad; m. Ludwig Kornel, May 27, 1952; children: Ezriel Edward, Amiel Mark. BA, Roosevelt U., 1971, MA, 1973; PsyD, Ill. Sch. Profl. Psychology, 1979. Fellow and diplomate Am. Bd. Med. Psychologists. Clin. psychologist Luth. Gen. Hosp., Park Ridge, Ill., 1973-74; unit coordinator Luth. Gen. Hosp., Park Ridge, 1974-82; pvt. practice psychologist Des Plaines, Ill., 1974—; clin. assoc. Dept. Psychiatry, Abraham Lincoln Sch. Medicine, U. Ill., 1974-82; cons. oncology, group leader oncology staff Luth. Gen. Hosp., 1975-82, coord. psychology tng., 1981-82; group leader mastectomy counseling project, Northwestern U. Cancer Ctr., Chgo., 1981-82; clin. tng. cons. Forest Inst. Profl. Psychology, Des Plaines, Ill., 1985-90. Mem. Amnesty Internat., N.Y.C., Women's Am. Orgn. for Rehab. through Tng., N.Y.C., Women's Internat. Zionist Orgn., N.Y.C., Common Cause, Washington. Recipient Experimental Family Therapist award Inst. Juv. Research State of Ill., 1984. Mem. Am. Psychol. Assn., Assn. for Advancement of Psychology, Am. Soc. Clin. and Exptl. Hypnosis (assoc.),. Democrat. Jewish. Office: Landings Profl Ctr 2604 E Dempster St Ste 409 Des Plaines IL 60016-5328

KORNFEIN, PEGGY ELLEN, social studies educator; b. Denver, June 17, 1949; d. Robert Stanley Goalstone and Jeanne Yvette (Levine) Hardie; m. William Kornfein, June 6, 1971; children: Kimberly, Amanda. BS in Edn., U. Mo., 1971; postgrad., Webster U., 1980-81, Maryville U., St. Louis, 1994—. Cert. gifted edn. tchr., Mo. Tchrs. asst. Hazelwood (Mo.) Sch. Dist., 1972-74; tchr. social studies Hazelwood Jr. H.S., Florissant, Mo., 1974—; mem. Hazelwood social studies curriculum com., Florissant, 1982, 85, 94; mem. Hazelwood criterion referenced test com., Florissant, 1985; mem. Mo. Coun. SS Membership Com., 1979; mem. Hazelwood Performance Goals Com., Florissant, 1993; sponsor Nat. Jr. Honors Soc., Hazelwood Jr. H.S., Florissant, 1985-91; sponsor, coach Odessey of the Mind, Hazelwood Jr. H.S., Florissant, 1992—; officer Families Through Adoption, St. Louis, 1985-89; SAIL coord. Hazelwood Sch. Dist. Mem. Mo. State Tchrs. Assn., Nat. Coun. Social Studies, Tchrs. Applying Whole Lang., Mo. Mid. Sch. Assn., Gifted Assn. Mo., Mo. Coun. Social Studies. Home: 835 Weatherwood Dr Ballwin MO 63021-7128 Office: Hazelwood Jr HS 1605 Shackelford Rd Florissant MO 63031-3530

KORNIEWICZ, DENISE M., nursing educator; b. Detroit, Dec. 21, 1951; d. Edward John and Roseline Marie (Luczak) K. BS, Madonna Univ., 1974; MS in Nursing, Tex. Woman's U., 1977; DNSc in Nursing, Cath. U. of Am., 1986; postdoctoral, Johns Hopkins U., 1989. RN, Mich., Md., D.C. Dir. nurse practitioner program East Carolina U., Greenville, N.C., 1978-82; rsch. assoc. Cath. U. of Am., Washington, 1984-87; postdoctoral fellowship Johns Hopkins U., Balt., 1987-89, dir. acute care program, 1989-92; assoc. dean for acad. devel. Georgetown U., Washington, 1992—; adv. bd. Ansell Cares, Sydney, Australia, 1993—, Regent Hosp. Products, Greenville, 1992—; chair, cons. Johns Hopkins U., Balt., 1993-94. Author: Pocket Guide to Infection Control, 1995; contbr. articles to profl. jours. Vol. probation officer, Washington, 1991. Capt. U.S. Army, 1973-77. Fellow Am. Acad. in Nursing; mem. So. Coun. on Colls. and Edn. (mentor 1992-94, Cert. 1994), Madonna U. Alumni (Plaque 1992), Am. Nurse Assn. Coun. of Nurse Rsch., Sigma Xi. Democrat. Roman Catholic. Home: 1569 Redhaven Dr Severn MD 21144 Office: Georgetown Univ Saint Mary's Hall 160 3700 Reservoir Rd NW Washington DC 20037

KOROW, ELINORE MARIA, artist, educator; b. Akron, Ohio, July 31, 1934; d. Alexander and Elizabeth Helen (Doszpoly) Vigh; m. John Henry Korow, Sept. 28, 1957 (div. Oct. 1980); children: Christopher, David, Daniel; m. Harry Edward Bieber, Aug. 1, 1982 (dec. May 1994). Student, Siena Heights Women's Coll., 1952-53; four yr. diploma, Cleve. Inst. Art, 1957; diploma, Sawyer Coll. Bus., 1976. Staff artist Am. Greetings Corp., Cleve., 1957-58, designer, 1970-73; owner Elinore Korow: Portraits, Shaker Heights, Ohio, 1973-94, Akron, 1994—; painting instr. Cuyahoga C.C., Cleve., 1979—, chmn. sr. excellence in art exhbn., 1985-96; painting instr. U. Akron, 1995—. Represented in permanent collections Blue Cross/Blue Shield of N.E. Ohio, Am. Greetings Corp.; one woman-shows include Akron (Ohio) Woman's City Club, 1996, Cuyahoga Valley Art Ctr., Cuyahoga Falls, Ohio,

1995, others; group shows include Ohio Regional Painting Exhbn., 1993, Beck Ctr. for the Cultural Arts, Lakewood, Ohio, 1993, 17th Ann. Russell Art Exhibit, Novelty, Ohio, 1992, others. Recipient 2d place 17th Annual Russell Show, Novelty, Ohio, 1992, first place 17th Annual Russell Show, Novelty, 1993, third place Valley Art Ctr., Cuyahoga Falls, Ohio, 1994. Mem. Am. Soc. Portrait Artists (assoc.), Am. Pastel Soc., Nat. League Am. Pen Women, Women's Art Club Cleve. (past pres. 1970-71), Ohio Watercolor Soc. (charter), Akron Soc. Artists (signature), Women's Network, Boardroom Group. Home: 923 Mayfair Rd Akron OH 44303

KORSGAARD, CHRISTINE MARION, philosophy educator; b. Chgo., Apr. 9, 1952; d. Albert and Marion Hangaard (Kortbek) K.; m. Timothy David Gould, June 1980 (div. Sept. 1984). BA, U. Ill., 1974; PhD, Harvard U., 1981. Instr. Yale U., New Haven, 1979-80; asst. prof. U. Calif., Santa Barbara, 1980-83; from asst. prof. to prof. U. Chgo., 1983-91; prof. Harvard U., Cambridge, Mass., 1991—; vis. assoc. prof. Berkeley, 1989, UCLA, 1990; Tanner lectr. human values, 1992. Author: The Sources of Normativity, 1996, Creating the Kingdom of Ends, 1996; contbr. chpts. to books, articles to profl. jours. Whiting fellow, 1978-79. Mem. Am. Philos. Assn., N.Am. Kant Soc., Hume Soc., Am. Soc. for Polit. and Legal Philosophy.

KORSHAK, YVONNE, art historian; b. Chgo., May 30, 1936; d. Donald Korshak and Irma B. Jaffe; m. Robert J. Ruben; 1 child, Karin. BA cum laude, Radcliffe Coll., Cambridge, Mass., 1958; MA, U. Calif. Berkeley, 1966; PhD, U. Calif., 1973. Asst. prof. U. Md., College Park, 1972-74, Fordham U., N.Y.C., 1974-75; from asst. prof. to prof. Adelphi U., Garden City, N.Y., 1975—, chairperson Dept. Art and Art History, 1978-81, dir. honors program, dir. mus. studies, 1979—; project dir. seminar on the modern condition NEH, 1990. Author: Frontal Faces in Attic Vase Painting, 1987, co-editor: Selections from Permanent Collection, 1983. Recipient Pres.'s award for excellence in teaching, 1990. Mem. Coll. Art Assn. Am., Archaeological Inst. Am., Long Island Art Historians Assn., American Soc. for Eighteenth Century Studies, American Philological Assn. Office: Adelphi U Dept Art And Art History Garden City NY 11530

KORT, MICHELE FAYE, journalist; b. L.A., Jan. 30, 1950; d. Norman Elliott and Shirley Jean (Cohen) K. BA, UCLA, 1971, MBA, 1975. Freelance writer, 1977—; assoc. and acting editor Grantsmanship Center News, L.A., 1977-78; asst. editor Songwriter Mag., L.A., 1980-81; sr. writer UCLA Mag. UCLA, 1990-94; sr. editor Living Fit and Fit Pregnancy mags. Weider Publs., Woodland Hills, Calif., 1994—. Mentor The Fulfillment Fund, L.A., 1993—. Recipient L.A. Press Club Journalism awards, L.A. Press Club, 1994, Miller Lite Women's Sports Journalism award Women's Sports Found., N.Y., 1993, Case Gold medal for Best Article of the Yr., Coun. for Advancment of Support of Edn., 1991, Deems Taylor award for Music Journalism, ASCAP, 1980. Democrat. Jewish.

KORTH, CHARLOTTE BROOKS, furniture and interior design firm executive; b. Milw.; d. Lewis C. and Marguerite Peil Brooks; m. Robert Lee Williams, Jr., Oct. 25, 1944 (dec.); children: Patricia Williams, Melissa Williams O'Rourke, Brooks Williams; m. Fred Korth, Aug. 23, 1980. Student, U. Wis., 1941. Owner Charlotte's Inc., El Paso, Tex., 1951—, chmn., CEO, 1979—; pres. Paso del Norte Design, Inc., El Paso, 1978-81, 83—; mem. adv. com. for interior design program El Paso C.C., 1981—; mem. adv. bd. Southwest Design Inst., 1982—; ptnr. Wilko Partnership, 1981—; mem. adv. bd. Mountain Bell Telephone Co., 1976-79; mem. Sch. Architecture Found. Adv. Coun. U. Tex. Austin, 1985-91. Charter mem. Com. of 200, 1982—, Nat. Mus. Women in the Arts, 1985—; mem. Renaissance 400, El Paso, El Paso Women's Symphony Guild, El Paso Mus. Art. Recipient of Silver plaque Gifts and Decorative Accessories Mag., 1978; named Woman of Yr. by El Paso Am. Bus. Women's Assn., 1978, Outstanding Woman of Yr. by Women's Polit. Caucus, 1979. Mem. Am. Soc. Interior Designers (bd. dirs. Tex. chpt. 1977-82), El Paso Women's C. of C. (hon.), El Paso C. of C. (dir. 1976-82), Coronado Country Club (El Paso), Internat. Club (El Paso), Santa Teresa Country Club (N.Mex.). Avocations: travel, antiques, collectibles. Home: 6041 Torrey Pines Dr El Paso TX 79912-2029 also: Apt 101 4200 Massachusetts Ave NW Washington DC 20016-4753 Office: Charlotte's Inc 5411 N Mesa St El Paso TX 79912-5438

KORTH, PENNE PERCY, ambassador; b. Hattiesburg, Miss., Nov. 3, 1942; m. Fritz-Alan Korth, Dec. 15, 1965; children: Fritz Jr., Maria, James. Sr. Washington assoc., client liaison and rep. trust and estate div. Sotheby's, 1986-89; amb. to Mauritius, Port Louis, 1989-92; pres., CEO Firestone and Korth Ltd., Washington, 1993—; bd. dirs. Chevy Chase Bank. Bd. dirs. Meridian Internat. Ctr., Coun. of Am. ambs., Van Cliburn Found., Hillwood Mus.; co-chmn. Am. Bicentennial Presdl. Inauguration, 1988-89. Mem. Sulgrave Club, Chevy Chase Club. Office: Firestone and Korth Ltd 1035 30th St NW Washington DC 20007

KORY, MARIANNE GREENE, lawyer; b. N.Y.C.; d. Hyman Louis and Belle (Rome) Greene; children: Erich Marcel, Lisa. BA, CCNY; JD, N.Y. Law Sch., 1976; LLM, U. Wash., 1986. Bar: Ohio 1977, D.C. 1979, N.Y. 1983, Vt. 1994, U.S. Dist. Ct. (so. and ea. dists.) N.Y. 1983, U.S. Dist. Ct. Vt. 1994. Hearing examiner Ohio Bd. Employee Compensation, Columbus, 1977; atty. advisor Office Hearings and Appeals, Social Security Adminstrn., Cin. and N.Y.C., 1977-78; gen. atty. labor Office of Solicitor, U.S. Dept. of Labor, N.Y.C., 1978-82; sole practice, N.Y.C., 1983-89, Seattle, 1989-91, Burlington, Vt., 1994—. Founder Cin. chpt. Amnesty Internat., 1977. Alvin Johnson fellow; grad. faculty New Sch. for Social Rsch. Mem. NOW, Nat. Orgn. Social Security Claimants' Reps., Nat. Abortion Rights Action League, Vt. Bar Assn., Chittenden County Women's Bar Assn., Common Cause Vt. (bd. dirs.), Vt. Trial Lawyers Assn., Phi Beta Kappa. Office: 3 Northshore Dr Burlington VT 05401-1248

KORZELIUS, LINDA DIANE, church lay worker, financial specialist, artist; b. Teaneck, N.J., June 8, 1955; d. Joseph Robertson and Beatrice (Hoyt) K. BFA, Ramapo Coll. N.J., 1977. Mem. parish coun. and pastor's adv. coun. St. Joseph's Ch., Oradell, New Milford, N.J., 1985—; eucharistic min., mem. various coms. St. Joseph's Ch., Oradell/New Milford, N.J., 1985—; catechist St. Joseph's Ch., Oradell/New Milford, 1985-87, St. Theresa Ch., Cresskill, N.J., 1987—; chairperson spiritual life com. St. Joseph Ch., Oradell, New Milford, 1991—; asst. to treas. Yegen Assocs., Paramus, N.J., 1991; accounts receivable dept. clk. Mokrynski & Assocs., Hackensack, N.J., 1993-95; accts. receivable clk. Sportcraft, Ltd., 1995—; instr. Christian Founds. for Ministry Program Archdiocese of Newark, 1993. Exhibiting artist, 1973—. Mem. Ladies of Knights Bowling League (pres. Northvale, N.J. club 1991—). Home: 153 River Rd New Milford NJ 07646-1703

KOS, STACEY ANN, pediatric nurse; b. Dearborn, Mich., Mar. 24, 1967; d. Robert S. and Diane H. (Gdowski) K. BSN, Madonna U., 1989. Cert. pediatric nurse; RN, Mich. Nursing asst. Children's Hosp. Mich., Detroit, 1988-89, staff nurse, preceptor, 1989—. Camp counselor, camp nurse Mich. Pulmonary Disease Camp, Inc., 1991-96. Mem. Assn. of the Care of Children's Health, Soc. Pediatric Nurses. Republican. Roman Catholic. Home: 6561 N Lafayette Dearborn Heights MI 48127 Office: Childrens Hosp Mich 3901 Beaubien St Detroit MI 48201-2119

KOS/DEMPSEY, SUSAN MICHAELINA, registered nurse, visual artist; b. N.Y.C., July 8, 1951; d. Walter Bohdon and Evelyn Theresa (Yakiemchuk) Kosmij; m. John Robert Dempsey, June 1, 1975; children: John Joseph, Nicholas Walter, Kristin Suzanne. AAS, Fashion Inst. Tech., N.Y.C., 1971; diploma, Queens Hosp. Ctr. Sch. Nursing, N.Y.C., 1975; BS Liberal Studies (Art, Psychology), SUNY, Albany, 1992. Registered profl. nurse, 1975. Staff nurse ICU, CCU Crouse Irving Hosp., Syracuse, N.Y., 1975-76; charge staff nurse ICU Cortland (N.Y.) Meml. Hosp., 1976-79; pediatrics nurse Cortland (N.Y.) Meml. Hosp., Cortland, N.Y., 1986-91; sch. nurse Hartnett Elem. Sch., Truxton, N.Y., 1991—. One woman show includes Diversities, for Cortland (N.Y.) State U., 1992; prin. works include Our Lady of Lourdes ceiling panels for Cancer Treatment Rm., Binghaamton, N.Y., 1994, Long Island U. C. W. Post Campus slides, 1993, Truxton paintinting, 1995; Designer Showroom Exhbn., Salt Lake City, group art shows in Conn., N.C. and N.Y.C.; also private and pub. collections. Democrat. Roman Catholic. Home: 12 Parker Ave Cortland NY 13045

KOSHLAND, CATHERINE PRESTON, mechanical engineer, educator; b. Phila., May 11, 1950; d. Edmond III and Elizabeth Miriam (Johnston) Preston; m. James Marcus Koshland, May 17, 1975; children: Sarah, Margrethe, Jacob. Student, Smith Coll., Northampton, Mass., 1968-70; BA in Fine Arts, Haverford (Pa.) Coll., 1972; MS in Mech. Engring., Stanford U., Palo Alto, Calif., 1978, PhD in Mech. Engring., 1985. Mgmt. asst. Energy Rsch. and Devel. Adminstrn., Washington, 1974-75; tech. editor Stanford U., Palo Alto, 1977-78, rsch. asst., 1980-85; asst. prof. U. Calif., Berkeley, 1985—, assoc. prof., 1992—, Wood-Calvert chair in Engring., 1995—; mem. Bay Area Air Quality Mgmt. Dist. Adv. Coun., San Francisco, 1988-94, chair, 1991-92; bd. mgrs. Haverford (Pa.) Coll., 1994—. Co-editor: Incineration of Hazardous Waste 1 and 2, 1992, 94; contbr. over 40 articles to profl. jours. Mem. site coun. Hillview Mid. Sch., Menlo Park, Calif., 1989-91; mem. site coun. Menlo-Atherton (Calif.) H.S., 1993-95. Recipient base rsch. award Nat. Inst. Environ. Health Sci., 1988—. Mem. Combustion Inst. (dir. 1994—, exec. bd. Western states sect. 1988—), Am. Chem. Soc. Office: U Calif 140 Warren Hall Berkeley CA 94720

KOSHLAND, MARIAN ELLIOTT, immunologist, educator; b. New Haven, Oct. 25, 1921; d. Waller Watkins and Margaret Ann (Smith) Elliott; m. Daniel Edward Koshland, Jr., May 25, 1945; children: Ellen R., Phyllis A., James M., Gail F., Douglas E. B.A., Vassar Coll., 1942, M.S., 1943; Ph.D., U. Chgo., 1949. Research asst. Manhattan Dist. Atomic Bomb Project, 1945-46; fellow dept. bacteriology Harvard Med. Sch., 1949-51; asso. bacteriologist biology dept. Brookhaven Nat. Lab., 1952-62, bacteriologist, 1963-65; assoc. research immunologist virus lab. U. Calif., Berkeley, 1965-69, lectr. dept. molecular biology, 1966-70, prof. dept. microbiology and immunology, 1970-89, chmn. dept., 1982-89, prof. dept. molecular and cell biology, 1989—; mem. Nat. Sci. Bd., 1976-82; mem. adv. com. to dir. NIH, 1972-75; mem. coun. Nat. Inst. Allergy and Infectious Diseases, NIH, 1991-95. Contbr. articles to profl. jours. Mem. NAS (coun. 1985-88), Nat. Acad. Arts and Scis. (coun. 1994—), Am. Assn. Immunologists (pres. 1982-83), Am. Soc. Biol. Chemists. Home: 3991 Happy Valley Rd Lafayette CA 94549-2423 Office: U Calif Dept Molecular and Cell Biology 439 LSA Berkeley CA 94720

KOSINSKY, BARBARA TIMM, librarian; b. St. Louis, July 4, 1942; d. Paul E. and Virginia L. (Borcherding) T.; m. John P. Kosinsky, July 25, 1964; children: James Alan, Bethany Anne. BS in Edn., Concordia Coll., River Forest, Ill., 1964; BA in Computer Sci., North Cen. Coll., Naperville, Ill., 1986; MLS, SUNY, Buffalo, 1972. Cert. tchr., Ill., N.Y. Tchr. St. Paul Luth. Sch., North Tonawanda, N.Y., 1964-67; libr. Trinity Luth. Sch., West Seneca, N.Y., 1971-80, North Cen. Coll., Naperville, 1981-89; regional mktg. rep. Online Computer Libr. Ctr., Dublin, Ohio, 1990—; free-lance writer West Seneca and Naperville, 1978—. Contbr. articles to religious mags. and general interest publs. Mem. ALA, Am. Soc. Info. Sci., Nat. Writers Club, Wis. Libr. Assn. Home: 225 Carlin Ct Hartland WI 53029-1805 Office: PO Box 138 Hartland WI 53029-0138

KOSKE, CHARLOTTE MAE, real estate broker; b. Longview, Tex., Dec. 23, 1937; d. Charles William and Margaret Charlottie (Cassady) Snyder; m. Keith Thorsen Koske, June 20, 1965 (dec. Feb. 1989); 1 child, Charles Franz. BS, Okla. State U., 1963. Broker, owner Charlotte M. Koske, Realtor, Canon City, Colo., 1983—; ins. saleswoman, Colo., 1985—. Active The Guild, Children's Disbetic Coun., Denver. Mem. AAUW, NAFE, Colo. Assn. Realtors (ethics panel 1996—), Women's Coun. Realtors, Royal Gorge Assn. Realtors, Canon City C. of C., Alpha Delta Pi. Democrat. Lutheran. Home: 763 Tyrolean Way Canon City CO 81212 Office: 107 S 9th St Ste D Canon City CO 81212

KOSKELLA, LUCRETIA C., real estate broker, appraiser; b. Newburgh, N.Y., Aug. 29, 1928; d. Vincent George and Josephine Anita (Gross) Canadé; m. John Archie Koskella, June 13, 1954 (div. May 1961); 1 child, Judith Ann. Grad. h.s., Newburgh. Lic. real estate, N.Y., lic. real estate broker, N.Y., lic. real estate appraiser, N.Y. Real estate salesperson, 1961-71, real estate broker, 1971—; chair adv. bd. real estate appraisal L.K.R.B., Newburgh, 1971—; active C.L.E.A.N. Chadwick Lake, Newburgh, 1980-96. Charter mem., organizer Scenic Hudson, Newburgh, 1980-96; Orange County Rep. committeewoman Rep. Party, 1980-92; campaign mgr., chmn., coord. local, state, and nat. campaigns, N.Y., 1980-96; publicist senate campaigns, Orange County and Newburgh, 1980-96; mem. exec. bd., speechwriter, spkr. Orange County Rep. Com., 1992-94; vol. Am. Cancer Soc., Heart Assn., March of Dimes, PTA. Mem. NRA, NOW, Nat. Mus. Women in Arts, N.Y. State Sheriffs Assn. (bus. mem.). Home and Office: 19 Pat Rd Newburgh NY 12550

KOSLOW, SALLY, editor-in-chief. Editor-in-chief McCall's mag., N.Y.C., 1994—. Office: McCalls 110 5th Ave New York NY 10011-5601*

KOSMIN, LINDA J., librarian; b. Phila., Nov. 7, 1939; d. Edward I. and Ruth (Blumfield) K.; m. Jonathan P. Myerson, Aug. 7, 1960 (div.). BA, U. Pa., 1961; MSLS, Drexel U., 1966, MS in Environ. Sci., 1974. Chemistry instr. U. Md., College Park, 1961-63; libr. sci. instr., engring. libr. Drexel U., Phila., 1963-78; dep. dir. biomed. libr. U. Pa., Phila., 1979-80; sect. supervisor applied physics lab. The Johns Hopkins U., Laurel, Md., 1980-94; sec. mgr. libr./archives/records NASA Jet Propulsion Lab., Pasadena, Calif., 1994—. Nat. sec. Friends of Danilo Dolci, Inc., Phila., 1971-72, bd. dirs., Short Hills, N.J., 1972-73. Mem. IEEE (PCS adminstrv. comm. 1995-96), Spl. Librs. Assn. (v.p., pres.-elect Phila. chpt. 968-69). Home: 135 E Holly St Apt 301 Pasadena CA 91103 Office: NASA Jet Propulsion Lab Calif Inst Tech MS111-113 4800 Oak Grove Dr Pasadena CA 91109

KOSMOSKI, MARY LOU TERESA, special education educator; b. Perth Amboy, N.J., Mar. 14, 1962; d. Benjamin Walter and Frances Dolores Kosmoski. BA, Georgian Ct. Coll., Lakewood, N.J., 1984, MEd, 1995. Cert. elem. tchr., N.J. Tchr. 2d grade Holy Spirit Sch., Perth Amboy, N.J., 1984-85; tchr. 3d grade Sacred Heart Sch., South Amboy, N.J., 1985-90; tchr. 1st grade St. Mary Sch., South Amboy, N.J., 1990-92; substitute tchr. South Amboy Elem. Sch., 1993, tchr. 1st and 4th grades resource rm., 1994—; tchr. 6th thru 8th grades resource rm. South Amboy Mid. Sch., 1993-94; isntr. drawing and watercolor Matawan (N.J.) Student Enrichment Program, 1989—; presenter workshops. Contbr. article to profl. jour. Georgian Ct. Coll. dean's scholar, 1982-84. Mem. ASCD, Nat. Assn. Mediation in Edn., Nat. Coun. Tchrs. English, N.J. Edn. Assn., N.J. Maths. Coalition, Delta Tau Kappa (Gamma Kappa chpt.). Roman Catholic. Home: 12 Kearney Ave South Amboy NJ 08879 Office: South Amboy Elem Sch John St South Amboy NJ 08879

KOSS, ROSABEL STEINHAUER, retired education educator; b. Phila., Sept. 3, 1913; d. Arthur H. and Agnes (Temple) Steinhauer; m. Franklyn C. Koss, July 6, 1947 (dec. 1987); children: C. Lynn Knauff, Susan Kreiner, Carolyn Ruef, Rosalind Diehl. BS, Trenton State Coll., 1935; MA, Teachers Coll., N.Y.C., 1942; DEd, Columbia U., 1964. Cert. health edn. specialist, 1989. Supr. health and phys. edn. Flemington (N.J.) Pub. Schs., 1935-37; tchr. health and phys. edn. Ridgewood (N.J.) High Sch., 1937-40, Passaic Valley Regional High Sch., Little Falls, N.J., 1940-48; asst. prof. Montclair State Coll., Upper Montclair, N.J., 1958-61, Upsala Coll., East Ornge, N.J., 1964-71; assoc. to full prof. Ramapo Coll of N.J., Mahwah, N.J., 1971-84; dir. tchr. edn. Ramapo Coll of N.J., Mahwah, 1974-79, prof. emeritus, 1985; adj. prof. Stockton State Coll., Pomona, N.J., 1985-95; asst. sport attachee Royal Swedish Embassy, N.Y.C., 1964-74. Author: (with others) Dance for Older Adults, 1988, Mature Stuff. Physical Activity for Older Adults, 1989; contbr. articles profl. jours. Mem. Little Falls (N.J.) Bd. Edn., 1954-63; trustee, treas. Bergen County (N.J.) Ret. Sr. Vol. Program, 1979-84; mem. recreation adv. com. Stone Harbor Bd. Health, v.p., 1995; mem. Cape May County Freeholders Adv. Commn. on Women, 1986—, Cape May County Human Svcs. Adv. Coun., 1989—; vestrywoman St. Mary's Episcopal Ch., Stone Harbor; mem. N.J. Comm. on Aging, 1991, 94; del. White House Conf. Aging, 1995. Recipient Work Study grants to Sweden, The Royal Swedish Consulate, N.Y.C., 1968, 70, 72, Athletic Alumni Women's award Trenton State Coll., 1976, State of N.J. Senate and Gen. Assembly citation, 1994; named to Trenton State Coll. Alumni Athletic Hall of Fame, 1987, Nat. Women's Wall of Fame, 1994, Cape Women's Resource Honor award, 1994, Disting. Leadership award N.J. AHPERD; named Gerontologist of Yr., Soc. on Aging N.J., 1993; Rosabel Koss ann. award in her honor AAHPERD. Mem. AAHPERD (life mem., profl. achievement award, N.J., 1973, honor award fellow 1979, merit award Ea. Dist. 1980, coun. on aging and adult devel., disting. leadership award, 1996), Gerontol. Soc. N.J. (parliamentatian 1988-89), AAUW, N.J. AHPERD, Nat. Coun. on the Aging, Assn. Gerontology in Higher Edn., Internat. Soc. of Comparative Phys. Edn. and Sport, Cape May County LWV, Garden Club, Wetlands Inst. (docent), Stone Harbor Women's Civic Club. Home: 150 91st St Stone Harbor NJ 08247-2016

KOSSAETH, TAMMY GALE, intensive care nurse; b. San Antonio, Feb. 18, 1969; d. Kenneth Roland and Hermina Marie (Hilzfelder) K. BSN, U. Tex., San Antonio, 1991. RN, Tex.; cert. BLS instr.; cert. ACLS; cert. cardiac rehab. Staff nurse surg. ICU Audie L. Murphy VA Hosp., San Antonio, 1991—. Altar server St. Antony Claret, San Antonio, 1980—. Mem. ANA, Women's Internat. Bowling Congress (local league pres. and league sec. 1994-95, 95-96, 96—). Roman Catholic. Home: 12379 W Fm 471 # 3 San Antonio TX 78253-4808

KOT, MARTA VIOLETTE, artist, art educator; b. Hartford, Conn., Nov. 27, 1963; d. Edward Anthony and Maria (Cermak) Kot. Fulbright student, Royal U. of Malta, 1985; BA in Graphic Design/Art, Ctrl Conn. State U., 1985; pvt. art studies Studio Antoine Camilleri, Valletta, Malta, 1985; pvt. art studies, Studio Adam Wsiolkowski, Cracow, Poland, 1988; studied with Zbylut Grzywacz, Cracow, 1988; MS in Adminstrn., Supervision and Curriculum Devel., Ctrl Conn. State U., 1988; cert. in Polish Art History, Jagiellonian U., Cracow, Poland, 1988; MA in Studio Art and Environ. Art, NYU, 1990; student, Acad. de la Grande Chaumiere, Paris, 1990-93; cert. French lang. and Civilization, U. Paris - Sorbonne, 1992; cert. Polish lang., Cath. U. of Lublin, Poland, 1993; postgrad., Tchrs. Coll., Columbia U., 1994—. Art cons. gifted and talented programs Consol. Sch. Dist. of City of New Britain, Conn., 1987-88. One-person shows include 80 Washington Sq. East Galleries, N.Y.C., 1990, Conn. Ho. of Reps., Hartford, 1995, City Hall, New Britain, Conn., 1996, Macy Gallery, N.Y.C., 1996, Cen. Conn. State U. Elihu Burritt Libr., 1996; exhibited in group shows at Slocumb Gallery, Tenn., 1985, Ctrl. Conn. State U., New Britain, 1982, 84-88, Macy Art Gallery, N.Y.C., 1994-96, Presdl. Inauguration, Tchrs. Coll., Columbia U., 1994, Nat. Arts Club, N.Y.C., 1995, Pumphouse Gallery, Hartford, 1995, Student Lounge Tchrs. Coll., Columbia U., 1996, John Jay Gallery, N.Y.C., 1996, others. Corp. mem. Boys and Girls Club, New Britain; bd. dirs. Camp Schade Program Affiliated United Way, New Britain. Recipient award for graphic design Advt. Club Greater Hartford, 1984, mural project (with Dave Burke) Incarnation Ctr. for Children with AIDS Tamarand Found., N.Y.C., 1995. Mem. ASCD, AAUW, Nat. Art Edn. Assn. Home: PO Box 2697 165 Monroe St New Britain CT 06050-2697

KOTCHER, SHIRLEY J. W., lawyer; m. Harry A. Kotcher; children: Leslie Susan, Dana Anne. BA, NYU; JD, Columbia U. Bar: N.Y. In-house counsel Booth Meml. Med. Ctr., Flushing, N.Y., 1975-83, gen. counsel, 1983-91; v.p., gen. counsel The N.Y. Hosp. Med. Ctr. Queens, 1991—; advisor health care Borough Pres. Queens, N.Y., 1978. Author: Hidden Gold and Pitfalls in New Tax Law, 1970. Mem. ABA (health law forum com.), Nat. Health Lawyers Assn., Am. Acad. Hosp. Attys., Am. Soc. Law and Medicine, Am. Soc. Health Care Risk Mgmt., Assn. for Hosp. Risk Mgmt. N.Y., Greater N.Y. Hosp. Assn. (legal adv. com. 1976—). Office: NY Hosp Med Ctr of Queens Flushing NY 11355

KOTEFF, ELLEN, periodical editor; b. Harvey, Ill.; d. Walter Peter and Florence (Walz) K. BS in Journalism, U.. Fla., 1977. Editor Palm Beach (Fla.) Daily News, 1977-90; met. editor Daily Record, Parsippany, N.J., 1990-92; exec. editor Nation's Restaurant News, N.Y.C., 1992—. Office: Nations Restaurant News 425 Park Ave New York NY 10022-3506

KOTHERA, LYNNE MAXINE, clinical psychologist; b. Cleve., Dec. 18, 1938; d. Leonard Frank and Lillian (Shackleton) K.; m. Richard Litwin, Oct. 24, 1965 (dec.). BA with hons., Denison U., Granville, Ohio, 1960; MA, NYU, 1983; PhD, L.I. U., Bklyn., 1989; postgrad. psychotherapy/psychoanalysis, NYU, 1992—. Dancer Martha Graham Dance Co., N.Y.C., 1961-62, Carmen DeLavallade Dance Co., N.Y.C., 1965-68, Glen Tetley Dance Co., N.Y.C., 1965-69; prin. dancer John Butler's, N.Y.C., 1971; artist-in-residence Boston High Schs. - Title III, 1969-71, Hobart-Smith Coll./Denison U., 1973; auditor N.Y. State Council of the Arts, N.Y.C., 1974-78; predoctoral fellow clin. psychology Yale-New Haven Hosp., 1987-88; postdoctoral fellow neuropsychology Inst. of Living, Hartford, Conn., 1989-91; with dept. rehab. medicine Mt. Sinai Med. Ctr., N.Y.C., 1991—, co-dir. tng. in-patient, 1995—. Mem. APA (divsn. 39, 40, 42 and 49), Internat. Neuropsychol. Soc. Democrat. Home: 23 E 11th St New York NY 10003-4450 Office: Mt Sinai Med Ctr Rehab Med KCC-365-G PO Box 1674 1 Gustave Levy Pl New York NY 10029

KOTLER, HELEN ANN, psychotherapist, consultant; b. Manchester, Conn., Aug. 16, 1935; d. William Nicholas and Rose Ellen (Tulin) Kronick; m. Paul Jay Gartzman, June 3, 1956 (div. 1970); children: Jeff Gartzman, Debra Gartzman; m. Richard Michael Kotler. Attended, Boston U., 1953-56; BS in Edn., So. Conn. State U., 1973, MS in Counseling, 1975; PhD in Psychology, Heed U., 1986. Cert. drug counselor. Tchr. Pomperang Elem. Sch., Southbury, Conn., 1973-84; pvt. practice Waterbury, 1975—; psychiat. technician Waterbury (Conn.) Hosp., 1980-86; program dir., clin. dir. Conn. Counseling Ctrs., Waterbury, 1984-89; counselor Waterbury Sch. Sys., 1988-89; spkr. Naugatuck Valley Tech. Sch., Waterbury, 1996; cons. Elmcrest Hosp., Cromwell, Conn., 1996; lectr. in field. Sec. Am. Heart Assn., Waterbury, 1967-84; pres. Women's Health Alliance, Waterbury, 1990-95; pres., v.p. Temple Israel Sisterhood, 1966-69; active Cancer Fund, Waterbury, 1967-80, Cultural Events, Middlebury, 1970-73. Mem. ACA, Am. Mental Health Counselors Assn., Conn. Counseling Assn., Phi Delta Kappa (sec. 1982-84). Home: 205 Lovely St Farmington CT 06085 Office: 134 Grandview Ave Waterbury CT 06708

KOTT, BEVERLY PARAT, financial counselor; b. Chgo., Sept. 7, 1936; d. Louis Joseph and Marie Elizabeth (Katich) Parat; m. Russell Kott; children: Vinson V., Donna M., James L., Michael A. Grad., Life Underwritr Tng. Coun., Washington, 1977. Mem. mgmt. ea. region Met. Life Ins. Co., Balt., 1977; ins. broker, 1979-85; pres. Kott & Assocs. Fin. Counseling Svc., Joppa, Md., 1985—; fin. counselor coop. extension svc. U. Md., Bel Air, 1987—, mem. Harford extension adv. coun., 1988-93; dir. Prison Ministry, 1983—; lay minister Roman Catholic Ch., 1995—. Commr. Harford County Commn. for Women, Bel Air, 1981-87; v.p. Joppa Friends of the Libr., 1988—; mem. Rumsey Island Civic Assn., 1980—; dir. Joppatowne Civic Assn., Joppa, 1990—, Padre Rio Rosary Makers, 1993—, Postal Adv. Coun., 1992—. Named one of Most Beautiful People, Harford County, 1990. Mem. Hunt Valley Bus. and Profl. Woman's Club (charter), Aux. VFW (pres. 1988-90, legis., youth, publicity and cancer aid coms. 1989, 90), Mensa Internat. Roman Catholic. Home: 661 Towne Center Dr Joppa MD 21085-4439 Office: PO Box 349 Joppa MD 21085-0349

KOTUK, ANDREA MIKOTAJUK, public relations executive, writer; b. New Brunswick, N.J., Oct. 19, 1948; d. Michael and Julia Dorothy (Muka) Mikotajuk. BA, Douglass Coll., Rutgers U., 1970. Pub. relations asst. Wall St. Jour. Newspaper Fund, Princeton, N.J., 1970; editorial asst. Redbook mag., N.Y.C., 1970-71; asst. pub. relations dir. Children's Aid Soc., N.Y.C., 1971-75; assoc. pub. relations dir. Planned Parenthood, N.Y.C., 1975-80; pres. Andrea & Assocs., N.Y.C., 1980—. Writer publicist for non-profit agys.; contbg. editor Arts Mag., 1970-75. Office: Andrea & Assocs 112 E 23rd St New York NY 10010-4518

KOUBA, LISA MARCO, lawyer; b. Chgo., July 1, 1957; d. Edward Samuel and Phyllis Lavergne (Pincus) Marco; m. Kenneth Edward Kouba, Sept. 24, 1983. BA with honors, U. Ill., 1978; JD cum laude, Loyola U., Chgo., 1981. Bar: Ill. 1981, U.S. Dist. Ct. (no. dist.) Ill. 1981, U.S. Ct. Appeals (6th, 7th, 8th and 10th cirs.) 1982, U.S. Supreme Ct. 1985, U.S. Dist. Ct. (cen. dist.) 1991. Ptnr. Clausen, Miller, Gorman, Caffrey & Witous, P.C., Chgo., 1981-87, ptnr., 1987—. Editor Loyola Law Jour., 1981. Bd. dirs. Mordine & Co. Dance Troupe, 1988. Mem. Ill. Bar Assn., Chgo. Bar Assn. (chmn. young lawyers sect. on appellate law 1982-83), Appellate Lawyers Assn. (bd. dirs. 1986-88). Office: Clausen Miller PC 10 S La Salle St Chicago IL 60603-1002

KOUFFMAN, MIRIAM, psychotherapist; b. Chotin, Romania, Feb. 17, 1941; came to U.S., Sept. 12, 1962; d. Avrum and Riva (Nussenbaum) Wolkove; m. Marc L. Kouffman, Aug. 16, 1964 (div. Oct. 24, 1989); children: Avra, Paulette. BA in English Lit., Sir George Williams U., 1962; MA in Early Childhood, Hunter Coll., 1975; Cert. in Psychoanalytic Psychotherapy, New Hope Guild, N.Y.C., 1979; MSW, Adelphi U., 1983. Tchr. various pub. schs., Montreal, Can., 1957-58; actress N.Y.C., 1962—; tchr. early childhood Emanuel Nursery Sch., N.Y.C., 1964-74; adj. lectr. early childhood Cmty. Coll., Bklyn., 1974-75; psychotherapist, clinician New Hope Guild Ctr., N.Y.C., 1979-81; intake dir., clinician Insts. of Religion and Health, N.Y.C., 1983-84; pschotherapist N.Y.C., 1984—; faculty, supr. New Hope Guild Ctr., N.Y.C., 1990—; dir. day care on-site therapy program C.I.S. Counseling Ctr., N.Y.C., 1992-94. Author: (book) Myths and Madness. Mem. People for the Am. Way, Warsaw Gathering of Holocaust Survivors. Recipient Hebrew prize Sir George Williams U., 1962; recommended for English prize Concordia U. Fellow Nat. Orgn. Social Work, Soc. for Clin. Social Work Psychotherapists (edn. com.); mem. New Hope Grad. Soc. (steering com.), Am. Bd. Examiners in Clin. Social Work. Jewish. Home and Office: 320 E 25th St #8EE New York NY 10010

KOURIDES, IONE ANNE, endocrinologist, researcher, educator; b. N.Y.C., Sept. 1, 1942; d. Peter T. and Anne E. (Spetseris) K.; m. Charles G. Zaroulis, Nov. 30, 1974; children: Anna Larisa, Andrew, Christina, Peter. BA, Wellesley Coll., 1963; MD, Harvard U., 1967. Diplomate Am. Bd. Internal Medicine, Am. Bd. Endocrinology and Metabolism. Intern Jewish Hosp., Wash. U., St. Louis, 1967-68; resident Montefiore, Albert Einstein Med. Sch., Bronx, N.Y., 1968-69; fellow Beth Israel, Harvard U., Boston, 1970-72; assoc. prof. medicine Cornell U. Med. Coll., N.Y.C., 1981—; sr. assoc. med. dir. Pfizer Pharms., N.Y.C., 1990—. Mem. editorial bd. Endocrinology, Jour. Clin. Endocrinol Metabolism, also others; contbr. over 100 articles to sci. jours., chpts. to books. Mem. nat. campaign Harvard Med. Sch., Boston, 1986-92; nat. bd. dirs. Philoptochos Soc. Greek Orthodox Archdiocese. Grantee NIH, 1979-84. Fellow ACP; mem. Am. Soc. Clin. Investigation, Am. Assn. Physicians, Am. Thyroid Assn. (coms.), Endocrine Soc. (coms.). Home: 1070 Park Ave New York NY 10128-1000 Office: Pfizer Pharms 235 E 42nd St New York NY 10017-5703

KOURLIS, REBECCA LOVE, judge; b. Colorado Springs, Colo., Nov. 11, 1952; d. John Arthur and Ann (Daniels) Love; m. Thomas Aristithis Kourlis, Aug. 19, 1978; children: Stacy Ann, Katherine Love. BA with distinction in English, Stanford U., 1973, JD, 1976. Bar: Colo. 1976, D.C. 1979, U.S. Dist. Ct. Colo. 1976, U.S. Ct. Appeals (10th cir.) 1976, Colo. Supreme Ct., U.S. Ct. Appeals (D.C. cir.), U.S. Claims Ct., U.S. Supreme Ct. Assoc. Davis, Graham & Stubbs, Denver, 1976-78; sole practice, Craig, Colo., 1978-87; assoc. Gibson, Dunn & Crutcher, Denver, part time 1981-87; judge 14th Jud. Dist. Ct., 1987-94; arbiter Jud. Arbiter Group, Inc., 1994-95; justice Colo. Supreme Ct., 1995—; water judge Divsn. 6, 1987-94; lectr. to profl. groups. Contbr. articles to profl. jours. Chmn. Moffat County Arts and Humanities, Craig, 1979; mem. Colo. Commn. on Higher Edn., Denver, 1980-81; mem. adv. bd. Colo. Divsn. Youth Svcs., 1988-91; mem. com. adminstrv. restructure Colo. Supreme Ct., 1992, mem. com. civil jury instructions, 1990-95, standing com. gender & justice, 1994—; mem. state ct. adminstr. selection com., 1992; mem. long range planning com. Moffat County Sch., 1990; bd. visitors Stanford U., 1989-94; mem. Colo. Commn. Higher Edn., 1980-81. Fellow Am. Bar Found., Colo. Bar Found.; mem. Rocky Mountain Mineral Found., Colo. Bar Assn. (bd. govs. 1983-85, mineral law sect. bd. dirs. 1985, sr. v.p. 1987-88), Dist. Ct. Judges' Assn. (pres. 1993-94), N.W. Colo. Bar Assn. (Cmty. Svc. award 1993-94), Denver Bar Assn. Republican. Greek Orthodox. Home: 303 Sandrock Dr Craig CO 81625-2339 Office: State Jud Bldg 2 E 14th Ave Rm 415 Denver CO 80203

KOURY, AGNES LILLIAN, real estate property manager; b. Denver, Oct. 16, 1935; d. John Joseph and Lucy Maria (Plomteaux) K.; m. William L. May, July 21, 1958 (div. 1961); 1 child, Tia Leslie Koury. BSBA, U. Denver, 1958; protocol cert., Southeastern U., 1964; paralegal cert., Georgetown U., 1978; MA, Marymount U., 1991. Registered profl. realtor, Va. Com. sec. N.Mex. Ho. of Reps., Santa Fe, 1959; contracts sec. Atomic Energy Commn., Albuquerque, 1959-63; ptnr. legal sec. Sughrue, Rothwell, Washington, 1963-65; legal asst. McClure & Trotter, Washington, 1965-67; case worker U.S. Ho. of Reps., Washington, 1968; adminstrv., rsch. asst. Harvard U., Washington, 1969-73; asst. mgr. Koury's Real Estate, Sant Fe, 1974-85; owner, mgr. various realty properties, Santa Fe and Arlington, 1985—. Pres. Yorktown Condominium, Arlington, 1972-74, bd. dirs.; treas. Birches Homeowners Assn., Arlington, 1987-90; coord., vol. spkrs. bur. Hospice of No. Va., Arlington, 1993—, spkrs. bur., 1985—; bd. dirs. Arlington Symphony Assn., 1990—, chmn. music scholarship for no. Va. high sch. students, 1994—. Mem. Delta Sigma Epsilon, Phi Gamma Nu (Outstanding Mem. 1958). Roman Catholic. Home and Office: 4741 N 23rd St Arlington VA 22207

KOVACH, BARBARA ELLEN, management and psychology educator; b. Ann Arbor, Mich., Dec. 28, 1941; d. Harry Arnold and Margaret Mayne (Buell) Lusk; m. Craig Randall Duncan, Dec. 28, 1963 (div. 1973); children: Deborah Louise, Mark Randall; m. Randall Louis Kovach, May 2, 1981; 1 child, Jennifer Elizabeth. BA magna cum laude, Stanford U., 1963, MA, 1964; PhD, U. Md., 1973. Asst. prof. psychology U. Mich., Dearborn, 1973-77, assoc. prof., 1977-82, prof., 1982-84, chair Dept. Behavioral Scis., 1980-83; dean Univ. Coll. Rutgers U., New Brunswick, N.J., 1984-88, prof. mgmt. and psychology, 1984—, dir. leadership devel. program, 1988—; pres. Leadership Devel. Inst., Princeton, N.J., 1990—; cons. Rochester (N.Y.) Products-GM, Grand Rapids, Mich., 1982-87, Ford Motor Co., Dearborn, 1981-82, Mich. Bell Telephone, 1980-81, Rockwell Internat., Troy, Mich, 1993—, Johnson & Johnson, 1995—. Author: Sex Roles and Personal Awareness, 1978, 90, Power and Love, 1982, Organizational Synch, 1983, Adolescent Experience, 1983, The Flexible Organization, 1984, Survival on the Fast Track, 1988, 93, Organization Gameboard, 1989, Leaders in Place, 1994, More About Survival on the Fast Track, 1996; producer (videotape series) Keys to Leadership I, 1991-93, II, 1993-94, III, 1995-96; contbr. articles to profl. jours.. Daniel E. Prescott fellow U. Md., 1972; recipient Susan B. Anthony and Faculty Recognition awards U. Mich., 1980. Mem. Am. Psychol. Assn., Acad. Mgmt., Organizational Devel. Network, Phi Beta Kappa. Republican. Episcopalian. Home: 95 Cuyler Rd Princeton NJ 08540-3460 Office: Rutgers U Sch of Bus New Brunswick NJ 08903

KOVACHEVICH, ELIZABETH ANNE, federal judge; b. Canton, Ill., Dec. 14, 1936; d. Dan and Emilie (Kuchan) Kovachevich. AA, St. Petersburg Jr. Coll., 1956; BBA in Fin. magna cum laude, U. Miami, 1958; JD, Stetson U., 1961. Bar: Fla. 1961, U.S. Dist. Ct. (mid. and so. dists.) Fla. 1961, U.S. Ct. Appeals (5th cir.) 1961, U.S. Supreme Ct. 1968. Research and adminstrv. aide Pinellas County Legis. Del., Fla., 1961; assoc. DiVito & Speer, St. Petersburg, Fla., 1961-62; house counsel Rieck & Fleece Builders Supplies, Inc., St. Petersburg, 1962; pvt. practice law St. Petersburg, 1962-73; judge 6th Jud. Cir., Pinellas and Pasco Counties, Fla., 1973-82, U.S. Dist. Ct. (mid. dist.) Fla., St. Petersburg, 1982—; chmn. St. Petersburg Profl. Legal Project-Days in Court, 1967; chmn. Supreme Ct. Bicentennial Com. 6th Jud. Circuit, 1975-76. prodr., coord. TV prodn. A Race to Judgement. Bd. regents State of Fla., 1970-72; legal advisor, bd. dirs. Young Women's Residence Inc., 1968; mem. Fla. Gov.'s Commn. on Status of Women, 1968-71; mem. Pres.'s Commn. on White House Fellowships, 1973-77; mem. def. adv. com. on Women in Service, Dept. Def., 1973-76; Fla. conf. publicity chmn. 18th Nat. Republican Women's Conf., Atlanta, 1971; lifetime mem. Children's Hosp. Guild, YWCA of St. Petersburg; charter mem. Golden Notes, St. Petersburg Symphony; hon. mem. bd. of overseers Stetson U. Coll. of Law, 1986. Recipient Disting. Alumni award Stetson U., 1970, Woman of Yr. award Fla. Fedn. Bus. and Profl. Women, 1981, ann. Ben C. Willard Meml. award, Stetson Lawyers Assn., 1983, St. Petersburg Panhellenic Appreciation award, 1964, Mrs. Charles Ulrick Bay award, St. Petersburg Rotary award, St. Petersburg Quarterback Club award, Pinellas United Fund award in recognition of concern and meritorious effort, 1968, Woman of Yr. award Beta Sigma Phi, 1970, Am. Legion Aux. Unit 14 Pres. award cmty. svc., 1970, Dedication to Christian Ideals award and Man of Yr. award KC Dists. 20-21, 1972. Mem. ABA, Fla. Bar Assn., Pinellas County Trial Lawyers, Assn. Trial Lawyers Am., Am. Judicature Soc., St. Petersburg Bar Assn. (chmn. bench and bar com., sec. 1969). Office: US Dist Ct 611 N Florida Ave Tampa FL 33602*

KOVACIC-FLEISCHER, CANDACE SAARI, law educator; b. Washington, Mar. 19, 1947; d. Donald George and Martha Eleanora (Saari) K.; m. Walter H. Fleischer; 1 child, Ilona Saari Fleischer. AB, Wellesley Coll., 1969; JD, Northeastern U., 1974. Law clk. to Judge James L. Oakes U.S. Ct. Appeals (2d Cir.), Brattleboro, Vt., 1974-75; law clk. to Chief Justice Warren Burger U.S. Supreme Ct., Washington, 1975-76; assoc. Wilmer, Cutler & Pickering, Washington, 1976-80, Cole & Groner, Washington, 1980-81; prof. Coll. of Law Am. U., Washington, 1981—; vis. prof. UCLA, 1988; moot ct. panelist Nat. Assn. of Attys. Gen., Washington, 1986-90; mediator U.S. Ct. Appeals (D.C. cir.). Author: (with Leavell, Love and Nelson) Equitable Remedies, Restitution and Damages 5th edit.; contbr. to profl. publs. Officer Eisenhower Found. for Prevention of Violence, 1977-81; mem. D.C. Cir. Com. on the Bicentennial of the Constn., 1986-92. Pauline Ruyle Moore scholar Coll. Law Am. U., Washington, Wellesley Scholar Wellesly Coll., 1968, 69; recipient U. Faculty award for outstanding teaching, Am. U., 1987, student award for outstanding teaching, 1994. Mem. ABA, Am. Assn. Law Schs. (chair remedies sect. 1990). Office: Am U Coll Law 4400 Massachusetts Ave NW Washington DC 20016-8001

KOVACS, DEBORAH, writer, editor; b. Chgo., Oct. 2, 1954; d. Stanton H. K. and Judith Genesen, (adoptive father) Louis Genesen; m. Nicholas Sullivan; children: Sarah J., Lucy. BA cum laude, Middlebury Coll., 1975. Toy, game and record developer Sesame Street Children's TV Workshop, N.Y.C., 1975-80; also editor Sesame Street Mag., 1975-80; founder, creative dir. software divsn. Sholastic, Inc., N.Y.C., 1982-85; editor Ocean Explorer mag., 1991-95; freelance writer for book, mag., computer software publs. including Nat. Audubon Soc., Jim Henson Prodns., Children's TV Workshop. Author: Frazzle's Fantastic Day, 1980, When Is Saturday?, 1981, A Day Underwater, 1987, Moondreamers: The Evening Song, 1988, Meet the Authors and Illustrators Vol. I, 1991, Vol. 2, 1993, Meet the Authors of Middle School Books, 1995, Brewster's Courage, 1992, Moonlight by the River, 1993; (with Kate Madin) Beneath Blue Waters, 1996; author computer based interactive fiction stories for Nat. Audubon Soc., Microzine series, (with Patricia Relf) Snooper Troops 2: The Disappearing Dolphin. Grantee Mass. Cultural Coun. in support of writing, 1990; recipient EdPress award Best News Story, 1981, Family Computing Software award, 1985, Appreciation cert. Mass. Marine Edn. Assn., 1992. *

KOVALCIK, STEPHANIE MARIE, special education educator; b. Cleve., Sept. 27, 1957; d. Vincent James and Myrtle Irene (Steckel) K.; m. Jeffrey Thomas Grothaus, June 23, 1990; 1 child, Laura Elizabeth. BA, Xavier U., 1979; MA, Ohio State U., 1982. Cert. spl. edn. tchr., Ohio. Tchr. of deaf Monroe County Bd. Edn., Woodsfield, Ohio, 1982-84, Hamilton County Ednl. Svc. Ctr., Cin., 1984—; telephone interpreter, Relay Sys. for the Deaf, Cin., 1985-87; presenter workshops, 1989-91, 93, 96. Author poetry; contbr. articles to profl. jours. Choir mem. Western Hill. Ch. of Christ, Cin., 1987-88; camp counselor Easter Seals, Eastern Ky., 1984. Recipient grant. 1991. Mem. Coun. Exceptional Children (sec. 1987-91, Tchr. of Yr. award 1990), Conv. Am. Instructors of Deaf (math. treas. 1985-87), Nat. Assn. Deaf (advancing mem.), Internat. Reading Assn., Alexander Graham Bell Assn., Am. Assn. Univ. Women. Roman Catholic. Office: Hamilton County Ednl Svc Ctr 11083 Hamilton Ave Cincinnati OH 45231

KOVELESKI, KATHRYN DELANE, retired special education educator; b. Detroit, Aug. 12, 1925; d. Edward Albert Vogt and Delane (Bender) Vogt; BA, Olivet (Mich.) Coll., 1947; MA, Wayne State U., Detroit, 1955; m. Casper Koveleski, July 18, 1952; children: Martha, Ann. Tchr. schs. in Mich., 1947-88; tchr. Garden City Schs., 1955-56, 59-88, resource and learning disabilities tchr., 1970-88, ret. 1988. Sec. bd. Christian edn. Congl. Ch., 1988-89, chmn., 1988-90, mem. Mem. BPW (Woman of Yr. 1985-86 Garden City), Mich. Assn. Ret. Sch. Pers. , Wayne Hist. Soc., Wayne Garden Club, Wayne Lit. Club (past pres., treas. 1988-89), Sch. Masters Bowling League (v.p. 1984-88), Odd Couples Bowling League (pres. 82-83, treas. 1995-96).

KOVNER, KATHLEEN JANE, civic worker, portrait artist; b. Cambridge, Mass., Nov. 25, 1919; d. David Leo and Kathleen Elizabeth (Lalley) Lane; m. Benjamin Kovner, June 20, 1938; children: Kathleen Barbara (dec.), Michael Anthony, Peter Christopher. Student, Art Students League, N.Y.C., 1937-40. Owner, CEO Helen Bennett Ltd., Stamford, Conn., 1948-59; cons. Bride's Mag., N.Y.C., 1967-70; co-chair membership com. Women's Nat. Rep. Club, N.Y.C., 1980-81, chmn. membership com., 1981-87, v.p., 1986-87, also bd. dirs.; ltd. ptnr. 519 8th Ave Corp., N.Y.C., 18-19th St. Corp., N.Y.C., Kaufman Arcade Bldg., N.Y.C., 19th St. Assn., N.Y.C. Portrait artist in oils, with various portraits in pvt. collections. Fundraiser St. Ignatius Loyola, N.Y.C., 1960-61, Jeanine Pirro-Campaign for Dist. Atty., Westchester County, N.Y., 1993. Roman Catholic. Address: 923 Fifth Ave New York NY 10021-2649

KOWAL, RUTH ELIZABETH, library administrator; b. Amherst, Mass., Mar. 16, 1948; d. Alfred Alexander and Mary Arandale (Tomlinson) Brown; m. Florian F. Kowal, June 19, 1989; children: Elizabeth Ann, Susannah Terry. BS, Syracuse U., 1970; MLS, Simmons Coll., 1971. Reference libr. Falmouth (Mass.) Pub. Libr., 1971-74; sch. libr. Nauset High Sch., Eastham, Mass., 1974-75; asst. dir. Plymouth (Mass.) Pub. Librs., 1975, dir., 1976-83; exec. dir. Southeastern 3R's, Highland, N.Y., 1983-86; regional adminstr. Ctrl. Mass. Libr. System, Worcester, 1987-91, Ea. Mass. Libr. System, Boston, 1991—; instr. Northeastern U., Boston, 1980-83, SUNY, Albany, 1984-86. Mem. ALA. Office: Ea Mass Reg Libr Boston Pub Libr Boston MA 02117

KOWALCZYK, ELIZABETH ANN, lawyer; b. Grove City, Pa., Aug. 12, 1968; d. Matthew Michael and Barbara Ann (Artzerounian) K. BA summa cum laude, Kent State U., 1990; JD, NYU, 1993. Bar: Ohio 1993, U.S. Dist. Ct. (so. dist.) Ohio, 1994. Legal intern NOW Legal Def. and Edn. Fund, N.Y.C., 1992-93; staff atty. Southeastern Ohio Legal Svcs., Steubenville, 1993-96; state support atty. Ohio State Legal Svcs., Columbus, 1996—. Author: (short story) Armenia's Last Son, 1990 (Univ. honors). Mem. Hutton House Adv. Bd., Steubenville, 1994—. Mem. ABA, Ohio NOW Edn. & Legal Fund, Phi Beta Kappa.

KOWALSKI, EILEEN MARIE, accountant; b. Reading, Pa., Apr. 4, 1964; d. Frederick Henry Yerger and Barbara Ann Koch; m. Edward Joseph Kowalski, Jr., Apr. 22, 1995. BSBA, Kutztown U., 1986; MBA, St. Joseph's U., 1996. Acctg. clk. Morgan Corp., Morgantown, Pa., 1987-89; staff acctg. Penske Truck Leasing Co., Green Hills, Pa., 1989-90; corp. banking officer, field auditor Dauphin Deposit Corp., Reading, Pa., 1990—. Chair United Way at Work, Reading, 1995, 96; cons., tchr. Jr. Achievement, Reading, 1996, advisor, 1987-89; mentor YES program, 1995-96. Mem. Inst. Mgmt. Accts. Republican. Roman Catholic. Office: Dauphin Deposit Corp PO Box 15210 Reading PA 19612-5210

KOWALSKI, HEATHER TERESA, customer service representative; b. Wheat Ridge, Colo., Jan. 27, 1968; d. Michael Anthony and Sara (Murphy) K. BA, Wells Coll.; cert., U. Grenoble, France, 1989; MBA, U. Hartford, Paris, France. Elevator operator U.S. Capital Senate, Washington, 1991-92; asst. to dir. finance City of Sugar Land, Tex., 1993-95; sales assoc. Crate & Barrel, Houston, 1993-95; customer svc. profl. MCI, Sugar Land, Tex., 1995—. Vol. for Kay Bailey Hutchison, Houston, 1993-94, campaign for P. Owen, 1994. Mem. NAFE, AAUW (recording sec. local chpt. 1993-94).

KOWALSKI, ROBIN MARIE, psychology educator; b. Anderson, S.C., May 23, 1964; d. Paul Randolph and Mary Frances (Bagwell) K. BA, Furman U., 1985; MA, Wake Forest U., 1987; PhD, U. N.C., Greensboro, 1990. Vis. instr. Wake Forest U., Winston-Salem, N.C., 1989-90; assoc. prof. psychology Western Carolina U., Cullowhee, N.C., 1990—; statis. cons. U. N.C., Charlotte, 1991. Contbr. articles to profl. jours. Recipient award Com. on Equality Profl. Opportunity, 1991; rsch. grantee Western Carolina U., 1991. Mem. APA, Am. Psychol. Soc., Southeastern Psychol. Assn. (award 1991), Soc. for Personality and Social Psychology, Soc. Southeastern Social Psychologists, Soc. for Advancement Social Psychology, Sigma Xi.

KOWLESSAR, MURIEL, retired pediatric educator; b. Bklyn., Jan. 2, 1926; d. John Henry and Arene (Driver) Chevious; m. O. Dhodanand Kowlessar, Dec. 27, 1952; 1 child, Indrani. AB, Barnard Coll., 1947; MD, Columbia U., 1951. Diplomate Am. Bd. Pediatrics. Instr. Downstate Med. Ctr., Bklyn., 1958-64, asst. prof., 1965-66; asst. prof. clin. pediatrics Temple U., Phila., 1967-70; assoc. prof. Med. Coll. Pa., Phila., 1971-83, dir. pediatric group svcs., 1975-90, acting chmn. pediatrics dept., 1981-83, vice chair pediatrics dept., 1982-91, prof., 1983-91, prof. emeritus, 1991—. Contbr. articles to med. jours. Mem. Pa. Gov.'s Task Force on Spl. Supplemental Food Program for Women, Infants and Children, Harrisburg, 1981-83, Phila. Bd. Health, 1982-86; vol. Phila. Com. for Homeless, 1991-92, Gateway Literacy Program, YMCA, Germantown Bridge, Pa., 1992-93. Fellow Am. Acad. Pediatrics (emeritus); mem. Phila. Pediatric Soc., Cosmopolitan Club Phila., Phi Beta Kappa. Democrat.

KOZA, JOAN LORRAINE, fabric manufacturing company executive; b. Berwyn, Ill., Apr. 28, 1941; d. Frank Louis and Lorraine Frances (Thomas) K.; BS in Communications, U. Ill., 1963. Office mgr. Dwan Med. Ctr., Summit, Ill., 1959-64; law office mgr. firm Gordon, Reicin & West, Chgo., 1964-73; sales mgr. Ambassador Hotels, Chgo., 1973-76; exec. v.p. MPC Industries, In., Chgo., 1976-96; owner, mgr. JK Advt., 1977—; pres. Chgo. Legal Secs. Assn., 1970-72; v.p. Ill. Assn. Legal Secs., 1970-73. Pres., chmn. bd. Children's Research Found., 1963-66. Contbg. author: New American Poetry Anthology (Golden Poet award 1988, 89). Named Chgo. Legal Sec. of Yr., 1972, Ill. Legal Sec. of Yr., 1972. Mem. Alpha Lambda Delta, Theta Sigma Pi. Roman Catholic. Home: 546 Banyon Ln La Grange IL 60525-1962 Office: 4834 S Oakley Ave Chicago IL 60609-4036

KOZBERG, DONNA WALTERS, rehabilitation administration executive; b. Milford, Del., Jan. 1, 1952; d. Robert Glyndwr and Gailey Ruth (Bedorf) Walters; m. Ronald Paul Kozberg, June 8, 1974; 1 child, Mariel Gailey. BA, U. Fla., 1973, M in Rehab. Counseling, 1974; MFA, CUNY, 1979; MBA, Rutgers U., 1986. Cert. rehab. counselor. Rehab. counselor Office Vocat. Rehab., N.Y.C., 1975-81; area dir. Lift, Inc., Staten Island, N.Y., 1981-83; ea. region dir. pub. relations, advt. Lift, Inc., Mountainside, N.J., 1983-85, v.p., 1985—, v.p., chief fin. officer, 1988, exec. v.p., 1991-93, pres., 1993; co-founder, mng. dir. Expert Strategies, Inc., Mountainside, N.J., 1992—; self-employed writer, editor, 1975—; adv. bd. Rutgers Exec. Master Bus. Adminstrn. Contbr. articles to profl. jours.; assoc. editor Parachute mag., 1978; editor-in-chief (newsletter) Counselor Adv, 1980. Pres. Com. on Employment of People with Disabilities; trustee Ctr. for Creative Living; bd. dirs. N.J. Adv. Coun. for Independent Living, adv. panel NYU. Mem. Nat. Rehab. Assn. (Spl. citation 1974, grantee 1973), Nat. Rehab. Adminstrs. Assn., Nat. Rehab. Counselors Assn., N.J. Rehab. Counselors Assn. (pres. 1996), Poets and Writers. Home: 45 Dug Way Watchung NJ 07060-6011 Office: Lift Inc PO Box 1072 Mountainside NJ 07092-0072

KOZDEMBA, KATHLEEN MARY, news executive; b. Elmira, N.Y., Jan. 24, 1954; d. Thomas Edward and Helen Bernadette (Janeski) K. BA in Journalism, St. Bonaventure U., Olean, N.Y., 1975; MBA, Syracuse U., 1984. Reporter Star-Gazette, Elmira, 1975-77, family news editor, 1977-80, Sunday editor, 1980-81, regional news editor, 1981-82, asst. mng. editor, 1982-83, mng. editor/news, 1983-85; mng. editor The Ithaca (N.Y.) Jour., 1985-87, The Springfield (Mo.) News-Leader, 1987-89; news exec. Gannett Co., Inc., Arlington, Va., 1989-92; editor The Jour. Newspapers, Springfield, Va., 1991; pres., chief exec. officer North Hills News Record, Warrendale, Pa., 1992-96; dir. NEWS 2000, Gannett Co., Inc., Arlington, Va., 1996—. Mem. bd. Pa. Newspaper Pubs. Found., 1995-96. Mem. AP Mng. Editors (bd. dirs. 1988-95), N.Y. AP Assn. (bd. dirs. 1986-87), N.Y. State Soc. Newspaper Editors (treas. 1986-87), Am. Soc. Newspaper Editors, Soc. Profl. Journalists, Women in Communications (com. chmn. 1988), Pa. Newspaper Publishers Assn. (govt. affairs com. 1994-96). Roman Catholic. Office: Gannett Co, Inc 1100 Wilson Blvd Arlington VA 22234

KOZICKY, TANJA L., lawyer; b. Mpls., Jan. 26, 1966; d. Richard and Carmen (Velasquez) K. BA, Cornell Coll., 1988; JD, Georgetown U., 1991. Bar: Minn. 1991. Lawyer environ. Popham Haik Law Firm, Mpls., 1991-93, Greene Espel Law Firm, Mpls., 1993-95; legal counsel to Gov. Arne H. Carlson St. Paul, 1996—. Bd. dirs. Suburban Rep. Women, Mpls. Mem. Mpls. Club, Phi Beta Kappa. Roman Catholic. Home: 623 W Ferndale Rd Wayzata MN 55319 Office: Governor's Office 130 State Capitol Saint Paul MN 55155

KOZLOW, BEVERLY KAY, physical therapist, clinical psychologist; b. Detroit, Aug. 10, 1931; d. Samuel and Genevieve Ione (Griffin) K.; m. Roy Carl Gleaves, Apr. 16, 1959 (div. 1975). BS, Eastern Mich. U., 1953; MS, UCLA, 1959; PhD, Sierra U., 1987. Registered physical therapist. Physical therapist Walter Reed Army Med. Ctr., Washington, 1953-55, Crippled Children's Soc., Rockville, Md., 1955-56, San Bernardino (Calif.) County Hosp., 1957-59; coord. physical therapy program UCLA, 1959-67; home health physical therapist Vis. Nurses Assn. L.A., 1967-68; from staff to dir. physical therapy L.A. County Med. Dept., 1968-73; dir. in-patient/out-patient acute & rehab. svcs. Valley Med. Ctr., Van Nuys, Calif., 1973-81; contract physical therapist L.A., 1981-89; home health physical therapist Vis. Nurses Assn., Stuart, Fla., 1992-96; adj. faculty U.S. Army Command and Gen. Staff Coll., Ft. Leavenworth, Kans., 1986-92. Ret. col. U.S. Army. Mem. Am. Physical Therapy Assn., Ret. Officers Assn., Fla. Master Gardeners, Med. Specialists Corps Assn. Democrat. Jewish. Home: 3307 Ironwood Ave Port Saint Lucie FL 34952

KOZMA, HELENE JOYCE MARIE, adult education educator; b. Bridgeport, Conn.; d. Ernest A. and Helen C. (Skurski) K. BA in English, Adelphi U.; MBA in Bus. Mgmt., Sacred Heart U., 1986, postgrad., 1990. Cert. English and bus. tchr., Conn. Tchr. bus. Town of Stratford, Conn., Acad. of Our Lady of Mercy, Milford, Conn.; Gateway Comty./Tech. Coll., New Haven, Conn. Eucharistic min. Holy Name of Jesus Ch., 1991, lectr., reader, 1991, catechist tchr., 1990-91; min. Secular Franciscan Order, Coun. of Holy Spirit Fraternity, 1991-94; mem. town com.; bd. dirs. Libr. Assn. Mme. Nat. Coun. Tchrs. of English, Shakespeare Guild, Toastmasters (charter, treas. 1984, adminstrv. v.p. 1986).

KOZY, KAREN EILEEN, primary grades educator; b. Akron, Ohio. BS in Early Childhood Edn., Kent State U., 1987, BS in Computer Sci., Math., 1988; MS in Reading Edn., U. Ctrl. Fla., 1992. Cert. tchr. early childhood, elem. 1-6, math. 5-9, reading k-12, Fla. Primary multi-age tchr. Golfview Elem. Sch., Rockledge, Fla., 1992—. Mem. ASCD, Internat. Reading Assn., Nat. Coun. Tchrs. of Math., Nat. Assn. for Edn. of Young Children, Jr. League of Ctrl. and N. Brevard County. Home: 1327 George Edwards Ct Merritt Island FL 32953-4458

KRA, PAULINE SKORNICKI, French language educator; b. Lodz, Poland, July 30, 1934; came to U.S., 1950, naturalized, 1955; d. Edward and Nathalie Skornicki; m. Leo Dietrich Kra, Mar. 10, 1955; children: David Theodore, Andrew Jason. Student Radcliffe Coll., 1951-53; BA, Barnard Coll., 1955; MA, Columbia U., 1963, PhD, 1968; MA, Queens Coll., 1990. Lectr., Queens Coll., City U. N.Y., 1964-65; asst. prof. French, Yeshiva U., N.Y.C., 1968-74, assoc. prof. French, 1974-82, prof., 1982—. Mem. MLA, Am. Assn. Tchrs. French, Am. Soc. 18th Century Studies, Société française d'étude du XVIII siècle, Soc. Montesquieu, Assn. for Computers and Humanities, Assn. for Literary and Linguistic Computing, Phi Beta Kappa. Author: Religion in Montesquieu's Lettres persanes, 1970; contbr. articles to profl. jours. Home: 109-14 Ascan Ave Forest Hills NY 11375-5370 Office: 500 W 185th St New York NY 10033-3201

KRACH, MARGARET Q., nursing educator, researcher; b. Balt., Feb. 8, 1936; d. Christopher Quinn and Margaret Lord; m. Frank Louis Krach; children: Frank, Kathleen, Michael, Theresa. Diploma, Mercy Hosp. Sch. Nursing, 1957; student, U. Md., 1969-71; BS in Nursing, Ohio State U., 1974, MS in Cmty. Mental Health Nursing, 1975, PhD in Family Rels. & Human Devel., 1985. Teaching asst. Ohio State U., Columbus, 1974-75; asst. prof. Capital U., Columbus, 1975-81, U. Hawaii, Honolulu, 1981-85, Meth. Coll. Nursing, Omaha, 1986-87, U. Iowa, Iowa City, 1987-90, Ball State U., Muncie, Ind., 1991-92; asst. prof. Purdue U., West Lafayette, Ind., 1992-93, assoc. prof., 1994—; staff nurse, med.-surg. nurse Mercy Hosp., Balt., 1957-59; staff nurse Provident Hosp., Washington, 1965-71; staff nurse oncology Ohio State U., 1975, staff nurse psychiatry, 1980-81; group facilitator Parents Unltd., Omaha, 1986-87; supr. U. Iowa, 1987-90, Purdue U., 1993—; presenter in field. Author: Differences in Nursing: A Study Guide; contbr. numerous articles to profl. jours.; subject of numerous interviews and TV/newspaper stories. Vol. Sr. Citizen Group, Indpls., 1993, Blessed Sacrament Ch., West Lafayette, 1993, Christian Nurses' Assn., West Lafayette, 1993, Home Health Nurses Kathryn Weil Ctr., Lafayette, Ind., 1994. Grantee U. Iowa, 1988, Ball State U., 1991, Purdue U., 1993-94, PRF Internat., 1995, Sigma Theta Tau, 1995. Mem. Psychiat. Nurses' Assn., Cmty. Health Nurses' Assn. Ind., Ind. Nurses Assn., Midwest Nursing Rsch. Soc., Sigma Theta Tau (Outstanding Nursing Educator award 1996). Home: 200 Navajo West Lafayette IN 47901

KRACKE, LORRAINE M.S., mental health therapist; b. Wagner, S.D., Aug. 14, 1940; d. John E. and Mary A. Syrovatka; m. Merlyn G. Kracke, June 11, 1961 (dec. Oct. 1979). BS, S.D. State U., 1990, MS in Counseling/Human Resource Devel., 1993. Nat. cert. gerontology counselor. Vol. gerontology intern Human Svcs. Ctr., Yankton, S.D., 1994; vol., chair Naval Relief Soc., 1968-69. Participant Nat. Conf. for Older Women, Washington, 1993; first participant and contestant from S.D. in Ms. Nat. Sr. Citizen Pageant, Joliet, Ill., 1995; Stephen min., 1985—; vol. line dance instr. sr. citizens, 1995. Mem. ACA, VFW Aux., Am. Legion Aux. (pres. 1979-80), Widowed Persons Svc. Lutheran. Home: 300 S Medary Ave # 105 Brookings SD 57006

KRAEMER, LILLIAN ELIZABETH, lawyer; b. N.Y.C., Apr. 18, 1940; d. Frederick Joseph and Edmee Elizabeth (de Watteville) K.; m. John W. Vincent, June 22, 1962 (div. 1964). BA, Swarthmore Coll., 1961; JD, U. Chgo., 1964. Bar: N.Y. 1965, U.S. Dist. Ct. (so. dist.) N.Y. 1967, U.S. Dist. Ct. (ea. dist.) N.Y. 1971. Assoc. Cleary, Gottlieb, Steen & Hamilton, N.Y.C., 1964-71; assoc. Simpson Thacher & Bartlett, N.Y.C., 1971-74, ptnr., 1974—; mem. vis. com. U. Chgo. Law Sch., 1988-90, 91-94. Bd. mgrs. Swarthmore Coll., 1993—. Fellow Am. Coll. Bankruptcy; mem. Lawyers Alliance N.Y. (bd. dirs. 1996—), Assn. of Bar of City of N.Y. (mem. various coms.), Coun. on Fgn. Rels., N.Y. State Bar Assn., Order of Coif, Phi Beta Kappa. Democrat. Episcopalian. Home: 2 Beekman Pl New York NY 10022-8058 also: 62 Pheasant Ln Stamford CT 06903-4428 Office: Simpson Thacher & Bartlett 425 Lexington Ave New York NY 10017-3903

KRAEMER, SYLVIA KATHARINE, government official, historian; b. Neisse, Silesia, Germany, Feb. 24, 1944; came to U.S., 1948; d. Thomas Paramore and Dorothea Freihube (Kraemer) Doughty; m. Russell Inslee Fries, Apr. 11, 1970 (div. Nov. 1991); children: Thomas Mount, Gwyneth Buchanan. BA in English, Hollins Coll., 1965; PhD in History, Johns Hopkins U., 1969. Instr. Johns Hopkins U., Balt., 1969; asst. prof. history Vassar Coll., Poughkeepsie, N.Y., 1969-70, So. Meth. U., Dallas, 1970-73; rsch. assoc. prof. U. Maine, Orono, 1975-78; mem. vis. faculty Bangor (Maine) Theol. Sem., 1981-83; chief historian NASA, Washington, 1983-89, dir. Office Spl. Studies, 1989—, mem. adv. coun., 1981-83. Author: Urban Idea in Colonial America, 1977, NASA Engineers in the Age of Apollo, 1992; also essays. Mem. Maine Humanities Coun., 1979-83; cons. on edn. issues, Va., 1993—. Fellow Coun. Humanities, So. Meth. U., 1973; rsch. grantee NSF, 1978-80. Fellow Internat. Acad. Astronautics; mem. Women in Aerospace, Exec. Women in Govt., Soc. for History in Fed. Govt. (exec. coun. 1988-91, James Madison award 1989), AAUW. Office: NASA 300 E St NW Washington DC 20546-0001

KRAETZER, MARY C., sociologist, educator, consultant; b. N.Y.C., Sept. 12, 1943; d. Kenneth G. and Adele L. Kraetzer; m. Kestas E. Silunas. AB, Coll. New Rochelle, 1965; MA, Fordham U., 1967, PhD, 1975. Instr. Mercy Coll., Dobbs Ferry, N.Y., 1969-70, asst. prof., 1970-75, assoc. prof., 1975-79, prof., 1979—; research asst. Fordham U., Bronx, N.Y., 1965-67, teaching asst., 1967-68, teaching fellow, 1968-69, adj. instr., 1971-75, adj. asst. prof., 1975-76; adj. assoc. prof. L.I. U. Grad. Br. Campus Mercy Coll., 1976-79, adj. prof., 1979-81, coordinator M.S. in Community Health Program, 1976-81, adj. prof. Westchester campus, 1988—; rsch. cons. elem. schoolbooks Nat. Council of Chs./Church Women United Task Force on Global Consciousness, N.Y.C., 1971; mem. adv. com. edn. and society div. Nat. Council Chs., 1975-78; mem. evaluation team Middle States Assn. Colls. and Secondary Schs. Commn. on Higher Edn., Monmouth, N.J., 1976. Contbr. chpts. to books, articles to profl. jours. Recipient citation Am. Men and Women of Sci., 1978; Bd. Regents scholar, 1961-65, Fordham U. scholar, 1965-68; Fordham U. fellow, 1968-69; grantee Mercy Coll., 1984, 85, 86, 88, 92; NSF summer intern, 1967. Mem. Am. Sociol. Assn., Am. Pub. Health Assn. Office: Mercy Coll 555 Broadway Dobbs Ferry NY 10522-1134

KRAFKA, MARY BAIRD, lawyer; b. Ottumwa, Iowa, Jan. 4, 1942; d. Glenn Leroy and Alice Erna (Krebill) B.; m. Jerry Lee Krafka, Oct. 14, 1962; children: Lisa M., Gregory D., Jeffrey A., Amy J. BS in English and Human Rels., William Penn Coll., Oskaloosa, Iowa, 1990; JD, U. Iowa, 1993. Bar: Iowa 1993. Vol. lawyer Legal Svcs. Corp., Ottumwa, 1993-94; pvt. practice, Ottumwa, 1994—. Mem. ABA, Iowa Bar Assn., Wapello County Bar Assn., PEO (Iowa chpt. HC 1973). Democrat. Lutheran. Home: 931 W Mary St Ottumwa IA 52501 Office: 101 S Market St Ste 203 Ottumwa IA 52501

KRAFT, BARBARA LENORE, public relations consultant; b. Hollywood, Calif., June 19, 1939; d. Emil Herman and Helen Josephine (Friedrich) Schauerte; m. William Kraft, June 15, 1960 (div. 1980); 1 child, Jennifer Nicole. BA, UCLA, 1962; PhD, Internat. Coll., 1976. Producer KPFK, North Hollywood, Calif., 1972-80; prof., profl. writing program U. So. Calif., L.A., 1981; program devel. assoc. Calif. Inst. Arts, 1984-85; reporter Time mag., L.A., 1982-86; dir. pub. rels. Mus. Contemporary Art, L.A., 1986-89; founder Barbara Kraft Comm. & Pub. Rels., 1989—; freelance writer, 1981—; program annotator L.S. Philharmonic at Hollywood Bowl; opera reviewer L.A. Daily News, 1976-77. Author: The Restless Spirit: Journal of a Gemini, 1976, (play, drama) Maud Gonne, 1973 (Ohio State U. award for original radio drama); contbr. essays to profl. publs.; writer The Innocents: Witch Trial at Salem for chorus and chamber orgn., 1976, The Dream Tunnel: A Musical Journey through America for orch. and narrator, 1976; commd. for Bicentennial, L.A. Philharm. Recipient Piano scholarship Immaculate Heart Coll., 1957, Goethe Inst. fellowship, 1988; named register scholar Huntington Libr., 1980-84, to the bd. of advisors Marilyn Horne Found., 1994—. Home and Office: 4369 Camellia Ave Studio City CA 91604

KRAFT, ELAINE JOY, community relations and communications official; b. Seattle, Sept. 1, 1951; d. Harry J. and Leatrice M. (Hanan) K.; m. Lee Somerstein, Aug. 2, 1980; children: Paul Kraft, Leslie Jo. BA, U. Wash., 1973; MPA, U. Puget Sound, 1979. Reporter Jour. Am. Newspaper, Bellevue, Wash., 1972-76; editor Jour./Enterprise Newspapers, Wash. State, 1976; mem. staff Wash. State Senate, 1976-78, Wash. Ho. of Reps., 1978-82, pub. info. officer, 1976-78, mem. leadership staff, asst. to caucus chmn., 1980—; ptnr., pres. Media Kraft Communications; mgr. corp. info., advt. and mktg. communications Weyerhaeuser Co., 1982-85; dir. communications Weyerhaeuser Paper Co., 1985-87; dir. community rels. N.W. region Coors Brewing Co. 1987-95; dir. Ctr. for Literacy Advocacy Seattle Pub. Library, 1996—. Recipient state and nat. journalism design and advt. awards. Mem. Nat. Fedn. Press Women, Women in Communications, Wash. Press Assn. Home: 14329 SE 63rd St Bellevue WA 98006-4802 Office: Seattle Pub Library 1000 4th Ave Seattle WA 98104

KRAFT, JANICE KAY, accounting educator; b. Casper, Wyo., Mar. 8, 1947; d. Milo Todd and Margaret Leary Buckingham; m. Edwin David Kraft, June 26, 1965; children: Brad, Brian. BS in Bus. Edn., U. Wyo., 1974, MBA with Acctg. Emphasis, 1976. Instr. U. Wyo., Laramie, 1974-76, staff prof., 1978-80; prof. Casper Coll., 1976-77; adj. prof. Ea. Mont. Coll., Billings, 1982-83; assoc. prof. acctg. S.W. State U., Marshall, Minn., 1984—. Coach Marshall Little League, 1985-91; treas. AAU Baseball, Marshall, 1992-94; mem. parent coun. Marshall Sr. H.S., 1995-96; mem. Marshall Music Booster, Marshall Speech Booster. Mem. Inst. Mgmt. Accts. (cert.), Minn. Coun. Acctg. Educators (treas.). Home: 232 N Hill St Marshall MN 56258

KRAFT, RITA ANNE, realtor; b. Dayton, Ohio, Mar. 19, 1943; d. John Russell and Frances Elizabeth (Reese) Lawyer; m. Leland Milo Kraft, Jr., Sept. 2, 1967; children: Lisa Anne, Michelle Leigh. BS, Ohio State U., 1965. Lic. real estate broker, Calif. Lab. asst. Good Samaritan Hosp., Zanesville, Ohio, 1961-63; med. technologist Ohio State U. Hosp., Columbus, 1964-68, Lee County Hosp., Opelika, Ala., 1970-72; rsch. asst. Uncle Ben's Foods, Houston, 1978-83; assoc. broker Kraft Properties, Camarillo, Calif., 1989-90, Century 21 Ctrl. Coast, Camarillo, 1990-92, Prudential-Jon Douglas Co., Camarillo, 1992—; state dir. Calif. Assn. Realtors, L.A., 1991-94. Blood dr. coord. St. Mary Magdalen Ch., Camarillo, 1993—. Mem. AAUW (fashion show chair bd. dirs. 1986, 87, named grant honoree 1991), Camarillo Assn. Realtors (dir. 1991-95, v.p. 1992, pres.-elect 1993, pres. 1994, program chair 1992, multiple listing chair 1993, by-laws chair 1995, Realtor of Yr. 1992), Camarillo C. of C. (edn. com. coord. 1989—, dir. 1990-93, installation dinner chair 1992, 93, coord. Educator of Month award 1990—). Roman Catholic. Home: 2497 Parkway Dr Camarillo CA 93010

KRAG, OLGA, interior designer; b. St. Louis, Nov. 27, 1937; d. Jovica Todor and Milka (Slijepcevic) Golubovic. AA, U. Mo., 1958; cert. interior design UCLA, 1979. Interior designer William L. Pereira Assocs., L.A., 1977-80; assoc. Reel/Grobman Assocs., L.A., 1980-81; project mgr. Kaneko/Laff Assocs., L.A., 1982; project mgr. Stuart Laff Assocs., L.A., 1983-85; restaurateur The Edge, St. Louis, 1983-84; pvt. practice comml. interior design, L.A., 1981—, pres., R.I., 1989—. Mem. invitation and ticket com. Calif. Chamber Symphony Soc., 1980-81; vol. Westside Rep. Coun., Proposition 1, 1971; asst. inaugural presentation Mus. of Childhood, L.A., 1985. Recipient Carole Eichen design award U. Calif., 1979. Mem. Am. Soc. Interior Designers, Inst. Bus. Designers, Phi Chi Theta, Beta Sigma Phi. Republican. Serbian Orthodox. Home and Office: 700 Levering Ave Apt 10 Los Angeles CA 90024-2797

KRAHNKE, BETTY ANN, county official; b. Washington, Sept. 27, 1942; d. Richard George Jr. and Mary (McLaughlin) Fletcher; m. Wilson Norris Krahnke, July 11, 1964; children: Carolyn, Catherine, Margaret. BA in Political Sci. with highest honors, U. Calif., Santa Barbara, 1964; postgrad., Johns Hopkins U., 1964-65. Columnist The Planning Game, The Montgomery Jour.; moderator Montgomery Week in Review, Montgomery Cmty. TV. Mem. Montgomery County Planning Bd., 1979-87; vol. coord. Congresswoman Connie Morella's re-election campaign, 1988; Bush del. Rep. Nat. Conv., 1988, 92; chmn. Citizen's Coord. Com. on Friendship Heights; active mem. LWV; former exec. v.p. Montgomery County Hist. Soc.; mem. coun. Montgomery United Way, 1986-96; elected mem. Montgomery County Coun., 1990, 94, chair Coun. pub. safety com., coun. health & human svcs. com., coun. govt's. com. on noise abatement at Nat. and Dulles Airport; mem. Nat. Assn. County Ofcls. land use and environ. com.; treas., mem. bd. dirs. Nat. Orgn. to Insure a Sound-Controlled Environment. Office: Office County Coun Coun Office Bldg 6th Fl 100 Maryland Ave Rockville MD 20850-2367

KRAINIK, ARDIS, opera company executive; b. Manitowoc, Wis., Mar. 8, 1929; d. Arthur Stephen and Clara (Bracken) K. BS cum laude, Northwestern U., 1951, postgrad., 1953-54, DFA (hon.), 1984; LHD (hon.), DePaul U., 1985, Loyola U., 1986, U. Wis., 1986; DFA (hon.), St. Xavier Coll., 1986, Knox Coll., 1987, Columbia Coll., Chgo., 1988, Lake Forest Coll., 1989, Roosevelt U., 1989; LLD (hon.), Albion Coll., 1990; D Mus. Arts (hon.), U. Ill., Chgo., 1990; LHD (hon.), No. Ill. U., 1990; HHD (hon.), Lewis U., 1991; MusD (hon.), Ind. U. N.W., 1992, Barat Coll., 1993; LHD honoris causa, Lawrence U., 1993; DFA (hon.), St. Mary's Coll., 1994. Tchr. drama, pub. speaking Horlick High Sch., Racine, Wis., 1951-53; exec. sec., office mgr. Lyric Opera, Chgo., 1954-59; asst. mgr. Lyric Opera, 1960-75, artistic adminstr., 1975-80, awd. mgr., 1981—, gen. dir., 1987—; bd. dirs. No. Trust Co. Trustee Northwestern U., mem. women's bd., mem. adv. coun. Kellogg Sch. Mgmt.; mem. governing bd. Ill. Arts Alliance; bd. dirs. Opera Am.;. Recipient commendator Italian Order Merit, 1983, Ill. Order Lincoln, 1985, Appdt. Rector, 1993, Grand Decoration of Honor in Silver, Republic of Austria, 1994, Alumni Merit award Northwestern U., 1986, award of Achievement Girl Scouts U.S., 1987, Dushkin Svc. award Music Ctr. of North Shore, 1987, Thomas de Gaetani award U.S. Inst. for Theatre Tech., 1990, Bravo award Rosary Coll., 1991, Career Svc. award Arts Mgmt. News Svc., 1992, Edward Moss Martin award Union League Club, 1993, Crystal award Chgo. Drama League, 1994, Exemplary Woman award Women in Charge, 1994, Sara Lee Frontrunner award 1994, Friendship award European Union, 1994, award Abraham Lincoln Ctr., 1995, Women of Achievement award Antidefamation League, 1995, Govt. of France/officier des L'ordre de Arts et Lettres, 1996; named to Crain's Chgo. Bus./Top 100 Business Women in Chgo., 1996, Exec. of Yr., 1990, Tribute to Chgo. Women Honoree Midwest Women's Ctr., 1986, one of Chicagoans of Yr. Boys and Girls Club, 1987. Mem. Ill. Arts Alliance (governing bd.), Internat. Assn. Opera Dirs., Opera Am. (bd. dirs.), Chgo. Hist. Soc. Guild, Northwestern U. Women's Bd., Northwestern U. Assocs., Northwestern U. Kellogg Sch. Mgmt. (adv. coun.), Mortar Bd., Econ. Club (bd. dirs.), Comml. Club (past pres.), Lake Geneva Country Club, Pi Kappa Lambda. Christian Scientist. Office: Lyric Opera of Chgo 20 N Wacker Dr Ste 860 Chicago IL 60606-2805

KRAKER, DEBORAH SCHOVANEC, special education educator; b. Enid, Okla., May 28, 1960; d. Charles Raymond and Marcella Ruth (Mack) Schovanec; m. Kevin Mark Kraker, July 10, 1987. BS, U. Ctrl. Okla., 1982; postgrad., Okla. State U., Stillwater, 1995—. Cert. tchr. spl. edn., learning disability/mentally handicapped. Customer svc. mgr. Skaggs, Oklahoma City, 1982-92; tchr. spl. edn. Edmond (Okla.) Pub. Schs., 1993—; tchr. Francis Tuttle Vocat. Tech. Ctr., Oklahoma City, 1993, 94, 95, mem. adv. bd., 1993-96. Mem. adv. bd. Francis Tuttle Vocat. Tech. Ctr., 1993—. Mem. NEA, Okla. Edn. Assn. (del. nat. assembly 1996), Edmond Assn. Classroom Tchrs., Coun. for Exceptional Children, Assn. Classroom Mems. (exec. bd.), Learning Disabilities Assn. Republican. Roman Catholic. Home: 2721 Berkshire Way Oklahoma City OK 73120-2704

KRAKORA-LOOBY, JANICE MARIE, pediatrician; b. Chgo., Jan. 14, 1951; d. Joseph George and Marie Adele (Doleshek) Krakora; m. John Augustus Looby III, July 21, 1979; children: Eileen Loretta, John Augustus IV, James Patrick. BS with honors, Mich. State U., 1972, DVM with honors, 1973; MD with honors, Rush Med. Coll., Chgo., 1987. Diplomate Am. Bd. of Pediatrics. Assoc. vet. Kohn Animal Hosp., Highland Park, Ill., 1973-75; assoc. vet. Libertyville (Ill.) Animal Hosp., 1976-77, hosp. dir., 1977-82; assoc. vet. Mundelein (Ill.) Animal Hosp., 1982-85; intern and resident in pediatrics Rush-Presbyn.-St. Luke's Med. Ctr., Chgo., 1987-90; pediatrician Vernon Hills (Ill.) Pediatric Assoc. Ltd., 1990—; bd. dirs. Sun Room, Inc., Lake Forest, Ill. Active St. Mary Parish Coun., editor newsletter, 1991-94, sch. parents club. Paul Harris fellow Rotary, 1988. Fellow Am. Acad. Pediatrics; mem. AMA, AVMA, Am. Med. Women's Assn., Chgo. Med. Soc., Ill. Med. Assn., Chgo. Pediatric Soc., Lake County Pediatric Soc., Aerospace Medicine Assn., Rotary Club Lake Forest/Lake Bluff. Home: 1764 Bowling Green Dr Lake Forest IL 60045-3504 Office: Vernon Hills Pediatric Assocs Inc 10 W Phillip Rd Vernon Hills IL 60061-1730 also: 36100 Brookside Dr Gurnee IL 60031-4571

KRAKOW, AMY GINZIG, advertising and marketing executive, writer; b. Bklyn., Feb. 25, 1950; d. Nathan and Iris (Minkowitz) Ginzig. BA, Bklyn. Coll., 1971, postgrad. in TV prodn., 1974. Copy mgr. U.S. News & World Report, N.Y.C., 1977-80; promotion mgr. Sta. WINS-Radio, N.Y.C., 1980-82; promotion dir. CBS Mags., N.Y.C., 1982-84, The Village Voice, N.Y.C., 1984-85, N.Y. Woman (Am. Express Pub.), N.Y.C., 1987-89; cons. Silverman Collection, Santa Fe, 1985—; sem. leader Radcliffe Pub. workshop, 1986-92, Mag. Pubs. Congress, 1989. Author: Total Tattoo Book, 1994; prodr. Festival of Street Entertainers, N.Y.C., 1984-93, Albuquerque, 1980, Obies-Off-Broadway Theater Awards, 1984-86; creator, prodr. Ann. Coney Island Tattoo Festival, 1986-93, The Psychedelic Festival, 1988; exec. dir. Radio Creative Mercury Awards, 1991-93; curator American Style: New York's Tattoo Roots, South St. Seaport Mus., 1995. Bd. dirs. Sideshows by the Seashore, Coney Island, U.S.A., Bklyn., 1985-92, Bond St. Theater Coalition, 1985—, City Lore, N.Y.C., 1987—, Princeton Bio Ctr., 1991-93. Recipient BPA award, 1981, Addy award, 1985, AAF Crystal Prism award, 1994. Mem. Advt. Women N.Y., Delta Phi Epsilon.

KRAKOWSKI, LINDA S., computer coordinator, consultant; b. Chgo., May 23, 1949; d. Edward J. and Geraldine (Prohaska) Tesarek; children: Ian, Olivia. BA, U. Ill., 1971; Cert. Advanced Studies, Lewis U., 1977; MA, Nat. Coll. Edn., 1985, EdD, 1987. Tchr. English High Sch. Dist. 230, Palos Hills, Ill., 1976-87, coord., instr. computers, 1987—; owner, cons. Ill. Computing Educators Consortium, Palos Hills, 1987—; presenter Ill. Gifted Edn. Coun., 1984-87; designer computer systems Banco Argentina, Buenos Aires, 1988; mem. strategic planning com. and intervention team High Sch. dist 230, Palos Hills, 1989—; judge Educationis Lumen award com., Lewis U., 1991—. Vol. Crisis Ctr. for South Suburbia, 1985—; active Hartigan for Gov. campaign, Chgo., 1989-90, Clinton/Gore Presdl. Campaign, Ill., Carol Moseley Braun for Senator Campaign, Chgo.; del. Dem. Nat. Conv., N.Y.C., 1992; mem. Fourth Presbyn. Ch. of Chgo., Legion of Young Polish Women. Ill. Dept. Edn. grantee, 1984-85; named Suburban Educator of Yr., Lewis U., 1990. Mem. AAUW (bd. dirs., past pres.), NEA (bd. dirs. 1979—, adv. pub. rels. 1979—, Excellence in Gifted Edn. Design award 1985), Ill. Edn. Assn. (bd. dirs. 1979—). Office: Ill Computing Educators Consortium 10705 S Roberts Rd Ste 21 Palos Hills IL 60465-3300

KRAL, NANCY BOLIN, political science educator; b. St. Louis, Oct. 4, 1958; d. Alpha E. Jr. and Shirley Judith (Wiseman) Bolin; m. Kenneth Joseph Kral, June 12, 1982; 1 child, Kelly Ann. BS, U. Tex., 1979; MA, U. Houston, 1989. Tchr. govt. Round Rock Ind. Sch. Dist., Austin, Tex., 1980-84, Spring Ind. Sch. Dist., Houston, 1984-85, Klein Ind. Sch. Dist., Houston, 1985-88; instr. polit. sci. Houston Community Coll., 1987-88; prof. polit. sci., program coord. North Harris Montgomery Coll. Dist., Tomball, Tex., 1988—; asst. to chancellor North Harris Montgomery Coll. dist., Tomball, Tex., 1993; edn. chair Tomball Regional Arts Coun., 1991-93, bd. dirs.; bd. dirs. Tri-Magna Industries, Waco; del. U.S. Inst. of Peace Seminar, Washington, 1996. Co-author: Texas Government, 1995. Bd. dirs. Champion Forest Civic Assn., Houston, 1986-88, North Area chpt. Houston Symphony League, 1989—, Performing Arts Coun. North Houston, 1994-96; chair Tomball Coll. Law Day; pres. Northampton Homeowners Assn., 1985-86; del. Tex. Rep. Conv., Ft. worth, 1990, Dallas, 1992; faculty advisor Coll. Reps., Tomball Coll.; panelist Nat. Inst. Staff and Orgnl. Devel. Conf., 1992; mem. March of Dimes Guild; charter mem. Houston Holocaust Mus.; legis. chair N.W. Rep. Women, 1988-90, campaign chair, 1990-92. Taft fellow Abilene Christian U., 1988. Mem. NOW, AAUW, Am. Assn. Women in C.C., Tex. Jr. Coll. Tchrs. Assn. (chair govt. sect. 1991-92, legis. com. 1992—, sec. 1994, 95), Tex. Women's Polit. Caucus, Soc. Prevention Cruelty to Animals, Midwest Polit. Sci. Assn., Ctr. for Study of Presidency, U. Houston Alumni Assn., U. Tex. Austin Ex-Students' Assn., LWV, Alpha Xi Delta North Houston Alumnae (pres. 1990-92). Presbyterian. Home: 9319 Appin Falls Dr Spring TX 77379-6554 Office: North Harris Montgomery Coll Dist 30555 Tomball Pky Tomball TX 77375-4096

KRAM, SHIRLEY WOHL, federal judge; b. N.Y.C., 1922. Student, Hunter Coll., 1940-41, CUNY, 1940-47; LLB, Bklyn. Law Sch., 1950. Atty. Legal Aid Soc. N.Y., 1951-53, 1962-71; assoc. Simons & Hardy, 1954-55; pvt. practice law, 1955-60; judge Family Ct., N.Y.C., 1971-83; judge U.S. Dist. Ct. (so. dist.) N.Y., N.Y.C., 1983-93, sr. judge, 1993—. Author: (with Neil A. Frank) The Law of Child Custody, Development of the Substantive Law. Office: US Dist Ct US Courthouse 40 Centre St, Rm 2601 New York NY 10007-1502*

KRAMER, ANN V., lawyer; b. N.Y.C., July 14, 1958. BA cum laude, CUNY, 1980; JD cum laude, U. Mich., 1984. Bar: N.Y. 1985, U.S. Dist. Ct. (so., ea. and no dists.) N.Y. 1985, U.S. Ct. Appeals (2d cir.) 1989, U.S. Supreme Ct. 1993. Ptnr. Anderson, Kill, Olick & Oshinsky, P.C., N.Y.C. Assoc. editor U. Mich. Jour. Law Reform. Office: Anderson Kill Olick & Oshinsky PC 1251 Avenue of the Americas New York NY 10020-1182*

KRAMER, ANNE PEARCE, writer, communications and film executive, educator, psychotherapist, research psychoanalyst; m. Stanley Kramer (div.); children: Larry David, Casey Lise. BA magna cum laude, U. So. Calif., MA, 1965, PhD, 1972. Gen. exec. asst. to producer/dir. Stanley Kramer Prodns., prodn. exec., assoc. producer, story editor, casting dir., dialogue dir.; sr. lectr. cinema and comparative lit. U. So. Calif., L.A.; acting asst. prof. comparative lit. and film Calif. State U., Long Beach; pres. Cathexis 3, L.A.; story editor, v.p. creative affairs Castle Hill Prodns., Inc., L.A., 1978-80; story editor Columbia Pictures, 1981-83, exec. story editor, 1985-88, exec. creative dir., 1983-86, creative cons. to the chmn., 1987—; free-lance cons. film prodn. and editorial pub., 1986—; creative collaborator Clifton Fadiman, Ency. Brit. Films; judge Focus Award for Screenwriting; cons. communications Sta. KPFK-Radio, govt., others. Author: (with others) Directors at Work, 1970, Neo-Metamorphoses-A Cyclical Study, Comparative Transformations in Ovidian Myth and Modern Literature, 1972, Interview with Elia Kazan, 1974, Focus on Film and Theatre, Minorities in Media: A Psychoanalytic Focus, 1990. Bd. dirs. Model UN; expert witness on censorship for Los Angeles Dist. Atty.; nurses aide ARC, Children's Hosp.; former pres. Recovery Found. for Disturbed Children; edn. cons., instr. Camarillo State Mental Hosp.; mem. Psychoanalytic Ctr. Calif. (clin. affiliate). Mem. MLA, AAUP, APA (div. 39 psychoanalysis), Women in Film, Women In Psychoanalysis, Delta Kappa Alpha, Phi Kappa Phi, Pi Beta Phi.

KRAMER, CAROL GERTRUDE, marriage and family counselor; b. Grand Rapids, Mich., Jan. 14, 1939; d. Wilson John and Katherine Joanne (Wasdyke) Rottschafer; m. Peter William Kramer, July 1, 1960; children: Connie R. Kramer Sattler, Paul Wilson Kramer. AB, Calvin Coll., 1960; MA, U. Mich., 1969; PhD, Holy Cross Coll., 1973; MSW, Grand Valley State U., 1985. Diplomate Internat. Acad. Behavioral Medicine, Counseling and Psychotherapy; cert. addictions/substance abuse counselor, Mich.; cert. hypnotist/psychotherapist. Elem. tchr. Jenison (Mich.) Pub. Sch., 1960-64; sch. social worker Grand Rapids Pub. Sch., 1964-81; pvt. practice marriage and family counselor Grand Rapids, 1973—; v.p. Human Resource Assocs., Grand Rapids, 1983-88; pres. Telecounseling, 1996—; guest lectr. Calvin Coll., Mich. State U., Grand Valley State U., 1975-85. Co-author: Parent Involvement Program, 1993, Stop Sexual Abuse for Everyone, 1996. Ruling elder 1st Presbyn. Ch., Grand Rapids, 1975-78; mem. Gerald R. Ford Rep. Women, Grand Rapids, 1980-87; mem. Mich. Bd. of Licensing Marriage Counselors, 1985-88, co-chair pastoral rels. com. Gun Lake Community Ch., 1989-91, v.p. consistory, 1991-93. Named one of Outstanding Young Women in Am., 1974; recipient Meritorious Svc. award Kent County Family Life Coun., 1983. Fellow Am. Assn. Marriage and Family Therapists; mem. NASW, Mich. Assn. Marriage Counselors (awards com. 1988, chmn. 1991, nominations com. 1992—), Kent County Family Life Coun. (pres. 1975), Voters Against Sexual Abuse (pres., bd. dirs. 1992—). Home: 12622 Park Dr Wayland MI 49348-9322 Office: Psychology Ctr 2059 Lake Michigan Dr NW Grand Rapids MI 49504-4742

KRAMER, CECILE E., retired medical librarian; b. N.Y.C., Jan. 6, 1927; d. Marcus and Henrietta (Marks) K. B.S., CCNY, 1956; M.S. in L.S., Columbia U., 1960. Reference asst. Columbia U. Health Scis. Library, N.Y.C., 1957-61, asst. librarian, 1961-75; dir. Health Scis. Libr. Northwestern U., Chgo., 1975-91; asst. prof. edn. Northwestern U., 1975-91, prof. emeritus, 1991—; instr. library and info. sci. Rosary Coll., 1981-85; cons. Francis A. Countway Library Medicine, Harvard U., 1974. Pres. Friends of Libr., Fla. Atlantic U., Boca Raton. Fellow Med. Libr. Assn. (chmn. med. sch. librs. group 1975-76, editor newsletter 1975-77, instr. continuing edn. 1966-75, mem. panel cons. editors Bull. 1987-90, disting. mem. Acad. Health Info. Profls. 1993—); mem. Biomed. Comm. Network (chmn. 1979-80). Home: 9184 Flynn Cir Apt 4 Boca Raton FL 33496-6675

KRAMER, CONSTANCE ANN, songwriter; b. Aug. 1, 1945; d. Isadore Arthur and Evelyn Antoinette (Hart) K.; m. Jerry Preston Raepdale, June 2, 1966 (div. 1979). BA in Psychology, Bklyn. Coll., 1995. In teletype dept. All Metal Nuts & Bolts Factory, Garden City, N.Y., 1965-66; med. receptionist Isadore Arthur Kramer, M.D., Hempstead, N.Y., 1966, 76-83; file clk. Ashforth Real Estate Corp., N.Y.C., 1967; with Vantage Press, Inc., N.Y.C., 1994—. Mem. Animals & The Environment, 1980—, Farm Sanctuary, 1993—, Ctr. Marine Conservation, 1994—, World Wildlife Fund, In Def. of Animals, 1993—, Physicians Com. for Responsible Medicine, 1994, The Fund for Animals, 1995, The Gorilla Found., 1995.

KRAMER, DIANA R., human resources executive; b. N.Y.C., Mar. 10, 1949; d. Joseph and Gloria S.; m. Steven Kramer, May 7, 1975. BA, Glassboro (N.J.) State Coll., 1972; MA, New Sch. Social Research, N.Y.C., 1975; PhD, Fordham U., 1979. Tchr. N.Y.C. Bd. Edn., 1972-80; mgr. human resources and tng. AT&T, Basking Ridge, N.J., 1980-87; mgr. human resources, planning and devel. BASF Corp., Parsippany, N.J., 1987-90; dir. human resources and tng. Miles Inc., Ridgefield Park, N.J., 1990-93; pres. Kramer Cons. Solutions, Chatham, N.J., 1993—. Mem. APA, ASTD, Am.

Psychol. Soc., Exec. Women N.J., N.J. Human Resource Planning Soc., N.Y. Human Resource Planning Soc., N.Y. Assn. Applied Psychology, Met. N.Y. Assn. for Applied Psychology, Orgn. Devel. Network of Greater N.Y., Soc. for Human Resource Mgmt., Soc. for Indsl. and Organizational Psychology. Home and Office: Kramer Consulting Solutions 1 Colonial Way Chatham NJ 07928-2757

KRAMER, JUDITH ANN, elementary education educator; b. Atlanta, Jan. 17, 1945; d. William Walter and Sara Jane (Blount) Blanton (dec.); m. James Anthony Kramer, Oct. 13, 1973; children: Kristopher J., Rebecca S. BS in Journalism, U. Fla., 1969; MEd in Elem. Edn., U. Houston, 1983. Pub. info. officer Fla. Dept. Edn., Tallahassee, 1970-73; tchr. kindergarten, 1st and 2d grades Galena Park Ind. Sch. Dist., Houston, 1983-87; tchr. 1st grade DeSoto (Tex.) Ind. Sch. Dist., 1987-88; tchr. 2d and 3d grades Cedar Hill (Tex.) Ind. Sch. Dist., 1988—; comdg. officer Coast Guard Res. Unit, Dallas, 1994-95; ret., 1995; freelance writer, photographer Gainesville Sun, Houston, Post, Dallas Morning News, Houston Bus. Jour., S.W. Life Mag., others, 1974—. Founder, bd. dirs., vol. Cedar Hill Food Pantry, 1989—. Mem. Assn. Tex. Profl. Educators (sec./bldg. rep., treas.), PTA of High Point Elem. Sch. Methodist. Office: Cedar Hill Ind Sch Dist High Pointe Elem Sch 1351 High Pointe Ln Cedar Hill TX 75104-5067

KRAMER, KAREN, documentary filmmaker; b. New Haven, July 8, 1948; d. Herbert and Sonia (Ginzberg) K. BFA, NYU, 1974. vis. lectr. various univs., 1978—; prfo. New Sch. for Social Rsch., N.Y.C., 1987—. Filmmaker The Jolo Serpent Handlers, 1978, Haitian Song, 1981, Legacy of the Spirits, 1986, Celebration!, 1988, Moko Jumbie, 1990, Rice and Peas, 1990, The Cigar Rollers, 1990, Coney Island Mermaid, 1990, Days of Awe, Days of Joy, 1996. Mem. Haiti Support Com., N.Y.C.; copy editor Haiti Insight, N.Y.C. Recipient awards Nat. Endowment Arts, Washington, 1980, 86, 90, 95, N.Y. Coun. for Humanities, 1980, N.Y. State Coun. on Arts, 1986, 90, 95, Alda Hartley award Noetics Found., Sausalito, Calif., 1995. Mem. Assn. Ind. Filmmakers, Filmmakers' Coop. (v.p. 1993—). Home: 22 Leroy St New York NY 10014

KRAMER, KAREN LEE VAN BRUNT, business administration educator; b. Milw., May 1, 1934; D. Roy Charles and Viola Marguerita (Yerges) Van Brunt; m. Allen Lloyd Weitermann (div. 1963); 1 child, Tera Lee Johnson; m. Keith Kramer (div. 1979); children: Holden Jon, Stafford James. BS, U. Wis., 1956; MA, NYU, 1976; PhD, Ohio State U., 1992. Owner Design By Karen Lee, Larchmont, N.Y., 1975-82; interior designer Maurice Vallency Design, N.Y.C., 1976-79; grad. research assoc. Ctr. on Edn. and Tng. for Employment, Columbus, Ohio, 1987-92; assoc. prof. bus. adminstrn. St. Joseph Coll., West Hartford, Conn., 1992—; lectr. and curriculum developer entrepreneurship state vocat. schs., high schs., colls., and univs. throughout U.S. and Ea. Europe, 1987-92; instr. Berkeley Sch., White Plains, N.Y., 1968-82; adj. prof. N.Y.C. C.C., 1979-83, Milw. Area Tech. Coll., 1983-85, Columbus (Ohio) State C.C., 1986-90, Capital U., Columbus. Mem. Women's Guild 1st Cmty. Ch., Columbus, 1985-92, Wadsworth Atheneum, Hartford, 1992—, West Hartford Art League, 1993—; vol. U. Conn. Health Ctr., Farmington; docent Columbus Symphony Orch., 1986-92. Mem. AAUP (membership chair 1993—), AAUW (past social chair Wis. br.), Am. Vocat. Assn., Ohio Vocat. Assn., Coalition for Effective Orgns., Am. Mktg. Assn., Phi Beta Kappa, Phi Kappa Phi, Phi Lambda Theta, Phi Delta Kappa, Delta Pi Epsilon, Omicron Tau Theta. Home: 30 Woodland St Hartford CT 06105 Office: St Joseph Coll 1698 Asylum Ave Hartford CT 06117

KRAMER, KAREN SUE, mind-body psychologist; b. L.A., Sept. 6, 1942; d. Frank Pacheco Kramer and Velma Eileen (Devlin) Moore; m. Stewart A. Sterling, Dec. 30, 1965 (div. 1974); 1 child, Scott Kramer Sterling. BA, U. Calif., Berkeley, 1966; MA, U.S. Internat. U., 1976; PhD, Profl. Sch. Psychology, 1980. Psychometrist U. Calif. Counseling Ctr., Berkeley, 1966-67; social worker Alameda County Welfare Dept., Oakland, Calif., 1967-69; vol. coord. San. Diego County Probation Dept., 1971-73; officer San Diego County Probation Dept., 1973-76; counselor and coord. clin. and outreach programs Western Inst., San Diego, 1976-77; program coord. and counselor Women's Resource Ctr., Oceanside, Calif., 1977-78; pvt. practice psychology San Diego, 1978-81; planner/analyst San Diego County Dept. Health Svcs., 1979-81; social svcs. program cons. Calif. Dept. Social Svcs., Emeryville, 1981-83; affirmative action officer State Compensation Ins. Fund, San Francisco, 1983-87; regional property mgr. Compensation Ins. Fund, San Francisco, 1991—; community psychologist Calif. Dept. Mental Health, 1987-89; pvt. practice psychology Berkeley, 1990—; cons. psychologist Calif. Dept. Mental Health, 1987-89; personal analyst State Comp. Ins. Fund, 1989-91; regional property mgr. State Compensation Ins. Fund, San Francisco, 1991-95; prof. Nat. U. San Diego, 1979-81; pres. North County Coun. Social Concerns, Vista, Calif., 1977-78; advisor USMC Camp Pendleton Human Svcs., 1978-87; mem. adv. bd. Chinatown Resources Devel. Ctr., San Francisco, 1984-87, San Francisco Rehab., 1984-87; bd. dirs. Network Cons. Svcs., Napa, Calif.; founder Qi Gong in China-Ednl. Svcs., 1994. Mem. Peer Counselors Assn. (adv. bd. 1987-90), Calif. Prevention Network (bd. dirs. 1989-93, editorial advisor jour. 1992-93).

KRAMER, LAURA MICHELLE BOEHNLEIN, psychology educator; b. Washington, May 7, 1969; d. Paul Herbert and Linda Jeanne (Melton) B. BA, Case Western Res. U., 1990, MA, 1990; PhD in Quantitative Psychology, U. N.C., 1994. Rsch. asst. U. N.C., Chapel Hill, 1990-91, teaching asst., 1991-93, instr. psychology, 1993-94; cons., rsch. analyst Research Triangle Inst., Research Triangle Park, N.C., 1991-95; test measurement specialist N.C. State U., Raleigh, 1994—. Mem. Am. Psychol. Soc., Am. Statis. Assn., Mortar Bd., Phi Beta Kappa, Phi Alpha Theta, Psi Chi, Phi Mu. Home: 3514 West Ten Rd Efland NC 27243 Office: NC State Univ Box 8616 1500 Blue Ridge Rd Raleigh NC 27695-8616

KRAMER, LINDA LEWIS, sculptor; b. N.Y.C., Mar. 25, 1937; d. Monty and Mary Ida (Ellis) Lewis; children: Kathryn Kramer Walley, Valerie, Michele. BA, Scripps Coll., 1959; MFA, Sch. of the Art Inst., Chgo., 1981. founding mem. Artemisia Gallery, Chgo., 1973-78, Mid-West Clay Guild, Evanston, Ill., 1973-96; mem. exhbns. com. Evanston Art Ctr., 1992—; councilor Urban Gateways, Chgo., 1996—. Artist: (installation sculptures) Solo American, 1993, Luminous Light, 1993, Pool, 1994, JOY, 1996. Grantee Ill. Arts Coun., 1984, 96, Karolyi grantee, 1989; Artists fellow Dorland Colony, 1986. Home: 370 Glendale Ave Winnetka IL 60093 Office: Midwest Clay Guild 1236 Sherman Ave Evanston IL 60202

KRAMER, MARSHA LOUISE ENDAHL, psychotherapist; b. Davenport, Iowa, Feb. 18, 1948; d. John Charles Sr. and Etta M. (Johnson) Endahl; m. Hugh Thomas Kramer, July 10, 1983; children: Jennifer Michelle Cressy, Jillian Nicole Cressy. Student, U. Minn.; diploma in social welfare, Ryerson Inst., 1969; BA in Sociology, U. Toronto, 1978; MS in Counseling, U. Bridgeport, 1986. Counselor Family Svc. Assn., Toronto, Ont., Can.; pvt. practice New Canaan, Conn.; psychotherapist Christian Counseling Ctr., Norwalk, New Canaan, Conn.; dir. congregational care First Presbyn. Ch., Boca Raton, Fla., 1995—; cons. in field; serve on numerous bd. dirs. Author: (with Fowler) Guide to Homemade Toys; also articles in field. Mem. AACD, Adult Devel. Assn. Address: 23371 Water Cir Boca Raton FL 33486-8542

KRAMER, MARY ELIZABETH, health services executive, state legislator; b. Burlington, Iowa, June 14, 1935; d. Ross L. and Geneva M. (McElhinney) Barnett; m. Kay Frederick Kramer, June 13, 1958; children: Kent, Krista. BA, U. Iowa, 1957, MA, 1971. Cert. tchr., Iowa. Tchr. Newton (Iowa) Pub. Schs., 1957-61; tchr. Iowa City Pub. Schs., 1961-67, tchr., asst. supt., 1971-75; dir. pers. Younkers, Inc., Des Moines, 1975-81; v.p. human resources IASD Health Svcs Inc., Des Moines, 1981—; mem., asst. minority leader Iowa State Senate, Des Moines, 1990—. Bd. dirs. Polk County Child Care Rsch. Ctr., Des Moines, 1986—, YWCA, Des Moines, 1989-94; mem. Olympic adv. com. Blue Cross and Blue Shield Assn., Chgo., 1988-92. Named Mgr. of Yr. Iowa Mgmt. Assocs., 1985, Woman of Achievement YWCA, 1986, Woman of Vision Young Women's Resource Ctr., 1989. Mem. Soc. Human Resource Mgmt. (Profl. of Yr. 1996), Iowa Mgmt. Assn. (pres. 1988), Greater Des Moines C. of C. (bd. dirs. 1986—), Nexus, Rotary Internat. Republican. Presbyterian. Home: 1209 Ashworth Rd West Des Moines IA 50265-3546 Office: IASD Health Svcs Corp 636 Grand Ave Des Moines IA 50309-2502 also: Iowa State Senate State Capitol Des Moines IA 50319

KRAMER, MARY LOUISE, journalist; b. Grand Rapids, Mich., Apr. 18, 1953; d. Vincent Paul and Solina Josephine (Langhals) K. BS, Grand Valley State U., 1979. Asst. city editor, reporter Grand Rapids Press, 1974-82; city editor Greenwich (Conn.) Time, 1982-83; assignment editor Ann Arbor (Mich.) News, 1983-86; city editor Kalamazoo (Mich.) Gazette, 1986-89; assoc. pub., editor Crain's Detroit Bus., 1989—; bd. dirs., ex chair Leadership Detroit, 1991—; bd. dirs. Mich. Ctr. High Tech., 1994—. Named Internat. Woman of Yr. Women in Internat. Trade, 1991, Role Model of Yr. Alternatives Girls, 1996. Mem. Detroit Athletic Club, Women's Econ. Club (adv. com., 30 Most Dynamic Women 1992). Office: Crain's Detroit Bus 1400 Woodbridge Detroit MI 48207-3187

KRAMER, MARY VINCENT, information specialist; b. Rochester, N.Y., Sept. 30, 1957; d. Leonard Patterson and Ruth Helen (Farrell) Vincent; m. Dusty Kramer, Nov. 4, 1989; children: Morgan Lindsay, Matthew Aaron. AS in Bus. Adminstrn., Monroe Community Coll., Rochester, 1981; BS in Mgmt., St. John Fisher Coll., 1989. Tech. info. asst. Xerox Corp., Rochester, N.Y., 1979-89; tech. info specialist Xerox Corp., Rochester, 1989—; steering com. Treas. Employee Involvement, 1987-94. Recipient cert. of appreciation Assn. Info. and Image Mgmt., 1985. Mem. Assn. for Quality and Participation, Xerox Mgmt. Assn., Am. Mgmt. Assn., Alpha Sigma Lambda. Roman Catholic. Office: Xerox Corp 800 Phillips Rd Bldg 105-66C Webster NY 14580-9720

KRAMER, MONICA, psychologist, educator, therapist; b. North Platte, Nebr., Nov. 13, 1953; d. Wayne Charles and Mary Eloise (Karn) K.; m. Randy Joe Kramer; children: Moriah Elizabeth, Nathan Nicholas, Joshua Joseph. BS in Edn., Chadron State Coll., 1975; MS in Elem. Guidance & Counseling, U. Nebr., Kearney, 1991, EdS, 1996. Educator elem. sch. St. Paul (Nebr.) Schs., 1975-77, North Platte (Nebr.) Cath. Schs., 1979-96; mental health practitioner Luth. Family Svcs., North Platte, 1996—; facilitator student assistance team North Platte Cath. Schs., 1994-95; coord. summer tutorial program North Platte Schs., 1993; presenter rsch. Nat. Sch. Psychology Conv., Atlanta, 1996; spkr. in field. Mem. North Platte Cmty. Playhouse, 1990-95; co-facilitator, group counselor Children from Alcoholic Homes, McKinley Edn. Ctr., North Platte, 1991; onsite coord., facilitator Rainbows "A Support Group for Children from Divorced Homes", North Platte, 1993. Rsch. Svc. Coun. grantee, U. Nebr., Kearney, 1994. Mem. ACA, Nat. Assn. Sch. Psychologists, Nat. Cath. Edn. Assn., Nebr. Sch. Psychology Assn., Am. Legion Aux., Alpha Phi Sigma. Democrat. Roman Catholic. Home: Rt 1 Box 406 B North Platte NE 69101 Office: McDaid Elem Sch 415 E 4th North Platte NE 69101

KRAMER, WEEZIE CRAWFORD, broadcast executive. Student, U. Ky., 1977, Wheaton Coll. Sales/local sales mgr. WKQQ, Lexington, Ky., 1977-80; local sales mgr. WHBQ, Memphis, 1980-81; gen. sales mgr. KBPI/KNUS, Denver, 1981-85, WFYR, Chgo., 1985-88; gen. sales mgr. WMAQ All News 67, Chgo., 1988-94, sta. mgr., 1994, v.p., gen. mgr., 1994—. Office: WMAQ-AM 455 N Cityfront Plaza Chicago IL 60611

KRAMER-DUCHARME, NANCY JOAN, calligrapher, designer, educator; b. Kew Gardens, N.Y., July 5, 1953; d. Franklin and Barbara (Richter) K.; m. Kenneth Ducharme, Apr. 13, 1996; children: Allison, Eric. AB, Goucher Coll., 1975; MBA, Northeastern U., 1980; postgrad., Eastern Nazarene Coll. Cert. tchr., Mass.; engr. trainee. Owner, mgr., designer Notes Unltd., Randolph, Mass., 1984—; with Randolph Pub. Sch., 1985—; calligraphy instr. M.E. Young P.T.O. Elem. Sch., Randolph, 1987—; tchr., tchrs. aide Randolph Pub. Sch. System, 1991—; calligraphy instr. Massasoit Community Coll., Brockton, Mass., 1988—; with Brockton (Mass.) Pub. Schs. Reporter (Goucher quarterly) Class Rep., 1987—. Mem. AAUW (v.p. 1987—). Home: 8 Bonnie Ln Randolph MA 02368-5227 Office: Notes Unltd Randolph MA 02368

KRAMM, DEBORAH LUCILLE, lawyer; b. Milw.; d. Hartzell McDonald and Alice Lucille (Johnson) K.; m. Gary Baiz, June 19, 1988. Student, Trinity Coll., Deerfield, Ill., 1971-73; BS, Bradley U., 1974; JD, New Eng. Sch. of Law, 1977; postgrad., Georgetown U., 1978. Bar: N.Y. 1982, Ill. 1980, Mass. 1978. Trademark atty U.S. Trademark Office, Washington, 1977-78; assoc. Hume, Clement, Willian, Brinks & Olds, Chgo., 1978-81; atty. Avon Products, Inc., N.Y.C., 1981-84; atty. Tiffany & Co., N.Y.C., 1981-84, v.p., sec., 1984-85; counsel Am. Brands, Inc., Old Greenwich, Conn., 1986—. Bd. dirs. Nat. Found. for Advancement for Arts, 1987-91; chmn. Martha Graham Guild, 1988—; trustee Martha Graham Ctr. for Contemporary Dance, Inc., N.Y.C., 1989—. Curt Tiege scholar, 1973. Mem. U.S. Trademark Assn. (bd. dirs. 1984-87), Cosmetic, Toiletry and Fragrance Assn. (chmn. trademark com. 1984). Office: Am Brands Inc 1700 E Putnam Ave Old Greenwich CT 06870-1321

KRANIS, LISA ANNE, healthcare administrator; b. Passaic, N.J., Aug. 22, 1964; d. Marinus Thomas and Vivian Mary (Granito) Lalumia; m. Jeffrey Mark Kranis, Sept. 21, 1991. BS in Allied Health, Slippery Rock U., 1987; BA in Pub. Adminstrn., Kean Coll., 1996, postgrad., 1995—. Staffing coord. Morristown (N.J.) Meml. Hosp., 1989-95; staffing and budget mgr. JFK Med. Ctr., Edison, N.J., 1995—. Mem. ASPA, Am. Coll. Healthcare Execs. (treas. 1996—), N.J. Jaycees (sec. Clifton chpt.), Sigma Sigma Sigma. Democrat. Roman Catholic. Office: JFK Med Ctr 65 James St Edison NJ 08817

KRANITZKY, MARY LISA, finance company executive; b. Schenectady, N.Y., July 20, 1955; d. Charles William Kranitzky, and Shirley Ann (Thomas) Ballou. BS in Fin., U. Ala., 1982. Fin. specialist GE Co., Birmingham, Ala., 1981-83, supv. acctg. adminstrn., Atlanta, 1984-85, corp. auditor, Schenectady, 1985-87; mgr. fin. analysis and auditing GE Constrn. Svcs., Burkville, Ala., 1988-90; mgr. fin. Manheim Auctions Inc., Atlanta, 1990-92; program fin. mgr. Latin Am. sales Gen. Electric Indsl. & Power Systems, Schenectady, 1992-94; dir. fin. GE Capital/PT Astra Sedaya Finance, Jakarta, Indonesia, 1995—. Bd. dirs. Birmingham Opera Theater, 1980—. Recipient Acad. Excellence medal Fin. Execs. Inst., 1982. Mem. Beta Gamma Sigma, Phi Kappa Phi, Omicron Delta Epsilon. Episcopalian. Avocations: music; water skiing; reading. Home: care Getsco Distbn PO Box 6027 Schenectady NY 12301 Office: PT Astra Sedaya Finance, JL R.S. Fatmawati No 9, Jakarta 12420, Indonesia

KRANKING, MARGARET GRAHAM, artist; b. Florence, S.C., Dec. 21, 1930; d. Stephen Wayne and Madge Williams (Dawes) Graham; BA summa cum laude (Clendenin fellow), Am. U., 1952; m. James David Kranking, Aug. 23, 1952; children: James Andrew, Ann Marie Kranking Eggleton, David Wayne. Asst. to head publs. Nat. Gallery Art, Washington, 1952-53; profl. artist, 1966—; tchr. art Woman's Club Chevy Chase (Md.), 1976-88; guest instr. Amherst Coll., 1985; one-woman shows: Spectrum Gallery, Washington, 1974, 76, 78, 79, 83, 85, 87, 90, 92, 95, Philip Morris U.S.A., Richmond, Va., 1982, 83, 86, Florence (S.C.) Mus., 1991, Lombardi Cancer Treatment Ctr., Washington, 1992; group shows include: Balt. Mus., 1974, 76, Corcoran Gallery Art, Washington, 1952, 72, USIA Traveling Exhibit, C. Am., 1978-79, AARP Traveling Exhibition, 1986; represented in permanent collection U. Va., 1979, Philip Morris U.S.A., 1982, 83, USCG, 1986-93, 95, AT&T, 1986, 88, Freddie Mac, 1987, 88, Florence Mus., S.C., 1994; traveling exhbn. Nat. Watercolor Soc., 1985-86, Watercolor U.S.A., 1987, 92, 95, Am. Watercolor Soc., 1988, Am. Artist mag., 1988, 91, 92, North Light Mag., 1990, Adirondacks Nat. Exhbn. of Am. Watercolor, 1988, 89, Artitude 7th Internat. Art Competition, N.Y., 1989, Shada Gallery, Riyadh, Saudi Arabia, 1991, Belle Grove Plantation Invitational, Middletown, Va., 1994, Washington County Mus. of Fine Arts Invitational, Hagerstown, Md., 1996; ofcl. artist USCG; contbr. reproductions and text to numerous books. Mem. Spectrum Gallery Washington, So. Watercolor Soc., Artists Equity, Washington Watercolor Assn., M.W. Watercolor Soc., Potomac Valley Watercolorists (pres. 1981-83), Nat. Watercolor Soc, Southwestern Watercolor Soc. Roman Catholic. Home: 3504 Taylor St Bethesda MD 20815-4022

KRANTZ, CLAIRE WOLF, artist; b. Chgo., June 22, 1938; d. George and Etta (Shtriker) Kaplan; m. San Robert Wolf, Mar. 8, 1959 (dec. 1973); children: Richard Wolf, Deborah Wolf Blanks, Rachel Wolf; m. David L. Krantz, Dec. 19, 1976. BS in Occpl. Therapy, U. Ill., 1961; post grad., Stanford U., 1977-78; BFA, Sch. Inst. of Chgo., 1979, postgrad., 1980-83. Occpl. therapist, 1961-76; freelance art critic for nat. art publs. Solo Exhbns. include: Artemesia Gallery, Chgo., 1988, Gallerie S&H De Buck, Belgium, 1989, Galerie Paula Kouwenhoven, Delft, The Netherlands, 1990, Galerie Blankenese, Germany, 1991, Sazama Gallery, Chgo., 1992, Chgo. Cultural Ctr., 1993, various others; group exhbns. include: Walker Gallery Art, 1981, Art Inst. Chgo., 1981, Hokin Kaufman Gallery, Chgo., 1988, A.I.R. Gallery, N.Y.C., 1991-95, Spertus Mus., Chgo., 1994, various others; numerous publs. Mem. Phi Kappa Phi. Home: 903 W Roscoe Chicago IL 60657 Studio: 1538 N Oakley Chicago IL 60622

KRANTZ, JUDITH TARCHER, novelist; b. N.Y.C., Jan. 9, 1928; d. Jack David and Mary (Brager) Tarcher; m. Stephen Falk Krantz, Feb. 19, 1954; children: Nicholas, Anthony. B.A., Wellesley Coll., 1948. Fashion publicist Paris, 1948-49; fashion editor Good Housekeeping mag., N.Y.C., 1949-56; contbg. writer McCalls, 1956-59, Ladies Home Jour., 1959-71; contbg. west coast editor Cosmopolitan mag., 1971-79. Author: Scruples, 1978, Princess Daisy, 1980, Mistral's Daughter, 1982, I'll Take Manhattan, 1986, Till We Meet Again, 1988, Dazzle, 1990, Scruples Two, 1992, Lovers, 1994, Spring Collection, 1996.

KRANTZ, MELISSA MARIANNE, public relations company executive; b. Cornwall, N.Y., Sept. 19, 1954; d. Abraham and Jane (Steinheimer) K.; m. David Michael Fleisher, Nov. 19, 1978; children: Jenny Rachel, Sara Rose. BA in Polit. Sci., SUNY Coll., Purchase, 1976. Account exec. Pub. Interest Pub. Relations, Inc., N.Y.C., 1975-77; assoc. Kekst & Co., N.Y.C., 1977-83, ptnr., 1983-91; v.p. corp. comm. JWP Inc., 1991-92; pres. Krantz Group, Inc., 1992—. Trustee Beth Am Shalom Synagogue, White Plains, N.Y., 1985-87, Mazon; bd. dirs. Project Ezra, N.Y.C., 1986-95; bd. dirs. BBB Met. N.Y., Inc., 1988—, mem. exec. com., 1989—. Democrat. Jewish. Home: 15 Franklin Ln Harrison NY 10528-1105

KRANZ, TRUDY J., food products executive; b. Carlsbad, Calif., Feb. 24, 1963; d. Jerry R. and Marie Antionette (Giesen) K. BS in Bus. Mgmt., Calif. Poly Inst., 1986. Dir. devel. Treats U.S.A., Bakersfield, Calif.; dist. mgr. Oh La La!, San Francisco; dir. devel. Cocolat, Berkeley, Calif.; pres. Pandora's Confections, San Francisco. Mem. Internat. Assn. Specialty Food & Trade.

KRASSA, KATHY BOLTREK, molecular biologist; b. N.Y.C., Dec. 6, 1946; d. Henry and Gloria Beatrice (Poliakoff) Boltrek; m. Robert Frederick Taylor Krassa; children: Josh Boltrek, Vicky Krassa. BS, Cornell U., 1968; postgrad., L.I. U., 1973-74; PhD, U. Colo., 1987. Lab. tech. U. Colo., Boulder, 1968-70; teaching asst. C.W. Post Coll., L.I. U., Glen Cove, N.Y., 1973-74; rsch. assoc. Nassau County Med. Ctr., East Meadow, N.Y., 1975-79; teaching asst. U. Colo., Boulder, 1980-81, rsch. asst., 1981-87, postdoctoral rschr., 1988-91; CEO Molecular Jeanetics, Boulder, 1991—. Author: Structure and Function of the Single-Stranded DNA Binding Protein of the Bacteriophage T4, 1987; contbr. articles to profl. jours. NIH grantee, 1974, 82, Am. Cancer Soc. rsch. grantee, 1988, 89.

KRAUS, HILDA, designer, artist; b. N.Y.C., Jan. 26, 1915; d. Isaac and Sadie (Langer) K. BA, Hunter Coll., 1935; postgrad., Internat. Acad. Art, Salzburg, Austria, 1967, 72, 77. Jewelry, enamels and metalwork designer, 1935—; tchr., instr. Brookfield (Conn.) Craft Ctr., 1965, 87, Silvermine Coll., New Canaan, Conn., 1975-76, Stamford (Conn.) Mus., 1979. Exhibited in shows at Cork Gallery, N.Y.C., Phila. Art Alliance, Gesellschaft fur goldschmiedekunst, Hamburg, Germany, Slater Meml. Mus., Norwich, Sarah Squeri Gallery, Cin., Mattatuck Mus., Waterbury, Conn., 1990, Berkshire Mus., Pittsfield, Mass., 1993, Worcester (Mass.) Ctr. for Crafts, 1993, Fuller Mus., Brockton, Mass., 1993, Silvermine Guild ARts Ctr., 1995, Coburg Germany, 1995, Ctr. for Arts, Wichita, Kans., 1995. Vol. Conn. Literacy, Norwalk, 1985—. Recipient Purchase prize Cooper-Hewitt Mus., 1969, Del. Art Ctr., Best in Show award Art on the Mountain, Wilmington, Vt., 1985, Pen and Brush Club, N.Y.C., 1965-76, 1st prize Craftsman of N.Y., 1974, 76, 91, Medaille de la Ville de Limoges (France) Troisieme Biennale internat., 1975. Mem. Soc. Conn. Craftsmen (bd. dirs. 1950-70), Enamel Guild N.E., Silvermine Guild of Artists (bd. dirs. 1970's), Soc. Am. Craftsmen, Brookfield Crafts Ctr. Office: Po Box 305 Westport CT 06881

KRAUS, JENNIFER ELAINE, microbiologist, musician; b. Saginaw, Mich., Sept. 20, 1955; d. Kenneth George and Ruth Gwendolyn (Hodder) Kraus; m. Paul David Scheerer (div. Nov. 1991); children: Stephanie Ruth Kraus-Scheerer, Phoebe Laurel Kraus-Scheerer. BS in Biology, Mich. State U., 1978, BS in Botany and Plant Pathology, 1981; PhD in Genetics and Cell Biology, Wash. State U., Pullman, 1987. Tech. asst. dept. botany and plant pathology Mich. State U., East Lansing, 1975-78; rsch. technician Dept. Energy Plant Rsch. Lab., East Lansing, 1979-81; rsch. assoc. program in genetics and cell biology Wash. State U., Pullman, 1981-88; plant pathologist Hort. Crops Rsch. Lab., ARS, USDA, Corvallis, Oreg., 1988-89; faculty rsch. assoc. dept. botany and plant pathology Oreg. State U., Corvallis, 1989-95, faculty rsch. assoc. dept. microbiology, 1995—. Contbr. chpts. to books, articles to profl. jours. Pres. Palouse Folklore Soc., Moscow, Idaho, 1985-86. NSF grad. fellow, 1982-85. Democrat. Office: Oreg State U Dept Microbiology Corvallis OR 97333

KRAUS, JOY ELAINE, respiratory therapist; b. Giddings, Tex., Mar. 11, 1957; d. Elvis William and Idell Amelia (Schoenberg) Kraus. AAS in Respiratory Therapy, S.W. Tex. State U., 1980, BS in Health Professions, 1980. Registered respiratory therapist, cert. respiratory therapist, Tex. Staff respiratory therapist Brackenridge Hosp., Austin, 1980-81; supr. respiratory therapy Hermann Hosp., Houston, 1981-83; staff respiratory therapist St. Luke's Episcopal Hosp., Houston, 1983-84, mgr. patient care svcs. respiratory care, 1984—. Mem. Am. Assn. for Respiratory Therapy, Tex. Soc. for Respiratory Therapy (sec.-treas. S. Tex. region 1983-84). Episcopalian. Office: St Lukes Episcopal Hosp 4-247 Bertner Houston TX 77030

KRAUS, NORMA JEAN, industrial relations executive; b. Pitts., Feb. 11, 1931; d. Edward Karl and Alli Alexandra (Hermanson) K. BA, U. Pitts., 1954; postgrad. NYU , 1959-61, Cornell U., 1969-70. Pers. mgr. for several cos., 1957-70; corp. dir. personnel TelePrompter Corp., N.Y.C., 1970-73; exec. asst., speech writer to lt. gov. N.Y. State, Office Lt. Gov., Albany, 1974-79; v.p. human resources, labor relations and stockholder relations Volt Info. Scis., Inc., N.Y.C., 1979—. Co-founder, Manhattan Women's Polit. Caucus, 1971, N.Y. State Women's Polit. Caucus, 1972, vice chair N.Y. State Women's Polit. Caucus, 1978; bd. dirs. Ctr. for Women in Govt., 1977-79. Lt. (s.g.) USNR, 1954-57. Pa. State Senatorial scholar, 1950-54. Mem. Women's Econ. Roundtable, Indsl. Relations Research Assn. Democrat. Avocations: politics, women's rights. Office: Volt Info Scis Inc 47th Fl 1221 Avenue of the Americas New York NY 10020-1579

KRAUS, PANSY DAEGLING, gemology consultant, editor, writer; b. Santa Paula, Calif., Sept. 21, 1916; d. Arthur David and Elsie (Pardee) Daegling; m. Charles Frederick Kraus, Mar. 1, 1941 (div. Nov. 1961). AA, San Bernardino Valley Jr. Coll., 1938; student Longmeyer's Bus. Coll., 1940; grad. gemologist diploma Gemological Assn. Gt. Britain, 1960, Gemological Inst. Am., 1966. Clk. Convair, San Diego, 1943-48; clk. San Diego County Schs. Publs., 1948-57; mgr. Rogers and Boblet Art-Craft, San Diego, 1958-64; part-time editorial asst. Lapidary Jour., San Diego, 1963-64, assoc. editor, 1964-69, editor, 1970-94, sr. editor, 1984-85; pvt. practice cons., San Diego, 1985—; lectr. gems, gemology local gem, mineral groups; gem & mineral club bull. editor groups. Mem. San Diego Mineral & Gem Soc., Gemol. Soc. San Diego, Gemol. Assn. Great Britain, Mineral. Soc. Am., Epsilon Sigma Alpha. Author: Introduction to Lapidary, 1987; editor, layout dir.: Gem. Cutting Shop Helps, 1964, The Fundamentals of Gemstone Carving, 1967, Appalachian Mineral and Gem Trails, 1968, Practical Gem Knowledge for the Amateur, 1969, Southwest Mineral and Gem Trails, 1972, Introduction to Lapidary, 1987; revision editor Gemcraft (Quick and Leiper), 1977; contbr. articles to Lapidary jour., Keystone Mktg. catalog. Home and Office: PO Box 600908 San Diego CA 92160-0908

KRAUS, SHERRY STOKES, lawyer; b. Richmond, Ky., Aug. 11, 1945; d. Thomas Alexander and Callie (Ratliff) Stokes; m. Eugene John Kraus, Aug.

27, 1966. Student, U. Ky., 1962-64; BS, Roosevelt U., 1966; JD cum laude, Albany Law Sch., 1975; LLM in Taxation, NYU, 1981. Bar: N.Y. 1976, U.S. Dist. Ct. (we. dist.) N.Y. 1976, U.S. Tax Ct. 1986. Law clk. U.S. Tax Ct., Washington, summer 1974, 4th dept. Appellate div. N.Y. State Supreme Ct., Rochester, 1975-77; assoc. Nixon, Hargrave, Devans & Doyle, Rochester, 1977-81, 83-84, Harter, Secrest & Emery, Rochester, 1984-86; pvt. practice Rochester, 1986—; faculty grad. tax program Sch. Law, NYU, N.Y.C., 1981-82; prin. tech. adv. to assoc. chief counsel - tech. IRS, Washington, 1983-84. Articles editor ABA Tax Articles Periodical, The Tax Lawyer, 1984-88; mng. editor NYU Tax Articles Periodical, NYU Tax Law Rev., 1981-82; lead articles editor Tax Articles Periodical, Albany Law Rev., 1973-75; contbr. articles to profl. jours. David J. Brewer scholar Albany Law Sch., 1973. Mem. ABA, N.Y. State Bar Assn. (tax sect. exec. com. 1984—), Monroe County Bar Assn. (treas. 1990-92), Monroe County Bar Found. (pres. 1994-95), Justinian Soc. Office: 513 Times Square Bldg Rochester NY 14614-2078

KRAUSCHE-MARTIN, KAREN, social services administrator, clinical social worker; b. N.Y.C., Sept. 2, 1947; d. John Francis and Gladys Rose (Cure) K.; m. John Charles Martin, Oct. 16, 1977; children: Stacey Elizabeth, Sean Patrick. BA, Sacred Heart U., 1984; MSW, Fordham U., 1985; cert. family therapy, Smith Coll., 1989. Cert. social worker, N.Y., Conn.; cert. sch. social worker, regular and spl. edn. tchr., Conn. Social worker United Cerebral Palsy, Bridgeport, Conn., 1983, Norwalk (Conn.) Sch. Sys., 1983-84, Cath. Family Services, Bridgeport, 1984-89; pvt. practice social work Ctr. Family Guidance, Stratford, Conn., 1986-90; social worker Fairfield (Conn.) Bd. Edn., 1993—, Olsten-Kimberly Quality Care, 1994-95; substitute tchr. Norwalk Sch. Sys., 1994-95; cons. Apple Tree Nursery Sch., Trumbull, Conn., 1989-91, Shelton (Conn.) Bd. Edn., 1989-92. Bd. dirs. Trumbull Counseling Ctr., 1984-89; mem. Regional Youth Substance Abuse Prevention Coun., Trumbull, 1988-89. Mem. Nat. Assn. Social Workers (register of clin. social work), Conn. Assn. Sch. Social Workers, Acad. Cert. Social Workers. Roman Catholic. Home: 50 Friar Ln Trumbull CT 06611-4014

KRAUSE, HEATHER DAWN, data processing executive; b. Kansas City, Kans., May 6, 1956; d. Jack E. Firth and Bonnie Jo (Reeves) Cupps; m. Kerry Murray Krause, May 23, 1981. Cert., Kansas City Skill Ctr., 1980. Cert. drafting tchr.; cert. in bus. supervision; cert. in Novell Netware system adminstrn. Assoc. drafter Black & Veatch, Kansas City, Mo., 1980; technician mech. design Wilcox Electric, Kansas City, 1980; coord. CAD design systems Smith & Loveless, Inc., Lenexa, Kans., 1980—; owner Digital Design Technologies, Kansas City, Mo., 1989—; tech. editor Que Books Macmillan Computer Pub., 1994—; instr. Longview C.C., Lee's Summit, Mo., 1987-93. Mem. NAFE, Kansas City Area AutoCAD Users Group, Heartland Windows User Group, Phi Theta Kappa. Democrat. Home: PO Box 11319 Kansas City MO 64112-0319

KRAUSE, HELEN FOX, physician, otolaryngologist; b. Boston, Mar. 20, 1932; d. Nathan and Frances Lena (Rich) Fox; children: Merrick Eli, Beth Reva Krause-Harper, Kim Debra Codd. BS, U. Maine, 1954; MD, Tuft U., 1958. Diplomate Am. Bd. Otolaryngology. Intern Health Ctr. Hosps. Pitts., 1958-59; resident Eye & Ear Hosp., Children's Hosp., VA Hosp., 1959-62; pvt. practice Pitts., 1962—; pres. Am. Acad. of Otolaryngic Allergy, 1984-85, Pa. Acad. of Otolaryngology, 1989-90; pres. Pitts. Otological Soc., 1983-85; chmn. otolaryngology adv. bd. U.S. Pharmacopea, 1991—; bd. govs. Am. Acad. Otolaryngology H & N Surgery, 1982-89, 90—; clin. assoc. prof. U. Pitts. Sch. Medicine, Pa. State U. Hershey Med. Coll.; vis. prof. Pan Hellenic Otorhinolaryngology Soc., Crete, Greece, 1993. Author, editor: Otolaryngic Allergy and Immunology, 1989; lectr., vis. prof. Singapore, Bangkok, Hong Kong (multiple tng. programs 1990); contbr. chpts. to books and articles to profl. jours. Pres. North Hills Jewish Community Ctr., Pitts., 1973-74; cons. North Allegheny Sch. Bd., Pitts., 1977; lectr. North Allegheny Sr. High Sch., Wexford, 1979-84; chmn. Desert Storm Project, North Hills Bus. and Profl. Women, 1991. Rsch. scholar Jackson Meml. Labs., Bar Harbor, Maine, 1954; recipient Disting. Svc. award Pa. Acad. Otolaryngology, 1993, Hon. Achievement award Am. Acad. Otolaryngology Head and Neck Surgery, 1993. Fellow ACS, Am. Acad. Otolaryngologic Allergy (Svc. award 1990, cert. appreciation 1991), Am. Acad. Facial Plastic and Rsch. Surgery; mem. Internat. Soc. Otorhinolaryngic Allergy and Immunology (pres. 1995—), Phi Beta Kappa, Phi Kappa Phi. Office: 9104 Babcock Blvd Ste 4110 Pittsburgh PA 15237-5818

KRAUSE, JUDITH MARILYN RICKENBACKER, career officer; b. Orangeburg, S.C., June 12, 1967; d. Robert Carroll and Judith Marilyn Rickenbacker; m. Paul Andrew Krause, May 25, 1989; children: Christopher Andrew, Daniel Paul. BS in Civil Engring., U.S. Mil. Acad., 1989; various mil. courses. Engr. in tng., Mo., 1994. Commd. 2d lt. U.S. Army, 1989, advanced through grades to capt., 1993; platoon leader 13th Engr. Co. U.S. Army, Ft. Knox, Ky., 1989-91; exec. officer 13th Engr. Co. U.S. Army, Ft. Knox, 1992, brigade asst. 194th Separate Armored Brigade, 1993; battalion adjutant 46th Engr. Battalion U.S. Army, Ft. Polk, La., 1994-96; co. comdr. 814th Engr. Co. U.S. Army, Ft. Polk, 1996—. Mem. Army Engr. Assn. (lifetime), Soc. Am. Mil. Engrs. Office: 814th Engineer Company Fort Polk LA 71459

KRAUSE, LOIS RUTH BREUR, chemistry educator; b. Paterson, N.J., Mar. 26, 1946; d. George L. and Ruth Margaret (Farquhar) Breur; m. Bruce N. Pritchard, 1968 (div. May 1982); children: John Douglas, Tiffany Anne,; m. Robert H. Krause, June 16, 1990. Student, Keuka Coll., 1964-65; BS in Chemistry cum laude, Fairleigh Dickinson U., 1980, MAT summa cum laude, 1994; postgrad., Stevens Inst. Tech.; PhD, Clemson U., 1996. With dept. R & D UniRoyal, Wayne, N.J., 1966-68, Jersey State Chem. Co., North Haledon, 1968-69, Inmont, Clifton, N.J., 1969; from chemist to sr. analyst Lever Bros., Edgewater, N.J., 1976-80; process engr. Bell Telephone Labs., Murray Hill, N.J., 1980-84, RCA, Somerville, N.J., 1984-86; sr. engr. electron beam lithography ops. Gain Electronics Corp., Somerville, 1986-88, ind. tech. cons. Pritchard Assocs., Budd Lake, N.J., 1988-92; tchr. of math. and scis. Mt. Olive Bd. Edn. (temporary assignments), 1990-92; tchr. chemistry Morris Hills Regional Dist., 1992-93; instr. chemistry, vis. asst. prof. edn. Clemson U., 1994-95; instr. chem. labs., 1994-96, vis. asst. prof. edn., 1995-96, vis. asst. prof. chemistry, 1996—; presenter workshops and profl. papers for profl. confs. Patentee package design. Troop leader, trainer, cons. Bergen County council Girl Scouts U.S., 1969-80, troop leader Morris Area council, 1980-83, head com. Mt. Olive twp., 1980-81; den leader, den leader coach, trainer Boy Scouts Am., 1973-76. Peter Sammartino scholar, 1994. Fellow Am. Inst. Chemists; mem. IEEE (sr., Components, Hybrids and Mfg. Tech. Soc. semicondr. tech. subcom. electronic components conf. program com. 1981-86), NEA, NRA (life), AAAS, ASCD, APA, Am. Soc. Quality Control, Soc. Women Engrs., Am. Chem. Soc., Assn. Women in Sci., N.Y. Acad. Scis., Nat. Woodlot Owners Assn., Arbor Day Found., Mensa, Marine Corps League Aux., Phi Omega Epsilon, Phi Delta Kappa (editor Clemson Kappan), Alpha Epsilon Lambda. Republican. Episcopalian. Home and Office: 303 Cherokee Hills Dr Pickens SC 29671-8619

KRAUS-FRIEDMANN, NAOMI, biochemistry educator; b. Budapest, Hungary, July 4, 1933; came to U.S., 1965; d. Jacob and Vilma (Schvartz) K.; (div.); 1 child, Daphna. MS, Hebrew U., Jerusalem, Israel, 1960; PhD, Hebrew U., 1966. Instr. U. Pa., Phila., 1968-74; asst. prof. U. Tex. Sch. Medicine, Houston, 1974-76, assoc. prof., 1976-86; prof. U. Tex. Sch. Medicine, 1986—. Editor: Hormonal Control of Gluconeogenesis, 1986. Pres. Assn. Women in Sci. (Gulf Coast chpt.), 1974-76, v.p., 1989-90. Recipient grants from NIH, NSF. Mem. Am. Soc. Cell Biology. Office: U Tex Med Sch Houston Dept Integrative Biology 6431 Fannin St Houston TX 77030

KRAUS-RAUBVOGEL, ANNETTE MARIE, illustrator; b. Carroll, Iowa, Oct. 4, 1963; d. Merlin Joseph and Mary Lou (Schettler) Kraus; m. David Robert Raubvogel, Oct. 6, 1990; 1 child, Alexander. BA, Buena Vista Coll., 1986. Intern, artists in newsroom Ariz. Republic, Phoenix, 1986; intern, graphic artist Newsday, Melville, N.Y., 1986-87; staff artist Gannett Newspapers, White Plains, N.Y., 1987-91; staff artist, newsroom Jour. Am., Bellevue, Wash., 1991-95; contractor, illustrator Microsoft Corp., Redmond, Wash., 1996—; freelance illustrator A. Kraus Illustration/Design, Seattle, 1996—. Recipient 1st place award Aldus Design Contest, 1992, Wash. Press Assn., 1992, 94. Mem. Soc. Newspaper Design, Graphic Artist Guild. Home and Office: A Kraus Illustration and Design 530 31st Ave E Seattle WA 98112

KRAUSS, EILEEN S., bank executive. Grad. magna cum laude, Mt. Holyoke Coll.; MA, Trinity Coll.; D Comml. Sci. (hon.), U. Hartford, 1995. Chmn. Fleet Bank, Hartford, Conn.; pres. Career Search Resources; v.p. human resources planning and devel. Shawmut Nat. Corp., vice chmn., bd. dirs.; bd. dirs. CPC Internat., Kaman Corp., Stanley Works, Yankee Energy Sys. Mem. exec. com., v.p. Bushnell Meml. Hall; chmn. Cmty. Econ. Devel. Found., Inc.; mem. exec. com. Conn. Bus. and Industry Assn.; bd. dirs. Yale New Haven Hosp. Named Conn. Bus. Leader of Yr., Hartford Courant, 1990; recipient Leadership award to women in bus. New Eng. Coun., 1993, Woman of Merit award Conn. Valley Coun. Girl Scouts U.S., 1994. Mem. Greater Hartford C. of C. (chmn.). Office: Fleet Bank 777 Main St Hartford CT 06115

KRAUSS, JUDITH BELLIVEAU, nursing educator; b. Malden, Mass., Apr. 11, 1947; d. Leo F. and Dorothy (Conners) Belliveau; m. Ronald L. Krauss, Sept. 5, 1970; children: Jennifer Leigh, Sarah Elizabeth. BS, Boston Coll., 1968; MSN, Yale U., 1970. RN, Conn. Clinical specialist Conn. Mental Health Ctr., New Haven, 1971-73; clin. specialist Yale Sch. Nursing, New Haven, 1971-73; asst. prof. rsch. Yale U. Sch. Nursing, New Haven, 1973-78, assoc. dean, 1978-85; prof., dean Yale U. Sch. Nursing, New Haven, Conn., 1985—; cons. pharm. and pub. cons., sch., govt. agys. Author: The Chronically Ill Psychiatric Patient and the Community, 1982 (Am. Jour. Nursing Book of Yr. 1982); editor Archives of Psychiat. Nursing, 1986—; mem. editorial bd. Issues in Mental Health Nursing, Psychosocial Rehab., Psychiat. Nursing Forum, Psychiat. Svcs.; contbr. articles to profl. jours. Am. Nurses Found. scholar, 1978; recipient Chamberlain award Soc. Edn. and Rsch. in Nursing, 1994; named Disting. Alumna Yale Sch. Nursing, 1984. Mem. ANA (Disting. Contbn. to Psychiat. Nursing award 1992), Am. Acad. Nursing, Conn. Nurses Assn. (mem. cabinet on edn. 1987-89, bd. dirs. 1988-91, rep. to ANA house of dels. 1988-91, Josephine Dolan award 1989), Sigma Theta Tau (Disting. Lectr. award 1987), Delta Mu (Founders award 1987). Office: Yale U Sch Nursing PO Box 9740 New Haven CT 06536-0740

KRAUT, JOANNE LENORA, computer programmer, analyst; b. Watertown, Wis., Oct. 29, 1949; d. Gilbert Arthur and Dorothy Ann (Gebel) K.; BA in Russian, U. Wis., Madison, 1971, MS in Computer Sci., 1973. Computer programmer U. Wis. Sch. Bus., Madison, 1969-72, Milw. Ins. Co., 1973-74; tech. coord. Wis. Dept. Justice, Madison, 1974-83; tech. svcs. supr. CRC Telecommunications (formerly Benchmark Criminal Justice Systems), New Berlin, Wis., 1983-89; sr. programmer/analyst Info. Communications Corp., Pub. Safety Software, Inc., 1989-91; advanced systems engr. EDS, 1991-93; technical specialist Time Ins., Milw., 1993-96; staff analyst Exacta Corp., Brookfield, Wis., 1996—. Mem. Lakewood Gardens Assn. (dir. 1981-83), Dundee Terrs. Condominium Assn. (officer 1983—). Mem. Phi Beta Kappa. Home: 609 Dundee Ln Hartland WI 53029-2722 Office: Exacta Corp 16595 W Bluemound Rd Brookfield WI 53005

KRAVITCH, PHYLLIS A., federal judge; b. Savannah, Ga., Aug. 23, 1920; d. Aaron and Ella (Wiseman) K. B.A., Goucher Coll., 1941; LL.B., U. Pa., 1943; LL.D. (hon.), Goucher Coll., 1981. Bar: Ga. 1943, U.S. Dist. Ct. 1944, U.S. Supreme Ct. 1948, U.S. Ct. Appeals (5th cir.) 1962. Practice law Savannah, 1944-76; judge Superior Ct., Eastern Jud. Circuit of Ga., 1977-79, U.S. Ct. Appeals (5th cir.), Atlanta, 1979-81, U.S. Ct. Appeals (11th cir.), 1981—; mem. Jud. Conf. Standing Com. on Rules, 1994—. Trustee Inst. Continuing Legal Edn. in Ga., 1979-82; mem. Bd. Edn., Chatham County, Ga., 1949-55; mem. coun. Law Sch., Emory U., Atlanta, 1986—; mem. vis. com. Law Sch., U. Chgo., 1990-93; mem. regional rev. panel Truman Scholarship Found., 1992—. Recipient Hannah G. Solomon award Nat. Coun., Jewish Women, 1978, James Wilson award U. Pa. Law Alumni Soc., 1992. Fellow Am. Bar Found.; mem. ABA (Margaret Brent award 1991), Savannah Bar Assn. (pres. 1976), State Bar Ga., Am. Judicature Soc., Am. Law Inst, U. Pa. Law Soc. Office: US Ct Appeals 11th Cir 56 Forsyth St NW # 202 Atlanta GA 30303-2205

KRAWITZ, MANDY JANE, urban planning manager; b. Johannesburg, South Africa, Apr. 19, 1969; came to U.S., 1978; d. Colin Michael and Ethel Ann (Lerman) K. BA in Sociology, U. Calif., Santa Barbara, 1990; MA in Sociology, U. Colo., Colorado Springs, 1995. Pub. rels. cons. Re/Max of Irvine, Calif., 1990-93; dir. response specialist DoubleCase Corp., Colorado Springs, 1993-94; grad. student coord. sociology dept. U. Colo., Colorado Springs, 1995, profl. rsch. asst. instnl. rsch., 1994-95; dept. mgr. urban planning U. Calif., Irvine, 1996—; staff rsch. asst. VCI Health Promotion Ctr., 1996—. Fellow AAUW, Applied Sociology Assn., Am. Planning Assn., Am. Jour. Sociology, Am. Sociol. Assn., Alpha Kappa Delta. Jewish. Office: U Calif Dept Urban and Regional Planning 202 Social Ecology I Irvine CA 92697-7075

KREADER, CAROL A., molecular biologist; b. St. Louis, May 5, 1956; d. Lester D. and Elizabeth M (Stewart) K.; Brian A. Wrenn, June 10, 1988. BS in Biology, S. E. Mo. State U., 1978; MS in marine biology, U. Miami, 1983; PhD in Biochemistry, Ind. U., 1988. Postdoctoral rsch. assoc. U. Ill., Urbana, 1988-92; rsch. asst. U.S. Environ. Protection Agy., Cin., 1992-95; rsch. sci. clin. diagnostics Johnson & Johnson, Rochester, N.Y., 1995—. Contbr. articles to profl. jours. Recipient assoc. instr. award IU Chem. Dept., 1986, lubrizol fellow Ind. U. Chem Dept., 1986-87, postdoctoral fellow NIH, 1988-90, postgrad. rsch. fellow Oakridge Inst. for Sci & Edn., 1992-95. Mem. Am. Soc. for Microbiology, Sigma Xi. Office: J & J CD NAD Bldg 82 4th Fl RL Rochester NY 14650-2117

KREAGER, EILEEN DAVIS, administrative consultant; b. Caldwell, Ohio, Mar. 2, 1924; d. Fred Raymond and Esther (Farson) Davis. BBA, Ohio State U., 1945. With accounts receivable dept. M & R Dietetic, Columbus, Ohio, 1945-50; complete charge bookkeeper Magic Seal Paper Products, Columbus, 1950-53, A. Walt Runglin Co., L.A., 1953-54; office mgr. Roy C. Haddox and Son, Columbus, 1954-60; bursar Meth. Theol. Sch. Ohio, Delaware, 1961-86; adminstrv. cons. Fin. Ltd., 1986—; ptnr. Coll. Administrv. Sci., Ohio State U., 1975-80; seminar participant Paperwork Systems and Computer Sci., 1965, Computer Systems, 1964, Griffith Found. Seminar Working Women, 1975; pres. Altrusa Club of Delaware, Ohio, 1972-73. Del. Altrusa Internat., Montreal, 1972, Altrusa Regional, Greenbrier, 1973. Mem. AAUW, Assoc. Am. Inst. Mgmt. (exec. council of Inst., 1979); Am. Soc. Profl. Cons., Internat. Platform Assn., Ohio State U. Alumna Assn., Columbus Computer Soc., Innovation Alliance, Toastmasters Internat., Ohio State U. Faculty Club, Univ. Club of Columbus, Delaware Country Club, Columbus Met. Club, Friends Hist. Costume & Textile Collection Ohio State U., Kappa Delta. Methodist. Home: PO Box 214 Columbus OH 43085-0214

KREAR, GAIL RICHARDSON, elementary education educator, consultant; b. Little Rock, July 24, 1942; d. Floyd E. Richardson and Selmarie (Hart) VanDerGriff; m. Bill J. Eason, May 17, 1963 (dec. 1985); 1 child, Kari V.; m. J. David Krear, Feb. 14, 1993. BA, U. Ark., 1964; MS, George Washington U., 1974; PhD in Elem. Edn., Montgomery County Pub. Schs., 1976. Ednl. cons., 1976-77, 85—; acting prin. Montgomery County Pub. Schs., Rockville, Md., 1974-76; tchr. in an award sch. State Sch. of Excellence, Rockville, Md., 1991=92; tchr. Nat. Sch. Excellence, 1994-95. Coach Montgomery County Recreational Dept., Rockville, 1978-81, Olney Boys & Girls Club, 1982. Mem. Am. Contract Bridge League (life master), Washington Bridge League, Alpha Delta Pi. Republican. Office: Montgomery County Pub Schs Rockville MD 20850

KREBS, ARLENE, communications educator; b. Bklyn., Sept. 25, 1945; d. Murray and Muriel (Epstein) K. BA, Bard Coll., 1967; MA, NYU, 1976, postgrad., 1995. Tchr. N.Y.C. Bd. Edn., 1968-76; pres. New Orbit Comm., Bklyn., 1985—; instr. comm. arts dept. Marymount Manhattan Coll., NYU. Author: The Distance Learning Funding Sourcebook, 1996. Mem. Partnership for Homeless, N.Y.C., Greenpeace, Washington, Amnesty Internat., N.Y.C. Vis. fellow Royal Melbourne (Australia) Inst. Tech., 1983; IDA Bodman scholar NYU, 1978; Rsch. grantee GTE Telephone Ops., Irving, Tex., 1993, 94, Bell South, 1994. Mem. AAUW, U.S. Distance Learning Assn., Soc. Satellite Profls. Internat. (v.p. edn. 1987—), Women's Inst. Freedom of Press, Union Dem. Communications. Home and Office: New Orbit Comm 39 Plaza St W Brooklyn NY 11217-3906

KREBS, MARGARET ELOISE, publishing executive; b. Clearfield, Pa., Apr. 20, 1927; d. Henry Louis and Delia Louise (Beahan) K.; grad. high sch. With Progressive Pub. Co., Inc., Clearfield, 1945—, bus. office mgr., 1956-60, bus. mgr., 1960-63, asst. to pub., 1963-69, assoc. pub., 1981—, dir., exec. v.p., 1969-77, pres., 1977—; v.p./sec. Clearfield Broadcasters, Inc., Stas. WCPA-AM and WQYX-FM, 1965—, dir., 1971—. Mem. Pa. Newspaper Women's Assn., Clearfield Bus. and Profl. Women's Club (pres. 1952-53, dist. membership chmn. 1952-53), Sigma Delta Chi. Democrat. Roman Catholic. Club: Lake Glendale Sailing (sec. 1966—). Home: 526 Ogden Ave Clearfield PA 16830-2146 Office: 206 E Locust St Clearfield PA 16830-2423

KREBS, MARTHA, physicist, federal agency administrator. Ph.D., theoretical physics, Catholic U. of America, Washington, D.C., 1966. Staff dir. House subcommittee on energy development and applications, Washington, D.C., 1977-83; assoc. dir. planning and development Lawrence Berkeley Lab., 1983-93; dir., office of energy research Dept. of Energy, 1993—. Office: Office of Energy Rsch Dept Energy 1000 Independence Ave SW Washington DC 20585-0001

KREBSBACH, KAREN ANTON, editor; b. Fond du Lac, Wis., Oct. 21, 1957; d. Orville Edward and Evelyn Rose (Sukowaty) K. BA in Journalism, English, U. Wis., Eau Claire, 1980; M of Latin Am. Studies, Harvard U., 1991. Reporter, bur. chief, asst. met. editor, asst. Sunday editor The Middlesex News, Framingham, Mass.; copy editor, fgn. desk The Boston Globe; reporter The Daily Jour., Caracas, Venezuela; mng. editor Bus. Venezuela, Caracas; editor Fgn. Svc. Jour., Washington, 1993—; fellow Knight Ctr. for Fgn. Journalists, Bolivia, 1996. Recipient ACE award, 1993; Knight Internat. Journalism fellow, 1996. Mem. Inter-Am. Press Assn., Nat. Writers Union, Washington Ind. Writers. Home: 1503 R St NW Apt 3 Washington DC 20009-3817 Office: Fgn Svc Jour 2101 E St NW Washington DC 20037-2916

KREIN, CATHERINE CECILIA, public relations professional; b. N.Y.C., July 2, 1938; d. Timothy T. and Catherine A. (Lavery) Mitchell; m. Robert Krein, Apr. 18, 1970; 1 child, Karen Elise. BS, Fordham U., 1960; film cert., NYU, 1974; MA, Queens Coll., 1994. Various positions including prodr., editl. dir., writer CBS News, N.Y.C., 1963-86; chief spokesperson Bklyn. Dist. Atty., 1986-87; v.p. coll. rels. Molloy Coll., Rockville Centre, N.Y., 1987—. Mem. Coun. for Advancement and Support of Edn., Internat. Assn. Bus. Communicators, Nat. Acad. TV Arts and Scis., Pub. Rels. Soc. Am., Profl. Pub. Rels. of L.I., L.I. Coalition Fair Broadcasting, L.I. Communicators Assn. Home: 151-20 88th St Apt 6J Howard Beach NY 11414-2008

KREINBERG, PENELOPE PETTIT, counselor; b. N.Y.C., Aug. 3, 1946; d. William Dutton and Carole (Earle) P.; m. Robert Lee Kreinberg, July 4, 1968; children: Joshua Adam, Patricia Dawn, Sarah Lynn. BA in Psychology/Sociology/Anthropology, Cornell U., 1968; MA in Counseling Psychology, Lewis & Clark Coll., 1993. Portland (Oreg.) chair Candlelighters for Children, 1982, 87, Oreg. pres., 1988-90; instr., counselor Clackama C.C., Portland, 1993—; pvt. practice counselor Portland, 1994-96; bd. dirs. Candlelighters for Children, Oreg., 1984-96; bd. dirs. Candlelighters Childhood Cancer Found., Washington, 1990-96. Bd. dirs. Camp Ukandu, Am. Cancer Found., Portland, 1985-89, mem. adv. bd. svc. and rehab. com., 1987-89; mem. local sch. adv. com. Grant H.S. PTA, Portland, 1984-88, 92-96; vol. U.S. Peace Corps, Colombia, 1968-70; vol. facilitator Dougy Ctr. for Grieving Children, Portland, 1994-96; vol. Ronald McDonald House, Portland, 1988-89; People to People Citizen Ambassador to South Africa, 1996. Recipient Cmty. Svc. award J. C. Penney, 1990, Met. Family Svc. award City of Portland, 1988. Mem. Nat. Counseling Assn., Oreg. Counseling Assn., Am. Assn. Mental Health Counselors, Oreg. Assn. Aging and Devel., Assn. for Psychol. Type, Am. Assn. Women in C.C.s, Oreg. Career Devel. Assn., Phi Beta Kappa, Delta Gamma. Democrat. Episcopalian. Home: 3145 NE 20th Ave Portland OR 97212-2410

KREITNER-CAIN, JANICE MARIE, minister, marriage and family therapist; b. Niagara Falls, N.Y., Sept. 24, 1943; d. Harold Lewis and Edith Viola (Grauer) Kreitner; children: James, Melissa. MusB, U. North Tex., 1970; MDiv, TCU, 1979, D of Ministry, 1984. Lic. marriage and family therapist, Tex. Music tchr., band dir. Italy (Tx.) Ind. Sch. Dist., 1967-69; choral music tchr. Halton Jr. High, Ft. Worth, 1970-75; exec. dir. Southside Area Ministries, 1976-88; chaplain Cook Ft. Worth Childrens Med. Ctr., 1989-91; chaplain, marriage and family therapist Charter Hosp., Ft. Worth, 1991-93; pastor Eureka United Meth. Ch., Corsicana, Tex., 1993-96, St. John's United Meth. Ch., Georgetown, Tex., 1996—. Chair Southside Sector Planning Coun., 1980-83, Cmty. Devel. Coun., 1985-86; vice-chair Tarrant Area Cmty. Chs., Ft. Worth, 1991-93. Named one of Outstanding Young Women of Am., 1980. United Methodist.

KREITZ, HELEN MARIE, retired elementary education educator; b. Taylor, Tex., Aug. 22, 1929; d. Joseph Jr. and Mary Lena (Miller) K. BA, U. Mary Hardin-Baylor, 1950; MEd, U. Tex., 1959. Cert. tchr., Tex. Bookkeeper Singer Sewing Machine Co., Taylor, 1950-51; advt. salesperson Taylor Times, 1951-52; tchr. Temple (Tex.) Ind. Sch. Dist., 1952-88. Lector, eucharistic min. St. Mary's Cath. Ch., Temple, 1974—. Mem. Tex. Ret. Tchrs. (life, treas. Temple chpt. 1991—), Tex. State Tchrs. Assn. (life, treas. Temple chpt. 1954-55), Tex. Classroom Tchrs. Assn. (life, pres. Temple chpt. 1967-69), U. Tex. Execs. (life), Pi Lambda Theta. Roman Catholic. Home: PO Box 3446 Temple TX 76505-3446

KREJCSI, CYNTHIA ANN, textbook editor; b. Chgo., Dec. 28, 1948; d. Charles and Dorothea Bertha (Hahn) K.; m. Daniel Neil Ehlebracht, May 16, 1986 (div. Nov. 1988). BA, North Park Coll., 1970; postgrad. Nat. Coll. Edn., 1989—. Prodn. editor Ency. Brit., Chgo., 1970-71, style editor, 1971-72; asst. editor Scott, Foresman & Co., Glenview, Ill., 1972-77, assoc. editor, 1977, editor, 1978-84, sr. editor, 1984-95; sr. editor Benefic Press, Westchester, Ill., 1977-78; editl. mgr. Ligature, Chgo., 1995-96, Contemporary Books, Chgo., 1996—; editl. dir. NTC/Contemporary Pub., Lincolnwood, Ill., 1996—. Mem. ASCD, Nat. Council of Tchrs. of English, Internat. Reading Assn. (program com., suburban coun.), Nat. Reading Conf., Assn. Ill. Mid. Schs. Home: 1425 Partridge Ln Arlington Heights IL 60004-7988 Office: Contemporary Pub Co 2 Prudential Plz Ste 1200 Chicago IL 60601

KRELOFF, BEATRICE, art educator; b. N.Y.C., Sept. 11, 1925; d. William and Celia (Singer) Magit; m. Bernard Kreloff (div. Jan., 1970); children: Elliot, Charles.; life ptnr. Edith Isaac-Rose, March, 1979. Artist pvt. practice, N.Y.C., 1941-75; chair art dept. Fieldston Sch., N.Y.C., 1973-89; instr., co-dir. Art Workshop, Assisi, Italy, 1980—; interior design cons. pvt. practice, N.Y.C., 1950-70; art cons., 1970—, curator, pvt. practice, 1985—. Painter; exhibited in one woman and group shows in N.Y.C. and nationally; many permanent collections including Joseph H. Hirshhorn Mus. Mem. Comty. Funding Bd., North Star Fund, N.Y.C., 1987-90; bd. dirs. N.Y.C. Commn. on the Status of Women, 1992-94; mem. Women's Action Coalition, 1992-94. Mem. ASTRAEA, Coll. Art Assn., Women's Caucus for Art. Jewish. Home and Office: Art Workshop Internat 463 West St 1028H New York NY 10014

KREMENTZ, JILL, photographer, author; b. N.Y.C., Feb. 19, 1940; d. Walter and Virginia (Hyde) K.; m. Kurt Vonnegut, Jr., Nov. 1979; 1 child, Lily. Student, Drew U., 1958-59; attended Art Students League. With Harper's Bazaar mag., 1959-60, Glamour mag., 1960-61; pub. relations staff Indian Industries Fair, New Delhi, 1961; reporter Show mag., 1962-64; staff photographer N.Y. Herald Tribune, 1964-65, staff photographer Vietnam, 1965-66; assoc. editor Status-Diplomat mag., 1966-67; contbg. editor N.Y. mag., 1967-68; corr. Time-Life Inc., 1969-70; contbg. photographer People mag., 1974—. Contbr. photography numerous U.S. and fgn. periodicals.; one-woman photography shows Madison (Wis.) Art Center, 1973, U. Mass., Boston, 1974, Nikon Gallery, N.Y.C., 1974, Del. Art Mus., Wilmington, 1975, Newark Mus., 1994; represented in permanent collections Mus. Modern Art, Library of Congress; photographer: The Face of South Vietnam (text by Dean Brelis), 1968, Words and Their Masters (text by Israel Shenker), 1974; photographer, author: Sweet Pea: A Black Girl Growing Up in the Rural South (foreword by Margaret Mead), 1969, A Very Young Dancer, 1976, A Very Young Rider, 1977, A Very Young Gymnast, 1978, A Very Young Circus Flyer, 1979, A Very Young Skater, 1979, The Writer's Image, 1980, How It Feels When a Parent Dies, 1981, How It Feels to be

Adopted, 1982, How It Feels When Parents Divorce, 1984, The Fun of Cooking, 1985, Lily Goes to the Playground, 1986, Jack Goes to the Beach, 1986, Katherine Goes to Nursery School, 1986, Jamie Goes on an Airplane, 1986, Tanya Goes to the Dentist, 1986, Benjy Goes to a Restaurant, 1986, Holly's Farm Animals, 1986, Zachary Goes to the Zoo, 1986, A Visit to Washington, D.C., 1987, How It Feels to Fight For Your Life, 1989, A Very Young Skier, 1990, A Very Young Musician, 1990, A Very Young Gardener, 1990, A Very Young Actress, 1991, How It Feels to Live With a Physical Disability, 1992. Recipient Nonfiction award Washington Post/Children's Book Guild, 1984, ACCH Joan Fassler Meml. Book award, 1990, Equality, Dignity, Independence award Nat. Easter Seals, 1992. Mem. PEN. Address: care Alfred A Knopf Inc 201 E 50th St New York NY 10022-7703*

KREMER, HONOR FRANCES (NOREEN KREMER), real estate broker, small business owner; b. Ireland, Aug. 9, 1939; came to U.S., 1961; m. Manny Kremer, May 17, 1963; 1 child, Patrick David. BS, CUNY; MS, Baruch Coll. Group sec. Bentalls, Ltd., Kingston-On-Thames, Surrey, Eng., 1954-58, Cen. Secondary Sch., Hamilton, Ont., Can., 1959-61; office mgr. Aschner Assocs., N.Y.C., 1961-63; pub. rels. asst. McMaster U., Hamilton, 1963-64; office mgr. Packaging Components, N.Y.C., 1965-67; head acctg. Shaller Rubin Assocs., N.Y.C., 1967-72, v.p. fin. and adminstrn., 1972-79, sr. v.p., 1979-82, sr. v.p., mem. exec. com., 1982—, sec.-treas. multi-media div., 1972-75; pvt. practice bus. cons., 1986-89; sr. v.p., exec. v.p., fin. officer Lewis & Gace Med. Advt., N.Y.C., 1989-91; broker, owner Malone Kremer Realty, Leonia, N.J., 1991—; bus. cons., 1991—. Mem. Nat. Fedn. Bus. and Profl. Women (bd. dirs., v.p.), Advt. Fin. Mgmt. Group. Roman Catholic.

KREMER, MICHELLE CELESTE, lawyer, environmental organization administrator; b. Laguna Beach, Calif., July 21, 1966; d. William Jacob and Carol Jean (Arcoli) K. BA in Journalism, U. So. Calif., 1988, BA in Polit. Sci., 1989; JD, Western State U., 1992. Bar: Calif. Environ. affairs dir. Surfrider Found., San Clemente, Calif., 1992—. Office: Surfrider Found 122 S El Camino Real # 67 San Clemente CA 92672

KRENEK, MARY LOUISE, political science researcher, educator; b. Wharton, Tex., Dec. 8, 1951; d. George P. Jr. and Vlasta (Zahn) K. AA, Wharton County Jr. Coll., 1972; BA, Tex. A&I U., Corpus Christi, 1974; MA, St. Mary's U., San Antonio, 1992; Czech lang. cert., Charles U., Prague, Czech Republic, 1994. Cert. secondary and elem. tchr., Tex. Polygraph examiner, San Antonio, 1979-81; ind. contractor market, polit. and social rsch., San Antonio and Houston, 1982—; substitute tchr., tchr. San Antonio Ins. Sch. Dist., 1981-82, Houston, 1991—. Del. Tex. Dem. Conv., 1971-72. 1st lt. U.S. Army, 1975-78; lt. col. USAR, 1978—. Mem. Nat. Assn. of Self-Employed, Res. Officers Assn. (sec.-treas. Alamo chpt., jr. v.p. Dept. Tex.), St. Mary's U. Alumni Assn., Alumni Assn. Presdl. Classroom for Young Ams., Polit. Sci. Hon. Soc., Am. Legion, Pi Sigma Alpha. Roman Catholic. Home: Box 310 Egypt TX 77436

KREPS, JUANITA MORRIS, economics educator, former government official; b. Lynch, Ky., Jan. 11, 1921; d. Elmer M. and Cenia (Blair) Morris; m. Clifton H. Kreps, Jr., Aug. 11, 1944; children: Sarah, Laura, Clifton. AB, Berea Coll., 1942; MA, Duke U., 1944; PhD, 1948; hon. degrees, Bryant Coll., 1972, U. N.C. at Chapel Hill, Denison U., Cornell Coll., 1973, U. Ky., Queens Coll., St. Lawrence U., 1975, Wheaton Coll., 1976, Claremont Grad. Sch., Berea Coll., 1979, Tulane U., Colgate U., 1980, Trinity Coll., 1981, U. Rochester, Grove City Coll., 1984, Davidson Coll., 1990; hon. degree, Lenoir-Rhyne Coll., 1991, U. Notre Dame, 1992, Duke U., 1993, Western Md. Coll., 1982. Instr. econs. Denison U., 1945-46, asst. prof., 1948-50; mem. faculty Duke U., 1955-77, assoc. prof., 1962-68, prof. econs., 1968-77, James B. Duke prof., 1972-77, James B. Duke prof. emerita, 1979—, asst. provost, 1969-72, v.p., 1973-77, v.p. emerita, 1979—; sec. U.S. Dept. Commerce, 1977-79; mem. adv. com. Congl. Commn. for the Future of Worker Mgmt. Rels., Secs. of Commerce and Labor, 1993-94. Author: (with C.E. Ferguson) Principles of Economics, 2d rev. edit. 1965, Lifetime Allocation of Work and Income, 1971, Sex in the Marketplace: American Women at Work, 1971, Women and the American Economy, 1976; co-author: (with Richard Perlman and Gerald Somers) Contemporary Labor Economics, 1973; Editor: Employment, Income and Retirement Problems of the Aged, 1963, Technology, Manpower and Retirement Policy, 1966, Sex, Age and Work, 1975. Bd. dirs. Am. Coun. on Germany, Rsch. Triangle Found., Ednl. Testing Svc., 1972-77; mem. Nat. Manpower Policy Task Force; trustee Berea Coll., 1972-78, 80—, Duke Endowment, 1979—, Nat. Humanities Ctr., 1983-86, U. N.C., Wilmington, 1993—, HumRRO, 1980-83, Coun. Fgn. Rels., 1983-89, Kenan Inst. Pvt. Enterprise of U. N.C., Chapel Hill, 1995—; pres. bd. overseers Tchrs. Ins. and Annuity Assn. and Coll. Retirement Equities Fund, 1985—; trustee Kenan Inst. of Pvt. Enterprise of U. N.C., Chapel Hill, 1995—. Named to Presl. Commn. on Nat. Agenda for the 80's, 1979; recipient N.C. Pub. Svc. award, 1976, Stephen Wise award, 1978, Woman of Yr. award Ladies Home Jour., 1978, Duke U. Alumni award, 1983, Haskins award Coll. Bus. and Pub. Adminstrn., NYU, 1984, First Corp. Governance award Nat. Assn. Corp. Dirs., 1987, Dir.'s Choice Leadership award Nat. Women's Econ. Alliance Found., 1987, Disting. Meritorious Svc. medal Duke U. Alumni, 1987. Fellow Gerontol. Soc. (v.p. 1971-72), Am. Acad. Arts and Scis.; mem. AAUP, AAUW (Achievement award 1981), Am. Econ. Assn. (v.p. 1983-84), So. Econ. Assn. (pres. 1975-76), Indsl. Rels. Rsch. Assn. (exec. com.). Office: Duke U 115 E Duke Bldg Durham NC 27708-0768

KRESNOFF, PHYLLIS MOLIN, artist; b. Chgo.; d. Samuel W. and Hilda (Freeman) Molin; m. Charles S. Kresnoff (dec. Dec. 1988); 1 child. Student, U. Chgo., 1950-53; BFA, Sch. Art Inst. Chgo., 1970. One-woman shows include Adele Beonarz, L.A., 1966, Kasha Heman, Chgo., 1960-62, Kovler Gallery, Chgo., 1962-71, Chgo. Pub. Libr., 1961, 71, Saks Gallery, Denver, 1996; group shows include Art Inst. Chgo., 1963, Smithsonian Inst., 1964, Old Orchard Invited Show, 1960, 61, 62, Ringling Mus., Sarasota, Fla., 1960. Chgo. Renaissance Soc., 1962, Ball State Tchrs. Coll., 1993. Mem. Arts Club Chgo., Mus. Contemporary Art, Art Inst. Home: 20 E Cedar St Chicago IL 60611

KRESS, NORMA L., manufacturing company executive. Exec. v.p. info. sys. Kimball Internat. Inc., Jasper, Ind. Office: Kimball Internat Inc 1600 Royal St Jasper IN 47549-1001*

KRESSIN, SANDRA KAY, accountant; b. Bloomer, Wis., May 1, 1962; d. Arnold Clayton and Marlene Margaret Windsor; 1 child, Grace. BSBA, U. Wis. Eau Claire, 1984. CPA, Wis. Sr. acct. Wipell Ullrich Bertelson CPA, Eau Claire, 1984-91; bus. mgr. U. Wis. Facilities Mgmt., Eau Claire, 1991—. Mem. IMA, Wis. Inst. CPA (continuing edn. com. 1995-96). Office: Univ Wis - Eau Claire 1425 Devney Dr Altoona WI 54720-2515

KRETZSCHMAR, ANGELINA GENZER, small business owner; b. San Antonio, Tex., July 19, 1946; d. Louis J. Genzer and Alma K. (Krause) Haase; m. Charles H. Kretzschmar, July 31, 1971. BBA cum laude, St. Mary's U., San Antonio, 1974. Budget analyst Fed. Govt., San Antonio, Tex., 1974-92; EEO specialist Fed. Govt., San Antonio, 1992—; owner, operator Kretzschmar Prop., San Antonio, 1971—; fed. women's program mgr. Fed. Govt., San Antonio, 1992—. Campaign treas. Citizens for Open Govt., San Antonio, 1988; polit. action com. Women's Polit. Caucas, San Antonio, 1993. Mem. Bus. & Profl. Women Inc. (com. chair), AAUW (public policy com. 1994), San Antonio Coun. of Fed. Womans Program Mgrs. (sec.), Federally Employed Women, Inc. (legis. chair). Democrat. Lutheran. Home: 6314 Meadow Grove San Antonio TX 78239

KREUTZER, RITA KAY, speech and language pathologist; b. West Point, Nebr., Jan. 19, 1966; d. Raymond G. and Genevieve C. (Stalp) Meiergerd; m. Mark Eugene Kreutzer, Aug. 19, 1988; children: Jonathan, Matthew, Nathan, Megan. BS in Communication Disorders, Kearney State Coll., 1988, MS, 1990. Cert. tchr., Nebr. Speech/lang. pathologist Holdrege (Nebr.) City Schs., 1989—. Active All Sts. Ch. Altar Soc., Holdrege, 1988—. Mem. Am. Speech/Lang./Hearing Assn., Nebr. State Speech/Lang./Hearing Assn. (conv. presenter 1990). Roman Catholic.

KREZ, DENICE, lawyer; b. Chgo., BSN, St. Louis U., 1971; JD with high honors, DePaul U., 1985. Bar: N.Y. 1985. Ptnr. Cadwalader, Wickersham & Taft, N.Y.C. Office: Cadwalader Wickersham & Taft 100 Maiden Ln New York NY 10006*

KRIDLER, JAMIE BRANAM, children's advocate, social psychologist; b. Newport, Tenn., Jan. 23, 1955; d. Floyd A. and Mary Leslie (Carlisle) Branam; m. Thomas Lee Kridler, Mar. 19, 1989; children: Brittani Audra, Houston Scott, Clark Eaton, Sabrina Morrow. BS, U. Tenn., 1976, MS, 1977; PhD, Ohio State U., 1985; cert. retailing, profl. modeling, Bauder Fashion Coll., Atlanta, 1973. Fashion coord. Bill's Wear House, Newport, Tenn., 1969-77; buyer Shane's Boutique, Gatlinburg, Tenn., 1977-78; instr. Miami U., Oxford, Ohio, 1978-81; asst. prof. U. Tenn., Knoxville, 1985-89; mktg. dir. Profitt's Dept. Stores, Alcoa, Tenn., 1989-90; mktg. cons. Kridler & Kridler Mktg., Newport, Tenn., 1990-93; children's advocate Safe Space, Newport, Tenn., 1993-95; adj. faculty U. Tenn., Knoxville, 1990—, Walters State Coll., Morristown, Tenn., 1990—, Carson Newman Coll., Jefferson City, Tenn., 1993—; founding mem. Cmty. House Coop., 1995—; mem. Nation Funding Collaborative on Violence Protection; participant Children's Defense Fund, Washington, 1992—; founding mem. Cmty. House Co-op. Costume designer Newport Theatre Guild: Guys and Dolls, Carousel, Fiddler on the Roof, Music Man, Crimes of the Heart, Rumors, Come Back to the Five and Dime, Jimmy Dean, Oliver, The Odd Couple, 1991—, The Sunshine Boys, 1991—, Miami U. Dance Theatre, Ice Show. Bd. dirs. Safe Space, 1991-92; v.p. Newport Theatre Guild, 1991-92, pres. 1992—. Named Outstanding Tchr., Miami U., Oxford, 1981, Outstanding Educator, U. Tenn., Knoxville, 1989; recipient numerous grants from univ. and non-profit orgns. Mem. NAACP, Lioness Club, Kappa Omicorn Nu. Democrat. Episcopalian. Home: 112 Woodlawn Ave Newport TN 37821-3031

KRIEG, DOROTHEA MURRAY, artist; b. Detroit, Feb. 16, 1931; d. Louis Edward and Ann Beatrice (Conlon) Murray; m. William H. Krieg, July 17, 1954; children: Charles, William, Dorothea, John (dec.), James. BA, Marygrove Coll., 1952; postgrad., Wayne State U., 1987-88. Tchr. Detroit Bd. of Edn., 1952-54; artist Grosse Pointe, Mich., 1989—. One-person shows include Saginaw Valley State U., 1995, Ashley-Chris Gallery, 1995, Ann Arbor Art Assn., 1994. Bd. dirs. Gross Point Friends of Libr., 1979-81; chmn. Children's Home of Detroit, Grosse Point Artists Benefit, 1995, featured artist meml. festival, 1994; hostess, lectr. Marygrove Coll. Alumni Tea, 1995. Recipient Pres. Purchase award Alma Coll. State Competition, 1994, (2) Purchase awards Gross Point Libr., 1993, 94. Mem. Detroit Soc. Women Painter and Sculptures (bd. dirs.), Printers Consortium, Gross Pointe Artists (bd. dirs.), Grosse Pointe 10.

KRIEGER, ERIKA, architect; b. Mt. Vernon, N.Y., Jan. 2, 1957; d. Arno and Kaethe (Intelmann) Talesnik; m. David Krieger, July 19, 1985; children: Yonathan, Benyamin. BS, McGill U., 1979, BArch, 1980. Registered architect, N.Y., N.J., Conn. Pvt. practice Mt. Vernon, 1986—. Commr. Dept. Bldgs. City of Mt. Vernon, 1992-96; vice chair Planning Bd., Mt. Vernon, 1992-96; chair Archtl. Rev. Bd., Mt. Vernon, 1988-92. Mem. AIA (sec. 1991), N.Y. Stte Bldg. Ofcls. Conf., Westchester Assn. Women Bus. Owners. Office: Krieger Architecture and Planning 221 Summit Ave Mount Vernon NY 10552

KRIEGER, MARCIA SMITH, judge; b. Denver, Mar. 3, 1954; d. Donald P. Jr. and Marjorie Craig (Gearhart) Smith; m. Michael S. Krieger, Aug. 26, 1976 (div. July 1988); children: Miriam Anna, Matthias Edward; m. Frank H. Roberts, Jr., Mar. 9, 1991; stepchildren: Melissa Noel Roberts, Kelly Suzanne Roberts, Heidi Marie Roberts. BA, Lewis & Clark Coll., 1975; postgrad., U. Munich, 1975-76; JD, U. Colo., 1979. Bar: Colo. 1979, U.S. Dist. Ct. Colo. 1979, U.S. Ct. Appeals (10th cir.) 1979. Assoc. Mason, Reuler & Peek, P.C., Denver, 1976-83, Smart, DeFurio Brooks, Eklund & McClure, Denver, 1983-84; ptnr. Brooks & Krieger, P.C., Denver, 1984-88, Wood, Ris & Hames, P.C., Denver, 1988-90; pvt. practice U.S. Bankruptcy Court, 10th Circuit, Denver, 1990-94, judge, 1994—; lectr. U. Denver Grad. Tax Program, 1987—, Colo. Soc. CPA's, Denver, 1984-87, Colo. Continuing Legal Edn., Denver, 1980—, Colo. Trial Lawyers Assn., Denver, 1987—. Contbr. articles to profl. publs. Vestry person Good Shepherd Episcopal Ch., Englewood, 1986—. Mem. Colo. Bar Assn., Arapahoe Bar Assn., Arraj Inn of Ct. (sec.), Nat. Conf. Bankruptcy Judges, Littleton Adv. Coun. Gifted and Talented. Republican. Office: US Custom House 721 19th St Denver CO 80202-2513

KRIEGMAN, SUSAN L., artist, art educator; b. Newark, June 6, 1950; d. Leonard W. and Frances (Pearl) K. BS in Art Edn., U. Vt., 1972; MFA, Washington U., St. Louis, 1976; postgrad., Columbia U. Cert. tchr. art K-12. Instr. art, metalsmithing and jewelry design Washington U., St. Louis, 1974-76; instr. art No. Mich. U., Marquette, 1976-77; art specialist of metalsmithing and jewelry N.J. Pub. Schs., Piscataway, Somerville, Roosevelt and Montgomery Twps., 1979-89; art specialist So. Brunswick (N.J.) Pub. Schs., 1989—; vis. prof. Ctr. for Creative Studies, Detroit, 1987-88; adj. art edn. prof. Kean Coll., Union, N.J., 1994-95; bd. dirs. Peters Valley Craft Ctr., Layton, N.J., 1988-94; cons. Ednl. Testing Svc., 1994—; bd. dirs. The Craft Experience in Art Edn. Conf., 1993—; adj. art educator Columbia U., 1993—; dir., curator The Craft Experience in Art Edn. ann. nat. conf. at TC Columbia U., 1993, 94, 95, 96. Exhbns. include Washington U. Sch. Art, 1979, Morris Mus., Morristown, N.J., 1984, 91, 94, Noyes Mus., N.J., 1984, Downey Mus. Art, Calif., 1986, N.J. State Mus., 1986, 92, 96, Montclair Art Mus., N.J., 1986, Nabisco Corp. Hdqs. Art Invitational, 1986, N.J. Arts Anns., 1986, 91, 93, 95, 96, Nat. Ornamental Metal Mus., Memphis, 1989, 92, 93, Johnson & Johnson Corp. Hdqs. Art Invitational, 1991, Schering-Plough Corp. Hdqs. Art Invitational, 1991, Pro Art Heikki Seppa Art Invitational, St. Louis, 1992, Newark Mus., 1995, Zimmerli Art Mus., N.J.; presenter of workshops and seminars in field. VISTA vol., early childhood curriculum specialist Honolulu Cmty. Action Program Head Start, 1972-73; test developer, reader Praxis series for art Ednl. Testing Svc., 1994—. Fellow Jewish Mus., 1986, N.J. State Coun. Arts, 1983, 86, 89; recipient Geraldine Dodge Found. Artist/Educator award, 1993-94, Craft Concepts award of distinction, 1986; Profl. Devel. grantee S. Brunswick Bd. of Edn., 1992, 93, 94, 95, 96. Mem. NEA, Nat. Art Edn. Assn., Am. Craft Coun., Soc. N.Am. Goldsmiths (life disting.), N.J. Edn. Assn., Art Educators N.J. Home: 5018 Quail Ridge Dr Plainsboro NJ 08536 Office: Greenbrook Sch 30 Roberts St Kendall Park NJ 08824

KRIENKE, CAROL BELLE MANIKOWSKE (MRS. OLIVER KENNETH KRIENKE), realtor; b. Oakland, Calif., June 19, 1917; d. George and Ethel (Purdon) Manikowske; student U. Mo., 1937; BS, U. Minn., 1940; postgrad. UCLA, 1949; m. Oliver Kenneth Krienke, June 4, 1941 (dec. Dec. 1988); children: Diane (Mrs. Robert Denny), Judith (Mrs. Kenneth A. Giss), Debra Louise (Mrs. Ed Paul Davalos). Demonstrator, Gen. Foods Corp., Mpls., 1940; youth leadership State of Minn. Congl. Conf., U. Minn., Mpls. 1940-41; war prodn. worker Airesearch Mfg. Co., Los Angeles, 1944; tchr. L.A. City Schs., 1945-49; realtor DBA Ethel Purdon, Manhattan Beach, Calif., 1949; buyer Purdon Furniture & Appliances, Manhattan Beach, 1950-58; realtor O.K. Krienke Realty, Manhattan Beach, 1958—. Manhattan Beach bd. rep. Community Chest for Girl Scouts U.S., 1957; bd. dirs. South Bay council Girl Scouts U.S.A., 1957-62, mem. Manhattan Beach Coordinating Coun., 1956-68, South Coast Botanic Garden Found., 1989—; v.p. Long Beach Area Childrens Home Soc., 1967-68, pres. 1979; charter mem. Beach Pixies, 1957-93, pres. 1967; chmn. United Way, 1967; sponsor Beach Cities Symphony, 1953—, Little League Umpires, 1981-91. Recipient Long-standing Local Bus. award City of Manhattan Beach, 1993. Mem. DAR (life, citizenship chmn. 1972-73, v.p. 1979, 83—), Calif. Retired Tchrs. Assn. (life), Colonial Dames XVII Century (charter mem. Jared Eliot chpt. 1977, v.p., pres. 1979-81, 83-84), Friends of Library, South Bay Bd. Realtors, Nat. Soc. New England Women (life, Calif. Poppy Colony), Internat. Platform Assn., Soc. Descs. of Founders of Hartford (life), Friends of Banning Mus., Hist. Soc. of Centinela Valley, Manhattan Beach Hist. Soc., Manhattan Beach C. of C. (Rose and Scroll award 1985), U. Minn. Alumni (life). Republican. Mem. Community Ch. (pres. Women's Fellowship 1970-71). Home: 924 Highview Ave Manhattan Beach CA 90266-5813 Office: OK Krienke Realty 1716 Manhattan Beach Blvd Manhattan Beach CA 90266-6220

KRIER, CYNTHIA TAYLOR, state legislator, lawyer; b. Beeville, Tex., July 12, 1950; m. Joseph Krier, 1982. B.J., U. Tex., 1971, J.D., 1975. Bar: Tex. 1975. Of Counsel Matthews & Branscomb, San Antonio; mem. Tex. State Senate from 26th dist., 1985—; judge Bexar County Courthouse, San Antonio. Mem. ABA, Tex. Bar Assn., San Antonio Bar Assn., Omicron Delta Kappa, Phi Kappa Phi, Phi Delta Phi. Republican. Office: Office County Judge Bexar County Courthouse San Antonio TX 78205-3002 also: 301 S Frio St San Antonio TX 78207-4421*

KRIESEL, DIANE M., vocational evaluator; b. Michigan City, Ind., Nov. 1, 1949; d. Richard B. and Dorothy M. (Barnoski) Geyer; m. Richard J. Kriesel, Sept. 2, 1972; children: Renee Ellen, John Richard, Stephanie Marie. BA in English, Ind. U., 1971, MS in Edn., 1976; MS in Vocational Evaln., East Carolina U., 1992. Cert. vocational evaluator. Tchr. elem. sch. St. Mary Sch., Michigan City, Ind., 1971-79; instr. Wilson (N.C.) Tech. C.C., 1979-85; program mgr., dep. dir. Diversified Opportunities, Inc., Wilson, N.C., 1985—; adj. prof. East Carolina U., Greenville, N.C., 1995—; chmn. Wilson County Transp. Svcs., Wilson, 1987—. Bd. dirs. Wilson County Residential Svcs., Wilson, N.C., 1992—; vol. United Way, Wilson County, 1987-92; leader Girl Scouts Am., Wilson County, 1985-93; mem. Transp. Adv. Bd., Wilson, 1990-93. Grantee transp. vehicle N.C. Dept. Transp., 1990-96. Mem. AAUW, ARC (Profl. of Yr. 1990), Ind. U. Alumni Assn. Office: Diversified Opportunities Inc 1010 Herring Ave Wilson NC 27896

KRIGSMAN, NAOMI, psychologist, consultant, photographer; b. Haifa, Israel; came to U.S., 1953, naturalized, 1961; d. Bezalel and Regina (Yacobi) Goussinsky; m. Ruben Krigsman; children—Michael W., Richard G., Jonathan H. MS, CCNY; PhD, Hofstra U.. Lic. psychologist, N.Y. State. Psychologist Mental Retardation Clinic, Flower-Fifth Avenue Hosp., N.Y.C., Children's Ctr., N.Y.C. Dept. Welfare, Rehab. Clinic, St. Barnabas Hosp., Newark, United Cerebral Palsy Ctr., Roosevelt, N.Y., Burke Rehab. Ctr., White Plains, N.Y., New Rochelle City Sch. Dist., N.Y., 1970-95; adj. asst. prof. grad. psychology dept. Coll. of New Rochelle, 1992-93; employment selection, career devel., employee relocation, quality circles, U.S. and Israel; psychol. evaluations and consultation in family ct.; feature writer N.Y. Womensweek, 1978-79; mem. bus. adv. com. dept. rehab. medicine, Mt. Sinai Med. Ctr., 1991—. Co-author tng. materials for quality circles; also author articles; exhibited in 2-person photography shows, 1990, 91, 1-person show, 1993, Israel, 1996; exhibited in group show at Mus. Photography, 1996; represented in permanent collection Mus. of Photography, Israel. Fellow N.Y. State Mental Health Dept., 1958-59. Mem. Am. Psychol. Assn., Westchester County Psychol. Assn. (chmn. profl. edn. com. sch. psychology div. 1976-78, founder, pres. div. indsl./orgnl. psychology 1988-90, bd. dirs 1990), Westchester Photographic Soc. Home: 13 Dupont Ave White Plains NY 10605-3537

KRILL, CAROLE L. ALDERSON, foreign language educator; b. Canonsburg, Pa., Nov. 3, 1945; d. George Herbert and Nellie Romaine (Weaver) Alderson; m. Dennis John Krill, Jan. 7, 1969. BA in Liberal Arts, Pa. State U., 1967. Cert. secondary edn., Pa., N.J. French tchr. Bald Eagle Are Sch. Dist., Wingate, Pa., 1967—, fgn. lang. dept. coord., 1975-95; translator for French auto racing teams Autoworld, Scranton, Pa., 1975-80. Contbr. articles to profl. jours. Mem. NEA, Pa. State Edn. Assn., Bald Eagle Area Edn. Assn., Pa. State Modern Lang. Assn., Am. Coun. on Teaching of Fgn. Lang., Am. Assn. Tchrs. French, Delta Kappa Gamma. Office: Bald Eagle Area Sch Dist S Eagle Valley Rd Wingate PA 16880

KRIM, MATHILDE, medical educator; b. Como, Italy, July 9, 1926; came to U.S.; BS, U. Geneva, Switzerland, 1948, PhD, 1953; DSc (hon.), Long Island U., 1987; LLD (hon.), Columbia U., 1988; DSc (hon.), Brandeis U., 1989; DHL (hon.), Southeastern Mass. U., 1990; DSc. (hon.), Tulane U., 1990; DHL (hon.), SUNY, Stonybrook, 1991; DSc(hon.), Columbia Coll., 1992. Asst. genetic sect., dept. exptl. biology Weizmann Inst. Sci., Rehovot, Israel, 1953-54, jr. scientist, 1954-57, rsch. assoc., 1957-59; rsch. assoc.divsn. virus rsch. Cornell Med. Coll., N.Y.C., 1959-62; rsch. assoc. Sloan Kettering Inst. Cancer Rsch., N.Y.C., 1962-68, assoc., 1968-75, assoc. mem., 1975-85, co-head interferon evaluation program, 1975-81, head interferon lab, 1981-85; assoc. rsch. scientist dept. pediatrics St. Luke's-Roosevelt Hosp. Ctr. and Columbia U., N.Y.C., 1986-90; adjunct prof. pub. health Columbia U., N.Y.C., 1990—; founding co-chair, chmn. bd., CEO Am. Found. for AIDS Rsch., N.Y.C.; bd. dirs. AIDSFILMS, Am. Com. for Weizmann Inst. Sci., Nat. Biomed. Rsch. Found.; trustee Scientists' Inst. for Pub. Information, Feinberg Grad. Sch. Weizmann Inst. Sci., African-Am. Inst.; mem. adv. panel on higher edn., New York, 1965, President's Com. on Mental Retardation, 1966-69, jury Albert D. Lasker Rsch. awards 1968-71, 78—, adv. bd. Health Profls. for Polit. Action, 1968-70, adv. com. to Sec. of HEW on Health Proteciton and Disease Prevention, 1969-70, Coun. NEH, 1969-73, Panel of Cons. on Cancer, Com. Labor and Pub. Welfare, U.S.Senate, 1970-71, adv. com. Nat. Colorectal Cancer Program NIH, 1971-73, working group develo. rsch. segment Virus Cancer Program NIH, 1971-74, review com. "A" Virus Cancer Program NIH, 1974-77, adv. com. Inst. Internat. Edn., 1974—, adv. com. Program of Sci., Tech., and Human Values NEH, 1974-78, U.S. Nat. Commn. for UNESCO, 1979-80, adv. com. World Rehabilitation Fund, 1978-82, Interferon Clin. Adv. Com. Schering-Plough Corp., 1980-85, Bristol Labs. Adv. Panel on Biological Response Modifiers, 1981-84, sci. adv. com. Am. Found. AIDS Rsch., 1985—, Com. of 100 for Nat. Health Ins., AIDS task force Am. Assn. Sex Educators, Counselors and Therapists, 1985—, rsch. adv. coun. Nat. Orgn. for Rare Disorders Inc., 1985—, AIDS Health Edn. Risk Reduction Consultation, Ctrs. for Disease Control, 1986, task force on Chemotherapeutics, Nat. Inst. of Allergy and Infectious Diseases, NIH, 1986, met. area adv. com. Lower Manhattan AIDS consortium, 1986—, scientific adv. bd. Nat. Coalition on Immune System Disorders, 1986—, adv. com. The Village Nursing Home, 1986—, sect. for the study of ethical, legal and social issues HIV Ctr. for Clin. and Behavioral Studies, 1987—, AIDS Rsch. Ctr., 1987—, bd. advisors Nat. Lawyers Guild AIDS Network, 1987—, AIDS adv. panel Planned Parenthood Fed. Am., 1988—, nat. adv. com. Nat. Communtiy AIDS Partnership, 1988—, adv. com. Women and AIDS Resource Network, 1988—; commr. Pres.'s Commn. for the Study of Ethical Problems in Medicine and Biomedical and Behavioral Rsch., adv. bd. LOVE HEALS, 1989—, adv. bd. Internat. Alliance for Haiti, 1989—, adv. bd. AIDS-AUF-KLARUNG, Frankfurt, Germany, 1990—, internat. com. Lottare Informare Formare Educare, Rome, Italy, 1990—, adv. coun. Columbia Sch. Pub. Health, 1990—, AIDS adv. panel, Med. Soc. State of New York, 1992—. Editor (with others) Mediation of Cellular Immunity in Cancer by Immune Modifiers: Progress in Cancer Research and Therapy, 1981;mem. editorial bd. The Aids Record; assoc. editor Cancer Investigation, Interferon Newsletter, Aids Care; contbr. articles to profl. jours. Bd. dirs. Nat. Med. Assn. Found., 1968-69, Inst. of Soc., Ethics, and the Life Scis. (The Hastings Ctr.), 1979-89; trustee Nat. Urban League, 1966-72, The Rockefeller Found., 1971-84, AIDS Med. Found. 1983-89, chairperson; vice chmn. Citizens Organized Against Drug Abuse, 1966; exec. sec. Am. Com. for Assistance to Tunisia, 1968-69; dir. at large Am. Cancer Soc., 1970-72. Fellow NAS, 1977; scholar U. Geneva, 1947-52; recipient Spirit of Achievement award Nat. Women's Divsn. Albert Einstein Coll. Medicine, 1972, Humanitarian award Fund for Human Dignity, 1985, award for contbns. to civic life Women's City Club, 1986, John and Samuel Bard award in medicine and sci., 1986, Human Rights Campaign Fund award, 1986, Elizabeth Cutter Morrow award, City of New York YWCA, 1986, Jack Dempsey Humanitarian award St. Clare's Hosp. and Health Ctr., 1986, 10 Ams. Who've Made a Difference award Better Health and Living Mag., 1987, Eleanor Roosevelt Leadership award NOW, 1987, Achievement award Am. Assn. of Physicians for Human Rights, 1987, Humanist Disting. Svc. award Am. Humanist Assn., 1987, Hall of Fame award Internat. Women's Forum, 1987, Commitment to Life award, AIDS project L.A., 1987, Frontrunner award Sara Lee Corp., 1988, Exceptional achievement award, Women's Project and Prodns., 1988, Pres.'s award Am. Equity Assn., 1988, Medical award Hassadah, New York, 1988, award for Pioneering Achievements in Health and Higher Edn. Charles A. Dana Found., 1988, gold medal of honor Casita Maria, 1988, Caring award Stewart McKinney Found., 1988, Outstanding Mother award Nat. Mother's Day Com., 1989, Myrtle Wreath Humantiarian award Nat. Hassadah, 1991, Edwin C. Whitehead award Nat. Ctr. Health Edn., 1991, M. Carey Thomas award Bryn Mawr Coll., 1991, Scientic Freedom and Responsibility award AAAS, 1994; named Woman of Distinction Birmingham (Ala.) So. Coll., 1987, Dallas Cares Benefit honoree, 1989, 100 New York Women Barnard Coll., 1989. Mem. NAS, NAACP, Am. Assn. Advancement of Sci., Soc. Biological Therapy, Am. Soc. Microbiology, Internat. Soc. for Interferon Rsch., Am. Humanists Assn. Office: Am Found AIDS Rsch 733 3rd Ave 12th fl New York NY 10017*

KRINER, SALLY GLADYS PEARL, artist; b. Bradford, Ohio, Jan. 29, 1911; d. Henry Walter and Pearl Rebecca (Brubaker) Brant; m. Leo Louis

Kriner, Feb. 28, 1933; children—Patricia Staab, Jane Palombo. Grad. Arsenal Tech. sch. Indpls.; student Ind. U.-Indpls., 1954, Herron Sch. Art, Indpls., 1958. Exhibited in one woman shows Hoosier Salon, Indpls., 1960, Village Art Gallery, Southport, Ind., 1967, 70, 73, Brown County Art Guild, Nashville, Ind., 1970, 74, 77, 80, 83, 87, 92; group shows include South Side Art League, Indpls., 1959-74, Indpls. Art League, 1959-64, Brown County Art Guild, 1969—, Hoosier Salon, 1961, 65, 67, 68, 73, 75, 76, 77, 82, 86, 87, 91, 95, Frames and Things Gallery, 1995; represented in permanent collections Riley Hosp., Indpls., others. Founder Southside Women's Symphony Com., Indpls., 1958; treas. Perry Twp. Republican Club, Ind., 1960-65; pres. State Assembly Women's Club, 1965-67; bd. dirs. ARC, Indpls., 1942-45, Southside Civic Orgn., Indpls., 1954, Clowes Hall Women's Com., Indpls., 1963. Recipient citation ARC, 1946; citation Marion County Meritorious Service Award, 1959; citation Greater Southside Civic Orgn., 1961; Art award Kappa Kappa Kappa, 1967, 68, 70, 71. Fellow Indpls. Art League Found. (numerous awards 1960-66); mem. Southside Art League, Inc. (pres. 1964-65, numerous awards 1964-75, founder), Ind. Artists Club, Inc. (Purchases award 1978), Ind. Heritage Arts, Inc., Rutland Art Assn., Brown County Art Guild (pres. 1980-83, v.p. 1983—), Ind. fedn. Arts Clubs (bd. dirs. 1963-73), Ind. Artist (chmn. prize fund 1974-75), Consignment and appraisal of fine arts, Hoosier Salon, Indpls. Mus. Arts, Nat. Soc. Arts and Letters, Nat. Mus. Women in Arts, Hoosier Group Women in Arts, Oil Painters of America. Presbyterian. Avocation: growing flowers. Home and Studio: 394 E Freeman Ridge Rd Nashville IN 47448-8871

KRINEY, MARILYN WALKER, publishing executive; b. Montclair, N.J., June 12, 1938; d. James Griffin and Grace Dagnall (Scott) Walker; m. Gordon Arthur Kriney, 1966; 1 child, Alexander Walker. AB in English, Douglass Coll., 1960; MBA in Fin., NYU, 1986. Editor T.Y. Crowell Publishers, N.Y.C., 1967-77; sr. editor Children's Books HarperCollins, N.Y.C., 1977-83, editor-in-chief Harper Trophy, 1983-89, sr. v.p., publisher, 1989—. Office: Harper Collins Pub 10 E 53rd St New York NY 10022-5244

KRINSKY, CAROL HERSELLE, art history educator; b. N.Y.C., June 2, 1937; d. David and Jane (Gartman) Herselle; m. Robert Daniel Krinsky, Jan. 25, 1959; 2 children. BA, Smith Coll., 1957; MA, NYU, 1960, PhD, 1965. Mem. faculty NYU, 1965—, assoc. prof. art history, 1973-78, prof., 1978—. Author: Vitruvius de Architectura, 1521. 1969, Rockefeller Center, 1978, Synagogues of Europe, 1985, rev. edit., 1996, Gordon Bunshaft of Skidmore, Owings & Merrill, 1988, Europas Synagogen, 1988, Contemporary Native American Architecture, 1996; contbr. articles to profl. jours. Bd. dirs. Internat. Survey Jewish Monuments, Urbana, Ill., 1981—, Soc. Archtl. Historians, 1978-80, 86-89, The Mac Dowell Colony, Inc., 1989—, Jewish Heritage Coun. World Monuments Fund; co-chair seminar on the city Columbia U., 1993-95. Am. Coun. Learned Socs. grantee, 1981, Nat. Endowment for the Arts grantee, 1993; recipient Arnold Brunner award N.Y.C. chpt. AIA, 1990. Mem. Soc. Archtl. Historians (pres. 1984-86, pres. N.Y.C. chpt. 1977-79), Coll. Art Assn., Planning History Group, Am. Urban History Assn., Women's City Club, Century Assn., Phi Beta Kappa. Office: NYU Dept Fine Arts 100 Washington Sq E New York NY 10003-6688

KRINSKY, SHARON FRANCES, librarian, editor, writer; b. Bronx, N.Y., June 5, 1945; d. Nathan and Dorothy (Rosen) K. BA, Queens Coll., 1966; MLS, Pratt Inst., 1993. Registration supr. New Sch. Social Rsch., N.Y.C., 1975-78; nursery sch. tchr. Everett Sch., N.Y.C., 1978-80; copy editor, proofreader N.Y.C., 1980-93; indexer H.W. Wilson Co., Bronx, 1993-96. Author: The Ruddy Duck, 1995; contbr. Best American Poetry of 1992; contbr. poetry to jours.; contbg author: Twenty Stories by Eighteen Authors, 1996. Vol. Am. Coun. Arts Libr., 1990-91, Poets House, 1992. Mem. ALA, Internat. Women's Writing Guild. Office: H W Wilson Co 950 University Ave Bronx NY 10452

KRINTZLINE, DEBORAH ANN, financial analyst; b. Dayton, Ohio, Nov. 30, 1967; d. Billy Joe and Ann Barbara (Wohlhueter) K. BS in Fin., Miami U., Oxford, Ohio, 1990; MBA, Wright State U., 1993. Fin. analyst intern Mead Data Ctrl./Lexis-Nexis, Miamisburg, Ohio, 1987-90, fin. analyst asset acctg., 1990-91, fin. analyst bus. planning, 1991-95, fin. analyst corp. bus. mgmt., 1995-96, fin. analyst legal info. svcs. bus. mgmt., 1996—. Vol. Kettering (Ohio) Med. Ctr., 1994—; vol, mentor West Carrollton (Ohio) City Schs. Mem. Inst. Mgmt. Accts., South Metro Dayton C. of C. (exec. bd., treas. 1996—), Gamma Phi Beta. Lutheran. Home: 2334 Promenade Way Miamisburg OH 45342 Office: Lexis-Nexis 9443 Springboro Pike Miamisburg OH 45342

KRISE, PATRICIA LOVE, automotive industry executive; b. Indpls., July 28, 1959; d. John Bernard and Ann (Emmons) Love; m. Thomas Warren Krise, Sept. 5, 1987. BA magna cum laude, Hanover Coll., Ind., 1981; MBA with hons., Miami U., Oxford, Ohio, 1982. Substitute tchr. Henry County Sch. Dist., Knightstown, Ind., 1982-83; project mgr. Servaas Labs., Inc., Indpls., 1983-84; sales analyst Ford Motor Co., Mpls., 1984, outstate field mgr., 1984-86, met. field mgr., 1986-87, truck merchandising mgr., 1987-88, merchandising mgr., 1988-89; met. field dir. Denver dist. Ford Motor Co., 1989, market representation specialist Denver dist., 1990-91; regional market rep. mgr. Infiniti divsn. Nissan Motor Corp., Naperville, Ill., 1991-92, regional merchandising mgr., 1992-93, dealer ops. cons., 1993—, dealer ops. mgr., 1995—; advisor/presenter Ford Dealer Advt. Fund, Mpls., 1987-88. Tutor adult literacy. Recipient Outstanding Mktg. award Ctrl. Region Ford Motor Co., 1987, Wall St. Jour. award, 1982; named Internat. Woman of Yr., 1992. Mem. Twin Cities Sales Mgrs. Club, Hanover Coll. Alumni Assn., Women's Athletic Assn. (treas. 1979-80), Pre-Law Club (pres. 1980-81), Nat. Assn. Female Execs., Alpha Delta Pi. Republican. Roman Catholic.

KRISS, M(ARY) ELISE, religious organization administrator, educator; b. LaPorte, Ind., June 8, 1947; d. Joseph Henry and Marcella Mae (Sramek) K. BS in Edn., St. Francis Coll., Ft. Wayne, Ind., 1973, MS in Edn., 1978; PhD, St. Louis U., 1984. Cert. tchr., Ind. Tchr. various elem. schs., 1969-77; prin. St. Mary Sch., Griffith, 1977-81; v.p. acad. affairs St. Francis Coll., Ft. Wayne, 1983-91, v.p. adminstrn., 1991-93, pres., 1993—; mem. provincial coun. Sisters of St. Francis of Perpetual Adoration, Mishawaka, Ind., 1990—. Treas. St. Francis Coll. Bd. Trustees, 1991-93, St. Francis Coll. Foun.d Bd., 1991-93, trustee, 1991—; bd. dirs. Stop Child Abuse & Neglect, 1988—, Sisters of St. Francis Health Svcs., Inc., 1990—; bd. dirs. Greater Fort Wayne Consensus Com., Inc., 1991—. Office: St Francis Coll 2701 Spring St Fort Wayne IN 46808-3994*

KRIST, CYNTHIA HELEN ARNOLD, accountant; b. Galveston, Tex., June 20, 1960; d. E.C. "Gene" and Barbara Jo (Fry) Arnold; m. Kennedy Kirk Krist, May 14, 1988; children: Kendall Paige, Kennedy Nicole. BBA, Tex. A & M Univ., College Station, 1982. CPA, Tex. Tax staff acct. Arthur Andersen & Co., Houston, 1982-84, sr. tax acct., 1984-87; dir. of taxation Mariner Corp., Houston, 1987-88; tax mgr. Hines Interests, Houston, 1988-94, sr. tax mgr., 1994—. Fundraiser/dinner sponsor Bob Lanier Mayoral Campaign, Houston; fundraiser The Children's Museum of Houston, 1992; dinner and auction com. United Cerebral Palsy, Houston, 1996—. Mem. Tex. Soc. of CPA's, Am. Inst. of CPA's, The Junior League of Houston. Episcopal. Office: Hines Interests 2800 Post Oak Blvd Houston TX 77056

KRISTALL-SCLAR, ANITA JOY, speech pathologist; b. Buffalo, Mar. 24, 1954; d. Alfred and Mildred (Rachman) Kristall; m. Gordon Sclar, July 1, 1979; children: Jennifer, Emily. BA, SUNY, Buffalo, 1976, BS, 1978. Cert. clin. competence; lic. speech pathologist, N.Y. Speech therapist City Sch. Dist., Buffalo, 1978-79; speech pathologist Rochester (N.Y.) City Sch. Dist., 1979-84, N.Y. State Bd. Cooperative Ednl. Svcs., 1986-90, North Syracuse (N.Y.) Ctrl. Schs., 1990—. Screenwriter: Dear Jane, 1994, Miss Abbey, 1994, An Ordinary Life, 1995, Change of Face, 996, Divided Waters, 1996. Active NOW. Mem. Am. Speech-Lang. Hearing Assn. Home: 5010 Lakeview Dr Fayetteville NY 13066 Office: care Dykeman Assocs Inc 4115 Rawlins Dallas TX 75219-3661

KRITSONIS, MARY ALICE, special education educator, consultant; b. Alexandria, La., Oct. 10, 1955; d. Thomas Elmo Jr. and Alice (Evans) Hill; m. William Allan Kritsonis, Sept. 20, 1984; children: Alicia Leigh, Amanda Clare. BS, La. State U., 1976, MEd, 1986; EdS, McNeese State U., 1991; EdD, Memphis State U., 1992. Cert. speech and lang. therapy, learning disability, generic mild/moderate tchr., spl. edn. prin., dir. spl. edn., elem. prin., supr., spl. edn. supr. Speech and lang. pathologist Rapides Parish Sch. Bd., Alexandria, 1977-82, spl. edn. educator, 1982-91; pupil appraisal Calcasieu Parish Sch. Bd., Lake Charles, La., 1991-92; asst. prof. McNeese State U., Lake Charles, La., 1992—; mem. La. Interagy. Coord. Coun., Baton Rouge, 1994—; mem. Comprehensive Sys. of Profl. Devel., Lake Charles, 1993—; mentor mem. Spl. Edn. Mentorship Program, Lake Charles, 1993-94; on-site coord. La. Non-Categorical and Early Intervention Pers. Recruitment and Enhancement Program. Author: Fostering Affective Development in Students with Mild Disabilities, 1993; contbr. articles to profl. jours. Mem. La. Assn. for Children Under Six, La. Speech and Hearing Assn., Coun. for Exceptional Children (div. Early Childhood), Phi Delta Kappa, Phi Kappa Phi. Office: McNeese State U Burton Coll Edn Dept Spl Edn Lake Charles LA 70609

KRIZMAN, DONNA MARTINSON, engineer, researcher; b. Washington, D.C., Nov. 11, 1960; d. Allen Powell and Betty (Stephenson) Martinson; m. Kevin Joseph Krizman, Oct. 1, 1988. BSEE, Va. Tech., Blacksburg, 1983, MSEE, 1992. Elec. engr. Naval Undersea Warfare Ctr., Norfolk, Va., 1983-92; rsch. asst. Va. Tech., Blacksburg, 1993—. Tutor Christiansburg (Va.) Cmty. Ctr., 1994—. Recipient Patricia Roberts Harris fellow Va. Tech., Blacksburg, 1993. Mem. IEEE, AAUW, ASEE, Eta Kappa Nu. Office: Mobile and Portable Radio Rsch Group Bradley Dept Elec Engring Pointe W Commons Ste 1-840 Univ City Blv Blacksburg VA 24061-0350

KRIZMIS, RENA PANCHERI, psychologist, educator; b. Schram City, Ill., May 1, 1923; d. Louis and Laura (Dalla Piazza) Pancheri; m. William James Krizmis, Sept. 3, 1945; children: William James Jr., Laura Jean. BA, Roosevelt U., 1965; MA, U. Chgo., 1967, cert. advanced studies, 1970; PhD, Loyola U., 1978. Tchr. Thornton Twp. H.S., Harvey, Ill., 1965-66; prof. Chgo. State U., 1967—; acting dir. Coun. Ctr. Chgo. State U., 1981-84. Mem. Toastmasters Internat., Inc.

KROBATH, KRISTA ANN, pharmacist; b. Pottsville, Pa., July 8, 1962; d. James Joseph and Gaye Diane (Anderson) E.; m. Gilbert Krobath. BS in Pharmacy, Temple U., 1985. Registered pharmacist. Pharmacist People's Drug, Harrisburg, Pa., 1985-86; pharmacist, mgr. Amcare Health Svcs., Harrisburg, 1986-96; pharmacist Pharmacy Corp. Am., Harrisburg, 1996—. Mem. Pa. Pharm. Assn., Capital Area Pharm. Assn. Office: Pharmacy Corp Am 440 Lewis Rd Harrisburg PA 17111

KROEGER, BROOKE W., journalist, writer; b. Kansas City, Mo., Feb. 18, 1949; d. David S. and Helen (Bratt) Weinstein; m. John C. Kroeger, Jan. 29, 1972 (div. 1983); children: Brett S. Kroeger; m. Alexander M. Goren, June 24, 1984; stepchildren: Andrea Goren, Elisabeth J. Goren. BS in Journalism, Polit. Sci., Boston U., 1971; MS in Journalism, Columbia U., 1972. UN corr. N.Y. Newsday, N.Y.C., 1984-85; dep. met. editor New York Newsday, N.Y.C., 1985-86; editor Europe, Middle East and Africa UPI, London, 1983-84; bureau chief Israel UPI, Tel Aviv, 1981-83, corr., 1979-81; corr. UPI, London, 1978-79, Brussels, 1977, Chgo., 1973-76. Author: (biography) Nellie Bly: Daredevil, Reporter, Feminist, 1994; contbr. numerous articles to various newspapers and mags., 1987—. Home: 1175 Park Ave New York NY 10128

KROGMANN, JOAN L., horse trainer, writer; b. Queens, N.Y., Oct. 12, 1936; d. Milton Irving and Hazel Darling (Diefenbacher) Andres; divorced; 1 child, Kimberley. Studied with Vladimer Littauer, Luis de La Vellette, George Brush, Frank Collins, others, 1958-75. Lic. real estate agent, N.Y. Owner Little Plains Stable and Little Plains Breeding Farm, L.I., N.Y., 1957-94; lic. real estate agent Century 21, N.Y., 1984-88; freelance writer N.Y., 1980-94; owner La Petite Cheval Farm, Loxahatchee, Fla., 1994—; organizer, creator L.I. High Score Awards, 1959-94; tchr. phys. edn., L.I., 1980-90; organizer L.I. Mini Circuit, 1984-90, Showcase Series, 1992 Galaxy Champions. Contbr. articles to various publs. Tchr., advisor Girl Scouts U.S., L.I., 1970-94, Boy Scouts Am., L.I., 1970-94; mem. bd. advisors Bd. Coop. Edn. Spl., L.I., 1979-94; pk. steward Town of Huntington, L.I., 1988-94, mem. conservation bd., 1988-94; active intensive care program Suffolk County Handicapped, L.I., 1993-94. Named Trainer of Yr., L.I. Mini Circuit, 1989-90, Pleasure Horse Champion, Nassau Suffolk Horsemans, 1991, 92, 93, 94, Trainer of Yr., North Shore Horse Shows, 1994. Mem. Am. Horse Show Assn. (show mgr.), Nat. Hunter Jumper Assn., Palm Beach Horse Industry Coun. (bd. dirs.), Palm Beach County Horseman's Assn. (bd. dirs.). Home: 13678 14th Pl Loxahatchee FL 33470-4905

KROHLEY, PATRICIA ANNE, realtor, artist, writer; b. N.Y.C., Feb. 13, 1954; d. Casper and Ann Marie (Calise) Inzerillo; m. Richard John Krohley Sr., June 10, 1977 (separated Mar. 1994); 1 child, Richard John Jr. Student, Bklyn. Mus. Art Sch., 1971, Queens Coll., 1972, Fashion Inst. Tech., 1974. Lic. real estate salesperson, N.Y. Realtor Century 21 Bonus RE, Woodhaven, N.Y., 1988-93, Re/Max Bonus Realty, Woodhaven, N.Y., 1993-96, Re/Max Liberty Realty, Ozone Park, N.Y., 1996; with Met. Life Ins. Co., Lake Success, N.Y., 1996—; mem. Agt. Adv. Panel, Century 21 Broker's Coun., L.I., N.Y., 1990; Key Communicator Re/Max Bonus Realty, Woodhaven, 1993-96. Recipient scholarship Bklyn. Mus. Art, 1971. Mem. Nat. Assn. Life Underwriters, Nat. Assn. Realtors, N.Y. State Assn. Realtors, N.Y.C. Assn. Life Underwriters, L.I. Bd. Realtors, Women in Transition (founder, pres. 1993—), Nat. Art League, Alliance of Queens Artists. Office: Met Life Inst Co # 253 Summit Agy Ste 107 3333 New Hyde Park Rd Lake Success NY 11042

KROIS, AUDREY, artist; b. Boston, Mar. 14, 1934; d. Henry and Lillian Marie (Mueller) Haeberle; m. Richard Gamage, May 14, 1966 (div. Mar. 1975); m. Joseph E. Krois Jr., June 17, 1978. BA, Syracuse U., 1956; MSW, Columbia U., 1958; postgrad., Fashion Inst. Tech., 1964-66, Art Students League, 1973-76. Social worker Pleasantville (N.Y.) Cottage Sch., 1958-62; cons. to UNICEF UN, Bangkok, Thailand, 1963; supr. vol. program Henry St. Settlement, N.Y.C., 1964-66; dir. cmty. devel. program Anti Poverty Funding, N.Y.C., 1966-88; supervising dir., asst. v.p., cons. Divsn. Homemaker, Home Health Care, G.H.I., Inc., N.Y.C., 1969-78. One-woman shows at Clayton Liberatore Gallery, Bridgehampton, N.Y., 1995, 96; exhibited in group shows at Access to the Arts, Jamestown, N.Y., 1981, Embroiders Guild and Abigail Adams Smith Mus., N.Y.C., 1982, Arrowmont Sch., Gatlinburg, Tenn., 1982, Gayle Willson Gallery, Southampton, N.Y., 1983, 88, Discovery Art Gallery, Glen Cove, N.Y., 1989, Decatur House, Washington, 1990, Mus. Am. Quilter Soc., Paducah, Ky., 1992, Vanderbilt Mus., Centerport, n.Y., 1992, 94, Wellspring Gallery, Santa Monica, Calif., 1993, 94, Aullwood Audubon Ctr., Dayton, Ohio, 1996 (Best of Show). Mem. South Fork Craft Assn., Southampton Artists Assn. (bd. dirs. 1990-91, fin. dir. 1992-93, pres. 1994, Award of Excellence in Watercolor, 1994, 95, Award of Merit in Watercolor 1993), Studio Art Quilts Calif., Armory Art Ctr. Fla. Home: Box 2482 Palm Beach FL 33480 also: Box 960 Southampton NY 11969

KROMINGA, LYNN, cosmetic and health care company executive, lawyer; b. L.A., May 16, 1950; d. Dale E. and Phyllis M. Krominga; m. Amnon Shiboleth, Apr. 9, 1992; 1 child, Karen Lee Shiboleth. B.A. in German, U. Minn., 1972, J.D., 1974. Bar: Minn. 1974, N.Y. 1976. Assoc. firms in Mpls. and N.Y.C., 1974-77; assoc. counsel Am. Express Co., N.Y.C., 1977-80; sr. internat. counsel Revlon, Inc., N.Y.C., 1981-92, v.p. law, 1988-92, gen. counsel to exec. com., 1991-92, pres. licensing div., 1992—, mem. exec. com., 1993—. Mem. ABA, Internat. Bar Assn., Cosmetic, Toiletry and Fragance Assn. (vice chmn. govt. rels. com. 1991-92), Am. Arbitration Assn. (corp. counsel com. 1986-92; panel of arbitrators for large complex cases 1993—), Phi Beta Kappa. Home: 333 E 57th St New York NY 10022-2950 Office: Revlon Inc 625 Madison Ave New York NY 10022-1801

KROMM, JANE E., art history educator; b. Phila., May 11, 1949; d. William A. and Nell (Wolfgang) K. BS in Edn., Wheelock Coll., 1970; MDiv, Harvard U., 1976; PhD, Emory U., 1984. Asst. prof. U. Ala., Huntsville, 1984-89; asst. prof. SUNY, Purchase, 1989-94, assoc. prof., 1994—; lectr. Cooper Hewitt Mus., 1989-93; cons. Ednl. Testing Svc., Princeton, N.J., 1990—. Contbr. articles to profl. jours. Rsch. fellow AAUW, 1981-82. Mem. Am. Assn. 18th Century Studies, Coll. Art Assn. Office: Purchase Coll Humanities Divsn 435 Anderson Hill Rd Purchase NY 10577-1400

KRONE, JULIE, jockey; b. Benton Harbor, Mich., July 24, 1963; d. Don and Judy Krone. Began as profl. jockey Tampa Bay (Fla.) Downs, 1980; first female jockey to win a Triple Crown race; first woman to win 5 races in a day at Saratoga, N.Y.; leading woman jockey in U.S., 1986-88; leading woman jockey money won, 1986—; winningest female jockey in history with nearly 3,100 victories. Author: (with Nancy Ann Richardson) Riding for My Life, 1995. Winner of 15 Grade I races including $67 Million in purses; races won include Cornhusker Handicap, AK-Star Ben Racetrack, Omaha, 1988, Flower Bowl Handicap, Belmont Park, 1988, Modesty Stakes, Arlington Park, Ill., 1989, Budweiser Md. Classic, Pimlico, 1989, Belmont Stakes, Elmont, N.Y., 1993, The Molson Millian, Toronto, Can., 1995, The Meadowlands Cup, East Rutherford, N.J., 1995, The Ill. Derby, Chgo., 1995, N.J. Derby, Cherry Hill, 1995; first rode in Ky. Derby, 1992; recipient Comeback award Am. Sportscasters Assn., 1994. Office: care Jockeys' Guild 250 W Main St Ste 1820 Lexington KY 40507-1733

KRONEN, JERILYN, psychologist; b. N.Y.C., July 17, 1947; d. Morris and Hester (Engel) Levy; m. Kenneth Kronen, Apr. 11, 1976; children: Ari, Joshua. PhD, Yeshiva U., 1982; cert. in psychotherapy & psychoanalysis, N.Y.U., 1988. Lic. psychologist, N.Y. Tchr. Pub. Sch. 119, N.Y.C., 1969-72; sch. psychologist Bd. Coop. Edn. Svc., N.Y.C., 1972-82; pvt. practice N.Y.C., 1982—; mem. faculty Resolve, N.Y.C., 1989—; adj. clin. supr. Ferkauf-Yeshiva U., N.Y.C., 1989—; lectr. in field. Bd. dirs. Couples Club Kehilat Jeshurun Synagogue, N.Y.C., 1989-91, adoption resource person, 1990—; liaison mem. Lower Sch. Ramaz, N.Y.C., 1990-92. Mem. APA, Div. 39 Psychoanalysis. Home and Office: 137 E 36th St Ste 14 New York NY 10016-3528

KRONENBERG, JANET LOIS, lawyer; b. Cleve., Jan. 13, 1948; d. Louis David and Shirley Evelyn (Weiskopf) K. Student, George Washington U., 1966-68; BA, NYU, 1970, MPA, 1976; JD, Cleve. State U., 1978. Bar: Ohio 1979, U.S. Dist. Ct. 1979, U.S. Ct. Appeals 1983, U.S. Supreme Ct. 1988. Rsch. asst. Cleve. State U., 1977-78, adj. lectr. law, 1980-91; dep. treas. Cuyahoga County, Cleve., 1977-78; ptnr. Kronenberg & Kronenberg, Cleve., 1979—; asst. to sr. v.p. Curtis Brown, Ltd., N.Y.C., 1970-75; presenter various continuing edn. programs; life del. 8th Jud. Conf., Cleve. Pres., trustee Ctr. for Prevention Domestic Violence, Cleve., 1988-89, N.E. Ohio Health Svcs., Cleve., 1992-95; trustee Womenspace, Cleve., 1989-91, N.E. Ohio Health Svcs., 1990—; mem. citizens adv. bd. Broadview Devel. Ctr., Broadview Heights, Ohio, 1990-91; mem. Cuyahoga County Child Protection Coun., Cleve., 1993-95; mem. Cuyahoga County Women's Polit. Caucus. Named Vol. Lawyer of Yr., Legal Aid Soc., Cleve., 1987, honoree Coalition To End Domestic Violence, Cleve., 1989. Mem. Ohio Bar Assn., Cuyahoga County Bar Assn., Cleve. Bar Assn. Home: 16729 Fernway Shaker Heights OH 44120 Office: 410 Midland Bldg Cleveland OH 44115

KRONENGOLD, PENNY, artist; b. N.Y.C., Apr. 14, 1932; d. Samuel and Augusta (Bohmart) Drexler; m. Jack S. Kronengold, Apr. 29, 1964; children: Charles S., Matthew S. BFA cum laude, Syracuse U., 1953. publicity dir. First Street Gallery, 1987—; tchr. printmaking and life drawing for sr. citizens, N.Y., 1964, 83—. Solo exhbns. include First St. Gallery, N.Y.C., 1983, 85, 88, 91, 93, 96, Books & Co., N.Y.C., 1994; museums group exhbns. include Stamford Mus., 1989, Trenton City Mus., 1993, Albright-Knox Mems. Gallery, 1994-95; work collected by Mobil Oil, MCI Telecomms., Dunwoodie Comms., Calif. Coll. of Fine Arts, Printmaking Workshop, The Russian Tea Room, and more than 40 pvt. collections. Recipient Hon. Mention award Gallery 57, Fullerton, Calif., 1992, curator award Kerry Brougher, Curator L.A. MOCA. Mem. Coll. Art Assn., Empire State Masters Swim Club (1st, 2d and 3d place awards 1993, 94, 95, 96), U.S. Masters Swimming Assn., Asphalt Green Swim Team, YWCA Metro Marlins Swim Team. Office: First Street Gallery 560 Broadway New York NY 10012

KRONHOLM, MARTHA MARY, elementary education educator; b. Wisconsin Rapids, Wis., July 28, 1952; d. Donald Edward and Ruth Marie (Albert) K. BS, U. Wis., LaCrosse, 1974; MEPD, U. Wis., Stevens Point, 1980; PhD, So. Ill. U., 1993. Elem. tchr. grades 4-6 Wisconsin Rapids Pub. Schs., 1974-88, sci. coord., 1986-88; ad hoc faculty U. Wis., Stevens Point, 1986-88; instr. sci. methods So. Ill. U., Carbondale, 1989-91; 6th grade tchr. Wisconsin Rapids (Wis.) Pub. Schs., 1992—, action rsch. team, 1993—; mem. environ. edn. task force Wis. Dept. Pub. Instrn., Madison, 1983-85; rsch. asst. Earthwatch, Ethiopia, 1984, Borneo, 1985, Minn., Alaska, 1987; mem. bd. visitors U. Wis., Stevens Point, 1987—; mem. tchr. certification rev. com. Wis. Environ. Edn., State of Wis., 1981-83; ad hoc faculty U. Wis., Stevens Point, 1986-88, 96—. Co-author: (curriculum guides) Wisconsin Environmental Education Curriculum Planning Guide, 1985, Wisconsin Rapids Environmental Education Guide, 1989, Wisconsin Rapids Science Guide, 1988; author articles, abstracts in field. Mentor; mem. Habitat Restoration Com., 1992—; edn. chairperson Aldo Leopold chpt. Audubon Soc., Stevens Point, 1983-88; tchr. amb. Russian Expedition, 1995. Christa McAuliffe fellow U.S. Dept. Edn., 1987; Delta Kappa Gamma Soc. Internat. scholar, 1989; Lifetouch Enrichment grantee, 1994; recipient Kohl fellowship award, 1994; named Wisconsin Rapids Tchr. of Yr., 1994, 95, Wood County Conervation Tchr. of the Year. Mem. Wis. Assn. for Environ. Edn. (sec., Aldo Leopold award 1990), AAUW (newsletter co-editor Wisconsin Rapids chpt. 1986-88, Project Renew scholar 1990), Ruffed Grouse Soc. (banquet com. 1983-87, Edn. and Conservation award 1986), Delta Kappa Gamma (sec. Gamma chpt., Golden award 1988), Phi Kappa Phi, Kappa Delta Pi, Phi Delta Kappa (Howard M. Soule Ednl. Leadership fellow 1992). Democrat. Lutheran. Home: 1430 23rd St N Ste G Wisconsin Rapids WI 54494-2192

KRONKE, DORENE EMMA, pharmaceutical executive; b. Tyler, Minn., May 20, 1950; d. Arthur John and Elaine Irene (Wendorff) K.; m. Jonathan Krim, June 21, 1980 (div. Oct. 1983); m. Michael William Rossi, Nov. 19, 1983 (separated). BA in Bus. Adminstrn., SW State U., 1973; MBA, Ariz. State U., 1981. Unit mgr. Good Samaritan Hosp., Phoenix, 1973-75; waitress Phoenix Country Club, 1976-77; sales rep. Treasure Chem. Co., Billings, Mont., 1977; profl. rep. Merck Sharp & Dohme, Missoula, Mont., 1978-80; program coord. Merck Sharp & Dohme, West Point, Pa., 1981-83; dist. mgr. Merck Sharp & Dohme, San Diego, 1983-86; product mgr. Merck Sharp & Dohme, West Point, 1986-88; region dir. Merck Sharp & Dohme, Mpls., 1988-91; v.p. sales and mktg. MGI Pharma, Inc., Mpls., 1991-92; exec. dir. info. edn. and svcs. Astra Merck, Inc., Wayne, Pa., 1992-95, exec. dir. field sales, 1995—. Bd. dirs. Nat. Soc. for Prevention of Blindness, Orange, Calif., 1986; trustee First Unitarian Soc., Mpls., 1990; mem. St. David's Episcopal Ch., Phila. Mus. Art, Nat. Parks & Conservation Assn., Washington, Nature Conservancy, Nat. Mus. of Women in the Arts, Washington. Mem. NOW, Ariz. State U. Alumni Assn., S.W. State U. Alumni Assn. (Childreach sponsor). Office: 725 Chesterbrook Blvd Wayne PA 19087-5637

KROPF, SUSAN J., cosmetics company executive; married. BA in English, St. John's U.; MBA in Fin., NYU. Adminstrv. asst. Avon Products, Inc., N.Y.C., 1970, various mgmt. positions, 1970-85, v.p. purchasing and package devel., 1985-90, v.p., sr. officer product devel., 1990—, v.p. R&D and mfg., 1992—, sr. v.p. global ops. and bus. devel., 1992—; bd. dirs. Green Point Savs. Bank. Mem. Cosmetic Exec. Women, Fashion Group Internat. Office: Avon Products Inc 9 W 57th St New York NY 10019

KROTSENG, MARSHA VAN DYKE, higher education administrator; b. Indiana, Pa., May 10, 1955; d. Chester James and Helen Louise (Gibson) Van Dyke; m. Morgan Lee Krotseng, June 24, 1978. BA in Spanish, Coll. of William and Mary, 1977, MEd in Ednl. Adminstrn., 1981, EdD in Higher Edn., 1987. Spanish, journalism tchr. Lancaster County Pub. Schs., Irvington, Va., 1977-79; office mgr., computer programmer SEMCO, Inc., Newport News, Va., 1979-80; Spanish, German tchr. Newport News Pub. Schs., 1980-82; rsch. asst. Coll. of William and Mary, Williamsburg, Va., 1982-87; Gov.'s fellow Office of Sec. of Edn. Commonwealth of Va., Richmond, 1984; instnl. rsch. assoc., asst. prof. higher edn. U. Miss., Oxford, 1987-89; asst. dir., planning and inst. rsch. U. Hartford, West Hartford, Conn., 1989-91; dir. rsch. and info. systems State Coll. and Univ. Systems, Charleston, W.Va., 1991—; proposal review panel mem. Assn. for Study of Higher Edn.-Ednl. Resource Info. Ctr. Higher Edn. Report Series, 1992—. Author: (chpt.) Politics and Policy in the Age of Education, 1990; co-editor: Developing Executive Information Systems in Higher Education, 1993; mem. editl. adv. bd. Ednl. Studies, 1990-93; assoc. editor Review of Higher Edn.,

1991-94. Unit coord. United Way Fund Drive, Hartford, 1989, 90; choir mem., soloist First Presbyn. Ch., Charleston, 1992—; mem. Charleston Women's Forum, 1994—; mem. Leadership W.Va., 1995. Recipient Outstanding Doctoral Rsch. award Va. Poly. Inst., 1988; named one of Outstanding Young Women of Am., 1985, 86, Outstanding West Virginian, Gov. of W.V.a, 1994, Leadership W.Va., 1995. Mem. Assn. for Study of Higher Edn. (bd. dirs. 1987-90, site selection com. chair 1990-93), Am. Assn. for Higher Edn., Am. Ednl. Rsch. Assn. (program co-chair divsn. J 1988-89), Assn. for Instnl. Rsch. (publs. bd. 1990-92, exec. com., forum chair 1992-94), Nat. Postsecondary Edn. Coop. Coun. on Postsecondary Edn. Stats., Phi Beta Kappa, Kappa Delta Pi (Nat. Essay award 1987). Office: State Coll and Univ Sys Ctrl Office 1018 Kanawha Blvd E Charleston WV 25301-2827

KROUSE, HELENE JUNE, nursing educator; b. Bklyn., Mar. 24, 1955; d. Sidney and Gertrude (Silver) Kempner; m. John H. Krouse, May 6, 1979; children: Beth Melissa, Daniel Jacob. BS cum laude, SUNY, Bklyn., 1976; MS, U. Rochester, 1979; PhD, Boston Coll., 1984. Staff nurse Downstate Med. Ctr., Bklyn., 1976-77; instr. in nursing Hunter Coll.-Bellevue Sch. Nursing, N.Y.C., 1979-80; asst. prof., coord. med.-surg. nursing Emmanuel Coll., Boston, 1980-84; asst. prof. nursing Boston Coll., Chestnut Hill, Mass., 1984-89; adult nurse practitioner Mass. Eye and Ear Infirmary, Boston; adminstr., nurse practitioner Fla. Ear, Nose & Throat Specialists, Ormond Beach, 1989-94; assoc. prof. U. N. Fla., Jacksonville, 1995—; faculty fellow Boston Coll., 1988, rsch. fellow, 1987. Contbr. articles to profl. publs. Grantee U. Rochester Alumni Seed Found., 1978-79, Emmanuel Coll., 1981-83. Mem. Oncology Nurse Soc., Am. Cancer Soc. (svc. and rehab. com. South Essex chpt., vol. phone bank), So. Nursing Rsch. Soc., Soc. Otorhinolaryngology and Head-Neck Nurses, Inc., Sigma Theta Tau (Clin. Rsch. award 1986-87, chair nominating com., eligibility com. Alpha Chi chpt.).

KROUSE, JENNY LYNN, elementary school educator; b. Houston, Oct. 9, 1956; d. Thomas Raymond and Anna Margaret (Davis) K. BS, U. Houston, 1979; postgrad., Sam Houston State U. Cert. tchr., Tex. 4th grade tchr. Orange Grove Elem. Sch., Houston, 1979-86, pre-kindergarten tchr., 1986-88, 3d grade tchr., 1988-89; 5th grade tchr. lang. arts Oleson Elem. Sch., Houston, 1989-93, pre-1st grade tchr., 1993-94, 4th grade tchr., 1994-95; 5th grade sci. tchr. Drew Magnet Sch. Acad. Math., Sci. and Arts, Houston, 1995—; coop. learning facilitator Johns Hopkins U., Houston, 1993; GESA facilitator Gray Hill, Houston, 1995; mentor Region IV, Houston, 1996. Mem. Women's Action Coalition, Houston, 1992-95. Mem. tex. PTA (life). Home: 910 Cypress Station Dr #918 Houston TX 77090 Office: Drew Academy 1910 W Little York Houston TX 77091

KROWN, SUSAN ELLEN, physician, researcher; b. Bronx, N.Y., Sept. 8, 1946; d. Frederick B. and Paula (Hauser) K.; m. Roger E. Pitt, May 18, 1980 (div. 1988); 1 child, Catherine Krown Pitt. AB, Barnard Coll., 1967; MD, SUNY, Bklyn., 1971. Diplomate Am. Bd. Internal Medicine. Intern, then jr. and sr. resident in internal medicine Mt. Sinai Hosp., N.Y.C., 1971-74; with Meml. Sloan-Kettering Cancer Ctr., N.Y.C., 1974—, assoc. mem., 1984-94, mem., 1994—; clin. asst. Meml. Hosp., N.Y.C., 1977-78, asst. attending physician, 1978-82; assoc. attending physician Meml. Sloan-Kettering Cancer Ctr., N.Y.C., 1982-94, attending physician, 1994—; asst. prof. Med. Coll. Cornell U., N.Y.C., 1977-83; assoc. prof. Med. Coll. Cornell U., N.Y.C., 1983-94, prof., 1994—; mem. oncologic drugs adv. com. FDA, Rockville, Md., 1986-90, cons., 1990—; chair oncology com. AIDS Clin. Trials Group, Bethesda, Md., 1990-92, mem. exec. com., 1992-94; mem. res. agenda com., 1995—; co-chair steering com. AIDS malignancy consortium NCI, Bethesda, 1995—; chair task force on Kaposi's Sarcoma staging Am. Joint Com. on Cancer, Chgo., 1991-93. Mem. editorial bd. Jour. Interferon Rsch., 1985—, Jour. AIDS, 1988—; contbr. numerous articles to profl. jours. NIH Rsch. grantee; Am. Cancer Soc. Jr. Faculty fellow, 1978-81. Mem. Internat. Soc. for Interferon Rsch. (coun. 1986-92, bd. dirs. 1995—), Soc. for Biol. Therapy (bd. dirs. 1987-89), AIDS Task Force (chmn. Meml. Sloan Kettering Cancer Ctr. 1989—), Alpha Omega Alpha. Office: Meml Sloan Kettering Ctr 1275 York Ave New York NY 10021-6007

KROWN-NEVINS, ELEANOR THEADORA, retired computer software editor, researcher, educator; b. Bklyn., Feb. 21, 1930; d. Benjamin and Alice (Rosenblum) Krown; m. Alfred Nevins, Feb. 4, 1951 (div. 1978); children: Sherry Nevins Dudley, Roni Nevins Prescott, Barry Jay, Phyllis. B.A. in Biology and Physiology, Hunter Coll., N.Y.C., 1951; M.S. in Edn., L.I.U., 1977. Cert. tchr., Fla., N.Y., cert. lab. technologist. Tchr. Dade County Sch. System, Miami, 1980-87, N.Y.C. Sch. 1987-88; freelance computer programmer, Miami, N.Y.C., 1982-87; pres. Cancer Care, Inc., Nat. Cancer Found., Baldwin chpt., N.Y., 1973-74, v.p. pub. relations Nassau/Suffolk regional bd., 1974-75, publicity chmn., 1969-73; active Crime Watch, North Miami Beach, Fla., 1982-85. Mem. Nat. Audubon Soc., Planetary Soc., Nature Conservancy, World Wildlife Fund. Democrat. Jewish. Avocations: needle point, crocheting, knitting.

KRUCK, DONNA JEAN, special education educator, consultant; b. Peoria, Ill., Jan. 26, 1930; d. Walter George and Lois Irene (Newburn) Hagemeyer; m. Michael Roy Kruck Jr., June 27, 1948; children: Pamela Ann Kruck Hokanson, Michael Roy III, Quentin Robert. BS, Ill. State U., 1961; MEd, U. Ill., 1968. Cert. spl. edn. tchr. and adminstr., Ill. Tchr. New Lenox Dist. 122, Ill., 1956-61; tchr. spl. edn. Lincoln Way Area Joint Agreement, New Lenox, 1961-66; tchr. spl. edn., coord. Joliet Twp. High Sch. Dist. 204, Ill., 1966-86; pvt. practice cons. and diagnostician New Lenox, 1986-92; child adv. New Lenox Dist. 122, 1986-88; instr. Chapel Christian U., 1994—. Author: Let's Learn to Cook, 1971. Pres. Joliet Twp. Edn. Assn., 1971-76; donar Aurora Area Blood Bank, Joliet, 1974-90. Mem. AAUW, NEA (life), Nat. Ret. Tchr. Assn., Am. Assn. Retired Persons, Am. Assn. Mental Retardation, Am. Bus. Women's Assn., Coun. Exceptional Children (life), Coun. Adminstrs. Spl. Edn., Christian Edn. Assn., Ill. Edn. Assn. (life), Ill. Div. Learning Disabilities, Coun. for Ednl. Diagnostic Svcs. (div. learning disabilities), Lutherans for Life, Kappa Delta Pi, Delta Kappa Gamma. Lutheran.

KRUEGER, BETTY JANE, telecommunications company executive; b. Indpls., Oct. 4, 1923; d. Forrest Glen and Hazel Luellen (Taylor) Burns; student Butler U., 1948-49; m. Alan Douglas Krueger, Apr. 4, 1975; 1 son by previous marriage—Michael J. Vornehm. Supr., instr. Ind. Bell Telephone Co., Indpls., 1941-54; supr. communications Jones & Laughlin Steel Co., Indpls., 1954-56, Ford Motor Co., Indpls., 1956-64, U.S. Govt., Camp Atterbury, Ind., 1964-66; dir. communications Meth. Hosp. of Ind., Indpls., 1966-79; pres. owner Rent-A-Radio, Inc. of Ind., Indpls., after 1979; sec.-treas. Communications Unltd., Inc. Former pres. Am. Legion Aux.; chmn. for Ind., Girls State U.S.A., 1972-77; probation officer vol., 1973-74; suicide prevention counselor, 1972-73. Recipient award for outstanding community service Ford Motor Co., 1961. Mem. Am. Soc. Hosp. Engring., Am. Hosp. Assn., Nat. Assn. Bus. and Ednl. Radio, Inc., Internat. Teletypewriters for the Deaf, Asso. Public Safety Communications Officers, Inc., Am. Bus. Women. Methodist. Home: RR 2 Box 119 Franklin IN 46131-9538 Office: 4032 Southeastern Ave Indianapolis IN 46203-1563

KRUEGER, BONNIE LEE, editor, writer; b. Chgo., Feb. 3, 1950; d. Harry Bernard and Lillian (Soyak) Krueger; m. James Lawrence Spurlock, Mar. 8, 1972. Student Morraine Valley Coll., 1970. Adminstrv. asst. Carson Pirie Scott & Co., Chgo., 1969-72; traffic coord. Tatham Laird & Kudner, Chgo., 1973-74; traffic coord. J. Walter Thompson, Chgo., 1974-76; prodn. coord., 1976-78; editor-in-chief Assoc. Pubs., Chgo., 1978—; editor-in-chief Sophisticate's Hairstyle Guide, 1978—, Sophisticate's Beauty Guide, 1978—, Complete Woman, 1981—, Sophisticate's Soap Star Hair Styles, 1995; pub., editorial svcs. dir. Sophisticate's Black Hair Guide, 1983—, Sophisticate's Soap Star Styles, 1994. Mem. Statue of Liberty Restoration Com., N.Y.C., 1983; campaign worker Cook County State's Atty., Chgo., 1982; poll watcher Cook County Dem. Orgn., 1983; mem. Chgo. Architecture Found. Mem. Soc. Profl. Journalists, Am. Health and Beauty Aids Inst. (assoc. mem.), Lincoln Park Zool. Soc., Landmarks Preservation Coun. of Ill., Art Inst. Chgo., Sigma Delta Chi. Lutheran. Clubs: Sierra, Headline Club. Office: Complete Woman 875 N Michigan Ave Chicago IL 60611-1803

KRUEGER, DIANA SUE, accountant; b. Ennis, Tex., Feb. 17, 1964; d. John Milton and Margaret Mary (Gerich) Haskovec; m. Todd Mitchell Krueger, April 20, 1986; children: Kristina, Kory. AAS, Navarro Jr., Corsicana, Tex., 1990; BBA in Acctg., U. Tex., Arlington, 1994. CPA, Tex. Acct. Lane, Gorman, Trubitt, L.L.P., Dallas, 1990—, Weaver & Tidwell, L.L.P., Dallas, 1993—. Mem. AICPA, Tex. Soc. CPAs, Inst. Mgmt. Accts. Home: 307 E Waco Ennis TX 75119

KRUEGER, JENNIFER ANN, librarian; b. New Orleans, Aug. 17, 1963; d. William Charles Jr. and Carol Ann (Koock) K.; m. Mitchell Craig, Stein, Oct. 22, 1989; 1 child, Zoe Rebecca. BS in Math., Tufts U., 1985; MLS, Simmons Coll., 1988; MBA in Mktg., Columbia U., 1993. Libr. Somerville (Mass.) Pub. Libr., 1985-87; info. asst. Lotus Devel. Corp., Cambridge, Mass., 1987; rsch. analyst PA Cons. Group, Hightstown, N.J., 1988-90; info. specialist AIG, N.Y.C., 1990-91; head info. svcs. N.Y. Pub. Libr., N.Y.C., 1993—. Named One of Top 40 New Yorkers under 40, Daily News, 1995. Mem. NAFE, Am. Soc. Info. Sci., Columbia U. Bus. Sch. Alumni Assn. Office: New York Pub Libr SIBL 188 Madison Ave New York NY 10016

KRUEGER, KATHERYN ELIZABETH, principal, retired; b. Chgo., June 23, 1938; d. Ralph A. and Katheryn E. (Lebsock) Logan; m. William August Krueger, Apr. 26, 1958; children: Lynda Katheryn, William Carl. BS, Ill. State U., 1972, MS, 1978. Cert tchr. physically handicapped, mentally handicapped, learning disabled, severely handicapped, multiple handicapped, elem., gen. adminstrn., Ill. Tchr. State of Ill., Lincoln, 1972-73, Mason City (Ill.) Elem. Sch., 1973-80, Kaskaskia Spl. Edn. Dist., Centralia, Ill., 1980-82; tchr. spl. edn., adj. dean students Mt. Vernon (Ill.) Twp. H.S., 1982-90; prin. jr./sr. H.S. Ford Ctrl. Sch. Dist., Piper City, Ill., 1990-91; prin. H.S. Forreston (Ill.) Valley Sch. Dist., 1991-93; ret., 1993. Author: Getting Ready for School, 1985. Mem. AAUW. Home: 5415 Tangelo St Leesburg FL 34748

KRUEGER, NANCY ASTA, physical therapist; b. Manhattan Beach, Calif., Jan. 8, 1947; d. Henry Adolph and Asta Ida (Harrison) Graef; m. Gary Patrick Krueger, June 14, 1969. Student, Lewis & Clark Coll., 1964-66; BS, U. So. Calif., L.A., 1969; postgrad., U. So. Calif., Downey, 1980-81. Staff phys. therapist Los Angeles County-U. So. Calif. Med. Ctr., L.A., 1969-71, Stockton (Calif.) State Hosp., 1971; pediatric phys. therapist Calif. Childrens Svcs.-San Joaquin County, Stockton, 1972-73; sr. phys. therapist Calif. Childrens Svcs.-San Diego County, San Diego, 1974-80; mng. dir. therapy svcs. Sharp-Cabrillo Hosp., San Diego, 1981-83; sr. phys. therapist El Cajon (Calif.) Valley Hosp., 1983-84; prin. El Cajon Therapy Assocs., 1984—; cons. Teledyne Ryan Aero., San Diego County, 1984—, San Diego Marriott Hotel, 1995—; speaker in field. Singer Old Globe Madrigal Singers, 1983; vice chair adv. com. Maternal, Child and Adolescent Health, San Diego County, 1987-89; active local polit. campaigns; advisor Mesa Coll., 1985—; mem. edn. and sci. com. Arthritis Found., 1986-87; chairperson adv. com. Mesa Coll., 1994-96. Fellow Am. Acad. Sports Medicine, Orthopedic Soc.; mem. Am. Phys. Therapy Assn. (chmn. San Diego dist. 1977-78, bd. dirs. Calif. chpt. 1983-84, mem. nominating com. 1989-91, chmn. 1991, v.p. 1994—, fin. com. Orthopedic sect. 1993—), Aux. Am. Optometric Assn., Arthritis Health Profls. Assn. (v.p. 1991-93), Jrs. of Social Svc. (treas. 1991-93), Soroptimists (sec. El Cajon chpt. 1982, chmn. 1994), Rotary Internat. Republican. Episcopalian. Home: 4657 Rancho Park Ave San Diego CA 92120 Office: El Cajon Therapy Assocs 590 S Magnolia Ave El Cajon CA 92020-6011

KRUG, KAREN-ANN, healthcare financial executive, accountant; b. Riverdale, N.D., Apr. 22, 1951; d. C. and Elsie (Eide) K.; m. C. Scott James, Aug. 19, 1978. BS, N.D. State U., 1980; MBA, U. Phoenix, 1996. CPA. Mgr. proof transit 1st Nat. Bank Grand Forks (N.D.); sr. acct. Leo E. Bell & Assocs., Grand Forks, 1978-80; dir. project rev. Agassiz Health Systems Agy., Grand Forks, 1980-82; sr. adminstrv. asst. St. Mary's Hosp., Reno; dir. planning and devel. St. Mary's Health Care Corp., Reno, 1982-87; contr. Pacific Presbyn. Med. Ctr., San Francisco, 1987-89, corp. contr. Daughters of Charity Nat. Healthcare System Seton Med. Ctr., Daly City, Calif., 1989-93; CFO, v.p. fin. Howard Cmty. Hosp., Kokomo, Ind., 1994—. Vol. Jr. Achievement, Reno, 1984-87, Project Literacy U.S., San Francisco, 1987-88. Fellow Healthcare Fin. Mgmt. Assn. (cert. managed care profl. 1995, chmn. Pressler Managed Care com. 1996, cert. mgr. Pt. Accts. 1996, HFMA Jour. editl. bd. 1996); mem. AICPA (bd. trustees Benevolent Fund 1983-93), Calif. Soc. CPAs (healthcare com. 1989-93, chmn. 1991-93), Delta Gamma (treas. San Francisco alumni chpt. 1992-93).

KRUGER, LOUISE, sculptor; b. L.A., Aug. 5, 1924, d. Otto H. and Elizabeth Mary (Spinner) K. Student, Scripps Coll., Claremont, Calif., 1942-45, Art Students League, N.Y.C., 1945-46, Guastini Foundry, Pistola, Italy, 1957-58, Chief Opoku Dwumfuor, Kumasi, Ghana, 1969-70. Sculptor: one-woman shows include Artists' Gallery, N.Y.C., 1949, Brown U., Mass., Farnsworth Mus., Maine, Martha Jackson Gallery, N.Y.C., Schoelkopf Gallery, N.Y.C., Bowdoin Mus., Maine, Martin Sumers Gallery, N.Y.C., 1986—; represented in group exhibitions Mus. Modern Art, N.Y.C., Whitney Mus., N.Y.C., Met. Mus., N.Y.C., Bklyn. Mus., Modern Mus., Sao Paulo, Kunsthaus, Zurich, Riksgalleriet, Oslo, Libr. Congress, Washington, Chgo. Art Inst.; included in collections Mus. Modern Art, N.Y.C., Prudential Ins. Collection, Rutgers U., New Britain Mus. Am. Art, Conn., Bowdoin Mus., Maine, N.Y.C. Pub. Libr. Home: 30 E 2d St New York NY 10003 Office: Martin Sumers Gallery 50 W 57th St New York NY 10019

KRUGER, MOLLEE COPPEL, writer; b. Bel Air, Md., Mar. 28, 1929; d. Benjamin and Mary (Hoffman) Coppel; m. Jerome Kruger, Feb. 20, 1955; children: Lennard Gideon, Joseph Avrum. BA, U. Md., 1950. Columnist The Harford Gazette, Bel Air, Md., 1945-47; advt. copywriter Joseph Katz Co., Balt., 1951-55; TV scriptwriter Jewish Community Coun., Washington, 1960-72; columnist, feature writer various newspapers, Washington and N.Y.C., 1967-88; freelance writer various nat. publs., 1980—; condr. writing workshop Montgomery County Community Svcs., Rockville, Md., 1982; cons. Buddemeir Co., Balt., 1958-59; pres. Maryben Books, Rockville, 1970—; tchr. creative writing Jewish Community Ctr., Rockville, 1974-78, cons. editor sr. adult publs., 1975, 76, 77; cons. editor Standards Alumni Assn., 1992. Author: Unholy Writ, 1970, More Unholy Writ, 1973, Yankee Shoes, 1975 (Gold Ribbon Bicentennial award 1976), Daughters of Chutzpah, 1983, Admiral of the Mosquitoes, 1990, Ladies First, 1995; mus. adaptation of Ladies First (book and lyrics, staging, performance), 1995-96; editor Standard newsletter Nat. Bur. Standards, 1978-80 (award of excellence 1979); playwright, prodr. hist. show for Md. 350 Com., Montgomery County, Rockville, 1982-84; playwright, prodr., dir. (musical adaption) Ladies First, 1995-96. Founding mem. Humanities Commn. Montgomery County, 1984-91; judge Md. Writing Contest for Sr. Citizens, Annapolis, 1987-91, Montgomery County Bd. Elections,l 1990-92. Recipient Cert. of Recognition U.S. Dept. Commerce, Washington, 1979, Alice Sherry Meml. award Poetry Soc. Va., Charlottesville, 1988; profiled as Outstanding Md. Woman Writer Md. State Dept. Edn., Md. Commn. for Women, Balt., 1989. Mem. Nat. League Am. Pen Women (Md. state letters chmn. 1990-92, br. pres. elect 1992-94, nat. letters bd. 1992-94, chmn. nat. letters com. 1994-95, nat. membership chmn. 1994-95, nat. exec. bd. 1994-95, writing awards 1983, 85, 87, 89, 1st prize Nat. Adult Short Story contest 1994, 1st prize Nat. Catherine Leach Poetry competition 1994, 1st prize Nat. Miriam S. Rogers letters contest, 1995, contbr. stories, poems, articles to The Pen Woman mag., 1992-96), Mortar Bd. Alumni Club (pres. 1977-78). Democrat. Jewish.

KRULFELD, RUTH MARILYN, anthropologist, educator; b. N.Y.C., Apr. 15, 1931; d. Leon and Frances (Rosenberg) Pulwers; m. Jacob Mendel Krulfeld, Aug. 28, 1964; 1 child, Michael David. BA cum laude, Brandeis U., 1956; PhD, Yale U., 1974. Field rschr. micro-geog. rsch. farms, Singapore, Malaya, 1951-53; anthropol. rsch. Jamaica, 1957, Costa Rica, Nicaragua, Panama, 1958, Lombok, Indonesia, 1960-62, 93, N.E. Thailand, 1993; asst. prof. anthropology, dir. grad. students George Washington U., Washington, 1964-72, 93—, assoc. prof., 1973-76, prof., 1976—, chmn. dept. anthropology, 1984-87, founder spl. grad. program in 3d world devel.; mem. Judaic studies com. George Washington U.; bd. dirs. No. Va. Humanities Coun.; v.p., bd. dirs. Ctr. Multicultural Human Resources; rschr. S.E. Asian refugees, 1981—, Laotian refugees in U.S., 1981—, also rsch. on culture change in villages in Indonesia. Contbr. articles to profl. jours.; co-author several books. Bd. dirs. No. Va. Regional Humanities Coun. Currier scholar Yale U., 1958; Ford fellow, 1960-62; grantee Found. for Study of Man, 1957, Am. Coun., 1963, Cotlow faculty rsch. grantee, 1992-93, faculty rsch. grantee George Washington U., 1992-93, rsch. grantee Va. Found. for Humanities and Pub. Policy, 1995-96; recipient Banneker award Ctr. for Washington Area Studies, 1996. Mem. Anthrop. Soc. Washington, Am. Anthrop. Assn. (nominating com., com. on refugee issues gen. anthropology divsn., vice chair com. on refugees issues 1992-94, gen. anthropology divsn. 1993-94, Cori award for best paper on refugees issues 1992, Pedagogical Rsch. and Innovative Devel. in Edn. award 1994). Jewish. Office: George Washington U Dept Anthropology Washington DC 20052

KRULIK, BARBARA S., director, curator; b. N.Y.C., June 13, 1955; d. Herbert Arnold and Irene Sylvia (Lichterman) K. BA in Art History, Pa. State U., 1976. Asst. to dir. NAD, N.Y.C., 1976-77, acting dir., 1977-78, coord. exhbns., 1978-83, asst. dir., 1983-89, interim dir., 1989-90, dep. dir., 1990-92; assoc. dir. Forum Gallery, 1992-94; dir. Grad. Sch. Figurative Art New York Acad. Art, N.Y.C., 1994—. Author, editor exhbn. catalogues. Mem. Am. Assn. Mus. (curators and registrars coms.), Internat. Coun. on Mus. Office: NY Acad Art 111 Franklin St New York NY 10013-2911

KRULIK, GLORIA LEE ANCELL, guidance counselor, educator, retired; b. Bklyn., Dec. 29, 1926; d. Samuel and Thelma (Lerner) Ancell; m. David Krulik, Dec. 25, 1948 (dec. July 1988); 1 child, Eleanor Jane Krulik Levitt. BA in Art, Bklyn. Coll., 1948, MS in Guidance Counseling, 1972; MA in Art Edn., Tchr.'s Coll. Columbia Coll., 1950. Cert. tchr., N.Y. Elem. tchr. Ctr. Acad., Bklyn., 1950-54; tchr. jr. h.s. N.Y.C. Bd. Edn., N.Y.C., 1960-66, guidance counselor, 1966-86; retired, 1986; lectr. Inst. of Retired Profls. & Execs. Bklyn. Coll., Bklyn., 1990-91. Co-contbr. numerous articles to Guidance mag., 1985. Founding mem. Bnai Brith Schoolwomen's Post, 1950-94; mem. East Medwood Jewish Ctr., 1989—; founding mem. Mus. of Women Artists, Washington, 1991—, Holocaust Mus., Washington, 1992—. Democrat.

KRULWICH, TERRY ANN, biochemistry researcher; b. N.Y.C., Apr. 7, 1943; d. Lester S. and Beatrice (Cohen) K.; m. S. Paul Posner, June 10, 1973; children: Jeremy Michael, Adam Jared, Amos Allen. BA, Goucher Coll., 1964; MS, U. Wis., 1966, PhD, 1968; DSc (hon.), Goucher Coll., 1987. Postdoctoral fellow in molecular biology Albert Einstein Coll. Medicine, Bronx, 1968-70; asst. prof. biochemistry Mount Sinai Sch. Medicine CUNY, N.Y.C., 1970-74, assoc. prof., 1974-81, prof. biochemistry, 1981—, dean, grad. sch. biol. sci., 1981—; mem. cellular and molecular com., basis of disease review com. NIH, 1978-81, mem. microbiology, physiology and genetics study sect., 1983-87, mem. nat. gen. med. scis. adv. coun., 1991-94. Editor: The Bacteria, Vol. XII, 1990; mem. editorial bd. Jour. Bacteriology, 1985—, Microbiol. Revs., 1983-88, Jour. Bioenergetic Biomembranes, 1991—, BBA Revs. Bioenergetics, 1992—. Trustee Ramaz Sch., N.Y.C., 1981-91, Heschel Sch., 1991— (pres. 1996—), Congregation Or Zarua, 1992—. Predoctoral fellow NSF, 1964-68, postdoctoral fellow NSF, 1968-70; recipient Rsch. Career Devel. award NIH, 1975-80. Fellow Am. Acad. Microbiology; mem. Am. Soc. Microbiology (div. chmn. physiol. 1990-91), Am. Soc. for Biochemistry and Molecular Biology, Biophys. Soc., N.Y. Acad. Scis., Harvey Soc. Office: Mt Sinai Sch Dept Biochem 1 Gustave L Levy Pl New York NY 10029-6504

KRUPNIK, VEE M., financial company executive; b. Chgo.; d. Phillip and Jane (Glickman) K.; m. Melvin Drury, Sept. 24, 1978. BS, Northwestern U., CPA, cert. fin. planner, real estate broker, ins. broker, Ill. Assoc. dir. corp. fin. Weis, Voisin, Cannon, Chgo., 1967-68; pres. PEC Industries Inc., Ft. Lauderdale, Fla., 1969-71; acct., real estate and ins. broker Vee M. Krupnik & Co., Chgo., 1971-73; sales cons. Baird & Warner Inc., Chgo., 1973-81, asst. v.p. comml.-investment div., 1981-85, v.p. corp. group, 1985-89; comml./investment specialist, 1990-91; v.p. comml. investment sales, 1992—. Mem. Internat. Assn. Fin. Planning (bd. dirs. 1985-87), Internat. Council Shopping Ctrs., Nat. Assn. Corp. Real Estate Execs., Nat. Assn. Securities Dealers, Women's Exec. Network, Nat. Assn. Realtors (bd. dirs. 1983-84, comml. investment council), Cert. Comml. Investment Mems. (pres. Ill. chpt. 1983-84), Ill. Assn. Realtors (bd. dirs. 1983-84), Chgo. Bd. Realtors (bd. dirs. 1982-85, 88-91), Chgo. Assn. Realtors (bd. dirs. 1992-94), Chgo. Assn. Realtors Multiple Listing Svc. (bd. dirs. 1992—), Chgo. Assn. Commerce and Industry, Chgo. Assn. Realtors Comml. Investment Multiple Listing Svc. (chmn. 1991-94), Comml. Investment Multiple Listing Service (pres. 1982-84), Comml. Real Estate Orgn., Chgo. Real Estate Exec. Women. Home: 5757 N Sheridan Rd Apt 7A Chicago IL 60660-4751 Office: Baird & Warner Inc 4040 N Lincoln Ave Chicago IL 60618-3038

KRUPP, CHARLA M., magazine editor, television correspondent; b. Chgo., Jan. 29, 1953; d. Walter M. and Esther Terry (Permut) K.; m. Richard Zoglin, Aug. 1, 1992. BS in Journalism, U. Ill., 1975. Editl. asst. Mademoiselle Mag., N.Y.C., 1975-76, prodn. dir., 1977-79; asst. editor Seventeen Mag. Triangle Publs., N.Y.C., 1976-77; mng. editor Talk Mag., N.Y.C., 1979-80; editor Glamour Entertainment Conde Nast Publs., N.Y.C., 1980-95; sr. editor In Style Time Inc., N.Y.C., 1995—; TV corr. E!, Entertainment TV, L.A., 1994—, The Today Show, N.Y.C., 1996—. Bd. dirs. Why Me?, Chgo., 1994-95, U. Ill. Resource Devel. Bd., Champaign, 1995, 96. Mem. NOW, AFTRA, NARAL, Am. Soc. Mag. Editors, Fund for Feminist Majority, Planned Parenthood, Emily's List. Office: In Style Mag 1271 6th Ave New York NY 10020

KRUPSKA, DANYA (MRS. TED THURSTON), theater director, choreographer; b. Fall River, Mass., Aug. 13, 1921; d. Bronislaw and Anna (Niementowska) Krupski; m. James M. Hanrihan (div. 1953); 1 child, Brion; m. Ted Thurston, May 27, 1954; 1 child, Tina Lyn. Student, Lankenau Sch. for Girls, Phila.; studied with, Ethel Phillips Dance Studio, Catherine Littlefield Ballet Studio, L. Egorova, Paris, Mikhail Mordkin, N.Y.C. and Phila.; studied, Aubrey Hitchens Studio, N.Y.C., Bobby Lewis Dir.'s Studio, N.Y.C. Performed concerts and toured in Poland, Roumania, Balkan Countries, Hungary, Vienna, Palestine, 1929-36; joined Phila. Ballet (Littlefield) for European tour, 1937, Chgo. Opera Season, 1938, Am. Ballet (Ballanchine), N.Y.C., 1938; soloist Broadway prodn.: Frank Fay Show, Radio City Music Hall Ballet; leading role on nat. tour: Johnny Belinda 1941; soloist in: Chouve Souris, 1943; dancer in role of Dream Laurie, 1st Nat. Co. of Okla., later Broadway Co., 1945; asst. to choreographer Agnes de Mille on Rodgers and Hammerstein prodn.: Allegro; asst. to choreographer on ballet prodn.: Fall River Legend, opera prodn.: Rape of Lucrece, Broadway prodns.: Girl in Pink Tights, Gentlemen Prefer Blonds, Paint Your Wagon; assisted Michael Kidd on Broadway prodn.: Can Can; choreographer Broadway prodn.: Most Happy Fella (Tony award nomination), Seventeen, 1st Shoestring Revue, Carefree Heart, Happiest Girl in the World (Tony award nomination), Her First Roman, 1968, Apollo and Miss Agnes; choreographer Met. Opera prodn.: The Gypsy Baron; choreographer Italian mus.: Rugantino, 1962; choreographer: TV Salute to the Peace Corps, 1965; guest choreographer: Zorba, Nat. Theatre, Reykjavik, Iceland, 1971, Company for Stora Teatern, Gothenburg, Sweden, 1971, Fantastiks, Little Theatre, Gothenburg, 1971, Okla. Nat. Theatre, Reykjavik, 1972, No No Nanette, Malmö Stadsteater, Sweden, 1973, Richard Rodger's Prodn. of Rex, Broadway, N.Y.C., 1976, Showboat, Malmö Stadsteater, 1976, Empress of China, Cin. Playhouse, 1984; dir., choreographer: Porgy and Bess, Malmö Stadsteater, Sweden, 1973, Bernstein's The Mass, Malmö Stadsteater, 1975, Chicago, Det Danske Teater, Denmark, 1977, Our Man in Havana, Poland, 1977, Cabaret, Helsingborg Stadsteater, Sweden, 1978, Guys and Dolls, Aarhus Teater, Denmark, 1978, Once Upon a Mattress, Nat. Theater Reykjavik, Iceland, 1981, Animalen, Malmö Stadsteater, Sweden, 1985, Papushko, Colonade Theatre, N.Y.C., 1985; producer, dir.; choreographer: The King and I, Malmö Stadsteater, Sweden, 1984; produced, directed, choreographed Sound of Music, Malmo Stadsteater, Sweden, 1990; directed, choreographed Lerner and Loewe lost musical Day before Spring, N.Y.C., 1990; dance and mus. staging How it Was Done in Odessa, Walnut St. Theatre, Phila., 1991; dir. mus. prodns., N.Y. City Center; Most Happy Fella, 1959, Showboat, 1961, Fiorello, 1962 (also White House prodn. for gov.'s conf. 1968), Oklahoma; choreographer for Buick Hour, 1952, Colgate Comedy Hour, 1953, Omnibus; dir. U.S. Steel Theatre Guild Prodns; Ballets Outlook for Three (Ellington), Pointes on Jazz (Brubeck), Am. Ballet Theatre. Mem. Actors Equity Assn., Soc. Stage Dirs. and Choreographers (exec. bd. mem.), Actors Studio (playwrights and dirs. unit), Dramatist's Guild. Office: 564 W 52nd St New York NY 10019-5009

KRUSE, ANN GRAY, computer programmer; b. Oklahoma City, Jan. 4, 1941; d. Floyd and Bernice Florence (Follansbee) Gray; A.B., Randolph Macon Woman's Coll., 1963; M.B.A., U. Chgo., 1973; m. Roy Edwin Kruse,

Mar. 20, 1971 (dec.). Programming mgr. Ind. Info. Controls, Valparaiso, Ind., 1966-67; systems programmer Nat. Bus. Lists, Inc., Chgo., 1968-69, Am. Steel Foundries, Hammond, Ind., 1970-73; engr. applications programming Bell Helicopter Textron, Fort Worth, 1974-76; lead systems programmer Harris Data Communications, Dallas, 1976-81; sr. systems programmer Lone Star Gas Co., Dallas, 1981-82; sr. software specialist E-Systems, Dallas, 1982—. Republican. Episcopalian. Home: 6128 Black Berry Ln Dallas TX 75248-4909 Office: PO Box 660023 Dallas TX 75266-0023

KRUSE, ROSALEE EVELYN, accountant; b. Muscatine, Iowa, Aug. 23, 1953; d. Burr Arthur Beeding and Mary Ellen (Phillips) McGourty; m. Michael Raymond Kruse, May 20, 1972; children: Lauretta Kathleen, Matthew William. A in Gen. Studies, Muscatine C.C., 1986; BBA, U. Iowa, 1988; M of Acctg., St. Ambrose U., 1993. CPA, Iowa. Acct. Rock Island (Ill.) Arsenal, 1989—. Mem. AICPAs, Am. Soc. Mil. Comptrs. (chairperson chpt. competition 1991-92, treas. 1993-94, 1st v.p. 1994-95), Iowa Soc. CPAs (membership com. 1995-96, auditing stds. and acctg. prin. com. 1996—, pub. and profl. rels. com. 1996—), Inst. Mgmt. Accts (program roster com. Illowa chpt. 1995-96, acad. rels. and ednl. project student affairs com.), Inst. Internal Auditors (bd. govs. 1996—). Methodist. Home: 324 Fletcher Ave Muscatine IA 52761-2043 Office: Rock Island Arsenal Attn Rosalee E Kruse Bldg 390 SE Wing Rock Island IL 61299-5000

KRUSICK, MARGARET ANN, state legislator; b. Milw., Oct. 26, 1956; d. Ronald J. and Maxine C. K. BA, U. Wis., 1978; postgrad., U. Wis., Madison, 1979-82. Legal asst. Milw. Law Office, 1973-78; teaching asst. U. Wis., Milw., 1978-79; staff mem. Govs. Ombudsman Program for the Aging & Disabled, Madison, Wis., 1980; administrv. asst. Wis. Higher Ednl. Aids Bd., Madison, 1981; legis. aide Wis. Assembly, Madison, 1982-83, state rep., 1983—. Author: Wisconsin Youth Suicide Prevention Act, 1985, Wisconsin Nursing Home Reform Act, 1987, Wisconsin Truancy Reform Act, 1988, Elder Abuse Fund, 1989, Lyme Disease Fund, 1989, Stolen Goods Recovery Act, 1990, Fair Prescription Drug Pricing Act, 1994. Mem. St. Gregory Great Cath. Ch., Milw., 1960—, Dem. Party, Milw., 1980—, Layton Park Assn.; bd. dirs. Alzheimer's Disease Assn., 1986-88. Named Legislator of Yr. award Wis. Sch. Counselors, Madison, 1986; recipient Sr. Citizen Appreciation Allied Coun. for Sr. Milw., 1987, Crime Prevention award Milw. Police Dept., Milw., 1988, Cert. Appreciation, Milw. Pub. Sch., 1989, Friends of Homecare award, 1989, Environ. Decades' Clean 16 award, 1986-90, Badger State Sheriff's Law and Order award, 1993. Mem. Jackson Park Neighborhood Assn., U. Milw. Alumni Assn. (trustee 1986-90). Home: 3426 S 69th St Milwaukee WI 53219-4037 Office: Wis Assembly State Capitol Madison WI 53702

KRUSZEWSKA, MALGORZATA (MEG KRUSZEWSKA), theater director, writer; b. Bialystok, Poland, Apr. 9, 1960; came to U.S., 1964; d. Jozef and Irene (Sklodowska) K. BFA, UCLA, 1984; cert. in filmmaking, NYU, 1991. Founder, editor poetsfeet, lit. mag., N.Y.C., L.A., 1988-94; founder, artistic dir. Winter Solstice Theater, L.A., 1994—; resident artist Mabou Mines Theater, N.Y.C., 1994; dir. Lincoln Ctr. Theater Dirs. Lab., N.Y.C., 1995—. Dir. The Lady from the Sea, Fountain Theater, L.A., 1988, The Trap, New Europe Arts Festival, Pitts., 1993, Three Sisters, L.A. Theater Ctr., 1996; co-dir. Never Still, Mus. Theater Works, N.Y.C., 1995; writer, dir. plays MotherGhost, 1989, Daddy Meets Durga, 1994. Vol. Artstart, N.Y.C., 1995—. Mem. Women Make Movies (program facilitator 1994—). Home: 412 W 44th St Apt 5 New York NY 10036

KRZESINSKI, MARIBETH, dentist, maxillofacial prosthodontist; b. Elmira, N.Y., Feb. 22, 1960; d. Edwin Paul and Emily Alice (Brzeski); m. Gregory M. Semashko, June 7, 1986. BA, Coll. of the Holy Cross, 1982; DDS, Georgetown U., 1986; cert. in prosthodontics, U. Medicine & Dentistry N.J., 1992; cert. in maxillofacial prosthetics, U. Pitts., 1994. Resident in gen. practice Jersey City Med. Ctr., 1986-87; gen. dentist U.S.A. DENTAC, Ft. Benning, Ga., 1987-90; prosthodontist Howard Charlebois Corp., Monroeville, Pa., 1993-96; asst. prof. dept. maxillofacial prosthetics U. Pitts. Sch. Dental Medicine, 1995—. Recipient Commdr.'s award for Pub. Svc., U.S. Dental Corps, 1990. Mem. Am. Coll. Prosthodontics, Nat. Med. Dental Assn., Acad. Maxillofacial Prosthetics (award 1995), Delta Sigma Delta. Roman Catholic. Home: 202 Hillside Dr Zelienople PA 16063

KRZYZAN, JUDY LYNN, automotive executive; b. Buffalo, Sept. 1, 1951; d. James Lambert and Janet Lucille (Grabau) McKellar; m. Ronald Edward Krzyzan, Dec. 21, 1974 (div. Jan. 1989); 1 child, Brian Edward. Student, Erie Community Coll., 1969-70. With counter and delivery M & H Auto Supply, Orchard Park, N.Y., 1973-75; parts counter person Crest Dodge Inc., Orchard Park, 1975-81; parts mgr. Case Chrysler Plymouth, Hamburg, N.Y., 1981-87, Mancuso Chrysler Plymouth, Hamburg, 1987-91, Transitowne Dodge, Williamsville, N.Y., 1991—; supr. Profl. Inventory Assn., N.H., 1976-85. Mem. Chrysler Parts and Svc. Mgrs. Guild (v.p., sec. 1986-87, 89-92), The Greater Buffalo Auto Body Guild. Home: 2801 Creek Rd Hamburg NY 14075 Office: Transitowne Dodge 7408 Transit Rd Williamsville NY 14221-6019

K-TURKEL, JUDITH LEAH ROSENTHAL (JUDI K-TURKEL), writer, editor, publisher; b. N.Y.C., Jan. 3, 1934; d. Samuel S. and Pauline (Turkel) Rosenthal; divorced; children: Joseph, Jeffrey Kesselman, David, Kevin Peterson. BA, Bklyn. Coll., 1955. Story and mng. editor Dell Publs., N.Y.C., 1955-58, 62-65; editor-in-chief Sterling, Stearn & KMR Publs., N.Y.C., 1959-62; sr. editor Macfadden-Bartell Publs., N.Y.C., 1966-68; freelance writer N.Y.C. and Wis., 1968-89; pres. P/K Assocs., Inc., Madison, Wis., 1977—; instr. adult edn. Great Neck (N.Y.) Pub. Schs., 1973-76, U. Wis., Madison, 1977-82; instr. journalism Madison Area Tech. Coll., 1984-87; lectr. nonfiction writing CW Post Ctr., L.I. U., Manhasset, N.Y., 1976-77; tchr.-in-residence Rhinelander (Wis.) Sch. Arts, 1984-86. Author: (writing as Judi Kesselman) Stopping Out, 1976, (writing as Judi Kesselman-Turkel with Franklynn Peterson) The Do-It-Yourself Custom Van Book, 1977, Vans, 1979, (with others) Eat Anything Exercise Diet, 1979, Snowmobile Maintenance and Repair, 1979, I Can Use Tools, 1981, (textbook) Good Writing, 1980, Test Taking Strategies, 1981, Study Smarts, 1981, Homeowner's Book of Lists, 1981, How to Improve Damn Near Everything Around Your Home, 1981, The Author's Handbook, 1982, rev., 1986, The Grammar Crammer, 1982, Research Shortcuts, 1982, Note-Taking Made Easy, 1982, The Vocabulary Builder, 1982, Getting it Down: How to Get Your Ideas on Paper, 1983, Spelling Simplified, 1983, The Magazine Writer's Handbook, 1983, rev. edit., 1986; syndicated computer newspaper columnist, 1983—; editor (newsletter) CPA Micro Report, 1985-92, CPA's PC Network Advisor, 1991-92; pub. CPA Computer Report, 1994—; contbr. articles to profl. jours. Chmn. non-partisan Citizens Nominating Com., Great Neck, 1972-75. Recipient Bus. Press. award, 1977, Nat. Press Club award, 1984, 85. Mem. Am. Soc. Journalists and Authors, Coun. Wis. Writers (pres. 1982-85), Authors Guild, Authors League, Nat. Press Club, Pen & Brush Club (Madison, publ. chmn. 1978-89). Home and Office: P K Assocs Inc 3006 Gregory St Madison WI 53711-1847

KUBA, DANIELLE L., special education educator; b. Glens Falls, N.Y., Dec. 12, 1969; d. Michael C. and Donna M. (Moreau) Graham; m. William C. Kuba, Jan. 16, 1993. AA in Liberal Arts, Adirondack C.C., 1990; BS in Spl. Edn., SUNY, Plattsburgh, 1992. Cert. spl. edn. tchr., N.Y. Spl. edn. asst. Hudson Falls (N.Y.) Ctrl. Schs., 1993, spl. edn. tchr., 1993—. Roman Catholic. Office: Maple Street Elem Sch 135 Maple St Hudson Falls NY 12839

KUBAS, CYNTHIA M., sales executive; b. Somerset, Pa., May 18, 1956; d. Joseph and Irene (Segedy) Kubas; m. Roger W. Hackett, June 6, 1984 (div. Jan. 1993). BS, Cornell U., 1978; MBA, Pepperdine U., 1990. Lab. technician Cornell U., Ithaca, N.Y., 1978-80; pharm. salesperson Stuart Pharms., Jamestown, N.Y., 1980-83, Adria Labs., Ithaca, 1983-85, T.A.P. Pharms., L.A., 1985-86, Schering Corp., L.A., 1986-89, Ortho Biotech, Honolulu, 1989—. Bd. dirs. The Life Found., Honolulu, 1994—; mem. "Race for the Cure" Com., Honolulu, 1995—; chairperson 1995 AIDS Walk, Honolulu. Mem. Cornell U. Alumni Assn.

KUBECKA, RONNA DENISE, English language and art educator; b. Freeport, Tex., Oct. 31, 1960; d. Warren Melvin and Bernice (Maroney) K. BS in Edn., Baylor U., 1983; MEd, U. North Tex., 1996. Cert. educator, Tex., cert. peer assistance leadership tchr. Tchr. English and art Martin H.S., Arlington, Tex., 1983—; sponsor Young Life, Arlington, 1984-85, The Care Team, 1988-89, Peer Assistance Leadership, Arlington, 1994; founder, co-facilitator New Wings Coda, Irving, Tex., 1991—. Counselor Womens Haven, Ft. Worth, Tex.; active Womens Chorus of Dallas, 1995—; sponsor Christian Childrens Fund, Brazil, 1986—. PTA scholar Martin High PTA, 1990. Mem. ACA, Internat. Assn. Marriage and Family Counselors, United Educators Assn., Womens Bus. Network, Womens Cmty. Assn. Republican. Home: 8620 Brushy Creek Trail Fort Worth TX 76118 Office: Martin H S 4501 W Pleasant Ridge Arlington TX 76016

KUBIDA, JUDITH ANN, museum administrator; b. Chgo., Aug. 29, 1948; d. William and Julia Ann (Kun) K.; m. Benjamin Kocolowski, Nov. 22, 1980. Attended, Southeast Coll. Adminstrn. asst. in Visitor Svcs. Dept. Mus. Sci. and Industry, Chgo. Columnist monthly community newspaper Pullman Flyer. Vice-pres. pub. rels. Hist. Pullman Found., Hist. Pullman Dist., Chgo., editor quarterly newsletter Update, create publicity brochures, liaison with Ill., Chgo. Film Offices, publ. chmn., mem. annual house tour com., prodr. commemorative plate. Democrat. Home: 11334 S Langley Ave Chicago IL 60628-5126 Office: Hist Pullman Found Hotel Florence 11111 S Forrestville Ave Chicago IL 60628-4649

KUBISTAL, PATRICIA BERNICE, educational consultant; b. Chgo., Jan. 19, 1938; d. Edward John and Bernice Mildred (Lenz) Kubistal. AB cum laude, Loyola U., Chgo., 1959, AM, 1964, AM, 1965, PhD, 1968; postgrad. Chgo. State Coll., 1962, Ill. Inst. Tech., 1963, State U. Iowa, 1963, Nat. Coll. Edn., 1974-75. With Chgo. Bd. Edn., 1959-93, tchr., 1959-63, counselor, 1963-65, adminstrv. intern, 1965-66, asst. to dist. supt., 1966-69, prin. spl. edn. sch., 1969-75, prin. Simpson Sch., 1975-76, Brentano Sch., 1975-87, Roosevelt High Sch., 1987, Haugan Sch., 1989; Cook County Juvenile Temporary Detention Ctr. Sch., Jones Met. High Sch. Bus. and Commerce, 1988-89, Cook County Juvenile Temporary Detention Ctr., 1989-90, adminstr. dept. spl. edn., 1990-93; supr. Lake View Evening Sch., 1982-92, ednl. cons. 1993—; lectr. Loyola U. Sch. Edn., Nat. Coll. Edn. Grad. Sch., Mundelein Coll., 1982-91; coord. Upper Bound Program of U. Ill. Circle Campus, 1966-68. Book rev. editor of Chgo. Prins. Jour., 1970-76, gen. editor, 1982-90. Active Crusade of Mercy; mem. com. Ill. Constnl. Conv., 1967-69; mem. Citizens Sch. Com., 1969-71; mem. edn. com. Field Mus., 1971; ednl. advisor North Side Chgo. PTA Region, 1975; gov. Loyola U., 1961-87. Recipient Outstanding Intern award Nat. Assn. Secondary Sch. Prins., 1966, Outstanding Prin. award Citizen's Shc. Com. of Chgo., 1986; named Outstanding History Tchr., Chgo. Pub. Schs., 1963, Outstanding Ill. Educator, 1970, one of Outstanding Women of Ill., 1970, St. Luke's-Logan Sq. Community Person of Yr., 1977; NDEA grantee, 1963, NSF grantee, 1965, HEW Region 5 grantee for drug edn., 1974, Chgo. Bd. Edn. Prins.' grantee for study robotics in elem. schs.; U. Chgo. adminstrv. fellow, 1984. Mem. Ill. Personnel and Guidance Assn., NEA, Ill. Edn. Assn., Chgo. Edn. Assn., Am. Acad. Polit. and Social Sci., Chgo. Prins. Club (pres. aux.), Nat. Council Adminstrv. Women, Chgo. Council Exceptional Children, Chgo. Council Fgn. Relations, Chgo. Urban League, Loyal Christian Benevolent Assn., Kappa Gamma Pi, Pi Gamma Mu, Phi Delta Kappa, Delta Kappa Gamma (parliamentarian 1979-80, pres. Kappa chpt. 1988-90, Lambda state editor 1982-92, chmn. Lambda state comm. com. 1992, Internat. Golden Gift Fund award), Delta Sigma Rho, Phi Sigma Tau. Home and Office: 5111 N Oakley Ave Chicago IL 60625-1829

KÜBLER-ROSS, ELISABETH, physician; b. Zurich, Switzerland, July 8, 1926; came to U.S., 1958, naturalized, 1961; d. Ernst and Emma (Villiger) K.; m. Emanuel Robert Ross, Feb. 7, 1958; children: Kenneth Lawrence, Barbara Lee. M.D., U. Zurich, 1957; D.Sc. (hon.), Albany (N.Y.) Med. Coll., 1974, Smith Coll., 1975, Molloy Coll., Rockville Centre, N.Y., 1976, Regis Coll., Weston, Mass., 1977, Fairleigh Dickinson U., 1979; LL.D., U. Notre Dame, 1974, Hamline U., 1975; hon. degree, Med. Coll. Pa., 1975, Anna Maria Coll., Paxton, Mass., 1978; Litt.D. (hon.), St. Mary's Coll., Notre Dame, Ind., 1975, Hood Coll., 1976, Rosary Coll., River Forest, Ill., 1976; L.H.D. (hon.), Amherst Coll., 1975, Loyola U., Chgo., 1975, Bard Coll., Annandale-on-Hudson, N.Y., 1977, Union Coll., Schenectady, 1978, D'Youville Coll., Buffalo, 1979, U. Miami, Fla., 1976; D.Pedagogy, Keuka Coll., Keuka Park, N.Y., 1976. Rotating intern Community Hosp., Glen Cove, N.Y., 1958-59; rsch. fellow Manhattan State Hosp., 1959-62; resident Montefiore Hosp., N.Y.C., 1961-62; fellow psychiatry Psychopathic Hosp., U. Colo. Med. Sch., 1962-63; instr. psychiatry Colo. Gen. Hosp., U. Colo. Med. Sch., 1962-65; mem. staff LaRabida Children's Hosp. and Rsch. Ctr., Chgo., 1965-70; asst. prof. psychiatry, asst. dir. psychiatric consultation and liaison service Billings Hosp., U. Chgo., 1965-71; chief cons. and rsch. liaison sect. LaRabida Children's Hosp. and Rsch. Ctr., 1969-70; med. dir. Family Service and Mental Health Ctr. S. Cook County, Chicago Heights, Ill., 1970-73; pres. Ross Med. Assos. (S.C.), Flossmoor, Ill., 1973-77; pres., chmn. bd. Shanti Nilaya Growth and Health Ctr., Escondido, Calif., 1977—; consulting psychiatrist Chicago Lighthouse for the Blind, 1965-71; consultant Peace Corps, 1965-71, Illinois State Psychiatric Inst., 1965-71; mem. numerous adv., cons. bds. in field. Author: On Death and Dying, 1969, Questions and Answers on Death and Dying, 1972, Death: The Final Stage, 1974, To Live Until We Say Goodbye, 1978, Working It Through, 1981, Living With Death and Dying, 1981, Remember The Secret, 1981, On Children and Death, 1985, AIDS: The Ultimate Challenge, 1988, On Life After Death, 1991, Death is of Vital Inportance: On Life, Death and Life After Death, 1994; contbr. chpts. to books, articles to profl. jours. Recipient Teilhard prize Teilhard Found., 1981; Golden Plate award Am. Acad. Achievement, 1980; Modern Samaritan award Elk Grove Village, Ill., 1976; named Woman of the Decade Ladies Home Jour., 1979; numerous others. Mem. AAAS, Am. Holistic Med. Assn. (founder), Am. Med. Women's Assn., Am. Psychiat. Assn., Am. Psychosomatic Soc., Assn. Cancer Victims and Friends, Ill. Psychiat. Soc., Soc. Swiss Physicians, Soc. Psychophysiol. Research, Second Attempt at Living. Address: PO Box 6168 Scottsdale AZ 85261

KUBY, BARBARA ELEANOR, personnel executive, management consultant; b. Medford, Mass., Sept. 1, 1944; d. Robert William and Eleanor (Frasca) Asdell; m. Thomas Kuby, July 12, 1969. BS in Edn./ Psychology, Kent State U., 1966, MEd, 1987. Tchr. Nordonia/Euclid (Ohio) Pub. Schs., 1966-78; mgr. tng. and devel. United Bldg. Factories, Manama, Bahrain, 1979-81, Norton Co., Akron, Ohio, 1981-85; v.p. Kuby and Assocs. Inc., Chagrin Falls, Ohio, 1973-91, pres., 1992—; corp. dir. human resource devel. and systems TransOhio Savs. Bank, Cleve., 1985-88; asst. v.p. human resources and adminstrv. systems Leasing Dynamics, Inc., Cleve., 1988-90; dir. human resources, organizational devel. GOJO Industries, Akron, 1990-93, v.p. human resources and orgnl. devel., 1993—; adj. faculty, cons. Buffalo State U., 1972-92, Lake Erie Coll., Cleve., 1985-95; lectr., cons. Cleve. State U., 1978—; program dir. Ctr. Profl. Adv., East Brunswick, N.J., 1978—. Cons., lectr. Girl Scouts U.S.A., Cleve., 1981-90; colleague Creative Edn. Found.; cons. project bus. Jr. Achievement, 1992-93; bd. trustees Ohio Ballet, 1996. Mem. Am. Mgmt. Assn., Human Resource Planning Soc., Soc. for Human Resource Mgmt., Gestalt Inst. of Cleve., Greenpeace, ACLU. Home: 7236 Chagrin Rd Chagrin Falls OH 44023-1102

KUCK, MARIE ELIZABETH BUKOVSKY, retired pharmacist; b. Milw., Aug. 3, 1910; d. Frank Joseph and Marie (Nozina) Bukovsky; Ph.C., U. Ill., 1933; m. John A. Kuck, Sept. 20, 1945 (div. Nov. 1954). Pharmacist, tchr. Am. Hosp., Chgo., 1936-38, St. Joseph Hosp., Chgo., 1938-40, Ill. Masonic Hosp., Chgo., 1940-45; chief pharmacist St. Vincent Hosp., Los Angeles, 1946-48, St. Joseph Hosp., Santa Fe, 1949-51; dir. pharm. services St. Luke's Hosp., San Francisco, 1951-76; pharmacist Mission Neighborhood Health Center, San Francisco, 1968-72; docent Calif. Acad. Sci., 1977—, DeYoung Mus., 1989—; mem. peer rev. com. Drug Utilization Com., Blue Shield Calif. and Pharm. Soc. San Francisco. Recipient Bowl of Hygeia award Calif. Pharm. Assn., 1966. Mem. No., Calif. (legis. chmn. aux. 1967-69, chmn. fund raising luncheon 1953-71, pres. San Francisco aux. 1974), Nat., Am., No. Calif. (pres. 1955-56, pres. San Francisco aux. 1965-66, editor ofcl. publ. 1967-70), San Francisco (sec. 1977-79, treas. 1979-80, pres. 1982-83; Pharmacist of Yr. award 1978) pharm. socs., Am. Pharm. Assn. (pres. No. Calif. br. 1956-57, nat. sec. women's aux. 1970-72, hon. pres. aux. 1975—), Calif. Council Hosp. Pharmacists (organizer 1962, sec.-treas. 1962-66), Am. Soc. Hosp. Pharmacists, Assn. Western Hosps. (gen. chmn. hosp. pharmacy sect. conv. San Francisco 1958), Internat. Pharmacy Congress (U.S. del. Brussels 1958, Copenhagen 1960), Fedn. Internationale Pharmaceutique, Lambda Kappa Sigma. Home: 2261 33rd Ave San Francisco CA 94116-1606

KUDROW, LISA, actress; b. Encino, Calif., July 30. BS in Biology, Vassar Coll., Poughkeepsie, N.Y. TV appearances include Bob, Cheers, Coach, Newhart, Flying Blind, Mad About You, 1991—, Freinds, 1994—. Office: care CAA 9830 Wilshire Blvd Beverly Hills CA 90212

KUEHNE, HELENIRENE ANNE, art educator; b. Douglasville, Pa., Nov. 7, 1941; d. John Julius Dusco and Helen Kathryn Rogosky; m. Paul Howard Kuehne, June 28, 1980; 1 child, John Paul. BS, Kutztown U., 1964, MEd, 1968; postgrad., U. No. Colo., 1978, LaSalle U., 1994. Tchr. elem. art Kutztown (Pa.) Area Schs., 1964-83, tchr. secondary art, 1983—, chair fine arts dept., mem. curriculum coun., 1993—; tchr. coop. tchr. program Kutztown U., 1970—, mem. program adv. com., 1972. Works exhibited in various art shows, 1978-81. Sec. Muhlenberg Twp. Arts Bd., Laureldale, Pa., 1991—; merit badge counselor Boy Scouts Am., Laureldale, 1993—; active Friends of Reading Pub. Mus., 1991. Grantee Pa. Coun. Arts, 1993-94. Mem. AAUW (chair 1979-80, 88-89), Wyomissing Inst. Fine Arts, Delta Kappa Gamma. Home: 3512 Kent Ave Laureldale PA 19605 Office: Kutztown Area Sr High 50 Trexler Ave Kutztown PA 19530-9700

KUEHNERT, DEBORAH ANNE, medical center administrator; b. Raleigh, N.C., Nov. 21, 1949; d. Eldor Paul and Lila Catherine (Gilbert) K. Student, Valparaiso (Ind.) U., 1967-69; BS in Biology, Lenior Rhyne Coll., Hickory, N.C., 1977. Cert. med. technologist. Rsch. asst. Strong Meml. Hosp., Rochester, N.Y., 1967-68; lab. technician Richard Baker Hosp., Hickory, N.C., 1969-76; med. technician, shift supr. Glenn R. Frye Hosp., Hickory, 1977-83; lab. tech. dir. Frye Regional Med. Ctr., Hickory, 1983-85, adminstrv. dir. lab. svcs., 1986-92; sr. tech. dir. lab. svcs. Al-Fanateer Hosp., Jubail, Saudia Arabia, 1993; med. technologist lab. Chinle (Ariz.) Health Care Facility, Navajo Indian Reservation USPHS Hosp., 1993; instr. microbiology Catawba Valley Tech. Coll., Hickory, 1977-94, Lenoir Rhyne Coll., Hickory, 1978-94; chief tech. lab. No. Area Armed Forces Hosp., Hafr Al Batin, Saudi Arabia, 1994—; cons. Frye Physicians, Hickory, 1985—; lab. cons. Am. Med. Internat., New Orleans, 1986, Lake City, Fla., 1984-85; cons. Med. Lab. Observer, Chgo., 1989; spkr. in field. Recipient Svc. of Appreciation award Govt. Saudi Arabia, 1996. Mem. Am. Soc. Clin. Pathologists, N.C. Soc. Blood Bankers. Lutheran. Home: 58 Penny Ln Hickory NC 28601-9341 Office: Providence Alaska Med Ctr Anchorage AK 99504

KUENSTER, KAREN A., lawyer; b. Chgo., Nov. 12, 1955. BBA, U. Notre Dame, 1977; JD, DePaul U., 1980. Bar: Ill. 1980. Ptnr. Baker & McKenzie, Chgo. Office: Baker & McKenzie 130 E Randolph Dr Chicago IL 60601*

KUERLEY-SCHAFFER, DAWN R., medical/surgical nurse; b. Bay City, Mich., June 8, 1959; d. Edward J. and Leaella Mae (Jacob) Kuerley; m. Michael B. Schaffer, May 30, 1986; 1 child, Randi Lea. Lic. practical nurse, Bay Practical Nurse Ctr., 1980; ADNB, Alpena Community Coll., 1986. RN. Mich., La., 1994. Practical nurse Tawas St. Joseph Hosp., Tawas City, Mich., staff nurse; RN, clinic head nurse Neurosurgery Tulane U. Med. Ctr., New Orleans. Clark Sawyer meml. scholar. Mem. Assn. Operating Room Nurses (cert. operating room nurse), Alpena Cmty. Coll. ADN Alumni Assn. (past pres.).

KUFFEL, JOAN ELIZABETH, school nurse; b. Madison, Wis., Dec. 25, 1931; d. Carl John and Elizabeth Catherine (Fettes) Robers; m. Eugene Francis Kuffel, July 31, 1954 (dec. Aug. 1992); children: Jane, Le Roy, Suzanne. Diploma, Mercy Hosp. Sch. Nursing, 1953; BA in Liberal Arts, Northeastern U., 1982; M Health Scis., Governor State U., 1993. Cert. sch. nurse, Ill. Sch. nurse River Trails Sch. Dist. # 26, Mount Prospect, Ill., 1965—; first aid nurse Marriotts Gt. Am. Theme Park, Gurnee, Ill., summer 1976; floor nurse Americana Nursing Home, Arlington Heights, Ill., summers 1973-75; mem. adv. task force Ambulatory Care Ctr., Luth. Gen. Hosp., Park Ridge, Ill., 1977-80. Designer ofcl. flag for Village of Buffalo Grove, Ill. Commr. Buffalo Grove Bd. Health, 1969—; disaster nurse ARC, 1968; organizer Buffalo Grove Disaster Nurse Corps, 1971 (now unit Ill. CD Agy.); mem. ministry of care, St. Mary's Parish, 1987—. Recipient Unsung Hero's award Village of Mt. Prospect Spl. Events Commn., 1995. Mem. NEA, River Trails Edn. Assn., Nat. Assn. Sch. Nurses, Ill. Assn. Sch. Nurses (north dist. area rep. lake Shore Calumet Valley div. 1990-94), Buffalo Grove Nurses Club (pres. 1964-66). Roman Catholic. Home: 119 Glendale Rd Buffalo Grove IL 60089-2125 Office: River Trails Sch Dist 1900 E Kensington Mount Prospect IL 60056

KUGELMASS, JUDY, special education educator, researcher, consultant; b. N.Y.C., Oct. 13, 1942; d. Mark and Hilda Waldman; m. Harold Kugelmass, Aug. 16, 1963; children: Eve, Noam. BA, CCNY, 1964; MA, U. Oreg., 1967; PhD, Syracuse U., 1983. Counselor U. Oreg., Eugene, 1966-67; spl. edn. tchr. Erie County Bd. Coop. Edn. Svcs., Buffalo, N.Y., 1967-68, Sullivan County Bd. Coop. Edn. Svcs., Liberty, N.Y., 1971-73; sch. psychologist Sullivan County BOCES, Liberty, N.Y., 1973-78; program dir. Spl. Children's Ctr., Ithaca, N.Y., 1981-86; lectr. Cornell U., Ithaca, N.Y., 1986-90; asst. prof. Hobart and Wm. Smith Colls., Geneva, N.Y., 1989-91; assoc. faculty Goddard Coll., Plainfield, Vt., 1993-94; coord. NEST: Foxfire Tchr. Outreach, Mountain City, Ga., 1990-94; asst. prof. Binghamton (N.Y.) U., 1994—; liaison 4 Seasons Project, Nat. Ctr. Restructuring Edn., Schs. and Teaching Columbia U. Tchr. Coll., N.Y.C., 1992-94; bd. dirs. N.Y. Folklore Soc. Author: Behavior, Bias and Handicaps, 1987; author chpt. to book. Community rep. Tompkins County HeadStart, Ithaca, 1983-87; mem. Tompkins County Mental Health Assn., Ithaca, 1985-94, Spl. Children's Ctr., Ithaca, 1992—. Recipient Fulbright lectureship Fulbright Commn., 1989, 93, Internat. Exch. Experts in Rehab. fellowship World Rehab. Fund, 1990. Mem. Coun. for Exceptional Children (N.Y. div. for early childhood regional rep. 1989—, v.p. 1989-90), Am. Edn. Rsch. Assn., Nat. Assn. Edn. of Young Children. Office: Binghamton Univ Dept Edn Binghamton NY 13902

KUH, JOYCE DATTEL, education administrator; b. Greenville, Miss., Mar. 10, 1937; d. Milton Joseph and Hannah (Marks) Dattel; m. Richard Henry Kuh, Jul. 31, 1966; children: Michael Joseph, Jody Ellen. BA, Newcomb Coll. Tulane U., 1959. Asst. to treas. Dynatech. Corp., Cambridge, Mass., 1959-63; editorial asst. McCall's Mag., N.Y.C., 1963-64; asst. editor Ladies's Home Jour., N.Y.C., 1964-73; freelance writer, editor N.Y.C., 1973-89; dir. of devel. Grace Ch. Sch., N.Y.C., 1989—. Del. Dem. County Com., N.Y.C., 1993—; bd. trustees The Dome Project. Jewish. Home: 14 Washington Pl New York NY 10003-6609 Office: Grace Ch Sch 86 4th Ave New York NY 10003-5246

KUHAR, JUNE CAROLYNN, retired fiberglass manufacturing company executive; b. Chgo., Sept. 20, 1935; d. Kurt Ludwig and Dorothy Julia (Lewand) Stier; m. G. James Kuhar, Feb. 5, 1953; children: Kathleen Lee, Debra Suzanne. Lic. real estate salesperson. Student William Rainey Harper Coll., Chgo. Engaged in fiberglass mfg., 1970—; sec.-treas. Q-R Fiber Glass Industries Inc., Rolling Meadows, Ill., 1970—. Leader Girl Scouts U.S.; mem. Civil Def. Disaster and Rescue Team, 1965-70, Rolling Meadows Golden Yrs. Coun., Arlington Heights Concerned People Helping to Understand Multiple Sclerosis; chmn. benefit fashion show William Rainey Harper Coll.- Sch. of Fashion Design, 1983. Mem. Multiple Sclerosis Soc., Nat. Fedn. Ileitis and Colitis, Bus. and Profl. Women N.W., Bus. and Profl. Woman's Club (pres. 1984—), Am. Legion Aux., Women in the Arts (charter). Home: 2303 Meadow Dr Rolling Meadows IL 60008-1546

KUHLER, DEBORAH GAIL, grief counselor, former state legislator; b. Moorhead, Minn., Oct. 12, 1952; d. Robert Edgar and Beverly Maxine (Buechler) Ecker; m. George Henry Kuhler, Dec. 28, 1973; children: Karen Elizabeth, Ellen Christine. BA, Dakota Wesleyan U., 1974; MA, U. N.D., 1977. Cert, grief counselor; lic. profl. counselor, S.D. Outpatient therapist Ctr. for Human Devel., Grand Forks, N.D., 1975-77; mental health counselor Community Counseling Services, Huron, S.D., 1978-88, 91-93; owner, dir. bereavement svcs. Kuhler Funeral Home, Huron, 1978—; adj. prof. Huron U., 1979-83, 90—; mem. from dist. 23 S.D. Ho. Reps., Pierre, 1987-90; mem. House Judiciary com., chair House Health and Welfare Com., Pierre, 1990. Active Beadle County Rep. Women, 1st United Meth. Ch. Named Young Alumnus of the Yr., Dakota Wesleyan U., 1989, Bus. and Profl. Women, 1989. Mem. ACA, AAUW (Achievement in Politics award 1987), Am. Mental Health Counselors Assn., Women Execs. and Adminstrs., Assn. for Death Edn. and Counseling, Phi Kappa Phi. Home: 1360 Dakota Ave S Huron SD 57350-3660

KUHLJUERGEN, NANCY LYNNE, secondary education educator; b. Fort Madison, Iowa, Aug. 6, 1954; d. Ira and Doris Eileen (Gutting) Johnson; m. Richard Alan Kuhljuergen, June 14, 1975; children: Kaitlin Alison, Evan Richard. BA, Iowa Wesleyan Coll., 1975. Cert. tchr., Iowa. Food svc. supr. Fort Madison Cmty. Hosp., 1975-76; dir. food svcs. Ft. Madison Cmty. Schs., 1976-79, substitute tchr., 1981-83; lab. tech. Consol. Packaging Inc., Fort Madison, 1984-94; exec. dir. Friends Reach Out, Inc., Fort Madison, 1995-96; H.S. sci. tchr. Fort Madison Cmty. Sch. Dist., 1996—. Mem. AAUW. Home: 2313 263rd Ave Fort Madison IA 52627-9528

KUHLMAN, GLORIA JEAN, mental health and geriatric nurse, educator; b. Wichita, Nov. 9, 1949; d. Virgil D. and Gladys (Plett) Coleman; m. Thomas A. Kuhlman, Sept. 12, 1969; 1 child, Jeffrey Paul. Diploma, St. Francis Sch. Nursing, Wichita, 1974; BSN, Wichita State U., 1976, MN, 1979; D. in Nursing Sci., U. Calif., San Francisco, 1992. Cert. community coll. instr. Prof., clin. coord. Ohlone Coll., Fremont, Calif., 1979—. Mem. NLN, Alzheimers Disease Assn., Am. Soc. on Aging, Gerontol. Soc. Am., Calif. Coun. on Gerontology and Geriatrics, Nat. Coun. on Aging. Home: 674 Giraudo Dr San Jose CA 95111-2680 Office: Ohlone Coll 43600 Mission Blvd Fremont CA 94539

KUHN, ANNE NAOMI WICKER (MRS. HAROLD B. KUHN), foreign language educator; b. Lynchburg, Va.; d. George Barnett and Annie (Hicks) Wicker; m. Harold B. Kuhn. Diploma Malone Coll., 1933, Trinity Coll. Music, London, 1937; AB, John Fletcher Coll., 1939; MA, Boston U., 1942, postgrad., 1965-70; postgrad. (fellow) Harvard U., 1942-44, 66-68; hon. grad. Asbury Coll., 1978. Instr., Emmanuel Bible Coll., Birkenhead, Eng., 1936-37; asst. in history John Fletcher Coll., University Park, Iowa, 1938-39; librarian Harvard U., 1939-44; tchr. adult edn. program U.S. Armed Forces, Fuerstenfeldbruck Air Base, Germany, 1951-52; prof. Union Bibl. Sem., Yeotmal, India, 1957-58; lectr. Armenian Bible Inst., Beirut, Lebanon, 1958; prof. German, Asbury Coll., Wilmore, Ky., 1962—, co-dir. coll. study tour to East Germany and West Germany, 1976, 77, 78, co-dir. acad. tours, 1979, 80; dir. acad. tour, Russia, 1981, 85, Scandanavia, 1982, Indonesia, Singapore, 1983, Hong Kong and Thailand, 1983, 85, East Germany, West Germany, France and Austria, 1983, Russia and Finland, 1984, 85, 89, China, 1979, 84, 85, 89, Estonia, Latvia, 1985, 89, Poland, 1989, 91, 92, Portugal, Spain, France, Ireland, Scotland, Norway, England, 1987, The Balkans, Hungary, Czech Republic, Slovak Republic, Bulgaria, Romania and Turkey, 1992, alumni academic tour Malta, Sicily, Greece, Macedonia, 1995; tchr. Seoul Theol. Sem., fall 1978. Author: (pamphlet) The Impact of the Transition to Modern Education Upon Religious Education, 1950; The Influence of Paul Gerhardt upon Wesleyan Hymnody, 1960, Light to Dispel Fear, 1987; transl. German ch. records, poems, letters; contbr. articles to profl. jours. Del. Youth for Christ World Conf., 1948, 50, London Yearly Meeting of Friends, Edinburgh, Scotland, 1948, World Council Chs., Amsterdam, 1948, World Friends Conf., Oxford, Eng., 1952, World Methodist Conf., Oslo, Norway, 1961, Deutscher Kirchentag, Dortmund, Germany, 1963, German Lang. Congress, Bonn, W. Ger., 1974, Internat. Conf. Religion, Amsterdam, Netherlands, Poland, West Berlin, Fed. Republic Germany, 1986, Internat. Missionary Conf., Eng., 1987, Congress on the Bible II, Washington, 1987; participant Internat. Congress World Evangelization, Lausanne, Switzerland, 1974; del., speaker Internat. Conf. on Holocaust and Genocide, Oxford and London, 1988; speaker Founders Week Malone Coll., Ohio, 1989, Nat. Quaker Conf., Denver; mem. acad. tour Poland, 1988; vol. of various special assignments in Ctrl. and Eastern Europe. Recipient German Consular award, Boston, 1965, Thomas Mann award Boston U., 1967; named Ky. Col., 1978. Fellow Goethe-Institut for Germanisten, Munich, 1966-68, 70-71. Mem. AAUW, Am. Assn. Tchrs. German, NEA, Ky. Ednl. Assn., Lincoln Lit. Soc., Protestant Women of Chapel, Harvard Univ. Faculty Club (Cambridge, Mass.), Harvard Univ. Club Eastern and Ctrl. Ky. (Lexington), United Daughters of the Confederacy, Delta Phi Alpha (award 1963, 65). Mem. Soc. of Friends. Home: 406 Kenyon Ave Wilmore KY 40390-1033

KUHN, JEANNIE, artist, archaeologist; b. Natrona Heights, Pa., Apr. 21, 1957; d. Willie Earnest and Jean Marie (Craig) K. BFA, W.Va. U., Morgantown, 1981, MFA, 1988. Drawing instr. WVa. U., Morgantown, 1988; gallery dir. Only Art, Morgantown, 1991-92, Appalachian Gallery, Morgantown, 1992-95; archaeologist Horizon Rsch. Cons., Morgantown, 1995-96; artist Resevoir Cats Studio, Independence, WVa., 1995—; chair Downtown Gallery Walk Com., Morgantown, W.Va., 1992-95; exhbn. review panel mem. Stifle Fine Arts Ctr., Wheeling, W.Va., 1993; chairperson Internat. Artist Mkt. Wine & Jazz Festival, Morgantown, 1993-94; exhbn. com. mem. Women & Creativity Conf. W.Va. U., Morgantown, 1994. Artist: (linocut prints) Celebration of West Virginia Women in the Arts, YMCA, 1995, Metamorphosis-Invitational Exhibit of W.Va. Women Artists, 1995, 937-Open Assoc. Artists of Pitts. Exhibit, 1995, W.Va. Juried Exhibit, 1995. Artist Arts Day at the Legislature, Charleston, W.Va., 1993; com. mem. Vision 2000-arts & creative initiative Morgantown Area of C. of C., 1994-96; artist mem. Arts Advocacy of W.Va., Kearneyville, W.Va., 1995-96. Recipient Underserved Area Artist's grant W.Va. Commn. on the Arts & Nat. Endowments For the Arts, 1995; fellow Vt. Studio Ctr., Johnson, 1994. Mem. Associated Artists of Pitts., Pitts. Ctr. for the Arts, Women's Caucus for Art (W.Va. chpt.). Democrat. Home: Rt 1 Box 290 Independence WV 26374 Office: Reservoir Cats Studio Rt 1 Box 290 Independence WV 26374

KUHN, KATHLEEN JO, accountant; b. Springfield, Ill., Aug. 9, 1947; d. Henry Elmer and Norma Florene (Niehaus) Burge; m. Gerald L. Kuhn, June 22, 1968; children: Gerald Lynn, Brett Anthony. BS in Bus., Bradley U., 1969. CPA, Ill. Controller Byerly Music Co., Peoria, Ill., 1969-70; staff acct. Clifton Gunderson & Co., Columbus, Ind., 1970-71; acct. Dept. of Transp., State of Ill., Springfield, 1972-76; acct. Gerald L. Kuhn & Assocs., Springfield, 1976-78, ptnr., 1979—, quality control mgr., 1990—; grad. asst. in Dale Carnegie courses, 1979-80. Writer, editor co. policy guideline, 1979-80; editor co. quality control manual, 1990. Recipient Attendance award Continuing Profl. Edn. for Accts., 1979—. Mem. Am. Inst. CPAs, Springfield Art Assn., Ill. Soc. CPAs, Am. Woman's Soc. CPAs, Nat. Bus. & Motivational Assn. Lutheran. Clubs: Olympic Swim, Metro. Federated Jr. Women's. Home: 2511 Westchester Blvd Springfield IL 62704-5406 Office: 2659 Farragut Dr Springfield IL 62704-1462

KUHNER, ARLENE ELIZABETH, English language educator, reviewer, academic administrator; b. Victoria, B.C., Can., May 1, 1939; d. Theodore Foort and Gladys Virginia (Evans) Huggins; m. Robert Henry Kuhner, Dec. 17, 1971; children: Mary Kathleen, Gwynne Elizabeth, Benjamin David. BA in English, Seattle U., 1960; postgrad., U. Calif., Berkeley, 1960-61; MA in English, U. Wash., 1966, PhD in English, 1978. Editor English dept. U. Wash., Seattle, 1964-66; instr. Seattle U., 1966-69, asst. prof., 1969-72; mem. adj. faculty Anchorage Community Coll., 1972-81, tchr., 1981-87; assoc. prof. U. Alaska, Anchorage, 1987-90, chair women's studies dept., 1989-93, prof., chair English dept., 1990-93, assoc. dean for acad. program & curriculum, prof. English, 1993—. Contbr. numerous papers to profl. confs. Contbg. mem. Oreg. Shakespeare Festival; nat. assoc. Folger Shakespeare Libr., Washington, 1987—; ptnr. in conscience Amnesty Internat., 1985—; bd. dirs. Tudor Community Sch., Anchorage, 1975-77. Woodrow Wilson Found. fellow, 1960; Western State Project grantee, 1986, 87, various others. Mem. MLA, Women's Caucus for Modern Langs., Nat. Coun. Tchrs. of English, Renaissance Soc. Am., Nat. Women's Studies Assn., N.W. Women's Studies Assn., Philos. Assn. of the Pacific Coast, Assn. for Can. Studies in U.S., Marlowe Soc. Am., Margaret Atwood Soc., Phi Kappa Phi. Democrat. Roman Catholic. Office: U Alaska Coll Arts and Scis 3211 Providence Dr Anchorage AK 99508-4614

KUHRT, SHARON LEE, nursing administrator; b. Denver, July 20, 1957; d. John Wilfred and Yoshiko (Ueda) K. BSN, Loretto Heights Coll., 1982; MSN, Regis U., 1992. RN, Colo., Hawaii, Mass., Maine. RN level III Porter Meml. Hosp., Denver, 1981-87; transport supr. Kapiolani Med. Ctr. for Women & Children, Honolulu, 1987-89; dir. patient care unit Aspen Valley Hosp., Colo., 1989-91; dir. clin. practice Ctrl. Maine Med. Ctr., Lewiston, 1991—. Mem. ANA (cert. in pediat. nursing and nursing adminstrn.). Home: 27 Chandler Mill Rd New Gloucester ME 04260-9999

KUIPERS, JUDITH L., academic administrator. Chancellor U. Wis., La Crosse. Office: U Wis Office of the Chancellor 1725 State St La Crosse WI 54601-3742

KUISEL, SALLY M., archivist, researcher; b. Lynchburg, Va., June 27, 1947; d. Charles H. and Anna Hewitt (Langhorne) McCarthy; m. Richard F. Kuisel, Nov. 11, 1989. BA, Stratford Coll., Danville, Va., 1969; MA, Va. Polytechnic Inst., Blackburg, 1971; attended, Corcoran Sch. of Art, Washington D.C., 1982-88. Writer Office of Presdl. Papers White House, Washington, D.C., 1972-75; archivist Diplomatic Branch Nat. Archives, Washington, D.C., 1975-88, cons. Reference Svcs. Branch, 1988-89, asst. branch chief Civil Reference, 1989-90; dir. of rsch. for devel. SUNY, Stony Brook, 1990—. Author: (book) The Covert War in South America: Intelligence, Counterintelligence and Military Deception During World War II Era, 1989. Recipient Westmoreland Davis Found. fellow VPI, 1970. Mem. Am. Prospect Rsch. Assn. (N.Y. chpt.). Episcopalian. Office: SUNY-Stony Brook Rm 328 Adminstrn Bldg Stony Brook NY 11794

KUKLA, CYNTHIA MARY, artist; b. Chgo., June 23, 1952; d. Stanley A. and Eugenia (Markowski) Cukla; children: Glenn D., Garth A. BFA, Sch. of Art Inst. Chgo., 1973; MFA, U. Wis., 1983. Asst. prof. art No. Ky. U., Highland Heights, 1983-89, assoc. prof. art, 1989-93; assoc. prof. art Ill. State U., Normal, 1993—; lectr. art U. London, 1985, 87, All Hallows Coll., Dublin, 1993; art reviewer Dialogue, Arts in the Midwest, Columbus, Ohio, 1989-92; book reviewer Prentice-Hall, Inc.; art juror Regional Art Exhibits, 1984—; chmn. ann. conf. panel Nat. Coll. Art Assn., 1989, Mid-Am. Coll. Art Assn., 1986, 95,S.E. Coll. Art Assn., 1986, 95. One woman shows at Kortman Ctr. for Design, Rockford, Ill., 1996, Chautauqua (N.Y.) Art Ctr., 1995, Kent State U., Canton, Ohio, 1992, Liberty Gallery, Louisville, 1992, Market Gallery, Rockford, Ill., 1991, Rosewood Art Ctr., Kettering, Ohio, 1990, Headley-Whitney Mus., Lexington, 1987, Cin. Commn. on Arts, 1986, Armory Art Gallery, Blacksburg, Va., 1985, others; exhibited in group shows at Rockford (Ill.) Art Mus., 1995, Peoria (Ill.) Art Ctr., 1995, U. Ky. Art Mus., Lexington, 1995, Arrowmont Ctr. for Arts & Crafts, Gatlinburg, Tenn., 1993-95, Kharkov (Ukraine) Art Mus., 1993, Liberty Gallery, Louisville, 1993, Canton Art Inst., 1992, Galerie Hertz, Louisville, Ohio, 1992, Mus. Ctr. at Union Terminal, Cin., 1991, Mayor's Office Commn. on Culture and Arts, Honolulu, 1991, Solway Coll. Complex, Cin., 1991, Grand European Nat. Ctr. of Arts and Letters, Nationale des Artes, Nice, France, 1990, Am. Embassy, Quito, Ecuador, 1989, Fine Arts Acad., Warsaw, Poland, 1988, Knox Coll. Gallery, Galesburg, Ill., 1988, U. Tenn. travelling exhbn., Knoxville, 1987-89, Ctr. for Contemporary Art, U. Ky., Lexington, 1987, Watertower Art Ctr., Louisville, 1987, Laguna Beach (Calif.) Art Mus., 1983, Springfield (Mo.) Art Mus., 1980, 83, 86, numerous others; works reviewed in (art jour. R.A.M., 1996) New Art Examiner, 1994, Dialogue, 1989, 90, Cin. Enquirer, 1986, 88, 89, Atlanta Art Papers, 1988, Montgomery Ala. Jour., 1987, Louisville Courier-Jour., 1987, 91, 92, Lexington Herald-Leader, 1987, St. Louis Post-Dispatch, 1986, others. Conf. developer, panel chair Gender and Ethnicity in Art, Cin. Art Mus., 1992; mem. exec. bd. Women's Studies program No. Ky. U., 1985-92; mem. Art Inst. Chgo., Contemporary Art Ctr., Cin., Nat. Mus. Women in Art, Washington. Grantee Ill. State U., 1995, Ky. Found. for Women, 1987, 90, Ky. Art Coun., 1988, No. Ky. U., 1985, 87, 90-91, 93, Ill. State U., 1995; Millay Colony/Studios Midwest fellow, 1986, 88; named One of Outstanding Young Women Am., Jaycees, 1983. Mem. AAUW, Nat. Mus. Women in Art (Washington), Art Inst. Chgo., CAC Cin., Coll. Art Assn., Nature Conservancy, Wilderness Soc., Greenpeace Action League. Office: Dept Art 5620 Ill State U Normal IL 61790-5620

KUKLINSKI, JOAN LINDSEY, librarian; b. Lynn, Mass., Nov. 28, 1950; d. Richard Jay and M. Claire (Murphy) Card; B.A. cum laude, Mass. State Coll., Salem, 1972; M.L.S., U. R.I., 1976; m. Walter S. Kuklinski, June 17, 1972. Classified librarian U. R.I. Extension Div. Library, Providence, 1974-75, U. R.I. Cataloging Dept., Kingston, 1975-79; original cataloger Tex. A&M U. Library, College Station, 1979-82; cataloger Goldfarb Library, Brandeis U., Waltham, Mass., 1982-83; automation coordinator, 1983-85; exec. dir. Minuteman Library Network, Framingham, Mass., 1985-96; exec. dir. C/W Mars, Inc., 1996—. Mem. Town of South Kingstown (R.I.) Women's Adv. Commn., 1977-79; trustee Princeton (Mass.) Pub. Libr., 1994—; mem. strategic planning com. for libr. svc. in yr. 2000 Mass. Bd. Libr. Commrs. Mem. ALA (resources and tech. services div. 1980—), Mass. Librs. Assn., New Eng. Libr. Assn., Libr. Info. Tech. Assn., Assn. Specialized Librs. and Coop. Groups, Am. Contract Bridge League, Delta Tau Kappa. Office: Minuteman Library Network 4 California Ave Framingham MA 01701-8867

KUKULINSKY, NANCY ELAINE, academic administrator; b. Pitts., Feb. 22, 1950; d. Henry Herman and Jennie Loretta (Guzeli) K.; children: Jeremy David Patches, Melissa Ann Patches. BS, U. Pitts., 1971; MPA, Pa. State U., 1981; PhD, U. Pitts., 1987. Rsch. project asst. Penn State U., University Park, Pa., 1971-80; exec. dir. Pathology Edn. & Rsch. Found., Pitts., 1980-90; dir. bus. ops. sch. medicine U. Cin., 1991—; exec. dir. Acad. Pathology Assocs. Inc., Cin., 1991—; cons. Physicians' Adv. Network, Pitts., 1990-91; trustee No. Allegheny Found. for Excellence, Pitts., 1989-91, Path-Tek Diagnostics, Inc., Pitts., 1987-88. Contbr. articles to profl. jours. Mem. Med. Group Mgmt. Assn., Acad. Practice Assn., Pathology Mgmt. Assn., Assn. Women Adminstrs., Grad. Women in Sci. (pres. 1978-79). Democrat. Roman Catholic. Home: 7880 Stonegate Dr # 1208 Cincinnati OH 45255-3181

KUKURA, RITA ANNE, elementary school educator; b. Tulsa, July 18, 1947; d. James Albert and Carmen Alberta (Parsons) Hayden; m. Joel Richard Graft, Oct. 28, 1967 (dec. Apr. 1969); m. Raymond Richard Kukura, Dec. 18, 1971 (div. 1981); children: Tiffany Carmen Noel, Austin Raymond. BS, Kent. State U., 1971; MS, Okla. State U., 1991. Cert. early childhood, nursery, elem. tchr., Okla., spl. edn. tchr. for emotionally disturbed. Tchr. kindergarten Southlyn Elem. Sch., Lyndhurst, Ohio, 1971-73; elem. tchr. Wakefield Acad., Tulsa, 1981-83, tchr. kindergarten, 1983-87; reg. early intervention coord. Okla. Dept. Edn., Tulsa, 1990-92; tchr. devel. delayed children, coord. integrated program Child Devel. Inst. Children's Med. Ctr., Tulsa, 1992-93; tchr. elem. sch. Prue (Okla.) Schs., 1993-95, Tulsa Pub. Schs., 1995—; manuscript reviewer for profl. orgns., 1989-91; mem. human rights com. Ind. Opportunities of Okla., 1995—; del. Okla. Edn. Assembly, 1995; grant reviewer for spl. grants State Dept. Edn., 1996; presenter and lectr. in field. Den leader Cub Scouts Am., Tulsa, 1984-88; com. mem. Boy Scouts Am., Tulsa, 1984-88; vol. officer worker Met. Tulsa Citizen Crime Commn., 1986; adv. com. Latchkey Project, Tulsa County, 1985; ad hoc task force on day care Interagy. Coord. Coun., 1989-91; nat. rep. Tourette Syndrome Assn. to Nat. Broadcasting Assn. AERho, 1990-93; mem. resource com. Ronald McDonald House, 1990-92, vol. Tulsa area, 1991—, STARBASE, 1993—, Drug Edn. for Youth, 1994; mem. adv. bd. Tulsa Regional Coordinating Coun. for Svcs. to Children and Youth and Families, 1991-92; planning com. symposium Magic Coun. Girl Scouts Am.; lt. sr. mem. Tulsa Composite Squadron CAP, 1992-94; active Human Rights Com. for Ind. Opportunities, 1995—; presenter numerous confs. Recipient Den Leader Tng. award Boy Scouts Am., 1988. Mem. AAUW (bd. dirs. Tulsa county chpt. 1991-93, mem. nomination com.), Fedn. Families for Children's Mental Health, Assn. for Care of Children's Health, Nat. Assn. Early Childhood Tchr. Educators, Nat. Tourette Syndrome Assn. (state pres. 1987-92, state dir. 1992-93, hon. mem. bd. dirs. 1993, area coord., fundraiser 1988-90), Gold Star Wives Am., Kappa Delta Pi, Omicron Nu, Alpha Epsilon Rho (hon. mem. S.W. region). Roman Catholic. Office: Anderson Elem Sch 1921 E 29th Pl N Tulsa OK 74110

KULIK, ROSALYN FRANTA, food company executive, consultant; b. Wilmington, Del., Aug. 29, 1951; d. William Alfred and Virginia Louise (Ellis) Franta. BS in Voc. Home Econs. Edn., Purdue U., 1972, MS in Foods and Nutrition, 1974. Registered dietitian. Home economist Kellogg Co., Battle Creek, Mich., 1974-75, nutrition and consumer specialist, 1975-77, mgr. advt. to children, 1977-79, corp. adminstrv. asst., 1979, dir. nutrition, 1979-82, dir. nutrition and analytical services, 1982, v.p. nutrition and chemistry, 1983, v.p. quality and nutrition, 1983-87, v.p., asst. to chmn., 1987-88; exec. v.p., gen. mgr. Fearn Internat., Franklin Park, Ill., 1988-90; cons., 1991—; chmn. tech. com. Grocery Mfrs. Am., Washington, 1985-87, mem. tech. com. planning group, 1982-88; trustee Internat. Life Scis. Inst., Washington, 1982-88; v.p. Internat. Life Scis. Inst. Nutrition Found., Washington, 1985-88, exec. com., 1985-88; mem. of corp. Culinary Inst. Am. Contbr. articles on food sci. and nutrition to profl. jours. Bd. dirs. State Arthritis Found., County Vol. Ctr. Recipient Ada Decker Malott Meml. scholarship, Purdue U., 1970. Mem. Inst. Food Technologists, Am. Dietetic Assn., Phi Kappa Phi, Gamma Sigma Delta, Omicron Nu, Alpha Omicron Pi (mem. Phi Upsilon chpt.). Republican. Lutheran.

KULISHECK, MEREDITH ANDERSON, mathematics educator; b. Wadena, Minn., Jan. 23, 1944; d. Donald Norris and Frances Jeanette (Stiller) Anderson; m. Robert John Kulisheck, June 11, 1966; children: Michael, Amy. BS, Mankato State Coll., 1965; MS, U. Iowa, 1975. Tchr. Hutchinson (Minn.) Schs., 1965-66, Lone Tree (Iowa) Schs., 1966-68; grad. asst. U. Iowa, Iowa City, 1968-69; asst. prof. No. Mich. U., Marquette, 1976—. Mem. LWV, Marquette County, Mich. Mem. AAUP (bd. dirs. No. Mich. U. chpt. 1983—), Am. Math. Assn. of 2-Yr. Colls., Nat. Coun. Tchrs. of Math., Math. Assn. Am., Mich. Coun. Tchrs. of Math. Office: No Mich U Marquette MI 49855

KULP, BETTE JONEVE, retired educator, wallpaper installation business owner; b. Pomona, Calif., Jan. 5, 1936; d. John M. and Eva Kathleen (Lynch) Beck; m. Edwin Hanaway Kulp, Sept. 12, 1957 (div. Apr. 1972); m. Frank Harold Little, Oct. 8, 1977. BS in Home Econs., UCLA, 1957, GPPS credential, 1972. Cert. C.C. counselor, gen. sch. svcs., tchr. homemaking. Social worker L.A. County DPSS, 1957-59; tchr., counselor L.A. City Sch. Dist., 1959-81; wallpaper installer West Los Angeles, Calif., 1981-87; mem. UCLA Scholarship Com. West L.A., San Luis Obispo, Calif., 1978—; judge Acad. Decathalon, San Luis Obispo County, 1989, 90, 92. Vol. Daffodil Days Am. Cancer Soc., San Luis Obispo, 1992-96, Am. Heart Assn., San Luis Obispo, 1992, Sr. Nutrition Program, San Luis Obispo, 1993—; runner Spl. Olympics, San Luis Obispo, 1992; participant Audubon Bird-A-Thon, San Luis Obispo, 1993; locator nesting birds Audubon Breeding Bird Atlas, San Luis Obispo, 1992; fundraiser Womens Shelter Program, San Luis Obispo, 1993-94; precinct clk., judge San Luis Obispo County Election Bd., 1989—; sch. dist. orgn. com. San Luis Obispo County Schs., 1995—; aide dist. 3 San Luis Obispo County Bd. Suprs., 1994—; campaign com. Marie Kiersch for Cuesta Coll. Bd. Trustees, 1994. Recipient Appreciation award Women's Shelter Program, 1993, Unsing Heroine award San Luis Obispo Commn. Status Women, 1995. Mem. AAUW (treas. San Luis Obispo br. 1989-91, pres.-elect 1991-92, pres. 1992-93, bylaws revision com. 1993, San Luis Obispo Interbr. chair 1993-94, chair state resolutions 1994-95, Grant Honoree 1994, membership co-v.p. 1994-95, herstory coord., 1995—, Cuesta scholarship chair 1995-96, parliamentarian 1993-94), Santa Lucia Bridge Club, Phi Mu Alumnae (founder Calif. Ctrl. Coast chpt.), Newcomers Club, Morro Coast Audubon Soc. Home: 2362 Meadow St San Luis Obispo CA 93401

KULP, SHERRILL IRENE, business educator, consultant; b. Lebanon, Kans., Jan. 27, 1944; d. Richard E. and Dorothy I. (Weems) Fisher; m. John W. Rabe Jr., Sept. 4, 1965 (div. June 1995); 1 child, Natasha R.; m. Edwin H. Kulp, Aug. 26, 1995. BA in Bus., Western State Coll., Gunnison, Colo., 1966, MA in Bus. Edn., 1968. Total quality mgmt. cert. Tchr. bus. Woodland (Calif.) H.S., 1967-84; prof. bus. Los Rios C.C., Sacramento, 1984—; cons. Source of Success, Folsom, Calif., 1993—. Author: Macintosh Lab Manual, 1989—. Recipient Outstanding Teaching award Bd. Trustees of City of Woodland, 1983. Mem. Calif. Bus. Edn. Assn. (legis. com.), Delta Kappa Gamma (pres.). Democrat. Methodist. Office: American River College 4700 College Oak Dr Sacramento CA 95841

KULPA, MARY FRANCES, elementary education educator; b. Portsmouth, Va., Mar. 7, 1947; d. Norman Francis and Mary Evelyn (Quinn) Tureman; m. Joseph John Kulpa, Aug. 23, 1969; 1 child, Frances Evelyn. BA, Rowan Coll. of N.J., Glassboro, 1991. Cert. elem. tchr., N.J. Substitute tchr. Washington Twp. (N.J.) Sch. Dsit., 1991-93, 95—; long-term substitute tchr. 2d grade John Fenwick Sch., Salem, N.J., 1992-93; sci. tchr. 7th grade Willingboro (N.J.) Jr. H.S., 1993-94; tchr. sci. and math, 7th and 8th grades Berlin (N.J.) Cmty. Sch., 1994-95. Mem. Kappa Delta Pi, Alpha Kappa Delta. Democrat. Roman Catholic.

KUMAR, MARTHA JOYNT, political science educator; b. Washington, July 4, 1941; d. John Howard and May Aberdeen (Lepley) Joynt; m. Vijayendra Kumar, June 12, 1970; 1 child, Zal Alexander. BA, Conn. Coll., 1963; MA, Columbia U., 1965, PhD, 1972. Rschr. NBC, News Dept., Election Unit, N.Y.C., 1965-66; instr. Tenn. State U., Nashville, 1967, U. Md., Balt., 1970-71; instr. Towson State U., Balt., 1971-72, asst. prof., 1972-75, assoc. prof., 1975-81, prof., 1981—; sr. fellow Ctr. on Polit. Leadership and Participation U. Md., College Park; cons. in field; mem. adv. bd. series presdl. leadership Tex. A&M Press; bd. dirs. Ctr. Presdl. Studies, Tex. A&M U. Co-author: Portraying the President: The White House and the News Media, 1981; co-editor: (jour.) Congress and the Presidency, 1996—; assoc. editor: Presdl. Studies Quar., 1986-89, co-chair editl. bd., 1994-96; editl. bd. Am. Jour. Polit. Sci.; contbr. articles to profl. jours. Mem. City Mgmt. Com., New Castle, Del., 1990-91. Ford Found. grantee, 1978-80. Mem. Am. Polit. Sci. Assn. (Kirkpatrick fund bd. 1990-93), Presidency Rsch. Group (sec., treas. 1989-93, v.p. 1993-95, pres. 1995—), Am. Polit. Sci. Assn. (rep. nat. archives), Phi Beta Kappa. Home: 53 The Strand New Castle DE 19720-4825 Office: Towson State U Dept Polit Sci Baltimore MD 21204

KUMIN, LIBBY BARBARA, speech language pathologist, educator; b. Bklyn., Nov. 11, 1945; d. Herbert H. and Berniece (Shuch) K.; m. Martin J. Lazar, Jan. 18, 1969; 1 child, Jonathan Kumin. BA summa cum laude, LIU, 1965; MA, NYU, 1966, PhD, 1969. Lic. speech pathologist, Md.; cert. clin. competence in speech-lang. pathology. Asst. prof. speech pathology U. Md., College Park, 1972-76; cons., 1976-80; adj. prof. Loyola Coll., Balt., 1976-80, assoc. prof., 1980-88, chmn. dept. speech and lang. pathology, 1983—, prof., 1988—; specialist in speech and language in Down Syndrome; mem. profl. adv. bd. Nat. Down Syndrome Cong; mem. Down Syndrome Med. Interest Group. Author: Aphasia, 1978, Communication Skills in Children with Down Syndrom, 1994; therapies editor: Down Syndrome Qtrly.; chief editor: Communicating Together; contbr. articles on Down Syndrome, others. Vol. cons. Howard County Office on Aging, 1977-83. Recipient Outstanding Individual of Year award Howard County Assn. Retarded Citizens, Nat. Meritorious Service award Nat. Down Syndrome Congress, 1987, Svc. Learning award Shriver Ctr., 1996. Aaron and Lillie Straus Found. grantee, 1983-89; Columbia Found. grantee, Joseph P. Kennedy Found. Faculty Innovation grantee, 1995; recipient summer research award Loyola Coll., 1983, 91. Mem. Am. Speech/Lang./Hearing Assn. (cert.), Md. Speech and Hearing Assn., ARC, Sigma Tau Delta, Pi Lambda Theta. Office: Loyola Coll Dept Speech Pathology 4501 N Charles St Baltimore MD 21210-2601

KUMIN, MAXINE WINOKUR, poet, author; b. Phila., June 6, 1925; d. Peter and Doll (Simon) Winokur; m. Victor Montwid Kumin, June 29, 1946; children: Jane Simon, Judith Montwid, Daniel David. AB, Radcliffe Coll., 1946, MA, 1948; LHD (hon.), Centre Coll., 1976, Davis and Elkins Coll., 1977, Regis Coll., 1979, New England Coll., 1982, Claremont Grad. Sch., 1983, U. N.H., 1984. Instr. Tufts U., Medford, Mass., 1958-61, lectr. English, 1965-68; scholar Radcliffe Inst. for Ind. Study, 1961-63; vis. lectr. U. Mass., Amherst, 1973, Princeton U., 1979, 81-82; adj. prof. Columbia U., 1975; Fannie Hurst prof. of literature Brandeis U., 1975, Wash. U., St. Louis, 1977; vis. sr. fellow, lectr. Princeton U., 1977; Carolyn Wilkerson Bell vis. scholar Randolph-Macon Woman's Coll., 1978; poet in residence Bucknell U., 1983; vis. prof. MIT, 1984; master artist Atlantic Ctr. for Arts, New Smyrna Beach, Fla., 1984; staff mem. Bread Loaf Writers' Conf., 1969-71, 73, 75, 77; poetry cons. Library of Congress, 1981-82; elector The Poet's Corner, The Cathedral of St. John the Divine, 1990—. Author: (poetry) Halfway, 1961, The Privilege, 1965, The Nightmare Factory, 1970, Up Country: Poems of New England, 1972 (Pulitzer Prize for poetry 1973), House, Bridge, Fountain, Gate, 1975, The Retrieval System, 1978, Our Ground Time Here Will Be Brief, 1982, Closing the Ring, 1984, The Long Approach, 1985, Nurture, 1989, Looking for Luck, 1992, Connecting the Dots, 1996; (novels) Through Dooms of Love, 1965, The Passions of Uxport, 1968, The Abduction, 1971, The Designated Heir, 1974; (essays) To Make A Prairie: Essays on Poets, Poetry, and Country Living, 1980, In Deep: Country Essays, 1987, Women, Animals and Vegetables: Essays and Stories, 1994; (short stories) Why Can't We Live Together Like Civilized Human Beings?, 1982; (juvenile) Sebastian and the Dragon, 1960, Spring Things, 1961, A Summer Story, 1961, Follow the Fall, 1961, A Winter Friend, 1961,

Mittens in May, 1962, No One Writes a Letter to the Snail, 1962, (with Anne Sexton) Eggs of Things, 1963, Archibald the Traveling Poodle, 1963, (with Sexton) More Eggs of Things, 1964, Speedy Digs Downside Up, 1964, The Beach Before Breakfast, 1964, Paul Bunyan, 1966, Faraway Farm, 1967, The Wonderful Babies of 1809 and Other Years, 1968, When Grandmother Was Young, 1970, When Great-Grandmother Was Young, 1971, (with Sexton) Joey and the Birthday Present, 1971, (with Sexton) The Wizard's Tears, 1975, What Color Is Caesar?, 1978, The Microscope, 1984; contbr. poems to nat. mags. Recipient Lowell Mason Palmer award, 1960, William Marion Reedy award, 1968, Eunice Tietjens Meml. prize Poetry Mag., 1972, Borestone Mountain award, 1976, Radcliffe Coll. Alumnae Recognition award, 1978, Am. Acad. and Inst. Arts and Letters award for excellence in literature, 1980, Levinson award Poetry mag., 1987, The Poets' prize, 1994; grantee Nat. Endowment for the Arts, 1966; fellow Nat. Coun. on Arts and Humanities, 1967-68; fellow Acad. Am. Poets, 1986; fellow Woodrow Wilson, 1979-80, 91-93. Mem. Acad. Am. Poets (chancellor), Poetry Soc. Am., PEN Am., Authors Guild, The Writers Union. Address: Curtis Brown Assoc 10 Astor Pl New York NY 10003-6935

KUNCE, AVON ESTES, vocational rehabilitation counselor; b. Sarasota, Fla., Apr. 20, 1927; d. William Breckinridge and Avon Mary (Zahlten) Estes; m. Henry Warren Kunce, May 26, 1948; children: Catherine Avon Hilton, Nancy Lynn Evers, Christopher Warren, Cynthia Tyree Kent, James Breckinridge. BEd in Secondary Edn., U. Miami, 1972; MS in Mgmt., Fla. Internat. U., 1977. Social worker State of Fla. Health & Rehab. Svcs., Miami, 1972-76; social and rehab. svcs. supr. State Disabled Adult Abuse Investigation Unit Adult Congregate Living Lic., Miami, 1976-82; med. disability specialist State of Fla. Health & Rehab. Svcs., Miami, 1982-89; sr. vocat. rehab. counselor State of Fla. Dept. of Labor, Miami, 1989—. Pres. LWV, Rockhill, Mo., 1955, mem., Miami, 1965-69; mem. South Dade Dem. Women's Club, Miami, 1967-69. Mem. ASPA, Nat. Assn. Disability Examiners, Nat. Rehab. Assn., Phi Lambda Pi, Gamma Theta Upsilon, Epsilon Tau Lambda, Pi Alpha Alpha. Democrat. Quaker. Home: 5025 SW 74th Ter Miami FL 33143-6003 Office: State of Fla Vocat Rehabilitation 5040 NW 7th St Ste 330 Miami FL 33126-3422

KUNDU, SMRITI KANA, biomedical scientist; b. Asansol, India, Mar. 5, 1959; came to U.S., 1989; d. Mrityunjoy and Uma (Mondal) K.; m. Siba P. Raychaudhuri, June 7, 1987; children: Suravi Raychaudhuri, Sanchita Raychaudhuri. MD, All India Inst. Med. Scis., New Delhi, 1987. Postdoctoral fellow Stanford (Calif.) U. Med. Ctr., 1989-92, rsch. assoc., 1992-94, sr. rsch. assoc., 1995—; mem. AIDS clin. trials unit NIH, Bethesda, Md., 1989—; mem. sci. rev. bd. FDA, 1995. Contbr. articles to profl. jours. Mem. Am. Assn. Immunologists, New Acad. Scis., N.Y. Acad. Scis., Am. Soc. for Microbiologists. Home: 510 Ashton Ave Palo Alto CA 94306 Office: Stanford U Med Ctr Rm S 156 Divsn Infectious Diseases 300 Pasteur Dr Stanford CA 94305

KUNIN, JACQUELINE BARLOW, art educator; b. Harrisburg, Pa., Apr. 20, 1941; d. Rodney Kipton and Marie (Trunk) Barlow; m. Richard Henry Kunin, June 17, 1967. BFA, Pratt Inst., 1963; MEd, Temple U., 1967. Comml. artist Dock and Kinney Co., N.Y.C., 1963-64; art libr. Norcross, Inc., N.Y.C., 1964; tchr. graphic arts Jones Jr. H.S., Phila., 1964-66; tchr. art John Bartram H.S., Phila., 1966-86; tchr. painting and drawing H.S. for Creative and Performing Arts, Phila., 1986—. Named Disting Tchr. White House Commn. Presdl. Scholars, Washington, 1994. Mem. AAUW, Pa. Art Edn. Assn., Victorian Soc. Am. (Phila. chpt. bd. dirs. 1986—), Valley Forge Civic Assn.

KUNIN, MADELEINE MAY, federal agency administrator, former governor; b. Zurich, Switzerland, Sept. 28, 1933; came to U.S., 1940, naturalized, 1947; d. Ferdinand and Renee (Bloch) May; children: Julia, Peter, Adam, Daniel. B.A., U. Mass., 1956; M.S., Columbia U., 1957; M.A., U. Vt., 1967; numerous hon. degrees. Newspaper reporter Burlington Free Press, Vt., 1957-58; guide Brussels World's Fair, Belgium, 1958; TV asst. producer Sta. WCAX-TV, Burlington, 1960-61; freelance writer, instr. English Trinity Coll., Burlington, 1969-70; mem. Vt. Ho. of Reps., 1973-78; lt. gov. State of Vt., Montpelier, 1979-82, gov., 1985-91; disting. vis. in Pub. Policy Bunting Inst., Cambridge, Mass., 1991-92, Dartmouth Coll., Hanover, N.H., 1992; deputy sec. of education Dept. Education, Washington, D.C., 1993—; fellow Inst. Politics, Kennedy Sch. Govt., Harvard U., 1983; lectr. Middlebury Coll., St. Michael's Coll., 1984; disting. pub. policy visitor Rockefeller Ctr., Dartmouth Coll., 1992; pub. policy fellow Bunting Inst., Radcliffe Coll., Harvard U., 1991-92; Vt. Joint Fiscal Com., 1977-78; mem. exec. com. Nat. Conf. Lt. Govs., 1979-80; founder, pres. Inst. Sustainable Cmtys., Montpelier, Vt., 1991. Author: Living a Political Life: A Memoir, 1994, The Big Green Book, 1976; contbr. articles to profl. jours., mags. and newspapers. Named Outstanding State Legislator, Eagleton Inst. Politics, Rutgers U., 1975; Montgomery fellow Dartmouth Coll., 1991. Fellow Am. Acad. Arts & Scis.; mem. Nat. Gov.'s Assn. (mem. exec. com.), Nat. Govs.' Conf. (chair com. on energy and the environ.), New Eng. Gov.'s Conf. (chairperson). Democrat. Office: Office of Dep Sec Edn 400 Maryland Ave SW Washington DC 20202-0001

KUNKA, LIANNE N., administrative assistant; b. Hammond, Ind., July 21, 1961; d. Dean L. and Marleen J. (Belza) Hunter; m. Richard T. Kunka, June 3, 1989; 1 child, Shannon. AS, Vincennes U., 1981; BS, Purdue U. Calumet, Hammond, 1993. Bookkeeper Trade Winds Rehab. Ctr., Gary, Ind., 1981-85; adminstrv. support Sand Ridge Bank, Schererville, Ind., 1985—. Mem. Inst. Mgmt. Accts., Highland Dollars for Scholars (treas. 1995—). Methodist. Home: 702 E Elm St Griffith IN 46319 Office: Sand Ridge Bank 450 W Lincoln Hwy Schererville IN 46375

KUNKEL, BARBARA, psychotherapist, consultant; b. Garfield, N.J., Mar. 17, 1945; d. Everett Edward and Florence Hilda (Davidsen) K.; children: Tasha Jade Decker, Lara Ashley Decker; m. John E. Carr. BA in Psychology and Pre-Theology, Elmira Coll., N.Y., 1966; MA in Human Devel., Fairleigh Dickinson U., 1983; PhD in Transpersonal Psychology and Alcholism Studies, Union Inst., 1988; grad. Postdoctoral Tng. Program N.E. Soc. Group Psychotherapy, 1993. Mgmt., human relations cons. pvt. practice, N.J., Mass., Maine, N.Y., 1983—; co-founder, psychologist Carr Counseling, Waltham, Mass., 1989—, teacher of A Course in Miracles, 1991—; clk. Supreme Jud. and Superior Cts., York County, Maine, 1985-88; clin. supr. Mass. Correctional Inst., Shirley, Mass., 1992-93; cons. Ctr. for Addictive Behaviors, Inc., Salem, Mass., 1988-91; mem. faculty Nasson Coll., Springvale, Maine, 1986-87. Teaching fellow Fairleigh Dickinson U., 1983-84. Recipient Beyond Excellence award, 1993. Mem. Am. Psychol. Practitioners Assn. (founding mem.), Am. Acad. Healthcare Providers in Addictive Disorders, Northeastern Soc. for Group Psychotherapy (affiliate mem.). Avocations: carpentry, photography, study Krishnamurti, furniture restoration. Home: 264 Delaware Dr Narrowsburg NY 12764-6030 Office: Carr Counseling 371 Moody St Ste 102 Waltham MA 02154-5239

KUNKEL, CHARLOTTE ANN, sociology educator; b. St. Cloud, Minn., Mar. 10, 1966; d. Andrew Paul and Celine Therese (Foley) K.; m. Steve J. Billig, Aug. 31, 1991. BA summa cum laude, St. Cloud State U., 1988; PhD, U. Colo., 1995. Instr. dept. sociology U. Colo., Boulder, 1991-95, instr. continuing edn., 1991-94; asst. prof. sociology Luther Coll., Decorah, Iowa, 1995—, facilitator diversity project, 1996; mem. adv. bd. Women's Resource Ctr., Boulder, 1994-95; cons. Women in Cmty. Svc., Denver, 1993. Contbr. articles and book revs. to profl. jours., chpt. to book. Vol. adv. Safehouse, battered women's shelter, St. Cloud, 1988; vol. Svcs. for Abused Women, Decorah, 1995—. Recipient Elizabeth Mathiot Meml. award Feminist Scholars in Sociology, 1995; scholar Women's Ctr., Boulder, 1993; grantee U. Colo., 1994. Mem. Sociologists for Women in Soc. (program com. 1996—). Office: Luther Coll Dept Sociology Koren 310 Decorah IA 52101

KUNKEL, DOROTHY ANN, music educator; b. Weeping Water, Nebr., Nov. 24, 1934; d. Lloyd Nelson and Dorothy Grace (Holman) K. Student, Nebr. Wesleyan U., 1952-54; MusB, Am. Conservatory of Music, Chgo., 1958, B of Music Edn., 1960, M of Music Edn. cum laude, 1970. Cert. music instr. K-12, Mich. Music supr., orch. dir. Sch. Dist. 48, Villa Park, Ill., 1960-80; orch. condr. Nat. Music Camp, Interlochen, Mich., 1970-84; dir. of orchs. Traverse City (Mich.) Area Pub. Schs., 1983-96; dir., founder Galena (Ill.) Music Acad., 1961-69; string methods instr. Sherwood Sch. of Music, Chgo., 1969-73, Am. Conservatory of Music, Chgo., 1978-79; guest condr. Ga. All-State Orch., 1976, 81, 93, Fla. All-State Orch., 1977, 82, Ill. All-State Orch., 1982, Mich. Youth Arts Honors Orch., 1995; condr. Petito Promonades concerts Chgo. Symphony Orch. Choir dir. Oakbrook (Ill.) Christian Ctr., 1977-80, Lake Ann (Mich.) Meth. Ch., 1981-90. Recipient They Are Making Am. Mus. award Sch. Musician, 1981, Best in Class award Adjudicators Nat. Invitational, Kennedy Ctr., Washington, 1992, 95. Mem. Am. String Tchrs. Assn. (pres. Ill. chpt. 1979-80), Nat. Sch. Orch. Assn., Mid-West Internat. Band and Orch. Clinic (bd. dirs. 1980—, Medal of Honor 1966, 70, 74), Mich. Sch. Band and Orch. Assn. (adjudicator 1990—, Orch. Tchr. of Yr. 1994), Music Educators Nat. Conf., Sigma Alpha Iota, Willard Sorority. Home: 2426 E Kasson Rd Cedar MI 49621-8673 Office: Traverse City HS 1150 Milliken Dr Traverse City MI 49684

KUNKEL, GEORGIE MYRTIA, writer, retired school counselor; b. Chehalis, Wash.; d. George Riley and Myrtia (McLaughlin) Bright; m. Norman C. Kunkel, Apr. 25, 1946; children: N. Joseph D.C., Stephen Gregory, Susan Ann, Kimberly Jane Waligorska. BA in Edn., Western Wash. U., 1944; MEd, U. Wash., 1968. Typist, clk. FHA, Seattle, 1940; tchr. pub. schs. Vader, Centralia, Wash., Seattle, 1941-67; pvt. cons., Seattle, 1970—; counselor Highline Pub. Schs., Seattle, 1967-82; sch. counselor rep. State of Art Conf., Balt., 1980. Editor Women and Girls in Edn., 1972-75. Author (under pseudonym Dorothy Bright): My Sex Secrets, 1989, How Do You Know You're Dying, 1991, Grandma's Holiday Greetings, 1992; contbr. articles to profl. jours. Organizer Women and Girls in Edn., Wash. state, 1971; pres. Wash. State NOW, 1973; mem. West Seattle Community Council, 1980. Grantee Women Adminstrs. Wash. State, 1971, Edn. Service Dist., Seattle, 1980. Mem. NEA (sec. pub. relations), Am. Assn. Counseling and Devel. (pres. state br. 1982-83), Am. Sch. Counseling Assn. (pres. state divsn. 1980-81), Seattle Counselors Assn. (organizer, past pres. office exec., Counselor of Yr. 1990), Holmes Harbor Homeowners Assn. (organizer and pres.), West Seattle C. of C., Past Pres. Assembly, West Seattle Dem. Women's Club (pres.). Unitarian Universalist. Avocation: singing. Home and Office: 3409 SW Trenton St Seattle WA 98126-3743

KUNS, NANCY LEE, office manager, pharmacist; b. Ashtabula, Ohio, Apr. 16, 1960; d. Frank Joseph Nappi Jr. and Wanda Gay (Britton) Mackey; m. Bryan P. Kuns, July 30, 1983; children: Kaitlyn, Brianne, Derek. BS, U. Toledo, 1983. Office mgr. Kuns Family Medicine, Inc., Castalia, Ohio, 1987—; pharmacist Firelands Community Hosp., Sandusky, Ohio, 1989-91, Walmart Pharmacy, Sandusky, 1991—. Com. chmn. Aux. to 5th Dist. Ohio Osteo. Assn., 1990—, treas., 1987-90, pres., 1991-93, v.p., 1993—. Mem. Ohio Pharmacists' Assn., N.W. Ohio Hosp. Pharmacists, Ohio Soc. Hosp. Pharmacists, Beta Sigma Phi (v.p. Xi Iota Eta chpt. 1990-91, pres. 1994—). Roman Catholic. Home: 6105 Deyo Rd Castalia OH 44824-9762

KUNSMAN, CYNTHIA LOUISE MULLEN, critical care nurse; b. Allentown, Pa., Sept. 29, 1966; d. Donald Lee and Phyllis Ann (Herbert) Mullen; m. Gary Wayne Kunsman, May 5, 1990. ASN, Gwynedd-Mercy Coll., 1986, BSN, 1987; MMin, Chesapeake Bible Seminary, 1994; D of Naturopathy, Clayton Sch. Natural Healing, 1995. CCRN. Staff nurse oncology/urology med./surg. Lehigh Valley Hosp. Ctr., Allentown, 1986; staff nurse PCCU Lehigh Valley Hosp. Ctr., 1987-88, staff nurse ICU, 1989; staff nurse MICU La. State U., Shreveport, La., 1990-91; asst. head nurse cardiovascular svcs. HCA Presbyn. Hosp., Oklahoma City, 1992-93; staff nurse cardiothoracic ICU U. Md. Med. Sys., Balt., 1993-95; dir. R & D, prof. biol. sci. Chesapeake Bible Coll., 1993—; sole proprietor Gilead Health Assocs., Pasadena, Md., 1995—; staff nurse Hospice of the Chesapeake, Millersville, Md., 1995—. Author: (book) Arrhythmia Interpretation: A Guide for Nurses, 1991; contbr. articles to profl. jours. Mem. AACN, Pa. Nurses Assn. (chair nominations com. local dist. 1988-90), Orgn. for the Advancement of ASN, Ctr. for Bioethics and Human Dignity. Office: Gilead Health Assocs 672 Old Mill Rd # 169 Millersville MD 21108

KUNSTADTER, GERALDINE SAPOLSKY, foundation executive; b. Boston, Jan. 6, 1928; d. Harry Herman and Nettie Sapolsky; m. John W. Kunstadter, Apr. 23, 1949; children: John W., Lisa, Christopher, Elizabeth. Student, MIT, 1945-48. Draftsman U. Chgo. Cyclotron Project, 1948; engring. asst. Gen. Electric Corp., Lynn, Mass., 1948-49; pres. Capricorn Investments Corp., 1971—; chmn., dir. A. Kunstadter Family Found., N.Y.C., 1966—; host family program dir. N.Y.C. Commn. for UN, 1971-86; pres. Nat. Inst. Social Scis., 1979-81. Bd. dirs. Friends of N.Y.C. Commn. for UN and Consular Corps, Bridge to Asia Found., Menninger Found., Internat. Devel. Enterprises, Atlantic Council of the U.S., Nat. Com. on U.S.-China Rels., Yale-China Assn., Feld Ballets, N.Y.C., Ctr. U.S.-China Arts Exch., Inst. World Affairs; mem. adv. coun. East Asian studies program MIT Sch. Architecture; mem. Peace Links Leadership Network, Overseas Devel. Coun., N.Y.-Beijing Friendship City Com.; mem. internat. hospitality com. Nat. Coun. Women. Recipient Windham award, 1970, silver medal Nat. Inst. Social Sci., 1981. Mem. Inst. Current World Affairs, Coun. on Fgn. Rels., Am. Women's Club, Hurlingham Club, Lansdowne Club (London).

KUNTZ, MARION LUCILE LEATHERS, classicist, historian, educator; b. Atlanta, Sept. 6, 1924; d. Otto Asa and Lucile (Parks) Leathers; m. Paul G. Kuntz, Nov. 26, 1970; children by previous marriage: Charles, Otto Alan (Daniels). BA, Agnes Scott Coll., 1945; MA, Emory U., 1964, PhD, 1969. Lectr. Latin Lovett Sch., Atlanta, 1963-66; mem. faculty Ga. State U., 1966—, assoc. prof., 1969-73, prof. Latin and Greek, 1973—, Regents' Prof., 1975—, chmn. dept. fgn. langs., 1975-84, research prof., 1984—, Fuller E. Callaway disting. prof., 1985—, alumni disting. prof., 1994. Author: Colloquim of the Seven About Secrets of the Sublime of Jean Bodin, 1975, Guillaume Postel, Prophet of the Restitution of All Things: His Life and Thought, 1981, Jacob's Ladder and the Tree of Life: Concepts of Hierarchy and the Great Chain of Being, 1987, Postello, Venezia e Il Suo Mondo, 1988; also scholarly articles; mem. editorial bd. Library of Renaissance Humanism. Named Latin Tchr. of Yr. State Ga., 1965; Semple scholar, 1965, Am. Classical League scholar, 1966, Gladys Krieble Delmas scholar, 1991; Am. Coun. Learned Socs. grantee, 1970, 73, 76, 81, 87, 90; recipient medal for excellence in Renaissance studies Pres. of Coun. Gen., Tours, France, 1995, Disting. Career Alumna award Agnes Scott Coll., 1995. Mem. Am. Philol. Assn., Renaissance Soc. Am. (coun. 1994—), Am. Soc. Aesthetics, Am. Cath. Philos. Assn., Soc. for Values in Higher Edn., Philosophy and Religion, Am. Soc. Ch. History, Am. Hist. Assn., Internat. Soc. Neo-Platonic Studies, Internat. Soc. Neo-Latin Studies, Soc. Christian Philosophers (exec. bd. 1987—), Sociètè des Seiziémistes, Medieval Acad. Sociètè de Culture Europèenne, Soc. Medieval and Renaissance Philosophy (exec. bd. 1988—), Soc. di Philosophique Medievale, Archaeol. Inst. Am., Am. Philological Assn., Classical Assn. Midwest and South (Semple award 1965), Am. Acad. Rome (sec.-treas. 1970-74), Friends of the Vatican Libr., Italia Nostra, Fondazione Ambiente Italiana, Amici di Querini-Stampalia Galleria e Biblioteca, Italian Cultural Soc., Nat. Trust Hist. Preservation, Atlanta Hist. Soc., High Mus. of Art (patron), The Commerce Club, Friends of the Warburg Inst., World Monuments Fund, Phi Beta Kappa, Phi Kappa Phi, Omicron Delta Kappa. Roman Catholic. Home: Villa Veneziana 1655 Ponce De Leon Ave Atlanta GA 30307 also: Dorsoduro, 714 Venice Italy

KUNZ, MARGARET MCCARTHY, realtor; b. Woodbury, N.J.; m. Lyle Bernard Kunz, July 31, 1965; children: Carolyn Louise, Elizabeth Anne, Paul Bernard. BA, U. Miami, 1957; MSW, Tulane U., 1962. Realtor Byrne-Rinehart & Co., South Miami, Fla., 1990—. Past pres., bd. mem. The Villagers, Inc., Miami; bd. dirs. Theatre Arts League, Miami. Mem. Miami Bd. Realtors, Med. Faculty Assn. U. Miami (bd. dirs.), Women's Guild U. Miami, Powerhouse Miami. Home: 7245 SW 142nd Ter Miami FL 33158-1610

KUNZ, MICHELLE LYNN, soprano; b. Rantoul, Ill., Feb. 4, 1964; d. DelRay and MaryAnn (Gonzales) K.; divorced; children: Katharine Leigh Thomas, Jonathan Wesley Thomas. BMus, Cath. U. Am., Washington, 1994, MMus, 1995. Pers. asst. Gian Carlo Menotti, Charleston, S.C., 1991; soloist, accompanist The Summer Opera Theatre Co., Washington, 1991-96; pianist The Washington Opera, 1994-96, children's chorus master, 1995—; condr. Tessitura, 1995. Arranger works for mixed chorus, men's chorus, women's chorus. Presser scholar Theodore Pesser Co., Pa., 1993-94, Furfey scholar Bd. Trustees Cath. U., Washington, 1994—; winner grad. women Nat. Assn. Tchrs. Singing-State of Va., 1995. Mem. Pi Kappa Lambda. Republican. Roman Catholic. Home: 4205 Hatton Ct Alexandria VA 22311

KUNZE, DOLORES JOHANNA, veterinarian; b. Waltham, Mass., Mar. 29, 1950; d. John Herman and Dorothy (Angiulo) K.; m. Morrow Bradford Thompson, Mar. 20, 1976 (div. 1985). BS in Agriculture, U. Ga., 1972, DVM, 1976; MS, Mich. State U., 1980. Lic. veterinarian, N.C., S.C. Resident large animal dept. Coll. Vet. Medicine, Mich. State U., Lansing, 1977-80, asst. prof. vet. medicine, 1980-81; asst. prof. vet. medicine N.C. State U., Raleigh, 1981-84; staff veterinarian Aiken (S.C.) Animal Hosp., 1985-87, East Side Vet. Clinic, Spartanburg, S.C., 1987-88; pvt. practice Boiling Springs Animal Clinic, P.A., Inman, S.C., 1988—; bd. dirs. Spartanburg Vet. Emergency Clinic, sec., 1990-91, pres., 1994-96. Contbr. articles to profl. publs., 2 chpts. to books. Mem. AVMA, S.C. Vet. Med. Assn., Phi Zeta (Zeta chpt.). Presbyterian. Home: PO Box 16014 Spartanburg SC 29316-6014 Office: Boiling Springs Animal Clin 4370 Highway 9 Inman SC 29349-8582

KUO, NINA, artist. lectr. in field. One woman shows include Basement Workshop, N.Y.C., 1982; exhibited in group shows at Kathryn Markel Gallery, N.Y.C., 1978-79, La Foret Gallery, Tokyo, 1980, The New Mus., N.Y., 1981, Floating Found. of Photography, N.Y.C., 1982, Kenkeleba House, N.Y.C., 1983, Bklyn. Mus., 1984, L.S. County Art Mus., 1984, P.S. 1 Gallery, L.I., N.Y., 1984, Asian Am. Arts Ctr., N.Y.C., 1986, Elaine Benson Gallery, Bridgehampton, N.Y., 1987, Harlem Sch. of Arts, N.Y.C., 1987, P.P.O.W. Gallery, N.Y.C., 1987, P.S. 39 Longwood Gallery, Bronx, N.Y., 1988, 89, Intar Gallery, N.Y.C., 1988, Camerawork Gallery, London, 1988, En Foco Gallery, Bronx, 1990, The Clocktower Gallery, N.Y.C., 1990, Woodstock Ctr. for Photography, N.Y.C., 1991, Wunsch Art Ctr., Glen Cove, N.Y., 1991, Chinatown History Mus., N.Y.C., 1992-93, Artist Space, N.Y.C., 1993, New Mus., N.Y.C., 1994, 95; exhibited in travelling show with Women of Color Artists' Book Show, Houston, 1988; pub. photography in American Born and Fgn. Anthology of Poetry, 1979, Super Art GoCoo mag., Tokyo, 1980, Obsolete Body Suspensions, Stelarc, 1984, Heresies mag., 1986-87, Ikon Mag.: Art Against Apartheid, 1986-88, Portable Lower East Side Jour., 1990, Mixed Blessing: Art in a Multicultural America, 1990, Downtown, 1993, Daily News, 1993; permanenet collections include Libr. of Congress, Washington, Bibliotheque Nationale, Paris, Bklyn. Mus., Chgo. Art Inst. Libr., Franklin Furnace Archives, N.Y.C., Chinatown History Mus., N.Y.C., Visual Comm., L.A. Recipient Artist-in-residence grant N.Y. State Coun. on Arts, 1984, Artist-in-residence book grant Women's Graphic Ctr., 1984, Aritst Space Emergency grant, 1988, Light Work Artist Grant Residency, 1988, grant Art Matters Inc., 1990, 93, Artist grant N.Y. State Coun. Arts, 1990, Travel grant Arts Internat., China, 1993, Artist book grant N.Y. Found. for Arts, 1993. Studio: 233 E 88th St # 3W New York NY 10129

KUPCINET, ESSEE SOLOMON, performing arts producer; b. Chgo., Dec. 7; d. Joseph David and Doris (Schoke) Solomon; m. Irv Kupcinet, Feb. 12, 1939; children: Karyn (dec.), Jerry S. PhB, Northwestern U., 1937. Asst. to dir. psychology dept. Michael Reese Hosp., Chgo., 1939-41; exec. producer eight Jefferson Award Shows; producer 1st Literary Arts Ball, Cultural Center, Chgo., 1979; talent coordinator Kup's Show, Chgo., 1964-84; producer for spl. events, 1978—. Mem. adv. bd., bd. dirs. Free St. Theater; prodn. chmn. Acad. Honors, 1984-87; chmn. bd. trustees Acad. Sch. Performing Arts, 1984-86, hon. lifetime chair, 1986—; prodn. chmn. Variety Club Telethon, 1984, 85; bd. dirs. Mus. Broadcasting Commn.; exec. com. Chgo. Tourism Coun., 1984-88; exec. bd. Internat. Theatre Festival, 1985-86; mem. sponsors com. Chgo. Pub. Libr., 1985-86; co-founder Chgo. Acad. Arts. Decorated Knight of Orange Nassau (The Netherlands); recipient Spl. award Jefferson Com., 1976; Cliff Dwellers award, 1975; Emmy award CBS, 1977, 79; Artisan award Acad. Theatre Arts and Friends, 1977; Prime Minister's medal for service to Israel, 1974; Woman of Yr. award Facets Multimedia, 1982, Mass Media award NCCJ, 1988, others; named (with Irv Kupcinet) Mr. and Mrs. Chgo., Greater North Michigan Ave. Assn., 1987, Chgo. Acad. for the Arts, 1988, Woman of Yr., Variety Club #26, 1988; honored by Mus. Brekest, Conn., 1989; honored (with Irv Kupcinet) 10th Anniversary Chgo. Acad. for Arts, 1992. Mem. NATAS (governing bd., program chmn. 1982-91, Govs. awards 1986, 91), Arts Club. Jewish.

KUPPERMAN, HELEN SLOTNICK, lawyer; b. Boston; d. Morris Louis and Minnie (Kaplan) Slotnick; B.A., Smith Coll.; postgrad. Royal Acad. Dramatic Art, London; J.D., Boston Coll., 1966; m. Robert H. Kupperman, Dec. 23, 1967; 1 dau., Tamara. Bar: Mass. 1966, D.C. 1986. Atty., advisor NASA, Washington, 1966-73, sr. atty., 1973-77, asst. gen. counsel for gen. law, 1977-86, assoc. gen. counsel, 1986, spl. asst. gen. counsel space station, 1986-87, chairperson contract adjustment bd., 1974-87, exec. v.p. Robert H. Kupperman & Assocs. Inc., 1987—; adj. fellow space policy study Ctr. Strategic and Internat. Studies, 1987-88; rep. on U.S. delegation to legal subcomittee of UN Com. on Peaceful Uses of Outer Space, 1977-87. Recipient NASA Sustained Superior Performance award, 1977, Exceptional Service medal, 1983, NASA Ses Bonus, 1980, 85, Space Station Task Force Group Achivement award NASA, 1984. Mem. U.S. Assn. of Internat. Inst. Space Law (sec. 1981, bd. dirs. 1989—), ABA, Fed., Mass., D.C., Boston bar assns., Internat. Women Lawyers Assn., Am. Astronautical Assn. (gen. counsel 1986-87). Jewish. Bus. editor Boston Coll. Indsl. and Comml. Law Rev., 1965-66. Home: 2832 Ellicott St NW Washington DC 20008-1019

KUPST, MARY JO, psychologist, researcher; b. Chgo., Oct. 4, 1945; d. George Eugene and Winifred Mary (Hughes) K.; m. Alfred Procter Stresen-Reuter Jr., Aug. 21, 1977. BS, Loyola U., 1967, MA, 1969, PhD, 1972. Lic. psychologist, Ill., Wis. Postdoctoral fellow U. Ill. Med. Ctr., Chgo., 1971-72; rsch. psychologist Children's Meml. Hosp., Chgo., 1972-89; assoc. prof. psychiatry and pediatrics Northwestern U. Med. Sch., Chgo., 1981-89; prof. pediatrics Med. Coll. Wis., Milw., 1989—, dir. pediatric psychology, 1995—; practice clin. psychology, Chgo., 1975-89, McHenry, Ill., 1987-89. Editor: (with others) The Child with Cancer, 1980; contbr. articles to profl. jours. Mem. APA, Wis. Psychol. Assn., Soc. Pediatric Psychology. Office: Med Coll Wis Dept Pediats 8701 W Watertown Plank Rd Milwaukee WI 53226-3548

KURAS, JEAN MARY, educator; b. Jersey City, Jan. 30, 1944; d. Stanley Richard and Ann (Tyra) K. BA, N.J. State Tchrs. Coll., 1960, MA, 1966. Tchr. Bloomfield (N.J.) Bd. Edn., 1962—. Pres. Big Bros.-Big Sisters Essex and Newark, Bloomfield, 1982-84, Bloomfield Hist. Soc., 1981—; vol. office staff Senator Bradley, N.J., 1984; trustee League for Family Svc., Bloomfield, 1988—, v.p., 1990-94. Art for Kids grantee Sta. WOR-TV, N.J., 1990. Mem. NEA, AAUW (Bloomfield and Glen Ridge chpt. edn. chairperson 1995-96), N.J. Edn. Assn., Essex County Edn. Assn., Bloomfield Edn. Assn. (sec. 1987-90, v.p. 1990—). Home: 11 Hawthorne Ave Glen Ridge NJ 07028-2010 Office: Oak View Sch 150 Garrabrant Ave Bloomfield NJ 07003-4510

KURETZA, MARY ANN, counselor adolescents; b. Fairmont, W.Va., Apr. 22, 1951; d. Thomas and Norma Jean (Welch) K. BA, La. State U., 1974, U. Southwestern La., 1977; MEd, U. Southwestern La., 1983. Nat. cert. counselor. Counselor North Marion H.S., Marion County Tech. Ctr., Miller Sch., Fairmont; instr. behavior disorders Marion County Bd. Edn., Fairmont; adminstrv. asst. Northside High Sch., Lafayette, La.; counselor North Marion High Sch., Farmington, W.Va. Mem. AAUW, NEA, ACA, Am. Sch. Counselor Assn., Assn. Specialists Group Work, Assn. Humanistic Edn. & Devel., W.Va. Assn. Counseling Assn., W.Va. Sch. Counselor Assn., Eastern Star. Home: PO Box 401 Grant Town WV 26574-0401

KURIANSKY, JUDY, television and radio talk show host, reporter, psychologist, writer, lecturer; b. N.Y.C., Jan. 31, 1947; d. Abraham and Sylvia (Feld) Brodsky; m. Edward Kuriansky, Aug. 24, 1969. BA, Smith Coll., 1968; MEd, Boston U., 1970; PhD, NYU, 1980. Reporter Sta. WABC-TV, N.Y.C., 1980-82, Sta. WBZ-TV, Boston, 1981-82, Sta. WCBS-TV, 1982-86, CBS-TV, N.Y.C., 1986-88, Sta. WPIX-TV, N.Y.C., 1987-89, Sta. CNBC-TV, Ft. Lee, N.J., 1989-93; host Total Wellness for Women program Sta. WDBB-TV, Birmingham, Ala., 1988-89; program host Sta. WABC-AM, N.Y.C., 1980-87, Sta. WOR-AM, 1987-88; temp. program host ABC Talk Radio, N.Y.C., 1988-90; host Modern Satellite Network, 1981; TV host J.C. Penney Golden Rule Network, Dallas, 1988-90; feature contbr.

Attitudes Show LifeTime, 1992-94; host Love Phones Sta. WHTZ Radio, Westwood One Radio, N.Y.C., 1992—; spokesperson Universal Studios Fla., 1993-94; cons. Lily of France, Val Mode Lingerie, Charles of the Ritz, The Rolland Co., Taylor-Gordon Arons Advt., Clairol; tchr. Columbia U. Med. Sch., 1974-79, Inst. for Health and Religion, 1980-82; adj. prof. psychology NYU, 1989-90; judge Most Unforgettable Women contest Revlon, 1990, Close-Up Rap N Roll Contest, 1993; therapy coord. Nat. Inst. for Psychotherapists, 1977-79; therapist Ctr. for Marital and Family Therapy, 1986—; v.p. Quezon Corp., 1978-79; sr. rsch. scientist N.Y. State Psychiat. Inst., 1970-78; lectr. Blanton Peale Inst., 1979-81. Author: Sex, Now That I've Got Your Attention, Let Me Answer Your Questions, 1984, How to Love a Nice Guy, 1990, Italian and Japanese transls., Generation Sex, 1995, The Complete Idiots Guide to Dating, 1996; columnist Family Circle mag., 1984-89, Whole Life Times, 1986-87, King Features Newspaper, 1984-86, N.Y. and L.I. Newsday, 1993—, Penthouse mag., 1995—, Soap Opera Update, 1995—, Telluride Daily Planet, 1995—; writer New Woman, Ad Age, Boardroom Reports, Am. Advt. Fedn. mag., Chgo. Tribune Woman News; contbg. editor Beauty Mag., 1989-90; guest editor Ladies Home Jour., 1993. Bd. dirs. Scientists Com. for Pub. Info., 1977-79; mem. adv. bd. N.Y. City Self Help Orgn., 1983-85; mem. benefits com. Mental Health Svcs. for Deaf, 1980-82. Recipient Civilian Commendation, N.Y.C. Police Dept., 1984, Cert. for Unique Pub. Svc., AWRT, 1984, Maggie award Planned Parenthood, 1985, 93, Freedoms Found. award Children for a Better Soc., 1986, Olive award Coun. of Chs., 1986, Mercury award Larimi Communications, 1987. Fellow APA; mem. Am. Women in Radio and TV (pres. N.Y. chpt. 1988-89, nat. found. vice chair 1988-90, nat. bd. treas. 1995—), Soc. Sex Therapy and Rsch. (charter), TV Acad. of N.Y. (gov. 1987-91), Friars Club.

KURONYA, CAROL GASCO, tour guide; b. Trenton, N.J., Dec. 23, 1935; d. Daniel A. and Amelia M. (Kovacs) Gasco; m. Géza Charles Kuronya, July 8, 1961; children: Kimberly Krajci, Thomas Daniel, Robert Charles. BA, Rutgers U., 1959; Tchr. Cert., Trenton State Coll., 1960. Lab. tech. N.J. State Health Dept., Trenton, 1956-59; tchr. Trenton Schs., 1959-62; owner, designer 18th Century Bouquet, Trenton, 1981-87; tour guide The Contemporary & Others, Bucks County, Pa., 1991—. Apptd. mem. Morrisville (Pa.) Econ. Devel. Corp., 1993-96; mem. edn. com. Mayor's Cultural Resource Com., Trenton, 1994—; pres. The Contemporary of Trenton, 1976-80, 96—. Mem. N.J. Children's Home Soc. (program policies chmn. 1990-93), Morrisville Bus. Assn. (pres. 1992-96), Morrisville Task Force (grant chmn. 1995—), Bucks County Children's Home Soc. Aux. (pres. 1972-74), Historic Morrisville Soc. (bd. dirs.). Home: 1230 Evergreen Rd Morrisville PA 19067

KURP, MELISSA MARIE, lawyer; b. Arlington Heights, Ill., Aug. 30, 1968. BS in Indsl. Engring., Northwestern U., 1990; JD, Loyola U., Chgo., 1994. Bar: Ill., U.S. Dist. Ct. (no. dist.) Ill. Staff cons. Anderson Consulting Co., Chgo., 1991; summer assoc. Shefsky & Froelich Ltd., Chgo., 1993, law clk., 1993-94, assoc., 1994—. Mem. ABA, Delta Gamma Chgo. Alumni Assn. Office: Shefsky & Froelich Ltd 444 N Michigan Ave Chicago IL 60611

KURTZ, DOLORES MAY, civic worker; b. Reading, Pa., Oct. 27, 1933; d. Harry Claude and Ethel Gertrude (Fields) Filbert; m. William McKillips Kurtz, Oct. 26, 1957. Cert. secretarial program, Pa. State U., 1980. Legal sec. Snyder, Balmer & Kershner, Reading, 1951-53; head teletype operator E.I. duPont de Nemours, Reading, 1953-56; exec. sec. Ford New Holland (Pa.) Inc. (formerly Sperry New Holland div. Sperry Corp.),, 1956-91, ret., 1991. Mem. Lancaster County Rep. Com., 1983-85; pres. New Holland Area Woman's Club, 1982-84; bd. dirs. Lancaster County Fedn. Women's Clubs, 1982—, 2d v.p., 1984-86, 1st v.p., 1986-88, pres. 1988-90; founding mem. Summer Arts Festival, New Holland, 1980—, bd. dirs., 1985-91; membership chmn S.E. dist. Pa. Fedn. Women's Clubs, 1984-86; bd. dirs. Community Meml. Park Assn., New Holland, 1957-82; area rep., bd. dirs. Woman's Rep. Club Lancaster County, 1982-84; committeewoman New Holland Boro 1983-85; v.p. Lancaster-Lebanon Arthritis Found. Guild, 1992, pres., 1993. Recipient Outstanding Vol. for Pa. award Pa. Fedn. Women's Clubs, 1984. Mem. Gen. Fedn. Women's Clubs Pa (conservation divsn. chmn. 1996). Methodist. Avocations: arts and crafts, travel, photography.

KURTZ, JOAN HELENE, pediatrician; b. N.Y.C., Apr. 23, 1937; d. Joseph G. and Catherine (Jacobs) Kurtz; m. Anthony M. Suriano, Oct. 15, 1960; children: Michael J., Anthony C., Catherine M. BA cum laude, NYU, 1958, MD, 1962. Diplomate Am. Bd. Pediatrics. Intern in pediatrics Bellevue Hosp., N.Y.C., 1962-63; resident in pediatrics Bronx Mcpl. Hosp. Ctr., N.Y., 1963-65; pvt. practice Carmel, N.Y., 1965-80; pediatrician Cigna Healthcare of Ariz., Phoenix, 1980—. Recipient Physicians Recognition award AMA, 1994. Fellow Am. Acad. Pediatrics; mem. Phoenix Pediatrics Soc., Phi Beta Kappa. Office: Cigna Healthcare of Ariz 12635 N 42d St Phoenix AZ 85032

KURTZ, KAREN BARBARA, writer, editor, administrator, consultant; b. Ft. Dodge, Iowa, July 21, 1948; d. Clifford Wenger and Eleanor Marie (Ulrich) Swartzendruber; m. Mark Allen Kurtz, June 25, 1977. AA, Hesston Coll., 1968; BA in Edn., Goshen (Ind.) Coll., 1970; MA in Elem. Edn., Ind. U., 1975. Lifetime cert. elem. tchr. First grade tchr. Fairfield Community Sch., Goshen, 1970-79; asst. editor and advt. copywriter Barth and Assocs., Middlebury, Ind., 1986-87; freelance writer, editor, cons. Kurtz Lens and Pen, Inc., Goshen, 1979-94, pres., 1994—; asst. dir. info. svcs. Goshen Coll., 1987-89; dir. found. rels., 1990-93; founder The Kurtz Kollection (stationery products). Author: Paper, Paint and Stuff, 1984, More Paper, Paint and Stuff, 1989; asst. editor Heritage Country Mag., 1986-87; contbr. articles to various mags. Mem. NEA, NAFE, Nat. Soc. Fund Raising Execs.$DInd. State Tchrs. Assn., Fairfield Educators Assn., Soc. Children's Book Writers and Illustrators. Republican.

KURTZ, MAXINE, personnel consultant, lawyer; b. Mpls., Oct. 17, 1921; d. Jack Isadore and Beatrice (Cohen) K. BA, U. Minn., 1942; MS in Govt. Mgmt., U. Denver, 1945, JD, 1962; postdoctoral student, U. Calif., San Diego, 1978. Bar: Colo. 1962; U.S. Dist. Ct., Colo., 1992. Analyst Tri-County Regional Planning, Denver, 1945-47; chief rsch. and spl. projects Planning Office, City and County of Denver, 1947-66, dir. tech. and evaluation Model Cities Program, 1966-71; pers. rsch. officer Denver Career Service Auth., 1972-86, dir. pers. svcs., 1986-88, sr. pers. specialist, 1988-90; pub. sector pers. cons., 1990-95, atty., 1990—, pers. and human resources cons., 1996—; expert witness nat. com. on urban problems U.S. Ho. of Reps., U.S. Senate. Author: Law of Planning and Land Use Regulations in Colorado, 1966; co-author: Care and Feeding of Witnesses, Expert and Otherwise, 1974; bd. editors: Pub. Adminstrn. Rev., Washington, 1980-83, 88-92; editorial adv. bd. Internat. Pers. Mgmt. Assn.; prin. investigator: Employment: An American Enigma, 1979. Active Women's Forum of Colo.; Denver Dem. Com.; chair Colo. adv. com. to U.S. Civil Rights Commn., 1985-89, mem. 1989—. Sloan fellow, U. Denver, 1944-45; recipient Outstanding Achievement award U. Minn., 1971, Alumni of Notable Achievement award, 1994. Mem. ABA, Am. Inst. Planners (sec. treas. 1968-70, bd. govs. 1972-75), Am. Soc. Pub. Adminstrn. (nat. council 1978-81, Donald Stone award), Colo. Bar Assn., Denver Bar Assn., Order St. Ives., Pi Alpha Alpha. Jewish. Home and Office: 2361 Monaco Pky Denver CO 80207-3453

KURTZ, MYRA BERMAN, microbiologist; b. N.Y.C., July 20, 1945; d. Milton Robert and Shirley (Letzter) Berman; m. Stuart Jacob Kurtz, Aug. 16, 1970; 1 child, Rachel Linda. AB, Goucher Coll., 1966; PhD, Harvard U., 1971. Rsch. assoc. SUNY, Albany, 1971-72; assoc. prof. microbiology Universidade Fed. de Sao Carlos, Brazil, 1972-74; rsch. assoc. Waksman Inst. Microbiology, Piscataway, N.J., 1975-76, asst. rsch. prof., 1976-82; sr. rsch. scientist E.R. Squibb & Sons, Princeton, N.J., 1982-87; sr. rsch. fellow Merck Rsch. Labs., Rahway, N.J., 1987-89, dir., 1989-95, sr. dir., 1995—; reviewer various jours. and granting orgns.; chmn. Gordon Rsch. Conf., 1992. Editor: Genetics of Candida; assoc. editor: Expl. Mycology Jour. (name changed to Fungal Genetics & Biology 1996), 1988—; contbr. articles to profl. jours. Del. Dem. Nat. Conv., Miami, Fla., 1970. Mem. AAAS, Am. Soc. for Microbiology.

KURTZ, RUTH G., lawyer; b. Forest Hills, N.Y., Nov. 18, 1950; d. Arthur and Madeline (Goldman) Goldberg; m. Robert Joseph Kurtz, June 20, 1973; children: Michael, Anne. BA, U. Rochester, 1972; JD, Columbia U., 1975. Bar: N.Y. 1976. Assoc. Tufo, Johnston, Allegaert, N.Y.C., 1976-79, Morris & McVeigh, N.Y.C., 1979-86; counsel BioRsch., Inc., Farmingdale, N.Y., 1986-95; assoc. Stapper & Van Doren, N.Y.C., 1996—. Mem. ABA, Am. Arbitration Assn. (arbitrator comml. and securities panels 1987—), Assn. of Bar of City of N.Y. (lawyer Monday Night Legal Clinic 1993-95), Phi Beta Kappa (U. Rochester chpt.). Office: Staper & Van Doren 10 Rockefeller Plz New York NY 10020

KURTZ, SWOOSIE, actress; b. Omaha; d. Frank and Margo (Rogers) K. Student, Acad. Music and Dramatic Arts, London, U. So. Calif. Appeared on TV series Mary, 1978, Love, Sidney, 1981-83 (nominated Best Actress in Comedy Series 1982-83), Sisters, 1991— (Emmy nominee Lead Actress in Drama 1993, 94, SAG award nominee 1995); (TV spls.) Uncommon Women and Others, Ah, Wilderness!, Fifth of July, The House of Blue Leaves, The Visit, Walking Through the Fire, The Mating Season; (TV films) Guilty Conscience, A Time to Live, Terror on Track 9, Baja, Oklahoma (Golden Globe nominee 1987), The Image (Emmy nominee, Ace award nominee), The Positively True Adventures of the Alleged Texas Cheerleader-Murdering Mom, And the Band Played On (Emmy award nominee 1994, Ace award nominee), Truman Capote's One Christmas, Betrayed: A Story of Three Women, A Promise to Carolyn; TV guest appearances on Kojak, Carol and Co. (Emmy award); (films) Slap Shot, 1977, The World According to Garp, 1982, Against All Odds, 1984, Wild Cats, 1986, True Stories, 1986, Vice Versa, 1988, Bright Lights, Big City, 1988, Dangerous Liaisons, 1988, Stanley and Iris, 1989, A Shock to the System, 1990, Reality Bites, 1994, The Devil Inside; (theater) Ah Wilderness!, 1975, Children, 1976, Tartuffe, 1977 (Tony award nominee), A History of the American Film, 1978 (Drama Desk award), Uncommon Women and Others, 1978 (Obie award, Drama Desk award), Fifth of July, 1980-81 (Tony award, Drama Desk award, Outer Critics Circle award), Michael Bennett's Scandal, 1985, The House of Blue Leaves, 1986 (Tony award, Obie award), Who's Afraid of Virginia Woolf, 1980, Summer, 1980, Beach House, 1986, Hunting Cockroaches, 1987 (Drama Logue award nominee), Love Letters, 1989, Six Degrees of Separation, 1990. Recipient Emmy award Outstanding Guest Performer in Comedy or Drama series. Office: The Sterling Winters Co 1900 Ave of the Stars # 1640 Los Angeles CA 90067

KURZ, KELLI MCDONALD, advertising executive; b. Torrance, Calif., Aug. 30, 1955; d. Henry James and Jimmie Lois (Manning) McDonald; m. Michael Dennis Kurz, Oct. 4, 1986. BJ with honors, Tex. Tech U., 1977. Media buyer Ranck-Ross-Moore Advt., Denver, 1977-79; media planner, buyer Tracy-Locke/BBDO Advt., Denver, 1979-81; media dir. Barnhart & Co. Advt., Denver, 1981-83; v.p., media dir. Evans/Bartholomew Pollack Norman, Denver, 1983—; pres. Evans Group, Denver, 1992—. Media liaison, mem. fund raising com. Excelsior Youth Ctr., Aurora, Colo., 1984—, Am. Lung Assn., Denver, 1984—; media coordinator, mem. mmktg. task force com. ARTREACH, Denver, 1983—. Mem. Denver Advt. Fedn. (social chmn. 1985-86, ad expo chmn. 1985-87, v.p., bd. dirs. 1986—), ADZ (chmn. membership com. 1979-82), Chi Omega, Beta Theta Pi. Republican. Methodist. Office: Evans Denver Inc Prudential Plz 1050 17th St Ste 700 Denver CO 80265-0701*

KURZWEIL, EDITH, sociology educator, editor; b. Vienna; d. Ernest W. and Wilhelmine M. (Fischer) Weiss; m. Charles H. Schmidt, June 24, 1945 (div. 1958); children: Ronald J., Vivien A.; m. Mr. Kurzweil, Aug. 2, 1958 (dec. 1966); 1 child, Allen J. B.A., Queens Coll., CUNY, 1967; M.A., New Sch. Social Rsch., 1969, Ph.D., 1973. Asst. prof. sociology Hunter Coll., N.Y.C., 1972-75, Montclair State Coll., Upper Montclair, N.J., 1973-78; assoc. prof. sociology Rutgers U., Newark, 1979-85, prof. sociology, chmn., 1985-92; Disting. Olin. Prof. Adelphi U., 1993, univ. prof., 1994—; vis. prof. Goethe U., 1984. Author: The Age of Structuralism, 1980, Italian Entrepreneurs, 1983, The Freudians: A Comparative Perspective, 1989, Freudians and Feminists, 1995; editor: The Partisan Century: 60 Years of Partisan Review, 1996, (with others) Literature and Psychoanalysis, 1983, Writers and Politics, 1983, Cultural Analysis, 1984; exec. editor Partisan Rev., Boston, 1978-94, editor, 1994—; editl. bd. Psyche, 1990—, Psychoanalytic Books, 1996—; series editor Psychiatry and Psychology, 1995. Rockefeller Humanities fellow, 1982-83, NEH fellow, 1987-88; NEH grantee, 1989-90, 91-92; NYCH grantee, 1995. Mem. Am. Sociol. Assn., Tocqueville Soc., Internat. Assn. History of Psychoanalysis, Internat. Sociol. Assn., Women's Freedom Network (bd. dirs. 1994—), P.E.N. Home: 1 Lincoln Plz New York NY 10023-7129 Office: Partisan Review 236 Bay State Rd Boston MA 02215-1403

KUSCHEL, ROBERTA DOUGLAS, architect, artist; b. Everett, Wash., Dec. 10, 1939; d. Alexander Robert Haherquist and Kathryn Havana (Jackson) Rankin; m. William Henry Fraser, Mar. 15, 1960 (div. June 1967); children: Mark William, Ian Douglas, Evan Stuart; m. Robert Herman, May 28, 1984. Student, Foothill Coll., 1959, Olympic Coll., 1961-63, U. Wash., 1964-67. Registered arch., Calif. With Daniel Mann Johnson, Honolulu, 1974; planner Marshall,Kaplan, Gans, Kahn & Yamamoto, Honolulu, 1975-80; project designer Develco Archs., Honolulu, 1980-82; arch. M & E Pacific, Honolulu, 1982-83; Michelle Belden, Arch., Palo Alto, Calif., 1988-90, Panko Archs., San Mateo, Calif., 1990-92; owner, pres. Roberta Douglas Kuschel, Arch., Redwood City, Calif., 1982-85, 92—; bd. dirs. 13th Regional Corp., Anchorage and Portland, Oreg. One-woman shows inlude Intermountain Arts, 1979, 80, 96; exhibited in group shows at Intermountain Arts, 1995; represented in pvt. collections. Chmn., mem. Commn. on Culture and Arts, Honolulu, 1975-81; pres. Friends of Agee House, Honolulu, 1978-80; bd. dirs. Laniolu Retirement Home, Honolulu, 1980-84, Sojourn Chaplaincy, San Francisco, 1995; deacon Episcopal Ch., 1984—; chaplain Stanford U. Hosp., 1989-91; mem. bishop's bd. for diaconate Episcopal Diocese of Calif., 1995—. Grantee Nat. Trust for Hist. Preservation, Honolulu, 1979. Mem. Pacific Art League. Democrat. Office: PO Box 5449 Redwood City CA 94063

KUSEK, (CAROL) JOAN, genealogist, publisher, distribution executive; b. Ottawa, Kans., Feb. 1, 1955; d. Ronald Eugene and Veda Doris (Geiss) Elliott; m. Gary Gerard Kusek, Sept. 10, 1977; children: Jacquelyn Ruth, David Michael. Student, Johnson County Community Coll., Overland Park, Kans., 1973-76, 88. Cert. geneal. records specialist. Office mgr. Lenexa (Kans.) Animal Hosp., 1973-82; journeyman, sign painter Elliott Custom Signs, Overland Park, 1982-92; owner Kusek Geneal. Svcs., Overland Park, 1985—; instr. Johnson County Community Coll., Overland Park, 1989—; researcher; contbr. gen. publs. Contbr. articles to geneal. publs. Mem. Johnson County Geneal. Soc. (pres. 1991-92), Assn. of Profl. Genealogists. Home: 9640 Walmer Lane Shawnee Mission KS 66212-1554

KUSHNER, EVE, writer, small business owner; b. Winston-Salem, N.C., Sept. 22, 1968; d. Jack and Annetta Esther (Horwitz) Kushner; m. Haroon Khalid Chaudhri, Apr. 12, 1992. Student, U. Calif., San Diego, 1988, U. London, 1988-89, U. Denver, 1990; BA summa cum laude, Dartmouth Coll., 1990. Proofreader Dharma Enterprises, Oakland, Calif., 1991-92; pres. Spruced Up Manuscripts, Berkeley, Calif., 1991—. Editor: Pleasures of the Canary Islands, 1992, Napa Wine, 1993, Social Policy, 1994, Computer Graphics, 1994, Windows 95 Fundamentals, 1996, Teaching Students with Learning and Behavior Problems, 1996. Dartmouth Gen. Award Com. fellow, 1991. Mem. NOW, Sane/Freeze, Phi Beta Kappa.

KUSHNER, MARILYN SATIN, curator; b. Chgo., Oct. 2, 1948; d. Marvin and Naomi L. (Gould) Satin; m. Richard Frank Weil, July 12, 1969 (div. 1980); children: Stephanie Weil, Daniel Weil; m. Steven Carter Kushner, June 21, 1983; children: Aviva, Hannah. BA, U. Wis., Milw., 1971, MA, 1979; PhD, Northwestern U., 1991. Rsch. asst. Whitney Mus. Am. Art, N.Y.C., 1985-87; curator of collections Montclair (N.J.) Art Mus., 1988-91; rsch. curator Whitney Mus. Am. Art, 1993-94; curator, dept. head The Bklyn. Mus., 1994—; adj. prof. Rutgers U., New Brunswick, N.J., 1993—; cons. Mary and Leigh Block Gallery, Evanston, Ill., 1993-94. Author: Morgan Russell, 1990, The Modernist Tradition in American Watercolors, 1991. Whitney Mus. Am. Art fellow, 1985. Mem. Am. Assn. Mus., Prin. Coun. Am., Coll. Art Assn., ArtTable. Home: 381 Essex Ave Bloomfield NJ 07003 Office: Bklyn Mus 200 Eastern Pky Brooklyn NY 11238-6052

KUSMIN, ELLYN SUE, music administrator; b. Boston, May 13, 1960; d. Murray and Phyllis (Nannis) K. BA, Oberlin Coll., 1982. Press assoc. Carnegie Hall, N.Y.C., 1982-83; gen. mgr. Sheldon Soffer Mgmt., N.Y.C., 1983-90; ops. mgr. N.Y. Philharmonic, N.Y.C., 1990-95; personal asst. Maestro Andre Previn, N.Y.C., 1995—; freelance cons. Boston Symphony Orch., 1982—, mgmt. fellow Nat. Endowment for the Arts, Washington, 1987. Democrat. Jewish. Home: 33 W 81st #3R New York NY 10024 Office: Manderville Enterprises 459 Columbus Ave #249 New York NY 10024

KUSSMAN, ELEANOR (ELLIE KUSSMAN), retired educational superintendent; b. Bklyn., Mar. 17, 1934; d. Mortimer Joseph and Eleanor Mary (O'Brien) Gleeson; m. Karl Kussman, June 30, 1956 (dec. Oct. 1988); children: Katherine Ann, Kristine Sue. BA, Wheaton Coll., Norton, Mass., 1955; MS, LaVerne Coll., Claremont, Calif., 1974. Cert. tchr. K-C.C., cert. in pupil pers. and adminstrn., Calif. Tchr. sci. and math. Norwood (Mass.) Jr. High Sch., 1955-56; tchr. phys. edn. Brawley (Calif.) Union High Sch., 1956-58; tchr. phys. edn. Ctrl. Union High Sch., El Centro, Calif., 1958-74, tchr. health careers, 1974-80, state and fed. project dir., 1980-85; instr. horse husbandry and equitation Imperial Valley Coll., Imperial, Calif., 1974-76; supr. Imperial Valley (Calif.) Regional Occupational Program, 1985-95; cons. E.E. Kussman Cons., El Centro, 1992—, Calif. Joint Gender Equity Com., Sacramento, 1991—, State of Calif. Gender Equity, Sacramento, 1986—; instr. program in counseling and guidance U.Calif., Redlands, 1989. Mem. fin. com. United Way, El Centro, 1987-93; sec.-treas. Pvt. Industry Coun., El Centro, 1985-95; past sec.-treas. Calif. Regional Occupational Ctrs./ Programs, 1986-88. Mem. AAUW, ASCD, Assn. Calif. Sch. Adminstrs. (past local and regional officer), Rotary Internat. (bd. dirs. 1994—), Phi Delta Kappa. Home and Office: PO Box 83 El Centro CA 92244-0083

KUSTER, DOREEN KAY, manufacturing executive; b. Amherst, Ohio, Feb. 26, 1956; d. Kenneth Edward and Doris Jean Mary (Rosenbusch) Williams; m. Richard James Kuster, Sept. 14, 1985. B.Acctg., Kent State U., 1978. CPA, Ohio; CMA. Sr. acct. gen. products divsn. Goodyear Tire & Rubber Co., Akron, Ohio, 1980-86; computer analyst Goodyear Tire & Rubber Co., Luxembourg, 1986-87; fin. analyst tire divsn. Goodyear Tire & Rubber Co., Akron, 1987-94, sect. mgr. payroll tax and acctg., 1994-95; bus. fin. mgr. Goodyear Tire & Rubber Co., Brook Park, Ohio, 1995—. Chairperson Heather Hills Woman's Club, Stow, Ohio, 1990-96. Mem. Inst. Mgmt. Accts. Republican. Methodist. Home: 1341 Whippoorwill Tr Stow OH 44224 Office: Goodyear Tire & Rubber Co 18901 Snow Rd Brook Park OH 44142

KUSTER, JANICE ELIZABETH, biology educator, researcher; b. Thunder Bay, Ont., Can., Nov. 22, 1951; d. Norman Walter Kuster and Anne Hill Allan; m. Robert J. Keenan, June 6, 1981; children: Melissa Kuster Keenan, Tyler Kuster Keenan. BSc in Biology, Lakehead U., Thunder Bay, 1973; PhD in Entomology, U. Alta., Can., 1978. Undergrad. lab. demonstrator dept. biology U. Lakehead, 1973; grad. student teaching asst. dept. entomology U. Alta., Edmonton, 1974-76, lectr., lab. coord. dept. zoology, dept. physiology, 1983-84; lectr. George Brown Coll., Toronto, Can., 1986; lectr., lab. instr. Ryerson Polytech. Inst., Toronto, Can., 1986; lab. instr. dept. biol. scis. U. Pitts., 1989-91, lectr. dept. biol. scis., 1994-95; instr. Williamson Rd. Elem. Sch., Toronto, 1992, Kerr Elem. Sch., Pitts., 1993, Boyd Cmty. Ctr., Fox Chapel, Pa., 1993, 1995; instr. Fairview Elem. Sch., Pitts., 1994-95, 1996; instr. Beechwood Farms Audubon Soc. Western Pa., 1993-95; post-doctoral rsch. fellow York U., Toronto, 1978-80, U. Alta., 1980-84; mem. edn. enhancement awards com. Fairview Elem. Sch., 1993, coord. sci. fair, 1994, chmn. great expectations, 1995-96. Contbr. articles to profl. jours. Instr. Summer Sci. Safari Camp Good Shepherd Luth. Ch., Fox Chapel, 1994, coord. Harvest Fair, 1993; mem. Integra Family House Polo com., Pitts., 1993-96. Alta. Heritage Found. Med. Rsch. fellow, 1981-84; Lakehead U. Alumni scholar, 1972, Gulf Oil Can. Ltd. scholar, 1973. Mem. AAUW (edn. com. 1992-96). Presbyterian. Home: 207 Highland Rd Pittsburgh PA 15238-2111

KUSTER, SYLVIA LEWIS, elementary school educator; b. N.C., June 28, 1947; d. James V. and Blanche (Ballance) Lewis; m. Dewey Kuster III, Sept. 30, 1972; children: Maria Lyne, Sarah Jane. BS in Edn., East Carolina U., 1970; postgrad., Georgetown Coll., 1979. Cert. tchr., N.C., Ky. Tchr. Craven County Bd. Edn., New Bern, N.C., 1970-71, 73, Myrtle Beach (S.C.) AFB Sch., 1971-73, Harrison County Bd. Edn., Cynthiana, Ky., 1974-94; elem. resource tchr. Harrison, Fayette and Bourbon County Bd. Edn., Cynthiana, Ky., 1994-96. Mem. adv. coun. Ky. Hist. Soc., Frankfort, 1991-94, Ky. Dept. Edn., 1994. Grantee South Ctrl. Bell, 1993, Harrison County Conservation Dist., 1988-94. Office: Southside Elem Sch 125 Education Dr Cynthiana KY 41031

KUTNER, JANET, art critic, book reviewer; b. Dallas, Sept. 20, 1937; m. Jonathan D. Kutner, Jan. 15, 1961. Student, Stanford U., 1955-57; BA in English, So. Meth. U., 1959. Asst. dir. Dallas Mus. Contemporary Arts, 1959-61; art critic, book reviewer Dallas Morning News, 1970—; Dallas/Ft. Worth corr. ARTnews Mag., 1975—; mem. arts adv. panel Dallas Mcpl. Libr., 1981-91; mem. adv. bd. Arts Magnet H.S. of Dallas, 1980-92; mem. adv. com. Sch. Architecture and Environ. Design, U. Tex., Arlington, 1985-87; mem. long range planning com. Dallas Mus. Art, 1985-86; mem. visual arts and architecture adv. panel Tex. Com. on Arts, 1980-82. Contbr. articles to profl. jours.; juror various art exhbns. Bd. trustees Greenhill Sch., Dallas, 1980-81. Art critic's grantee Nat. Endowment for Arts, 1976-77, art critic's fellow Nat. Gallery Art, 1991—. Mem. Am. Assn. Museums, Dallas Mus. Art, Internat. Coun. Museums, ArtTable. Office: Dallas Morning News POB 655237 Dallas TX 75265

KUTVIRT, DUDA CHYTILOVA (RUZENA), scientific translator; b. Pilsen, Czechoslovakia, Sept. 17, 1919; came to U.S., 1949; d. Frantisek and Ruzena (Vitousek) Chytil; m. Otakar Kutvirt, July 10, 1942 (dec.); children: Thomas (dec.), Daniel. BA, Smith Coll., 1940; MA, Mills Coll., 1942. Rsch. asst. U. Rochester Med. Sch., 1942-44; scientific translator Eastman Kodak Rsch. Labs., Rochester, 1944-45, 61-78. Voter registrar LWV, Albuquerque, 1980—, Rochester, 1955-70; vol. U. N.Mex. Hosp. Svc. League, Albuquerque, 1979—; mem. Albuquerque com. for fgn. affairs. Home: 5 Pool St NW Albuquerque NM 87120-1809

KUVSHINOFF, BERTHA HORNE, painter, sculptor; b. Dungeness, Wash., Aug. 29, 1915; d. Mellon Tobias and Mariamagdalena (Volnagel) Horne; m. Nicolai V. Kuvshinoff. Represented in numerous mus., pvt. and pub. collections, including Evansville (INd.) Art Mus., Miami Mus. Modern Art, Seattle Art Mus., World's Fair, Seattle, 1962-63; exhibited in group and one-woman shows in France and England. Recipient Diploma of Merit of Univ. of Arts, Univ. Delle Arti, Rome, Italy. Studio: 121 1/2 Yale Ave N Seattle WA 98109-5428

KUYKENDALL, TEMPEST ANNE, elementary education educator; b. Waverly, Iowa, Jan. 12, 1949; d. Arlo M. and Dorothy F. (Munson) Baker; m. David Erwin Kuykendall, Aug. 3, 1974; children: Carrie Anne, Cory David. BFA, Mpls. Coll. Art and Design, 1971; tchg. cert., Wartburg Coll., 1972; MA in Art and Design, Iowa State U., 1994. Lic. tchr., Iowa. Tchr. art Webster City (Iowa) Schs., 1972-78, Roland (Iowa)-Story Schs., 1979—; participant new art basics pilot program Iowa State U., Ames, 1986—, mem. new art basics adv. bd., 1989—, coop. pub. sch. art tchr. in conjunction with tchr. edn. program, 1973-77. Recipient God and Country award Girl Scouts U.S.A., Waverly, 1967. Mem. Nat. Art Edn. Assn., Iowa Edn. Assn., Art Educators Iowa (lectr., presenter state confs. 1973-94, membership chmn. 1979-81, elem. rep. 1981-83, Iowa Christmas Seals rep. 1974-75, ctrl. rep. 1976-78, Presdl. citation for outstanding svc. 1976, Iowa Elem. Art Tchr. of Yr. award 1988). Republican. Lutheran. Home: RR 1 Box 112 Roland IA 50236

KUYPER, JOAN CAROLYN, foundation administrator; b. Balt., Oct. 22, 1941; d. Irving Charles and Ethel Mae (Pritchett) O'Connor; m. L. William Kuyper, Dec. 20, 1964; children: Susan Carol, Edward Philip. BA in Edn., Salisbury State U., 1963; postgrad. Columbia U., 1978; MA in Arts Mgmt. and Bus., NYU, 1988. Elem. sch. tchr. Prince Georges County Schs., Md., 1963-68; free lance singer, opera, oratorio, chamber music Amato Opera, N.Y.C., 1967-80; owner, mgr. Privette Artists' Registry, Placement Service for Singers, Teaneck, N.J., 1969-78; exec. dir. Teaneck Artists Performing Chamber Music Series, 1975-80; program dir. Vols. in Arts & Humanities, Vol. Bur. Bergen County, N.J., 1978-81; dir. Bergen Mus. Art and Sci., 1981-83; cons. Am. Soc. Prevention Cruelty to Animals, 1984, Am. Council for the Arts, 1987; dir. ops. Isabel O'Neil Found. and Studio, 1981-85. Dir. vol. services March of Dimes Birth Defects Found. of Greater N.Y., 1985-88; dir. chpt. devel. Huntington's Disease Soc. Am., 1988-91; bd. dirs Pro Arte Chorale and adv. bd. on the arts, Teaneck, 1976-81; mgmt. cons. Girl Scouts U.S., 1992—. Mem. N.Y. Soc. Assn. Execs. (membership com. 1991-94, Cert. Assn. Execs. chair 1995-96, program planning com. 1996—), Am. Soc. Assn. Execs. (cert. 1992, 96), Assn. Mus., Mus. Coun. N.J., Am. Mktg. Assn. (bd. dirs. 1990—), Assn. for Vol. Adminstrn. (author handbook), Nat. Soc. Fund Raising Execs., Orgnl. Devel. Network, SearchNet. Democrat. Presbyterian. Clubs: Altrusa (bd. dirs. 1984-86, 90-93, 96—, pres. 1986-88), P.E.O., Phi Alpha Theta. Home: 345 W 58th St Apt 14X New York NY 10019-1142 also: 1275 Pebble Beach Rd Tobyhanna PA 18466-9119

KVETKO, NELL PATTERSON, elementary school educator; b. Ft. Lee, Va., Nov. 2, 1950; d. Alford August and Pattie Ray (Chandler) Patterson; m. James George Kvetko, Nov. 18, 1989; 1 child, Emily Caitlann. AA, Richard Bland Coll., 1970; BA, Coll. of William and Mary, 1972; MEd, Va. State U., 1989. Cert. tchr., Va. Tchr. Petersburg (Va.) Pub. Schs., 1972-75, chpt. I reading specialist, 1976-89; reading specialist Chesterfield County Pub. Schs., Chester, Va., 1989—. Mem. Delta Kappa Gamma, Phi Delta Kappa. Home: 4803 Lynbrook Ln Richmond VA 23237

KWAN, LILIAN C.H., research chemist; b. Xiamen, Peoples Republic of China, Aug. 9, 1943; d. Eugene and Meng Chin (Hwang) Chong; m. Hok Wai Kwan, July 19, 1969; 1 child, Julian G.H. BSc with hons. in Chemistry, U. Manchester Inst. Sci. Tech., Manchester, Eng., 1964, PhD in Polymer Chemistry, 1967; MS in Pharm. Chemistry, Temple U., 1977. Postdoctoral rsch. chemist Shell Rsch. Ltd., Manchester, Eng., 1968; rsch. officer Rsch. Assn. for Packaging Industries, Leatherhead, Eng., 1968-69; project mgr. Standard Packaging Corp., Clifton, N.J., 1970-73; analytical, pharm. chemist Rhone-Poulenc Rorer, Fort Washington, Pa., 1977-82; mgr. drug deliver, project leader SmithKline Beecham Animal Health, West Chester, Pa., 1982-95; pres. Innova Consulting Svcs., Ltd., Wayne, Pa., 1995—; treas. Monte Jade Sci. & Tech. Assn. of Greater Phila., Radnor, Pa., 1995-96, Bio/Pharm Sci. Divsn. Soc. Chinese Biosci. in Am., Rockville, Md., 1994. Co-inventor oral, controlled-release delivery system for animal use; contbr. various articles to sci. jours. and chpt. to book. Vis. judge Del. Valley Sci. Fair, The Franklin Inst., 1981—; vis. sci. for Vis. Sci. Program for Schs. in Phila., SmithKline Beecham Pharm., 1989-91; bd. mem. Radnor (Pa.) H.S. Scholarship Fund, 1990—. Mem. Am. Chem. Soc., Controlled Release Soc. Inst. Packaging Profls., Am. Pharm. Assn., Am. Acad. Pharm. Sci., Soc. Chem. Industry.

KWAN, MARY P., retail company executive; b. Hong Kong, Dec. 20, 1952; came to U.S., 1971; d. Rocco and Mary (Wong) Y.; m. Tony P. Kwan, June 22, 1974; children: Tammy M., Jonathan M. BS, U. San Francisco, 1974. Sr. mdse. mgr. J.C. Penney, San Francisco, 1974-83; sr. analyst Mervyn's, Hayward, Calif., 1983-84, unit control mgr., 1984-85, buyer, 1985-87, unit control dir., 1987-90, divisional mdse. mgr., 1990-92, divisional v.p., 1992-93; v.p., gen. mdse. mgr. Sears Roebuck & Co., Hoffman Estates, Ill., 1993—. Office: Sears Roebuck & Co 3333 Beverly Rd Hoffman Estates IL 60179

KWIK-KOSTEK, CHRISTINE IRENE, physician, air force officer; b. Lvov, Poland, Sept. 12, 1939; d. Karol Stanislaus and Leonarda Fryderica (Seniuk) Kostek; widowed; children: Christine, Catherine. Grad. summa cum laude, Med. Acad. Cracow, Poland, 1956-62; student primary aerospace medicine course, Brooks AFB, Tex., 1985; student chief of profl. staff course, Sheppard AFB, Tex., 1988. Diplomate Am. Bd. Emergency Medicine; cert. Bd. Internal Medicine, Poland; cert. Ednl. Coun. Fgn. Med. Grads.; recert. Extended Allergy Care Provider. Intern. Med. Acad. Cracow, Poland, 1962-63; residency in internal medicine II-Clinic of Internal Diseases, Cracow, Poland, 1963-66, staff mem., 1966-69; gen. med. officer Gen. Hosp., Sokoto, Nigeria, 1969-72; intern. Frankford Hosp., Phila., 1972-73; house physician Holy Redeemer Hosp., Meadowbrook, Pa., 1973-74; emergency room physician John F. Kennedy Hosp., Phila., 1974-76, emergency room dir., 1976-78; commd. capt. USAF Med. Corps, 1978, advanced through grades to col., 1993; emergency rm. and primary care physician USAF Clinic, Ramstein, West Germany, 1978-81; officer in charge Emergency Room and Gen. Practice Clinic, Peterson Field, Colo., 1981-84; primary care physician Malcolm Grow Med. Ctr., Andrews AFB, Md., 1984-88; chief clinic svcs. 63d Med. Group/SGH, Norton AFB, Calif., 1988-93; staff physician 60th Med. Group, Travis AFB, Calif., 1993—; asst. tchr., sr. asst. tchr. Inst. Descriptive Anatomy, Cracow, 1963-69; emergency physician on call First Aid Sta., Cracow, 1966-69. Fellow Am. Coll. Emergency Physicians; mem. AMA, Am. Coll. Emergency Physicians, World Med. Assn., Am. Coll. Physician Execs. Office: 694 Inteligence Group AIA Fort George G Meade MD 20755

KYLE, GENE MAGERL, merchandise presentation artist; b. Phila., Oct. 11, 1919; d. Elmer Langham and Muriel Heleen (Magerl) K. Student Center for Creative Studies, Detroit, 1938-45. Mdse. presentation artist D. J. Healy Shops, Detroit, 1946-50, Saks Fifth Ave., Detroit, 1950-58, J.L. Hudson Co., Detroit, 1958-84; freelance merchandise presentations for windows, Grosse Pointe, Mich., 1989—; tchr. workshop classes. Exhibited in group shows at Mich. Water Color Soc., 1944, 53, 74, Mich. Artists Exhbn., 1962, 64, Scarab Club, 1948-49, 52, Detroit Artists Market, 1946—, Michigan Gallery, 1989-92, Coach House Gallery, 1980, 90, Cmty. House, Birmingham, Mich., 1993-94, First Fed. Mich. Bank, 1994, 95. Vol. presentation work. Recipient various art awards. Mem. Detroit Inst. Arts Founders Soc., Mich. Water Color Soc., Windsor Art Gallery.

KYLE, PENELOPE WARD, state administrator, lawyer; b. Hampton, Va., Aug. 6, 1947; d. Lanny Astor and Penelope (Ward) K.; m. Charles L. Menges, Oct. 10, 1981; children: Kyle Ward, Penelope Whitley, Patricia Lee. BA, Guilford Coll., 1969; postgrad., So. Meth. U., 1969-71; JD, U. Va., 1979; MBA, Coll. William and Mary, 1987. Bar: Va. 1979, U.S. Ct. Appeals (4th cir.) 1979. Asst prof. Thomas Nelson C.C., Hampton, 1970-76; assoc. McGuire, Woods Battle & Boothe, Richmond, Va., 1979-81; assoc. counsel CSX Realty, Inc., Richmond, 1981-83, asst. v.p. and asst. to pres., 1987-89, v.p., 1989-92; asst. corp. sec. CSX Corp., Richmond, 1983-87, v.p., 1993-94; exec. dir. Va. Lottery, Richmond, 1994—. Trustee Hist. Richmond Found., 1983-94, 1st v.p., 1987-89, pres., 1989-91, chmn., 1991-93; mem. bd. visitors James Madison U., Harrisburg, Va., 1984-92; mem. Port of Richmond Commn., 1985-94; bd. dirs. Ctrl. Richmond Assn., 1988—, vice chmn., 1991-93, chmn., 1993—; mem. Indsl. Devel. Authority City of Richmond, 1990-94, vice chmn., 1991-93, chmn., 1993-94, bd. dirs. Richmond Childrens Mus., 1992—, sec., 1995—; bd. dirs. Cornerstone Realty Income Trust, 1993—; commr. Richmond Redevel. and Housing Authority, 1994—; trustee Richmond United Way, 1996—, mem. exec. com. 1996—; trustee Va. Commonwealth U. Found., 1994—. Mem. ABA, Va. Bar Assn. (pres. young lawyers conf. 1984-85, mem. coun. 1984-85), Richmond Bar Assn., Jr. League Richmond, Bear and Bull Club (bd. dirs. 1986-89, sec. bd. dirs. 1987-88), The Country Club of Va. Home: 4706 Charmian Rd Richmond VA 23226-1706 Office: Va Lottery 900 E Main St Richmond VA 23219

KYMAN, WENDY, sex therapist, health educator; b. N.Y.C., Mar. 29, 1947; d. Jack and Tess (Starman) K.; 1 child, Jesse. BS, CCNY, 1968; MS, Bklyn. Coll., 1971; PhD, NYU, 1984. Diplomate, cert. sex therapist and educator Am. Bd. Sexology. Tchr. N.Y.C. Bd. Edn., 1968-74; coord., supr. YWCA Women's Ctr., 1977-78; instr. health edn. SUNY, Old Westbury, 1980-81; instr. allied health SUNY, Nanuet, 1982; family planning counselor NYU Health Svc., N.Y.C., 1984; asst. prof. health edn. CUNY Hunter Coll., 1984-85; sr. pub. health educator Gouverneur Hosp., 1984-87; asst. prof. health edn. CUNY Baruch Coll., 1985—; pvt. practice sex therapy and sex educator, cons., N.Y.C.; teaching fellow NYU, 1980. Contbr. articles to profl. jours. Profl. Staff Congress of CUNY rsch. grantee, 1988-89. Mem. Am. Assn. Sex Educators, Counselors and Therapists (cert. sex educator), Nat. Coun. Women in Medicine, Am. Pub. Health Assn., Nat. Women's Health Network. Home: 272 6th Ave Brooklyn NY 11215-2547 Office: CUNY Baruch Coll 17 Lexington Ave New York NY 10010-5526

KYPRIOS, TINA SLOCUM, auditor; b. Schenectady, N.Y., June 1, 1967; d. Gilbert Allen Slocum and Elizabeth Ann Ford; m. Gregory P. Kyprios, Oct. 8, 1994. BBA, St. Bonaventure U., 1989. CPA. Cost analyst Met Life, Troy, N.Y., 1992-93; auditor U.S. Army Audit Agy., Fort Belvoir, Va., 1993—; regional rep. Fed. Women's Program, Alexandria, Va., 1994; cmty. tax advisor Darmstadt Mil. Com., Germany, 1992. 1st lt. U.S. Army, 1989-92. Mem. Assn. Govt. Accts., Inst. Mgmt. Accts., Inst. CPAs. Greek Orthodox. Home: 7700 Havenbrook Way Springfield VA 22153

KYRIAKOU, LINDA GRACE, communications executive; b. N.Y.C., Dec. 5, 1943; d. Frank T. and Dolores Helen (Coscia) Lagamma; m. Konstantinos G. Kyriakou, May 7, 1967; 1 child, Christina Elena. BA, Hunter Coll., 1965. Acct. exec., dir. rsch. Booke and Co., N.Y.C., 1969-75; mgr. pub. rels. CIT Fin. Corp., N.Y.C., 1975-79; dir. corp. comm. Sequa Corp., N.Y.C., 1979-88, v.p. corp. comm., 1988—. Recipient Twin award, 1985. Mem. Pub. Rels. Soc. Am., Nat. Investor Rels. Inc. (bd. dirs. 1981-82), Women's Bond Club N.Y. (bd. govs. 1978-80). Office: Sequa Corp 200 Park Ave New York NY 10166-0005

LAARTZ, ESTHER ELIZABETH, interior designer; b. Adair, Iowa, May 28, 1913; d. Christian Henry and Pearl Ethel (Hardenbrook) L. BA, Riverside Jr. Coll., 1933; grad., N.Y. Sch. Design, 1943, Parsons Sch. Interior Design, 1994. Designer, mgr. studio interior design Bloomingdales, N.Y.C., 1944-51; mgr. studio interior design Gimbel Bros., Pitts., 1951-61; pvt. practice interior design Los Angeles, 1963-70; interior designer Ross Thiele & Son, La Jolla, Calif., 1970-74, Wiseman & Gale, Scottsdale, Ariz., 1977-88; pvt. practice Phoenix, 1988—; mem. faculty Scottsdale Coll. Docent mem. Phoenix Art Mus., 1986—. Fellow Am. Inst. Interior Designers (pres. Western Pa. chpt. 1955-59, N.E. regional v.p. 1958, pres. Los Angeles chpt. 1967-69, nat. sec. 1959, regional v.p. southern Calif. 1968-70); mem. Am. Soc. Interior Designers (life). Republican. Home and Office: 811 W Indianola Ave Phoenix AZ 85013-3338

LABALME, PATRICIA HOCHSCHILD, educational administrator; b. N.Y.C., Feb. 26, 1927; d. Walter and Kathrin (Samstag) Hochschild; m. George Labalme, Jr., June 6, 1958; children: Jennifer R., Henry G., Lisa G., Victoria A. B.A. magna cum laude, Bryn Mawr Coll., 1948; M.A., Harvard U., 1950, Ph.D., 1958. Instr. history Wellesley Coll., Mass., 1952-57; tchr. history Brearley Sch., N.Y.C., 1957-59; lectr. Barnard Coll., N.Y.C., 1961-77; adj. assoc. prof. history Hunter Coll., N.Y.C., 1979; lectr. NYU, N.Y.C., 1980-82; adj. prof. history NYU, 1986-87; assoc. dir. Inst. for Advanced Study, Princeton, N.J., 1982-88; sec. corp. Inst. for Advanced Study, Princeton, 1982-92, asst. to dir., 1992—; mem. adv. bd. G. K. Delmas Found., N.Y.C., 1976-79, trustee, 1979; trustee Am. Acad. in Rome, N.Y.C., 1979—; exec. dir. Renaissance Soc. Am., N.Y.C., 1982-85, trustee, 1982-89; bd. dirs. Quantum Chem. Corp., 1990-93. Author: Bernardo Giustiniani: A Venetian of the Quattrocento, 1969; contbg. editor: Beyond Their Sex: Learned Women of the European Past, 1980, A Century Recalled: Essays in Honor of Bryn Mawr College, 1987; contbr. articles to profl. jours. and publs. Trustee Brearley Sch., 1975-83, pres., 1978-82, hon. trustee, 1983—; trustee Lawrenceville Sch., 1986-96. Recipient Caroline A. Wilby prize Radcliffe Coll., 1958. Mem. Am. Hist. Assn., Soc. for Renaissance Studies, Renaissance Soc. Am., Ateneo Veneto, Cosmopolitan Club, Harvard Club (N.Y.C.), Cream Hill Lake Assn. (West Cornwall, Conn.), Phi Beta Kappa. Office: Inst for Advanced Study Olden Ln Princeton NJ 08540-4920

LA BARE, MARTHA JANE, dean; b. Springfield, Mo., Dec. 3, 1948; d. R.L. and Floriece (Horn) La B.; m. Michael McEvoy, July 5, 1991. BA cum laude, Vanderbilt U., 1971; MA, U. Tulsa, 1975. Dir. Street Sch., Tulsa, 1972-74; developer, demonstrator Alternate Learning Project, Providence, 1974-75; program officer Bloomfield (N.J.) Coll., 1975-77, dir. programs, 1977-80, asst. dean of coll., 1980-88, assoc. dean acad. affairs, 1988-94, dean acad. affairs, 1994—, acting v.p. acad. affairs, 1995; adj. assoc. prof. NYU, N.Y.C., 1977—; cons. in field. Author: (poetry) Shooting Star and Other Poems, 1984, (chpts.) Promoting Diversity in College Classrooms, 1995. Woodrow Wilson fellow Princeton U., 1989. Mem. AAC&U, Am. Assn. Higher Edn., Acad. Am. Poets, N.J. Faculty Devel. Network, Friends of PEN, Profl. & Orgnl. Devel. NEtwork. Office: Bloomfield Coll 467 Liberty St Bloomfield NJ 07003

LABBE-WEBB, ELIZABETH GERALYN, arts administrator, theatre artist; b. Akron, Ohio, Oct. 7, 1966; d. Edward James and Ruth Carolyn (Petree) L. BA in Theatre Arts, Kent State U., 1989. Contract prodn. technician Players' Theatre Columbus, Ohio, 1989-91; asst. prodn./co. mgr. Phila. Festival Theatre, 1991-92; costume asst. Am. Music Theatre Festival, Phila., 1991-92; office asst. Players' Theatre Columbus, 1992-93; asst., audio description coord. Ohio Theatre Alliance, Columbus, 1993-94; asst. to devel. dir. Opera Assn. Ctrl. Ohio, Columbus, 1994—; freelance stage mgr., 1994—; bldg. diverse audiences panel mem., mem. artists with disability adv. com. Ohio Arts Coun., Columbus; bd. mem., corr. sec. Accessable Arts Inc., Columbus, 1993—; v.p., pres.-elect Rosebriar Shakespeare Co., Columbus, 1995—. Dep. chpt. leader, chpt. arts officer Soc. for Creative Anachronism; adv., vol. Canine Companions for Independence. Personal Devel. grantee Jefferson Ctr. for the Arts, 1994. Mem. Ohio Prospect Rsch. Network.

LABELLE, ANN D., legislative staff member; b. Chelmsford, Mass., Jan. 23, 1950. BSN, D'Youville Coll., 1970; BS in Biology, Southeastern Mass. U., 1974; MS in Health Policy and Mgmt., Harvard U., 1976; DDS, U. Md., 1983. Health svcs. cons. Johns Hopkins U. Ctr. Hosp. Fin. and Mgmt., 1980-86; sr. health policy advisor to sec. Dept. Health and Human Svcs., 1986-89; mem. staff House Ways and Means Com., Washington, 1989-90, minority health counsel, 1993—; exec. dir. Adv. Coun. Social Security, 1990-92; chief health counsel, staff dir. Senate Labor and Human Resources Com., 1992-93; now prof. staff Oversight Subcom. Office: Com Ways and Means 1136 Longworth House Office Bldg Washington DC 20515*

LABELLE, GINGER SULLIVAN, pediatric nurse practitioner; b. Jamaica, N.Y., Apr. 28, 1950; d. Thomas Robert and Betty (Steeg) Sullivan; m. James D. LaBelle (dec. 1988); children: Erin, Sean. BSN, Georgetown U., Washington, 1972; practitioner cert., U. Va., 1974. Cert. pediat. nurse practitioner. Pediat. nurse practitioner Richmond, Va., 1975-78; sr. nurse Duke Med. Ctr., Durham, N.C., 1978—. Mem. Nat. Assn. Pediat. Nurse Assocs. and Practitioners (pres. N.C. chpt. 1988-90, treas. 1990-96). Home: 413 Lochside Dr Cary NC 27511

LABELLE, PATTI, singer; b. Phila., Oct. 4, 1944; d. Henry Holte; m. Armstead Edwards; children: Zuri, Stanley, Dodd. Singer Patti LaBelle and the Bluebelles, 1962-70; lead singer musical group LaBelle, 1970-76; solo performer, 1977—. Albums include Over the Rainbow, 1967, La Belle, 1971, Moon Shadows, 1972, Pressure Cookin', 1974, Chameleon, 1976, Patti LaBelle, 1977, Live at the Apollo, 1980, Gonna Take A Miracle-The Spirit's in It, 1982, I'm in Love Again, 1984, Winner in You, 1986, The Best of Patti LaBelle, Patti, Be Yourself, Burnin', 1991, Live (Apollo Theater), 1993, Gems, 1994; appeared in films A Soldier's Story, 1985, Beverly Hills Cop, 1985; appeared in TV movie Unnatural Causes, 1986, TV series A Different World, Out All Night, 1992. Recipient award of Merit, Phila. Art Alliance, 1987.Recipient Grammy award: best Rhythm & Blues vocal for "Burnin'", 1991, Grammy nomination (Best Rhythym & Blues Female Vocal, 1994) for "All Right Now". Home: 8730 W Sunset Blvd Ph W Los Angeles CA 90069-2210 Office: care MCA Records Inc 100 Universal City Plz Universal City CA 91608*

LABODA, AMY SUE, writer; b. Phila., Sept. 10, 1962; d. Gerald and Sheila Lois (Plasky) L.; mem. Barry Lee Marz, Mar. 5, 1987; children: Rose Marie, Leah Ann. BA, Sarah Lawrence Coll., 1984. Vol. U.S. Peace Corps, Togo, 1985; flight instr., pilot Redwood Aviation, Santa Rosa, Calif., 1986, Qualiflight Tng., Ft. Worth, 1987-88; depts. editor Flying mag., N.Y.C., 1988-90; free-lance writer, mktg. cons. Ft. Myers, Fla., 1990—; mem. selection com. Am. Flyers Scholarship, Pal-Walkee, Ill., 1990-96. Cons. editor textbook series: The Pilot's Manual, 2d edit., 1993; editor: Flying Ultralights, U.S. edit., Principles of Helicopter Flight; contbr. articles to various mags. Mem. NAFE, Exptl. Aircraft Assn., Aircraft Owners and Pilots Assn., Women in Aviation (internat. exec. bd. dirs.), Women's Scuba Assn., Diver's Alert Network.

LABONNE, PATRICIA TETI, college administrator, educator; b. Chester, Pa., Jan. 5, 1948; d. Nicholas and Elizabeth (Albano) Teti; m. L. Eugene Labonne, June 21, 1969; children: Christopher, Brian, Michelle. BA in Math., U. Del., 1969; MA in C.C. Edn./Math., Glassboro (N.J.) State Coll., 1990. Systems rep./programmer Burroughs Corp., Pitts., 1969-71; math. lab. asst. Atlantic C.C., Mays Landing, N.J., 1972-73; math. lab. asst. Cumberland County Coll., Vineland, N.J., 1981, Nat. teaching fellow, 1982; acting dir. learning lab. Cumberland County Coll., Vineland, 1983, teaching asst. in math., 1983-92, prof. math., 1992—, chair math./phys. sci./tech. div., 1993—. Author: (booklet) A Guidebook to Nim's Getting Started in Electronics, 1992. Office: Cumberland County Coll College Dr Vineland NJ 08360

LABORIEL, LYN, pediatrician; b. Boston, Dec. 21, 1948; d. Patrick Francis and Madeline Rose (Webb) McCauley; m. Abraham Laboriel, Sept. 6, 1970; children: Abraham Jr., Mateo. BS, MD, Boston U., 1974. Lic. physician, Calif. Pvt. practice Tarzana, Calif., 1978-82, Burbank, Calif., 1990-94. Spl. task force L.A. County Commn. for Women, 1988-92. Mem. Calif. Profl. Soc., L.A. Pediat. Soc. Democrat. Presbyterian.

LABOUSIER, SUSAN EVELYN, choreographer, dancer; b. Boston, Mar. 25, 1954; d. Harry E. and Evelyn M. (Durant) Neeves; m. Richard L. Labousier, June 16, 1973; children: Michelle Lee, Wendy Ann. Student, MIT, Boston Conservatory, Boston Sch. Ballet, Brookline (Mass.) Ballet, Natick (Mass.) Sch. Ballet and Theatre Arts, Le Ctr. De Danse, Newton, Mass.; studies with Mme. Tatiana Ouroussoff and Pamela E. Feri; student in psychology and theatercraft, MIT, 1970-71; student, Boston Sch. Ballet, 1968-70, Natick Sch. Ballet, 1973, Le Centre de Dance, 1973-79, Edison Coll., Punta Gorda, Fla., 1995—. Cert. to teach, Dance Masters of Am., 1979, cert. for studies in prevention of dance injuries, Boston Children's Hosp., Div. Sports Medicine, 1979. Owner, dir. Susan Neeves Dance Studio, Roxbury, Mass, 1968-70, Fidelis Way Dance Workshop, Brighton, Mass., 1970-73; founder Franklin (Mass.) Dance Workshop, 1977—, Fla. Dance Workshop, 1991—. Dir./choreographer numerous Showtime prodns., 1968-92, A Family Affair, Brighton, Mass., 1970, Christmas Prodn., Franklin, 1984; choreographer The Unsinkable Molly Brown, Roxbury, Mass., 1968, The Drunkard, Franklin, 1979, My Fair Lady, South Boston, 1971, Franklin, 1987, Peter Pan, Summer Arts Sch., Pt. Charlotte, Fla., 1992, Oliver, Pt. Charlotte, 1992; choreographer, co-prodr. My Fair Lady, Pt. Charlotte, 1996. Choreographer Summerthing, Boston, 1968; dir./choreographer benefit prodn. Arthritis Found., 1983; founder, operator Susan Neeves Dance Studio, Mission Ch., Boston, 1968-70, Fidelis Way Dance Workshop, Brighton, Mass., 1970-73; model, dancer Mayor's Youth Activity Commn. Fashion Show, Boston, 1972; bd. dirs. Dance Masters Am., 1986-87; founder The Franklin Dance Co. Inc. as a charitable performing troupe, 1979—; active Franklin Arts Coun., 1986-87; founder, dir. Dance Badge Edn. Program, Girl Scouts Am., 1991—. Recipient Outstanding Citizenship award DAR, 1972, Brotherhood award Jewish War Vets. Am., 1972; recipient Award for Outstanding Performance at Boston City Hall, Mayor Kevin White, 1972. Mem. ASCAP, Charlotte County Arts & Humanities Coun., Charlotte County C. of C. Home and Office: 3357 Vassar St Port Charlotte FL 33980

LABRIE, JANET MARY, English language educator; b. Wisconsin Rapids, Wis., Nov. 12, 1942; d. Leo Joseph and Eva Marie (Liebenstein) Crotteau; children: Christopher, Lara, Sheila. BA, U. Wis., Whitewater, 1978; MA, U. Wis., 1981, Phd, 1993. Tchg. asst. U. Wis., Madison, 1983-88; assoc. lectr. U. Wis. Ctr. Rock County, Janesville, 1988-96, lectr., 1996—; mem. steering com. U. Wis. Ctr. Rock County, Janesville, 1993-95, chair design for diversity com. Contbr. articles and essays to profl. publs. Mem. MLA, NOW, Nat. Coun. Tchrs. English, Midwestern Modern Lang. Assn., Wis. Women Entrepreneurs (chair comms. Rock Valley chpt. 1995-96, mem. program com. 1993-95). Roman Catholic. Office: U Wis Ctr Rock County 2909 Kellogg Ave Janesville WI 53545

LACAS, TRACY CHRISTINE, mathematics educator; b. Bayshore, N.Y., July 13, 1971; d. Michael Edward and Rosanna Marguerite (Reid) Stapleton; m. Robert Wilfred Lacas, Jr., Nov. 26, 1994. BS in Math. and Secondary Edn., Springfield Coll., 1993. Chpt. 1 math. and reading tchr. West Springfield (Mass.) Jr. H.S., 1993-94, 7th grade math. tchr., 1994—. Mem. Nat. Coun. Tchrs. of Math. Office: West Springfield Jr HS 115 Southworth St West Springfield MA 01089

LACEBAL, CHRISTINA LEONA, accountant, financial consultant; b. San Jose, Calif., Oct. 25, 1959; d. Romualdo Estoesta Lacebal and Hattie Elizabeth (Bates) Rea; m. Alexander Mazon, Dec. 27, 1986 (div. Mar. 1994); children: Krissy Michelle Lacebal, Marissa Mazon; m. Allison Doyle Arender, Sept. 4, 1994; 1 child, Heather Marie Cuevas. AS in Acctg./Bus., Fresno City Coll.; postgrad. in Acctg./Bus., Chabot Coll., 1989-90. Corp. office mgr. Valley Grain Products, Madera, Calif., 1980-85; acctg. mgr. Saulsbury Orchards, Madera, Calif., 1985-87; purchasing mgr. Lambertson Industries, Hayward, Calif., 1988-89; staff acct. So. Wine and Spirits, Union City, Calif., 1989-91; personnel dir. Prather Meth. Homes, Alameda, Calif., 1991-92; office mgr. Tidy Bldg. Svcs., New Orleans, 1994-95; staff acct. Brorson, Kay and Stone, Dallas, 1995—. Counselor Crisis Pregnancy Ctr., Duncanville, Tex., 1996. With USN, 1992—. Republican. Mem. Ch. of God. Office: CLL and Assocs PO Box 671271 Dallas TX 75367

LACERTE, JUDITH J., social worker; b. Boston, June 2, 1943; d. Brydon Soper and Virginia (Hitchcock) Greene; m. Robert K. Lacerte, June 15, 1968 (div. 1990). BA, U. of the Pacific, 1965; MSW, Case Western Res., 1968. Lic. for ind. practice of social work, S.C.; cert. geriatric specialist S.C. Dept. Mental Health. Instr. U. Ky., Lexington, 1973-75; chief social worker Austin (Tex.) Evaluation Ctr., 1970-73; prin. tng. officer Ch. of Eng. Children's Soc., London, 1975-77; asst. prof. Ea. Wash. U., Cheney, 1978-83, assoc. prof., 1984-90, dir. alcohol/drug studies, 1989-90; family therapist Deaconess Med. Ctr., Spokane, Wash., 1983-84; clin. specialist N.C. Dept. Social Svcs., Hickory, N.C., 1990-93; team leader Home Health S.C. Health Dept., Anderson, S.C., 1993—. Contbr. articles to profl. jours. Mem. steering com., pres. Peace and Justice Action League, Spokane, 1987-90; sponsor Com. for Human Rights Inquiry, N.Y.C., 1989. Named S.C. Pub. Health Social Worker of Yr., 1995. Mem. NASW. Roman Catholic. Home: 109 Creekview Dr Clemson SC 29631 Office: Dept Health 220 McGee Rd Anderson SC 29625

LACEY, BEATRICE CATES, psychophysiologist; b. N.Y.C., July 22, 1919; d. Louis Henry and Mollie (Libowitz) Cates; m. John I. Lacey, Apr. 16, 1938; children: Robert Arnold, Carolyn Ellen. Student, Columbia U., 1935-38; A.B. with distinction, Cornell U., 1940; M.A., Antioch Coll., 1958. Mem. staff Fels Research Inst., Yellow Springs, Ohio, 1953-82; sr. investigator Fels Research Inst., 1966-72, sr. scientist, 1972-82; instr. Antioch Coll., Yellow Springs, 1956-63, asst. prof., 1963-68, assoc. prof., 1968-73, prof., 1973-82; Fels prof. psychiatry Wright State U. Sch. Medicine, 1977-82, clin. prof. psychiatry, 1982-89, Fels prof. emeritus, 1989—; acting sci. dir. Fels Research Inst., 1979-82. Assoc. editor Psychophysiology, 1975-78; reviewer Jour. Abnormal Psychology, Psychophysiology, Biol. Psychology, Cognitive Psychology, Sci.; contbr. articles to profl. jours.; researcher, author numerous publs. in psychophysiology of the autonomic nervous system. Recipient Disting. Sci. Contbn. award, Am. Psychol. Assn., 1976, Psychol. Sci. Gold Medal award, Am. Psychol. Found., 1985. Fellow Acad. Behavioral Medicine Research, Soc. Exptl. Psychologists, Am. Psychol. Soc. (William James fellow 1989); mem. Soc. Psychophysiol. Research (dir. 1972-75, pres. 1978-79), Soc. Neurosci., Phi Kappa Phi. Home: 1425 Meadow Ln Yellow Springs OH 45387-1221

LACEY, CANDACE H., school system administrator; b. N.Y.C., Jan. 14, 1949; d. Robert J. and Veronica L.; 1 child, James A. Kramer. BFA, Fla. Atlantic U., 1972; MBA, Nova U., 1982; Cert. Edn. Leadership, Barry U., 1991. Dir. mktg. AMI, Palm Beach Gardens, Fla., 1977-84; asst. prin. Msgr. Pace High Sch., Miami, 1985—; prof. St. Thomas U., Miami, 1993—, Miami-Dade C.C., 1989-94. Mem. Nat. Cath. Edn. Assn., AAUW, Nat. Assn. Secondary Sch. Prins. Roman Catholic. Office: MSGR Edward Pace High Sch 15600 NW 32 Ave Miami FL 33054

LACEY, ROBERTA BALAAM, pediatrics nurse; b. Houston, Aug. 22, 1970; d. Edwin Carnall and Clara Hideko (Fujita) Balaam; m. Wayne Robert Lacey, Dec. 31, 1991. BSN, U. Wash., 1993. RN, Wash., Hawaii; CNA, Wash.; cert. PALS. CNA Valley Health Care Ctr., Renton, Wash., 1990; clinic nurse Valley Family Practice Clinic, Renton, 1991-93; nursing unit asst. Swedish Hosp., Seattle, 1991-92, nursing technician II, 1992-93;

staff RN Kapiolani Med. Ctr. for Women and Children, Honolulu, 1993—. Mem. Sigma Theta Tau, Hui Wa'a Kaukahi Kayak Club. Democrat. Home: 1476 Begonia Pl Apt H Honolulu HI 96818-4104

LACH, ALMA ELIZABETH, food and cooking writer, consultant; b. Petersburg, Ill.; d. John H. and Clara E. (Boeker) Satorius; diplome de Cordon Bleu, Paris, 1956; m. Donald F. Lach, Mar. 18, 1939; 1 dau., Sandra Judith. Feature writer Children's Activities mag., 1954-55; creator, performer TV show Let's Cook, children's cooking show, 1955; hostess weekly food program on CBS, 1962-66, performer TV show Over Easy, PBS, 1977-78; food editor Chgo. Daily Sun-Times, 1957-65; pres. Alma Lach Kitchens Inc., Chgo., 1966—; dir. Alma Lach Cooking Sch., Chgo.; lectr. U. Chgo. Downtown Coll., Gourmet Inst., U. Md., 1963, Modesto (Calif.) Coll., 1978, U. Chgo., 1981; resident master Shoreland Hall, U. Chgo., 1978-81; food cons. Food Bus. Mag., 1964-66, Chgo.'s New Pump Room, Lettuce Entertain You, Bitter End Resort, Brit. V.I., Midway Airlines, Flying Food Fare, Inc., Berghoff Restaurant, Hans' Bavarian Lodge, Unocal '76, Univ. Club Chgo.; columnist Modern Packaging, 1967-68, Travel & Camera, 1969, Venture, 1970, Chicago mag., 1978, Bon Appetit, 1980, Tribune Syndicate, 1982; inventor: Curly-Dog Cutting Bd., 1995. Recipient Pillsbury award, 1958; Grocery Mfrs. Am. Trophy award, 1959, certificate of Honor, 1961; Chevalier du Tastevin, 1962; Commanderie de l'Ordre des Anysetiers du Roy, 1963; Confrerie de la Chaine des Rotisseurs, 1964; Les Dames D'Escoffier, 1982, Culinary Historians of Chgo., 1993. Mem. Am. Assn. Food Editors (chmn. 1959). Clubs: Tavern, Quadrangle (Chgo.). Author: A Child's First Cookbook, 1950; The Campbell Kids Have a Party, 1953; The Campbell Kids at Home, 1953; Let's Cook, 1956; Candlelight Cookbook, 1959; Cooking a la Cordon Bleu, 1970; Alma's Almanac, 1972; Hows and Whys of French Cooking, 1974; contbr. to World Book Yearbook, 1961-75, Grolier Soc. Yearbook, 1962. Home and Office: 5750 S Kenwood Ave Chicago IL 60637-1744

LACHANCE, JANICE RACHEL, federal agency administrator, lawyer; b. Biddeford, Maine, June 17, 1953; d. Ralph L. and Rachel A. (Desnoyers) L. BA, Manhattanville Coll., 1974; JD, Tulane U., 1978. Bar: Maine 1978, D.C. 1982. Staff dir. subcom. on antitrust Ho. of Reps., Washington, 1982-83; adminstrv. asst. Congresswoman Katie Hall, 1983-84; asst. pres. sec. Mondale-Ferraro Campaign, Washington, 1984; press sec. Congressman Tom Daschle, 1985; ptnr. Lachance and Assocs., Washington, 1985-87; dir. communications and polit. action Am. Fedn. Govt. Employees (AFL-CIO), Washington, 1987-93; dir. policy and communications U.S. Office Pers. Mgmt., Washington, 1993-96, chief of staff, 1996—; vis. scholar Cornell U., 1972-73. Editor newsletter Govt. Standard, 1987-93. Mem. Delta Delta Delta, Phi Alpha Delta. Democrat. Roman Catholic. Office: US Office Pers Mgmt 1900 E St NW Washington DC 20415-0001

LACHENICHT-BERKELEY, ANGELA MARIE, marketing professional; b. St. Louis, Feb. 3, 1955; d. Bernard J. and Dolores B. (Vaughn) L.; m. David L. Fuller, Sept. 6, 1974 (div. Mar. 1987); m. John Berkeley, Apr. 22, 1991. A in Bus. Adminstrn., Meremac Community Coll., St. Louis, 1983; chancellor cert., U. Mo., St. Louis, 1989; cert. of tng. in employment law, U. Mo. St. Louis, St. Louis, 1990. P.B.X. operator Arthur Enterprises, St. Louis, 1971-73; credit mgr. Watson Furniture, St. Louis, 1973-80; owner, operator Action Video World, St. Louis, 1980-85; regional telemktg. mgr. Charter Comms., St. Louis, 1985—; coord. Am. Cablevision, St. Louis, 1988; cons. Thomas Construction, St. Louis, 1987-90. Author, editor: (guide) Cencom Insider, 1989-91. Telemarketing coord. Comic Relief/Health Care for Homeless Coalition, St. Louis, 1988-92; cons. Non-Profit Employment Liaison Com., St. Louis, 1989-90. Recipient Emmy award, St. Louis chpt. NATAS, 1988, Civic Commendation, Health Care for the Homeless Coalition, St. Louis, 1989, 90, 91, 92. Mem. Women in Cable, Nat. Cable TV Assn. Democrat. Roman Catholic. Office: Charter Comms 9358 Dielman Industrial Dr Saint Louis MO 63132-2205

LACKEY, MARY MICHELE, physician assistant; b. Johnson City, N.Y., Dec. 22, 1955; d. Joseph Charles and Jane Ann (Weston) Reardon; m. Donald V. Lackey Jr., Oct. 27, 1979 (div. Nov., 1995). AAS in Nursing, Broome Community Coll., Binghamton, N.Y., 1978, cert. family nurse practitioner, Albany Med. Coll., 1982; BS in Psychology and Sociology, U. State of N.Y., Albany, 1989. Cert. physician asst., family nurse practitioner, nurse midwife; RN, N.Y., Conn. Physician asst. Streit, Hickey & Lasky MD, P.C., Saratoga Springs, N.Y., 1982-85, Litchfield Hills Ob/Gyn., Sharon, Conn., 1986-89, Foothills Family Health Ctr., Amenia, N.Y., 1991—; physican asst. Vassar Coll. Health Svcs., Poughkeepise, N.Y., 1990—. Leader, instr. Girl Scouts U.S.A., Dutchess County, N.Y., 1990—. Lt. col. U.S. Army, 1975—. Fellow Am. Acad. Physician Assts., Am. Coll. Nurse Midwives; mem. Nat. Guard Assn. U.S., Malitia Assn. N.Y., Phi Theta Kappa. Roman Catholic. Home: RR 1 Box 222 Salt Point NY 12578-9801

LACOMB-WILLIAMS, LINDA LOU, community health nurse; b. Galion, Ohio, Oct. 1, 1948; d. Horace Allen and Roberta May (Black) Braden; m. Robert Earl LaComb, Feb. 1, 1970 (div. Aug. 1984); children: Robin Marie, Patrick Alan; m. Robert Allen Williams, Aug. 30. 1991; children Erin, Megan. BSN, Capital U., 1970. RN, Fla., Ohio. Staff nurse St. Anne's Hosp., Columbus, Ohio, 1970; pub. health nurse Hillsborough County Dept. Health, Tampa, Fla., 1970-80, community health nurse supr., 1980-87; sr. community health nurse Polk County Dept. Health, Lakeland, Fla., 1987-88; sr. RN supr. Children's Med. Svcs., Tampa, 1988-91, Lakeland, 1991—. 1st lt. flight nurse res. USAF, 1971-75. Recipient Boss of Yr. award Stawberry Chpt. of Am. Bus. Women's Assn., 1985. Mem. ANA, ARC, Fla. Nurses Assn. (grievance rep. state employees profl. bargaining unit 1976-87, pres. 1984-87, 1st v.p. 1989-91, Undine Sams award 1987, Nurse of Yr. award Dist. Four 1987), Sigma Theta Tau (Delta Beta chpt.). Republican. Presbyterian. Home: 502 Shamrock Rd Brandon FL 33511-5548 Office: Children's Med Svcs 1417 Lakeland Hills Blvd Lakeland FL 33805-3200

LACY, ANN MATTHEWS, geneticist, educator, researcher; b. Boston, May 29, 1932; d. Clive Willoughby and Mona Bellingham (Matthews) L. BA in Botany, Wellesley Coll., 1953; MS in Microbiology, Yale U., 1956, PhD in Microbiology, 1959. Rsch. asst. Carnegie Inst. Washington, Cold Spring Harbor, N.Y., 1953-54; instr. genetics Goucher Coll., Towson, Md., 1959-61, asst. prof. genetics, 1961-67, assoc. prof. genetics, 1967-73, prof. genetics, 1973—, Elizabeth Connolly Todd prof., 1994—, chmn. dept. biol. sci., 1969-72, 86-87, 89, chmn. faculty natural sci. & math., 1988-91; sr. rsch. fellow U. Glasgow, Scotland, 1968-69; sr. investigator NSF rsch. grants Goucher Coll., 1960-70. Contbr. articles to profl. jours. Mem. AAAS, Genetics Soc. Am., Am. Inst. Biol. Scis., Sigma Xi. Unitarian. Office: Goucher Coll Dept Biol Scis Dulaney Valley Rd Baltimore MD 21204

LACY, CAROLYN JEAN, elementary education educator, secondary education educator; b. Marshall, Ark., Apr. 6, 1944; d. Charles Ira Bolch and Edna Rebecca Cherry; 1 child, Kelli Jean. AA with distinction, Riverside City Coll., 1980; BA, U. Calif., Riverside, 1982, postgrad., 1983; MEd, U.S. Internat. U., 1993. Cert. social sci. tchr., Calif. Educator Perris (Calif.) Elem. Sch. Dist., 1984-89, Rialto (Calif.) Unified Sch. Dist., 1989—; instr. Developing Capable People, Riverside, Calif., 1986-89; presenter, lectr. Jurupa Unified Sch. Dist., Riverside, 1990, Rialto Unified Sch. Dist., 1990; developer peer tutor program Perris Elem. Sch. Dist., 1989; dir. chess club Dollahan Elem. Sch., 1995, computer chmn., 1995—. Editor: (newsletter) Perris Lights, 1989. Active Students in Environ. Action, Riverside, 1978; mem. Riverside County Task Force for Self-Esteem. Named Mentor Tchr. State of Calif., 1988. Mem. AAUW, NEA, Calif. Tchrs. Assn., Internat. Reading Assn., U. Calif. Alumni Assn., Phi Delta Kappa, Alpha Gamma Sigma. Democrat. Mem. LDS Ch. Home: 4044 Wallace St Riverside CA 92509-6809

LACY, ELIZABETH BERMINGHAM, state supreme court justice; b. 1945. BA cum laude, St. Mary's Coll., Notre Dame, Ind., 1966; JD, U. Tex., 1969; LLM, U. Va., 1992. Bar: Tex. 1969, Va. 1977. Staff atty. Tex. Legis. Coun., Austin, 1969-72; atty. Office of Atty. Gen., State of Tex., Austin, 1973-76; legis. aide Va. Del. Carrington Williams, Richmond, 1976-77; dep. atty. gen. jud. affairs div. Va. Office Atty. Gen., Richmond, 1982-85; mem. Va. State Corp. Commn., Richmond, 1985-89; justice Supreme Ct. Va., Richmond, 1989—. Office: Va Supreme Ct PO Box 1315 100 N 9th St Richmond VA 23210

LADANYI, BRANKA MARIA, chemist, educator; b. Zagreb, Croatia, Sept. 7, 1947; came to U.S., 1969; d. Branko and Nevenka (Zilic) L.; m. Marshall Fixman, Dec. 7, 1974. BSc, McGill U., Montreal, Can., 1969; M in Philosophy, Yale U., 1971, PhD, 1973. Vis. prof. of chemistry U. Ill., 1974; postdoctoral research assoc. Yale U., 1974-77, research assoc., 1977-79; asst. prof. chemistry Colo. State U., Ft. Collins, 1979-84, assoc. prof. chemistry, 1985-87, prof. chemistry, 1987—; vis. fellow Joint Inst. for Lab. Astrophysics, 1993-94. Assoc. editor Jour. Chem. Physics, 1994—; referee and contbr. articles to profl. jours. Fellow Sloan Found., 1982-84, Dreyfus Found., 1983-87; vis. fellow JILA, 1993-94; grantee NSF, NATO, 1983-89. Mem. AAAS, Am. Chem. Soc. (PRF grantee 1979-82, 1989-91, 95—), Am. Phys. Soc., Sigma Xi. Home: 1100 E Pitkin St Fort Collins CO 80524-3909 Office: Colo State U Dept Chemistry Fort Collins CO 80523

LADAS-GASKIN, CAROL, therapist, educator, artist; b. San Bernardino, Calif., Feb. 15, 1941; d. George Haralambus and Cecelia Marie (Axdahl) Ladas; m. Stephen F. Gaskin (div. 1965); 1 child, Dana Gaskin Wenig. BA, Columbia Pacific U., Calif., 1986, MA, 1988. Reg. counselor. Clay artist Winlaw, B.C., 1973—; Progoff Intensive jour. cons. U.S. and Can., 1986—; massage practitioner, 1989—, creative process instr., 1990-94; massage instr. Brenneke Sch. Massage, Seattle, 1990—; reg. therapist integrative therapy Seattle, 1990—; integrative psychology tchr. Leadership Inst. Seattle, 1995—; dir. and founding mem. Paradise Valley New Family Soc., Winlaw, 1968—, Kootenay Boundary Artisan's Alliance, Winlaw, 1980-84. Sculptor: clay murals, 1993-95; clay artist: vases, 1980-95; poet: (poems) Metro Arts Program, various mags. Democrat. Taoist. Home: 6051 Seward Park Ave S Seattle WA 98118

LADD, DIANE, actress; b. Meridian, Miss., Nov. 29, 1943; m. Bruce Dern (div.); 1 child, Laura; m. William Shay, Jr. (div.). Grad., St. Aloysius Acad. Appearances include (films) The Wild Angels, 1966, The Reivers, 1969, Macho Callahan, 1970, Rebel Rousers, 1970, WUSA, 1970, White Lightning, 1973, Alice Doesn't Live Here Anymore, 1974, Chinatown, 1974, Embryo, 1976, The November Plan, 1976, All Night Long, 1981, Something Wicked This Way Comes, 1983, Black Widow, 1987, Plain Clothes, 1988, National Lampoon's Christmas Vacation, 1989, Wild at Heart, 1990, A Kiss Before Dying, 1991, Rambling Rose, 1991, Cemetery Club, 1992, Hold Me, Thrill Me, Kiss Me, 1992, Code Name: Chaos, 1992, Carnosaur, 1993, Father Hood, 1993, Spirit Realm, 1993, Obsession, 1994, Mrs. Milnck (also dir.), 1994, The Haunted Heart, 1995; (TV series) Alice, 1980-81; (TV movies) The Devil's Daughter, 1973, Thaddeus Rose and Eddie, 1978, Black Beauty, 1978, Willa, 1979, Guyana Tragedy: The Story of Jim Jones, 1980, Desperate Lives, 1982, Grace Kelly, 1983, I Married a Centerfold, 1984, Crime of Innocence, 1985, Celebration Family, 1987, Bluegrass, 1988, The Lookalike, 1990, Rock Hudson, 1990, Shadow of a Doubt, 1991, Hush Little Baby, 1994. Recipient award Brit. Acad., Spirit award, Golden Globe award, 3 Acad. award nominations, 4 Golden Globe nominations, Emmy nomination for Guest Actress in a Comedy Series (Grace Under Fire), 1994. Office: Abrams Artists 9200 Sunset Blvd Ste 1130 Beverly Hills CA 90069*

LADD, MARCIA LEE, medical equipment and supplies company executive; b. Bryn Mawr, Pa., July 22, 1950; d. Edward Wingate and Virginia Lee (McGinnes) Mullinix; children: Joshua Wingate, McGinnes Lee. BA, U. Pa., 1972; MEd, U. Va., 1973; MA, Emory U., 1979. Rsch. assoc. N.C. Tng. and Standards Coun., Raleigh, 1973-75; dir. counseling svc. N.C. State Youth Svcs. Agy., Raleigh, 1975-76; acad. dean Duke U., Durham, N.C., 1976-77; prin. Ladd & Assocs. Mgmt. Cons., Chapel Hill, N.C., 1979-88; v.p. adminstrn. CompuChem Corp., Research Triangle Park, N.C., 1988-91; v.p. mktg. Prentke Romich Co., Wooster, Ohio, 1991-94; v.p. ops. Exec. Staffing Svcs., Inc., Cary, N.C., 1994; pres., CEO, owner Triangle Aftercare, Durham, N.C., 1994—. Bd. dirs. Wayne County Arts Coun., Wooster, 1992, Stoneridge/Sedgefield Swim/Racquet Club, Chapel Hill, N.C., 1985-88, Oakwood Hist. Soc., Raleigh, 1981-84; mem. bd. visitors Carolina Friends Sch., Durham, 1986-89; Stephen min. Univ. Presbyn. Ch., Chapel Hill, 1994—, youth group leader, 1995—. Decorated Order of Long Leaf Pine Gov. of N.C., 1976. Presbyterian. Office: Triangle Aftercare 249 W Hwy 54 Durham NC 27713

LADD-POWELL, ROBERTA KAY, horsebreeder, marketing executive; b. Clearwater Beach, Fla., July 24, 1953; d. F. Robert and Marguerite Elizabeth (Ethier) Ladd; m. Michael Moore Powell, Jan. 13, 1992. BA in Indsl. Pyschology, Calif. State U., Long Beach, 1975. Lic. seminar facilitator. Sales trainer western region GTE Directories Corp., Los Alamitos, Calif., 1977-84; breeder, mktg. dir. Liberty West Arabians, Calif., 1978—; dir. mktg., tng. and promotions Guam Cable TV, Yellow Pages Ink, 1990-94; mktg. & advt. sales mgr. Marianas Cablevision, Tamuning, Guam, 1994—. Pub. Desert Horse Directory, 1984-86; editor Arabian Horse Jour., 1982-83, Animal Air Transport mag., 1988-89; contbr. articles to trade jours. and newspapers. Dir. promotions Ride Across Am. Benefit, Tucson, 1988-89; fund raiser Rainforest Action Network, San Francisco, 1988-89; supporter Orange County Riders, 1980-81, Therapeutic Riding Orgn. Tucson, 1988-89. Mem. NAFE, Internat. Arabian Horse Assn. (conf. del. 1987, 88), Am. Horse Shows Assn., Arabian Racing Assn. Calif. (Top 10 Arabian Race Mare award for LWA Khlassy Lady 1988, region 2 res. Champion Mare 1989, Can. Top 20 Mare 1989), Arabian Jockey Club (vice chmn., mem. exec. com. 1988—), So. Ariz. Arabian Horse Assn. (racing chmn. Tucson chpt. 1988-89), Sierra Pacific Arabian Racing Coun. (pres. 1987-88), Guam Equestrian Fedn. (bd. dirs. 1990-93), Hawaii Combined Tng. Assn., Arabian Horse Registry, U.S. Dressage Fedn., Cable TV Advt. & Mktg. Methodist. Home and Office: 1270 N Marine Dr #101-154 Tamuning GU 96911

LADEN, SUSAN, publisher, consultant; b. Washington, Aug. 3, 1942; d. Louis and Irene (Berenter) Sherman; m. Ben E. Laden, Aug. 16, 1964; children: Francine, Jonathan, Paul. AB, Vassar Coll., 1964. Caseworker Dept. Welfare, Balt., 1964-66; publ. Biblical Archaeology rev., Washington, 1976-94, Bible rev., Washington, 1984-94, Moment mag., Washington, 1987-94; pres. Laden & Assocs., 1994, Jewish Family & Life, Washington, 1996—, Rejevenation, Inc., 1995—; bd. dirs. Portfolio Travel, Washington. Treas. Lafayette Home and Sch. Assn., Washington, 1973-75; v.p. Jewish Ednl. Ventures, Boston, 1987-94; sec. Jewish Coun. for the Aging, Rockville, Md., 1992-94, treas., 1994; sec.-treas., Bibl. Archeology Soc., 1977-94. Democrat. Home and Office: Jewish Family Life 3111 Rittenhouse St NW Washington DC 20015-1614

LADIGES, LORI JEAN, learning disabilities specialist; b. Sheboygan, Wis., Feb. 25, 1956; d. Donald William and Marion Margaret (Henning) L. BS in Edn., U. Wis., 1978; MA in Learning Disabilities, Cardinal Stritch Coll., 1984. Cert. tchr. elem. (grades 1-8), Cognitive disorders (K-12) and learning disabilities (K-12). Learning disabilities specialist Kohler (Wis.) Pub. Sch., 1978—; part-time instr. Silver Lake Coll., Manitowoc, Wis., 1984-92; tchr. Cardinal Stritch Coll., Milw., 1989, adj. asst. prof., 1996—; sch. evaluation consortium chair spl. edn. Kohler Pub. Schs., 1989—, learning disabilities specialist, rep. long-range planning com., 1992—, cheerleading advisor, 1981-84, yearbook advisor, 1985-86; reviewer Sch. Evaluation Consortium, 1995, adj. asst. prof., Cardinal Stritch Coll. Mem. Sch. to Work com., Alpha Sigma (Grace Alvord award 1978). Lutheran. Home: 2236 N 23rd St Sheboygan WI 53083-4443

LADNER, ANN-MARIE CALVO, special education educator; b. Hartford, Conn., Feb. 6, 1949; d. Vincent J. and Mary S. (Santangelo) Calvo; m. R. Martin Ladner, June 19, 1971; children: Mary-Lorraine Amy Cox, R. Vincent, Michelle A. AS, Belleville Area Coll., 1983; BS in Speech and Theater, So. Ill. U., Edwardsville, 1985, MS in Edn., 1986; EdS, Auburn U. Montgomery, 1993. Cert. specific learning disabilities, Ala., psychometrist, Ala., sch. adminstr., Ala. Tchr. merchandising Skadron Coll. Bus., San Bernardino, Calif., 1981-82; tchr. English as second lang. Turkish-Am. Assn., Ankara, Turkey, 1986; tchr. speech and computers Ozel Atilim Lisesi, Ankara, 1987-88; tchr. English and reading St. Jude H.S., Selma, Ala., 1989-90; tchr. spl. edn. Selma Sch. Dist., 1990-92, Montgomery (Ala.) County Schs., 1992-93, 95—, Dept. Youth Svcs., Jemison, Ala., 1993-95. Libr. bd. dirs. City of Millbrook, Ala., 1992-94; bd. dirs. Turkish-Am. Assn., Ankara, 1987-88, Millbrook YMCA, 1993—; judge, coach Nat. Forensics League, Belleville, Ill., 1985. Named Competent Toastmaster, Toastmasters Internat., 1985; mini-grantee Montgomery Area Comty. Found., 1992. Mem. NEA, ASCD, Coun. Exceptional Children, Nat. Coun. Tchrs. Math., Ala. Edn. Assn., Mensa, Kappa Delta Pi. Home: 200 River Oaks Dr Apt 1D Wetumpka AL 36092 Office: Project Upward Madison Park Alt Sch Montgomery AL 36110

LADUKE, NANCIE, lawyer, corporate executive; b. Mayfield, Ky.; m. Daniel E. LaDuke, 1978. BA, Wayne State U., 1962; JD, U. Detroit, 1976. Pvt. practice Detroit, 1976; atty. KMart, Troy, Mich., 1977-84, comml. law counsel, 1984-90, v.p., sec., 1991—. Office: KMart Corp 3100 W Big Beaver Rd Troy MI 48084-3004

LADUKE, WINONA, activist; b. L.A., 1959; d. Vincent and Betty Bernstein; m. Randy Kapashesit (div.); children: Waseyabin, Aajuawak. Diploma, Harvard U.; attended, MIT; MA, Antioch Coll. Activist, founder White Earth (Minn.) Land Recovery Project. Office: White Earth Land Recovery Project PO Box 327 White Earth MN 56591*

LADWIG, PATTI HEIDLER, lawyer; b. Harleysville, Pa., Aug. 28, 1958; d. L. Donald and Joan E. (Wright) Heidler; m. Manfred Friedrich Ladwig, July 30, 1983; 1 child, Brittney Nichole. BA in Psychology, U. Miami, 1980, JD, 1988. Bar: Fla. 1988, U.S. Dist. Ct. (so. dist.) Fla. 1988. Assoc. atty. Taplin, Howard & Shaw, West Palm Beach, Fla., 1988-92; ptnr. Shaw, St. James, & Ladwig, West Palm Beach, Fla., 1992, St. James & Ladwig, P.A., West Palm Beach, Fla., 1992-93; pvt. practice Patti Heidler Ladwig, P.A., West Palm Beach, 1993—; bd. dirs. Cmty. Assns. Inst., West Palm Beach, First Wellington, Inc.; mem. condominium and planned devel. com., real property, probate and trust law sect. Fla. Bar. Pres., bd. dirs. Treasure Coast Communities Assn., West Palm Beach, 1990—, Pine Lake Condominium Assn. Inc., Pembroke Pines, Fla., 1986-88; mem. community appearance com. ACME Improvement Dist., Wellington, Fla., 1990—, Condominium Owners Fla., 1991—, Fedn. Mobile Home Owners Fla., 1990—; del. Fla. Legis. Action Com., 1989-91. Mem. Fla. Bar Assn. (bus. law sect., mem. condominium and planned devel. com. real property, probate and trust law sect.). Lutheran. Office: Ste 640 1645 Palm Beach Lakes Blvd West Palm Beach FL 33401-2216

LAETHEM, FERN MELODY, lawyer; b. N.Y.C., Jan. 11, 1946; d. Herbert Irving and Cherie Claire (Stern) Lifton; m. Robert Malcolm Segal, Oct. 8, 1980 (div.); children: David Benjamin Laethem, Jared Matthew Laethem. BA in Econs., CUNY, 1968; JD, U. of the Pacific, 1976. Bar: Calif., 1976. Dep. dist. atty. Dist. Atty.'s Office, Sacramento, 1976-79; asst. U.S. atty. U.S. Atty.'s Office, Sacramento, 1979-80; pvt. practice Sacramento, 1981-89; state pub. defender of Calif. Office of the State Pub. Defender, Sacramento, 1989—; co-chair Justice and Technology Forum, Sacramento, 1994-96; adv. bd. Citizen and Law-Related Edn. Ctr., Sacramento, 1995-96. Active Cub Scouts Am., Sacramento, 1994-96. Recipient Profl. Achievement award McGeorge Sch. of Law Alumni Assn., 1989. Mem. Calif. Coun. on Criminal Justice (bd. dirs. 1989—), Calif. Pub. Defenders Assn., Nat. Legal Aid and Defender Assn., Calif. Justice Coun. Democrat. Jewish. Office: Office of the State Pub Defender 801 K St # 1100 Sacramento CA 95814

LAFAVE, LEANN LARSON, lawyer; b. Ramona, S.D., May 31, 1953; d. Floyd Burdette and Janice Anne (Quist) L.; m. Richard Curtis Finke, May 19, 1973 (div. Jan. 1978); 1 child, Timothy; m. Dwayne Jeffery LaFave, May 31, 1981 (div. 1992); children: Jeffrey, Allison. BS, U. S.D., 1974, JD with honors, 1977. Bar: S.D. 1977, U.S. Dist. Ct. S.D. 1977, U.S. Ct. Appeals (8th cir.) 1977, N.D. 1978, U.S. Dist. Ct. N.D. 1978. Asst. atty. gen. State of S.D., Pierre, 1977-78, 79-81; assoc. Bjella, Neff, Rathert & Wahl, Williston, N.D., 1978-79, Tobin Law Offices, P.C., Winner, S.D., 1981-83; assoc. dean, asst. prof. U. S.D. Sch. Law, Vermillion, 1983-86, dir. continuing legal edn., 1983-89, assoc. prof. law, 1986-89; ptnr. Aho & LaFave, Brookings, S.D., 1990-91; pvt. practice Brookings, 1991-92; asst. U.S. atty. U.S. Dist. S.D., 1992—; mem. S.D. Bd. Pardons and Paroles, 1987-90, chmn., 1989-90; comml. arbitrator Am. Arbitration Assn., 1985—; prof. Kilian C.C. Contbr. articles to profl. jours. Mem. planning coun. Nat. Identification Program for Advancement Women in Higher Edn. Adminstrn., Am. Coun. on Edn., S.D., 1984-90; bd. dirs. Mo. Shores Women's Resource Ctr., Pierre, 1980, W.H. Over Mus., Vermillion, 1986-87, S.D. Vol. Lawyers for Arts, 1987—, Brookings Interagy. Coun., 1990-91, Brookings Women's Ctr., 1990-94; sec. Mediation Ctr., Inc. Named S.D. Woman Atty. of Yr. Women in Law U. S.D., 1985. Mem. S.D. Bar Assn. (bd. govs. young lawyers sect. 1983-84), S.D. Mediation Assn., Epsilon Sigma Alpha (S.D. coun. sect. 1985-86). Republican. Episcopalian. Home: 1808 S Jefferson Ave Sioux Falls SD 57105-2415 Office: PO Box 5073 Sioux Falls SD 57117-5073

LA FEVER, LYNNE ANNE, human services administrator; b. East Lansing, Mich., Dec. 18, 1964; d. Carl Hale and Sharon Lynne (Feller) Mensing; m. Michael James La Fever, May 16, 1987 (dec. 1990). BA in Broadcasting, U. Wyo., 1986, BA in Psychology, 1989; MEd in Counseling, U. N.H., 1992. Youth specialist N.H. Job Tng. Coun., Concord, 1992—; cons. Optima Day Spa, Newmarket, N.H., 1994—. Active Dover (N.H.) Sch. to Career Partnership, 1994—. Mem. Rotary. Methodist. Office: NH Job Tng Coun Dover HS Alumni Dr Dover NH 03820

LAFFERTON, MACKIE V. (MAKKI V. LAFFERTON), artist; b. Gallina, N.Mex., Dec. 11, 1933; d. Jose Melquiades and Maria Ruperta (Serrano) Valdez; m. Henry Imre Lafferton, July 31, 1959 (div. Dec. 1983); children: Sandra Marie, Henry James, Jacqueline Margit. Student, N.Mex. State U., 1977, 82, San Juan Coll., 1983, 84, Art Masters Acad., Albuquerque, N. Mex., 1995. Owner, mgr. Bloomfield (N.Mex.) Plumbing and Heating, Inc., 1971-83, Central Apts., Bloomfield, 1981-93, Makki Fine Art Studio, Albuquerque, 1995—; mem., fundraiser Bloomfield C. of C., 1972-84. Tailor, designer ready-made clothing (numerous awards 1971-80); artist: represented in private and pub. collections throughout the U.S. and abroad; in permanent collections: Multi-Cultural Ctr. of Bloomfield, N. Mex., Cath. Social Svcs. of Albuquerque, Casa Esperanza, Inc., Albuquerque, Salmon Ruins Mus., Bloomfield; exhbns. and awards include: Portraiture and figurative painting and drawings: 1st prize, Farmington, N. Mex., 1987, numerous shows at the Civic Ctr. of Farmington, N. Mex., 1993, People's Choice award, N. Mex. Art League, Albuquerque, 1995, Hon. Mention Maro Polo Art Exhibit, Nairobi, Kenya, 1995, Jurors Selection award of recognition Minature Arts Bardean, Albuquerque, 1996, 25th Nat. Small Painting Exhibition Jurors Selection N. Mex. Art League, Albuquerque, 1996. Mem. N.Mex. Watercolor Soc. (mem. social com. 1995-96), N.Mex. Art League (mem. hanging com. 1995-96), Knickerbocker Artists, Pastel Soc. N. Mex. Republican. Roman Catholic. Home and Studio: Makki Fine Art Studio 6128 Alderman Dr NW Albuquerque NM 87120-5415

LAFFERTY, BEVERLY LOU BROOKOVER, retired physician, consultant; b. Newark, Ohio, Aug. 15, 1938; d. Lawrence William and Rosie (Rey) Brookover; B.S., Ohio State U., 1959, M.D., 1963; diplomate Am. Bd. Family Practice; children—Marla Michele, William Brookover, Wesley Voris, Latour Rey. Intern Grant Hosp., Columbus, Ohio, 1963-64; practice medicine, West Union, Ohio, 1964-75, Sun City Center, Fla., 1975-79, Brandon, Fla., 1979-95; mem. staff Adams County Hosp., v.p., 1971-72, chief of staff, 1973-75; mem. staff Humana Hosp., Brandon, 1977-95, chmn. dept. family practice, 1984-86, hosp. trustee, 1984-92, chief of staff elect, 1986-88, chief of staff, 1988-90; physician adv. utilization mgmt. dept. South Bay Hosp., Sun City Ctr., Fla., 1995—. Mem. AMA, Fla., Hillsborough County med. assns., Am. Acad. Family Physicians, Fla. Acad. Family Physicians, Alpha Lambda Delta, Alpha Epsilon Iota, Alpha Epsilon Delta (sec. 1958-59). Home: 3913 John Moore Rd Brandon FL 33511-8020

LAFILI, ELLEN YOST See YOST, ELLEN G.

LAFLEUR, AMANDA ROZAS, counselor; b. Eunice, La., Jan. 31, 1940; d. Stewart P. and Florence (Fontenot) R.; m. Gary J. Lafleur, Aug. 18, 1962; children: Gary Jr., Michelle, Holly, Claire. BBA, St. Mary's Dominican Coll., 1961; MEd in Counseling, La. State U., 1980. Lic. profl. counselor, La. Head dept. counseling St. Edmund High Sch., Eunice, 1981-89; sexuality educator Diocese of Lafayette, La., 1987-89; pvt. practice Altanta, 1989—. Speaker Diocese of Baton Rouge Youth Rally, 1989; founder Gold Card program, 1986. Mem. Am. Sch. Counselors Assn., AACD (conv. presenter 1988), Nat. Bd. Cert. Counselors, La. Profl. Counselors Bd. Republican. Roman Catholic. Office: 3379 Peachtree Rd NE Ste 800 Atlanta GA 30326-1020

LAFON, CHARLOTTE ANNE, art educator; b. Welch, W.Va., Mar. 7, 1951; d. Charles LeRoy and Georgia Anne (Mullins) Byrd; m. Charles Willard LaFon, Sept. 6, 1970; children: Shane, Todd. BA in Art Edn., Marshall U., 1984, MFA, 1989. Cert. art tchr., W.Va. Elem. art tchr. Spring Hill Elem. Sch., Huntington, W.Va., 1985-86, 89—; art tchr. Lincoln Jr. High Sch., Huntington, 1986-87; traveling elem. art tchr. Cabell County, Huntington, 1987-89; art tchr. Marshall U. Children's Coll., Huntington, 1987-90, Marshall U. Art Opportunity, 1988-90; art cons. for tchrs. Lawrence County Bd. Edn., Ironton, Ohio, 1993; art tchr. Acad. of Excellence Ohio U., Ironton, 1994-95; co-owner LaFon's Window Cleaning, South Point, Ohio, 1974—. Jr. Sunday sch. tchr. LDS Ch., Huntington, 1968-87, active, 1964—; cub scout leader Boy Scouts Am., Huntington, 1981-88, co-program dir. cub scout day camp, Barboursville, W.Va., 1984-85. Mem. Huntington Mus. Art, Nat. Art Edn. Assn., W.Va. Art Edn. Assn., NEA, W.Va. Edn. Assn., Delta Kappa Gamma. Home: 4694 County Rd 15 South Point OH 45680-9618 Office: Spring Hill Elem Sch 1901 Hall Ave Huntington WV 25701-3938

LAFORS, JEANETTE RENÉE, secondary school educator; b. Rutherford County, Tenn., May 19, 1969; d. Kary René and Nanette Keener (Hebert) LaF. BA in Am. Studies with distinction, Stanford U., 1991, MA in Edn. in Secondary Tchg., 1992. Cert. tchr. social studies, Calif.; cert. in rape trauma svcs., San Mateo County. Tchr. social studies Carlmont H.S., Belmont, Calif., 1991—; advisor Jr. State of Am. Orgn., advisor peer helping program, mem. governing coun., 1996—; intern N.J. Dept. Edn., Trenton, 1989, Office of Rsch., U.S. Dept. Edn., Washington, 1989; cons. Edn. and Human Resources Directorate AAAS, 1990-91; mem. rev. panel of vol. nat. history stds. Coun. for Basic Edn., 1995; panelist on gender equity in schs. AAUW, 1993; co-condr. workshop series Cross-Cultural Lang. Acquisition and Devel., 1992; presenter, participant various workshops and confs. in field. Sexual assault counselor San Mateo County, 1993—; vol. tutor literacy project Stanford U., 1989-91; coach girls' soccer Carlmont H.S., 1993-95. Andrew Mellon scholar Stanford U., 1989-92. Democrat. Office: Carlmont HS 1400 Alameda de las Pulgas Belmont CA 94002

LAFOUNTAIN, JEANNE KAY, nurse; b. Defiance, Ohio, Sept. 26, 1953; d. Paul Albert and Mary Ann (Hanlin) Dobbelaere; m. Michael Thomas LaFountain; children: Courtney Marie, Danielle René. ADN, Purdue U., Ft. Wayne, Ind., 1974; BS, Eastern Ill. U., Charleston, 1993. RN, Ohio; CNOR, cert. nurse 1st asst.; cert. ACLS, basic cardiac life support instr. Office nurse Dr. Gerald Huber, Defiance, Ohio, 1974-75; indsl. health nurse Gould Inc., Napoleon, Ohio, 1975-77; supr. Putnam Regional Health, Continental, Ohio, 1978-81; office nurse, surg. asst. Oral & Maxillofacial Surgeons N.W. Ohio, Defiance, 1981-84; perioperative nurse Defiance Hosp., 1984-86; first asst., perioperative nurse Carle Found. Hosp., Urbana, Ill., 1986-94, Doctors Hosp. N., Columbus, Ohio, 1994; nurse 1st asst. Grady Meml. Hosp., Delaware, Ohio, 1994—; RN 1st asst. John D. DeWalt, 1996—; cons., coord. Inst. RN first asst. program, Columbus State Coll., 1994—; item reviewer Nat. Cert. Exam Nat. Cert. Bd.-Perioperative Nursing Inc., Denver, 1994. Lector St. Patrick's Ch., Tolono, Ill., 1988-94. Mem. ABA, Assn. Oper. Rm. Nurses (bd. dirs. local chpt. 1992-93, pres. 1990-92, v.p. 1994—, governing coun. RN first asst. specialty assembly 1992—, adv. panel RN first asst. task force 1992, nat. chair RN first asst. specialty assembly), Am. Heart Assn. (cardiovasc. sci. coun. 1993—), Alpha Sigma Lambda. Roman Catholic. Home: 537 Pollyanna Dr Delaware OH 43015-9393 Office: Dr John D DeWalt 100 W Third Ave Columbus OH 43201

LAFOUREST, JUDITH ELLEN, editor, publisher, lecturer, writer, educator; b. Indpls., Jan. 10; d. Edward Elston and Dorothy Jeanette (Parker) LaFourest; BA, Ind. U.-Purdue U., Indpls., 1972; MAT, Ind. U., 1980; m. William E. Lugar; children: Beth Anne Gruner, Paul Christopher Stewart Pitts Lugar LaFourest. Lead pre-vocat. instr., ednl. adminstr. Opportunities Industrialization Ctr., Indpls., 1972-76; part-time English and human rels. instr. Profl. Careers Inst., Indpls., 1975-78; editor, pub. Womankind, Indpls., 1977-83; co-dir. Womankind Ctr., 1981-82; editor, creative writer, photographer Bio-Feed-Back Bio Dynamics/BMC, Indpls., 1977-80; mem. assoc. faculty, creative writing inst. and composition Ind. U.-Purdue U., Indpls., 1979-87, supr. student tchrs. of English, 1983-89; adj. faculty dept. English, Butler U., 1984-95; also lectr., free-lance editor. Editor The Pen Woman, 1994-96. Ind. sec. NOW, 1978-80. Campaign mgr. Jill Chambers for Ind. State Senator Dist. 30, 1996. Recipient Disting. Alumni award Ind. U.-Indpls., 1980; Jessamyn West scholar. Mem. Nat. League Am. Pen Women (Ind. br., co-pres. 1990-92, pres. 1992-94, nat. 2nd v.p. 1994-96, 1st v.p. 1996—), Ind. U.-Indpls. Liberal Arts Alumni Assn. (pres. 1982), Sigma Tau Delta. Office: Nat League Am Pen Women 1300 17th St NW Washington DC 20036-1973

LAFRAMBOISE, JOAN CAROL, middle school educator; b. Bklyn., June 23, 1934; d. Anthony Peter and Nellie Eva (Zaleski) Ruggles; m. Albert George Laframboise, Aug. 5, 1961; children: Laura J., Brian A. BS in Edn., Springfield (Mass.) Coll., 1956. Cert. tchr. social sci., and mid. sch.; cert. tchr. support specialist. Tchr. Meml. Jr. H.S., Wilbraham, Mass., 1956-61, Midland Park (N.J.) Jr./Sr. H.S., 1961-63, Luke Garrett Middle Sch., Austell, Ga., 1983-93; tchr. lang. arts Pine Mountain Middle Sch., Kennesaw, Ga., 1993—. Coun. pres. Knights of Lithuania, Westfield, Mass., 1973-75, Holyoke, Mass., 1975-76, New Eng. dist. pres., 1976-77; mem. Wistariahurst Mus. Assocs., Holyoke, 1975-77. Jr. League mini-grantee, 1991. Mem. ASCD, NEA, Ga. Assn. Educators, Cobb County Assn. Educators, Nat. Coun. Tchrs. English, Nat. Coun. Social Studies. Home: 2891 Dara Dr Marietta GA 30066-4009

LAGANGA, DONNA BRANDEIS, sales and marketing executive; b. Bklyn., June 27, 1949; d. Sidney L. and Sylvia (Herman) Brandeis; B.S. in Bus. Edn., Central Conn. State Coll., New Britain, 1972, M.S., 1975; m. Thomas LaGanga, Aug. 11, 1974. Various secretarial positions, 1969-72; tchr. bus. Lewis S. Mills Regional High Sch., Burlington, Conn., 1972-78; cons. nat. accounts Southwestern Pub. Co., Pelham Manor, N.Y., 1978-84, dist. sales mgr., 1984-89; pres. DBL Industries, Inc., 1989—; nat. accounts mgr. South-Western Pub. Co., Cin., 1989-93, from sr. sales and mktg. mgr. to nat. career sch. mgr., 1993-95; dir. admissions and records Tunxis Cmty. Tech. Coll., Farmington, Conn., 1995—; v.p. adminstrv. svcs. Human Resource Devel. Assocs., 1996—; co-owner Colonial Welding Svc.; seminar condr., 1980—; pres. DBL Industries, Inc. Mem. adv. bd. secretarial sci. dept. LaGuardia Community Coll., Long Island City, N.Y., 1982—; adv. bd. Krissler Bus. Inst. EDPA grantee, 1973; mem. non-partisan ednl. reform task force Pres. George Bush; cert. profl. sec. Mem. NAFE, Assn. Info./Systems Profls., Am. Mgmt. Assn., Nat. Bus. Edn. Assn., Profl. Secs. Internat., Eastern Bus. Edn. Assn., Conn. Bus. Edn. Assn., New Eng. Bus. Edn. Assn., Profl. Secs. Assn. N.Y., Nat. Assn. Cert. Profl. Secs., U.S. Golf Assn., Delta Pi Epsilon. Avocations: knitting, sewing, reading, bicycling, golf. Home: 2929 Torringford St Torrington CT 06790-2332

LAGORIA, GEORGIANNA MARIE, curator, writer, editor, visual art consultant; b. Oakland, Calif., Nov. 3, 1953; d. Charles Wilson and Margaret Claire (Vella) L.; m. David Joseph de la Torre, May 15, 1982; 1 child, Mateo Joseph. BA in Philosophy, Santa Clara U., 1975; MA in Museology, U. San Francisco, 1978. Exhbn. coordinator Allrich Gallery, San Francisco, 1977-78; asst. registrar Fine Arts Mus., San Francisco, 1978-79; gallery coordinator de Saisset Mus., Santa Clara, Calif., 1979-80, asst. dir., 1980-83, dir., 1983-86; dir. Palo Alto (Calif.) Cultural Ctr., 1986-91; ind. writer, editor and cons. mus. and visual arts orgns., Hawaii, 1991-95; dir. The Contemporary Mus., Honolulu, 1995—; V.p. Non-Profit Gallery Assn., San Francisco, 1980-82; bd. dirs. Fiberworks, Berkeley, Calif., 1981-85; field reviewer Inst. Mus. Services, Washington, 1985-87; adv. bd. Hearst Art Gallery, Moraga, Calif., 1986-89, Womens Caucus for Art, San Francisco, 1987—; mem. adv. bd. Weigand Art Gallery, Notre Dame Coll., Belmont, Calif. Curator exhbns. The Candy Store Gallery, 1980, Fiber '81, 1981; curator, author exhbn. catalogue Contemporary Hand Colored Photographs, 1981, Northern Calif. Art of the Sixties, 1982, The Artist and the Machine: 1910-1940, 1986; author catalogue, guide Persis Collection of Contemporary Art at Honolulu Advertiser, 1993; co-author: The Little Hawaiian Cookbook, 1994; coord. exhbn. selections Laila and Thurston Twigg-Smith Collection and Toshiko Takaezu ceramics for Hui No'eau Visual Arts Ctr., Maui, 1993; editor Nuhou (newsletter Hawaii State Mus. Assn.), 1991-94; spl. exhbn. coord. Honolulu Acad. Arts, 1995; dir. The Contemporary Mus., Honolulu, 1995—. Mem. Arts Adv. Alliance, Santa Clara County, 1985-86; grant panelist Santa Clara County Arts Council, 1987. Exhbn. grantee Ahmanson Found., 1981, NEA, 1984, Calif. Arts Coun., 1985-89. Mem. Am. Assn. Mus., ArtTable, 1983—, Calif. Assn. Mus. (bd. dirs. 1987-89), Hawaiian Craftsmen (bd. dirs. 1994-95), Honolulu Jr. League, Key Project (bd. dirs. 1993-94). Democrat. Roman Catholic. Home and Office: 47-665 Mapele Rd Kaneohe HI 96744-4918

LAGRANGE, CLAIRE MAE, special education educator; b. Tarkio, Mo., Oct. 11, 1937; d. Floyd Gerald and Phyllis Geneva (Wilson) McElfish; m. Irving Joseph LaGrange, May 20, 1955; children: Raymond, Robert, Rhonda, Roger. BA, U. Southwestern La., 1983; MEd, Northwestern State U., 1990. Cert. English, spl. edn., K-12 mild and moderate, assessment tchr., libr. sci., La. Tchr.'s aide St. Martin Parish Sch. Bd., Cecilia, La., 1979-82; tchr. English Florien (La.) High Sch., 1984-86; tchr. Zwolle (La.) High Sch., 1986-90, Cecilia Jr. High Sch., 1990-92, Cecilia High Sch., 1992—. Den mother Cub Scouts-Boy Scouts Am., Spokane, Wash., 1967-69; Sunday sch. tchr. First Friends Ch., Spokane, 1968-69. Fellow U. S.W. La Alumni Assn., Northwestern State U. Alumni Assn.; mem. ASCD, Coun. Exceptional Children, Nat. Educators Am., Nat. English Honor Soc., Internat. Reading Assn., La. Assn. Educators, La. Ednl. Assessment Tchrs. Assn., La. Reading Assn., St. Martin Assn. Educators. Home: 1052 Charles Marks Rd Arnaudville LA 70512-3820

LAGRONE, ELIZABETH WOODFORD DUFFY, psychotherapist; b. Washington, Jan. 15, 1952; d. Douglas M. and Betty (Minor) Duffy; m. Don Michael LaGrone, Jan. 27, 1990. BS with distinction, U. Ariz., 1974; M Degree, U. Md., 1976. Lic. master social worker advanced clin. practitioner, marriage and family therapist, chem. dependency counselor, profl. counselor; cert. chem. dependency specialist. Clin. dir. HCA, Houston, 1979-93; program dir. Kelsey-Seybold Clinic, Houston, 1993—. Mem. Tex. Assn. Partial Hospitalization Assns. (sec. 1992-94), Mental Health Assn. Ft. Bend County (sec. 1991-93, adv. coun. 1993—). Office: Kelsey-Seybold Clinic 5757 Woodway Ste 180 Houston TX 77057

LAGRONE, LAVENIA WHIDDON, chemist, real estate broker; b. Conroe, Tex., Feb. 27, 1940; d. James Lewis and Cora Lee (DeLuish) Whiddon; A.A., Kilgore Coll., 1960; B.S., North Tex. State U., 1962; grad. med. tech. Baylor U. Med. Center, 1962; m. Doyle W. LaGrone, June 26, 1959 (div. Sept. 1965); 1 child, Russell Randal. Sr. technologist in spl. chemistry Baylor U. Med. Center, Dallas, 1962-63; research chemist, supr. labs., cardiovascular surgery Southwestern Med. Sch., Dallas, 1964-69, Upstate Med. Center, SUNY, Syracuse, 1969-70; research assoc., supr. lab., dept. surgery U. Tex. Med. Br., Galveston, 1970-74, research assoc., supr. labs., pediatric nephrology, 1974—, mem. chem. safety com., 1984-87; real estate broker DeLanney & Assocs., realtors, 1979-83; owner La Grone & Assocs., Realtors, 1983—. Chmn. student activities PTA Galveston, Tex., 1976-77. Recipient Top Real Estate Sales award, Top Real Estate Producer award, DeLanney & Assocs., 1979, also named Broker's Excellence award and Top Real Estate Commn. award, 1980, also Million Dollar Producer 1980-91. Mem. Am. Soc. Clin. Pathologists (registered med. technologist), Nat. Assn. Realtors, Tex. Assn. Realtors, Galveston Bd. Realtors, Multiple Listing Service (budget com., MLS com.), Phi Theta Kappa. Club: Bus. and Profl. Women's (pub. relations officer 1985-86, chmn. Young Careerist Award 1987, chmn. Woman of Yr. Award 1989, scholarship com. 1988). Contbr. articles to chemistry and med. jours. Home: 142 San Fernando Dr Galveston TX 77550-5712 Office: U Tex Med Br 301 University Blvd Galveston TX 77550-2708

LAHAYE, BEVERLY, cultural organization administrator. Pres. Concerned Women for Am., Washington. Office: Concerned Women For America 370 L'Enfant Promenade SW Ste 800 Washington DC 20024*

LAHIFF, MARILYN J., nursing administrator; b. Youngstown, Ohio; d. Jack L. and Lila J. (Webb) Mills; m. Lawrence C. Lahiff, Apr. 26, 1974. AAS, Lorain County C.C., Elyria, Ohio, 1973; student, Youngstown U., 1960-61. RN, Fla., Ohio; lic. rehab. svc. provider, Fla.; cert. rehab. nurse, cert. ins. rehab. specialist, cert. case mgr. Team leader pediatrics Lakewood (Ohio) Hosp., 1973-75; adminstr. Upjohn HealthCare Svcs., Reno, N.Y., 1977-78, 83-84; occupational health/sch. nurse Medina (Ohio) County Achievement Ctr., 1979-83; regional mgr. Beverly Enterprises, Torrance, Calif., 1984-87; program mgr. RehabCare Corp., Cleve., 1988-89; supr. med./vocat.rehab Feisco, Sarasota, Fla., 1989-92; cons., med. case mgmt. Riscorp, Sarasota, 1993-94; chief operating officer Prime Managed Care Svcs., Inc., Sarasota, 1994—. Mem. editl. bd. Directions in Rehab. Counseling, 1994. Mem. Assn. Rehab. Nurses, Fla. State Assn. Rehab. Nurses, Phi Theta Kappa. Home: 18 Stonesthrow Way Englewood FL 34223-1939

LAHTI, CHRISTINE, actress; b. Detroit, Apr. 5, 1950; d. Paul Theodore and Elizabeth Margaret (Tabar) L.; m. Thomas Schlamme, Sept. 4, 1983; 1 child, Wilson Lahti. BA in Speech, U. Mich., 1972; postgrad., Fla. State U., 1972-73; studies with William Esper, Uta Hagen, Herbert Berghof Studios. Actress: (stage prodns.) The Woods, 1978 (Theater World award 1979), Division Street, 1980, Loose Ends, 1981, Present Laughter, 1983, Landscape of the Body, 1984, The Country Girl, 1984, Cat on a Hot Tin Roof, 1985, Little Murders, 1987, The Heidi Chronicles, 1989, Three Hotels, 1993; regular mem. cast (TV series) Dr. Scorpion, 1978, The Harvey Korman Show, 1978, Chicago Hope, 1995—, (TV films) The Last Tenant, 1978, The Henderson Monster, 1980, The Executioner's Song, 1982, Single Bars, Single Women, 1984, Love Lives On, 1985, Amerika, 1987, No Place Like Home, 1989, Crazy from the Heart, 1991, The Fear Inside, 1992, The Good Fight, 1985, The Four Diamonds, 1995, (feature films) And Justice For All, 1979, Whose Life Is It, Anyway?, 1981, Swing Shift, 1984 (N.Y. Film Critics Circle award for best supporting actress 1985, Acad. award nominee 1985, Golden Globe award nominee 1985), Ladies and Gentlemen: The Fabulous Stains, 1985, Just Between Friends, 1986, Housekeeping, 1987, Season of Dreams, 1987, Stacking, 1988, Running on Empty, 1988, Gross Anatomy, 1989, Miss Firecracker, 1989, Funny About Love, 1990, The Doctor, 1991, Leaving Normal, 1992, Hideaway, 1995, Pie in the Sky, 1995, A Weekend in the Country, 1996; prodr. short action film, actress: Lieberman in Love, 1995 (Acad. award nominee for best live action short film 1996). Recipient Golden Globe award for Best Actress in a Miniseries or Motion picture Made for TV. Office: ICM 8942 Wilshire Blvd Beverly Hills CA 90211*

LAIKIND, DONNA, psychotherapist, consultant; b. N.Y.C., Oct. 29, 1944; d. Charles and Eleanor (Boyarsky) Ressler; m. Jeffrey Laikind, June 29, 1969; children: Rachel Kate, Daniel Aaron. BA, Cornell U., 1965; MS in Counseling, Bank St. Coll. Edn., 1984; cert. in family therapy, Ackerman Inst. Family Therapy, 1990. Behavioral trainer McDermott & Assocs., N.Y.C., 1982-84; dir. orgnl. devel. Altro Health and Rehab., N.Y.C., 1985-86; family therapy cons. Family Dynamics, N.Y.C., 1987-90; psychosocial cons. Food Allergy Ctr., N.Y.C., 1990-91; family therapy cons. SCAN, N.Y.C., 1990—; pvt. practice N.Y.C. and Weston, Conn., 1987—; co-dir. The Marriage Ctr.; dir. Family Dynamics Inc., 1985—, chmn., bd. dirs, 1990-94; guest lectr. workshops in field. Contbr. articles to profl. jours. Bd. dirs. U.S. Com. Sports for Israel, Maccabiah Games, N.Y.C., 1990—, mission dir., 1989, Ackerman Inst. Family Therapy, 1991-96, chmn. bd. 1996—. Address: 37 Cedar Hls Weston CT 06883-2948

LAINCZ, BETSY ANN, nurse; b. Phila., Feb. 7, 1949; d. Harry Ellsworth and Betty Mary (Minton) Henderson; m. Douglas Dardaris, 1968 (div. 1975); children: Amy, Christopher; m. Fred J. Laincz, Jan. 12, 1982; children: Joshua, Emily, Michael. Student, Bucks County C.C., Newtown, 1969-87, Temple U., Phila., 1973, Upper Bucks Sch. of Nursing, Perkasie, 1983, Internat. Sch. of Shiatsu, Doylestown, 1995-96. Lic. practical nurse, Pa. Staff nurse, mental health technician Doylestown (Penn.) Hosp., 1983-85, data abstractor med. records, 1988-89; nurse, coun., asst. mgr. NutriSystem, Warrington, Penn., 1985-88; nurse Independence Court, Quakertown, Pa., 1991; health svcs. supr. Bucks County Assn. Retarded Citizens, Quakerstown, 1992-95; owner, operator Complimentary Healing Arts Agency, Perkasie, Pa., 1996—; supports and standards com. Bucks County Assn. Retarded Citizens, 1995. Mem. United Friends Sch. (fundraising chair 1989—; nominating com., 1995-96; ann. audition com. 1990—; devel. com, 1991-92); mem. Individual's Person Centered Planning Team, 1994—; mem. Inst. of Noetic Scis., 1993—. Mem. Buck Womens Investment Club (v.p. 1995), Moon Lodge, The Smithsonian Instn., Libr. of Congress Assn., Nat. Assn. of Investers Corp. Republican. Mem. United Ch. Christ. Home: 532 W Market St Perkasie PA 18944

LAINE, KATIE MYERS, communications consultant; b. Bluffton, Ohio, Oct. 2, 1947; d. George Emerson and Elanore (Keeney) Myers; m. Donald Edward Laine (div. Feb. 1990); 1 child, Brett Edward. BS in Edn., S.W. Tex. State U., 1970. Dir. vols. Austin (Tex.) Ctr. for Attitudinal Healing, 1983-86; talk show host Austin Cablevision, 1986-89; community rels. officer Laguna Gloria Art Mus., Austin, 1989-90; spl. events mgr. Ann Richards for Gov. Campaign, Austin, 1990—. Profl. TV talk show host Katie Laine and Friends. Mem. Mayor's Adv. Coun., Austin, 1989—, Austin Women's Polit. Caucus, 1989—, Emily's List, 1989—; vol. Mayor Lee Cooke Campaign, 1988, Ann Richards Campaign for Gov., 1989; tchr. Divorce Recovery Clinic. Mem. NOW, Women in Communications, Nat. Assn. for Corp. Speaker Activities, Paramount Producers. Home: 8703 United Kingdom Dr Austin TX 78748-6400 Office: Katie Laine Comms 8703 United Kingdom Austin TX 78748

LAING, BEVERLY ANN, sports administrator; b. Newark, Mar. 13, 1959; d. Gustave Raymond Hicks and Gloria Mildred (Bellina) Hicks-Prestinari; m. James Thomas Laing Sr., Mar. 10, 1979; children: Christina Marie, James Thomas Jr. A degree, Lab. Inst. Merchandising, N.Y.C., 1979. Pension adminstr. Prudential Ins. Co., Florham Park, N.J., 1976-79; paralegal O'Donnell, Kennedy, Esqs., West Orange, N.J., 1986-90, Greenberg, Mellinger, Esqs., Morris Plains, N.J., 1991; asst. mgr. U.S. Golf Assn., Far Hills, N.J., 1991—, mgr. women's adminstrn. and competitions; apptd. to steering com. Women in Golf Summits, LPGA Hdqs., Daytona Beach, Fla., 1996—. Vol. player registration Children's Miracle Network for golf tournament, 1992. Recipient 1st pl. ribbon N.J. Ceramic Show, 1984. Mem. U.S. Golf Assn., Exec. Women's Golf League. Republican. Roman Catholic. Office: US Golf Assn Golf House Liberty Corner Rd Far Hills NJ 07931

LAING, KAREL ANN, magazine publishing executive; b. Mpls., July 5, 1939; d. Edward Francis and Elizabeth Jane Karel (Templeton) Hannon; m. G. R. Cheesebrough, Dec. 19, 1959 (div. 1969); 1 child, Jennifer Read; m. Ronald Harris Laing, Jan. 6, 1973; 1 child, Christopher Harris. Grad., U. Minn., 1960. With Guthrie Symphony Opera Program, Mpls., 1969-71; account supr. Colle & McVoy Advt. Agy., Richfield, Minn., 1971-74; owner The Cottage, Edina, Minn., 1974-75; salespromotion rep. Robert Meyers & Assocs., St. Louis Park, Minn., 1975-76; cons. Webb Co., St. Paul, 1976-77, custom pub. dir., 1977-89; pres. K.L. Publs., Inc., Bloomington, Minn., 1989—. Contbr. articles to profl. jours. Community vol. Am. Heart Assn., Am. Cancer Soc., Edina PTA; charter sponsor Walk Around Am., St. Paul, 1985. Mem. Bank Mktg. Assn., Fin. Instn. Mktg. Assn., Advt. Fedn. Am., Am. Bankers Assn., Direct Mail Mktg. Assn., St. Andrews Soc. Republican. Presbyterian. Office: KL Publs 2001 Killebrew Dr Minneapolis MN 55425-1865

LAING, PENELOPE GAMBLE, art educator; b. Dallas, July 24, 1944; d. William Oscar and Beth (Robertson) G.; m. Richard Harlow Laing, June 29, 1970; children: Scott Emerson, Lindsey Elizabeth. BA in Art, N. Tex. State U., 1966; MFA, Edinboro State Coll., 1979. Cert. tchr., Tex. (life), N.C. (Art all-level). Art cons. Lawrence (Kans.) Unified Sch. Dist., 1966-68; instr. art Ball State U., Muncie, Ind., 1969-71, Edinboro (Pa.) State U., 1976-77, Pitt C.C., Greenville, N.C., 1980-83; exec. dir. Pitt-Greenville Arts Coun., Greenville, 1983-84; free-lance designer, 1984-90; art tchr., head dept. art Pitt County Schs., 1990—; seminar participant N.C. Ctr. for Advancement of Teaching, 1993, tchr.-scholar, 1994, 95. Bd. dirs., v.p. Pitt-Greenville Arts Coun., 1979-82; mem. adv. bd. Pitt County Schs., Greenville, 1985-87; pres. PTA S. Greenville Sch., 1986-87. Named fellow Tchr. Exec. Inst., Pitts County Edn. Found., Greenville, 1992; grantee Pitt County Edn. Found., 1991, 92, 93. Mem. Nat. Art Edn. Assn., N.C. Art Edn. Assn. (bd. dirs., chmn. elem. divsn. 1992-94), Surface Design Assocs. (N.C. rep.), Phi Delta Kappa. Democrat. Home: 204 Pineview Dr Greenville NC 27834-6434 Office: 1325 Red Banks Rd Greenville NC 27858-5315

LAING-MALCOLMSON, SALLY ANNE, enrolled tax agent, tax consultant; b. Seattle, Sept. 25, 1957; d. Ian Laing-Malcolmson and Frances Rutherford (Arold) Cook; children: Rhiannon Ethel Quandt, Peter Eugene Stone, Benjamin Elliott Stone. AS in Bus., SUNY, 1989. With accounts payable dept. King County Airport, Seattle, 1984-86; bookkeeper Driftmeir Architects, P.S., Kirkland, Wash., 1986; pvt. practice tax cons. Bellevue, Wash., 1987—; tax specialist Puget Sound Nat. Bank, Tacoma, 1990-92; bookkeeper Papillon, Inc.; sec. Washington State Tax Cons., Bellevue, 1991—, Am. Bus. Women's Assn., Bellevue, 1992—. Active Word of His Grace Fellowship, PTA, newsletter editor, 1991—. Mem. Pentecostal Ch. Home and Office: 3170 Kinsler Ln Stevensville MT 59870

LAIOU, ANGELIKI EVANGELOS, history educator; b. Athens, Greece, Apr. 6, 1941; came to U.S., 1959; d. Evangelos K. and Virginia I. (Apostolides) Laios; m. Stavros B. Thomadakis, July 14, 1973; 1 son, Vassili N. B.A., Brandeis U., 1961; M.A., Harvard U., 1962, Ph.D., 1966. Asst. prof. history Harvard U., Cambridge, Mass., 1969-72, Dumbarton Oaks prof. Byzantine history, 1981—; assoc. prof. Brandeis U., Waltham, 1972-75; prof. Rutgers U., New Brunswick, N.J., 1975-79, disting. prof., 1979-81; chmn. Gennadeion com. (Am. Sch. Classical Studies), Athens, Greece, 1981-84; dir. Dumbarton Oaks, 1989—. Author: Constantinople and the Latins, 1972, Peasant Society in the Late Byzantine Empire, 1977, Mariage, amour et parenté à Byznace, XIe-XIIIe siècles, 1992, Gender, Society and Economic Life in Byzantium, 1992, Consent and Coercion to Sex and Marriage in Ancient and Medieval Societies, 1993. Guggenheim Found. fellow, 1971-72, 79-80, Dumbarton Oaks sr. fellow, 1983-88, Am. Coun. Learned Socs. fellow, 1988-89. Fellow Am. Acad. Arts and Scis., Medieval Acad.; mem. Am. Hist. Assn., Medieval Acad. Am., Societa Ligure di Storia Patria, Greek Com. Study of South Eastern Europe. Office: Dumbarton Oaks 1703 32nd St NW Washington DC 20007-2934

LAIPSON, HANNAH KARP, retired English language educator; b. Haverhill, Mass., Apr. 27, 1925; d. Edward Baruch and Inda (Kelce) Karp; m. Myron Ralph Laipson, Sept. 18, 1946; children: Deborah Payne, Ellen, Adam. BA in English, Colby Coll., 1946; MA in English, Assumption Coll., 1968. Lectr. in English U. Mass., Amherst, 1947; instr. English Worcester (Mass.) Jr. Coll., 1968, Assumption Coll., Worcester, 1968-71; from asst. prof. to assoc. prof. to prof. English Quinsigamond C.C., Worcester, 1971-91; cons. New Eng. Bd. Higher Edn., 1977, Butler County (Pa.) C.C., 1983; project dir. NEH grants, Worcester, 1979-82. Co-author: Research Papers, Plain and Simple, 1992; author: (book chpt.) Writing Across Curriculum in Community Colleges, 1991. State chair Common Cause, Boston, 1993-95; founder's group, v.p. Worcester Inst. for Sr. Edn., 1994-96; alumni coun. Colby Coll., Waterville, Maine, 1991-96; exec. com. bd. dirs. Jewish Family Svc. Worcester, 1977—. Recipient Mary Tobin award for leadership and women's advocacy Mass. Assn. Women Deans, Adminstrs. and Counselors, 1990. Mem. NEA, Nat. Coun. Tchrs. English, Mass. Tchrs. Assn., Jewish Family Svc. (bd. dirs., exec. com. 1977—), Coun. Jewish women (v.p. edn. 1957-59, co-pres. 1960), Phi Beta Kappa. Democrat. Jewish. Home: 25 Pomona Rd Worcester MA 01602

LAIRD, JEAN ELOUISE RYDESKI (MRS. JACK E. LAIRD), author, adult education educator; b. Wakefield, Mich., Jan. 18, 1930; d. Chester A. and Agnes A. (Petranek) Rydeski; m. Jack E. Laird, June 9, 1951; children: John E., Jayne E., Joan Ann P., Jerilyn S., Jacquelyn T. Bus. Edn. degree Duluth (Minn.) Bus. U., 1948; posgrad. U. Minn., 1949-50. Tchr. Oak Lawn (Ill.) High Sch. Adult Evening Sch., 1964-72, St. Xavier Coll., Chgo., 1974—; lectr., commencement address cir. Writer newspaper column Around The House With Jean, A Woman's Work, 1965-70, Chicagotown News column The World As I See It, 1969, hobby column Modern Maturity mag., travel column Travel/Leisure mag., beauty column Ladycom mag., Time and Money Savers column Lady's Circle mag., consumerism column Ladies' Home Jour. Mem. Canterbury Writers Club Chgo. (past. pres.), Oak Lawn Bus. and Profl. Women's Club (Woman of Yr. award 1987), St. Linus Guild, Mt. Assisi Acad., Marist, Queen of Peace parents clubs. Roman Catholic. Author: Lost in the Department Store, 1964; Around The House Like Magic, 1968; Around The Kitchen Like Magic, 1969; How To Get the Most From Your Appliances, 1967; Hundreds of Hints for Harrassed Homemakers, 1971; The Alphabet Zoo, 1972; The Plump Ballerina, 1971; The Porcupine Story Book, 1974; Fried Marbles and Other Fun Things To

Do, 1975; Hundreds of Hints for Harassed Homemakers; The Homemaker's Book of Time and Money Savers, 1979; Homemaker's Book of Energy Savers, 1981; also 348 paperback booklets. Contbr. numerous articles to mags. Home: 10540 Lockwood Ave Oak Lawn IL 60453-5161 also: 1 Magnificent Mile Bldg Chicago IL 60600 also: Vista De Lago Lake Geneva WI 53147

LAIRD, MARY See WOOD, LARRY

LAJINESS-POLOSKY, DANINE THERESA, psychiatric-mental health nurse, pediatric nurse; b. Toledo, Oct. 16, 1961; d. Ambrose Joseph and Sharon Joyce (Montrie) Lajiness; m. John Daniel Polosky III, Apr. 21, 1990. BSN, U. Detroit-Mercy, 1984; student, U. Toledo, 1988, Med. Coll. of Ohio, 1988; MN, U. Phoenix, 1994. Cert. psychiat.-mental health; RN cert. Adult psychiat. nurse St. Charles Hosp., Oregon, Ohio, 1984-87; adult psychiat. clin. instr. Med. Coll. of Ohio, Toledo, 1987-88; crisis unit supr. New Rescue Crisis Svcs., Toledo, 1987-88; adult med. nurse Mercy-Meml. Hosp., Monroe, Mich., 1988; child pscyhiat. nurse Charter Hosp. of Aurora (Colo.), 1989-90, asst. dir. nursing, 1990; pediatric float nurse Children's Hosp., Denver, 1991, clin. coord. After Hours Care Program, 1991-95; v.p. quality improvement Six County, Inc., Zanesville, Ohio, 1995—. Republican. Roman Catholic.

LAKAH, JACQUELINE RABBAT, political scientist, educator; b. Cairo, Apr. 14, 1933; came to U.S., 1969, naturalized, 1975; d. Victor Boutros and Alice (Mounayer) Rabbat; m. Antoine K. Lakah, Apr. 8, 1951; children: Micheline, Mireille, Caroline. BA, Am. U. Beirut, 1968; MPh, Columbia U., 1974, cert. Mid. East Inst., 1975, PhD, 1978. Assoc. prof. polit. sci. and world affairs Fashion Inst. Tech., N.Y.C., 1978—, asst. chairperson social scis. dept., 1989-95, chairperson social scis. dept., 1995—; asst. prof. grad. faculty polit. sci. Columbia U., N.Y.C., summer 1979, vis. scholar, 1982-83, also mem. seminar on Mid. East; guest faculty Sarah Lawrence Coll., 1981-82; cons. on Mid. East; faculty rsch. fellow SUNY, summer 1982. Fellow Columbia Faculty, 1970-73, NDEA Title IV, 1971-72; Mid. East Inst. scholar, 1976; Rockefeller Found. scholar, 1967-69. Mem. European Cmty. Studies Assn., Am. Polit. Sci. Assn., Fgn. Policy Assn., Internat. Studies Assn., Internat. Polit. Sci. Assn. Roman Catholic. Home: 41-15 94th St Flushing NY 11373-1745 Office: 7th Ave At 27th St New York NY 10001-5992

LAKE, KATHLEEN C., lawyer; b. San Antonio, Jan. 11, 1955; d. Herschel Taliaferro and Virginia Mae (Hylton) Cooper; m. Randall Brent Lake, Apr. 9, 1977; 1 child, Ethan Taliaferro. AB magna cum laude in Polit. Sci. with high honors, Middlebury Coll., 1977; JD with high honors, U. Tex., 1980. Bar: Tex. 1980, U.S. Ct. Appeals (5th cir.) 1981, U.S. Ct. Appeals (D.C. and 3d cirs.) 1984. Assoc. atty. Vinson & Elkins, Houston, 1980-88; ptnr. Vinson & Elkins, LLP, Houston, 1989—. Mem. pack com., den leader Sam Houston Area Coun.-Golden Arrow dist. Boys Scouts Am., 1993— . Recipient Unit Svc. award Sam Houston Area Coun.-Golden Arrow dist. Boy Scouts Am. Fellow Tex. Bar Found., Houston Bar Found.; mem. ABA, Fed. Energy Bar Assn., State Bar Tex., Tex. Law Rev. Assn. (life), Houston Bar Assn., Middlebury Coll. Alumni Assn. (com. mem. 1980—), Phi Beta Kappa, Phi Kappa Phi, Order of the Coif. Office: Vinson & Elkins LLP 2300 First City Twr 1001 Fannin St Houston TX 77002-6760

LAKE, RICKI, talk show host, actress; b. N.Y.C., Sept. 21, 1968. Syndicated talk show host Ricki Lake. Movie appearances include: Hairspray, 1988, Working Girl, 1988, Cookie, 1989, Cry-Baby, 11990, Last Exit to Brooklyn, 1989, Where the Day Takes You, Inside Monkey Zetterland, Skinner, Cabin Boy, Serial Mom, Mrs. Winterbourne; TV appearances include (series) China Beach, 1990, Kate and Allie, Fame, (spls.) A Family Again, 1988, Starting Now, 1989, Gravedale High, 1990, (movies) Babycakes, 1989, The Chase, 1991, Basedon an Untrue Story, (pilot) Starting Now; stage actress: A Girl's Guide to Chaos, 1990, (off-Broadway) The Early Show, Youngsters, 1983. Office: Entrada Prodns 401 Fifth Ave 7th Fl New York NY 10016*

LAKE, SUZANNE PHILENA, singer, teacher; b. Palisade, N.J., June 26, 1929; d. Mayhew Lester and Suzanne Louise (Robin) L.; m. George A. De Vos, Nov. 19, 1974. pvt. tchr., Oakland, Calif., 1976-86, univ. extension U. Calif., Sacramento State U., 1981-84. Featured roles opera, N.Y.C., 1948-51; appeared in Broadway plays The King and I, 1951-54, Flower Drum Song, 1960-61; concert and supper club appearances in U.S., Can., Carribbean, Japan, and Europe, 1955-91, also TV appearances. Mem. Actors Equity, AFTRA, Am. Guild Mus. Artists, Am. Guild Variety Artists. Home: 2835 Morley Dr Piedmont CA 94611-2547

LAKIN, JOAN FIELD, water treatment plant manager; b. Long Branch, N.J., Dec. 29, 1949; d. Norman J. and Gladys (Katz) Field; m. Alan Ray Lakin, June 6, 1971; children: Brian Matthew, Sara Lorraine. BA in Psychology, Wells Coll., 1971; MS in Environ. Sci., U. New Haven, 1992. Lic. water treatment plant operator class IV, State of Conn. Dept. Health Svcs., lic. distbn. sys. operator class II, State of Conn. Dept. Health Svcs. Collections rep. Regional Water Authority, New Haven, 1982-84, water quality control technician, 1984, water treatment plant operator, 1985 . Commr., planning sect. chairperson Planning and Zoning Commn., Hamden, Conn., 1982-86, chairperson long range planning com., chairperson personnel com.; mem. bldg. and grounds com., ritual com. Congregation Mishkan Israel Bd. Trustees, Hamden, 1994—. Mem. LWV (pres., natural resources chairperson), Am. Water Works Assn., Conn. Safety Soc. Home: 182 Eramo Ter Hamden CT 06518 Office: Regional Water Authority 90 Sargent Dr New Haven CT 06511

LALA, PATRICIA LUCILLE, accountant; b. Monterey Park, Calif., June 1, 1939; d. John J. and Ruth M. Lala; m. Vincent G. Pugliese Jr., Dec. 1957 (div. 1968); 1 child, Alan W.; m. E. Ruben Yuriar, Oct. 1969 (div. 1974). BA cum laude, Nat. U., San Diego, 1985, postgrad., 1993. Cert. govt. fin. mgr. Assn. Govt. Accts. Acct. Fed. Govt.-Exec. Br., 1989—; auditor Def. Contract Audit Agy., Orange County, Calif., 1989-90; resource mgr. Marine Corps Air Sta., Iwakuni, Japan, 1990-91; auditor Office of the Inspector Gen., U.S. Dept. Energy, Idaho Falls, Idaho, 1991-93; acct. Fed. Comm. Commn. Cable Divsn., 1994-95; revenue agt. IRS, Laguna Nigel, Calif., 1995; fin. analyst TRICARE, USN, San Diego, 1995-96; expert witness U.S. Senate, 1992; pvt. practice acct. and bus. cons., Carlsbad, Calif., 1985-89, 93-94. Organizer, coord. Women's Crisis Line, Salinas, Calif., 1975-76, ERA Coalition of Monterey County, 1981-82; coord. NOW Monterey/Salinas chpt., 1981-82. Recipient Award of Merit for Outstanding Achievement, Women's Crisis Line, Salinas, 1977, Letter of Appreciation, Handicapped Students Program, Mira Costa Coll., Oceanside, Calif., 1984, Cert. of Recognition, VISTA Program, Tutor in the Literacy Project, Ea. Idaho Tech. Coll., 1992, Cert. of Appreciation, Idaho Nat. Engring. Lab.-Office of Acad. Programs, 1993, Cert. of Achievement, Japanese Am. Soc., Iwakuni, others. Mem. NAACP (treas. Idaho Falls chpt. 1993), Assn. Govt. Accts., Nat. Contract Mgmt. Assn., Nat. Women's Polit. Caucus (San Diego chpt.), Inland Soc. Tax Cons. (San Diego chpt.), Calif. Soc. Mpcl. Fin. Officers, Pub. Employees for Environ. Responsibility (supporter), Nat. Univ. Alumni Assn. (North San Diego County chpt. treas. 1993). Home: 3744 Pershing Ave #2 San Diego CA 92104

LALE, CISSY STEWART (LLOYD LALE), freelance writer; b. Port Arthur, Tex., Jan. 15, 1924; d. Lloyd M. and May (Cowart) Stewart; m. Max Sims Lale, Oct. 9, 1983. BJ, U. Tex., 1945. Reporter Record-News, Wichita Falls, Tex., 1945, News-Messenger, Marshall, Tex., 1945-47; editor Times-Rev., Cleburne, Tex., 1947-49; women's editor, columnist Star-Telegram, Ft. Worth, 1949-87; freelance writer, Ft. Worth mag., Ft. Worth, 1987—. Bd. dirs. Trinity Terr. Retirement Community, 1991-94; active Jewel Charity Ball. Cissy Stewart Day proclaimed by Ft. Worth City Coun., 1987, portrayed in outdoor mural City of Ft. Worth, 1987. Mem. Women in Comm., Inc. (nat. pres. 1968-71), Tex. State Hist. Assn. (pres. 1996-97), East Tex. Hist. Assn. (pres. 1994), Tex. Heritage, Inc. (bd. dirs. Ft. Worth chpt. 1990), Womans Club Ft. Worth, Ft. Worth Garden Club (v.p. 1995-96). Episcopalian. Home: # 101 3900 White Settlement Rd Fort Worth TX 76107-7822

LA LIBERTE, ANN GILLIS, graphic artist, consultant, designer, educator; b. St. Paul, Nov. 10, 1942; d. Edward Robert and Frances Caroline (Sullivan) Gillis; m. Paul Henry La Liberte, Aug. 22, 1964; children: Paul E., Elizabeth La Liberte Collins, Stephen A., Helen C., Peter N., Marc H. Student, Am U., 1963-64, Cardinal Stritch Coll., Milw., 1960-63; BA, Coll. St. Catherine, St. Paul, 1985. Artist, owner Ann La Liberte Papers and Posters, Minnetonka, Minn., 1968-71, A.L. Graphic Design and Drawings, Minnetonka, Minn., 1983-93; artist-in-residence Tara Tonka Studio, Minnetonka, 1988—; artist Arts in Schs., Minn., 1985—; pvt. art tchr., dir. creativity and problem solving seminars, 1991—. Liturgical designer Christian Chs., Mpls. and St. Paul, 1977—; paintings, drawings, photography and sculpture exhibited Mpls. and St. Paul area, 1983—; sculpture Life Exhibit, Paul VI Inst. for the Arts, Washington, 1988, on tour Vt., Ohio, Mo., Ill., Wis., 1988. Del. Minn. Ind. Reps., 1969, vice chmn., 1970; promotional artist Soc. for Preservation Human Dignity, Palatine, Ill., 1973, Minn. Citizens Concerned for Life, 1980-88, Secular Franciscans, St. Paul, 1985; deanery rep. pastoral coun. Archdiocese of St. Paul, Mpls., 1978-82; chmn. devel. task force out-reach program Resurrection Ch., Mpls., 1980-81, cons. artist, 1983—; mem. worship bd. Ch. of Immaculate Heart of Mary, Minnetonka, 1991-95; liturgical art and environ. cons. Mem. Nat. Assn. Liturgical Mins., Mpls. Soc. Fine Arts, Nat. Mus. Women in Arts (charter), Walker Art Ctr., Minnetonka Ctr. for Arts, Coll. of St. Catherine Alumna Assn., Artist for Life Nat. Slide Registry, Delta Phi Delta. Roman Catholic. Home: 13418 Excelsior Blvd Minnetonka MN 55345-4910

LALLI, CELE GOLDSMITH, editor; b. Scranton, Pa., Apr. 8, 1933; d. Arthur Langfeld and Viola Catherine (Wolfort) Goldsmith; m. Michael Anthony Lalli, Apr. 4, 1964; children—Francesca Ann, Erica Catherine. BA, Vassar Coll., 1955. From asst. editor to editor Amazing Sci. Fiction Stories, N.Y.C., 1955-65; mng. editor Modern Bride's Guide to Decorating Your First Home, N.Y.C., 1965-69; exec. editor Modern Bride, N.Y.C., 1969-81, editor-in-chief, v.p., 1982—. Co-author: Modern Bride Guide to Your Wedding and Marriage, 1984, Modern Bride Wedding Celebrations, 1992; author: Modern Bride Guide to Etiquette, 1993. Bd. dirs. Conn. Assn. for Children with Learning Disabilities, 1984-93. Recipient Invisible Little Man award West Coast Sci. Fiction Orgn., 1961; named to YWCA Acad. of Women Achievers, 1986. Mem. Am. Soc. Mag. Editors, Fashion Group. Republican. Roman Catholic. Office: Modern Bride K-III Comms 249 W 17th St New York NY 10011-5300

LALLI, MARY SCHWEITZER, writer, artist; b. Newark, Ohio, June 24, 1925; d. Clemence Sylvester and Ethel Ann (Deem) Schilling; m. Francis Edward Schweitzer, Aug. 23, 1947 (div. Oct. 1974); children: Dale Francis, Darrell Charles, David Edward; m. Joseph G. Lalli, June 21, 1975. BA, Denison U., 1947. Lic. tchr. English. Tchr. English Ctrl. Jr. High, Newark, 1947-48; profl. artist Nat. Forum Profl. Artists, Phila., 1968-75; dir. art shows Phila., 1968—. Writer Doll Castle News, Doll Times, Doll Reader, Antique Doll World, Doll Collector's Price Guide, Doll World, 1983—; photojournalist Doll Times; columnist Doll Designs. Recipient 125 art awards Phila. Plastic Club, 1972, 73, 78, award of honor Inst. Pub. Edn., Drexel Hill, Pa., 1980. Mem. Nat. League Am. Pen Women (1st v.p. 1985-89), DaVinci Art Alliance (sec.), Plastic Club (pres., v.p.), Chester County Art Assn.

LALLY, NORMA ROSS, federal agency administrator, retired; b. Crawford, Nebr., Aug. 10, 1932; d. Roy Anderson and Alma Leona (Barber) Lively; m. Robert Edward Lally, Dec. 4, 1953 (div. Mar. 1986); children: Robyn Carol Murch, Jeffrey Alan, Gregory Roy. BA, Boise (Idaho) State U., 1974, MA, 1976; postgrad., Columbia Pacific U., 1988—. With grad. admissions Boise State U., 1971-74; with officer programs USN Recruiting, Boise, 1974; pub. affairs officer IRS, Boise and Las Vegas, 1975-94; ret., 1994; speaker in field, Boise and Las Vegas, 1977— Contbr. articles to newspapers. Mem. task force Clark County Sch. Dist., Las Vegas. Staff sgt. USAF, 1950-54. Mem. NAFE, Internat. Assn. Bus. Communicators, Women in Mil. Svc. Am., Mensa, Toastmasters (Las Vegas), Marine's Meml. Club (life), Am. Legion. Home: 3013 Hawksdale Dr Las Vegas NV 89134-8967

LAM, KAI-LUAN HELEN, accountant, small business owner; b. Saigon, Vietnam, May 5, 1963; came to U.S., 1981; d. Pok Wo and Kwok-Ying (Tang) L.; m. Jui Tai Richard Wang, Dec. 25, 1987; children: Young Sheng Josiah Wang, Ling-Zhi Joyce Wang. BS in Bus. Adminstrn., Boston U., 1985. CPA. Auditor in charge Deloitte, Haskins & Sells, Toronto, 1985-88; v.p. Yu Feng Internat. Corp., N.Y.C., 1988-90, I.K.I. New York Am. Clothing and Fashion Ltd., N.Y.C., 1990-94. Pianist Queen's Herald Ch., Flushing, N.Y., 1990, Sunday Sch. coord., 1991; counselor North End Youth Program, N.Y.C., 1991—; treas., trustee Trevor Pl. Home Owners Assn. Mem. AICPA, N.J. Soc. CPAs, N.Y.C. of C., Toronto Chinese Profl. Assn. (treas. 1986—), Alpha Beta Psi.

LAMAR, MARTHA LEE, chaplain; b. Birmingham, Jan. 2, 1935; d. Alco L. and Anne Lee (Morris) Lee; m. William Fred Lamar, Jr., June 7, 1986; children: Barbara Gayle Martin, Owen Parker Jr. BS, Auburn U., 1955; MA, Christian Theol. Sem., Indpls., 1992. From adminstv. asst. to rsch. coord. Ala. Affiliate Am. Heart Assn., Birmingham, 1977-86; adminstrv. asst. alumni office De Pauw U., Greencastle, Ind., 1986-89; nursing home chaplain Heritage House Health and Rehab. Ctr., Greencastle, 1989 ; nursing home chaplain Garfield Park Health Facility, Indpls., 1992-94, Heritage House Health and Rehab. Ctr., Martinsville, Ind., 1992-95; chaplain cons. Oakwood Corp., Indpls., 1991—. Vol. chaplain's office De Pauw U., 1986—, community work for homeless, Greencastle, 1986—, Fountain Sq. Devel. Corp., Indpls., 1992. Mem. ACA, Nat. Interfaith Coalition on Aging, Am. Soc. on Aging, Mental Health and Aging Network and Forum on Religion, Spirituality and Aging, Ind. Health Care Chaplains Assn. Methodist. Office: Heritage House Health & Rehab Ctr 1601 Hosp Dr Greencastle IN 46135

LAMAR, MICHELLE MARIE, lawyer; b. Inglewood, Calif., July 8, 1962; d. Edward Blake and Alice Blanche (Leggett) LaM. BA in History/Art cum laude, UCLA, 1988; JD, Loyola U., 1992. Bar: Calif. 1992. Atty. Inland Countries Legal Svcs., San Bernardino, Calif., 1992-93, Booth, Mitchel & Strange, L.A., 1994—. Mem. Calif. Bar Assn. Office: Booth Mitchel & Strange 3435 Wilshire Blvd 30th Fl Los Angeles CA 90010

LAMB, DARLIS CAROL, sculptor; b. Wausa, Nebr.; d. Lindor Soren and June Berniece (Skalberg) Nelson; m. James Robert Lamb; children: Sherry Lamb Sobh, Michael, Mitchell. BA in Fine Arts, Columbia Pacific U., San Rafael, Calif., 1988; MA in Fine Arts, Columbia Pacific U., 1989. Exhibited in group shows at Nat. Arts Club, N.Y.C., 1983, 85, 89, 91, 92, 93, 95, 96 (Catherine Lorillard Wolfe award sculpture 1983, C.L. Wolfe Horse's Head award 1994, Anna Hyatt Huntington cash award 1995), N.Am. Sculpture Exhibit, Foothills Art Ctr., Golden, Colo., 1983-84, 86-87, 90-91 (Pub. Svc. Co. of Colo. sculpture award 1990), Nat. Sculpture Soc., 1985, 91, 95 (C. Percival Dietch Sculpture prize 1991), Loveland Mus. and Gallery, 1990-91, Audubon Artists, 1991, Allied Artists Am., 1992, 95, Pen and Brush, 1993, 95-96 (Roman Bronze award 1995), Colorado Springs Fine Arts Mus., 1996, others; represented in permanent collections in Nebr. Hist. Soc., Am. Lung Assn. of Colo., Benson Park Sculpture Garden, Loveland, others. Mem. Catherine Lorillard Wolfe Art Club, N.Am. Sculpture Soc. Office: PO Box 9043 Englewood CO 80111-0301

LAMB, DEBORAH A., federal and state government lawyer; b. Missoula, Mont., May 31, 1953; d. George E. and Ingeburg (Teckenburg) L.; m. Joseph Valenza, 1989. BA summa cum laude, Lewis and Clark Coll., 1975; MA with distinction, John Hopkins Sch., 1977; JD cum laude, Georgetown U., 1988. Bar: D.C., 1989. Economist Bur. of East West Trade, Dept. Commerce, Washington, 1978-82; dir. Korea and Taiwan Internat. Trade Adminstrn., Dept. Commerce, 1982-88; atty. Steptoe & Johnson, Washington, 1988-90; internat. trade counsel Senate Com. on Fin., Washington, 1990—. Mem. ABA, D.C. Bar Assn., Amnesty Internat. Office: Com on Finance 203 Hart Senate Office Bldg Washington DC 20510

LAMB, GINGER LOUISE, editor; b. Newfane, N.Y., May 26, 1967; d. Ronald LaVerne Sr. and Caroline Ann (Diez) Tucker; m. David Carl Lamb, Aug. 6, 1988. AS in Journalism, Niagara C.C., 1987; BS in Communications, SUNY, Brockport, 1990. Editor family page Lockport (N.Y.) Union-Sun & Jour., 1985; anchor, reporter 1340 AM WLVL, Lockport, 1987-88; bus. editor, reporter The Greece Post, Rochester, N.Y., 1990-91; anchor, reporter 1030 AM WYSL, Avon, N.Y., 1992-94, 1180 AM WHAM, Rochester, 1993-94; communications coord. The Daily Record, Rochester, 1994, editorial dir., 1994—; chair Daily Record Adv. Panel, Rochester, 1996—; presenter in field. Recipient Pres.'s medallion Niagara County C.C., Sanborn, N.Y., 1987. Mem. Nat. Newspaper Assn., Am. Ct. & Comml. Newspaper Assn., Women in Communications, Niagara County C.C. Alumni Assn. Office: The Daily Record PO Box 6 11 Centre Park Rochester NY 14601

LAMB, IRENE HENDRICKS, medical researcher; b. Ky., May 9, 1940; d. Daily P. and Bertha (Hendricks) Lamb; m. Edward B. Meadows. Diploma in nursing, Ky. Bapt. Hosp., Louisville; student, Berea (Ky.) Coll., Calif. State U., L.A. RN, Ky. Charge nurse, head nurse acute medicine, med. ICU, surgical ICU, emergency room various med. ctrs., 1963-67; staff nurse rsch. CCU U. So. Calif./L.A. County Med. Ctr., 1968; nurse coord. clin. rsch. ctr. U. So. Calif./Los Angeles County Med. Ctr., L.A., 1969-74; sr. rsch. nurse cardiology Stanford (Calif.) U. Sch. Medicine, 1974-85, rsch. coord. pvt. clin., 1988; dir. clin. rsch. San Diego Cardiac Ctr., 1989-92; sr. cmty. health nurse Madison County Health Dept., Berea, 1993—; clin. rsch. cons., 1988—. Co-contbr. numerous articles to med. jours.; contbr. articles to nursing jours., chpts. to med. books. Mem. Am. Heart Assn. (cardiovasc. nursing sect.). Home: 107 Lorraine Ct Berea KY 40403-1317

LAMB, JOANN ISABEL, adult nurse practitioner; b. Ottawa, Ont., Can., Oct. 18, 1939; came to U.S., 1961; d. Joseph Gordon and Amelia Marguerite (Gillis) L. BSN, SUNY, Albany, 1980; MA in Nursing Edn., Columbia U., 1980, MSN, 1987. RN, N.Y. Surg. ICU head nurse Columbia-Presbyn. Med. Ctr., N.Y.C., 1973-79, procurement coord. Organ Bank, 1979-80, cardiac transplant coord., 1980-87, nurse practitioner Cardiothoracic Transplant Program, 1987-91, mgr. Cardiothoracic Transplant Program, 1991; v.p. patient svcs. The Dobelle Inst., N.Y.C., 1991—; co-owner Carlam Consultants, Inc., N.Y.C., 1979-83; mem. com. for the devel. of critical care stds. Emergency Med. Svcs. Sys., City of N.Y., 1978-79; mem. planning task force 3d Internat. Intensive Care Nursing Meeting, Montreal, 1985-88; site visitor U. Alta. Hosps., Edmonton, 1988; mem. expert panel selecting cardiac transplant ctrs. managed care program John Hancock Ins. Co., 1990, 91; participant Partnership for Organ Donation, Inc., Washington, 1990; lectr. in the field. Author: (with others) Cardiovascular Nursing, 1986, Pediatric Cardiology, 1986, Standrads for Critical Care Nursing, 3d edit., 1988, Organ & Tissue Transplantation: Nursing Care from Procurement through Rehabilitation, 1991, SCCM Textbook of Critical Care Medicine, 1995, Pocket Companion to: Textbook of Critical Care, 1996; mem. editl. bd. Heart & Lung: The Jour. of Critical Care, 1978-81, Life Support Nursing, 1981-83, Critical Care Communique, 1978-81; contbr. more than 30 articles to profl. jours. Recipient Norma J. Shoemaker award for Critical Care Nursing Excellence, Soc. of Critical Care Medicine, 1996. Fellow Am. Coll. Critical Care Medicine; mem. AACN (co-chair program com. N.Y.C. chpt. 1977-78, scholarship com. 1977-78, chair symposium com. 1979-80, bd. dirs. 1981-83, membership com. 1983-88), Soc. for Critical Care Medicine (external affairs com., 1980-81, chair nursing section, 1983, coun. mem., 1984-87, sec., 1987-89, selection panel 1988-89, co-chair mem. com., 1990-94), Columbia U. Sch. Nursing Alumni Assn., Ottawa Civic Hosp. Sch. Nursing Alumni Assn., Am. Assn. Neuroscis. Nurses, Am. Assn. Physician Assts., Internat. Soc. for Heart Transplantation, RNs Assn. Ont. (Can.). Office: 3960 Broadway New York NY 10032

LAMB, STACIE THOMPSON, elementary school educator; b. Abilene, Tex., Nov. 9, 1965; d. George Lyman and Shirley Elizabeth (Burton) T.; m. Dennis A. Lamb; children: Lane, Logann. BS in Edn., Lubbock Christian Coll., 1986; postgrad., Tex. Tech U. Elem. Edn. grades 1-6, Tex. 1st grade tchr. Lubbock (Tex.) I.S.D. Brown Elem., 1986-87; 3rd grade tchr., chairperson Morton (Tex.) I.S.D., 1987-89; 5th grade lang. arts tchr. Whiteface (Tex.) C.I.S.D., 1990—. Mem. ASCD, Classroom Tchrs. Assn. (sec. 1988-89, elem. rep. 1991-92). Home: 2104 Tech Dr Levelland TX 79336-7035 Office: PO Box 117 Whiteface TX 79379-0117

LAMB, WENDY KAREN LAURENT, secondary school mathematics educator; b. N.Y.C., Mar. 26, 1952; d. Randolph William and Anne (Adam) Laurent; m. Gerald Elliot Lamb, Aug. 24, 1974; children: Jeremy Michael, Timothy Matthew. BA, SUNY, Oswego, 1974; MA, Montclair State Coll., 1979. Tchr. Grover Cleveland Jr. H.S., Caldwell, N.J., 1975-85; tchr. James Caldwell H.S., 1985—, coord. math. dept., 1994-95, freshman class advisor, 1994—. Sunday sch. tchr. Cmty. Ch. of Cedar Grove, N.J., 1986-94; chair phone squad Meml. Middle Sch. Faculty Assn., Cedar Grove, 1992-94. Mem. N.J. Edn. Assn., Assn. Math. Tchrs. N.J., Nat. Coun. Tchrs. Math. Office: James Caldwell HS Westville Ave Caldwell NJ 07006

LAMBARTH, JANET KISER, academic administrator; b. Indiana, Pa., Dec. 16, 1943; d. Kenneth Williams and Winnifred (Weamer) Davis; m. Larry Leroy Kiser, Aug. 11, 1966 (div. 1984); m. Douglas Don Lambarth, Oct. 10, 1992. BS, Indiana U. of Pa., 1965; MA in Child Devel., Wash. State U., 1976; postgrad., Gonzaga U. Cert. mediator dispute resolution; cert. home econs. vocat. tchr. Tchr. Watchung Hills Regional H.S., Warren, N.J., 1965-68; editor Macmillan Pub., N.Y.C., 1968-70; author McGraw-Hill Books, N.Y.C., 1973, 78, EMC Pub. Co., 1987, 90; county ext. agt. Wash. State U., Pend Oreille County, Wash., 1976—; curriculum devel. profl. Spokane Falls C.C., Spokane, 1973; bd. dirs. Dispute Resolution Ctr. Spokane; mem. adv. bd. N.E. Wash. Dispute Resolution Ctr.; organizer women's confs., 1989—; presenter Nat. Coun. Family Rels., 1975; invited presenter Nat. Assn. Ext. 4-H Agts., 1994, Oreg. Sch. Age Coalition and Wash. Sch. Age Care Alliance Nat. Conf., 1994; chair ext. dir.'s adv. com. Wash. State U., 1992-94. Co-author: (textbook) Resources for Living, 1987, 90, Personal Perspectives, 1973, 78. Mem. Soroptimist. Office: Wash State U Ext Box 5000 Newport WA 99156

LAMBDIN, DOROTHY DOWNING, educator; b. Bryn Mawr, Pa., Oct. 10, 1951; d. Charles Ernest and Dorothy Diana (Carlson) L.; m. Lawrence Dagger Abraham, Aug. 16, 1975; children: Andrew Carson, Rebecca Diana. BS, U. Mass., 1973; MA, Columbia U., 1974; EdD, U. Mass., 1992. Tchr. The Town Sch., N.Y.C., 1973-74, The Cathedral Sch., N.Y.C., 1974-75, St. Andrew's Episcopal. Sch., Austin, Tex., 1976-86, U. Tex., Austin, 1976—, Blanton Elem. Sch., Austin, 1993-95. Contbr. articles to profl. jours. Recipient AAPER Svc. award Austin Assn. Phys. Edn. and Dance, 1987, Oak Tree award Austin PTA, 1994. Mem. Am. Alliance Health, Physi. Edn., Recreation and Dance, Am. Ednl. Rsch. Assn., U.S. Phys. Edn., Nat. Assn. Phys. Edn. Higher Edn., Tex. Assn. Health, Phys. Edn., Recreation and Dance, Phi Delta Kappa. Office: U Tex Dept Kinesology & Health Anna Hiss 107 A2000 Austin TX 78772

LAMBERG, JOAN BERNICE, purchasing agent; b. St. Paul, July 5, 1935; d. Gustave William and Anna Marie (Steinhilpert) L.; 1 child, Mary Lamberg King. Student, U. Mo., Rolla, 1971. Payroll clk. Continental Baking Co., Mpls., 1953-54; mgr. prodn. scheduling, purchasing and inventory control Stewart Paint Mfg. Co., Mpls., 1954-72; with purchasing, accounts payable and sales dept. Horton-Earl Co., South St. Paul, Minn., 1972—. Mem. Northwestern Soc. for Coatings Tech. (treas. 1984-85, sec. 1985-86, v.p. 1986-87, pres. 1987-88, tech. com. 1985-90, membership chmn. 1985—, advt. mgr. 1988—, symposium com. 1985—, monthly meeting notice editor 1988—, Trigg award 1986), Fedn. Socs. for Coatings Tech. (bd. dirs. 1987-89). Home: 6949 Macbeth Cir Saint Paul MN 55125-2408 Office: Horton-Earl Co 949 Concord St S South Saint Paul MN 55075-5912

LAMBERT, CHERYL M., accountant, controller; b. Newark, Feb. 28, 1965; d. John Wayne and Mary Anna M.; m. Michael Timothy Lambert, Mar. 20, 1993; 1 child, Alexander Semina Lambert. BA, Rutgers U., 1987; postgrad., Kean Coll., 1995—. Acct. CPC Behavioral Healthcare, Morganville, N.J., 1987-90, sr. acct., 1990-94, asst. controller, 1994-96. Home: 617 Brinley Ave Bradley Beach NJ 07720 Office: CPC Behavioral Healthcare Inc 1 High Point Center Way Morganville NJ 07751

LAMBERT, DEBORAH KETCHUM, public relations executive; b. Greenwich, Conn., Jan. 22, 1942; d. Alton Harrington and Robyna (Neilson) Ketchum; m. Harvey R. Lambert, Nov. 23, 1963 (div. 1985); children: Harvey Richard Jr., Eric Harrington. BS, Columbia U., 1965. Researcher, writer The Nowland Orgn., Greenwich, Conn., 1964-67, model Country Fashions, Greenwich, Conn., 1964-67; freelance writer to various newspapers and mags., 1977-82; press sec. Va. Del. Gwen Cody, Annandale, Va., 1981-82; assoc. editor Campus Report, Washington, 1985—; adminstrv. asst. Accuracy in Media, Inc., Washington, 1983-84, dir. pub. affairs, 1985—; TV producer weekly program The Other Side of the Story, 1994—; bd. dirs. Accuracy in Academia, Washington; film script cons. The Seductive Illusion, 1988-89. Columnist: The Eye, The Washington Inquirer, 1984—, Squeaky Chalk, Campus Report, 1985—; contbr. articles to various mags.; producer: The Other Side of the Story, 1993—. Co-founder, mem. Va. Rep. Forum, McLean, 1983—; mem. Rep. Women's Fed. Forum. Mem. Am. Bell Assn., Pub. Rels. Soc. Am., DAR., World Media Assn., Am. Platform Assn. Republican. Presbyterian. Home: 1945 Lorraine Ave Mc Lean VA 22101-5331 Office: Accuracy in Media Inc 4455 Connecticut Ave NW Washington DC 20008-2328

LAMBERT, ETHEL GIBSON CLARK, secondary school educator; b. Atlanta, Apr. 18, 1943; d. Robert Harold and Ethel (Gibson) Clark; m. Hugh Felder Lambert, June 27, 1964 (div. Nov. 3, 1988); children: Courtney, Elizabeth, Hugh Lambert Jr. BA, Oglethorpe U., Atlanta, 1965; MEd, Kennesaw State Coll., Marietta, Ga., 1992; postgrad., State U. West Ga., Carrollton, 1995—. Lic. tchr. T-5, Ga. Tchr. Clayton County Bd. Edn., Jonesboro, Ga., 1965-66, Fulton County Bd. Edn., Atlanta, 1966-67; tchr. pre-sch. weekday program First Bapt. Ch., Gainesville, Ga., 1984-88; tchr. remedial edn. program Riverdale High Sch./Clayton County Bd. Edn., 1990—. Author: The Impact of Geography on the Campaigns of the Civil War Fought in Georgia, 1993, The Utilization of Georgia Historical Sites as Teaching Methodology in MIddle Grades Education, 1993, (juvenile) Obnoxious Bill, 1993, Research on Academic Motivation of Elementary, Middle and Secondary School Students in America, 1993, Reading Strategies that Address the Reluctant Reader in America's Public Middle and High Schools, 1995. Den leader Cub Scouts Am., Gainesville, 1980-83; mem. Christian Businessmen's Prayer Breakfast, Atlanta, 1990-95, 96. Mem. Profl. Assn. Ga. Educators, Order Ea. Star, College Park Women's Club, College Park Hist. Soc. Baptist. Home: 1881 Myrtle Dr SW Apt 711 Atlanta GA 30311-4919 Office: Riverdale High Sch 160 Roberts Dr Riverdale GA 30274

LAMBERT, JEAN MARJORIE, health care executive; b. Bay City, Mich., Mar. 19, 1943; d. Richard William and Fidelis Rena (LeVasseur) L. BA, Madonna U., Livonia, Mich., 1967; MA, Eastern Mich. U., 1975. Dir. religious edn. Archdiocese of Detroit, 1970-75, dir. of evaluation, 1975-77; assoc. dir. programming Intermedia Found., Santa Monica, Calif., 1977-78; acad. dean St. John Provincial Sem., Plymouth, Mich., 1978-84; asst. dir. quality mgmt. Sisters of Mercy Health Corp., Farmington Hills, Mich., 1984-87; sr. cons. Mercy Collaborative, Livonia., Mich., 1987-88; v.p. Mission Mercy Health System, Cin., 1988-91; v.p. Mission Sisters Providence Health System, Springfield, Mass., 1991—; asst. prof. homiletics St. John Sem., Plymouth, Mich., 1978-85, St. Mary of the Woods Coll., Terre Haute, Ind., summer 1985, St. Meinrad Sem., Ind., summer 1984; bd. dirs. Combined Health Appeal of Mass. Editor Religious Edn., 1975-77. Nat. Cath. Edn. Assn.-Assn. Theol. Schs. for U.S. and Can. grantee, 1983. Mem. NAFE, Groundwork, Network, Am. Hosp. Assn., Am. Mgmt. Assn., Mental Health Assn., Cath. Health Assn. (bd. dirs. New Eng. Conf.), Acad. Leadership in Cath. Health Care. Roman Catholic. Avocations: woodcarving, photography, continuing education. Office: Sisters of Providence Health System 146 Chestnut St Springfield MA 01103-1539

LAMBERT, JOAN DORETY, elementary education educator; b. Trenton, N.J., Oct. 21, 1937; d. John William and Margaret (Fagan) Dorety; m. James E. Lambert Sr., June 25, 1960; children: Margi, Karen, James E., Kevin. BA, Georgian Ct. Coll., Lakewood, N.J., 1958. Cert. tchr., Pa., N.J. Tchr. 2d and 3d grades combined Washington Elem. Sch., Trenton, 1958-61; tchr. kindergarten music St. Genevieve Sch., Flourtown, Pa., 1968-78, tchr. 3d grade, 1978—; producer, dir. musical shows for St. Genevieve Sch., 1970-78; demonstration classroom for writing process on computers Chestnut Hill Coll. Mem. Jr. League of Trenton, 1960-68, Jr. League of Phila., 1968-70. Teleflex Internat. grantee, 1989-92, Anna B. Stokes Meml. scholar, 1960, Met. Opera grantee, 1958-60. Mem. NEA. Republican. Roman Catholic. Home: 33 Coventry Ct Blue Bell PA 19422-2528 Office: St Genevieve Sch 1237 Bethlehem Pike Flourtown PA 19031-1902

LAMBERT, JUDITH A. UNGAR, lawyer; b. N.Y.C., Apr. 13, 1943; d. Alexander Lawrence and Helene (Rosenson) Ungar; m. Peter D. Leibowits, Aug. 22, 1965 (div. 1971); 1 child, David Gary. BS, U. Pa., 1964; JD magna cum laude, U. Miami, 1984. Bar: N.Y. 1985, Fla. 1990. Assoc. Proskauer Rose Goetz & Mendelsohn, N.Y.C., 1984-86, Taub & Fasciana, N.Y.C., 1986-87, Hoffinger Friedland Dobrish Bernfeld & Hasen, N.Y.C., 1987-88; pvt. practice N.Y.C., 1988—. Mem. ABA, N.Y. State Bar Assn., Assn. Bar of City of N.Y., N.Y. Women's Bar Assn. (family law and trusts and estates com.), N.Y. County Lawyers Assn. Office: 245 E 54th St New York NY 10022-4707

LAMBERT, LINDA MARGARET, reading specialist; b. Livingston County, Ky., Jan. 17, 1941; d. Wiley Jackson and Florence Allie (Davidson) Stallions; m. Leland Dawson Lambert; children: Sharon Kay, Sheila Lynn, Wiley Lee. AA, Yuba Coll., 1970; BLS, Mary Washington Coll., 1980; MEd, U. Va., 1986. Cert. tchr., Va. Elem. tchr. Stafford (Va.) County Schs., 1979-91, reading specialist, 1991—; mem. com. Devel. Elem. Counselors, Stafford, 1987-89, Devel. Appropriate Assessment, Stafford, 1993-94. Sponsor Ghostwriter Mystery Club, Garrisonwoods Estates, 1993—; mem. Falmouth Bapt. Ch., Stafford Dem. Com., 1996—; del. Va. State Dem. Convention. Mem. NEA, Va. Edn. Assn., Stafford County Edn. Assn., Internat. Reading Assn., Va. State Reading Assn., Rappahannock Reading Coun., Hist. Fredericksburg Antique Automobile Club. Democrat. Home: 203 Rumford Rd Fredericksburg VA 22405-3206 Office: Hampton Oaks Elem Sch 107 Northampton Blvd Stafford VA 22554-7660

LAMBERT, PEGGY LYNNE BAILEY, lawyer; b. Seattle, Oct. 15, 1948; d. John Thomas and Doris Mae (Lindgren) Bailey; m. Tom Kenneth Newton, May 25, 1975 (div. 1980); m. Allan Gregory Lambert, Aug. 3, 1980 (div. May 1996); children: Eli Raven, Joshua Alec. BA in Psychology, Beloit Coll., 1970; MS in Counseling Psychology, Ill. Inst. Tech., 1973; JD, Syracuse (N.Y.) U., 1978. Bar: D.C. 1983. Mental health specialist Ill. Dept. Mental Health, Chgo., 1971-72; mem. rsch. faculty Cornell U., Ithaca, N.Y., 1973-75; assoc. O'Connor, Sovocool, Pfann and Greenburg, Ithaca, 1978, Dacy, Richin & Meyers, Silver Springs, Md., 1979-81; ins. adminstr. Nat. Assn. Broadcasters, Washington, 1981-86, dir. ins. programs, 1986-90; assoc. Architect of the Capitol, Washington, 1990—. Co-author, editor: Broadcaster's Property and Liability Insurance Buying Guide, 1989. Mem. ABA, D.C. Bar Assn. (mem. steering com. of arts entertainment, sports law sect. 1989-90, sect. editor newsletter 1989-90). Democrat. Jewish. Office: Architect of the Capitol Office of Gen Coun Rm H2-265A Ford House Office Bldg Washington DC 20515

LAMBERT, SALLY HARDIN, lawyer; b. Ashland, Ky., Mar. 13, 1948; d. Josiah and Bess Arjyra (Hood) L.; m. Robert William Keats, June 16, 1973 (Apr. 1995); 1 child, Josiah. BA with honors, Denison U., 1970; JD with high honors, U. Louisville, 1974; MBA, Ind. U., 1989. Tchr. Bullen Jr. H.S., Kenosha, Wis., 1970-71; law clk. Ewen, MacKenzie & PEden, Louisville, 1972-74; staff atty. KFC Corp., Louisville, 1974-87; assoc. Ray and Morris, Louisville, 1987-88; ptnr. Nicolas, Welsh & Brooks, Louisville, 1988-91, Keats, Hibbs & Brooks, Louisville, 1991-92, Keats, Schwietz & O'Donnell, Louisville, 1992-93; mng. ptnr. Conliffe, Sandmann & Sullivan, Louisville, 1993—; gen. counsel Kentuckiana Chinese Sch., Inc. Louisville, 1991—, bd. dirs. Mem. editl. bd. Trademark Reporter, 1979. Sec. Louisville Ballet, 1993-95, bd. dirs., 1991—. Mem. Ky. Bar Assn., Louisville Astronomical Soc. (bd. chair 1996), Astronomical League (co-chair nat. conv. 1996—), Zonta Club Louisville (pres. 1985). Office: Conliffe Sandmann Sullivan 621 W Main St Louisville KY 40202-2967

LAMBERT, SHARON WHITE WILLIS, microbiologist; b. Greensboro, N.C., Mar. 15, 1964; d. Roy Frank and LaVerne (Gilchrest) White. BS, N.C. State U., 1986. Tech. asst. III CIBA-Geigy, Greensboro, N.C., 1986-87; asst. rsch. microbiologist CIBA Vision, Alpharetta, Ga., 1987-92; rsch. microbiologist Ciba Vision, Alpharetta, Ga., 1992—; Presenter in field. Mem. Am. Soc. Microbiology. Office: CIBA Vision 11460 Johns Creek Duluth GA 30155-1518

LAMBERTH, REBECCA MCLEMORE, lawyer; b. Louisville, Sept. 12, 1960. BA summa cum laude, Vanderbilt U., 1982; JD, U. Va., 1985. Bar: Ga. 1985, U.S. Dist. Ct. (no. dist.) Ga. 1986, U.S. Ct. Appeals (11th cir.) 1990, U.S. Dist. Ct. (mid. dist.) Ga. 1990. Ptnr. Alston & Bird, Atlanta. Mem. ABA, State Bar Ga., Atlanta Bar Assb. (bd. dirs. and younger lawyers sects.), Phi Beta Kappa. Office: Alston & Bird 1 Atlantic Ctr 1201 W Peachtree St Atlanta GA 30309-3424*

LAMBERTI, MARJORIE, history educator; b. New Haven, Sept. 30, 1937; d. James and Anna (Vanacore) L. B.A., Smith Coll., 1959; M.A., Yale U., 1960, Ph.D., 1965. Prof. history Middlebury Coll., Vt., 1964—, Charles A. Dana prof., 1984—. Author: Jewish Activism in Imperial Germany, 1978, State, Society and the Elementary School in Imperial Germany, 1989; edtl. bd. History of Edn. Quar., 1992-94; contbr. articles to profl. jours. NEH fellow, 1968-69, 81-82; German Acad. Exch. Svc. rsch. grant, 1988. Fellow Inst. for Advanced Study (Princeton 1992-93); mem. Am. Hist. Assn., Conf. Group for Ctrl. European History, Leo Baeck Inst., Phi Beta Kappa. Home: 8 S Gorham Ln Middlebury VT 05753-1016 Office: Middlebury Coll Dept History Middlebury VT 05753

LAMBETH, ALYCE FLORAINE, secondary school educator; b. Tulsa, Sept. 18, 1930; d. James W. and Mai Lillian (Ellis) Cox; m. James D. Lambeth, July 5, 1953 (div. July 1964); 1 child, J. Eric. B Journalism, U. Tex., 1952; MA in Mass. Comms., U. Tex., Odessa, 1981. Amusements editor Ft. Worth Star-Telegram, 1951-52; asst. account exec. Beaumont/Holman Advt. Agy., Dallas, 1953-56; account exec. Anges Compton, Inc., Dallas, 1957-59; English tchr. Permian H.S., Odessa, 1964-83, dir. publs., 1983-91, govt. tchr., 1992—. Mem. Dem. Exec. Com., Edor County, 1968-70; mem. Pres. Clinton's Nat. Adv. Com.; adult Sunday sch. tchr. local Presbyn. ch.; 1st woman's area gov. Toastmasters Internat., Tex., 1978-79. Democrat. Home: 2457 Idlewood Ln Odessa TX 79761 Office: Permian HS 1806 E 42d Odessa TX 79761

LAMBIRD, MONA SALYER, lawyer; b. Oklahoma City, July 19, 1938; d. B.M. Jr. and Pauline A. Salyer; m. Perry A. Lambird, July 30, 1960; children: Allison Lambird Watson, Jennifer Salyer, Elizabeth Gard, Susannah Johnson. BA, Wellesley Coll., 1960; LLB, U. Md., 1963. Bar: Okla. 1968, Md. Ct. Appeals 1963, U.S. Supreme Ct. 1967. Atty. civil div. Dept. Justice, Washington, 1963-65; sole practice law Balt. and Oklahoma City, 1965-71; mem. firm Andrews Davis Legg Bixler Milsten & Price, Inc. and predecessor firm, Oklahoma City, 1971—; minority mem. Okla. Election Bd., 1984—, vice chmn., 1990-94; mem. profl. responsibility tribunal Okla. Supreme Ct., 1984-90; Master of Bench, sec.-treas. Luther Bohanan Am. Inn of Ct., Oklahoma City, 1986—, pres., 1994—. Editor: Briefcase, Oklahoma County Bar Assn., 1976. Profl. liaison com. City Oklahoma City, 1974-80; mem. Hist. Preservation of Oklahoma City, Inc., 1970—; del. Oklahoma County and Okla. State Republican Party Conv., 1971—; Okla. City Orch. League Inc., legal advisor, 1973—, bd. dirs., 1973—; incorporator, bd. dirs. R.S.V.P. of Oklahoma County, pres., 1982-83; bd. dirs. Congregate Housing for Elderly, 1978—, Vis. Nurses Assn., 1983-86, Oklahoma County Friends of Library, 1980-91, The Support Ctrs., Inc., 1989—. Mem. Okla. Women's Hall of Fame, 1995. Mem. ABA, Okla. Bar Assn. (pres. labor and employment law sect., bd. govs. 1992-94, pres. 1996), Oklahoma County Bar Assn. (bd. dirs. 1986—, pres. 1990), Oklahoma County Bar Found. (pres. 1988), Jr. League Oklahoma City (bd. dirs. 1973-76, legal advisor), Oklahoma County and State Med. Assn. Aux. (bd. dirs.), Seven Sisters Colls. Club (pres. 1972-76), Women's Econ. Club (steering com. 1981-86). Methodist. Home: 419 NW 14th St Oklahoma City OK 73103-3510 Office: 500 W Main St Oklahoma City OK 73102-2220

LAMBRIGHT HOWELL, NATALIE ANN, special education educator; b. Bluefield, W.Va., July 12, 1956; d. Alonzo and Etta Eleanor (Bennett) L. BS, W.Va. U., 1978; MA, W.Va. Coll. Grad. Studies, 1982; EdS, Ga. State U., 1996. Cert. tchr. support specialist, Ga. Tchr. mildly intellectual disabled McDowell County Bd. Edn., Welch, W.Va., 1978-82; tchr. interrelated resource Fulton County Bd. Edn., Atlanta, 1982-85; tchr. learning disabled Fulton Bd. Edn., Atlanta, 1985—; cons. Ga. Learning Resource Ctr., Atlanta, 1993; coord. McDowell County Spl. Olympics, Welch, W.Va., 1977; task force mem. Regional Ednl. Svc. Agy., Beckley, W.Va., 1980-81. Pres. Greater Atlanta Pan Hellenic Coun., Atlanta, 1992; corr. sec. Greater Atlanta Pan Hellenic, Atlanta, 1991; vol. United Negro Coll. Fund, Atlanta, 1989. Named to Outstanding Young Women of Am., 1982. Mem. Coun. for Exceptional Children, Oak Nkoll PTA, NAACP, Delta Sigma Theta (Pres.'s award 1992). Democrat. Baptist. Home: 7059 Whitfield Dr Riverdale GA 30296

LAMDEN, LILLIAN K., artist; b. Cleve., Mar. 9, 1921; m. Sidney K. Lamden, Nov. 22, 1943 (dec. Sept. 1993); children: Amy Lamden Burton, Margery Lamden. BFA, Dayton Art Inst., 1975. Animation film maker Bell Aircraft, Buffalo, 1943; sculptor in residence Living Arts Program, Dayton, Ohio, 1968-70; adj. faculty Cleve. Art Mus., 1940-41; faculty U. Dayton, 1970-74, Sinclair Coll., Dayton, 1976-80; mem. artist com. Miami Valley Coop. Gallery, Dayton, 1988—. Active Dayton Visual Arts Ctr., 1991—, Contemporary Art Ctr., Cin., 1992-95. Recipient 1st prize sculpture award Cleve. Mus. May Show, 1959, 1st prize Ind. U. E., 1978. Studio: 1121 E 2d St Dayton OH 45402

LAMEL, LINDA HELEN, insurance company executive, former college president, lawyer; b. N.Y.C., Sept. 10, 1943; d. Maurice and Sylvia (Abrams) Treppel; 1 child, Diana Ruth Sands. BA magna cum laude, Queens Coll., 1964; MA, NYU, 1968; JD, Bklyn. Law Sch., 1976. Bar: N.Y. 1977, U.S. Dist. Ct. (3d dist.) N.Y. 1977. Mgmt. analyst U.S. Navy, Bayonne, N.J., 1964-65; secondary sch. tchr. Farmingdale Pub. Sch., N.Y., 1965-73; curriculum specialist Yonkers Bd. Edn., N.Y., 1973-75; program dir. Office of Lt. Gov., Albany, N.Y., 1975-77; dep. supt. N.Y. State Ins. Dept., N.Y.C., 1977-83; pres., chief exec. officer Coll. of Ins., N.Y.C., 1983-88; v.p. Tchr.'s Ins. and Annuity Assn., N.Y.C., 1988-96; dir. Seneca (N.Y.) Ins. Co. Contbr. articles to profl. jours. Campaign mgr. lt. gov.'s primary race, N.Y. State, 1974. Mem. ABA (tort and ins. sect. com. chmn. 1985-86), N.Y. State Bar Assn. (exec. com. ins. sect. 1984-88), Assn. of Bar of City of N.Y. (chmn. med. malpractice com. 1989-91), Am. Mgmt. Assn. (ins. and risk mgmt. council), Fin. Women's Assn., Assn. Profl. Ins. Women (Woman of Yr. award 1988), Phi Beta Kappa (v.p. Phi Beta Kappa Assoc. 1992—).

LAMFERS, DEBRA K., creative director; b. Salina, Kans., July 1, 1957; d. G. Harold and Ruth I. (Anderson) L. BA, U. Kans., 1979. Owner, creative dir. Debra Lamfers Design, Kansas City, San Francisco, 1980—. Supporting vol. Zen Hospice Project, San Francisco, 1991—; art therapy vol. San Francisco Gen. Hosp., 1992-93. Recipient award of excellence in logo design Am. Corp. Identity, 1996. Mem. Am. Inst. Graphic Arts (events coord. 1995-96). Office: 665 3d St Ste 513 San Francisco CA 94107

LAMM, BARBARA HAVILAND, writer, researcher; b. Waynesville, N.C., May 28, 1920; d. Willis Bradley and Mary Lucile (Satterthwaite) Haviland; 1 child, Willis Haviland Lamm. AB, Stanford U., 1942; MEd, U. N.C., 1959. Model John Powers, N.Y.C., 1943, 1947-48; civilian employee Econ. and Fin. Directorates Office of Mil. Govt. U.S., Berlin, 1945-47; civilian employee in cryptography Signal Sect., 6th Army Hdqrs., San Francisco; instr. social studies, counselor N.C. Pub. Schs., 1954-64; instr. history and govt., rehab. counselor spl. svcs. Calif. Pub. Schs., 1964-79; creator REACH Abuse and Rape Ctr., Haywood County, N.C., 1985; instr. adult edn. Haywood C.C., N.C., 1985-88. Author: This Is You, America!, 1996; also articles. Mem. Inner Wheel Internat. Home: 500 Killian St #E15 Waynesville NC 28786

LAMM, CAROLYN BETH, lawyer; b. Buffalo, Aug. 22, 1948; d. Daniel John and Helen Barbara (Tatakis) L.; m. Peter Edward Halle, Aug. 12, 1972; children: Alexander P., Daniel E. BS, SUNY Coll. at Buffalo, 1970; JD, U. Miami (Fla.), 1973. Bar: Fla., 1973, D.C., 1976, N.Y. 1983. Trial atty. frauds sect. civil div. U.S. Dept. Justice, Washington, 1973-78, asst. chief comml. litigation sect. civil div., 1978, asst. dir., 1978-80; assoc. White & Case, Washington, 1980-84, ptnr., 1984—; mem. Sec. State's Adv. Com. Pvt. Internat. law, 1988-91; arbitrator U.S. Panel of Arbitrators, Internat. Ctr. Settlement of Investment Disputes, 1995—. Mem. bd. editors Can./U.S. Rev. Bus. Law, 1987-92; mem. editorial adv. bd. Inside Litigation; contbr. articles to legal publs. Fellow Am. Bar Found.; mem. ABA (chmn. young lawyers divsn., rules and calendar com., chmn. house membership com., chmn. assembly resolution com., sec. 1984-85, chmn. internat. litigation com. coun. 1991-94, sect. litigation, ho. dels. 1982—, nominating com. 1984-87, chair, past D.C. Cir. mem., standing com. fed. judiciary 1993—, com. scope and correlation of work), Am. Arbitration Assn. (arbitrator, com. on fed. arbitration act), Fed. Bar Assn. (chmn. sect. on antitrust and trade regulation), Bar Assn. D.C. (bd. dirs., sec.), D.C. Bar (pres.-elect, bd. govs. 1987-93, steering com. litigation sect.), Am. Law Inst., Women's Bar Assn. D.C., Am. Soc. Internat. Law, Internat. Bar Assn. (bus. law sect., internat. litigation com.), Am. Turkish Friendship Coun. (bd. dirs., chair dirs., sec., gen. counsel), Nat. Women's Forum, Columbia Country Club. Democrat. Home: 2801 Chesterfield Pl NW Washington DC 20008-1015 Office: White and Case 601 Thirteenth St NW Washington DC 20005

LAMMA, CANDACE MCDANIEL, guidance counselor, primary school educator, elementary school educator; b. Warrenton, Va., Oct. 1, 1955; d. Roy Franklin and Bette Anne (Slusher) McD.; m. Philip Daniel Lamma, Jan. 2, 1988; children: Anne-Ashleigh, Paige. BS, Longwood Coll., 1977; MA, Va. Tech., 1991. Cert. elem. tchr. K-3, Va., elem. guidance counselor. Tchr. Craig County Schs., New Castle, Va., 1977-79; tchr. Rappahannock County Schs., Washington, Va., 1979-88, counselor, 1989—; chmn. gifted and talented screening com., Rappahannock County Schs., Washington, Va., 1989—, mem. gifted and talented adv. bd., 1989—, cons., 1989—, chmn. food drive, 1989—, child study team, 1989, virtue curriculum com., 1994—. Mem. choir Flint Hill (Va.) United Methodist Ch., 1982, Sunday sch. tchr., 1983—, supt., 1986—, pres. Women's Mission Group, 1995—; asst. leader 4-H Cloverbuds, Rappahannock County, 1992—; com. mem. 10K Fodderstack Race Rappahannock County, 1983—; helper Brownies, Flint Hill, Va., 1994—. Mem. Am. Counseling Assn., Va. Counseling Assn., Va. Sch. Counseling Assn., Apple Valley Counseling Assn., Rappahannock County Heart Assn. (resdl. chmn. 1992-94), Alpha Delta Kappa (recording sec. 1994—), Alpha Delta Pi. Methodist. Home: P O Box 368 Flint Hill VA 22627 Office: Rappahannock County Elem Sch 34 School House Rd Washington VA 22747

LAMON, KATHY LYNN, nursing administrator; b. Moultrie, Ga., July 24, 1961; d. James Daniel and Sammie Ruth (Fletcher) Miles; m. Thomas Eldred Lamon, Aug. 23, 1980. BSN, Valdosta State U., 1983. RN, Fla. Surg. staff nurse Putnam Cmty. Hosp., Palatka, Fla., 1983-84, surg. charge nurse, 1984-86, surg. asst. nurse mgr., 1986-87, nurse mgr. progressive care unit, 1987-90; sr. cmty. health nurse Putnam County Pub. Health Dept., Palatka, 1990; DON Palatka Health Care Ctr., 1991-94; asst. regional nurse North Fla. region Nat. Healthcare, Ocala, 1994—. Author: Pockety Buddy for Nurses PCH, 1991. Youth group leader Palatka Bapt. Temple, 1992-95. Recipient Dr. Frist Humanitarian award Hosp. Corp. of Am., 1988, others; named Outstanding Young Med. Profl., Jaycees, 1988. Mem. Nat. Assn. DON, Intravenous Nurses Soc., N.E. Fla. DON. Republican. Office: Nat Healthcare 3400 SW 27th Ave Ocala FL 34474

LAMONT, ALICE, accountant, consultant; b. Houston, July 19; d. Harold and Bessie Bliss (Knight) L. BS, Mont. State U.; MBA in Taxation, Golden Gate U., 1983; CPA. Tchr. London Central High Sch., 1971-80; acct. Signetics, Sunnyvale, Calif., 1980-82; propr. Alice Lamont Ltd., 1985—. Mem. Atlanta Hist. Soc., High Mus. Art, Atlanta Botanical Garden, Brit. Amer. Bus. Group (mem. com., 1993—), Friend of Atlanta Opera, Atlanta Opera Guild, St. Philips Planned Giving Com. Fellow Ga. Soc. CPAs (chmn. Acctg. Inst. 1995—); mem. AAUW (life mem., audit chmn. 1993-95, mem. scholarship com. 1994—), Atlanta Tax Study Assn., Inst. Internal Auditors, English Speaking Union, Women Bus. Owners, Buckhead Bus. Assn., Atlanta Woman's Club (co-chair ways and means com. 1985-86, asst. treas. 1986-88, treas. 1990, 92-94), Women's Commerce Club (mem. adv. bd. 1994—).

LAMONT, LEE, music management executive; b. Queens, N.Y.; m. August Tagliamonte, Apr. 30, 1951; 1 child, Leslie Lamont. With Nat. Concerts & Artists Group, N.Y.C., 1955-58; asst. Sol Hurok Concerts, N.Y.C., 1958-67; person rep. for concerts, rec. and TV Isaac Stern, N.Y.C., 1968-76; v.p. ICM Artists Ltd., N.Y.C., 1976-85; pres. ICM Artists Ltd. and ICM Artists (London) Ltd., N.Y.C., 1985-95, chmn. bd. dirs., 1995—; Mem. adv. com. Hannover (Germany) Internat. Violin Competition. Mem. Am. Coun. on the Arts, Japan Soc., Asia Soc., Am. Symphony Orch. League (bd. dirs.), Bohemian Club. Office: ICM Artists Ltd 40 W 57th St Fl 16 New York NY 10019-4001

LAMONT, ROSETTE CLEMENTINE, Romance languages educator, theatre journalist, translator; b. Paris; came to U.S., 1941, naturalized, 1946; d. Alexandre and Loudmilla (Lamont) L.; m. Frederick Hyde Farmer, Aug. 9, 1969. B.A., Hunter Coll., 1947; M.A., Yale U., 1948, Ph.D., 1954. Tutor Romance langs. Queens Coll., CUNY, 1950-54, instr., 1954-61, asst. prof., 1961-64, assoc. prof., 1965-67, prof., 1967—; mem. doctoral faculties, comparative lit., theatre, French and women's studies cert. program CUNY, 1968—; State Dept. envoy Scholar Exch. Program, USSR, 1974; rsch. fellow, 1976; lectr. Alliance Francaise, Maison Francaise of NYU; vis. prof. Sorbonne, Paris, 1985-86; vis. prof. theatre Sarah Lawrence Coll., 1994, 95, 96. Author: The Life and Works of Boris Pasternak, 1964, De Vive Voix, 1971, Ionesco, 1973, The Two Faces of Ionesco, 1978, Ionesco's Imperatives: The Politics of Culture, 1993, Women on the Verge, 1993; translator: Days and Memory, 1990, Auschwitz and After, 1995, Brazen, 1996; also contbr. to various books; author, guest editor The Metaphysical Farce issue Collages and Bricolages, 1996-97; mem. editl. bd. Western European Stages, also contbg. editor; European corr. Theatre Week: Columbia Dictionary of Modern European Literature; fgn. corr. Stages. Decorated chevalier, then officier des Palmes Academiques, officier des Arts et Lettres (France); named to Hunter Coll. Hall of Fame, 1991; Guggenheim fellow, 1973-74; Rockefeller Found. humanities fellow, 1983-84. Mem. PEN, MLA, Am. Soc. Theatre Research, Internat. Brecht Soc., Drama Desk (voting mem.), Internat. Assn. Theatre Critics, Phi Beta Kappa, Sigma Tau Delta, Pi Delta Phi. Club: Yale. Home: 260 W 72nd St Apt 9D New York NY 10023-2822 Office: CUNY Queens Coll Dept European Langs Flushing NY 11367

LA MONT-WELLS, TAWANA FAYE, camera operator and video director, public relations executive; b. Ft. Worth, May 12, 1948; d. Jerry James and Roberta Ann (Wilkinson) La M. AA, Antelope Coll., 1979; BA in Anthropology, UCLA, 1982. Forest technician, trail constrn. supr. Angeles Nat. Forest, Region 9 U.S. Forest Svc., Pear Blossom, Calif., 1974-79; trail constrn. supr., maintenance asst. Calif. State Parks, 1979-81; cable TV installer Sammons Comm., Glendale, Calif., 1981-83; camera operator Sammons Comm., San Fernando, Calif., 1983-87; video studio and ENG remotes dir., mgr., program mgr. channels 6 and 21 Marcus Cable, Glendale, Calif., 1987—; video dir., prodr. LBW & Assocs. Internat., Ltd., 1988—; mem. ednl. access channel satellite program evaluation com., Glendale and Burbank, 1990-92; mem. Foothill Cmty. TV Network, Glendale and Burbank, 1987—; pres./CEO Chamblee Found., Ltd., 1995—. Prodr., dir. (homeless video) Bittersweet Streets, 1988; cameraperson Rockin in A Hard Place, 1988-93; dir., editor over 1000 videos. Active Glendale Hist. Soc., 1992—; bd. dirs. Am. Heart Assn., 1992—, comms. chair; bd. dirs. ARC, 1993—, mem. disaster svcs. team, cultural diversity chair, 1994—; mem. mktg. com. Burbank YMCA, 1994—; bd. dirs. Glendale Rose Float Assn., 1995—. Recipient award of appreciation LBW and Assocs. Internat., 1988, Bur. Census, 1990, USMC, 1991, Verdugo Disaster Recovery Project, 1995, ARC, 1995, ARC Spl. citation for exceptional vol. svc., 1995, award of outstanding pub. svc. Social Security Adminstrn. HHS, 1989, dedicated svc. award Am. Heart Assn., 1992, cert. of appreciation, 1994, 95. Mem. NFA, NRA, Am. Women in Radio and TV, Am. Bus. Women Assn., UCLA Alumni ASsn. (lfie), Wildlife Waystation, Alpha Gamma. Democrat. Home: 46209 Kings Caynon Rd Lancaster CA 93536

LAMORE, BETTE, rehabilitation counselor, motivational speaker; b. Chgo., Oct. 1, 1948. BA in Polit. Sci., U. Ariz., 1971, MS in Rehab. Counseling, 1974. Cert. rehab. counselor & ins. rehab. specialist. Social worker Pima County Welfare Dept., Tuscon, 1971-72; residential therapist So. Arix. Mental Health Clinic, Tuscon, 1972-73; drug counselor Awareness House Drug Clinics, Tuscon, 1973-74; dir. residential intervention ctr. YWCA,

Tuscon, 1974-75; rehab. counselor Calif. State Dept. Rehab., Ventura and Thousand Oaks, 1975-77; job placement specialist, counselor Moorpark (Calif.) C.C., 1977-81; co-owner, rehab. counselor Experienced Rehab. Advisors, Atascadero, Calif., 1981—; breeder Arabian horses Whispering Oaks Arabians, Atascadero, 1987—; cons. for drug abuse programs Ventura (Calif.) County Health Svcs., 1975; expert witness in field. Author: My Friend Joe, 1984; co-author: Injured Workers Guide to California Workers Compensation System, 1988. Scholar NIMH, 1973. Mem. Calif. Assn. Rehab. Profls., Internat. Arabian Horse Assn. (v.p. Los Robles chpt. 1991), Am. Horseshow Assn., Phi Kappa Phi, Phi Beta Kappa, Pi Lambda Theta. Democrat. Home: PO Box 2863 Atascadero CA 93423-2863 Office: Experienced Rehab Advisors PO Box 1521 Paso Robles CA 93446

LAMOREAUX, LAURA ELÁN, artist; b. Manhattan, N.Y., Nov. 5, 1955; d. Marilyn Jeanne L.; m. Michael Edward Hilleman. AS (with honors), Columbia Greene Coll., 1973; student, UCLA, Westwood, 1983, Otis Palson Sch. Design, L.A., 1984-88. RN, Calif. Design artist (CD cover and 8 record labels) The Message Is in the Music, 1994. Recipient Creative award Internat. Art Show, Paris, 1994. Home and Office: 151 Westlake Blvd Malibu CA 90265

LAMOTTE, JANET ALLISON, management specialist; b. Norfolk, Va., Mar. 3, 1942; d. Charles Nelson Jr. and Geneva Elizabeth (Baird) Johnson; m. Larry LaMotte, Aug. 30, 1964 (div. Aug. 1979); children: Lisa Renee LaMotte Buchholz, Lori Louise. AA, Rose State Coll., 1982; BA, U. Ctrl. Okla., 1984; MA in Human Rels., U. Okla., 1986. Clk./typist U.S. Army, Washington, 1960, Fort Belvoir, Va., 1961, Dallas, 1961; clk./typist IRS, Dallas, 1962, Richmond, Va., 1962-63; clk./typist DLA, Alexandria, Va., 1978, IRS, Oklahoma City, 1978-79, Tinker AFB, 1979; sec. IRS, Richmond, 1963-64, Tinker AFB, 1981-82; pers. asst. State Bd. Control, Austin, Tex., 1964-65; procurement clk. FAA, Oklahoma City, 1965-66; acctg. clk. Tinker AFB, 1980-81, clk./stenographer, 1980-81, supply specialist, 1982-87, recoverable inventory mgmt. specialist, 1987—. Mem. NAFE, AAUW, Am. Bus. Women's Assn. (v.p. membership downtown reflections chpt. 1992-93), Air Force Assn. (v.p. pub. rels. Gerrity chpt., Medal of Merit 1995, exceptional svc. award 1996), Okla. Air Force Assn. (v.p. 1995-96, mem. of yr. award 1996, exec. sec. 1996—), Tinker (Okla.) Mgmt. Assn. (membership, ticket monitor 1994—, 1st place new mem. recruitment), Toastmasters (area gov. 1991-92). Home: 9525 Ridgeview Dr Oklahoma City OK 73120

LAMOUREUX, GLORIA KATHLEEN, nurse, air force officer; b. Billings, Mont., Nov. 2, 1947; d. Laurits Bungaard and Florence Esther (Nielsen) Nielsen; m. Kenneth Earl Lamoureux, Aug. 31, 1973 (div. Feb. 1979). BS, U. Wyo., 1970; MS, U. Md., 1984. Staff nurse, ob-gyn DePaul Hosp., Cheyenne, Wyo., 1970; enrolled USAF, 1970, advanced through grades to col.; staff nurse ob-gyn dept. 57th Tactical Hosp., Nellis AFB, Nev., 1970-71, USAF Hosp., Clark AB, Republic Philippines, 1971-73; charge nurse ob-gyn dept. USAF Regional Hosp., Sheppard AFB, Tex., 1973-75; staff nurse ob-gyn dept. USAF Regional Hosp., MacDill AFB, Fla., 1976-79; charge nurse ob-gyn dept. USAF Med. Ctr., Andrews AFB, Md., 1979-80, MCH coord., 1980-82; chief nurse USAF Clinic, Eielson AFB, Alaska, 1984-86, Air Force Systems Command Hosp., Edwards AFB, Calif., 1986-90; comdr. 7275th Air Base Group Clinic, Italy, 1990-92, 42d Med. Group, Loring AFB, Maine, 1992-94; 347th Med. Group, Moody AFB, Ga., 1994-96; chief nursing svcs. divsn. Hdqrs. Air Edn. and Tng. Command, Randolph AFB, Tex., 1996—. Mem. Assn. Women's Health, Obstetric, and Neonatal Nurses (sec.-treas. armed forces dist. 1986-88, vice-chmn. armed forces dist. 1989-91), Air Force Assn., Assn. Mil. Surgeons U.S., Bus. and Profl. Women's Assn. (pub. rels. chair Prince George's County chpt. 1981-82), Assn. Healthcare Execs., Sigma Theta Tau. Republican. Lutheran. Home: 13515 ThessalyRd Universal City TX 78148

LAMPE, HARRIETT RICHMOND, retired educator, artist; b. Pitts., June 5, 1906; d. David Philip and Harriet Calhoun (Colwell) Richmond; m. William Seth Lampe, Apr. 12, 1930; children: Keith, Elin, Seth, Karen. BA, Carnegie-Mellon U., 1927; postgrad., Columbia U., 1927, 28, Fairleigh Dickinson U., 1959, U. Mich., Dearborn, 1961. Cert. art tchr., Pa., N.J., Mich. Tchr. elem. art Bayard Sch., Pitts., 1927-29; tchr. art Frick Tchr.'s Tng., Pitts., 1929-31, Tenafly (N.J.) High Sch., 1959-61; tchr. art, English, French jr. and sr. high schs. Birmingham, Mich., 1962-71. One-woman shows include Maitland Gallery of Art and the Ormond War Meml. Art Gallery; exhibited in group shows at U. Miami Lowe Gallery, Winter Park Art Festival, Halifax Art Festival, Images and others; represented in pvt. collections, Fla., Mich., Pa., N.Y. Mem. AAUW, Detroit Women Painters and Sculptors, Detroit Fine Arts Alliance, Birmingham Art Assn., Pitts. Art League, Nat. League of Am. Pen Women, Art League of Volusia County (Fla.), Artist Group, Beaux Art of Volusia. Republican. Presbyterian. Home: 9 Hialeah Dr Apt 102 Daytona Beach FL 32117-2531

LAMPEL, ANITA KAY, psychologist; b. L.A., May 25, 1946; d. Jack Murray and Rose (Maltun) L.; m. Stanley David Mishook, Dec. 21, 1975; children: Jacob, David. PhD, Stanford U., 1969. Diplomate Am. Bd. Profl. Psychology; lic. psychologist, Calif. Staff psychologist Children's Meml. Hosp., Chgo., 1970-73; mgr. children's program San Bernardino (Calif.) County Dept. of Mental Health, 1973-79; pvt. practice San Bernardino, 1979—; instr. various univs., Calif., 1973— Author: (with others) Group Psychotherapy with Children and Adolescents, 1987; contbr. articles to profl. jours. Chair Gifted Edn. Adv. Commn., San Bernardino, 1988-90; mem. Family Life Edn. Adv. Commn., San Bernardino, 1988-91. Mem. Am. Psychology Assn., Calif. State Psychology Assn., Inland Counties Psychol. Assn. (sec. 1988-89), Am. Bd. Profl. Psychology (western regional bd. dirs. 1988-93).

LAMPERT, ZOHRA, actress; b. N.Y.C.; d. Morris and Rachil (Eriss) L. Student, U. Chgo.; studies with Mira Rostova. Actress: (stage prodns.) Dancing in the Chequered Shade, 1955, Venice Preserv'd, 1955-56, Diary of a Scoundrel, 1956, Major Barbara, 1956, Maybe Tuesday, 1958, Look: We've Come Through, 1961, First Love, 1961, Mother Courage and Her Children, 1963 (N.Y. Drama Critics Poll award 1973), After the Fall, 1964, Marco Millions, 1964, The Natural Look, 1967, Lovers and Other Strangers, 1968, Drinks Before Dinner, 1978-79, Gifted Children, 1983, My Poppa's Wine, 1986, The Diary of Anne Frank, 1987, Mr. Gogol and Mr. Preen, 1991, A Day in New York, 1994-95, (feature films) Splendor in the Grass, 1961, A Fine Madness, 1966, Bye Bye Braverman, 1968, Let's Scare Jessica to Death, 1971, Alphabet City, 1984, Fakebook, 1989, Alan and Naomi, 1991, The Cafeteria, 1986, (TV series) Where the Heart is, 1970-71, The Girl with Something Extra, 1973-74, Doctors' Hospital, 1975-76, (TV movies) The Connection, 1972, Izzy & Moe, 1985, (TV spl.) Leonard Bernstein's Carmen for Omnibus; (TV episodes) Better Luck Next Time, 1964, The F.B.I., 1970, Love, American Style, 1972-73, Kojak (Emmy award), others, also radio and TV commls. (Andy awards). Recipient Ralph Weiler prize for painting, Louis La Beaume prize for painting Nat. Acad. Design. Mem. Actors' Equity Assn., AFTRA, AGVA. Address: care David Williams Don Buchwald Agy 10 E 44th St New York NY 10017

LAMSON, EVONNE VIOLA, therapist, computer software company executive, consultant, pastor, Christian education administrator; b. Ithaca, Mich., July 8, 1946; d. Donald and Mildred (Perdew) Guild; m. James E. Lamson, Nov. 2, 1968; 1 child, Lillie D. Assoc. in Math., Washtenaw C.C., Ypsilanti, Mich., 1977; BS, Ea. Mich. U., 1989; MA in Pastoral Counseling Ashland (Ohio) Theol. Sem., 1993. Lic. profl. counselor, Mich. Data base mgr. ERIM, Ann Arbor, Mich., 1978-81; mgr. product svcs. Comshare, Ann Arbor, 1981-90, project leader, tng. course designer info. techs., 1991-93; founder, pres. G & L Consultants, Brighton, Mich., 1982—; tng. specialist Comshare, Ann Arbor, 1990-93; Assoc. Pastor, dir. Christian edn. Keystone Cmty. Ch., Saline, Mich., 1993-95; founder Living Waters Counseling, 1993—. Study leader Brighton Wesleyan Ch., 1981-93; lic. minister Weseleyan Ch. Am., 1993—; program dir. Wesleyan Womens Assn. of Brighton, 1983-91; clin. staff counselor Women's Resource Ctr., Howell, Mich., 1991-94; clin. counselor Livingston Counseling and Assessment, 1994—, clin. team leader, 1995—. Mem. AACD, NAFE, AACC, Am. Mgmt. Assn., Fairbanks Family of Am., Internat. Platform Assn. Avocations: skiing, motivational speaking, reading. Home: 6708 Calfhill Ct Brighton MI 48116-7419

LANAHAN, ELLEN ANN DOTY, human resources specialist; b. Boston, May 13, 1941; d. Bradford and Grace Ann (Shay) Doty; m. Mario Roberto Perez-Avoca, Dec. 19, 1964 (div. June 1975); 1 child, Elena Nicole; m. Frank B. Lanahan, Apr. 2, 1980; 1 child, Kate. BA, Smith Coll., 1963; MA, Fla. State U., 1965; ABD, U. Fla., 1975. Cert. tchr. English/guidance K-14, Fla. Internat. edn. cons. Am. Assn. State Colls. and Univs., Washington, 1975-76, 81-83; minority student counselor Coppin State Coll., Balt., 1976-77; core faculty mem. Goddard Coll. Program, Washington, 1976-78; dir. student affairs Calif. Sch. Profl. Psychology, L.A., 1979-80; coord. internat. student svcs. U. Wis., Stout, Menomonie, 1983-85; east coast mktg. dir. Whispers from Nature, Silver Spring, Md., 1985-86; dir. student svcs. Southeastern U., Washington, 1986-87; sr. rsch. assoc. Westat, Rockville, Md., 1987-88; sr. cons. Rsch. & Evaluation Assocs., Washington, 1988-90; mgmt. devel. specialist FDIC, Washington, 1990—; lectr. in field. Author: Values, Beliefs and Goals of Education, 1973. County rep. PTA, Pasadena, Calif., 1979-80; vol. coord. RSBBA Satsang, Washington, 1986-94; vol. Gaithersburg (Md.) Help, 1988-90; leader Girl Scouts, Gaithersburg, 1989—. Mem. NAFE, ASTD (conf. com. 1990-91), Orgn. Devel. Network. Democrat. Office: FDIC 550 17th St NW VASQ 2065 Washington DC 20019

LANAM, LINDA LEE, lawyer; b. Ft. Lauderdale, Fla., Nov. 21, 1948; d. Carl Edward and Evelyn (Bolton) L. BS, Ind. U., 1970, JD, 1975. Bar: Ind. 1975, Pa. 1979, U.S. Dist. Ct. (no. and so. dists.) Ind. 1975, U.S. Supreme Ct. 1982, Va. 1990. Atty., asst. counsel Lincoln Nat. Life Ins. Co., Ft. Wayne, Ind., 1975-76, 76-78; atty., mng. atty. Ins. Co. of N.Am., Phila., 1978-79, 80-81; legis. liaison Pa. Ins. Dept., Harrisburg, 1981-82, dep. ins. commr., 1982-84; exec. dir., Washington rep. Blue Cross and Blue Shield Assn., Washington, 1984-86; v.p. and sr. counsel Union Fidelity Life Ins. Co., Am. Patriot Health Ins. Co., etc., Trevose, Pa., 1986-89; v.p., gen. counsel, corp. sec. Life Ins. Co. Va., Richmond, 1989—, also bd. dirs.; chmn. adv. com. health care legis. Nat. Assn. Ins. Commrs., 1985-87, chmn. long term care, 1986-87, mem. tech. resource com. on cost disclosure and genetic testing, 1993-95; mem. tech. adv. com. Health Ins. Assn. Am., 1986-89; mem. legis. com. Am. Coun. Life Ins., 1994—. Contbr. articles to profl. jours. Pres. Phila. Women's Network, 1980-81; chmn. city housing code bd. appeals Harrisburg, 1985-86. Mem. ABA, Richmond Bar Assn. Republican. Presbyterian. Office: Life Ins Co Va GE Capital C 6610 W Broad St Richmond VA 23230-1702

LANCASTER, B. JEANETTE, dean, nursing educator. BSN, U. Tenn.; MSN, Case Western Res. U.; PhD, U. Okla. Staff nurse U. Tenn.; nurse clinician Univ. Hosps. of Cleve.; assoc. prof. psychiat. nursing Tex. Christian U.; coord. cmty. health nursing U. Ala., Birmingham, chair master's degree program Sch. Nursing; dean, prof. Sch. Nursing Wright State U., Dayton, Ohio; now dean, prof. nursing U. Va., Charlottesville; assoc. dir. patient care svcs. U. Va. Health Scis. Ctr., Charlottesville; assoc. Va. Health Policy Rsch. Ctr.; chmn. bd. dirs. Statewide Area Health Edn. Ctr. Program; mem. study group for nurse practitioners Va. Gen. Assembly; presenter in field. Author 4 books, including Community Health Nursing: Processes and Practices for Promoting Health; editor Family and Cmty. Health; contbr. articles to profl. jours. Recipient Disting. Alumni award Frances Payne Bolton Sch. Nursing-Case Western Res. U., 1984, Outstanding Alumni award U. Tenn. Coll. Nursing, 1985. Fellow Am. Acad. Nursing; mem. Am. Assn. Colls. Nursing (bd. dirs.). Office: U Va Sch Nursing Charlottesville VA 22903

LANCASTER, KATHY JO, medical, surgical nurse; b. Anderson, S.C., Jan. 17, 1957; d. William Elijah Morris and Betty Jo Blalock; m. Terry Wayne Lancaster, Dec. 11, 1976 (div. June 1994); children: Aaron Daniel, Jonah Elias. ADN, U. S.C., Spartanburg, 1984. EMS, CCRN, AACN, Cert. critical care nurse. Staff nurse Mary Black Meml. Hosp., Spartanburg, 1984-86; staff nurse ICU Spartanburg Regional Med. Ctr., 1986-88, staff nurse, charge nurse cardiovascular recovery unit, 1988-96; staff nurse St. Lukes Free Clinic, Spartanburg, 1992-93. Kitchen worker Soup Kithche 1st Presbyn., Spartanburg, 1986-88. Democrat. Soc. of Friends. Home: 835 Old Melvin Hill Rd Campobello SC 29322

LANCASTER, LISA MARIE, law enforcement officer; b. Worcester, Mass., Nov. 13, 1966; d. William Peter Ben and Willie Mae (Blyther) L.; m. James T. Spencer, Jr., July 15, 1987 (div. July 1988). Student, Lincoln U., 1984-85, U. S.C., 1986; B, Community Coll., Dover, Del., 1991; A in Criminal Justice, C.C. of the Air Force, Wilmington Coll., 1990; BS in Behavioral Sci., Wilmington Coll., 1996; postgrad., Wesley Coll., 1991—. E-1 3743 BMTS USAF, Lackland AFB, Tex., 1985-86; E-2, E-3 363 SPS USAF, Shaw AFB, S.C., 1986-88; E-4 8th SPS USAF, Kunsan Air Base, Korea, 1989-90; E-5 436 SPS USAF, Dover, 1990—; D.A.R.E. instr. Sch. Ill. Police Acad., 1993; police officer New Castle County Police, New Castle, Del., 1994—; pres. dorm coun. 363 SPS, Shaw AFB, 1986-88; K-55 radar cert. 436 SPS, Dover, 1991—; drug identifier Del. State Police Acad., Dover, 1991—. Rep. Worcester (Mass.) Youth Games, 1982-84; counselor Worcester City Boys & Girls Camp, 1983-84; social worker Shelter for Abused Children, Sumter, S.C., 1987-88; vol. Shelter for Homeless, Kunsan, 1989-90; tchr. Drug Abuse Resistance Edn., 1993; active Big Sister program. Mem. NAACP (Del. charter), 436 Security Policy Bouster Club (sec. 1990—). Democrat. Baptist. Home: Newtowne Village 4 Stephanie Dr Bear DE 19701 Office: 3601 N DuPont Hwy New Castle DE 19720

LANCASTER, PEGGY, advertising agency executive. Prin., creative dir. Scott/Lancaster (formerly Scott Lancaster Mills Atha), L.A., 1976—. Recipient numerous creative awards; named Woman of Yr., Am. Advt. Fedn., 1973. Office: Scott/Lancaster 27520 Hawthorne Blvd Ste 240 Rolling Hills Estates CA 90274

LANCASTER, RUTH VYSOKY, tax training manager; b. Cleve., May 28, 1937; d. John and Agnes Ann (Mehalko) Vysoky; m. William Dean Lancaster, Aug. 13, 1960; 1 child, Leslie Renée. BS in English, Carnegie Inst. Tech., 1959. Tchr. English Cleve. Bd. Edn., 1959-64; asst. editor Am. Ceramic Soc., Columbus, Ohio, 1973-77, Edutronics, Inc., Kansas City, Mo., 1978-80; programmed instrn. specialist H&R Block, Inc., Kansas City, Mo., 1980-82, tax rsch. and tng. specialist, 1982-92; mgr. tax tng. H&R Block Tax Svcs., Inc., Kansas City, Mo., 1992—. Office: H&R Block 4400 Main St Kansas City MO 64111

LANCASTER, SALLY RHODUS, non-profit consultant; b. Gladewater, Tex., June 28, 1938; d. George Lee and Milly Maria (Meadows) Rhodus; m. Olin C. Lancaster Jr., Dec. 23, 1960; children: Olin C. III, George Charles, Julie Meadows. BA magna cum laude, So. Meth. U., 1960, MA, 1979; PhD, East Tex. State U., 1983. Tchr. English, Tex. pub. schs., 1960-61, 78-79; sr. advisor Meadows Found., Inc., Dallas, 1979-96, also trustee and dir.; cons. to non-profit sector, 1996—. Trustee So. Meth. U., 1980-88, East Tex. State U., regent 1987-93; Tex. del. White House Conf. on Tourism, 1995; adv. dir. Los Caminos del Rio Inc.; dir. Inst. Nautical Archaeology; dir. emeritus Meadows Found.; mem. adv. bd. Communities Found. Tex. Office: Meadows Foundation Inc Wilson Historic Block 4802 Cole # 1301 Dallas TX 75205

LANCASTER, WYNNE ELAINE, air traffic contol assistant; b. Winchester, Va., Oct. 15, 1947; d. George William and Audry Lucille (Keckley) Keeler; 1 child, Aimee Lynne. AA, Shenandoah Coll., Winchester, Va., 1968; EEG cert., Med. Coll. Va., 1969; student, Fed. Aviation Acad., Oklahoma City, 1978-79, CAP Regional Staff Coll., Raleigh, N.C., 1989. Cert. Ross landscape painting instr. 1995. Computer info. specialist AUS, Leavenworth, Kans., 1979-80; text cons. USAF, Lowry AFB, Colo., 1980-81, tng. technician, 1981-83; exec. asst. U.S. Customs, Dulles Airport, Washington, 1983-86; air traffic control asst. FAA, Leesburg, Va., 1986-88; wilderness searcher, rescue team leader CAP, Va. wing, 1989-92, electronic DF leader 1989-92, comm. officer 1989-92, pub. rels. officer CAP, Front Royal, Va., 1989-91. water safety coord. and instr., U.S. Govt./ARC, West Germany, 1966-69; CPR trainer, trainer reviewer U.S. Govt., Lowry AFB, 1981-82; level I field team leader CAP, Front Royal, 1989-92; vol. Winchester (Va.) Med. Ctr., 1992—. Recipient Chuck Yeager Aerospace Edn. Achievement award CAP, Va. wing, 1990, Air Search and Rescue Ribbon 1988.

LANCOUR, KAREN LOUISE, secondary education educator; b. Cheboygan, Mich., June 2, 1946; d. Clinton Howard and Dorothy Marie (Passeno) L. AA, Alpena Community Coll., 1966; BA, Ea. Mich. U., 1968, MS, 1970. Teaching asst. Ea. Mich. U., Ypsilanti, 1968-70; tchr. sci. Utica (Mich.) Community Schs., 1970—. Nat. event supr. Sci. Olympiad, 1986—, mem. nat. rules com., 1987—, state event supr., 1986-91, regional dir., 1987. Recipient Disting. Svc. award Nat. Sci. Olympiad, 1995. Mem. Nat. Sci. Tchrs. Assn., Mich. Sci. Tchrs. Assn., Nat. Assn. Biology Tchrs., Met. Detroit Sci. Tchrs. Assn., Smithsonian Inst., Nat. Geographic Soc., Edison Inst., Mortar Bd., Internat. Biograph. Soc., Am. Biograph. Inst. Rsch. Assn. (dep. gov.), Internat. Platform Assn., Phi Theta Kappa, Kappa Delta Phi. Home: 8378 18 Mile Rd Apt 202 Sterling Heights MI 48313-3034 Office: Henry Ford II High Sch 11911 Clinton River Rd Sterling Heights MI 48313-2420

LAND, JUDITH BROTEN, stockbroker; b. Newark, July 27, 1951; d. Robert Allan and Marjorie (Frederickson) Broten; m. Andre Paul Land, Jan. 6, 1973; children: Ian Sherard, Margo Caryn. Student, Hood Coll., 1969-70, Denver U., 1970-71, Monmouth Coll., 1971-72, Fla. Atlantic U., 1976-77. Lic. ins. agt., Fla. Ops. dept. Fahnestock & Co., Red Bank, N.J., 1973; with ops. dept. Thomson McKinnon, South Orange, N.J., 1973-75; br. ops. rep. Thomson McKinnon, Boca Raton, Fla., 1977-80; sales asst., trainee Butcher & Singer Inc., Boca Raton, 1980-81, stockbroker, 1981-85; stockbroker A.G. Edwards & Sons, Inc., Boca Raton, 1985—; lectr. Palm Beach County Schs., Boca Raton, 1987-95, Palm Beach County Librs., 1990-91; daily stock market radio reporter Sta. WDBF-AM, Delray Beach, Fla., 1979-81. Community theatre performer; song composer. Mem. Whispering Pines PTA, 1986—, Singing Pines Children's Mus., Boca Raton, 1985-89, Young Women of the Arts, Boca Raton, 1989, C. of C., 1990-92. Republican. Episcopalian. Office: AG Edwards & Sons Inc 1900 Glades Rd Ste 451 Boca Raton FL 33431-7331

LANDAU, LAURI BETH, accountant, tax consultant; b. Bklyn., July 21, 1952; d. Jack and Audrey Carolyn (Zuckernick) L. BA, Skidmore Coll., 1973; postgrad., Pace. U., 1977-79. CPA, N.Y., Oreg. Mem. staff Audrey Z. Landau, CPA, Suffern, N.Y., 1976-78; mem. staff Ernst & Whinney, N.Y.C., 1979-80, mem. sr. staff, 1980-82, supr., 1982-84; mgr. Arthur Young & Co., N.Y.C., 1984-87, prin., 1987-89; sr. mgr. Ernst & Young, N.Y.C., 1989-92; ptnr. Landau & Landau, Pomona, N.Y., 1992—; ptnr. Audrey Z. Landau & Co., Wilmington, Vt., 1995—; spkr. World Trade Inst., N.Y.C., 1987—, Nat. Fgn. Trade Coun., N.Y.C., 1989—. Composer songs. Career counselor Skidmore Coll., Saratoga Springs, N.Y., 1977—; mem. leadership com. Class of 1973, 83-85, pres., 1985-93, fund chmn., 1987-88, mem. planned gift com., 1989—. N.Y. State Regents scholar, 1970. Mem. Nat. Conf. CPA Practitioners, N.Y. State Soc. CPAs, Skidmore Coll. Alumni Assn. (mem. nominating com. 1989-92). Skidmore Alumni Club, German Shepherd Dog Am. Club. Democrat. Office: Ste 205B 26 Firemens Memorial Dr Pomona NY 10970

LANDAU, MARILYN JOY, school counselor; b. Cleve., Apr. 3, 1942; d. Rubin Lawrence and Dorothy (Silver) L. BS, Ohio State U., 1964; MS in Sch. Counseling, U. LaVerne, 1991. Cert. tchr. K-8 Calif. Tchr. Cleve. Schs., 1964-65, Sulphur Springs Union Sch. Dist., Saugus, Calif., 1965-69; tchr., counselor L.A. Unified Sch. Dist., 1970—; v.p. secondary, United Tchrs. L.A., 1984-88. Regional dir. Calif. Dem. Party, 1992—; mem. L.A. County Dem. Com., 1976—, Calif. State Ctrl. Dem. Com., 1980—. Recipient Tchr. in Politics award United Tchrs. L.A., 1983; grantee Calif. Dept. Edn. Mem. LWV, AAUW, NOW, NEA (Pacific region coord. women's caucus 1994—), Nat. Women's Political Caucus, Anti Defamation League, L.A. Jewish Fedn. Coun. (Israel Commn. 1995—), Calif. Tchrs. Assn. (bd. dirs. 1992—), Am. Israel Pub. Affairs Com., Nat. Coun. Jewish Women, L.A. Sch. Counselors Assn., Calif. Sch. Counselors Assn., Calif. Assn. Counseling and Devel. Office: Calif Tchrs Assn 1705 Murchison Dr Burlingame CA 94010

LANDAU-CRAWFORD, DOROTHY RUTH, local social service executive; b. S.I., N.Y., Oct. 5, 1957; d. Robert August and Dorothy Faith (Schaut) Landau; m. John W. Crawford, Oct. 21, 1989. AS in Applied Sci., SUNY-Farmingdale, 1977; BS in Biology, Wagner Coll., 1979. Sci. tchr. Bais Yaakov, S.I., 1979-81; dental asst. Dr. Marvin Freeman, S.I., 1981-82; office mgr. Dr. Bennett C. Fidlow, S.I., 1982-85; polit. aide to S.I. Borough Pres., 1985-89; exec. dir. Richmond Sr. Svcs. Project Share, 1990—; v.p. N.J. Shared Housing Assn., regional dir. Nat. Shared Housing Resouces Ctr., 1995—. Environ. chmn. S.I. League for Better Govt., 1984—; pres. Tottenville Improvement Council Inc., Staten Island, 1985—; Dem. candidate for N.Y. State Assembly 60th dist., 1986, dist. leader; dir. community bds. S.I. Borough Pres.' Office; founder, pres. environ. group S.I.L.E.N.T., S.I., 1985; 1st v.p. 123d Community Council, S.I., 1986; social chmn. S. Shore Democratic Club; founding mem. Friends of Clay Pit Pond Park; mem. Protectors of Pine Oak Woods Inc., Roserio Alliotta Dem. Club, Dem. Orgn. of Richmond; trustee S.I. Bd. Leukemia Soc. Am., 1988—, chair Celebrity Waiters Luncheon; spl. election candidate for 51st Councilmatic Dist., 1994. Recipient Community Activist Award Office of Pres. S.I. Borough, 1987. Mem. NAFE, Bus. and Profl. Women (Young Careerist for S.I.). Roman Catholic. Avocations: photography, sports, ceramics, youth programs. Home: 168 Bedell Ave Staten Island NY 10307-2057 Office: 500 Jewett Ave Staten Island NY 10302-2613

LANDAUER, JERAMY LANIGAN, publishing company executive; b. Medford, Mass., Dec. 27, 1939; d. William Nicholas and Marion Elizabeth (Dorman) L. BA, Trinity Coll., Washington, 1961; cert., Harvard U., 1962; MBA, Columbia U., 1964. From mgr. direct mktg. to sr. v.p. direct mktg. Funk & Wagnalls, Inc., Ramsey, N.J., 1973-80; pres. Book Div. Times-Mirror Mags., N.Y.C., 1980-87; v.p., gen. mgr. Book Group Meredith Corp., Des Moines, 1987-88, pres. Book Group, 1988-91; pres. Landauer Corp., Des Moines, 1991—; bd. dirs. D.M.I.X., N.Y.C. Pres., bd. dirs. Girls' Club N.Y.C., 1986-87; bd. dirs. Trinity Coll., Washington, 1981-87, Des Moines Met. Opera, 1988—, Des Moines Symphony, 1989-91. Mem. Direct Mktg. Assn. (bd. dirs. 1984-91), Rotary. *

LANDBERG, ANN LAUREL, nurse, psychotherapist; b. Chgo., June 20, 1926; d. Carl Ryno and Ebba Sadie Elvira (Engstrom) Granlund; m. Harry Morton Landberg, Apr. 1, 1953 (dec. Feb. 1967); stepchildren: Rosabel, Marcene. RN, Swedish Hosp. Sch. Nursing, Seattle, 1948. Asst. head nurse Halcyon Hosp., Seattle, 1948; doctor's asst. Office of H.M. Landberg, M.D., Seattle, 1948-50, psychotherapist, 1950-67; pvt. practice psychotherapy, Seattle, 1967—; cons. Good Shepherd Sch. for Disturbed Girls, Seattle, 1954—, bd. dirs., 1954-60. Mem. Am. Psychotherapy Assn., King County Med. Aux., Stevens Hosp. Aux. (life), Swedish Hosp. Alumni (pres. 1952-53), Nat. Council Jewish Women, City of Hope, Edmonds Arts Assn. (life patron), Seattle Forensic Inst. (charter). Club: Swedish (Seattle). Home: 16900 Talbot Rd Edmonds WA 98026-5051 Office: 1007 Spring St Seattle WA 98104-1235

LANDECKER, ANITA EMILY, community developer, city planner; b. L.A., Jan. 16, 1958; d. Fred Klaus Landecker and Eva Miriam (Fuchs) Menkin; m. Gary William Squier, June 3, 1989; children: Aaron Squier, Hannah Squier, Jacob Squier. Bachelor's degree, U. Calif., Santa Barbara, 1979; M of City Planning, MIT, 1982. Planner L.A. Cmty. Design Ctr., 1982-83, exec. dir., 1983-87; Calif. dir. Local Initiatives Support Corp., L.A., 1987, regional v.p., 1989—; bd. dirs., chair 12th dist. Fed. Res. Bank, L.A.; mem. adv. bd. Fed. Home Loan Bank Bd. Mem. Mayor's Blue Ribbon Com. on Housing, L.A., 1988. Jewish. Office: Local Initiatives Ste 1600 1055 Wilshire Blvd Los Angeles CA 90017-2499

LANDEN, SANDRA JOYCE, psychologist, educator; b. L.A., May 8, 1960; m. Bernard B. Reifkind, Aug. 15, 1981. BA, UCLA, 1982, MA, 1984, PhD, 1988. Lic. clin. psychologist, Calif. Rsch. asst. UCLA Autism Clinic, 1980-82, UCLA Teaching Homes for Devel. Disabilities Project, 1981-82; rsch. assoc. UCLA Project for Devel. Disabilities, 1982-87; co-coord. parent tng. program UCI-UCLA Program for ADHD Children, 1984; teaching assoc. psychology dept. UCLA, 1984-87; psychology intern Hathaway Home for Children, Lakeview Terrace, Calif., 1985-86, clin. staff, 1986-87; clin. postdoctoral fellow Childrens Hosp. L.A., 1987-88; adj. faculty Grad. Sch. Edn. and Psychology Pepperdine U., L.A., 1988—; psychologist L.A., 1987—; dir. Westside Parenting Ctr., L.A., 1992—. Contbr. articles to profl. jours. Recipient scholarship UCLA, 1978-82, fellowship UCLA, 1982-85, dissertation rsch. grant UCLA, 1985-87. Mem. APA (div. psychoanalysis), Calif. Psychol. Assn., L.A. Psychol. Assn., Am. Assn. Mental Retardation. Office: 11340 W Olympic Blvd Ste 245 Los Angeles CA 90064-1612

LANDER, JOYCE ANN, nursing educator, medical/surgical nurse; b. Benton Harbor, Mich., July 27, 1942; d. James E. and Anna Mae (Versaw) Remus. LPN, Kalamazoo Practical Nursing, Ctr., 1967; AAS, Kalamazoo Valley C.C., 1981, Grad. Massage Therapy Program, 1995. LPN-RN Bronson Meth. Hosp., Kalamazoo, 1972-82; RN med./surg. unit Borgess Med. Ctr., Kalamazoo, 1982-84; RN pediatrics Upjohn Home Health Care, Kalamazoo, 1984-88; supr. nursing lab Kalamazoo Valley Community Coll., 1982—; nursing asst., instr. State of Mich. Observer, 1996—. Author: What Is A Nurse, 1980. Address: 3834 Greenleaf Cir Kalamazoo MI 49008-2509

LANDERS, ANN (MRS. ESTHER P. LEDERER), columnist; b. Sioux City, Iowa, July 4, 1918; d. Abraham B. and Rebecca (Rushall) Friedman; m. Jules W. Lederer, July 2, 1939 (div. 1975); 1 dau., Margo Lederer Howard. Student, Morningside Coll., 1936-39, LHD (hon.), 1964; hon. degree, Wilberforce (Ohio) Coll., 1972, Am. Coll. Greece, 1979, Meharry Med. Coll., 1981, Jacksonville U., 1983, St. Leo Coll., 1984, Fla. Internat. U., 1984, Med. Coll. Pa., 1985, New Eng. Coll., 1985, U. Wis., 1985, Lincoln Coll., 1986, Nat. Coll. Edn., 1986, Southwestern Adventist Coll., 1987, Duke U., 1987, Rosary Coll., 1989, U. Hartford, 1989, L.I. U., 1989, Med. Coll. Ohio, 1989, Roosevelt U., 1991, Ind. U., 1991, Howard U., 1991, Bellevue U., 1992, DePaul U., 1992, Ursinus Coll., 1992, Hillsdale Coll., 1993, St. Xavier U., 1993, Chgo. Theol. Sem., 1993, Barry U., 1993, Northwestern U., 1994, Columbia Coll., 1995. Syndicated columnist Chgo., 1955—; pres. Eppie Co., Inc., Chgo. Author: Since You Asked Me, 1962, Ann Landers Talks to Teen-agers about Sex, 1964, Truth is Stranger, 1968, Ann Landers Speaks Out, 1975, The Ann Landers Encyclopedia, 1978; also pub. svc. booklets and numerous mag. articles; syndicated columnist Los Angeles Times-Creators Syndicates. Chmn. Eau Claire (Wis.) Gray-Lady Corps, ARC, 1947-53; chmn. Minn.-Wis. council Anti-Defamation League, 1945-49; asst. Wis. chmn. Nat. Found. Infantile Paralysis, 1951-53; hon. nat. chmn. 1963 Tb Christmas Seal Campaign; bd. sponsors Mayo Clinic, 1970; mem. sponsors com. Mayo Found.; nat. adv. bd. Dialogue for the Blind, 1972; adv. com. on better health services AMA; county chmn. Democratic Party Eau Claire; bd. dirs. Rehab. Inst. Chgo.; nat. bd. dirs. Am. Cancer Soc., Nat. Cancer Inst.; vis. com. bd. overseers Harvard Med. Sch.; mem. Pres.'s Commn. Drunk Driving; trustee Menninger Found., Nat. Dermatology Found., Am. Coll. Greece, Deree-Pierce Coll., Athens, Meharry Med. Sch., Hereditary Disease Found.; dirs. adv. bd. Yale Comprehensive Cancer Ctr. Recipient award Nat. Family Service Assn., 1965, Adolf Meyer award Assn. Mental Health N.Y., 1965, Pres.'s Citation and nat. award Nat. Council on Alcoholism, 1966, 2d nat. award, 1975, Golden Stethoscope award Ill. Med. Soc., 1967, Humanitarianism award Internat. Lions Club, 1967; plaque of honor Am. Friends of Hebrew U., 1968, Gold Plate award Acad. Achievement, 1969; Nat. Service award Am. Cancer Soc., 1971, Robert T. Morse award Am. Psychiat. Assn., 1972; plaque recognizing establishment of chair in chem. immunology Weizmann Inst., 1974, Jane Addams Public Service award Hull House, 1977, Health Achievement award Nat. Kidney Found., 1978, Nat. award Epilepsy Found. Am., 1978, James Ewing Layman's award Soc. Surg. Oncologists, 1979, citation for disting. service AMA, 1979, Thomas More medal Thomas More Assn., 1979, NEA award, 1979, Margaret Sanger award, 1979, Stanley G. Kay medal Am. Cancer Soc., 1983, 1st William C. Menninger medal for achievement in mental health, 1984, Albert Lasker pub. service award, 1985, Edwin C. Whitehead award, 1988, Community Svc. award Gateway Found.'s Citizen's Coun., 1989, Pub. Svc. award NIMH, 1989, award for outstanding pub. edn. Nat. Alliance for the Mentally Ill, 1990, Outstanding Pub. Svc. to Sci. award Nat. Assn. for Biomed. Rsch., 1990, World of Children award UNICEF, 1993, Auxiliary Pub. Spirit award Am. Legion, 1995. Fellow Chgo. Gynecol. Soc. (citizen hon.); mem. LWV (pres. 1948), Brandeis U. Women (pres. 1960), Chgo. Econs. Club (dir. 1975), Harvard Club (Award 1994), Sigma Delta Chi. Clubs: Chgo. Econs. (dir. 1975), Harvard, Sigma Delta Chi. Office: Chgo Tribune 435 N Michigan Ave Chicago IL 60611-4001

LANDERS, SUSAN MAE, psychotherapist, professional counselor; b. Houston; d. James Edward and Frances Pauline (Braunagel) L. BS in Advt., U. Tex.; MS in Psychol. Counseling, U. Houston, Clearlake, 1994; cert. in sales, Dale Carnegie Inst. Lic. profl. counselor. Mktg. rep. K.C. Products, Houston, 1981-83; account exec. Williamson County Express, Austin, Tex., 1984; advt. cons. Stas. KMMM/KOKE, Austin, 1985; key account sales rep. GranTree Furniture Rental, Austin, 1986-89; individual habilitation counselor Ctr. for the Retarded Inc., Houston, 1990; case mgr. Mental Health and Mental Retardation Authority Harris County, Houston, 1991-92; primary therapist Riceland Psychiat. Hosp., 1994—. Mem. ACA, Am. Mental Health Counselors Assn., Tex. Counseling Assn., Tex. Mental Health Counselors Assn., Houston LPC Assn., Houston Group Psychotherapy Soc. Home: 4615 N Braeswood Blvd # 311D Houston TX 77096-2841 Office: Riceland Psychiat Hosp 4910 Airport Rosenberg TX 77471

LANDERS, VERNETTE TROSPER, writer, educator, association executive; b. Lawton, Okla., May 3, 1912; d. Fred Gilbert and LaVerne Hamilton (Stevens) Trosper; m. Paul Albert Lum, Aug. 29, 1952 (dec. May 1955); 1 child, William Tappan; m. 2d, Newlin Landers, May 2, 1959 (dec. Apr. 1990); children: Lawrence, Marlin. AB with honors, UCLA, 1933, MA, 1935, EdD, 1953; Cultural doctorate (hon.) Lit. World U., Tucson, 1985. Tchr. secondary schs., Montebello, Calif., 1935-45, 48-50, 51-59; prof. Long Beach City Coll., 1946-47; asst. prof. Los Angeles State Coll., 1950; dean girls Twenty Nine Palms (Calif.) High Sch., 1960-65; dist. counselor Morongo (Calif.) Unified Sch. Dist., 1965-72, coordinator adult edn., 1965-67, guidance project dir., 1967; clk.-in-charge Landers (Calif.) Post Office, 1962-82; ret., 1982. V.p., sec. Landers Assn., 1965—; sec. Landers Vol. Fire Dept., 1972—; life mem. Hi-Desert Playhouse Guild, Hi-Desert Meml. Hosp. Guild; bd. friends Copper Mountain Coll., 1990-91; bd. dirs., sec. Desert Emergency Radio Service; mem. Rep. Senatorial Inner Circle, 1990-92, Regent Nat. Fedn. Rep. Women, 1990-92, Nat. Rep. Congl. Com., 1990-91, Presdl. Task Force, 1990-92; lifetime mem. Girl Scouts U.S., 1991. Recipient internat. diploma of honor for community service, 1973; Creativity award Internat. Personnel Research Assn., 1972, award Goat Mt. Grange No. 818, 1987; cert. of merit for disting. svc. to edn., 1973; Order of Rose, 1978, Order of Pearl, 1989, Alpha Xi Delta; poet laureate Center of Internat. Studies and Exchanges, 1981; diploma of merit in letters U. Arts, Parma, Italy, 1982; Golden Yr. Bruin UCLA, 1983; World Culture prize Nat. Ctr. for Studies and Research, Italian Acad., 1984; Golden Palm Diploma of Honor in poetry Leonardo Da Vinci Acad., 1984; Diploma of Merit and titular mem. internat. com. Internat. Ctr. Studies and Exchanges, Rome, 1984; Recognition award San Gorgonio council Girl Scouts U.S., 1984—; Cert. of appreciation Morongo Unified Sch. Dist., 1984, 89; plaque for contribution to postal service and community U.S. Postal Service, 1984; Biographee of Yr. award for outstanding achievement in the field of edn. and service to community Hist. Preservations of Am.; named Princess of Poetry of Internat. Ctr. Cultural Studies and Exchange, Italy, 1985; community dinner held in her honor for achievement and service to Community, 1984; Star of Contemporary Poetry Masters of Contemporary Poetry, Internat. Ctr. Cultural Studies and Exchanges, Italy, 1984; named to honor list of leaders of contemporary art and lit. and apptd. titular mem. of Internat. High Com. for World Culture & Arts Leonardo Da Vinci Acad., 1987; named to honor list Foremost Women 20th Century for Outstanding Contbn. to Rsch., IBC, 1987; Presdl. Order of Merit Pres. George Bush-Exec. Coun. of Nat. Rep. Senatorial Com., Congl. cert. of Appreciation U.S. Ho. of Reps.; other awards and certs. Life fellow Internat. Acad. Poets, World Lit. Acad.; mem. Am. Personnel and Guidance Assn., Internat. Platform Assn., Nat. Ret. Tchrs. Assn., Calif. and Nat. Assn. for Counseling and Devel., Am. Assn. for Counseling and Devel. (25 yr. membership pin 1991), Nat. Assn. Women Deans and Adminstrs., Montebello Bus. and Profl. Women's Club (pres.), Nat. League Am. Pen Women (sec. 1985-86), Leonardo Da Vinci Acad. Internat. Winged Glory diploma of honor in letters 1982), Landers Area C. of C. (sec. 1985-86, Presdl. award for outstanding service, Internat. Honors Cup 1992-93), Desert Nature Mus., Phi Beta Kappa, Pi Lambda Theta (Mortar Bd., Prytanean UCLA, UCLA Golden Yr. Bruin 1983), Sigma Delta Pi, Pi Delta Phi. Clubs: Whittier Toastmistress (Calif.) (pres. 1957); Homestead Valley Women's (Landers). Lodge: Soroptimists (sec. 29 Palms chpt. 1962, life mem., Soroptimist of Yr. local chpt. 19, Woman of Distinction local chpt. 1987-88). Author: Impy, 1974, Talkie, 1975, Impy's Children, 1975; Nineteen O Four, 1976, Little Brown Bat, 1976; Slo-Go, 1977; Owls Who and Who Who, 1978; Sandy, The Coydog, 1979; The Kit Fox and the Walking Stick, 1980; contbr. articles to profl. jours., poems to anthologies. Guest of honor ground-breaking ceremony Landers Elem. Sch., 1989, dedication ceremony, 1991. Home: 632 N Landers Ln PO Box 3839 Landers CA 92285

LANDGRAF, MAUREEN MICHEL, auditor; b. Freeport, N.Y., Feb. 5, 1964; d. Robert Louis and Edith Marie (Tommas) Walsh; m. Albert F. Landgraf, Jr. AS, Seminole C.C., Sanford, Fla., 1985, AA, 1988; BSBA, U. Ctrl. Fla., Orlando, 1992. Sr. acctg. clk. Seminole County Govt., Sanford, 1992—. Recipient Pub. Svc. commendation U.S. Dept. Commerce/Dept. Census, 1992. Mem. Am. Motorcyclist Assn., Harley Owners Group (life), Golden Key, Beta Gamma Sigma, Phi Kappa Phi.

LANDIS, DONNA MARIE, nursing administrator, women's health nurse; b. Lebanon, Pa., Sept. 5, 1944; d. James O.A. and Helen Joan (Fritz) Muench; m. David J. Landis, 1967 (div. 1985); children: Danielle M. Landis Farley, David J., Derek J.; m. John C. Broderick, 1990 (div. 1995). Diploma, St. Joseph's Hosp. Sch. Nursing, Reading, Pa., 1965. RN, Md.; cert. densitometry technologist. Head nurse med.-surg. unit Hosp. of U. Pa., 1965-67; nurse various hosps. and physician's offices, Md., Pa., 1965-85; clin. dir., clin. rsch. study coord., dual energy xray absorptiometry technologist Osteoporosis Diagnostic and Monitoring Ctr., Laurel, Md., 1985-95, owner, 1995—; clin. dir., clin. rsch. study coord. Osteoporosis Assessment Ctr., Wheaton, Md., 1985-95; clin. dir./owner Women's Health Rsch. Ctr., Laurel, Md., 1996—; cons. on osteoporosis and DEXA, Merck Pharm., 1995. Mem. Balt. Bone Club, Soc. Clin. Densitometry (steering com. 1993-96, assoc. editor SCAN 1994—, sci. adv. bd. 1996, certification & credentialing com. technologists & physicians 1995-96), Nat. Osteoporosis Found., Sandoz Women's Speakers Bur., Allied Health Profls./Arthritis Found., St. Joseph's Hosp. Alumni Assn. Office: 14201 Laurel Park Dr Ste 104 Laurel MD 20707-5203

LANDIS, LINDA KAY, music educator; b. Keyser, W. Va., May 2, 1950; d. Donald Avis L. and Uldene May Mongold Duke. BS, West Chester State U., 1972, MM in Voice, 1976. Registered music educator; cert. profl. II. Music educator Phoenixville (Pa.) Area Middle Sch., 1972—; soprano soloist St. John's Lutheran Ch., Phoenixville, Pa., 1972—. Composer: As The Daisy Fields Grow, 1984, God's Rainbow, 1985, Wedding Song, 1995. Sunday sch. tchr. St. John's Luth. Ch., Phoenixville, Pa., 1966—, mem. Christian edn. com., 1983-93, Stephen ministry leader mem., 1990—, mem. ch. coun., 1985-93. Mem. NEA, Pa. State Edn. Assn., Phoenixville Area Edn. Assn., Music Educators Nat Conf., Pa. Music Edn. Assn., Bus. and Profl. Women (past dist. dir.), Acad. Boosters Club, Order Eastern Star (past matron), Delta Kappa Gamma. Lutheran. Home: 1018 Pothouse Rd Phoenixville PA 19460-2242 Office: Phoenixvill Area Middle Sch 1330 S Main St Phoenixville PA 19460-2242

LANDIS, SARA MARGARET SHEPPARD, editorial consultant; b. Badin, N.C., May 20, 1920; d. Thomas Coates and Ouida (Watson) Sheppard; m. Williard Griffith Landis, Dec. 7, 1945; children: Susan Sheppard, Timothy Joseph, Margaret Carol. Student, Flora MacDonald Coll. Women, 1937-38, Rice Bus. Coll., 1939; AB in Journalism, U. N.C., 1942. Editorial asst. Redbook Mag., N.Y.C., 1942-43; with Doubleday and Co., N.Y.C., 1944-46, Eagle Pencil Co., N.Y.C., 1953-54; mgr. personnel Workman Service, N.Y.C., 1955-56, Clay Adams Co., N.Y.C., 1957-58; job analyst Bigelow Carpet Co., N.Y.C., 1959-60; asst. to guidance dir. Childrens Village, Dobbs Ferry, N.Y., 1960-61; dir. promotions, advt. Oceans Publs., Dobbs Ferry, 1961-66; mgr. promotions Reinhold Pub. Co., N.Y.C., 1967-68, Watson Guptil Pub. Co., N.Y.C., 1968, Chilton Book Co., Phila., 1968-69; cons. editorial, promotions Sheppard-Landis Ink, N.Y.C., 1969—; cons. Parker, Rebel Without Rights, Millbrook, 1996. Collaborator: (with Tereso Pregnall) Treasured Recipes from the Chrleston Cake Lady, 1996; abridgement editor Kente Books on Tape, 1996. Mem. St. George Episc. Ch. Mem. English Speaking Union (head book discussion group 1989—), Friends Ephiphany chpt. N.Y. Pub. Library, United Daughters Confederacy. Home and Office: 271 Ave C Peter Cooper-Stuyvesant Town New York NY 10009

LANDIS, VIRGINIA HEARD, accountant, small business consultant; b. New Bedford, Mass., Aug. 27, 1953; d. Hamilton Jr. and Virginia Thayer (Scott) Heard; m. Nelson Patrick Landis, Apr. 30, 1983; children: Heather Landis Wohl, Shannon Rachelle, Patrick Hamilton. AA, Pine Manor Jr. Coll., Chestnut Hill, Mass., 1973; BSBA, Boston U., 1978. Acctg. clk. N.E. Investors Trust, Boston, 1974-78; real estate broker, office mgr. Century 21 Baystate Properties, Brighton, Mass., 1978-81; bookkeeper Ezra J. Leboff Co., Inc., Brighton, 1981-84; contr., acctg. dir. Arrow Pub. Co., Inc., Taunton, Mass., 1984-91; owner, mgr. Can-Do Bus. Svcs., Middleborough, Mass., 1990—; acct. Shevalier Assocs., Inc., archs., Taunton, 1991—; prof. Kinyon-Campbell Bus. Sch., 1992; bd. dirs. Naturally Nantucket (Mass.), Inc. Mem. Middleborough Charter Study Com., 1990-95; chmn. data processing rev. com. City of Middleborough, 1994-95. Mem. Cranberry County C. of C. Republican. Episcopalian.

LANDMAN, BETTE EMELINE, academic administrator; b. Piqua, Ohio, July 18, 1937; d. Wilson Richard and Lois (Wilson) L. BS, Bowling Green State U., 1959; MA, Ohio State U., 1961, PhD, 1972. From instr. to asst. prof. anthropology Springfield (Mass.) Coll., 1963-67; asst. prof. Temple U., 1967-71; asst. prof. anthropology Beaver Coll., Glenside, Pa., 1971-76, dean, 1976-85, v.p. acad. affairs, 1980-85, acting pres., 1982-83, 85, pres., 1985—. Bd. dirs. Abington (Pa.) Meml. Hosp., 1986-93, Abington Meml. Hosp. Found., 1993—; mem. blood donor campaign ARC, chair Pa.-Jersey Region Higher Edn., 1990-91; bd. advisors Coll. Physicians of Phila., 1994—. Recipient Disting. Teaching award Christian R. and Mary F. Lindback Found., 1973; NSF fellow, 1961-63, Wenner-Gren Found. for Anthrop. Rsch. fellow, 1965-66; named Disting. Dau. of Pa., 1992; Ann. Pa. Am. Coun. on Edn.-NIP award established in her honor, 1992. Mem. Am. Coun. Edn. (state coord. 1980-84, commn. on leadership devel. 1989-94, chmn. 1991-92, bd. dirs. 1993—), Assn. Am. Colls. (bd. dirs. 1986-91, vice chair 1989-90, chair 1990-91), Assn. Presbyn. Colls. and Univs. (exec. com. 1988-93, 95—, sec. 1989-90, v.p. 1990-91, pres. 1991-92), Pa. Assn. Colls. and Univs. (exec. com. 1992-93), Nat. Assn. Ind. Colls. and Univs. (commn. on campus concerns 1991—, vice chmn. 1992, chmn. 1993), Sigma Xi, Phi Kappa Phi, Kappa Delta Pi. Office: Beaver Coll Office of Pres 450 S Easton Rd Glenside PA 19038-3295*

LANDOVSKY, ROSEMARY REID, figure skating school director, coach; b. Chgo., July 26, 1933; d. Samuel Stuart and Audrey Todd (Lyons) Reid; m. John Indulis Landovsky, Feb. 20, 1960; children: David John, Linette. BA in Psychology, Colo. Coll., 1956. Profl. skater Holiday on Ice Touring Show, U.S., Mex., Cuba, 1956-58; skating dir. and coach Paradice Arena, Birmingham, 1958-62, Les Patineurs, Huntsville, Ala., 1960-62; coach competitive (Ice Skating Inst. Am., U.S. Figure Skating Assn.) Michael Kirby and Assocs., River Forest, Chgo., Ill., 1962-63; rink mgr., skating dir. Lake Meadows Ice Arena, Chgo., 1963-68; coach (ISIA, USFSA) Rainbo Arena, Chgo., 1968-73; skating dir. Northwestern U. Skating Sch., Evanston, Ill., 1968-73, Robert Crown Ice Ctr., Evanston, 1973-75; dir. instl. programs Skokie (Ill.) Park Dist., 1975-87; competition dir. ISIA All America Competition, 1985-86. Dir., producer, choreographer Ice Show: Nutcracker Ballet, 1973, Ice Extravaganza III, 1985, Ice Lights '86, '87. Election judge, worker, Ind. Dems., Chgo., 1964-68. Mem. Profl. Skaters Guild, Ice Skating Inst. Am., Coll. Coll. Alumni Assn. (mem. Chgo. area com.), Gamma Phi Beta.

LANDRAM, CHRISTINA LOUELLA, librarian; b. Paragould, Ark., Dec. 10, 1922; d. James Ralph and Bertie Louella (Jordan) Oliver; m. Robert Ellis Landram, Aug. 7, 1948; 1 child, Mark Owen. BA, Tex. Woman's U., 1945, B.L.S., 1946, M.L.S., 1951. Preliminary cataloger Library of Congress, Washington, 1946-48; cataloger U.S. Info. Ctr., Tokyo, Japan, 1948-50, U.S. Dept. Agr., Washington, 1953-54; librarian Yokota AFB, Yokota, Japan, 1954-55; librarian St. Mary's Hosp., West Palm Beach, Fla., 1957-59; librarian Jacksonville (Ark.) High Sch., 1959-61; coord. Shelby County Libraries, Memphis, 1961-63; head catalog dept. Ga. State U. Library, 1963-86, librarian, assoc. prof. emeritus, 1986—. Contbr. articles to library jours. Mem. Ga. Library Assn. (chmn. resources and tech. services sect. 1969-71), Metro-Atlanta Library Assn. (pres. 1967-68), ALA (chmn. cataloging norms 1979-80, nominating com. 1977-78), Southeastern Library Assn. (mem. govtl. rels. com. 1975-78, intellectual freedom com. 1984-86, mem. Rothrock awards com. 1987-90). Presbyterian. Home: 1478 Leafmore Rdg Decatur GA 30033-2110

LANDRUM, BEVERLY HOLLOWELL, nurse; b. Goldsboro, N.C., Jan. 28, 1960; d. Joseph Bryant and Doris Helen (Barnett) Hollowell; m. William Timothy Landrum; children: Amber, Justin, Caitlyn. ADN with honors, Florence-Darlington Tech., 1989; BSN summa cum laude, Med. U. S.C., 1995. RN, S.C.; cert. BLS, ACLS, NALS. Charge nurse Carolinas Hosp. System, Florence, S.C., 1989—. Neighborhood campaign organizer March of Dimes, Am. Heart Assn., Atlantic Beach, Fla. and Florence, 1982—; active Assn. Parents and Tchrs., Florence, 1993—. Mem. ANA, S.C. Nurses Assn., Sigma Theta Tau.

LANDRY, ABBIE VESTAL, librarian; b. Martinsville, Va., Oct. 29, 1954; d. Samuel Raynor and Grace Loraine (Cochrane) Vestal; m. Michael Ray Landry, Aug. 4, 1979. Assoc. Gen. Edn., Patrick Henry C.C., Martinsville, Va., 1975; BA in History, Longwood Coll., Farmville, Va., 1977; M in Libr. and Info. Sci., U. Tenn., Knoxville, 1981. Grad. asst. history dept. U. Tenn., Knoxville, 1977-78, grad. teaching asst., 1978-80, grad. asst. libr. and info. sci., 1980-81; reference libr., coord. online svcs., coord. biog. instrn. Watson Libr., Northwestern State U., Natchitoches, La., 1981-87, head reference divsn., supr. reference, 1987—; mem. adv. bd. Bowker Publ. Topical Reference Books, Princeton, N.J., 1988-89; sec. La. Assn. for Acad. Competition, 1991—; chair faculty-staff devel. com. Watson Libr., 1983-88, chair devel. com. collection, 1988-89, chair quiz bowl com., 1989—, mem. automated circulation sys. com., 1984-85, mem. centennial com. 1983-84. Contbr. articles to profl. jours. and encys.; mem. editl. bd. Alumni Reviewer for Reference Books Bull., 1991—, mem. edit. bd., 1987-91; co-editor newsletter Libr. Users Edn., 1991-92; editor Online Svcs. Interest Group Newsletter, 1986-87; editor Watson Libr. Newsletter Ex Libris, 1983-93. Mem. Assn. for Preservation Historic Natchitoches, 1985—, Natchitoches Humane Soc., 1983—. Recipient Sigma Xi award, Natchitoches, 1986. Mem. ALA, La. Libr. Assn. (vice chair acad. sect. 1988-89, chair 1989-90, mem. exec. bd. 1988-90, coord. online svcs. interest group 1985-86), Southeastern Libr. Assn., Apple Libr. Users Group, Phi Kappa Phi, Beta Phi Mu, Phi Alpha Theta. Episcopalian. Office: Northwestern State U Natchitoches LA 71497

LANDRY, BRENDA LEE, securities analyst; b. Wolfboro, N.H., June 24, 1942; d. Christopher Lee and Barbara F. (Sullivan) L. B.A., Vassar Coll., 1964. Sales analyst Polaroid Co., Cambridge, Mass., 1966-70; 1st v.p. White Weld, N.Y.C., 1970-78, Merrill Lynch, N.Y.C., 1978-80; prin. Morgan Stanley & Co., Inc., N.Y.C., 1980—. Contbr. articles to profl. jours.; various TV appearances. Mem. N.Y. Soc. Security Analysts, Women's Fin. Assn., Photo Mfrs. Assn., Vassar Club. Republican. Home: PO Box 10 Water Mill NY 11976-0010 Office: Morgan Stanley 1585 Broadway New York NY 10036

LANDRY, DEBBY ANN, computer programmer; b. Tacoma, July 27, 1963; d. Israel Joseph and Joyce Ann (Franzella) L.; 1 child, Jessica Elizabeth. BS, S.E. La. U., 1987; postgrad., U. So. Miss., 1994. Computer programmer Lockheed Engring. and Scis., Bay St. Louis, Miss., 1988-92; programmer/analyst I Sverdrup Techs., Inc., 1992-94; computer assoc. sr. Lockheed Engring. & Scis., Stennis Space Center, Miss., 1994—. Mem. Beta Sigma Phi. Democrat. Roman Catholic. Home: 1107 Rose Meadow Loop Slidell LA 70460-5105 Office: Lockheed Engring & Scis Co Bldg 2105 Bay Saint Louis MS 39529

LANDRY, ESTHER FRANCES, health services executive; b. Swampscott, Mass., Aug. 13, 1935; d. George Murdock Landry and Esther Louise (Gott) Hopkins; m. James Joseph Fernald (div. 1981); children: Scott Edward, Esther Louise; m. David Elmer Howes (div. 1963); 1 child, David Ralph. BS, Fitchburg State U., 1957; student, U. Mass., 1990-91. Cert. RN. Pvt. practice Cape Cod, Mass., 1959-63; operating room nurse Cape Cod Hosp., Hyannis, Mass., 1963-64; dir. health svcs. Cape Cod Community Coll., W. Barnstable, Mass., 1967—, acting chair div. life fitness/wellness edn., 1988—; active Health Promotion Resource Ctr., Barnstable, 1986—; cons. health svc. devel. Mass. Bd. Regional Community Colls., 1969-76; pres. bd. dirs. Cape Cod Coun. Alcoholism and Drug Dependence, Hyannis, Mass., 1989-94. Author: Jour. Am. Coll. Health Assn., 1975. Sec. Cape & Islands Area Bd. Mental Health, 1978; active Substance Abuse Prevention Com., CC Baseball League, Cape Cod, 1988; chair com. svc. March of Dimes, S.E. Mass., 1988; smoking cessation instr. Am. Lung Assn., 1987-94; safety svcs. com. sec. ARC, 1985. Recipient governors Pride in Performance award Commonwealth of Mass., 1987, S. Louise Gazzara award for excellence in coll. health nursing, 1994. Mem. Am. Coll. Health Assn. (chair nurse directed health svcs. 1986-88), New England Coll. Health Assn., Mass. Women in Higher Edn. Home: 17 Hampshire Ave Hyannis MA 02601-2627 Office: Cape Cod CC Rte 132 West Barnstable MA 02668

LANDRY, SARA GRIFFIN, social worker; b. Thomaston, Ga., Sept. 17, 1920; d. John Carl and Mary Thelma (Abercrombie) Griffin; m. Thomas Leonard Perkins, Dec. 22, 1939 (dec. Jan. 27, 1945); 1 child, Thomas Leonard Perkins Jr.; m. George Kimball Landry, Dec. 19, 1949 (dec. Aug. 30, 1971). AB in Social Work magna cum laude, Wesleyan Coll., 1980; MS in Family Counseling, Mercer U., 1981. Receptionist Social Security Adminstrn., Macon, Ga., 1945-50, clerical, 1960-65, svc. rep., 1965-78; dir., organizer Bibb County Foster Grandparent Program, Macon, Ga., 1981-84; coord. rsch. project Med. Ctr. of Cen. Ga., Macon, Ga., 1986-87; social worker, bd. dirs. Bibb County Sr. Citizens Inc., Macon, Ga., 1984—; sec. bd. dirs. Bibb County Sr. Citizens, Inc., Macon, Ga., 1989-90, pres. bd. dirs., 1990-91; bd. dirs. grant chmn. Family Counseling Ctr., Macon, 1986-92, 94—. Contbr. articles, poems and various short stories to profl. jours. Bd. dirs., v.p., com. chmn. Am. Cancer Soc., Macon, 1956—, hon. life mem., 1993—; sec., com. chmn. Dem. Women Bibb County, 1979—; mem., sec. Civic Woman's Club, Macon, 1955-61; mem. Coun. Cath. Women, St. Joseph's Parish, pres., 1956-58; mem., bd. dirs. Savannah Diocesan Coun. Cath. Women, 1957-59; bd. dirs. Macon Little Theatre, 1994-96. Recipient Disting. Alumnae award for cmty. svc. Wesleyan Coll., 1996, Svc. to Mankind award Sertoma Club of Macon, 1995; named Vol. of Yr., Bibb County Sr. Citizens, Inc., 1988, Am. Cancer Soc., 1987-88, Cherry Blossom Sr. Queen for Cmty. Svc., 1986; Fundraiser honoree Am. Cancer Soc., 1991; Sara Landry Day proclaimed in her honor Mayor of Macon, 1991. Mem. LWV, AAUW (pres. 1991-93), Wesleyan Coll. Alumnae Assn. (Sara Griffin Perkins Landry scholarship established for non-traditional age students 1994, Disting. Alumnae award for cmty. svc. 1996), Nat. Honor Soc., Macon Little Theatre. Democrat. Roman Catholic. Home: 3807 Drury Dr Macon GA 31204-1313

LANDSBERG, JILL WARREN, state government lawyer; b. N.Y.C., Oct. 11, 1942; d. George Richard and Evelyn (Schepps) Warren; m. Lewis Landsberg, June 14, 1964; children: Alison, Judd Warren. BA, George Washington U., Washington, 1964; MAT, Yale U., 1965; JD, Boston Coll., 1976. Bar: Mass., 1977, Ill., 1991. Assoc., dir. (ptnr.) Widett, Slater & Goldman PC, Boston, 1976-90; pvt. practice Chgo., 1991-94; faculty Med. Sch. Ethics and Human Values Dept. Northwestern U., Chgo., 1991-94; exec. asst. spl. counsel for child welfare svcs. Office of the Gov., Chgo., 1994-95, acting spl. counsel for child welfare svcs., 1995—; mem. Legis. Com. on Juvenile Justice, Chgo., 1995—, Task Force on Violence Against Children, Chgo., 1995—, Citizens Com. on the Juvenile Ct., Chgo., 1995-96. Tutor Ptnrs. in Edn., 4th Presbyn. Ch., Chgo., 1993—; adv. bd. Libr. Internat. Rels., Chgo., 1993-94. Mem. ABA, Chgo. Bar Assn., Women's Bar Assn., Ill. State Bar Assn., Abraham Lincoln Marovitz Inn of Ct., Phi Beta Kappa, Order of the Coif. Home: 70 E Cedar St Chicago IL 60611

LANDSMAN, SANDRA GILBERT, psychologist, transactional analyst, hypnotherapist; b. Detroit, Jan. 5, 1933; d. Arthur Bernard (dec.) and Ida Myra (Finkelstone) (dec.) G.; BS, Wayne State U., 1955, MA, 1970, PhD, 1984. Ordained to ministry, 1994; cert. hypnotherapist, spiritual healer. m. Rodney Glenn Landsman, Apr. 3, 1955; children: Victoria Louise Landsman Peterson, Jonathan Gilbert, Faith Susan, Jill Barbara. Cons., counselor Continuum Center for Women, Oakland U., Rochester, Mich., 1970-77; pvt. practice Transactional Analysis, Farmington Hills, Mich., 1966-87; clin. cons., U.S., Can., Europe, South Am.; Transactional Analysis, clin. supr. North Metro & Dearborn Downriver Growth Centers, Rochester and Allen Park, Mich., 1975-78; mem. faculty Macomb County (Mich.) Community Coll., 1976-79; dir. clin. and edn. services Landsman/Foner & Assocs., West Bloomfield, Mich., 1977-82; disting. lectr. Sch. Social Work, Mich. State U., 1975-78; dir. Coastal Hypnosis Ctr.; cons. in field; mem. faculty dept. psychology Columbia Pacific U.; internat. lectr. on psychopathology and pre and peri-natal psychology and metaphysics, U.S., Can., Europe, S.Am., 1966—. Cert. social worker, Mich.; trustee Temple Beth Am; nat. women's com. Brandeis U. Mem. NOW, Am. Counseling Assn., Nat. Mus. Women in the Arts, Orgn. Rehab. and Tng., U.S. Power Squadrons, Universal Holistic Healers Assn., Assn. Pastlife Rsch. and Therapies Internat. Transactional Analysis Assn. (mem. editorial bd.), U.S. Transactional Analysis Assn. (clin. teaching mem.), Nat. Guild Hypnotists, Am. Coun. Hypnotist Examiners, Women's Am. Orgn. for Rehab. and Tng., Alternative Edn. Assn., European Transactional Analysis Assn., Pre & Peri-Natal Assn. N.Am., Nat. Assn. Social Workers, Am. Coll. Personnel Assn., Fla. Soc. Profl. Hypnotists, Assn. Specialists in Group Work, Mich. Assn. for Counseling and Devel., Mich. Coll. Personnel Assn., Mich. Assn. Specialist Group Work (past pres.), Mich. Assn. Women Deans, Adminstrs. and Counselors, New Directions in Edn. and Psychotherapy (charter, trustee), Pre and Perinatal Assn. of N.Am. Author: Affective Disorders: The Assessment, Development, and Treatment Strategies of Manic-Depressive Structure; I'm Special: An Experiential Workbook for the Child in Us All, Found: A Place for Me-the Development Diagnosis and Treatment of Manic-Depressive Structure, (with others) Secret Places; contbr. articles to profl. publs. Office: 810 Saturn St Ste 16 Jupiter FL 33477-4456

LANDSTROM, ELSIE HAYES, editor; b. Kuling, Kiangsi, China, June 22, 1923; came to the U.S., 1935; d. Paul Goodman and Helen Mae (Wolf) Hayes; m. Victor Norman Landstrom, Jan. 21, 1953 (dec. Oct. 1989); children: Peter S., Ruth H. BA, Hamline U., 1945. Writer, editor adminstrv. staff Am. Friends Svc. Com., Phila., 1946-52, M.I.T., Cambridge, Mass., 1952-53; mem. editl. bd. Approach Mag., Phila. and Needham, 1947-67; sr. editor Word Guild, 1976-82; freelance writer and editor Conway, Mass., 1976—. Author: Closing the Circle-An American Family in China, 1996; editor: Propaganda and Aesthetics, 1979, Taoism and Chinese Religion, 1981, Hyla Doc in China 1924-1949, 1991, Hyla Doc in Africa 1950-1961, 1994; exhibited Chinese paintings in show, 1996. Newsletter editor, draft resisters support com. Wellesley (Mass.) Friends Meeting; chair Fair Housing Com., Needham. Home: 2036 Roaring Brook Rd Conway MA 01341-9767

LANDVOGT, PENNY LUCILLE, psychotherapist, educator; b. Janesville, Wis., May 19, 1946; d. John Lenard and Marion Lucille (Scholinski) Piekarski; m. William G. Landvogt. BS, U. Wis., 1968, MS, 1969, PhD, 1986. Assoc. prof. U. Wis., Madison, 1969-83, evaluation specialist, 1983-86; psychotherapist pvt. practice, Madison, 1985—. Office: 6402 Odana Madison WI 53545

LANDY, JOANNE VEIT, foreign policy analyst; b. Chgo., Oct. 15, 1941; d. Fritz and Lucille (Stearns) Veit; m. Seymour Landy, Mar., 1959 (div. 1962); m. Nelson Lichtenstein, Mar., 1972 (div. 1976). BA in History, U. Calif., Berkeley, 1968; MA in History, U. Calif., Berkley, 1970; MPH, Columbia U., 1982. Dir. N.Y. Met. Office, U. Chgo., N.Y.C., 1977-80; pres. Campaign for Peace and Democracy, N.Y.C., 1982—; bd. dirs. Human Rights Watch, Helsinki. Editor: Peace & Democracy, 1984—. Recipient grant for rsch. and writing John D. and Catherine T. Mac Arthur Fedn., Program on Peace and Internat. Cooperation, Chgo., 1990-91. Mem. Coun. on Fgn. Rels., Phi Beta Kappa. Home: 2785 Broadway Apt 7A New York NY 10025-2850 Office: Campaign for Peace and Democracy PO Box 1640 New York NY 10025-1560

LANDY, LISA ANNE, lawyer; b. Miami, Fla., Apr. 20, 1963; d. Burton Aaron and Eleonora Maria (Simmel) L. BA, Brown U., 1985; JD cum laude, U. Miami, 1988. Bar: Fla. 1988, U.S. Dist. Ct. (so. dist.) Fla. 1988. Atty. Paul, Landy, Beiley & Harper, P.A., Miami, Fla., 1988-94, Steel Hector & Davis, Miami, Fla., 1994—. Bd. dirs. Miami City Ballet, 1992—, pres., 1996; bd. dirs. Women in Internat. Trade, Miami, 1992—, pres., 1994. Mem. ABA, Inter-Am. Bar Assn. (sec. young lawyers divsn. 1992).

LANE, AVA-LYNN, art educator, jewelry designer; b. Laconia, N.H., Dec. 20, 1956; d. Harry and Joyce Doreen (Mardell) Sonsky; m. Dennis E. Lane, Aug. 15, 1980; 1 child, Britton Kyle. BS in Art Edn. cum laude, Plymouth State Coll., 1978. Cert. art tchr., N.H. Art tchr., dept. chairperson Goffstown (N.H.) Area High Sch., 1979—; owner, designer Kaleidoscope Jewelry, Londonderry, N.H., 1991—; adv. bd. N.H.-Boston Globe Scholastic Art, 1992—; juror Mass./Boston Globe Scholastic Art Award Program, 1992—, N.H. Federated Arts, 1996—. Co-author: (booklet) Artfully Selling Youth Art Program, 1989, 91—. Mem. NEA, Nat. Art Educators Assn., ASCD, N.H. ASCD, N.H. Art Educators Assn. (regional v.p. 1986-92, pres.-elect 1993-94, pres. 1994-95, past pres. 1995-96, mem. state conf. com. 1988—, N.H. Art Educator of Yr. award 1994, N.H. Art Educator of the Month awards 1988, 94), Goffstown Edn. Assn. Office: Goffstown Area H S Art Dept 27 Wallace Rd Goffstown NH 03045-1824

LANE, BARBARA ANN, environmental company official, systems analyst; b. Boston, Nov. 1, 1939; d. William James and Marguerite Jean (Lawler) Ohrenberger; m. David Joseph Lane, Nov. 2, 1963; children: David Joseph Jr., William Francis. BS summa cum laude, Northeastern U., 1989. Cert. in personal protection and safety for hazardous waste site ops. OSHA. Supr. facility lab. quality assurance and control Clean Harbors Environ. Svcs. Cos., Braintree, Mass., 1988-89, facility sys. analyst, 1989-90, sys. analyst, mgr. facilty quality assurance, 1990-93, sr. mgr. nat. facilities quality assurance, 1993-94, mem. bus. process reengring. core team, 1994—. Co-author: Resource Guide to State Agencies Serving Children and Adolescents, 1983. Bd. dirs. Pro-Arte Singers, Scituate, Mass., 1979-81, Scituate Arts Assn., 1981-83; founder, bd. dirs. Prelude Internat. Concert Series, Scituate, 1981-89, Young Performers Music Guild, Scituate, 1981-83. Recipient cmty. svc. citation Mass. Ho. of Reps., 1985, outstanding cmty. svc. citation Scituate Bd. Selectmen, 1986. Mem. AAUW, Phi Kappa Phi. Home: 59 Creelman Dr Scituate MA 02066 Office: Clear Harbors Environ Svcs Co 1501 Washington St Braintree MA 02185-0327

LANE, CAROLYN BROOKS, school counselor; b. Phila., Nov. 11, 1948; 1 child, Brett A. BS, Millersville U., 1970; MEd, Xavier U., 1976; EdS, U. Ga., 1993. Nat. cert. counselor. Adminstrv. asst. State Govt., Harrisburg, Pa., 1970-71, Cen. Mich. U., Mt. Pleasant, Mich., 1971-72; reading specialist Princeton City Schs., Cin., 1972-79, Hamilton County Bd. of Edn., Cin., 1979-85, DeKalb County Schs., Ga., 1985-92; sch. counselor Gwinnett County Schs., Ga., 1992—; level chair M.S. Sch. Counselors, Gwinnett County, 1995-96; mem. peer leadership conf. steering com. Gwinnett County Schs., 1993-95. Vol. Christ Hosp., Cin., 1980-82. Mem. Am. Sch. Counselor Assn., Ga. Sch. Counselor Assn., Phi Kappa Phi. Office: Lilburn Mid Sch 4994 Lawrenceville Hwy Lilburn GA 30087

LANE, DOROTHY SPIEGEL, physician; b. Bklyn., Feb. 17, 1940; d. Milton Barton and Rosalie (Jacobson) Spiegel; m. Bernard Paul Lane, Aug. 5, 1962; children: Erika, Andrew, Matthew. BA, Vassar Coll., 1961; MD, Columbia U., 1965, MPH, 1968. Diplomate Am. Bd. Preventive Medicine, Am. Bd. Family Practice. Resident preventive medicine N.Y.C. Dept. Health Dist., 1966-68; project dir. children and youth project Title V, HHS N.Y.C. Dept. Health Dist., Rockaway, N.Y., 1968-69; med. cons. Maternal and Child Health Svc. HHS, Rockville, Md., 1970-71; asst. prof. preventive medicine Sch. Medicine SUNY, Stony Brook, 1971-76, assoc. prof., 1976-92; prof., 1992—; assoc. dean Sch. Medicine SUNY, Stony Brook, 1986—; chair dept. community medicine, dir. med. edn. Brookhaven Meml. Hosp. Med. Ctr., Patchogue, N.Y., 1972-86. Contbr. numerous articles to profl. jours. Mem. exec. com. Am. Cancer Soc., L.I. divsn., 1975—; mem. nat. bd. dirs. Am. Cancer Soc.; corp. mem. Nassau Suffolk Health Systems Agy., L.I., 1977—; bd. dirs. Community Health Plan Suffolk, Hauppauge, 1986-91. Grantee HHS-USPHS, 1977-85, 83—, Nat. Cancer Inst., 1987—. Fellow APHA, Am. Coll. Preventive Medicine (regent 1988-96, sec.-treas. 1994-96), Am. Acad. Family Physicians, N.Y. Acad. Medicine, Am. Bd. Preventive Medicine (trustee), Assn. Tchrs. Preventive Medicine (pres. 1996—). Office: SUNY at Stony Brook Sch Medicine Health Scis Ctr L-4 Stony Brook NY 11794-8437

LANE, GLORIA JULIAN, foundation administrator; b. Chgo., Oct. 6, 1932; d. Coy Berry and Katherine (McDowell) Julian; m. William Gordon Lane (div. Oct. 1958); 1 child, Julie Kay Rosewood. BS in Edn., Cen. Mo. State U., 1958; MA, Bowling Green State U., 1959; PhD, No. Ill. U., 1972. Cert. tchr. Assoc. prof. William Jewell Coll., Liberty, Mo., 1959-60; chair forensic div. Coral Gables (Fla.) High Sch., 1960-64; assoc. prof. No. Ill. U., DeKalb, 1964-70; prof. Elgin (Ill.) Community Coll., 1970-72; owner, pub. Lane and Assocs, Inc., San Diego, 1972-78; prof. Nat. U., San Diego, 1978-90; pres., chief exec. officer Women's Internat. Ctr., San Diego, 1982—; founder, dir. Living Legacy Awards, San Diego, 1984—. Author: Project Text for Effective Communications, 1972, Project Text for Executive Communication, 1980, Positive Concepts for Success, 1983; editor Who's Who Among San Diego Women, 1984, 85, 86, 90—, Systems and Structure, 1984. Named Woman of Accomplishment, Soroptimist Internat., 1985, Pres.'s Coun. San Diego, 1986, Center City Assn., 1986, Bus. and Profl. Women, San Diego, 1991, Woman of Yr., Girls' Clubs San Diego, 1986, Woman of Vision, Women's Internat. Ctr., 1990, Wonderwoman 2000 Women's Times Newspaper, 1991; recipient Independence award Ctr. for Disabled, 1986, Founder's award Children's Hosp. Internat., Washington, 1986. Home and Office: 6202 Friars Rd Apt 311 San Diego CA 92108-1008

LANE, HANA UMLAUF, editor; b. Stockholm, Mar. 14, 1946; came to U.S., 1951, naturalized, 1957; d. Karel Hugo Antonin and Anatolia (Spitel) Umlauf; m. John Richard Lane, Feb. 16, 1980; 1 stepchild, Matthew John. A.B. magna cum laude, Vassar Coll., 1968; A.M. in Russian and East European Studies, Yale U., 1970. Asst. to exec. editor Newspaper Enterprise Assn., N.Y.C., 1970-72, sr. asst., asst. editor World Almanac div., 1972-75, assoc. editor World Almanac, 1975-80, spl. project editor, 1977-80; editor World Almanac and World Almanac Publs., N.Y.C., 1980-85; editor in chief Pharos Books, N.Y.C., 1984-91; editor Pharos Books, 1991-93; sr. editor John Wiley & Sons, 1993—. Editor: World Almanac Book of Who, 1980, World Almanac and Book of Facts, 1981-85; (with others) The Woman's Almanac, 1977. Democrat. Home: 140 Fairview Ave Stamford CT 06902-8040

LANE, HOLLY DIANA, artist; b. Cleve., Sept. 13, 1954; d. Edwin Joseph and Ursula Anna (Neustadt) Selyem; m. L.A. Lane, Apr. 20, 1975. AA in 2-Dimensional Art, Cuesta Coll., San Luis Obispo, Calif., 1992; BFA with great distinction, San Jose State U., 1986, MFA in Pictorial Art, 1988. One-woman shows include Ivory/Kimpton Gallery, San Francisco, 1989, Rutgers Barclay Gallery, Santa Fe, 1990, Bingham Kurts Gallery, Memphis, 1992, (solo survey show with catalog) Art Mus. of S.E. Tex., Beaumont, 1995, (3 major solo shows) Schmidt Bingham Gallery, N.Y.C., 1991, 93, 95; group mus. shows include Eiteljorg Mus., Indpls., 1995, Yerba Buena Ctr. for the Arts, San Francisco, 1944, Knoxville (Tenn.) Mus. Art, 1993-94, Fine Arts Ctr. U. R.I., Kingston, 1992, Calif. Ctr. for the Arts Escondido Mus., 1996, Samuel P. Harn Mus., U. Fla., Gainesville, 1996; represented in permanent collections in Art Mus. S.E. Tex., A.R.A. Svcs., Phila., Dow Jones & Co., N.Y.C., Detroit Zool. Gardens, Prin. Fin. Group, Des Moines, IDS, Mpls., Memphis Cancer Ctr.; works reproduced in books, mags., calendars, jours., including ARTNews, Art in America, Art Papers, Art & Antiques, New Yorker Mag., Women Artists calendar 1996, San Raphael, Calif., The Sciences, N.Y. Acad. Scis., 1992, 93, (textbook) Artist and Audience, (London) 1996; works presented and discussed in TV documentaries, including "Wlcome to Nocturnia", 1993, Women in Art, 1993, Time-Warner, 1993, Manhattan Cable, 1993, N.Y.C., 1993, 94; in books accompanying TV show Bill Moyers Genesis, A Living Tradition, PBS, 1996, Healing and the Mind, 1993. Named Alumna of Yr., Cuesta Coll., 1992; pres.'s scholar, San Jose State U., 1986, Johanna Rietz scholar, Art Assn. of Morro Bay, Calif., 1981; recipient honorable mention Western States Arts Fedn., Santa Fe, 1994. Mem. Coll. Art Assn. Home and Studio: PO Box 154 Los Gatos CA 95031-0154 Address: care Schmidt Bingham Gallery 41 East 57th St 5th Fl New York NY 10022

LANE, JULIA A., nursing educator; b. Chgo., June 29, 1927; d. James and Julia (Ivins) L. BSN, DePaul U., 1956; MSN, Cath. U. Am., 1961; PhD, Loyola U., Chgo., 1974. Cert. nurse midwife. Staff nurse St. Joseph Hosp., 1954-55, Chgo. Bd. of Health, 1955-57; instr. South Chgo. Hosp. Sch. Nursing, 1957-58, dir. edn., 1960-63; prof. Loyola U. Sch. Nursing, 1963—, dean, 1974-91; prof., 1992-94, ret., 1994. Home: 300 N State St Apt 4532 Chicago IL 60610-4807 Office: Loyola U Marcella Neihoff Sch Nursing 6525 N Sheridan Rd Chicago IL 60626-5311

LANE, KATHLEEN MARGARET, optical company administrator; b. Mpls., Oct. 25, 1946; d. Bernard Melvin and Margaret (Beck) Aanerud; m. Kenneth LeRoy Lane, Sept. 1, 1979; 1 child, Dennis Leon. Cost acct. Honeywell, Mpls., 1964-66; bank bookkeeper Columbia Heights State Bank, Minn., 1968-71; inventory control mgr. Hodes Optical Inc., Torrance, Calif., 1972-75, office mgr., 1975-79; lens supr. Coburn Optical Industries, Inc., Carson, Calif., 1979-85, br. mgr., St. Paul, 1985-93; office mgr. J.M. Refrigeration, St. Croix Falls, Wis., 1993; customer rels. Opti Fair, Aneheim, Calif., 1978-83. Mem. Am. Inst. Banking, NAFE. Avocations: restoring old furniture, camping, knitting. Office: JM Refrigeration 132 Middle School Dr Saint Croix Falls WI 54024-9189

LANE, LAURA ALICE, librarian; b. N.Y.C.; d. Cedric R. and Alice J. (Lay) Lane; m. David R. DeVoe; 1 child, Charles. AB, Lake Erie Coll., Painesville, Ohio, 1963; MLS, U. Calif., Berkeley, 1964. Fine arts libr. acquisitions dept. Fogg Art Mus./Harvard U., Cambridge, Mass., 1964-67; humanities cataloger U. Minn., Mpls., 1967-69; head libr. Am. Heritage Pub. Co., N.Y.C., 1969-82; ref. libr. Mt. Sinai Sch. Medicine, N.Y.C., 1983-87; bibliographer Temple U., Phila., 1991—. Mem. ALA. Office: Temple U Paley Library Philadelphia PA 19122

LANE, LILLY KATHERINE, museum staff member; b. Inverness, Fla., Mar. 25, 1934; d. Robert Joseph and Edna Lee (Rooks) Lane; m. James A. Nichols, Dec. 28, 1955 (div. Feb. 28, 1986); children: James D. Nichols, Gayle Patricia Nichols. RN, St. Luke's Hosp., Jacksonville, Fla., 1955; BFA cum laude in Ceramics, U. Fla., 1984, BA in Asian Studies, 1985, MFA in Ceramics, 1994; postgrad., Fla. State U., 1996. RN, Fla., Va., Ill., Morocco. Swimming tchr. Port Lyautey, Morocco, 1962-63; RN various, 1955-83; English tchr. South China Normal U., Guangzhou, 1987-88; Chinese Calligraphy tchr. St. Augustine, Fla., 1992-93; asst. collections Harn Mus. Art, Gainesville, Fla., 1994—. Den mother Cub Scouts, Bear Lake, Fla., 1964-65; asst. leader Brownies, 1963-64, PTA (del. to state legis., 1964-65); pres. Naval Officers Wives Club, Washington, 1973-74. Recipient Fed. Nursing traineeship, 1964, Fla. State Nursing scholarship, 1963, Winn-Lovett Nursing scholarship, 1950, Balfour award Baldwin (Fla.) H.S., 1952. Mem. AAUW, Asia Soc., Fla. Craftsmen, Asian Ceramic Rsch. Orgn., Phi Delta Kappa. Democrat.

LANE, MARGARET ANNA SMITH, property manager developer; b. Aspinwall, Pa., Nov. 26, 1918; d. Max Charles and Mary Ann (Jones) Smith; m. Frank A. Lane Jr., Feb. 7, 1954; 1 child, Alan Michael. AB, UCLA, 1940; MS, U. So. Calif., 1949. Cert. secondary tchr., Calif. Demonstration and tng. tchr. UCLA and U. Calif., Northridge, 1948-74; pvt. practice Cottonwood, Ariz., 1975—; tchr. dept. chmn. L.A. City Schs., 1948-74; sec.-treas. Silver Hoof, Inc., Sedona, Stone Pine Gallery, Ltd., Sedona. Mem. Pi Gamma Mu. Home: PO Box I-I West Sedona AZ 86340

LANE, MARGARET BEYNON TAYLOR, librarian; b. St. Louis, Feb. 6, 1919; d. Archer and Alice (Jones) Taylor; B.A., La. State U., 1939, J.D., 1942; B.S. in Library Sci., Columbia U., 1941; m. Horace C. Lane, Jan. 6, 1945; children—Margaret Elizabeth, Thomas Archer. Reference and circulation asst. Columbia Law Library, N.Y.C., 1942-44; law librarian, asst. prof. U. Conn. Sch. Law, Hartford, 1944-46; law librarian La. State U. Law Sch., Baton Rouge, 1946-48; recorder documents La. Sec. of State's Office, Baton Rouge, 1949-75; law librarian Lane Fertitta, Lane Janney & Thomas, 1976—. Author: State Publications and Depository Libraries, 1981, Selecting And Organizing State Government Publications, 1987. Mem. depository library council to Pub. Printer, 1972-77; mem. plan devel. com. La. Fed. Depository Library, 1982-83. Treas. Delta Iota House Bd. of Kappa Kappa Gamma, 1965-68; mem. La. Adv. Coun. State Documents Depository Program, 1991—. Inducted into La. State U. Law Ctr. Hall of Fame, 1987. Mem. ALA (interdivisional com. public documents 1967-74, chmn. 1967-70; govt. documents round table, state and local documents task force 1972—, coordinator 1980-82; James Bennett Childs award 1981, anniv. honor roll 1996), La. Library Assn. (Essae M. Culver Disting. Service award 1976; chmn. documents com. 1982-83, Lucy B. Foote award subject specialist sect. 1986, Named in Her honor Margaret T. Lane Award 1994), La., Baton Rouge Bar Assns., Mortar Bd., Phi Delta Delta, Kappa Kappa Gamma. Club: Baton Rouge Library. Home: 7545 Richards Dr Baton Rouge LA 70809-1547 Office: PO Box 3335 Baton Rouge LA 70821-3335

LANE, ROBIN, lawyer; b. Kerrville, Tex., Nov. 28 1947; d. Rowland and Gloria (Benson) Richards; m. Stanley Lane, Aug. 22, 1971 (div. 1979); m. Anthony W. Cunningham, Nov. 22, 1980; children: Joshua Lane, Alexandra Cunningham. BA with honors in Econs., U. Fla., 1969; MA, George Washington U., 1971; JD, Stetson U. Coll. Law, 1978. Bar: Fla. 1979, U.S. Ct. Appeals (11th cir.) 1981, U.S. Supreme Ct. 1986, U.S. Ct. Appeals (D.C. cir.) 1992, U.S. Ct. Appeals (3rd cir.) N.Y. 1993. Mgmt. trainee internat. banking Gulf Western Industries, N.Y.C.; internat. rsch. specialist Ryder Systems, Inc., Miami, Fla., 1973, project mgr., 1974; assoc. Wagner, Cunningham, Vaughan & McLaughlin, Tampa, Fla., 1979-85; pvt. practice law, 1985—; guest lectr. med. jurisprudence Stetson U. Coll. Law, 1982-91, also mem. exec. coun. law alumni bd. Contbr. articles to various revs. Recipient Am. Jurisprudence award-torts Lawyers Co-op. Fla., 1979; Scottish Rite fellow, 1968-69. Mem. ABA, Acad. Fla. Trial Lawyers (mem. com. 1983-84), Assn. Trial Lawyers Am., Fla. Bar Assn., Fla. Women's Alliance, Omicron Delta Epsilon. Home: 4934 Saint Croix Dr Tampa FL 33629 Office: PO Box 10155 Tampa FL 33679-0155

LANE, SARAH MARIE CLARK, elementary education educator; b. Conneaut, Ohio, July 27, 1946; d. Robert George and Julia Ellen (Sanford) Clark; m. Ralph Donaldson Lane, May 28, 1977; children: Richard, Laura. BS in Edn., Kent State U., 1977; MS in Edn., Coll. Mt. St. Joseph, 1988. Cert. tchr., Ohio. Coord. newspaper in edn. Tribune Chronicle, Warren, Ohio, 1986-89; tutor MacArthur Found. Project, Warren, Ohio, 1988-89; tchr. chpt. I Lakeview Local Schs., Cortland, Ohio, 1989—. Freelance writer newspaper Conn. News Herald, 1963-64, Tribune Chronicle, 1980-89; contbr. articles to profl. jours.; author: A Walk Through Historic Cortland, 1994. V.p. Bazetta Cortland Hist. Soc., 1983-85; chmn. com. local history project Lakeview Schs., Cortland, 1992—. George Record Found. scholar, 1964-66. Mem. Internat. Reading Assn. (Ohio coun.), Cortland Community Concert Band (pres. 1991-92),. Mem. Christian Ch. (Disciples of Christ). Home: 298 Corriedale Dr Cortland OH 44410-1622 Office: Cortland Elem Sch 264 Park Ave Cortland OH 44410-1047

LANE, SHERRY See UNGER, SHARON LOUISE

LANE, STEPHANIE EILEENMIDDLETON, counselor, musician; b. Oklahoma City, Jan. 18, 1950; d. James Allen and Doris Ione (Gugler) Middleton; m. John Atherton Lane, June 10, 1988 (div. Jan. 1992). B of Music Edn., Okla. U., 1973; M of Music Edn., U. Louisville, 1981, MEd in Counseling, 1984. Cert. sch. counselor, Mo. Musician Louisville Orch., 1973-88; music tchr. Ky. Country Day Sch., Louisville, 1976-81; music instr. U. Louisville, 1981-86; counselor Ctr. Schs., Kansas City, Mo., 1993-94, Kansas City (Mo.) Schs., 1994—. Musician/performer numerous recitals, 1981-86. Mem. ACA, Am. Sch. Counselors Assn., Mo. Sch. Tchrs. Assn. Home: PO Box 8461 Kansas City MO 64114

LANE-MAHER, MAUREEN DOROTHEA, marketing educator, consultant; b. West Point, N.Y., June 26, 1943; d. John Joseph and Dorothea (Fennell) L. BA, St. Louis U., 1965; MEd, U. Va., 1972, EdD, 1977. High sch. history tchr. Va., Okinawa, Japan, 1965-69; published products coord. 3M Bus. Products Sales, Inc., Springfield, Va., 1969-71; program mgr. U. Va., Charlottesville, 1971-77, asst. prof., 1977-78; mktg. svcs. mgr. Westinghouse, Iowa City, 1978-83; mktg. mgr. Nat. Computer Systems, Washington, 1983-87; prof. Nat.-Louis U., McLean (Va.) Acad. Ctr., 1989—; gen. ptnr. The ML Group, Washington, 1987—; spl. asst. USIA, Washington, 1982-83. Contbg. editor, contbr. Ednl. IRM Quar., 1990-92. Exch. exec. class XIII Pres.'s Commn. on Exec. Exch., 1982. Mem. Global Bus. Assn., Am. Mktg. Assn., Mid-Atlantic Women Studies Assn. Roman Catholic. Office: Nat Louis U 8000 Westpark Dr Mc Lean VA 22102-3105

LANE-OREIRO, LAVERNE TERESA, former tribal official; b. Bellingham, Wash., Aug. 29, 1951; d. Vernon Adrian and Nancy Ann (Solomon) Lane; m. David William Cagey Oreiro, Oct. 27, 1979; children: Tyson Hawk, Cody Lane. Student, Grenoble, France, 1972-73; BA in Humanities, Seattle U., 1974. Asst. dir. social svcs. Lummi Indian Tribe, Bellingham, 1974-77, dir. fed. contracts, 1977-78, exec. dir., 1978-81; real estate agt. Ron Bennett & Assocs., Bellingham, 1982-86; Indian edn. coord. Ferndale (Wash.) Pub. Schs., 1984—; vice-chairperson Lummi Indian Nation, 1991-93; pub. spkr. and presenter for local confs., media press confs., talk shows and cmty. functions; bd. chmn. Lummi Tribal Enterprises, Bellingham, 1978-80; bd. dirs. minority sch. and engring. adv. bd. U. Wash., Seattle, 1987-91; mem. minority cmty. adv. bd. Western Wash. U., Bellingham, 1989-93; Wash. state del.-at-large White House Conf. on Indian Edn., Washington, 1992. Writer eulogies for variety of tribal mems. including tribal leaders, elders, etc. Co-chairperson Nat. Indian Women's Fast Pitch, Lummi Indian Reservation, 1978, co-MC Nat. Indian Edn. Opening Rec., Spokane, Wash., 1985; mem. cmty. adv. bd. U. Wash. Women's Ctr., 1995—. Recipient Cmty. Svc. Diversity award Western Wash. U., 1994. Mem. Wash. State Indian Edn. Assn. (bd. sec. 1985-86, 1st v.p. 1986-87), Western Wash. Native Am. Edn. Consortium (vice-chairperson 1985-86, chairperson 1986-87). Democrat. Roman Catholic. Home: 2210 Lummi View Dr Bellingham WA 98226-9208 Office: Ferndale Sch Dist # 502 PO Box 428 Ferndale WA 98248-0428

LANE STONE, NANCY ANN, educator; b. Montague, Mass., Oct. 23, 1945; d. John Henry Adams and Helen Ann (Yez) Lane; m. Richard F. Koscinski, June 8, 1968 (dec. June 1980); children: Todd Lane Koscinski, Michael Lane Koscinski; m. David Lewis Stone, Feb. 26, 1984. BA, U. Mass., 1981; M. Human Svcs., Keene State Coll., 1990. Cert. tchr., Mass.; cert. experienced educator, N.H. Substitute tchr. Montague Pub. Schs., 1981-84, Keene (N.H.) Pub. Schs., 1985-86; v.p. Beck Mfg., Keene, 1986—; dir. Good Mourning Children, Keene, 1988—; dir. children's svcs. Hospice of Monadnock Region, Keene, 1992-94; cons. to staff adv. com. Franklin County Tech. Sch., Turners Falls, Mass., 1977-84; intern, vol. Hospice of Cheshire County, Keene, 1989-90; mem. adj. clin. faculty Antioch New Eng. Grad. Sch., 1993-94; mem. adj. faculty Keene State Coll., 1990—. Dir. Big Bro./Big Sister Orgn. Recipient Sch. Vol. award Symonds Sch., Keene, 1984-85. Mem. AAUW, Assn. for Death Edn. and Counseling, Keene Woman's Club (v.p. 1986-88), Keene Bus. and Profl. Women's Club, N.H. Hospice Orgn., Children's Hospice Internat. Roman Catholic. Office: Good Mourning Children Program 54 Blackberry Ln Keene NH 03431-2120

LANEY, SANDRA EILEEN, chemical company executive; b. Cin., Sept. 17, 1943; d. Raymond Oliver and Henrietta Rose (Huber) H.; m. Dennis Michael Laney, Sept. 30, 1968; children: Geoffrey Michael, Melissa Ann. AS in Bus. Adminstrn., Thomas More Coll., 1988. Adminstrv. asst. to chief exec. officer Chemed Corp., Cin., 1982, asst. v.p., 1982-84, v.p., 1984-91, v.p., chief adminstrv. officer, 1991-93, sr. v.p., chief adminstrv. officer, 1993—, bd. dirs., 1986—; bd. dirs. Roto-Rooter, Cin., Nat. San. Supply Co., L.A., Omnicare, Inc., Cin., Chemed Corp., Cin. Bd. advisors Sch. Nursing and Health U. Cin., 1992. Mem. Cin. Club. Roman Catholic. *

LANG, CATHERINE LOU, small business owner; b. Hugo, Okla., June 12, 1946; d. John Wilburn Sr. and Velma Lou (Evans) Freeman; m. Laurence Larry Lang, Nov. 20, 1974; children: Tana Louise, Henry Nathan, Gina Elise; 1 stepchild, Michael. BA in Sociology and Econs., Northeastern State U., 1970. Co-owner C&L Jewelry, Waterford, Mich., 1980—; landlord of rental home, Novi, Mich., 1977-93. Active Northwest Child Rescue Women Jr. League, 1975—, League of Women of Detroit; mem. PTA Mercy Sch. for Girls, Farmington, Mich., 1990-94, Walled Lake Mich. Schs., 1981—; mem. Great Decisions, active in leadership, 1988; team parent Team Elan Skating Team, 1991-92; mem. Lakes Assn., Novi, 1992; mem. Covenant Bapt. Ch., 1977—, Am. Bapt. Women. Recipient (with son) Arrow of Light pin Cub Scouts. Mem. AAUW (charter Novi-Northville br.), MADD, Internat. Fedn. Univ. Women, Nat. Assn. Investors Corp., Detroit Skating Club, Top Stock Stock Club. Democrat. Home: 1369 E Lake Dr Novi MI 48377-1442 Office: C&L Jewelry 924 W Huron St Waterford MI 48328-3726

LANG, ELISSA, psychiatric rehabilitation administrator, consultant; b. St. Cloud, Minn., July 3, 1950; d. Vincent and Joan (Coughlin) L.; m. John J. Rio, Nov. 23, 1984; 1 child, Nicholas Matthew. BA in Psychology, Japanese

Studies, Manhattanville Coll., Purchase, N.Y., 1972; MA in Psychol. Counseling and MEd in Vocat. Psychology and Rehab., Columbia U., N.Y., 1974. Cert. rehab. counselor, psychiatric rehab. trainer. Supr. L.I. Jewish Hillside Med. Ctr., Glen Oaks, N.Y., 1974-77; program coord. Adult Day Hosp. N.Y. Hosp.-Cornell, White Plains, N.Y., 1977-81; dir. vocat. rehab./intensive rehab. N.Y. Hosp.-Cornell, White Plains, 1981-87; pres. Careerscope, Inc., White Plains, 1975—; dir. psychiat. rehab. Westchester divsn. N.Y. Hosp./Cornell Med. Ctr., White Plains, 1987-95; lectr. in psychiatry Cornell Med. Coll., N.Y., 1987—; sec. faculty coun. Cornell Med. Coll., White Plains, 1982-85, 89-95; coord. NIMH grant Psychiatric Rehab. Dissemination grant, Cornell U.; vocat. expert cons. Dept. Health & Human Svcs., SSA, Balt., 1982—; project adv. Cornell U., Am. Indian Rehab. Rsch. Ctr., 1994—; dir. spl. program YWCA, White Palins, 1996—. Contbr. chpts. to books, articles to profl. jours. Vol. coord. Project Steppingstone Vol. Svc. Bur., White Plains, 1979-84; den parent Boy Scouts of Am., White Plains, 1993—. Recipient Innovations in Vol. Opportunities for Mentally Ill award Am. Red Cross, 1988. Mem. ACA, Am. Rehab. Counseling Assn., Internat. Assn. Psychosocial Rehab. Svcs. Office: Careerscope PO Box 229 White Plains NY 10605

LANG, JEAN MCKINNEY, editor, business educator; b. Cherokee, Iowa, Nov. 6, 1921; d. Roy Clarence and Verna Harvey (Smith) McKinney; BS, Iowa State U., 1945; MA, Ohio State U., 1969; postgrad. U. South Fla., 1972; m. Thomas E. Greef; 1 dau., Barbara Jean Wilcox; step-children: Mary McDonald, Daniel A. Greef. Merchandiser, jewelry buyer Rike-Kumler Co., Dayton, Ohio, 1952-59, Met. Co., Dayton, 1959-64; tchr. DeVilbiss High Sch., Toledo, 1966-67; chmn. dept. retailing Webber Coll., Babson Park, Fla., 1967-72; assoc. editor Wet Set Illustrated, 1972-75; sr. editor Pleasure Boating, Largo, Fla., 1975-84; tchr. bus. adminstrn. St. Petersburg (Fla.) Jr. Coll., 1974-88; adj. prof. bus. adminstrn., 1988—, securities arbitrator, 1992—; editor Suncoast Woman, 1986-88. Mem. U.S. Senatorial Bus. Adv. Bd.; mem. Nat. Boating Safety Adv. Council, 1979-81; Recipient recognition Nat. Retail Mchts. Assn., 1971, certs. of appreciation U.S. Power Squadron, 1976, Webber Coll., 1972. Mem. AAWU, Fla. Women's Alliance, Greater Tampa C. of C., Tampa Aux. Power Squadron, USCG Aux., Sales and Mktg. Execs. of Tampa (pres.'s award 1973), Fla. Freelance Writers Assn., Am. Mktg. Assn., Gulf Coast Symphony, Internat. Platform Assn., The Fashion Group, Fla. Coun. Yacht Clubs, Toledo Yacht Club (hon.), Tampa Yacht and Country Club, Chi Omega. Republican. Presbyterian. First woman to cruise solo from Fla. to Lake Erie in single-engine inboard, 1969, to be accepted into Fla. Council Yacht Clubs; yachting accomplishments published in The Ensign, Lakeland Boating, Yachting, Boote mags. Office: PO Box 402 Largo FL 34649-0402

LANG, LENORE SCHULMAN, visual artist; b. N.Y.C., Nov. 23, 1927; d. Samuel Woolf and Rose (Horowitz) Rosenberg; m. Jerome Lewis Schulman, June 12, 1948 (div. Oct. 1973); children: Ellen Frances Schulman, Martha Sue Schulman; m. Fred Fulton Lang, Jan. 28, 1975 (dec. Nov. 1991); m. Carl Abraham Auerbach, June 11, 1993. Student, Pratt Inst., Bklyn., 1948, Balt. Mus. Art, 1953-54, IIT Sch. Design, Chgo., 1966-67. Designer Norcross, Inc., N.Y.C., 1948-50; tchr. printmaking North Shore Art League, Winnetka, Ill., 1971-73; juror Art Inst. Chgo., 1985-87. Solo exhbns. include U. Ill. Med. Ctr., Chgo., 1971, Federal Jewish Orgn., Chgo., 1972, Mishkenot Sha'ananim, Jerusalem, 1974, Unicorn Gallery, N.Y.C., 1975, Botanic Gardens, Glencoe, Ill., 1977, Evanston (Ill.) Pub. Libr., 1982, Gruen Gallery, Chgo., 1st Ill. Ctr. bldg. lobby, Chgo., 1985, 101 N. Wacker Dr. bldg. lobby, 1986, East/West Gallery, 1988, Gallery 416, Mpls., 1995; group shows include Art Inst. Chgo., 1978, 79, 87, Peace Mus., Chgo., 1981, Northwestern U., Evanston, 1982, WFMT-Chgo. Mag., 1983, Evanston Art Ctr., 1985, NAB Gallery, Chgo., 1986, Suburban Fine Arts Ctr., Highland Park, Ill., 1988, Spertus Mus., Chgo., 1988, Countryside Gallery, Arlington Heights, Ill., 1989, Chgo. Post Gallery, 1989, Evanston Art Ctr., 1989, State of Ill. Bldg., Chgo., 1989, Artemisia Gallery, Chgo., 1990, Sabbeth Gallery, Glen Cove, N.Y., 1990, Arts Club Chgo., 1991, SCAN Exhibit, Chgo., 1991, Chgo. Cultural Ctr., 1992, Riggs Gallery, La Jolla, Calif., 1992, Beacon St. Gallery, Chgo., 1994, Triangle Gallery, 1995, Ill. State Mus., Springfield, 1995, Mus. Sci. and Industry, Chgo., 1995, Athaneum Music & Art Libr., La Jolla, Calif., 1995, Loyola U., Chgo., 1995, Ancient Traditions Gallery, 1996. Mem. Arts Club Chgo. (profl. mem.), Chgo. Artists Coalition, Cliffdweller's Club (profl. mem.). Home: 1530 Tower Rd Winnetka IL 60093

LANG, PEARL, dancer, choreographer; b. Chgo., May 1922; d. Jacob and Frieda (Feder) Lack; m. Joseph Wiseman, Nov. 22, 1963. Student, Wright Jr. Coll., U. Chgo.; D (hon.), Juilliard Sch. Music, 1995. Formed own co., 1953; faculty Yale, 1954-68; tchr., lectr. Juilliard, 1953-69; tchr., lectr. Jacobs Pillow, Conn. Coll., Neighborhood Playhouse, 1963-68, Israel, Sweden, Netherlands. Soloist, Martha Graham Dance Co., 1944-54; featured roles on Broadway include Carousel, 1945-47, Finian's Rainbow, 1947-48, Danced Marth Graham's roles in Appalachian Spring, 1974-76, Primitive Mysteries, 1978-79, Diversion of Angels, 1948-70, Herodiade, 1977-79; role of Solvieg opposite John Garfield Broadway include, ANTA Peer Gynt; choreographer: TV shows CBC Folio; co-dir. T.S. Eliot's Murder in the Cathedral, Stratford, Conn., Direction, 1964-66, 67, Lamp Unto Your Feet, 158, Look Up and Live TV, 1957; co-dir., choreographer: full length prodn. Dybbuk for CBC; dir. numerous Israel Bond programs; assumed roles Emily Dickinson: Letter to the World, 1970; Clytemnestra, 1973; Jocasta in: Night Journey, 1974, for Martha Graham Dance Co.; choreographer: dance works Song of Deborah, 1952, Moonsung and Windsung, 1952, Legend, 1953, Rites, 1953, And Joy Is My Witness, 1954, Nightflight, 1954, Sky Chant, 1957, Persephone, 1958, Black Marigolds, 1959, Shirah, 1960, Apasionada, 1961, Broken Dialogues, 1962, Shore Bourne, 1964, Dismembered Fable, 1965, Pray for Dark Birds, 1966, Tongues of Fire, 1967, Piece for Brass, 1969, Moonways and Dark Tides, 1970, Sharjuhm, 1971, At That Point in Place and Time, 1973, The Possessed, 1974, Prairie Steps, 1975, Bach Rondelays, 1977, I Never Saw Another Butterfly, 1977, A Seder Night, 1977, Kaddish, 1977, Icarus, 1978, Cantigas Ladino, 1978, Notturno, 1980, Gypsy Ballad, 1981, Hanele The Orphan, 1981, The Tailor's Megilleh, 1981, Bridal Veil, 1982, Stravinsky's opera Oedipus Rex, 1982, Song of Songs, 1983, Shiru L'adonay, 1983, Tehillim, 1983, Sephardic Romance and Tfila, 1989, Koros, 1990, Eyn Keloheynu, 1991, Schubert Quartetsatz No. 12, 1993, Schubert Quartet 15 1st Mov., 1994. Founder Pearl Lang Dance Found.; mem. Boston Symphony, Tanglewood Fest. Recipient 2 Guggenheim fellowships; recipient Goldfadden award Congress for Jewish Culture, Achievement award Artists and Writers for Peace in the Middle East, Cultural award Workmen's Circle, Queens Coll. award, 1991, Jewish Cultural achievement award Nat. Found. for Jewish Culture, 1992. Mem. Am. Guild Mus. Artists. Home: 382 Central Park W New York NY 10025-6054

LANG, SUZANNE P., city administrator; b. Phila., June 5, 1951; d. Charles Henry and Ann (Lonardo) Lang. BS, N.H. Coll., 1981, MS, 1984. Group leader Hartford (Conn.) Neighborhood Ctrs., 1971-73; dir. The Arts Café, Hartford, 1973-78; program developer Cmty. Renewal Team, Hartford, 1978-80, ops. adminstr., 1980-81; adminstrv. analyst City of Hartford Police Dept., 1981-82; sr. adminstrv. analyst various depts. City of Hartford, 1982-87; program supr. City of Hartford Housing and Cmty. Devel., 1987—; exec. v.p. Hartford Mcpl. Employees Assn., 1993—. Bd. dirs. Legis. Electoral Action Program, Hartford, 1990—; mem. Mayor's Blue Ribbon Panel on Taxes, Hartford, 1994; treas. Broad-Park Devel. Corp., Hartford, 1981-83; pres. Vols., Inc., Hartford, 1973-78. Mem. Henry George Inst., Mt. Laurel Ski Club. Democrat. Home: 272 Grandview Terr Hartford CT 06114 Office: City of Hartford Dept Housing and Cmty Devel 10 Prospect St Hartford CT 06103

LANG, THERESA, investment banker; b. Hochhausen, Germany, Aug. 25, 1952; d. John and Theresa (Wendler) L.; m. Scott David St. Marie, Nov. 12, 1977; 1 child, Hanna. BA in Econs., Fordham U., 1974; MBA in Finance, UCLA, 1982. Assoc. investment banking A.G. Becker Paribas, N.Y.C., 1982-84; assoc. investment banking Merrill Lynch Capital Markets, N.Y.C., 1984-86, v.p. investment banking, 1986-89, dir. investment banking, 1989-92; sr. v.p., treas. Merrill Lynch & Co., Inc., 1992—. Office: Merrill Lynch and Co World Financial Ctr 250 Vesey St New York NY 10281-1012

LANGBORT, POLLY, retired advertising executive; b. N.Y.C.; d. Julius and Nettie (Berman) L. BA, Adelphi U. Sec. Young & Rubicam, Inc., N.Y.C., media buyer, media planner, 1960-65, planning supr., 1965-70, v.p. group supr., 1970-75, v.p. dir. planning devel., 1975-80, sr. v.p., dir. planning, 1980-85, sr. v.p. direct mktg. and media services Wunderman, Worldwide div., 1985-86, exec. v.p. dir. mktg. & media services Wunderman, Worldwide div., 1986-90; assoc. pub. Lear's Mag., N.Y.C., 1990-91; ret., 1991. Author: DMA Factbook, 1986; contbr. articles to profl. jours. Spl. gifts chairperson Am. Cancer Soc., N.Y.C., 1985-90. Jewish. Home: 7614 La Corniche Cir Boca Raton FL 33433

LANGDON, VICKI N., public information coordinator; b. Sherman, Tex., Apr. 22, 1960; d. Sue N. (Campbell) L. BS in Journalism with acad. distinction, East Tex. State U., 1982. Asst. news dir. Sta. KSEO/KLBC Radio, Durant, Okla., 1982-83, news dir., 1983; entertainment editor, staff writer The Denison (Tex.) Herald, 1983-93; coord. pub. info. Denison (Tex.) Ind. Sch. Dist., 1993—. Publicist (documentary) Mother Maybelle's Carter Scratch, 1989-90; photographer (cover videocassette tape) Johnny Cash Live in London, 1985, (souvenir concert program) Johnny Cash, 1985, (cookbook) Mother Maybelle's Cookbook, 1989, (feature story) Country Music People mag., 1991, (album cover) Helen Carter Clinch Mountain Memories, 1993, (album cover) Anita Carter Yesterday, 1995. Recipient award Tex. State Teachers Assn., Tex. Classroom Teachers Assn., Am. Cancer Soc. Tex. Div., Galveston County Press Club, Texoma Music Assn. Mem. Tex. Sch. Pub. Rels. Assn., Carter Family Fan Club (area rep.), John and June Cash Fan Club (Tex. co-rep.), Alpha Chi. Office: Denison Ind Sch Dist 1201 S Rusk Ave Denison TX 75020-6340

LANGE, BILLIE CAROLA, aquatic exercise video creator and specialist; b. Cullman, Ala.; d. John George and Josephine (richard) Luyben; m. Harry E. Lange (div.); children: JoAnne Lange Graham, Linda Jean Lange Reeve; m. Melvin A. Coble (div.). Grad., Long Beach City (Calif.) Coll.; BMus, U. So. Calif. Chief piano accompanist Long Beach Civic Opera Assn.; tchr./creator aquatic exercise program U. Ala., Huntsville, 1984-87; advisor Aquatic Exercise Assn., Port Washington, Wis., 1988—; creator, prodr. aquatic video exercise tapes Billie C. Lange's Aquatics, Palm Beach, Fla., 1979—. Creator: (aquatic exercise video tapes) Slim and Trim Yoga with Billie In and Out of Pool, 1979, Slim and Trim with Billie In Pool, 1994 (televised on Today Show, NBC 1995); pianist Organ-Piano Duo and various audio tapes; instrumental, audio Tranquility, 1992. Mem. Nat. Acad. Recording Arts and Scis. Home: PO Box 822 Umatilla FL 32784-0822 Office: PO Box 822 Umatilla FL 32784-0822

LANGE, JESSICA, actress; b. Minn., Apr. 20, 1949; d. Al and Dorothy Lange; m. Paco Grande, 1970 (div. 1982); 1 child with Mikhail Baryshnikov, Alexandra; children with Sam Shepard: Hannah Jane, Samuel Walker. Student, U. Minn.; student mime, with Etienne DeCroux, Paris. Dancer Opera Comique, Paris; model Wilhelmina Agy., N.Y.C. Film appearances include King Kong, 1976, All That Jazz, 1979, How to Beat the High Cost of Living, 1980, The Postman Always Rings Twice, 1981, Frances, 1982 (Acad. award nominee 1982), Tootsie, 1982 (Acad. award 1983), Country, 1984, Sweet Dreams, 1985, Crimes of the Heart, 1986 (Acad. award nominee 1987), Everybody's All American, 1988, Far North, 1988, Music Box, 1989 (Acad. award nominee 1990), Men Don't Leave, 1990, Cape Fear, 1991, Night and the City, 1992, Blue Sky, 1994 (Golden Globe award Best Actress in a Drama 1995, Acad. award for Best Actress 1995), Losing Isaiah, 1995, Rob Roy, 1995; TV movies: Cat on a Hot Tin Roof, 1984, O' Pioneers!, 1992, A Streetcar Named Desire, 1995 (Golden Globe award 1996); in summer stock prodn. Angel on My Shoulder, N.C., 1980, A Streetcar Named Desire, 1992. Office: Creative Artists Agy care Ron Meyer 9830 Wilshire Blvd Beverly Hills CA 90212-1804*

LANGE, KATHERINE J., writer; b. Wyandotte, Mich., Feb. 8, 1957; d. James DiDi and Margaret Ann (Kirk) Putman. Student, Normandale Coll., 1980-82. V.p., artist mgr. The T.S.J. Prodns. Inc., Richfield, Minn., 1975—; mgr., agt. The T.S.J. Booking Agy., Richfield, 1980-96; asst. editor, author Songwriter U.S.A. mag., Atlanta, 1986-87; staff writer Music Mgmt. and Internat. Promotion mag., Copenhagen, 1983—; pres. Katherine's Greetings, 1994—, Internat. Literary Concepts, Mpls., 1996—. Contbr. articles to Sun Newspapers, Songwriter Connection, Woman's Press. Mem. ASCAP, NAFE, Am. Fedn. Musicians. Democrat. Lutheran. Home and Office: Internat Literary Concepts 422 Pierce St NE Minneapolis MN 55413-2514

LANGE, LINDA DIANE, education educator, researcher; b. Muskegon, Mich., Jan. 28, 1950. AB in Edn., U. Mich., 1974, EdS in Edn. and Psychology, 1978, PhD in Edn., 1991. Cert. sch. psychologist, N.J. Dance coach Huron (Mich.) H.S., 1974-75; sch. psychologist Lenawee County Schs., Adrian, Mich., 1979-80; rsch. asst. The Psychol. Corp., San Antonio, 1986-88; asst. prof. edn. Marshall U., Huntington, W.Va., 1991-95; vis. asst. prof. edn. Sacred Heart U. Fairfield, Conn., 1995-96; ednl. rschr. Collaborative Rsch. Bd. Marshall U., 1992-93; presenter in field. Contbr. articles to profl. jours. Mem. ASCD, APA, Am. Assn. Tchg. and Curriculum, Am. Ednl. Rsch. Assn., Assn. Tchr. Educators, Ea. Ednl. Rsch. Assn., Soc. Rsch. on Adolescence, Soc. for Study of Social Problems, Southeastern Assn. Ednl. Studies, New England Edn. Rsch. Orgn. Lutheran. Address: PO Box 416 Huntington WV 25705

LANGE, LYNETTE PATRICIA, real estate agent, marketing professional, nurse; b. St. Cloud, Minn., Sept. 20, 1964; d. Daniel Herbert and Patricia Barbara (Berg) Schulist. Student, Bemidji State U., 1982, Anoka Ramsey C.C., 1982-95; student in naturopathic medicine, 1993—. RN, Minn. Acct., bus. mgr. Hannon Security Svcs., Golden Valley, Minn., 1988-91; real estate agt. Sundial Realty, Mpls., 1990-95; prin. Lange Enterprises, Inc., Golden Valley, 1991—. Fundraiser, vol. Am. Heart Assn./Diabetes Found. Home: 121 83d Ave NE Fridley MN 55432

LANGE, MARILYN, social worker; b. Milw., Dec. 6, 1936; d. Edward F. and Erna E. (Karstaedt) L.; divorced; children: Lara McKelvie, Gregory Cash. B of Social Work, U. Wis., Milw., 1962, MSW, 1974. Cert. ind. clin. social worker. Recreation specialist Dept. Army, Europe, 1962-63; social worker Family Svc. Milw., 1967-75, dir. homecare divsn., 1975-85; nat. field rep. Alzheimers Assn., Chgo., 1986-90; exec. dir. Village Adult Day Ctr., Milw., 1991—. Mem. Nat. Coun. Aging, Wis. Adult Daycare Assn. (pres.), Dementia Care Network, Older Adult Svc. Providers Consortium, West Allis Bus. & Profl. Women, U. Wis.-Milw. Alumni Assn. Home: 5727 W Fillmore Dr Milwaukee WI 53219-2219 Office: Village Adult Day Ctr Inc 130 E Juneau Ave Milwaukee WI 53202-2552

LANGE, PAMELA SANDFORD PARKER, English educator; b. S.I., N.Y., Feb. 23, 1939; d. Harold Rothe Sandford and Mary Isabel (Hewitt) Parker; m. John H. Lange Jr., Dec. 7, 1957; children: Linda Anne Lange McDonald, Jacqueline Sandford Lange McMurrey. Student, Moravian Coll., 1956-58; BA in English with high honors, So. Meth. U., 1971, MA in English, 1973; postgrad., Rice U., 1978. Tchg. fellow in English So. Meth. U., Dallas, 1971-73, English instr., 1973-78, lectr. in English, 1993—; humanist in residence Dallas Pub. Libr., 1978-80, editl. dir., 1980-86; pres. Eidos Publs., Dallas, 1986-88; mktg. dir. Taylor Pub. Co., Dallas, 1988-91; exec. dir. Book Pubs. Tex., Dallas, 1991—; cons., editor F. Mason Assocs., Dallas, 1992—; condr. workshops in field. Host, prodr. TV program Conversations, Irving (Tex.) Cmty. TV, 1987—; author: Family Business in Dallas, 1979, In Beauty it is Finished, 1981; editor periodical Moving to Dallas-Ft. Worth, 1979-81; contbr. articles, poems to profl. publs.; co-originator, editor: Criteria: A Journal of Freshman Writing, 1976; co-editor jour. Revisions, 1978-79, Jour. Freshman Writing, 1978-79; editor: Remembering and Writing: An Ahthology, 1981, Dreams Crowded with Families, 1982. Mem. PEN (treas. Tex. chpt. 1993—), Women's Nat. Book Assn. (bd. dirs., v.p. 1995—). Democrat. Presbyterian. Home: 1629 Junior Dr Dallas TX 75208

LANGE, SUSAN KAYE, musician; b. Valparaiso, Ind., July 21, 1958; d. Donald Dwayne and Jeannette Paula (Gilkeson) Buyze; m. Lawrence Lange, Apr. 1980 (div. Dec. 1985). BS in Chemistry & Biology cum laude, Western Mich. U., 1981. Chemistry technician Consumers Power, Covert, Mich., 1981-85, chemistry lab. supr., 1985-87; bandleader CeLange, N.Y.C., 1992—. Songwriter, recording artist: (CD recording) New Day Comin', 1996. Mem. ASCAP. Home: 624 E 11th St 5C New York NY 10009 Office: IEEE Communications Soc 345 E 47th St New York NY 10017

LANGELAN, MARTHA JANE, sexual harassment expert; b. Toledo, May 16, 1949; d. Harry C. and Severina (Gurzynski) L.; m. William M. LeoGrande, July 20, 1985. BA in Econs. and Polit. Sci., Syracuse U., 1973. Economist U.S. Civil Aeronautics Bd., Washington, 1976-84; sr. economist U.S. Dept. Transp., Washington, 1985-94; self-def. instr. D.C. Rape Crisis Ctr., Washington, 1980—, sexual harassment prevention, 1981—; pres. Langelan & Assocs., Chevy Chase, Md., 1994—; prof. justice and law Am. U., Washington, 1995—; nonviolence instr. Washington Peace Ctr., 1983-93; assoc. Nat. Coun. for Rsch. on Women, N.Y.C., 1993—; judge expert panel Puget Sound Regional Coun., Seattle, Wash., 1994-96; sexual harassment expert Am. Friends Svc. Com., Budapest, Hungary, 1995. Author: Back Off! How to Confront and Stop Sexual Harassment and Harassers, 1993; contbr. articles to profl. jours. Pres. D.C. Rape Crisis Ctr., Washington, 1982-86; nat. bd. mem. Nat. Woman's Party, Washington, 1993—; keynote spkr. ALA Nat. Conf., Miami, Fla., 1995, Women's Leadership Conf., Fairfax, Va., 1996. Recipient Lifetime Achievement award D.C. Rape Crisis Ctr., Washington, 1994. Fellow Coun. Excellence in Govt.; mem. NAFE, NOW, AAUW, Women's Transp. Seminar (spkr.), Internat. Assn. in Feminist Econs., Com. on the Status of Women in the Econs. Profession. Office: Langelan & Assocs 7215 Chestnut St Chevy Chase MD 20815

LANGELOH, JEAN KLEPPINGER, interior designer; b. Allentown, Pa., Aug. 2, 1921; d. Samuel Adam Kleppinger and Elsie Mae Herman; m. Robert H. Langeloh, Feb. 7, 1959 (div. 1986); children: Geoffrey Robert (dec.), Gail Elizabeth. BS in Art Edn., Skidmore Coll., 1943; postgrad., Columbia U., 1945-46, N.Y. Sch. Interior Design, 1945-46. Interior designer James McCreary, N.Y.C., 1946-47; showroom, sales staff Katzenbach & Warren, 1947-48; owner, interior designer, cons. Jean K. Langeloh Interiors, Beals Island, Maine, 1950—; interior design instr. YWCA, Greenwich, Conn., 1975-86. Mem. Am. Soc. Interior Designers (assoc. New England chpt.). Republican. Lutheran. Home and Office: Box 189 Beals Island ME 04611

LANGEN, KATHLEEN SUMMERS, sales professional; b. Buffalo, N.Y., Aug. 2, 1946; d. Matthew Arthur and Elanor Daws (Summers) Cullen; m. Joseph Gill Langen, Aug. 2, 1946; children: Susan, Peter, Becky. Grad., U. Buffalo, 1969; student, Genesee C.C., Batavia, N.Y., 1982. Clk., law libr. U. Buffalo, 1967-69; clk., camera shop North Wales, Pa., 1969-71, Batavia, N.Y.; rep. Watkins Co., Batavia, 1995—, Discovery Toys, Batavia, 1995—, Partylite, Batavia, 1995—. Pres. bd. dirs. YWCA, Genesee County. Mem. St. Mary's Ch., Batavia, 1974—. Roman Catholic.

LANGENBAHN, STACIA, research analyst; b. Midland, Tex., Nov. 14, 1962; d. William Edward and Joanne Elaine (Cathey) L. BA in Am. Studies and Dance, Wesleyan U., 1985. Rsch. asst. Abt Assocs. Inc., Cambridge, Mass., 1991-94; analyst Abt Assocs. Inc., Cambridge, 1994—. Co-author: (White House White Paper) Substance Abuse Prevention: What Works, and Why, 1993, (monograph) The Criminal Justice and Community Response to Rape, 1994. Oral historian, interviewer Somerville (Mass.) Arts Coun., 1994, 95. Democrat. Zen Buddhist. Office: Abt Assocs Inc 55 Wheeler St Cambridge MA 02138

LANGENHEIM, JEAN HARMON, biology educator; b. Homer, La., Sept. 5, 1925; d. Vergil Wilson and Jeanette (Smith) H.; m. Ralph Louis Langenheim, Dec. 1946 (div. Mar. 1961). BS, U. Tulsa, 1946; MS, U. Minn., 1949, PhD, 1953. Rsch. assoc. botany U. Calif., Berkeley, 1954-59, U. Ill., Urbana, 1959-61; rsch. fellow biology Harvard U., Cambridge, Mass., 1962-66; asst. prof. biology U. Calif., Santa Cruz, 1966-68, assoc. prof. biology, 1968-73, prof. biology, 1973—; academic v.p. Orgn. Tropical Studies, San Jose, Costa Rica, 1975-78; mem. sci.adv. bd. EPA, Washington, 1977-81; chmn. com. on humid tropics U.S. Nat. Acad. Nat. Research Council, 1975-77; mem. com. floral inventory Amazon NSF, Washington, 1975-87. Author: Botany-Plant Biology in Relation to Human Affairs.; Contbr. articles to profl. jours. Grantee NSF, 1966-88; recipient Disting. Alumni award U. Tulsa, 1979. Fellow AAAS, AAUW, Calif. Acad. Scis., Bunting Inst.; mem. Bot. Soc. Am., Ecol. Soc. Am. (pres. 1986-87), Internat. Soc. Chem. Ecology (pres. 1986-87), Assn. for Tropical Biology (pres. 1985-86), Soc. for Econ. Botany (pres. 1993-94). Home: 191 Palo Verde Ter Santa Cruz CA 95060-3214 Office: U Calif Dept Biology Sinsheimer Labs Santa Cruz CA 95064

LANGENKAMP, SANDRA CARROLL, retired healthcare policy executive; b. St. Joseph, Mo., Feb. 10, 1939; d. William Harry Minger and Beverly (Carroll) Lee; m. R. Hayden Downie, June 1, 1963 (div. Feb. 1979); children: Whitney, Timothy, Allyson. BS, Tex. Women's U., 1960. Adjunctive therapist Menninger Meml. Hosp., Topeka, 1960-66; asst. adminstr. Hillcrest Med. Ctr., Tulsa, 1977-82; dir. Vol. Action Agy., Tulsa, 1982-83; exec. dir. Tulsa Bus. Health Group, 1983—; v.p. Met. Tulsa C. of C., 1985—; exec. dir. Tulsa Program for Affordable Health Care, 1986-96; ret., 1996; cons. mem. Okla. Employment Security Commn., Oklahoma City, 1988—; exec. dir. Tulsa Cmty. Found. for Indigent Health Care, 1986-96; officer State of Okla. Basic Health Benefits Bd., 1985-96, chmn., 1992-93; exec. dir. Tulsa Program for Affordable Health Care, 1989—; mem. health benefit com. State of Okla. Ins. Commn., 1994—; Gov. Com. Health Care, 1993. Author: editorial column Point of View, 1985—, Tulsa mag., 1985—. Count commn. appointee Tulsa Met. Area Planning Commn., 1973-81; mayor's appointee Tulsa Housing Authority, 1985-88; pres. Tulsa Met. Ministry, 1980-83; bd. dirs. ARC, Tulsa, 1971-73, 84-85. Mem. Am. C. of C. (exec. dir. Okla. chpt.), Met. Tulsa C. of C. (v.p. 1983-95), Tulsa Tennis Club. Democrat. Roman Catholic. Office: Met Tulsa C of C 616 S Boston Ave Tulsa OK 74119

LANGER, ELLEN JANE, psychologist, educator, writer; b. N.Y.C., Mar. 25, 1947; d. Norman and Sylvia (Tobias) L. BA, NYU, 1970; PhD, Yale U., 1974. Cert. clin. psychologist. Asst. prof. psychology The Grad. Ctr. CUNY, 1974-77; assoc. prof. psychology Harvard U., Cambridge, Mass., 1977-81; prof. Harvard U., 1981—; cons. NAS, 1979-81, NASA; mem. div. on aging Harvard U. Med. Sch., 1979—, mem. psychiat. epidemiology steering com., 1982-90; chair social psychology program Harvard U., 1982—, chair Faculty Arts and Scis. Com. of Women, 1984-88. Author: Personal Politics, 1973, Psychology of Control, 1983, Mindfulness, 1989; editor: (with Charles Alexander) Higher Stages of Human Development, 1990, (with Roger Schank) Beliefs, Reasoning and Decision-Making, 1994); contbr. articles to profl. anc scholarly jours. Guggenheim fellow; grantee NIMH, NSF, Soc. for Psychol. Study of Social Issues, Milton Fund, Sloan Found., 1982; recipient Disting. Contbn. of Basic to Applied Psychology award APS, 1995. Fellow Computers and Soc. Inst., Am. Psychol. Assn. (Disting. Contributions to Psychology in Public Interest award 1988, Disting. Contributions of Basic Sci. to Applied Psychology 1995); mem. Soc. Exptl. Social Psychology, Phi Beta Kappa, Sigma Xi. Democrat. Jewish. Office: Harvard U Dept Psychology 33 Kirkland St Cambridge MA 02138-2044

LANGER, JUDITH ANN, education educator; b. N.Y.C.. BA, CUNY, 1962, MSEd, 1965; PhD, Hofstra U., 1978. Asst. prof. L.I. U., 1973-78; asst. prof. dept. ednl. psychology NYU, 1978-80; sr. rschr. lang. behavior rsch. lab. U. Calif., Berkeley, 1980-84; assoc. prof. sch. of edn. Stanford U., 1984-87; prof. SUNY, Albany, 1987—; co-dir. Nat. Rsch. Ctr. of Lit. Tchg. and Learning; dir. Nat. Rsch. Ctr. on English Learning & Achievement; trustee Rsch. Found., Nat. Coun. of Tchrs. of English; task force mem. Nat. Commn. on Edn. Stds. and Testing; adv. com. New Stds. in Edn. Project, Literacy Unit, LRDC and Nat. Ctr. on Edn. and the Economy; adv. bd. Nat. Coun. of Chief State Sch. Officers, Nat. Objective in Reading; adv. bds., Nat. Assessment of Ednl. Progress, Reading and Writing Assessments, 1980—; cons. Calif. Assessment Program, Calif. State Dept. Edn., Ctr. for Lang. Edn. and Rsch., Ctr. for the Study of Writing, Rev. of Rsch. on Reading and Writing Relationships, Mich. State Edn. Dept., others. Author: Reader Meets Author/Bridging the Gap, 1982, Understanding Reading and Writing Research, 1985, Children Reading and Writing: Structures and Strategies, 1986, Language, Literacy, and Culture, 1987, Issues of Society and Schooling, How Writing Shapes Thinking: Studies of Teaching and Learning, 1987, Literature Instruction: A Focus on Student Response, 1992, Literature Instruction: Practice & Policy, 1994, Envisioning Literature, 1995; contbr. numerous articles to profl. jours.; editor: Research in the Teaching of English, 1984-92; editl. bd. English Internat., Jour. of Reading Behavior, Newsletter, Lab. of Comparative Human Cognition, Jour. of Reading and Writing, Internat. Jour. of Reading and Writing; reviewer numerous jours.

Recipient numerous grants; fellow Rockefeller Found., Benton fellow U. Chgo. Fellow Am. Psychol. Assn., Nat. Conf. on Rsch. in English; mem. MLA, Am. Ednl. Rsch. Assn., Am. Psychol. Soc., Conf. on Coll. Composition and Comm., Internat. Reading Assn., Nat. REading Conf., Nat. Coun. of Tchrs. of English, Soc. for Rsch. in Child Devel., Soc. for Text and Discourse.Kappa Delta Pi. Office: Univ at Albany 1400 Washington Ave Albany NY 12222

LANGFIELD, HELEN ELION, artist, radio commentator; b. New London, Conn., July 6, 1924; d. Harry Robert and Ida Fannie Elion; m. Raymond Lee Langfield, Oct. 6, 1952; 1 child, Joanna Langfield Rose. BA in English, Ohio State U., 1946; MA in Studio Art, Conn. Coll., 1972. Interviewer, commentator Sta. WNLC/WTYD, Waterford, Conn., 1971-88; instr. Lyman Allyn Mus., New London, Conn., 1984-86; chmn., art instr. Conn. Coll. Summer Program in Humanities, New London, 1968-72; TV interviewer, New London, 1970. Columnist New London Day, 1972; exhibited in one-woman and group shows at Wadsworth Atheneum, Hartford, 1974, Aldrich Mus. of Art, Ridgefield, Conn., 1976, 55 Mercer, N.Y.C., 1977, Whitney Counterweight, N.Y.C., 1981, Pastel Soc. Am., N.Y.C., 1982, Adam Gimbel Gallery, N.Y.C., 1982, 83, Cummings Art Ctr., New London, 1979, 83, 85, Brouhaha Gallery, Providence, 1986, Vangarde Gallery, New London, 1986, 87, 88, NOHO Gallery, N.Y.C., 1981, 85, 88, Conn. Commn. on Arts Showplace, Hartford, 1987, Lyman Allyn Mus., New London, Conn., 1988, 92, Conn. Coll., New London, 1988, MS Gallery, Hartford, 1988, Mark Humphrey Gallery, Southhampton, N.Y., 1991, Boca Raton (Fla.) Mus. Art, 1992, Hoxie Gallery, Westerly, R.I., 1994, Habitat Gallery, West Palm Beach, Fla., 1996; represented in permanent collections Michael DeSantis, Inc., N.Y.C., Radisson Hotel, New London, 1st Nat. Bank Danbury, Conn., Conn. Savings Bank, New Haven, Suisman, Shapiro, Wool, Brennan, Gray and Faulkner, P.C., New London, Citicorp, Boston, Otis Elevator, Hartford, State Ct. House, New London, pvt. collections. Commr. Conn. Commn. on the Arts, Hartford, 1983-85. Jewish.

LANGFORD, KAREN SOLTIS, counselor, family therapist; b. Amarillo, Tex., Jan. 18, 1955; d. Raymond John and Gladys Gloria (Ross) Soltis; m. Earl Louis Gardner, June 23, 1973 (div. Aug. 1976); 1 child, Kristina Marie; m. John Stephen Langford, Nov. 5, 1982; children: Stephen Joshua, Thomas Gregory. BS, West Tex. State U., 1980; MEd, West Tex. A&M U., 1993. Tchr., coach Amarillo (Tex.) Ind. Sch. Dist., 1980-91; owner Raindancer Lawn Sprinkler Sys., Amarillo and Hereford, Tex., 1985—; sch. counselor Hereford Ind. Sch. Dist., 1992-96; therapist Quest Hosp., Amarillo, 1992—; juvenile probation counselor Deaf Smith County, Hereford, 1996—; presenter in field. Vol. counselor O'Brien House Cath. Family Svcs., Amarillo, 1993-94; vol. family counselor Child Protective Svcs., Hereford, 1994-95; vol. Cub Scout leader Boy Scouts Am., Hereford, 1995—, Hereford Health Care Alliance. Mem. ACA, Am. Assn. Christian Counselors, Tex. Counseling Assn., High Plains Counseling Assn., Kappa Delta Pi, Delta Psi Kappa. Republican. Methodist. Home: 305 Hickory Hereford TX 79045 Office: Deaf Smith County Juvenile Probation 126 E 3d Hereford TX 79045

LANGFORD, LAURA SUE, ratings analyst; b. Evansville, Ind., Sept. 28, 1961; d. Lee Denmar Miller and Susan E. (Morton) Reitz; m. John E. Langford, May 15, 1992; 1 child, Rowan Diane. BFA in Drama, U. So. Calif., L.A., 1983; MBA in Fin. & Pub./Non-Profit, Columbia U., 1992. Credit mgr. Super-Freeze Co., Inc., Burbank, Calif., 1984-86; asst. Salomon Bros. Inc., L.A., 1986-87; rsch. analyst Bank of Calif., N.A., L.A., 1987, pub. fin. officer, 1988-90; intern Citizens Budget Commn., N.Y.C., 1991; analyst Standard & Poor's Ratings Group, N.Y.C., 1992-93, assoc., 1993-94, assoc. dir., 1994-95, dir., 1996—. Contbr. to periodical Standard & Poor's Credit Week, 1993—; founding mem., editor GAA Gazette, 1985—. Pres.'s scholar U. Evansville, 1979-81; Divsn. Rsch. Assn. student officer fellow Columbia U., 1991-92. Office: Standard & Poor's Ratings 25 Broadway Fl 13 New York NY 10004-1010

LANGGOOD, JUDITH ANN, secondary level art educator; b. Buffalo, Feb. 2, 1950; d. Alfred Victor Canetti and Irma Frances (Oakes) Reitz; m. Mark Gerald Langgood, Nov. 27, 1985. BA, Geneseo (N.Y.) State Coll., 1972; tchg. certification, Buffalo State Coll., 1995, MS in Edn., 1996. Cert. elem. and secondary sch. art tchr., N.Y. Sales mgr. Globe Advt. Co., Buffalo, 1980—; tchr. art various dists., N.Y., 1995—; dir. art Camp Agape, Buffalo, 1978-80; cons. art activities Camp Fresh Horizons, Buffalo, 1995. Freelance jewelry designer and fabricator, 1975—; exhibited paintings in area art shows, 1977—. Mem. Nat. Art Edn. Assn., N.Y. State Art Tchrs. Assn., Buffalo Fine Arts Acad., Kappa Delta Pi, Alpha Sigma Lambda.

LANGHAM, NORMA, playwright, educator, poet, composer, inventor; b. California, Pa.; d. Alfred Scrivener and Mary Edith (Carter) L. BS, Ohio State U., 1942; B in Theatre Arts, Pasadena Playhouse Coll. Theatre Arts, 1944; MA, Stanford U., 1956; postgrad., Summer Radio-TV Inst., 1960, Pasadena Inst. Radio, 1944-45. Tchr. sci. California High Sch., 1942-43; asst. office pub. info. Denison U., Granville, Ohio, 1955; instr. speech dept. Westminster Coll., New Wilmington, Pa., 1957-58; instr. theatre. California U., Pa., 1959, asst. prof., 1960-62, assoc. prof., 1962-79, prof. emeritus, 1979—, co-founder, sponsor, dir. Children's Theatre, 1962-79; founder, producer, dir. Food Bank Players, 1985, Patriot Players, 1986, Noel Prodns., 1993. Writer: (plays) Magic in the Sky, 1963, Founding Daughters (Pa., Nat. DAR awards 1991), Women Whisky Rebels (Pa. Nat. DAR awards 1992), John Dough (Freedoms Found. award 1968), Who Am I?, Hippocrates Oath, Gandhi, Clementine of '49, Soul Force, Dutch Painting, Purim, Music in Freedom, The Day the Moon Fell, Norma Langham's Job Johnson; composer, lyricist (plays) Why Me, Lord?, (text) Public Speaking; co-inventor (computer game) Highway Champion. Recipient Exceptional Acad. Svc. award Pa. Dept. Edn., 1975, Appreciation award Bicentennial Commn. Pa., 1976, Gregg award Calif. U. of Pa. Alumni Assn., 1992; Henry C. Frick Ednl. Commn. grantee. Mem. AAUW (co-founder Calif. br., 1st v.p. 1971-72, pres. 1972-73, Outstanding Woman of Yr. 1986), DAR, Theatre Assn. Pa., Internat. Platform Assn. (Poetry award 1993-94, Monologue award 1995), Calif. U. Pa. Assn. Women Faculty (founder, pres. 1972-73), Calif. Cmty. Choir, Calif. Hist. Soc., Washington County Hist. Soc., Dramatists Guild, Ctr. in Woods, Mensa, Alpha Psi Omega, Omicron Nu. Presbyterian (elder). Home: PO Box 459 California PA 15419-0459

LANGHOUT-NIX, NELLEKE, artist; b. Utrecht, The Netherlands, Mar. 27, 1939; came to U.S., 1968, naturalized, 1978; d. Louis Wilhelm Frederick and Geertruida Nix; m. Ernst Langhout, July 26, 1958; 1 child, Klaas-Jan Marnix. MFA, The Hague, 1958. Head art dept. Bush Sch., Seattle, 1969-71; dir. creative projects Project Reach, Seattle, 1971-72; artist-in-residence Fairhaven Coll., Bellingham, Wash., 1974, Jefferson Cmty. Ctr., Seattle, 1978-82, Lennox Sch., N.Y.C., 1982; dir. NN Gallery, Seattle, 1970—; guest curator Holland-U.S.A. Bicentennial show U. Wash., 1982; project dir. Women in Art Today, Wash., 1989, Wash. State Centennial Celebration; Washington to Washington traveling exhibition, 1989. Executed wall hanging for King County Courthouse, Seattle, 1974; one-woman shows include: Nat. Art Center, N.Y.C., 1980, Gail Chase Gallery, Bellevue, Wash., 1979, 80, 83, 84, Original Graphics Gallery, Seattle, 1981, Bon Nat. Gallery, Seattle, 1981, Kathleen Ewing Gallery, Washington, 1986, Ina Broerse Laren, Holland, 1992, Charlotte Daneel Gallery, Holland, 1992, Christopher Gallery, Tucson, 1992, Mercer Island Cmty. Arts Ctr., 1992, Lisa Harris Gallery, Seattle, 1994, Jacques Marchais Mus. Tibetan, S.I., N.Y., 1995, 4th World Conf. on Women, China, 1995, Global Focus, Beijing, 1995, Elite Gallery, Moscow, 1995; group shows include: Cheney Cowles Mus., Spokane, 1977, Bellevue Art Mus., 1978, 86, Renwick Gallery, Washington, 1978, Kleinert Gallery, Woodstock, N.Y., 1979, Artcore Meltdown, Sydney, Australia, 1979, Tacoma Art Mus., 1979, 83, 86, 87, Ill. State Mus., Springfield, 1979, Plener Sandomierz, Poland, 1980, Plener Kielce, Poland, 1980, Western Assn. Art Museums traveling show, 1979-80, Madison Square Garden, N.Y.C., 1981, Exhbn. Space, N.Y.C., 1982, Lisa Harris Gallery, 1985, 87, 88, Wash. State Centennial, Tacoma, 1989, Nordic Heritage Mus., Seattle, 1994; represented in permanent collections Plener Collection, Sandomierz, Poland, Bell Telephone Co. Collection, Seattle, Wash. U., Seattle, Children's Orthopedic Hosp., Seattle, Nat. Mus. Women in Arts, Washington; installations Tacoma Art Mus. Bd. dirs. Wing Luke Mus., Seattle, 1978-81, Wash. State Trust Hist. Preservation, 1990-93; v.p. Denny Regrade Cmty. Coun., 1978-79; mem. Seattle Planning Commn., 1978-84. Author (with others) Step Inside the Sacred Circle, 1989, An Artist's Book 1940-45 Remembered, 1991; designer, editor Papua New Guinea-Where She Invented Bow and Arow, 1996. Recipient Wallhanging award City of Edmonds (Wash.), 1974; Renton 83 merit award, 1984; Merit award Internat. Platform Assn. Art Exhibit, 1984, Silver medal 1st place, 1985, 87, Gold medal, Internat. Platform Assn., 1989. Mem. Denny Regrade Arts Coun. (co-founder), Internat. Platform Assn., Women in Arts N.Y.C., Nat. Mus. Women in Arts (founding mem., Libr. fellow, chairperson Wash. State com. 1988-89, mem. nat. adv. bd. 1993—), Internat. Platform Assn., Seattle-King County Cmty. Arts Network (bd. dirs. 1983-85, chmn. 1984-85), Nat. Artist Equity Assn. Address: PO Box 375 Mercer Island WA 98040-0375

LANGLEY, CHIARA MARIA BINI, society executive, research scientist; b. Castelfranco Emilia, Mo, Italy, June 26, 1934; came to the U.S., 1954; d. Giovanni and Maria (Cavallini) Bini; m. Robert B. Sexton, Aug. 20, 1958 (div. June 1969); children: John Andrew, Marta A., Michael R.; m. Rolland A. Langley, Apr. 12, 1978. Student, U. Bologna, Italy, 1954-55; BS in Biology, Kans. State U., 1959; postgrad., Sonoma State Coll., 1974-75, San Francisco State U., 1976-80. Histology lab. tech., rsch. assoc. Nat. Cancer Found. Kans. State U., Manhattan, Kans., 1955-60; radiochem. technician Aerojet-Gen. Nucleonics, San Ramon, Calif., 1968-69; med. lab. tech. various orgns., Calif., 1969-71; sr. med. tech., microbiology supr. Ukiah (Calif.) Gen. Hosp., 1971-75; bacteriologist Pediatric Clinic, Ukiah, 1972-75; sr. med. tech. Clin. Labs., VA Med. Ctr., San Francisco, 1976; adminstrv. asst. to the chief, lab. mgr., sr. technician Immunology Rsch., VA. Med. Ctr., San Francisco, 1976-82; rsch. adminstr., rsch. scientist Kuzell Inst Arthritis Rsch. Inst. Med. Scis., Pacific Med. Ctr., San Francisco, 1981-82; pres. GCBL Enterprises, Inc., 1984-86; dir. internat. rels. IDEA of San Francisco, Calif., 1986-90; vis. scholar Dr. Peter Witschi's Lab., Oak Ridge (Tenn.) Nat. Lab./Biology Divsn., 1982; fundraiser Loudon Healthcare Found., Leesburg, Va., 1993; mem., advisor World Meml. Fund for Disaster Relief, London, 1993; advisor internat. exchanges Notre Dame Acad., Middleburg, Va., 1994; bd. dirs. Fund Internat. Youth Coop., Ctr. Profl. Tng. and Internat. Exchanges, Moscow. chairperson fin. com. Oak Ridge Art Ctr., 1982-83, v.p., 1983-84; active Italian Regional Events, 1984-87, San Francisco/Moscow Med. Exchange Program, 1987-89; bd. dirs. Juvenile Diabetes Found. Internat. of San Francisco, 1988-90; establisher The Clara Lux Found., 1988-90; amb. Internat. Fedn. Keystone Youth Orgns., 1991—; mem. bd., internat. coor., amb. Internat. Fedn. Multiple Sclerosis Socs., 1991—; amb. and v.p. World Meml. Fund for Disaster Relief USA, 1994—. Recipient U.S. Govt. Fulbright scholarship, Pi Beta Phi scholarship, Kans. State Fedn. Women scholarship, 1955-56, AAUW scholarship, 1955-57, Pvt. commendation Chief of Surgery, Ukiah Gen. Hosp., 1972, Am. Soc. Med. Techs./Mgmt. Tng. grant, 1973. Republican. Roman Catholic. Home and Office: 1341 28th St NW Washington DC 20007-3101

LANGLEY, PATRICIA ANN, lobbyist; b. Butler, Pa., Feb. 13, 1938; d. F.J. and Ella (Serafine) Piccola; m. Harold D. Langley, June 12, 1965; children: Erika, David. BA, U. Pitts., 1961; postgrad., Georgetown U., 1967, Cath. U. Am., 1985, George Mason U., 1990—. Legis. staff U.S. Congress, Washington, 1961-63; dir. social studies Am. Polit. Sci. Assn., Washington, 1963-65; legis. specialist U.S. Congress, Washington, 1965-67, caseworker, 1967-68; polit. staff Dem. Study Group U.S. Congress, Washington, 1969; Washington rep. Family Services Am., 1975-82, dir. Washington hdqrs., 1989-92, v.p. for govt. rels., 1992; pres. Policy Directions, Arlington, Va., 1992—; vis. lectr. George Mason U., Fairfax, Va., 1994; vis. lectr. in sociology George Mason U., Fairfax, Va., 1994; bd. dirs. Coalition for Children and Youth, Washington, 1977-78; chmn. steering com. for the Coalition on White House Conf. on Families, 1979-80, Ad Hoc Coalition on A.F.D.C., 1981-82. Mem. Donaldson Run Civic Assn., Arlington, Va., 1980—; bd. mem. Va. Chamber Orch. Recipient Service Recognition U.S. Dept. Health and Human Services, 1980. Mem. Am. Soc. Assn. Execs., Women in Govt. Rels., Nat. Coun. Family Rels., North Va. Assn. Female Execs., Arnova, Groves Conf. Roman Catholic. Home and Office: 2515 N Utah St Arlington VA 22207-4031

LANGLEY, PATRICIA COFFROTH, psychiatric social worker; b. Pitts., Mar. 1, 1924; d. John Kimmel and Anna (McDonald) Coffroth; m. George J. Langley, May 1, 1946; children: George Julius III, Mary Patricia, Kelly Joan; stepchildren: Robin Spencer, Veronica Bell. BA, Empire State Coll., 1976; MSW, Hunter Coll., 1980. Diplomate Clin. Social Worker; lic. social worker, Conn.; cert. Conn. Psychiat. rehab. worker. Credentialed alcoholism treatment counselor, supervisor, Bronx Mcpl. Hosp. Center, Albert Einstein Med. Coll., 1970-74, case worker, comprehensive alcoholism treatment center, dept. psychiatry, 1974-80; asst. coordinator outpatient psychiat. alcoholism Meridian Ctr., Stamford, Conn., 1980-83; dir. family treatment Meridian Ctr.; pvt. practice and consultation. Vol., DuBois Day Clinic, Stamford, 1966-67, Greenwich Hosp., 1966-67. Mem. NASW, Conn. Soc. for Clin. Social Workers. Home and Office: 50 Lafayette Place Greenwich CT 06830

LANGLEY, SHARON THRASHER, computer programmer; b. Booneville, Miss., Nov. 24, 1942; d. Tom Goodman and Dorothy J. (Wright) Thrasher; m. Robert Warren Langley, Aug. 28, 1965 (div. May 1989); children: Anne Sharon, Kathryn Clay. BA, Hollins Coll., 1965; AA, Pikes Peak C.C., Colo., 1987. Libr. No. Rsch. & Engring., Boston, 1966; tchr. Chaparral Jr. H.S., Alamogordo, N.Mex., 1967; adminstr. database Ultran, adventure travel, Colorado Springs, Colo., 1987; mgr. statis. process engring. Holly Sugar Corp., Colorado Springs, 1988-92; mgr. tech. reporting Imperial Holly Corp., Colorado Springs, 1992—. Mem. Data Processing Mgrs. Assn. (pres. Colorado Springs chpt. 1991), Jr. League Colorado Springs. Home: 390 Buckeye Dr Colorado Springs CO 80919 Office: Imperial Holly Corp PO Box 1052 Colorado Springs CO 80901

LANGREHR, JOCELYN CLARE, counselor; b. Barton-on-Sea, Eng., Sept. 12, 1963; came to U.S., 1964; d. Peter Glynn and Geraldine Ann (Williams) Hibbert; m. Jeffrey Dale Langrehr, Mar. 27, 1994; 1 child, Mae Elizabeth. BS in Edn., U. Del., 1986; MS Counseling with highest distinction, San Diego State U., 1988. Assoc. lic. profl. counselor; lic. elem. tchr., spl. edn. tchr. K-12, guidance counselor K-12, Del.; nationally cert. counselor; cert. ins. rehab. specialist; cert. case mgr. Spl. edn. tchr. Christina Sch. Dist., New Castle County, Del., 1986; career svcs. advisor U. Calif., San Diego, 1987; counselor San Diego City Schs., 1987; grad. program advisor San Diego State U., 1987-88; vocat. cons. Del. Valley Rehab., Wilmington, Del., 1989-90; vocat. cons. sr. Olsten/Upjohn Inc., Wilmington, 1990-92; dir. vocat. svc. Phoenix Cons. Svc., Chadds Ford, Pa., 1992—. Leader Sr. High Youth Group, 1st Unitarian-Universalist Ch., 1990-93. Mem. ACA, Nat. Rehab. Assn., Del. Rehab. Assn., FSRCA (sec. 1990, pres. 1991, past pres. 1992), NARPPS, Del. Claims Assn. Home: 614 W 28th St Wilmington DE 19802-3034

LANGRICK, MARGARET, actress; b. Vancouver, B.C., Can., May 4, 1971; came to the U.S., 1991; d. Roger and Helena Langrick. Appeared in (films) My American Cousin, 1984, Harry & The Hendersons, 1986, Cold Comfort, 1988, Sweet Angel Mine, 1995, (tv) Camp Wilder, 1992-94. Recipient Best Actress Genie award Acad. Can. Cinema, Toronto, 1985.

LANGSAM, IDA S., press agent, consultant; b. N.Y.C., Apr. 5, 1951; d. Sydney and Mary (Goldberg) L. AAS in Photography, Fashion Inst. Tech., 1971; BA in Mass Communications, Queens Coll., 1973. Publicity dir. Mike's Artist Mgmt., N.Y.C., 1978-79; sr. account exec. Howard Bloom Orgn., N.Y.C., 1979-81; publicity dir. Aucoin Mgmt., N.Y.C., 1981-82; pres. Pub. I Publicity Svcs., N.Y.C., 1982-91; exec. v.p. music divsn. Middleberg & Assocs., N.Y.C., 1991-95; pres. ISL Pub. Rels., N.Y.C., 1995—; guest panelist New Music Seminar, N.Y.C., 1985-88, CMJ/MM Seminar, N.Y.C., 1987-88, Founds. Forum, L.A., 1989, Platinum Seminar, Hoboken, N.J., 1990; instr. Discovery Ctr., N.Y.C., 1988-90; adj. profl mus. bus. profls. program grad. level NYU, 1995, music bus. professions program NYU, N.Y.C. Office: ISL # 1003 333 W Fifty-second St New York NY 10019

LANGSLEY, PAULINE ROYAL, psychiatrist; b. Lincoln, Nebr., July 2, 1927; d. Paul Ambrose and Dorothy (Sibley) Royal; m. Donald G. Langsley, Sept. 9, 1955; children: Karen Jean, Dorothy Ruth Langsley Runman, Susan Louise. BA, Mills Coll., 1949; MD, U. Nebr., 1953. Cert. psychiatrist, Am. Bd. Psychiatry and Neurology. Intern Mt. Zion Hosp., San Francisco, 1954; resident U. Calif., San Francisco, 1954-57; student health psychiatrist U. Calif., Berkeley, 1957-61, U. Colo., Boulder, 1961-68; assoc. clin. prof. psychiatry U. Calif. Med. Sch., Davis, 1968-76; student health psychiatrist U. Calif., Davis, 1968-76; assoc. clin. prof. psychiatry U. Cin., 1976-82; pvt. practice psychiatry Cin., 1976-82; cons. psychiatrist Federated States of Micronesia, Pohnpei, 1984-87; resident in geriatric psychiatry Rush-Presbyn./St. Luke Hosp., Chgo., 1989-91; mem. accreditation rev. com. Accreditation Coun. for Continuing Med. Edn. Trustee Mills Coll., Oakland, 1974-78; bd. dirs. Evanston Women's Club. Fellow Am. Psychiat. Assn. (chair continuing med. edn. 1990-96); mem. AMA, Am. Med. Womens Assn., Acad. Medicine Cin., Ohio State Med. Assn., Ill. Psychiat. Assn. (sec. 1993-95, pres.-elect 1995-96, pres. 1996—, accreditation coun. 1996—). Home: 9445 Monticello Ave Evanston IL 60203-1117

LANGUM, W. SUE, civic worker; b. Kennett, Mo., Jan. 10, 1934; d. Howard S. and Lucille (Hubble) Walker; m. Norman H. Nelson, June 22, 1957 (dec. Sept. 1969); 1 child, Kirby Walker Nelson; m. John K. Langum, Dec. 28, 1972. Student, Northwestern U., 1952-53, Crane Jr. Coll., 1953-54. Svc. rep. Ill. Bell Tel. Co., Chgo., 1956-57; receptionist Tri-City Animal Hosp., Elgin, Ill., 1967-69; rsch. asst. Bus. Econs. Inc., Chgo., 1969-73, dir., 1973—. V.p. Elgin Coun. PTA, 1969-73; bd. dirs. OEO, 1972-73, Meals on Wheels, Elgin, 1972-93, Coloquy Coffee House, 1968-70, Judson Coll. Friends, 1976-87, Elgin Area Hist. Soc., 1982—, Elgin Symphony Orch. Assn., 1984-93, Elgin Symphony League, 1982-93, pres. 1984-86; bd. dirs. United Meth. Women, 1978-93, pres., 1980-84; vol. Fish, 1974-76; bd. dirs., treas. Easter Seal Assn. for Crippled Children, 1977-90; mem. Elgin Beautification Commn., 1986-88, Tuesday Morning Bible Study Club. Mem. Sister Cities Assn. Elgin (bd. dirs. 1990), LWV (v.p. Elgin Club 1965), Tucson Women's Club, Current History Forum Club. Home: Diamond T Ranch 9820 E Old Spanish Trl Tucson AZ 85748-7547 also: Balsam Bay Is Manitowish Waters WI 54545

LANGWORTHY, AUDREY HANSEN, state legislator; b. Grand Forks, N.D., Apr. 1, 1938; d. Edward H. and Arla (Kuhlman) Hansen; m. Asher C. Langworthy Jr., Sept. 8, 1962; children: Kristin H., Julia H. BS, U. Kans., 1960, MS, 1962; postgrad., Harvard U., 1989. Tchr. jr. high sch. Shawnee Mission Sch. Dist., Johnson County, Kans., 1963-65; councilperson City of Prairie Village, Kans., 1981-85; mem. Kans. State Senate, 1985—; alt. del. Nat. Conf. State Legislatures, 1985-87, del., 1987—, nominating com., 1990-92, vice chair fed. budget and taxation com., 1994, chair fed. budget and taxation com., 1995-96; del. Midwestern Conf. State Legislatures, 1989. City co-chmn. Kassebaum for U.S. Senate, Prairie Village, 1978; pres. Jr. League Kansas City, Mo., 1977, Kansas City Eye Bank, 1980-82, chmn., 1983-85, bd. mem., 1977—; mem. bd. Greater Kansas City ARC, 1975—, pres., 1984, chmn. midwestern adv. coun., 1985-86, nat. bd. govs., 1987-93; mem. Johnson County C.C. Found., 1989—; mem. Leadership Kans., Germany Today Program, 1991; bd. dirs. Kans. Wildlife & Parks Fund; trustee Found. on Aging, 1992—; mem. nat. adv. panel Child Care Action Campaign, 1988—; mem. adv. com. Coro Found., 1989—; mem. adv. bd. Kans. Alliance for Mentally Ill., 1994—; hon. chair Fund Raiser for Health Partnership of Johnson County, 1995. Recipient Outstanding Vol. award Cmty. Svcs. Award Found., 1983, Confidence in Edn. award Friends of Edn., 1984, Pub. Svc. award as Kans. Legislator of Yr., Hallmark Polit. Action Com., 1991, Clara Barton Honor award Greater Kans. City ARC, Intergovtl. Leadership award League Kans. Mcpls., 1994, Disting. Pub. Svc. award United Cmty. Svcs. of Johnson County, 1995, Outstanding Achievement in Hist. Preservation award Alexander Majors Hist. House, 1995, Kansas City Spirit award, 1996. Mem. LWV, Women's Pub. Svc. Network, U. Kans. Alumni Assn. Episcopalian. Home: 6324 Ash St Prairie Village KS 66208-1369

LANIER, ANITA SUZANNE, musician, piano educator; b. Talladega, Ala., May 21, 1946; d. Luther Dwight and Elva (Hornsby) L. BS in Music Edn., Jacksonville (Ala.) State U., 1969. Elem. music tchr. Talladega City Schs., 1969-81; librarian, elem. music tchr. Talladega Acad., 1981-84, tchr. piano and organ Talladega, 1981—. Organist Trinity United Meth. Ch., Talladega, 1981—. Recipient Commemorative Honor medallion, 1990, World Decoration of Excellence medallion, 1990; named Woman of the Yr., 1990, Rsch. Adv. of Yr., 1990, ABI, 1990. Mem. NAFE, AAUW, Am. Pianists Assn., Pilot Club (sec. 1977-78), World Inst. Achievement, Women's Inner Circle Achievement, Internat. Platform Assn., Delta Omicron. Home: 601 North St E Talladega AL 35160-2525

LANIER, JACQUELINE RUTH, curator, artist; b. Boston, Dec. 15, 1947; d. John Stanley and Mary Elizabeth (Porter) L.; 1 child, Raymond Rashad Lanier. BS in Edn., Morgan State U., 1976. Drama specialist Day in Arts Boston Symphony, 1971; drama specialist Balt. City Cultural Arts & Urban Svcs., 1974-78; prodr. Sta. WEAA-FM, 1985-90; with ACTION, 1987-89; R & D implementer Abell Found., 1988-89; developer, curator Lanier Mus. African-Am. History, 1983—; seminar staff developer dept. edn. Balt. Cith Sch., 1988; lectr., presenter IRS, 1988; R & D implementer Lady Md. Found., 1989; lectr. D.C. Pub. Libr., 1990; asst. devel. coord., collections mgr. Heritage Mus. Art, 1990—; lectr. in field. Prodr. Call of the Ancestor, 1992; exhbts. include Counciling Ctr., 1992, Internat. Black Women Congress, 1992, Morgan State U., 1992, Busterizing, Inc., Md. Commn. African Am. History & Culture, 1992, City Life Mus., 1992, Encore Theatre Co., 1992, Social Security Adminstrn., 1992, New Shiloh Bapt. Ch., 1992, Enon Bapt. Ch., 1992, St. Peter Clavers Ch., 1992, Immaculate Conception Ch., 1994, Martin Luther King Ch., 1994, Heritage Mus. Art, 1994, Chesapeake Coll., 1994, Native Am. Mus., 1994, Nat. Assn. Black Vets., 1994, Dept. Equal Employment Devel., 1994, Perry Point Vets. Hosp., 1994, UN, 1995, D.C. Country Club, 1995, Howard County C.C., 1995, Cambridge Coll., 1995, Johns Hopkins Rsch. Inst., 1995, Hist. Sharp. St. Ch., 1995, Balt. Aquarium, 1996, Chesapeake Coll., 1996, Allaganey County Arts Coun., 1996, Heritage Mus., 1996, Md. Humanities Coun., 1996. Mem. exec. com. Broadway East Cmty. Assn.; bd. dirs., 2d dist. rep. Citizen Planning & Housing Assn.; chmn. East Balt. Coun. Neighborhoods, Inc.; mem. Empowerment Zone Devel. Bd.; gen. ptnr. Gay St. Housing Partnership Ltd.; bd. dirs., pres. Housing Assistance Corp.; v.p. Mid. East Cmty. Devel. Corp.; vol. Balt. City Commn. Women, Urban Svcs. Agy., Balt. City Youth Fair, WAVR Radio; com. mem. Democratic State Ctrl. Com.; mem. substance abuse prevention coun. Mayor's Coordinating Coun. Criminal Justice, Voices of Electorate; mem. Black Single Parents; mem., pres. Ira Aldridge Players; adv. com. minority bus. tourism Md. Dept. Econ. Employment Devel. Office Tourism; mem. Sankofa exhb. adv. com. Md. Hist. Soc., bd. dirs. Seventh Sons Prodn. Co. Recipient Outstanding Svc. award Campfire, Inc., Fifteen Yr. Svc. award, 100 Hours Vol. Svc. award VA, Outstanding Svc. award Md. House Dels., Citation City of Balt. Citizens, Svcs. Agy. & Citizens Balt. award Urban Svcs. Agy., Svc. to Jazz Cmty. award Gemini Prodns., Inc., Outstanding Cmty. Svc. award African Am. Women's Expo, Outstanding Leadership award AFRAM, 1995; inducted into Black Collectors Hall of Fame, Wall of Fame. Mem. Nat. Assn. Fundraising Execs., Nat. Assn. Black Collectors & Dealers, New Gay St. Improvement Assn. (pres.), Black Ethnic Collectibles Mag. (adv. bd.), Transitional Housing Program (adv. com.). Democrat. Lutheran. Home: 3817 Clifton Ave Baltimore MD 21216

LANIER, NANCY MCDANIEL, researcher; b. Hinton, W.Va., Mar. 10, 1944; d. Roy Edward and Mary Elizabeth (Hulme) McDaniel; m. Dawson Edward Watkins III, Aug. 29, 1964 (div. Aug. 1978); children: Patricia Ann, Benjamin Edward; m. Moultrie Shrewsbury Lanier II, May 5, 1989. BA, Lynchburg Coll., 1965; postgrad., Va. Commonwealth U., 1980-83. Adminstrv. asst. to dean of grad. studies Lynchburg (Va.) Coll., 1966-69; sec. engring. dept. AMF Bakery Sys., Richmond, Va., 1977-80; office mgr. behavioral svcs. unit, divsn. youth svcs. Va. Dept. Corrections, Richmond, 1981-83; asst. to the pres. Va. Found. for Ind. Colls., Richmond, 1983-89; mgr. donor info. Union Theol. Sem., Richmond, 1989—; cons. in computer tng. Tenn. Ind. Coll. Fund, Nashville, 1987. Active Jay-C-Ettes, Lynchburg, 1967-69; mem., chmn. fine arts Jr. Women's Club, Staunton, 1970-73; choir mem., tchr. Covenant Presbyn. Ch., Staunton, 1969-77; elder, choir mem. The Gayton Kirk Presbyn. Ch., 1985—; sec. Northside Sch. PTA, Staunton, 1977; former mem. Richmond Choral Soc., 1988-94; mem., former pres. ACCA Temple Chantettes, Richmond, 1989—. Mem. Assn. for Profl. Rschrs. for Advancement, The Hollows Golf Club. Office: Union Theol Sem 3401 Brook Rd Richmond VA 23227

LANIS, VIOLET ANN, business educator; b. Gary, Ind., Sept. 10, 1948; d. Steve and Danica (Arbutina) Bayus; m. Barry S. Lanis, Dec. 1, 1973. BS, Ball State U., 1970, MEd, 1972. Cert. elem. sch. adminstr., secondary sch. adminstr. Tchr. Thornton Twp High Schs., Harvey, Ill., 1970-73; lectr.

Katharine Gibbs Secretarial Sch., Norwalk, Conn., 1974-78; adj lectr. Sacred Heart U., Bridgeport, Conn., 1974-79; adj. asst. prof. U. Bridgeport, 1974-81; tchr. Darien (Conn.) Pub. Schs., 1981-83; instr. Norwalk C.C., 1983-87; adj. lectr. Dekalb Coll., Dunwoody, Ga., 1988; lectr., asst. to dir. student teaching supervision and field experience Ind. U. N.W., Gary, 1989-96; lectr. dept. edn. Purdue U., Hammond, Ind., 1996—. Author secretarial procedures manual, 1979. Mem. NEA, Norwalk Jr. Woman's Club (v.p. 1980-81), Delta Pi Epsilon, Kappa Delta Pi (pres. 1993—). Roman Catholic. Office: Purdue U Hammond IN 46323-2094

LANK, EDITH HANDLEMAN, columnist, educator; b. Boston, Feb. 27, 1926; m. Norman Lank; children: Avrum, David, Anna. BA magna cum laude, Syracuse U., 1947. Columnist L.A. Times Syndicate, 1976—; TV host Sta. WOKR-TV, Rochester, N.Y., 1983-84; radio host Sta. WBBF-AM, Rochester, 1984-85; lectr. St. John Fisher Coll., Rochester, 1977-89; commentator Sta. WXXI-FM, Rochester, 1977—; guest Pub. Radio Internat., St. Paul, 1987—; speaker in field. Author: Home Buying, 1981, Selling Your Home, 1982, Modern Real Estate Practice in New York, 1983, rev. 5th edit. 1995, The Complete Home Seller's Kit, 1988, rev. 3rd edit. 1994, The Complete Home Buyer's Kit, 1989, rev. 3rd edit., 1994, Dear Edith, 1990, Essentials of New Jersey Real Estate, 201 Questions Every Homebuyer and Seller Must Ask, 1996; co-author: Your Home as a Tax Shelter, 1993; contbr. articles to Time, New Yorker, McCall's, Real Estate Today, Persuasions, Modern Maturity, others. Recipient media award Bar Assn. Monroe County, 1982, Matrix award Women in Ommunications, 1984, Woman of Distinction award Gov. Mario Cumo, N.Y., 1985; named Communicator of Yr., SUNY, Brockport, 1986. Mem. Real Estate Educators Assn. (bd. dirs., Consumer Edn. award 1982, 83, 86, 96, Real Estate Educator of Yr. 1984), Nat. Assn. Real Estate Editors (bd. dirs), Jane Austen Soc. N.Am. (dir.), Phi Beta Kappa. Home and Office: 240 Hemingway Dr Rochester NY 14620-3316

LANSBERRY, LILLIAN BROOKS, social worker; b. Balt., July 29, 1941; m. W.A. James, Jan. 27, 1963 (div. Dec. 1975); 1 child, Michael Kevin; m. Charles Lansberry Jr., May 14, 1976. Lic. cert. social worker. Tng. specialist Dept. Social Svcs., Balt., 1975-81; chief Child Protective Svcs., Dept. Social Svcs., Balt., 1983-84; tng. coord. Balt. Blueprint, Office of the Mayor, Balt., 1981; coord. Wednesday's Child, Dept. Human Resources, Balt., 1982-83, Md. Adoption Resource Exch., Dept. Human Resources, Balt., 1984-95, Mutual Consent Adoption Registry, Dept. Human Resources, Balt., 1990-95; child welfare cons., trainer LBL Assocs., Balt., 1995—; adj. instr. U. Md. Sch. Social Work, Balt., 1995—; spkr., presenter in field. Mem. Child Welfare League of Am. Nat. Adv. Com. on Adoption, Washington, 1993—; bd. dir. Adoption Exchange Assn., 1984—, v.p., 1991—; pres. Black Adoption Recruitment Network, Balt., 1990—; sec., bd. dirs. Katharine of Alexandria Cmty. Svcs., Inc., Balt., 1993—; bd. dirs. Planned Parenthood of Md., Balt., 1983-88; sec., v.p., bd. dirs. Grace and St. Peter's Sch., Balt., 1973-83; steering com. mem. Md. Telethon-United Negro Coll. Fund, Balt., 1980-88. Recipient Svc. award Congressman Kweisi Mfume, 1995, Adoption Exchange Assn., 1995; Cert. of Appreciation Adoptee-Birthparent Support Network, 1995, Dept. of Health and Human Svcs., 1994. Mem. Delta Sigma Theta (life mem., Pub. Svc. award 1988). Home: 6004 Sycamore Rd Baltimore MD 21212 Office: LBL Assocs 6004 Sycamore Rd Baltimore MD 21212

LANSBURY, ANGELA BRIGID, actress; b. London, Oct. 16, 1925; came to U.S., 1940; d. Edgar and Moyna (Macgill) L.; m. Peter Shaw, Aug. 12, 1949; children: Anthony, Deirdre. Student, Webber-Douglas Sch. Drama, London, 1939-40, Feagin Sch. Drama, N.Y.C., 1940-42; LHD (hon.), Boston U., 1990. Host 41st, 42d and 43d Ann. Tony Awards, 45th Ann. Emmy Awards. Actress with Metro-Goldwyn-Mayer, 1943-50; films include: Gaslight, 1944 (Acad. award nomination), National Velvet, 1944, The Picture of Dorian Gray, 1944 (Golden Globe award, Acad. award nomination), The Harvey Girls, 1946, The Hoodlum Saint, 1946, Till the Clouds Roll By, 1946, The Private Affairs of Bel Ami, 1947, If Winter Comes, 1948, Tenth Avenue Angel, 1948, State of the Union, 1948, The Three Musketeers, 1948, The Red Danube, 1949, Samson and Delilah, 1949, Kind Lady, 1951, Mutiny, 1952, Remains to be Seen, 1953, A Life at Stake, 1955, The Purple Mask, 1956, A Lawless Street, 1956, Please Murder Me, 1956, The Court Jester, 1956, The Long Hot Summer, 1958, Reluctant Debutante, 1958, A Breath of Scandal, 1960, Dark at the Top of the Stairs, 1960, Season of Passion, 1961, Blue Hawaii, 1961, All Fall Down, 1962, Manchurian Candidate, 1962 (Golden Globe award, Acad. award nomination), In the Cool of the Day, 1963, Dear Heart, 1964, The World of Henry Orient, 1964, The Greatest Story Ever Told, 1965, Harlow, 1965, The Amorous Adventures of Moll Flanders, 1965, Mister Buddwing, 1966, Something for Everyone, 1970, Bedknobs and Broomsticks, 1971, Death on the Nile, 1978, The Lady Vanishes, 1980, The Mirror Crack'd, 1980, The Pirates of Penzance, 1982, The Company of Wolves, 1983, Beauty and the Beast, 1991; star TV series Murder She Wrote, 1984— (Golden Globe awards 1984, 86, 91, 92, 11 Emmy nominations, Lead Actress - Drama); appeared in TV mini-series Little Gloria, Happy at Last, 1982, Lace, 1984, Rage of Angels, part II, 1986; other TV movies include: The First Olympics-Athens 1896, A Talent for Murder, Gift of Love, 1982, Shootdown, 1988, The Shell Seekers, 1989, The Love She Sought, 1990, Mrs. 'Arris Goes to Paris, 1992; appeared in plays Hotel Paradiso, 1957, A Taste of Honey, 1960, Anyone Can Whistle, 1964, Mame (on Broadway), 1966, 83 (Tony award for Best Mus. Actress 1966), Dear World, 1968 (Tony award for Best Mus. Actress 1969), All Over (London Royal Shakespeare Co.), 1971, Prettybelle, 1971, Gypsy, 1974 (Tony award for Best Mus. Actress 1975, Sarah Siddons award), The King and I, 1978, Sweeney Todd, 1979 (Tony award for Best Mus. Actress 1979, Sarah Siddons award), Hamlet, Nat. Theatre, London, 1976, A Little Family Business, 1983. Named Woman of Yr., Harvard Hasty Pudding Theatricals, 1968, Comdr. of British Empire by Queen Elizabeth II, 1994; inducted Theatre Hall of Fame, 1982; recipient British Acad. award, 1991. Office: Bldg 426 100 Universal City Plz Universal City CA 91608

LANSDOWNE, KAREN MYRTLE, retired English language and literature educator; b. Twin Falls, Idaho, Aug. 11, 1926; d. George and Effie Myrtle (Ayotte) Martin; BA in English with honors, U. Oreg., 1948, MEd, 1958, MA with honors, 1960; m. Paul L. Lansdowne, Sept. 12, 1948; children: Michele Lynn, Larry Alan. Tchr., Newfield (N.Y.) H.S., 1948-50, S. Eugene (Oreg.) H.S., 1952; mem. faculty U. Oreg., Eugene, 1958-65; asst. prof. English, Lane C.C., Eugene, 1965-82, ret., 1982; cons. Oreg. Curriculum Study Center. Rep., Cal Young Neighborhood Assn., 1978—; mem. scholarship com. First Congl. Ch., 1950-70. Mem. MLA, Pacific N.W. Regional Conf. C.C.s, Nat. Council Tchrs. English, U. Oreg. Women, AAUW (sec.), Jaycettes, Pi Lambda Theta (pres.), Phi Beta Patronesses (pres.), Delta Kappa Gamma. Co-author: The Oregon Curriculum: Language/Rhetoric, I, II, III and IV, 1970. Home: 15757 Rim Dr La Pine OR 97739-9412

LANSFORD, TERRI SETLIFF, real estate agent; b. Altus, Okla.; d. Louis S. and Treva N. (Emberton) Setliff; m. Alonzo Ray Lansford, Aug. 25, 1980; children: Danny Kale Blaskowsky, Nathaniel R., Elizabeth J. ABA, Rose State Coll., 1982; ABA in Real Estate, Houston C.C., 1996. Cert. apt. mgr. Nat. Apt. Assn. Property mgr. Boston Fin. Property Mgmt., 1988-89; sr. property mgr. Casa Caribe Apts., Galveston, Tex., 1989-95; real estate agt. Jefferson Investments Associated Bus., Houston, 1995—. Vol. Ronald McDonald House, Galveston, 1989-90. Mem. Tex. Apt. Assn. (bd. dirs. 1995-96, Top Producing Mem. Go Getters com. 1993-94), Galveston Apt. Assn. (sec.-treas. 1991-92, 93-94, Mgr. of Yr. 1993). Republican. Lutheran.

LANSING, KATHY ANN, elementary school educator; b. Plymouth, Mass., Jan. 16, 1952; d. Richard William and Mary Ann (Quintal) Correa; m. George Harding Warren, June 28, 1975 (div. Aug. 1979); m. Richard Francis Lansing, Aug. 4, 1981; children: Julie Noelle, Neil Christopher, Ben Richard, Brett Christian, Ashley Faith. Student, Emmanuel Coll., Boston, 1969-71; BA, U. Mass., Boston, 1973; MEd, Cambridge (Mass.) Coll., 1993. Computer programmer Liberty Mut. Ins. Co., Boston, 1973; elem. tchr. Plymouth (Mass.) Pub. Schs., 1974—. Pres., Plymouth Lupus Support Group, Jordan Hosp., 1985-92; troop leader brownies Girl Scouts U.S., 1991-94; tchr. St. Joseph's Ch., Kingston, 1992-94. Roman Catholic.

LANSING, SHERRY LEE, motion picture production executive; b. Chgo., July 31, 1944; d. Norton and Margo L.; m. William Friedkin. BS summa cum laude in Theatre, Northwestern U., 1966. Tchr. math. public high schs. Los Angeles, 1966-69; model TV commls. Max Factor Co., 1969-70, Alberto-Culver Co., 1969-70; story editor Wagner Internat. Prodn. Co., 1972-74, dir. west coast devel., 1974-75; story editor MGM, 1975-77, v.p. creative affairs, 1977; v.p. prodn. Columbia Pictures, 1977-80; pres. 20th Century Fox Prodns., 1980-82; founder Jaffee-Lansing Prodns., 1982—; chmn. Paramount Pictures' Motion Picture Group, 1992—. Appeared in movies Loving, 1970, Rio Lobo, 1970; exec. story editor movies, Wagner Internat., 1970-73; v.p. prodn., Heyday Prodns., Universal City, Calif., 1973-75; exec. story editor, then v.p. creative affairs, MGM Studios, Culver City, Calif., 1975-77; sr. v.p. prodn., Columbia Pictures, Burbank, Calif., 1977-80, pres., 20th Century-Fox Prodns., Beverly Hills, Calif., 1980-83; ind. producer., Jaffe-Lansing Prodns., Los Angeles, 1983-91; producer Racing With the Moon, 1984,Firstborn, 1984, Fatal Attraction, 1987, The Accused, 1988, Black Rain, 1989, School Ties, 1992, Indecent Proposal, 1993; TV exec. producer When the Time Comes,1987, Mistress, 1992. Office: Paramount Pictures Corp 5555 Melrose Ave Los Angeles CA 90038-3197*

LANSKY, VICKI LEE, publishing executive; b. Louisville, Jan. 6, 1942; d. Arthur and Mary (Kaplan) Rogosin; children: Douglas, Dana. BA, Conn. Coll., 1963. Asst. buyer Lord n Taylor, N.Y.C., 1963-65; sportswear buyer Mercantile Stores, N.Y.C., 1965-68; v.p. Meadowbrook Press, Deephaven, Minn., 1975-83; pres. Book Peddlers, Deephaven, 1984—; columnist Sesame Street Parents Mag., 1988—, Family Circle Mag., 1988—. Author: Feed Me I'm Yours, 1974, Taming of the Candy Monster, 1978, Practical Parenting Tips, 1980, Games Babies Play, 1993, others. Home: 3342 Robinson Bay Rd Deephaven MN 55391

LANSKY, ZENA, surgeon; b. Phila., Apr. 18, 1942; d. Jacob and Thelma Lansky. BA summa cum laude, U. Pa., 1963; MD, Med. Coll. Pa., 1967. Diplomate Am. Bd. Surgery, 1975. Intern Montefiore Hosp., 1968-69; resident in surgery Bellevue Hosp., 1968-72, chief resident in surgery, 1971-72, instr. surgery, 1971-72; teaching asst. NIH, 1970, 71; mem. med. staff Morton F. Plant Hosp., Largo Med. Ctr., Clearwater Community Hosp.; staff mem. Morton Plant Hosp., Largo Med. Ctr., Clearwater Cmty. Hosp., Mease Hosp., Northside Hosp., Bayonet Point Hosp., Health South Rehab. Ctr., New Port Richey Cmty. Hosp., Riverside Hosp., HCA Oak Hill Hosp., Univ. Cmty. Hosp., Dade City Hosp., Helen Ellis Meml. Hosp., St. Anthony's Hosp., St. Joseph Hosp., North Bay Hosp., Brooksville Regional Hosp., Bartow Meml. Hosp.; pres. Metabolic Cons. Inc. Infusion Co., pharmacy; mem. nat. med. adv. bd. New Eng. Critical Care, 1985. Mem. editorial bd. Nutritional Support mag., 1987; contbr. articles to profl. jours.; inventor gastrostomy tube, long term venous catheter repair kit, gastrostomy tube and percutaneous endoscopic kit. Fellow ACS, Southeastern Surg. Congress; mem. Am. Soc. Parenteral and Enteral Nutrition (bd. dirs. 1989), Fla. Med. Assn., Fla. Assn. Nutritional Support (pres. 1986-87), Pinellas County Med. Soc. Office: Metabolic Cons Inc 412 S Missouri Ave Clearwater FL 34616-5836

LANTZ, CAROL RAE, interior designer; b. Elkins, W.Va., Oct. 22, 1953; d. George Raymond and P. Marguerite (Duckworth) L. BS in Comm./Theater Arts, Davis & Elkins Coll., 1976, BA in Art and Design, 1977; MA Counseling Guidance, MS Rehab. Psych., W.Va. U., Morgantown, 1981. Owner Animal Kingdom Inc., Falls Church, Va., 1981; CEO L&J Enterprises, Washington, 1981-91; regional mgr. east coast ACI Systems Inc., Langhorne, Pa., 1991—; owner, CEO Free Lantz Solutions, Inc. Artist, author (cook book) Tastee Elegance, 1993; artist (children's book) School Room Manners, 1992. Art dir., stage dir. Easter Seals, Elkins, 1987; art dir. Jennings Randolph Campaign, Washington, 1989; fundraising leader Juvenile Diabetic Assn., Washington, 1993. Mem. NEA, Nat. Assn. Rehab. Counselors, Nat. Tchr.'s Assn., Mensa, Spotsylvania Writer's Club, Alpha Psi Omega, Zeta Tau Alpha (v.p. 1972—).

LANTZ, JOANNE BALDWIN, academic administrator emeritus; b. Defiance, Ohio, Jan. 26, 1932; d. Hiram J. and Ethel A. (Smith) Baldwin; m. Wayne E. Lantz. BS in Physics and Math., U. Indpls., 1953; MS in Counseling and Guidance, Ind. U., 1957; PhD in Counseling and Psychology, Mich. State U., 1969; LittD (hon.), U. Indpls., 1985; LHD (hon.), Purdue U., 1994; LLD (hon.), Manchester Coll., 1994. Tchr. physics and math. Arcola (Ind.) High Sch., 1953-57; guidance dir. New Haven (Ind.) Sr. High Sch., 1957-65; with Ind. U.-Purdue U., Fort Wayne, 1965—, interim chancellor, 1988-89, chancellor, 1989-94, chancellor emeritus, 1994—; bd. dirs. Ft. Wayne Nat. Corp., Foellinger Found. Contbr. articles to profl. jours. Mem. Ft. Wayne Econ. Devel. Adv. Bd. and Task Force, 1988-91, Corp. Coun., 1988-94; bd. advisors Leadership Ft. Wayne, 1988-94; mem. adv. bd. Ind. Sml. Bus. Devel. Ctr., 1988-90; trustee Ancilla System, Inc., 1984-89, chmn. human resources com., 1985-89, exec. com., 1985-89; trustee St. Joseph's Med. Ctr., 1983-84, pers. adv. com. to bd. dirs., 1978-84, chmn., 1980-84; bd. dirs. United Way Allen County, sec., 1979-80; bd. dirs. Anthony Wayne Vocat. Rehab. Ctr., 1969-75. Mem. Fort Wayne Ind.-Purdue Alumni Soc. (hon. mem. 1987), Am. Psychol. Assn., AAUW (internat. fellowship com. 1986-88, prog. com. 1981-83, Am. women fellowship com. 1978-83, chmn. 1981-83, trust rsch. grantee 1980), Southeastern Psychol. Assn. (referee conv. papers 1987, 88), Ind. Sch. Women's Club (v.p. prog. chair 1979-81), Pi Lambda Theta, Sigma Xi, Delta Kappa Gamma (editorial bd. 1986-88, gen. chair conv. 1985-86, dir. N.E. region 1982-84, adminstrv. bd., exec. bd. 1982-84, leadership devel. com.).

LANTZ, VICKI T., agricultural education teacher; b. Harrisburg, Pa., May 30, 1964; d. Paul J. and Virginia E. (Calaman) Basehore; m. William H. Lantz, July 28, 1990. BS Agr. Edn., Pa. State U., 1987. Agr. tchr. Manheim (Pa.) Cen. High Sch., 1987, Big Spring High Sch., Newville, Pa., 1987—; adv. bd. Pa. State U. Ag. & Ext. Edn. Dept., State College, Pa. Dept. head beef dept. Shippensburg Fair, Pa., 1995; pres. Cumberland-Dauphin-Perry Ag Tchrs., Mechanicsburg, Pa., 1993-94. Mem. Pa. Vocat. Agr. Tchrs. Assn. (pres. 1994-95, Outstanding Young Mem. 1994), Nat. Vocat. Agr. Tchrs. Assn., Pa. State Edn. Assn./Vocat. and Practical Arts Edn. (exec. bd. 1994-95), Pa. State FFA Assn. (bd. dirs. 1994—). Democrat. Presbyterian. Home: 215 Strohm Rd Shippensburg PA 17257 Office: Big Spring Sch Dist 45 Mount Rock Rd Newville PA 17241

LANYON, ELLEN (MRS. ROLAND GINZEL), artist, educator; b. Chgo., Dec. 21, 1926; d. Howard Wesley and Ellen (Aspinwall) L.; m. Roland Ginzel, Sept. 4, 1948; children: Andrew, Lisa. BFA, Art Inst. Chgo., 1948; MFA, U. Iowa, 1950; Fulbright fellow, Courtauld Inst., U. London, 1950-51. Tchr. jr. sch. Art Inst. Chgo., 1952-54; past tchr. day sch., tchr. Rockford Coll., summer 1953, Oxbow Summer Sch. Painting, Saugatuck, Mich., 1961-62, 67-70, 71-72, 78, 88, 94, U. Ill., Chgo., 1970, U. Wis. Extension, 1971-72, Pa. State U., 1974, U. Calif., 1974, Sacramento State U., 1974, Stanford U., 1974, Boston U., 1975, Kans. State U., 1976, U. Mo., 1976, U. Houston, 1977; assoc. prof. Cooper Union, N.Y.C., 1980-93; ret., 1993; founder, sec.-treas. Chgo. Graphic Workshop, 1952-55; participant Yaddo, 1973, 75, 76, Ossobow Island Project, 1976; adj. vis. prof. So. Ill. U., 1978, No. Ill. U., 1978, SUNY, Purchase, 1978, Cooper Union, N.Y.C., 1978-79, Parsons Sch. Design, N.Y.C., 1979; disting. vis. prof. U. S.D., 1980, U. Calif. Davis, 1980, Sch. Visual Arts, N.Y.C., 1980-83; vis. artist U. N.Mex., 1981, So. Ill. U., 1984, Sch. Art Inst., Chgo., 1985, U. Tenn., Md. Inst., Northwestern Grad. Sch., 1988, U. Pa., U. Iowa, 1991, 92; instr. workshops Anderson Ranch Workshop, Snow Mass, Colo., 1994, 96, Aspen Design Conf., 1994; vis. prof. U. Iowa, 1991-92; bd. dirs. Oxbow Summer Sch. Painting, 1972-82, emeritus, 1982—, instr., 1960, 72-82, 88, 94; vis. artist, instr. workshops Vt. Studio Sch., 1995, U. Costa Rica, San Pedro and San Ramon, 1995; instr. Interlaken Sch. of Art, 1996. One woman shows, Superior St. Gallery, Chgo., 1960, Stewart Richart Gallery, San Antonio, 1962, 65, Fairweather Hardin Gallery, Chgo., 1962, Zabriskie Gallery, N.Y.C., 1962, 64, 69, 72, B.C. Holland Gallery, Chgo., 1965, 68, Ft. Wayne Art Mus., 1967, Richard Gray Gallery, Chgo., 1970, 73, 76, 79, 82, 85, Madison Art Center, 1972, Nat. Collection at Smithsonian Instn., 1972, Odyssia Gallery, Rome, 1975, Krannert Performing Arts Center, 1976, Oshkosh Pub. Mus., 1976, U. Mo., 1976, Harcus Krakow, Boston, 1977—, Fendrick Gallery, Washington, 1978, Ky. State U., 1979, Ill. Wesleyan U., 1979, U. Calif., Davis, 1980, Odyssia Gallery, N.Y., 1980, Landfall Press, 1980, Alverno Coll., Milw., 1981, Susan Caldwell, Inc., N.Y.C., 1983, N.A.M.E. Gallery, Chgo., 1983, Printworks, Ltd., Chgo., 1989, 93 Pretto Berland Hall, N.Y.C., 1989, Struve Gallery, Chgo., 1990, 93, Berland Hall Gallery, N.Y.C., 1992, Sioux City Art Mus., Iowa, 1992, U. Iowa Mus. Art, 1994, Andre Zarre Gallery, N.Y.C., 1994, TBA, Chgo., 1996; retrospective exhibitions, Krannert Art Mus., McNay Art Mus., Chgo. Cultural Ctr., Stamford Mus., U. Tenn.; exhibited group shows, 1946—, including traveling exhbns., Am. Fedn. Arts, 1946-48, 50, 53, 57, 65, 66, 69; Art Inst. Chgo., 1946-47, 51-53, 55, 57-58, 60-62, 64, 66, 67, 68, 69, 71, 73, Corcoran Gallery Art, 1961, 76, Denver Art Mus., 1950, 52, Exhbn. Momentum, Chgo., 1948, 50, 52, 54, 56, Library of Congress, 1950, 52, Met. Mus. Art, 1952, Mus. Modern Art, 1953, 62, Phila. Mus. Art, 1946, 47, 50, 54, San Francisco Mus. Art, 1946, 50, U. Ill., 1953, 54, 57, Drawing Soc., Nat. Traveling Exhbn., 1965-66, The Painter and The Photograph traveling exhbn., 1964-65; Nostalgia traveling show, 1968-69, Violence,, Mus. Contemporary Art, Chgo., 1969, Birds and Beasts,, Graham Gallery, N.Y.C., 1969-71; Ill. Painters, Ill. Arts Council, 1968-71; Ill. painters: Beyond Illustration, HMH Publs. Europe, 1971, Chgo. Imagists, 1972, Chgo. Sch, 1972, Am. Women, 1972, Artists Books, 1973; Bicentennial America 76 traveling exhibit, 1976; Chgo. Connection, 1976-77, Downtown Whitney, N.Y.C., 1978—, Queens Mus., 1978, Dayton Art Inst., 1978, Odyssia Gallery, N.Y.C., 1979, Chgo. Cultural Center, 1979, Aldrich Mus. Contemporary Art, 1980, Bklyn. Mus., 1980, Walker Art Center, 1981, also Lisbon, Venice biennales, Voorhees Mus. Rutgers U., Mus. Contemporary Art, Chgo., Milw. Art. Mus., Art of the Quilt traveling exhibition, 1985—, Made In America Berkeley Art Mus., 1987, Art of the Screen traveling exhibition, 1986—, Lines of Vision: Drawings by Contemporary Women, 1989, Symbolism: Cooper Union, 1989, Randall Gallery, St. Louis, 1991, Printworks Ltd., Chgo., 1989-96, Berland/Hall, N.Y.C., 1991, The Cultural Ctr., Chgo., 1992, Matnan Locks Gallery, Phila., 1992, Art Inst. Chgo., 1992, Andre Zarre Gallery, N.Y.C., 1993-96, Nat. Mus. Women in Arts, Washington, 1994-95, Wadsworth Atheneum, Hartford, Conn., 1996, Mus. Contemporary Art, 1996, Block Gallery, Northwestern U., 1996, Rockford Art Museum., represented in permanent collections Art Inst. Chgo., Denver Art Mus., Library of Congress, Inst. Internat. Edn., London, Finch Coll., N.Y., Krannert Mus., U. Ill., U. Mass., N.J. State Mus., Ill. State Mus., Bklyn. Mus., Mus. Contemporary Art, Chgo., Nat. Coll. Fine Arts, Walker Art Ctr., Mpls., Boston Pub. Library, Des Moines Art Center, Albion Coll., Met. Mus., McNay Art Inst., Albion Coll., Kans. State U., U. Dallas, U. Houston, Cornell U., CUNY, Nat. Mus. Women in Arts, also numerous pvt. collections.; mural paintings: Working Men's Coop. Bank Boston, 1979, State of Ill. Bldg., Chgo., 1985, State Capitol, Springfield, Ill., 1989, City of Miami Beach, Art in Public Places project, Police and Court Facility, 1993; published: Wonder Production Vol. I, 1971, Jataka Tales, 1975, Transformations, 1976, Transformations II (Endangered), 1983 ; editorial bd.: Coll. Art Jour., 1982-92; illustrator: The Wandering Tattler, 1975, Perishible Press, 1976—, Red Ozier Press, 1980—. Recipient Armstrong prize Art Inst. Chgo., 1946, 55, 77, Town and Country purchase prize, 1947, Blair prize, 1958, Palmer prize, 1962, 64, Chan prize, 1961, Vielehr prize, 1967, Logan prize, 1981; purchase prize Denver Art Mus., 1950; purchase prize Library of Congress, 1950; Cassandra Found. award, 1970; Nat. Endowment for Arts grantee, 1974, 87; Herewood Lester Cook Found. grantee, 1981. Mem. Coll. Art Assn. (dir., exec. com. 1977-80), Delta Phi Delta. Address: 138 Prince St New York NY 10012-3135 also: PO Box 1045 Stockbridge MA 01262

LANZONE, DEBORAH VON HOFFMANN, state legislative staff member; b. Montclair, N.J., Apr. 23, 1952; d. Robert Ferdinand and Anne Marie (Perdue) von Hoffmann; m. Dale Martin Lanzone, Oct. 17, 1981; 1 child, Dominic Peter. BA in Liberal Arts, Colgate U., 1974. Legis. aide Mass. Legislature, Boston, 1975; mem. advance staff Nat. Dem. Com., Washington, 1976; congrl. liaison officer Land Use Planning Commn., Washington, 1977-79, Heritage Conservation Recreation Svc., Washington, 1979-81; planner natural resources Nat. Park Svc., Washington, 1981-86; spl. asst. to dir. Fish and Wildlife Svc., Washington, 1986-88; sr. regulatory analyst Bur. Land Mgmt., Washington, 1988-89, congrl. liaison officer, 1989-91; staff dir. subcom. energy and natural resources U.S. Ho. Reps., Washington, 1992-94, mem. legis. staff Com. on Resources, 1994—. Del. Mass. Nat. Dem. Conv., 1976; mem. advance staff Nat. Dem. Campaign, 1976, inaugural staff Nat. Dem. Com., 1977. Episcopalian. Office: US Ho Reps Com on Resources 1329 Longworth HOB Washington DC 20515*

LAPADOT, SONEE SPINNER, automobile manufacturing company official; b. Sidney, Ohio, Apr. 19, 1936; d. Kenneth Lee and Helyn Kathryn (Hobby) Spinner; m. Jan. 13, 1955 (div. Apr. 1970); 1 child, Douglas Cameron Proud; m. Robert Stephen Lapadot, May 4, 1974 (div. Mar. 1994). Student, U. Cin., 1954-56, U. Akron, 1966; BS in Mgt. Human Resources, Spring Arbor Coll., 1991. Mgr. engrng. change implementation Terex div. GM, Hudson, Ohio, 1975-77, mgr. prodn. scheduling, 1977-78, gen. adminstr. product purchasing, 1978-79; sr. staff asst. non-ferrous metals GM, Detroit, 1979-80, mgr. tires and wheels, 1980-83, mgr. staff purchasing, 1983-85, mgr. corp. constrn. contracting, 1985-86; mfg. techs. adminstr. Chrysler Motors, Detroit, 1986-87, mgr. mfg. prodn. control adminstrn. and svcs., 1988, mgr. advanced planning and prodn. systems, 1988-89, mgr. advanced planning and control power train, 1989-90, mgr. Mound Rd. Engine Prodn. Control, 1990-95, MGR Corp Project Sys., 1995—. Active fundraising Boy Scouts Am., Grosse Pointe, Mich., 1980-82, Detroit, 1985-96, United Fund, Detroit, 1980-96, Jr. Achievement, Detroit, 1984, 90-96. Mem. NAFE, Soc. Automotive Engrs., Am. Soc. Profl. and Exec. Women, Am. Prodn. and Inventory Control Soc., Automotive Industry Action Group (returnable containers and packaging team), Mensa, Women's Econ. Club of Detroit. Home: 1941 Squirrel Rd Bloomfield Hills MI 48304-1162 Office: Chrysler Motors Corp 800 Chrysler Dr E Auburn Hills MI 48326

LAPENSEE, DAPHNE CHARMAYNE, automotive designer, consultant; b. Detroit, Nov. 13, 1963; d. Paul M. Lapensee and Dolores J. (Leidy) DiMaggio; m. Joseph M. Reiss, Jr. Dec. 8, 1993 (div. Dec. 1995). Student, Mich. State U., 1981-83; cert., Batavia Sch. Drafting, 1990, Philpot Sch. Automotive Body Design, 1991, Edgar Desmet Planography Course, 1995. Designer GM, Warren, Mich., 1989-91; cons. GM-Opel, Russelsheim, Germany, 1991-92; sr. designer GM-Midsize, Warren, 1992-94, GM-Cadillac Luxury Car Divsn., Flint, Mich., 1994-95; cons. Saab, Trollhottan, Sweden, 1995; sr. designer United Techs. Automotive/Chrysler, Troy, 1995—. Mem. Desmet Alumni Assn.

LAPIDUS, JACQUELINE, writer, editor; b. N.Y.C., Sept. 6, 1941; d. Joseph and Edith Judith (Friedman) L. BA, Swarthmore Coll., 1962; M.Theol. Studies, Harvard U., 1992. Letters corr. Life Mag., N.Y.C., 1962-64; English tchr. Greek-Am. Cultural Inst., Iraklion, Crete, 1964-67, U. Paris and CESTI, France, 1977-80; editor, translator Selection du Reader's Digest, Paris, 1981-85; rsch. editor Walking Mag., Boston, 1986-89; sr. editor The Boston Reader, Boston, 1992-93; editl. cons. Boston, 1992—. Author: Ready to Survive, 1975, Starting Over, 1977, Ultimate Conspiracy, 1987; co-author: Yantras of Womanlove, 1982; contbr. articles to profl. jours.

LAPIN, SHARON JOYCE VAUGHN, interior designer; b. Lagrange, Mo., July 28, 1938; d. John Nolan and Wilma Emma (Huebotter) Vaughn; BA summa cum laude, U. Wash., Seattle, 1960; m. Byron Richard Lapin, Oct. 14, 1972. Appeared in various Broadway shows, TV commls. and TV shows, 1962-72; mgr. arts and crafts div.,Convenience Products Clayton Corp., Fenton, Mo. Bd. dirs. St. Louis Conservatory and Schs. for Arts, 1977-92, v.p., 1982-87; chmn. bd. Studio Set, 1978-81, pres., 1975-78, bd. dirs., 1975-83; bd. dirs. Friends of Sci. Mus., 1980-90, v.p., 1984-85; pres. Assocs. Bd. Dirs., St. Louis Sci. Ctr., Inc., 1986-87; bd. dirs. Jr. Div., St. Louis Symphony Women's Assn., 1973-75; bd. dirs. Womens Assn. St. Louis Symphony, 1988-90. Mem. AFTRA, SAG, AEA, Am. Soc. Interior Designers, Pi Beta Phi, Mu Phi Epsilon.

LA POINTE, DIANNE POLLY, art educator, sculptor; b. Mt. Clemens, Mich., Aug. 25, 1944; d. Lester John and Doris Olwilda (Suhr) Schutt; m. David Anthony La Pointe, Aug. 22, 1964; children: Hunter David, Heather Dianne. BA, Mich. State U., 1966, MA, 1969. Cert. secondary tchr. art, Mich., Ariz. Adult edn. art tchr. Linden (Mich.) Adult Edn., 1966-68; art tchr. Linden Area Schs., 1966-68, Laingsburg (Mich.) Schs., 1968-69, Bergland (Mich.) Schs., 1969-70, Ontonagon (Mich.) Area Schs., 1972-73, Copper Harbor (Mich.) Schs., 1973-80; painting instr. Mohave C.C., Lake Havasu City, Ariz., 1985-88; art specialist Lake Havasu Unified Sch. Dist., 1982—, fine arts and fitness coord. festival, 1994, 95; interviewee Sta. WLUC-TV, Marquette, Mich., 1978. Exhbns. include Mich. Tech. U., 1978; contbr. Copper Country Anthem mag., 1977. Reflections coord. Starline PTA, Lake Havasu, 1992-94; sec. Copper Country Artists Assn., Calumet, Mich,. 1975-80; mem. Cmty. Art Day for Children, Eagle Harbor, Mich.,

1977; mem. performing arts adv. bd. Mohave C.C., Lake Havasu, 1993—; mem. sch. bd., sec. Grant Twp. Schs., Copper Harbor, 1978-80; mem. adv. coun. for gifted Keweenaw County, Hancock, Mich., 1977-78; mem., sec. Mut. Investors of Lake Havasu, 1990—. Recipient 1st pl. in photography Mohave County Fair, 1989; Grantee Ariz. Commn. on the Arts, 1993. Mem. NEA, Nat. Art Edn. Assn. (assoc.), Ariz. Art Edn. Assn. (assoc.), Ariz. Art Edn. Coun. (coun., regional rep. 1992—), Lake Havasu Edn. Assn. (meet and confer team 1992, 94, Tchr. of Yr. 1990-91), Ariz. Edn. Assn.

LAPOINTE-PETERSON, KITTIE VADIS, choreographer, ballet school director, educator; b. Chgo., June 4, 1915; d. Samuel Joseph and Katie (Parbst) Andrew; m. Arthur Joseph LaPointe, Dec. 17, 1938 (dec. Apr. 1985); children: Janice Deane, Suzanne Meta; m. Ray Burt Peterson, Feb. 2, 1992 (dec. Nov. 1995). Studies with, Marie Zvolanek, Chgo., 1921-28, Laurent Novikoff, Chgo., 1928-35, Edward Caton, Chgo., 1928-35; student, Royal Danish Ballet, Copenhagen, 1926. Dancer Chgo. Civic Opera, 1929-32, Century of Progress, Chgo., 1933-34, Stone-Camryn Ballet, Chgo., 1934-35, Mary Vandas Dancers, Chgo., 1935-38, Balaban-Katz Theaters, Chgo., 1935-36; tchr., choreographer Studio of Dance Arts, Chgo., 1952-68, Herrstrom Sch., Chgo., 1968-72; dir. Le Ballet Petit Sch., Chgo., 1972-92. Soloist in Michael Fokine's Co., 1935. Mem. Danish Brotherhood and Sisterhood (pres. 1962-65, 72-75, Midwest dist. pres. 1972-74), Chgo. Outdoor Art League (sec. 1975-79, Manor Garden Club. Home: 5843 W Peterson Ave Chicago IL 60646-3907

LAPP, SUSAN BOLSTER, learning disability educator; b. Washington, Nov. 23, 1945; d. Robert Fay and Nona (Peifly) Bolster; m. Richard Gordon Lapp, Apr. 22, 1967. BS in Edn., Miami U., Oxford, Ohio, 1967; MEd, Xavier U., Cin., 1977. Cert. tchr. English; cert. in learning disabilities and behavior disorders K-12. Sec. Penta Tech. Coll., Perrysburg, Ohio, 1965-67; tchr. 3d grade Toledo Pub. Schs., 1966-67; thcr. 7th and 8th grades Fairfield (Ohio) City Schs., 1967-78, 6th, 7th and 8th grade learning disabilities tchr., 1978—, spl. svcs. coordinator, 1984—, career edn. coordinator, 1987—; career edn. coordinator Butler County Joint Vocat. Sch., Hamilton, Ohio, 1987—; student vol. dir. Fairfield Middle Sch., 1990—. Vice chair S.W. Ohio Profl. Devel. Ctr., 1993-94, co-sec., 1994. Named Spl. Edn. Tchr. of Yr., S.W. Ohio Spl. Edn. Regional Resource Ctr., 1989, Ohio Career Educator of Yr., Career Edn. Assn., 1991, Outstanding Sch. Vol.-Ptnr. award, 1991, Ohio Mid. Sch. Career Planning Team of Yr., 1994. Mem. NEA, S.W. Ohio Edn. Assn., Fairfield Classroom Tchrs. Assn., Ohio Mid. Sch. Assn., Nat. Assn. for Career Edn., Career Edn. Assn. (Ohio Career Planning Team of Yr. 1994), Orton Soc. Home: 900 Harrison Ave Hamilton OH 45013-3511 Office: Fairfield Middle Sch 255 Donald Dr Fairfield OH 45014-3006

LAPPE, FRANCES MOORE, author, lecturer; b. Pendleton, Oreg., Feb. 10, 1944; d. John and Ina (Skrifvars) Moore; m. Marc Lappe, Nov. 11, 1967 (div. 1977); children: Anthony, Anna; m. J. Baird Callicott, Dec. 1, 1985 (div. 1991); m. Paul Martin DuBois, Aug. 19, 1991. BA in History, Earlham Coll., 1966; PhD (hon.), St. Mary's Coll., 1983, Lewis and Clark Coll., 1983, Macalester Coll., 1986, Hamline U., 1987, Earlham Coll., 1988, Kenyon Coll., 1989, U. Mich., 1990, Nazareth Coll., 1990, Niagara Coll., 1993. Co-founder, mem. staff Inst. for Food and Devel. Policy, Oakland, 1975-90; co-founder, co-dir. Ctr. for Living Democracy, Brattleboro, Vt., 1990—. Author: Diet for A Small Planet, 1971, 75, 82, 91, Mozambique and Tanzania: Asking the Big Questions, 1979, What To Do After You Turn Off the T.V., 1985, Rediscovering America's Values, 1989; (with Joseph Collins) Food First: Beyond the Myth of Scarcity, 1977, Aid as Obstacle, 1980, Now We Can Speak, 1984, Nicaragua: What Difference Could a Revolution Make?, 1984, World Hunger: Twelve Myths, 1986; (with Rachel Schurman and Kevin Danaher) Betraying the National Interest, 1987, (with Schurman) Taking Population Seriously, 1990, (with Paul Martin Du Bois) The Quickening of America: Rebuilding Our Nation, Remaking Our Lives, 1994. Named to Nutrition Hall of Fame Ctr. for Sci. and Pub. Interest, 1981; recipient Mademoiselle Mag. award, 1977; World Hunger Media award, 1982, Right Livelihood award, 1987. Office: Ctr Living Democracy RR 1 Black Fox Rd Brattleboro VT 05301-9801

LARAYA-CUASAY, LOURDES REDUBLO, pediatric pulmonologist, educator; b. Baguio, Philippines, Dec. 8, 1941; came to U.S., 1966; d. Jose Marquez and Lolita (Redublo) Laraya; m. Ramon Serrano Cuasay, Aug. 7, 1965; children: Raymond Peter, Catherine Anne, Margaret Rose, Joseph Paul. AA, U. Santo Tomas, Manila, Philippines, 1958, MD cum laude, 1963. Diplomate Am. Bd. Pediatrics. Resident in pediatrics U. Santo Tomas Hosp., 1963-65, Children's Hosp. Louisville, 1966-67, Charity Hosp. New Orleans-Tulane U., 1967-68; fellow child growth and devel. Children's Hosp. Phila., 1968-69; fellow pediatric pulmonary and cystic fibrosis programs St. Christopher's Hosp. for Children, Phila., 1969-71, rsch. assoc., 1971-72; clin. instr. Tulane U., New Orleans, 1967-68; asst. prof. pediatrics Temple Health Scis. Ctr., Phila., 1972-77; assoc. prof. pediatrics Thomas Jefferson Med. Sch., Phila., 1977-79; assoc. prof. pediatrics U. Medicine & Dentistry N. J., Robert Wood Johnson Med. Sch., New Brunswick, 1980-85, prof. clin. pediatrics, 1985—; dir. pediatric pulmonary and cystic fibrosis program U. Medicine and Dentistry, Robert Wood Johnson Med. Sch., New Brunswick, 1981—. Co-editor: Interstitial Lung Diseases in Children, 1988. Recipient Pediatric Rsch. award Mead Johnson Pharm. Co., Manila, 1965. Fellow Am. Coll. Chest Physicians (steering com., chmn. cardiopulmonary diseases in children 1976—), Am. Acad. Pediatrics (tobacco free generation rep. 1986-92); mem. Am. Ambulatory Pediatric Soc., Am. Thoracic Soc., Am. Sleep Disorder Assn., N.J. Thoracic Soc. (chmn. pediatric pulmonary com. 1986-91, governing coun. mem. 1981-94), Am. Coll. Physician Execs., European Respiratory Soc., Lung Club. Home: 100 Mercer Ave Spring Lake NJ 07762-1208 Office: UMDNJ Robert Wood Johnson Med Sch CN19 New Brunswick NJ 08903

LARCH, BILLIE BENTLEY, nursing administrator; b. Texarkana, Tex., Aug. 26, 1919; d. William Calvin and Lula Marie (Cowley) Bentley; m. Monroe P. Larch, Mar. 26, 1936; children: James Monroe, Michael B. BSN, U. Ark., Little Rock, 1962; MSN, U. Cen. Ark., Conway, 1971; MA in Gerontology, U. Little Rock, 1987. Cert. gerontol. nurse, psychiat. clin. nurse; registered lobbyist legis. gen. assembly, 1996—. Nurse cons. Ark. Dept. Mental Health, Little Rock, 1978-89; assoc. chief nursing svc. for edn. John L. McClellan VA Hosp., Little Rock, 1972-85; exec. dir. Ark. State Nurses Assn., Little Rock, 1989-92; nurse cons. Larch Cons. Svcs., 1992—; health care specialist Children and Family Divsn. Ark. Dept. Human Svcs., 1993-96; nurse cons., registered lobbyist Ark. Legis., 1995—; mem. nursing faculty Allied Health, U. Ark., 1973-76; med. rschr. for pros. and def. trial lawyers, 1992—. Developer small group work program Chronically and Mentally Ill, Ark., 1966—; organizer Ark. affiliate chpt. Am. Diabetes Assn., 1973, bd. dirs. 1973-79; healthcare specialist Ark. Dept. Human Svcs., Children's and Family Divsn., 1993—. Recipient Gold Star award Atty. Gen.'s Office, 1989; named to Hall of Fame in Nursing, Ark. State Nurses Assn., 1988. Mem. Nat. League for Nursing (Linda Richards award 1969), Ark. Gerontol. Soc. (bd. dirs. 1982-92, 93—).

LARKIN, JOAN PATRICIA, secondary education educator; b. Bronx, N.Y., Jan. 17, 1930; d. John and Elizabeth (Dooley) Loonam; m. William Joseph Larkin, Nov. 26, 1949; children: Deirdre, Dympna, William James, Eithne. BA, William Patterson Coll., Paterson, N.J., 1968; MA in Tchg., Rutgers U., 1971. Real estate saleswoman Edgar Reilly Real Estate, Ridgewood, N.J., 1962-64; English tchr. Ridgewood Bd. Edn., 1968-90; ret., 1990-96; tour lectr. TraveLearn, Lakeville, Pa., 1992—. Chief negotiator Ridgewood Edn. Assn., 1980-82, pres. 1984-86; vol. negotiator Alt. Dispute Resolution Divsn., Newark, N.J., 1994-95; candidate Democratic Assembly, Bergen County, N.J., 1995. Coun. for the Humanities fellow, Washington, 1984. Mem. NEA, AAUW, N.J. Edn. Assn., Bergen County Edn. Assn.

LARKIN, MARY, chemist, consultant; b. Mt. Vernon, N.Y., Oct. 8, 1950; d. Frederick Joseph and Dorothy Patricia (Sillery) Larkin; m. Alfred Karl Jung, June 11, 1983 (div. Jan. 1994). BA in Chemistry, Coll. of New Rochelle, 1976. Cert. color and image cons. From technician to assoc. rsch. chemist Stauffer Chem. Co., Dobbs Ferry, N.Y., 1971-86; rsch. chemist Chesebrough-Ponds Inc., Shelton, Conn., 1986-87; tech. mktg. asst. Ganes Chems. Inc., N.Y.C., 1988; rsch. chemist Rhone-Poulenc, Cranbury, N.Y., 1989-91; devel. specialist UOP, Tarrytown, N.Y., 1991-95; sr. rsch. scientist Clairol, Inc., Stamford, Conn., 1995—. Patentee in field (2); contbr. articles to profl. jours. Mentor Pace U. Rsch. Project, Tarrytown, 1993. Mem. ASTM, Soc. Cosmetic Chemists. Roman Catholic. Office: Clairol Inc 2 Blachley Rd Stamford CT 06922

LARKIN, MARY SUE, financial planner; b. Kansas City, Kans., Sept. 29, 1948; d. Claude Dewey Jr. and Mildred Elaine (Foster) Wyrick; m. James Donald Larkin, June 5, 1971; children: Michael James, David Kirk. BA in Elem. Edn., Baker U., 1970; MA in Edn., Ariz. State U., 1980. Tchr. Bonner Springs (Kans.) Unified Sch. Dist., 1970-71, Finney County Unified Sch. Dist., Garden City, Kans., 1971-73, Deer Valley Unified Sch. Dist., Phoenix, 1974-80; fin. planner Larkin & Assocs., Sun City, Ariz., 1980—; co-founder, registered rep. Fin. Network Investment Corp., Torrance, Calif., 1983. Co-author: The Larkin Guide-Enjoying the Riches of Retirement, 1987. Bd. dirs. Mingus Mountain Estate Residential Ctr., Incc., 1993, sec., 1994—. Recipient creative programming award Nat. Univ. Continuing Edn. Assn., 1994. Mem. Internat. Assn. Fin. Planning (pres. greater Phoenix chpt. 1994-95), Altrusa (pres. Sun City 1987-89). Republican. Roman Catholic. Office: 17220 N Boswell Blvd Ste L200 Sun City AZ 85373-2000

LARKIN, NELLE JEAN, computer programmer, analyst; b. Ralston, Okla., July 4, 1925; d. Charles Eugene and Jennivea Pearl (Lane) Reed; m. Burr Oakley Larkin, Dec. 28, 1948 (div. Aug. 1969); children: John Timothy, Kenneth James, Donald Jerome, Valerie Jean Larkin Rouse. Student, UCLA, 1944, El Camino Jr. Coll., 1946-49, San Jose (Calif.) City Coll., 1961-62. Sr. programmer, analyst III Santa Clara County, San Jose, Calif., 1963-69; sr. analyst, programmer Blue Cross of No. Calif., Oakland, 1971-73; sr. programmer, analyst Optimum Systems, Inc., Santa Clara, Calif., 1973-75, Crocker Bank, San Francisco, 1975-77, Greyhound Fin. Service, San Francisco, 1977-78; analyst, programmer TRW, Mountain View, Calif., 1978-79; sr. programer analyst Memorex, Santa Clara, 1979-80; staff mgmt. cons. Am. Mgmt. System, Foster City, Calif., 1980-82; sr. programmer, analyst, project leader Tymeshare, Cupertino, Calif., 1982-83; sr. programmer, analyst Beckman Instruments, Palo Alto, Calif., 1983-89; analyst, programmer U.S. Postal Svc., San Mateo, Calif., 1989—. Mem. Calif. Scholarship Fedn. (life mem. 1943), Alpha Sigma Gamma. Home: 3493 Londonderry Dr Santa Clara CA 95050-6632 Office: US Postal Svc 2700 Campus Dr San Mateo CA 94497-0001

LARMORE, CATHERINE CHRISTINE, university official; b. West Chester, Pa., Apr. 8, 1947; d. Ashby Morton and Catherine (Burns) L.; m. Thomas Henry Beddall, May 2, 1994. BA, Earlham Coll., 1969. Tchr. Westtown (Pa.) Sch., 1969-75, asst. dean girls, 1971-73, dean girls, 1973-75; sec. U. Pa., Kennett Square, 1976-78; media coord. New Bolton Ctr U. Pa. Sch. Vet. Medicine, Kennett Square, 1978-83, dir. external affairs, 1983-88, dir. devel., 1988—. Mem. London Grove (Pa.) Twp. Planning Commn., 1990—, Chester County (Pa.) Women's Task Force, 1992-93, Chester County Women's Commn., 1994-95; v.p. White Clay Watershed Assn., Landenburg, Pa., 1994-95; mem. White Clay Creek bi-state adv. coun. Commonwealth of Pa., 1996—; chmn. steering com. for Ad Hoc Task Force on White Clay Creek. Recipient Take Pride in Pa. award Commonwealth of Pa., 1991. Mem. Nat. Soc. Fund Raising Execs., So. Chester County C. of C. (bd. dirs. 1989-91), Am. Horse Coun., Nat. Steeplechase and Hunt Assn., Thoroughbred Owners and Breeders Assn., Chester-Delaware County Farm Bur. Office: U Pa New Bolton Ctr 382 West Street Rd Kennett Square PA 19348

LA ROCCA, ISABELLA, artist, educator; b. El Paso, Apr. 14, 1960; d. Remo and Alicia Estela (Gonzalez) La R. BA, U. Pa., 1984; MFA, Ind. U., 1993. Freelance photographer N.Y.C., 1986-90; assoc. instr. Ind. U., Bloomington, 1991-93; instr. Herron Sch. Art, Indpls., 1992; vis. asst. prof. Ind. U., 1994—; asst. prof. DePauw U., Greencastle, Omd/, 1994-95; vis. asst. prof. Bloomsburg (Pa.) U., 1995—. One-woman shows include Haas Gallery, Bloomsburg, Pa., 1996, Ctr. Photography Woodstock, N.Y., Moore Coll., Pa., 1994, Emison Art Ctr., Greencastle, Ind., 1996; exhibited in group shows at Bellevue Gallery, 1992, 494 Gallery, N.Y.C., 1993. Ind. U. CIC Minority fellow, 1990-91; Jewish Found. Edn. Women scholar, 1990; recipient Friends Photography Ferguson award, 1993.

LAROCCO, ELIZABETH ANNE, management information systems professional; b. Bethpage, N.Y., Feb. 15, 1957; d. Alfred Joseph and Teresa Lucille (Scalzo) Bott; m. Michael Gerard LaRocco, May 17, 1980. BBA, Hofstra U., 1979, postgrad., 1992. Programmer Computerland, Westbury, N.Y., 1980-82; software cons., propr. E.A. LaRocco, Ronkonkoma, N.Y., 1982-85; from bus. programmer to supr. corporate applications NEC America, Inc., Melville, N.Y., 1984—. Mem. Huntington Twp. Art League. Mem. IEEE, NAFE, Assn. Computing Machinery. Roman Catholic. Office: NEC Am Inc/MIS Div 8 Corporate Center Dr Melville NY 11747-3148

LA ROCHE, MARIE-ELAINE, investment banker; b. N.Y.C., Aug. 17, 1949; d. Andre and Madeleine (Hanin) LaR.; 3 children. BS in Internat. Affairs, Georgetown U., 1971; MBA, Am. U., 1978. With equity sales dept. Morgan Stanely Investment Banking Co., N.Y.C., 1978-81, v.p. investment banking, 1981-84; v.p. investment banking Morgan Stanely Investment Banking Co., London, 1984-85; prin. mktg. dir. fixed income div. Morgan Stanely Investment Banking Co., N.Y.C., 1985-86, mng. dir. fixed income div., 1986—, mng. dir., dir. worldwide fixed income mktg., 1986-89, mng. dir., dir. pub. fin. dept., 1989-94, firm mgr.; now mng. dir. Morgan Stanely Investment Banking Co. Nat. co-chair Women's Campaign Fund; mem. Com. of 200, 1991—; founder WISH List. Named to YWCA Acad. Women Achievers, 1983. Mem. Forum for Women Dirs., Fin. Womens Assn. of N.Y. Republican. Roman Catholic. Office: Morgan Stanley & Co Inc 1585 Broadway New York NY 10036*

LAROSA, LISA ANN, accountant; b. Lawrence, Mass.; d. Antonino and Susan Ann (Bohne) L. BSBA in Acctg., Merrimack Coll., 1993. Mutual fund acct. State St. Bank and Trust, Quincy, Mass., 1993-95; acct. Foto Fantasy, Inc., Windham, N.H., 1995—. Mem. Inst. Mgmt. Accts. Office: Foto Fantasy Inc 57 Range Rd Windham NH 03087

LARRABEE, KELLY DIANE, women's health nurse; b. Charleston, W.Va., Sept. 12, 1968; d. Conrad Renick Jr. and Joyce Diana (Rowlands) L. BS in Nursing, W.Va. U., 1990. Staff nurse antepartum St. Luke's Episc. Hosp., Houston, 1990; perinatal nurse Tokos Clin. Svcs., Atlanta, 1992; prenatal nurse Tokos Clin. Svcs., Houston, 1992—; staff nurse labor and delivery Piedmont Hosp., Atlanta, 1991-92; rsch. nurse U. Tex. Med. Sch., Houston, 1992, high risk obstetric coord., 1993, sr. rsch. nurse, 1993—; com. mem. Planned Parenthood Pub. Rels., Houston, 1993-94; presenter at Womens Health Issues confs. and symposiums, NIH Ctr., 1995, W.Va. Univ., 1995, Am. Coll. Ob/Gyn., 1995, Coll. Problems in Drug Dependence, 1995, U. Tex., 1995, Soc. Perinatal Obstetricians, Soc. For Gynecologic Investigation. Mem. Assn. Am. Coll. Women, Assn. Women's Health, Obstetrics, Neonatal Nurses. Office: U Tex Houst Med Sch 6431 Fannin St Ste 3 204 Houston TX 77030-1501

LARREY, INGE HARRIETTE, jazz and blues freelance photographer; b. Freiburg, Germany, Jan. 21, 1934; came to U.S., 1983; d. Friedrich W. and Claerle I. (Mueller) Luger; m. Toni Halter, Aug. 5, 1967 (div. 1977); m. Louis A. Larrey, June 13, 1981. Student, N.Y. Inst. Photography, Saudi Arabia, 1983. Au Pair, Finland, 1952; Various assignments Federal Republic of Germany in Turkey, Spain, Belgium, England, 1956-82; audit student in journalism, photography U. Houston, 1984; substitute employee with consulate gen. Federal Republic of Germany, Houston, 1985; visitors' Relations German real estate company, Houston, 1985—; internat. network mktg. Interior Design Nutritionals, 1995—. Works shown in more than a dozen exhbns., 1986-91; photographs in pvt. collections, in various publs., on cassette, record covers. Vol. Houston FotoFest, Women's Caucus for Art. Mem. Nat. Mus. of Women in the Arts (charter), Am. Image News Svc., Cultural Arts Coun. of Houston, Friends of Photography, Houston Ctr. for Photography, Jazz Heritage Soc. Tex., Milt Larkin Jazz Soc. (founding). Office: Sueba USA Corp 1800 West Loop S Ste 1323 Houston TX 77027-3211

LARRIMORE, PATSY GADD, nursing administrator; b. Knoxville, Tenn., Feb. 18, 1933; d. Harry Collins and Frances (Irwin) Gadd; m. Walter Eugene Larrimore; children: Patricia J. Titus, Walter Eugene Jr., Beverly Calderon. BS, Johns Hopkins U., 1976, MEd, 1977. RN. Pediatric supr. Johns Hopkins Hosp., Balt., 1960-68; supr. critical care South Balt. Gen. Hosp., 1968-78; DON Hosp. for Sick Children, Washington, 1978-84; field rep. Joint Commn. Accreditation Hosp., Chgo., 1984-95; dir. nursing Bon Secours Hosp., Balt., 1987-88; assoc. dir. clin. affairs Paralyzed Vets. Am., Washington, 1989-92; pres. Diabetes Action Rsch. and Edn. Found., Inc., Washington, 1991-92, Larrimore and Assocs., Inc., Linthicum, Md., 1991-95; clin. auditor Vencor, Inc., Lousville, 1995—; asst. prof. nursing and allied health Catonsville Community Coll., Balt. Contbr. articles to profl. jours. Bd. dirs. Christian Relief Svcs., Alexandria, Va., 1987-92. Recipient Bronze Svc. award Am. Heart Assn., 1981, Md. affiliate Silver Disting. Svc. award, 1980, Cen. Md. chpt. Bronze Svc. Recognition medallion, 1982, Md. chpt. Founder's award Am. Heart Assn., 1978, D.C. Hosp. Svc. award, 1982. Mem. Am. Heart Assn. (bd. dirs. Balt. chpt. 1972-84, Md. chpt. 1978-85, Bronze Service award Md. affiliate 1981, Silver Disting. Service Cen. Md. chpt. 1980, Bronze Service Recognition award, 1979), Am. Assn. Critical Care Nurses, Am. Nurses Assn., Advanced Nursing Adminstrn., Assn. Care Children's Health (bd. dirs. 1981-82), Am. Soc. Nursing Service Adminstrs., Am. Assn. Spinal Cord Injury Nurses, Phi Delta Kappa.

LARSEN, ANNA KARUS, medical practice administrator; b. Howell, Mich., June 6, 1932; d. Arthur Emil Karus and Alida Lucile (Schoenhals) Loring; m. James Patrick Larsen, Apr. 22, 1955 (div. Oct. 1973); children: K. Stephan, Kirsten Larsen Babcock. Diploma, Mercy Sch. Nursing, Ann Arbor, Mich., 1953; BA, Stephens Coll., Columbia, Mo., 1979; MBA, Ariz. State U., Tempe, 1980. Nurse Houston, 1956-58, Coromoto Hosp., Maracaibo, Venezuela, 1960-62; program coord. St. Joseph's Hosp., Phoenix, 1973-79; owner Larsen & Assocs., Phoenix, 1982-89; project mgr. Harris Labs., Lincoln, Nebr., 1989-90; adminstr. Hope Eye Ctr., Phoenix, 1990—; owner, shareholder Pearlsen, Inc., Phoenix, 1994—; owner, developer Corhealth, Phoenix, 1986-88; editor, pub. Ariz. Mgmt. Newsletter, Phoenix, 1983-86; med. practice mgmt. cons., Phoenix, 1980—. Mem. Med. Group Mgmt. Assn., Am. Assn. Ophthalmic Adminstrs., Ariz. Treasury Mgmt. Assn. Office: Hope Eye Ctr 1530 W Glendale Ave Ste 103 Phoenix AZ 85021-8578

LARSEN, ELIZABETH B. (LIBBY LARSEN), composer; b. Wilmington, Del., Dec. 24, 1950; m. James Reece, Sept. 6, 1975; 1 child. BA, U. Minn., 1971, MA, 1975, PhD, 1978. co-founder Minn. Composers Forum. Composer operas Silver Fox, 1979, Tumbledown Dick, 1980, Clair de Lune, 1984, Frankenstein, The Modern Prometheus, 1990, A Wrinkle in Time, 1992, Mrs. Dalloway, 1993; orchestral and chamber works Symphony: Water Music, 1985, Four on the Floor, 1983, Overture: Parachute Dancing, 1983, Symphony No. 3, 1992, Ring of Fire, 1995, Blue Fiddler, 1995; choral and solo vocal works: Coming Forth into Day, 1986, Missa Gaia, 1992. RecipientDisting. Alumni award U. Minn., 1987, Catherine Steward award, 1991, Grammy award, 1994; named Exxon/Rockefeller composer in residence, Minn. Orch., 1983-87. Address: 2205 Kenwood Pky Minneapolis MN 55405-2329

LARSEN, ETHEL PAULSON, retired secondary school educator; b. Superior, Wis., Jan. 24, 1918; d. Ole Peter Paulson and Petra Marie (Boardsen) Gilbertson; m. James Eugene Larsen, June 13, 1943; children: Robert, Karen Larsen DePalermo, Deborah Larsen Farmer, Candice Larsen Herrera. AA, Kendall Coll., 1940; student, U. Wis., 1940-44; BS, SW Tex. U., 1960; postgrad., U. Tex., 1961-67. Tchr. Lakefield (Minn.) Pub. Schs., 1944-46; credit mgr. Sagebiel's Automotive Parts, Seguin, Tex., 1948-49, supervisory clk. supply Edward Gary AFB, San Marcos, Tex., 1951-56; property/acctg. chief Gary Army Air Field, San Marcos, 1956-59; tchr. Seguin High Sch., 1960-80; substitute tchr. Seguin Pub. Schs., 1981-83; reporter, photographer Seguin Citizen newspaper, 1981; now ret.; developer speech-journalism curriculum, Minn. State Bd. Edn., 1945; pres. AAUW, Seguin, 1965-66, Seguin Classroom Tchrs., 1971-72; del. to Tex. State Tchrs. Assn., Austin, 1970. Founding mem. York Creek Flood Prevention Dist. for Hays, Comal and Guadalupe counties, 1953-54; Voice of Democracy chair VFW Aux., Geronimo, Tex., 1970-78; writer radio scripts for improved farm-city rels., 1956; vol. tax aide, Seguin, 1987-90; Circle leader 1st United Meth. Ch., Seguin, 1989—; mem. T.B. Bd. Guadalupe County, 1954-57. Mem. Nat. Writers Club, Seguin Garden Club, Seguin-Guadalupe County Ret. Tchrs. (pres. 1990—), Nat. Coun. State Garden Clubs, Inc. (life), Tex. Garden Clubs, Inc. (life), Tex. State Garden Clubs (life, Tex. dist. VII), Tex. Agrl. Ext. Svc. (master gardener), Order Ea. Star, Oakwood Art Group, Delta Kappa Gamma (Theta Kappa chpt. pres. 1978-80). Home: 1619 Driftwood St Seguin TX 78155-5211

LARSEN, GWYNNE E., computer information systems educator; b. Omaha, Sept. 10, 1934; d. Melvin and Vernetta (Allen) Bannister; m. John M. Larsen, June 8, 1958; children: Bradley Allen, Blair Kevin, Randall Lawrence. A in Bus. Adminstrn., Denver U., 1956, MBA, 1975, PhD, 1979; BS, Met. State Coll., 1971. Instr. Met. State Coll. Denver, 1979-81, asst. prof., 1981-85, assoc. prof., 1985-88, prof., 1989—, acting chair computer dept., 1991-92; book reviewer McGraw Hill, 1991, Harcourt Brace Jovanovich, 1991, Macmillan Pub. Co., 1993, Southwestern Pub. Co., 1993; presenter Mountain Plains Mgmt. conf., Denver, 1982, Rocky Mountain Bus. Expo, Denver, 1982, Red Rocks C.C., 1984, Colo.-Wyo. Acad. Sci. conf., 1985, Boulder, 1986, Colorado Springs, 1987; local coord. John Wiley & Sons, Denver, 1982, 83; panel chmn. on office automation Assn. for Computing Machinery, Denver, 1985; spkr. ASTD, 1986, Am. Pub. Works Assn., 1986; participant numerous presentations and confs. Author: (with others) Computerized Business Information Systems Workbook, 1983, Collegiate Microcomputer, 1992, (with Verlene Leeberg) Word Processing: Using WordPerfect 5.0, 1989, Word Processing: Using WordPerfect 5.1, 1991, First Look at WordPerfect 5.1, 1991, First Look at DOS, 1991, First Look at NetWare, 1992, Using WordPerfect for Windows, 1993, (with Marold and Shaw) Using Microsoft Works: An Introduction to Computing, 1993, Using Microsoft Works, An Introduction to Computing, 1993, First Look at WordPerfect 6.0 for Windows, 1994, Using WordPerfect 6.0 for Windows, 1994, Using Microsoft Works for Windows, An Introduction to Computing, 1996, Beyond the Internet, 1996; apptd. editl. bd. Jour. Mgmt. Systems, 1988, Jour. Microcomputer Systems Mgmt., 1989, Info. Resources Mgmt. Jour., 1991; mem. editl. review bd. Jour. Info. Resources Mgmt. Systems, 1985—, Jour. Mgmt. Info. Systems, 1986—, Jour. Database Mgmt. Systems, Jour. Database Mgmt. Systems, 1987—, Jour. End User Computing, 1990—; contbr. articles to profl. jours. Mem. Info. Resources Mgmt. Assn., Colo.-Wyo. Acad. Scis., Office Automation Soc. Internat., Internat. Acad. for Info. Mgmt., panel part., 1995. Home: 8083 S Adams Way Littleton CO 80122 Office: Met State Coll Denver Campus Box 45 PO Box 173362 Denver CO 80217-3362

LARSEN, KAREN LYNN, secondary education educator; b. Fergus Falls, Minn., Jan. 22, 1949; d. Hans Peder and Garnette Imogene (Strissel) L. BA in English Edn., U. No. Colo., Greeley, 1971; M in English, Gonzaga U., 1990. Cert. in edn. K-Adult. Instr. Tchg. English as Fgn. Lang. Peace Corps, Bangkok, 1971-74; tchr. English Gordon (Nebr.) H.S., 1974-76, Joliet (Mont.) H.S., 1976-88; Costello fellow in English Gonzaga U., Spokane, 1988-90; tchr. English Lake Elsinore (Calif.) H.S., 1990-91, Temescal Canyon H.S., Lake Elsinore, 1991-95, Lake Stevens (Wash.) H.S., 1995—; vis. project cons. Mont. Writing Project, Missoula, 1986—. Contbr. articles to profl. jours. Named Tchr. of Yr. Joliet/Lake Elsinore, 1986, 87, 92, 94. Mem. NEA, AAUW, Wash. Tchrs. Assn., Lake Stevens Tchrs. Assn., Nat. Coun. Tchrs. English, Nat. Assn. Secondary Sch. Prins. Democrat. Lutheran. Home: 11615 Hwy 99 S D103 Everett WA 98204 Office: Lake Stevens HS 2908 113th Ave NE Lake Stevens WA 98258

LARSEN, LILA DUNCAN, curator; b. Neola, Utah, Nov. 18, 1929; d. Joseph Roger and Katie (Petersen) Duncan; m. Richard Bryce Larsen, Dec. 20, 1950 (dec. Nov. 1990); children: Nancy Ann, David, Bryce, Kathryn, Samuel. Student, Brigham Young U., 1947-50; BS in Comm./English/Bus., Weber State U., 1979; MA in Art History, U. Utah, 1987. Asst. dir. Springville (Utah) Mus. of Art, 1987-92; curator of edn. Eccles Cmty. Art Ctr., Ogden, Utah, 1992—; state mus. rep., bd. mem. Utah Art Educators Assn., 1990-92; bd. mem. arts commn. City of Ogden, 1992—; mem. visual arts adv. bd. Utah Arts Coun., Salt Lake City, 1993—. Bd. dirs. Eccles Cmty. Art Ctr., Ogden, 1974-78, Utah Mus. Vols. Assn., Salt Lake City, 1987-93; bd. mem., arts & crafts chmn. Federated Women's Clubs, Utah, 1992-94; bd. mem. Acad. Lifelong Learning-Weber State U., Ogden, 1992—. Ednl. Outreach grantee Marriner S. Eccles Found., 1988, 89, 90, 91; named

Utah Art Educator of Yr., Utah Art Educators Assn., 1992. Mem. Nat. Art Educators Assn. (Utah rep. lifelong learning 1992—), Kiwanis Club, Mystae Lit. Club (pres., sec.), Fine Arts Club. Mem. LDS Ch. Office: 1360 32nd St Ogden UT 84403-0902

LARSEN, PAULA ANNE, operating room nurse; b. Norfolk, Va., Oct. 2, 1962; d. Larry Gene and Sue Frances (Williams) P. ADN, Labette C.C., 1982. RN, Mo.; CNOR, TNCC. Lab. asst. Labette County Med. Ctr., Parsons, Kans., 1979-82; RN operating rm. St. John's Regional Med. Ctr., Joplin, Mo., 1982-85, RN oper. rm., shift coord., 1989-94; head nurse Mason Gen. Hosp., Shelton, Wash., 1994—; with Mo. Lions Eye Bank, 1989-94. Mem. Assn. Operating Rm. Nurses (del. 1991). Republican. Baptist. Office: Mason Gen Hosp 901 Mountain View Dr Bldg 1 Shelton WA 98584-4401

LARSON, DIANE LAVERNE KUSLER, principal; b. Fredonia, N.D., July 28, 1942; d. Raymond Edwin and LaVerne (Mayer) Kusler; m. Donald Floyd Larson, Aug. 14, 1965. BS, Valley City (N.D.) State U., 1964; MS, Mankato (Minn.) State U., 1977; EdS, U. Minn., 1987. Cert. tchr., Minn. Tchr. elem. Cokato (Minn.) Elem. Sch., 1962-64, Lakeview Elem. Sch., Robbinsdale, Minn., 1964-66; vocal tchr. Wheaton (Minn.) High Sch., 1966-67; tchr. Owatonna (Minn.) Elem. Sch., 1967-88, prin., 1988—; v.p. Cannon Valley Uniserv, Mankato, 1981-83; NEA del. World Confederation of Orgns. of the Teaching Professions, Melbourne, 1988. Named Woman of Yr., Owatonna Bus. and Profl. Women, 1990. Mem. NEA (bd. dirs. 1986-88), Minn. Edn. Assn. (bd. dirs. 1983-88, Outstanding Woman in Leadership award 1983), Minn. Reading Assn. (bd. dirs. 1983—, Pres. award 1984), Internat. Reading Assn. (coord. for Minn. 1990—), Minn. Elem. Prins. Assn., Delta Kappa Gamma (legis. chmn. 1986—, pres. 1992, Woman of Achievement award 1989, Tau leadership chair). Congregationalist. Home: 19654 Bagley Ave Faribault MN 55021-2246 Office: Washington Sch 338 E Main St Owatonna MN 55060-3037

LARSON, GAYLE ELIZABETH, public relations professional; b. Vancouver, Wash., Nov. 5, 1942; d. Edwin Ellis and Lois Marguerite (Wilson) L. Student, U. Mex., 1963; BA in Spanish lang. and lit., Wash. State U., 1964; cert. in Hispanic studies, U. Madrid, 1970; postgrad., City U. Portland, 1983. Flight attendant, purser Pan Am. Airlines, N.Y.C., 1965-69; bilingual asst. Touche, Ross Internat., Madrid, 1969-73; mgr. sales and pub. rels. Westin Hotels, Portland, Oreg., 1979-84; dir. pub. rels. Columbia River coun. Girl Scouts U.S., Portland, 1986-89; freelance writer, cons. Vancouver, 1989—; workshop presenter Women in Communications, 1984; pub. rels. cons. Make a Wish Found., Portland, 1989; mentor talented and gifted program Portland Pub. Schs., 1989; tchr. English as 2d lang. Mangold Inst., Madrid, 1970. Novelist: Senorita Blonde, 1989, The Fraudulent Monk, 1991. Mem. Pub. Rels. Soc. Am. (Silver Anvil commendation 1989), Women in Communications (v.p. spl. events 1987), Willamette Writers, Quill and Scroll. Home: 9832 N Willamette Blvd Portland OR 97203

LARSON, JANE RUTH SCHAEDIGER, non-profit organization administrator; b. Englewood, N.J., Sept. 27, 1939; d. Alvin Henry and Ruth Louise (Otterbein) S.; m. James Roderick Larson, Oct. 21, 1961 (dec. Mar. 1995); children: Linda Jane Larson Daniel, Debra Jane Larson. BS in Edn., Wittenberg U., 1961; postgrad., U. Toledo, 1970. p. 6th grade classroom tchr. Toledo Pub. Schs., 1961-63; elem. sch. music tchr. Sylvania (Ohio) City Schs., 1970-86; staff aide part-time Nat. Abortion and Reproductive Rights Action League of Ohio, Columbus, 1986-88, interim exec. dir., 1992, data organizer, office mgr., 1988—. Recipient Dedicated Svc. award Nat. Abortion and Reproductive Rights Action League, 1989. Mem. ACLU, NOW, LWV, AAUW (program and policy chair, Ohio campaign for choice coord. 1989-91, testified for women's reproductive rights 1991, Community Svc. award 1990), People for The American Way, Ohio Women, Inc. (exec. bd., equality day award com. 1992—, 1st recipient Ann. Women's Equality Day award 1991), Religious Coalition for Reproductive Rights, Parents and Friends of Lesbians and Gays. Home: 3111 Rivermill Dr Columbus OH 43220-2258 Office: NARAL Ohio 760 E Broad St Columbus OH 43205-1015

LARSON, JANICE TALLEY, computer science educator; b. Houston, Sept. 29, 1948; d. Hiram Peak Talley and Jennie Edna (Forbes) Donahoo; m. Harold Vernon Larson, Apr. 8, 1977; children: Randall Neil, Christopher Lee. AA in Computer Sci., San Jacinto Coll., 1981; BA in Computer Info. Systems, U. Houston, Clear Lake, 1984, MA in Computer Info. Systems, 1988; postgrad. in instructional tech., U. Houston, 1994—. Programmer Control Applications, Houston, 1985-86, Tex. Eastern Pipeline, Houston, 1988-90; instr. computer sci. San Jacinto Coll., Houston, 1990-94; sponsor Computer Sci. Club, Houston, 1992-94. Mem. IEEE, U. Houston Alumni Assn., Phi Delta Kappa, Kappa Delta Pi.

LARSON, MARGARET ANNE, bed and breakfast owner, food service executive; b. Dodge City, Kans., Nov. 25, 1944; d. John Archibald and Elma (Phillips) Fogarty; m. Robert O'Neal Brewer, June 16, 1963 (dec. Feb. 1986); children: Robert O'Neal Brewer II, Anne Michelle Brewer Davison; m. David James Larson, Apr. 25, 1992; children: Thomas David, James Matthew, Jennnifer Elizabeth. AS, Seminole Jr. Coll., 1980. Owner, operator Functions, Inc., Shawnee, Okla., 1991—, Mayne Harber Inn, Shawnee, Okla., 1994—; caterer St. Paul's United Methodist Ch., Shawnee, Okla., 1995. Pres. St. Paul's United Meth. Women, Shawnee, Okla., 1995, v.p., 1996; workshop facilitator Liberty Bapt. Ch., Shawnee, 1989-92. Mem. Okla. Bed and Breakfast Assn. Republican. Methodist. Home and Office: Mayne Harber Inn 2401 E Highland PO Box 1114 Shawnee OK 74802-1114

LARSON, NANCY CELESTE, computer systems manager; b. Chgo., July 17, 1951; d. Melvin Ellsworth and Ruth Margaret (Carlson) L. BS in Music Ed., U. Ill., 1973, MS in Music Edn., 1976; postgrad., Purdue Univ., 1982-86. Vocal music educator Consol. Sch. Dist., Gilman, Ill., 1975-77; elem. vocal music tchr. Sch. Dist. 161, Flossmoor, Ill., 1977-87; instr. Vander Cook Coll., Chgo., 1980-88; systems programmer analyst Sears, Roebuck & Co., Chgo., 1987-92, tech. instr., 1989-90, project leader, 1990-91, sr. systems analyst, 1991-92; sr. systems analyst Trans Union Corp., Chgo., 1992—, project mgr., 1994, mgr., 1994—; tchr. adult computer edn. Homewood-Flossmoor High Sch., 1986-90. Chmn. Faith Luth. Ch., 1982-87, pres. bd., 1988-91, vocal soloist and voice-over performer. Mem. Ill. Music Educators Assn., Music Educators Nat. Conf., Ill. Educators Assn., Nat. Educators Assn., Am. ORFF Schulwerk Assn., Flossmoor Edn. Assn. (negotiator 1983-86). Republican. Lutheran. Office: Trans Union Corp 555 W Adams St Chicago IL 60661-3601

LARSON, SALLY, educator; b. Sioux Falls, S.D., June 13, 1949; m. Gary D. Larson; children: Blane, Brock Garett, Gannon, Joelle. AA, U. N.D., Devils Lake, 1987; BS in Elem. Edn., Minot (N.D.) State U., 1988; MS in Edn., No. State U., Aberdeen, S.D., 1995. Cert. tchr., N.D. Instr. grade 2 Four Winds Elem. Sch., Ft. Totten, N.D., 1988-89; instr. grade 5 Prairie View Elem. Sch., Devils Lake, 1989-92; instr. grades 7 and 8 Ctrl. Mid. Sch., Devils Lake, 1992-96, assoc. prin., 1995—; mem. Tchr. Ctr. Adv. Bd., Devils Lake Dist., 1992-95, pres., 1994-95; Title II bd. mem. Devils Lake Pub. Schs., 1993-96; grant writer Devils Lake Dist. Math. and Sci. Title II Program, 1992-94, Lake Region Area Found., 1992; insvc. presenter Devils Lake Sch. Dist. Math. Curriculum, 1993-94; mem. Sch. Wide Student Assistance Team, 1993-96; 504 case mgr., 1993-96. Bd. mem. U. N.D., Lake Region, Devils Lake, 1994—. Mem. Nat. Coun. Tchrs. Math., N.D. Coun. Tchrs. Math. Home: PO Box 347 Leeds ND 58346-0347 Office: Ctrl Mid Sch Devils Lake Pub Schs 325 7th St Devils Lake ND 58301-2488

LARUE, LAURA ELLEN, family nurse practitioner; b. Grayson County, Va., Dec. 29, 1951; d. Wayne and Margaret (Rakes) Mitchell; m. Raymond LaRue Sr.; children: J.W., Eddie. Student, Radford U., 1970-71; AAS in Nursing, Wytheville C.C., 1980; BSN summa cum laude, Med. Coll. Va./Va. Cmty. U., 1991, MS, 1995. RN, Va.; cert. ACLS instr., pediatric advanced life support, TNCC, EMT-CT, BLS instr., family nurse practitioner. Staff/charge nurse surg. floor Twin County Regional Hosp., Galax, Va., 1980-84, charge nurse emergency nurse, recovery rm. relief nurse, 1980-84, emergency dept. nurse, 1986-90, home health case mgr., admissions mgr., 1990-91, nursing supr., 1991-92, insvc. coord., 1992-96; office nurse Primary Care Ctr., Independence, Va., 1984-88; family nurse practitioner Twin County Health Clinics, 1996—; mem. infection control com., quality assurance nursing com., TB and case mgmt. task force Twin County Regional Hosp., 1992—; mem. adj. faculty Old Dominion U. EMT-CT Fries (Va.) Rescue Squad, 1992—; nurse Bapt. Free Clinic, Galax, 1993; vol. nurse for sports physicals for local sch. dists.; tchr. EMT defibrillation classes, BLS. Mem. Health Care Educators Assn., Golden Key Nat. Honor Soc., Sigma Theta Tau. Republican. Methodist. Home: 369 Stevens Creek Rd Fries VA 24330 Office: Twin County Health Clinic Fries VA 24330

LARWOOD, LAURIE, psychologist; b. N.Y., 1941; PhD, Tulane U., 1974. Pres., Davis Instruments Corp., San Leandro, Calif., 1966-71, cons., 1969—; asst. prof. orgnl. behavior SUNY, Binghamton, 1974-76; assoc. prof. psychology, chairperson dept., assoc. prof. bus. adminstrn. Claremont (Calif.) McKenna Coll., 1976-83, Claremont Grad. Sch., 1976-85; prof., head dept. mgmt. U. Ill.-Chgo., 1983-87; dean sch. bus. SUNY, Albany, 1987-90; dean Coll. Bus. Adminstrn., U. Nev., Reno, 1990-92; dir. Inst. Strategic Bus. Issues, 1992—; mem. western regional advisory coun. SBA, 1976-81; dir. The Mgmt. Team; pres. Mystic Games, Inc. Mem. Acad. Mgmt. (editl. rev. bd. Rev. 1977-82, past chmn. women in mgmt. div., managerial consultation divsn., tech. and innovation mgmt. divsn.), Am. Psychol. Assn., Assn. Women in Psychology. Author: (with M.M. Wood) Women in Management, 1977; Organizational Behavior and Management, 1984, Women's Career Development, 1987, Strategies-Successes-Senior Executives Speak Out, 1988, Women's Careers, 1988, Managing Technological Development, 1988; mem. editl. bd. Sex Roles, 1979—, Consultation, 1986-91, Jour. Orgnl. Behavior, 1987—, Group and Orgn. Mgmt., 1982-84, editor, 1986—; founding editor Women and Work, 1983, Jour. Mgmt. Case Studies, 1983-87; contbr. numerous articles, papers to profl. jours. Home: 2855 Sagittarius Dr Reno NV 89509-3885 Office: U Nev Coll Bus Adminstrn Reno NV 89557

LARY, JANICE HARRISON, accountant; b. National City, Calif., Nov. 2, 1942; d. E. T. and Mildred Floye (Carter) Harrison; m. Alton Leon Lary, May 11, 1970; children: Joseph Trayle, Elizabeth Elaine, Michelle Ruth. BBA, Tex. Tech. U., 1995. CPA, Tex. Bus. owner Lubbock, Tex., 1965-75, 80—; cons. Yellowhouse Canyon River Ranch, Lubbock, 1989-96. Foster parent Tex. Dept. Human Svc., Lubbock, 1984. Mem. AICPA (mem. pvt. practice sect. 1994-96), Tex. Soc. CPAs. Mem. Ch. of Christ.

LARY, MARILYN SEARSON, library director; b. Walterboro, S.C., Sept. 3, 1943; d. Charles Baring and Julia Caroline (Rizer) Searson; AB, Newberry Coll., 1964; MLS, U. N.C., 1965; PhD, Fla. State U., 1975; m. Jahangir Lary, Oct. 27, 1975; children: Sara, Heidi. Young adult librarian Greenville County (S.C.) Libr., 1965-66; libr. dir. U. S.C., Sumter, 1966-69; instr. Radford (Va.) U., 1969-70; asst. prof. East Carolina U., Greenville, 1970-72; reference librarian Clemson U., S.C., 1972-73; asst. prof. U. Mich., Ann Arbor, 1975-78, U. South Fla., Tampa, 1978-84; librarian Hillsborough Community Coll.-Brandon, Tampa, 1984-86; dir. libr. resource ctr. Dalton (Ga.) Coll., 1986-96; dir libr. North Ga. Coll., 1996—. Mem. ALA, Ga. Libr. Assn. Home: 104B Walker Dr 8D Dahlonega GA 30533 Office: North Ga Coll Stewart Library Dahlonega GA 30597

LA SALA, CAROLANN MARIE, educational administrator, education educator; b. Bklyn., Apr. 25, 1957; d. Vincent Joseph and Carole (Tricomi) La S.; divorced; children: Lisa Michelle, Gina Maria. BA, Adelphi U., Garden City, N.Y., 1978; MS in Edn., L.I. U., Brookville, N.Y., 1989, profl. diploma, 1996. Cert. elem. tchr., sch. dist. adminstr. Elem. tchr. L.I., N.Y., 1988-94; supr. student tchrs. L.I. U.-C.W. Post Campus, Brookville, 1994—, adj. prof. edn., 1994—, honors thesis advisor, 1994—; dir. instrnl. and recreation programs Summer Ctr. Manhasset (N.Y.) Union Free Sch. Dist., 1994—; ednl. cons. N.C.H.E., 1992-94, Harcourt Brace & Co., 1994—; presenter Am. dental Soc. conv., 1994. Author ednl. rsch. Alternativees to Pull-Out Programs, 1995. Vol. Am. Cancer Soc., L.I., N.Y., 1988—, Greenpeace U.S.A., 1988—; mem. Salisbury Civic Assn., L.I., 1988—. Mem. AAUW, ASCD, Nat. Coun. Tchrs. Math., Phi Delta Kappa. Office: LI U Sch Edn C W Post Campus Brookville NY 11548

LASALLE-TARANTIN, SERAFINA A., director primary school, educator; b. Phila., Pa., Jan. 12, 1954; d. Michael and Norma (Pugliese) LaS.; m. John Richard Tarantin, Apr. 24, 1976; children: Justin, Marissa, Meredith. BA in Elem. Edn., Holy Family Coll., 1975; MA Early Childhood Edn., Columbia U., 1979. Cert. elem. sch. tchr., N.J., Pa., early childhood edn., Pa. Tchr. kindergarten Alpha House/Holy Family Coll., Phila., 1975—, dir., 1993—. Mem. Nat. Assn. Edn. Young Children, Assn. Childhood Edn. Internat. Home: 144 Mountain Oaks Rd Yardley PA 19067 Office: Alpha House Early Childhood Learning Ctr Grant & Frankfort Aves Philadelphia PA 19114

LASATER, SANDRA JO, nurse; b. Cookeville, Tenn., Jan. 20, 1948; d. Herbert Hershel and Bunola Christine (Jones) Garrett; m. Richard Lee Lasater Jr., July 21, 1973; children: Becky, Beth, Bonnie, Lee, Scott. Diploma, St. Thomas Sch. Nursing, 1970; BSN, Vanderbilt U., 1972, MSN, 1973. Cert. urology registered nurse. Child psychiatry head nurse, coord. Vanderbilt Univ. Hosp., Nashville, 1970-73; clin. instr. Univ. Tenn., Nashville, 1975-77; asst. dir. nursing, RN operating rm. Cookeville (Tenn.) Gen. Hosp., 1977-81; adminstrv. dir., drug info. and treatment Cumberland Med. Ctr., Crossville, Tenn., 1981-82; DON White County Community Hosp., Sparta, Tenn., 1982-84; clin. instr. Columbia (Tenn.) State Community Coll., 1984-85; supr. operating rm. Bedford County Hosp., Shelbyville, Tenn., 1984-85; RN ambulatory care Alvin C. York VA Med. Ctr., Murfreesboro, Tenn., 1985—. Author: poetry; contbr. articles to profl. jours. Lt. col. USAR Nurse Corp., 1979—, with Operation Desert Storm, 1991. Mem. USAR Officer Assn., Assn. Mil. Surgeons. Home: 705 Cason Ln Murfreesboro TN 37129-4832

LASHER, ESTHER LU, minister; b. Denver, June 1, 1923; d. Lindley Aubrey and Irma Jane (Rust) Pim; m. Donald T. Lasher, Apr. 9, 1950 (dec. Mar. 1982); children: Patricia Sue Becker, Donald T., Keith Alan, Jennifer Luanne Oliver. Assoc. Fine Arts, Colo. Women's Coll., 1943; BA, Denver U., 1945; MA Religious Edn., Ea. Bapt. Sem., 1948; MA, Denver U., 1967. Ordained to ministry Bapt. Ch., 1988. Christian edn. dir. 1st Bapt., Evansville, Ind., 1948-52; min. Perrysburg Bapt. Ch., Macy, Ind., 1988-95; min.-at-large Am. Baptist Conv./USA, 1996—; libr. Peru (Ind.) Pub. Schs., 1990-91; sec. Ind. Ministerial Coun., Indpls., 1990-92; chairperson Women in Ministry, Indpls., 1988-93; chmn. Fellowship Mission Circle, Rochester, Ind., 1988-93; mem. Partnership in Ministry, Indpls., 1990-94; bd. mgrs. Am. Bapts./Ind., 1991-93; asst. dir. Greenwood Pub. Library, 1978-84; dir. Fulton County Pub. Library, 1984-90. Pres. Toastmasters, Rochester, 1984-90, 95, edn. v.p., 1992-93; asst. dir. Greenwood Pub. Libr., 1977-85; dir. Fulton County Pub. Libr., 1985-90; bd. dirs. Manitau Tng. Ctr., Rochester, 1988-90; v.p. Mental Health Ctr., Rochester, 1987-90; founder Fulton County Literacy Coalition, Rochester, 1989-90; tutor/trainer Peru Literacy Coalition of Peru Pub. Libr., 1994-95; sec. Northwest Area ABC/IN, 1994-95; sec.-treas. North Miami County Mins. Fellowship, 1993-95; bd. dirs. Peru Civic Ctr., 1995; active CASA Lincoln County, 1995—; chair Christian Edn. Bd., 1995—. Named Outstanding Libr., Biog. Inst., 1989. Mem. Leadership Acad. (bd. dir., sec.), Bus. and Profl. Women (pres. Greenwood, Ind. chpt. 1984-86), Rochester Women's Club (pres. 1989-92), Fulton County Mins. Assn. (treas. 1993-95), Logansport Assn. Bapt. Women, Peru Lit. Club (v.p.-elect 1995), Christian Women's Club (hostess chair 1995—), CASA Miami County, Rotary, Sigma Alpha Iota (adv.), Christian Edn. (chmn. 1996—). Republican. Home and Office: HC 64 Box 768 South Bristol ME 04568

LASHER, HARRIET PINSKER, director, educator; b. Bay Shore, N.Y.; d. Albert and Irene (Kuchlik) Pinsker; children: Heather Lasher, Todd Lasher. BA, Conn. Coll., 1965; MEd, N.C. State U., 1986. Cert. prin., tchr. N.C. State Dept. Pub. Instrn. Tchr. Yonkers (N.Y.) Bd. Edn., 1966-72; dir. The Raleigh (N.C.) Sch., 1982—; mem. adv. bd. Triangle Meld, Raleigh, Meredith Child Devel. Adv. Bd., Raleigh; exec. bd. Wake Assn. for the Edn. Young Children, Raleigh, 1993-94. Mem. ASCD, Nat. Assn. for the Edn. Young Children, Nat. Coun. Tchrs. Math., N.C. Assn. for the Edn. Young Children. Office: The Raleigh Sch 1215 Ridge Rd Raleigh NC 27607

LASHLEY, BARBARA NORMAN, artist, educator; b. Martinsville, Va., Mar. 4, 1939; d. Clay Dewey Norman and Evelyn Virginia Spencer; m. Kirkland Hastings Lashley, Sept. 3, 1960; children: Kimberly Sutliff, Eric P., Mark G. AS, Bluefield (Va.) Coll., 1959; BA, Averett Coll., Danville, Va., 1977; MALS, Hollins Coll., 1994; student, Penland (N.C.) Sch. Crafts, 1994. Artist Vinton, Va., 1977-95; instr. art Averett Coll., Danville, Va., dir. Women's Resource Ctr., 1988, sec., asst. dean, 1983-88. Solo and group shows include Averett Coll. Gallery, Sommerhill Gallery, Chapel Hill, N.C., Danville Cmty. Coll., Sovran Bank, Danville, Danville Pub. Libr., Danville Mus. Fine Arts and History, Mus. York County, Rock Hill, S.C., Caswell County Civic Ctr., Yanceyville, N.C., Y.M.C.A., Roanoke, Va., Hollins Coll. Gallery, Roanoke, Reynolds Homestead, Critz Va., Roanoke United Meth. Home, Rainbow News and Cafe, Winston-Salem, N.C.; exhibited in group shows at Foot of Hills, Martinsville, Va., 1976 (best in show), Lynchburg Art Festival, 1976 (Gen. Elec. award), Lynchburg Fine Arts Ctr., 1977 (Denny Found. award), The Va. Mus., 1983 (C & P Purchase award and United Va. Bank Purchase award), Caswell County Civic Ctr. Juried Art Show (1st place 1982, 83, 89), League of Roanoke Artists, 1993 (Pres.'s Choice award), Piedmont Arts Assn., Martinsville (Merit award), The 1994 Bath County Art Show, Hot Springs, Ark. (2d place award, hon. mention award), Carnegie Hall 6th Ann. Juried Art Exhibit, Lewisburg, W.V., 1994 (2d place award, hon. mention award), 21st Ann. Foot of Hills Show, 1994 (Merit award, Purchase award), Danville Art League Juried Show, 1994 (Goodyear Tire and Rubber Co. Cash award), Danville Mus. Summer Select Biennial, 1995 (Merit award), The 1995 Bath County Art Show, Hot Springs (1st place watercolor award, 1st place mixed media award), The 22d Ann. Foot of the Hills Arts and Craft Show (Merit award), Vinton Dogwood Festival, 1996 (award of distinction), Bedford AAUW Art Show, 1996 (award); represented in numerous pub. and private collections Va. Nat. Bank, Bad. Tobakmanufaktur Roth-Haendle Gmbh & Co., A.C. Monk Tobacco Co., Averett Coll. Lib., Miller Breing Co., First & Merchants Bank, First Fed. Savings and Loan, C & P Telephone Co., others; pub. in Henley Southeastern Spectrum, Artemis Jour., others. Bd. dirs. Artemis Jour., Roanoke, 1994-95; mem. adv. panel Va. Commn. Arts, Richmond, 1986-87; guide Mus. Western Va., Roanoke, 1995; area coord. Gov.'s Awards for the Arts, Richmond, 1988. Mem. League Roanoke Artists (v.p. 1993-95), Piedmont Arts, Danville Art League (v.p. 1987). Baptist. Home: 4260 Twin Mountains Dr Vinton VA 24179

LASHOF, JOYCE C., public health educator; b. Phila.; d. Harry and Rose (Brodsky) Cohen; m. Richard K. Lashof, June 11, 1950; children: Judith, Carol, Dan. AB, Duke U., 1946; MD, Women's Med. Coll., 1950; DSc (hon.), Med. Coll. Pa., 1983. Dir. Ill. State Dept. Pub. Health, 1973-77; dep. asst. sec. for health programs and population affairs Dept. Health, Edn., and Welfare, Washington, 1977-78; sr. scholar in residence IOM, Washington, 1978; asst. dir. office of tech. assessment U.S. Congress, Washington, 1978-81; dean sch. pub. health U. Calif., Berkeley, 1981-91, prof. pub. health Sch. Pub. Health, 1981-94, prof. emerita, 1994—; co-chair Commn. on Am. after Roe vs. Wade, 1991-92; mem. Sec.'s Coun. Health Promotion and Disease Prevention, 1988-91; pres. APHA, 1992; chair Pres.'s Adv. Com. on Gulf War Vets. Illnesses, 1995-96. Vice chairperson editl. bd. Wellness Letter, 1983—; mem. editl. com. Ann. Rev. of Pub. Health, 1987-90. Recipient Alumni Achievement award Med. Coll. Pa., 1975, Sedgewick Meml. medal APHA, 1995. Home: 601 Euclid Ave Berkeley CA 94708-1331 Office: U Calif-Berkeley Sch Pub Health 140 Earl Warren Hall Berkeley CA 94720

LASKIN, BARBARA VIRGINIA, legal association administrator; b. Chgo., July 2, 1939; d. Cyril Krieps and Gertrude Katherine (Kujawa) Szymanski; children: Dawn Katherine Doherty, Amy Lynn Anderson. BA, U. Ill., Chgo., 1967; MA, Am. U. Beirut, 1978, Georgetown U., 1985. Asst. buyer Carson, Pirie, Scott & Co., Chgo., 1967-69; fgn. svc. officer Dept. State, Washington, 1969-79; mgr. gift shops Marriott Hotels, Washington, 1979-81; office mgr. Robt Schwinn & Assoc., Bethesda, Md., 1983-85; exec. dir. Internat. Acad. Trial Lawyers, San Jose, Calif., 1985—. Fellow Rotary Club San Jose; mem. AAUW (v.p. 1987), Am. Soc. Assn. Execs., Meeting Planners Internat., Internat. Spl. Events Soc. (v.p. membership 1996), Internat. Spl. Events Found. (dir.), Profl. Conservation Mgrs. Assn. Roman Catholic. Office: Internat Acad Trial Lawyers 4 N 2nd St Ste 175 San Jose CA 95113-1306

LASKIN, CYNTHIA MICHAEL, business manager; b. Balt., May 13, 1952; d. Ellward Laskin and Ruth Rita Laskin Engelman; 1 child, Rebecca Bradley Lavinson. BS, Boston U., 1974; MEd, Duke U., 1976; postgrad., Loyola Coll., 1982-86. Lic. real estate salesperson, Md. Educator Balt. County Pub. Schs., 1976-81; ops. analyst/mktg. assoc. Md. Cup Corp., Balt., 1981-86; asst. v.p. Md. Nat. Bank, Balt., 1986-91; bus. mgr. Lawrenceville (N.J.) Assocs., 1991—; spkr. in field. Com. chair Home for the Aged, Ewing, N.J., 1993—. Home: 2 Dorchester Ct Princeton NJ 08540

LASKIN, PAMELA L., writing educator; b. Bklyn., Sept. 4, 1954; d. Carl and Frances (Kornbluh) L.; m. Ira Reiser; children: Craig, Samantha. BA, Harper Coll., 1975, MA, 1981. Editor McGraw-Hill, N.Y.C., 1978-81; instr. CCNY, 1984—; instr. Kingsborough Coll., N.Y.C., 1995—; film critic Nassau Herald, N.Y., 1996—; writer Parachute Press, N.Y.C., 1989. Author: Music from the Heart, 1990, A Wish Upon a Star, 1991, In a Glass Ball, 1992, Dear Hades, 1994. Mem. Children's Book Soc., Poets & Writers, Poetry Soc. Am. Home: 414 5th St New York NY 11215

LASSER, GAIL MARIA, psychologist, educator; b. Saddle River, N.J., Feb. 29, 1956; d. Dominick A. and Genevieve M. Sanzo; children: Michael, Jason, Jonathan. B.A., Seton Hall U., 1971; teaching cert. William Paterson Coll., 1973; M.A., Montclair State Coll., 1975; postgrad. Seton Hall U., 1977; cert. staff psychologist, N.J., 1977; lic. real estate agt., N.J.; notary pub. Public relations rep. European Health Spa, 1970-71; med. asst. Sci. Prevention and Rehab. Assn., 1973; grad. teaching and research asst. Montclair State Coll., 1973-74; clin. asst. Dr. Brower, 1974; instr. psychology Essex County Coll., 1976-77; clin. psychologist intern Community Mental Health Center, Mt. Carmel Guild, Newark, 1976-77; lectr. St. Michaels Med. Center-N.J. Coll. Medicine, 1977-80; instr. psychology Bergen Community Coll., Paramus, N.J., 1977—; asst. to ct. adminstr. Bergen County Cts., 1977-78; cons. telecom., 1994—. Active Am. Heart Assn. Mem. Am. Psychol. Assn., Am. Soc. for Psychical Research, Pi Lambda Theta, Psi Chi. Home: 7 Westwind Ct Saddle River NJ 07458-3211

LASSESEN, CATHERINE AVERY CLAY, small business owner, manager/trainer; b. Corte Madera, CA, Nov. 8, 1961; d. Ralph Kindel Boyland Clay and Susan Avery (Kendall) Clay; m. B. Rune Lassesen, Mar. 2, 1991. BA in Hotel Adminstrn., U. Nev., 1985. Promotions asst. Tropicana Hotel, Las Vegas, Nev., 1985; front desk mgr. Marriott Corp., various locations, 1986-88; mgr. Six Ravens Ranch, Boonville, Calif., 1988-96, CEO, 1988-92; owner/mgr. Custom Engraving by Catherine, Boonville, Calif., 1989—; co-owner, trainer Bridgegate Stables & Tack Barn One, Boonville, 1991-93; owner, instr. Flying Colors An Equine Edn. Svc. Six Ravens Ranch, Boonville, Calif., 1994—; mgr. Hestehaven, 1996—; coach Mendocino County vaulting team, 1994—. Publicity dir. Mendocino County Fair and Apple Show, 1992-94. Named one of the Women of Yr., Clark County, Las Vegas, Nev., 1986. Mem. Ind. Career Women (historian 1991-92, v.p. 1992-93), U. Nev. Las Vegas Alumni Assn., Delta Zeta (province alumnae dir. 1991-93, nat. alumnae/collegiate rels. chmn. 1995—), Am. Vaulting Assn., Am. Quarter Horse Assn., Am. Paint Horse Assn., N.Am. Horseman Assn., Am. Horse Show Assn., Calif. Gymkhana Assn. (judge 1992—, dist. 37 pres. 1992-93, co-chmn. 1993-94), N.Am. Riding for the Handicapped Assn., Inc. Office: Hestehaven PO Box 160 Days Creek OR 97429

LASSITER, BETTIE WATFORD, retired elementary education educator; b. Colerain, N.C., Nov. 12, 1941; d. Hunter and Mary (Freeman) Watford; m. James Lassiter Jr., Dec. 30, 1963; children: Kimberly Arnet Lassiter, Tracy Arnez Lassiter. BS, Fayetteville (N.C.) State U., 1963. Cert. elem. tchr., N.C. Tchr. Bertie County Sch. Sys., Powellsville, N.C., 1963-64, 65-67; tchr. Hertford County Sch. Sys., Winton, N.C., 1967-95, ret., 1995. Mem. N.C. Edn. Assn., Retired Employees Assn. Democrat. Baptist. Home: 110 Doll Hill Rd PO Box 374 Powellsville NC 27967

LASSITER, KATRINA ANN, medical/surgical nurse; b. N.Y.C., Dec. 6, 1958; d. James Thomas and Wilhelmina (Belfield) L. BS, Hampton (Va.) U., 1982; MS, Hunter Coll., 1990. Staff nurse NYU Med. Ctr., N.Y.C., 1983-84; staff nurse Mary Immaculate Hosp., Jamaica, N.Y., 1984-85, charge nurse, 1985-88, clin. nurse mgr., 1988-90, nursing unit dir., 1990—. Bd. dirs. Am. Heart Assn., N.Y.C., 1992—; mem. NAACP; Cadette leader Girl Scouts U.S., 1983—; mem. nurses unit Calvary Bapt. Ch., 1983—. Named

Outstanding Vol. Mentor, N.Y. Mentoring, 1990. Mem. Nat. Black Nurses Assn., Progressive Women Inc. (sec. 1990-91), Sigma Theta Tau, Delta Sigma Theta. Home: 727 Beech St Baldwin NY 11510-2724 Office: Mary Immaculate Hosp 152-11 89th Ave Jamaica NY 11432-3723

LASSMANN, MARIE ELIZABETH, education educator, consultant; b. San Antonio, Mar. 13, 1945; d. William Taft and Ruby Elizabeth (Ward) Henry; children: Angela Smith, Molly Michaels, Honee Aylmer; m. Richard Allan Lassmann, Jan. 2, 1993. BS, Tex. A&I U., 1973, MS, 1979; PhD, U. Tex., 1991. Tchr. Sinton (Tex.) Ind. Sch. Dist., 1974-78, Kingsville (Tex.) Ind. Sch. Dist., 1978-89; tchg. asst. U. Tex., Austin, 1989-91; counselor Presbyn. Pan Am. Sch., Kingsville, 1992-94; asst. prof. dept. edn. Tex. A&M U., Kingsville, 1992—, asst. prof. continuing edn., 1984-95; asst. adj. prof. Embry-Riddle Aero. U., Kingsville, 1992-94; author test questions for dental and optometry schs., 1991-92. Recipient scholarship Tex. Woman's Club, 1990-91. Mem. ASCD, Nat. Coun. Tchrs. Math. (referee 1994), Phi Kappa Phi, Delta Kappa Pi.

LAST, DIANNA LINN SCHNEIDER, marketing company executive; b. Canton, Ohio, Dec. 29, 1944; d. Ld Mervyn and Veronica Lee Schneider; m. David D. Last, Nov. 29, 1969; 1 child, Jason Holden. BA in German, Ohio State U., 1966. Rsch. asst., programmer trainee high-energy physics dept. Ohio State U., Columbus, 1964-66; mfg. programmer RANCO, Inc., Columbus, 1966-68; sr. edn. rep. Honeywell Info. Systems, Cleve., 1968-72; dist. mgr. Honeywell Info. Systems, Orlando, Fla., 1972-78, telecommunications cons., 1978-79; mgr. networking edn. Honeywell Info. Systems, Phoenix, 1979-81, mgr. distributed systems, 1981-84; account and tech. mgr. Honeywell Info. Systems, Beijing, People's Republic of China, 1985; resident dir., chief rep. Honeywell Bull (formerly Honeywell Info. Systems), Beijing, People's Republic of China, 1985-87; dir. Integrated Info. Architecture Honeywell Bull, Phoenix, 1987-88; dir. info. mgmt. U.S. mktg. Bull (formerly Honeywell Bull), Phoenix, 1988-90; pres. Last Concepts Internat. Mktg. & Export Mgmt. Co., Phoenix, 1990—; bd. advisors Internat. Bus. Orgn., Am. Grad. Sch. Internat. Mgmt., 1981-84, 90—; cons., speaker in field; co-founder, co-chair Ariz. Internat. Trade Orgn., 1992—; co-founder, chmn. Am. High-Tech Forum, Beijing, 1985-87; co-chair mktg. com. Enterprise Network, 1990—; adj. faculty internat. bus. Maricopa Colls., 1994—; mem. governing bd. Internat. Studies Acad. 7-12 Charter Sch.; bd. dirs. Digital Network Access, 1995—. Chalice bearer, lay reader St. John Baptist Episcopal Ch., Phoenix, 1983—, mem. bishop's com., 1980-83, mem. vestry, 1991-92; adv. bd. Ariz. Assn. Children and Adults with Learning Disabilities, 1983-84; design task force Maricopa C.Cs., 1984; active World Trade Ctr. Ariz., 1992—; mem. internat. adv. coun. Paradise Valley Coll., 1994—; bd. dirs. Ctr. for New Dirs., Phoenix, 1987-90. Mem. IEEE (past vice chmn. programs), Coun. Fgn. Rels. (mem. Phoenix com. 1994—), Ariz. Software Assn. (internat. com. 1990-92). Home: 1274 E Marconi Ave Phoenix AZ 85022-3232

LAST, MARIAN HELEN, social services administrator; b. L.A., July 2, 1953; d. Henry and Renee (Kahan) Last. BA, Pitzer Coll., 1975; postgrad., U. So. Calif., 1975-84; MS, Long Beach State U., 1980. Lic. marriage therapist. Coordinator City of El Monte, Calif., 1975-76, project dir., 1976—; pvt. practice psychotherapist Long Beach, Calif., 1982—; div. mgr. City of El Monte, 1982—; cons. U. So. Calif. Andrus Ctr., L.A., 1977-78; bd. dirs. Coord. Coun., City of El Monte, 1975—, Sr. Pres.'s Coun., 1982—; Congl. del. White House Conf. on Aging, 1995; chair Nutrition Focus Group, L.A. Co. Area Agy. On Aging, 1993—. Co-author rape survival guide, 1971. Dir., co-founder Rape Response Program, Pomona, San Gabriel Valley, Calif., 1971-80; cons. on sexual assault Pitzer Coll., Claremont, Calif., 1975-78; past pres. El Monte-South El Monte Coord. Coun. Recipient Susan B. Anthony award NOW, Pomona, 1976, Gold award Calif. Emergency Svcs. Assn., 1995. Mem. Am. Soc. on Aging, Calif. Assn. Sr. Ctr. Dirs. (dist. dir. XIII), Calif. Parks and Recreation Soc. (Profl. Citation award 1993), Calif. Assn. Marriage and Family Therapists, Emergency Resources Assn. (bd. dirs.), Women's Club, Civitan, Chi Kappa Rho Gamma. Democrat. Jewish. Office: City of El Monte 3120 N Tyler Ave El Monte CA 91731-3354

LAST, SUSAN WALKER, curriculum developer; b. Waterbury, Conn., Sept. 26, 1962; d. Harold Alfred and Mary (Alferie) Hull; m. Michael Allen Walker, Feb. 11, 1984 (div. July 1988); 1 child, Cassandra Mary; m. Robert Lee Last, Sept. 26, 1992. BS, Ind. U., 1983. Ctr. dir. Sylvan Learning Corp., Arlington, Tex., 1984-88, franchise cons., 1988-89, dist. mgr., 1989-90; coord. of program devel. Sylvan Learning Systems, Arlington, 1991—; trainer, cons. Charles R. Hobbs Corp., Salt Lake City, 1989—; cons. Highpointe, Arlington, 1988—. Author: (curriculum) Study Skills Program, 1990, Study Power Video, 1991, Basic Math Program (K-8), 1994, Adult Reading Program, 1993, ESL program, 1995. Mem., speaker Parents Without Ptnrs., Arlington, 1991. Mem. ASCD, Children and Adults with Attention Deficient Disorder, Nat. Coun. Tchrs. of Math., Nat. Coun. Tchrs. of English. Home: 3902 Wrentham Dr Arlington TX 76016-2746 Office: Sylvan Learning Systems 4101 W Green Oaks Blvd Ste 327 Arlington TX 76016-4463

LASTER-SPROUSE, CHARLINE HIGGINS, health care facility administrator, educator, family therapist; b. San Angelo, Tex., Jan. 13, 1942; d. Charles Cleophus and Eunice Maxine (Frey) Higgins; m. Marvin Earl Sprouse Jr., July 29, 1988; children: Marvin Earl III, Amber Leigh, Lisa Kauai, Carleen Danielle McGuffy, John Paul, Alicia Denise Slaton, Angela Desiree Cooke, Robin C.D. De La Garza. Student, West Tex. U., 1964-65, 80-81, Columbus (Ga.) Coll., 1978-79, U. Tex. Med. Br., 1981-82; MA, U. Houston, 1988; postgrad., Trinity U., 1996—. Internat. lic. drug and alcohol counselor; lic. profl. counselor, Tex.; cert. hypnobehavioral therapist, neurolinguistic programmer practitioner. Mgr., hostess and waitress Spencecliff Restaurants, Honolulu, 1965-67; office mgr. Polly Grigg Designs, 1966-68; psychiat. occupational therapist, technician N.W. Tex. Psychiat. Pavilion, Amarillo, 1968-74; career placement specialist Snelling & Snelling, Amarillo, 1971-72; psycho-social dysfunction specialist U.S. Army Med. Corps, Ft. Benning, Ga., 1974-78; dispatcher League City (Tex.) Police and Fire Depts., 1981-82; chiropractic trainer, office mgr. Clear Lake, Tex., 1981-82; property mgr. Houston, 1984-88; J.T.P.A. addictions counselor, life skills tchr. Ed White Youth Ctr., Seabrook, Tex., 1987-88; family addictions therapist, educator, dir. family restoration Chemical Dependency Ctr., Las Cruces, N.Mex., 1990-94; rehab. dir. The Profl. Assessment Outpatient Treatment Ctr., Las Cruces, 1991—; case analyst II TYC Bootcamp Sheffield (Tex.) Youth Leadership Acad., 1991-96; primary svc. worker supr. chem. dependency treatment program Gainesville (Tex.) State Sch., 1996—; co-owner Bootcamp Cons., 1995-96; presenter N.Mex. Gov.'s Conf., Las Cruces, 1990, Western N.Mex. U., Silver City, 1991; facilitator MVH Community Edn., Las Cruces, 1990-91; addictions counselor, developer family edn. program St. Mary's Hosp., Galveston, 1987-90. Co-author: Human Phallacies, 1988, Streatcare Named Codependency, 1989, Connecting-A Guide to Great Relationship, 1990, Love at the Drive-Through Window, 1991, Political Correctness Exposed-The Pirahna in Your Bathtub, 1995, Championship Group Workbook. Provider Support Group Families of Desert Storm Troops, Las Cruces, 1990-91, His Holy Name Cath. Apostolic Ch., Las Cruces, 1990-91. Mem. ACA, NAFE, NRA, Soc. Ams. for Recovery, Concerned Women for Am., Nat. Assn. Alcohol and Drug Abuse Counselors, Vietnam Vets Am. (pres. Las Cruces chpt.), Vietnam Vets War on Drugs (v.p.), Tex. Assn. for Counseling and Devel., Tex. Assn. Alcoholism and Drug Abuse Counselors, N.Mex. Alcohol and Drug Abuse Counselors, N.Mex. Counseling Assn., El Paso Profl. Growth Assocs., Christian Counselors of Tex., Am. Assn. Christian Counselors, Trinity Coll. and Sem. Alumni, Trinity Ctr. Conflict, Am. Correctional Assn., Am. Ctr. for Law and Justice, Independent Order of Foresters. Office: 12840 Hillcrest Ste H-100 Dallas TX 75230 also: 15889 Preston Rd Ste 1035 Dallas TX 75248 also: 3417 N Midland Dr Ste 1908 Midland TX 79707

LASTINE, BETH CHRISTINE, copywriter; b. Morristown, N.J., Nov. 21, 1967; d. Ronald Willis and Dolores Rae (Reindollar) Onnen; m. Doug Lyle Lastine, July 17, 1993. BA, Augustana Coll., 1990. Advt. asst. Fort Dodge (Iowa) Labs., 1990-91; proofreading editor Kragie Newell Advt., Des Moines, 1991-92; proofreader, copywriter Kirke-Van Orsdel, Inc., West Des Moines, 1992-94; copywriter ITA Group, Inc., West Des Moines, 1994—. Mem. Women in Comms. Inc. Democrat. Lutheran.

LATESSA, MARGARET MARY, accountant; b. Concord, Mass., Oct. 11, 1957; d. Edward Anthony and Olive Ruth (Cullinane) Lalli; m. James Gerard Latessa, Nov. 4, 1995. AS in Bus. Adminstrn., Middlesex C.C., Bedford, Mass., 1982; BS in Accountancy, Bentley Coll., 1988. Accounts payable processor Hillhaven Corp., Bedford, 1982-88, acctg. asst., 1988, field acct., 1988-89; sr. investment acct. Allmerica Fin., Worcester, Mass., 1989-96, accounts payable supr., 1996—. Leader Patriots Trail coun. Girl Scouts U.S.A., 1980-84; chmn. fin. com. Town of Maynard, Mass., 1990. Mem. Inst. Mgmt. Accts. (dir. comm. 1993-94, v.p. membership 1994-95, v.p. adminstrn. 1995-96, pres. 1996-97). Roman Catholic. Home: 9 Collins St Worcester MA 01606 Office: Allmerica Fin 440 Lincoln St Worcester MA 01653

LATHAM, ELEANOR RUTH EARTHROWL, neuropsychology therapist; b. Enfield, Conn., Jan. 12, 1924; d. Francis Henry and Ruth Mary (Harris) Earthrowl; m.Vaughan Milton Latham, July 20, 1946; children: Rebecca Ann, Carol Joan, Jennifer Howe, Vaughan Milton Jr. BA, Vassar Coll., 1945; MA, Smith Coll., 1947, Clark U., Worcester, Mass., 1974; EdD, Clark U., Worcester, Mass., 1979. Lic. psychologist, Mass. Guidance counselor Worcester Pub. Schs., 1967-74, sch. psychologist, 1975-80; pvt. practice neuropsychology Worcester, 1981—; postdoctoral trainee Children's Hosp.-Harvard Med. Sch., Boston, 1980-81; mem. staff The Med. Ctr. of Ctrl. Mass. Meml.-Hahnemann, Worcester, St. Vincent Hosp., Worcester; assoc. in pediats. U. Mass. Med. Ctr. and Med. Sch., Worcester, 1982—. Author: Neuropsychological Impairment in Duchene Muscular Dystrophy, 1985, Motor Coordination and Visual-Motor Development in Duchenne Muscular Dystrophy, 1991, Developmental Considerations in Educational Planning for Boys with Duchenne Muscular Dystrophy; contbr. chpt.: Children and Death, 1987. Mem. Internat. Neuropsychology Soc., Am. Psychol. Assn. Republican. Unitarian. Home: 59 Berwick St Worcester MA 01602-1442 Office: Vernon Med Ctr 10 Winthrop St Worcester MA 01604-4435

LATHAM, MARGARET PECK, former nurse, poet; b. Lexington, Mo., June 23, 1920; d. Herbert Massey and Frances McCoy (Sawyer) Peck; m. Ralph Wellington Latham, Jr., June 3, 1943; children: Susan L. Klein, Nancy Page, Stephen M. BS, Coll. William and Mary, 1941; M Nursing, Frances Payne Bolton Sch. Nursing, 1944. Office nurse Ventura, Calif., 1944-45. Author (poetry) The Poet's Domain, 1995, 96, The National Library of Poetry, 1996. Vol. Red Cross, Roslyn Heights, N.Y., 1960-62, Hospice of Piedmont, 1984-93; troop leader, cons. Girl Scouts, Roslyn Heights, 1953-62; foster grandparent, Charlottesville, Va., 1991-93. Mem. Boar's Head Sports Club. Democrat. Episcopalian. Home: 1715 King Mountain Rd Charlottesville VA 22901

LATHAM, PATRICIA SUZANNE, pathology and medicine educator; b. Annapolis, Md., Aug. 22, 1946. BS, Simmons Coll., 1968; MD, U. So. Calif., 1972. Diplomate Am. Bd. Pathology, Am. Bd. Internal Medicine. Fellow in hepatology YNHH; assoc. prof. pathology and medicine George Washington U. Med. Sch., Washington, 1992—. Home: 5008 Fulton St NW Washington DC 20016-3447

LATHROP, ANN, librarian, educator; b. L.A., Nov. 30, 1935; d. Paul Ray and Margaret (Redfield) W.; divorced; children: Richard Harold, John Randolph, Rodney Grant. BA in History summa cum laude, Ea. N.Mex. U., 1957; MLS, Rutgers U., 1964; PhD, U. Oreg., 1988. Cert. elem. tchr., Calif.; cert. libr., Calif; adminstrv. credential, Calif. Elem. sch. tchr. Chalfont (Pa.) Boro Sch., 1960-61, Livingston Elem. Sch., New Brunswick, N.J., 1961-63, Rosedale Elem. Sch., Chico, Calif., 1964-65; libr. Chico (Calif.) H.S., 1965-72, Princeton (Calif.) H.S., 1972-73, Santa Maria (Calif.) H.S., 1973-77; libr. coord. San Mateo County Office Edn., Redwood City, Calif., 1977-89; assoc. prof. Calif. State U., Long Beach, 1989-92, prof., 1993—, dir. Calif. Software Clearinghouse, Calif. State U. Long Beach. Author: Online Information Retrieval as a Research Tool in Secondary School Libraries, 1988; co-author: Courseware in the Classroom, 1983; editor: Online and CD-ROM Databases in School Libraries, 1989, The 1988-89 Educational Software Preview Guide, 1988, Technology in the Curriculum Resource Guides, 1988; editor, founder: (jours.) The Digest of Software Reviews: Education, 1983-86, Software Reviews on File, 1985-86; editor: (database) California Online Resources in Education, 1989-94, Technology in the Curriculum Online, 1995—; contbr. chpts. to books, articles to profl. jours. Mem. ALA, NEA, Am. Assn. Sch. Librs., Assn. State Tech. Using Tchr. Educators, Calif. Faculty Assn., Calif. Sch. Libr. Assn., Computer Using Educators, Internat. Soc. for Tech. in Edn. Office: Calif State U 1250 N Bellflower Blvd Long Beach CA 90840-0006

LATHROP, GERTRUDE ADAMS, chemist, consultant; b. Norwich, Conn., Apr. 28, 1921; d. Williams Barrows and Lena (Adams) L. B.S., U. Conn., 1944; M.A., Tex. Woman's U., 1953, Ph.D., 1955. Devel. chemist on textiles/Alexander Smith & Sons Carpet Co. Yonkers, N.Y., 1944-52; research assoc. textiles Tex. Woman's U., 1952-56; chief chemist Glasgo Finishing Plant div. United Mchts. & Mfrs., Inc., Conn., 1956-57; chief chemist Old Fort Finishing Plant div. United Mchts. & Mfrs., Inc., N.C., 1957-63; research chemist United Mchts. Research Ctr., Langley, S.C., 1963-64; lab. mgr. automotive div. Collins & Aikman Corp., Albemarle, N.C., 1964-78; chief chemist, lab. mgr. Old Fort Finishing Plant div. United Mchts., 1979-82. Treas. 1st Congl. Ch., Asheville, N.C., 1985-87, bd. deacons, 1990-93; tax-aide counselor to elderly IRS, 1984—, Am. Assn. Ret. Person, Widowed Person Svcs., Asheville-Buncombe County, Inc., 1990-91, pres. Widowed Persons Svcs., 1992—; active RSVP Land of Sky, 1989-92; pub. Rels. com. Swannanoa Valley, N.C., Am. Assn. Ret. Persons, 1984-92, v.p., 1992, treas., 1993-94. Recipient Nat. Cmty. Svc. award Am. Assn. Ret. Persons, 1989, 96, Widowed Person's Outstanding Individual Achievement award, 1994, Disting. Alumni award U. Conn. Sch. Family Studies, 1980-81, Woman of Yr. award, 1979, Bus. and Profl. Women's Club, Albemarle, Woman of Yr. award Bus. and Profl. Women's Club Asheville, 1980. Mem. ASTM (chmn. transp. fabrics on flammability com. 1973-75), Am. Chem. Soc. (emeritus), Am. Assn. Textile Chemists and Colorists (emeritus, sec., rsch. chmn., treas., vice chmn. 1962-64, chmn. edn. com. Piedmont sect. 1977-78), Bus. and Profl. Women's Club (chpt. pres. 1974-76), Iota Sigma Pi (emeritus mem.-at-large). Home and Office: PO Box 1166 Black Mountain NC 28711-1166

LATHROP, JENNIFER FARGO, audiologist; b. Corning, N.Y., Oct. 8, 1950; d. Jarvis Jerome and Gloria Mary (Christy) Fargo; m. Steve Cate, 1977 (div. 1983); m. John Walter Lathrop, Jan. 26, 1985; children: Laurel, Ellen. BA, U. Redlands, 1972; MA, Kent State U., 1973. Audiologist Behavioral Scis. Inst., Monterey, Calif., 1973; pvt. practice audiologist, 1973-79; audiologist, owner Pacific Hearing Svc., Los Altos, Calif., 1979—. Mem. adv. bd. Self Help for the Hard of Hearing; sec. Calif. Speech Pathologists and Audiologists in Pvt. Practice, 1989-91. Fellow Am. Acad. Audiology; mem. Am. Speech, Lang. and Hearing Assn. (cert. in audiology), Calif. Speech, Lang. and Hearing Assn., Calif. Acad. Audiology (treas. 1993—, chair 1995—), Audiology Assn. Calif. Democrat. Congregationalist. Home: 575 Los Altos Ave Los Altos CA 94022 Office: Pacific Hearing Svc 960 N San Antonio Ste 101 Los Altos CA 94022

LATIMER, ALLIE B., lawyer, government official; b. Coraopolis, Pa.; d. Lawnye S. and Bennie Latimer. BS, Hampton Inst., 1947; JD, Howard U., 1953, MDiv, 1986, DMin, 1988; LLM, Cath. U., 1958; postgrad., Am. U., 1960-61. Bar: N.C. bar 1955, D.C. bar 1960. Vol. in projects Am. Friends Service Com., N.J. and, Europe, 1948-49; correctional officer Fed. Reformatory for Women, Alderson, W.Va., 1949-51; personnel clk. NIH, Bethesda, 1953-55; realty officer Mitchell AFB, N.Y., 1955-56; with Office Gen. Counsel, GSA, Washington, 1957-76; chief counsel Office Gen. Counsel, GSA, after 1966, asst. gen. counsel, 1971-76, gen. counsel, 1977-87; asst. gen. counsel NASA, 1976-77; spl. counsel Gen. Svcs. Adminstrn., Washington, 1987—; past chmn. central office com. Fed. Women's Program, GSA; mem. membership and budget com. Health and Welfare Council, 1967-72. Bd. dirs. D.C. Mental Health Assn., pres., 1977-79; bd. dirs. Friendship House, Washington; elder Presbyn. Ch.; pres. Interacial Council, 1964-75; chmn. Presbyn. Econ. Devel. Corp., 1975-81; mem. governing bd. Nat. Council Chs. of Christ in U.S.A. Recipient GSA Sustained Superior Service award, 1959, Meritorious Service award, 1964, Commendable Service award, 1964, Pub. Service award, 1971, Outstanding Performance award, 1971, Presdl. Rank award, 1983, Disting. Service award, 1984. Mem. ABA, Nat. Bar Assn. (sec. 1966-74), Fed. Bar Assn., Washington Bar Assn., N.C. Bar Assn., Nat. Bar Found. (dir. 1970-71, pres. 1974-75), Hampton Alumni Assn. (pres. Washington chpt. 1970-71), Howard Law Alumni Assn. (v.p. 1962-63) alumni assns), Links (pres. Washington chpt. 1971-74, nat. v.p. 1976-80), Federally Employed Women (founder, 1st pres.). Home: 1721 S St NW Washington DC 20009-6117

LATIMER, HELEN, information resource manager, writer, researcher; b. Elizabeth, N.J.; d. Raymond O. and Minna A. Mercner; divorced; children: Alexander, Victoria. AB, Duke U.; MS in Journalism, Columbia U.; cert. in bus. adminstrn., Harvard-Radcliffe; MBA in Mktg., Am. U.; postgrad., U. Calif., Berkeley, Rutgers U.; MBA upgrade, Syracuse U., 1995. Instr. mktg. Am. U., Washington; mgr. info. resources Burdeshaw Assocs., Ltd., Bethesda, Md., 1985-94, assoc., 1994—; commr. Commn. for Women, Washington, 1996—; initiated publ. specialists program George Washington U., Washington; officer alumni bds. Harvard-Radcliffe Program in Adminstrn., Am. U.; comm., info. resource mgmt. cons., tech. editor MIT Servomechanisms Lab.; AA to editor Reinhold Pub. (former subs. McGraw-Hill); facilitator, subgroup on mktg. The White House Conf. on Libr. and Info. Svcs., 1991. Contbr. articles to newspapers and mags. Past leader Troop 1907, Girl Scouts Am.; mem. Troop 100 com. Boy Scouts Am. Named to D.C. Commn. for Women, 1996. Mem. Spl. Librs. Assn., Harvard Bus. Sch. Club D.C. (initiated admission of women, v.p., bd. dirs.).

LATIMER, MARGARET PETTA, nutrition and dietetics educator; b. Sacramento, Aug. 17, 1932; d. Rosario and Helen (Sclafani) Petta; m. Westford Ramos Latimer, June 18, 1978. BS, U. Calif., Berkeley, 1954; MA, Calif. State U., Sacramento, 1982. Registered dietitian, Calif.; life teaching credential, Calif. Therapeutic dietitian U. Calif. Med. Ctr., San Francisco, 1955-65; dietitian Roseville (Calif.) Community Hosp., 1966-67, Mercy San Juan Hosp., Carmichael, Calif., 1967-69; substitute tchr. San Juan Unified Sch. Dist., Sacramento, 1970-75, tchr. adult edn., 1971-74; instr. dietetics American River Coll., Sacramento, 1975-77, San Joaquin Delta Coll., Stockton, Calif., 1975-95; cons. dietitian, Sacramento, 1973-78. Mem. Am. Dietetic Assn., Nutrition Today, Calif. Dietetic Assn. (pres. Golden Empire dist. 1974-75), AAUW (gourmet chmn. 1981-82, editor AAUW Book of Favorite Recipes 1982), SOc. Nutrition Edn. Republican. Roman Catholic.

LATSIOS, BARBARA LYNN, government official; b. Phila., Jan. 25, 1954; d. Stephen and Helen Valentina (Matweychuk) Samereck; m. George Latsios, Aug. 29, 1976; 1 child, Cassandra. Clk., stenographer Nat. Park Svc., Phila., 1971-72, park ranger, 1972-79, supervisory park ranger, 1979-85, purchasing agt., 1985-87; contract specialist EPA, Phila., 1987-90, program analyst, 1990—. Mem. Nat. Contract Mgmt. Assn., AFL-CIO (sec. Local 2058 Phila. 1973-75, 2d v.p. 1976-79). Republican. Russian Orthodox. Office: EPA Region III 841 Chestnut St Bldg Philadelphia PA 19107-4414

LATTIMORE, JOY POWELL, preschool administrator; b. Goldsboro, N.C., Jan. 18, 1954; d. Albert and Zudora (Baldwin) P.; m. Vergel L. Lattimore, Dec. 16, 1978; children: V. Alston, Adam V., Alia Joy. BS in Early Child Edn., Barber-Scotia Coll., 1976; MEd in Early and Mid. Child Edn., The Ohio State U., 1977. Dir. alumni affairs Barber-Scotia Coll., Concord, N.C., 1977-79; tchra. Concord Mid. Sch., 1979-80; asst. dir. admissions Kendall Coll., Evanston, Ill., 1980-83; dir. pre-K program Dunbar Ctr. United Way Agy., Syracuse, N.Y., 1987-89; tchr. Hughes Magnet Sch., Syracuse, 1989-90; dir. Busy Bee Day Care, Westerville, Ohio, 1991—. Mem. race adv. com. United Way, 1995-96; vol. benefit com. Columbus Works. Mem. Nat. Assn. Edn. of Young Children, AAUW, NAFE, Internat. Reading Assn., Phi Delta Kappa. Methodist. Home: 610 Olde N Church Dr Westerville OH 43081 Office: Busy Bee Day Care 610 Olde N Church Dr Westerville OH 43081

LATZA, BEVERLY ANN, accountant; b. Pompton Plains, N.J., June 10, 1960; d. George and Helen Mae (Ryan) L. BA in Acctg., Bus. Adminstrn., Thiel Coll., 1982. Internal auditor Monroe Systems for Bus., Morris Plains, N.J., 1983-85; acct. Am. Airlines, Tulsa, 1985-86, Accountemps, Tulsa, 1986-87; credit investigator Demich Leasing, Inc., Kansas City, Mo., 1987-89; tax examining asst. IRS, Kansas City, Mo., 1989—. Vol., disaster action team mem. ARC, 1996—. Lutheran. Home: 13148 W 88th Ct Apt 141 Lenexa KS 66215-4923 Office: IRS 2306 E Bannister Rd Kansas City MO 64131-3011

LATZEL, LYNN MARINA, college administrator; b. Chgo., June 15, 1955; d. Frank William and Ruth Wyatt (Sieber) L. AA, Coll. DuPage, 1986; BA, Elmhurst Coll., 1988. Asst. dir. adult and transfer admissions Elmhurst (Ill.) Coll., 1993—, coord. internat. admissions, 1993—. Mem. ACLU, Assn. Internat. Educators, Ill. Assn. Coll. Registrars and Admission Counselors, Ill. Assn. Coll. Admission Counselors, U.S. Holocaust Meml. Mus. (founding mem.), Chgo. Geneal. Soc., Jewish Geneal. Soc., Mensa, Psi Chi, Phi Theta Kappa. Office: Elmhurst Coll 190 Prospect Ave Elmhurst IL 60126

LAU, CHERYL A., former state official. BM, Ind. U.; JD, U. San Francisco. Bar: 1986. Formerly dep. atty. gen. Nev. Motor Vehicles and Pub. Safety Dept., Carson City, Nev.; sec. of state, State of Nev. State of Nev., Carson City, 1991-94; gen. coun. U.S. Ho. of Reps., Washington, 1995—. Office: House of Reps 219 Cannon House Office Bldg Washington DC 20515

LAU, MICHELE DENISE, advertising consultant, sales trainer, television personality; b. St. Paul, Dec. 6, 1960; d. Dwyane Udell and Patricia Ann (Yri) L. Student, U. Minn., 1979-82. Pub. rels. coord. Stillwater (Minn.) C. of C., 1977-79; asst. mgr. Salkin & Linoff, Mpls., 1982, store merchandiser, sales trainer, 1982-83; rental agt. Sentinel Mgmt. Co., St. Paul, 1983-84; account exec. Community Svc. Publs., Mpls., 1984-85, frwy. news supr., 1985, asst. sales mgr., 1985-86; asst. sales mgr. St. Paul Pioneer Press Dispatch, 1986-91; pres. Promotional Ptnrs., Eden Prairie, Minn., 1991-96; on-air show host Home Shopping Network, Eden Prairie, 1996—; on-air personality Sta. WCCO II Cable TV Mpls., 1988-89, co-host Afternoon Midwest, 1989-93; co-host Home Shopping Show, host Minn. Voices, Fox 29, 1995; cons. U. Minn. Alumni mag., 1986-89. Author mechandising and sales tng. manuals. Fund-raiser sustaining program YMCA, Mpls., 1986, Jr. Achievement, St. Paul, 1988; cons. Muscular Dystrophy Assn., St. Paul, 1988-89; bd. dirs. St. Paul Jaycees. Mem. NAFE, Nat. Assn. Home Builders, Mpls. Builder Assn. (amb.), Metro-East Profl. Builders Assn. (spl. events com.), Advt. Fedn., The Newspaper Guild, Internat. Platform Assn., Speakeasy Club. Lutheran. Home: Bldg D # 101 4750 Dolphin Cay Ln S Saint Petersburg FL 33711

LAUBER, MIGNON DIANE, food processing company executive; b. Detroit, Dec. 21; d. Charles Edmond and Maud Lillian (Foster) Donaker. Student Kelsey Jenny U., 1958, Brigham Young U., 1959; m. Richard Brian Lauber, Sept. 13, 1963; 1 child, Leslie Viane (dec.). Owner, operator Alaska World Travel, Ketchikan, 1964-67; founder, owner, pres. Oosick Soup Co., Juneau, Alaska, 1969—. Treas., Pioneer Alaska Lobbyists Soc., Juneau, 1977—. Mem. Bus. and Profl. Women, Alaska C. of C. Libertarian, Washington Athletic Club. Author: Down at the Water Works with Jesus, 1982; Failure Through Prayer, 1983, We All Want to Go to Heaven But Nobody Wants to Die, 1988. Home: 321 Highland Dr Juneau AK 99801-1442 Office: PO Box 1625 Juneau AK 99802-0078

LAUBER, PATRICIA GRACE, writer; b. N.Y.C., Feb. 5, 1924; d. Hubert Crow and Florence (Walker) L.; m. Russell Frost III, Apr. 11, 1981. BA, Wellesley Coll., 1945. Rsch., writer Look Mag. Book Dept., N.Y.C., 1945-46; staff writer Scholastic Mags., N.Y.C., 1946-48, editor, 1948-54, freelance editor, 1954-56; freelance editor Challenge Books, Coward-McCann, N.Y.C., 1955-59; founding editor, editor-in-chief Science World, Street & Smith, N.Y.C., 1956-59; chief editor Science and Mathematics, The New Book of Knowledge, Grolier, N.Y.C., 1961-67; freelance editor Good Earth Books, Garrard, Scarsdale, N.Y., 1973-79; cons. editor Sci. Am. Books, N.Y.C., 1977-80; cons. Nat. Sci. Resources Ctr., NAS-Smithsonian Instn., 1992-94. Author numerous children's books including Volcano: The Eruption and Healing of Mount St. Helens, 1986 (Newbery honor Book 1987, N.Y. Acad. Scis. Hon. Mention 1987), From Flower to Flower: Animals and Pollination, 1986 (N.Y. Acad. Scis. Hon. Mention 1988), Dinosaurs Walked Here and Other Stories Fossils Tell, 1987, Snakes Are Hunters, 1988, Lost Star, the

Story of Amelia Earhart, 1988, Yellowstone, 1988, Meteors and Meteorites: Voyagers from Space, 1989, The News About Dinosaurs, 1989 (N.Y. Acad. Scis. Hon. Mention 1990), Living with Dinosaurs, 1989 (Orbis Pictus hon. mention Nat. Coun. Tchrs. English 1990), Seeing Earth from Space, 1990 (Orbis Pictus hon. mention Nat. Coun. Tchrs. English 1991), Summer of Fire, 1991, Great Whales-The Gentle Giants, 1991, Fur, Feathers, and Flippers, 1994, What Do You See?, 1994, How Dinosaurs Came To Be, 1996, Hurricanes, 1996, Flood: Wrestling with the Mississippi, 1996, others. Recipient award for Overall Contbn. to Children's Lit., Washington Post/ Children's Book Guild, 1983, Eva L. Gordon award Am. Nature Study Soc., 1988, Lit. award Cen. Mo. State U., 1989, Lifetime Achievement commendation Nat. Forum on Children's Sci. Books, Carnegie-Mellon U., 1992. Mem. PEN, The Authors Guild, Soc. Children's Book Writers. Democrat. Congregationalist. Office: care Scholastic Trade Books 555 Broadway New York NY 10012-3919

LAUCK, SARANAN MCCUNE, city commissioner, marketing professional; b. Piqua, Ohio, Aug. 3, 1940; d. James Augustus and Bernice Eileen (Morgan) McCune; m. Theodore Edward Lauck, Dec. 30, 1961; children: Liz-Beth, Deanna, Ronice, Patricia. Student, Fla. State U., 1958-60; BA in Bus. Mgmt., Eckerd Coll., 1987. Exec. sec. Fla. Power Corp./Fla. Progress, St. Petersburg, 1981-89, mgr. spkrs. bur., 1989-90, govtl. coord., 1990-94; dir. mktg. and sales Pollution Prevention Svcs., Tampa, Fla., 1994-95; commr. City of St. Petersburg Beach, Fla., 1990—; sales adminstr. Linn and Assocs., St. Petersburg, 1995—; trustee Fire Pension Bd., St. Petersburg Beach, 1992-96; author, pub. slide presentation Hurricane Preparedness, 1990. Bd. dirs. YMCA, West Bend, Wis., 197-74, Jr. Woman's Club, West Bend, 1963-74, United Way, West Bend, 1971-74, Keep South Pinellas Beautiful, 1991-96; participant St. Petersburg Beach Vol. Response; mem. Barrier Islands Govtl. Coun., 1990—. Recipient Leadership Fla. award Fla. C. of C., 1996. Mem. Fla. League Cities (trustee workers compensation 1994—, trustee 1990—, Leadership Fla. award 1996), St. Petersburg Beach Area C. of C., Gulf Beaches Hist. Soc., Kappa Alpha Theta. Republican. Roman Catholic. Home: 650 79th Ave Saint Petersburg Beach FL 33706 Office: City of St Petersburg Beach 7701 Boca Ciega Way Saint Petersburg Beach FL 33706

LAUDER, ESTÉE, cosmetics company executive; b. N.Y.C.; m. Joseph Lauder (dec.); children: Leonard, Ronald. LLD (hon.), U. Pa., 1986. Chmn. bd. Estée Lauder Inc., 1946—. Author: Estée: A Success Story, 1985. Named One of 100 Women of Achievement Harpers Bazaar, 1967, Top Ten Outstanding Women in Business, 1970; recipient Neiman-Marcus Fashion award, 1962; Spirit of Achievement award Albert Einstein Coll. Medicine, 1968; Kaufmann's Fashion Fortnight award, 1969; Bamberger's Designer's award, 1969; Gimbel's Fashion Forum award, 1969; Internat. Achievement award Frost Bros., 1971; Pogue's Ann. Fashion award, 1975, Golda Meir 90th Anniversary Tribute award, 1988; decorated chevalier Legion of Honor France, 1978; medaille de Vermeil de la Ville de Paris, 9, 1979; 4th Ann. award for Humanitarian Service Girls' Club N.Y., 1979; 25th Anniversary award Greater N.Y. council Boy Scouts Am., 1979; L.S. Ayres award, 1981; Achievement award Girl Scouts U.S.A., 1983; Outstanding Mother award, 1984; Athena award, 1985; Pres. award Cosmetic Exec. Women, 1989, Neiman-Marcus Fashion award, 1992; honored Lincoln Ctr., World of Style, 1986; 1988 Laureate Nat. Bus. Hall of Fame. Office: Estée Lauder Cos 767 Fifth Ave New York NY 10153-0002*

LAUDER, VALARIE ANNE, editor, educator; b. Detroit, Mar. 1; d. William J. and Murza Valerie (Mann) L. AA, Stephens Coll., Columbia, Mo., 1944; postgrad. Northwestern U. With Chgo. Daily News, 1944-52, columnist, 1946-52; lectr. Sch. Assembly Svc., also Redpath lectr., 1952-55; freelance writer for mags. and newspapers including N.Y. Times, Yankee, Ford Times, Travel & Leisure, Am. Heritage, 1955—; editor-in-chief Scholastic Roto, 1962; editor U. N.C., 1975-80, lectr. Sch. Journalism, 1980—; gen. sec. World Assn. for Pub. Opinion Rsch., 1988-95; nat. chmn. student writing project Ford Times, 1981-86; pub. rels. dir. Am. Dance Festival, Duke U., 1982-83, lectr., instr. continuing edn. program, 1984; contbg. editor So. Accents mag., 1982-86. Mem. nat. fund raising bd. Kennedy Ctr., 1962-63; bd. dirs. Chapel Hill Mus., Inc. Recipient 1st place award Nat. Fedn. Press Women, 1981; 1st place awards Ill. Women's Press Assn., 1950, 1951. Mem. Pub. Rels. Soc. Am. (treas. N.C. chpt. 1982, sec. 1983, v.p. 1984, pres.-elect 1985, pres. 1986, chmn. council of past pres., chmn. 25th Ann. event 1987, del. Nat. Assembly 1988-94, S.E. dist. officer, nat. nominating com. 1991, 1st Pres.'s award 1993), Women in Communications (v.p. matrix N.C. Triangle chpt. 1984-85), N.C. Pub. Rels. Hall of Fame Com., DAR, Soc. Mayflower Desc. (bd. dir. Ill. Soc. 1946-52), Chapel Hill Hist. Soc. (bd. dir. 1981-85, 94—, pres. 1996—, chmn. publs. com. 1980-85), Chapel Hill Preservation Soc. (bd. trustees 1993-96, nominating com. 1994), N.C. Press Club (3d v.p. 1981-83, 2d v.p. 1983-85, pres. 1985, 1st pl. awards 1981, 82, 83, 84), Univ. Woman's Club (2d v.p. 1988), The Carolina Club, The Nat. Press Club. Office: U NC Sch Journalism and Mass Comm CB 3365 Chapel Hill NC 27599-3365

LAUDERDALE, KATHERINE SUE, lawyer; b. Wright-Patterson AFB, Ohio, May 30, 1954; d. Azo and Helen Ceola (Davis) L. BA in Soviet Studies, Ohio State U., 1975; JD, NYU, 1978. Bar: Ill. 1978, U.S. Dist. Ct. (no. dist.) Ill. 1978, Calif. 1987. Assoc. Schiff, Hardin & Waite, Chgo., 1978-82; dir. bus. and legal affairs Sta. WTTW-TV, Chgo., 1982-83, gen. counsel, 1983—, also v.p., sr. v.p., gen. counsel legal and bus. affairs, 1993—; acting sr. v.p. Prodn. Ctr., 1994; sr. v.p. New Ventures, 1995—. Mem. Lawyers Com. for Harold Washington, Chgo., 1983; bd. dirs. Midwest Women's Ctr., Chgo., 1985-94; active Chgo. Coun. Fgn. Rels., 1981—, mem. fgn. affairs com., 1985—; pres.'s mem. nat. adv. coun. on pub. affairs Ohio Stae U., 1994—; mem. U. Chgo. Women's Bd., 1996—. mem. ABA, Chgo. Bar Assn. (bd. dirs. TV Prodns., Inc. 1986—), Lawyers for Creative Arts (bd. dir. 1984—), ACLU (bd. dirs. 1987-94), Nat. Acad. TV Arts and Scis., NYU Law Alumni Assn. Midwest (mem. exec. bd. 1982—), The Ohio State U. Pres.'s Nat. Adv. Coun. on Pub. Affairs (Chgo. com., 1994—), The U. Chicago Women's Bd., 1996—. Democrat. Office: Sta WTTW-TV 5400 N Saint Louis Ave Chicago IL 60625-4623

LAUDERDALE, VICKI BUNTING, elementary education educator; b. Geneva, Ill., July 23, 1936; d. William Emerson and Nell (McMillen) Bunting; m. William Burt Lauderdale, June 21, 1958 (div. Mar. 1983); children: Burt Emerson, Jennifer Bea. BS in Home Econs., U. Ill., 1958; MEd, Auburn U., 1978, EdD in Reading, 1989. Cert. elem. and secondary tchr., Ala. Tchr. home econs. and sci. East Lansing (Mich.) Jr. H.S., 1961-63; reading tchr. Auburn (Ala.) Pub. Schs., 1978-83; instr. So. Union State Jr. Coll., Opelika, Ala., 1984; computer coord., tchr. Eufaula (Ala.) City Sch. System, 1985-91; asst. prof. Troy State U., Montgomery, 1991-96, assoc. prof., 1996—; cons. high risk grant program Troy State U., Montgomery, 1992-95; adv. bd. Ctrl. Ala. Region Insvc. Ctr., Montgomery, 1991—; cons. computer video prodn. Troy State U., 1986. Contbr. articles to profl. publs. Judge tchr. awards Montgomery County PTA, 1992, 93; conf. on technology Gov.'s Office, Montgomery, 1994. Mem. Internat. Reading Assn., Ala. Reading Assn. (dir., membership 1982—), Ala. Coun. for Technology Edn. (treas. 1985-92), Post Secondary Reading Coun., Phi Delta Kappa, Delta Kappa Gamma. Democrat. Methodist. Office: Troy State U Montgomery PO Drawer 4419 Montgomery AL 36103

LAUENSTEIN, ANN GAIL, librarian; b. Milw., Nov. 8, 1949; d. Elmer Lester Herbert and Elizabeth Renatta (Bovee) Zaeske; m. Mark Lauenstein, Aug. 16, 1986; 1 child, Maria. MA, U. Wis., 1972. Asst. libr. U. Wis., Wausau, 1972-73; cataloger, libr. MacMurray Coll., Jacksonville, Ill., 1973-76; corp. libr. Anheuser-Busch Cos. Inc., St. Louis, 1976—; facilitator Anheuser-Busch Quality Circle, St. Louis, 1984—. Treas. Friends of Kirkwood Libr., 1986—; mem. adv. coun. Sch. Info. Sci. U. Mo., 1987—. Mem. AAUW (editor jour. 1981-84, publicity chmn. 1985-87, scholar 1984), Spl. Librs. Assn. (network liaison 1981-83, chmn. employment com. 1983-84, chmn. hospitality com. 1984-85, membership chmn. 1988-89, newsletter editor 1992-94, advt. editor 1995—), St. Louis Regional Libr. Network (coun. 1981-83), St. Louis Online Users Group, Women in Bus. Network (adv. panel 1980-82, 86-87, programs planner 1987-88, asst. coord. 1988-89), Ohio Coll. Libr. Consortium Acquisitions Users Coun. Office: Anheuser-Busch Co Inc 1 Busch Pl Saint Louis MO 63118-1849

LAUER, JEANETTE CAROL, college dean, history educator, author; b. St. Louis, July 14, 1935; d. Clinton Jones and Blanche Aldine (Gideon) Pentecost; m. Robert Harold Lauer, July 2, 1954; children: Jon, Julie, Jeffrey. BS, U. Mo., St. Louis, 1970; MA, Washington U., St. Louis, 1973, PhD, 1975. Assoc. prof. history St. Louis Community Coll., 1974-82; assoc. prof. history U.S. Internat. U., San Diego, 1982-90, prof., 1990-94; dean Coll. of Arts and Scis., San Diego. Author: Fashion Power, 1981, The Spirit and the Flesh, 1983, Til Death Do Us Part, 1986, Watersheds, 1988, The Quest for Intimacy, 1991, 2d edit., 1993, No Secrets, 1993, The Joy Ride, 1993, For Better of Better, 1995, True Intimacy, 1996, Intimacy on the Run, 1996. Woodrow Wilson fellow, 1970, Washington U. fellow, 1971-75. Mem. Am. Hist. Assn., Orgn. Am. Historians. Democrat. Presbyterian. Home: 18147 Sun Maiden Ct San Diego CA 92127-3102

LAUFMAN, LESLIE RODGERS, hematologist, oncologist; b. Pitts., Dec. 13, 1946; d. Marshall Charles and Ruth Rodgers; m. Harry B. Laufman, Apr. 25, 1970 (div. Apr. 1984); children: Hal, Holly; m. Rodger Mitchell, Oct. 9, 1987. BA in Chemistry, Ohio Wesleyan U., 1968; MD, U. Pitts., 1972. Diplomate Am. Bd. Internal Medicine and Hematology. Intern Montefiore Hosp., Pitts., 1972-73, resident in internal medicine, 1973-74; fellow in hemotology and oncology Ohio State Hosp., Columbus, 1974-76; dir. med. oncology Grant Med. Ctr., Columbus, 1977-92; practice medicine specializing in hematology and oncology Columbus, 1977—; bd. dirs. Columbus Cancer Clinic; prin. investigator Columbus Cmty. Clin. Oncology Program, 1989—. Contbr. articles to profl. jours. Mem. AMA, Am. Women Med. Assn. (sec./treas. 1985-86, pres. 1986-87), Am. Soc. Clin. Oncology, Southwest Oncology Group, Nat. Surg. Adjuvant Project for Breast and Bowel Cancers. Office: 393 E Town St # 109 Columbus OH 43215-4741 also: 8100 Ravine'S Edge Ct Worthington OH 43235

LAUGHAM-MCNALLY, GAY PATTERSON, nutritionist; b. Beaumont, Tex., Nov. 1, 1945; d. Bert Raymond and Virginia Estelle (Wood) Patterson; m. Lindsay L. Laugham, Dec. 28, 1978 (div. Sept. 1983); 1 child, Annalee; m. Charles Richard McNally, July 11, 1995. BS, U. Tex., 1978. Cons., owner New You Workshop, San ANtonio, 1978-86; clin. nutritionist pvt. practice, Dallas, 1986—; instr. Tyler (Tex.) Jr. Coll., 1974-78; cons. in field. Vol. ARC, 1969-72; bd.dirs. RESTART, Dallas, 1989-92; charter mem. NAt. Mus. Women in Arts, Washington, 1987—; sustaining mem. Jr. League San Antonio, 1978—. Fellow Am. Coun. Applied Clin. Nutrition; mem. Am. Preventive Medicine Assn., Internat. Assn. Clin. Nutritionists (nat. v.p. 1994—, state pres. 1994—). Home: 5909 Luther Ln #1807 Dallas TX 75225 Office: Exec Profiles 3102 Oak Lawn Ste 810 Dallas TX 75219

LAUGHLIN, BARBARA L., bank executive. Past exec. v.p. Seaman's Bank for Savs., N.Y.C.; now exec. v.p. First Empire State Corp., Buffalo, N.Y. Office: First Empire State Corp One M & T Plaza Buffalo NY 14240*

LAUGHTON, DORIS ELIZABETH, artist; b. S.I., N.Y., Aug. 18, 1951; d. Frank Gordon and Ernestine Elizabeth (Accettola) L.; m. Martin L. Smith, June 20, 1990. BA, Drew U., 1973; student, Parsons Sch. Design, N.Y.C., 1974-79, Inst. Arch. & Urban Studies, 1976-79, Internat. Ctr. Photography, N.Y.C., 1982, N.Y. Acad. Art, 1985. owner, designer, mfr. Personal Adornment, 1985—; rschr. film It Came From Hollywood, 1979-83; designer Nat. Assn. Display Industries Showrooms, 1977-79; illustrator Holt, Rinehart, Winston Joy of Crafts, 1974. One-person shows include Commenda dei Cavalieri di Malta, Centignano, Italy, 1991, Galleria Miralli, Palazzo, Ghigi, Viterbo, Italy, 1993, Galleria Steffanoni d'Arte Comtemporanea, Milan, 1993, Open Press, Denver, 1996; two-person shows include Galerie Taub, Phila., 1984, Gallery 10, Ltd., Washington, 1987; exhibited in group shows include Lever House Gallery, 1968, Sandos Gallery, Morristown, N.J., 1970, 71, Korn Gallery, Madison, N.J., 1973, 78, 90, Mark. A. Gallery, Teaneck, N.J., 1982, Marie Pellicone Gallery, N.Y., 1983, Hudson Valley '85, Poughkeepsie, N.Y., 1985, Hudson Valley '86, Poughkeepsie, 1986, N.Y. Open Ctr., N.Y.C., 1988, Fondazione d'Arte Moderna Vittorio Caporella, Rome, 1993, Areoporto Maremma, Montalto di Castro, Italy, 1994, LDDI, Alley Painting, Denver, 1995, CSK Gallery, Denver, 1995, Univ. Meml. Ctr. Art Gallery, U. Colo., Boulder, 1995; subject of articles and revs. popular mags. and jours. Home and Studio: Doris Laughton Studio PO Box 696 Bailey CO 80421

LAUGHTON, KATHARINE L., career officer; b. L.A., Dec. 9, 1942; d. Herman and Mary-Alice (McCunniff) H.; m. Robert James Laughton, Oct. 16, 1972. Attended, Vassar Coll., 1960-61; BA, U. Calif., Riverside, 1964; dist. grad., Navy War Coll., 1986. Dep. dir. mgmt. info. svcs. Military Sealift Command, 1977-79; commdg. officer Military Sealift Command, Pt. Canaveral, 1979-82; program mgr. Naval Data Automation Command, 1982-84; spl. asst. inspector gen. U.S. Navy, 1984-86; head ADP svcs. commdr. n chief U.S. Atlantic, Norfolk, Va., 1986-87; commander Navy Space Command, Dahlgren, Va., 1995—. Recipient medal of merit for excellence in tech. Armed Forces Communications & Elecs. Assn., 1991, Parsons award for scientific and Tech. progress Navy League, 1990. Mem. AFCEA (internat. v.p.), Vassar Club. Episcopalian. Office: Navy Dept. 5820 4th St Dahlgren VA 22448-5300*

LAUNDER, YOLANDA MARIE, graphic design director; b. Columbus, Ohio, Mar. 21, 1957; d. Wilbur Winfield and Julia Mary (Moretti) Reifein; m. David Paul Launder, Oct. 14, 1989; 1 child, Jonathan David. BFA in Design Comm., Tex. Tech. U., 1979. Graphic designer Perception, Inc., Chgo., 1980-81; graphic designer Source, Inc., Chgo., 1982-83, assoc. design mgr., 1983-84; sr. graphic designer Oscar Mayer Foods Corp., Madison, Wis., 1984-85, design mgr., 1986-88, group design mgr., 1989-95; assoc. dir., 1995—; lectr. Wis. Dept. Agr., Madison, 1988, Design Mgmt. Inst., Martha's Vineyard, Mass., 1991, Oscar Mayer Foods Corp., Women Career Devel., Madison, 1993-94, Philip Morris Packaging Roundtable, 1995. Co-inventor in field of Oscar Mayer Lunchables Packaging, 1989—. Sunday sch. tchr. St. Bernard's Ch., Dallas, 1973-75; evaluated high sch. portfolios Tex. Tech. U., Chgo., 1982-83; poll watcher David Patt Alderman campaign, Chgo., 1982; graphic design vol. Mental Health Assn Dane County, 1986, United Way of Wis., Madison, 1992. Recipient Snack Food Package of the Yr. award Food & Drug Packaging Mag., 1989, Sial D'or award Salon International de L'alimentation, Paris, 1990, Bronze award for Excellence in Packaging for Oscar Mayer Lunchables, The Nat. Paperboard Packaging Coun., 1990, Mktg. Creativity award Kraft U.S.A., 1992, 93. Mem. Women in Design/Chgo. (program dir. 1982-83, membership dir. 1983-84, pres. 1984-85), Madison Advt. Fedn. (Addy awards com. 1985, voluntary action com. 1986), Design Madison (programs com. 1989-92), Package Designers Coun. Internat., Design Mgmt. Inst. Office: Oscar Mayer Foods Corp 910 Mayer Ave Madison WI 53704-4256

LAUNIUS, BEATRICE KAY, critical care nurse, educator; b. Chisledon, Wiltshire, Eng., Dec. 14, 1954; came to the U.S., 1956; d. Wendell Arthur and Susie (Wright) L. Diploma, Charity Hosp. Sch. Nursing, New Orleans, 1975; BS in Biology, La. State U., Shreveport, 1990; BSN, Northwestern State U., 1996. RN, La.; CCRN, ANCC; cert. ACLS instr., pediatric advanced life support instr. Staff nurse surg. ICU Charity Hosp., New Orleans, 1976; staff nurse emergency room Schumpert Med. Ctr., Shreveport, 1975-76, 77-82, asst. head nurse surg. ICU, 1982-83, staff nurse surg. ICU, 1983-87; staff nurse surg. ICU La. State U. Med. Ctr., 1987-88, asst. supr. surg. ICU, 1988-90, supr. surg. ICU, 1990-92, critical care edn. coord., 1992—; spkr. in field. Mem. AACN (chpt. pres. N.W. La. 1994-96, spl. interest cons. for edn. region 12 1995-97, Reporter fellow 1993), Soc. for Crit. Care Medicine, Soc. Trauma Nursing, So. Nurses Rsch. Soc., Sigma Theta Tau Internat. Office: La State U Med Ctr 1501 Kings Hwy Shreveport LA 71103-4228

LAU-PATTERSON, MAYIN, psychotherapist; b. N.Y.C., May 13, 1940; d. Justin S. and Susan (Lee) Lau; m. Oscar H. L. Bing, Dec. 26, 1962 (div. Dec. 1974); children: David C., Michael H.; m. Michael Morrow Patterson, Nov. 8, 1989. BA, Goucher Coll., 1962; MA, George Washington U., 1966; postgrad., Boston Coll., 1977. Lic. psychologist, Mass.; lic. profl. counselor, Tex.; diplomate in managed mental health care; chem. dependency specialist, marriage and family therapist, criminal justice specialist; compulsive gambling counselor, hypnotherapist, Tex.; cert. criminal justice specialist. Psychologist children's unit Met. State Hosp., Waltham, Mass., 1966-67, clin. psychologist, 1967-68, prin. psychologist, 1968-70, chief psychologist 1970-76; chief psychologist South Cove Community Health Ctr., Boston, 1976-78; pvt. practice Newton, Mass., 1974-78, Gateway Counseling, Framington, Mass., 1975-78, Alamo Mental Health, San Antonio, 1978-92, The Patterson Relationship and Counseling Ctr., San Antonio, 1992—; clin. instr. psychology Dept. Psychiatry Harvard U. Med. Sch., Cambridge, MAss., 1974-76; instr. Tufts New Eng. Med. Ctr. Hosp., Boston, 1975-78, presenter Am. Acad. Child Psychiatry, 1973, 74. Contbr. articles to profl. jours. Office: Ste 200 3510 N St Marys St Ste 200 San Antonio TX 78212-3164

LAUREANO, ANNE BRIGA, management consultant; b. Bonn, Germany, Oct. 31, 1961. BS, U. So. Calif., 1981; MBA, U. Ill., Chgo., 1983. Ind. contractor various orgns., 1983-84, 85-87; with Arthur Young & Co., Sacramento, 1984-85; cons. The Warner Group, Woodland Hills, Calif., 1987-91, Delphin Internat., Monterey Park, Calif., 1991-92, Western Trade Adjustment Assistance Ctr., L.A., 1992-95; owner Laureano, Beverly Hills, Calif., 1995—. Bd. dirs. City Hearts, L.A., 1993—; com. chmn. Am. Cancer Soc., L.A., 1990; chair Ea. European com. L.A. Jr. Chamber, 1991-92. Mem. NAFE. Office: Laureano 235 S Gale Dr Ste 203 Beverly Hills CA 90211

LAURENT, J(ERRY) SUZANNA, technical communications specialist; b. Oklahoma City, Okla., Dec. 28, 1942; d. Harry Austin and M. LaVerne (Barker) Minick; m. Leroy E. Laurent, July 2, 1960; children: Steven, Sandra, David, Debra. AS in Tech. Writing, Okla. State U., 1986. With Technically Write, Mustang, Okla., 1960-75, acctg. adminstr., 1976-80, retail bus. mgr., 1981-87, owner, CEO, 1989-95; sr. tech. comms. specialist Applied Intelligence Group, Edmond, Okla., 1995—. Mem. Soc. Tech. Comm. (Superscript editor 1985, feature editor 1986, v.p., 1985, student chpt. pres. 1986, program coord. Okla. chpt. 1992-93, sec. 1993-94, v.p. 1994-95, state pres. 1995-96, other honors), Am. Bus. Women's Assn. (Dist. III v.p. 1988-89, conf. gen. chair 1992, editor Smoke Signals 1993-95, chmn. bd. dirs. Help Us Grow Spiritually 1993-95, Bull. award 1977, 81, 83, 84, 93, 95, Woman of Yr. 1977, 96, Bus. Assoc. of Yr. 1983-84). Democrat. Baptist. Home: 347 W Forest Dr Mustang OK 73064-3430

LAURICELLA, JANET MAY, association administrator; b. Fitchburg, Mass., Dec. 9, 1944; d. Ronald George and Pauline Janet (Perodeau) LeClair; m. David Lauricella, Apr. 3, 1987; children: Thomas II, Kristine, Beth, Robert, Heather, Cheryl. BA in Biology, Fitchburg State Coll., 1974, postgrad., 1974-80. Owner, operator nursery sch. Westminster, Mass., 1980-82; assoc. dir. Mental Health Assn. North Cen. Mass., Fitchburg, 1982-83; job specialist Jobs for Bay State Grads., Fitchburg, 1983-84; state dir. student activities Jobs for Bay State Grads., Boston, 1984-87; pres., chief profl. officer United Way Greater Gardner, Mass., 1987—. Contbr. articles to profl. jours. Mem., past pres. Oakmont Music Parents Assn., Ashburnham, Mass.; bd. dirs. Montachusett Coun. Girl Scouts U.S., 1987-90; dir. Emanuel Singers. Mem. NAFE, Rotary (pres. Gardner Club 1992), Greater Gardner C. of C. (Cmty. Svc. award for Leadership in AIDS). Lutheran. Office: United Way of Greater Gardner 161 Chestnut St # A Gardner MA 01440-2703

LAURIE, MARGARET SANDERS, retired English educator; b. Phila., Oct. 11, 1926; d. Joseph A. and Elizabeth Esther (Simmons) Sanders; m. Dominic Laurie, Jan. 30, 1945 (dec. Sept. 1995); children: Lucille M., Donald J. AB, Alfred U., 1948; MA, Niagara U., 1967. Engr. Remington div. I.E. DuPont, Ilion, N.Y., 1943-47; English tchr. Lewiston (N.Y.)-Porter H.S., 1961-63; English prof. Niagara County C.C., Sanborn, N.Y., 1966-87. Author: Centering: Your Guide to Inner Growth, 1995. Chmn. Lewiston Hist. Preservation Commn., 1988-92; pres. YWCA Niagara Falls, 1972-78. Named woman of yr. Niagara Falls Assn., 1972, woman of week WHLD Radio Sta., Niagara Falls, 1973, vol. of yr. Niagara Falls YWCA. Mem. Assn. Profl. Women Writers (v.p., pres. 1988—), Nat. League Am. Pen Women (v.p., pres. 1986-94). Republican. Roman Catholic. Home: 310 N 4th St Lewiston NY 14092

LAURIE, MARILYN, communications and computer company executive; b. N.Y.C.; d. Abraham and Irene Gold; m. Robert Laurie; children: Amy, Lisa. BA in English, Barnard Coll., 1959; MBA, Pace U., 1975. Responsible for environ. programs AT&T, N.Y.C., 1971-75, established electronic media program, 1975-78, exec. speeches, policy statements, 1978-79, advt. mgr., 1979-80; exec. dir. AT&T Bell Labs., 1980-83; v.p. AT&T Bell Labs., N.J., 1983-84, AT&T, N.J., 1984-85; group v.p. AT&T, 1986-87; exec. v.p. pub. rels. info. AT&T, Basking Ridge, N.J., 1987—; chmn. AT&T Found., N.Y.C. Author articles on environ. issues. Co-founder Environ. Action Coalition, 1970; co-originator Earth Day, 1970; bd. dirs. N.Y.C. Ballet, N.Y.C. Pub. Edn. Fund. Recipient Gold Key award Pub. Rels. News, WEAL award Women's Equity Action League, 1985, Women in Comm. Matrix award, 1988, Human Rels. award Am. Jewish Com., 1995; named to YWCA Acad. Women Achievers, 1984; named Pub. Rels. All Star, Inside Pub. Rels. Mag., 1993. Mem. Pub. Rels. Seminar (officer), Arthur Page Soc. (bd. officer), N.Y.C. Partnership (mem. exec. com.), Women's Forum. Office: AT&T 295 N Maple Ave RM 4342I3 Basking Ridge NJ 07920 also: AT&T Foundation 1301 Avenue Of The Americas New York NY 10019-6022*

LAURIE, PIPER (ROSETTA JACOBS), actress; b. Detroit, Jan. 22, 1932; 1 child. Motion picture debut in Louisa; other motion pictures include The Prince Who Was A Thief, Until They Sail, The Hustler (Acad. award nominee 1962), Carrie, 1976 (Acad. award nominee 1976), Tim, 1978, Return to Oz, 1985, Children of a Lesser God, 1986 (Acad. award nominee 1986), Appointment with Death, 1988, Other People's Money, 1990, Rich in Love, 1992, Trauma, 1993, Wrestling Ernest Hemingway, 1993, The Grass Harp, 1995; TV appearances include Days of Wine and Roses, Playhouse 90, The Deaf Heart, The Ninth Day, G.E. Theatre, Play of the Week, Hallmark Hall of Fame, Nova: Margaret Sanger, The Woman Rebel, In The Matter of Karen Ann Quinlan, Rainbow, Skag, The Thorn Birds, 1983; TV films include The Bunker, 1981, Love, Mary, 1985, Mae West, 1985, Promise, 1986, Toughlove, 1985, Lies and Lullabies, 1993, Shadows of Desire, 1994, Fighting for My Daughter, 1995; TV series: Twin Peaks, 1990-91 (Golden Globe award 1990), Traps, 1994; appeared Broadway play Glass Menagerie, 1965, off-Broadway plays Rosemary and the Alligators, 1961, The Innocents, 1971, Biography, 1980, Zelda, 1986, The Destiny of Me, 1992, The Cherry Orchard, 1993. Recipient Emmy award Acad. TV Arts and Scis., 1987; named Woman of Yr., Harvard U. Hasty Pudding, 1962. Mem. Acad. Motion Picture Arts and Scis. Address: William Morris Agy care Jonathan Howard 151 S El Camino Dr Beverly Hills CA 90212-2704*

LAUTENSCHLAGER, PEGGY ANN, prosecutor; b. Fond du Lac, Wis., Nov. 22, 1955; d. Milton A. and Patsy R. (Oleson) L.; m. Rajiv M. Kaul, Dec. 29, 1979 (div. Dec. 1986); children: Joshua Lautenschlager Kaul, Ryan Lautenschlager Kaul; m. William P. Rippl, May 26, 1989; 1 child, Rebecca Lautenschlager Rippl. BA, Lake Forest Coll., 1977; JD, U. Wis., 1980. Bar: Wis., U.S. Dist. Ct. (we. dist.). Pvt. practice atty. Oshkosh, Wis., 1981-85; dist. atty. Winnebago County Wis., Oshkosh, 1985-88; rep. Wis. Assembly, Fond du Lac, 1988-92; U.S. atty. U.S. Dept. of Justice, Madison, Wis., 1992—; apptd. mem. Govs. Coun. on Domestic Violence, Madison, State Elections Bd., Madison; bd. dirs. Blandine House, Inc. Active Dem. Nat. Com., Washington, 1992-93; com. Wis., 1989-92. Named Legislator of Yr., Wis. Sch. Counselors, 1992, Legislator of Yr., Wis. Corrections Coalition, 1992. Mem. Wis. Bar Assn., Dane County Bar Assn., Western Dist. Bar Assn., Fond du lac County Bar Assn., Phi Beta Kappa. Home: 1 Langdon St Apt 211 Madison WI 53703-1314

LAUVER, EDITH BARBOUR, nonprofit organization administrator; b. Tarrytown, N.Y., Mar. 2, 1933; d. John Alan and Adelaide Cora (Marden) Barbour; m. Robert Mitchell Lauver, Dec. 16, 1961; children: Alan Jackson, Donald Marden, Robert Barbour. BSN, Skidmore Coll., 1954; MA, Columbia U., 1957; postgrad., U. Ariz., 1980—. Sch. nurse, tchr. Pub. Schs. of Tarrytowns, North Tarrytown, N.Y., 1956-60; instr. St. Mary's Hosp. Sch. Nursing, Tucson, 1960-62; asst. prof. Coll. Nursing U. Ariz., Tucson, 1969-73, grad. teaching, rsch. assoc., 1980-85; asst. dir. nursing for pediatrics U. Ariz. Med. Ctr., Tucson, 1973-74; asst. adminstr. patient care Pima County/Kino Community Hosp., Tucson, 1974-77; asst. dir. nursing for staff devel. U. Ariz. Health Scis. Ctr., Tucson, 1978-80; dir. Interfaith Coalition for Homeless, Tucson, 1987—; mem. staff Thomas-Davis Clinic, Tucson, 1963-64; staff nurse surg. unit St. Joseph's Hosp., Tucson, 1964-65; adminstrv. asst. Tucson Ecumenical Coun., 1987; weekend relief staff nurse Handmaker Jewish Geriatric Ctr., Tucson, 1988-89. Active Accord Interfaith Soc. Action Group, 1983-94, St. Mark's Prebyn. Presch. and

Kindergarten, 1965-87, St. Mark's Presbyn. Ch., 1986—, elder, 1986-92; bd. dirs. Ariz. Coalition for Human Svcs., 1987—; Mobile Meals Tucson, Inc., 1976-87, sec. 1981-83; bd. dirs. Interfaith Coalition for Homeless 1987—; participant Ariz. Women's Town Hall, 1986, 87; mem. adv. bd. Tucson Met. Ministry's Cmty. Closet, 1988-92; bd. dirs. Tucson Met. Ministry, 1989-92; active various other civic activities. Mem. ANA, Ariz. League Nursing (bd. dirs. 1982-84, legis. liaison 1984-85, long-term care task force 1986), Ariz. Nurses' Assn. (fin. com. 1985-87, ANA del. 1986-87, dist. bd. dirs. 1982-84, pres.-elect, pres. dist. 1985-87, various coms.), Skidmore Coll. Alumni Assn., Sigma Theta Tau (mem. nat. fin. com. 1981-83, treas. local chpt. 1978-81, fin. com. 1974-88, pres.-elect 1990—, pres. 1988-92), Pi Lambda Theta, Phi Delta Kappa. Home and Office: 445 S Craycroft Rd Tucson AZ 85711-4549

LAUZON, MARCIA LOUISE, performing company executive; b. Evanston, Ill., July 17, 1948; d. Charles William and Marguerite Agnes (Postill) L.; m. Edward Anthony Schalk, Oct. 24, 1970 (div. Aug. 1992); children: Kenneth Charles Schalk, Elizabeth Margaret Schalk. BA in Theatre, Western Ill. U., 1970; MA, Columbia Coll., 1992. Sec. Arthur Andersen & Co., St. Charles, Ill., 1984-88; gen. mgr. Elgin (Ill.) Choral Union, 1988-90; adminstrv. asst., concert mgr. Glen Ellyn (Ill.) Childrens Chorus, 1990-91; exec. dir. Mont. Chorale, Great Falls, 1992—; bus. mgr. Elgin Childrens Chorus, 1989-91; adv. bd. Fox Valley Arts Coun., St. Charles, 1991-92. Bd. dirs. Elgin Choral Union, 1979-88; active People for the Am. Way, 1985—; chalice bearer, lector Episcopal Ch. of the Incarnation, Great Falls, 1994—. Follett fellow Columbia Coll., 1988. Mem. NOW, Am. Symphony Orch. League (profl. affiliate), l'Association des familles Lauzon d'Amerique (regional del. 1992—). Episcopalian. Home: 1600 4th Ave N Great Falls MT 59401

LAVAGNINO, AYN R., manufacturing engineer; b. Bangkok, Thailand, May 27, 1964; m. Albert M. Lavagnino, Aug. 7, 1994. BS in Materials Sci. and Engring., Rice U., 1986; MS in Materials Sci. and Engring., Stanford U., 1991. Materials scientist Mosaic Industries, Newark, Calif., 1989-91; math. and sci. tchr. Pinewood Sch., Los Altos Hills, Calif., 1991-95, chair math. dept., 1992-95; mfg. devel. engr. Hewlett-Packard, Palo Alto, Calif., 1995—; contest team coach Jr. Engring. Tech. Soc., Stanford, Calif., 1992-94; coach, advisor Santa Clara (Calif.) Valley Sci. and Engring. Fair, 1994. Coach, mem. Palo Alto (Calif.) Women's Ultimate Team, 1987-88; asst. coach U-19 Woodside (Calif.) Men's Select Soccer, 1986; counselor youth camp City Team Ministries, East Palo Alto, Calif., 1988; assoc. tchr. to learning disabled teenagers Rancho Santa Maria Children's Home, Mex., 1988. Horace Lucich Meml. fellow, 1994, Stanford Materials Sci. Tchr. fellow Stanford U., 1986-87; recipient Outstanding Tchr. award Santa Clara Valley Sci. and Engring. Fair, 1994, Best Craftsmanship award Santa Clara Valley Sci. and Engring. Fair, 1994. Presbyterian.

LAVALLEE, DEIRDRE JUSTINE, marketing professional; b. Woonsocket, R.I., June 14, 1962; d. Albert Paul and Margaret Justine (O'Brien) L. BS in Chem. Engring., U. R.I., 1984; MBA, U. Denver, 1995. Sales engr. NGS Assocs. Inc., Canton, Mass., 1985-87; mgr. dist. sales MKS Instruments Inc., Balt., also Boulder, Colo., 1987-96; sales and mktg. mgr. API divsn. MKS Instruments Inc., Phoenix, 1996—. V.p., bd. dirs. Nat. Conf. Standards Labs.; mem. adv. bd. Tex. State Tech. Coll. Mem. AIChE (sec. chpt.), Am. Soc. Materials, Am. Inst. Physics, Am. Vacuum Soc. Home: 845 13th St Boulder CO 80302-7503 Office: MKS Instruments Inc 5330 Sterling Dr Boulder CO 80301-2351

LAVALLEE-LOESCH, MICHELLE RENEÉ, counselor; b. Springfield, Mass., Jan. 1, 1970; d. Charles Raymond and Phyllis Ann (Abdow) LaVallee; m. Robert Kendrick Loesch, Oct. 6, 1995. BS, Am. Internat. Coll., 1991; MEd, Suffolk U., 1993. Cert. sch. counselor, 1993, adjustment counselor, 1994. Pers. asst. Abdow Corp., Springfield, Mass., 1983 93; counselor Ctr. for Human Devel., Springfield, 1993—; sch. counselor Ware (Mass.) H.S., 1995—; admissions asst. Russell Sage Coll., Troy, N.Y., 1987-88; rsch. and teaching asst. Am. Internat. Coll., Springfield, 1989-91; adjustment counselor Palmer (Mass.) H.S., 1994-95; entertainer Strawberry Prodns., Chicopee, Mass., 1992—. Mem. ACA, ASCD, APA, NOW, NEA, Am. Sch. Counselors Assn., We. Mass. Pers. and Guidance Assn., Mass. Sch. Counselor Assn., Mass. Tchrs. Assn., Ware Tchrs. Assn. Home: 25 Sherwood Rd Springfield MA 01119

LAVE, JUDITH RICE, economics educator; came to U.S., 1961; d. J.H. Melville and G.A. Pauline (Lister) Rice; m. Lester Bernard Lave, June 21, 1965; children: Tamara Rice, Jonathan Melville. BA in Econs., Queen's U., Kingston, Ont., Can., 1957-61; MA in Econs., Harvard U., 1964, PhD, 1967; LLD, Queen's U., 1994. Lectr., asst. prof. econs. Carnegie Mellon U., Pitts., 1966-73, assoc. prof., 1973-78; dir. econ. analysis Office of Sec., Dep. of Asst. Sec. Planning and Evaluation, Washington, 1978-79; dir. office of rsch. Health Care Fin. Adminstrn., Washington, 1980-82; prof. health econs. U. Pitts., 1982—, co-dir. Ctr. for Rsch. on Health Care, 1996—; cons. Nat. Study Internal Medicine Manpower, Chgo., 1976, Wash. State Hosp. Assn., 1984, Horty, Springer & Mattern, Pitts., 1984, Hogan and Hartson, Washington, 1989, Ont. Hosp. Assn., Conn. Hosp. Assn., 1991; cons. various agys. U.S. HHS (formerly U.S. HEW), 1971-89; mem. adv. panel Robert Wood Johnson Found., Princeton, N.J., 1983-84, 96—, Leonard Davis Inst., Phila., 1984, U.S. Congress, 1977, 82, 83—; com. mem. Inst. Medicine Coms., Washington, 1975-91, Project 2000 Commn. on Future of Podiatry, Washington, 1985-86. Edtl. bd. Wiley Series in Health Svcs., 1989-90, Health Svcs. Rsch., 1970-74, Inquiry, 1979-82, AUPHA Press, 1986, Jour. of Health Policy Politics and Law; co-author: Hospital Construction Act - An Evaluation of the Hill Burton Program, 1948-73, 74, Health Status, Medical Care Utilization and Outcome: A Bibliography of Empirical Studies (4 vols.) 1989, Providing Hospital Services, 1989; contbr. numerous articles to profl. jours. Mem. Prospective Payment Assessment Commn., 1993—, planning com. ARC, Pitts., 1986—; mem. rev. com. United Way, Pitts., 1988-90; bd. dirs. Craig Ho., Pitts., 1976-77. Woodrow Wilson fellow, 1961-62. Fellow Assn. Health Svcs. Rsch. (pres. 1977-88, bd. dirs. 1983-93); mem. Found. for Health Svcs. Rsch. (pres. 1988-89, bd. dirs. 1983—), Am. Pub. Health Soc., Am. Econ. Soc. (com. mem.), Inst. Medicine, Nat. Acad. Social Ins., Robert wood Johnson Found. (coun. on econ. impact of health sys. change 1996—). Democrat. Home: 1008 Devonshire Rd Pittsburgh PA 15213-2914 Office: U Pitts A649 Pub Health Pittsburgh PA 15213

LA VECCHIA, JEAN M., telecommunications executive. Sr. v.p. orgn. devel. So. New Eng. Telecom. Corp., New Haven. Office: So New Eng Telecom Corp 227 Church St New Haven CT 06510*

LAVELLE, PHILLIS D., real estate property manager; b. Johnstown, Pa., Nov. 17, 1948; d. Russell P. and Grace C. (Young) Daniel; m. Robert M. Lavelle, Dec. 11, 1971; children: Jacquelyn G., Robert D. BSN, U. Pitts., 1969, MPH, 1973. Cert. property mgr., Inst. Real Estate Mgmt. Pub. health nurse Allegheny County Health Dept., Pitts., 1971-72; team leader Vis. Nurse Assn. of Allegheny County, Pitts., 1973-74, supr., 1975-84; property mgr. Lavelle Real Estate, Inc., Pitts., 1984—. Sch. vol. Pitts. Pub. Schs., 1978-95; trustee, Pitts. Presbytery; treas. Grace Meml. Presbyn. Ch., Pitts. Presbyterian.

LAVENAS, SUZANNE, writer, editor, consultant; b. Buenos Aires, Dec. 17, 1942; came to U.S., 1955; d. Carlos Fernando and Mary (Sharp) Lavenas; m. Wesley First, Jan. 9, 1982. Student, Antioch Coll., 1960-64, 65-66. Computer programmer N.Y. Telephone, N.Y.C., 1966-68; prodn. editor, then copy editor Travel Weekly, N.Y.C., 1968-76, chief copy editor, 1976-79; mng. editor Indsl. Chem. News, N.Y.C., 1981-82; editor, writer, cons. N.Y.C., 1986—. Author numerous articles. Mem. Overseas Press Club, Soc. Silurians. Republican. Episcopalian. Home: 236 Edgemere St Montauk NY 11954-5249

LAVENSON, SUSAN BARKER, hotel corporate executive, consultant; b. L.A., July 26, 1936; d. Percy Morton and Rosalie Laura (Donner) Barker; m. James H. Lavenson, Apr. 22, 1973; 1 child, Ellen Ruth Stanclift. BA, Stanford U., 1958, MA, 1959; PhD (hon.), Thomas Coll., 1994. Cert. gen. secondary credential tchr., Calif. Tchr. Benjamin Franklin Jr. High Sch., San Francisco, 1960; tchr. French dept. Lowell High Sch., San Francisco, 1960-61; v.p. Monogram Co., San Francisco, 1961-62; creative dir. Monogram Co., N.Y.C., 1973-86; pres. SYR Corp., Santa Barbara, Calif., 1976-89; ptnr. Lavenson Ptnrs., Camden, Maine, 1989—; mem. commn. on co-edn. Wheaton Coll., Norton, Mass., 1985-87; mem. Relais et Chateaux, Paris, 1978-89; cons. World Bank Recruit Divsn., 1993. Author: Greening of San Ysidro, 1977 (Conf. award 1977). Trustee Camden Pub. Libr., 1989-95, v.p. 1991-93; vice chair bd. trustees Thomas Coll., Waterville, Maine; trustee Atlantic Ave. Trust; founding pres. Maine chpt. Internat. Women's Forum, 1991—; mem. Coun. of Advisors Coll. of the Atlantic. Bar Harbor, Maine, 1996—. Mem. Advice Inc., Camden Yacht Club, Stanford Alumni Assn., Com. of 200 (treas. 1985-86), Phi Delta Kappa. Home and Office: 12 Norumbega Dr Camden ME 04843-1746

LAVID, JEAN STERN, school director; b. Roanoke, Va., Jan. 4, 1943; d. Ernest George and Marianne (Stamm) Stern; m. Aug. 26, 1968 (div. 1989); children: Nathan, Eric, Craig, Brian, Laura. BA, Coll. William and Mary, 1965; MA, Wichita State U., 1986, specialist degree, 1989. Cert. permanent tchr. German, N.Y.; cert. supt., bldg. adminstr., Kans., Colo., N.Y., Va., N.H., Ohio, Ariz., Pa., Ky. Rural community devel. vol. Peace Corps, Turkey, 1965-67; tchr. German, Spanish and English Kenmore (N.Y.)-Tonawanda Sch. Dist., 1967-70; tchr. German Grand Island (N.Y.) Sch. Dist., 1978-82, coord. adult edn., prin., 1982; grad. rsch. asst. Wichita (Kans.) State U., 1984-86, instr. German, 1985; asst. prin. Unified Sch. Dist. 259, Wichita, 1986-88; supt., high sch. prin. Unified Sch. Dist. 314, Brewster, Kans., 1988-91; supt. Unified Sch. Dist. 271, Stockton, Kans., 1991-93; dir. edn. Computer Learning Ctr., Alexandria, Va., 1993; sr. dir. distbr. Nat. Safety Assocs., Lorton, Va., 1993-96; dir. KinderCare Learning Ctr., Alexandria, 1994; dir. edn. Gesher Jewish Day Sch. of No. Va., Fairfax, 1994; dir. Kinder Care Learning Ctr., Vienna, Va., 1994-95, Children's World Learning Ctr., Lake Ridge, Va., 1995—; mem. sch. community adv. coms., N.Y., Kans., 1975-86; chmn. Com. To Revise Fgn. Lang. Curriculum, Grand Island, 1981-83; judge Kans. Fgn. Lang. Competition, 1987. Contbr. numerous articles on ednl. leadership to profl. jours. Pres. Grand Island Food Coop., 1978-83, Waterford Food Coop., Wichita, 1983-88. mem. Am. Assn. Sch. Adminstrs., Assn. for Supervision and Curriculum Devel., Nat. Assn Secondary and Elem. Sch. Prins., Am. Assn. Tchrs. German, Kans. Assn. Sch. Adminstrs., Kans. Unitied Sch. Adminstrs., AAUW (active local, regional and state levels 1973—), Phi Kappa Phi, Phi Delta Kappa, Nat. Supts. Acad. Home: 9734 Hagel Cir Lorton VA 22079-4314 Office: Children's World Learning Ctrs 12781 Harbor Dr Woodbridge VA 22192

LAVIN, BERNICE E., cosmetics executive; b. 1925; m. Leonard H. Lavin, Oct. 30, 1947; children: Scott Jay, Carol Marie, Karen Sue. Student, Northwestern U. Vice chairperson of bd., sec.- treas. Alberto-Culver Co.; dir., v.p., sec.- treas. Alberto-Culver U.S.A., Inc.; sec.- treas., dir. Alberto-Culver Internat., Inc.; v.p., sec.-treas. Sally Beauty Co., Inc. Office: Alberto-Culver Co 2525 Armitage Ave Melrose Park IL 6016C 1125

LAVIN, LINDA, actress; b. Portland, Maine, Oct. 15, 1937; d. David J. and Lucille (Potter) L. BA, Coll. William and Mary, Williamsburg, Va., 1959. Debut: (Off-Broadway) Oh, Kay!, 1960, (Broadway) A Family Affairs, 1962; appearances in revues Wet Paint, 1965, The Game Is Up, 1965, The Mad Show, 1966; with nat. touring company On a Clear Day You Can See Forever, 1966-67; mem. acting company Eugene O'Neil Playwrights' Unit, 1968; other stage appearances include It's a Bird... It's a Plane... It's Superman, 1966, Something Different, 1967, Little Murders, 1969, Cop-Out, 1969, The Last of the Red Hot Lovers, 1969 (Tony nominee), Story Theatre, 1970, The Enemy is Dead, 1973, Love Two, 1974, The Comedy of Errors, 1975, Dynamite Tonite!, 1975, Six Characters in Search of an Author, Am. Repertory Theatre, Cambridge, Mass., 1983-84 season, Broadway Bound, 1986 (Tony award 1987), Gypsy, 1990, The Sisters Rosensweig, 1993, Death Defying Acts, 1995; film appearances: See You In The Morning, 1989, I Want to Go Back Home, 1989; star: (TV series) Alice, 1976-85 (Golden Globe award 1979); star and prodr.: (TV series) Room for Two, 1992—; prodr.: (PBS TV miniseries) The Sunset Gang, 1991; other TV appearances on Phyllis, Family, Rhoda, Harry O; TV movies include: The Morning After, 1974, Like Mom, Like Me, 1978, A Matter of Life and Death, 1981, Another Woman's Child, 1983, A Place To Call Home, Lena: My One Hundred Children. Recipient Sat. Rev., Outer Critics Circle awards for Little Murders, Theater World award for Wet Paint. Office: Metropolitan Talent Agy 4526 Wilshire Blvd Los Angeles CA 90010-3801*

LAVIN, ROXANNA MARIE, finance executive; b. San Antonio, Sept. 8, 1952; d. Teddy Harold and Cora Ann (Ames) Maddox; m. Michael Paul Lavin, July 11, 1971; children: Sharon Renai, Christopher Michael, Katherine Marie. Student, Ea. Mich. U., 1985, 86, 70; BBA magna cum laude, Cleary Coll., 1992; postgrad, Ctr. Mich. U., 1993, Madonna Univ., 1994; postgrad., U. Mich., 1996. Sales clk. Children's Fashion Shop, Livonia, Mich., 1970; bookkeeping clk. Ypsilanti (Mich.) Savs. Bank, 1970-73; receptionist, acctg. clk. Maize & Blue Properties, Ann Arbor, Mich., 1986-87; acctg. clk. Sensors, Saline, Mich., 1987; office supr., fin. mgr. Great Lakes Coll. Assn., Ann Arbor, 1988-94; fin., pers. mgr. Jackson (Mich.) Libr., 1994—, interim co-dir., 1995. Sec., treas. Old Mill Hills Assn., Pinckney, Mich., 1990-93; mem. Pinckney High and Mid. Sch. Parents, 1990-92; parent vol. Lincoln Cons. Schs., Ypsilanti, 1985-86; mem. Jackson County Literacy Coun. Recipient scholarship Ea. Mich. U., 1970. Mem. AAUW, Mich. Libr. Assn. Office: Jackson Dist Libr 244 W Michigan Ave Jackson MI 49201-2230

LAVINO, JANE PETRICK, museum curator, art educator; b. Boston, July 8, 1960; d. Stanley Roy and Mary (Buxton) Petrick; m. Edwin Lavino, Aug. 9, 1986; 1 child, Hillary. BA magna cum laude, Bowdoin Coll., 1982; cert., SUNY, New Paltz, 1984, U. Wyo., 1994. Cert. tchr., N.Y., Wyo. Photography and art tchr. The Knox Sch., St. James, N.Y., 1983-84; art dept. head, art tchr. Tuxedo Park (N.Y.) Sch., 1985-90; curator of edn. Nat. Mus. Wildlife Art, Jackson, Wyo., 1991—; instr., EMT Nat. Outdoor Leadership Sch., Lander, Wyo., summers 1985-90; part-time instr. Cmty. Visual Art Edn., Jackson, 1991—; part-time art educator Teton County Sch. Dist., Jackson, 1990-92. Named scholar-athlete Maine Hall of Fame, 1982, All-Am. Cross-Country Runner, NCAA, 1979, 80, 81. Mem. Nat. Art Edn. Assn., Wyo. Alliance for Art Edn., Phi Beta Kappa. Office: Nat Mus Wildlife Art PO Box 6825 2820 Rungius Rd Jackson WY 83002

LAVOIE, CHERYL AUDET, real estate agent, computer technician; b. Salem, Mass., Mar. 7, 1939; d. Albert Alfred and Dorothy Parker (Wilde) Audet; m. Wilfred George Lavoie, Aug. 6, 1961 (div. Jan. 1995); children: J. Andre, Elena R., Glenn A., J. Loron. BFA, Mass. Coll. Art, 1960. Lic. real estate agt., Va. Real estate agt. Weichert Realtors, Arlington, Va., 1993—. Sec. Arlington Art Ctr., 1973. Mem. VA. MAC Users Group. Home: 1608 W Abingdon Dr # 302 Alexandria VA 22314 Address: Weichert Realtors 4701 Old Dominion Dr Arlington VA 22207

LAVOIE, NOELLA, advertising agency executive; b. Rimouski, Que., Can., Dec. 25, 1953; d. Gerard Lavoie and Emma Ruest. Cert. in mktg., U. Laval, Quebec City, Que., Can., 1992. Media dir. Publim, Québec, 1981-85, account supr., 1985-87; rep. Radio Can., Québec, 1987-89, sales mgr., 1989; v.p. client svcs. Marketel, Québec, 1989-91, v.p., gen. mgr., 1991-94; pres., gen. mgr. Cargo Marketel, Québec, 1994—; cons. Theatre du Gros Mecano, Quebec, 1990-91, Quebec 2002, 1992. Mem. Ste-Foy C. of C., Québec Met. C. of C., Cercle de la Garnison, Lions (v.p. Québec Centre club 1989-92). Office: Cargo Marketel, 871 Chemin Saint-Louis, Québec, PQ Canada G1S 1C1

LAVOY, DIANNE ALLISON, physical education educator; b. Aurora, Ill., Aug. 12, 1955; d. Charles Miles and JoAnne Elizabeth (Doan) McDuffee; m. Richard C. LaVoy, July 17, 1981. BA in Edn., North Ctrl. Coll., 1991. Substitute tchr. McWayne Sch., Batavia High Sch., 1991-92, tchg. asst. spl. edn., 1992-93, tchr. phys. edn., 1993—, girls soccer coach, 1994—. Richter fellow North Ctrl. Coll., 1990. Mem. AAHPERD (del. nat. conv. 1991). Home: 552 Apache Dr Batavia IL 60510 Office: Batavia High Sch 1200 W Wilson Batavia IL 60510

LAW, CAROL JUDITH, medical psychotherapist; b. N.Y.C., May 1, 1940; d. Aldo and Jennie (Feldman) Settimo; m. Perry J. Koll, Dec. 26, 1967 (div. Nov. 1974); 1 son, Perry J.; m. Edwin B. Law, June 1, 1979. BA, Upsala Coll., 1962; postgrad., Rutgers U., 1964-66; MA, Columbia Pacific U., 1982, PhD, 1984. Diplomate Am. Bd. Med. Psychotherapy. Pers. dir. Hotel Manhattan, N.Y.C., 1961; supr. social work Essex County, Newark, 1962-67; exec. dir. USO, Vung Tau, South Vietnam, 1967-68; dir. Dept. Health and Rehab. Svcs., Pensacola, Fla., 1968-79; therapist, tchr. Franciscan Renewal Ctr., Scottsdale, Ariz., 1982-92; pvt. practice Scottsdale, 1982-92; drug free workforce cons. Pensacola C. of C., Fla., 1992—; pres. Drug Free Workplaces, Inc., 1993—; mem. Healthy Start of N.W. Fla.; dist 1 chmn. Alcohol, Drug Abuse and Mental Health Planning Coun. Mem. state adv. bd. Parents Anonymous, Phoenix, 1982; chmn. Gov.'s Adv. Commn. Drugs and the Elderly, Tallahassee, 1978; pres. Jaycettes, Pensacola, 1969; chmn. social com. United Way Fund, Pensacola, 1977; mem. adv. bd. USO, Pensacola, 1973, H.R.S. Dist. 1 Community Collaboration Project; trustee ORME Sch. Fellow Am. Acad. Polit. and Social Sci.; mem. Am. Assn. Pub. Adminstrs., Pensacola Country Club, Escambia County Drug Court Coalition, Fla. State C. of C. (drug issues com.,), Nat. Drugs Don't Work (Fla. rep.), Partnership for a Drug Free Fla. (bd. dirs.), Pensacola Downtown Rotary. Roman Catholic. Home: 3386 Chantarene Dr Pensacola FL 32507-3586

LAW, CLARENE ALTA, innkeeper, state legislator; b. Thornton, Idaho, July 22, 1933; d. Clarence Riley and Alta (Simmons) Webb; m. Franklin Kelso Meadows, Dec. 2, 1953 (div. July 1973); children: Teresa Meadows Jillson, Charisse Meadows Haws, Steven Riley; m. Creed Law, Aug. 18, 1973. Student, Idaho State Coll., 1953. Sec., sub. tchr. Grand County Schs., Cedar City, Utah, 1954-57; UPI rep. newspaper agy. Moab, Utah Regional Papers, Salt Lake City and Denver; auditor Wort Hotel, Jackson, Wyo., 1960-62; innkeeper, CEO Elk Country Motels, Inc., Jackson, Wyo., 1962—; rep. Wyo. Ho. of Reps., Cheyenne, 1991—, chmn. house travel com., 1993—, mem. bank bd. State of Wyo., 1991—; bd. dirs. Jackson State Bank, Snow King Resort. Chmn. sch. bd. dirs. Teton County Schs., Jackson, 1983-86. Named Citizen of Yr. Jackson C. of C., 1976, Bus. Person of Yr. Jackson Hole Realtors, 1987, Wyo. Small Bus. Person SBA, 1977. Mem. Wyo. Lodging and Restaurant Assn. (pres., chmn. bd. dirs. 1988-89, Big Wyo. award 1987), Internat. Leisure Hosts (bd. dirs. Phoenix chpt. 1991-94), Soroptimists (charter), BPW (Woman of Yr. 1975). Republican. Mem. LDS Ch. Home: Box 575 43 W Pearl Jackson WY 83001 Office: Elk County Motels Inc 43 W Pearl Jackson WY 83001

LAW, JANET MARY, music educator; b. East Orange, N.J., Mar. 8, 1931; d. Charles and Mary Ellen (Keavy) Maitland; m. William Howard Law, Dec. 13, 1952; children: Robert Alan, Gail Ellen. Lic. Practical Nurse, St. Barnabas Sch., 1971; BA magna cum laude, Fairleigh Dickinson U., Rutherford, N.J., 1981; tchr. tng. course, Westminster Choir Coll., 1990—, Queens U., Canada, 1993. Registered Suzuki tchr., Suzuki piano tchr., traditional piano tchr. Staff nurse psychiat. unit St. Barnabas Med. Ctr., Livingston, N.J., 1972-78; office nurse, asst. to pvt. physician North Arlington, N.J., 1978-79; dir., owner B Sharp Acad., Rutherford, N.J., 1979-83; founder, tchr. piano music preparatory div. Fairleigh Dickinson U., Rutherford, 1983-89; founder, coord. piano divsn. Garden State Acad. Music, Rutherford, N.J., 1989-94; tchr. piano divsn. Garden State Acad. Music, Rutherford, 1989-95; Suzuki piano coord., tchr. Suzuki piano program, coord. Suzuki piano divsn. Montclair (N.J.) State U., 1994—. Author: Keyboard Kapers, 1983; inventor music games, 1983. Mem. Music and Performing Arts Club, Profl. Music Tchrs. Guild N.J. Inc., Suzuki Assn. of the Ams. Home: 169 Hillcrest Dr Wayne NJ 07470-5629 also: Montclair State U Valley Rd and Normal Ave Upper Montclair NJ 07043

LAW, MELINDA JANE, adult nurse practitioner; b. Columbus, Ohio, Dec. 22, 1951; d. L. E. and Jane (Hinton) L.; m. J.D. Russell, Feb. 18, 1994; children: Emily Talbot, Ashley Talbot. BSN, Kent State U., 1973. RN, N.Mex.; cert. adult nurse practitioner. Camp nurse WGM Inc. Anchorage Alaska, Brooks Range, Alaska, 1978; asst. supr. cmty. health Anchorage Alaska, 1978-82; adult nurse practitioner William Talbot, M.D., Albuquerque, 1983-86, Health Care for the Homeless, Albuquerque, 1986-91, Steven Hsi, M.D., Albuquerque, 1991—; pres. bd. dirs. S.W. Maternity Ctr., Albuquerque, 1984-86; preceptor BSN Students, U. N.Mex., 1992—. Mem. N.Mex. Nurse Practitioner Coun. Episcopalian. Office: Steven Hsi MD 717 Encino Pl NE Albuquerque NM 87102

LAW, NANCY ENELL, school system administrator; b. South Gate, Calif., Jan. 12, 1935; d. Frank Ronald Cruickshank and Grace Margaret (Wright) Brotherton; m. George Otto Enell, Aug. 26, 1955; children: George, Grace; m. Alexander Inglis Law, Feb. 1, 1987. BS, U. So. Calif., 1956, MEd, 1961, PhD, 1977. Tchr. El Monte (Calif.) City Schs., 1956-58, Pasadena (Calif.) City Schs., 1958-62; from tchr. to project cons. Fullerton (Calif.) Elem. Sch. Dist., 1966-76; evaluation specialist San Juan Unified Sch. Dist., Carmichael, Calif., 1976-84; from dir. evaluation svcs. to adminstr. accountability Sacramento (Calif.) City Schs., 1984—; officer divsn. H Am. Ednl. Rsch. Assn., 1995—. Mem. Phi Delta Kappa. Home: 9045 Laguna Lake Way Elk Grove CA 95758-4219 Office: Sacramento City Schs 520 Capitol Mall Sacramento CA 95814-4704

LAW, SARA ANN LUDWIG, occupational therapist, organization executive; b. Bklyn., Apr. 1, 1948; d. Meyer and Miriam (Zimmerman) Ludwig; m. P. Law, June 1, 1969 (div. Oct. 1977); 1 child, Daniel Aaron. BS, SUNY, Buffalo, 1969; MS, D'Youville Coll., 1990. Registered occupl. therapist. Occupl. therapist E.J. Meyer Meml. Hosp., Buffalo, N.Y., 1970-74; sr. occupl. therapist Erie County Med. Ctr., Buffalo, 1974-78, supr. occupl. therapy, 1978-81; dir. occupl. therapy Vis. Nursing Assn. Buffalo, 1981-83, patient svc mgr. rehab., 1983 87; v.p. rehab. Blind Assn. Western N.Y., Buffalo, 1987—; asst. clin. prof. SUNY, Buffalo, 1973—, adj. clin. instr. Sch. Nursing, 1980—, clin. rep. to health rels. profl. exec. com., 1980-81, profl. adv. bd. rehab. nursing program, 1985-89; adj. clin. faculty dept. occupl. therapy Erie C.C., 1976—; mem. adv. bd. tchrs. of visually impaired program P'Youville Coll., Buffalo, 1987—; cmty. cons. Fred Sammons, Inc., Burr Ridge, Ill., 1974—; occupl. therapy cons. N.Y. State Divsn. Am. Cancer Soc., Buffalo, 1978; utilization rev. bd. Episcopal Ch. Home, Buffalo, 1980—; profl. adv. com. Long Term Home Health Program, Episcopal Gen. Cert. Home Health, Buffalo, 1980—. Mem. Am. Occupl. Therapy Assn. (content reviewer home health practice guidelines 1986-87), Assn. Edn. and Rehab. of Blind, N.Y. State Occupl. Therapy Assn. (annual exhibit chair, state conf. 1976, 92).

LAWHON, SUSAN HARVIN, lawyer; b. Houston, Oct. 10, 1947; d. William Charles and Ruth Helen (Beck) Harvin; m. Robert Ashton, July 25, 1970 (dec. Dec. 1992); children: Bryan Ashton, Harvin Griffith. AB, Smith Coll., Northampton, Mass., 1970; MEd, U. Tex., 1973; JD, U. Houston, 1990. Bar: Tex. 1990, U.S. Dist. Ct. (so. dist.) Tex. 1991, U.S. Ct. Appeals (5th cir.) 1993. Tchr. Nat. Cathedral Sch., Washington, 1970-71, Austin (Tex.) Ind. Sch. Dist., 1973-74, Spring Branch Ind. Sch. Dist., Houston, 1974-76; assoc. Fulbright & Jaworski, LLP, Houston, 1990—. Editor-in-chief: Houston Jour. Internat. Law, 1989-90. Mem. devel. coun. Tex. Children's Hosp., Houston, 1986—; mem. devel. bd. U. Tex. Health Sci. Ctr., Houston, 1984-87; sponsor Children's Fund, Inc., Houston, 1979-87; bd. dirs. Houston Child Guidance Ctr., 1977-80; bd. dirs., treas., fin. v.p. Jr. League Houston, 1984-86; docent Bayou Bend, 1977-84. Mem. ABA, State Bar Tex., Houston Bar Assn., Houston Country Club, Smith Coll. Club (Houston) (Seven Coll fund rep. 1982-87). Episcopalian. Home: 6222 Holly Springs Dr Houston TX 77057-1137 Office: Fulbright & Jaworski LLP 1301 McKinney St Ste 5100 Houston TX 77010-3095

LAWHON, TOMMIE COLLINS MONTGOMERY, child development and family living educator; b. Shelby County, Tex., Mar. 15; d. Marland Walker and Lillian (Tinsley) Collins; m. David Baldwin Montgomery, Mar. 31, 1962 (dec. Aug. 1964); m. John Lawhon, Aug. 27, 1967; 1 child, David Collins. B.S., Baylor U., 1954; M in Home Econs. Edn. in Home Econs., Tex. Woman's U., 1964, Ph.D., 1966. Cert. tchr., Tex., home economist, family life educator. Tchr., Victoria Pub. Schs. (Tex.), 1954-55; stewardess, supr. Am. Airlines, Dallas/Fort Worth, 1955-62; prof. home econs. Ea. Ky. U., Richmond, 1966-67, U. North Tex., Denton, 1968—; profl. presenter Profl. Devel. Inst., U. North Tex., 1981-84, mem. faculty senate 1984-90, chmn. com. on coms., 1987-88, com. status of women, 1984-87, mem. faculty salary study com., 1989-95, chmn., 1989-91, mem. tradition com., 1989-95, recorder, 1989-91; bd. dirs. Univ. union, 1985-88, mem. Status of Women Com., 1984-87, mem. Com. on Coms., 1986-89, chmn. 1987-88, vice chmn., 1988-89, mem. student mentor com., 1990-96, mem. benefits com., 1994—, vice chair, 1994-95, mem. faculty senate mentor com., 1990-96. Co-author: Children are Artists, 1971; Hidden Hazards for Children and Families, 1982; editor: What to do with Children, 1974; Field Trips for Children, 1984; contbr. articles to profl. jours. Chmn., United Way North Tex. State U.,

1980-81; chmn. crusade Am. Cancer Soc., Denton County, 1982-83; chmn. nominating com. First Bapt. Ch., Denton, 1983-84, 84-85; advisor North Tex. Student Coun. on Family Rels., 1994—. Recipient Presdl. award Tex. Council on Family Rels., 1979, Fessor Graham award North Tex. State U., 1980, Svc. award Am. Cancer Soc., 1983, Outstanding Home Economists Alumni award Baylor U., 1985, Moore-Bowman award, 1994; named Honor Prof. North Tex. State U., 1975. Mem. Tex. Council on Family Rels. (pres. 1977-79, chmn. policy advisor com. 1986-88, nominating com. 1986-88, 94-96, chair 1994-96, mem. family life edn. com. 1994—), Denton Assn. for Edn. of Young Children (pres. 1970-72, 84-85, 85-86, v.p. 1986-87), Tex. Assn. Coll. Tchrs. (nominating com. 1988-89, 89-90, v.p. 1990-92, v.p. U. North Tex. chpt. 1987-88, pres. 1988-89, 89-90), Tex. Home Econs. Assn. (chmn. FLCD nominating com. 1983-84, chmn. child devel. and family rels. sect. 1988-90, sect. rep. THEA bd. 1989-90), Nat. Council on Family Rels. (com. 1982-83, cert. family life edn. com. 1996—), Nat. Assn. Early Childhood Tchr. Educators (mem. membership com. 1995—), North Tex. Home Econs. Inter-orgnl. Council (adviser 1983-85), Phi Delta Kappa (pres. local chpt. 1991-92), Alpha Iota/Phi Upsilon Omicron (advisor 1970-82, chmn. nat. com. 1984-87, nat. bd. dirs. edn. found. 1990-94, com. pubs. 1991-92, vice chair ednl. found. 1992-94). Democrat. Clubs: Tri D (v.p. Baylor U. 1953-54); Univ. Grad. (pres. Tex. Woman's U. 1965-66). Office: U North Tex Coll Edn Denton TX 76203

LAWLAH, GLORIA GARY, state legislator, educator; b. Newberry, S.C., Mar. 12, 1939; d. Eugene Calvin and Erline (Guess) Gary; m. John Wesley Lawlah III, 1960; children: John Wesley IV, Gloria Gene, Gary McCarrell. BS, Hampton U., 1960; MA, Trinity Coll., Washington, 1970; postgrad., George Washington U., 1968-81. Formerly mem. Md. Ho. of Dels.; mem. Md. State Senate, Annapolis, Md., 1991—; mem. Dem. State Cen. Com., 1982-86; mem. coordinating com. 26th Legis. Dist., Prince Georges, Md., 1982-87; mem. Black Dem. Council, Md. Bd. dirs. Nat. Polit. Congress Black Women, 1984-87, Coalition on Black Affairs, 1980-82, Pub. Access Cable Corp., Prince Georges City, 1980-85, Hillcrest-Marlow Planning Bd., Prince Georges City, 1982-87, Family Crisis Ctr., Prince Georges City, 1982-84; co-chair Rev. Task Force for Pub. Safety, Prince Georges City, 1982; del. Dem. Nat. Conv.; co-chair Prince Georges City Exec. 7th Councilmanic Dist. Campaign, 1982; mem. Ctr. for Aging Greater S.E. Community Found. Mem. Nat. Council Negro Women (life), NAACP (3d v.p. Prince Georges City chpt. 1980-82). Club: Links. Home: 3801 24th Ave Temple Hills MD 20748-3003 Address: State House 314 James Senate Bldg Annapolis MD 21401*

LAWLER-EVANS, PATRICIA ELLEN, nursing administrator; b. Mt. Kisco, N.Y., Aug. 12, 1957; d. Joseph James and Sally Eileen (Gincel) Lawler; m. Jeffrey Allen Evans, Oct. 3, 1981; 1 child, Laura Sylyea. BSN, Keuka Coll., Keuka Park, N.Y., 1979; postgrad., St. Josephs Coll., Standish, Maine, 1995—. RN. Staff nurse med.-surg. United Hosp., Portchester, N.Y., 1979-80; staff nurse ICU Rome (N.Y.) City Hosp., 1980-81; staff nurse ICU St. Elizabeth's Hosp., Utica, N.Y., 1981, charge nurse med.-surg., 1981-83; evening supr. Falmouth (Mass.) Home, 1983; charge nurse orthopedics Cape Cod Hosp., Hyannis, Mass., 1983-90; staff nurse home care Vis. Nurse Assn. of Ctrl. and Outer Cape Cod, South Dennis, Mass., 1990, nursing mgr., 1990—; faculty mem. Med. Edn. Systems, East Falmouth, Mass., 1988-90; owner History in the Making, 1994—; com. mem. creating computerized patient acuity system Cape Cod Hosp., Hyannis, Mass., 1986; mem. Dacum com. developing nursing curriculum Cape Cod C.C., Barnstable, 1988; developer series of lectures on orthopedic patients for Cape Cod Hosp., 1988. Mem. fundraising com. Alzheimer's Assn., Barnstable, 1994; usher, mem. com. on human sexuality First Luth. Ch., Barnstable, 1992—; civilian re-enactor First Mass. Vol. del of U.S. Christian Commn. Cavalry Co. B, 1992—. Republican. Lutheran. Office: Vis Nurse Assn Ctrl & Outer Cape Cod 434 Route 134 South Dennis MA 02660-3433

LAWLEY, ELIZABETH, artist; b. N.Y.C., Apr. 17, 1956; d. Robert K. and Anna (Tino) L.; m. Gary Basaraba, Dec. 17, 1984; 1 child, Cale Basaraba. BFA, Cooper Union U., 1976; MFA, Yale U., 1982. Two person show at Painting Ctr., 1996; exhibited in numerous group shows, including Beitzel Gallery, N.Y.C., 1981-85, Twining Gallery, N.Y.C., 1982-86, Nassau County Fine Arts, 1982. Dir. homeless advocacy orgn. Hands in Outreach, Nepal, 1994-96; co-founder non-profit gallery Painting Ctr., N.Y.C., 1992—; bd. dirs. Shire Village, Mass., 1991—; dir. children's summer cmty. program, Cummington, Mass., 1991-96. Fellow Greenshield Found., Montreal, Can., 1977, Alice Kimball English fellow Yale U., 1982.

LAWLEY, KAREN R., health and safety officer; b. Lakehurst, N.J., July 24, 1947; d. Marsden Jr. and Ruth (Nichols) L.; m. Steven A. Coval, July 20, 1985; 1 child, Elick M. BS, Pa. State U., University Park, 1969. Sr. rsch. technician Mass. Gen. Hosp., Boston, Mass., 1973-81; sr. rsch. asst. Harvard U., Cambridge, Mass., 1981-84; lab. coord. Harvard U., Cambridge, 1984-87, facilities coord. and safety officer, 1987-92, health and safety officer, 1992—. Contbr. articles to profl. jours. Recipient Outstanding Contbr. award Ctr. for Astrophysics, 1995. Office: 16 Divinity Ave Rm 151 Cambridge MA 02138-2020

LAWLIS, PATRICIA KITE, air force officer, computer consultant; b. Greensburg, Pa., May 5, 1945; d. Joseph Powell, Jr., and Dorothy Theresa (Allshouse) Kite; m. Mark Craig Lawlis, Sept. 17, 1976 (div. 1983); 1 child, Elizabeth Marie. BS, East Carolina U., 1967; MS in Computer Sci., Air Force Inst. Tech., 1982; PhD in Computer Sci., Ariz. State U., 1989. Cert. secondary math. tchr. Employment counselor Pa. State Employment Service, Washington, Pa., 1967-69; math. tchr. Fort Cherry Sch. Dist., McDonald, Pa., 1969-74; commd. 2d lt. USAF, 1974, advanced through grades to lt. col., 1994, data base mgr. Air Force Space Command, Colorado Springs, Colo., 1974-77, computer systems analyst, USAF in Europe, Birkenfeld, Germany, 1977-80, prof. computer sci. Air Force Inst. Tech., Wright-Patterson AFB, Ohio, 1982-86, 89-94, ret. 1994; computer cons., pres. C.J. Kemp Systems, Inc., Huber Heights, Ohio, 1983—; Ada cons., Ada Joint Program Office, Washington, 1984-94. State treas. NOW, Pa., 1973-74. Recipient Mervin E. Gross award Air Force Inst. Tech., 1982, Prof. Ezra Kotcher award, 1985. Mem. Computer Soc. of IEEE, Assn. Computing Machinery, Tau Beta Pi (v.p. Ohio Eta chpt. 1981-82), Upsilon Pi Epsilon. Office: CJ Kemp Systems Inc PO Box 24363 Huber Heights OH 45424-0363

LAWRENCE, ALICE LAUFFER, artist, educator; b. Cleve., Mar. 2, 1916; d. Erwin Otis and Florence Mary (Menough) Lauffer; m. Walter Ernest Lawrence, Sept. 27, 1941; 1 child, Phillip Lauffer. Diploma in art, Cleve. Inst. Art, 1938; BS in Art Edn., Case Western Res. U., 1938. Grad. asst. in art edn. Kent (Ohio) State U., 1939-40; art tchr. Akron (Ohio) and Cleve. Pub. Schs.; comml. artist B.F. Goodrich Co., Akron, 1942-44; sub. art tchr. Akron Pub. Schs.; sketch artist numerous events Akron, 1945-91. Author numerous poems. Mem. Cuyahoga Valley Art Ctr., Women's Art Mus., Akron Art Mus., 1963-94. Recipient 1st pl., 2d pl. in drawing, Butler Mus. Am. Arts, 1940-41, Cleve. Mus. Art, 1944. Mem. Woman's Art League Akron (sec. 1962), Ohio Watercolor Soc., Internat. Soc. Poets (life). Republican. Home: 861 Clearview Ave Akron OH 44314-2969

LAWRENCE, CHRISTINE ELIZABETH, counselor, consultant; b. Fairhaven, Mass.; m. Stephen Anthony Lawrence, Sr.; children: Stephen Anthony Jr., Shauna L. BA in History, U. Mass., Dartmouth, 1985; MEd in Counseling, Bridgewater State U., 1990. Cert. guidance counselor, Mass. Counselor Office for Job Partnership, New Bedford, Mass., 1985; job specialist Jobs for Bay State Grads., New Bedford, Mass., 1986-88; career counselor Displaced Homemakers, New Bedford, Mass., 1989-90; clinet svc. coord. Bristol C.C., Fall River, Mass., 1990—; owner, pvt. cons. SEEC Career Counselor, Fairhaven, 1990—; cons. Charlton Meml. Hosp., Fall River, 1994; sr. instr. Divsn. of Continuing Edn./Bristol C.C., 1993—. Mem. Am. Bus. Woman's Assn. (ednl. chair 1991-94, sec. 1995-96, v.p. 1996—).

LAWRENCE, DEBORAH JEAN, statistician; b. San Jose, Calif., June 25, 1960. BA in Math., San Jose State U., 1982; MS in Stats., Stanford U., 1985. Math. aide Info. Mgmt. Internat., Moffet Field, Calif., 1980-82; group engr. Lockheed Missiles and Space Co., Sunnyvale, Calif., 1982-89; total quality mgmt. mgr. Analog Devices, Inc., Santa Clara, Calif., 1989—; reengring. spl. interest group leader Coun. for Contiuous Improvement, 1994—, QS 9000 spl. interest group leader, 1995—. Author tech. papers. Mem. Am. Soc. for Quality Control (sr. mem., cert. engr.), Am. Statis. Assn. Office: Analog Devices Inc. 1500 Space Park Dr Santa Clara CA 95052

LAWRENCE, DEIRDRE ELIZABETH, librarian, coordinator research services; b. Lawton, Okla., Mar. 15, 1952; d. Herbert Thomas and Joan Roberta (McDonald) L. BA in Art History, Richmond Coll., 1974; MLS, Pratt Inst., 1979; postgrad., Harvard U., 1981-82. Prin. libr. mus. librs. and archives, coord. rsch. svcs. Bklyn. Mus., 1983—; head cataloging and tech. scvs. Mus. Fine Arts, Boston, 1980-83; mem. preservation task force Rsch. Librs. Group, 1985-91, steering com. 1986-88, art and architecture com.; mem. conservation/preservation adv. coun. Met. Reference and Rsch. Agy., N.Y., 1988-92; grant reviewer fed. and state agys.; cons. in field. Author: New York and Hollywood Fashion, 1986, Dressing the Part: Costume Sket, 1989, Modern Art--The Production, 1989, Culin: Collector and Documentor of the World He Saw, Fashion and How It Was Influenced by Ethnographic Collections in Museums, Native American Art and Culture: Documentary Resources, Access to Visual Images-Past and Present; contbr. articles to profl. jours. Mem. Art Librs. Soc. N.Am., Spl. Librs. Assn., Native Am. Art Studies Assn., Internat. Fedn. Libr. Assns. Office: Brooklyn Mus 200 Eastern Pky Brooklyn NY 11238-6052

LAWRENCE, ESTELENE YVONNE, transportation executive, musician; b. Lynch, Ky., Aug. 10, 1933; d. Samuel Coleridge and Florence Estelle (Gardner) Taylor; m. Otto Lee Lawrence, Sept. 14, 1957; children: Stuart, Neil, Adelbert. Student Fenn Coll., 1953-60, Cleve. Inst. Music, 1955-56, John Carroll U., 1977-78, Northeastern U., 1979-80; BA Cleve. State U., 1993. Stenographer Cleve. Transit System/Regional Transit Authority, 1951-76, tng. asst., 1976-78, pers. devel. asst., 1978-82, dist. adminstr., 1983-86; supr./mgmt. skills instr. RTA, 1976-86, dir. tng. and career devel., 1986-88. Dir. music Friendly United Baptist Ch., 1947-95; piano tchr., 1953-73; minister of music Mt. Nebo Baptist Ch., 1995—; pianist/organist Nat. Bapt. Conv., 1971, 80. Publicity chmn. Moses Cleve. Sch. PTA, 1965-75; audit chmn. RTA Main Office Credit Union, 1980-83; dist. sec. Boy Scouts Am., 1982-83; chmn. adv. bd. Baldwin Wallace Coll., 1984-88; mem. adv. bd. Cleve. Mgmt. Devel. Consortium, 1985-88; chief musician RTA Choir; mem. Cleve. Choral Union, 1992-96. Mem. Am. Choral Dirs. Assn., Cleve. Mgmt. Seminars (treas. 1979-81, pres. 1981-83), Conf. Minority Transp. Ofcls., Phi Kappa Gamma (pres. 1966-69), Mu Phi Epsilon (historian 1990-91, chorister 1991-92, pres. 1992-93), Alpha Kappa Alpha. Mem. A.M.E. Ch. Clubs: East 153d St. (v.p. 1980—), East Ky. Social. Home: 4066 E 153rd St Cleveland OH 44128-1926

LAWRENCE, EVELYN THOMPSON, retired music educator, researcher; b. Marion, Va., Nov. 13, 1919; d. John Emmett and Susie Barnett (Madison) Thompson; m. Joseph John Lawrence, Oct. 5, 1946; 1 child, Sheila Ann (dec.). BS in Edn., W. Va. State Coll., 1941; student, Va. State U., 1946, Hampton U., 1948; M of Music, U. Mich., 1952. Elem. sch. tchr., music tchr. Carnegie High Sch., Marion, Va., 1941-65; tchr. Marion Primary Sch., 1965-84; judge art, storytelling, and creative writing Smyth County Schs., Marion, Chilhowie, Va., 1984-96; rocking reader Smyth County Schs., Marion, 1994—; producer, dir. plays Supporters Enriched Edn. and Knowledge, Marion, 1983-92; music and recreation dir. Douglass Ctr., Toledo, Ohio, summer, 1953; instr. ch. music Va. Union U., Richmond, summer 1960, 61; judge Sherwood Anderson Lit. Contest, 1989-91. Author: Directoty of African-American Students and Teachers in all Smyth County Schools, 1906-1965. Organist and choir dir. Mt. Pleasant Meth. Ch., Marion, 1994—; bd. dirs. Blue Ridge Job Corps., Marion, 1994—; v.p., past pres. Church Women United, Marion, 1985-86. Recipient 2 nominations Tchr. of Yr. award, S.W. Va. Coun. of Internat. Reading Assn., Abingdon, Va., 1981, 82, Svc. to Youth aard Carnegie Sch. Alumni, Marion, 1983, Citizen of Yr. award Marion Rotary Club, 1985. Mem. AAUW (chmn. cultural rels. com. 1966-96), Alpha Kappa Alpha (1940—), Alpha Delta Kappa (tchrs. sor. 1987—). Home: 312 Broad St Marion VA 24354-2804

LAWRENCE, JEAN HOPE, writer, marketing consultant, film producer; b. Waukegan, Ill., Mar. 5, 1944; d. George Herbert and Hope Delinda (Warren) L.; 1 child, Kelsey Hope. BA, George Washington U., 1966. Tech. editor, Am. Chem. Soc., Washington, 1966; proposal writer Krohn-Rhodes Inst., Washington, 1966-67; legislative counsel Aerospace Industries Assn., Washington, 1967-82; v.p., co-owner Data Specific, Washington, 1985-86; pres. Angel Watch Prodn., 1992, Success Stories, 1996—. Contbg. editor: Communications Concepts, 1983-86; editor, pub., creator: (newsletters) Get It Done!, 1987-88, Cheap Relief, 1988—; film prodr. OMNIFAX, 1994. Mem. Washington Film and Video Coun. Mem. Washington Ind. Writers, Women's Direct Response Group, Women in Film and Video. Recipient Winner Bronze Telly award, 1995. Democrat. Methodist. Avocation: essayist. Address: 734 W El Alba Way Chandler AZ 85224

LAWRENCE, KELLY JOY, federal agency administrator; b. Amsterdam, N.Y., May 2, 1958; d. Carl Douglas and Patricia Louise (Brown) Pearson; m. Lawrence J. Lawrence, June 19, 1982; 1 child, Christopher Carl. BA in Orgnl. Adminstrn., Alaska Pacific U., 1994. Clk. U.S. Postal Svc., Anchorage, 1980-87, account rep., 1987-90, mgr. comml. accounts, 1990-92, mgr. postal bus. ctr., 1992—; coord. Postal Customer Coun., Anchorage, 1990-92. Dir. hospitality Am. Mktg. Assn., Anchorage, 1992-93; v.p. Bus. Profl. Women's Assn., Anchorage, 1991. With U.S. Army, 1976-79. Named Profl. Bus. Woman of Yr., Bus. Profl. Women's Orgn., 1991. Office: US Postal Svc 3201 C St Ste 505 Anchorage AK 99503-3934

LAWRENCE, LAUREN, psychoanalytical theorist, psychoanalyst; b. N.Y.C., June 26, 1950; d. Jack and Elaine (Gaumont) Soever; m. D. Henry Lawrence, June 24, 1972; 1 child, Graham. MA in Psychology, New Sch. for Social Rsch., 1993. Psychoanalyst N.Y.C., 1992—. Contbr. articles to profl. jours. Mem. N.Y. Psychoanalytic Soc. Home: 31 E 72d St New York NY 10021

LAWRENCE, LINDA HIETT, retired school system administrator, writer; b. Phoenix, July 26, 1939; d. Lydle and Hazeldell (Sutton) Hiett; children: Pamela Lee Reardon, Annabel Virginia Urrea. BA, U. Ariz., 1961; MA, Ariz. State U., 1985, EdD, 1986. Cert. sch. supt., prin., tchr., Ariz. Prin. Washington Elem. Sch. Dist. 6, Phoenix, 1980-83; prin. Dysart Unified Sch. Dist. 89, Peoria, Ariz., 1985-87, asst. supt., 1987-88; supt. Cottonwood Ariz. Oak Creek Sch. Dist. 6, 1988-91; cons., writer, 1991—; owner Lawrence Properties and Enterprises; adj. prof. No. Ariz. U., 1990-91. Author: Adventures in Arizona, 1991; co-author: History of Jerome and Verde Valley, 1991. Trustee Marcus J. Lawrence Hosp.; pres. bd. dirs. Children's Advocacy Ctr. NSF grantee for Math; recipient USC's 100 Outstanding Supts. award. Mem. AAUW, Ariz. Hist. Soc., Ariz. Ctr. for the Book, Sacred Heart Alumni Assn., Ariz. State U. Alumni Assn. Ariz. Humanities Coun., Phoenix Zoo, Friends of Our Bros. and Sisters, Phi Delta Kappa.

LAWRENCE, LOIS MARIE, art educator; b. Slaton, Tex., Jan. 6, 1928; d. Brent Gaston and Octavia Louis (Satterwhite) Thompson; m. Troy Odel Lawrence, Sept. 27, 1945; children: Teresa, Joni. BS, Tex. Tech U., 1970, MS, 1977. Art tchr., 1970-90; art textbook advisor, 1989. One woman shows include Sand Hills Mus., Monahans State Pk., 1965, South Plains Coll., Levelland, Tex., 1980, YWCA, Lubbock, Tex., 1996. Mem. Western Fedn., S.W. Watercolor, West Tex. Watercolor Soc. (pres., sec. 1985, news editor 1986, nat. show chmn. 1980, scholarship com. 1995-96), Lubbock Art Assn. (scholarship chair 1995-96).

LAWRENCE, MARILYN EDITH (GUTHRIE), association executive; b. Auburn, N.Y., Oct. 5, 1946; d. George Nelson and Marjorie Estelle (Field) G.; AAS, SUNY, Morrisville, 1966. Various secretarial positions, 1966-75; exec. asst. Northeastern Retail Lumbermens Assn., Rochester, N.Y., 1975-79, sr. v.p., Wellesley, Mass. and Rochester, 1979-86; placement specialist Renda Personnel Cons., Rochester, N.Y., 1986-89; exec. dir. Oil Heat Inst. Upstate N.Y., Rochester, 1989-92; owner Profl. Bus. Svcs., Newark, N.Y., 1992-94; program dir. Assn. Mgmt. Svc., Rochester, 1992-94; exec. dir. Internat. Mcpl. Signal Assn., 1994-95, Newark, N.Y., exec. dir., 1995—. Mem. Am. Soc. Assn. Execs. Republican.

LAWRENCE, MARY JOSEPHINE (JOSIE LAWRENCE), library official, artist; b. Carbondale, Pa., Mar. 9, 1932; d. Domenick Anthony and Teresa Rose (Zaccone) Gentile; m. John Paul Lawrence, Apr. 25, 1953 (dec. June 1977); children: Mary Josephine, Jane Therese, Susan Michele. BFA, Mass. Coll. Art, 1989; postgrad, Chelsea (Eng.) Sch. Art, 1989, San Pancrazio Art Sch., Tuscany, Italy, 1990, 91, 92; cert. in grad. studies, Guangzhou Acad. Fine Arts, China, 1993; postgrad., Md. Inst. Fine Art, Sorrento, Italy, 1994. Sales clk. Gorins, 5&10, Jordan Marsh, Boston, 1946-49; clk.-typist, sec. John Hancock Ins. Co., Boston, 1950-53; machine operator, quality control supr. Rust Craft Greeting Cards, Dedham, Mass., 1961-69; restaurant hostess Tony's Villa, Waltham, Mass., 1972-73; mus. sales clk., artist John F. Kennedy Libr., Boston, 1979-87, mgr. mus. store, supr., 1988—; tchr.'s asst. San Pancrazio Art Sch., 1992; guest appearance TAKE TWO cable TV, Channel 11, 1996. One woman shows include de Havilland Fine Art Gallery, Boston, 1993; exhibited in group shows including South Shore Arts Ctr., Cohasset, Mass., 1991, North River Arts Soc., Marshfield Hills, Mass, Boston Visual Artists Union, 1996; works in permanent collection Dr. James McDermott, Boston, 1996. Juror Quincy Art Assn., 1996. Recipient Outstanding Achievement awards Nat. Archives and Rsch. Adminstrn., 1989, 94, Svc. award, 1990, Hon. Mention award South Shore Arts Ctr., 1991, Best of Show award de Havilland Fine Art Gallery, 1992, Best of Show North River Arts Soc., 1994, Honorium Weymouth Art Assn., 1995. Mem. Boston Visual Artist Union, de Havilland Fine Art Gallery, South Shore Art Ctr., North River Arts Soc., Nat. Mus. Women in Arts (charter), Weymouth Art Assn. (honorium). Democrat. Roman Catholic. Office: John F Kennedy Libr and Mus Columbia Pt Boston MA 02125

LAWRENCE, PAULA DENISE, physical therapist; b. Ft. Worth, May 21, 1959; d. Roddy Paul and Kay Frances (Spivey) Gillis; m. Mark Jayson Lawrence, Apr. 20, 1985. BS, Tex. Women's U., 1982. Lic. phys. therapist, Tex., Calif. Sales mgr. R. and K Camping Ctr., Garland, Tex., 1977-82; staff physical therapist Longview (Tex.) Regional Hosp., 1982-83, dir. phys. therapy, 1983-87, dir. rehab. svcs., 1987-88; staff phys. therapist MPH Home Health, Longview, Tex., 1983-84; owner, pres. Phys. Rehabil. Ctr., Hemet, Calif., 1988—; mem. adv. com. div. health occupations Kilgore (Tex.) Coll., 1985-88; mem. profl. adv. bd. Hospice Longview, 1985-88. Bd. dirs. V.I.P. Tots. Mem. NAFE, Am. Phys. Therapy Assn., Calif. Phys. Therapy Assn., Am. Bus. Women's Assn. (v.p. 1987, 89, pres. 1990, Woman of Yr. 1988, 91), Assistance League Aux., Soroptimist (corr. sec. 1992, dir. 1993-95, sec. 1995-97), Hemet C. of C. (bd. dirs.), Psi Chi, Omega Rho Alpha. Home: 43725 Mandarin Dr Hemet CA 92544 Office: 901 S State St Ste 500 Hemet CA 92543-7127

LAWRENCE, RUTH ANDERSON, pediatrician, clinical toxicologist; b. N.Y.C.; d. Stephen Hayes and Loretta (Harvey) A.; m. Robert Marshall Lawrence, July 4, 1950; children, Robert Michael, Barbara Asselin, Timothy Lee, Kathleen Ann, David McDonald, Mary Khalil, Joan Margaret, John Charles, Stephen Harvey. BS in Biology summa cum laude, Antioch Coll., 1945; MD, U. Rochester, 1949. Internship and residency in pediatrics Yale New Haven (Conn.) Hosp., 1949-50; asst. resident in Medicine Yale New Haven (Conn.) Community Hosp., 1950-51; postdoctoral fellow Yale New Haven Hosp., 1951, chief resident newborn svc., 1951; cons. in medicine U.S. Army, Ft. Dix, N.J., 1952; from clin. instr. to sr. instr. in pediatrics U. Rochester, N.Y., 1952-64, assoc. resident, 1957-58, asst. prof., 1964-70, assoc. prof., 1970-85, prof. pediatrics, ob.-gyn., 1985—; rsch. pediatrician, Monroe County Health Dept., Rochester, 1952-58; dir. Finger Lakes Regional Poison Control Ctr., 1958—; chief nursery svc. Strong Meml. Hosp., Rochester, 1960-73, chief dept. pediatrics, The Highland Hosp., Rochester, 1960-91; rsch. in field. Author: (book with others) Caring for Your Baby and Young Child, 1991, What to Expect in the First Year, 1989, Breastfeeding: A Guide for the Medical Profession, 4th edit. 1994; editor various periodicals; contbr. numerous articles to profl. publs. Recipient Gold Medal award U. Rochester Alumni Assn., 1979, William Keeler award Rochester Safety Coun., 1982, Civic Contribution citation Rochester Safety Coun., 1984, Career Achievement award Girl Scouts U.S. of Genesee Valley, 1987, Rochester Diocesan award for women, St. Bernard's Inst., 1989, Albert David Kaiser medal, 1991, Chamber Civic Health Care award, 1996, numerous svc. awards; named Woman of Yr. Girl Scouts U.S. of Monroe County, 1968; hon. fellow Am. Sch. Health Assn., 1960, rsch. fellow Jackson Meml. Rsch. Labs., 1945. Fellow Am. Pediatric Soc., Am. Acad. Clin. Toxicology (trustee, chair com. on rsch. fellowship, com. sci. rev.); mem. Human Milk Banking Assn. N.Am. (adv. bd.), Nat. Acad. Sci. (subcom. on nutrition during lactation), Physicians for Social Responsibility, Acad. Breastfeeding Medicine (founding bd. dirs. 1994—), Safety Coun. Rochester and Monroe County (past pres.), Bd. of Life Line (past pres.), Alpha Omega Alpha. Roman Catholic. Office: U Rochester Sch Medicine 601 Elmwood Ave Rochester NY 14620

LAWRENCE, SALLY CLARK, academic administrator; b. San Francisco, Dec. 29, 1930; d. George Dickson and Martha Marie Alice (Smith) Clark; m. Henry Clay Judd, July 1, 1950 (div. Dec. 1972); children: Rebecca, David, Nancy; m. John I. Lawrence, Aug. 12, 1976; stepchildren: Maia, Dylan. Docent Portland Art Mus., Oreg., 1958-68; gallery owner, dir., Sally Judd Gallery, Portland, 1968-75; art ins. appraiser, cons. Portland, 1975-81; interim dir. Mus. Art Sch., Pacific Northwest Coll. Art, Portland, 1981, asst. dir., 1981-82, acting dir., 1982-84, dir., 1984-94, pres., 1994—; bd. dirs. Art Coll. Exch. Nat. Consortium, 1982-91, pres., 1983-84. Bd. dirs. Portland Arts Alliance, 1987—, Assn. Ind. Colls. of Art and Design, 1991—, pres., 1995—. Mem. Nat. Assn. Schs. Art and Design (bd. dirs. 1984-91, treas. bd. dirs. 1994—), Oreg. Ind. Coll. Assn. (bd. dirs. 1981—, exec. com. 1989-94, pres. 1992-93). Office: Pacific NW Coll of Art 1219 SW Park Ave Portland OR 97205-2430

LAWRENCE, SHARON, actress. Appeared in (TV series) NYPD Blue. Office: care Steven Bochco Prodns PO Box 900 Beverly Hills CA 90213*

LAWRENCE, SHIRLEY JOAN, graphic designer, artist; b. Mattoon, Ill., July 19, 1937; d. Paul Theodore and Regina Elizabeth (Moran) Wolke; m. Donald John Lawrence, Feb. 17, 1955; children: Debbie Jean, Randolph David. Student, U. Ill., Ea. U., Lakeland Coll. Graphic and advertisement designer Goodlife Chems., Effingham, Ill.; draftsman, art designer Best Homes, Effingham, Ill., Superior Equip., Mattoon, Fedders Corp., Effingham; graphic designer Stevens Ind. Inc., Teutopolis, Ill. Mem. NAFE, Assn. Stds. Testing Materials, Soc. Mfg. Engrs., Nat. Assn. Desktop Pubs., Women in Arts, Effingham Art Guild. Home: RR1 Box 67 Sigel IL 62462 Office: Stevens Ind Inc 704 W Main Teutopolis IL 62467

LAWRENCE, SUSAN, art dealer; b. N.Y.C., Dec. 10, 1939; d. Sidney and Anne (Marom) L.; m. Charles David Nicol, July 1, 1962 (div. Sept. 1973); 1 child, David Lawrence. BA in English, U. Kans., 1961; student art history, U. Mo., 1974-76. Art dealer Lawrence Gallery, Kansas City, Mo., 1976-84, Batz/Lawrence Gallery, Kansas City, Mo., 1984-88, Susan Lawrence Fine Arts, Kansas City, Mo., 1988—; coord. film prodn., Kansas City, 1988-90; coord. med. edn. Trinity Luth. Hosp., Kansas City, 1990—. Mem. Kansas City Film Soc. (founder, bd. dirs., dir. membership 1990—). Office: Susan Lawrence Fine Arts 804 W 48th St Ste 305 Kansas City MO 64112-1817

LAWRENCE, SYLVIA YVONNE, critical care nurse; b. Danville, Pa., July 11, 1937; d. John Jacob and Florence Rebecca (Fenstermacher) Tanner; m. Davey Leon House, Oct. 4, 1958 (div. 1980); children: Susan D., Gayle Y. House Troxell; m. William C. Lawrence (div.). Diploma, Thomas Jefferson U., 1958; BSN, Lycoming Coll., 1991. RN, Pa.; cert. emergency nurse. Nurse various med. facilities, Pa., 1958-70; ho. supr. Sycamore Manor Nursing Home, Williamsport, Pa., 1970-71; gen. duty staff nurse Evangelical Community Hosp., Lewisburg, Pa., 1971-82, surg. staff nurse, 1983-87; surg. staff nurse Twelve Oaks Hosp., Houston, 1982-83; staff nurse emergency dept. Muncy Valley Hosp., 1985-91; patient care mgr. asst. Geisinger Med. Ctr., Danville, 1987—. Mem. Sigma Theta Tau. Republican. Home: PO Box 338 Riverside PA 17868-0338

LAWRY, SYLVIA (MRS. STANLEY ENGLANDER), association executive; b. N.Y.C.; d. Jack and Sonia (Tager) Friedman; m. Michael Lawry, Mar. 1944 (div. 1946); m. Stanley Englander, Apr. 1957 (dec. 1968); children: Franklin Miles, Steven Jon. A.B., Hunter Coll., 1936. Law practice and hearing reporter for State Arbitrator, 1937-40; sponsored by N.Y.C., 1942-43; Law practice and hearing reporter for U.S. Atty.'s office, N.Y., 1943-44; asst. dir. radio prodn. Civilian Def. Reporting; founded Nat. Multiple Sclerosis Soc., N.Y.C., 1946; exec. dir. Nat. Multiple Sclerosis Soc., until 1982, now founder-dir., 1982—; sec. Internat. Fedn. Multiple Sclerosis

Soc., 1967—. Mem. President's Com. on Employment of Handicapped. Recipient Disting. Svc. award Nat. Health Coun., Pres. Reagan's Volunteer Action award, 1987. Mem. APHA, Acad. Polit. Sci., Am. Judicature Soc., Rehab. Internat. Office: Nat Multiple Sclerosis Soc 733 3rd Ave New York NY 10017-3288

LAWS, PRISCILLA WATSON, physics educator; b. N.Y.C., Jan. 18, 1940; d. Morris Clemens and Frances (Fetterinan) Watson; m. Kenneth Lee Laws, June 3, 1965; children: Kevin Allen, Virginia. BA, Reed Coll., 1961; MA, Bryn Mawr Coll., 1963, PhD, 1966. Asst. prof. physics Dickinson Coll., Carlisle, Pa., 1965-70; assoc. prof. Dickinson Coll., Carlisle, 1970-79, prof. physics, 1979—, chmn. dept. physics and astronomy, 1982-83; cons. in field. Author: X Rays: More Harm than Good?, 1977, The X-Ray Information Book, 1983; contbr. numerous articles to profl. jours.; assoc. editor Am. Jour. Physics, 1989—. Vice-pres. Cumberland Conservancy, 1972-73, pres. 1973; bd. dirs. Pa. Alliance for Returnables, 1974-77; asst. sec., treas. Carlisle Hosp. Authority, 1973-76; pres. bd. Carlisle Day Care Ctr., 1973-74. Fellow NSF, 1963-64, grantee, 1989-95, Commonwealth of Pa., 1985-86, U.S. Dept. Edn. Fund for Improvement of Post-Secondary Edn., 1986-89, 89-93, AEC; recipient Innovation award Merck Found., 1989, Educom Incriptal award for curriculum innovation in sci. labs., 1989, award Sears Roebuck and Co., 1990, award Outstanding Software Devel. Computers in Physics Jour., 1991, Pioneering Achievement in Edn. award Dana Found., 1993. Mem. Am. Assn. Physics Tchrs. (Disting Svc. citation 1992, Robert A. Milliken award for Outstanding Contbns. to Physics Tchg., 1996), Fedn. Am. Scientist, Sigma Xi, Sigma Pi Sigma, Omicron Delta Kappa. Democrat. Home: 10 Douglas Ct Carlisle PA 17013-1714 Office: Dickinson Coll PO Box 1773 Carlisle PA 17013

LAWSON, BARBARA ELIZABETH, nurse educator; b. Milw., June 10, 1952; d. George Michael and Elizabeth Jane (Kranz) Fleming; m. Patrick George Gray Lawson, Dec. 14, 1974; children: Robert, Margaret. BSN, Viterbo Coll., LaCrosse, Wis., 1974; MSC Nurse Edn., Edinburgh U., Scotland, 1985. RN, Wis., registered gen. nurse, Scotland. RN Milw. Children's Hosp., 1974; RGN Foresterhill Hosp., Aberdeen, Scotland, 1975-77; head nurse Cairo Hosp., Maadi, Cairo, Egypt, 1983; NURSE tchr. Foresterhill Coll., Aberdeen, Scotland, 1984-88; RN St. Francis Hosp., LaCrosse, Wis., 1989-90; nurse educator Northcentral Tech. Coll., Wausau, Wis., 1990—; staff nurse Wausau Hosp., 1990—. Mem. Vocat. Tech. Assn. Edn. (cert.), Midstate Dist. Nurses Assn., Northcentral Tech. Coll. Nursing Club (advisor 1990-96). Roman Catholic. Home: 1980 River Vista Dr Mosinee WI 54455-8638 Office: North Central Tech College 1000 W Campus Dr Wausau WI 54401-1880

LAWSON, BECKY ANN, government official; b. Washington, Aug. 5, 1957; d. Luther Roy and Julia (Dameron) Pounds; m. Gerald W. Lawson, Oct. 26, 1985; 1 child, Holly Jo. Student, Montgomery Coll., Rockville, Md., 1975, 87. Com. mgmt. officer Office Recombinant DNA Activities, NIH, Bethesda, Md., 1976—. Co-chmn. reasonable accommodations and facilities accessibility subcom., 1993-96; mem. adv. com. for employees with disabilities, 1993-96. Recipient Exceptional Svc. award NIH Recreation and Welfare Assn., 1983. Office: NIH Office Recombinant DNA Activities 6000 Executive Blvd Ste 302 Bethesda MD 20892-7010

LAWSON, BETH ANN REID, strategic planner; b. N.Y.C., Jan. 9, 1954; d. Raymond Theodore and Jean Elizabeth (Frinks) Reid; m. Michael Berry Lawson, Jan. 29, 1983; children: Rayna, Sydney. BA, Va. Tech., 1976; MPA, Golden Gate U., 1983. From systems analyst I to support ops. asst. City of Virginia Beach, Va., 1977-93; water conservation coord. City of Virginia Beach, 1993-94; owner Strategic Planning and Teamwork, Virginia Beach, 1993—; U.S. Army Corps. Engring. Va. Beach Cmty. Devel. Corp.; cons. Va. Beach Cmty. Devel. Corp., 1996, Lifesaving Mus. Va., 1994, Virginia Beach C.A.R.E. Com., 1995, Virginia Beach Rescue Squad, 1992—, Virginia Beach Mcpl. Employees Fed. Credit Union, 1992—, Virginia Beach Resort Area Adv. Commn., 1993, Virginia Beach Conv. and Visitors Devel. Bur., 1991-93. Sunday sch. tchr. Wycliffe Presbyn. Ch., Virginia Beach. Mem. Virginia Beach Rotary Club (Outstanding Employee 1993), Va. Tech. Alumni Assn. (pres. 1982-83). Home: 701 Earl Of Warwick Ct Virginia Beach VA 23454-2910 Office: Strategic Planning and Teamwork 701 Earl Of Warwick Ct Virginia Beach VA 23454-2910

LAWSON, CELESTE MONETTE, non-profit administrator; b. Columbus, Ohio, May 17, 1952; d. Marian Louis Wright Harrison; children: Ginger Eleanor, Georann Noel Lawson Muharram. AS, Bryant & Stratton Bus. Inst., Buffalo, 1974; student, SUNY, Buffalo, 1980, Empire State Coll., Buffalo, 1986-88. Spl. projects coord. Buffalo Philharmonic Orch., 1974-79; mktg. dir. Empire State Ballet, Buffalo; program coord. Buffal State Coll. Performing Arts Ctr.; adminstr., co. mgr. Buffalo Inner City Ballet; dir. Eastside Coalition of the Arts, Buffalo; cultural edn. specialist Shiloh Summer Fun, Buffalo; exec. dir. King Urban Life Ctr., Buffalo; owner/operator Sir-Rah Pub., Buffalo, Sunflower Prodns., Buffalo. Choreographer (fusion dance) African Arabesque, 1988, Coffee House Dances of the East, 1987. Dir. adv. bd. Erie County Cultural Resources, Buffalo, 1995—, Arts Commn., City of Buffalo, 1995—, Arts coun. of Buffalo and Erie County, Western N.Y. Family Literacy Consortium, Buffalo; past chmn. spl. svcs. N.Y. State Coun. on the Arts, Manhatten, 1993, 94, 95; del. N.Y. State Coalition on Women's Issues, Buffalo, 1994-96, UN 4th World Conf. on Women, 1995; mem. El Museo Fancisco Oller y Diego Rivera Gallery, 1994—; grad. Leadership 2000 - A Program, 1992; mem. Manchester Crafts Guild, Rockefeller Found., Nat. Endowment on the Arts. Grantee N.Y. State Arts Dencentralization, 1988, 89. Home: 506 Linwood Ave Buffalo NY 14209

LAWSON, DIANE MARIE, counselor; b. Dallas, July 21, 1947; d. Michael and Clara Mae (McGuire) Maida; m. Howard Lynn Lawson, July 22, 1966; children: Scott M., Stephen L. BA, North Tex. State U., 1971, MEd. Cert. secondary English, history, learning disabilities tchr., secondary sch. counselor, vocational counselor, spl. edn. counselor, mid-mgmt. adminstr., Tex. Tchr. Italy (Tex.) Ind. Sch. Dist., 1972-80, instrnl. leader, 1984-89, elem. prin., 1989-91, h.s. counselor, 1992—; tchr. Red Oak (Tex.) Ind. Sch. Dist., 1980-81; instrnl. leader ESC Region 10, Richardson, Tex., 1981-84; GED instr. Navarro Coll., Coriscana, Tex., 1991-92. City election judge, City of Italy, 1993-95, sch. election judge, Italy, 1992; primary election clk., Ellis County, Italy, 1991. Mem. Am. Counseling Assn., Assn. Tex. Profl. Educators. Office: Italy ISD 300 S College Italy TX 76651

LAWSON, JANE ELIZABETH, bank executive; b. Cornwall, Ont., Can.; d. Leonard J. and Margaret L. BA, LLB, U. N.B., Can., 1971. With law dept. Royal Bank Can., Montreal, Que., Can., 1974-78, sr. counsel, 1978-84; v.p., corp. sec. Royal Bank Can., Montreal, Que., 1988-92, sr. v.p., sec., 1992—. Mem. Can. Bar Assn., N.B. Bar Assn., Que. Bar Assn., Inst. Chartered Secs. and Adminstrs., Inst. Corp. Dirs., Inst. Donations and Pub. Affairs Rsch. (fin. com.), Am. Soc. Corp. Secs., Mt. Royal Tennis Club. Office: Royal Bank Can PO Box 6001, 1 Place Ville Marie, Montreal, PQ Canada H3C 3A9

LAWSON, JENNIFER, broadcast executive; b. Birmingham, Ala., June 8, 1946; d. Willie DeLeon and Velma Theresa (Foster) L.; m. Elbert Sampson, June 1, 1979 (div. Sept. 1980); m. Anthony Gittens, May 29, 1982: children: Kai, Zachary. Student, Tuskegee U., 1963-65; MFA, Columbia U., 1974; LHD (hon.), Teikyo Post U., Hartford, Conn., 1991. Assoc. producer William Greaves Prodns., N.Y.C., 1974-75; asst. prof. film studies Bklyn. Coll., 1975-77; exec. dir. The Film Fund, N.Y.C., 1977-80; TV coord. Program Fund Corp. for Pub. Broadcasting, Washington, 1980-83, assoc. dir. TV Program Fund, 1983-89, dir. TV Program Fund, 1989; exec. v.p. programming PBS, Alexandria, Va., 1989-95; broadcast cons. Md. Pub. TV, 1995—, exec. cons., 1996—; v.p. Internat. Pub. TV, Washington, 1984-88; panelist Fulbright Fellowships, Washington, 1988-90. Author, illustrator: Children of Africa, 1970; illustrator: Our Folktales, 1968, African Folktales: A Calabash of Wisdom, 1973. Coord. Nat. Coun. Negro Women, Washington, 1969. Office: 1838 Ontario Pl Washington DC 20009

LAWSON, KATHERINE ELAINE, minister, counselor; b. Cleve, Feb. 8, 1950; d. Fred and Cora Belle Cole; m. Gerald Edward Lawson, Mar. 24, 1973; 1 child, Jordan Edward. BA, Bowling Green State U., 1972, MEd, 1974; EdD, Memphis State U., 1991. Cert. sch. psychologist, 1991. Intern sch. psychologist Wood County Schs., Bowling Green, Ohio, 1973-74; sch. psychologist Lucas County Schs., Toledo, Ohio, 1974-77; project psychologist Cin. Public Schs., 1978-79; psychometrist adolescent program Oak Tree Children's Ctr., Albany, Ga., 1979-81; sustitute tchr. Memphis State U. Early Childhood Sch., 1985; grad. asst. Memphis State U., 1986-91, adj. asst. prof., 1991-94; dir. counseling and support Abundant Grace Fellowship, Memphis, 1994—; cons. violence reduction program Memphis Area Neighborhood Watch, 1990, 91; organizing com., chair pers. The Shepherd's Sch., Memphis, 1991; adv. bd. The Healing Ctr., Memphis, 1992—; pastoral care adv. bd. Regional Med. Ctr. Memphis, 1993—. Coord. Adopt a Sch. Program, Abundant Grace and Fellowship, Memphis, 1990—; spkr. leadership panel Mid-South Regional Black Family Reunion, Memphis, 1991; mem. student achievement citizenship task force Memphis 2000, 1991-92, conf. spkr. W. Tenn. Br. Nat. Assn. of Social Workers, Shelby County Govt. Victims Assistance Ctr., Memphis, 1996; founder Victims to Victory, 1995, Victims of Crime Act, 1996; devel. team coord. Memphis Neighbors Who Care, 1996; conf. spkr. Neighbors Who Care, 1996. Mem. Assn. Clin. Pastoral Edn., Am. Assn. Christian Counselors, Nat. Assn. for Edn. Young Children. Office: Abundant Grace Fellowship 843 W Raines Rd Memphis TN 38109

LAWSON, KAY DONAHUE, music educator; b. Olean, N.Y., May 16, 1954; d. Norman Kay and Louise Lucille (Carter) Donahue; m. Stephen James Lawson, July 1, 1978; children: Erin Louise, Erika Rose. BMus, Crane Sch. Music, 1976; MMus in Edn., Mich. State U., 1983, MMus in Bassoon Performance, 1991. Music tchr. grades 7-8 Pittsfield (Mass.) City Schs., 1976-78; dir. choral music grades 7-12 Schuylerville (N.Y.) Ctrl. Sch., 1978-80; instr. bassoon & oboe Western Carolina U., Cullowhee, N.C., 1983-89; instr. woodwinds Brevard (N.C.) Coll., 1984-89; adj. prof. bassoon & oboe Minot (N.D.) State U., 1991—; bassoonist Asheville (N.C.) Symphony, 1983-89, Brevard Chamber Orch., 1983-89, Audubon Chamber Ensemble, Minot, 1991—; prin. bassoonist Minot Symphony, 1991—. Mem. Minot Symphony Assn. Bd., 1994-96. Mem. Internat. Double Reed Soc. Home: 100 Eleventh Ave SE Minot ND 58701

LAWSON, MELANIE KAY, management administrator, early childhood consultant; b. Fort Valley, Ga., Feb. 8, 1955; d. William C. and Mamie Nell (Brown) Chapman; m. Robert Scott Lawson, Dec. 18, 1975; children: Robert Scott Jr., Joshua Cody, Ashley Jeanell. AA, Cisco Jr. Coll., 1984; BE in Elem./Spl. Edn., Hardin-Simmons U., 1988, MEd in Reading, 1990; MEd in Sch. Adminstrn., Abilene Christian U., 1992; MEd in Higher Edn., Tex. Tech. U., 1996. Cert. reading specialist, supr., mid-mgmt. tchr. Speech pathology asst. Head Start/Abilene Ind. Sch. Dist., Abilene, Tex., 1983-84; assoc. tchr. Head Start/AISD, Abilene, Tex., 1984-88, cert. tchr., 1988-90; English as second lang. tchr. AISD-Curriculum div., Abilene, Tex., 1990-92; kindergarten tchr. AISD-Long Elem. Sch., Abilene, Tex., 1992-93; asst. dir. Child Devel. Ctr., Dyess AFB, Tex., 1993-94; tng. mgr. 7 SVS Squadron, Dyess AFB, Tex., 1994—. Mem. Youth Task Force, Abilene City Govt., 1994-95, Higher Edn. Working Group, Tex. Head Start Collaboration Project. Recipient Key City Reading award Reading Coun., 1988. Mem. AAUW, Internat. Reading Assn., Nat. Assn. Edn. of Young Children (Membership Affiliate grant 1994, academy mentor 1995—, validator 1993—), Tex. Assn. Edn. of Young Children (at-large, Tex. Affiliate grant, 1993, 94, exec. bd., chair accreditation), Big Country Assn. for Edn. of Young children (membership chair 1988-90, pres. 1992-94, state repl 1992-94), Tex. Assn. for Gifted/Talented (grant 1991), Coun. Early Childhood Profl. Recognition (rep. 1993—), Golden Key Honor Soc., Kappa Delta Phi, Phi Delta Kappa. Baptist. Home: 1702 Yorktown Dr Abilene TX 79603-4216 Office: 7 SVS Squadron 309 Fifth St Dyess AFB TX 79607

LAWSON, NANCY LOUISE, computer scientist, educator; b. Boston, Sept. 22, 1943; d. James Llewellyn and Jane Hancock (Kraft) L.; m. Michael Douglass Marvin, June 14, 1965 (div. Oct., 1985); children: Heidi Jo Newburg, Russel Hugh Marvin, Daryl James Marvin; m. Peter William Henner, June 6, 1992. BA, Oberlin Coll., 1965; MS in Math. Edn., U. Pa., 1973; MS in Computer Sci., Rensselaer Poly. Inst., 1986; PhD in Computer Sci., Rensselaer Polytech. E., 1996. Cert. tchr. math., gen. sci., chemistry, N.Y. Math. tchr. various schs., N.Y., 1973-79; farmer, 1976-84; software engr. GE & Rensselaer Poly. Inst., 1984-92; teaching asst., lectr. Rensselaer Poly. Inst., Troy, N.Y., 1992-95; prof. Coll. St. Rose, 1996—; vis. prof. Union Coll., 1996-97. Mem. Emergency Med. Tech. Scho-Wright Ambulance Corps, Schoharie, N.Y., 1979-81. Mem. Alliance for Environ. Renewal (bd. dirs., v.p.), Adirondack 46ers, Schoharie Valley Concert Band, Pi Mu Epsilon. Home: 60 Scutt Rd Feura Bush NY 12067

LAWSON, SUSAN COLEMAN, lawyer; b. Covington, Ky., Dec. 4, 1949; d. John Clifford and Louise Carter Coleman; m. William Henry Lawson, June 6, 1980; 1 child, Philip. BA, U. Ky., 1971, JD, 1979. Bar: Ky. 1979. Ptnr. Lawson & Lawson, P.S.C., Harlan, 1995—; atty. Stoll, Keenon & Park, Lexington, Ky., 1979-80; atty., Harbert Constrn. Co., Middlesboro, Ky., 1980-81; ptnr. Buttermore, Turner, Lawson & Boggs, P.S.C., Harlan, Ky., 1981-94. Elder 1st Presbyn. Ch., Pineville, Ky., 1986—. Mem. ABA, Ky. Bar Assn., Harlan County Bar Assn. (pres. 1983), Order of Coif. Democrat. Home: 511 W Kentucky Ave Pineville KY 40977-1307 Office: PO Box 837 103 N 1st St Harlan KY 40831

LAWSON, SUZANNE, religious organization administrator. Exec. dir. programming Anglican Ch. of Can., Toronto. Office: Anglican Ch of Can, 600 Jarvis St, Toronto, ON Canada M4Y 2J6*

LAWSON-JOWETT, M. JULIET, lawyer; b. Mobile, Ala., May 26, 1959; d. William Max Lawson and Perina Juliet (Barich) Franc. BA, U. Miss., 1981, JD, 1987. Bar: Miss. 1988, U.S. Dist. Ct. (no. and so. dists.) Miss. 1988. Tchr. Ocean Springs (Miss.) Sch. System, 1981-85; atty. Ronald W. Lewis & Assocs., Oxford, Miss., 1988-89; atty. occupl. hearing loss and hand-arm vibration syndrome Scruggs, Millette, Lawson, Bozeman & Dent, P.A., Pascagoula, Miss., 1989—; cons. Occupational Hearing Loss, P.A., 1989—. Contbr. articles to profl. jours. Mem. Walter Anderson Players, Ocean Springs, 1973-96. Mem. ABA, ATLA (chmn. occupational hearing loss litigation group 1990-94), Miss. Trial Lawyers Assn. (editor 1990-92), Magnolia Bar Assn. Democrat. Roman Catholic. Office: Scruggs Millette Lawson Bozeman & Dent PA 610 Delmas St Pascagoula MS 39567-4345 Office: Scruggs Millette Lawson Bozeman & Dent PA 934 Jackson Ave Pascagoula MS 39567-4345

LAWTON, JACQUELINE AGNES, retired communications company executive, management consultant; b. Bklyn., June 9, 1933; d. Thomas G. and Agnes R. (McLaughlin) Maguire; m. George W. Lawton, Feb. 14, 1954; children: George, Victoria, Thomas. With N.Y. Telephone, 1954-82, mktg. mgr. govt., edn. and med. Mid State, 1978-81, mktg. mgr. health care, N.Y.C., 1981-82; dist. field market mgr. health care and lodging; region 1 N.E. and Region 2 Mid Atlantic, AT&T-Am. Bell, N.Y.C., 1982-83; ea. region mgr. pers., mktg. and sales AT&T Info. Systems, Parsippany, N.J., 1983-86, pvt. practice mgmt. and travel cons., Cornish Flat, N.H., 1986-96; diocesan dir. Medjugirje in Am., Manchester, N.H. Republican. Roman Catholic. Home and Office: PO Box 385 Cornish Flat NH 03746-0385

LAWTON, LORILEE ANN, pipeline supply company owner, accountant; b. Morrisville, Vt., July 17, 1947; d. Philip Wyman Sr. and Margaret Elaine (Ather) Noyes; m. Lee Henry Lawton, Dec. 6, 1969; children: Deborah Ann, Jeffrey Lee. BBA, U. Vt., 1969. Sr. acct., staff asst. IBM, Essex Junction, Vt., 1969-72; owner, pres., chmn. bd. Red-Hed Supply Inc, Colchester, Vt., 1972—; owner, treas. Firetech Sprinkler Corp., Colchester, 1992—; treas. Greater Burlington Indsl. Corp.; bd. dirs. Merchants Bank, Burlington, Cynosure Corp., Burlington. Mem. Assn. Gen. Contractors Am., Assn. Gen. Contractors Vt., Am. Water Works Assn., Vt. Water Works Assn., New Eng. Water Works Assn., No. Vt. Homebuilders Assn., Water and Sewer Distbrs. Am., Am. Fire Sprinkler Assn., Nat. Fire Protection Assn. Republican. Home: 53 Middle Rd Colchester VT 05446-1117 Office: Firetech Sprinkler Corp 1720 Hegeman Ave Colchester VT 05446-3173

LAWTON, NANCY, artist; b. Gilroy, Calif., Feb. 28, 1950; d. Edward Henry and Marilyn Kelly (Boyd) L.; m. Richard Enemark, Aug. 4, 1984; children: Faith Lawton, Forrest Lawton. BA in Fine Art, Calif. State U., San Jose, 1971; MFA, Mass. Coll. Art, 1980. artist-in-residence Villa Montalvo Ctr. Arts, Los Gatos, Calif., 1971, Noble & Greenough Sch., Dedham, Mass., 1990. One-woman shows include The Bklyn. Mus., 1983, Victoria Munroe Gallery, N.Y.C., 1993; group shows include San Francisco Mus. Modern Art, 1973, The Bklyn. Mus., 1980, 83, Staempfli Gallery, N.Y.C., 1984, The Ark. Art Ctr. Mus., Little Rock, 1984, 88, 92, 93, Victoria Munroe Gallery, 1985, 87, 88, 92, Butler Inst. Am. Art, Ohio, 1988, Smith Coll. Mus. Art, Mass., 1988, NAD, N.Y.C., 1988, Reynolds Gallery, Richmond, 1994, Nancy Solomon Gallery, Atlanta, 1995; public collections include The Ark. Art Ctr. Mus., Art Inst. Chgo., Bklyn. Mus., Nat. Mus. Am. Art, Smithsonian Inst., Washington. Scholar Mellon Found., 1982; N.Y. State Creative Artists grantee, 1983, N.Y. State Arts Devel. Fund grantee, 1989. Home and Office: 49 Monument Rd Orleans MA 02653-3511

LAWYER, VIVIAN JURY, lawyer; b. Farmington, Iowa, Jan. 7, 1932; d. Jewell Everett Jury and Ruby Mae (Schumaker) Brewer; m. Verne Lawyer, Oct. 25, 1959; children: Michael Jury, Steven Verne. Tchr.'s cert. U. No. Iowa, 1951; BS with honors, Iowa State U., 1953; JD with honors, Drake U., 1968. Bar: Iowa 1968, U.S. Supreme Ct. 1986. Home econs. tchr. Waukee High Sch. (Iowa), 1953-55; home econs. tchr. jr. high sch. and high sch., Des Moines Pub. Schs., 1955-61; pvt. practice law, Des Moines, 1972—; chmn. juvenile code tng. sessions Iowa Crime Commn., Des Moines, 1978-79, coord. workshops, 1980; assoc. Lawyer, Lawyer & Assocs., Des Moines, 1981—; co-founder, bd. dirs. Youth Law Center, Des Moines, 1977—; mem. com. rules of juvenile procedure Supreme Ct. Iowa, 1981-87, adv. com. on costs of ct. appointed counsel Supreme Ct. Iowa, 1985-88; trustee Polk County Legal Aid Svcs., Des Moines, 1980-82; mem. Iowa Dept. Human Svcs. and Supreme Ct. Juvenile Justice County Base Joint Study Com., 1984—. Mem. Iowa Task Force permanent families project Nat. Coun. Juvenile and Family Ct. Judges, 1984-88; mem. substance abuse com. Commn. Children, Youth and Families, 1985—; co-chair Polk County Juvenile Detention Task Force, 1988. Editor: Iowa Juvenile Code Manual, 1979, Iowa Juvenile Code Workshop Manual, 1980; co-editor: 1987 Cumulative Supplement, 1993 supplement, Iowa Academy of Trial Lawyers Trial Handbook; author booklet in field, 1981. Mem. Polk County Citizens Commn. on Corrections, 1977. Iowa Dept. Social Svcs. grantee, 1980. Mem. Purple Arrow, Phi Kappa Phi, Omicron Nu. Republican. Home: 5831 N Waterbury Rd Des Moines IA 50312-1339 Office: 427 Fleming Building Des Moines IA 50309-4011

LAX, KATHLEEN THOMPSON, federal judge. BA, U. Kans., 1967; JD, U. Calif., L.A., 1980. Law clk. U.S. Bankruptcy Ct., L.A., 1980-82; assoc. Gibson, Dunn & Crutcher, L.A., 1982-88; judge ctrl. dist. U.S. Bankruptcy Ct., L.A., 1988—; bd. dirs. L.A. Bankruptcy Forum, 1988—; bd. govs. Fin. Lawyers Conf., L.A., 1991-92, 94—. Bd. editors: Calif. Bankruptcy Jour., 1988—. Office: US Bankruptcy Court 255 E Temple St Rm 1334 Los Angeles CA 90012-3334*

LAY, ELIZABETH MARIAN, health association administrator; b. Reading, Eng., Oct. 11, 1949; d. John Hunter and Brigid Mary (Maas) L. BS in Biology, SUNY, Albany, 1976; Cert. in Exec. Devel., George Washington U., 1989. mem. adv. coun. No. Va. Mental Health Inst.; puppeteer Smithsonian Instn., 1970-71. Sec. Touche Ross & Co., Washington, 1971-73, para-cons., 1974-75, assoc. cons., 1975-82; fin. systems liason Student Loan Mktg. Assn., Washington, 1982-84, mgr. fin. systems, 1985-87, dir. fin. systems, 1988-95. Mem. Am. Assn. Suicidology, Nat. Mental Health Assn. (life, pres. 1994-95), Alexandria Mental Health Assn. (pres. 1984-86, 95-96, treas. 1993-94, exec. dir. 1996—, Disting. Svc. award 1994), Am. Mensa. Democrat.

LAYBOURNE, GERALDINE, broadcasting executive; b. Plainfield, N.J., 1947; married; 2 children. BA, Vassar Coll., 1969; MS, U. Pa., 1971. Former high sch. tchr.; with Nickelodeon, 1980—, creator Nick at Nite, 1985—, pres.; also vice chmn. MTV Networks; now pres. Disney/ABC Cable Networks, N.Y.C. Office: 77 W 66th St New York NY 10023*

LAYCHAK, ANN ELEANOR, school counselor; b. N.Y.C., Nov. 19, 1946; d. George and Eleanor (Weismann) O'Day; m. Kenneth Joseph Laychak, June 22, 1968; children: Christopher, Bryan, Courtney. BA, Hunter Coll., 1968; MS, Purdue U., 1991. Cert. Counselor. Elem. tchr. Good Shepherd Sch., N.Y.C., 1967-68, Tippecanoe Sch. Corp., Lafayette, Ind., 1984-85; rsch. asst. Purdue U., W. Lafayette, 1985-88; sch. counselor Caesar Rodney Sch. Dist., Camden, Del., 1991—. Named Sch. Counselor of the Year Kent County, Del., 1994-95. Mem. Am. Counseling Assn., Am. Sch. Counselors Assn., Nat. Bd. Cert. Counselors, Delta Delta Delta. Roman Catholic. Home: 303 Quail Run Camden Wyoming DE 19934 Office: Caesar Sch Corp 5 Old North Rd Camden Wyoming DE 19934

LAYER, MEREDITH MITCHUM, retired financial services company executive, public responsibility professional; b. Rutherfordton, N.C., July 26, 1946; d. Lee Wallace and Ellie (Saine) Mitchum; m. Charles Layer, 1990. BS, U. N.C., Greensboro, 1968; MS, U. Md., 1972. Tchr. home econs. Prince Georges County pub. schs., Md., 1968-72; assoc. dir. market research H.J. Kaufman Advt., Washington, 1972-74; dir. consumer edn. Washington Consumer Affairs Office, 1974-76; dir. consumer affairs U.S. Dept. Commerce, Washington, 1976-80; v.p. consumer affairs Am. Express Co., N.Y.C., 1980-82, sr. v.p.-pub. responsibility, 1982-96; former mem. consumer adv. coun. Fed. Res. System, Washington; bd. dirs. Nat. Consumers League, Washington, N.Y. Met. Better Bus. Bur., N.Y.C. Contbr. articles to profl. jours. Trustee Inst. for Future, 1986—; bd. dirs. Women's Forum N.Y., 1987-88; former bd. overseers Malcolm Baldridge Nat. Quality Award; commr. Nat. Commn. Working Women, 1987—. Recipient Consumer Edn. award Nat. Found. Consumer Credit Fedn., 1981, Disting. Woman award Northwood Inst., 1985, Matrix award N.Y. Women in Communications, Inc., 1986, Acad. Women Achievers award N.Y.C. YWCA, 1989, N.Y. Women's Agenda Star award, 1992. Mem. Soc. Consumer Affairs Profls. (pres. 1985, individual achievement award 1990), Advt. Women N.Y. (Advt. Woman of the Yr. award 1987), Fin. Women's Assn., Am. Home Econs. Assn., Internat. Credit Assn. (bd. dirs. 1984—).

LAYUG, LYNNE PORTER, laboratory scientist; b. Washington, Aug. 15, 1963; d. Earl John and Mary Agnes (De Bonig) Porter; m. Joseph Michael Layug, Oct. 20, 1990; 1 child, Patrick Joseph. BS, Loyola Coll., Balt., 1985; MPH, George Washington U., 1994. Technologist NIH, Bethesda, Md., 1985-86, ARC-Nat. Reference lab. for Infectious Diseases, Rockville, Md., 1986-90; reference assoc. ARC-Nat. Reference lab. for Infectious Diseases, Rockville, 1990-92, mgr., 1992-93, dir., 1993-94, tech. officer, 1994—. Contbr. articles and abstracts to profl. publs. Mem. APHA, Am. Soc. Clin. Pathologists (cert. med. tech.), Am. Soc. for Clin. Lab. Sci., Am. Assn. Blood Banks, Am. Assn. Bioanalysts. Republican. Roman Catholic. Office: ARC 15601 Crabbs Branch Way Rockville MD 20855

LAZAR, FERN, public relations executive; b. N.Y.C., May 30, 1961. BS in internat. fin., Georgetown U., 1983; postgrad. in securities analysis, N.Y. Inst. Fin. Commodities analyst Lonconex, N.Y.C., 1983-85; account supr. Triad Internat., N.Y.C., 1985-86; account supr. Dewe Rogerson, N.Y.C., 1986-88, v.p., 1988-90, sr. v.p., 1990-91, exec. v.p., 1991—. Mem. NIRI, Internat. Assn. Bus. Communicators. Office: Dewe Rogerson Inc 850 3rd Ave New York NY 10022-6222*

LAZAR, KATHY PITTAK, lawyer; b. Lorain, Ohio, Nov. 12, 1955. BA summa cum laude, Kent State U., 1978; JD, Case Western Res. U., 1982. Bar: Ohio 1982. Ptnr. Arter & Hadden, Cleve. Rsch. editor Case Western Res. U. Law Rev., 1981-82. Mem. ABA, Ohio State Bar Assn., Cleve. Bar Assn., Order of Coif, Phi Beta Kappa. Office: Arter & Hadden 1100 Huntington Bldg 925 Euclid Ave Cleveland OH 44115-1475*

LAZARIS, PAMELA ADRIANE, municipal agency administrator; b. Dixon, Ill., Oct. 13, 1956; d. Michael Christ and Ellen Euridice (Eftax) L.; m. Eugene Dale Monson, Oct. 17, 1987; children: Anthony Edward, Anna Adriane. BFA in Fine Arts, U. Wis., Milw., 1978; MS in Urban and Regional Planning, U. Wis., 1982; MBA, U. St. Thomas, 1992. Analyst planning Wis. Dept. Natural Resources, Madison, 1979-82; asst. city planner City of Albert Lea, Minn., 1982-83; specialist community devel. City of Winona, Minn., 1983-85; dir. community devel. City of Waseca, Minn., 1985—. Vol. spl. events Farmam-Minn. Agrl. Interpretive Ctr., Waseca, 1985-86; sec., comm. dir. Waseca Area Cmty. Fund, 1989-95; mem. Waseca

County Econ. Devel. Commn., 1989-96; com. dir. Waseca Area Found., 1989-96. Named one of Oustanding Young Women of Am., 1986. Mem. Am. Inst. Cert. Planners (cert.), Am. Planning Assn. (chpt. bd. dirs. 1986-89), Minn. Planning Assn. (v.p. 1989-90, dist. bd. dirs. 1985-89), Toastmasters (chpt. sgt.-at-arms 1987, ednl. v.p. 1988, 91-96). Home: PO Box 325 110 6th Ave NE Waseca MN 56093 Office: City of Waseca 508 S State St Waseca MN 56093-3033

LAZARNICK, SYLVIA, secondary education educator; b. Bklyn., Feb. 6, 1949; d. Emanuel and Karin Lazarnick; m. Timothy Taylor Beaman, June 18, 1973. BA, Bklyn. Coll., 1969; MA, Pa. State U., 1971. Math. tchr. Class. High Sch., Springfield, Mass., 1971-72, Alternative High Sch., Lakewood, N.J., 1972-73, Broadmeadows (Australia) Tech. Sch., 1975-77, Neshaminy-Langhorne (Pa.) High Sch., 1979, Rice Meml. High Sch., Burlington, Vt., 1979-80, Bellows Free Acad., St. Albans, Vt., 1980—. Bd. dirs. Franklin County Food Coop., St. Albans; coach Vt. All Stars; mem. BFA Math League Team. Mem. Nat. Coun. Tchrs. Math., Assn. Tchrs. Math. in New Eng. (program co-chair fall meeting 1994), Vt. Coun. Tchrs. Math. (pres.-elect 1994-95, pres. 1995-97). Home: RR 1 Box 2120 Fairfield VT 05455-9733 Office: Bellows Free Acad 71 S Main St Saint Albans VT 05478-2209

LAZARUS, ROCHELLE BRAFF, advertising executive; b. N.Y.C., Sept. 1, 1947; d. Lewis L. and Sylvia Ruth (Eisenberg) Braff; m. George M. Lazarus, Mar. 22, 1970; children: Theodore, Samantha, Benjamin. AB, Smith Coll., 1968; MBA, Columbia U., 1970. Product mgr. Clairol, N.Y.C., 1970-71; account exec. Ogilvy & Mather, N.Y.C., 1971-73, account supr., 1973-77, mgmt. supr., 1977-84, sr. v.p., 1981—, account group dir., 1984-87; gen. mgr. Ogilvy & Mather Direct, N.Y.C., 1987-88, mng. dir., 1988-89, pres., 1989-91; pres. Ogilvy & Mather, N.Y.C., 1991-94, pres. N. Am., 1991-94; pres., COO Ogilvy & Mather Worldwide, N.Y.C., 1995—, CEO, 1996. Bd. dirs. Ann Taylor, Advt. Edn. Found., YMCA, Nat. Women's Law Ctr., World Wildlife Fund; mem. Com. of 200; mem. bus. com. Solomon R. Guggenheim Mus.; mem. bd. overseers Columbus Bus. Sch.; trustee Smith Coll., Columbia Presbyn. Hosp. Recipient YWCA Women Achievers award, 1985, Matrix award, 1995. Mem. Am. Assn. Advt. Agys. (bd. dirs.), Advt. Women N.Y. (Woman of Yr. 1994). Home: 106 E 78th St New York NY 10021-0302 Office: Ogilvy & Mather Worldwide 309 W 49th St New York NY 10019-7316

LAZARUS, SARA LOUISE, theatre director and educator; b. Bklyn., Apr. 15, 1948; d. Laurence and Bella (Sollender) L.; m. David Seader, June 5, 1988. BS, Northwestern U., 1968; cert. in acting, Royal Acad. Dramatic Art, London, 1975. Actress, singer Broadway, Off-Broadway, nat. tours, regional theatre, 1968-78; actor, instr. Durham (N.H.) Summer Theatre, U. N.H., 1978; announcer, moderator New Eng. Forum, Sta. WHEB-AM-FM, Portsmouth, N.H., 1979; dir. Hangar Theatre, Cornell U., Ithaca, N.Y., 1981; founder, tchr. Sara Lazarus Studio for Mus. Theatre Studies, N.Y.C., 1982—; dir. 137th and 138th Ann. Hasty Pudding Shows, Harvard U., Cambridge, Mass., 1985, 86, Centenary Stage Co., Hackettstown, N.J., 1987, 89, Yale U. Dramatic Assn., New Haven, 1988, guest instr. master classes, 1991; instr. Am. Mus. and Dramatic Acad., N.Y.C., 1985-86, 92. Dir. Babes in Arms concert, Avery Fisher Hall, Lincoln Ctr., N.Y.C., 1989 (Back Stage Bistro award 1989), Carried Away-Eighty Eights and the Ballroom, 1989, Ridin' High, Eighty-Eights (Back Stage Bistro award 1990), Hollywood Opera, The Ballroom, 1990, The 1959 Broadway Songbook, The Oak Room, Algonquin Hotel, 1991 (Manhattan Assn. Cabarets award 1991), Cabaret Comes to Carnegie, Weill Recital Hall, 1991, Oliver, Chiswick Park Theatre, Sudbury, Mass., 1992, Plaisir D'Amour, 1992, Dancing in the Dark Oak Room Algonquin Hotel, 1993, Weill at Weill Carnegie Weill Recital Hall, 1992, Shauna Hicks and Her 60's Chicks, 1993-94 (Bistro award, Manhattan Assn. Cabarets award), Havana BC, 1993-94 (Bistro award), Hoagy On My Mind-A Carmichael Revue-The Ballroom, 1994, The Blindfold-Working Lights Unlimited, 1994, Backstage Bistro Awards Show, 1995, 96, Starting Here, Starting Now-New American Theatre, 1995, Awakening on Santa Monica: Poems from L.A., 1995, A House on a Hill, 1995, Off The Record, Town Hall, 1996, 50's Gold, Rainbow and Stars, 1996, Tovahioutof Her Mind, Playhouse 91, 1996 (recordings) The 1959 Broadway Songbook, Live at the Algonquin, Babes in Arms. Outstanding Dir. award CAB Mag., 1992, Outstanding Dir. award Cabaret Hotline, 1992. Mem. Soc. Stage Dirs. and Choreographers, Actors Equity Assn., Manhattan Assn. Cabarets (Outstanding Dir. 1991), League of Profl. Theatre Women. Home and Office: 535 Cathedral Pky New York NY 10025-2086

LAZECHKO, D. M. (MOLLY LAZECHKO), former state legislator; b. Innisfail, Alta., June 3, 1926; came to U.S., 1960; d. Archibald Donald and Violet Georgina (Adams) Manuel; m. Walter Vladmir Lazechko, Apr. 16, 1960; children: William Donald, Robert James. BA, Boise State U., 1976. Cert. elem. tchr. Tchr. Olds Sch. Dist., Stewart Sch., Alta., 1945-46, Innisfail (Alta.) Sch. Dist., 1946-50; tchr., vice prin. Calgary (Alta.) Sch. Dist., 1950-59; exchange tchr. Edinburgh, Scotland, 1954-55; math tutor mgr. Title I, Boise, Idaho, 1974-76; elem. tchr. Boise (Idaho) Sch. Dist., 1976-87; jr. high tchr. Chpt. I, Boise, 1987-88; ret., 1988-90; mem. Idaho Ho. of Reps., Boise, 1991, 92; pres. div. I Alta. Tchrs. Assn., Calgary, 1958-59, Whittier PTA, Boise, 1969-70, 73-74; pres., 3d v.p. Dist. 8 Idaho State PTA, 1973-75; sec., elem. dir. Boise (Idaho) Edn. Assn., 1978-81. Treas. LWV, Boise, 1988-90, Ho. Dems. Campaign Com., Boise, 1991-92; precinct capt. Ada County Dems. Dist. 16, Boise, 1988-90; sec. Boise Ret. Tchrs., 1989-90, pres., 1993-94; bd. dirs. Boise Neighborhood Housing Svcs., 1990-92, Cmty. Contbn. Ctr., 1991-94, Idaho Housing Coalition, 1991-94, Epilepsy League Idaho, 1993-95; gubernatorial appointee to bd. dirs. Idaho Coun. on Domestic Violence, 1994—; candidate Idaho Legis. Ho. Reps., 1994. Mem. NEA, Idaho Edn. Assn., Idaho Conservation League, Idaho Women's Network, Grassroots Women's Lobby, Idaho Citzen's Network. Episcopalian.

LAZENBY, GAIL R., library director; b. Charlotte, N.C., May 6, 1947; d. James Yates and Marian Elizabeth (Church) Rogers. BA, Salem Coll., 1969; MLS, U. N.C., 1971. Cert. libr., Ga. Br. libr. Atlanta Pub. Libr., 1970-77; br. coord. Dekalb Libr. System, Decatur, Ga., 1977-82; asst. dir. West Ga. Regional Libr., Carrollton, 1982-83; asst. dir. Cobb County Pub. Libr., Marietta, Ga., 1983-90, dir., 1991—. Mem. Leadership Cobb, Cobb County, 1985-86. Mem. ALA, Ga. Libr. Assn. (2d v.p. 1987-89), Southeastern Libr. Assn. (v.p.-pres. elect. 1990-92, pres. 1992-94), Urban Librs. Coun., Kiwanis Club Marietta (bd. dirs. 1991-92, sec. 1992-93, sec.-treas. 1993-94, pres. 1995-96). Office: Cobb County Public Lib 266 Roswell St SE Marietta GA 30060-2005

LAZIN, LAUREN, filmmaker, broadcast executive. BA magna cum laude, Smith Coll., 1982; MA in Documentary Film Prodn., Stanford U. Exec. producer MTV news and spls. MTV, N.Y.C., 1992—; v.p. Spls. divsn. MTV News, N.Y.C., 1994—. Prodr., dir., writer editor more than 40 documentary, rockumentary, entertainment and hard news spls. for MTV. Recipient numerous awards for her documentaries and shows; named one of four Role Models, Women's Coll. Coalition, 1995. Office: MTV Networks 1515 Broadway New York NY 10036*

LAZOR, PAMELA ALEXANDREA, public relations executive; b. New Brunswick, N.J., July 29, 1960; d. Alexander and Patricia Ann (La Gattuta) L. AA, Mt. Vernon Coll., Washington, 1980. Freelance cons. in pub. rels., 1987-89; owner, dir. Pamela A. Lazor Pub. Rels., N.Y.C., 1989—. Com. mem./vol. Kips Bay Boys and Girls Club, N.Y. Republican. Episcopalian. Office: 9 E 97th St Ste 4D New York NY 10029-6924

LAZOR, PATRICIA ANN, interior designer; d. Charles A. and Grace E. (Siegrist) LaGattuta; m. E. Alexander Lazor, Aug. 22, 1959; children: Pamela A., Carolyn L., Charles L., Peter A. BA, Chestnut Hill Coll., 1957; MEd, Rutgers Coll., 1962; cert., N.Y. Sch. Interior Design, 1972. Tchr. Bridgewater (N.J.) Raritan Schs., 1958-69; designer Patricia A. Lazor Interior Design, Bernardsville, N.J., 1975-85; pres. Alexander Abry, Inc., Washington, 1985-87; owner, designer Patricia A. Lazor Interior Design Antiques, Inc., Bernardsville, 1985—. Rep. com. woman, Somerset County, N.J., 1978; chmn. Family Counseling Svc. Somerset County, 1972-78. Mem. Essex Hunt Club (Peapack, N.J.), Somerset Hills Country Club (Bernardsville), Garden Club Morristown, Morristown Club, Kappa Delta Phi. Republican. Home and Office: Interior Design/Antiques Inc Roebling Rd Bernardsville NJ 07924

LAZZARA, BERNADETTE See **PETERS, BERNADETTE**

LE, DONG PHUONG NGUYEN, travel agency executive, hospital official; b. Saigon, Vietnam, Mar. 15, 1971; d. Dat Hien Le and Thuyen Thi. BA, U. Md., Balt., 1995. Mem. med. records staff Columbia (Md.) Med. Plan, 1992-94; patient receptionist Kaiser Permanente, Kensington, Md., 1994-95, human resources asst., 1995-96; mgr. Colt Enterprises, Columbia, 1993-94; with admitting dept., contr. Suburban Hosp., Bethesda, Md., 1989-96, adminstrv. coord., 1996——; mng. ptnr., cons. Atlas Travel, Inc., Wheaton, Md., 1994—; health adv. specialist Atty. Gen.'s Office, Balt., 1995. Author: The Lost Boy, 1984 (merit award 1984). Charity asst. Washington Area Wheelchair Soc., Silver Spring, Md., 1990-91. Mem. Women of Arts (assoc.).

LE, YVONNE DIEMVAN, chemist; b. Vietnam, Nov. 21, 1961; d. Hien Trung and Thanh-Hoa Thi (Luu) L. BA in Chemistry, Math., San Jose State U., 1984. Chem. technician Hewlett Packard Co., Palo Alto, Calif., 1983; assoc. chemist Ampex Corp., Sunnyvale, Calif., 1984-86; chemist II Info. Memory Corp., Santa Clara, Calif., 1986-88; R&D project engr. Komag, Inc., Milpitas, Calif., 1988—. Mem. Am. Chem. Soc. Roman Catholic. Office: Komag Inc 275 S Hillview Dr Milpitas CA 95035

LEA, ELEANOR LUCILLE, retired state agency administrator; b. Diller, Nebr., Nov. 6, 1916; d. Edward Richard and Gertrude (Loock) Henrichs; m. Stanley Guy Lea, Mar. 6, 1936; children: Dianna Evenson, Cylesta Peters, Jeffrey, Chad. Student, Fairbury State Coll. Owner Modern Furniture Store, Fairbury, Nebr., 1945-80; dist. mgr. Field Enterprises, Chgo., 1966-80; libr. resource person Fairbury Pub. Libr., 1982-85; job coord. Blue River Area Agy. on Aging, Lincoln, Nebr., 1985-87; Bd. mem. Operation ABLE, Lincoln, 1987-92, Nat. Grandparent Program, Beatrice, Nebr., 1985-87. Pres., dist. v.p. United Meth. Women; Sunday Sch. supt. Meth. Ch., Fairbury; v.p. sch. bd. Fairbury Pub. Sch. Bd., 1956-62; bd. mem. Girl Scouts U.S.A., 1950-56. Mem. Toastmasters (v.p. pub. rels. Lincoln 1992-94). Republican. Home: 2920 S 72nd St Apt 85 Lincoln NE 68506-3681

LEACH, DEBRA ANN, alcohol beverage association executive; b. Kokomo, Ind., Dec. 27, 1952; d. William Thomas and Mary Ellen (Clarke) L.; m. Gary Simpkins Widdowson, Aug. 9, 1974 (dec. Feb. 1980). BS, U. Md., 1975. Home econs. tchr. Wicomico County Schs., Salisbury, Md., Balt. City Schs., 1976-81; bartender, cocktail server Md., Va., 1982-88; nat. program dir. Techniques of Alcohol Mgmt., Alexandria, Va., 1988—; exec. dir. Nat. Licensed Beverage Assn., 1992—. Contbr. articles to profl. jours. Active Sky Ranch for Boys, N.Am. Partnership for Responsible Hospitality, Leadership Advantage. Mem. NOW, Am. Soc. Assn. Execs., Greater Washington Soc. Assn. Execs., Assn. Chief Exec. Coun., World Assn. Alcohol Beverage Industries (mem. adv. bd.), Nat. Lic. Beverage Assn. (exec. dir. 1992—), Nat. Abortion Rights Action League, Nat. Wildlife Fedn., World Wildlife Fund, Responsible Hospitality Inst. (mem. exec. bd.). Home: 5120 Maris Ave # 401 Alexandria VA 22304-1961 Office: NLBA/TAM 4214 King St Alexandria VA 22302-1507

LEACH, MARY JANE, composer; b. St. Johnsburh, Vt., June 12, 1949; d. Benjamin George Leach and Juliet Anne (Cooke Barton. BA, U. Vt., 1972; postgrad., Columbia U., 1977-78. Composer, 1978—; co-dir. Re:Soundings, N.Y.C., 1993—. Composer (choral works) Ariadne's Lament, 1993, Song of Sorrows, 1995, Bruckstück, 1989, (piece for oboe) Xantippe's Rebuke, 1994. Recipient commn. Mary Flagler Cary Charitable Trust, 1994, 96; Found. for Contemporary Performing Arts career grantee, 1995-96; Nat. Endowment for Arts composers fellow, 1995. Mem. Am. Music Ctr., Am. Composers Forum. Home: 90 LaSalle St #13H New York NY 10027

LEACH, SHAWNA, food service director; b. Lehi, Utah, July 9, 1949; d. Lloyd D. and Dawna Mae (Marrott) Boren; m. Micheal Merrell Wiley, Feb. 11, 1967 (div.); children: Shannon Wiley Espinoza, Cyndie Wiley Anderson, Michael Shane, Stacie Lee; m. Calvin Donald Leach, Feb. 18, 1983. Cert. in dietary managing, Ctrl. Ariz. Coll., 1993. Mgr. cafeteria Provo (Utah) Sch. Dist., 1976-86; supply clk. Bur. of Reclamation, Page, Ariz., 1987-88; dir. food svc. Page Unified Sch. Dist., 1988—. Mem. Am. Sch. Food Svc. Assn. (dir., adminstr. I 1992—, instr. 1993—), Am. Sch. Bus. Officials, Ariz. Sch. Bus. Officials, Ariz. Sch. Food Svc. Assn. (chair certification 1992, state v.p. 1995-96, state pres. elect 1996-97, state officer), Dietary Mgrs. Assn., Page Recycles. Democrat. LDS. Home: PO Box 3618 Page AZ 86040-3618 Office: Page Unified Sch Dist PO Box 1927 Page AZ 86040-1927

LEACHMAN, CLORIS, actress; b. Des Moines, June 30, 1930; m. George England, 1953 (div. 1979); 5 children. Ed., Northwestern U. Actress: (films) including Kiss Me Deadly, 1955, Butch Cassidy and the Sundance Kid, 1969, W.U.S.A., 1970, The People Next Door, 1970, Lovers and Other Strangers, 1970, The Steagle, 1971, The Last Picture Show, 1971 (Acad. award for best supporting actress 1971), Charles and the Angel, 1972, Happy Mother's Day...Love, George, 1973, Dillinger, 1973, Daisy Miller, 1974, Young Frankenstein, 1974, Crazy Mama, 1975, High Anxiety, 1977, The Mouse and His Child, 1977 (voice), Foolin' Around, 1979, The North Avenue Irregulars, 1979, The Muppet Movie, 1979, Scavenger Hunt, 1979, Yesterday, 1979, Herbie Goes Bananas, 1980, History of the World, Part 1, 1982, Shadow Play, 1986, My Little Pony, 1986 (voice), Walk Like a Man, 1987, Hansel and Gretel, 1987, Prancer, 1989, Love Hurts, 1990, Texasville, 1990, Walter and Emily, 1991, My Boyfriend's Back, 1993, The Beverly Hillbillies, 1993, A Troll in Central Park, 1994 (voice), Storytime, 1994, Nobody's Girls, 1994; TV series including Lassie, 1957, Route 66, Laramie, Trials of O'Brien, Mary Tyler Moore Show, Phyllis, 1975-77, Facts of Life, The Nutt House, 1989; (TV movies) including Silent Night, Lonely Night, 1969, Suddenly Single, 1971, Haunts of the Very Rich, 1972, Brand New Life, 1973, Dying Room Only, 1973, Crime Club, 1973, Death Sentence, 1974, Thursday's Game, 1974, Hitchhike!, 1974, The Migrants, 1974, A Girl Named Sooner, 1975, Ladies of the Corridor, The New Original Wonder Woman, 1975, Death Scream, 1975, Someone I Touched, 1975, It Happened One Christmas, 1977, Long Journey Back, 1978, Mrs. R.'s Daughter, 1979, Willa, 1979, S.O.S. Titanic, 1979, The Acorn People, 1981, Advice to the Lovelorn, 1981, Miss All-American Beauty, 1982, Dixie: Changing Habits, 1983, The Demon Murder Case, 1983, Ernie Kovacs, Between the Laughter, 1984, Deadly Intentions, 1985, Love is Never Silent, Danielle Steele's Fine Things, 1990, In Broad Daylight, 1991, A Little Piece of Heaven, 1991, Fade to Black, 1993, Without a Kiss Goodbye, 1993, Spies, 1993, Miracle Child, 1993, Double, Double, Toil and Trouble, 1993, Between Love and Honor, 1995; (TV miniseries) Backstairs at the White House, 1979; theater appearance in Grandma Moses: An American Primitive, Washington, 1990; guest appearance: The Love Boat, 1976. Recipient 6 Emmy awards. *

LEAHEY, LYNN, editor-in-chief. Editor-in-chief Soap Opera Digest, N.Y.C. Office: Soap Opera Digest 45 West 25th St 8th Fl New York NY 10010*

LEAK, MARGARET ELIZABETH, insurance company executive; b. Atlanta, Sept. 9, 1946; d. William Whitehurst and Margaret Elizabeth (Whitsitt) L. BS in Psychology, Okla. State U., 1968; postgrad., U. Okla., 1968-69, Cornell U., 1976-78; grad. advanced mgmt. program, Harvard U., 1983-84. Editor communications Eastern State Bankcard Assn., N.Y.C., 1969-71; sr. edn. specialist Citibank, N.Y.C., 1971-73; adminstr. orgn. devel. NBC, N.Y.C., 1973-74; mgr. tng. and devel. Atlantic Mut. Cos., Property/Casualty Ins., N.Y.C., 1974-76, sec. human resources, 1976-78, v.p. human resources, 1978-84, v.p. human resources and corp. communications, 1984-86, sr. v.p. adminstrv. services, 1987—. Office: Atlantic Mut Cos 3 Giralda Farms Madison NJ 07940-1027

LEAK, NANCY MARIE, artist; b. Takoma Park, Md., Nov. 24, 1931; d. George Morton and Ella (Oberholtzer) Hinkson; m. Thomas Clayton Leak Jr., Dec. 30, 1950; children: Suzanne, Sharon, Stephen, Scott. Grad. high sch., Washington. Co-illustrator: The Kissing Hand, 1993; exhbns. include Olney Art Assn. Ann. Show, Internat. Exhbn. of the Miniature, Cider Painters Am. Nat. Exhbn., Hunterdon Art Ctr., N.J., Sumner Mus., Washington, Gurmukhs Gallery, Aspen Hill, Md., Nev. Miniature Art Soc., Hoffberger Gallery, Balt., Ocean City (Md.) Art League, Rockville (Md.) Art League, Md. Printmakers, Worldwide Miniature Exhbn. Recipient numerous awards for art. Mem. Nat. League Am. Pen Women, Md. Printmakers Assn., Miniature Painters, Sculptors & Gravers Soc. Washington, Miniature Art Soc. Fla., Rockville Art League, Olney Art Assn., Cider Painters Am., Miniature Artists Am. Democrat. Methodist.

LEAKE, BRENDA GAIL, enterostomal therapist nurse practitioner; b. Harriman, Tenn., Aug. 5, 1950; d. James Frank and Pauline Ruby (McGuffey) Judd; m. Lee Leake, Aug. 1, 1970 (div. Apr. 1974). AS in Nursing, U. Nev., Las Vegas, 1971, BN, 1986; cert. enterostomal therapist, U. Calif., San Diego, 1975. RN, Nev.; cert. enterostomal therapist, urol. nurse. Staff nurse Humana Hosp. Sunrise, Las Vegas, 1971-73, relief charge nurse, 1973-76, enterostomal therapist, 1976—; speaker Hospice Vol. program, Las Vegas, 1982—, I Can Cope program, Las Vegas, 1984—. Author instructional guide. Vol. Am. Cancer Soc., 1983—, mem. program devel. nurse edn. com. Mem. Intenat. Assn. Enterostomal Therapists (cert.), Nat. Assn. Pediatric Pseudobstructure Soc., Am. Nurses Assn., So. Nev. Nurses Assn., World Council Enterostomal Therapists, Am. Urol. Assn. (cert.), So. Nev. Ostomy Assn. (med. advisor 1976—), Crohns & Colitis Assn., Advanced Practitioners Nursing (cert., program chmn. 1986—), Wound Healing Soc. Republican. Presbyterian. Office: Sunrise Hosp 3186 S Maryland Pky Las Vegas NV 89109-2317

LEAL, BARBARA JEAN PETERS, fundraising executive; b. Hartford, Ala., Oct. 24, 1948; d. Clarence Lee and Syble (Simmons) Peters; m. Michael Wayne Foster, 1966 (div.); children: Michaelle, Jonathan; m. Ramon Leal, 1991. AA, Enterprise State Jr. Coll., 1970; BA, U. South Fla., 1974; MA, Trinity U., San Antonio, 1975; postgrad. Universidad Nacional Autonoma de Mexico, 1982. Cert. fund raising exec. Instr., San Antonio Coll., 1975; planner Econ. Opportunities Devel. Corp., San Antonio, 1976, Alamo Area Council Govts., San Antonio, 1977-82; dir. planned giving Oblate Missions, San Antonio, 1982—; spkr. in field. Author: Paratransit Provider Handbook, 1978; contbg. author: Human Responses to Aging, 1976; Transportation for Elderly Handicapped Programs and Problems, 1978; contbr. articles to profl. publs. Named one of Outstanding Young Women of Am., 1985. Founding mem. Nat. Soc. Fund Raising Execs. (past pres. San Antonio chpt.), Am. Coun. on Gift Annuities, Coun. Advancement and Support Edn., San Antonio Planned Giving Coun. Democrat. Roman Catholic. Office: Oblate Missions PO Box 96 San Antonio TX 78291-0096

LEALE, OLIVIA MASON, import marketing company executive; b. Boston, May 5, 1944; d. William Mason and Jane Chapin (Prouty) Smith; m. Euan Harvie-Watt, Mar. ll, 1967 (div. Aug. 1979); children: Katrina, Jennifer; m. Douglas Marshall Leale, Aug. 29, 1980. BA, Vassar Coll., 1966. Cert. paralegal. Sec. to dir. Met. Opera Guild, N.Y.C., 1966; sec. to pres. Friesons Printers, London, 1974-75; guide, trainer Autoguide, London, 1977-79; ptnr. Inmark Internat. Mktg. Inc., Seattle, 1980—. Social case worker Inner London Ednl. Authority, 1975-76. Democrat. Presbyterian. Home and Office: 5427 NE Penrith Rd Seattle WA 98105-2842

LEAR, EVELYN, soprano; b. Bklyn., Jan. 8, 1930; m. Thomas Stewart; children: Jan, Bonni. Vocal student in, N.Y.C.; student, N.Y. U., Hunter Coll. Song recitals, Phillips Gallery, Washington; mem. Juilliard Sch. Music Workshop; recital, Town Hall, N.Y.C., 1955; lead in Marc Blitzstein's Reuben, Reuben; performed Strauss's Four Last Songs with London Symphony Orch., 1959; mem. Deutsche Opera, 1959, appeared in Lulu at Vienna Festival, 1962, The Marriage of Figaro at Salzburg Festival, 1962, debut, Vienna State Opera, 1964, Frankfurt Opera, 1965, Covent Garden, 1965, Kansas City (Mo.) Performing Arts Found., 1965, Chgo. Lyric Opera, 1966, La Scala Opera, 1971, also in Brussels, San Francisco, Los Angeles, Buenos Aires, debut at Met. Opera as Lavinia in Mourning Becomes Electra, 1967, mem. co., 1967—; roles include Tosca, Manon, Marshallin, Desdemona, Mimi, Dido, Donna Elvira, Marina, Tatiana: TV appearance in La Boheme, 1965; numerous solo appearances, 1960—; appeared in film Buffalo Bill, 1976; rec. artist Angel Records, Deutsche Grammophon. Recipient Concert Artists Guild award 1955, Liederabend, Salzburg Festival 1964, Grammy award for best operatic recording (Marie in Wozzeck) 1965; Fulbright scholar, 1957.

LEAR, FRANCES LOEB, writer; b. Hudson, N.Y., July 14, 1923; d. Herbert Adam and Aline (Friedman) Loeb; m. Norman Milton Lear, 1956 (div. 1985); children: Kate, Maggie. Grad. high sch., Northampton, Mass. Asst. buyer Bloomingdales, N.Y.C., 1945-51; buyer Lord & Taylor, N.Y.C., 1952-59; owner Woman's Pl., Inc., L.A., 1965-84; founder Lear's Mag., N.Y.C., 1988-94; editor-in-chief Lear's Magazine, 1992-94; pres. Lear Television, N.Y.C., 1994—. Author: (autobiography) The Second Seduction, 1992; prodr., appeared video Take Control of Your Money, 1995; contbr. articles to jours. Office: Lear Television 785 Fifth Ave New York NY 10021

LEARMANN, JUDITH MARILYN, secondary education educator; b. Charleston, Ill., Feb. 1, 1938; d. Charles P. and Estelle M. (DeWitt) Swan; m. Paul C. Learmann, Aug. 29, 1958 (dec.); children: Kevin L., Michael P. (dec.). BS, Wis. State Coll., Oshkosh, 1960; MA, Pacific Western U., 1994. Tchr. Monona (Wis.) Grove H.S., 1960-62, U.S. Army Coll. Program, Denver, 1967, Wood Mid. Sch., Ft. Leonard Wood, Mo., 1983-85; tchr., chmn. dept. lang. arts Waynesville (Mo.) H.S., 1985—; presenter in field; chmn. North Ctrl. Philosophy Com., Waynesville, 1987-88; reviewer textbook Adventures in English Literature, 1994; reviewer sci. curriculum, 1994-95, math. curriculum, 1995, social studies curriculum, 1996; mem. evaluation steering com. Mo. Sch. Improvement Program, 1996—, chair instrn. process com., 1996—. Named Most Influential Tchr. award U. Mo., 1991; recipient influential tchr. recognition letter Westminster Coll., 1992, 95. Mem. Nat. Coun. Tchrs. English, Mo. Tchrs. Assn., Mo. Tchrs. English (meeting chmn. dist. conv. 1989, 90), Cmty. Tchrs. Assn. (chmn. legal svcs. 1991-95, sick leave pool com. 1996—), Phi Delta Kappa (tchr. awards, officer nomination, constn. revision coms.). Home: 1737 J C St Waynesville MO 65583-2450 Office: Waynesville HS Historic Rt 66 West Waynesville MO 65583

LEARY, CAROL ANN, academic administrator; b. Niagara Falls, N.Y., Mar. 29, 1947; d. Angelo Andrew and Mary Josephine (Pullano) Gigliotti; m. Noel Robert Leary, Dec. 30, 1972. BA, Boston U., 1969; MS, SUNY, Albany, 1970; PhD, Am. Univ., 1988. Asst. to v.p. for student affairs, dir. women's programs Siena Coll., Loudonville, N.Y., 1970-72; asst. dir. housing Boston U., 1972-78; dir. residence Simmons Coll., Boston, 1978-84, assoc. dean, 1984-85; assoc. dir. The Washington Campus, Washington, 1985-86; adminstrv. v.p., asst. to pres. Simmons Coll., Boston, 1988-94; pres. Bay Path Coll., Longmeadow, Mass., 1995—. Bd. dirs. Bay State Med. Ctr., Carew Hill Girls Club, Colony Club, STCC Assistance Corp., 1996—. Fellow Ednl. Policy Fellowship Program, 1990-91. Mem. Am. Coun. Edn. (rep. Mass. divsn. 1991—), Greater Springfield C. of C. Office: Bay Path Coll Office of the President 588 Longmeadow St Longmeadow MA 01106-2212

LEARY, ROBIN JANELL, administrative secretary, county government official; b. Hudson, Wis., July 9, 1954; d. Edward James and Marlys Marie (Ensign) L. BA in History, U. Wis., Eau Claire, 1976. From stenographer I to program asst. 3 U. Wis., Eau Claire, 1977—; elected sec. 3rd Congl. Dist./Dem. Party of Wis., 1993-95; elected bd. suprs. Dist. 23, Eau Claire County, 1996—; elected Eau Clair County Bd. of Suprs., Dist. 23. Chmn. Eau Claire County Dem. Party, 1990-92, sec., 1986-90, mem. ex-officio exec. bd., 1993-95; elected mem. dist. 23 Eau Claire County Bd. Suprs., 1996-98; elected mem. exec. bd. Eau Claire County Dem. Party, 1995—; mem. credentials com. Wis. Dem. Party, 1990-95, chmn. com., 1990-92; mem. elections commn. Wis. Dem. Party, 1990—; del. Dem. Nat. Conv., Atlanta, 1988, N.Y.C., 1992, Chgo., 1996. Named Female Dem. Vol. of Yr., Eau Claire County Dem. Party, 1989. Mem. AFL-CIO (Eau Claire area labor coun., treas. 1986-94, trustee 1994—, sec. 3d congl. dist. com. on polit. edn. 1993—), AFSCME Pub. Employees Organized to Promote Legis. Equality (vice chmn. 3d congl. dist. 1992-93, chair com. 1993-95, elected vice-chair 3d confl. P.E.O.P.L.E. 1995—, coun. 24 family and gender com. 1990—, tricoun. state woman's com.). Home: 2104 Providence Ct Eau Claire WI 54703-4103 Office: U Wis 105 Garfield Ave Eau Claire WI 54701-4811

LEASE, JANE ETTA, environmental science consultant, retired librarian; b. Kansas City, Kans., Apr. 10, 1924; d. Joy Alva and Emma (Jaggard) Omer; B.S. in Home Econs., U. Ariz., 1957; M.S. in Edn., Ind. U., 1962; M.S. in L.S., U. Denver, 1967; m. Richard J. Lease, Jan. 16, 1960; children—Janet

(Mrs. Jacky B. Radifera), Joyce (Mrs. Robert J. Carson), Julia (Mrs. Earle D. Marvin), Cathy (Mrs. Edward F. Warren); stepchildren—Richard Jay II, William Harley. Newspaper reporter Ariz. Daily Star, Tucson, 1937-39; asst. home agt. Dept. Agr., 1957; homemaking tchr., Ft. Huachuca, Ariz., 1957-60; head tchr. Stonebelt Council Retarded Children, Bloomington, Ind., 1960-61; reference clk. Ariz. State U. Library, 1964-66; edn. and psychology librarian N.Mex. State U., 1967-71; Amway distbr., 1973—; cons. solid wastes, distressed land problems reference remedies, 1967; ecology lit. research and cons., 1966—. Ind. observer 1st World Conf. Human Environment, 1972; mem. Las Cruces Community Devel. Priorities Adv. Bd. Mem. ALA, Regional Environ. Edn. Research Info. Orgn., NAFE, P.E.O., D.A.R., Internat. Platform Assn., Las Cruces Antique Car Club, Las Cruces Story League, N.Mex. Library Assn. Methodist (lay leader). Address: 2145 Boise Dr Las Cruces NM 88001-5149

LEASOR, JANE, religion and philosophy educator, musician; b. Portsmouth, Ohio, Aug. 10, 1922; d. Paul Raymond Leasor and Rana Kathryn (Bayer) Leasor-McDonald. BA, Wheaton Coll., 1944; MRE, N.Y. Theol. Sem., 1952; PhD, NYU, 1969. Asst. prof. Belhaven Coll., Jackson, Miss., 1952-54; dept. chmn. Beirut Coll. for Women, 1954-59; asst. to pres. Wheaton (Ill.) Coll., 1961-63; dean of women N.Y. Theol. Sem., N.Y.C., 1963-67; counselor CUNY, Bklyn., 1967-74; assoc. prof. Beirut U. Coll., 1978-80; tchr. internat. sch., Les Cayes, Haiti, 1984-85; pvt. tutor, 1985—; tchr. Fayette County (W.Va.) Schs., 1993—. Author religious text for use in Syria and Lebanon, 1960; editor books by V.R. Edman, 1961-63, Time and Life mags. Mem. Am. Assn. Counselors, Am. Guild Organists. Episcopalian. Home and Office: 606 Driftwood Dr Charleston WV 25306

LEATH, MARY ELIZABETH, medical/surgical nurse; b. Cochran, Ga., Aug. 12, 1949; d. Warren Shaw Leath and Hattie Mae (Blackshear) Sterling; divorced; children: Myisha Renee, Shamara Antonea. Diploma, City Hosp., 1972; BS, Johns Hopkins U., 1988; ADN, Catonsville Community Coll., 1990; BSN, U. Md., 1993; MS, Johns Hopkins U., 1995. Cert. ACLS, critical care, ICU/trauma specialist, med./surg., PICC lines, IV therapy and maintenance, cardiac care. LPN staff MIEMSS, Balt., 1973-80, Ft. Howard (Md.) VA Med. Ctr., 1981-90; staff nurse Ft. Howard (Va.) VA Med. Ctr., 1990—. Mem. ANA, Black Nurses' Assn., Woodmoor Community Health Assn. (instr. 1984—), Alpha Kappa Phi.

LEATHER, VICTORIA POTTS, college librarian; b. Chattanooga, June 12, 1947; d. James Elmer Potts and Ruby Lea (Bettis) Potts Wilmoth; m. Jack Edward Leather; children: Stephen, Sean. BA cum laude, U. Chattanooga, 1968; MSLS, U. Tenn., 1978. Libr. asst. East New Orleans Regional Libr., 1969-71; libr. Erlanger Nursing Sch., Chattanooga, 1971-75; chief libr. Erlanger Hosp., Chattanooga, 1975-77; dir. Eastgate Br. Libr., Chattanooga, 1977-81; dir. libr. svcs. Chattanooga State Tech. Community Coll., 1981-95, dean libr. svcs., 1996—. Mem. Allied Arts, Hunter Mus., High Mus. Art. Mem. ALA, Southeastern Libr. Assn., Tenn. Libr. Assn. (chair legislation com.), Chattanooga Area Libr. Assn. (pres. 1978-79), Tenn. Bd. Regents Media Consortium (chair 1994-95), Phi Delta Kappa. Episcopalian.

LEATHERBERRY, ANNE KNOX CLARK, interior designer, architectural designer; b. Geneva, Ill., Jan. 19, 1953; d. Donald William and Margaret Lorraine (Johnson) Clark; m. David Boyd Leatherberry, Aug. 5, 1978; children: Elizabeth Anne, Laura Knox. BS in Bus., Miami U., Oxford, Ohio, 1975. With Carson, Pirie, Scott & Co., Chgo., 1975-77; health care sales specialist Gen. Foods Corp., Northlake, Ill., 1977-78; account mgr. Cin., 1978-79; pres., owner Annie's Originals/Kids Collectables, Ltd., Waukesha, Wis., 1979—; mktg. rep./demonstrator mktg. Waukesha, 1988-91; owner Dreamhouse Designs, Waukesha, 1990—, Creative Enterprises Inc., 1990—; cons. Lamb's Quarters, Hartford, Wis., 1982-83, Ungerwear, West Alexandria, Ohio, 1982-84, Little Bits, Waukeshaw, 1984-90, Evelyn's Creations, East Troy, Wis., 1986-90, The Queen's Empire, Inc., Pitts., 1989-90, DRC Co., Mukwonago, Wis., 1990—, Don Belman Builders, 1991-92, Millikin Homes, 1992—, Opportunity Homes, 1993—, Affordable Homes, 1993—, Gemini Homes, 1993, Nelson Remodeling, 1993. Active Waukesha Area Symphonic Band, 1979-93, sec. bd. dirs., 1987-89; active Carroll Coll. Cmty. Orch., 1985-86; vol. tchr.'s aide Clarendon Avenue Sch., Mukwonago, 1988-89; asst. leader Girl Scouts U.S.A., 1988, leader, 1988-89; vol. staff aide Jim Thompson for Gov. Campaign, 1975-76; dir. Children's Choir, 1986; summer music dir. Luth. Ch., 1986, 88; events chmn. Edgewood Golf League, 1988-92; vol. Rose Glen Reading Rams, Waukesha, 1990-92, Health Room, 1990-91, tchr.'s aid, 1991-92; pres. archtl. rev. bd. Red Wing Hills Assn., 1993-96; instr. architecture mentor program Waukesha Sch. Dist., 1995—. Mem. NAFE, PEO (officer 1980-82), Direct Mktg. Assn., Soc. Craft Designers, Met. Builders Assn., Nat. Assn. of Remodeling Industry, Kappa Kappa Gamma. Republican. Lutheran. Home and Office: W241 S5910 Autumn Haze Ct Waukesha WI 53186-9512

LEATHERS, MARGARET WEIL, foundation administrator; b. Princeton, Ind., Dec. 22, 1949; d. Albert J. and Nora Jewel (Franklin) Weil; m. Charles L. Leathers, June 19, 1971 (div. Dec. 1987); children: Julianna L., Kevin Sean. AB, U. Ill., 1971; MS, Russell Sage Coll., 1979. Cert. tchr., N.Y., health edn. specialist. Employment counselor Snelling & Snelling, Schenectady, N.Y., 1972-76; substitute tchr. Monahasen High/Jr. High Sch., Schenectady, 1978-79; grant abstractor State of N.Y., Albany, 1979, program coordinator Am. Lung Assn. Santa Clara-San Benito Counties, San Jose, Calif., 1982-84, dir. programs, 1984-87, nat. clinic leader trainer, 1986—, acting exec. dir., 1987-88, exec. dir., 1988—. Author: Camp Superstuff Workbook and Teachers Manual, 1983; contbr. articles to profl. publs. and mags. Bd. dirs., officer Santa Clara Valley Coun. Parent-Participating Nursery Schs., 1980-81; resource vol. Lyceum Santa Clara Valley, 1983-87; leader Explorer post Boy Scouts Am., San Jose, 1988; mem. adminstrv. bd. coun. ministries United Meth. Ch.; mem. staff 1st asthma camp Young Tchrs. of Health, Soviet Union, 1989, Seattle, 1990; mem. citizen's oversight com. Local Transp. Commn. for Santa Clara County, 1993—; mem. steering com. for Measure A., 1992. Mem. APHA, Soc. Pub. Health Educators, Am. Sch. Health Assn., Assn. of United Way Agys. (exec. bd. 1993), ALA Calif. Coun. Execs. (v.p. 1994). Democrat. Home: 341 Springpark Cir San Jose CA 95136-2144 Office: Am Lung Assn 1469 Park Ave San Jose CA 95126-2530

LEATON, MARCELLA KAY, insurance representative, business owner; b. Eugene, Oreg., Oct. 9, 1952; d. Robert A. and Wanda Jo (Garner) Boehm; m. Michael G. Schlegel, Aug. 9, 1975; children: Kaellen June, Krystalynn Michele. Grad. high sch., Springfield, Oreg. Sales rep. The Prudential, Novato, Calif., 1973—; bus. owner Marcella Enterprises, Novato, 1983—; owner, operator Meetings Extraordinaire, 1987—; owner Mastermind Escapes, 1990—; ind. travel agt., 1995—. Contbr. articles, poetry to profl. pubs. Mem. Nat. Assn. Life Underwriters (nat. quality award 1978, 80, 84), Marin Life Underwriters, Nat. Assn. Profl. Saleswomen (founder Marin chpt., pres. 1982-85, 91-93, chmn. 1985-87, nat. v.p. 1985-86, awards and recognition chmn. 1985-88, nat. pres. 1987-90, exec. dir. 1988-91, regional v.p. 1991-92, N.W. region conf. chmn. 1993), Leading Life Producers No. Calif., Million Dollar Round Table (qualifying), Marin Rowing Assn. (travel chmn. 1992-93), President's Club, Western Star Club. Office: Marcella Enterprises 1929 Benton Ln Novato CA 94945

LEAVER, BETTY LOU, educational administrator, writer; b. Rochester, N.H., Feb. 16, 1950; d. Herman Nathan and Mary Elizabeth (Germon) Ham; m. Carl Don Leaver, Mar. 20, 1970; children: Echo Elizabeth, Fawn Noelle, Shawn Thomas, Shenan Carl. BA, Pa. State U., 1971, MA, 1978. Officer U.S. Army, 1974-82; tchg. fellow U. Pitts., 1978-82; instr. Allegheny County (Pa.) C.C., Monroeville, 1982-83; lang. tng. supr. Fgn. Svc. Inst. U.S. Dept. State, Arlington, Va., 1983-89; dean Sch. Ctrl. European Langs. Def. Lang. Inst., 1992-93; dean Sch. Slavic Langs. Def. Lang. Inst., Monterey, Calif., 1989-92; pres. Am. Global Studies Inst., Salinas, Calif., 1993—; vis. prof. Middlebury (Vt.) Coll., 1994, Bryn Mawr (Pa.) Coll., 1995, 96, U. Helsinki, 1989; cons. Portland (Oreg.) Pub. Schs., Accels and Uzbekistan Ministry of Justice, 1995, Ctr. for Advancement of Lang. Learning, Washington, 1994, 95, pub. schs., Krasnoyarsk, Siberia, 1993—, joint U.S./Russian Space Agy. projects, 1996, Soros Founds., Belarus, 1993, Russia, 1993-94, Ukraine, 1994, Ohio State U., 1988-91, 93, numerous others; interpreter in U.S. and Russia; mem. fgn. lang. adv. com. Arlington County (Va.) Pub. Schs., 1985-88, chmn. 1988; founder consortia CIFLI Georgetown U., Am. Global Studies Inst., Columbia U., UCLA, Harvard U., Middlebury Coll., Bryn Mawr Coll., U. Md., 1994—, U.S. Nval Acad., West Point, N.Y., CIA, NSA, Def. Lang. Inst., Fgn. Svc. Inst., U.S. Air Force Acad., others. 1st lt. U.S. Army, 1974-78. Mem. Am. Assn. for Advancement of Slavic Studies (coord. open house 1985 World Congress), Am. Coun. Tchrs. of Russian (bd. dirs. 1988—, editor newsletter 1987-92), Am. Coun. Tchg. Fgn. Langs., Prunedale Grange, Profl. Women's Network. Home: 747 St Regis Way Salinas CA 93905 Office: Am Global Studies Inst 14 Spreckels Ln Salinas CA 93908

LEAVITT, JUDITH WALZER, history of medicine educator; b. N.Y.C., July 22, 1940; d. Joseph Phillip and Sally (Hochman) Walzer; m. Lewis Arger Leavitt, July 2, 1966; children: Sarah Abigail, David Isaac. BA, Antioch Coll., 1963; MA, U. Chgo., 1966, PhD, 1975. Asst. prof. history of medicine U. Wis., Madison, 1975-81, assoc. prof., 1981-86, prof., 1986—; Evjue-Bascom prof. U. Wis., 1990-95, chmn. dept., 1981-93, assoc. dean for faculty, 1996—. Author: The Healthiest City, 1982, Brought to Bed, 1986, Typhoid Mary, 1996; editor: Women and Health, 1984, Sickness and Health in America, 1985. Office: U Wis Dept History Medicine 1300 University Ave Madison WI 53706-1510

LEAVITT, MARY JANICE DEIMEL, special education educator, civic worker; b. Washington, Aug. 21, 1924; d. Henry L. and Ruth (Grady) Deimel; BA, Am. U., Washington, 1946; postgrad. U. Md., 1963-65, U. Va., 1965-67, 72-73, 78-79, George Washington U., 1966-67; tchr.'s cert. spl. edn., 1968; m. Robert Walker Leavitt, Mar. 30, 1945; children: Michael Deimel, Robert Walker, Caroline Ann Leavitt Snyder. Tchr., Rothery Sch., Arlington, Va., 1947; dir. Sunnyside, Children's House, Washington, 1949; asst. dir. Coop. Sch. for Handicapped Children, Arlington, 1962, dir., Arlington, Springfield, Va., 1963-66; tchr. mentally retarded children Fairfax (Va.) County Pub. Schs., 1966-68; asst. dir. Burgundy Farm Country Day Sch., Alexandria, Va., 1968-69; tchr., substitute tchr. specific learning problem children Accotink Acad., Springfield, Va., 1970-80; substitute tchr. learning disabilities Children's Achievement Ctr., McLean, Va., 1973-82, Psychiat. Inst., Washington and Rockville, Md., 1976-82, Home-Bound and Substitute Program, Fairfax, Va., 1978-84; asst. info. specialist Ednl. Rsch. Svc., Inc., Rosslyn, Va., 1974-76; docent Sully Plantation, Fairfax County (Va.) Park Authority, 1981-87, 88-94, Childrens Learning Ctrs., vol. Honor Roll, 1987, Walney-Collections Fairfax County (Va.) Park Authority, 1989—; sec. Widowed Persons Svc., 1983-85, mem., 1985—. Mem. edn. subcom. Va. Commn. Children and Youth, 1973-74; den mother Nat. Capital Area Cub Scouts, Boy Scouts Am., 1962; troop fund raising chmn. Nat. Capitol coun. Girl Scouts U.S.A., 1968-69; capt. amblyopia team No. Va. chpt. Delta Gamma Alumnae, 1969; vol. Prevention of Blindness, 1980—; fund raiser Martha Movement, 1977-78; mem. St. John's Mus. Art, Wilmington, N.C., 1989—, Corcoran Gallery Art, Washington, 1989-90, 94—, Brunswick County Literacy Coun., N.C., 1989—; sunday sch. tchr. St. Andrews Episc. Ch., Burke, Va., 1995—, mem. search com., 1996. Recipient award Nat. Assn. for Retarded Citizens, 1975, Sully Recognition gift, 1989, Ten Yr. recognition pin Honor Roll, 1990. Mem. AAUW (co-chmn. met. area mass media com. D.C. chpt. 1973-75, v.p. Alexandria br. 1974-76, fellowship co-chmn., historian Springfield-Annandale br. 1979-80, 89-94, 94-95, name grantee ednl. found. 1980, cultural co-chmn. 1983-84), Assn. Part-Time Profls. (co-chmn. Va. local groups, job devel. and membership asst. 1981), Older Women's League, Nat. Mus. of Women in the Arts (charter mem.), Delta Gamma (treas. No. Va. alumnae chpt. 1973-75, pres. 1977-79, found. chmn. 1979-81, Katie Hale award 1989, treas. House Corp. Am. U. Beta Epsilon chpt. 1994—). Club: Mil. Dist. of Washington Officer's Clubs (Ft. McNair, Ft. Myer). Episcopalian. Home: 7129 Rolling Forest Ave Springfield VA 22152-3622

LEAVITT, RHODA VICTORIA, educator; b. Funk, Nebr., Mar. 29, 1921; d. Victor Emmanuel and Bessie Luella (Anderson) Almquist; m. Elton Jay Leavitt, Mar. 24, 1951; children: Daphne Sue Leavitt Sowers, Jill Renee Leavitt Swagerty. BA, Colo. State Coll., Greeley, 1949. Life cert. tchr., Colo. Tchr. Kearney County, Nebr., 1939-42; 3rd & 4th grade tchr. Paxton (Nebr.) Pub. Sch., 1942-45; 3rd grade tchr. Sidney (Nebr.) Pub. Sch., 1945-48; 2nd grade tchr. Denver Pub. Sch., 1949-51; substitute tchr. Clayton (N.Mex.) Pub. Schs., 1959-73; pvt. tutor Clayton, 1973-94; bookkeeper Leavitt Constrn. Co., Clayton, 1955-85. Author: 40 Years - Sierra Grande Camp Meeting, 1992; (poetry) On Death of Friend, 1994, Hummingbird and Eagle, 1995, Rain, 1995. Leader, recruiter Girl Scouts Am., Clayton, 1959-64; facilitator First Offender Program, Jud. Ct., Clayton, 1980-82; bd. mem. Shelter for Domestic Violence, Clovis, N.Mex., 1994—; tutor Literacy Coun., Clayton. Recipient 40 Yr. Tchg. Pin First United Meth. Ch., Clayton, 1990, Woman in Arts award Nat. Mus. Women in Arts, Washington, 1994, 1st pl. watercolor Cimarron County Art Assn., Boise City, Okla., 1995. Mem. PEO Sisterhood, Belle Lettres Book Rev. Club, Tex-Mex Investment Club, Clayton Art Coun., Pi Lambda Theta, Kappa Delta Pi. Republican. Methodist. Home: RR 1 Box 39 Clayton NM 88415

LEAVITT, SANDRA B., editor; b. Chgo., Nov. 27, 1933; d. Sidney S. and Jean (Goldberg) Bloch; m. Arnold Keith Leavitt, July 5, 1953; children: Debbie Leavitt Castleberry, Gail Leavitt Culberson. BA, Northeastern Ill. U., 1974, MA, 1978. Asst. editor Irving-Cloud Pub., Lincolnwood, Ill., 1979-82; assoc. editor Cahners Pub., Des Plaines, Ill., 1982-85; mng. editor Vance Pub., Lincolnshire, Ill., 1985 86; ret. Freelance feature writer in the field. Editor, newsletter Brandeis U. Nat. Women's Com., North Shore, Ill., 1994—. Mem. Am. Contract Bridge League (Master bridge player, winner nat. women's knock-out team, 1981), Brandeis U. Nat. Women's Com. (bd. dirs. 1993—). Home: 195 Linden Park Pl Highland Park IL 60035

LEBAN, CELESTE CASDIA, elementary school educator; b. Que., Can., July 24, 1953; d. Carl Vincent and Maria del Carmen (Rodriguez) Casdia; m. Brian John Leban, Oct. 29, 1976; children: Carla Casiopia, Brianne Gem. BE, U. Miami, 1975. Cert. elem. tchr., Fla. Tchr. 4th and 6th grades Inter Am. Mil. Acad., Miami, Fla., 1975-76; legal investigator Lloyds of Legals & Property Searchers Inc., Miami, 1977-79; tchr. 1st and 2nd grades Shady Acres Sch., North Miami, Fla., 1982-83; med. receptionist Drs. Nichols, Phillips, Elias et al, Miami, 1983-86; tchr. 1st grade Archdiocese of Miami, 1976-77, tchr. 2nd, 5th and 6th grades, 1986-89, tchr. 6th grade, 1989-90; tchr. 6th grade Dade County Pub. Schs., Miami, 1990—; mem. adv. com., co-writer sch. improvement plan Natural Bridge Elem. Sch., North Miami, 1991—, peer tchr., 1996-97; advisor Future Educators of Am. club Natural Bridge Elem. Sch./Dade County Pub. Schs. and State of Fla., 1993—; participant Buddy Reading grant program Dade County Pub. Edn. Fund, 1993-94, chair testing com., 1995-96; co-chair Multicultural com., co-planner Cultural Fair, 1994—; directing tchr. for student tchrs., 1992-93, 95-96.

LEBBY, GLORIA C., history educator; b. Orangeburg, S.C., July 12, 1956; d. Clarence Vivian and Eddie (Mitchell) L. BA, St. Augustine's Coll., 1976; MEd, S.C. State Coll., 1978; EdS, U. So. Miss., 1981; EdD, Nova Southeastern U., 1994. Cert. tchr., S.C., N.C., Miss., La. Instr. history Denmark (S.C.) Tech. Coll., 1993—; vis. instr. history S.C. State Coll., Orangeburg, 1991—. Cert. lay speaker U. Meth. Ch., Orangeburg, S.C., 1986-93. Named Outstanding Young Woman of Am., 1982, 84. Mem. AAUW (life), ASCD, S.C. Hist. Assn., Bamberg County Mental Health Assn., Nat. Coun. for Social Studies, U. So. Miss. Alumni Assn. (life), Order of Ea. Star, Order Golden Cir., Nat. Geographic Soc., Am. Legion Aux., Delta Sigma Theta (Denmark alumnae chpt. Dedicated Svc. award 1984, 90), Phi Alpha Theta. Methodist. Office: Denmark Tech Coll Dept History Denmark SC 29042

LEBEDOFF, RANDY MILLER, lawyer; b. Washington, Oct. 16, 1949; m. David Lebedoff; children: Caroline, Jonathan, Nicholas. BA, Smith Coll., 1971; JD magna cum laude, Ind. U., 1975. Assoc. Faegre & Benson, Mpls., 1975-82, ptnr., 1983-86; v.p., gen. counsel Star Tribune, Mpls., 1989—; asst. sec. Star Tribune Cowles Media Co., Mpls., 1990—; Bd. dirs. Milkweed Editions. Bd. dirs. Minn. Opera, 1986-90, YWCA, 1984-90, Planned Parenthood Minn., 1985-90, Fund for Legal Aid Soc., 1988—, Abbott-Northwestern Hosp., 1990-94. Mem. Newspaper Assn. Am. (legal affairs com. 1991—), Minn. Newspapers Assn. (bd. dirs. 1995—). Home: 1738 Oliver Ave S Minneapolis MN 55405-2222 Office: Star Tribune 425 Portland Ave Minneapolis MN 55488-0001

LEBER, CELIA KETLEY, patent lawyer; b. Washington, Sept. 10, 1964; d. Arthur Donald and Celia May (Swift) Ketley. BS in Mfg. Engring., Boston U., 1989; JD cum laude, Suffolk U., 1994. Bar: Mass. 1994; registered patent atty. Technician W.R. Grace & Co.-Conn., Lexington, Mass., 1983-86, tech. svc. specialist, 1986-88, patent agt., 1988-91; patent agt. Fish & Richardson, Boston, 1991-94, patent atty., 1994—. Mem. Boston Patent Law Assn. Democrat. Office: Fish & Richardson 225 Franklin St Boston MA 02110

LEBER, DEIRDRE ANNE, artist; b. N.Y.C., Sept. 22, 1959; d. Alexander Boris and Madeleine Patricia (Vaneerde) L.; m. David Wolcott Daub, June 27, 1987; children: Ariana, Lucas. Student, Art Students League, N.Y.C., 1973-74, Bowdoin Coll., Brunswick, Maine, 1977-79; BA sigma cum laude, U. Pa., Phila., 1981; postgrad., Showhegan Sch. Painting, Maine, 1981; MFA, Bklyn. Coll., 1986. teaching asst. Bklyn. Coll., 1986; substitute art instr. St. Ann's, Bklyn., 1989. One-person shows at Amsterdam's, N.Y.C., 1992, Hampshire Coll., Amherst, Mass., 1993; exhibited in group shows at Barrett House, Poughkeepsie, N.Y., 1986, Albany (N.Y.) Inst. Art, 1986, Ward-Nasse Gallery, N.Y.C., 1987, 88, Chuck Levitan Gallery, N.Y.C., 1987, Acad. Arts, Easton, Md., 1988, Ariel Gallery, N.Y.C., 1988, Ceres Gallery, N.Y.C., 1988, Marie Galleries, Westchester, N.Y., 1988, East Hampton (N.Y.) Ctr. for Contemporary Art, 1988, Bronx (N.Y.)Mus., 1988, Owl 57 Gallery, Woodmere, N.Y., 1988, 89, 94, Lintas Worldwide, N.Y.C., 1989, Waterworks Visual Art Ctr., Salisbury, N.C., 1990, Cork Gallery, N.Y.C., 1990, Salena Gallery, L.I. U., Bklyn., 1990, Nat. Acad. Design, N.Y.C., 1990, Oreg. State U., Corvallis, 1990, G.W. Einstein Gallery, N.Y.C., 1990, 95, 148 Duane St. Gallery, N.Y.C., 1991, Watchung (N.J.) Art Ctr., 1991, Washington & Jefferson Coll., Washington, Pa., 1992, Hera Gallery, Wakefield, R.I., 1992, Prince St. Gallery, N.Y.C., 1992, , Wycoff (N.J.) Gallery, 1992, 93, Waterside Artists Studios, Stamford, Conn., 1992, Passaic C.C., Paterson, N.J., 1993, Elaine Benson Gallery, Bridgehampton, N.Y., 1993, Bowery Gallery, N.Y.C., 1993, Bklyn. Coll. Gallery, 1994, Metaphor Fine Arts, N.Y.C., 1994. Home: 6 Greene St New York NY 10013

LEBLANC, EUGENIA TALBERT, counselor, educator; b. Gainesville, Fla., July 17, 1947; d. Samuel Stubbs and Francis Eleandor (Selzer) T.; m. Randall Joseph LeBlanc, children: Samuel Joseph, Joshua Randall, Virginia Adeline. BA in Edn., U. Miss., 1969, MEd in Guidance & Counseling, 1972; postgrad., Memphis State U., 1972-74. Cert. counselor; type "A" La. tchg. cert.; nat. cert. counselor; lic. profl. counselor, La. Liaison-tchr. counselor Western State Psych. Hosp., 1972-74; educator St. Charles Sch. Dist., Luling, La., 1986-93; counselor Nicholls State U., Thibodaux, La., 1993—. Coach various recreational youth soccer teams, Luling, La., 1987-91, Youth Softball, Baseball & Track, Luling, La., 1987-91. Mem. ACA, Am. Coll. Counseling Assn., La. Counseling Assn., La. Career Devel. Assn., La. Sch. Counselors Assn., Southwest Assn. Student Assistance Program, La. Assn. Student Assistance Program.

LEBLANC, JEAN EVA, writer, poet; b. Leominster, Mass., Apr. 16, 1961; d. J. Camille and Sydne Grace (Lloyd) LeB. BS in Biology, Fitchburg State Coll., 1986; MA in English, Middlebury Coll., 1993. Contbr. poetry and essays to various periodicals, mus. revs. to Classical disCDigest.

LEBLANC, JEANETTE AMY, psychotherapist, educator, writer, consultant; b. Blytheville, Ark., Mar. 31, 1968; d. Bob Gene and Joan Ann (Hall) Ash; m. Robert Louis LeBlanc, May 27, 1987. BS in Liberal Arts and Psychology, SUNY, Albany, 1989; MS in Cmty. Counseling, Ga. State U., 1991; PhD in Adminstrn. and Mgmt., Walden U., 1994. Libr. technician Civil Svc., Munich, 1988-89; crisis counselor U.S. Army Community Svc., Munich, 1988-89; adolescent counselor Bradley Ctr. Hosp., Inc., Columbus, Ga., 1990-91; group therapist children of alcoholics, 1991-92; social svcs. coord., therapist Anne Elizabeth Shepherd Home, Inc., Columbus, 1991-93; instr. Upper Iowa U., Ft. Polk, La., 1993—; cons., trainer, speaker, 1995—; group therapist for womens group Vernon Cmty. Action Coun., Leesville, La., 1994-96. With U.S. Army, 1986-88. Mem. ACA, NAFE, Assn. for Counselor Edn. and Supr., Internat. Assn. Marriage and Family Counselors, Sierra Club, Toastmasters.

LEBLANC, TINA, dancer; b. Erie, Pa.; m. Marco Jerkunica, May 1988. Trained, Carlisle, Pa. Dancer Joffrey II Dancers, N.Y.C., 1982-83, The Joffrey Ballet, N.Y.C., 1984-92; prin. dancer San Francisco Ballet, 1992—; guest tchr. Ctrl. Pa. Youth Ballet, 1992, 94—. Work includes roles in (with San Francisco Ballet) Con Brio, Bizet Pas de Deux, Swan Lake, Nanna's Lied, Handel -- A Celebration, La fille mal gardée, Rubies, Tchaikovsky Pas de Deux, Seeing Stars, The Nutcracker, La Pavane Rouge, Company B, Romeo and Juliet, Sleeping Beauty, The Dance House, Terra Firma, Lambarena, Fly by Night, In the Night, Ballo della Regina, The Lesson, The Tuning Game, Quartette; (with other companies) The Green Table, Les Presages, Le sacre du printemps, Les Noces, Light Rain, Romeo and Juliet, Runaway Train, Empyrean Dances, La Vivandière, L'air D'esprit, Corsaire Pas de deux, Don Quixote pas de deux. Recipient Princess Grace Found. award, 1988, Princess Grace Statuette award, 1995. Office: San Francisco Ballet 455 Franklin St San Francisco CA 94102-4438

LEBLANC, VICTORIA ANNE, educator; b. Port Arthur, Tex., May 17, 1952; d. Carl Nelson and Vera Adoree (Langworthy) LeB. BS in Theatre/speech, Lamar U., 1974; MA in Theatre/speech, U. Ala., 1977. Voice and diction tchr. asst. U. Ala., Tscaloosa, 1974-76; theatre, speech instr. Lamar U., Beaumont, Tex., 1976-78, 82-83, 93-94, Port Arthur, Tex., 1978-81, 94-95; 1st grade tchr. L.A. Unified, 1985-86; performer My Fair Lady, 1973, 81, The Belle of Amherst, 1982, Little Broadway, L.A., 1986-88, Rock Salt Co., L.A., 1989-91, Imagination Co., L.A., 1991-92, Am. Family Theatre, 1994, Man of La Mancha, 1995. Mem. Mensa.

LEBOUTILLIER, JANET ELA, real estate investment asset manager, writer; b. Marshfield, Mass., May 10, 1936; d. Preston Carleton and Barbara (Higgins) Ela; m. John Walter McNeill, Oct. 10, 1959 (div. 1970); children: Duncan Davis McNeill, Sarah McNeill Treffry; m. Martin LeBoutillier, May 10, 1986. AA, Briarcliff Jr. Coll., 1956; BA in English Lit., U. Colo., 1958; postgrad. Real Estate/Mortgage Banking, NYU, 1973-78. Lic. N.Y. and Conn. real estate broker; cert. property mgr. Sales, leasing agt. L.B. Kaye Assocs., Ltd., N.Y.C., 1969-74; comml. leasing agt. Kenneth D. Laub & Co., N.Y.C., 1975; dir. leasing, asst. bldg. mgr. Douglas Elliman Gibbons & Ives Co., N.Y.C., 1975-76; adminstr. REIT adv. unit Chase Manhattan Bank, N.A., N.Y.C., 1976-78; asst. dir. real estate investments Mass. Mut. Life Ins. Co., Springfield, Mass., 1978-80; dir. real estate investments Yale U., New Haven, Conn., 1980-81; ind. cons. N.Y.C., 1981-83; sr. analyst, equity mgmt., sales and devel. Aetna Realty Investors, Inc., Hartford, Conn., 1983-84; dir. pub. involvement unit Aetna Realty Investors, Inc., 1984-86; sr. asset mgr. Cigna Investments, Inc., Hartford, 1986-87; v.p. Wm. M. Hotchkiss Co., New Haven, Conn., 1987-88; pres., prin. LeBoutillier & LeBoutillier, Inc., Lyme, Conn., 1989-93. Author: Mediations on Joy, 1995. Mem. Grace Episcopal Ch., mem. pastoral care and healing commn., coord. prayer team ministry. Mem. Internat. Order of St. Luke the Physician (co-founder, convener Heart of COmpassion Conn. Shoreline, Conn. area chpt. 1993—), Soc. Mayflower Descendants, Nat. Soc. of Colonial Dames of Am. Democrat. Episcopalian. Home and Office: 8 Laurel Dr Old Lyme CT 06371-1462

LEBOWITZ, CATHARINE KOCH, state legislator; b. Winchester, Mass., June 30, 1915; d. William John and Carolyn Sophia (Kistinger) Koch; m. Murray Lebowitz, Sept. 21, 1971 (dec. Oct. 1978). Student Northeastern U., 1948-49, Boston Coll., 1949-52. Sec. ERA, Bangor, Augusta, Maine, 1935-38, WPA, Portland, Maine, 1938-42; personnel officer, exec. sec. USN, Portland, 1942-47; exec. sec. Clark Babbitt, Boston, 1947-48; adminstrv. asst. Moore Bus. Forms, Boston, 1948-52; apt. mgr., wholesale appliance div. Coffin-Wimple Inc., 1952-62, clerk U.S. Dist. Ct. Bangor (No. dist), 1962-79; sec. Portland Credit Bur., 1980-86; mem. Bangor City Council, 1985-87; mem. Maine State Legislature, 1982-92; bd. dirs. Eastern Transportation, 1989-94; mem. Bus. Adv. Coun., 1991—; active Program Rev. Subcom., 1991—; mem. adv. com. RSVP, 1987—, bd. dir., bus. adv. coun., and chmn. sub com. project with industry, 1992—; mem. adv. coun. Eastern Maine Tech. Coll., 1992—; bd. dirs. Rural Health Ctrs. Maine, Inc., 1992—; adv. bd. Maine Ctr. for the Arts, U. Maine, 1992—. Sec. Symphony Women, Bangor, 1964-84; bd. dirs. Opera House Com., Bangor, 1978-94; del. Rep. Nat. Conv., 1984, 88; mem. Spl. Task Force to Study Child Abuse, 1985-92; legis. com. United Way of Penobscot Valley, 1988-93, bd. mem., 1993—, subcom. strategic planning cmty. leadership fund distbn.; adv. com. Maine

Devel. Found., 1984-92; adv. bd. Aftercare, 1990, planning bd. St. Joseph Hosp., 1987-92, dir., v.p. St. Joseph Hosp. Aux., 1994—, Maine Ctr. Arts adv. bd., 1994; Bangor City Hosp. Aux., 1988—; bd. dirs. Penobscot Theater, 1990; accredited Beauty Pageant judge, 1986—. Recipient Civilian Meritorious Service award USN, Portland Maine, 1946; named Hon. Alumnus Secretarial Sci., Husson Coll., 1980; mem. Eastern Maine Commn. Cmty. Svc., 1996. Mem. Credit Women Internat. (treas. 1975-77, Credit Woman of Yr. 1969), Credit Profls., 1988-92, Bangor Community Theater (treas. 1973—, award 1973), U. Maine Maine Masque Theater (judge 1983-90), Maine N.G. Assn. (hon.), Maine Air N.G. (hon.), Nat. Assn. Retired Fed. Employers (v.p. bd. dirs. 1993—, sec. 1994), Credit Women Bangor (sec. 1965-67), Bangor Dist. Nursing Assn. (corp. mem. at large), Bangor C. of C. (mem. consumer rels. coun. 1981-90, coord. 150th anniversary prodn. Music Man 1984), Bangor Hist. Soc. (bd. dirs. 1993—, exec. bd. sec. 1994—), Penobscot County Extension Svc. (bd. dir. 1995), Penobscot County Republicans, Penobscot County Rep. Women's Club (sec. 1979), Bangor City Rep. Club (bd. dirs., treas. 1993—), Newcomb Soc., Ret. Fed. Employees (v.p. 1994—, pres. 1996), Zonta Club (pres. Bangor 1962-64, 80-82, v.p. 1994, Outstanding Leader 1991), Mgmt. Club, Easdtern Maine Med. Ctr. Aux.

LEBRECHT, THELMA JANE MOSSMAN, reporter; b. Indpls., Feb. 21, 1946; d. Elmore Somerville and Lois Thelma (Johnson) Mossman; m. Roger Dublon LeBrecht, May 4, 1968. BS in Journalism, U. Fla., 1968. Pub. affairs reporter WBT and WBTV, Charlotte, N.C., 1967-72; freelance reporter Toronto and N.Y.C., 1972-76; reporter KYW Newsradio, Phila., 1976-80; editor ABC Radio Network, N.Y.C., 1980-81; reporter AP Broadcast, Washington, 1981—. Bd. dirs. Washignton Press Club Found., 1995—. Mem. Radio and TV Corrs. Assn. in U.S. Capitol (chmn. 1991, AP Oliver S. Gramling Disting. Reporter award 1996). Office: AP Broadcast 1825 K St NW Washington DC 20006-1202

LECHTANSKI, CHERYL LEE, chiropractor; b. Elizabeth, N.J., Dec. 27, 1961; d. Leo Joseph and Barbara Frances (Sullivan) L. BA in Biology and Journalism, NYU, 1985; DC, N.Y. Chiropractic Coll., 1989. Lic. chiropractor, N.J., N.Y., Pa., Del., Mich. Chiropractic assoc. Chiropractic Arts Ctr., Downingtown, Pa., 1990-91; pvt. practice, Newark, 1992-93, Morganville (N.J.) Family Chiropractic Office, 1993—. Mem. N.J. Chiropractic Soc., Pa. Chiropractic Soc., NOW, World Wildlife Fund, Save the Manatee Club, Ctr. for Marine Conservation, Phi Chi Omega. Unitarian. Home: 42 Hutchinson Dr Port Monmouth NJ 07758 Office: Morganville Family Chiropractic Office 52 Tennent Rd Morganville NJ 07751

LECHTENBERGER, DEANN, special education educator; b. Okarche, Okla., June 24, 1954; d. William Joseph and Peggy Jo (Huston) Lechtenberger; 1 child, Mark Earl William. BS, U. Tex., Austin, 1976; MS, U. Tex., Richardson, 1981. Cert. in elem. edn. and spl. edn., Tex. Spl. edn. tchr. Briarwood Sch., Houston, 1976-77, Dickinson (Tex.) Ind. Sch. Dist., 1977-78, Dallas Ind. Sch. Dist., 1978-83, Grand Prairie (Tex.) Schs., 1983-93; Univ. teaching fellow U. North Tex., Denton, 1993-96; grad. intern Office of Spl. Edn. Programs U.S. Dept. Edn., 1996—; cons. Mansfield (Tex.) Ind. Sch. Dist., 1994; cons., tchr. Natural History Mus., Dallas, 1984—. Co-author monograph; presenter workshops. Sch. Bd. reporter South Grand Prairie PTA, 1990-91. Mem. aSCD, Coun. Exceptional Children, Tex. Classroom Tchrs. Assn. (bd. dirs. 1992-93), tex. Student Coun. Exceptional Children (pres.-elect 1994-95, pres. 1995-96). Christian. Office: U North Tex Sta PO Box 9865 Denton TX 76203-4865

LECKIE, CAROL MAVIS, retired state government administrator; b. Watertown, Wis., Feb. 25, 1929; d. Arthur Walter Bessel and Effie Vada (Squires) Downs; m. Ralph Junior Judd, Sept. 27, 1947 (div. Dec. 1952); children: Russell Howard, Barbara Rae; m. Leonard John Leckie, Sept. 30, 1977 (dec. May. 1990); stepchildren: Leonard John, Gordon Armstrong, Lorna Jean. Grad. high sch. Madison, Wis. Mgr. data processing Dept. Justice, State of Wis., Madison, 1971-79, mgr. Records Mgmt. Program, 1979-83, mgr. Typography Sect., 1983-90; ret. Mem. com. State of Wis. Employees Combined Campaign, Madison, 1986, 88-91, co-chair, 1987. Mem. Assn. Records Mgrs. and Adminstrs. (pres. 1983-84), Bus. Forms Mgmt. Assn. Lutheran. Avocations: travel, church work. Home: 810 Ziegler Rd Madison WI 53714-1342

LECLAIR, SUSAN JEAN, hematologist, clinical laboratory scientist, educator; b. New Bedford, Mass., Feb. 17, 1947; d. Joseph A. and Beatrice (Perry) L.; m. James T. Griffith; 1 child, Kimberly A. BS in med. tech., Stonehill Coll., 1968; postgrad., Northeastern U., Boston, 1972-74; MS in Med. Lab. Sci., U. Mass., Dartmouth, 1977. Cert. clin. lab. scientist; cert. med. technologist. Med. technologist Union Hosp., New Bedford, Mass., 1968-70; supr. hematology Morton Hosp., Taunton, Mass., 1970-72; edn. coord., program dir. Sch. Med. Tech. Miriam Hosp., Providence, 1972-79; hematology technologist R.I. Hosp., Providence, 1979-80; asst. prof. med. lab. sci. U. Mass., Dartmouth, 1980-84, assoc. prof. med. lab. sci., 1984-92, prof. med. lab. sci., 1992—; instr. hematology courses Brown U., Providence, 1978-80; cons. Bd. R.I. Schs. Med. Tech., R.I. Hosp. Div. Clin. Hematology, Cardinal Cushing Gen. Hosp., Charlton Meml. Hosp., St. Luke's Hosp., VA Med. Ctr., Providence, 1984—, Nemasket Group, Inc., 1984-87, Gateway Health Alliance, 1985-87; chair hematology/hemostasis com. Nat. Cert. Agy. for Med. Lab. Pers. Exam. Coun., 1994—. Contbr. articles to profl. jours.; contbr. articles to jours and chpts. to books; author computer software in hematology. Reviewer Nat. Commn. Clin. Lab. Scis., 1986-89; chairperson Mass. Assn. Health Planning Agys., 1986-87; bd. dirs. Southeastern Mass. Health Planning Devel. Inc., (1975-88, numerous other offices and coms.); planning subcom. AIDS Edn. (presentor Info Series). Mem. Am. Soc. Clin. Lab. Sci., Nat. Cert. Agy. for Med. Lab. Pers. (chair Hematology Com. of Exam Coun. 1994—), Am. Soc. Med. Tech. Edn. and Rsch. Fund, Inc. (chairperson 1983-85), Mass. Assn. for Med. Tech. (pres. 1977-78), Southeastern Mass. Soc. Med. Tech. (pres. 1975-76), Alpha Mu Tau (pres. 1993-94). Office: U Mass Dept Med Lab Sci Dartmouth MA 02747

LECOCQ, KAREN ELIZABETH, artist; b. Santa Rosa, Calif., Nov. 4, 1949; d. Maynard Rodney and Lois May (Lessard) LeC.; m. David Lawrence Medley, Sept. 7, 1995. BA, Calif. State U., Fresno, 1971, MA, 1975; postgrad., Calif. Inst. of the Arts, L.A., 1971-72. Founding mem. Feminist Art Program, Fresno, Calif., 1971, Calif. Inst. of the Arts, L.A., 1972; One woman shows include Calif. State U. Art Gallery, Fresno, 1970, 76, Merced (Calif.) Coll., 1969, 77, 91, Calif. Inst. of the Arts, L.A., 1972, Recent Sculptures, Fresno, 1977, 78, Womanart Gallery, N.Y.C., 1980, Merced, 1987, Arts Coun. Gallery, Merced, 1989, Amos Eno Gallery, N.Y.C., 1994, 750 Gallery, Sacramento, 1995, Meridian Gallery, San Francisco, 1996, others; commissions include Absolut Vodka, 1993; vis. artist Merced County Schs., 1977-78, 79-82, 88-91; grad. instr. Calif. State U., Fresno, 1976-78, Merced Coll., 1973-76. Group shows include Womanhouse, L.A., 1972, Off Centre Centre, Calgary, Alta., Can., 1985, 86, Ryosuke Gallery, Osaka, Japan, 1986, Gallery Six Oh One, San Francisco, 1989, Fresno Art Mus., 1989, Ann Saunders Gallery, Jamestown, Calif., 1991, Pro arts Gallery, Oakland, Calif., 1991, Calif. Mus. Art, Santa Rosa, 1991, Harbs Gallery, Lexington, Va., 1992, Russell Sage Gallery, Troy, N.Y., 1992, Amos Eno Gallery, 1992-96, ARC Gallery, Chgo., 1993, 96, Lengyel Gallery, San Francisco, 1995, 750 Gallery, Sacramento, 1994-96, L.A. Mus. Contemporary Art, 1995, Armand Hammer Mus., L.A., 1996, many others. Docent Gallery Guide Art Train, Merced, 1983; artistic dir. Black and White Ball, Merced Regional Arts Coun., 1989-96. Cora T. McCord scholar; CETA grantee, Merced, 1978, Fresno, 1977; Calif. Inst. Arts scholar, 1972. Mem. Internat. Sculpture Source, No. Calif. Women's Caucus for Art, Pro Arts of Oakland, San Francisco Mus. Art. Democrat. Home and Office: PO Box 2204 Merced CA 95344

LE COUNT, VIRGINIA G., communications company executive; b. Long Island City, N.Y., Nov. 22, 1917; d. Clifford R. and Luella (Meier) LeCount. BA, Barnard Coll., 1937; MA, Columbia U., 1940. Tchr. pub. schs. P.R., 1937-38; supr. HOLC, N.Y.C., 1938-40; translator Guildhall Publs., N.Y.C., 1940-41; office mgr. Sperry Gyroscope Co., Garden City, Lake Success, Bklyn. (all N.Y.), 1941-45; billing mgr. McCann Erickson, Inc., N.Y.C., 1945-56; v.p., bus. mgr., bd. dirs. Infoplan Internat, Inc., N.Y.C., 1956-69; v.p., bus. mgr. Communications Affiliates Ltd., Communications Affiliates (Bahamas) Ltd., N.Y.C., 1964-69; bus. mgr. Jack Tinker & Ptnrs., Inc., N.Y.C., 1969-70; mgr. office services Interpublic Group of Cos., Inc., N.Y.C., 1971-72, corp. records mgr., 1972-83, mktg. intelligence data mgr., 1975-83. Mem. Alumnae Barnard Coll., N.Y. Health and Racquet Club Spa. Mem. Marble Collegiate Ch. Home: 136 E 55th St Apt 10Q New York NY 10022-4534

LEDBETTER, DEIDRE LEDAY, special education educator; b. New Orleans, Oct. 16, 1959; d. Felton Clark Augusta and Frances Ada (Norman) Provost; m. Robert Leday, June 8, 1975 (dec. Aug. 1976); 1 child, Demetria Marie; m. George Dallas Ledbetter, Jr., Feb. 7, 1981. B Gen. Studies in Behavioral Scis., U. Southwestern La., 1982, BA in Spl. Edn., 1993, MEd in Guidance and Counseling, 1996. Resource tchr. Iberia Parish Sch. Bd., New Iberia, La., 1982-94, link cons., 1994—; mem. core com. Very Spl. Arts Festival, New Iberia, 1990-94. Active Coun. for Exceptional Children. Named Tchr. of Yr., Lee Street Elem. Sch., 1994. Mem. NEA, La. Assn. Educators, Iberia Assn. Educators (sec. 1989-90), Order Ea. Star, Order of Cyrene (royal Magdalene 1991—), Heroines of Jericho (vice ancient matron 1990—). Democrat. Methodist. Home: 1007 Bank Ave New Iberia LA 70560 Office: Iberia Parish Spl Edn Dept PO Box 200 New Iberia LA 70560

LEDBETTER, RANDI RAE, obstetrician/gynecologist; b. Portland, Oreg., June 24, 1952; d. James Edward Wagenblast and Shiela Faye (Mathis) Rhyne; m. Gordon Kirk Ledbetter, Feb. 14, 1971. BA in Biology, Linfield Coll., 1974; MD, Oreg. Health Scis. U., 1978. Diplomate Am. Bd. Ob-Gyn., Am. Bd. Family Practice. Intern, resident Family Practice Residency of Idaho, Boise, 1978-81; pvt. practice Boise Family Practice, 1981-88; resident in ob-gyn. Kaiser Found. Hosp., San Francisco, 1988-91; pvt. practice Women's Healthcare Assocs., Portland, Oreg., 1991—; chmn. laparoscopy com. ob-gyn. dept. St. Vincent's Hosp., Portland, 1993—. Mem. women's task force Women's Life, Boise, 1985-88. Fellow Am. Coll. Ob-Gyn.; mem. Oreg. Med. Assn., Washington County Med. Soc. (bd. dirs.), Porsche Club Am., Sports Car Club Am., Team Continental (dir. med.). Republican. Home: 12929 NW Laidlaw Rd Portland OR 97229-2413 Office: Women's Healthcare Assocs 9155 SW Barnes Rd Ste 340 Portland OR 97225-6630

LEDBETTER, SHARON FAYE WELCH, educational consultant; b. L.A., Jan. 14, 1941; d. James Herbert and Verdie V. (Mattox) Welch; m. Robert A. Ledbetter, Feb. 15, 1964; children: Kimberly Ann, Scott Allen. BA, U. Tex.-Austin, 1963; learning disabilities cert. Southwestern U., Tex., 1974; MEd, Southwest Tex. State U., 1979, prin. cert., 1980, supt. cert., 1984. Speech pathologist Midland Ind. Sch. Dist., Tex., 1963, Austin Ind. Sch. Dist., Tex., 1964-72; speech pathologist, asst. prin. Round Rock Ind. Sch. Dist., Tex., 1972-84; prin. Hutto Ind. Sch. Dist., 1984-88; asst. dir. div. mid. sch. edn. Tex. Edn. Agy., 1989-94; educational cons. 1994—. Pres. Berkman PTA, 1983-84; sponsor Jr. Woman's Club, 1980-82; mistress ceremonies Hutto Beauty Pageant, 1986, 87. Recipient Appreciation award Round Rock Sch. Dist., 1984, St. Judes Children's Research Hosp., 1985, Soc. Disting. Am. High Sch. Students, 1985, Disting. Svc. award Tex. Edn. Agy, 1994. Mem. ASCD, Nat. Mid. Sch. Assn., Tex. Mid. Sch. Assn., Tex. Assn. Community Schs., Tex. Assn. Secondary Sch. Prins., Phi Delta Kappa. Avocations: horses, spectator sports. Home: 43 Woodland Loop Round Rock TX 78664-9776

LEDBURY, DIANA GRETCHEN, adult education educator; b. Denver, Mar. 7, 1931; d. Francis Kenneth and Gretchen (Harry) Van Ausdall; m. Chander Parkash Lall, Dec. 26, 1953 (div. Aug. 1973); children: Anne, Neil, Kris; m. Eugene Augustus Ledbury, Sept. 13, 1976; stepchildren: Mark, Cindy, Rob. BA in Sociology, Colo. U., 1953. Instr. Home, and Family Life Seattle Pub. Schs. Adult Edn., 1957-62, Seattle C.C., Seattle, 1962-69, Green River C.C., 1969-71; asst. tchr. Renton Sch. Dist., Wash., 1974-83; adult edn. instr. Mental Health Network, Renton, 1984—; coord. Inter-Study, Renton, 1985—, program dir. Crossroads Child Care, 1985-86, family svcs. coord. , 1986-87, program supr. Candyland Too Child Care Ctr., 1987—, Candyland Also, 1987-90; coord. child care staff Washington Fitness Ctr., 1991-93. Mem. Renton Area Youth Svcs. Bd., Sch. and Community Drug Prevention Program, Renton dist. coun. PTA, Renton Citizen's Com. on Recreation; vol. Griffin Home for Boys; coord. Modern Dance Prodn., Carco Theater; adult leader Camp Fire Girls' Horizon Club; mem. bd. Allied Arts of Renton; mem. Bicentennial Com. for a Cultural Arts, Edn. and Recreation Ctr.; PTA rep. Dimmit Jr. High Sch.; mem. Sch. and Community Recreation Com.; founder Handicapped Helping Themselves, Mental Health Network; precinct committeeperson 11th dist. Republican party, Wash., 1976-85. Recipient Golden Acorn award Wash. State Congress PTA, Renton, 1972. Mem. AAUW (legis. chair 1983-87, mem. com. on strategic sch. policy safety in schs. 1993-94, com. on getting parents involved. 1994-95, pub. policy chair AAUW 1994-96), Assn. Social and Health Services (mem. com. 1984-85). Episcopalian. Avocations: arts; culture; recreation; child and family advocate.

LEDDY, SUSAN, nursing educator; b. N.J., Feb. 23, 1939; d. Bert B. and Helen (Neumann) Kun; children: Deborah, Erin. BS, Skidmore Coll., 1960; MS, Boston U., 1965; PhD, NYU, 1973; cert., Harvard U., 1985. Chair dept. nursing Mercy Coll., Debbs Ferry, N.Y.; dean sch. nursing U. Wyo., Laramie, dean coll. health scis.; prof. Widener U. Sch. Nursing, Chester, Pa., 1988—, dean, 1988-93. Author: (with M. Pepper) Conceptual Bases of Professional Nursing, 1985, 3d edit., 1993. Bd. dirs. Springfield Hosp., 1992-94. Postdoctoral fellow U. Pa., 1994-96. Mem. NLN (bd. dirs. and 1st v.p. 1985-87).

LEDER, MIMI, television director; b. N.Y.C., Jan. 26, 1952; d. Paul and Etyl Leder; m. Gary Werntz, Feb. 6, 1986; 1 child, Hannah. Student, Los Angeles City College, Am. Film Inst. Dir. TV movies A Little Piece of Heaven (also known as Honor Bright), 1991, Woman with a Past, 1992, Rio Shannon, 1992, Marked for Murder, 1992, There Was a Little Boy, 1993, House of Secrets, 1993, The Sandman, 1993; dir. TV series L.A. Law, 1986, Midnight Caller, 1988, A Year in the Life, 1988, Buck James, 1988, Just in Time, 1988, Crime Story, 1988; supervising prodr. China Beach, 1988-91 (Emmy nominations for outstanding drama series 1989, 90, and outstanding directing in drama series 1990, 91), Nightingales, 1989, ER, 1994— (Emmy award 1995). Mem. Dirs. Guild Am. *

LEDER, SANDRA JUANITA, elementary school educator; b. Stuttgart, Ark., Apr. 17, 1942; d. Everett Samuel and Lorene (Payer) L. BS, U. Cen. Ark., 1963; MEd, McNeese State U., 1976, EdS, 1979; PhD, Fla. State U., 1984. Cert. tchr. grades 1-8, supr., prin., aerospace edn., supr. student tchrs., La.; cert. pvt. pilot. Elem. tchr. DeWitt (Ark.) Pub. Schs., 1963-66, Gillett (Ark.) Pub. Schs., 1966-69; math. tchr. Tulsa County, Tulsa, Okla., 1970; tchr. Calcasieu Parish, Lake Charles, La., 1971-94, Episcopal Day Sch., Lake Charles, La., 1994—; guest instr. McNeese State U., 1995; condr., dir. numerous aerospace camps, 1980—; chmn., judge sci. fairs; com. mem. and chmn. self-study com. So. Assn. Colls. and Schs., 1985-86; arranger numerous tours and workshops in field. Manuscript rev. panel Sci. Scope, 1988-91, writer, 1992; TV interviews, 1991—; radio and ednl. TV appearances, Tchr. in Space applicant, 1985; contbr. Metric Curriculum Guide for La., 1978; presenter in field; contbr. articles to profl. jours. Vol. reader NEA, 1990; active outreach com. Episcopal Ch. of Good Shepherd, 1994; pres. Lake Charles Regional Airport Authority, 1991, 95, sec., 1993, v.p. 1994, pres., 1995; mem. gen. adv. coun. Sowela Tech. Inst., 1990; active Mayor's Commn. for Women, 1986-91, fall conf. chmn. resource fair, 1988; founder Lake Charles Ninety-Nines Challenger Ctr.; pres. La. Nat. Airshow Bd., 1993-95, sec. 1993—; bd. dirs. Chenault Airpark Aviation Mus., 1994—; tour organizer. Recipient S.W. Region Frank Brewer Aerospace Edn. award CAP, 1990, Excellence in Aviation Edn. Championship award S.W. region FAA, 1989, Acad. Edn. award Women's History Month, Lake Charles, Great Expectations Tchr. award Sta. KPLC-TV, 1993, Pinnacle award, 1993, NEWMAST award NASA, 1986, STEP award, 1993, Outstanding Young Astronaut Chpt. Leader award, 1993; grantee Space Acad., 1988, South Cen. Bell, 1991, 93, Olin Corp., 1994; Olin Corp. grantee, 1995. Mem. Nat. Sci. Tchrs. Assn., Nat. Space Soc., La. Assn. Educators (del. to convs. 1977-79, 84, 86), Aircraft Owners and Pilots Assn., Delta Kappa Gamma (pres. 1992-94, legis. com. 1985-86, chair social com. 1987-89, comms. com. chair 1990, 94-95), Kappa Kappa Iota, Phi Delta Kappa. Republican. Episcopalian. Office: Episcopal Day Sch Ch of Good Shepherd 715 Kirkman St Lake Charles LA 70601-4350

LEDERBERG, VICTORIA, judge, former state legislator, lawyer, psychology educator; b. Providence, July 7, 1937; d. Frank and Victoria (Marzilli) Santopietro; m. Seymour Lederberg, 1959; children: Tobias, Sarah. AB, Pembroke Coll., 1959; AM, Brown U., 1961, PhD, 1966; JD, Suffolk U., 1976, LLD, 1995. Mem. R.I. Ho. of Reps., 1975-82, chmn. subcom. on edn., fin. com., 1975-82, subcom. on mental health, retardation and hosps. and health, spl. legis. commns pub. sch. funding and funding handicapped edn. programs; chmn. nat. adv. panel on financing elem. and sec. edn., Washington, 1979-82; mem. R.I. State Senate, 1985-91, chmn. fin. com. subcom. on social svcs., 1985-89, dep. majority leader, 1989-91; prof. psychology R.I. Coll., 1978-93; pvt. practice, Providence; mcpl. ct. judge, Providence, 1991-93; justice R.I. Supreme Court, Providence, 1993—, chmn. com. on judicial performance evaluation, 1993—, chmn. com. on user-friendly cts., 1994—. USPHS Fellow physiol. psychology, 1964-66. Trustee Brown U., 1983-89, Roger Williams U., 1980—, vice chmn. corp., dir. Sch. Law, Butler Hosp., 1985-93, also sec. of corp. Mem. New Eng. Psychol. Assn., ABA, R.I. Bar Assn., Am. Judicature Soc., Nat. Assn. Women Judges, Sigma Xi. Office: 250 Benefit St Providence RI 02903-2719

LEDERER, MRS. ESTHER P. See LANDERS, ANN

LEDERER, MARION IRVINE, cultural administrator; b. Brampton, Ont., Can., Feb. 10, 1920; d. Oliver Bateman and Eva Jane (MacMurdo) L.; m. Francis Lederer, July 10, 1941. Student, U. Toronto, 1938, UCLA, 1942-45. Owner Canoga Mission Gallery, Canoga Park, Calif., 1967—; cultural heritage monument Canoga Mission Gallery, 1974—; Vice pres. Screen Smart Set women's aux. Motion Picture and TV Fund, 1973—; founder sister city program Canoga Park-Taxco, Mexico, 1963; Mem. mayor's cultural task force San Fernando Valley, 1973—; mem. Los Angeles Cultural Affairs Commn., 1980-85. Mem. Los Angeles Cultural Affairs Commn., 1980-85. Recipient numerous pub. service awards from mayor, city council, C. of C. Mem. Canoga Park C. of C. (cultural chmn. 1973-75, dir. 1973-75). Presbyn. Home: PO Box 32 Canoga Park CA 91305-0032 Office: Canoga Mission Gallery 23130 Sherman Way Canoga Park CA 91307-1402

LEDERMAN, STEPHANIE BRODY, artist; b. N.Y.C.; d. Maxwell and Ann (Rockett) Brody. Student, U. Mich.; BS in Design, Finch Coll.; MA in Painting, L.I. U., 1975. One-person exhbns. Franklin Furnace, N.Y.C., 1979, Kathryn Markel Fine Arts, N.Y.C., 1979, 81, 83, Katzen/Brown Gallery, N.Y.C., 1988, 89, Real Artways, Hartford, Conn., 1984, Alfred U., 1990, Hal Katzen Gallery, N.Y.C., 1992, Hillwood Art Mus., Brookville, N.Y., 1992, Casements Mus., Ormond Beach, Fla., 1994, Broward Cmty. Coll., Ft. Lauderdale, Fla., 1994, Hebrew Home for the Aged, N.Y.C., 1994-95, Galerie Caroline Corre, Paris, 1995, La. State U., Shreveport, 1995; exhibited in numerous group shows including Newark Mus., 1983, Met. Mus. Art, N.Y.C., 1986, Queens Mus., 1989, Basel Art Fair, 1989, Caroline Corre, Paris, 1991, R.I. Mus. Art, 1991, Am. Acad. Arts & Letters, N.Y.C., 1992, Guild Hall Mus., East Hampton, N.Y., 1993, Ind. U, Terre Haute, 1993, Jewish Mus., N.Y.C., 1993, Nat. Mus. Women in Arts, Washington, 1994, Ronald Feldman Gallery, N.Y.C., 1995, Alternative Mus., N.Y.C., 1995, Eugenia Cucalon, Gallery, N.Y.C., 1995; represented in permanent collections Newark Mus., Mus. Modern Art, Prudential Ins., Bertelsmann Music Group, Guild Hall Mus., East Hampton, L.I., Chase Manhattan Bank, N.Y. Health and Hosp. Corp., Victoria & Albert Mus., London, Doubleday Books. Recipient Hassam and Speicher purchase award Am. Acad. and Inst. Arts and Letters, 1988, purchase award Arts in Hosps., Richmond, Va.; grantee Creative Artists Pub. Svc., 1977, Ariana Found. for Arts, 1985, Artists Space, 1987, E.D. Found., 1991, Lancaster Group., U.S. A. Comm. award, 1991, spl. opportunity stipend N.Y. State Coun. Arts, 1992, 94, Heuss House project Lower Manhattan Cultural Coun., 1992. Studio: 85 N 3rd St Fl 5 Brooklyn NY 11211-3923

LEDING, ANNE DIXON, artist, educator; b. Fort Smith, Ark., Jan. 29, 1947; d. Charles Victor Dixon and Elizabeth Johanna (Mitchell) Dixon Roderick; m. Larry Joseph Peters (dec), Jan. 6, 1967; m. John Thomas Leding, June 24, 1978; children: Jonathan Brian (Peters) Leding, Caroline Kristen Leding. Student, Memphis State U., Memphis, 1964-66, Westark C.C., Fort Smith, 1976-78. Art instr. Fort Smith (Ark.) Art Ctr., 1976; pvt. practice art instr. Fort Smith, 1977-78; classical guitar instr. Paul Mendy Guitar Studio, Fort Smith, 1978-79; cmty. svc. classical guitar instr. Westmark C.C., 1976. One-woman shows include Ariel Gallery, Fort Smith Art Ctr., Cafe Bliss, La Cima Club; group shows include Del Mar Coll., Ariel Gallery, N.Y.C.; featured in Ency. of Living Artists in Am., 1986-87; listed in N.Y. Art Rev., S.W. Art Rev., 1990-91; critiqued in Artspeak, N.Y., 1990. Recipient 1st place Fort Smith Sch. Dist., 1955; letter of recognition Seventeen Mag., 1963; hon. mention Fort Smith Art Ctr. Bicentennial, 1976, Del Mar Coll., 1985, Trinity Arts Competition, 1992, Mid Cities Fine Artists Competition, 1994. Mem. Nat. Mus. Women in the Arts, Dallas Mus. Art, Kimbel Art Mus., Trinity Arts Guild, Ft. Smith Art Ctr. Republican. Anglican. Home: 402 Walden Tr Euless TX 76039-3870 Office: Anne Leding Illustrations 402 Walden Tr Euless TX 76039-3870

LEDKOVSKY, MARINA, Slavic languages and literature educator; b. Berlin, May 12, 1924; came to U.S., 1951; d. Victor Fasolt and Sophie Dimitrievna Nabokov; m. Boris Mikhailovich Ledkovsky, Nov. 24, 1943 (dec. Aug. 1975); children: Alexander, Dimitri, Tatiana, Michael; m. William W. Astman, July 17, 1980 (div. 1992). Cert., highest (superiore) diploma, U. Perugia, Italy, 1942; BA magna cum laude, Columbia U., 1956, PhD, 1969. Chmn. lang. dept. St. Hilda's and St. Hughs's H.S., N.Y.C., 1955-58; chmn. French dept. Chapin Sch., N.Y.C., 1958-62; instr. slavic langs. and lits. Columbia U., N.Y.C., 1958-69, asst. prof., 1969-73, assoc. prof., 1973-79; prof. Barnard Coll./Columbia U., N.Y.C., 1979-96, prof. emerita, 1996—; mem. corp., trustee, asst. treas., editl. bd. New Rev., 1991—; nominator Booker Russian Novel Prize, 1994-95, juror, 1994; cons. mem. Transfiguration Women's Club, Moscow, 1990—. Author: The Other Turgenev: From Romanticism to Symbolism, 1973; editor: (anthology) Russia According to Women, 1989, (dictionary) Russian Women Writers, 1994 (Assn. Women in Slavic Studies Best Book award 1994); contbr. chpts. to books, articles to profl. jours. Active Congress Russian-Ams., Inc., Washington, 1960—; bd. dirs. Russian Orthodox Ch. Musicians' Fund, N.Y.C., 1986—, Russian-Am. Scholars in the U.S.A., 1995. Recipient East European and Slavic Lang. award Am. Assn. Tchrs. Slavic and East European Lang. for outstanding achievement in scholarship, 1995; grantee NEH, 1975-76, Am. Philos. Soc., 1989, travel grantee IREX, 1989, numerous others. Mem. Am. Assn. for Advancement Slavic Studies, Am. Assn. Tchrs. Slavics, Assn. for Women in Slavic Studies (Lifetime Achievement award 1994), Assn. Russian-Am. Scholars (bd. dirs. 1994—), Phi Beta Kappa. Eastern Orthodox. Home: 110 Brooklyn Ave Apt 2-A Freeport NY 11520-2998 Office: Columbia U Barnard Coll 3009 Broadway New York NY 10027

LEDLEY, TAMARA SHAPIRO, earth system scientist, climatologist; b. Washington, May 18, 1954; d. Murray Daniel and Ina Harriet (Gordon) Shapiro; m. Fred David Ledley, June 6, 1976; children: Miriam Esther, Johanna Sharon. BS, U. Md., 1976; PhD, MIT, 1983. Rsch. assoc. Rice U., Houston, 1983-85, asst. rsch. scientist, 1985-90, sr. faculty fellow, 1990—; assoc. rsch. scientist Tex. A&M U., 1995—; mem. Alaska SAR facility archive working team NASA, Pasadena, Calif., 1988, McMurdo SAR facility sci. working team, 1990; participant workshop of Arctic leads initiative Office Naval Rsch., Seattle, 1988, 1st DeLange Conf. on Human Impact on Environ., Houston, 1991; cons. Houston Mus. Natural Sci., 1989-90, Broader Perspectives, Houston, 1989; dir. weather project for tchr. tng. program George Obs., Rice U., 1990-92; co-dir. Rice Houston Mus. Natural Sci. Summer Solar Inst., 1993; mem. rev. panels NSF, 1993, 95. Contbr. articles to profl. publs. Spl. judge Houston Area Sci. and Engring. Fair, 1985; judge S.W. Tex. Region H.S. Debates, 1986, Houston Area Sci. and Engring. Fair, 1990, 91, 92, 95; guest expert Great Decisions '88 Polit. Discussion Group, 1988; participant U.S. Global Change Rsch. Program's Climate Modeling Forum, 1994. Fellow sci. computing Nat. Ctr. for Atmospheric Rsch., 1978, Fed. Jr. fellow, 1972-74; senatorial scholar State of Md., 1972-76; grantee NSF, 1985-87, 89-92, 92-94, 94—, Tex. Higher Edn. Coordinating Bd., 1988-90, 90-92, Univ. Space Rsch. Assn., NASA, 1991-93, 92-94. Mem. AAAS (mem. electorate nominating com. 1995—), Am. Geophys. Union (com. global environ. change 1993-96, assoc. editor Jour. Geophys. Rsch.-Atmospheres 1993-96), Am. Meteorol. Soc., Oceanography Soc., Sigma Xi, Phi Beta Kappa, Phi Kappa Phi, Alpha Lambda Delta. Office: Rice U Dept Space Physics & Astronomy 6100 Main St Houston TX 77005-1827

LEDNICKY, DONNA CAROL, art educator; b. Houston, Aug. 13, 1965; d. Donald Gene and Carol Ann (Clark) L. BS in Recreation and Pks., Tex. A&M U., 1987; MA, U. Tex., 1993. Project specialist/family involvement Bryan (Tex.) Ind. Sch. Dist., 1989-91, art smart coord., 1991-94; art smart coord. Pathways Cmty. Counseling, Bryan, 1994-96; artistic dir. Art's For Everyone, Inc., 1996—; vol. coord. Forsyth Ctr. Galleries, College Station, 1989-91; festival vol. coord. Arts Coun., College Station, 1990-91. Founder Extravaganic Art Smart Gallery, Bryan, 1994. Prevention grantee Tex. Commn. on Alcohol and Drug Abuse, 1991-94; Arts grantee Tex. Commn. on Arts, 1994, 95. Mem. Nat. Art Edn. Assn., Tex. Art Edn. Assn., Brazos Valley Art Edn. Assn. (founding mem.), Am. Sch. Health Assn., Arts Coun. Brazos Valley (art space chair 1993—, Arts grantee 1994, 95, 96). Home: PO Box 206 Snook TX 77878-0206 Office: Arts For Everyone 1307 Memorial Ste 606 Bryan TX 77802

LEDO, MARLENE, dialysis staff nurse; b. Miami Beach, Fla., Dec. 21, 1963; d. Manuel and Georgina (Sobrino) L.; m. Anthony Quinones, Apr. 24, 1992. Nursing diploma with honors, Jackson Meml. Hosp., 1991; AS, Miami Dade C.C., 1991; BSN with honors, Fla. Internat. U., 1996. AACN, BLS, ACLS; cert. nephrology nurse, clin. nurse II. Nursing asst. Mercy Hosp., Miami, Fla., 1980-83; sec. Palm Springs Hosp., Hialeah, Fla., 1983-85, Wilfredo Alvarez, M.D., Hialeah, 1985-87; ICU sec. Bapt. Hosp., Miami, 1988-91, ICU staff nurse, 1991-93, dialysis staff nurse, 1993—; adv. bd. Bapt. Hosp. of Miami, 1993-95, adj. faculty, 1996, clin. practice coun., 1996. Named to Am. acad. of Disting. Students, 1996; Nephrology Nursing Cert. Bd. Career Mobility scholar, 1996. Mem. AACN, Am. Nephrology Nurses Assn. (sec. 1994-96, pres.-elect 1996, ESRD seminar coord. 1995—). Republican. Roman Catholic. Home: 10615 SW 129th Ct Miami FL 33186 Office: Bapt Hosp of Miami 8900 N Wendall Dr Miami FL 33176

LEE, ANGELA DEANN, optometrist; b. Ada, Okla., June 28, 1960; d. Gerald Wayne and Janice Kay (Thompson) L. BS, Cameron U., 1983; OD, Northeastern U., 1987. cert. nat. and internat. bds. Assoc. doctor Lawton, Okla., 1987-89, Atlanta Eye Surgery Group, 1989-93; owner Atlanta Eye Care Ctr., 1993—; dir. Hope for Kids, Atlanta, 1995—. Republican. Mem. Internat. Ch. of Christ. Home: 2472 Becky Ln Atlanta GA 30319

LEE, ANN MCKEIGHAN, secondary school educator; b. Harlan, Iowa, Nov. 18, 1939; d. Earl Edward and Dorothy Elizabeth (Kaufman) McK.; m. Duane Edward Compton, Aug. 13, 1960 (div. 1985); children: Kathleen, David, Anne-Marie, John. Cert. in med. tech., Creighton U., 1960; BA in Art History, Ind. U., 1984; MA, U. South Fla., 1992, postgrad. Cert. secondary tchr., Fla.; cert. med. technologist. Realtor Savage/Landrian Realty, Indpls., 1978-84; lectr. Marian Coll., Indpls., 1987-88; tchr. Sarasota (Fla.) County Schs., 1989-92, rep. faculty coun., 1991-92; lectr. curriculum & instrn. U. South Fla., 1993—; docent Historic Spanish Point, Osprey, Fla., 1989-93, Ringling Mus. Art, 1993—; presenter panel Bibliographic Intstruction in Art History. Contbr. articles to profl. jours. V.p. fin. LWV, Indpls., 1971-73; v.p. dist. IV aux. ADA, 1976-78, comptroller, 1978-89; coord. Gold Coun. and Ambs. U. South Fla., 1990-92. Recipient Silver Svc. award Crossroads Guild, 1981. Mem. AAUW, Coll. Art Assn., Soc. Archtl. Historians, Gulf Coast Heritage Assn. (co-chmn. pub. rels.), Sarasota Arts Coun. (tchr. rep. 1990), Phi Kappa Phi, Phi Delta Kappa. Roman Catholic. Home and Office: 3617 Shady Brook Ln Sarasota FL 34243-4840

LEE, ANNE NATALIE, nurse; b. Bklyn.; d. Taras Pavlovich and Maria (Jukovskaya) Dubovick; B.A., Hunter Coll., 1940; M.A., N.Y.U., 1948; R.N., McLean Hosp. Sch. Nursing, Waverly, Mass., 1946; M.S., Boston U., 1958; m. Henry Lee, Feb. 20, 1945; adopted children: Alice, Jennifer, Philip. Pvt. duty nurse, N.Y.C., 1946-48; staff nurse Vis. Nurse Service, 1947-48; staff nurse health dept. Schoharie Co., N.Y., 1948-51; supervising nurse N.Y. Dept. Health, Syracuse, 1951-53, cons. hosp. nursing, Albany, 1958-63, cons. nurse in epidemiology, 1963-65, cons. nurse in svc. edn., 1965-72, cons. nursing svcs. and adminstrn., 1972-75, dir. Office Hosp. Nursing Svcs. N.Y. State Dept. Health, 1975-80; dir., coord. nursing service instr. program co-sponsored N.Y. State Dept. Health, N.Y. State Hosp. Assn., N.Y. State League Nursing, N.Y. State Nurses Assn., 1954-57; sometimes lectr. Mem. Am. Nurses Assn. (cert. advanced nursing administrn.), Sigma Theta Tau. Contbr. articles to profl. jours. Home and Office: 1149 Hillsboro Mile Pompano Beach FL 33062-1724

LEE, BARBARA A., retired federal magistrate judge. AB, Boston U., 1959; LLB, Harvard Law Sch., 1962. Bar: Conn. 1962, N.Y. 1966. Atty. Poletti Freidin Prashker Feldman & Gartner, 1968-74, ptnr., 1974-82; pvt. practice N.Y.C., 1983-87; U.S. magistrate judge U.S. Dist. Ct. (so. dist.), N.Y., 1988-96; ret., 1996; adj. prof. law Seton Hall U., So. Orange, N.J., 1984-87. Mem. com. on ecumenical and inter-religious affairs of Roman Cath. Archdoicese of N.Y., 1983—. Mem. Fed. Magistrate Judges Assn., Assn. of Bar of City of N.Y. (mem. adminstrv. law com. 1973-74, mem. fed. cts. com. 1981-84, mem. com. on state cts. of superior jurisdiction 1984-87, mem. libr. com. 1989-92).

LEE, BARBARA CATHERINE, career counselor; b. Augusta, Ga., Apr. 30, 1931; d. Walter Charles and Dorothy Fulgum (Sasser) L.; married, Dec. 23, 1951 (div. Feb. 1959); 1 child, William Lee Hooton. BS in Vocat. Hom Econs., Winthrop Coll., 1952; MEd, U. Ga., 1960, MS in Family and Child Devel., 1968, EdS in Counselor Edn., Ga. Southern U., 1991. Cert. Nat. Bd. Cert. Counselors. Vocat. hom econs. tchr. Evans (Ga.) High Sch., 1955-56; vocat. home econs. tchr. Murphey Jr. High Sch., Augusta, Ga., 1956-63; vocat. consumer home econs. tchr. Butler High Sch., Augusta, 1963-75, Josey High Sch., Augusta, 1975-81; vocat. child devel. tchr. Hephzibah High Sch., Augusta, 1981-85; elem. and middle sch. counselor Ridge Spring-Monetta Elem. and Middle schs., 1986-87; part-time grad. rsch. asst. Ga. Southern U., Statesboro, 1990; career counselor St. John's High Sch., Charleston, S.C., 1991—; part-time tchr. Augusta Coll., 1972-73; part-time child devel. tchr. Augusta Tech. Sch., 1985-86; part-time edl. dir. adolescent program Human Hosp., 1988-89. Recipient Ga. Six-Yr. Study scholarships Richmond County Bd. Edn., 1958; recipient Augusta Woman's Club scholarship, 1990. Mem. AAUW (scholarship chmn. Ga. chpt. 1983), AACD, Am. Sch. Counselor Assn. Am. Vocat. Assn., Nat. Career Devel. Assn., S.C. Assn. Counseling Devel., S.C. Career Devel. Assn., Kappa Delta Pi, Phi Upsilon Omicron, Phi Kappa Phi. Office: St Johns High Sch 1518 Main Rd Johns Island SC 29455-3437

LEE, BETTY REDDING, architect; b. Shreveport, La., Dec. 6, 1919; d. Joseph Alsop and Mary (Byrd) Redding; m. Frank Cayce Lee, Nov. 22, 1940 (dec. Aug. 1978); children: Cayce Redding, Clifton Monroe, Mary Byrd (Mrs. Kent Ray). Student La. State U., 1936-37, 37-38, U. Calif. War Extension Coll., San Diego, 1942-43; student Centenary Coll., 1937; attended Roofing Industry Ednl. Inst., 1980-82, 84, 86-88, 89-90, 93, Better Understanding Roofing Systems Inst., 1989. Sheetmetal worker Consol.-Vultee, San Diego, 1942; engring. draftsman, 1943-45; jr. to sr. archtl. draftsman Bodman & Murrell, Baton Rouge, 1945-55; sr. archtl. draftsman to architect Post & Harelson, Baton Rouge, 1955-58; assoc. arch. G. Ross Murrell, Jr., Baton Rouge, 1960-66; staff arch. Charles E. Schwing & Assos., Baton Rouge, 1966-71, Kenneth C. Landry, Baton Rouge, 1971, 73-74; design draftsman Rayner & McKenzie, Baton Rouge, 1972-73; cons. arch. and planner Office Engring. and Cons. Svcs., La. Dept. Health and Human Resources, Baton Rouge, 1974-82; arch. roofing and waterproofing sect. La. Dept. Facility Planning and Control, 1982—. Author Instructions to Designers for Roofing Systems for Louisiana Public Buildings; co-author: Building Owners Guide for Protecting and Maintaining Built-Up Roofing Systems, 1981; designed typical La. country store for La. Arts and Sci. Ctr. Mus. Recipient Honor award Schuller BURSI Group, 1989, 90, 91, 92, 93. Mem. La. Assn. Children with Learning Disabilities, 1967-69, Multiple Sclerosis Soc., 1963—, CPA Aux., 1969-70, PTA, 1953-66; troop leader Brownies and Girl Scouts U.S.A., 1959-60; asst. den mother Cub Scouts, 1955-57. Licensed architect. Mem. ASTM, Nat. AIA, AIA La., AIA Baton Rouge (first woman mem.), DAR, Constrn. Specifications Inst. (charter mem. Baton Rouge chpt.) So. Bldg. Code Congress Internat., Miss. Roofing Contractors Assn. (first woman hon.), Nat. Roofing Contractors Assn., La. Inst. Bldg. Scis. (founding mem. 1980), Roof Cons. Inst. (govt. liaison mem.), Inst. Roofing and Waterproofing Consultants, Jr. League Baton Rouge., Le Salon du Livre Club, Kappa Delta. Republican. Episcopalian. Home: 1994 Longwood Dr Baton Rouge LA 70808-1247 Office: Capitol Sta 281 Kenmore Ave Baton Rouge LA 70806-5521

LEE, CARLA ANN BOUSKA, nursing educator; b. Ellsworth, Kans., Nov. 26, 1943; d. Frank J. and Christine Rose (Vopat) Bouska; m. Gordon Larry Lee, July 8, 1967. RN, Marymount Coll., Salina, Kans., 1964; BSN, U. Kans., 1967; MA, Wichita State U., 1972, EdS, 1975, M in Nursing, 1984; PhD, Kans. State U., 1988. RN; cert. family and adult nurse practitioner, advanced nurse adminstr., health edn. specialist. Staff, charge nurse Ellsworth (Kans.) County Vet. Meml. Hosp., 1964-65; critical, coronary, and surg. nurse Med. Ctr. U. Kans., Kansas City, 1966-67; Watkins Meml. Hosp. and Student Health Ctr., 1965-55; asst. dir., chief instr. sch. nursing Wesley Sch. Nursing, Wichita, Kans., 1967-74; asst prof., chairperson Nurse Clinician/Practitioner Dept. Wichita State U., 1974-84; assoc. prof., dir. nurse practitioner program Ft. Hays State U., Hays, Kans., 1992-95; assoc. prof., coord. postgrad. nursing studies Clark Coll., Omaha, 1995—; cons. GRCI's CE Providership, 1994-96; lectr. Wichita State U., 1972-74, mem. grad. faculty, 1993-95; cons. Hays Med. Ctr.-Family Healthcare Ctr., 1993-96, Baker U., Northeastern U., Boston; mem. adv. coun. Kans. Newman Coll.; mem. adv. bd. Kans. Originals, Kans. Dept. Econ. Devel. Project, Wilson; mem. grad. faculty U. Kans. 1993-95; rschr. in field. Author: (with Stroot & Barrett) Fluids and Electrolytes: A Basic Approach, 3d edit., 1984, 4th ed., 1996 (poetry) Seasons: Marks of Life, 1991 (Golden Poet award 1991), Winter Tree, 1995 (Internat. Poet of Merit award 1995), (booklet) Czechoslovakian History, 1988 (honor room Czech Mus. and Opera House, Wilson); author, editor: History of Kansas Nursing, 1987; contbr. articles to profl. jours. Co-founder Kans. Nurses Found., pres., trustee, 1978-93, vol. ARC, 1967-92, bd. dirs., 1977-90; mem. rschr. Gov.'s Commn. Health Care, Topeka, 1990; mem. State of Kans. health care agenda Kans. Pub. Health Assn., 1995; city coord. campaign Sec. State, 1986; vol., lectr. Am. Heart Assn., Am. Cancer Soc., 1967—; election judge Sedgwick County, Kans., 1989-94; chair Nat. Task Force on Care Competence of Nurse Practitioners, 1995; mem. Nat. Task Force on Feasibility of Care Exam. for Nurse Practitioners, 1995. Nurse Practitioner Tng. grantee U.S. Health and Human Svcs.; named Outstanding Cmty. Leader, jaycees, Alumnus of Yr., Kansas U, 1979, marymount Coll., 1987, Poet of Yr., 1995; recipient Tchr. award Mortar Bd. Fellow Am. Acad. Nursing, Am. Acad. Nursing; mem. ANA (nat. and site visitor ANCC), Kans. Nurses Assn. (bd. dirs., treas.), Kans. Alliance Advanced Nurse Practitioners (founder, pres., 1986), Gt. Plains Nurse Practitioners Soc., (founder, pres. 1993), Internat. Soc. Poets (disting.), Alpha Eta (pres. Wichita State U. chpt.), Sigma Theta Tau Internat., Internat. Woman of Yr. Republican. Roman Catholic. Home: 1367 N Westlink St Wichita KS 67212-4238 Office: Clarkson Coll Dept Nursing 101 S 42nd St Omaha NE 68131

LEE, CAROL FRANCES, lawyer; b. Montreal, Que., Can., Sept. 17, 1955; came to U.S., 1966; d. Frank B. and Mary Lee; m. David John Seipp, Sept. 10, 1994. BA, Yale U., 1976, JD, 1981; BA, Oxford (Eng.) U., 1978. Bar: D.C. 1982, U.S. Ct. Appeals (D.C. cir.) 1982, U.S. Dist. Ct. D.C. 1984, U.S. Supreme Ct. 1986. Law clk. to judge U.S. Ct. Appeals (D.C. cir.), Washington, 1981-82; law clk. to justice U.S. Supreme Ct., Washington, 1982-83; assoc. Wilmer, Cutler & Pickering, Washington, 1983-88, ptnr., 1989-93; gen. counsel Export-Import Bank U.S., Washington, 1993-95; v.p., gen. counsel Internat. Fin. Corp. (World Bank Group), Washington, 1995—; lectr. law Harvard U., Cambridge, Mass., 1989-90, 92, Yale U., New Haven, Conn., 1991. Contbr. articles to profl. jours. Marshall scholar U.K., Oxford, 1976. Fellow Am. Bar Found.; mem. ABA, Am. Soc. Internat. Law, Am. Soc. Legal History, Phi Beta Kappa. Office: Internat Fin Corp 1850 I St NW Washington DC 20433

LEE, CARVEL ANITA, author, artist; b. Mpls., Apr. 2, 1910; d. Abraham Lincoln and Rebecca Theodora (Lung) Bigham; m. Kermit Anton Lee, May 18, 1934; children: Kermit Anton Jr., Lorita Gail Nelson. Student, Mpls. Sch. Art, 1929, U. Minn., 192. Artist, copywriter Bigham Print Shop, Mpls., 1926-28; head artist, advt. mgr. Strutwear Knitting Co., Mpls., 1928-41; cons. Bloomington Sr. Adv. Group, Bloomington, Minn., 1992-94. Author, illustrator, 1961-96; graphic artist Bloomington TOOL TV, Time of Our Lives TV; artist Nat. WCTU, 1952-53. Recipient Citation Eleven Who Care TV, 1992. Mem. Nat. League Am. Pen Women, Nat. Assn. Ret. Persons (activity dir. Richfield chpt., citation 1994), Richfield Ret. Edn. Assn., Federated Garden Clubs. Baptist. Home: 8830 Logan Ave S Minneapolis MN 55423-2065

LEE, CATHERINE A., librarian, educator; b. Jersey City, N.J., Dec. 4, 1961; d. Peter John and Catherine (Powell) Apicella; m. Roger Alan Lee, Sept. 10, 1988. BA in English, U. South Fla., 1988, MLS, 1990; MA in English, Eastern Ky. U., 1993. Crisis counselor Alternative Human Svcs., St. Petersburg, Fla., 1985-90; libr. dir. Greenbrier C.C., Lewisburg, W.Va., 1990-91; pub. svcs. libr. Eastern Ky. U., Richmond, 1991-94; head libr. Pa. State U., DuBois, 1994—; mem. libr. adv. bd. DuBois Bus. Coll., Pa., 1995—. Contbr. articles to profl. jours., chpts. to books; editor: Nat. Coun. Learning Resources Newsletter, 1996—. Friend DuBois Pub. Libr., 1994—. Recipient Acad. Excellence grants Pa. State DuBois Ednl. Found., 1995, 96; Continuing Edn. scholarship Pa. State Libr., 1994. Mem. AAUW (program chair 1995—, woman of yr. award 1996), ALA, Assn. Coll. & Rsch. Librs., Golden Key Nat. Honor Soc., Phi Kappa Phi (pres. eastern Ky. U. br.), Sigma Tau Delta. Republican. Office: Pa State U DuBois Campus College Pl Du Bois PA 15801

LEE, CHARLYN YVONNE, chemical engineer; b. Washington, May 1, 1960; d. James Charles and Beverly Mae (Williams) L. BSChemE, MIT, 1982; MSChemE, Ga. Inst. Tech., 1984. Cert. environ. mgr. Engring. intern Naval Surface Weapons Ctr., Silver Spring, Md., 1977-78; engring. aid VA, Washington, 1978-81; engr. Dupont Savannah River Lab, Aiken, S.C., 1982-83, Dupont Exptl. Sta., Wilmington, Del., 1984-86; mfg. engr. Dupont Spruance Plant, Richmond, Va., 1986-89; rsch. engr. Dupont Jackson Lab., Deepwater, N.J., 1989-91; process engr. Dupont Pontchartrain Works, LaPlace, La., 1991-93; environ. protection specialist NIH, Bethesda, Md., 1995—. Bd. mem. Richmond Area Program for Minorities in Engring., 1987-89; corp. advisor Nat. Action Coun. for Minorities in Engring., Wilmington, 1991; mem. D.C. Youth Adv. Bd. for Mental Health, Washington. Recipient Merit award VA, 1981; Proctor and Gamble grantee, 1981; Gem fellow Nat. Consortium for Grad. Degrees for Minorities in Engring., Inc., 1982, Fed. Jr. fellow, 1978. Mem. AIChE, NAFE. Home: 4812 Illinois Ave NW Washington DC 20011-4578

LEE, CORINNE ADAMS, retired educator; b. Cuba, N.Y., Mar. 18, 1910; d. Duston Emery and Florence Eugenia (Butts) Adams; m. Glenn Max Lee, Oct. 30, 1936 (dec. Feb. 1964). BA, Alfred U., 1931. Cert. tchr., N.Y. Tchr. English Lodi (N.Y.) High Sch., 1931-36, Ovid (N.Y.) Cen. Sch., 1936-67. Author: (light verse) A Little Leeway, 1983, (anecedotes, light verse, quips) A Little More Leeway, 1984, (essays, short stories, poems) Still More Leeway, 1986. Trustee Montour Falls Meml. Libr. Mem. life PTA. Mem. Nat. Ret. Tchrs. Assn., N.Y. State Ret. Tchrs. Assn., Schuyler County Ret. Tchrs. Assn., Elmira and Area Ret. Tchrs. Assn., LWV. Avocations: reading, travel, writing.

LEE, DEBORA ANN, elementary school educator, reading specialist; b. Beckley, W. Va., May 2, 1958; d. David Lavon and Edith (Graham) L. AB in Bus. Adminstrn., Beckley Coll., 1978; AB in Arts, Beckley Coll. (Coll. W. Va.), 1982; BS, Concord Coll., 1984; MA, U. W. VA., 1990. Cert. tchr. elem. edn. 1-8, reading specialist k-12, adult. Sec. United Mine Workers Assn., Mullens, W. Va., 1978; receptionist, sec. Ashland Fin., Mullens, 1978-79; tchr. Wyoming County Bd. Edn., Pineville, W. Va., 1984—. Mem. NEA, W. Va. Edn. Assn., Internat. Reading Assn., W. Va. State Reading Coun., Wyoming County Reading Coun. (charter, pres. 1990), Kappa Delta Pi. Democrat. Baptist. Office: Mullens Elem Sch 300 Front St Mullens WV 25882-1304

LEE, DENISE TERI, tax specialist; b. Burlingame, Calif., Jan. 12, 1966; d. Edwin Theodore and Lillian (Wong) L.; m. Rodney Lum, May 20, 1995. BS, San Francisco State U., 1990, MS in Taxation, 1996. Tax auditor Franchise Tax Bd., Oakland, Calif., 1990—. Office: Franchise Tax Bd 1970 Broadway Ste 550 Oakland CA 94612

LEE, ELIZABETH BOBBITT, architect; b. Lumberton, N.C., July 9, 1928; d. William Osborne and Catharine Wilder (Bobbitt) Lee. Student Salem Coll., 1945-47; B.Arch. with honors, N.C. State Coll., 1952. Registered architect, N.C., 1955, S.C., 1964. Assoc. William Coleman, Architect, Kinston, N.C., 1952-55; Skidmore, Owens & Merrill, N.Y.C., 1955-56; prin. Elizabeth B. Lee, FAIA, Architect, Lumberton, N.C., 1956-73, 82—; sr. ptnr. Lee & Thompson, Architects, Lumberton, 1973-82. Bd. dirs. Robeson Little Theatre, Lumberton, 1977-80, N.C. Dance Theatre, Winston-Salem, N.C., 1980-85, Robeson County Community Concerts, Lumberton, 1980-87; trustee N.C. State U., Raleigh, 1983-92; mem. bd. endowment N.C. State U., 1993—. Recipient cert. recognition Randolph E. Dumont Design Program, 1970, Disting. Alumna award, Salem Coll., 1989. Fellow AIA (nat. dir. 1983-85; officeholder N.C. chpt., 1959, v.p., 1978, pres. 1979, bd. dirs. 1980, pres. eastern sect. N.C. chpt., 1975, bd. dirs. S. Atlantic Regional Council, 1977-79); mem. Jr. League (pres. Lumberton chpt., 1968), Robeson County Heart Assn. (pres. 1970), N.C. Design Found., N.C. Archtl. Found. (pres. 1982-83), Lumberton Jr. Service League (pres. 1968), N.C. State Alumni Assn. (bd. dirs. 1982-85, chmn. Robeson county chpt.), Phi Kappa Phi. Democrat. Presbyterian. Home: 906 N Chestnut St Lumberton NC 28358-4801 Office: 407 Elm St PO Box 1067 Lumberton NC 28359

LEE, EMMA MCCAIN, social worker; b. McCormick, S.C., July 8, 1948; d. John Walker and Emma Eliza (Nealous) McCain; m. Lannis Bernard Lee, Dec. 27, 1986; children: Nefertiti McCain, Jasmine Lee; stepchildren: LaTonia, LaStacia, Lannis Bernard Jr., Laterra. BS in Sociology, Paine Coll., 1970; MA in Sociology, Am. U., 1975; EdS, U. S.C., 1995. Cert. criminal justice specialist. Caseworker II Phila. County Bd. Assts., 1972-75; social worker II, human svcs. sr. provider Ga. Dept. Human Resources, Augusta, 1976—. Mem. AACD, Nat. Orgn. Forensic Counselors, Alpha Kappa Mu. Democrat. Office: Ga Dept Human Resources Ga Regional Hosp 3405 Old Savannah Rd Augusta GA 30906-3815

LEE, ESTHER, advertising executive. Exec. v.p., group acct. dir. Deutsch, Inc., N.Y.C. Office: Deutsch Inc 215 Park Ave S New York NY 10003*

LEE, EVE, actress; b. N.Y.C., Mar. 17; d. Everett and Sylvia Ward (Olden) L. BA, U. Cin., 1969, MA, 1970; PhD, Vanderbilt U., 1974. Asst. prof. German Fisk U., Nashville, 1971-76; asst. prof. German and Swedish U. Md., College Park, 1976-78; area coord. Christian Sci. Ctr., Boston, 1978-81; instr. German, U. So. Calif., L.A., 1982; instr. German Goethe Inst., L.A., 1985-89; sr. rsch. assoc. U. N.Y., Albany, 1989-92. Appeared in (TV series) Days of Our Lives, NBC, 1984-91, General Hospital, 1988—, Santa Barbara, NBC, 1990-92, The Bold and the Beautiful, CBS, 1991-94. Del. to Dem. State Party Conv., 1995, 96; vol. coord. Broadview, L.A., 1995—. Mem. New Frontier Dem. Club (exec. bd. 1994—), Beverly Hills Dem. Club (v.p. 1994—). Office: PO Box 77134 Los Angeles CA 90007-0134

LEE, EVELYN MARIE, secondary education educator; b. Germantown, Ohio, Dec. 17, 1931; d. Robert Orlandus and Edna Cathern (Durr) Stump; m. John Henry Lee, Dec. 16, 1956; children: Mark Douglas, David Matthew, Lori Ann Lee Delehoy. BS in Edn., Otterbein Coll., 1954; MEd with emphasis in reading, U. Alaska, 1979. Dept. store tng. supr., asst. mdse. mgr. The Home Store, Dayton, Ohio, 1954-55; tchr. Parma (Ohio) Pub. Schs., 1955-56; math aide civil svc. Nat. Adv. Com. for Aeros. Ames Lab., Moffett Field, Calif., 1956-57; substitute tchr. Warren (Ohio) Pub. Schs., 1957-59, tchr., 1969-60; tchr. Gwinn (Mich.) Pub. Schs., 1960-64; tchr. Anchorage Sch. Dist., 1964-65, 68-87, substitute tchr., 1987-96. Hon. life mem. Alaska PTA. Mem. NEA (life), NEA-Alaska (ret. v.p., bd. dirs., life), Anchorage Concert Assn. (coun. of dirs.), Alaska Hist. Soc. (life). United Methodist. Home: 1521 Park Dr Loveland CO 80538-4285

LEE, FRANCES HELEN, editor; b. N.Y.C., Jan. 6, 1936; d. Murray and Rose (Rothman) Lee; BA, Queens Coll., 1957; MA, NYU, 1962. Editorial asst. Christian Herald Family Bookshelf, N.Y.C., 1957-62; with Gordon and Breach Sci. Pubs., Inc., N.Y.C., 1964-66, Am. Electric Power Svc. Corp. AEP Operating Ideas, N.Y.C., 1966-69, Indsl. Water Engring. Mag., N.Y.C., 1969-71; directory editor Photographic div. United Bus. Publs., N.Y.C., 1971-80; editor Am. Druggist Blue Book, Hearst Books/Bus. Publs. Group, 1980-81, spl. projects coord. motor manuals Hearst Book div., 1981-82, editor New Price Report, 1982-84; editor Am. Druggist Blue Book, 1982-88; freelance editor, cons., 1988—. Supr. Bronx div. N.Y. State CD, 1953-59. Mem. com. on N.Y.C. charter revision Citizens Union, 1975, com. on city personnel practices, 1975-76, com. on city mgmt., 1977—, bd. dirs., 1978—, co-chmn. com. on N.Y.C. Cultural Concerns, 1979—; vol. N.Y. City Opera, 1988—, N.Y. Opera Guild, 1990—, N.Y.C. Opera, 1992—. Recipient cert. of honor NYU Alumni Fedn., 1985, Meritorious Serv. award, 1986. Mem. N.Y. Bus. Press Editors (bd. dirs. 1988-90, sec. 1990-91), Women's Equity Action League (chmn. rsch. com.), NYU Alumnae Club (dir. 1976-78, rec. sec. 1978-80, v.p. 1980-82, pres. 1982-84, rep. to bd. dirs. fedn. 1984-86), NYU Alumni Fedn. (dir.-at-large 1986-96), Villa-Lobos Music Soc. (sec. 1989-91, treas. 1992-95), NYU Club (bd. govs. 1987-89.) Home: 170 2nd Ave New York NY 10003-5779

LEE, GLENDA DIANNE, accountant; b. Anniston, Ala., Dec. 10, 1953; d. Viola (Williams) Walker; children: Tashira Johnson, Bobby Lee II. BS in Acctg., Ala. State U., 1980. CMA. Co-pub. Metro Forum, Jackson, Tenn., 1989-93; acct. Housing Dept., Fort Worth, 1995—; dir. of roster advt. Inst. of Mgmt. Accts., 1996—; v.p. pub. affairs Speak n Eat Toastmasters, Fort Worth, 1995. Grantee Poynter Inst., 1991. Home: PO Box 123176 Fort Worth TX 76121 Office: Housing Dept 1000 Throckmorton Fort Worth TX 76102

LEE, JANET ELAINE, educational administrator; b. Ames, Iowa, July 9, 1968; d. Harry Donald and Virginia Marie (Sydnes) Lee. BA, Wartburg Coll., Waverly, Iowa, 1990; MS in Edn., Ea. Ill. U., 1991. Grad. asst. Ea. Ill. U., Charleston, 1990-91; dir. programs/activities Morningside Coll., Sioux City, Iowa, 1991-96, dir. orientation and student leadership, 1996—; conf. chair Iowa Student Pers. Assn., 1994-96; profl. devel. chair for nat. conv. Nat. Assn. for Campus Act, Nashville, 1996; spl. programs chair for nat. conv. Nat. Assn. for Campus Act, Anaheim, Calif., 1995. Mem allocations com. Sioux City United Way, 1995—. Named Outstanding New Profl. Iowa Student Pers. Assn., 1995, Toastmaster of Yr. Area Toastmasters, Sioux City, 1994, Divsn. Toastmasters, Storm Lake, 1994; recipient Founder's award Nat. Assn. for Campus Act, Upper Midwest Region, 1990. Mem. AAUW, Toastmasters Internat. (Sioux City club pres. 1994-95, Toastmaster of Yr. 1994, Divsn. Toastmaster of Yr. 1994), Jr. League of Sioux City (parliamentarian 1996-97), Delta Zeta. Democrat. Lutheran. Office: Morningside College 1501 Morningside Ave Sioux City IA 51106-1717

LEE, JANICE ALTA, university official; b. Stoddard, Wis., July 27, 1932; d. Edwin Julius and Josephine Cecila (Knutson) Stylen; m. Burton Christian Lee, June 21, 1930; children: James, Toby, Jody. Diploma in rural edn., U. Wis., LaCrosse, 1952, BS in Elem. Edn., 1960; MS in Psychology of Edn., U. Mich., 1964; postgrad., U. Wis., Madison, 1988. Tchr. elem. sch. Onward Sch., Coon Valley, Wis., 1952-54, McFarland (Wis.) Sch. Dist., 1954-55, Columbus (Wis.) Sch. Dist., 1958-59, Sparta (Wis.) Pub. Sch. Dist., 1961-62, Beloit (Wis.) Sch. Dist., 1962-66; tchr. lang. arts Westby Area Sch. Dist., Coon Valley, 1966-75; curriculum/reading specialist Westby Area Sch. Dist., 1975-87, prin., 1987-90; supr. U. Wis., LaCrosse, 1990—; founder, pres., treas., v.p. Coulee Region Literacy Coun., 1975—. Pres. Luth. Brotherhood Fraternal Br., Westby, 1992—, Women of Evangl. Luth. Ch. Am., Coon Valley, 1992—. Rena Angell scholar U. Wis., 1956. Mem. ASCD, Delta Kappa Gamma. Lutheran. Home: S 185 A Lee Ln Coon Valley MI 54623

LEE, JANINE ANDREA, elementary and middle school educator; b. Queens, N.Y., Nov. 21, 1961; d. Ryland Wilson and Audrey Elizabeth (Brown) Gaines; m. Peter DuVal Lee, Aug. 11, 1984; children: Andra Danielle, Alexus Andrea. B in Music Therapy, Shenandoah U., 1983. Registered, cert. music therapist. Choir dir. The Music Sch., Providence, 1990-91, 93—; dir. edn. Cmty. Prep. Sch., Providence, 1990-94, creative arts dir., 1987—; mem. adv. bd. Everett Dance Theatre, Providence, 1994-95. Membership and conf. coord. Cmty. Bus. Network, Providence, 1989; children's choir dir. Pond St. Bapt. Ch., Providence, 1986-90. Grantee R.I. State Coun. on the Arts, 1990, 91, 92, 93, 94, 95. Mem. Nat. Assn. for Music Therapy (New Eng. chpt. for music therapy), R.I. Music Educators, Nat. Art Edn. Assn., Music Educators Nat. Conf., Nat. Theatre Edn. Assn., R.I. Artists for Advocacy, R.I. Alliance for Edn. Home: 110 Grand View St Providence RI 02906-1860 Office: Cmty Prep Sch 126 Somerset St Providence RI 02907-1034

LEE, JANIS K., state legislator; b. Kensington, Kans., July 11, 1945; m. Lyn Lee; children: David, Brian, Daniel. BA, Kans. State U., 1970. Mem. from dist. 36 Kans. State Senate, 1988—. Mem. Kappa Delta Pi, Phi Kappa Phi. Democrat. Home: RR 1 RR 1 Box 145 Kensington KS 66951-9745 Office: State Senate State House Topeka KS 66612*

LEE, JEANNE KIT YEW, administrative officer; b. N.Y.C., July 31, 1959; d. Tat Yuen and Yow Seum (Chu) Lee. BBA, Baruch Coll., 1982. Clk. typist U.S. Dept. Health and Human Svcs., N.Y.C., 1980-83; clk. typist U.S. Consumer Product Safety Commn., N.Y.C., 1983-85, adminstrv. asst., 1985-90; sys. adminstr. U.S. Consumer Product Safety Commn., 1986-93; adminstrv. officer U.S. Consumer Product Safety Commn., N.Y.C., 1990—. Mem. NAFE, Humane Soc., Nat. Wildlife Fedn. (assoc.), Am. Humane, DAV (Commanders Club 1988—).

LEE, JOYCE ANN, administrative assistant; b. Safford, Ariz., Sept. 18, 1942; d. Roy and Minnie R. (Mobley) Brewer; m. Eugene W. Gaddy Jr., Mar. 16, 1970 (div. 1985); children: Carol, Kevin, Aaron; m. Glenn A. Lee, Oct. 16, 1992. AA, Ea. Ariz. Coll., 1980, AAS, 1993; BA in Mgmt., U. Phoenix, 1995. Dispatcher Mohave County Sheriff's Office, Kingman, Ariz., 1969-74; sec. Globe (Ariz.) Mobile Home Sales, 1975-83; data entry supr. SMC & Assocs., Globe, 1985-88; tax preparer H&R Block Co., Globe, 1992; adminstrv. asst. Am. Pub. Co., Globe, 1994—; instr. computer, bus. classes Ea. Ariz. Coll. Gila Pueblo campus, Globe, 1996—. Girls camp dir. LDS Ch., Globe, 1985-90; mem. com. Boy Scouts Am., Globe. Mem. NAFE, Phi Theta Kappa. Democrat. Home: Rte 1 CC # 179 Globe AZ 85501 Office: Ea Ariz Coll Gila Pueblo Campus Globe AZ 85501-1416

LEE, JUNE WARREN, dentist; b. Boston, Feb. 24, 1952; d. Earl Arnold and Rosemary Regina (Leary) Warren; m. William Lee, July 25, 1976; children: Jaime Michelle, Daniel William. BA, Brandeis U., 1973; DDS, Georgetown U., 1977; student, U.S. Dental Inst., 1985-87. Pvt. practice, Boston, 1977—; chair gen. arrangements YDC 21, Yankee Dental Congress, chair sci. com. YDC 23. Mem. Altrusa Club of Quincy, Mass., 1979—, Cunningham Sch. PTO, Milton, Mass., 1987—, Parent-Adv. Coun., Collicot Elem. Sch., Milton, 1986-87; dental instr. Cunningham Sch., 1987—; dental screening, Healthworks, Neponset Health Ctr., Boston, 1981-84; bd. dirs. Delta Dental Plan Mass., 1995—. Master Acad. Gen. Dentistry (coun. ann. meetings and internat. confs., past pres. New Eng. Mastertrack program, pres.-elect Mass. chpt., past chmn. editl. rev. bd. Audiodent); fellow Am. Coll. Dentists, Internat. Coll. Dentists, Acad. Dentistry Internat.; mem. ADA, Mass. Dental Soc., South Shore Dist. Dental Soc. (chmn.-elect 1991, chmn. 1992, chmn. program com. 1995-96), Am. Orthodontic Soc., Am. Acad. Gnathologic Orthopedics, Am. Assn. for Functional Orthodontics, Am. Assn. Women Dentists (sec. 1987, v.p. 1988, pres.-elect 1989, pres. 1990, A.T. Cross Co. Women of Achievement award 1985, bd. dirs. Gillette Hayden Meml. Found.), Women's Dental Soc. Mass. (sec. 1978, v.p. 1979-81, pres. 1981-83), Mass. Dentists Interested in Legislation, Chestnut Hill Rsch. Study Club. Roman Catholic. Office: 383 Neponset Ave Dorchester MA 02122-3104

LEE, LAURIE NEILSON, lawyer; b. Portland, Oreg., Jan. 22, 1947; d. Duncan Reese and Lilian (Schwichtenberg) Neilson; m. Douglas Caldwell, Sept. 13, 1968 (div. Aug. 1987); children: Jessica, Ashley; m. Alan M. Lee, Jan. 1, 1988; stepchildren: Erin Lee, Sam Lee. BA, U. Oreg., 1969; JD, Lewis & Clark Coll., 1980. Bar: Oreg. 1980, U.S. Dist. Ct. Oreg. 1980. Assoc. Urbigkeit, Hinson & Abele, Oregon City, Oreg., 1980-85, Gleason, Scarborough, McNeese, O'Brien & Barnes, P.C., Portland, Oreg., 1985-88; ptnr. Bullivant, Houser, Bailey, Pendergrass & Hoffman, Portland, 1989-94, Foster Pepper & Shefelman, Portland, 1994—; spkr. legal seminars Oreg. State Bar, 1984-86, 88, 90, 92, 93, 94, 95, Oreg. Law Inst., 1989, Oreg. Soc. CPAs, 1986-90, 92, 95, Nat. Bus. Inst., 1990, Portland Tax Forum, 1991. Contbr. articles to profl. jours.; contbg. author: Administering Trusts in Oregon, 1994. Mem. activities coun. Portland Art Mus., 1989-91, Nature Conservancy, Portland, 1990; bd. dirs. The Dougy Ctr., Portland, 1989-91; mem. N.W. Planned Giving Roundtable, 1992—; past chair, past sec., com. mem. exec. com. estate planning and adminstrn. sect. Oreg. State Bar, Lake Oswego, 1982-88. Fellow Am. Coll. Trust and Estate Coun.; mem. ABA, Oreg. Women Lawyers (charter), Estate Planning Coun. Portland Inc. (bd. dirs. 1992—, chair planning com. 22d Ann. Estate Planning Seminar 1992, sec. 1995), Oreg. State Bar, Multnomah County Bar Assn. Office: Foster Pepper & Shefelman 1 Main Pl 15th flr 101 SW Main St Portland OR 97204-3228

LEE, LEILA, interior designer, artist; b. Chgo., Aug. 6; d. George Mitchell and Jen (Klein) Gollin; children: Boni Joy Weinstein, David Steven Slack. Student, Chgo. Art Inst., Inst. Design, Loyola U. chair interior design seminar U. Wis., 1993; design cons. Mdse. Mart, 1990-95. Exhbns. include Unique Accent, Chgo., 1995, Mead Gallery, Oak Park, Ill., 1995, Warner Showroom, Chgo., 1995, Acad. Fine Arts, Beijing, Textile Mus. & Inst., Moscow, Russia Ethnographic Mus., St. Petersburg, various juried art fairs; contbr. to publs. including Parade Mag., Chgo. Sun-Times, HFD Fairchild Publ., Chgo., Profile News, Chgo., Interior Design Mag., River North News, Oak Park News, The Skyline; editor: (newsletter) No Space Like Home, Hi There, This is Lee; on radio show No Space Like Home; represented in pvt. collections. Mem. Internat. Interior Design Assn., Nat. Assn. Women Bus. Owners, Chgo. Artists Coalition. Home and Office: 21 W Goethe Ste 15L Chicago IL 60610

LEE, LILY KIANG, scientific research company executive; b. Shanghai, China, Nov. 23, 1946; came to U.S., 1967, naturalized, 1974; d. Chi-Wu and An-Teh (Shih) Kiang; m. Robert Edward Lee; children: Jeffrey Anthony, Michelle Adrienne, Stephanie Amanda, Christina Alison. BS, Nat. Cheng-Chi U., 1967; MBA, Golden Gate U., San Francisco, 1969. Acct., then acctg. supr. Am. Data Systems, Inc., Canoga Park, Calif., 1969-73; sr. acct. Pertec Peripheral Equipment div. Pertec Corp., Chatsworth, Calif., 1973-76; mgr. fin. planning and acctg., then mgr. fin. planning, program and internal control Sci. Ctr. div. Rockwell Sci. Ctr., Thousand Oaks, Calif., 1976—. Mem. NAFE, Am. Mgmt. Assn., Nat. Mgmt. Assn., Nat. Property Mgrs. Assn. Republican. Baptist. Office: Rockwell Sci Ctr PO Box 1085 1049 Camino Dos Rios Thousand Oaks CA 91358

LEE, MARGARET ANNE, social worker, psychotherapist; b. Scribner, Nebr., Nov. 23, 1930; d. William Christian and Caroline Bertha (Benner) Joens; m. Robert Kelly Lee, May 21, 1950 (div. 1972); children: Lawrence Robert, James Kelly, Daniel Richard. AA, Napa Coll., 1949; student, U. Calif., Berkeley, 1949-50; BA, Calif. State Coll., Sonoma, 1975; MSW, Calif. State U., Sacramento, 1977. Diplomate clin. social worker; lic. clin. social worker, Calif.; lic. marriage and family counselor, Calif.; tchr. Columnist, stringer Napa (Calif.) Register, 1946-50; eligibility worker, supr. Napa County Dept. Social Services, 1968-75; instr. Napa Valley Community Coll., 1978-83; practice psychotherapy Napa, 1977—; oral commr. Calif. Dept. Consumer Affairs, Bd. Behavioral Sci., 1984—; bd. dirs. Project Access, 1978-79. Trustee Napa Valley C.C., 1983—, v.p. bd., 1984-85, pres. bd., 1986, 90, 95, clk., 1988-89; bd. dirs. Napa County Coun. Econ. Opportunity, 1984-85, Napa chpt. March of Dimes, 1957-71, Mental Health Assn. Napa County, 1983-87; vice chmn. edn. com. Calif. C.C. Trustees, 1987-88, chmn. edn. com., 1988-89, legis. com., 1985-87, bd. dirs., 1989—, 2d v.p., 1991, 1st v.p., 1992, pres., 1993; mem. student equity rev. group Calif. C.C. Chancellors, 1992; bd. dirs. C.C. League Calif., 1992-95, 1st v.p., 1992. Recipient Fresh Start award Self mag., award Congl. Caucus on Women's Issues, 1984. Mem. NASW, Mental Health Assn. Napa County, Calif. Assn. Physically and Handicapped, Women's Polit. Caucus, Calif. Elected Women's Assn. Edn. and Rsch., Am. Assn. Women in Community and Jr. Colls. Democrat. Lutheran. Office: 1100 Trancas St Napa CA 94558-2908

LEE, MARIANNA, editor; b. N.Y.C., Aug. 23, 1930; d. Isaac and Charlotte (Steiner) Lubow; m. Edward Lee, June 17, 1968 (div. 1978); 1 child, Susanna. BA, Smith Coll., 1952; postgrad, Columbia U., 1952-53; postgrad., Oxford (Eng.) U., 1957-58. Asst. editor Watson-Guptill Publs., N.Y.C., 1958-59; chief copy editor Grolier, Inc., N.Y.C., 1960-61; mng. editor Portfolio & Art News Ann., N.Y.C., 1961-62; assoc. editor Parade Publs., N.Y.C., 1962-66; mng. editor The Johns Hopkins Press, Balt., 1966-68, U. Tex. Press, Austin, 1968-69; sr. publs. mgr. Scripps Inst. of Oceanography, La Jolla, Calif., 1979-82; mng. editor Harcourt Brace and Co., San Diego, 1982—. Contbr. articles to profl. jours. Democrat. Jewish. Office: Harcourt Brace and Co 525 B St San Diego CA 92101-4403

LEE, MARIE G., writer; b. Hibbing, Minn., Apr. 25, 1964; d. William Chae-Sik and Grace Koom-Soon L. AB, Brown U., 1986. Cons. Data Resources/Standard and Poor's, N.Y.C., 1986-88; editor equity rsch. Goldman Sachs and Co., N.Y.C., 1988-90; mem. Read Aloud N.Y.C. sch. vol. program. Author: Finding My Voice, 1992 (Best Book award Friends of Am. Writers, Best Book for Reluctant Readers citation ALA, N.Y. Pub. Libr. Books for the Teen Age citation, 1992, Children's Choice citation Internat. Reading Assn. 1994), If It Hadn't Been for Yoon Jun, 1993 (Books for the Teen Age citation N.Y. Pub. Libr.), Saying Goodbye, 1994. Mem. PEN, Soc. of Children's Book Writers and Illustrators, Authors Guild, Authors Leage of Am., Asian Am. Arts Alliance, Com. Against Anti-Asian Violence, Nat. Coalition Against Censorship, Asian Am. Writer's Workshop (v.p., bd. dirs., 1992). Roman Catholic. Office: care Wendy Schmaltz Harold Ober Assoc 425 Madison Ave New York NY 10017*

LEE, MARILYN (IRMA) MODARELLI, law librarian; b. Jersey City, Dec. 8, 1934; d. Alfred E. and Florence Olga (Koment) Modarelli; m. Alfred McClung Lee III, June 8, 1957 (div. July 1985); children: Leslie Lee Ekstrand, Alfred McClung IV, Andrew Modarelli. BA, Swarthmore (Pa.) Coll., 1956; JD, Western New Eng. Sch. of Law, 1985. Bar: Mass. 1986. Claims rep., supr. region II Social Security Adminstrn., Jersey City, 1956-59; law libr. County of Franklin, Greenfield, Mass., 1972-78; head law libr. Mass. Trial Ct., Greenfield, 1978—; mem. Franklin County Futures Lab Task Force (Mass. Cts.), 1994—. Chmn. Franklin County (Mass.) Regional Tech., Turners Falls, 1974-76, Sch. Bldg. Com., 1974-76; mem. Franklin County Planning Bd., 1988—, mem. exec. bd., 1992-95; clk. Franklin County Tech. Sch., 1976-81; vice chmn. Greenfield Planning Bd., 1987-95; mem. Greenfield Sch. Bldg. Com., 1995—; mem. Greenfield C.C. Found., 1990—. Mem. Mass. Bar Assn., Franklin County Bar Assn. (chmn. lawyer referral com. 1992-94, vice chmn. 1994—, chmn. libr. com. 1992—), Law Librs. of New Eng. (treas. 1993—), Am. Assn. Law Librs., Greenfield Charter (com. clk. 1979-83), Swarthmore Alumni Coun. Office: Mass Trial Ct Franklin Law Libr 425 Main St Greenfield MA 01301-3313

LEE, MARTHA, artist, writer; b. Chehalis, Wash., Aug. 23, 1946; d. William Robert and Phyllis Ann (Herzog) L.; m. Peter Reynolds Lockwood, Jan. 25, 1974 (div. 1982). BA in English Lit., U. Wash., 1968; student, Factory of Visual Art, 1980-82. Reporter Seattle Post-Intelligencer, 1970; personnel counselor Theresa Snow Employment, 1971-72; receptionist Northwest Kidney Ctr., 1972-73; proprietress The Reliquary, 1974-77; travel agt. Cathay Express, 1977-79; artist, 1980—; represented by Lucia Douglas Gallery, Bellingham, Wash., WhiteBird Gallery, Cannon Beach, Oreg. Painter various oil paintings; exhibitor group and one-person shows. Home and Studio: 24309 Pacific Way Ocean Park WA 98640-3823

LEE, MARTHA FRANCES, political science educator; b. Toronto, Ont., Can., Mar. 26, 1962; d. L. Frank and Margaret Lee. BA in Polit. Sci., U. Calgary, 1985, MA in Polit. Sci., 1987; PhD in Polit. Sci., Syracuse U. Doctoral fellow Social Scis. and Humanities Rsch. Coun. Can., 90-91; prof. polit. sci. U. Windsor (Ont.), 1992—. Author: The Nation of Islam, 1988, rev. edit., 1996, Earth First!, Environmental Apocalypse, 1995. Mem. Can. Polit. Sci. Assn. Office: U Windsor Dept Polit Sci, 401 Sunset, Windsor, ON Canada W9B 4P1

LEE, MAUREEN T., engineer; b. Chgo., Feb. 4, 1963; d. Edward R. and Kathleen T. (Hopkins) Smith; m. Melvin E. Lee, Sept. 10, 1992. BS in Civil/Ocean Engring., U. R.I., 1987; MS in Civil/Geotech. Engring., U. Hawaii, 1996. Registered profl. engr., Hawaii. Engr. Naval Facilities Engring. Command, Washington, 1987-92; rsch. asst. U. R.I., Kingston, 1992-93; engr. Oceanit Labs., Inc., Honolulu, 1994-95; rsch. asst. U. Hawaii, Manoa, 1995-96; engr. Geolabs, Hawaii, 1996—. Mem. ASCE, Marine Tech. Soc., Soc. Women Engrs. (student chpt. v.p. 1985-86), Chi Epsilon (student chpt. pres. 1986-87), Tau Beta Pi. Home: 38 McGrew Loop Aiea HI 96701

LEE, MICHELE, actress; b. L.A., June 24, 1942; d. Jack and Sylvia Helen (Silverstein) Dusick; m. James Farentino, Feb. 20, 1966 (div. 1983); 1 son, David Michael; m. Fred Rappoport, Sept. 27, 1987. Actress roles include (Broadway play) How to Succeed in Business Without Trying, 1962-64, Seesaw, 1973, (movies) How to Succeed in Business With Really Trying, 1967, The Love Bug, 1969, Dark Victory, 1975, Bud and Low, 1976, A Letter to Three Wives, 1985, Single Women, Married Men, 1989, The Fatal Image, 1990, My Son Johnny, 1991, (TV movie) Broadway Bound, 1992, When No One Would Listen, 1993, Big Dreams Broken Hearts: The Dottie West Story, 1995, (TV series) Knots Landing, 1979-93 (Outstanding Lead Actress award Soap Opera awards 1992). Recipient Top Star of Tomorrow award Motion Picture Exhibitors of U.S. and Can., 1967, Drama Desk award Broadway Critics, 1973, Outer Critics Circle award, 1973; nominated for Antoinette Perry award, 1973-74, Emmy for Knots Landing, 1981-82.

LEE, MONA DUH-WEI, pharmacologist; b. L.A., Nov. 24, 1970; d. Steven Ying-Yuan and Sandy Ping-Ping (Hu) L. BA in Molecular and Cell Biology, U. Calif. Berkeley, 1992; MS in Toxicology, San Diego State U., 1995. Rsch. assoc. Houghten Pharm., Inc., San Diego, 1992—. Vol. Habitat for Humanity, San Diego, 1994, Amnesty Internat., Berkeley, 1990. Mem. Soc. Toxicology (so. Calif. chpt.), San Diego Toxicol. Assn., Calif. Alumni Assn., Sierra Club, Sigma Kappa (activities chair), Sigma Xi. Democrat. Office: Houghten Pharm Inc 3550 General Atomics Ct San Diego CA 92121

LEE, NELDA S., art appraiser and dealer, film producer; b. Gorman, Tex., July 3, 1941; d. Olan C. and Onis L.; A.S. (Franklin Lindsay Found. grantee), Tarleton State U., Tex., 1961; B.A. in Fine Arts, N. Tex. State U., 1963; postgrad. Tex. Tech. U., 1964, San Miguel de Allende Art Inst., Mexico, 1965; 1 dau., Jeanna Lea Pool. Head dept. art Ector High Sch., Odessa, Tex., 1963-68. Bd. dirs. Odessa YMCA, 1970, bd. dirs. Am. Heart Assn., Odessa, 1975; fund raiser Easter Seal Telethon, Odessa, 1978-79; bd. dirs. Ector County (Tex.) Cultural Center, 1979—, Tex. Bus. Hall of Fame, 1980-85; bd. dirs., mem. acquisition com. Permian Basin Presdl. Mus., Odessa, 1978; bd. dirs., chairperson acquisition com. Odessa Art Mus., 1979—; pres. Mega-Tex. Prodns., TV and movie producers; pres. Ector County Democratic Women's Club, 1975, Nelda Lee, Inc., Odessa; appointee Tex. Commn. Arts, 1993—. Group exhbns. include El Paso, Tex., New Orleans. Recipient Designer-Craftsman award El Paso Mus. Fine Arts, 1964. Mem. Am. Soc. Appraisers (sr.), Nat. Tex. Assn. Art Dealers (pres. 1978—), Odessa C. of C. Contbr. articles to profl. jours. Office: Nelda Lee Inc PO Box 4268 Odessa TX 79760-4268

LEE, NORA L., epidemiologist. BS in Physiology, U. Calif., Davis, 1987. Rsch. assoc. Health & Environ. Scis. Group, Washington, 1989-90, tech. rsch. coord., 1990-92, assoc. scientist, 1992-93, sr. assoc. scientist, 1993-95; dir. edn. The Carlo Inst., Washington, 1994—; rsch. asst. The Ctr. for Epidemiology and Policy, Johns Hopkins U., Balt., 1995—. Contbr. articles to profl. jours. Vol. tutor Washington Literacy Coun., 1992-94, bd. dirs., 1992-93, com. chair, 1993. Mem. AAAS, APHA, Internat. Soc. for Environ. Epidemiology, Soc. Risk Analysis, Soc. for Epidemiologic Rsch. Office: Health & Environ Scis Group 1711 N St NW Ste 200 Washington DC 20036-2811

LEE, PAMELA ANNE, accountant, business analyst; b. San Francisco, May 30, 1960; d. Larry D. and Alice Mary (Reece) L. BBA, San Francisco State U., 1981. CPA, Calif. Typist, bookkeeper, tax acct. James G. Woo, CPA, San Francisco, 1979-85; tutor bus. math. and statistics San Francisco State U., 1979-80; teller to ops. officer Gibraltar Savs. and Loan, San Francisco, 1978-81; sr. acct. Price Waterhouse, San Francisco, 1981-86; corp. acctg. mgr. First Nationwide Bank, Daly City, Calif., 1986-89, v.p., 1989-91, v.p., project mgr., 1991-92, sr. conversion and bus. analyst, 1992-93; sr. bus. analyst, asst. v.p. Bank of Am., 1993-96, sr. bus. analyst, v.p. Bank of Am., 1996—; v.p. Bank Am., 1996—; acctg. cons. New Performance Gallery, San Francisco, 1985, San Francisco Chamber Orch., 1986. Founding mem., chair bd. trustees Asian Acctg. Students Career Day, 1988-89. Mem. NAFE, Am. Inst. CPA's, Calif. Soc. CPA's, Nat. Assn. Asian-Am. CPA's (bd. dirs. 1986, news editor 1987, pres. 1988). Republican. Avocations: reading, music, travel, personal computing, needlework. Office: 50 California St Fl 11 San Francisco CA 94111-4624

LEE, REBECCA LAWRENCE, writer, retired real estate broker; b. Washington, Oct. 6, 1915; d. Lawrence Rust and Alexandra (McDannold) L.; m. Philip Bennett Lukei, Apr. 7, 1956; children: Arthur Lee, Ronald Van R., Virginia Lee. Student, Vassar Coll., 1933-35; AB, Stanford U., 1937. With Lucky Realty, Redlands, Calif., 1956-74. Author: Concha-My Dancing Saint, 1966, My Friend Father Ignacio, 1971, Kori and the Island of Enchantment, 1991; contbr. articles to Calif. history to newspapers and mags.

LEE, ROBERTA KARI, nursing educator, science researcher; b. Red Wing, Minn., Nov. 30, 1947; d. Merlin H. and Margaret F. (Ackermann) L.; m. Carl R Marquart (div.); children: Joshua, Timothy, William. BSN, St. Olaf Coll., Northfield, Minn., 1969; MPH, U. Minn., Mpls., 1975; DrPH, U. Tex., Houston, 1988. From pub. health nurse I to pub. health nurse II Combined Nursing Service, Mpls., 1969-73; instr. nursing Sch. Pub. Health U. Minn., Mpls., 1975-80; mem. profl. staff St. Mary's Jr. Coll., Mpls., 1980-81; asst. prof. Ball State U., Muncie, Ind., 1981-83; assoc. prof., injury epidemiology Sch. Nursing Med. Br. U. Tex., Galveston, 1983-92, prof., 1992—; with intentional injury sect., epidemiology br. Div. Injury Control, CDC, 1989-91, prof., 1992—; cons. Galveston Health Dept., 1986-92; with Ministries of Health, Barbados, Dominica, Trinidad. Contbr. Chpt. to book, articles to profl. jours. Bd. dirs. Galveston YMCA, 1987—. Bush Found. Leadership fellow, 1979, Kempner Found. fellow; grantee USPHS, 1974-75. Fellow Am. Acad. Nursing; mem. APHA, AAS, Tex. Pub. Health Assn. Soc. for Epidemiologic Rsch., Sigma Theta Tau. Office: U Tex Medical Branch 301 University Blvd Galveston TX 77555

LEE, RUBY BEI-LOH, multimedia and computer systems architect; b. Singapore; came to the U.S., 1970, naturalized, 1996; m. Howard F. Lee, July 27, 1974; children: Patrick, Josephine. AB in Computer Sci. and Comparative Lit. with distinction, Cornell U., 1973; MS in Computer Sci., Stanford U., 1975, PhDEE, 1980. Asst. prof. elec. engring. Stanford (Calif.) U., 1980-81; lead architect Hewlett Packard Co., Palo Alto, Calif., 1982-84, lead designer microprocessors, 1984-86; project mgr. Hewlett Packard Co., Cupertino, Calif., 1987-90, chief architect computer sys. architecture, multimedia, 1991—; cons. assoc. prof. elec. engring. Stanford U., 1990-95, cons. prof., 1995—. Designer PA-RISC (Precision Architecture-Reduced Instrn. Set Computer) architecture, Multimedia Acceleration EXtensions (MAX) architecture; contbr. articles to profl. jours.; inventor, patentee in field, including 12 U.S. patents and several foreign ones. Mem. IEEE (mem. exec. com., mem. tech. com. on microprocessors, mem. program com. Compcon conf. San Francisco 1991—, program chairperson Hot-Chips Symposium, Stanford 1992-93, mem. editl. bd. IEEE Micro and Spectrum, guest editor spl. issue IEEE MICRO 1996), Assn. for Computing Machinery, Phi Beta Kappa, Alpha Lambda Delta. Methodist. Office: Hewlett-Packard Co 19410 Homestead Rd Cupertino CA 95014-0606

LEE, SALLY A., editor-in-chief; m. Rob Niosi. Grad., Durham U., Eng., Clark U., Mass. Reporter Worcester (Mass.) Telegram; mng. editor Worcester (Mass.) Monthly; spl. features editor Woman's World mag., N.Y.C.; articles editor Woman's Day mag., N.Y.C.; sr. editor Redbook mag., N.Y.C.; editor-in-chief YM/Young & Modern mag., N.Y.C., 1994-96, Fitness Mag., N.Y.C., 1996—; corr. E! Entertainment Network. Office: Fitness Mag 110 Fifth Ave New York NY 10011

LEE, SUSAN A., librarian; b. N.Y.C., Jan. 11, 1947; d. Richard William and Maria A. (Rice) L. BA, C.W. Post Coll., 1968; MA, Long Is. U., 1970; MLS, Simmons Coll., 1972, ArtsD in Lib. Adminstrn., 1976; MBA, Nichols Coll., 1981. Grad. asst. English dept. Long Island U., Greenvale, N.Y., 1968-70; tchr. English grade 7, 8, 9 Watertown (Mass.) Pub. Schs., 1970-71; circulation, res. book asst. Baker Lib. Harvard Bus. Sch., Boston, 1971-72; dir. reference, audiovisual svcs. Newton (Mass.) Coll., 1972-75; coll. librarian Nichols Coll., Dudley, Mass., 1976-79; lib. dir., asst. prof. mgmt. MBA program Am. Internat. Coll., Springfield, Mass., 1979-83; assoc. librarian adminstrv. svcs. U. Conn., Storrs, 1983-89; assoc. librarian personnel Harvard Coll. Lib. Harvard U., Cambridge, Mass., 1989-91, assoc. librarian adminstrv. svcs., faculty arts and scis. Harvard Coll. Lib., 1991—; cons. lib. facilities an space utilization Am. Internat. Coll., 1988; mem. leadership devel program adv. com. Lib. of Congress, 1994—; participant Sr. Fellow profgram Grad Sch. Lib. and Info. Sci. UCLA, 1993; spkr. in field. Editor: The New Library Legacy, 1996; contbr. chpts. to book, articles to profl. jours. Mem. ALA, Assn. Coll. and Rsch. Libs. (mem. budget and fin. com. 1992, planning, 1995), New Eng. Deposit Lib. (v.p. 1990—). Home: 43 Linnaean St #47 Cambridge MA 02138 Office: Harvard U Widener Lib Cambridge MA 02138

LEE, YEU-TSU MARGARET, surgeon, educator; b. Xian, Shensi, China, Mar. 18, 1936; m. Thomas V. Lee, Dec. 29, 1962 (div. 1987); 1 child, Maxwell M. AB in Microbiology, U. S.D., 1957; MD, Harvard U., 1961. Cert. Am. Bd. Surgery. Assoc. prof. surgery Med. Sch., U. So. Calif., L.A., 1973-83; commd. lt. col. U.S. Army Med. Corps, 1983, advanced through grades to col., 1989; chief surg. oncology Tripler Army Med. Ctr., Honolulu, 1983—; assoc. clin. prof. surgery Med. Sch., U. Hawaii, Honolulu, 1984-92, clin. prof. surgery, 1992—. Author: Malignant Lymphoma, 1974; author chpts to books; contbr. articles to profl. jours. Pres. Orgn. Chinese-Am. Women, L.A., 1981; active U.S.-China Friendship Assn., 1991—. Recipient Chinese-Am. Engrs. and Scis. Assn., 1987; named Sci. Woman Warrior, Asian-Pacific Womens Network, 1983. Mem. ACS, Soc. Surg. Oncology, Assn. Women Surgeons. Office: Tripler Army Med Ctr Dept Surgery Honolulu HI 96859

LEEDER, ELAINE, sociologist, educator; b. Lynn, Mass., July 7, 1944; d. Samuel and Ida (Rosenfield) Sneierson; m. David Leeder, July 15, 1971 (separated 1986); 1 child, Abigail. BA, Northeastern U., Boston, 1967; MSW, Yeshiva U., 1969; MPH, U. Calif., Berkeley, 1975; PhD, Cornell U., 1985. Cert. Soc. Worker. Psychiat. soc. worker Elmira (N.Y.) Psychiat. Ctr., 1971-72; clin. psychiat. soc. worker Elmira, 1972-80; assoc. prof. Ithaca (N.Y.) Coll., 1977—; pvt/ practice Ithaca, 1980-92; dept. chair Ithaca Coll., 1992-95. Author: The Gentle General: Rose Pesotta, Anarchist & Labor Organizer, 1993, Treating Abuse in Families: A Feminist & Community Approach, 1994; contbr. articles to profl. jours. Feminist Therapy Inst. (steering com. 1990—). Jewish. Home: 112 Bundy Rd Ithaca NY 14850 Office: Ithaca Coll Muller 112 Ithaca NY 14850

LEEDER, ELLEN LISMORE, language and literature educator, literary critic; b. Vedado, Havana, Cuba, July 8, 1931; came to U.S., 1959; d. Thomas and Josefina (Jorge) Lismore; m. Robert Henry Leeder, Dec. 20, 1957 (dec.); 1 child, Thomas Henry. D of Pedagogy, U. Havana, Cuba, 1955; MA, U. Miami, 1966, PhD, 1973. Lang. tchr. St. George's Sch., Havana, 1952-59; from part-time instr. to full prof. Spanish Barry U., Miami Shores, Fla., 1960-75, prof. Spanish, 1975—, chmn. dept. for lang., 1975-76, coord. of Fgn. Lang., 1976-89; dir. Spanish immersion program, 1986-88; part-time prof. Miami-Dade C.C., 1974-75; vis. prof. U. Madrid, 1982; prof. Forspro Program Studies Abroad, 1989, 90; cons. HEH, 1981-83; judge Assiación Críticos y Comentaristas del Arte, Miami, 1985—; judge Silver Knight Awards, 1979-83; oral examiner juror Dade County Pub. Schs., Miami, 1986-87. Author: El Desarraigo en Las Novelas de Angel María de Lera, 1978, Justo Sierra y el Mar, 1979, Dimensión Existencial en la Narrativa de Lera, 1992. Bd. dirs. Vis. Nurse Assn., 1978-80. Mem. MLA, South Atlantic MLA, Am. Coun. Tchg. Fgn. Langs., Am. Assn. Tchrs. Spanish and Portuguese (pres. 1978-84, v.p. 1984-87, pres. Southeastern Fla. chpt.), Fla. Fgn. Assn., Círculo de Cultura Panamericano, Assn. Internat. Hispanistas, Assn. Cubana de Mujeres Universitarias (pres.), Cuban Women Assn., Phi Alpha Theta, Kappa Delta Pi, Sigma Delta Xi, Alpha Mu Gamma, Coral Gables Country Club. Home: 830 SW 101st Ave Miami FL 33174-2836 Office: Barry Univ 11300 NE 2d Ave Miami FL 33161-6628

LEEDS, ELIZABETH LOUISE, miniature collectibles executive; b. L.A., July 24, 1925; d. Charles Furnival and Etta Louise (Jackson) Mayes; m. Walter Albert Leeds, Jan. 20, 1973 (dec.); children: Pam Ravey Lewis, Linda Ravey McCallam, Diane Ravey Lathrop, Tom Ravey. Student pub. sch., Prescott, Ariz. Lic. real estate agt., Ariz., cert. motel mgr. Real estate agt., Prescott, Ariz., 1962-64; sec. to mgr. Kon Tiki Hotel, Phoenix, 1964-65; draftsman Goleta Water Dist., Calif., 1965-68; asst. to v.p. rsch. and design

House of Mosaics, Santa Barbara, Calif., 1968-69; exec. chmn. poster design, dept. music U. Calif.-Santa Barbara, 1969-74; v.p. Colorform West, Inc., Santa Barbara, 1974-75; pres. Leeds Miniatures, Inc., Lincoln City, Oreg., 1975-86, Leed's Co., Inc., 1989—; cert. instr. Technologies for Creating, DMA, Inc., 1986—; lamp and silk screen designer Colorform West, Inc.; ind. assoc. The Environ. Network. Illustrator: Just A Story by Gustav Coenod, 1964. Active Global Vols., 1993, Oceanic Soc. Expeditions, 1993. Mem. Hobby Industry Am., Miniatures Industry Assn. Am., Nat. Assn. Female Execs., Eugene C. of C., Eugene Bus. and Profl. Women (cert. practitioner neuro-linguistic programming, trainer values realization). Republican. Clubs: Assn. Humanistic Psychology, Internat. New Thought Alliance, Assn. Transpersonal Psychology. Home: 2290 Arthur Ct Eugene OR 97405-1525

LEEDS, NANCY BRECKER, sculptor, lyricist; b. N.Y.C., Dec. 22, 1924; d. Louis Julius and Dorothy (Faggen) Brecker; m. Richard Henry Leeds, May 9, 1945; children: Douglas Brecker, Constance Leeds Bennett. BA, Pine Manor Coll., 1944. Pres. Roseland Ballroom, N.Y.C., 1977-81. One-woman shows: Andrew Crispo Gallery, N.Y.C., 1979, Jeannette McIntyre Gallery Fine Arts, Palm Springs, Calif., 1987-88; exhibited in group shows at Bond Street Gallery, Great Neck, N.Y., Gallery Ranieri, N.Y.C., 1978, Country Art Gallery, 1984, Nature Conservatory Show, Country Art Gallery, 1985, Bonwit Teller, Manhasset, N.Y., 1985, Jeanette C. McIntyre Gallery, Palm Springs, Calif., 1987, The Empire Collection, N.Y.C., 1988, 89, Nassau County Mus. of Art, 1992; permanent collections include New Orleans Mus. of Art. Writer lyrics for musical Great Scot, 1965, score for Scrooge Musical Theatre of Ariz., 1989; lyricist for popular music. Trustee The Floating Hosp., N.Y.C., 1975—, v.p. Mem. ASCAP, The Dramatist Guild, The Songwriters Guild. Avocations: tennis; skiing.

LEEDY, EMILY L. FOSTER (MRS. WILLIAM N. LEEDY), retired education educator, consultant; b. Jackson, Ohio, Sept. 24, 1921; d. Raymond S. and Grace (Garrett) Foster; MEd, Ohio U., 1957; postgrad. Ohio State U., 1956, Mich. State U., 1958-59, Case Western Res. U., 1963-65; m. William N. Leedy, Jan. 1, 1943; 1 son. Dwight A. tchr. Frankfort (Ohio) schs., 1941-46, Ross County Schs., Chillicothe, Ohio, 1948-53; elem. and supervising tchr. Chillicothe City Schs., 1953-56; dean of girls, secondary tchr. Berea City Schs., 1956-57; vis. tchr. Parma City Schs., 1957-59; counselor Homewood-Flossmoor High Sch., Flossmoor, Ill., 1959-60; teaching fellow Ohio U., 1960-62; asst. prof. edn., 1962-64; assoc. prof., counselor Cuyahoga Community Coll., 1964-66; dean of women Cleve. State U., 1966-67, assoc. dean student affairs, 1967-69; guidance dir. Cathedral Latin Sch., 1969-71; dir. women's service div. Ohio Bur. Employment Svcs., 1971-83; cons. in edn., 1983-87. Mem. adv. com. S.W. Community Info. Svc., 1959-60; youth com. S.W. YWCA, 1963-70, chmn., 1964-70, bd. mgmt., 1964-70; group svcs. coun. Cleve. Welfare Fedn., 1964-66; chmn. Met. YWCA Youth Program study com., 1966, bd. dirs., 1966-72, v.p., 1967-68; chmn. adv. coun. Ohio State U. Sch. Home Econs., 1977-80, chmn., 1978-80. Named Cleve. area Woman of Achievement, 1969; named to Ohio Women's Hall of Fame, 1979, Chillicothe Ross Women's Hall of Fame, 1988; recipient Outstanding Contbn. special award Nat. Assn. Commns. for Women, 1983, Meritorious Svc. award Nat. Assn. Women Deans, Adminstrs. and Counselors, 1984. Mem. AAUW (Berea-Parma br. v.p. 1995—), Am., Northeastern Ohio (sec. 1958-59, exec. com. 1963-64, pub. rel. chmn. 1962-64, newsletter chmn., editor 1963-64, del. nat. assembly 1959-63) personnel and guidance assns., LWV, Am. Assn. Retired Persons (Ohio women's initiative spokesperson 1987-89, state legis. com. 1989-90, AARP/VOTE state coord. Ohio 1990-94), Nat. Assn. Women Deans and Counselors (publs. com. 1967-69, profl. employment practices com. 1980-82, Meritorious Svc. award 1984), Ohio (program chmn. 1967, editor Newsletter 1968-71), Cleve. Counselors Assn. (pres. 1966), Zonta Internat. (exec. bd. 1968-70, treas. 1970-72, chmn. dist. V Status of Women 1980-81), Nat. Assn. Commns. for Women (dir. 1980-81, sec. 1981-83), Rio Grande Coll. Alumni Assn. (Atwood Achievement award 1975), Bus. and Profl. Women's Club (Nike award 1973, Berea treas. 1996—), Ohio Retired Tchrs. Assn., Svc. Corps of Retired Execs. Delta Kappa Gamma, Women's City Club (Cleve.). Home: 580 Lindberg Blvd Berea OH 44017-1418 Office: 699 Rocky Rd Chillicothe OH 45601-9469

LEESMAN, BARBARA ELAINE ATTAYA, sales executive and trainer; b. New Orleans, May 11, 1963; d. Moses and Barbara Jean (Campbell) A.; m. Brad W. Leesman. Student, La. State U., 1981, U. New Orleans, 1982-83. Lic. life ins. salesperson; registered securities sales rep. Teller Oak Tree Savs. Bank, Metairie, La., 1983-84, customer svc. rep., 1984-86; customer svc. rep. Oak Tree Savs. Bank, Baton Rouge, 1986, tng. instr., 1987-89; account exec. Landmark Fin. Svcs., Shreveport, La., 1989-91; nat. tng. instr. Fin. Horizons Distributors, Columbus, Ohio, 1991-92; dir. tng. IFS Fin. Svcs., Cin., 1992-93, dir. tng. and comms., 1993-95, dir. mktg. support svcs, 1995—. Republican. Baptist. Home: 1413 Cheltenham Dr Loveland OH 45140

LEESMAN, BEVERLY, artist, art critic, art educator; b. Lincoln, Ill., Apr. 22, 1953; d. Robert Eugene and Jean (Bruner) L.; m. Paul A. Martin, Nov. 28, 1987; 1 child, Danielle. AS in Fine Art, Springfield Coll., 1973; BS in Art History, Graphics Design, Painting, Ill. State U., 1976; postgrad., U. Grenoble, France, 1980, L'Ecole de Louvre, Paris, 1980, U. Ill., 1986. Dept. mgr. J.C. Penney, Springfield, Ill., 1979; head asst. to curator Slide Libr. Ill. State U., Normal, 1981-82; teaching asst. U. Ill., Urbana-Champaign, 1983-84, instr., 1984-85; art instr. North Syracuse Adult Edn. Program, 1992-94; guest lectr. U. Ill., 1981-85; layout, past-up artist Dynamic Graphics, Inc., Peoria, Ill., 1976-78; tech. illustrator I-270 Project, St. Louis, 1984-85; freelance artist, 1986—. One-woman shows include Paine Br. Libr., Syracuse, N.Y., 1993, Liverpool Pub. Libr., 1994, Manlius (N.Y.) Libr., 1995, Roaster's Corner Cafe, Fayetteville, N.Y., 1995; group shows include SUNY Inst. Tech., Utica, Rome, N.Y., 1990, 92-94, Skaneateles (N.Y.) Arts Expn., 1990, 93, Everson Mus., Syracuse, 1994-95, Canastota (N.Y.) Canal Town Mus., 1991-95, Cooperstown (N.Y.) Art Assn., 1992, 94-95, Rome Art & Cmty. Ctr., 1994, Great N.Y. State Fair, Syracuse, 1994-95, CNY Art Open, DeWitt, N.Y., 1995, North East Watercolor Soc., Goshen, N.Y., 1994, Pitts. Watercolor Soc., 1995. Recipient Cooperstown Vet. Clinic prize, 1995, Dick Blick award Pitts. Watercolor Soc., 1995. Mem. Nat. League Am. Pen Women, N.Y.C. Art Guild, Inc. (founding pres. 1994-95, 2d v.p. 1995-96), Nashua Art Assn. Home: 18 Kessler Farm Dr Nashua NH 03063

LEET, MILDRED ROBBINS, corporate executive, consultant; b. N.Y.C., Aug. 9, 1922; d. Samuel Milton and Isabella (Zeitz) Elowsky; m. Louis J. Robbins, Feb. 23, 1941 (dec. 1970); children: Jane, Aileen; m. Glen Leet, Aug. 9, 1974. BA, NYU, 1942; LHD (hon.), Coll. Human Svcs., 1988, Conn. Coll., 1996; LLD honoris causa, Marymount Coll., Tarrytown, N.Y., 1991; HHD, Lynn U., 1993; D Humanitarian Svc. (hon.), Norwich U., 1994; DHL, Conn. Coll., 1996. Pres. women's div. United Cerebral Palsy, N.Y.C., 1951-52; bd. dirs. United Cerebral Palsy, 1953-55; rep. Nat. Coun. Women U.S. at UN, 1957-64, 1st v.p., 1959-64, pres., 1964-68, hon. pres., 1968-70; sec., v.p. conf. group U.S. Nat. Orgns. at UN, 1961-64, 76-78, vice chmn., sec., 1962-64, mem. exec. com., 1961-65, 75—, chmn. hospitality info. svc., 1960-66; vice chmn. exec. com. NGO's UN Office Public Info., 1976-78, chmn. ann. conf., 1977; chmn. com. on water, desertification, habitat and environment Conf. NGO's with consultative status with UN/ECOSOC, 1976—; mem. exec. com. Internat. Coun. Women, 1960-73, v.p., 1970-73; chmn. program planning com., women's com. OEO, 1967-72; chmn. com. on natural disasters N.Am. Com. on Environment, 1973-77; N.Y. State chmn. UN Day, 1975; ptnr. Leet & Leet (cons. women in devel.), 1978—; co-founder Trickle Up Program, 1979—, co-pres., 1991—; mem. task force on Africa UN, 1995—. Contbr. articles to profl. jours.; editor UN Calendar & Digest, 1959-64, Measure of Mankind, 1963; editorial bd.: Peace & Change. Co-chmn. Vols. for Stevenson, N.Y.C., 1956; vice chmn. task force Nat. Dem. Com., 1969-72; commr. N.Y. State Commn. on Powers Local Govt., 1970-73; chmn. Coll. for Human Svcs. Audrey Colten Coll., 1985—; former mem. bd. dirs. Am. Arbitration Assn., New Directions, Inst. for Mediation and Conflict Resolution, Spirit of Stockholm; bd. dirs. Hotline Internat.; v.p. Save the Children Fedn., 1986-93; rep. Internat. Peace Acad. at UN, 1974-77, Internat. Soc. Cmty. Devel., 1977—; del. at large 1st Nat. Women's Conf., Houston, 1977; chmn. task force on internat. interdependence N.Y. State Women's Meeting, 1977; mem. Task Force on Poverty, 1977—; chmn. Task Force on Women, Sci. and Tech. for Devel., 1978; U.S. del. UN Status of Women Commn., 1978, UN Conf. Sci. and Tech. for Devel., 1979, co-dir. Trickle Up Program, Inc., 1979—; Brazzaville Centennial Celebration, 1980; mem. global adv. bd. Internat. Expn. Rural Devel., 1981—; mem. Coun. Internat. Fellows U. Bridgeport, 1982-88; trustee overseas edn. fund LWV, 1983-91; v.p. U.S. Com. UN Devel. Fund for Women, 1983—; mem. Nat. Consultative Com. Planning for Nairobi, 1984-85; co-chmn. women in devel. com. Interaction, 1985-91; mem. com. of cooperation Interam. Commn. of Women, 1986; bd. dirs. Internat. Devel. Conf., 1991—; mem. UN task force informal sector devel Africa,1995—. Recipient Crystal award Coll. Human Svcs., 1983, Ann. award Inst. Mediation and Conflict Resolution, 1985, Woman of Conscience award Nat. Coun. Women, 1986, Temple award Inst. Noetic Scis., 1987, Presdl. Edn Hunger award, 1987, Giraffe award Giraffe Project, 1987, Woman of the World award Eng.'s Women Aid, 1989, Mildred Robbins Left award Interaction, 1995; co-recipient Rose award World Media Inst., 1987, Human Rights award UN Devel. Fund for Women, 1987, (with Glen Leet) Pres.'s medal Marymount Manhattan Coll., 1988, Leadership award U.S. Peace Corps, Woman of Vision award N.Y.C. NOW, 1990, Matrix award Women in Comm., Inc., Spirit of Enterprise award Rolex Industries, 1990, Ann. award Interaction, 1990, Citation, Pres. Bush's Ann. Points of Light Award, 1992, Internat. Humanity award ARC Overseas Assn., 1992, Excellence award U.S. Com. for UNIFEM, 1992, Champion of Enterprise award Avon, 1994, Achievement award NYU-Washington Square Coll. Alumni Assn., 1995, Lizette H. Sarnoff Vol. Svc. award Yeshiva U , 1996, Disting. Svc. award N.Y. African Studies Assn., 1996. Mem. AAAS, Women's Nat. Dem. Club, Women's Forum Inc., Cosmopolitan Club, Princeton Club. Home and Office: 54 Riverside Dr New York NY 10024-6509

LEETCH, NANCY WIKOFF, artist; b. Muncie, Ind., Apr. 11, 1934; d. Charles Henry and Hazel Annetta (Bidlack) Wikoff; m. James Frederick Leetch, Sept. 6, 1958; children: Alice Annette, Elaine Marie. BS in Home Econs., Ohio State U., 1955; MA in Painting, Bowling Green State U., 1986. Home svc. advisor Cols. & S. Ohio Electric Co., Columbus, 1955-59; presch. head tchr. North Broadway Meth. Ch., Columbus, 1959-61; artist, poet Bowling Green, Ohio, 1984-95; tchr. gifted students Bowling Green Schs., 1991-93. One woman exhibits include Ohio Citizens Bank, Toledo, 1987, Obetz Gallery, Columbus, 1987, Currents Gallery, 1988, Images Gallery, 1990, 92, Cable Gallery, 1992, Millikin Hotel Lobby, Bowling Green, 1994, Court House Gallery, 1995, Wile-Kovach Gallery, Columbus, Ohio, 1996; group shows include Owens Ill., 1983, 86, Toledo Mus. Art, 1983, Gallery 200, Columbus, Obetz Gallery, 1987-89, Images Gallery, Toledo, 1985-94, Currents Gallery, 1990, And Beautiful Baskets Gallery, Lyme Regis, Eng., 1990, Medici Gallery, London, 1991, Cable Gallery, San Diego, 1992, Art Moves Gallery, 1993, Angelwood Gallery, 1994, Studio 129, 1995, Lafayette Gallery, Adrian, Mich., 1995, Main Street Gallery, 1995, American Gallery, Sylvania, 1995. Recipient Purchase award Toledo Mus. of Art, 1983. Studio: #213 Huntington Bank Bldg Bowling Green OH 43402

LEFCO, KATHY NAN, law librarian; b. Bethesda, Md., Feb. 24, 1949; d. Ted Lefco and Dorothy Rose (Fox) Harris; m. Stephen Gary Katz, Sept. 2, 1973 (div. May 1984); m. John Alfred Price, Nov. 24, 1984 (dec. Jan. 1989). BA, U. Wis., 1971; MLS, U. Wis., Milw., 1975. Rsch. asst. Ctr. Auto Safety, Washington, 1971-73; asst. to dir. Ctr. Consumer Affairs, Milw., 1973-74; legis. librarian Morgan, Lewis & Bockius, Washington, 1976-78; dir. library Mulcahy & Wherry, Milw., 1978; paralegal Land of Lincoln Legal Assistance, Springfield, Ill., 1979-80; reference and interlibrary loan librarian Sch. Medicine So. Ill. U., Springfield, 1980; reader svcs. librarian Wis. State Law Library, Madison, 1981-83; ref. librarian Mudge Rose Guthrie Alexander & Ferdon, N.Y.C., 1983-85; sr. legal info. specialist Cravath, Swaine & Moore, N.Y.C., 1985-86; asst. librarian Kaye, Scholer, Fierman, Hays & Handler, N.Y.C., 1986-89; head libr. Parker Chapin Flattau & Klimpl, N.Y.C., 1989-94; dir. library svcs. Winston & Strawn, Chgo., 1994—. Author: (with others) Mobile Homes: The Low-Cost Housing Hoax, 1973. Mem. Law Libr. Assn. Greater N.Y. (sec. 1989-91), Chgo. Assn. Law Librs., Am. Assn. Law Librs. Democrat. Jewish. Home: Apt 2504 474 N Lake Shore Dr Chicago IL 60611 Office: Winston & Strawn 35 W Wacker Dr Chicago IL 60601

LEFEBVRE, DENISE HAASE, packaging engineer; b. Bayshore, N.Y., Apr. 1, 1969; d. Edward Alexander and Ida Frances (Ganga) Haase; m. Christopher Joseph Lefebvre, Apr. 24, 1993. BS, Rochester Inst. Tech., 1991. Packaging engr. Colgate-Palmolive Co., Piscataway, N.J., 1991-92; packaging technologist Beech-Nut Nutrition Corp., Canajoharie, N.Y., 1992-96, sr. packaging technologist, 1996—.

LEFEBVRE, PEGGY ANDERSON, advertising executive; b. Springfield, Mo., Dec. 2, 1951; d. Paul William and Norma Jean (Turk) Anderson; m. Donald E. Lefebvre, July 25, 1980. BA in Graphic Arts cum laude, U. Ill., 1974; MBA, Pacific Western U., 1993. Coord. advt. and trade show Bell & Howell, Salt Lake City, 1971-74; designer, prodn. asst. Sta. KUTV, Salt Lake City, 1974; art dir. Associated Advt., Salt Lake City, 1977-80; owner, creative dir. Lefebvre Advt., Anaheim, Calif., 1980—; freelance designer various advt. agys., Chgo.; bd. dirs. Delmark Corp.; past guest lectr. advt. copywriting and bus. devel. Nat. U., Inc. Mag., Orange Coast Coll. One woman shows Ward Gallery, Chgo., 1974, Atrium Gallery, Salt Lake City, 1976. Past bd. dirs. MADD, Orange County Sexual Assault Network; mem. Anaheim Area Visitor and Conv. Bd., Western States Advt. Agy. Assn. Recipient Excellence in Creative Direction award, Bus. and Profl. Advt. Assn., 1989, 94, Outstanding Achievement in Advt. award Western Assn. Conv. & Visitor Burs, Award of Merit Bus. Comms. and Mktg. Assn. L.A., 1991, 95, Award of Excellence, 1995. Mem. DAR. Republican. Office: Lefebvre Advt 1547 E La Palma Ave Anaheim CA 92805-1614

LEFF, ILENE J(OAN), management consultant, corporate and government executive,; b. N.Y.C., Mar. 29, 1942; d. Abraham and Rose (Levy) L.; BA cum laude, U. Pa., 1964; MA with honors, Columbia U., 1969. Statis./computer analyst McKinsey & Co., N.Y.C., 1969-70, rsch. cons., 1971-74, mgmt. cons., N.Y.C. and Europe, 1974-78; dir. exec. resources Revlon, Inc., N.Y.C., 1978-81, dir. human resources, 1981-83, dir. personnel, 1983-86; cons. APM Inc., 1986-88, ind. mgmt. cons., 1988-93, 95—; dep. asst. sec. for mgmt. HUD, Washington, 1993-94; rsch. asst. U. Pa., Phila., 1964-65; employment counselor State of N.J., Newark, 1965-66; tchr., Newark, 1966-69; lectr. Grad. Program in Pub. Policy, New Sch. for Social Rsch., Wharton Sch., Duke U.; chmn. com. on employment and unemployment, mem. exec. com. Bus. Rsch. Adv. Coun., U.S. Bur. Labor Stats., 1980; sr. del. econ. rels. and trade Sino-U.S. Conf., 1986. Ops. coun. Jr. Achievement Greater N.Y., 1975-78; cons. Com. for Econ. Devel., N.Y. Hosp., Regional Plan Assn., Am. Cancer Soc.; vol. for dep. mayor for ops. N.Y.C., 1977-78. Mem. N.Y. Human Resource Planners (treas. 1984), Fin. Women's Assn. N.Y. (exec. bd., 1977-78, 83-84), The Fashion Group (treas. 1989). Contbr. issue papers and program recommendations to candidates for U.S. Pres., U.S. Senate and Congress, N.Y. State Gov., mayor N.Y.C. Office: 767 5th Ave New York NY 10153

LEFF, NOHRA MARGARITA, nursing adminstrator, educator; d. Rafael and Regina (Ballestas) Gonzalez; m. Kenneth M. Leff, Mar. 25, 1984; children: Kenneth, Karen. ASS, Rockland C.C.; BSN, SUNY, 1984; MS, Columbia U., 1989, MPH, 1990; postgrad., 1996—. RN, N.Y., N.J.; cert. continuing edn. and staff devel.; cert. cmty. health nurse. Nursing svc. assoc. Montefiore Med. Ctr., Bronx, N.Y.; asst. DON Beth Abraham Hosp., Bronx; prof. Rockland Cmty. Coll.; with St. Luke's Roosevelt Homecare, 1996; cons. Leff's Health Edn. Svcs. Apptd. Am. Cancer Soc's. Rockland County Nurse of Hope; pres. Orangetown Jewish Ctr. Sisterhood. Mem. APHA, ANA, Nat. Assn. Hispanic Nurses, Hadassah Nurses Coun., N.Y. State Nurses Assn., Columbia U. Sch. Nursing Alumni Assn. (bd. dirs.), Sigma Theta Tau.

LEFF, SANDRA H., gallery director, consultant; b. N.Y.C., Dec. 24, 1939; d. I. Bernard and Rose (Kupfer) L. BA, Cornell U., 1960; MA, Inst. Fine Arts, N.Y.C., 1969. Editorial asst. Indsl. Design Mag., N.Y.C., 1960-61; instr., asst. Mus. of City of N.Y., 1962-65; assoc. print dept. Sotheby Parke Bernet, N.Y.C., 1969-73; rsch. asst. Daniel Chester French Exhibit, Washington, 1975-77; dir. Am. painting Graham Gallery, N.Y.C., 1977-93. Author: (exhbn. catalogs) Thomas Anshutz: Paintings, Watercolors and Pastels, 1979, Guy Pène du Bois: Painter, Draftsman and Critic, 1979, Helen Torr, 1980, John White Alexander: Fin-de-Siècle American, 1980, Jan Matulka & Vaclav Vytlacil, 1992. Ford Found. fellow, 1967. Mem. Phi Beta Kappa.

LEFFLER, CAROLE ELIZABETH, mental health nurse, women's health nurse; b. Sidney, Ohio, Feb. 18, 1942; d. August B. and Delores K. Aselage; children: Veronica, Christopher. ADN, Sinclair Community Coll., Dayton, Ohio, 1975. Cert. psychiat. nurse coord. Nurse Grandview Hosp, Dayton, 1961-76; substitute sch. nurse Fairborn (Ohio) City Schs., 1981-82; dir. nursing Fairborn Nursing Home, 1983; psychiat. nurse coord. Dayton Mental Health Ctr., 1984—; mem. exec. bd. 1199. Vol., instr., disaster health nurse ARC; officer, leader, camp nurse for Girl Scouts, Boy Scouts; Ch. Parish Coun. Recipient Fleur de Lis award Girl and Boy Scouts, Svc. award ARC, Fairborn Mayor's Cert. of Merit for Civic Pride, State of Ohio Govs. award Innovation Ohio. Mem. ANA, Ohio Nurses Assn. Home: 29 W Bonomo Dr Fairborn OH 45324-3407

LEFKOW, JOAN HUMPHREY, judge; b. Kans., Jan. 9, 1944; d. Otis L. and Donna Grace (Glenn) Humphrey; m. Michael F. Lefkow, June 21, 1975; children: Maria Aithne, Helena Claiborne, Laura Bethany, Margaret Frances. AB, Wheaton Coll., 1965; JD, Northwestern U., 1971. Bar: Ill. 1971, U.S. Dist. Ct. (no. dist.) Ill. 1972, U.S. Ct. Appeals (7th cir.) 1972, U.S. Ct. Appeals (5th cir.) 1980. Law clerk to Hon. Thomas E. Fairchild U.S. Ct. Appeals (7th cir.), 1971-72; atty. Legal Assistance Found. Chgo., 1972-75; adminstrv. law judge Ill. Fair Employment Practices Commn., 1975-77, chief adminstrv. law judge, 1977-79; instr. sch. law U. Miami, Fla., 1980-81; exec. dir. Cook County Legal Assistance Found., 1981-82; now magistrate judge U.S. Dist. Ct. (no. dist.) Ill. Editor Northwestern U. Law Rev. Active PTA. Mem. Chgo. Bar Assn. (legal aid com. 1982, Alliance for Women 1992—), Chgo. Coun. Lawyers (gov. bd. 1975-77), 7th Cir. Bar Assn. Episcopalian. Office: Everett McKinley Dirksen Bldg 219 S Dearborn St Ste 2402 Chicago IL 60604-1802

LEFLY, DIANNE LOUISE, research psychologist; b. Denver, July 17, 1946; d. Gordon Eugene Boen and Elizabeth (Welsh) Tuveson. AB, U. No. Colo., 1968; MA, U. Colo., 1980; PhD, U. Denver, 1994. Classroom tchr. Adam County Sch. Dist. #12, Thornton, Colo., 1968-77; rschr. John F. Kennedy Child Devel. Ctr., Denver, 1979-81, U. Colo. Health Scis. Ctr., 1981-89, U. Denver, 1989—. Contbr. articles to profl. jours. Mem. Colo. Rep. Party, Denver, 1968—. Scholarship U. No. Colo., 1964-68; fellowship U. Denver, 1989. Mem. Mensa. Republican. Home: 8650 W 79th Ave Arvada CO 80005-4321 Office: U Denver 2155 S Race St Denver CO 80210-4633

LEFRANC, MARGARET (MARGARET SCHOONOVER), artist, illustrator, editor, writer; b. N.Y.C., Mar. 15, 1907; d. Abraham and Sophie (Teplitz) Frankel; m. Raymond Schoonover, 1942 (div. 1945). Student, Art Students League, N.Y.C., Kunstschule des Westerns, Berlin, NYU Grad. Sch., Andre L'Hote, Paris, Acad. Grande Chaumiere, Paris. Tchr. art Adult Edn., Los Alamos, 1946, Miami (Fla.) Mus. Modern Art, 1975-76. Exhibited in one-person shows at Mus. N.Mex., Santa Fe, 1948, 51, 53, Philbrook Art Ctr., Tulsa, 1949, 51,, Okla. Art Ctr., 1950, Recorder WOrkshop, Miami, 1958, St. John's Coll., Santa Fe, 1993, A Lifetime of Imaging, 1921-95; group shows include Salon de Tuileries, Paris, 1928, 29, 30, Art Inst. Chgo., 1936, El Paso Mus. Art, 1964, Mus. Modern Art, 1974, North Miami Mus. Contemporary Art, 1984, Miami Collects, 1989, Women's Caucus Invitational, 1990, Gov.'s Gallery, Santa Fe, 1992, Gene Autry Western Heritage Mus, 1995, Gilcrease Mus., Tulsa, 1996, Mus. N.Mex. Santa Fe, 1996, Brigham Young U., Provo, Utah, 1996; in collections at Beiles Artes, Mexico City, Mus. Fine Arts, Santa Fe. Bd. dirs., pres. Artist Equity of Fla., 1964-68; v.p. Miami Art Assn., 1958-60; founder, bd. dirs. Guild Art Gallery, N.Y.C., 1935-37. Recipient Illustration award Fifty Best Books of Yr., Libr. of Congress; Honorable Mention award Rodeo of Santa Fe, Mus. N.Mex., others.

LEFTWICH, WILMA JEAN, education research analyst; b. Kansas City, Kans., Oct. 1, 1929; d. Albert George and Flossie Mae (Hibbert) Andrews; m. James Dale Leftwich, Mar. 26, 1929; children: Brion Scot, Brenna Renée Leftwich Wolfe. Grad. h.s., Kansas City, Kans. USAF civil svcs. sec. commdg. gen.'s office Walker Air Force Strategic Air Command Base, Roswell, N.Mex., 1950-52; sec. Earhart Lab. Calif. Inst. Tech., Pasadena, 1953-56; sec. packers and stockyards USDA, L.A., 1956-60; edn. rsch. analyst, 1961—; writer, spkr., rschr. on pro family issues. Mem. nat. adv. bd. Am. Life League, Stafford, Va.; mem. citizen's adv. panel on edn. to former Sen. Henry Bellmon, Okla., 1970s; mem. citizen's adv. com. on edn. Broken Arrow (Okla.) Sch. Sys., 1976; coord. Okla. Coalition on Preservation of Family, Tulsa, 1978; Tulsa County vice-chair Rep. Party, Tulsa, 1978-80; presenter polit. seminars programs Sand Springs (Okla.) Sch. Sys., 1977. Named Okla. Outstanding Eagle, Eagle Forum. Home: 905 W Lansing Broken Arrow OK 74012

LEGAN, PEGGY LYNN, nurse practitioner; b. Appleton, Wis., Apr. 19, 1953; d. Michael John and Lucille A. (DeGroot) Kolosso; m. Greg M. Legan, Nov. 5, 1982; children: John, Joseph, Kathleen. Student, Luth. Gen./Concordia Coll., 1978, Grant Hosp. and Med. Ctr., 1981. RN, Ill.; cert. adult nurse pracitioner ANCC. Nurse ICU U. Ill. Med. Ctr., Chgo., 1978-80; adult nurse practitioner surg. dept. Grant Med. Ctr., Chgo., 1980-84; adult nurse practitioner women's health Tecumseh Area Planned Parenthood, Lafayette, Ind., 1987-92, Purdue U., West Lafayette, Ind., 1992-93; adult nurse practitioner So. Ill. U., 1994—. Healthcare provider Migrant Med. Clinic, Cobden, Ill., summers 1994, 95. Mem. NOW. Democrat. Home: 167 Misty Lake Dr Murphysboro IL 62966 Office: So Ill U Student Health Clinic Carbondale IL 62906

LEGASPI, ELEANOR FLORIDA, childcare provider; b. Tamuning, Guam, July 18, 1960; d. Eddie DeGracia and Concepcion Balajadia Duenas; m. Lorenzo Santos Legaspi; children: Leticia, Lorenze. BA in Polit. Sci., Calif. State U., Hayward, 1992, MS in Edn., 1995. Credit analyst Assn. Nat. Bank, Pleasanton, Calif., 1984-91; childcare provider At Eleanor's, Castro Valley, Calif., 1991—. Area dir. girls' basketball Transfiguration Ch.; chmn. ways and means Palomares' Parents Club, 1992-93, 2d v.p., 1994-95; fundraising chmn. Jensen Rance PTA, 1995-96; sec. Cath. Yough Orgn. Metro League, 1996. Mem. Nat. Women Polit. Caucus (sec. 1992-94). Home: 19002 Carson Ln Castro Valley CA 94552

LEGASPI, JESUSA CRISOSTOMO, agricultural scientist, entomologist; b. Pasay, Manila, Philippines, Oct. 26, 1958; came to U.S., 1987; d. Benjamin Buencamino and Rosalinda Nieto (Manikis) Crisostomo; m. Benjamin Antonio Legaspi Jr., Jan. 2, 1987; 1 child, Michelle Elaine. BS, U. Philippines, Los Banos, 1978; MSc, U. Newcastle-Upon-Tyne, Eng., 1984; PhD, Purdue U., 1991. Rsch. asst. Philippine Coun. for Agr., Los Banos, 1980-82, Internat. Rice Rsch. Inst., Los Banos, 1985-86; grad. rsch. asst. Purdue U., West Lafayette, Ind., 1987-91; rsch. assoc. USDA, Weslaco, Tex., 1992-95; asst. prof. Tex. Agrl. Experiment Sta., Weslaco, 1995—. Contbr. articles to profl. jours. Sci. judge Jackson Elem. Sch., McAllen, Tex., 1992; vol. Ind. State Fair, Indpls., 1990; mem. Fil-Am Assn., Rio Grande Valley, Tex., 1993. David Ross fellow Purdue U., 1987; Colombo Plan scholar Brit. Coun., 1982. Mem. Entomol. Soc. Am., Philippine Assn. of Entomologists, Sigma Xi, Gamma Sigma Delta. Roman Catholic. Office: Tex Agrl Experiment Sta 2415 E Hwy 83 Weslaco TX 78596-8344

LEGAULT, JEANNE EMMA, paralegal; b. Washington, Aug. 11, 1952; d. Oscar and Louise (Munishor) L. AA in English, Finch Coll., 1970; BA in Psychology, Newcomb Coll., 1973; MS in Exptl. Psychology, Tulane U., 1980. Cert. paralegal, Wash. King County field dir. Washington State Pro-Choice Initiative, Seattle, 1991; Wash. State campaign coord. Harkin Presdl. Campaign, Seattle, 1992; paralegal Schroeter, Goldmark & Bender, Seattle, 1992—; legis. analyst Wash. State Senate, Olympia, 1993. Chair King County Rainbow Coalition, Seattle, 1990-94; committeewoman Wash. State Dems., Seattle, 1994—; treas. King County Dems., Seattle, 1992—; mem. candidate evaluation com. Mcpl. League, Seattle, 1989-90; vol. legal dept. ACLU, Seattle, 1986-88; precinct com. officer, Seattle, 1988—; vol. coord. Tom Weeks City Coun. Campaign, 1989; mem. King County Dem. Legis. Action Com., 1988-90; mgr. Helen Sommers State Rep. Campaign, 1990, Jeanne Kohl State Rep. Campaign, 1992; mem. steering com. Ctr. for Dem. Renewal, 1988-91; mem. Wash. State Dem. Legis. Action Com., 1991—; mem. exec. bd., now state committeewoman 36th Dist. Dems., 1989—; vol. Mike Lowry Gubernatorial Campaign, Wash., 1992; treas. Michael Spearman for King County Superior Ct. Campaign, 1993; dist. coord. Com. for Wash.'s Future Campaign, 1993; mem. steering com. Larry Gossett for County Coun. Campaign, 1994, Gary Locke for King County Exec. Campaign, 1994, Tina Podlodowski for City Coun. Campaign, 1995, Margaret Pageler for City

Coun Campaign, 1995, Roselle Pekelis for State Supreme Ct. Campaign, 1995. Named Dem. of Yr., King County Dems., 1994. Mem. Met. Dem. Club (bd. dirs. 1993—). Home: 625 Queen Anne Ave N # 201 Seattle WA 98109 Office: Schroeter Goldmark & Bender 810 3d Ave 5th Fl Seattle WA 98104

LEGERE, DIANE J., art association administrator, alpaca breeder; b. Inglewood, Calif., July 18, 1952; d. Charles E. and June L. Brown; m. Richard M. Legere, July 21, 1984. BA, San Jose State U., 1976. Regional mgr. Am. Internat. Grou Subs., Seattle, 1987-92; exec. dir. Western Art Assn., Ellensburg, Wash., 1992—; bd. dirs., past 2d v.p., past chair human resources The Clymer Mus. and Gallery, Ellensburg, Wash., 1992-95; bd. dirs., chair promotions com. Laughing Horse Summer Theatre, 1995. Author, editor: (newsletter) Brush Strokes, 1993—. Mem. Tourism Task Force, 1992, Tourism C. of C., Ellensburg, Wash., 1995. Theatre Arts scholar Kiwanas, 1970. Mem. Alpaca Breeders of Am., Wash. Athletic Club. Office: Western Art Assn PO Box 893 Ellensburg WA 98926-3112

LEGGETT, GLORIA JEAN, minister; b. Buffalo, June 6, 1941; d. Richard Howard and Mary Alice (Jumper) Pope; m. Arthur William Leggett, June 17, 1961; children: Wendy Irene, Pamela Jean. MusB, Va. Commonwealth U., 1986; MDiv, Wesley Theol. Sem., 1991. Ordained to ministry, Christian Ch., 1991. Choir dir. St. Mark's United Meth. Ch., Richmond, Va., 1974-80; hosp. chaplain Johnston-Willis Hosp., Richmond, Va., 1991—; interim minister Westville Christian Ch., Mathews, Va., 1992-93, Crewe (Va.) Christian Ch.; police chaplain Chesterfield County (Va.) Police Dept., 1995—; tchr. music, Richmond, 1972—; supply preacher, keynote speaker Main Line Denomination Chs., Va., 1990—. Rape crisis counselor YWCA, Richmond, 1992; bd. dirs. Va. Wildlife Fedn., 1986-92. Recipient Achievement award Dale Carnegie Course, Richmond, 1979. Mem. NOW, AAUW, Phi Kappa Phi. Home and office: 9216 Groomfield Rd Richmond VA 23236

LEGGETT, RUBENIA MARIE (RUBY LEGGETT), nursing administrator; b. Nordenham, Germany, Jan. 5, 1948; d. Charles Joseph and Elfreda Marie (Houfek) L.; children: Betty, Louise. Diploma, Phelps Meml. Hosp., 1969; AAS, Rockland C.C., 1973. RN N.Y. Nurses aide Phelps Meml. Hosp., North Tarrytown, N.Y., 1966-68, staff nurse med., surg., 1969-73, staff nurse ICU/CCU, 1973-87; dir. student health Guiding Eyes for the Blind, Yorktown Heights, N.Y., 1990—; home care nurse Unltd. Care, White Plains, N.Y., 1992-93; mem. adv. bd. Phelps Meml. Hosp. Ctr., 1980-81. Leader 4H Club Am., Westchester County, N.Y., 1992—; bd. dirs. Mt. Carmel Bapt. Ch., Carmel, N.Y. Mem. Emblem Club. Republican. Baptist. Home: 426 Croton Ave Cortlandt Manor NY 10566 Office: Guiding Eyes for the Blind 611 Granite Springs Rd Yorktown Heights NY 10598-3411

LEGINGTON, GLORIA R., middle school educator. BS, Tex. So. U, Houston, 1967; MS, U. So. Calif., L.A., 1973. Cert. adminstr. (life). Tchr., mentor L.A. Unified Sch. Dist., 1991-93; grade level chair L.A. Unified Schs., 1975-78, faculty chairperson, 1978, 80, 84, Black history/Martin Luther King program chair, 1978, 80, 83, 86, 88, 90-92, social chair, bus. coord., svc. club sponsor, 1978-80, Indian edn. chair, 1980-84, opportunity chair, 1976-78, grade level chair, 1984; Black edn. commn. liaison, 1989-90, impact tchr., 1991-92, human rels. sponsor, 1991-92, coun. Black adminstrs.-student conf. facilitator, 1992, tchr. inservice classes for area colloquim, parents, tchrs., faculty shared decision making coun., 1993-94, mem. faculty senate, 1992-93, mem. sch. improvement, 1993-94, mem. discipline com., 1993-94; del. U.S.-Spain Joint. Conf. on Edn., Barcelona, 1995. Chair United Way, 1988, 90; sponsor, 8th Grade, 1994-96; del. US/Spain Joint Conf. on Edn., Barcelona, 1995. Mem. NEA, Internat. Reading Assn., United Tchrs. L.A., Calif. League of Mid. Schs.

LEGUE, LAURA ELIZABETH, resort and recreational facility executive; b. Towanda, Pa., Oct. 11, 1954; d. William Frederick and Frances Lorraine (Cease) Goeckel; m. Stephen Wheeler, Nov. 9, 1974 (div. June 1989); m. Brian E. Legue, Mar. 17, 1990. AA, Mt. Ida Jr. Coll., Newton Ctr., Mass., 1974. Gen. mgr. Towanda Motel & Restaurant, Inc., 1974-82; mgr. Wilson's Suede & Leather, Lawrenceville, N.J., 1982-83; front office mgr. Park Shore Resort Hotel, Naples, Fla., 1985-87; property mgr. World Tennis Ctr. and Resort, Naples, 1987—; pres. World Tennis Club, Inc., Naples, 1991-95, World Tennis Cmty. Assn., Inc., 1994—; notary pub. State of Fla., 1987—. Mem. Collier County Hotel Assn. (sec. 1988, v.p. 1989), Fla. Vacation Rental Mgrs. Assn., Naples Area Accomodations Assn., Hospitality Sales and Mktg. Assn. Internat. (lic. cmty. assn. mgr.). Office: World Tennis Ctr. 4800 Airport Rd Naples FL 33942

LE GUIN, URSULA KROEBER, author; b. Berkeley, Calif., Oct. 21, 1929; d. Alfred Louis and Theodora (Kracaw) Kroeber; m. Charles A. Le Guin, Dec. 22, 1953; children: Elisabeth, Caroline, Theodore. B.A., Radcliffe Coll., 1951; M.A., Columbia, 1952. Vis. lectr. or writer in residence numerous workshops and univs., U.S. and abroad. Author: Rocannon's World, 1966, Planet of Exile, 1966, City of Illusion, 1967, The Word For World is Forest, 1967, A Wizard of Earthsea, 1968, The Left Hand of Darkness, 1969, The Tombs of Atuan, 1971, The Lathe of Heaven, 1971, The Farthest Shore, 1972, The Dispossessed, 1974, The Wind's Twelve Quarters, 1975, A Very Long Way from Anywhere Else, 1976, Orsinian Tales, 1976, The Language of the Night, 1979, Leese Webster, 1979, Malafrena, 1979, The Beginning Place, 1980, Hard Words, 1981, The Eye of the Heron, 1982, The Compass Rose, 1982, King Dog, 1985, Always Coming Home, 1985, Buffalo Gals, 1987, Wild Oats and Fireweed, 1988, A Visit from Dr. Katz, 1988, Catwings, 1988, Solomon Leviathan, 1988, Fire and Stone, 1989, Catwings Return, 1989, Dancing at the Edge of the World, 1989, Tehanu, 1990, Searoad, 1991, Blue Moon Over Thurman Street, 1993, Wonderful Alexander and the Catwings, 1994, Going Out With Peacocks, 1994, A Fisherman of the Inland Sea, 1994, Four Ways to Forgiveness, 1995, Unlocking the Air, 1996; also numerous short stories, poems, criticism, screenplays. Recipient Howard D. Vursell award Am. Acad. Arts and Letters, 1991, Pushcart prize, 1991, Boston Globe-Hornbook award for excellence in juvenile fiction, 1968, Nebula award (novel) 1969, (novel and story) 1975, (story) 1975, (novel) 1990, Hugo award (novel) 1969, (story) 1973, (novella) 1973, (novelette) 1988, Gandalf award, 1979, Kafka award, 1986, Newbery honor medal, 1972, Nat. Book award, 1972, H.L. Davis award Oreg. Inst. Literary Arts, 1992, Hubbub annual poetry award, 1995, Asimov's Reader's award, 1995. Mem. Sci. Fiction Research Assn., Sci. Fiction Writers Assn., Authors League, PEN, Writers Guild West, NOW, NARAL, Phi Beta Kappa. Office: care Virginia Kidd PO Box 278 Milford PA 18337-0278 also: care Matthew Bialer William Morris Agy 1350 Avenue Of The Americas New York NY 10019-4702

LEHMAN, BARBARA JUNE, elementary education educator; b. Waukegan, Ill., June 8, 1940; d. Ralph Jasen and Eleanor Helen Kollars; m. James Eugene Lehman, June 15, 1963 (div. Nov. 1972); 1 child, Jeanette Barbara Lehman Tobin. BA in Edn., Blackburn Coll., 1962; MS in Early Childhood Edn., Nat. Lewis U., 1988. Tchr. kindergarten Cmty. Unit Dist. 300, Carpentersville, Ill., 1962-66; tchr. kindergarten, 1st & 2d grades Cmty. Unit. Dist. 118, Wauconda, Ill., 1972—; mem. spl. edn. team Inclusion Class Dist. 118, 1994-95; speaker in field. Support group facilitator Lovelton Acad., Elgin, Ill., 1989-92; adult sponsor, mem. founding bd. ALAKIDS, Barrington, Ill., 1990-94. Mem. NEA, Nat. Assn. for Edn. of Young Children, Ill. Edn. Assn. Ill. Assn. for Edn. of Young Children, Wauconda Edn. Assn., ACEI. Home: 420 Asbury Ave Fox River Grove IL 60021-1813 Office: Cmty Unit Sch Dist 118 555 N Main St Wauconda IL 60084-1229

LEHMAN, JOAN ALICE, real estate executive; b. Jamaica Queens, N.Y., May 8, 1938; d. Hans Newman and Margot (Deutsch) Senen; m. Eugene Lehman, June 17, 1956 (div. Mar. 1990); children: Joel, Peter, Alan, Ira, Helen Ann, Helen Beth, Robert, Jacqueline, John, Steven, Robin, Elizabeth, Jody, Lisa, David, Andy, Jeremy, Jay. AA, Nassau C.C., East Meadow, N.Y., 1971; BS, Nova U., 1982. Lic. real estate broker, Fla. Owner Joan Lehman Real Estate Mgmt. Co., Old Bethpage, N.Y., 1961-82; tchr. Broward County Schs., Ft. Lauderdale, Fla., 1982-86; owner Joan Lehman Real Estate, Plantation, Fla., 1986—; pres. Jo Al 1 Inc., Plantation, —%. Mem. Sunset Sch. Adv. Bd., Ft. Lauderdale, 1994-96; bd. dirs. Property Owners Ctrl. Lauderhill, Fla., 1996; den mother Boy Scouts Am., Old Bethpage, N.Y.; leader Girl Scouts U.S., Old Bethpage. Office: 1841 S W 68th Ave Plantation FL 33317

LEHMAN, KATHERINE MEGEE, Episcopal priest; b. Austin, Tex., Feb. 7, 1946; d. Robert Ernest and Nancy (Stover) Megee; m. Henry Clay Lehman, June 11, 1966;; children: Gwen Stover, Kate Marshall. BA in English, U. Santa Clara, 1970; MDiv, Church Div. Sch., Berkeley, Calif., 1982, D of Ministry, 1996—. Ordained to ministry Episcopal Ch. Dir. edn. Trinity Episc. Ch., Fort Worth, 1976-78; seminarian St. Anselm's Episc. Ch., Lafayette, Calif., 1978-80; seminarian St. Stephen's Episc. Ch., Orinda, Calif., 1980-82, asst. rector, 1982-84; assoc. rector St. Stephen's Episc. Ch., Belvedere, Calif., 1984-90; rector St. Bede's Episc. Ch., Menlo Pk., Calif., 1990—; trustee, chaplain Trinity Episc. Sch., Menlo Pk., 1990—; coun. mem. Associated Parishes, Ft. Worth, 1990—, Coll. of Preachers, Washington, 1993—; deputation co-chair Episc. Diocese of Calif., San Francisco, 1993—. Office: Saint Bede's Episc Ch 2650 Sand Hill Rd Menlo Park CA 94025

LEHMAN, LOIS JOAN, medical librarian; b. Danville, Pa., Apr. 25, 1932; d. Harold M. and Leona (Shuey) L. B.A., Pa. State U., University Park, 1954; M.S., Columbia U., 1959. Librarian Lankenau Hosp., Phila., 1959-66; reference librarian Sch. Medicine, U. Pa., Phila., 1966-68; asst. librarian head pub. services Coll. Medicine, Pa. State U., Hershey, 1968-71, acting librarian, 1971-72, librarian, 1972—. Mem. Med. Libr. Assn., Assn. Acad. Health Scis. Libr. Dirs., Health Scis. Librs. Consortium (bd. dirs.), Interlibr. Delivery Svc. of Pa. (bd. dirs.), Quentin Riding Club. Office: Pa State U Coll Medicine George T Harrell Libr The Hershey Med Ctr Hershey PA 17033

LEHMAN, SHARON LEE, special education educator; b. Yakima, Wash., Jan. 27, 1938; d. Nephi Ballard and Lelah Margaret (Miller) Walruff; m. Melvin Edwin Lehman, Feb. 24, 1957; children: Stanley, Sheldon, Lani, Spencer, Debra, Crystal. BA, U. Hawaii, Hilo, 1985; MS in Edn., Western Oreg. State Coll., 1989. Cert. spl. educator, elem. edn. educator, Hawaii. Counselor, spl. edn. tchr. Naalehu (Hawaii) Sch., 1985-86, spl. edn. tchr., 1986-89; spl. edn. tchr. pre-kindergarten Keaau (Hawaii) Sch., 1989-92, spl. edn. tchr. prekindergarten thru primary, 1992-93; spl. edn. tchr.- elem. Mt. View (Hawaii) Sch., 1993-94; spl. edn. tchr. and sci. tchr. Keaau Sch., 1994-95, second grade tchr., 1995—; rschr. in field. Author, editor: Communication Sponge, Language Lightbulbs, 1993. Named Hawaii Dist. Tchr. of Yr., 1993. Mem. Phi Delta Kappa. Home: PO Box 69 Mountain View HI 96771-0069 Office: Keaau Sch 16-565 Pahoo Rd Keaau HI 96749

LEHMANN, ESTHER STRAUSS, investment company executive; b. Binghamton, N.Y., Apr. 19, 1944; d. Julius and Betty (Lind) Strauss; m. Aaron Lehmann, Feb. 27, 1966; children: Shanna, Shira, Marc, David. BS, Cornell U., 1966; cert. in vol. and non-profit orgn. mgmt., U. Conn., 1976; cert. employee benefits specialist, U. Pa., 1983. V.p. Fairway Mgmt., West Hartford, Conn., 1976-80; investment exec. Herzfeld & Stern, Paramus, N.J., 1980-86; assoc. v.p. Gruntal & Co., Inc., Ft. Lee, 1988—. Home: 1632 Dover Ct Teaneck NJ 07666-2965

LEHMANN-CARSSOW, NANCY BETH, educator, coach; b. Kingsville, Tex., Sept. 9, 1949; d. Valgene William and Ella Mae (Zajicek) Lehmann; m. William Benton Carssow, Jr., Aug. 1, 1981. BS, U. Tex., 1971, MA, 1979. Freelance photographer, Austin, Tex., 1971—; geography tchr., tennis coach Austin Ind. Sch. Dist., Tex., 1974—; salesperson, mgr. What's Going On Clothing, Austin, 1972-78; area adminstr. Am. Inst. Fgn. Study, Austin, 1974-81; area rep. World Encounters, Austin, 1981—, tour guide, Egypt, Kenya, 1977, 79, 81, 87, 92; participant 1st summer inst. Nat. Geog. Soc., Washington, 1986; tchr. Leader for People in Soviet Union, 1989, 90; vol. First Internat. Environ. Expedition to Antarctica. Author curriculum materials; photographer (book) Bobwhites, 1984. Recipient Merit award Nat. Coun. Geog. Edn., 1975, Creative Teaching award Austin Assn. Tchrs., 1978; Fulbright scholar, Israel, 1983; recipient study grant to Malaysia & Indonesia, 1990. Mem. NEA, Nat. Coun. Social Studies, Nat. Coun. Geog. Edn., Earthwatch (participant archaeol. dig. in Swaziland 1984), World Wildlife Fund, Rotary, Delta Kappa Gamma (pres. 1986-88), Phi Kappa Phi. Democrat. Roman Catholic. Avocations: stained glass, photography, tennis, gardening, needlepoint. Home: 1025 Quail Park Dr Austin TX 78758-6749 Office: Lanier High Sch 1201 Payton Gin Rd Austin TX 78758-6616

LEHOVEN, SUSAN HYLTON, video producer; b. Knoxville, Tenn., Dec. 5, 1960; d. Clyde D. and Josie (Kester) Hylton; m. Anthony C. LeHoven, Mar. 21, 1986. BS, U. Tenn., 1983, MA, 1986. Fitness instr. Norwegian Cruise Line, 1984-85; grad. tchg. asst. U. Tenn., Knoxville, 1983-86; owner VideoCard Prodns., Kauai, Hawaii, 1986—. Author: Collection of Poetry, 1994. Dir. Kauai Concert Assn., 1995-98. Office: VideoCard Prodns PO Box 843 Kilauea HI 96754-0843

LEHRHAUPT, KAREN, elementary and secondary education educator; b. Detroit, Feb. 4, 1942; d. Karl M. and Evelyn (Hubbell) Kuechenmeister; m. James Allen Youngling, Aug. 22, 1964 (div. 1976); 1 child, Lisa Youngling Howard; m. Michael Lehrhaupt, Aug. 25, 1978; stepchildren: Gwen, David, Nancy, Amy (dec.). BA, Hood Coll., 1964; MA, Fairleigh Dickinson U., 1977. Tchr. Old Bridge (N.J.) Bd. of Edn., 1968—. Home: 35 Lakeridge Dr Matawan NJ 07747 Office: Old Bridge Bd of Edn Rte 516 Old Bridge NJ 08857

LEHRMAN, MARGARET MCBRIDE, television news executive, producer; b. Spokane, Wash., Sept. 25, 1944; d. John P. and Ruth A. (Score) McBride; m. Michael Lloyd Lehrman, June 27, 1970. BA, U. Oreg., 1966; MS, Columbia U., 1970. Dir. coll. desk Peace Corps, Washington, 1966-69; asst. to exec. editor The Morning News Co., Washington, 1970-72; reporter Albright Communications, Washington, 1973-74; tv assignment editor ABC News, Washington, 1974; press asst. Senator Robert P. Griffin, Washington, 1975-79; researcher Today Show, NBC News, Washington, 1979, assoc. producer, 1979-83, Washington producer, 1983-89, dep. bur. chief, 1989-95, Washington producer, spec. coverage and events, 1995—. Trustee U. Oreg. Found., 1990—. Recipient Edwin M. Hood award for diplomatic reporting (China) adv. bd. Internat. Women's Media Found., Women's Fgn. Policy Group. Office: NBC News 4001 Nebraska Ave NW Washington DC 20016-2733

LEHTINEN, MERJA HELEN KOKKONEN, journalist, researcher, publisher; b. N.Y., Feb. 25, 1954; d. Osmo Ilmari and Hilkka Annikki (Kokkonen-Lind) L. AB in Am. Studies, Mt. Holyoke Coll., 1976; student, Dartmouth Coll., 1975; cert. in Finnish and Scandinavian, U. Helsinki, 1978. Assoc. tech. writer The Travelers Ins. Co., Hartford; mng. editor ASHRAE, N.Y.; internat. editor ASCE, N.Y.; dir. publs. Am. Assn. Engring., N.Y.; mng. editor Bill Comms., Inc., N.Y.; news editor McGraw Hill Co., N.Y.; exec. editor Mng. Automation Mag., N.Y.; editor-in-chief, pub. Indsl. Computing Mag. Kruger, McCarthy & Lehtinen, N.Y., 1987-93; founder, pres. Westisle Pub. Co., Westford, Mass., 1993; owner, pub. Discover Conn. Mag. and The Conn. Chronicles, 1993—; intern for Sen. Strom Thurmond U.S. Senate, Washington, 1973; dir. career guidance Am. Assn. Engring. Scis., N.Y., 1983-84; commr. Econ. Devel. Commn. of Colchester, Conn., 1992-96, hearing officer, 1994—; bd. dirs. Indsl. Computing Soc., Rsch. Triangle Park, N.C., 1993-95. Author (book) Quality Control, 1977 (recipient award of excellence Soc. Tech. Comms., 1977); contbr. articles to profl. jours. and mags. Vice chmn. Rep. Town Com., 1993-96; Rep. candidate for nomination to U.S. Congress 2d dist., 1992; hearing officer Justice of the Peace, Colchester, Conn., 1996—; bd. incorporators Eliza Huntington Meml. Home, Inc., 1993—; co-chair Internat. Conf. on Indsl. Computing, Toronto, 1992. Recipient rsch. fellow Rep. National Com., Washington, 1975. Mem. Instrument Soc. Am., Indsl. Computing Soc. (founder, mem. bd. dirs. 1993-95). Republican.

LEHTO, ALISON RAGNA, middle school educator; b. Klamath Falls, Oreg., Aug. 26, 1943; d. Lyle Frank and Alice Montana (Madison) Glenn; m. Glenn Alan Lehto, Dec. 24, 1973; 1 child, Glison Angela; 1 stepson, Bruce Alan. BA in English, San Diego State U., 1969, MA in English Lit., 1978; Cert. of Advanced Study, U. Maine, 1994. Cert. tchr., adminstr., Maine, jr. coll. tchr., Calif. Acctg. clerk GMAC, San Diego, 1963-65, Chrysler Credit Corp., San Diego, 1967-69; tchr. San Diego Unified Sch. Dist., 1969-80; instr. U. Maine, Farmington, 1980-82; substitute tchr. Mt. Blue H.S., Farmington, 1980-82; tchr. Williams Jr. H.S., Oakland, Maine, 1982—; facilitator Messalonskee Summer Inst. for Tchrs. and Adminstrs., Maine Sch. Adminstrv. Dist. # 47, Oakland, 1993, 94, 95. Author essays and poems. Mem. NEA, Nat. Coun. English, Maine Tchrs. Assn., Oakland PTA. Home: PO Box 495 Oakland ME 04963-0495 Office: Williams Jr HS Pleasant St Oakland ME 04963

LEIBOVITZ, ANNIE, photographer; b. Conn., Oct. 2, 1949. Student, San Francisco Art Inst. Chief photographer Rolling Stone, from 1973, photographer, 1970-83; photographer Vanity Fair, 1983—; photographer for advertisements, 1987—; proprietor Ann Leibovitz Studio, N.Y.C. Works exhibited various galleries; author: Photographs 1970-90, 1992. Recipient Innovation in Photography award Am. Soc. Mag. Photographers, 1987. Office: Annie Leibovitz Studio 55 Vandam St New York NY 10013-1104 also: Annie Leibovitz Studio 101 W 18th St New York NY 10013-4124*

LEIBOWITZ, ANN GALPERIN, lawyer; b. Balt., Oct. 11, 1940; d. Harold Marcy and Dorothy Rebecca (Trivas) Galperin; m. Howard Marvin Leibowitz, July 3, 1960; children: Ellen Ann, Katherine Leibowitz Kotkin. AB, Goucher Coll., 1960; LLB, U. Md., 1964. Bar: Mass. 1964, U.S. Ct. Appeals (1st cir.) 1984. Patent agt. W.R. Grace & Co., Clarkesville, Md., 1960-63; patent atty. Polaroid Corp., Cambridge, Mass., 1963-72, corporate atty., 1972-77, sr. corporate atty. and labor counsel, 1977-95; prin., founder AGL Assocs., Weston, Mass., 1995—; lectr. Coun. Edn. in Mgmt., Walnut Creek, Calif., 1987—; mem. faculty Mass. Continuing Legal Edn., Boston, 1991—. Bd. trustees Goucher Coll., Towson, Md., 1983-89; chmn. fin. com. Town of Weston, 1989-91, active, 1984-91, chmn. bd. selectmen, 1993—, active, 1991—; mem. exec. adv. bd. Ctr. House, Boston, 1990—; exec. com. bd. trustees Deaconess Waltham Hosp., 1995—. Mem. ABA, Am. Corporate Counsel Assn. (bd. dirs. N.E. chpt. 1988-91), Mass. Bar Assn. (lectr. 1987—), Boston Bar Assn., Indsl. Rels. Rsch. Assn.

LEIBOWITZ, FLORA LYNN, philosophy educator; b. Bklyn., Jan. 22, 1951; d. Joseph and Shirley Ellen (Bogen) L.; m. Loren Kenneth Russell, Jan. 22, 1986. BA, SUNY, Stony Brook, 1973; MA, Johns Hopkins U., 1975, PhD, 1979. Asst. prof. philosophy Oreg. State U., Corvallis, 1977-84, assoc. prof., 1984-93, prof., 1993—, dir. grad. studies dept. philosophy, 1994—; vis. asst. prof. U. Tex., Austin, 1983-84; vis. rsch. fellow Ctr. Philosophy and Lit. U. Warwick, Eng., 1993. Contbr. articles to profl. jours. Publicity dir. Friends of Chamber Music, Corvallis, 1994—. Mem. Am. Soc. Aesthetics, Brit. Soc. Aesthetics, Am. Philos. Assn. (program com. pacific divsn. 1996—). Office: Philosophy Dept Oreg State U Hovland Hall 208B Corvallis OR 97331

LEIDERMAN-CORBETT, RONI COHEN, university facility director; b. Bklyn., Nov. 7, 1951; d. Abraham and Selma Marsha (Berlly) Cohen; m. Richard Leiderman, June 24, 1972 (div.); children: Rachel, Ryan; m. Anthony Corbett, Dec. 12, 1992. BS in Edn., Boston U., 1973; MS in Edn., Lesley Coll., 1974; PhD in Psychology, Nova U., 1986. Tchr. family programs Nova Southeastern U., Ft. Lauderdale, Fla., 1983-86, asst. dir. family programs, 1983-86, instr., 1989-90, rsch. assoc., 1990—, dir. high risk infant program, 1985—, coord. parenting svcs., 1986—, assoc. dir. family ctr., 1986—, dir. family inst., 1991—; bd. dirs. Love Jen Children's Cancer Fund, Broward County, Gilda's Club Cancer Support Cmty., Hollywood. Co-author: In Time With Love-Caring for the Special Needs Baby, 1981, Your Child at Play, 1983. Mem., bd. dirs. State of Fla. Resource Coalition, Orlando, 1990-92. Mem. Broward County Supreme Ct. Mediation, East/West Found., Telford Club (v.p. 1988-90). Office: Nova Southeastern U 3301 College Ave Fort Lauderdale FL 33314-7721

LEIFELD, ELLEN M., publishing executive; b. Columbus, Nebr., Oct. 17, 1954; d. Donald Matthew and Dolores Ann (Ullrich) Emanuel; m. Randall Dean Trahan, Mar. 10, 1973 (div. 1980); 1 child, Ann Marie; m. Ronald Joseph Leifeld, Aug. 21, 1982; 1 child, Michael Emanuel. Reporter, lifestyle editor Fremont (Nebr.) Tribune, 1974-80; city editor Hastings (Nebr.) Daily Tribune, 1980-82; mng. editor Lake County Record-Bee, Lakeport, Calif., 1982-86; city editor Lansing (Mich.) State Jour., 1986-88, mng. editor, 1988-90; exec. editor Battle Creek (Mich.) Enquirer, 1990-92; mng. editor Gannett Rochester (N.Y.) Newspapers, 1992-94; pres., pub. The Ithaca (N.Y.) Jour., 1994—; adv. com. journalism Ctrl. Mich. U., Mt. Pleasant, 1992; vice chair membership & readership com., AP Mng. Editors, 1992-93; mem. Sciencenter Adv. Bd., 1996—. Chair 1996 campaign Tompkins County United Way, Ithaca, 1996—. Recipient runner-up editor of yr. Gannett Co., Inc., Battle Creek, 1991. Mem. Tompkins County C. of C., Rotary Club of Ithaca, Ithaca Coll. Bd. of Publs. Roman Catholic. Office: The Ithaca Jour 123 W State St Ithaca NY 14850

LEIGH, JENNIFER JASON (JENNIFER LEIGH MORROW), actress; b. L.A., Feb. 5, 1962; d. Barbara Turner and Vic Morrow. Student, Lee Strasberg Inst. Appearances include (films) Eyes of a Stranger, 1980, Fast Times at Ridgemont High, 1982, Wrong is Right, 1982, Easy Money, 1983, Grandview U.S.A., 1984, Flesh + Blood, 1985, The Hitcher, 1986, The Men's Club, 1986, Sister, Sister, 1987, Under Cover, 1987, Heart of Midnight, 1988, The Big Picture, 1989, Last Exit to Brooklyn, 1989, Miami Blues, 1990, Crooked Hearts, 1991, Backdraft, 1991, Rush, 1992, Single White Female, 1992, Short Cuts, 1993, The Hudsucker Proxy, 1994, Mrs. Parker and the Vicious Circle, 1994, Dolores Claiborne, 1994, Kansas City, 1996, Bastard Out of Carolina, 1996; (TV movies) Angel City, 1980, The Killing of Randy Webster, 1981, The Best Little Girl in the World, 1981, The First Time, 1982, Girls of the White Orchid, 1983, Buried Alive, 1990; prodr., actress Georgia, 1995. Office: ICM c/o Tracey Jacobs 8942 Wilshire Blvd Beverly Hills CA 90211 also: care Elaine Rich 2400 Whitman Pl Los Angeles CA 90068-2464*

LEIGH, SHARI GREER, software consulting firm executive; b. Reading, Pa., Mar. 1, 1959; d. Martin and Francine Rita (Gross) Rothenstein; m. Martin Brad Greer, Dec. 31, 1979; children: Shannon Leigh, Krista Heather. BA in Biochemistry, Wellesley Coll.-MIT, 1980; postgrad. in bus. adminstrn., Colo. State U., 1982-83. Lead thermal engr. Rockwell Internat. Space div., Downey, Calif., 1980-81; systems engr. Martin Marietta Aerospace, Denver, 1981-82, aerospace new bus. analyst, 1982-84; v.p. Miaco Corp. (Micro Automation Cons.), Englewood, Colo., 1984-87, pres., CEO, 1987—. Co-designer life systems monitor for Sudden Infant Death Syndrome, 1980. Exec. bd. dirs. Mile High chpt. ARC, 1991—. Recipient Recognition award for 500 fastest growing cos. Inc. Mag., 1990, 91, Blue Chip Enterprise award Am.'s Best Small Bus., U.S. C. of C., 1991; named Bus. Leader to Watch in the 90's Corp. Connection; finalist Colo. Small Bus. of the Yr. award C. of C., 1992-93, Person of Yr., U.S. Small Bus. Bus. Adminstrn., South Metro Small Bus. Person of Yr., 1992-93. Mem. Greater Denver Chamber (coun. mem. small bus. bd. 1991-93), So. Met. C. of C. (bd. dirs. 1994—). Office: Miaco Corp 6300 S Syracuse Way Ste 415 Englewood CO 80111-6724

LEIGH, SHERREN, communications executive, editor, publisher; b. Cleve., Dec. 22, 1942; d. Walter Carl Maurushat and Treva Eldora (Burke) Morris; m. Norman J. Hickey Jr., Aug. 23, 1969 (div. 1985). BS, Ohio U., 1965. Communications dir. Metal Lath Assn., Cleve., 1965-67; creative dir. O'Toole Inc., Chgo., 1967-69; sr. v.p. RLC Inc., Chgo., 1969-77; pres. Leigh Communications Inc., Chgo., 1978—; chmn. Today's Chgo. Woman mag., 1982—; pres. Ill. Ambassadors, Chgo., 1985-86; bd. dirs. Chgo. Fin. Exchange, 1985-87. Author: How to Write a Winning Resume, How to Negotiate for Top Dollar, How to Find, Get and Keep the Job You Want. Bd. dirs. Midwest Women's Ctr., Chgo., 1984-86, Girl Scouts Chgo., 1985-87, Black Women's Hall of Fame Found., Chgo., 1986—, Apparel Industry Bd., Chgo., 1988, Auditorium Theater of Roosevelt U. Recipient Corp. Leadership award YWCA Met. Chgo., 1979, Entrepreneurship award, 1988, Media Advocate of Yr. award U.S. SBA, 1994; named one of 10 Women of Achievement Midwest Women's Ctr., Chgo., 1987, Advt. Woman of Yr. Women's Advt. Club, Chgo., 1988; inducted City of Chgo. Women's Hall of Fame, 1988. Mem. Chgo. Network, Econ. Club Chgo., Execs. Club Chgo., Com. of 200 (founding mem.). Office: Leigh Communications, Inc 150 E Huron St # 1225 Chicago IL 60611

LEIGHTON, FRANCES SPATZ, writer, journalist; b. Geauga County, Ohio; m. Kendall King Hoyt, Feb. 1, 1984. Student, Ohio State U. Washington corr. Am. Weekly; corr. and Washington editor This Week Mag.; Washington corr. Met. Group Sunday Mags.; contbg. editor Family Weekly; free-lance journalist Metro Sunday Group, Washington; lectr. summer confs. Dellbrook-Shenandoah Coll., Georgetown U., Washington. Author over 30 books on hist. figures, celebrities, Hollywood, psychiatry, the White House and Capitol Hill, 1957—; (with Louise Pfister) I Married a Psychiatrist, 1961, (with Francois Rysovy) A Treasury of White House Cooking, 1968, (with Frank S. Caprio) How to Avoid a Nervous Breakdown, 1969, (with Mary B. Gallagher) My Life with Jacqueline Kennedy, 1969, (with Traphes Bryant) Dog Days at the White House, 1975, (with William Fishbait Miller) Fishbait—the Memoirs of the Congressional Doorkeeper, 1977, (with Lillian Rogers Parks) My 30 Years Backstairs at the White House (made into TV mini-series), 1979, (with Hugh Carter) Cousin Beedie, Cousin Hot--, My Life with the Carter Family of Plains, Georgia, 1978, (with Jerry Cammarata) The Fun Book of Fatherhood-or How the Animal Kingdom is Helping to Raise the Wild Kids at Our House, 1978, (with Natalie Golos) Coping with Your Allergies, 1979, (with Ken Hoyt) Drunk Before Noon—The Behind the Scenes Story of the Washington Press Corps, 1979, (with Louis Hurst) The Sweetest Little Club in the World, The Memoirs of the Senate Restaurateur, 1980, (with John M. Szostak) In the Footsteps of Pope John Paul II, 1980, (with Lillian Rogers Parks) The Roosevelts, a Family in Turmoil, 1981, (with June Allyson) June Allyson, 1982, (with Beverly Slater) Stranger in My Bed, 1985 (made into TV movie, 1987), (with Oscar Collier) How to Write and Sell Your First Novel, 1986, The Search for the Real Nancy Reagan, 1987, (with Oscar Collier) How To Write and Sell Your First Nonfiction Book, 1990, (with Stephen M. Bauer) At Ease at the White House, 1991; contbr. numerous feature stories on polit., social and govtl. personalities to various publs. Bd. dirs. Nat. Found., from 1963. Recipient Edgar award, 1961. Mem. Senate Periodical Corr. Assn., White House Corr. Assn., Am. News Women's Club, The Writers Club, Nat. Press Club, Writers League of Washington (pres.), Washington League Am. Pen Women (pres.), Washington Ind. Writers, Smithsonian Assocs., Nat. Trust Historic Preservation, Lake Barcroft Women's Club, Delta Phi Delta, Sigma Delta Chi. Unitarian. Office: Lake Barcroft 6336 Lakeview Dr Falls Church VA 22041-1331

LEIGHTON, MIRIAM, artist, consultant; b. N.Y.C.; d. Nathan and Rose (Unger) Kaback; m. Bruce Leighton, Feb. 22, 1965 (dec.); children: Elayne Joyce, Jo-Ann Helene. Student, NYU, 1934, 45. Cons. Saks Fifth Ave., N.Y.C., 1954-56; freelance cons. Ft. Lee, N.J., 1973-80; cons. in field; rep. Artists and Sculptors, N.J., 1984—. Active vol. various charitable orgns. Honored by Am. Cancer Soc., Technion, Univ. of Tech., United Jewish Community of Bergen County, Holly Ctr. (adv. for abused children), others.

LEIH, GRACE JANET See **FORELLE, HELEN**

LEINO, DEANNA ROSE, business educator; b. Leadville, Colo., Dec. 15, 1937; d. Arvo Ensio Leino and Edith Mary (Bonan) Leino Malenck; adopted child, Michael Charles Bonan. BSBA, U. Denver, 1959, MS in Bus. Adminstrn., 1967; postgrad. Community Coll. Denver, U. No. Colo., Colo. State U., U. Colo., Met. State Coll. Cert. tchr., vocat. tchr., Colo. Tchr. Jefferson County Adult Edn., Lakewood, Colo., 1963-67; retired tchr. bus., coordinator coop. office edn., Jefferson High Sch., Edgewater, Colo., 1959-93, ret., 1993; sales assoc. Joslins Dept. Store, Denver, 1978—; mem. ea. team, clk. office automation Denver Svc. Ctr. Nat. Park Svc, 1993-94, U.S. Dept. Labor, 1994—, wage hour asst.; instr. Community Coll. Denver, Red Rocks, 1967-81, U. Colo. Denver, 1976-79, Parks Coll. Bus. (name now Parks Jr. Coll.), 1983—; dist. adviser Future Bus. Leaders Am. Active City of Edgewater Sister City Project Student Exchange Com.; pres. Career Women's Symphony Guild; treas. Phantoms of Opera, 1982—; active Opera Colo. Assocs. & Guild, I Pagliacci; ex-officio trustee Denver Symphony Assn., 1980-82. Recipient Disting. Svc. award Jefferson County Sch. Bd. 1980, Tchr. Who Makes A Difference award Sta. KCNC/Rocky Mountain News, 1990, Youth Leader award Lakewood Optimist Club, 1993; inducted into Jefferson High Sch. Wall of Fame 1981 Mem. NEA (life), Colo. Edn. Assn., Jefferson County Edn. Assn., Colo. Vocat. Assn., Am. Vocat. Assn., Colo. Educators for and about Bus., Profl. Secs. Internat., Career Women's Symphony Guild, Profl. Panhellenic Assn., Colo. Congress Fgn. Lang. Tchrs., Wheat Ridge C. of C. (edn. and scholarship com.), Federally Employed Women, Delta Pi Epsilon, Phi Chi Theta, Beta Gamma Sigma, Alpha Lambda Delta. Republican. Roman Catholic. Club: Tyrolean Soc. Denver. Avocations: decorating wedding cakes, crocheting, sewing, music, world travel. Home: 3712 Allison St Wheat Ridge CO 80033-6124

LEISENRING, CAROL A., bank executive. Exec. v.p., chief economist CoreStates Fin. Corp., Phila., 1987—. Office: CoreStates Fin Corp 1500 Market St PO Box 7618 Philadelphia PA 19102-7618*

LEISER, JO ANN, artist; b. Burlington, Iowa, Sept. 17, 1935; d. Phillip E. and Ottie Amy (Mossman) Fichtner. BA, Western Coll., Oxford, Ohio, 1957; student, Art Students League, N.Y.C. Curator art exhibits 1st N.Y. Bank. One-woman shows 1st N.Y. Bank for Bus., N.Y.C., 1990, Rsch. Found., CUNY, 1992, James Beard Found., N.Y.C., 1994; exhibited in group shows Broome Street Gallery, N.Y.C., 1990, 92, Salmagundi Club, N.Y.C., 1992, 93, 95, 96, Ch. of Covenant, N.Y.C., 1992, 93, 94, Pen and Brush, 92, 93, 94, 95, Catharine Lorillard Wolfe Art Club, N.Y.C., 1992, 93, Pastel Soc. Am., N.Y.C., 1994, 95, Hammond Mus., North Salem, N.Y., 1995, Sharon (N.H.) Art Ctr., Joanne Chappell Gallery, San Francisco, also others. Recipient Freida Jensen award Ch. of Covenant, 1993. Mem. Salmagundi Club (Martin Hannon Meml. award 1993, 94, Alice B. McReynolds award 1993, Salmagundi Club award 1994, hon. mention 1995), Pastel Soc. Am. (Hahnemuhle award 1995), Pen and Brush (Margery Soroka Meml. award 1991, hon. mention 1992, 94, 96, Elizabeth Morse Genius award 1992, 2 Philip Isenberg awards 1995, 96), Catharine Lorrilard Wolfe Art Club, Allied Artists, Am. Artists Profl. League, Artists Fellowship, Pastel Soc. Am. (signature mem.). Home and Studio: 145 4th Ave Apt 7J New York NY 10003

LEISETH, PATRICIA SCHUTZ, educational district administrator; b. Menomonie, Wis., Dec. 13, 1942; d. Herb D. and Dorothy F. (Husby) Schutz; m. Keith M. Leiseth, June 12, 1964; children: Kjrsten Leiseth Bobb, Jon. BA, Macalester Coll., 1964, MEd, 1972; MS, St. Cloud State U., 1994. Elem. music coord. Hopkins (Minn.) Pub. Schs., 1964-65; English instr. Bloomington (Minn.) Pub. Schs., 1965-67; English instr. Maple Lake (Minn.) Pub. Schs., 1974-90, vocal instr. music, 1990-93, K-12 technology coord., 1993—. Vol., Buffalo (Minn.) Pub. Libr., 1993-94. Mem. NEA, Minn. Edn. Assn., Internat. Soc. for Tech. in Edn., Minn. Soc. for Tech. in Edn., Minn. Ednl. Media Orgn., Phi Kappa Phi. Home: 1510 Anderson Ave # 223 Buffalo MN 55313-4403 Office: Maple Lake Pub Schs PO Box 820 Maple Lake MN 55358-0820

LEISHMAN, HELEN TERESA, elementary school educator; b. Jersey City, July 16, 1965; d. Donald B. and Barbara A. (Kopilok) L. BS in Math. and Sci. Edn., West Ga. Coll., 1988; MEd in Math. and Social Studies Edn., Ga. State U., 1992. Cert. mid. sch. tchr., Ga. Math. lab. paraprofl. Gresham Park Elem. Sch. DeKalb County, Atlanta, 1985-86; 5th and 7th grade tchr. Terry Mill Elem. Sch., DeKalb County, 1988-94, grade chairperson, 1989-91, supervising tchr. for student tchrs., 1990-92, mem. exec. com. Future Tchrs., 1990-91, acad. bowl coach, 1990-94, student/tchr. support team, 1990-93; 5th grade tchr. Norcross (Ga.) Elem. Sch., 1994—, grade level mgr., 1995—; curriculum writer Atlanta Com. for the Olympic Games, 1992. Sch. sponsor ARC, Atlanta, 1991-94; mem. Friends of Fernbank, 1994. Gender Equity Mentor Program at Ga. Tech., 1994-95. Mem. Nat. Coun. Tchrs. Math., Ga. Assn. Educators, Ga. Indsl. Fellowship for Tchrs., Chi Omega (Greek Woman of Yr. 1988). Democrat. Roman Catholic. Home: 3230-320 Mercer Univ Dr Chamblee GA 30341 Office: Norcross Elem Sch 150 Hunt St Norcross GA 30071-3939

LEISING, JEAN, state legislator. Farm owner and operator; indls. nurse Good Samaritan Hosp. Sch. Nursing; state senator from dist. 42 Ind. Senate, 1988—. Trustee Cath. Community Found. Mem. Ind. Corn Growers Assn., Batesville (Ind.) C. of C., Soybean Assn., Pork Producers and Cattlemen's Assn. Republican. Home: 5268 Stockpile Rd Oldenburg IN 47036-9713 Office: Ind State Senate State Capitol Indianapolis IN 46204*

LEIST, ELISABETH PASEK, retail executive, retired; b. Hastings, Nebr., July 1, 1927; d. Joseph Edwin and Ethel (Anderson) Pasek; m. Frederick Morris Leist Sr., Nov. 26, 1949 (dec. 1976); children: Frederick Morris, Laurette Elisabeth. AA, Stephens Coll., 1947; BS, Ind. U., 1949. Ordained elder Presbyn. Ch., 1984. Electronics and camera merchandiser treasury div. J.C. Penney, Niles, Ill., 1974-79; with K-Mart, Des Plaines, Ill., 1979-94, camera and jewelry dept. mgr., 1981-88, jewelry and cosmetic dept. mgr., 1988-91; jewelry dept. mgr. K-Mart, Des Plaines, 1991-94; ret., 1994. Chmn. pub. rel. coun. Girl Scouts Am., LaPorte, Ind., 1950-52, from organizer to svc. unit chmn., Ill., 1968-84, alt. del., publicity chmn., 1984-88.

LEIST, MARILYN THOMAS, computer programmer; b. Glen Ridge, N.J., Nov. 4, 1942; d. William and Lucy Elizabeth (Perry) Thomas; m. Charles Albert Leist, June 30, 1963; children: Rosemary Alice, Lorraine Elizabeth. BS in Elem. Edn., Ohio State U., 1963; MS in Reading Edn., Towson State U., 1973; MS in Adminstrn. and Mgmt., Hood Coll., 1982. Tchr. 1st grade Talcott St. Sch., Owego, N.Y., 1963-65; title I tchr. Montgomery County Pub. Schs., Rockville, Md., 1968-70; second tchr. 3rd grade Barnesville (Md.) Primary, 1975-76; programmer Sperry Syss. Mgmt., Reston, Va., 1977-80, GE Info. Syss., Rockville, Md., 1980-83, IBM, Gaithersburg, Md., 1983-94, Loral Fed. Syss., Gaithersburg, Md., 1994; Indsl. adv. bd. Embry Riddle U., Daytona Beach, Fla., 1993-94. Commr. Cmty. Ministries of Montgomery County, Rockville, Md., 1993—. Mem. AAUW (pres. Md. chpt. 1994-96). Democrat. Methodist. Home: 19201 Forest Brook Rd Germantown MD 20874-2566 Office: Loral Fed Syss 9201 Corporate Blvd Rockville MD 20850

LEITER, ELAINE CAROL, technical writer; b. Pitts., Jan. 12, 1942; d. Joseph and Ruth Grumer; m. Kenneth C.W. Leiter, May 20, 1984. BS in English and Tech. Writing & Editing, Carnegie-Mellon U., 1963. Tech. pubs. editor U.S. Geol. Survey, Silver Spring, Md., 1963-72; tech. writer Otis Engrng. Corp., Carrollton, Tex., 1979-82, Syntech Internat., Inc., Richardson, Tex., 1982-87; cons. Dallas, 1987-96; tech. writer EDS, Plano, Tex., 1996—. Del. Senatorial Dist. Conv., Dallas, 1992, 96. Frances Camp Parry Meml. Book grantee, 1959-63; Carnegie scholar, 1959-63, C.S. May scholar, 1959-63. Mem. Soc. Tech. Comm., Bus. & Profl. Women, Hadassah. Jewish.

LEITES, SUSAN, artist, educator; b. N.Y.C., July 23, 1938; d. A.A. Miller and Mildred L. Levine; m. Edmund Leites, Feb. 3, 1963 (div. 1985); 1 child, Justin. BA, Smith Coll., 1960. Tchr. in drawing Hispanic Ctr. for the Treatment of Drug Addiction, Bronx, N.Y., 1970-71; instr. in painting and drawing Smith Coll., Northampton, Mass., 1981-82; vis. artist Smith Coll., Northampton, 1985; vis. critic to grad. students U. Pa., Phila., 1979-82, art tchr., 1982-93, dir. BFA program, 1984-90; referee Cultural Coun. Found. Artist Project, N.Y.C., 1979. Editor: The Rule of The Taewon'gun 1864-73, Resoration in Yi Korea, 1964-68; one-woman shows include Artists Space, N.Y.C., 1976, Belfast Pub. Libr., Maine, 1982, John Szoke Gallery, N.Y.C., 1992, B.A.I. Gallery, Soho, 1995; exhibited in group shows at Green Mountain Gallery, N.Y.C., 1971, 77, Genesis Gallery, N.Y.C., 1976, Artists Space, N.Y.C., 1977, 92, John Szoke Gallery, N.Y.C., 1990, Maine Coast Artists, 1990, 92, 94, 45th Ann. Mus. Acad. Arts & Letters, N.Y.C., Portland Mus. Art, 1993, 94, Gallery Swan, Soho, 1995, others; stage designer Strays set for Conn. Ballet, 1990; executed mural Hispanic Ctr. for the Treatment of Drug Addiction, Bronx, N.Y.; commd. painting World Trade Ctr., N.Y.C., 1976-79. Mem. AAUP, AAUW, Coll. Art Assn. Studio: 280 Riverside Dr # 13K New York NY 10025-9033

LEITZ, ELIZABETH RENÉE, bookkeeper; b. Columbia, Mo., Sept. 18, 1961; d. George Matthus and Renee Jewel (Holm) Pavey; m. Richard Warren Leitz, Aug. 27, 1983; children: Matthus R., Audra E., Katharina R. BA in Bus. Adminstrn., Eastern Wash. U., 1984. Clk., treas. Town of Mattawa (Wash.), 1984-85; full charge bookkeeper Agri-Bus. Svc., Mattawa, 1986—. Chmn. Family Policy Network, Grant County, Wash., 1995—; pres. Vol. Involved Parents, Mattawa, 1994-95, com. chmn. Cub Scouts Am., Mattawa, 1994-95; goal setting facilitator Wahluke Sch. Dist., 1995, vocat. edn. adv., 1996—. Home: 22758 U 2 SW Mattawa WA 99349 Office: 72 W Government Way Mattawa WA 99349

LEITZEL, JOAN RUTH, university president. BA in Math., Hanover Coll., 1958; MA in Math., Brown U., 1961; PhD in Math., Ind. U., 1965. Instr. math. Oberlin (Ohio) Coll., 1961-62; asst. prof. math. Ohio State U., Columbus, 1965-70, assoc. prof., 1970-84, prof., 1984-92, vice chmn. dept., 1973-79, acting chmn., 1978, assoc. provost, 1985-90; prof. dept. math. and stats. U. Nebr., Lincoln, 1992-96, sr. vice chancellor for acad. affairs, 1992-96, interim chancellor, 1995-96; pres. U. N.H., Durham, 1996—; mem. adv. com. Griffith Ins. Found., 1979-82; cons. Ohio Dept. Edn., 1980-83; participant Am. Coun. on Edn., 1980, 82; cons. Nat. Commn. on Excellence in Edn., U.S. Dept. Edn., 1982; mem. univ. math. edn. del. to China, 1983; dir. divsn. materials devel., rsch. and info. sci. edn. NSF, 1990-92; presenter in field, 1980—; bd. dirs. Am. Assn. Higher Edn., chmn.-elect, 1996-97; mem. interpretive reports adv. bd. Nat. ssessment Ednl. Progress, 1995-98; trustee Consortium on Math. and Its Applications, 1994-95; mem. exec. coun. com. on acad. affairs Nat. Assn. State Univs. and Land-Grant Colls., 1994-96, chmn. com. on faculty, 1994-96; mem. coordinating coun. for edn. NRC, 1993-95, mem. bd. on math. scis. edn., 1985-87; numerous others. Bd. dirs. United Way Lincoln, 1995-96, 1st Plymouth Ch., 1996, Lincoln Partnership for Econ. Devel., 1996. Recipient Disting. Alumni award Hanover Coll., 1986, dir.'s award for mgmt. excellence NSF, 1991; grantee NSF, 1976-79, 84-88, Battelle Found., 1981-83, SOHIO, 1983-85. Mem. AAAS (edn. com. 1981-84), Am. Math. Soc. (com. on excellence in scholarship 1993-95), Assn. for Women in Math., Math. Assn. Am. (nominating com. 1978-79, com. on tchr. tng. and accreditation Ohio sect. 1976-79, nat. com. on undergrad programs 1982-85, chmn. joint task force on curriculum for grades 11-13 with Nat. Coun. Tchrs. Math. 1986-88), Nat. Coun. Tchrs. Math., Mortar Bd., Sigma Xi, Phi Kappa Phi. Office: U NH Office of Pres Durham NH 03824

LEKAS, MARY DESPINA, otolaryngologist; b. Worcester, Mass., May 13, 1930; d. Spyridon Peter and Merciny S. (Manoliou) L.; m. Harold William Picozzi. BA, Clark U., 1949; MD, Athens (Greece) U., 1957; MA, Brown U., 1986; student, Boston U. Diplomate Am. Bd. Otolaryngology. Sci. instr. Hahnemann Hosp. Sch. Nursing; rotating intern Meml. Hosp., Worcester, 1957-58; resident in otolaryngology R.I. Hosp., Providence, 1958-62; resident in otolaryngology and otorhinolaryngology U. Pa. Grad. Sch. Medicine, 1960; surgeon in chief, dept. otolaryngology R.I. Hosp., 1984—; pvt. practice Providence, 1962—; chmn. dept. otolaryngology Brown U., Providence, 1984—; cons. Cleft Palate Clin. and Craniofacial of R.I. Hosp., 1964—, VA Hosp., Providence, 1967—, St. Joseph Hosp., Providence, 1983—, Miriam Hosp., Providence, 1984—; lectr. profl. orgns. Europe, U.S. Mem. editorial bd. Am. Jour. Rhinology, 1987—; contbr. articles to profl. jours. Mem. alumni coun. Clark U. Clark V./Jonas Clark fellow; named R.I. Woman Physician of Yr., 1992. Fellow ACS, Soc. Univ. Otolaryngologists-Head and Neck Surgeons, Triological Soc. (ea. sect. sec., Presdl. Citation 1993), Am. Acad. Otolaryngology-Head and Neck Surgeons, Am. Acad. Facial Plastic and Reconstructive Surgeons, Am. Acad. Broncho-Esophagology (treas., v.p. 1990); mem. AMA, Assn. Acad. Dept. Otolaryngology-Head and Neck Surgery, Deafness Rsch. Found., Am. Cleft Palate Assn., Am. Med. Women's Assn. (R.I. Woman Physician of Yr. 1992), Centurian Club, New Eng. Otolaryng. Soc. (pres. 1987-88). Greek Orthodox. Home: 129 Terrace Ave Riverside RI 02915-4726 Office: Physicians Office Bldg 110 Lockwood St Providence RI 02903-4801

LELAND, PAULA SUSAN, educational administrator, educator; b. Duluth, Minn., Feb. 10, 1953; d. Clarence Henry and Agnes Gudrun (Feiring) L. BS in Elem. Edn. and Music with honors, U. Minn., Duluth, 1975, BS in English, Lang. Arts and Sec. Edn. with honors, 1979; MS in Edn. Adminstrn. and Edn. summa cum laude, U. Wis., Superior, 1982, MEd in Profl. Devel., English and Language Arts summa cum laude, 1984, Spl. degree in Edn. Adminstrn. summa cum laude, 1988, postgrad., 1988—; postgrad., U. St. Thomas, 1989, U. Minn., Mpls., 1996—. Tchr. elem. gifted children U. Minn., Mpls., 1980; tchr. Hermantown (Minn.) Cmty. Schs. Dist. 700, 1975—, substitute adminstr., 1982-92; mem. staff devel. com. Hermantown (Minn.) Cmty. Schs. Dist. 700, Hermantown, 1987—; dist. coord. and chairperson, planning, evaluating and reporting com., adminstrv. rep. State Dept. of Edn. for Minn. #700, Hermantown, 1984-86; supr. student tchrs. U. Wis., Superior, 1977—, adminstr. practicum, 1981-82; supr. student tchrs. U. Minn., Duluth, 1977—; mem. faculty community adv. com. for student tchrs., 1985—; Coll. St. Scholastica, 1977—; supr. tchr. aides, parent vols., and interpreters, 1980—; fgn. exch. tchr. host, 1982-83; profl. edn. tutor, 1989-90; mem. textbook com. Hermantown Schs., 1977—; writer, reporter Hermantown Star, 1978. Curriculum writer Hermantown Community Schs.; music arranger, composer, lyricist. Mem. Dem. Nat. Conv. supporter, Dem. Party Local Affiliation, Duluth, 1972—, Lake Superior Ctr. Non-Profit Orgn.; choir dir., dir. music Zion Luth. Ch., 1980—, dir./coord. music and handbell, 1983—, asst. dir. 1976-79, co-chair music and co-author music tape for Centennial Celebration, 1988, mem. nominating and worship coms. chairperson, 1992-94, recorder, sec. and choir sec., pastor-selected com. for assoc. in ministry, 1980—, vocalist, 1967—, Sunday Sch. tchr., Bible sch. tchr. 1968-75, substitute asst. dir., 1976-80, coun. mem. 1992—, v.p. 1993-94, pres. 1994—, chair call com. pastor-elect, 1994—, found. bd. dirs., 1994—; supporter Reading is Fundamental, 1975—, United Way of Greater Duluth, 1975—; mem. Dairy Coun., Hermantown Arts Coun.; active Goodwill Industries, Salvation Army, Clean Water Action, Minn. Dept. Natural Resource-Wildlife, U. Minn. Legis. Network, 1992—; Archtl. Planner Ednl. Facilities and Creative Activity, 1984; bd. dirs. Duluth Fed. Employees Credit Union, 1994-95. Named to The Nat. Women's Hall of Fame, 1995; Alworth scholar, 1971-75, Denfeld scholar, 1968-71. Mem. AAUW, NAFE, Am. Mus. Nat. Hist., Assn. Lutheran Ch. Musicians (invited), Future Tchrs. Orgn., Red Cross Club (pres, former v.p., svc. award), Sons of Norway (Viking Ship Project), N.Am. Assn. for Environ. Edn., Norwegian Am. Heritage Fund, Minn. Valley Nat. Wildlife Refuge, N.D. Parks and Recreation, Friends of Deep Portage, Arrowhead Reading Coun., Minn. Reading Assn., Hermantown Fedn. Tchrs., Hermantown Sch. Dist. Cont. Edn. (co-chair, former sec., cert. of appreciation 1990), Hermantown Fedn. Tchrs., Minn. Hist. Soc., Midwest Fed. Banking Consortium, U. Minn.-Duluth Alumni Assn., U. Wis.-Superior Alumni Assn., Minn. Naturalists Assn., Tweed Mus. Art, Mpls. Soc. of the Arts, Mpls. Soc. of Fine Arts, Minn. Inst. Art, Internat. Platform Assn., Smithsonian Nat. Assocs., Smithsonian Inst., Charles F. Menninger Soc., Laura Ingalls Wilder Meml. Soc., Midwesterners Club, Alpine Club, Zoofari Club, Queen Mary and Spruce Goose Voyager Club, Kappa Delta Pi, Sigma Alpha Iota, Phi Kappa Phi, Phi Delta Kappa, Delta Kappa Gamma, Beta Sigma Phi, Alpha Delta Kappa. Office: 4289 Ugstad Rd Hermantown MN 55811-3615

LELAND, VIRGINIA ROSE, pharmacist; b. Wenatchee, Wash., Dec. 8, 1945; d. Theodore Roosevelt and Edith Rose (Tews) Ballard; m. Paul D. Leland, Dec. 27, 1969 (div. Sept. 1985). BS in Pharmacy, U. Wash., 1969. Registered pharmacist, Wash. Pharmacist Seattle Pharm. Svcs., 1972-73; clin. staff pharmacist U. Wash. Med. Ctr., Seattle, 1974-88, lead pharmacist, 1988-93, drug svcs. lead pharmacist, 1993—. Mem. Am. Soc. Health Sys. Pharmacists, Wash. State Soc. Health Sys. Pharmacists, Seattle Area Soc. Health Sys. Pharmacists, U. Wash. Sch. Pharmacy Alumni Assn. Home: 1348 E Interlaken Blvd Seattle WA 98102 Office: Univ Wash Med Ctr 1959 Pacific Ave Seattle WA 98195

LELE, AMOL SHASHIKANT, obstetrician and gynecologist; b. Chhindnara, India, May 23, 1944; came to U.S., 1970; d. Gajanan S. and Sarala S. (Manjrekar) Karahde; m. Shashikant Lele, Feb. 28, 1970; children: Kedar, Rajal. MBBS, Bombay U., 1967, MD, 1970; DGO, Coll. Physicians, Bombay, 1969. Diplomate Am. Bd. Ob-Gyn. Clinician ob-gyn. clinic St. Luke's Hosp., Cleve., 1974; instr. SUNY, Buffalo, 1974-76, asst. prof., 1978-84, clin. assoc. prof., 1984—; fellow Children's Hosp., Buffalo, 1976-78, dir. women's svcs., 1976—, dir. outreach program, 1991—; dir. prenatal care Erie County Med. Ctr., Buffalo, 1979—; mem. health com. Planned Parenthood, Buffalo, 1992—; mem. infant mortality task force Health Systems Agy., Buffalo, 1994—. Home: 75 Nottingham Ter Buffalo NY 14216 Office: Children's Hosp Buffalo 239 Bryant St Buffalo NY 14222

LELEWICZ, DEBORAH GATLIN (DEBBI LELEWICZ), artist; b. Dallas, Dec. 22, 1951; d. Herman Maurice and Irene (Evans) Gatlin; m. Kenneth Frank Lelewicz, May 17, 1975; 1 child, Veronica Sarah. AA in Edn., Tyler (Tex.) Jr. Coll., 1971; student, So. Meth. U., Dallas, 1971-74. Educator Richardson (Tex.) Montessori Sch., 1975-78; owner, operator Gold Mine Gallery, Plano, Tex., 1979-87; instr. art Heights Recreation Ctr., Richardson, 1987—; cons Wildflower Festival, Richardson, 1993-95, Dallas Christmas Parade, 1993. Troop leader, recruiter Girl Scouts, Richardson, 1988-93, mem. adv. bd. Tex. coun., 1989-91; docent The Sixth Fl. Mus., Dallas, 1995—. Named Outstanding Leader Tex. Girl Scout Coun., Dallas, 1990, Green Angel award, 1991. Mem. Richardson Civic Art Soc., Vinyl Goddess Club Dallas (pres. bd. dirs. 1994—). Democrat. Methodist. Home: 911 Wayside Way Richardson TX 75080

LELYVELD, GAIL ANNICK, actress; b. Boston, May 22, 1948; d. Edward I. and Beatrice Elizabeth (Hewitt) L. BA in Polit. Sci., Boston U., 1970; MA in Polit. Sci., Goddard Coll., 1974; studies with Paul Barry, Peter Donat, Ray Reinhardt, Darrell Lauer, others. Actress, 1970—; tech. staff USA Prodns. and Midseason, Hempstead, N.Y., 1986-87, prodn. stage mgr., 1987—; tech. staff Gray Wig, Hempstead, 1986, 87; cons. Talking With prodn. M.A., C.W. Post. Appeared in numerous films including Frances, Halloween III, Children on Their Birthdays, Project 1917, Rocky II, Happy Endings, Seeds of Innocence, Bonfire of the Vanities, The Bird's Eye View, Insomnia, Monster Math, The Lesson, I'm Not Rappaport, City Hall; (TV shows): Archie Bunker's Place, Mister Clown Says, White Noise, The Gentle Creature, (ABC Afterschool Spl.) Summer Stories: The Mall, Mathnet, Bill Cosby Murder Mystery; actor (theatre) Alice in Wonderland, Not so Grimm Fairytale Players; actress (Littletop Theatre Co.) Toby Tyler, Marmalade Gumdrops, (theatre) Bohemian Lights, King Lear - Tenant, Doctor & Knight Plainedge Playhouse, The Hostage, USA Prodns.; reader Yom Kippur Svcs., Temple Emanuel San Francisco; singer Musicum Collegium Hofstra U., Pala Opera Assn., St. Patrick's Cathedral Choir, Temple Emanual New Hyde Park Choir; theatre tech. involvement includes stage mgr., sound asst. Wings; sound asst. Danton's Death; asst. stage mgr. Endgame, Breaker Morant; lighting, stage mgr. The Foreigner; lighting asst. Midnight Waltz, Broadhollow Theatre; asst. stage mgr. props., fx, dresser Accomplice; cons. on reading The Sisters Rosensweig. Mem. AFTRA. Jewish. Home: 291 Saville Rd Mineola NY 11501-1345

LEMASTER, SHERRY RENEE, fundraising administrator; b. Lexington, Ky., June 25, 1953; d. John William and Mary Charles (Thompson) LeM.; BS, U. Ky., 1975, MS in Health Edn. Adminstrn., Bryn Mawr Coll. Inst. for Women, 1984. Cert. fund raising exec. Lab. technician in virology, serology Cen. Ky. Animal Disease Diagnostic Lab., Lexington, 1975-76; grant coord., environ. specialist Commonwealth Ky. Dept. for Natural Resources and Environ. Protection, Frankfort, 1976-78; coord. residence hall program Murray (Ky.) State U., 1978-80; dean students Midway (Ky.) Coll., 1980-81, v.p. devel., alumnae affairs, 1981-86; dir. devel. Wilderness Road Coun. Girl Scouts U.S., Lexington, 1986-88, Coll. of Agr. and Life Scis. Va. Tech., Blacksburg, Va. 1988-94; sr. major gifts officer Bowman Gray Sch. Medicine Wake Forest U. and N.C. Baptist Hosp., Inc., Winston-Salem, N.C., 1994—. amb. U. Ky. Coll. Agr.; cons. U.S. Dept. Edn., 1987—; chmn. Midway chpt. Am. Heart Assn., 1981; mem. adminstrv. bd. First United Meth. Ch., Lexington, 1982-84, 87; mem. Coun. for Advancement and Support Edn., 1981—, chmn. Ky. conf., 1982; planning com. charter mem. Nat. Disciples Devel. Execs. Conf., 1984; mem. East Ky. First Quality of Life Com., 1987-88. Recipient Young Career Woman award Bus. and Profl. Women's Club, Frankfort, 1981; named to Hon. Order of Ky. col., 1977, hon. sec. state, 1984. Mem. Nat. Soc. Fund Raising Execs. (bd. dirs. Lexington chpt. 1986), Advancement Women in Higher Edn. Adminstrn. (former state planning com. Ky.), U. Ky. Alumni Assn. (life), P.E.O. (charter, chpt. X-Ky., sec. chpt. AU-Va. 1991-93, Va. state chpt., amendments and accommendation com. 1990-92), Ninety-Nines Internat. Assn. Women Pilots (vice chmn. Ky. Bluegrass chpt. 1986-87, chmn. and chmn. bd. 1987-88), Kentuckians N.Y., Jr. League, Nat. Agriculture Alumni and Devel. Assn. (awards com. 1992-94), Pi Beta Phi Nat. Alumnae Assn. (alumnae province pres. 1980-81, sec. bd. dirs. Ky. Beta chpt. 1982-84, pres. Va. Zeta chpt. house corp. 1991-94). Avocations: private pilot, needlecrafts, swimming, equitation, racquetball. Office: Bowman Gray Baptist Hosp Wake Forest U The Med Ctr Medical Center Blvd Winston Salem NC 27157

LEMAY, NANCY, graphic designer, painter; b. N.Y.C., Sept. 7, 1956; d. Michael and Mary (Lombardozzi) Potenzano; m. Harry Adrian LeMay, Jan. 24, 1986. BFA with honors, Sch. Visual Arts, 1978; postgrad., NYU, 1981-84. Admissions counselor Sch. Visual Arts, N.Y.C., 1979-81, acad. advisor, 1981-84; asst. art dir. NYU, N.Y.C., 1984-87; graphic designer J. C. Penney, N.Y.C., 1987-89; art dir. Catch A Rising Star, N.Y.C., 1989; graphic designer WNBC TV News Graphics, N.Y.C., 1989-90; graphics engr. NBC Network News Graphics, N.Y.C., 1990-91; graphics engr. KCOP TV News, L.A., 1991-94, art dir., 1994—; adv. commn. High Sch. Art and Design,

N.Y.C., 1984-91; judge Washington and Balt. Area Emmy Awards for Graphics. Exhibited in group show Wings N Water Festival (poster winner), 1990; designer: (logotype design) Art Direction Mag. (Award of Merit), 1985; contbr. MacWeek Mag., 1989. Recipient Sch. Art League full scholarship, 1974, Rhodes Family award, 1978, Master Eagle Gallery Award of Merit, 1976, 77, 78, L.A. Area Emmy award, 1996. Mem. Broadcast Designers Assn. (Silver award 1995). Office: KCOP TV 915 N La Brea Ave Los Angeles CA 90038-2321

LEMESHOW, ALISON, advertising executive; b. Kendall Park, N.J., Nov. 7, 1961; d. Seymour and Judith (Feinstein) L. BA, Hamilton Coll., 1984. Rsch. asst. Opinioin Rsch. Corp., Princeton, N.J., 1984-86; with W.B. Doner's Co., Balt., 1986—, rsch. project mgr., rsch. mgr., v.p. rsch. mgr., v.p. rsch. dir., sr. v.p. rsch. dir., sr. v.p., dir. strategic planning and rsch. Mem. Am. Mktg. Assn. (Gold Effie award 1989). Office: 400 E Pratt St Baltimore MD 21202

LEMIEUX, LINDA DAILEY, museum director; b. Cleve., Sept. 6, 1953; d. Leslie Leo LeMieux Jr. and Mildred Edna (Dailey) Tutt. BA, Beloit Coll., 1975; MA, U. Mich., 1979; assoc. cert., Mus. Mgmt. Program, Boulder, Colo., 1987. Asst. curator Old Salem, Inc., Winston-Salem, N.C., 1979-82; curator Clarke House, Chgo., 1982-84; curator Western Mus. Mining and Industry, Colorado Springs, Colo., 1985-86, dir., 1987—. Author: Prairie Avenue Guidebook, 1985; editor: The Golden Years--Mines in the Cripple Creek District, 1987; contbr. articles to mags. and newspapers. Fellow Hist. Deerfield, Mass., 1974—. Research grantee Early Am. Industries Assn., 1978. Mem. Am. Assn. Mus., Am. Assn. State and Local History, Colo.-Wyo. Mus. Assn., Colo. Mining Assn., Nev. Mining Assn., Mountain Plains Assn. Mus., Women in Mining. Congregationalist. Home: 1337 Hermosa Way Colorado Springs CO 80906-3050 Office: Western Mus of Mining & Industry 1025 N Gate Rd Colorado Springs CO 80921-3018

LEMKE, LAURA ANN, assistant principal, foreign language educator; b. Hollis, L.I., N.Y., May 4, 1964; d. Ronald Louis Zarobinski and Donna Jean (Strayer) Williams; m. David Michael Lemke, Aug. 25, 1984; 1 child, Kelsey Marie. BA in French and Bus. with honors, Mich. State U., 1987, M in Edn. Adminstrn., 1993. Cert. secondary tchr., vocat. and adminstrn. Teaching asst. East Lansing (Mich.) Pub. Schs., 1985-87, French and bus. tchr. comty. edn., 1985-87; tchr. French and bus. Grand Blanc (Mich.) Comty. Schs., 1987&, coord. elem. fgn. lang., 1990-91, coord. K-12 fgn. lang., 1991—; chair North Cen. accreditation Grand Blanc Mid. Sch., 1990—. Vol. Flint Internat. Inst., 1987-91, United Way, Flint, 1992. Mem. Nat. Bus. Edn. Assn. (Award of Merit 1987), Am. Assn. of Tchrs. of French, Mich. Fgn. Lang. Assn. (presider's chair 1994-95), Mich. Bus. Edn. Assn. (Outstanding Bus. Educator award 1986-87), Phi Kappa Phi. Home: 6057 E Maple Ave Grand Blanc MI 48439-9003 Office: Grand Blanc Comty Schs 11920 S Saginaw St Grand Blanc MI 48439-1402

LEMMEY, DOROTHY ELLA, nursing educator; b. Pitts., Oct. 17, 1947; d. Donald A. and Rosmarie Cline; m. Harold Cheadle, Feb. 4, 1967 (dec. 1968); m. Kenneth Lemmey Jr., Oct. 17, 1970 (div. 1976); 1 child, Dawn Michelle. BSN, Kent State U., 1982; MSN, Case Western Res., 1988. Staff nurse MICU Univ. Hosps., Cleve., 1982-83, staff nurse radiology, 1983-86; clin. instr. Lorain (Ohio) C.C., 1988; staff nurse labor and delivery Mt. Sinai Med. Ctr., Cleve., 1988—; lab instr. Cuyahoga C.C., Cleve., 1989; clin. instr., course coord. Huron Rd. Sch. of Nursing, Cleve., 1989; asst. prof. maternity Lakeland C.C., Mentor, Ohio, 1989—; dir. edn. Greater Cleve. Nurses, 1991-93; presenter workshops, 1989—. Pres. bd. trustees Forbes House, Painesville, Ohio, 1994—;. Recipient Vol. of Yr. Health and Human Svcs., 1992, Nursing Now, 1991, Outstanding Vol. Cmty. Svcs. March of Dimes, 1990, Lake County Prosecutors Victim Sensitivity award, 1996. Mem. ANA, Nursing Network on Violence Against Women, OAADN, NOW, ToastMaster, Nat. League for Nursing, Am. Holistic Nurses Assn., Sigma Theta Tau. Democrat. Home: 536 South Bay Cove Painesville OH 44077 Office: Lakeland Cmty Coll 7700 Clocktower Mentor OH 44077

LEMMON, JEAN MARIE, editor-in-chief; b. Duluth, Minn., Nov. 11, 1932; d. Lawrence Howard and Marie Julien (Gunderson) H.; m. Richard LuVerne LemMon, Apr. 17, 1965 (div. 1976); 1 child, Rebecca Jean. BA, U. Minn., 1954. Editor Better Homes and Gardens Mag., Des Moines, 1961-63, dept. head crafts, 1985-86, editor-in-chief, 1993—; women's editor Successful Farming, Des Moines, 1963-68; pres. Jean LemMon & Assocs., Des Moines, 1968-84; project editor Meredith Pub. Svcs., Des Moines, 1984-85; editor-in-chief Country Home Mag., Des Moines, 1986-93; adv. bd. Drake U. Journalism Sch., 1991—. Mem. ASCAP, Mensa Internat., Am. Soc. Interior Designers. Office: Better Homes and Gardens 1716 Locust St Des Moines IA 50309-3023*

LE MONS, KATHLEEN ANN, portfolio manager, investment broker; b. Trenton, N.J., Apr. 6, 1952; d. Albert Martin and Veronica Grace (Kerr) LeM.; m. Walter Everett Faircloth, Apr. 15, 1978 (div. Dec. 1988); m. Jeffery West Benedict, June 29, 1991. Attended, Rollins Coll., 1970-71, Fla. State U., 1971-76; BSBA magna cum laude, Christopher Newport U., 1995; post-grad., Coll. William and Mary, 1995—. Registered rep. NASD/NYSE, investment advisor; cert. portfolio mgr. Sci. rsch. assoc. NASA, Hampton, Va., 1973-76; fin. cons. Merrill Lynch Pierce Fenner Smith, Hampton, 1985-88; cert. portfolio mgr. Wheat First Butcher Singer, Newport News, Va., 1988—. Pres. James Landing Assn., 1991-95; life mem. Capital Dist. Found., 1992; mem. exec. panel fund distbn. Va. Peninsula United Way, 1996—; Hampton Rds. chair March of Dimes Walk Am., 1996—. George F. Hixson fellow Kiwanis Internat., 1996. Mem. Am. Mktg. Assn., Va. Peninsula C. of C. (transp. task force 1993—, govtl. affairs task force 1993—), Oyster Point Kiwanis (charter), Coll. of William and Mary Part-Time MBA Assn. (charter, curriculum com. chair 1995—, v.p. 1996—), Christopher Newport U. Pres.' Coun., Christopher Newport Univ. Alumni Soc. (bd. dirs. 1996—), James River Country Club (9-hole golf group), Alpha Chi. Republican. Home: 61 Queens Ct Newport News VA 23606-2034 Office: Wheat First Butcher Singer 11817 Canon Blvd Newport News VA 23606-2569

LEMONS, TERI COPELAND, fundraising executive; b. Edenton, N.C., Aug. 29, 1959; d. Preston M. and Margaret Neelly (Chappell) Copeland; m. Charles Ray Lemons, Oct. 14, 1986. BA in Social Scis., U. N.C., Elizabeth City, 1980, BS in History, 1981; MA in Edn., History, East Carolina U., 1986; Cert., Leadership Catawba, 1994. Cert. tchr., N.C. Dropout prevention cons. N.C. Dept. Pub. Instrn., Raleigh, 1982-85, spl. asst. JTPA, 1985-89; dir. annual fund Roanoke Coll., Salem, Va., 1989-90, dir. alumni rels., 1990-93; mktg. cons. Kings Coll., Charlotte, N.C., 1993-94; dir. maj. gifts Lenoir-Rhyne Coll., Hickory, N.C., 1994-96, dir. devel., 1996—; dir. Catawba Med. Found., Hickory, 1995—. Vol. Meals on Wheels, Roanoke, 1992-93, Hickory, 1994—; amb. United Way, Hickory, 1995; vol. ARC, Roanoke, 1993. Mem. Nat. Soc. Fund-Raising Execs., Newcomen Soc. Am., N.C. Planned Giving Coun., Catawba Valley Execs. Club, Greensboro Coll. Young Alumni Coun. (bd. dirs. 1992—), Phi Beta Lambda. Office: Lenoir Rhyne Coll LRC Box 7467 Hickory NC 28603

LEMPNER, KELLIE ANN, elementary school counselor; b. Manhasset, N.Y., Jan. 18, 1969; d. John Anthony and Anne (Muehlbauer) Knoerzer; m. Michael Stephen Lempner, Oct. 9, 1993. BA, U. Richmond, 1991; MEd, Loyola Coll., Balt., 1993. Cert. counselor. Elem. sch. counselor Montgomery County Pub. Schs., Rockville, Md., 1993—. Mem. Am. Counseling Assn., Am. Sch. Counselors Assn. Office: Montgomery County Pub Schs Twinbrook Elem 5911 Ridgway Ave Rockville MD 20851

LENAGHAN, DONNA DISMUKE, educational and management consultant; b. Atlanta, Nov. 28, 1954; d. William Thomas Dismuke and Elizabeth (Taylor) Dismuke Fraser; m. Michael J. Lenaghan, Sept. 18, 1982. BA in Psychology, Salem Coll., Winston-Salem, N.C., 1976; BS in Mgmt. and Cmty. Devel., U. Md., 1983; EdD in Adult and Continuing Edn., Va. Poly. Inst., 1990. Dir. leadership project Nat. Hemophilia Found., N.Y.C., 1983-85; dir. project ARC, Washington, 1985-88; pres. Lenaghan Group, Chevy Chase, Md., 1988-92; v.p., curricula and devel. svcs. Ctr. for Profl. Devel., Shawnee, Kans., 1993-94; pres. I.Q. Enterprises, Miami, Fla., 1994—; vis. prof. U. Coll. Galway, Ireland, 1985; strategic planner Campfire Nat. Hdqrs., Kansas City, Mo., 1989-92; prof. edn. and psychology Maimi (Fla.)-Dade C.C., 1993—; curriculum and tng. specialist nat. sems., 1992-93; cons. in field. Contbr. articles to profl. jours. Deacon, educator Presbyn. Chs., N.C., Md., Kans. and Fla., 1976—; leadership vol. Gril Scouts U.S.A., 1976—; bd. dirs. Campfire Coun., Washington, 1983-87; vol. Laubach Literacy Coun., Lee's Summit, Mo., 1992-94. Named to Young Profls. Hall of Fame, Am. Hist. Archives, 1987. Mem. Midwest Leadership Inst. Presbyterian. Office: IQ Enterprises 8900 NW 194th Ter Hialeah FL 33015-6218

LENG, MARGUERITE LAMBERT, regulatory consultant, biochemist; b. Edmonton, Alta., Can., Sept. 25, 1926; came to the U.S., 1950; d. Joseph Edouard and Marie (Kiwit) Lambert; m. Douglas Ellis Leng, June 18, 1955; children: Ronald Bruce, Janet Elaine, Douglas Lambert. BSc in Honours Chemistry, U. Alta., 1947; MSc, U. Sask., 1950; PhD, Purdue U., 1956. Rsch. asst. U. Mich. Med. Rsch. Inst., Ann Arbor, 1950-53; sr. rsch. chemist bioproducts Dow Chem. Co., Midland, Mich., 1956-59, sr. registration specialist, product registration mgr., 1966-73, rsch. assoc. for internat. registration agrochems., 1973-86, mgr. internat. regulatory affairs, 1986-90; pres., cons. Leng Assocs., Midland, 1991—. Editor: Pesticide Chemist and Modern Toxicology, 1981, Agrochemical Environmental Fate Studies: State of the Art, 1995; contbr. articles to profl. jours., chpts. in books and encys. Life ins. med. rsch. fellow Equitable Life Assurance Co., 1949-50. Fellow Am. Inst. Chemists (bd. dirs., vice chmn. bd. dirs., exec. com. 1993-95), Am. Chem. Soc. (agrochems. divsn. fellow 1976, chmn. 1981, program chmn. 1980, alt. councilor 1984-91, councilor 1992—); mem. Internat. Soc. for Study Xenobiotics, Assn. Ofcl. Analytical Chemists Internat., Soc. Environ. Toxicology and Chemistry, Sigma Xi. Home and Office: 1714 Sylvan Ln Midland MI 48640-2538

L'ENGLE, MADELEINE (MRS. HUGH FRANKLIN), author; b. N.Y.C., Nov. 29, 1918; d. Charles Wadsworth and Madeleine (Barnett) Camp; m. Hugh Franklin, Jan. 26, 1946; children: Josephine Franklin Jones, Maria Franklin Rooney, Bion. A.B., Smith Coll., 1941; postgrad., New Sch., 1941-42, Columbia U., 1960-61; holder 19 hon. degrees. Tchr. St. Hilda's and St. Hugh's Sch., 1960—; mem. faculty U. Ind., 1965-66, 71; writer-in-residence Ohio State U., 1970, U. Rochester, 1972, Wheaton Coll., 1976—, Cathedral St. John the Divine, N.Y.C., 1965—. Author: The Small Rain, 1945, Ilsa, 1946, Camilla Dickinson, 1951, A Winter's Love, 1957, And Both Were Young, 1949, Meet the Austins, 1960, A Wrinkle in Time, 1962, The Moon by Night, 1963, The 24 Days Before Christmas, 1964, The Arm of the Starfish, 1965, The Love Letters, 1966, The Journey with Jonah, 1968, The Young Unicorns, 1968, Dance in the Desert, 1969, Lines Scribbled on an Envelope, 1969, The Other Side of the Sun, 1971, A Circle of Quiet, 1972, A Wind in the Door, 1973, The Summer of the Great-Grandmother, 1974, Dragons in the Waters, 1976, The Irrational Season, 1977, A Swiftly Tilting Planet, 1978, The Weather of the Heart, 1978, Ladder of Angels, 1980, A Ring of Endless Light, 1980, Walking on Water, 1980, A Severed Wasp, 1982, And It Was Good, 1983, A House Like a Lotus, 1984, Trailing Clouds of Glory, 1985, A Stone for a Pillow, 1986, Many Waters, 1986, Two-Part Invention, 1988, A Cry Like a Bell, 1987, Sole Into Egypt, 1989, From This Day Forward, 1988, An Acceptable Time, 1989, The Glorious Impossible, 1990, Certain Women, 1992, The Rock That Is Higher: Story As Truth, 1993, Anytime Prayers, 1994, Troubling a Star, 1994, Penguins and Golden Calves, 1996, A Live Coal in the Sea, 1996. Pres. Crosswicks Found. Recipient Newbery medal, 1963, Sequoyah award, 1965, runner-up Hans Christian Andersen Internat. award, 1964, Lewis Carroll Shelf award, 1965, Austrian State Lit. award, 1969, Bishop's Cross, 1970, U. South Miss. medal, 1978, Regina medal, 1985, Alan award Nat. Coun. Tchrs. English, 1986, Kerlan award, 1990; collection of papers at Wheaton Coll. Mem. Authors Guild (pres., mem. council, mem. membership com.), Authors League (mem. council), Writers Guild Am., Colonial Dames. Episcopalian. Home: 924 W End Ave Apt 95 New York NY 10025-3534 Office: care Cath St John the Divine 1047 Amsterdam Ave New York NY 10025

LENK, MARGARITA MARIA, educator; b. Buenos Aires, Argentina, Apr. 5, 1960; came to U.S., 1960, naturalized, 1983; d. Peter Alfred and Maria del Rosario (Bianchi) Lenk; m. George McCelvey Hester, June 27, 1992; children: Nicholas Lenk, Andy Hester. BSBA, U. Ctrl. Fla., 1981; MACC, U. N.C., 1987; PhD, U. S.C., 1991. Acct. Fla. Software Svcs., Altamonte Springs, 1979-80, Gen. Mills/Red Lobster, Orlando, Fla., 1980-81, Import Music SA, Buenos Aires, 1983-84; instr./teaching asst. U. N.C., Chapel Hill, 1982-87; faculty in residence Plymouth (N.H.) State Coll., 1987-88; cost acct. Standard Products Inc., Winnsboro, S.C., 1990; instr./teaching asst. U. S.C., Columbia, 1988-91; asst. prof. Colo. State U., Fort Collins, 1991—; costing advisor Storage Tech., Louisville, Colo., 1995; bd. dirs. Village Green Homeowners, Ft. Collins, 1993-95, Bi-City Day Care, Chapel Hill, 1984-87. Contbr. articles to ency. and jours. Spanish vol. tchr. Bauder Elem. Sch., Ft. Collins, 1993-95, geography vol. tchr., 1994-95. Mem. Am. Acctg. Assn., Colo. Soc. CPAs, Inst. Mgmt. Accts. Office: Colo State U 252 Rockwell Hall Fort Collins CO 80523

LENNON, AMY JO, elementary school educator; b. Watertown, N.Y., Feb. 28, 1958; d. William Arnold and Evelyn Louise (Timerman) L. A in Edn., Cazenovia (N.Y.) Coll., 1978; BS in Edn., SUNY, Cortland, 1980; MS in Edn., U. N.Mex., 1982. Cert. tchr., N.Y. Lifeguard Gloversville (N.Y.) City Dept. Recreation, 1977-83; tchr. phys. edn. Middleburgh (N.Y.) Ctrl. Sch., 1983—; curriculum coord. Middleburgh Ctrl. Sch., 1990—, citizen mgrs. cons., 1993—, mem. discipline task force, 1995—. Mem. ARC, 1976—; fund raiser Cmty. Playground Project, Middleburgh, 1990-91; co-organizer Cmty. Girls Basketball Camp, Middleburgh, 1990—. Recipient award for 300 hours of svc. ARC, 1984. Mem. AAHPERD (profl.), Nat. Assn. Girls and Women's Sports (profl.), N.Y. State Alliance Health, Phys. Edn., Recreation and Dance (profl.). Office: Middleburgh Ctrl Sch RR 2 Box 78 Middleburgh NY 12122

LENNOX, ANNIE, rock musician; b. Aberdeen, Scotland, Dec. 25, 1954; m. Radha Raman, Mar. 1984 (div. 1985). Student, Royal Acad. Music, London. Mem. musical group Catch, Tourists, 1977-80; founding mem. Eurythmics. Albums: (with Eurythmics) In The Garden, 1980, Sweet Dreams, 1983, Touch, 1984, 1984 (For the Love of Big Brother), 1984, Be Yourself Tonight, 1985, Revenge, 1986, Savage, 1988, We Too Are One, 1989, Greatest Hits, 1991, Eurythmics Live, 1993; (solo) Diva, 1992, Medusa, 1994; actress (film) Revolution. Office: care Simon Fuller Mgmt Unit 32, 35-37 Parkgate Rd, London England SW11 4NP

LENOIR, GLORIA CISNEROS, small business owner, business executive; b. Monterrey, Nuevo Leon, Mex., Aug. 18, 1951; came to U.S., 1956, naturalized; d. Juan Antonio and Maria Gloria (Flores) Cisneros; m. Walter Frank Lenoir, June 6, 1975; children: Lucy Gloria, Katherine Judith, Walter Frank IV. Student, Inst. Am. Univs., 1971-72; BA in French Art, Austin Coll., 1973, MA in French Art, 1974; MBA in Fin., U. Tex., 1979. French tchr. Sherman (Tex.) High Sch., 1973-74; French/Spanish tchr, dept. chmn. Lyndon Baines Johnson High Sch., Austin, 1974-77; legis. aide Tex. State Capitol, Austin, Tex., 1977-81; stock broker Merrill Lynch, Austin, 1981-83, Schneider, Bernet and Hickman, Austin, 1983-84; bus. mgr. Holleman Photographic Labs., Inc., Austin, 1984-87, 88-90; account exec., stock broker Eppler, Guerin & Turner, 1987-88; ind. distbr. Austin, 1990-93; owner, cons. Profl. Cons. Svcs., Austin, 1991—; adj. faculty Spanish, internat. bus. St. Edwards U., 1991--; group counselor, organizer Inst. Fgn. Studies, U. Strasbourg, France, summer 1976; mktg. intern IBM, Austin, summer 1978; mktg. cons. Creative Ednl. Enterprises, Austin, 1980-81; hon. speaker Mex.-Am. U. of Tex., Austin, 1984; speaker various orgns., bus. classes, Austin, 1981-84; speaker, coord. small bus. workshops, 1985. Photographs pub. in Women in Space, 1979, Review, 1988; exhibited in group shows throughout Tex., 1979, 88-89. Neighborhood capt. Am. Cancer Soc., Austin, 1982-86, 90, Am. Heart Assn., 1989; active PTA, 1989—, mem. Bryker Woods Elem. PTA Bd., 1990-92, pres., 1990-91, mem. Kealing Jr. H.S. PTA Bd., 1992-94, chair 50th anniversary celebration com., 1990, hospitality chmn., 1st grade coord., Austin, 1986, mem. legis. com. Tex. State, 1990-92; vol. liaison leads program Austin Coll., 1983—; mem. advantage Austin, 1988; peer panelist Major Art Insts. Austin, 1989-90; co-chair fin. Ctrl. Presbyn. Ch., elder, 1988-90, session clk., 1989, chair membership com., 1990, mem. staff com., 1991-92; megaskills leader Austin Ind. Sch. Dist., 1991—; bd. dirs. Magnet Parents Coalition, 1995—; mem. Austin City coun. PTA Bd., 1991-96, Dist. 7 PTA Bd., 1996—. Recipient Night on the Town award IBM, 1978. Republican. Home and Office: 1202 W 29th St Austin TX 78703-1917

LENOIR, MARIA ANNETTE, management consultant; b. St. Louis, June 11, 1950; d. Jack and Beatrice (Brown) Doyle; m. Howard L. Williams, Sept. 29, 1969 (div. Aug. 1981); 1 child, Howard L. Jr.; m. Aguinaldo Alphonse Lenoir Jr., June 28, 1985; 1 stepchild, Aguinaldo Alphonse III. Student, Florissant (Mo.) Valley Community Coll., 1974-76; BA in Mgmt., Webster U., 1980. Stenographer Internat. Shoe Co., St. Louis, 1968-69; office mgr. Chemplastics Inc., St. Louis, 1969-71; advt./media coord. Ralston Purina Co., St. Louis, 1971-73, sec., 1973-76, adminstrv. asst., 1976-79, sales/mktg. adminstr., 1979-84; pres., chief exec. officer, owner Corp. Image, Inc., St. Louis, 1984—; instr. St. Louis Univ., 1987, St. Louis Community Coll.; pub. rels. advisor Mo. White House Conf. Small Bus., St. Louis, 1986; mem. adv. panel Omni Internat. Hotel, St. Louis, 1986. Contbr. articles to profl. jours. Mktg. advisor Jr. Achievement of Miss. Valley, Hazelwood, Mo., 1983—; mem. Women's Assn. St. Louis Symphony, 1984—, ACE (div. of SCORE), St. Louis, 1985—; role model St. Louis Pub. Schs., 1987; bd. dirs. Community Commitment, Greeley Community Ctr. Youth Emergency Svcs. (YES), St. Louis, 1988—. Named Outstanding Young Women Am., 1987. Mem. Meeting Planners Internat., Nat. Speakers Assn., Am. Soc. Tng. and Devel., Assn. Ind. Meeting Planners (adv. com., bd. dirs.), Florissant Valley Community Coll. Alumni Assn. (v.p. 1985-86, sec./treas. 1987, Alumna of Yr. award 1986 Hall of Fame), Women in Leadership Alumni, NAFE, St. Louis Regional Commerce & Growth Assn., Boulder Yacht Club. Democrat. Pentecostal. Office: Corp Image Inc 4825 Lockwig Trl Florissant MO 63033-7521

LENOX, ANGELA COUSINEAU, healthcare consultant; b. Vergennes, Vt., Dec. 12, 1946; d. Romeo Joseph and Colombe Mary (Gevry) C.; m. Donald Allen Lenox, Oct. 5, 1969 (div.); 1 child, Tiffanie Jae. RN diploma, Albany Med. Ctr. Sch. Nursing, 1969; BS, Barry U., 1982; M of Health Mgmt., St. Thomas U., 1990. Cert. in profl. healthcare quality. Intravenous therapist Holy Cross Hosp., Ft. Lauderdale, Fla., 1979-91; utilization review coord. North Borward Hosp., Pompano Beach, Fla., 1984-89; med. staff quality mgr. Humana Bennett, Plantation, Fla., 1990-91; med. resource analyst Hermann Hosp., Houston, 1991-93; assoc. mgr. quality improvement The Prudential, Sugarland, Tex., 1993-95; cons. ACL Cons., Houston, 1995—. Contbr. articles to profl. jours. 1st lt. U.S. Army res., 1991—. Mem. Tex. Gold Coast Assn. Healthcare Quality, Tex. Soc. Quality Assurance, Nat. Assn. Healthcare Quality. Home & Office: 8523 Dawnridge Dr Houston TX 77071-2441

LENTINI, RUTH HASSEL, reading consultant; b. Hartford, Conn., Oct. 30, 1948; d. William Parker and Muriel Esther (Morehead) Hassel; m. Thomas Lentini, Apr. 21, 1989. BS, Cen. Conn. State U., 1970, MEd., 1975, Sixth Yr. Cert., 1977. Cert. tchr. reading/lang. arts cons. K-12, Conn. Elem. tchr. Ellington (Conn.) Pub. Schs., 1970-75; reading/lang. arts cons. South Windsor (Conn.) Pub. Schs., 1975—; adj. univ. faculty reading, Cen. Conn. State U., New Britain, Conn., 1994—; presenter coop. learning Conn. Reading Conf., Waterbury, 1990-93, New Eng. Reading Conf., Nashua, N.H., 1992, workshop presenter Bloomfield (Conn.) Pub. Schs., 1992, West Hartford (Conn.) Pub. Schs., 1993-94. Author: (pamphlet) Cooperative Learning for Substitute Teachers, 1992. Informational speaker Arthritis Found. of Conn., Rocky Hill, 1991—, mem. pub. rels. com. 1993—. Grantee New Eng. Reading Assn., 1993. Mem. Conn. Assn. Reading Rsch., Conn. Reading Coun., Internat. Reading Assn. Roman Catholic. Office: Philip R Smith Elem Sch 949 Avery St South Windsor CT 06074

LENTZ, CONSTANCE MARCHAND, accountant; b. Tampa, Fla., May 6, 1948; d. George Ray and Allie Mae (Renner) L. BSBA, Calif. State U., Northridge, 1970, MSBA, 1974. CPA, Nev. Staff acct. Laventhol & Horwath CPA, Las Vegas, Nev., 1981-84; sr. mgr., acct. Deloitte, Haskins & Sells, Las Vegas, 1984-90; acct., pres. Constance M. Lentz, CPA, Ltd., Las Vegas, 1990—. Treas., bd. dirs. Warm Springs Res. Homeowners Assn., Henderson, Nev., 1990-94; trustee New Vista Ranch, Las Vegas, 1990—; treas. bd. trustees Las Vegas Natural History Mus., 1989-94; treas., bd. dirs. Clark County unit/Nev. divsn. Am. Cancer Soc., Las Vegas, 1978-85; treas. New Vista Ranch, Las Vegas, 1995—. Mem. AICPA, Nev. Soc. CPAs, Las Vegas C. of C. (Leadership Las Vegas grad. 1991), Leadership Las Vegas Alumni Assn. Office: 930 S 3rd St Ste 100A Las Vegas NV 89101-6843

LENTZ, DEBORAH LYNN, telemetry, thoracic surgery nurse; b. Greenport, N.Y., Oct. 24, 1971; d. Stanley Antone Jr. and Linda Ann (Bernhard) C.; m. Stephen C. Lentz III, Dec. 1993; 1 child, Stephen C. Lentz IV. Cert. LPN, Harry Ward Tech. Ctr., Riverhead, N.Y., 1989; ADN, SUNY, Alfred, 1991. RN, N.Y.; cert. BLS, ACLS. LPN San Simeon By the Sound, Greenport, 1989-91; RN Meml. Sloan Kettering Cancer Ctr., Manhattan, N.Y., 1991-92, L.I. Jewish Hosp., New Hyde Park, N.Y., 1992-94, Ctrl. Suffolk Hosp., 1994—. Mem. N.Y. State Nurses Assn. Roman Catholic. Home: 68750 Route 48 Greenport NY 11944-2217

LENZEN, LAURA ELAINE, civil engineer; b. Lincoln, Nebr., Apr. 6, 1947; d. George Harry and Esther Ruth (Gies) DeBus; children: Timothy A., Amy L.; m. Louis W. Lenzen, Feb. 15, 1980. Registered profl. engr., Nebr.; cert. profl. mgr. From sec. to traffic engr. supr. Nebr. Dept. Rds., Lincoln, 1969-89, wetlands engr. unit head, 1989—. Recipient Environ. award Fed. Hwy. Adminstrn., 1995, Environ. Excellence award U.S. Dept. Transp., 1995. Mem. Nebr. Mgrs. Assn., Engrs. Club Lincoln (bd. dirs., sec.-treas.). Home: 2017 N 57th St Lincoln NE 68505-1107 Office: Nebr Dept Roads PO Box 94759 Lincoln NE 68509-4759

LENZI, LINDA JEAN, gifted education educator; b. New Eagle, Pa., May 2, 1948; d. Joseph Samuel and Wilma Louise (Turri) L. BS Edn., U. Steubenville, 1970; MS Edn., U. Dayton, 1976. Reading tchr. 2-6 Elizabeth Forward (Pa.) Schs., summer 1971; tchr. fifth and sixth grade Indan Creek Schs., Mingo Junction, Ohio, 1970-82, elem. gifted tchr., 1982-94, tchr. 7th and 8th grade gifted edn., 1994-95, tchr. elem. gifted edn., 1995-96; negotiation chmn. Indian Creek Edn. Assn., 1990-96, negotiation team, 1988-96; chairperson Ohio Valley Uniserv, Stuebenville, Ohio, 1983-96; co-presenter at various convs., workshops, seminars in field, 1983-96. Exec. com. Dem. Party, Jefferson County, 1985-95, mem. Dem. Nat. Com., 1994-96, mem. congl. campaign com., 1995-96. Grantee Jefferson County S.E. Dist., Steubenville, Ohio. Mem. NEA, ASCD, AAUW, Ohio Edn. Assn., Ohio Assn. Gifted Children, Consortium of Coords. of Gifted. Home: Apt 2 2239 1/2 Cherry Ave Steubenville OH 43952

LEONARD, ANGELINE JANE, psychotherapist; b. McKeesport, Pa., Dec. 9, 1940; d. Paul James Franklin and Jane Angeline (McKee) L.; m. Tom L. Kregel, Aug. 25, 1962 (div. 1970). BFA, U. Okla., 1962; MA in Art History, UCLA, 1965; MA in Clin. Art Therapy, Immaculate Heart Coll., 1980; PhD in Clin. Psychology, Cambridge Grad. Sch., 1991. Lic. marriage, family, child counselor, Calif., marriage and family counselor, N.C.; registered, bd. cert. art therapist; cert. hypnotherapist, guided imagery; lic. sci. of mind practitioner. Tchr. San Gabriel (Calif.) Mission High Sch., 1964-66, L.A. Valley Coll., Van Nuys, 1966-90, L.A. Unified Sch. Dist., 1980-90; pvt. practice psychotherapy, Reseda, Calif., 1982—; spkr. in field. Author: California Art Therapy Trends, 1993; author of poems. Bd. dirs., v.p. Ch. of Religious Sci., North Hollywood, Calif., 1989-93. Mem. Am. Art Therapy Assn., Am. Assn. Marriage and Family Therapists, Artist Equity Assn. (sec.), Calif. Assn. Marriage and Family Therapists, So. Calif. Art Therapy Assn. (bd. dirs.), No. Calif. Art Therapy Assn. Democrat. Home and Office: 19520 Vose St Reseda CA 91335-3637

LEONARD, CAROLYN J., special education educator; b. Youngstown, Ohio, Aug. 21, 1950; d. William L. Rothbauer and Delores M. Micklas; m. Albert E. Leonard, June 17, 1972; children: Ryan E. Leonard, Carrie M. Leonard. BSEd/Spl. Edn., Youngstown State U., 1972, M Spl. Edn., 1994. Spl. edn. tchr. Boardman (Ohio) H.S., 1985—. Named Outstanding Spl. Educator of the Yr., Dept. of Spl. Edn., State of Ohio, Columbus, 1994. Mem. Coun. for Exceptional Children (v.p. 1991-95, adv. student club 1990-95). Roman Catholic. Office: Boardman HS 7777 Glenwood Ave Boardman OH 44512

LEONARD, CLAIRE OFFUTT, pediatric geneticist educator; b. Rochester, N.Y., Apr. 1, 1945; d. Edward Preble and Virginia Leoma (Williams) Offutt; divorced; children: Christopher Edward, Kathleen. BA, Mount Holyoke Coll., 1967; MD, John Hopkins U., 1971. Diplomate Am. Bd. Pediatrics, Am. Bd. Med. Genetics. Intern and resident in pediat. U. Colo., 1971-74, fellow in genetics and birth defects, 1974-75; fellow in genetics Johns Hopkins Hosp., Balt., 1978-80; asst. prof. pediatrics John Hopkins U., Balt., 1980-81; asst. prof. pediatrics U. Utah, Salt Lake City, 1981-87, assoc. prof. pediatrics, 1987—. Mem. Am. Soc. Human Genetics, Am. Acad. Pediatrics, Am. Coll. Med. Genetics, Inherited Metabolic Disorders. Mem. Soc. of Friends. Office: U Utah Dept Peds 50 N Medical Dr Salt Lake City UT 84112-1122

LEONARD, DOROTHY LOUISE, fisheries administrator; b. Newark, Aug. 30, 1932; d. Joseph Peter and Charlotte Mary (Dinkel) L.; m. Gary Lawrence Fellows, Sept. 4, 1954 (div. Mar. 1978); children: Mark Leonard, Paige Charlotte Wright, Scott Lawrence, Joy Dorothy. BA, Syracuse U., 1954; postgrad., SUNY, Brockport, 1976, George Washington U., 1982-84. Asst. planner Monroe County Dept. Planning, Rochester, N.Y., 1975-77; specialist coastal resources N.Y. Dept. State, Albany, 1977-80; program analyst Office Coastal Zone Mgmt. Nat. Oceanic & Atmospheric Adminstrn. div. U.S. Dept. Commerce, Washington, 1980-83, specialist fisheries devel. Nat. Marine Fisheries Svc., 1983-86; program mgr. shellfish water quality projects Nat. Oceanic & Atmospheric Adminstrn., Washington, 1986-96; pres. Dorothy Leonard Assocs., Washington, 1985—; dir. fisheries Md. Dept. Natural Resources, 1996—; bd. dirs. Charleston Maritime Inst.; cons. Charleston Harbor Project. Mem. com. N.Y. Legis. Com. on Women, Albany, 1975-77; pres. Washington Area Waterfront Action Group, 1986-90; mem. bd. advisors Inst. for Coastal and Marine Recovery, 1988-90. Mem. Am. Fisheries Soc., Nat. Fisheries Assn., World Aquaculture Soc., Interstate Shellfish Sanitation Conf., Nat. Shellfisheries Assn., Am. Soc. Limnology and Oceanography, AIA (urban design com. 1986-90), Chesapeake Bay Citizen Adv. Com., Waterfront Washington Assn., Survival of the Sea Soc. (bd. advisors 1987-89), LWV, Phi Kappa Phi. Home: 776 Rolling View Dr Annapolis MD 21401-4655 Office: Md Dept Natural Resources Tawes Office Bldg Annapolis MD 21401

LEONARD, ELIZABETH LIPMAN, psychologist; b. Phila., Sept. 5, 1947; d. M. Irvin and Natalie Claire (Seidmann) Lipman; m. Sept. 5, 1969; children: Noah, Emily. BS, Boston U., 1969; MS, Va. Commonwealth U., 1975; PhD, Tufts U., 1986. Lic. phys. therapist, psychologist. Dir. phys. and occupational therapy Crotched Mountain Rehab. Ctr., Greenfield, N.H., 1977-80; dir. child devel. unit Child Health Svcs., Manchester, N.H., 1980-85; rsch. assoc. Cath. Med. Ctr., Manchester, 1985-87; psychologist Barrow Neurol. Inst./St. Joseph's Hosp. and Med. Ctr., Phoenix, 1987—; cons. biomed. engrng. MOCO, Inc., Scituate, Mass., 1986—. Editorial bd.: Phys. and Occupational Therapy in Pediatrics; contbr. articles to profl. jours. Recipient traineeship Vocat. Rehab. Adminstrn., Boston U., 1967-68; scholarship award Found. for Phys. Therapy, 1982; grantee March of Dimes, N.H. Devel. Disabilies Coun., 1981, Div. Health and Human Svcs.-Maternal and Child Health, State of N.H., 1980, Bur. for Health Promotion, State of N.H., 1986, Ariz. Disease Rsch. Control Commn., 1990. Mem. APA, Internat. Soc. for Infant Studies, Internat. Neuropsychol. Soc., Soc. for Rsch. in Child Devel., Soc. Pediatric Psychology, Nat. Acad. Neuropsychology. Office: Barrow Neurol Inst 222 W Thomas Rd Ste 412 Phoenix AZ 85013-4423

LEONARD, JANET ERWIN, director of development; b. Johnson City, Tenn., Nov. 4, 1946; d. Richard Martin and Myrtle Beatrice (Buck) Erwin; m. Thomas E. Leonard, July 1, 1964; children: Angelia Hunt, Thomas B. BS, Milligan Coll., 1996. Purchasing agt. Bristol (Va.) Utilities Bd., 1974-76; benefits coord., buyer Valleydale Packers, Inc., Bristol, 1976-90; coord. spl. events Bristol Regional Med. Ctr. Found., Bristol, 1990—, supervisory com. chairperson Valleydale Fed. Credit Union, Bristol, 1984-90; grad. Dale Carnegie Effective Speaking and Human Rels., 1986. Named Vol. of Yr. for State of Va., Va. Credit Union League, Alexandria, 1988, Competent Toastmaster, Toastmasters Internat., Bristol, 1989, Effective Spkrs. award Toastmasters Internat., 1990. Mem. Assn. for Healthcare Philanthropy (presenter conf. 1994), Nat. Soc. Fund Raising Execs., Bristol Orgns., Bristol C. of C., Rotary. Office: Bristol Reg Med Ctr Found 1 Medical Park Blvd Bristol TN 37620

LEONARD, SUSAN RUTH, psychologist, consultant; b. Mineola, N.Y., June 15, 1955; d. Donald Edward Leonard and Jane (Solomon) Hertzberg. BA, L.I. U., 1977; MA, U. N.C., 1980, PhD, 1985. Lic. psychologist, N.C. From instr. to asst. prof. psychology dept. Wake Forest U., Winston Salem, N.C., 1984-86, staff psychologist counseling ctr., 1985-89; clin. psychologist Manoogian Psychol. Assocs., Winston-Salem, 1986—; cons. Ctr. for Creative Leadership, Greensboro, N.C., 1985-92. Vol. United Way, Winston-Salem, 1990-91; mem. adv. com. Family Svcs., Family Violence, Winston-Salem, 1987-90; trustee Resource Ctr. for Women and Ministry in South, 1989-91; bd. dirs. AIDS Task Force, Winston-Salem, 1989-92, Youth Opportunities Inc., Winston-Salem, 1990-92, 93—, AIDS Care Svc., Winston-Salem, 1991-95, Cancer Svcs., Winston-Salem, 1996—. Mem. APA, AAUW, Assn. Women in Psychology, N.C. Psychol. Assn. Office: Manoogian Psychol Assocs 1338 Ashley Sq Winston Salem NC 27103

LEONARD, SUZANNE LOUISE, artist; b. San Francisco, Feb. 27, 1951; d. Randall Clarence and Elizabeth Louise (Humphrey) L.; m. Lloyd Bernerd Dykes, June 1, 1980. BA in Psychology, St. Mary's Coll., Moraga, Calif., 1973; acctg. cert., Heald Bus. Coll., 1977. Owner Purple Pony, Vacaville, Calif., 1992—. Mem. Calif. Dressage Soc. Office: Purple Pony PO Box 398 Vacaville CA 95696

LEONARD, VIRGINIA KATHRYN, public financial manager; b. Street, Md., Aug. 31, 1944; d. Elbert Monroe and Mildred Rudolph (Patrick) Joines; m. James Richard Leonard, Aug. 31, 1963; children: James Richard II, Raymun Bradley. Student, Ea. Nazarene Coll., 1962-63; AA, Harford Community Coll., 1976; BS in Bus. Mgmt., U. Md., 1983; grad., U.S. Army Mgmt. Staff Coll., 1988, Fed. Exec. Inst., 1992, Harvard/JFK Sch. Govt., 1996. Program analyst Facilities Engring., Aberdeen Proving Ground, Md., 1976-79; budget analyst Aberdeen Proving Ground Command, 1980; program analyst officer Facilities Engring., Aberdeen Proving Ground, Md., 1981; budget analyst Test and Evaluation Command, Aberdeen Proving Ground, Md., 1982-83; budget analyst, budget officer Dept. of Army, Washington, 1984; budget officer test and evaluation command U.S. Army, Aberdeen Proving Ground, Md., 1985-89; fin. mgr. test and evaluation command U.S. Army, Aberdeen Proving Ground, 1989-94, dir. resource mgmt. test and evaluation command, 1994—. Mem. Am. Soc. Mil. Comptrollers, Assn. U.S. Army, Fed. Exec. Inst. Alumni Assn. Office: Test and Evaluation Command AMSTE-RM Dept of Army Aberdeen Proving Ground MD 21005

LEONARD, VIRGINIA WAUGH, history educator, writer, researcher; b. Willimantic, Conn., Dec. 9, 1941; d. William Norris and Elizabeth Flora (Waugh) L.; m. James Madison Ewing, May 14, 1978. BA in Internat. Rels., U. Calif., Berkeley, 1963; MA in Social Scis., Hofstra U., 1967; PhD in History, U. Fla., 1975. Cert. social studies tchr., N.Y.; cert. bilingual social studies tchr., N.Y.; lic. pvt. pilot. Civilian recreation officer U.S. Army Spl. Svcs., Nuremburg, West Germany, 1963-64; tchr. social studies Colegio Lincoln, La Lucila, Argentina, 1970, Seward Park H.S., N.Y.C., 1975-77; asst. prof. history Western Ill. U., Macomb, 1977-83, assoc. prof. history, 1983-90, prof. history, 1990—; sr. program mgr. Nat. Faculty Exchange-Dept. of Edn., Washington, 1986-87; chairperson Univ. Personnel Commn., Western Ill. U., 1990-91; mem. internat. adv. bd. 5th Internat. Interdisciplinary Congress on Women, San Jose, 1992-93. Author: Politicians, Pupils and Priests: Argentine Education since 1943, 1989; author: (chpt.) Los Ensayistas, 1989. Treas. Bus. and Profl. Women, Macomb, 1994-95; seminar leader Project Democracy, LWV, Dubna, Russia, summer 1995; coord. Grassroots, LWV, McDonough County, Ill., 1995. Recipient grant Orgn. Am. States, 1971-72, Fulbright Rsch. award Fulbright Office-Argentina, 1983, Grassroots Democracy grant LWV/USAID, 1995. Mem. Am. Hist. Assn., Midwest Assn. for Latin Am. Studies (pres. 1984-85), North Ctrl. Coun. Latin Am. (chair nominating com. 1990-91, Tchg. award 1990), Berkshire Conf. of Women Historians (book prize com. 1990-95), Charlevoix Hist. Soc., Phi Kappa Phi, Delta Kappa Gamma (legis. com. 1993-94). Unitarian. Office: Western Ill Univ Dept History Macomb IL 61455

LEONE, EMILIA RITA, business consultant; b. Cleve., Apr. 19, 1961; d. Emidio and Nicoletta (Amatangelo) L. AAB in Mktg., Cuyahoga C.C., 1982; BS in Tech. Edn., U. Akron, 1993. Budget sec. Cuyahoga C.C., Parma, Ohio, 1984-86, rsch. asst. physician asst. program, 1986-92; rsch. coord. Fairview Gen. Hosp., Cleve., 1992-94; sr. cons. Ernst & Young, LLP, Cleve., 1994—. Comty. rep. adv. com. physician asst. program Cuyahoga C.C., Parma, 1986—; vol. Cleanland, Cleve., 1995, Janet Saringer State Rep. Campaign, Cleve., 1992, Juvenile Diabetes Assn., Cleve., 1991, Cuyahoga C.C. Levy Campaign, Cleve., 1990, 92; presenter in field; workshop facilitator. Mem. ASTD, Internat. Soc. for Performance Improvement, Assn. of Physician Asst. Programs. Roman Catholic. Office: Ernst & Young 1200 Skylight Office Tower 1660 W 2d St Cleveland OH 44113

LEONE, JANIS MARIE, social worker; b. Niagara Falls, N.Y., Jan. 5, 1954; d. Casmer E. and Elpina P. (Marinello) L. BA, Niagara U., 1976, MSEd in Counseling, 1978. Registered social worker, N.S.; cert. tchr., N.Y.; cert. in feminist therapy, orgnl. mgmt., supervisory devel. Project coord. Niagara Rape Crisis, Niagara Falls, Ont., Can., 1978-79; counseling coord. Planned Parenthood, Niagara Falls, N.Y., 1979-80; exec. dir. Big Bros./Big Sisters, Yarmouth, N.S., Can., 1981-84; key counselor Jubien House, Halifax, N.S., Can., 1985-86; exec. dir. Phoenix House, Halifax, N.S., Can., 1986-90; clin. supr. Drug Dependency, Halifax, N.S., Can., 1990-95; mem. Family Violence Prevention, Halifax, 1993-95; chair Mgmt./Union Consultation, Halifax, 1993-95; bd. dirs. Planned Parenthood, Halifax, 1991-94; chair bd. Stepping Stone, Halifax, 1988-89. Vol. Single Mothers Support Group, Yarmouth, 1983-84; bd. dirs. Big Bros./Big Sisters, Yarmouth, 1985; mem. Transition House Assn., Yarmouth, 1984. Mem. ACA, Internat. Assn. Marriage and Family Counselors, Can. Assn. Social Workers, N.S. Assn. Social Workers. Democrat. Roman Catholic. Home: 451 College Ave Niagara Falls NY 14305

LEONE, JUDITH GIBSON, educational media specialist, video production company executive; b. Toms River, N.J., Sept. 27, 1945; d. James Delaney and Louise Gertrude (Eberhardt) Gibson; m. Stephan Robert Leone, Nov. 27, 1971; stepchildren: Cheryl, Debra. BA, Kean Coll., 1970; MLS, Rutgers U., 1980. Cert. edn. media specialist. Tchr. Toms River Schs., 1970-84, media specialist, 1984-89; v.p., owner Prodn. House, Toms River, 1985-94; libr. coord. Amb. Christian Acad., Toms River, 1989-95; exec. dir. Designer Showcase, 1995-96; mem. region 5 book evaluation com. N.J. State Libr. System, 1986-90. Sec., bd. dirs. The Shelter, Inc., Bricktown, N.J., 1979—; past pres. Open Arms, Inc.; past pres., bd. dirs. Harbor House; v.p., bd. dirs. Ocean County chpt. United Way; v.p. Garden State Philharm.; bd. dirs. Italian-Am. Cultural and Heritage Soc. Honoree for cmty. svc. Italian Am. Cultural Soc., 1995; named Vol. of Yr., United Way of Ocean County, 1996. Mem. N.J. Ednl. Assn., Ednl. Media Assn. N.J., Ocean County Libr. Assn., Internat. Assn. Sch. Librarianship, Toms River Country Club. Democrat. Home: 143 Cranmoor Dr Toms River NJ 08753-6805

LEONG, HELEN VANESSA, systems programmer; b. Chgo., Dec. 14, 1949; d. Linton and Sue Lin (Hong) L.; m. Stephen Occhuizzo, Aug. 28, 1993. BS in Liberal Arts/Math., Ill. Inst. Tech., 1971. Computer sys. analyst Ill. Bell Tel., Chgo., 1971-76; commd. ensign USN, 1977, advanced through grades to lt. comdr., 1992; pers. officer NAS Glenview, Ill., 1977-78; pub. affairs officer NAS Glenview, 1979-80; computer sys. analyst Space and Naval Warfare Sys. Command, Washington Navy Yard, Washington, 1980-83; program mgr. asst. Dept. of Navy (OP-942) Pentagon, Washington, 1983-86; joint action officer Office Joint Chiefs of Staff (J-6), Pentagon, Washington, 1986-87; exec. officer Naval Regional Data Automation Ctr., Newport, R.I., 1987-89; sys. programmer Stanford (Calif.) Health Svcs., 1989—. mem. Svc. Acad. Adv. Bd. Frank Wolf, 11th Dist., Va., 1985-87; chairperson energy com. Skyline Condo Assn., Falls Church, Va., 1986. Decorated Navy Achievement medal, 1982, Joint Commendation medal, 1987, Navy Commendation medal, 1989, Nat. Def. medal, 1992. Mem. NAFE, Nat. Sys. Programmers Assn. Office: Stanford Health Svcs 300 Pasteur Dr N2B Stanford CA 94305

LEONG, JO-ANN CHING, microbiologist, educator; b. Honolulu, May 15, 1942; d. Raymond and Josephine Ching; m. Oren T.H. Leong; children: Kara Elise, Jonathan Raymond. BA in Zoology, U. Calif., Berkeley, 1964; PhD in Microbiology, San Francisco Sch. Medicine, 1971. Postdoctoral rsch. assoc. dept. biochemistry U. Calif., San Francisco, 1971-75, asst. rsch. virologist Cancer Rsch. Inst., 1975; asst. prof. Oreg. State U., Corvallis, 1975-80, assoc. prof., 1980-86, prof., 1986-92, disting. prof., 1992—, chairperson, 1996—; grant reviewer Sea Grant, NSF, CRIS, USDA, NIH; cons. Am. Microscan, 1986. Co-author: Retroviruses and Differentiation, 1982, Molecular Approaches to Bacteria and Viral Diseases of Fish, 1983, Fish Vaccination, 1988, Viral Vaccines for Aquaculture, 1993, Human Endogenous Retroviruses, 1994, DNA Vaccines for Fish, 1996; virology editor Diseases of Aquatic Organisms. Coord. Women in Sci. Career Workshop, Portland (Oreg.) State U., 1977. Recipient Dernham Rsch. Fellowship, Am. Cancer Soc., 1973-75, fellowship Giannini Found. for Med. Rsch., 1973, Rsch. award Sigma Xi, 1990; named NORCAS prof. Battelle NW Labs, 1976, Disting Prof. Oreg. State U. Alumni Assn., 1991. Fellow Am. Acad. Microbiology; mem. AAAS, AAUP (exec. bd. 1982), European Assn. of Fish Pathologists, Am. Soc. Microbiology, Am. Soc. Virology, Am. Fisheries Soc. (fish health sect.), Assn. Women in Sci., Am. Assn. Cancer Rsch. Office: Oreg State U Dept Microbiology Corvallis OR 97331

LEONG, SUE, retired community health and pediatrics nurse; b. Alameda, Calif., Feb. 15, 1930; d. Leong Dai Sun and Leong San See. BS, U. Calif., San Francisco, 1953; MPH, U. Mich., 1963; MA, San Francisco Theol. Sem., 1958. Cert. sch. nurse, sch. nurse practitioner, nurse specialist. Head nurse Lafayette Clinic, Detroit; pub. health nurse San Francisco Health Dept.; assoc. dir. Ecumenical Campus Ctr., Ann Arbor, Mich.; sch. nurse practitioner Ann Arbor Pub. Schs.; adj. asst. prof. U. Mich. Contbr. articles to profl. jours. Mem. NEA, Mich. Assn. Sch. Nurses (Disting. Svc. award 1990, Dorothy Christy award 1993). Home: 1506 Golden Ave Ann Arbor MI 48104-4327

LEPARD, SANDRA LEE, credit executive; b. Marion, Ohio, June 17, 1941; d. Ralph Leroy and Audrey Janice (Williams) Gaster; m. Daniel D. Lepard, June 11, 1959; children: Sunday D., Scott D., Schelley L. Grad. high sch., Prospect, Ohio. Parts mgr. Holiday Motors, Forrest City, Ark., 1974-76; credit mgr. Wyandot, Inc., Marion, Ohio, 1978—. Mem. budget com. United Way Marion County, 1985-88; program dir. Jr. Achievement, Marion, 1984—. Mem. Nat. Assn. Accts. (dir. 1986-88, local pres. 1983-84), Inst. Mgmt. Accts. (pres. local chpt. 1993—), Marion Indsl. Club (pres. 1988-89, 1st v.p. 1987-88), Federated Women Club (pres. Red Oak chpt. 1973-74). Republican. Lutheran. Home: 1984 Smeltzer Rd Marion OH 43302-7354 Office: Wyandot Inc 135 Wyandot Ave Marion OH 43302

LEPERI, KARIN A., government official; b. St. Louis, May 12, 1952; d. Edwin Oral and Alice Louise Reed; m. Dominic Thomas Leperi, Jr., Nov. 1, 1990; children: Karson Troy, Kosette Dominique. BA in Polit. Sci., Calif. State U., L.A., 1973, MS in Pub. Adminstrn., 1974; postgrad., U. Md., 1980-85. Registered profl. flight engr.; CFP. Presidential intern Dept. Navy, Washington, 1973-74; sr. budget analyst Dept. Energy, Germantown, Md., 1974-83; chief fin. control br. USDA, Washington, 1983-84; systems acct. Nat. Fin. Ctr., New Orleans, 1987; dept. fin. adv. Office Internat. Cooperation and Devel., Washington, 1987-88; chief fin. mgmt. branch U.S. Dept. Agriculture, Washington, 1984-88, dep. dir. budget and acctg. div., 1988-91; asst. dep. adminstr. for resource mgmt. support Internat. Svcs., U.S. Dept. Agr., 1992—; flight engr. U.S. Naval Air Res., Washington, 1983-86; advisor/mentor Women's Exec. Leadership Program, Washington, 1991-92. Mem. Naval Res. Assn., Am. Coun. of Exercise (cert. personal trainer, aerobics instr., lifestyle and weight mgmt. cons.), Internat. Dance and Exercise Assn. (master), Carpathia Soc., Taipan, Oxford Club. Republican. Home: 6006 Greenbelt Rd Ste 329 Greenbelt MD 20770-1019 Office: USDA Rm 5A-21 4700 River Rd Riverdale MD 20737

L'EPLATTENIER, NORA SWEENY HICKEY, nursing educator; b. N.Y.C., Mar. 16, 1945; 1 child, Brendan Sweeny Hickey. Diploma, Bellevue Mills Sch. Nursing, 1965; BS in Health Sci. summa cum laude, Bklyn. Coll., 1978; MS in Psychiat.-Mental Health Nursing, Adelphi U., 1982, PhD, 1988. RN, N.Y., N.J.; cert. specialist in adult mental health; cert. group therapist; Reiki therapist. Dir. psychiat. staff devel. Bellevue Hosp. Ctr., N.Y.C., 1980-82; group psychotherapist Jewish Inst. Geriatric Care, New Hyde Park, N.Y., 1983; staff psychotherapist New Hope Guild, N.Y.C., 1984; assoc. prof. grad. and undergrad. L.I. U. Bklyn., N.Y.C., 1986—; nurse rschr. Englewood (N.J.) Hosp. and Med. Ctr., N.Y.; pvt. practice N.Y., 1982—. Maj. USAR, 1977—. Isabel McIsaac scholar, 1983, Am. Legion scholar, 1962. Mem. Ea. Group Psychotherapy Soc., Sigma Theta Tau.

LEPORE, DAWN GOULD, stock brokerage executive. BA, Smith Coll. With Cin. Bell, Informatics, San Francisco; with Charles Schwab Corp., San Francisco, now exec. v.p., chief info. officer. Named One of Bay Area's Most Powerful Corp. Women San Francisco Chronicle, One of Top 100 Women in Computing Open Computing mag. Office: Charles Schwab Corp 101 Montgomery St San Francisco CA 94104

LEPORE, MARIE ANN, home care nurse; b. Bronx, N.Y., Aug. 21, 1946; d. John Paul and Lillian Josephine (Lucenta) LePore; 1 child, Marie Ann Bank. Student, Cambridge Acad., 1982, S.I., N.Y., 1983, Barton Sch., 1986; med. asst. diploma, Laurel Sch., 1986; A of Specialized Bus., I.C.S., Scranton, Pa., 1995, A in Computer Specialist in Sci., 1996; DegreeMed. Dental Asst., Laurel Sch. for Med. Recruit, N.Y. Home care nurse Dept. Social Svcs., N.Y.C., 1975-78; home health care worker Massive Home Health Svcs., Bronx, N.Y., 1978-82; home careworker Puerto Rican Home Care Svcs., Bronx, N.Y., 1982-84; home care nurse Entea Home Care, Bronx, N.Y., 1986-89, Montefiore Hosp., Bronx, 1989—; dental asst. Recipient numerous professional awards. Home: 3304 White Plains Rd Bronx NY 10467-5703 Office: 925 Oak St Scranton PA 18515

LEPPIG, MARY LOUISE, artist; b. McCurtain, Okla., Dec. 14, 1910; d. John Henigman and Louse Rom; m. Gordon Jack Leppig, June 20, 1931 (dec. 1990); children: Ron, Donna. Student, Chgo. Art Inst. Comml. artist Chgo., illustrator, designer. Mem. Nat. Mus. Women in Arts, West Suburbium Art League, West Alexander Art Club, Middle Ga. Art Club.

LEPPIK, MARGARET WHITE, state legislator; b. Newark, N.J., June 5, 1943; d. John Underhill and Laura Schaefer White; m. Ilo Elmar Leppik, June 18, 1967; children: Peter, David, Karina. BA, Smith Coll., 1965. Rsch. asst. Wistar Inst., U. Pa., Phila., 1967-68, U. Wis., Madison, 1968-69; mem. Minn. Ho. Reps., St. Paul, 1990, 92, 94. Commr. Golden Valley (Minn.) Planning Com., 1982-90; mem. Golden Valley Bd. Zoning Appeals, 1985-87. Recipient Citizen of Distinction award Hennepin County Human Svcs. Planning Bd. 1992; named Legislator of Yr., U. Minn. Alumni Assn., 1995. Mem. LWV (v.p., dir. 1984-90), Minn. Opera Assn. (pres. 1986-88), Rotary Internat., Optimists Internat. Republican. Home: 7500 Western Ave Golden Valley MN 55427-4849 Office: 393 State Office Bldg Saint Paul MN 55155

LEPPO, TAMARA ELIZABETH MARKS, account executive; b. San Jose, Costa Rica, Dec. 12, 1962; came to U.S., 1968; d. Russell Edward and Patricia (Hunt) Marks; m. Michael Leppo, Apr. 23, 1994. Student, Wheaton Coll., Norton, Mass., 1981-83; BA in Spanish Lang. and Lit., Boston U., 1985. Research analyst Coopers & Lybrand, N.Y.C., 1985-87; project coordinator Healthcare Communications, Inc., Princeton, N.J., 1987-88, product mgr., 1988-89; electronic product rep. Commerce Clearing House, Inc., Boston, 1990-91; sales rep., 1991-94; Wiltel/Comlink, Marlborough, Mass., 1996—. Pres. Boston U. South Campus Govt., 1984-85; mem. June Opera Festival N.J., Princeton, 1986-90. Mem. Am. Mus. of Natural History, Boston U. Alumni Assn., Wheaton Coll. Alumni. Home: 141 Parker Rd Framingham MA 01701

LE QUIRE, LOUISE LASSETER, artist, writer; b. Nashville, Sept. 9, 1924; d. Rollin Amos and Lista Lillian (Kendrick) Lasseter; m. Virgil Shields LeQuire, Aug. 20, 1946; children: Nancy, Paul, Alan, Lista. Diploma, Ward-Belmont Jr. Coll., 1943; BA, George Peabody Coll., 1945, MA, 1946. Art tchr. Monroe H.S., Rochester, N.Y., 1946-47, Eastern H.S., Washington, 1947-49; art history, English tchr. Ward-Belmont Jr. Coll., 1949-52; art, English tchr. Franklin (Tenn.) H.S., 1965-67, Montgomery Bell Acad., Nashville, 1967-79; artist, tchr. Nashville Inst. Arts, 1980—; art critic Nashville Banner, 1960-70; art cons. Farris, Warfield, and Canaday, Nashville, 1988; curator Carl Sublett Exhbn. Tenn. State Mus., 1984. Arts editor Nashville Life mag., 1994-95. bd. dirs. Watkins Inst. Coll. Art and Design. Recipient Gov. award Arts, 1984. Mem. Tenn. Arts Acad. (bd. dirs.), Nashville Artist Guild (pres. 1950—), Visual Artists Alliance Nashville (bd. dirs.). Home: 698 Sneed Rd W Franklin TN 37069

LERITTE, JENNIFER JONES, social worker, mental health administrator; b. Ville Platte, La., Feb. 26, 1953; d. John Clifton and Marie Clamie (Richard) Jones; m. John Downs Hutchins, Dec. 18, 1971 (div. Apr. 1977); m. George Alan Leritte, Nov. 22, 1980; children: Jonathan Christopher, Jeremy Wilton. BA in Sociology, N.E. La. State U., 1975; MSW, La. State U., 1981. Cert. social worker, La., social work clin. practitioner, Tex. Food stamp eligibility worker I Bossier Parish Office of Family Security, Benton, La., 1978-79; food stamp eligibility worker II Caddo Parish Office of Family Security, Shreveport, La., 1979; student intern Family Counseling and Children's Svcs., Shreveport, 1979-80; housing insp. I Shreveport Dept. Urban Devel., 1980; social worker supr. I Ellisville (Miss.) State Sch., 1982; program coord. Sabine Valley Regional Mental Health/Mental Retardation Ctr., Longview, Tex., 1982-84; residential coord., social worker supr. Normal Life La., Layfayette, 1984-86; exec. coord. supr. ACCESS, Shreveport, 1986-90; mental health spl. svcs. dir. I, La. dept. health/hosps. Office Human Svcs., Div. Mental Health, Shreveport, 1990-94; exec. dir. Cmty. Interaction Svc., Inc., Bossier City, La., 1994—; group co-therapist Sexual Behavior Modification Program, 1994-96; active parent, tchr. Family Counseling and Children Svcs., Shreveport., 1989-91. Field Day coord. St. Joseph Sch. Home-Sch. Assn., Shreveport, 1990; mem. Mayor's Citizens Adv. Group on Disabilities, City of Shreveport. Mem. NASW (bd. sec. 1989-91, treas. 1990-92, sec. La. state chpt. 1992-94, Shreveport region rep. 1995—, registered, qualified clin.social worker, diplomate in clin. social work, Dorothy Schenthal Leadership award La.-Shreveport region 1996), Acad. Cert. Social Workers, Civitan Internat. (Shreveport club). Republican. Roman Catholic. Office: Triple J Mgmt, Inc 915 Barksdale Blvd 1-K Bossier City LA 71111

LERMAN, CARLA LINSCHEID, urban planner; b. Bklyn., Sept. 15, 1932; d. Carl William and Mabelle Angeline (Kirgan) Linscheid; m. Paul Lerman, June 15, 1956; children: Nina Evelyn, Joshua Carl. BA, Vassar Coll., 1954; MA, U. Chgo., 1956. Lic. planner, N.J. Planning cons. Candeub Fleissig & Assoc., Newark, 1958-76; dir. Bergen County Home Improvement Program, Hackensack, N.J., 1976-77; exec. dir. Housing Authority of Bergen County, Hackensack, 1977-87; asst. dir. N.J. Dept. Cmty. Affairs, Trenton, 1987-91; exec. dir. Episcopal Cmty. Devel. Inc., Newark, 1991—; commr. Teaneck Redevel. Agy., 1976-96; bd. dirs. Nat. Housing Conf., Washington, 1979—; spl. master, expert witness N.J. Superior Ct., Toms River, N.J., 1983-87; bd. mem. N.J. Cmty. Loan Fund, 1991—, pres., 1995—; mem. adv. bd. Midlantic Nat. Bank, Edison, N.J., 1991—; housing cons. Stockton St. Devel. Corp., Trenton, 1991—, Newark Fighting Back Partnership, 1993-96. V.p., bd. dirs. Nat. Multiple Sclerosis Soc., Bergen-Passaic Chpt., N.J., 1978-84, Gimbel Multiple Sclerosis Ctr., Teaneck, N.J., 1984-94; chairperson Affordable Housing Adv. Bd., Teaneck, 1990—. Recipeint award of honor for achievements in the pub. interest N.J. Soc. Archs., 1987, Gov.'s Alice Paul Humanitarian award Gov. Christine Todd Whitman, 1994-95. Mem. Am. Inst. Cert. Planners, Nat. Congress on Cmty. Econ. Devel., Nat. Assn. Housing and Redevel. Ofcls. (N.J. bd. mem. 1979-84), Women in Housing and Fin.

LERMAN, EILEEN R., lawyer; b. N.Y.C., May 6, 1947; d. Alex and Beatrice (Kline) L. BA, Syracuse U., 1969; JD, Rutgers U., 1972; MBA, U. Denver, 1983. Bar: N.Y. 1973, Colo. 1976. atty. FTC, N.Y.C., 1972-74; corp. atty. RCA, N.Y.C., 1974-76; corp. atty. Samsonite Corp. and consumer products div. Beatrice Foods Co., Denver, 1976-78, assoc. gen. counsel, 1978-85, asst. sec., 1979-85; ptnr. Davis, Lerman, & Weinstein, Denver, 1985-92, Eileen R. Lerman & Assocs., 1993—; bd. dir. Legal Aid Soc. of Met. Denver, 1979-80. Bd. dirs., vice chmn. Colo. Postsecondary Ednl. Facilities Authority, 1981-89; bd. dirs., pres. Am. Jewish Com., 1989-92; mem. Leadership Denver, 1983. Mem. ABA, Colo. Women's Bar Assn. (bd. dir. 1980-81), Colo. Bar Assn. (bd. govs.), Denver Bar Assn. (trustee), N.Y. State Bar Assn., Rhone Brackett Inn (pres.-elect 1996), Denver Law Club, Rutgers U. Alumni Assn., University Club. Home: 1018 Fillmore St Denver CO 80206-3332 Office: Eileen R Lerman & Assocs 50 S Steele St Ste 420 Denver CO 80209-2809

LERNER, GERDA, historian, educator, author; b. Vienna, Austria, Apr. 30, 1920; came to U.S., 1939, naturalized, 1943; d. Robert and Ilona (Neumann) Kronstein; m. Carl Lerner, Oct. 6, 1941 (dec.); children: Stephanie, Daniel. B.A., New Sch. Social Research, 1963; M.A. (faculty scholar), Columbia U., 1965, Ph.D., 1966. Lectr. New Sch. Social Research, N.Y.C., 1963-65; asst. prof. L.I. U., 1965-67, assoc. prof., 1967-68; mem. faculty Sarah Lawrence Coll., Bronxville, N.Y., 1968-80; dir. Master's Program in Women's History, 1972-76, 78-79; ednl. dir. Summer Inst. in Women's History, 1976, 79; scholar-in-residence Rockefeller Found. Conf. Center, Bellagio, Italy, 1975, 91; Robinson-Edwards prof. history U. Wis., Madison, 1980—, Wis. Alumni Research Found. sr. disting. research prof., 1984; co-dir. FIPSE grant for Promoting Black Women's History, 1980-83. Author: screenplay Black Like Me, 1964; novel No Farewell, 1955, The Grimke Sisters from South Carolina: Rebels Against Slavery, 1967; The Woman in American History, 1971, Black Women in White America: A Documentary History, 1972, The Female Experience: Documents in American History, 1976, A Death of One's Own, 1978, The Majority Finds its Past: Placing Women in History, 1979, Teaching Women's History, 1981, The Creation of Patriarchy, 1986, The Creation of Feminist Consciousness, 1993. Social Sci. Research Council research fellow, 1970-71; Ford Found. grantee, 1978-79; Guggenheim fellow, 1980-81; Ednl. Found. Achievement award AAUW, 1986. Mem. Am. Hist. Assn., Orgn. Am. Historians (pres. 1981-82), AAUP, Authors League, Am. Studies Assn., PEN. Office: U Wis Dept History 5123 Humanities Bldg 455 N Park St Madison WI 53706-1405

LERNER, IRENE KARPMAN, elementary school educator, education educator; b. Chgo., Feb. 24, 1944. BA in Edn., Roosevelt U., 1964, MA in Edn., 1967; postgrad., various univs. and seminars. Cert. tchr. grades kindergarten through 9, Ill.; cert. gifted/spl. edn. tchr. Tchr. 1st grade Pub. Sch. Dist. 123, Oak Lawn, Ill., 1964-67; tchr. Head Start program Chgo. Cath. Archdiocese, 1966; tchr. 3rd grade Pub. Sch. Dist. 74, Lincolnwood, Ill., 1967-68; tchr. kindergarten Pub. Sch. Dist. 21, Wheeling, Ill., 1970-71, instr. summer gifted edn. program; instr. early childhood edn. Harper Coll., Palatine, Ill., 1986; tchr. pull-out programs Pub. Sch. Dist. 96, Buffalo Grove, Ill., 1987; tchr. 5th grade Pub. Sch. Dist. 70, Libertyville, Ill., 1988—; mem. adj. faculty dept. edn. Nat.-Louis U., Evanston, Ill., 1994—; tchr. gifted program and resource enrichment, 1995—; participant elem. level Newspapers in Edn., Arlington Heights, Ill.; mem. profl. devel. partnership com. Pub. Sch. Dist. 70, Nat. Louis U.; mem. adv. bd. Nat.-Louis U. Ednl. Partnership, Wheeling. Nominee Tchr. Excellence award Kohl Ctr., Wilmette, Ill. Mem. NEA, Assn. Supervision & Curriculum Devel., Ill. Edn. Assn., Libertyville Edn. Assn. (mem. adminstrv. bd. 1992-94), Ill. Assn. Gifted Children.

LERNER, JILL KAREN, music educator; b. Bklyn., Apr. 23, 1962; d. Frank Lerner and Elaine Myrna (Schwartz) Montes. BA magna cum laude, Barry U., 1983; MS, SUNY, New Paltz, 1992. Cert. elem. edn. tchr., N.Y.; cert. music tchr., N.Y.; cert. social studies tchr., N.Y.; cert. EMT and instr. coord., N.Y. Asst. dir. of music Pub. Sch. 149 Dist. 19, Bklyn., 1986-87; music tchr., choral dir. Monticello (N.Y.) Cen. Sch. Dist., 1987-88, Livingston Manor (N.Y.) Cen. Sch., 1988-90; instr. coord. EMT Sullivan County C.C., Loch Sheldrake, N.Y., 1993—; music tchr. Pub. Sch. 149, Bklyn., 1990—; piano tchr., Woodbourne, N.Y., 1987—. Instr. CPR, Sullivan County C.C., Loch Sheldrake, 1993—; Fallsburg Rescue Squad vol. Fallsburg First Aid and Rescue, South Fallsburg, N.Y., 1994—; bd. dirs. Am. Heart Assn., Monticello, 1995-96; EMS vol. Sullivan County EMS, 1990-96; mem. Tri-Valley Volleyball Players. Democrat. Home: PO Box 251 Woodbourne NY 12788

LERNER, LINDA JOYCE, human resources executive; b. N.Y.C., Aug. 19, 1944; d. Morris and Victoria (Mizrahi) L. BS in Bus., U. Bridgeport, 1966. Asst. dir. pers. Bridgeport (Conn.) Hosp., 1969-73; dir. pers. Tufts U., Boston, 1973-80; sr. v.p. human resources Provident Instn. Savs., Boston, 1981-88; sr. v.p. UST Corp. Bank Holding Co., Boston, 1988—. Mem. allocations com. Combined Jewish Philanthropies; v.p. bd. dirs. Horizons for Youth, Boston, 1991—; bd. dirs. Operation A.B.L.E. Fellow Internat. Mktg. Inst., Boston, 1978. Mem. ASTD, N.E. Human Resources Assn., Am. Bankers Assn. (human resources exec. com. 1991—), Mass. Bankers Assn. (human resources com. 1989—, chmn. human resources com. 1993-94), Fin. Women Internat., Boston Human Resources Assn. (chmn. sr. practitioners, bd. dirs.), The Boston Club. Office: UST Corp 40 Court St Boston MA 02108-2202

LERNER, MARCIA, graphic designer, new media specialist; b. Bklyn., May 7, 1955; d. Leo J. and Pauline (Rice) Lerner. BFA, The Cooper Union, N.Y.C., 1976; MFA, Syracuse U., 1980. Art dir. Princeton Gamma-Tech., Princeton Junction, N.J., 1976-79, Quality Comm., San Diego, 1979-84; assoc. art dir. Smart Living Mag., N.Y.C., 1984-85; art dir. Power & Motoryacht Mag., Stamford, Conn., 1985-88, Second Wind Mag., Westport, Conn., 1988-89, Mill Hollow Publishing, N.Y.C., 1989-90, NYU, N.Y.C., 1990-92, Hadassah, Inc., N.Y.C., 1992-95; digital media specialist R.R. Donnelley & Sons, N.Y.C., 1995—; creative dir. Pro-Bono Law Inst., N.Y.C., 1995—; cons. designer San Diego Dept. Socal Svcs., 1979-85. Editor, designer (web site) Pro Bono Law for Laymen, 1996; designer (curriculum) Crazy Clients, 1990; author (booklets) Guide to Digital Production, 1996. Cons. designer Vol. Opportunities, N.Y.C., 1987, Women's Ctr. of San Diego, 1984. Recipient Creativity award Art Dir. Mag., 1995, Excellence award The Visual Club, 1995, Apex Excellence award Comm. Concepts, 1995, Excellence in Journalism Design Simon Rockower award, 1995. Mem. NAFE, Am. Inst. Graphic Art, Women in Comm., Soc. Publication Designers, Nat. Assn. Desktop Publishers. Office: RR Donnelly & Sons 99 Park Ave New York NY 10016

LEROY, CATHERINE A., legislative counsel; b. Houston, Oct. 26, 1946. BA, Smith Coll., 1968; JD, U. Mich., 1973. Staff atty. U.S. Equal Employment Opportunity Commn., 1973-75, asst. counsel, 1975-80; chief counsel subcom. on civil and constitutional rights, com. on the judiciary, 1980-95; now. fed. agy. coord. dir. Dept. HUD, Washington, 1995—. Office: HUD 451 7th St SW Washington DC 20410*

LEROY, MISS JOY, model, designer; b. Riverdale, Ill., Sept. 8, 1927; d. Gerald and Dorothea (Wingebach) Reasor. BS, Purdue U., 1949. Model, sales rep. Jacques, Lafayette, Ind., 1950; book dept. sales rep. Loebs, Lafayette, 1951-52; window trimmer Marshall Field's and Co., Evanston, Ill., 1952-53; sales and display rep. Emerald Ho., Evanston, 1954-55; model, narrator, designer J.L. Hudson Co., GM Corp., Coca Cola Co., Hoover Vacuum Co., Jam Handy Orgn., Am. Motors Corp., Speedway Petroleum Corp., Ford Motors Tractor & Implement Divsn.-The Sykes Co., Detroit, 1958-61; tour guide, model The Christian Sci. Publ. Soc., spl. events coord. Prudential Ins. Co., model Copley 7, Boston, 1962-70. Author: Puzz-its, 1986-96. Founding angel Asolo Theatre, Sarasota, 1960s; mem. Ft. Lauderdale Internat. Film Festival, 1990, Mus. of Art, 1978, Fla. Conservation Assn., Rep. Senatorial Com. Inner Cir., 1990, Congl. Com., 1990, Nat. Trust for Hist. Preservation, 1986, Fla. Trust for Hist. Preservation, 1987, Nat. Wildflower Rsch. Ctr., 1992; one of founding friends 1000 Friends of Fla., 1991; mem. Rep. Presdl. Task Force, 1993; founding mem. Rep. Campaign Coun., 1994. Mem. Purdue U. Gold Coast Club, Stratford Shakespearean Festival of Am., USS Constn. Mus. (charter mem. 1993), Purdue U. Alumni Assn., Walt Disney's Magic Kingdom Club, Wilderness Soc., Magic Kingdom Entertainment Club, Maupin Alumni, Nat. Wildlife Fedn., Fla. Wildlife Fedn., Internat. Wildlife Fedn., Ducks Unltd., Paddlewheel Steamboatin' Soc. Am., Cunard World Club, Skald Club, Yacht Club, The Crystal Soc., The Cousteau Soc., Covette Club, Coastal Conservatoin Assn., Captain's Cir., Intravler Club, Internat. Marine Animal Trainers Assn., Am. Queen Inaugural Soc., Zeta Tau Alpha. Home: 2100 S Ocean Ln Apt 2104 Fort Lauderdale FL 33316-3827

LERSCH, DELYNDEN RIFE, computer engineering executive; b. Grundy, Va., Mar. 22, 1949; d. Woodrow and Eunice Louise (Atwell) Rife; m. John Robert Lersch, May 9, 1976; children: Desmond, Kristofer. BSEE, Va. Poly. Inst. and State U., 1970; postgrad. Boston U., 1975—. With Stone & Webster Engring. Corp., 1970-91, elec. engr., supr. computer applications, Boston, 1978-80, mgr. computer graphics, 1980-84, mgr. engring. systems and computer graphics, 1984-87, div. chief info. techs., 1987-90, v.p., 1990-91; chief A.D.P. officer Univ. Rsch. Assocs., 1991-94; CARE Pvt. Mortgage Ins. Sys. Corp. account mgr. Perot Sys. Corp., Dallas, 1994—. Named Stone and Webster's Woman Engr. of Yr., 1976, 79; Mass. Solar Energy Research grantee, 1978; honored by Engring. News Record mag. for contbns. to constrn. industry, 1983. Mem. IEEE (sr.), Assn. Women in Sci., Soc. Women Engrs. (sr.), Women in Sci. and Engring., Energy Communicators, Nat. Computer Graphics Assn., Profl. Council New Eng., Women in Energy (dir. Mass. chpt. 1978, New Eng. region 1979), LWV, Rotary (Rotarian of Yr. 1993-94). Congregationalist. Club: Boston Bus. and Profl. Women's. Author: Cable Schedule Information Systems As Used in Power Plant Construction, 1973, 2d edit., 1975; Information Systems Available for Use by Electrical Engineers, 1976; contbr. articles in field of computer aided design and engring. Home: 1106 Bristol Cir De Soto TX 75115-2818 Office: Perot Sys Corp 12377 Merit Dr Ste 1100 Dallas TX 75251-3233

LERUD, JOANNE VAN ORNUM, library administrator; b. Jamestown, N.D., Nov. 21, 1949; d. Elbert Hiel and Dorothy Arlene (Littrick) Van Ornum; m. Gerald Henry Groenewold, Jan. 15, 1971 (div. Nov. 1978); 1 child, Gerd Heil Groenewold; m. Jeffrey Craig Lerud, Aug. 30, 1980; 1 child, Jesse Currier. BS in Geology, U. N.D., 1971, MS in Geology, 1979; MA in Librarianship and Info. Mgmt., U. Denver, 1979. Assoc. tech. info. specialist Marathon Oil Co., Littleton, Colo., 1980-86; libr. dir. Mont. Coll. Mineral Sci. and Tech., Butte, 1986-89, Colo. Sch. Mines, Golden, 1989—; report investigator in field. NSF grantee, 1970. Mem. Geosci. Info. Soc. (v.p. 1988, pres. 1989). Office: Colo Sch Mines Arthur Lakes Libr Golden CO 80401

LESESNE, TERI STEWART, educational consultant; b. Pitts., Oct. 16, 1952; d. Floyd William Stewart and Mary (Angel) Letwin; m. Henry Hilton Lesesne, May 18, 1973; children: Henry Hilton, Meredith Elizabeth. BA, U. Houston, 1976, MEd, 1983, EdD, 1991. Cert. tchr., gifted & talented tchr., Tex. Tchr. St. Peter the Apostle Sch., Houston, 1976-79; tchr., dept. chair Alief Mid. Sch., Houston, 1979-83; tchr., gifted coord. Albright Mid. Sch., Houston, 1983-89; asst. prof. Sam Houston State U., Huntsville, Tex., 1989—; cons. various sch. dists., Tex., 1989—; mem. Tchrs. Choices Com., Newark, Del., 1996—. Editor column Jour. Adolescent & Adult Literacy, 1993-96; columnist MAGC, 1995-96, R & E, 1996. Rsch. grantee Tex. Coun. Tchrs. English, 1995, Tex. State Reading Assn., 1995, Sam Houston State U., 1996, ALAN Found., 1996. Mem. ALA, Nat. Coun. Tchrs. English, Internat. Reading Assn., Tex. Coun. Tchrs. English (pres. 1995-96), Tex. Libr. Assn. (chair membership com. 1995-96), Phi Delta Kappa. Roman Catholic. Office: Sam Houston State U PO Box 2236 Huntsville TX 77341

LESH, KATHRYN ANN, nursing researcher; b. Harrisburg, Pa., Nov. 26, 1955; d. Roy Layton and Dorothy Jean (Jones) L.; m. Charles LaVerne Wilkerson, Nov. 17, 1981 (div. Feb. 1993); children: Nicholas Ryan, Alexandra Lynn. BS, Wilkes Coll., 1978; MEd, Boston U., 1986; MS, U. Ill., 1992; postgrad., Johns Hopkins U., 1993—. Registered profl. nurse N.Y., Md. Program coord., instr. City Colls. Chgo., Wiesbaden, Germany, 1984-86; vol. safety instr. ARC, Wiesbaden, Germany, 1984-88, asst. sta. mgr., 1987-88; head nurse St. John's Hosp., San Angelo, Tex., 1988-89; nursing instr. Crouse Irving Meml. Hosp., Syracuse, N.Y., 1989-90; staff devel. coord. Elmhurst (Ill.) Meml. Hosp., 1990-92; rsch. nurse, program coord. Johns Hopkins U., Balt., 1992-96; sci. editor Kevric Co., Nat. Libr. Medicine, Silver Spring, Md., 1996—; nurse cons. County North Children's Ctr., Syracuse, 1989-90. Vol. firefighter, vol. ambulance Chinchilla Vol. Fire Dept., Pa., 1972-78; vol. instr., chair, ARC, Wiesbaden, 1984-88; vol. instr. Am. Heart Assn., 1985-95; mem. Lipid Nurse Task Force, 1995—. Capt. USAF, 1979-84. Mem. ANA, AAUW, APHA, Sigma Theta Tau. Democrat. Home: 12419 Sandal Ln Bowie MD 20715

LESIKAR, MELISSA ELAINE, exercise physiologist; b. Dugway, Utah, Mar. 16, 1969; d. Frederick Melvin and Gayle Elaine (Essington) Mohr. BS in Kinesiology, U. Ill., 1991; MS in Phys. Edn., Ea. Ill. U., Charleston, 1992. Exercise physiologist Covenant Med. Ctr., Urbana, Ill., 1992—; vol. Covenant Med. Ctr., Urbana, 1991—, Sarah Bush Lincoln Health Ctr., Mattoon, Ill., 1992. Mem. Am. Coll. Sports Medicine, Ill. Soc. for Cardiopulmonary Health and Rehab., Am. Assn. Cardiovascular and Pulmonary Rehab. Home: 1715 B Lawyer St College Station TX 77840 Office: Covenant Med Ctr 1400 W Park Urbana IL 61801

LESLIE, CLARE WALKER, artist, naturalist educator; b. Phila., Jan. 3, 1947; d. Robert Miller and Alice Stimson (Smith) Walker; m. David Robert Leslie; children: Eric Roger, Anna Elizabeth. BA, Carleton Coll., 1968. Tchr. K-12 various schs., 1976—; vis. faculty Williams Coll., Coll. of the Atlantic, Carleton Coll., Middlebury Coll., Harvard/Radcliffe Continuing Edn., Cambridge, 1985—; adj. faculty Cambridge (Mass.) Ctr. for Adult Edn., 1974—, Antioch/New England Grad. Sch., Keene, N.H., 1978—, Mass. Coll. of Art, Boston, 1989—; ednl. adv. bd. Cambridge Ctr. for Adult Edn.; cons. Glenbrook Nature Wrtiers Soc., Battleboro, 1995, Guild of Scientific Illustrators, Washington, 1979—. Author, artist: Nature Drawing: A Tool for Learning, 1979, 95, The Art of Field Sketching, 1984, 95, A Naturalist's Sketchbook, 1987, Nature All Year Long, 1991. Vol. Agassiz Pre-Sch., Cambridge, 1982-91, Cambridge Friends Sch., 1984—; mem., organizer The Artist's Guild, Rochester, Vt., 1992—. Mem. Guild of Scientific Illustrators, Cambridge Art Assn. (exhibn. coord. 1994—), N.Am. Assn. of Environ. Educators, Mass. Environ. of Educators Soc. Home and Office: 76 Garfield St Cambridge MA 02138

LESLIE, KATHLEEN BONNEMA, artist; b. Ft. Collins, Colo., Apr. 21, 1963; d. Calvin Joel and Janet Frances (Bender) Bonnema; m. Mark Chad Leslie, Nov. 23, 1991. BFA, U. No. Colo., Greeley, 1985. Exhibited paintings in solo show Sleeping Bear Gallery, Ketchum, Idaho, 1996, two-woman show, 1995, group shows Interlochen Ctr. for the Arts, 1981, Midwest Watercolor Soc. Nat. Exhibit, 1994, Taos Nat. Exhibit, 1995, Gallery by the Lake Coeur d'Alene, Idaho, 1995, others. Fine Art Scholar U. No. Colo., 1982. Mem. Nat. Mus. of Women in the Arts, Nat. Assn. Univ. Women.

LESLIE, LISA, basketball player. Student, U. So. Calif. Basketball player USA Women's Nat. Team; mem. gold medal winning 1994 Goodwill Games Team. Named 1993 USA Basketball Female Athlete of Yr.; recipient gold medal Atlanta Olympics, 1996. Office: USA Basketball 5465 Mark Dabling Blvd Colorado Springs CO 80918-3842

LESLIE, LYNN MARIE, secondary education educator; b. Lake City, Fla., Nov. 17, 1948; d. Billy Verlyn Spooner and Dorothy Marie (Odom) Loomis; m. Roy Hamner Leslie, Nov. 25, 1967; children: Kim Ball, Billy Leslie, Dodi Leslie. BS in Edn., Trevecca U., 1970; ME in Spl. Edn., Tenn. State U., 1987. Cert. career ladder III, Tenn. Tchr. Leesburg (Fla.) Elem. Sch., 1970-71, Wessington Pl. Elem. Sch., Hendersonville, Tenn., 1974-87, Knox Doss Mid. Sch., Hendersonville, 1987—; mem. Sumner County Ins. Trust, Gallatin, Tenn., 1991-96. Mem. Sumner County Edn. Assn. (pres. 1991-92, 95-96, sec. 1992-95, sec., treas. 1996—). Mem. Ch. of Nazarene. Home: 1032 Carriage Hill Pl Hendersonville TN 37075-8728

LESONSKY, RIEVA, editor-in-chief; b. N.Y.C., June 20, 1952; d. Gerald and Muriel (Cash) L. BJ, U. Mo., 1974. Researcher Doubleday & Co., N.Y.C., 1975-78; researcher Entrepreneur Mag., L.A., 1978-80, rsch. dir., 1983-84, mng. editor, 1985-86, exec. editor, 1986-87; editor Entrepreneur Mag., Irvine, Calif., 1987-90; editor-in-chief Entrepreneur Mag. Bus. Start-Ups Entrepreneur Group, Irvine, Calif., 1990—; rsch. dir. LFP Inc., L.A., 1980-82; speaker, lect. in field. Editor: 184 Businesses Anyone Can Start, 1990, Complete Guide to Owning a Home-based Business, 1990, 168 More Businesses Anyone Can Start, 1991, 111 Businesses You Can Start for Under $10,000, 1991; contbr. articles to mags. Apptd. SBA Nat. Adv. Coun., 1994-96, 96—. Named Dist. Media Advocate of Yr., Small Bus. Adminstrn., 1993, Dist. Women in Bus. Advocate, Small Bus. Adminstrn., 1995. Mem. Women's Network for Entrepreneurial Tng. (bd. dirs., advisor, nat. steering com.), Nat. Assn. Women's Bus. Advocates (bd. dirs.). Office: Entrepreneur Mag Group 2392 Morse Ave Irvine CA 92614-6234

LESSARD, SUZANNAH TERRY, writer; b. Islip, N.Y., Dec. 1, 1944; d. John Ayres and Alida Mary (White) L.; m. David Victor Soeiro (div.); 1 child, Julian Soeiro. BA, Columbia U., 1969. Editor, writer The Washington Monthly, 1969-75; staff writer The New Yorker, N.Y.C., 1975-94. Author: The Architect of Desire: Beauty and Danger in the Stanford White Family, 1996. Recipient Whiting award Giles Whiting Found., 1995. Democrat.

LESSER, JOAN L., lawyer; b. L.A.. BA, Brandeis U., 1969; JD, U. So. Calif., 1973. Bar: Calif. 1973, U.S. Dist. Ct. (cen. dist.) Calif. 1974. Assoc. Irell and Manella, L.A., 1973-80, ptnr., 1980—; mem. planning com. Ann. Real Property Inst., Continuing Edn. of Bar, Berkeley, 1990—; speaker at profl. confs. Trustee Windward Sch.; grad. Leadership L.A., 1992. Mem. Orgn. Women Execs., Order of Coif. Office: Irell and Manella LLP 1800 Avenue of the Stars Ste 900 Los Angeles CA 90067-4211

LESSER, RIKA ELLEN, writer, translator; b. Bklyn., July 21, 1953; d. Milton S. and Celia (Fogelhut)L. BA summa cum laude, Yale U., 1974; MFA, Columbia U., 1977. Freelance writer, translator from German and Swedish Bklyn., 1976—; editl. and graphic asst. Barron's Bus. and Fin. Weekly, N.Y.C., 1976-84; vis. lect. Yale Coll., 1976, 78, 87, 88; sec./researcher/editor The Local Fin. Project Assn. Bar of the City of N.Y., 1977-78; adj. lectr. English CUNY, 1979; workshop instr. Poetry Ctr.of 92d St Y, N.Y.C., 1982-85; Jenny McKean Moore vis. lectr. George Washington U., 1985-86. Author: (books) Etruscan Things, 1983, All We Need of Hell, 1995. Mem. ASCAP, Acad. Am. Poets, Associated Writing Programs, Poetry Soc. Am., Poets and Writers, PEN Am. Ctr. (exec. bd. 1991-96), Phi Beta Kappa. Home and Office: 133 Henry St #5 Brooklyn NY 11201

LESSER, WENDY, literary magazine editor, writer, consultant; b. Santa Monica, Calif., Mar. 20, 1952; d. Murray Leon Lesser and Millicent (Gerson) Dillon; m. Richard Rizzo, Jan. 18, 1985; 1 stepchild, Dov Antonio; 1 child, Nicholas. BA, Harvard U., 1973; MA, Cambridge (Eng.) U., 1975; PhD, U. Calif., Berkeley, 1982. Founding ptnr. Lesser & Ogden Assocs., Berkeley, 1977-81; founding editor The Threepenny Rev., Berkeley, 1980—; Bellagio resident Rockefeller Found, Italy, 1984. Author: The Life Below the Ground, 1987, His Other Half, 1991, Pictures at an Execution, 1994; editor: Hiding in Plain Sight, 1993. Fellow NEH, 1983, 92, Guggenheim fellow, 1988. Fellow NEH, 1983, 92, Guggenheim Found, 1988, ACLS, 1996. Democrat. Office: The Threepenny Rev PO Box 9131 Berkeley CA 94709-0131

LESSICK, MIRA LEE, nursing educator; b. Hazleton, Pa., Jan. 25, 1949; d. Jack H. and Shirley E. (Frumkin) L. Diploma in nursing, Albany (N.Y.) Med. Ctr., 1969; BSN, Boston U., 1972; MS, U. Colo., 1973; PhD, U. Tex., 1986. Staff nurse Boston City Hosp. and Mass. Gen. Hosp., 1969-72; instr. to asst. prof. nursing, genetics clinician U. Rochester, N.Y., 1973-79; asst. prof. nursing, practitioner Rush U., Chgo., 1986-91, assoc. prof. nursing, 1992—. Contbr. articles to profl. jours. Recipient Bd. of Govs. award, Excellence in Pediatric Nursing award Albany Med. Ctr., 1969, Outstanding Nurse Recognition award March of Dimes Birth Defects Found., 1991, Recognition award for Individual Contbn. to Maternal-Child Health Nat. Perinatal Assn., 1993. Mem. AAAS, ANA, APHA, Internat. Soc. Nurses in Genetics (chair rsch. com.), Assn. Women's Health, Obstetric, and Neonatal Nurses, Am. Soc. Human Genetics, Chgo. Nurses Assn. (legis. com. 1990-91), N.Y. Acad. Scis., Midwest Nursing Rsch. Soc., Sigma Theta Tau (Luther Christman award for excellence in published writing 1993), Phi Kappa Phi. Home: 4180 N Marine Dr Apt 612 Chicago IL 60613-2210 Office: Rush U Coll Nursing 301 SSH Chicago IL 60612

LESSOR, EDITH SCHROEDER, educator; b. Chgo., Aug. 5, 1930; d. William and Hanna Maria (Ingwersen) S.; m. Arthur Eugene Lessor Jr., Nov. 20, 1955 (dec.); children: Ralph Arthur, Karen Lessor Moran. BS, Valparaiso U., 1952; PhD, Ind. U., 1955. Instr. Ulster County Community Coll., Kingston, N.Y., 1965-66, SUNY, Binghamton, 1966-68; from instr. to assoc. prof. Mt. St. Mary Coll., Newburgh, N.Y., 1968-76, prof., 1976-93, prof. emerita, 1994. Mem. AAAS, NOW, AAUW, Am. Chem. Soc., Older Women's League, Sigma Xi. Home: 7F Knightsbridge Poughkeepsie NY 12603-3617

LESTER, DEBORAH LOUISE, elementary education educator; b. Athens, Ga., Nov. 27, 1951; d. Wallace Lampkin and Ann M. (Walker) Lester; 1 child, Aimee Danielle. AS in Edn., Young Harris Jr. Coll., 1972; BS in Edn., Ga. So. U., 1974; MEd, U. Ga., 1977. Cert. elem. educator, supervising tchr. svc., instrnl. supr., data collector, Ga. Elem. tchr. Alps Rd. Elem. Sch., Athens, Ga., 1974-83; summer sch. reading tchr. Oglethorpe Ave. Elem. Sch., Athens, Ga., 1980; elem. tchr. David C. Barrow Elem. Sch., Athens, Ga., 1983-94, chpt. 1 reading tchr., 1994-95, SIA/Title I tchr., 1995—; staff devel. rep. Alps Rd. Elem. Sch., David C. Barrow Elem. Sch., Athens, 1981-86; dir. after sch. program, David C. Barrow Elem. Sch., 1991, student support team coord. Chmn. pastor parish rels. com. Princeton United Meth. Ch., Athens, 1995-97, chmn. parsonage com. Mem. NEA, Clarke County Assn. Educators, Ga. Assn. Educators, Clarke County Adoption Resource Exch. Republican. Methodist. Home: 114 Clifton Dr Athens GA 30606 Office: David C Barrow Elem Sch 100 Pinecrest Dr Athens GA 30605-1459

LESTER, PAMELA ROBIN, lawyer; b. N.Y.C., Aug. 5, 1958; d. Howard M. and Patricia Barbara (Briger) L. Student, Princeton U., 1978-79; BA cum laude, Amherst Coll., 1980; JD, Fordham U., 1983. Bar: N.Y. 1984, D.C. 1985. With Advantage Internat., Inc., Washington, 1984-89, gen. counsel, 1987-89; assoc. Akin, Gump, Strauss, Hauer & Feld, Washington, 1989-90; sr. v.p. bus. affairs and gen. counsel Time Warner Sports, N.Y.C., 1991—; adj. lectr. sports law Am. U. Law Sch., 1989-91; adj. faculty sports law Fordham U. Law Sch., 1992—; bd. advisors Ctr. for Protection of Athletes Rights. Contbr. chpt. to: The Law of Professional and Amateur Sports, 1989, 95. Mem. ABA (program and sports divsn. chair forum entertainment and sports industries' governing com. 1992-96, chair elect 1996, governing com. standing com. on forum-coms. 1994—), Assn. Bar City N.Y. (sports law com. 1991-95), Sports Lawyers Assn. (bd. dirs.), N.Y. State Bar Assn., Women's Sports Found. (mem. bd. adv.). Office: Time Warner Sports 1100 Avenue Of The Americas New York NY 10036-6712

LETCHER, NAOMI JEWELL, quality engineer, educator, counselor; b. Belle Point, W. Va., Dec. 29, 1924; d. Andrew Glen and Ollie Pearl (Meadows) Presley; m. Frank Philip Johnson, Oct. 5, 1945 (div. Dec. 1953); m. Paul Arthur Letcher, Mar. 6, 1954; children: Frank, Edwin, Richard, David. AA, El Camino Jr. Coll., 1964; BA, Calif. State U., 1971. Inspector N. Am. Aviation, Downey, Calif., 1964-71; substitute tchr. ABC Unified sch. Dist., Artesia, Calif., 1971-72; recurrence control rep. Rockwell Internat., Downey, Calif., 1972-80, quality engr., 1981-86; counselor Forest Lawn Cemeteries, Cerritos, Calif., 1980-81; tech. analyst Northrop, Pico Rivera, Calif., 1986-89; gov. divsn. D-2 area T.M. Internat., Downey, Calif., 1978-79. Author: History of the Letcher Family, 1995. Docent Temecula (Calif.) Valley Mus., 1994—. Mem. AAUW, Nat. Mgmt. Assn., NOW, Srs. Golden Yrs. Club, Alpha Gamma Sigma. Democrat. Baptist.

LETT, CYNTHIA ELLEN WEIN, marketing executive; b. Takoma Park, Md., Dec. 24, 1957; d. Arthur Benjamin and Mary Louise (Barker) Wein; m. Gerald Lee Lett, June 1, 1991. BS, Purdue U., 1979; M, Antioch Sch. Law, 1982-83. Mktg. researcher Sheraton, Washington, 1979-80; sales mgr. Sea Pines Plantation Co., Hilton Head Island, S.C., 1980-81; dir. sales Sheraton Potomac Hotel, Rockville, Md., 1981-82, Ritz Carlton Hotel, Washington, 1982-83; pres. Creative Planning Internat., Washington, 1983—; dir. mem. Great Inns Am., Annapolis, 1987-89; etiquette cons., 1989—; dir. meetings Am. Healthcare Inst., 1991-92; corp. affairs mgr. MCI Telecom Corp., 1992-95. Author: Getaway Innstyle, America's Fifty Best Inns, 1990; editor Travel Inn Style Newsletter, 1990-91. Mem. Exec. Women Internat., Profl. Conf. Mgmt. Assn., Washington Conv. and Visitors Assn., Greater Washington Soc. Assn. Execs., Found. for Internat. Meetings (bd. govs. 1985-86), Purdue Club (1982-93). Office: Creative Planning Internat 13116 Hutchinson Way Ste 100 Silver Spring MD 20906-5947

LETT, ROSALIND KIMBER, infomation scientist; b. Tuscaloosa, Ala., Feb. 28, 1956; d. William Lincoln and James Ella (Toney) Kimber; m. Victor Lemond Lett, June 28, 1986; children: Victor Lemond Jr., Victoria L'erin. BS, Ala. A&M U., 1978; MS, Atlanta U., 1983. Info. specialists Morris Brown Coll., Atlanta, 1983-86; reference specialist Ga. State U., Atlanta, 1986; reference libr. Morehouse Sch. Medicine, Atlanta, 1986-87; med. libr. Kennestone Hosp., Marietta, Ga., 1987-90; dir. librs. Ga. Mental Health

Inst., Atlanta, 1990-92; med. libr. dir. Crawford Long Hosp., Atlanta, 1992—; med. libr. cons Henry Med. Ctr., Stockbridge, Ga., 1988—, Northside Hosp., Atlanta, 1990-92, Gwinnett Med. Ctr., Lawrenceville, Ga., 1994—, Parkway Med. Ctr., Lithia Springs, Ga., 1995. Author: Consumer Health Resource Guide, 1996. Voter registrar Dekalb County Voter Registration, 1993; info. advocate Libr.'s on the Info. Superhighway Advocacy Network, 1995—; mem. NN/LM Reg. Adv. Coun., 1992-94. Recipient Mktg. divsn. PR award Spl. Libr. Assn., 1995, 96, Diversity Leader Devel. award Spl. Libr. Assn., 1996. Mem. MLA (leadership award 1994, chair hosp. libr. com. So. chpt. 1996—), Med. Libr. Assn. (disting. level Acad. Health Info. Profls.), Ga. Health Sci. Libr. Assn. (pres. 1993-94), Spl. Libr. Assn. (pres. Ga. chpt. 1995-96), Southeastern Conf. Hosp. Libr. Assn. (pres. 1992-93), Atlanta Health Sci. Libr. Assn. (pres. 1990-92). Mem. AME Ch. Home: 931 Andiron Ct Stone Mountain GA 30083

LETZIG, BETTY JEAN, association executive; b. Hardin, Mo., Feb. 18, 1926; d. Robert H. and Alina Violet (Mayes) L. BA, Scarritt Coll., 1950, MA, 1968. Ednl. staff The Methodist Ch., Ark., Okla. Tex., 1953-60; with Internat. Deaconess Exchange Program, London, 1961-62; staff exec. Nat. Div. United Meth. Ch., N.Y.C., 1962-95, ret. 1995; coord. Mission Pers. Support Svcs., 1984-88; exec. sec. Deaconess Program Office, 1989-95. Contbr. articles to profl. jours. Bd. dirs. Internat. Svcs. Assn. for Health, Inc., Atlanta, 1974-88, Vellore Christian Med. Coll., N.Y.C., 1984-94; mem. U.S. com. Internat. Coun. Social Welfare, Washington, 1983-89; active Nat. Interfaith Coalition on Aging, Athens, Ga. and Washington, 1972—, pres., 1981-85. Recipient Deaconess Exch. award Commn. Deaconess Work, 1961-62. Mem. Nat. Coun. Aging, Nat. Voluntary Orgns. Ind. Living for Aging (exec. com. 1978-84), Nat. Coun. Social Welfare, Older Women's League. United Methodist. Avocations: travel, beachcombing, photography, needlework. Home: 235 E 22nd St Apt 1U New York NY 10010-4630 Office: Nat Program Divsn Gen Bd Global Ministries 475 Riverside Dr Ste 300 New York NY 10115-0122

LEUKUMA, MARY ANN, physician, pediatrician; b. Litchfield, Minn., Sept. 14, 1948; d. Joseph Fredrick and Adelyne Mabel (Salmonson) L.; m. Richard Edwin Manthey, Feb. 25, 1978. BA, U. Minn., 1970, BS, 1972, MD, 1982. Diplomate Am. Acad. Pediats. Intern, resident pediat. U. Minn., 1982-85; with Margaret J. Hustad, P.A., White Bear Lake, Minn., 1985-90; CEO, staff pediatrician Northeast Pediat. Clinic, St. Paul, 1990-95. Mem. Ramsey County Med. Soc. Office: Northeast Pediat Clinic 4520 Centerville Rd Saint Paul MN 55127

LEUPP, EDYTHE PETERSON, retired education educator, administrator; b. Mpls., Nov. 27, 1921; d. Reynold H. and Lillian (Aldridge) Peterson; m. Thomas A. Leupp, Jan. 29, 1944 (dec.); children: DeEtte (dec.), Patrice, Stacia, Roderick, Braden. BS, U. Oreg., 1947, MS, 1951, EdD, 1972. Diplomate Am. Bd. Profl. Neuropsychology, Am. Bd. Forensic Examiners. Tchr. various pub. schs. Idaho, 1941-45, Portland, Oreg., 1945-55; dir. tchr. edn. Northwest Nazarene Coll., Nampa, Idaho, 1955-61; sch. adminstr. Portland Pub. Schs., 1963-84; dir. tchr. edn. George Fox Coll., Newberg, Oreg., 1984-87; ret., 1987; vis. prof. So. Nazarene U., Bethany, Okla., 1988-95; pres. Portland Assn. Pub. Sch. Adminstrs., 1973-75; dir.-at-large Nat. Coun. Adminstrv. Women in Edn., Washington, 1973-76; state chmn. Oreg. Sch. Prins. Spl. Project, 1978-79; chair Confdn. Oreg. Sch. Adminstrs. Ann. Conf.; rschr. 40 tchr. edn. programs in colls. and univs.; designer tchr. edn. program George Fox Coll.; adj. prof. Warner Pacific Coll., Portland, 1996. Author tchr. edn. materials. Pres. Idaho State Aux. Mcpl. League, 1957, Nampa PTA, 1958, Nampa unit AAUW, 1956; bd. dirs. Portland Fedn. Women's Clubs, 1963. Idea fellow Charles Kettering Found., 1978, 80, 87, 91, 92, 93, 94. Fellow Am. Coll. Forensic Examiners; mem. APA (mem. exec. bd.), Assn. Women in Psychology (mem. steering com.), Ea. Psychol. Assn. (chmn. 1980 conv.), Conn. Psychol. Assn. (mem. coun. 1978-79), R.I. Psychol. Assn., N.Y. Acad. Scis., Sigma Xi, Psi Chi. Republican. Nazarene. Home: 8100 SW 2nd Ave Portland OR 97219-4602

LEV, ESTHER SUSAN, restoration ecologist; b. Cleve., May 9, 1955. BS, Evergreen State Coll., 1977. Botanist, wildlife ecologist U.S. Fish and Wildlife Svc., Alaska Peninsula, 1977-78; wildlife biologist Nat. Park Svc., Yellowstone, Mont., 1978; botanist U.S. Forest Svc., LaGrande, Oreg., 1981; wildlife ecologist U. Wis., Apostel Islands, 1983-84, U. N.Mex., Loreto BCS Mex., 1984-85, various planning burs., 1987-93; cons. to Metro regional govt. Portland, 1989-93; restoration ecologist Portland/Vancouver Metro Region, Vancouver, 1991-95; scientific dir., restoration ecologist The Wetlands Conservancy, Portland, 1993-96; sci. dir. Corps Restoring the Urban Environ., Portland, 1993-95; adv. bd. City of Portland Planning Bur., 1994-95, Unified Sewerage Agy., Beaverton, Oreg., 1994-95. Author (Daniel Mathews) Cascade Olympic Natural History, 1987; contbr. articles to profl. jours.; editor (newsletter) Freshet-The Wetlands Conservancy, 1994-95. Founder Annetta Carter Meml. Botanical Park, Loreto, BCS Mex., 1993—; vol. local citizen stream groups, 1991-96, Rainbow Coalition, Portland, 1990-93. Recipient Mamie Cambell award Audubon Soc. of Portland, 1994. Mem. Soc. of Ecol. Restoration, Pronatura, Soc. of Wetlands Scientists, Am. Ornithol. Union, Coalition to Restore Urban Waters. Office: The Wetlands Conservancy PO Box 1195 Tualatin OR 97062

LE VA, BRITTA, photographer; b. Cologne, Germany, Jan. 1, 1949. Student, Women's Coll., Germany, 1966. Design asst. Kohlhammer Pub. House, Cologne, 1967; gallery asst. Winfred Reckermann Gallery, Cologne, 1967, Wilbrandt Gallery, Cologne, 1967; gallery dir. Rene Block Gallery, Berlin and N.Y.C., 1973-89, Max Protech Gallery, Washington and N.Y.C., 1973-89; spl. events photographer Mus. Modern Art; lectr. in field; appeared on radio programs Radio Cairo, 1992, Cairo TV, 1992, Nile TV, 1994; rschr. various projects in field; intern with Prof. B.V. Bothmer on photographing Corpus of Ancient Egyptian Sculpture, Inst. Fine Arts N.Y., 1990; photographer at excavations of Giza and Saqqara Pyramids. Author: Pyramids of Egupt, 1995; contbr. photography: Women in Ancient Egypt, 1996; exhbns. at ETA, N.Y., 1992, Al-Ahram Exhbn. Hall, Cairo, 1992, Parrish Art Mus., 1994, Ashwagh Hall, 1994; contbr. articles to profl. publs., photographs to various mags. Home: PO Box 1642 East Hampton NY 11937

LEVALLEY, JOAN CATHERINE, accountant; b. Decatur, Ill., Nov. 27, 1931; d. Clarence and Pearl Mae (McClure) Krall; m. Charles R. LeValley, Apr. 13, 1958 (div.); children: Curtis Ray, Cara Marie. BA in Bus., Manchester Coll., 1957. Accredited tax advisor, Ill. Acct. with various firms, 1960-76; pvt. practice acctg., Park Ridge, Ill., 1964-79; pres., dir. LeValley & Assocs., Inc., Park Ridge, 1979—; mem. tax adv. com. Chgo. IRS Dirs.; mem. com. United Way of Park Ridge, 1991, co-chmn., 1992. Mem. Nat. Assn. Pub. Accts., Ind. Acct. Assn. Ill. (2d woman pres. 1987-88, Person of Yr. award 1990), Bus. and Profl. Women Park Ridge (pres. 1974-75, Bus. Woman of Yr. 1983), Park Ridge C. of C. (treas. 1985-87). Baptist. Avocations: baking; sewing; gardening. Home: 2200 Bouterse St Apt 101 Park Ridge IL 60068-2367 Office: LeValley & Assocs Inc 6215 S 44th St Lincoln NE 68516-5506

LEVASSEUR, SUSAN LEE SALISBURY, secondary education educator; b. Wyandotte, Mich., Nov. 20, 1967; d. David Henry and Lynda Lee (Macaulay) Salisbury; m. John Peter LeVasseur, Dec. 19, 1992. BS in Edn., Ctrl. Mich. U., 1990; postgrad., Wayne State U., 1991—. Cert. secondary tchr., Mich. Substitute tchr. Dearborn (Mich.) Schs., 1991, Allen Park (Mich.) Schs., 1991; tchr. sci. Berkley (Mich.) Schs., 1991—. Instr. Mich. Red Cross, Detroit, 1983—; deacon Allen Park Presbyn. Ch., 1991-93; mem. Colitis Found. Am. Mem. ASCD, AAUW, Nat. Counseling Assn., Am. Kennel Club, Nat. Sci. Tchrs. Assn., Mich. Sci. Tchrs. Assn., Mich. Counseling Assn., Mich. Edn. Assn., Kappa Delta Pi, Alpha Phi Omega. Presbyterian. Home: 22436 Cobb Dearborn MI 48128

LEVAY, PATRICIA MINTZ, school administrator; b. N.Y.C., Sept. 1, 1934; d. Emil and Bertha (Armel) Pomboy; m. Edward Allen LeVay, Jr.; 1 child by previous marriage, Peter Graham Mintz. AB in History with honors, Columbia U., 1956, AM in English, 1967, EdD in Curriculum and Supervision, 1980. Cert. tchr. English, adminstr. and supr., N.Y. Tchr. English and history Fieldston Sch., N.Y.C., 1960-67; dir. Upward Bound English program Fieldston Sch., 1967; chmn. dept. English Bryan Hills Sch., Armonk, N.Y., 1967-72; dist. supr. English North Shore Schs., Glen Head, N.Y., 1972—; instr. English Columbia U., N.Y.C., 1966; program chair N.Y. State English Coun. Conf., 1993, L.I. Writing Conf., 1984-90. Editor: America, the Melting Pot, 1969; author: Film Guide for Educational Films, 1972-73. N.Y. Found. Arts grantee, 1988, Title III Matching grante Writing Program for North Shore Sch., 1977-78. Mem. ASCD, Nat. Coun. Tchrs. English (presenter ann. conf. 1994), N.Y. State English Coun., L.I. Lang. Arts Coun., Coun. of Supers. and Adminstrs.

LEVE, SHIRLEY BOOK, jewelry designer; b. N.Y.C., July 21, 1917; d. Isidor and Malvina (Karp) Book; m. Samuel Leve, Sept. 26; 1 child, Teri. BA, Bklyn. Coll., 1938; postgrad., Hunter Coll., Columbia U., NYU, Syracuse U., U. Colo., 1961, U. R.I., 1962-63. Cert. secondary art tchr. Advt. artist Ben Lewis Studio, N.Y.C., 1939-41; asst. art dir. Art News, Art Tech. mags., N.Y.C., 1942-44; prodn. mgr. Mademoiselle mag., N.Y.C., 1945; TV and theatre advertiser N.Y.C., 1945-56; art tchr. James Kieran Jr. H.S., N.Y.C., 1961, Inwood Jr. H.S., N.Y.C., 1964; art tchr. George Washington H.S., N.Y.C., 1965, acting chmn. art dept., 1980-83; ret., 1983; case worker in art therapy New Sch. Social Rsch., N.Y.C., 1965-70. Jewelry designer, 1985—. Mem. N.Y.C. Art Tchrs. Assn., Coun. of Suprs. and Adminstrs.

LEVELT SENGERS, JOHANNA MARIA HENRICA, research physicist; b. Amsterdam, The Netherlands, Mar. 4, 1929; came to U.S., 1963; d. Wilhelmus Henricus and Maria Antonia Josephine (Berger) Levelt; m. Jan V. Sengers, Feb. 21, 1963; children: Rachel Teresa, Adriaan Jan, Maarten Willem, Phoebe Josephine. BS, Municipal U., Amsterdam, 1950, MS, 1954, PhD in Physics, 1958; hon. doctorate, Delft U. Tech., 1992. Rsch. asst. Municipal U., Amsterdam, 1954-63; postdoctoral assoc. U. Wis., Madison, 1958-59; rsch. physicist Nat. Bur. Standards, Gaithersburg, Md., 1963-95, group leader, 1978-88, scientist emeritus, 1995—; vis. prof. U. Louvain, Belgium, 1971; vis. scientist Mcpl. U., Amsterdam, 1974-75; Regents prof. UCLA, 1982; sr. fellow Nat. Inst. Standards and Tech., Gaithersburg, 1983-95, scientist emeritus, 1995—. Contbr. 12 chpts. to books and over 100 articles to profl. jours. Recipient DOC silver medal, 1972, DOC gold medal, 1978, WISE award U.S. Interagy. Com., Women in Sci. and Engring., Washington, 1985, A.V. Humboldt Rsch. award Ruhr-U., Bochum, Germany, 1991. Fellow Am. Phys. Soc.; mem. ASME (nat. del. rsch. com. water and steam 1988—), AIChE, AAAS, NAE, NAS, Royal Netherlands Acad. Scis., Internat. Assn. Properties Water and Steam (v.p. 1988-90, pres. 1990-91, hon. fellow 1994), European Phys. Soc., Am. Chem. Soc. (divsn. phys. chemistry), Sigma Xi. Democrat. Home: 110 N Van Buren St Rockville MD 20850-1861 Office: Nat Inst Standards & Tech Gaithersburg MD 20899

LEVENDOSKY, CHARLOTTE ANNE, elementary educator; b. N.Y.C., Dec. 8, 1934; d. George Christopher and Emelie Nicolene (Schultz) Jaeger; m. Charles Leonard Levendosky, Aug. 15, 1961; children: Alytia Akiko, Ixchel Nicole. BA, Mt. Holyoke Coll., 1956; MA in Edn., NYU, 1957. Tchr. George M. Davis Elem. Sch., New Rochelle, N.Y., 1957-59; tchr. Greenacres Elem. Sch., Scarsdale, N.Y., 1959-61, tchr., libr., 1962-63; tchr. Aberdeen (Md.) Elem. Sch., 1961-62, Christiansted (V.I.) Elem. Sch., 1963-65; adminstrv. dir. Greenwich Village Montessori Sch., N.Y.C., 1971-72; tchr. Crest Hill Elem. Sch., Casper, Wyo., 1973—; cons. Tchr. Ctr., Cheyenne, Wyo., Am. Enterprise Inst. Conf., Washington, 1985; dir. Nat. History Day, Casper, 1985-86; co-creator program for gifted edn. Escalate, 1975. Dir. childrens conf. Wyo. Assn. for Gifted Edn., Casper, 1982; bd. dirs. Wyo. State Bd. Edn., 1987-93. Named Tchr. of Yr., Wyo. State Dept. Edn., 1984, Outstanding Tchr., Casper Coll., 1984. Mem. NEA, Wyo. Edn. Assn. (commr. instruction and profl. devel. 1982-83), Wyo. Tchrs. Math., Wyo. Tchrs. Soo St., Natrona County Edn. Assn. (sch. rep.), Casper REading Coun. (sch. rep. 1994-95), Murie Audubon Soc. (bd. dirs. 1995—). Democrat. Lutheran. Home: 3120 S Poplar St Casper WY 82601

LEVENSON, MARIA NIJOLE, retired medical technologist; b. Kaunas, Lithuania, Mar. 24, 1940; came to U.S., 1948; d. Zigmas and Monika (Galbuogis) Sabataitis; m. Coleman Levenson, Nov. 21, 1975. BA, Annhurst Coll., 1962. Sr. rsch. technician Case Western Res. U., Cleve., 1962-69; phys. sci. technician Nat. Oceanographic Data Ctr., Washington, 1969-70; biologist NIH, Bethesda, Md., 1970-76; nuclear medicine technologist VA Med. Ctr., New Orleans, 1977-79; paramed. examiner Hooper Industries, New Orleans, 1980-82; assoc. chemist Computer Scis. Corp., Stennis Space Ctr., Miss., 1982-83; med. technologist VA Med. Ctr., New Orleans, 1984-96; sec. Lithuanian Cath. Youth Assn., Putnam, Conn., 1960-62, Lithuanian Club, Annhurst Coll., South Woodstock, Conn., 1960-62. Participant Freedom Movement for Baltic Independence, Slidell, La., 1990-91; counselor Life with Cancer, Slidell, 1989—. La. State Nursing Sch. scholar, 1989. Mem. Daus. of Lithuania, Internat. Platform Assn. Home: PO Box 593 Dauphin Island AL 36528-5130

LEVENTHAL, RUTH, academic administrator, dean emeritus, educator; b. Phila., May 23, 1940; d. Harry Louis Mongin and Bertha (Rosenberg) Mongin Blai; children: Sheryl Anne, David Alan. BS, U. Pa., 1961, PhD, 1973, MBA, 1981; HHD (hon.), Thomas Jefferson U., 1995. Cert. med. technologist, clin. lab. scientist. Trainee NSF, 1971, USPHS, 1969-70, 73; asst. prof. med. tech. U. Pa., Phila., 1974-77; acting dean U. Pa., 1977-81; dean Hunter Coll., N.Y.C., 1981-84; provost, dean, prof. biology Capital Coll. Pa. State U., Middletown, 1984-95; prof. biology Pa. State Hershey Med. Ctr., 1996—; site visitor Middle State Assn. Colls. and Secondary Schs., Phila., 1983—. Author: (with Cheadle) Medical Parasitology: A Self Instructional Text, 1979, 2d edit., 1985, 3rd edit., 1991, 4th edit., 1995; contbr. chpt. to book and articles to profl. jours. Chmn. pub. service div. Tri-County United Way, South Central Pa., 1985; mem. health found. bd. Harrisburg Hosp., Pa., 1984-92; bd. dirs. Tri-County Planned Parenthood, 1984-87 , Harrisburg Acad., Wormleysburg, Pa., 1984-88, Metro Arts of Harrisburg, 1984-87, Pa. Power and Light, Inc., 1988—, Mellon Bank Commonwealth Region, 1990—; founding chair Coun. Pub. Edn., 1984—. Recipient Alice Paul award Women's Faculty Club, U. Pa., 1981; Recognition award NE Deans of Schs. of Allied Health, 1984, Athena award Capital Region C. of C., 1992, John Baum Humanitarian award Am. Cancer Soc., 1992; named Disting. Dau. Pa. by Gov. Thomas Ridge, 1995. Mem. Am. Soc. Parasitologists, AAUW (bd. dirs. Pa. br. 1985—), Sigma Xi. Office: Pa State U Milton S Hershey Med Ctr 500 University Dr PO Box 850 Hershey PA 17033

LEVERENZ, JUDITH ROBERTA, accountant; b. Lackawanna, N.Y., Oct. 25, 1942; d. Irwin Henry and Lillian (Hall) Wesp; m. Carl Leo Leverenz, Feb. 10, 1962; children: Mark Carl, Karen Lynne Hahn. Student, U. Fla., 1960-61. FC bookkeeper Leverenz-Eblen Ace Hardware, Lake Worth, Fla., 1977-84, Spectrum Interior Design, West Palm Beach, Fla., 1984-85, N.Am. Comms. Sys., Palm Beach, Fla., 1985-86, Rosner's, Inc., West Palm Beach, 1986-87; acct. Profl. Group Svcs., Inc., Boynton Beach, Fla., 1987-94, Michael S. Kokol, CPA, Boca Raton, Fla., 1994—, Lewis Longman & Walker, West Palm Beach, FL, 1996—. Treas. Profits. for Children's Charities, Boca Raton, 1995; bd. dirs. Palm Beach County Women's Coalition, West Palm Beach, 1995; fundraiser Am. Cancer Soc., Boca Raton, 1995; mem. Evening Herb Soc., West Palm Beach, 1995. Mem. Am. Soc. Women Accts. (pres. 1995-1996), Am. Bus. Women's Assn. (program chmn. 1994-95), Women's Exec. Club, Wings of the Palm Beaches (NAFE). Democrat. Lutheran. Home: 305 Riverdale Rd Lake Worth FL 33461-2411 Office: Lewis Longman & Walker Ste 900 2000 Park Beach Lake Blvd West Palm Beach FL 33409

LEVI, BARBARA GOSS, physicist, editor; b. Washington, May 5, 1943; d. Wilbur H. and Mildred C. (Wallin) Goss; m. Ilan M. Levi, Sept. 10, 1966; children: Daniel S., Sharon R. BA, Carleton Coll., 1965; MS, Stanford U., 1967, PhD, 1971. Assoc. editor Physics Today Am. Inst. Physics, N.Y.C., 1969-70, cons. editor Physics Today, 1970-89, assoc. editor Physics Today, 1987-88; sr. assoc. editor Physics Today, N.Y.C., 1989-93, sr. editor, 1993—; mem. tech. staff Bell Labs, Holmdel, N.J., 1982-83; mem. rsch. staff Ctr. for Energy and Environ. Studies Princeton U., 1981-82, 83-87; lectr. Ga. Tech., Atlanta, 1976-80, Fairleigh Dickinson U., Madison, N.J., 1970-75; vis. prof. Rutgers U., Piscataway, N.J., 1988-89; cons. U.S. Office Tech. Assessment, Washington, 1976-93. Editor: (with others) Energy Sources: Conservation and Renewables, 1985, The Future of Land-Based Strategie Missiles, 1989, Global Warming: Physics and Facts, 1992. Treas. LWV, Holmdel and Colts Neck, N.J., 1983-94. Fellow AAAS, Am. Phys.Soc. (edn. com. 1989-91, chmn. forum on physics and soc. 1988-89, forum councilor, 1992-95, mem. exec. bd. 1994-95, Lilienfeld prize com. 1993-95, chair 1995, com. on coms. 1994-96, chair 1996); mem. AAUW (nuclear energy task force 1975-77), Fedn. Am. Scientists (gov. bd. 1985-89), Am. Assn. Physics Tchrs.

LEVI, VICKI GOLD, magazine editor, historical consultant, actress; b. Atlantic City, Sept. 16, 1941; d. Albert and Beverly Valentine Gold; m. Alexander Hecht Levi, May 31, 1970; 1 child, Adam Hecht Levi. Student, Montclair State Coll., 1959-60, New Sch. Social Rsch., N.Y.C., 1970-73, Sch. Visual Arts, N.Y.C., 1972, Lee Strass Berg Sch. Acting, N.Y.C., 1961. Actress Atlantic City, N.Y.C and L.A., 1945—; asst. to pres. Family Fare, Inc., N.Y.C., 1966; advt. rep. Cosmopolitan Mag., N.Y.C., 1967; publicity dir. Misty Harbor, Ltd., N.Y.C., 1968; freelance picture researcher, 1972—; contbg. picture editor Esquire Mag., N.Y.C., 1980—, Mirabella Mag., N.Y.C., 1991—, Atlantic City Mag., 1988—, New Woman Mag., 1995—; story cons. Alvin Cooperman Prodns., N.Y.C., 1985—; hist. cons. various Atlantic City, N.Y.C., 1994—; lectr. on Atlantic City, 1979—; guest exhibitor Internat. Ctr. Photography, N.Y.C., 1979; guest exhibitor and lectr. Cooper Hewitt, N.Y.C., 1980; guest curator Songwriters Hall of Fame, N.Y.C., 1979; guest lectr. Mcpl. Art Soc., N.Y.C., 1979; co-founder Atlantic City Hist. Mus., 1985—, bd. dirs., exhibit dir., 1995—; hist. cons. Toast to Times Square Com., N.Y.C., 1988—; curator Atlantic City Playground of the Nation, Atlantic City Hist. Mus., 1994; co-curator Charles K. Doble's Atlantic City, 1994, Images of African Americans in Atlantic City, 1995, Severty-Five Years of Miss America in Pictures, 1995, The Al Gold Years, 1996, Atlantic City Hist. Mus., 1996; bd. dirs. Hecht-Levi Found. Co-author: Atlantic City: 125 Years of Ocean Madness, 1979, rev. edit., 1994, Live and Be Well: A Celebration of Yiddish Culture in America, 1982, You Must Have Been a Beautiful Baby, 1992; columnist Phila. Bull., The Way It Was, 1980; prodr., dir. (hist. video) Boardwalk Ballyhoo, 1992 (Am. Assn. State and Local History award 1995, Atlantic City Tourism Coun. Resolution award 1995, Tourism Advocacy award Greater Atlantic City Region Tourism Coun. 1996); rschr.: Miss America, The Dream Lives On, 1995; hist. cons. (prodn.) Atlantic City Experience, 1995, (Broadway prodn.) Having Our Say, 1995; hist. image cons. (PBS prodn.) I Hear America Singing, 1996; hist. rschr. (Disney World prodn.) BoardWalk, 1996. Reviewer of grants, Nat. Endowment for Humanities, Washington. Recipient Author's Citation, N.J. Inst. Tech., Div. Continuing Edn., 1980, Senate Resolution, N.J. State Senate, 1979, Outstanding Achievement award, Atlantic City Women's C. of C., 1981, Proclamation from mayor of Atlantic City, 1981, Key Club award Atlantic City, 1995; named An Atlantic City Treasure, Atlantic City Women's C. of C., 1989. Mem. Nat. Acad. TV Arts and Scis. (Emmy judge 1987—, spl. events com. 1989-90), Screen Actors Guild, Am. Fedn. TV and Radio Artists, Am. Soc. Picture Profls. (bd. dirs. 1984), Ziegfeld Club. Democrat. Jewish. Home and Office: 211 Central Park W New York NY 10024-6020

LEVIN, BETSY, lawyer, educator, university dean; b. Balt., Dec. 25, 1935; d. M. Jastrow and Alexandra (Lee) L. AB, Bryn Mawr (Pa.) Coll., 1956; LLB, Yale U., 1966. Bar: D.C. 1967, Colo. 1982. Research geologist U.S. Geol. Survey, Washington, 1956-63; law clk. to judge U.S. Ct. Appeals (4th cir.), Balt., 1966-67; spl. asst. to U.S. Amb. to UN, Arthur J. Goldberg N.Y.C., 1967-68; dir. edn. studies Urban Inst., Washington, 1968-73; prof. law Duke U., Durham, N.C., 1973-80; gen. counsel U.S. Dept. Edn., Washington, 1980-81; dean, prof. law U. Colo., Boulder, 1981-87; exec. v.p. Assn. Am. Law Schs., Washington, 1987-92; Arch T. Allen vis. disting. prof. law U. N.C. Sch. Law, Chapel Hill, 1993; vis. prof. law Am. U. Washington Coll. Law, 1994, Georgetown U. Law Ctr., Washington, 1994; disting. vis. prof. sch. law U. Balt., 1995-96; vis. prof. law Howard U. Sch. Law, Washington, 1996—; mem. Nat. Coun. Ednl. Rsch., 1978-79; mem. civil rights reviewing authority HEW, 1979-80. Co-author: Educational Policy and the Law, 2d edit., 1982, 3d edit., 1991; editor: Future Directions for School Finance Reform, 1975; co-editor: The Courts, Social Science and School Desegregation, 1977, School Desegregation: Lessons of the First 25 Years, 1979. Bd. dirs. Nat. Inst. for Dispute Resolution. White House fellow, 1967-68. Fellow Am. Bar Found.; mem. ABA, Nat. Assn. Women Judges (program com. 1985-92), Am. Law Inst. (coun.), Order of Coif. Office: Howard U Sch Law 2900 Van Ness St NW Washington DC 20008

LEVIN, CAROL ARLENE, educator; b. L.A., Apr. 4, 1945; d. Harold Allen and Sally (Salter) L. AA, Santa Monica Coll., 1965; BA, UCLA, 1967; MS, Pepperdine U., 1990. Cert. tchr., 1969, bilingual tchr., 1977. Tchr. L.A. Unified Sch. Dist., 1969-89; master tchr. UCLA, 1985-89; tchr., adviser bilingual editor newspaper D.A.R.E. to Read, 1989-94; adviser drug, alcohol and tobacco edn., 1994—; pres., v.p. Calif. Assn. Childhood Edn., Los Angeles, 1977-81; chmn. workshop Calif. State Assn. for Childhood Edn. Internat. Conf., Universal City, 1979; invited observer Assn. for Childhood Edn. Internat. White House Conf.-Families, Los Angeles, 1980; tchr., adviser elem. news Sta. KTTV, Los Angeles, 1980-82. Editor: (with others) Our Los Angeles, 1976; contbr. articles to profl. jours. Treas. Dickens Towers Homeowners Assn., Sherman Oaks, Calif., 1978-80; sec. Sherman Villas Homeowners Assn., Sherman Oaks, 1981-83; mem. Sherman Oaks Homeowners Assn., 1986—, Palm Springs (Calif.) Tennis Club Owners Assn., 1981—; mem. Los Angeles Music Ctr. Theatre Group Vols., 1987—. Recipient P.I.E. award Los Angeles Schs., 1978, 79, 80, 81. Mem. NEA, Calif. Tchrs. Assn., Women in Ednl. Leadership, Delta Kappa Gamma (sec. Epsilon chpt.), Unihi Edn. Found. (bd. dirs., sec.). Office: LA Unified Sch Dist Office Instrn 2151 N Soto St Los Angeles CA 90032-3629

LEVIN, CHERYL JOY, lawyer; b. Phila., Apr. 5, 1956; d. Norman Leonard and Audrey Herberta (Herman) L. BA, Brandeis U., 1978; JD, Nova U., 1981. Bar: Fla. 1982, U.S. Dist. Ct. (so. dist.) Fla. 1983, Trial Bar, U.S. Dist. Ct. (so. dist.) Fla. 1985. Assoc. Donald J. Vestal, P.A., Hollywood, Fla., 1983-85, Bacen & Kaplan, P.A., Ft. Lauderdale, Fla., 1985-87, Siegfried, Kipnis, Rivera et al, Coral Gables, Fla., 1987-90, Garfield & Assocs., P.A., Lauderdale Lakes, Fla., 1990-92; ptnr. Garfield & Levin, P.A., Lauderdale Lakes, 1992-94; pres., ptnr. Cheryl J. Levin, P.A., Sunrise, Fla., 1994—; adj. lectr. Fla. Internat. U., Miami, 1990-92. Contbr. chpts. to books. Vol. Habitat for Humanity, Pompano Beach, Fla., 1995. Winner Let Freedom Ring Photography Contest, 1991. Democrat. Jewish. Office: Courtyard Bus Ctr 10226 NW 47th St Sunrise FL 33351

LEVIN, DEBBE ANN, lawyer; b. Cin., Mar. 11, 1954; d. Abram Asher and Selma Ruth (Herlands) L. BA, Washington U., St. Louis, 1976; JD, U. Cin., 1979; LLM, NYU, 1983. Bar: Ohio 1979. Staff atty. U.S. Ct. Appeals (6th cir.), Cin., 1979-82; shareholder Schwartz, Manes & Ruby, Cin., 1983—; lectr. tax conf. U. Cin., 1984-86, adj. prof. coll. of bus., 1987-89. Editor: U. Cin. Law Rev., 1972-79. Mem. ABA, Ohio Bar Assn., Cin. Bar Assn., Women Entrepreneurs, Inc., Order of Coif. Jewish. Office: Schwartz Manes & Ruby 2900 Carew Tower Cincinnati OH 45202

LEVIN, HELEN WEINBLATT, visual artist, educator; b. N.Y.C., Feb. 7, 1940; d. Isadore and Yetta Weinblatt; m. Shane Levin, Sept. 15, 1968 (div. Mar. 1989); 1 child, Golan. BFA, CUNY, N.Y.C., 1962; MFA, Columbia U., 1963. Tchr. adult studio art N.Y.C. Bd. Edn., 1980-86, tchr. homebound children, 1988—; tchr. adult edn. lang. arts N.Y.C. Bd. Edn., 1984-86, developer, demonstrator art pilot project, 1985-86; field rep. N.Y. State Coun. on Arts, N.Y.C., 1981-83; art cons., 1988—; resident Artpark Kidspace, Lewiston, N.Y., 1983, Palenville (N.Y.) Interarts Colony, 1991, 92. Author: Brainstorms, 1978; art reviewer Staten Island Register, 1978-79; one-woman shows include Edn. Testing Svc., Princeton, N.J., 1984, N.Y. Open Ctr., N.Y.C., 1986, Staten Island Cmtyl TV Gallery, 1993, Wagner Coll. Gallery, Staten Island, 1994; exhibited in group shows at Cork Gallery Lincoln Ctr., N.Y.C., 1984, 90, 91, 94, Janco Dada Mus., Ein Hod, Israel, 1985, Ammo Gallery, Bklyn., 1986, Phoenix Gallery, N.Y.C., 1988, Provident Nat. Bank, Phila., 1988, Macy Gallery Tchrs. Coll., Columbia Univ., 1989, 91, Broome St. Gallery, N.Y.C., 1991, Rosenthal Libr., Queens Coll. Art Ctr., 1991, 92, 26 Fed. Plaza, 1992, Art Lab, Snug Harbor, Staten Island, 1992, Bank St. Coll., 1993, Westbeth (N.Y.) Gallery, 1994, Schering-Plough Corp., Madison, N.J., 1995; represented in permanent collection Mus. of City of N.Y.; subject of numerous magazine and newspaper articles; contbr. articles to profl. publs. Columbia U. scholar, 1963; exhibition grantee Artists' Space, N.Y.C., 1980, Greater N.Y. Arts Devel. Fund, 1993, 94. Mem. Women in Arts, Univ. Coun. Art Edn., Women's Caucus for Art, N.Y.C. Art Tchrs. Assn. (Art Advocacy award 1994), N.Y. State Art Tchrs. Assn., United Fedn. Tchrs.

LEVIN, JANA RUTH, veterinary dentist; b. Phila., May 14, 1957; d. Daniel Leonard and Gloria Burness (Tomita) L.; 1 child, Robert Daniel. BS, U. Calif., Davis, 1991, DVM, 1993. Resident in vet. dentistry Am. Vet. Dental Coll., Denver, 1993-96; pres. Mew Chews Inc., Denver, 1996—; v.p. Pachay Labs., Inc., Denver, 1995—; faculty affiliate Colo. State U., Ft. Collins, 1995—; cons. VRX Labs., Harbor City, Calif., 1995—, ASI Med., Denver, 1995—. Mem. People for Ethical Treatment of Animals, Am. Vet. Dental Soc., Assn. Vets. for Animal Rights, Physicians Com. for Responsible Medicine, Animal Def. League.

LEVIN, LINDA ROSE, mental health counselor; b. Des Moines, June 29, 1951; d. Morris Sam and Betty Francis (Burns) Nemirovski; m. Michael Arthur Levin, Feb. 25, 1971; children: David Bradley, Shane Michael. Student, Grandview Jr. Coll., 1969-70; BS in Psychology, Ottawa Univ., 1992, MA in Counseling, 1994. Cert. hypnotherapist, advanced hypnotherapist. Asst. dir. trade practice Better Bus. Bur., Phoenix, 1980-83; program coord. Carnation Health and Nutrition Ctr., Phoenix, 1983-85; v.p. AAA Telephone Answering Svc., Phoenix, 1985-90; past state of Ariz. rep. Toughlove, Phoenix, 1988-90; counselor level II, resident advisor Wayland Family Ctrs., Phoenix, 1990-91; case mgr. for the seriously mentally ill Community Care Network, Phoenix, 1991-92; pvt. practice in hypnotherapy Counseling Ctr. for Personal Growth, Phoenix, 1992—. Vol. arbitrator Better Bus. Bur., 1983—. Mem. Am. Arbitration Assn. Democrat. Jewish. Office: Counseling Ctr for Personal Growth 13231 N 35th Ave A-10 Phoenix AZ 85029-1233

LEVIN, MARLENE, human resources executive, educator; b. Detroit, Oct. 7, 1934; d. Louis and Cele (Drapkin) Bertman; m. Jerome J. Goodman, Apr. 4, 1954 (dec. Mar. 1962); children: Bennett J., Marc R.; m. Herbert R. Levin, June 7, 1967. Student U. Miami, 1952-53; BA, Coll. of New Rochelle, 1975; MPA, NYU, 1978. Cert. human resource mgr. Asst. administr. Richmond Children Ctr., Yonkers, N.Y., 1973-74; research assoc. Westchester Country Dept. Mental Health, N.Y., 1975-80, clinic administr., 1980-82; founder, pres. The Phoenix Group, Armonk, N.Y., 1982-88; v.p. human resources and adminstrn. Ensign Bank, N.Y.C., 1988-92; adj. prof. Iona Coll., New Rochelle, N.Y., 1978-88; cons. Social Area Research, Scarsdale, N.Y., 1983-84; lectr./trainer Volvo of Am., Inc., Rockleigh, N.J., 1983-84, Lederle Labs., Spring Valley, N.Y., 1984-88. Contbr. articles on sociol. subjects to profl. jours. Mem. Mental Health Council, Mount Kisco, N.Y., 1981-83, Council for Youth, Armonk, 1984-92; mem. legis. adv. com. N.Y. State 37th Dist., 1991. Mem. Nat. Staff Devel. Council, NOW (v.p. White Plains 1978-80). Democrat. Jewish. Avocation: stamp collecting. Home: 2576 NW 63rd St Boca Raton FL 33496-2029

LEVIN, NANETTE JANEL, marketing consultant; b. Washington, Apr. 12, 1964; d. Michael Richard and Nancy Rita (King) L.; m. Richard Robert Dimperio, Sept. 4, 1993. BA in English and Polit. Sci., U. Rochester, 1986. Writer Southside Cmty. News, Rochester, N.Y., 1985-86, Farmington Valley Herald, Simsbury, Conn., 1987-88; editl. asst. Democrat & Chronicle, Rochester, 1988-90; assoc. Wanda Miller & Assocs., Rochester, 1988-89; pub. affairs dir. Sta. WZSH, Rochester, 1990-92, Sta. WMAX, Rochester, 1992-95; owner Fulcrum Comm., Rochester, 1990—; mktg. dir. Internat. Resource Group, 1994—; bd. dirs., treas. Lake Ont. Sport Fishing Promotions Coun., N.Y., 1994-96; bd. dirs. Rochester Profl. Cons. Network, Rochester, East House, Rochester. Contbr. articles to profl. jours. del. White House Conf. Small Bus., Washington, 1995; mem. com. Yates County Chamber, Penn Yan, N.Y., 1994—; presenter Small Bus. Adminstrn., Rochester, 1995-96. Mem. Nat. Assn. Women Bus. Owners. Republican. Office: Fulcrum Comm 996 State Rt 247 Rushville NY 14544

LEVIN, SHERI BETH, nurse; b. Queens, N.Y., Jan. 15, 1961; d. Stanley and Yvonne Rochelle (Collier) Reichler; m. Marc Louis Levin, May 25, 1988; children Jared, Andrew. BS in Nursing, U. Bridgeport, 1984. RN, Pa. Registered nurse Mt. Sinai Hosp., N.Y.C., 1984-88, Hosp. Univ. Pa., Phila., 1988—. Mem. Assn. Oper. Rm. Nurses, Am. Soc. Plastic and Reconstructive Nurses (program coord. local chpt.). Republican. Jewish. Office: Hosp Univ Pa 4th Fl 3400 Spruce St Philadelphia PA 19104

LEVIN, SUSAN BASS, lawyer; b. Wilmington, Del., July 18, 1952; d. Max S. and Harriet C. (Rubin) Bass; children: Lisa, Amy. BA, U. of Rochester, 1972; JD, George Washington U., 1975. Bar: D.C. 1975, U.S. Ct. Claims 1975, N.J. 1976, Pa. 1981, U.S. Ct. Appeals (3d cir.) 1983, U.S. Supreme Ct. 1984. Law clk. to assoc. justice U.S. Ct. Claims, Washington, 1975-76; assoc. Covington & Burling, Washington, 1976-79; pvt. practice Cherry Hill, N.J., 1979-87; counsel Ballard, Spahr, Andrews & Ingersoll, Phila., Camden (N.J.), 1993—. Pres. Cherry Hill (N.J.) Twp. Council, 1986-88; mayor City of Cherry Hill, 1988—; trustee N.J. Coalition of Small Bus. Orgns., 1985-87; del. Dem. Presdl. Conv., 1992, 96; nat. fin. bd. Dem. Nat. Conv., also exec. bd. women's leadership forum; chair Pam's List; trustee N.J. Alliance for Action, South Jersey Devel. Coun. Recipient Woman of Achievement award Camden County Girl Scouts, 1986. Mem. Tri County Women Lawyers (pres. 1984-85), N.J. Assn. Women Bus. Owners (state pres. 1984-85 named Woman of Yr. 1985), Phi Beta Kappa, Order of Coif. Office: Ballard Spahr Andrews & Ingersoll 1735 Market St Philadelphia PA 19103-7501

LEVINE, ELLEN R., magazine editor; b. N.Y.C., Feb. 19, 1943; d. Eugene Jack and Jean (Zuckman) Jacobson; m. Richard U. Levine, Dec. 21, 1964; children: Daniel, Peter. Student, Wellesley Coll. Reporter The Record, Hackensack, N.J., 1964-70; editor Cosmopolitan mag., N.Y.C., 1976-82; editor in chief Cosmopolitan Living mag., N.Y.C., 1980-81, Woman's Day mag., N.Y.C., 1982-91, Redbook mag., N.Y.C., 1991-94, Good Housekeeping, N.Y.C., 1994—; dir. N.J. Bell, Newark; commr. U.S. Atty. Gen.'s Commn. on Pornography, 1985-86. Author: Planning Your Wedding, Waiting for Baby, Rooms That Grow With Your Child. Mem. exec. com. Senator Bill Bradley, 1984—. Named to Writers Hall of Fame, 1981, Acad. Women Achievers, YWCA, 1982; recipient Outstanding Profl. Achievement award N.J. coun. Girl Scouts U.S., 1984, Woman of Achievement award N.J. Fedn. Women's Clubs, 1984, Matrix award N.Y. Women in Communications, Inc., 1989, honor award Birmigham So. Coll., 1991. Office: Good Housekeeping 959 8th Ave New York NY 10019-3767*

LEVINE, FRANCINE ADLER, early childhood education educator, bookseller; b. Detroit, Jan. 28, 1954. BS, Wayne State U., 1976; MA in Tchg., Oakland U., 1982. Tchr.'s asst. Children's Orthogenic Ctr., Detroit, 1977-78; head tchr. United Children and Families Head Start, Detroit, 1978-80; edn. coord. Franklin-Wright Settlements Parent Child Ctr., Detroit, 1980—; bookseller The Olive Press, West Bloomfield, Mich., 1986—. Author: Beyond Bows and Arrows, 1988, Cultural Routes, 1993; contbg. author: Global Journeys, 1996. Mem. Nat. Assn. for Edn. of Young Children, Assn. Child Edn. Inc., Metro-Detroit Assn. Edn. of Young Children (sec. 1984-92). Home: 5727 Dunmore Dr West Bloomfield MI 48322-1613 Office: FWS Parent Child Ctr 5245 Concord Detroit MI 48211

LEVINE, JANIS E., financial analyst; b. Akron, Ohio, Apr. 7, 1953; d. Paul and Sarah (Levin) L.; student U. Cin., 1971-73; B.S. in Acctg., U. Akron, 1975; M.B.A., Xavier U., 1978. Acctg. intern Price Waterhouse & Co., Cleve., 1974-75; systems acct. Mead Corp., Cin., 1975-77; internal auditor, sr. capital expenditures analyst Champion Internat. Corp., Stamford, Conn., 1977—. Vol., Headstart and ARC; adv. Jr. Achievement; active Nat. Young Leadership Conf. Wash., 1994, 96. Recipient Young Citizens Achievement award for Headstart, 1969. Mem. AAUW, NAFE, Jewish Fedn. Stamford (cmty. rels. com., leadership devel. divsn., programs com., events com., Israel com., Washington conf. com.), Bus. and Profl. Women, Young Leadership Coun., Stamford Forum for World Affairs, Assn. MBA Execs., Inst. Mgmt. Accts. (community programs dir.), Am. Jewish Congress, B'nai B'rith Women, Beta Alpha Psi (sec.). Office: Champion Internat Corp 1 Champion Plz Stamford CT 06921-0001

LEVINE, KATHY, artist, educator; b. N.Y.C., Apr. 16, 1958; d. Irving Levine and Dorothy Rothbard. BA, Potsdam Coll. SUNY, 1980; MFA, Pratt Inst., 1983. Drawing instr. Pratt Inst., Bklyn., 1983-89; photography instr. The Photography Ctr., N.Y.C., 1986-91; workshop instr. The New Sch., N.Y.C., 1990-95; seminar instr. Fashion Inst. Tech., N.Y.C., 1991-94; drawing and photography instr. Suffolk C.C., Brentwood, N.Y., 1992—; adj. prof. photography Nassau C.C., Garden City, N.Y., 1990-91; adj. asst. prof.visual arts Dowling Coll., Oakdale, N.Y., 1991—, darkroom supr., 1993—; artist in residence Yellowstone Nat. Park, Madison Junction, Wyo., 1993, Millay Colony Arts, Austerlitz, N.Y., 1995. One or two-person exhibitions include Pratt Inst., Brooklyn, N.Y., 1983, The Photography Ctr., N.Y.C., 1987, Esta Robinson Contemporary Art Gallery, N.Y.C., 1988, St. Joseph's Coll., Patchogue, N.Y., 1991, Madison Art Mus., Yellowstone Nat. Park, Wyo., 1993, Open Studio Show, N.Y.C., 1995; group exhibitions include Richard F. Brush Gallery, Canton, N.Y., 1980, Bush Terminal Loft, Brooklyn, 1985, Seneres on Sixth, N.Y.C., 1987, N.J. Ctr. Visual Arts, Summit, 1988, Soho Ctr. Visual Artists, N.Y.C., 1989, Kurtz Cultural Ctr., Winchester, Va., 1992, Tribeca 148 Gallery, N.Y.C., 1992, 94, Multi-Media Arts Gallery, N.Y.C., 1993, It's A Mod World, N.Y.C., 1994-95, The Anthony Giordano Gallery, Oakdale, N.Y., 1994, 96, The N.Y. Law Sch., N.Y.C., 1995; corporate exhibitions at Fed. Plz., N.Y.C., 1986, Ibex Internat., Washington, 1987, The Steelcase Design Partnership, N.Y.C., 1989, Fed. Bldg. at 209 Varick St., N.Y.C., 1990, Pan Am Bldg., N.Y.C., 1991; commns. include Fed. Res. Bank, East Rutherford, N.J., 1992, Paradigm Power, Inc., Wall, N.J., 1994. Mem. Brooklyn Loft Tenants, 1985, Parkslope Artists' Coun., Brooklyn, 1984-87, Brooklyn Art and Cultural Assn., 1993-95. Intern Corcoran Gallery, Washington, 1980; fellow Pratt Inst., 1983; recipient Women's Caucus for Art honorarium, 1987. Mem. Coll. Arts Assn., The Alternative Mus., Art Initiatives. Studio: 425 W 13th St 4th Flr New York NY 10014

LEVINE, LEDA DALE, secondary school educator; b. Elizabeth, N.J.; d. Bernard Joseph and Mildred Beverly (Samuel) Sipress; divorced; 1 child, Ronald Joseph. BS, Northeastern U., Boston, 1970. Tchr. Holbrook (Mass.) Pub. Schs., 1970-81, coach field hockey, basketball, softball, 1974-81; coach field hockey Mansfield (Mass.) Pub. Schs., 1981—, tchr., 1986—. Named Coach of the Yr., Boston Globe, 1993; recipient New Agenda: Northeast. Mem. Mass. South Sect. Field Hockey Assn. (pres. 1989—), Mass. State Field Hockey Coaches Assn. (pres. 1993—). Jewish. Home: 106 Armiston St Brockton MA 02402-1900 Office: Mansfield HS 250 East St Mansfield MA 02048

LEVINE, LINDA ELAINE, elementary school principal; b. N.Y.C., June 18, 1942; d. Harold I. and Betty (Horowitz) Pearlman; m. David Barry Levine, June 2, 1962; children: Seth, Michele. BS, Bklyn. Coll., 1963; MA, CUNY, Bronx, 1973. Cert. in spl. edn., sch. adminstrn., reading, N.Y. Grade 3-4 tchr. P.S. 94, Bronx, 1963-65; reading specialist Anne M. Dorner Mid. Sch., Ossining, N.Y., 1971-73; reading specialist—LD/TC East Hanover (N.J.) Mid. Sch., 1973-79; dir. spl. svcs. Mountainside (N.J.) Sch. Dist., 1979-83; child study supr. N.J. Dept. Edn., Union County, 1983-91; dir. spl. svcs. Clifton (N.J.) Bd. Edn., 1991, Midland Park (N.J.) Sch. Dist., 1991-94; prin. Hehnly Sch., Clark, N.J., 1994—; advisor, bd. dirs. N.J. Staff Devel. Coun., 1995—. Mem. ASCD, N.J. Prins. and Suprs. Assn. (edn. com.), N.J. Coun. Edn., N.J. Elem. Sch. Prins.' Assn. Home: 210 Mayhew Dr South Orange NJ 07079

LEVINE, MADELINE GELTMAN, Slavic literatures educator, translator; b. N.Y.C., Feb. 23, 1942; d. Herman and Nettie (Kritman) Geltman; m. Steven I. Levine; children: Elaine, Daniel. B.A., Brandeis U., 1962; M.A., Harvard U., 1964, Ph.D., 1971. Asst. prof. Grad Sch. CUNY, N.Y.C., 1971-74; assoc. prof. U. N.C., Chapel Hill, 1974-80, prof., 1980-94, Kenan prof. Slavic lits., 1994—, chmn. dept. Slavic langs., 1979-87, 94—; chmn. joint com. on Ea. Europe, Am. Coun. Learned Socs.-Social Sci. Rsch. Coun., 1989-92. Translator: A Memoir of the Warsaw Uprising (Miron Bialoszewski), 1977, 2d edit. 1991, The Poetry of Osip Mandelstam: God's Grateful Guest (Ryszard Przybylski), 1987, Beginning With My Streets: Essays and Recollections (Czeslaw Milosz), 1992, A Year of the Hunter (Czeslaw Milosz), 1994; translator with Francine Prose: A Scrap of Time and Other Stories (Ida Fink), 1986, 2d edit., 1995; author: Contemporary Polish Poetry, 1925-75, 1981. NEH fellow, 1984; recipient (with Francine Prose) award for lit. translation PEN-America, 1988. Mem. Am. Assn. for Advancement of Slavic Studies, Polish Inst. of Arts and Scis. Am., Am. Assn. Tchrs. of Slavic and East European Langs., Am. Literary Translators Assn., Pen-Am. Home: 5001 Whitehorse Rd Hillsborough NC 27278-9399 Office: U NC 421 Dey Hall CB # 3165 Chapel Hill NC 27599

LEVINE, MARILYN MARKOVICH, lawyer, arbitrator; b. Bklyn., Aug. 9, 1930; d. Harry P. and Fannie L. (Hymowitz) Markovich; m. Louis L. Levine. June 24, 1950; children: Steven R., Ronald J., Linda J. Morgenstern. BS summa cum laude, Columbia U., 1950; MA, Adelphi U., 1967; JD, Hofstra U., 1977. Bar: N.Y. 1978, U.S. Dist. Ct. (so. and ea. dists.) N.Y. 1978, D.C. 1979, U.S. Supreme Ct. 1982. Sole practice Valley Stream, N.Y., 1978—; contract arbitrator bldg. svc. industry, N.Y.C., 1982—; panel arbitrator retail food industry, N.Y.C., 1980—; arbitrator N.Y. dist. cts., Nassau County, 1981—; mem. Nat. Acad. Arbitrators, 1992—. Panel arbitrator Suffolk County Pub. Employee Relations Bd., 1979—, Nassau County Pub. Employee Relations Bd., 1980—, Nat. Mediation Bd., 1986—, N.Y. State Pub. Employee Relations Bd., 1984—; mem. adv. council Ctr. Labor and Industrial Relations, N.Y. Inst. Tech., N.Y., 1985—; counsel Nassau Civic Club, 1978—. Mem. ABA, N.Y. State Bar Assn., D.C. Bar Assn., Nassau County Bar Assn., N.J. Bd. Mediation (panel arbitrator), Am. Arbitration Assn. (arbitrator 1979—), Fed. Mediation Bd. (arbitrator 1980—). Home and Office: 1057 Linden St Valley Stream NY 11580-2135

LEVINE, MELISSA SMITH, lawyer; b. New Haven, Oct. 10, 1964; d. Stanley B. Smith and Meredith (Joy) Weiland; m. Glenn S. Levine, Aug. 26, 1989. BA, Emory U., 1986; JD, U. Miami Sch. Law, 1989. Bar: Va. 1991. Dir. advt. New Art Examiner mag., Washington, 1989-90; contract negotiator, bus. activities Smithsonian Inst., Washington, 1990-95; legal adviser nat. digital libr. project Libr. of Congress, Washington, 1996—. Mem. Arts Club Washington (co-chair literary com. 1991-95), Am. Assn. Mus.

LEVINE, MONA, administrator, educator; b. Washington, Apr. 15, 1950; d. Isaac E. and Beatrice C. (Cohen) Friedlander; m. Kenneth Michael Levine, Oct. 21, 1973; children: Martin Louis, Amy Schoen. BA in Govt. and Politics, U. Md., 1972, MBA, 1984. Internat. economist U.S. Dept. Commerce, Washington, 1972-81; assoc. prof. bus. adminstrn. and econs. Montgomery Coll., Rockville, Md., 1986-96, asst. chief adminstr. for acad. and student affairs, 1996—; adminstrv. assoc. office of pres. Office of Pres., Rockville, Md., 1994-95; chair self-study comprehensive work team Mid. States Assn., 1996—; adj. prof. Montgomery Coll., 1985-86; cons. Adams, Duque & HAzeltine, Washington, 1985. Contbr. to books and articles to profl. jours. Pres. Coll. Gardens PTA, Rockville, 1987-88; chair Israel scholar com. B'nai Israel Congregation, Rockville, 1993-95; chair band fund raiser R. Montgomery H.S., Rockville, 1993-94, mem. open lunch com., 1995. Mem. Am. Mktg. Assn., Phi Beta Kappa. Democrat. Jewish. Home: 1529 Baylor Ave Rockville MD 20850 Office: Montgomery Coll 900 Hungerford Dr Rockville MD 20850

LEVINE, NAOMI BRONHEIM, university administrator; b. N.Y.C., Apr. 15, 1923; d. Nathan and Malvina (Mermelstein) Bronheim; m. Leonard Levine, Apr. 11, 1948; 1 dau., Joan. B.A., Hunter Coll., 1944; LL.B., Columbia, 1946, J.D., 1970. Bar: N.Y. bar 1946. With firm Scaadrett, Tuttle & Chalaire, N.Y.C., 1946-48, Charles Gottleib, N.Y.C., 1948-50; with Am. Jewish Congress, 1950-78, exec. dir., 1972-78; v.p. to sr. v.p. external affairs NYU, 1978—; asst. prof. law and police sci. John Jay Coll., N.Y.C., 1969-73, L.I. U., 1965-69. Author: Schools in Crisis, 1969, The Jewish Poor-an American Awakening, 1974, Politics, Religion and Love, 1990; mem. editorial staff Columbia Law Rev., 1945-46. Bd. dirs. Interracial Council Bus. Opportunities, Am. Women's Econ. Devel. Council; trustee N.Y. UJA-Fedn. Recipient Constl. Law prize Hunter Coll., 1944; named to Hall of Fame, 1972. Office: 70 Washington Sq S New York NY 10012-1019

LEVINE, PAMELA GAIL, business owner; b. Alameda, Calif., Nov. 20, 1942; d. Carl B. and Lucille N. (Lua) Leverenz; m. George David Barth (div. 1974); children, Claudia Anne, Shanette Michelle; m. Leonard Stuart Levine; children: Leslie, Julie, Susan, Stuart Carl. BA in Archtl. Design/Fine Arts, U. Calif., Berkeley, 1965. Designer Trude of Calif., San Francisco, 1965-66; tchr. TWA, Kansas City, Mo., 1966-69; ptnr., owner, archtl. designer Leverenz of N.Y., 1970—; owner, designer Ressco, Katonah, N.Y., 1974—; cons. archtl. design and real estate devel.; founder, owner Sintec-Internat. Bus. Opportunities, 1989—. Designer of Sets/Costumes, Chappaqua Drama Group, 1973—. Devel. com. Mount Holyoke Coll., S. Hadley, Mass., 1987—; co-founder Looking Glass Players, Mt. Kisco, N.Y., 1985—; active Jr. League, Caramoor, Katonah Mus. Mem. No. Westchester Ctr. for the Arts (exec. com., v.p. bd. dirs., bd. dirs. devel. com., co-chmn. bldg. com.), Chappaqua Drama Group (bd. dirs.). Republican. Home: RR 6 Katonah NY 10536-9806 Office: Real Estate Support Svcs PO Box 574 Katonah NY 10536-0574

LEVINE, PATTI, public relations executive. Pres. pub. rels., graphics firm Pleasanton, Calif.; dir. comm. Stoorza, Ziegaus & Metzger, Sacramento, Calif., 1985-87; v.p. Stoorza, Ziegaus & Metzger, Sacramento, 1987-91, sr. exec. v.p., 1993—. Office: Stoorza Ziegaus Metzger & Hunt 555 Capitol Mall Ste 600 Sacramento CA 95814-4502*

LEVINE, PEGGY AYLSWORTH, psychotherapist; b. Newark, May 2, 1921; d. Roscoe Nichols and Helen (Dorsen) Aylsworth; m. Samuel Schultz, Mar. 29, 1950 (div. 1979); children: Christie Romero, Ron M. Schultz; m. Norman Philip Levine, Sept. 20, 1986. BA in Psychology, Lindenwood Coll., 1977; MA in Psychology, Antioch West Coll., L.A., 1978. Rschr. Carl Byoir & Assocs., N.Y.C., 1941-43; rsch. editor True Mag., Fawcett Publs., N.Y.C., 1944-45; adminstr. Valley Ctr. of Arts, Encino, Calif., 1966-69; pub. rels. dir. Comsky Gallery, L.A., 1970; pvt. practice psychotherapy Santa Monica, Calif., 1980—. Author: (children's album) The Glooby Game, 1949, (poetry) Letters to the Same Address, 1989, Along These Lines, 1995, (novels) Morning in the Long Night City, 1992, Among These Several, 1996; contbr. poems to various mags., revs. V.p. Valley Ctr. of Arts, 1956-57, publicity dir., 1955-65; publicity dir. Alliance for Survival, Santa Monica, 1979-81. Home and Office: 606 Raymond Ave No 1 Santa Monica CA 90405

LEVINE, RHEA JOY COTTLER, anatomy educator; b. N.Y.C., Nov. 26, 1939; d. Zachary Robert Cottler and Hildreth (Abramson) Cottler Rosenfeld; m. Stephen Maxwell Levine, June 16, 1960; children: Elizabeth, Michael Gordon, Zachary Thomas. AB summa cum laude, Smith Coll., 1960; MS, NYU, 1963, PhD, 1966. Lab. instr. NYU Sch. Commerce, N.Y.C., 1963-64; postdoctoral fellow, instr. histology Yale U. Sch. Medicine, New Haven, 1966-68; rsch. assoc. U. Pa. Sch. Medicine, Phila., 1968-69; asst. prof. anatomy Med. Coll. Pa., Phila., 1969-74, assoc. prof. anatomy, 1974-80, prof. anatomy, 1980—, vice chmn., 1988-89; manuscript reviewer numerous sci. journals, Washington and N.Y.C., 1975—; reviewer grant proposals NSF, Washington, 1975—, mem. NIH Study Sect., 1980-84. Contbr. sci. articles to profl. jours. Trustee Richard Stockton Coll. N.J., Pomona, 1983—, chmn. bd. trustees, 1991-94; trustee Smith Coll., 1996—; bd. dirs. Hollybush Festival, Glassboro, N.J., 1987-91, Smith Coll. Friends of Libr., Northampton, Mass., 1968-72. NYU Sch. Medicine summer rsch. fellow, 1960, NSF grad. fellow, 1960-65, A.H. Robins rsch. fellow, 1966, USPHS fellow, 1966-68; grantee Women's and Program project NIH, NSF, 1973—; recipient Founder's Day award NYU, 1966, Smith Coll. medal, 1994. Mem. AAAS, Coalition Jewish Profl. Women South N.J. (steering com.), Am. Assn. Anatomists, Am Soc. Cell Biology, Biophys. Soc. (coun. 1991-94, chair pub. sci. policy com. 1992-94), Histochem. Soc., Soc. Gen. Physiology, Wilderness Med. Soc., N.Y. Acad. Scis., Smith Coll. Club, Woodcrest Country Club (house chair 1983-84), Phi Beta Kappa, Sigma Xi. Jewish. Office: Med Coll Pa/Hahnemann Univ Dept Neurobiology/Anatomy 3200 Henry Ave Philadelphia PA 19129-1137

LEVINE, ROSANNE See HEPBURN, ROSANNA LEVINE

LEVINE, SHEREE FAITH, lawyer; b. Springfield, Mass., May 21, 1956; d. Irving H. and Lillian I. (Sugarman) L. BA, U. Pa., 1976; JD, Boston Coll., 1979. Bar: N.Y. 1980, Mass. 1980. Intern U.S. Atty. for the So. Dist. of N.Y. bus. frauds section, N.Y.C., 1978; atty. U.S. Securities & Exchange Commn., N.Y.C., 1979-82, 1982-85; br. chief Securities Industry Assn., N.Y.C., 1985-86, asst. gen. counsel, 1986-87, asst. v.p., asst. gen. counsel, 1988-89, v.p., assoc. gen. counsel, 1990—, v.p., sec., assoc. gen. counsel. Editor: looseleaf jour. Uniform Commercial Code, 1977-79. Mem. ABA, Assn. Bar City N.Y. Office: Securities Industry Assn 120 Broadway Fl 35 New York NY 10271-3599

LEVINE, SUZANNE BRAUN, magazine editor; b. N.Y.C., June 21, 1941; d. Imre and Esther (Bernson) Braun; m. Robert F. Levine, Apr. 2, 1967; children: Joshua, Joanna. BA with honors, Radcliffe Coll., 1963. Reporter Seattle mag., 1963-65; reporter, researcher Time/Life Books, N.Y.C., 1965-67; features editor Mademoiselle, N.Y.C., 1967-68, McCalls mag., N.Y.C., 1968-69; free-lance writer, 1970; mng. editor Sexual Behavior mag., 1971-72, MS. mag., N.Y.C., 1972-88; editor Columbia Journalism Rev., N.Y.C., 1989—; adj. prof. Columbia Grad. Sch. Journalism. Co-editor: The Decade of Women, A Ms History of the Seventies, 1980; exec. producer: Ms. HBO TV spl., 1981, She's Nobody's Baby, TV documentary, 1981 (Peabody award). Woodrow Wilson guest lectr. coord. Chautauqua Conf. on Families. Mem. Am. Soc. Mag. Editors (v.p.), Women's Media Group. Office: Columbia U Columbia Journalism Rev 700 Journalism Bldg New York NY 10027

LEVINE, TOBY KLEBAN, communications executive, educational media developer; b. N.Y.C., Apr. 12, 1944; d. Julian Milton and Sylvia (Kandel) Kleban; m. Andrew Seth Levine, Feb. 4, 1964; children: Caren Beth Pelletier, Amy Ruth. BS, Cornell U., 1964; MEd, Boston U., 1965. Rsch. asst. Synetics, Inc., Cambridge, Mass., 1964-66; project dir. The Children's Mus., Boston, 1965-66; rsch. assoc. Creative Studies, Inc., Boston, 1968-69, curriculum coord., 1969-71, v.p. ednl. devel., 1971-73; founder, pres. Levine Rsch. Assocs., Brookline, Mass., 1973-78; curriculum dir. WETA-TV, Washington, 1978-81, dir. ednl. activities, 1981-84; founder, pres. Toby Levine Comm., Inc., Bethesda, Md., 1984—. Author: (handbook) Telecourses: Opportunities and Options, Everyone Wins! Quality Care Without Restraints, The World of Abnormal Psychology, Chicano: History of the Mexican American Civil Rights Movement, The Africans. Trustee, sch. com. chair Temple Israel, Boston; founding bds. dirs. 2 after-school day care ctrs. Recipient Gold plaque Chgo. Internat. Film Festival, 1992, Mental Health Media award Nat. Mental Health Assn., 1993, Gold award Washington Ednl. Press, 1993, Spl. Achievement OWL award Retirement Rsch. Found., 1996. Mem. Assn. Ednl. Comm. and Tech., Pres.'s Coun. Cornell Women (program chair), Cornell Univ. Coun. Home: 7906 Inverness Ridge Rd Potomac MD 20854 Office: Toby Levine Comm, Inc 7910 Woodmont Ave # 910 Bethesda MD 20814

LEVINE, YARI, artist, jewelry designer; b. Minsk, Russia; came to U.S. 1927; d. Samuel and Lillian (Lapidus) Turboff; m. Samuel S. Levine, June 10, 1945; children—Steven Robert, Mark Eric. Cert. in Fine Arts, Pratt Inst., 1939; student Am. Artists Sch., 1941, New Sch. Social Research, 1942-43. One-woman shows at: Ward Egleston Galleries, 1964, Washington Hebrew Congregation, N.Y.C., 1959, Brandeis U., 1966, U. Wis., 1969, Union of Am. Hebrew Congregations, 1953, 66, Nassau Community Coll., 1970, Art and Design Atelier, 1980, Hebrew Tabernacle, 1981; exhibited in group shows at: Creative Gallery, John Myers Gallery, 1952, A.C.A. Gallery, 1954, 55, 56, Nat. Acad. Galleries, 1953-78, Internat. Jewish Conf. Exhibit, Los Angeles, 1955, Suffolk Mus., 1957, 300th Houston Commemorative Exhibit, 1957, Art League of L.I., 1957, Heckscher Mus., 1962, Lido Gallery, 1970, Harbor Gallery, 1974, Hudson Guild Gallery, 1980, Artists Equity of N.Y., 1980, Lever House, 1983, Jacob K. Javits Fed. Bldg., 1984, 85; works represented in permanent collections at House of Living Judaism of Union of Am. Hebrew Congregations, N.Y.C., Westchester Reform Temple, Temple Sinai of Washington, U. Wis., others. Named Artist of Jewish Yr., Union of Am. Hebrew Congregations, 1966. Fellow Internat. Inst. Arts and Letters; mem. Artists Equity of N.Y., Nat. Assn. Women Artists, Jewish Visual Artists Assn. of Nat. Council on Arts in Jewish Life, Internat. Platform Assn. Studio: 24 Fifth Ave Apt 214 New York NY 10011

LEVINSON, BETTY ZITMAN, artist; b. Chgo., May 14, 1908; d. Samuel and Ella (Block) Z.; m. Julius Yale Levinson, Aug. 19, 1928 (dec. Dec., 1981); children: Lila Scher, Joyce Levinson, Robin Boushie. Student, U. Chgo., 1966, Art Inst. Chgo., 1972. Exhibitions include N. Shore Art League, Chgo., Spertus Mus., 57th St. Art Festival, Old Town Chamber Art Festival, Oak Park Art Festival; represented in collections at Deer Path Gallery, Lake Forest, Camino Real Gallery, Boca Raton, Fla., Prism Gallery, Evanston, Ill., Fort Wayne (Ind.) Mus. Art Alliance; juried group shows include Palm Springs (Calif.) Mus. Founder, mem. United Cerebral Palsy Assn. N.Y.C., 1949, pres. Stamford, Conn., 1954-58, v.p. Chgo.,

1968—; patron Mus. Contemporary Art, Chgo. Historic Soc.; trustee Spertus Mus., Chgo.; active supporter print and drawing club Art Inst. Chgo. Recipient Honor Mother of Yr. Conn. Mother of Yr., N.Y., 1954, Award of Excellence Chgo. Soc. Artists, 1980, 1st prize David Adler Cultural Ctr., Libertyville, Ill., 1986, award of excellence, 1988, 2d prize Am. Jewish Art Club, Chgo., 1990, award of excellence Deer Path Gallery, Lake Forest, Ill., 1994, award for excellence, Cultural Ctr. for Abstract Painting, 1995, 96, award United Cerebral Palsy Chgo., 1996. Mem. English Speaking Union, Shakespeare Globe Ctr., Chgo. Soc. Artists, United Cerbral Palsy Chgo. (life v.p.). Home: Casa Dorinda 300 Hot Springs Rd Apt 89 Monticeto CA 93108

LEVINSON, RASCHA, psychotherapist; b. N.Y.C., Nov. 27, 1930; d. Frank Alfred and Goldye Dena (Preiser) Cohen; m. Monroe Louis Levinson, Oct. 6, 1955 (div. 1973); 1 child, Nadia Levinson Fogel. BA, NYU, 1960; MSW, Columbia U., 1962; Tng. in Hypnosis, Milton Erickson Soc., N.Y.C., 1992-93. Lic. social worker, N.Y. Pvt. practice N.Y.C., 1970—; psychotherapist Wasington Sq. Inst., N.Y.C., 1973-74; intake therapist Women's Psychotherapy Referral Svcs., N.Y.C., 1973-76; supr. psychotherapy Mid-Hudson Cons. Ctr., Wappinger Falls, N.Y., 1974-83; workshop leader New Sch. Social Rsch., N.Y.C., 1980-87. Fellow Soc. Clin. Social Workers (pres. Westchester chpt. 1986-88); mem. Assn. for Women in Psychology, N.Y.C. Coalition for Women's Mental Health (bd. dirs. 1986-89), Advanced Feminist Therapy Inst. (editor newsletter 1990-92). Office: 55 Central Park W # 1B New York NY 10023-6003

LEVINSON, ROSLYN GOODMAN, public relations executive; b. Dubuque, Iowa; d. Meyer P. Goodman and Libbey Pauline (Epstein) Rotman; m. Harold Lawrence Levinson (dec.); children: Barbara Ott, Mark J. Levinson, David Levinson Lewis. BS in English, Northwestern U., 1950. Theater publicist Balaban & Katz, Chgo., 1951-52; campaign publicist March of Dimes, Chgo., 1952; dir. pub. rels. Evanston (Ill.) Dept. Parks, Recreation and Forestry, 1964-67; pub. info. dirs. Evanston Dist. 65 Lab. Sch., 1967-71; owner, founder Levinson Assocs., Evanston, Ill., 1971-94, ptnr., 1994-96. Bd. dirs. Dem. Orgn., Evanston, Ill., 1955-64, St. Francis Hosp. Adult and Child Guidance Ctr., 1968, YWCA, 1984-86. Recipient Golden Trumpet award 1st Place Publicity Club of Chgo., 1973, 75, 80, Disting. Svc. award, 1975, Best Campaign award Suburban Press Chgo., 1979. Mem. Pub. Rels. Soc. Am. (mem. counselors acad. 1985-87, mem. internat. com. 1989-91). Democrat. Jewish. Office: Levinson Assocs Pub Rels 1325 Howard St #204 Evanston IL 60202

LEVINSON, SHAUNA T., bank and financial services marketing executive; b. Denver, Aug. 1, 1954; d. Charles and Geraldine D. Titus; m. Kenneth L. Levinson, Dec. 21, 1986. BA cum laude, U. Puget Sound, 1976; M Bank Mktg. with honors, U. Colo., 1986. Cert. fin. planner. Fin. planning analyst Swift and Co., Chgo., 1977-79; from credit analyst to asst. v.p. Ctrl. Bank of Denver, 1979-84; v.p. fin. svcs. First Nat. Bank S.E. Denver, 1984-94; dir. mktg. First Nat. Banks, 1991-94; pres., CEO Fin. Directions, Inc., Denver, 1994—; mem. bankers edn. com. Colo. Bankers Assn., Denver, 1992-94. Chmn. human resources com., mem. adminstrv. coun. Jr. League of Denver, 1983—; mem. cmty. assistance fund, placement adv. com., fundraiser Women's Libr. Assn. U. Denver, 1990-94, 96—; fundraiser Good Shepherd Cath. Sch., 1986-95, Jewish Cmty. Ctr., Denver, 1990-95, St. Mary's Acad., 1995—. Recipient Gold Peak award Am. Bankers Assn.-Bank Mktg. Assn., 1987; named Businessperson of Week Denver Bus. Jour., 1995. Mem. AAUW, Am. Inst. Banking, Jr. League Denver, U. Denver Pioneer Hockey Club, Kappa Alpha Theta (program chair Northwest Chgo. alumnae 1977-79), Phi Kappa Phi. Office: 1624 Market St # 475 Denver CO 80202

LEVIN-WIXMAN, IRENE STAUB, librarian; b. Bklyn., Sept. 30, 1928; d. Harry and Regina (Klein) Staub; BA, Hunter Coll., CUNY, 1949; MLS, L.I. U., 1969; m. Harold E. Levin, Nov. 19, 1950 (dec. June 1984); children: Alan, Leslie, Kim, Paula; m. Lee Wixman, June 5, 1989. Reference librarian and young adults Henry Waldinger Library, Valley Stream, N.Y., 1969-87, program coordinator public relations, 1976-87; free-lance info. specialist, Boynton Beach, Fla., 1988—; cons. on Jewish books and libraries; librarian Judaica Libr. Temple Emanu El, Palm Beach., Fla., 1988—; active Palm Beach Libr. Adv. Bd., 1993—; lectr. books with Judiac themes. Trustee, Sisterhood Temple B'nai Israel of Elmont, 1969-71, 87, Temple B'nai Israel of Elmont, 1982; libr. Temple Emanuel, Palm Beach, Fla., 1988—. Recipient Library Public Relations Council award, 1973. Mem. Assn. Jewish Librs. (editor Bull. 1973-83, Newsletter 1978—, Fanny Goldstein Merit award 1992), Am. Mizrachi Women, Hadassah. Contbr. to Contemporary Literary Criticism, Vol. 13, 1979.

LEVISON-MARCUS, PEGGY LEE, psychologist; b. Mitchell, S.D., June 24, 1942; d. Eugene Keith and Berenice Pauline (Stuart) Snow; m. Stuart Allen Levison, June 3, 1933 (div. 1987); children: Derek, Gregory, Rebecca; m. Peter Colton Marcus, July 19, 1991 (dec.). BA in Russian Lang., San Diego State U., 1969; MA in Human Behavior, U.S. Internat. U., 1975, PhD in Clin. Psychology, 1978. Counselor LaJolla (Calif.) Pub. Sch., 1976; psychotherapist The Marks Clinic, San Diego, 1976-78; staff psychotherapist Fifth Ave. Ctr. for Counseling and Psychotherapy, N.Y.C., 1978-81, Ctr. for Stress Disorders, Bayside, N.Y., 1978-85; pvt. practice Bayside and N.Y.C., 1985—; cons. in field; pvt. tutor Russian lang., San Diego, 1975-77. Author: Manual for GPI, 1979. Pres. Scripps Clinic and Rsch. Found. Women's Group, LaJolla, 1968-69. Mem. APA, NOW, MADD, Internat. Psychol. Assn., N.Y. State Psychol. Assn., Amnesty Internat., Sierra Club. Office: 35 W 9th St # 1B New York NY 10011-8973

LEVIT, EDITHE JUDITH, physician, medical association administrator; b. Wilkes-Barre, Pa., Nov. 29, 1926; m. Samuel M. Levit, Mar. 2, 1952; children: Harry M., David B. BS in Biology, Bucknell U., 1946; MD, Woman's Med. Coll. of Pa., 1951; DMS (hon.), Med. Coll. Pa., 1978; DSc (hon.), Wilkes U., 1990. Grad. asst. in psychology Bucknell U., 1946-47; intern Phila. Gen. Hosp., 1951-52, fellow in endocrinology, 1952-53, clin. instr., assoc. in endocrinology, 1953-57, dir. med. edn., 1957-61, cons. med. edn., 1961-65; asst. dir. Nat. Bd. Med. Examiners, Phila., 1961-67; assoc. dir., sec. bd. Nat. Bd. Med. Examiners, 1967-75, v.p., sec. bd., 1975-77, pres., chief exec. officer, 1977-86, pres. emeritus, life mem. bd., 1987—; cons. in field, 1964—; mem. adv. coun. Inst. for Nuclear Power Ops., Atlanta, 1988-93; bd. dir. Phila. Electric Co. Contbr. articles to profl. jours. Bd. dirs. Phila. Gen. Hosp. Found., 1964-70; bd. dirs. Phila. Council for Internat. Visitors, 1966-72; bd. sci. counselors Nat. Library Medicine, 1981-85. Recipient award for outstanding contbns. in field of med. edn. Commonwealth Com. of Woman's Med. Coll., 1970; Alumni award Bucknell U., 1978; Disting. Dau. of Pa. award, 1981; Spl. Recognition award Assn. Am. Med. Colls., 1986; Disting. Service award Fedn. State Med. Bds., 1987; Master A.C.P. Fellow Coll. Physicians of Phila.; mem. Inst. Medicine of Nat. Acad. Scis., AMA, Pa., Phila. County med. socs., Assn. Am. Med. Colls., Phi Beta Kappa, Alpha Omega Alpha, Phi Sigma. Home: The Rittenhouse 210 W Rittenhouse Sq Philadelphia PA 19103-5726

LEVIT, HELOISE B. (GINGER LEVIT), arts administrator, fine arts and media consultant; b. Phila., Apr. 2, 1937; d. Elmer and Claire Frances (Schwartz) Bertman; m. Jay Joseph Levit, July 14, 1962; children: Richard Bertman, Robert Edward, Darcy Francine. BA in French Literature, U. Pa., 1959; MA in French Literature, U. Richmond, 1975; Cert., Alliance Française, Paris, 1991, Chambre de Commerce et d'Industrie de Paris, 1991, La Sorbonne, Paris, 1994, Instituto Lorenzo di Medici Firenze, Italy, 1996; post grad., art history, Commonwealth U., Richmond. Arts broadcaster Richmond, Va., 1976-82; dir. Fine Arts Am., Inc., Richmond, 1982-84; tchr. Henrico County Pub. Schs., Richmond, 1984-88; dir. devel. Sta. WVST-FM Va. State U., Petersburg, 1987-88; mgr., dir. devel. Richmond Philharm. Orch., 1988-94; fine arts and media cons. Art-I-Facts, Richmond, 1988—. Author: Moments, Monuments & Monarchs, 1986 (Star award 1986); arts writer Richmond Rev., 1989-90; anchor, producer (syndicated radio series) Va. Arts Report, 1978-83, Va. Women, 1984 (Va. Press Women award 1986). V.p. Va. Mus. Collector's Cir., Richmond, 1986-91, mem. steering com.; pres. Richmond Area Dem. Women's Club, 1992-93; mem. Va. Mus. Coun., Richmond; mem. Richmond Symphony Orch. League. Mem. Am. Assn. Tchrs. of French, Va. Capitol Corrs. Assn., Va. Press Women, U. Pa. Alumni Club (v.p. 1980-90, Ben Franklin award 1990), Am. Symphony Orch. League, Amicale Francaise, Alliance Francaise (cert. 1989, 91), La Table Francaise (pres. 1996), Va. Writers Club. Home and Office: Art-I-Facts 1608 Harborough Rd Richmond VA 23233-4720

LEVITAS, MIRIAM C. STRICKMAN, events coordinator, realtor, television producer; b. Phila., Aug. 3, 1936; d. Morris and Bella (Barsky) Cherrin; m. Bernard Strickman, June 3, 1956 (dec. 1975); children: Andrew, Brian, Craig, Deron; m. Theodore Clinton Levitas, Apr. 25, 1976; children: Steven, Leslie, Anthony. Student Temple U., 1953-56, LaSalle U., Chgo., 1968; cert. in Gerontology Ga. State U., 1988, coord. Intergenerational Connections, State of Ga., 1989—. V.p. programming interior design Nat. Home Fashions League, Atlanta, 1974-75; Ga. Bd. Realtors, 1971—; adminstr. Stanley H. Kaplan Ednl. Ctr., Atlanta, 1974-84; owner, pres. Levitas Svcs., Inc. (Internat. Destinations), Atlanta, 1984-85; owner, v.p. Nat. Travel Svcs. and Internat. Destinations, Atlanta, 1984-85; realtor Philip White Properties Inc./Sotheby's Internat. Realty, 1985-91; realtor Coldwell Banker Previews, 1991—. Exec. producer, host community svc. videos TV cable broadcast, Atlanta, 1988—; solo pianist Paul Whiteman TV, Phila. Youth Orch., Frankford Symphony Orch., 1950. Pres. Ahavath Achim Sisterhood, Atlanta, 1977-79, co-pres., 1996—; bd. dirs. Jewish Family Svcs., 1993-96, Atlanta chpt. Nat. Osteoporosis Found., 1990-91, Outings in the Park, 1989-91; chmn. Tea at the Ritz Scottish Rite Children's Med. Ctr., 1987-90, women's div. Israel Bond, Atlanta, 1987, 88, 89, mem. aux.; chmn. Who's Bringing in the Great Chefs Scottish Rite Childrens Med. Ctr., 1990, 91, 92; mem. Atlanta Symphony, High Mus. Art, Nat. Mus. of Women in Arts (charter), Alliance Theater Atlanta. Phila. Bd. Edn. scholar, 1952, Atlanta Hist. Ctr.-Atlanta Hist. Soc., Alliance No. Dist. Dental Soc.; charter mem. U.S. Holocaust Mus.; bd. dirs. Jewish Family Svcs., nat. bd. advisors Brevard Music Ctr., 1993—. Named Woman of Achievement, Atlanta Jewish Fedn., 1993. Mem. Ga. Gerontology Soc., Atlanta Bd. Realtors, Spl. Children of the South (chmn. 1991-93), Internat. Furnishings and Design Assn. (Atlanta chpt.), Women in Film, Am. Women in Radio and TV, Children's Med. Ctr. Aux., Brandeis Nat. Women (life), Hadassah (life), Nat. Council Jewish Women (life), B'nai Brith (life), Scots (life).

LEVITEN, SARA BESS, word processing operator; b. Miami, Fla., Dec. 8, 1947; d. Sam Frank and Esther (Leavitt) L. AA, Miami-Dade C.C., 1970; BA, Fla. Atlantic U., 1972. Clk. typist I Miami-Dade Pub. Libr., 1972-74; substitute tchr. Dade County Pub. Schs., Miami, 1978-79; clk. typist II Dade County Bldg. & Zoning, Miami, 1979-81, word processor operator II, 1981—. Committeewoman Dade County Dem. Exec. Com., Miami, 1974-76; commr., program chair Dade County Commn. on Status Women, Miami, 1985-90; historian, bd. dirs. Young Dem. Club Dade County, Miami, 1971-73, 76; active Friends of Miami-Dade Libr., 1985—, Miami Book Fair Internat., 1995, Dade County Womens Polit. Caucus, Miami, 1971-77, 80-89, 92-96, corr. sec., bd. dirs., 1973-77, 80-89; vol. tutor L.E.A.D. Program, Miami, 1987-90; vol. usher Maurice Gusman Ctr. for Performing Arts, Miami, 1983—, petition initiator, 1995; bd. dirs. Beth David Congregation, Miami, social action chair, 1988-90, adult edn. com., 1995-96; vol. WLRN-FM, WLRN Radio Reading Svc., Miami, 1992-93; sec.-treas. Heritage Condo Assn., Miami, 1990-96; centennial amb. City of Miami, 1996—; vol. Dem. Nat. Conv., 1996. Recipient Outstanding Svc. award Young Dem. Club Dade County, Miami, 1970, Caring and Sharing award Metro-Dade Women's Assn., Miami, 1992; named Outstanding Usher Maurice Gusman Ctr. for Performing Arts, Miami, 1987. Mem. Metro Dade Women's Assn. (co-chair program 1993-94), Hist. Assn.So. Fla. (docent 1990), Heritage Condo Assn. (sec.-treas. 1990—). Home: 645 NE 121st St Apt 408 North Miami FL 33161

LEVITT, B. BLAKE, medical and science writer; b. Bridgeport, Conn., Mar. 25, 1948; d. John Joseph and Beatrice Dolores (Rozanski) Blake; m. Andrew Levitt, Dec. 20, 1968 (div. May 1977); m. Jon P. Garvey, Nov. 19, 1983. BA in English magna cum laude, BA in History summa cum laude, Quinnipiac Coll., 1972; postgrad., Yale U., 1988. Instr. English as fgn. lang. U. Khon Kaen, Thailand, 1968-69; market researcher Lyons Bakeries Ltd., London, summer 1971; traffic mgr., copywriter Provocatives Advt. Agy., Danbury, Conn., 1976-78; tech. writer tng. divsn. Jack Morton Prodns., N.Y.C., 1978-82; freelance feature and med. writer Litchfield County Times, New Milford, Conn., 1982-85, N.Y. Times, N.Y.C., 1985-89; freelance writer med. and sci. books, 1989—. Author: Electromagnetic Fields: A Consumer's Guide to the Issues and How to Protect Ourselves, 1995 (Will Solimene Book award for excellence 1996), 50 Essential Things to Do When the Doctor Says It's Infertility, 1995; co-author: (with John R. Sussman) Before You Conceive, The Complete Pre-Pregnancy Guide, 1989 (Will Solimene Book Award of Excellence 1991); contbr. articles to N.W. Hills mag., New Eng. Monthly, Conn. Mag. Founding mem., bd. dirs. Warren (Conn.) Land Trust, 1989-91; mem. Dem. Town Com., Warren, 1993—; vice-chmn. zoning bd. appeals Town of Warren, 1993-95. Mem. Nat. Assn. Sci. Writers, Am. Med. Writers Assn., Author's Guild, Author's League.

LEVITT, GERTRUDE H. KAPLAN, real estate broker, volunteer; b. New York, Jan. 18, 1919; d. Jacob Kaplan and Dora Laskey; m. Jack Levitt, June 15, 1978. BA, Hunter Coll., 1939. Real estate broker N.Y. State BD. of Realtors. Exec. sec. Coca-Cola Co., N.Y.C., 1940-43; censor Censorship Bur., N.Y.C., 1943-45; exec. sec. Netherlands Info. Bur., N.Y.C., 1945-47, Burlington Mills, N.Y.C., 1974-55; asst. to pres. Lumber Industries Inc., Brooklyn, N.Y., 1956-66; real estate broker N.Y.C., 1966—. Fundraiser Women's Am. O.R.T. Internat., 1975-90; vol. Canine Companions. Mem. Hunter Coll. Alumni Assn. Jewish. Home: Hathaway Dr 14 Escondido Altamonte Springs FL 32701

LEVITT, IRENE HANSEN, sales associate, writer, artist; b. Berkeley, Calif., Aug. 18, 1953; d. Alvin Kenneth and Bertha (Schiff) Hansen; m. Kim De Wayne, Oct. 22, 1983. BA in Art, Calif. Luth. U., 1976. Bookkeeper, data processor, sec. pvt. contractor, 1984-95; sales assoc. Dayton Hudson Corp., 1995—. Photographer with exhibits of greeting card and prints in numerous art galleries in the Seattle area; exhibited in art show, Oakland, Calif., 1972, L.A., 1986, Seattle, 1994; author: (plays) A Cancer of Proximity, 1987, The Price of the Retreat, 1987, Sacrifices to the Compromise, 1987, In Order to Bury Our Dead, 1987, Foxtrot, 1993, The Loom, 1993, (novel) The Renaissance of the Poppy, 1991, (anthology) Diaries of the Affluent, 1993. Vol., alumni rep. Calif. Luth. U., Thousand Oaks, Calif., 1987; vol. Am. Cancer Soc., Modesto, Calif., 1991-92; vol. Remond Cmty. Celebration of the Arts, 1995. Recipient award in art Alameda County Art Com., 1972, Mark Van Doren Meml. Poetry prize Calif. Luth. U., 1976; Undergrad. scholar VA, 1972-76, U.S. Civil Svc. Commn., 1972-75.

LEVITT, MADELYN MAE, philanthropist, fund raiser; b. Des Moines, Nov. 23, 1924; d. Ellis I. and Nelle (Seff) L.; divorced; children: Linda Toohey, Jeffrey Glazer, Susan Burt, Ellen Ziegler. BS, Ohio State U., 1946; LHD (hon.), Drake U., 1993. Exec. com. United Way, Des Moines, 1968-95; bd. dirs. exec. com. Drake U., Des Moines; exec. com. Network of Women in Philanthropy, Madison, Wis., Des Moines Art Ctr.; mem. gov. bd. Blank Children's Hosp. Recipient Nat. award for philanthropy Nat. Soc. Fund Raising Execs., 1995. Home: # 903 3131 Fleur Dr Des Moines IA 50321 Office: Drake U Des Moines IA 50511

LEVITT, MIRIAM, pediatrician; b. Lampertheim, Germany, June 10, 1946; came to U.S., 1948; d. Eli and Esther (Kingston) L.; m. Harvey Flisser, June 25, 1967; children: Adam, Elizabeth, Eric. AB, NYU, 1967; MD, Albert Einstein Coll. Medicine, Yeshiva U., 1971. Diplomate Am. Bd. Pediatrics. Intern Montefiore Med. Ctr., Bronx, N.Y., 1970-71, resident in pediatrics, 1971-73, attending pediatrician, 1975—; dir. outpatient svcs. pediatrics Bronx-Lebanon Hosp., N.Y.C., 1973-77; instr. pediatrics Albert Einstein Coll. Medicine, N.Y.C., 1973-76, asst. prof. clin., 1976—; med. staff Lawrence Hosp., Bronxville, N.Y., 1978—, dir. pediatrics, 1988—; sch. physician Bronxville Bd. Edn., 1983—. Fellow Am. Acad. Pediatrics; mem. Westchester County Med. Soc. Office: 1 Pondfield Rd Bronxville NY 10708-3706

LEVITT, SERENA FARR, nursing administrator; b. Washington, June 10, 1938; d. James Franklin and Evelyn Estelle (Richards) Farr; m. Edward Isaac Levitt, Jan. 2, 1966; children: Daniel Clifford, Richard Curtis, Lynette Cecelia, David Samuel Charles. AAS in Nursing, N. Va. C.C., Annandale, Va., 1977. Registered nurse. Clk. typist U.S. Dept. of Agr., Washington, 1956-58; pubs. asst. Jansky & Bailey Atlantic Rsch., Springfield, Va., 1960-61; spl. asst. avionics pubs., prodn. supr. Howard Rsch., Arlington, Va., 1962-64; tech. writer Computer Usage, Washington, Va., 1964-65; pubs. supr. Tracor, Rockville, Md., 1965; pubs. engr. Fairchild-Hiller, Bladensburg, Md., 1965-66; dir. documentation, program mgr. Krohn-Rhodes Rsch. Inst., Washington, 1966-67, Documentation Logistics Corp., Fairfax, Va., 1967-74; supr. Leewood Nursing Home, Annandale, Va., 1977-78; med. liaison Dept. Navy, Yokosuka, Japan, 1986-88; nursing supr., office mgr. Dr. Bruce E. Lessin, MD, McLean, Va., 1990-94. Recipient scholarship Zonta Club of Arlington, 1956. Mem. ANA, AAAS, IEEE, Am. Assn. Office Nurses, Nat. League Nursing, Soc. Tech. Writers and Pubs. Jewish. Home: 9920 Farr Dr Fairfax VA 22030-2020

LEVITZ, I. S., artist, educator, curator; b. Bklyn., Aug. 24, 1943; d. Irving Jacob and Mary (Matts) Steiner; m. Martin N. Levitz, June 19, 1965; children: Robin, David, Jodi. Student, Vesper George Sch. Art, Boston, Hartford Art Sch., Trinity Coll., Hartford, Wesleyan U., Middletown, Conn. artist-in-residence Brandeis U. Women's Commn.,1994. Juried exhibits include Mattatuck Mus. "Conn. Vision", 1992, Silvermine Guild, Norwalk, Conn., 1983, New Britain Mus. Am. Art, 1982, 85, 87, 90, Conn. Acad. Fine Arts, 1988-91, 95, 96, Three Women Artists - Chase Freedom Gallery, Hartford Jewish Ctr., 1994, Women in the Arts, Wave Gallery, New Haven, 1995, Yale-New Haven Hosp. The Arts in Health Care, 1995. Vol. Toys for Tots, Bloomfield, 1989-92; bd. dirs. Hartford Arts Coun., 1976; chmn. Ann Randall Arts Com., 1978-80. Recipient Purchase award Town of Bloomfield, 1991. Mem. West Hartford Art League (chmn. selection com. for exhbns. 1983-84), Conn. Watercolor Soc.(vol.), Conn. Acad. Fine Arts (bd. dirs. 1995-96), New Britain Mus. Am. Art. Home: 1011 N Main St West Hartford CT 06117-2055

LEVY, BARBARA MINA WEXNER, writer, publisher, editor; b. Hot Springs, Ark., Jan. 30, 1927; d. Henry David and Helen Ruth (Loeb) Wexner; A.A., Lindenwood Coll., 1945; student U. Houston, 1958-59; m. Herbert E. Levy, July 25, 1945; children: Barbara Dian, Richard H., Lauren. Feature writer Houston Town, 1957-58; regional editor Boot & Shoe Recorder, Houston, 1958-65; with customer service Scholastic Mag., Englewood Cliffs, N.J., 1966-67; fashion shoe editor Window Shopping World, N.Y.C., 1967-68; women's fashion editor Boot & Shoe Recorder, N.Y.C., 1968-74; pub., editor Barbara's Report/Shoes and. . . , Miami, Fla., 1974—, Barbara's View Travel Guides, 1976—; lectr. in field. Mem. alumnae bd. Lindenwood Coll., 1967-68, v.p., 1969. Mem. Footwear and Accessories Council N.Y.C. (pres. 1973, chmn. bd. 1974, honored for creative contbn. to industry 1982), Fashion Group, Women in Communications. Contbr. articles to profl. jours. Address: 1236 NE 92nd St Miami FL 33138-2937

LEVY, BARBARA RIFKIN, executive director; b. Schenectady, Apr. 25, 1941; d. Sam and Jane (Goodman) Rifkin; m. Martin Ray Levy, July 21, 1963; children: Douglas Marc, Mitchell Brent. BS, U. Vt., 1962; postgrad., Ithaca Coll. Music, 1962, Ohio U., 1964-65, U. Ariz., 1973-75. Tchr. music Vernon Pub. Schs., Rockville, Conn., 1962-63, Northwood Pub. Schs., Toledo, 1963-64; supr. music therapy Athens (Ohio) State Hosp., 1964-66; dir. devel. Ariz. Opera Co., Tucson, 1974-78, Ariz. Theatre Co., Tucson, 1978-89; devel. officer U. Ariz. Mus. Art, Tucson, 1989-90; dir. of devel. Arts & Libraries, Tucson, 1990-94; executive dir. Ariz. Children's Home Found., Tucson, 1994—; cons. Ariz. Commn. on Arts, 1984—, Found. for Extension and Devel. Am. Profl. Theatre, 1985—; mem. pvt. sector adv. com. Nat. Assn. Attys. Gen. Model Law, 1986-87; mem. ad hoc com. to devel. state legis. Phoenix Solicitation Bd., 1988-90, bd. mem. U. Ariz. Coll. of Fine Arts Dean's Bd., 1994—, Greater Tucson Leadership, 1996—. Editor: NSFRE Fund-Raising Dictionary, 1996. Mem. NSFRE (cert. bd. 1994—, mem. nat. found. bd., vice chmn. 1987-88, sec. found. bd. chair ann. fund campaign 1991, Outstanding Fund Raising Exec. 1988). Office: Arizona Children's Home Found 2700 South 8th Ave Tucson AZ 85725-7277

LEVY, BEVERLY KENNARD, college administrator; b. Salt Lake City, Oct. 5, 1949; d. Lon H. and Irma T. (Smith) Kennard; m. Marc B. Levy, Nov. 26, 1990; children: Ryan D. Giles, Brooke R. Miller-Levy. BS in Orgnl. Comms., U. Utah, 1988; MA in Profl. Comms., Westminster Coll., 1995. Comm. mgr. U. Utah Rsch. Inst., Salt Lake City, 1988-90; asst. coord. supplemental instrn. U. Utah, Salt Lake City, 1988-90; assoc. dir. admissions Westminster Coll., Salt Lake City, 1990—; developed curriculum for supplemental instrn. program Westminster Coll., Salt Lake City, 1994-96. Mem. Internat. Assn. Bus. Communicators, Soc. for Tech. Comm., Women in Comm. (membership v.p., bd. dirs.). Office: Westminster Coll 1840 S 1300 E Salt Lake City UT 84105

LEVY, CYNTHIA ANN, software engineer; b. Bethpage, N.Y., June 10, 1958; d. Richard Edwin and Miriam Lee (Gottlieb) Bergman; m. Mark Allan Levy, Nov. 27, 1983. BSEE, U. Rochester, 1980; MSEE and Computer Sci., Marquette U., 1985. Edison engr. GE, Pittsfield, Mass., 1980-81; Edison engr. GE Med. Sys., Waukesha, Wis., 1981-82, software engr., 1982-86, software sys. engr., 1986-92; program mgr. Critcare Sys., Inc., Waukesha, 1992-93, Catalyst USA, Brown Deer, Wis., 1994-95; dir. info. tech. project mgr. E.H. Boeckh, New Berlin, Wis., 1995—. Pres. Congregation Sisterhood, Waukesha, 1987-89; v.p. Milw. Assn. for Jewish Edn., 1989-95, co-pres., 1995—. Mem. Tau Beta Pi. Home: 905 Weston Hills Dr Brookfield WI 53045 Office: EH Boeckh 2885 S Calhoun Rd New Berlin WI 53151

LEVY, DALE PENNEYS, lawyer; b. Phila., Sept. 10, 1940; d. Harry M. and Rosalind (Fried) Penneys; m. Richard D. Levy, Dec. 20, 1970; children: Jonathan D., Michael Z. BA, Wellesley Coll., 1962; JD, U. Pa., 1967. Bar: Pa. 1967, U.S. Ct. Appeals (3rd cir.) 1971. Assoc. Blank, Rome, Comisky & McCauley, Phila., 1967-76, ptnr., 1976—; bd. dirs. Phila. Sch., Phila. Indsl. Devel. Corp. Contbr. articles to profl. jours. Bd. dirs., chair Women in Transition, 1983-85, active adv. bd., 1985—; chair Women's Rights Com., 1978; bd. dirs. Phila. Sr. Ctr., 1994—, Phila. Theatre. Co., 195—. Mem. ABA, Pa. Bar Assn., Phila. Bar Assn. (past chair women's rights com.). Mem. ABA (real property, probate and trust law sect., vice chairperson com. on pub.-pvt. ventures/privatization internat. law and practice sect.), Phila. Bar Assn. (real estate, corp., banking and bus. law sect., mem. women's rights com.). Office: Blank Rome Comisky & McCauley 4 Penn Center Plz Philadelphia PA 19103-2521

LEVY, LEAH GARRIGAN, federal official; b. Miami, Fla., Apr. 29, 1947; d. Thomas Leo and Mary (Flaherty) Garrigan; m. Roger N. Levy, May 2, 1977; children: Philip, Aaron. Student, George Mason U. Mem. legis. staff U.S. Ho. Reps., 1973-75; mem. scheduling staff U.S. Senate, 1975-77, mem. adminstrv. scheduling staff, 1977-81; staff asst. pub. liaison The White House, 1982-84; spl. asst. U.S Dept. Transport, Washington, 1984-89, U.S. Dept. Housing, Washington, 1989—; scheduling asst. Empower Am., Washington, 1993-94; scheduler majority leader Dick Armey U.S. Ho. of Reps., Washington, 1995—. Contbr. to Rep. Nat. Com., Washington. Contbr. Rep. Nat. Conv. Va. Rep. Party, Washington; del. Va. State GOP Conv., Richmond, 1994. Roman Catholic.

LEVY, MAUREEN MCRAE, college administrator; b. El Paso, Tex., Feb. 1, 1963; d. James Gordon McRae and Anne Elizabeth (Spickard) Law; m. David Steven Levy, Dec. 17, 1995. BA, U. Redlands, 1985; MA, Sheffield (Eng.) U., 1988. Fin. aid counselor Western State U., San Diego, 1985-86; fin. aid counselor Hastings Coll. of the Law U. Calif., San Francisco, 1989-90; dir. fin. aid Grad. Theol. Union, Berkeley, Calif., 1990-93; assoc. dean, fin. aid Glendale (Calif.) C.C., 1993—; presenter at confs. of fin. aid orgns., 1989—. Mem. selection com. for adminstrv. fellowship Calif. Student Aid Commn., 1996, com. on grants, 1994-96, regional coord. 1993-94, ops. com. 1994. Mem. AAUW, Calif. Assn. Student Fin. Aid Adminstrs. (pres. 1995, nominating com. chair 1996—, exec. coun. 1992-96, mem. numerous other coms. in past and presentincluding fiscal planning and nominations coms.) Western Assn. Student Fin. Aid Adminstrs. (moderator conf. 1989, mem. fed. issues com. 1993, exec. coun. Calif. rep., newsletter editor, 1996-97), Nat. Assn. Student Financial Aid Adminstrs. (participant leadership retreat 1994, moderator conf. 1994, task force on fin. aid standards), Phi Beta Kappa, Phi Alpha Theta, Omicron Delta Kappa. Democrat. Jewish. Office: Glendale Comty Coll 1500 N Verdugo Rd Glendale CA 91208

LEVY, ROBIN CAROLE, elementary guidance counselor; b. Berlin, Apr. 13, 1964; parents Am. citizens; d. Kenneth and Henrietta Nan (Weithorn) Kaplan; m. Guy Glickson Levy, July 27, 1986; 1 chld, Clare Sydney. BS,

Fla. State U., 1986; MEd, Coll. William and Mary, 1991. Cert. tchr. Presch. tchr. Talent House Pvt. Sch., Fairfax, Va., 1986-87; 4th grade tchr. Mt. Vernon Elem., Tabb, Va., 1987-92; elem. counselor Bethel Manor Elem., LAFB, Va., 1992-95; family mediator Dispute Settlement Ctr., Norfolk, Va., 1993—, Dispute Resolution Ctr., Richmond, Va., 1994—. Past pres., v.p. Denbigh Jaycees, Va., 1987-94 (Project Mgr. of Yr. 1991, 93, Outstanding Local Pres. 1994), sec., treas. Mem. ASCD, ACA, Va. Counselors Assn., Va. Sch. Counselors Assn., Peninsula Counselors Assn. Democrat. Jewish. Home: 463 Cheshire Ct Newport News VA 23602-6404

LEVY, ROCHELLE FELDMAN, artist; b. N.Y.C., Aug. 4, 1937; d. S. Harry and Eva (Krause) Feldman; m. Robert Paley Levy, June 4, 1955; children: Kathryn Tracey, Wendy Paige, Robert Paley, Angela Brooke, Michael Tyler. Student Barnard Coll., 1954-55, U. Pa., 1955-56; BFA, Moore Coll. Art, 1979. Mgmt. cons. Woodlyne Sch., Rosemont, Pa., 1983-84; sr. ptnr. DRT Interiors, Phila., 1983—; ptnr. Phila. Phillies, 1981-94. One-woman shows: Watson Gallery, Wheaton Coll., Norton, Mass., 1977, U. Pa., 1977, Med. Coll. Pa., Phila., 1982, Aqueduct Race Track, Long Island, N.Y., 1982, 68, Phila. Art Alliance, 1983, Moore Coll. Art, Phila., 1984, Phila. Art Alliance, 1994. Pres., League of Children's Hosp., Phila., 1969-70; bd. overseers Ctr. for Judaic Studies U. Pa., 1993-96. Recipient G. Allen Smith Prize, Woodmere Art Gallery, Chestnut Hill, Pa., 1979; Woman honoree Samuel Paley Day Care Ctr., Phila., 1990, Jefferson Bank Declaration award, 1991, Nat. Philanthropy honoree The Nat. Soc. of Fund Raising Execs. Greater Phila. chpt., 1994. Trustee Moore Coll. Art, 1979—, chmn. bd. trustees, 1988—; mem. selections and acquisitions com. Pa. Acad. Fine Arts, 1979—; bd. mgrs., 1975—, chmn. exec. com., 1982—, bd. trustees, 1990—. Mem. Allied Artists Am., Artist's Equity, Phila. Art Alliance, Phila. Mus. Art (assoc.), Phila. Print Club. Office: 2 Logan Sq Ste 2525 Philadelphia PA 19103

LEVY, (ALEXANDRA) SUSAN, construction company executive; b. Rockville Centre, N.Y., Apr. 26, 1949; d. Alexander Stanley and Anna Charlotte (Galasieski) Jankoski; m. William Mack Levy, Aug. 12, 1977. Student, Suffolk Community Coll., Brentwood, N.Y., 1976. Cert. constrn. assoc. Supr. N.Y. Telephone Co., Babylon, 1970-74; v.p. Aabbacco Equipment Leasing Corp., Lindenhurst, N.Y., 1974-81; pres., owner Femi-9 Contracting Corp., Lindenhurst, 1981—. Mem. affirmative action adv. coun. N.Y. State Dept. Transp., Albany, 1984-88, human resources adv. panel Long Island Project 2000; mem. Presdl. Task Force, Washington, 1982—; mem. Leadership Am., 1994-95. With U.S. Army, 1967-69. Recipient Henri Dunant Corp. award ARC Suffolk County, 1986, Race to the Top award Bridgestone Tire Corp., 1992, Nawbo award Nat. Assn. Women Bus. Owners, 1993; named honoree Women on the Job, 1989. Mem. Nat. Assn. Women in Constrn. (founder L.I. chpt., pres. 1983-85, regional chmn. woman-owned bus. enterprise com., nat. chmn. pub. rels. and mktg. com., nat. dir. Region 1 1988-89, Mem. of Yr. L.I. chpt. 1987, Exec. of Yr. L.I. chpt., nat. dir., 1988-89, nat. treas. 1991-93, nat. v.p. 1993-94, nat. pres.-elect 1994-95, pres. 1995-96), Nassau Suffolk Contractors Assn. (sec. 1984-87, sec.-treas. 1987-96, bd. dirs.), Nat. Assn. Women Bus. Owners (charter, Top Woman Bus. Owner award 1993), Am. Plat form Assn. Republican. Roman Catholic. Avocations: reading, writing, golf. Home: 133 Hollins Ln East Islip NY 11730-3006 Office: Femi-9 Contracting Corp 305 E Sunrise Hwy Lindenhurst NY 11757-2521

LEVY, VALERY, publisher; b. Khartoum, Sudan, Feb. 16, 1946; came to U.S., 1959; d. Robert and Victorine (Malka) Braunstein; m. Joseph Levy, Aug. 24, 1968; children: Nomi, Berti. BA in political sci., Fairleigh Dickinson U., 1976, MA in internat. studies, 1978. Eng. tchr. Am. Inst. Cultural Affairs, Barcelona, Spain, 1965-66; Montessori tchr. Ft. Lee (N.J.) Community Ctr., 1974-81; project coord. Friends of Hebrew U., N.Y.C., 1981-83; devel. cons. Ft. Lee, 1983-85; editor, sr. editor Holt, Rinehart & Winston, N.Y.C., 1986-88; sr. editor, exec. editor Simon & Schuster Edn. Co., Morristown, Englewood, N.J., 1988-90; pres. Wonder Well Publishers, Ft. Lee, 1990—. Author: Alphabet Connections, 1990; editor: Room Of Mirrors, 1991. Address: 2100 Linwood Ave Fort Lee NJ 07024-3186

LEW, D(UKHEE) BETTY, physician; b. Seoul, Korea, June 1, 1952; came to U.S., 1972; d. H.S. and M.S. Lew. BS, Temple U., 1976, MD, 1980. Intern, resident Shands Med. Ctr., Gainesville, Fla., 1980-83; fellow Nat. Jewish Ctr. for Immunology and Respiratory Medicine, Denver, 1983-86; asst. prof. U. Tenn., Memphis, 1986-92; assoc. prof. U. Tenn., 1992—. Grantee Am. Lung Assn., 1991—, Am. Lung Assn. Tenn., 1990-91; recipient 1st award NIH, 1991—. Mem. Am. Acad. Allergy & Immunology, Am. Coll. Allergy & Immunology, Ten. Soc. Allergy & Immunology, Tenn. Thoracic Soc., Soc. Pediat. Rsch., Soc. Leukocyte Biology. Methodist. Home: 2490 Ayrshire Cv Memphis TN 38119-7506 Office: LeBonheur Children's Med Ctr 1 Children's Plz Memphis TN 38105

LEW, FRAN, artist. BA in Art with honors, Bklyn. Coll., 1966; MFA, Boston U., 1968; postgrad., Internat. Ctr. Painting and Costume Design, Venice, Italy, 1978, Art Student's League, N.Y.C., 1978-79, Reilly League of Artists, White Plains, N.Y., 1979-84. One-man shows include Grand Ctrl. Art Galleries, N.Y.C., 1990, Manhattan Borough Pres.'s Art Gallery, N.Y.C., 1989, Pen and Brush Club, N.Y.C., 1989, Columbus Club, N.Y.C., 1982; group shows include John Pence Gallery, San Francisco, 1987, Salmagundi Club, Nat. Arts Club, Am. Artists Profl. League; represented in public collections Gov.'s Mansion, Albany, N.Y., Consulate of Israel, N.Y.C.; represented in permanent collection Fenster Mus., Tulsa, Okla., Maitland Art Ctr., Fla., Cornell Mus., Delray Beach, Fla.; portraits include Gov. Mario M. Cuomo, First Lady Matilda Cuomo, Nobel Laureate Dr. Vincent duVigneaud, Philip H. Geier Jr., Daniel Damiano, trilogy Golda Meir, David Ben Gurion, and Moshe Dayan. Artist, cons. Westchester 2000, White Plains, 1989. Recipient Crescent Cardboard Corp. prize Am. Artist Mag., 1987. Mem. Art Students' League (life), Reilly League Artists, Knickerbocker Artists (Gold medal 1984), Hudson Valley Art Assn. (Mrs John Newington award 1989), Catherine Lorillard Wolfe Art Club (Margaret Dole award 1988), Pen and Brush Club (Solo award 1987). Home and Studio: 150 Lake St Apt 3F White Plains NY 10604-2469

LEW, JOYCELYNE MAE, actress; b. Santa Monica, Calif., Feb. 25, 1962; d. George and Mabel Florence (Lum) L. BA in Theatre Arts, UCLA, 1981, teaching credential, 1982; MA in Urban Edn., Pepperdine U., 1984; bilingual cert., U. So. Calif., 1983; postgrad., Stella Adler Acad., 1988; studied with, The Groundlings Improv Group, 1987. Appeared in films Tai-Pan, 1987, Fatal Beauty, 1989, The Royal Affair, 1993, Shattered Image, 1993, Dr. Boris and Mrs. Duluth, 1994, Hindsight, 1996, Fire in My Heart, 1996, TV programs The Young and the Restless, 1990, Phil Donahue Show, 1993, Hard Copy, 1994, Current Affair, 1995, Gordon Elliott, 1995; voice over artist, mag. model, body double, dancer; appeared in comml. Good Seasons, 1996, Pillsbury Doughboy, 1996, Pacific Bell, 1996; co-writer film script They Still Call Me Bruce, 1986 (award); song lyricist Nighttime Blues. Mem. judging com. for film grants Nat. Endowment for Arts, 1986; mem. L.A. Beautiful, 1993. Mem. AFTRA, SAG, NATAS (blue ribbon com. for Emmy awards 1986-90), Assn. Asian Pacific Am. Artists (treas. 1983-89), Nat. Asian Am. Telecomms. Assn., Am. Film Inst. Conservatory Workshop, Calif. PTA (life). Home and Office: 1958 N Van Ness Ave Los Angeles CA 90068-3625

LEW, REBECCA MARIE, horticulturalist, landscape designer; b. Groton, Conn., Feb. 3, 1970; d. Girard Thomas and Annette Theresa (Sollée) Lew. BS in Landscape Horticulture, N.C. State U., 1992. N.C. Assn. Nurserymen cert. plant profl., 1993; Ga. Green Industry cert. plant profl., 1995. Landscape mgmt. foreman Greenscapes, Inc., Holly Springs, N.C., 1992-93; landscape estimator The Briar Patch, Apex, N.C., 1993; nursery mgr. Hastings Garden Ctr., Atlanta, 1994-96, Kiefer Landscaping, Durham, N.C., 1996—. Cons. horticulturalist for computer program The Right Landscape Plant Program, 1991.

LEWANDOWSKI, JULIA ELIZABETH, secondary school educator, retired; b. Toledo, Jan. 25, 1934; d. Alex E. Farkas and Julia (Vargo) Kowalski; m. Richard John Lewandowski, Aug. 20, 1955; children: Richard A., Douglas J., Gregory S., Bradley E., Juliana R. BS in Edn., Toledo U., 1959, postgrad., 1982. Tchr. Brittany Jr. H.S., University City, Mo., 1955-59, Vista (Calif.) H.S., 1960-61, St. John's Elem., Toledo, 1977-79, Whitmer H.S., Toledo, 1979-94; supr. of student tchrs. in maths. U. Toledo; owner Pleasures & Treasures ceramic shop, Toledo, 1974-76. Founder paper recycling program, Whitmer H.S., 1990-94. Named Woman of Toledo St. Vincent Hosp., 1970. Mem. Toledo Dental Aux. (pres. 1972-73), KC (pres. 1973-74), Zeta Tau Alpha (pres. 1970-71). Home: 5804 Staghorn Dr Toledo OH 43614-4563

LEWANDOWSKI, MICHALENE MARIA, human service consultant, lecturer; b. Hamilton, Ont., Can., June 2, 1920; d. Stanley Casmere and Winifred (Kolodziejski) Doskotch; m. Henry Adam Schultz, Aug. 30, 1939 (dec. July 1940); m. Matthew John Lewandowski, July 27, 1941 (dec. Jan. 1987); children: Adrian, Christopher. Student, Wayne State U. Cert. med. asst.; cert. Am. Coll. Nursing Home Adminstrs., Mich. Health Facilities Assn., various other state health assns. Activity-patient affairs dir. Abbey Nursing Home, Warren, Mich., 1963-70; designated social worker Good Shepherd Nursing Home, Detroit, 1970, Rose-Villa Nursing Home, Roseville, Mich., 1970-81; instr. rehab. and devel. various nursing homes, Warren, 1976—; originator Day Care Ctrs., Macomb County, Mich., 1990-91; cons. various nursing homes, Mich., 1984-87; profl. lectr., 1990—; instr. rehab. and human rels. devel. in nursing homes Macomb County Community Coll., 1976; pres. Macomb County Activity Dirs. Assn., 1975; panelist in field; human svc. cons., 1984-86. Author: The Human Island, 1970 (Outstanding Cultural Achievement award, 1976); contbr. articles to profl. pubns. Del. White House Conf. on Aging, Lansing, Mich., Washington, 1971; state commr. on aging State of Mich., Lansing, 1975-80; bd. dirs. Macomb County (Mich.) Coun. on Aging, 1973, spl. cons., 1976. Recipient citation for Care and Therapy of Aged, City of Warren, 1964, Polish Nat. Alliance for Complete Dedication to the Aged, 1970, Spl. Tribute State of Mich., 1974; named Citizen of Week WBRB, 1970; honored for Contbns. to Mankind, Macomb County Commrs., 1973; recipient personal letter from Pres. Nixon for her work; documentary on her work with elderly presented on Sta. WXYZ-TV.

LEWANDOWSKI, TERESA MARIE, civil engineer; b. Wilmington, Del.. BSCE, U. Del., 1986. Registered profl. engr., Del. Design engr. pvt. cons., 1986-92; civil engr. Del. Dept. Transp., Dover, 1992—. Bd. dirs. alumni engring. bd. U. Del., Newark, 1995—. Mem. ASCE, Am. Soc. Hwy. Engrs. Office: Del Dept Transp PO Box 778 Dover DE 19903

LEWARK, CAROL ANN, special education educator; b. Fort Wayne, Ind., Mar. 8, 1935; d. Lloyd L. and Elizabeth J. (Arthur) Meads; m. Paul N. Lewark, Aug. 20, 1955; children: David P., Laura, Beth, Daniel A. BA, St. mary of Woods, 1978; MS, Ind. U., 1981. Cert. elem. educator, spl. educator mentally retarded K-12, learning disabilities K-12, Ind.; cert. home tng. specialist, Wis. Home tng. specialist Madison Wis. ARC, Madison, 1968-70; nursery sch. cons. Allen County ARC, Ft. Wayne, Ind., 1971-73; early childhood spl. edn. dir. Allen County ARC, Ft. Wayne, 1973—; cons. in field; presenter in field; apptd. by Ind. Gov. to State Interagy. Coordinating Coun. for Infants and Toddlers, 1992-95; apptd. to Higher Ed Coun. for Early Childhood and Spl. Edn. Contbr. articles to profl. jours. Apptd. to Leadership Ft. Wayne, 1994. Named Model Project Site 99-457 Early Intervention Ind. State Dept. Mental Health, 1987; Tech. Assistance grantee Georgetown U., 1991-93. Mem. Ind. Coun. for Exceptional Children (sec. 1990-94), First Steps of Allen County (facilitator 1989—), Leadership Fort Wayne. Home: 910 Kensington Blvd Fort Wayne IN 46805-5312 Office: ARC of Allen County 2542 Thompson Ave Fort Wayne IN 46807-1051

LEWENT, JUDY CAROL, pharmaceutical executive; b. Jan. 13, 1949. BA, Goucher Coll., 1970; MS in Mgmt., MIT, 1972. With corp. fin. dept. E.F. Hutton & Co., Inc., 1972-74; asst. v.p. for strategic planning Bankers Trust Co., 1974-75; sr. fin. analyst corp. planning Norton Simon, 1975-76; div. contr. Pfizer, Inc., 1976-80; dir. acquisitions and capital analysis Merck & Co., Inc., Whitehouse Station, N.J., 1980-83, asst. contr., 1983-85, exec. dir. fin. evaluation and analysis, 1985-87, v.p., treas., 1987-90, v.p. fin., CFO, 1990-92, sr. v.p., CFO, 1993—. Office: Merck & Co Inc PO Box 100 One Merck Dr Whitehouse Station NJ 08889-0100

LEWIN, PEARL GOLDMAN, psychologist; b. Bklyn., Apr. 25, 1923; d. Frank and Anna (Simon) Goldman; m. Seymour Z. Lewin, Oct. 17, 1943; children: David, Jonathan. BA, Hunter Coll., 1943; MS, U. Mich., 1947; PhD, NYU, 1980. Lic. psychologist, N.Y. Insp. chemist quarter master corps U.S. Army, 1943-45; chemist chem. warfare U.S. Army, Edgewood Arsenal, Md., 1945; asst. psychologist Bur. Psychol. Svcs., U. Mich., Ann Arbor, 1947-48; freelance rsch. asst. chemistry N.Y.C., 1955-71; adj. lectr. CUNY, Bklyn., 1973-74, instr., 1974-79, asst. prof., 1979-80; psychologist Creedmore Psychiat. Ctr., N.Y.C., 1980-82; sr. psychologist Manhattan Family Ct., N.Y.C., 1982-87; cons., 1987—; mentor Peer Counseling Orgn., Bklyn. Coll., 1976-80, coord. student svcs. New Sch. Liberal Arts, 1974-76, adminstr. acad. regulations, 1974-76. Author: Sexist Humor, 1979. Mem. APA, Pi Lambda Theta, Phi Kappa Phi. Home and Office: 4231 N Walnut Ave Arlington Heights IL 60004-1302

LEWIN, SUSAN GRANT, creative director advertising and public relations; b. Phila., Feb. 25, 1939; d. Benj Gerald Winig and May (Lipsky) Feman; m. Chester Grant, Aug. 7, 1960 (div. 1966); m. Harold F. Lewin, June 4, 1967; children: Adam, Gabrielle. BA, U. Pa. Reporter and columnist Home Furnishing Daily, 1962-65, design editor, 1965-70; sr. editor architecture House Beautiful Mag. Hearst Publs., 1970-82; creative dir. Formica Corp., N.Y.C., 1982-96; pres. Design Communications Internat., N.Y.C., 1988-96, global creative dir., 1994-96; pres. Susan Grant Lewin Assocs., N.Y.C., 1996—; exhbn. curator Surface and Ornament, 1983-88, Table to Tablescape, Kansas City Art Inst., et al, 1988-91, Found Futures, 1992; bd. dirs. Archtl. League. Author: Formica and Design, 1991, One Of A Kind American Art Jewelry Today, 1994. Chmn. corp. adv. com. Am. Craft Mus., 1995—. Recipient Disting. Editl. award Am. Soc. Interior Designers, 1967, Nat. Endowment for Arts, 1978, Pres.' award Inst. Bus. Designers, 1983, Circle of Excellence award Internat. Furnishings & Design Assocs., 1993; felow Internat. Design Conf., Aspen, 1990. Mem. AIA (com. on design), Archtl. League, World Design, Am. Inst. Graphic Arts, Indsl. Designers Soc., Mcpl. Arts Soc., IFDA.

LEWINGER, JEAN ELIZABETH, pediatrics nurse, neonatal intensive care nurse; b. Bklyn., Oct. 30, 1946; d. Donald and Grace W. (Mowat) Gordon; m. Arnold A. Lewinger, Nov. 4, 1967; children: William Anthony, Andrea Jean. Diploma in nursing, Kings County Hosp. Ctr., Bklyn., 1967; BSN, Cedar Crest Coll., 1986; MSN, U. Pa., 1988. Staff nurse neonatal ICU Southside Hosp., Bayshore, N.Y., 1973-76; staff nurse, charge nurse pediatric spl. care unit Ea. Maine Med. Ctr., Bangor, 1976-81, transport nurse, 1977-81; neonatal transport nurse Allentown (Pa.) Hosp., 1981-88, neonatal ICU, 1981-88; neonatal nurse practitioner Pa. Hosp., Phila., 1988-89, Episc. Hosp., Phila., 1989-95, Thomas Jefferson U. Hosp., Phila., 1995—; CPR instr.; nurse laision for neonatal support group, Phila.; regional instr. neonatal resuscitation program. Contbr. articles to profl. publs. Mem. NAACOG (cert. neonatal intensive care practitioner, cert. neonatal intensive care nurse), AHWONN, Nat. Assn. Neonatal Nurses, Am. Bd. Examiners, Ob-Gyn. Nurses, Nat. Perinatal Assn., Pa. Perinatal Assn., Phila. Perinatal Assn., Delaware Valley Assn. Neonatal Nurses.

LEWIS, ANNE MCCUTCHEON, architect; b. New Orleans, Oct. 15, 1943; d. John Tinney and Susan (Dart) McCutcheon; m. Ronald Burton Lewis, Oct. 2, 1971; children: Matthew, Oliver. BA magna cum laude, Radcliffe Coll., 1965; MArch, Harvard U., 1970. Registered architect, D.C. Designer and planner Skidmore, Owings & Merrill, Washington, 1969-72, Keyes, Lethbridge & Condon, Washington, 1972-75; prin. Anne McCutcheon Lewis AIA, Washington, 1976-81; ptnr. McCartney Lewis Architects, Washington, 1981—. Mem. Harvard U. Grad. Sch. Design Alumni Coun., Cambridge, Mass., 1979-82; bd. dirs. Friends Non-Profit Housing, Washington, 1981—, Washington Humane Soc., 1990—. Fellow AIA (Design awards 1979, 83, 89, 90, 91, 92, 93, dir.-at-large Washington chpt. 1982-84). Mem. Soc. of Friends. Office: McCartney Lewis Architects 1503 Connecticut Ave NW Washington DC 20036-1103

LEWIS, AUDREY GERSH, financial marketing/public relations consultant; b. Phila., Dec. 1, 1933; d. Benjamin and Augusta (Fine) Gersh; divorced; children: Jamie Lewis Keith, Ruth-Ellen. Student, Temple U., 1951-53. Asst. mgr. accounts payable/receivable Turner Constrn. Co., Louisville, 1953-55; rep. sales, mktg., fin. depts. Benjamin Gersh Wholesaler Jeweler, Wyncote, Pa., 1955-69; registered rep. Seaboard Planning Corp. (formerly B.C. Morton Broker Del.), Greenwich, Conn. and Wyncote, 1969-72; placement counselor sales and mktg. dept. Greyhound Permanent Pers. subs. Greyhound Corp., Stamford, Conn., 1974-77; asst. v.p. Am. Investors Corp., Greenwich, 1977-85; founder, pres. Audrey Gersh Lewis Cons. Ltd., Greenwich, 1985—. Chair Cancer Fund, Wyncote, United Fund Leadership Award, Wyncote; asst. treas. Republican Town Com., Greenwich, 1981-82; mem. Greenwich Town Alarm Appeals Bd., 1985—. Mem. Assn. Corp. Growth (bd. dirs., v.p. mktg. and pub. rels. N.Y. chpt. 1989-92, mem. nat. ann. meeting planning com. 1992, 93, 94), Fin. Women's Assn., Women's Econ. Round Table, Greenwich C. of C. (mem. pub. rels. com. 1990—, corp. devel. com. 1991—), Centre for the Study of the Presidency (nat. adv. coun.), N.Y. Hong Kong Assn., Am. C. of C. in Hong Kong, World Trade Centres in Can. Office: Audrey Gersh Lewis Cons Ltd PO Box 4644 Greenwich CT 06830-8644

LEWIS, BARBARA G., accountant; b. Hamilton, Ohio, Nov. 26, 1964; d. Albert L. and Lois A. (Rosencrans) Gorrell; 1 child, Taira. BS, U. Louisville, 1989. Cert. mgmt. acct. Acct. Gen. Welding, Louisville, 1990-91; staff acct. CompDent Corp., Louisville, 1991-95; fin. analyst ARM Fin., Louisville, 1995—; cons. in field. Mem. Inst. Mgmt. Accts. Office: ARM Fin Group 515 W Market St Louisville KY 40202

LEWIS, BARBARA GRIMES, financial administrator; b. Prescott, Ark., Aug. 22, 1941; d. Benjamin Franklin and Dorothy Fay (Barnes) Grimes; m. Ronald B. Lewis, Sept. 5, 1959 (div. Oct. 1981); children: Ginger, Billy. B of Bus. Adminstrn., So. Ark. U., 1983; M of Comty. Svcs., Henderson State U., 1995. Lic. preacher United Meth. Ch. Adminstrv. asst. Talbot's Inc., Magnolia, Ark., 1967-80; computer ops. mgr. So. Ark. U., Magnolia, 1981-83; tchr. Draughon Sch. Bus., Little Rock, 1983-85; acct. Am. Cancer Soc., Little Rock, 1985-86; contr. Am. Contract Svcs., Little Rock, 1986-89; treas. Pulaski Heights United Meth. Ch., Little Rock, 1989-92; adminstr. Boatmen's Trust Co., Little Rock, 1993-96; contr. Beach Abstract & Guaranty, 1996—. Part-time pastor Floyd/Garner United Meth. Ch., Floyd, Ark., 1994—; mem. Dem. Nat. Com., 1992, Clinton/Gore Steering Com., 1995-99. E. Craig Brandenberg scholar United Meth. Ch., 1994. Mem. Bus. and Profl. Women (numerous offices held, Woman of Yr. 1990), Cen. Ark. So. Ark. U. Alumni Assn. (dir., pres.), Order of Ea. Star (Worthy Matron 1996). Home: 217-C W 20th Little Rock AR 72206

LEWIS, BARBARA JEAN, occupational therapist; b. Hugoton, Kans., Nov. 16, 1965; d. ERnest Howard and Selola Belle (Wilson) L. AS, Seward County C.C., Liberal, Kans., 1986; B of Occupl. Therapy, U. Kans., 1990. Staff occupl. therapist High Plains Bapt. Hosp., Amarillo, Tex., 1990-94, sr. hand therapist sports and occupl. medicine, 1993-94; staff occupl. therapist Mariner Rehab., Nashville, 1994-96. Mem. Am. Occupl. Therapy Assn. (registered occupl. therapist). Office: SunSpectrum Outpatient Rehab Ste 126 2410 Charlotte Ave Nashville TN 37023

LEWIS, BERNADETTE, primary school educator; b. N.Y.C., May 21, 1930; d. George A. and Frances Marie (Andrews) Miller; m. George J. Lewis, Dec. 14, 1952; children: George J. IV, Richard, Laura, Charles, Douglas, Carol. BA in Sci. and Math., Ctrl. Wash. U., 1974, MA in Reading, 1980. Cert. primary sch. tchr., Wash. Tchr. 1st grade Highland Sch. Dist., Tieton, Wash., 1974-80; tchr. Naches Valley Sch. Dist., Naches, Wash., 1980—; reading methods instr. Heritage Coll., Toppenish, 1993; sci. thru lit. instr. Heritage Inst., Seattle, summer 1994; organizer, dir. after-sch. tutorial program for jr. high/h.s. students, Naches, 1988-91. Editor: The Idea Book, 1987. Dir. Cmty. Concert Series, Yakima, Wash., 1978-88, Naches Libr., 1972—; charter mem. Yakima Literacy Coalition, 1995; exec. bd. Wash. Orgn. Reading Devel., 1983—, East v.p., 1990-92, pres.-elect, 1995-96, pres., 1996—, coun. pres., 1983-84; mem. Wash. State Com. for Yr. of the Leader, 1996—. Migrant grantee, 1982, Rotary grantee, 1993; named Outstanding Tchr., PTA/Sch. Dist. Highland, 1978; recipient Wash. State Outstanding Tchrs. award, Christa McAuliffe award, 1995. Mem. Internat. Reading Assn., Wash. Orgn. Reading Devel. (exec. bd. 1983—, coun. pres., 1983-84, Pres. award 1993, pres. 1996—), Yakima Valley Reading Coun. (past sec., v.p., pres.), Philanthropic Edn. Orgn. (chaplain, sec., v.p., pres.), PEO (chair scholarship bd.), Naches Women's Club (chair scholarship bd 1983), Phi Delta Kappa (found. chair 1986—, sec., v.p., pres. 1986-93), Alpha Phi Alumni Assn. (treas. 1989). Presbyterian. Home: 13471 Old Naches Hwy Naches WA 98937-9733

LEWIS, CAROL JEANNE, poet; b. Chgo., Jan. 12, 1930; d. Walter van Hagen and Edith Marie (Chatelaine) Weiss; m. Ross Duane Lewis, June 1959 (div. 1985); 1 child, Anthony Ross. AA, Wright Jr. Coll.; student, Santa Monica Jr. Coll. Contbr. poetry to profl. publs. Recipient First Pl. award Bridge Mag. Poetry Contest, 1994, Finalist Allen Jay Freedman Poetry Contest, 1994. Mem. Midnight Spl. Poetry Workshop (monitor). Democrat. Home: 9622 Lucerne Ave #302 Culver City CA 90232-2925

LEWIS, CHERIE SUE, attorney, author, language & journalism educator; b. Cleve., Feb. 6, 1951; d. Samuel D. and Evelyne P. L. BA, U. Mich., 1973; MS, Boston U., 1975; PhD, U. Minn., 1986; JD, Southwestern U., 1996. Cert. ESL tchr., Calif. Prof. Pa. State U., State College, 1988-89, Nat. Chengchi U., Taipei, Taiwan, 1989-91, Syracuse U., 1992-93, Nat. U., L.A., 1993—; cons. Pacific Rim Inst., L.A., 1992-95. Author: (book chpt.) Disability Rights, International, 1994, ednl. brochures, 1994; mng. editor Southwestern U. Jour. Law and Trade, 1995-96. Mem. AAUP, ABA. Office: 6 Kenwood Ct Beachwood OH 44122-7501

LEWIS, CHRISTINA LYNN, human services administrator; b. Brook Park, Ohio, June 19, 1963; d. Albert Joseph and Gail Ann (Kohler) Urbas; m. Timothy Allen Lewis, Aug. 3, 1989; 1 child, Cherie Ann. AA, Pasco Hernando C.C., Brooksville, Fla., 1996; student, Thomas Edison State Coll., 1996—. Owner, operator Spl. Touch Day Care, Olmsted Twp., Ohio, 1986-89, Spring Hill, Fla., 1989-94; dir., tng. coord. United Cerebral Palsy, Brooksville, 1994-96; mentor, tng. advisor child care outreach program United Cerebral Palsy, Brooksville, Fla., 1993—; advisor, instr. Child Devel. Assn. Credential Program, Brooksville, 1991—; coun. mem. Pre-K Interagy. Coun., Brooksville, 1994—; CPR, First Aid instr. ARC, 1994—; area supr. Head Start, Inverness, Fla., 1996—. Author (tng. packet) CDA: Everything You Need to Know to Get Started, 1992. Dep. registrar Supr. Elections, Hernando County, 1994; vol. instr. ARC. Recipient Resolution 91-70 award Hernando County Commr., Brooksville, 1991. Mem. Nat. Assn. for the Edn. Young Children, Assn. for Better Child Care (founding mem., newsletter editor 1990, sec., resource and referral 1989-93, Tchr. of Yr. 1990), Phi Theta Kappa. Republican. Home: 9063 Spring Hill Dr Spring Hill FL 34608-6241 Office: Childhood Devel Svcs US 41 Inverness FL 34450

LEWIS, DEBORAH GAIL, personnel management specialist; b. Burlington, Iowa, Oct. 5, 1953; d. James Howard Jr. and Evelyn Merle (Leinart) L.; m. Walter Scott Fargo, Sept. 20, 1950 (div. Mar. 1983, dec. Sept. 1995). BS in Biomed. Sci., Tex. A&M U., 1978, MPA, 1988. Technician Tex. Forest Svc., Lufkin, 1972-73; technician Tex. A&M U., College Station, 1973-75, student technician, 1975-78; biol. technician Agrl. Rsch. Svc., College Station, 1978-81, pers. asst., 1984-89; biol. technician Agrl. Rsch. Svc., Stillwater, Okla., 1981-84; pers. staffing and classification specialist Bur. of Engring. and Printing, Washington, 1989-90; pers. mgmt. specialist Nat. Oceanic and Atmospheric Adminstrn., Silver Spring, Md., 1990-94, Dept. of Energy, Washington, 1994—. Mem. bd. dirs. Long Reach House Condominiums, Columbia, 1993—; sec. Dem. Women of Howard County, Columbia, 1996. Mem. AAUW, NOW, Internat. Pers. Mgmt. Assn., Columbia Ski Club, Nat. Mus. for Women in the Arts, Columbia (Md.) Dem. Club (bd. dirs. 1996). Home: 8729 Hayshed Ln #21 Columbia MD 21045

LEWIS, ELEANOR ROBERTS, lawyer; b. Detroit, Jan. 5, 1944; d. David Edward and Patricia Mary (Easterbrook) Roberts; m. Roger Kutnow Lewis, June 24, 1967; 1 child, Kevin Michael. B.A., Wellesley Coll., 1965; MA, Harvard U., 1966; JD, Georgetown U., 1974. Bar: D.C. 1975, U.S. Dist. Ct. D.C. 1975, U.S. Ct. Appeals (D.C. cir.) 1975, U.S. Ct. Appeals (10th cir.) 1976, U.S. Supreme Ct. 1980. Secondary sch. tchr., Mass., Md., 1966-71; atty. HUD, Washington, 1974-76, asst. gen. counsel, 1979-82; atty. Brownstein Zeidman & Schomer, Washington, 1976-79; chief counsel internat. commerce U.S. Dept. Commerce, Washington, 1982—. Author, editor (with others) Street Law, 1975. Contbr. chpts. to books, articles to legal and fin. jours. Commr. D.C. Adv. Neighborhhod Commn. Bd. dirs. Dana Place Condominium, Washington. Mem. ABA (U.S. govt. liaison to internat. sect.), D.C. Bar Assn., Sr. Execs. Assn. (nat. bd. dirs.). Home: 5034 1/2 Dana Pl NW Washington DC 20016-3441 Office: US Dept Commerce 14th & Constitution Ave NW Washington DC 20230-0002

LEWIS, ENID SELENA, educator; b. Jamaica, W.I., Aug. 6, 1928; arrived in U.S., 1989; d. Thomas Vivian and Carlena Agatha (Hemmings) Davis; m. George Nathaniel Lewis, Aug. 12, 1953; children: Patrick, Heather, Peter, Charmaine, George Jr., Suzanne. BA in Early Childhood Edn., Univ. Coll. W.I., 1983. Primary sch. tchr. Ministry of Edn., Jamaica, 1949-70, trainer tchr. early childhood and spl. edn., 1970-80, edn. officer early childhood and spl. edn., 1980-83, edn. officer spl. edn., 1983-88; tchr. Archdiocese of N.Y., 1989—; field work in edn. Swasiland, Africa, 1976; adv. bd. Edn., Jamaice, 1986-88. Recipient Nat. award scholarships Jamaica Gov., 1982, Israel Assn. Internat Coop. to Israel, 1974-75, U. Kans., 1983, U. West Indies, 1979, 80. Baptist. Home: 391A Decator St Brooklyn NY 11233 Office: Sacred Heart of Jesus Sch 456 W 52d St New York NY 10019

LEWIS, EVELYN, management consultant; b. Goslar, Germany, Sept. 19, 1946; came to U.S. 1952, naturalized 1957; d. Gerson Emanuel and Sala (Mendlowicz) L. BA, U. Ill.-Chgo., 1968; MA, Ball State U., 1973, PhD, 1976. Rsch. analyst Comptr. State Ill., Chgo., 1977-78; lectr. polit. sci. dept. Loyola U., Chgo., 1977; asst. to commr. Dept. Human Svcs., Chgo., 1978-81; group mgr. communications Arthur Andersen & Co., Chgo., 1981-84; dir. communications and pub. rels. Heidrick and Struggles, Inc., Chgo., 1984-88; assoc. ptnr. change mgmt. svcs. practice Andersen Cons., 1989—; adj. faculty sch. bus. adminstrn. Roosevelt U., 1988. Mem. Children of the Holocaust, Chgo., 1982; bd. dirs. Internat. Children's Benefit Fund. Mem. Internat. Communication Assn., Coun. of Communication Mgmt, B'nai Brith. Jewish. Avocations: writing, poetry, bicycling, hiking. Office: Andersen Cons 33 W Monroe Chicago IL 60603

LEWIS, FELICE FLANERY, lawyer, educator; b. Plaquemine, La., Oct. 5, 1920; d. Lowell Baird and E. Elizabeth (Lee) Flanery; m. Francis Russell Lewis, Dec. 22, 1944. BA, U. Wash., 1947; PhD, NYU, 1974; JD, Georgetown U., 1981. Bar: N.Y. 1982. Dean L.I. Univ., Liberal Arts & Scis., Bklyn., 1974-78; assoc. Harry G. English, Bklyn., 1983-85, 91—; adj. prof., polit. sci. L.I. Univ., Bklyn., 1983—. Author: Literature, Obscenity and Law, 1976; co-editor: Henry Miller, Years of Trial & Triumph, 1962-64, 1978. Home: 28 Whitney Cir Glen Cove NY 11542-1316 Office: Harry G English 7219 3rd Ave Brooklyn NY 11209-2131

LEWIS, GLADYS SHERMAN, nurse, educator; b. Wynnewood, Okla., Mar. 20, 1933; d. Andrew and Minnie Elva (Halsey) Sherman; R.N., St. Anthony's Sch. Nursing, 1953; student Okla. Bapt. U., 1953-55; AB, Tex. Christian U., 1956; postgrad. Southwestern Bapt. Theol. Sem., 1959-60, Escuela de Idiomas, San Jose, Costa Rica, 1960-61; MA in Creative Writing, Central (Okla.) State U., 1985; PhD in English Okla. State U. 1992; m. Wilbur Curtis Lewis, Jan. 28, 1955; children: Karen, David, Leanne, Cristen. Mem. nursing staff various facilities, Okla., 1953-57; instr. nursing, med. missionary Bapt. mission and hosp., Paraguay, 1961-70; vice-chmn. edn. commn. Paraguay Bapt. Conv., 1962-65; sec. bd. trustees Bapt. Hosp., Paraguay, 1962-65; chmn. personnel com., handbook and policy book officer Bapt. Mission in Paraguay, 1967-70; trustee Southwestern Bapt. Theol. Sem., 1974-84, chmn. student affairs com., 1976-78, vice-chmn. bd. 1978-80; ptnr. Las Amigas Tours, 1978-80; writer, conference leader, campus lectr., 1959—; adj. prof. English Cen. State U., Okla. (name changed to U. Cen. Okla.), 1990-91; faculty mem., asst. prof. English U. Cen. Okla., 1991-95, assoc. prof., 1996—. Active Dem. com., Evang. Women's Caucus, 1979-80; leader Girl Scouts U.S.A., 1965-75; Okla. co-chmn. Nat. Religious Com. for Equal Rights Amendment, 1977-79; tour host Meier Internat. Study League, 1978-81. Mem. AAUW, Internat. and Am. colls. surgeons women's auxiliaries, Okla. State, Okla. County med. auxiliaries, Am. Nurse Assn., Nat. Women's Polit. Caucus, 1979-80. Author: On Earth As It Is, 1983; Two Dreams and a Promise, 1984, Message, Messenger and Response, 1994; also religious instructional texts in English and Spanish; editor Sooner Physician's Heartbeat, 1979-82; contbr. articles to So. Bapt. and secular periodicals. Home: 14501 N Western Ave Edmond OK 73013-1828

LEWIS, GOLDY SARAH, real estate developer, corporation executive; b. West Selkirk, Man., Can., June 15, 1921; d. David and Rose (Dwor) Kimmel; m. Ralph Milton Lewis, June 12, 1941; children: Richard Alan, Robert Edward, Roger Gordon, Randall Wayne. B.S., UCLA, 1943; postgrad., U. So. Calif., 1944-45. Pvt. practice acctg. L.A., 1945-57, law office mgr., 1953-55; dir., exec. v.p. Lewis Homes, Upland, Calif., 1955—, Lewis Construction Co. Inc., Upland, 1959—, Lewis Bldg. Co., Inc., Las Vegas, 1960—, Republic Sales Co., Inc., 1956—, Kimmel Enterprises, Inc., 1959—; mng. partner Lewis Homes of Calif., 1973—; mng. ptnr. Lewis Homes of Nev., 1972—, Western Properties, 1972—, Foothill Investment Co., 1971—, Republic Mgmt. Co., 1978—. Contbr. articles to mags., jours. Mem. Dean's Coun. UCLA Grad. Sch. Architecture and Urban Planning; mem. UCLA Found., Chancellor's Assocs.; endowed Ralph and Goldy Lewis Ctr. for Regional Policy at UCLA, 1989, Ralph and Goldy Lewis Hall of Planning and Devel. at U. S.C., 1989, others. Recipient 1st award of distinction Am. Builder mag., 1963, Homer Briggs Svc. to Youth award West End YMCA, 1990, Spirit of Life award City of Hope, 1993; co-recipient Builder of Yr. award Profl. Builder Mag., 1988, Housing Person of Yr. award Nat. Housing Conf., 1990, Entrepreneur of Yr. award Inland Empire, 1990; Ralph and Goldy Lewis Sports Ctr. named in their honor City of Rancho Cucamonga, 1988, also several other parks and sports fields including Lewis Park in Claremont.; named one of Woman of Yr. Calif. 25th Senate Dist., 1989, (with husband Ralph M. Lewis) Disting. Chief Exec. Officer, Calif. State U., San Bernadino, 1991, Mgmt. Leaders of the Yr. Univ. Calif., Riverside, 1993. Mem. Nat. Assn. Home Builders, Bldg. Industry Assn. So. Calif. (Builder of Yr. award Baldy View chpt. 1988), Internat. Coun. Shopping Ctrs., Urban Land Inst. Office: Lewis Homes PO Box 670 Upland CA 91785-0670

LEWIS, JANET K., university dean; b. Yankton, S.D., Aug. 13, 1950; d. Merle and Barbara Jean (Stafford) Kautson; m. Keith E. Larsen, May 16, 1970 (div. Apr. 1983); children: Ryan K., Stafford J.; m. James J. Lewis, May 17, 1986. BA, Sioux Falls Coll., 1972; MA, U. S.D., 1977; PhD, U. Nebr., 1986; postgrad., Harvard U., 1991. Instr. speech comm. dept. U. S.D., Vermillion, 1977-85, dir. speech com. program, 1986-90, spl. asst. to the pres., 1990-91, chmn. speech com. dept., 1991-95, 1991-95, dir. M.S. adminstrv. studies, 1992-95, dean continuing edn., 1995—; tchg. asst. U. Nebr., Lincoln, 1985-86; cons., tng. exec. bds. over 40 cos. Radio program host: Poets Five, 1977-80; numerous oral interpretation performances. Mem. exec. bd. Vermillion Coalition Against Domestic Violence, 1990-95, Tri-State Grad. Ctr., ; support group facilitator Support Group for Battered Women, Vermillion, 1983-85. Fellow Danforth Found., 1979-85, others. Mem. Nat. U. Continuing Edn., NAFE, Acad. Mgmt. Office: U SD 414 E Clark St Vermillion SD 57069

LEWIS, JENNIFER CRAWLEY, lawyer, banker; b. Honolulu, Dec. 1, 1965; d. Ned Wayne and Carol Elizabeth (Kingsolver) Crawley; m. Max Robert Lewis, Dec. 16, 1995. BA, Sweet Briar Coll., 1988; JD, George Mason U., 1995. Office adminstr. Manarin & Odle Realtors, Alexandria, Va., 1988; regulatory compliance rep. Ind. Bankers Assn., Washington, 1989-92; law clk. Dept. Justice, Arlington, Va., 1994; asst. v.p., sec. Approved Residential Mortgage, Inc., Virginia Beach, Va., 1995—; asst. v.p. Am. Indsl. Loan Assn., Virginia Beach, 1995—. Editor: IBAA Compliance Deskbook, 1991-92; contbr. articles to profl. jours. Mem. Arlington County Rep. Com., Arlington, 1993; precinct capt. Jim Miller for Senate Campaign, Fairfax, Va., 1994; mem. policy com. Tom Davis for Congress, Fairfax, 1994; del. Rep. Conv., Richmond, Va., 1993, 94. Mem. Fairfax County Young Reps. Roman Catholic. Home: 1800 Old Meadow Rd # 109 Mc Lean VA 22102

LEWIS, JOAN, lawyer; b. Trenton, N.J., July 13, 1953. BA in Econs. with honors, U. Wis., 1975; MA, Johns Hopkins U., 1977; postgrad., Fordham U.; JD cum laude, U. San Francisco, 1985. Ptnr. Anderson, Kill, Olick & Oshinsky, P.C., N.Y.C. Contbr. articles to profl. jours. Office: Anderson Kill Olick & Oshinsky PC 1251 Avenue of the Americas New York NY 10020-1182*

LEWIS, JOSEPHINE VICTORIA, marketing executive; b. Chgo., Dec. 3, 1936; d. Wincenty and Helena (Francysczak) Gurbacki; m. Laurence Warren Lewis, Jan. 8, 1955; children: Laurence Michael, Michaleen Kay, Gregory Michael. AS, Triton Coll., 1979. Sec. Marsh & McLennan, Chgo., 1953-57; with factory prodn. Motorola, Franklin Park, Ill., 1969-70; with inventory control Reflector Hardware, Melrose Park, Ill., 1970-71; distbn./inventory supr. Jewel Imports (Osco Drug, Inc.), Oakbrook, Ill., 1971-83; Midwest regional mgr. Port of Seattle, 1983—. Leader Dupage County Girl Scouts U.S.A., 1968-71; den mother Thatcher County Boy Scouts Am., 1974-75; fundraiser United Way Northlake, Ill., 1972-74; active Christian Family Movement, Marriage Encounter. Mem. Women in Internat. Trade, Internat. Trade Assn. Greater Chgo., Customs Brokers and Fgn. Freight Forwarders Assn., Ocean Freight Agts. (sec. 1993, treas. 1994, v.p. 1995, pres. 1996), Piggyback Assn. Chgo., Midwest Fgn. Commerce Club (bd. govs.), Chgo. Transp. Club. Office: Port of Seattle 184 Shuman Blvd Ste 200 Naperville IL 60563-1219

LEWIS, JULIETTE, actress; b. Fernando Valley, Calif., June 21, 1973; d. Geoffrey and Glenis Batley L. TV appearances include Homefires (Showtime miniseries), I Married Dora, 1988, A Family For Joe, 1990; TV Movies include Too Young To Die, 1989; films include My Stepmother is an Alien, 1988, Meet the Hollowheads, 1989, National Lampoons Christmas Vacation, 1989, Cape Fear, 1991 (Academy Award nomination best supporting actress 1991), Crooked Hearts, 1991, Husbands and Wives, 1992, Kalifornia, 1993, That Night, 1993, What's Eating Gilbert Grape, 1993, Romeo is Bleeding, 1994, Natural Born Killers, 1994, Mixed Nuts, 1994, Strange Days, 1995, The Basketball Diaries, 1995, From Dusk Till Dawn, 1996, The Evening Star, 1996, The Audition, 1996. Office: William Morris Agy 151 S El Camino Dr Beverly Hills CA 90212-2704*

LEWIS, KAREN DEWITT, English language educator; b. N.Y.C., June 1, 1942; d. William DeWitt and Rosalind (Walter) Smith; m. Tom J. Lewis, Jan. 30, 1965 (div. Apr. 1992); 1 child, Gregory William. BA in English, U. Ill., 1964, MA in Tchg. of English, 1966. Tchr. English Crispus Attucks H.S., Indpls., 1968-70; instr. ESL English Lang. Svcs. Lang. Ctr., Norman, Okla., 1975; instr. adult edn. and ESL Lincoln Parish Sch., Ruston, La., 1975-77; instr. ESL La. Tech. U., Ruston, 1977-92, instr. English, 1992—. Vol. Peace Corps, Guatemala, 1966-68. Mem. La. TESOL (pres. 1991-92), South Cen. MLA, Conf. on Coll. Composition and Comm. Office: La Tech U English Dept PO Box 3162 Ruston LA 71272

LEWIS, KAREN MARIE, writer, editor; b. Syracuse, N.Y., Oct. 29, 1965; d. Stephan Joseph and Mary Josephine (Scully) L. Student, Simon's Rock of Bard Coll., 1982-83; BA cum laude, Barnard Coll., 1986; MA, Brandeis U., 1989. Prodn. asst. Claremont Rsch. and Pub., N.Y.C., 1984-86; tchg. asst. Barnard Coll., N.Y.C., 1984-86; teaching asst. Brandeis U., Waltham, Mass., 1988; freelance writer Great Barrington, Mass., 1989-95; editl. asst. o.blek, Great Barrington, 1992-93; ESL algebra tutor Lenox (Mass.) Meml. High, 1995; editor Construct, Inc., Great Barrington, 1994—. Contbr. articles to anthologies, newspapers and poetry jours. Bd. dirs. Construct Inc., Great Barrington, 1995—. Mem. Poets and Writers. Roman Catholic. Home: PO Box 1094 Great Barrington MA 01230

LEWIS, LINDA CHRISTINE, executive search firm executive; b. St. Paul, Oct. 7, 1949; d. Richard Lewis and Gloria Christine (Dickey) Williams; m. John T. Housladen, Dec. 12, 1971 (div. Dec. 1978); children: Matthew, Joshua; m. Douglas Scott Lewis, July 21, 1979. BS with honors, Southwest Tex. State U., 1971. Area sales mgr. AM Internat., Austin, Tex., 1978-82; nat. sales mgr. Auscom Inc., Austin, 1982-85, v.p. sales, 1985; v.p. sales KMW Systems Corp., Austin, 1985-89; original equipment mfr. sales mgr. Intel Corp., Austin, 1989-90; dir. of sales Tadpole Tech. Inc., Austin, 1990-92; dist. sales mgr. Rocal-Datacom, 1992-95; assoc. Hardie & Crowley, Austin, 1995—. Asst. scoutmaster, Boy Scouts Am. Mem. Am. Contract Bridge League. Republican. Lutheran. Home: 3509 Carla Dr Austin TX 78754-4917 Office: Hardie & Crowley LLC 600 Sabine Ste 100 Austin TX 78701

LEWIS, LINDA DENISE, artist, educator; b. Battle Creek, Mich., Feb. 9, 1949; d. Harmon Edwin and Dorothy May (Holcomb) Chamberlin; m. A. Fuat Firat, June 21, 1985; 1 child, Matthew Clay Lewis. BGS cum laude, U. Tex., Dallas, 1982; MA, Appalachian State U., Boone, N.C., 1986. Rsch. asst. sociology Appalachian State U., Boone, 1985, program devel. asst. for women's studies, 1987-90, adj. prof. women's studies, 1987-90; adminstrv. and studio asst. Janet Taylor Designs, Tempe, Ariz., 1992; rsch. asst. fine arts Ariz. State U., Tempe, 1994-95. Exhibited in group shows at Nelson Fine Arts Mus., Tempe, Ariz., 1992, Downey (Calif.) Mus. Art, 1993, Nev. State Mus., Las Vegas, 1993, Dallas Women's Caucus for Art, 1993, Matrix Internat., Sacramento, 1994, Shemer Art Ctr., Phoenix, 1994, Women's Caucus for Art, San Antonio,1995, others; artwork included in book: Fiberarts Design Book Five, 1995. Fulbright scholar, 1995-96. Mem. Women's Caucus for Art, Ariz. Designer Craftsmen, Pi Gamma Mu. Home: 1857 E Tulane Dr Tempe AZ 85283-2217

LEWIS, LINDA MARIE, district court commissioner, community activist; b. Baltimore, June 22, 1959; d. Leslie Levi and Esther Marie L.; 1 child, Assata Jecolia. BS in Polit. Sci., Towson State Univ., 1993. Legal sec. Md. Real Estate Comm., Balt., 1982 85; paralegal, sec. Nat. Assn. the Advancement of Colored People, Balt., 1987-89; paralegal Office of the States Aty., Balt., 1989-93; court commissioner Dist. Ct. of Balt., 1993—; choreographer To The Glory of God Dancers, 1993; actress El Hajj Malik, 1989; radio talk show host Morgan State Jazz Radio The Sister Cir., Morgan State U., 1993; spkr. in field; coun. mem., UN intern Akosua Visions Global Ministry; workshop presentor Global Sisterhood Meet in Bahamas, 1994, co-organizer, 1994—. Author: Sister Songs, 1993, (play) Is Jesue Lord?, 1992. Chairperson Adele Carr Prison Mission, Bethel Ch., Balt., 1985, Interdenominational Peace, Love, Sisterhood, Balt., 1986; empowerment speaker Women in Prison, 1993-95; youth leader Young People Dept. of Missionary Group, Balt., 1993; speaker, workshop presentor Woman of Excellence Campaign, Tex., 1992; asst. to com. chairperson, Campaign to Elect Councilman to Congress, Balt., 1986; organizer/chairperson Ain't I A Woman Day, Balt., 1989, organizer Ujima Collective, Balt., 1983; guest speaker Kingdom Women Broadcast Ministries, Balt., 1988. Recipient Merit award for Poetry, World of Poetry, Sacramento, Calif., 1990. Home: PO Box 4646 Baltimore MD 21212-0646

LEWIS, L(INDA) MAUREEN, publishing executive; b. Culver City, Calif., May 22, 1948; d. Richard Harold and Nada Maureen (Kimball) Eastwood; m. James T. Mayer, Apr. 29, 1970 (div. Mar. 1985); children: Theodore Duke, Kirk Ryan; m. John S. Lewis, July 23, 1988. BA, UCLA, 1969; elem. teaching credential, Calif. State U., Northridge, 1972; postgrad., Calif. State U., Fullerton, 1986. Instr. journalism Saddleback Community Coll., Mission Viejo, Calif., 1981-83; mgr. advt. and mktg. communications Kim Lighting, Industry, Calif., 1985-87; adminstr. mktg. dir. Approved Products, Santa Ana, Calif., 1987-88; asst. to pres., mgr. advt. and spl. projects Republic Capital Holding Corp., Burbank, Calif., 1988-89; exec. dir. The Dalton Press, Corona del Mar, Calif., 1989-90; mgr. Forensic Publs. L.A. County Bar Assn., 1990—; assoc. editor Preface mag., Laguna Hills, Calif., 1982, Saddleback Alive mag., Laguna Hills, 1983. Mem. AAUW (publs. editor Mission Viejo br. 1979-80, chmn. pub. info. 1980-81, 1st v.p. 1981-82, pres. 1982-83, named grant honoree 1981, communications officer publs. and pub. info. Calif. div. 1981-83).

LEWIS, LORRAINE, general counsel; b. Springfield, Mass., Feb. 25, 1956; d. Richard N. and Janet Claire (Howard) Pratte; m. Jacob M. Lewis, Sept. 28, 1985; 2 children. BA in History magna cum laude, Yale Coll., 1978; JD, Harvard Law Sch., 1981. Bar: D.C., Ill., 1982. Field atty. NLRB, Chgo., 1982-84; assoc. Feder & Edes, Washington, 1984-85; vol. atty. Washington Lawyer's Com. for Civil Rights, 1986; staff asst. Sen. John Glenn, 1986; asst. counsel then counsel and gen. counsel sen. com. on govtl. affairs, 1987-93; gen. counsel Office of Personnel Mgmt., 1993—. Office: Office of Personnel Mgmt 1900 E St NW Rm 7353 Washington DC 20415-0001

LEWIS, MARCILE RENEÉ, nursing educator; b. Kansas City, Mo.; m. Autry E. Lewis, Aug. 28, 1965; children: C. Renee, Kevin E. Diploma, Trinity Luth. Hosp., 1965; BS in Trade, Tech. & Health Occupation Edn., Ctrl. Mo. State U., 1983, MS in Vocat. Edn., 1992. RN Mo. Staff nurse, supr. Wetzel Hosp. Inc., Clinton, Mo., 1965-70, dir. nurses, 1970-71; staff nurse ICU Golden Valley Meml. Hosp., Clinton, Mo., 1972-74; head nurse ICU Western Mo. Med. Ctr., Warrensburg, 1974-75, staff nurse med./surg. ICU, 1982-90; practical nurse educator Warrensburg Area Vocat. Tech. Sch., 1976-88, practical nurse coord., 1988—. Mem. Heart of Mo. Tech.-Pre. Consortium, Sedalia, 1992—; mem. community health adv. bd. Johnson County Health Dept., Warrensburg, 1990—; curriculum writer Mo. Dept. Edn., Jefferson County, 1986-88, practical nurse statewide, 1992 (Outstanding Adult Vocat. Edn. Program, 1992, 94). Mem. Am. Vocat. Assn. (del., Nat. Tchr. of Yr. Nat. Health Occupl. Edn. divsn. 1994), Vocat. Indsl. Clubs Am. (advisor), Mo. Vocat. Assn. (bd. dirs. 1977—), Mo. State Assn. Health Educators (pres., treas., bd. dirs. 1977—), Mo. Coun. Practical Nurse Educators (treas., sec.), Warrensburg C. of C., Phi Kappa Phi. Methodist. Office: Warrensburg Area Vocat & Tech Sch 205 S Ridgeview Dr Warrensburg MO 64093-2019

LEWIS, MARGARET M., marketing professional; b. Bridgeport, Conn., Sept. 27, 1959; d. Raymond Phillip and Catherine Helen (Gayda) Palovchak; m. William A. Lewis Jr., Oct. 4, 1980. BS summa cum laude, Sacred Heart U., 1986; postgrad., U. Bridgeport; AS, Katherine Gibbs Sch., 1980. Program mgr. sales svc. group Newspaper Coop. Couponing, Inc., Westport, Conn., 1985-87; sales adminstr. Supermarket Communication Systems, Inc., Norwalk, Conn., 1987-88, mgr. mktg. support, 1988-89; asst. project mgr. sales promotion Mktg. Corp. Am., Westport, 1989-91, account exec., 1991-92; mgr. program svcs. Ryan Partnership, Westport, 1992-93, sr. program mgr., 1993-95, mng. dir., 1995-96; account dir. Creative Alliance, Westport, Conn., 1996—. Mem. NAFE, Direct Mktg. Assn., Am. Mgmt. Assn. Democrat. Roman Catholic. Home: 16 Nickel Pl Monroe CT 06468-3005 Office: 55 Post Rd W Westport CT 06880-4205

LEWIS, MARIANNE H., psychiatric nurse practitioner; b. Frankfurt, Germany, Feb. 8, 1921; d. Emil B. and Jessie (Falk) Horkheimer; m. Harold S. Lewis, July 10, 1943; children: Harold S., Jr., Dale G. AAS in Nursing, Pace U., White Plains, N.Y., 1970; BS, 1976; MSN in Adult Psychiatric Nursing, Yale U., 1980. Registered profl. nurse, Conn., advance nurse practitioner, Fla., cert. ANA specialist in psychiatric-mental health nursing, 1983. Sr. staff nurse Psychiatry N.Y.U. Med. Ctr., 1971-73; dir. White Plains (N.Y.) Med. Ctr. Day Hosp., 1973-78; asst. clin. prof. Yale U. Sch. Nursing, 1981-91; clin. specialist Dept. Psychiatry VA Med. Ctr., West Haven, Conn., 1980-83; nurse counseling group Northwalk, Conn., 1983-88; clin. specialist Grand View Psychiatric Resource Ctr. Waterbury (Conn.) Hosp., 1988-90; psychiatric review specialist Aetna Life and Casualty Ins. Co., Middletown, Conn., 1991-92; advanced registered nurse practitioner Vis. Nurse Asn. of Southwest Fla., 1995-96. Speaker Pace U. Dedication of Lienhard Sch. Nursing Bldg., Pleasantville, N.Y., 1974. Mem. ANA, Coun. Clin. Specialists, Fla. Nurses Assn. Home: 3030 Binnacle Dr Apt 309 Naples FL 34103

LEWIS, MARILYN WARE, water company executive; b. 1943. Former pres. Solanco Pub. Co.; vice chmn. Am. Water Works Co., Inc., Voorhees, N.J., now chmn., also bd. dirs.; bd. dirs. Penn Fuel Gas Co., Cigna Corp. Office: Am Water Works Co Inc 2 East Main St Strasburg PA 17579

LEWIS, MARION ELIZABETH, social worker; b. Los Alamos, Calif., Dec. 7, 1920; d. James Henry and Carolina Sophia (Niemann) Eddy; m. William Ernest Lewis, May 30, 1943 (dec. Oct. 1954); children: Doris Lenita Lewis Terrill, Paul William. Student, Jr. Coll., Santa Maria, Calif., 1939-40, Bus. Coll., Santa Barbara, Calif., 1940-41, Alan Hancock Coll., 1958-61; BA in Sociology cum laude, Westminster Coll., Salt Lake City, 1964. Office clk. Met. Life Ins. Co., Santa Barbara, 1942-43; sales clk. Sprouse Reitz Co., Laguna Beach, Calif., 1943-44; office clk. U.S. Army, Santa Maria AFB, 1944-45; sch. crossing guard Calif. Hwy. Patrol, Los Alamos, 1956-58; office clk. Holaday Children's Ctr., Salt Lake City, 1964; social worker Sonoma County Social Svc., Santa Rosa, Calif., 1964-78, ret., 1978; sales rep. Avon Products, Los Alamos, 1957-61; sales clk. Gen. Store, Los Alamos, 1957-59; office clk. Sonoma County Pub. Health Dept., 1979-80. Deacon Presbyn. Ch., 1956—, moderator Presbyn. Women, 1990-91, vice moderator, 1989-90, sem. rep., 1978-80, 92-94. Mem. AAUW, R.I. Geneal. Soc., Sonoma County Geneal. Soc., Calif. Automobile Assn., Nat. Geographic Soc., Sonoma County Assn. Ret. Employees, Commonwealth Club Calif., Sequoia Club, Westminster Coll. Alumni Assn., Alpha Chi (alumni chpt.). Republican. Home: 61 Sequoia Cir Santa Rosa CA 95401-4992

LEWIS, MARTHA ANDREÉ, special education educator, counselor; b. Chattanooga, Dec. 26, 1949; m. Jerry D. Lewis. AA in Liberal Arts Edn., St. Leo (Fla.) Coll., BA in Sociology, Social Svcs., 1979; BS in Edn., Occupl. and Vocat. Tchg., So. Ill. U., Carbondale, 1983; MS in Edn. and Applied Psychology, Social Svcs., Ea. Wash. U., 1984; PhD in Human Ecology, Vocat. Home Econs., and Sociology Tchg., U. Tenn., 1991. Cert. vocat. tchr., Tenn. Tchr., counselor Tacoma Urban League, 1981-84; instr. Knapp Bus. Coll., Tacoma, 1984; instr., counselor Career Com Bus. Coll., Knoxville, Tenn., 1985-88; asst. prof. Knoxville Coll., 1989-91, Alcorn State U., Lorman, Miss., 1991-92; spl. edn. assoc. tchr., counselor Knoxville Adaptive Edn. Ctr., 1992—; grad. tchr., asst. instr. U. Tenn., Knoxville, 1986-89; mem. adj. faculty Bristol U., Knoxville, 1988-89, Pellissippi State Tech. C.C., Knoxville, 1992. Author: Elementary Design Made Simple, 1981, 82. Dir. nursery Sunday sch., pres. nursery com. Mt. Olive Bapt. Ch., Knoxville, 1994—; staff writer Knoxville Enlightener, cmty. newspaper, 1993, asst. mng. editor, 1992-93. Recipient cert. of tchr. appreciation Tacoma Urban League, 1984, Outstanding and Dedicated Tchg. award Career Com Bus. Coll., 1987, All-Am. Scholar award, 1994; fellow U. Tenn. and State of Tenn., 1986. Mem. ASCD, NEA, NAFE, Am. Assn. Family and Consumer Scis., Tenn. Assn. Family and Consumer Scis., Tenn. Edn. Assn., Knox County Edn. Assn. Home: PO Box 11581 Knoxville TN 37939-1581

LEWIS, MARTHA NELL, expressive arts therapist, massage therapist, counselor, director; b. Atlanta, Mar. 4, 1944; d. Clifford Edward and Nell (Shropshire) Wilkie; m. Jeffrey Clark Lewis, Aug. 20, 1966 (div. Aug. 1986); children: John Martin, Janet Michelle Teal. BA, Tex. Tech. U., 1966; massage therapy, The Winters Sch., 1991; MA, Norwich U., 1994. Registered expressive therapist, massage therapist, therapeutic massage and bodywork, massage therapist instr. Geophys. analyst Shell Oil Co., Houston, 1966-68; photogravity specialist Photogravity, Inc., Houston, 1972-80; tchr. music Little Red Sch. House, Houston, 1974-75; sec., treas. Lewis Enterprises, Inc., Houston, 1976-83; regulatory supr. Transco Energy Co., Houston, 1983-92; expressive arts therapist Shalom Renewal Ctr., Splendora, Tex., 1995—, River Oaks Health Alliance, Houston, 1995—; also bd. dirs. Shalom Renewal Ctr. and River Oaks Health Alliance, 1995—; nat. exec. dir., pres. Music for Healing and Transition Program, Houston, 1994—; massage therapist, Houston, 1991—. Advisor youth Corpus Christi Ch., Houston, 1970-80; vocalist, instrumentalist Sounds of Faith Folk Group, Houston, 1978—; harpist Houston Harpers Harp Ensemble, 1990-92; instr. exercise, body awareness Transco Energy Co. Fitness Ctr., Houston, 1990-92; vol. The Inst. for Rehab. and Rsch., Houston, 1989-90, Houston Hospice, 1992—, Houston Healing Healthcare Project, 1993—; vol. Healing Environ. Coun. St. Luke's Episc. Hosp., 1993—, lay chaplain, 1994—; founder The Winters Sch. Massage Therapy Care Team, Houston, 1991—. Mem. Internat. Expressive Arts Therapy Assn., Am. Holistic Nurses Assn., Am. Harp Soc., Internat. Folk Harp Assn., Am. Massage Therapy Assn., Nat. Soc. Fund Raising Execs., Exec. Dir.'s Forum, Space City Ski Club (asst. trip coord. 1991-92), Houston Sigma Kappa Found. (bd. dirs.), Sigma Kappa Alumnae Assn. (pres. Houston chpt. 1974-76, nat. collegiate province officer 1981-85, Houston Alumnae of Yr. 1981, Tex. Alumnae of Yr. 1980, Pearl Ct. award 1991). Roman Catholic. Home: 6400 Christie Ave # 4202 Emeryville CA 94608

LEWIS, MARY BETH, merchandise manager; b. Bloomington, Ind., July 21, 1965; d. John Patrick and Judith (Weaver) L. BA in Comms., BS in Psychology, U. So. Calif., L.A., 1987. Dept. mgr. O'Neil's (May Co.), Akron, Ohio, 1987-89; asst. buyer May Ohio (May Co.), Cleve., 1989-91, buyer accessories, 1991-93; buyer-logo apparel Princess Cruises, L.A., 1993, merchandise mgr., 1993—. Recipient Acad. Scholarship award U. So. Calif., L.A., 1983-87. Home: 423 28th St Hermosa Beach CA 90254 Office: Princess Cruises 10100 Santa Monica Blvd Los Angeles CA 90067

LEWIS, MARY JANE, communication educator, writer; b. Kansas City, Mo., July 22, 1950; d. J.W. Jr. and Hilda (Miller) L. BA, Stephens Coll., Columbia, Mo., 1971; MA, NYU, 1984, PhD, 1996. Cert. video prodr. Corp. for Cmty. TV, Honolulu. Office mgr. Crazy Shirts, Inc., Honolulu, 1974-79; creator Exotic Exports, Honolulu, 1979-80; asst. buyer Bloomingdale's, N.Y.C., 1980-82; office mgr., media dir. Andiamo, Inc., N.Y.C., 1982-85; freelance stylist Condé Nast, Inc., N.Y.C., 1985-86; lectr. U. Hawaii, Honolulu, 1986-89; tchg. fellow NYU, 1989-90, asst. prof., 1990-92; prof. U. Hawaii, Kapiolani C.C., Honolulu, 1992—, U. Hawaii, Honolulu C.C., 1994—; mem. adj. faculty Fashion Inst. Tech., N.Y.C., 1983; lectr. U. Hawaii, Kapiolani C.C. adult edn. programs, 1986—, NYU Sch. Continuing Edn., 1991-94; video stylist, asst. prodr. State of Hawaii Dept. Edn., Honolulu, 1994—; video prodr. Ólelo: The Corp. for Cmty. TV, Honolulu, 1995—; developer numerous adult edn. comm. courses. Author: (book) Careers in Fashion Manual, 1994, (TV/movie script) The Last Rose of Summer, 1992. Mem. AAUW, NEA, The Fashion Group Internat., Inc., U. Hawaii Profl. Assn., Cmty. TV Prodrs. Assn. State of Hawaii, Kappa Alpha Theta (pres. pledge class 1968—). Home: 91-513 B Hapalua St Ewa Beach HI 96706 Office: U Hawaii Kapiolani C C 4303 Diamond Head Rd Honolulu HI 96816

LEWIS, MARY LAUREN, medical company executive; b. Birmingham, Ala., Sept. 22, 1967; d. Frederick Stearns and Judith Williams (Parker) L. BS in Psychology, U. Ga., 1989. Exec. trainee Macy's South, Atlanta, 1990; asst. dept. mgr. Macy's South, Athens, Ga., 1990; sales mgr. Macy's South, Atlanta, 1991-93; account exec. Tallahassee Med. Corp., Jacksonville, Fla., 1993-94; sr. acct. exec. Capital Med. Corp., Jacksonville, 1995—. Tutor Ch. of Good Shepherd Cmty. Outreach, Jacksonville, 1993-94; group leader Children's Enrichment Workshop, Jacksonville, 1993-94; bd. dirs. Childbirth and Parenting Edn. Assn., 1995-96; mem. Willing Hands of Jacksonville. Mem. NOW, North Fla. Hunter Jumper Assn., Assn. Rehab. Technologies. Episcopalian. Home: 911 LaSalle St Jacksonville FL 32207 Office: Capital Med Corp PO Box 15013 Tallahassee FL 32317-5013

LEWIS, MARY SALS, social services administrator, educator; b. Detroit, Dec. 6, 1942; d. Robert James and Charlotte Christine (Brasch) Sals; m. James Allen Lewis, Sept. 9, 1964; children: Robert Blacklock, Christine Rozelle, Laura Marie. BS, Tex. Ea. U., 1976; MA, U. Tex., 1979. Exec. dir. Smith County ARC, Tyler, Tex., 1976-78; drug abuse planner NETHSA, Marshall, Tex., 1979; legal asst. Tyler, 1980-87; contr. Western Map & Pub. Co., Bullard, Tex., 1988-92, Burchfield Pipe, Tyler, 1992-94; owner/ptnr. Theatre on Tour, Tyler, 1994—; instr. Tyler Jr. Coll., 1988—; exec. dir. Family Violence & Sexual Assault Inst., Tyler, 1994—; conf. coord. 1st nat. conf. on children exposed to domestic violence, Austin, Tex., 1996., 6th nat. conf. on trauma, abuse and dissociation, Austin, 1995. Editor: Trauma, Amnesia and Denial of Abuse, 1995; mng. editor Family Violence and Sexual Assault Bulletin, 1994—. Cmty. rels. com. Tyler United Way, 1996; prodn. dir. summer musicals Lake County Playhouse, Mineola, Tex., 1995, 96; pres. Tyler Interagency Projects, 1979; participant Synergy 95, Chgo., 1995. Recipient History honors Phi Alpha Theta, 1977, Acad. honors Alpha Chi, 1977, Theatre honors Alpha Psi Omega, 1994. Mem. Brickstreet Playhouse (adminstrv. v.p. 1991-93), Tyler Civic Chorale Assn. (bd. dirs. 1979—, pres.), Tyler Music Coterie/Nat. Fedn. Music Clubs. Democrat. Methodist. Home: 3024 Terilinga Tyler TX 75701 Office: Family Violence & Sexual Assault Inst 1121 ESE Loop 323 Ste 130 Tyler TX 75701

LEWIS, MELVA JEAN, language arts educator; b. Davenport, Iowa, Dec. 28, 1942; d. Melvin Earl and Hanna Barbara (Engler) Quick; m. John William Lewis, June 24, 1966; 1 child, Nicole Lewis Sodawasser. BA, U. Northern Iowa, 1965; MA, Western Ill. U., 1985. Cert. English & lang. arts 7-16 tchr. Iowa. Tchr. lang. arts North Scott Schs., Eldridge, Iowa, 1965—; adj. instr. Teikyo Marycrest U., Davenport, Iowa, 1992-93; team tchr. Kollege for Kids, Bettendorf, Iowa, 1983-89; assessor Nat. Standards Bd., Princeton, N.J., 1995. Contbr. articles to profl. jours.; author of poems. Asst. camp dir. Girl Scouts Am., Rock Isl., Ill., 1983-87; vol. coord. Eastern Iowa Spl. Olympics, 1988-92; vol. Spl. Olympics, 1994-95. Recipient Women in the Workplace award Women's Encouragement Bd., 1990, Golden Apple award Scott County Tchr. Recognition Program, 1989. Mem. NCTE, NOW, United Tchg. Profession, Iowa State Edn. Assn. (mem. exec. bd. 1994—), Iowa Coun. Tchrs. of Lang. Arts/Reading, 1970—. Office: North Scott Jr HS 502 S 5th St Eldridge IA 52748

LEWIS, MICHELLE NICOLE, curator, exhibit designer; b. Phila., June 2, 1963; d. John Michael and Genevieve Nicole (Dumont) L. MA, U. Edinburgh, Scotland, 1987; MFA, U. Arts, 1996. Exhbn. developer Creese Gallery, Phila., 1992-93; intern Phila. Mus. Art, 1995; freelance exhbn. developer, Phila., 1994-96; web site designer. Mem. Am. Assn. Mus., Nat. Assn. Mus. Exhbn., Internat. Com. Mus., Soc. Environ. Graphic Design, Assn. Asian Studies. Home: 2321 Perot St Philadelphia PA 19130

LEWIS, MOIRA EALASAID, sculptor, researcher, nurse/research coordinator; b. St. Louis, Oct. 18, 1952; d. William Rapheal and Rita Elizabeth (Lynch) L.; m. Alan Steven Weinstock, July 2, 1971 (div. 1989); 1 child, Rita Gail. BS cum laude, Southern Ill. U., 1979; MFA in Sculpture, Washington U., 1990. Teaching asst. chemistry, anatomy and physiology So. Ill. U., Edwardsville, 1977-79; pub. health nurse Vis. Nurse Assn., St. Louis, 1979-81; oncology nurse Barnes Hosp., St. Louis, 1981-85; mem. nursing faculty Barnes Coll., St. Louis, 1985-89; mem. art faculty St. Louis C.C., 1991—; study coord. rsch. into treatments for recurrent miscarriage NIH, 1992-96; rsch. nurse sch. medicine Washington U., St. Louis, 1992—; asst. to Judy Pfaff, St. Louis Art Mus., 1989; study coord. rsch. into treatments for recurrent miscarriage NIH, 1992-96; instr. Florissant Valley, 1990-93. One-woman shows include The sea of Maximillian Kolbe: Installation, St. Louis C.C., 1996, Dromedary Mirth, So. Ill. U., Edwardsville, 1992, 93, Master of the Mercies, Maastricht, The Netherlands, 1991; group shows include: The Living Arts Festival, Tulsa, 1995, The Lake Gallery, Bainbridge Island, Wash., 1994, SOHO 20 Gallery, N.Y.C., 1991, Steinberg Gallery, St. Louis, 1990. Mem. Coll. Art Assn., Internat. Sculpture Soc., Amnesty Internat. Democrat. Roman Catholic.

LEWIS, NANCEE ELAINE, photojournalist; b. New Orleans, Jan. 31, 1962; d. Allen E. and Elaine Joy (Weferling) L. BA, Loyola U., New Orleans, 1985. Freelance photographer New Orleans, 1985-89; staff photographer The Times, Shreveport, La., 1989-92, Chgo. Tribune, 1992-94, San Diego Union-Tribune, 1994. Recipient various photo contest awards Ill. Press Photographer Assn., 1992, 93; Rotary grad. studies scholarship, 1985. Mem. Nat. Press Photographers Assn. (various monthly regional clip contest awards 1990—). Office: San Diego Union-Tribune 350 Camino de la Reina San Diego CA 92108

LEWIS, NANCI VICEDOMINI, investment advisor; b. Springfield, Mass., Apr. 26, 1962; d. Roland Benito and Ann Ernestine (Desmone) Vicedomini; m. Jonathan Joseph Lewis, May 20, 1990. BA in Econs., Boston Coll., 1984; MBA, Rollins Coll., 1986. Fin. analyst Sikorsky Aircraft div. United Technologies, Stratford, Conn., 1986-87, fin. program analyst, 1987-88; corp. planning analyst Sprague Technologies, Stratford, 1988; cons. Total Planning Concept, East Haven, Conn., 1989—; v.p. ROANN Electronics, Wolcott, Conn., 1989—; fin. advisor Prudential Securities Inc., N.Y.C., 1995—. Fundraiser New Haven Symphony Orch., 1991. Mem. Women in Sales.

LEWIS, NANCY LOUINE LAMBERT, school counselor; b. Austin, Tex., Jan. 28, 1938; d. Claud Standard and Audrey Louine (Jackson) Lambert; m. Raymond Clyde Lewis, Dec. 27, 1958; children: Laura Lewis Maloy, John Lambert. BA in English with highest honors, U. Tex., 1958, MEd in Guidance and Counseling, 1964. Lic. tchr. secondary English, counselor; lic. profl. counselor. Tchr. English Allan Jr. High Sch. Austin Ind. Sch. Dist., 1958-62, counselor Univ. Jr. High Sch., 1963-65; counselor Gary Job Corps Ctr., San Marcos, Tex., 1965-67; supr. student tchrs. English dept. curriculum and instrn. U. Tex., Austin, 1968-69, editor, writer, group leader Ctr. Pub. Sch. Ethnic Studies, 1969-76; counselor Allan Jr. High Sch. Austin Ind. Sch. Dist., 1976-80, counselor Martin Jr. High Sch., 1980-86, counselor Fulmore Mid. Sch., 1986-87, counselor Mendez Mid. Sch., 1987—; instr. corr. studies U. Tex., Austin, 1968—. Contbr. articles to profl. jours. Vol. Dem. party, Austin, 1973—, First United Meth. Ch., Austin, 1955—; mem. Mayor's Task Force on Gangs, Crime and Drugs, City of Austin, 1990-91. Mem. ACA, NEA, Am. Sch. Counselors Assn. (editl. bd. Sch. Counselor 1989 96), Tex. State Tchrs. Assn., Tex. Sch. Counselors Assn. (senator 1981-84, pres. 1985-86, chair counseling advocacy com. 1991-93, Mid. Sch. Counselor of Yr. 1993), Tex. Counseling Assn. (senator 1981-84, publs. com. chair 1981-84, membership com. chair 1994-96), Ctrl. Tex. Counseling Assn. (pres. 1982-83), Austin Assn. Tchrs. (cons. com. 1990-93, Human Rels. award 1989-90), Pathways (bd. dirs.), Delta Kappa Gamma (pres. Lambda Iota chpt. 1990-92), Phi Beta Kappa, Phi Delta Kappa. Home: 1427 Salem Meadow Cir Austin TX 78745-2911 Office: Mendez Mid Sch 5106 Village Square Dr Austin TX 78744-4462

LEWIS, PENELOPE POST (PENNY LEWIS), development director, nurse; b. Oak Park, Ill., July 5, 1940; d. Edgar August and Elisabeth (Esten) Post; m. Robert Donald Lewis, Jan 23, 1965 (div. Dec. 1989); children: Karen, Greg. Student, Williamette U., 1958-60; BS, Columbia U., 1963; postgrad., U. Wash., 1994. Creator, mgr. Lion & Assocs. Gift Shop, Seattle, 1982-84; mgr. support systems PLUMS Corp. Gift Co., Seattle, 1984-88; mgr. retail outlet, 1989-93; capital campaign coord. The Overlake Sch., Redmond, Wash., 1993-94, coord. devel., 1994-95, assoc. dir. devel., 1995—; trustee Lakeside Sch., Seattle, 1981-90; pres. McGilvra Sch., Seattle, 1984. Mem. Northwest Devel. Officers Assn., U.S. Rowing Assn. (bd. dirs. 1988-94), Pocock Rowing Assn. (bd. dirs. 1986—). Office: The Overlake Sch 20301 NE 108th St Redmond WA 98053

LEWIS, REBECCA ANNE HEWSON, farmer; b. Manhattan, Kans., Feb. 5, 1949; d. Kenneth Dean and Mary Elizabeth (McDonald) Hewson; m. Robert Walter Lewis, Nov. 8, 1980; children: Lincoln Landon, Hamilton Hewson. BS, Kans. State U., 1971; MA in Curriculum and Instrn., U. Kans., 1974. Tchr. Topeka Pub. Schs., 1971-72, Shawnee Mission (Kans.) Sch. Dist., 1972-77; grain merchandiser Continental Grain Co., N.Y.C., 1977-80; v.p. Lewis Land & Livestock, Ltd., Larned, Kans., 1980—. Youth leader 4-H Club, Larned, 1980-86; bd. dirs. Girl Scouts U.S.A., Hutchinson, Kans., 1980—, PTA, Larned, 1987—; elder Presbyn. Ch., Larned, 1989-92; active adopt a hwy. and clean-up project AAUW, Larned, 1993; campaigner for new sch. Citizens for Better Schs., Larned, 1994-95. Mem. PEO (state treas. 1995-96), Kappa Kappa Gamma. Home and Office: RR 3 Larned KS 67550

LEWIS, RITA HOFFMAN, plastic products manufacturing company executive; b. Phila., Aug. 6, 1947; d. Robert John and Helen Anna (Dugan) Hoffman; 1 child, Stephanie Blake. Student Jefferson Med. Coll. Sch. Nursing, 1965-67, Gloucester County Coll., 1993—; Gen. mgr. Sheets & Co., Inc. (now Flower World, Inc.), Woodbury, N.J., 1968-72; dir., exec. v.p., treas. Hoffman Precision Plastics, Inc., Blackwood, N.J., 1973—; ptnr. Timber Assocs.; commr. N.J. Expressway Authority, 1990—, sec., 1990-91, treas., 1991—, chmn. pers., 1991—; apptd. mem. N.J. Senate Forum on Budget and Revenue Alternatives, 1991; guest speaker various civic groups, 1974; poetry editor SPOTLIGHTER Innovative Singles Mag. Author: That Part of Me I Never Really Meant to Share, 1979; In Retrospect: Caught Between Running and Loving; columnist Innovative Singles mag., 1989—. Mem. Com. for Citizens of Glen Oaks (N.J.), 1979—, Gloucester Twp. Econ. Devel. Com., 1981—, Gloucester Twp. Day Scholarship Com., 1984—; mem. adv. coun. Gloucester Twp. Econ. Devel., 1995—; chairperson Gloucester Twp. Day Scholarship Found., 1985—; bd. dirs. Diane Hull Dance Co. Recipient Winning Edge award, 1982, Mayor's award for Womens' Achievement, 1987, Outstanding Cmty. Svc. award Mayor, Coun. and Com., 1987. Mem. NAFE, Sales Assn. Chem. Industry, Blackwood Businessmen's Assn., Soc. Plastic Engrs. Roman Catholic.

LEWIS, SANDRA JEAN, cardiologist; b. Portland, Oreg., Apr. 11, 1949; d. Stanley Bernard and Susanne Laurel (White) L.; m. James Todd Rosenbaum, June 27, 1970; children: Lisa Rosenbaum, Jennifer Rosenbaum. BA, Stanford U., 1971, MD, 1977. Diplomate Am. Bd. Cardiology. Intern Stanford (Calif.) Univ. Hosp., 1977-78, resident, 1978-80, fellow cardiology, 1980-83; cardiologist Kaiser Permanente, San Francisco, 1983-85, The Heart Clinic, Portland, 1985-94, Portland Cardiovascular Inst., 1995—; chief cardiology Good Samaritan Hosp., Portland, 1990-93. Fellow Am. Coll. Cardiology; mem. AMA, Am. Med. Womens Assn., Am. Heart Assn.

LEWIS, SHARI, puppeteer, entertainer; b. N.Y.C., Jan. 17, 1934; d. Abraham B. and Ann (Ritz) Hurwitz; m. Jeremy Tarcher, Mar. 15, 1958; 1 child, Mallory. Star weekly NBC-TV show The Shari Lewis Show, 1960-63, weekly syndicated series Lambchop's Play-Along (named TV Guide's Best of Best for Children), 1975-77, weekly TV show BBC, London, 1969-75, weekly TV show for ind. network in Gt. Britain, 1970, daily TV show PBS, 1992—; writer, producer, star NBC spl. A Picture of Us, 1971; performer or condr. with over 100 symphonies in U.S., Can., Japan, 1977—; command performances, London, 1970, 73, 78; author 60 pub. books including 15 One Minute Bedtime Stories (bestselling series); 24 home video cassettes: including 101 Things for Kids to do Shari's Christmas Concert, Don't Wake Your Mom, 1992, Let's Make Music, 1994; appeared in shows including Bye Bye Birdie, Funny Girl. Past mem. nat. bd. dirs. Girl Scouts U.S.; past internat. bd. dirs. Boy Scouts Am.; past pres. Am. Ctr. Films for Children; past hon. chmn. bd. trustees Internat. Reading Found.; trustee Greater L.A. Zoo Assn. Recipient 11 Emmy awards, including award for best program and outstanding female personality, 1989, for outstanding performer in a children's program, 1992, outstanding writing in children's series, 1993, outstanding performer in a children's series, 1993, 94, 95, daytime Emmy for performer in a children's series; Peabody award, 1960, 50th Anniversary Dir.'s award Ohio State Award Com., 1988, Monte Carlo Internat. TV award, 1963, Radio-TV Mirror award, 1960, Kennedy Ctr. award for excellence in arts for young people, 1986, Video Choice award, 1988, Parents Choice award, 1992, Calif. Media award, 1992, Dir. Choice Recognition award, 1992, Assn. Visual Communicators Gold Cindy award, 1992, Parents Mag. prize, 1993, Gemini award for LambChop's Play Along, 1994; TV Guide Top Ten Children's Shows, 1993. Office: care Jim Golden 3128 Cavendish Dr Los Angeles CA 90064-4743*

LEWIS, SHEILA MURIEL O'NEIL, retired communications management specialist; b. Glendive, Mont., Sept. 23, 1937; d. John Edward and Muriel Christine (Johnson) O'Neil; m. Lyndell W. Lewis, Dec. 14, 1957 (div. 1973); children: Sheri Lynne, Debra Lynne, Linda Marie, Valerie Jean. AA, Colo. Women's Coll., 1957; BS, U. No. Colo., 1976; postgrad., Stanford U. Adminstrv. asst. DAFC/Dept. Defense DOT/FAA, Denver, 1956-64; substitute tchr. Portland (Oreg.) Public Schs., 1964-72; communications operator Denver Air Rt. Traffic Control Ctr., 1972-78, communications specialist, 1978-80, computer programmer, 1980-82, air traffic controller, 1982-86; communications specialist Air Force Space Command, Falcon AFB, Colo., 1986-95, retired, 1995. Troop leader Campfire Girls, Las Vagas, 1964-72, pres. PTA, Las Vagas, 1964-72. .. Mem. AAUW, Armed Forces Communications and Electronics Assn., Aviation Space Edn. Assn., Civil Air Patrol, Univ. Aviation Assn., Order of Eastern Star, Order of White Shrine Jerusalem, Chi Omega. Democrat. Lutheran. Home: 4934 Daybreak Cir Colorado Springs CO 80917-2657

LEWIS, SHIRLEY, artist; b. Bklyn., Oct. 13, 1921; d. Nathan Shapiro and Jennie (Zimmerman) Schwartz; m. Alfred E. Lewis, Aug. 16, 1953 (dec. Mar. 1968); children: Leora, Sanford, Roland, Elena; m. Hananiah Harari, Sept. 1, 1979. Art therapist, New Sch. for Social Rsch., 1968; BFA, Manhattanville Coll., 1972; MA, NYU, 1976, cert. art tchr., 1976. Tchr. fine arts Our Lady of Sorrows Sch., White Plains, N.Y., 1972-74, Blythedale Children's Hosp., Valhalla, N.Y., 1972—; counselor art therapy Albert Einstein Med. Ctr., Bronx, N.Y., 1978, Wiltwyck, Ossining, 1980. One-man shows include Manhattanville Coll., Purchase, N.Y., 1972, Town Hall, Greenburgh, N.Y., 1975, Hudson River Gallery, Ossining, N.Y., 1989; exhibited in group shows at Cork Gallery Lincoln Ctr., N.Y.C., 1989, Rotunda Gallery, Bklyn., 1991, Nat. Acad. Design, N.Y.C., 1992, Putnam Arts Coun., Mahopac, N.Y., 1993, Susan Teller Gallery, N.Y.C., 1992. Recipient First prize Beaux Arts Westchester, 1990. Mem. Art Students League (life), Garrison Art Ctr., Artists Equity, Audubon Artists (nat. juried ann. exhbns. 1991-96). Home: 34 Prospect Pl Croton On Hudson NY 10520

LEWIS, SUSAN D., lawyer; b. N.Y.C., Jan. 26, 1952. BA, NYU, 1973, MBA, 1977, JD, 1977. Bar: N.Y. 1978. Ptnr. Brown & Wood, N.Y.C. Office: Brown & Wood 1 World Trade Ctr New York NY 10048-0557*

LEWIS, SYLVIA DAVIDSON, association executive; b. Akron, Ohio, Apr. 28; d. Harry I. and Helen E. (Stein) Davidson; m. Allen D. Lewis, Oct. 12, 1947; children: Pamela Lewis Kanfer, Randy, Daniel, Cynthia. Student, U. Mich., 1945-47, U. Akron, 1961-62. Editor Akron Jewish News, 1948-50; tchr. Revere Rd. Congregation, Akron, 1964-70; office mgr. Acme Lumber & Fence Co., Akron, 1970-85; nat. pres. NA'AMAT (Movement of Working Women & Vols.), N.Y.C., 1993—. Mem. Planned Parenthood Summit County, bd. dirs., 1994—; founding mem. Govt. Affairs Com., Columbus, Ohio, 1981—, mem. exec. com., 1988-89; v.p. Akron Jewish Cmty. Fedn., 1988-95, pres. women's divsn., 1987-90. Inducted into Ohio Women's Hall of Fame, 1995; recipient Golden Rule award J.C. Penney, 1994, Vol. of Yr. award Lippman Cmty. Day Sch., 1992, Commendation of Honor award Ohio Gen. Assembly, 1993. Democrat. Jewish. Home: 277 Keith Ave Akron OH 44313-5301 Office: NA'AMAT USA 200 Madison Ave New York NY 10016

LEWITZKY, BELLA, choreographer; b. Los Angeles, Jan. 13, 1916; d. Joseph and Nina (Ossman) L.; m. Newell Taylor Reynolds, June 22, 1940; 1 child, Nora Elizabeth. Student, San Bernardino Valley (Calif.) Jr. Coll., 1933-34; hon. doctorate, Calif. Inst. Arts, 1981; PhD (hon.), Occidental Coll., 1984, Otis Parsons Coll., 1989, Juilliard Sch., 1993; DFA, Santa Clara U., 1995. Chmn. dance dept., chmn. adv. panel U. So. Calif., Idyllwild, 1956-74; founder Sch. Dance, Calif. Inst. Arts, 1969, dean, 1969-74; vice chmn. dance adv. panel Nat. Endowment Arts, 1974-77, mem. artists-in-schs. adv. panel, 1974-75; mem. Nat. Adv. Bd. Young Audiences, 1974—, Joint Commn. Dance and Theater Accreditation, 1979; com. mem. Am. chpt. Internat. Dance Coun. of UNESCO, 1974—; trustee Calif. Assn. Dance Cos., 1976—, Idyllwild Sch. Music and Arts, 1986-95, Dance/USA, 1988-95, Calif. State Summer Sch. of Arts, 1988—; cons. the dance project WNET, 1987—. Co-founder, co-dir. Dance Dance Assocs., L.A., 1951-55; founder, 1966; artistic dir. Lewitzky Dance Co., L.A.; choreographer, 1948—; founder, former artistic dir. The Dance Gallery, L.A.; contbr. articles in field; choreographed works include Trio for Saki, 1967, Orrenda, 1969, Kinaesonata, 1971, Pietas, 1971, Ceremony for Three, 1972, Game Plan, 1973, Five, 1974, Spaces Between, 1975, Jigsaw, 1975, Inscape, 1976, Pas de Bach, 1977, Suite Satie, 1980, Changes and Choices, 1981, Confines, 1982, Continuum, 1982, The Song of the Woman, 1983, Nos Duraturi, 1984, 8 Dancers/8 Lights, 1985, Facets, 1986, Impressions #1, 1987, Impressions #3, 1988, Agitime, 1989, Impressions #3, 1989, Episode #1, 1990, Glass Canyons, 1991, Episode #2, 1992, Episode #3, 1992, Episode #4, 1993, Meta 4, 1994, Four Women in Time, 1996. Mem. adv. com. Actors' Fund of Am., 1986—, Women's Bldg. Adv. Council, 1985-91, Calif. Arts Council, 1983-86, City of Los Angeles Task Force on the Arts, 1986—; mem. artistic adv. bd. Interlochen Ctr. for Arts, 1988—. Recipient Mayoral Proclamation, City of L.A., 1976, 1982, ann. award Dance mag., 1978, Dir.'s award Calif. Dance Educators Assn., 1978, Plaudit Award, Nat. Dance Assn., 1979, Labor's Award of Honor for Community Svc., L.A. County AFL-CIO, 1979, L.A. Area Dance Alliance and L.A. Junior C. of C. Honoree, 1980, City of L.A. Resolution, 1980, Distguished Artist Award, City of L.A. and Music Ctr., 1982, Silver Achievement award YWCA, 1982, California State Senate Resolution, 1982, 1984, Award of Recognition, Olympic Black Dance Festival, 1984, Distinguished Women's Award, Northwood Inst., 1984, California State U. Distinguished Artist, 1984, Vesta Award, Woman's Bldg, L.A., 1985, L.A. City Council Honors for Outstanding Contributions, 1985, Woman of the Year, Palm Springs Desert Museum, Women's Committee, 1986, Disting. Svc. award Western Alliance Arts Adminstrs., 1987, Woman of Achievement award, 1988, Am. Dance Guild Ann. award, 1989, So. Calif. Libr. for Social Studies & Rsch. award, 1990, Am. Soc. Journalists & Authors Open Book award, 1990, Internat. Soc. Performing Arts Adminstrs. Tiffany award, 1990, Burning Bush award U. of Judaism, 1991, 1st recipient Calif. Gov.'s award in arts for individual lifetime achievement, 1989; honoree L.A. Arts Coun., 1989, Heritage honoree, Nat. Dance Assn., 1991, Vaslav Nijinsky award, 1991, Hugh M. Hefner First Amendment award, 1991, Artistic Excellence award Ctr. Performing Arts U. Calif., 1992, Lester Horton Lifetime Achievement award Dance Resource Ctr. of L.A., 1992, Occidental Coll. Founders' award, 1992, Dance/USA honor, 1992, Visual Arts Freedom of Expression award Andy Warhol Found., 1993, Artist of Yr. award L.A. County High Sch. Arts, 1993, Freedom of Expression honor Andy Warhol Found. Visual Arts, 1993, Calif. Alliance Edn. award, 1994, Lester Horton Sustained Achievement award, 1995 Danie Resource Ctr. of L.A.; grantee Mellon Found., 1975, 81, 86, Guggenheim Found., 1977-78, NEA, 1969-94; honoree Women's Internat. League Peace and Freedom, 1995. Mem. Am. Arts Alliance (bd. dirs. 1977), Internat. Dance Alliance (adv. council 1984—), Dance/USA (bd. dirs. 1988). Office: Lewitzky Dance Co 1055 Wilshire Blvd Ste 1140 Los Angeles CA 90017-2498

LEWKOWITZ, KAREN HELENE, orthodontist; b. Bklyn., Dec. 26, 1956; d. William A. and Janet B. (Kagan) L.; m. Robert Louis Shpuntoff, Dec. 18, 1983; children: Hilana Megan, Ariana Elizabeth. BA magna cum laude, CUNY, 1978; DDS, Columbia U., 1982; cert. in orthodontics, NYU, 1984. Researcher W. M. Krogman Ctr., Children's Hosp. Phila., Pa., 1976; ptnr. Bayside (N.Y.) Orthodontic Assocs., 1984—; pres. med. awareness com. Queens Coll.-CUNY, 1977-78; attending orthodontist, lectr. Jamaica (N.Y.) Hosp., 1984—. Mem. Temple Torah, Little Neck, N.Y., 1988-94, Temple Israel, Great Neck, N.Y., 1994—, Hadassah, Great Neck, 1990—; v.p. of programming Orgn. Rehab. Thru Tng., Lake Success, N.Y., 1991. Mem. ADA, Acad. Gen. Dentistry, Am. Assn. Women Dentists, Am. Assn. Orthodontists, Queens County Dental Soc. (trustee 1985—, historian 1990, treas. 1991, sec. 1992, v.p. 1993, pres.-elect 1994, pres. 1995), Alpha Omega (pres. Columbia U. chpt. 1980-82, pres. Queens-Nassau chpt. 1984-87, Presdl. citation 1986, regent N.Y. met. area 1990, 91). Office: Bayside Orthodontic Assocs 59-01 Springfield Blvd Bayside NY 11364

LEWTER, HELEN CLARK, elementary education educator; b. Millis, Mass., Jan. 14, 1936; d. Waldimar Kenville and Ida Mills (Currier) Clark; m. Alvin Council Lewter, June 18, 1966; children: Lois Ida, David Paul, Jonathan Clark. BA, U. Mass., 1958; MS, Old Dominion U., 1978. Postgrad. profl. cert. reading specialist, sociology, elem. grades 1-7. Tchr. Juniper Hill Sch., Framingham, Mass., 1960-63, Aragona Elem. Sch., Virginia Beach, Va., 1963-65, Park Elem., Chesapeake, Va., 1965-67; edn. specialist Riverview Sch., Portsmouth, Va., 1977-78; reading tchr. Truitt Jr. H.S., Chesapeake, 1979-83; reading resource tchr. Southeastern Elem., Chesapeake, 1983-86; tchr. Deep Creek Elem. Sch., Chesapeake, 1986—; pers. task force Chesapeake (Va.) Pub. Schs., 1984-85, textbook adoption com., 1984-85, employee handbook com., 1986-87, K-6 writing curriculum com., 1988-89. Tchr., workshop leader, dir., mem. various coms. Fairview Heights Bapt. Ch., Deep Creek Bapt. Ch., Va. So. Bapt. Retreats, 1968—; mem. mayor's adv. coun. City of Chesapeake, Va., 1988-89; mem. summer missionary Va. So. Bapts., 1993; active PTA. Mem. NEA, Va. Edn. Assn., Chesapeake Edn. Assn., Chesapeake Reading Assn. (v.p., pres., honor and merit coun., chmn. various coms.), Internat. Reading Assn., Va. Reading Assn., Delta Kappa Gamma (legis. chmn.), Kappa Delta Pi, Phi Kappa Phi. Republican. Home: 428 Plummer Dr Chesapeake VA 23323-3116 Office: Deep Creek Elem Sch 2809 Forehand Dr Chesapeake VA 23323-2005

LEWY, PHYLLIS, English educator; d. Leonard and Rosalie (Solomon) L. BA, Temple U., 1968, MA, 1971, reading specialist cert., 1979. Cert. secondary tchr., Pa. English instr. Mercer C.C., Trenton, N.J., 1971; English tchr. Lansdowne (Pa.) Aldan H.S., 1972-74; English instr. C.C. of Phila., 1975; reading specialist, grades K-12 Montgomery County Intermediate Unit, Norristown, Pa., 1979—; part-time English instr. Delaware County C.C., 1991-94, Villanova U., Pa. State U., 1979-83, Temple U., 1968-71; pvt. tutor. Freelance editor for Lea & Febiger, Amsco Sch. Publs. Recipient teaching assistantship Temple U., 1968-71, summer fellowship Temple U., 1980.

LEY, LINDA SUE, employee benefits company executive; b. Franklin, Ind., Nov. 27, 1949; d. Jiles Rex and Naomi Katherine (Van Horn) Riggs; m. Thomas Alan Ley, Feb. 28, 1987. BS in Edn. with distinction, Ind. U.-Purdue U., 1971, MS in Edn. with highest distinction, 1975. Cert. paralegal; lic. life, accident, health, property and casualty ins. agt., Ind. Elem. tchr. Indpls. Pub. Schs., 1972-74, Center Grove Community Schs., Greenwood, Ind., 1974-81; dir. adminstrn. Brougher Agy., Inc., Greenwood, 1981-84; mgr. claims/customer svc. The Associated Group, Inc., Indpls., 1984-89; v.p. team ops. Key Benefit Adminstrs., Inc., Indpls., 1989-92; regional mgr. ops. rev. Anthem Benefit Svcs. Corp., Indpls., 1992—. Mem. cotillion com. Humane Soc. Indpls., 1991; vol. Riley Run for Children, Indpls., 1985-92.

Recipient Good Girl Citizenship award Women's Aux. of Am. Legion, 1968. Mem. Am. Mgmt. Assn., Nat. Assn. Life Underwriters, Nat. Assn. Health Underwriters, Inst. Internal Auditors, Indpls. Paralegal Assn., Toastmasters Internat. Republican. Episcopalian. Home: 6358 Bluff Acres Dr Greenwood IN 46143-9037 Office: Anthem Health Cos 4040 Vincennes Cir Indianapolis IN 46268

LEYBOURN, CAROL, musician, educator; b. Toledo, Dec. 15, 1933; d. Charles Wilson and Esther Lenore (McCaughey) L.; m. Donald Herbert Kenney, Aug. 21, 1954 (div. 1981); children: James Herbert, Paul McLean, Laura Elizabeth, Matthew McLean; m. Jerry Frederick Janssen, May 26, 1984. MusB, U. Mich., 1955, MusM, 1957. Tchg. asst. U. Mich., Ann Arbor, 1955-57; concert pianist USIA, Kaiserslautern, Germany, 1957-61; dir., instr. Leybourn Studios, Ann Arbor, 1961-90; solo pianist, harpsichordist Ann Arbor, 1961-90; keyboardist, mgr. Sterling Chamber Players, Ann Arbor, 1975-90; keyboardist Ann Arbor Chamber Orch., 1980-90, Ann Arbor Symphony, 1980-90; pianist Leybourn Trio, 1986—, Janssen Trio, 1986—; solo pianist, harpsichordist Libertyville, Ill., 1990-96; pianist Camerata Singers, Lake Forest, Ill., 1990-91, with cellist Laura Kenney, 1993—; lectr., cons. various piano tchr. groups, 1975—; dir. Jr. Chamber Players, Ann Arbor, 1978-90, Junior Dixieland Jazz Players, Ann Arbor, 1984-90, St. Gilbert's Elem. Sch. Grayslake, Ill., 1990-91; performer Nat. Conf. Women in Music, U. Mich., 1981, 83; adj. music instr. Ann Arbor Community Edn., 1984-90; instrumental music dir. Greenhills Sch., Ann Arbor, 1988-90; mem. piano faculty David Adler Cultural Ctr., Libertyville, Ill., 1990-96; adj. piano faculty Coll. of Lake County, 1993-94. Arranger (Dixieland music books) for 6th Graders--Combo!, 1987; concert appearances include (with cellist Laura Kenney) Mich., Ill., Wis., Fla. Oreg., B.C., Canada, 1993—. Bd. dirs. Ann Arbor Soc. Mus. Arts, 1962-90; dir. chamber music and jazz workshops David Adler Cultural Ctr., Libertyville, 1991-96; founder, chmn. bd. dirs. Lake County Youth Orch., 1994—. Regents scholar U. Mich., 1951-55. Mem. Nat. Music Tchrs. Assn., Mich. Music Tchrs. Assn., Ind. Music Tchrs. Assn., Washtenaw Coun. for Arts, Women's City Club (Ann Arbor), Suzuki Assn. of the Ams., Mu Phi Epsilon (pres. Ann Arbor alumnae chpt. 1964-66), Pi Kappa Lambda. Republican. Presbyterian. Office: 5835 Manning Rd Indianapolis IN 46228

L'HEUREUX-DUBÉ, CLAIRE, judge; b. Quebec City, Que., Can., Sept. 7, 1927; d. Paul H. and Marguerite (Dion) L'H.; m. Arthur Dubé (dec. 197u); children: Louise, Pierre (dec. 1994). BA magna cum laude, Coll. Notre-Dame de Bellevue, Que., 1946; LLL cum laude, Laval U., Que., 1951, LLD (hon.), 1984; LLD (hon.), Dalhousie U., 1981, Montreal U., 1983, Ottawa U., 1988, U. Que., 1989, U. Toronto, 1994. Bar: Que. 1952. Ptnr. Bard, L'Heureux & Philippon, 1952-73; sr. ptnr. L'Heureux, Philippon, Garneau, Tourigny, St.Arnaud & Assocs., from 1969; Puisne judge Superior Ct. Que., 1973-79, Ct. Appeal of Que., 1979-87, Supreme Ct. Can., Ottawa, 1987—; commr. Part II Inquiries Act Dept. Manpower and Immigration, Montreal, 1973-76; del. Gen. Coun. Bar of Que., 1968-70, com. on adminstrn. justice, 1968-73, others; pres. family law com. Family Ct. com. Que Civil Code Rev. Office, 1972-76; pres. Can. sect. Internat. Commn. Jurists, 1981-83, v.p., 1992—. Editor: (with Rosalie S. Abella) Family Law - Dimensions of Justice, 1983; chmn. editorial bd. Can. Bar Rev., 1985-88; author articles, conf. proc., book chpt. Bd. dirs. YWCA, Que., 1969-73, Ctr. des Loisirs St. Sacrement, 1969-73, Ctr. Jeunesse de Tilly-Ctr. des Jeunes, 1971-77; v.p. Can. Consumers Coun., 1970-73; v.p. Vanier Inst. of the Family, 1972-73; lifetime gov. Found. Univ. Laval, 1980, bd. dirs., 1984-85; mem. Comité des grandes orientations de l'Univ. Laval, 1971-72; mem. nat. coun. Can. Human Rights Found., 1980-82, 82-84; mem. Can. del. to Peoples Republic China on Status of Women, 1981; pres. Can. sect. Internat. Commn. Jurists, 1981-83, v.p. internat. bd., 1992—. Apptd. Queen's Counsel, 1969; recipient Medal of the Alumni, U. Laval, 1986, Médaille du Barreau de Que., 1987. Mem. Can. Bar Assn. Can. Inst. Adminstrn. Justice, Internat. Soc. Family Law (bd. dirs. 1977-88, v.p. 1981-88), Internat. Fedn. Women Lawyers, Fedn. Internat. des Femmes Juristes, L'Assn. des Femmes Diplômées d'Univ., Assn. Québécoise pour l'Étude Comparative du Droit (pres. 1984-90), Am. Coll. Trial Lawyers (hon.), Am. Law Inst., Phi Delta Phi. Roman Catholic. Office: Supreme Ct Can, Wellington St, Ottawa, ON Canada K1A 0J1

LI, GRACE CHIA-CHIAN, accountant, business planning manager; b. Taipei, Taiwan, Republic of China, Aug. 7, 1963; came to U.S., 1987; d. Chuan-Chun and Yu-Lin (Hsueh) L.; m. Michael H. Chang, Dec. 21, 1993. BA, Nat. Cheng Chi U., Taipei, 1985; MBA, Wash. U., 1989. CPA, Calif. Acct. Cosa Libermann LTD, Taipei, 1985-86; cost acctg. supr. Johnson & Johnson, Taipei, 1988; planning and control specialist IBM Corp., Taipei, 1986-87; fin. analyst Ameritech Cellular, St. Louis, 1989-92; mgr. market planning Ameritech Internat., Hoffman Estates, Ill., 1992-94; internat. mktg. mgr. Pactel Internat., Walnut Creek, Calif., 1994; bus. cons. Decision Consulting, San Ramon, Calif., 1994-95; bus. planning mgr. Mitsubishi Wireless Comms., Inc., Sunnyvale, Calif., 1995—; guest spkr. on China telecom. industry devel. Nat. Comm. Forum, Chgo., 1993. Mem. NAFE, AICPA, Ill. CPA Soc., Chgo. Com. Fgn. Rels. Office: Mitsubishi Wireless Comm Inc 1050 E Arques Ave Sunnyvale CA 94086

LI, JESSIE WAI-LING, textile industry executive; b. Hong Kong, Feb. 3, 1959; d. Ping Choi and Sam Mui (Chan) Lee. BS, Metro. State Coll. Denver, 1994. Bookkeeper Union Plastic Mfg. Co., Hong Kong, 1980-81; shipping exec. garment export industry, Hong Kong, 1981-89; acct. specialist III Weyerhouser Co., Denver, 1989—. Mem. Phi Theta Kappa. Office: Weyerhauser Co 5315 Race Ct Denver CO 80216

LI, MICHELLE AIMEE, secondary education educator; b. Brandon, Man., Can., Apr. 9, 1970; came to U.S., 1976; d. Kai Tung and So Kuen (Leung) L. BA in English, U. Tex., 1992, MEd, 1993. Cert. tchr., reading specialist, Tex. English tchr. Newman Smith H.S., Carrollton, Tex., 1993—; mentor New Tchrs., Newman Smith H.S., Carrollton, 1994-95; workshop leader Carrollton Ind. Sch. Dist., 1994. Recipient Henderson Edn. scholarship, U. Tex., 1991, Grad. fellowship, 1992-93. Mem. Nat. Coun. Tchrs. of English, Phi Beta Kappa. Office: Newman Smith HS 2335 N Josey Ln Carrollton TX 75006

LI, PEARL NEI-CHIEN CHU, information specialist, executive; b. Jiangsu, China, June 17, 1946; came to U.S., 1968; d. Ping-Yung and Yao-Hwa (Li) Chu; m. Terry Teng-Fang Li, Sept. 20, 1969; children: Ina Ying, Ping Li. BA, Nat. Taiwan U., Taipei, 1968; MA, W.Va. U., 1971; cert. advanced study in info. studies, Drexel U., 1983. Cert. sr. libr., N.J. Instr. Nat. Tchr.'s Coll., Chang-Hua, Taiwan, 1977-78; reference libr. Camden County Libr., Voorhees, N.J., 1981-82; libr. Kulzer and Dipadova, P.A., Haddonfield, N.J., 1982-87; libr. dir. Am. Law Inst., Phila., 1987-92; gen. mgr., info. specialist Unitek Internat. Corp. (Am.), Mt. Laurel, N.J., 1992—; tchr. South Jersey Chinese Sch., Cherry Hill, N.J., 1978-82. Editor: CLE Around the Cuontry (annually), 1988-92; contbr. articles to profl. jours. Bus. mgr. Chinese Community Ctr., Voorhees, 1981. Mem. NAFE, N.J. Entrepreneurial Network, Inc., Spl. Librs. Assn., Soc. Competitive Intelligence Profls. Home: 1132 Sea Gull Ln Cherry Hill NJ 08003-3113 Office: Unitek Internat Corp 131A Gaither Dr Mount Laurel NJ 08054

LIANG, VERA BEH-YUIN TSAI, psychiatrist, educator; b. Shanghai, China, July 29, 1946; came to U.S., 1970, naturalized, 1978; d. Ming Sang and Mea Ling Chu Tsai; m. Hanson Liang, Nov. 6, 1971; children: Eric G., Jason G. MBBS, U. Hong Kong, 1969. Diplomate Am. Bd. Psychiatry and Neurology. Intern Cambridge Hosp. (Mass.), 1970-71; resident Hillside div. L.I. Jewish Med. Ctr., New Hyde Park, N.Y., 1971-73; fellow Albert Einstein Coll. Medicine, Bronx, N.Y., 1973-75, asst. clin. prof., 1989-95; instr. SUNY, Bklyn., 1975-79; asst. prof. SUNY, Stony Brook, 1979-86; med. dir. Hillside Ea. Queens Ctr., Queens Village, N.Y., 1977-90, 91-92; staff child psychiatrist Schneider Children's Hosp., New Hyde Park, N.Y., 1990-92; sr. psychiatrist South Oaks Hosp., Amityville, N.Y., 1992—; cons. in field. Contbr. articles to profl. jours. Mem. Am. Psychiat. Assn., Am. Acad. Child Psychiatry. Office: South Oaks Hosp 400 Sunrise Hwy Amityville NY 11701-2508

LIANZI, THERESA LOUISE, librarian; b. Sycamore, Ill., Oct. 23, 1939; d. Frank and Margaret Emma (Boettcher) L. BA, No. Ill. U., 1961, MS in Edn., 1965; MS, Fla. State U., 1967. Tchr. Leland (Ill.) Pub. Schs., 1963-64, Sandwich (Ill.) Pub. Schs., 1964-65, Carson City-Crystal River (Mich.) Pub. Schs., 1965-66; asst. libr. Fla. Keys C.C., Key West, 1967-69; catalog libr. Miami-Dade C.C., Miami, Fla., 1969-75, libr.III, 1975—, sec. faculty senate, 1972-74. Sec. LWV, Dade County, 1989-92; usher, vol. Gusman Theater of the Pub. Arts, 1982-94, Coconut Grove (Fla.) Playhouse, 1980-91. Mem. ALA, Dade County Libr. Assn., Alumni Assn. Fla. State U. Office: Miami-Dade Public Libr 101 W Flagler Miami FL 33130

LIAO, IRENE JOAN, medical documents specialist; b. Hartford, Conn., Aug. 23, 1970; d. Paul S.H. and Janice T.Y. (chang) L. BS in Journalism with honors, U. Kans., 1993. Intern KSNT-TV, Topeka, Kans., 1992; rsch. asst. Beach Ctr. on Families and Disability, Lawrence, Kans., 1992-93; sec. The Gerson Co., Mission, Kans., 1994-95; med. documents specialist IMTCI, Lenexa, Kans., 1995—. Editor newsletter MCM Update, 1995—, co. newsletter IMTCI Matters, 1996. Mem. Asian-Am. Profls. Journal Project. Univ. scholar U. Mo., 1989, journalism scholar U. Kans., 1992. Office: IMTCI 16300 College Blvd Lenexa KS 66219

LIAO, MEI-JUNE, biopharmaceutical company executive; came to U.S., 1974; BS, Nat. Tsing-Hua U. Taiwan, 1973; MPh, Yale U., 1977, PhD, 1980. Tchg. asst. Nat. Taiwan U., 1973-74, Temple U., Phila., 1974-75; tchg. asst. Yale U., New Haven, 1975-76, rsch. asst., 1976-79; postdoctoral assoc. MIT, Cambridge, 1980-83; sr. scientist Interferon Scis., Inc., New Brunswick, N.J., 1983-84; group leader Interferon Scis. Inc., New Brunswick, N.J., 1984-85, dir. cell biology, 1985-87; dir. R&D Interferon Scis., Inc., New Brunswick, N.J., 1987-94, v.p. rsch. & deve., 1995—. Contbr. articles to profl. jours.; inventor in field. Mem. Am. Soc. Biochemistry and Molecular Biology, Internat. Soc. Interferon and Cytokine Rsch., Soc. Chinese Bioscientists in Am., N.Y. Acad. Scis. Office: Interferon Sci Inc 783 Jersey Ave New Brunswick NJ 08901-3605

LIBBEY, DARLENE HENSLEY, artist, educator; b. La Follettee, Tenn., Jan. 9, 1952; d. Charles Franklin and Geneva (Chitwood) Hensley; children: Michael Damon McLaughlin, Marina Auston. BFA in Painting, San Francisco Art Inst., 1989; MFA in Painting/Drawing, U. Tenn., 1994. Grad. asst. Alliance of Ind. Colls., N.Y.C., 1989; gallery asst. Holley Solomon Gallery, N.Y.C., 1989; teaching assoc., instr. U. Tenn., Knoxville, 1991-94; lectr., instr. U. Tex.-Pan Am., 1994—, South Tex. Cmty. Coll., 1995—; curator Belleza Salon, Knoxville, 1993—; invitational rep. San Francisco Art Inst., N.Y. Studio Program, Alliance Ind. Colls., 1989; organizer Multi-Media Group Exhbn.; lectr., instr. South Tex. C.C., McAllen. One-woman shows include U. Tex.-Pan Am., 1995, 96; exhibited in group shows at San Francisco Art Inst., 1985, 86, 87, 88, 89, Pacific Ctr., San Francisco, 1988, alliance of Ind. Colls., N.Y.C., 1989, San Francisco Mus. Modern Art, 1990, Bluxom Studios, San Francisco, 1991, Gallery 1010, Knoxville, 1991, 92, Ewing Gallery, U. Tenn., Knoxville, 1991, 92, 93, 94, SUNY, Syracuse, 1992, Printers Mark, Knoxville, 1993, Unitarian Ch., Knoxville, 1993, Tomato Head, Knoxville, 1994, Belleza Salon, Knoxville, 1994, U. Pan Am., 1995, 96; group show Museo Historico de Reynosa, Tamalipus, Mex., 1996. Vol. San Francisco Mus. Modern Art, 1990-91; founding mem. Grad. Student Union, U. Tenn., Knoxville, 1993; vol. instr. Knox County Schs., Knoxville, 1992-93; vis. artist Marin County Schs., San Anselmo, Calif., 1989. Tuition scholar San Francisco Art Inst., 1987; materials grantee U. Tenn., 1993, grantee Buck Found., 1987-89. Mem. Coll. Art Assn. Democrat. Unitarian. Home: 1118 W Upas Ave Mcallen TX 78501 Office: U Tex-Pan Am Art Dept 1201 W University Dr Edinburg TX 78539-2909

LIBBIN, ANNE EDNA, lawyer; b. Phila., Aug. 25, 1950; d. Edwin M. and Marianne (Herz) L.; m. Christopher J. Cannon, July 20, 1985; children: Abigail Libbin Cannon, Rebecca Libbin Cannon. AB, Radcliffe Coll., 1971; JD, Harvard U., 1975. Bar: Calif. 1975, U.S. Dist. Ct. (cen. dist.) Calif. 1977, U.S. Dist. Ct. (no. dist.) Calif. 1979, U.S. Dist. Ct. (ea. dist.) Calif. 1985, U.S. Ct. Appeals (2d cir.) 1977, U.S. Ct. Appeals (5th cir.) 1982, U.S. Ct. Appeals (7th cir.) 1976, U.S. Ct. Appeals (9th cir.) 1976, U.S. Ct. Appeals (D.C. cir.) 1978. Appellate atty. NLRB, Washington, 1975-78; assoc. Pillsbury Madison & Sutro LLP, San Francisco, 1978-83, ptnr., 1984—; dir. Alumnae Resources, San Francisco. Mem. ABA (labor and employment sect.), State Bar Calif. (labor law sect.), Bar Assn. San Francisco (labor law sect.), Anti-Defamation League (ctrl. Pacific regional adv. bd.), Radcliffe Club (San Francisco). Office: Pillsbury Madison & Sutro 235 Montgomery St San Francisco CA 94104-2902

LIBBY, SANDRA CHIAVARAS, special education educator; b. Clinton, Mass., Apr. 8, 1949; B.S. in Spl. Edn., Fitchburg (Mass.) State Coll., 1970, M.Ed. in Reading, 1976; postgrad. (fellow) Clark U., 1981-83; 2 children. Tchr. spl. class Webster (Mass.) Schs., 1970-73, asst. coord. program materials, resource room, 1974, tchr./coord. primary spl. needs program, 1975-78, tchr. jr. high English, 1978-79, reading tchr. jr. high, 1979-80 adminstrv. asst. intern Shepherd Hill Regional Sch., Dudley, Mass., 1980-81; dir., owner Teddy Bear Day Care Ctr., Dudley, Mass., 1983-85; devel. specialist Ft. Devens Post Learning Ctr., Shirley, Mass., 1985-86; resource room tchr. Murdock High Sch., Winchendon, Mass., 1986; tchr. behavioral modification Middle Sch., Winchendon, 1986-87; coord., tchr. gifted and talented Lancaster Pub. Schs., 1987-90; tchr. learning disabilities Leominster Pub. Sch., 1990-91, tchr. primary level behavior modification, 1991—. V.p. Samoset Sch. PTO, Leominister, Mass., 1995—; mem. Edn. Reform Change Team, 1996—. Mem. Nat. Edn. Assn., Mass. Tchrs. Assn., Leominster Tchrs. Assn. (bldg. rep. 1992-95, negotiating com. 1993—, sec. 1995—), Internat. Reading Assn. (v.p. 1994-95, chairperson celebrate literacy award 1994-95), Mass. Reading Assn. (mem. North Worcester County coun. 1994-95), Webster Emblem Club (pres. 1984-85), Phi Delta Kappa (Horace Mann grant 1989-90). Cert. in elem. and spl. edn., reading, reading supervision, learning disabilities, English (secondary), Mass. Home: 29 Chapman Pl Leominster MA 01453

LIBERTOSKI, AMY LYNNE, accountant; b. Wakefield, Mich., Sept. 30, 1970; d. Ralph Howard and Lorraine Gay (Bailey) Fruik; m. Kenneth Allan Libertoski, June 22, 1991; 1 child, Justin Allan. BS, U. Wis., Superior. CPA, Minn. Acct. John J. Tomasi, CPA, Bergland, Mich., 1993-94, Schweitzer Rubin Karon & Bremer, Mpls., 1994—. Office: 1400 TCF Tower 121 S 8th St Minneapolis MN 55402

LIBERTY, LEONA HELEN, rehabilitation services professional; b. Troy, N.Y., Nov. 2, 1940. BS cum laude, Syracuse U., 1976, MS, 1979; EdD, La. State U., 1985. Asst. prof. St. John's U., Jamaica, N.Y., 1984-91; rehab. coord. Capabilities Evaluation Ctr., Albany, N.Y., 1991—; adj. prof. SUNY, Albany, 1991—. Office: Capabilities Evaluation Ctr 16 Corporate Words Blvd Albany NY 12211

LIBERTY, SUSAN SPENCE, community college official; b. Lincoln, Nebr., Sept. 15, 1937; d. William Morton and Catherine (Crancer) Spence; m. Robert J. Liberty, Sept. 13, 1958 (div. 1971); children: Jay Andrew, Joel Adrian, Jena Sue; m. James Walter Warwick, July 4, 1996. BA, U. Colo., 1959; MA, Calif. State U., Northridge, 1971; postgrad., UCLA, 1972-76. Lectr. English, Calaif. State U., 1970-74, L.A. Valley Coll., Van Nuys, Calif., 1971-76; coord. tutorial svcs. Fresno (Calif.) City Coll., 1976-87, dir. arts, honors and devel. edn., 1987—; mem. exec. com. acad. senate Calif. C.C.'s, 1981-83, rep. chancellor's adv. on telecom., 1982-85. Contbr. articles to profl. jours., chpt. to book. Mem. Calif. Coll. Tutorial and Learning Assistance Assn. (pres.-elect, pres. 1980-82), Coll. Reading and Learning Assts. Assn. Democrat. Congregationalaist. Office: Fresno City Coll 1101 E University Ave Fresno CA 93714

LIBKIND, JEAN SUE JOHNSON (JEAN SUE JOHNSON-LIBKIND), publishing executive; b. Racine, Wis., Apr. 4, 1944; d. John Bert and Loretta Laura (Richards) Johnson; m. D.M. Spradling, June 5, 1966 (div. Nov. 1971); 1 child, Eric David (dec.); m. Robert Lawrence Libkind, Oct. 13, 1991. Student, U. Oslo, Norway, 1965; BA in Journalism, U. Wis., 1966. Libr. asst. Racine (Wis.) Pub. Libr., 1962-64; mng. editor Daily Cardinal, Madison, 1965-66; project assoc. U. Wis.-Journalism Extension, Madison, 1966-68; office mgr. Senrac Enterprises, Madison, 1968-71; prodn. mgr. U. Wis. Press, Madison, 1971-72, asst. journs. mgr., 1972-77, asst. mktg. mgr., 1977-80; mktg. mgr. U. Ga. Press, Athens, 1980-84; sales, mktg. mgr. U. Penn Press, Phila., 1984-88; mktg. dir. Jewish Publ. Soc., Phila., 1988-91, mktg. dir. pub. ops., 1991-94; owner Johnson Libkind Pubs.' Agy.; speaker and cons. in field. Program chair Unitarian Universalist Fellowship, Athens, 1982-84; pres. Friends of Ea. State Penitentiary Park. Recipient Svc. award USMC, 1966, Svc. award After Sch. Day Care Assn., 1976; named Hon. Lt. Col., Ga. Militia, 1985. Mem. Women in Scholarly Pub. (treas. 1990-91, sec. 1989-90, pres. 1970-71), Phila. Pub. Group (pres. 1990-92), Women in Scholarly Pub. (newsletter editor 1981-83, mentoring co-chair 1993-94), Religious Pub. Group, Soc. Scholarly Pub., Internat. Assn. Scholarly Pub. Home: 837 N Woodstock St Philadelphia PA 19130-1408

LIBOV, CHARLOTTE ANN, author, speaker; b. New Haven, Conn., Mar. 5, 1950; d. Benjamin and Henrietta (Stark) L. BA with hons., U. Conn., 1973; MS, U. Oreg., 1979. Reporter The Milford (Conn.) Citizen, 1974-76, Jour. Enquirer, Manchester, Conn., 1980-81; bur. chief The Daily News, Springfield, Mass., 1981-85; freelance writer Bethlehem, Conn., 1985—; counselor Battered Women's Shelter, Eugene, Oreg., 1977-79;lectr. U. Conn. Sch. of Journalism, 1982-83; judge Assn. of Schs. of Journalism and Mass Comm., Journalist in Space Project, 1986; program cons., featured expert (TV documentary) Women's Hearts at Risk, 1996; mem. med. adv. bd. The Difference in a Woman's Heart, Women and Heart Disease: A Neglected Epidemic, The Older Women's League. Co-author The Woman's Heart Book: The Complete Guide to Keeping a Healthy Heart and What to Do if Things Go Wrong, 1994 (Will Solimene award of excellence, Am. Med. Writers Assn. 1994), 50 Essential Things To Do if the Doctor Says It's Heart Disease, 1995; founder and editor (newsletter) Woman's Health Hotline, 1994—; editor: (commemorative book) Hands Across America, 1986; contbr. articles to newspapers and mags. including the New York Times. Vol. Am. Heart Assn., Wallingford, Conn., 1993—, Animal Rescue Found., Middlebury, Conn., 1990—. Recipient 3rd place award in-depth spl. section Conn. Soc. Profl. Journalists, 1990, Outstanding Comm. Vol. award, Am. Heart Assn. Conn. Affiliate, 1993, Annual Media award Combined Health Appeal, 1994. Mem. NOW, The Authors Guild, Profl. Speakers Assn., Nat. Assn. Sci. Writers, Am. Med. Writers Assn., Nat. Writers Union, Am. Soc. Journalists and Authors, Acad. Radio and TV Health Communicators.

LIBRIZZI, ROSE MARIE MEOLA, library administrator, counselor; b. Newark, Apr. 15, 1940; d. Salvatore J. and Marie (Consoli) Meola; m. Vincent F. LiBrizzi, June 25, 1965 (div. 1983); children: Vincent, Steve. BA in History and Pre-law magna cum laude, Bloomfield (N.J.) Coll., 1965; MLS, Rutgers U., 1967; JD, Seton Hall U., 1989; MA in Counseling, MontclairState U., 1992. Cert. tchr., N.J.; cert. sch. libr.; profl libr. cert. Acting children's libr. Newark Pub. Libr., 1965-66; head children's svcs. Belleville (N.J.) Pub. Libr., 1966-68; asst. dir. Kearny (N.J.) Pub. Libr., 1969; mem. adj. faculty Kean Coll., Union, N.J., 1969-73; supr. children's svcs. Jersey City Pub. Libr., 1973-87, asst. dir., 1987-90, 91—, libr. dir., 1990-91. Mem. ABA, ALA, N.J. Libr. Assn. (v.p. 1988, mem.-at-large 1982, sec. 1981, pres. and founder adminstr. sect. 1978, chairperson pers. adminstrn. com., chairperson resolutions, nominations and honor and awards coms., chairperson NJLA Centennial Celebration com. 1984-89, Adminstrn. section award), Hudson County Libr. Dirs. Assn. (pres. 1990—), Exxex-Hudson Region Exec. Bd. (mem-at-large, sec. 1990-93, chairperson continuing edn. com. 1986-88), Rutgers Alumni Assn. (pres., senator, mem. alumni fedn. bd. 1990—), Infolink (mem-at-large). Home: 5 Squier Ct Livingston NJ 07039-2506 Office: Jersey City Pub Libr 472 Jersey Ave Jersey City NJ 07302-3499

LICENS, LILA LOUISE, administrative assistant; b. Puyallup, Wash., Feb. 18, 1949; d. C.L. and Joan L. (Rubert) Vormestrand. Cert., Knapp Bus. Coll., 1968. Cert. profl. sec. Adminstrv. asst. Weyerhaeuser Co., Tacoma, 1968-93, adminstrv. asst. bleached paperboard, 1993—. Mem. adv. bd. Bates Tech. Coll., 1994—. Mem. Profl. Sec. Internat. (pres. Mt. Rainier chpt. 1994—, pres. Wash.-Alaska divsn. 1990-91, pres.-elect 1989-90, sec. 1987-89, pres. Sea-Tac chpt. 1985-87), Fed. Way Women's Network (treas. 1988, sec. 1989, pres. 1995, 96). Home: 771 108th St S Tacoma WA 98444-5666

LICETTI, MARY ELIZABETH, business analysis director; b. N.Y.C., Nov. 2, 1954; d. Philip Carmelo and JoAnn (Milner) Licetti; m. George Guy Colagreco, Apr. 22, 1995. BS in Acctg., Rutgers U., 1985; postgrad., Duke U., 1991, 92, Kenan Flagler Bus. Sch., Chapel Hill, N.C., 1995. Sr. acct. Johns-Manville, Manville, N.J., 1972-80; acctg. supr. Ortho Diagnostic Syss. (Johnson & Johnson), Raritan, N.J., 1981-87, bus. unit fin. mgr., 1988-90, project mgr., 1991-92, USA contr., 1992-95, dir. bus. analysis and fin. sys., 1995—; chmn. supervisory com. Johns-Manville Employees Credit Union, Manville, 1977-80. Treas. Johns-Manville Employee Club; vol. audit com. United Way, Somerset, N.J., 1991-92; dir. Am. Liver Found., Commack, N.Y., 1995—. Mem. NAFE, Am. Mgmt. Assn., Soc. Competitive Intelligence Profls., Somerset County Art Assn. Home: 30 Madison Ave Flemington NJ 08822-3306 Office: Ortho Diagnostic Sys US Hwy 202 Raritan NJ 08869

LICHT, ALICE VESS (ALICE O'NEILL), publishing executive, journalist; b. Caroleen, N.C., May 28, 1937; d. Troy Cleet Vess and Clara Ella Lee (Johnson) Littleton; m. Gennaro Pietro Di Biase, Nov. 12, 1955 (div. 1971); children: Stephen Eugene, Michael Antonio; m. Raymond Licht, Feb. 11, 1989. BA in English, Theatre, R.I. Coll., 1969, MA in English, 1976; postgrad., Emerson Coll., 1982-83, Southwestern U., 1984. Cert. secondary sch. English tchr. English tchr. Scituate (R.I.) High Sch., 1969-83; actress films and TV L.A., 1984-86, freelance journalist, 1984-86; pres., journalist Los Angeles Features Syndicate, 1986—. Mem. AAUW, NAFE, Internat. Platform Assn., Chgo. Internat. Press Club. Home: 650 Winnetka Mews Winnetka IL 60093-1967

LICHTENBERG, JUDITH A., philosophy educator; b. N.Y.C., Apr. 19, 1948; d. Al and Friedel (Rothschild) L.; m. David J. Luban, Mar. 5, 1983; children: Daniel, Rachel. BA, U. Wis., 1968, MA, 1971; PhD, CUNY, 1978. Asst. prof. philosophy U. N.C., Chapel Hill, 1978-81; rsch. scholar Inst. Philosophy and Pub. Policy U. Md., College Park, 1981—, assoc. prof., 1991—. Editor: Democracy and the Mass Media, 1990; contbr. articles to profl. jours. Mem. Am. Philos. Assn., Am. Soc. Polit. and Legal Philosophy. Office: U Md Dept Philosophy College Park MD 20742

LICHTENBERG, MARGARET KLEE, publishing company executive; b. N.Y.C., Nov. 19, 1941; d. Lawrence and Shirley Jane (Wicksman) Klee; m. James Lester Lichtenberg, Mar. 31, 1963 (div. 1982); children: Gregory Lawrence, Amanda Zoe. BA, U. Mich., 1963; postgrad., Harvard U., 1963. Book rev. editor New Woman mag., 1972-73; assoc. editor children's books Parents Mag. Press, 1974; editor, rights dir. Books for Young People, Frederick Warne & Co., N.Y.C., 1975-78; sr. editor Simon & Schuster, N.Y.C., 1979-80; dir. sales promotion Grosset & Dunlap, N.Y.C., 1980-81; ednl. sales mgr. Bantam Books, N.Y.C., 1982-84; dir. mktg. and sales Grove Press, N.Y.C., 1984-86; dir. of sales Grove Press, 1986-87; dir. sales Weidenfeld & Nicolson, N.Y.C., 1986-87; mktg. dir. Beacon Press, Boston, 1988-95; book mktg. coach, pers. bus. coach, 1995—; writer, freelance critic, 1961—. Contbr. articles, essays, stories, poetry, revs. to mags., newspapers and anthologies. Bd. dirs. Children's Book Council, 1978. Recipient 2 Avery Hopwood awards in drama and fiction, 1962, 2 in drama and poetry, 1963; coll. fiction contest award Mademoiselle mag., 1963; Woodrow Wilson fellow, 1963. Mem. Women's Nat. Book Assn. (past pres. N.Y. chpt.). Home and Office: PO Box 268 Santa Fe NM 87504

LICHTENSTEIN, ELISSA CHARLENE, legal association executive; b. Trenton, N.J., Oct. 23, 1954; d. Mark and Rita (Field) L. AB cum laude, Smith Coll., Northampton, Mass., 1976; JD, George Washington U., 1979. Bar: D.C. 1980, U.S. Dist. Ct. (D.C. dist.) 1980, U.S. Ct. Appeals (D.C. cir.) 1980. Law clk. U.S. EPA, Washington, 1978-79; staff dir. ABA, Washington, 1979—, assoc. dir. pub. svcs. div., 1981-85, dir., 1985—. Editor, contbr.: Common Boundary/Common Problems: The Environmental Consequences of Energy Production, 1982, Exit Polls and Early Election Projections, 1984, The Global Environment: Challenges, Choices and Will, 1986, (newsletter) Environ. Law; co-editor, contbr. The Environ. Network; co-editor: Determining Competency in Guardianship Proceedings, 1990, Due Process Protections for Juveniles in Civil Commitment Proceedings, 1991, Environmental Regulation in Pacific Rim Nations, 1993, The Role of Law in the 1992 UN Conference on Environment and Development, 1992, Trade and the Environment in Pacific Rim Nations, 1994, Public Participation in Environmental Decisionmaking, 1995, Endangered Species Act Reauthorization: A Biocentric Approach, 1996, Sustainable Development in the Americas: The Emerging Role of the Private Sector, 1996. Mem. Nat. Trust for

Hist. Preservation. Named Outstanding Young Woman of Am., 1982. Mem. ABA, NAFE, Am. Soc. Assn. Execs., Washington Coun. Lawyers, Women in Communications, Inc., Environ. Law Inst. (assoc.), Met. Washington Environ. Profls. (pres. 1986-96), D.C. Bar Assn. Democrat. Jewish. Office: ABA Div Pub Svcs 740 15th St NW Washington DC 20005

LICHTMAN, SUSAN A., English language educator, artist; b. Chgo., Mar. 30, 1952; d. James Anthony Saviano and Lorraine Ruth (Menichetti) Dilsaver; m. Stephen R. Lichtman, Dec. 5, 1971; children: Rachel, Sarah, Elijah. BA in English, Purdue U., 1987; MA in English, U. Notre Dame, 1990. Freelance comml. artist Michigan City, Ind., 1975-81; dir., tchr. Sunday sch. Sinai Temple, Michigan City, Ind., 1978-81; English tutor North Ctrl. Writing Ctr. Purdue U., Westville, Ind., 1982-87, asst. supr., 1985-87, prof., 1990-96. Author: Lifestages of Woman's Heroic Journey, 1991, The Female Hero in Women's Literature and Poetry, 1996. co-chair Sinai Sunday Evening Forum Michigan City, 1985-95; group facilitator Impact Drug Abuse Program, Michigan City, 1985-86. John J. Stanfield scholar Purdue U. North Ctrl., 1987. Mem. MLA, Midwest MLA, North Ctrl. Women's Studies Assn. Jewish. Home: 101 Orchard Michigan City IN 46360 Office: Purdue U North Ctrl US Hwy 421 Westville IN 46391-9528

LICK, SUE FAGALDE, journalist; b. San Jose, Calif., Mar. 9, 1952; d. Clarence Edwin and Elaine Veronica (Avina) Fagalde; m. James Brian Barnard, June 22, 1974 (div. May 1980); m. Fred Allan Lick, May 18, 1985; children: Ted William, Gretchen Lick Hedgecock, Michael Douglas. AA in Journalism, West Valley C.C., 1972; BA, San Jose State U., 1974, postgrad., 1978-80, 88-90. Reporter Meredith Sun Newspapers, Cupertino, Calif., 1973-76, 78-80; editl. asst. Calif. Sch. Employees Assn., San Jose, 1976-78; reporter, feature editor Pacifica (Calif.) Tribune, 1981-83; assoc. editor CMP Publs., San Jose, 1984-85; copyeditor Hayward (Calif.) Daily Review, 1985-86; editor Advocate Jour. Post-Record Co., San Jose, 1986-87; freelance writer, 1987-94; reporter, editor Saratoga News/Metro Newspapers, San Jose, 1993-96. Author: The Iberian-Americans, 1990; co-author, editor: Living in San Jose, 1987. Music min. St. Julie's Ch., San Jose, 1989—; singer Valley Chorale, Sunnyvale, Calif., 1975-83, 87-95; co-dir. Singers Anonymous, San Jose, 1985-88; newsletter editor Cabrilho Cultural Ctr., San Jose, 1989-91; vol. San Jose Hist. Mus., 198796. Mem. Nat. League Am. Pen Women, Calif. Writers Club (South Bay pres. 1991-92, 1st prize short story 1993), Calif. Coast Music Camp, South Bay Folks. Democrat. Roman Catholic. Home and Office: 2126 NW Inlet Ave Lincoln City OR 97367

LIDDELL, JANE HAWLEY HAWKES, civic worker; b. Newark, Dec. 8, 1907; d. Edward Zeh and Mary Everett (Hawley) Hawkes; AB, Smith Coll., 1931; postgrad. in art history, Harvard U., 1933-35; MA, Columbia U., 1940; Carnegie fellow Sorbonne, Paris, 1937; m. Donald M. Liddell, Jr., Mar. 30, 1940; children: Jane Boyer, D. Roger Brooke. Pres., Planned Parenthood Essex County (N.J.), 1947-50; trustee Prospect Hill Sch. Girls, Newark, 1946-50; mem. adv. bd., publicity and public relations chmn. N.J. State Mus., Trenton, 1952-60; sec., then v.p. women's br. N.J. Hist. Soc.; women's aux. prodn. chmn. Englewood (N.J.) Hosp., 1959-61; pres. Dwight Sch. Girls Parents Assn., 1955-57; v.p. Englewood Sch. Boys Parents Assn., 1958-60; mem. Altar Guild, women's aux. bd., rector's adv. council St. Paul's Episcopal Ch., Englewood, 1954-59; bd. dir. N.Y. State Soc. of Nat. Soc. Colonial Dames, 1961-67, rep. conf. Patriotic and Hist. Socs., 1964—; bd. dirs. Huguenot Soc. Am., 1979-86, regional v.p., 1979-82, historian, 1983-84, co-chmn. Tercentennial Book, 1983-85; bd. dirs. Soc. Daus. Holland Dames, 1965-82; nat. jr. v.p. Dames of Loyal Legion, USA; bd. dirs., mem. publs. com. Daus. Cin., 1966-72; bd. dirs. Ch. Women's League Patriotic Service, 1962—, pres., 1968-70, 72-74; bd. dirs., chmn. grants com. Youth Found., N.Y.C., 1974—; chmn. for Newark, Smith Coll. 75th Ann. Fund, 1948-50; pres. North N.J. Smith Club, 1956-58; pres. Smith Coll. Class 1931, 1946-51, 76-81, editor 50th anniversary book, 1980-81. Author: (with others) Huguenot Refugees in the Settling of Colonial America, 1982-85; contbr. The Dutch Contribution to the Development of Early Manhattan, 1969. Recipient various commendation awards. Republican. Mem. Colonial Dames Am. (N.Y.C. chpt.). Clubs: Colony, City Gardens, Church (N.Y.C.); Jr. League N.Y.; N.Y. Jr. League; Needle and Bobbin, Nat. Farm and Garden . Editor: Maine Echoes, 1961; research and editor asst., Wartime Writings of American Revolution Officers, 1972-75.

LIDE, NEOMA JEWELL LAWHON (MRS. MARTIN JAMES LIDE, JR.), poet; b. Levelland, Tex., Apr. 1, 1926; d. Charles Samuel and Juel (Yeager) Lawhon; Secretarial cert. Draughon's Bus. Coll., 1943; student U. Tex., 1944-46; R.N., Jefferson-Hillman Sch. Nursing, 1950; m. Martin James Lide, Jr., Nov. 12, 1950; children: Martin James, III, Brooks Nathaniel, Gardner Lawhon. Writer column Baldwin Times, Bay Minette, Ala., 1964-68, Shades Valley Sun newspapers, Birmingham, Ala., 1974-75; v.p., sec. Martin J. Lide Assocs., Inc., Birmingham, 1977-81; R.N. supr. St. Martin's in the Pines, 1984. Mem. def. adv. com. Women in Services, for Ala., 1961-63; coordinator women's activities Nat. Vets. Day, Birmingham, 1961-68; mem. exec. com., 1968-70; exec. bd. Women's Com. of 100 for Birmingham, 1964-65, 84-85; spkr. Arlington Hist. Assn., 1983; mem. Gorgas bd. U. Ala., Tuscaloosa, 1959. Recipient citation Merit, Muscular Dystrophy Assn. Am., 1961. Mem. Christian Women's Soc. Mountain Brook (bd. dirs. 1993), Nat. Soc. DAR (regent Princess Sehoy chpt. 1983-85, 91-92, chpt. spkr. 1988, 92, chpt. exec. bd. 1991-95), Cauldron Club (spkr. 1989, 2d v.p. 1992-93). Author: (poetry) Instead of Sunset, 1973; (narrative) Life of Service-These are My Jewels, 1979; Music in the Wind - The Story of Lady Arlington, 1980; Brother James Bryan-Hope Lives Eternal, 1981; Music of the Soul, 1982; The Past and Psyche of Arlington, 1983, The Light Side of Life in the American Colonies, 1988, The American Woman, 1989, revised, 1992, The Lawhons of Texas, 1995. Home: 3536 Brookwood Rd Birmingham AL 35223-1446

LIDEN, SUSAN JEANINE, secondary education educator; b. Crookston, Minn., Dec. 22, 1948; d. Jens Raymond and Jacqueline Henriette (Fayola) Ree; m. Gary Merle Liden, Nov. 22, 1969 (dec. Jan. 1994); children: Allison Ree, Lindsey Ree. BS, Moorhead State U., 1970; MA, St. Cloud State U., 1989. Edn. counselor U.S. Army, Schweinfurt, Germany, 1970-71; French tchr. Willmar (Minn.) Pub. Sch., 1971—, dept. chair, 1978—; presenter in field. Pres. NOW, Willmar, 1978-82; bd. dirs. Kandiyohi County United Way, Willmar, 1989-90. Named Ashland Tchr. of Achievement, Ashland Oil, St. Paul, 1992. Democrat. Lutheran. Home: Box 295 Clara City MN 56222 Office: Willmar Sr High 2701 30th St NE Willmar MN 56201

LIDSTROM, PEGGY RAY, mental health administrator, psychotherapist; b. Oxford, N.C., Apr. 8, 1949; d. Robert Marsh and Margaret (O'Brian) Ray; m. Paul D. Lidstrom (div.); 1 child, Kristin. BA, Stratford Coll., Danville, Va., 1971; MSW, Norfolk (Va.) State U., 1979. Lic. clin. social worker, Va.; cert. social worker; diplomate in clin. social work. Coord. social work Tidewater Psychiat. Inst., Norfolk, 1983-85; dir. substance abuse Southside Community Svc. Bd., South Boston, Va., 1985-88; dir. mental health svcs. Hampton (Va.) Newport News Community Svcs. Bd., 1988-95; clin. mgr., psychotherapist Chessen and Assocs., Newport News, Va., 1995—; adj. prof. St. Leo Coll., Langley AFB, Hampton, Va. Named Boss of Yr., Am. Bus. Women's Assn., 1986; Va. Gov.'s Coun. on Substance Abuse grantee, 1988. Fellow Am. Bd. Managed Care Providers; mem. NASW, Peninsula Mental Health Assn. (pres. 1991-92, Rollins award 1996), Mental Health Assn. Va. (pres. 1996—), C.G. Jung Soc. of Tidewater. Quaker. Office: Chessen and Assocs 12420 Warwick Blvd Ste C Newport News VA 23606-3001

LIDTKE, DORIS KEEFE, computer science educator; b. Bottineau County, N.D., Dec. 6, 1929; d. Michael J. and Josephine (McDaniels) Keefe; m. Vernon L. Lidtke, Apr. 21, 1951. BS, U. Oreg., 1952; MEd cum laude, Johns Hopkins U., 1974; PhD, U. Oreg., 1979. Programmer analyst Shell Devel. Co., Emeryville, Calif., 1955-59, U. Calif., Berkeley, 1960-62; asst. prof. Lansing (Mich.) Community Coll., 1963-68; ednl. specialist Johns Hopkins U., Balt., 1968; assoc. program mgr. NSF, Washington, 1984-85; program dir., 1992-93; sr. mem. tech. staff Software Productivity Consortium, Reston, Va., 1987-88; asst. prof. Towson State U., Balt., 1968-80, assoc. prof., 1980-90, prof. computer sci., 1990—. Named Outstanding Educator, Assn. for Ednl. Data Systems, 1986. Mem. Assn. for Computing Machinery (edn. bd. 1980—, coun. 1984-86, 94—, spl. interest group bd. 1985—, chair 1994—, Recognition Svc. award 1978, 83, 85, 86, 90, 91, Outstanding Contbn. award 1995), Computer Soc. of IEEE (Outstanding Contbn. award 1986, 92, Golden Core), Nat. Ednl. Computer Conf. (steering com., vice chmn. 1983-85, chmn. 1985-89, Recognition award 1988, 92, 95), Computing Scis. Accreditation Bd. (v.p. 1993-95, pres. 1995—). Home: 4806 Wilmslow Rd Baltimore MD 21210-2328 Office: Towson State U Computer & Info Scis Baltimore MD 21204

LIEBELER, SUSAN WITTENBERG, lawyer; b. New Castle, Pa., July 3, 1942; d. Sherman K. and Eleanor (Klivans) Levine; BA, U. Mich., 1963, postgrad. U. Mich., 1963-64; LLB (Stein scholar), UCLA, 1966; m. Wesley J. Liebeler, Oct. 21, 1971; 1 child, Jennifer. Bar: Calif. 1967, Vt. 1972, D.C. 1988. Law clk. Calif. Ct. of Appeals, 1966-67; assoc. Gang, Tyre & Brown, 1967-68, Greenberg, Bernhard, Weiss & Karma, L.A., 1968-70; assoc. gen. counsel Rep. Corp., L.A., 1970-72; gen. counsel Verit Industries, L.A., 1972-73; prof. of law law sch. Loyola U., L.A., 1973-84; spl. counsel, chmn. John S. R. Shad, SEC, Washington, 1981-82; commr. U.S. Internat. Trade Commn. Washington, 1984-88, vice chmn., 1984-86, chmn., 1986-88; ptnr. Irell & Manella, L.A., 1988-94; sr. v.p. Legal Rsch. Network, Inc., L.A., 1994-95; pres. Lexpert Rsch. Svcs., L.A., 1995—; vis. prof. U. Tex., summer 1982; cons. Office of Policy Coordination, office of Pres.-elect, 1981-82; cons. U.S. Ry. Assn., 1975, U.S. EPA, 1974, U.S. Price Commn., 1972; mem. Adminstrv. Conf. U.S., 1986-88. Mem. editorial adv. bd. Regulation mag. CATO Inst. Mem. ABA, State Bar Calif. (treas., vice chair, chair exec. com. internat. law sect.), L.A. County Bar Assn., Practicing Law Inst. (internat. law adv. com.), Washington Legal Found. (acad. adv. bd.), bd. dirs. Century City Hosp., adv. bd. U. Calif. Orientation in U.S.A. Law, Order of Coif. Jewish. Sr. editor UCLA Law Review, 1965-66; contbr. articles to legal publ.

LIEBERMAN, CAROL, healthcare marketing communications consultant, city planning administrator; b. St. Louis, June 14, 1938; d. Norman Leonard and Ethel (Silver) Mistachkin; m. Malcolm P. Cooper, Aug. 25, 1962 (div. June 1977); children: Lawrence, Edward, Marcus; m. Edward Lieberman, Apr. 1992. BS, U. Wis., 1959; MA, N.Y. Inst. Tech., 1992. Media buyer Lennen and Newell, Los Angeles, 1959-61; advt. mgr. Hartfield-Zodys, Los Angeles, 1961-62, Haggarty's, L.A., 1962-63; sales rep. Abbott Labs., Bklyn., 1974-75; edn. dir. N.Y. and N.J. Regional Transp. Program, N.Y.C., 1975-78; account exec. Med. Edn. Dynamics, Woodbridge, N.J., 1978-79; dir. program devel. Kallir, Phillips & Ross Info. Media, N.Y.C., 1979-81; exec. v.p. sales and mktg. Audio Visual Med. Mktg., N.Y.C., 1981-85; exec. v.p. Park Row Pubs./John Wiley & Sons Med. Div., N.Y.C., 1985-88; pres., prin. Park Row Pubs., N.Y.C., 1988-91; healthcare mktg. communications cons., Southampton, N.Y., 1991—; cons., prof. comms. and speech N.Y. Inst. Tech., 1991—; exec. dir. Bus. Improvement Dist., Riverhead, N.Y., 1994-95; exec. sec. Cardiopulmonary Bypass Consensus Panel, 1994—; cons. Am. Acad. Physician Assts., Washington, 1986-87, Am. Soc. Anesthesiologists, Chgo., 1986-88, Am. Acad. Family Physicians, 1987-91, Am. Psychiat. Assn., 1988, Am. Coll. Gen. Practitioners, 1988, N.Am. Soc. pacing and Electrophysiology, 1988-91, Cardiopulmonary Bypass Consensus Panel, 1993—. Editor pub. med. papers, med. films, med. jours. for pharmaceutical cos. Mem. Am. Women in Radio and TV, Soc. Tchrs. Family Medicine (cons.), Pharm. Advt. Council, Nat. Council Jewish Women, Hadassah. Home and Office: 41 Barkers Island Rd Southampton NY 11968-2702

LIEBERMAN, CAROLE ILENE, media psychiatrist, consultant. BA in Psychology with honors, SUNY, Stony Brook; MD, U. de Louvain, Belgium. Diplomate Am. Bd. Psychiatry and Neurology. Intern Mt. Sinai Hosp., Hartford, Conn., N.Y. Infirmary, N.Y.C.; resident in psychiatry NYU/Bellevue Psychiatry Hosp., N.Y.C.; ednl. cons. Met. State Hosp., L.A.; mem. attending staff Motion Picture and TV Hosp., L.A.; mem. assoc. staff Cedars Sinai Hosp./Thalians Mental Health Ctr., L.A.; pvt. practice Beverly Hills; asst. clin. prof. psychiatry UCLA/Neuropsychiat. Inst.; med. advisor/med. editor (cable TV programs) Your Mental Health-Informathon, 1984, Depression Informathon, 1985, The Nephronauts, 1986; lectr. in field. Author: Love Transplant: A High Risk Affairs of the Heart, 1990; columnist Show Biz Shrink Nat. Examiner, 1994—; columnist, contbr. The Malibu Times, 1986—, Malibu Surfside News, 1984-89, Working World mag., 1990, Ency. Britannica, 1990, Michael Jackson, The Magic and the Madness, Your View, 1991, Health Net News, 1992, Doctors Book of Home Remedies for Children, Glam Scam, Abuse of Discretion: The Rodney King Story; (TV scripts) Stranger Dangers, My House to Yours, Seeds of Success, What If It Were Real?, Feeling Female and Fine, Feelings Behind the Masks, (with Ginny Weissman) America's Un-Wanted and Mouseketeers Become Imagineers...And You Can Too!; contbr. articles to profl. jours., mags., and newspapers; host/prodr. (cable TV series) Real Talk about Reel Life, 1992, What You Always Wanted to Know about Psychiatry...But Were Afraid to Ask, The Seven Warning Signals of Mental Illness, (dramatic therapy) Psycho-Theatre; host Understanding Asthma, Lifetime TV, 1987-88, (weekly radio series) Life Perspectives with Dr. Carole Lieberman, 1990, Dr. Carole Lieberman with Real Talk about Reel Life, 1990-91, Real Talk about Reel Life with Dr. Carole Lieberman, Sta. KWNK, 1991-92, Sta. KGIL, 1992; host (radio shows) Psychiatry and the Media, 1990-92, Hollywood Correspondent, 1993—; numerous TV, radio appearances and psychology call-in shows. Mem. Pub. Access Producer's Acad., 1985-87, Calif. Theater Coun., 1985-87. Recipient Film Adv. Bd. Excellence award, 1990, Mayor Bradley commendation for scipt consulting, City of L.A., Emmy award, 1992, 93, O'Henry prize for lit. N.Y. Mem. Am. Psychiat. Assn., So. Calif. Psychiat. Soc. (pub. info. com. 1980—, co-chair 1982-85), Malibu Med. Soc. (chair pub. info. com. 1986-89), Nat. Insts. for Profl. Edn. (bd. govs. 1983-86, NYU/Bellevue Psychiat. Soc., Los Angeles County Med. Women's Assn., Am. Assn. Dirs. Psychiat. Residency Tng., Soc. for Liaison Psychiatry, Nat. Coalition on TV Violence (chair 1992-93, bd. dirs. 1990-93, spokesperson 1987-93), Writers Guild Am. (Outstanding Achievement TV Children's Script award 1992), AFTRA, Motion Picture Assn. Am. (press credentials), Acad. TV Arts and Scis.

LIEBERMAN, GAIL FORMAN, investment company executive; b. Phila., May 26, 1943; d. Joseph and Rita (Groder) Forman. BA in Physics and Math., Temple U., 1964, MBA in Fin., 1977. Dir. internat. fin. Standard Brands Inc., N.Y.C., 1977-79; staff v.p. fin. and capital planning RCA Corp., 1979-82; CFO, exec. v.p. Scali McCabe Sloves, Inc., 1982-93; v.p. finance, CFO, mng. dir. Moody's Investors Svc., N.Y.C., 1994—; bd. dirs. Allied Devices, Inc. Bd. dirs. Vineyard Theater Group, N.Y.C. Mem. Fin. Execs. Inst. Office: Moody's Investor Svcs 99 Church St New York NY 10007-2701

LIEBERMAN, ILENE D., art history and humanities educator; b. L.A., Aug. 18, 1954; m. Thomas M. McCavera, 1982. BA, U. Calif., Berkeley, 1976; PhD, Princeton U., 1983. Lectr. Princeton (N.J.) U., 1983, Villanova (Pa.) U., 1983-84; assoc. prof. Gabriel Lucas Chair Fine Arts Widener U., Chester, Pa., 1985—, head humanities maj., art history and humanities, 1995—. Contbg. author: The Memorial Redefined: New Dimensions of Public Memory, 1989; contbr. articles to profl. jours. Grantee Am. Coun. Learned Socs., 1984-86, NEH, 1985. Mem. Coll. Art Assn., Historians Brit. Art, Assn. Historians 19th Century Art, Walpole Soc., Womens Caucus for Art, Phi Kappa Phi. Office: Widener U Humanities Div One Univesity Pl Chester PA 19013

LIEBERMAN, NANCY ANN, lawyer; b. N.Y.C., Dec. 30, 1956; d. Elias and Elayne Hildegarde (Fox) L. BA summa cum laude, U. Rochester, 1977; JD, U. Chgo., 1979; LLM in Taxation, NYU, 1981. Bar: N.Y. 1980. White House intern, 1975; law clk. to chief judge Henry A. Politz U.S. Ct. Appeals 5th Cir., Shreveport, La., 1979-80; assoc. ptnr. Skadden Arps Slate Meagher & Flom, N.Y.C., 1981-87, ptnr., 1987—; bd. dirs. Rite Aid Corp. Bd. trustees U. Rochester, 1994—. Recipient McGill prize, 1977; N.Y. State Regents' scholar, 1973. Mem. ABA, Assn. Bar City N.Y., Coun Fgn. Rels., Phi Beta Kappa. Republican. Jewish. Home: 935 Park Ave # 7A New York NY 10028-0212 Office: Skadden Arps Slate Meagher & Flom 919 3rd Ave New York NY 10022

LIEBERMAN, RITA LEAH, psychologist; b. Poland, Aug. 16, 1945; came to U.S., 1950; d. Isaac and Dora (Apfelbaum) L.; m. Martin Ira Becker, Dec. 18, 1994; children: Adam Seth Ziffer, Matthew Jed Ziffer. BS, Fairleigh Dickinson U., 1967; cert. in journalism, Sarah Lawrence Coll., 1978; MS, L.I. U., 1984; PhD, NYU, 1990; postgrad., 1992—. Lic. psychologist Nat. Register Health Svc. Providers in Psychology; cert. English tchr., N.Y., N.J. Tchr. secondary and alternative schs. N.Y.C. Bd. Edn., 1967-76; freelance writer, 1976-80; adminstr., clinician ROPEC, Spring Valley, N.Y., 1980-84; asst. coord. Adult Ctr. Orange-Ulster Bd. Coop. Ednl. Svcs., N.Y., 1985-87; psychologist Edwin Gould Acad., Chestnut Ridge, N.Y., 1990-92; pvt. practice, Nyack, 1991—; dir. Rockland County Guidance Ctr., Nyack, N.Y., 1992—; adj. prof. NYU, N.Y.C., 1990-91, mem. adult edn. adv. bd. BOCES, Nyack, N.Y.; mem. exec. bd. Nyack Literacy Coop., 1992-94, Westchester-Rockland Assn. for Adult and Continuing Edn., 1994; cons. N.J. Unemployment Coalition, 1993-94; presenter in field. Contbr. articles to profl. jours. and newspapers. Chmn. Pomona (N.Y.) Parks and Recreation Commn., 19776-79; mem. Rockland County women's com. Rockland Legislature, 1992. Mem. APA, N.Y. State Psychol. Assn., Rockland County Psychol. Assn., NOW, Rockland County Women's Network (columnist), Women Entrepreneurs. Office: 100 S Broadway Nyack NY 10960 also: Rockland County Guidance Ctr 83 Main St Nyack NY 10960

LIEBERMAN, RUTH SEGAL, atmospheric scientist; b. Hampton, Va., Jan. 13, 1958; d. Lionel M. and Mara (Eneman) L.; m. Joel David Rogers, Oct. 29, 1991; 1 child, Ari Benjamin. BS, U. Wis., 1981; MS, UCLA, 1983; PhD, U. Wash., 1992. Sci. programmer NOAA, Boulder, Colo., 1984-85; rsch. asst. U. Wash., Seattle, 1985-92; postdoctoral rsch. assoc. U. Mich., Ann Arbor, 1992-94, asst. rsch. scientist, 1994—. Contbr. rsch. articles to profl. jours. Rsch. grantee NSF. Mem. Am. Meteorol. Soc., Am. Geophys. Union (student mem.). Democrat. Jewish. Office: U Mich 2455 Hayward Ann Arbor MI 48109

LIEBES, RAQUEL, import/export company executive, educator; b. San Salvador, El Salvador, Aug. 28, 1938; came to the U.S., 1952, naturalized, 1964; d. Ernesto Martin and Alice (Philip) L.; m. Richard Paisley Kinkade, June 2, 1962 (div. 1977); children: Kathleen Paisley, Richard Paisley Jr., Scott Philip. BA, Sarah Lawrence Coll., 1960; MEd, Harvard U., 1961; MA, Yale U., 1963, postgrad., 1963-65; PhD in English, Oxford (Eng.) U., 1994. Teaching fellow in Spanish Sarah Lawrence Coll., Bronxville, N.Y., 1958-60; econ. teaching fellow Yale U., New Haven, 1964-65, instr. Spanish dept., 1964-66; exec. stockholder Import Export Co., San Salvador, 1968-89, also bd. dirs.; adj. prof. Am. U., Washington, 1989-91, dept. fgn. lang. and linguistics dept. fgn. studies Georgetown U., Washington, 1989-93. Contbr. glossary of Spanish med. terms. Hon. consul Govt. of El Salvador, 1977-80; docent High Mus. of Art, Atlanta, 1972-77; vol. Grady Hosp., Atlanta, 1966-71; instr. Spanish for med. drs. Tucson Med. Ctr., 1966-71; chmn. Atlanta Coun. for Internat. Visitors, 1966-71; mem. Outreach Group on Latin Am., Washington, 1982-86; founding mem. John Kennedy Ctr. for Performing Arts, 1980—; mem. Folger/Shakespeare Libr., Smithsonian Inst., Agape, El Salvador. Econ. fellow Yale U., 1964-65; Corcoran Mus. Art fellow, 1984-85; Smithsonian Mus. awardee, 1981-96. Mem. MLA, Am. Biog. Inst. Rsch. Assn. (hon. consul of El Salvador, dep. gov. 1978-80, bd. advisors 1994), Jr. League of Washington, Harvard Club, Yale Club. Republican. Home: 700 New Hampshire Ave NW Washington DC 20037-2406

LIEBICH, MARCIA TRATHEN, community volunteer; b. Troy, N.Y., Mar. 10, 1942; d. Roland Henry and Ida Mae (Horsfall) Trathen; m. Donald Herbert Liebich, May 13, 1941; children: Kurt Roland, Mark Christian. BA, Elmira Coll., 1964. With Sunnyview Hosp. and Rehab. Ctr., Schenectady, 1982—, dir. devel., 1992-94; CEO Sunnyview Hosp. Found., 1994-96. Co-founder Parent Anonymous Lay Therapy, Schenectady, 1974-80; trustee Elmira (N.Y.) Coll., 1978-94; bd. dirs. United Way, Schenctady, 1980-81, pres. 1985, bd. dirs. United Way, N.Y., 1991—, Sunnyview Rehab. Hosp., Schenectady, 1982, pres. 1988-91; social svcs. Women's Legis. Forum, Albany, 1984-91; bd. dirs. Leadership Schenectady, 1987-92, Schenectady C. of C., 1987-90, YMCA Capital Dist., 1991-94, WMHT Pub. Radio and TV, 1991—; pres. Samaritan Counseling Ctr., Schenectady, 1988-91; bd. dirs., treas. Bridge Ctr. Drug Treatment, Schenectady, 1988-91. Recipient YWCA Community Vol. award, 1986, K.S. Rozendaal award Community Svc. Schenectady, 1987, Liberty Bell award Schenectady Bar Assn., 1990, Women of Vision Betty Bean award YWCA, 1990. Mem. AAUW (pres. 1978), Jr. league Schenectady (Vol. of Yr. award 1981), Phi Beta Kappa. Republican. Lutheran. Home: 6 Brian Dr Rexford NY 12148-1415

LIEBMAN, JUDITH RAE STENZEL, operations research educator; b. Denver, July 2, 1936; d. Raymond Oscar and Mary Madelyn (Galloup) Stenzel; m. Jon Charles Liebman, Dec. 27, 1958; children: Christopher Brian, Rebecca Anne, Michael Jon. BA in Physics, U. Colo., Boulder, 1958; PhD in Ops. Rsch., Johns Hopkins U., 1971. Successively asst. prof., head indsl. systems, assoc. prof. U. Ill., Urbana, 1972-84, prof., 1984—, chmn. bd. Ill. Resource Network, 1987-90, acting vice chancellor for rsch., 1986-87, vice chancellor for rsch., 1987-92, acting dean Grad. Coll., 1987-92, dean, 1987-92, prof. ops. rsch., 1992—; vis. prof. Tianjin (China) U., 1985; charter mem. Ill. Gov.'s Sci. Adv. Com., Ill. Exec. Com., 1989-92; mem. adv. com. for engrng. NSF, 1988-92, chmn., 1991-92. Author: Modeling and Optimization with GINO, 1986; author numerous articles in field. Bd. dirs. United Way, Champaign, Ill., 1986-91; bd. dirs. East Cen. Ill. Health Systems Agy., Champaign, 1977-82, pres., 1980-82. Mem. Ops. Rsch. Soc. Am. (pres. 1987-88), Nat. Assn. State Univs. and Land Grant Colls. (exec. bd. 1990-92), Rotary, Sigma Xi, Sigma Pi Sigma, Alpha Pi Mu, Phi Kappa Phi. Home: 110 W Whitehall Ct Urbana IL 61801-6664 Office: U Ill 1206 W Green St Urbana IL 61801-2906

LIEBMAN, NINA R., economic developer; b. Toledo, Ohio, May 27, 1941; d. Jules Jay and Phyllis Gertrude (Kasle) Roskin; m. Theodore Liebman, Oct. 27, 1968; children: Sophie, Hanna, Tessa. Student, U. Marseilles, Aix-en-Provence, France, 1959-60, Skidmore Coll., 1960-61, NYU, 1961-63; cert. labor negotiator, Cornell U., 1993. Pub. info. officer Young Adult Inst., N.Y.C., 1978-81; U.S.A. dir. Rhone-Alps Econ. Devel. Assn., N.Y.C. and Lyon, France, 1981-85; internat. mktg. specialist N.Y. State Dept. Econ. Devel., N.Y.C., 1985-89, chief internat. programs, 1989-95; cons. Russian Fedn. Housing Project-The World Bank, Moscow, 1995—. Co-author: Biz Speak: A Dictionary of Business Terms, Slang and Jargon, 1986. Vol., trained mediator Bklyn. Mediation Ctr.; mem. internat. adv. coun. Eisenhower Found.; mem. internat. adv. bd. Nat. Minority Bus. Coun. Fellow Eisenhower Exch. Fellowship Program, 1993. Mem. Alliance Am. and Russian Women, U.S. Com. for UN Devel. Fund for Women, Minority Internat. Network for Trade, Bklyn. C. of C. (bd. dirs., internat. advisor), Bklyn. Heights Assn., Mcpl. Arts Soc., Grace Choral Soc. (bd. dirs. 1993—). Democrat. Jewish.

LIEBOW, JOANNE ELISABETH, marketing communication coordinator; b. Cleve., May 15, 1926; d. Arnold S. and Rhea Eunice (Levy) King; m. Irving M. Liebow, June 30, 1947 (div. Jan. 1972); children: Katherine Ann Liebow Frank, Peter. Student, Smith Coll., 1944-47; BA, Case Western Res. U., 1948. Cleve. reporter Fairchild Publs., N.Y.C., 1950-51; freelance pub. rels., Cleve., 1972-78; pub. info. specialist Cuyahoga Community Coll., Cleve., 1979—. Founder, pres. Mt. Sinai Hosp. Jr. Women's Aux., Cleve., 1948-50; pres. PTA, Bryden Elem. Sch., Beachwood, Ohio, 1964; mem. bd., pres. Beachwood Bd. Edn., 1968-76. Recipient Exceptional Achievement award Coun. for Advance Edn., 1982, Citation award, 1982, Grand Prize, 1983; Sophia Smith scholar Smith Coll., 1946, Cleve. Communicator's award Women in Communications, Inc., 1982. Home: 23511 Chagrin Blvd Apt 211 Cleveland OH 44122-5538 Office: Cuyahoga Community Coll Ea Campus 4250 Richmond Rd Cleveland OH 44122-6104

LIEF, NINA RAYEVSKY, psychiatrist, educator; b. Liberty, N.Y., Feb. 12, 1907; d. Charles and Lucy (Kalina) Rayevsky; m. Victor F. Lief (dec.); 1 child, Carlotta Lief Schuster. BA, Barnard Coll., 1927; MD, NYU, 1931. Asst. prof. psychiatry Tulane U., New Orleans, 1960-63; assoc. prof. psychiatry N.Y. Sch. Psychiatry, N.Y.C., 1963-68, N.Y. Med. Coll., N.Y.C., 1968-87; pvt. practice specializing in child psychiatry N.Y.C.; cons. prof. psychiatry N.Y. Med. Coll., 1987—. Author: First Year of Life, 1979, Second Year of Life, 1983, Third Year of Life, 1991. Fellow Am. Acad. Psychoanalysis, Am. Acad. Child Psychiatry, Am. Psychiat. Assn., AMA, Am. Acad. Pediatrics; mem. N.Y. Med. Soc. Democrat. Jewish. Office: Ctr for Comprehnsive Health 167 E 97th St New York NY 10029-7305

LIEM, ANNIE, pediatrician; b. Kluang, Johore, Malaysia, May 26, 1941; d. Daniel and Ellen (Phuah) L. BA, Union Coll., 1966; MD, Loma Linda U., 1970. Diplomate Am. Bd. Pediatrics. Intern Glendale (Calif.) Adventist Hosp., 1970-71; resident in pediatrics Children's Hosp. of Los Angeles, 1971-73; pediatrician Children's Med. Group, Anaheim, Calif., 1973-75, Anaheim Pediatric Med. Group, 1975-79; practice medicine specializing in pediatrics

Anaheim, 1979-96, Camas, Wash., 1996—. Fellow Am. Acad. Pediatrics; mem. Los Angeles Pediatric Soc., Orange County Pediatric Soc., Adventist Internat. Med. Soc., Chinese Adventist Physicians' Assn. Office: 411 NE 6th Ave Camas WA 98607

LIEM, DARLENE MARIE, secondary education educator; b. Lorain, Ohio, June 25, 1941; d. Frederick August and Mary Jane (Derby) Kubishke; m. Frans Robert Liem; children: Dorothea Saliba, Frans Liem, Raymond Liem, Bryan Liem, Shannon Daniel. BS in Edn., Ohio State U., 1963; ME, Wright State U., 1980. Cert. secondary tchr., Ohio. Sci. tchr. Southwestern City Schs., Grove City, Ohio, 1963-66, Greeneview High Sch., Jamestown, Ohio, 1973—; advisor Quick Recall Team, Jamestown, 1984—, NASA Student Shuttle Projects, Regional winners, 1981, 82; dir. Ramblers Drill Team, Jamestown, 1973-77; adv. TEAMS, 1991—. Contbr. articles to profl. jours. Mem. Huber Heights (Ohio) Community Chorus, 1989-90; girl scout leader Huber Heights Girl Scout Troop, 1976-78; children's choir dir., Huber Heights, 1980-84, Sunday sch. tchr., Huber Heights, 1978-83; summer camp dir. Kirkmont Presbyn. Camp, Bellefontaine, Ohio, 1978-83; ordained elder Presbyn. Ch. Named Outstanding Educator Green County Bd. Edn., 1988-89, 92, Woman of Yr. Am. Bus. Women's Assn., 1988, West Region Project Discovery Tchr.-Leader, 1992—, Tandy Tech. Hon. Mention Tchr., 1994. Mem. Nat. Sci. Tchrs. Assn., Sci. Edn. Coun. Ohio (bd. dirs. 1981-83), Am. Assn. Physics Tchrs. (South Ohio sect.), Western Ohio Sci. Tchrs. Assn. (pres. 1981-83), Delta Kappa Gamma, Phi Delta Kappa, Kappa Delta Pi. Home: 7056 Montague Rd Dayton OH 45424-3044 Office: Greeneview High Sch 53 N Limestone St Jamestown OH 45335-1550

LIETZ, DIANE KATHRYN, artist; b. Wausau, Wis., Apr. 19, 1933; d. John Joseph and Marie (Myshka-Bennett) L. Student, U. Wis., 1951-53, Prospect Hall, 1953-55. Air hostess Trans World Airlines, Kans. City, Mo., 1955-60; freelance sec. L.A., 1955-70; freelance artist Laguna Beach, Calif., 1970—; mem. Art-A-Fair Festival, 1970-80, 93-96. Recipient Wrigley award Catalina Art Assoc, 1974, 2d prize Catalina Art Festival, 1975, spl. award, 1976. Home: 1060 Flamingo Rd Laguna Beach CA 92651 Office: Ivan Anderson/Diane Lietz Studio 1060 Flamingo Rd Laguna Beach CA 92651

LIFKA, MARY LAURANNE, history educator; b. Oak Park, Ill., Oct. 31, 1937; d. Aloysius William and Loretta Catherine (Juric) L. B.A., Mundelein Coll., 1960; M.A., Loyola U., Los Angeles, 1965; Ph.D., U. Mich., 1974; postdoctoral student London U., 1975. Life teaching cert. Prof. history Mundelein Coll., Chgo., 1976-84, coordinator acad. computer, 1983-84, prof. history Coll. St. Teresa, Winona, Minn., 1984-89, Lewis U., Romeoville, Ill., 1989—; chief reader in history Ednl. Testing Service, Princeton, N.J., 1980-84; cons. world history project Longman, Inc., 1983—; cons. in European history Coll. Bd., Evanston, Ill., 1983—; mem. Com. on History in the Classroom. Author: Instructor's Guide to European History, 1983; contbr. articles to publs. Mem. Am. Hist. Assn., Ednl. Testing Service Devel. Com. of History. Democrat. Roman Catholic. Office: Lewis U RR 53 Romeoville IL 60446

LIFTON, DIANE E., lawyer; b. Stamford, Conn., May 3, 1965. BA, Cornell U., 1986; JD, U. Mich., 1990. Bar: N.Y. 1992, U.S. Dist. Ct. (so. and ea. dists.) N.Y. 1992, U.S. Dist. Ct. (no. dist.) Calif. 1992. Law clk. to Hon. Jerry Buchmeyer U.S. Dist. Ct. (no. dist.) Tex., 1990-91; ptnr. Anderson, Kill, Olick & Oshinsky, P.C., N.Y.C. Assoc. editor U. Mich. Jour. Law Reform, 1988-89, exec. editor, 1989-90; contbr. articles to profl. jours. Mem. ABA, Assn. Bar of City of N.Y. (transp. com.). Office: Anderson Kill Olick & Oshinsky PC 1251 Avenue of the Americas New York NY 10020-1182*

LIGENZA, ANDREA ANGELA, nurse; b. Lansford, Pa., Apr. 7, 1952; d. Stanley Walter and Mary (Porambo) L. Diploma in Nursing, Hosp. of U. Pa., 1973; BS in Nursing, U. Pa., 1976. RN; cert. nurse practitioner, Pa. Staff nurse Hosp. of U. Pa., Phila., 1973-79, nurse practitioner cardiothoracic surgery sect., 1979-88; preceptor nursing students U. Pa., 1985-91; founder, group leader Self Esteem Workshops, 1986-87; nurse practitioner Cardiothoracic Surg. Assocs. Pa. Hosp., 1988-91, Bryn Mawr Hosp., 1991-93, Primary Care, Drexel Hill, Pa., 1992—. Eucharistic min. Roman Cath. Ch. Mem. Puccini Inst., Sigma Theta Tau. Republican. Avocations: classical music, tennis, travel. Office: 2235 Garrett Rd Drexel Hill PA 19026-1130

LIGGETT, TWILA MARIE CHRISTENSEN, academic administrator, public television company executive; b. Pipestone, Minn., Mar. 25, 1944; d. Donald L. Christensen and Irene E. (Zweigle) Christensen Flesher. BS, Union Coll., Lincoln, Nebr., 1966; MA, U. Nebr., 1971, PhD, 1977. Dir. vocal and instrumental music Sprague (Nebr.)-Martell Pub. Sch., 1966-67; tchr. vocal music, pub. schs., Syracuse, Nebr., 1967-69; tchr. Norris Pub. Sch., Firth, Nebr., 1969-71; cons. fed. reading project, pub. schs., Lincoln, 1971-72; curriculum coord. Westside Community Schs., Omaha, 1972-74; dir. State program Right-to-Read, Nebr. Dept. Edn., 1974-76; asst. dir. Nebr. Commn. on Status of Women, 1976-80; asst. dir. project adminstrn./devel. Great Plains Nat. Instructional TV Libr., U. Nebr., Lincoln, 1980—; exec. prodr. Reading Rainbow, PBS nat. children's series, 1980— (9 Emmy awards 1990-96); cons. U.S. Dept. Edn., 1981; Far West Regional Lab., San Francisco, 1978-79; panelist, presenter AAAS, NEA, NEH, NSF, Corp. Pub. Broadcasting, Internat. Reading Assn., Blue Ribbon panelist, Acad. TV Arts & Scis., 1991-96, final judge Nat. Cable Programming Awards, 1991-92. Author: Reading Rainbow's Guide to Children's Books: The 101 Best Titles, 1994. Bd. dirs. Planned Parenthood, Lincoln, 1979-81. Recipient Grand award N.Y., 1993, Gold medal award Internat. Film and TV Festival, 1996, World Gold medal N.Y. Internat. Film & TV, 1995, Coun. on Internat. Nontheatrical Events Golden Eagle award, 1995, 2 Image awards NAACP, 1996. Mem. NATAS, Internat. Reading Assn. (Spl. award Contbns. Worldwide Literacy 1992), Am. Women in Film and TV,Phi Delta Kappa. Presbyterian. Home: 649 S 18th St Lincoln NE 68508-2681 also: 301 E 79th St Apt 23P New York NY 10021-0944 Office: PO Box 80669 Lincoln NE 68501-0669

LIGGIO, JEAN VINCENZA, adult education educator, artist; b. N.Y.C., Nov. 5, 1927; d. Vincenzo and Bernada (Terrusa) Verro; m. John Liggio, June 6, 1948; children: Jean Constance, Joan Bernadette. Student, N.Y. Inst. Photography, 1965, Elizabeth Seton Coll., 1984, Parsons Sch. of Design, 1985. Hairdresser Beauty Shoppe, N.Y.C., 1947-65; freelance oil colors and portraits N.Y.C., 1958-75; instr. watercolor N.Y. Dept. Pks., Recreation and Conservation, Yonkers, 1985-89, Bronxville (N.Y.) Adult Sch., 1989—; substitute tchr. cosmetology Yonkers Bd. Edn., 1988-89. Paintings pub. by Donald Art Co., C.R. Gibson Greeting Card Co.; 12 watercolor paintins for Avon Calendar, Avon Cosmetics Co., 1994, 96; 12 florals for Avon-Can. Publ., 1996, 97; 12 floral paintings published by Enesco Corp., 1996; 2 floral greeting cards published by C.R. Gibson Co. Publ., 1996; floral and still life images on mesh interlock canvas and sold in needlework kits published by Candamar Designs Inc., 1997. Recipient numerous awards. Mem. Mt. Vernon Art Assn. (pres. membership com. 1983—), Mamaroneck Artist's Guild, Hudson River Contemporary Artist's, Scarsdale Art Assn. (publicity chmn. 1984-89), New Rochelle (N.Y.) Art Assn. Home and Office: 166 Helena Ave Yonkers NY 10710-2524

LIGHT, BETTY JENSEN PRITCHETT, former college dean; b. Omaha, Sept. 14, 1924; d. Lars Peter and Ruth (Norby) Jensen; m. Morgan S. Pritchett, June 27, 1944 (dec. 1982); children: Randall Wayne, Robin Kay Pritchett Church, Royce Marie Pritchett Creech; m. Kenneth F. Light, Nov. 23, 1985. B.S., Portland State U., 1965; M.B.A., U. Oreg., 1966; Ed.D., Oreg. State U., 1973. Buyer Rodgers Stores, Inc., Portland, Oreg., 1947-62; chmn. bus. div. Mt. Hood Community Coll., Gresham, Oreg., 1966-70, dir. evening coll., 1970-71, assoc. dean instn., 1972-77, dean humanities and behavioral scis., 1977-79, dean devel. and spl. programs, 1979-83; dean communication arts, humanities and social scis. Mt. Hood Community Coll., 1983-86; mem. state com. for articulation between cmty. colls. and higher edn., 1976-78; mem. Gov.'s Coun. on Career and Vocat. Edn., 1977-86; owner Effective Real Estate Mgmt., 1982—. Author: Values and Perceptions of Community College Professional Staff in Oregon, 1973; contbg. author: (case study) The Pritchett Study in Retailing, An Economic View, 1969. Mem. Gresham City Council, 1983-86. Mem. Oreg. Bus. Edn. Assn., Am. Assn. Higher Edn., Nat. Assn. Staff and Oreg. Devel., Oreg. Women's Polit. Caucus, Am. Vocat. Assn., Oreg. Vocat Assn., Danish Heritage Soc. Club: Soroptimist (pres. 1974-75, 81-82). Home: 1635 NE Country Club Ave Gresham OR 97030-4432

LIGHT, CHERYL ELLEN, lawyer; b. Kingsport, Tenn., June 24, 1958; d. Bob Leonard and Juanita Irene (Dykes) L.; m. Michael Jarrell Searcy, Oct. 15, 1983; children: Cameron Light, Aaron Michael. BS, East Tenn. State U., 1980; JD, Wake Forest U., 1983. Assoc. Campbell and Hooper, Newport, Tenn., 1984-88, Morton, Lewis, King & Krieg, Knoxville, Tenn., 1989; assoc. gen. coun. 1st Am. Nat. Bank, Knoxville, 1989—; mem. moot ct. bd. Sch. Law Wake Forest U., Winston-Salem, N.C., 1981-83. Mem. ABA, Tenn. Bar Assn., Omicron Delta Kappa. Methodist. Office: 1st Am Nat Bank 505 S Gay St Knoxville TN 37902-1502*

LIGHT, MARION JESSEL, retired elementary education educator; b. San Antonio, Dec. 5, 1915; d. Marion Jackson and Kate Jessel (Cox) Parr; m. Marion Russell Light, Nov. 8, 1958 (dec. July 1983); children: Russell Jeffers, Paul Love. BA, So. Meth. U., 1936; MA, U. Tex., 1947. Cert. elem. and secondary sch. tchr., Tex. Elem. tchr. Dallas Ind. Sch. Dist., 1936-72; 1st v.p. The Cosmos Rev. Class, 1991-92. Del. to 16th Senatorial Dist. Dem. Conv., 1988; moderator Presbyn. Women, 1st Ch., Dallas, 1989-90, co-moderator, 1994-95. Mem. AAUW (chmn. hobbies and crafts Dallas br. 1970s), Dallas Ret. Tchrs. Assn. (corr. sec. 1984-90), Dallas Women's Forum (rec. sec. Friday study 1987-89), Bay View Century Club (corr. sec. 1988-89, pres. 1993-95), Dallas Symphony Orch. League, Delta Kappa Gamma (pres. Delta Sigma chpt. 1956-58, Chpt. Achievement award 1979, Marion Parr Light Recruitment grantee named in her honor Delta Sigma chpt. 1958). Democrat.

LIGHTFOOT, JAN LINDA, artist, photographer; b. Middletown, Conn., Dec. 3, 1949; d. Francis St. Martin and Isabella Carta-Fairfield Me. AS, U. Maine at Orono, 1977. Freelance artist, photographer Maine, 1978-83; bd. coordinator Hospitality House Inc., Fairfield, Maine, 1982—; program coordinator Hospitality House Inc., Hickley, Maine, 1986—; speaker in field. Impressionistic artist; photographer wildlife. Adv. for civil rights and better life for the poor. Office: Hospitality House Inc PO Box 62 Hinckley ME 04944-0062

LIGHTFOOT, MARJORIE JEAN, English educator; b. Oak Park, Ill., Apr. 24, 1933; d. Cecil Dane and Maybelle June (Doyle) L. BA, Brown U., 1955; MA, Northwestern U., 1956, PhD, 1964. Tchg. asst. Northwestern U., Evanston, Ill., 1957-60; instr. U. Ariz., Tucson, 1960-63; asst. prof. English Ariz. State U., Tempe, 1964-69, assoc. prof. English, 1969-74, prof. English, 1974—. Author: Glimpses of the Brontes: A Biography on Stage, 1980; dramatist: (Chaucer) Troilus and Criseyde, 1978, Belinda: Oh, What a Fine Confusion, 1995. Mem. Am. Soc. for 18th Century Studies, Rocky Mountain Modern Lang. Assn. Office: Ariz State U English Dept Tempe AZ 85287

LIGHTFOOT, TEDDI, music school director, composer, singer; b. Poteau, Okla., Apr. 29, 1946; d. Charles Fredrick and Frances Mary (Stucin) Zirbel; m. Jon Charles Lightfoot, Feb. 5, 1970 (div. June 1978). MusB, San Francisco State Coll., 1968, MA, 1972; postgrad., Conservatorio, Florence, Italy, 1968-69. Designer mfg. Lightfoot Fyne Leather Clothing, San Francisco, 1970-88; supr. Police Fire Communications, South San Francisco, Calif., 1977-85; dir., tchr. Yamaha Music Sch., South San Francisco, 1986-90; co-owner Lightweight Music Pub. Co., San Francisco and L.A., 1990—, Radical Prodns. Rec. Co., San Francisco and L.A., 1990—; sr. exec. v.p. Hello Tomorrow Music Group, 1991-92; dir., artist and repetoire Growing Up Music, 1991-92; music dir. Ctr. Stage U.S.A., San Francisco, 1994, Burlingame Enrichment Acad., 1994, Into the Woods, San Mateo, Calif., 1994; choral dir. Bayside Mid. Sch., San Mateo, 1985-86; dir. sch. for music and mus. entertainment Lightfoot Studio, South San Francisco, 1984—; actress in commls. and TV, San Francisco, 1978—, Italy, 1968-69; dir. Razzle Dazzle Kids Performance Troupe, South San Francisco, 1985—; creative/mus. cons. schs. and orgns., Bay Area, Calif., 1984—. Composer, arranger shows, original works, prodns., San Francisco, 1978—; composer, singer: Let Me Sing, 1989; composer Heroes Are Just Ordinary People, Eyes of God, A Star Spangled Odyssey, 1996; co-producer, mus. dir. albums P.J. Ford and Something New, 1992, Children Care, 1992; music dir. rock opera Love's Destiny, 1990; lead actor, singer theatrical prodn. Stroll Down Broadway, San Mateo, 1994; music dir. Rags, 1995, Grease, 1995, And the World Goes Round, 1996, Happy Birthday America, An Historical Review, 1996, Joseph and the Amazing Technicolor Dreamcoat, 1996—. Dir. Barbara Neal Prodns., San Francisco, 1987; lay min. Unity Christ Ch., San Francisco, 1988—, dir. Unity Angels Choir, 1985—; tchr. musical theatre San Mateo High Sch., 1992—. Named State Grand Champion Calif. State Talent Assn., 1986-94; inducted into Calif. Youth Hall of Fame, 1993. Mem. Nat. Assn. Tchrs. Singing, Music Tchrs. Assn. Calif., No. Calif. Songwriters Assn., Theatre Bay Area, Internat. New Thought Music Alliance Com. Democrat. Office: Lightfoot Studio 574 Commercial Ave South San Francisco CA 94080-3410

LIGHTNER, PATRICIA PAYNE, elementary education educator; b. Danville, Va., May 8, 1953; d. William Harvey and Viola Agnes (Tenney) Payne; m. John Steven Rotz, May 31, 1975 (div. June 1990); children: Jason Andrew Rotz, Cory Adair Rotz; m. Bruce Wayne Lightner, Apr. 12, 1991. BA in Elem. Edn., Va. Poly. Inst. and State U., 1975; MS in Libr. Sci., Shippensburg U., 1992. Cert. K-7, Va. Tchr. 4th grade Caroline County, Bowling Green, Va., 1975-76; tchr. 7th grade English Clarke County, Berryville, Va., 1976-77, tchr. 5th and 6th grade, 1977-79; tchr. 3d grade Frederick County, Winchester, Va., 1986—. Mem. Va. Edn. Assn. (pres. dist. 21), Frederick County Edn. Assn. (pres. 1992-94), Phi Delta Kappa. Methodist. Home: 271 Deer Creek Rd Winchester VA 22602-1648 Office: Indian Hollow Elem Sch 1548 N Hayfield Rd Winchester VA 22603-3420

LIGON, PATTI-LOU E., real estate investor, educator; b. Riverside, Calif., Feb. 28, 1953; d. Munford Ernest and Patsy Hazel (Bynum) L. BS, San Diego State U., 1976; BBA, Nat. U., San Diego, 1983, MA in Bus. Adminstrn., 1984; Clear Profl. Credential, Nat. U., 1986. Cert. profl. counselor. Escrow asst. Cajon Valley Escrow, El Cajon, Calif., 1978-79; escrow asst. Summit Escrow, San Diego, 1979-81; escrow officer Fidelity Nat. Title, San Diego, 1982-84, Dawson Escrow, San Diego, 1984; owner, property mgr., investment adviser Ligon Enterprises., San Diego, 1980—, cons., 1982—. Chmn. com., alumnae and assocs. San Diego State U., 1983, 84, 85; com. chmn. San Diego Zool. soc., 1985; pres. Friends of Symphony, Riverside, Calif., 1978. Recipient commendation City and County of Honolulu, 1981. Mem. Nat. Notary Assn., Calif. Escrow Assn., Am. Home Econs. Assn., Nat. Assn. Female Execs, Internat. Platform Assn., Calif. Bus. Edn. Assn., Jr. League of San Diego, Sigma Kappa (pres. 1974, v.p. sorority corp. 1976—). Republican. Methodist. Club: Spinster (pres. 1981), Univ. (San Diego). Avocations: racquetball; clothing design; photography; travel. Home and Office: Ligon Enterprises 7937 Wetherley St La Mesa CA 91941-6335

LIGUORI, JO ANN, editor; b. Bklyn., Feb. 2, 1970; d. Anthony J. and Marilyn J. (Grosso) L. BA summa cum laude, Bklyn. Coll., 1992. From editl. asst. to mng. copy editor early childhood divsn. Scholastic Inc., N.Y.C., 1989-95; sr. copy chief Good Housekeeping Mag., N.Y.C., 1995—. Mem. NOW, Columbus Citizens Found. Democrat. Roman Catholic. Office: Hearst Corp 959 8th Ave New York NY 10019

LILES, BETH KIRKLAND, media specialist; b. Waycross, Ga., Feb. 17, 1955; d. Broughton Parker and Mavis (Higgs) Kirkland; m. B. Philip Liles, Sept. 14, 1981; children: B. Parker, Kira E. Bs in Edn., Valdosta State Coll., 1978; MEd, Ga. Southwestern Coll., 1982, Valdosta State Coll., 1990. Tchr. Atkinson County, Pearson, Ga., 1978-90; media specialist Atkinson County, 1990—. Office: Atkinson County Schs PO Box 608 Pearson GA 31642-0608

LILIENTHAL, WENDY, artist; b. N.Y.C., Dec. 20, 1919; d. Milton and Doris (Sternberg) Hecht; m. Theodore Max Lilienthal, Mar. 6, 1941; children: Peggy, Thomas, Vicky. Student, Parsons Sch. Design, 1939-41, Richmond Art Ctr., 1968-70, U. Calif. Ext., Mill Valley, 1967-74, Calif. Coll. Arts and Crafts, 1970. Cert. tchr., Calif. Artist, tchr., lectr. San Anselmo, Calif., 1970—; team tchr. U. Calif. Ext., 1970-72; with tchrs. workshop Dominican Coll., San Rafael, Calif., 1975; tchr., lectr. Art Sch., Belvedere, Calif., 1977-78; judge, lectr., exhibitor 30th No. Calif. Handweavers Conf., Ukiah, 1980; team tchr. Imaginarium Nat. Childrens Festival, San Rafael, 1980; judge Marin County Fine Craft Fair, San Rafael, 1981, Coll./Marin Art Exhibit, Kentfield, Calif., 1983; seminar leader, exhibitor Handweavers of Am., San Jose, Calif., 1990. Guest artist PBS, 1982-84. Bd. dirs. blood bank ARC, San Rafael, 1969-74, Drake High Scholarship Found., San Anselm, 1967-95; capt. Am. Heart Assn., San Anselmo, 1985-95; mem. humanities adv. coun. Marin Gen. Hosp., 1996. Recipient Marcelle Laboudt award San Francisco Women Artists, 1973, Merit award Sausalito Arts Festival, 1987, Sculpture award Marin Soc. Artists, 1995. Mem. Legend Club (pres. 1978-79), Marin Soc. Artists (v.p. 1971), Fibermania (co-founder 1984). Home: 740 Butterfield Rd San Anselmo CA 94960

LILJESTRAND, ANGELA YVONNE, geriatrics nurse; b. Traverse City, Mich., Feb. 1, 1969; d. Timothy Charles and Jeanne Marie (Markey) L. Diploma in Nursing, Washtenaw C.C., Ann Arbor, Mich., 1991. LPN, Mich. Geriatric charge nurse Evergreen Hills Nursing Ctr., Ypsilanti, Mich., 1992-94; neurol. staff nurse VA Hosp., Ann Arbor, Mich., 1992-93, med.-surg. staff nurse, 1993-94; geriatric charge nurse Evangelical Home, Saline, Mich., 1994-95, The Julia Temple Ctr., Englewood, Colo., 1995—; AIDS patient care pvt. and hosps., Ypsilanti, 1992—. Republican.

LILLESTOL, ANN MARIE, special education educator; b. San Francisco, Sept. 10, 1953; d. Jack Kenneth and Marylouise (Dechery) L. AA, Fresno City Coll., 1977; BA, Sonoma State Coll., Rohnert Park, Calif., 1987; postgrad., Dominican Coll., San Rafael, Calif., 1988; MEd, U. San Francisco, 1995, MEd, MA in Curriculum and Instrn. Cert. tchr. learning handicapped, Calif. Reading specialist, dir. Tamalpais Valley Edna McGuire, Mill Valley, Calif., 1988-91; ESL instr. Mill Valley, Sausalito Sch. Dist., 1988-90; bilingual resource specialist West Contra Costa Unified Sch. Dist., Richmond, Calif., 1992-93; learning handicapped specialist Star Acad., San Anselmo, Calif., 1993—; bilingual tutor Oracle, San Rafael, 1993; student study team leader Grant Elem. Sch., Richmond, 1992-93. Mem. women's div., mem. culture dept. Soka Gakkai Internat., San Francisco, 1994. Mem. Coun. for Exceptional Children (v.p. 1993—). Buddhist.

LILLESTOL, JANE BRUSH, career development company executive; b. Jamestown, N.D., July 20, 1936; d. Harper J. and Doris (Mikkelson) Brush; m. Harvey Lillestol, Sept. 29, 1956; children: Kim, Kevin, Erik. BS, U. Minn., 1969, MS, 1973, PhD, 1977; grad. Inst. Ednl. Mgmt., Harvard U., 1984. Dir. placement, asst. to dean U. Minn., St. Paul, 1975-77; assoc. dean, dir. student acad. affairs N.D. State U., Fargo, 1977-80; dean Coll. Human Devel. Syracuse (N.Y.) U., 1980-89, v.p. for alumni rels., 1989-95, project dir. IBM Computer Aided Design Lab., 1989-92; prin. Lillestol Assocs.; charter mem. Mayor's Commn. on Women, 1986-90; NAFTA White House Conf. for Women Leaders, 1993. Bd. dirs. Univ. Hill Corp. Syracuse, 1983-93; mem. steering com. Consortium for Cultural Founds. of Medicine, 1980-89; trustee Pebble Hill Sch., 1990-94, Archbold Theatre, 1990-95, N.D. State U., 1992—. Recipient award U.S. Consumer Product Safety Commn., 1983, Woman of Yr. award AAUW, 1984, svc. award Syracuse U., 1992. Roman Catholic.

LILLEY, EVELYN LEWIS, operating room nurse; b. Jackson, Miss., Jan. 10, 1962; d. Robert B. and Clara Mae (Thompson) Lewis; m. Bobby Frank Lilley, Mar. 16, 1985 (dec. Sept. 1991); children: Phillip James, Latasha Nicole. BSN, Miss. Coll., 1987. RN, Miss.; cert. nurse operating rm. Med-surg. staff nurse Miss. Bapt. Med. Ctr., Jackson, 1987-88; operating rm. staff nurse U. Miss. Med. Ctr., Jackson, 1988-90; staff nurse Nightingale Nursing Agy., Jackson, Miss., 1991-92; staff devel. instr. U. Miss. Med. Ctr., Jackson, 1992-94; head nurse U. Miss. Med. Ctr., 1994—. Dir. youth choir Mt. Hood Ch. Mem. Assn. Oper. Rm. Nurses (bd. dirs. 1995—), Elizar Pillar Nurses Assn. (Toastmasters Internat. (pres. local chpt. 1995-96, competent toastmaster, advanced toastmaster). Baptist. Home: 112 Casa Grande Dr Clinton MS 39056 Office: U Miss Med Ctr 2500 N State St Jackson MS 39216-4500

LILLEY, MILI DELLA, insurance company executive, entertainment management consultant; b. Valley Forge, Pa., Aug. 29; d. Leon Hanover and Della Beaver (Jones) L. MBA, Tex. Christian U., 1957, PhD, 1959. Various positions G & G Cons. Inc., Ft. Lauderdale, Fla., 1971-75; v.p. AMEX, Inc., Beverly Hills, Calif. and Acapulco, Mex., 1976-80; pres. The Hanover Group, Ft. Lauderdale, 1981—; personal and bus. mgr. entertainers including Ink Spots, Ft. Lauderdale, 1984—, Lanny Poffo, Ft. Lauderdale, 1990—; dist. agt. ITT Life Ins. Corp., also other leading cos. Named to All Stars Honor Roll Nat. Ins. Sales Mag., 1989. Mem. Fla. Assn. Theatrical Agents, Fla. Guild of Talent Agts., Mgrs., Producers and Orchestras. Office: The Hanover Group PO Box 70218 Fort Lauderdale FL 33307-0218

LILLICH, ALICE LOUISE, retired secondary education educator; b. East Cleveland, Ohio, Aug. 18, 1940; d. Robert Earl and Charlotte Louise (Stewart) L. BS in Home Econs. Edn., Ohio U., 1968. Cert. tchr., Ohio. Quality control Stouffer's Frozen Foods, Cleve., 1961-67; head home econs. dept. Wellston (Ohio) City Schs., 1969-94; with children's dept. Kaufman's Dept. Store, 1995—; Ohio reference person Wagons West tours of Afton, Wyo. Vol. Willoughby Hills United Meth. Ch., mem. nurture com., chair adv. com. Mem. AAUW (2d vice chair 77-80, publicity chair 1985-86, issue chair 1987-90), Ohio Ret. Tchrs. Assn. (Lake County chpt.), Cleve. Audubon Soc., Republican Optimist Club (flag chair 1987-88, 2d v.p. 1989-90), Phi Delta Kappa (found. rep. 1986-87), Delta Kappa Gamma (former v.p., pres. Jackson chpt., mem. Iota-Lake County chpt.). Methodist. Home: 37570 Milann Dr Willoughby OH 44094

LILLIE, CHARISSE RANIELLE, lawyer, educator; b. Houston, Apr. 7, 1952; d. Richard Lysander and Vernell Audrey (Watson) L.; m. Thomas L. McGill, Jr., Dec. 4, 1982. B.A. cum laude, Conn. Wesleyan U., 1973; J.D., Temple U., 1976; LL.M., Yale U., 1982. Bar: Pa. 1976, U.S. Dist. Ct. (ea. dist.) Pa. 1977, U.S. Ct. Appeals (3d cir.) 1980. Law clk. U.S. Dist. Ct. (ea. dist.) Pa., Phila., 1976-78; trial atty., honors program, civil rights div. Dept. Justice, Washington, 1978-80; dep. dir. Community Legal Services, Phila., 1980-81; asst. prof. law Villanova U. Law Sch., Pa., 1982-83, assoc. prof., 1983-84, prof., 1984-85; asst. U.S. atty. U.S. Dist. Ct. (ea. dist.) Pa., 1985-88; gen. counsel Redevel. Authority City of Phila., 1988-90; city solicitor Law Dept. City of Phila., 1990-92; ptnr. litigation dept. Ballard, Spahr, Andrew and Ingersoll, 1992—, exec. com. bd. dirs., 1994—; mem. 3d Cir. Lawyers Adv. Com., 1982-85, legal counsel Pa. Coalition of 100 Black Women, Phila., 1983-88; bd. dirs. Juvenile Law Center, Phila., 1982—, Pa. Intergovernmental Coop. Authority, 1992—, Fed. Res. Bank Phila., 1996—; commr. Phila. Ind. City Charter Commn., 1991-94; trustee Women's Law Project, Phila., 1984—; mem. Mayor's Commn. on May 13 MOVE Incident, 1985—. Bd. dirs. Women's Way, Phila. Davenport fellow, 1973; Yale Law Sch. fellow, 1981; recipient Equal Justice award Community Legal Svcs., Inc, 1991, J. Austin Norris award Barristers Assn., 1991, Outstanding Alumna award Wesleyan U., 1993, Elizabeth Dole Glass Ceiling award ARC, Phila. chpt., 1994; named One of the Top Three Phila. Labor Mgmt. Attys. Phila. Mag., 1994. Mem. ABA, Nat. Bar Assn., Fed. Bar Assn. (1st v.p. Phila. chpt. 1982-84, pres. Phila. chpt.1984-86, 3rd cir. rep. 1991—), Nat. Conf. Black Lawyers (pres. 1976-78, Outstanding Service award 1978), Am. Law Inst., Phila. Bar Assn. (vice chair bd. govs. 1994, chair, bd. of govs., 1995—), Hist. Soc. U.S. Dist. Ct. (ea. dist.) Pa. (dir. 1983—), Barristers Assn. (J. Austin Norris award 1991). Home: 7000 Emlen St Philadelphia PA 19119-2556 Office: Ballard Spahr Andrews Ingersoll 1735 Market St Ste 51 Philadelphia PA 19103-7501

LILLIE, HELEN, journalist, novelist; b. Glasgow, Scotland, Sept. 13, 1915; came to U.S., 1938; d. Thomas and Helen Barbara (Lillie) L.; m. Charles S. Marwick, Sept. 20, 1956. MA, U. Glasgow, 1938; postgrad., Yale U., 1938-40. Rsch. asst. info. divsn. Brit. Info. Svcs., N.Y.C., 1942-45, Brit. Security Coord., N.Y.C., 1945-46; asst. U.S. mgr., writer Media Reps., Inc., N.Y.C., 1947-54; with advt. dept. Family Cir. Mag., N.Y.C., 1955-56; Am. corr. The Glasgow Herald (name now The Herald), 1956-94; freelance feature writer, book reviewer Detroit Free Press, 1965-66. Author: The Listening Silence, 1970, Call Down the Sky, 1973, Home to Strathblane, 1993, (columns) Inside USA, Helen Lillie's Washington Letter. V.p., acting pres. Cosmopolitan B PM Club of DC, 1972-73. Mem. Am. News Women's Club D.C., Soc. Women Geographers, Advt. Women of N.Y. (various coms.).

Presbyterian. Home and Office: 3219 Volta Pl NW Washington DC 20007-2732

LILLY, ELIZABETH GILES, mobile park executive; b. Bozeman, Mont., Aug. 5, 1916; d. Samuel John and Luella Elizabeth (Reed) Abegg; m. William Lilly, July 1, 1976; children: Samuel Colborn Giles, Elizabeth Giles. RN, Good Samaritan Hosp., Portland, Oreg., 1941; student, Walla Walla Coll., Lewis and Clark Coll. Bus., Portland. ARC nurse area high schs., Portland; owner Welton Studio Interior Design, Portland; in pub. rels. Chas. Eckelman, Portland, Fairview Farms-Dairy Industry; owner, builder Mobile Park Plaza, Inc., Portland. Del. platform planning com. Rep. Party; mem. Sunnyside Seventh Day Adventist Ch. Recipient Svc. award Multnomah County Commrs., 1984. Mem. Soroptimist Internat. (local bd. dirs., bd. dirs. Women in Transition), Rep. Women's Club (pres.), C. of C., World Affairs Coun., Toastmistress (pres.), Oreg. Logging Assn. (pres. bd. dirs.), Rep. Inner Circle (life). Address: 19825 SE Stark St Portland OR 97233-6039

LILLY, KRISTINE MARIE, soccer player; b. Wilton, Conn., July 27, 1971. Grad., U. N.C., 1993. Midfielder Washington Warthog, Landover, Md. Named U.S. Soccer's Female Athlete of the Yr., 1993, U.S. Nat. Team All-Time Appearance Leader (more than 90 games). Office: care Marc Goldman US Air Arena Harry S Truman Dr Landover MD 20765

LILLY, SHANNON JEANNE, dancer; b. Alexandria, Va., Feb. 18, 1966; d. John Howard Lilly and Barbara Lynn (Root) Graham. Student, Contra Costa Ballet Centre, San Francisco Ballet Sch. Dancer Phoenix Ballet Co., 1985-86; mem. of Corps de Ballet San Francisco Ballet, 1986-88, soloist, 1988-91, prin. dancer, 1991-94; prin. dancer Northern Ballet Theatre, Birmingham, England, 1994—; Performed with San Francisco Opera, 1993; performed at the Reykjavik Arts Festival, Iceland, 1990. Performed with Jean Charles Gil and Friends, Paris, 1988, Tanantella, 1989, In the Middle Somewhat Elevated, 1990, Rubies, 1991, Bagaku, 1991, Sleeping Beauty, 1991; ballets include New Sleep, Connotations, Narcisse, Interplay, The Concert, Handel-a Celebration, Ballet d'Isoline, Menuetto, Giuliani: Variations on a Theme, Contredanses, Concerto in d: Poulenc, Con Brio, Intimate Voices, Calcium Light Night, Krazy Kat, Serenade, Swan Lake, Flower Festival at Genzano, Dark Elegies, Who Cares?, Theme and Variations, Airs de Ballet, Pulcinella, The Wanderer Fantasy, The Sons of Horus, Ballo Della Regina, The Theme Variations, Dreams of Harmony, Nutcracker, La Fille mal gardee, Rodeo, La Sylphide, The Sleeping Beauty, Meistens Mozart, Bugaju, Rubies, Symphony in C, The Four Temperaments, Star and Stripes, In the middle, somewhat elevated, Seeing Stars, Company B, La Pavane Rouge, Job, Harvest Moon, Tagore, Romeo and Juliet, Il Distratto, Divertissement d'Auber, Sinfonia, Scarlatti, Portfolio, The Comfort Zone, Dreams of Harmony, The End, Forgotten Land, Napoli. Episcopalian. Office: Northern Ballet Company, Spring Hall Huddersfield Rd, Halifax HX3 0AQ, England*

LILLY-HERSLEY, JANE ANNE FEELEY, nursing researcher; b. Palo Alto, Calif., May 31, 1947; d. Daniel Morris Sr. and Suzanne (Agnew) Feeley; children: Cary Jane, Laura Blachree, Claire Foale; m. Dennis C. Hersley, Jan. 16, 1993. BS, U. Oreg., 1968; student, U. Hawaii, 1970; BSN, Sacramento City Coll., 1975. Cert. ACLS, BCLS. Staff and charge nurse, acute rehab. Santa Clara Valley Med. Ctr., San Jose, Calif., staff nurse, surg. ICU and trauma unit; clin. project leader mycophenolate mofetil program team Syntex Rsch., Palo Alto; pres. Clin. Rsch. Consultation, Santa Cruz, Calif. Co-founder, CFO and dir. scientific rsch. Citizens United Responsible Environmentalism, Inc., CURE (internat. non-profit edn./rsch. orgn.). Mem. AACN.

LIM, JASMINE LEONG, township official; b. N.Y.C., May 25, 1952; d. Gim Chu and May Yok (Chan) L.; children: Matthew Warren Leong Young, Jana Megan Leong Young. BA in Urban Studies, Wellesley Coll., 1974; M Urban Planning, U. Wash., 1978. From intern, cmty. planner to planner City of Everett, Wash., 1977-80; adminstr. cmty. devel. City of Ithaca, N.Y., 1980-81; cons. in housing-cmty. devel., planning and grants mgmt., 1982-91; adminstr. grants and cmty. devel. Twp. of Parsippany (N.Y.)-Troy Hills, 1984-86, dir. purchasing and contracts adminstrn., 1986-87, dir. mcpl. svcs., 1987-88, bus. adminstr., 1988-91; twp. adminstr. Twp. of Vernon, N.J., 1992-95; mgr. Twp. of Randolph, N.J., 1995—; trustee, sec. Morris County Employees Fed. Credit Union, Morristown, N.J., 1988-91; bd. dirs. Statewide Excess Liability Fund, Parsippany, 1993-95, mem. exec. com., 1993—; Morris County League Municipalities, 1996—. Trustee Craftsman Farms Found., Inc., Parsippany, 1991-95, pres., 1992-95; bd. dirs. Mental Health Assn. Morris County, Madison, 1991-95, 1st v.p., 1993-94. Mem. Internat. City and County Mgmt. Assn., N.J. Mcpl. Mgmt. Assn. Office: Twp of Randolph 502 Millbrook Ave Randolph NJ 07869-3799

LIM, SALLY-JANE, insurance consultant; b. Manila; came to U.S., 1990; d. Teddy and Sonia (Yii) L.; children: Robin Michael, Rodney Jovin, Romelle Gavin Lim Velasco. BA, BS in Commerce magna cum laude, Coll. of Holy Spirit, Manila. CPA, The Philippines. Treas, contr. Ky. Fried Chicken, Makati, Philippines, 1968-73; ins. rep. Insular Life Assurance Co., Makati, 1972-82; project analyst Pvt. Devel. Corp. of Philippines, Makati, 1972-78; account exec. Genbancor Devel. Corp., Makati, 1978-80; risk mgr. Filcapital Devel. Corp., Makati, 1978-82; pres., gen. mgr., ins. broker Sally-Jane Multiline Insce., Inc., Makati, 1978-90; real estate broker Sally-Jane Realty, Inc., Manila, 1980-90; ins. rep. Sun Life of Can./AIU (Philippines) AFIA/CIGNA, Makati, 1982-91; rep. Prudential Ins. & Fin. Svcs., Prudential Property & Casualty, PruCare of Calif.; registered rep. Pruco Securities Corp. L.A. Dist., South Pasadena, Calif., 1990-92, Pruco Securities Corp. Asian Pacific Dist., 1992—. Recipient Young Achiever award Young Achiever Found., Quezon City, Philippines, 1988, Golden Scroll award Philippine Ednl. Youth Devel., Inc., Quezon City, 1988, Young Famous Celebrity Mother's award Golden Mother/Father Found., Quezon City, 1990, Recognition of Excellence cert. San Gabriel Valley YWCA, 1992, Most Outstanding Ins. Exec. of The Philippines bronze trophy Consumers' Union of Philippines, Manila, 1983, 88, Ten Outstanding Profl. Svc. award Achievement Rsch. Soc., Manila, 1988, numerous others. Fellow Life Underwriters Tng. Coun.; mem. Nat. Assn. Life Underwriters, Arcadia C. of C., Asian Bus. Assn., Filipino-Am. C. of C., Million Dollar Round Table (life mem.), Greater Pasadena Assn. Life Underwriters, Chinese C. of C. (bd. dirs. L.A. 1992—). Home: 1006 A Royal Oaks Dr Monrovia CA 91016-3737 Office: Prudential of Am Penthouse 1255 Corporate Center Dr Monterey Park CA 91754

LIMA, MARILYNNE, foreign language educator, consultant; b. Murray, Utah, Aug. 20, 1938; d. John William and Mary Elsie (Barr) Fitzgerald; m. Marco Antonio Lima, Aug. 22, 1959 (div. 1986); children: Maria Lorraine, Shawn Antonio. BA, Brigham Young U., Provo, Utah, 1962, MA, 1972. Cert. tchr. Utah. Tchr. Spanish/English Jordan Sch. Dist, West Jordan (Utah) Jr. High, 1962-67; supr. student tchrs. Brigham Young U., 1967-68; tchr. Spanish/English Granite Sch. Dist., Evergreen Jr. High, Salt Lake City, 1968-69; tchr. Spanish Brigham Young U., 1978-79, Granite Sch. Dist., Cottonwood High Sch., Salt Lake City, 1969—; sales cons. Scott Foresman Pub., Salt Lake City, 1993-96; presider, presenter numerous adv. placement seminars in Spanish, 1976-86. Mem. Am. Fedn. Tchrs., Utah Fgn. Lang. Assn., Sigma Delta Pi. Mem. Ch. Latter Day Saints. Office: Cottonwood HS 5717 S 1300 E Salt Lake City UT 84121

LIMACHER, MARIAN CECILE, cardiologist; b. Joliet, Ill., May 4, 1952; d. Joseph John and Shirley A. (Smith) L.; m. Timothy C. Flynn, May 17, 1980; children: Mary Katherine Flynn, Brian Patrick Flynn. AB in Chemistry, St. Louis U., 1973, MD, 1977. Diplomate Am. Bd. Internal Medicine, Am. Bd. Cardiovascular Diseases. Resident in internal medicine Baylor Coll. Medicine, Houston, 1977-80, cardiology fellow, 1980-83, instr. medicine, 1983-84; dir. cardiology non-invasive labs. Ben Taub Hosp., Houston, 1983-84; asst. prof. medicine U. Fla., Gainesville, 1984-91, assoc. prof., 1991—; dir. non-invasive labs. Gainesville VA Med. Ctr., 1984—, chief cardiology, 1995—; dir. preventive cardiology program U. Fla., 1987—. Author: (with others) Cardiac Transplantation: A Manual for Health Care Professionals, 1990, Geriatric Cardiology, 1992, The Role of Food in Sickness and in Health, 1993, Clinical Anesthesia Practice, 1994, Primary Care, 1994; mem. editorial bd. Clin. Cardiology, 1990—; contbr. articles to profl. jours. Mem. bioethics commn. Diocese of St. Augustine, Jacksonville, Fla., 1990-94. Recipient Preventive Cardiology Acad. award NIH, 1987-92; grantee for Women's Health Initiative, NIH, 1994—. Fellow ACP, Am. Coll. Cardiology (chair ad hoc com. women cardiology 1994—), Coun. Geriatric Cardiology; mem. Am. Soc. Preventive Cardiology (pres.-elect 1996—), Am. Heart Assn. (fellow coun. clin. cardiology, bd. dirs., pres. Alachua County divsn. 1986-89). Roman Catholic. Office: U Fla Coll Medicine PO Box 100277 Gainesville FL 32610-0277

LIMAN, ELLEN, painter, writer, arts advocate; b. N.Y.C., Jan. 4, 1936; d. David and Gertrude (Edelman) Fogelson; m. Arthur Liman, Sept. 20, 1959; children: Lewis, Emily, Doug. BA, Barnard Coll., 1957; student, N.Y. Sch. Interior Design, 1959. In pub. rels. Tex McCrary, Inc., 1957; interior designer Malanie Kahane Assocs., 1958-60; cons. on grants to the arts The Joe and Emily Lowe Found., 1975-92, pres./trustee, 1993—; exec. asst. Adv. Commn. for Cultural Affairs, N.Y.C., 1981-82; dir. spl. projects, dir. City Gallery for N.Y.C. Dept. Cultural Affairs, 1980-84; chair N.Y.C. Adv. Commn. for Cultural Affairs, 1991-93. Author: The Money Savers Guide to Decorating, 1972, Decorating Your Country Place, 1973, Decorating Your Room, 1974, The Spacemaker Book, 1977, The Collecting Book, 1980, Babyspace, 1984, others; contbr. editor: Kid Smart Mag., 1995—; contbr. articles to nat. mags. Founding trustee Internat. Ctr. of Photography, 1973—; trustee The Jewish Mus., 1974—, hon. trustee, 1993—, The Ctr. for Arts Info., 1985-86; mem. N.Y.C. Commn. for Cultural Affairs, 1986-89; bd. dirs. Art Table, Inc., 1987-90, Trust for Cultural Resources, 1993-96, Am. Fedn. of Arts, 1994—.

LIMBACH, BARBARA JUNE, management educator; b. Crawford, Nebr., June 29, 1958; d. William Bruce and Joann (Whipple) Corbin; m. Robert S. Limbach, Aug. 6, 1977; children: Zachary, Zane, Zalie. B, Chadron State Coll., 1979, M, 1985, specialist, 1992; PhD, U. Wyo., 1994. Loan officer Occidental Nebr. Fed. Sav. Bank, Crawford, 1981-86; instr., registrar Chadron (Nebr.) State Coll., 1987-92, asst. prof., 1992—; chair self-study com. North Ctrl. Accreditation, Chadron, 1995—. Mem. editl. bd. Collegiate Press, 1994. Mem. parish coun. St. John's Cath. Ch., Crawford, 1992—; sec.-treas. Music Boosters, Crawford, 1995—. Mem. NEA, AAUW, Nat. Bus. Edn. Assn. (presenter 1995), Nebr. State Edn. Assn., Chadron State Edn. Assn. (treas. 1992—), Phi Delta Kappa. Home: 719 6th St Crawford NE 69339 Office: Chadron State Coll 1000 Main St Chadron NE 69337

LIMBACK, E(DNA) REBECCA, vocational education educator; b. Higginsville, Mo., Mar. 23, 1945; d. Henry Shobe and Martha Pauline Rebecca (Willard) Ernstmeyer; m. Duane Paul Limback, Nov. 9, 1963; children: Lisa Christine, Derek Duane. BE, Cen. Mo. State U., 1968, MEd, 1969, EdS, 1976; EdD, U. Mo., 1981. Cert. bus., English and vocat. tchr. Supervising tchr. Lab. Sch. Cen. Mo. State U., Warrensburg, 1969-76, asst. to grad. dean, 1977-79, asst. prof., asst. to bus. dean, 1981-83, assoc. prof. computer and office info. systems, 1984-95, prof. computer and office info. systems, 1986—; mem. manual editing/revision staff State of Mo., Jefferson City, 1989-90; textbook reviewer Prentice-Hall, Englewood Cliffs, N.J., 1990-91. Author various curriculum guides; mem. editl. bd. Cen. Mo. State U. Rsch., 1982-92. Active Warrensburg Band Aides, 1989-93. Grantee RightSoft Corp., 1988. Mem. DAR, Nat. Bus. Edn. Assn. (mem. conf. profl. opportunities com. 1989, info. processing editor Bus. Edn. Forum 1991), Am. Vocat. Assn., North Cen. Bus. Edn. Assn. (Mo. rep., Collegiate Disting. Svc. award 1993), Mo. Bus. Edn. Assn. (all-chpt. pres. 1988-89, Postsecondary Tchr. of Yr. 1992), Assn. Bus. Comms., Warrensburg Athletic Booster Club, Phi Delta Kappa (all-chpt. pres. 1985), Delta Pi Epsilon (rsch. rep. 1989-92, nat. publs. com. 1993—). Lutheran. Home: 1102 Tyler Ave Warrensburg MO 64093-2049 Office: Dockery 200-I/COIS Dept Cen Mo State U Warrensburg MO 64093

LIMMROTH, KARIN LEIGH, international design consultant, television correspondent; b. New Orleans, Oct. 4, 1949; d. Weldon Eugene and Cora Elizabeth (Graby) L. BA, Bryn Mawr Coll., 1969; BFA, Sch. Visual Arts, N.Y.C., 1970. Designer, assoc. art dir. Essence mag., N.Y.C., 1973-74; designer RCA Records, N.Y.C., 1970-72; asst. art dir. Seventeen mag., N.Y.C., 1970-72; designer CBS Records, N.Y.C., 1974-75, Fantasy Records & Filmworks, Berkeley, Calif., 1975-76; asst. art dir., set designer CBS TV, L.A., 1979-81; art dir. CBS News, N.Y.C., 1981-83, CBS Entertainment, L.A., 1981-83; art dir., design cons. Ogilvy & Mather, N.Y.C., L.A., 1983-87; assoc. creative dir. E&J Gallo Winery, Modesto, Calif., 1987-89; dir. Image Assocs., Paris and N.Y.C., 1989—; mktg. cons. U.S. Embassy, Paris, 1991—; design cons. San Francisco Opera, 1975-76, U.S. Olympic Com., Boulder, Colo., 1978-79, Internat. Olympic Com., Barcelona, Spain, 1989—; art dir., design cons. Ogilvy & Mather, N.Y.C. and L.A., Young & Rubicom, L.A., Saatchi & Saatchi/Compton, N.Y.C., Scali McCabe Sloves, N.Y.C., 1983-87; field prodr.-dir. VOX-TV, Germany, 1993—. Co-star talk show La 5 TV, Paris, 1990-92; European corr./prodr. City-TV show MediaTV (seen in 68 countries), 1992—; European music corr. BET Network (USA), 1993—; French corr. NBC Super Channel, 1993-94, RTL-TV Germany, 1994—, Worldwide TV News, 1995—; field prodr./dir. Nat. Geog. TV Explorer; field prodr. NBC Access Hollywood, 1996—. Fundraiser Martha Graham Dance Co., N.Y.C., 1985, Amnesty Internat., Paris, 1989. Recipient award N.Y. Art Dirs. Club, 1977-78; nomination Internat. Emmy, 1993, N.Y. Festival, 1993. Mem. NARAS (bd. dirs. 1976-78, Grammy nomination 1973, Internat. Emmy nomination 1993, N.Y. Festival nomination 1993), Am. Film Inst. (art direction fellow 1976, 77), Am. Inst. Graphics Arts, La Maison des Artists (France), La Donne Vino (Italy), Internat. Design and Advt., Women in Film, Cinefilles (France), Anglo-am. Press Assoc. (Paris). Office: Image Assocs, 5 Rue du Foin, 75003 Paris France

LIMOGES-GILMORE, KATHLEEN ANN, social service executive, therapist; b. Lakewood, Ohio, Dec. 12, 1940; d. Joseph Frederick and Corrine Dahlmeyer Limoges; m. Gregory L. Gilmore (div. 1978); children: Hunter, Barton, Matthew. BS, Bowling Green State U., 1962; MS, No. Ill. U., 1978. Tchr. Wakefield (Mass.) Schs., 1962-63, Piedmont (Calif.) Schs., 1963-64, Swarthmore (Pa.) Schs., 1964-66; owner Indoor Greenery, Balt., 1969-75; therapist, program dir. Family Support, Aurora, Ill., 1979-82; exec. dir. Family Counseling Svc., Aurora, 1982—; dir. Plum Landing Retirement Ctr., Aurora, Ill., 1992—; mem. adv. coun. Aurora U. Sch. Social Work, 1992—; mem. adv. bd. Mercy Healthcare Ctr., 1996—; active Ill. Family Policy Coun., Chgo., 1993—. Active Jr. League of Balt., 1970-76; commr. Aurora Pub. Art Commn. Named Women of Yr., Aurora YWCA, 1993. Mem. ACA, Ill. Assn. Family Svc. Agys., Kiwanis (pres. 1993-94). Episcopalian. Home: 302 Cobbleston Ct Oswego IL 60543 Office: Family Counseling Svc 70 S River Aurora IL 60506

LIMON, LAVINIA, social services administrator; b. Compton, Calif., Mar. 5, 1950; d. Peter T. and Marie W. Limon; m. Mohamad Hanon. BA in Sociology, U. Calif., Berkeley, 1972. Asst. dir., office mgr. Ch. World Svc., Camp Pendleton, Calif., 1975-77; chief Vietnamese refugee sect. Internat. Rescue Com., Bangkok, 1977-79; dir. Internat. Rescue Com., L.A., 1983-86, 1983-86; asst. dir. ops. Am. Coun. for Nationalities Svcs., L.A., 1979-83; exec. dir. Internat. Inst., L.A., 1986-93; dir. office refugee resettlement and office family assistance Adminstrn. for Children and Families Dept. HHS, Washington, 1993—; bd. dirs. Am. Coun. for Nationalities Svc., 1992, chair standing com. of profl. coun., 1992; organizer U.S. refugee conf. Am. Coun. Vol. Agys., Manila, 1982; cons. Dept. of State, 1979, 80. Mem. bd. human rels. hate violence response alliance City of L.A., 1992; chair corp. coun. execs. United Way of L.A., 1992, mem. task force fund on devel., 1990; mem. citizen's adv. com. Eastside Neighborhoods Revitilazation Study, 1992; mem. steering com. Coalition for Humane Immigration Rights of L.A., 1992; mem. steering com. Jerusalem Coop. Cities Project, 1991; chair Refugee Forum L.A. County, 1984-85, chair vol. agy. com., 1983-84; treas. Calif. Refugee Forum, 1985-86. Democrat. Home: 4508 Flintstone Rd Alexandria VA 22306-1204 Office: Refugee Resettlement Office 370 Lenfant Plz SW Washington DC 20447-0001

LIMPERT, ALEXANDRA MICHELLE, artist, computer designer; b. N.Y.C., May 28, 1967; d. John Harold Jr. and Michelle (Van Der Leur) L. Student, Yale U., 1988; BFA, Parsons Sch. Design, N.Y.C., 1989. Book buyer Guggenheim Mus., N.Y.C., 1989-93; pres. Atomex Design Mus. Jewelry, N.Y.C., 1991—; artist's asst. Blythe Bohnen, N.Y.C., 1993; freelance designer, Bklyn., 1989—. One-woman shows Ceres, N.Y.C., 1994, 96; exhibited in group shows Erector Square Gallery, New Haven, 1992, Goddard-Riverside Inst. Cmty. Ctr., N.Y.C., 1993, Stuart Levy Gallery, N.Y.C., 1994, Art N.Y. Internat., N.Y.C., 1994, 4th UN Conf. on Women, Beijing, 1995, Snug Harbor Cultural Ctr., S.I., N.Y., 1995; work featured in catalogues and articles. Fellow Yale U. Sch. Fine Arts, 1988. Mem. Women's Caucus for Art, Ceres. Home: 63 S 3d St Brooklyn NY 11211 Studio: 338 Berry St Brooklyn NY 11211

LIN, ALICE LEE LAN, physicist, researcher, educator; b. Shanghai, China, Oct. 28, 1937; came to U.S., 1960, naturalized, 1974; m. A. Marcus, Dec. 19, 1962 (div. Feb. 1972); 1 child, Peter A. AB in Physics, U. Calif., Berkeley, 1963; MA in Physics, George Washington U., 1974. Statis. asst. dept. math. U. Calif., Berkeley, 1962-63; rsch. asst. in radiation damage Cavendish Lab. Cambridge (Eng.) U., 1965-66; info. analysis specialist Nat. Acad. Scis., Washington, 1970-71; teaching fellow, rsch. asst. George Washington U., Catholic U. Am., Washington, 1971-75; physicist NASA/Goddard Space Flight Ctr., Greenbelt, Md., 1975-80, Army Materials Tech. Lab., Watertown, Mass., 1980—. Contbr. articles to profl. jours. Mencius Ednl. Found. grantee, 1959-60. Mem. AAAS, N.Y. Acad. Scis., Am. Phys. Soc., Am. Ceramics Soc., Am. Acoustical Soc., Am. Men and Women of Sci., Optical Soc. Am. Democrat. Home: 28 Hallett Hill Rd Weston MA 02193-1753 Office: Army Materials Tech Lab Bldg 39 Watertown MA 02172

LINBURG, SUSANNA, sculptor, educator; b. Dayton, Ohio, Nov. 9, 1935; d. E.E. and Irene Ruth (Magnie) Linburg; m. Morris Brose, June 18, 1966; 1 child, Jillian Linburg Brose. AB cum laude, Ind. U., 1958; MFA, Wayne State U., 1974. Prof. fine arts Ctr. for Creative Studies, Detroit, 1962-91, exhbn. dir., 1975-85; exhbn. dir. Detroit Focus Gallery, 1983-87; cons. Mfrs. Nat. Bank, Livonia, Mich., 1989. Author: Bronze Sculpture in Detroit, 1986, Robert Champigny: Poete et Philosophe, 1987; subject of books and articles; exhibited sculpture at Alexander Milliken Gallery, N.Y.C., 1981-90, Jane Haslem Gallery, Washington, 1993—, Xochipilli Gallery, Birmingham, Mich., 1995—, Galerie Rytz, Nyon, Switzerland, 1988—, Bay Street Gallery, Northport, Mich., Barbara Bunting Gallery, Royal Oak, Mich.; selected pub. commns. include Arch VII: Valley, Grand Valley State U., Allendale, Mich., 1995, Arch: Montrose, Ctr. for Creative Studies, Detroit, 1991. Recipient Disting. Sculptor award Mich. Women's Found., 1988; Fulbright-Hays scholar, 1959-60; Andrew Mellon Found. grantee, 1983. Home: 14886 E Acadia Woods Rd Northport MI 49670

LINCOLN, ANNA, company executive, foreign languages educator; b. Warsaw, Poland, Dec. 13, 1932; came to U.S., 1948; d. Wigdor Aron and Genia (Zalkind) Szpiro; m. Adrian Courtney Lincoln Jr., Sept. 22, 1951; children: Irene Anne, Sally Linda, Allen, Kirk. Student, U. Calif., Berkeley, 1949-50; BA in French and Russian with honors, NYU, 1965; student, Columbia Tchrs. Coll., 1966-67. Tchr. Waldwick (N.J.) H.S., 1966-69; chmn. Tuxedo Park (N.Y.) Red Cross, 1969-71; pres. Red Cross divsn. Vets. Hosp.; pres. China Pictures U.S.A. Inc., Princeton, N.J., 1994—; prof. fgn. rels. Fudan U., Shanghai, 1994—, prof. English and humanitarian studies, 1996—; adv. bd. guidance dept. Waldwick (N.J.) H.S., 1966-69; hon. bd. dirs. Shanghai Fgn. Lang. Assn., 1994; hon. prof. Fudan U., Shanghai, 1994; leader seminars pm Chinat at top univs., 1996—. Author: Escape to China, 1940-48, 1985, Chinese transl., 1985, The Art of Peace, 1995; dir. devel. of film The Bridge, 1996—. Hon. U.S. Goodwill amb. for peace and friendship, China, 1984, 85, 86, 88. Named Woman of Yr. Am. Biog. Soc., 1993; recipient Peace Through the Arts prize Assn. Internat. Mujeres en las Artes, Madrid, 1993. Mem. AAUW, Women's Coll. Club (publicity chmn. 1991-96), Lit. Club Princeton (chmn.), Present Day Club. Home and Office: China Pictures USA Inc 550 Rosedale Rd Princeton NJ 08540

LINCOLN, BLANCHE LAMBERT, congresswoman. Mem. U.S. Ho. of Reps., Washington. Office: US Ho of Reps 1204 Longworth Ho Off Bldg Washington DC 20515*

LINDBERG, M. BETH DIETRICH, operations planning manager; b. Pitts., Apr. 15, 1965; d. Albert Edward III and Marilyn (Babb) Dietrich; m. Robert Brierly Lindberg, Oct. 6, 1990; 1 child, Brierly Dietrich. BS, Pa. State U., 1987; postgrad., Calif. State U., 1992—. Cert. inventory mgmt. and master planning. Mgmt. assoc. USS-Posco Industries, Pittsburg, Calif., 1987-88, ops. planning mgr., 1988-90, customer svc. mgr., 1991-92, st. products mgr., 1993-94, prodn. scheduling & shipping mgr., 1995—. Mem. NAFE, Am. Mgmt. Assn., Assn. Women in Metals Industry. Republican. Methodist. Home: 824 Falcon Ct Antioch CA 94509 Office: USS-Posco Industries PO Box 471 Pittsburg CA 94565

LINDBERGH, ANNE SPENCER MORROW (MRS. CHARLES AUGUSTUS LINDBERGH), author; b. Englewood, N.J., 1906; d. Dwight Whitney and Elizabeth Reeve (Cutter) Morrow; m. Charles Augustus Lindbergh, May 27, 1929 (dec. 1974); children: Charles Augustus (dec.), Jon Morrow, Land Morrow, Anne Spencer, Scott Morrow, Reeve Morrow. Grad., Miss Chapin's Sch., N.Y.C., Smith Coll., Northampton, Mass., 1928; MA (hon.), Smith Coll., Northampton, Mass., 1935; LLD (hon.), Amherst Coll., 1939, Univ. Rochester, 1939. Author: North to the Orient, 1935, Listen! The Wind, 1938, The Wave of the Future, 1940, The Steep Ascent, 1944, Gift from the Sea, 1955, The Unicorn and Other Poems, 1935-1955, 1956, Dearly Beloved, 1962, Earth Shine, 1969, Christmas in Mexico: 1972, 1971, Bring Me a Unicorn: Diaries and Letters of Anne Morrow Lindbergh, 1972, Hour of Gold, Hour of Lead: Diaries and Letters of Anne Morrow Lindbergh, 1929-2932, 1973, Locked Rooms and Open Doors: Diaries and Letters of Anne Morrow Lindbergh, 1932-1935, 1974, The Flower and the Nettle: Diaries and Letters of Anne Morrow Lindbergh, 1936-1939, 1976, War Within and Without: Diaries and Letters of Anne Morrow Lindbergh, 1939-1944, 1980, The People in Pineapple Place, 1982, Bailey's Window, 1984, The Worry Week, 1985, The Hunky-Dory Diary, 1986, The Shadow on the Dial, 1987, Nobody's Orphan, 1987, The Prisoner of Pineapple Place, 1988, Next Time, Take Care, 1988, Tidy Lady, 1989, Travel Far, Pay No Fare, 1992, Three Lives to Live, 1992, Nick of Time, 1994. Recipient two prizes for lit. work Smith Coll.; cross of honor (for part in survey of trans-Atlantic air route) U.S. Flag Assn., 1933; Hubbard gold medal (for work as co-pilot and radio operator in flight of 40,000 miles over five continents) Nat. Geog. Soc., 1934. *

LINDBLOM, MARJORIE PRESS, lawyer; b. Chgo., Mar. 17, 1950; d. John E. and Betty (Grace) P.; m. Lance E. Lindblom, June 13, 1971; children: Derek, Ian. AB cum laude, Radcliffe Coll., 1971; JD with honors, U. Chgo., 1978. Bar: Ill. 1978, U.S. Dist. Ct. (no. dist.) Ill. 1978, U.S. Ct. Appeals (7th cir.) 1978, U.S. Ct. Appeals (10th cir.) 1983, U.S. Supreme Ct. 1983, U.S. Ct. Appeals (5th cir.) 1984, N.Y. 1995, U.S. Dist. Ct. (so. and ea. dist.) N.Y. 1995, U.S. Ct. Appeals (2d cir.) 1995. Assoc. Kirkland & Ellis, Chgo., 1978-84, ptnr., 1984-94; N.Y.C., 1994—; asst. dir. fiscal affairs Ill. Bd. Higher Edn., 1973-75; budget analyst Ill. Bur. Budget, Office of Gov., 1972-73; admissions officer Princeton U., 1971-72; adj. prof. Northwestern U., Evanston, Ill., 1994. Comment editor U. Chgo. Law Rev., 1977-78. Bd. dirs. Chgo. Lawyers Com. for Civil Rights Under Law, 1989-94, Pub. Interest Law Initiative, 1989-94. Mem. ABA, Chgo. Coun. Lawyers (bd. govs. 1987-91, legal counsel 1986-87), 7th Cir. Bar Assn., Women's Bar Assn. of Ill. Office: Kirkland & Ellis Citicorp Ctr 153 E 53rd St New York NY 10022-4602

LINDBURG, DAYTHA EILEEN, physician assistant; b. Emporia, Kans., June 24, 1952; d. Kenneth Eugene and Elsie Eileen (Smith) L. BS cum laude, Kans. State U., 1974; BS magna cum laude, Wichita State U., 1976. Registered cert. physician asst. Physician asst. in family practice Fredrickson Clinic, Lindsborg, Kans., 1976-93; physician asst. in ob/gyn. Mowery Clinic, Salina, Kans., 1993—; cons. McPherson County (Kans.) Health Dept., 1983—. Mem. adv. bd. Riverview Estates Nursing Home, 1980-86; bd. dirs. McPherson County Humane Soc., 1989-93; choir mem. Messiah Luth. Ch., Lindsborg, 1981—, liturgist, 1991—, mem. Altar Guild, 1976—, mem. music and worship com., 1981-88. Kans. Bd. Regents scholar, 1970-71, Kans. State U. scholar, 1972, 73, Smurthwaite scholar, 1970-74. Mem. Assn. of Physician Assts. in Obstetrics and Gynecology, Kans. Acad. Physician Assts., Am. Acad. Physician Asst.

LINDE, LUCILLE MAE (JACOBSON), motor-perceptual specialist; b. Greeley, Colo., May 5, 1919; d. John Alfred and Anna Julia (Anderson) Jacobson; m. Ernest Emil Linde, July 5, 1946 (dec. Jan. 27, 1959). BA, U. No. Colo., 1941, MA, 1947, EdD, 1974. Cert. tchr. Calif., Colo., Iowa,

N.Y.; cert. ednl. psychologist; guidance counselor. Dean of women, dir. residence C.W. Post Coll. of L.I. Univ., 1965-66; asst. dean of students SUNY, Farmingdale, 1966-67; counselor, tchr. West High Sch., Davenport, Iowa, 1967-68; instr. grad. tchrs. and counselors, univ. counselor, researcher No. Ariz. U., Flagstaff, 1968-69; vocat. edn. and counseling coord. Fed. Exemplary Project, Council Bluffs, Iowa, 1970-71; sch. psychologist, counselor Oakdale Sch. Dist., Calif., 1971-73; sch. psychologist, intern Learning and Counseling Ctr., Stockton, Calif., 1972-74; pvt. practice rsch. in motor-perceptual tng. Greeley, 1975—; rschr. ocumeter survey Lincoln Unified Sch. Dist., Stockton, 1980, 81, 82, Manteca (Calif.) H.S., 1981; spkr. Social Sci. Edn. Consortium, U. Colo., Boulder, 1993; presenter seminars in field. Author: Psychological Services and Motor Perceptual Training, 1974, Guidebook for Psychological Services and Motor Perceptual Training (How One May Improve in Ten Easy Lessons!), 1992, Manual for the Lucille Linde Ocumeter: Ocular Pursuit Measuring Instrument, 1992, Motor-Perceptual Training and Visual Perceptual Research (How Students Improved in Seven Lessons!), 1992, Effects of Motor Perceptual Training on Academic Achievement and Ocular Pursuit Ability, 1992; inventor ocumeter, instrument for measuring ocular tracking ability, 1989, target for use, 1991; patentee in field. Mem. Rep. Presdl. Task Force, 1989-96, trustee, 1991-92, charter mem., 1994—, life mem., 1994-95; mem. Rep. Nat. Com., 1990, 93-96, Rep. Nat. Com. on Am. Agenda, 1993, Nat. Rep. Congl. Com., 1990, 92, 93, 95, 96, Nat. Fedn. Rep. Women, Greeley Rep. Women, 1996; advisor Senator Bob Dole for Pres.; charter mem. Rep. Newt Gingrich's Speaker's Task Force, Senator Phil Gramm's Presdl. Steering Com.; at-large- del. Rep. Platform Planning Com.; team leader Nat. Rep. Rapid Response Network, Campaign America, 1996; active Heritage Found., Attention Deficit Disorder Adv. Group, Christian Bus. Men's Assn., Friends U. N.C. Librs., Citizens Against Govt. Waste, 1996, Concerns of Police Survivors, 1996, Nat. Assn. of Police Org. Recipient Presdl. medal of merit and lapel insignia, 1990, Nat. Rep. Senatorial Com., 1991-96, cert. of appreciation Nat. Rep. Congl. Com., 1992, 95, lapel pin Rep. Senatorial Inner Circle, 1990-96, Rep. Presdl. commemorative honor roll, 1993, Rep. Senatorial Freedom medal, 1994, Rep. Legion of Merit award, 1994, 96, Rep. Congl. Order of Freedom award, 1995, Convention medallion Rep. Senatrioal Inner Cir., 1996, Lapel Pin award RNC, 1996, Leadership citation Rep. Senatorial Inner Cir./ Rep. Nat. Conv., 1996, Legion of Merit Rep. Presdl. exec. com., 1996, Honor cert. House Spkr. Newt Gingrich, 1996; named to Rep. Nat. Hall of Honor, 1992. Mem. AAUP, NAFE, Nat. Assn. Sch. Psychologists and Psychometrists (spkr. at conf. 1976), Nat. Fedn. Rep. Women (name engraved on Ronald Wilson Reagan Eternal Flame of Freedom, 1995, on the Nat. Rep. Victory Monument, Washington, 1996, Rep. Sen. Inner Cir. Conv. Medallion 1996, RNG Mems. Only pin 1996), The Smithsonian Assocs., Nat. Trust for Hist. Preservation, Am. Pers. and Guidance Assn., Nat. Assn. Student Pers. Adminstrs., Nat. Assn. Women Deans and Counselors, Calif. Tchrs. Assn., Internat. Platform Assn., Independence Inst., Assn. Children Learning Disabilities (conf. spkr. 1976), Learning Disabilities Assn. (spkr. internat. conv. 1976), Greeley Rep. Women's Club, Pi Omega Pi, Pi Lambda Theta. Home: 1954 18th Ave Greeley CO 80631-5208

LINDELL, ANDREA REGINA, dean, nurse; b. Warren, Pa., Aug., 21, 1943; d. Andrew D. and Irene M. (Fabry) Lefik; m. Warner E. Lindell, May 7, 1966; children: Jennifer I., Jason M. B.S., Villa Maria Coll., 1970; M.S.N. Catholic U., 1975, D.N.Sc., 1976; diploma R.N., St. Vincent's Hosp., Erie, Pa. Instr. St. Vincent Hosp. Sch. Nursing, 1964-66; dir. Rouse Hosp., Youngsville, Pa., 1966-69; supr. Vis. Nurses Assn., Warren, Pa., 1969-70; dir. grad. program Cath. U., Washington, 1975-77; chmn., assoc. dean U. N.H., Durham, 1977-81; dean, prof. Oakland U., Rochester, Mich., 1981-90, dean, Schmidlapp prof. nursing U. Cin., 1990—; bd. dirs. CHEMED Corp.; cons. Moorehead U., Ky., 1983. Editor; Jour. Profl. Nursing, 1985; contbr. articles to profl. jours. Mem. sch. bd. Strafford Sch. Dist., N.H., 1977-80; Gov.'s Blue Ribbon Commn. Direct Health Policies, Concord, N.H., 1979-81; vice chmn. New England Commn. Higher Edn. in Nursing, 1977-81; mem. Mich. Assn. Colls. Nursing, 1981—. Named Outstanding Young Woman Am., 1980. Mem. Nat. League Nursing, Am. Assn. Colls. Nursing, Sigma Theta Tau. Democrat. Roman Catholic. Avocations: water skiing, roller skating, reading, fishing, camping.

LINDEMAN, CAROLYNN ANDERSON, music educator; b. Kane, Pa., June 5, 1940; d. David Julius and Aralaine Elizabeth (Wagstaff) Anderson; m. Alfred Lindeman, June 29, 1963; 1 child, David Henry. MusB, Oberlin Coll., 1962; MA in Music, San Francisco State U., 1972; D of Mus. Arts, Stanford U., 1979. Elem. music cons. Commack (N.Y.) Unified Sch. Dist., 1962-67; from lectr. in music to prof. music San Francisco (Calif.) State U., 1973—; mem. nat. bd. examiners Ednl. Testing Svc. NTE-Music, Princeton, N.J., 1990—; mem. Nat. Task Force on Music Standards. Author: PianoLab.: An Introduction to Class Piano, 3rd edit., 1996; co-author: MusicLab.: An Introduction to Music Fundamentals, 1989, The Musical Classroom, 3rd edit., 1995; editor: Strategies for Teaching Series, 1995-96; mem. editl. bd. Jour. Music Tchrs., 1991-94; compiler: Women Composers of Ragtime, 1985. Chair Nat. Women's Polit. Caucus, Marin County. Mem. Music Educators Nat. Conf. (nat. pres. 1996-98, pres.-elect western divsn. 1992-94), Calif. Coalition for Music (chair 1991-94), Calif. Music Educators Assn. (pres. 1990-92), Calif. Coun. Music Tchr. Edn. (chair 1987-90). Office: San Francisco State Univ Music Dept 1600 Holloway Ave San Francisco CA 94132-1722

LINDEMANN, JAN RUTH, social worker, governmental affairs consultant; b. Kankakee, Ill., Dec. 26, 1948; d. George A. and Ruth E. (Danker) Noffke; m. Paul F. Lindemann, May 22, 1971; children: Andrea, Jessica. BA, Valparaiso U., 1971; MSW, Ind. U., 1973. Cert. clin. social worker. Psychiat. social worker Larue Carter Hosp., Indpls., 1973-78; exec. dir. Ind. chpt. NASW, Indpls., 1978-80; lobbyist, cons. Ind. Coalition Human Svcs., Indpls., 1984—, Ind. Primary Health Care Assn., Indpls., 1993—; adj. field instr. Sch. Social Work Ind. U., Indpls., 1973-95. Mem. pub. policy com. Mental Health Assn. Ind., Indpls., 1994—; mem. steering com. Kids Count, Indpls., 1994—; mem. Planned Parenthood, Indpls., 1987—; mem. adv. com. social svc. block grant State of Ind., 1987-90; del. White House Conf. Families, 1980. Named Social Worker of Yr. Ind. chpt. NASW, 1995. Mem. NOW, Govt. Affairs Soc. Ind. (bd. dirs. 1995—), Women's Polit. Caucus, Acad. Cert. Social Workers, Indpls. Press Club. Home and Office: 8132 Meadowbrook Dr Indianapolis IN 46240

LINDEN, MOLLY KATHLEEN, nursing administrator, educator; b. Spokane, Wash., Dec. 30, 1952; d. Robert Michael and Agnes Patricia (Gill) L. Student, Wash. State U., 1971-73; BSN magna cum laude, Seattle U., 1976; MS in Nursing, U. Wash., 1983. RN, Wash.; cert. case mgr. Staff nurse Univ. Hosp. Med. Ctr., Seattle, 1976-83; clin. nurse specialist Pacific Med. Ctr., Seattle, 1983-87, supr. adminstrv. nursing; supr. clin. nursing Swedish Med Ctr., Seattle, nursing adminstr., 1987-94, coord. care specialist, case mgr., 1994—; adj./part-time faculty Seattle U. Contbr. articles to profl. jours. Mem. ANA, King County Nurses Assn. (Nurse of Day award), Wash. State Nurses Assn., Seattle U. Alumni Assn. (bd. dirs., pres. 1991-93), Sigma Theta Tau (Outstanding Leader award 1992, pres. 1994-96).

LINDEN, SUSAN PYLES, marketing executive; b. Mt. Clemens, Mich., Apr. 29, 1954; d. Paul James Pyles and Charlotte Ettalene Snowden. BA cum laude, U. South Fla., 1976. Copywriter Denton & French, Tampa, Fla., 1977-79, account exec., 1979-81; account rep. J. Walter Thompson, Atlanta, 1981-82; account exec. Liller Neal, Atlanta, 1982-83; account exec. The Bloom Agy., Dallas, 1983-85, sr. account exec., 1985-86, v.p., account supr., 1986-89; sales and mktg. dir. Sta. KSPN-FM, Aspen, Colo., 1989-91, World Wide Ski Corp., Aspen, 1991-93; owner Susan Pyles Mktg., 1993—. Mem. Women's Forum, Aspen. Mem. Phi Kappa Phi. Home: PO Box 8264 Aspen CO 81612-8264 Office: PO Box 8264 Aspen CO 81612-8264

LINDENFIELD, NAOMI, ceramic artist; b. Princeton, N.J., May 14, 1958; d. Peter and Lore (Kadden) L. BA, Boston U., 1980. Apprentice Fred Tregaskis, Kent, Conn., 1980, Elizabeth McDonald, Bridgewater, Conn., 1981, Carol Sevick, Westminster W., Vt., 1981; baker Innisfree Farms Bakery, Brattleboro, Vt., 1982; potter Brattleboro Clayworks, 1983—; pres. Brattleboro Clayworks, 1988—; workshop instr. in field. Bd. dirs. Windham Citizens for Responsible Growth, Brattleboro, 1993-94. Mem. League N.H. Craftmen, Vt. Craftsmen., N.H. Potter's Guild, Am. Crafts Coun.

LINDERMAN, CHARLENE RUTH, media specialist; b. Charleroi, Pa., May 25, 1955; d. C. Cecil and Louise E. (Annis) L. AA, Delta Coll., 1974; BA, Mich. State U., 1975; MA, Ctrl. Mich. U., 1981; postgrad., various univs. Cert. tchr. and libr. sci., Mich. Exec. sec. Marshall Appraisal & Co., Midland, Mich., 1972-73; tchr. 2d-5th grades Midland Pub. Schs., 1975-87, media specialist K-6th grades, 1987—; instr. adult edn. Meridian Pub. Schs., Sanford, Mich., 1984-86; presenter confs. Co-author and producer video Antarctica, 1992; co-producer photography Antarctica Photographs, 1993. Grantee Midland Jaycees, 1992, Rotary, 1992, Midland Found., 1992, J.C. Penney Co., Inc., 1992, Target Stores, 1993; recipient Women's Book Project award AAUW, Celebrate Literacy award Midland County Reading Coun., 1995. Mem. NEA, Mich. Edn. Assn. Mich. Assn. for Media Edn., Midland City Edn. Assn. (bldg. rep. 1988-95, exec. com. 1995—), Friends of the Libr., Delta Kappa Gamma (sec. 1994-96, Woman of Distinction 1994). Office: Midland Pub Schs 600 E Carpenter St Midland MI 48640-5417

LINDERMAN, JEANNE HERRON, priest; b. Erie, Pa., Nov. 14, 1931; d. Robert Leslie and Ella Marie (Stearns) Herron; m. James Stephens Linderman; children: Mary Susan, John Randolph, Richard Webster, Craig Stephens, Mark Herron, Elizabeth Stewart. BS in Indsl. and Labor Rels., Cornell U., 1953; MDiv magna cum laude, Lancaster Theol. Sem., 1981; postgrad., clin. pastoral edn., Del. State Hosp., New Castle, 1981. Ordained priest, Episcopal Ch. Mem. pers. staff Hengerer Co., Buffalo, 1953-55; chaplain Cathedral Ch. St. John, Wilmington, Del., 1981-82; priest-in-charge Christ Episcopal Ch., Delaware City, Del., 1982-87; vicar Christ Episcopal Ch., 1987-91; assoc. rector St. Andrew's Episcopal Ch., Wilmington, Del., 1991-95, priest in charge, 1995—; chair human sexuality task force, Diocese of Del., 1981-82, mem. clergy compensation com. and diocesan coun., 1982-86, pres. standing com., 1991—, com. on constitution and canons, 1989. Author, editor hist. study papers. Bd. dirs. St. Michael's Day Nursery, Wilmington, 1985-88; mem. secondary schs. com. Cornell U.; bd. dirs., chmn. pers. com. Geriatrics Svcs. of Del., 1989—, sec. bd., 1993—. Mem. Episcopal Women's Caucus, Del. Episcopal Clergy Assn., Nat. Assn. Episcopal Clergy, DAR, Mayflower (elder, surgeon 1983—), Dutch Colonial Soc. Del., Stoney Run Questers (pres.), Cornell Women's Club Del. (pres. 1966), Women of St. James the Less (pres. 1972-73), Women's Witnessing Community at Lambeth, Patriotic Soc. in Del. (sec.-treas. conv. 1965-68), Chi Omega. Republican. Home: 307 Springhouse Ln Hockessin DE 19707-9691 Office: St Andrews's Episcopal Ch Eighth And Shipley St Wilmington DE 19801

LINDERS, MARTINA RYAN, tax specialist; b. Chgo., Aug. 27, 1968; d. John Joseph and Anne Theresa (Power) Ryan; m. Timm Alan Linders, Aug. 5, 1995. BS in Acctg., U. Ill., 1990. CPA, Ill. Tax sr. Ernst & Young LLP, Chgo., 1990-93; tax specialist Mfd. Home Communities, Inc., Chgo., 1993—. Treas. Chgo. Gaelic Park, Oak Forest, Ill., 1992—. Mem. AICPA. Roman Catholic. Office: Mfd Home Communities Inc Two N Riverside Plz Chicago IL 60606

LINDGREN, ELIZABETH MALY, banker; b. San Francisco, Dec. 15, 1965; d. Richard Wendell and Mary Jo (Fanning) Maly; m. John Stanley Lindgren, Nov. 6, 1993. BS, Duke U., 1988; MBA, U. Calif., Berkeley, 1992. Sales asst. Westin Hotels & Resorts, Washington, 1988-89, account mgr., 1989-90; fin. analyst Banknorth Group, Inc., Burlington, Vt., 1993-94, mgmt. acctg. mgr., 1995, fin. planning mgr., 1995—. Mem. Inst. Cert. Mgmt. Accts. Republican. Roman Catholic. Home: Bostwick Farm PO Box 105 Shelburne VT 05482 Office: Banknorth Group Inc St George Rd at Taft Corner Williston VT 05495

LINDH, PATRICIA SULLIVAN, banker, former government official; b. Toledo, Oct. 2, 1928; d. Lawrence Walsh and Lillian Winifred (Devlin) Sullivan; m. H. Robert Lindh, Jr., Nov. 12, 1955; children: Sheila, Deborah, Robert. B.A., Trinity Coll., Washington, 1950, LL.D., 1975; LL.D., Walsh Coll., Canton, Ohio, 1975, U. Jacksonville, 1975. Editor Singapore Am. Newspaper, 1957-62; spl. asst. to counsellor to Pres., 1974, spl. asst. to Pres., 1975-76; dep. asst. sec. state for ednl. and cultural affairs Dept. State, 1976-77; v.p., dir. corp. comms. Bank Am., L.A., 1978-84; corp. pub. rels. Bank Am., San Francisco, 1985-93. Trustee La. Arts and Sci. Center, 1970-73, Calif. Hosp. Med. Ctr., 1979-84; bd. dirs. Jr. League of Baton Rouge, 1969, Children's Bur. Los Angeles, 1979, 84, USO Northern Calif.; Rep. state vice chairwoman La., 1970-74; Rep. nat. committeewoman, La., 1974; mem. pub. affairs com. San Francisco World Affairs Coun., 1985; adv. bd. Jr. League Los Angeles, 1980-84; bd. visitors Southwestern U. Sch. Law. Roman Catholic. Home: 850 Powell St San Francisco CA 94108-2051

LINDQUIST, SUSAN PRATZNER, museum executive; b. San Francisco, Dec. 20, 1940; d. Carleton Edward Pratzner and Edith Crane (Johnson) Cox; m. Philip George Lindquist, Oct. 27, 1962; children: Tucker D., Travis C. BS in Edn., Lesley Coll., 1962; MEd, Northeastern U., Boston, 1979; postgrad., U. Calif., Berkeley, 1994. Tchr. local sch. Marshfield, Mass., 1962-63, Peabody, Mass., 1963-66; coord. early intervention Dept. Mental Health, Hyannis, Mass., 1976-79; supr. Dept. Social Svcs., Hyannis, 1981; program dir. Latham Sch., Brewster, Mass., 1982-85; vol. coord. Cape Cod Mus. Natural History, Brewster, 1986—, assoc. dir., 1987, pres., CEO, 1987—; corp. trustee Cape Cod Five Bank, 1992. Bd. dirs. Cape Cod C. of C., 1993, Mus. Inst. for Teaching Sci., Boston; trustee Cape Cod Acad., 1994; mem. Brewstr Bd. Appeals, 1977-87; founder, trustee Cape Cod Lighthouse Charter Sch., 1994—. Office: Cape Cod Mus Natural History PO Box 1710 Rte 6A Brewster MA 02631

LINDSAY, BARBARA JEANNE, human services manager; b. Mansfield, Ohio, Mar. 23, 1965; d. John Ronald and Marilyn Ruth (Waldman) Mertler; m. Craig Charles Lindsay, Dec. 29, 1990. BS, U. Akron, 1987; MBA, Case Western Res. U., 1993. Dialysis technician Ctrs. Dialysis Care, Cleve., 1987-89, St. Vincent Charity Hosp., Cleve., 1989; chief dialysis technician Home Intensive Care, Inc., Cleve., 1989-92; spl. asst. v.p. & CFO Home Intensive Care, Inc., Miami, Fla., 1989-92; gen. mgr. Cleve. br. Home Intensive Care, Inc., 1989-92; dist. dir. bus. devel. Home Intensive Care, Inc., Cleve., 1989-92; territory mgr., gen mgr. Option Care, Inc., Lorain, Mansfield, Ohio, 1993—; ind. cons., Cleve., 1994—. Com. mem. Am. Cancer Soc., Lorain, 1994—; bd. dirs. Ohio Continuum Care Coun., Lorain County, 1994—; mem. edn. com. North East Ohio Case Mgmt. Network, Cleve., 1995—; vol. Cuyahoga County Commr. Re-election Campaign, 1996. Mem. Promise (flight leader 1995-96, chair gala event 1996), Phi Sigma Alpha. Home: 5252 Linda Dr Medina OH 44256

LINDSAY, BEVERLY, university dean, education educator; b. San Antonio, Dec. 21, 1948; d. of Joseph Bass Benson and Ruth Edna (Roberts) L. BA, St. Mary's U., San Antonio, 1969; MA, U. Mass., 1971, EdD, 1974; PhD, Am. U., 1986. Asst. prof. Pa. State U., University Park, 1974-79; Am. Coun. on Edn. fellow Nat. Inst. Edn., Washington, 1979-81, sr. rschr., sr. staff, 1981-83; spl. asst. to v.p. Pa. State U., University Park, 1983-86; adminstr., coord. USIA, Washington, 1983-86; assoc. dean, prof. edn. U. Ga., Athens, 1986-92; dean internat. edn. and policy studies, prof., exec. dir. Hampton (Va.) U., 1992—; mem. nat. adv. and rev. bd. Fulbright Programs, Washington, 1993—; mem. nat. adv. bd. So. Ctr. for Study in Pub. Policy, Atlanta, 1990; cons. AID, Washington, 1990—, Acad. for Ednl. Devel., Washington, 1990—. Editor: Comparative Perspectives of Third World Women, 1980, 83, Migration and National Development in Africa, 1985; co-editor: Political Dimension in Education, 1995; mem. eidtorial bd. Comparative Edn., 1994—, New Edn.: Internat. Jour., 1994—. Coord. United Way/Coll. Edn., Athens, 1989-92; treas., bd. dirs. Winston/Beers Cmty. Sch., Washington, 1979-84, aerobics instr., 1981-82. Grantee U. Ga., 1987, 90, Ministry of Edn./U. Montreal, 1989, Charles Sturt U., Australia, 1996; A Coun. on Edn. fellow, 1979-81, 90. Mem. NAACP (life), Comparative Internat. Edn. Soc. (pres. 1988-89), World Coun. on Comparative Edn. Socs. (bd. dirs., exec. coun. 1986-89), Am. Ednl. Rsch. Assn. (presdl. com. 1987-90), Am. Assn. Colls. for Tchr. Edn. (univ. rep. 1990-94).

LINDSAY, DIANNA MARIE, educational administrator; b. Boston, Dec. 7, 1948; d. Albert Joseph and June Hazelton (Mitchell) Raggi; m. James William Lindsay III, Feb. 14, 1981. BA in Anthropology, Ea. Nazarene Coll., 1971; MEd in Curriculum and Instrn., Wright State U., 1973, MEd in Social Studies Edn., 1974, MEd in Edn. Adminstrn., 1977; EdD in Edn. Adminstrn., Ball State U., 1976. Supr. social edn. Ohio Dept. Edn., Columbus, 1976-77; asst. prin. Orange City Schs., Pepper Pike, Ohio, 1977-79; prin. North Olmsted (Ohio) Jr. High Sch., 1979-81; dir. secondary edn. North Olmsted City SChs., 1981-82; supt. Copley (Ohio)-Fairlawn City Schs., 1982-85; prin. North Olmsted High Sch., 1985-89, New Trier High Sch., Winnetka, Ill., 1989-96, Worthington Kilbourne H.S., Columbus, Ohio, 1996—; bd. dirs. Harvard Prins. Ctr., Cambridge, Mass. Contbr. articles to profl. jours. Bd. dirs. Nat. PTA, Chgo., 1987-89 (Educator of Yr. 1989). Named Prin. of Yr. Ohio Art Tchrs., 1989, one of 100 Up and Coming Educators, Exec. Educator Mag., 1988; recipient John Vaughn Achievements in Edn. North Cen. Assn., 1988. Mem. AAUW, Ill. Tchrs. Fgn. Lang., Rotary Internat., Phi Delta Kappa. Methodist. Office: Worthington Kilbourne High Sch 1499 Hard Rd Columbus OH 43235

LINDSAY, HELEN MILLS, psychotherapist; b. Cleve., June 2; d. Don Parmenter Mills and Grace Elidah Stroup; m. Harry Anderson Lindsay, July 21, 1991; stepchildren: Bruce, Evan, Dean. BA, Case Western Ress. U., 1932; MS of Social Sci., Boston U., 1947. Lic. clin. social worker. Sr. sen. Calif. Sr. Legislature, 1985—; pres. Aux. Laguna Hills Adult Day Health Care, 1993—. Mem. Leisure World Dem. Club (pres. 1984-85). Address: Unit A 801 Ronda Mendoza Laguna Hills CA 92653-5902

LINDSAY, SHARON WINNETT, lawyer, consultant; b. N.Y.C., Apr. 10, 1949; d. William Richardson and Rosemary (Walton) Winnett; m. George Peter Lindsay, Sept. 8, 1973; children: William Charles, Kimberly Michelle. BA, MA, Fordham U., 1970; JD, Harvard U., 1973. Bar: N.Y. 1974, U.S. Dist. Ct. (fed. dist.), U.S. Ct. Appeals 1974. Atty. Milbank, Tweed, Hadley & McCloy, N.Y.C., 1973-83; v.p., asst. gen. counsel J.P. Morgan & Co., Inc., N.Y.C., 1983-95. Trustee Fordham U., Bronx, N.Y., 1994—; bd. dirs. Scarsdale Middle Sch., N.Y., 1990—, Scarsdale High Sch., N.Y., 1995—; mem. spl. events com. Carnegie Hall, 1995—. Mem. ABA, N.Y. State Bar Assn., Bar Assn. City of N.Y., Scarsdale Golf Club, Stockbridge Golf Club, Phi Beta Kappa. Roman Catholic. Home and Office: 25 Mamaroneck Rd Scarsdale NY 10583-2811

LINDSEY, ANNE ELIZABETH, communication educator; b. Bitburg, Germany, Feb. 10, 1959; came to U.S., 1961; d. Kemp Gibson and Valerie Hilda (Briscoe) L. BA, Boise State U., 1982; MA, U. Conn., 1985; PhD, Purdue U., 1993. Instr. U. Conn., Storrs, 1983-85, Purdue U., West Lafayette, Ind., 1985-90; asst. prof. U. Ga., Athens, 1990-93, N.Mex. State U., Las Cruces, 1993—; cons. City of Las Cruces, N.Mex., 1995—, N.Mex. State U. Alumni Assn., Las Cruces, 1995—. Contbr. chpt. to book and articles to profl. jours. Mentoring fellow Inst. Behavioral Rsch., U. Ga., 1991; grantee N.Mex. Dept. Pub. Health, 1995. Mem. Internat. Comm. Assn., Speech Comm. Assn., Western States Comm. Assn. Democrat. Office: NMex State Univ Box 30001 Las Cruces NM 88003

LINDSEY, BONNIE JOAN, vocational school educator; b. Oklahoma City, May 4, 1935; d. David DeWitt and Genevieve Catherine (Rucinski) Bevans; m. Donald G. Lindsey, Apr. 3, 1963 (div. 1974): 1 child, Jon Erik. AS, Mt. San Jacinto Coll., 1973; BA Vocat. Edn., Long Beach State U., 1975, MA Vocat. Edn., 1977. Tchr. Riverside (Calif.) Regional Occupation program, 1972-74, mem. adv. com., 1983-85; supr. Colton-Redlands-Yucaipa Regional Occupation Program, Redlands, Calif., 1974-75; assoc. prof. Riverside Community Coll., 1975-89, prof. emeritus, 1989—; tchr. Idaho State U., Pocatello, 1990-93, chmn. dept. health occupations, 1990—. Author: Medical Assisting, 1974, 75, 89; co-author Professional Medical Assistant: Clinical Assisting, 1990. Mem. Am. Assn. Med. Transcription (pres. Orange Empire chpt. 1985-88), Am. Assn. Med. Assts., Calif. Assn. Med. Assisting Instrs., Vocat. Indsl. Clubs of Am. (named Advisor of Yr. 1974), Epsilon Pi Tau. Democrat. Roman Catholic. Home: 1506 Meadowhill Dr Mountain Home AR 72653-5063 Office: Ark State U 213 E 6th St Mountain Home AR 72653

LINDSEY, D. RUTH, physical education educator; b. Kingfisher, Okla., Oct. 26, 1926; d. Lewis Howard and Kenyon (King) L. BS, Okla. State U., 1948; MS, U. Wis., 1954; PEd, Ind. U., 1965. Registered kinesiotherapist, 1970. Instr. Okla. State U., Stillwater, 1948-50, Monticello Coll., Alton, Ill., 1951-54, DePauw U., Greencastle, Ind., 1954-56; prof. Okla. State U., Stillwater, 1956-75; vis. prof. U. Utah, Salt Lake City, 1975-76; prof. phys. edn. Calif. State U., Long Beach, 1976-88; prof. emeritus phys. edn. Calif. State U., 1988—; freelance author, cons. Westminster, Calif. Co-author: Fitness for the Health of It, 6th edit., 1989, Concepts of Physical Fitness, 8th edit., 1993, Fitness for Life, 3d edit., 1993, Concepts of Physical Fitness and Wellness, 1993, The Ultimate Fitness Book, 1984, Survival Kit for Those Who Sit, 1989, A Menu of Concepts: Physical Fitness Concepts, Toward Active Lifestyles and Fitness and Wellness Concepts, Toward Health Lifestyles, 1996; editor: Perspectives: Jour. of Western Soc. for Phys. Edn. Coll. Women, 1988-95. Amy Morris Homans scholar, 1964; recipient Disting. and Meritorious Svc. Honor award Okla. Assn. Health, Phys. Edn. and Recreation, 1970, Meritorious Performance award Calif. State U., 1987, Julian Vogel Meml. award Am. Kinesiotherapy Assn., 1988. Fellow AAHPERD, Am. Kinesiotherapy Assn., Calif. Assn. Health, Phys. Edn., Recreation and Dance, Nat. Coun. Against Health Fraud, Orange County Nutrition Coun., Tex. and Acad. Authors Assn., Western Soc. for Phys. Edn. of Coll. Women (hon. mem.), Phi Kappa Phi. Republican. Baptist.

LINDSEY, DOTTYE JEAN, marketing executive; b. Temple Hill, Ky., Nov. 4, 1929; d. Jesse D. and Ethel Ellen (Bailey) Nuckols; m. Willard W. Lindsey, June 14, 1952 (div.). BS, Western Ky. U., 1953, MA, 1959. Owner, Bonanza Restaurant, Charleston, W.Va., 1965; tchr. remedial reading Alice Waller Elem. Sch., Louisville, 1967-75, tchr., 1953-67, 1975-84, contact person for remedial reading, 1968—; regional mgr. A.L. Williams Fin. Mktg. Co., 1988—; profl. model Cosmo/Casablancas Modeling Agy., Louisville, 1984-89; with Primerica Fin. Svcs. (formerly A.L. Willams Fin. Svcs.), Louisville, 1988—; model, 1984-89; regional mgr. Primerica Fin. Svcs., 1988—. Treas. Met. Louisville Women's Polit. Caucus, 1980-88, Ky. Women's Polit. Caucus, 1988-91; bd. sponsor ROTC Western Ky. U., 1950; local precinct capt., 1987—; election officer, 1984—; treas. Ky. Women's Polit. Caucus, 1988-91. Named Miss Ky., 1951. Mem. NEA, Ky. Edn. Assn., Jefferson County Tchrs. Assn., various polit. action coms., Internat. Reading Assn., Am. Childhood Edn. Assn. Democrat. Baptist.

LINDSEY, JACQUELYN MARIA, editor; b. Buffalo, June 6, 1952; d. George Henry and Patricia Ann (Rott) Bilkey; m. Timothy Paul Murphy, Jan. 29, 1970 (div. May 1981); children: Paul Jeffrey, Jeremy Michael; m. Warren Lee Eckert, Dec. 5, 1987 (div. June 1992); m. Donald J. Lindsey, Nov. 5, 1994. Student, Ind. U., 1984. Adminstrv. asst. Western N.Y. Cath. Visitor, Buffalo, 1979-81; sec. religious edn. Our Sunday Visitor, Huntington, Ind., 1981-84, editorial asst. periodicals dept., 1985, staff editor periodicals and books, editor My Daily Visitor, 1985-91, coord. Diocesan edits., 1986-88, assoc. editor books, 1987-90, editor trade books, 1990-93, acquisitions editor trade books, 1991—, acquisitions editor religious edn., 1991—; co-founder, co-owner Specialty Tool & Engring., LLC, 1995—. Editor, compiler: Photo Directory of U.S. Catholic Hierarchy, 1987, 90, 93; editor Leaves Marianhill Missionaries, 1991—. Candidate for rep. Ind. Gen. Assembly 21st Dist., 1984; mem. LaFontaine Arts Coun., Huntington County, 1985-88; mem. Huntington County Dems., 1986-88. Mem. Cath. Press Assn. Office: Our Sunday Visitor Pub 200 Noll Plz Huntington IN 46750-4310

LINDSEY, LYDIA, education educator, researcher; b. Trenton, N.J., Jan. 10, 1951; d. Charles and Ollie S. Lindsey. BA, Howard U., 1972, MA, 1974; PhD, U. N.C., 1992. Asst. prof. N.C. Ctrl. U., Durham, 1974-92, archivist, 1992—; adj. prof. U. N.C., Chapel Hill, 1992—; cons. A Philip Randolph Ednl. Found., 1975-78; rsch. assoc. U. Warwick, Coventry, Engr., 1985-86; Rockefeller doctoral fellow Duke-U.N.C. Women's Studies Rsch. Ctr., 1985-886; bd. dirs. Carolina Wren Press, Durham, Stagville Plantation, 1992—; minority postdoctoral fellow U. N.C., 1994-96, participant in nat. land interaction confs. Contbr. articles to profl. jours. Campaign mgr. Beverly Jones Sch. Bd., Durham, 1991-92; active People's Alliance, Durham, 1991-92, Durham Hist. Preservation Soc., 1991-92. Recipient DAR History award; N.C. Minority Postdoctoral fellow, 1994—, N.C. Bd. Gov.'s Doctoral fellow, 1986-87, NEH fellow for coll. tchrs. of historically black colls., 1985-86, U. N.C.-Chapel Hill Reynolds Overseas Grad. fellow, 1985-86, Rockefeller fellow from Duke-U. N.C. Women's Studies Rsch. Ctr. Doctoral fellow, 1985-86; N.J. State scholar, 1968-72, Fulbright scholar, 1995; NEH grantee, 1979. Mem. Assn. Black Women Historians, Assn. for

Study African, Caribbean and Asian Culture in Britain, Assn. for Study of Afro-Am. Life and History, Assn. Caribbean Studies, Assn. So. Women Historians, Assn. Social and Behavioral Scis., Collegium for African Am. Studies, Am. Hist. Assn., Nat. Coun. Black Studies, Nat. Coun. Black Women, Carolina Symposium Brit. Study, So. Confs. Brit. Studies, Golden Key (hon.), Delta Sigma Theta, Pi Gamma Mu, Phi Alpha Theta. Democrat. Baptist. Home: 2210 Alpine Rd Durham NC 27707-3970 Office: NC Ctrl U Durham NC 27707

LINDSEY, ROBERTA LEWISE, music researcher, historian; b. Munich, Apr. 23, 1958; d. Fred S. and Elsie E. (White) L. BMus, Butler U., 1980, MMus, 1987; PhD, Ohio State U., 1996. Pres., owner Profl. Typing Svcs./Indpls., 1980-84; mktg. specialist Merchants Mortgage Corp., Indpls., 1985-87; exec. asst. Ind. Arts Commn., Indpls., 1988-90; GTA Ohio State U., Columbus, 1990-94, music libr. asst., 1991-93, student coord. music in Ohio festival, 1993, vol. tutor coord., 1994-95; lectr. Ohio State U., Marion, 1995; rep. Susan Prter Meml. symposium Ohio State U., Columbus, 1995. Reader Ctrl. Ind. Radio Reading, Inc., Indpls., 1985-90; co-founder, mem. Grad. Music Students Assn., Ohio State U., Columbus; mem. multicultural diversity com. Coun. of Grad. Students, Columbus, 1992, mem. orgns. and elections com., 1992, co-chair orientation com., 1993. Sinfonia Rsch. grantee Sinfonia Found., 1993; recipient Grad. Student Alumni Rsch. award Ohio State U., 1993. Mem. Sonneck Soc., Am. Musicological Soc., Coll. Music Soc., Soc. of Ethnomusicology. Presbyterian.

LINDSKOG, MARJORIE OTILDA, elementary school educator; b. Rochester, Minn., Oct. 13, 1937; d. Miles Emery and Otilda Elvina (Hagre) L. BA, Colo. Coll., 1959, MA in Teaching, 1972. Field advisor/camp dir. Columbine council Girl Scouts U.S., Pueblo, Colo., 1959-65; staff mem. Wyo. Girl Scout Camp, Casper, 1966, dir., 1967; tchr. Sch. Dist. 60, Pueblo, 1966—; asst. dir. camp Pacific Peaks Girl Scouts U.S., Olympia, Wash., 1968, dir., 1969; instr. Jr. Gt. Books Program, 1981—; mem. adv. bd. Newspapers in Edn., 1988—; mem. supervisory com. Pueblo Tchr.'s Credit com.; lectr., instr. edn. U. So. Colo., 1990-96; instr. math. Adams State Coll., 1991; mem. adv. bd. ctr. for advancement teaching sci., math, and tech. U. So. Colo., 1992-94; apptd. by Gov. to Colo. Standards Assessment Devel. and Implementation Coun., 1993—. Author: (series of math. lessons) Bronco Mathmania, 1987, 88, 89, 90, 91, 92, 93, 94, 95, Welcome to Wall Street, 1992, 93, 94, 95, 96, Day to Day Math, 1994, Mental Math, 1995, Everyday Math, vol. 1 and 2, 1996, Word Problems, 1996; area co-chair Channel 8 Pub. TV Auction, Pueblo, 1983-87; contbr. articles to profl. jours. Bd. dirs. Columbine Girl Scout Council, 1983-85, Dist. #60 Blood Bank, 1985—; mem. Pueblo Greenway and Nature Ctr., 1981—. Recipient Thanks badge Girl Scouts U.S., Presdl. award for Outstanding Tchg. in Elem. Math., 1995. Mem. Nat. Council for Tchrs. Math., Colo. Coun. Tchrs. Math. (Outstanding Elem. Math Tchr. of Yr. 1989), Intertel, Mensa, Phi Delta Kappa, Alpha Phi. Lutheran. Club: Pueblo Country. Lodge: Sons of Norway. Home: 2810 7th Ave Pueblo CO 81003-1625 Office: Baca Elem Sch 2800 E 17th St Pueblo CO 81001

LINDSTEDT-SIVA, (KAREN) JUNE, marine biologist, environmental consultant; b. Mpls., Sept. 24, 1941; d. Stanley L. and Lila (Mills) Lindstedt; m. Ernest Howard Siva, Dec. 20, 1969. Student, U. Calif.-Santa Barbara, 1959-60, U. Calif.-Davis, 1960-62; B.A., U. So. Calif., 1963, M.S., 1967, Ph.D., 1971. Asst. coordinator Office Sea Grant Programs U. So. Calif., 1971; environ. specialist So. Calif. Edison Co., Rosemead, 1971-72; asst. prof. biology Calif. Luth. U., 1972-73; sci. advisor Atlantic Richfield Co., Los Angeles, 1973-77, sr. sci. advisor, 1977-81, mgr. environ. scis., 1981-86, mgr. environ. protection, 1986-96; environ. cons., 1996—; mem. Nat. Sci. Bd., 1984-90; mem. panels on environ. issues Nat. Rsch. Coun.; mem. Polar Rsch. Bd., 1994—; mem. EPA Panel on Environ. Risk Reduction, 1992-94; mem. NAS Alaska Panel; mem. biology adv. coun. Calif. State U.-Long Beach, 1980-92; bd. dirs. So. Calif. Acad. Scis., 1983-93, pres., 1990-92; mem. Marine Scis.; adv. coun. U. So. Calif. Inst. Coastal and Marine Scis.; trustee Bermuda Biol. Sta. for Rsch.; chmn. Oil Spill Conf., San Antonio, 1989, API Oil Spills Com. Contbr. articles to profl. jours. Recipient Calif. Mus. Sci. and Industry Achievement award, 1976, Trident award for Marine Scis., 11th Ann. Rev. Underwater Activites, Italy, 1970, Achievement award for Advancing Career Opportunities for Women, Career Planning Council, 1978; research grantee; distg. scholar biology Calif. Lut. U. Colloquim Scholars, 1988. Fellow AAAS, ASTM (award of merit 1990), So. Calif. Acad. Scis., Soc. Petroleum Industry Biologists (pres. 1976-80); mem. Marine Tech. Soc., Calif. Native Plant Soc., Am. Inst. Biol. Sci., Phi Beta Kappa, Sigma Xi, Phi Kappa Phi.

LINDSTROM, JANET ELENA, non-profit executive; b. Erie, Pa., Jan. 27, 1934; d. Charles and Emma Marie (Brummer) Ramandanes; m. Gary Edward Lindstrom, June 19, 1958 (wid. Jan. 1980); children: Maren, Jennifer. BS, Pa. State U., 1956; MA, Columbia U., 1960. Tchr. Erie Sch. Dist., 1956-58, New Canaan (Conn.) Schs., 1958-62, Foxglove Sch., New Canaan, 1982-83; exec. dir. New Canaan Hist. Soc., 1983—; sec., 1992-94, v.p., 1994, dir. vol., Stamford, Conn., 1990—; commr. Hist. Dist. Commn., New Canaan, 1989-95, sec. 1989-93, v.p. 1989-95; sec. Day Care Ctr. of New Canaan, 1992—; pres. New Canaan High Sch. Parent Facility, 1980-85, New Canaan Hist. Soc. (bd. govs.), 1983-85; co-chmn. NCHS Scholarship Found, New Canaan, 1982-84. Sec. Dirs. of Vols., Stamford, Conn., 1990-94, v.p. 1994-95, pres. 1996—. Commr. Hist. Dist. Commn., New Canaan, 1989—; sec. Day Care Ctr. of New Canaan, 1984—, vice-chmn., 1992—; pres. New Canaan High Sch. Parent Facility, 1980-81, New Canaan Hist. Soc., 1983-85; co-chmn. NCHS Scholarship Found., New Canaan, 1982-84; bd. dirs. New Canaan C. of C., 1996; mem. bd. Lower Hudson Conf., 1996. Mem. AAUW (pres. 1971-73, grantee 1973), Rep. Woman's Club, New Canaan Field Club. Republican. Presbyterian. Office: The New Canaan Hist Soc 13 Oenoke Rdg New Canaan CT 06840-4104

LINEBERRY, SANDRA BEECH, accountant; b. Battle Creek, Mich., Nov. 22, 1946; d. Raymond August and Betty Jean (Bailey) Wank; m. James E. Beech, June 19, 1964 (div. June 1977); children: James Michael, Daniel Lee, Christina Rena; m. Terry Lineberry, Sept. 10, 1977 (div. June 1983). AA, Kellogg C.C., 1976; BA, Fla. Atlantic U., 1981. Bookkeeper Henry D. Bogaton, Lantana, Fla., 1978-81; acct. Darling & Rosasco CPA's, Palm Beach Garden, Fla., 1981-84, Rosasco & Lineberry CPA's, Royal Palm Beach, Fla., 1984-86, Peterson, Peterson & Rioux, Lake Worth, Fla., 1987—. Mem. AICPA, Fla. Inst. of CPA's. Republican. Methodist. Home: 200 NE 5th Ct Delray Beach FL 33444 Office: Peterson Peterson & Rioux CPAs 3003 S Congress Ave 2C Palm Springs FL 33461

LINERT, SUSAN MARIE, cattle breeder; b. Seattle, May 18, 1949; d. Edwin Joseph and Gilda Leah (Taylor) L. Diploma, Skagit Valley Coll., Mt. Vernon, Wash., 1969; BS in Petroleum Engring., N.Mex. Inst. Mining and Tech., 1984. Rsch. and devel. equipment operator Petroleum Tech. Corp., Redmond, Wash., 1977-79; well completion supr. William Perlman Co., Ignacio, Colo., 1985; asst. dept. mgr. Best Products, Lynnwood, Wash., 1986-87; prodn. supt. Kimbell Oil Co. Tex., Farmington, N.Mex., 1987-95; Red Angus cattle breeder Fair Well Farm, Koshkonong, Mo., 1995—. Mem. Soc. Petroleum Engrs. Home and Office: Fair Well Farm RR 1 Box 69 Koshkonong MO 65692

LING, DOROTHY HUEI-LIN, physician; b. Tulsa, Okla., Aug. 10, 1961; d. Hsin Yi and Suyu Ling. BS summa cum laude, U. Ill., 1983; MD, Northwestern U., 1987. Ptnr. Physicians Anesthesia Svc., Inc., Seattle, 1991—; physician staff mem. Swedish Med. Ctr., Seattle, 1991—; asst. clin. prof. dept. of anesthesiology U. of Wash. Sch. of Medicine, 1995—. Bd. trustees Intiman Theatre, 1996—. Mem. Am. Soc. of Anesthesiologists, Internat. Anesthesia Rsch. Soc., Jr. League of Seattle, Phi Beta Kappa, Phi Kappa Phi.

LING, KATHRYN WROLSTAD, health association administrator; b. Watertown, Wis., Aug. 3, 1943; d. Jeffrey Harold and Constance Devina (Egre) Wrolstad; stepchildren: Renee Rainey, Roz Harper. BS in History and Polit. Sci., U. Wis., 1965. Supr. recreation ARC, DaNang, Cam Ran Bay, VietNam, 1968; assoc. exec. dir. Am. Cancer Soc., Evanston, Ill., 1968-71, exec. dir., 1971-73; exec. dir. Montgomery County Unit Am. Cancer Soc., Md., 1973-76, cons. income devel., 1976, dir., profl. edn. cancer incidence and end results, 1976-78, dir. income devel., 1978-82; exec. dir. Am. Cancer Soc., Chgo., 1982-84; assoc. exec. dir. Alzheimer's Disease and Related Disorders Assn., Chgo., 1985-87, v.p. community svcs., 1988-91, sr. v.p. chpt. Family Svcs. and Edn. divsn., 1991-93; cons. Nat. Aphasia Assn.; pres. The Leadership Edge, Chgo.; chmn. bd. dirs. Kaleidoscope. Mem. Soc. Non-Profit Orgn. (chmn. bd. dirs.). Home: 1255 N Sandburg Ter Chicago IL 60610

LINGLE, KATHLEEN MCCALL, consultant, marketing executive, entrepreneur; b. Berea, Ohio, Aug. 24, 1944; d. Arthur Vivian McCall and Mary M. (Maxwell) Miller; m. John Hunter Lingle, Sept. 3, 1968 (div. 1991); 1 child, Michael Cameron; m. Sam F. Serrapede, Aug. 15, 1993. BA, Occidental Coll., 1966; MS, Ohio State U., 1977. Project dir. Ohio State U. Hosp., Columbus, 1977-78; rsch. assoc. Ednl. Testing Service, Princeton, N.J., 1978-82; mgr. mktg. services Gulton Industries, Princeton, 1982-84; rsch. dir. Rsch. 100, Princeton, 1984-85; dir. mktg. planning and rsch. Applied Data Research, Princeton, 1985-88; Western European sales mgr. Heuristics Software, Inc., Sacramento, 1988-89; pres., chief exec. officer Princeton Leadership Dynamics, 1989-90; rsch. dir. Families & Work Inst., N.Y.C., 1990-91; dir. tng. Families & Work Inst., 1991-93; cons. Wyatt Co., N.Y.C., 1994-96; mgr. HR solutions KPMG Peat Marwick LLP, Short Hills, N.J., 1996—. Vice pres. ops. Unitarian Ch. of New Brunswick (N.J.), 1983-84; served with Peace Corps, Chile and Venezuela, 1966, 69-72. Mem. NAFE, Am. Mktg. Assn., Am. Mgmt. Assn., Bus. and Profl. Women (chairperson membership com., 1990-91), N.J. Assn. Women Bus. Owners, Princeton Network Profl. Women, Princeton Area C. of C. (mem. membership com.), Am. Field Svc. (Princeton chpt.). Democrat. Home: 50 Coriander Dr Princeton NJ 08540-9434

LINGLE, MARILYN FELKEL, freelance writer, columnist; b. Hillsboro, Ill., Aug. 16, 1932; d. Clarence Frederick and Anna Cecelia (Stank) Felkel; m. Ivan L. Lingle, Oct. 4, 1950; children: Ivan Dale, Aimee Lee Lingle Galligan, Clarence Craig. Sec. Ill. State Police, 1950; with welfare dept. Ill. Pub. Aid, Hillsboro, 1951-52; rschr. Small Homes Council, Champaign, 1952-53; sec. Hillsboro Schs., 1954; office, payroll clk. Eagle Picher Zinc, Hillsboro, 1955-56; continuity dir. Sta. WSMI, Litchfield, Hillsboro, 1966-87; adv. bd. Am. Savs. Bank/Citizens Savs. Bank, vice chmn., 1986-93; cmty. edn. bridge instr. Lincoln Land C.C. Contbr. poetry to profl. jours. Fin. chmn. Hillsboro Hosp. Aux., 1972; literacy vol. Graham Correctional Ctr., Hillsboro, 1986—; pres., bd. dirs. Montgomery Players and Encore Play Theatre, 1954-70. Recipient Vol. of Yr. award Graham. Correctional Ctr., 1995, award of Merit Ill. State Bd. Edn., 1994-95. Mem. Cousteau Soc., Internat. Wildlife Fedn., Nat. Wildlife Fedn., Phi Theta Kappa Internat. Democrat. Lutheran. Club: Hillsboro Country. Avocations: bridge, golf, gardening, travel, reading.

LINGLE, MURIEL ELLEN, elementary education educator; b. Sundown Twp., Minn.; d. Harold O. and Carrie H. (Ewald) Anderson; m. Dale A. Lingle, Aug. 21, 1946; children: Barbara Jean, Tamara Jane. BS with distinction, Union Coll., Lincoln, Nebr., 1968; MA, U. Nebr., Lincoln, 1976. Cert. tchr., Nebr. Elem. tchr. Hallam, Nebr., 1959-62; tchr. Cen. Elem. and High Sch., Sprague-Martell, Nebr., 1963-67, Helen Hyatt Elem. Sch., Lincoln, 1968-70; elem. tchr. Crete (Nebr.) Sch. System, 1970-91; ret., 1991. Recipient award for excellence in teaching Cooper Found., 1990-91, Internat. Woman of Yr. award, 1993-94. Home: 4730 Hillside St Lincoln NE 68506-6431

LINHART, LETTY LEMON, editor; b. Pittsburg, Kans., Sept. 22, 1933; d. Robert Sheldon and Lois (Wise) Lemon; m. Robert Spayde Kennedy, June 8, 1955 (div. 1978); children: Carole Shea, Nancy Schrimpf, Nina Kennedy; m. Daniel Julian Linhart, June 9, 1986. BS, BA in English and Journalism, U.Kans., 1955; MS in Journalism, Boston U., 1975. Reporter Leavenworth (Kans.) Times, 1954; editor Human Resources Rsch. Office George Washington U., Washington, 1955-56; editor Behavior Rsch. Lab. Harvard Med. Sch., Boston, 1956-58; instr. Boston YMCA, 1960-64; freelance writer and columnist, 1975—; editor Somerville (Mass.) Times, 1975-77; pub. rels. dir. Lettermen of Lexington, Mass., 1978; instr. English Rollins Coll., Winter Park, Fla., 1978-79, Valencia Community Coll., Orlando, Fla., 1978-82, U. Cen. Fla., Orlando, 1979-82; tech. writer Kirschman Software, Altamonto Springs, Mass., 1980-81, Dynamic Control Software, Winter Park, Fla., 1981-82; editor Fla. Specifier, Winter Park, 1982-85, Mobile Home News, Maitland, Fla., 1985-86; instr. English Seminole C.C., Sanford, Fla., 1986-94; Elderhostel instr. Canterbury Rsch. Ctr., 1994—; editor Oviedo (Fla.) Voice, 1994-95, 96. Author: Are These Extravagant Promises, 1989, Clues for the Clueless, 1996; contbr. articles to profl. jours. Pres. MIT Dames Boston, 1958-59, Boston Alumnae of Delta Delta Delta, 1959-62; dist. pres Delta Delta Delta, Tex., 1962-65; mem. Friends of Cornell Mus., Winter Park, Fla. Named Outstanding Collegiate Delta Delta Delta, 1955. Mem. NAFE, Ctrl. Fla. Jazz Soc. (bd. dirs. 1983-93), Internat. Platform Soc., Soc. Women Execs., Altrusa Club (publicity com. 1980-83), Orlando Press Club (bd. dirs.), Univ. Club Winter Park, Mortar Bd., Phi Beta Kappa (Belmont, Mass. pres. 1965-78), Theta Sigma Phi, Sigma Delta Chi, Delta Sigma Rho. Home: PO Box 621131 Oviedo FL 32762-1131

LINK, PATRIC G., legislative staff executive; married; 2 children. BA, Mary Washington Coll., 1972. Legis. dir. to Rep. Larry Pressler, 1975-81, then spl. asst. to Rep. Larry Pressler; congl. liaison officer Office of Sec. NOAA Dept. of Commerce, 1981, dep. then dir. Office Legis. Affairs NOAA, 1982-89; cons. subcom. on tech., environment and aviation House Com. on Sci., Space and Tech., 1989-92, Rep. legis. asst. subcom. on tech., environment and aviation, 1992-93; staff dir. to Senator Larry Pressler, 1993-95; chief of staff U.S. Senate Com. on Commerce, Sci. and Transp., Washington, 1995—. Office: US Senat Com on Commerce Sci and Transp 254 Senate Russell Office Washington DC 20510

LINK, SHIRLEY ANN, telecommunications executive; b. Cleve., Apr. 22, 1946; d. Walter John and Margaret Irene (Kurtz) Korniet; m. Charles H. Martin, Sept. 10, 1965 (div. 1969); m. Gerald Smelko, Dec. 26, 1970 (div. 1979); children: Brian Martin, James Martin, Paul Smelko; m. Steven William Link, Nov. 15, 1985 (div. 1993). Student, Cuyahoga Community Coll., 1979-80, 82, Cleve. State U., 1981, 83. Sales mgr. Grolier, Strongsville, Ohio, 1978-80; sec. Lessem Glass, Cleve., 1980-82; interior designer Cleve., 1981-83; bookkeeper N&H, Inc., Cleve., 1983-84; asst. to project mgr. DeBartolo Corp., Northfield, Ohio, 1984-86; v.p. Clifton Phone Systems, Cleve., 1986-93; with Vista Communications, Westlake, Ohio, 1993—. Mem. NAFE, Soc. Telecommunications Profls., Smithsonian Instn. (assoc.). Democrat. Office: Vista Communications 821 West Point Pkwy Ste 920 Westlake OH 44145

LINKER, NANCY SUE, information systems executive; b. Toledo, May 15, 1956; d. Charles Edward and Dorothy Ruth (Bittner) Linker; m. Donald Thomas Kerner, June 20, 1975 (div. June 1980); children: Brittni Mae, Stephanie Noelle. AS with high honors, U. Toledo, 1980; BSM cum laude, Pepperdine U., 1983. Cert. systems profl.; cert. aerobics instr. Programmer, Owens-Ill., Toledo, 1973-80; programmer analyst Smith Tool Co., Irvine, Calif., 1980-82; systems analyst Denny's, Inc., La Mirada, Calif., 1982-83; sr. corp. systems analyst, mgr. corp. systems group Libbey-Owens-Ford Co., Toledo, 1983-86, pres. Seagate Systems Cons., 1986—. Participant ToledoScape. Mem. NAFE, Nat. Mgmt. Assn., Assn. Systems Mgmt., Inst. for Cert. of Sys. Profls. Republican. Roman Catholic. Avocations: travel, skiing, scuba, bicycling.

LINKONIS, SUZANNE NEWBOLD, pretrial case manager, counselor; b. Phila., Aug. 24, 1945; d. William Bartram and Kathryn (Taylor) Newbold; m. Bertram Lawrence Linkonis, May 29, 1966; children: Robert William, Deborah Anne, Richard Anthony. AA in Psychology, Albany (Ga.) Jr. Coll., 1979; BA in Psychology, Albany (Ga.) State Coll., 1981; MS in Indsl. Psychology, Va. Commonwealth U., 1986. Office mgr., media buyer Long Advt. Agy., Richmond, Va., 1981-84; media mgr. Clarke & Assocs., Richmond, 1984-85; human resources asst. Continental Ins., Richmond, 1985; rsch. assoc. Signet Bank, N.A., Richmond, 1986-87; program coord. Med. Coll. Va., Richmond, 1988; personnel mgr. Bur. Microbiology, Richmond, 1988; pers. specialist Va. State Dept. Corrections, Richmond, 1989-90; human rights adv. Va. State Dept. Youth and Family Svcs., Richmond, 1990-92, rehab. counselor, 1992-94, sr. rehab. counselor, 1994; pre-trial case mgr./counselor Henrico County Govt., 1995—; future dir., cons. Mary Kay Cosmetics, Springfield, Va., 1975-77. Mem. NAFE, APA. Republican. Roman Catholic. Home: 401 Saybrook Dr Richmond VA 23236-3621 Office: 8600 Dixon Powers Dr Richmond VA 23228-2737

LINN, CAROLE ANNE, dietitian; b. Portland, Oreg., Mar. 3, 1945; d. James Leslie and Alice Mae (Thorburn) L. Intern, U. Minn., 1967-68; BS, Oreg. State U., 1963-67. Nutrition cons. licensing and cert. sect. Oreg. State Bd. Health, Portland, 1968-70; chief clin. dietitian Rogue Valley Med. Ctr., Medford, Oreg., 1970—; cons. Hillhaven Health Care Ctr., Medford, 1971-83; lectr. Local Speakers Bur., Medford. Mem. ASPEN, Am. Dietetic Assn., Am. Diabetic Assn., Oreg. Dietetic Assn. (sec. 1973-75, nominating com. 1974-75, Young Dietitian of Yr. 1976), So. Oreg. Dietetic Assn., Alpha Lambda Delta, Omicron Nu. Democrat. Mem. Christ Unity Ch. Office: Rogue Valley Med Ctr 2825 E Barnett Rd Medford OR 97504-8332

LINNAN, JUDITH ANN, psychologist; b. Pasadena, Calif., July 11, 1940; d. Robert Emmet Linnan and Jane Thomas (Shutz) H.; m. Ralph Theodore Comito, Feb. 1, 1964 (div. Mar. 1975); children: Matthew, Andrew, Kristine. BA, U. Portland, 1962; MS, Calif. State U., Long Beach, 1974; PhD, CCI Internat. U., 1982; postgrad., Newport Psychoanalytical Inst., 1984-87, 95—. Lic. MFCC pupil pers., lic. rsch. psychoanalyst. Probation officer L.A. County Probation Dept., 1962-63; social worker L.A. County Dept. Probation and Social Svcs., 1963-69; counselor Huntington Beach (Calif.) Free Clinic, 1970-73, counseling ctr., Calif. State U., Long Beach, 1973-74; psychologist Fullerton (Calif.) Union High Sch. Dist., 1975-80, Psychiat. Med. Group, Orange County, Calif., 1981-82; psychologist, dir. Berkeley Psychol. Svcs., Placentia, Calif., 1982—; pvt. practice psychotherapist Huntington Beach, 1975—; founder, dir. Pacific Acad., Fullerton, 1981-82; dir. human resources So. Calif. Coll. Optometry, Fullerton, 1986—; cons., expert witness Orange County Social Svcs., 1992—; dir. student parent program Placentia Sch. Dist., 1993—. Democrat. Roman Catholic. Office: Berkeley Psychol Svcs 101 N Kraemer Blvd Ste 125 Placentia CA 92670-5000

LINNANSALO, VERA, engineer; b. Helsinki, Finland, Oct. 9, 1950; came to U.S., 1960, naturalized, 1969; d. Boris and Vera (Schkurat-Schkuropatsky) L. BS in Computer and Info. Sci., Cleve. State U., 1974, BME, 1974; MBA, U. Akron, 1983. Engring. assoc. B.F. Goodrich Co., Akron, Ohio, 1974-75, assoc. product engr., 1975-77, tire devel. engr., 1977-79, advanced tire devel. engr., 1979-84, quality devel. engr., 1984-85, sr. quality devel. engr., 1985-86; coordinator GM-10 Uniroyal Goodrich Tire Co., Akron, 1986-88, sr. tire devel. scientist, 1988-89; mgr. design and product quality Pirelli Armstrong Tire Corp., New Haven, 1989-90; product design engr. truck ops. Ford Motor Co., Dearborn, 1990-93, vehicle quality and process specialist, corp. quality office, 1993-94, supr. economie quality and reliability comml. truck vehicle ctr., 1995-96, supr. ranger quality & reliability light truck vehicle ctr., 1996—. Mem. Am. Soc. Quality Control (sr., cert. quality engr.), Soc. Automotive Engrs., Mensa. Home: 9234 Mayflower Plymouth MI 48170 Office: Ford Motor Co PDC Mail Drop 233 20901 Oakwood Blvd Dearborn MI 48121

LINNÉA, SHARON, writer, playwright; d. William Diderichsen and Marilynn Joyce Webber; m. Robert Owens Scott; 1 child, Jonathan Brendan. Student, Wheaton Coll., 1974-76; BA, NYU, 1978. Editor William Morrow and Co., N.Y.C., 1977-78, Taplinger and Assocs., N.Y.C., 1978-80; staff writer Flying Magazine, N.Y.C., 1982-83, Scholastic Voice, N.Y.C., 1983-85; staff writer Guideposts Mag., N.Y.C., 1985-91, contbg. editor, 1991—; contbg. editor Angels on Earth, 1995—; v.p. Imagining Things Enterprises, N.Y.C.; spkr. in field. Producer (film) Knowing Lisa, 1991 (Silver award Worldfest/Houston film festival); author: (study guide) Romeo and Juliet by William Shakespeare, 1984, Hedda Gabbler and A Doll's House by Henrik Ibsen, 1985, (book) Raoul Wallenberg: The Man Who Stopped Death, 1993 (Best Book of 1993 Jewish World, Dayton Jewish Chronicle, The Speaker), (plays), Clown of God, 1977, The Singer, 1978, A Matter of Time, 1981, Tales from the Vermont Woods, 1982, (screenplays) Missouri, Ma Cheri, Tomorrow Is My Dancing Day; ghostwriter articles in Reader's Digest and Guideposts Mag.; profile biographer World of Heroes Sch. Curriculum; freelancer Marvel Comics, Children's TV Workship, Hallmark Hall of Fame; contbr. articles to popular publs. Mem. Soc. Children's Book Writers and Illustrators, N.Y. Arts Group. Office: Imagining Things Enterprises 43 West 16th St Ste 7G New York NY 10011*

LINNEHAN, SHARON ANNE, visual artist, educator; b. Chgo., July 27, 1946; d. John Joseph and Lois Florence (Rickerman) Linnehan; m. John Thomas Gassmann, Oct. 4, 1969 (div. Feb. 1993); 1 child, Margaret Anne. BFA, St. Mary's Coll., Notre Dame, Ind., 1968; MA, Mich. State U., 1969; MFA, U. N.D., 1993—. Cert. tchr. secondary edn., N.D. Instr. Valley City (N.D.) State U., 1984-85, 92, 93; grad. teaching asst. U. N.D., Grand Forks, 1993, 95; artist-in-residence N.D. Coun. on the Arts, Fargo, 1992—; artist-in-residence U. N.D., Grand Forks, 1993-95, artist-in-the-classroom, 1993-95; docent; artist Artist-in-the-Classroom, Grand Forks, 1993—; docent N.D. Mus. Art, 1994—. Solo exhbn. The Color of Life, 1986. Roman Catholic. Home: 1603 11th Ave North Grand Forks ND 58203 Office: Univ of North Dakota Hughes Fine Art Ctr Dept Visual Arts Grand Forks ND 58203

LINNEY, BEVERLY See HALLAM, BEVERLY

LINTELMAN, JOY KATHLEEN, history educator; b. Fairmont, Minn., Oct. 16, 1957; d. Arthur H. and Clarice M. (Barke) L.; m. Richard Mark Chapman, Sept. 15, 1984; children: Emma, Hannah, Noah. BA, Gustavus Adolphus Coll., 1980; MA, U. Minn., 1983, PhD, 1991. Assoc. prof. history Concordia Coll., Moorhead, Minn., 1989—, dir. women's studies program, 1994—; guest curator U. Minn. Art Mus., Mpls., 1985-86. Author chpts. to books. Bd. dirs. Children and Adults with Attention Deficit Disorders, Fargo, N.D., 1995—. Rsch. grantee Minn. Hist. Soc., 1995; rsch. scholar Fulbright Commn., 1986-87. Office: Concordia Coll 901 S 8th St Moorhead MN 56562

LIOI, MARGARET M., performing company executive, educator; b. Rochester, N.Y., Feb. 24, 1952; d. Anthony L. and Mary Jane (Coiro) L.; m. Michael E. Ziemski, June 7, 1992; 1 child, Anna Margaret Ziemski. BMus, Marymount Coll., Tarrytown, N.Y., 1974; MMus, New England Conservatory, Boston, 1976; MBA, Binghamton (N.Y.) U., 1984. Asst. dir. devel. Spoleto Festival USA, Charleston, S.C., 1984-85, dir. devel., 1985-89; exec. dir. Eleanor Naylor Dana Charitable Trust, N.Y.C., 1989-93; dir. planning & devel. The Public Theater/N.Y. Shakespeare Festival, N.Y.C., 1993—; presenting and commissioning program cons. Nat. Endowment for the Arts, 1993; mem. adv. panel The Arts Forward Fund, N.Y.C., 1992-93; mem. Binghamton U. Found., 1993—. Prin. keyboard Binghamton Symphony Orchestra, 1979-83; asst. conductor and accompanist Binghamton Choral Soc., 1979-83. Sec. Arts Comm. Com. on Advocacy, Columbia, 1985-89; mem. adv. com. Joint Legis. Com. on Cultural Affairs, Columbia, 1985-89. Mem. Pi Kappa Lambda. Office: The Public Theater/NYSF 425 Lafayette St New York NY 10003

LIONE, GAIL ANN, lawyer; b. N.Y.C., Oct. 22, 1949; d. James G. and Dorothy Ann (Marsino) L.; 1 child, Margo A. Peyton. BA, U. Rochester, 1971; JD, U. Pa., 1974. Bar: Pa. 1974, Ga. 1975, D.C. 1990. Atty. Morgan, Lewis & Bockius, Phila., 1974-75, Hansell & Post, Atlanta, 1975-80; v.p. 1st Nat. Bank of Atlanta, 1980-86; sr. v.p., corp. sec., gen. counsel Sun Life Group of Am., Inc., Atlanta, 1986-89; v.p. Md. Nat. Bank, Balt., 1989-90; gen. counsel, sec. U.S. News & World Report, L.P., Applied Graphics Technologies, Atlantic Monthly Co., Washington, 1990—; bd. mgrs. U. Pa. Law Sch., 1982-85. Chmn. bd. Spl. Audiences, Inc., 1983-85, bd. dirs., 1975-89; vice chmn. Metro Atlanta United Way Campaign, 1986-87; chmn. bd. Atlanta Ballet, 1985-86, bd. dirs., 1975-89; mem. U. Rochester Trustee Coun., 1994—; bd. dirs. YMCA Balt., 1989-90; past bd. dirs. Metro YMCA, Sudden Infant Death Syndrome Inst., Atlanta Cmty. Food Bank; mem. Leadership Atlanta, 1988. Named Top 20 Women in Atlanta by Atlanta Bus. Chronicle, 1987, Top 40 Under 40 Atlanta Mag., 1984; teaching fellow Salzburg Inst., 1989. Mem. ABA (co-chair litigation sect. com. fed. legis. 1994-95, chmn. standing com. comm. on assn. comms. 1995-96, ho. of dels. 1980-84), Copyright Soc. USA (trustee 1996—), State Bar Ga. (sec., dir., chair com. young lawyer's sect. 1976-84, trustee client security fund 1985-89). Office: U S News & World Report 2400 N St NW Washington DC 20037-1153

LIONE, SUSAN GARRETT, sales executive; b. Boston, May 23, 1945; d. Charles Gerard and Josephine (Galgano) Garrett; m. Gerald Frederick Lione, Nov. 9, 1968; children: Mark Garrett, Christina Marie. BA in Econs., Immaculata Coll., 1966. Investment asst. Morgan Guaranty Trust, N.Y.C., 1966-69; portfolio mgr. Union Trust Co., Stamford, Conn., 1969-72; sales coord. Japan Air Lines, Hong Kong, 1977-84; mktg. coord. Hong Kong Tennis Patron Assn., 1982-84; ind. study on schs. Cen. Pk. Task Force, N.Y.C., 1990; sales assoc. Preferred Properties, New Canaan, Conn., 1991—; pres. Am. Women's Assn., Hong Kong, 1977-78; sec. New Canaan CARES, 1989-90, v.p., 1990-91, pres., 1991-93. Bd. dirs. United Way New Canaan, 1994—, bd. sec., 1996—, mem. allocations com., 1994—, chmn., 1995-96; mem. lay adv. bd. St. Aloysius Ch., New Canaan, 1994, 95—. Mem. AAUW. Office: Preferred Properties 170 Main St New Canaan CT 06840-5513

LIPINSKI, ANN MARIE, newspaper editor. Assoc. mng. editor for met. news. Chgo. Tribune, now dep. mng. editor, now mng. editor, 1995—. Recipient Pulitzer prize for series on politics and conflicts of interest Chgo. City Coun., 1988. Office: Chgo Tribune 435 N Michigan Ave Chicago IL 60611*

LIPINSKI, BARBARA JANINA, psychotherapist, psychology educator; b. Chgo., Feb. 29, 1956; d. Janek and Alicja (Brzozkiewicz) L.; m. Bernard Joseph Burns, Feb. 14, 1976 (div. 1985). B of Social Work, U. Ill., Chgo., 1978; MFCC, MA, U. Calif., Santa Barbara, 1982; PhD, U. So. Calif., 1992. Diplomate Am. Bd. Forensic Medicine; cert. tchr., Calif., psychology tchr., Calif.; cert. adminstr., non-pub. agent; lic. marriage, family and child therapist; bd. cert. forensic examiner. Police svc. officer Santa Barbara (Calif.) Police Dept., 1978-79; peace officer Airport Police, Santa Barbara, 1979-80; emergency comms. Univ. Police, Santa Barbara, 1980-82; facilitator, instr. Nat. Traffic Safety Inst., San Jose, Calif., 1981-87; assoc. dir. Community Health Task Force on Alcohol and Drug Abuse, Santa Barbara, 1982-86; instr. Santa Barbara C.C., 1987-88; patients' rights adv. Santa Barbara County Calif. Mental Health Adminstrn., 1986-89; pvt. practice psychotherapist Santa Barbara, 1985—; faculty mem., clin. coord. Pacifica Grad. Inst., Carpinteria, Calif., 1989—; intern clin. psychology L.A. County Sheriff's Dept., 1991-92, cons. Devereaux Found., Santa Barbara, 1993-95, Ctr. for Law Related Edn., Santa Barbara, 1986; cons., trainer Univ. Police Dept., Santa Barbara, 1982, 89. Vol. crisis work Nat. Assn. Children of Alcoholics, L.A., 1987; crisis intervention worker Women in Crisis Can Act, Chgo., 1975-76; vol. counselor Santa Barbara Child Sexual Assault Treatment Ctr.-PACT, Santa Barbara, 1981-82. Recipient Grad. Teaching assistanship U. So. Calif., 1990-92. Mem. APA, Am. Profl. Soc. on Abuse of Children, Am. Coll. Forensic Examiners, Internat. Critical Incident Stress Found., Calif. Assn. Marriage and Family Therapists, Internat. Soc. for Traumatic Stress Studies. Home: 301 Los Cabos Ln Ventura CA 93001 Office: Pacifica Grad Inst 249 Lambert Rd Carpinteria CA 93013-3019

LIPITZ, ELAINE KAPPEL, secondary education fine arts educator; b. N.Y.C., Oct. 5, 1924; d. Herman Kappel and Ceil (Friedson) Ferester; m. Elliott Alan Lipitz, Mar. 20, 1945; children: Linda Marsha Schreiber, Alice Lynn Lindholm. BFA, Pratt Coll., 1946; MA, Columbia U., 1955; MA in Adminstrn., St. Johns U., 1974. Fine art tchr. Art & Design High Sch., N.Y.C., 1946-47; fine art tchr. Jamaica High Sch., Queens, N.Y., 1949-70, fin art supr., 1970-75; coord. student affairs John Bowne High Sch., Queens, 1979-90, dir. community rels., 1990-93; interior design cons., 1950-80; jewelry designer, 1950-62. One woman shows include Gallery of Manhasset, 1968, Booth Meml. Art Gallery, Queens, 1989; exhibited in group shows at Ctr. Kew Gardens Hills, 1966, Bklyn. Mus. Art, 1969, Park Ave. Christian Ch., 1969, N.Y. Regional Exhbn. Painting and Sculpture, 1969, Newsday Fed. Art Show, 1969 (1st Prize), 70 (2d Place award), Norfolk Mus., 1970, Gallery North, Setauket, N.Y., 1994, 95, Art Guild of Coconut Creek, 1995, 96. Recipient Mayor's Honor award for Cmty. Svc., 1989, 1st prize sculpture Govt. Ctr. Art Guild of Coconut Creek, Fla., 1994. Home: 3 Princess Tree Ct Port Jefferson NY 11777-1742

LIPKIN, JANET L., artist, educator; b. Jersey City, July 24, 1948; d. Milton Sonny and Ruth (Jacobson) L.; m. Arthur Decker, June 10, 1969 (div. Aug. 1974); m. Barry Lee Shapiro, Apr. 16, 1981; children: Max, Ruby. BFA with honors, Pratt Inst., 1970. Artist, lectr. workshops Sheridan Coll. Tech., Caledon East, Can., 1970-71; artist-in-residence Peters Valley Craftsman, Layton, N.J., 1972-73, DeYoung Mus., San Francisco, 1974-75; textile designer Tami Sportswear, San Francisco, 1978-80; head artist designer Janet Lipkin Knits, Berkeley, Calif., 1982-92; art tchr. Berkeley Adult Sch., 1992—, Tehiyah Day Sch., El Cerrito, Calif., 1993—; art tchr. U. Minn., Duluth, summers 1992, 95, Mendocino (Calif.) Art Ctr., summers 1992-96; lectr., presenter workshops in field; creator curriculum for art program Berkeley-Richmond Jewish Cmty. Ctr., 1991; tchr. Oakes Children's Ctr., Francisco, 1975-76, Bessie Carmichael Sch., San Francisco, 1986; vis. artist Tehiyah Day Sch., 1991-92. Artist for book: Art to Wear, 1986; feature artist various publs.; one-woman shows at Julie Artisans Gallery, N.Y.C., 1973—, Mobilia, Cambridge, Mass., 1973—, OBIKO, San Francisco, 1973—, Palo Alto (Calif.) Cultural Ctr., 1979, Kurland/Summers, L.A., 1988—; exhibited in group shows at Oreg. Sch. Arts and Crafts, Portland, Oreg., 1984, Albright Knox Gallery, Buffalo, 1984, Fiberworks, Berkeley, 1984, Am. Crafts Mus., N.Y.C., 1983-85, 89, 90, 92, Janis Studio, Chgo., 1985, Internat. Gallery, San Diego, 1985, Calif. Crafts Mus., San Francisco, 1985, Cambridge Art Coun., Soc. Arts and Crafts, Boston, 1985, OBIKO, 1985, U.S. Info. Svc., 1984-86, Redding (Calif.) Mus. and Art Ctr., 1986, Cleve. Ctr. Contemporary Art, 1987, 92, Columbus (Ohio) Cultura Arts Ctr., 1987, Textile Coun. of Mpls. Inst. Art, 1987, Hibberd McGrath Gallery, Breckenridge, Colo., 1988, U. Calif.-Davis, 1988, N.C. State U., Raleigh, 1988, Visual Arts Mus., N.Y.C., 1989, Kurland/Summers Gallery, L.A., 1989, Hand and Spirit Gallery, Scottsdale, Ariz., 1990, Art Ginza Space, Tokyo, 1990, Gulbenkian Mus., Lisbon, Portugal, 1990, Columbus Cultura Arts Ctr., 1990, Crocker Mus. Art, Sacramento, 1991, Katie Gingrass Gallery, Milw., 1992, Sun Gallery, Hayward, Calif., 1992, Navy Pier, Chgo., 1992, Julie Artisans Gallery, N.Y.C., 1994, Textile Mus., Washington, 1996, others; appeared on TV documentary Artwear, The Body Adorned, 1991, People Art Talking. Fulbright Hays scholar, 1976; grantee San Francisco Pub. Funds, 1974, Artist in Schs., 1975. Mem. U. Calif. Berkeley Mus., Berkeley Art Ctr., Richmond Art Ctr., Oakland Mus., San Francisco Modern Mus., Mendocino Art Ctr. Democrat. Jewish. Home: 625 Sonoma St Richmond CA 94805

LIPMAN, CAROL KOCH, designer; b. Lincoln, Nebr., Mar. 23, 1960; d. Robert Carl and Gertrude Evelyn (Kornmuller) Koch; m. Ken Lipman, Dec. 16, 1989. B.S., Drexel U., 1982. Design asst. Sydney Carvin Milliken, N.Y.C., 1981, 82-83, Jones New York, N.Y.C., 1983-84; sales rep., designer Asymmetry, N.Y.C., 1984-85; designer Rayman/Ridless, N.Y.C., 1985-87; designer Echo Design Group, Albert Nipon Belts, 1987-88; designer Philip Sand Belts, 1988; designer, mgr. product devel. Karl Lagerfeld Bijoux div. Victoria Internat., 1988-89; designer The 1928 Jewelry Co., 1989-91; brand mgr. Hair Jewelry divsn. Crystals, 1991-92; brand mgr. Aurora R.S.V.P. Collection, 1993, vice pres. design, 1994; mgr. design dept. Leegin Creative Leather Products, Inc., 1994-95; sole proprieter, designer C.K. Lipman, 1995—. Avocations: art, art history, mosaic tile art, jewelry making.

LIPMAN, DEBORAH S., federal agency administrator; b. Pitts., Sept. 20, 1953; d. Lawrence and Helene Swartz; m. Andrew D. Lipman, Jan. 7, 1982; 2 children. BA, U. Pa., 1975; MA in City and Regional Planning, U. N.C., 1977. Transp. planner Dept. Transp., 1977; sr. cons. Ernst & Whinney, 1977-79; prof. staff subcom. on commerce, transp. and tourism House com. on energy and commerce, 1979-81; group leader nat. resources, sr. transp. analyst Sen. com. on budget, 1981-86; pres. Women's Transp. Seminar, 1986—. Recipient Mellon fellow, 1975-77. Office: Office of Govt Relations Wash Metro Area Transit Authority 600 5th St NW Rm 2a 14 Washington DC 20001-2651

LIPMAN, WYNONA M., state legislator; b. Ga.; children: Karyne Anne, William (dec.). BA, Talladega Coll.; MA, Atlanta U.; Ph.D., Columbia U.; LL.D. (hon.), Kean Coll., Bloomfield Coll. Former high sch. tchr., lectr. Seton Hall U., Assoc. prof. Essex County Coll.; mem. N.J. State Senate, 1971—, Human Svcs. com., budget and appropriation com., Women, Children Family Svcs com. chmn., Commn. on Sex Discrimination in the Statutes. Mem. NAACP, Nat. Coun. Negro Women, Women's Polit. Caucus, Essex County Urban League. Recipient Outstanding Woman award Assn. Women Bus Owners, 1983. Democrat. Office: NY State Senate 29th Legislative Dist Newark NJ 07102-4301 Also: NJ State Senate State Capitol Trenton NJ 08625*

LIPNER, ROBYN, legislative staff director. BA, Evergreen State Coll., 1978; MA, U. Calif., Berkeley, 1983. Fellow Women's Rsch. and Edn. Inst. Office of Rep. Patricia Schroeder, 1985-86, legis. asst., 1986-89; policy assoc. Am. Pub. Welfare Assn., 1989-90; mem. profl. staff Sen. Brock Adams, 1990-93; staff dir. Subcom. Aging Senate Labor & Human Resources Com., 1993-95; now Wash. rep. U. Calif., 1995; mem. health and human svcs. cluster Clinton-Gore Transition Team, 1992. Office: U Calif 1523 New Hampshire Ave NW Washington DC 20036*

LIPPIATT, SHANNA KAY, secondary geography educator; b. Ft. Hood, Tex., Oct. 14, 1965; d. Howard Denton and Marjorie Mildred (Hayton) Hudgeons; m. Michael James Lippiatt, Aug. 12, 1984; children: Dustin Lee, Patrick Vincent. BS in Secondary Edn., U. of Tex., 1987; MS in Earth Sci./Geography, East Tex. State U., 1995. Cert. tchr., Tex., composite social studies. Tchr. world geography and econs. Rockwall (Tex.) H.S., 1989-92; tchr. history Pittsburg (Tex.) H.S., 1992-93; tchr. world geography Chisum H.S., Paris, Tex., 1993—; tchr., cons. Nat. Geographic, Tex., 1992. Mem. adminstrv. bd. 1st United Meth. Ch., Paris, 1993-94. Mem. Nat. Coun. for Geographic Edn., Nat. Coun. for Social Studies, Am. Lung Assn., Mothers of Asthmatic Children, Tex. Coun. for Social Studies, Tex. Alliance for Geographic Edn. (presenter 1992—), Tex. Exe's Alumni Group. Republican. Home: 3210 Cleveland St Paris TX 75460-6404 Office: Chisum Ind Sch Dist 3250 S Church St Paris TX 75462-8909

LIPPIG, VIRGINIA ELLEN, tax accountant; b. Oak Park, Ill., Sept. 22, 1934; d. Walter C. and Irene Katherine Grottke; m. George Kenneth Lippig, Dec. 14, 1957; children: Larry, Ray, Sandra, Laura. Student Bus. and Fin., Valparaiso (Ind.) U., 1952-55, Northwestern U., Chgo., 1956-57. Acct. pvt. practice, Lombard, Ill.; v.p. Police Pension Bd., Lombard, Ill., 1976-84, v.p. Davea Bd. of Accountancy, Addison, Ill., 1976-84, Good Samaritan Hosp. Adv. Bd., Downers Grove, Ill., 1980-84. Treas. Lombard Parade Com., 1970-84, Lombard Hist. Soc. 1980-84; mem. rep. Lombard Hist. Commn., 1976-80; chmn. bd. fin. St. John, 1976-92. Named Woman of Yr., Lombard (Ill.) Svc. League, 1978; recipient cert. appreciation, YWCA, 1976-95, Day Care Action Coun., Evanston, DeKalb, 1976-93, Davea Bd. of Accountancy. State of Ill., Downers Grove, Skokie, Wheaton, 1984. Mem. Nat. Soc. Pub. Accts. (Ill. chpt.), Ind. Accts. Assn. of Ill. (sec. 1978-80), Lombard C. of C. (pres. 1978). Republican. Lutheran. Office: Lombard Fin Svc Inc 425 S Main St Lombard IL 60148

LIPPITT, ELIZABETH CHARLOTTE, writer; b. San Francisco; d. Sidney Grant and Stella L. Student Mills Coll., U. Calif.-Berkeley. Writer, performer own satirical monologues, nat. and polit. affairs for 85 newspapers including Muncie Star, St. Louis Globe-Dem., Washington Times, Utah Ind., Jackson News, State Dept. Watch. Singer debut album Songs From the Heart; contbr. articles to 85 newspapers including N.Y. Post, L.A. Examiner, Orlando Sentinel, Phoenix Rep., The Blue Book; author: 40 Years of American History in Published Letters 1952-1992. Mem. Commn. for Free China, Conservative Caucus, Jefferson Ednl. Assn., Presdl. Adv. Commn. Recipient Congress of Freedom award, 1959, 71-73. Mem. Amvets, Nat. Trust for Hist. Preservation, Am. Security Coun., Internat. Platform Assn., Am. Conservative Union, Nat. Antivivisection Soc., High Frontier, For Our Children, Childhelp U.S.A., Free Afghanistan Com., Humane Soc. U.S., Young Ams. for Freedom, Coun. for Inter.-Am. Security, Internat. Med. Corps, Assn. Vets for Animal Rights, Met. Club, Olympic Club. Home: 2414 Pacific Ave San Francisco CA 94115-1238

LIPPMAN, MURIEL MARIANNE, biomedical scientist; b. N.Y.C., Oct. 16, 1930; d. Louis George and Erna (Hirsch) L. BA, Syracuse U., 1951; MS, U. Pa., 1955; postgrad., Tufts U., 1965-66, Yale U., 1966-67; PhD, U. Chgo., 1970. Chmn. sci. dept. St. Agnes High Sch., Roshester, N.Y., 1957-59, Nazareth Acad., Rochester, 1959-63; asst. prof. biology, research dir. Nazareth Coll., Rochester, 1963-65; scientist Retina Found., Boston, 1965-66; vis. scientist Karolinska Inst., Stockholm, 1967; assoc. prof. biology Seton Hall U., South Orange, N.J., 1970-71; sr. staff fellow Nat. Cancer Inst., Bethesda, Md., 1971-76; sr. scientist Food and Drug Adminstrn. Bur. Med. Devices, Silver Spring, Md., 1976-77; sr. staff scientist Nat. Acad. Scis., Washington, 1977-78; dir. scientific planning and review Clement Assocs., Washington, 1978-79; pres. ERNACO, Inc., Silver Spring, 1979—; adj. prof. biology Am. U., Washington, 1981-83; vis. prof. Cook Coll., Tugers State U., N.J., 1985-86; adj. prof. anatomy Frederick (Md.) C.C., 1991, No. Va. C.C., Sterling, 1992-96; vis. prof. biology U. Md., 1996. Contbr. articles to profl. jours. Commr. Human Relations Commn. Montgomery County, Md., 1982-83. Recipient numerous grants and fellowships including Cancer Rsch. grantee Damon Runyon Found., 1964, Am. Cancer Soc. grantee, 1969-70, Biomedical rsch. grantee Evans Found., 1984-91, Nat. Heart, Lung and Blood Inst. NIH, 1986-87; U.S. Pub. Health fellow, 1965-66, KC Rsch. fellow, 1967, Danforth Teaching fellow U. Chgo., 1970; Teaching Excellence award Rochester Acad. Scis., 1963. Mem. N.Y. Acad. Scis., Soc. for Complex Carbohydrates, Sigma Xi. Home: 3740 Capulet Ter Silver Spring MD 20906-2644 Office: ERNACO Inc PO Box 6522 Silver Spring MD 20906-6522

LIPPMAN, SHARON ROCHELLE, cultural organization educator, artist, writer; b. N.Y.C., Apr. 9, 1950; d. Emanuel and Sara (Goldberg) L. Student, Mills Coll., 1968; BFA, New Sch. Social Rsch., 1970, CCNY, 1972; MA in Cinema Studies, NYU, 1976, postgrad., 1987. Cert. secondary tchr., N.Y. Instr., dir. Sara Sch. of Creative Art, Sayville, N.Y., 1976-85; founder, exec. dir., tchr. Art Without Walls, Inc., Sayville and N.Y.C., 1985—; exec. dir., curator Profl. Artist Network for Artists Internationally; organizer Profl. Artist Network for Nat./Internat. Artists, 1994. Author: Patterns, 1968, College Poetry Press Anthology, 1970; contbr. articles to profl. jours. Vol. Schneider Children's Hosp., New Hyde Park, N.Y., 1992, New Light-AIDS Patients, Smithtown, N.Y., 1993, Helen Keller Svcs. for the Blind, Hempstead, N.Y., 1993-94. Recipient Suffolk County New Inspiration award, 1990, Am. Artist Art Svc. award Am. Artists mag., 1993, Suffolk County Legis. proclamation, 1993, Newsday Leadership Vol. award Newsday newspaper, 1994, Nat. Women's Month award Town of Islip, 1996, Disting. Women's award Town of Islip, 1996. Mem. Orgn. Through Rehab. and Tng., Coll. Art Assn., Met. Mus. Art, Mus. Modern Art Univ. Film Assn. Office: Art Without Walls Inc PO Box 341 Sayville NY 11782-0341 also: PO Box 6344FDR Sta New York NY 10150-1902

LIPSCOMB, ANNA ROSE FEENY, small business owner, arts organizer, fundraiser b. Greensboro, N.C., Oct. 29, 1945; d. Nathan and Matilda (Carotenuto) L. Student langs., Alliance Francaise, Paris, 1967-68; BA in English and French summa cum laude, Queens Coll., 1977; diploma advanced Spanish, Forester Instituto Internacional, San Jose, Costa Rica, 1990; postgrad. Inst. Allende San Miguel de Allende, Mex., 1991. Reservations agt. Am. Airlines, St. Louis, 1968-69, ticket agt., 1969-71; coll. rep. CBS, Holt Rinehart Winston, Providence, 1977-79, sr. acquisitions editor Dryden Press, Chgo., 1979-81; owner, mgr. Historic Taos (N.Mex.) Inn, 1981-89, Southwest Moccasin and Drum, Taos; pres., co-owner Southwest Products, Ltd., 1991—; fundraiser Taos Arts Celebrations, 1989—; bd. dirs. N.Mex. Hotel and Motel Assn., 1986—; sem. leader Taos Women Together, 1989; founder All One Tribe Found., 1994, All One Tribe Fall Drumming Workshop Series, 1992—; mem. adv. bd. Drum Bus. Mag., 1996—. Editor: Intermediate Accounting, 1980; Business Law, 1981. Contbr. articles to profl. jours.; patentee in field. Bd. dirs., 1st v.p. Taos Arts Assn., 1982-85; founder, bd. dirs. Taos Spring Arts Celebration, 1983—; founder, dir. Meet-the-Artist Series, 1983—; bd. dirs. and co-founder Spring Arts N.Mex., 1986; founder Yuletide in Taos, 1988, A Taste of Taos, 1988; bd. dirs. Music from Angel Fire, 1988—; founding mem. Assn. Hist. Hotels, Boulder, 1983—; organizer Internat. Symposium on Arts, 1985; bd. dirs. Arts in Taos, 1983, Taoschool, Inc., 1985—; mem. adv. bd. Chamisa Mesa Ednl. Ctr., Taos, 1990—; founder All One Tribe Found., 1994; bd. dirs. Roadrunner Recyclers, 1995—. Recipient Outstanding English Student of Yr. award Queens Coll., 1977; named Single Outstanding Contbr. to the Arts in Taos, 1986. Mem. Millicent Rogers Mus. Assn., Taos Lodgers Assn. (mktg. task force 1989), Taos County C. of C. (1st v.p. 1988-89, bd. dirs. 1987-89, advt. com. 1986-89, chmn. nominating com. 1989), Internat. Platform Assn., Taos Women Bus. Owners, Phi Beta Kappa. Home: Talpa Rte Taos NM 87571 Office: PO Drawer N Taos NM 87571

LIPSCOMB, ROSALIND TARVER, artist; b. Spartanburg, S.C., Apr. 12, 1920; d. Virgil Wood and Rosalind (Tarver) L.; m. Richard Bethune Zimmerman, Sr., June 24, 1941 (div. Jan. 1969); children: Richard Bethune Jr., Rosalind; m. Alfred Alonzo Forrest, Jan. 25, 1971 (div. June 1972). BFA, U. Ga., 1940; MA, Auburn U., 1968. Tchr. English Ga. Southwestern Coll., Americus, 1965-75, Sumter County H.S., Americus, 1975-80; profl. artist Americus, 1980—. Portrait artist of Drs. of Sumter Regional Hosp., 1994—. Mem. Nat. Mus. Women in Arts (charter), Portrait Soc. Atlanta (charter), Jr. Svc. League. Republican. Episcopalian.

LIPSCOMB-BROWN, EDRA EVADEAN, retired childhood educator; b. Marion, Ill., Aug. 3, 1919; d. Edgar and Anna Josephine (Wiesbrodt) Turnage; m. July 5, 1939 (div. Sept. 1950); 1 son, H. Alan; m. Mark S. Brown, 1981. B.S., So. Ill. U., 1955; M.A., U. Mich., 1955; Ed.D., Ind. U., 1962; postgrad., U. Minn. Tchr. Benton (Ill.) Elem. Schs., 1939-54, DeKalb (Ill.) Consol. Schs., 1955-56; mem. faculty No. Ill. U., DeKalb, 1956-81; prof. elem. edn. No. Ill. U., 1967-81, chmn. elem. and childhood edn., 1978-81, ret., 1981; ednl. cons. to various schs., No. Ill.; mem. vis. accreditation com. Nat. Council Accreditation Tchr. Edn., Kent State U., 1974, U. Wis.-Stout, 1975; co-author, director numerous projects sponsored by U.S. Office Spl. Edn., 1979-81. Author: Lipscomb Teacher Attitude Scale; Contbr. articles to profl. jours. Research grantee No. Ill. U., 1965, 73; Research grantee State of Ill., 1972-73. Mem. Internat. Reading Assn., Internat. Assn. Supervision and Curriculum Devel., NEA, Ill. Edn. Assn., Assn. Higher Edn., Am. Ednl. Research Assn., Pi Lambda Theta. Democrat.

LIPSHUTZ, LAUREL SPRUNG, psychiatrist; b. Easton, Pa., Dec. 11, 1946; d. Joseph A. and Helen A. (Rochlin) S.; m. Robert M. Lipshutz, June 15, 1975; 1 child, Jonathan. BA, U. Pa., 1968; MD, Albany Med. Coll. of Union U., 1972. Diplomate Am. Bd. Psychiatry and Neurology. Resident in psychiatry Johns Hopkins Hosp., Balt., 1972-75; unit chief psychiatric inpatient unit Phila. Gen. Hosp., 1975-77; dir. psychiatric inpatient svc. Pa. Hosp., Phila., 1977-96; assoc. dir. residency tng. Inst. of Pa. Hosp., Phila., 1983-96; coord. psychiatric clerkship for U. Pa. med. students Pa. Hosp., Phila., 1982-95; sr. examiner Am. Bd. Psychiatry and Neurology, 1979—; sr. attending psychiatrist Inst. Pa. Hosp., Phila., 1989—, psychiatrist, 1984—; clin. assoc. prof. psychiatry U. Pa. Sch. Medicine, Phila., 1987-95, Thomas Jefferson Med. Coll., Phila. 1994—. Mem. Am. Psychiatric Assn., Pa. Psychiatric Assn. (mem. com. on women), Phila. Psychiatry Soc., Assn. Acad. Psychiatry (region III Excellence in Teaching award 1995). Office: 210 W Washington Sq 7th Fl Philadelphia PA 19106

LIPSKY, LINDA ETHEL, business executive; b. Bklyn., June 2, 1939; d. Irving Julius and Florence (Stern) Ellman; m. Warren Lipsky, June 12, 1960 (div. Sept. 1968); 1 child, Phillip Bruce; m. Jerome Friedman, Jan. 17, 1988. BA in Psychology, Hofstra U., 1960; MPS in Health Care Adminstrn., Long Island U., 1979. Child welfare social worker Nassau County Dept. Social Service, N.Y., 1960-64; adminstr. La Guardia Med. Group of Health Ins. Plan of Greater N.Y., Queens, 1969-72; cons. Neighborhood Service Ctr., Bronx, N.Y., 1973-78; dir. ODA Health Ctr., Bklyn., 1978-82; pres. Millin Assocs., Inc., Nassau, N.Y., 1982—. Mem. Health Care Fin. Mgmt. Assn., Nat. Assn. Community Health Ctrs., Nat. Assn. Female Execs., Cmty. Health Ctr. Assoc. of N.Y., Hofstra U. Alumni Assn. (mem. senate 1984—, chairperson membership com. 1985—), Pi Alpha Alpha. Republican. Jewish. Avocations: cooking, writing, reading. Office: Millin Assocs Inc 521 Chestnut St Cedarhurst NY 11516-2223

LIPSON, ROBERTA LYNN, marketing professional, entrepreneur; b. N.Y.C., June 17, 1955; d. Morris and Dorothy (Newman) L. BA, Brandeis U., 1976; MBA, Columbia U., N.Y.C., 1977. Mktg. trainee Schering Plough Corp., Kennilworth, N.J., 1977, product promotion mgr., 1978-79; mktg. rep. Sobin Chems., Boston, 1979-81; pres. U.S.-China Indsl. Exch. Inc., N.Y.C., 1981—, also chmn. bd. dirs. Mem. Am. C. of C. (Beijing), Am. Club (Beijing). Home: PO Box 9065, Xiao Paifang Hutong #7, Beijing 100010, Republic of China*

LIPSZYC, ANNIE, French and English language educator; b. Paris, Feb. 1, 1950; d. Abraham and Rachelle (Fajn) L. BA, U. Ill., 1972; postgrad., NE Ill. U. Cert. Tchr. Ill. Tchr. Bd. of Edn., Chgo., 1974; tutor Albany Park Cmty. Ctr., Chgo. 1995. Ward worker Dem. Org. 44th Ward, Chgo. 1983. Mem. Am. Fed. of Tchrs., ITBE BE.

LIPTAK, IRENE FRANCES, retired business executive; b. Clifton, N.J., Feb. 22, 1926; d. George J. and Anna J. (Strelec) L. Student, U. Newark, 1944-45; BS, Rutgers U., 1950, MBA, 1955, EdM, 1964; postgrad., Montclair State Coll., 1960-61, Fairleigh Dickinson U., 1963-64. Exec. sec., adminstrv. asst. to pres. and chmn. bd. Botany Mills, Inc., Passaic, N.J., 1942-53; treas., sec. Rowland-Johnson Co., Clifton, 1953-80; exec. sec. to chief exec. officer Edison Parking Corp., Newark, 1983; bldg. adminstr. Hippodrome Bldg., N.Y.C., 1984; office mgr. Decor Structure, Inc., Carlstadt, N.J., 1984-85. Editor: Ch. News, 1958-68. Mem. conf. planning com. N.J. Commn. on Women, 1972; treas. Slovak Nat. Cath. Cathedral, Passaic, 1976-77; sec., dir., trustee Charles Jr. and Dorothy Johnson Found., 1957-80. Mem. AAUW (life, corr. sec. Nutley br. 1972-74, treas. 1974-76, pres. 1979-81, dir. N.J. divsn. 1975-76), Grad. Sch. Edn. Alumni Assn. Rutgers, Rutgers U. Coll. Honor Soc. (life), Rutgers U. Coll. Alumni Assn. (life, mem. ctrl. coun. 1971-74, v.p. Paterson regional coun. 1986-94), Am. Soc. Notaries (life), Am. Friends Arts, S.W. Bergen Stroke and Disabled Club (founder, pres. 1987-88), Phi Chi Theta (chmn. nat. conv. 1972). Republican. Home: 106 Ridge Rd Rutherford NJ 07070-2422

LIPTON, AMY N., lawyer; b. Flushing, N.Y., July 9, 1954; d. Mortimer J. and Lucille (Goldberg) Natkins; m. Richard B. Lipton; children: Lianna, Justin. BA, Brandeis U., 1976; JD, Boston U., 1979. Bar: Ill. 1979, N.Y. 1981. Assoc. Baker & McKenzie, Chgo. and N.Y., 1979-87; gen. counsel, sr. v.p. CUC Internat., Inc., Stamford, Conn., 1987—. Trustee, dir. Am. Craft Mus., N.Y.C., 1994-96. Office: CUC International Inc 707 Summer St Stamford CT 06901-1026

LIPTON, BARBARA, museum director, curator; b. Newark, N.J.; m. Milton Lipton; children: Joshua, Sara, Beth. BA, U. Iowa; MA, U. Mich.; MLS, Rutgers U. Library dir. Newark Mus., 1970-75, spl. projects cons., 1975-82; asst. dir. Castle Gallery Coll. of New Rochelle, N.Y., 1982-83; guest curator Dept. Indian and No. Officers, Ottawa, Ont., Can., 1983-85; dir. Jacques Marchais Mus. Tibetan Art, S.I., N.Y., 1985—; tchr., lectr. various schs. and mus. including Mus. Natural History, Smithsonian Inst., Washington, 1976—; former guest curator many mus. Author: (catalogs) Survival Art Life of the Alaskian Eskimo, 1976, Arctic Vision, 1984, Treasures of Tibetan Art: Collections of the Jacques Marchais Museum of Tibetan Art, 1996; (bibliography) Westerners in Tibet, 1972; exec. producer, writer documentary film: Village of No River, 1981. Grantee NEH, 1976, 79, 80, 87, 91. Mem. Am. Assn. Museums. Office: Jacques Marchais Mus Tibetan Art PO Box 060198 Staten Island NY 10306

LIPTON, BRONNA JANE, marketing communications executive; b. Newark, May 10, 1951; d. Julius and Arlene (Davis) L.; m. Sheldon Robert Lipton, Sept. 23, 1984. BA in Spanish, Northwestern U., 1973. Tchr. Spanish Livingston (N.J.) High Sch., 1973-78; profl. dancer Broadway theater, film, TV, N.Y.C., 1978-82; v.p., mgr. Hispanic mktg. svcs. Burson-Marsteller Pub. Rels., N.Y.C., 1982-89; exec. v.p. Lipton Communications Group, Inc., N.Y.C., 1989—; mem. minority initiatives task force Am. Diabetes Assn., Alexandria, Va., 1987-90, mem. pub. rels. com., 1990-91, mem. visibility and image task force, 1991-92, bd. dirs. N.Y. Downstate affiliate, chmn. visibility and image com., 1992-93. Mem. rev. panel Hispanic Designers, Inc. Recipient Pinnacle award Am. Women in Radio and TV (N.Y. Chpt.), 1984, Value Added awards Burson-Marsteller, N.Y.C., 1982, 83, 84. Mem. Hispanic Pub. Rels. Assn. Home: 1402 Chapel Hill Rd Mountainside NJ 07092-1405

LIPTON, LEAH, art historian, educator, museum curator; b. Kearny, N.J., Mar. 22, 1928; d. Abraham and Rose (Berman) Shneyer; m. Herbert Lipton, Sep. 19, 1951 (dec. 1979); children: David, Ivan, Rachel. BA, Douglass

Coll. Rutgers U., New Brunswick, N.J., 1949; MA, Harvard U., Cambridge, Mass., 1950; postgrad., Harvard U., 1970-73, Wellesley Coll., 1970-73. Photo, library researcher Mus. Fine Arts, Boston, 1950-53, lectr., division edn., 1965-70; instr. Boston Coll., 1968-69; faculty, full prof. Framingham State Coll., Mass., 1969-94; ret., 1994; interim dir. Danforth Mus. Art, 1994-95; mem. bd. trustees Danforth Mus. Art, Framingham Mass., 1975—; curator Am. art Danforth Mus. Art, Framingham Mass., 1994—; chair exhibitions Com.; Collections Com. Danforth Mus., Framingham Mass., 1988, guest curator Nat. Portrait, Wash., 1985. Author: Book, 1985, Exhibition Catalogues, 1988-94; contbr. articles to profl. jours., 1981—. Co-Founder Danforth Mus. Art., Mass. 1973-75. Recipient Distinguished Service award Framingham State Coll., Mass. 1978, 87. Mem. Coll. Art Assn., Am. Studies Assn. Office: Danforth Mus of Art 123 Union Ave Framingham MA 01701-8223

LIPTON, NINA ANNE, marketing executive; b. N.Y.C., Oct. 6, 1959; d. Robert and Rita Kay (Wolfman) L. BA in Econs., Wellesley Coll., 1981; postgrad., London Sch. Econs., 1981-82. Rsch. asst. Nat. Econ. Rsch. Assocs., White Plains, N.Y., 1983-84; cons. A.T. Hudson and Co., Paramus, N.J., 1984; asst. economist Dean Witter Reynolds, N.Y.C., 1984-89; dir. market rsch. Platinum Guild Internat., N.Y.C., 1989-94; pres. Alternative Med. Ctrs., Inc., Charlotte, N.C., 1995—; exec. dir. Summit Med. Group, Conn., Ga., Ala., Mich., 1995—; bd. dirs. RRI Industries, Boca Raton, Fla., Aztec Mgmt. Co. Writer This Week in Platinum weekly, 1989-94; contbr. articles to profl. jours. Recruiter, fundraiser, reunion com. chair Wellesley (Mass.) Coll. Alumnae Assn.,1982—. Mem. Internat. Precious Metals Inst., Nat. Assn. Bus. Economists, Futures Industry Assn.

LISA, ISABELLE O'NEILL, law firm administrator, mergers and acquisitions executive; b. Phila., Mar. 12, 1934; d. Thomas Daniel and Margaret Marie (Hayes) O'Neill; m. Donald Julius Lisa, June 15, 1957; children: Richard Allan, Steven Gregory. Student, Harper Community Coll., Rolling Meadows, Ill., 1976, Scottsdale Community Coll., 1980, Ariz. State U., 1981-82. Cost control clk. Curtis Pub. Co., Phila., 1952-56; sec. United Ins. Co., Annapolis, Md., 1956-57; firm adminstr., legal sec. Law Offices Donald J. Lisa, Bloomingdale, Ill., 1987; legal sec. Lisa & Kubida, P.C., Phoenix, 1987-88, firm adminstr., 1987-89; firm adminstr. Lisa & Assocs., Phoenix, 1989-90, Lisa & Lisa, Phoenix, 1990-91, Lisa & Assocs., Scottsdale, Ariz., 1991-95, Law Offices of Donald J. Lisa, Scottsdale, 1995—; Law Offices of Donald J. Lisa, 1995—; v.p. adminstrn. Lisa & Co., Scottsdale, 1987-91, 1991—. Den mother Cub Scouts Am., Millburn, N.J., 1965; founder, pres. Pro-Tem Rutgers U. Law Wives Assn., 1962-63; bd. advisors Am. Inst., Phoenix, 1991—. Mem. NAFE, Maricopa County Bar Assn. (legal adminstrs. sect. 1992-95), Internat. Platform Assn., Rotary. Republican. Roman Catholic. Home and Office: 8661 E Carol Way Scottsdale AZ 85260

LISANDRELLI, ELAINE SLIVINSKI, secondary education educator; b. Pittston, Pa., July 11, 1951; d. Leo Joseph and Gabriella Alexandra (Sharek) Slivinski; m. Carl A. Lisandrelli, June 20, 1980. BA, Marywood Coll., Scranton, Pa., 1973, MS, 1976. Cert. secondary tchr. English and counselor, Pa. Tchr. English, North Pocono Mid. Sch., Moscow, Pa., 1973—; part-time instr. Marywood Coll., 1986—; ednl. cons., Pa., 1988--93. Author: Maya Angelou: More Than a Poet, 1996; contbr. articles to lit. mags. Mem. Nat. Coun. Tchrs. English, Soc. Children's Book Writers and Illustrators, Pa. Edn., Assn., Kosciuszko Found., Polish Arts and Cultural Found. Home: 3501 Lawrence Ave Moosic PA 18507 Office: North Pocono Mid Sch Church St Moscow PA 18507

LISANTI, DIANE, religious studies educator; b. Mineola, N.Y., Mar. 28, 1952; d. Gerald Thomas and Florence Ann Lisanti. BSEE, Adelphi U., 1974; MA in Religions, Fordham U., 1978; MA in Counseling, Gallaudet U., 1995. Cert. N-6th grade tchr., N.Y. Educator, tchr. St. Catharine Acad., Bronx, 1978-82, 86-93; pastorial assoc. John XXIII Newman Ctr., Plattsburgh, N.Y., 1982-86; instr. Archdiocese of N.Y., 1988-93; info. asst. Nat. Info. Ctr. on Deafness, Washington, 1993-95; diocesan dir. of campus min. Diocese of Ogdensburg, N.Y., 1984-86. Contbr. articles to profl. jours. corr. sec. Plattsburgh (N.Y.) Inter Faith Coun., 1983-85, musician St. Benedict's Parish, Bronx, 1988-93, vol. Silver Spring Takoma Park (Md.) Food Co-op, 1993-94. Mem. Am. Counseling Assn. Democrat. Roman Catholic.

LISBOA-FARROW, ELIZABETH OLIVER, public and government relations consultant; b. N.Y.C., Nov. 25, 1947; d. Eleuterio and Esperanza Oliver; student pvt. schs., N.Y.C.; m. Jeffrey Lloyd Farrow, Dec. 31, 1980; 1 child, Hamilton Oliver Farrow; 1 stepchild, Maximillian Robbins Farrow. With Harold Rand & Co. and various other public rels. firms, N.Y.C., 1966-75; dir. pub. rels. N.Y. Playboy Club and Playboy Clubs Internat., 1975-79; pres., CEO Lisboa Assocs., Inc., N.Y.C., 1979—; founder, pres. Lisboa Prodns., Inc., Washington, 1994—; counselor Am. Woman's Devel. Corp. Sec. Nat. Acad. Concert and Cabaret Arts; mem. nat. adv. coun. SBA, 1980-81, apptd., 1994—; exec. dir. Variety Club of Greater Washington, Inc., 1985-90, Children's Charity; bd. dirs. Variety Myoelectric Limb Bank Found., 1990-91; trustee Hispanic Bus. Scholarship Fund, 1995—; vice chairperson bd. trustees Southea. U., 1996—; mem. adv. bd. Indsl. Bank, N.A., 1996; active Women and Heart Disease Task Force. Recipient Disting. award of Excellence SBA, 1992, Women Bus. Enterprise award U.S. Dept. Transp. Nat. Hwy. Transp. Safety Adminstrn., 1994, Excellence in Entrepreneurship award Dialogue on Diversity, Inc., 1995; named Pub. Rels. Woman of Yr., Women in Pub. Rels., Hispanic Bus. Woman of Yr., Nat. Hispanic Bus. Coun., 1996.. Mem. SAG, NATAS, U.S. Hispanic C. of C. (Blue Chip Enterprise award 1993, Hispanic Bus. Woman of Yr. 1996), Small Bus. Advisory Coun., U.S. C. of C., Advt. Coun., Am. Heart Assn., Hispanic Bus. and Profl. Women's Assn., Ibero-Am. C. of C. (bd. dirs. 1993—, v.p. 1995—, Small Bus. award 1993), City Club Washington. Office: 1317 F St NW Washington DC 20004-1105

LISENBY, DORRECE EDENFIELD, realtor; b. Sneads, Fla., Dec. 2, 1942; d. Neal McLendon and Linnie (McCroan) Edenfield; m. Wallace Lamar Lisenby, Nov. 18, 1961; children: Pamela Ann, Wallace Neal. BS in Tech. Bus. magna cum laude, Athens (Ala.) State Coll., 1991. Stenographer State of Fla., Tallahassee and Miami, Fla., 1960-62, Gulf Oil Corp., Coral Gables, Fla., 1962-64, Gulf Power Co., Pensacola, Fla., 1965-68; loan svc. asst. First Fed. Savs. and Loan Assn., Greenville, S.C., 1969-70; various real estate positions Greenville, 1978-85; adminstrv. asst. Charter Retreat Hosp., Decatur, Ala., 1986-91; realtor assoc. Ferrell Realty Plus, Inc., Tallahassee, Fla., 1995—. Mem. Am. Legion (Citizenship award 1957), Tallahassee Symphony Soc., Avondale Forest Cmty. Club (pres. Taylors, S.C. chpt. 1969), Taylor's Garden Club (pres. Taylor's chpt. 1975-76), P.E.O. Sisterhood, Killearn Ladies Club. Republican. Baptist. Home: 2925 Shamrock St S Tallahassee FL 32308-3226

LISH, JENNIFER D., psychologist; b. Tucson, Ariz., Oct. 5, 1957; d. Gordon Jay and Frances (Fokes) L.; m. Frederic Henry Schwartz, Oct. 3, 1993. AB, Brown U., 1979; PhD, NYU, 1986. Lic. psychologist, N.Y., Pa. Postdoctoral fellow Columbia U., 1986-88, asst. prof., 1988-91; asst. prof. U. Pa., Phila., 1991-93, Med. Coll. of Pa. and Hahnemann U., 1993—; rsch. scientist Compass Info. Svcs., King of Prussia, Pa., 1995—. Contbr. articles to profl. jours. Recipient Lebensohn award Am. Assn. Gen. Hosp. Psychiatrists, 1994, Best Poster award Acad. Psychosomatic Medicine, 1994. Mem. Am. Psychol. Assn., Am. Psychol. Soc. Democrat. Jewish. Home: 154 Weatherstone Dr Worcester MA 01640 Office: Compass Info Svcs 1060 1st Ave King Of Prussia PA 19406

LISI, MARY M., federal judge. BA, U. R.I., 1972; JD, Temple U., 1977. Tchr. history Prout Meml. High Sch., Wakefield, R.I., 1972-73; hall dir. U. R.I., 1973-74; law clerk to Prof. Jerome Sloan Temple U., Phila., 1975-76; law clerk U.S. Atty., Providence, R.I., 1976, Phila., 1976-77; asst. pub. defender R.I. Office Pub. Defender, 1977-81; asst. child advocate Office Child Advocate, 1981-82; also. pvt. practice atty. Providence, 1981-82; dir. office ct. appointed spl. advocate R.I. Family Ct., 1982-87; dep. disciplinary counsel office disciplinary counsel R.I. Supreme Ct., 1988-90, chief disciplinary counsel, 1990-94; mem. Select Com. to Investigate Failure of R.I. Share and Deposit Indemnity Corp., 1991-92. Recipient Providence 350 award, 1986, Meritorious Svc. to Children of Am. award, 1987. Office: Fed Bldg and US Courthouse 1 Exchange Ter Rm 113 Providence RI 02903-1720*

LISK, MARTHA ANN, vocational rehabilitation counselor; b. Manchester, Conn., Jan. 20, 1956; d. Burton Roy and Ruth Elizabeth (Coe) L. BA, Colo. State U., 1978; MA, U. No. Colo., 1983. Rehab. counselor State of Colo. Rehab. Ins. Svcs. for Employment, Loveland, 1984-86; owner, mgr. Pro-Three One Wear, Loveland, 1986-89; coord. employment and tng. Epilepsy Found. Am., Denver, 1989-93; vocat. rehab. counselor II, Kans. Rehab. Svcs., Garden City, 1993—; summer youth counselor Colo. Job Svc., Aurora, 1984; adv. Colo. Rehab. Svcs. Adv. Bd., Denver, 1991-93; pres. Job Developers Network, Denver, 1992. Vol. Hist. Ft. Hays, Kans., 1994—. Mem. Nat. Rehab. Assn., Nat. Trust for Hist. Preservation, Finney County Hist. Soc. Home: 2103 Commanche Dr Garden City KS 67846-3827

LISK, PAMELA KONIECZKA, lawyer; b. Chgo., Oct. 8, 1959; m. Thomas Joseph Lisk; 1 child, Sarah. BA, Northwestern U., 1980; M of Pub. Policy, JD, Harvard U., 1984. Staff atty. SEC, Washington, 1984-86; assoc. Lord, Bissell & Brook, Chgo., 1986-89; sr. atty. Sundstrand Corp., Rockford, Ill., 1989—. Mem. Ill. Bar Assn., Phi Beta Kappa.

LISKA, MARGARET NAYLOR, retired small business owner; b. Callaway, Nebr., July 27, 1922; d. James Corban and Ruth Frances (Snodgrass) Naylor; m. Arthur Joseph Liska, Apr. 5, 1946; children: Jo, A. James. BS, U. Denver, 1944. Auditor Conn. Gen. Life Ins., Hartford, 1944-45; mgr. Conn. Gen. Life Ins., Denver, 1945-46; co-owner Broadview (Ill.) Hardware, 1946-60, Ben Franklin Store, Batavia, Ill., 1962-93; pres. Liska Enterprises, Inc., Batavia, 1962-93; owner Wedding Wisdom, Batavia, 1982-93. Mem. AAUW (Rsch. and Project Endowment namee 1986), AARP, PEO (pres.), Am. Needlework Guild, Embroiders Guild of Am., St. Charles Country Club, Order of Eastern Star. Home: 310 Woodridge Cir Apt B South Elgin IL 60177-2366

LISNEK, MARGARET DEBBELER, artist, educator; b. Covington, Ky., Sept. 26, 1940; d. Aloysius Frank and Mary Elizabeth (Haubold) Debbeler; m. Schiller William Lisnek, June 26, 1966 (dec. May 1995); 1 child, Kimberly Anne. AA with honors, Mt. San Antonio Coll., 1985; BA in Art with honors, Calif. State U., Fullerton, 1991. Cert. substitute tchr. Freelance artist, 1985—; tchr. art Rorimer Elem. Sch., La Puente, Calif., 1992-93, City of Walnut (Calif.) Recreation Svcs., 1992—, Christ Luth. Sch., West Covina, Calif., 1993—, Los Molinos Elem. Sch., Hacienda Heights, Calif., 1993—, Los Altos Elem. Sch., Hacienda Heights, 1993—; mem. Getty Inst. Insvc. Resource Team. One-woman shows include Calif. State U., Fullerton, 1990; exhibited in group shows. Sec., treas., social chair PTA, Los Altos Elem. Sch., Hacienda Heights, 1972-73; membership and social chair Friends of Libr., Hacienda Heights, 1974-75; active Nat. Mus. Women in the Arts, L.A. County Art Mus., Norton Simon Mus., Pasadena, Calif. Mem. Calif. Art Edn. Assn.

LISS, MARCIA, psychologist; b. Yonkers, N.Y., Jan. 27, 1961; d. Ernest and Pauline (Jacobs) L.; m. John Nicholas O'del. BA in History & Psychology, SUNY, Stony Brook, 1984; EdM in Counseling and Ednl. Psychology, Harvard Univ., 1986; PhD in Counseling Psychology, SUNY, Buffalo, 1991. Lic. psychologist. Postdoctoral fellow Rehabilitation Inst. Mich., Detroit, 1991-92; staff psychologist Nat. Rehabilitation Hosp., Wash., 1992—. Contbr. articles to profl. jours. Mem. Am. Psychological Assn., Phi Alpha Theta. Home: 14440 Parkvale Rd # 5 Rockville MD 20853 Office: Nat Rehabilitation Hosp 102 Irving St NW Washington DC 20010

LISSAKERS, KARIN MARGARETA, federal agency administrator; b. Aug. 16, 1944; married; 2 children. BA in Internat. Affairs, Ohio State U., 1967; MA in Internat. Affairs, Johns Hopkins U., 1969. Mem. staff com. fgn. rels. U.S. Senate, Washington, 1972-78, mem. staff subcom. multinat. corps., 1972, staff dir. subcom. fgn. econ. policy, 1977; dep. dir. econ. policy planning staff U.S. Dept. State, Washington, 1978-80; sr. assoc. Carnegie Endowment for Internat. Peace, N.Y.C., 1981-83; lectr. internat. banking, dir. internat. bus. and banking program Sch. Internat. Pub. Affairs Columbia U., N.Y.C., 1985-93; U.S. exec. dir. Internat. Monetary Fund, Washington, 1993—. Author: Banks, Borrowers and the Establishment, 1991; contbr. articles to profl. jours. Office: Internat Monetary Fund 700 19th St NW Rm 13-320 Washington DC 20431-0001

LISSENDEN, CAROLKAY, pediatrician; b. Newark, Aug. 22, 1937; d. George Cyrus Sr. and Irene Elizabeth (Hempel) L.; m. Bart Albert Barré, June 13, 1964; children: Lisa Kim Barré-Quick, Bart Christopher Barré. BA, U. Pa., 1959; MD, Med. Coll. Pa., 1964. Pediat. intern St. Luke's Hosp., N.Y.C., 1964-65; pediat. resident Columbia-Presbyn. Hosp., N.Y.C., 1965-67; pvt. practice Mountainside, N.J., 1967—. Fellow Am. Acad. Pediats.; mem. AMA, N.J. Med. Assn., Union County Med. Assn. Republican. Presbyterian. Home and Office: 135 Wild Hedge Ln Mountainside NJ 07092-2520

LISSMAN, JUDY ANN, primary school educator; b. Bayard, Nebr., Oct. 22, 1942; d. Harry B. and Anne (Schwartz) Bowers; children: Kathy Marie, Paul Lorn. AA, Ea. Wyo. Coll., 1962; BA, U. Wyo., 1964, MEd, 1989. Cert. elem. tchr., Wyo. Tchr. elem. grades, learning disabilities, libr. Southeast Elem. Sch., Goshen County Sch. Dist., Huntley, Wyo., 1964—. Named Milken Nat. Educator for Wyo., Calif. Milken Found., 1994-95, Outstanding Tchr., Goshen County Edn. Assn., 1991. Mem. Wyo. Reading Coun. (pres. 1995—), Order Ea. Star (Star Point 1991), Delta Kappa Gamma, Beta Sigma Phi. Presbyterian. Home: 231 Willow Ct Torrington WY 82240-3702 Office: SE Elem Sch 1 Lacey St Yoder WY 82244

LIST, ILKA KATHERINE, art educator, sculptor, writer, psychotherapist; b. Orange, N.J., Nov. 22, 1935; d. Albert and Phyllis Howells (Carrington) L; children: Lee Maidoff, Jonah Maidoff, Natasha Maidoff. BS, U. Maine, Orono, 1976; MFA, SUNY, 1978; postgrad., NYU, 1987—. Cert. art tchr., N.Y. Freelance artist New Paltz, N.Y., 1978-87; adj. prof. SUNY, New Paltz, 1992-94; pvt. sculpture tchr., also sculpture tchr. Woodstock Sch. of Art, 1993-96; dir. edn. The Mohonk Preserve, New Paltz, 1987-95. Author/illustrator: Let's Explore the Shore, 1962, Grandma's Beach Surprise, 1975, Questions and Answers about Seashore Life (Children's Book Coun. award) 1976, A Walk in the Forest (Children's Book Coun., Nat. Sci. Tchrs. Assn. Joint Com. for best books) 1976; illustrator: (coloring/activity book) What's in the Woods, 1995; exhibited in group shows at Nat. Arts Club (Grand Ctrl. Galleries award, 1983), Pen and Brush Women Sculptors (Roman Bronze Foundry award, 1983); executed sculpted and painted commns., also 3 murals at River Run Elderly Housing, New Haven, Conn. Recipient Educator of Yr. award Outdoor Environ. Edn. Assn., 1995; resident fellowships to Yaddo, Saratoga Springs, N.Y., 1972, 78. Mem. Nat. Art Edn. Assn., Amnesty Internat., N.Y. State Outdoor Edn. Assn. Home: 427 Springtown Rd New Paltz NY 12561 Office: 77 Cornell St Kingston NY 12561

LIST, KAREN K., communications educator; b. Burlington, Iowa, Apr. 3, 1948; d. Herman H. and Jeri I. (Hellenthal) Kuntz; m. Jacob P. List, May 22, 1976; children: Emily Caroline, Madeleine Elizabeth. BJ, U. Mo., 1970; MA in Journalism, Pa. State U., 1974, MA in History, 1975; PhD in Comm., U. Wis., 1980. Reporter Metro-East Jour., East St. Louis, Ill., 1970-72; instr. Pa. State U., State College, 1975-77; asst. prof. U. R.I., Kingston, 1980-81; assoc. prof. U. Mo., Columbia, 1981-88; prof. U. Mass., Amherst, 1988—; faculty assoc. U. Mass. Ctr. for Teaching, 1993-95. Author: (with others) Significance of Media in American History, 1993; contbg. editor Journalism History, 1981—; mem. editl. bd. Am. Journalism, Jour. Mass Media Ethics, 1984—; contbr. articles to profl. jours. Recipient Disting. Teaching award U. Mass., 1993; Lilly Teaching fellow U. Mass., 1990. Mem. Assn. Edn. in Journalism and Mass Comm. (history and law divsns., Covert Rsch. award 1995), U. Mo. Mystical Seven Honorary, U. Mo. QEBH Honor Soc., Kappa Tau Alpha (nat. pres.). Democrat. Home: 1671 S East St Amherst MA 01002 Office: U Mass 108 Bartlett Amherst MA 01003

LISTON, MARY FRANCES, retired nursing educator; b. N.Y.C., Dec. 17, 1920; d. Michael Joseph and Ellen Theresa (Shaughnessy) L. BS, Coll. Mt. St. Vincent, 1944; MS, Catholic U. Am., 1945; EdD, Columbia, 1962; HHD (hon.), Allentown Coll., 1987. Dir. psychiat. nursing and edn. Nat. League for Nursing, N.Y.C., 1958-66; prof. Sch. Nursing, Cath. U. Am., Washington, 1966-78; dean Sch. Nursing, Cath. U. Am., 1966-73; prof. Marywood Coll., 1984-87; spl. assignment Imperial Med. Center, Tehran, Iran, 1975-78; dep. dir. for program affairs Nat. League for Nursing, N.Y.C., 1978-84. Mem. Sigma Theta Tau. Home: 182 Garth Rd Scarsdale NY 10583-3863

LISTROM, LINDA L., lawyer; b. Topeka, Kans., Mar. 17, 1952. BA magna cum laude, U. Houston, 1974; JD, Harvard U., 1977. Bar: Ill. 1977. Ptnr. Jenner & Block, Chgo. Bd. dirs. Cook County Court Watching Project, Inc., 1983-92. Mem. ABA. Office: Jenner & Block 1 E Ibm Plz Chicago IL 60611*

LITCHFIELD, JEAN ANNE, nurse; b. Gary, Ind., Oct. 6, 1942; d. Donald Kleine and Helen Louise (Sweet) Eller; m. Norman E. Stone, Dec. 27, 1965 (div. Aug. 1973); children: Diana, David, Julie; m. Frank Litchfield, Jan. 26, 1974. Lic. practical nurse, Ind. U. Vocat. Tech. Coll., 1973; AS in Biology, Richland C.C., 1991; BSN, Millikin U., 1993; MSN, Ind. State U., 1995. RN, Ind., Ill. Nurse asst. St. Anthony Hosp., Terre Haute, Ind., 1960-73, nurse, 1973-74; charge nurse psychiatric ward St. Mary's Hosp., Decatur, Ill., 1974—; instr. allied nursing and health divsn. Richland C.C., Decatur, 1995—; mem. student welfare com. Millikin U., Decatur, 1991-92. Recipient 1st place art award 1984, 85, 86, 2d place art award 1984, 85, 2d place County Fair, 1985, Gold Poet award World of Poetry, 1989, Silver Poet award, 1990; named Most Caring Nurse St. Mary's Hosp. 1990, Clara Compton scholar, St. Mary's Hosp., 1993, 94, scholar Am. Legion, 1992. Mem. Internat. Platform Assn., Barn Colony Artists (treas. 1986-88), Phi Theta Kappa, Beta Sigma Phi (treas. 1976-78), Alpha Tau Delta (treas. 1991-92, pres. 1992-93), Sigma Theta Tau Internat. Home: 1680 N 30th St Decatur IL 62526-5416

LITER, AMY MORRIS, university administrator; b. Batesville, Ind., June 3, 1966; d. Paul Jacob and Anita (Burton) Morris; m. R. Jeffery Liter, Oct. 29, 1988. BS, Butler U., 1987. Pers. asst. The Provident Bank, Cin., 1988-89; spl. projects coord. Inst. for Pub. Safety Pers., Indpls., 1989-90; assoc. dir. devel. and alumni rels. Consumer & Family Scis. Purdue U., West Lafayette, Ind., 1990—; com. mem., workshop participant Advancement for Family and Consumer Scis., 1993—. Com. mem., chmn. planning com. United Way, Lafayette, Ind., 1991—; mem. exec. com. United Meth. Women, Congress St. Ch., Lafayette, 1993—, pres., 1994; publicity com., chair Home Hosp. Fair, Lafayette, 1990-92; com. chair Nat. Family Week, Family Svcs., Lafayette, 1991. Recipient Gold medal Coun. for Advancement and Support of Edn. Dist. 5, 1995, Mead 60 cert. of honor, 1996. Mem. Nat. Assn. Fund Raising Execs. Republican. Office: Purdue U Sch Consumer & Family Scis 1260 Stone Hall West Lafayette IN 47907

LITMAN, DIANE JUDITH, computer scientist; b. N.Y.C., Mar. 5, 1958; d. Philip and Freda Rae (Grumet) L.; m. Mark William Kahrs, May 17, 1987. BA, Coll. William and Mary, 1980; MS, U. Rochester, 1982, PhD, 1986. Mem. tech. staff AT&T Bell Labs., Murray Hill, N.J., 1985-90, 92—; asst. prof. Columbia U., N.Y.C., 1990-92. Editl. bd. Computational Linguistics, 1991-93; book rev. editor: User Modeling, User-Adapted Interaction; contbr. articles to profl. jours. Mem. Assn. for Computational Linguistics, Am. Assn. of Artificial Intelligence, Phi Beta Kappa. Office: AT&T Bell Labs 600 Mountain Ave New Providence NJ 07974-2008

LITMAN, ROSLYN MARGOLIS, lawyer, educator; b. N.Y.C., Sept. 30, 1928; d. Harry and Dorothy (Perlow) Margolis; m. S. David Litman, Nov. 22, 1950; children: Jessica, Hannah, Harry. B.A., U. Pitts., 1949, J.D., 1952. Bar: Pa. 1952. Practiced in Pitts., 1952—; partner firm Litman, Litman, Harris & Brown, P.C., 1952—; adj. prof. U. Pitts. Law Sch., 1958—; permanent del. Conf. U.S. Circuit Ct. Appeals for 3d Circuit; past chair dist. adv. group U.S. Dist. Ct. (we. dist.) Pa., 1991-94, mem. steering com. for dist. adv. group, 1991—; chmn. Pitts. Pub. Parking Authority, 1970-74; mem. curriculum com. Pa. Bar Inst., 1986—, bd. dirs., 1972-82. Recipient Roscoe Pound Found. award for Excellence in Tchg. Trial Advocacy, 1996. Mem. ABA (del., litigation sect., anti-trust health care com.), ACLU (nat. bd. dirs..), Pa. Bar Assn. (bd. govs. 1976-79), Allegheny County Bar Assn. (bd. govs. 1972-74, pres. 1975), Allegheny County Acad. Trial Lawyers (charter), United Jewish Fedn. (cmty. rels. com.). Home: 5023 Frew Ave Pittsburgh PA 15213 Office: 3600 One Oxford Centre Pittsburgh PA 15219

LITRENTA, FRANCES MARIE, psychiatrist; b. Balt., June 25, 1928; d. Frank P. and Josephine (DeLuca) L. AB, Coll. Notre Dame Md., 1950; MD, Georgetown U., 1954. Diplomate Am. Bd. Psychiatry and Neurology. Rotating intern St. Agnes Hosp., Balt., 1954-55, asst. resident in psychiatry, 1955-56; fellow in psychiatry Univ. Hosp., Balt., 1956-57; fellow in child psychiatry Georgetown U. Hosp., Washington, 1957-59; clin. instr. psychiatry Med. Ctr. Georgetown U., Washington, 1959-63; clin. asst. prof. Med. Ctr. Georgetown U., 1963-72, clin. assoc. prof. psychiatry Med. Ctr., 1972-87; pvt. practice Balt., 1959—; cons. St. Vincent's Infant Home, Balt., 1965-75; mem. coun. to dean Georgetown U. Sch. Medicine, 1977-93. Fellow Am. Acad. Child and Adolescent Psychiatry, Am. Orthopsychiat. Assn. (life); mem. Am. Psychiat. Assn. (life), Md. Psychiat. Soc. (life), Georgetown Med. Alumni Assn. (nat. comm. chmn. 1987-90, class co-chmn. 1974-87, class comm. chmn. 1987—, bd. dirs. 1989—, gov. 1989-95, senator 1995—, Founder's award 1994). Office: 6110 York Rd Baltimore MD 21212-2697

LITT, IRIS FIGARSKY, pediatrics educator; b. N.Y.C., Dec. 25, 1940; d. Jacob and Bertha (Berson) Figarsky; m. Victor C. Vaughan, June 14, 1987; children from previous marriage: William M., Robert B. AB, Cornell U., 1961; MD, SUNY, Bklyn., 1965. Diplomate Am. Bd. Pediatrics (bd. dirs. 1989-94), sub-specialty bd. cert. in adolescent medicine. Intern, then resident in pediat. N.Y. Hosp., N.Y.C., 1965-68; assoc. prof. pediat. Stanford U. Sch. Medicine, Palo Alto, Calif., 1982-87, prof., 1987—, dir. divsn. adolescent medicine, 1976—, dir. Inst. for Rsch. on Women and Gender, 1990—; bd. dirs. Youth Law Ctr., San Francisco. Editor Jour. Adolescent Health. Mem. Soc. for Adolescent Medicine (charter), Am. Acad. Pediatrics (award sect. on adolescent health), Western Soc. Pediatric Rsch., Soc. Pediatric Rsch., Am. Pediatric Soc., Inst. of Medicine/NAS. Office: 750 Welch Rd Ste 325 Palo Alto CA 94304

LITTELL, MARCIA SACHS, educator, educational administrator; b. Phila., July 12, 1937; d. Leon Harry Sobel and Selma Fisher Goldstein Lipson; m. Robert L. Sachs, Apr. 3, 1955 (div. June 1978); children: Jonathan R., Robert L. Jr., Jennifer Sachs-Dahnert; m. Franklin H. Littell, Mar. 23, 1980; children: Jennith Lawrence, Karen, Miriam, Stephen. BS in Edn., Temple U., 1971, MS in Edn., 1975, EdD, 1990. Cert. tchr. secondary and social studies, Pa. Tchr. Lower Merion Sch. Dist., Ardmore, Pa., 1972-74; regional exec. dir. Brit. European Ctr., Paris, 1974-78; dir. confs. Bryn Mawr (Pa.) Coll., 1976-80; internat. exec. dir. Anne Frank Inst., Phila., 1981-89; adj. prof. Temple U., Phila., 1990—; exec. dir. Ann. Scholars' Conf. on the Holocaust & the Chs., Merion, Pa., 1990—; vis. prof. Phila. C.C., 1974-76; dir. Phila. Ctr. on the Holocaust, Genocide and Human Rights, 1989—; exec. com. Remembering for the Future, Oxford, Eng. and Berlin, 1986—; mem. edn. com. U.S. Holocaust Meml. Mus., Washington, 1987—, chmn.'s adv. com., 1985. Editl. adv. bd. Holocaust & Genocide Studies, Oxford U. Press, volume I, 1987—, Bridges: An Interdisciplinary Journal of Theology, Philosophy, History and Science, 1995—; editor: Holocaust Education: A Resource for Teachers and Professional Leaders, 1985, Liturgies on the Holocaust: An Interfaith Anthology, 1986, rev. edit., 1996 (Merit of Distinction award), The Holocaust: Forty Years After, 1989, The Netherlands and Nazi Genocide, 1992, From Prejudice to Destruction: Western Civilization in the Shadow of Auschwitz, 1995, Remembrance and Recollection: Essays on the Centennial Year of Martin Neimoller and Reinhold Niebuhr, 1995, The Uses and Abuses of Knowledge: The Holocaust and the German Church Struggle, 1996, The Holocaust: Lessons For The Third Generation, 1996, Holocause and Church Struggle: Religion, Power and the Politics of Resistance, 1996. Exec. com. YM/YWHA Arts Coun., Phila., 1980—; adv. bd. Child Welfare, Montgomery County, 1975-80; bd. govs. Lower Merion Scholarship Fund, 1972-80. Named Woman of the Yr., Brith Sholom Women, Phila., 1993, Eternal Flame award Anne Frank Inst., 1988, Hall of Fame award Sch. Dist. of Phila., 1988. Fellow Nat. Assn. Holocaust Educators, Assn. of Holocaust Orgns. (founding sec. 1985-88), Nat. Coun. for the Social Studies. Democrat. Jewish. Home: PO Box 10 Merion Station PA 19066

LITTEN, CHARLOTTE ELAINE, contractor, counselor, small business owner; b. Salyersville, Ky., Jan. 9, 1944; d. Henry Sterling and Lela May (Reed) Bailey; m. Arthur G. Litten, Sept. 23, 1962 (div. Jan. 1980); 1 child,

Robert Mark Litten. Assoc. in Math. and Scis., Shawnee State U., 1986; BBA, Ohio U., 1987, MEd, 1990. Cert. counselor; cert. sec. With indsl. rel. Goodyear Atomic Corp., Piketon, Ohio, 1980-87; labor rels. specialist Martin Marietta Energy Sys., Inc., Piketon, 1987-90, asst. to divsn. mgr., 1990-92, dept. mgr. cascade svcs., 1992—; counselor, co-owner Hope Counseling Ctr., South Shore, Ky., 1991—. Bd. dirs. Pike County Joint Vocat. Sch. Adv. Bd., 1980—, Scioto County Vocat. Sch. Adv. Bd., Lucasville, 1980—, Atomic Employees Credit Union, Piketon, 1993-96. Mem. Chi Sigma Iota, Phi Kappa Phi. Democrat. Home: 2928 N Hill Rd Portsmouth OH 45662-2419 Office: Martin Marietta Energy System Inc PO Box 628 Piketon OH 45661-0628

LITTLE, GRACE RUIZ, computer services administrator; b. Habana, Cuba, Aug. 16, 1956; d. Abelardo A. and Marta E. (Nodarse) Ruiz; m. Michael S. Little, Mar. 1, 1980; children: Kristina, Christopher. BS, Coll. William & Mary, 1978. Programmer Old Dominion U., Norfolk, Va., 1978-79, programmer, analyst, 1979-80, sr. programmer, analyst, 1980-82, systems analyst, 1982-84, asst. dir., 1984—; coord. Great Computer Challenge, Norfolk, 1982—; mem. Help Desk Inst., 1995—. Sec. St. Gregory PTG, Virginia Beach, 1992-95; tchr. St. Gregory Ch., Virginia Beach, 1989—, asst. soccer coach, 1996—. Roman Catholic. Office: Old Dominion U 128 Hughes Hall Norfolk VA 23529

LITTLE, SYLVIA FORD, oil industry executive. Student, So. Meth. U., Scottsdale Community Coll., Ariz. Owner, operator gas and oil properties San Juan Basin, N.Mex., 1977—; pres. Little Oil & Gas, Inc., San Juan Basin, N.Mex. Founder Farmington (N.Mex.) Totah Festival of Authentic Indian Art; chmn. residential com. Town Forum 2000, 1980; mem. exec. com., state ctrl. com. N.Mex. Rep. Com., 1984-86; bd. dirs. N.Mex. Fedn. Rep. Women, 1984-90, Farmington LWV, Four Corners Better Bus. Bur., 1993—; mem. industry adv. com. to N.Mex. Dept. Energy, 1993; mem. N.Mex. Bd. Econ. Devel. Commrs., 1994—. mem. Ind. Petroleum Assn. N.Mex. (pres.-elect 1990, pres. 1991-93), N.Mex. Oil and Gas Assn. (exec. com. 1993-96), Assn. Commerce and Industry N.Mex. (bd. dirs. 1988-92), Farmington C. of C. (pres. 1996, redcoats amb. com.), Rotary. Office: 2346 E 20th St Farmington NM 87401-8906

LITTLEFIELD, VIVIAN MOORE, nursing educator, administrator; b. Princeton, Ky., Jan. 24, 1938; children: Darrell, Virginia. B.S. magna cum laude, Tex. Christian U., 1960; M.S., U. Colo., 1964; Ph.D., U. Denver, 1979. Staff nurse USPHS Hosp., Ft. Worth, Tex., 1960-61; instr. nursing Tex. Christian U., Ft. Worth, 1961-62; nursing supr. Colo. Gen. Hosp., Denver, 1964-65, pvt. patient practitioner, 1974-78; asst. prof. nursing U. Colo., Denver, 1965-69, asst. prof., clin. instr., 1971-74, asst. prof., 1974-76, acting asst. dean, assoc. prof. continuing edn., regional perinatal project, 1976-78; assoc. prof., chair dept. women's health care nursing U. Rochester Sch. Nursing, N.Y., 1979-84; clin. chief ob-gyn., nursing U. Rochester Strong Meml. Hosp., N.Y., 1979-84; prof., dean U. Wis. Sch. Nursing, Madison, 1984—; cons. and lectr. in field. Author: Maternity Nursing Today, 1973, 76, Health Education for Women: A guide for Nurses and Other Health Professionals, 1986; mem. editorial bd. Jour. Profl. Nursing; contbr. articles to profl. jours. Bur. Health Professions Fed. trainee, 1963-64; Nat. Sci. Service award, 1976-79. Mem. MAIN, AACN (bd. dirs.), NLN (bd. dirs.), Am. Acad. Nursing, Am. Nurses Assn., Consortium Prime Care Wis. (chair), Health Care for Women Internat., Midwest Nursing Research Soc., Sigma Theta Tau (pres. Beta Eta chpt., co-chair coun nursing practice and edn. 1995). Avocations: golf, biking. Office: U Wis Sch Nursing 600 Highland Ave # H6 150 Madison WI 53792-0001

LITTLETON, GAYE DARLENE, nonprofit executive director; b. Parma, Idaho, Nov. 1, 1938; d. Donald Lyle and June E. (Shelton) Graham; m. Jerry M. Littleton, June 11, 1960; children: Leslie, Clark, Laura, Stacey. BS in Edn., U. Idaho, 1960; MS in Ednl. Adminstrn., Utah State U., 1980. Tchr. Seattle, 1960-62; tchr. jr. high sch. Ogden (Utah) Sch. Dist., 1975-76; tchr. Utah State Sch. for the Blind, Ogden, 1976 80; cdnl. equity program coord. Weber State Coll., Ogden, 1979-81; councilwoman Ogden City Coun., 1983—; exec. dir. Your Cmty. Connection, 1981—; bd. dirs. Zion's State Bank, First Security Bank Housing Com.; rschr. in field. Contbr. articles to profl. jours. Commr. Ogden Redevel. Agy., Ogden Housing Agy., 1993; mem. human devel. com. Nat. League of Cities; bd. dirs. Weber County Dept. Aging, City Parks and Recreation, Nature Ctr., Arts Commn., Equal Employment Opportunity; mem. Weber County Social Svcs. Coordinating Coun.; past chair Weber County Title XX Coun.; mem. Weber County Resource Coalition, Weber County Human Rights Coalition, Weber County Homeless Coordinating Com.; mem. ethics com. McKay Dee Hosp., 1990—. Recipient Acad. scholarship for Cmty. Svc., 1956, Thesian award U. Idaho, 1959, LWV Cmty. Svc. award Weber County Mental Health, 1974, Cmty. Svc. award, VIP award Hill AFB, Utah, 1977, Liberty Bell award Utah Bar Assn., 1977, Leadership award Nat. YWCA, 1979, Susa Young Gates award Utah Women's Polit. Caucus for Outstanding Contbn. to Women and Minorities, 1980, Jane Addams award, 1982, Women Helpin Women award, 1983, Utah Women of Achievement award, 1984, Golden Deeds award, 1988, Athena award, Disting. Alumni award WSU, 1994, Outstanding Rotarian Housing Commr., 1990. Mem. LWV, AAUW (Woman of Yr. 1988), Ogden Rotary Club (First Woman Rotarian 1992), Ogden C. of C. (Athenia award 1992). Home: 1708 Hislop Dr Ogden UT 84404-5320 Office: Your Cmty Connection 2261 Adams Ave Ogden UT 84401-1510

LITTRELL, ANN ROBERTA, lawyer; b. Douglas, Ariz., Oct. 13, 1952; d. Norman M. and Marjorie T. (Lammers) L.;m. Edward J. Shisslak; children: Zachary S., Erik D., Sara E. Student, U. Autonoma de Guadalajara, Mexico, 1974-75; BA in Journalism and Anthropology with high honors, U. Ariz., Tucson, 1975, JD with highest honors, 1979; cert. in Internat. Law, Stockholm U., 1978. Bar: Ariz. 1979, U.S. Dist. Ct. Ariz. 1979, White Mt. Apache Tribal Ct., 1980. Mng. atty. Apache Legal Aid, Whiteriver, Ariz., 1980-83; pvt. practice Pinetop, Ariz., 1983-86; owner Littrell & Weyrauch, P.C., Lakeside, Ariz., 1986-88; ptnr. Greer, Littrell & Winters, Lakeside, 1988; pub. fiduciary Cochise County Pub. Fiduciary, Bisbee, Ariz., 1988-94; pvt. practice Bisbee, 1994-95; elder law atty. Cochise County Pub. Fiduciary, Bisbee, 1994-95; city atty. City of Douglas, Ariz., 1995—; vol. judge, coach Ariz. Mock Trial competition, 1990, 94, 96; presenter nat. conf. Nat. Guardianship Assn., 1990-94; mem. Southeastern Ariz. Govts. Orgn. Title XX Planning Com., 1991-94; bd. dirs So. Ariz. Legal Aid, 1989-90, Fort Apache Legal Aid, 1988-89; bd. dirs. DNA People's Legal Svcs., 1987-88. Co-founder White Mt. Safe House for Battered Women, Pinetop, 1985; dir., incorporator Save our Stairs, Bisbee, 1991-94; chairperson City of Bisbee Jud. Selection Com., 1995; mem. Bisbee Sch. Facilities Needs Com., 1995. Fulbright-Hays fellow Fulbright Found., Sweden, 1977-78; recipient Ariz. Alumni scholastic award U. Ariz., Tucson, 1979. Mem. Ariz. Assn. Pub. and Pvt. Fiduciaries (pres. 1991-93), Nat. Acad. Elder Law Attys. (Ariz. chpt. treas. 1992-95), State Bar Ariz. (treas. mental health and elder law com. 1993-94, dir. 1993-95, legal scs. com. 1988-89), Nat. Inst. Mcpl. Law Officers, Bisbee Hist. Soc., World Wildlife Fund, Amnesty Internat., Bowhunters Club So. Ariz., Phi Beta Kappa. Home: 508 San Jose Dr Bisbee AZ 85603 Office: PO Box 4127 Bisbee AZ 85603

LITWIN, LINDA JOAN, laboratory executive, medical illustrator; b. Hartford, Conn., Aug. 18, 1944; d. Robert Davis and Greta (Westerfeld) Moses; m. Paul Gary Litwin, Apr. 12, 1969 (dec. Apr. 1986); children: Seth Eaton, Jared Stix. Diploma, Mt. Ida Jr. Coll., Boston, 1965; BS, U. Ky., 1968. Med. illustrator U. Ky. Med. Ctr., Lexington, 1966-68, U. Cin. Coll. Medicine, 1969-72, Mayo Inst. of Jewish Hosp., Cin., 1970-76, USDA, 1978—; pvt. swimming instr., 1960-90; freelance horse trainer, instr., 1966—; instr., trainer obedience Capitol Dog Tng. Club, Washington, 1979-85; v.p., co-owner Orthodyne Lab., Inc., Rockville, Md., 1982—. Mem. Jr. Women's Club, Wyoming, Ohio, 1972-77. Recipient awards U.S. Dressage Fedn., 1969-87, U.S. Kennel Club, 1978-85, Pvt. Pilot lic. Airplane SEL, 1986, Instrument Rating, 1992, Wings I award FAA, 1988, Wings II, 1991, Wings III, 1993, Wings IV, 1994, Cert. of Recognition FAA, 1989. Mem. NAFE, Aircraft Owners and Pilots Assn., Internat. Women Pilots Assn. (membership chmn., vice chmn., chmn. Washington chpt. 1993—), Montgomery County Airport Assn. (bd. dirs. 1995—), U.S. Hunter, Jumper Assn., Am. Horse Show Assn., Potomac Valley Dressage Assn. (treas. 1984-86). Office: Orthodyne Lab Inc 771 E Gude Dr Rockville MD 20850-1329

LITYNSKI, DIANE MARIE, marketing and business professional; b. Schenectady, N.Y., Jan. 22, 1962; d. John Gregory and Anne Marie (Trejderowski) L.; m. Karlin Boyington Jessen, Nov. 7, 1987 (div. Dec. 1994). BSChemE, Rensselaer Poly. Inst., 1984, MS in Psychology, 1992, PhD, 1992; MBA, Boston U., 1987. New products mktg. mgr. Polaroid Corp., Cambridge, Mass., 1988-90; pvt. cons. Albany, N.Y., 1990-92; prof. Auckland (New Zealand) U., 1992-94; prof. mktg. and bus. Marist Coll., Poughkeepsie, N.Y., 1993-95; mktg. mgr. Ryan-Biggs Assocs., P.C., 1996—; cons. The Saratoga Assocs., Saratoga Springs, N.Y., 1990-92. Author: (poetry) The Gordon, 1983-84, Nat. Book of Poetry, 1992, Rainbow's End, 1996. Eucharistic minister Albany Diocese, Troy, N.Y., 1980-84; blood donor adminstr. ARC, Troy, 1980-84; student counselor Marist Coll., Poughkeepsie, 1994—; church lectern, vol. Our Lady of Mt. Carmel, Poughkeepsie, 1994—. Capt. USAF, 1984-88. Mem. Am. Mktg. Assn., Am. Psychology Assn., Am. Mgmt. Assn. Roman Catholic.

LITZ, JORDAN S., virologist; b. Roswell, N.Mex., Mar. 4, 1941; d. Douglas Todd and Kayla Alyssa White; m. Kurt Darreck Litz; children: Donald Robert, Vivian Lois. BS, N.Mex. State U., 1963, MD, 1967. Virologist St. Catherine's Health Clinic, Roswell, 1967-78, Werik Clinic, St. Joseph's Meml. Hosp., Clovis, N.Mex., 1978—. Vol. Meml. Hosp. AIDS ward, N.Mex., 1990—; den mother Boy Scouts, 1978-83. Mem. N.Mex. Virologists Assn. (sec. 1993-95, treas. 1995—). Office: Werik Clinic 121 W 4th St Clovis NM 88101-7405

LIU, ALICE YEE-CHANG, biology educator; b. Hunan, China, July 12, 1948; came to U.S., 1970; d. Tin-Kai and Te-Ming (Young) L.; m. Kuang Yu Chen, Aug. 26, 1978; children: Andrew T-H, Winston T-C. BS, Chinese U., Hong Kong, 1969; PhD, Mount Sinai Sch. Med., 1974. Postdoctoral fellow Yale U. Med. Sch., New Haven, Conn., 1974-77; asst. prof. Harvard Med. Sch., Boston, 1977-84; assoc. prof. Rutgers U., Piscataway, N.J., 1984-89, prof., 1989—; dir. grad. program in cell and devel. biology Rutgers U.-U. Medicine-Dentistry N.J.-R.W. Johnson Med. Sch., 1994—; mem. pharmacological scis. rev. com. NIH, 1984-88; mem. cell biology panel NSF, 1989-93, 94-95; mem. basic rsch. adv. group N.J. Commn. on Cancer Rsch., 1989-93, 94—. Author: Receptors Again, 1985; editorial bd. Biol. Signals, 1991—. Recipient N.Y.C. Bd. of Higher Edn. award, 1972, Am. Cancer Soc. Scholar award, Boston, 1982-85; NIH postdoctoral fellow, 1974-77, Medical Found. fellow, Boston, 1977-79. Mem. Am. Soc. Biochemistry and Molecular Biology, Am. Soc. Pharmacology and Experimental Therapeutics. Home: 20 Woodlake Dr Piscataway NJ 08854-5148 Office: Rutgers U PO Box 1059 Nelson Biology Labs Piscataway NJ 08855-1059

LIU, CLARICE C., lawyer; b. Hong Kong, May 10, 1963; d. Charles and Yu Bei (Fu) Liu. BA, U. Calif., Berkeley, 1985; JD, UCLA, 1992. Bar: Calif. 1992. Assoc. Gronemeier & Barker, Pasadena, Calif., 1993-95, Thelen, Marrin, Johnson & Bridges, San Francisco, 1995—. Bd. govs. Lawyers for Human Rights, L.A., 1994-95; treas. Campaign for James Lomako for City Councilman, Pasadena, 1996; vol. atty. Gay and Lesbian Cmty. Svcs. Ctr., L.A., 1993—. Mem. San Francisco Bar Assn., Bay Area Lawyers for Individual Freedom. Office: Thelen Marrin Johnson & Bridges 2 Embarcadero Ctr San Francisco CA 94111

LIU, JING-QIU, education educator; b. Beijing, China, Sept. 15, 1951; came to U.S., 1987; m. Luzheng Shen, June 26, 1979; 1 child, Yu Lisa. MS, Iowa State U., 1989, PhD, 1992. Sr. tchr. Baoding H.S., China, 1977-87; rsch. asst. Iowa State U., Ames, 1987-92, rsch. assoc. Rsch. Inst. for Studies in Edn., 1993, temp. instr. Sch. Edn., 1993-94; asst. prof. edn. Troy (Ala.) State U., 1994—. Contbr. articles to profl. jours. Recipient Women Tchr. Awards for excellence in instrn. Baoding Dist., China, 1979, 86; Ctr. for Internat. Edn., Coll. of Edn., Iowa State U. Grad. Asst. award, 1992; Internat. Peace scholar, 1988-89. Mem. Nat. Assn. Multicultural Edn., Am. Edn. Assn., Phi Kappa Phi, Phi Delta Kappa. Office: Troy State U Sch Edn Troy AL 36081

LIU, MARGARET M., fabric company executive; b. China, July 24, 1946; d. I-Yung and K-Ming (Huan) L.; m. Shau-Chung Hu, Feb. 14, 1984; 1 child. Z.G. BA, Christian Coll., Taipei, Taiwan, 1974; MBA, Lincoln U., 1983; BBA, Nat. Acad. Mgmt., Taipei, 1980. Dir., pres. Am. Hubei Assoc., N.Y.C.; dir. Nat. Acad. Mgmt., Taipei; dir., pres. China Natural Fabric Corp., Bklyn.; hostess TV and radio program Computer and You, China TV Co., Cen. Radio Sta., 1970-73. Mem. Nat. Rep. Congl. Com. Recipient award Fend Chia U., Taipei, Taiwan Internat. Conf. on Computerized Bus. Simulations, 1976, Taiwan Merchants Assn. N.Y., Inc. Home: 1025 45th St Apt 1D Brooklyn NY 11219-1904

LIU, PAMELA PEI-LING, graphic designer; b. Taipei, Taiwan, Republic of China, Jan. 31, 1951; came to U.S., 1968; d. Hoh-Tu and Julia C.Y. (Sheng) L. BS, Marywood Coll., 1972. Calligrapher Geyer Studio, N.Y.C., 1972-74; artist James Bell Graphic Design, N.Y.C., 1974-75; freelance artist, designer, art dir. N.Y.C., 1975-82; ptnr. Triptic Graphics Inc., N.Y.C., 1982-92; pres. LIU Communications & Design, Inc., N.Y.C., 1992—. Mem. NOW, Am. Assn. Bot. Gardens and Arbarita, Am. Hort. Soc., Women in The Arts (charter), Smithsonian Inst., China Inst. Am., Sierra Club. Office: LIU Comm & Design Inc 126 W 96th St New York NY 10025

LIU, PEGGY, internet executive; b. Ann Arbor, Mich., Oct. 15, 1968; d. Leonard and Ann (Hwa) L. BS CSEE, MIT, 1990. Mgmt. cons. McKinsey, L.A., 1990-92; OEM product mgr. Symantec, Cupertino, Calif., 1992, product mgr., 1993; product mgr. NetManage, Cupertino, 1994-96; pres. Channel A, Los Altos Hills, Calif., 1996—. Mem. Asian Am. Mfg. Assn. (exec. com. 1996), Orgn. of Chinese Am. Women (bd. dirs. 1992-93). Office: Channel A 26937 Almaden Ct Los Altos Hills CA 94022

LIU, RHONDA LOUISE, librarian; b. Honolulu; d. David Yuk Fong Liu and Shirley May Chong. BA, U. Hawaii at Manoa, Honolulu, 1974, MLS, 1991. Outreach libr. Alu Like Native Hawaiian Libr. Project, 1992; libr. II Hawaii State Libr., 1992; fgn. expert Beijing Fgn. Studies U., 1992-93; libr. Savs. & Cmty.. Bankers of Am., Washington, 1993-94; tech. libr. Md. State Libr. for Blind & Physically Handicapped, Balt., 1995—; grad. student intern East-West Ctr. Resource Materials Collection, 1991-92; libr. asst. Legis. Reference Bur. Libr., 1989-90; asst. rschr. Legis. Info. Sys. Office, 1984-85; English-as-second lang. tutor Keimei Gakuen, Tokyo, 1979. Active Friends of Md. State Libr. for Blind and Physically Handicapped, 1994—; v.p., sec. Sch. Libr. and Info. Studies, 1990-91. Alu Like Native Hawaiian Libr. fellow, 1990-91; Kamehameha Schs./Bishop Estate scholar, 1991. Mem. ALA, U. Hawaii Alumni Assn. Office: Md State Libr for Blind & Phys Handicapped 415 Park Ave Baltimore MD 21201

LIVENGOOD, CHARLOTTE LOUISE, employee development specialist; b. L.A., June 18, 1944; d. James Zollie and Zela (Cogburn) L. BS in Secondary Edn., Tex. A & I U., 1968; MEd in Pers. Guidance and Counseling, North Tex. U., 1971. Cert. secondary teaching, Tex.; cert. counselor, Tex. Counselor Gus Grissom H.S., Huntsville, Ala., 1971-72; tchr. West Springfield H.S., Springfield, Va., 1972-73; edn. specialist U.S. Dept. Def., El Paso, Tex., 1975-78; instr. El Paso (Tex.) C.C., 1977-78; employee devel. specialist U.S. Office Pers. Mgmt., Dallas, 1978-79; pers. mgmt. specialist Dept. Vets. Affairs, Houston, 1979-87; labor rels. specialist Dept. Vets. Affairs, VA Med. Ctr., Houston, 1987-89; pers. staffing specialist Dept. Vets. Affairs, Houston, 1989-90; employee devel. specialist, acad. tng. officer HUD, Ft. Worth, 1990—; assoc. prof. Ariz. State U., 1995—; Bur. of Engraving and Printing univ. tng. officer Dept. Treasury, Ft. Worth, 1995—; EEO investigator Dept. Vet. Affairs, 1984-87, fed. women's program mgr., 1984-85; mem. standing panel for pers. specialists/fed. suprs./mgrs. Merit Systems Protection Bd., 1996—; speaker in field. Editor: (monthly office newspaper) Pipeline, 1980-87. Chairperson, forensics coach Jr. High Sch. Speech Dept., 1968-69; tchr. S. Grand Prarie H.S., 1969-71; mem. Dallas/Ft. Worth Quality Control Coun., Tex. War on Drugs Com., 1990—; hon. mem. Dallas/Ft. Worth Fed. Exec. Bd., 1993-94. Recipient Future Secs. of Am. scholarship, 1962. Mem. ASTD, AAUW, Am. Pers. and Guidance Assn., Assn. for Quality Participation, Internat. Transactional Analysis Assn., Tex. State Tchrs. Assn., Tex. Classroom Tchrs. Assn., Fed. Bus. Assn., VA Employee Assn., Intergovernmental Tng. Assn., Intergovernmental Tng. Coun. (chairperson 1993-94), Federal Women's Program Mgr., Merit Sys. Protection Bd. Standing Panel for Personnel Specialists, Federal Supv., Mgrs. Mem. Church of Christ. Office: US Dept Treasury Bur Engraving & Printing Western Currency Facility 9000 Blue Mound Rd Fort Worth TX 76131-3304

LIVENGOOD, VICTORIA ANN, opera singer; b. Thomasville, N.C., Aug. 8, 1959; d. Gerald Winston and Carolyn Ann (Young) L. MusB in Voice, U. N.C., 1983; MusM in Opera, Boston Conservatory, 1985. tchr. master classes Pittsburg U., Kans., 1990, Temple U., Phila., 1993, U. N.C., Chapel Hill, 1994. Appeared as Queen Gertrude in Hamlet, Greater Miami (Fla.) Opera Co., 1987, Beauty in Beauty and the Beast, Opera Theater St. Louis, 1987, Mercy Kirke in Hazel Kirke, Lake George (N.Y.) Opera, 1987, Giulietta in Les Contes d'Hoffmann, Cleve. Opera Co., Charlotte in Werther, Seattle Opera Co., 1989, Carmen in Carmen, Conn. Opera Co., Hartford, 1990, Dalila in Samson and Dalila, Lyric Opera, Kansas City, 1990, Dorabella in Cosi Fan Tutti, Hawaii Opera Theater, 1990, Carmen in Carmen, Oper der Stadt Köln, Cologne, Germany, 1992, 94, Meg Page in Falstaff, Calgary (Can.) Opera Co., 1991, Idamante in Idomeneo, and Sesto in La Clemenza, L'Opera de Nice, France, 1991, Laura in Louisa Miller, Met. Opera Co., N.Y.C., 1991, Mrs. Grose in Turn of the Screw, Edmonton Opera, Can., 1993, Isolier in Il Conte Ory with Charleston's Spoleto Festival, 1993, Maddalena in Rigoletto, Oper der Stadt Köln and Edmonton Opera, 1994, Desideria in the Saint of Bleeker Street, Kansas City Lyric Opera, 1994, Lola in Cavalleria Rusticana, Met. Opera, 1994, Sonetka in Lady Macbeth of Mtsensk, Met. Opera, 1994, Dalila, Balt. Opera, 1995, Carmen, Edmonton Opera, Can., Giulietta in Les Contes d'Hoffmann, Santiago (Chile) Opera, 1995, girl in Mahogany, Met. Opera Co., 1995; soloist at J.F. Kennedy Ctr., Washington, 1986; performed with Am. Symphony Orch., Carnegie Hall, N.Y., 1986, N.C. Symphony Orch., Carnegie Hall, 1987, Nat. Symphony Orch., Washington, 1990, Atlanta Symphony Orch., 1991, Honolulu Symphony, 1991, Balt. Symphony Orch., 1991, Cologne Symphony, Germany, 1992, Minn. Symphony, 1992, Columbus Symphony, 1993, Buffalo Philharm., 1994, Northwest Chamber Mus. Soc., Portland, Oreg., 1994, Am. Composers Orch., 1995, San Diego Symphony, 1995, Rochester Philharmonic, 1995, others; solo recitalist in numerous locations including Boston, N.Y., N.C., Kans., Mo., Washington, others; EMI recs. include Oberon (soloist), 1992; subject of article Mus. Am. mag., 1986, Opera News Mag., 1987, 94, 95. Min. music Mills Home Bapt. Ch., Thomasville, 1980-81; recitalist Hosp. Guild, Thomasville, 1980-82, 87, 92, Epilepsy Benefit, Kansas City, Mo., 1989, Aids Benefit-Buffalo Philharmonic N.Y., 1994. Recipient Nat. award Met. Opera Auditions, N.Y.C., 1985, Internat. award Rosa Ponselle Competition, N.Y.C., 1987, D'Angelo Competition award, 1987, Recipient of the U. N.C. Disting. Young Alumnus award, Luciano Pavarotti Competition, Phila., 1988, Key to City of Thomasville, 1992; grantee Sullivan Found., 1987, Nat. Inst. Music Theater, 1989. Office: care Herbert Barrett Mgmt 1776 Broadway Ste 1610 New York NY 10019-2002

LIVERIGHT, BETTY FOUCH, actress, director, writer; b. La Grange, Ill., Oct. 20, 1913; d. Squire and Edna Amanda (Wright) Fouch; m. Herman Elsas Liveright, Feb. 1, 1936; children: Beth, Timothy. BA, Temple U., 1963. Actress L'Aiglon, N.Y.C., 1934, White Plains (N.Y.) Comty. Theater, 1947-52; coord., actress TV Tulane U., New Orleans, 1953-56; actress TV Commercials, New Orleans, 1954-56; rschr. Friends Libr. Swarthmore (Pa.) Coll., 1956-69; pub. rels. agt. Highlander Rsch. and Edn. Ctr., Knoxville, Tenn., 1969-71; co-dir. Berkshire Forum, Stephentown, N.Y., 1972-90; rschr., author pvt. practice, Pittsfield Mass., 1990—. Co-coord. This Just In bull. Pres. Yorkville Peace Coun., N.Y.C., 1940-42; bd. dirs. Women's Internat. League for Peace and Freedom, Phila., 1965-85. Home and Office: 103 Bartlett Ave Pittsfield MA 01201

LIVERMAN, LYNDA M., community health nurse; b. Bogalusa, La., Mar. 26, 1941; d. Warren LeRoy and Verdine jane (McTaggart) Mizell; m. Merlin C. Liverman, Jan. 28, 1962; children: David, Debra, Donna. Student, La. State U., 1959-61, Our Lady Holy Cross Coll., 1972-74; ADN, Northwestern State U., 1979. Cert. care mgmt. Staff nurse Schumpert Med. Ctr., Shreveport, La., 1979; staff, charge nurse North Caddo Meml. Hosp., Vivian, La., 1979 81, Highland Hosp., Shreveport, 1982-85; patient care supr. for home health MAS Nursing, Shreveport, 1985-87, dir. pers., Medicare adminstr., 1987-89; br. mgr. Kimberly Quality Care, Shreveport, 1989-92; established Premier Family Healthcare, Inc., Shreveport, La., 1992—, Glen Home Health, Inc. (subs. Premier Healthcare Mgmt. Inc.), Shreveport, La., 1995—; v.p. clin. svcs. Premier Healthcare Mgmt., Inc., Shreveport, La., 1995—. Mem. Riverside Bapt. Ch. Named Nurse of the Yr. Shreveport Dist. Nurses Assn., 1989. Mem. ANA, NAHC, Shreveport Dist. Nurses Assn., Am. Soc. Parenteral and Enteral Nutrition, Ark.-La.-Tex. Assn. Home Health and Hospice Agys., Homecare Assn. La.

LIVERMORE, BETH ANNE, freelance journalist, photographer; b. Waterbury, Conn., Jan. 10, 1962; d. Robert Allen and Anne Elizabeth (DeGrote) L. BJ, U. Mo., 1986. Writer, editor Health mag., N.Y.C., 1987-90; assoc. editor Sea Frontiers, Miami, Fla., 1993-96. Contbr. numerous articles to Sea Frontiers (1st place award 1991, 93), Smithsonian, Glamour, Self, Destination Discovery, Omni, Nat. Geog. World, Travel Holiday, E: The Environ. Mag., Popular Sci., Snow Country, Mademoiselle. Recipient gold award Nat. Health Info. Awards, 1995; internat. enrichment scholar, 1985, Virginia McElroy Schwartz journalism scholar, 1986, Nat. Arts Club, 1992; sci. writing fellow Marine Biol. Labs., 1990, APA, 1996. Mem. Am. Soc. Journalists and Authors, Nat. Press Photographers Assn., Soc. Environ. Journalists, Nat. Assn. Sci. Writers, N.Y. Newswomen's Assn. Home and Office: 27 W 86th St Apt 15D New York NY 10024

LIVERMORE, JEANNE M., insurance company executive; b. Salem, Mass., 1948. Grad., Lake Forest Coll., 1970. Sr. v.p. invest and pension John Hancock Fin. Svcs.; sr. v.p. Ctr. for Quality Control John Hancock Mut. Life Ins. Co., Boston; bd. dirs. The Berkely Fin. Group. Office: John Hancock Mut Life Ins Co John Hancock Pl 200 Clarendon St PO Box 111 Boston MA 02117*

LIVESAY, VALORIE ANN, lead security analyst; b. Greeley, Colo., Sept. 9, 1959; d. John Albert and Mary Magdalene Yurchak. BA in Edn., U. No. Colo., 1981; M in Computer Info. Sys., U. Denver, 1991. Drafter Computer Graphics, Denver, 1981, Advanced Cable Sys., Inc., Denver, 1981-82, Am. TV Comm. Corp., Englewood, Colo., 1982-83; janitor Rockwell Internat., Golden, Colo., 1983-84, analytical lab tech., 1984-86, metall. operator, 1986-88; nuclear material coord. EG&G Rocky Flats Inc., Golden, 1988-92, lead security analyst, 1992-95. Active Channel 6, Denver, 1985, World Wildlife Fund, Westminster, Colo., 1987, Denver Dumb Friends League, 1987, The Nature Conservancy, Boulder, Colo., 1989. Mem. NAFE, Am. Soc. Insdl. Security. Home: 6344 W 115th Ave Broomfield CO 80020-3034 Office: EG&G Rocky Flats Inc PO Box 464 Rocky Flats Plant Golden CO 80402-0464

LIVINGSTON, MARGARET GRESHAM, civic leader; b. Birmingham, Ala., Aug. 16, 1924; d. Owen Garside and Katherine Molton (Morrow) Gresham; m. James Archibald Livingston, Jr., July 16, 1947; children: Mary Margaret, James Archibald, Katherine Wiley, Elizabeth Gresham. Grad. The Baldwin Sch., Phila., 1942; AB, Vassar Coll., 1945; MA, U. Ala., 1946. Acting dir. Birmingham Mus. Art, 1978-79, 81, chmn. bd. dirs., 1978-86; bd. dirs. Birmingham Civic Ctr. Authority, 1988-95; bd. dirs. Altamont Sch., Birmingham, 1963—, chmn. bd. 1986. Named Woman of Yr., Birmingham, 1986; named to Ala. Tennis Hall of Fame, 1994. Mem. Am. Assn. Mus. Episcopalian. Clubs: Jr. League, Ala. State Tennis Assn.

LIVINGSTON, MYRA COHN, poet, writer, educator; b. Omaha, Aug. 17, 1926; d. Mayer L. and Gertrude (Marks) Cohn; m. Richard Roland Livingston, Apr. 14, 1952 (dec. 1990); children: Joshua, Jonas Cohn, Jennie Marks. BA, Sarah Lawrence Coll., 1948. Profl. horn player, 1941-48; book reviewer Los Angeles Daily News, 1948-49, Los Angeles Mirror, 1949-50; asst. editor Campus Mag., 1949-50; various public relations positions and pvt. sec. to Hollywood (Calif.) personalities, 1950-52; tchr. creative writing Dallas (Tex.) public library and schs., 1958-63; poet-in-residence Beverly Hills (Calif.) Unified Sch. Dist., 1966-84; sr. instr. UCLA Extension, 1973-96; cons. to various sch. dists., 1966-84, cons. poetry to publishers children's lit., 1975-96. Author: Whispers and Other Poems, 1958, Wide Awake and Other Poems, 1959, I'm Hiding, 1961, See What I Found, 1962, I Talk to Elephants, 1962, I'm Not Me, 1963, Happy Birthday, 1964, The Moon and a Star and Other Poems, 1965, I'm Waiting, 1966, Old Mrs. Twindlytart and

Other Rhymes, 1967, A Crazy Flight and Other Poems, 1968, The Malibu and Other Poems, 1972, When You Are Alone/It Keeps You Capone: An Approach to Creative Writing with Children, 1973, Come Away, 1974, The Way Things Are and Other Poems, 1974, 4-Way Stop and Other Poems, 1976, A Lollygag of Limericks, 1978, O Sliver of Liver and Other Poems, 1979, No Way of Knowing: Dallas Poems, 1980, A Circle of Seasons, 1982, How Pleasant to Know Mr. Lear!, 1982, Sky Songs, 1984, A Song I Sang to You, 1984, Monkey Puzzle, 1984, The Child as Poet: Myth or Reality?, 1984, Celebrations, 1985, Worlds I Know and Other Poems, 1985, Sea Songs, 1986, Earth Songs, 1986, 1987, Higgledy-Piggledy, 1986, Space Songs, 1988, There Was a Place and Other Poems, 1988, Up in the Air, 1989, Birthday Poems, 1989, Remembering and Other Poems, 1989, My Head Is Red and Other Riddle Rhymes, 1990, Climb Into the Bell Tower: Essays on Poetry, 1990, Poem-making: Ways to Begin Writing Poetry, 1991, Light and Shadow, 1992, I Never Told and Other Poems, 1992, Let Freedom Ring: A Ballad of Martin Luther King, Jr., 1992, Abraham Lincoln, A Man for All the People, 1993, Platero Y Yo/Platero and I (trans. 1994, Flights of Fancy and other poems, 1994, Keep on Singing: A Ballad of Marian Anderson, 1994; The Writing of Poetry, film strips; co-editor: The Scott-Foresman Anthology, 1984, Festivals, 1996, B is for Baby, 1996; editor 37 anthologies of poetry; contbr. articles on children's lit. to ednl. publs., essays on lit. and reading in edn. to various books; mem. editorial adv. bd. The New Advocate, The Reading Teacher. Officer Beverly Hills PTA Council, 1966-75; pres. Friends of Beverly Hills Public Library, 1979-81; bd. dirs. Poetry Therapy Inst., 1975-96, Reading is Fundamental of So. Calif., 1981-96. Recipient honor award N.Y. Herald Tribune Spring Book Festival, 1958, excellence in poetry award Nat. Coun. Tchrs. of English, 1980, Commonwealth Club award, 1984, Nat. Jewish Book award, 1987, Kerlan award U. Minn., 1994, Transl. award Internat. Bd. on Books for Young People, 1994, Claremont Reading Inst. award, 1996. Mem. Authors Guild, Internat. Reading Assn., Soc. Children's Book Writers (honor award 1975), Tex. Inst. Letters (awards 1961, 80), So. Calif. Council on Lit. for Children and Young People (Comprehensive Contribution award 1968, Notable Book award 1972, Poetry Quartet award 89), PEN, Nat. Acad. Recording Arts & Scis. (Best Historical Album, 1995 The Heifetz Collection).

LIVINGSTON, PAMELA ANNA, corporate image and marketing management consultant; b. Richmond Hill, N.Y., Nov. 21, 1930; d. Paul Yount and Anna Margaret (Altland) L.; B.A., Adelphi U., 1951; postgrad. NYU, 1952, Columbia U., 1959, Am. Acad. Dramatic Art, 1954, IBM Systems and Mktg. Schs., 1967-70, Brandon Sch. Electronic Data Processing, 1973, Penn State U., 1993. Personnel and public relations depts. Am. Can Co., N.Y.C., 1951-60; exec. sec. to pres. York (Pa.) div. Borg-Warner Corp., 1962-65; freelance writer, 1965-67; mktg. ofcl. IBM Corp., 1967-70; research analyst, dir. new EDP bus. Ins. Co. N. Am., 1971-74; asst. to v.p. corp. affairs IU Internt., Phila., 1974-75; communications and mktg. mgmt. cons. specializing in corp. identity, 1975—; corp. image cons., 1984—; freelance writer, speaker on identity, 1994—. Recipient various journalism awards, award in mktg. and sales IBM, 1969-70, award for innovative product application, 1969. Mem. Sales/Mktg. Execs. Internat., Art Alliance, Public Relations Soc. Am., Econs. Club of York C. of C., Phila. Club Advt. Women, AAUW, Phila. Acad. Fine Arts, World Affairs Council, English-Speaking Union, Kappa Kappa Gamma. Contbr. articles to tech. jours. Home and Office: 108 S Rockburn St York PA 17402-3467

LIVINGSTON, SUSAN, occupational therapist, consultant; b. Boulder, Colo., Oct. 24, 1947; d. Ward Albert and Eleanor Jeanne (Carmack) Rogers; children: Greg, Christopher, Sue. BS in Occupl. Therapy, U. Kans., 1970. Registered occupl. therapist, N.Mex. Dir. rehab. clinic Ctrl. Kans. Med. Ctr., Great Bend, 1970-72; pvt. practice Great Bend, 1972-77; dir. occupl. therapy curriculum Burton County Coll., Great Bend, Kans., 1978-81; dir. tribal early childhood So. Ute tribe, Ignacio, Colo., 1981-88; owner, dir. Livingston Assocs., Durango, Colo., 1994—; cons. Bur. Indian Affairs, Crownpoint, N.Mex., 1995—. Recipient Spl. Svc. award Kans. Occupl. Therapy Assn.; named BPW Woman of Yr. Mem. Sensory Integration Internat., Assn. Psychol. Type, Am. Occupl. Therapy Assn., Bus. and Profl. Women, Colo. Occupl. Therapy Assn., N.Mex. Occupl. Therapy Assn.

LIVINGSTON, VICKI MAY, artist; b. Norfolk, Va., May 8, 1942; d. Willard Crandall and Pauline Mae (Cleveland) Rheubottom; m. Domingo Polimeni, Dec. 31, 1966 (div. Feb. 1974); m. Brian Alexander Livingston, Oct. 4, 1974. BFA, Va. Commonwealth U., 1963. Solo exhibitions include Zodiac Gallery, Richmond, Va., 1963, Va. Commonwealth U., 1963, Ruth Sherman Gallery, N.Y.C., 1965, Mondragon Corp. Offices, L.A., 1986, Orlando Gallery, L.A., 1988, 90, 93, Torrance (Calif.) Cultural Arts Ctr., Joslyn Gallery, 1992, Palos Verdes Art Ctr., Stewart Gallery, 1993; exhibited in group shows at Va. Mus. Fine Arts, 1963, Va. Union, U., 1962, Richmond Artists Assn., 1962, Carillon Gallery, 1963, Va. Commonwealth U. Gallery, 1962, 63, Twentieth Century Gallery, 1963, 62, Westhampton Coll., 1962, 63, U. Va., 1963, Va. Commonwealth U. Fine Art Dept. Travelling Exhbn., 1962, 63, Ruth Sherman Gallery, 1965 (Best in Show and Solo Exhibit 1965), Sarasota Art Assn. Gallery, 1979, 80, Burbank Fine Arts Fedn. Sixth Ann. Multimedia, 1981, Santa Paula 45th Ann. Juried Exhibit, 1981, Wing Gallery, L.A., 1982, Orange County Ctr. for Contemporary Art, 1982, LA Harbor Coll. Gallery, 1984, Laguna Beach Mus. Art, 1983, 84, Bowers Mus., 1985, Radius Gallery, 1984, 85, Carnegie Art Mus., 1986, Brea Civic-Cultural Ctr. Gallery, 1982, 84, 85, 86, Riverside Mus. of Art, 1987, Brand Art Libr. Gallery, 1987, Long Beach Arts, 1988, Palos Verdes Art Ctr., 1989, S.I.T.E., 1989, Finegood Art Gallery, 1990, Orlando Gallery, 1987, 88, 89, 90, 91, 92, Artspace, L.A. Mcpl. Satellite Gallery at Woodland Hills, 1991; work reviewed in various art mags. Recipient Best in Show and Solo Exhibit award Ruth Sherman Gallery, 1965, Merit award, Annual Juried Open, Sarasota, Fla., 1980, Second Place/First Painting award Bowers Mus., 1985, Hon. Mention Ann. Juried Exhbn., Palos Verdes, 1989, Merit award 84th Open Juried Exhbn., Long Beach, Calif., 1989, Bronze award Mixed Media and Silver award Contemporary Painting, Discovery 1993, Art of California Mag. Competition. Democrat. Home: 1723 Hollifield Ct Rancho Palos Verdes CA 90275 Studio: 1723 Hollifield Ct Rancho Palos Verdes CA 90275

LIVINGSTONE, CHARLEEN THOMPSON, furniture manufacturer; b. Utica, N.Y., Dec. 13, 1929; d. Charles Alva and Edith Elizabeth (Wagner) Thompson; m. James Richard Livingtone, Apr.12, 1952; children: Charleen E. Steers, Edith A., Jane Roberts. Grad., Mohawk Valley Community Coll., 1949. Asst. prodn. Time Inc., N.Y.C., 1951-52; advt. prodn. Hoag & Provandie, Boston, 1953-55; sales cons. Guy P. Livingstone Co., Winchester, Mass., 1964-95; v.p. Livingstone Mfg. Co. Mass. Inc., Winchester, 1978-95. Apptd. mem. Wellington Sch. Bldg. Com., Belmont, Mass., 1968, elected sec., 1969, elected. chmn. Pro Tem, 1972. Episcopalian. Home: 90 Agassiz Ave Belmont MA 02178-1324 Office: Livingstone Mfg Co Mass Inc 28 Church St Winchester MA 01890-2538

LIVINGSTONE, SUSAN MORRISEY, nonprofit administrator; b. Carthage, Mo., Jan. 13, 1946; d. Richard John II and Catherine Newell (Carmean) Morrisey; m. Neil C. Livingstone III, Aug. 30, 1968. AB, Coll. William and Mary, 1968; MA, U. Mont., 1973; postgrad., Tufts U., 1973, Fletcher Sch. Law and Diplomacy, 1973—. Researcher Senator Mark O. Hatfield, Washington, 1969-70; chief legis. and press asst. Congressman Richard H. Ichord, Washington, 1973-75, adminstrv. asst., 1975-81; cons. Congressman Wendell Bailey, Washington, 1981; exec. asst. VA, Washington, 1981-85, assoc. dep. adminstr. logistics and mgmt., 1985-86, sr. procurement exec., 1985-89, assoc. dep. adminstr. logistics, 1986-89; asst. sec. Army Dept. of Def., Washington, 1989-93; v.p. health and safety svcs. ARC, Washington, 1993—; mem interagy. com. on women's bus. enterprise The White House, 1985-89; mem. Pres.'s Coun. on Mgmt. Improvement, 1985-86. NDEA fellow. Mem. Exec. Women in Govt., Procurement Round Table (bd. dirs. 1994—), Assn. U.S. Army (bd. dirs. 1994-96, coun. trustees 1996—), Women in Internat. Security (adv. bd. 1994—). Republican. Episcopalian. Office: ARC 8111 Gatehouse Rd Falls Church VA 22042

LIVINGSTONE, TRUDY DOROTHY ZWEIG, dancer, educator; b. N.Y.C., June 9, 1946; d. Joseph and Anna (Feinberg) Zweig; m. John Leslie Livingstone, Aug. 7, 1977; 1 child, Robert Edward. Student, Charles Lowe Studios, N.Y.C., 1950-52, Nina Tinova Studio, N.Y.C., 1953-56, Ballet Russe de Monte Carlo, N.Y.C., 1956-57, Bklyn. Coll., 1964-66; BA in Psychology cum laude, Boston U., 1968, MEd, 1969; postgrad., Serena Studios, Carnegie Hall Ballet Arts, N.Y.C., 1973-74. Tchr. Millis (Mass.) Pub. Schs., 1969-72, Hebrew Acad. Atlanta, 1974-76; profl. dancer various orgns. including Rivermont Country Club, Jewish Community Ctr., Callanwolde Performing Arts Ctr., Atlanta, 1974-84; founder, owner, instr. dance Sasha Studios, Atlanta, 1974-77; owner Trudy Zweig Livingstone Studios, Wellesley, Needham, Mass., 1987-88, Palm Beach, Fla., 1989—; judge dance competition Atlanta Council Run-Offs, 1976. Vol. League Sch., Bklyn., 1965, Kennedy Meml. Hosp., Brighton, Mass., 1969, Nat. Affiliation for Literacy Advances, Santa Monica, Calif., 1982. Mem. Am. Alliance for Health, Phys. Edn., Recreation and Dance, Poets of the Palm Beaches, L.A. Athletic Club, Wellesley Coll. Club, Governor's Club (West Palm Beach). Jewish.

LIZE, JOANNE ELLEN, librarian; b. Chgo., Oct. 10, 1948; d. George Edward and Dorothy Eleanor (Kunc) Hauri; m. Henry Teodor Lize, July 11, 1970; children: Steven Edward, Andrew Teodor. BS in Elem. Edn., U. Wis., Whitewater, 1970; cert. in gifted edn., Aurora U., 1986; postgrad., Rosary Coll., 1995—. Cert. elem. tchr., Ill. 1st grade tchr. Janesville (Wis.) Pub. Schs., 1970-73, Wood Dale (Ill.) Sch. Dist., 1973-75; tchg. asst. Lombard (Ill.) Sch. Dist., 1984-88, learning ctr. asst., 1990-94; substitute tchr. Collier County Pub. Sch., Naples, Fla., 1988-89; tchg. asst. Naperville (Ill.) Sch. Dist., 1989-90; tchr. of gifted LaGrange Park (Ill.) Schs., 1987-88, Worlds of Wisdom and Wonder/Nat. Louis U., Evanston, Ill., 1990; children's libr. Helen M. Plum Meml. Libr., Lombard. Pres. gifted advocacy for children and parents PALS, Lombard, 1990-91; chmn. pack 40 Boy Scouts Am., Lombard, 1986-88; soloist First Ch. United Ch. of Christ, Lombard, 1990—. Ill. State Libr. edn. and tng. grantee, 1994, Gifted Edn. Fellowship grantee Aurora U., 1986-88. Mem. AAUW (Grad. Edn. award 1995), ALA, Ill. Libr. Assn., Prairie State Storytelling League, Lombard Hist. Soc. (ednl. com. 1994—). Home: 130 W Washington Blvd Lombard IL 60148 Office: Helen Plum Meml Libr 110 W Maple St Lombard IL 60148

LJUNG, ELLEN JO, secondary school educator, writer, storyteller; b. White Plains, N.Y., Aug. 29, 1947; d. George Michael and Shirley Florence (Meyers) Szabad; m. Donovan Allen Ljung, Sept. 5, 1968; children: Michael Allen, David Jeffrey. BS with honors, U. Wis., 1970; MS, So. Conn. State U., 1979. Tchr. St. James Sch., Madison, Wis., 1970-71, North Haven (Conn.) Schs., 1978-79, Batavia (Ill.) H.S., 1979-80; tchr., grant writer, fine arts sponsor, internet trainer Glenbard West H.S., Glen Ellyn, Ill., 1980—; mem. tchr. edn. adv. bd. Ill. Benedictine Coll., Lisle, 1993—; charter mem. Ill. Problem-Based Learning Network. Author: Writing with Apple Works, 1992, Writing with Microsoft Works, 1994; contbr. articles to profl. jours. Curriculum advisor Temple B'Nai Israel, Aurora, Ill., 1992-94; soccer coach, ref., commr. Tri-Cities Soccer, Geneva, 1981-87, varsity soccer announcer, 1988—; mem. parent adv. coun. Geneva Cmty. H.S., 1986-89. Named Master Tchr., State of Ill., 1984. Mem. ASCD, Nat. Coun. Tchrs. English (presenter 1991, 92, program award 1987), Ill. Assn. Tchrs. English, Nat. Storytelling Assn., Internat. Reading Assn. Home: 2257 Clover Ln Geneva IL 60134-1013 Office: Glenbard W HS 670 Crescent Blvd Glen Ellyn IL 60137-4281

LLOVERAS, CONNIE, artist; b. Havana, Cuba, Oct. 16, 1958; came to U.S., 1960; d. Gaston Andres and Conchita (Freyre) de Zarraga; m. Robert Lloveras, Oct. 5, 1979; children: Christianne, Robert, Michael. AA, Miami Dade C.C., 1979; BFA, Fla. Internat. U., 1981. Gallery artist Barbara Gillman Gallery, Miami, 1981-93, Americas Collection, Coral Gables, Fla., 1993-95; represented by Forum of the Arts, San Juan, Puerto Rico, Arte Consult, Panama; juror Coconut Grove Arts Festival, Miami, 1994, Fla. Internat. U. ann. student exhibit, Miami, 1993. One-woman shows at Barbara Gillman Gallery, Miami, 1984, 90, Galeria Matisse, Barcelona, Spain, 1992, The Americas Collection, Coral Gables, Fla., 1993, 96, The Cultural Resource Ctr., Miami, 1994, Forum of the Arts, San Juan, P.R., 1994, Wheeler Gallery, Art Inst., Ft. Lauderdale, Fla., 1995, Nexus Contemporary Art Ctr., Ga., 1996; exhibited in group shows at Mus. Contemporary Hispanic Art, N.Y.C., 1985, Sibi Art Gallery, Miami, 1985, 86, Miami-Dade C.C. South Campus Art Gallery, 1985, Barbara Gillman Gallery, Miami, 1986, 88, 92, Gillman/Stein Gallery, Tampa, 1986, Centre Cultural Paul Dumais, Tonneins, France, 1987, Jane Voorehees Zimmerman Art Mus., Rutgers U., New Brunswick, N.J., Mus. Contemporary Hispanic Art, N.Y.C., Miami U., Oxford, Ohio, Museo de Arte de Ponce, P.R., Ctr. for fine Arts, Miami, 1987-89, The Continuum Art Ctr., Miami Beach, Fla., 1987, Leigh U. Art Galleries, Bethlehem, Pa., 1987, Contemporary Arts Ctr., New Orleans, Art and Culture Ctr., Hollywood, Calif., 1988, Cultural Resource Ctr., Miami, Gillman/Baker Gallery, Boca Raton, Fla., 1989, City Hall, Orlando, 1992, South Dade Regional Libr., Miami, 1992, Main Libr., Metro Dade Cultural Resource Ctr., Miami, 1992, 93, Mus. Art, Inc., Ft. Lauderdale, 1993, The Americas Collection, Coral Gables, 1994, Cuban Mus., Miami, 1995, Miami Dade Libr., 1995, Ground Level Gallery, Miami, 1995, others; represented in permanent collections at Mus. of Art, Inc., Ft. Lauderdale, Boca Raton Mus. Art, Cuban Mus., Miami, Pa. Conv. Ctr., Phila., Palm Beach County Coun. Arts, Palm Beach, Wash. State Arts Commn., Seattle, State of Fla. Divsn. of Cultural Affairs, Confort, Barcelona, Atlanta U. Ctr., others. Recipient scholarships Fla. Internat. U., 1980, 81, Merit award U. Miami, 1981, Best Sculptor award Metro Dade Ctr. for Fine Arts, Miami, 1987, Equal Merit award Ga.Mus. Art, Miami, 1987, Silver medal Les Plus Grands Peintres Latins D'Amerique, 1987, Artist in Residency grant Fla. Dept. State, Divsn. Cultural Affairs, Miami, 1992. Roman Catholic. Home: 8800 Old Cutler Rd Miami FL 33156

LLOYD, DEBRA WOOD, banker; b. Anderson, Ind., Apr. 21, 1951; d. Wilburn H. and Mary L. (Robbins) Wood; m. Stephen Michael Lloyd, Oct. 9, 1992. BA, Anderson (Ind.) U., 1973; MBA, Butler U., Indpls., 1982. Comml. lender Merchants Nat. Bank, Indpls., 1976-85, Irving Trust Co., N.Y.C., 1985-86; v.p., comml. real estate lender Peoples Bank & Trust Co., Indpls., 1986—; part-time instr. comml. lending U. Indpls., 1991. Vol. Conner Prairie, Noblesville, Ind., 1985—, Pan Am Games, Indpls., 1987, U.S. Rowing, Indpls., 1988—; del. 1st Japan-Am. Grassroots Summit, Tokyo, 1991; bd. dirs. YWCA of Indpls., grad. Exec. Women's Leadership Program; mem. adv. coun. Bus. Women's Ctr. Mem. Japan Am. Soc., Columbia Club (new dimensions com.), Robert Morris Assocs., English Speaking Union, Contemporary Club. Republican. Office: Peoples Bank & Trust Co 130 E Market St Indianapolis IN 46204-3234

LLOYD, JACQUELINE, English language educator; b. N.Y.C., Aug. 21, 1950; d. R.G. and Hortense (Collins) L. BA, Fisk U., 1972; MEd, U. North Fla., 1989. Instr. English Edward Waters Coll., Jacksonville, Fla., 1983, 90—. Mem. Nat. Coun. Tchrs. English. Democrat. Presbyterian. Home: 5006 Andrew Robinson Dr Jacksonville FL 32209-1002

LLOYD, JUNE DICKSON, vocational school educator; b. Monaca, Pa., June 17, 1936; d. Harry Ross and Mabel Pearl (Yoho) Dickson;m. william Howard Lloyd Sr., Jan. 24, 1957 (separated); children: Kathleen Gay, William Howard Jr., Richard Lewellyn. BS in Home Econs., Carnegie Mellon U., 1971; MEd in Vocat. Edn., U. Pitts., 1976; PhD in Vocat. Edn., Pa. State U., 1994. Cert. tchr. home econs., cert. vocat. tchr., Pa. Instr. Pitts. Sch. Dist., 1973—; sec. Future Directions Task Force, Home Econ. in Pa., 1990-91; trainer Pa. Home Econs. Leadership Training, 1991. Mem. league of Women Voters, Churchill, Pa., 1965-70; chmn. PTA, Churchill, 1968-80, Beulah Women's Orgn., Churchill, 1968-80. Recipient grant Pa. Dept. Edn., 1987-88, 93-94. Mem. Am. Vocat. Assn., Am. Family and Consumer Scis. Assn., Pa. Vocat. Assn. (bd. dirs. 1990-91, 94—), Pa. Vocat. Family and Consumer Scis. Assn. (pres. 1989-91), Phi Delta Kappa, Kappa Omicron Phi. Home: 3 Waterside Pl Pittsburgh PA 15222-4707 Office: Schenley High Tchrs Ctr 4410 Bigelow Blvd Pittsburgh PA 15213-2661

LLOYD, LAUREN, film company executive. Sr. pres. Hollywood Pictures, Burbank, Calif. Office: Hollywood Pictures 500 S Buena Vista St Burbank CA 91521*

LLOYD, MARTHA, artist; b. Washington, Aug. 24, 1927; d. James Aubrey Powell and Mary Helen Jones; m. Donal B. Lloyd, Aug. 28, 1948; children: Deborah, Nancy. BFA, Am. U., 1965; postgrad., Yale U., 1982; MFA, Simons Rock Coll. of Bard, 1991. vis. lectr. Montserrat Coll. Art, Beverly, Mass.; artist-in-residence Decordova Mus., Lincoln, Mass. One person shows include Georgetown Ctr. for Arts, Washington, 1963, Wheeler Gallery, Concord, Mass., 1974, Tufts U., Medford, Mass., 1980, Merrimack Coll., North Andover, Mass., 1989, The Harcus Gallery, Boston, 1991, Kimball Bourgault Gallery, Boston, 1993; exhibited in group shows Watkins Gallery Exhibit, Am. U., Washington, 1964, Inst. Contemporary Art, Boston, 1970, Rockwell Gallery, Cambridge, Mass., 1976, Inst. Art, Beijing, China, 1981, Northeastern U., Boston, 1983, The Harcus Gallery, Boston, 1991, Harbor Gallery, U. Mass., Boston, 1992, Fed. Res. Gallery De Cordova Mus., Boston, 1992, Attleboro (Mass.) Mus., 1992, Warren St. Gallery, Hudson, N.Y., 1994; represented in permanent collections Merrimack Coll., North Andover, Linsky, Finnegan and Stanzler, Boston, Cigna, Phila., others. Recipient Painting award curator Nat. Gallery Art, Phillips Gallery, painting award fine art dept. U. Minn. Home: PO Box 250 East Nassau NY 12062

LLOYD, SUSAN ELAINE, middle school educator; b. Sioux Falls, S.D., Aug. 25, 1942; d. Travis Monroe and Lois Elaine (Herridge) Hetherington; m. Jerry Glynn Lloyd, Mar. 13, 1982; children: Joseph Sanders Rogers III, Melissa Elaine Rogers. BS in Edn., SW Tex. State U., 1965; MA, U. Tex., San Antonio, 1979; AA, Stephens Coll., 1962. Cert. reading specialist, supervisory, art (all levels), secondary English, elem. edn. Art tchr. South Park Ind. Sch. Dist., Beaumont, Tex., 1965-68; reading specialist John Jay High Sch., San Antonio, 1979-84; reading dept. coord. Sul Ross Mid. Sch., Northside Ind. Sch. Dist., San Antonio, 1984—, remedial reading tchr., 1990; developer reading curricula, cons.; advisor Scholastic TAB Book Club, 1992-94. Author: Reading Education in Texas, 1992, 93. Named Sul Ross Middle Sch. Tchr. of Yr., 1993, Trinity U. Disting. Educator, 1993. Mem. ASCD, Internat. Reading Assn. (hon. chmn. 14th ann. SW regional meeting, presenter 19th 1991, 20th 1992), Tex. Reading Coun., Alamo Reading Assn., Assn. Tex. Profl. Educators, San Antonio Watercolor Group. Home: 7614 Tippit Trl San Antonio TX 78240-3627 Office: Sul Ross Mid Sch 3630 Callaghan Rd San Antonio TX 78228-4323

LLOYD, WANDA SMALLS, newspaper editor; b. Columbus, Ohio, July 12, 1949; d. Gloria Walker; m. Willie Burk Lloyd, May 25, 1975; 1 child, Shelby Renee. BA, Spelman Coll., Atlanta, 1971. Copy editor Providence Evening Bull., R.I., 1971-73, Miami Herald, Fla., 1973-74, Atlanta Jour., Ga., 1974-75, Washington Post, 1975-76; instr. program for minority journalists Columbia U., N.Y.C., summer 1972; dep. Washington editor Times-Post News Service, 1976-86; dpt. mng. editor cover stories, USA Today, 1986-87, mng. editor/adminstrn., 1987-88, sr. editor, 1988-96; mng. editor The Greenville News, 1996—; cons. So. Regional Press Inst., Savannah State Coll., Ga., 1973—; mem. adv. bd. urban journalism workshop Howard U., Washington, 1983—. Mem., bd. dirs. Nation's Capital council, Girl Scouts U.S., Washington 1985; trustee Spelman Coll., 1988—; mem. adv. com. Alfred Friendly Found., 1992—; bd. dirs. Dow Jones Newspaper Fund, 1992—. Mem. Washington Assn. Black Journalists, Nat. Assn. Black Journalists, Washington Spelman Alumnae Assn. (v.p. 1984-86; Named Alumna of Yr. 1985), Am. Soc. of Newspaper Editors, Delta Sigma Theta. Baptist. Office: The Greenville News PO Box 1688 Greenville SC 29602

LO, THERESA NONG, health science administrator; b. Hai Phong, Vietnam, Mar. 16, 1945; d. Dang Van and Boi Thuy (Lam) Nong; m. Chu Shek Lo, Dec.27, 1969; 1 child, Francesca Che Lo. Student, Ottumwa Heights Coll., 1964-65; BA, Clarke Coll., 1968; PhD, Ind. U., Indpls., 1974. Lab. asst. Clarke Coll., Dubuque, Iowa, 1966-68; teaching/rsch. asst. Med. Ctr. Ind. U., Indpls., 1968-73; USPHS postdoctoral trainee U. Calif., San Francisco, 1973-75; vis. fellow Nat. Heart, Lung & Blood Inst., Bethesda, Md., 1975-77; vis. fellow Nat. Cancer Inst. NIH, Bethesda, 1977-78; rsch. chemist Lab. of Cellular Metabolism, Nat. Heart, Lung & Blood Inst., Bethesda, 1979-82, Lab. Chem. Pharmacology, Nat. Heart, Lung & Blood Inst., Bethesda, 1982-88; health sci. adminstr. trainee div. blood diseases & resource Nat. Heart, Lung & Blood Inst., Bethesda, 1988-89; chemist rev. logistics br. NIH, Bethesda, 1989-91; scientific review adminstr., review br. Nat. Inst. Arthritis & Musculoskeletal & Skin Diseases, Bethesda, Md., 1991—; trainee NIH health scientist adminstr. assocs. program Office of Dir.; liaison to Drug Enforcement Adminstrn., U.S. Dept. Justice; liaison to lab. chem. pharmacology Nat. Heart, Lung and Blood Inst., Bethesda, 1982-83, coord. sci. seminar program, 1982-83; role model NIH career day divsn. equal opportunity NIH, Bethesda, 1988, 90, 91; U.S. savs. bond canvasser, 1989; exec. sec. NIH Asian/Pacific Island Am. Adv. Com., 1991, vice chair, 1992-94, NIAMS EEO Adv. Com., 1992-94; invited speaker Chinese Acad. Med. Scis., Beijing, 1982, others. Contbr. articles and abstracts to profl. jours. Sec. Orgn. Chinese Ams., Inc., Greater Washington, 1984, woman rep. White House briefing, Washington, 1985; participant women's mgmt. tng. initiative HHS Pers. Adminstrn., 1987-88; bd. dirs. Orgn. of Chinese Ams., Greater Washington, 1991-92. Ottumwa Quota Club scholr, 1965, Clarke Coll. scholar, 1965-68; named hon. citizen City of Indpls., 1968, hon. speedway ambassador Civil Town of Speedway (Ind.), 1972; recipient Spl. Achievement award Nat. Cancer Inst., div. extramural activities, 1990. Mem. Am. Soc. for Biochemistry and Molecular Biology, Am. Soc. for Pharmacology and Exptl. Therapeutics, Inflammation Rsch. Assn., Cardiovascular Rsch. Inst. Alumni Assn., Ind. U. Alumni Assn., Clarke Coll. Alumni Assn., Sigma Xi. Home: 5304 Elsmere Ave Bethesda MD 20814-1647 Office: NIAMS Review Br Natcher Bldg Rm 5AS-37B Bethesda MD 20892-6500

LO, WENDY WAI YAN, financial analyst; b. Stamford, Conn., May 5, 1968. BA in Econs., Boston U., 1990. Statis. specialist Pitney-Bowes, Inc., Stamford, Conn., 1990-91; fin. analyst Pitney-Bowes, Inc., 1991-94; EDP auditor Pitney Bowes, Inc., 1994-95; sr. fin. analyst Perrier Group of Am., Greenwich, Conn., 1995—; divsn. rep. Minorities Resource Group, sec., chair comm. com., 1992-95, co-chair Diversity Task Force, 1993-95. Mem. NAFE.

LOBIG, JANIE HOWELL, special education educator; b. Peoria, Ill., June 10, 1945; d. Thomas Edwin and Elizabeth Jane (Higdon) Howell; m. James Frederick Lobig, Aug. 16, 1970; 1 child, Jill Christina. BS in Elem. Edn., So. Ill. U., 1969; MA in Spl. Edn. Severely Handicapped, San Jose State U., 1989. Cert. elem. tchr., Calif., Mo., Ill., handicapped edn., Calif., Mo.; ordained to ministry Presbyn. Ch. as deacon, 1984. Tchr. trainable mentally retarded children Spl. Luth. Sch., St. Louis, 1967-68; tchr. trainable mentally retarded and severly handicapped children Spl. Sch. Dist. St. Louis, 1969-80, head tchr., 1980-83; tchr. severly handicapped children San Jose (calif.) Unifed Sch. Dist., 1983-86; tchr. autistic students Santa Clara County Office Edn., San Jose, 1986—; tchr. Suzanne Dancers, 1991-92. Vol. Am. Cancer Soc., San Jose, 1986-89, 92, St. Louis Reps., 1976-82, Am. Heart Assn., 1985—, Multiple Sclerosis Soc., 1990—; troop leader Camp Fire Girls, San Jose, 1984-85; moderator bd. deacons Evergreen Presbyn. Ch., 1986-89; mem. exec. bd. Norwood Creek Elem. Sch. PTA, 1983-86. Mem. Council for Exceptional Children, Assn. for Severly Handicapped, Nat. Edn. Assn., Calif. Tchrs. Assn. Independent. Home: 3131 Creekmore Way San Jose CA 95148-2805 Office: Weller Elem Sch 345 Boulder Dr Milpitas CA 95035

LOBO, KORLIN KAE, marketing professional; b. Cedar Rapids, Iowa, Jan. 18, 1963; d. Robert F. and Janis L. (Stodola) Kazimour; m. J. Philip Lobo, Nov. 16, 1991. BBA, Iowa State U., 1985; MBA, So. Meth. U., 1986, M in Liberal Arts, 1993. Asst. account exec. The Bloom Agy., Dallas, 1986-88, account exec., 1988-90, sr. account exec., 1990-92; product mgr. popcorn divsn. Nat. Oats Co., Cedar Rapids, 1992-93, group product mgr., 1993-94; customer mktg. mgr. Ralston Foods (formerly Nat. Oats Co.), Cedar Rapids, 1994—; bd. dirs. Tex. Club, Dallas, 1990-92; pres. Tri-K Transp., Cedar Rapids, 1986-96. Vol. Dallas Heart Assn., 1989-91, Dallas Internat. Sports Commn., 1991; fund raiser Jr. Achievment, Cedar Rapids, 1992—, classroom cons. econ., 1995; co. coord. United Way fundraising, Cedar Rapids, 1993. N.C.H. Corp. Merit scholar So. Meth. U., 1985. Mem. Tri-Delta Alumnae Group (alumnae panhellenic rep. 1993—, alumnae newsletter com. 1995-96). Home: 2041 Forest Dr SE Cedar Rapids IA 52403

LOBO, REBECCA, basketball player; b. Southwick, Mass.. Student, U. Conn. Basketball player USA Women's Nat. Team; mem. 1992 U.S. Olympic Festival East Team, 1992 Jr. World Championship Qualifying Team, 1993 USA Jr. World Championship Team. Recipient Wade trophy and named Nat. Player of Yr., Naismith, U.S. Basketball Writers Assn., 1995, 1994 and 1995 Kodak All-Am. First Team, Big East Conf. Player of Yr., Big East Tournament Most Outstanding Player, 1994 and 1995 Big East Conf. Women's Basketball Scholar Athlete of Yr. Office: USA Basketball 5465 Mark Dabling Blvd Colorado Springs CO 80918-3842

LOBOSCO, ANNA FRANCES, state development disabilities program planner; b. Binghamton, N.Y., Nov. 13, 1952; d. James H. and Marie A. (Wilcox) Mee; m. Charles M. Lobosco, Apr. 27, 1974; children: Charles Jr., Amanda, Nicholas, Dennis. BA in History, Marist Coll., Poughkeepsie, N.Y., 1974; MS in Edn./Spl. Edn., Coll. St. Rose, Albany, 1978; PhD in Curriculum and Instrn., SUNY, Albany, 1989. Cert. tchr. elem., secondary and spl. edn., N.Y. Diagnostic remedial tchr. Orange County Assn. for Help of Retarded Children, Middletown/Newburgh, N.Y., 1973-78; instr., supr. student tchrs. Mt. St. Mary Coll., Newburgh, 1980-82; rsch. asst., assoc. dir. evaluation consortium SUNY, Albany, 1985-89; devel. disability program planner/prevention specialist N.Y. State Developmental Disabilities Planning Coun., Albany, 1989—; cons. N.Y. State Edn. Dept. Edn., 1987-89, N.Y. State Unified Tchrs., 1988-89, N.Y. State Coun. on Children's Families, 1986-88, N.Y. State Assn. Counties, 1987-88; instr. Coll. St. Rose, Albany, 1989-90. Contbr. articles to profl. jours; exec. producer viedeos Mary's Choice: The Effects of Prenatal Exposure to Alcohol and Other Drugs, 1992, Its Up to You, 1995. Named Advocate of the Yr., N.Y. Libr. Assn., 1993. Mem. Coun. Exceptional Children, Am. Evaluation Assn., Am. Ednl. Rsch. Assn., Am. Assn. Mental Retardation, Kappa Delta Pi. Office: NYS Devel Disabilities Planning Coun 155 Washington Ave 2d Fl Albany NY 12210-2329

LOBRON, BARBARA L., speech educator, writer, editor, photographer; b. Phila., Mar. 19, 1944; d. Martin Aaron and Elizabeth (Gots) L.; student Pa. State U., 1962-63; B.A. cum laude, Temple U., Phila., 1966; student photography Harold Feinstein, N.Y.C., 1970, 79-80; student art therapy Erika Steinberger, N.Y.C., 1994—. Reporter, writer Camden (N.J.) Courier-Post, 1966-68; editorial asst. Med. Insight mag., N.Y.C., 1970-71; mng. editor Camera 35 mag., N.Y.C., 1971-75, also assoc. editor photog. anns. for U.S. Camera/Camera 35, 1972, 73; freelance editor as Word Woman, N.Y.C., 1975-77, 79—; acct. exec. Bozell & Jacobs, N.Y.C., 1977-79; copy editor Camera Arts mag., N.Y.C., 1981-83; editorial coord. Center mag., Nat. Ctr. Health Edn., 1985; editorial coord. Popular Photography mag., 1986-95; assoc. editor Sony Style, 1995; tchr. speech improvement N.Y.C. Bd. Edn., 1995—; contbg. editor Photograph; participant 3M Editor's Conf. (1st woman), 1972. Photographs: group exhbns. include Internat. Women's Art Festival, N.Y.C., 1975, Rockefeller Ctr., N.Y.C., 1976, Photograph Gallery, N.Y.C., 1981 ; acrylic painting exhbns. at Tchrs. Coll., N.Y.C., 1994, Warwick Hotel, N.Y.C., 1995; represented in collection Library of Calif. Inst. Arts, Valencia. Tchr. Sch. Vol. Program, N.Y.C., 1994—. Recipient 1st pl. honors Dist. 1, Internat. Assn. Bus. Communicators, 1977. Copy editor: The Complete Guide to Cibachrome Printing, 1980, The Popular Photography Question and Answer Book, 1979, The Photography Catalog, 1976, Strand: Sixty Years of Photography, 1976, You and Your Lens, 1975; contbr. articles to comml. publs., chpts. to books. Dist. leader SGI-USA. Buddhist. Avocations: dancing, reading, photography, singing, walking. Home: 85 Hicks St Apt 7 Brooklyn NY 11201-6825

LOCEY, ANN PEDERSEN, interior designer; b. Buffalo, May 21, 1944; d. Gilbert John and Carmen (Ogden) Pedersen; m. Dave Ryan Locey, Aug. 27, 1966; children: Allison, Jennifer. BA, U. Ariz., 1966. Owner, mgr. APL Design, St. Paul, 1986—. Co-chmn. benefit adv. com. Pacer Ctr., Mpls., 1991-93, 95-96; chmn. benefit Wilderness Inquiry, Mpls., 1993, 95; bd. dirs. Jr. League St. Paul, 1995—; chmn. capital campaign Summit Leadership Soc., United Way St. Paul, 1995; pres. Port Superior Village Assn., 1994—. Named Sustainer of Yr., Jr. League St. Paul, 1990. Mem. Ind. Designers Assn., St. Paul Yacht Club, Minn. Club. Republican. Presbyterian. Home and Office: 168 E 6th St Apt 4202 Saint Paul MN 55101

LOCHALA, SUSAN DIANE, accountant; b. Graysville, Ala., Aug. 28, 1973; d. Vertis Thomas and Naomi (Perkins) Sides; m. Mark Allen Lochala, June 3, 1995. BS in Acctg., Miss. U. for Women, 1994. Bookkeeper Fashion Barn, Inc., Columbus, Miss., 1993-94; fin. mgr. Universal Health Svcs., Columbus, 1994—. Fellow Inst. Mgmt. Accts., Am. Soc. Women Accts. Ch. of God of Prophecy. Office: Universal Health Svcs 1505 1/2 Hwy 45 N PO Box 703 Columbus MS 39701

LOCHER, ELIZABETH AIKEN, elementary education educator; b. N.Y.C., Oct. 10, 1943; d. Richard Eustace Jr. and Marjorie Armstrong (Siebers) Aiken; m. Peyton Ring Neal Jr., June 20, 1964 (div.); children: Melissa Davis Neal Reed, Peyton Ring Neal III; m. Baldwin Gerard Locher Jr., Dec. 21, 1979; 1 child, Baldwin Locher III. AA, Peace Coll., 1964; BA, Mary Baldwin Coll., 1980; MEd, U. Va., 1991. Cataloger, asst. libr. Georgetown Law Ctr., Washington, 1965-71; asst. libr. Lexington (Va.) High Sch., 1976-79; reading specialist, tchr. Nat. Bridge Elem./Rockbridge County Schs., Lexington, 1989—; bd. dirs. Literacy Vols. Rockbridge, Lexington; presenter in field. Editor: Union List of Legal Periodicals, 1971; contbr. articles to newspapers and jours. Bd. dirs. Rockbridge Regional Libr., Lexington, 1994—; corr. sec. Colonial Dames XVII Century, Lexington, 1993-94; bd. dirs., sec. Lexington Downtown Devel., 1985-91; libr., docent Stonewall Jackson House, Lexington, 1979-89. U. Va. fellow, Charlottesville, 1991. Mem. NEA, DAR, Internat. Reading Assn., Nat. Coun. Tchrs. English, Va. Edn. Assn., Va. State Reading Assn., Rockbridge Edn. Assn. (treas. 1995—), Shenandoah Valley Reading Coun. (rec. sec. 1994-96, Tchr. of Yr. 1994), Phi Alpha Theta, Delta Kappa Gamma (rec. sec. 1996—). Episcopalian. Home: RR 2 Box 70 Lexington VA 24450-9407 Office: Natural Bridge Elem PO Box 280 Natural Bridge Station VA 24579

LOCKE, ELIZABETH HUGHES, foundation administrator; b. Norfolk, Va., June 30, 1939; d. George Morris and Sallie Epps (Moss) Hughes; m. John Rae Locke, Jr., Sept. 13, 1958 (div. 1981); children: John Rae III, Sallie Curtis. BA magna cum laude with honors in English, Duke U., 1964, PhD, 1972; MA, U. N.C., 1966. Instr. English, U. N.C., Chapel Hill, 1970-72; vis. prof. English, Duke U., Durham, N.C., 1972-73, dir. univ. pubs., 1973-79; corp. contbns. officer Bethlehem Steel Corp., Pa., 1979-82; dir. edn. div. and comm. Duke Endowment, Charlotte, N.C., 1982-96, exec. dir., 1996—; past pres. Comm. Philanthropy, Washington; mem. comms. com. Coun. on Founds., Washington, 1995—. Editor: Duke Encounters, 1977, Prospectus for Change: American Private Higher Education, 1985, (mag.) Issues, 1985-96. Pres., Jr. League, Durham, 1976, Hist. Preservation Soc., Durham, 1977, Pub. Rels. Soc. Am., Charlotte chpt., 1988, Charlotte Area Donors Forum; past pres. Sch. of Arts, Charlotte; bd. visitors Davidson Coll., Charlotte Country Day Sch., Duke U., Johnson C. Smith U. Recipient Leadership award Charlotte C. of C., 1984; Danforth fellow, 1972. Mem. Nat. Task Force, English Speaking Union, The Most Venerable Order of St. John of Jerusalem (officer sister), Phi Beta Kappa. Democrat. Episcopalian. Club: Charlotte City. Office: 100 N Tryon St Ste 3500 Charlotte NC 28202-4000

LOCKE, MAMIE EVELYN, dean; b. Brandon, Miss., Mar. 19, 1954; d. Ennis and Amanda Jean (McMahon) L. BA, Tougaloo Coll., 1976; MA, Atlanta U., 1978, PhD, 1984; cert. in archives adminstrn., Emory U.; cert. in mgmt. devel., Harvard U. Archivist Dept. Archives and History, Jackson, Miss., 1976-79, Atlanta Hist. Soc., 1979-81; instr. in polit. sci. Hampton (Va.) U., 1981-84, asst. prof., 1984-88, assoc. prof., 1988—, asst. dean, 1991—; rsch. historian Aberdeen (Md.) Proving Ground, summer 1988; mem. NEH summer seminar Spelman Coll., 1985; mem. Fulbright Hays summer seminar U.S. Dept. Edn., Egypt, 1986. Contbr. articles to profl. publs., chpts. to books. Bd. dirs. Girls, Inc., Hampton; chmn. pvt. schs. campaign Peninsula United Way, Hampton, 1994; vol. Big Bros./Big Sisters, Hampton, Peninsula Coun. on Domestic Violence, Hampton; mem. Hampton City Coun., 1996-2000; commr. Hampton Redevel. and Housing Authority; mem. Va. Mcpl. League. Curriculum devel. grantee Ford Found., 1987, 88. Mem. NAACP (exec. coun.), Nat. Conf. Black Polit. Scientists (mem. coun. 1989-95, pres. 1993-94), Am. Polit. Sci. Assn. (mem. coun. 1993-95), So. Polit. Sci. Assn., Nat. Women's Studies Assn., Alpha Kappa Alpha (v.p.). Democrat. Roman Catholic. Home: 20 Gayle Sty Dr Hampton VA 23669 Office: Hampton U 119 Armstrong Hall Hampton VA 23668

LOCKE, VIRGINIA OTIS, textbook editor, behavioral sciences writer; b. Tiffin, Ohio, Sept. 4, 1930; d. Charles Otis and Frances Virginia (Sherer) L. BA, Barnard Coll., 1953; MA in Psychology, Duke U., 1972, postgrad. Program officer, asst. corp. sec. Agrl. Devel. Coun., N.Y.C., 1954-66; staff psychologist St. Luke's-Roosevelt Med. Ctr., N.Y.C., 1973-75; freelance writer and editor N.Y.C., 1976-85; writer-editor Cornell U. Med. Coll./N.Y. Hosp. Med. Ctr., N.Y.C., 1986-89; sr. editor humanities and social scis. coll. divsn. Prentice Hall divsn. Simon & Schuster, Upper Saddle River, N.J., 1989—. Co-author: (coll. textbook) Introduction to Theories of Personality, 1985, The Agricultural Development Council: A History, 1989. Founder Help Our Neighbors Eat Year-Round (H.O.N.E.Y.), Inc., N.Y.C., chmn., 1983-87, vol., 1987—, newsletter editor, 1992—; reader Recording for the Blind, N.Y.C., 1978-84; vol. Reach to Recovery program Am. Cancer Soc., Bergen County, N.J., 1990—. Recipient Our Town Thanks You award, N.Y.C., 1984, Mayor's Vol. Svc. award, N.Y.C., 1986, Cert. of Appreciation for Community Svc. Manhattan Borough, 1986, Jefferson award Am. Ins. Pub. Svc., Washington, 1986.

LOCKE MONDA, ROBIN, graphic designer, artist; b. Lowell, Mass., Apr. 17, 1950; d. Newton and Jean Woodman (Emery) Locke; m. Robert Monda, July 15, 1972. Student, Cooper Union, 1968-69; BA in English and Art summa cum laude, Bklyn. Coll., 1989. Prodn./rsch. asst. Arthur Young & Co., N.Y.C., 1973-74; graphic artist Williamhouse Regency, N.Y.C., 1974-77, Steelograph Co., N.Y.C., 1977-78; studio mgr. Harcourt Brace Jovanovich, N.Y.C., 1978-80; graphic artist Bozell & Jacobs, N.Y.C., 1981-84; cons. in graphic prodn. Wells, Rich, Greene, N.Y.C., 1989-91; designer Penguin U.S.A., N.Y.C., 1991-92, sr. designer, 1993-94; cons., graphic designer Robin Locke Monda: Grafik: Arts, N.Y.C., 1994—. Illustrator jour. Menninger Perspective, 1993; editor, art dir. for book: Bloody Wymmin Comix, I, 1994, II, 1995; author: A to Z: An Adult Alphabet, 1990; artist for book: Crash: Nostalgia for the Absence of Cyberspace, 1994. Bd. dirs., mem. visual arts adv. bd. Snug Harbor Cultural Ctr., S.I., N.Y., 1995—. Grantee Artist Space, 1990. Mem. Women's Caucus for Art, Coun. on Arts and Humanities for S.I., N.Y. Mac Users Group, Alpha Sigma Lambda. Democrat. Home and Office: Robin Locke Monda: Grafik Arts 36 Hamilton Ave Staten Island NY 10301

LOCKHART, AILEENE SIMPSON, retired dance, kinesiology and physical education educator; b. Atlanta, Mar. 18, 1911; d. Thomas Ellis and Aileene Reeves (Simpson) L. B.S., Tex. Woman's U., 1932; M.S., U. Wis., 1937, Ph.D., 1942; D.Sc. (hon.), U. Nebr., 1967. Mem. faculty Mary Hardin Baylor Coll., Belton, Tex., 1937-42, U. Wis., 1941-42; asst. prof., then assoc. prof. phys. edn. and pharmacology U. Nebr., 1942-49; assoc. prof., then prof. U. So. Calif., 1949-73; dean Coll. Health, Phys. Edn., Recreation and Dance Tex. Woman's U., 1973-78, prof. dance and phys. edn., chmn. dept. dance, 1978-83, adj. prof., 1983-88; Clare Small lectr. U. Colo., 1975; Ethel Martus Lawther lectr. U. N.C., 1978; Amy Morris Homans lectr., Milw., 1976; Donna Mae Miller Humanities scholar/lectr. , U. Ariz., Tucson, 1989; vis. prof./lectr. Iowa State U., univs., Wash., Oreg., Wis., Mass.; N.H., Calif. State U., Long Beach, Springfield (Mass.) Coll., Smith Coll., Wellesley Coll., U. Maine-Presque Isle, Dunfermline Coll., Edinburgh, Scotland, U. Brazil, Brasilia; cons. editor William C. Brown Publishing Co., Dubuque, Iowa, 1954—. Author or co-author 12 books; contbr. numerous articles profl. jours.; cons. editor or editor over 200 books. Recipient Disting. Alumnae award Tex. Woman's U., 1971, Disting. Alumnae award U. Wis.-Madison, 1981, Cornaro award, 1980, Honor award Ministry Edn., Taiwan, 1981, Minnie Stevens Piper Found. award State of Tex., 1983, Nat. Dance Assn. Heritage award, 1985, Amy Morris Homans fellow, 1961-62; honra ao Merito Ministerio de Educato and Cultura Brazilia, Brazil, 1977; Nat. Dance Assn. scholar, 1986-87; Tex. Assn. Health, Phys. Edn., Recreation and Dance scholar, 1986. Fellow Am. Coll. Sports Medicine, Am. Alliance Health, Phys. Edn., Recreation and Dance (Honor award 1963, Luther Halsey Gulick award 1980), Am. Acad. Phys. Edn. (pres. 1980-81, Hetherington award 1992); mem. Nat. Assn. Girls and Women in Sports (honor award 1991), Nat. Dance Assn., So. Assn. Phys. Edn. Coll. Women, Nat. Assn. Phys. Edn. in Higher Edn., Phi Kappa Phi. Presbyterian.

LOCKHART, GEMMA, producer, writer; b. Rapid City, S.D., Dec. 5, 1956; d. Jim and Tcena L.; children: Mica, Nakca, Aaron. BA in English, Creative Writing, Dartmouth Coll., 1979. TV news reporter Duhamel Broadcasting Enterprises, Rapid City, S.D., 1974-80; TV producer Rural Ethnic Inst., Rapid City, 1981-83; instr. Oglala Lakota Coll., Kyle, S.D., 1983-86; horse rider Black Hills, S.D.; TV producer S.D. Pub. TV, Vermillion, 1989-90; ind. producer, 1990—; CEO Wambli Win Prodns., 1994 , Anpao Studio, Rapid City, 1995—; auditor Lakota Elders, Dakota Land, 1975—; freelance columnist various publs. including USA Today. Presdl. scholar, 1975, 85. Mem. NAFE, Dartmouth Coll. Alumni Coun., Nature Conservancy (bd. dirs. 1995-96). Republican. Home: Box 8044 Rapid City SD 57709-8044 also: Dark Canyon Rapid City SD 57702

LOCKHART, LILLIE WALKER, retired primary school educator; b. Anderson, S.C., Mar. 19, 1931; d. Luther James and Katy Lee (Evans) Walker; m. Rufus Nelson Lockhart, Mar. 29, 1953. BA cum laude, Johnson C. Smith U., 1958; MA, Appalachian State U., 1981; Advanced MA, U. N.C., Charlotte, 1986. Cert. primary tchr., N.C. Prin. Airline Sch., Anderson, S.C., 1952-55; tchr. primary sch. Alexander St. Sch., Charlotte, N.C., 1956-60, First Ward, Charlotte, 1961-69, Lansdowne Sch., Charlotte, 1970-88; dir. music Rising Star Missionary Assn., 1988-92; team leader, grade chmn., supr. student tchrs., com. chmn., tchr. Charlotte-Mechlenburg Sch. System, 1958-88. Active Nat. Sunday Sch. Congress Christian Edn. Nat. Bapt. Conv. USA, The Lott Carey Missionary Conv., Gen. Bapt. Conv., N.C., All Bapt. World Alliance; vol. March of Dimes; pres. Mountain and Catawba Missionary Women's Aux., 1960-64, supr., 1965-78; tchr. Fairview Heights Bapt. Ch., Salisbury, N.C., 1980-88, com. chair Womens Home and Fgn. Missionary Convention N.C., 1988-92, chair pres.'s address, 1990-93; pianist, supr., tchr. Sunday sch. Fairview Heights Bapt. Ch., Salisbury, 1978-92, program coord., 1986-93; tchr., pianist Rising Star Sunday Sch. Conv., Thomasville, N.C., 1989-92; tutor Enrichment Program of the Oaklawn Park and McCrocery Heights Cmty. Orgn., Charlotte, N.C. Recipient Svc. award Mountain and Catawba Women's Aux., 1964, Christ Call to Youth, 1970, Womens Home and Fgn. Missionary Conv., 1992, Fairview Heights Bapt. Ch., 1990-92, Recognition cert., 1990, Recognition cert. Time and Place, 1995; named N.C. Minister's Wife of Yr., N.C. Assn. Minister's Wives and Widows Interdenominational, Cert. of Appreciation Salisbury-Rowan County Missionary Union, 1996. Mem. NEA, Assn. Childhood Edn. Internat., Interdenominational Mins. Wives (pres., sec. 1966-76, chair budget com. 1992—, Silver Tray award 1988), Charlotte-Mecklenburg Assn. Educators (sch. rep. 1980-88), Charlotte Ret. Sch. Pers., Alumnae J.C. Smith and Appalachian State Univs., Dean St. Cmty. Club (sec. 1990-92), Order Eastern Star, Am. Diebetic Assn. Democrat. Home: 1315 Dean St Charlotte NC 28216-5132

LOCKHART, MADGE CLEMENTS, educational organization executive; b. Soddy, Tenn., May 22, 1920; d. James Arlie and Ollie (Sparks) Clements; m. Andre J. Lockhart, Apr. 24, 1942 (div. 1973); children: Jacqueline, Andrew, Janice, Jill. Student, East Tenn. U., 1938-39; BS, U. Tenn., Chattanooga and Knoxville, 1955, MEd, 1962. Elem. tchr. Tenn. and Ga., 1947-60, Brainerd High Sch., Chattanooga, 1960-64, Cleveland (Tenn.) City Schs., 1966-88; owner, operator Lockhart's Learning Ctr., Inc., Cleveland and Chattanooga, 1975—; co-founder, pres. Hermes, Inc., 1973-79; co-founder Dawn Ctr., Hamilton County, Tenn., 1974; apptd. mem. Tenn. Gov.'s Acad. for Writers. AuthAor poetry, short stories and fiction; contbr. articles to profl. jours. and newspapers. Pres. Cleveland Assn. Retarded Citizens, 1970, state v.p., 1976; pres. Cherokee Easter Seal Soc., 1973-76, Cleveland Creative Arts Guild, 1980; bd. dirs. Tenn. Easter Seal Soc., 1974-77, 80-83; chair Bradley County Internat. Yr. of Child; mem. panel for grants Coun. Govts. S.E. Tenn. Devel. Dist., 1990-92; mem. Internat. Biog. Centre Adv. Coun., Cambridge, Eng., 1991-92; mem. mayor's com. Mus. for Bradley County, Tenn., 1992—. Recipient Service to Mankind award Sertoma, 1978, Gov.'s award for service to handicapped, 1979; mental health home named in her honor, Tenn., 1987. Mem. NEA (life), Tenn. Edn. Assn., Am. Assn. Rehab. Therapy, S.E. Tenn. Arts Coun., Cleveland Edn. Assn. (Service to Humanity award 1987). Mem. Ch. of Christ. Clubs: Byliners, Fantastiks. Home: 3007 Oakland Dr NW Cleveland TN 37312-5281

LOCKLEAR, HEATHER, actress; b. L.A., Sept. 25, 1961; d. Bill and Diane L.; m. Tommy Lee, 1986 (div. 1994); m. Richie Sambora, 1994. Appeared in (TV series) Dynasty, 1981-89, T.J. Hooker, 1982-87, Going Places, 1990, Melrose Place, 1992—, (films) Firestarter, 1986, Return of the Swamp Thing, 1990, Wayne's World 2, 1993, A Dangerous Woman, 1993, The First Wives Club, 1996; (TV movies) Twil, 1981, City Killer, 1984, Blood Sport, 1986, Rich Men, Single Women, 1990, Fade to Black, 1993, Texas Justice, 1995, Shattered Mind, 1996. Office: William Morris Agy 151 S El Camino Dr Beverly Hills CA 90212-2704*

LOCKNER, VERA JOANNE, farmer, rancher, legislator; b. St. Lawrence, S.D., May 19, 1937; d. Leonard and Zona R. (Ford) Verdugt; m. Frank O. Lockner, Aug. 7, 1955; children: Dean M., Clifford A. Grad., St. Lawrence (S.D.) High Sch., 1955. Bank teller/bookkeeper First Nat. Bank, Miller, S.D., 1963-66, Bank of Wessington, S.D., 1968-74; farmer/rancher Wessington, 1955—. Sunday sch. tchr. Trinity Luth. Ch., Miller, 1968-72; treas. PTO, Wessington, 1969-70; treas., vice chmn., chmn., state com. woman Hand County Dems., Miller, 1978—. Named one of Outstanding Young Women of Am., Women's Study Club, Wessington, 1970. Mem. Order of Ea. Star (warder, marshall, chaplain 1970—). Home and Office: RR 2 Box 102 Wessington SD 57381-8932

LOCKWOOD, FRANCINE PATRICK, air force officer, mathematician; b. Jamaica, N.Y., Nov. 29, 1957; d. Richard Jerome and Frances Mae Patrick; 1 child, Kellee F.P.; m. Edward Joseph Goode, Sept. 2, 1996. BS in Math., Western Oreg. State Coll., 1981; MS in Math., Fla. Inst. Tech., 1989. Commd. 2d lt. USAF, 1983—, advanced through grades to maj., 1995; meteorologist DET 11/2 Weather Squadron, Patrick AFB, Fla., 1984-87; asst. prof. math. USAF Acad., Colorado Springs, Colo., 1989-92; mathematician 694th Intelligence Group, Ft. Meade, Md., 1992-95; student Air Command and Staff Coll., Maxwell AFB, Ala., 1995-96; analyst USAF Hdqs., Washington, 1996—; mentor/tutor Sibanye, Washington, 1994-95, Brewbaker Mid. Sch., Montgomery, Ala., 1995-96; sec. Air Force Cadet Officer Mentor Action Program, 1994-95. Democrat. Home: 7856 Emilys Way Greenbelt MD 20770

LOCKWOOD, JOANNE SMITH, mathematician educator; b. Quebec City, Can., Nov. 9, 1946; d. Donald William MacKay and Sylvia Eleanor (Howard) Smith; m. Bryce M. Lockwood Jr., Aug. 10, 1968; children: Daren MacKay, Keith McLellan. BA in English, St. Lawrence U., 1968; MBA, Plymouth State Coll., 1980, BA in Math., 1985. Editor Houghton Mifflin Co., Boston, 1969-86; tchr. New Hampton (N.H.) Sch., 1974-76, 80-81; lectr. Plymouth (N.H.) State Coll., 1988—. Author: (textbooks) Beginning Algebra with Applications, 1989, 92, 96, Intermediate Algebra with Applications, 1989, 92, 96, Business Mathematics, 1988, 94, Introductory Algebra with Basic Mathematics, 1989, 96, Algebra with Trigonometry for College Students, 1991, A Review of Geometry, 1993, Prealgebra, 1994, Algebra for College Students: A Functions Approach, 1994. Mem. Am. Math. Assn. of Two Yr. Colls., Text and Acad. Authors Assn. Home: RR 1 Box 180 New Hampton NH 03256-9717

LOCKWOOD, RHONDA J., mental health services professional; b. Jacksonville, N.C., Apr. 4, 1960; d. George Barton and Sally Lynn (Hassell) L. BA, Newberry Coll., 1982; MS in Edn., Youngstown State U., 1988. nat. cert. counselor. Corrections/tng. officer Geauga County Sheriff's Dept., Chardon, Ohio, 1982-87; forensic counselor Human Svcs. Ctrs., Inc., New Castle, Pa., 1987-89; dir. children & family svcs. Marion Citrus Mental Health Ctrs., Inc., Ocala, Fla., 1989-96; clin. social worker Fla. Dept. Juvenile Justice, Alachua Halfway House, 1996—; co-founder Sexual Abuse Intervention Network, Ocala, 1990-96, chair, 1990-92, Family Svcs. Planning Team, 1992-94; cons. Health & Human Svcs. Bd. Dist. 13, 1993-96. Pol. vol. state campaigns Dem. Party, Warren, Ohio, 1978-85; mem. Sexual Abuse Prevention Edn. Network, New Castle, 1987-88; cons. to gov.'s task force Sex Offenders and Their Victims; cons. Mad Dads Orgn., Ocala, 1993; mem. Juvenile Justice Coun., Ocala, 1993-94; children's svc. rep. Fla. Coun. for Cmty. Mental Health, 1995-96. Recipient Outstanding Teen Vol. award Am. Red Cross, 1977. Fellow N. Eastern Ohio Police Benevolent Assn.; mem. Nat. Mus. for Women in the Arts, Nat. Bd. Cert. Counselors, NGLTF, Human Rights Campaign Fund, Chi Sigma Iota, Phi Kappa Phi. Democrat. Home: 201 E Main St Archer FL 32618-5517

LODER, VICTORIA KOSIOREK, information broker; b. Batavia, N.Y., May 27, 1945; d. Leon Stanley and Jennie Joann (Amatrano) Kosiorek; m. Ronald Raymond Loder, Nov. 6, 1965. BS in Bus. Mgmt., Roberts-Wesleyan Coll., Rochester, N.Y., 1989; MLS, SUNY, Buffalo, 1992; postgrad. in Religious Study, Liberty U., 1993—. Tech. info. specialist Eastman Kodak Co., Rochester, 1985-92; reference libr. Xerox Corp., Webster, N.Y., 1993-95; mgr. XPS strategy and integration libr. Xerox Corp., Fairport, N.Y., 1995-96, in PSG new bus. and mktg., 1006—; v.p., treas. Victron Design Svc. USA, Kent, N.Y., 1988—; pres., owner Alpha Omega Info Source, Kent, N.Y., 1993—. Republican.

LODOWSKI, RUTH ELLEN, physician; b. Dallas, Feb. 15, 1951; s. Charles Harry and Genevieve (Gowaty) L. BS, U. Tex., 1972; MBA, North Tex. State U., Denton, 1976; MD, U.Tex.-San Antonio, 1986. Resident asst., then head resident Castilian Dormitory, Austin, Tex., 1971-73; singer self-employed band, Austin, 1972-74; teller Greenville Ave. Bank, Dallas, 1974-75; employment interviewer Tex. Employment Commn., Grand Prairie, 1975-76; personnel intern U.S. Dept. Justice, Seagoville, Tex., 1976-77; personnel asst. Army and Air Force Exchange Service, San Antonio, 1977-78; staffing adminstr., personnel adminstr. Tex. Instruments Inc., Dallas, 1978-81, U. Tex. Med. Sch. at San Antonio, 1982-86; intern, then resident Parkland Meml. Hosp., Dallas, 1986-90; pvt. practice medicine specializing in psychiatry, Dallas, 1990—; clin. faculty psychiatry dept. U. Tex. Southwestern Med. Sch., Dallas, 1991—. Mem. AMA, Am. Psychiat. Assn., Tex. Med. Assn., Tex. Soc. Psychiat. Physicians, Dallas County Med. Soc., Kiwanis Internat. (top ten medal of honor). Address: 12201 Merit Dr Ste 660 Dallas TX 75251-2262

LOE, LINDA JANE, cultural association administrator; b. Dallas, May 24, 1936; d. Donald Riley and Louise Grissom (Faulkner) L.; m. Curtis E. Tyler, July 1, 1955 (dec. Jan., 1978); children: Joycelynn Tyler, Curtis E. II. BA in Comm. Studies Summa Cum Laude, UCLA, 1996. Dir. membership and activities Acad. TV Arts and Scis., North Hollywood, Calif., 1985—. Mem. AAUW, Women in Comm. (v.p. membership L.A. 1994-95), UCLA Alumni Assn. (Disting. Scholar award 1995, Outstanding Sr. 1996, Chancellor's award 1996), Golden Key, Mortar Board. Democrat. Home: 12701 Moorpark Apt 109 Studio City CA 91604 Office: Acad TV Arts & Scis 5220 Lankershim Blvd North Hollywood CA 91604

LOEB, FRANCES LEHMAN, civic leader; b. N.Y.C., Sept. 25, 1906; d. Arthur and Adele (Lewisohn) Lehman; student Vassar Coll., 1924-26; L.H.D. (hon.), NYU, 1977; m. John L. Loeb, Nov. 18, 1926; children: Judith Loeb Chiara, John L., Ann Loeb Bronfman, Arthur Lehman, Deborah Loeb Brice. N.Y.C. commr. for UN and Consular Corps, 1966-78. Exec. com. Population Action Com., Washington; life mem. bd. Children of Bellevue, Inc., 1974-96; bd. dirs. Internat. Presch., Inc., N.Y. Landmarks Conservancy; chmn. bd. East Side Internat. Community Ctr., Inc.; mem. UN Devel. Corp., 1972-94; life trustee Collegiate Sch. for Boys, N.Y.C.; trustee Cornell U., 1979-88, trustee emeritus, 1988-96; trustee Vassar Coll., 1988-96; bd. overseers Cornell U. Med. Coll., 1983-88 (life mem. 1988-96), Inst. Internat. Edn. (life). Mem. UN Assn. (dir.). Clubs: Cosmopolitan, Vassar, Women's City (N.Y.C.). Died May 17, 1996.

LOEB, JANE RUPLEY, university administrator, educator; b. Chgo., Feb. 22, 1938; d. John Edwards and Virginia Pentland (Marthens) Watkins; m. Peter Albert Loeb, June 14, 1958; children: Eric Peter, Gwendolyn Lisl, Aaron John. BA, Rider Coll., 1961; PhD, U. So. Calif., 1969. Clin. psychology intern Univ. Hosp., Seattle, 1966-67; asst. prof. ednl. psychology U. Ill., Urbana, 1968-69, asst. coord. rsch. and testing, 1968-69, coord. rsch. and testing, 1969-72, asst. to vice chancellor acad. affairs, 1971-72, dir. admissions and records, 1972-81, assoc. prof. ednl. psychology, 1973-82, assoc. vice chancellor acad. affairs, 1981-94, prof. edn. psychology, 1982—. Author: College Board Project: the Future of College Admissions, 1989. Chmn. Coll. Bd. Coun. on Entrance Svcs., 1977-82; bd. govs. Alliance for Undergrad. Edn., 1988-93; active charter com. Coll. Bd. Acad. Assembly, 1992-93. HEW grantee, 1975-76. Mem. APA, Am. Ednl. Rsch. Assn., Nat. Coun. Measurement in Edn., Harvard Inst. Ednl. Mgmt. Home: 1405 N Coler Ave Urbana IL 61801-1625 Office: U Ill 1310 S 6th St Champaign IL 61820-6925

LOEB, JEANETTE WINTER, investment banker; b. N.Y.C., June 18, 1952; d. Leon and Fay (Rotenberg) Winter; m. Peter Kenneth Loeb, Nov. 1, 1980; 1 child, Alexander Winter. BA, Wellesley Coll., 1974; MBA, Harvard U., 1977. Assoc. Goldman, Sachs & Co., N.Y.C., 1977-81, v.p., 1981—, ptnr. 1986—. Wellesley Coll. Devel. Fund chmn. for N.Y. Mem. Phi Beta Kappa. Club: India House. Office: Goldman Sachs & Co 85 Broad St New York NY 10004-2434*

LOEB, MARA C., communications educator, artist; b. Des Moines, Iowa, Apr. 8, 1950; d. Frederic William and Rosemary Frances (Urban) L. BA, U. No. Iowa, Cedar Falls, 1983, MA, 1985; PhD, So. Ill. U., Carbondale, 1996. Pres., designer Firesign Designs, Vancouver, Canada, 1980-81; asst. prof. theater Northeast La. U., Monroe, 1985-91; grad. asst. speech commn. So. Ill. U., Carbondale, 1991-95; asst. prof. speech comm. and theater Northeast La. U., Monroe, 1995—; mem. bd. dirs., treas. Sumus Theater Ensemble, Portland, 1978-80; mem. bd. dirs. Vancouver Little Theater Assn., Vancouver, 1980-81. Recipient Doctoral fellow So. Ill. U., 1992-93; Outstanding Svc. to Students of Theater award Alpha Psi Omega, Northeast La. U., 1991, Outstanding Rschr. award Northeast La. U. Dept. Speech, Comms. & Theater, 1989, Outstanding Artist award, 1990, Marian Kleinau Theater award So. Ill. U., 1995. Mem. Nat. Storytelling Assn., So. States Commn. Assn., Speech Commn. Assn. Home: 3904 Harrison Monroe LA 71203 Office: Dept Speech Commns & Theater Northeast La U Monroe LA 71203

LOEBLICH, HELEN NINA TAPPAN, paleontologist, educator; b. Norman, Okla., Oct. 12, 1917; d. Frank Girard and Mary (Jenks) Tappan; m. Alfred Richard Loeblich, Jr., June 18, 1939; children: Alfred Richard III, Karen Elizabeth Loeblich, Judith Anne Loeblich Covey, Daryl Louise Loeblich Valenzuela. BS, U. Okla., 1937, MS, 1939; PhD, U. Chgo., 1942. Instr. geology Tulane U., New Orleans, 1942-43; geologist U.S. Geol. Survey, Washington, 1943-45, 47-59; mem. faculty UCLA, 1958—, prof. geology, 1966-84, prof. emeritus, 1985—, vice chmn. dept. geology, 1973-75; research assoc. Smithsonian Instn., 1954-57; assoc. editor Cushman Found. Foraminiferal Research, 1950-51, incorporator, hon. dir., 1950—. Author: (with A.R. Loeblich Jr.) Treatise on Invertebrate Paleontology, part C, Protista 2, Foraminiferida, 2 vols., 1964, Foraminiferal Genera and Their Classification, 2 vols., 1987, Foraminifera of the Sahul Shelf and Timor Sea, 1994; author: The Paleobiology of Plant Protists, 1980; mem. editl. bd. Palaeoecology, 1972-82, Paleobiology, 1975-81; contbr. articles to profl. jours., govt. publs. and encys. Recipient Joseph A. Cushman award Cushman Found., 1982; named Woman of Yr. in Sci. Palm Springs Desert Mus., 1987; Guggenheim fellow, 1953-54. Fellow Geol. Soc. Am. (sr., councilor 1979-81); mem. Paleontol. Soc. (pres. 1984-85, patron 1987, medal 1982), Soc. Sedimentary Geology (councilor 1975-77, hon. mem. 1978, Raymond C. Moore medal 1984), UCLA Med. Ctr. Aux. (Woman of Yr. medal), AAUP, Internat. Paleontological Assn., Paleontol. Rsch. Inst., Am. Microscopical Soc., Am. Inst. Biol. Scis., Phi Beta Kappa, Sigma Xi. Home: 1556 W Crone Ave Anaheim CA 92802-1303

LOEB-MUNSON, STELLA MARIE, school system administrator; b. Cleve., Feb. 14, 1943; d. Charles Harold and Beulah Hortense (Franklin) Loeb; children: Charles William, Maisha Kwetu. BS in Elem. Edn., Kent State U., 1969; MS in Ednl. Adminstrn., St. John Coll., 1974. Tchr. Cleve. Pub. Schs., 1969-72; freshman advisor spl. svcs., dir. peer counseling Case Western Res. U., Cleve., 1977-80, asst. dir. spl. svcs., 1977-80; classroom tchr. East Cleveland (Ohio) City Schs., 1981-84, curriculum specialist, 1984-85, bldg. prin., 1985—; mem. adv. bd. Young Audiences of Greater Cleve., Inc.; dist. chair East Cleve. Computer Com., 1988—; facilitator, presenter Ohio Dept. Edn., 1991, Ohio Acad. for Prins., 1987-91; presenter Cleve. State U., Lakeland C.C., 1991. Mem. program adv. com. Young Audiences Greater Cleve., 1991. Stella Loeb-Munson day proclaimed by East Cleve. City Coun. and Mayor, 1991; recipient Disting. Arts Educator award Ohio Arts Edn. Assn., 1994, Ohio N.E. Regional Disting. Arts Educator award, 1994; named Nat. Disting. Prin. U.S. Secondary Edn., 1991, Prin. Leadership Nat. Safety Ctr., Nat. Assn. Elem. Sch. Prins., Nat. Assn. Secondary Sch. Prins., 1992. Mem. N.E. Ohio Computer Consortium (bd. dirs. 1988—), ASCD, Nat. Assn. Elem. Sch. Adminstrs., Ohio Assn. Elem. Sch. Adminstrs. (Disting. Prin. Ohio 1991), Phi Delta Kappa (greater Cleve. inter-univ. chpt., named Disting. Educator of Yr. 1992). Democrat. Office: Caledonia Sch 914 Caledonia Ave Cleveland OH 44112-2319

LOEH, CORINNE GENEVIEVE, artist; b. Livingston, Ill., Apr. 6, 1918; d. Tipmer Charles and Mae Leona (Batemon) Rachow; m. Hugo William Loeh (dec.); children: Sandra Mae Blaeser, Danna Clare Koschkee (dec.). Grad., Blackburn Coll., 1937; BS in Edn., Greenville Coll., 1950; MS in Art Edn., So. Ill. U., 1958. Tchr. pub. schs., Ill., 1937-52; art supr. Unit Dist. #1, Carlyle, Ill., 1952-55; tchr. art high sch., supr. K-9 Unit Dist. #2, Greenville, Ill., 1955-65, title one author, dir., 1965-69; prof. art Greenville Coll., 1956-65; art dir. Unit Dist. #46, Elgin, Ill., 1969-77; freelance artist Oro Valley, Ariz., 1982—; art collector CLO Art Gallery, Oro Valley, 1982—; cons. in field. Author: Prescription for Titans, 1971; editor: Ill. Art Edn. Assn. News, 1972, 77; one-woman shows include Judson Coll., Elgin, 1979, Western Gallery, Tucson, Ariz., 1985. Mem. AAUW, Ill. Art Edn. Assn., Nat. Mus. Women in Arts, Surpace Designers. Republican. Home and office: 151 E Carolwood Dr Oro Valley AZ 85737

LOESCH, KATHARINE TAYLOR (MRS. JOHN GEORGE LOESCH), communication and theatre educator; b. Berkeley, Calif., Apr. 13, 1922; d. Paul Schuster and Katharine (Whiteside) Taylor; student Swarthmore Coll., 1939-41, U. Wash., 1942; BA, Columbia U., 1944, MA, 1949; grad. Neighborhood Playhouse Sch. of Theatre, 1946; postgrad. Ind. U., 1953; PhD, Northwestern U., 1961; m. John George Loesch, Aug. 28, 1948; 1 child, William Ross. Instr. speech Wellesley (Mass.) Coll., 1949-52, Loyola U., Chgo., 1956; asst. prof. English and speech Roosevelt U., Chgo., 1957, 62-65; assoc. prof. communication and theatre U. Ill. at Chgo., 1968—; assoc. prof. emerita speech in communication and theater, U. Ill., Chgo., 1987—. Contbr. writings to profl. jours.; poetry performances. Active ERA, Ill., 1975-76. Am. Philos. Soc. grantee, 1970; U. Ill., Chgo., grantee, 1970. Mem. MLA, Speech Communication Assn. (Golden Anniversary prize award 1969, chmn. interpretation div. 1979-80), Celtic Studies Assn. N.Am., Pi Beta Phi. Episcopalian. Home: 2129 N Sedgwick St Chicago IL 60614-4619 Office: U Ill Dept Performing Arts M/C 255 1040 W Harrison St Chicago IL 60607-7130

LOESCH, MABEL LORRAINE, social worker; b. Annandale, Minn., July 1, 1925; d. Rudolph and Hedwig (Zeidler) Treichler; m. Harold Carl Loesch, Oct. 19, 1945; children: Stephen, Gretchen, Jonathan, Frederick. BS, La. State U., 1972, MSW, 1974. Cert. Acad. Cert. Social Worker, bd. cert. diplomate. Tchr. Am. schs. Tegucigalpa, Honduras, 1960-61; Guayaquil, Ecuador, 1962-66, La Ceiba, Honduras, 1966-67; supr. clin. svc. Blundon Home, Baton Rouge, 1974-81; social worker, cons. Dhaka, Bangladesh, 1981-85; social worker Manna Food Bank, Pensacola, Fla., 1986—; adj. instr. social work dept. Southern U., Baton Rouge, 1976-81. Author: Generations in Germany and America, 1996; editor: Making Do, 1989, Making Do II, 1994. Mem. adv. com. Luth. Ministries of Fla., 1993—. Mem. NASW, Mensa (local sec. 1986-90, chair scholarships com.), Phi Kappa Phi. Democrat. Lutheran. Home: 2140 E Scott St Pensacola FL 32503-4957

LOESCHER, BARBARA ANN, auditing executive; b. Mauston, Wis., Aug. 20, 1953; d. Arnold John Loescher and Carol Jeanne (Vinopal) Gross. BS in Bus. and Acctg., Edgewood Coll., 1988. CPA, Wis; cert. internal auditor, fraud examiner. Acct. Harco Ins. Co., Milw., 1977-78; corp. acct. Blunt Ellis and Loewi, Milw., 1978-79; fin. technician Cumis Ins. Soc., Inc., Madison, Wis., 1979-81; budget, tax and cost specialist Cumis Ins. Soc., Inc., Madison, 1981-83, risk mgmt. investment specialist, 1983-84, fraud auditing mgr., 1984-90; asst. to sr. v.p. individual life and health mktg. CUNA Mut. Fin. Svcs. Corp., Inc., Madison, 1990-91; pres., COO, Fin. Standards Group, Inc., Boca Raton, Fla., 1991-94; pres. Loescher & Assocs., Boca Raton, 1994—; lectr. seminars on auditing, risk mgmt. and fraud. Author of numerous articles in field. Mem. AICPA, Wis. Inst. CPAs, Inst. Internal Auditors (sec. 1987), Nat. Assn. Cert. Fraud Examiners. Republican. Roman Catholic. Home: 21479 Sweetwater Ln S Boca Raton FL 33428 Office: 20423 State Rd 7 Ste 295 Boca Raton FL 33498

LOEVINGER, JANE, psychologist, educator; b. St. Paul, Feb. 6, 1918; d. Gustavus and Millie (Strauss) L.; m. Samuel I. Weissman, July 13, 1943; children: Judith, Michael B. BA in Psychology, U. Minn., 1937, MS in Psychometrics, 1938; PhD. in Psychology, U. Calif., Berkeley, 1944. Instr. psychology and edn. Stanford (Calif.) U., 1941-42; lectr. psychology U. Calif., Berkeley, 1942-43; part-time instr. in stats. and sociology Washington U., St. Louis, 1946-47, research psychologist and cons. air force projects, 1950-53, research assoc. prof. child psychiatry, 1960-64, research assoc. prof., Grad. Inst. Edn., 1964-71, research assoc., Social Sci. Inst., 1964-70, research prof., 1971-74, prof., 1974-88, Stuckenberg prof. human values and moral devel., 1984-88, prof. emeritus dept. psychology, 1988—; rsch. assoc. Jewish Hosp., St. Louis, 1954-60; mem. personality and cognition research rev. com. NIMH, 1970-74; ad hoc reviewer U. Witwatersrand, Johannesburg, Republic of South Africa, 1985, NSF, NIMH, various other orgns.; mem. various coms. Washington U.; lectr. in field. Author: (with R. Wessler) Measuring Ego Development 1: Construction and Use of a Sentence Completion Test, 1970, (with R. Wessler and C. Redmore) Measuring Ego Development 2: Scoring Manual for Women and Girls, 1970, Ego Development: Conceptions and Theories, 1976, Scientific Ways in the Study of Ego Development, 1979, Paradigms of Personality, 1987; cons. editor: Psychol. Rev., 1983—, Jour. Personality and Social Psychology, 1984—, Jour. Personality Assessment 1987—; contbr. articles to profl. jours., book revs., letters and abstracts. Recipient Research Sci. award NIMH, 1968-73, 74-79; Ednl. Testing Service Disting. Vis. scholar, 1969; Margaret M. Justin fellow, 1955-56, NIMH grantee, 1956-79. Fellow Am. Psychol. Assn. (pres. Div. 5 1962-63, mem. com. on tests, mem. policy and planning bd. 1969-72, mem. policy task force on psychologists in criminal justice system 1976-77, pres. Div. 24 1982-83, com. on early career award in personality 1985), Phi Beta Kappa, Sigma Xi (assoc.). Democrat. Home: 6 Princeton Ave Saint Louis MO 63130-3136 Office: Washington U Dept Of Psychology Campus Box 1125 #1 Brookings Dr Saint Louis MO 63130-4899*

LOEWENTHAL, NESSA PARKER, communications educator; b. Chgo., Oct. 13, 1930; d. Abner and Frances (Ness) Parker; m. Martin Moshe Loewenthal, July 7, 1951 (dec. Aug. 1973); children: Dann Marcus, Ronn Carl, Deena Miriam; m. Gerson B. Selk, Apr. 17, 1982 (dec. June 1987). BA in Edn. and Psychology, Stanford U., 1952. Faculty Stanford Inst. for Intercultural Communication, Palo Alto, Calif., 1973-87; dir. Trans Cultural Svcs., San Francisco, 1981-86, Portland, Oreg., 1986—; dir. dependent svcs. and internat. edn. Bechtel Group, San Francisco, 1973-81, internat. edn. cons., 1981-84; mem. adv. com. dept. internat. studies Lesley Coll., Cambridge, Mass., 1986—; mem. Oreg. Ethics Commons, 1990—; mem. Bay Area Ethics Consortium, Berkeley, 1985-90; chmn. ethics com. Sietar Internat., Washington, 1987—, mem. governing bd., 1992-95; mem. faculty Summer Inst. for Internat. Comms., Portland, Oreg., 1987—; core faculty Oreg.'s Gov.'s Sch. for Social Leadership, 1995—. Author: Professional Integration, 1987, Update: Federal Republic of Germany, 1990, Update: Great Britain, 1987; author, editor book series Your International Assignment, 1973-81; contbr. articles to profl. jours. Mem. equal opportunity and social justice task force Nat. Jewish Rels. Adv. Coun.; bd. dirs. Kids on the Block, Portland, Portland Jewish Acad., 1996—, Portland-Ashkalon Sister City Assn., Soc. Humanistic Judaism, 1996—; mem. Lafayette (Calif.) Traffic Commn., 1974-80; bd. dirs. Ctr. for Ethics and Social Policy, 1988-91; mem. exec. bd. and planning com. Temple Isaiah, Lafayette, 1978-82; bd. dirs. Calif. Symphony, Orinda, 1988-90; mem. exec. com. overseas schs. adv. com. U.S. Dept. State, 1976-82; mem. cmty. rels. com. Portland Jewish Fedn.; mem. Nat. Jewish Cmty. Rels. task force: Social Justice and Econ. Opportunity, 1995—. Named Sr. Interculturalist, Sietar Internat., 1986. Mem. ASTD (exec. bd. internat. profl. performance area 1993—), Soc. for Intercultural Edn., Tng. and Rsch. (chmn. 1986-87, nomination com. 1985-86, co-chmn. 1989-90, chmn. ethics com. 1989—, governing bd. 1992-95), World Affairs Coun., Am. Women for Internat. Understanding, Portland City Club. Democrat. Office: TransCultural Svcs 712 NW Westover Ter Portland OR 97210-3136

LOEWI, LYN HELEN HUBLER, musician, choral director; b. Cleve., Sept. 10, 1957; d. Myron Jewell and Sarah Ann (Ramsey) H.; m. David Matthew Loewi, June 18, 1982; children: Alexander Martin, Peter Abraham, Ethan Gabriel. BMus, U. Mich., 1978; M Musical Arts, Stanford U., 1982, D Musical Arts, 1983; postgrad., U. Tex., 1986-87. Mus. dir. Hyde Park Meth. Ch., Austin, Tex., 1985-89; min. music Webster Presbyn. Ch., St. Louis, 1989-94; dir. music ministries First Presbyn. Ch., Portland, Oreg., 1994—; organist, lectr. Presbytery Cascades, Oreg., 1995-96. Recitalist Germany, France, Sweden, The Netherland, Japan, U.S., 1980—; contbr. articles to profl. jours. Fund raiser Habitat for Humanity, St. Louis, 1991; benefit concert performer Rm. at Inn, St. Louis, 1993. Recipient Deutscher Akademischer Austausch Dienst German Govt., 1979-80, First prize Organ Nat. Conservatory France, 1985; grantee AAUW, 1984, Harriet Hale Woolley, 1984-85; Annette Kade Performing Arts fellow French Govt., 1983-84. Mem. Am. Guild Organists (adjudicator 1995, scholarship tutor 1995-96), Presbyn. Assn. Musicans. Democrat. Office: First Presbyn Ch 1200 SW Alder St Portland OR 97205

LOEWITH, CAROL A., educational consultant; b. N.Y.C., Mar. 27, 1944; d. Milton P. and Martha W. (Weinberg) Adler; m. David A. Huchital, July 10, 1965 (div. June 1982); children: Jill Huchital, Alana Huchital; m. Howard Loewith, May 6, 1984; stepchildren: Jason, Margaret, David. BA, Russell Sage Coll., Troy, N.Y., 1964; MA, Columbia U. Tchrs. Coll., N.Y., 1965; MS, U. Bridgeport, Conn., 1984. Nat. cert. counselor. Tchr. N.Y.C., 1964-65, Niskayuna, N.Y., 1965-66, Westport, Conn., 1966-67; tchr. Jewish Cmty. Ctr., Bridgeport, 1975-81; pvt. ednl. cons. Steinbrecher Assocs., Westport, Conn., 1984-89; ednl. cons. Fairfield and Westport, Conn., 1989—. Hostess: (TV talk show) Bringing Up Kids, 1989-94. Mem. exec. bd. Cong. Beth El, Fairfield, Conn., 1990-94, Ind. Edn. Cons. Assn., Fairfax, Va., 1986—, bd. dirs., 1992—; mem. bd. dirs. Jewish Family Svcs., Bridgeport, 1992-94. Mem. Conn. Assn. for Children With Learning Disabilities. Democrat. Jewish. Office: 191 Fairfield Woods Rd Fairfield CT 06432

LOFGREN, DONNA LEE, geneticist; b. Bay Shore, N.Y., Apr. 13, 1957; d. Carl Oscar and Esther Louise (Kustes) L. BS, Cornell U., 1979; MS, Va. Polytech. Inst. and State U., 1981, PhD, 1984. Postdoctoral rsch. assoc. Dept. Animal Scis. Purdue U., West Lafayette, Ind., 1985-90; prof. assoc. in animal breeding Dept. Animal Scis. Purdue U., 1990—. Mem. Am. Soc. Animal Sci., Am. Dairy Sci. Assn., Sigma Xi (rsch. award 1985). Office: Dept Animal Sci Purdue U 1151 Lilly Hall West Lafayette IN 47907-1151

LOFGREN, ZOE, congresswoman; b. San Mateo, Calif., Dec. 21, 1947; d. Milton R. and Mary Violet L.; m. John Marshall Collins, Oct. 22, 1978; children: Sheila Zoe Lofgren Collins, John Charles Lofgren Collins. BA in Polit. Sci., Stanford U., 1970; JD cum laude, U. Santa Clara, 1975. Bar: Calif., 1975. D.C. Adminstrv. asst. to Congressman Don Edwards, San Jose, Calif., 1970-79; ptnr. Webber and Lofgren, San Jose, 1979-81; mem. Santa Clara County Bd. Suprs., 1981-94; congresswoman 104th U.S. Congress, Calif. 16th Dist., 1995—; part-time prof. Law, U. Santa Clara, 1978-80; jud. com., judiciary subcom. on comml. and adminstrv. law, subcom. on crime, sci. com. subcoms. on basic rsch. & tech.; house com. on sci., subcommittee on tech., basic rsch. Exec. dir. Community Housing Developers, Inc., 1979-80; trustee San Jose Community Coll. Dist., 1979-81; bd. dirs. Community Legal Svcs., 1978-81, San Jose Housing Svc. Ctr., 1978-79; mem. steering com. sr. citizens housing referendum, 1978; del. Calif. State Bar Conv., 1979-82, Dem. Nat. Conv., 1976; active Assn. Immigration and Nationality Lawyers, 1976-82, Calif. State Dem. Cen. Com., 1975-78, Santa Clara County Dem. Cen. Com., 1974-78, Notre Dame High Sch. Blue Ribbon Com., 1981-84, Victim-Witness Adv. Bd., 1981-94. Recipient Bancroft-Whitney award for Excellence in Criminal Procedure, 1973. Mem. Santa Clara County Bar Assn. (trustee 1979—), Santa Clara County Women Lawyers Com. (exec. bd. 1979-80), Sanata Clara Law Sch. Alumni Assn. (v.p. 1977, pres. 1978), Nat. Women's Polit. Caucus, Assn. of Bay Area Govts. (exec. bd. 1981-86). Office: US House Reps 118 Cannon House Office Bldg Washington DC 20515-0516 also: 635 N First St Ste B San Jose CA 95112

LÖFGREN-CHUNG, BARBRO ANITA, minister; b. Lycke, Sweden, Oct. 16, 1940; came to U.S., 1980; d. S. Harald and Sigrid C. (Johansson) Löfgren; m. J.f. Bart Nubuer, July 17, 1965 (div. Nov. 1988); children: Charlotta, Elisabeth Nuboer-Ranjhan, Franciscus, Carolina; m. Paul C.P. Chung, Nov. 22, 1989. MDiv, Andover Newton Theol. Sch., 1984. Ordained to ministry of Word and Sacrament Luth. Ch., 1986. Worship leader Djursholms Kapell, Sweden, 1978-80; parish min. Luth. Ch. Newtons, Newton, Mass., 1983; parish minister intern Faith Luth. Ch., Cambridge, Mass., 1984-85; protestant chaplain Boston Coll., 1986-89; asst. Luth. chaplain Tufts U., Boston, 1990-91; visitation pastor Luth. Ch. of the Redeemer, Woburn, Mass., 1992—; mem. coun. Met. Luth. Coun., Boston, 1988-90; chair older adult ministry task force New Eng. Synod Luth. Ch., 1996—. Mem. Winchester Interfaith Clergy Coun., 1993—; mem. Holocaust remembrance panel Mus. of Fine Arts, Boston, 1995; mem. Jewish-Christian Dialog of Mass. Coun. Chs., Boston, 1993—. Home: 14 Sussex Rd Winchester MA 01890

LOFTIS, KAREN, public relations executive; b. Lincoln, Nebr., Nov. 17, 1964; d. Alan G. and Frances M. L. BA in Polit. Sci., U. Nebr., 1987, M of Comm. and Regional Planning, 1995. Coord. pub. info. State of Nebr., Lincoln, 1988-92; program coord. U. Nebr., Lincoln, 1992-96; mgr. publs. Century Tel. Enterprises, Pinconning, Mich., 1996—; cons. Loftis Flowers & Farms, Lincoln, 1995—. Author: The Internet: A Tool for Community Development, 1994, Internet Guide for Small Business, 1995. Rep. precinct coord. Lancaster County, Lincoln, 1990-96. Mem. Cmty. Devel. Soc., FBLA-PBL Profl. Divsn., Kiwanis Internat. Office: Century Tel Enterprises 4399 N Huron Rd Pinconning MI 48650

LOFTIS-STONE, LISA DIANE, special education educator; b. Greer, S.C., Oct. 6, 1964; d. Larry Earl and Nellie Elizabeth (Eppley) L.; m. Fred Barron Stone, Feb. 28, 1988; 1 child, Brandon. Student, Lander U., 1982-86; BA in Early Childhood Edn., U. S.C., 1990; MA, Furman U., 1996. Tchr. Greenwood (S.C.) County Sch. Dist. #50; team coord., direct care supr. Pickens County Dept. Disabilities & Spl. Needs, Easley, S.C., 1988-91; tchr., chair spl. edn. Easley Jr. High Sch., 1990-92; tchr. profoundly mentally handicapped Belton (S.C.) Elem. Sch., 1992-96; tchr. trainable/profoundly mentally handicapped Belton-Honea Path (S.C.) H.S., 1996—. Vol. Spl. Olympics, Piedmont, S.C., 1981—. Mem. ASCD, NEA, Coun. Exceptional Children. Home: 203 Somerset Ln Anderson SC 29625 Office: Belton-Honea Path HS Honea Path SC 29654

LOGAN, NANCY ALLEN, library media specialist; b. Rochester, N.Y., Mar. 27, 1933; d. Warren William and Dorothea Amelia (Pund) Allen; m. Joseph Skinner Logan, Dec. 29, 1952; children: Jennifer Martha, Joseph Skinner Jr., Susan Logan Huber, Annette Logan Miller. Student, Middlebury Coll., 1951-52; BA, Cornell U., 1955; MLS, SUNY, Albany, 1967; cert. legal asst., Marist Coll., 1983. Cert. libr. media specialist, tchr., social studies tchr., N.Y. Libr. media specialist Hyde Park (N.Y.) Sch. Dist., 1971-93. Editor: Dear Friends, 1989; editor newsletter Sch. Libr. Media Specialists, 1984-85; contbr. articles to profl. publs. Arts chmn. Jr. League, Poughkeepsie, N.Y., 1967-69, dir. Jr. Arts Ctr., 1967-69, edn. chmn., 1970-71; sec. bd. dirs. Poughkeepsie (N.Y.) Tennis Club, 1973-79; indexer periodicals Dutchess County Hist. Soc., Poughkeepsie, 1979-93; county rep. Sch. Libr. Media Specialists, S.E. N.Y., 1982, exhibits chmn. ann. meeting, 1983, 84; vol. libr., indexer Jamestown (R.I.) Philomenian Libr., 1993—; bd. dirs. Friends of Jamestown Philomenian Libr., 1994—. Mem. Newport Hist. Soc., Beavertail Lighthouse Assn. (bd. dirs. 1994—), New Eng. Hist. Geneal. Soc., Phi Delta Kappa. Home: 149 Seaside Dr Jamestown RI 02835-3117

LOGAN, SHARON BROOKS, lawyer; b. Easton, Md., Nov. 19, 1945; d. Blake Elmer and Esther N. (Statum) Brooks; children: John W. III, Troy Blake. BS in Econs., U. Md., 1967, MBA in Mktg., 1969; JD, U. Fla., 1979. Bar: Fla. 1979. Ptnr. Raymond Wilson, Esq., Ormond Beach, Fla., 1980, Landis, Graham & French, Daytona Beach, Fla., 1981, Watson & Assocs., Daytona Beach, 1982-84; prin. Sharon B. Logan, Esq., Ormond Beach, 1984—; legal advisor to paralegal program Daytona Beach Community Coll., 1984—. Sponsor Ea. Surfing Assn., Daytona Beach, 1983—, Nat. Scholastic Surfing Assn., 1987—; bd. dirs. Ctr. for Visually Impaired, Daytona Beach, 1991—; mem. Fla. Supreme Ct. Hist. Soc. Recipient Citizenship award Rotary Club, 1962-63; Woodrow Wilson fellow U. Md., 1967. Mem. ABA, Fla. Bar Assn. (real property and probate sect., cert. real estate atty.), Volusia County Bar Assn. (bd. dirs.), Volusia County Real Property Council, Inc. (bd. dirs. 1987—, sec. 1987-88, v.p. 1988-89, pres. 1989-90, sec. 1990-91), Ducks Unlimited, Mus. Arts and Scis., Volusia County Estate Planning Council, Daytona Beach Area Bd. Realtors, Ormond Beach C. of C., Gator Club, Halifax Club, Tomoka Oaks Country Club, Daytona Boat Club, Md. Club, Beta Gamma Sigma, Alpha Lamba Delta, Phi Kappa Phi, Omicron Delta Epsilon, Delta Delta Delta (Scholarship award 1964), Sigma Alpha Epsilon. Democrat. Episcopalian. Avocations: cooking, sewing, golf, tennis, aerobics. Office: Sharon B Logan Esq 400 S Atlantic Ave Ste 110 Ormond Beach FL 32176-7142

LOGAN, VERYLE JEAN, retail executive, realtor; b. St. Louis, Oct. 24; d. Benjamin Bishop and Eddie Mae (Williams) Logan. BS, Mo. U., 1968; postgrad. Wayne State U., 1974, 76, U. Mich.-Detroit, 1978, 80. Cert. residential specialist. With Hudson Dept. Store, Detroit, 1968-84, Dayton Hudson, Mpls., 1984-86, div. mdse. mgr., 1983-84, retail exec. div. mdse. mgr. Coats and Dresses, 1984-86; pres. Ultimate Connection, Inc., Mpls., 1987—. Mem. Golden Valley Black History Month Com., 1987—, co-chair, 1991-92, also bd. dirs., 1993-95; trustee Harry Davis Found., 1988-94, mem. exec. bd., 1990, v.p., 1991-92; chair equal opportunity com. Mpls. Bd. Realtors, also bd. dirs., 1993—. Named Woman of Yr., Am. Bus. Women, 1984. Mem. Grad. Realtors Inst., Am. Bus. Womens Assn. (v.p. 1983-84, named Woman of Yr. 1984), Minn. Black Networking (exec. bd. 1985-90), Delta Sigma Theta (life, Mpls.-St. Paul alumnae chpt., recording sec. 1985-87, chmn. arts and letters, corresponding sec. 1987-88, chmn. heritage and archives 1988-89, 1st v.p. 1991-93, pres. 1993-95, named Delta of the Yr., 1988), Grad. Realtors Inst., M.L. King Tennis Buffs Club. Office: Burnet Realty Lakes 3033 Excelsior Blvd Minneapolis MN 55416-4688

LOGAN PRINCE, KATHLEEN, clinical social worker; b. Quincy, Mass., June 9, 1932; d. George Washington and Mary Margaret (Pheney) Arbuckle; m. Louis L. Logan, Feb. 8, 1964 (div. Feb. 1988); m. George Mather Prince, Dec. 9, 1989. AB, Coll. New Rochelle, 1954; MSW, Boston Coll., 1957. Lic. ind. clin. social worker, marriage and family therapist, Mass. Social worker Peter Bent Brigham Hosp., Boston, 1957-59, St. Vincent's Hosp., N.Y.C., 1959-61, New England Med. Ctr., Boston, 1961-65; psychotherapist New England Inst. Family Rels., Framingham, Mass., 1976-86; pvt. practice Weston, Mass., 1986—; founding mem. Pathfinders: Ctr. for Sexual Health, Newton, 1991—, Mind Free Inc., Weston, 1992—; sex therapist Diagnostic Ctr. for Men, Woburn, Mass., 1994—. Author: (with others) Mind-Free - A Group Process of Renegotiating Self Imposed Limitations, 1993, Divorce Handbook, 1996. Dir. Divorce Ctr. of Framingham, 1989—. Mem. Am. Assn. Sex Educators, Counselors and Therapists (cert., chair Boston sect., chair dist. VII/New Eng. 1996). Roman Catholic. Office: 40 Bakers Hill Rd Weston MA 02193

LOGGIE, JENNIFER MARY HILDRETH, medical educator, physician; b. Lusaka, Zambia, Feb. 4, 1936; came to U.S., 1964, naturalized, 1972; d. John and Jenny (Beattie) L. M.B., B.Ch., U. Witwatersrand, Johannesburg, South Africa, 1959. Intern Harare Hosp., Salisbury, Rhodesia, 1960-61; gen. practice medicine Lusaka, 1961-62; sr. pediatric house officer Derby Children's Hosp., also St. John's Hosp., Chelmsford, Eng., 1962-64; resident in pediatrics Children's Hosp., Louisville, 1964, Cin., 1964-65; fellow clin. pharmacology Cin. Coll. Medicine, 1965-67; mem. faculty U. Cin. Med. Sch., 1967—, prof. pediatrics, 1975, asso. prof. pharmacology, 1972-77. Contbr. articles to med. publs.; editor Pediatric and Adolescent Hypertension, 1991. Grantee Am. Heart Assn., 1970-72, 89-90. Mem. Am. Pediatric Soc. (elected, Founder's award 1996), Midwest Soc. Pediatric Research. Episcopalian. Home: 1133 Herschel Ave Cincinnati OH 45208-3112 Office: Children's Hosp Med Ctr Children's Hosp Rsch Found 3300 Burnet Ave Cincinnati OH 45229

LOGGIODICE, SUSAN REBECCA, small business owner; b. Chadron, Nebr., Mar. 8, 1969; d. Charles Alan and Crystal Eve (Licthe) Staetz; m. Walter Edward Bancroft, June 18, 1988 (div. Oct. 1991); 1 child, Crystal Marie;/ m. Omar Raphael Loggiodice Adrian, Apr. 15, 1993. BA, LaSalle U., 1991, MA, 1992; MS in Computer Tech., Cleve. Inst. Electronics, 1993; JD, LaSalle U., 1996. Field rschr. Networking Agy., Inc., Richboro, Pa.,

1988-90; sys. designer CMG Internat., Inc., Boonton, N.J., 1991-93; graphic designer Chadron Record, Inc., 1992-93; Internet site adminstr., owner TOPS BBS, Smyrna, Ga., 1993—; team leader Software Devel. Group, Santa Ana, Calif., 1992—; advisor Team/OS2, Smyrna, 1994—. Author: Undocumented OS Calls, 1991, Society's Ghost: Manic Depression, 1993. Advocate Pendulum, 1992—. Mem. NAFE, Internat. Shareware Group.

LOGRASSO, CATHLEEN AGNES, elementary school and preschool educator; b. Bklyn., July 5, 1952; d. John Joseph and Olga Gertrude (Suydam) Williams; m. Thomas Gerard LoGrasso, June 30, 1973; children: Timothy, Sean, John, Susan, Christina. BS in Elem. Edn., Harris Stowe State Coll., 1989; MA in Ednl. Processes, Maryville U., 1996. Cert. elem. tchr. and early childhood tchr., Mo. Adminstr., tchr. Hilltop Acad. (formerly Apple Sch.), Olivette, Mo., 1980-82; dir. Apple Sch., Olivette, Mo., 1982-93, tchr., 1993—. Mem. Nat. Assn. Edn. of Young Children.

LOGSDON, JUDITH KAY, merchandiser, small business owner; b. Tulia, Tex., Dec. 5, 1947; d. Bill and Audrey Lee (Hendrix) Humphrey; m. Muriel Frazier Bussey, Mar. 19, 1965 (div.); children: Jeffrey Eldon Bussey, Shawn DeWitt Bussey; m. Leon Francis Logsdon, Nov. 28, 1980. Attended, South Plains Coll., 1987-88. Lic. cosmetologist. Cosmetologist K-K Beauty Shop, Dimmitt, Tex., 1966-67, The Blue Room, Dimmitt, 1967-68; reporter, interviewer Tex. Crop & Livestock Reporting Svc., Austin, 1972-74; bookkeeper Kearn Machine Shop, Hereford, Tex., 1975-76, Tex. Sesame divsn. ADM, Muleshoe, Tex., 1978-88; merchandiser, owner J&L Fashions, Muleshoe, 1988—. Sec.-treas. Muleshoe Activities Com., 1992-94; vol. Hospice of the Plains, 1996, The Heart Assn., 1985-86. Office: J&L Fashions 202 Main St Muleshoe TX 79347

LOGUE, JUDITH R., psychoanalyst, educator; b. Phila., Aug. 21, 1942; d. Martin and Laura (Goldman) Kirshenbaum; AB in Govt., Wheaton (Mass.) Coll., 1963; MSW, Rutgers U., 1966, PhD, Rutgers U. Grad. Sch. Arts and Scis., 1983; grad. N.Y. Center for Psychoanalytic Tng., 1978; m. Stephen Felton, Feb. 8, 1966 (div. Aug. 1989); 1 dau., Jane Jennifer; m. A. Douglas Logue, Feb. 14, 1990. Clin. social worker VA, Newark, 1967; psychotherapist Santa Barbara (Calif.) Mental Health Services, 1967-69; supr. Santa Barbara Counselling Center, 1967-69; pvt. practice psychoanalysis, 1969—; psychoanalyst, therapist Fifth Ave. Center for Psychotherapy, N.Y.C., 1969-72; instr. Marymount Manhattan Coll., 1971; psychotherapy supr. clin. faculty, dept. psychiatry Rutgers U. Med. Sch., New Brunswick, N.J., 1972-75, teaching asst. Grad. Sch. Social Work, 1974-76; vis. lectr. Bryn Mawr Coll. Sch. Social Work and Social Research, 1980; mem. faculty N.Y. Center for Psychoanalytic Tng., 1980—, N.J. Inst. Psychoanalysis and Psychotherapy, 1982—. Bd. dirs. N.Y. Ctr. for Psychoanalytic Tng., Inst. for Psychoanalysis and Psychotherapy N.J. Faculty, 1982—. NIMH fellow, 1965; diplomate Am. Bd. Psychotherapy. Recipient Disting. Faculty award Atlantic County Psychoanalytic Soc., 1987. Fellow N.J. Soc. for Clin. Social Work; mem. AAUP, APA (div. 39, sect. 1), NASW, Conf. Psychoanalytic Psychotherapists, Nat. Assn. for Advancement Psychoanalysis, Groves Conf. on Family, Acad. Cert. Social Workers, Soc. for Psychoanalytic Tng. (bd. dirs. 1983—, dir. social sci. program 1983-86). Mem. editorial bd. jour. Current Issues in Psychoanalytic Practice, 1983—; contbr. articles to profl. jours. Home and Office: 159 Valley Rd Princeton NJ 08540-3442

LOGUE-KINDER, JOAN, alcoholic beverages company executive; b. Richmond, Va., Oct. 26, 1943; d. John T. and Helen (Harvey) Logue; m. Lowell A. Henry Jr., Oct. 6, 1963 (div. Sept. 1981); children: Lowell A. Henry III, Catherine D. Henry, Christopher Logue Henry; m. Randolph S. Kinder, Dec. 13, 1986 (div. Nov. 1995). Student, Wheaton Coll., 1959-62; BA in Sociology, Adelphi U., 1964; cert. in edn., Mercy Coll., Dobbs Ferry, N.Y., 1971; postgrad., NYU, 1973; cert. in edn., St. John's U., 1974. Asst. to dist. mgr. U.S. Census Bur., N.Y.C., 1970; tchr. and adminstr. social studies Yonkers (N.Y.) Bd. Edn., 1971-75; dir. pub. rels. Nat. Black Network, N.Y.C., 1976-83; corp. v.p. NBN Broadcasting (formerly Nat. Black Network), N.Y.C., 1984-90; sr. v.p. The Mingo Group/Plus, N.Y.C., 1990-91; v.p. Edelman Pub. Rels. Worldwide, N.Y.C., 1991-93; dep. asst. sec. pub. affairs U.S. Dept. Treasury, Washington, 1993-94, asst. sec. pub. affairs, 1994-95; dir. corp. comm. programs The Seagram Co., N.Y.C., 1995—; cons. in field. Mem. alumnae recruitment coun. Wheaton Coll.; mem. Nigerian-Am. Friendship Soc., 1978-81; bd. dirs. Westchester Civil Liberties Union, 1974-77, Greater N.Y. coun. Girl Scouts U.S.A., 1985-93, Operation PUSH, 1985-93; del. White House Conf. on Small Bus.; active polit. campaigns, including Morris Udall for U.S. Pres., Howard Samuels for Gov.; sr. black media advisor Dukakis/Bentsen presdl. campaign, 1988; conv. del. N.Y. State Women's Polit. Caucus, 1975, pres. black caucus, 1976-77. Recipient Excellence in Media award Inst. New Cinema Artists, 1984. Mem. World Inst. Black Comm. (bd. dirs. 1983-91). Home: 1800 7th Ave Apt 9B New York NY 10026 Office: Seagram Corp Comm 375 Park Ave New York NY 10152

LOH, EDITH KWOK-YUEN, oncology nurse; b. Hong Kong, May 1, 1948; came to U.S., 1972; d. Chun Wing and Pui King (Chan) Lee; m. Kevin Kai-Tsu Loh, Mar. 30, 1972; children: Elizabeth, Jennifer, Jeffrey. RN, Hong Kong Govt. Nursing Sch., 1971, Tex. Woman's U., 1976; BSN magna cum laude, Hawaii Loa Coll., 1989; MPH, U. Hawaii, 1990, postgrad., 1994—. Cert. health edn. specialist; RN, Hawaii, Tex., Hong Kong, Eng. Student gen. nurse Hong Kong Govt. Hosps., 1968-70; pediatric nurse Queen Elizabeth Hosp., Hong Kong, 1971-72; head nurse oncology Ctr. Pavillion Hosp., Houston, 1972-75; oncology nurse Dr. Kevin Loh, Inc., Honolulu, 1978-90; nurse coord., health instr. Hawaii Hematology, Oncology, Inc., Honolulu, 1991-92; vol. rschr. immunol. studies U. Hawaii, 1990, health educator Baby S.A.F.E., Adminstrv. Office Dept. Health, Honolulu, 1993-94; presenter Am. Indian and Alaska Native Caucus 123d ann. meeting APHA, San Diego, 1995; guest lectr. U. Hawaii Sch. Pub. Health. Vol. recruitor Hawaii Bone Marrow Donor Registry, Honolulu, 1992; chmn. cmty. svc. com., Honolulu, 1992—; dir. Health Svcs. for Sr. Citizens, 1993; bd. dirs. Hawaii Cancer Children Found., 1992-94. Recipient Award of Merit, Nat. Dean's List, Nat. Collegiate Nursing award, 1989; named All American Scholar, 1989. Mem. AMA, Hawaii Pacific U. Nursing Honor Soc., Am. Cancer Soc., Soc. for Pub. Health Edn.-Hawaii (bd. dirs., sec., life), Orgn. Chinese Am. Women, Assoc. Chinese Univ. Women Inc. (chmn. welfare com. 1992, chmn. cmty. svc. com. 1991-95, mem. in parliamentary procedure legis. com. 1992, v.p. 1996), Soc. Pub. Health Edn. (bd. dirs. 1992-96, sec. 1992-93), Hawaii Soc. for Health Care Edn. and Tng. (planner, fundraiser and subcom. chair), Sigma Theta Tau. Home: 1815 Kumakani Pl Honolulu HI 96821-1327

LOHMAN, LORETTA CECELIA, social scientist, consultant; b. Joliet, Ill., Sept. 25, 1944; d. John Thomas and Marjorie Mary (Brennan) L. BA in Polit. Sci., U. Denver, 1966, PhD in Am. History, 1996; MA in Social Sci., U. No. Colo., 1975. Lectr. Ariz. State U., Tempe, 1966-67; survey researcher Merrill-Werthlin Co., Tempe, 1967-68; edn. asst. Am. Humane Assn., Denver, 1969-70; econ. cons. Lohman & Assocs., Littleton, Colo., 1971-75; rsch. assoc. Denver Rsch. Inst., 1976-86; rsch. scientist Milliken Chapman Rsch. Group, Littleton, 1986-89; owner Lohman & Assocs., Littleton, 1989—; affiliate Colo. Water Resources Rsch. Inst., Ft. Collins, Colo., 1989-91; tech. adv. com. Denver Potable Wastewater Demo Plant, 1986-90; cons. Constrn. Engrng. Rsch. Lab., 1984—; peer reviewer NSF, 1985-86, Univs. Coun. Water Resources, 1989—; WERC consortium reviewer N.Mex. Univs.-U.S. Dept. Energy, 1989—; course cons. Regis Coll., Denver, 1992—. Contbr. articles to profl. jours. Vol. Metro Water Conservation Projects, Denver, 1986-90; vol. handicapped fitness So. Suburban Parks and Recreation. Recipient Huffsmith award Denver Rsch. Inst., 1983; Nat. Ctr. for Edn. in Politics grantee, 1964-65. Mem. ASCE (social and environ. objectives com.), Am. Water Works Assn., Am. Water Resources Assn., Orgn. Am. Historians, Pub. Hist. Assn., Colo. Water Congress, Water Environ. Fedn., Sigma Xi, Pi Gamma Mu, Phi Alpha Theta. Democrat. Home and Office: 3375 W Aqueduct Ave Littleton CO 80123-2903

LOHMANN, JUDITH LEITH, secondary education educator; b. Bryn Mawr, Pa., Jan. 13, 1940; d. Harvey Bruce and Elizabeth A. (Abernethy) Leith; m. Watson M. Lohmann, July 22, 1960; children: Watson M. Jr., David, Kimberly. BS, Lebanon Valley Coll., Annville, Pa., 1961. Tchr. Pitman (N.J.) Sch. Dist., 1978—; cons. State of N.J., 1987—; mem. adv. bd. Gloucester County Inst. Tech., Sewell, N.J., 1987—. Mem. coun. Borough of Pitman, 1976-78; trustee McCowan Libr., pres., 1986—. Named Tchr. of Yr., Gov.'s award Pitman Sch. Dist., 1987. Mem. Reading Coun. South N.J., Delta Kappa Gamma (sec.). Republican. Presbyterian. Home: 330 Pitman Ave Pitman NJ 08071-1646 Office: Pitman Mid Sch E Holly Ave Pitman NJ 08071

LOIOCANO, BARBARA J., bilingual education educator; b. Dunkirk, N.Y., Feb. 13, 1953; d. Carl Russell and Jean Eleanor (Bowker) L. BS in Edn., SUNY, Fredonia, 1975; MS in Edn., SUNY, Plattsburgh, 1980; CAS, SUNY, New Paltz, 1993. Cert. tchr. Spanish edn. and bilingual edn., sch. adminstr./supr., sch. dist. adminstr., N.Y. Spanish tchr. Delaware Valley Ctrl. Sch., Callicoon, N.Y., 1984-85, Monticello (N.Y.) Ctrl. Sch., 1985-86; bilingual tchr. Otisville (N.Y.) Correctional Facility, 1986—; bilingual tchr. Marist Coll., Poughkeepsie, N.Y., 1987; Spanish tchr. Mercy Coll., Dobbs Ferry, N.Y., 1988; adult edn. tchr. Sullivan County Bd. Coop. Ednl. Svcs., Liberty, N.Y., 1985, 89-90; sec. literacy coun. Otisville Correctional Facility, 1992—, supr. literacy vols., 1992-93; acting edn. supr. Otishill Sch., 1989-94. Mem. Am. Legion Aux., Fredonia. Mem. Nat. Assn. Bilingual Edn., N.Y. State Assn. Fgn. Lang. Tchrs., State Assn. Bilingual Edn. Office: Otisville Correctional Facility PO Box 8 Otisville NY 10963

LOKEN, BARBARA, marketing educator, social psychologist; b. Owatonna, Minn., Aug. 22, 1951; d. Gordon Keith and June Rosaline (Iverson) Anderson; m. B. Michael Diebel, Apr. 7, 1991; 1 child, Elizabeth Loken Diebel. BA in Psychology magna cum laude, U. Minn., 1973; MA, NYU, 1976; PhD in Social Psychology, U. Ill., 1981. Rsch. and statis. asst. Nat. Soc. Prevention Blindness, N.Y.C., 1974-76; rsch. asst. dept. psychology U. Ill., 1976, 78-80, instr., 1977-78; NIMH trainee in measurement, 1979-80, asst. prof. dept. mktg. U. Minn., 1980-86, assoc. prof., 1986-92, prof., 1992—, co-dir. edn. evaluation Minn. heart health project Sch. Pub. Health, 1982-88, adj. assoc. prof. dept. psychology, 1987-92, adj. prof., 1992—; vis. assoc. prof. mktg. UCLA, 1988. Assoc. editor: Jour. Consumer Rsch., 1996—; contbr. articles to profl. jours. Rsch. grantee Sch. Mgmt., U. Minn., 1981-84, 86, 88-93. Mem. Am. Psychol. Assn., Am. Mktg. Assn., Assn. Consumer Rsch. Office: U Minn Carlson Sch Mgmt 271 19th Ave S Minneapolis MN 55455-0430

LOKMER, STEPHANIE ANN, public relations counselor; b. Wheeling, W.Va., Nov. 14, 1957; d. Joseph Steven and Mary Ann (Mozney) L. BA in Comm., Bethany Coll., 1980; cert., U. Tübingen, Germany, 1980, Sprach Inst. Tübingen, Germany 1980. V.p., Wheeling Coffee and Spice, W.Va., 1981—; pres. Lokmer & Assocs., Inc., McLean, Va., 1986—; pharm. mktg. rep. Bristol Labs., Wheeling, 1982-84, pharm. hosp. mktg. rep., 1984-85; pharm. mktg. rep. Boehringer Ingelheim, Nashville, 1985-87. V.p., bd. dirs. Wheeling Coffee & Spice, 1981—. Mem. Pub. Rels. Soc. Am. (accredited), Pub. Rels. Soc. Am. Internat., Counselors Acad., Zeta Tau Alpha. Republican. Roman Catholic. Avocations: flying, sailing, tennis, reading.

LOLLAR, KATHERINE LOUISE, social worker, therapist; b. Cin., Nov. 1, 1944; d. Robert Miller and Dorothy Marie L.; div.; 2 children. BA, U. Kans., 1966; MSW, Loyola U., 1971. Lic. clin. social worker, Oreg.; cert. social worker, Wash.; bd. cert. diplomate clin. social work. Head activity therapy dept. Fox Children's Ctr., Dwight, Ill., 1966-68; child care worker Madden Mental Health Ctr., Hines, Ill., 1968-69, social worker, 1971-74; pvt. practice therapy Wheaton and Oakbrook, Ill., 1977-82; intern Monticello Care Unit alcohol and drug treatment program, 1983; cons. Residential Facility for Developmentally Disabled Adults, Battle Ground, Wash., 1983-85; therapist Cath. Community Svcs., Vancouver, Wash., 1983-88; outsta. mgr. Wash. Div. Devel. Disabilities, Vancouver, 1987—; pvt. practice therapy Vancouver, 1988—. Troop cons. Columbia River coun. Girl Scouts Am., 1984-86, internat. trip leader, 1993, alt. leader, 1995-96, life mem.; com. mem. Friends of Sangam Internat. Com., 1994—; mem. Internat. Field Selection Team, 1994-96; mem. Unity of Vancouver. Mem. NASW (sec. Vancouver chpt. 1982-84, co-chair 1985-87, unit rep. Wash. state unit 1990-92), Singles on Sat. Sq. Dance Club, Recycles Sq. Dance Club (pres. 1995—). Office: 650 Officers Row Vancouver WA 98661-3836

LOMAN, MARY LAVERNE, retired mathematics educator; b. Stratford, Okla., June 10, 1928; d. Thomas D. and Mary Ellen (Goodwin) Glass; m. Coy E. Loman, Dec. 23, 1944; 1 child, Sandra Leigh Loman Easton. BS, U. Okla., 1956, MA, 1957, PhD, 1961. Grad. asst., then instr. U. Okla., Norman, 1956-61; asst. prof. math. U. Ctrl. Okla., Edmond, 1961-62; assoc. prof. U. Cen. Okla., Edmond, 1962-66, prof., 1966-93; prof. emeritus U. Ctrl. Okla., Edmond, 1993—; ret., 1993. NSF fellow, 1965-67. Mem. Math. Assn. Am., Nat. Coun. Tchrs. Math., Okla. Coun. Tchrs. Math. (v.p. 1972-76), Higher Edn Alumni Coun. Okla., VFW Aux., Delta Kappa Gamma. Home: 2201 Tall Oaks Trl Edmond OK 73003-2325

LOMBARD, DEBORAH LYNN, nurse midwife; b. Toledo, Ohio, Mar. 15, 1950; d. Raymond S. Jr. and Eleanor K. (Rakestraw) Metzger; m. Bernard E. Lombard, Aug. 7, 1976; children: Travis Alan, Craig Kinkade. BA, Bowling Green State U., 1972; BSN, U. South Fla., 1980; MSN, U. Fla., 1984. RN, Fla.; CNM. Staff RN St. Joseph's Hosp., Tampa, Fla., 1980-81, Tampa (Fla.) Gen. Hosp., 1982-84; nurse midwife Polk Gen. Hosp., Bartow, Fla., 1984-87; nurse midwife-ARNP Hillsborough County Health Dept., Tampa, 1987-88; nurse midwife Turner & Muir, M.D., PA, Cocoa Beach, Fla., 1988-94, Brevard Ob-Gyn. Assocs., Titusville, Fla., 1994-96, A Place for Women, Inc., Port St. John, Fla., 1996—; adj. faculty, clin. instr. Polk County C.C., Lakeland, Fla., 1985-86, Brevard C.C., Cocoa, Fla., 1989—; adj. faculty, preceptor for masters level nursing students U. Fla., Gainesville, Fla., 1988—; adj. faculty, preceptor for masters level nurse-midwifery students U. Fla., Jacksonville, Fla., 1991—; clin. instr. Polk Gen. Hosp., Bartow, Fla., 1985-86; instr. in childbirth edn. classes Tampa Gen. Hosp., 1982-83. Den leader Cub Scouts Pack 397, Merritt Island, 1993—. Named Best Midwife of Brevard County Fla. Today Newspaper, 1990. Mem. Am. Coll. of Nurse Midwives, Fla. Perinatal Assn., Am. Coll. of Nurse-Midwives (Fla. chpt. scholarship com. 1991—), Sigma Theta Tau. Home: 1830 Newfound Harbor Dr Merritt Island FL 32952 Office: A Place For Women A Place for Women Inc Port Saint John FL 32927

LOMBARD, JUDITH MARIE, human resource policy specialist; b. Harmony, Maine, June 7, 1944; d. Clayton Selden and Helen Mae (Wentworth) L. BA, U. Maine, 1966; MPA, U. So. Calif., 1982, D of Pub. Adminstrn., 1987. Psychodramatist HEW, Washington, 1966-68; creative arts therapist U.S. Health and Human Svcs., Washington, 1968-87; sr. therapist Mental Health Svcs., Washington, 1987-88; tng. officer USDA, Washington, 1988-92; mem. adj. faculty U. So. Calif., L.A., 1988-92, Shenandoah U., Winchester, Va., 1993—; employee devel. specialist U.S. Office Personnel Mgmt., Washington, 1992—; pvt. cons., Alexandria, Va., 1988—. Author (book chpt.) How Public Organizations Work, 1991, (handbook) Supervisor's Guide, 1993; contbr. articles to profl. jours. Active Maine State Soc., Washington, 1980—; mem. fundraising bd. doctorial assn. U. So. Calif., Washington, 1986—; active Del Ray Citizens Assn., Alexandria, 1982—. Recipient Dorothy Dix award St. Elizabeth's Hosp., Washington, 1982. Mem. Am. Soc. Pub. Adminstrn., Am. Soc. Tng. and Devel., Nat. Therapeutic Recreation Soc., Am. Therapeutic Recreation Assn. (pres. Washington chpt. 1990), Med. Soc. Washington (pres. 1990), Nat. Recreation and Parks Assn. (elections chair 1990, 91), D.C. Jungian Soc., Chesapeake Bay Orgnl. Devel. Network. Office: US Office Personnel Mgmt 1900 E St NW Washington DC 20415

LOMBARD, MARJORIE ANN, business manager; b. Stoughton, Mass., Feb. 25, 1956; d. John Joseph and Marie Josephine (Hopkins) Lombard; children: Katie Marie Burt, Elizabeth Ann Burt. BSBA with honors, Northeastern U., 1979. Acctg. trainee HEW Audit, Boston, 1976-78; staff acct. Etonic, Inc., Brockton, Mass., 1979-81; ops. acct. Foxboro Co., East Bridgewater, Mass., 1981-82, 86-87; chief acct. New Eng. Structures, Inc., Avon, Mass., 1983-84; bus. mgr. Mutron Corp., Brockton, Mass., 1988-92; contr. Connector Tech. Corp., Warwick, R.I., 1992-94; bus. mgr. Cath. Charities-Laboure Ctr., South Boston, Mass., 1994—. Tchr. confraternity Christian doctrine program St. Thomas Aquinas Ch., Bridgewater, 1988-94; keyperson Old Colony United Way, Brockton, 1988-91, mem. funds allocation com., 1991—; vol. tchr. You and Me drug prevention program, Bridgewater, 1990-92, Parents for Edn., Bridgewater, 1990—; vol. Am. Electronics Assn.-Brockton Jr. High Sch. Alliance, 1990-92; mem. Bridgewater Parents Collaborative, 1991—. Mem. Am. Electronics Assn., Small Bus. Assn. New Eng. Roman Catholic.

LOMBARDI, CELESTE, zoological park administrator; b. Columbus, Ohio, Feb. 16, 1955; d. Adam Dominic and Frances Elizabeth (Varda) L.; m. Terence Lawrence Smith, Mar. 26, 1990; 1 child Matthew Peachey. BS in Zoology, Ohio State U., 1978. Zoo keeper Children's Zoo Columbus Zoo, 1978-83, supr. Children's Zoo, 1983-90, asst. curator mammals, 1990-93, gen. curator, 1993—. TV appearances include David Letterman Show, Good Morning America, PM Magazine, and various local news shows. Mem. Am. Assn. Zool. Parks and Aquariums, Am. Assn. Zoo Keepers. Roman Catholic. Home: 4190 Rutherford Rd Powell OH 43065-9733 Office: Columbus Zoo PO Box 400 9990 Riverside Dr Powell OH 43065-9606

LOMBARDI, TRACEY ANNE, financial administrator, medical assistant; b. Teaneck, N.J., Sept. 26, 1965; d. John David and Dianne T. (Regina) Lisch; m. Eugene Nicholas Lombardi, May 20, 1995; 1 child, Aracelis Gianna. Student in Ophthalmic/Surg. Asst., Bergen C.C./Mercy Coll. and, Manhattan Eye and Ear. Cert. ophthalmic technologist, N.Y. Ophthalmic technologist, fin. adminstr. Cliffside Eye Ctr., Cliffside Park, N.J., 1992—. Office: Cliffside Eye Ctr 663 Palisade Ave Cliffside Park NJ 07010

LOMBARDINI, CAROL ANN, lawyer; b. Framingham, Mass., Dec. 29, 1954; d. Harry and Sarah (Scarano) L. m. William L. Cole, Apr. 23, 1983; children: Kevin Daniel, Kristin Elizabeth. BA, U. Chgo., 1976; JD, Stanford U., 1979. Bar: Calif. 1979. Assoc. Meserve, Mumper & Hughes, L.A., 1979-80, Proskauer Rose Goetz & Mendelsohn, L.A., 1980-82; from counsel to sr. v.p. legal and bus. affairs Alliance of Motion Picture and TV Prodrs., Encino, Calif., 1982—; trustee Dirs. Guild Contract Adminstrn., Encino, 1982—, Prodr.-Writers Guild Pension & Health Plans, Burbank, Calif., 1983—, SAG-Prodr. Pension & Health Plans, Burbank, 1986—, Dirs. Guild-Prodr. Pension & Health Plans, L.A., 1987—. Office: Alliance Motion Picture & TV Prodrs 15503 Ventura Blvd Encino CA 91436-3103

LOMELI, MARTA, elementary education educator; b. Tijuana, Baja Calif, Mex., Oct. 28, 1952; came to U.S. 1954; d. Jesus and Guadalupe (Ascencio) Lomeli; m. Rudolph Benitez, 1978 (div. 1982); children: Pascual Lomeli Benitez; m. David E. Miller, Aug. 16, 1991. BA, San Diego State U., 1977. With M & N Tree Nursery, Vista, Calif., 1957-70; libr. Vista Boys Club, 1969-70; vol. tutor MECHA U. Calif. San Diego, La Jolla, 1971-73; tchr. aide San Diego City Schs., 1976-77; bilingual educator National City (Calif.) Schs., 1978—; mem. restructuring com. Lincoln Acres Sch., 1991. Author numerous poems. Mem. Lincoln Acres Com. to Advise the Prin., National City, 1986-88, Com. to Advise the Supt., National City, 1986-88; art editor Lincoln Jr. H.S., Vista, Calif., 1964-65, Third World U. Calif., San Diego, 1970-73; mem. Lincoln Acres Sch. Site Coun., 1988-89; mem. high tech. com. Nat. Sch. Dist., 1993-94; vol. tchr. St. Vincent de Paul's Ctr. for Homeless, San Diego, 1991-93, Shaolin Kempo Karate (black belt 1st degree); mem. Paradise Hills Citizens Patrol, 1994—. Mem. Calif. Tchrs. Assn. (site rep. Nat. City 1985), Calif. Assn. Bilingual Edn. (sec. 1986), Nat. Assn. Bilingual Edn., La Raza Club (pres., co-founder 1970). Democrat. Home: 6920 Alsacia St San Diego CA 92139-2101

LOMMATSCH, I. LAVON, retired business administration consultant; b. Denver, June 6, 1940; d. William Theodore and Iro (Watenpaugh) Fisher; m. Lynn Lommatsch, June 1, 1985; children: James Waldorf, Lance Waldorf, Stacy Waldorf, Eric, Keith. Student, U. Colo., 1960-61, Front Range C.C., Denver, 1984, Don Kagy Real Estate Sch., Denver, 1985. Lic. realtor, Colo. With juvenile divsn. Adams County Dist. Atty., Brighton, Colo., 1983-86; with Adams County Parks and Cmty. Resources, Brighton, 1986-95; ret. Charter mem. bd. dirs. Women In Crisis, Adams County, 1983; prodr., dir. walk-a-thons Adams County Trails and Greenway Found.; active fundraising Amaranth Diabetes Found., Alternatives to Domestic Violence, Cmty. Health Svcs., Hearing/Seeing Dogs, Santa's Workshop, Shriner's Burn Ctrs. Recipient Excellence award Nat. Assn. County Info. Officers, 1986, State Recognition award Heart Assn. Mem. Order Ea. Star (worthy matron 1977-78), Order Amaranth, Inc. (grand royal matron 1991-92), White Shrine Jerusalem. Lutheran.

LONDON, CHARLOTTE ISABELLA, secondary education educator, reading specialist; b. Guyana, S.Am., June 11, 1946; came to U.S., 1966, naturalized, 1980; d. Samuel Alphonso and Diana Dallett (Daniels) Edwards; m. David Timothy London, May 26, 1968 (div. May 1983); children: David Tshombe, Douglas Tshaka. BS, Fort Hays State U., 1971; MS, Pa. State U., 1974, PhD, 1977. Elem. sch. tch., Guyana, 1962-66, secondary sch. tchr., 1971-72; instr. lang. arts Pa. State U., University Park, 1973-74; reading specialist/ednl. cons. N.Y.C. Community Coll., 1975; dir. skills acquisition and devel. center Stockton (N.J.) State Coll., 1975-77; reading specialist Pleasantville (N.J.) Public Schs., 1977—; ind. specialist United Nations Devel. Programme , Guyana, 1988—; v.p. Atlantic County PTA, 1980-82; del. N.J. Gov.'s Conf. Future Edn. N.J., 1981; founder, pres. Guyana Assn. Reading and Lang. Devel., 1987. Sec. Atlantic County Minority Polit. Women's Caucus. Mem. Internat. Reading Assn., Nat. Council Tchrs. English, Assn. Supervision and Curriculum Devel., NEA, N.J. Ednl. Assn., AAUW, Pi Lambda Theta, Phi Delta Kappa (sec.). Mem. African Methodist Episcopal Ch. Home: 6319 Crocus St Mays Landing NJ 08330-1107 Office: Pleasantville Pub Schs W Decatur Ave Pleasantville NJ 08232

LONEY, MARY ROSE, airport administrator. Dir. aviation Phila. Internat. Airport. Office: Phila Dept of Commerce Aviation Div 3751 Island Ave Phila Intl Airport TrmlE Philadelphia PA 19153*

LONG, CECELIA MORENE, religious organization administrator. Cert. in German Lit., Goethe Inst., Bad Reichenhall, Germany, 1968; BA in German, Hollins Coll., 1970; MSW, U. Mich., 1973; postgrad., Garrett Evang. Theol. Sem., 1995. Adminstrv. intern Cedar Crest Coll., Allentown, Pa., 1975-76; adminstrv. asst. in Continuing Edn. Bishop Coll., Dallas, 1976-78; mgr. residence svc. ctr. Southwestern Bell Telephone Co., Ft. Worth, 1978-84; dir. programs and ops. St. Luke Cmty. United Meth. Ch., Dallas, 1984-89; gen. secretariat of gen. commn. on status and role of women United Meth. Ch., Evanston, Ill., 1989—; facilitator No. Ill. Black Clergywomen. workshops for Ch. Bus. Adminstrs. of United Meth. Ch.; mem. Bishop's Task Force on Theology of Compensation for No. Ill. Conf.; facilitator of workshops on sexual harassment for Bishops of United Meth. Ch., Nat. Assn. of Asian Am. United Methodists; speaker and workshop leader Western N.C. Tng. Event for Women of Color, WomenVision, Detroit, W. Mich., E. Ohi and W. Ohio Ann. Confs.; mem. Ctr. for Prevention of Sexual and Domestic Violence Task Force on the Black Ch. and Sexual Abuse, Ala.-West Fla. Commn. on Statis and Role of Women; speaker at numerous U.S. Confs. concerning women's issues; co-chairperson No. Ill. Conf. Bd. of Ch. and Soc.; lay mem. No. Ill. Ann. Conf. Bd. dirs. Shalom Edn., Chgo.; bd. trustees Hollins Coll., Roanoke, Va., Founders Day Spkr., 1995; chairperson adminstrv. coun. Sherman United Meth. Ch., Evanston, Ill., mem. Pastor Parish Rels. com., Trustee com., Youth Advisor, Jail and Care Ministries; chairperson Worship Com., Nurture. Mem. NAACP, Black Methodists for Church Renewal, Hollins Coll. Alumnae Club, Chgo. Office: United Methodist Ch Comm Status/Role of Women 1200 Davis St Evanston IL 60201-4118

LONG, DEBORAH JOYCE, lawyer; b. Oct. 26, 1953; d. Thomas C. and Margaret N. (Falks) L.; m. William Daniel Sockwell, May 26, 1979; 1 child, Daniel Long. BA, Auburn U., 1975; JD, U. Ala., 1980. Bar: Ala. 1980, U.S. Ct. Appeals (5th cir.) 1980, U.S. Ct. Appeals (11th cir.) 1981, U.S. Dist. Ct. (no. dist.) Ala. 1981. Law clk. U.S. Ct. Appeals for 5th Cir., Montgomery, Ala., 1980-81; assoc. Cabaniss, Johnston, Gardner, Dumas & O'Neal, Birmingham, Ala., 1981-84, Maynard, Cooper, Frierson & Gale, P.C., Birmingham, 1984—; mem.; sr. v.p., gen. counsel Protective Life Ins. Co., Birmingham, Ala., 1994—. Recipient Cert. of Appreciation, Ala. Bar Assn., Montgomery. Mem. Farrah Soc., Ala. State Bar (bd. bar examiners 1987—, bd. editors 1991—), Birmingham Bar Assn. (bd. editors 1989-90). Office: Protective Life Ins Co 2801 Hwy 280 S Birmingham AL 35223*

LONG, DEE, state legislator; b. 1939; m. Nicholas Long; 2 children. BA, Northwestern U.; postgrad., U. Minn. Legislator State of Minn., St. Paul, 1978—; speaker of House; mem. rules and legis. adminstrn. com., taxes com., ways and means com. Home: 2409 Humboldt Ave S Minneapolis MN 55405-2540 Office: Minn Ho of Reps State Capital Building Saint Paul MN 55155-1606*

LONG, ELIZABETH VALK, magazine publisher; b. Winston-Salem, N.C., Apr. 29, 1950; d. Henry Lewis and Elizabeth (Fuller) V. BA, Hollins Coll., 1972; MBA, Harvard Bus. Sch., 1979. Clin. adminstr. Mass. Gen. Hosp., Boston, 1973-77; asst. to circulation dir. Time Mag.-Time Inc., N.Y.C., 1979-80, 81-82; circulation dir. Fortune Mag.-Time Inc., N.Y.C., 1982-84, Sports Illustrated-Time Inc., N.Y.C., 1984-85, Time Mag.-Time Inc., N.Y.C., 1985-86; publisher Life Mag.-Time Inc., N.Y.C., 1987-93; pres. Time Mag., 1993-95; exec. v.p. Time Inc., N.Y.C., 1995. Trustee Hollins Coll., 1987—; mem. bus. com. Mus. Modern Art, N.Y.C.; mem. bd. visitors Wake Forest U., Winston-Salem, N.C.; bd. dirs. Hanover Direct, Inc., Weehawken, N.J.; mem. Com. of 200. Recipient Matrix award N.Y. Women in Comms., 1992, Silver Medal award Am. Advt. Fedn., 1993. Mem. Phi Beta Kappa. Office: Time Inc Time & Life Bldg 1271 Avenue Of The Americas New York NY 10020*

LONG, ELLEN JOYCE, accounting/business educator; b. Clarence, Mo., Apr. 28, 1938; d. Paul L. and Phoebe M. (Hill) Baker; m. Everett Lee Long, June 10, 1961; children: Paula Dawn, Laura Ruth, Jay Douglas. BS, U. Mo., 1960, MS in Bus. Edn., 1963; MS in Acctg., U. Wis., 1986. Bus. edn. tchr. Warren County R-111, Warrentown, Mo., 1960-62, Sturgeon (Mo.) Sch. Dist. No-RV, 1962-64; staff acct. Virchow Krause & Co., Whitewater, Wis., 1987; cost acct. Albert Trostel Packing, Ltd., Lake Geneva, Wis., 1988; sec.-treas. BL Farms, Inc., Whitewater, 1982—; lectr. U. Wis., Whitewater, 1965-92, mem. cultural affairs com., 1991-96. Pres., treas., bd. dirs., newsletter editor Cmty. of Christ Ch., 1986—; bd. dirs. Habitat for Humanity, dir. pub. rels. and fin., City of Whitewater, 1978—, chair devel. com. 1994-95, v.p. 1995-96. Mem. Wis. Inst. of Cert. Pub. Accts. (assoc.), PEO (pres., v.p., newsletter editor), LWV, Delta Pi Epsilon (v.p. 1980, corr. sec. 1979), Phi Kappa Phi. Home: 1259 W Satinwood Ln Whitewater WI 53190-1601

LONG, FLEUR LAIRD, artist, art teacher; b. San Francisco, Mar. 16, 1931; d. John Parry Laird and Deborah Emma Sampson; m. John Allen Long, Sept. 29, 1956; children: Terry Francis, Deborah Anne, John Michael, Jolie Marie. AA, U. Calif., Berkeley, 1950; BA in Visual Arts, Coll. Santa Fe, 1981; postgrad., John Tyler, UCLA. Stewardess Pan Am. World Airways, 1952-56; dir. Flowers & Fantasies Studio & Gallery, Dinwiddie, Va., 1981-95; art tchr. Ghost Ranch, N.Mex., 1991-94, Bascom-Louise Gallery, Highlands, N.C., 1993-95, Petersburg Area Art League for Va. Mus., 1993; pvt. art tchr. Highlands, N.C., 1993-94. One-woman shows include Greer Garson Ctr., Santa Fe, 1981, Eric Schindler Gallery, Richmond, Va., 1985, 86, 88, Philip Morris, Richmond, Va., 1987, 88; group shows include Am. Watercolor Soc., Salamungundi Club, N.Y.C., 1985, Bascom-Louise Gallery, Highlands, N.C. (blue ribbon mixed media 1994), Art League of Va. Mus., Petersburg, Ariz. Aqueous, Tubac, Ctr. Gallery, Chapel Hill, N.C., Festival of the Masters Disney World, W.Va. Watercolor Soc., U.S. Art, San Francisco, Winter Park Art Show, Fla., Works on Paper, Annapolis, Md., Limited Edition Expo, Charlotte Conv. Ctr., N.C., 45th Nat. Colo. Springs; represented in permanent collections at Mus. Fine Arts, Santa Fe. Mem. Am. Watercolor Soc. (N.Y.C., assoc.), Allied Artists Am. (N.Y.C., assoc.), Nat. Mus. of Women in the Arts (Washington, charter mem.), Art League of Highlands, N.C. (artist mem.), Va. Watercolor Soc. (artist mem., sec. 1987), Kappa Delta Phi. Home: 15030 Boydton Plank Rd Dinwiddie VA 23841

LONG, JEANINE HUNDLEY, state legislator; b. Provo, Utah, Sept. 21, 1928; d. Ralph Conrad and Hazel Laurine (Snow) Hundley; m. McKay W. Christensen, Oct. 28, 1949 (div. 1967); children: Cathy Schuyler, Julie Schulleri, Kelly M. Christensen, C. Brett Christensen, Harold A. Christensen; m. Kenneth D. Long, Sept. 6, 1968. AA, Shoreline C.C., Seattle, 1975; BA in Psychology, U. Wash., 1977. Mem. Wash. Ho. of Reps., 1983-87, 93-94, mem. bd. joint com. pension policy, Inst. Pub. Policy; mem. Wash. Senate, 1995—. Mayor protem, mem. city coun. City of Brier, Wash., 1977-80. Republican. Office: PO Box 40482 Olympia WA 98504-0482

LONG, JOANN MOREY, publishing company executive, editor; b. Dallas; d. David and Mary Q. Morey; m. James W. Long, Aug. 15, 1946; children: Mary Joan, Michael. BA, So. Meth. U., 1946. Editor, v.p. Hendrick-Long Pub. Co., Dallas, 1969—; bd. dirs., sec. Book Pubs. of Tex., 1980s; bd. dirs., treas. Southwestern Booksellers Assn., 1980s. Bd. dirs. Jr. League of Dallas, 1977-78, Cath. Charities, 1970-79. Mem. Dallas Mus. Art, Dallas Zool. Soc., Dallas County Heritage Soc., Dallas Woman's Club, Pi Beta Phi Alumnae. Roman Catholic. Home: 3513 Villanova St Dallas TX 75225-5008 Office: Hendrick-Long Pub Co 4811 W Lovers Ln Dallas TX 75209-3137

LONG, KATHLEEN ANNE, dean. BS, Catholic U.; MS in Child Psychiatric Nursing and Nursing Education, Wayne State U.; PhD in Behavorial Scis., Johns Hopkins U. Prof., dean Coll. Nursing U. Fla., Gainesville, 1995—; adv. bd. U.S. Office Rural Health Policy, Nat. League Nursing; mem. adv. group Deans Schs. Nursing U.S. Pres.'s Task Force Nat. Health Care Reform. Fellow ANA, Am. Acad. Nursing; mem. Am. Assn. Colls. Nursing (bd. dirs.), Western Inst. Nursing (past chair), Sigma Theta Tau (past-pres. Zeta Upsilon chpt.). Office: Univ of Florida College of Nursing PO Box 100197 Gainesville FL 32610-0197*

LONG, LEVITHA OWENS, special education educator; b. Washington, Aug. 5, 1951; d. Otha and Lola Mary (Robinson) Owens; m. Johnnie Edward Long, Aug. 22, 1987; 1 child, Owen Edward Robinson. BS, Va. State U., 1980; MA, U. D.C., 1983. Tchr., adminstrv. asst. Friendship House Inc., Washington, 1980-82; spl. edn. educator Prince George's County (Md.) Pub. Sch., 1982-84, Davis Elem. Sch., Washington, 1984-86; spl. edn. educator Weatherless Elem. Sch., Washington, 1986-92, co-chmn. gifted and talented com., 1989-92; spl. edn. educator Ketcham Elem. Sch., Washington, 1992-95, Roper Middle Sch. of Science and Math Technology; coord. spelling bee Ketcham Elem. Sch., Washington, 1992-94, chairperson music/drama club. Dir. summer program Girl Scouts Am., Washington, 1985-93; mem. voter registration com. Prince George's County, 1991-94, voter registration ward 7 Rylan-Epworth Civiv Assn., Washington, 1977-85; mem. polit. action com., Kaypark Civic Assn., Sutland, Md., 1985—. Mem. ASCD, Coun. for Exceptional Children, Black Child Devel. Inst., Va. State U. Alumni Assn. (chair 1991-93), Va. State U. Alumni Assn. (chair scholarship fundraising), Alpha Kappa Alpha (co-chair 1985-87, cotillion co-chair). Democrat. Methodist. Home: 2531 Fairhill Dr Suitland MD 20746-2306 Office: Roper Middle Sch/DC Pub Sch 415 12th St NW Washington DC 20001

LONG, LISA ANN, publishing supervisor, business owner; b. Springfield, Mo., Jan. 28, 1965; d. Charles Wayne and Clara Belle (Matney) L.; life ptnr. Jari Gwen Wilson, Sept. 16, 1987. Student, Mo. Western State Coll., 1987-91. Graphic artist Kuehne br. YMCA, Topeka, 1991—, Today's Printing Svc., Topeka, 1994-96; owner, designer LaLong Designs, Topeka, 1996—; pub. supr. Comty. Resource Coun., Topeka, 1996—. Author, editor, designer: Breaking the Silence, 1996. House mgr., supr. Florence Crittenton Home for Girls, Topeka, 1992-95; active Nat. Gay and Lesbian Task Force. Scholar Challenging Opression Conf., Conf. Bd., Chgo., 1990. Mem. NOW, ACLU. Democrat. Office: LALong Designs PO Box 1392 Topeka KS 66601

LONG, MARY LOUISE, retired government official; b. Macon, Ga., Aug. 25, 1922; d. Willie and Sarah (Sparks) Tyson; A.B., Morris Brown Coll., Atlanta, 1946; m. Samuel F. Long, Apr. 14, 1962. Supervisory procurement clk. Dept. Def., N.Y., 1954-62, purchasing agt. Phila. Procurement Dist., 1962-64, Army Electronic Command, Phila., 1964-66, Med. Directorate, Def. Personnel Support Center, Phila., 1966-75, contracting officer, 1975-80, sect. chief/contracting officer, 1980-83. Active NAACP, YMCA; established Mary Louise Tyson Long Scholarship Fund, Morris Brown Coll., 1986; mem. Phila Inter-alumni coun. United Negro Coll. Fund. Named Alumna of Yr. Morris Brown Coll., 1987, 50th Reunion Cert., 1996. Mem. Beta Omicron, Iota Phi Lambda. Congregationalist. Home: 617 E Mt Airy Ave Philadelphia PA 19119-1147

LONG, MAXINE MASTER, lawyer; b. Pensacola, Fla., Oct. 20, 1943; d. Maxwell L. and Claudine E. (Smith) M.; m. Anthony Byrd Long, Aug. 27, 1966; children: Deborah E., David M. AB, Bryn Mawr Coll., 1965; MS, Georgetown U., 1971; JD, U. Miami, 1979. Bar: Fla. 1979, U.S. Ct. Appeals (5th cir.) 1980, U.S. Dist. Ct. (so. dist.) Fla. 1980, U.S. Ct. Appeals (11th cir.) 1981, U.S. Dist. Ct. (mid. and no. dists.) Fla. 1987. Law clk. to U.S. dist. judge U.S. Dist. Ct. (so. dist.) Fla., Miami, 1979-80; assoc. Shutts & Bowen, Miami, 1980-90, of counsel, 1990-92, ptnr., 1992—. Mem. Fla. Bar Assn. (vice chair bus. litigation cert. com. 1996—, past chair bus. litigation com., exec. coun. bus. law sect.), Dade County Bar Assn. (mem. fed. cts. com., recipient pro bono award/Vol. Lawyers for the Arts 1989). Office: Shutts & Bowen 201 S Biscayne Blvd Miami FL 33131-4332

LONG, NANCY L., counselor; b. Fayetteville, Tenn., Dec. 8, 1954; d. Curtis and Fannie (Gaunt) L. BS, Tenn. State U., Nashville, 1976, MS, 1979; MDiv, So. Sem., Louisville, 1987; postgrad., Va. Union U., Richmond, 1994—. Searcher Chgo. Title Co., Nashville, 1976-77; claims adjuster Hartford Ins. Co., Nashville, 1977-84; chaplain intern Humana Hosp., Louisville, 1985; counselor Interfaith Counseling Svc., Scottsdale, Ariz., 1988-90, Va. Inst. Pastoral Care, Richmond, 1990-95, Chesterfield County Mental Health, Richmond, 1991—; adj. prof. Va. Union U., Richmond, 1992—. Bd. mem. Richmond AIDS Ministry, 1993-94, Richmond Housing Corp., 1995. Fellow Am. Assn. Pastoral Counseling; mem. Lic. Profl. Counselors, Alpha Kappa Alpha. Baptist. Office: Chesterfield County Mental Health 6801 Lucy Corr Dr Chesterfield VA 23834

LONG, NICHOLA Y., technical writer; b. Walnut Creek, Calif., Jan. 4, 1955; d. Shogo and Elizabeth (Hughes) Yamaguchi. BS in Indsl. Tech./Electronics, Tuskegee U., 1978. From spl. tech. asst. to tech. writing specialist Western Electric Corp., Winston-Salem, N.C., 1977-86; sr. tech. documentation specialist AT&T Network Systems, Winston-Salem, 1986-96. Friend, The Arts Council, Inc., Winston-Salem, 1984-86. Mem. NAFE, Am. Soc. Profl. and Exec. Women, Tuskegee Nat. Alumni Assn. (pres. Winston-Salem chpt. 1984-85), Alliance Black Telecommunications Employees, Alpha Kappa Mu. Home: 168 Carrisbrooke Ln Winston Salem NC 27104-2528

LONG, PRISCILLA, writer; b. Quakertown, Pa., Mar. 17, 1943; d. Winslow Nielson and Barbara Jane (Henry) L. BA, Antioch Coll., Yellow Springs, Ohio, 1967; MFA, U. Wash., 1990. Author: Where the Sun Never Shines: A History of America's Bloody Coal Industry, 1989; contbr. short fiction to profl. publs.

LONG, SARAH ANN, librarian; b. Atlanta, May 20, 1943; d. Jones Lloyd and Lelia Maria (Mitchell) Sanders; m. James Allen Long, 1961 (div. 1985); children: Andrew C., James Allen IV; m. Donald J. Sager, May 23, 1987. BA, Oglethorpe U., 1966; M in Librarianship, Emory U., 1967. Asst. libr. Coll. of St. Matthias, Bristol, Eng., 1970-74; cons. State Libr. of Ohio, Columbus, 1975-77; coord. Pub. Libr. of Columbus and Franklin County, Columbus, 1977-79, dir. Fairfield County Dist. Libr., Lancaster, Ohio, 1979-82, Dauphin County Libr. System, Harrisburg, Pa., 1982-85, Multnomah County Libr., Portland, Oreg., 1985-89; system dir. North Suburban Libr. System, Wheeling, Ill., 1989—; chmn. Portland State U. Libr. Adv. Coun., 1987-89. Contbr. articles to profl. jours. Bd. dirs. Dauphin County Hist. Soc., Harrisburg, 1983-85, ARC, Harrisburg, 1984-85; pres. Lancaster-Fairfield County YWCA, Lancaster, 1981-82; vice-chmn. govt. and edn. div. Lancaster-Fairfield County United Way, Lancaster, 1981-82; sec. Fairfield County Arts Coun., 1981-82; adv. bd. Portland State U., 1987-89; mentor Ohio Libr. Leadership Inst., 1993, 95. Recipient Dir.'s award Ohio Program in Humanities, Columbus, 1982; Sarah Long Day established in her honor Fairfield County, Lancaster, Bd. Commrs., 1982. Mem. ALA (elected coun. 1993—), Pub. Libr. Assn. (pres. 1989-90, chair legis. com. 1991-95, chair 1998 nat. conf. com. 1995—), Ill. Libr. Assn. (pub. policy com. 1991—). Office: N Suburban Libr Systems 200 W Dundee Rd Wheeling IL 60090-4750

LONG, SARAH ELIZABETH BRACKNEY, physician; b. Sidney, Ohio, Dec. 5, 1926; d. Robert LeRoy and Caroline Josephine (Shue) Brackney; m. John Frederick Long, June 15, 1948; children: George Lynas, Helen Lucille Corcoran, Harold Roy, Clara Alice Lawrence, Nancy Carol Sieber. BA, Ohio State U., 1948, MD, 1952. Intern Grant Hosp., Columbus, Ohio, 1952-53; resident internal medicine Mt. Carmel Med. Ctr., Columbus, 1966-69, chief resident internal medicine, 1968-69; med. cons. Ohio Bur. Disability Determination, Columbus, 1970—; physician student health Ohio State U., Columbus, 1970-73; sch. physician Bexley (Ohio) City Schs., 1973-83; physician advisor to peer rev. Mt. Carmel East Hosp., Columbus, 1979-86, med. dir. employee health, 1981-96; physician cons. Fed. Black Lung program U.S. Dept. Labor, Columbus, 1979—. Mem. AMA, Gerontol. Soc. Am., Ohio Hist. Soc., Ohio State Med. Assn., Franklin County Acad. Medicine, Alpha Epsilon Delta, Phi Beta Kappa. Home: 2765 Bexley Park Rd Columbus OH 43209-2231

LONG, SARAH S., pediatrician; b. Portland, Oreg., Oct. 31, 1944. MD, Jefferson Med. Coll., 1970. Intern St. Christopher Hosp. for Children, Phila., 1970-71, resident, 1971-73; fellow pediatric and infant depts. Temple U. Sch. Medicine, Phila., 1973-75; staff St. Christopher Hosp. for Children, Phila., 1975—; prof. Temple U. Sch. Medicine, 1975—; Diplomate Am. Bd. Pediatrics. Office: St Christopher Child Hosp Erie Ave at Front St Philadelphia PA 19134

LONG, SHELLEY, actress; b. Fort Wayne, Ind., Aug. 23, 1949; m. Bruce Tyson; 1 child, Juliana. Student, Northwestern U. Writer, assoc. prodr., co-host Chgo. TV program Sorting It Out, 1970s (3 local Emmys 1970); mem. Second City, Chgo.; guest TV appearances various shows including M.A.S.H., Love Boat, Family, Frasier; regular TV series Cheers, 1982-87, Good Advice, 1993-94; motion pictures include A Small Circle of Friends, 1980, Caveman, 1981, Night Shift, 1982, Losin' It, 1983, Irreconciliable Differences, 1984, The Money Pit, 1986, Outrageous Fortune, 1987, Hello Again, 1987, Troop Beverly Hills, 1989, Don't Tell Her It's Me, 1990, Frozen Assets, 1992, The Brady Bunch Movie, 1995, A Very Brady Sequel, 1996; TV films include The Cracker Factory, 1979, The Promise of Love, 1980, The Princess and the Cabbie, 1981, Memory of a Murder, 1992, A Message from Holly, 1992, The Women of Spring Break, 1995, Freaky Friday, 1995; TV mini-series, Voices Within: The Lives of Trudy Chase, 1990. Recipient Emmy award Outstanding Actress in a Comedy Series for Cheers, 1983. Office: Creative Artists Agy Ron Meyer 9830 Wilshire Blvd Beverly Hills CA 90212-1804*

LONGBERG, DEBRA LYNN, dietitian, nutrition consultant; b. Queens, N.Y., May 2, 1960; d. Seymour Longberg and Gail Toby (Funk) Borock; m. Stuart Soycher, Aug. 18, 1991; 1 child, Nikki Samantha. BS in Dietetics, U. Del., 1982; MS in Dietetics, N.Y. Inst. Tech., 1987. Registered dietitian, N.Y.; cert. dietitian/nutritionist N.Y. Clin. dietitian A. Holly Patterson Nursing Home, Uniondale, N.Y., 1984-85; dir. dietary Grace Plaza Nursing Home, Gt. Neck, N.Y., 1986-89; asst. dir. dietary Beth Israel Nursing Home, White Plains, N.Y., 1989-91; chief clin. dietitian New Rochelle (N.Y.) Hosp., 1991-93; adminstrv. dietitian Ramapo Manor Nursing Ctr., Suffern, N.Y., 1993—; counselor Sharon Saka Assocs., Suffern, 1991—; nutrition cons. Metro Mosaic segment, NBC-TV, N.Y.C., 1992; nutrition cons. Sta. WVOX, Westchester, N.Y., 1991-93. Mem. T.O.U.C.H., AIDS orgn., Rockland, N.Y., 1994—; mem. subcom. on health issues Spl. Com. on Women's Issues, Clarkstown Legislature, N.Y., 1995. Mem. NOW, Am. Dietetic Assn., Westchester-Rockland Dietetic Assn., Planned Parenthood. Democrat. Jewish. Home: 201 Richard Ct Pomona NY 10970 Office: Ramapo Manor Nursing Ctr 30 Cragmere Rd Suffern NY 10901

LONGDEN, CLAIRE SUZANNE, financial planner, investment advisor; b. Sheffield, Yorkshire, Eng., June 2, 1938; came to U.S., 1964; d. John Stewart and Daisy (Heath) L. Diploma in pvt. sec., Coll. Commerce & Tech., Sheffield, 1956; cert. in Fin. Planning, Coll. Fin. Planning, 1979. Sec. Sheffield, 1956-62; G-4 asst. UN/WHO, Geneva, Switzerland, 1962-64; pvt. sec. Arthur Wiesenberger, N.Y.C., 1966-70; v.p. Alex Brown & Sons, N.Y.C., 1970-75; 1st v.p. Butcher & Singer, N.Y.C., 1975-89; pres. Claire Longden Assocs., Rhinebeck, N.Y., 1989—; adj. prof. fin. planning NYU, 1981-82. Conf. speaker 1980-86; contbr. articles to profl. jours. Bd. dirs. No. Dutchess Hosp., Rhinebeck, 1989, pres., 1995-97. Named one of Top Planners Nationwide, Money mag., 1987. Mem. Inst. Cert. Fin. Planners (nat. bd. dirs. 1984-86, founder, N.Y.C. chpt. 1982-86, N.E. regional dir. 1985-86, bd. of ethics 1993-95, Cert. Fin. Planner of Yr. 1984), Womens Bond Club N.Y. (pres. 1982-84), Inst. Am. Fin. Planners (bd. dirs. 1983-85), Registry Fin. Planning Practitioners, Rotary (pres. Rhinebeck chpt. 1993-94). Office: Claire Longden Assocs 30 E Market St Rhinebeck NY 12572-1606

LONGINO, THERESA CHILDERS, nurse; b. Jacksonville, Fla., Feb. 17, 1959; d. Harold David and Eleanor Theresa (McHarg) Childers; m. Matthew Ray Longino, July 11, 1987. Student, Stetson U., 1977-78; ADN, Fla. C.C., Jacksonville, 1981; student, U. North Fla., 1985—. RN, Fla. RN Meth. Hosp., Jacksonville, 1981, Meml. Med. Ctr., Jacksonville, 1981-86, Good Samaritan Home Health, Jacksonville, 1986, Kimberly Nurses, Jacksonville, 1986, St. Vincents Med. Ctr., Jacksonville, 1986—. Catechist Prince of Peace Cath. Ch., Jacksonville, 1990-91, lectr., reader, 1991—, youth min., 1996. Mem. Jacksonville Jaguars Booster Club. Republican. Roman Catholic. Home: 4135 Hudnall Rd Jacksonville FL 32207-5766

LONGLEY, MARJORIE WATTERS, newspaper executive; b. Lockport, N.Y., Nov. 2, 1925; d. J. Randolph and Florence Lucille (Craine) Watters; m. Ralph R. Longley, Oct. 1, 1949 (dec.). B.A. in English with highest honors cum laude, St. Lawrence U., 1947. Sports editor, feature writer Lockport Union Sun and Jour., 1945; with N.Y. Times, N.Y.C., 1948-88, asst. to v.p. consumer mktg., 1975-78, circulation sales mgr., 1978-79, sales dir., 1979-81, dir. pub. affairs, 1981-88; pres. Gramercy Internat., Inc. (mktg. and pub. rels.), N.Y.C., 1988—; dir. pub. affairs and pub. info., N.Y.C. Off-Track Betting Corp., 1990-94; mem. Nat. Newspapers' Readership Coun., 1979-82; mem. adv. coun. API, 1980-85. Author: America's Taste, 1960. Trustee St. Lawrence U., 1969-75, 77—; chmn. bd. dirs. Am. Forum for Global Edn., 1977—; pres. N.Y. City Adult Edn. Coun., 1974-77; mem. N.Y. State Adv. Coun. for Vocat. Edn., 1976-81, postsecondary edn., 1978-81, Mayor's Coun. Environment of N.Y.C., 1983-96; bd. dirs. Nat. Charities Info. Bur., 1983-96, Literacy Ptnrs., Inc., 1996—; chmn. 42d St. Edn., Theatre, Culture, 1984-88, chmn. emeritus, 1988—. Mem. Nat. Inst. Social Scis., Am. Mgmt. Assn. (nat. mktg. coun. 1972-89, bd. dirs. 1986-88), Nat. Arts Club, Overseas Press Club, Phi Beta Kappa. Democrat. Baptist. Office: Gramercy Internat Inc 34 Gramercy Park E New York NY 10003-1731

LONGLEY, SUSAN WALSH, state senator, educator, lawyer; b. Lewiston, Maine, Dec. 15, 1955; d. James B. and Helen W. (Walsh) L. BA in History, Mt. Holyoke U., 1978; JD, Cath. U., 1988; MA in History, U. Maine, 1992. Bar: Maine, Mass., D.C.; cert. tchr., Maine. Law clk. Tureen and Margolin, Portland, Maine, summer 1986, Lawyers' Com. on Civil Rights, Washington, fall 1986, NEA, Washington, 1987, Monaghan, Leahy, Hochadel and Libby, Portland, summer 1987; student lawyer Columbus Cmty. Legal Svcs., Washington, 1987-88; legal affairs rschr. Nat. Pub. Radio, Washington, 1987-88; law clk. Superior Ct. Clerkship, Bangor, Maine, 1988-89; prof. dept. conservation law Unity (Maine) Coll., 1989—; lawyer Law Office of Susan W. Longley, P.A., 1989—. State senator, Maine, 1994—; mem. Sen. Margaret Chase Smith Libr. Bd., State Ct. Libr. Com., Pine Tree Legal Bd., Waldo County Pre-sch. Summer Bd., Maine Women's Lobby, Maine Pub. Radio, Town of Liberty Planning Bd., Waldo County (Food) Share Program Bd., Maine Freewheeler's Bicycling Club, Maine Children's Trust Bd. Mem. Maine Assn. Dispute Resolution Profls., U. Maine Alumni Assn., Sportsmen Alliance of Maine. Home: RR 1 Box 1108 Liberty ME 04949 Office: Unity Coll State Senate Augusta ME 04330*

LONGO, KATHRYN MILANI, pension consultant; b. Jersey City, N.J., July 22, 1946; d. Joseph John Baptiste and Kathryn (Sacco) Milani; BA, Adelphi U., 1969; postgrad. N.Y. U., 1968-69, Hunter Coll., 1969-70; m. John Carmine Longo, Mar. 15, 1970 (div. June 1984). Pension cons. Laiken, Siegel & Co., N.Y.C., 1967-84, ptnr., 1977-84; mng. ptnr. Laventhol & Horwath Retirement and Employee Benefit Cons. Div., 1984-88; pres. Pension Alternatives Inc., 1988—, mgmt. cons. Creative Pension Systems, Inc., 1988—. cons., 1988—; pres., creative cons. Pinch-Hitters, Inc., North Bergen, N.J., 1978-82; Teaneck Econ. Devel. Corp., 1993-96. Co-founder, co-chmn. Greater N.Y. Pension Cons. Workshop, 1974-96; jazz dance tchr. Kay Marie Sch. Dance Arts, Hammonton, N.J., 1976-83; guest choreographer Regis Drama Soc., Regis High Sch., N.Y.C., 1978-79; choreographer The Garage Theater, Tenafly, N.J., 1993—. Bd. dirs. Phila. Chamber Orch., 1988, Cultural Exch. Arts, Englewood, N.J., 1994—. Adelphi U. scholar, 1964-68. Mem. Am. Soc. Pension Actuaries (assoc.), N.J. Network of Bus. and Profl. Women, Women Entrepreneurs of N.J., Women Bus. Ownership Ednl. Coalition, Inc. (bd. dirs. 1988), Ft. Lee C. of C., Teaneck C. of C. (pres. 1993-94). Roman Catholic.

LONGSWORTH, ELLEN LOUISE, art historian, consultant; b. Auburn, Ind., Aug. 21, 1949; d. Robert Smith and Alice Louise (Whitten) L.; m. Frederic Sanderson Stott, Sept. 1, 1973 (div. 1981); m. Joseph Nicholas Teta, June 15, 1991. BA, Mt. Holyoke Coll., 1971; MA, U. Chgo., 1976; PhD, Boston U., 1987. Trainer, designer Polaris Enterprises Corp., Quincy, Mass., 1981-82, asst. v.p., 1982-84, cons., 1989-93; from asst. prof. to assoc. prof. Merrimack Coll., N. Andover, Mass., 1985-95, prof., 1995—, chmn. dept., 1993—; adj. instr. art and art history Bradford Coll., Haverhill, Mass., 1975-80; vis. lectr. art history Lowell (Mass.) U., 1981-82, Boston U., 1982-86, 88, 91, Babson Coll., Wellesley, Mass., 1984-85. Mem. Merrimack Valley Coun. on the Arts and Humanities, Haverhill, 1975-78, Friends of Kimball Tavern, Bradford Coll., Haverhill, 1975-80; bd. dirs. Winnekenni Found., Haverhill, 1990—; mem. Haverhill Arts Commn., 1996—. Grantee Faculty Devel., Merrimack Coll., 1989-90, 92-93, 95, Kress Summer Travel, Boston U., summers 1980, 86; fellowship Boston U., 1980-82, 85; recipient internship Isabella Stewart Gardner Mus., Boston, 1979-80. Mem. AAUW, Coll. Art Assn., South-Ctrl. Renaissance Conf., Am. Assn. Italian Studies, Italian Art Soc., Renaissance Soc. Am. Republican. Methodist. Home: 62 Arlington St Haverhill MA 01830-5922 Office: Merrimack Coll North Andover MA 01845

LONGUENESSE, BÉATRICE MARGUERITE, philosophy educator, researcher; b. Dieulefit, France, Sept. 6, 1950; d. Max Léon and Madeleine Jeanne (Bertrand) L.; m. Wayne Allen Waxman, July 20, 1989. Agrégation philosophie, U. Paris, Sorbonne, 1973, PhD, 1980, Doctorat d'Etat Philosophie, 1992. Prof. de lycee Edn. Nationale, Carvin, France, 1975-78, Lens, France, 1980-81; lectr. U. Paris-Sorbonne, 1978-79, Ecole Normale Superieure, Paris, 1981-83; asst. prof. U. de Franche.Comte, Besançon, France, 1983-85; maitre de confs. U. Blaise Pascal, Clermont-Ferrand, France, 1985-93; assoc. prof. Princeton (N.J.) U., 1993—; mem. adv. com. philosophy Ctr. Nationale des Lettres, Paris, 1989-93. Author: Hegel et la Critique de la Metaphysique, 1981, Kant et le Pouvoir de Juger, 1993; author, editor: Hegel: Notes et Fragments, 1991; contbr. articles to profl. jours. Mem. Soc. Française de Philosophie. Office: Princeton U Dept Phil 1879 Hall Princeton NJ 08544-1006

LONOFF, ALICE SESSIONS, lawyer; b. Detroit, May 14, 1950; d. Cecil Robert and Geneva Mae (Mann) Sessions; m. Mark J. Lonoff, July 14, 1973; children: Julia Rachel, David Sessions. BA, Oberlin Coll., 1972; JD cum laude, Boston Coll., 1977; LLM in Taxation, Boston U., 1983. Bar: Mass. 1977, Ill. 1985. Assoc. Tyler and Reynolds, Boston, 1977-81, Foley, Hoag and Eliot, Boston, 1981-84; assoc. Bell, Boyd and Lloyd, Chgo., 1984-87, ptnr., 1987—; mem. lawyers adv. coun. Chgo. Comty. Trust, 1995—; mem. planned giving adv. coun. Ravinia Festival Assn., Highland Park, Ill., 1996—. Mem. ABA, Chgo. Bar Assn., Chgo. Estate Planning Coun. United Methodist. Office: Bell Boyd and Lloyd 70 W Madison St Chicago IL 60602

LONSDALE, DIANE, advertising executive. Office: 400 E Pratt St Baltimore MD 21202*

LOOK, ALICE, writer, producer; b. N.Y.C., Aug. 2, 1952; D. Walter F. W. and Soak Har (Ho) L.; m. Donald (Sandy) Forbes McGill, May 26, 1984; 1 child, Ian Look McGill. BA, NYU, 1974. Producer, news writer NBC Radio, N.Y.C., 1976-77; producer, news writer WNBC TV, N.Y.C., 1977-87, reporter, 1987; owner LOOK TV, Darien, Conn., 1989-94; bd. dirs. YWCA of Darien (Conn.)-Norwalk, pub. rels. cons., 1990—. Bd. trustees Darien Libr., 1994—; TV host Darien Dateline, 1991; coord. Christmas In April Program, Darien YWCA, 1992. Recipient Emmy for best news broadcast NATAS, 1983-84. Mem. ITVA, Conn. Press Club (1st Pl. award 1996), Nat. Fedn. of Press Women. Home and Office: 36 Walmsley Rd Darien CT 06820-5129

LOOK, JANET K., psychologist; b. Bklyn., Mar. 11, 1944; d. Harry and Isabelle (Chernoff) Kaplan; divorced; children: Howard, Erika (dec.). AB, NYU, 1964; EdM, Rutgers U., 1967, EdD, 1976. Lic. psychologist; cert. sch. psychologist. Asst. examiner Ednl. Testing Svc., Princeton, N.J., 1964-

66; instr. Rutgers U., New Brunswick, N.J., 1968-69; psychologist Seattle Pub. Schs., 1991—; pvt. practice Kirkland, Wash., 1993—; adj. instr. U. Conn., Waterbury, 1973-91; appearances on various TV and radio shows including the Today Show; interviews include Litchfield County Times, 1987, Waterbury Rep.-Am., 1983-87, Manchester Jour. Inquirer, 1986, Danbury News-Times, 1985; presenter APA, San Francisco, 1991, Nation's Concern and Its Response, U. Wis., Milw., 1991, Nat. Assn. Sch. Psychologists, Dallas, 1991, Divorce Issues Inst., So. Conn. State U., New Haven, 1989. Author: (with others) The Troubled Adolescent, 1991; contbr. articles to newspapers, including N.Y. Times. Mem. APA, Wash. State Psychol. Assn., Nat. Assn. Sch. Psychologists, Wash. State Assn. Sch. Psychologists (area rep., bd. dirs. 1991-93). Office: 1104 Market St Kirkland WA 98033-5441

LOOMANITZ, CLARA, early childhood education educator, consultant; b. N.Y.C., Aug. 13, 1922; d. Benjamin and Anna (Kotick) L. BA, Hunter Coll., 1943; MA, NYU, 1950; EdD, Yeshiva U., 1964. Cert. in early childhood edn. and spl. edn., N.Y. Tchr. nursery schs., N.Y.C., 1943-46; ednl. dir. Day Care Ctrs., N.Y.C., 1946-50, dir., 1950-54; dir. Parent Coop. Nursery Sch., N.Y.C., 1954-58; prof., dir. Washburne Early Childhood Ctr. of Bklyn. Coll., N.Y.C., 1958-91; cons. in child devel., early childhood edn., spl. edn. Bklyn., 1990—; cons. Bd. Jewish Edn., N.Y.C., 1970-83, pub. schs., N.Y.C., 1970—, Project of Bruner Found., N.Y.C., 1991-93, parents and parent groups, N.Y.C., 1968—. Vol. The Lighthouse Inc., N.Y.C., 1994—; mem. Riverside Choral Soc. Mem. Internat. Assn. for Edn. of Pre-schoolers, Nat. Assn. for Edn. of Young Children, N.Y. Assn. for Edn. of Young Children.

LOOMIS, CAROL J., journalist; b. Marshfield, Mo., June 25, 1929; d. Harold and Mildred (Case) Junge; m. John R. Loomis, Mar. 19, 1960; children: Barbara, Mark. Student, Drury Coll., 1947-49; B in Journalism, U. Mo., 1951. Editor Maytag News, Maytag Co., Newton, Iowa, 1951-54; rsch. assoc. Fortune mag., N.Y.C., 1954-58, assoc. editor, 1958-68, mem. bd. editors, 1968—. Office: Fortune Mag 1271 Avenue Of The Americas New York NY 10020

LOOMIS, JACQUELINE CHALMERS, photographer; b. Hong Kong, Mar. 9, 1930 (parents Am. citizens); d. Earl John and Jennie Bell (Sherwood) Chalmers; m. Charles Judson Williams III, Dec. 2, 1950 (div. Aug. 1973); children: Charles Judson IV, John C., David F., Robert W.; m. Henry Loomis, Jan. 19, 1974; stepchildren: Henry S., Mary Loomis Hankinson, Lucy F., Gordon M. Student, U. Oreg., 1948-50, Nat. Geog. Soc., 1978-79, Winona Sch. Profl. Photography, 1979, Sch. Photo Journalism, U. Mo., 1979. Pres. J. Sherwood Chalmers Photographer, Jacksonville, Fla., 1979—, Windward Corp., Washington, 1984—. Contbr. photos to Nat. Geog. books and mag., Fortune mag., Nat. Newspapers, Ducks Unltd., Living Bird Quar., Orvis News, Frontiers Internat., others, also calendars; one-woman show Woodbury-Blair Mansion, Washington, 1980; rep. in pub. and pvt. collections. Trustee Sta. WJCT-TV, Jacksonville, Fla., 1965-73, mem. exec. com., chmn., 1965-66; co-chmn. Arts Festival, Jacksonville, 1970, chmn., 1971; bd. dirs., mem. exec. com. Nat. Friends Pub. Broadcasting, N.Y.C., 1970-73; bd. dirs. Washington Opera, 1976—, Pub. Broadcasting Svcs., Washington, 1972-73, Planned Parenthood of North Fla., 1968-70; bd. dirs. Jacksonville Art Mus., 1968-70, treas., 1968; bd. dirs. Jacksonville Symphony Assn., 1988-94; mem. bd. Children's Home Soc. of Fla., 1988-96. Recipient Cultural Arts award Jacksonville Coun. Arts, 1971, award Easton Waterfowl Festival, 1982, 1st and 2d prizes, 1984. Mem. Profl. Photographers Am. (Merit award 1982), Photog. Soc. Am., Am. Soc. Picture Profls., Jr. League Jacksonville Inc., Fla. Yacht Club (Jacksonville), Amelia Island Plantation Club (Fla.), Timuquana Country Club (Fla.), Chattooga Club (N.C.). Republican. Presbyterian. Avocations: travel, golf, sailing, skiing, riding. Home and Office: 4661 Ortega Island Dr Jacksonville FL 32210-7500

LOOMIS, NORMA IRENE, marriage and family therapist; b. Dunlap, Ind., May 6, 1941; d. Edwin Clifford and Lucille DeVere (Hall) Dick; m. Edwin Dale Loomis; children: William Dale, James Vernon. BS in Edn., Western Mich. U., 1973, MA in Edn., 1976; PhD in Christian Counseling, Rocky Mountin Inc., 1990. Cert. marriage and family therapist. Tchr. Cassopolis (Mich.) Schs., 1973-95; counseling Christian Counseling Svcs., Goshen, Ind., 1985—; presenter Elkhart (Ind.) Pub. Schs., 1992-95, Middlebury (Ind.) Pub. Schs., 1992-94, Elkhart Ct., 1995; pres. Champion Reality Inc., Elkhart, 1983-95. Contbr. articles to profl. publs.; author tchg. materials Hot Shots Prodns. Mem. Cmty. Corrections Adv. Bd., Elkhart County, 1994-95; pres. Juniper Beach Assn., Mears, Mich., 1985—, Women in Action, Elkhart, 1985-94. Mem. ACA, Am. Mental Health Counselors Assn., Ind. Counselors Assn. for Alcohol and Drug Abuse, Am. Assn. Christian Counselors, Christian Assn. Psychol. Studies. Republican. Mem. Bretheran Ch. Home: 22650 Lake Shore Dr Elkhart IN 46514 Office: Christian Counseling Svcs 333 E Madison Goshen IN 46526

LOONEY, CLAUDIA ARLENE, academic administrator; b. Fullerton, Calif., June 13, 1946; d. Donald F. and Mildred B. (Gage) Schneider; m. James K. Looney, Oct. 8, 1967; 1 child, Christopher K. BA, Calif. State U., 1969. Dir. youth YWCA No. Orange County, Fullerton, Calif., 1967-70; dir. dist. Camp Fire Girls, San Francisco, 1971-73; asst. exec. dir. Camp Fire Girls, Los Angeles, 1973-77; asst. dir. community resources Childrens Hosp., Los Angeles, 1977-80; dir. community devel. Orthopaedic Hosp., Los Angeles, 1980-82, sr. v.p. Saddleback Meml. Found./Saddleback Meml. Med. Ctr., Laguna Hills, Calif., 1982-92; v.p. planning and advancement Calif. Inst. Arts, Santa Clarita, Calif., 1992—; pres. NW Meml. Found., Chicago, Ill., 1996—; instr. U. Calif., Irvine, Univ. Irvine; mem. steering com. U. Irvine. Mem. steering com. United Way, Los Angeles, 1984-86. Fellow Assn. Healthcare Philanthropy (nat. chair-elect, chmn. program Nat. Edn. Conf. 1986, regional dir. 1985-89, fin. com. 1988—, pres., com. chn. 1987—, Give To Life com. chmn. 1987-91, Orange County Fund Raiser of Yr. 1992, L.A. County fund raisier of yr. 1996); mem. Nat. Soc. Fund Raising Execs. Found. (cert., vice chmn. 1985-90, chair 1993—), So. Calif. Assn. Hosp. Devel. (past pres., bd. dirs.), Profl. Ptnrs. (chmn. 1986, instr. 1988—), Philanthropic Ednl. Orgn. (past pres.). Office: Calif Inst of the Arts 24700 Mcbean Pky Valencia CA 91355-2340

LOPAT, ROMALDA REGINA, publisher, editor; b. Bridgeport, Conn., Aug. 2, 1954; d. Francis George and Susan Jane (Hermenze) L.; m. Larry R. Sorensen (div. 1983); m. John Dobyns Drummond, June 11, 1988; children: Danielle Ferree, Leah Michelle. BA, U. Conn., 1976; M Urban Planning & Policy, U. Ill., Chgo., 1979. Dir. programs Ill.-Ind. Bi-State Commn., Chgo., 1979-80, dep. dir., 1981; dir. pub. & cmty. rels. Chgo. Dept. Aviation, 1981-85; prin. R. Lopat Comm., 1985—; dep. dir. Chgo. Econ. Devel. Commn., 1986-89. Pub. Weedpath Gazette, 1992—. Recipient Recognition cert. FAA, 1985. Mem. Ill.-Ind. Bi-State Commn. (hon.), Garden Writers Assn. Office: The Weedpath Gazette PO Box 339 Richmond IL 60071

LOPATA, HELENA ZNANIECKA, sociologist, researcher, educator; b. Poznan, Poland, Oct. 1, 1925; d. Florian Witold and Eileen (Markley) Znaniecki; m. Richard Stefan Lopata, Feb. 8, 1946 (wid. July 1994); children: Theodora Karen Lopata-Menasco, Stefan Richard. B.A., U. Ill., 1946, M.A., 1947; Ph.D., U. Chgo., 1954; DSc (hon.), Guelph U., Can., 1995. Lectr. U. Va. Extension, Langley AFB, 1951-52, DePaul U., 1956-60; lectr. Roosevelt U., 1960-64, asst. prof. sociology, 1964-67, assoc. prof., 1967-69; prof. sociology Loyola U., Chgo., 1969—; chmn. dept. sociology Loyola U., 1970-72, dir. Center for Comparative Study of Social Roles, 1972—; mem. NIMH Rev. Bd., 1977-79; mem. Mayor's Council Manpower and Econ. Devel., 1974-79; mem. adv. com., chair tech. com. White House Conf. on Aging, 1979-81; adv. council Nat. Inst. Aging, 1978-83. Author: Occupation: Housewife, 1971, Widowhood in an American City, 1973, Polish Americans: Status Competition in an Ethnic Community, 1976, (with Debra Barnewolt and Cheryl Miller) City Women: Work, Jobs, Occupations, Careers, Vol. I, America, 1984, Vol. II, Chicago, 1985, City Women in America, 1986, (with Henry Brehm) Widows and Dependent Wives: From Social Problem to Federal Policy, 1986, Polish Americans, 1994, Circles and Settings: Role Changes of American Women, 1994, Current Widowhood: Myths and Realities, 1996; adv. editor: Sociologist Quar., 1969-72, Jour. Marriage and Family, 1978-82, Symbolic Interaction, 1989—; editor: Marriages and Families, 1973, (with Nona Glazer and Judith Wittner) Research on the Interweave of Social Roles: vol. I, Women and Men, 1980, (with David Maines) vol. 2, Friendship, 1981, (with Joseph Pleck) vol. 3, Families and Jobs, 1983, vol. 4, Current Research on Occupations and Professions, 1987, vol. 5, 1987, Widows: The Middle East, Asia and the Pacific, 1987, Widows: North America, 1987, (with Anne Figert) Current Research on Occupations and Professions: Vol. 9: Getting Down to Business, 1996, (with David Maines) Friendship in Context, 1990; adv. bd. Symbolic Interaction, 1977-89; contbr. articles to profl. jours. Bd. overseers Wellesley Ctr. of Rsch. and Women, 1979-84. Recipient Research award Radcliffe Coll., 1982; grantee Chgo. Tribune, 1956, Midwest Coun. Social Research on Aging, 1964-65, Adminstrn. on Aging, 1967-69, 68-71, Social Security Adminstrn., 1971-75, also 1975-79, Indo-Am. Fellowship Program: Coun. for Internat. Exchange Scholars, 1987-88, Rsch. Stimulation grantee Loyola U. Chgo., 1988, 92, Am. Coun. Learned Soc. travel grant, 1995, Internat. Rsch. Exchange Bd. short term travel grant, 1995; named Faculty Mem. of Yr., Loyola U., 1975. Fellow Midwest Coun. for Social Rsch. on Aging (pres. 1969-70, 91-92, postdoctoral tng. dir. 1971-77), Ill. Sociol. Assn. (pres. 1969-70), Gerontol. Soc. Am. (chmn. social and behavioral sci. sect. 1980-81, Mentoring award 1995), Internat. Gerontol. Assn.: mem. Soc. for Study Social Problems (chmn. spl. problems com. 1971, v.p. 1975, coun. 1978-80, pres. 1983, Disting. Scholar award family div. 1989), Am. Sociol. Assn. (coun. 1978-81, chmn. sect. family 1976, chmn. sect. sex roles 1975, Sorokin awwards com. 1970-73, publs. com. 1972-73, nominations com. 1977, chmn. sect. on aging 1982-83 (Disting. Career award, 1992 Section on Aging), Cooley-Blumer awards com., 1984, Jessie Bernard awards com. 1984-86, disting. scholarly publ. awards selection com. 1988-89, awards policy com. 1990-92, co-chair com. on internat. sociology, 1992-95), Soc. for the Study of Symbolic Interaction (mem 1977—, Mead award for Life Time Achievement, 1993), Internat. Sociol. Soc. (com. on family rsch., bd. dirs. 1991-94, com. on work 1972—, rsch. com. on aging 1990—), Midwest Sociol. Assn. (state dir. 1972-74, pres. 1975-76, chair 1994—, publs. com. 1993-95), Nat. Coun. Family Rels. (Burgess award 1990, chair internat. sect. 1991-93), Polish Inst. of Arts and Scis. in Am. (dir. 1976-82, with Zbigniew Brzezinski, Bronislaw Malinowski award in social scis. 1995), Polish Welfare Assn. (bd. dirs. 1988-91), Internat. Inst. Sociology, 1994—, Sociologists for Women in Society (mem. task force alternative work patterns, pres. 1993-94, adv. editor Gender and Soc. 1993-94). Home: 5815 N Sheridan Rd Apt 917 Chicago IL 60660-3829 Office: Loyola Univ Dept Sociology 6525 N Sheridan Rd Chicago IL 60626-5311

LOPATIN, CAROL KEESLER, artist; b. Spring Valley, N.Y., Oct. 16, 1934; d. Irving Verdin and Jessie Louise (Day) Keesler; m. Milton Lopatin, Apr. 5, 1963; 1 child, John David. BS, Skidmore Coll., 1956. Artist mem. Spectrum Gallery, Washington, 1985-93, Touchstone Gallery, Washington, 1996; juried studio artist Arlington (Va.) Art Ctr., 1984-93, Torpedo Factory Art Ctr., Alexandria, Va., 1988—; participating artist Women in Art and Culture, Beijing, 1995. One-woman shows Spectrum Gallery, Washington, 1988, 91, 93, 20th Century Gallery, Williamsburg, Va., 1989, 95, Charles County C.C., La Plata, Md., 1992, Arlington (Va.) Art Ctr., 1993, Holden Gallery, Warren Wilson Coll., Swannanoa, N.C., 1996, Art Assn. Harrisburg, Pa., 1996; exhibited in group shows Art League Gallery, Alexandria, Va., 1985-96, Chrysler Mus., Norfolk, Va., 1990, 92, Strathmore Hall Found. Inc., Rockville, Md., 1991, 92, 94, Assoc. Artists and Milton Rhodes Galleries, Winston-Salem, N.C., 1992, Greater Reston (Va.) Arts Ctr., 1992, 94, 95, Delaplaine Visual Arts Ctr., Frederick, Md., 1994, 95, Adirondacks Art Ctr., Old Forge, N.Y., 1995, Foothills Art Ctr., Golden, Colo., 1995, Global Focus, Beijing, 1995, Gadsden (Ala.) Ctr. for Cultural Arts, 1995, Olin Fine Arts Gallery, Washington, Pa., 1996, Moss-Thoms Gallery Art, Ft. Hays U., Hays, Kans., 1996; represented in permanent collections No. Va. C.C., George Washington U. Med. Coll., also corp. and pvt. collections. Recipient purchase award Watercolor Soc. Ala., 1995. Mem. Nat. Watercolor Soc. (signature mem.), Artists Equity (1st place award 1992, juror's award 1994), Art League Alexandria (numerous awards), Greater Reston Art Ctr. Presbyterian. Home: 6118 Beachway Dr Falls Church VA 22041-1410 Office: Torpedo Factory Art Ctr 105 N Union St Ste 301 Alexandria VA 22314

LOPATKA, SUSANA BEAIRD, maternal, child health nurse consultant; b. White Plains, N.Y., May 1, 1937; d. Paul J. and Dorothy V.L. (Jewell) Grueninger; m. John Rudolph Lopatka, Sept. 6, 1975. AB in Polit. Sci., Duke U., 1959; BSN, Columbia U., N.Y.C., 1962; MA in Parent/Child Nursing, NYU, N.Y.C., 1975. RN, Ill. Staff nurse Columbia-Presbyn. Med. Ctr., N.Y.C., 1962; pub. health nurse Dept. of Health, City of N.Y., 1962-66; pub. health nurse high-risk maternal and infant care project N.Y. Med. Coll., N.Y.C., 1966-67; nursing coord. Brownsville East N.Y. Ctr. Maternal and Infant Care Project City of N.Y., 1967-69; asst. supr. ambulatory care Mt. Sinai Med. Ctr., N.Y.C., 1969-70, sr. supr. ambulatory care, 1970-72, asst. DON ambulatory care, 1972-75; clin. specialist in maternity Chgo. Lying-In Hosp., U. Chgo. Med. Ctr., 1976-80, DON, 1980-86; maternal/child health nurse cons. Ill. Dept. Pub. Health, Chgo., 1986—; mem. perinatal nursing adv. coun. Greater Ill. chpt. March of Dimes, Chgo., 1979—. Founding pres., bd. dirs. Am. Scandinavian Assn. Ill., Chgo., 1983-95; active Chgo. Coun. Fgn. Rels., 1976—, Chgo. Hist. Soc., 1994—. Recipient Nurses Recognition award Greater Ill. chpt. March of Dimes, 1993. Mem. ANA, APHA, Ill. Nurses Assn., Chgo. Nurses Assn. (dist. 1), Ill. Pub. Health Assn. (chairperson maternal/child health sect. 1992-94, asst. chairperson 1990-92), Ill. Assn. Maternal/Child Health (pres. 1992-94, bd. dirs. 1989-96), Sigma Theta Tau, Pi Sigma Alpha. Office: Ill Dept Pub Health 33 E Congress Pky Chicago IL 60605-1223

LOPER, CHARLENE MARIE, army officer; b. Allentown, Pa., Mar. 11, 1958; d. Henry Noe and Pauline E.L. (Hubbard) Magnon; m. Leonard J. Loper, Mar. 29, 1985; 1 child, John W. BS, N.E. La. U., 1979; MS, U. So. Calif., 1989. Commd. 2d lt. U.S. Army, 1979, advanced through grades to major, 1993, platoon leader to exec. officer 101st M.I. Bn., 1979-81; assignments officer 1st Inf. Div. U.S. Army, Ft. Riley, Kans., 1981-83; pers. staff officer MS ARNG, 184th Trans Bde, Laurel, Miss., 1983-86; from tng. officer to brigade electronic warfare officer to bn. ops. officer then co. comdr. 103d M.I. Bn. U.S. Army, Wurzburg, Fed. Republic Germany, 1986-90; chief ops. and resource mgmt. Field Sta. Berlin U.S. Army, 1990-91, selected Acquistions Corps, 1991; with Combined Arms Command U.S. Army, Ft. Leavenworth, Kans., 1991-93; command gen. staff U.S. Army, Ft. Leavenworth, 1993-94, Mil. Dist., Washington, 1994—. Decorated Army Achievement medal, Army Commendation medal, Meritorious Svc. medal with 3 oak leaf clusters. Mem. Marne Assn., Phi Kappa Phi. Roman Catholic. Address: 7853 Michael Ct Fort George G Meade MD 20755-1132

LOPER, LINDA SUE, learning resources center director; b. Wakefield, R.I., Jan. 28, 1945; d. Delmas Field and Dora Belle (Hanna) Sneed; children: Matthew Lee Mathany, Amanda Virginia Mathany, Morgan Lynnclare Loper. BA, Peabody Coll., Nashville, 1966, MLS, 1979; EdD in Ednl. Adminstrn., Vanderbilt U., Nashville, 1988. Tchr. Parkway Sch., Chesterfield, Mo., 1966-68, Charlotte Mecklenburg Schs., Charlotte, N.C., 1968-71; dir. city libr. Jackson George Regional Libr. System, Pascagoula, Miss., 1979-82; media ctr. specialist Pascagoula Mcpl. Sch. Dist., 1982-83, Moore County Sch. System, Lynchburg, Tenn., 1983-91; ref. libr. Motlow State Community Coll., Tullahoma, Tenn., 1983-85; dir. learning resource ctr. Columbia (Tenn.) State C.C., 1991-96; exec. dir. Tenn. Bd. Regents Media Consortium, 1993-96; pres., CEO Grant Seekers, Inc., 1996—; pres./CEO Grant Seekers, Inc.; presenter TLA Ann. Conv., Knoxville, Tenn., LEAP State Dept. Edn. Conf. for Libr., Chattanooga; career ladder participant Tenn. Edn. Dept. Level II; TIM trainer Dept. Edn., Nashville; exec. dir. Tenn. Bd. of Regents Media Consortium, 1993-96. Author: Bibliography for Tennessee Commission on Status of Women, 1979; contbr. article to profl jour. Pres. Moore County Friends of Libr., Lynchburg, Tenn., 1991; bd. dirs. Moore County Hist. and Geneal. Soc., Lynchburg, 1991; mem. Tenn. Bicentennial Com., Giles County; co-dir. So. Tapestry, a Bicentennial oral history project; sec., mem. exec. bd. Hope House Domestic Violence Shelter, 1993-96, mem. adv. bd., 1996—; mem. steering com. Bus., Industry, Edn. Coun. Recipient Gov.'s Acad. award State Dept. of Edn., U. Tenn., 1988, Inst. for Writing Tenn. History, U. Tenn., 1990, Gov.'s Conf. on Info. Sci., Nashville, 1990. Mem. ASCD, ALA, S.E. Libr. Assn., Tenn. Libr. Assn., Moore County Edn. Assn. (treas., chair tchrs. study coun., chair polit. action commn. 1989-91), Giles County Edn. Found. (bus., industry, edn. steering com.), UDC (historian), DAR, Phi Delta Kappa, Beta Phi Mu, Delta Kappa Gamma. Democrat. Methodist. Office: Columbia State Cmty Coll PO Box 1315 Columbia TN 38402-1315

LOPES, LISA, singer; b. Phila., May 27, 1971. Singer, mem. TLC, 1991—. Recipient Grammy for "Creep", 1995. Office: LaFace Records One Capital City Plz 3350 Peachtree Rd Ste 1500 Atlanta GA 30326-1040*

LOPES, MARIA FERNANDINA, commissioner; b. Ganda, Angola, Portugal, Dec. 12, 1934; came to U.S., 1963; d. Rodrigo do Carmo and Maria Jose Fernandes (Mendes) Marques; m. Fernandes Esteves Lopes, Aug. 11, 1962; children: Lisa Maria Lopes Moss, Mark Esteves. Student, Lisbon (Portugal) Comml. Inst., 1953, Massasoit Community Coll., Brockton, Mass., 1988. With archives dept. Portuguese Govt., Lisbon, 1958-62; congl. aide Congresswoman Margaret M. Heckler, Fall River, Taunton, Mass., 1972-74; mem. Taunton (Mass.) Sch. Com., 1976-93; commr., chairperson Bristol County, Mass., 1991—. Founder Day of Portugal, 1974. Home: 28 Worcester St Taunton MA 02780-2041 Office: Office County Commissioners Superior Courthouse Nine Court St PO Box 208 Taunton MA 02780

LOPES, MYRA AMELIA, educational administrator; b. Nantucket, Mass., July 9, 1931; d. Leo Joseph and Mary Ellen (Moriarty) Powers; m. Curtis Linwood Lopes, June 25, 1955; children: Dennis, Sherry, Kathy, Curtis, Becky. BS, Bridgewater, 1954; diploma, Inst. Children's Lit., 1982, N.Y. Inst. Journalism, 1984. Cert. elem. educator, Mass. Tchr. Fairhaven (Mass.) Sch. System, 1954-58; prin. Sheri Ka Kindergarten, Fairhaven, 1960-76; market promotion Store Systems, Greater New Bedford, Mass., 1976-82; writer Fairhaven Sch. System, 1987-95, fund raiser, reading promoter, 1987-92. Author: Look Around You, 1990, Looking Back, 1991, Seeing It All, 1992, But Then There Was More, 1993, Captain Joshua Slocum: A Centennial Tribute, 1994. Bd. dirs. Fairhaven Improvement Assn., 1986-94, chmn. membership, 1986-96, pres., 1990-93; bd. dirs. YWCA, Fairhaven, 1982-88, chmn. cmty. rels., 1982-83, nominating chmn., 1983-84, chmn. pers. bd., 1984-88; bd. trustees Millicent Libr., 1993-96. Democrat. Roman Catholic. Home: 71 Fort St Fairhaven MA 02719-2811

LOPEZ, JUDITH CARROLL, lawyer; b. Boulder, Colo., Dec. 22, 1945; d. Robert Warren and Irene Caroll (Young) Adams; m. Richard Manuel Lopez, Mar. 19, 1967 (div. Nov. 1975); children: Heather Linn, Amber Elise. BA, Colo. Coll., 1967; JD, U. Wyo., 1979. Assoc. R. Michael Mullikin, Jackson Hole, Wyo., 1979-81; pvt. practice Jackson Hole, 1981-82; atty. KN Energy, Inc., Lakewood, Colo., 1982-88; assoc. Hawley & Vanderwerf, Denver, 1988-89; corp. counsel ANR Freight System, Inc., Golden, Colo., 1990-96; with Coastal States Mgmt. Corp., Houston, 1996—; bd. dirs. Edit, Inc. Bd. mgrs. Stonebridge Townhomes Homeowners Assn., Lakewood, 1993—. Office: Ste 888 Nine Greenway Pl Houston TX 77045-0995

LOPEZ, MARIA ELENA CHELALA, principal, educator; b. Miami, Fla., Aug. 18, 1963; d. Rosendo and Dora (Mestril) Chelala; m. William John Lopez, Mar. 2, 1985. BS, U. Miami, 1984; MS, Nova U., 1989; postgrad. in Edn., Greenwich U., 1990—. Cert. elem. edn., middle grade edn., tchr., Fla.; cert. childcare trainer; notary. Tchr.'s aide Children's Garden, Miami, 1983-84; 7th and 8th grade lit. tchr. Sts. Peter & Paul Sch., Miami, 1984-86; K-5 fgn. lang. tchr. Williams Elem., Gainesville, Fla., 1988-90; 2d grade tchr. Epiphany Sch., Miami, 1990-91, asst. prin., 1991-94, prin., 1994-95; project developer, prin. Our Lady of Lourdes Elem. Sch., Miami, 1995—; bd. dirs. Sch. Tech. Adv. Bd., Miami; adj. prof. Miami Dade C.C., 1994—. Fellow ASCD, South Fla. Assn. for Young Children, Nat. Assn. for Edn. of Young Children, Rotary. Office: Our Lady of Lourdes Elem 11291 SW 142 Ave Miami FL 33186

LOPEZ, NANCY, professional golfer; b. Torrance, Calif., Jan. 6, 1957; d. Domingo and Marina (Griego) L.; m. Ray Knight, Oct. 25, 1982; children: Ashley Marie, Erinn Shea, Torri Heather. Student, U. Tulsa, 1976-78. Author: The Education of a Woman Golfer, 1979. First victory at Bent Tree Classic, Sarasota, Fla., 1978; named AP Athlete for 1978; admitted to Ladies Profl. Golf Assn. Hall of Fame, 1987, to PGA World Golf Hall of Fame, 1989. Mem. Ladies Profl. Golf Assn. (Player and Rookie of Yr. 1978). Republican. Baptist. Office: care Internat Mgmt Group 1 Erieview Plz Ste 1300 Cleveland OH 44114-1715*

LOPEZ-MORILLAS, FRANCES M., translator; b. Fulton, Mo., Sept. 3, 1918; d. Erwin Kempton and Laura (Hinkhouse) Mapes; m. Juan Lopez-Morillas, Aug. 12, 1937; children: Martin Morell, Consuelo, Julian. BA, U. Iowa, 1939, MA, 1940. Translator Collins Radio Co., Cedar Rapids, Iowa, 1940-43; tchr. Spanish Lincoln Sch., Providence, 1943-44; tchr. French, Spanish Mary C. Wheeler Sch., Providence, 1951-64; tchr. ESL Internat. Inst., Madrid, 1957-58; freelance translator, 1964—; Co-editor: (with E.K. Mapes) J.J. Fernandez de Lizardi, El periquillo sarniento, 1952; translator over 25 books and articles. Grantee NEH, 1984, NEA, 1986; recipient translation prize Tex. Inst. Letters, 1991. Mem. Internat. Assn. Hispanists, Am. Literary Translators Assn., Phi Beta Kappa. Home: 2200 Hartford Rd Austin TX 78703*

LOPEZ-MUNOZ, MARIA ROSA P., land development company executive; b. Havana, Cuba, Jan. 28, 1938; came to U.S., 1960; d. Eleuterio Perfecto and Bertha (Carmenati Colon) Perez Rodriguez; m. Gustavo Lopez-Munoz, Sept. 9, 1973. Student, Candler Coll., Havana, 1951-53; Sch. Langs., U. Jose Marti, Havana, 1954-55. Lic. interior designer, real estate broker. Pres. Fantasy World Acres, Inc., Coral Gables, Fla., 1970-84, pres., dir., 1984—; sec. Sandhills Corp., Coral Gables, Fla., 1978-85, dir., 1978—. Treas. Am. Cancer Soc., Miami, Fla., 1981, sec. Hispanic Bd., 1987, pres. Hispanic div., 1989, bd. dirs., aux. treas.; bd. dirs. Am. Heart Assn., Miami, 1985, chmn. Hispanic div.; bd. dirs. YMCA, Young Patronesses of Opera, Miami, 1985, Lowe Mus. of U. Miami, 1986—, Linda Ray Infant Ctr.; ex-pres. Ladies Aux. Little Havana Child Care Ctr.; trustee Ronald McDonald House, sec. exec. bd., 1992; mem exec. bd. Young Patronesses of the Opera; cabinet mem. Children's Cardiac Found., New Horizons Cmty. Devel., Transplant Ctr. Sch. Medicine U. Miami-Jackson Meml. Hosp, 1992; dir. Cultura Italiana, Inc.; v.p. Messenger of Peace. Recipient Merit award Am. Cancer Soc., 1980, 81, 82, 83, 84, Dynamic Woman award, 1992; Woman with Heart Award, Am. Heart Assn., 1985, Merit awards, 1980-84, Women of Yr., 1986, Outstanding Ladry award Greater Miami Opera, 1992; named Woman of Yr., Children's Hosp., 1993; named to Gt. Order of José Marti, 1988; named Leading Miami's Beautiful Couples for ACS, 1995. Mem. Real Estate Bd. Realtors, Coral Gables Real Estate Assn. Republican. Roman Catholic. Clubs: YPO, Vail 50, Ocean Reef (Key Largo, Fla.); Opera Guild (Miami); Key Biscayne Yacht; Regine's Internat. Bath Club (Paris). Avocations: yachting, snow skiing, scuba diving, guitar, piano. Office: Fantasy World Acres Inc 147 Alhambra Cir # 22021 Miami FL 33134-4524

LOPKER, ANITA MAE, psychiatrist; b. San Diego, May 25, 1955; d. Louis Donald and Betty Jean (Sayman-Campbell) L. BA magna cum laude, U. Calif., San Diego, 1978; MD, U. Rochester, 1982. Diplomate Nat. Bd. Med. Examiners, Am. Bd. Forensic Examiners. Intern in internal medicine Yale U. Sch. Medicine-Greenwich Hosp., 1982-83; resident in psychiatry Yale U. Sch. of Medicine, 1983-86; postdoctoral fellow Yale U. Sch. Medicine, New Haven, Conn., 1982-86; clin. instr. Yale U. Sch. Medicine, New Haven, 1986-88; pvt. practice specializing eating disorders and Lyme disease Westport, Conn., 1987—; cons. psychiatrist Yale-New Haven Hosp Lyme Disease Study Clinic, 1987—, Yale U. Lyme Disease Rsch. Project, 1986—, Alcoholism and Drug Dependency Coun., Inc., 1989-90; internat. lectr. on Lyme psychiat. syndrome; nat. lectr. on eating disorders, substance abuse. Contbr. articles to profl. jours. Founding mem. Nat. Mus. for Women in the Arts, Washington, 1986; patron Menninger Found.; bd. dirs. The Fairfield Orch., 1993-96. Recipient Benjamin Rush prize in psychiatry U. Rochester Sch. Medicine, 1982. Mem. AAAS, Am. Psychiat. Assn., Conn. Psychiat. Soc., World Fedn. Mental Health (life), N.Y. Acad. Scis., Menninger Found., Alpha Omega Alpha, Phi Beta Kappa. Home: 27 Strathmore Ln Westport CT 06880-4700 Office: 7 Whitney Street Ext Westport CT 06880-3761

LOPO, DIANA M., lawyer; b. Havana, Cuba, 1957. BS cum laude, U. Miami, 1978; JD, U. Mich., 1981; LLM, NYU, 1982. Bar: N.Y. 1984. Ptnr. Skadden, Arps, Slate, Meagher & Flom, N.Y.C. Office: Skadden Arps Slate Meagher & Flom 919 3rd Ave New York NY 10022*

LOPP, SUSAN JANE, insurance underwriter; b. Billings, Mont., Feb. 16, 1944; d. Russell and Edith (Trapp) Wallace; m. Robert J. Lopp, June 2,

1963; children: Robert J. Jr., Cheryl J. BA, U. Mont., 1972. CLU, ChFC; registered rep. Reporter Park County News, Livingston, Mont., 1965-66; tchr. Sch. Dist. #5, Kalispell, Mont., 1968-73; planner Areawide Planning Orgn., Kalispell, 1974-77; econ. devel. dir. NW MT HRDC, Inc., Kalispell, 1978-79; ins. underwriter The Equitable, Kalispell, 1979-88, The Prudential, Kalispell, 1989—; mem. Mont. Supreme Ct. Gender Bias Task Force, Helena, 1990—, Mont. Pvt. Industry Coun., Helena, 1988—; commr. Mont. Human Rights Commn., 1993—, chair, 1995—; dir., sec.-treas. Mont. Life and Health Ins. Guaranty Assn. Bd., 1994—; Govs. Coun. for Monts. Future, Helena, 1992; chair Govs. Coun.-Women & Employment, Helena, 1981-83, Mont. Bd. Printing, Helena, 1991-92. Active Flathead City-County Health Bd., Kalispell, 1987-95, chair, 1989-95; mem. Flathead Coop. Planning Coalition Campaign Bd., 1993-94, Mont. Sch. for Deaf and Blind Found., Great Falls, 1988-96, Mont. Rep. Women Bd., 1980-85; exec. com. United Way Flathead County, Kalispell, 1986-92; chair Mont. Womens Prison Site Selection Com., Helena, 1991. Recipient Great Chief award Kalispell C. of C., 1995, Carrying the Torch award Mont. Women's Lobby, 1995, Mont. Centennial Equity award Mont. Depts. Labor and Pub. Instrn. and Higher Edn., 1989, 4-H Silver Clover award Mont. State U./Mont. Ext. Svc., 1980. Mem. AAUW (Mont. pres. 1980-82, Named Gift 1982, 93), N.W. Mont. Life Underwriters (pres. 1988-89), Flathead County Rep. Women (pres. 1985), Am. Soc. CLU and ChFC, Glacier County Pachyderm Club. Republican. Mem. Seventh Day Adventist. Office: The Prudential 295-3d Ave EN Box 7547 Kalispell MT 59904

LOPRESTO, BIRGITA GUNNEL, writer; b. Stora Levene, Sweden, June 29, 1941; came to U.S., 1971; d. Ivar Antonius and Eva Dagmar (Flink) Anderson; m. Vincent LoPresto, Apr. 24, 1971; 1 child, Catherine. Florist assoc. Stora Levene, 1959-71. Author: (poetry) The Big Darkness, 1994, Anthalagion, 1995. Recipient Pres.'s award of lit. excellence Iliad, 1994, 95. Mem. Nat. Mus. Women in the Arts.

LORBER, BARBARA HEYMAN, communications executive; b. N.Y.C.; d. David Benjamin and Gertrude (Meyer) Heyman; divorced. AB in Polit. Sci., Skidmore Coll., 1966; MA, Columbia U., 1973, postgrad., 1973-76. Asst. dir. young citizens divsn. Dem. Party, 1966-68; exec. asst. to dean Albert Einstein Coll. Medicine, Bronx, N.Y., 1968-72; exec. asst. to v.p. devel. Vanderbilt U., Nashville, 1976-77; spl. projects dir. Am. Acad. in Rome, N.Y.C., 1977-78; pub. affairs dir., assoc. devel. dir. Met. Opera, N.Y.C., 1978-84; sr. v.p. Hill and Knowlton, N.Y.C., 1985-88; pres. Lorber Group, Ltd., N.Y.C., 1989-95; v.p. comms. and planning N.Y.C. Partnership and C. of C., 1996—; guest lectr. Arts and Bus. Coun., N.Y.C., Internat. Soc. Performing Arts Adminstrs., N.Y.C., NYU Sch. Continuing Edn., Nat. Media Conf., Nat. Soc. Fund Raising Execs., N.Y.C.; exec. prodr., prodr., writer N.Y. Internat. Festival Arts, N.Y.C., 1988. Author chpts. to book; contbr. articles to profl. jours. Office: NYC Partnership and C of C One Battery Pk Plz New York NY 10004

LORCH, MARISTELLA DE PANIZZA (MRS. INAMA VON BRUNNENWALD), Romance languages educator, writer, lecturer; b. Bolzano, Italy, Dec. 8, 1919; came to U.S., 1947, naturalized, 1951; d. Gino and Giuseppina (Cristoforetti) de Panizza Tuama von Brunnenwald; m. Claude Bové, Feb. 10, 1944 (div. 1955); 1 dau., Claudia; m. Edgar R. Lorch, Mar. 25, 1956; children: Lavinia Edgarda, Donatella Livia. Ed., Liceo Classico, Merano, 1929-37; Dott. in Lettere e Filosofia, U. Rome, 1942; DHL (hon.), Lehman Coll., CUNY, 1993. Prof. Latin and Greek Liceo Virgilio, Rome, 1941-44; assoc. prof. Italian and German Coll. St. Elizabeth, Convent Station, N.J., 1947-51; faculty Barnard Coll., 1951-90, prof., 1967—, chmn. dept., 1951—, chmn. medieval and renaissance program, 1972-86; founder, dir. Ctr. for Internat. Scholarly Exch., Barnard Coll., 1980-90; dir. Casa Italiana, Columbia U., 1969-76, chmn. exec. com. Italian studies, 1980-90, founding dir. Italian Acad. Advanced Studies in Am., 1991—. Author: Critical edit. L. Valla, De vero falsoque bono, Bari, 1970, (with W. Ludwig) critical edit. Michaelida, (with K. Hieatt), 1976, On Pleasure, 1981, A Defense of Life: L. Valla's Theory of Pleasure, 1985, (with E. Grassi) Folly and Insanity in Renaissance Literature, 1986, (with F. Colombo, M. Spaziani, Sinisca) All' America, 1990; editor: Il Teatro Italiano del Renascimento, 1981, Humanism in Rome, 1983, La Scuola, New York, 1987; mem. editorial bd. Italian jour. Romanic Review; also articles on Renaissance lit. and theater. Chmn. Am. Ariosto Centennial Celebration, 1974; chmn. bd. trustees La Scuola N.Y., 1986-91; trustee Lycée Française de N.Y., 1986—. Decorated Cavaliere della Repubblica Italiana, 1973, Commendatore della Repubblica Italiana, 1988, Grande ulfale della Republican Italiana, 1996; recipient AMITA award for Woman of Yr. in Italian Lit., 1973, Columbus '92 Countdown prize of excellence in humanities, 1990, Elen Cornaro award Sons of Italy Woman of Yr., 1990, Father Ford award, 1994. Mem. Medieval Acad. Am., Renaissance Soc. Am., Am. Assn. Tchrs. Italian, Am. Assn. Italian Studies (hon. pres. 1990-91), Internat. Assn. for Study of Italian Lit. (Am. rep., assoc. pres. 8th Congress 1973), Acad. Polit. Sci. (life), Pirandello Soc. (pres. 1972-78), Arcadia Acad. (Asteria Aretusa 1976). Home: 445 Riverside Dr New York NY 10027-6842

LORD, BETTE BAO, writer; b. Shanghai, China, Nov. 3, 1938; came to U.S., 1946, naturalized, 1964; d. Sandys and Dora (Fang) Bao; B.A., Tufts U., 1959, M.A., 1960, hon. doctorate, 1982; hon. doctorate, U. Notre Dame, 1985, Bryant Coll., Domincan Coll., 1990, Skidmore Coll., 1992, Marymount Coll., 1992, Pepperdine U., 1995; m. Winston Lord, May 4, 1963; children: Elizabeth Pillsbury, Winston Bao. Asst. to dir. East-West Cultural Center, Honolulu, 1961-62; program officer Fulbright Exchange Program for Sr. Scholars, 1962-63; dancer, tchr. modern dance, Geneva and Washington, 1964-73; conf. dir. Assoc. Councils of the Arts, N.Y.C., 1970-71; writer, lectr., 1982—; author: (non-fiction) Eighth Moon, 1964 (Readers' Digest Condensed Books), (novel) Spring Moon, a novel of China (Lit. Guild selection), 1981, In the Year of the Boar and Jackie Robinson (named one of best books for children AIH), 1984, Legacies: A Chinese Mosaic, 1990 (one of 10 best nonfiction books of 1990 Time mag.), The Middle Heart, 1996. Mem. selection bd. White House Fellows, 1979-81; former bds. trustees Asia Found., Asia Soc., Nat. Com. on U.S.-China Rels., Com. of 100; chairperson Freedom House; trustee Kennedy Ctr. Community and Friends, Nat. Portrait Gallery; trustee Freedom Forum; apptd. by Pres. Clinton to Broadcasting Bd. of Govs., 1995. Named Woman of Yr., Chinatown Planning Coun., 1982; recipient Disting. Am. award, 1984, Am. Women for Internat. Understanding award, 1988, U.S.I.A. award, 1988, Women's Project & Prodns. Exceptional Achievement award, 1992, Lit. Lion award N.Y. Pub. Libr., 1992, Medal of Distinction, Barnard Coll., 1993, Gala 12 Women of Distinction award Birmingham-So. Coll., 1995; named to Internat. Women's Hall of Fame, 1989. Mem. Orgn. Chinese Ams., Coun. on Fgn. Rels., PEN, Freedom Forum Selection Com. Free Spirit Awards, Authors Guild.

LORD, EVELYN MARLIN, former mayor; b. Melrose, Mass., Dec. 8, 1926; d. John Joseph and Mary Janette (Nourse) Marlin; m. Samuel Smith Lord Jr., Feb. 28, 1948; children: Steven Arthur, Jonathan Peter, Nathaniel Edward, Victoria Marlin, William Kenneth. BA, Boston U., 1948; MA, U. Del., 1956; JD, U. Louisville, 1969. Bar: Ky. 1969, U.S. Supreme Ct. 1973. Exec. dir. Block Blight Inc., Wilmington, Del., 1956-60; mem. Del. Senate, Dover, 1960-62; administrv. asst. county judge Jefferson County, Louisville, 1968-71; corr. No. Ireland News Jour. Co., Wilmington, 1972-74; legal adminstr. Orgain, Bell & Tucker, Beaumont, Tex., 1978-83; v.p. Tex. Commerce Bank, Beaumont, 1983-84; councilman City of Beaumont, 1980-82, mayor pro tem, 1982-84, mayor, 1990-94; tourism chmn. U.S. Conf. Mayors, 1994, mem. adv. bd., chmn. arts, culture and recreation, 1992-94; bd. dirs. Tex. Commerce Bank. Bd. dirs. Symphony Soc. S.E. Tex., 1990—, Beaumont Cmty. Found., 1990-96, S.E. Tex. Art Mus., 1990-96, Lincoln Inst. Land Policy, Beaumont Pub. Schs. Found., Cmtys. in Schs.; trustee, pres. United Way, Beaumont, 1995; exec. bd. Boy Scouts Am., Three Rivers, 1978-84, 89-96; pres. Girl Scouts Am., Louisville, 1966-70, Tex. Energy Mus.; active Sister City Commn. Recipient Silver Beaver award Boy Scouts Am., Beaumont, 1979, Disting. Alumni award Boston U., 1983, Disting. Leadership award Nat. Assn. Leadership Orgns., Indpls., 1991, Labor-Mgmt. Pub. Sector award, 1991, Disting. Grad. award Leadership Beaumont, 1993, Rotary Svc. Above Self award, 1994; named Citizen of Yr., Sales and Mktg. Assn., 1990, Beaumont "Man of Yr.", 1993. Mem. LWV (Del. state pres. 1960-62, bd. dirs. Tex. 1978-80), Bus. and Profl. Women Assns. (Woman of Yr. 1983), 100 Club (pres. 1995—), Girl Scouts Am. (life), Rotary (hon.), Sigma Kappa (life), Phi Kappa Phi, Delta Kappa Gamma (hon.), Sigma Iota Epsilon (hon.). Home: 1240 Nottingham Ln Beaumont TX 77706-4316

LORD, JACQUELINE WARD, accountant, photographer, artist; b. Andalusia, Ala., May 16, 1936; d. Marron J. and Minnie V. (Owen) Ward; m. Curtis Gaynor, Nov. 23, 1968. Student U. Ala., 1966, Auburn U., 1977, Huntingdon Coll., 1980, Troy State U., 1980; BA in Bus. Adminstrn., Dallas Bapt. U., 1985. News photographer corr. Andalusia (Ala.) Star-News, 1954-59, Sta. WSFA-TV, Montgomery, Ala., 1954-60; acct., bus. mgr. Reihardt Motors, Inc., Montgomery, 1962-69; office mgr., acct. Cen. Ala. Supply, Montgomery, 1969-71; acct. Chambers Constrn. Co., Montgomery, 1972-75; pres. Foxy Lady Apparel, Inc., Montgomery, 1973-76; acct. Rushton, Stakely, Johnston & Garrett, attys., Montgomery, 1975-81; acctg. supr. Arthur Andersen & Co., Dallas, 1981-82; staff acct. Burgess Co., C.P.A.s, Dallas, 1983; owner Lord & Assocs. Acctg. Svc., Dallas, 1983—; tax acct. John Hasse, C.P.A., Dallas, 1984-86; Dallas Bapt. Assn., 1986—. Vol. election law commr. Sec. of State of Ala. Don Siegelman, Montgomery, 1979-80; mem. Montgomery Art Guild, 1964-65, Ala. Art League, 1964-65, Montgomery Little Theatre, 1963-65, Montgomery Choral Soc., 1965. Recipient Outstanding Achievement Bus. Mgmt. award Am. Motors, 1968. Mem. Am. Soc. Women Accts. (pres. Montgomery chpt. 1976-77, area day chmn. 1978, del. ann. meeting 1975-78), Soroptimists Internat. (pres. elect Montgomery chpt. 1975-76), Nat. Assn. Ch. Bus. Adminstrn. Home: 5209 Meadowside Dr Garland TX 75043-2731

LORD, M. G., writer; b. La Jolla, Calif., Nov. 18, 1955; d. Charles Carroll and Mary (Pfister) L.; m. Glenn Horowitz, May 19, 1985. B.A., Yale U., 1977. Reporter N.Y. Bur. Wall St. Jour., N.Y.C., summer 1976; editorial artist Chgo. Tribune, 1977-78; editorial cartoonist, columnist Newsday, N.Y.C., 1978-94; cartoons syndicated L.A. Times Syndicate, 1984-89; column syndicated Copley News Svc., 1989-94. Author: Mean Sheets, 1982, Prig Tales, 1990, Forever Barbie: The Unauthorized Biography of a Real Doll, 1994. Resident humanities fellow U. Mich., 1986-87. Club: Yale (N.Y.C.). Office: care Eric Simonoff Janklow & Nesbit Assoc 598 Madison Ave New York NY 10022

LORD, MARIA ELENA, financial analyst, quality management specialist; b. Hammonton, N.J., Sept. 29, 1967; d. David and Jean (Panarello) L.; m. Michael Miranda, May 1993. BS, Fairleigh Dickinson U., Teaneck, N.J., 1989; MBA, Fordham U., N.Y., 1994. Fin. analyst Empire Blue Cross Blue Shield, N.Y.C., 1989—. Mem. Inst. Mgmt. Accts. Office: Empire Blue Cross Blue Shield 622 3rd Ave 27th Fl New York NY 10017

LORD, MARION MANNS, retired academic director; b. Fort Huachuca, Ariz., Dec. 17, 1914; d. George Wiley and Annie May (Pellett) Manns; children: Caroline L. Gross (dec.), Polly Steadman, Jane Chapin Humphries. BS, Northwestern U., 1936; MEd, Harvard U., 1962; MA, U. Wis., 1968, PhD, 1968. Columnist, exec. sec. Boston Am., 1936-38; dean women, dir. counseling Henniker, N.H., 1962-64; psychology tchr. Cen. Mich. U., Washington, 1975-79; higher edn. adminstr. U.S. Office Edn., Washington, 1968-75; dean faculty Borough of Manhattan Community Coll., CUNY, 1975-79, Cottey Coll., Nevada, Mo., 1979-80; English tchr. high sch., 1982-84, realtor, 1984-90; asst. dir. Franklin Pierce Coll., Concord, N.H., 1992; mem. faculty N.H. Coll., 1994-95; ednl. cons. N.H. Coll. and Univ. Coun., 1974-80, David W. Smith & Assocs., Washington, U.S. Office Edn., 1975-80. Editor, contbr.: A Survey of Women's Experiences and Perceptions Concerning Barriers to Their Continuing Education, Review of the Literature. State rep. Gen. Ct. N.H., 1957-62; active various polit. campaigns; active in past numerous civic orgns. E.B. Fred fellow, 1964-68; Breadloaf Coll. scholar, 1936, Northwestern U. scholar, 1933-36. Mem. Am. Psychol. Assn., Pi Lambda Theta. Republican. Home: RR 4 Box 402 Laconia NH 03246-8907

LORD, MIA W., world peace activist; b. N.Y.C., Dec. 2, 1920; m. Robert P. Lord (dec. Nov. 1977); children: Marcia Louise, Alison Jane. BA in Liberal Arts cum laude, Bklyn. Coll., 1940; postgrad., San Francisco State U., 1984—. Hon. sec. Commonwealth of World Citizens, London; membership sec. Brit. Assn. for World Govt., London; sec. Ams. in Brit. for U.S. Withdrawal from S.E. Asia, Eng.; organizer Vietnam Vigil to End the War, London; pres. Let's Abolish War chpt. World Federalist Assn., San Francisco State U.; appointed hon. sec. Commonwealth of World Citizens, London; officially invited to Vietnam, 1973; organizer Vietnam Vigil to End the War, London. Author: The Practical Way to End Wars and Other World Crises: the case for World Federal Government: listed in World Peace through World Law, 1984, and in Strengthening the United Nations, 1987, War: The Biggest Con Game in the World, 1980. Hon. sec., nat. exec. mem. Assn. of World Federalists-U.K.; founder, bd. dirs. Crusade to Abolish War and Armaments by World Law. Nominated for the Nobel Peace Prize, 1975, 92, 93; recipient four Merit awards Pres. San Francisco State U. Mem. Secretariat of World Citizens USA (life), Assn. of World Federalists USA, Brit. Assn. for World Govt. (membership sec.), Crusade to Abolish War and Armaments by World Law (founder, dir.), World Govt. Orgn. Coord. Com., World Fed. Authority Com., Campaign for UN Reform, Citizens Global Action, World Constitution and Parliament Assn., World Pub. Forum, Internat. Registry of World Citizens. Home: 174 Majestic Ave San Francisco CA 94112-3022

LORD, SHIRLEY, cosmetics magazine executive, novelist; b. London, Aug. 28; came to U.S., 1971; d. Francis J. and Mabel Florence (Williamson) Stringer; m. Cyril Lord; m. David Anderson; m. A.M. Rosenthal, June 10, 1987; children: Mark, Richard. Matriculation, S.W. Essex Coll., London, 1948. Reporter London Daily Mirror; fiction editor Woman's Own, 1950-53; features editor Good Taste mag., 1953-56; features, fiction editor Woman and Beauty, 1956-59; fashion editor Star Evening newspaper, 1959-60; women's editor London Evening Standard, 1960-63, London Evening News, 1963-68; beauty editor Harper's Bazaar, London, 1963-71, N.Y.C., 1971-73; beauty, health editor Vogue mag., Condé Nast Publs., N.Y.C., 1973-75; v.p. corp. rels. Helena Rubinstein, N.Y.C., 1975-80; beauty dir. Vogue mag., 1980-94, contbg. editor, 1994—; chairwoman media coun. The Am. Acad. Dermatology, 1995—. Syndicated Field columnist on beauty, health; author 3 beauty books; also novels: Golden Hill, 1982; One of My Very Best Friends, (Lit. Guild Selection), 1985; Faces, 1989; My Sister's Keeper, 1993. City commr. Craigavon City, No. Ireland, 1963-68.

LORD, VICTORIA LYNN, artist; b. Danville, Ill., May 29, 1956; d. Delno and Merlyn LaDonna (Gillis) Gilliland; m. Maurice Powers Lord II, Dec. 1, 1987. Student, Purdue U., 1974-77. host, instr. painting series PBS, Learning Channel, U.S., Can., Mexico, 1990—; instr. various orgns. Author: Techniques in Acrylics, Alkyds, Oils, 1987, Painting with Alkyds and Oils, 1989, First Steps in Acrylics, 1996. Named one of Top 100 Wildlife Artists, Artist Mag., 1990, Sponsor Artist, Ducks Unltd., Ind., 1991, Featured Ad Artist, Winsor & Newton, 1990-91. Mem. Soc. of Layerists in Multimedia, Soc. Exptl. Artists, Soc. Decorative Painters, Am. Craft Coun., Ind. Wildlife Artists, Soc. of Painters in Casein and Acrylic, Tippecanoe Arts Fedn. (bd. dirs. 1992-95). Office: PO Box 2195 West Lafayette IN 47906

LORDS, TRACI, actress, singer; b. W.Va., 1968; m. Brook Yeaton. Film appearances include Not of This Earth, Shock 'Em Dead, Raw Nerve, MacGyver, Cry-Baby, Tommyknockers; TV appearances include Roseanne, Wiseguy, MacGyver, Married...With Children, Melrose Place. Office: MCA 3d Fl 70 Universal City Plaza Universal City CA 91608*

LOREN, MARY ROONEY, controller; b. Monaghan, Ireland, Nov. 18, 1939; came to U.S., 1957; d. Peter Paul and Mary Alice (McKenna) Rooney; m. Thomas Leroy Loren, Aug. 22, 1959; children: Mary Teresa, Aileen Frances, Susan Marie. AAS in Acctg., Adirondack C.C., 1976; BS in Bus., Skidmore Coll., 1979; postgrad., SUNY, Plattsburgh, 1995—. Acctg. supr. Neles-Jamesbury, Glens Falls, N.Y., 1979-88; contr. Queensbury Hotel, Glens Falls, 1988-89; mgmt. acct. Ahlstrom Screen Pl., Glens Falls, 1989-92; mill contr. Hollingsworth & Vose, Greenwich, N.Y., 1993—; owner Heritage Heirlooms. Treas. Every Woman's Coun., Glens Falls, 1985—; lectr., eucharistic min. St. Michael's Roman Cath. Ch., Glens Falls, 1980—. Mem. Inst. Mgmt. Accts. (corp., acad. dir. 1993-94, pres. 1992-93, Achievement award 1992-93, Cmty. Svc. award 1993). Republican.

LORENZ, ANNE PARTEE, special education educator, consultant; b. Nashville, Aug. 6, 1943; d. McCullough and Mary Elizabeth (Shemwell) Partee; m. Philip Jack Lorenz, Jr., Nov. 26, 1970; stepchildren: Brenna Ellen, Philip Jack III. Student, Rhodes Coll., 1961-63, 64; BS, George Peabody Coll., 1966; postgrad., Ga. State U., 1967-68; MS, George Peabody Coll., 1969. Clerk Tenn. State Libr. Archives, Nashville, 1963-64; tchr. learning disabilities Howard Sch., Atlanta, 1966-68; prin., tchr. learning disabilities Sewanee (Tenn.) Learning Ctr., 1969-78; tchr. learning disabilities Clark Meml. Sch., Winchester, Tenn., 1978-79; tutor, cons. learning disabilities Anne Partee Lorenz Tutoring Consultation Svc., Sewanee, 1979—; psychol. cons. U. of South, 1974-78; cons. St. Andrew's-Sewanee Sch., Tenn., 1980—; vol. presenter Effective Adv. for Citizens With Handicaps, Inc. workshop, 1986. Active Coun. for Exceptional Children, 1968-79; treas. Franklin County Dem. Party; sec. Sewanee Precinct Dem. Party, 1974-76; del. dist. and state Dem. Conf.; judge John M. Templeton Laws of Life Essay Contest; vol. Cordelle-Lorenz Obs., U. of the South, 1970—; bd. dirs. Franklin County Adult Activities Ctr., 1979-82; vol. presenter E.A.C.H., Inc. (Effective Advocacy for Citizens with Handicaps), 1986. Recipient letter of commendation Gov. Tenn., 1974. Mem. Tenn. LWV (pres., bd. dirs.), Franklin County LWV (pres.), Learning Disabilities Assn. Tenn. (1st Tchr. Yr. 1975), Children and Adults with Attention Deficit Disorders. Home and Office: 390 Onteora Ln Sewanee TN 37375-2639

LORENZ, BETTY FIELDEN, management consultant, health policy analyst; b. New London, Conn., June 7, 1947; d. Robert William and Bernice (Simpson) Fielden; m. Laurence T. Lorenz, June 14, 1969; 1 child, Brian James. BA magna cum laude, U. Md., 1969. Tchr. Montgomery County Pub. Schs., Rockville, Md., 1969; dir. human resources Geomet, Inc., Rockville, 1969-70; edn. cons., Rockville, 1970-83; sr. cons. Birch & Davis Assocs., Inc., Silver Spring, Md., 1983-94; div. dir. Houston Assocs., Inc., Silver Spring, 1994—. Dept. chmn. Met. Cmty. Club Montgomery County, 1981—, sec., 1988-90, v.p., 1990-92, pres., 1992-94. Recipient Outstanding Vol. of Yr. award Montgomery County Pub. Schs., 1981. Mem. APHA, NAFE, Md. Pub. Health Assn., Phi Kappa Phi. Home: 2404 Glenmore Ter Rockville MD 20850 Office: Houston Assocs Inc 1010 Wayne Ave Ste 240 Silver Spring MD 20910

LORENZ, KATHERINE MARY, banker; b. Barrington, Ill., May 1, 1946; d. David George and Mary (Hogan) L. BA cum laude, Trinity Coll., 1968; MBA, Northwestern U., 1971; grad., Grad. Sch. for Bank Adminstrn., 1977. Ops. analyst Continental Bank, Chgo., 1968-69, supr. ops. analysis, 1969-71, asst. mgr. customer profitability analysis, 1971-73, acctg. officer, mgr. customer profitability analysis, 1973-77, 2d v.p., 1976, asst. gen. mgr. contr.'s dept., 1977-80, v.p., 1980, contr. ops. and mgmt. svcs. dept., 1981-84, v.p., sector contr. retail banking, corp. staff and ops. depts., 1984-88, v.p., sr. sector contr. pvt. banking, centralized ops. and corp. staff, 1988-90, v.p., sr. sector contr. bus. analysis group/mgmt. acctg., 1990-94, mgr. contrs. dept. adminstrn. and tng., 1990-94; v.p., chief of staff to chief adminstrv. officer Bank of Am. Ill., Chgo., 1994-96, sr. v.p., mgr. adminstrv. svcs., 1996—. Mem. Execs. Club Chgo. Office: Bank of Am Ill 231 S La Salle St Rm 1320 Chicago IL 60697

LORFANO, PAULINE DAVIS, artist; b. Westbrook, Maine; d. Paul A. and Nellie R. (Robinson) Davis; m. Joseph James Lorfano, Apr. 18, 1952; children: Mary-Jo, Paula, Julie-Ann, Joseph III. Student, Westbrook Coll., 1946-48; Assoc. degree, Maine Coll. Art, 1950; BS, U. Maine, 1951. Tchr. Riggs Sch., Gloucester, Mass., 1951-52; art tchr. Westbriar Elem., Vienna, Va., 1969-76, George Mason U., Fairfax, Va., 1976-80; art tchr., workshop instr. Va., 1980—, juror, lectr. art, 1980—. Illustrator: (book) Visiting Historic Vienna...A Child's Book to Color, 1995; one person shows include Summer Sch. Mus., 1988, Nat. Wildlife Fedn., 1989; works featured for mag. covers. Mem. Vienna Arts Soc. Inc. (permanent mem., bd. dirs. 1990-96, pres. 1979-81, 88-90, Stillwell award 1988, Gold medal 1987), Nat. League Am. PEN Women (juried-in mem., cons. art bd. 1994-96, chmn. art bd. 1982-84, 2d Pl. award Biennial Art Exhibit 1992), Potomac Valley Watercolorists (juried-in mem., bd. dirs. 1990-95, pres. 1989-90), Washington Watercolor Assn. (juried-in mem.). Home: 402 Old Courthouse Rd NE Vienna VA 22180-3603

LORIMER, LINDA KOCH, college official; m. Ernest McFaul Lorimer; children: Katharine Elizabeth, Peter Brailler. AB, Hollins Coll., 1974; JD, Yale U., 1977; DHL, Green Mountain Coll., 1981, Washington Coll., 1992, Randolph-Macon Coll., 1992. Bar: N.Y. 1978, Conn. 1982. Assoc. Davis Polk and Wardwell, N.Y.C., 1977-78; asst. gen. counsel Yale U., New Haven, 1978-79, assoc. gen. counsel, 1979-84, assoc. provost, 1983-87, acting assoc. v.p. human resources, 1984-85; prof. law, pres. Randolph-Macon Woman's Coll., Lynchburg, Va., 1987-93; v.p., sec. Yale Univ., New Haven, 1993—; lectr. Yale Coll. Undergrad. Seminars, 1980, 83; bd. dirs. Spring, McGraw Hill; past pres., mem. exec. com. Women's Coll. Coalition; mem. corp. Yale U., 1990-93, chair Virginia Rhodes scholarship com., 1991-93. Chair editorial bd. Jour. Coll. and Univ. Law, 1983-87. Former trustee Hollins Coll., Berkeley Div. Sch.; mem. com. on responsible conduct rsch. Inst. Medicine, NAS, 1988; bd. dirs. Norfolk Acad.; cabinet mem. United Way of Greater New Haven. Mem. Nat. Assn. Coll. and Univ. Attys. (exec. bd. 1981-84), Nat. Assn. Schs. and Colls. of United Meth. Ch. (1st v.p.), Assn. Am. Colls.,(bd. dirs., chmn. bd.), Am. Assn. Theol. Schs. (bd. dirs.), Mory's Assn., Phi Beta Kappa. Episcopalian. Home: 87 Trumbull St New Haven CT 06511-3723 Office: Woodbridge Hall Yale Univ New Haven CT 06520-9999

LORING, GLORIA JEAN, singer, actress; b. N.Y.C., Dec. 10, 1946; d. Gerald Louis and Dorothy Ann (Tobin) Goff; m. Alan Willis Thicke, Aug. 22, 1970 (div. 1986); children: Brennan Todd, Robin Alan; m. Christopher Beaumont, June 18, 1988 (div. 1993); m. René Lagler, Dec. 20, 1994. Grad. high sch. Owner Glitz Records, L.A., 1984—; pres. Only Silk Prodns., L.A., 1985-90; owner Silk Purse Prodns., 1992—. Began profl. singing, Miami Beach, 1965; appeared in numerous TV shows; featured singer: Bob Hope's Ann. Armed Forces Christmas Tour, 1970; featured several record albums; featured actress: Days of Our Lives, 1980-86; composer: TV themes Facts of Life, 1979, Diff'rent Strokes, 1978; author: Days of Our Lives Celebrity Cookbook, 1981, Vol. II, 1983, Living the Days of Our Lives, 1984, Kids, Food and Diabetes, 1986, Parenting a Diabetic Child, 1991, The Kids Food and Diabetes Family Cookbook, 1991. Celebrity chmn. Juvenile Diabetes Found. Recipient Humanitarian of Yr. award Juvenile Diabetes Found., 1982, 88, Parents of Yr. award, 1984, Woman of Yr. award Jeweler's Assn. Am., 1986. Mem. Nat. Acad. Songwriters (gold mem.).

LORING, HONEY, small business owner; b. Phila.. BA in Psychology, U. Md., 1970; MEd, Wash. U., St. Louis, 1971. Lic. psychologist-master Vt.; directress cert. Assn. Montessori Internat. Counselor Gardenville Diagnostic Ctr., St. Louis, 1971-72; tchr. Early Learning Pre-Sch., St. Louis, 1972-74; music dir., cabin counselor Follow Through Day Camp, Brattleboro, Vt., 1972-74; tchr. Montessori Sch., Dublin, 1974-75; ednl. cons. children's books Left Bank Books, St. Louis, 1975-76; program dir. day camp Brattleboro Child Devel., 1975-79; behavioral therapist Behavioral Medicine Unit, Dartmouth Med. Sch., 1979-84; pvt. therapist Brattleboro, Vt., 1984-85; founder, pres. Gone to the Dogs, Inc., Putney, Vt., 1984—; dog groomer, 1979-92; founder, dir. Camp Come to the Dogs, 1990—; mfr. dog collars, 1984-96; founder Tails Up Inn, 1995—. Author: (with Jeremy Birch) You're On. . .Teaching Communication Skills, 1984, The Big Good Wolf; contbr. articles to profl. jours. Leader 4-H Dog Club; helper Riding for the Physically Handicapped, St. Louis, 1974. Home and Office: RR 1 Box 958 Putney VT 05346-9748

LORMAN, BARBARA K., state senator; b. Madison, Wis., July 31, 1932; 3 children. Student U. Wis., Whitewater and Madison. Pres. Lorman Iron and Metal Recycling Co., 1979-87; mem. Wis. State Senate from 13th Dist., 1980—; chair edn. com.; mem. health, human svc. and aging com., mem. fin. insts. and cultural affairs com., mem. select com. on healthcare reform; sec. Legis. Coun., also mem. spl. com. on farm safety, mem. spl. com. on women offenders in correctional system; mem. spl. com. study sch. aid formula; commr. Edn. Commn. of States. Bd. dirs. Rainbow Hospice Care, Inc., Ft. Atkinson (Wis.) Devel. Coun., Ft. Atkinson (Wis.) Meml. Hosp.; mem. exec. bd. Sinissippi Coun. Boy Scouts Am.; mem. govs. commn. U.S.S. Wisconsin; active Edn. Block Grant Com., Edn. Comm. Bd., Chronic Renal Disease Adv. Com., Dept. Corrections Community Rels. Bd., Nat. Kidney Foun. Wis., Dept. Devel. Forward Wisconsin, Prison Overcrowding Task Force, Rep. Party Wis. Mem. Rotary Internat. Address: 1245 Janette St Fort Atkinson WI 53538-1526*

LOSADA-PAISEY, GLORIA, psychologist; b. Havana, Cuba, Apr. 20, 1957; came to U.S., 1962; d. Manuel Benito and Maria del Pilar (Fernandez) Losada; m. Timothy John Henry Paisey, June 4, 1983 (div. June 1989); 1 child, Monica Paisey. BA, Fla. Internat. U., 1980; D Psychology, Nova U., 1984. Lic. psychologist, Conn. Pre-doctoral pyschology fellow Yale U., New Haven, 1983-84; clin. psychologist State of Conn. Dept. Mental Retardation Southbury Tng. Sch., Southbury, Conn., 1984-86, State of Conn. Dept. Mental Retardation New Haven Ctr., New Haven, 1986-88; dir. psychol. svcs. State of Conn. Dept. Mental Retardation Region 6, Waterford, Conn., 1988-92; clin. psychologist Conn. Dept. Children and Youth Svcs., Middletown, Conn., 1992—; pvt. practice psychology, Waterbury, 1986—; dir. treatment program for mentally retarded offenders Southbury Tng. Sch., State of Conn., 1984-86. Mem. APA, New Eng. Psychol. Assn. Democrat. Roman Catholic. Office: 265 Meriden Rd Waterbury CT 06705-2001

LOSCAVIO, ELIZABETH, dancer; b. Jacksonville, Fla.. Student, Contra Costa Ballet Sch., Pacific N.W. Ballet Sch., San Francisco Ballet Sch. Co. apprentice San Francisco Ballet, 1986, mem. corps de ballet, 1986-88, soloist, 1988-90, prin. dancer, 1990—. Performances include Romeo and Juliet, The Sleeping Beauty, Swan Lake, Nanna's Lied, Haffner Symphony, Con Brio, Handel-a Celebration, Menuetto, Contradanses, Ballet D'Isoline, Intimate Voices, La Fille mal gardée, Ballo della Regina, Tchaikovsky Pas de Deux, Theme and Variations, Who Cares?, Symphony in C, Tarantella, Rubies, Stars and Stripes, The Four Temperaments, A Midsummer Night's Dream, Rodeo, Maelstrom, La Pavane Rouge, Dark Elegies, Grand Pas de Deux, Flower Festival at Genzano, Rodin, Connotations, Le Corsaire Pas de Deux, Sunset, In the Night, Interplay, The End, The Comfort Zone, Dreams of Harmony, The Wanderer Fantasy, The Sons of Horus, Nutcracker, Divertissemet d'Auber, Vivaldi Concerto Grosso, New Sleep, La Sylphide. Recipient Isadora Duncan award, 1991. Office: San Francisco Ballet 455 Franklin St San Francisco CA 94102-4438

LOSCHIAVO, LINDA BOSCO, library director; b. Rockville Ctr., N.Y., Aug. 31, 1950; d. Joseph and Jennie (DelRegno) Bosco; m. Joseph A. LoSchiavo, Sept. 7, 1974. BA, Fordham U., 1972, MA, 1990; MLS, Pratt Inst., 1974. Picture cataloguer Frick Art Reference Libr., N.Y.C., 1972-75; sr. cataloguer Fordham U. Libr., Bronx, N.Y., 1975-87, head of retrospective conversion, 1987-90, systems libr., 1990-91, dir. libr. at Lincoln Ctr., 1991—; libr. cons. Mus. Am. Folk Art Libr., N.Y.C., 1985-90; indexer Arco Books, N.Y.C., 1974. Editor: Macbeth, 1990, Julius Caesar, 1990, Romeo and Juliet, 1990. Mng. producer Vineyard Opera, N.Y.C., 1981-88. Mem. ALA, N.Y. Tech. Svcs. Librs., Beta Phi Mu, Alpha Sigma Nu. Home: 317 Collins Ave Mount Vernon NY 10552-1601 Office: Fordham Univ Library 113 W 60th St New York NY 10023-7471

LOSSE, CATHERINE ANN, pediatric nurse, critical care nurse, educator, clinical nurse specialist; b. Mount Holly, N.J., Mar. 12, 1959; d. David C. and Bernice (Lewis) L. Diploma, Helene Fuld Sch. Nursing, 1980; BSN magna cum laude, Thomas Jefferson U., 1986; MSN, U. Pa., 1989; postgrad., Widener U., 1995—. RN, N.J., Pa., Del.; cert. pediatric nurse, cert. pediatric critical care nurse; cert. PALS provider, BLS instr. Staff nurse adult med.-surg. Meml. Hosp. Burlington County, Mount Holly, N.J., 1980-81; staff nurse pediatric home care Newborn Nurses, Moorestown, N.J., 1986-87; clin. nurse II surg. intensive care Deborah Heart & Lung Ctr., Browns Mills, N.J., 1986-87, clin. nurse III pediatric cardiology, 1981-86, 87—; ednl. nurse specialist critical care The Children's Hosp., Phila., 1992-94; instr. nursing of families, maternal-child health, pediat., geriatrics Burlington County Coll., 1994-96; staff nurse pediatric home care Bayada Nurses, Burlington, N.J., 1995—; clin. instr. pediatrics Thomas Jefferson U., 1990; clin. instr. adult med. surg. Burlington County Coll., 1991. Mem. ANA, AACN (CCRN, pediat. spl. interest cons. 1995-96), Nat. Assn. Pediatric Nurse Assocs. and Practitioners, Am. Acad. Nurse Practitioners, Soc. Pediat. Nurses, N.J. State Nurses Assn. (mem. cabinet on continuing edn. rev. team III 1992-96, mem. forum for nursing in advanced practice 1994—), Am. Heart Assn. (cert. instr. PALS and BLS, bd. dirs. Burlington County br. 1995—, vice chairperson cmty. site com. 1995—), Sigma Theta Tau. Home: 253 Spout Spring Ave Mount Holly NJ 08060-2041

LOSTY, BARBARA PAUL, college official; b. Norwich, N.Y., June 16, 1942; d. Henry Edward and Mary Frances (Crowell) Paul; m. Thomas August Losty, Nov. 27, 1965; children: Ellen Christine, Amanda Elizabeth. BA, Wellesley Coll., 1964; MA, U. Conn., 1969, PhD, 1971. Asst. prof. psychology Westminster Coll., Fulton, Mo., 1971-73; asst. prof. psychology Stephens Coll., Columbia, Mo., 1973-75, assoc. dir. sch. liberal and profl. studies, 1975-79, assoc. dean of faculty, 1979-85; dean U. Wis. Ctr.-Sheboygan County, Sheboygan, 1985-91; coord. human svcs. degrees Thomas Edison State Coll., Trenton, N.J., 1992-94, assoc. dean human svcs. degrees, 1994-96; pres. Waycross (Ga.) Coll., 1996—. Home: 922 Wood Valley Dr Waycross GA 31503 Office: Waycross Coll 2001 S Ga Pky Waycross GA 31503

LOTAS, JUDITH PATTON, advertising executive; b. Iowa City, Apr. 23, 1942; d. John Henry and Jane (Vandike) Patton; children: Amanda Bell, Alexandra Vandike. BA, Fla. State U., 1964. Copywriter Liller, Neal, Battle and Lindsey Advt., Atlanta, 1964-67, Grey Advt., N.Y.C., 1967-72; creative group head SSC&B Advt., N.Y.C., 1972-74, assoc. creative dir., 1974-79, v.p., 1975-79, sr. v.p., 1979-82, exec. creative dir., 1982-86; founding ptnr. Lotas Minard Patton McIver, Inc., N.Y.C., 1986—. Active scholarship fund raising; bd. dirs. Samuel Eaxman Cancer Rsch., Found., N.Y.C., 1981-88; fundraiser Nat. Coalition for the Homeless, N.Y.C., 1986—. Recipient Clio award, Venice Film Festival award, Graphics award Am. Inst. Graphic Artists, 1970, Effie award, Grad. of Distinction award Fla. State U., 1993; named Woman of Achievement, YWCA, One of Advt. Agys. 100 Best Women Ad Age, 1989. Mem. Advt. Women N.Y. (1st v.p. 1984-87, bd. dirs. 1981-87, Advt. Woman of Yr. 1993), The Ad Coun. (mem. creative rev. bd. 1994—, bd. dirs. 1995—), Women's Venture Fund (bd. dirs. 1995—), Kappa Alpha Theta. Democrat. Home: 45 E 89th St New York NY 10128-1251

LOTEMPIO, JULIA MATILD, accountant; b. Budapest, Hungary, Oct. 14, 1934; came to U.S., 1958, naturalized 1962; d. Istvan and Irma (Sandor) Fejos; m. Anthony Joseph LoTempio, Mar. 11, 1958. AAS in Lab. Tech. summa cum laude, Niagara County C.C., Sanborn, N.Y., 1967; BS in Tech. and Vocat. Edn. summa cum laude, SUNY, Buffalo, 1970; MEd in Guidance and Counseling, Niagara U., 1973, BBA in Acctg. summa cum laude, 1983. Sr. analyst, rschr. Gt. Lakes Carbon Co., Niagara Falls, N.Y., 1967-71; tchr. sci. Niagara Falls Schs., 1973-75; tchr. sci. and English Starpoint Sch. System, Lockport, N.Y., 1975-77; instr. acctg. principles Niagara County Community Coll., Sanborn, N.Y., 1989—; club adminstr., acct. Twinlo Racquetball, Inc., Niagara Falls, 1979-81; bus. cons. Twinlo Beverage, Inc., Niagara Falls, 1981-85; staff acct. J.D. Elliott & Co. PC, CPAs, Buffalo, 1986-87; acct., Lewiston, N.Y., 1988—; instr. applied chemistry Niagara County C.C., 1979, instr. acctg. principles, 1989—; bd. dirs. Niagara Frontier Meth. Home Inc., Niagara Frontier Nursing Home Inc., The Blocher Homes Inc., Buffalo. Mem. faculty continuing edn., speaker, chairperson fin. and community rels. coms. United Meth. Ch., Dickersonville, N.Y., 1985-90; guest speaker, counselor, tchr. Beechwood Svc. Guild, Buffalo, 1987-91; bd. dirs. Niagara Frontier Meth. Home, Inc., Getzville, N.Y., 1988—; bd. dirs., mem. fin., investment, pension, ins., and community rels. coms. Niagara Frontier Nursing Home Co., Inc., Getzville, 1988—, Blocher Homes, Inc., Williamsville, N.Y., 1988—; asst. sec., bd. dirs., mem. exec., quality and assurance coms., chmn. community rels. com. Beechwood/Blocher Community, Buffalo, 1990—; mem. Coop. Parish Coun., Sanborn, N.Y., 1991—; mem. adminstrv. bd., chmn. outreach com. Pekin (N.Y.) United Meth. Ch., 1992—; sec. to bd. dirs. Beechwood/Blocher Found., Amherst, N.Y., 1992—, asst. treas., 1993-94, treas., 1994, vice chmn., 1994—. Mem. NAFE, Nat. Soc. Pub. Accts., Nat. Assn. Accts., Nat. Fedn. Bus. and Profl. Women's Club, Internat. Platform Assn., Niagara U. Alumni Assn., SUNY Coll. Buffalo Alumni Assn., Niagara County C.C. Alumni Assn. Home and Office: 1026 Ridge Rd Lewiston NY 14092-9704

LOTEYRO, CORAZON BIGATA, physician; b. Manila, Apr. 9, 1951; came to U.S., 1979; d. Victor G. Loteyro and Emilia Bigata; 1 child, Elizabeth. BS, Mindanao State U., Marawi City, The Philippines, 1972; MD, U. of East, Manila, 1976. Diplomate Am. Bd. Family Physicians. Physician Humana Medfirst, Peoria, Ill., 1984-85, Family Health Plan, Elm Grove, Wis., 1985-96, Covenant Health, Pewaukee, Wis., 1996—. Vol. Salvation Army, Milw., 1993. Fellow Am. Acad. Family Physicians; mem. Filipino-Am. Med. Assn. (pres. 1994-95), U. of East Alumni Assn. Midwest (treas. 1990-94). Republican. Roman Catholic. Home: 16965 Beverly Dr Brookfield WI 53005 Office: Covenant Health Care Pewaukee WI 53072

LOTHROP, MONICA WARD, finance administrator; b. Norristown, Pa., May 9, 1958; d. Thomas F. and Elizabeth Mary (Marino) Ward; m. Howard J. Lothrop, June 22, 1980 (div. Nov. 1991). BS, St. Joseph's U., 1980; MBA, Memphis State U., 1990. Cert. mgmt. acct. Trainee York (Pa.) Bank and Trust Co., 1980-81; acct. Volvo White Truck Corp., Greensboro, N.C., 1981-84; fin. analyst Dairymen Inc., Greensboro, N.C., 1984-86; acctg. mgr. Kraft Dairy Group, Memphis, 1986-88; contr. Green Duck Corp., Hernando, Miss., 1988-89; divisional contr. Am. Signature, Olive Branch, Miss., 1992-93; plant contr. Smurfit Recycling, Memphis, 1992-94; fin. dir. Borough of Norristown, Pa., 1995—; instr. Data Processing Trainers, Phila., 1995—; dir. Dairymen Credit Union, Greensboro, 1986. Chpt. treas. Amigos de las Americas, Memphis, 1994-95. Mem. AAUW, Inst. Cert. Mgmt. Accts. (cert.), Govt. Fin. Officers Assn., Assn. Cert. Fraud Examiners. Home: B-1 1015 W Beech St Norristown PA 19401

LOTITO, LISA ANN, secondary education educator; b. Crawley, Eng., Apr. 1, 1968; d. Lawrence Aloysius and Ramona Marie (Fugee) L. BA in History, U. Calif., Irvine, 1991; Cert. Social Sci. Tchr., Calif. State U., Fullerton, 1993. Tchr. social sci. Morongo Unified Sch. Dist., Yucca Valley, Calif., 1993—; pres. Student Activities Com., Fullerton, 1993; mem. Staff Devel., Yucca Valley, 1993—. Mem. ASCD, Smithsonian Inst. Democrat. Roman Catholic. Home: 62238 Verbena Rd # 46 Joshua Tree CA 92252-4023 Office: Morongo Unified Sch Dist 7600 Sage Ave Yucca Valley CA 92284

LOTSPEICH, ELLIN SUE, art specialist, educator; b. Spring Valley, Ill., July 2, 1952; d. Donald Robert and Mary Rita (Smith) Mason; m. Thomas Grant Weaver, Jan. 26, 1974 (dec. July 1989); children: Jennifer, Michelle, Patrick; m. Michael Charles Lotspeich, Apr. 9, 1994; 1 child, Michael Charles II. BS, Western Ill. U., 1974, M Ednl. Adminstrn., 1995. Unit art specialist Winola Unit Dist., Viola, Ill., 1974-84, Al Wood Unit Dist., Woodhull, Ill., 1984—; discipline based art cons. Getty Ctr. for Edn. in Arts, 1989—; exec. bd. Commn. on Edn. Diocese of Peoria, Ill., 1993—, exec. chmn. Religious Edn. Com., 1994—. Mem. Nat. Art Edn. Assn., Ill. Art Edn. Assn. (exec. bd. 1980—, state youth art chmn. 1990-93), Ill. Rembrandt State Assn. (editor newsletter 1987-90, bd. dirs.), Ill. Alliance for Arts, Henry Stark H.S. Art Tchrs. (pres. 1984-94). Home: 212 N 3d Ave New Windsor IL 61465 Office: Al Wood Unit Dist 201 E 5th Ave Woodhull IL 61490

LOTT, BRENDA LOUISE, insurance company executive; b. Clinton, Ind., July 29, 1955; d. John and Thelma Louise (Anderson) Pastore; m. Robert Ralph Rundle, June 16, 1974 (div. July 1985); children: Danielle Marie Rundle, John Robert Rundle; m. Mark Lee Lott, July 4, 1985. BA in Polit. Sci., Colo. Women's Coll., Denver, 1976; student, Ins. Inst. of Am. Claim adjuster Allstate Ins. Co., Englewood, Colo., 1973-83; field claim adjuster Transamerica Ins. Co., Englewood, 1983-86; claim examiner Colonial Ins. Co., Denver, 1986-87, examiner/supr., 1987-89, regional claim mgr., 1990-92; programs mgr. Innovative Svcs. Am., Golden, Colo., 1992—; staff speaker Western Ins. Info. Svc., Denver, 1983-85; participant, invited faculty mem. 5-day lecture series Colonial Univ., Anaheim, Calif., 1990. Sponsor Plan Internat. foster parents program, 1989—. Mem. NAFE, LWV, NAACP (mem.-at-large), Ins. Women of Denver, Internat. Customer Svc. Assn., Colo. Claims Assn. (bd. dirs. 1986-88), Claim Mgrs. Coun., Denver Claims Assn., PGA Tours Ptnrs.

LOTT, JOYCE GREENBERG, English language educator; b. Atlantic City, Jan. 27, 1938; d. David E. and Florence (Steinig) Feinstein; m. Morton I. Greenberg, June 30, 1956 (div. 1983); m. Gary C. Lott, Sept. 30, 1984; children: Elizabeth Greenberg, Suzanne Greenberg, Larry Greenberg. BA, Douglass Coll., 1976; MA, Rutgers U., 1979. Tchr. English South Brunswick H.S., N.J., 1978-80; mem. adj. English faculty Somerset County C.C., N.J., 1978-80; leader, cons. in-svc. workshops in pub. schs., N.J., 1992—; spkr. on portfolios, reflective writing, multicultural lit. at nat. convs., Milw., San Diego, Pitts., Seattle, 1990—. Author: When Kids Dare to Question Their Education, 1995, A Teacher's Stories, Reflections on High School Writers, 1994; contbr. stories and articles to mags. and jours. Recipient N.J. Poetry Monthly prize; co-winner Acad. of Am. Poets Contest. Mem. ASCD, Nat. Coun. Tchrs. English, N.J. Edn. Assn. Home: 5 Toth Ln Rocky Hill NJ 08553

LOTT, LESLIE JEAN, lawyer; b. Louisville, Nov. 12, 1950; d. Emmett Russell Jr. and Allene (Barbee) L.; m. Michael T. Moore, Dec. 28, 1977; children: Michael T. Jr., Emmett Russell Lott. BA, U. Fla., 1972, JD, 1974; postgrad., Escuela Libre de Derecho, Mexico City, 1973. Bar: Fla. 1974, D.C. 1975, U.S. Ct. Appeals (fed. cir.) 1975, N.Y. 1977, U.S. Dist. Ct. (so. dist.) Fla. 1981, U.S. Dist. Ct. (so. dist.) Trial Bar 1981, U.S. Dist. Ct. (mid. dist.) Fla. 1995. Trademark examiner U.S. Patent and Trademark Office, Arlington, Va., 1974-76; assoc. Pennie & Edmonds, N.Y.C., 1976-80, Hassan Mahassni/Burlingham, Underwood & Lord, Jeddah, Saudi Arabia, 1978-79, Floyd, Pearson, Stewart, Richman, Greer, Weil & Zack, Miami, Fla., 1981-83; pvt. practice Leslie J. Lott & Assocs., P.A., Coral Gables, Fla., 1983-94, Lott & Friedland, PA, Coral Gables, 1994—; judge Moot Ct., Trial Advocacy U. Miami, 1981, 82, 84, 85, 87; lectr. continuing legal edn., 1987—. Editor So. Dist. Digest, 1981-84; contbr. articles to profl. jours. Recipient Am. Jurisprudence Book Award in Fed. Practice, 1973. Mem. U.S. Trademark Assn. (chmn. com. 1986-88), Am. Intellectual Property Law Assn., Fla. Bar Assn. (chmn. 1983—), South Fla. Patent Law Assn. Office: Lott & Friedland PA 255 Alhambra Cir Ste 555 Coral Gables FL 33134

LOTTES, PATRICIA JOETTE HICKS, foundation administrator, retired nurse; b. Balt., Aug. 18, 1955; d. James Thomas and Linda Belle (Cadd) Hicks; m. Jeffrey Grant Gross, Aug. 18, 1979 (div. 1981); m. William Melamet Lottes, Sept. 10, 1983. Diploma in practical nursing, Union Meml. Hosp., 1978. Staff nurse Union Meml. Hosp., Balt., 1978-79, critical care nurse, 1979-81; vis. critical care nurse Balt., 1981-84; head nurse Pharmakinetics, Inc., Balt., 1984-85; dir. Arachnoiditis Info. and Support Network, Inc., Ballwin, Mo., 1991—, dir. nat. support groups, 1992—; nat. support group leader Arachnoid, 1993—. Sec., treas. O'Fallon (Mo.) Elks Ladies Aux., 1989-91, treas., 1991-92, incorporator, 1991, bd. dirs., 1991-94; co-chairperson 303d Field Hosp., U.S. Army Family Support Group, St. Louis, 1990-94. Mem. Nat. Disaster Med. Systems (assoc.), Elks Benevolent Trust, Elks Nat. Home Perpetual Trust. Republican. Baptist. Home: 606 Barbara Dr O'Fallon MO 63366-1306

LOTUS, LINDA, carpentry educator; b. Chgo., June 14, 1947; d. David LEslie and Dorothy Jean (McCleery) Johnson; m. Frank Joseph Miller, Aug. 1969 (div. 1977); 1 child, Sonam Tsering Leslie; life ptnr. Barbara Jean Smith. Student, U. Wash., 1996—. Collective mem., worker Soup & Salad Restaurant, Little Bread Co., Seattle, 1970-73; owner, waitress Sound Food Restaurant, Vashon, Wash., 1974-76; carpenter Happy Homes, Vashon, Wash., 1977-79; carpenter, owner Lotus Constrn., Vashon, Wash., 1980-90; lumber sales Henry Bacon, Kent, Wash., 1991; housing adminstr, inspector Pierce Co. Housing Repair, Tacoma, Wash., 1992; instr. carpentry Green River C.C., Auburn, Wash., 1993—. Office: Green River C C 12401 SW 320th St Auburn WA 98092-3699

LOTZ, AILEEN ROBERTS, government consultant, author, photographer, travel consultant; b. Orange, N.J., Dec. 11, 1924; d. Paul R. and Aileen (Jeandron) Roberts; children: Alexandra Virginia, David William. BA, U. Miami, 1971. Exec. dir. Miami Beach Taxpayers Assn., 1954-60; exec. dir. Govt. Rsch. Coun., Miami, Fla. 1960-66; sr. adminstrv. asst. to mgr. Dade County, Miami, 1966-72; dir. Dade County Dept. Human Resources, 1975-82; cons. to local govt., 1982-90. Candidate Fla. Ho. of Reps., 1974. Author: Metropolitan Dade County: Two-Tier Government in Action, 1984, Birding Around the World, 1987, Birding Around the Year, 1989; contbr. articles to profl. jours. Mem. N.Am. Nature Photography Assn. (charter dir.), Zool. Soc. of Fla. (exec. dir. 1983-84), The Explorers Club. Democrat. Address: 2804 Bookcliff Ave Grand Junction CO 81501-4950

LOTZ, JOAN THERESA, public relations company executive; b. N.Y.C., Feb. 22, 1948; d. Andrew J. and Joan (McCartney) L. BA, Lehman Coll., 1970. Libr. asst. Met. Mus. Art, N.Y.C., 1969-74; office mgr. York Cable Corp., Inc., N.Y.C., 1974-77, Mobile Communications, Inc., N.Y.C., 1977-78; lease mgr. Major Muffler Ctrs., Inc., N.Y.C., 1978-81; v.p., asst. to chmn. Rowland Worldwide, N.Y.C., 1981-93; pres. JL Enterprises, N.Y.C., 1993—. N.Y. State Regent's scholar, 1965-69. Mem. Nat. Scholastic Soc. Democrat. Roman Catholic.

LOTZE, BARBARA, physicist; b. Mezokovesd, Hungary, Jan. 4, 1924; d. Matyas and Borbala (Toth) Kalo; came to U.S., 1961, naturalized, 1967; Applied Mathematician Diploma with honors, Eotvos Lorand U. Scis., Budapest, Hungary, 1956; PhD, Innsbruck (Austria) U., 1961; m. Dieter P. Lotze, Oct. 6, 1958. Mathematician, Hungarian Cen. Statis. Bur., Budapest, 1955-56; tchr. math., Iselsberg, Austria, 1959-60; asst. prof. physics Allegheny Coll., 1963-69, assoc. prof., 1969-77, prof., 1977-90, prof. emeritus, 1990—, chmn. dept., 1981-84; lectr. in history of physics; speaker to civic groups. Mem. Am. Phys. Soc. (mem. com. internat. freedom of scientists 1993-95), Am. Inst. Physics (mem. adv. com. history of physics 1994—), Am. Assn. Physics Tchrs. (coun., sect. rep. Western Pa., chmn. nat. com. on women in physics 1983-84, com. internat. physics edn. 1991-93, com. history and philosophy of physics 1996—, Disting. Svc. award 1986, cert. of appreciation 1988), AAUW, N.Y. Acad. Scis., Am. Hungarian Educators Assn. (pres. 1980-82), Wilhelm Busch Gesellschaft (Hanover). Editor: Making Contributions: An Historical Overview of Women's Role in Physics, 1984; co-editor The First War Between Socialist States: The Hungarian Revolution of 1956 and Its Impact, 1984; contbr. articles to profl. jours. Home: 462 Hartz Ave Meadville PA 16335-1325 Office: Allegheny Coll Dept Physics Meadville PA 16335

LOTZE, EVIE DANIEL, psychodramatist; b. Roswell, N.Mex., Mar. 6, 1943; d. Wadsworth Richard and Lee Ora (Norrell) Daniel; m. Christian Dieter Lotze, June 9, 1963; children: Conrad, Monica. BA cum laude, La. State U., 1964; MA, Goddard Coll., 1975; PhD, Union Inst., Cin., 1990. Dir. Casa Alegre, Hogares, Albuquerque, 1979-80; pvt. practice Riyadh, Saudi Arabia, 1980-83, Silver Spring, Md., 1983-85; dir. Gulf States Psychodrama Tng., Houston, 1986-88; founder, dir. Innerstages Psychodrama Tng., Houston, 1988-94; program devel. cons. in tng. Children's Nat. Med. Ctr., Washington, 1994-96; pvt. practice Paris, 1996—; supr. Houston Area psychodramatists, 1988—; tng. cons. Assn. Applied Psychologists, Moscow, 1992—; cons. in field. Author: (tng. manual) Clinical Psychodrama Training Manual, 3 vols., 1990. Bd. dirs. Interact Theater, Houston, 1992. Mem. Am. Group Psychotherapy Assn., Internat. Coun. Psychologists. Democrat. Lutheran. Home and Office: 1 rue Georges Appay, 92152 Suresnes France

LOUCK, LISA ANN, lawyer; b. Davenport, Iowa, July 16, 1963; d. Richard Lane and Jo Ann (Frerkes) L. BSBA, Iowa State U., 1985; JD, South Tex. Coll. Law, 1991. Bar: Tex. 1992. Atty. Woodard, Hall & Primm, Houston, 1994—; mediator Tex. Registry Alt. Dispute Resolution Profls., 1992—. Recipient Am. Jurisprudence award Lawyers Coop. Pub., 1991. Mem. ABA, State Bar Tex., Houston Young Lawyers Assn., Phi Alpha Delta. Office: Woodard Hall & Primm PC 7100 Texas Commerce Tower Houston TX 77002

LOUCK, LORI ANN, speech-language pathologist; b. Davenport, Iowa, Sept. 5, 1965; d. Richard Lane and JoAnn (Frerkes) L.; m. John Joseph Stankus III, July 10, 1993. BS in Edn., U. Houston, 1990; MS in Speech Pathology, Nova Southeastern U., 1995. Tchr. Broward County Schs., Hollywood, Fla., 1990-95; speech pathologist Dade County Pub. Schs., Miami, Fla., 1996—; interview com. Dade County Schs., 1996—, child study team, 1996—. Col. Humane Soc.-Broward, Ft. Lauderdale, 1995—, Coconut Grove Arts Festival, Miami, 1996. Mem. Am. Speech-Lang.-Hearing Assn. (cert. clin. competency 1996). Home: 501 El Dorado Pky Plantation FL 33317

LOUDEN, JENNIFER MARIE, writer; b. Bloomington, Ind., Nov. 30, 1962; d. Doyle Paul and Betty Marie (Lowery) L.; m. Christopher Martin Mosio, Dec. 31, 1989; 1 child, Lillian Louden-Mosio. BA, U. So. Calif., 1985. cons. Canadian Imperial Bank, Toronto, 1995; spkr. in health field. Author: The Woman's Comfort Book, 1992, The Couple's Comfort Book, 1994, The Pregnant Woman's Comfort Book, 1995. Mem. Unitarian Soc. Santa Barbara. Home: 369 Paso Robles Dr Santa Barbara CA 93108

LOUDERMILK, PEGGY JOYCE, pediatrics nurse, public health nurse; b. Mar. 1, 1944; d. Marshall Brown and Esther Rebecca (Gaines) Fisher; m. George E. Loudermilk, Dec. 21, 1968; children: Darrell Wayne, Donna Lynn. ADN, Dabney S. Lancaster C.C., 1985. Nursing asst. Alleghany Regional Hosp., Low Moor, Va., 1980-84, nursing extern, 1984-85, staff nurse med./surg., 1985-87, staff nurse ICU, 1987-92; nurse pediatrics Alleghany County/Covington (Va.) Health Dept., 1992—; CPR instr. ARC, Covington, 1984-92. Mem. sch. adv. bd. Alleghany County Sch. System, 1994; local interagy. coun. (State Mandated Orgn.), Clifton Forge, Va., 1993—. Nursing grantee Alleghany Regional Hosp., 1983-85. Fellow Nursing Coun. Alleghany Dist. Republican. Baptist. Home: 2700 Sugar Maple Dr PO Box 52 Low Moor VA 24457

LOUDON, DOROTHY, actress; b. Boston, Sept. 17, 1933; d. James E. and Dorothy Helen (Shaw) L.; m. Norman Paris, Dec. 18, 1971 (dec.). Student, Syracuse U., 1950-51, Emerson Coll., summers 1950, 51, Alviene Sch. Dramatic Art, 1952, 53, The Am. Acad. Dramatic Art. Appeared in nat. repertory cos. of The Effect of Gamma Rays on Man in the Moon Marigolds, 1970, Plaza Suite, 1971, Luv, 1965, Anything Goes, 1967; appeared in Broadway prodns. Nowhere to Go But Up, 1962 (Theatre World award), Sweet Potato, 1968, Fig Leaves Are Falling, 1969 (Tony nominee), Three Men on a Horse, 1969 (Drama Desk award), The Women, 1973, Annie (Tony award, Drama Desk award, Outer Critics Circle award), 1976 (Dance Educators Am. award), Ballroom, 1979 (Tony nominee), Sweeney Todd, 1980, West Side Waltz, 1981 (Sarah Siddons award), Noises Off, 1983 (Tony nomination), Jerry's Girls, 1985 (Tony nomination), Driving Miss Daisy, 1988, Annie 2, 1990, Comedy Tonight, 1994; appeared in film Garbo Talks, 1984; numerous appearances on TV variety and talk shows; latest TV appearances In Performance at the White House, A Salute to Stephen Sondheim at Carnegie Hall, 1992; star TV show Dorothy, 1979; appeared in supper clubs The Blue Angel, Le Ruban Bleu, Persian Room; rec.: (CDs) Saloon, Broadway Baby. Mem. Actors Equity, Screen Actors Guild, AFTRA. Office: Lionel Larner Ltd 119 W 57th St Ste 1412 New York NY 10019*

LOUIS-DREYFUS, JULIA, actress. TV appearances include Saturday Night Live, 1982-85, Day by Day, 1986-89, Seinfield, 1990— (Emmy nomination Supporting Actress-Comedy, 1993, 94); films include Soul Man, 1986, Troll, 1986, Hannah and Her Sisters, 1986, National Lampoon's Christmas Vacation, 1989, Jack the Bear, 1993, North, 1994. Emmy nominations 1992, 93, 94, 95. Office: TPEG Mgmt 9150 Wilshire Blvd Ste 205 Beverly Hills CA 90212-3429

LOUNSBERRY, JOYCE BEVERLY, occupational health consultant; b. Cloquet, Minn., Jan. 31; d. Eino Harold and Lempi Maria (Maijala) Halmet-Sohn; m. Richard Harrington Lounsberry, Mar. 17; children: Teresa, Mark, Kenneth. BA, U. Redlands, 1981; MA, U. Phoenix, 1992, Inst. Transpersonal Psychology, 1995; postgrad., Inst. Transpersonal Psychology, 1996. RN, Minn.; cert. occupl. health nurse, creative expression. Instr. Lawton Sch. Med. Assts., 1968-73; occupational health nurse, pers. generalist Teledyne Semiconductor, 1973-78; corp. dir., occupl. health cons. Calif. Indsl. Med. Clinic, Inc., 1978-84; pres. Lounsberry Cons. Svcs., Cupertino, Calif., 1984—; occupational health cons. Digital Equipment Corp., 1988-92. Sec. Santa Clara (Calif.) Vanguard, 1979-81; bd. dirs. Prince of Peace Ch., Saratoga, Calif., 1993-94; ambassador People to People, China and Mongolia, 1994. Recipient Occupl. Health Nurse award Schering Corp., 1989. Mem. AAOHN (past chmn. coms., bd. dirs.), Am. Holistic Nurses Assn., Calif. Assn. Occupl. Health Nurses (2d v.p., chmn. coms.), Western Assn. Occupl. Health Nurses (pres., v.p., bd. dirs. mem. coms.), El Camino Real Assn. Occupl. Health Nurses (bd. dirs., v.p. chmn. com.), Assn. Transpersonal Psychology. Home: 1598 James Town Dr Cupertino CA

95014 Office: Lounsberry Cons Svcs 1598 James Town Dr Cupertino CA 95014

LOUNSBURY, HELEN MARIE, education educator, consultant; b. Dumont, N.J., Mar. 14, 1939; d. Joseph Anthony Sr. and Helen Teresa (Byrne) Golden; m. Patrick Lounsbury Sr., Jan. 30, 1960; children: Patrick Jr., Elaine Teresa, Amy Jo. BS with distinction, SUNY, 1960; MA in Lit., Vt. Coll., 1993. Tchr. Mohanasen Ctrl. Sch., Rotterdam, N.Y., 1960-62, Berne-Knox-Westerlo Ctrl. Sch., Berne, N.Y., 1962-96; clin. edn. regional supr. SUNY, Oneonta, 1996—; instr. Coll. St. Rose, Albany, N.Y., 1996—; presenter in field; cons. U.S. Dept. Edn.; bd. dirs. Albany County Reading Assn. Co-author: DeBeers, A Factory Family, 1985, Chances Are: Investigations in Probability, 1995. Bd. dirs. Hilltown Cmty. Rsch. Ctr., Berne, 1982-94, Albany County (N.Y.) Rural Housing Alliance, 1984—, Albany City Reading Coun.; coord. Arts Connection Learning Partnership, Albany, 1992-95; active PTA. Named N.Y. Tchr. of Excellence, 1993; NEH Masterworks Study grantee, 1995, N.Y. Found. of the Arts grantee, 1993, 94, Pioneering Partnership grantee PTA, 1996. Mem. PTA (hon. life), N.Y. State Reading Assn. (presenter), N.Y. State Math. Assn. (presenter), Internat. Reading Assn. (presenter), Assn. Math. Tchrs. N.Y. State, N.Y. State English Tchrs. (presenter), Hodge Podge Soc., Civil War Roundtable, Kiwanis, Kappa Delta Pi. Office: Berne-Knox-Westerlo Ctr Sch 1738 Helderberg Trail Berne NY 12023

LOUREY, BECKY J., state legislator; b. 1943; m. Gene Lourey; 11 children. Student, Asbury Coll., U. Minn. Mem. Minn. Ho. of Reps., 1990—, mem. various coms., vice-chair health and housing fin. divsn., mem. internat. trade, tech. and econ. devel. divsn., mem. Legis. Commn. Health Care Access. Democrat. Home: Box 100 Star Rte Kerrick MN 55756 Office: Minn Ho of Reps 421 State Office Bldg Saint Paul MN 55155-1606

LOVE, ADELLE LODZIA, English as second language educator; b. N.Y.C., Aug. 28, 1944; d. Stanley W. and Rose M. (Perlak) Stonina; m. Robert J. Love, Apr. 22, 1967; children: Robert S., Jessica L. BA in Sociology, Elms Coll., 1966, MA in Tchg. ESL, 1990. Cert. elem. edn. grades K-8, ESL secondary edn. grades 5-9, 9-12, bilingual cert. Elem. tchr. Chicopee (Mass.) Pub. Schs., 1966-68, bilingual tutor, 1980-88, adult edn. tchr., 1980—, ESL tchr., coord., 1988—; lectr. Elms. Coll., Chicopee, 1995. Commr. Chicopee (Mass.) Housing Authority, 1984—, vice chair, 1994-95, chair, 1996-97. Mem. Mass. Assn. TESOL, Mass. Assn. Bilingual Educators, St. Vincent de Paul Soc. (v.p.), Polish Jr. League. Democrat. Roman Catholic. Home: 45 Saratoga Ave Chicopee MA 01013-2931

LOVE, AMY DUNDON, business executive, marketing and sales executive; b. Atlanta, Mar. 6, 1966; d. David Milton and Jo Ann (Pleak) L. BBA in Mktg., BBA in Mgmt., Tex. Tech. U., Lubbock, 1988; MBA, Harvard U., Boston, 1993. Unit mgr. Procter & Gamble, Cin., 1988-91; asst. to pres. SLT Environ. Inc., Conroe, Tex., 1992; sr. assoc. Booz, Allen & Hamilton, San Francisco, 1993-95; v.p. sales and mktg. Navigation Technologies, Sunnyvale, Calif., 1995—. Founder Tex. State Student Govt. Pres. Coun., Austin, Tex., 1987; exec. adv. Jr. Achievement, Houston, 1989; mem. exec. bd. Taft/HBS Partnership, Boston, 1989. Mem. Stanford Fast Break Club, Harvard Alumni Club. Democrat. Home: 712 Partridge Ave Menlo Park CA 94025

LOVE, BERLINDA ANIETA, assistant principal, minister; b. Valdosta, Ga., Feb. 3, 1953; d. William Howard and Parrie Bernice (Hart) L. BS in Edn., Trenton State Coll. (now Coll. N.J.), 1978; MA in Ednl. Adminstrn., Rider Coll. (now Rider U.), 1987; ed. clin. pastoral edn. program, Robert Wood Johnson U., 1990; MDiv, Princeton Theol. Sem., 1992; DST (hon.), Ea. N.C. Theol. Inst., 1995. Cert. sch. prin./supr., cert. tchr. nursery sch., elem. sch., elem. and secondary health, elem. and secondary comprehensive sci., N.J.; ordained to ministry Am. Bapt. Chs., 1995. Asst. min. New Hope Bapt. Ch., Newark, 1990-93; assoc. pastor, asst. min. Union Bapt. Ch., Trenton, N.J., 1993—; substitute tchr. Trenton Bd. Edn., 1978-80, tchr. math. and sci., 1980-92, asst. prin., 1994—, tchr. math., sci., 1980-94; project leader extended day program, project leader Better Edn. through Alternatives program Trenton Bd. Edn.; Sunday sch. tchr., supt., dir. Christian edn., tutorial dir. Union Bapt. Ch.; organizer, 1st youth dir. N.J. Conv. Progressive Bapts.; spkr. Women's Day and Prayer Retreat; chaplain Robert Wood Johnson U. Hosp.; premarital/marital counselor Prepare-Enrich, Inc.; guest lectr. Georgian Ct. Coll., 1996. Author: (with others) Women at the Well, Meditations for Healing and Wholeness; writer, pub. (Christian hymns) Holding Me So Dear, Bind Us Together, Lord. Stakeholder Cmty. Ptnrs. for Trenton Youth; counselor Womanspace Ctr. for Battered Women; pregnancy counselor Planned Parenthood, Trenton; mem. exec. com. Capital Assn., Am. Bapt. Chs. N.J.; bd. dirs. Trenton Ecumenical Area Ministry; mem. pulpit com., mem. ch. coun., mem. Bible study Union Bapt. Ch. Honoree, N.J. Conv. Progressive Bapts., 1987, Top Ladies of Distinction, Trenton, 1990; recipient citation The Rare Pages, The Window to the World of Black Bus., N.J., Princeton Theol. Sem. Rev., 1980, proclamation N.J. Gen. Assembly, 1990, commendation, 1992, proclamation Mercer County Bd. Chosen Freeholders, 1987, Mayor Douglas H. Palmer, City of Trenton, 1992. Mem. NAESP, ASCD, NAFE, NAACP (life), Nat. Assn. Secondary Sch. Prins., Nat. Notary Assn., Am. Acad. Religion, Soc. Bibl. Lit., Internat. Platform Assn., N.J. Alliance Black Sch. Educators, N.J. Assn. Female Execs., Trenton Adminstrs. and Suprs. Assn., Zeta Phi Beta (Epsilon Xi Zeta chpt.), Phi Delta Kappa (Pi chpt.), Tau Gamma Delta (Nu Omega charter chpt.). Home: 8 Bittersweet Rd Trenton NJ 08638 Office: Trenton Bd Edn 108 N Clinton Ave Trenton NJ 08618

LOVE, COURTNEY, singer, actress; b. San Francisco, 1964; d. Hank Harrison and Linda Carroll; m. Kurt Cobain, Feb. 1992 (dec.); 1 child, Frances Bean. Singer, writer, musician Hole. Albums include Pretty on the Inside, 1991, Live Through This, 1994; appeared in film Side and Nancy, 1986; television appearance on MTV Unplugged, 1995. Office: care David Geffen Co 9130 Sunset Blvd Los Angeles CA 90069*

LOVE, DIAN, interior architect, educator; b. Bluffton, Ind., Feb. 18, 1940; d. James Edmound and Juaniece (Delight) Morrison L.; 1 child. BS in Interior Design, Purdue U., 1962; student, Toledo U., 1964, Lawrence Inst. Tech., 1964-66; MS in Arch., U. Mich., 1996. Registered interior designer, Ill. With Silver's Bus. Interiors, Detroit, 1964-65, Newell B. Newton Co. Bus. Interiors, Toledo, Ohio, 1963, Benche Assocs. Bus. Interiors, Schenectady, N.Y., 1962; designer, planner interior dept. Giffels and Rossetti Archs., Engrs., Detroit, 1965-66; sr. staff interior designer U. Mich., Ann ARbor, 1966-70, mgr. coord. interior design dept., 1971-73; acting head interior design Univ. Hosp., Ann ARbor, 1978-80; head interior design dept. Samborn, Steketee, Otis and Evans, Toledo, Ohio, 1970; establisher Design Collective, Ann Arbor, Mich., 1974-88; mgr., coord. interior design Kessler, Zeidler, Giffels Joint Venture, Detroit, 1976-77; mgr., coord. interior design for Detroit Gen. Hosp. project Gunnar Birkerts & Assocs., Birmingham, Mich., 1979-80; mgr., coord. interior planning and design Cambridge (Mass.) Seven Assocs., 1984-86; sr. interior designer The Robinson Green Beretta Corp., Providence, 1987; interior designer Dian Love Design Assocs., Providence, 1988-89; sr. staff interior design Payette Assocs., Boston, 1990—; instr. interior design Ea. Mich. U., Ypsilanti, 1977-78; vis. lectr. interior design Sch. Art U. Mich., Ann Arbor, 1978-80; head dept. interior arch. RISD, Providence, 1980-84; coord. interior design curriculum Endicott Coll., Beverly, Mass., 1989-90; facilitator Archeworks Design Lab., Chgo., 1995; spkr., presenter in field. Works include The Children's Hosp., Boston, The New Detroit Gen. Hosp., Edgehill Newport (R.I.) Rehab. Ctr., Genesis Health Syss., Davenport, Iowa, Good Samaritan Med. Ctr., West Palm Beach, Fla., Greewich (Conn.) Hosp. Assn., Lab. for Atmospheric Rsch. Harvard U., Cambridge, Mass., The Jackson Lib., Bar Harbor, Me., Johns Hopkins Hosp. Outpatient Med. Ctr., Balt., Moffet Lab. Molecular Biology Lab., Princeton (N.J.) U., R.I. Hosp., Providence, Rush-Prudential Health Plans, Chgo., Inst. Advanced Scis. and Tech. U. Pa., Phila., New Ctr. Study Human Disease, Yale U., numerous bldgs. U. Mich.; restorations include: Atlantic City Conv. Ctr. and Exhbn. Hall, Tennis Hall of Fame, Newport, R.I.; exhbns. include Ann Arbor Art Assn., 1974, Ella Sharp Mus., Jackson, Mich., 1975; featured in Interiors mag. (Health Care Category Design award 1981), Newsweek mag., others. Office: JNV Assocs/Dian Love 2084 South State St Ann Arbor MI 48104

LOVE, DIANE, painter, designer; b. N.Y.C., Dec. 11, 1939; d. George and Ethel (Gilbert) Stewart; m. Stanley J. Love, Nov. 25, 1959 (div. June 1974); children: Victoria, William Kennedy; m. Robert Emmet Frye, Aug. 6, 1994. BA, Barnard Coll., 1961. Pres. Diane Love Inc., N.Y.C., 1968-85; ind. painter, jewelry designer and home furnishings designer. Author: Flowers and Fabulous, 1975; actor: Part of My Vacation.

LOVE, EDITH HOLMES, theater producer; b. Boston, Oct. 17, 1950; d. Theodore Rufus and Mary (Holmes) L. Student, Denison U., 1968-72; BFA, U. Colo., 1973. Freelance designer various orgns., Atlanta, 1974-75; costumer Atlanta Children's Theatre, 1975-77; prodn. acct. David Gerber Co., L.A., 1980-81; bus. mgr. Alliance Theatre/Atlanta Children's Theatre, 1977-79, adminstrv. dir., 1981-83, gen. mgr., 1983-85, mng. dir., 1985—; bd. dirs. Midtown Bus. Assocs., 1988-94; mem. adv. bd. Stage Hands, Inc., Atlanta, 1983-89; mem. exec. com. Prodn. Valves, Inc., Atlanta, 1985-89; mem. adv. com. arts mgmt. program Carnegie Mellon U.; panelist Nat. Endowment for Arts, 1994-96. Mem. Cultural Olympiad Task Force, 1996 Summer Olympic Games, 1992-96, Met. Atlanta Arts Fund Bd.; bd. dirs. Atlanta Convention and Visitor's Bur., 1993-95. Recipient Deca award for Outstanding Bus. Women in Atlanta, 1992. Mem. League Resident Theatres (treas. 1987—), Atlanta Theatre Coalition (exec. com. 1987-91, pres. 1989), Atlanta C. of C. (bd. dirs. bus. coun. for arts 1988—), Leadership Atlanta. Office: Alliance Theatre Co 1280 Peachtree St NE Atlanta GA 30309-3502

LOVE, GAYLE MAGALENE, special education educator, adult education educat; b. New Orleans, July 25, 1953; d. Lowell F. Sr. and Nathalie Mae (Adams) L.; children: Nathanael Dillard, Raphael. BMEd, Loyola U., New Orleans, 1975, MMEd, 1981. Cert. learning disabled, emotionally disturbed, gifted-talented, adult edn., mild-moderate, elem.-secondary vocal music, prin., spl. sch. prin., parish/city sch. supr. instrn., supervision of student tchg., supr. adult edn. & spl. edn., child search coord. Dean student svcs. Jefferson Parish Sch. Bd., Harvey, La., chmn. spl. edn. dept., 1990-93; adult educator instr.; chmn. Sch. Bldg. Level Com., 1994-96; presenter St. Joseph the Worker Cath. Ch., 1988, Very Spl. Arts Week Jefferson Parish Pub. Sch. Sys., 1989, 90, 91, 92, 93, 94, 95, 96; mem. spl. edn. alternative curriculum com., 1990—, Urban Ctr. Tchrs. Devel. com. U. New Orleans, 1990-91. Mem. NAFE, ASCD, Coun. Exceptional Children (workshop presenter 1990), Jefferson Assn. Pub. Sch. Adminstrs., East Bank Jefferson Parish Parent Adv. Coun., New Orleans C. of C. (com. Alliance for Quality, small bus. improvement team), La. Assn. Sch. Execs., Phi Beta, Kappa Delta Pi, Alpha Kappa Alpha. Home: 1740 Burnley Dr Marrero LA 70072-4522

LOVE, MARGARET COLGATE, lawyer; b. Balt., June 9, 1942; d. H.A. and Margaret West (Dennis) L.; 1 child, Jenny West. BA, Sarah Lawrence Coll., 1963; MA, U. Pa., 1969; JD, Yale U., 1977. Bar: Washington, 1977. Lawyer Shea & Gardner, Washington, 1977-79; spl. counsel office of legal counsel U.S. Dept. Justice, Washington, 1979-88, dep. assoc. atty. gen., 1988-89, assoc. dep. atty. gen., 1989-90, pardon atty., 1990—. Mem. ABA (standing com. on ethics and profl. responsibility chair 1994—). Office: Dept Justice 500 1st St NW Fl 4 Washington DC 20530*

LOVE, SANDRA RAE, information specialist; b. San Francisco, Feb. 20, 1947; d. Benjamin Raymond and Charlotte C. Martin; B.A. in English, Calif. State U., Hayward, 1968; M.S. in L.S., U. So. Calif., 1969; m. Michael D. Love, Feb. 14, 1971. Tech. info. specialist Lawrence Livermore (Calif.) Nat. Lab., 1969—. Mem. Spl. Libraries Assn. (sec. nuclear sci. div. 1980-82, chmn. 1983-84, bull. editor 1987-89), Beta Sigma Phi. Democrat. Episcopalian. Office: Lawrence Livermore Nat Lab PO Box 808 # L387 Livermore CA 94551-0808

LOVE, SHARON IRENE, elementary education educator; b. Pontiac, Mich., July 27, 1950; d. James and Ethlyn (Cole) M.; married; 1 child, Sheralyn Reneé. BS, Western Mich. U., 1964; postgrad., Oakland U., Rochester, Mich. Cert. elem. educator, early childhood educator, Mich. Tchr. kindergarten Pontiac Bd. Edn., 1964-69, 76-83, 87—, tchr. 1st grade, 1965-66, tchr. 4th grade, 1983-84, tchr. 2d grade, 1984-87; tchr. trainer triple I.E. classroom instruction Emerson Elem. Sch., Pontiac, 1988-89; trainer Math Their Way, Pontiac Sch. Sys., 1989, leadership, 1990; trainer Mich. Health Model Oakland Schs., Waterfort, 1987; co-chair com. for developing and writing new Fine Arts curriculum for Pontiac Sch. Dist., 1993-94; head tchr. kindergarten pilot Bethune Elem. Sch., 1995-96. Chair coord. coun. Walt Whitman Elem. Schs., Pontiac, 1987-91; mem. PTA, 1970-90; chair coord. coun. Webster Elem. Sch., 1993-94. Creative Art grantee Pontiac PTA, 1965; recipient cert. Appreciation Pontiac Blue Ribbon Com., 1991, cert. for outstanding educatorMich. Gov. Engler, 1991. Mem. NAACP, Mich. Edn. Assn., Pontiac Edn. Assn. (del. 1965-66). Office: Pontiac Bd Edn 350 Wide Track Dr E Pontiac MI 48342-2243

LOVE, SUSAN DENISE, accountant, consultant, small business owner; b. Portland, Oreg., Aug. 5, 1954; d. Charles Richard and Betty Lou (Reynolds) Beck; m. Daniel G. Oliveros, Dec. 21, 1979 (div. Nov. 1983); m. Michael Dean Love, Aug. 24, 1984 (div. Mar. 1989); m. Michael Eugene Watson, July 28, 1990 (div. Dec. 1994). BA in Graphic Design, Portland State U., 1976. Office mgr. Rogers Machinery Co., Portland, 1972-77; exec. sec. Creighton Shirtmakers, N.Y.C., 1977-80; dir. adminstrn. Henry Grethel div. Manhattan Industries, N.Y.C., 1980-81; exec. asst. S.B. Tanger and Assocs., N.Y.C., 1981-83; exec. asst., bookkeeper M Life Ins. Co., Portland, 1983-84; acct. cons., owner Office Assistance, Portland, 1984—; owner WE LOVE KIDS Clothing Store, Portland, 1985—; owner, pres. Oreg. Music and Entertainment, 1989—; sec./treas. Designers' Roundtable, Portland, 1985-88; co-owner, The Tuxedo Club, 1992—. Mem. Oreg. State Pub. Interest Rsch. Group, Portland, 1985-90, Oreg. Fair Share,Salem, 1987, mem. adv. bd. career and life options program Clackamas Community Coll., 1989-91. Mem. Women Entrepreneurs Oreg. (bd. dirs. 1988-92, pres. 1992-95, Mem. of Yr. award 1991, 95), Brentwood-Darlington Neighborhood Assn. (treas. 1993—), North Clackamas County C. of C., Nat. Fedn. Ind. Bus., Outer S.E. Coalition. Democrat. Office: Oreg Music & Entertainment PO Box 1784 Clackamas OR 97015-1784

LOVEJOY, ANN LOUISE, development director, insurance company executive; b. Baker, Oreg., Aug. 18, 1949; d. Victor and Norma (Peters) Lovejoy; m. Pierre Ventur, June 9, 1975; 1 child, Conrad Ventur. Bachelors, U. Wash., 1971, Masters, 1975. Bot. field asst. (grant) Yale U., San Luis, Guatemala, 1975-77; editorial asst., micro personal computer trainer Yale U., New Haven, Conn., 1977-86; tech. trainer Bunker Ramo/Allied Signal, Shelton, Conn., 1984-86; sr. training specialist Bank of Boston, Springfield, Mass., 1986-87, MassMutual Life Ins., Springfield, Mass., 1987-96, CIGNA, Hartford, Conn., 1996—. Mem. bd. corporators Springfield Metro YMCA, 1994—. Mem. ASTD (bd. dirs. Pioneer Valley 1986-91), Assn. for Computing Machinery. Office: CIGNA 900 Cottage Grove Rd A145 Hartford CT 06152-1011

LOVEJOY, JEAN HASTINGS, social services counselor; b. Battle Creek, Mich., July 1, 1913; d. William Walter and Elizabeth (Fairbank) H.; m. Allen Perry, March 27, 1912; children: Isabel L. Best, Linda L. Ewald, Elizabeth L. Fulton, Margaret L. Baldwin, Helen L. Battad. BA, Mt. Holyoke Coll., So. Hadley, Mass., 1935. Traveling sec. Student Volun. Movement, N.Y.C., 1935; bookkeeper Hartford Consumers Co-operative, Conn., 1944; tchr. Pre-School, Congl. Ch., W Hartford, Conn., 1944-45; instr. St. John's U., Shanghai, China; tchr. Edn., 1st Congl. Ch., Berkeley, Calif., 1958-59; instr. Tunghai U., Taiwan, 1960-63; sec. Pres. Tunghai U., Taichung, Taiwan, 1960-63. Pres. Ecumenical Assn. for Housing, San Rafael, 1971, 78-80; founding mem. Hospice of Havasu, 1982, pres. bd. dirs., 1985-87, vol. trainer, 1987-92, bereavement coord., 1989-92; bereavement vol. Cmty. Hospice, Tucson; vol. friendly visitor N.W. Interfaith Ctr., Tucson, 1995—. Recipient OACC Sr. Achievement award, 1991; named Vol. of Yr., Marin County, Calif., 1970, 79; street named Lovejoy Way in her honor Novato (Calif.) City Coun., 1980. Mem. LWV (program v.p. Pierce County chpt. 1967, pres. cen. Marin County chpt. 1973-75, legis. analyst land use 1979-80, Calif. chpt.). Mem. United Ch. of Christ (Stephen min.). Home: Apt 8208 7500 N Calle Sin Envidia Tucson AZ 85718-7306

LOVELACE, KATHLEEN, librarian, art educator; b. Anna, Ill., Apr. 23, 1953; d. Bryan Wood and Frances P. (Perkins) Lovelace; m. Ronald A. Canada, June, 1978 (div. 1980); m. Mark Arthur Kennedy, Oct. 1, 1982; children: Gwenn, Christine, Hugh, Andrew. BA, Augustana Coll., Rock Island, Ill., 1976; MA, U. Ill., 1978, No. Ill. U., 1988. Vol. and advocate coord. Lake County Ct. Svcs., Waukegan, Ill., 1980-84, juvenile/intake counselor, 1986-87; ref. assoc. Warren-Newport Pub. Libr., Gurnee, Ill., 1987-90; pub. svc. libr. Donnelley Libr., Lake Forest, Ill., summer 1994; head ref. and instrn. Barat Coll. Libr., Lake Forest, 1990—; head ceramics dept., figure drawing coord. David Adler Cultural Ctr., Libertyville, Ill., 1981-83; free-lance art instr., 1991—; continuing edn. coord. LIBRAS, Inc., 1996—, bibliographic instrn. SIG-chair, 1993-94, ref. SIG chair, 1992-93. Vol. Woodland Sch. Dist. 50, Gages Lake, Ill., 1989-95, Art Inst. Chgo., 1982-83; vol., mem. art bd. David Adler cultural Ctr., Libertyville, 1982-83, judge Festival of the Arts, 1982. Ill. State Libr. L.S.C.A. Libr. Tng. grantee, 1995; Charles Merriam fellow U. Ill., 1976. Mem. ALA, Am. Assn. Mus. Office: Barat College Library 700 E Westleigh Rd Lake Forest IL 60031

LOVELACE, ROSE MARIE SNIEGON, federal space agency administrator; b. Sweet Hall, Va., Feb. 19, 1937; d. Adolph and Annie (Mickel) Sniegon; m. William Wayne Lovelace, Aug. 11, 1962. Degree in bus., Longwood Coll., 1957. Adminstrv. aide Dept. of Navy, Washington, 1957-60; adminstrv. asst. Joint Blood Coun.-Pvt., Washington, 1960-63; exec. staff NASA, Washington, 1963-73, program analyst-specialist, 1973-80, chief adminstrv. ops. and Congl. affairs br., 1980-92; ret., 1992; cons. NASA, 1992—. Editor, author: (pamphlet) Space Operations, 1989, (video) Space Communications, 1991. Pres. Jr. Achievement Co., 1953-55, Kettering Recreation Coun., Largo, Md., 1974-76; league coord. U.S. Tennis Assn., Anne Arundel County, Md., 1989-91, team capt., 1985—; active various civic orgns. including LWV, ch., community and county functions, 1957—. Recipient Jr. Achievement Exec. award and Nat. Speakers award, 1954, Gold medal Parks and Planning, Prince Georges County, Md., 1976, Exceptional Svc. award NASA, 1983, Exceptional Svc. medal NASA, 1992. Mem. U.S. Tennis Assn. (county coord. 1989-91), Anne Arundel County Tennis Assn., Big Vanilla Raquet Club, Severn Town Club (pres. 1996—). Republican. Methodist. Office: NASA 600 Independence Ave SW Washington DC 20546-0002

LOVELACE, SUSAN GARACH, social worker, researcher; b. Hartford, Conn., Dec. 22, 1964; d. Mark Bernard and Patricia Ann (Beaudin) Garach; m. Edward Carl Francis Lovelace, June 18, 1994. BA in Sociology, Wheaton Coll., 1986; MSW, Boston U., 1992. Milieu counselor Kennedy Meml. Hosp., Boston, 1986-87; afterschool program coord. Bay Cove Elem. Sch., Boston, 1988-89; sr. svc. analyst AETNA Ins. Co., Hartford, 1989-90; rsch. dir. Mass. Joint Com. on Human Svcs., Boston, 1992—; steering com. mem. Spl. Com. on Family Support and the Child Welfare Sys., Boston, 1994—. Foster care reviewer Dept. Social Svcs., Boston, 1991-92; vol. Tax Equity Alliance of Mass., Boston, 1992—. Tina J. Howell scholar Boston U. Sch. Social Work, 1991-92. Mem. Nat. Assn. Social Work Mgrs. Democrat. Roman Catholic. Office: Joint Com on Human Svcs & Elderly Affairs State House Rm 22 Boston MA 02133

LOVELAND, CHRISTINE ANN, anthropology educator; b. Watertown, S.D., July 28, 1946; d. Earl Joseph and Grace Leanore (Philp) Brown; m. Franklin Olds Loveland III, Nov. 22, 1969; children: Elizbeth Rachel, David Franklin. BA, Carleton Coll., 1968; MA, Duke U., 1973, PhD, 1975. Adj. instr. Wilson Coll., Chambersburg, Pa., 1976-84; asst. prof. sociology and anthropology Shippensburg (Pa.) U., 1985-86, assoc. prof. anthropology, 1986-91, prof., 1991—; mem. nat. panel profl. advisors Nat. Multiple Sclerosis Soc., N.Y.C., 1994—. Editor, author: Sex Roles and Social Change in Native Lower Central American Societies, 1982; contbg. author: End Results and Starting Points: Expanding the Field of Disability Studies, 1996; contbr. articles to profl. jours. Vol. Pa. Assn. for Blind, Gettysburg, 1984-91. Named Vol. of Yr., Gettysburg chpt. Pa. Assn. for Blind, 1988; Title VI fellow NDEA, 1968-70; grantee Shippensburg U., 1987-91, Nat. Multiple Sclerosis Soc., 1992-93. Fellow Am. Anthrop. Assn.; mem. Soc. for Disability Studies, Am. Ethnol. Soc., Soc. for Med. Anthropology. Office: Shippensburg U 1871 Old Main Dr Shippensburg PA 17257-2299

LOVELAND, JACQUELINE JANE, neuroscientist, biologist; b. Point Pleasant Borough, N.J., Feb. 16, 1952; d. George Clark and Virginia Mae (Skimmons) L.; m. Alan Dale Nunes, Aug. 22, 1974 (div. Aug. 1978); 1 child, Emmett Todd Nunes. BA, San Jose State U., 1981, MA, 1987. Rsch. assoc. NASA-Ames Rsch. Ctr., Mt. View, Calif., 1980-83; supr., sr. case mgr. Cmty. Companions, Inc., San Jose, Calif., 1983-85, cons., 1985; neurosci. biologist Syntex Rsch. Inst. of Pharmacology, San Jose, Calif., 1985-93; safety pharmacology biologist Syntex Rsch. Inst. of Pathology, Toxicology & Metabolism, Palo Alto, 1993-95; clin. rsch. assoc. Roche Global Devel., Palo Alto, 1995—. Contbr. articles to profl. jours.; author abstracts. Mem. AAAS, Soc. Neurosci., Drug Info. Assn., Psi Chi, Phi Theta Kappa. Office: Roche Global Devel 3401 Hillview Ave Palo Alto CA 94304-1397

LOVELESS, KATHY LYNNE, client services executive; b. Corsicana, Tex., Mar. 7, 1961; d. Vernon Ray and Barbara Alice (Brown) L. BA, Baylor U., 1983. Adminstrv. asst. InterFirst Bank, Dallas, 1983-85; adminstrv. asst. Chaparral Steel Co., Midlothian, Tex., 1985-89, audio/visual coord., 1989-93; freelance computer instr. Duncanville, Tex., 1993-94; tng. specialist U. Tex. Southwestern Med. Ctr., Dallas, 1994-95, supr. client svcs. ctr., 1995—. Pres., v.p. Midlothian Cmty. Theatre, 1990-93, mem., 1987-94; v.p. Lovers Ln. United Meth. Ch. Choir, Dallas, 1994, 95, Adminstrv. Bd., 1995-96; chmn. worship and mem. care com. Elmwood United Meth. Ch., 1990, 91; bd. dirs. Trinity River Mission, Dallas, 1994, 95, 96. Mem. NAFE, AAUW, USA Film Festival, Am. Film Inst. Home: 8903 San Benito Way Dallas TX 75218

LOVELESS, PEGGY ANN, social work administrator; b. Decatur, Ill., June 9, 1952; d. William Walter and Rose Marie (Sheppard) L. Student, Ill. State U., 1970-72; BA, U. Ill., 1974, MSW, 1976. Cert. lic. clin. social worker; cert. in health care ethics; diplomate Am. Bd. Examiners in Clin. Social Work. Social worker Met.-Police Social Svcs., Urbana, Ill., 1976-80; clin. supr. Ctr. Children's Svcs., Danville, Ill., 1980-84; med. social worker Sarah Bush Lincoln Health Ctr., Mattoon, Ill., 1984-86, Portland (Oreg.) Adventist Med. Ctr., 1986-88; dept. supr., social worker Oreg. Health Scis. U., Portland, 1988-92, interim dir. social work, 1992-93, asst. dir. social work Ctr. Ethics, 1993-96, mem. ethics consulting svc., 1991-96; behavioral health case mgr. PacifiCare Behavioral Health, 1996—. Vol. Goose Hollow Family Homeless Shelter, Portland, 1993-94, vol. supr., 1994-95. Mem. Soc. Social Work Adminstrs. Health Care (com. nominations 1995-96, chair, pres. meeting planning com. 1994), Oreg. Soc. Social Work Adminstrs. Health Care (pres. elect 1993, pres. 1994, chair/conf. com. 1995). Office: PacifiCare Behavioral Health 5 Centerpoint Dr Lake Oswego OR 97035

LOVELL, EMILY KALLED, journalist; b. Grand Rapids, Mich., Feb. 25, 1920; d. Abdo Rham and Louise (Claussen) Kalled; student Grand Rapids Jr. Coll., 1937-39; BA, Mich. State U., 1944; MA, U. Ariz., 1971; m. Robert Edmund Lovell, July 4, 1947. Copywriter, asst. traffic mgr. Sta. WOOD, Grand Rapids, 1944-46; traffic mgr. KOPO, Tucson, 1946-47; reporter, city editor Alamogordo (N.Mex.) News, 1948-51; Alamogordo corr., feature writer Internat. News Service, Denver, 1950-54; Alamogordo corr., feature writer El Paso Herald-Post, 1954-65; Alamogordo news dir., feature writer Tularosa (N.Mex.) Basin Times, 1957-59; co-founder, editor, pub. Otero County Star, Alamogordo, 1961-65; newscaster KALG, Alamogordo, 1964-65; free lance feature writer Denver Post, N.Mex. Mag., 1949-69; corr. Electronics News, N.Y.C., 1959-63, 65-69; Sierra Vista (Ariz.) corr. Ariz. Republic, 1966; free lance editor N.Mex. Pioneer Interviews, 1967-69; asst. dir. English skills program Ariz. State U., 1976; free-lance editor, writer, 1977—; part-time tchr., lectr. U. Pacific, 1981-86; part-time interpreter Calif., 1983-91, Interpreters Unlimited, Oakland, 1985-91; sec., dir. Star Pub. Co., Inc., 1961-64, pres., 1964-65. 3d v.p., publicity chmn. Otero County Community Concert Assn., 1950-65; mem. Alamogordo Zoning Commn., 1955-57; mem. founding com. Alamogordo Central Youth Activities Com., 1957; vice chmn. Otero County chpt. Nat. Found. Infantile Paralysis, 1958-61; charter mem. N.M. Citizens Council for Traffic Safety, 1959-61; pres. Sierra Vista Hosp. Aux., 1966; pub. rels. chmn. Ft. Huachuca chpt. ARC, 1966. Mem. nat. bd. Hospitalized Vets. Writing Project, 1972—; vol. instr. autobiography & creative writing, 1991—. Recipient 1st Pl. awards N.Mex. Press Assn., 1961, 62. Pub. Interest award Nat. Safety Council, 1962. 1st Pl. award Nat. Fedn. Press Women, 1960, 62; named Woman of Year Alamogordo, 1960. Editor of Week Pubs. Aux., 1962, adm. N.Mex. Navy,

1962, col. a.d.c. Staff Gov. N.Mex., 1963, Woman of Yr., Ariz. Press Women, 1973. Mem. N.Mex. (past sec.), Ariz. (past pres.) press women, N.Mex. Fedn. Womens Clubs (past dist. pub. rels. chmn., hon. life Alamogordo), N.Mex. Hist. Soc. (life), N.Mex. Fedn. Bus. and Profl. Womens Clubs (past pres., hon. life Alamogordo), Pan Am. Round Table Alamogordo, Theta Sigma Phi (past nat. 3d v.p.), Phi Kappa Phi. Democrat. Moslem. Author: A Personalized History of Otero County, New Mexico, 1963; Weekend Away, 1964; Lebanese Cooking, Streamlined, 1972; A Reference Handbook for Arabic Grammar, 1974, 77; contbg. author: The Muslim Community in North America, 1983. Home: 3400 Wagner Height Rd # 226 Stockton CA 95209

LOVELL, KATHRYN SHEEHY, elementary education educator; b. Butte, Mont., Sept. 16, 1948; d. Michael Joseph and Frances Marie (Boyle) Sheehy; m. Willard Francis Lovell, Dec. 27, 1980. BS, Western Mont. Coll., 1970; MEd, Lesley Coll., 1993. 3d grade tchr. Sherman Sch., Butte, 1970-73, kindergarten tchr., 1973-77; kindergarten tchr. McKinley Sch., Butte, 1977-80, 3d grade tchr., 1980-86; 3d grade tchr. West Elem. Sch., Butte, 1986-88; 2d grade tchr. Margaret Leary Sch., Butte, 1988-93, tchr. STEP lead, 1993—; mem. student tchg. partnership We. Mont. Coll., 1992—; Keystone mentor, 1995—. Keystone grantee NSF, 1995—. Mem. AAUW, S.W. Mont. Reading Coun., Alpha Delta Kappa. Home: 4 Mile Vue Butte MT 59701

LOVELL, SHARON JANE, accountant, consultant; b. Collegeville, Ark., July 2, 1943; d Henry Homer and Hazel Jane (Batchelor) Rosencrans; m. John Lovell, Dec. 1961 (div. Jan., 1974); children: J. Richard, Jeffrey Scott. Student, Little Rock U., 1961-62, BS in Acctg., 1973; student, Henderson U., Arkadelphia, Ark., 1963-64. CPA, Ark. Rev. agt. IRS, Little Rock, 1974-90; various mgmt. positions IRS, Washington, 1990-93, team mgr. coord. examination program, 1993-94, dir. corp. specialties, 1994-96; nat. tax svcs. mgr. Coopers & Lybrand, Washington, 1996—; instr. in Russia, U.S. Treasury Dept., 1994-95.

LOVELL-ALBERT, JOAN ELLEN, mental health professional; b. Alton, Ill., Oct. 24, 1955; d. Lee Roy and Arlou (Brown) Waller; 1 child, Frank. AS, RN, Monticello Coll., Godfrey, Ill., 1974; BA in Social Work, Calif. State U., Northridge, 1977; MA in Psychology, Calif. Grad. Inst., Westwood, 1988, PhD in Psychology, 1996. RN, Calif., psychol. asst., Calif. Nurse, asst. head nurse St. Francis Med. Ctr., 1977-80; crisis resolution unit nurse Dept. Mental Health L.A. County, L.A., 1983-85, homeless coord., 1985-87, patient rights advocate, 1987-92, children and youth svc. coord., 1993—; mental health cons. Fed. Project 90044, L.A., 1992-93; owner Medi Fact Rsch., Huntington Beach, Calif., 1992—; cons. Philippine-Am. Orgn., Long Beach, Calif., 1985-87. Ct. advocate for victims of rape L.A. Commn. Against Assaults on Women, L.A., 1977, rape hotline counselor, 1976-77. Mem. APA (affiliate), Calif. Psychol. Assn.

LOVENHEIM, BARBARA IRENE, editor, writer; b. Rochester, N.Y., July 19, 1940; d. Clifford Norman and May (Yampolsky) L. BA, Barnard Coll., 1962; MA in Eng. Lit., U. Wis., 1963; PhD in Eng. Lit., U. Rochester, 1970. Lectr. in Eng. Queens Coll., Flushing, N.Y., 1966-70; asst. prof. Eng. Baruch Coll., N.Y.C., 1971-75; account exec. Ruder & Finn, N.Y.C., 1976-78; London arts corr. The Internat. Herald Tribune, Paris, 1979-80; text editor Glamour Mag., N.Y.C., 1980-82; writer, editor, media cons. various pubs., N.Y.C., 1982-95; editor-in-chief, founder NYcitylife, 1995—; adj. asst. prof. journalism NYU, 1990-95. Author: The Marriage Odds, 1990; contbr. articles to pubs. including The N.Y. Times, The L.A. Times, McCalls Mag., The Wall St. Jour., Elle, N.Y. Mag., The Village Voice, Redbook, Working Mother, Working Woman, others. Founder, pres. Barnard Columbia Alumni Social Com. Inc., N.Y.C., 1973-83. N.Y. State Regents fellow, 1958-62, U. Rochester Tchg. fellow, 1964-66. Home: 315 E 65th St New York NY 10021

LOVE-SCHIMENTI, CHERYL D., scientist, researcher; b. Ft. Worth, Tex., Oct. 1, 1951; d. Curtis Leroy and Ella Catherine (Patterson) Love; m. Scott Micheal Shelley, Oct. 27, 1972 (div. May 1974); m. Dan Schimenti, July 21, 1979. BS in Cell & Molecular Biology, San Francisco State U., 1985; PhD in Biomed. Scis., U. Tex., 1993. Rsch. asst. Medi-Physics, Emeryville, Calif., 1985-86; staff rsch. assoc. VAMC, San Francisco, 1986-89; postdoctoral fellow U. Calif. San Francisco, 1994, U. Calif. San Francisco, VA Med. Ctr., 1994—. Contbr. articles to profl. jours. NCI Tng. grantee NIH, 1990, 91, 92; postdoctoral fellow U.S. Army Breast Cancer Rsch. Program, 1996—. Mem. AAUW, Am. Assn. Cancer Rsch. Home: 16 28th St San Francisco CA 94110 Office: UCSF/VAMC Endocrine Unit 111N 4150 Clement St San Francisco CA 94121

LOVETRI, JEANNETTE LOUISE, voice educator; b. Southampton, N.Y., Apr. 2, 1949; d. James John and Aline Rita (Zimmer) L. Student, Manhattan Sch. Music, 1967-68, Juilliard Sch., 1971-72; pvt. dance, piano and vocal study. Singer opera, cabaret, summer stock, oratorios, jazz, 1966-80; owner voice studio, Greenwich, Conn., 1970-75, N.Y.C., 1975—; tchr. voice music dept. Upsala Coll., East Orange, N.J., 1976-81; founder, dir. The Voice Workshop, pub. speaking seminar, 1983—; guest lectr. Boston Conservatory of Music, 1987-89, Faculty Internat. Symposium Care of Profl. Voice, N.Y., 1987—, 1st Internat. Congress Arts Medicine, N.Y.C., 1992, British Voice Assn., Actors Ctr., London, 1993, 1st Internat. Music Theatre Tng., Australia, Wagner Coll., N.Y., 1994, Loyola Coll. Balt., 1994, Towson State Coll., Balt., 1996, N.A.T.S. Va. Chpt., 1996; lectr., workshop leader, various U.S. cities, Amsterdam, and Copenhagen; sci. rschr. on vocal acoustics Royal Swedish Tech. Inst., 1990, master classes, 1991; guest vocal coach for Meredith Monk at Houston Grand Opera, 1991. Mem. N.Y. Singing Tchrs. Assn. (bd. dir., pres., former chmn. Music Theatre Com. Am. Symposium), Nat. Assn. Tchrs. Singing.

LOVETT, CLARA MARIA, university administrator, historian; b. Trieste, Italy, Aug. 4, 1939; came to U.S., 1962; m. Benjamin F. Brown. BA equivalent, U. Trieste, 1962; MA, U. Tex.-Austin, 1967, PhD, 1970. Prof. history Baruch Coll., CUNY, N.Y.C., 1971-82, asst. provost, 1980-82; chief European div. Library of Congress, Washington, 1982-84; dean Coll. Arts and Scis., George Washington U., Washington, 1984-88; provost, v.p. academic affairs, George Mason U., Fairfax, Va., 1988-93; on leave from George Mason U.; dir. Forum on Faculty Roles and Rewards Am. Assn. for Higher Edn., 1993-94; pres. No. Ariz. U., Flagstaff, 1994—; vis. lectr. Fgn. Service Inst., Washington, 1979-85; bd. dirs. Inst. for Research in History, N.Y.C., 1981-82; exec. council Conf. Group on Italian Politics, 1980-83, others; lectr., cons. Fgn. Service Inst. State Dept., 1979—; adv. bd. European program Wilson Ctr., 1986—; bd. dirs. Assn. Am. Colls., 1990—. Author: The Democratic Movement in Italy 1830-1876, 1982 (H.R. Marraro Prize, Soc. Italian Hist. Studies); Giuseppe Ferrari and the Italian Revolution, 1979 (Phi Alpha Theta book award); Carlo Cattaneo and the Politics of Risorgimento, 1972 (Soc. for Italian Hist. Studies Dissertation award), (bibliography) Contemporary Italy, 1985; co-editor: Women, War, and Revolution, 1980, (essays) State of Western European Studies, 1984; contbr. sects. to publs. U.S., Italy. Organizer Dem. clubs Bklyn., 1972-76; exec. com. Palisades Citizens Assn., Washington, 1985-87; vestry mem. St. David's Episc. Ch., Washington, 1986-89. Fellow Guggenheim Found., 1978-79, Woodrow Wilson Internat. Ctr. for Scholars, 1979 (adv. bd. West European program), Am. Council Learned Socs., 1976, Bunting Inst. of Radcliffe Coll., 1975-76, others. Named Educator of Yr., Va. Fedn. of Bus. and Profl. Women, 1992. Mem. Am. Hist. Assn. (officer 1984-87), Am. Assn. Higher Edn. (cons. 1979—), Council for European Studies, Soc. for Italian Hist. Studies, Conf. Group on Italian Politics, others. Avocations: choral singing, swimming. Office: No Ariz U Office of Pres PO Box 4092 Flagstaff AZ 86011

LOVING, SUSAN B., lawyer, former state official; m. Dan Loving; children: Lindsay, Andrew, Kendall. BA with distinction, U. Okla., 1972, JD, 1979. Asst. atty. gen. Office of Atty. Gen., 1983-87, first asst. atty. gen., 1987-91; atty. gen. State of Okla., Oklahoma City, 1991-94; atty. Lester & Bryant, P.C., Oklahoma City, 1995—; with Lester, Loving & Davies, Edmond, Okla., 1996—; Master Ruth Bader Ginsburg Inn of Ct.; bd. dirs. Bd. for Freedom of Info., Okla., Inc., Boy Scouts Am., Legal Aid of West Okla., Okla. Com. for Prevention of Child Abuse, Inst. for Ch. Adv.; mem. med. steering com. Partnership for Drug Free Okla., 1993—; adv. bd. Law and You Found. Vice chmn. Pardon and Parole Bd., 1995—; bd. dirs. Bd. for Freedom of Info., Okla. Inc., Boy Scouts Am., Legal Aid of West Okla., Okla. Com. for Prevention of Child Abuse; mem. med. steering com. Partnership for Drug Free Okla., Inst. for Child Advocacy, 1996—; mem. adv. bd. Law and You Found. Recipient Nat. Red Ribbon Leadership award Nat. Fedn. Parents, Headliner award, By-liner award Okla. City and Tulsa Women in Comm., First Friend of Freedom award, Freedom of Info., Okla., Dir. award Okla. Dist. Attys. Assn. Mem. Okla. Bar Assn. (past chmn. adminstrv. law sect., mem. adminstrn. of justice com., profl. responsibility commn.), Phi Beta Kappa. Office: Lester Loving & Davies PLLC Ste 102 601 N Kelly Edmond OK 73003

LOVINGER, SOPHIE LEHNER, child psychologist; b. N.Y.C., Jan. 15, 1932; d. Nathaniel Harris and Anne (Rosen) Lehner; m. Robert Jay Lovinger, June 18, 1957; children: David Fredrick, Mark Andrew. BA, Bklyn. Coll., 1954; MS, City Coll., N.Y.C., 1959; PhD, NYU, 1967. Sr. clin. psychologist Bklyn. State Hosp., 1960-61; grad. fellow NYU, N.Y.C., 1961-67; psychotherapy trainee Jamaica (N.Y.) Ctr., 1964-67; asst. prof. Hofstra U., Hempstead, N.Y., 1967-70; prof. Cen. Mich. U., Mt. Pleasant, 1970—; psychotherapist, psychoanalyst N.Y.C. and Mt. Pleasant, Mich., 1964—. Author: Learning Disabilities and Games, 1978, Language-Learning Disabilities, 1991; contbr. articles to profl. jours. Fellow Am. Orthopsychiat. Assn.; mem. Am. Psychol. Assn., Nat. Register Health Svc. Providers. Office: 405 S Main St Mount Pleasant MI 48858-2522

LOVINS, L. HUNTER, public policy institute executive; b. Middlebury, Vt., Feb. 26, 1950; d. Paul Millard and Farley (Hunter) Sheldon; m. Amory Bloch Lovins, Dept. 6, 1979; 1 child, Nanuq. BA in Sociology, Pitzer Coll., 1972, BA in Polit. Sci., 1972; JD, Loyola U., L.A., 1975; LHD, U. Maine, 1982. Bar: Calif. 1975. Asst. dir. Calif. Conservation Project, L.A., 1973-79; exec. dir., co-founder Rocky Mountain Inst., Snowmass, Colo., 1982—; vis. prof. U. Colo., Boulder, 1982; Henry R. Luce vis. prof. Dartmouth Coll., Hanover, N.H., 1982; pres. Nighthawk Horse Co., 1993, Lovins Group, 1994. Co-author: Brittle Power, 1982, Energy Unbound, 1986, Least-Cost Energy Solving the CO2 Problem, 2d edit., 1989. Bd. dirs. Renew Am., Basalt and Rural Fire Protection Dist., E Source, Roaring Fork Polocrosse Assn.; vol. EMT and firefighter. Recipient Mitchell prize Woodlands Inst., 1982, Right Livelihood Found. award, 1983, Best of the New Generation award Esquire Mag., 1984. Mem. Calif. Bar Assn., Am. Quarter Horse Assn., Am. Polocrosse Assn. Office: Rocky Mountain Inst 1739 Snowmass Creek Rd Snowmass CO 81654-9199

LOVIO-RODRIGUEZ, JESSICA BERTHA, accountant; b. Miami, Fla., Apr. 29, 1971; d. Hector Jose and Sonia (Sanchez) L.; m. David Rodriguez. B in Acctg. with honors, Fla. Internat. U., 88-92, MS in Taxation, 93. CPA, Fla. Bookkeeper Internat. Devel. & Investment Corp., Miami, 88-90; mgmt. intern Pan Am. World Airways, Miami, 90; contr. Capital Devel. & Investment Corp., Miami, 91-93; sr. tax acct. Morrison, Brown, Argiz & Co., Miami, 1993-96; with Price Waterhouse LLP, Miami, 1996—. Mem. AICPA, Fla. Inst. CPAs, Cuban Am. CPA Assn., Miami Bd. Realtors. Republican. Roman Catholic. Office: Price Waterhouse LLP Ste 3000 First Union Fin Ctr Miami FL 33131

LOVRICH, KATHERINE MARIE, education professional; b. Salt Lake City, Dec. 22, 1944; d. Charles Hansen and Ruth Marie (Chaney) Ackerson; m. Nicholas Peter Lovrich, Jr., Sept. 9, 1967; 1 child, Nichole Ruth. BS Psychology, Stanford U., 1967; Tchg. Cert., Metro. State Coll., Denver, 1972; MAT, DePauw Univ., 1977. AFDC social worker L.A. County, 1967-70; early childhood tchr. Denver Pub. Schs., 1972-74; remedial reading and math. tchr. Greencastle (Ind.) Pub. Schs., 1974-77; reading instr. Wash. State U., Pullman, 1978-91, acad. advisor, learning strategies instr., coord. tutorial, 1990—, guest lectr. Wash. State U., 1978—. Editor: Traveling in America, 1984. Mem. AAUW, Nat. Assn. Devel. Edn., Internat. Reading Assn., Wash. Assn. Devel. Edn. (sec. 1992—, named Outstanding Educator of the Yr. 1995), Coll. Reading and Learning Assn. (sec. Wash. chpt. 1993-94, pres.-elect 1994-95, pres. 1996). Democrat. Mem. Ch. of Christ. Office: SALC Washington State U Lighty St Serv Bldg 260 Pullman WA 99164-2105

LOW, BARBARA WHARTON, biochemist, biophysicist; b. Lancaster, Eng., Mar. 23, 1920; came to U.S., 1946, naturalized, 1956; d. Matthew and Mary Jane (Wharton) L.; m. Metchie J.E. Budka, July 13, 1950 (dec. 1995). B.A. (Coll. scholar), Somerville Coll., Oxford (Eng.) U., 1942, M.A., 1946, DPhil, 1948. Research fellow Calif. Inst. Tech., 1946-47; research assoc. in phys. chemistry Harvard U. Med. Sch., 1948, assoc. in phys. chemistry, 1948-50; assoc. mem. Univ. Lab. Phys. Chemistry Related to Medicine and Public Health, 1950-54; asst. prof. phys. chemistry Harvard U., 1950-56; assoc. prof. biochemistry Columbia U. Coll. Physicians and Surgeons, 1956-66, prof., 1966-90, prof. emeritus, 1990—; cons. USPHS; mem. biophysics and biophys. chemistry study sect. div. rsch. grants NIH, 1961, spl. study sect., 1966-69, 1988, 90; rsch. coun. Pub. Health Rsch. Inst. City N.Y., 1973-78, bd. dirs., 1974-78; assoc. prof. U. Strasbourg, France, 1965; vis. prof. Japan Soc. Promotion Sci., Tohoku U., Sendai, Japan, 1975; invited lectr. Chinese Acad. Scis. 1981, Soviet Acad. Scis., 1988; mem. seminar on archaeology of Ea. Mediterranean, Ea. Europe and near East, Columbia U. Contbr. articles to chem., biochem., biophys., and crystallographic jours., also chpts. in books. Recipient Career Devel. award NIH, 1963-68; NIH sr. research fellow, 1959-63. Fellow Am. Acad. Arts and Scis.; mem. AAAS, Am. Crystallographic Assn., Am. Inst. Physics, Am. Soc. Biol. Chemists, Biophys. Soc., Royal Soc. Chemistry, Harvey Soc., Internat. Soc. Toxinology, Protein Soc., Soc. Neurosci. Office: Columbia U Dept Biochem & Mo Bio 630 W 168th St New York NY 10032-3702

LOW, LOUISE ANDERSON, consulting company executive; b. Saline, Mich., May 1, 1944; d. Harry Linné and Rose Josephine (Chvala) Anderson; m. James Thomas Low, Dec. 30, 1967; children: James William, Eric Linné, Kari Louise, Antony Anderson. BA in Biology, U. Mich., 1966. Permanent teaching cert., Mich.; cert. master gardener Coop. Ext. Svc. Tchr. secondary sci. Novi (Mich.) Community Schs., 1966-67; rsch. asst. U. Mich. Med. Sch., Ann Arbor, 1967-68; tchr. secondary sci. Livonia (Mich.) Pub. Schs., 1968-72; tax preparer H&R Block, Saline, 1991; sr. exec. asst. Low & Assocs., Saline, 1991—. apptd. mem. long-range planning com. Saline Area Schs., 1990-94, apptd. mem. gifted and talented com., 1996—; mem. Saline H.S. PTO, 1995—, mem. Saline Middle Sch. PTO, 1996; treas. youth bd. Zion Luth. Ch., Ann Arbor, 1993—; mem. St. Joseph Hosp. Ball Com., 1994; active Friends of the Saline Dist. Libr.; apptd. mem. Saline Area Schs. Project, 1997, bldg. com., parent advisor, 1996. Mem. AAUW (life, bd. dirs., com. chairperson), Washtenaw County Alliance for Gifted Edn. (v.p., bd. dirs.), U. Mich. Conger Alumnae Group (bd. dirs., mem. exec. bd.), Alumni Assn. U. Mich. (life), Interlochen Ctr. for Arts Alumni Orgn. (life), Ann Arbor Area Panhellenic Alumnae (pres. 1976-77), Wayne State U. Faculty Wives, Travis Pointe Country Club, Huron Valley Swim Club, Sigma Kappa (alumnae pres. 1970-72), Alpha Mu Sigma Kappa (mem. corp. bd., mem. adv. bd.). Lutheran. Home and Office: Low & Assocs 3431 Surrey Dr Saline MI 48176-9571

LOW, MARISSA E., health care administrator; b. San Francisco; d. Fred and Winifred L. AA, Fashion Inst. of Design and Mdse., 1979; Cert. Corp. Communications, Calif. State U.-Long Beach, 1987; BSBA, U. Redlands, 1992. Assoc. area mgr. Buffums, Glendale, Calif., 1979-80; asst. buyer Buffums, Long Beach, Calif., 1981-83; mdse. control mgr. Buffums, Long Beach, 1983-86, advt. mgr., 1987-89; account rep. CompuMed, Culver City, Calif., 1989-91; physician recruiter Pioneer Ind. Physician Network, Artesia, Calif., 1991-92; provider rels. mgr. Mullikin Ind. Physician Assn., Long Beach, Calif., 1992-93; dir. provider rels. Mullikin Ind. Physician Assn., Daly City, 1993-94; dir., payor, provider rels., regional network mgr. AHI Healthcare Systems, Inc., San Mateo, Calif., 1994-95; regional contracts mgr. Nat. Med., Inc., Modesto, Calif., 1996—. Judge Miss Lakewood Pageant of Beauty, 1987; vol. Long Beach Conv. and Visitors Coun., 1987, Am. Cancer Soc. 1996; pub. rels. chmn. March of Dimes, Calif., 1986; v.p. programs, spl. projects, chmn. bd. dirs., nomination com. chmn. Women's Coun., 1985-91; sec. Women's Bus. Conf., 1985; com. mem. Interval House Le Bal des Papillons. Recipient Cert. Appreciation Orange County Commn. on Status of Women, 1991, Interval House, 1991. Mem. NAFE, Am. Mktg. Assn., Group Health Assn. of Am., Acad. Health Svcs. Mktg. (chmn. managed care com. Health Futures Forum 1992), Healthcare Fin. Mgmt. Assn. Office: 1005 W Orangeburg Ave Ste B Modesto CA 95350-4163

LOW, MARY LOUISE (MOLLY LOW), documentary photographer; b. Quakertown, Pa., Jan. 3, 1926; d. James Harry and Dorothy Collyer (Krewson) Thomas; m. Antoine Francois Gagné, Nov. 3, 1945 (div.); children: James L., David W., Stephen J., Jeannie Wolff-Gagné; m. Paul Low, July 11, 1969 (dec. July 1991). Student, Oberlin Conservatory of Music, 1943-44, Oberlin Coll., 1944; cert., Katharine Gibbs Sec. Sch., 1945; degree in psychiat. rehab. work, Einstein Coll. Medicine, 1968-70. Sec. Dept. Store, N.Y.C., 1945; sec., treas. Gagné Assocs., Consulting Engrs., Binghamton, N.Y., 1951-66; psychiat. rsch. asst. Jacobi Hosp., Bronx, 1969-70; asst. to head of sch. Brearley Sch., N.Y.C., 1976-78; pvt. practice documentary photographer San Diego, 1984—. Contbr. articles to profl. jours. Pres., bd. trustees Unitarian-Universalist Ch. Recipient Dir.'s award for excellence Area Agy. on Aging, San Diego, 1993, Citizen Recognition award County of San Diego, Calif., 1993. Office: Molly Low Photography 5576 Caminito Herminia La Jolla CA 92037-7222

LOW, MERRY COOK, civic worker; b. Uniontown, Pa., Sept. 3, 1925; d. Howard Vance and Eleanora (Lynch) Mullan; m. William R. Cook, 1947 (div. 1979); m. John Wayland Low, July 8, 1979; children: Karen, Cindy, Bob, Jan. Diploma in nursing, Allegheny Gen. Hosp., Pitts., 1946; BS summa cum laude, Colo. Women's Coll., 1976. RN, Colo. Dir. patient edn. Med. Care and Rsch. Found., Denver, 1976-78. Contbr. chpt. to Pattern for Distribution of Patient Education, 1981. Bd. dirs. women's libr. assn. U. Denver, 1982—, vice chmn., 1985-86, chmn., 1986-87, co-chmn. spl. event, 1992; bd. dirs. Humanities Inst., 1993—, co-chair Founder's Day, 1994, 95, 96; mem. adv. com. U. Denver Women's Coll., 1995—; docent Denver Art Mus., 1979—, mem. vol. exec. bd., 1988-94, mem. nat. docent symposium com., 1991, chmn. collectors' choice benefits, 1988, pres. vols., trustee 1988-90; mem. alumni assn. bd. U. Denver, 1994—, sec., 1996—; bd. dirs. Lamont Sch. Music Assocs., 1990-96; mem. search com. for dir. Penrose Libr., 1991-92; trustee ch. coun., chmn. invitational art show 1st Plymouth Congl. Ch., Englewood, Colo., 1981-84; co-chmn. art auction Colo. Alliance Bus., 1992, 93, com., 1994—. Recipient Disting. Svc. award U. Denver Coll. Law, 1988, King Soopers Vol. of Week award, 1989, Citizen of Arts award Fine Arts Found., 1993, Outstanding Vol. Colo. Alliance of Bus., 1994, U. Denver Cmty. Svc. award, 1996. Mem. Am. Assn. Mus. (vol. meeting coord. 1990-91), P.E.O. (pres. Colo. chpt. DX 1982-84), U. Denver Alumni Assn. (bd. dirs., sec. 1996—). Republican. Congregationalist. Home: 2552 E Alameda Ave Apt 11 Denver CO 80209-3324

LOWDEN, SUZANNE, state legislator; b. Camden, N.J., Feb. 8, 1952; m. Paul W. Lowden; children: Christopher, Jennifer, Paul, William. BA magna cum laude, Am. U.; MA cum laude, Fairleigh Dickinson U. Resort industry exec.; mem. Nev. State Senate, 1993—, majority whip, 1993—. Active Juvenile Diabetes Found., United Way of So. Nev. With USO, 1971, Vietnam. Recipient Woman of Achievement award Women's Coun. of Las Vegas C. of C. Republican. Home: 992 Pinehurst Dr Las Vegas NV 89109-1569 Office: Nev State Senate State Capitol Carson City NV 89710 also Office: 4949 N Ranelo Dr Las Vegas NV 89130*

LOWE, KATHLENE WINN, lawyer; b. San Diego, Dec. 1, 1949; d. Ralph and Grace (Rodes) Winn; m. Russell Howells Lowe, Oct. 7, 1977; 1 child, Taylor Rhodes. BA in English magna cum laude, U. Utah, 1971, MA in English, 1973, JD, 1976. Bar: Utah 1976, U.S. Dist. Ct. Utah 1976, U.S. Ct. Appeals (10th cir.) 1980, Calif. 1989, U.S. Dist. Ct. (ctrl. dist.) Calif. 1990. Assoc. Parsons, Behle & Latimer, Salt Lake City, 1976-80, ptnr., 1980-84; v.p. law Skaggs Alpha Beta Inc., Salt Lake City; now ptnr. Brobeck, Phleger & Harrison, Newport Beach, Calif. Contbg. editor Utah Law Rev., 1975-76. Mem. ABA, Utah Bar Assn., Salt Lake City Bar Assn., Phi Kappa Phi. Office: Brobeck Phleger & Harrison 4675 Macarthur Ct Ste 1000 Newport Beach CA 92660-1846

LOWE, LYNN RAE, sculptor, educator, small business owner; b. Detroit, Dec. 24, 1946; d. Sidney Lewis and Beverly Monica (Shapero) Cohn; m. Sherwood Saul Swartz, Feb. 25, 1968 (div. Nov. 1978); children: Bradley, Damion; m. Buck Lowe (Dennis Michael Mellin), May 24, 1981; children: Persephone, Dustin. Student, U. Colo., 1965-67; cert. master gardener, U. Ariz., 1990, BFA in Mixed Media summa cum laude, 1993. Gen. mgr. Sta. KOTO-FM, Telluride, Colo., 1981-83; publicity dir., actor SRO Theatre Troupe, Telluride, 1982-87; exec. dir. Gov.'s Cup and Pioneers of Skiing Internat., Telluride, 1984-88; tchr. art San Xavier Mission Sch., Tucson, 1990-93; founding pres. Lowe Co Motion, Telluride and Tucson, 1979—; prodr. Telluride Jazz Festival, 1984-88, Ariz. Theatre Co. Temple of Music: Art Celebration, Tucson, 1988; dir. design and events Telluride Film Festival, 1977—; cons. Colo. Coun. Arts and Humanities, Denver, 1980-81; mem. grants panel Tucson-Pima Arts Coun., 1991; bd. dirs. Nat. Film Preserve, Hanover, N.H., 1991—; mem. adv. bd. Global Arts Project, Tucson, 1995-96; mem. adj. faculty Pima C.C., 1992—. One-woman shows Cathedral Heritage Found., Louisville, 1996, Sun Cities Mus., Ariz., 1997; author: Call Someplace Paradise, 1989; illustrator: Inner Journey, 1994; commns. include logo Am. Holistic Med. Nurses Assn., Boone, N.C., 1995; work featured in jours., mags. and newspapers. Moderator Town of Telluride, 1984-88; bd. dirs. Project Graduation, Tucson, 1989; sponsor Tucson Med. Ctr. Aux.; coord. Meals on Wheels, Tucson, 1990-91; mem. adv. bd. Tucson Mayor's Task Force on Cultural Tourism, 1991; mem. fundraising steering com. Tucson Jewish Cmty. Ctr., 1994—. Mem. Internat. Sculpture Ctr., Nat. Mus. Women in the Arts, Rosicrucian Soc., Golden Key, Phi Kappa Phi. Home and Studio: 2425 E Caminito de los Ranchos Tucson AZ 85718

LOWE, MARY JOHNSON, federal judge; b. N.Y.C., June 10, 1924; m. Ivan A. Michael, Nov. 4, 1961; children: Edward H. Lowe, Leslie H. Lowe, Bess J. Michael. BA, Hunter Coll., 1952; LLB, Bklyn. Law Sch., 1954; LLM, Columbia U., 1955; LLD, CUNY, 1990. Bar: N.Y. 1955. Pvt. practice law N.Y.C., 1955-71; judge N.Y.C. Criminal Ct., 1971-72; acting justice N.Y. State Supreme Ct., 1972-74; judge Bronx County Supreme Ct., 1974; justice N.Y. State Supreme Ct., 1977, 1st Jud. Dist., 1978; judge U.S. Dist. Ct. (so. dist.) N.Y., 1978-91, sr. judge, 1991—. Recipient award for outstanding service to criminal justice system Bronx County Criminal Cts. Bar Assn., 1974, award for work on narcotics cases Asst. Dist. Attys., 1974. Mem. Women in Criminal Justice, Harlem Lawyers Assn., Bronx Criminal Lawyers Assn., N.Y. County Lawyers Assn., Bronx County Bar Assn., N.Y. State Bar Assn. (award for outstanding jud. contbn. to criminal justice Sect. Criminal Justice 1978), NAACP, Nat. Urban League, Nat. Council Negro Women, NOW. Office: US Dist Ct US Courthouse 40 Foley Sq New York NY 10007*

LOWE, SARAH MARGARET, curator, writer; b. Buffalo, Sept. 1, 1956; d. Charles Upton and Eileen Lowe. BA, Vassar Coll., 1979; MPhil, CUNY, 1989, PhD, 1996. Adj. instr. Adelphi U., Garden City, N.J., 1986, 90, Kean Coll. N.J., Union, 1987, Montclair State Coll., Upper Montclair, N.J., 1988, SUNY, Purchase, 1988. Author: Frida Kahlo, 1991, Tina Modotti: Photographs, 1995, The Diary of Frida Kahlo: An Intimate Self-Portrait, 1995; co-author: Consuelo Kanaga: An American Photographer, 1992. Bd. dirs. Lower East Side Printshop, N.Y.C., 1995—; chair doctoral students' coun. CUNY, 1985-86. Kristie A. Jayne fellow CUNY, 1991-92, dissertation fellow, 1988-89, Eliza Buffington fellow for grad. rsch. Vassar Coll., 1986-87. Home and Office: 497 Pacific St Brooklyn NY 11217

LOWELL, NICOLE ELLEN, lawyer; b. Phila., May 27, 1963; d. Robert Mitchell and Danielle Constance (Roberts) L. BA, Temple U., 1986; JD, Widener U., 1992. Bar: Pa. 1992. Broker, sales asst. Smith Barney, Mt. Laurel, N.J., 1988-89; paralegal Barbara Montgomery, P.C., Phila., 1990; intern L.S. Environ. Clinic Widener U., Wilmington, Del., 1991; law clk., intern divil divsn. Ct. Common Pleas, Phila., 1992, law clk., intern criminal divsn., 1993; vol. atty. Commonwealth of Pa. Dept. Environment, Conshohocken, 1993-94; office mgr. Mike Rosen & Assocs., Phila., 1994-95; paralegal litigation support Thomas P. Reeves & Assocs., San Francisco, 1995-96; dir. eviction def. svc. Tenderloin Housing Clinic, San Francisco, 1996—; broker, sales asst. Wilt Newbold & Sons, Inc., Phila., 1987-88; customer svc. agt. Van-Kampen-Merritt, Phila., 1986-87. tenant counselor San Francisco Housing Rights Com., 1995-96; atty. cons. San Francisco Alliance for Environ. Justice, 1995-96, San Francisco Baykeeper, 1996. Mem. Pa. Bar Assn. Democrat. Jewish. Home: 1365 Alabama St San Francisco CA 94110 Office: Tenderloin Housing Clinic 995 Market St # 5416 San Francisco CA 94103

LOWENBERG, GEORGINA GRACE, elementary school educator; b. El Paso, Tex., Feb. 15, 1944; d. Eduardo Antonio and Grace Elizabeth (Fletcher) Orellana; m. Edward Daniel Lowenberg, June 14, 1968, 1968 (div. 1985); 1 child, Jennifer Anne. BSEd, U. Tex., El Paso, 1965, postgrad., 1965-66; postgrad., U. St. Thomas, 1983. Permanent profl. teaching cert., Tex. Tchr. 5th grade El Paso Pub. Sch. Dist., 1965-70; tchr. 3d grade gifted, talented Ysleta Ind. Sch. Dist., El Paso, 1980—; mem. com. Tex. State Textbook Selection Com., Austin, 1984-85, Tex. State TEAMS Math Adv. Com., Austin, 1986-87; sci. presentor Silver Burdett, Albuquerque, 1985-86; critic reader Scott-Foresman, Dallas, 1986; pres., v.p. Scotsdale Elem. Sch. PTA, El Paso, 1976-83; v.p. Eastwood Middle Sch. PTA, El Paso, 1984-85; mem. Eastwood Heights Elem. Sch. PTA, 1985-87; sec. Eastwood High Sch. Band Boosters, El Paso, 1985-89, Speech Boosters, 1986-88; life mem. Tex. State PTA, 1981—. Troop leader Brownie and Jr. Girl Scouts Am., El Paso, 1977-82; dir. Eaglette Dance Team, 1994—. Mem. Assn. Tex. Profl. Educators (regional treas. 1987-88). Roman Catholic.

LOWENBRAUN, RENATA DIANE, lawyer; b. Kew Gardens, N.Y., July 18, 1964. BA, SUNY, Albany, 1986; MA, Montclair State U., 1993; JD, Rutgers Sch. Law, 1989. Bar: N.J. 1989, N.Y. 1990. Law clk. to Hon. George Farrell III Superior Ct. of N.J. Law Divsn., Salem, N.J., 1989-90; assoc. Suarez & Suarez, Jersey City, N.J., 1990-91, Law Offices of Richard Thiele, Somerville, N.J., 1991-93, Cooper Perskie April Niedelman Wagenheim & Levenson, Atlantic City, N.J., 1993-95; pvt. practice law Camden, N.J., 1995—; dir. bus. legal affairs Omni 2000, Inc., Camden, N.J., 1995—; guest lectr. Montclair (N.J.) State U., 1993-95. Contbr. article to profl. jour. Trustee South Jersey Regional Theatre, Somers Point, 1995, Stageworks Touring Co., Glassboro, N.J., 1995. Mem. N.J. State Bar Assn. (mem. exec. com. young lawyers divsn. 1994—, chairperson1995—), Inn of Ct., N.J. Assn. Women Bus. Owners (v.p. pub. affairs, publicity Atlantic County chpt. 1995—). Home: 3851 Boardwalk PH106 Atlantic City NJ 08401

LOWENSTEIN, AMY GANULIN, public relations professional; b. Chgo., May 2, 1937; d. Alvin and Sadie (Reingold) Landis; m. James Ganulin, June 23, 1957; children: Stacy, Amy Ganulin Lowenstein. BA in Journalism, U. Calif., Berkeley, 1958. Copywriter-sec. Joe Connor Advt., Berkeley, 1958; exec. sec. Prescolite Mfg. Co., Berkeley, 1958-59; info. officer Office of Consumer Counsel, Sacramento, 1959-61; pub. rels. positions various polit. campaigns, Fresno, Calif., 1966; adminstrv. asst., editor, mktg. Valley Pubs., Fresno, 1971-80; staff asst. to county supr. Bd. Suprs., Fresno, 1980-82; field rep. Assemblyman Bruce Bronzan, Fresno, 1982-84; prin. Judy Ganulin Pub. Rels., Fresno, 1984—; speaker new bus. workshop SBA/Svc. Corps Ret. Persons, Fresno, 1990—. Active Hadassah, Fresno, 1975—; pres. Temple Beth Israel Sisterhood, Fresno, 1976; panelist campaign workshop Nat. Women's Polit. Caucus, Fresno, 1994; bd. dirs. Temple Beth Israel, Fresno, 1972-75, Planned Parenthood Ctrl. Calif., Fresno, 1986-91. Mem. Pub. Rels. Soc. Am. (accredited pub. rels. practitioner, pres. Fresno/Ctrl. Valley chpt. 1994), Am. Mktg. Assn. (pres. ctrl. Calif. chpt.-ctrl. 1987-88), Calif. Press Women, Fresno Advt. Fedn., Pub. Rels. Roundtable (v.p., pres. 1991-93), Fresno C. of C. (mem. mktg. com. 1988—). Democrat. Office: Judy Ganulin Pub Rels 1117 W San Jose Ave Fresno CA 93711-3112

LOWENTHAL, CONSTANCE, art historian; b. N.Y.C., Aug. 29, 1945; d. Jesse and Helen (Oberstein) L. BA cum laude, Brandeis U., 1967; AM, Inst. Fine Arts, NYU, 1969; PhD, Inst. Fine Arts, NYU, N.Y.C., 1976. Mem. faculty Sarah Lawrence Coll., Bronxville, N.Y., 1975-78; asst. mus. educator Met. Mus. Art, N.Y.C., 1978-85; exec. dir. Internat. Found. Art Research, N.Y.C., 1985—; bd. dirs. Ctr. for Edn. Studies, Inc. Regular contbr. Art Crime Update column Wall Street Jour., 1988—; contbr. articles to Mus. News and other profl. publs. Office: Internat. Found. for Art Rsch Ste 1234 500 Fifth Ave New York NY 10110

LOWENTHAL, SUSAN, finance company executive; b. Munich, Nov. 30, 1946; came to U.S., 1949; d. Jerry and Gertrude (Wiestreich) L.; m. Alex J. Stolitzka, Oct. ll, 1987. BA, Bklyn. Coll., 1969. Exec. dir. Manhattan Girls Club, N.Y.C., 1969-73; conf. coord. Orton Soc., N.Y.C., 1973-77; v.p. Gemtique, N.Y.C., 1977-81; broker Prudential Bache, N.Y.C., 1981-83, Smith Barney, N.Y.C., 1983-85; pres., chief exec. officer Lowenthal Fin. Svcs., Inc., N.Y.C., 1985-89, fin. cons., money mgr., 1990—; realtor, exclusive buyer agt. March Buyers Realty, 1995—. Jewish.

LOWERS, GINA CATTANI, process and instrumentation engineer; b. Evanston, Ill., Oct. 16, 1961; d. Lawrence F. and Arlene Bernice (Phillips) Cattani; m. Robert Judson Lowers, Oct. 10, 1984. BS in Math., U. Calif., Riverside, 1984; BS in Physics, Carnegie-Mellon U., 1987, MS in Physics, 1989; postgrad., W.Va. U. Test systems engr. Aerojet Electrosystems Co., Azusa, Calif., 1983-85; instr. calculus Carnegie Mellon U., Pitts., 1986-88; product devel. engr. Philips Lighting Co., Fairmont, W.Va., 1988—; instr. physics Fairmont State Coll., 1990-91, instr. electronics, 1992—. Judge physics and math. orals and presentations W. Va. State Sci. and Engring. Fair, 1989-91, judge physics projects, 1989, 91, 92; co-chair covenants and restrictions com. Greystone-on-the-Cheat Property Owner's Assn., sec. Mem. Electrochem. Soc., Soc. Mfg. Engrs., Soc. Tech. Comm. Office: Philips Lighting Co RR 3 Box 505 Fairmont WV 26554-9484

LOWERY, LEONA FAITH, retired secondary school and college educator; b. Killbuck, Ohio, Mar. 19, 1921; d. Frederick William and Sybil Anna (Middaugh) Duncan; m. Robert Charles Lowery, June 10, 1942 (dec.); 1 child, James Keith. BS, Ohio No. U., 1942; MA, Vanderbilt U., 1958, EdS, 1970. Cert. social sci., speech, drama, English and Latin tchr., Ohio. Tchr. Middle Point H.S., Ohio, 1943-45, Beaver H.S., Pa., 1952-56, Huntsville (Ala.) H.S., 1956-67, 68-70, Prince George County (Md.) Schs., 1967-68, Long Branch (N.J.) H.S., 1970-71, Marlboro (N.J.) H.S., 1971-87, Brookdale Coll. Br., Guayaquil, Ecuador, 1987-88, Mississippi Gulf Coast Coll., 1989-94; civil svc. Panama Canal Zone, 1945-46, Ohio State U., 1947-48. Contbr. articles to profl. jours. Pres. Ala. Classroom Tchrs., 1975-76. Recipient Minuteman Debating award Newark Acad., 1979; named Profl. Tchr. of Yr., Huntsville, Ala., 1970. Mem. DAR (state chmn. vet.-patients 1995—), Daus. Am. Colonists (parliamentarian 1995—), Ocean Springs Geneal. Soc. (pres. 1975-76), Friends of Libr. (pres. 1995—), Colonial Dames of 17th Century (2d v.p. 1995—), Alpha Delta Kappa (pres. N.J. chpt. 1983-85, chaplain Zeta chpt. 1996—, internat. v.p. 1985-87, Honored Mem. of Yr. 1988, Pres.'s award Miss. chpt. 1995). Democrat. Presbyterian. Home: 110 Springtree Dr Brandon MS 39042

LOWERY, MARION MARGARET, retired rehabilitation counselor; b. Phila., Dec. 19, 1934; d. Harry Galleghar and Margaret (Sauer) R.; children: Pamela A., James D., Stephen L. BA, U. North Colo., Greeley, 1967-70; MEd magna cum laude, Oreg. State U., 1974. Coord.-adult basic Edn. Rogue Com. Coll., Grants Pass, 1971-75; dir.-loaves and fishes Fed. Title VII Programme, Medford, 1975-79; child abuse caseworker State Oregon, Medford, 1979-81; adult caseworker State of Oregon, Medford, employment spec., 1982-87; rehab. counselor State of Oreg., Medford, 1987—; mem. Sch. Transition Team; CEO The Cooking Connection, The Disability Specialist. Author: (pub. rsch.) Changing Status of Women in Middle East. Bd. dirs. Crisis Intervention Svc., Parents Anonymous, Supported Work Coun., Interagy. Coun., Medford, 1980-90. Mem. Regional Vocat. Ednl. Planning Com., Ednl. Svcs. Dist. Representing Vocat. Rehab., Lions (1st v.p.). Home: 830 Carol Rae Medford OR 97501-1729

LOWERY, SHARON A., travel industry executive; b. Chgo., Sept. 27, 1943; d. James William and Alice Dorothy (Buckley) L. BA, Knox Coll., 1965. Pres. Expert Visa Svcs. Inc., Chgo. Mem. Nat. Assn. Women Bus. Owners, NAt. Bus. Travel Assn., Ohio Valley Bus. Travel Assn., 410 Club (Chgo.). Home: 1430 Sandstone Dr Wheeling IL 60090-5923 Office: 28 E Jackson Blvd Chicago IL 60604-2215

LOWERY, VIRGINIA GAIL, human resources professional; b. Knoxville, Tenn., Mar. 17, 1955; d. James Powell and Johnnie Mae (McConnell) L. BMus summa cum laude, U. Tenn., 1976; MMus, Juilliard Sch., 1979; dipl. human resources mgmt., NYU, 1994. Supr. Battle Fowler, N.Y.C., 1986-93; co-founder, v.p. The Human Equation, Inc., N.Y.C., 1993—; mgr. employment The Bklyn. Hosp. Ctr., 1993—; profl. mentor L.I. U., N.Y., 1994—. Team leader AIDS Walk, N.Y.C., 1993—. Named Outstanding Young Women of Am., 1977. Mem. Soc. Human Resource Mgmt., Assn. Hosp. Human Resource Adminstrs., Employment Mgmt. Consortium, Mensa Soc., Sigma Alpha Iota (corr. sec. 1974-75), Pi Kappa Lambda, Phi Kappa Phi. Office: The Human Equation Inc 649 E 14th St Ste ME New York NY 10009

LOWERY, WILLA DEAN, obstetrician-gynecologist; b. Caryville, Fla., Apr. 16, 1927; d. Ernest and Nadine (Fowler) L. BS in Chemistry, Stetson U., 1948; MS in Microbiology, U. Fla., 1952; MD, U. Miami, 1959; MPH, U. Pitts., 1963; MDiv in Theology, Pitt. Theol. Sem., 1995. Diplomate Am. Bd. Ob-Gyn.; ordained to ministry Presbyn. Ch. Microbiologist Fla. Dept. Pub. Health, Jacksonville, 1948-52, pub. health officer, 1959-65; microbiologist U. S. Operation Mission to Brazil, Belém, 1952-55; rotating intern Jackson Meml. Hosp., Miami, Fla., 1959-60; resident in ob-gyn. Magee Women's Hosp., Pitts., 1965-68; asst. prof. ob-gyn. Sch. Medicine, U. Pitts., 1968-69; pvt. practice Pitts., 1970-88; cons. Med. Mission in Brazil, Teresina, 1986-89. Contbr. articles to profl. jours. Mem. AMA, ACOG, Pa. State Med. Soc., Allegheny County Med. Soc. Home: 119 Sunnyhill Dr Pittsburgh PA 15237-3666

LOWEY, NITA M., congresswoman; b. N.Y., July 5, 1937; m. Stephen Lowey, 1961; children: Dona, Jacqueline, Douglas. BS, Mt. Holyoke Coll., 1959. Community activist, prior to 1975; asst. sec. state State of N.Y., 1975-87; former mem. 101st-102nd Congresses from 20th N.Y. dist., 1989-92; mem. 103rd-104th Congresses from 18th N.Y. dist., 1993—; mem. appropriations com., 1993—. Democrat. Office: US Ho of Reps 2421 Rayburn HOB Washington DC 20515*

LOWITZ, ROBIN ADELE, nurse administrator; b. Balt., May 29, 1954; d. Irving Robert and Sonia Dean (Krulevitz) L. BSN, U. Md., 1976; postgrad., U. Miami, Fla., 1986; cert. health mgmt., St. Thomas U., Miami, 1995; MS in Mgmt., St. Thomas U., Miami, Fla., 1996. CCRN. Staff nurse Sinai Hosp., Balt., 1976-80, Mt. Sinai Med. Ctr., Miami Beach, Fla., 1980-84; educator critical care Cedars Med. Ctr., Miami, Fla., 1984-85, nurse mgr., 1985-86; nurse pvt. duty Allied Nurses and Health Care Svcs., Miami, Fla., 1986-88, coord. mini ICU, 1988-89, dir. profl. svcs., 1989-91; staff nurse Surg. Park, Inc., Miami, Fla., 1990-91; case mgr. PayMed/Ontario Blue Cross, Bay Harbor Islands, Fla., 1991-92; nursing supr. HRS/Hurricane Andrew Relief Project, Miami, 1992-94; pre-authorization coord. Av Med Health Plan, Miami, 1994-96, mgmt. info. sys. project implementation team mem., 1996—; cons. in field. Mem. AACN, Emergency Nurses Assn. Home: 8315 SW 72nd Ave # 216 Miami FL 33143-7694 Office: AV Med Health Plan 9400 S Dadeland Blvd Miami FL 33156-2823

LOWLEY, SUSAN ANNETTE, educator, coach; b. Detroit, July 23, 1963; d. Paul Edmund and Virginia K. (Parkhurst) L. BS, U. Iowa, 1985; MS, U. Tex. Health Sci. Ctr., 1990. Rsch. asst. Baylor Coll. Medicine, Houston, 1985-86; med. tech. Methodist Hosp., Houston, 1988-90; clin. coord. Health Quest Rsch., Austin, Tex., 1990-93; faculty, coach St. Stephen's Episcopal Sch., Austin, 1993-96; coach, dir. field hockey camp St. Stephen's Episcopal Sch., 1993-96; head coach field hockey Bridgewater Coll., Va., 1996. Mem. U.S. Field Hockey Assn., Women's Sports Found., Austin Ridge Riders.. Methodist. Office: St Stephen's Episcopal Sch 2900 Bunny Run Austin TX 78767

LOWNDES, JANINE MARIE HERBERT, journalist; b. Albany, N.Y., May 15, 1958; d. Bernard and Wanda E. (Ahrens) H.; m. Jeffrey D. Lowndes; children: Nicholas, Grant, Victoria, Jeffrey Lee (dec.). BS in Adminstrn. of Justice, MacMurray Coll., 1984. Pvt. investigator Springfield, Ill., 1984-85; ins. claims investigator Tulsa, 1985; self-employed paralegal investigator Springfield, Ill. and Norfolk, Va., 1985-90; pvt. investigator Dayton, Ohio, 1990-91; freelance author, investigative reporter, journalist, 1976—; self-employed paralegal investigator Brunswick, Maine, 1996—. Author: Crystal Images (poetry), 1976; contbr. articles to newspaper, poetry to anthology; editor coll. newspaper: Spectator, 1982. Vol. chmn. Mental Health Assn., Springfield, 1969-76; pres. World Dem. Family Club Internat., 1979—. Recipient Golden Poets award, 1989-95. Mem. Maine Writers and Publishers Alliance. Home: Writer's Garret Gen Delivery Brunswick ME 04011

LOWRANCE, MURIEL EDWARDS, program specialist; b. Ada, Okla., Dec. 28, 1922; d. Warren E. and Mayme E. (Barrick) Edwards; B.S. in Edn., East Central State U., Ada, 1954; 1 dau., Kathy Lynn Lowrance Gutierrez. Accountant, adminstrv. asst. to bus. mgr. East Central State U., 1950-68; grants and contracts specialist U. N.Mex. Sch. Medicine, Albuquerque, 1968-72, program specialist IV, dept. orthopaedics, 1975-86; asst. adminstrv. officer N.Mex. Regional Med. Program, 1972-75. Bd. dirs. Vocat. Rehab. Center, 1980-84. Cert. profl. contract mgr. Nat. Contract Assn. Mem. Am. Bus. Women's Assn. (past pres. El Segundo chpt., Woman of Yr. 1974), AAUW, Amigos de las Americas (dir.). Democrat. Methodist. Club: Pilot (Albuquerque) (pres. 1979-80, dir. 1983-84, dist. treas. 1984-86, treas. S.W. dist., 1984-86, gov.-elect S.W. dist. 1986-87, gov. S.W. dist. 1987-88). Home: 3028 Mackland Ave NE Albuquerque NM 87106-2018

LOWRIE, KATHRYN YANACEK, manufacturing company executive; b. Midland, Mich., Nov. 23, 1958; d. Frank Joseph and Jacqueline Ann (Sipko) Yanacek; m. David Bruce Lowrie, Mar. 14, 1987; 1 child, Alexandra Yanacek. BA in Psychology, Northea. U., 1980. Psychology technician Rsch. Inst. of Environ. Medicine, U.S. Army, Natick, Mass., 1980-81, computer programmer, 1981-83; assoc. recruiter Mgmt. Adv. Svcs., Burlington, Mass., 1983-85, v.p. mgmt. info. sys., 1985-86, exec. v.p., 1986-89; CEO Computer Careers, Raynham, Mass., 1989-90; v.p. G.R.S.I. Corp., Middleboro, Mass., 1990-94; owner S.B. Industries, Taunton, Mass., 1994-96; pres. Enviro-Screen, Inc., Taunton, 1996—. Bd. dirs. MSPCC. Roman Catholic.

LOWRY, LINDA ELEANOR, artist, educator; b. Lubbock, Tex., June 30, 1956; d. David Auld and Stella (West) L. BA, Colo. Coll., 1978; postgrad., Sch. Visual Arts, 1978-79, Tyler Sch. Art, 1979-80; MFA, U. Colo., 1983. Instr. U. Colo., Boulder, 1982-91, Colo. State U., Ft. Collins, 1983-84, Rocky Mountain Coll. Art and Design, Denver, 1984-85, Colo. Coll., Colorado Springs, 1989-90, U. Colo., Denver, 1990; chair art dept. Arapahoe Cmty. Coll., Littleton, Colo., 1990—; instr. Artreach, Denver, 1983-90; vis. artist Denver Art Mus., 1985; chair exhibition com. Colo. Gallery of Arts, Littleton, 1993—; juror The Eleventh Congl. Art Competition, Denver, 1993, Congressman Shaeffer's Nat Scholarship Award, Denver, 1994, U. No. Colo. Student Show, Greeley, 1994. Author, illustrator: (book) Inside Colorado: An Artist's View of Colorado Interiors, 1993; one-person shows include Gallery 44, Boulder, 1993, Martin County Arts Mus., Stuart, Fla., 1994; exhibited in group shows at Indpls. Mus. Art, 1984, Viridian Gallery, N.Y.C., 1988, Denver Art Mus., 1983. Recipient Merit award Henry Hopkins, Artreach '88, Salt Lake City, 1988, Excellence award Artists of Colo., Denver, 1996; artist-in-residence Rocky Mountain Nat. Park, 1990. Mem. Coll. Art Assn., Arapahoe Cmty. Coll. Art Club (advisor 1990-96, Appreciation award 1990-95). Office: Arapahoe Cmty Coll Art Dept 2500 W College Dr Littleton CO 80160

LOWRY, LOIS (HAMMERSBERG), author; b. 1937. Author: A Summer to Die, 1977, Find A Stranger, Say Goodbye, 1978, Anastasia Krupnik, 1979, Autumn Street, 1980, Anastasia Again, 1981, Anastasia at Your Service, 1982, The One Hundredth Thing About Caroline, 1983, Taking Care of Terrific, 1983, Anastasia, Ask Your Analyst, 1984, Us and Uncle Fraud, 1984, Anastasia on Her Own, 1985, Switcharound, 1985, Anastasia Has the Answers, 1986, Anastasia's Chosen Career, 1987, Rabbie Starkey, 1987, All About Sam, 1988, Number the Stars, 1989 (John Newbery medal 1990), Your Move, J.P.!, 1990, Anastasia at This Address, 1991, Attaboy, Sam!, 1992, The Giver, 1993 (John Newbery medal 1994), Anastasia Absolutely, 1995, See You Around, Sam!, 1996. Address: 205 Brattle St Cambridge MA 02138-3319 Office: care Houghton Mifflin 222 Berkeley St Boston MA 02116-3748

LOWRY MALONEY, MARCIA, mental health counselor; b. L.A., Feb. 17, 1963; d. Ralph William Lowry and Linda Marcy Rasmussen; Richard Gerard Maloney, Jr., Oct. 14, 1989. BA, Bates Coll., 1985; MA, Lesley Coll., 1991. lic. mental health counselor, Mass., 1996. Ast. to dir. Anorexia Bulimia Care, Inc., Lincoln, Mass., 1986-92; Milieu therapist Hahnemann Hosp. Eating Disorders Unit, Brighton, Mass., 1989; child care worker New England Home for Little Wanderers, Boston, 1992; intern Lesley Coll. Counseling Ctr., Cambridge, Mass., 1990-91; dir. counseling Newbury Coll., Brookline, Mass., 1992—. Bd. mem. League of Women Voters of Newton, Mass., 1992-96; mem. Domestic Violence Action Com, Newton, Mass., 1994—. Recipient Bates Key Bates Coll., Lewiston, Maine, 1990, Point of Light award Pres. of U.S. Anorexia Bulimia Care, Inc., Lincoln, Mass., 1992. Mem. ACA, Am. Mental Health Counselors Assn., Mass. Mental Health Counselors Assn., Mass. Assn. for Women in Edn., Bates Coll. Key. Democrat. Episcopalian. Office: Newbury College Counseling Ctr 129 Fisher Ave Box 442 Brookline MA 02146

LOZAUSKAS, DOROTHY MILLER, supervisor educational programs; b. N.J., Apr. 11, 1947; m. Ronald Lozauskas, Nov. 9, 1969; 1 child, Eric. BA in Sci., Montclair State U., 1969, MA in Biology, 1972, postgrad. in ednl. adminstrn. and supervision. Tchr. sci. Verona (N.J.) H.S., 1969-92; supr. of instrn. Mountain Lakes (N.J.) Pub. Schs., 1992—; adj. instr. Seton Hall U., 1990-92, Montclair State U., 1991-92; tchr. trainer Hoffmann La Roche Co., Nutley, N.J., 1995—; spkr. various confs. Recipient N.J. Gov.'s Tchr. Recognition award N.J. Dept. Edn., 1990. Mem. AAUW, ASCD, NSTA, Nat. Assn. Biology Tchrs., Nat. Coun. Tchrs. Math., Nat. Assn. Secondary Sch. Prins. Office: Mountain Lakes HS Powerville Rd Mountain Lakes NJ 07046

LOZEAU, DONNALEE M., state legislator; b. Nashua, N.H., Sept. 15, 1960; m. David Lozeau; 3 children. Attended, Rivier Coll. Mem. N.H. Ho. of Reps.; vice chair corrections and criminal justice com. Former chair ward five Rep. City Com.; commr. Nashua Airport Authority. Home: 125 Shore Dr Nashua NH 03062-1339 Office: NH Ho of Reps State Capitol Concord NH 03301

LOZITO, GILDA LELIA, artist, painter; b. N.Y.C., Dec. 20; d. Massimo and Concetta (D'Amico) Greco; m. Rocco Jerome Lozito, Aug. 19, 1941. Student, Bono Hall Acad Fine Arts, 1937-41, Norton Sch. Art, 1949-53, Palm Beach Community Coll., 1960. Art instr. nat. Youth Adminstrn. Art Ctr., N.Y.C., 1939-41; Fed. Civil Svc., Eglin Field, Fla., 1942-45, Morrison Field, Fla., 1946; Architect Agnes Ballard, West Palm Beach, Fla., 1947-52; art instr. pvt. practice West Palm Beach, Fla., 1953—; artist Bagatelle Art Shop, Palm Beach, Fla., 1960-65; art consignments Gallery Gemini, Palm Beach, Fla., 1962-69; art judge City of West Palm Beach, 1968; lectr., cons. Fla., 1953—; cons. in art Pub. Civic Activities, 1970s; dir. exhibitions Nat. League of Am. Pen Women, Palm Beach, 1980s; lectr. in field. One woman shows at Norton Mus. Art, West Palm Beach, 1954, Hobbelink Kaastra Art Gallery, Palm Beach, 1955, Upstairs Art Gallery, Palm Beach, 1959, 1st Nat. In Palm Beach, 1970, 71, 72, 73, 74, 76, 90, 91, 92, 93, 94; exhibited in group shows at Palm Beach Coun. Arts; contbr. illustratins to mags. and jour., art reprodns. for book covers, art revs. in Palm Beach Today, Palm Beach's Pictorial P.B. with photograph, Palm Beach Daily News, Photo. of Paintings. Chairperson 20th Anniversary Celebration of Nat. League of Arts & Pen, 1985. Recipient Hon. Diploma awarded in the 2,000 Women of Achievement, 1972, First Prize award Palm Beach Art League Juried Art Exhibition, 1953, First Prize award Lake Worth Art League, 1954, Awards of merit Norton Sch. of Art, 1951, 52, Award of Merit, Palm Beach Nat. League of Art & Pen Women, 1975. Mem. Fla. Artists Group Inc., Soc. Four Arts, Fla. Fedn. Art, Artists Equity Nat., Nat. League Am. Arts and Pen Women (pres.), Palm Beach Quills and Artists, Northwood's Women Aux. in Arts, Nat. Mus. Women Artists, Fla. Watercolor Soc., Nat. League Am. Women (pres. Palm Beach branch 1985, chairperson anniversary celebration), Norton Mus. Art. Home and Office: 307 Cordova Rd West Palm Beach FL 33401-7907

LOZOFF, BETSY, pediatrician; b. Milw., Dec. 19, 1943; d. Milton and Marjorie (Morse) L.; 1 child, Claudia Brittenham. BA, Radcliffe Coll., 1965; MD, Case Western Res. U., 1971, MS, 1981. Diplomate Am. Bd. Pediat. From asst. prof. to prof. pediatrics Case Western Res. U., Cleve., 1974-93; prof. pediatrics U. Mich., Ann Arbor, 1993—, dir. Ctr. for Human Growth and Devel., 1993—. Recipient Rsch. Career Devel. award Nat. Inst. Child Health and Human Devel., 1984-88. Fellow Am. Acad. Pediatrics; mem. Soc. for Pediatric Rsch., Soc. Rsch. in Child Devel. (program com. 1988—), Soc. Behavioral Pediatrics (exec. com. 1985-88), Ambulatory Pediatric Soc. Office: Univ Mich Ctr Human Growth and Devel 300 N Ingalls St Ann Arbor MI 48109-2007

LUALDI, NINA MARY, marketing executive; b. Caracas, Venezuela, Feb. 6, 1965; came to U.S., 1992; d. Giuseppe and Maria (Aina) Lualdi; m. Dana Karl De Nault, Apr. 6, 1996. BS in Computer Sci., U. Caracas, 1987; MBA, U. San Francisco, 1993. Software support engr. Olivetti Sys. and Networks, Ivrea, Italy, 1988-90; tech. software support cons. Olivetti Sys. and Networks, Caracas, 1991; prof. computer sci. U. Ctrl. Venezuela, Caracas, 1991; mktg. analyst, cons. Cisco Sys., San Jose, 1994-95, 96—; strategic analyst, mgr. Omnitel, Milan, Italy, 1995. Author: (manual) Model of Segmentation and Corresponding Strategies for the Internetworking Market, 1994. L.Am. Studes Program/Am. U. scholar, 1991. Roman Catholic. Home: 18760 Devon Ave Saratoga CA 95070

LUBBERS, TERESA S., state senator, public relations executive; b. Indpls., July 5, 1951; d. Richard and Evelyn (Ent) Smith; m. R. Mark Lubbers, Oct. 7, 1978; children: Elizabeth Stone, Margaret Smith. AB, Ind. U., 1973; MPA, Harvard U., 1981. Tchr. English Warren Ctrl. High Sch., 1973-74; pub. info. officer Office of Mayor Richard Lugar, 1974-75; dep. press sec., legis. asst. Office of U.S. Senator Richard Lugar, 1976-78; legis. rep. Nat. Fedn. Ind. Bus., 1978-80; dir. info. INC. Mag., 1981-82; press sec. Dielmann for Congress, 1982-83; pres. pub. rels. firm Capitol Communications, 1983—; state senator State of Ind., Indpls., 1992—; co-founder, v.p. Richard G. Lugar Excellence in Pub. Svc. Series, 1990—; bd. dirs. Young Audiences Ind., Nat. Policy Forum. Bd. deacons Tabernacle Presbyn. Ch.; mem. cultural enrichment com. Immaculate Heart Sch., Meridian Kessler Neighborhood Assn., Rep. Profl. Women's Roundtable; mem. steering com. Forum Series, Girls Inc.; bus. mem. Broad Ripple Village Assn.; vol. Dick Lugar's 1974 Senate Campaign; pub. info. officer Mayor's Office, 1974-75; office mgr., Friends of Dick Lugar, 1976; senate staff Office of Senator Richard Lugar, 1976-78. Republican. Home: 5425 N New Jersey St Indianapolis IN 46220-3019 Office: State Senate State Capitol Indianapolis IN 46204*

LUBBOCK, MILDRED MARCELLE (MIDGE LUBBOCK), former small business owner; b. Clebourne, Tex., Apr. 9, 1920; d. Richard Talmadge and Nell Bouregarde (Boykin) Hardin; m. Wilson Niebuhr Munz (div. July 26, 1990); children: Pamela Ann Sanders, Timothy Ray Munz, Phyllis Glasscock; m. Charles William Lubbock, Aug. 12, 1990. Grad. high sch. and bus. sch., Houston. Asst. photographer Robinson Portraits, Houston; clk.-typist U.S. Naval Lighter-Than-Air Base, Houma, La., U.S. Naval Air Sta., Norfolk, Va.; sales distbr. Nina Ross Cosmetiques, Brenham, Tex., Midge's Health Food Store, Brenham, 1992-95. Contbr. poetry to various anthologies. Mem. libr. bd. Fortnightly Club, Brenham, 1970—, pres. arts dept.; pres. Brenham Fine Arts League, 1985. Recipient Golden Poet award, 1987-90, medal of honor World of Poetry, 1990. Mem. UDC, Am. Legion Aux. (past pres.). Baptist. Home: 1501 E Stone St Brenham TX 77833

LUBER, AMANDA KIMMER, public relations executive, marketing professional; b. Aliquippa, Pa., June 21, 1961; d. William Cephus Jr. and Joan Elizabeth (Phillips) Kimmer; m. Jay Lance Luber, Dec. 10, 1988; 1 child, Matthew William. BA in Pub. Rels., Journalism, Econs., Fla. So. Coll., 1983. Cert. pub. rels. profl. Asst. dir. Ctrl. Fla. Health Fair, Orlando, 1983-84; prodn. editor Harcourt Brace Pub., Orlando, 1984-86; features writer The Independent, Winter Haven, Fla., 1986; pub. rels. dir. Palmview Hosp., Lakeland, Fla., 1986-87, Fantastic Sam's Regional Office, Tampa, Fla., 1987-90; mktg. supr. Manatee Community Blood Ctr., Bradenton, Fla., 1991-94; freelance writer, graphic artist Luber Comms. and Design, Riverview, Fla., 1993—; pub. affairs dir. ARC, Tampa Bay chpt., 1995—, state lead for pub. affairs, Fla., 1995—. Founder Reneé Turbeville Meml. Scholarship, Fla. So. Coll., Lakeland, 1984. Mem. Fla. Pub. Rels. Assn. (bd. dirs. 1993-94, newsletter editor 1993-94, Most Improved Chpt. Newsletter state award 1994, PR Profl. of Yr. 1994, Judges award 1993, Award of Distinction 1992). Democrat. Roman Catholic. Home: 10408 Deepbrook

Dr Riverview FL 33569 Office: ARC Tampa Bay Chpt Pub Affairs PO Box 4236 Tampa FL 33677

LUBETSKI, EDITH ESTHER, librarian; b. Bklyn., July 16, 1940; d. David and Leah (Aronson) Slomowitz; m. Meir Lubetski, Dec. 23, 1968; children: Shaul, Uriel, Leah. BA, Bklyn. Coll., 1962; MS in L.S., Columbia U., 1965; MA in Jewish Studies, Yeshiva U., 1968. Judaica librarian Stern Coll., N.Y.C., 1965-66, acquisitions librarian, 1966-69, head librarian, 1969—; Author: (with Meir Lubetski) Building a Judaica Library Collection, 1983; contbr. articles to profl. jours. Mem. ALA, Assn. Jewish Libraries (corr. sec. 1980-84, pres. N.Y. chpt. 1984-86, nat. v.p. 1984-86, nat. pres. 1986-88, Fanny Goldstein Merit award 1993), N.Y. Library Assn. Home: 1219 E 27th St Brooklyn NY 11210-4622 Office: Yeshiva U Hedi Steinberg Libr 245 Lexington Ave New York NY 10016-4605

LUBIC, RUTH WATSON, association executive, nurse midwife; b. Bucks County, Pa., Jan. 18, 1927; d. John Russell and Lillian (Kraft) Watson; m. William James Lubic, May 28, 1955; 1 son, Douglas Watson. Diploma, Sch. Nursing Hosp. U. Pa., 1955; BS, Columbia U., 1959, MA, 1961, EdD in Applied Anthropology, 1979; Cert. in Nurse Midwifery, SUNY, Bklyn., 1962; LLD (hon.), U. Pa., 1985; DSc (hon.), U. Medicine and Dentistry, N.J., 1986; LHD (hon.), Coll. New Rochelle, 1992; DSc (hon.), SUNY, Bklyn., 1993; LHD (hon.), Pace U., 1994. RN, Pa. Mem. faculty Sch. Nursing, N.Y. Med. Coll.; mem. faculty Maternity Ctr. Assn., SUNY Sch. Nurse-Midwifery, Downstate Med. Ctr.; staff nurse through head nurse Meml. Hosp. for Cancer and Allied Disease, N.Y.C., 1955-58; clin. assoc. Grad. Sch. Nursing N.Y. Med. Coll., N.Y.C., 1962-63; parent educator, cons. Maternity Ctr. Assn., N.Y.C., 1963-67, gen. dir., 1970-95; dir. clin. projects., 1995—; cons. in midwifery, nursing and maternal and child health Office of Pub. Health and Sci. HHS, 1995—; adj. prof. divsn. nursing, NYU, 1995—; bd. dirs., v.p. Am. Assn. for World Health U.S. Com. for WHO, 1975-94, pres. 1980-81; mem. bd. maternal child and family health NRC, 1974-80; mem. Commn. on Grads. Fgn. Nursing Schs., 1979-83, v.p. 1980-91, treas., 1982-83; bd. govs. Frontier Nursing Svc., 1982-92; bd. dirs. Pan Am. Health Edn. Found., pres. 1987-88; vis. prof. King Edward Meml. Hosp., Perth, Australia, 1991; Kate Hanna Harvey vis. prof. cmty. health nursing Frances Payne Bolton Sch. Nursing Case Western Res., 1991; Lansdowne lectr. U. Victoria, B.C., Can., 1992. Author: (with Gene Hawes) Childbearing: A Book of Choices, 1987; contbr. articles to profl. jours. Recipient Letitia White award, Florence Nightingale medal, 1955, Rockefeller Pub. Svc. award, 1981, Hattie Hemschemeyer award, 1983, Alumnae award Sch. Nursing U. Pa., 1986, Tchrs. Coll. Columbia U., 1992, Disting. Svc. award Francis Payne Bolton Sch. Nursing, 1993, MacArthur Fellowship award, 1993, Hon. Recognition N.Y. State Nurses Assn., 1993, Nurse-Midwifery Faculty award Columbia U., 1993, Spirit of Nursing award Vis. Nurses Svc. N.Y., 1994, Maes-MacInnes award Divsn. Nursing NYU, 1994, Hon. recognition ANA, 1994; named Maternal-Child Health Nurse of Yr., ANA, 1985. Fellow AAAS, Am. Acad. Nursing, N.Y. Acad. Medicine, Soc. for Applied Anthropology, Am. Coll. of Nurse Midwives; mem. APHA (mem. com. on internat. health, sec. maternal and child health coun. 1982, mem. governing coun. 1986-89, mem. nominating com. 1987, mem. action bd. 1988-90), Am. Coll. Nurse-Midwives (v.p. 1964-66, pres.-elect 1969-70), Soc. Applied Anthropology, Inst. Medicine of NAS, Nat. Assn. Childbearing Ctrs. (pres. 1983-91), Herman Biggs Soc. (sec., treas. 1989-90), Cosmopolitan Club, Sigma Theta Tau.

LUBIN, CAROL RIEGELMAN, political scientist; b. Montclair, N.J., Sept. 23, 1909; d. Charles A. and Lilian (Ehrich) Riegelman; m. Isador Lubin, Jan. 30, 1952 (dec. July 1978); 1 child, Ann L. Buttenwieser. BA, Smith Coll., 1930; MA, Columbia U., 1933, PhD, 1950. Rschr. Carnegie Endowment for Internat. Peace, N.Y.C., 1930-35; mem. internat. staff Internat. Labor Office, Geneva, Switzerland, 1935-52; social policy dir. United Neighborhood Houses, N.Y.C., 1970-80; editl. bd. Unemployment Compensation Commn., Washington, 1979-81; rep. Internat. Fedn. Settlements and Neighborhood Ctrs., 1982—; also bd. dirs. Internat. Fedn. Settlements ans Neighborhood Ctrs.; rep. UN. Co-author: Social Justice for Women: The International Labour Orgn. and Women, 1991. Bd. dirs. Franklin and Eleanor, 1990—, v.p.; exec. com. Roosevelt Inst.; bd. dirs., sec. William Hodson Cmty. Ctr., 1960—. Mem. Nat. Women's Dem. Club, Cosmopolitan Club, Women's City Club, Phi Beta Kappa. Democrat. Home and Office: 1095 Park Ave New York NY 10128

LUBKIN, GLORIA BECKER, physicist; b. Phila., May 16, 1933; d. Samuel Albert and Anne (Gorrin) B.; m. Yale Jay Lubkin, June 14, 1953 (div. Apr. 1968); children: David Craig, Sharon Rebecca. AB, Temple U., 1953; MA, Boston U., 1957; postgrad., Harvard U., 1974-75. Mathematician Fairchild Stratos Co., Hagerstown, Md., 1954, Letterkenny Ordnance Depot, Chambersburg, Pa., 1955-56; physicist TRG Inc., N.Y.C., 1956-58; acting chmn. dept. physics Sarah Lawrence Coll., Bronxville, N.Y., 1961-62; v.p. Lubkin Assocs., electronic cons., Port Washington, N.Y., 1962-68; assoc. editor Physics Today Am. Inst. Physics, N.Y.C., 1963-69; sr. editor Physics Today Am. Inst. Physics, 1970-84, editor, 1985-94, editl. dir., 1994—; cons. in field; mem. Nieman adv. com. Harvard U., 1978-82; co-chmn. search/adv. com. Theoretical Physics Inst., U. Minn., 1987-89, co-chmn. oversight com. 1989—; mem. mng. com. Westinghouse Sci. Writing Prizes, 1988-91; mem. selection com. Knight Fellowships, 1990. Contbr. articles to profl. publs. Gloria Becker Lubkin Professorship of Theoretical Physics established in her honor U. Minn., 1990; Nieman fellow, 1974-75. Fellow AAAS (mem. nominating com. for sect. B phusics 1987-89, chair 1989), Am. Phys. Soc. (exec. com. history of physics divsn. 1983-86, 92-95, exec. com. forum on physics and soc. 1977-78); mem. N.Y. Acad. Scis. (chair The Scis. pub. com. 1992-93), Nat. assn. Sci. Writers, D.C. Science Writers Assn., Sigma Pi Sigma. Jewish. Office: Am Inst Physics One Physics Ellipse College Park MD 20740

LUBKIN, VIRGINIA LEILA, ophthalmologist; b. N.Y.C., Oct. 26, 1914; d. Joseph and Anna Fredericka (Stern) L.; m. Arnold Malkan, June 6, 1944 (div. 1949); m. Martin Bernstein, Aug. 28, 1949; children: Ellen Henrietta, James Ernst, Roger Joel, John Conrad. BS summa cum laude, NYU, 1933; MD, Columbia U., 1937. Diplomate Am. Bd. Ophthalmology. Intern Harlem Hosp., N.Y.C., 1938-40; asst. resident neurology Montefiore Hosp., N.Y.C., 1940, asst. resident pathology, 1940-41, fellow in ophthalmology, 1941-42; resident ophthalmology Kings County Hosp., Bklyn., 1942-43, Mt. Sinai Hosp., N.Y.C., 1943-44; attending ophthalmologist, assoc. clin. prof. emeritus Mt. Sinai Sch. Medicine, 1944—; also sr. attending surgeon N.Y. Eye and Ear Infirmary, Mt. Sinai Sch. Medicine; pvt. practice N.Y.C., 1945-90; surgeon, now sr. surgeon N.Y. Eye and Ear Infirmary, 1945—; rsch. prof. N.Y. Med. Coll., 1986—; co-creator, now chief of rsch. bioengineering lab. N.Y. Eye and Ear Infirmary (name now The Aborn), N.Y.C., 1978—; creator first grad. course in oculoplastics and bi-yearly symposia in devel. dyslexia Mt. Sinai Sch. Medicine; educator courses in psychosomatic ophthalmology Am. Acad. Ophthalmology, 1950-60, educator course in complications of blepharoplasty, 1980-90; bd. dirs. Jewish Guild for the Blind; tchr. surg. ophthalmology in French Cameroon, Presbyn. Mission, 1951; lectr. in numerous countries including India, 1976, 92, Pakistan, 1976, 84, China, 1978, Sri Lanka, 1979, South Africa, 1982, Singapore, 1984, Thailand, 1984, Argentina, 1986, Peru, 1987. Author: (with others) Ophthalmic Plastic and Reconstructive Surgery, 1989; contbr. articles to profl. jours. Bd. dirs. Ctr. fo Environ. Therapeutics, 1995. Grantee Intraocular Lens Implant Mfrs., 1989. Fellow AMA, AAAS, Am. Soc. Ophthalmic Plastic and Reconstructive Surgery (founding), Am. Coll. Surgeons, N.Y. Acad. Medicine, N.Y. Acad. Scis., Am. Acad. Ophthalmology, Am. Soc. Cataract and Refractive Surgery, PanAm. Soc. Ophthalmology, N.Y. Soc. Clin. Ophthalmology (pres. 1975), Soc. Light Treatment and Biol. Rhythms, Phi Beta Kappa, Alpha Omega Alpha. Home: 1 Blackstone Pl Bronx NY 10471-3607 Office: NY Eye and Ear Infirmary Res Bldg 2C 310 E 14th St New York NY 10003-4200

LUBY, JODI ANN, graphic designer; b. N.Y.C., May 20, 1957; d. Chester J. and Joan (Sparer) L.; m. Kent B. Dolan, July 1, 1990; 1 child, Nola Lee Luby Dolan. BFA, Rochester Inst. Tech., 1978; postgrad., Parsons Sch. Design, 1987-90. Designer Jeheber and Peace, N.Y.C., 1978-79, Anspach, Grossman, Portugal, N.Y.C., 1979-81; packaging designer Gerstman and Meyers, N.Y.C., 1981; dir. graphics The Space Design Group, N.Y.C., 1981-83; pres. Jodi Luby and Co., Inc., N.Y.C., 1983—. designer logo type (design award 1980), direct mail package (Folio award 1994). Mem. Am. Inst. of Graphic Arts, WNYC, Sierra Club. Democrat. Home and Office: 808 Broadway New York NY 10003

LUCAL, MARTHA JANE, judge; b. Weston, Va., June 9, 1938; d. James Cledith and Mary Elizabeth (Ocheltree) Bleigh; m. Dean S. Lucal, May 4, 1962; children: Katherine Ann, Mary Elizabeth. AA, Stephens Coll., Columbia, Mo., 1958; BA, Ohio State U., 1961, JD, 1961. Atty. ICC, Washington, 1962-63; tchr. Erie County Sch. Sys., Ohio, 1964-67; asst. pros. atty. Erie County, Sandusky, Ohio, 1976-78; solicitor Village of Berlin Heights, Ohio, 1983-84; pvt. practice law Sandusky, 1972-84; judge probate divsn. Erie County Common Pleas Ct., Sandusky, 1985—. Contbr. articles to profl. publs. Recipient Superior Judicial award Ohio Supreme Ct., 1986. Mem. AAUW, Nat. Judicial Coll., Ohio Bar Assn., Nat. Coll. Probate Judges, Ohio Probate Judges Assn.(chair 1985, legis. com. 1988-89), Delta Kappa Gamma. Methodist. Office: Erie County Common Pleas Court Probate Divsn 323 Columbus Ave Sandusky OH 44870-2602

LUCAS, BARBARA B., electrical equipment manufacturing executive; b. 1945. BA, U. Md., 1967; MA, Johns Hopkins U., 1968. V.p., sec. Equitable Bancorp, 1977-85; v.p. pub. affairs, corp. sec. Black & Decker Corp., Balt., 1985—; bd. dirs. Goulds Pumps, Inc. Office: Black & Decker Corp 701 E Joppa Rd Baltimore MD 21286-5559*

LUCAS, BARBARA N., lawyer; b. Bklyn., Mar. 4, 1946. BA, Cornell U., 1966; JD, Am. U., 1971. Bar: Md. 1971, D.C. 1973, N.Y. 1984. Ptnr. Cadwalader, Wickersham & Taft. Mem. Am. Bankers Assn. (chair lawyers com. 1990). Office: Cadwalader Wickersham & Taft 100 Maiden Ave New York NY 10006*

LUCAS, BETH ANNE, television producer; b. Grand Rapids, Mich., Sept. 15, 1960; d. Gordon Patrick and Phyllis (Sablack) Galka; m. Mark Fordham, Mar. 19, 1982 (div. 1985); m. Gus Lucas, June 3, 1991. BA in Psychology, Antioch U., 1995. Segment producer Breakaway, Metromedia TV, Hollywood, Calif., 1983; asst. dir. Anything for Money, Paramount TV, Hollywood, 1984; post prodn. supr. Heathcliff DIC, Hollywood, 1984; post prodn. supr. Beauty and the Beast, Witt-Thomas Prodns., Hollywood, 1986-88; assoc. producer Anything But Love, 20th Century Fox, Hollywood, 1989; assoc. producer Easy Street Viacom Prodns., Hollywood, 1984-85; mgr. post prodn. Matlock, Perry Mason, Father Dowling, Jack and the Fatman, Hollywood, 1990-91; project coord. Teen Dating Violence Prevention Team, Haven Hills, Inc. Vol. Children Are Our Future, Haven Hills Battered Woman's Shelter; mem. AIDS Project, L.A., L.A. Mission, Children Def. Fund. Mem. APA, NOW, Amnesty Internat., Am. Profl. Soc. on the Abuse of Children, Calif. Profl. Soc. on the Abuse of Children, Nature Conservancy, Nat. Parks and Conservation Assn., Feminist Majority, Nat. Abortion Rights Action League, Greenpeace, Smithsonian Assocs., Mus. Contemporary Art, Los Angeles County Mus., Sta. KCET, UCLA Alumni Assn., Child Help USA, Childreach, Mus. of Tolerance.

LUCAS, ELIZABETH COUGHLIN, educator; b. Youngstown, Ohio, May 5, 1918; d. Joseph Anthony and Gertrude Elizabeth (Handel) Coughlin; m. Charles Edward Lucas, Apr. 7, 1945. BS magna cum laude, Notre Dame Coll. of Ohio, 1940; Diploma, Harvard U., 1944; MA in Edn., Calif. State Poly U., 1980. Cert. tchr., Calif. (life), secondary tchr., Pa., Ohio. Tech. sec. for v.p. engring and purchasing Patterson Foundry and Machine Co., East Liverpool, Ohio, 1941-42; tchr. chemistry Point Marion (Pa.) High Sch., 1942, Lincoln High Sch., Midland, Pa., 1942-44; radar specialist Thunderstorm Project U.S. Weather Bur., St. Cloud, Fla., 1946, Wilmington, Ohio, 1947; substitute tchr. math, sci. Chaffey (Calif.) Union High Schs., 1971-75; tchr. math Claremont (Calif.) High Sch., 1975-80; tchr., counselor, head sci. dept. San Antonio High Sch., Claremont, 1980-88; substitute tchr. Claremont Unified Sch. Dist., Claremont, 1988—; mem. dist. adv. com. for math. and sci., Claremont, 1983-85; substitute tchr. San Antonio (Calif.) High Sch., 1988—, Upland (Calif.) High Sch., 1988-89, Hillside High Sch., 1988-89. Author, editor: A Descriptive Study of the Effects of the New Math Syndrome on the Average High School Student, 1980. Lt. (j.g.) USNR, 1944-48. Mem. NAFE, Nat. Coun. of Tchrs. of Math., Nat. Sci. Tchrs. Assn., Assn. for Supervision and Curriculum Devel., Cath. Daus. of the Ams. (regent 1975-77, diocesan chmn. 1979-81). Republican. Roman Catholic. Home and Office: 9185 Regency Way Alta Loma CA 91701-3439

LUCAS, GEORGETTA MARIE SNELL, retired educator, artist; b. Harmony, Ind., July 25, 1920; d. Ernest Clermont and Sarah Ann (McIntyre) Snell; m. Joseph William Lucas, Jan. 29, 1943; children:Carleen Anita Lucas Underwood-Scrougham, Thomas Joseph, Joetta Jeanne Lucas Allgood. BS, Ind. State U., 1942; MS in Edn., Butler U., 1964; postgrad. Herron Sch. of Art, Indpls., 1961-65, Ind. U., Indpls. and Bloomington, 1960, 61, 62, 65. Music, art tchr. Jasonville City Schs., Ind., 1942-43, Van Buren High Sch., Brazil, Ind., 1943-46, Plainfield City Schs., Ind., 1946-52, Met. Sch. Dist. Wayne Twp., Indpls., 1952-56, 1959-68; art tchr. Met. Sch. Dist. Perry Twp., Indpls., 1968-81. Illustrator: (book) Why So Sad, Little Rag Doll, 1963; artist (painting) Ethereal Season, 1966, (lithograph) Bird of Time, 1965-66; exhibited in group shows Hoosier Salon Art Exhibit 1956, 60, 62-65, 67, 70, 72, 87, 94, N.Y. Lincoln Ctr., N.Y.C., 1994; represented in permanent collections Ind. State U., Ind.-Purdue U.-Indpls., GM Inst., Detroit; lectr. Art Educators Assn. Ind., Ind. U.-Bloomington, 1976. Mem. NEA (life), Nat. Assn. Women Artist, Ind. Artist Craftsmen, Inc. (hon., pres. 1979-85, 87, 88), Ind. Fedn. Art Clubs (hon., pres. 1986-87, counselor 1988-91, bd. dirs. 1991—, parliamentarian 1992—), Hoosier Salon, Ind. State U. Mortar Bd. 1982, Alumni, 1988, Art Edn. Assn. Ind. (life), Nat. League Am. Pen Women (Ind. state art chmn. 1984—, Best of Show award 1983, pres. Indpls. branch 1994-96, front cover drawing Pen-Woman Mag. 1994), Fine Art for State Ind. (Internat. Women's Yr. fine art chmn. 1977), Internat. Platform Assn. (bd. dirs. 1983—, chmn. art com. 1987—, lectr. 1975, 78, 82, 84, Silver award 1978, appointed gov. 1983—), Cen. Ind. Artists (hon.), Alpha Delta Kappa (life, Ind. state chmn. of art 1973-77, pres. 1972-74, represented by painting in nat. hdqrs.-Kansas City, Mo., Fidelis Delta first v.p.), Retired Educators Sorority (1st v.p.), Order of Eastern Star. Republican. Methodist. Avocations: genealogy, travel, numismatics. Home and Office: 3192 E Main St Plainfield IN 46168-2621

LUCAS, JUANITA GLASSCO, realtor, systems analyst; b. Waverly, Ohio; d. Harold Frank and Lillie Meredith (Harris) Glassco; 1 child, Carol Brynne. BS, Franklin U., Columbus, Ohio, 1976; grad., Def. Logistics Supply Mgmt. Program, U.S. Dept. Def., 1978; MA, Cen. Mich. U., Mt. Pleasant, Mich., 1979; postgrad., Columbia Pacific U., 1993—. Sec. State of Ohio, Columbus, 1951-57; registration clk. Wittenberg U., Springfield, Ohio, 1957-60; asst. to registrar U. Chgo., 1960-62; local bd. clk. Selective Svc. Sys., Columbus, 1962-66; supply sys. analyst Def. Sys. Automation Ctr., U.S. Dept. Def., Columbus, 1966-89; realtor Saxton Real Estate, Columbus, 1976—, Saxton Realtors, 1993—; interior designer Transdesigns, Atlanta, 1983-87; fashion cons. Worldwide Images, Boston, 1989-94; cons. Mary Kay Cosmetics, 1994—. Mem. Hope Luth. Ch., Columbus, 1969—, Impressarios Opera, Columbus, 1988—. Mem. Nat. Assn. Realtors, Ohio Assn. Realtors, Women's Coun. Realtors (mem. leadership tng. designation program), Ctrl. Mich. U. Alumni, Am. Contract Bridge League, Internat. Platform Assn., Internat. Pageant Assn. (cert. pageant judge), Sigma Iota Epsilon. Home: PO Box 30127 Gahanna OH 43230-0127

LUCAS, JUDITH ANN, secondary school educator; b. Waterloo, Iowa, Aug. 12, 1939; d. Edward Newton and Ona Norine (Carter) Foster; m. Paul Robert Lucas, Apr. 14, 1962; children: Rebecca Ann, Robert Corydon. BA, Simpson Coll., 1962; MS, Ind. U., 1982. Cert. English and Spanish tchr., Minn., English and Reading tchr., Ind. English and Spanish tchr. Mpls. Pub. Schs., 1962-67, Monroe County Pub. Schs., Bloomington, Ind., 1967-69; English tchr. Richland-Bean Blossom Cmty. Schs., Ellettsville, Ind., 1978—. Recipient Shining Star award for Excellence in Teaching, Sta. WTHR-TV and Star Fin. Bank Indpls., 1994, Prentice Hall/Nat. Mid. Sch. Teaching Team award, 1995; Tchr. Creativity fellow Lilly Endowment, Inc. Mem. NEA, Nat. Coun. Tchrs. English, Ind. Coun. Tchrs. English, Nat. Mid. Sch. Assn., Ind. State Tchrs. Assn., Richland Bean Blossom Tchrs. Assn. (negotiation team 1985-95). Home: 3921 Sugar Ln Bloomington IN 47404 Office: Edgewood Mid Sch Reeves Rd Ellettsville IN 47429

LUCAS, JUNE H., state legislator; children: Deven Armeni, Adrien. Student, Youngstown State U. Mem. Ohio Ho. of Reps., 1986—, mem. energy and environment, judiciary and criminal justice coms.; Mem. adv. com. ohio child support guidelines, women's policy and rsch. Com.; ranking minority mem. family svcs. com. Contbr. articles to Warren Tribune Chronicle. Active Animal Welfare League. Named Woman of Yr., Coalition Labor Union Women, YWCA, 1988. Mem. NOW (Trumbull County chpt.), LWV, Ohio Bus. and Profl. Women, Ohio Farm Bur., Mosquito Creek Devel. Assn., Farmer's Union, Sierra Club. Democrat. Home: 1435 Locust St Mineral Ridge OH 44440-9721 Office: Ohio House of Reps Office of House Mems Columbus OH 43215

LUCAS, SHARI, musician, educator; b. Ridgewood, N.J., Sept. 5, 1960; d. Donald and Irene (Van de Veen) L. MusB, Baldwin-Wallace Coll., 1982; MusM, Yale U., 1984. Organist, choir dir. Spring Glen Congrl. Ch., Hamden, Conn., 1983-85; asst. sec. Yale Alumni Fund, New Haven, 1984-86; organist North Haven (Conn.) Congl. Ch., 1985; dir. music First Congl. Ch., Madison, Conn., 1986—. Mem. Am. Guild Organists (dean New Haven chpt. 1996—), Organ Hist. Soc. Democrat. Office: First Congl Ch 26 Meetinghouse Ln Madison CT 06443

LUCAS, SHIRLEY AGNES HOYT, management executive; b. Chicago, Aug. 21, 1921; d. Howard L. and Lucille P. (Von Krippenstapel) Hoyt; m. William H. Lucas, Feb. 2, 1952; 1 child, Lucille Shirley. Student, Northwestern U., 1941-42. V.p. Lucas Co., Chgo., 1980—. Mem. Ill. Hosp. Assn. (Leadership award 1975), Aux. Christ Hosp. and Med. Ctr. (life, past bd. dirs., cotillion chmn., housewalk chmn.). Republican. Lutheran. Office: Lucas Co 9127 S Kedzie Ave Evergreen Park IL 60642-1606

LUCAS, THERESA EILEEN, elementary education educator; b. Bellingham, Wash., Jan. 6, 1948; d. John M. and Lillian Sigrid (Westford) Cairns; m. Paul T. Lucas, 1970 (div. June 1987); children: Jeffrey Thomas, Aimee Michelle. BA, U. No. Colo., 1970, MA, 1985. Cert. elem. edn. grades K-6, spl. edn. grades K-12, Colo. Tchr. spl. edn. Baker Elem. Sch. Adams County Sch. Dist. 50, Westminster, Colo., 1970-77, tchr. 1st grade Berkeley Gardens Elem. Sch., 1978-84, tchr. kindergarten Harris Park Elem. Sch., 1984-87, tchr. kindergarten Tennyson Knolls Elem. Sch., 1987—; mem. sch. coms. Baker Elem. Sch., Berkeley Gardens Elem. Sch., Harris Park Elem. Sch., Tennyson Knolls Elem. Sch., Adams County Sch. Dist. 50, Westminster, 1970—; co-author literacy grant Adams County Ednl. Found., 1994, Gov.'s Creativity grant Tennyson Knolls Elem. Sch., 1989-90. Vol. Rainbows for All God's Children, Spirit of Christ Ch., Arvada, Colo., 1988-90, vol. crisis hotline, 1990-91; campaign vol. pro-edn. candidates, Arvada, 1992. Mem. ASCD, NEA, Internat. Reading Assn., Colo. Edn. Assn., Colo. Coun. Internat. Reading Assn., West Adams County Coun. Internat. Reading Assn., Westminster Edn. Assn. (membership rep. Tennyson Knolls Elem. Sch. 1990-95). Democrat. Home: 8279 Iris St Arvada CO 80005-2136

LUCCHETTI, LYNN L., career officer; b. San Francisco, Calif., Aug. 21, 1939; d. Dante and Lillian (Bergeron) L. AB, San Jose State U., 1961; MS, San Francisco State U., 1967; grad. U.S. Army Basic Officer's Course, 1971, U.S. Army Advanced Officer Course, 1976, grad. U.S. Air Force Command and Staff Coll., 1982, U.S. Air Force War Coll., 1983, Sr. Pub. Affairs Officer Course, 1984. Media buyer Batten, Barton, Durstine & Osborn, Inc., San Francisco, 1961-67; producer-dir. Sta. KTVA-TV, Anchorage, 1967-68; media supr. Bennett, Luke and Teawell Advt., Phoenix, 1968-71; commd. 1st lt. U.S. Army, 1971; advanced through ranks to lt. col., 1985, col., 1989, brig. gen. nom. 1993; officer U.S. Army, 1971-74, D.C. N.G., , 1974-78, U.S. Air Force Res., 1978—, program advt. mgr. U.S. Navy Recruiting Command, 1974-76; exec. coordinator for the Joint Advt. Dirs. of Recruiting (JADOR), 1976-79; dir. U.S. Armed Forces Joint Recruiting Advt. Program (JRAP), Dept. Def., Washington, 1979-91; resources mgr. Exec. Leadership Devel. Program Dept. Def., Washington, 1991-94. Author: Broadcasting in Alaska, 1924-1966. Decorated U.S. Army Meritorious Svc. medal, Nat. Def. medal, U.S. Air Force Longevity Ribbon, U.S. Navy Meritorious Unit Commendation, Dept. Def. Joint Achievement medal, 1984. Sigma Delta Chi journalism scholar, 1960. Mem. Women in Def., Sr. Profl. Womens Assn. Home: 11401 Malaguena Ln NE Albuquerque NM 87111-6899

LUCCI, SUSAN, actress; b. Scarsdale, N.Y., Dec. 23, 1946; d. Victor and Jeanette L.; m. Helmut Huber, 1969; children: Liza Victoria, Andreas Martin. BA, Marymount Coll., 1968. Portrays Erica in TV series All My Children, 1970—; appearances in other series include: Fantasy Island, The Love Boat, The Fall Guy; TV films: Invitation to Hell, 1985, Mafia Princess, 1985, (mini-series) Anastasia: The Mystery of Anna Anderson, 1986, Haunted by Her Past, 1988, Lady Mobster, 1988, The Bride in Black, 1990, The Woman Who Sinned, 1991, Double Edge, 1992, Between Love and Hate, 1993, French Silk, 1994; host of spl. with Tony Danza 99 Ways to Attract the Right Man. Recipient 13 Emmy nominations for best actress in daytime drama series, numerous other awards. Office: All My Children 320 W 66th St New York NY 10023-6338 also: ICM care Sylvia Gold 8942 Wilshire Blvd Beverly Hills CA 90211-1934*

LUCE, MARGARET MARY, electrical engineer; b. Ft. George Meade, Md., June 11, 1959; d. Howard John and Esther Ruth (Snow) L. BA in Physics, Ea. Wash. U., 1989; BSEE, Gonzaga U., 1992. Stenographer Spokane (Wash.) County Sheriff Dept., 1978-87; elec. engr. Hewlett Packard, Spokane, 1992—. Vol. presenter hands on sci. local schs., Spokane County, Wash. Office: Hewlett Packard 24001 E Mission Liberty Lake WA 99025

LUCE, PRISCILLA MARK, public affairs executive; b. N.Y.C., Feb. 4, 1947; d. S. Carl and Patricia (Greenfield) Mark; m. Robert Warren Luce, July 19, 1969; children: James Warren, David Mark. BA, U. Pa., 1968. Adminstrv. asst. Phila. Mus. Art, 1968-69; asst. dir. pub. info. Mt. Holyoke Coll., South Hadley, Mass., 1969-71; v.p. Barnes & Roche, Inc., Phila., 1971-82; mgr. civic programs TRW Inc., Cleve., 1982-85; mgr. community relations TRW Inc., 1985-88, mgr. external communications, 1988-90, dir., pub. affairs and advt., 1990-92; v.p. info. sys. and svcs. comms., cons. United Way Svcs., Cleve., 1983-85, 92-94, v.p. mktg. and orgn. comms., 1994—; cons. United Way Svcs., Cleve., 1983-85. Trustee New Orgn. for the Visual Arts, Cleve., 1983—, Community Info. Vol. Action Ctr., Cleve., 1984-86, Albert M. Greenfield Found., Phila., 1989—; trustee Ohio Chamber Orch., Cleve., 1986-92, chmn. devel. com. 1987-88, chmn., trustee, 1991-92, exec. v.p., 1990-91; pres. New Orgn. for the Visual Arts, Cleve., 1984-86; mem. steering com. Cleve. Art Festival, 1983-84, Mayor's Cultural Arts Planning Task Force, Cleve., 1985-87; trustee Ret. Sr. Vol. Prog., 1991; leadership devel. prog. participant United Way Svcs., Cleve., 1983; mem. steering com. Bus. Volunteerism Coun. of Cleve., 1984-92, comm. adv. com. Work in NE Ohio Coun., 1991-94. Recipient Woman of Profl. Excellence award YWCA of Cleve., 1990. Mem. Pub. Rels. Soc. Am., Cleve. Advt. Club. Republican. Office: TRW Inc 1900 Richmond Rd Cleveland OH 44124-3719

LUCENTE, ROSEMARY DOLORES, educational administrator; b. Renton, Wash., Jan. 11, 1935; d. Joseph Anthony and Erminia Antoinette (Argano) Lucente; BA, Mt. St. Mary's Coll., 1956, MS, 1963. Tchr. pub. schs., Los Angeles, 1956-65, supr. tchr., 1958-65, asst. prin., 1965-69, prin. elem. sch., 1969-85, 86—, dir. instrn., 1985-86, 1986—; nat. cons., lectr. Dr. William Glasser's Educator Tng. Ctr., 1968—; nat. workshop leader Nat. Acad. for Sch. Execs.-Am. Assn. Sch. Adminstrs., 1980; L.A. Unified Sch. Dist. rep. for nat. pilot of Getty Inst. for Visual Arts, 1983-85, 92—, site coord., 1983-86, team leader, mem. supt.'s adv. cabinet, 1987—. Recipient Golden Apple award Stanford Ave. Sch. PTA, Faculty and Community Adv. Council, 1976, resolution for outstanding service South Gate City Council, 1976. Mem. Nat. Assn. Elem. Sch. Prins., L.A. Elem. Prins. Orgn. (v.p. 1979-80), Assn. Calif. Sch. Adminstrs (charter mem.), Assn. Elem. Sch. Adminstrs. (vice-chmn. chpt. 1972-75, city-wide exec. bd., steering com. 1972-75, 79-80), Asso. Adminstrs. Los Angeles (charter), Pi Theta Mu, Kappa Delta Pi (v.p. 1982-84), Delta Kappa Gamma. Democrat. Roman Catholic. Home: 6501 Lindenhurst Ave Los Angeles CA 90048-4733 Office: Figueroa St Sch 510 W 111th St Los Angeles CA 90044-4231

LUCI, DEB, data analyst; b. Winter Haven, Fla., June 7, 1966; d. James Luci and Elizabeth Milbrae McKinley. BA in English and Writing, Denison U., 1988. Writing instr. Marshall U., Huntington, W.Va., 1989-91; direct care counselor Autism Svcs. Ctr., Huntington, 1990-91; data analyst Filoli Info. Sys., Palo Alto, Calif., 1994—.

LUCIA, MARILYN REED, physician; b. Boston; m. Salvatore P. Lucia, 1959 (dec. 1984); m. C. Robert Russell; children: Elizabeth, Walter, Salvatore, Darryl. MD, U. Calif., San Francisco, 1956. Intern Stanford U. Hosps., 1956-57; NIMH fellow, resident in psychiatry Langley Porter, U. Calif., San Francisco, 1957-60; NIMH fellow, resident in child psychiatry Mt. Zion Hosp., San Francisco, 1964-66; NIMH fellow, resident in community psychiatry U. Calif., San Francisco, 1966-68, clin. prof. psychiatry, 1982—; founder, cons. Marilyn Reed Lucia Child Care Study Ctr., U. Calif., San Francisco; cons. Cranio-facial Ctr., U. Calif., San Francisco, No. Calif. Diagnostic Sch. for Neurologically Handicapped Children; dir. children's psychiat. svcs. Contra Costa County Hosp., Martinez. Fellow Am. Psychiat. Assn., Am. Acad. Child Psychiatry; mem. Am. Cleft Palate Assn. Office: 350 Parnassus Ave Ste 602 San Francisco CA 94117-3608

LUCIANO, GWENDOLYN KAYE, planning specialist, utility rates administrator; b. Cleve., Feb. 26, 1954; d. Charles Wayne and Lila (Cole) Rhodes. BA in Math. and Mktg., Lake Erie Coll., 1975, MBA, 1988. cert. project mgmt. profl. Scheduling engr. A.G. McKee & Co., Independence, Ohio, 1975-78; project scheduling supr. Perry Nuclear Plant Raymond Kaiser Engrs., Perry, Ohio, 1978-85; maintenance planning supr. Cleve. Electric Illuminating Co., 1985-89; mgmt. cons. Liberty Cons. Group, Balt., 1989-91; outage planning coord. Cleve. Electric Illuminating, 1991-94; mgr. fed. regulation Centerior Energy Corp., Independence, Ohio, 1994-96, mgr. fed. reg. and pricing, 1996—; instr. Inst. Nuclear Power Ops., Atlanta, 1993-94; bd. dirs. Learning About Bus., 1992-96. Mem. Am. Assn. Cost Engrs., Project Mgmt. Inst., Lake Erie Coll. Nat. Alumni Assn. (pres. 1996—). Republican. Episcopalian. Office: Centerior Energy Corp 6200 Oak Tree Blvd Independence OH 44131-2510

LUCIANO, ROSELLE PATRICIA, advertising executive, editor; b. Bklyn., Feb. 10, 1921; d. Giacomo Roberto and Francesca Rosa (Ruvolo) Rubino; m. Anthony Vincenzo Luciano, Nov. 24, 1946; 1 child, Nino Vincenzo Luciano. Attended, NYU. College shop mgr. Abraham & Straus, Bklyn., 1939-41, advtg. copywriter, 1941-44; fashion editor Syndicated MB Reports, N.Y.C., 1945-48; advtg. mgr., fashions copywriter Macy's 34th St., N.Y.C., 1949-54; publicist, adminstr. Fun With Prodns., N.Y.C., 1959-69; chair, adminstr. U.U. Plandome Forum, Manhasset, N.Y., 1970-78, UU Veatch Found., Manhasset, N.Y., 1979-84; dir. devel. IALRW Literacy For Women Program, Great Britain and India, 1984—; coord. numerous workshops in field for various orgns.; served as spkr., editor, writer, publicist, 1984—. Operator political booth Democratic Party, Garden City, 1984, 88, 92; founder R.P.L. Literacy Fund for Women, 1996—. Recipient Best Advtg. Ad of the Yr. award Women's Wear Daily, 1954, Citizen of the Yr. award Carle Place Schs., 1965, award for outstanding leadership and encouragement for working women Women-On-the-Job, Inc., N.Y., 1987. Unitarian Universalist.

LUCID, SHANNON W., biochemist, astronaut; b. Shanghai, China, Jan. 14, 1943; d. Joseph O. Wells; m. Michael F. Lucid; children: Kawai Dawn, Shandara Michelle, Michael Kermit. BS in Chemistry, U. Okla., 1963, MS in Biochemistry, 1970, PhD in Biochemistry, 1973. Sr. lab. technician Okla. Med. Rsch. Found., 1964-66, rsch. assoc., from 1974; chemist Kerr-McGee, Oklahoma City, 1966-68; astronaut NASA Lyndon B. Johnson Space Ctr., Houston, 1979—; mission specialist flights STS-51G and STS-34 NASA Lyndon B. Johnson Space Ctr., mission specialist on Shuttle Atlantis Flight, 1991; mission specialist flight STS-58 NASA, 1993, mission specialist flight STS 76 & 79, 1996; Mission Specialist Stationed on Space Station Mir, 1996. First woman to fly on the shuttle three times. Address: NASA Johnson Space Ctr CB-Astronaut Office Houston TX 77058*

LUCKE, BETTY JEAN, dressmaker; b. Pitts., July 6, 1926; d. George Michael and Emma Mae (Burris) Brilhart; m. Winston Slover Lucke, Sept. 13, 1947 (div. Sept. 1963); children: Nancy, Robert, Susan. ADN, St. Luke's Sch. Nursing, N.Y.C., 1947. RN, N.Y. Floor nurse orthopedics Mass. Gen. Hosp., Boston, 1947-49; nurse Palo Alto (Calif.) Med. Clinic, 1950-53; self-employed dressmaker Menlo Park, Calif., 1960—. Clothing Leader 4-H of San Mateo County, Calif., 1960-71; 4-H Club Leader, Alpine Valley 4-H, Calif., 1969-72. Democrat. Office: Bonasue 1172 Chestnut St Menlo Park CA 94025

LUCKEY, DORIS WARING, civic volunteer; b. Union City, N.J., Sept. 17, 1929; d. Jay Deloss and Edna May (Ware) Waring; m. George William Luckey, Mar. 29, 1958; children: G. Robert, Jana Elizabeth, John Andrew. AB, U. Rochester, 1950; CLU, Am. Coll., Bryn Mawr, Pa., 1957. With pers. dept., supr. life dept. Travelers Ins. Co., Rochester, N.Y., 1952-58; agt. asst. life underwriting Mass. Mut. Ins. Co., Rochester, 1958. Chairperson, various past offices Bd. Coop. Ednl. Svcs. and State Edn. Dept., Vocat. Tech. Adv. Com., Rochester and Albany, 1975—, pres. Rochester, 1975-85, Monroe County Sch. Bds. Assn., Rochester, 1980-81; v.p. Penfield (N.Y.) Schs., 1978-81; various fin. ednl. and speaking engagements LWV, 1983—; pres. ch. coun., chair ch. and min. com., co-chair United Ch. Christ denomination, Genesee Valley; pres. William Warfield Scholarship Fund Bd.; former adv. to bd. St. John's Home for Aging, mem. bd.; vol. numerous other civic, cultural, ch. and artistic orgns. Mem. AAUW (past pres., past bd. dirs., dist. 1 state rep.). Republican.

LUCKEY, MARGARET ANN, critical care nurse; b. Seymour, Ind., June 18, 1958; d. Paul Henry and Virginia Marilyn (Enzinger) L. BSN with honors, Ea. Ky. U., 1980. RN, Ind., N.C., Ariz., Fla., Calif.; cert. post anesthesia nurse; cert. ACLS instr. Staff nurse med.-surg. unit Columbus (Ind.) Regional Hosp., 1980-87; staff nurse acute care unit Duke U. Med. Ctr., Durham, N.C., 1987-89; staff nurse intensive care unit USAF Med. Ctr., Scott AFB, Ill., 1989-90, charge nurse post anesthesia care unit, 1990-92; staff nurse post anesthesia care unit Ind. Surgery Ctr., Indpls., 1993-95; traveling nurse post anesthesia care unit Am. Mobile Nurses, San Diego, 1995—. Capt. USAF, 1989-92. Mem. Am. Soc. Post Anesthesia Nurses, Sigma Theta Tau, Theta Nu.

LUCKMAN, SHARON GERSTEN, arts administrator; b. Sioux City, Iowa, Oct. 10, 1945; d. Robert S. and Libbie (Izen) Gersten; m. Peter Luckman, Nov. 22, 1968 (div. 1979); children: Melissa, Gregory; m. Paul Shapiro, Dec. 13, 1981. BS, U. Wis., 1967; cert. Inst. Not-For-Profit Mgmt., Columbia U., 1982. Dir. 92nd St YM/YHA Dance Ctr., N.Y.C., 1978-86; dir. devel. & new ventures Alvin Ailey Dance Found., N.Y.C., 1986-87, exec. dir., 1988; dir. Vol. Lawyers for the Arts, N.Y.C., 1988—; dance tchr. 92nd St. Y, N.Y.C., 1963-78, Nassau Community Coll., Garden City, N.Y., 1963-78, Long Beach (N.Y.) Pub. Schs., 1963-78; dir. Brant Lake (N.Y.) Dance and Sports Ctr., 1980-86. Chairperson Laban/Bartenieff Inst. Movement Studies, N.Y.C., 1984-87. Democrat. Jewish. Office: Volunteer Lawyers for Arts 1285 Ave of the Ams 3d Fl New York NY 10019 Office: Dance Theater Foundation Inc 211 West 61st St 3rd Flr New York NY 10023*

LUCKOW, ELIZABETH ELLEN, retired nurse; b. Stromsburg, Nebr., Jan. 31, 1934; d. Paul William and Lillian Marcella (Anderson) James; children: Michael, Erin Elizabeth. Diploma in nursing, Lincoln Gen. Hosp., 1954; BS, U. Colo., 1966, cert. pediatric nurse practitioner, 1967, MS, 1970. RN, Colo. Charge nurse sick baby nursery Children's Hosp., Fresno, Calif., 1955-56; pediatric nurse Pediatric Group, Fresno, 1956-62; emer. rm. nurse Gen. Rose Hosp., Denver, 1962; pediatric nurse emer. rm. Children's Hosp., Denver, 1963; pediatric nurse pvt. practice med. office, Denver, 1964; migrant nurse, child care nurse dept. pediatrics U. Colo., Boulder, 1967; clinic coord. Boulder County Devel. Evaluation Clinic, Boulder, 1969-82; child devel. cons. Boulder County Social Svcs., Boulder, 1983-84; staff nurse Boulder Psychiat. Inst., 1985-88; ret., 1988. Mem. Boulder County Child Abuse Team, 1978-79; bd. dirs. Boulder County Bd. Devel. Disabilities, 1980-82; mem., adviser Colo. Subcom. on Mental Retardation, Denver, 1969-78; pres. Colo. Nurses Assn., Boulder, 1973; treas. Boulder Valley Bd. Edn., 1973-76; mem. adv. bd. Boulder Valley Sch. Adv. Bd., 1970-82; mem. Boulder County Mental Health-Child Team, 1978-80. Mem. Non Practicing and Part Time Colo. Nurses Assn. (program com. 1991—), Sigma Theta Tau (life). Methodist. Home: 3111 14th St Boulder CO 80304-2611

LUCKS, LINDA CAROLE, community relations consultant, educator; b. N.Y.C., Mar. 31, 1943; d. Arthur and Paula (Schulman) L.; m. Jason D. Groode, Dec. 20, 1964 (div. 1973); children: Cameron Lynne, Justin Sanders; m. R. Michael Rosenfeld, June 22, 1986. BA, UCLA, 1965. Dir. Parallel Corp., L.A., 1980-83; mgr., dir. pub. rels. L.A. Olympic Orgn. Com. Olympic Torch Relay, 1983-85; v.p. Pvt. Entertainment Network, L.A., 1985-87; prin. Linda Lucks & Assoc., Venice, Calif., 1988—; mem. Calif. Bd. Psychology, Sacramento, 1986-95, Calif. Bd. Dental Examiners, Sacramento, 1995—. Dep. L.A. City Coun., 1991; mem. Los Angeles County Beach Adv. Com., 1992—; chmn. Venice Beach Area Police Adv. Coun., Calif., 1992—; fin. projects coord. Californians for Cranston, L.A., 1980; trustee Neighborhood Youth Assn., 1992—. Recipient Outstanding Contbn. award L.A. County Bd. Suprs., 1993, cert. of appreciation Neighborhood Youth Assn., 1993. Democrat. Home: 30 Wavecrest Venice CA 90291

LUCKY, ANNE WEISSMAN, dermatologist; b. N.Y.C., May 11, 1944; d. Jacob and Gertrude (Tetelman) Weissman; m. Paul A. Lucky, May 19, 1972; children: Jennifer, Andrea. BA, Brown U., 1966; MD, Yale U., 1970. Diplomate Nat. Bd. Med. Examiners, Am. Bd. Pediatrics/subspecialty of pediatric endocrinology, Am. Bd. Dermatology. Intern and resident in pediatrics The Children's Hosp. Med. Ctr., Boston, 1970-73; fellow in human genetics and pediatrics Yale U. Sch. Medicine, New Haven, Conn., 1973-74; resident in dermatology Yale U. Sch. Medicine, 1979-81, instr. pediatrics, 1980-81, assoc. prof. dermatology and pediatrics, 1981-83; clin. assoc. Reprodn. Rsch. Br./Nat. Inst. Child Health/NIH, Bethesda, Md., 1974-76; asst. prof. pediatrics Wyler Children's Hosp./Pritzker Sch. Med./U. Chgo. Hosps., 1976-79; assoc. prof. dermatology, pediatrics U. Cin. Coll. Medicine, 1983-88; pvt. practice Dermatology Assocs. of Cin, Inc., 1988—; pres. Dermatology Rsch. Assocs., Inc., Cin., 1988—; dir. Dermatology Clinic Children's Hosp. Med. Ctr., Cin., 1989—; vol. prof. dermatology and pediatrics U. Cin. Coll. Medicine, 1988-94. Editorial bd. Pediatric Dermatology, 1982—, Archives of Dermatology, 1983-94; contbr. numerous articles to profl. jours., publs. Recipient the Janet M. Glasgow Meml. Scholarship, Am. Women's Med. Assn., 1970, the Ramsey Meml. Scholarship award Yale U. Sch. Medicine, 1968, others; grantee USPHS, 1964-66, 67, 68-70, NIH, 1977-79, 79-82, 82-87, 84-87, 87-93, others. Mem. Lawson Wilkins Pediatric Endocrine Soc., Soc. for Pediatric Endocrinology (bd. dirs. 1984-87, pres. 1990-91), Am. Acad. Dermatology, Soc. Investigative Dermatology, Soc. for Dermatologic Genetics of the Am. Acad. Dermatology, Endocrine Soc., Acad. Medicine/Cin. Women's Faculty Assn./The Children's Hosp. Med. Ctr., Women's Derm. Soc. (bd. dirs. 1993—), Ohio State Med. Assn., Soc. Pediatric Rsch., Cin. Derm. Soc. (pres. elect 1995-96), Phi Beta Kappa, Sigma Xi, Alpha Omega Alpha. Office: Derm Assocs of Cin 7691 Five Mile Rd Cincinnati OH 45230

LUCOFF, KATHY ANN, art advisor; b. L.A., Jan. 28, 1953; d. Marvin and JoAnn Ruth (Blaugrund) Miller Lucoff; m. Martin Gary Godin, Apr. 26, 1992. BFA, Calif. Coll. Arts & Crafts, Oakland, 1974. Asst. dir. L.A. Louver Gallery, Venice, Calif., 1976-78; instr. Santa Monica (Calif.) Coll., 1977; prin. Kathy Lucoff Arts Adv. Svcs., 1978—; instr. Dept. of Continuing Edn. Rice U., Houston, 1987-88; bd. dirs. Univ. Art Mus., Long Beach, Calif. Art advisor: Poets Walk, Pub. Art Program, CBS Med. Art Ctr., L.A. C. of C. Pub. Art Program. Office: 10520 Wilshire Blvd Apt 604 Los Angeles CA 90024-4595

LUDES, REGINA ANN, editor, writer; b. Chgo., Aug. 22, 1961; d. Laurence P. and Marilyn (Bush) L. BS in Comms., Ill. State U., 1983. Asst. broadcase coord. BBDO Chgo., 1985-86; sales asst. Longman Fin. Svcs. Inst., Chgo., 1986-88, mktg. coord., 1988-89; course devel. editor Comml. Investment Real Estate Inst., Chgo., 1989-94; mng. editor Remy Pub. Co., Chgo., 1994-95; freelance editl. cons. Chgo., 1995—. Mng. editor Human Resource Mgmt. News, 1994-95; editor jour. articles. Mem. Internat. Assn. Bus. Communicators, Women in Comms. (media rels. com. 1993), Chgo. Women in Publishing. Home: 640 Waveland 3C Chicago IL 60613

LUDGUS, NANCY LUCKE, lawyer; b. Palo Alto, Calif., Oct. 28, 1953; d. Winston Slover and Betty Jean (Brilhart) Lucke; m. Lawrence John Ludgus, Apr. 8, 1983. BA in Polit. Sci. with highest honors, U. Calif., Berkeley, 1975; JD, U. Calif., Davis, 1978. Bar: Calif. 1978, U.S. Dist. Ct. (no. dist.) Calif. 1978. Staff atty. Crown Zellerbach Corp., San Francisco, 1978-80, Clorox Co., Oakland, Calif., 1980-82; staff atty. Nat. Semiconductor Corp., Santa Clara, Calif., 1982-85, corp. counsel, 1985-92, sr. corp. counsel, asst. sec., 1992—. Mem. ABA, Am. Corp. Counsel Assn., Calif. State Bar Assn., Phi Beta Kappa. Democrat. Office: Nat Semiconductor Corp 1090 Kifer Rd # 16 135 Sunnyvale CA 94086-5301

LUDLAM, HEATHER JO, veterinarian; b. Detroit, Dec. 17, 1965; d. H. Bernard and Joan Mabel (Reetz) Spafford; m. Michael Joseph Ludlam, July 22, 1989; 1 child, Samantha Jo. BS, Mich. State U., 1989, DVM, 1991. Lic. vet. State Mich. Bd. Vet. Medicine. Vet. intern Laurel East Vet. Svc., Laurel, Mont., 1991; assoc. vet. Allegan Vet. Clinic, Allegan, Mich., 1991-94; vet., owner, mgr. Monterey Vet. Ctr., Hopkins, Mich., 1994—; assoc. mem. Midwest Police Canine Assn., Mich., Ind., Ill. (1989-1991). Vol. conservation officer, Mich. Dept. Natural Resources, Allegan County, Mich., 1992—. Mem. AMVA, Am. Assn. Bovine Practitioners Assn., Am. Assn. Equine Practitioners, Assn. Women Veterinarians, Wester Mich. Vet. Med. Assn., Mich. Vet. Med. Assn. Home and Office: 3051 130th Ave Hopkins MI 49328

LUDWIG, MARGARET G., state legislator; m. Leland Ludwig; 3 children. BA, Colby Coll. Mem. Maine State Senate, 1994. Mem. Maine State Sch. Bd. Assn. Republican. Home: 3 Roger St Houlton ME 04730-1520 Office: Maine State Senate State Capitol Bldg Augusta ME 04330*

LUDWIG, ORA LEE KIRK, coal company executive; b. Morgantown, W.Va., June 25, 1925; d. Thomas Jefferson and Nora Belle (Browning) Johnson; m. Eugene P. Kirk, Dec. 6, 1947 (div. 1957); children: E. Phillip, Lisa Ann Kirk Wiese; m. August J. Ludwig, May 17, 1983. AA, Mt. State Coll., Parkersburg, W.Va. With Rosedale Coal Co., Morgantown, W.Va., 1945—; corp. sec. Rosedale Coal Co., 1954, v.p., 1971, pres., 1980—; with Mon Valley Coal & Lumber Co., Morgantown, 1945—; pres. Mon Valley Coal & Lumber Co., 1983—; with Mon-Valley Mining Co., 1945—, pres., 1980—. Pres. Monongalia Arts Ctr., Morgantown, 1960-83; bd. dirs., com. chmn. W.Va. Hosp. Aux., 1990—; treas. United Way, 1991—; bd. dirs. Lakeview Theatre. Mem. Tri-State Coal Assn., W.Va. Coal Assn., W.Va. Hosp. Assn. (exec. bd. aux., treas. 1991—), Morgantown C. of C. (treas. 1989-90), Women's Alliance, Rotary, White Shrine of Jerusalem, Order Eastern Star. Methodist. Home: 940 Riverview Dr Morgantown WV 26505-4634 Office: Rosedale Coal Co Morgantown WV 26507-0676

LUECKE, ELEANOR VIRGINIA ROHRBACHER, civic volunteer; b. St. Paul, Mar. 10, 1918; d. Adolph and Bertha (Lehman) Rohrbacher; m. Richard William Luecke, Nov. 1, 1941; children: Glenn Richard, Joan Eleanor Ratliff, Ruth Ann. Student, Macalester Coll., St. Paul, 1936-38, St. Paul Bus. U., 1938-40. Author lit. candidate and ballot issues, 1970—; producer TV local issues, 1981—; contbr. articles to profl. jours. Founder, officer, dir., pres. Liaison for Inter-Neighborhood Coop., Okemos, Mich., 1972—; chair countrywide special edn. millage proposals, 1958, 1969; trustee, v.p., pres. Ingham Intermediate Bd. Edn., 1959-83; sec., dir. Tri-County Cmty. Mental Health Bd., Lansing, 1964-72; founder, treas., pres. Concerned Citizens for Meridian Twp., Okemos, 1970-86; mental health rep. Partners of the Americas, Belize, Brit. Honduras, 1971; trustee Capital Area Comprehensive Health Planning, 1973-76; v.p., dir. Assn. Retarded Citizens Greater Lansing, 1973-83; chair, mem. Cmty. Svcs. for Developmentally Disabled Adv. Coun., 1973—; dir., founder, treas. Tacoma Hills Homeowners Assn., Okemos, 1985—; facilitator of mergers Lansing Child Guidance Clinic, Clinton and Eaton counties Tri-County Cmty. Mental Health Bd., Lansing Adult Mental Health Clinic, founder. Recipient Greater Lansing Cmty. Svcs. Coun. "Oscar," United Way, 1955, state grant Mich. Devel. Disabilities Coun., Lansing, 1983, Disting. award Mich. Assn. Sch. Bds., Lansing, 1983, Pub. Svc. award C.A.R.E.ing, Okemos, 1988, Earth Angel award WKAR-TV 23, Mich. State U., East Lansing, 1990, Cert. for Cmty. Betterment People for Meridian, Okemos, 1990, 2nd pl. video competition East Lansing/Meridian Twp. Cable Comm. Commn., 1990, 1st pl. award video competition, 1992; Ingham Med. Hosp. Commons Area named in her honor, Lansing, 1971. Mem. Advocacy Orgn. for Patients and Providers (dir. 1994—). Home: 1893 Birchwood Dr Okemos MI 48864-2766

LUECKING, JULIANA, artist; b. Balt.. Resident artist Dist. Columbia Urban Art Connection, 1989, Dist. Columbia Youth Outreach Program, 1991; on site artist Positive Peers, Dist. Columbia Bd. Edn., 1991; recs. on Simple Machines Records, Arlington, Va., 1991, Kill Rock Stars, Olympia, Wash., 1993—. Appeared in Mich. Women's Festival, Northern Mich., 1995, D.C. Riot Grrrl Conv., Washington, 1992, Internat. Underground Festival, Olympia, Wa., 1991 and numerous others; writer, performer, ind. prodr. of several recs. Grant panelist New Forms Reg. Grant Program, Painted Bride Arts Ctr., Phila., 1993; performance art grant recipient, Dist. of Columbia Commission on the Arts and Nat. Endowment for the Arts, 1992; residency grant recipient, New Forms Reg. Grant Program, Painted Brides Arts Ctr., Phila., 1990; media arts grants recipient, Dist. of Columbia Commission on the Arts, 1988.

LUEDERS, DEBRA MARIE, auditor; b. Portland, Oreg., Jan. 2, 1969; d. William C. and Sandra K. (Stanfill) L. BA in Bus. Mgmt., Portland State U., 1992. Property acct. Consolidated Freightways, Inc., Portland, 1989-93, internat. acct., 1993-94, internal auditor, 1994—. Lutheran. Home: 1580 SW Lillyben Ave Gresham OR 97080 Office: Consolidated Freightways 1717 NW 21st Portland OR 97208

LUEPKE, GRETCHEN, geologist; b. Tucson, Nov. 10, 1943; d. Gordon Maas and Janice (Campbell) Luepke; B.S., U. Ariz., 1965, M.S., 1967; U. Colo., summer, 1962. Geol. field asst. U.S. Geol. Survey, Flagstaff, Ariz., 1964; with U.S. Geol. Survey, Menlo Park, Calif., 1967—, geologist, Pacific Br. of Marine Geology, 1976—. Registered geologist, Ore. Mem. U.S. Congress Office Tech. Assessment Workshop, Mining and Processing Placers of EEZ, 1986. Fellow Geol. Soc. Am. (Interdisciplinary Perspectives on the Hist. Earth Scis., Penrose Conf. 1994); mem. Soc. Econ. Paleontologists and Mineralogists (chmn. com. libraries in developing countries 1988-91), Ariz. Geol. Soc., Peninsula Geol. Soc., Bay Area Mineralogists (chmn. 1979-80), History of the Earth Scis. Soc., Internat. Assn. Sedimentologists, Internat. Marine Minerals Soc. (charter), Geospeakers Toastmasters Club (charter), Sigma Xi. Editor: Stability of Heavy CTM Minerals in Sediments, 1995; Econ. Analysis of Heavy Minerals in Sediments; editor book rev. Earth Scis. History, 1989—. Contbr. articles on heavy-mineral analysis to profl. jours. Office: 345 Middlefield Rd Menlo Park CA 94025-3561

LUGBAUER, CATHERINE A., technical company executive. Grad., Trinity Coll.; degree in mgmt., Worcester Poly. Inst. Mktg. comms. mgr. Dresser Industries, 1971-81; with Creamer Dickson Basford, Providence, 1981-94, sr. v.p., dep. gen. mgr., exec. v.p., 1989-94; sr. v.p. Weber Group, Cambridge, Mass., 1994-95, exec. v.p., 1995—. Office: The Weber Group 101 Main St Cambridge MA 02142*

LUHRS, CARO ELISE, internal medicine physician, administrator, educator; b. Dover, N.J., Jan. 21, 1935; d. Albert Weigand and Ethel Adelaide (Voss) L. BA, Swarthmore Coll., 1956; MD, Harvard U., 1960. Diplomate Am. Bd. Internal Medicine; cert. personal fitness trainer, fitness instr., strength and conditioning specialist. Instr., asst. prof. medicine, dir. hematology labs. Georgetown Univ. Hosp., Washington, 1964-68; White House fellow USDA, Washington, 1968-69, spl. asst. to Sec. of Agr., 1969-73; dir. health and med. divsn. Booz, Allen & Hamilton, Washington, 1973-77; v.p., med. dir. EHE/Nat. Health Svcs., Washington, 1977-78; pvt. practice Washington, 1978—; med. dir. Hummer Assocs., Washington, 1989—; clin. prof. family medicine Georgetown U., Washington, 1991—. Trustee Swarthmore (Pa.) Coll., 1975-79; bd. dirs. USDA Grad. Sch., Washington, 1970-74, The Pillsbury Co., 1973-89, White House Fellow Found., Washington, 1979; bd. regents Uniformed Svcs. U. of Health Scis., Bethesda, Md., 1980-85; cons. Office Sci. and Tech. Policy, The White House, 1977-80; active D.C. Mayor's Adv. Com. on Emergency Med. Svcs., 1980-84. Recipient Disting. Svc. award Uniformed Svcs. U. Health Scis., 1985. Fellow ACP, Royal Soc. Medicine; mem. AMA, Am. Coll. Sports Medicine, Med. Soc. D.C. Office: Caro Luhrs Assocs 1100 Connecticut Ave NW Ste 720 Washington DC 20036-4101

LUHTA, CAROLINE NAUMANN, airport manager, flight educator; b. Cleve., Mar. 26, 1930; d. Karl Henry and Fannie Arletta (Harlan) Naumann; m. Fred Harlan Jones, July 2, 1955 (div. 1961); m. Adolph Jalmer Luhta, Dec. 12, 1968 (dec. 1993); 1 child, Katherine Louise. BA, Ohio Wesleyan U., 1952; BS magna cum laude, Lake Erie Coll., Painesville, Ohio, 1977. Rsch. chemist Standard Oil Co. Ohio, Cleve., 1952-68; office mgr. Adolph J. Luhta Constrn. Co., Painesville, 1968-83; acct. Thomas Y. Ellis, CPA, Painesville, 1978; bd. dirs. Painesville Flying Svc., Inc., 1968—, flight instr., 1970—, pres., 1993—, 1993—; bd. dirs. Concord Air Park, Inc., Painesville, 1968—, pres. 1993—; accident prevention counselor FAA, Cleve., 1975-85. Contbr. articles to profl. jours. Trustee Northeastern Ohio Gen. Hosp., Madison, 1973-83, chmn. bd. 1980-82; trustee Internat. Women's Air and Space Mus., Centerville, Ohio, 1989-96, treas. 1991-95; trustee Concord Twp., 1992—. Recipient Aerospace award Cleve. Squadron, Air Force Assn., 1966. Mem. Nat. Assn. Flight Instrs., Exptl. Aircraft Assn., Aircraft Owners and Pilots Assn., Ninety-Nines (life, chmn. All-Ohio chpt. 1969-70, Achievement award 1965, Amelia Earhart Meml. scholar 1970), Silver Wings (life), Order Ea. Star, Alpha Delta Pi (life). Office: Painesville Flying Svc Inc 12253 Concord Hambden Rd Painesville OH 44077-9566

LUI, AMY ROSENBLATT, development director; b. Toledo, Ohio, Nov. 20, 1962; d. Charles Alan and Mazal (Ben-Abraham) Rosenblatt; m. David H. Lui, June 3, 1990. BA, Ohio State U., 1986; MBA, U. Judaism, 1990. Regional youth dir. New Eng. Region Hadassah-Internat. Women's Zionist Orgn. of Am., Boston, 1986-88; dir. cmty. campaign U. Judaism, L.A., 1989-90; regional dir. No. Calif./Pacific N.W. U. Judaism, San Francisco, 1990-92; exec. dir. women's alliance Jewish Cmty. Fedn. San Francisco, 1992-95, dir. maj. gifts, 1995—. Mem. profl. women's task force United Jewish Appeal, L.A., 1994. Kitsis scholar, 1988-90, Greenberg scholar, 1990; grantee Hadassah Study Tour to Poland, 1986, World Zionist Orgn. Study Tour to USSR, 1987. Mem. Nat. Soc. Fundraising Execs. (new mem. com. 1992-93). Office: Jewish Cmty Fedn 121 Steuart St San Francisco CA 94105

LUKE, NANCY ANN, lawyer; b. L.A., May 15, 1957; d. Teddy Edward and Coriene (Pfaeffle) L. BA, U. Tenn., 1980; JD, Loyola U., L.A., 1983. Bar: Calif. 1983. Law clk., assoc. Thorpe, Sullivan, Workman & Thorp, L.A., 1981-84; assoc. Parkinson, Wolf, Lazar & Leo, L.A., 1984-86, Sedwick, Detert, Moran & Arnold, L.A., 1986-89; assoc. Kirtland & Packard, Irvine, Calif., 1989-95, ptnr., 1996—; cons. Assn. Calif. Cremationists. Mem. So. Calif. Assn. Health-Risk Mgrs. Office: Kirtland & Packard 18101 Von Karman Ste 1900 Irvine CA 92714

LUKER, JEAN KNARR, administrator; b. St. Petersburg, Fla., May 4, 1944; d. Harry M. Jr. and Mary M. (Insley) Knarr; m. Maurice S. Luker Jr., Mar. 1, 1976; children: Maurice S. III, Amy Luker Cloud, Marc A. Miller. AA, Manatee Jr. Coll., 1964; BS in Edn., Fla. State U., 1966; MS in Edn., U. Va., 1982. Tchr., 1st grade Sarasota (Fla.) County Pub. Schs., 1966-70, tchr. emotionally disturbed, 1974-76; tchr. mentally retarded Washington County Schs., Abingdon, Va., 1978-82; tchr. learning disabled Washington County Schs., 1982-89; coord. gifted secondary Washinton County Schs., 1990-91, coord. instructional technology, gifted, 1991—; chair, bd. dirs. Southwest Va. Edn. & Tng. Network, Abingdon, 1993—; founding mem. Electronic Village of Abingdon; mem. VESIS Bd., Richmond, Va., 1993—. Co-author, illustrator: Of Clay Metal and Stone: Objects for Life and Death in Ancient Palestine, 1979. Mem. Va. Assn. Edn. of Gifted, Delta Kappa Gamma (scholar com. chair 1991—, AK7 Founders scholar), Phi Delta Kappa, Kappa Delta Pi, Phi Theta Kappa. Methodist. Home: 216 Stonewall Hts NE Abingdon VA 24210-2924 Office: Washington County Schs 220 Stanley St Abingdon VA 24210-2346

LUKERT, CLAUDIA GRACE, business agent; b. Mendota, Ill., May 3, 1964; d. Michael Thomas and Emmalou (Rittmeyer) L.; m. David Brian Howell, May 25, 1991. BA in Polit. Sci., Edinboro U. of Pa., 1986; MA in Indsl. and Lab. Rels., Indiana U. of Pa., 1989; JD cum laude, Widener U., 1995. Bar: Pa. 1996. Residential counselor Brooke Hancock Group Home, Wellsburg, W.Va., 1986-87; bus. agt. Pa. Social Svc. Union, Harrisburg, Pa., 1989—. Mem. Stephens ministries United Meth. Ch., Harrisburg, 1995. Recipient Am. Jurisprudence award Lawyers Co-op Pub., 1993, John Fillion Meml. award Widener U., 1995. Mem. Union Employees Union (treas.

1991), Pa. Social Svcs. Union. Democrat. Home: 3027 Guineveers Dr Apt B3 Harrisburg PA 17110

LUKITSCH, CAROL TAYLOR, artist; b. Ft. Worth; d. Cecil Edward and Madge Lucille (Boswell) Taylor; m. Joseph Michael Lukitsch, Sept. 4, 1964; children: Courtney Michelle Lukitsch-Oymen, Joseph Michael Jr. BFA magna cum laude, So. Ill. U., 1982; MFA, U. Md., 1984. Lectr. Trinity Coll., Washington, 1984, U. Md., College Park, 1984; asst. prof. Middle East Tech. U., Ankara, Turkey, 1985, Hacettepe U., Ankara, Turkey, 1986, Pa. State U., University Park, Pa., 1987; adj. faculty No. Va. C.C., Annandale, 1990-96; Fulbright grantee, sr. lectr. Bilkent U., Ankara, Turkey, 1996—; bd. dirs. Gallery 10, Washington; resident artist Arlington (Va.) Arts Ctr., 1990-96; lectr. in field. One-woman shows include Gallery of the Turkish-Am. Assn., Ankara, Turkey, 1986, Arlington Arts Ctr. Satellite Gallery, 1989, 94, Greater Reston (Va.) Arts Ctr., 1990, Mont. Gallery, Alexandria, 1991, Gallery 10, Washington, 1992, 94, Gallery A-3, Moscow, 1994, Arlington Arts Ctr., 1995, Vartai Gallery, Vilnius, Lithuania, 1995; group exhibitions include Stadtische Galerie, Regensburg, West Germany, 1988, Westbeth Gallery, N.Y.C., 1990-91, Mont. Gallery, Alexandria, 1990, Ellipse Gallery, Arlington, 1990, Clary-Miner Gallery, Buffalo, 1991, MUSE Gallery, Phila., 1991, No. Va. C.C., Annandale, 1991, Washington Project for the Arts, 1992-94, Clark and Co. Gallery, Washington, 1993, Vartai Gallery, Vilnius, 1994, U.S. Embassy Am. Cultural Ctr, Vilnius, 1994, UN Womens Conf., Beijing, 1995; prin. works include Nat. Mus. Women in the Arts; contbr. articles to profl. jours. Va. Ctr. for the Creative Arts fellow, 1983, 88, Hilai Ctr. for Creative Arts, Má alot, Israel, 1987, Millay Colony for the Arts fellow, Austerlitz, N.Y., 1981; recipient Audrey Glassman award Washington Womens Arts Ctr., 1984, Joyce and Bob Jones award, 1989, Distingction award D'Art Ctr., Norfolk, Va., 1991. Mem. Artists Equity, Coll. Art Assn., Phi Kappa Phi. Office: PO Box 4668 Alexandria VA 22303-0668

LUKITSH, JOANNE MARY, art educator, curator; b. Pitts., July 16, 1954; d. Robert Albert and Mary Margaret (Rooney) L. BA in History, Wesleyan U., 1976; MA, U. N.Mex., 1981; PhD, U. Chgo., 1987. Curatorial intern George Eastman House, Rochester, N.Y., 1982-86; Mellon postdoctoral fellow Rice U., Houston, 1987-89; vis. asst. prof. SUNY, Buffalo, 1989-90, 91-92; vis. lectr. Ohio State U., Columbus, 1990-91; mem. faculty U. Mass., Lowell, 1993-95; asst. prof. Mass. Coll. of Art, Boston, 1995—; mem. adv. bd. Interdisciplinary 19th Century Studies, 1989-92; co-chmn. Feminist Art History Conf., N.Y.C., 1991. Author: Cameron: Her Work and Career, 1986. ACLS grantee, 1989; NEH summer inst. grantee, 1989, NEH summer seminar grantee, 1992. Mem. Coll. Art Assn. (session chair for ann. meeting 1995), Soc. for Lit. and Sci. Home: 73 Adams St Somerville MA 02145-2601

LULAY, GAIL C., human resources and corporative outplacement executive, consultant; b. Evanston, Ill., Feb. 13, 1938; d. Earl Albert and Helen Marie (Blackwell) Minnich; m. Wayne L. Lulay, Aug. 15, 1959; children: Michael Brent, Catherine Marie. BS, Elmhurst Coll., 1970; MS, Roosevelt U., 1972. Cert. counselor, Ill. Instr. Dist. #181, Hinsdale, Ill., 1970-74; corp. bus. devel. Continental Bank, Chgo., 1974-79; pres., owner Lulay & Assocs., Inc., Downers Grove, Ill., 1979—; instr. Elmhurst Coll. Adult Edn., 1982, Coll. of DuPage, Glen Ellyn, Ill., 1983-86; lectr., cons. in field., 1980—. Author: Nelson Eddy, America's Favorite Baratone, Authorized Biographical Tribute, 1992; contbr. articles to profl. jours. Bd. dirs. Crisis Homes, Des Plaines, Ill., 1984-86. Mem. Am. Assn. Counseling and Devel., Am. Soc. Personnel Adminstrn., Assn. Outplacement Cons. Firms, Inc., Human Resources Mgmt. Assn. of Chgo., Roosevelt U. Alumni Assn., Chi Omega. Office: Lulay & Assocs Inc 1431 Opus Pl Downers Grove IL 60515-1166

LULING-HAUGHTON, ROSEMARY E., writer, lecturer, non-profit organization executive; b. London, Apr. 13, 1927; d. Peter T. and Sylvia E. (Thompson) Luling; m. Algernon E. Houghton, June 19, 1948; children: Susanna, Benet and Barnabas (twins), Dominic, Mark and Andrew (twins), Philip, Luke, Elizabeth, Emma. Student, Slade Sch. of Art, London, 1944-45, La Grande Chaumiere, Paris, 1944-45, Holburn Sch. Arts and Crafts, London, 1945-46; DD (hon.), U. Notre Dame, 1977; DLitt (hon.), St. Mary's Coll., Ind., 1983. Founder, assoc. dir. Wellspring House, Inc., Gloucester, Mass., 1980—. Author 35 books, including The Passionate God, The Catholic Thing, Song in a Strange Land, over 200 articles. Active local polit. and econ. groups, Gloucester. Recipient Avila award, U. Dayton award. Roman Catholic. Home and Office: 302 Essex Ave Gloucester MA 01930

LUMPE, SHEILA, state legislator; b. Apr. 17, 1935; m. Gustav H. Lumpe, 1958. AB, Ind. U.; postgrad., Johns Hopkins U.; MA, U. Mo. Mem. Mo. of Reps. Trustee Mo. Consol. Health Care Plan; active Civil Liberties Union; bd. dirs. People to People. Democrat. Home: 6908 Amherst Ave Saint Louis MO 63130-3124 Office: Mo Ho of Reps State Capitol Building Jefferson City MO 65101-1556

LUNA, BARBARA CAROLE, expert witness, accountant, appraiser; b. N.Y.C., July 23, 1950; d. Edwin A. and Irma S. (Schub) Schlang; m. Dennis Rex Luna, Sept. 1, 1974; children: John S., Katherine E. BA, Wellesley Coll., 1971; MS in Applied Math. and Fin. Analysis, Harvard U., 1973, PhD in Applied Math. and Fin. Analysis, 1975. Investment banker Warburg Paribas Becker, L.A., 1975-77; cons./mgr. Price Waterhouse, L.A., 1977-83; sr. mgr. litigation Pannell Kerr Forster, L.A., 1983-86; nat. dir. litigation cons. Kenneth Leventhal & Co., L.A., 1986-88; ptnr. litigation svcs. Coopers & Lybrand, L.A., 1988-93; sr. ptnr. litigation svcs. White, Zuckerman, Warsavsky & Luna, Sherman Oaks, Calif., 1993—. Wellesley scholar, 1971. Mem. AICPA, Assn. Bus. Trial Lawyers (com. on experts), Am. Soc. Appraisers, Assn. Cert. Real Estate Apparaisers, Assn. Cert. Fraud Examiners, Assn. Insolvency Accts., Inst. Mgmt. Cons., Calif. Soc. CPAs (steering com. L.A. litigation svcs. com., com. econ. damages CIMS, fraud CIMS com., bus. violation CIMS com.), Am. Bd. Forensic Examiners. Home: 18026 Rodarte Way Encino CA 91316-4370 Office: White Zuckerman Warsavsky & Luna 14455 Ventura Blvd Ste 300 Sherman Oaks CA 91423

LUNA, PATRICIA ADELE, marketing executive; b. Charleston, S.C., July 22, 1956; d. Benjamin Curtis and Clara Elizabeth (McCrory) L. BS in History, Auburn U., 1978, MEd in History, 1980; MA in Adminstrn., U. Ala., 1981, EdS in Adminstrn., 1984, PhD, ABD in Adminstrn., 1986. Cert. tchr., Ga., Ala. History tchr. Harris County Middle Sch., Ga., 1978-79, head dept., 1979-81; residence hall dir. univ. housing U. Ala., 1981-83, asst. dir. residence life, 1983-85; intern Cornell U., Ithaca, N.Y., 1983; dir. of mktg. Golden Flake Snack Foods, Inc., Birmingham, Ala., 1985-89; sr. v.p. Quest U.S.A., Inc., Atlanta, 1989-90; pres. Promotion Mgmt. Group, Inc., 1990—; cons., lectr. in field. Author: Specialization: A Learning Module, 1979, Grantsmanship, 1981, Alcohol Awareness Programs, 1984; University Programming, 1984; Marketing Residential Life, 1985; The History of Golden Flake Snack Foods, 1986; Golden Flake Snack Foods, Inc., A Case Study, 1987, Cases in Strategic Marketing, 1989, Cases in Strategic Management, 1990, Frequency Marketing, 1992. Fundraiser, U. Ala. Alumni Scholarship Fund, Tuscaloosa, 1983, Am. Diabetes Assn., Tuscaloosa, 1984, Urban Ministries, Birmingham, 1985-88; fundraiser, com. chmn. Spl. Olympics, Tuscaloosa, 1985; fundraiser Am. Cinema Soc., 1988; chmn. Greene County Relief Project, 1982-89; bd. dirs. Cerebral Palsy Found., Tuscaloosa, 1985-86; lay rector and com. chmn. Kairos Prison Ministry, Tutwiler State Prison, Ala., 1986—; lobbyist, com. chmn. task force Justice Fellowship, 1988-91; bd dirs. Internat. Found. Ewha U., Seoul, Korea, 1988-91; chmn. bd. dirs. Epiphany Ministries, 1991—; bd. dir. Hunting Coll. of Fine Arts. Recipient Dir. of Yr. award U. Ala., 1982, 83; Skeets Simonis award, U. Ala., 1984, nat. award Joint Coun. on Econ. Edn., 1979, rsch. award NSF, 1979; named to Hon. Order Ky. Cols. Commonwealth of Ky., 1985—, Rep. Senatorial Inner Circle, 1986—; Com. chmn. Emmaus Ministry, 1985—; chmn. Chrysalis steering com., 1995-96. Mem. Sales and Mktg. Execs. (chmn. com. 1985-86), Leadership Ala. (pres. 1982-83), Am. Mktg. Assn. (Disting. Leadership award 1987, Commemorative Medal of Honor 1988), Assn. Coll. and Univ. Housing Officers (com. chmn. 1983-85), Nat. Assn. Student Personnel Officers, Snack Food Assn. (mem. mktg. com. and conf. presenter), Internat. Coun. Shopping Ctrs. (Merit award 1991, program com.), Commerce Exec. Soc., Snow Skiing Club, Sailing Club, Omega Rho Sigma (pres. 1983-84), Omicron Delta Kappa, Phi Delta Kappa, Kappa Delta Pi, Phi Alpha Theta. Republican. Methodist. Avocations: skiing, racquetball, tennis, community work, public speaking.

LUNA PADILLA, NITZA ENID, photography educator; b. San Juan, P.R., Mar. 13, 1959; d. Luis and Carmen Iris (Padilla) Luna. BFA, Pratt Inst., 1981; MS, Brooks Inst., 1985. Instr. U. P.R., Carolina, 1981-82, Cultural Inst., San Juan, 1988; asst. prof. photography U. Sacred Heart, Santurce, P.R., 1987—; assoc. dir. communication ctr. U. Sagrado Corazon, Santurce, P.R., 1989-90. Contbr. articles to profl. publs.; one-woman shows P.R. Inst. Culture, 1988, Art and History Mus., San Juan, 1989, 94, 96, U. P.R., 1989, 90, Brooks Inst. Phototography, Santa Barbara, Calif., 1990, Miriam Walsh Gallery, Glenwood Springs, Colo., 1991, Mus. Ponce, 1991; exhibited in group shows Santa Barbara Mus. Art, 1987, Coll. of Santa Fe, N.Mex., 1988, Durango (Colo.) Arts Ctr., 1988, 90, Laband Art Gallery, L.A., 1989, Cultural Ctr., Vercelli, Italy, 1989, Univ. Union Gallery Calif. Poly. State U., 1990, Coconino Ctr. Arts, Flagstaff, Ariz., 1990, Centro Cultural Washington Irving, Madrid, 1991, L.A. County Fair, 1991, Museo del Grabado Latinoamericano, San Juan, 1992, 93, 94, P.R. Inst. Culture, 1994, Hostos Art Gallery, N.Y.C., 1996, others; in permanent collections; juror Fotografia de prensa "Mandin,", 1991-92. MacDowell Colony grantee, Instituto de Cultural Puertorriqueña grantee, 1993, 94. Mem. Soc. Photog. Edn., Friends of Photography. Roman Catholic. Office: U Sagrado Corazón PO Box 12383 San Juan PR 00914-0383

LUND, SISTER CANDIDA, college chancellor; b. Chgo.; d. Fred S. Lund and Katharine (Murray) Lund Heck. BA, Rosary Coll., River Forest, Ill.; MA, Catholic U. Am.; PhD, U. Chgo., 1963; DLitt (hon.), Lincoln Coll., 1968; LLD (hon.), John Marshall Law Sch., 1979; LHD honoris causa, Marymount Coll., 1979; LittD (hon.), St. Mary-of-the Woods Coll., 1994. Pres. Rosary Coll., 1964-81, chancellor, 1981—. Editor: Moments to Remember, 1980, The Days and the Nights: Prayers for Today's Woman, In Joy and in Sorrow, 1984, Coming of Age, 1992, Nunsuch, 1982, God and Me, 1988, Praymates, 1993; author, editor: If I Were Pope, 1987; contbr.: Why Catholic. Mem. women's bd. U. Chgo., 1984—; bd. dirs. The Chgo. Network, 1983-86, The Park Ridge Ctr., 1987-93, Gottlieb Hosp., 1991—. Recipient Profl. Achievement award U. Chgo. Alumni, 1974, U.S. Catholic award, 1984. Fellow Royal Soc. Arts; mem. Thomas More Assn. (bd. dirs. 1975—), The Arts Club (bd. dirs. 1987—). Home and Office: Rosary Coll 7900 Division St River Forest IL 60305-1066

LUND, DORIS HIBBS, retired dietitian; b. Des Moines, Nov. 10, 1923; d. Loyal Burchard and Catharine Mae (McClymond) Hibbs; m. Richard Bodholdt Lund, Nov. 9, 1946; children: Laurel Anne, Richard Douglas, Kristi Jane Lund Lozier. Student, Duchesne Coll., Omaha, 1941-42; BS, Iowa State U., 1946; postgrad., Grand View Coll., Des Moines, 1965; MS, Iowa State U., 1968. Registered dietitian, lic. dietitian. Clk. Russell Stover Candies, Omaha, 1940-42; chemist Martin Bomber Plant, Omaha, 1942-43; dietitian Grand Lake (Colo.) Lodge, 1946; tailoring instr. Ottumwa Pub. Schs., 1952-53; cookery instr. Des Moines Pub. Schs., 1958-62; dietitian Calvin Manor, Des Moines, 1963; home economist Am. Wool Coun./Am. Lamb Coun., Denver, 1963-65, The Merchandising Group of N.Y., 1965-68, Thomas Wolff, Pub. Rels., 1968-70; home economist weekly TV program Iowa Power Co., 1968-70; cons. in child nutrition programs Iowa Dept. Edn., Des Moines, 1970-95; ret. Nutritioneering, Ltd., 1995; Mem. Iowa Home Economists in Bus. (pres. 1962-63), PEO, Pi Beta Phi (Iowa Gamma chpt. pres. 1945-46). Pres. Callanan Jr. H.S. PTA, 1964, Roosevelt H.S. PTA, 1966; pres., mem. Ctrl. Presbyn. Mariners, Des Moines; ruling elder, clk. of session Ctrl. Presbyn. Session, Des Moines, 1972-78; bd. dirs. Ctrl. Found., 1996; amb. Friendship Force Internat., 1982—. Duchesne Coll. 4 yr. scholar. Mem. Iowa Home Economists in Bus. (pres. 1962-63), PEO, Pi Beta Phi (pres. 1945-46). Republican. Home: 105 34th St Des Moines IA 50312-4526

LUND, LOIS A., food science and human nutrition educator; b. Thief River Falls, Minn., Aug. 9, 1927; d. Robert J. and E. Luella (Tosdal) L. BS, U. Minn., 1949, MS, 1954, PhD, 1966. Instr. foods U. Iowa, 1951-55, U. Minn., 1955-63; assoc. prof., dir. core studies program, asst. dir. Sch. Home Econs., 1966-68; research fellow U.S. Dept. Agrl., 1963-66; assoc. dean, dir. Sch. Home Econs. Ohio State U., 1969-72; dean Coll. Human Ecology Mich. State U., East Lansing, 1973-85, prof. food sci. and human nutrition, 1985—; bd. dirs. Consumers Power Co., Jackson, Mich., CMS Energy, Dearborn, Mich. Contbr. articles to profl. jours. Recipient Betty award for excellence in teaching U. Minn., 1958, 63, 68, Hon. Alumni award Mich. State U., 1977, Outstanding Achievement award U. Minn. Alumni Assn., 1977. Mem. Am. Coun. on Consumer Interest, Am. Assn. Cereal Chemists, Inst. Food Technologists, Am. Agrl. Econs. Assn., Soc. for Nutrition Edn., Pi Lambda Theta, Phi Kappa Phi, Phi Upsilon Omicron, Omicron Nu (nat. treas. 1971-74, 84-86), Sigma Delta Epsilon. Lutheran. Home: 5927 Shadowlawn Dr East Lansing MI 48823-2379 Office: Mich State U Dept Food Sci and Human Nutrition East Lansing MI 48824

LUND, MARY LOUISE, human resources director; b. Mauston, Wis., Mar. 9, 1950; d. L. Wallace and Helen I (Haschke) L. BS in Bus. and Psychology, U. Wis., River Falls, 1971; MS in Coll. Pers., U. Wis., La Crosse, 1979. Manpower specialist State of Wis. Job Svc., La Crosse, Wis., 1974-77; dir. human resources Dairyland Power Coop., La Crosse, 1977—; mem. del. to Russia Citizens Adv. Program, Washington, 1992, apprentice adv. coun., State of Wis. Dept. of Industry, Labor and Human Rels., Madison, 1995-99, utility benefits com. Nat. Rural Electric Coop. Assn., Washington, 1994-97. Solicitor large employers United Way, La Crosse, 1985—, co-chair registration Oktoberfest, USA, La Crosse, 1975-92. Recipient award United Way, La Crosse, 1993. Mem. Nat. Generation and Transmission Human Resources (sec.-treas. 1988-90, pres. 1991-92, past pres. 1992-93), Soc. Human Resource Mgmt. (cert. Sr. Profl. Human Resources, treas. La Crosse chpt. 1978-95), Avant, Rotary Internat. Office: Dairyland Power Coop PO Box 817 La Crosse WI 54602-0817

LUND, RITA POLLARD, aerospace consultant; b. Vallscreek, W.Va., Aug. 28, 1950; d. Willard Garfield and Faye Ethel (Perry) Pollard; m. James William Lund, Dec. 30, 1969. Student, Alexandria Sch. Nursing, 1989-90, Columbia Pacific U., 1989-91. Confidential asst. U.S. Ho. of Reps., Washington, 1975-76; exec. asst. White House Domestic Policy Staff, Washington, 1977-82, White House Sci. Office, Washington, 1982-83; asst. to pres. Telecom Futures Inc., Washington, 1983-84, v.p. for adminstrn., 1985-86; internat. accounts mgr. TFI Ltd., McLean, Va., 1987-89; ind. cons. telecom. Washington, 1989-90, aerospace cons., 1990—; rep. Scott Sci. & Tech., Washington, 1992—; cons. Vanguard Space Corp., Washington, 1992—; exec. dir. Puckett Bros. Co., Washington, 1995—; sec. ELS Corp., 1992; Washington rep. Scott Sci. & Tech., 1992—; cons. Vanguard Space Corp., 1992—; exec. dir. Puckett Brothers Corp., 1995—. Mem. AIAA, NAFE, Women in Aerospace, Am. Space Transp. Assn., Competitive Alliance Space Enterprise. Republican. Methodist. Home: 9020 Patton Blvd Alexandria VA 22309-3334

LUNDBERG, LOIS ANN, political consultant, property manager executive; b. Tulsa, Sept. 21, 1928; d. John T. and Anna M. (Patterson) McQuay; m. Ted W. Lundberg, Sept. 30, 1954; children: Linda Ann, Sharon Lynn. With Pacific Telephone, 1950-65; gen. ptnr. McLund Co. Property Mgmt., 1972—; realtor Morgan Realty, 1974—; with Nason, Lundberg and Assoc., Orange, Calif., 1983-85, pres., campaign cons., 1985—; pres. NLS Comm. Inc. Bd. dirs. Luth. Ch. of the Master, La Habra, Calif., 1970-75, v.p. of congregation, 1986-87; mem. bd. trustees Nixon Law Office Preservation, Inc., 1972-75, Regional Ctr. of Orange County, 1982; bd. dirs. UCI Med. Ctr./Burn Ctr., 1982; apptd. Council on Criminal Justice Com., 1983-91; mem. adv. bd. KOCE-TV, 1976—, La Habra Children's Mus., 1985—. Recipient Gov. Ronald Reagan award, 1967, Woman of Achievement award City of La Habra, 1979; named Outstanding Rep. of Orange County, 1978. Lutheran. Home: 1341 Carmela Ln La Habra CA 90631-3511 Office: Nason Lundberg and Assocs 320 W Whittier Blvd Ste 223 La Habra CA 90631-3886

LUNDBERG, SUSAN ONA, cultural organization administrator; b. Mandan, N.D., Mar. 15, 1947; d. Robert Henry and Evelyn (Olson) L.; m. Paul R. Wick, July 2, 1972 (div. May 1976); 1 child, Melissa. BA, Stephens Coll., 1969; MLS, Western Mich. U., 1970; MPA, Calif. State U., Fullerton, 1980. Children's and reference libr. Bismarck (N.D.) Pub. Libr., 1970-71; reference libr. U. Tenn., Knoxville, 1971-72; coord. children's svcs. Orange County (Calif.) Pub. Libr., 1972-75; exec. dir. Bismarck-Manda Orch. Assn., 1992—; exec. dir., founder Sleepy Hollow Summer Theatre, Bismarck, 1990—; trustee Gabriel J. Brown Trust, Bismarck, 1989—. Chair Nat. Music Week N.D., 1990—, Friends of the Belle, 1994—. Named Outstanding Leaders of Yr. Bismarck Tribune, 1995. Mem. Calif. Libr. Assn. (pres. children's svcs. 1971-72), Bismarck Art Assn. (pres. 1982-84), Bismarck Art and Galleries Assn. (bd. dirs. 1985-96, pres. 1986-88, Honor Citation award 1992), Jr. Svc. League. Lutheran. Home: 112 Ave E West Bismarck ND 58501

LUNDBLAD, KAREN KAY, social worker; b. Fargo, N.D., July 13, 1945; d. Stanley Elton and Marguerite (Mather) S.; m. Conrad Harry Lundblad, Dec. 27, 1967 (dec. Jan. 1975); children: Robert Conrad, Michael Stanley. BS, U. Minn., 1967, MSW, 1979; postgrad., Bryn Mawr, 1996—. Cert. social worker; lic. social worker, Pa. Tchr. Mpls. Pub. Schs., 1967-69, spl. edn. tchr., 1975-77; head day care tchr. Scotts Run Settlement House, Osage, W.Va., 1970-71; social worker Luth. Social Svcs., Mpls., 1979-81; dir. social svcs. and bereavement Wissahickon Hospice, Phila., 1981-83; patient care coord. Hospice Program of Pa. Hosp., Phila., 1983-86; pvt. practice Bryn Mawr (Pa.) Hosp., 1986-90; coord. radiation oncology social work U. Pa., Phila., 1990-95; edn. chair, bd. Action AIDS, Phila., 1986-89; social work adv. bd. Am. Cancer Soc., Phila., 1986-90; HIV/AIDS cons. dept. geriatric psychiatry Thomas Jefferson Med. Sch., Phila., 1988-90; profl. adv. bd. The Wellness Cmty., Phila., 1991-96; mem. faculty Pa./N.Y. AIDS Edn. Tng. Ctr., Hahnemann U., Phila., 1984-89. Mem. Women's Internat. League for Peace and Freedom, Phila., 1986-96. Recipient Peace and Justice scholarship on Jane Addams Pendle Hill, Wallingford, Pa., 1995-96, oncology fellow grant Am. Cancer Soc., 1992-93. Mem. NASW, Nat. Assn. Oncology Social Work, Am. Assn. Marriage and Family Therapists, Am. Assn. Sex Educators, Counselors, Therapists, Pa. Hospice Network. Democrat. Home: 1733 S Forge Mountain Dr Phoenixville PA 19460

LUNDBY, MARY A., state legislator; b. Carroll County, Feb. 2, 1948; d. Edward A. and Elizabeth Hoehl; m. Michael Lundby, 1971; 1 child, Daniel. BA in History, Upper Iowa U., 1971. Former staff asst. Senator Roger Jepsen; mem. Iowa State Senate, Des Moines, 1994. Active Solid Waste Adv. Com. Republican. Home: 1240 14th St Marion IA 52302-2562 Office: Iowa State Senate State Capitol Des Moines IA 50319*

LUNDE, KATHERINE LAMONTAGNE, educational consultant; b. Kankakee, Ill., May 3, 1947; d. James Armond and Frances Elizabeth (Maas) LaMontagne; m. Walter A. Lunde Jr., June 15,1969; children: Lisa Christine, Walter James. BS, No. Ill. U., 1969; postgrad., Jacksonville (Fla.) U., 1972. Cert. elem., secondary and early childhood educator. Tchr. 1st grade Kenwood Elem. Sch., Ft. Walton Beach, Fla.; kindergarten tchr., supr. Orange Park (Fla.) Kindergarten; asst. dir. Stoneway Sch., Stoneway Pvt. Sch., Plano, Tex.; former dir. Westminster Preschool and Kindergarten, Dallas; dep. gov. Am. Biog. Rsch. Inst. (life); internat. motivational spkr. spkr.'s bur. Assn. Childhood Edn. Internat. Track coach Spl. Olympics, 1981-83; learning disabilities tutor, 1978-85; bd. dirs. Mi Escuelita Preschs., Inc., 1985-90, v.p. bd. dirs., 1989-90. Grantee Sewell Fund, Lard Trust; recipient Christa McAuliffe Outstanding Educator award, 1994. Mem. ASCD, Nat. Assn. Edn. Young Children (life), Dallas Assn. Edn. Young Children, Kappa Delta Pi.

LUNDEN, JOAN, television personality; b. Fair Oaks, CA, Sept. 19, 1950; d. Erle Murray and Gladyce Lorraine (Somervill) Blunden; children: Jamie Beryl, Lindsay Leigh, Sarah Emily. Student, Universidad de Las Americas, Mexico City, U. Calif., Calif. State U., Am. River Coll., Sacramento, Calif. Began broadcasting career as co-anchor and prodr. at Sta. KCRA-TV and Radio, Sacramento, 1973-75; with Sta. WABC-TV, N.Y.C., 1975—, co-anchor, 1976-80; co-host Good Morning America, ABC-TV, 1980—; host spl. report TV for Whittle Comm.; host Everyday with Joan Lunden, 1989; (TV spl.) Behind Closed Doors With Joan Lunden, 1994, 95; film appearances include: Macho Callahan, 1970, What About Bob?, 1991; co-author: (with Andy Friedburg) Good Morning, I'm Joan Lunden, 1986, (with Michael Krauss) Joan Lunden's Mother's Minutes, 1986, Your Newborn Baby, Healthy Cooking For Your Family With Joan Lunden; syndicated columnist: Parent's Notes. Recipient Outstanding Mother of Yr. award, Nat. Mother's Day Com., 1982; Albert Einstein Coll. of Yeshiva U. Spirit of Achievement award; Nat. Women's Polit. Caucus award; NJ Divsn. of Civil Rights award; Baylor U. Outstanding Woman of the Year award. Office: Good Morning Am 147 Columbus Ave New York NY 10023-5900*

LUNDERGAN, BARBARA KEOUGH, lawyer; b. Chgo., Nov. 6, 1938; d. Edward E. and Eleanor A. (Erickson) Keough; m. James A. Lundergan, Dec. 29, 1962; children—Matthew K., Mary Alice. B.A., U. Ill., 1960; J.D., Loyola U., Chgo., 1964. Bar: Ill. 1964, U.S. Dist. Ct. (no. dist.) Ill. 1964, U.S. Tax Ct. 1974. With Seyfarth, Shaw, Fairweather & Geraldson, Chgo., 1964—, ptnr., 1971—. Fellow Am. Coll. Trust and Estate Counsel; mem. ABA (com. on fed. taxation), Ill. Bar Assn. (coun. sect. on fed. taxation 1983-91, chair 1989, coun. sect. on trusts and estates sect. coun. 1992—, sec. 1996—, editl. bd. Ill. Bar Jour. 1993-96), Chgo. Bar Assn. (chmn. trust law com. 1982-83, com. on fed. taxation). Office: Seyfarth Shaw Fairweather & Geraldson 55 E Monroe St Chicago IL 60603-5702

LUNDGREN, RUTH WILLIAMSON WOOD (RUTH LUNDGREN WILLIAMSON WOOD), public relations executive, writer; b. Bklyn.; d. William and Hanna (Carlson) L.; m. W. F. Williamson, Dec. 17, 1949 (dec.); children: John Ross (dec.), Mark Ward; m. John Earle Wood, Aug. 27, 1988 (dec.). Student, Bklyn. Coll., 1936-41, Columbia U., 1942. Assoc. editor Everywoman's mag., 1940-42; pub. relations staff exec. J.M. Mathes Advt. Agy., 1942-45; dir. pub. relations Pan-Am. Coffee Bur., 1945-48; pres. Ruth Lundgren Ltd., N.Y.C., 1948-92. Pub. Ruth Lundgren Newsletter, 1950-58; writer daily column St. Petersburg (Fla.) Times, 1956-60; contbg. editor, writer monthly column Motor Boating and Sailing mag., 1962-80; contbr. to popular profl. publs. Home and Office: 27 Meadowood Dr Stoughton MA 02072

LUNDQUIST, LINDA ANN JOHNSON, insurance professional; b. Iowa City, Iowa, Aug. 15, 1945; d. Elmer Clinton and Georgia Joan (Molloy) L.; m. Scott Arthur Johnson, Sept. 26, 1981. BA, U. Iowa, 1968. Civil engring. drafter firm Shive-Hattery & Assocs., Iowa City, 1968-78; dir. drafting svcs. firm Shoemaker & Haaland, Profl. Engrs., Coralville, Iowa, 1978-82; mktg. rep. Veenstra & Kimm, Inc., Engineers and Planners, Iowa City and West Des Moines, 1982-86; head mktg. support dept. Stanley Cons. Inc., Muscatine, Iowa, 1986-87; agt. State Farm Ins. Cos., 1988—. mem. spl. appointments Urban Environment Ad Hoc Com., Iowa City, 1985-86, groundwater protection ad hoc adv. com. State Iowa, 1987-88. Recipient Spl. Merit award Cedar Rapids Mus. Art, Iowa, 1979, Svc. award Epsilon Pi, 1993. Mem. Greater Iowa City Area C. of C. (environ. concerns com. 1982-87, chair 1984-86, govt. affairs com. 1988-95), Iowa Groundwater Assn. (bd. dirs. 1986-89), Nat. Assn. Life Underwriters (Nat. Sales Achievement award 1991, 93, Louis I. Dublin Nat. Cmty. award 1994, 95, Nat. Quality award 1995), Iowa Assn. Life Underwriters, Nat. Wildlife Fedn., Iowa Wildlife Fedn. (conservation issues com. 1987-88), Iowa City Assn. Life Underwriters (bd. dirs. 1993—, chmn. community svc. com. 1993-95, treas. 1995—), Internat. Fund Animal Welfare, Wilderness Soc., World Wildlife Fund, Nature Conservancy, The Humane Farming Assn., The Humane Soc. of USA, Physicians Com. Responsible Medicine, Alpha Gamma Delta (bd. dirs. house assn. 1986—, alumnae advisor 1991—). Avocations: drawing, watercolors, dance. Office: 405 Highway 1 W Iowa City IA 52246-4205

LUND-SEEDEN, KATHLEEN SANDRA, journalist, editor; b. Oakdale, Calif., Jan. 17, 1956; d. Donald Rawlings and Geraldine Irene (Whitley) Lund; m. Curtis William Seeden, Sept. 2, 1979; 1 child, Kristal Dawn Seeden. BA in Journalism and Polit. Sci., U. Calif., Berkeley, 1978. Staff writer, arts editor The Laguna News-Post, Laguna Hills, Calif., 1978-80; staff writer The Newport Ensign, Newport Beach, Calif., 1980-82; staff writer, sr. news editor Daily Sun/Post, San Clemente, Calif., 1982-84; staff writer The Orange County Register, Santa Ana, Calif., 1984-87; edn. writer The San Bernardino County Sun, San Bernardino, Calif., 1987; account exec. Nelson/Ralston, Costa Mesa, Calif., 1987-88; staff writer, acting asst. city editor The Outlook, Santa Monica, Calif., 1988-93; city editor The Whittier (Calif.) Daily News, 1993—. Campaign co-chair McGovern for Pres., Winters, Calif., 1972, other polit. activities. Recipient 2d place Copley Ring of Truth award, 1988, 2 1st place awrds Orange County Fair, 1987. Mem. Press Club So. Calif. (3d place award 1995), Calif. Newspaper Pubs. Assn.

(judge ann. state contest 1996, 2d place award 1989, 92). Democrat. Methodist.

LUNDSTROM, MARJIE, newspaper editor. Grad., U. Nebr. Columnist, editor, nat. corr. The Denver Post, 1981-89; with The Sacramento Bee, 1989-90, 91—; nat. corr. Gannett News Svc., Washington, 1990-91. Recipient Pulitzer Prize for nat. reporting, 1991. Office: The Sacramento Bee 2100 Q St PO Box 15779 Sacramento CA 95852

LUNDY, JESSICA, actress. Appeared in (films) Caddyshack 2, 1988, Madhouse, 1990, (TV series) Hope and Gloria, 1995—. Office: care NBC 3000 W Alameda Blvd Burbank CA 91523*

LUNDY, SADIE ALLEN, small business owner; b. Milton, Fla., Mar. 29, 1918; d. Stephen Grover and Martha Ellen (Harter) Allen; m. Wilson Tate Lundy, May 17, 1939 (dec. 1962); children: Wilson Tate Jr., Houston Allen, Michael David, Robert Douglas, Martha Jo-Ellen. Degree in acctg., Graceland Coll., 1938. Acct. Powers Furniture Co., Milton, Fla., 1939-40, Lundy Oil Co., Milton, 1941-52; controller First Fed. Savs. & Loan, Kansas City, Mo., 1953-55, Herald Pub. Co., Indepenence, Mo., 1956-58; mgr. Baird & Son Toy Co., Kansas City, Mo., 1959-62; regional mgr. Emmons Jewelers of N.Y., Kansas City, 1963-65; owner, pres. Lundy Tax Service, Independence, 1965-85; corporate sec., purchasing mgr. Optimation, Inc., Independence, 1974-85, mgr., 1985—; v.p. Lundy Oil Co., Milton, 1941-52. Contbr. articles to profl. jours. Mem. com. Neighborhood Council, Independence, 1985. Mem. Am. Bus. Women's Assn., Independence C. of C. (mem. com. 1965-85). Republican. Mem. Reorganized Ch. of Jesus Christ of Latter Day Saints. Club: Independence Women's. Home: PO Box 520238 Independence MO 64052-0238 Office: Optimation Inc 300 N Osage St Independence MO 64050-2705

LUNN, KITTY ELIZABETH, actress; b. New Orleans, Aug. 5, 1950; d. Hugh I. Morrison and Beatrice (McClung) Farrell; m. Andrew Macmillan, Dec. 21, 1989. Student, Washington Sch. Ballet, 1965-68, Neighborhood Playhouse Sch., 1968-70; degree summa cum laude, CUNY, 1995. Dancer Washington Ballet, 1965-68; radio producer WOR Radio, N.Y.C., 1983-85, WABC Talk Radio, N.Y.C., 1985-87; performer CBS TV, N.Y.C., 1990-93; founder, exec. dir. Infinity Dance Theatre, 1995. Prin. works include Agnes of God, 1992-95, Edinburgh Festival, Fan's False Face Soc., 1990, The Waiting, 1990, Sand Dragons, 1990, As the World Turns, 1990-92, Awakenings, 1990, Eyes of a Stranger, 1979, Loving, 1995, numerous TV appearances, 1978-86; dancer Cleve. Ballet, Dancing Wheels. Bd. dirs. Hosp. Audiences, Inc., N.Y.C., 1990—; dir. svcs. people with disabilities Actors' Work Program, N.Y.C., 1991—; mentor networking project YWCA, N.Y.C., 1991; mem. White House Conf. on Libr. and Info. Svcs., Washington, 1991; N.Y. State Libr. regent advisor; del. Dem. Nat. Conv., 1992. Named Belle Zeller scholar, CUNY, 1993, Woman of Excellence, 1994. Mem. SAG, AFTRA (nat. bd. dirs.), Nat. Alliance Broadcast Engrs. and Technicians, Actor's Equity Assn. (councillor Eastern Regional adv. bd. 1990—, chair performers with disabilities com. 1990—). Roman Catholic. Office: Actors' Equity Assn 165 W 46th St Fl 15 New York NY 10036-2501

LUNSFORD, BEVERLY KOEHLER, nursing educator; b. Hastings, Nebr., Nov. 11, 1951; d. Lawrence Calvin and Blanche Lola (Urwiller) Koehler; m. John Kyle Lunsford, June 3, 1981; children: Jeremy, Jayme; stepchildren: Lisa, Jefferson, Leah. BSN, Marymount Coll., 1974; M of Nursing, U. Kans., Kansas City, 1980; D of Nursing Sci., Cath. U. Am., 1994. Cert. clin. nurse specialist. Instr. Mid Am. Nazarene U., Olathe, Kans., 1978-81; dir. adolescent health and devel. Community Hope Health Svc., Washington, 1980-87, dir. community health advs., 1987-90, acting dir., 1988; asst. prof. Cath. U. Am., Washington, 1983-86; staff nurse Vis. Nurse Assn., Washington, 1989-92; adj. asst. prof. Bowie (Md.) State U., 1992-93; assoc. prof. Pittsburg (Kans.) State U., 1993—; nurse cons. Nurses Care Partnership, Washington, 1986-88, Cmty. Hope health Svc., 1988-93; devel. dir. Africa Nazarene U., Nairobi, Kenya, 1992; dir. Wellness Ctr., Pitts. Cmty. of Hope; resource mem. internat. nursing ctr. Am. Nurses Found., 1994—. Author: (with others) Psychiatric Mental Health Nursing, 1991, Pregnancy and Cocaine, 1995. Bd. dirs. Youth Ministries Crawford County, Pittsburg, 1994—. Adolescent Health and Devel. grantee George Preston Marshall, 1981. Mem. ANA (mem. legis. com., educator HIV/AIDS prevention and care 1994—), AAUW, Nursing Rsch. Club (dir. 1993—), Sigma Theta Tau (chpt. sec., disting. lectr. 1996—). Home: 1611 S College St Pittsburg KS 66762-5614 Office: Pittsburg State U 111 McPherson Pittsburg KS 66762

LUNZ, ELLEN DEITELBAUM, speech and language pathologist; b. Chgo., Dec. 18, 1950; d. Louis Walter and Marjorie Jaffe; m. Robert Edward Lunz, July 27, 1974; children: Rebecca Gwen, Jennifer Caitlin. BS with honors, U. Wis., 1972; MS with honors, U. Mich., 1973. Cert. speech-lang. pathologist, Ill.; cert. clin. competence speech-lang. pathology Am. Speech Hearing Assn.; cert. speech-lang. pathologist Chgo. Bd. Edn. Speech pathologist Chgo.-Read Mental Health Ctr., 1973-74, Ont. Ministry Health, Toronto, Can., 1974-76, Rimland Sch. for Autistic Children, Evanston, Ill., 1976-77, 3 C's Med. Ctr., Chgo., 1977-79, Chgo. Bd. Edn., 1979-1989, Julia Molloy Ctr., Morton Grove, Ill., 1989-91, Chgo. Home Health Care Groups, 1991—; pvt. practice Chgo., 1979—. Mem. Dem. Party of Ill., Wilmette, 1983—. Mem. Nat. Assn. Down Syndrome, Chgo. Down Syndrome Assn., League of Women Voters, North Suburban Speech-Lang. Assn., Ill. Speech Hearing Assn. Jewish. Home: 808 Leyden Ln Wilmette IL 60091 Office: Chgo Bd Edn Courtenay Sch 1726 W Berteau Chicago IL 60613

LUNZMAN, PAMELA JO, counselor; b. Madelia, Minn., Nov. 6, 1962; d. Lloyd Johan and Judy Mae (Noren) Christenson; m. Todd Alan Lunzman, Oct. 24, 1992. Student, Granite Falls (Minn.) Vocat., 1982; BA in Psychology Social Work, U.S.D. Vermillion, 1989; MEd in Guidance Counseling, No. State U., Aberdeen, S.D., 1994. Lic. social worker, S.D.; nat. cert. counselor. Vol. worker Coalition Against Domestic Violence, Vermillion, S.D., 1987-89; intern intake officer Woodbury County Juvenile Ct. Svcs., Sioux City, Iowa, 1989; social svcs. coord. Sunrise Retirement Cmty., Sioux City, 1989-92; family preservation/reunification worker Luth. Social Svcs. Iowa, Sioux City, 1992; intern counselor Luth. Social Svcs., Aberdeen, S.D., 1993-94, counselor dept. corrections, case mgr., 1995—; pub. adminstr. Dickey County, Ellendale, S.D., 1994—. Mem. ACA, S.D. Counseling Assn., Aberdeen Child Protection Team. Office: Luth Social Svcs 2020 3rd Ave SE Aberdeen SD 57401

LUONGO, LUCILLE FRANCESCA, communications company executive; b. N.Y.C., May 29, 1948; d. Carmine and Jean (Gubitosi) Ariniello. BA in English and Speech, Hofstra U., 1970, MA in Communications, 1975. Tchr. Roosevelt (N.Y.) High Sch.; exec. sec. Katz Communications, Inc., N.Y.C., 1978-79, asst. dir. corp. communications, 1979-81, dir. communication svcs., 1981-82, dir. corp. rels., 1982-85, v.p. corp. rels., 1985-96, sr. v.p. corp. communications, 1991—. Adv. bd. The Caption Ctr.; bd. dirs. Broadcasters Found. Mem. NAFE, Internat. Radio and TV Soc., Am. Women in Radio and TV (nat. pres., trustee, chair of found.), Broadcast Promotion and Mktg. Execs. Office: Katz Media Corp 125 W 55th St New York NY 10019-5369

LUPONE, PATTI, actress; b. Northport, L.I., N.Y., Apr. 21, 1949; d. Orlando Joseph and Angela Louise (Patti) LuP.; m. Matt Johnston; 1 child, Joshua Luke. BFA, The Juilliard Sch., 1972. Off-Broadway prodns. include: The Woods, School for Scandal, The Lower Depths, Stage Directions; appeared in Broadway prodns.: Next Time I'll Sing to You, The Time of Your Life, The Three Sisters, The Robber Bridegroom (Tony award nominee), The Water Engine, The Beggar's Opera, Edward II, The Baker's Wife, 1976, The Woods, 1977, Working, 1978, Catchpenny Twist, 1978, As You Like It, 1982, The Cradle Will Rock, 1983, Stars of Broadway, 1983, Edmond, 1982, Oliver, 1984; star Broadway musicals Evita, 1979 (Best Actress in Musical Tony award 1980), Anything Goes, 1987, Pal Joey, 1995; London prodns. Les Miserables, 1985, Sunset Boulevard, 1993; films include: King of the Gypsies, 1978, 1941, 1979, Fighting Back, 1982, Witness, 1985, Wise Guys, 1986, Driving Miss Daisy, 1989; TV appearances include: Kitty, The Time of Your Life, Lady Bird in LBJ, 1987, The Water Engine, 1992, Family Prayers, 1993, The Song Spinner, 1995, Her Last Chance, 1996; TV series, Life Goes On, 1989-93. Office: ICM 40 W 57th St New York NY 10019*

LUPTON, ELLEN, curator, graphic designer; b. Phila., Dec. 1, 1963; d. William La Rue and Mary Jane Laura (Hohman) L.; m. Jerry Abbott Miller, Sept. 22, 1990. BFA, Cooper Union, 1985. Curator Herb Lubalin Study Ctr, The Cooper Union, N.Y.C., 1985-92; curator of contemporary design Cooper-Hewitt Nat. Mus. of Design, Smithsonian Institution, N.Y.C., 1992—; ptnr., cons. Design Writing Rsch., N.Y.C., 1985—. Author: Mechanical Brides: Women and Machines from Home to Office, 1993, (with J.A. Miller) The Bathroom, The Kitchen and The Aesthetics of Waste, 1992; editor: (with Miller) The Bauhaus and Design Theory, 1991. Mem. Am. Inst. Graphic Arts (bd. dirs. 1992—). Democrat. *

LUPTON, MARY HOSMER, retired small business owner; b. Olympia, Wash., Jan. 2, 1914; d. Kenneth Winthrop and Mary Louise (Wheeler) Hosmer; student Gunston Hall Jr. Coll., 1932-33; BS in Edn., U. Va., 1940; m. Keith Brahe-Wiley, Oct. 12, 1940 (dec. Apr. 1955); children: Sarah Hosmer Wiley Guise, Victoria Brahe-Wiley; m. Thomas George Lupton, Nov. 27, 1965 (dec. Feb. 1989); 1 stepson, Andrew Henshaw. Ptnr., Wakefield Press, Earlysville, Va., 1940-55; owner, operator Wakefield Forest Bookshop, Earlysville, 1955-65, Forest Bookshop, Charlottesville, 1965-85, Wakefield Forest Tree Farm, 1955-85. Contbr. articles to profl. mags. Corr. sec. Charlottesville-Albemarle Civic League, 1963-64; sec. Instructive Vis. Nurses Assn., Charlottesville, 1961-62; chmn. pub. info. Charlottesville chpt. Va. Mus. Fine Arts, 1970-77; mem. writers' adv. panel Va. Center for Creative Arts, 1973-75, chmn. pub. info., 1976-77; mem. Albemarle County Forestry Com., 1961-62; bd. dirs. Charlottesville-Albemarle Mental Health Assn., 1980-82, 89-91. Mem. AAUW, DAR (Am. Heritage com. chmn. 1983-85, 89-91), Assns. of U. Va. Libr., New Eng. Hist. Geneal. Soc., Conn. Soc. Genealogists, Geneal. Soc. Va., Albemarle County hist. socs., Va. Soc. Mayflower Descs. (asst. state historian 1979-82), LWV, Soc. Mayflower Descs., Am. Soc. Psychical Research, Brit. Soc. Psychical Rsch., Nature Conservancy, Charlottesville Soc. of Friends, Jefferson Soc., Cornerstone Soc. (charter), Lawn Soc. (charter), Chi Omega. Unitarian. Address: 2600 Barracks Rd Apt 361 Charlottesville VA 22901-2195

LURENSKY, MARCIA ADELE, lawyer; b. Newton, Mass., May 4, 1948. BA magna cum laude, Wheaton Coll., 1970; JD, Boston Coll. Law Sch., 1973. Bar: Mass. 1973, D.C. 1990, U.S. Dist. Ct. (we. dist.) Wis. 1978, U.S. Dist. Ct. Mass. 1974, U.S. Ct. Appeals (1st cir.) 1974, U.S. Ct. Appeals (3d cir.) 1982, U.S. Ct. Appeals (4th cir.) 1984, U.S. Ct. Appeals (5th cir.) 1995, U.S. Ct. Appeals (8th cir.) 1985, U.S. Ct. Appeals (9th cir.) 1976, U.S. Ct. Appeals (10th cir.) 1995, U.S. Ct. Appeals (11th cir.) 1982, U.S. Ct. Appeals (fed. cir.) 1989, U.S. Claims Ct. 1989, U.S. Supreme Ct. 1979. Atty. U.S. Dept. Labor, Washington, 1974-90, Fed. Energy Regulatory Commn., U.S. Dept. Energy, Washington, 1990—. Mem. Phi Beta Kappa. Office: Fed Energy Regulatory Commn 888 First St NE Washington DC 20426

LURIA, ZELLA HURWITZ, psychology educator; b. N.Y.C., Feb. 18, 1924; d. Hyman Hurwitz and Dora (Garbarsky) H.; m. Salvador Edward Luria, Apr. 18, 1945; 1 child, Daniel David. BA, Bklyn., 1944; MA, Ind. U., 1947, PhD, 1951. lic. clin. psychologist, Mass. Ford Found. post-doctoral fellow U. Ill., Urbana, 1951-53, Russell Sage found. fellow, 1953-56, clin. researcher, 1954-58; asst. prof. psychology Tufts U., Medford, Mass., 1958-62, assoc. prof., 1962-70, prof., 1970—; psychiatry lectr. Mass. Gen. Hosp., Boston, 1970-79; vis. scholar Stanford U., 1977, 83; vis. prof. UCLA, 1992, 94, U. Mich., 1993. Sr. author: Psychology of Human Sexuality, 1979, Human Sexuality, 1987. Postdoctoral fellow USPHS, Paris, 1963-64, Bunting fellow Radcliffe Coll., 1989-90; Mellon Found. Faculty grantee Wellesley Coll., 1979-80. Mem. Tufts U. Am. Assn. Univ. Profs. (pres. 1986-87). Office: Tufts Univ Dept Of Psychology Medford MA 02155

LURIE, ALISON, author; b. Chgo., Sept. 3, 1926; children: John, Jeremy, Joshua. AB, Radcliffe Coll., 1947. Lectr. English Cornell U., 1969-73; adj. assoc. prof. English Cornell U., Ithaca, N.Y., 1973-76, assoc. prof., 1976-79, prof., 1979—. Author: V.R. Lang: A Memoir, 1959, Love and Friendship, 1962, The Nowhere City, 1965, Imaginary Friends, 1967, Real People, 1969, The War Between the Tates, 1974, Only Children, 1979, The Language of Clothes, 1981, Foreign Affairs, 1984, The Truth About Lorin Jones, 1988, Don't Tell the Grownups, 1990, Women and Ghosts, 1994. Recipient award in lit. Am. Acad. Arts and Letters, 1978, Pulitzer prize in fiction, 1985; fellow Yaddo Found., 1963-64, 66, Guggenheim Found., 1965, Rockefeller Found., 1967. Office: Cornell U Dept English Ithaca NY 14853

LUSBY, GRACE IRENE, infection control nurse practitioner; b. Huntington Park, Calif., Aug. 20, 1935; d. Fletcher Homer and Charlotte Ione (Hayden) L. BS in Nursing, U. Calif., San Francisco, 1964, MS, 1968; cert. program in epidemiology, U. Calif., San Diego, 1981. RN, pub. health nurse, psychiat. nurse. Staff nurse, head nurse cancer rsch. unit U. Calif., San Francisco, 1964-66; pvt. duty nurse open heart surgery Profl. Registry, San Francisco, 1966-68; infection control coord. San Francisco Gen. Hosp., 1969-92; infection control cons. Oakland, Calif., 1992—; infection control rep. Calif. Task Force on AIDS, Sacramento, 1983-87, U.S. AIDS Task Force, San Francisco, 1983-92; co-establisher 1st infection control program for AIDS, San Francisco Gen. Hosp., 1983; mem. infection control-adv. coms. Svc. Employees Internat. Union, Calif. Nurses Assn., Mayor's Homeless Com., CAL-OSHA, also others, San Francisco, 1985—; infection control cons. emergency, home care, skill nursing, psychiatry, San Francisco, 1985—. Contbr. chpts. to books. Recipient Founder's award U. Calif.-San Francisco AIDS/ARC Update, 1988. Mem. Assn. Practitioners Infection Control (past treas., rec. sec., chmn. AIDS resource group), Women's AIDS Network (charter), PEO (rec. sec., corr. sec.), Sigma Theta Tau. Home and Office: 5966 Chabolyn Ter Oakland CA 94618-1914

LUSHER, JEANNE MARIE, pediatric hematologist, educator; b. Toledo, June 9, 1935; d. Arnold Christian and Violet Cecilia (French) L. BS summa cum laude, U. Cin., 1956, MD, 1960. Lic. physician, Mich.; cert. in pediat. and hematology/oncology, Am. Bd. Pediat. Resident in pediat. Tulane divsn. Charity Hosp. La., New Orleans, 1961-64; fellow in pediat. hematology-oncology Child Rsch. Ctr. Mich., Detroit, 1964-65, St. Louis Children's Hosp./Washington U., 1965-66; instr. pediat. Washington U., St. Louis, 1965-66; from instr. to assoc. prof. Sch. Medicine Wayne State U., Detroit, 1966-74, prof., 1974—; dir. divsn. hematology-oncology Children's Hosp. Mich., Detroit, 1976—; Marion I. Barnhart prof. hemostasis rsch. Sch. Medicine Wayne State U., Detroit, 1989—; med. dir. Nat. Hemophilia Found., N.Y.C., 1987-94, chmn. med. and sci. adv. coun., 1994—. Author, editor: Treatment of Bleeding Disorders with Blood Components, 1980, Sickle Cell, 1974, 76, 81, Hemophilia and von Willebrand Disease in the 1990's, 1991, Acquired Bleeding Disorder in Children, 1981, F VIII/von Willebrand Factor and Platelets in Health and Disease, 1987, Inhibitors to Factor VIII, 1994, Blood Coagulation Innhibitors, 1996. Mem. Citizens Info. Com., Pontiac Township, Mich., 1980-82; apptd. mem. Hazardous Waste Incinerator Commn., Oakland County, Mich., 1981. Recipient Disting. Alumnus award U. Cin. Alumni Assn., 1990. Mem. Am. Bd. Pediat. (chmn. sub-bd. on hematology-oncology 1988-90), Am. Soc. Hematology (chmn. sci. com. pediat. 1991-92), Am. Pediat. Soc., Soc. Pediat. Rsch., Internat. Soc. Thrombosis-Hemostasis (chmn. factor VIII/IX subcom. 1985-90, sec., chmn. sci. and standardization com. 1996—), Mich. Humane Soc. Office: Children's Hosp Mich 3901 Beaubien St Detroit MI 48201-2119

LUSK, GLENNA RAE KNIGHT (MRS. EDWIN BRUCE LUSK), librarian; b. Franklinton, La., Aug. 16, 1935; d. Otis Harvey and Lou Zelle (Bahm) Knight; m. John Earle Uhler, Jr., May 26, 1956; children: Anne Knight, Camille Allana; m. 2d, Edwin Bruce Lusk, Nov. 28, 1970. BS, La. State U., 1956, MS, 1963. Asst. librarian Iberville Parish Library, Plaquemine, La., 1956-57, 1962-68; tchr. Iberville Parish Pub. Schs., Plaquemine, 1957-59, Plaquemines Parish Pub. Schs., Buras, La., 1959-61; dir. Iberville Parish Library, Plaquemine, 1969-89; chmn. La. State Bd. Library Examiners, 1979-89; pres. Camille Navarre Gallery, Ltd., Zachary, La., 1989-94. Mem. Iberville Parish Econ. Devel. Council, Plaquemine, 1970-71; sec. Iberville Parish Bicentennial Commn., 1973—; mem. La. Bicentennial Commn., 1974; bd dirs. McHugh House Mus., 1991-92. Named Outstanding Young Woman Plaquemine, La. Jr. C. of C., 1970. Mem. La. (sect. chmn. 1967-68), Riverland (sec. 1973-74) libraries assns., Capital Area Libraries (chmn. com. 1972-74). Republican. Episcopalian. Author: (with John E. Uhler, Jr.) Cajun Country Cookin', 1966, Rochester Clarke Bibliography of Louisiana Cookery, 1966, Royal Recipes from the Cajun Country, 1969, Iberville Parish, 1970. Home: 22736 Plainsland Dr Zachary LA 70791-9764

LUST, BARBARA C., psychology and linguistics educator; d. John Benedict and Virginia (Sleth) L. BA in English Lit., Manhattanville Coll., 1963; postgrad., Fairleigh Dickinson, 1965, The New Sch. for Social Rsch., 1965-66, U. Geneva, Switzerland, 1968-69; MA in English Lit., Fordham U., 1971; PhD Devel. Psychology, CUNY, 1975. Post doctoral fellow dept. linguistics and philosophy MIT, Cambridge, 1974-76; from asst. prof. to prof. dept. human development and family studies Cornell U., Ithaca, N.Y., 1976—, field rep. cognitive studies program, 1987—, co-dir., 1992—, prof. modern langs. & linguistics, 1990—; vis. prof. SUNY, Binghamton, 1977; vis. scientist MIT, 1984, 90; vis. scholar Kelaniya U., Sri Lanka, 1984, U.S. Ednl. Found., 1984; cons. in field, lectr. various colls. and univs. Author: Studies in the Acquisition of Anaphora (vol I 1986, II 1987); co-editor, author: Syntactic Theory & First Language Acquisition, 1994 (vol. I and II); co-author: Studies in the Cognitive Basis of Language Development, 1975; contbr. articles to prof. jours., chpts. to books. Grantee NIMH, 1976, NSF, 1979-88, 92-93, 95; fellow Nat. Inst. Health, 1990, NSF, 1989-91; Smithsonian grant Am. Inst. Indian Studies, 1980-81; recipient Travel award Linguistic Soc. Am. and NSF, 1982, Rsch. award NSF, 1988-89, James McKeen Cattell award, 1992-93, N.Y. State Coll. Human Ecology award, 1976-79, 83. Fellow AAAS (chair linguistics and the lang. scis. 1993-94); mem. APA, Linguistic Soc. Am. (del. to AAAS psychology sect. 1988—), Am. Psychological Soc., Internat. Assn. Study Child Language, Soc. Rsch. Child Devel., Internat. Soc. Woman in Cognitive Neuroscience, Internat. Soc. Korean Linguistics, New Eng. Child Lang. Assn., N.Y. Acad. Scis., Soc. Philosophy and Psychology, Linguistic Assn. Great Britian, Piaget Soc. Democrat. Office: Cornell U Human Devel & Family Studies Ng 28 Marth Van Rensse Ithaca NY 14853

LUST, ELENORE (NORLIST), artist; b. Chgo.; d. Herbert and Dora (Koumas) Lust; m. Robert Eising, Jan. 7, 1932 (div.). Student, Smith Coll., 1929-30; BA, NYU, 1935, MA, 1957. Cert. tchr., N.Y., N.J. Dir., co-founder Norlyst Art Gallery, N.Y.C., 1940-49; art tchr. Cape of Good Hope Sem., Capetown, South Africa, 1952-55, St. Siprian's Sch., Capetown, 1952-55, N.J. High Schs., 1957-79; art lectr. Herald Tribune N.Y.C., 1944-49, art tchr. Little Red Sch. House, N.Y.C., 1944-49, Bklyn. Mus. Art Sch., 1947-50, Rancocas Valley Region High Sch., 1959-68; spl. edn. tchr. Lenape High Sch. System, 1970-79. Exhibited in one-woman shows at Norlyst Art Gallery, 1944, Stuttaford's Gallery, Capetown, 1952, Cafe Gallery, Burlington, N.J., 1988, Ft. Dix, Pemberton, N.J., 1988; represented in permanent collections at Ft. Dix, Mus. Women in Arts, Washington, and 74 other pvt. and corp. collections. Vol. art asst. tchr. Walter Elem. Sch., Lumber, N.J.; vol. Meml. Hosp., Mt. Holly, N.J. Mem. AAUW, Burlington County Art Guild (pres. 1983-85, v.p. 1989), Atlantic City Art Ctr., Trenton Artists' Workshop Assn., So. N. J. Advocates for Arts, Artworks/Princeton. Democrat. Episcopalian. Studio: PO Box D Mount Holly NJ 08060

LUSTICA, KATHERINE GRACE, publisher, artist, marketing consultant; b. Bristol, Pa., Nov. 20, 1958; d. Thomas Lustica and Elizabeth Delores (Moyer) De Groat. Student, Hussian Sch. Art, Phila., 1976-78, Rider Coll., 1980-82, U. Utah, 1993—. Comml. artist, illustrator Bucks County Courier Times Newspapers, Levittown, Pa., 1978-82; account exec. Trenton (N.J.) Times Newspapers, 1982-84; promotions and account exec. Diversified Suburban Newspapers, Murray (Utah) Printing, 1984-88; pub. Barclays Ltd. Salt Lake City, 1988—; cover artists, illustrator Accent mag., Bristol, 1978-82; freelance artist, 1978—; advt. and creative cons. Everett & Winthrop Products Group, Salt Lake City, 1988-90, Multi Techs. Internat., Salt Lake City, 1990-91. Newcombe scholar, 1981-82. Mem. Art Dirs. Salt Lake City. Presbyterian. Office: 4640 Stratton Dr Salt Lake City UT 84117-5558

LUSTIG, JACQUELINE STANLEY, lawyer; b. N.Y.C., July 6, 1949; d. Morris and Queenie (Stanley) L.; m. Christopher J. Hallett, Feb. 19, 1984; children: Jessica, Vanessa. BA, CCNY, 1970; JD, DePaul U., 1979. Bar: Ill. 1979. Assoc. Stack & Filipi, Chgo., 1979-81; exec. dir. Gannon-Proctor Commn., Office of Gov., Chgo., 1982-84, counsel to gov., 1984-85; chief legal counsel Dept. Rehab. Svc., Chgo., 1985-91, Ill. Dept. Human Rights, Chgo., 1991—. Bd. dirs. Lakeview Citizens Coun., Chgo., 1983-88, Pro Bono Advs., Chgo., 1989-91; chmn. CLVN, Chgo., 1986-88. Named Woman of Yr., Na'amat U.S.A., 1988. Mem. Women's Bar Assn. Ill. (pres. 1988-89, bd. dirs. Found. 1990-92)), Chgo. Bar Assn. (bd. mgrs. 1989-91, bd. dirs. Found. 1986-92). Jewish. Office: Ill Dept Human Rights 100 W Randolph Ste 10-100 Chicago IL 60601

LUTHER, DARLENE, state legislator; b. 1947; m. Bill Luther; 2 children. BA, U. St. Thomas. Mem. Minn. Ho. of Reps., 1993—. Home: 6809 Shingle Creek Dr Brooklyn Park MN 55445-2647 Office: Minn Ho of Reps State Capital Building Saint Paul MN 55155-1606

LUTHER, FLORENCE JOAN (MRS. CHARLES W. LUTHER), lawyer; b. N.Y.C. June 28, 1928; d. John Phillip and Catherine Elizabeth (Duffy) Thomas ; J.D. magna cum laude, U. Pacific, 1963; m. William J. Regan (dec.); children—Kevin P., Brian T.; m. 2d, Charles W. Luther, June 11, 1961. Admitted to Calif. bar; mem. firm Luther, Luther, O'Connor & Johnson, Sacramento, 1964—. Mem. faculty McGeorge Sch. Law, U. Pacific, Sacramento, 1966-88, prof., 1968-88, prof. emeritus, 1988—. Judge Bank Am. Achievement awards, 1969-71. Bd. dirs. Sacramento Suicide Prevention League, 1969-70. Mem. ABA, Calif., Sacramento County bar assns., AAUP, Womens Legal Groups, Am. Judicature Soc., Order of Coif, Iota Tau Tau. Mem. bd. advisors Community Property Jour., 1974—, state decision editor, 1974—. Home: 11101 Fair Oaks Blvd Fair Oaks CA 95628-5136 Office: PO Box 1030 Fair Oaks CA 95628-1030

LUTHER, LUANA MAE, editor; b. L.A., Mar. 7, 1939; d. Chester Harry and Mildred P. (Knight) L.; m. O. Solorzano, Sept. 6, 1958 (div. 1974); children: Suzanne, Troy, Stephanie, Paul; m. Edwin J. Salzman, Apr. 4, 1981. BA, Calif. State U., Sacramento, 1974. Law indexer, legis. counsel State Calif., Sacramento, 1975-80, analyst, adminstrv. law, 1981-84; communications dir. Townsend & Co., Sacramento, 1985-87; adminstrv. asst., dept. justice State of Calif., Sacramento, 1987-88; editorial asst. Golden State Report Mag., Sacramento, 1986-88; mktg. cons. Lake Oswego, Oreg., 1989—; editor-in-chief Doral Pub., Wilsonville, Oreg., 1990—. Author: Red Mack Truck Massacre, 1981; contbr. articles to numerous publs.; columnist: Sacramento Bee, 1982-84; editor: (newsletter) Sacramento Youth Band, 1985. Dir. pub. rels., pres. LWV, West Clackamas County, Oreg., 1993-95; vol. numerous polit. campaigns, Sacramento; fundraiser Dem. Women's Com., Sacramento, 1986. Mem. Mex.-Am. Ednl. Assn. (treas. 1964, Cert. Appreciation 1971). Democrat. Home: 17239 Rebecca Ln Lake Oswego OR 97035

LUTHER, M. IDA, state legislator. Former mem. Maine Ho. of Reps., Augusta, past mem. labor com.; mem. Maine State Senate, Augusta, 1993-95, Maine Ho. of Reps., Augusta, 1995—. Democrat. Home: 160 Granite St Mexico ME 04257-1733 Office: Maine State Ho of Reps State House Sta #2 Augusta ME 04333*

LUTHER, MAXINE W., artist; b. L.A., Dec. 16, 1924; d. Maxwell J. and Alice Gertrude (Derrin) Williamson; m. Eldon Harmon Luther, June 12, 1948; children: Calvin Andrew, Scott Jarvis, Douglas William. Attended, Lasell Jr. Coll., 1943, Newton Wellesley Sch. Nursing, 1944-45; grad., Hartford Secretarial Sch., 1947. Pvt. sec. Immanuel Congl. Ch., Hartford, Conn., 1947-48; sec. U.S. Army-Navy Signal Corps, Washington, Arlington, Va., 1948-51. Exhibited in group shows at Beth El, East Hartford, Conn., Boynton Beach (Fla.) Art League, Canton (Conn.) Artists Guild, Inc., Conn. Watercolor Soc., Conn. Women Artists, Essex (Conn.) Art Assn., Lyme (Conn.) Art Assn., Mystic (Conn.) Art Assn., New Britain (Conn.) Mus. Am. Art, Shoreline Alliance for Arts, Conn., Slade Ely House, New Haven. Mem. Conn. Watercolor Soc. (juried), Canton Artist's Guild (juried), East Lyme Art League (juried), Essex Art Assn. (juried), Lyme Art Assn. (juried), Women in Visual Arts Fla. (juried). Republican. Congregational. Home: 491 Joshuatown Rd Lyme CT 06371 also: 800 SW 15th Boynton Beach FL 33426

LUTHER, SARA FLETCHER, political sociologist, communications researcher; b. Mpls., Dec. 6, 1918; d. Clark Robinson Fletcher and Alice Genevieve (Johnson) Fletcher Martin Taylor; m. Charles Hamilton Luther Febr. 28, 1941 (div. Aug. 1963); children: Charles H. Luther, Jr., Mark Fletcher Luther, Sara Lee Luther; m. John J. Neumaier, Sept. 2, 1969. BA,

Vassar Coll., Poughkeepsie, N.Y., 1940; MA, SUNY, New Paltz, 1974; PhD, CUNY, N.Y., 1986. With personnel dept. Mpls. Honeywell Co., 1943-47; newspaper reporter Mpls. Star Tribune, 1947-50; elected mem. Minn. State Legislature, St. Paul, 1950-62; campaign dir. Mayor Arthur Naftalin, Mpls., 1963; adminstrv. asst. Gov. Karl Rolvaag, St. Paul, 1963-66; sr. rschr. Am. Rehab. Found., Mpls., 1966-68; dir. off-campus studies Vassar Coll., 1968-70; tchr. Poughkeepsie Day Sch., 1970-74; rschr., writer Poughkeepsie, 1974—; assoc. Luther/Neumaier Assocs., Poughkeepsie and Mount Dora, Fla., 1986—. Author: The United States and the Direct Broadcast Satellite: The Politics of International Broadcasting in Space, 1988; editor: Diverse Perspectives on Marxist Philosophy - East and West, 1995; contbr. articles to profl. jours. Chair ACLU-Mid Hudson Branch, Poughkeepsie, 1974-75; co-chair Dutchess County Peace Ctr., Poughkeepsie, 1984-89; mem. internat. adv. bd. Radio for Peace Internat., Santa Ana, Costa Rica, 1989—; sec. No. Dutchess branch NAACP, Poughkeepsie, 1991-92, 94. Recipient Citizen Svc. award NAACP-No. Dutchess, 1995. Mem. AAUW, Am. Sociology Assn., Internat. Assn. Mass Comms. Rsch., Radical Philosophy Assn. Democrat. Home: 60 S Randolph Ave Poughkeepsie NY 12601 also: Apt 410 601 McDonald St Mount Dora FL 32757

LUTHER-LEMMON, CAROL LEN, middle school educator; b. Waverly, N.Y., May 8, 1955; d. Carl Ross and Mary Edith (Auge) Luther; m. Mark Kevin Lemmon, June 21, 1986; children: Matthew C., Cathryn M. BS, Ithaca Coll., 1976; MS in Edn., Elmira Coll., 1982. Cert. elem. and secondary tchr., Pa., N.Y. Reading aide Waverly (N.Y.) Central Schs., 1978-80; tchr. reading N.Y. State Div. for Youth, Lansing, 1981-82; tchr. title I reading, mem. student assistance program and instructional support team Rowe Mid. Sch., Athens (Pa.) Area Sch. Dist., 1982—; tchr. Title I reading Lynch Elem. Sch. Basketball coach Youth Activities Dept., Athens, 1982-85, asst. softball coach, 1990-91; mem. ad hoc com. Waverly Sch. Dist., 1990-91; mem. Goal G parents & edn. Mid. Sch. Implementation Team for WINGS-Waverly in a Global Soc. for Waverly Ctr. Sch. Dist. Strategic Plan; bd. dirs. SACC, 1995-96, Waverly Cmty. Ch., 1976-78; active Girls' Softball League Waverly, 1978-80, commr., 1980; choir mem. Meth. Ch., Wverly, 1976-90, adminstrv. bd., trustee, chmn. bd. trustees, 1995, 96; mem. Valley Chorus, Pa. and N.Y., 1983-86. With USAR, 1977-83. Mem. ASCD, AAUW (v.p. Waverly br. 1982-83, pres. Waverly br. 1992—), Am. Legion Aux. (girl's state rep. 1972, girl's state chmn. 1976-80 Waverly post, counselor 1977), Chemung Area Reading Coun., N.Y. State Reading Assn. Republican. Home: 490 Waverly St Waverly NY 14892-1102 Office: Athens Area Sch Dist Pennsylvania Ave Athens PA 18810-1440

LUTJENS, ELAINE WILHELMINA, insurance company professional; b. Honolulu, Jan. 7, 1960; d. Paul Richard and Frances Lorraine (Phillips) L.; m. Philip Dennis Cyr, Dec. 1, 1985. BA in Econs., U. Calif., Santa Barbara, 1981. Dept. mgr. May Co., San Diego, 1982-85; sales rep. ITT Hartford Ins., San Diego, 1985-86, svc. supr., 1986-91, ops. mgr., 1991-94, 96—, project mgr., 1994-96. Founder Partnership in Edn., San Diego, 1996; mem. Giant Steps-ITT Hartford, 1995-96. Mem. Toastmasters Internat. (treas. 1995—). Office: ITT Hartford Ins 3131 Camino Del Rio North San Diego CA 92129

LUTTRULL, SHIRLEY JOANN, protective services official; b. Fordland, Mo., Feb. 26, 1937; d. Thomas Marion and Pauline (Sherrow) Pirtle; m. Leslie Allen Luttrull, June 3, 1956 (div. May 1978); children: Vicki Lynn, Ricki Allen; m. Orben Lowell Clark, Dec. 31, 1982 (div. Oct. 1987); m. Barry Mabe, June 1992 (div. Oct. 1994). Student, Southwest Mo. State U., 1979. Checker person Lea's Market, Fordland, Mo., 1955-56; plant supr. Mellers Photo Lab., Springfield, Mo., 1968-82; shopper Hopper and Hawkins, Dallas, 1982-83; crew leader Sentinal Security, Okla. City, Shrink Control Corp., Houston, 1984-86; sales mgr. Shrink Control Corp., 1986-88; owner Internal Theft Control, Springfield, 1988--. Mem. Mo. Retail Grocers Assn., Springfield C. of C. Republican. Home and Office: 1347 S Airwood Dr Springfield MO 65804-0520

LUTZ, CARLENE, educational association administrator; b. Chgo., Feb. 4, 1946; d. John Calvin Sr. and Helen (Kwast) L. BS in Edn., No. Ill. U., 1967; MA in Edn., U. Conn., 1971; adminstrv. endorsement, Chgo. State U., 1988. Cert. early childhood edn., tchr. kindergarten-grade 9. 2d grade tchr. Chgo. Pub. Schs., 1967-73, reading resource tchr., 1973-79, ESEA coord., 1979-80, upper grade lang. arts, 1980-89, reading resource tchr., 1989-92, asst. dir. Chgo. Tchrs. Union Quest Ctr., 1992—; trainer ednl. rsch. and dissemination and critical thinking programs, Chgo., 1986—. Editor (pamphlet) EPDA Project, Pictorial Report, 1971. Ill. State scholar Ill. State Scholarship Commn., 1964; EPDA fellow U.S. Dept. Edn., 1971. Mem. ASCD, Internat. Reading Assn., Nat. Coun. Tchrs. English, Am. Fedn. Tchrs., Chgo. Tchr. Union, Ella Flagg Young Assn., Delta Kappa Gamma, Phi Delta Kappa. Home: 125 Acacia Dr Apt 613 Indianhead Park IL 60525-4409 Office: Chgo Tchrs Union Quest Ctr Fl 4 222 Merchandise Mart Plz Chicago IL 60654-1016

LUTZ, EDITH LEDFORD, state legislator; b. Lawndale, N.C., Oct. 20, 1914; d. Curtis and Annie Hoyle Ledford; m. M. Everett Lutz, 1933 (dec.); 1 child, E. Jacob. Farmer, horticulturist; mem. N.C. Ho. of Reps., 1975-93, chmn. local and regional govt. II, vice-chmn. agr., forestry, horticulture and wildlife subcom., mem. various coms. Active Sheltered Workshops Rutherford County; bd. dirs. Farm Bur. Named Farm Woman of Yr., S.W. Dist., Woman of Yr., Cleve. Times, Disting. Woman of Cleveland County. Mem. Am. Bus. Women, Cleveland County C. of C. (bd. dirs.), Apple Grower's Assn. Democrat. Methodist. Home: 1015 Carpenters Grove Church Rd Lawndale NC 28090-9803

LUTZ, GRETCHEN KAY, English language educator; b. Ft. Worth, Tex., Jan. 6, 1948. BA, Tex. Christian U., 1970; MA, U. Houston, 1974, Rice U., 1995; postgrad., Dartmouth Coll., 1994; MA, Rice U., 1995. High sch. and mid. sch. tchr. English Galveston and Deer Park (Tex.) Sch. Dists., 1970-77; instr. ESL and English Schreiner Coll., Kerrville, Tex., 1979-80; instr. English San Jacinto Coll. Ctr., Pasadena, Tex., 1981—; tchr. jr. and sr. English Sch. of the Talented and Gifted Townview Ctr., Dallas. Contbr. articles to profl. jours. Mem. MLA, Nat. Symposium for Coherence in Liberal Arts, C.C. Humanities Assn., Am. Culture and Popular Culture Assn., U.S. European Command Mil. to Mil. Program Conf., Am. Studies Assn. Tex., South Ctrl. MLA, Conf. Coll. Tchrs. English (exec. coun.), S.W. Conf. Christianity and Lit., Western Soc. 18th Century Studies, Tex. Folklore Soc., S.W. Regional Conf. English in Two-Year Colls., Tex. Voices Sesquicentennial Series, Rice English Symposium, San Jacinto Coll. Faculty Symposium. Home: 3946 Sherwood Forest #135E Dallas TX 75220

LUTZ, JULIE HAYNES, astronomy and mathematics educator; b. Mt. Vernon, Ohio, Dec. 17, 1944; d. Willard Damon and Julia Awilda (Way) Haynes; m. Thomas Edward Lutz, July 8, 1967 (dec. 1995); children: Melissa, Clea. BS, San Diego State U., 1965; MS, U. Ill., 1968, PhD, 1971. Asst. prof. astronomy Wash. State U., Pullman, 1972-78, asst. dean sci., 1978-79, assoc. prof., 1978-84, assoc. provost, 1981-82, prof., 1984—, chair math. and astronomy dept., 1992—; rsch. fellow Univ. Coll. London, England, 1976-77, 82-83; vis. resident astronomer Cerro Tololo Inter-Am. Obs., 1988-89; dir. div. astron. scis. NSF, 1990-92. Contbr. articles on astron. research to profl. jours. Fellow AAAS (mem. com. 1982-85, mem. nominating com. 1992—, chair sect. D 1993—), Royal Astron. Soc.; mem. Am. Astron., Soc. (chair publs. bd. 1986-88), Astron. Soc. Pacific (bd. dirs. 1988—, v.p. 1989, pres. 1990-92), Internat. Astron. Union. Home: 1200 NE Mcgee St Pullman WA 99163-3818 Office: Wash State U Program in Astronomy Pullman WA 99164-3113

LUTZE, RUTH LOUISE, retired textbook editor, public relations executive; b. Boston, Apr. 19, 1917; d. Frederick Clemons and Louise (Rausch) L. BA with honors, Radcliffe Coll., 1938; postgrad., Boston U., 1938-39. Tchr. Winthrop (Mass.) Pub. Schs., 1938-39; with pub. rels. dept. Boston City Club, 1939-42; sr. projects editor D.C. Heath & Co., Lexington, Mass., 1942-82; book reviewer, lectr., cons. on pub. rels., lectr. textbook publ. Bd. dirs. Winthrop Improvement and Hist. Assn., 1980—; vol. tchr. Boston Pub. Schs., 1967-77; mem. Winthrop Rep. Town Com., 1970—; v.p. 1st Luth. Ch. Boston, 1986, deacon, 1980—. Recipient cert. appreciation for vol. in edn., Kiwanis Club of East Boston, 1972. Mem. Radcliffe Club Boston. Home: 110 Circuit Rd Winthrop MA 02152-2819

LUZURIAGA, FRANCESCA, manufacturing executive; b. Boston, 1954. Grad., Pomona Coll., 1976, U. So. Calif., 1978. Exec. v.p. fin. and adminstrn. Mattel Inc., El Segundo, Calif. Mem. Fin. Execs. Inst. Office: Mattel Inc 333 Continental Blvd El Segundo CA 90245-5032*

LYALL, KATHARINE C(ULBERT), academic administrator, economics educator; b. Lancaster, Pa., Apr. 26, 1941; d. John D. and Eleanor G. Lyall. BA in Econs., Cornell U., 1963, PhD in Econs., 1969; MBA, NYU, 1965. Economist Chase Manhattan Bank, N.Y.C., 1963-65; asst. prof. econs. Syracuse U., 1969-72; prof. econs. Johns Hopkins U., Balt., 1972-77; dir. grad. program in public policy Johns Hopkins U., 1979-81; dep. asst. sec. for econs. Office Econ. Affairs, HUD, Washington, 1977-79; v.p. acad. affairs U. Wis. System, 1981-85; prof. of econ. U. Wis., Madison, 1982—; acting pres. U. Wis. System, Madison, 1985-86, 91-92, exec. v.p., 1986-91, pres., 1992—; bd. dirs. Kemper Ins. Cos.; mem. bd. Carnegie Found. for Advancement of Teaching. Author: Reforming Public Welfare, 1976, Microeconomic Issues of the 70s, 1978. Mem. Mcpl. Securities Rulemaking Bd., Washington, 1990-93. Mem. Am. Econ. Assn., Assn. Am. Univs., Phi Beta Kappa. Home: 6021 S Highlands Ave Madison WI 53705-1110 Office: U Wis System Office of Pres 1720 Van Hise Hall 1220 Linden Dr Madison WI 53706-1559

LYBARGER, ADRIENNE REYNOLDS (MRS. LEE FRANCIS), college administrator; b. Boston, Mar. 8, 1926; d. Joseph Anthony and Albertine (Mouton Drevet) Reynolds; BA, Mills Coll., Calif., 1947; cert. Katharine Gibbs Sch., 1948; m. Lee Francis Lybarger, Jr., Sept. 15, 1955 (dec); children: Linda, Lauretta, James (dec.), Lisa, Leslie (dec.), Jeffrey (dec.), Lucia, Lana. Asst. to dir. Mid-Century convocation M.I.T. Cambridge, 1949, asst. to dir. West Coast regional office Mid-Century devel. program, 1949-50, asst. dir. So. regional office, 1950-51; asst. to dir. convocation devel. program Ithaca (N.Y.) Coll., 1951; asst. to dir., devel. program U. Buffalo, 1951-52; asst. to dir. Diamond Jubilee program Case Inst. Tech., Cleve., 1952-54; asst. to dir., expansion and improvement program John D. Archbold Hosp., Thomasville, Ga., 1955-61; ptnr. Lybarger Prodns., comml. films, N.Y.C.; asst. dir., dir. regional campaigns, Ohio, Boston, Mass., N.Y.C., also supr. all other nat. regional campaigns Mount Holyoke Coll. Fund for Future, South Hadley, Mass., 1961-63; fund-raising cons. to capital programs, Vocation Svc. Ctr. and Bronx-Westchester YMCA, YMCA Greater N.Y., 1963-65; dir. devel. and pub. rels. Bank St. Coll. Edn., N.Y.C., 1965-79; cons. S. Bronx Overall Econ. Devel. Corp., 1978-79; v.p. devel. Wells Coll., 1979-92, dir. Wells Capital campaign; ednl. fund-raising cons., 1993—; cons. capital campaign Borough of Manhattan Community Coll., 1979-80; Realtor assoc./mktg. cons. Century 21, Clinton, N.J., 1978-81; Pres., Birch Island (Maine) Corp., 1979; mem. Nat. Women's Hall of Fame, 1987-90, bd. dirs., 1987—. Mem. Am. Prospect Rsch. Assn. Author: (with L. F. Lybarger) Proven Guides to Effective Soliciting (slide film), 1950, rev., 1960, 81; exec. producer, Scriptwriter Now More than Ever, Wells Coll. Home: Kings Manor 272 Pittstown Rd Pittstown NJ 08867

LYCAN, REBECCA TATUM, professional dog handler; b. Atlanta, Oct. 10, 1960; d. Clement Marduke and Ruth (Davenport) Tatum; m. Glenn Eugene Lycan, July 14, 1984. BS in Microbiology, U. Ga., 1982. Lab. technician Optimal Systems, Inc., Norcross, Ga., 1982-84; asst. dog handler Canine Country Club, Chattanooga, 1984-86; profl. dog handler Leading Edge Kennel, Griffin, Ga., 1986—. Nominee for Best New Female Profl. Handler, Kennel Rev. and IAMS, 1989, 90. Mem. Profl. Handlers Assn., Dog Handlers Guild, Griffin Kennel Club, Griffin Kennel Club (show chmn. Fall shows 1990-92), Conyers Kennel Club. Office: Leading Edge Kennel PO Box 849 Griffin GA 30224-0849

LYDAY, MARGARET M., associate dean; b. Sewickley, Pa., Oct. 29, 1946; d. Edward F. and Emma Jane (Acklin) Campbell; m. Leon F. Lyday, Nov. 28, 1992. BA, Carlow Coll., 1969; PhD, Cath. U. Am., 1973. Instr. Mohegan Coll., Norwich, Conn., 1974-78; asst. prof. Pa. State U., Hazelton, Pa., 1978-85, assoc. prof., 1985—, assoc. dean, 1990-95; dir. Lehigh Valley Writing Project, Allentown, Pa., 1988—. Mem. MLA, Nat. Coun. Tchrs. English, Modern Langs. Soc. Office: Pa State Univ 31 S. Burrowes Bldg State College PA 16802

LYDON, PATRICIA DIANE, secondary education educator; b. Parkersburg, W.Va., Sept. 29, 1946; d. Forrest Woodrow and Hazel Virginia (Bell) Walcutt; m. James Patrick Lydon, Nov. 10, 1967; children: Michael, Pamela. Student, Glenville State Coll., 1968; Master's degree, W.Va. U., 1984. Tchr. Marshall County Bd. of Edn., Moundsville, W.Va., 1967, Wirt County Bd. Edn., Elizabeth, W.Va., 1979—; trainer Appalachian Edn. Lab., Charleston, W.Va.; ptnr. in edn. Wesvaco, Parkersburg, W.Va. Mem. Am. Fedn. Tchrs., Nat. Geography Alliance, Delta Kappa Gamma (legis. chair), Woman's Club (past pres.). Roman Catholic. Home: PO Box 657 Elizabeth WV 26143-0657 Office: Wirt County H S PO Box 219 Elizabeth WV 26143-0219

LYERLY, ELAINE MYRICK, advertising executive; b. Charlotte, N.C., Nov. 26, 1951; d. J.M. and Annie Mary (Myrick) L.; m. Marc Rauch, Jan. 17, 1987. AA in Advt. and Comml. Design, Cen. Piedmont Community Coll., 1972. Freelance designer Sta. WBTV, Charlotte, N.C., 1972; fashion illustrator Matthews Belk, Gastonia, N.C., 1972-73; designer Monte Curry Mktg and Communication Svcs., Charlotte, 1973-74, exec. v.p., 1974-77; pres. Repro/Graphics, Charlotte, 1975-77, Lyerly Agy. Inc., Charlotte, 1977—; bd. dirs. SouthTrust Bank. Illustrator: Mister Cookie Breakfast Cookbook, 1985. Chmn. regional blood com. ARC, chmn. Greater Carolinas chpt., 1990-93, mem. nat. implementation com., 1991; bd. dirs. United Way; mem. exec. com. Ptnrs. in Quality. Named Bus. Woman of Yr., Shearson Lehman Hutton/Queens Coll., 1989, N.C. Young Careerist Bus. and Profl. Women's Club, 1981; recipient ACE award Women in Comms., 1993. Mem. Women Execs. (bd. dirs.), Women Bus. Owners (adv. coun., Leadership award 1990, Woman Bus. Owner of Yr. award 1994), Pub. Rels. Soc. Am. (Counselors Acad. 1985—), Charlotte C. of C. (bd. dirs., diversity coun., long-range planning com., Bus. Woman of Yr. award 1985), Hadassah. Republican. Jewish. Office: Lyerly Agy Inc 4819 Park Rd Charlotte NC 28209

LYJAK CHORAZY, ANNA JULIA, pediatrician, medical administrator, educator; b. Braddock, Pa., Feb. 25, 1936; d. Walter and Cecilia (Swiatkowski) Lyjak; m. Chester John Chorazy, May 6, 1961; children: Paula Ann Chorazy, Mary Ellen Chorazy-Cuccaro, Mark Edward Chorazy. BS, Waynesburg Coll., 1958; MD, Women's Med. Coll. Pa., 1960. Diplomate Am. Bd. Pediats. Intern St. Francis Gen. Hosp., Pitts., 1960-61; resident in pediats., tchg. fellow Children's Hosp. of Pitts., 1961-63, pediatrician, devel. clinic, 1966-75; pediat. house physician Western Pa. Hosp., Pitts., 1963-66; med. dir. Rehab. Instn. Pitts., 1975—; clin. asst. prof. pediats. Children's Hosp. Pitts. and U. Pitts. Sch. Medicine, 1971-94, clin. assoc. prof. pediats., 1994—; pediat. cons. Children's Home Pitts., 1985—. Author chpts. to books. Co-chmn. EACH Joint Planning and Assessment, Pitts., 1980-85; mem. adv. com. 10th Nat. Conf. on Child Abuse, Pitts., 1993. Recipient Miracle Maker award Children's Miracle Network, 1995. Fellow Am. Acad. Pediats.; mem. AMA, Pa. Med. Soc., Pitts. Pediat. Soc., Allegheny County Med. Soc. Home: 131 Washington Rd Pittsburgh PA 15221-4437 Office: Rehab Inst Pitts 6301 Northumberland St Pittsburgh PA 15217-1360

LYLE, CHARLOTTE ANN, cardiac rehabilitation services administrator; b. Sanford, Fla., Apr. 25, 1958; d. William Howard and Lavada Ann (Green) Bruce; m. Gary Daniel Lyle, Feb. 2, 1980 (div. Dec. 1990); children: Amanda, Jessica. ADN, Troy State U., 1980. RN, Ala.; cert. instr. ACLS and BCLS. With Jackson Hosp., Montgomery, Ala., 1980-81, Warren County Hosp., McMinnville, Tenn., 1981; RN Bapt. Med. Ctr., Montgomery, Ala., 1981—; RN, cardiac rehab. dir. Montgomery Cardiovascular Assn., 1994—. Active programs com. Am. Heart Assn., Ala., 1989-95, programs chair, 1994-95, bd. mem., 1994-95; coord. blood drive ARC, Ala., 1992-94. Named for Outstanding Svc., Am. Heart Assn., 1990, for Leadership Montgomery County Extension Svc., 1990. Baptist. Office: Bapt Med Ctr Cardiac Rehab PO Box 11010 Montgomery AL 36111-0010

LYLE, GLENDA SWANSON, state legislator; b. Knoxville, Tenn.; d. Richard and Olivia Swanson; Kipp Elise, Jennifer, Anthony. BA, U. Denver, 1964; MA, U. Colo., 1973. Former dir. cmty. and personal svcs., instr. early childhood edn., dir. preschool lab C.C. of Denver/Auraria; owner Planners, Etc.; mem. Colo. Ho. of Reps., 1992—, mem. various coms., 1993—. Del. White Ho. Conf. Small Bus., 1980-86; mem. Regional Transp. Dist. Bd., 1986-92, Regulatory Agy. Adv. Bd., Mayor's Planning Bd., Nat. Pub. Lands Adv. Coun., Gov.'s Small Bus. Coun., Colo. Mkt. and Distributive Edn. Adv. Coun., Va Neal Blue Ctr. Mem. Am. Planning Assn., Conf. Minority Transp. Ofcls. (nat. bd. dirs.), Black Women Polit. Action (founding mem.), Black C. of C. (bd. dirs.). Democrat. Office: Colo House of Reps State Capitol Denver CO 80203

LYLE, JEAN STUART, social worker; b. Rock Hill, S.C., Jan. 13, 1912; d. David and Martha (Nash) L.; BA, U. S.C., 1949; MS in Social Work, Columbia U., 1951. Recreation dir. City of Rock Hill, 1938-44; commd. 1st lt. Med. Svc. Corps, U.S. Army, 1951, advanced through grades to lt. col., 1966; asst. chief social worker, Ft. Benning, Ga., 1951-55; chief social worker Fort Jay, N.Y., 1955-58, Fort McClellan, Ala., 1958-62, female inpatient svc. Walter Reed Gen. Hosp., Washington, 1962-66; dir. Army Cmty. Svc., U.S. Army, Hawaii, 1966-68, Walter Reed Army Med. Ctr., 1968-70; cons. group work to Med. Field Svc. Sch., Fort Sam Houston, Tex., 1969; ret., 1970; dir. vol. svcs. S.C. Dept. Health and Environ. Control, Columbia, 1970-74; pvt. practice social work, Rock Hill, 1974—; tchr. and supr. social work students Catholic U. Am., Washington, 1960-62. Decorated Legion of Merit; recipient Cmty. Svc. award U.S. Army, 1968. Mem. Nat. Assn. Social Workers, Acad. Cert. Social Workers. Democrat. Address: PO Box 2553 Rock Hill SC 29732-4553

LYLES, JEAN ELIZABETH CAFFEY, journalist, church worker; b. Abilene, Tex., Mar. 2, 1942; d. Wiley Luther and Pauline Linn (Marlin) Caffey; m. James Vernon Lyles, Aug. 23, 1969 (div. Aug. 1987). Student, McMurry Coll., 1960-61; BA with honors, U. Tex., 1964. Copy editor Christian Century mag., Chgo., 1972-74, assoc. editor, 1974-84, editor at large, 1984—; assoc. editor Religious News Svc., N.Y.C., 1984-87; sr. news editor The Lutheran, Chgo., 1987-91; news dir. United Meth. News Svc., Evanston, Ill., 1991-94; freelance photojournalist, 1995—, freelance organist, 1995—. Author: A Practical Vision of Christian Unity, 1982; contbg. author: The First Amendment in a Free Society, 1979, Fearfully and Wonderfully Weird, 1990; contbg. editor Wittenburg Door, 1982-87; columnist Inside the Am. Religion Scene, 1985-87, The Underground Ecumenist, 1989-92; mem. editl. bd. Mid-Stream, Indpls., 1984—; mem. exec. com. Associated Ch. Press, 1989-91. Church organist. Mem. Religion Newswriters Assn., Am. Guild Organists, Hymn Soc. Am., United Meth. Assn. of Communicators. Democrat. Episcopalian. Home: 922 North Blvd Oak Park IL 60301-1243

LYMAN, JING, social activist; b. Phila., Feb. 23, 1925; d. Bennet Fellow and Marjorie (Page) Schauffler; m. Richard Wall Lyman, Aug. 20, 1947; children: Jennifer, Holly Lyman Antolini, Christopher M., Timothy R. BA, Swarthmore Coll., 1947. Carpentry tchr. Shady Hill Sch., Cambridge, Mass., 1948-50; founding mem., exec. dir. Midpeninsula Citizens for Fair Housing, Palo Alto, Calif., 1965-66; founding bd. mem., chmn. fair housing task force Stanford (Calif.) Midpeninsula Urban Coalition, 1968-74; founding bd. mem. Women & Philanthropy, N.Y.C., 1975-81; founder, pres. Nat. Coalition for Women's Enterprise, Inc., N.Y.C., 1983-89; trustee Citizen's Trust (formerly Working Assets Common Holdings), San Francisco, 1984-94; pres. HUB Co-Ventures, Palo Alto, 1989—; bd. chmn., CEO Am. Leadership Forum, Stanford, 1991-94; cons. Am. Enterprise Inst., Washington, 1982-83; mem. bd. overseers vis. com. Harvard and Radcliff Colls., 1973-79; bd. dirs. Rosenberg Found., San Francisco, 1973-80. Co-author: (handbook) Women's Economic Development Handbook: A Working Guid to Women's Self-Employment, 1987. Bd. dirs. Career Action Ctr., Palo Alto, 1974-80, Found Ctr., N.Y.C., 1976-82, vice-chmn. 1980-81, chmn. 1981-82,; adv. com. Coun. on Founds., Washington, 1977-82, SRI/HUD, 1978-80, Conf. of Mayors, 1980-81, bd. govs. Stanford Assocs., 1980-86; trustee The Enterprise Found., Columbia, Md., 1983—; mem. selection com. of John W. Gardner Leadership award, Washington, 1985-88; adv. coun. Global Fund for Women, Menlo Park, Calif., 1987, The Spring Found., Palo Alto, 1993—, Leadership Calif., Pasadena, 1994—; bd. dirs. Am. Leadership Forum, 1989—; numerous other civic activities. Recipient Wider Opportunities for Women award Jane Fleming Women's Employment award Washington, 1984, Uncommon Woman award Stanford U., 1991, others. Democrat.

LYMAN, PEGGY, dancer, choreographer, educator; b. Cin., June 28, 1950; d. James Louis and Anne Earlene (Weeks) Morner; m. David Stanley Lyman, Aug. 29, 1970 (div. 1979); m. Timothy Scott Lynch, June 21, 1982; 1 child, Kevin Kynch. Grad. high sch., Cin. Solo dancer Cin. Ballet Co., 1964-68, Contemporary Dance Theater, 1970-71; chorus dancer N.Y.C. Opera, 1969-70; Radio City Music Hall Ballet Co., 1970; chorus singer and dancer Sugar, Broadway musical, N.Y.C., 1971-73; prin. dancer Martha Graham Dance Co., N.Y.C., 1973-88, rehersal dir., 1989-90; artistic dir. Martha Graham Ensemble, N.Y.C., 1990-91; faculty Martha Graham Sch., 1975—; head dance div. No. Ky. U., 1977-78; artistic dir. Peggy Lyman Dance Co., N.Y.C., 1978-89; asst. prof. dance, guest choreographer Fla. State U., Tallahassee, 1982-89; guest choreographer So. Meth. U., Dallas, 1986; adjudicator Nat. Coll. Dance Festival Assn., 1983—; co-host To Make a Dance, QUBE cable TV, 1979; mem. guest faculty Am. Dance Festival, Durham, N.C., 1984; site adjudicator Nat. Endowment for Arts, 1982-84; tchr. Hartford Ballet Sch., 1992—, East Conn. Concert Ballet, 1992—; guest faculty Wesleyan U., Middletown, Conn., 1992; guest artist Conn. Coll., 1993; chair dance dept. Hartt sch. U. Hartford, Conn., 1994—; freelance master tch. internat. univs. Prin. dancer Dance in America, TV spls., 1976, 79, 84; guest with Rudolph Nureyev, Invitation to the Dance, CBS-TV, 1980; guest artist Theatre Choregraphique Rennes, Paris, 1981, Rennes, France, 1983, Adelaide U., 1991; site dir. Martha Graham's Diversion of Angels for student concert U. Mich., 1992, Martha Graham's Panorama, U. Ill., Champaign-Urbana, 1993, Martha Graham's Diversion of Angels for Dutch Nat. Ballet, 1995. Founding mem. Cin. Arts Coun., 1976-78. Mem. Am. Guild Mus. Artists. Office: Hartford Ballet 224 Farmington Ave Hartford CT 06105-3501

LYNCH, ANNETTE PETERS, educator; b. Marion, Ind., Oct. 23, 1922; d. Frank Robert and Delight Kindle (Simmons) Peters; m. Thomas Millard Lynch, Aug. 24, 1949 (div. Jan. 1975); children: Robert Millard, Susan D.L. Marks, David Barrett. BA, Ind. U., 1944, MA, 1945; PhD, Occidential Coll., 1961. Instr. Ind. U., Bloomington, 1945-49, Glendale (Calif.) Coll., 1949-50, Occidential Coll., L.A., 1950-55; prof. Mt. San Antonio Coll., Walnut, Calif., 1955-93; adj. assoc. prof. Calif. State U., L.A., 1954-58; treas. Coll. English Assn., So. Sect., Calif., 1956-57, v.p., 1957-58, pres., 1958-59' writer's day worker Mt. San Antonio Coll., Calif., 1972-93; leader poetry workshops. Author: Ways Around the Heart, 1988; author of poems; editor Mt. San Antonio Literary Mag., 1981-89. Vol. South Pasadena Pub. Libr., 1993—. Mem. Poetry Soc. Am., Acad. Am. Poets, Calif. State Poetry Soc., Beyond Baroque Literary Arts Ctr. Democrat. Home: 833 Garfield Ave South Pasadena CA 91030

LYNCH, BEVERLY PFEIFER, education and information studies educator; b. Moorhead, Minn., Dec. 27, 1935; d. Joseph B. and Nellie K. (Bailey) Pfeifer; m. John A. Lynch, Aug. 24, 1968. B.S., N.D. State U., 1957, L.H.D. (hon.); M.S., U. Ill., 1959; Ph.D., U. Wis., 1972. Librarian Marquette U., 1959-60, 62-63; exchange librarian Plymouth (Eng.) Pub. Library, 1960-61; asst. head serials div. Yale U. Library, 1963-65, head, 1965-68; vis. lectr. U. Wis., Madison, 1970-71, U. Chgo., 1975; exec. sec. Assn. Coll. and Research Libraries, 1972-76; univ. librarian U. Ill.-Chgo., 1977-89; dean Grad. Sch. Libr. and Info. Sci. UCLA, 1989-94, prof. Grad. Sch. Edn. and Info. Studies, 1989—. Author: (with Thomas J. Galvin) Priorities for Academic Libraries, 1982, Management Strategies for Libraries, 1985, Academic Library in Transition, 1989, Information Technology and the Remaking of the University Library, 1995. Named Acad. Libr. of Yr., 1982, one of top sixteen libr. leaders in Am., 1990. Mem. ALA (pres. 1985-86), Nat. Info. Standards Orgn. (bd. dirs. 1996—), Acad. Mgmt., Am. Sociol. Assn., Bibliog. Soc. Am., Caxton Club, The Chicago Network, Grolier Club, Arts Club Chgo., Phi Kappa Phi. Office: UCLA Grad Sch Edn and Info Mailbox 951521 Los Angeles CA 90095-1521

LYNCH, CAROL LEE, director special services, psychologist; b. Passaic, N.J., Sept. 22, 1943; d. Joseph Louis and Ellen (Birish) Dobkowski; m. Carl R. Grant, Feb. 16, 1969 (div. July 1987); m. Mervin Dean Lynch, Aug. 13, 1989; 1 child, Eric Alexander. BA, William Paterson Coll., 1966; MA,

NYU, 1970, D Psychology, 1984. Lic. psychologist, N.J., N.Y. Tchr. Bloomfield (N.J.) Pub. Schs., 1966-68, psychologist, 1970-87; dir. spl. svcs. Waldwick (N.J.) Pub. Schs., 1987—, acting supt. schs., 1995-96; adj. clin. prof. NYU, N.Y.C., 1983-86 adj. prof. Montclair (N.J.) State Coll., 1984-85. Mem. profl. alumni coun. Sch. Edn., Health and Nursing, NYU, 1989-91. NYU fellow, 1981-82; recipient Best Practice award N.J. State Dept. Edn. for Fast Families Program, 1995, Disting. Grad. Brian E. Tomlinson Meml. award NYU, 1995. Mem. APA (sch. psychology task force 1989-90), N.J. Psychol. Assn. (treas. 1985-86), Nat. Assn. Sch. Psychologists (del. 1984-88), N.J. Assn. Sch. Psychologists (pres. 1982-83), Ea. Ednl. Rsch. Assn. (pres. 1993-95), N.J. Coun. Edn., Bergen County Assn. Lic. Psychologists (bd. dirs. 1991-93), NYU Sch. Psychology Alumni Assn. (founder 1988-92), Ramapo Valley Adminstrs. (v.p. 1996—). Home: 124 Frank Ct Mahwah NJ 07430-2963 Office: Waldwick Pub Schs 155 Summit Ave Waldwick NJ 07463-2133

LYNCH, CATHERINE GORES, social work administrator; b. Waynesboro, Pa., Nov. 23, 1943; d. Landis and Pamela (Whitmarsh) Gores; BA magna cum laude and honors, Bryn Mawr Coll., 1965; Fulbright scholar, Universidad Central de Venezuela, Caracas, 1965-66; postgrad. (Lehman fellow), Cornell U., 1966-67; m. Joseph C. Keefe, Nov. 29, 1981; children: Shannon Maria, Lisa Alison, Gregory T. Keefe, Michael D. Keefe. Mayor's intern, Human Resources Adminstrn., N.Y.C., 1967; rsch. asst. Orgn. for Social and Tech. Innovation, Cambridge, Mass., 1967-69; cons. Ford Found., Bogota, Colombia, 1970; staff Nat. Housing Census, Nat. Bur. Statistics, Bogota, 1971; evaluator Foster Parent Plan, Bogota, 1973; rsch. staff FEDESARROLLO, Bogota, 1973-74; dir. Dade County Advocates for Victims, Miami, Fla., 1974-86; asst. to dep. dir. Dept. Human Resources, Miami, 1986-87, computer liaison, 1987-88, asst. adminstr. placement svcs. program, 1988-89; exec. dir. Health Crisis Network, 1989-96; liaison HIV cmty. svc. State of Fla. Disease Prevention and Control, 1996—; guest lectr. local univs. Participant, co-chmn. various task forces rape, child abuse, incest, family violence, elderly victims of crime, nat., state, local levels, 1974-86; developer workshops in field; participant, chair, co-chair task forces on HIV/AIDS impact, long term care, children and AIDS, AIDS orgnl. issues, 1991—; mem. gov.'s task force on victims and witnesses, gov.'s task force on sex offenders and their victims, gov.'s Red Ribbon panel on AIDS, 1992-93, gov.'s interdepartmental work group, 1993—; mem. ednl. review com. Am. Found. AIDS Rsch., 1991-96; vice chair Metro-Dade HIV Svcs. Planning Council, 1991-93; active Fla. HIV Svcs. Adv. Coun., 1991-94; review panel Fed. Spl. Projects of Nat. Significance; adv. coun. Metro Dade Social Svcs., 1995-96; cert. expert witness on battered women syndrome in civil and criminal cts. Recipient various public svc. awards including WINZ Citizen of Day, 1979, Outstanding Achievement award Fla. Network Victim Witness Svcs., 1982, Pioneer award Metro-Dade Women's Assn., 1989; cert. police instr. Mem. Nat. Orgn. of Victim Assistance Programs (bd. dirs. 1977-83; Outstanding Program award 1984). Fla. Network of Victim/Witness Programs (bd. dirs., treas., 1980-81), Nat. Assn. Social Workers, Am. Soc. Public Adminstrs., Dade County Fedn. Health and Welfare Workers, Fla. Assn. Health and Social Svcs. (Dade County chpt., treas., 1979-80), LWV (bd. dirs. Dade County chpt. 1989-92). Contbr. writings in field to publs. Office: Fla. HRS Office Dist Adminstr N-1007 401 NW 2d Ave Miami FL 33128

LYNCH, CHARLOTTE ANDREWS, communications executive; b. Fall River, Mass., Mar. 25, 1928; d. Alan Hall and Florence (Worthen) Andrews; m. Francis Bradley Lynch, June 7, 1952; children: Sarah, Richard, Stephen, William. AB in Philosophy, Radcliffe Coll., 1950; postgrad., U. Bridgeport, 1969-71. Adminstrv. asst. Mass. Congl. Confs. and Missionary Soc., Boston, 1951, 52; journalist Town Crier newspaper, Westport, Conn., 1968; asst. dir. devel. Cape Cod Hosp., Hyannis, Mass., 1975-76; parish adminstr. S. Congl. Ch., Centerville, Mass., 1977-83; cons. to ethnic advt. agy. Loiminchay, Inc., N.Y.C., 1992—. Mem. Toastmasters Club Cape Cod, Radcliffe Club Cape Cod (v.p. 1990—, exec. com. 1990—). Republican. Roman Catholic.

LYNCH, FRAN JACKIE, investment advisory company executive; b. Bklyn., Dec. 15, 1948; d. William R. and Ruth (Slaiman) Diamondstein; m. James P. Lynch, Jan. 8, 1969; children: Cheryl Ann, Christopher, Kevin. BA, Bklyn. Coll., 1969; student, Suffolk Community Coll., Brentwood, N.Y., 1980-82; postgrad, L.I. U., 1983. V.p. Castle Capital Corp., N.Y.C., 1971-74; agt. Jerome Castle Found., N.Y.C., 1970-74; dir. office services Penn-Dixie Industries, N.Y.C., 1970-74; exec. asst. Med. Fin. Advisor, N.Y.C., 1974; v.p. Sept. Capital Corp., Glen Cove, N.Y., 1977-80; controller Bobgar Inc., Wallweaves Inc. and N.Y. Twine, Syosset, N.Y., 1980-86, The Kapson Group, Commack, N.Y., 1987-91, Westbury Transport ETAL, Astoria, N.Y., 1991-93; ptnr. Econometric Capital Advisors Inc., Miami, Fla., 1992—; bus. mgr. Am-Pro Protective Agy., Columbia, S.C., 1994-96; cons. Women's Times, Queens, N.Y., 1987. Sec. Elwood Booster Club, East Northport, N.Y., 1987; mem. Harley Ave. PTA, 1980-87; coach Northport Youth Soccer, 1982; tchr. Confraternity Christian Doctrine Project St. Elizabeth's Ch., 1972-80, bd. dirs. Parish council, S. Huntington, N.Y., 1978-80. Home: 216 Camden Chase Columbia SC 29223-8416

LYNCH, LAURA ELLEN, parochial school educator; b. Chgo., June 25, 1965; d. Edgar Lewis and Loretta Ann (Sheehar) Hield; m. Terrence Michael Lynch, June 22, 1991; children: Dennis Edgar, Ellen Rose. BA in Edn., St. Xavier U., 1987. Cert. tchr., Ill. Tchr. Queen of Martyrs Sch., Chgo., 1987-92.

LYNCH, LUANN JOHNSON, accountant; b. Raleigh, N.C., June 20, 1962; d. James Vinson and Eloise (Edwards) Johnson; m. Byron Claude Lynch III, Oct. 3, 1987. BS in BA, Meredith Coll., Raleigh, 1984; MBA, Duke U., 1986; postgrad., U. N.C., 1993—. Fin. analyst Procter & Gamble, Cin., 1985; fin. mgmt. program No. Telecom, Inc., Research Triangle Park, N.C., 1986-89; mgr. corp. pricing Roche Biomed. Labs., Inc., Burlington, N.C., 1989-91, asst. v.p., 1991-93; Joseph E. Pogue doctoral fellow U. N.C., Chapel Hill, 1993—. Am. Acctg. Assn. Doctoral Consortium fellow, 1995, AICPA Doctoral fellow, 1993-95; Fuqua scholar, 1986. Mem. AAUW, NAFE, Inst. Mgmt. Accts., Am. Acctg. Assn. Home: 1622 Delaware Ave Durham NC 27705 Office: Kenan-Flagler Bus Sch U NC Chapel Hill NC 27599

LYNCH, MARGARET A., state legislator; b. Keene, N.H., Sept. 10, 1939; 4 children. BA, Keene State Coll., 1979. Ret. coll. adminstr.; mem. N.H. Ho. of Reps., mem. appropriations com., fin. com. Roman Catholic. Home: 37 Church St Keene NH 03431-4378 Office: NH Ho of Reps State Capitol Concord NH 03301

LYNCH, MARY BRITTEN, artist, educator; b. Pruden, Ky., Sept. 30, 1931; d. Fred Clarence and Mary Virginia (Strange) Hill; m. James Walton Lynch, Oct. 6, 1956; 1 child, Holly Kristen. BA, U. Tenn.-Chattanooga, 1956. Art instr. Hunter Mus. Art, Chattanooga, 1954-56, 65-75; Chattanooga Christian High Sch., Chattanooga, 1979-85; apptd. panel mem. Tenn. Arts Commn. Visual Arts Adv. Panel, 1972-76. Exhibited in group shows throughout U.S., 1974-77; represented by Art South, Inc., Phila. and Montgomery, Ala., Trinity Artgroup, Atlanta; featured in numerous art mags. & books, 1983-96. Founder Tenn. Watercolor Soc., 1969, Lenoir City Spring Arts Festival, Tenn., 1963; v.p. Hamilton County Republican Women's Club, 1969; bd. dirs. Chattanooga Symphony Guild, 1968-73, Little Miss Mag Day Nursery, 1977-85, Chattanooga Nature Ctr., 1983-84. Recipient award for Outstanding Contbn. to the State of Tenn. Tenn. Arts Commn., 1978, numerous purchase and cash awards Tenn. State Mus., Anchorage Mus., 1995. Mem. Am. Watercolor Soc., Nat. Watercolor Soc. (top award 1995). Episcopalian. Home: 1505 Woodnymph Trl Lookout Mountain GA 30750-2633

LYNCH, PATRICIA ANN, photographer, educator; b. Watsonville, Calif., Oct. 9, 1950; d. Edward P. and Mary (Sanchez) L. BA, Coll. Notre Dame, 1972; MA, U. San Francisco, 1994. Instr. photography Lincoln H.S., San Jose, Calif., 1982-93; instr. digital photography Lincoln H.S., San Jose, 1993—; new adviser trainer Jostens, Santa Barbara, Menlo Park, Calif., 1995—. Mem. NEA, Calif. Tchrs. Assn., San Jose Tchrs. Assn., Delta Kappa Gamma. Office: Lincoln HS 555 Dana Ave San Jose CA 95126

LYNCH, PATRICIA GATES, broadcasting organization executive consultant, former ambassador; b. Newark, Apr. 20, 1926; d. William Charles and Mary Frances (McNamee) Lawrence; m. Mahlon Eugene Gates, Dec. 19, 1942 (div. 1972); children: Pamela Townley Gates Sprague, Lawrence Alan; m. William Dennis Lynch. Student, Dartmouth Inst., 1975. Broadcaster Sta. WFAX-Radio, Falls Ch., Va., 1958-68; pub. TV host Sta. WETA, Washington, 1967-68; broadcaster NBC-Radio, Europe, Iran, USSR, 1960-61; internat. broadcaster, producer Voice of Am., Washington, 1962-69; staff asst. to First Lady The White House, Washington, 1969-70; host Voice of Am. Breakfast Show, Morning show, 1970-86; U.S. ambassador to Madagascar and the Comoros, 1986-89; dir. corp. affairs Radio Free Europe/Radio Liberty, Washington, 1989-94; worldwide lectr., 1968-86; adv. com. Ind. Fed. Savs. and Loan Assn., Washington, 1970-86. Author stories on Am. for English teaching dept. Radio Sweden, 1967-68, others on internat. broadcasting. Chair internat. svc. com. Washington chpt. ARC, 1979-86; bd. visitors Duke U. Primate Ctr., Durham, N.C. Grantee USIA, 1983; recipient Pub. Service award U.S. Army, 1960. Mem. Coun. Am. Ambs., (bd. dirs., v.p.), Assn. Diplomatic Studies and Tng. Dept. State (bd. dirs.), Am. Women in Radio and TV (pres. 1966-67), Am. News Women's Club, Washington Inst. Fgn. Affairs (bd. dirs.). Republican. Episcopalian.

LYNCH, PATRICIA MARIE, elementary education educator; b. Columbus, Ohio, Dec. 2, 1950; d. Ralph F. E. and Betty Lou (Rogers) Nicol; m. James Robert Lynch, June 17, 1972; children: Jason, Christopher. BEd, Capital U., 1972. Cert. tchr., Ohio. Tchr. Marion (Ohio) City Schs., 1972—; instr. math. workshops, other workshops Portland (Oreg.) State U., summers 1992—; math tchr. leader Cen. Ohio Reg. Profl. Devel. Ctr. Den leader Boy Scouts Am., Marion. Recipient Presdl. award for excellence in math., NSF, 1994, 95, 96; named Educator of Yr., PTA, 1993. Mem. Internat. Reading Assn., Ohio Coun. Tchrs. Math. (Outstanding Math. Tchr. Cen. Dist. 1993), Nat. Coun. Tchrs. of Math., NEA, Ohio Edn. Assn., Marion Edn. Assn., DAR, Craft Club, OES, Delta Kappa Gamma. Republican. Lutheran. Home: 1065 Barks Rd E Marion OH 43302-6718

LYNCH, PHYLLIS ANNE, stockbroker; b. Lakeville, Minn., Aug. 9, 1944; d. Eugene and Helen mary (Brown) L.; children from previous marriage: Evan Astrowsky, Amy Astrowsky. BS in Mktg., Fairfield U., 1983. Lic. securities broker, N.Y. Account exec. Blythe Eastman Dillon, N.Y.C., 1976-79, Great Western Fin., L.A., 1979-91, Smith Barney, L.A., 1991-92; fin. rep. Fidelity Investments, L.A., 1992-96; investment broker A.G. Edwards & Sons, Inc., Coral Gables, Fla., 1996—. Treas. L.A. Children's Hosp. Aux., Conejo Valley, Calif., 1988-90; bd. mem. L.A. County H.S. for the Arts, L.A., 1989-91. Recipient Parent of the Yr. award L.A. County Bd. Edn., 1991. Mem. Women's Polit. Action, NOW.

LYNCH, PRISCILLA A., nursing educator, therapist; b. Joliet, Ill., Jan. 8, 1949; d. LaVerne L. and Ann M. (Zamkovitz) L. BS, U. Wyo., 1973; MS, St. Xavier Coll., Coll., 1981. RN, Ill. Staff nurse Rush-Presbyn.-St. Luke's Med. Ctr., Chgo., 1977-81, psychiat.-liaison cons., 1981-83, asst. prof. nursing, unit leader, 1985—; mgr. and therapist Oakside Clinic, Kankakee, Ill., 1987—; mem. adv. bd. Depressive and Manic Depression Assn., Chgo., 1986—; mem. consultation and mental health unit Riverside Med. Ctr., Kankakee, 1987—; speaker numerous nat. orgns. Contbr. numerous abstracts to profl. jours., chpts. to books. Bd. dirs. Cornerstone Svcs. Recipient total quality mgmt. award Rush-Presbyn.-St. Luke's Med. Ctr., 1991. Mem. ANA, Ill. Nurses Assn. (coms.), Coun. Clin. Nurse Specialists, Profl. Nursing Staff (sec. 1985-87, mem. coms.). Presbyterian. Home: 606 Darcy Ave Joliet IL 60436-1673

LYNCH, ROSE PEABODY, retail executive; b. Dallas, June 6, 1949; d. Russell Vincent and Rose Peabody (Parsons) L.; m. Peter Stuart Milhaupt, Feb. 12, 1972 (div. 1977); m. James Alexander Torrey, Apr. 22, 1989. AAS, Bennett Coll., 1969; BA, Princeton U., 1971; MBA, Harvard U., 1982. Personal asst. Halston, Ltd., N.Y.C., 1975-76; assoc. dir. retail promotion Revlon, Inc., N.Y.C., 1976-80; dir. mktg. devel. Elizabeth Arden, N.Y.C., 1982-85; dir. mktg. Charles of the Ritz, N.Y.C., 1985-87; pres. Danskin, N.Y.C., 1987-89, Trowbridge Gallery, U.S., N.Y.C., 1989-93; cons., acting chief operating officer LeRoi Princeton Inc., 1991-92; v.p. merchandising-fragrance Victoria's Secret, Reynoldsburg, Ohio, 1993—. Republican. Episcopalian. Office: Three Limited Parkway Columbus OH 43218

LYNCH, SANDRA LEA, federal judge; b. Oak Park, Ill., July 31, 1946; d. Bernard Francis and Eugenia Tyus (Shepherd) L.; 1 child, Stephen Lynch Bowman. AB, Wellesley Coll., 1968; JD, Boston U., 1971. Bar: Mass. 1971, U.S. Dist. Ct. Mass. 1973, U.S. Dist. Ct. R.I., U.S. Ct. Appeals (1st cir.) 1974, U.S. Supreme Ct. 1974. Law clk. U.S. Dist. Ct., Providence, 1971-72; asst. atty. gen. Mass. Atty. Gen.'s Office, Boston, 1972-73; gen. counsel Mass. Dept. Edn., Boston, 1973-78; assoc. Foley, Hoag & Eliot, Boston, 1978-81, ptnr., 1981-95; apptd. U.S. cir. ct. judge U.S. Ct. of Appeals (1st cir.), Boston, 1995—; spl. counsel Jud. Conduct Commn., 1990-92. Contbr. articles to legal jours. Recipient Disting. Service award Planned Parenthood League of Mass., 1981. Mem. ABA (com. on partnership, ho. of dels. 1993-95), Boston Bar Assn. (pres. 1992-93, bd. bar overseers 1982-86, joint bar com. 1986). Office: US Ct Appeals 1st Cir 1617 US PO & CH Boston MA 02109

LYNCH, SHARON GLYNN, neurologist, educator; b. Lake Charles, La., July 23, 1958; d. Lynden Wayne and Martha (Schunke) L. BS, U. South Ala., 1979; MD, U. Ala., 1984. Diplomate Am. Bd. Psychiatry and Neurology. Intern in internal medicine U. Utah, 1984-85; resident in neurology U. Utah, Salt Lake City, 1985-88, postdoctoral fellow in immunogenetics, 1988-91; asst. prof., dir. multiple sclerosis clinic U. Kans. Med. Sch., Kansas City, 1991—. NIH grantee, 1996. Mem. AAAS, Am. Acad. Neurology, Nat. Multiple Sclerosis Soc. (bd. dirs. Mid-Am. chpt. 1995—, postdoctoral fellow 1988-91, Profl. Svcs. award 1993, grantee 1987, 91), Soc. for Creative Anachronism. Office: U Kans Med Sch Dept Neurology 3901 Rainbow Blvd Kansas City KS 66160

LYNCH, SHERRY KAY, counselor; b. Topeka, Kans., Nov. 20, 1957; d. Robert Emmett and Norma Lea Lynch. BA, Randolph-Macon Woman's Coll., 1979; MS, Emporia State U., 1980; PhD, Kans. State U., 1987. Vocat. rehab. counselor Rehab. Services, Topeka, 1980-81, community program cons., 1981-86. Mem. exec. com. Sexual Assault Counseling Program, Topeka, 1983-86, recruitment coordinator, 1983-86, counselor, 1981-86, Nat. Singles Conf. Planning Com., Green Lake, Wis., 1987-90; area admissions rep. Randolph-Macon Woman's Coll., Lynchburg, Va., 1981-87; counseling intern, Winthrop Coll., Rock Hill, S.C., 1986-87; counselor Ripon (Wis.) Coll., 1987-90, mem. Student Outreach Svcs. coun. Northbrooke Hosp., 1988-90; counselor Va. Poly. Inst. and State U., 1991—, mem. Student Affairs Staff Devel. com., 1991-94, chairperson, 1992-94, mem. Sexual Assault Victim Edn. and Support com., 1991-95, Wellness com., 1993—, Leadership Resource team, 1994—; bd. dirs., sec. Ripon Chem. Abuse and Awareness program, 1987-90; bd. dirs. Montgomery County Community Shelter, 1992—, also sec., 1993—, Haymarket Sq. Homeowners Assn., 1992—, also treas., 1993—; chairperson ch. and soc. com. Blacksburg United Meth. Ch., 1992-94, mem. coun. ministries, 1992-94. Recipient Kans. 4-H Key award Extension Service of Kans. State U., 1974; named Internat. 4-H Youth Exchange Ambassador to France, 1977. Mem. Nat. Rehab. Counseling Assn. (bd. dirs. 1982-88, chairperson br. devel. subcouncil 1982-87, chairperson policy and program council 1987-88), Gt. Plains Rehab. Counseling Assn. (newsletter editor 1982-85, bd. dirs. 1983-87, pres. 1984-85, sec. 1986-87), Gt. Plains Rehab. Assn. (bd. dirs. 1983-85, awards chairperson 1984-85), Kans. Rehab. Counseling Assn. (bd. dirs. 1983-86, pres. 1984-85), Kans. Rehab. Assn. (bd. dirs. 1982-85, advt. chairperson 1983-85), Topeka Rehab. Assn. (bd. dirs. 1982-85, sec. 1982-83, pres. 1983-84), Am. Assn. Counseling and Devel., Am. Coll. Personnel Assn. (chair-elect commn. VII counseling and psychol. svcs., 1995-96, chair, 1996—, directorate body, 1990-93, 95—, membership commn. 1990-93), Wis. Coll. Personnel Assn. (bd. dirs. 1988-90), Assn. for Specialists in Group Work, Va. Coll. Pers. Assn. Republican. Methodist. Avocation: tennis. Home: 2700 Newton Ct Blacksburg VA 24060-4112 Office: Va Tech U Counseling Ctr 152 Henderson Hall Blacksburg VA 24061

LYNCH, SONIA, data processing consultant; b. N.Y.C., Sept. 17, 1938; d. Espriela and Sadie Beatrice (Scales) Sarreals; m. Waldro Lynch, Sept. 18, 1981 (div. Oct. 1983). BA in Langs. summa cum laude, CCNY, 1960; cert. in French, Sorbonne, 1961. Systems engr. IBM, N.Y.C., 1963-69; cons. Babbage Systems, N.Y.C., 1969-70; project leader Touche Ross, N.Y.C., 1970-73; sr. programmer McGraw-Hill, Inc., Hightstown, N.J., 1973-78; staff data processing cons. Cin. Bell Info. Systems, 1978-89; sr. analyst AT&T, 1989-92; lead tech. analyst Automated Concepts Inc., Arlington, Va., 1992-96; tech. cons. Maxim Group, Reston, Va., 1996—. Elder St. Andrew Luth. Ch., Silver Spring, 1992-96. Downer scholar CUNY, 1960, Dickman Inst. fellow Columbia U., 1960-61. Mem. Assn. for Computing Machinery, Phi Beta Kappa. Democrat. Home: 13705 Beret Pl Silver Spring MD 20906-3030 Office: Maxim Group 11417 Sunset Hills Rd Reston VA 22090

LYNCH, SUSAN H., state legislator; b. Mpls., July 5, 1943; d. Lewis Mifflin and Helen Hayes; m. Thomas Vincent Lynch, June 14, 1969; children: Brian, Robin, Karen. BA in Biology, Cedar Crest Coll., 1965. Genetic rsch. technician NIH, Bethesda, Md., 1965-67, Children's Hosp., L.A., 1967-69; dir. summer arts and crafts City of Prescott, Ariz., 1976-78, dir. preschool, 1978-82; mem. Prescott City Coun., 1983-87; mem. Ariz. Ho. Reps., Phoenix, 1993—. Bd. dirs. Prescott Fine Arts, Phippen Mus. Western Art; mem. adv. bd. Anytown U.S.A., 1990-93. Mem. AAUW (br. pres. 1990-92), Ariz. Women's End. and Employment, Rep. Women Prescott (treas. 1991). Presbyterian. Office: Ariz State Legislature 1700 W Washington St Phoenix AZ 85007-2812*

LYNCH, SUSAN MCNEESE, communications executive; b. Lexington, Ky., Jan. 10, 1955; d. William B. and Mary Scott (Concannon) McNeese; m. Philip John Lynch, Sept. 4, 1982; children: Matthew, Alex. BA, U. Ky., 1978. Copywriter Southeast Comms., Lexington, Ky., 1979-81; acct. exec. Franklin Ross & Assocs., Louisville, 1981-82; creative dir. Bass Advt., Louisville, 1982-85; sr. writer, producer Fessel, Siegfriedt & Moeller, Louisville, 1985-88; v.p. creative svcs. wtr Group, Louisville, 1988-91; v.p. comms. Louisville Conv. Bur., 1991—. Writer, producer: (video) How You Say Louisville (Louie award 1994, Telly award 1995, PRSA award 1995, Cindy award 1996, Marty award 1995). Pres. Friends of the Waterfront, Louisville, 1996—; hospitality chair radio com. Ky. Derby Festival, Louisville, 1993-96; publ. chair Bourbon Ball, Louisville, 1995; auction chair Ky. Opera Assn., Louisville, 1995; mem. ann. dinner com. Louisville C. of C., 1993-95. Mem. Internat. Assn. Convs. and Vis. Burs., Ky. Tourism Coun., Pub. Rels. Soc. Am., Soc. Am. Travel Writers (com. chair 1995-96), Advt. Club (v.p. comms. 1995-96). Democrat. Roman Catholic. Office: Louisville Conv & Vis Bur 400 South First Louisville KY 40202

LYNCH, TERESA ANN, state legislator; b. Mpls., Jan. 15, 1954; d. Leslie Alvin Steinberg and Joanne (Pouliot) Brand; m. David C. Lynch, May 18, 1974; children: Emily, Erin, Anna, Tessa. Grad. interpreter tng. program, St. Paul Tech. Coll., 1983. Interpreter Anoka-Hennepin Sch. Dist., Mpls., 1983-87; state rep. Minn. Ho. of Reps. Dist. 50B, Andover, Minn., 1988—. Asst. caucus leader Rep. House Caucus, St. Paul, 1992-94; vice chair Rules & Legislative Adminstrn. Named Legislator of Yr., Assn. of Minn. Counties, St. Paul, 1992; recipient Legis. Recognitive award Nat. Assn. of the Deaf, 1992; named Legislator of Yr., Minn. Assn. Deaf Citizens, 1993. Republican. Office: Minn House of Reps 295 State Office Bldg Saint Paul MN 55155*

LYNCH, VIRGINIA ANNE (VIRGINIA A. RED HAWK), forensic nurse, educator, consultant; b. Weatherford, Tex., Jan. 27, 1941; m. Z. G. Standing Bear, Mar. 22, 1988; children from previous marriage: Kristi Lynch Hulme, Keri Lynch Kembel, Angela Lynch Thompson. AA, Weatherford Coll., 1979; BSN, Tex. Christian U., 1982; MSN, U. Tex., Arlington, 1990. RN, Tex., Ga.; cert. coroner, Ga.; cert. profl. instr. in forensic sci.; cert. sexual assault nurse examiner; cert. ARC disaster nurse; diplomate Am. Bd. Forensic Examiners. Asst. head nurse surgery All Saints Hosp., Ft. Worth, 1981-82; RN emergency surgery Campbell Meml. Hosp., Weatherford, Tex., 1983-84; med. investigator Tarrant-Parker Med. Examiners Dist., Ft. Worth, 1984-90; forensic clin. nurse specialist, addiction and forensic mental health substance abuse program psychiat. nurse Ga. Dept. Mental Health, Valdosta, 1990-91; dep. coroner Echols County, Ga., 1990-95; exec. dir. Forensic Nurse Cons., Valdosta, 1990-95, Ft. Collins, Colo., 1995—; tng. specialist Parker County Rape Crisis Program, Weatherford, 1982-88; facilitator in group therapy for sexual abuse, awareness tng., and in-svc. tng. for tchrs., 1984-85; mem. Tarrant County Multidisciplinary Inst. for Child Sexual Abuse, Intervention and Treatment, 1988-90; mem. curriculum devel. com. Nurse Sexual Assault Examiner Program John Peter Smith Hosp., Ft. Worth, 1989-90; instr. in rape crisis counseling dept. sociology, anthropology and criminal justice Valdosta (Ga.) State Coll., 1990; instr. in emergency dept. sexual assault protocol, hosp. instrn. Women's Health Ctr., Albany, Ga., 1990; mem. organizing com. for rape crisis ctr. Victim-Witness Assistance Program Valdosta-Lowndes County, Ga., 1990-92; nurse educator, forensic sci. cons. Barbara Clark Mims Assocs., Lewisville, Tex., 1991-94, Bearhawk Consulting Group, Valdosta, Ga., 1988-95, Fort Collins, Colo., 1995—; cons. Ga. Dept. Mental Health. 1991-95; adj. faculty Beth El Coll. Nursing, Colorado Springs, Colo., 1995—; presenter, lectr. in field. Editl. bd. Jour. Psychosocial Nursing & Mental Health Svcs., 1996—; editl. bd., cons. Jour. Trauma Nursing; internat. editl. bd. Jour. CLin. Forensic Medicine, 1994—; contbr. articles to profl. jours. Fellow Am. Acad. Forensic Scis. (program chair gen. sect. 1988-90, 95-96); mem. ANA, ASTM (co-coord. task group to devel. stds. for sexual assault protocol, mem. subcom. forensic scis.), Tex. Nursing Assn., Internat. Assn. Bloodstain Pattern Analysts, Am. Soc. Criminology, Am. Bd. Forensic Examiners (cert. forensic examiner, mem. exec. bd.), Am. Profl. Soc. on Abuse of Children, Internat. Assn. Forensic Nurses (founding mem., mem. exec. bd., pres. 1993-96, Virginia A. Lynch Pioneer award 1994), Internat. Homicide Investigators, Nurses Network on Violence Against Women.

LYNCH, VIRGINIA (LEE) M., art gallery director; b. Greenville, Tex., May 27, 1915; d. Oscar Roscoe and Catherine Claudine (Cooper) McGaughey; m. Eric Noble Dennard, June 16, 1938 (div. 1960); children: Katherine Fryer, Eric Jr. (dec.); m. William Stang Lynch, May 7, 1962 (dec. 1977); stepchildren: F. Bradley, James B., Mrs. Edward T. Barrett. BA, Baylor U., 1937, MA, 1960. Tchr. Tatum (Tex.) High Sch., 1937-38; part-time and substitute tchr. Waco (Tex.) Pub. Schs., Tyler (Tex.) Jr. Coll., 1950-60, Laselle Jr. Coll., Newton, Mass., 1959-60; dir. women Brandeis U., Waltham, Mass., 1960-62; owner Virginia Lynch Gallery, Tiverton, R.I., 1983—; guest curator Newport Art Mus., 1992-95. Trustee R.I. Sch. Design, Providence, 1980—; trustee Newport (R.I.) Art Mus., 1987-92, hon. life trustee, 1993—; mem. R.I. State com. Nat. Gallery Women in Arts, 1987—; mem. Town Planning Bd., Little Compton, R.I., 1980-86, Village Improvement Soc., Little Compton, 1963—, Save the Lighthouse Com., Little Compton; deacon United Congl. Ch., Little Compton, 1980-82; bd. dirs. Little Compton Hist. Soc., v.p., 1980-84. Recipient Citizen of Yr. award R.I. Sch. Design, 1983, State of the Arts award R.I. State Coun. on the Arts, 1992, Best Gallery award R.I. Monthly, 1992-94. Mem. Little Compton Garden Club (pres. 1975-77), Sakonnet Golf Club, Brown U. Faculty Club. Home: 54 S Of Commons Rd Little Compton RI 02837-1522 Office: Virginia Lynch Gallery 3883 Main Rd Tiverton RI 02878-4843

LYNE, DOROTHY-ARDEN, educator; b. Orangeburg, N.Y., Mar. 9, 1928; d. William Henry and Janet More (Freston) Dean; m. Thomas Delmar Lyne, Aug. 16, 1952 (div. June 1982); children: James Delmar, Peter Freston, Jennifer Dean. BA, Ursinus Coll., 1949; MA, Fletcher Sch. Law and Diplomacy, 1950. Assoc. editor World Peace Found., Boston, 1950-51; editorial assoc. Carnegie Endowment Internat. Peace, N.Y.C., 1951-52; dir. Assoc. of Internat. Rels. Clubs, N.Y.C., 1952-53; editor The Town Crier, Westport, Conn., 1966-68; editorial assoc. Machinery Allied Products Inst., Wash., 1959-63; tchr. Helen Keller Mid. Sch., Easton, Conn., 1967-89; vice chmn. Cooperative Ednl. Svcs., Fairfield, 1983-85. Editor: Documents in American Foreign Rels., 1950, Current Rsch. in Internat. Affairs, 1951. Chmn. Westport Zoning Bd. of Appeals, 1976-80, Westport Bd. of Edn., 1985-87; vice chmn. Westport Bd. of Edn., 1980-85; mem. Westport Charter Revision Commn., 1966-67. Republican. Episcopalian.

LYNES, ROSEMARIE ANNE, health facility administrator; b. Charleston, S.C., July 26, 1962; d. Gerald W. and Ruth (Boer) L. AA, York Tech. Coll., 1992; BS in Health Adminstrn., Winthrop U., 1993. Adminstrv. asst. Med. U.S.C., Charleston, 1984-86; reimbursement analyst Carolina Surg. Ctr., Rock Hills, S.C., 1993—; maternity care coord. Mercy Hosp. South, Charlotte, N.C., 1994—. Pell grantee York Tech. and Winthrop U., 1991-93. Mem. Am. Coll. Healthcare Execs. (sec. Winthrop chpt. 1993), MBA Winthrop. Home: # 2226 1924 Paces Landing Ave Rock Hill SC 29732

LYNN, CHERYL, critical care nurse; b. Phila., Oct. 24, 1963; d. Thomas E. and Shirley A. (Boldi) L. ASN, Hahnemann U., 1983; BSN, Widener U.,

1985. Staff nurse oncology unit Crozer-Chester (Pa.) Med. Ctr., 1983-86, staff nurse Burn Treatment Ctr., 1986-90, neonatal intensive care staff nurse, 1990-91, cardiovasc. ICU nurse, 1991—. Mem. AACN (CCRN, Sepa chpt.).

LYNN, DONNA MARIA, public relations and marketing executive, writer; b. Hollywood, Calif., Oct. 4, 1945; d. Kane Wallace Lynn and Rita (Piazza) Maxwell; m. Dennis D. Schreffler, 1965 (div. 1973); children: Scott G. Schreffler, Susan M. Schreffler. Student, UCLA, 1963-65, U. Utah, 1965-68; BA, U. Ark., 1970; postgrad. in law, U. Balt., 1973-74. Lobbyist, UniServ dir. NEA, Washington, 1970-77; pres., CEO Lynn Assocs., Inc., Westport, Conn., 1977—; mgr. media rels. Perrier/Great Waters of France, N.Y.C., 1978-79; sr. cons. The Nestle Co., Washington and White Plains, N.Y., 1979-83; dep. dir. sports div. Hill & Knowlton, N.Y.C., 1983-85; mgr. pub. relations Avon Products, Inc., N.Y.C., 1985-86; supr. account group Daniel J. Edelman, N.Y.C., 1979-81. Features editor: Flight Attendant mag., 1986-87; contbr. numerous articles to newspapers and mags. Founder, dir. Earth Day in Ark., 1970; del. White House Conf. on Children and Youth, Washington, 1970; nat. pres. Women's Aux. to Student AMA, 1971-73; liaision White House Press Office, Dem. Nat. Conf., N.Y.C., 1979; mem. Md. Commn. for Women, Annapolis, 1976-77; pres. Annapolis Summer Garden Theatre, 1976-78; mem. bus. adv. bd. Nat. Down Syndrome Soc., N.Y.C., 1985-89. Mem. Am. Mgmt. Assn., Boating Writers Internat., Pub. Rels. Soc. Am., NEA (life, legis. chair Ark. chpt. 1970-73), Rotary Internat., Cedar Point Yacht Club, The Superyacht Soc. (exec. dir. 1989-95), Nat. Fedn. Press Women, Conn. Press Club, Phi Alpha Theta. Office: 7 Punch Bowl Dr Westport CT 06880-2126

LYNN, EVADNA SAYWELL, investment analyst; b. Oakland, Calif., June 1935; d. Lawrence G. Saywell; m. Richard Keppie Lynn, Dec. 28, 1962; children: Douglas, Lisa. BA, U. Calif., Berkeley, MA in Econs. With Dean Witter, San Francisco, 1958-61, 70-71, Dodge & Cox, San Francisco, 1961-69; v.p. Clark, Dodge & Co., San Francisco, 1971-73; chartered fin. analyst. V.p. Paine Webber, N.Y.C., 1974-77, Wainwright Securities, N.Y.C., 1977-78; 1st v.p. Merrill Lynch Capital Markets, N.Y.C., 1978-90; sr. v.p. Dean Witter Reynolds, N.Y.C., 1990—. Mem. N.Y. Soc. Security Analysts, San Francisco Security Analysts (treas. 1973-74). Mem. Fin. Women's Club of San Francisco (pres. 1967). Office: Dean Witter Reynolds 2 World Trade Ctr New York NY 10048-0203

LYNN, GWENDOLYN RENAYE, educator; b. Monticello, Fla., Nov. 12, 1958; d. Elder Joe Gray and Beatrice W. Lynn-Gray. BS, Fla. A&M U., 1980, MEd, 1984. Cert. profl. educator, Fla. Playground dir. Tallahassee Parks & Recreation Dept., 1978-84, instr. and recreation leader, 1978-82; tchr. phys. edn. Leon County Schs., Tallahassee, 1984-89, tchr. health edn., 1990—; team leader Griffin Mid. Sch., Tallahassee, 1993-95, sch.-based mgmt. mem., 1995, Newton/learner profile trainer, 1994—. Bd. dirs., treas. New Hope New Faith Ministries, Tallahassee, 1993—; co-sponsor Fellowship of Christian Athletes, Tallahassee, 1994—. Mem. NEA, Fla. Alliance Health, Phys. Edn., Recreation, Dance. Office: Griffin Middle School 800 Alabama St Tallahassee FL 32304

LYNN, KRISTINA ANNE, journalist, actress, writer, producer; b. Dayton, Ohio, Apr. 18, 1954; d. Donald Louis Craddock and Carol Rose (Righthouse) Guthrie; m. Gerald Lee Diez, Oct. 19, 1985 (div. Aug. 1988). BA with honors in Speech, English and Theatre, West Ga. Coll., 1976; postgrad. in Psychology, Ga. State U., 1978. Tchr., drama dir. Redan H.S., Stone Mountain, Ga., 1976-78; co-hostess Am. Radio Network, Balt., 1978-90; co-host, interviewer WNTR Radio, Washington, 1988-91; pres., owner Lynn Prodns., L.A., Atlanta, N.Y.C., 1985—; spkr., tchr., coord. Learning Annex, Washington, 1987-91; corr. Joan Rivers Show, N.Y.C., 1992, Geraldo Show; corr., reporter Paramount TV., L.A., 1993—; corr., celebrity reporter Entertainment TV, L.A., 1995-96; corr., reporter, anchor Backstage Prodns., Nashville, 1994—; film festival chair Women in Film, Washington, N.Y.C., 1988-92. Dir. (theatre) Plaza Suite, 1977 (1st place region competition award 1977), Sorry Wrong Number, 1978 (2d place region competition award 1978). Bd. dirs. Child Savers, Inc., Rockville, Md., 1991-96, fund raiser, 1991-96. Mem. AFTRA (mem. outreach program 1996), N.Am. Rec. Industry and Songwriters Assn., Talk Radio Assn. (bd. dirs. 1996), Nashville Songwriters Assn., Screen Actors Guild (vol. womens com. 1985), Women in Music Bus. Assn. (chmn. com. 1994-95), Phi Kappa Phi, Phi Alpha Gamma. Democrat. Mem. Unity Ch. Home: 8750 Mt Rushmore Dr Alpharetta GA 30202 Office: Lynn Prodns 307 E 81st St Apt 5-RE New York NY 10028

LYNN, NAOMI B., academic administrator; b. N.Y.C., Apr. 16, 1933; d. Carmelo Burgos and Maria (Lebron) Berly; m. Robert A. Lynn, Aug. 28, 1954; children: Mary Louise, Nancy, Judy Lynn Chance, Jo-An. BA, Maryville (Tenn.) Coll., 1954; MA, U. Ill., 1958; PhD, U. Kans., 1970. Instr. polit. sci. Cen. Mo. State Coll., Warrensburg, Mo., 1966-68; asst. prof. Kans. State U., Manhattan, 1970-75, assoc. prof., 1975-80, acting dept. head, prof., 1980-81, head polit. sci. dept., prof., 1982-84; dean Coll. Pub. and Urban Affairs, prof. Ga. State U., Atlanta, 1984-91; chancellor u. Ill., Springfield, 1991—; cons. fed., state and local govts., Manhattan, Topeka, Altanta, 1981-91; bd. dirs. Bank One Springfield. Author: The Fulbright Premise, 1973; editor: Public Administration, The State of Discipline, 1990, Women, Politics and the Constitution, 1990; contbr. articles and textbook chpts. to profl. pubs. Bd. dirs. United Way of Sangamon County, 1991—, Ill. Symphony Orch., 1992-95; bd. dirs. Urban League, 1993—. Recipient Disting. Alumni award Maryville Coll., 1986; fellow Nat. Acad. Pub. Adminstrn. Mem. Nat. Assn. Schs. Pub. Affairs and Adminstrn. (nat. pres.), Am. Soc. Pub. Adminstrn. (nat. pres. 1985-86), Am. Polit. Sci. Assn. (mem. exec. coun. 1981-83, trustee 1993—), Am. Assn. State Colls. and Univs. (bd. dirs.), Midwest Polit. Sci. Assn. (mem. exec. coun. 1976-79), Women's Caucus Polit. Sci. (pres. 1975-76), Greater Springfield C. of C. (bd. dirs. 1991—, accreditation task force 1992), Pi Sigma Alpha (nat. pres.). Presbyterian. Office: U Ill at Springfield Office of Chancellor Springfield IL 62794-9243

LYNN, NORA CHARLENE, newspaper editor; b. N.Y.C., June 2, 1965; d. Harry Merchant, Jr. and Charlene (Robinson) L.; m. Daniel Andrew Martin, Apr. 16, 1988 (div. Feb. 1996). AA, Cosumnes River Coll., Sacremento, 1993; BA in govt. journalism, Calif. State U., Sacremento, 1996. Editor in chief State Hornet, Calif. State U., Sacramento, 1993-94, The Daily Recorder, Sacramento, 1995—; com. mem. Bench Bar Media, Sacramento, 1996—. Campaign asst. Randy Perry for Congress campaign, Sacramento, 1994; precinct captain United Dem. campaign, Sacramento, 1994; vol. letter writer Amnesty Internat., 1988—; phone mentor Women in Cmty. Svc., Sacramento, 1995—. Recipient Earl Warren prize Calif. State U., Sacramento Govt. Dept., 1995; Faculty merit scholar Calif. State U. Sacramento Acad. Senate, 1995, 2nd place gen. column, 1995, 2nd place satirical column Calif., 1995, Intercollegiate Press Assn. Fellow Knight Ctr. for Specialized Journalism U. Md. "Covering the Law", College Park, 1996; mem. Sacramento Press Club. Democrat. Roman Catholic.

LYNN, PHYLLIS JEAN, entrepreneur; b. Harrisburg, Ill., Feb. 14, 1936; d. Waldo Houston Basham and Ruth Pearl Irvin; m. Vincent Paul Kaduk, Feb. 21, 1958 (div. 1970); children: Kimberly, Tamara, Christopher; m. John M. Lynn, Oct. 8, 1982. AD in Psychology, George Williams Coll., Downers Grove, Ill., 1973. Lic. real estate salesperson. Real estate owner Birdsong Builders, Inc., Downers Grove, 1965-72; owner Charmills Restaurant & Bar, Clearwater, Fla., 1977-82, On Target Co., Indian Head Park, Ill., 1983-92; adminstrv. asst. J.S. James Co., Burr Ridge, Ill.; part owner Atocha Silver Mine, CoChBomba, Bolivia, 1980-81, Cleaves/Lynn, Inc., Western Springs, Ill., 1993—. Lobbyist for ERA, NOW, 1972-73. Home: 6418 Blackhawk Trl La Grange IL 60525-4316 Office: Cleaves/Lynn Inc PO Box 229 Western Springs IL 60558-0229

LYNN, SHEILAH ANN, service executive, consultant; b. Anderson, Ind., Jan. 28, 1947; d. John Benton and Kathleen (Taylor) Bussabarger; m. John Hoftyzer, Dec. 21, 1968 (div. June 1982); children: Melanie Kay, John Theo; m. Guy C. Lynn, May 20, 1984. BS, Ind. U., 1969; postgrad., U. N.C., Greensboro, 1970, Webster U., 1994; diploma, Data Processing Inst., Tampa, Fla., 1983; MS, Ctrl. Mich. U., 1993. Bookkeeper John Hancock Life Ins. Co., Greensboro, 1970-72; freelance seminar leader and devel. Dhahran, Saudi Arabia, 1978-82; dir. programming Fla. Tech. Inst., Jacksonville, 1983-84, instr. in computer sci., 1984-85; real estate sales assoc. Fla. Recreational Ranches, Gainesville, 1985; instrnl. program coord., workforce tng. coord. Fla. C.C., Jacksonville, 1986—; handwriting analyst, cons. Sheilah A. Lynn & Assocs., Jacksonville, 1989—; cons. programmer, analyst Postmasters Co., Jacksonville, 1986—; pres. Options Cons., Jacksonville, 1986-89, Sheilah A. Lynn & Assocs., Jacksonville, 1989—; 6L cons. assocs. Dacum facilitator and curriculum developer. Mem. Jacksonville Community Council, Inc., 1986-87, Fla. Literacy Coalition, 1986-87. Mem. NAFE, ASTD, Fla. Assn. Ednl. Data Systems, Bus. and Profl. Women, Jacksonville C. of C. (bd. dirs. south coun. 1987, sec. 1989, treas. 1990, v.p. 1991, pres. 1992). Democrat.

LYNNE, SANDRA JONES, elementary education educator; b. Richmond, Va., July 25, 1944; d. C. Hunter and Marcyne Jones; children: Allan Hunter, Joshua Joseph, John Andrew. BA, Mary Washington Coll., 1966. Tchr. elem. edn. San Diego City Schs., 1966-70, Hanover County Schs., Ashland, Va., 1987—; EXXON primary math. curriculum leader Hanover County Schs., 1989—; adj. prof. dept. edn. Randolph-Macon Coll., 1995—; lead tchr. math. V-Quest, Henry Clay Elem., 1994—. Va. State Math. elem. awardee Presdl. Excellence in Math. & Sci. Tchg. Award, 1993. Mem. NEA, Nat. Coun. Tchrs. of Math., Va. Edn. Assn., Va. Coun. Tchrs. of Math. (William C. Lowry Outstanding Va. Elem. Math. Tchr. of Yr. 1995), Hanover Edn. Assn., Greater Richmond Coun. Tchrs. of Math. (rec. sec. 1995-96), Alpha Delta Kappa (historian 1994-96). Mem. Christian Ch. (Disciples of Christ). Office: Henry Clay Elem Sch 310 S James St Ashland VA 23005-1925

LYON, BARBARA BROOKS, educational administrator; b. Galax, Va., Nov. 6, 1946; d. Reeves Mack and Hazel (Maines) Brooks; m. Danny Dean Lyon, Sept. 21, 1965; children: Noah Christopher, Danna Dianne. BS, Appalachian State U., 1972, MA, 1982. Cert. tchr., prin., N.C. Tchr Glade Creek Sch., Ennice, N.C., 1972-92; asst. prin. Alleghany H.S., Sparta, N.C., 1992—; active Work First, Sparta, 1994—. Named to Outstanding Young Women in Am., 1983. Mem. NEA, N.C. Assn. Educators, (sec. Alleghany County 1974), Boosters Club of Alleghany H.S., Delta Kappa Gamma. Baptist.

LYON, BERENICE IOLA CLARK, civic worker; b. Westfield, Pa., June 4, 1920; d. Stephen Artemus and Ruth Gertrude (Tubbs) Clark; m. Robert Louis Lyon, May 28, 1944. Pres., Twin Tiers Geneal. Soc., N.Y. and Pa., 1976-88, pub. jour. Gemini; Pa. state pres. Colonial Dames XVII Century, 1981-83, state chmn. heraldry, 1977-79, hon. state pres., 1983—, organizer-pres. Tyoga Gateway chpt., 1973-75, Treaty Elm chpt., 1975-77, state yearbook-directory compiler, 1979-81, Pa. state chmn. 1988—; N.Y. state chmn. DAR, 1968-71, pres. N.Y. coun. of regents, 1968-71, regent Corning (N.Y.) chpt. 1965-68, Wellsboro (Pa.) chpt., 1977-80, Pa. state vice chmn., 1980-83, Pa. dist. dir., 1983-88, Pa. state chmn., 1987—; N.Y. state chmn. Daus. Am. Colonists, 1965—, Atlantic Coast chmn., 1970-79, organizer-regent Forbidden Trail chpt., 1967-76, regent, 1974-76, 83-88, Pa. state chmn. 1987—; condr. geneal. seminars; speaker to convs., meetings, TV, radio; historian, researcher, writer; lectr., healthful family living, 1991—; contbr. articles on heraldry to 17th Century Rev., 1978-79. Recipient medal of appreciation SAR, 1966. Mem. Ams. of Royal Descent, Descs. Knights of Garter, Magna Carta Dames, Old Plymouth Colony Descs., Order of Crown, Order of Washington, Plantagenet Soc., Mansfield Friends of Library (pres. 1980-81). Clubs: Kiwanis Ladies, Clionian Circle (Corning); Mansfield (Pa.) Garden (pres. 1979-80), N.Y. Fedn. Garden Clubs (sect. chmn. 1969-73). Home: Lowenhof 168A Bailey Creek Rd Millerton PA 16936

LYON, CAROLYN BARTEL, civic worker; b. Richmond, Ind., Mar. 28, 1908; d. Frederick John and Cora Caroline (Eggemeyer) Bartel; m. E. Wilson Lyon, Aug. 26, 1933 (dec.); children: Elizabeth Lyon Webb, John Wilson. BA, Wellesley Coll., 1928; MA, U. Chgo., 1930; LHD (hon.), Pomona Coll., 1974. Editorial asst. U. Chgo. Press, 1930-33. Alumna trustee Wellesley Coll., 1958-65; bd. trustees United Bd. for Christian Higher Edn. in Asia, N.Y.C., 1966-83; mem. women's coun. KCET Pub. TV, L.A., 1965—; active LWV, Claremont, Calif., 1941—, bd. dirs., 1945-50; pres. Foothill Philharmonic Com., L.A. Philharmonic, 1970-72. Mem. UN Assn. U.S. Congregationalist. Home: 900 E Harrison Ave A17-18 Pomona CA 91767

LYON, CYNTHIA S., nursing executive; b. Jamestown, N.Y., Dec. 5, 1946; d. Rodger A. and Mia L. (Dahlquist) Gisslin; m. Richard Lyon, Aug. 8, 1975; children: Patricia, Michael, Sean. AS in Nursing, Arnot Ogden Hosp., 1968. RN, Calif. Staff nurse Long Beach (Calif.) Meml. Hosp., 1968-70, Orange County Med. Ctr., Orange, Calif., 1970-71, Children's Hosp. of Orange County, Orange, 1971-78, Children's Hosp. of San Diego, 1984-89, Mission Med. Home Care, Mission Viejo, Calif., 1989-93; exec. dir. Trauma Intervention Programs of San Diego County, Inc., Carlsbad, Calif., 1993—. Bd. dirs. Seagaze Concerts, Oceanside, Calif., 1990—; mem. sch. site coun. El Camino H.S., Oceanside, 1995—. Recipient Women Helping Women award Soroptomists, 1995. Mem. Ocean C. of C. (mem. Harbor Days com. 1988—). Episcopalian. Home: 4464 Inverness Dr Oceanside CA 92057 Office: Trauma Intervention Programs of San Diego County Inc 2560 Orion Way Carlsbad CA 92008

LYON, DIANA, counselor, art educator; b. Paragould, Ark., June 21, 1935; d. Wakeman Richard and Frances Jane Bell; m. Joseph Edward Dornbusch, Dec. 24, 1956 (div. 1974); children: Jeff Dornbusch, Dan K. Dornbusch. BA, U. No. Colo., 1958, MA, 1967. Lic. profl. counselor, N.Mex., 1994. Art instr. Island of Guam Edn. Dept., Agana, 1958-60; spl. edn. tchr. of the deaf Cedar Rapids (Iowa) Pub. Sch., 1967-69; dean, dir. Shapley Internat. House, Florence, Italy, 1974-79; chief classification officer N.Mex. Dept. Corrections, Radium Springs, 1979-83; pvt. practice D. Lyon Entepriss, Hillsboro, N.Mex., 1979-83; dir., counselor Domestic Abuse Intervention Ctr., Truth or Consequences, N.Mex., 1990-91; project dir. Cmty. Partnership for a Healthy Environment, Truth or Consequences, 1991-94; VISTA Vol. Corp. for Nat. and Cmty. Svc., Truth or Consequences, 1994-95; profl. counselor Domestic Abuse Intervention Ctr., Truth or Consequences, 1995—; bus. owner (D. Lyon Enterprises), Las Cruces and Truth or Consequences, N.Mex., 1983—; organizer/facilitat or Female and Fully Alive Workshop Series, Sierra County, N.Mex., 1986-88, Youth Leadership Tng., Truth or Consequences, 1988-90; facilitator/advisor Mayor's Drug and Alcohol Prevention Task Force, Truth or Consequences, 1989-90. Contbr. art to Present Time Jour., 1975-96; art works on exhbn. in U.S., Italy, Guam, 1975-96. Bd. dirs. Hillsboro (N.Mex.) Cmty. Ctr., 1986-89; county co-chair Dem. Party of Sierra County, Hillsboro, 1985-86; pres., charter mem. Sierra County Kiwanis, Hillsboro, 1986-91, Women's Caucus for Arts, So. N.Mex., 1984—. Recipient Exemplary Svc. award N.Mex. Dept. Corrections, 1983, Resourceful Women award, Resourceful Women, San Francisco, 1994; mem. 4th World Conf. on Women, UN, Beijing, China, 1995. Mem. Women's Caucus for the Arts, Black Range Artists, Inc., Sierra Art Soc., Optimist Club of Sierra County, Sierra County Arts Coun. (grant writer 1995-96). Home and Office: PO Box 211 Truth or Consequence NM 87901

LYON, JOANNE B., psychologist; b. Little Rock, June 2, 1943; d. F. Ike and Marie (Graham) Beyer; m. James S. Lyon, Dec. 1971 (div. Sept. 1975), m. John M. Lofton, May 22, 1983 (dec. Feb. 1990). BA, Webster U., 1966; MEd, U. Mo., St. Louis, 1976, PhD, 1986. Lic. psychologist, Kans. Reading specialist Rockwood Sch. Dist., St. Louis, 1976-79; psychology cons. handicapped component St. Louis Head Start, 1982-83; intern Topeka State Hosp., 1983-84; dir. partial hosp. programs Family Svc. & Guidance Ctr., Topeka, 1985-89; pvt. practitioner and joint owner Shadow Wood Clin. Assocs., Topeka, 1989—; clin. supr. Family Svc. & Guidance Ctr., Topeka, 1989-93; behavioral scis. regulatory bd. Psychology Adv. Com., 1996—. Mem. exec. bd. Interfaith of Topeka, 1995—, I Have a Dream Coalition, 1994—, Psychology Advisory Bd. Behavioral Sci. Regulatory Bd.; bd. dirs. Temple Beth Sholom Sisterhood, 1996—. Sherman scholar U. Mo., St. Louis, 1982. Mem. APA, Kans. Psychol. Assn., Am. Orthopsychiatric Assn., Soc. for Personality Assessment, Internat. Platform Assn. Jewish. Home: 3030 SW Arrowhead Rd Topeka KS 66614-4134 Office: Shadow Wood Clin Assocs 2933 SW Woodside Dr Topeka KS 66614-4181

LYON, MARTHA SUE, research engineer, retired military officer; b. Louisville, Oct. 3, 1935; d. Harry Bowman and Erma Louise (Moreland) Lyon. BA in Chemistry, U. Louisville, 1959; MEd in Math., Northeastern Ill. U., 1974. Cert. tchr. Ill., Ky. Rsch. assoc. U. Louisville Med. Sch., 1959-61, 62-63; commd. ensign, USNR, 1965, advanced through grades to comdr., 1983; instr. instrumentation chemistry Northwestern U., Evanston, Ill., 1968-70; tchr. sci., chemistry, gifted math. Waukegan (Ill.) pub. schs., 1970-75; phys. scientist Libr. of Congress, Washington, 1975-76; rsch. engr. Lockheed Missiles & Space Co., Sunnyvale, Calif., 1976-77; instr., assoc. chmn. dept. physics U.S. Naval Acad., Annapolis, Md., 1977-80; analyst Systems Analysis Div., Office of Chief of Naval Ops. Staff, Washington, 1980-81; comdg. officer Naval Res. Ctr., Stockton, Calif., 1981-83; mem. faculty Def. Intelligence Coll., 1983-85; program mgr. Space and Naval Warfare Systems Command, 1985-86, commanding officer PERSUPPACT Memphis, 1986-88; program mgr. Space and Naval Warfare Sys. Command, 1988-91; sect. chief Def. Intelligence Agy., 1991-95. Chief marching divsn. Nat. Homecoming Parade and N.Y.C. Regional Parade Task Force Desert Storm, 1991-95. Grantee Am. Heart Assn., 1960-62, NSF, 1971, 72. Mem. ACS, Soc. Women Engrs., Am. Fedn. Musicians, Am. Statis. Assn., Am. Soc. Photogrammetry, Internat. Conf. Women in Sci. Engrng. (protocol chair), Internat. Soc. Bassists, Mensa, Zeta Tau Alpha, Delta Phi Alpha. Club: Order of Ea. Star. Developer processes used in archival photography, carbon-14 analyses; presenter of papers at profl. confs.

LYONS, ELISABETH HELENE, peer counselor; b. Hanover, N.H., Dec. 19, 1950; d. John B. and Mary P. (Johnson) Lyons. BA in Sociology-Psychology, Annhurst Coll., 1973; MEd in Counseling and Psychotherapy, Notre Dame Coll., Manchester, N.H., 1990. Active supportive svcs. to elderly Hanover Terrace Healthcare, 1981-86; mem. Com. on Accessiblity for Persons with Disabilities, Town of Hanover, 1986; active supportive svcs. Hanover Hill Health Care Ctr., Manchester, 1989-91; vol. Manchester Mental Health Ctr., 1991-92; active supportive svcs. to elderly Mt. Carmel Nursing Home, Manchester, 1991-92; peer support facilitator Granite State Ind. Living Found., Concord, N.H., 1983-86, 89—, activities planning com., 1990—, devel. com., 1991-92, bd. dirs., 1991—, svc. com., 1991—, pers. com., 1992—, by-laws com., 1994—; vol. Hospice, 1984—; mem. parish liaison com. St. Marie's Parish, 1991—, chair, 1992; mem. Manchester Transit Authority Adv. Bd., 1992—; social svc. vol. McKerley Health Care Ctr., Ridgewood, Manchester, 1992-95; mem. evaluation and assessment com. Statewide Ind. Living Coun., Concord, 1994, adminstrn. com., 1994—, pub. info. and liaison com., 1994—, exec. com., 1995—; bd. trustees Crotched Mountain Found., 1995—, program and svc. com. Named Vol. of Yr., Gov. Sununu, Concord; recipient Peer Support Facilitator award, 1986, 89, 90, 91. Mem. ACA, N.H. Assn. Mental Health Counselors, N.H. Assn. Counseling and Devel. Roman Catholic. Home: Courtyard Apts # 9 245 Main St Manchester NH 03102

LYONS, MARY E., academic administrator. Pres. Calif. Maritime Acad., Vallejo, 1990-96, Coll. of St. Benedict, St. Joseph, Minn., 1967. Office: Office of the President College of St Benedict 37 College Ave South Saint Joseph MN 56374-2099*

LYONS, MOIRA K., state legislator; b. Trenton, N.J.. BA, Georgian Ct. Coll.; student, Miami U. Mem. Conn. Ho. of Reps., mem. appropriations com., chmn. transp. com. Democrat. Home: 37 Ocean Dr W Stamford CT 06902-8002 Office: Legislative Office Bldg Rm 4100 Capital Ave Hartford CT 06106*

LYONS, NATALIE BELLER, family counselor; b. Habana, Cuba, Apr. 3, 1926; d. Herman Lawrence and Jennie (Engler) B.; widowed, Apr. 18, 1986; children: Anne, Sara. BS in Surveying and Land Appraising, Inst. Vedado, Habana, Cuba, 1943; BA, U. Mich., 1946; MEd, U. Miami, Fla., 1967. Family counselor, mem. staff furniture design and mfg. co. George B. Bent, Gardner, Mass., 1953-58; tchr. H.S., Winchendon, Mass., Hollywood, Fla., 1962; tchr. parochial sch., Ft. Lauderdale, Fla., 1963-64; family counselor Miami, 1967—; project dir. Cen. Am. fisheries program Peace Corps, 1972-74; counselor Svc. Corp. of Ret. Execs., Miami, 1993, bd. dirs., 1994—; bd. dirs., mem. Com. for Accuracy in Mid East Reporting, 1990—. Pres. Miami region Hadassah, 1989-91; bd. dirs. Greater Miami Jewish Fedn., 1985—, mem. women's divsn., mem. cmty. rels. coun., 1985—; bd. dirs. Miami Civic Music Assn., 1985—; mem. nat. bd. dirs. nat. women's divsn. Am. Soc. for Technion, 1991—, pres. 1984-86; co-chair Pro-Israel Rally, Tri County, 1991, Joint Action Com., Miami, 1989-91; tng. dir. Los Amigos de las Ams., 1975—; founder, dir. Cmty. Inst. Jewish Studies, Hollywood, Fla., 1962-64. Recipient Leadership award Hadassah, 1987, honoree Am. Soc. for Technion Scholarship Fund, 1991; named Woman of Yr., Hadassah, 1991. Democrat.

LYONS, SHERRI ANN, educator; b. Chicago Heights, Ill., Aug. 2, 1966; d. Steven and Malina Jean (Laux) L. BS in Music Edn., U. Ill., 1988, MS in Music Edn., 1993. Band dir. Galesburg (Ill.) High Sch., 1988-92; grad. asst. U. Ill. Bands, Champaign-Urbana, 1992-93; band dir. Homer Jr. High Sch., Lockport, Ill., 1993—; guest conductor Ill. Summer Youth Music, Champaign, 1995; instr. pvt. practice, Lockport, 1993—, Galesburg, 1988-93; mem. trumpet sect. Wheaton (Ill.) Mcpl. Band, 1994—. Recipient Outstanding Tchr. award Ill. Math. and Sci. Acad., 1992, My Favorite Tchr. award Sta. WQAD-TV, 1992. Mem. Am. Fedn. Tchrs., Ill. Music Educators Assn., Music Educators Nat. Conf. Office: Homer Jr High Sch 15711 S Bell Rd Lockport IL 60441

LYONS, SUSAN MARIE, lawyer; b. Sarasota, Fla., Oct. 19, 1951; d. Richard Henry and Constance Joyce (Minnehan) L.; m. Nicholas Cowdery Webb, Sept. 28, 1989; 1 child, Sean. BA, U. Calif., San Diego, 1978; JD, U. San Diego, 1981. Bar: Calif., 1981. Assoc. Law Office John Adler, San Diego, 1981-82, Law Office James Miller, San Diego, 1981-82; law clk. Ct. Appeal, San Diego, 1982-83; lectr. City Coll. of Chgo., Huis-ter-Heide, Netherlands, 1983, Webster U., Leiden, Netherlands, 1985-89, U. Md., Huis-ter-Heide, 1984-88; editor Internat. Bur. of Fiscal Documentation, Amsterdam, 1987-95; editor, Tax Notes Internat. Tax Analysts, Arlington, Va., 1995—. Editor: (newsletter) Women's Internat. Network, Amsterdam, 1994, 96; author: International Tax Glossary, 1992, 95; contbr. articles to profl. jours. Social activities person/legal asst. Am. Women's Club, Amsterdam, 1990. Mem. Calif. Bar Assn., Internat. Fiscal Assn., Am. Tax Inst. in Europe, NAFE, Women's Internat. Network. Office: Tax Analysts 6830 N Fairfax Dr Arlington VA 22213

LYSHAK-STELZER, FRANCIE, artist; b. Detroit, June 3, 1948; d. Peter Paul and Frances Ellen (Harrington) Lyshak; m. Stephen Stelzer, Oct. 10, 1994. BFA, Wayne State U., 1970; MPS, Pratt Inst., 1978. Art therapist Creative Women's Collective, N.Y.C., 1978-79; asst. activities dir., dir. art therapy internship tng. Bronx Children's Psychiat. Ctr., 1979—. One woman shows include La Mama La Galleria, N.Y.C., 1993, 96, Pvt. Exhibn. Provincetown (Mass.) Art Assn. and Mus., 1983, Bill Rice Studio, N.Y.C., 1984, 88, Art Quest 86, L.A., Mus. of the Hudson Highlands, N.Y., 1985, Claire Dunphy's Studio, N.Y.C., 1985, W.O.W. Theatre/Gallery, N.Y.C., 1983; group exhbns. include Interart de St. Armand Gallery, 1983, Park Ave. Atrium, 1984, Cash/Newhouse Gallery, 1985, Marymount Manhattan Coll. Gallery, 1989, La Mama La Galleria, N.Y.C., 1985, 86, 92, Denise Bibro Fine Art, N.Y.C., 1996; co-author: Expressive Therapy: A Creative Arts Approach to Depth-Oriented Treatment, 1980, Psychoanalytic Review The Creative Act as a Means of Overcoming Resistance in Treatment; author: The Secret, 1994. Mem. Am. Art Therapy Assn., A.T.R.

LYSTAD, MARY HANEMANN (MRS. ROBERT LYSTAD), sociologist, author, consultant; b. New Orleans, Apr. 11, 1928; d. James and Mary (Douglass) Hanemann; m. Robert Lystad, June 20, 1953; children: Lisa Douglass, Anne Hanemann, Mary Lunde, Robert Douglass, James Hanemann. A.B. cum laude, Newcomb Coll., 1949; M.A., Columbia U., 1951; Ph.D., Tulane U., 1955. Postdoctoral fellow social psychology S.E. La. Hosp., Mandeville, 1955-57; field rsch. social psychology Ghana, 1957-58, South Africa and Swaziland, 1968, Peoples Republic of China, 1986; chief sociologist Collaborative Child Devel. Project, Charity Hosp. La., New Orleans, 1958-61; feature writer African div. Voice Am., Washington, 1964-73; program analyst NIMH, Washington, 1968-78; asso. dir. for planning and coordination div. spl. mental health programs NIMH, 1978-80; chief Nat. Ctr. for Prevention and Control of Rape, 1980-83, Ctr. Mental Health Studies of Emergencies, 1983-89; pvt. cons. specializing on mental health implications social and econ. problems Bethesda, Md., 1990—; cons. on youth Nat. Goals Research Staff, White House, Washington, 1969-70. Author: Millicent the Monster, 1968, Social Aspects of Alienation, 1969, Jennifer Takes Over P.S. 94, 1972, James the Jaguar, 1972, As They See It: Changing Values of College Youth, 1972, That New Boy, 1973, Halloween

Parade, 1973, Violence at Home, 1974, A Child's World As Seen in His Stories and Drawings, 1974, From Dr. Mather to Dr. Seuss: 200 Years of American Books for Children, 1980, At Home in America, 1983; editor: Innovations in Mental Health Services to Disaster Victims, 1985, Violence in the Home: Interdisciplinary Perspectives, 1986, Mental Health Response to Mass Emergencies: Theory and Practice, 1988. Recipient Spl. Recognition award USPHS, 1983, Alumna Centennial award Newcomb Coll., 1986. Home and Office: 4900 Scarsdale Rd Bethesda MD 20816-2440

LYTEL, ELAINE, municipal offical; b. Balt., Sept. 10, 1923; d. Arnold and Rose (Berliner) Greenbaum; m. Allan Lyntel, Oct. 24, 1954 (dec. July 1966); children: David, Laurie. BA in Psychology, Antioch Coll., Yellow Springs, Ohio, 1945; postgrad., NYU, 1947-49; cert. tchr., Bank St. Coll., 1950; MPA, Syracuse U., 1965. Tng. counselor Gimbel Bros., Phila., 1953-55; elem. sch. tchr. Syracuse (N.Y.) Bd. Edn., 1965-67; rschr. in edn. Syracuse U. Rsch. Corp., 1968-70; coord. youth theater Salt City Playhouse, Syracuse, 1971-73; county legislator Onondaga County, Syracuse, 1974-79, county clk., 1984-90; real estate sales agt. Galliger Real Estate, Syracuse, 1980-81; pub. affairs coord. Planned Parenthood, Syracuse, 1982-83; town councilor Town of De Witt, N.Y., 1992—. Co-author: Women's Encampment for A Future of Peace and Justice, 1987; contbr. articles to Chgo. Tribune. Mem. steering com. Onondaga County Women's Polit. Caucus, Syracuse, 1983—; bd. dirs. Contemporary Theater of Syracuse, 1992—. Recipient Woman of Achievement awar Post Std. Women of Achievement in Politics, 1982, Outstanding Polit. Person award Ams. for Dem. Action, 1984, Jeanette Rankin Day award Onondaga Women's Polit. Caucus, 1986, Dedicated Svc. award DeWitt Dem. Com., 1990. Mem. NOW (bd. dirs. 1974—), Nat. Coun. Jewish Women. Home: 222 Ambergate Rd DeWitt NY 13214 Office: Town of De Witt PO Box 159 De Witt NY 13214

LYTHCOTT, MARCIA A., newspaper editor. Op-ed editor Chicago Tribune, Ill. Office: Chicago Tribune 435 N Michigan Ave Chicago IL 60611-4001

LYTLE, EVELYN POMROY, Hispanic languages and literature educator, author; b. Indiana, Pa., Dec. 5, 1920; d. Joseph Bertram and Sarah Emma (Kunkle) L. BS, Indiana U. Pa., 1943; postgrad., Reformed Presbyn. Theol. Sem., 1944, N.Y. Theol. Sem., 1944-45; MA, Princeton Theol. Sem., 1947; student, U. de Sao Paulo, 1953-54; PhD, Tulane U., 1967. Ednl. missionary Presbyn. Ch., Sao Paulo, Brazil, 1949-50; vis. prof. English Pontificia U. Catolica de Sao Paulo, 1950-51; editor, translator IIAA, U.S. Dept. State, Washington, 1951-52; asst. prof. Spanish Randolph-Macon Woman's Coll., Lynchburg, Va., 1965-67; instr. Portuguese and Spanish U. New Orleans, 1958-65, asst. prof., 1967-71, assoc. prof., 1971-79, prof., 1979-87, prof. emerita, 1987; rschr., writer, lectr. U. Coimbra, Portugal, 1991, 92; translator, interpreter Consulate of Portugal, New Orleans, 1973-76; mem. Nat. Adv. Coun. on Bilingual Edn., U.S. Office of Edn., Washington, 1974-77, chair, 1976-77; translator USDA, New Orleans, 1982, U.S. Dept. Interior, New Orleans, 1983. Author: Os Novissimos do homem, 1970; pioneer developer, dir., producer: Spanish for Careers instrnl. videotape programs, 1975; contbr. articles to profl. jours. Cons. Jud. Conf. U.S. Bicentennial Com., Washington, 1977. Recipient Disting. Alumna award Princeton Theol. Sem., 1992; Brazilian Ministry Fgn. Affairs grantee, 1953-54; Fulbright fellow, 1962; Ford Found. Venture Fund grantee, 1975. Mem. Soc. for Spanish and Portuguese Hist. Studies.

LYTTON, LINDA ROUNTREE, marriage and family therapist, test consultant; b. Suffolk, Va., Mar. 30, 1951; d. John Thomas and Anne Carolyn (Edwards) Rountree; m. Daniel Michael Lytton, June 23, 1973; 1 child, Seth Daniel. BS, Radford U., 1973; MS, Va. Poly. Inst. and State U., 1992. Collegiate profl. cert. Tchr., cons. Fauquier County Pub. Schs., Warrenton, Va., 1973-74, Chesterfield County Pub. Schs., Richmond, Va., 1974-78, Williamsburg (Va.)-James City Pub. Schs., 1979-83, Prince William County Pub. Schs., Manassas, Va., 1983-89; hist. area interpreter Colonial Williamsburg Found., 1978-79; outpatient therapist Prince William County Community Svcs. Bd., 1989-91, emergency svcs. therapist, therapist cons., 1991-93; marriage and family therapist Employee Assistance Svc., Inc., Manassas, 1993—; pvt. practice Ashton Profl. Ctr., 1996—; cons. Horizons for LEarning, Inc., Richmond, 1989—. Great Books LEader, 1993—. Mem. Am. Assn. Marriage and Family Therapy, Va. Assn. Marriage and Family Therapy, Internat. Assn., Marriage and Family Counselors, Sigma Kappa (life). Home: 12046 Market Square Ct Manassas VA 20112-3214

MA, YAN, information science educator; b. Hangzhou, China, Apr. 27, 1957; came to U.S., 1986; d. Ru-jin Chen and Chao-ying Ma. BA in English, Hangzhou U., 1982; MLS in Libr. Sci., Kent State U., 1988; postgrad., U. Wis., 1990, PhD in Ednl. Tech., 1993. Tchr. English Qingchun H.S., Hangzhou, 1976-78; instr. English Zhejiang (China) Med. U., 1982-86; grad. asst. Kent (Ohio) State U., 1986-88; tchg. asst. U. Wis., Madison, 1989-91; cataloging libr. Northwestern U., Chgo., 1991-94; asst. prof. U. Wis., Milw., 1994—; presenter in field at local, nat., and internat. confs. Contbr. articles to profl. jours. Grad. Sch. Rsch. Incentive Program grantee U. Wis., 1995, grantee U. Wis. Sys., Inst. on Race and Ethnicity, 1996. Mem. Internat. Visual Lit. Assn. (bd. dirs. 1994—), Am. Ednl. Rsch. Assn., Assn. for Ednl. Comm. and Tech., Assn. for Libr. and Info. Sci. Edn., Chinese Am. Librs. Assn., Med. Libr. Assn. Home: 3909 N Murray Ave Apt 607 Shorewood WI 53211 Office: Univ Wis Milw PO Box 413 Sch Libr and Info Sci Milwaukee WI 53201

MAARBJERG, MARY PENZOLD, office equipment company executive; b. Norfolk, Va., Oct. 2, 1943; d. Edmund Theodore and Lucy Adelaide (Singleton) Penzold; m. John Peder Maarbjerg, Oct. 20, 1966; 1 son, Martin Peder. A.B., Hollins Coll., 1965; M.B.A., Wharton Sch., Pa., 1969. Cons. bus. and fin., Stamford, Conn., 1977-78; corp. staff analyst Pitney Bowes, Inc., Stamford, Conn., 1978-80, mgr. pension and benefit fin. 1980-81, dir. investor relations, 1981-85; v.p. planning and devel. Pitney Bowes Credit Corp., Norwalk, Conn., 1985-86; treas., v.p. planning Pitney Bowes Credit Corp., 1986-94; v.p. mkt. devel. and mng. dir. Asia Pacific Bowes Fin. Svcs., 1994-95, v.p. ops. and mng. dir., 1995—. Mem. adv. com. City of Stamford Mcpl. Employees Retirement Fund, 1980-85; mem. fin. adv. com. YWCA, Stamford, 1982-86; bd. dirs. Stamford Symphony, 1985-95, Vis. Nurses Assn., 1984-86, Am. Recorder Soc., 1986—. Fellow Royal Statis. Soc.; mem. Fin. Execs. Inst., Phi Beta Kappa. Congregationalist. Office: Pitney Bowes Credit Corp 201 Merritt Seven Norwalk CT 06856

MAAS, BARBARA E., nurse, retired, volunteer; b. Milw., July 15, 1933. BSN, U. Wis., Milw., 1965. RN, Wis. Staff nurse Milw. Luth., 1954-58, head nurse, 1958-61, supr., 1961-71; supr. infection control Luth./Good Samaritan, Milw., 1971-80; infection control/discharge planning Good Samaritan, Milw., 1980-88; infection control/utilization review Sinai-Samaritan Med. Ctr., Milw., 1988-93. Editor (newsletter) Rose Hybridizers Assoc., 1985—, Petals and Thorns, 1990—. Mem. Wauwatosa (Wis.) Beautification Com., 1992—. Mem. AAUW, Am. Rose Soc. (dir. 1985—, Outstanding Consulting Rosarian 1981, Silver medal 1984). Lutheran.

MAAS, JANE BROWN, advertising executive; b. Jersey City; d. Charles E. and Margaret (Beck) Brown; m. Michael Maas, Aug. 30, 1957; children: Katherine, Jennifer. BA, Bucknell U., 1953; postgrad., U. Dijon, France, 1954; MA, Cornell U., 1955; LittD, Ramapo Coll., 1986, St. John's U., 1988. Assoc. producer Name That Tune TV Program, N.Y.C., 1957-64; v.p. Ogilvy and Mather Inc., N.Y.C., 1964-76; sr. v.p. Wells, Rich, Greene, Inc., N.Y.C., 1976-82; pres. Muller Jordan Weiss Inc., N.Y.C., 1982-89; pres. Earle Palmer Brown Cos., N.Y.C., 1989-92, chmn., 1992-94, chmn. emeritus, 1994—. Co-author: How to Advertise, 1975, Better Brochures, 1981, Adventures of a Advertising Woman, 1986, The New How to Advertise, 1992, Christmas in Wales: a Homecoming, 1994. Trustee Bucknell U., Lewisburg, 1976-86, Fordham U., N.Y., 1983-91; bd. govs. com. Scholastic Achievement, 1985-92; active Girl Scouts U.S. Greater N.Y., 1970-76; mem. adv. bd. William E. Simon Grad. Sch. Bus. U. Rochester, 1989—, pub. dir. AIA, 1993-95. Recipient Matrix award Women in Communications, 1980, N.Y. Advt. Woman of Yr., 1986. Mem. AIA (hon.), Am. Archtl. Found. (regent 1993—), Am. Assn. Advt. Agys. (bd. govs.). Home: PO Box 1109 Westhampton Beach NY 11978-7109

MAAS, JOAN LOUISE, training and development consultant; b. San Jose, Calif., Apr. 26, 1961; d. Elmer Alvin Maas and Betty Lu Rowe. BA, Whitman Coll., 1983; MA in Psychology, U.S. Internat. U. Asst. mgr. New Times Clothing Co., Costa Mesa, Calif., 1984-85; bus. analyst Dun and Bradstreet, Long Beach, Calif., 1985-86; intern McDonnell Douglas, Huntington Beach, Calif., 1986; training and personnel asst. Western Digital, Irvine, Calif., 1986-88; instrl. designer Toastmasters Internat., Rancho Santa Margarita, Calif., 1988-91; prin. Maas Tng. and Devel., Mission Viejo, Calif., 1991-92; staff cons. Richard Chang Assocs., Irvine, 1992; orgnl. devel. specialist Anaheim Meml. Hosp., 1992-95. Author Orangespiel newsletter, 1991. Mem. Orange County (Calif.) Young Reps., 1986—, South Orange County Young Reps., 1991. Mem. ASTD (sec. 1992, dir. spl. interest groups 1993, Orange County Merit award 1994), Orange County Nat. Soc. for Performance and Instrn., Toastmasters (v.p. edn. 1991). Home and Office: 3463 State St # 354 Santa Barbara CA 93105

MAATSCH, DEBORAH JOAN, trust administrator, compliance officer, paralegal tax specialist; b. Lincoln, Nebr., Mar. 26, 1950; d. Leon F. Forst and Jarolyn J. Hoffman Forst Conrad; m. Gordon F. Maatsch, Mar. 14, 1969; children: Jason, Diana. BS, U. Nebr., 1976. Acct., supr. U.S. Civil Svc., Heidelberg, Ger., 1971-73; paralegal Mattson Rickets Davies et al, Lincoln, Nebr., 1976-87; tax cons. Lincoln and Denver, 1981—; pres. DGJD Inc.-Bleachers, 1993—; paralegal Wade Ash Woods & Hill, P.C., Denver, 1986-94; sr. trust adminstr. Investment Trust Co., Denver, 1994—; compliance officer Nelson, Benson and Zellmer, Inc., 1995—; mem. Denver Trust Officers Assocs., bus. adv. bd. Ponderosa H.S., 1994—; officer The "O" Streeters, Lincoln, 1984-87; spkr., coord. Nebr. Continuing Legal Edn. Seminars, 1976-86. Contbr. articles to profl. jours. Officer The Aurorians Synchronized Swim Team Parents Orgn., Rocky Mt. Spash Parents' Corp.; youth edn. staff Ave Maria Cath. Ch., Parker, Colo., 1990-91; vol., chmn. activities PTSA Ponderosa H.S. Mem. Doane Coll. Alumni Assn. (dir. 1989-93), Rocky Mt. Legal Assts. (dir., sect. chair 1990-94), Am. Soc. Women Accts. (officer, dir.), Nebr. Assn. Legal Assts. (officer, dir. 1976-87), Colo. Bar Assn. (computer probate sect.), Phi Chi Theta (treas. 1988-89). Office: DGSD, Inc 7533 Windford Parker CO 80134

MABIN, ANN MARIE, artist management executive, consultant; b. Memphis, Apr. 22; d. Jim and Pearline White; m. Robert Mabin (div. 1989); children: Camille, Diane. AA, Wayne State C.C., 1974, BS, 1977; postgrad., UCLA, 1979-81. Artist rels. Motown Records, Detroit, 1968-79; pres. artist mgmt. Mary Jane Prodn., L.A., N.Y.C., 1979-91, Klasact Entertainment, L.A., 1991—; tour cons. Mary Jane Girls, L.A., 1982-87. Author (poem) Smile, 1989 (Golden Poet award 1990); coord. (record album) Street Songs, 1981 (Am. Music award 1982), Mary Jane Girls, 1983 (Am. Music award 1984), Super Freak, 1981 (Grammy award 1991). Vol. Dem. Conv., Detroit, 1975. Mem. Prestigious Women Assn., Starlight Found. (vol.), Braille Inst. for Blind (vol.). Baptist.

MABRY, CATHY DARLENE, elementary school educator; b. Atlanta, Dec. 9, 1951; d. German William and Erma Isabel (Lyons) M. BA in Sociology and Psychology, U. Ga., 1975; Cert. in Edn., Oglethorpe U., Atlanta, 1983, MA in Elem. Edn., 1990. Cert. in early childhood edn., Ga. Charge account svcs. staff C&S Nat. Bank, Atlanta, 1974-75; with Rich's, Decatur, Ga., 1975-76, 79-84; mgr. trainee sales Sears Roebuck & Co., Decatur, 1974-75, 76-78; intermediate clk. Superior Ct. of DeKalb County, Decatur, 1978-81; paraprofl. kindergarten DeKalb County Sch. Sys., Decatur, 1979-81, tchr., 1984—; mem. sch.-based mgmt. com. Hooper Alexander Sch., Decatur, 1991-92, strategic planning com., 1990—; mem. social studies curriculum com. DeKalb County Sch. Sys., 1990-91, tchr. forum rep., 1992—. Author poetry in Am. Poetry Anthology, 1986. Sec. Lithonia Civic League, Inc., 1987—, Teen Scene, Inc., Lithonia, 1993-94; chair bd. dirs. DeKalb Econ. Opportunity Authority, Decatur, 1991-92, 93—; mem. Teach Well Wellness Program, Emory U. Sch. Pub. Health, 1994; active PTA. Mem. NAACP, Nat. Coun. of Negro Women, Inc., Nat. Geog. Soc., DeKalb Assn. Educators, Zeta Phi Beta. Democrat. Baptist. Home: 7109 Rhodes St Lithonia GA 30058-4235 Office: Hooper Alexander Sch 3414 Memorial Dr Decatur GA 30032-2708

MABRY, MARJORIE ANN, career counselor; b. Urbana, Ill., Apr. 11, 1934; d. George and Charlotte Elma (Priddy) Metz; m. John Daniel Mabry, Nov. 27, 1955; children: Max Andre, Monte Del, Daniel Stacy, Samuel Kirk, Katherine Elizabeth. BA, Baylor U., 1955; MA, Azusa Pacific U., 1985. Cert. secondary edn. tchr., Tex. High sch. algebra and biology tchr. Summer Inst. Linguistics, Ukarumpa, Papua New Guinea; mgr. publicity dept. Australian Aborigines and Islanders br. Summer Inst. Linguistics, Darwin, Australia; career counselor Wycliffe Bible Translators and Summer Inst. Linguistics, Waxhaw, N.C. and Darwin, Australia. Editor: Praise and Prayer Bull., Didjeridu, Personnel Development News and Views. Mem. Am. Assn. Christian Counselors, Assn. Psychol. Type, N.C. Counseling Assn., N.C. Career Devel. Assn., N.C. Assn. Assessment in Counseling, N.C. Assn. Adult Devel. and Aging, Internat. Assn. Invitational Edn. Address: PO Box 248 Waxhaw NC 28173-0248

MABUS, BARBARA JEAN, special needs educator; b. Cleve., Nov. 6, 1950; d. Elmer Wilhelm and Florence Pauline Witzke; m. Stephen Michael Mabus, June 29, 1974; 1 child, Mark Samuel. BS in Edn., Bowling Green U., 1973, postgrad., 1991, 94; postgrad., Baldwin-Wallace Coll., 1991. Cert. 7-12 English and earth sci. educator, provision grad. tchr., Ohio. Tchr. lang. arts Bellefontaine (Ohio) City Schs., 1973-74; substitute tchr. Bryan (Ohio) City Schs., 1974-76, 90-93, spl. needs tutor, 1993—, vol. art appreciation tchr., 1988-91; substitute tchr. Williams County Schs., Bryan, 1974-76, 90-92; tchr. sci., health and phys. edn. St. Patrick Sch., Bryan, 1991. Leader 4-H, Bryan, 1987—; active Clowns of Grace, Bryan, 1991—; youth leader Grace Cmty. Ch., Bryan, 1992-93. Co-recipient Disting. Citizen of Yr. award N.W. Ohio Art Edn. Assn., 1990, tchr. recognition award Supporting Our Challenged Kids, 1995. Mem. NEA, Ohio Edn. Assn., Bryan Edn. Assn. (scholarship com. 1993-94), Coun. for Learning Disabilities. Home: 115 W Trevitt St Bryan OH 43506-1229 Office: Bryan Mid Sch 1301 Center St Bryan OH 43506-9125

MACAFEE, SUSAN DIANE, reporter; b. Feb. 1944. Attended, Foothill Coll. Disc jockey with news, pub. affairs; engr., editor, producer KZSU-Stanford U., Calif., 1975-80; freelance reporter, broadcast journalist, 1975—. Writer, prodr., engr. editor, narrator 25 original nationwide news stories and furnished story material for numerous radio stas. and networks, TV stas. including NPR, Pacifica, ABC, NBC and CBS networks, BBC radio and TV, Channel 9 Australia, numerous newspapers and magazines; copyrighted stories include: Agent Orange Pilot Nutritional Detox Program, 1986, (5-part series) Food-Diet-Crime, Behavior and Learning Disability Connection, 1986; recorder, transcriber A Historical Prospective of Vitamin C With Linus Pauling, 1991; researcher, documentor, writer Postscipt: Interactions of Glutathione, Ascorbic Acid HIV and AIDS, 1992, Chromiun - A New Treatment for Adult Type II (Maturity Onset) Diabetes, 1996. V.p. Calif. Coll. Young Reps., 1967; sec., asst. to Nat. Field Dir. Coll. Young Reps., Rep. Nat. Com., Washington, 1968; dir. precinct orgn. Calif. State Assembly Campaign, San Francisco Rep. Ctrl. Com., 1968. Recipient 3 Nat. awards Young Rep. Nat. Com., 1967-68. Home and Office: PO Box 4644 Rockville MD 20849-4644

MACALISTER, KIM PORTER, advertising executive; b. Providence, Oct. 25, 1954; d. Bruce Barnes and Jeanne Marie (Cahill) Macalister; m. Bruce Phillip Person, Dec. 29, 1979 (div. June 1984); m. Arthur Gene Quinby, Feb. 19, 1988. BS, Skidmore Coll., Saratoga Springs, N.Y., 1976. Media planner, account exec. J.H. Dietz Advt., Providence, 1976-79; media planner Della Femina, Travisano, L.A., 1979-80; media planner J. Walter Thompson, L.A., 1980-82, assoc. media dir., 1982-83, v.p., media dir., 1983-85; v.p., media dir. Thompson Recruitment Advt. subs. J. Walter Thompson, 1985-86, mgr.and v.p., 1986-89, pres., COO, 1989-90, pres., CEO, 1990—; former faculty mem. AAAA Inst. Advanced Advt. Studies. Trustee Skidmore Coll. Mem. Young Pres.' Orgn., L.A. Advt. Club. Republican. Office: Int Specialized Comm 6500 Wilshire Blvd Ste 2100 Los Angeles CA 90048-4941

MACARLE, MARIA TERESE, physiologist; b. Brookhaven, N.Y., Jan. 3, 1958; d. Anthony J. and Josephine M. (Cappabianca) M. BA, SUNY Cortland, 1980; MA, Adelphi U., 1988; EdM, Columbia U., 1996. Cert. strength and conditioning specialist. Exercise physiologist Colony Hill Fitness Ctr., Hauppauge, N.Y., 1980-82, Off the Wall Fitness Ctr., Hauppauge, 1982-85, Mid Island Cmty. Ctr., Plainview, N.Y., 1985—; instr. Suffolk C.C., Selden, N.Y., 1990—. Contbr. articles to profl. jours. Instr. ARC, L.I., 1980—; mem. L.I. Ladies Soccer League, 1991—, Breast Cancer Action Coalition Sports Team, L.I., 1992—; capt. Am. Cancer Soc., L.I., 1995—. Mem. Nat. Strength and Conditioning Assn., Am. Coll. Sports Medicine (Greater N.Y. chpt.). Roman Catholic. Office: Mid Island Y Cmty Ctr 45 Manetto Hill Rd Plainview NY 11803

MACARTHUR, ELIZABETH WHITTEMORE, artist; b. Boston, Sept. 12, 1933; d. Arthur Easterbrook and Suvia Lanice (Paton) Whittemore; m. Robert Helmer MacArthur, June 14, 1952 (dec. Nov. 1972); children: Duncan, Alan, Elizabeth, Donald. BA in Botany, Smith Coll., 1954; postgrad., Princeton (N.J.) Art Assn., 1966-73, Windham Coll., 1975-76. One woman shows include Marlboro (Vt.) Coll., 1974, 82, 91, 93, West Village Meeting House, Brattleboro, Vt., 1979, 83, 88, Cafe Grad. Students, Berkeley, Calif., 1988. Home and Studio: PO Box 119 South Rd Marlboro VT 05344

MACARTHUR, SANDRA LEA, financial services executive; b. Springfield, Mass., July 21, 1946; d. John J. MacArthur and Catherine E. (Lantry) Mason; m. Edgar A. Dunn, June 23, 1973 (div. Mar. 1980); 1 child, Jonathan H.; m. Robert M. Cruickshank, Sept. 15, 1984. AA, Bradford Coll., 1966; BA, Simmons Coll., 1973; MBA, Babson Coll., 1983. Asst. dir. rental properties Wintergreen Resort, Charlottesville, Va., 1978-79; treas., ptnr. Elan, Inc., Boston, 1983-84; agt. State Mut. Am., Newton Center, Mass., 1985-86; sr. account officer Fidelity Investments Instl. Svcs., Boston, 1986-87, mgr. client svcs., 1987-88, assoc. market mgr., 1988-89; market mgr. Fidelity Instl. Retirement Svcs. Co., Boston, 1989-90, v.p. mktg., 1990-92, v.p. comm. prodn., 1992-96; v.p. Investment Cons. Svcs., Boston, 1996—. Fundraiser Babson Coll., Wellesley, Mass., 1988. Mem. Internat. Assn. Bus. Communicators, Internat. TV and Video Assn., New England Employee Benefits Coun., Alumni Bd. of MacDuffie Sch., Beta Gamma Sigma. Democrat. Episcopalian. Home: 47 Westchester Rd Jamaica Plain MA 02130-3451 Office: Investment Cons Svcs 82 Devonshire St Ste A2A Boston MA 02109-3614

MACAVINTA-TENAZAS, GEMORSITA, family physician; b. Numancia, Aklan, Phillippines, Dec. 18, 1938; came to U.S., 1967; d. Dominador Zalazar and Georgina Estrada (Tabanera) Macavinta; m. Salvador Torrefiel Tenazas Jr., Apr. 18, 1963; children: Alan, Alex, Albert, Alfred. BA, Far Ea. U., Manila, 1959, D of Medicine, 1964. Diplomate Am. Bd. Family Practice. Intern North Gen. Hosp., Manila, 1963-64; pvt. practice Manila, 1965-67; extern Chinese Gen. Hosp., Manila, 1965-67; with St. Joseph Med. Ctr., Burbank, Calif., 1967-69; chief cytotechnologist Cancer Screening Svcs., North Hollywood, Calif., 1969-73; resident in family practice medicine Health Scis. Ctr., Tex. Tech. U., Lubbock, 1974-75; staff physician VA Outpatient Clinic, L.A., 1975—. Recipient physician recognition awards AMA, 1973-85, 92-94; named Disting. Alumna, Aklan Acad., Philippines, 1991, Most Outstanding Parent award Builders Lions Club, 1995, Citizen of Yr. Builders Lions Club, 1996. Fellow Am. Acad. Family Physicians; mem. Calif. Acad. Family Physicians, Filipino Asian-Pacific VA Employees Soc. (pres. L.A. chpt. 1988—), Aklanons of Am. (pres. 1988—, 1st Mrs. Aklan 1986-89), Far Ea. U. Med. Alumni Assn. (asst. sec. 1988—). Roman Catholic. Office: VA Outpatient Clinic 425 S Hill St Los Angeles CA 90013-1110

MACCALLUM, (EDYTHE) LORENE, pharmacist; b. Monte Vista, Colo., Nov. 29, 1928; d. Francis Whittier and Berniece Viola (Martin) Scott; m. David Robertson MacCallum, June 12, 1952; children: Suzanne Rae MacCallum Barslund and Roxanne Kay MacCallum Batezel (twins), Tracy Scott, Tamara Lee MacCallum Johnson, Shauna Marie MacCallum Bost. BS in Pharmacy U. Colo., 1950. Registered pharmacist, Colo. Pharmacist Presbyn. Hosp., Denver, 1950, Corner Pharmacy, Lamar, Colo., 1950-53; rsch. pharmacist Nat. Chlorophyll Co., Lamar, 1953; relief pharmacist, various stores, Delta, Colo., 1957-59, Farmington, N.Mex., 1960-62, 71-79, Aztec, N.Mex., 1971-79; mgr. Med. Arts Pharmacy, Farmington, 1966-67; cons. pharmacist Navajo Hosp., Brethren in Christ Mission, Farmington, 1967-77; sales agt. Norris Realty, Farmington, 1977-78; pharmacist, owner, mgr. Lorene's Pharmacy, Farmington, 1979-88; tax cons. H&R Block, Farmington, 1968; cons. Pub. Svc. Co., N.Mex. Intermediate Clinic, Planned Parenthood, Farmington; first woman registered pharmacist apptd. N.Mex. Bd. Pharm., 1982-92. Author numerous poems for mag. Advisor Order Rainbow for Girls, Farmington, 1975-78. Mem. Nat. Assn. Bds. Pharmacy (com. on internship tng., com. edn., sec., treas. dist. 8, mem. impaired pharmacists adv. com., chmn. impaired pharmacists program N.Mex., 1987—, mem. law enforcement legis. com., chmn. nominating com. 1992), Nat. Assn. Retail Druggists, N.Mex. Pharm. Assn. (mem. exec. coun. 1977-81), Order Eastern Star (Farmington). Methodist. Home and Office: 1301 Camino Sol Farmington NM 87401-8075

MACCARTHY, TALBOT LELAND, civic volunteer; b. St. Louis, Jan. 28, 1936; d. Austin Porter Leland and Dorothy (Lund) Follansbee; m. John Peters MacCarthy, June 21, 1958; children: John Leland MacCarthy, Talbot MacCarthy Payne. BA, Vassar Coll., 1958. Sec., treas. Station List Pub. Co., St. Louis, 1975-85, pres., 1985-90. Trustee Robert E. Lee Meml. Assn., Arts and Edn. Coun. Greater St. Louis, pres., 1978-80, emerita; trustee St. Louis Art Mus.; past trsutee St. Louis Mercantile Libr. Assn., Family & Children's Svc. Greater St. Louis, Health and Welfare Coun., Greater St. Louis, Jr. Kindergarten St. Louis Page Park YMCA, Scholarship Found. St. Louis, Friends St. Louis Art Mus. Bd., Ch. St. Michael and St. George Sch. Bd., Mid-Am. Arts Alliance; chmn. Mo. Arts Coun., 1980-85; past chmn. Vol. Action Ctr. Greater St. Louis; past vice chmn. bd. dirs. Mary Inst.; past pres. Jr. League St. Louis; mem. Nat. Coun. Arts, 1985-91. Recipient Woman of Achievement citation St. Louis Globe Democrat, 1979, Mo. Citizens for Arts/Arts Advocacy award, 1987, Mo. Arts Award, 1993. Mem. Vassar Club St. Louis (past pres.), Mary Inst. Alumnae Assn. (past pres.), Colonial Dames Am., Garden Club St. Louis. Republican. Episcopalian.

MACCLOSKEY, RUTH BLAIR See PARRIS, REBECCA

MACCOBY, ELEANOR EMMONS, psychology educator; b. Tacoma, May 15, 1917; d. Harry Eugene and Viva May (Johnson) Emmons; m. Nathan Maccoby, Sept. 16, 1938 (dec. Apr. 1992); children: Janice Maccoby Carmichael, Sarah Maccoby Bellina, Mark. BS, U Wash., 1939; MA, U. Mich., 1949, PhD, 1950. Study dir. div. program surveys USDA, Washington, 1942-46; study dir. Survey Rsch. Ctr. U. Mich., Ann Arbor, 1946-48; lectr., rsch. assoc. dept. social rels. Harvard U., Cambridge, Mass., 1950-58; from assoc. to full prof. Stanford (Calif.) U., 1958-87, chmn. dept. psychology, 1973-76, prof. emeritus, 1987—; elected Nat. Acad. of Sci., 1993. Author: (with R. Sears and H. Levin) Patterns of Child-Rearing, 1957, (with Carol Jacklin) Psychology of Sex Differences, 1974, Social Development, 1980, (with R.H. Mnookin) Dividing the Child: Social and Legal Dilemmas of Custody, 1992; editor: (with Newcomb and Hartley) Readings in Social Psychology, 1957, The Development of Sex Differences, 1966. Recipient Gores award for Excellence in Teaching Stanford U., 1981, Disting. Contbn. to Ednl. Research award Am. Ednl. Research Assn., 1984, Disting. Sci. Contbn. to Child Devel. award Soc. for Research in Child Devel., 1987, Disting. Sci. Contbns. award Am. Psychol. Assn., 1988; named to Barbara Kimball Browning professorship Stanford U., 1979—. Fellow APA (pres. Divsn. 7, 1971-72, G. Stanley Hall award 1982), Soc. for Rsch. in Child Devel. (pres. 1981-83, mem. governing coun. 1963-66, Am. Psychol. Soc.; mem. NAS, Western Psychol. Assn. (pres. 1974-75), Inst. for Rsch. on Women and Gender, Social Sci. Rsch. Coun. (chmn. 1984-85), Inst. Medicine, Am. Acad. Arts and Scis., Consortium of Social Sci. Assns. Democrat. Home: 729 Mayfield Ave Palo Alto CA 94305-1016 Office: Stanford U Dept Psychology Stanford CA 94305-2130

MACCONKEY, DOROTHY I., academic administrator; b. New Brunswick, N.J.; d. Donald Thurston and Dorothy Bennett (Hill) Ingling; m. Joseph W. MacConkey, June 19, 1949 (dec. Aug. 1975); children: Donald Franklin, Diane Margaret, Dorothy Frances; m. Karl Schmeidler, May 26, 1994. BA, Beaver Coll., 1947; MA, Wichita State U., 1953; PhD, U. Md., 1974; LLD (hon.), Beaver Coll., 1988. Lectr. Wichita (Kans.) State U., 1950-51; rsch.-campaign assoc. United Fund and Council, Wichita, 1951-62; rsch.- com. coordination Health and Welfare Council of Nat. Capital Area, Washington, 1963-65; exec. dir. multi-program agy. Prince Georges County Assn. for Retarded Children, Hyattsville, Md., 1965-66; prof. George Mason U.,

Fairfax, Va., 1966-76, asst. vice pres., acting dean, 1976-82; v.p., dean of coll. Hiram (Ohio) Coll., 1982-85; pres. Davis & Elkins (W.Va.) Coll., 1985—; bd. dirs. Davis Trust Co., Elkins, 1987—; adv. bd. George Mason U. Found., Fairfax, 1976—; trustee Beaver Coll., Glenside, Pa., 1971-87; cons., evaluator North Cen. Assn., Chgo., 1985—, commr., 1993—; mem. exec. com., pres. Assn. Presbyn. Colls. and Univs.; mem. bd. Svc. Opportunity Colls., Presbyn. Found., trustee, 1993—; chmn. North Area Cen. Com.; treas. Coun. of Ind. Colls. Pres. County Chasers of Am., 1985—. Recipient Citizen award for service to handicapped, Fairfax County, 1981, Goddin Women Alumni award, 1985, Woman of Yr. in Edn. award W.Va. Fedn. Women's Clubs, 1986. Mem. Coun. of Pres.', Nat. Assn. Intercollegiate Athletics, Coun. Ind. Colls. (bd. dirs.). Office: Davis and Elkins Coll Office of Pres 100 Campus Dr Elkins WV 26241-3971

MACCOY, MARILYN, physical education educator, volleyball coach; b. Ossining, N.Y., Oct. 30, 1940; d. Cecil and Henrietta (Authouse) MacC. BS, Boston U., 1962; MA, Adelphi U., 1969. Permanent cert. in edn. and coaching, N.Y. Coach varsity girls volleyball Mepham H.S., Bellmore, N.Y., 1962—, coach varsity boys volleyball, 1987—, coach varsity girls badminton, 1980-86, coach varsity girls tennis, 1962-80; rep. Sect. 8 H.S. Sports Assn., 1990—; mem. Boys Volleyball Exec. Coun., Nassau County, 1990—; mem. Com. for Girls and Women in Sports Day, SUNY, 1995. Mem. PTA Bellmore Merrick Sch. Dist., 1962—. Named Girls Volleyball Coach of Yr., Nassau County, 1992; recipient Outstanding Achievement Coaches award N.Y. State Coaches Assn., 1992, Nat. Award for Outstanding Contbrns. to Girls' and Women's Sports, 1993; coached Nassau County volleyball championship teams, 1976, 88, 89, 92, 93. Mem. Nassau County H.S. Assn., Nassau County Boys and Girls Volleyball Coaches Assn. Republican. Congregational. Office: W C Mepham H S 2401 Camp Ave Bellmore NY 11701

MACDONALD, CAROLYN HELMS, gifted education educator; b. Leesburg, Va., Oct. 15, 1941; d. Edmund Davis and Mary Irene (Peters) Helms; m. John Mount MacDonald, July 27, 1963 (div. Dec. 1984); children: Christina Hope, Heather Laurel, Katherine Anne. BS, East Tenn. State U., 1964; MS, Nova U., 1979. Cert. elem. tchr., jr. coll. tchr., gifted tchr., Fla. Elem. tchr. Shoemaker Elem. Sch., Gate City, Va., 1964-65, Bakersfield Elem. Sch., Aberdeen, Md., 1965-66, Brookview Elem. Sch., Jacksonville, Fla., 1966-68, Holiday Hill Elem. Sch., Jacksonville, Fla., 1968-69, Arlington Annex 5th Grade Ctr., Jacksonville, 1972-73; elem. tchr., social studies, lang. arts specialist Loretto Elem. Sch., Jacksonville, 1973-81, tchr. gifted, 1981—; mem. steering com. for gifted edn. Duval County Sch. Bd., 1982-85; del to Murmansk, USSR, 1991, ESOL trainer, 1995—. Pres. Mandarin Cmty. Club, Jacksonville, 1980; mem. Panel on Sewage Treatment Problems, 1979, Neighborhood Cancer Drive Com., 1979-84, Com. to Assess Cmty. Recreation Needs, Jacksonville, 1981-82; sponsor ARC. Recipient placque Mandarin Community Club, Jacksonville, 1974-77; named Outstanding Safety Patrol Sponsor North Fla., 1993. Mem. Fla. Jr. Coll. Woman's Club (v.p. 1969-71, pres. 1971-72, Outstanding Young Woman Am. 1971), Southside Jr. Woman's Club (v.p. 1970-73), Phi Mu Alumnae (v.p. 1989-90), Delta Kappa Gamma. Democrat. Methodist. Home: 9439 San Jose Blvd Apt 228 Jacksonville FL 32257 Office: Loretto Elem Sch # 30 3900 Loretto Rd Jacksonville FL 32223-2055

MACDONALD, CHRISTINE, social worker; b. Lowell, Mass., Sept. 13, 1952; d. Robert Francis and Ruth Olvie (Breed) MacD.; children: Jessica Eireanne Craig Walters, Braea Walters. BGS in Behavioral Sci., Sch. of Life Long Learning, Conway, N.H., 1987; postgrad., N.H. Tech. Coll., Berlin, 1994-95. Family counselor Family Strength, Concord, N.H., 1987-90; resident mgr., family support consumer liaison The Ctr. of Hope, Conway, 1990—. bd. dirs. Big Bros./Big Sisters, Carroll County, N.H., 1988-89, 94; intern, trainer, vol. Carroll County Against Domestic Violence and Rape, Conway, 1983—; bd. alt. Carroll County Transport Alliance, 1994—. Mem. NOW, Mt. Washington Valley Bus. and Profl. Women. Office: COH Family Support Po Box 2048 Banfield Ln Conway NH 03818

MACDONALD, JANE CRONIN, elementary school educator; b. Bklyn., June 12, 1950; d. Joseph Victor and Edith Rita (Ferrari) Cronin; m. Kenneth Francis MacDonald, Dec. 22, 1973; 1 child, Amanda Jane. BA, Georgian Ct. Coll., 1971; MA, Kean Coll. N.J., 1975; EdD, Nova Southeastern U., 1984. Cert. elem. tchr., reading tchr., reading specialist, nursery sch. tchr., adminstr./supr., N.J. Elem. sch. tchr. Toms River (N.J.) Regional Schs., 1971—; instr. reading Brookdale C.C., Lincroft, N.J., 1994; instr. humanities Ocean County Coll., Toms River, 1992—; cons. DJ Mac Assocs., Island Heights, N.J., 1984—; internat. cons. Creative Pubs. Prodr., host Going Strong! Growing Straight! series, Toms River, 1982-85, Parent Express TV show, Toms River, 1994; rschr. in field. Bd. dirs. Parent Kid Tips, South Toms River, 1992-94; mem. com. N.J. Edn. Assn., 1984-86; assembly del. NEA, Washington, 1980-85. Hilda Maehling fellow NEA, 1984. Mem. AAUW, Assn. for Childhood Edn. Internat., Nat. Assn. for Edn. of Young Children, Georgian Ct. Coll. Alumni Assn. (v.p. of clubs 1981-87), Phi Delta Kappa. Republican. Roman Catholic. Home: 720 Dunedin St Toms River NJ 08753 Office: DJ Mac Assocs PO Box 908 Island Heights NJ 08732-0908

MACDONALD, JOAN SIBYL, chef, restaurant manager; b. Mpls., Nov. 10, 1944; d. William Porter and Jeanne Louise (Hall) MacD.; m. William Mathew Carlstrom, Dec. 18, 1968 (div.); 1 child, Eva-Lise Carlstrom. BA cum laude, U. Minn., 1967; Cordon Bleu cert., Cordon Bleu Sch. Cookery, London, 1973. Chef, mgr. U. Oreg. Univ. Club, Eugene, 1978—. Editor: (neighborhood newspaper) Westside News, 1977-80. Treas. Westside Neighborhood Quality Project, Eugene, 1992—; mem. Support Hult Ops., Eugene, 1992—, Friends of Eugene Ballet, 1993—, Ln. County Dems. Cen. Com., Eugene, 1990—. Mem. Oreg. Restaurant Assn. (legis. affairs com. 1994—). Democrat. Home: 1091 W Broadway Eugene OR 97402 Office: U Oreg Univ Club Collier House 1170 E 13th Ave Eugene OR 97403

MACDONALD, KAREN CRANE, occupational therapist, geriatric counselor; b. Denville, N.J., Feb. 24, 1955; d. Robert William and Jeanette Wilcox (Crane) M.; m. Geno Piacentini, Oct. 22, 1994. BS, Quinnipiac Coll., 1977; MS, U. Bridgeport, 1982; postgrad., NYU, 1983—. Cert. occupational therapist. Occupational therapist, coord. of spl. care unit Jewish Home for the Elderly, Conn., 1987-93, N.Y. Inst., N.Y.C., 1984-86; pvt. practice Fairfield County, Conn., 1977-88; occupl. therapist Rehab. Assocs., Fairfield, Conn., 1993—; instr. NYU, 1985-89, Quinnipiac Coll., 1986-92; lectr., cons. in field. Contbr. articles to profl. jours. Youth leader, deacon Union Meml. Ch., Stamford, Conn., 1980-88; deacon Southport Congl. Ch., 1992-94; chair consumer com. Alzheimer's Coalition of Conn., 1991-92. Teaching fellow NYU, 1983-86. Mem. World Fedn. Occupl. Therapy, Am. Occupl. Therapy Assn. (scholar 1985, coun. edn.), Conn. Occupl. Therapy Assn. (gerontology liaison 1980-83), Pi Lambda Theta. Office: Rehab Assocs 60 Katona Dr Fairfield CT 06430-3544

MACDONALD, LENNA RUTH, lawyer; b. Providence, July 16, 1962; d. Arthur Robert and Laina Ruth (Weake) M.; m. Robert Christopher Carew, Sept. 18, 1993. BA, Brown U., 1984; postgrad., London Sch. Econs., 1984-85; JD, Emory U., 1988. Bar: Ohio 1988, R.I., 1989, Mass. 1992. With Erikson Internat. Biog. Database, Providence, 1983-86; assoc. Smith & Schnacke, Dayton, Ohio, 1988-89, Edwards & Angell, Providence, 1989-91, McDermott, Will & Emery, Boston, 1991-93; asst. gen. counsel, group mgr. Banc One N.H. Asset Mgmt. Corp., Manchester, 1993-96, Banc One Corp., Bank One, Ky., NA, Louisville, 1996—. Mem. Mass. Bar Assn., R.I. Bar Assn., Am. Friends London Sch. Econs., Phi Alpha Delta. Republican. Episcopalian. Home: 1721 Devondale Dr Louisville KY 40222 Office: Bank One Ky NA Legal Dept 416 W Jefferson St Louisville KY 40202-3244

MACDONALD, MARGARET E., nonprofit organization administrator; b. Glendive, Mont., Aug. 31, 1951; d. Alexander Colin and Marie Christine (Peterson) MacD.; m. John Dickson Smillie, July 31, 1982; children: Siri Marie, Charles MacDonald. BS, U. Mont., Missoula, 1974. Librarian and editor Boulder River (Mont.) Sch. & Hosp., 1975-76; assoc. editor The Columbus (Mont.) News, 1976-77; cmty. organizer No. Plains Resource Coun., Glendive, 1977-78; rsch. editor, lobbyist No. Plains Resource Coun., Billings, Mont., 1979-82, staff dir., 1982-86; non-profit consulting, 1986-90; exec. dir. Mont. Assn. of Churches, Billings, 1990—; adv. Mont. CELMAPP, Helena, 1982-86; asst. moderator United Ch. of Chirst GS21, Cleve., 1995—; mem. exec. bd. Mont. Human Rights Network, Helena, 1993-96; mem. gov's. coun. on econ. devel. State of Mont., Helena, 1983-88. Recipient Just-Peace award United Ch. of Christ OCIS, 1995; honoree YWCA Salute to Women, 1996. Mem. Billings Coalition for Human Rights (bd. dirs.), St. John's Nursing Home Found. (bd. dirs.). Democrat. Office: Montana Assoc of Churches Ste G 100 24th St W Billings MT 59106

MACDONALD, SHARON ETHEL, dancer, choreographer, administrator; b. Pittsfield, Mass., Mar. 24, 1952; d. Harry and Angeline (Saracco) MacD. BA, Skidmore Coll., 1974; MA, Smith Coll., 1992. Faculty Smith Coll., Northampton, Mass., 1974-76; dancer, tchr. Berkshire Ballet, Pittsfield, 1976-77; dance dir. Becket (Mass.) Arts Ctr., Mass., 1977-80; faculty mem. Williams Coll., Williamstown, Mass., 1979-80; co-artistic dir., owner N.E. Am. Ballet, Northampton, 1980-85; devel. dir., tchr. Berkshire Ballet, Pittsfield, 1984-85; adminstr., tchr. Hartford (Conn.) Ballet, Inc., 1985-90; artistic dir., exec. dir. Am. Dance Inst., 1995—; freelance dir., choreographer, master tchr.; asst. choreographer Easthampton Mass. Community Theatre Assn., 1981-83, Project Opera, 1982; bd. dirs. Jacob's Pillow Dance Festival, Becket, 1978-81; bd. trustees Becket Arts Ctr., 1979-80; tchr. Trinity Coll., Hartford, Conn., 1990—; dir. mktg., bus. cons. Limelight Prodns., Inc., 1990-95; guest artist numerous pub schs., pvt. studios, colls., and univs. Pres. Friends of Jacob's Pillow, Becket, 1978-81, Friends of The Hartford Ballet, 1988-91, Jacob's Pillow Alumnae/Archives Com., 1988—, Dance History Scholars, 1976-78, 91—; chmn. Lee (Mass.) Cultural Coun., 1995—. Mass. Arts Lottery Grantee Mass. Arts Coun., 1984, Arts Lottery Grantee Northampton Arts Coun., 1984; Smith Coll. Fellow. Mem. AAHPERD, Nat. Dance Assn., Smith Coll. Club. Democrat. Baptist. Home: PO Box 697 Stockbridge MA 01262-0697

MACDONALD, SHEILA DE MARILLAC, transaction mamagement company executive; b. Santa Monica, Calif., Jan. 17; d. William Alan and M. Jane (Crotty) M. BS, Stanford U.; BA, U. San Francisco; MBA, Harvard U. Prin. Tex. Transaction Mgmt. Co., Houston, 1990—. Mem. Harvard Club N.Y., Met. Club, Petroleum Club.

MACDONALD GLENN, LINDA, lawyer; b. Perth Amboy, N.J., Sept. 29, 1955; d. John and Anna (Janocko) Stefanik; m. John Arch MacDonald, Sept. 17, 1983 (dec. Feb. 1984); m. Kim Garrett Glenn, Dec. 31, 1987; stepchildren: Katherine Glenn, Nicole Glenn. AB, Rutgers U., 1977; JD, Western New Eng. Law Sch., 1981. Bar: R.I. 1981, U.S. Dist. Ct. R.I. 1981. Assoc. Manning, West, Santianiello & Pari, Providence, 1981-82; spl. asst. atty., gen. sr. trial atty. Atty. Gen.'s Office State of R.I., Providence, 1982-87; legal counsel sp. legis. com. R.I. Ho. of Reps., Providence, 1986-88; legal counsel R.I. HEW Com., Providence, 1988—; assoc. Saunders, Dumas & Fleury, East Greenwich, R.I., 1987-89; ptnr. Dumas, MacDonald & Holland, East Greenwich, 1988-91, MacDonald and Holland, Ltd., East Greenwich, 1992-94, MacDonald Glenn & Assocs., East Greenwich, 1994—. Mem. Lambda Class Leadership R.I., 1991. Named one of Outstanding Women, YWCA, 1983, Outstanding Bd. Dirs., Leukemia Soc. of R.I., 1984. Mem. ABA, R.I. Bar Assn., R.I. Women's Bar Assn., Assn. Trial Lawyers Am., R.I. Trial Lawyers Assn., Warwick Bus. and Profl. Women's Assn. (Woman of Yr. 1988), R.I. Women's Network, East Greenwich C. of C. (v.p.). Democrat. Greek Catholic. Office: MacDonald-Glenn & Assocs 139 Main St East Greenwich RI 02818-3808

MACDONNELL, JOANNE CAPELLA, writer, editor, editorial consultant; b. Santa Rosa, Calif., Jan. 26, 1937; d. Joseph Lawrence and Mabel Alida (Strome) Capella; m. S.J. Cogliandro, Feb. 23, 1957 (div. 1963); 1 child, Cory; m. Ignacio Plancarte Lopez, June 2, 1964 (dec. 1971); children: Kenneth Lopez, Lauren Lopez; m. John Faust MacDonnell, Sept. 6, 1981. Student, U. Calif., Berkeley, 1955-56, San Jose (Calif.) State U., 1956-57. Advt. Palo Alto Times, Calif., 1960-62; columnist San Jose Mercury News, Calif., 1962-83; clk. Santa Clara County Superior Ct., San Jose, 1984—. Author six-part series on unsafe toys, 1968; humor columnist San Jose Mercury News, 1977-81. Writer fund-raising brochure Valley Med. Ctr., San Jose, 1964; vol. Alexian Bros. Hosp., San Jose, 1967; TV appearances local pub. TV, San Jose, 1967-70. Recipient 2nd Place feature series award San Francisco Press Club 1968 series entered into congl. record by Rep. Don Edwards, 1969, Achievement in writing award Santa Clara County Pen Women Los Gatos Calif. 1965, Santa Clara County Family Law award for excellence, 1995. Mem. San Francisco Press Club, San Jose Newspaper Guild. Democratic. Roman Catholic. Home: 3514 El Grande Dr San Jose CA 95132-3110

MACDOUGALL, PRISCILLA RUTH, lawyer; b. Evanston, Ill., Jan. 20, 1944; d. Curtis Daniel and Genevieve Maurine (Rockwood) MacDougall; m. Lester H. Brownlee, July 5, 1987. BA, Barnard Coll., 1965; grad. with honors, U. Paris, 1967; JD, U. Mich., 1970. Bar: Wis. 1970, Ill. 1970. Asst. atty. gen. State of Wis., 1970-74; instr. Law Sch. and undergrad. campuses U. Wis., 1973-75; staff counsel Wis. Edn. Assn. Council, Madison, 1975—; instr. Columbia Coll., Chgo., 1988—; litigator, writer, speaker, educator women's and children's names and women's rights and labor issues. Mem. ABA, Wis. State Bar (founder sect. on individual rights and responsibilities, chairperson, 1973-75, 78-79), Legal Assn. Women Wis. (co-founder). Author: Married Women's Common Law Right to Their Own Surnames, 1972, (with Terri P. Tepper) Booklet for Women Who Wish to Determine Their Own Names After Marriage, 1974, supplement, 1975, The Right of Women to Name Their Children, 1985; contbr. articles to profl. jours. Home: 502 Engelhart Dr Madison WI 53713-4742 Office: 33 Nob Hill Dr Madison WI 53713-2198

MACE, MARY ALICE, coal company administrator; b. Charleston, W.Va., Nov. 21, 1949; d. John Robert Leake and Georgia Alice (Wilhelm) Crist; m. Charles Michael Mace, May 20, 1968; 1 child, Christina Michelle. Student, U. Charleston, 1990—. Sec. Capitol Paper Supply, Inc., Charleston, 1967-68, Persingers, Inc., Charleston, 1968-77; benefits coordinator Elk Run Coal Co., Inc., Sylvester, W.Va., 1981—; notary public. Sec. PTA, Pettus, W.Va., 1981-83, pres. 1983-85. Mem. NAFE, Health Benefits Group, Women of Moose. Democrat. Home: 2741 Rose Lane Dr Charleston WV 25302-4923 Office: Elk Run Coal Co Inc PO Box 497 Sylvester WV 25193-0497

MACER-STORY, EUGENIA ANN, writer, artist; b. Mpls., Jan. 20, 1945; d. Dan Johnstone and Eugenia Loretta (Andrews) Macer; divorced; 1 child, Ezra Arthur Story. BS in Speech, Northwestern U., 1965; MFA, Columbia U., 1968. Writing instr. Polyarts, Boston, 1970-72; theater instr. Joy of Movement, Boston, 1972-75; artistic dir. Magik Mirror, Salem, Mass., 1975-76, Magick Mirror Comm., 1977—. Author: Congratulations: The UFO Reality, 1978, Angels of Time, 1982, Project Midas, 1986, Dr. Fu Man Chu Meets the Lonesome Cowboy: Sorcery and the UFO Experience, 1991, 3d edit., 1994, Gypsy Fair, 1991, The Strawberry Man, 1991, Sea Condor/Dusty Sun, 1994, Awakening to the Light-After the Longest Night, 1995; (short stories) Battles with Dragons: Certain Tales of Political Yoga, 1993, 2d edit., 1994, Legacy of Daedulus, 1995; (plays) Fetching the Tree, Archeological Politics, Strange Inquiries, Divine Appliance, 1989, The Zig Zag Wall, 1990, The Only Qualified Huntress, 1990, Telephone Taps Written Up for Tabloids, 1991, Wars With Pigeons, 1992, Conquest of the Asteroids, 1993, Commander Galacticon, 1993, Meister Hemmelin, 1994, Six Way Time Play, 1994, Radish, 1996, others; philosophy writer; contbr. articles to profl. jours.; author poetry in Woodstock Times, Lamia Ink!, Manhattan Poetry Rev., Sensations, Kore, others; feature writer Borderlands Mag., 1995; editor Magick Mirror Newsletter. Shubert fellow, 1968. Mem. Dramatists Guild, U.S. Psychotronics Assn., Internat. Guild of Occult Scis. Democrat. Office: Magick Mirror Comm PO Box 741 New York NY 10116-0741

MACEWAN, BARBARA ANN, middle school educator; b. Adams, Mass., Apr. 22, 1938; d. Thomas Lawrence and Vera (Ziemba) Gaskalka; m. George Louie MacEwan, Feb. 16, 1963; children: Rebecca, Debra. BS in Edn. cum laude, North Adams State Coll., 1959; MEd with honors, Plymouth State Coll., 1994. Cert. K-8, secondary social studies tchr., sch. libr., Mass. Tchr. Town of Valatie, N.Y., 1959-61, 62-63, Dept. Def., Aachefensburg, Germany, 1961-62, Town of East Longmeadow, Mass., 1964; asst. children's libr. Springfield (Mass.) Libr., 1964; tchr. history Southwick (Mass.)-Tolland Regional Schs., 1971—, tchr. history, curriculum coord. mid. sch., 1995—; state coord. Nat. History Day, 1989-92. Author: The Old Cemetery: Southwick, 1977, Shays Rebellion, 1987, The Princess, 1995. Sec. Southwick Hist. Soc., 1976-79, treas., 1979-86, pres., 1986-94; trustee Moore House, Southwick, 1989—; chair Southwick Hist. Commn., 1994—; active Mass. Curriculum Framework Focus Group, 1994-96. Recipient recognition New Eng. League Mid. Schs., 1991; Horace Mann grantee Southwick Sch. Com., 1982, Southwest Regional Alliance grantee. Mem. ASCD, NEA, Mass. Tchrs. Assn., New Eng. Oral History Assn., New Eng. Hisotry Tchrs. Assn., Nat. Coun. for Social Studies, Mass. Coun. Social Studies (recognition 1992), Western Mass. Coun. for Social Studies (bd. dirs. 1987-95), Mass. Assn. Ednl. Media, Nat. Mus. Am. Indian, New Eng. Native Am. Inst., Pioneer Valley Reading Coun., Historic Mass., Nat. Women's Hall Fame, Nat. Trust Historic Preservation, Phi Delta Kappa. Roman Catholic. Office: Powder Mill Mid Sch 94 Powder Mill Rd Southwick MA 01077-9324

MACFARLAND, MARY ELIZABETH, graphic designer; b. Bellevue, Wash., May 13, 1962; d. William Herbert and Phyllis Elaine (Frank) MacF. BA, Evergreen State Coll., 1986; BFA, Art Ctr. Coll. Design, Pasadena, Calif., 1990. Freelance graphic designer, illustrator N.Y.C., 1990—; art dir., sr. designer N.Y. Film and Animation, 1994—. Shows include Soc. of Illustrators, 1990. Office: NY Film and Animation 352 7th Ave New York NY 10009

MACGILLIVRAY, LOIS ANN, organization executive; b. Phila., July 8, 1937; d. Alexander and Mary Ethel (Crosby) MacG. BA in History, Holy Names Coll., 1966; MA in Sociology, U. N.C., 1971, PhD in Sociology, 1973. Joined Sisters of Holy Names of Jesus and Mary, 1955. Research asst. U. N.C., Chapel Hill, 1969-70, 71-72, instr. sociology, 1970-71; sociologist Rsch. Triangle Inst., Durham, N.C., 1973-75, sr. sociologist, 1975-81; dir. Ctr. for Population and Urban-Rural Studies, Research Triangle Inst., Durham, 1976-81; pres. Holy Names Coll., Oakland, Calif., 1982-92; mem. steering com. Symposium for Bus. Leaders Holy Names Coll., 1982-92; prin. owner Svc. Orgns.: Planning and Evaluation, Chapel Hill, 1994—; vis. scholar dept. sociology U. N.C., Chapel Hill, 1992-94; mem. policy bd. U. Oakland Met. Forum, co-convenor panel on edn. and youth. Bd. dirs. Oakland Coun. Econ. Devel., 1984-86; bd. dirs. Bay Area Biosci. Ctr., 1990-92, mem. adv. com., 1992-94. Mem. Am. Sociol. Assn., Assn. Ind. Calif. Colls. and Univs. (exec. com. 1985-92, vice chmn. 1989-92), Regional Assn. East Bay Colls. and Univs. (past pres., bd. dirs. 1982-92). Home and Office: 101 N Hamilton Rd Chapel Hill NC 27514-5627

MACGILLIVRAY, MARYANN LEVERONE, marketing professional; b. Mpls., Oct. 18, 1947; d. Joseph Paul and Genevieve Gertrude (Ozark) Leverone; B.S., Coll. of St. Catherine, St. Paul, 1969; Med. Technologist, Hennepin County Gen. Hosp., 1970; M.B.A., Pepperdine U., 1976; m. Duncan MacGillivray, Apr. 28, 1973; children: Duncan Michael, Catherine Mary and Monica Mary (twins), Andrew John. Med. technologist Mercy Hosp., San Diego, 1970-72; with Diagnostics div. Abbott Labs., South Pasadena, Calif., 1972-79, tech. service rep., 1972-74, sr. tech. service rep., 1974-75, product coordinator, mktg., 1975-77, mktg. product mgr., 1977-79; clin. diagnostic mktg. cons., Sierra Madre, Calif., 1979-88; founder, mktg. dir. Health Craft Internat., Pasadena, Calif., 1988—; elected council woman City of Sierra Madre, 1990-94, mayor, 1994-95, re-elected council women, 1994—. Recipient Pres.'s award Abbott Diagnostics Div., 1975. Mem. Biomed. Mktg. Assn., Am. Assn. Clin. Chemistry, Am. Assn. Clin. Pathologists, Am. Soc. Med. Tech., Calif. Assn. Med. Lab. Technologists, Pasadena Symphony Assn. Roman Catholic. Home: 608 Elm Ave Sierra Madre CA 91024-1245

MACGOWAN, MARY EUGENIA, lawyer; b. Turlock, Calif., Aug. 4, 1928; d. William Ray and Mary Bolling (Gilbert) Kern; m. Gordon Scott Millar, Jan. 2, 1970; 1 dau., Heather Mary. A.B., U. Calif., Berkeley, 1950; J.D., U. Calif., San Francisco, 1953. Bar: Calif. 1953; cert. family law specialist Calif. State Bar Bd. Legal Specialization. Research atty. Supreme Ct. Calif., 1954, Calif. Ct. Appeals, 1955; partner firm MacGowan & MacGowan, Calif., 1956-68; pvt. practice, San Francisco, 1968—. Bd. dirs. San Francisco Speech and Hearing Center, San Francisco Legal Aid Soc., J.A.C.K.I.E. Mem. Am., Calif., San Francisco bar assns., Queen's Bench. Clubs: San Francisco Lawyers, Forest Hill Garden. Office: 1 Sansome St Ste 1900 San Francisco CA 94104

MACGOWAN, SANDRA FIRELLI, publishing executive, publishing educator; b. Phila., Nov. 9, 1951; d. William Firelli and Barbara (Gimbel) Kapalcik. BS in Biology, BA in English, Pa. State U., 1973, MA in English Lit., 1978. Cert. supervisory analyst N.Y. Stock Exchange. Editor McGraw-Hill Pub. Co., N.Y.C., 1979-81; sr. acquisitions editor Harcourt Brace Jovanovich, Inc., N.Y.C., 1981-82; sr. editor The Coll. Bd., N.Y.C., 1982-88; v.p., head editorial CS First Boston Corp., N.Y.C., 1988-94; v.p. supervisory analyst internat. rsch. SBC Warburg, N.Y.C., 1994-96; v.p. supervising analyst internat. rsch. Arnhold and S. Bleichroeder, N.Y.C., 1996—; part time asst. prof. pub. NYU Sch. Continuing Edn., N.Y.C., 1985—. Author: 50 College Admission Directors Speak to Parents, 1988. Democrat. Office: SBC Warburg 277 Park Ave New York NY 10172

MACGUINNESS, ROSEMARY ANNE, lawyer; b. Newry, County Down, No. Ireland, June 26, 1957; came to U.S., 1981.; d. Micahel Gerald and Maureen Rosemary (Leavy) MacG.; m. Philip Martin Bellber, Dec. 5, 1987; children: Sam Martin Bellber, Rhys Patrick Bellber, Mason Philip Bellber. B in Civil Law, U. Coll. Dublin, 1978, diploma in European Law, 1979; MS in Criminal Justice, Northeastern U., 1982. Bar: Ireland 1981, Calif. 1994. Legal asst. Bronson, Bronson & McKinnon, San Francisco, 1983; atty. McInerney & Dillon, Oakland, Calif., 1984-87; sr. counsel Pacific Stock Exch., San Francisco, 1987-90, sr. counsel, dir. arbitration, 1990—. Mem. Queen's Bench. Office: Pacific Stock Exch 301 Pine St San Francisco CA 94104-3301

MACHIN, BARBARA E., lawyer; b. Kansas City, Mo., Mar. 26, 1947; d. Roger H. and Doris D. (Dunkel) Elliott; m. Peter A. Machin, June 1, 1969; 1 child, Andrew D. BS in Sec. Edn., U. Kans., 1969, MA in Curriculum Devel./Anthropology, 1973; JD, U. Toledo Coll., 1978. Bar: Ohio 1978, U.S. Dist. Ct. (no. dist.) Ohio 1978, U.S. Ct. Appeals (6th cir.) 1981, U.S. Supreme Ct. 1987. Instr. rsch. and writing U. Toledo Coll. of Law, 1978-79; law clerk Lucas County Ct. of Common Pleas, Toledo, 1979-80; assoc., ptnr. Doyle, Lewis & Warner, Toledo, 1980-87; assoc. Shumaker, Loop & Kendrick, Toledo, 1987-92; gen. counsel U. Toledo, 1993—; pres., v.p., mem. bd. trustees Toledo Legal Aid Soc., 1983—; pres. Toledo Civil Trial Attys., 1990-93. Contbr. articles to profl. jours. Mem. house corp. bd. Gamma Phi Beta Sorority, 1985—; mem. bd. trustees Epworth Found., 1993—, St. Luke's Hosp., 1994—. Mem. Ohio State Bar Assn., Toledo Bar Assn., Toledo Women's Bar Assn., Toledo Civil Trial Attys. (pres. 1983-92). Home: 5034 W Dauber Dr Toledo OH 43615-2172 Office: U of Toledo Office of the Gen Counsel 3620 University Hall 2801 W Bancroft Toledo OH 43606

MACHT, AMY, real estate executive, foundation manager; b. Balt., Mar. 18, 1954; d. Philip Romm and Lois Lerner (Kleiman) M.; m. George Richmond Grose II, June 7, 1981; children: Eloise Macht Grose, Madeleine Macht Grose. BA, U. Pa., 1974; BArch, U. Md., 1978. Archtl. designer, draftsperson Hord, Coplan & Macht, Balt., 1978-81; pres., mgr. Morton & Sophie Macht. Found., Balt., 1978—; real estate mgr. Regional Mgmt., Inc., Balt., 1981-86, real estate broker, v.p., CEO, 1986—. Mem. bd. Associated Jewish Cmty. of Balt. (1985-95), dir. Charles Crane Family Found., Balt., 1995—, adv. bd. Johns Hopkins Sch. of Pub. Health, Balt., 1995—. Home: 1412 LaBelle Ave Baltimore MD 21204 Office: Regional Management Inc 11 E Fayette St Baltimore MD 21202

MACHTIGER, HARRIET GORDON, psychoanalyst; b. N.Y.C., July 27, 1927; d. Michael J. and Miriam D. (Rand) Gordon; BA, Bklyn. Coll., 1947; dipl. with distinction, U. London, 1966, PhD, 1974; m. Sidney Machtiger, Feb. 7, 1948; children: Avram Coleman, Marcia Gordon, Bennett Rand. Tchr., Phila. Pub. Schs., 1962-64; ednl. therapist Child Guidance Tng. Center, London, 1966-68; ednl. therapist Sch. Psychol. Svc., Inner London Edn. Authority, 1968-70; therapist Paddington Day Hosp., London, 1970-71, London Centre for Psychotherapy, 1971-74, Staunton Clinic, U. Pitts., 1974-78; pvt. practice psychoanalysis, Pitts., 1976—; pres. C.G. Jung Ctr., Pitts., 1976-81; cons. in field. Mem. S.W. Pitts. Community Mental Health, 1976-78; past dir. Pitts. program Inter-Regional Soc. Jungian Analysts, 1975-85. Recipient award for Disting. Contributions to Advancement in Edn., Pa. Dept. Edn., 1962; Social Sci. Rsch. Coun. award, 1973; cert. psychologist, Pa. Fellow Am. Orthopsychiat. Assn.; mem. APA, N.Y. Assn. Analytical

Psychologists, Pa. Psychol. Assn., Brit. Psychol. Soc., Brit. Assn. Psychotherapists, Assn. Child Psychology and Child Psychiatry. Home: 207 Tennyson Ave Pittsburgh PA 15213-1415 Office: 123 Cathedral Mansions 4716 Ellsworth Ave Pittsburgh PA 15213-2851

MACIEIRA-KAUFMANN, REBECCA LYNN, marketing executive; b. San Francisco. BA in Semiotics, Brown U., 1986; MBA, Stanford U., 1989. Casewriter Stanford Grad. Sch. bus., Fall 1989; sr. cons. Aeris Cons. Group, London and Paris, 1990-91; sr engagement mgr. Retail Solutions Mgmt. Cons., London, 1992; product mgr. Providian Bancorp, San Francisco, 1993-94, dir. mktg., 1994-95, v.p. mktg., 1995-96; v.p. mktg. Wells Fargo Ins. Svcs., Brisbane, Calif., 1996—. Editor: Semiotics of Management, 1987, Semiotics of Culture, 1988; contbr. articles to profl. jours. Vol. JVS (non-profit agy. helping people find jobs), San Francisco, 1993—, bd. dirs., chmn. mktg. com., 1995—. Fulbright scholar, 1986-87. Home: 184 Parker Ave San Francisco CA 94118 Office: 1000 Marina Blvd 3d Fl Brisbane CA 94005

MACIEL, PATRICIA ANN, hospital administrator; b. Providence, Jan. 13, 1940; d. Raymond Wallace Sr. and Elizabeth Josephine (Kelly) Ross; m. John Maciel Jr., July 24, 1963; children: Kelly Patricia, Christopher John. BEd, R.I. Coll., 1961, MA in Tchg., 1976. Cert. tchr., R.I. 3d grade tchr. Pawtucket (R.I.) Pub. Schs., 1961-62; 5th and 6th grade tchr. Providence Pub. Schs., 1962-63; tchr. Pawtucket and Providence Pub. Schs., 1963-72; tchr., curriculum coord. Holy Name Sch., Providence, 1972-80; dir. ednl. programming Basic Skills, Inc., Providence, 1980-83; dir. devel./pub. rels. IN-SIGHT, Warwick, R.I., 1983-88; coord. ann. giving and spl. events St. Joseph Health Svcs. R.I., North Providence, R.I., 1988—. Editor, author newsletter IN-SIGHT News, 1980-83. Sec. exec. bd. Holy Name Sch., 1972-80; pres. employee activities com. St. Josephs Hosp., 1991-93; founding mem., pres. Friends of the Pawtucket Pub. Libr., 1966; pres. Pawtucket Jr. Woman's Club, 1965; publicity chair Middlebridge Assn., South Kingstown, R.I., 1989-90; mem. Narrow River Preservation Assn., South Kingstown, 1976—; mem. Save the Bay, State of R.I., 1987—; ex officio mem. R.I. Coll. Found., 1992-94, corporate bd. dirs., 1996—. Recipient Alumna of Yr award Rhode Island Coll., 1992. Mem. R.I. Coll. Alumni Assn. (treas. exec. bd. 1990-92, chair ann. fund dr. 1990-92, chair class reunion 1981, 86, 91, class news sec. 1972-78, pres. 1992-94). Roman Catholic. Office: St Joseph Health Svcs RI Devel Office 200 High Svc Ave North Providence RI 02904

MACINTYRE, MARY LOUISE, artist; b. Rochester, N.H., Feb. 21, 1952; d. Charles A. and Florence A. (Manley) MacI. Student, Franconia Coll., 1974; BFA, Md. Inst. Coll. Art, 1991; MFA, Wichita State U., 1994. Cert. tchr. N.H., Maine. Counselor KVMHC, Waterville, Maine, 1974-78; libr. asst.selor K.V.V.T.I., Waterville, 1978-79; career counselor CETA Program State of Maine, Augusta, 1979-81; account rep. WCSH-HYNZ Radio, Portland, Maine, 1980-82; computer sales rep. Computer Ctr., Falmouth, Maine, 1982-83; computer sales staff and mgr. Tandy Corp., Maine/Md., 1983-87; housing coord. Md. Inst. Coll. Art, Balt., 1987-92; tchg. asst. Wichita State U., 1992-94; student asst. Edwin A. Ulrich Mus. Art, Wichita, 1993-94. Works exhibited in 2 person show Student Gallery-MICA, Balt., 1987, Coll. Ctr., Balt., 1988, group shows Staples Gallery, 1993, McFarland Gallery, 1993, Literary Conf., CAC, WSU, 1993, McKnight Ctr., Wichita State U., 1993, Century II, Wichita, 1993. Democrat. Studio: Macin Art 1520 #4 Center Dr Santa Fe NM 87505

MACIUSZKO, KATHLEEN LYNN, librarian, educator; b. Nogales, Ariz., Apr. 8, 1947; d. Thomas and Stephanie (Horowski) Mart; m. Jerzy Janusz Maciuszko, Dec. 11, 1976; 1 child, Christinia Alexsandra. BA, Ea. Mich. U., 1969; MLS, Kent State U., 1974; PhD, Case Western Res. U., 1987. Reference libr. Baldwin-Wallace Coll. Libr., Berea, Ohio, 1974-77, dir. Conservatory of Music Libr., 1977-85; dir. bus. info. svcs. Harcourt Brace Jovanovich, Inc., Cleve., 1985-89; staff asst. to exec. dir. Cuyahoga County Pub. Libr., Cleve., 1989-90; dir. Cleve. Area Met. Library System, Beachwood, Ohio, 1990; media specialist Cleve. Pub. Schs., 1991-93, Berea (Ohio) City Sch. Dist., 1993—. Author: OCLC: A Decade of Development, 1967-77, 1984; contbr. articles to profl. jours. Named Plenum Pub. scholar, 1986. Mem. Spl. Librs. Assn. (pres. Cleve. chpt. 1989-90, v.p. 1988-89, editor newsletter 1988-89), Baldwin-Wallace Coll. Faculty Women's Club (pres. 1975),. Office: Midpark HS 7000 Paula Dr Middleburg Heights OH 44130

MACK, BRENDA LEE, sociologist, public relations consulting company executive; b. Peoria, Ill., Mar. 24; d. William James and Virginia Julia (Pickett) Palmer; m. Rozene Mack, Jan. 13 (div.); 1 child, Kevin Anthony. AA, L.A. City Coll.; BA in Sociology, Calif. State U., L.A., 1980. Ct. clk. City of Blythe, Calif.; ptnr. Mack Trucking Co., Blythe; owner Brenda Mack Enterprises, L.A., 1981—; conflict mediator, cultural sensitivity cons.; lectr., writer, radio and TV personality; cons. European cmty.; co-originator advt. concept View/Door Project; pub. News from the United States newsletter through U.S. and Europe; Cultural Sensitivity Cons.; Conflict Mediator. Past bd. dirs. Narcotic Symposium, L.A. With WAC, U.S. Army. Mem. Women For, Calif. State U. L.A. Alumni Assn., World Affairs Coun., German-Am. C. of C., European Cmty. Studies Assn. Home: 8749 Cattaraugus Ave Los Angeles CA 90034-2558 Office: Brenda Mack Enterprises/Mack Media Presents PO Box 5942 Los Angeles CA 90055-0942

MACK, JUDITH COLE SCHRIM, political science educator; b. Cin., Aug. 9, 1938; d. James Douglass and Cathleen (Cole) Schrim; m. Thomas H. Mack, Jan. 3, 1968; children: Robert Michael, Cathleen Cole. AB with high distinction, U. Ky., 1960; AM, Radcliffe Grad. Sch., 1962; MPhil, Columbia U., 1988, postgrad., 1986—. Tchr. The Lexington (Ky.) Sch., 1962-63; instr. Russian Emory U., Atlanta, 1963-64, Kent (Ohio) State U., 1964-65; instr. Hunter Coll., N.Y.C., 1988-90; adj. lectr. Barnard Coll., N.Y.C., spring 1991, 92; instr. Douglass Coll. Rutgers U., 1992-93; rsch. asst. sociology dept. U. Ky., summer 1961; rsch. asst. Russian and East European Studies Ctr., UCLA, 1965-67; rsch. asst. security studies ctr. UCLA, 1967-68; adj. lectr. Hunter Coll., N.Y.C., spring 1988; presenter in field. Chmn. State Pub. Affairs Com., N.J. Jr. Leagues, 1979-80; bd. dirs. Children's Aide Adoption Soc., Hackensack, N.J., 1979-90, v.p. 1985-90; bd. dirs. Assn. for Children N.J., Newark, 1982—, v.p. 1983-88; bd. trustees Div. of Youth and Family Svcs., Trenton, 1982-91, v.p. 1983-88, others; mem. Millburn-Short Hills County Com. Rep. Party, 1994—, corr. sec., 1994—; co-chair Rep. Party Campaign Millburn Township com., 1995. Recipient Woodrow Wilson fellowship Radcliffe Coll., 1960-61, Nat. Def. fellowship Radcliffe Coll., 1961-62. Mem. Phi Beta Kappa, Phi Sigma Iota, Mortar Bd. Episcopalian. Home: 47 Knollwood Rd Short Hills NJ 07078-2821

MACK, JULIA COOPER, judge; b. Fayetteville, N.C., July 17, 1920; d. Dallas L. and Emily (McKay) Perry; m. Jerry S. Cooper, July 30, 1943; 1 dau., Cheryl; m. Clifford S. Mack, Nov. 21, 1957. B.S., Hampton Inst., 1940; LL.B., Howard U., 1951. Bar: D.C. 1952. Legal cons. OPS, Washington, 1952-53; atty.-advisor office gen. counsel Gen. Svcs. Adminstrn., Washington, 1953-54; trial appellate atty. criminal div. Dept. Justice, Washington, 1954-68; civil rights atty. Office Gen. Counsel, Equal Employment Opportunity Commn., Washington, 1968-75; assoc. judge Ct. Appeals, Washington, 1975-89; sr. judge, 1989—. Mem. Am., Fed., Washington, Nat. Bar Assns., Nat. Assn. Women Judges. Home: 1610 Varnum St NW Washington DC 20011-4206 Office: DC Ct Appeals 500 Indiana Ave NW Ste 6 Washington DC 20001-2131

MACK, KIRBIE LYN, municipal official; b. Chgo., Jan. 3, 1953; d. Robert Lee and Luvonia (Cheatham) Green; m. Jeffery Frazier Mack, Aug. 10, 1974; children: Maaina, Jeffery Jr., Anisha. BA in Psychology, Northeastern Ill. U., 1975; MA in Policy Analysis and Pub. Adminstrn., U. Wis., 1995. Pers. specialist City of Madison, Wis., 1975-76; program asst. planning budget analysis dept. natural resource State of Wis., Madison, 1976-79, dir. conservation corps, 1979-80, equal opportunity officer, mgr., 1980-85, chief negotiator employment rels., 1985-89; dir. affirmative action dept. City of Madison, 1989—. Co-host, prodr. (cable TV program) Focus On Equality, 1989-95. Pres. Southside Raiders Football Booster Club, Madison, 1995. Recipient Gov.'s Orchid award State of Wis., 1987, Exemplary Leadership award Wis. Assn. Black State Employees, 1993, Leadership in Affirmative Action award Am. Soc. for Pub. Adminstrs., 1992, 93, Outstanding Cmty. Svc. award Prevention and Intervention Alcohol and Drug Abuse, 1992, Spirit of Am. Woman award Sta. WISC-TV, 1994, Pub. Svc. for Students award Links, Inc. and Madison Pub. Schs., 1994; named one of 100 Most Alluring Creative Influential and Entrepreneurial People Madison Mag., 1995. Mem. NAACP (life, 1st v.p. 1993-95, Outstanding Svc. award Madison br. 1990, 92, Unsung Heroine award 1993), Am. Contract Compliance Assn., Wis. Assn. Black State Employees (past pres 1985, Pres.'s award 1989-90). Office: City of Madison Ste 130/MMB 215 Martin Luther King Jr Blvd Madison WI 53701

MACK, PATRICIA JOHNSON, newspaper editor; b. New Brunswick, N.J., Oct. 4, 1942; d. Henry Francis and Ann May (Monahan) Johnson; m. Parker Horton Moore, July 22, 1961 (div. 1971); m. Lonnie Burnell Mack, May 23, 1973; children: Tevis Ann, Kelaine Dorothy, Aidan Ruth. Student, Alderson-Broaddus Coll., 1960-61, U. W.Va., 1961, Harvard U., 1961-62, U. Ky., 1962-64. Reporter The Sentinel Greater Media Newspapers, East Brunswick, N.J., 1971-77; reporter, food editor, restaurant critic News Tribune, Woodbridge, N.J., 1977-92; food editor News Tribune/The Record, Woodbridge and Hackensack, N.J., 1992-95; food editor, columnist, restaurant reviewer The Record, Hackensack, 1992-96. Bd. dirs. Parents for Deaf Awareness, 1985-87; active Ctrl. Jersey Health Planning Commn., Woodbridge, 1987, Middlesex County Commn. for Handicapped, New Brunswick, 1987-89. Recipient 7 awards N.J. Press Assn., 1987-92, Cardiac Reporting award N.J. divsn. Am. Heart Assn., 1987, Nutrition Writing award Nestle, 1992, Disting. Svc. award N.J. Dietetic Assn., 1993. Mem. Assn. Food Journalists (Best Food Sect. awards 1987, 92, 93), Dame de Canardier (France). Office: The Record 150 River St Hackensack NJ 07601-7110

MACK, SHIRLEY ANN, counseling educator, counselor; b. Detroit, Oct. 2, 1953; d. Leonard Anthony Zavorski and Florence Nora (Raymond) Zavorski Suszka; m. Russell David Mack, Oct. 23, 1983; 1 child, Russell. BS, Western Mich. U., 1980; MA, Wayne State U., 1993, postgrad., 1993—. Lic. profl. counselor, Mich. Mental health technician Psychiat. Ctr. of Mich. Hosp., New Baltimore, 1991-93; crisis interventionist Harbor Oaks, New Baltimore, 1992-94; cons. Oakland U., Rochester, Mich., 1994-95; supr. counseling lab. Wayne State U., Detroit, 1993—, career counselor univ. counseling svcs., 1993-94, grad. tchg. asst., 1994—, counselor Work First program, 1995; adj. asst. prof. counseling U. Detroit Mercy, 1995—; substance abuse counselor intern Harper Hosp., Detroit, 1993. Cub scout den leader Boy Scouts Am., Mt. Clemens, Mich., 1991-92; sch. rep. D.A.R.E. program, Mt. Clemens, 1991-92; facilitator Mayor's Conf. on Edn., Detroit, 1995. Scholar Wayne State U., 1993—. Mem. ACA, Assn. Counselor Educators and Suprs., Mich. Counselors Assn., Mich. Mental Health Counselors Assn. Office: Wayne State U Coll Edn 5429 Gullen Mall Detroit MI 48202

MACKAY, PATRICIA MCINTOSH, counselor; b. San Francisco, Sept. 12, 1922; d. William Carroll and Louise Edgerton (Keen) McIntosh; AB in Psychology, U. Calif., Berkeley, 1944, elem. teaching credential, 1951; MA in Psychology, John F. Kennedy U., Orinda, Calif., 1979; PhD in Nutrition, Donsbach U., Huntington Beach, Calif., 1981; m. Alden Thorndike Mackay, Dec. 15, 1945; children—Patricia Louise, James McIntosh, Donald Sage. Cert. marriage, family and child counselor. Elem. tchr. Mt. Diablo Unified Sch. Dist., Concord, Calif., 1950-60; exec. supr. No. Calif. Welcome Wagon Internat., 1960-67; wedding cons. Mackay Creative Svcs., Walnut Creek, Calif., 1969-70; co-owner Courtesy Calls, Greeters and Concord Welcoming Svcs., Walnut Creek, 1971-94; marriage, family and child counselor, nutrition cons., Walnut Creek, 1979—; coord. Alameda and Contra Costa County chpts. Parents United, 1985—, pres. region 2; bd. dirs. New Directions Counseling Ctr., Inc., 1975-81, founder, pres. aux., 1977-79. Bd. dirs. Ministry in the Marketplace, Inc.; founder, dir. Turning Point Counseling; active Walnut Creek Presbyn. Ch.; bd. dirs. counseling dir. Shepherd's Gate-shelter for homeless women and children, 1985-92, Contra Costa County Child Care Coun., 1993, 94, 95. Recipient Individual award New Directions Counseling Ctr., 1978, awards Neo-Life Co. Am. Prestige Club, yearly, 1977-86, Cmty. Svc. award Child Abuse Prevention Coun., 1990, 92, 94. Mem. Assn. Marriage and Family Therapists, Parents United Internat. (pres. region 2, bd. dirs. 1992), U. Calif. Berkeley Alumni (sec. 1979-94), C. of C., Prytanean Alumnae, Delta Gamma. Republican. Club: Soroptimist (dir. 1976, 86) (Walnut Creek). Home: 1101 Scots Ln Walnut Creek CA 94596-5432 Office: 1399 Ygnacio Valley Rd Ste 34 Walnut Creek CA 94598-2831

MACKENZIE, LINDA ALICE, alternative medicine and awareness company executive, entertainer, educator, hypnotherapist; b. Bronx, N.Y., June 24, 1949; d. Gino Joseph and Mary J. (Damon) Arale; m. John Michael Lassourreille, Aug. 7, 1968 (div. 1975); 1 child, Lisa Marie Lassourreille; m. Donald John Mackenzie, July 2, 1978 (div. 1982). Student Richmond Coll., 1967-68, West L.A. Community Coll., 1978-81. Spl. rep. N.Y. Telephone Co., White Plains, 1968-71; asst. mgr. Paul Holmes Real Estate Inc., Richmond, N.Y., 1974-77; telcom applications specialist engring. Continental Airlines, L.A., 1977-83; data transmission specialist Western Airlines, Los Angeles, 1983-87; owner Computers on Consignment, El Segundo, Calif., 1984-94; cons. Caleb Feb. Credit Union, Las Vegas, Nev., 1985, Nat. Dissemenators, Las Vegas, 1985, Vega & Assocs. Prodn. Div., 1987, Uptech/Downtech, 1986, Dollar Rent-a-Car, 1987, Pomona Sch. Dist., 1987, Advanced Digital Networks, 1987, State Senate, 1988, Nordstroms, 1988, Flying Tigers, 1988, Fed. Express, 1989, Sita/ITS, 1990-92, Neutrogena, 1991, B & B Computers, 1992; mktg. cons. AT&T, L.A., 1984-85, Radio KPSL, 1995—, Carter Broadcasting, Talk America, 1995—, WDRC, 1995, WXLW, 1995; host Creative Health and Spirit Radio Show, 1995—; owner Creative Health & Spirit, Manhattan Beach, Calif., 1995—. Author: The World Within, 1983, Inner Insights-The Book of Charts, 1995. Active Calif. Lobbyists for Conservation, 1986. Contbr.: Am. Anthology Poetry, 1987, 88., Poetic Voices of America, 1988. Recipient Alexander award Met. Mus. Art, N.Y., 1967. Mem. Nat. Assn. Female Execs., Am. Bd. Hypnotherapists, Am. Inst. Hypnotherapy, Manhattan Beach C. of C. Republican. Clubs: Marina City, Manhattan Beach Women's. Avocations: painting, creative writing, aerobic dance, skiing, travel.

MACKENZIE-WOOD, MELODY, entrepreneur; b. Portsmouth, Va., Dec. 13, 1955; d. Herbert Marion and Carolyn (Tarkenton) Criswell; m. David Mackenzie-Wood. BS in English & Speech Edn. with honors, U. Tenn., 1977. Pub. rels. Reliance Group Holdings, N.Y.C., 1981-85; human rels./employee rels. rep. Broad Inc./SunAmerica, L.A., 1985-92; CEO, founder, coach, entrepreneur, corp. trainer, spkr. Lifeworks Resources; motivational spkr., tchr. in field. Office: Lifeworks Resources 645 N Beau Chene Dr Ste 14 Mandeville LA 70471

MACKETY, CAROLYN JEAN, laser medicine and nursing consultant; b. Chgo., Feb. 27, 1932; d. Gerald J. and Minnette (Buis) Kruyf; m. Robert Martin, Oct. 3, 1952 (div.); m. Armand Mackety, Apr. 15, 1972 (div.); children: Daniel, David, Steven, Martin, Laura Fitzgerald. RN, Hackley Hosp., Muskegon, Mich., 1969; BA, Coll. St. Francis, Joliet, Ill., 1977; MA, Columbia Pacific U., San Rafael, Calif., 1987. Dir. surg. svcs. Grant Med. Ctr., Columbus, Ohio, 1981-84; pres. Laser Cons., Inc., Chgo., 1984-86; v.p. Laser Ctrs. Am., Cin., 1986-88; nursing adminstr. Med. Ctr. Hosp., Burlington, Vt., 1988-91; cons. Colan, Inc., Holland, Mich., 1991—; dir. perioperative svcs. Mercy Hosp., Muskegon, Mich., 1991-95, dir. critical care and emergency rm., 1996—, continuous quality improvement instr.; mgmt. infor. systems workgroup Sister O Mery Corp., Farmington, Mich. Contbr. articles to profl. jours. Deacon 1st Reformed Ch., Holland, Mich., 1992—, parish nurse, 1995—, leader children in worship, 1994—. Recipient nursing excellence award Am. Soc. for Lasers Medicine and Surgery, 1991. Mem. Assn. Operating Rm. Nurses (mem. nursing practice com., data element com.), Am. Soc. Laser Medicine (nursing excellence award 1992), Mich. Orgn. Nurse Execs.

MACKEY, NILOUFER V., mathematics educator; b. Bombay; d. Vishram and Kamela (Khan) Masoji; m. D. Steven Mackey. BS, St. Xavier's Coll., Bombay; PhD, SUNY, Buffalo, 1995. Asst. prof. Western Mich. U., Kalamazoo, 1995—. Contbr. articles to profl. jours. Am. fellow AAUW, 1996. Mem. Am. Math. Soc., Math. Assn. Am., Soc. for Indsl. and Applied Math., Assn. for Women in Math., Assn. for Women in Sci., Internat. Linear Algebra Soc. Office: Western Mich U Dept Math and Statistics Kalamazoo MI 49008

MACKEY, SALLY SCHEAR, retired religious organization administrator; b. Seattle, Feb. 17, 1930; d. Rillmond Weible and Helen Annajane (Bovee) Schear; m. Hallie Willis Mackey, May 22, 1953; children: Melinda Kay, John Mark, Heather Lynn. BA, U. Wash., 1951; postgrad., San Francisco Theol. Sem., 1951-53. Teenage program dir., camp dir. YWCA, Seattle, 1953-55; sponsor, devel. Wash. Assn. Chs. Immigration and Refugee Program (affiliate Ch. World Svc.), Seattle, 1979-85, dir., 1985-90; bd. dirs., v.p. Ch. Coun. Greater Seattle, 1974-84; bd. dirs. Wash. Assn. Chs., 1976-79; mem. Gen. Assembly Mission Coun. Presbyn. Ch., N.Y.C., 1979-83, adv. com. on ecumenical rels., Presbyn. Ch. (U.S.A.), Louisville, 1989-92; Presbyn. Ch. (U.S.A.); del. to Caribbean Area Coun. World Alliance Reformed Chs., 1987-92. Home: 2127 SW 162nd St Seattle WA 98166-2654

MAC'KIE, PAMELA S., lawyer; b. Jackson, Miss., Jan. 2, 1956; d. Charles Edward and Betty Jo (Moore) Spell; children: John Greene IV, Ann Katherine. BS, Delta State U., Cleveland, Miss., 1978; JD, U. Miss., Oxford, 1984. Bar: Miss. 1984, Fla. 1986. Assoc. Cummings & Lockwood, Naples, Fla., 1985-93; prin. Pamela S. Mac'Kie, P.A., Naples, 1993-95, pres., 1995—. Pres. Naples Better Govt., 1992-95; pres.-elect Women's Rep. Club, Naples, 1994; county commr. Collier County Bd., Naples, 1994—; dir. Youth Haven, 1992, YMCA, 1993, Collier County Women's Polit. Caucus, 1992—. Recipient Pro Bono award Fla. Bar, 1990, Leadership Collier C. of C., Naples, 1991. Recipient Pro Bono award Fla. Bar, 1990; grad. Leadership Collier, Naples, 1991, Leadership S.W. Fla., 1995. Republican. Episcopalian. Office: Ste 201 5551 Ridgewood Dr Naples FL 33963

MACKIEWICZ, LAURA, advertising agency executive. Formerly with D'Arcy Advt.; with BBDO, Chgo., 1973—, now sr. v.p., dir. broadcast and print svcs. Office: BBDO Chgo 410 N Michigan Ave Chicago IL 60611-4211*

MACKINNON, CATHARINE A., lawyer, law educator, legal scholar, writer; d. George E. and Elizabeth V. (Davis) MacKinnon. BA in Govt. magna cum laude with distinction, Smith Coll., 1969; JD, Yale U., 1977, PhD in Polit. Sci., 1987. Vis. prof. U Chgo., Harvard U., Stanford U, Yale U., others, Osgoode Hall, York U., Canada; prof. of law U. Mich., 1990—. Author: Sexual Harassment of Working Women, 1979, Feminism Unmodified, 1987, Toward a Feminist Theory of the State, 1989, Only Words, 1993. Office: U Michigan Law School Ann Arbor MI 48109-1215

MACKINNON, PEGGY LOUISE, public relations executive; b. Florence, Ariz., June 18, 1945; d. Lacy Donald Gay and Goldie Louise (Trotter) Martin; m. Ian Dixon Mackinnon, Oct. 20, 1973. BA, San Jose State U., 1967, postgrad., 1968. Cert. secondary tchr., Calif. Tchr. Las Lomas High Sch., Walnut Creek, Calif., 1968-69; edn. officer Ormond Sch., Sydney, Australia, 1970-72; tchr. Belconnen High Sch., Canberra, Australia, 1972-73; temp. exec. sec. various orgns., London, 1973-75; mktg. mgr. Roadtown Wholesale, Tortola, British Virgin Islands, 1975-80; sr. v.p., gen. mgr. Hill & Knowlton Inc., Denver, 1981-96; pres. Peggy Mackinnon Inc., Denver, 1996—. Bd. dirs. Rocky Mountain Poison and Drug Found., Denver, 1984-87, Denver C. of C., Boy Scouts Am., Denver coun. Mem. Pub. Relations Soc. Am. (accredited). Home and Office: Apt 21 9200 Cherry Creek South Dr Denver CO 80231-4018

MACKLIN, RUTH, bioethics educator; b. Newark, Mar. 27, 1938; d . Hyman and Frieda (Yaruss) Chimacoff; m. Martin Macklin, Sept. 1, 1957 (div. June 1969): children: Meryl, Shelley Macklin Taylor. BA with distinction, Cornell U., 1958; MA in Philosophy, Case Western Res. U., 1966, PhD in Philosophy, 1968. Instr. in philosophy Case Western Res. U., Cleve., 1967-68, asst. prof., 1968-71, assoc. prof., 1971-76; assoc. for behavioral studies The Hastings Ctr., Hastings-on-Hudson, N.Y., 1976-80; vis. assoc. prof. Albert Einstein Coll. Medicine, Bronx, N.Y., 1977-78, assoc. prof., 1978-84, prof. dept. epidemiology and social medicine, 1984—; cons. NIH, 1986—; advisor WHO, Geneva, 1989: apptd. mem. White House Adv. Com. on Human Radiation Experiments, Washington, 1994—. Author: Man, Mind and Morality, 1982, Mortal Choices, 1987, Enemies of Patients, 1993, Surrogates and Other Mothers, 1994; contbr. articles to ethics, law and med. jours. Fellow The Hastings Ctr., Inst. Medicine of NAS, Am. Philos. Assn. (life), Am. Pub. Health Assn., Am. Soc. Law, Medicine and Ethics; mem. Internat. Assn. Bioethics (bd. dirs.), Am. Assn. Bioethics (bd. dirs.), Phi Beta Kappa. Democrat. Office: A Einstein Coll Medicine Dept Epidemiology & Social Medicine 1300 Morris Park Ave Bronx NY 10461-1926

MACKNIGHT, CAROL BERNIER, educational administrator; b. Quincy, Mass., Apr. 12, 1938; d. Harold Nelson and Marguerite (Norris) Bernier; m. William J. MacKnight, Aug. 19, 1967. BS, Ithaca Coll., N.Y., 1960; MM, Manhattan Sch. Mus., N.Y.C., 1961; Dipl., Fontainebleau Sch. Music/Art, France, 1963; EdD, U. Mass., 1973. Asst. to supt. Falmouth (Mass.) pub. schs., 1975-76; dir. bus., mgmt., engring. prog. Sch. Bus. Adminstrn. U. Mass., Amherst, 1976-79; assoc. dir. continuing edn. U. Mass., 1979-82, dir. Office Instructional Tech., 1982—; trustee New Eng. Regional Computer Program, Inc., 1986-92; bd. dirs. Info. Sys. and Bus. Exch., 1992-93; keynote spkr. Australian Soc for Computers in Learning in Tertiary Edn. Conf., Adelaide, Australia, 1996. Editor Jour. Computing in Higher Edn., 1988—, Jour. Info. Sys. for Mgrs., 1992-93; mem. editorial rev. bd. Jour. of Computer-Based Instrn., 1988-91; author/editor computer progs.; contbr. articles to profl. jours. CDC grantee, 1986, Regents of Boston grantee, 1988, Lilly Fellow Mentor, 1991-92. Mem. ACM, Assn. for Computing Machinery, Educom, Soc. Applied Learning Tech., New England Regional Computer Program. Office: Office Info Tech U Mass Lederle Grad Res Ctr Amherst MA 01003

MACLACHLAN, PATRICIA, author. Tchr. English Bennett Jr. H.S., Manchester, Conn., 1973-79; vis. lectr. Smith Coll., 1968—. Author: Through Grandpa's Eyes, 1980, Arthur, For the Very First Time, 1980, Moon, Stars, Frogs, and Friends, 1980, Mama One, Mama Two, 1982, Cassie Binegar, 1982, Tomorrow's Wizard, 1982, Seven Kisses in a Row, 1983, Unclaimed Treasures, 1984, Sarah, Plain and Tall, 1985 (Newberry medal 1986), The Facts and Fictions of Minna Pratt, 1988, Journey, 1991, Baby, 1993, Three Names, 199, All the Places to Love, 1994, Skylark, 1994. Address: care HarperCollins 10 E 53d St New York NY 10022*

MACLAINE, SHIRLEY, actress; b. Richmond, Va., Apr. 24, 1934; d. Ira O. and Kathlyn (MacLean) Beatty; m. Steve Parker, Sept. 17, 1954 (div.); 1 child, Stephanie Sachiko. Ed. high sch. Appearances include (Broadway plays) Me and Juliet, 1953, Pajama Game, 1954, (films) The Trouble With Harry, 1954, Artists and Models, 1954, Around the World in 80 Days, 1955-56, Hot Spell, 1957, The Matchmaker, 1957, The Sheepman, 1957, Some Came Running, 1958 (Fgn. Press award 1959), Ask Any Girl, 1959 (Silver Bear award as best actress Internat. Berlin Film Festival), Career, 1959, Can-Can, 1959, The Apartment, 1959 (Best Actress prize Venice Film Festival), Children's Hour, 1960, The Apartment, 1960, Two for the Seesaw, 1962, Irma La Douce, 1963, What A Way to Go, The Yellow Rolls Royce, 1964, John Goldfarb Please Come Home, 1965, Gambit and Woman Times Seven, 1967, The Bliss of Mrs. Blossom, Sweet Charity, 1969, Two Mules for Sister Sara, 1969, Desperate Characters, 1971, The Possession of Joel Delaney, 1972, The Other Half of the Sky: A China Memoir, 1975, The Turning Point, 1977, Being There, 1979, A Change of Seasons, 1980, Loving Couples, 1980, Terms of Endearment, 1983 (Acad. award 1984, Golden Globe-Best Actress), Cannonball Run II, 1984, Madame Sousatzka, 1988 (Best Actress Venice Film Festival, Golden Globe-Best Actress), Steel Magnolias, 1989, Waiting For the Light, 1990, Postcards From the Edge, 1990, Defending Your Life, 1991, Used People, 1992, Wrestling Ernest Hemingway, 1993, Guarding Tess, 1994, Evening Star, 1995, Mrs. Winterbourne, 1996; (TV shows) Shirley's World, 1971-72, Shirley MacLaine: If They Could See Me Now, 1974-75, Gypsy in My Soul, 1975-76, Where Do We Go From Here?, 1976-77, Shirley MacLaine at the Lido, 1979, Shirley MacLaine...Every Little Movement, 1980 (Emmy award 1980), (TV movie) Out On A Limb, 1987; prodr., co-dir. documentary: China The Other Half of the Sky; star U.S. tour stage musical Out There Tonight, 1990; author: Don't Fall Off the Mountain, 1970, The New Celebrity Cookbook, 1973, You Can Get There From Here, 1975, Out on a Limb, 1983, Dancing in the Light, 1985, It's All in the Playing, 1987, Going Within: A Guide for Inner Transformation, 1989, Dance While You Can, 1991; editor: McGovern: The Man and His Beliefs, 1972. *

MAC LAM, HELEN, periodical editor; b. N.Y.C., Aug. 17, 1933; d. Forrest Mearl and Bertha Margaret (Herzberger) Keen; m. David Carlyle MacLam, Feb. 7, 1953; children: Timothy David, David Andrew. AB Sociology,

Heidelberg Coll., 1961; AMLS, U. Mich., 1967; MA African Am. Studies, Boston U., 1978. Dep. clerk Mcpl. Ct., Tiffin, Ohio, 1962-64; subprofessional asst. Heidelberg Coll. Libr., Tiffin, Ohio, 1964-66; collection devel. libr. social scis. Dartmouth Coll. Libr., Hanover, N.H., 1967-83; social scis. editor Choice Mag., Middletown, Conn., 1983—; cons. in field; spkr. in field. Editorial bd. Multicultural Review, 1992-95; contbr. articles to profl. jours. Bd. dirs. Headrest, 1976-80, Hanover Consumer Coop. Soc., 1969-72. Recipient Grant award Rsch. Program for Ethnic Studies Librarianship Fisk U., 1975. Mem. Nat. Assn. Ethnic Studies (pres. 1985-87, assoc. editor publs. 1980-83), African Studies Assn., Africana Libs. Coun. (exec. bd. 1989-91), Am. Soc. Indexers, Freelance Editorial Assn., Women in Scholarly Publishing, Assn. Coll. and Rsch. Librs. (New England chpt.). Home: 185 Upper Loveland Rd Norwich VT 05055-9724 Office: Choice Mag 100 Riverview Ctr Middletown CT 06457-3401

MACLEAN, JUDITH E., writer, editor; b. L.A., May 13, 1946; d. Fred M. and Dorothy C. (Schmidt) MacL. BA, Rice U., 1969; postgrad., Duquesne U., 1970-71; postgrad. lang. study, Sorbonne U., 1966. Family therapist Families Together, Pitts., 1974-76; reporter In These Times, Chgo., 1976-77; co-chmn. New Am. Movement, Chgo., 1977-79; editor Am. Soc. on Aging, San Francisco, 1980-85; freelance writer, editor San Francisco, 1986—; instr. U. Calif. Berkeley ext., San Francisco, 1994-95, Support Ctr., San Francisco, 1992-93. Co-author: (book) Women Take Care, 1986; contbr. articles/stories to publs. Newsletter editor: Harvey Milk Lesbian and Gay Dem. Club, San Francisco, 1982-85, polit. action chmn., 1986-87; mem. nat. com. New Am. Movement, Pitts., 1972-76; mem. Nicaragua Solidarity Brigarde, Leon, Nicaragua, 1986. Named Vol. of Yr. Harvey Milk Lesbian and Gay Dem. Club, San Francisco, 1986. Mem. Media Alliance.

MACLELLAND, JACKIE L., English educator; b. Kaufman, Tex., Nov. 13, 1940; d. Grady and Juanita (Richman) Hill; m. C.G. MacLelland III, Dec. 18, 1965; children: Charles G. IV, Russell, Stephanie. BA, U. Tex. Dallas, Richardson, 1980; MFA in Painting and Drawing, Tex. Woman's U., 1986, MA, 1990, PhD, 1995. Pres., co-owner Ambience, Mesquite, Tex., 1965-84; pres. MacLelland & Son, Inc., Mesquite, 1990-95; editor Women's Caucus for Art, Phila., 1990-92, asst. to nat. pres., 1990-92; instr. art history Trinity Valley C.C., Tirrell, Tex., 1990-95; dir. galleries Collin County C.C., Plano, Tex., 1994-95; prof. English Baiko Jo U., Shimonoseki, Japan, 1995—. Author: High Heels, 1994; contbr. articles to profl. jours. Planning mem. Planning and Zoning, Mesquite, 1970's; com. mem. Performing Arts Co., Mesquite, 1980's. Lavon B. Fulwiler scholar Tex. Woman's U., Denton, 1993. Mem. Phi Kappa Phi. Mailing: PO Box 852261 Mesquite TX 75185 Home: 2227 Berry Rd Mesquite TX 75181 Office: Baiko Jo Univ, Shimonoseki 751, Japan

MACMANUS, SUSAN ANN, political science educator, researcher; b. Tampa, Fla., Aug. 22, 1947; d. Harold Cameron and Elizabeth (Riegler) MacM. BA cum laude, Fla. State U., 1968, PhD, 1975; MA, U. Mich., 1969. Instr. Valencia Community Coll., Orlando, Fla., 1969-73; rsch. asst. Fla. State U., 1973-75; asst. prof. U. Houston, 1975-79, assoc. prof., 1979-85, dir. M of Pub. Adminstrn. program, 1983-85, rsch. assoc. Ctr Pub. Policy 1982-85; prof., dir. PhD program Cleve. State U., 1985-87; prof. pub. adminstrn. and polit. sci., U. South Fla., Tampa, 1987—, chairperson dept. govt. and internat. affairs, 1987-93; vis. prof. U. Okla., Norman, 1981—; field rsch. assoc. Brookings Instn., Washington, 1977-82, Columbia U., summer 1979, Princeton (N.J.) U., 1979—, Nat. Acad. Pub. Adminstrn., Washington, summer 1980, Cleve. State U., 1982-83, Westat, Inc., Washington, 1983—. Author: Revenue Patterns in U.S. Cities and Suburbs: A Comparative Analysis, 1978, Federal Aid to Houston, 1983, (with others) Governing A Changing America, 1984, (with Francis T. Borkowski) Visions for The Future: Creating New Institutional Relationships Among Academia, Business, Government, and Community, 1989, Reapportionment and Representation in Florida: A Historical Collection, 1991, Doing Business with Government: Federal, State, Local and Foreign Government Purchasing Practices for Every Business and Public Institution, 1992, Young v. Old: Generational Combat in the 21st Century, 1996; writer manuals in field; mem. editorial bds. various jours., contbr. articles to jours. and chpts. to books. Bd. dirs. Houston Area Women's Ctr., 1977, past pres., v.p. fin., treas.; mem. LWV, Gov.'s Coun. Econ. Advisers, 1988-90, Harris County (Tex.) Women's Polit. Caucus, Houston; bd. dirs. USF Rsch. Found., Inc. Recipient U. Houston Coll. Social Scis. Teaching Excellence award, 1977, Herbert J. Simon Award for best article in 3d vol. Internat. Jour. Pub. Adminstrn., 1981, Theodore & Venette Askounes-Ashford Disting. Scholar award U. South Fla., 1991, Disting. Rsch. Scholar award, 1991; Ford Found. fellow, 1967-68; grantee Valencia Community Coll. Faculty, 1972, U. Houston, 1976-77, 79, 83; Fulbright Rsch. scholar, Korea, 1989. Mem. Am. Polit. Sci. Assn. (program com. 1983-84, chair sect. intergovtl. rels., award 1989, mem. exec. coun. 1994—, pres.-elect sect. urban politics 1994-95, pres. sect. urban politics 1995-96), So. Polit. Sci. Assn. (v.p. 1990-91, pres.-elect 1992-93, pres. 1993-94, V.O. key award com. 1983-84, best paper on women and politics 1988), Midwest Polit. Sci. Assn., Western Polit. Sci. Assn., Southwestern Polit. Sci. Assn. (local arrangements com. 1982-83, profession com. 1977-80), ASPA (nominating com. Houston chpt. 1983, bd. mem. Suncoast chpt., pres.-elect 1991, Lilly award 1992), Policy Studies Orgn. (mem. editorial bd. jour. 1981—, exec. coun. 1983-85), Women's Caucus Polit. Sci. (portfolio pre-decision rev. com. 1982-83, projects and programs com. 1981, fin.-budget com. 1980-81), Acad. Polit. Sci., Mcpl. Fln. Officers Assn., Phi Beta Kappa, Phi Kappa Phi, Pi Sigma Alpha (mem. exec. coun. 1994—), Pi Alpha Alpha. Republican. Methodist. Home: 2506 Collier Pky Land O'Lakes FL 34639-5228 Office: U South Fla Dept Govt & Internat Affairs Soc 107 Tampa FL 33620

MACMANUS, YVONNE CRISTINA, editor, videoscripter, writer, consultant; b. L.A., Mar. 18, 1931; d. Daniel S. and Josefina Lydia (Pina) MacM. Student, UCLA, NYU, U. So. Calif., U. London. Assoc. editor Bobbs-Merrill, N.Y.C., 1960-63; TV producer Leo Burnett Ltd., London, 1965-66; founding editor, editor-in-chief Leisure Books, L.A., 1970-72; tchr. pub. course UCLA Extension, 1972; sr. editor Major Books, 1974-77; co-pub., editor in chief Timely Books, Chattanooga, 1977; co-owner Write On...!, Chattanooga, 1977—; corp. videoscripting PR & video tng., 1983—; tchr. writing workshop Chattanooga State C.C., 1996. Author: Better Luck Elsewhere, 1966, With Fate Conspire, 1974, Bequeath Them No Tumbled House, 1977, Deadly Legacy, 1981, The Presence, 1982, You Can Write A Romance, 1983, (updated and expanded) 1996, (play) Hugo, 1990; contbr. articles to profl. publs. Home and Office: 4040 Mountain Creek Rd Ste 1304 Chattanooga TN 37415-6025

MAC MASTER, HARRIETT SCHUYLER, retired elementary education educator; b. Maxbass, N.D., Nov. 5, 1916; d. Hugh Riley and Christine (Park) Schuyler; m. Jay Myron Mac Master, May 27, 1944; children: Jay Walter, Robert Hugh, Anne Schuyler. BS, Trenton State Coll., 1971, postgrad., 1971; grad., Inst. for Children's Lit., 1993. Tchr. Woodfern Elem. Sch., Neshanic, N.J., 1972-87; ret., 1987; freelance writer elem. sci. program Silver Burdett Co., 1983. Organizer, vol. Phone Friend for Latchkey Children, Somerset County; elder local Presbyn. Ch. Fellow AAUW, LWV, Older Women's League. Republican. Home: 24 Meadowbrook Dr Somerville NJ 08876-4810

MACMILLAN, CATHERINE COPE, restaurant owner; b. Sacramento, Mar. 3, 1947; d. Newton A. Cope and Marilyn (Jacobs) Combrink; m. Thomas C. MacMillan, Dec. 18, 1967 (div. Jan. 1984); children: Corey Jacobs, Andrew Cope. BA, U. Calif., 1969; MBA, Calif. State U., Sacramento, 1978; JD, McGeorge Sch. Law, 1993. Bar: Calif. 1994. Pub. health microbiologist County of Sacramento, 1969-74; pres., gen. mgr. The Firehouse Restaurant, Sacramento, 1980—; bd. dirs. Westamerica Bank, San Rafael, Calif. Chmn. Sacramento Conv. and Visitors Bur., 1987-88; pres. Old Sacramento Propery Owners Coun., 1987; mem. Sacramento Sports Commn, 1988-89. Mem. Calif. Restaurant Assn. (bd. dirs.), Sacramento Restaurant Assn. (restaurateur of yr. 1983), Old Sacramento Citizens and Merchants Assn. (chmn. bd. dirs. 1984), Sacramento Met. C. of C. (bus. woman of yr. 1992), Calif. State U.-Sacramento Alumni Assn. (sch. of bus. alumna award 1992), Sacramento Capital Club (pres. 1995). Office: The Firehouse Restaurant 1112 2nd St Sacramento CA 95814-3204

MACMINN, PAMELA LEE See KOPACK, PAMELA LEE

MACMURREN, MARGARET PATRICIA, secondary education educator, consultant; b. Newark, Nov. 4, 1947; d. Kenneth F. and Doris E. (Lounsberry) Bartro; m. Harold MacMurren, Nov. 21, 1970. BA, Paterson State U., 1969; MA, William Paterson Coll., 1976; postgrad., Jersey City State Coll., 1976—. Tchr. Byram (N.J.) Twp. Schs., 1969-77; learning cons., child study team coord. Andover Regional Schs., Newton, N.J., 1977—. Mem. NEA, N.J. Edn. Assn., N.J. Assn. Learning Cons., Sussex Coutny Assn. Learning Cons. (pres. 1982-83, 93-94, sec.-treas. 1991-92, v.p. 1992-93), Andover Regional Edn. Assn. (pres. 1986-87). Home: 4 Systema Pl Sussex NJ 07461-2833 Office: Andover Regional Schs 707 Limecrest Rd Newton NJ 07860-8801

MACO, TERI R., accountant; b. Allentown, Pa., Nov. 4, 1953; d. Francis M. and Jacqueline K. (Becker) Regan; m. Bruce F. Maco, Oct. 1, 1983; children: Adam S., Alex M. BSChemE with honors, Lehigh U., 1975; MBA with distinction, U. New Haven, 1979; cert. in sci., West Chester U., 1994. Supr. Ivory, Procter & Gamble Mfg. Co., S.I., N.Y., 1975-77; asst. mgr. processing Chesebrough-Ponds, Inc., Clinton, Conn., 1977-81, sec. and bd. dirs. credit union, 1980; group supr. Chesebrough-Ponds, Inc., Ft. Washington, Pa., 1981-83; mgr. processing Johnson & Johnson, Ft. Washington, Pa., 1983-84, mgr. nat. planning, 1984-87; group mgr. acctg. Johnson & Johnson, Ft. Washington, 1987-93; pres. Child Placement Network, Inc., Norristown, Pa., 1989-93; tchr. Phoenixville (Pa.) H.S., 1993-94; pres. T. Maco & Assocs., Inc., 1996—; treas. Borough of Collegeville, 1995—; treas. United Fund Collegeville-Trappe, Inc., 1996—; developer computer-based tng. program; pres, T. Maco & Assocs., 1996—. Author: Capital Asset Pricing Model: Capital Budgeting Applications (NAA Manuscript award 1979). Recipient Johnson & Johnson Achievement awards, 1989, 92. Democrat. Roman Catholic. Home: 4183 Ironbridge Dr Collegeville PA 19426-1189

MACON, CAROL ANN GLOECKLER, micro-computer data base management company executive; b. Milw., Mar. 25, 1942; d. William Theodore and Gwendolyn Martha (Rice) Gloeckler; m. Jerry Lyn Macon, Aug. 28, 1981; children: Christian, Marie. BS in Edn. cum laude, U. Wis., Milw., 1969; postgrad., Midwestern State U., Wichita Falls, Tex., 1977, U. Tex., San Antonio, 1978, U. Colo., Colorado Springs. Tchr. Lubbock, Tex.; patient affairs coord. Cardiac Assocs., Colorado Springs; founder, CFO Macon Systems, Inc., Colorado Springs. Artist, Australia, Tex., Colo. Mem. Software Pubs. Assn., Colorado Springs Better Bus. Bur., Colorado Springs Fine Arts Ctr., Pikes Peak Rose Soc. (v.p.), Glen Eyrie Garden Soc., Bontanic Garden (mem. steering com.), Colo. Mountain Club, Phi Kappa Phi, Kappa Delta Pi, Sigma Tau Delta, Psi Chi.

MACON, MYRA FAYE, retired library director; b. Slate Springs, Miss., Sept. 29, 1937; d. Thomas Howard and Reba Elizabeth (Edwards) M. BS in Edn., Delta State U., 1959; MLS, La. State U., 1965; postgrad., U. Akron, Ohio; EdD, Miss. State U., 1977. Librarian Greenwood (Miss.) Jr. High Sch., 1959-62, Greenwood High Sch., 1962-63, Grenada (Miss.) High Sch., 1963-64; library supr. Cuyahoga Falls (Ohio) City Schs., 1964-71; assoc. prof. U. Miss., Oxford, 1971-83; dir. libraries Delta State U., Cleve., 1983—. Editor: School Library Media Services for Handicapped; editor: ANRT Newsletter, Miss. Libraries; contbr. articles to profl. jours. Mem. ALA, Southeastern Library Assn., Miss. Library Assn., Exch. Club, Phi Delta Kappa, Beta Phi Mu, Delta Kappa Gamma, Omicron Delta Kappa. Home: Rt 3 Box 215A Calhoun City MS 38916 Office: WB Robers Library Delta State U Cleveland MS 38733

MACPIKE, LORALEE, literature educator; b. Beverly Hills, Calif., Mar. 6, 1939; d. Frederick Lea and Loretta Alice (Jazowick) MacP.; m. R. Craig D. Sawyer, June 6, 1960 (div. July 14, 1976); children: Gwynn Anne Sawyer Ostrom. BA, Bryn Mawr Coll., 1960; MA, Calif. State U., 1970; PhD, UCLA, 1976. Asst. prof. U. Hawaii, Honolulu, 1975-78; from assoc. prof. to prof. Calif. State U., San Bernardino, 1978—; editor, publisher The Lesbian Rev. of Books, Altadena, Calif., 1994—. Author: Dostoevsky's Dickens, 1981; editor: There's Something I've Been Meaning to Tell You, 1989; contbr. articles to profl. jours. AAUW fellow, 1974. Office: Calif State U 5500 University Pkwy San Bernardino CA 92407

MACQUEEN, CHER, newscaster, sportscaster; b. Kansas City, Mo., Mar. 20, 1952; . Ira Raymond and Peggy Estelle (Turner) Milks. AA in Liberal Arts, L.A. Valley Coll., 1982; BS in Broadcasting, U. New York, Albany, 1993; grad., Barbizon Sch. of Modeling, 1996. Lic. radio-TV operator. Personnel specialist U.S. Army, Honolulu, Hawaii, 1973-75; adminstrv. specialist U.S. Army, San Francisco, Calif., 1975-77; broadcast journalist U.S. Army, Vicenza, Italy, 1977-80; radio traffic specialist Armed Forces Radio & TV, L.A., 1980-84, radio prodn. specialist, 1984-86; supr. broadcast support specialist Armed Forces Radio & TV, Sun Valley, Calif., 1986-90; broadcast support mgr, Armed Forces Radio & TV, Sun Valley, 1990-91, internal info. mgr., 1991-94, news and sports specialist, 1994—. Mem. DAV (life), Armed Forces Broadcasters Assn. (v.p. L.A., 1991-93). Home: 23306 Stoneycreek Way Moreno Valley CA 92557 Office: Armed Forces Radio & TV Svc 1363 Z St Bldg 2730 Riverside CA 92518-1700

MACRO, LUCIA ANN, editor; b. Rhinebeck, N.Y., May 15, 1959; d. Virgil Jordan and Jeannette Anastasia (Jakelski) M.; m. Richard Marchione, 1992. BA, Fordham U., Bronx, 1981. Asst. editor, editor Silhouette Books, N.Y.C., 1985—, sr. editor, 1989—; speaker in field nat. convs. Romance Writers Am., 1985—; interviewed Bus. Week, 1987, CNN, 1991, Sta. WNBC, various newspapers including N.Y. Daily News, Washington Post. Author articles Romantic Times, 1988-89, 93, Romance Writers Report, 1988-89. Recipient Rita award Romance Writers Am., 1990, 92, 94, 95. Democrat. Office: Silhouette Books 300 E 42nd St New York NY 10017-5947

MAC WATTERS, VIRGINIA ELIZABETH, singer, music educator, actress; b. Phila.; d. Frederick-Kennedy and Idoleein (Hallowell) Mac W.; m. Paul Abée, June 10, 1960. Grad., Phila. Normal Sch. for Tchrs., 1933; student, Curtis Inst. Music, Phila., 1936. With New Opera Co., N.Y.C., 1941-42; artist-in-residence Ind. U. Sch. Music, 1957-58; assoc. prof. U. Ind. Sch. Music, 1958-68, prof. voice, 1968-82, prof. emeritus, 1982—. Singer: leading roles Broadway mus. Rosalinda, 1942-44, Mr. Strauss Goes to Boston, 1945, leading opera roles New Opera Co., N.Y.C., 1941-42, San Francisco, 1944, N.Y.C. Ctr., 1946-51; leading soprano for reopening of Royal Opera House, Covent Garden, London, 1947-48, Guatemala, El Salvador, Cen. Am., 1948-49; debut at Met. Opera, N.Y.C., 1952; TV spls. on NBC include Menotti's Old Maid and the Thief, 1949, Would-be Gentleman (R. Strauss), 1955; leading singer with Met. Opera Co. on coast to coast tour of Die Fledermaus, 1951-52,, Met. Opera debut, N.Y.C., 1952, leading soprano Cen. City Opera Festival, Colo., 1952-56; performed with symphony orchs. in U.S., Can., S.Am.; concert recitalist U.S., Can., 1950-62; opened N.Y. Empire State Music Festival in Ariadne auf Naxos (Strauss), 1959; soloist Mozart Festival, Ann Arbor, Mich. Recipient Mile award Album Familiar Music, 1949, Ind. U. Disting. Tchg. award, 1979; named One of 10 Outstanding Women of the Yr.; Zeckwer Hahn Phila. Mus. Acad. scholar, 1941-42; MacWatters chair donated by New Auer Grand Concert Hall, U. Ind. Sch. Music. Mem. Nat. Fedn. of Music Clubs, Nat. Soc. Arts and Letters, Nat. Soc. Lit. and Arts, Soc. Am. Musicians, Nat. Assn. Tchrs. of Singing, Internat. Platform Assn., Sigma Alpha Iota. Club: Matinee Musical (hon. mem. Phila., Indpls. chpts.). Home: 3800 Arlington Rd Bloomington IN 47404-1347 Office: Ind U Sch Music Bloomington IN 47401

MACZULSKI, MARGARET LOUISE, corporate executive; b. Detroit, Apr. 1; d. Bohdan Alexander and Olga Louise (Martinuick) M. BS, Mich. State U. Mgr. meetings Nat. Assn. Realtors, Mktg. Inst., Chgo., 1977-82, mgr. mktg., 1982-83; regional sales mgr. Fairmont Hotels, Chgo., 1982; dir., mgr. trade shows and confs. Am. Broadcasting Co./Pub. Div., Wheaton, Ill., 1983-85; mgr. meeting and conf. planning Am. Soc. Personnel Adminstrn., Alexandria, Va., 1985-90; mgr. meeting and conv. planning Kraft Foods, Glenview, Ill., 1990-95, cons. mtgs. and spl. events, 1996—. Mem. Meeting Planners Internat., Greater Washington Soc. Assn. Execs. (past chmn. site inspection com.), Soc. Corporate Meeting Planners, Am. Soc. Assn. Execs., Nat. Assn. Exposition Execs., Mich. State U. Alumni Assn. (treas. D.C. chpt. 1987-90), Soc. for Corp. Mtg. Planners. Republican. Roman Catholic. Avocations: piano, swimming. Home: 3150 N Sheridan Rd Apt 24C Chicago IL 60657-4839 Office: Kraft Foods 1 Kraft Ct Glenview IL 60025-5066

MADAY, CHRISTINE VERGA, artist, illustrator; b. Cedarhurst, N.Y.; d. John Richard and Joan Margaret Verga; m. Joseph Edward Maday III; 1 child, Sandra Lynn. AAS, Fashion Inst. Tech., SUNY, N.Y.C., 1974. Textile designer trainee Massaki Design Studio, N.Y.C., 1974; textile artist Farid Kahn Designs, Unlimited, N.Y.C., 1974-76; display asst. Sears, Roebuck & Co., Valley Stream, N.Y., 1983—; freelance artist for greeting cards, illustrations. Recipient Watercolor award State of N.Y., 1981, 92; Newsday Art contest award, 1996, Decorative Artist's Workbook Mag. award, 1996. Mem. Tri-County Artists (Art award of Excellence 1996), Lawrence High Sch. Art Alumni Assn. (bd. dirs. 1994—).

MADDALENA, LUCILLE ANN, management executive; b. Plainfield, N.J., Nov. 8, 1948; d. Mario Anthony and Josephine Dorothy (Longo) M.; m. James Samonte Hohn, Sept. 7, 1975; children: Vincent, Nicholas, Mitchell. AA, Rider Coll., 1968; BS, Monmouth Coll., 1971; EdD, Rutgers U., 1978. Newscaster, dir. pub. relations Sta. WBRW, Bridgewater, N.J., 1971-73; editor-in-chief Commerce mag., New Brunswick, N.J., 1973-74; dir. pub. relations Raritan Valley Regional C. of C., New Brunswick, N.J., 1973-74; aide pub. relations to mayor City of New Brunswick, 1974; dir. communications United Way Cen. Jersey, New Brunswick, 1974-77; mgmt. cons. United Way Am., Alexandria, Va., 1977-78; pres., owner Maddalena Assocs., Chester, N.J., 1978—; sr. cons. United Research Co., Morristown, N.J., 1980-81; sr. ptnr., dir. OCD Group, Parsippany, N.J., 1984-87; chmn. bd. dirs. OCD Group (subs. Xicom Inc.), Morristown, N.J., 1988; pres. Morris Bus. Group, Chester, 1989—; adj. faculty Somerset County Coll., Bridgewater, N.J., 1970, Fairleigh Dickinson U., 1980; guest lectr. Rutgers U., New Brunswick, N.J., 1975-80; designer publicly offered seminars for Bell Atlantic, 1992—; cons. change Howmet, Alloy, Dover, N.J., 1993; consortium trainer Johnson & Johnson, 1988—. Author: A Communications Manual for Non-Profit Organizations, 1980; editor New Directions for Instl. Advancement, 1980-81. Chmn. pers. com., police com. Chester Borough Coun., 1984-87; pres. Chester Consolidation Study Commn., 1990. Recipient Mayor's Commendation City of New Brunswick, 1973, Chester Borough, N.J., 1988. Mem. AAUW, LWV, Nat. Assn. Press Women, N.J. Elected Women Officials, Kappa Delta Pi. Republican. Roman Catholic. Club: N.J. Sled Dog Assn. Home: 75 Melrose Dr Chester NJ 07930-2321 Office: Morris Bus Group 415 State Route 24 Chester NJ 07930-2919

MADDEN, HEATHER ANN, aluminum company executive; b. Sharon, Pa., Dec. 20, 1967; d. Edward Arthur and Mary Ann (McWilliams) M. BS in Bus., Salisbury (Md.) State U., 1991; MS in Bus., Johns Hopkins U., 1994. With Delmarva Aluminum Co., Inc., Delmar, Del., 1984-95, exec.'s asst., 1987-95, also dir., 1990—; instr. office sys. tech. Del. Tech. & C.C., Georgetown, 1995—. Vol. The Holly Ctr., Salisbury, 1992-94. Recipient Holly Svc. award The Holly Found., Salisbury, 1994. Home: 8300 Robin Hood Dr Salisbury MD 21804

MADDEN, SUSAN BROOKS, librarian; b. Portland, Oreg., Aug. 7, 1944; d. Raymond E. and Lorna (Wahner) Brooks; m. John Michael Madden, Nov. 18, 1967; children: Laura K. Williams, Brooks M. Madden; m. John C. Thompson, Oct. 31. BA, U. Portland, 1966; MALS, U. Denver, 1967. Dean's asst. Libr. Sch. U. Denver, 1966-67; reference and bookmobile libr. Clackamas County libr., Oregon City, Oreg., 1967-70, asst. dir., acquisitions, 1970-71; juvenile ct. libr. King County Libr. Sys., Seattle, 1972-80, young adult svcs. coord., 1980-88; coord. human resources King County Libr. Sys., 5, 1988-90, coord. lit., 1990—; founding bd. dirs. King County Lit. Coalition, Seattle, 1990—,Wash. Coalition Against Censorship, Seattle, 1980-90; cons. and speaker in field. Contbr. chpt. to book, articles to profl. jours. Mem. comty. adv. bd. Highline Sch. Dist., Burien, Wash., 1993-94; pres. S.W. Alliance for outh, Burien, 1992-93; mem. adv. bd. Wash. Tech. Coll., Kirkland, 1994-95. Recipient Allie Beth Martin award Pub. Libr. Assn., 1988, Matrix Table award Women in Comms., 1989, Pres.'s award Wash. Libr. Media Assn., 1989, Oreg. State Libr. scholar, 1966-67. Mem. ALA (officer), Pacific N.W. Libr. Assn., Wash. Libr. Assn., Solinas Soc., Pirhana Orgn., PNW Bead Soc. Democrat. Office: King county Libr Sys 300 8th Ave N Seattle WA 98109

MADDEN, TERESA DARLEEN, insurance agency owner; b. Dallas, Aug. 4, 1960; d. Tommy Joe Frederick Dodd and Mary Helen (Sterner) Smith; m. Kim Ashley Madden, June 2, 1989. Student, Tex. Tech U., 1978-81. Cert. ins. counselor. With personal lines svc. Charles R. Ervin Ins., Midland, Tex., 1981, Bryant Scalf Ins., Richardson, Tex., 1981-82; with comml. ins. svc. Street & Assocs. Inc., Dallas, 1982-84; with comml. ins. sales/svc. Hotchkiss Ins., Dallas, 1984-85; mgr. sales Abbott-Rose Ins. Agy., Dallas, 1985-89; owner Glenn-Madden & Assocs. Ins., Dallas, 1990—. Methodist. Office: Glenn Madden & Assocs Inc Ste 1470 9330 Lyndon B Johnson Fwy Dallas TX 75243-3436

MADDEN, THERESA MARIE, elementary education educator; b. Phila., Feb. 12, 1950; d. James Anthony and Marie Margaret (Clark) M. BA in Social Sci., Neumann Coll., 1977; postgrad., Beaver Coll.; Immaculata Coll. Cert. tchr., Pa. Tchr. elem. grades St. Anthony Sch., Balt., 1971-73, St. Mary-St. Patrick Sch., Wilmington, Del., 1973-74, Queen of Heaven Sch., Cherry Hill, N.J., 1974-77, St. Bonaventure Sch., Phila., 1977-78, 79-83, St. Stanislaus Sch., Lansdale, Pa., 1978-79; substitute tchr. various schs. Phila., 1983-84; tchr. 8th grade math. St. Cecilia Sch., Phila., 1984-94; tchr. math., vice prin. Corpus Christi Sch., Lansdale, Pa., 1994—; mem. visiting team Mid. States Assn., Phila., 1992; presenter workshops. Mem. Nat. Coun. Tchrs. Math., Pa. Coun. Tchrs. Math., Assn. Tchrs. Math. of Phila. and Vicinity. Roman Catholic. Office: Corpus Christi Sch 920 Sumneytown Pike Lansdale PA 19446-5414

MADDOCK, BARBARA B., human resources professional. Sr. v.p. human resources McGraw-Hill, Inc., N.Y.C. Office: McGraw-Hill Inc 1221 Ave of the Americas New York NY 10020*

MADDOCK, CHERYL JOANNE, charge nurse; b. Sandusky, Mich., May 30, 1948; d. Clinton Gerald Herbert and Marilyn Katherine Ling; m. Stephen Douglas Maddock, July 21, 1972 (div. Feb. 1976). Assoc., El Centro C.C., 1986; student, U. Tex., 1995—. RN, Tex.; LPN, Tex.; ACLS. Nurse aide, LPN Pt. Huron (Mich.) Hosp., 1966-69; nurse coronary care unit, intermediate LPN Mercy Hosp., Pt. Huron, 1969-72; LPN CCU Lawrence Hosp., Port Huron, Mich., 1969-72; nurse critical care unit St. Lawrence Hosp., Lansing, Mich., 1976-81; nurse St. Paul Med. Ctr., Dallas, 1981-83, Med. Arts Hosp., Dallas, 1983-86; charge nurse intermediate care St. Paul Med. Ctr., Dallas, 1981-83; nurse CCU Parkland Meml. Hosp., Dallas, 1986-87; night supr. Tex. Women's U. Campus Clinic, 1987-88; home health nurse Ventilator Mgmt., 1988-90; staff nurse, 1990-95; charge nurse cardiology-telemetry unit St. Paul Med. Ctr., Dallas, 1991-95; nurse agy. nursing ICUs various S.W. Tex. hosps., 1987-88. nurse asst. physician exams. summer camp St. Paul Ctr.-Salvation Army, Dallas, 1993-94. Home: 202 Oak Knoll Cir Apt 352B Lewisville TX 75067-8889 Office: St Paul Med Ctr 5909 Harry Hines Dallas TX 75235

MADDOCK, DIANA GAIL, visual artist, educator; b. Chgo., Nov. 5, 1938; d. Clark Edward and Kathleen (Maston) M. AA with honors, Lorain County C.C., Elyria, Ohio, 1988; BA magna cum laude, Baldwin-Wallace Coll., 1995. With G.D. Searle Pharms., Skokie, Ill., Northrop Corp., Rilling Meadows, Ill., Vickers, Bensenville, Ill., Elmhurst (Ill.) Meml. Hosp., Glen Ellyn (Ill.) Clinic; developer visual arts program, art instr. Asbury's Save Our Children, Elyria, Ohio, 1995—; profl. visual artist, 1989—; adj. art instr. Lorain County C.C., Elyria, 1996—; art instr. Firelands Assn. for Visual Arts, Oberlin, Ohio, 1996—. Works exhibited Very Spl. Arts Gallery, Washington, 1991—. Founder, vice chmn., Share Christmas, Inc., 1991—; mem. nominating com. Asbury United Meth. Ch., Elyria, 1995—. Recipient 1st Pl. award in painting, 1989, Artists award Ohio Arts Coun., 1991, Drahos award for best painting, 1994.

MADDOX, IRIS CAROLYN CLARK, secondary education educator; b. Wardell, Mo., Apr. 20, 1936; d. Newman Walter and Mary Elizabeth (Edney) Clark; m. James P. Maddox, June 4, 1954; children: James Steven, Sandra Jean. BS cum laude, Prairie View A&M U., 1983, MEd in Indsl.

Edn., 1984, MEd in Counseling., 1990. Cert. counselor and tchr., Tex. Tchr. Spring Branch Ind. Sch. Dist., Houston, 1982—; sec. Bus. Office Svcs. Adv. Com., Houston, 1991-92. Mem. Am. Vocat. Assn., Tex. Assn. Continuing Adult Edn., Nat. Assn. Classroom Educators in Bus. Edn., Chi Sigma Iota. Home: PO Box 430791 Houston TX 77243-0791

MADDOX, MARJORIE LEE (MARJORIE LEE MADDOX-HAFER), English educator; b. Columbus, Ohio, Mar. 24, 1959; d. William Maddox and Roberta Lee (Clark) Scurlock; m. Gary R. Hafer, June 5, 1993. BA in Lit., Wheaton Coll., 1981; MA in English, U. Louisville, 1985; MFA in Poetry, Cornell U., 1989. Editor The Cobb Group, Louisville, 1983-87; instr. U. Louisville, 1982-85, Cornell U., Ithaca, N.Y., 1987-90; asst. prof. English Lock Haven (Pa.) U., 1990-95, assoc. prof. English, 1995—. Author: Perpendicular As I, 1994 (Sandstone Pub. Nat. Poetry Book award), How to Fit God into a Poem, 1993, Ecclesia, 1996; ; contbr. more than 200 poems to profl. publs. Bread Loaf scholarship, Catskill Poetry scholarship; recipient Acad. of Am. Poets prize, Cornell's Chasen award; Va. Ctr. for the Creative Arts fellowship; Pa. State System of Higher Edn. grant. Mem. AWP, MLA. Episcopalian.

MADDOX-TOUNGARA, JEANNE, history educator, researcher; b. L.A., Jan. 24, 1950; d. Willie and L'Bertice (Cain) Maddox; 1 child, Macani. BA, UCLA, 1971, MA, 1972, PhD, 1980. From asst. to assoc. prof. history Nat. U. Côte d'Ivoire, Abidjan, 1976-87; asst. prof. history, continuing edn. lectr. Global Change program U. Va., Charlottesville, 1988-94; asst. prof. Howard U., Washington, 1987-88, 94—; lectr. Fgn. Svc. Inst., Dept. State, Washington, 1989—; cons. assessment history dept. N.C. A&T U., 1994; cons. African Am. Inst., 1994, African Devel. Found., 1988-93. Contbr. articles to profl. jours. Mem. Dem. Nat. Com. Fulbright-Hayes grantee, 1992-93. Mem. African Studies Assn., West African Rsch. Assn. (sec. 1995-96, rsch. grantee 1991), Manding Studies Assn., LWV, NOW, Amnesty Internat. Office: Howard U Dept History 2441 6th St NW Washington DC 20059

MADDUX, DONNA R., superintendent of schools; b. Lewistown, Mont., Sept. 1, 1944; d. Donald and Alice (Levens) Smail; widowed; children: Anita Rae, Angela Renee Maddux LaRoque. BA, U. Mont., 1971, MEd, 1979. Cert. document examiner. Tchr. pub. schs., Mont.; supt. schs. Flathead County Schs., Whitefish, Mont. Contbr. articles to profl. jours. Councilor City of Whitefish, 1988-93; bd. dirs. Flathead CARE, 1987—, Sunrift Ctr. for Sustainable Cmtys., Kalispell, Mont., Flathead County Mus.; pres. Dick Maddux Found., Whitefish, 1994—. Recipient Golden Rule award J.C. Penney, 1996, Woman of Distinction award Soroptimist, 1995. Mem. Whitefish Lake Golf Assn. (tournament com. 1992-95, Men's State chmn. 1994), Daybreak Rotary Club (co-editor newsletter 1995—), Phi Delta Kappa. Office: Flathead County Supt Schs 723 5th Ave E Kalispell MT 59937

MADDY, JANET MARIE, educator, dean of students; b. Crestline, Ohio, Feb. 20, 1939; d. Hubert Franklin and Mabel May (Hotelling) M. AA, Pasadena City Coll, 1959; BA, Calif. State U., L.A., 1965, MA, 1972. Instr. Calif. State Coll., L.A., fall 1965; tchr. phys. edn. Irving Jr. High, L.A. Unified Sch. Dist., spring 1966, Bret Harte Jr. High Sch., L.A. Unified Sch. Dist., 1966-67; tchr., phys. edn. tchr., dept. chair Walton Jr. High Sch.-Compton (Calif.) Unified Sch. Dist., 1967-72; tchr. phys. edn./coach Dominguez H.S., Compton, 1972-78; prin. Westchester Luth. Schs., L.A., 1978-84; tchr. phys. edn., dept. chair Nimitz Middle Sch., L.A. Unified Sch. Dist., Huntington Park, Calif., 1985-94, dean of students-C Track, 1994—; mem. shared decision making coun. Nimitz Middle Sch., Huntington Park, 1992-96; mentor tchr. selection com. L.A. Unified Sch. Dist., 1993-94; women in sports delegation to China, Citizen Amb. Program, Spokane, Wash., 1994, U.S. China Joint Conf. on Women's Issues, China, 1995. Synod womens orgn. bd. ELCA Women, L.A., 1990-93, 94—, chair references and counsel com. triennial nat. conf., Washington, 1993, del. triennial conv., Mpls., 1996; chair cmty. com. Police Activity League, Inglewood, Calif., 1990-93; co-chair Neighborhood Watch, Inglewood, 1988—. Comdr. USNR, ret., 1960-83. Mem. CAHPER, AAHPER, CTA, UTLA. Democrat. Lutheran. Home: 412 W Spruce Ave Inglewood CA 90301 Office: Nimitz Middle Sch 6021 Carmelita Ave Huntington Park CA 90255-3320

MADER, ELIZABETH B., public art consultant, artist; b. Norman, Okla., July 12, 1966; d. Mervin Louis Jr. and Helen Claudia (Hicks) Brownsberger; m. Blake M. Mader, 1996. Student, Outward Bound Leadership Tng., Colorado Springs, Colo., 1984, Nat. Outdoor Leadership Sch., Wyo., 1988; BA, Colo. Coll., 1988; MFA, U. Denver, 1993. Prodn. asst. The Wheetley Co., Skokie, Ill., 1989; rsch./tchg. asst. U. Denver, 1990-93, printshop coord., 1990-93, instr. art camp, 1991; owner Tabby Ant Fine Art, Denver, 1993—, Tabby Ant Pub. Art Cons., Denver Internat. Airport, 1994-96; mem. interagy. maintenance task force Mayor's Office of Art, Culture, and Film, City and County of Denver, 1995—. Editor: (pub. art maintenance manual) Denver International Airport Public Art Collection Maintenance Manual, 1996; works featured in solo shows, group exhbns. and comms. Grad. rsch./tchg. scholar U. Denver, 1990-93. Mem. Nat. Assn. for Self-Employed, Coll. Art Assn. Office: Denver Int Airport Pub Art 8500 Pena Blvd Denver CO 80249

MADEYA, ELIZABETH CATHERINE, customer service represenative; b. Cleve., Sept. 6, 1969; d. Arthur Otto Madeya and Carol Ann Matsko Tiwari. Circulation data specialist Penton Pub., Cleve., 1987-88; claims processor Colonial Ins. Co., Cleve., 1988-89; customer svc. rep. Kaufmann's, Parma, Ohio, 1989; traffic asst. Nationwide Advt. Svc., Cleve., 1990-95; customer svc. rep. Ameritech, Cleve., 1995—. Home: 10031 Pleasant Lakes Blvd P9 Cleveland OH 44130

MADISON, DEBORAH LEAFY, author, chef; b. West Hartford, Conn., June 21, 1945; d. John Herbert and Winifred (Law) Madison; m. Dan Welch, Mar. 17, 1979 (div. Nov. 1986); m. J. Patrick McFarlin, May 29, 1991. BA, U. Calif., Santa Cruz, 1968. Founding chef The Greens Restaurant, San Francisco, 1978-83, Cafe Escalera, Santa Fe, N.Mex., 1990-93; menu cons. Rancho San Miguel, Baja Sur, Mex., 1996; cons. to various restaurants, 1986—. Author: The Greens Cookbook, 1986 (Andre Simon award 1987), The Savory Way, 1990 Best Cookbook of Yr. Julia Childs award 1991), The Vegetarian Table: America, 1996; adv. editor Saveor, 1994—; contbg. author books; contbr. articles to profl. jours. Bd. dirs. Santa Fe Area Farmers Mkt., 1990—; mem. Student Nutrition Action Com., Santa Fe, 1995—. Named to Food and Wine Mag. Honor Roll of Am. Chefs, 1983. Mem. Internat. Assn. Culinary Professions, The Chef's Collaborative (founder), Les Dames D'Escoffier (MFK Fisher Mid-Career award 1994). Home and Office: 230 Cibola Cir Santa Fe NM 87501

MADISON, MIRIAM FRANCES, educational administrator; b. Starkville, Miss., Nov. 29, 1937; d. Leonard and Minnie (Smith) Green; children: Harriet Madison Tuggle, Michael, Keshea L. BS, Stillman Coll., 1960; MS, Fort Valley State Coll., 1971; Cert. L6 Specialist Adminstrn., U. Ga., 1982. Tchr. Starkville Separate Mcpl., 1960-63; tchr. Pearl Stephens Elem. Sch., Warner Robins, Ga., 1964-87, prin., 1991-94; prin. Watson Elem. Sch., Warner Robins, Ga., 1988-91; coord. parent and family svcs. Houston County Sch. System, Perry, Ga., 1994—. Vice pres. Presbyn. Women, 1991, pres. Mem. AAUW, Profl. Assn. Educators, Nat. Assn. Elem. Prins., Ga. Assn. Educators, Phi Delta Kappa. Democrat. Presbyterian. Home: 9342 Feagin Rd Macon GA 31206-7944 Office: 305 Watson Blvd Warner Robins GA 31093-3405

MADISON, OCTAVIA DIANNE, mental health services professional; b. Lynchburg, Va., Mar. 28, 1960; d. Raymond Barlow Sr. Madison and Doreatha Madison Anderson. BA, Hampton U., 1982; MEd, Lynchburg Coll., 1983; postgrad., George Mason U., Fairfax, Va., 1989-94, Va. Poly. Inst. and State U., 1994—. Lic. profl. counselor, addiction counselor. Resource counselor Lynchburg Community Action Group, 1983, placement specialist, 1984; program mgr. Lynchburg 70001 Program, 1985; therapist, case mgr. Cen. Va. Community Svcs., Lynchburg, 1985-88; substance abuse counselor II Fairfax County Govt., 1988—; therapist Women's Ctr. No. Va., Vienna, 1990—; psychotherapist Dr. Carolyn Jackson-Sahni-Assocs., 1993; mental health therapist Arlington County Dept. Human Svcs., 1994—; grad. asst. Va. Polytechnic Inst. and State U., 1994. Asst. sec. So. Christian Leadership Conf., Lynchburg, 1983-84; mem. single ministry, asst. chair youth adv. bd. Mt. Pleasant Bapt. Ch., Alexandria, Va., 1991—; bd. examiners Profl. Counselors, 1991—. Recipient 2-Star award United Way (coord.), 1989. Mem. Am. Assn. for Counseling and Devel., Women's Ctr. Career Network, Advs. for Infants and Mothers, Inc., Nat. Black Alcoholism Coun., Va. Counselor's Assn., Washington Met. Area Addictions Counselors, Nat. Bd. Cert. Counselors, Psi Chi, Beta Kappa Chi. Home: 3890 Lyndhurst Dr Apt 303 Fairfax VA 22031-3722

MADISON, ROBERTA ELEANOR, epidemiologist, educator, consultant; b. Bklyn., Feb. 10, 1932; d. A.I. and Grace (Weinstein) M.; children: Jerry Solomon, Sue Vann. AB in History, UCLA, 1966, MA, 1969, MSPH in Environ. Health, 1972, DrPH, 1974. Chief epidemiological analyst Los Angeles County, L.A., 1972-75; from asst. prof. to assoc. prof. Calif. State U., Northridge, 1975-83, prof. epidemiology and biostatistics, 1983-89; part-time epidemiologist City of Hope, Duarte, Calif., 1977-85; instr. biostatistics UCLA Sch. Pub. Health, 1978-84; v.p. Enrich; cons., biostatistician Northridge Hosp., 1983-91; cons. epidemiology and biostats. Thrasher & Assocs., Northridge, 1988-91, Cytosystems, Cupertino, Calif., 1988-90; cons. epidemiology Warner Day Care Ctr., Woodland Hills, Calif., 1988-90; cons. to phys. therapy masters program Coll. Osteo Medicine of Pacific, 1992-93. Mem. editorial rev. bd. Alzheimers Disease and Assoc. Disorders, 1985—; contbr. articles to profl. jours.; cons. editor: Informed Consent mag., 1994—. Bd. dirs. Basehart Theatre, Woodland Hills, 1986-94. Grantee Am. Lung Assn., Health and Human Svcs., 1995, others. Fellow Am. Coll. Epidemiology, Cancer Rsch. Ctr.; mem. Am. Statis. Assn. (sec. state edn. sect. 1982, workshop organizing com. State Calif. chpt. 1986—), Golden Key Honor Soc. (hon.), Sigma Xi (sec. chpt. 1982). Office: Calif State U 18111 Nordhoff St Northridge CA 91330-0001

MADISON, TRINA SHAUNALDREA, lawyer; b. Tallahassee, Oct. 8, 1968; d. Harold and Marian Sabrina (Harris) M. BA, Smith Coll., 1990; Cert. in Musicology, U. Chgo., 1993; JD, Northwestern U., Evanston, Ill., 1996. Tax return processor Amalgamated Bank, Chgo., 1992-93; legal intern Shorebank Corp., Chgo., summer 1994; jud. clk. Cook County Cir. Ct., Chgo., 1994; intern Lawyers for Creative Arts, Chgo., 1994-95; legal cons. Phoenix Animation, Lombard, Ill., 1995; prodn. intern Faded Denim Prodns., Chgo., 1995—. Mem. Arts Censorship Project, ACLU, N.Y.C., 1995, Harper Ct. Arts Coun., Chgo., 1995. Recipient Grad. fellowship U. Chgo., 1990, grant Northwestern Law Sch., 1994, scholarship Baker & McKenzie, Chgo., 1994. Mem. ABA, Black Entertainment and Sports Lawyers Assn., Ctr. for Black Music Rsch., Nat. Acad. Recording Arts & Scis., Alpha Kappa Alpha. Democrat. Roman Catholic. Home: 1380 E Hyde Park Blvd Chicago IL 60615

MADONIA, VALERIE, dancer; b. Buffalo. Dancer Nat. Ballet of Can., 1979-81, Am. Ballet Theater, 1981-86, The Joffrey Ballet, N.Y.C., 1987—; mem. Baryshnikov and Co. Tour 1985; guest artist with The Armitage Ballet, 1987, Lines Contemporary Ballet, 1994; dir. Telluride (Colo.) Dance Gallery, 1995—. Office: Telluride Dance Gallery PO Box 1303 Telluride CO 81435

MADONICK, HELENE B., lawyer; b. N.Y.C., Aug. 5, 1960. BA magna cum laude, Tufts U., 1982; JD, Columbia U., 1986. Bar: N.Y. 1987, D.C. 1988. Ptnr. Arnold & Porter, Washington. Mem. Phi Beta Kappa. Office: Arnold & Porter 555 12th St NW Washington DC 20004*

MADONNA (MADONNA LOUISE VERONICA CICCONE), singer, actress; b. Bay City, Mich., Aug. 16, 1958; d. Sylvio and Madonna Ciccone; m. Sean Penn, Aug. 16, 1985 (div. 1989). Student, U. Mich., 1976-78. Dancer Alvin Ailey Dance Co., N.Y.C., 1979; CEO Maverick Records, L.A. Albums include Madonna, 1983, Like a Virgin, 1985, True Blue, 1986, (soundtrack)Who's That Girl, 1987, (with others) Vision Quest Soundtrack, 1983, You Can Dance, 1987, Like a Prayer, 1989, I'm Breathless: Music From and Inspired by the Film Dick Tracy, 1990, The Immaculate Collection, 1990, Erotica, 1992, Bedtime Stories, 1994, Something to Remember, 1995; film appearances include A Certain Sacrifice, 1980, Vision Quest, 1985, Desperately Seeking Susan, 1985, Shanghai Surprise, 1986, Who's That Girl, 1987, Bloodhounds of Broadway, 1989, Dick Tracy, 1990, Truth or Dare, 1991, Madonna, 1992, Body of Evidence, 1992, Dangerous Game, 1993, Blue in the Face, 1995, Four Rooms, 1996, Girl 6, 1996; Broadway theater debut in Speed-the-Plow, 1987; author: Sex, 1992. Roman Catholic. Office: Maverick Records 8000 Beverly Blvd Los Angeles CA 90048*

MADORE, SISTER BERNADETTE, retired academic administrator; b. Barnston, Que., Can., Jan. 24, 1918; came to U.S., 1920, naturalized; d. Joseph George and Mina Marie (Fontaine) M.; A.B., U. Montreal, 1942, B.Ed., 1943; M.S., Cath. U. Am., 1949, Ph.D., 1951. Joined Sisters of St. Anne, Roman Cath. Ch., 1935. Instr. math. and English, Marie Anne Coll., Montreal, Que., 1943-44; prof. biology, dean of coll. Anna Maria Coll., Paxton, Mass., 1952-76, v.p., 1975-77, pres., 1977-93, pres. emerita, 1995—; fund-raising cons.; corporator YWCA. Past bd. dirs. Central Mass. chpt. ARC; past bd. dirs. Worcester Coll. Consortium; former trustee Worcester Boys Club. Mem. AAAS, Am. Soc. Microbiology, Nat. Assn. Biology Tchrs., Am. Assn. Higher Edn., Worcester C. of C. Home and Office: Anna Maria Coll 10 Sunset Ln Worcester MA 01612-1198

MADORE, JOYCE LOUISE, gerontology nurse; b. Madison, Kans., Dec. 15, 1936; d. Lionel Wiedmer and Mary Elizabeth (Piley) Murphy; m. Robert Madore, Aug. 15, 1969; children: Carl, Clay. BS, Emporia State U., 1980; diploma, Newman Hosp., 1981. RN, Kans., Mo.; cert. gerontol. nurse, non profit adminstr., nursing home adminstr. Med. charge nurse St. Mary's Hosp., Emporia, Kans., 1971-72; dir. nursing Madison (Kans.) Manor, 1974-81, 82-83; staff nurse Newman Meml. Hosp., Emporia, 1981-82; dir. Daybreak Adult Day Svcs., dir. HELP program Springfield (Mo.) Area Coun. of Chs., 1983—; mem. Gov.'s Com. to Establish Rules and Regulations on Adult Day Care Patients State of Mo.; cons. U. Mo. Coop. Extension Svc. Program Guides on Adult Day Care. Contbr. video Understanding Aging Program; developer Home Guide for the Homebound, 1996. Named one of Outstanding Nurses in Mo. St. Louis U., 1989. Mem. NANA, AFE, Adult Day Care Assn. (past sec., exec. past v.p. 1989-91), Mo. Nurses Assn., Mo. Adult Day Care assn. (pres. 1991-95, Exec. award 1995), Mo. League of Nursing. Home: 171 Hilltop Oaks Ln Sparta MO 65753-8911

MADRID, OLGA HILDA GONZALEZ, retired elementary education educator, association executive; b. San Antonio, May 4, 1928; d. Victor A. and Elvira Ardilla Gonzalez; m. Sam Madrid, Jr., June 29, 1952; children: Ninette Marie, Samuel James. Student, U. Mex., San Antonio, St. Mary's U., San Antonio; BA, Our Lady of Lake U., 1956, MEd, 1963. Cert. bilingual tchr., adminstr., Tex. Sec. Lanier High Sch. San Antonio Ind. Sch. Dist., 1945-52, tchr. Collins Garden Elem. Sch., 1963-92; tutor Dayton, Ohio, 1952-54; bd. dirs., sch. rep. San Antonio Tchr.'s Coun., 1970-90; chair various coms. Collins Garden Elem., 1970-92. Elected dep. precinct, senatorial and state Dem. Convs., San Antonio, 1968—; apptd. commr. Keep San Antonio Beautiful, 1985; life mem., past pres. San Antonio YWCA; bd. dirs. Luth. Gen. Hosp., NCCJ, Cath. Family and Children's Svcs., St. Luke's Luth. Hosp.; nat. bd. dirs. YWCA, 1985—, also mem. exec. com.; mem. edn. commn. Holy Rosary Parish, 1994—; mem. bus. assocs. com. Our Lady of the Lake U., 1995—. Recipient Outstanding Our Lady Lake Alumni award Our Lady Lake U., 1975, Guadalupana medal San Antonio Cath. Archdiocese, 1975, Yellow Rose Tex. citation Gov. Briscoe, 1977; Olga H. Madrid Ctr. named in her honor, YWCA San Antonio and San Antonio City Coun., 1983; Lo Mejor De Lo Nuestro honoree San Antonio Light, 1991, honoree San Antonio Women's History Month Coalition, 1996. Mem. San Antonio Bus. and Profl. Women, Inc. (mem. exec. com.), Salute Quality Edn. (honoree 1993), Delta Kappa Gamma (Theta Beta chpt., mem. exec. com.). Home: 2726 Benrus Blvd San Antonio TX 78228-2319

MADRIL, LEE ANN, writer; b. Burbank, Calif., Sept. 16, 1944; d. George Mathew McDougall; 1 child, Francis Michael. Student, Granada Hills (Calif.) Coll., 1962. Freelance writer, 1986-90; shoot out artist, life mem. Bad Co., Auburn, Calif., 1990—; writer Idaho State Newspaper, Just Horses, Indian Valley, 1994—; cons. in authenticity, Calif. State Horsemen, Santa Rosea, 1988-90, Bad Co., 1990. Writer Idaho State Newspaper Just Horses; contbr. articles to profl. jours. Vol. Red Cross, Soques, Calif., 1982, Salinas (Calif.) Valley Meml. Hosp., 1979, Greenpeace, Humane Soc. U.S. Recipient Kodak KINSA award, 1989, winner County and State photo awards, 1993. Mem. Calif. State Horseman's Assn. (state champion 1989-90), Silver Spurs. Republican. Roman Catholic. Home and Office: PO Box 121 Newcastle CA 95658

MADSEN, BARBARA A, judge. Justice Washington Supreme Ct., Seattle. *

MADSEN, DOROTHY LOUISE (MEG MADSEN), writer; b. Rochester, N.Y.; d. Charles Robert and Louise Anna Agnes Meyer; BA, Mundelein Coll., Chgo., 1978; m. Frederick George Madsen, Feb. 17, 1945 (dec.). Pub. rels. rep. Rochester Telephone Corp., 1941-42; feature writer Rochester Democrat & Chronicle, 1939-41; exec. dir. LaPorte (Ind.) chpt. ARC, 1964; dir. adminstrv. svcs. Bank Mktg. Assn., Chgo., 1971-74; exec. dir. The Eleanor Found., Chgo., 1974-84; founder Meg Madsen Assocs., Chgo., 1984-88; women's career counselor; founder, Clearinghouse Internat. Newsletter; founder Eleanor Women's Forum, Clearinghouse Internat., Eleanor Intern Program Coll. Students and Returning Women. Served to lt. col. WAC, 1942-47, 67-70. Decorated Legion of Merit, Meritorious Svc. award. Mem. Res. Officers Assn., Mundelein Alumnae Assn., Phi Sigma Tau (charter mem. Ill. Kappa chpt.). Home and Office: 1030 N State St Chicago IL 60610-2844 also: 3902 Joliet Rd La Porte IN 46350

MADSEN, G. HOLLY, education professional; b. Kansas City, Mo., Mar. 20, 1962; d. Murphy W. and Jean Maxine (Edwards) Ford. BA, Hendrix Coll., 1984; MA, Vanderbilt U., 1996, postgrad., 1996—. Tchg. asst. Vanderbilt U., Nashville, 1987-90, 91-92; editor Assn. Am. Colls. and Univs., Washington, 1992-94; coord. spl. projects Assn. of Governing Bds. of Univs. and Colls., Washington, 1994—. Asst. editor Liberal Edn., 1992-94. Tutor, instr. ESL Carlos Rosario Ctr., Washington, 1993-95. German Acad. Exch. Program scholar, U. Calif., Berkeley, 1988, Fulbright scholar Inst. for Internat. Edn. of the U.S. Govt., Berlin, 1990-91. Mem. MLA. Democrat. Office: Assn Governing Bd U/Colls Ste 400 One Dupont Cir. Washington DC 20036

MADY, BEATRICE M., artist; b. N.Y.C., Dec. 30, 1953; d. Raymond J. and Beatrice A. Mady; m. David W. Cummings, Oct. 2, 1982. Student, Bklyn. Mus. Art Sch., 1971-72; BFA, U. Dayton, 1976; MFA, Pratt Inst., 1978. One-woman shows include Rockville Centre (N.Y.) Pub. Gallery, 1976, Jersey City (N.J.) Visual Art Gallery, 1988, Caldwell (N.J.) Coll., 1991, Johnson & Johnson Gallery, New Brunswick, N.J., 1992, Johnson & Johnson Consumer Products Divns., Skillman, N.J., 1993, Rabbet Gallery, New Brunswick, 1996; group shows include Newark Mus., 1982, Summit (N.J.) Art Ctr., 1985, Gallery Jupiter, Little Silver, N.J., 1986, Morris Mus., Morristown, N.J., 1987, Yuma (Ariz.) Art Ctr., 1989, Van Vorst Gallery, Jersey City, 1990, City Without Walls, Newark, 1993, Rabbet Gallery, New Brunwick, 1995; works in pub. collections at Janssen Pharmaceutia, Titusville, N.J., Bristol-Meyers Squibb, Plainsboro and Lawrenceville, N.J., Johnson & Johnson, New Brunswick, Sydney & Francis Lewis Found., Richmond, Va., Drew U. Mus., Madison, N.J., Arenol Chem. Corp., N.Y.C., Goetz and Mady-Grove, Jericho, N.Y. Painting fellow Pratt Inst., Bklyn., 1977-78, N.J. State Coun. on the Arts, 1985; grantee Ford Found., 1978. Mem. Coll. Art Assn.

MAEDA, J. A., data processing executive; b. Mansfield, Ohio, Aug. 24, 1940; d. James Shunso and Doris Lucille Maeda; m. Robert Lee Hayes; 1 child, Brian Sentaro Hayes. BS in Math., Purdue U., 1962, postgrad., 1962-63; postgrad., Calif. State U., Northridge, 1968-75; cert. profl. designation in tech. of computer operating systems and tech. of info. processing, UCLA, 1971. Cons., rsch. asst. computer ctr. Purdue U., West Lafayette, Ind., 1962-63; computer operator, sr. tab operator, mem. faculty Calif. State U., Northridge, 1969, programmer cons., tech. asst. II, 1969-70, supr. acad. applicatons, EDP supr. II, 1970-72, project tech. support coord. programmer II, office of the chancellor, 1972-73, tech. support coord. statewide timesharing tech. support, programmer II, 1973-74, acad. coord., tech. support coord. instrn., computer cons. III, 1974-83; coord. user svcs. info. ctr., mem. tech. staff IV CADAM INC subs. Lockheed Corp., Burbank, Calif., 1983-86, coord. user svcs., tech. specialist computing dept., 1986-87; v.p., bd. dirs. Rainbow Computing, Inc., Northridge, 1976-85; dir. Aki Tech./Design Cons., Northridge, 1976—; mktg. mgr. thaumaturge Taro Quipu Cons., Northridge, 1987—; tech. cons. Digital Computer Cons., Chatsworth, Calif., 1988; computer tech., fin. and bus. mgmt., sys. integration, 1988-90; tech. customer software support Collection Data Sys., Westlake, Calif., 1991; tech. writer Sterling Software Info. Mgmt. Divsn., 1992—. Author, editor more than 275 user publs., tutorials, reference manuals, user guides; contbr. articles and photos to profl. jours. Mem. IEEE, SHARE, DECUS (editor spl. interest group 1977-83, ednl. steering com. RSTS/E 1979-82). Office: Sterling Software Info Mgmt Divsn PO Box4237 5900 Canoga Ave Woodland Hills CA 91365-4237

MAEHL, NANCY R., client services supervisor; b. Clarinda, Iowa, Oct. 1, 1949; d. Charles H. and Edith L. (Bowen) Underwood; m. John F. Maehl, June 6, 1970; children: Jennifer L., J. Javan. BA, U. No. Iowa, 1971. Cert. elem. edn. tchr. Precinct chmn. Linn County (Iowa) Election Office, election asst.; asst. dept. head Coe Coll., Cedar Rapids, Iowa, 1988-94, asst. dept. head, acting dept. head, 1989-91; adminstrv. asst. Integra Health, Cedar Rapids, 1994-96; client svcs. supr. Kelly Assisted Living, Cedar Rapids, 1996—; mem. faculty grievance com. Coe Coll., faculty sponsor intervarsity Christian fellowship. Editor Pertinent Press, 1993-96. State del. State Rep. Conv., Des Moines, county del. County Rep. Conv., Cedar Rapids; telephone chmn. Christian Women's Club, Cedar Rapids. Mem. NAFE, Profl. Women's Network. Republican. Home: 3009 Stratford Ln SW Cedar Rapids IA 52404 Office: Kelly Assisted Living 4341 First Ave SE Cedar Rapids IA 52402

MAENE, CAREN DEBORAH GROSS, social planner; b. Morgantown, W.Va., Dec. 17, 1953; d. Stanley Burton and Ruth Doris (Brill) G.; m. Quentin Walker Nelson, Sept. 30, 1975 (div. Apr. 1980); m. Victor A. Maene, June 2, 1984; children: Shane David Brill, Chelsea Maria. BA, Wilmington Coll., 1974; MBA, Monmouth Coll., 1980; postgrad., Rutgers U., 1985. Cert. social worker, tchr. fine arts and bus. Dir. arts and crafts Cin. Jewish Cmty. Ctr., 1974; tchr. Wilmington (Ohio) City Schs., 1974-75; vol. tchr. Montreal, Can., 1975; tchr. Margate (N.J.) Jewish Cmty. Ctr., 1976; youth planner Atlantic County, Atlantic City, 1976-79, prin. planner, 1979-81; dir. planning C.A.P. Agy.-tri-County, Bridgeton, N.J., 1982-83; chief planner Cape May County, Irma, N.J., 1983-88; dir. sch. based youth svcs., asst. exec. dir. Cape Counseling Svcs., Cape May Court House, N.J., 1988—; cons. Hughes Assocs., Atlantic City, 1981-84; mediator Cape Mediation Svcs., Inc., Cape May Court House, 1991—, bd. treas., 1992—. Active Ch. of The Larger Fellowship; bd. dirs. ARC, Cape May County, 1986-89; adv. peace and disarmament Soc. of Friends, So. N.J., 1978—. Inst. Ednl. Leaders fellow, 1993-94; Sch. Bd. Youth Svcs. grantee, 1988—; Grantee Children's Trust Fund, N.J., State Aid, N.J., Black United Fund, 1993-94. Fellow N.J. Collaborative Leaders Program. Unitarian. Home: 414 Shore Rd Marmora NJ 08223 Office: Cape Counseling Svcs Inc 128 Crest Haven Rd Cape May Court House NJ 08210

MAERSCH, NANCY KAY, laboratory manager; b. Norfolk, Nebr., May 11, 1942; d. Ambrose Pryor and Angela Gertrude (Goergen) Jordan; m. Frank C. Maersch, May 11, 1968; 1 child, Todd F. BS in Med. Tech., Mt. Marty Coll., 1963; MA in Health Care Adminstrn., Cen. Mich. U., 1981. Diplomate Lab. Medicine; clin. lab. scientist; specialist in hematology. Med. technologist Madison (Wis.) Gen. Hosp. Lab., 1963-64, hematology sect. head, 1964-72, hematology specialist, 1973-79, hematology sect. head, 1979-80, lab. customer svc. rep., 1980-82, mgr. adminstrv. svc. and mktg., 1982-85; mgr. mobile diagnostics Meriter Gen. Med. Labs., Madison, 1985-87, mgr. client svcs., 1987-89, mgr. lab. ops., 1990—; bd. dirs. Dane County Cytology Ctr., Madison, Wis. chpt. of Clin. Lab. Mgmt. Assn., 1993—, pres., 1995-96. Chair Edgefest event Edgewood H.S. Aux., 1987-92; mem. Bus. Forum, Madison, 1989—; vol. Ronald McDonald House; bd. dirs. parents assn. Marquette U., 1993—. Mem. Am. Soc. Clin. Lab. Sci., Wis. Soc. Clin. Lab. Sci. (sec. 1967-70, 76-80), Clin. Lab. Mgmt. Assn. (coun. of chpt. pres. 1997-98), Wis. chpt. Clin. Lab. Mgmt. Assn. (bd. dirs., pres.-elect 1995-96, pres. 1997-98), Madison Area Lab. Suprs., Madison Civics Club. Roman Catholic. Home: 3105 Nottingham Way Madison WI 53713-3457 Office: Gen Med Labs 36 S Brooks St Madison WI 53715-1304

MAES, PETRA JIMENEZ, judge; widowed; 4 children. BA, U. N.Mex., 1970, JD, 1973. Bar: N.Mex. 1973. Pvt. pratice law Albuquerque, 1973-75; rep., then office mgr. No. N.Mex. Legal Svcs., 1975-81; dist. judge 1st Jud. Dist. Ct., Santa Fe, Los Alamos, 1981—; chief judge, 1984-87, 92-95. Active S.W. coun. Boy Scouts Am., mem. dist. coms.; presenter pre cana St. John's Cath. Ch.; bd. dirs. Nat. Ctr. on Women and Family Law; chairperson Tri-County Gang Task Force; mem. Gov.'s Task Force on Children and Families, 1991-92; mem. adv. com. Santa Fe County Jail, 1996. Mem. N.Mex. Bar Assn. (elderly law com. 1980-81, alternative dispute resolution com. 1987-92, code of jud. conduct com. 1992—, juvenile cmty. corrections svcs. com. chairperson), Hispanic Nat. Bar Assn., N.Mex. Dist. Judges Assn., N.Mex. Women's Bar Assn., Hispanic Women's Coun. (charter). Office: 1st Jud Dist Ct PO Box 2268 Santa Fe NM 87504-2268

MAFFRE, MURIEL, ballet dancer; b. Enghien, Val D'Oise, France, Mar. 19, 1966; came to U.S., 1990; d. Bernard and Monique (Berteaux) M. Diploma, Paris Opera Ballet Sch., 1981; Baccalauréat (hon.), France, 1984. Dancer Hamburg Ballet, Fed. Republic Germany, 1983-84; soloist Sarragoza Ballet, Spain; premiere danseuse Monte Carlo Ballet, Monaco, 1985-90; prin. dancer San Francisco Ballet, 1990—; guest artist with Berlinor Staatsoper and Lines Contemporary Ballet. Recipient 1st prize Nat. Conservatory, Paris, 1983, Grand prize and Gold medal Paris Internat. Ballet Competition, 1984, Isadora Duncan award, 1990. Office: San Francisco Ballet 455 Franklin St San Francisco CA 94102-4438

MAGARIAN, KAREN S., chiropractor, consultant; b. Bronx, N.Y., May 19, 1957; d. Nazareth and Phyllis (Wolkoff) M. BS in Rehab. Counseling, Boston U., 1979; BS in Human Biology, Nat. Coll. of Chiropractic, Lombard, Ill., 1984; DC, L.A. Coll. of Chiropractic, Whittier, Calif., 1987; MA in Family Therapy, Phillips Grad. Inst., North Hollywood, Calif., 1994. Lic. chiropractor, Calif., Mass.; cert. sex educator and counselor, Am. Assn. Sex Educators, Counselors & Therapists; diplomate Am. Acad. Pain Mgmt. Office mgr., counselor Women's Reproductive Health Ctr., Boston, 1978-82; pres., CEO Womanspirit Consulting, Boston, L.A., 1978—; med. tching. assoc. KASEP, Inc., L.A., 1990—; pres., CEO Advantage Representatives, L.A., 1993—; rschr. L.A. Coll. Chiropractic, 1986-87. Author: Turning Dreams Into Reality, 1995; editor: Chiropractic College Admissions and Curriculum Directory. Peer counselor Boston U. Speak Easy, 1976-79; pres., Woman's Health Coun., Nat. Coll. Chiropractic, 1982-83; v.p., Woman's Health Coun., L.A. Coll. of Chiropractic, 1986-87. Mem. AAUW, APHA, NOW, Nat. Coun. on Women's Health, Am. Assn. Sex Educators, Counselors and Therapists, Sexuality Info. and Edn. Coun. of the U.S.

MAGGIORE, SUSAN, geophysical oceanographer; b. Newark, Mar. 14, 1957; d. John James and Marietta Nancy (Testa) M.; m. Stephen P. Garreffa, Oct. 21, 1989; children: Julianna Garreffa, Marietta Garreffa. BS in Geosci., Montclair State U., 1978; postgrad., U. So. Miss., 1981-84. Supr. rsch. and communications The Cousteau Soc., N.Y.C. and Norfolk, Va., 1979-81; geophysicist Naval Oceanographic Office, Bay St. Louis, Miss., 1981-85, NE Consortium Oceanographic Research, Narragansett, R.I., 1985-86; mem. tech. staff Lucent Technologies (formerly AT&T Bell Labs.), Whippany, N.J., 1986—; writer, creative cons. The Cousteau Soc., Los Angeles, 1981-89. Researcher book The Cousteau Almanac of the Environment, 1981; contbr. articles to profl. jours. Vol. Dover (N.J.) Gen. Hosp., 1987-88. Mem. Am. Geophys. Union, Marine Tech. Soc., Nat. Assn. Female Execs. Roman Catholic. Office: Lucent Techs 67 Whippany Rd Whippany NJ 07981-1406

MAGIE, DIAN LEE, arts association administrator; b. Houston, July 23, 1943; d. James Madison and Ruth Imogene (McGowan) Goldsborough; m. James Ronald Shelley, Aug. 62 (div. Aug. 1969); children: Steven Madison, Carl Andrew; m. Roderic Greg Magie, Aug. 1974 (div. June 1979). Student, Stetson U., 1961-62, U. Fla., 1963-64; BA in Humanities, U. West Fla., 1970, MA in Am. History, 1971. Instr. art history Pensacola (Fla.) Sch. Liberal Arts, 1971-73; instr. Am. black history Pensacola (Fla.) Jr. Coll., 1973-77; instr. art Creative Learning Ctr., Pensacola, 1978-81; agt. Donavan Realty, Pensacola, 1979-81; exec. dir. Info. and Referral, Pensacola, 1981-82, Arts Coun. N.W. Fla., Pensacola, 1982-85, Coconino Ctr. for the Arts, Flagstaff, Ariz., 1985-88, Tucson (Ariz.)-Pima Arts Coun., 1988—; spkr., cons. and workshop presenter in field. Author: Arts Festival Work Kit, 1989, Untapped Public Funding for the Arts, 1995, (monographs) Summer Youth Employment Programs, 1993, Arts Programs that Revitalized a Downtown, 1993. Bd. mem. Arizonans for Cultural Devel., Phoenix, 1989-95, sec., 1990-91; bd. mem. Access Tucson, 1990-95, Tucson Cmty. Cable Corp., 1990-95, Desert Survivors, Tucson, 1991-94, Nat. Assembly for Local Arts Agys., Washington, 1991-94, Nat. Assembly of Local Arts Agys., 1991-94, co-chair 1992 annual conv. Recipient Gov.'s Arts award for Coconino Ctr. for Arts, Ariz. Gov./Ariz. Commn., Phoenix, 1992. Home: 3142 W Avenida Cresta Tucson AZ 85745 Office: Tucson-Pima Arts Coun 240 N Stone Tucson AZ 85701

MAGILL, DODIE BURNS, early childhood education educator; b. Greenwood, S.C., July 10, 1952; d. Byron Bernard and Dora Curry B.; m. Charles Towner Magill, May 4, 1974; children: Charles Towner II, Emily Curry. BA, Furman U., 1974; MEd, U. S.C., 1978. Cert. tchr., early childhood, elementary, elementary principal, supv., S.C. Kindergarten tchr. Sch. Dist. Greenville County, 1974-83; early childhood edn. instr. Valdosta (Ga.) State Univ., 1983-84; dir. lower sch. Valwood Sch., Valdosta, 1984-86; kindergarten tchr. Sch. Dist. Greenville County, 1986—; tchr.-in-residence S.C. Ctr. for Tchr. Recruitment, Rock Hill, 1993, mem. policy bd.; workshop presenter and lectr. in various schs. and sch. dists. throughout U.S., 1974—; chmn. S.C. Pub. Kindergarten Celebration, 1994; gir. S.C. State Readiness Policy Group; mem. Southeastern Region Vision for Edn. Adv. Bd., S.C. Coun. Ednl. Collaboration. Demonstration tchr. S.C. ETV (TV show) Sch. Begins with Kindergarten. Mem. Gov. of S.C.'s State Readiness Policy Group, Southeastern Regional Vision for Edn. Adv. Bd., South Carolina Ctr. Tchr. Recruitment Policy Bd. Recipient Ralph Witherspoon award S.C. Assn. for Children Under Six; named Tchr. of Yr., Greenville County, 1992, 93, State of S.C., 1993, S.C. Tchr. of Yr. Coun. of Chief State Sch. Officers, 1993, 94. Mem. Assn. for Childhood Edn. Internat., S.C. Tchr. Forum (chmn. 1993-94), S.C. Early Childhood Assn., Alpha Delta Kappa. Presbyterian. Office: Mountain Park Elem Sch 1500 Pounds Rd SW Lilburn GA 30247

MAGILL, NANCY GENE, microbiologist, researcher; b. Seneca Falls, N.Y., Sept. 3, 1957; d. Malcolm Eugene and Ruth Shirley (Holcomb) M. BS, Allegheny Coll., 1979; MS, Cornell U., 1982, PhD, 1988. Postdoctoral fellow dept. biochemistry health ctr. U. Conn., Farmington, 1988-95; rschr., microbiologist, molecular biologist divsn. of infectious diseases R.I. Hosp., Providence, 1995—. Vol. Macintosh tutor R.I. Libr., Providence, 1996. Mem. AAAS, Am. Soc. Microbiology, Am. Women Sci., Union Concerned Scientists. Home: 22 Blodgett Ave Pawtucket RI 02860 Office: RI Hosp Divsn Infectious Diseases 593 Eddy St Providence RI 02903

MAGILL, ROSALIND MAY, psychotherapist; b. Albany, N.Y., Apr. 27, 1944; d. Fenton Elliot Sr. and Rosalind Pearl (Gross) M.; m. Theodore T. Solomon, May 18, 1970 (div. 1980). Student, N.Y. Inst. Tech., 1963-64, Pace Coll., 1970-71; cert. in process piping design, Voorheese Tech. Inst., 1968; MEd in Counseling and Psychology, Cambridge Coll., 1994. Lic. master pipefitter, Mass.; EIT. Piping designer Badger Am., Inc., Cambridge, Mass., 1976-77; tchr. advanced math. Vision-in-Action, Natick, Mass., 1977-80; plumbing designer R. G. Vanderweil Assocs., Boston, 1980-81; vol. counselor alcohol/substance abuse social detox program Bergen County Hosp., Paramus, N.J., 1981-83; field engr. United Engrs. and Constructors, Phila., 1983-84; tchr. spl. edn. math. and sci. Amesbury (Mass.) High Sch., 1984-85; resident engr. Hoyle, Tanner Assocs., Londonderry, N.H., 1985-86; resident engr., constrn. mgr. dept. environ. mgmt. Commonwealth of Mass., Boston, 1986-89; clin. supr., counselor substance abuse Positive Lifestyles, Mattapan, Mass., 1990-93; dir. Respond Program, substance abuse therapist Ctr. for Family Devel., Lowell, Mass., 1993-94, dir. Respond Program, 1994—; counselor alcoholism and substance abuse Serenity House/Gift of Serenity, 1977-80; counselor substance abuse Baldpate Hosp., Georgetown, Mass., 1984.85. With USMC, 1962. N.Y. State Regent's scholar, 1962. Mem. ACA, Internat. Assn. Addictions and Offender Counselors, Women's Ordination Conf., Daus. Bilitis (pres. N.Y. chpt. 1968-70), Matachine Soc. (bd. dirs. 1968-70).

MAGLIOCCO, SABINA, anthropologist, folklorist; b. Topeka, Dec. 30, 1959; d. E. Bruno and Maria Teresa (Manente) M.; m. Uli Schamiloglu, May 21, 1988 (div. Mar. 1995). BA, Brown U., 1980; MA, Ind. U., 1983, PhD, 1988. Vis. asst. prof. U. Wis., Madison, 1990-94, UCLA, 1994; vis. asst. prof. U. Calif., Santa Barbara, 1995, Berkeley, 1995-96. Author: The Two Madonnas: The Politics of Festival in a Sardinian Community, 1993 (Chgo. Folklore prize 1994), Festa E Trasformazione Sociale in Sardegna, 1995; book rev. editor: Jour. Am. Folklore, 1996—. Pres., bd. dirs. Monroe County Humane Assn., Bloomington, Ind., 1984-85; bd. dirs. Monroe County Animal Control Commn., Bloomington, 1983-89. Fulbright-Hayes doctoral rsch. grantee, 1986, Fulbright postdoctoral grantee, 1989; Guggenheim fellow, 1996. Mem. MLA, Am. Anthropol. Assn., Am. Folklore Soc. (convenor Italian sect. 1996—, sec.-treas. Italian sect. 1993-96), Soc. for Anthropology of Europe, Soc. for Humanistic Anthropology. Office: U Calif Dept Anthropology 212 Kroeber Hall Berkeley CA 94720

MAGLIONE, LILI, fine artist, art consultant; b. Manhasset, N.Y., Jan. 30, 1929; d. Angelo and Mary (Marciano) M.; m. Bernhart H. Rumphorst, June 1, 1957; children: Catherine, Douglas. AD, Traphagen Sch., N.Y.C., 1950; studetn, Art Students League, N.Y.C., 1950-52. Fashion artist Butterick Pattern Co., N.Y.C., 1952-53; fashion art cons. Miss. America Inc., N.Y.C., 1953-54; dept. head fashion art office Simplicity Pattern Co., N.Y.C., 1953-58, fashion art cons., 1958-62; art dept. cons. Nassau County Mus., Roslyn, N.Y., 1984-86; dir. decorative affairs Harbor Acres Assn., Port Washington, N.Y., 1987-89, Sands Point (N.Y.) Mus., 1989-91; art cons. Horst Design Assocs., Huntington, N.Y., 1992—. Exhibited paintings in one-woman shows at Palm Gallery, Southampton, N.Y., 1980, Art Internat., Chgo., 1985, Isis Gallery, Port Washington, 1987, Gallery 84, N.Y.C., 1989, 91, 93; one woman retrospective shows include Harkness Gallery, 1978, James Hunt Barker Gallery, 1984, Sands Point Mus., 1988, Fairfield U., 995. Mem. Nat. Assn. Women Artists, Nat. Mus. Women in the Arts. Roman Catholic. Home: 7 Harmony Rd Huntington NY 11743

MAGNARELLI, SHARON DISHAW, educator; b. Seneca Falls, N.Y., Oct. 3, 1946; d. Claude Nathan and Joyce (Appleyard) Dishaw; m. Louis Magnarelli, June 28, 1969. BA, SUNY, Oswego, 1968; PhD, Cornell U., 1975. Prof. spanish Albertus Magnus Coll., New Haven, Conn., 1976-94; assoc. prof. spanish Quinnipiac Coll., Hamden, Conn., 1994—. Author: The Lost Rib, 1985, Reflections/Refractions, 1988, Understanding Jose Donoso, 1993; contbr. articles to profl. jours. Office: Quinnipiac Coll Hamden CT 06518

MAGNER, RACHEL HARRIS, banker; b. Lamar, S.C., Aug. 5; d. Garner Greer and Catherine Alice (Cloaninger) Harris; m. Fredric Michael Magner, May 14, 1972. BS in Fin., U. S.C., 1972; postgrad. UCLA, 1974, Calif. State U., 1975. Mgmt. trainee Union Bank, L.A., 1972-75, comml. loan officer, 1975-77; asst. v.p. comml. fin. Crocker Bank, L.A., 1978, asst. v.p., factoring account exec. subs. Crocker United Factors, Inc., 1978-81; v.p. comml. services div. Crocker Bank, 1981-82, v.p., sr. account mgr. bus. banking div., 1982-83; v.p. and mgr. corporate banking Office of Pres., Sumitomo Bank Calif., 1983—. Home: 2200 Pine Ave Manhattan Beach CA 90266-2833 Office: Sumitomo Bank Calif 15250 Ventura Blvd Sherman Oaks CA 91403

MAGNESS, PATRICIA, humanities and English educator; b. Kenton, Ohio, June 29, 1947; d. Calvin Luther and Gail Myrtle (German) Phillips; m. J. Lee Magness, June 3, 1967; children: Erik Lee, Ethan Lane. BA, Milligan Coll., 1969; MA, Vanderbilt U., 1974; PhD, Emory U., 1992. Tchr. h.s. Mountain Mission Sch., Grundy, Va., 1971-74; prof. English Boise (Idaho) Bible Coll., 1975-80; tchr. 6th grade Mt. Carmel Christian Sch., Decatur, Ga., 1980-83; tchr. mid. sch. Vance Jr. H.S., Bristol, Tenn., 1983-84; prof. humanities and English Milligan Coll., Tenn., 1984—; bd. dirs. Pioneer Bible Translators, Dallas, 1987—, CMF Internat., Indpls., 1994—. Author curriculum materials and articles. Dist. coord. Bread for the World, Washington. Mem. South Atlantic MLA, Nat. Assn. for Humanities Edn., Nat. Coun. Tchrs. English, Coun. on Christianity and Lit. Christian. Office: Milligan Coll PO Box 500 Milligan College TN 37682

MAGNESS, RHONDA ANN, microbiologist; b. Stockton, Calif., Jan. 30, 1946; d. John Pershing and Dorothy Waneta (Kelley) Wetter; m. Barney LeRoy Bender, Aug. 26, 1965 (div. 1977); m. Gary D. Magness, Mar. 5, 1977; children: Jay D. (dec.), Troy D. BS, Calif. State U., 1977. Lic. clin. lab. technologist, Calif., med. technologist; cert. clin. lab. scientist. Med. asst. C. Fred Wilcox, MD, Stockton, 1965-66; clk. typist Dept. of U.S. Army, Ft. Eustis, Va., 1967, Def. Supply Agy., New Orleans, 1967-68; med. asst. James G. Cross, MD, Lodi, Calif., 1969, Arthur A. Kemalyan, MD, Lodi, 1969-71, 72-77; med. sec. Lodi Meml. Hosp., 1972; lab. aide Calif. State U., Sacramento, 1977; phlebotomist St. Joseph's Hosp., Stockton, 1978-79; supr. microbiology Dameron Hosp. Assn., Stockton, 1980—. Active Concerned Women Am., Washington, 1987—. Mem. AAUW, Calif. Assn. Clin. Lab. Technologists, San Joaquin County Med. Assts. Assn., Nat. Geog. Soc., Nat. Audubon Soc. Baptist. Lodge: Jobs Daus. (chaplain 1962-63). Home: 9627 Knight Ln Stockton CA 95209-1961 Office: Dameron Hosp Lab 525 W Acacia St Stockton CA 95203-2405

MAGNUS, KATHY JO, religious organization executive; b. Brainerd, Minn., Oct. 22, 1946; d. Fred L. and Doris K. (Anderson) Kunkel; m. Richard A. Magnus, Dec. 17, 1966; children: Erica Jo, Cory Allan. BS, U. Minn., 1968. Tchr. St. Paul Schs., 1968-69, Denver Pub. Schs., 1969-75; dir. comm. St. Paul Luth. Ch., Denver, 1979-81; adminstrv. asst. to bishop Rocky Mountain Synod Luth. Ch. Am., Denver, 1981-87; exec. staff Rocky Mountain Synod Evang. Luth. Ch. Am., Denver, 1988—; v.p. Evangel. Luth. Ch. in Am., 1991—. Named exemplar of univ. Calif. Luth. U., 1992. Office: Evang Luthern Ch in Am 7000 Broadway #401 Denver CO 80221

MAGNUSON, NANCY, librarian; b. Seattle, Aug. 15, 1944; d. James Leslie and Jeanette (Thomas) M.; 2 sons, Daniel Johnson, Erik Johnson. BA in History, 1977; MLS, U. Wash., 1978. With. King County Libr. System, Seattle, 1973-80; rsch. asst. Free Libr. Phila., 1980-81; asst. libr. Haverford (Pa.) Coll., 1981-87; libr. dir. Goucher Coll., Balt., Md., 1987—. Contbr. to profl. publs. Mem. ALA (com. on status of women in librarianship, various others), Online Computer Libr. Ctr. Users Coun., Md. Libr. Assn., Congress Acad. Libr. Dirs., NOW, Women's Internat. League for Peace and Freedom, Balt. Bibliophiles, Jane Austen Soc. N.Am. Democrat. Office: Goucher Coll Julia Rogers Libr 1021 Dulaney Valley Rd Baltimore MD 21204-2753

MAGOON, NANCY AMELIA, art association administrator, philanthropist; b. N.Y.C., Apr. 19, 1941; d. Jack and Norma Harriet (Hirschl) Parker; m. Robert Cornelius Magoon, Mar. 16, 1978; children: Adam Glick, Peri Curnin. Student, Cornell U., 1958-59. Gallerist Hokin Gallery, Miami, 1986-89; sec. Nat. Found. Advancement in Arts, 1989-94; nat. coun. mem. Aspen Art Mus., 1985—, Aspen Ballet, 1985—; v.p. Ctr. for Fine Arts, Miami, 1984-94, Miami City Ballet, 1990-94. bd. dirs. Cmty. Alliance Against AIDS, 1990-92; coun. mem. Susan Komen Broast Cancer, Aspen, 1994—; hon. trustee Ctr. for Fine Arts, Miami Beach, 1996. Named one of Outstanding Women in Miami, 1992; NEA grantee, 1995.

MAGRILL, ROSE MARY, library director; b. Marshall, Tex., June 8, 1939; d. Joe Richard and Mary Belle (Chadwick) M. BS, E. Tex. State U., 1960, MA, 1961; MS, U. Ill., 1964, PhD, 1969. Asst. to dean women E. Tex. State U., Commerce, 1960-61, librarian II, 1961-63; teaching asst. U. Ill., Urbana, 1963-64; instr. to asst. prof. E. Tex. State U., Commerce, 1964-67; asst. prof. Ball State U., Muncie, 1969-70; asst. prof. to prof. U. Mich., Ann Arbor, 1970-81; prof. U. N. Tex., Denton, 1981—; dir. libr. E. Tex. Bapt. U., Marshall, 1987—; accreditation site visitor ALA, Chgo., 1975—; cons. in field. Co-author: Building Library Collections, 4th edit. 1974, Library Technical Services, 1977, Building Library Collections, 5th edit. 1979, Acquisition Management and Collection Development in Libraries, 2d edit. 1989. Trustee Memphis Theol. Sem., 1988—; treas. Mission Synod of Cumberland Presbyn. Ch., 1989—; bd. fin. Trinity Presbytery, 1989—; sec.-treas. Harrison County Hist. Commn., 1995—. Mem. ALA (RTSD Resources Sect. pub. award 1978), Tex. Libr. Assn. Home: 804 Caddo St Marshall TX 75670-2414 Office: E Tex Bapt Univ 1209 N Grove St Marshall TX 75670-1423

MAGSIG, JUDITH ANNE, early childhood education educator; b. Saginaw, Mich., Nov. 9, 1939; d. Harold Howard and Catherine Louise (Barstow) Gay; m. George Arthur Magsig, June 22, 1963; children: Amy Catherine, Karl Joseph. BA, Alma Coll., 1961. Cert. tchr., early childhood tchr., Mich. 1st grade tchr. Gaylord (Mich.) Schs., 1961-64, spl. edn. tchr., 1965-67, kindergarten tchr., 1968—. instr. Suzuki violin method; second violinist Traverse (Mich.) Symphony Orch., 1985-92. Mem. ASCD, NEA, Mich. Edn. Assn., Gaylord Edn. Assn., Assn. for the Edn. of Young Children, Assn. for Childhood Edn. Internat., Suzuki Assn. Am., Am. String Tchrs. Assn., Order Eastern Star, Voyageurs, Alpha Delta Kappa (pres. Beta Rho chpt. 1980-82, 84-86). Methodist. Home: 2130 Evergreen Dr Gaylord MI 49735 Office: S Maple Multi Age Program 590 W Fifth St Gaylord MI 49735

MAGUIRE, MARY, banking executive. Sr. v.p. Chase Manhattan Bank, N.Y.C. Office: Chase Manhattan Corp 1 Chase Manhattan Plz New York NY 10081-1000*

MAGUIRE-KRUPP, MARJORIE ANNE, corporate executive; b. Stamford, Conn., Apr. 29, 1955; d. Walter Reeves and Jean Elisabeth (Cook) Maguire; m. Joseph Michael Krupp, Jr., Nov. 26, 1983; children: Parnell Joseph Maguire Krupp; stepchildren: Theresa Margaret Krupp, Donna Marie Krupp Jepson, Maura Elizabeth Krupp. BA in Acctg. cum laude, Franklin and Marshall Coll., 1977; MBA in Fin. with honors, NYU, 1983, cert. in real estate, 1986; cert. in French, U. Strasbourg, France, 1971. CPA, Conn., N.J. Supervisory auditor Arthur Young & Co., Stamford, 1976-80; mgr. fin. planning Combustion Engring., Stamford, 1980-84; asst. v.p., mgr. fin. planning and analysis Kidder Peabody & Co., N.Y.C., 1984-87, fin. cons. to brokerage industry, 1988-90; dir. fin. svcs. Mass Mut. Life Ins. Co., 1990-91; pres. Parnell Devel. Corp., 1987—; v.p. fin. Jeremiah Devel. Co., 1987-89; v.p. acctg. Sumitomo Bank Ltd., 1991-92, v.p., dir. internal auditing 1992-94, v.p., dep. chief internal auditor, 1994; v.p./mgr. internal auditing Kidder Peabody & Co., Inc., N.Y.C., 1994-95, mgr. internal audit, fin. svcs. divsn. Am. Internat. Group, Inc., N.Y.C., 1995—. Advisor Jr. Achievement, Stamford, 1979-80; mem. Inst. Internal Auditors, Met. Opera Guild N.Y.C., 1985-89, Met. Mus. Art, N.Y.C., 1983-90, Mus. Modern Art, N.Y.C., 1983-90; treas., bd. dir. Cliffhouse Condo Assn., Cliffside Park, N.J., 1983-85; treas. 73 Madison St. Condo Assn., 1991—, 79 Monroe St. Condo Assn., 1991—; mem. exec. bd. Liberty Harbor Power Squadron, 1995—. Mem. AICPA, N.Y. State Soc. CPAs, Inst. Internal Auditors, Stamford Jaycee Women Club (pres. 1980-81, chmn. bd. 1981-82, Stamford Disting. Svc. award, Outstanding Young Woman of Yr. award, 1980), Phi Beta Kappa (honor soc.), Beta Gamma Sigma (bus. honor soc.). Republican. Presbyterian. Avocations: travel, skiing, sailing, gourmet cooking, golf. Home: 107 Shearwater Ct E Jersey City NJ 07305-5401

MAGUIRE-ZINNI, DEIRDRE, federal community development administrator; b. Bklyn., Oct. 21, 1954; d. James Michael and Dorothy Ursula (Gronske) Maguire; m. Nicholas A. Zinni, Aug. 27, 1977; 1 child, Miles Angelo. BA with honors, SUNY, Stony Brook, 1976; MS, Fla. State U., 1981. Housing specialist Suffolk Community Devel. Corp., Coram, N.Y., 1977-78; planner Palm Beach County Housing and Community Devel., West Palm Beach, Fla., 1980-83, sr. planner, 1983-84, mgr. adminstrn. and ops., 1984-87; fed. community planning and devel. rep. HUD, Jacksonville, Fla., 1987-88; community planning and devel. specialist entitlement cmtys. divsn. HUD, Washington, 1988-91, asst. dir. entitlement communities, 1991-94, dir. entitlement communities divsn., 1994—; staff liaison Affordable Housing Task Force, West Palm Beach, 1985-86, Fla. Community Devel. Assn., 1985-87. Democrat. Roman Catholic.

MAGYAR-BOLOGNA, JENIFER ANN, lawyer; b. Stamford, Conn., Sept. 18, 1967; d. Charles and Rita Louise (Pace) Magyar; m. Peter Joseph Bologna, June 25, 1994; 1 child, Andrew Peter Bologna. BA, Hamilton Coll., 1989; JD magna cum laude, Boston U., 1993. Bar: N.Y. 1994, Conn. 1994. Assoc. labor and employment law Weil, Gotshal & Manges, N.Y.C., 1993—. Editor Boston U. Law Rev., 1993. Mem. Jr. League of Greenwich. Republican. Roman Catholic. Office: Weil Gotshal & Mangers 767 Fifth Ave New York NY 10153

MAHAFFEY, MARCIA JEANNE HIXSON, retired educational administrator; b. Scobey, Mont.; d. Edward Goodell and Olga Marie (Frederickson) Hixson; m. Donald Harry Mahaffey (div. Aug. 1976); 1 child, Marcia Anne (dec.). BA in English, U. Wash.; MA in Secondary Edn., U. Hawaii, 1967. Cert. secondary and elem. tchr. and adminstr. Tchr. San Lorenzo (Calif.) Sch. Dist., 1958-59; tchr. Castro Valley (Calif.) Sch. Dist., 1959-63, vice prin., 1963-67; vice prin. Sequoia Union High Sch. Dist., Redwood City, Calif., 1967-77, asst. prin., 1977-91, ret., 1991; tchr. trainer Project Impact Sequoia Union Sch. Dist., Redwood City, 1986-91; mem. supr.'s task force for dropout prevention, 1987-91, Sequoia Dist. Goals Commn. (chair sub-com. staff devel. 1988); mentor tchr. selection com., 1987-91; mem. Stanford Program Devel. Ctr. Com., 1987-91; chairperson gifted and talented Castro Valley Sch. Dist.; mem. family svcs. bd., San Leandro, Calif. Vol. Am. Cancer Soc., San Mateo, Calif., 1967, Castro Valley, 1965; Sunday sch. tchr. Hope Luth. Ch., San Mateo, 1970-76; chair Carlmont H.S. Site Coun., Belmont, Calif., 1977-91; mem. Nat. Trust for Hist. Preservation. Recipient Life Mem. award Parent, Tchr., Student Assn., Belmont, 1984, Svc. award, 1989, Exemplary Svc award Carlmont High Sch., 1989; named Woman of the Week, Castro Valley, 1967, Outstanding Task Force Chair Adopt A Sch. Program San Mateo (Calif.) County, 1990. Mem. ASCD, AAUW, DAR, Assn. Calif. Sch. Adminstrs. (Project Leadership plaque 1985), Sequoia Dist. Mgmt.Assn. (pres. 1975, treas. 1984-85), Met. Mus. Art, Smithsonian Instn., Libr. of Congress Assocs. (charter), Am. Heritage - The Soc. of Am. Historians, Internat. Platform Assn., Animal Welfare Advocacy, Woodrow Wilson Internat. Ctr. Scholars, Nat. Geographic Soc., Libr. of Congress Assn., Am. Mus. Natural History (charter mem.), Delta Kappa Gamma, Alpha Xi Delta (Order of Rose award).

MAHAFFIE, LYNN BOYNTON, lawyer, government official; b. Bronxville, N.Y., Feb. 21, 1965; d. Edmund Stratton and Jane (Bodorff) Boynton; m. Matthew Barton Mahaffie, Aug. 4, 1990; 1 child, Shelby Alice. BBA, George Washington U., 1987; JD, U. Pa., 1990. Bar: Pa. 1990, D.C. 1991. Assoc. atty. Brownstein, Zeidman & Lore, Washington, 1990-93; mgmt. & program analyst U.S Dept. Edn., Washington, 1993—. George Washington U. Bd. Trustees scholar, 1984-86. Mem. Nat. Fin. Mgmt. Hon. Soc., Beta Gamma Sigma. Democrat. Home: 3020 Tilden St NW #404 Washington DC 20008 Office: US Dept Edn ROB-3 # 4060 600 Independence Ave Washington DC 20202

MAHER, FRAN, advertising agency executive; b. Chgo., June 22, 1938; d. Edward Stephan and Virginia Rose (Harrington) M.; m. Anthony Peter Petrella, Sept. 17, 1957; children: Roland, Louis, Marcus; m. Brian L. Coffey, June 19, 1993. Student (univ. scholar) U. Minn., 1956-57; student Spectrum Inst., 1968-71; BA summa cum laude, Kean Coll. N.J., 1979. Office mgr. Lead Supplies, Inc., Mpls., 1957-59; freelance artist and writer, Warren, N.J., 1968-72; prin. Visuals, Warren, N.J., 1974-79; pres. Fran Maher, Inc., Bound Brook, N.J., 1980—; dir. Parent Edn. Advocacy Tng. Center, Alexandria, Va., 1979-85. Officer Friends of Weigand Farm, Milton, N.J., 1977-80, Somerset County Assn. for Retarded Citizens, 1982—, pres., bd. dirs. 1987-89; officer, bd. dirs. Assn. Retarded Citizens N.J., 1989—, chair residential quality life com., 1991-94; trustee Peoplecare Ctr., Inc., 1990-93; bd. dirs. Somerset County Coalition on Affordable Housing, 1991-92; rep. Congress of States, The Arc of USA, 1993-95; founding mem. Flintlock Boys' Club. Recipient N.J. Art Dirs. Show award, 1978, 1st place award in graphics Watchung Art Center, 1980. Mem. Somerset County C. of C. (bd. dirs. 1989-94, chair affordable housing 1990-93). Office: 200 E Union Ave Bound Brook NJ 08805-1762

MAHER, FRANCESCA MARCINIAK, air transportation executive, lawyer; b. 1957. BA, Loyola U., 1978, JD, 1981. Ptnr. Mayer, Brown & Platt, Chgo., 1981-93; v.p., sec. UAL Corp., Elk Grove Village, Ill., 1993—. Bd. dirs. United Ctr. Mem. Ill. Humane Soc. (bd. dirs.). Office: UAL Corp PO Box 66100 Chicago IL 60666

MAHER, MIRANDA ALICE, artist; b. Ft. Levenworth, Kans., June 15, 1955; d. John Ralph and Jo Lynn (Blackburn) M. BFA, R.I. Sch. of Design, Providence, 1988; MFA, Cranbrook Acad. of Art, Detroit, 1990.

Pvt. practice artist N.Y.C., 1990—; art editor. Long News in the Short Century (lit. jour.), 1991—. Author/artist: Emergency Instructions I, II, III, 1990, 18 Self Portraits, 1991, Redbook: A Book of Hours, 1992, Girls! Girls! Girls! Madwomen & Murderesses, 1993, 100 Coordinates of Violence, 1995; one-woman shows include C.A.G.E., Cin., RMCAD, Denver, CEPA Gallery, Buffalo, 1996, Paramount Gallery, Long Island U., N.Y., 1996; exhibited in group shows at CEPA Gallery, Longwood Arts, Bronx, Plan B, Memphis, 1996, Soho20, N.Y.C., 1995, A.I.R. Gallery, N.Y.C., 1994, MMC Gallery, N.Y.C., Testsite Gallery, Brooklyn, 1992-93 and numerous others; represented in permanent book/print collections at the Museum of Modern Art, N.Y.C., The N.Y. Pub. Libr., N.Y.C., The Whitney Museum of Am. Art, N.Y.C., Nat. Museum of Women in the Arts, Washington, Museum of Contemporary Art, Chgo., Libr. of Congress, Washington, L.A. County Museum, Art Metropole, Toronto, and numerous others. Home and Office: 342 21st St # 1L Brooklyn NY 11215

MAHLBURG, NORINE ELIZABETH, retired nurse; b. Onawa, Iowa, June 16, 1917; d. James Erve and Florence Elizabeth (Larson) Zortman; m. Milton William Mahlburg, Mar. 4, 1946; children: Suzanne, William, Marie, Robert. RN, St. Joseph Coll. Nursing, 1945; BSN, St. Francis Coll., 1975. RN, Iowa, Ill. Pvt. duty nurse Third Dist., Sioux City, Iowa, 1945-46, Rockford, Ill., 1947-61; polio nurse ARC, Rockford (Ill.) Hosps., 1945; new born nursery Swedish-Am. Hosp., Rockford, 1962; shop nurse Giant Photos, Rockford, 1963-67; with Staff Relief Health Care Instns., Rockford, 1967-76; staff nurse of devel. disabilities Singer Zone Ctr., Ill. Dept. Mental Health, Rockford, 1976-91, ret., 1991. Author: (booklet) Birding in Rockford, 1952, (book) Larson-Fors History, 1993. Donor, advisor Rockford Peace and Justice, 1985—. Recipient Life Pin Nat. PTA, 1963, Scouter's Key Cub Scouts Am., 1967, Disaster pin ARC. Mem. ANA (50 Yr. mem.), Rockford Woman's Club (sec. 1994), North Ctrl. Ill. (life, pres. 1975-85), Ornithol. Soc. (bd. dirs. 1991-94), DAR (bd. dirs. 1987-89), Swedish Hist. Soc. (sec. 1993—), Moose Club (com. 1984—). Democrat. Roman Catholic. Home: 06 Johns Woods Dr Rockford IL 61103-1680

MAHMOUD, CINDY L., broadcast executive. Program exec. WBBM-TV, Chgo.; Midwest divsn. mgr. Group W Prodns., Chgo.; v.p. entertainment and children's programming Black Entertainment TV, Washington, v.p. devel. and spl. projects. Developer programs including Screen Scene, Teen Summit, Love Between the Sexes, Live from L.A., StoryPorch, Kimboo & Kids, Comic View; vol. of spls. for the NETWORK. Recipient Emmy awards, Iris awards, CEBA wards, Parent's Choice awards (3), NEA awards (5), San Francisco State awards (2). Office: Black Entertainment Tel Entertainment Orig Programming 1900 W Place NE Washington DC 20018

MAHONE, BARBARA JEAN, automotive company executive; b. Notasulga, Ala., Apr. 19, 1946; d. Freddie Douglas M. and Sarah Lou (Simpson). BS, Ohio State U., 1968; MBA, U. Mich., 1972; PMD, Harvard U., 1981. Sys. analyst GM, Detroit, 1968-71, sr. staff asst., 1972-74, mgr. career planning, 1975-78; dir. pers. adminstrn. GM, Rochester, N.Y., 1979-81; mgr. indsl. rels. GM, Warren, Ohio, 1982-83; dir. human resources mgmt. Chevrolet-Pontiac-Can. group GM, 1984-86; dir. gen. pers. and pub. affairs Inland divsn. GM, Dayton, Ohio, 1986-88; gen. dir. pers. Indland Fisher Guide divsn. GM, Detroit, 1989-91, gen. dir. employee benefits, 1991-93; dir. human resources truck group GM, Pontiac, Mich., 1994—; chmn. Fed. Labor Rels. Authority, Washington, 1983-84, Spl. Panel on Appeals; dir. Metro Youth; mem. bd. govs. U. Mich. Alumni. Bd. dirs. ARC, Rochester, 1979-82, Urban League Rochester, 1979-82, Rochester Aea Multiple Sclerosis; mem. human resources com. YMCA, Rochester, 1980-82; mem. exec. bd. Nat. Coun. Negro Women; mem. allocations com. United Way Greater Rochester. Recipient Pub. Rels. award Nat. Assn. Bus. and Profl. Women, 1976, Mary McLeod Bethune award Nat. Coun. Negro Women, 1977, Senate resolution Mich. State Legislature, 1980; named Outstanding Woman, Mich. Chronicle, 1975, Woman of Yr., Nat. Assn. Bus. and Profl. Women, 1978, Disting. Bus. Person, U. Mich., 1978, one of 11 Mich. Women, Redbook mag., 1978. Mem. Nat. Black MBA Assn. (bd. dirs., nat. pres. Disting. Svc. award, bd. dirs., nat. pres. Outstanding MBA), Women Econ. Club (bd. dirs.), Indsl. Rels. Rsch. Assn., Internat. Assn. for Pers. Women, Engring. Soc. Detroit. Republican. Home: 175 Kirkwood Ct Bloomfield Hills MI 48304-2927 Office: MC 483-512-8G3 2000 Centerpoint Pkwy Pontiac MI 48341-3147

MAHONEY, ANN DICKINSON, fundraiser; b. Topeka, Sept. 12, 1961; d. Jacob Alan II and Ruth (Curd) D.; m. Michael James Mahoney, May 29, 1993; 1 child, James Junius Castle Mahoney. AB in History, Grinnell Coll., 1983; postgrad., McGill U., Montreal, Quebec, Can., 1985. Analyst, corp. fin. dept. E.F. Hutton & Co., Inc., N.Y.C., 1983-85; pres., owner The Dark Side, N.Y.C., 1985-87; asst. dir. individual giving Meml. Sloan-Kettering Cancer Ctr., N.Y.C., 1987-88, dir. spl. gifts, 1988-91; assoc. dir. devel. Sch. Humanities and Scis. Stanford (Calif.) U., 1991—; devel. asst. regional office Brandeis U., N.Y.C., 1987. Vol. interviewer Grinnell Coll., N.Y.C., San Francisco, 1983—; vol. Tom Huening for Congress, Palo Alto, Calif., 1992. Mem. Nat. Soc. Fund Raising Execs., Jr. League San Francisco (com. chmn. 1996—), Pacific Rsch. Inst. for Pub. Policy, Hist. Topeka Assn., Friends of Filoli (Woodside, Calif.), Spokane Club (Washington). Republican. Episcopalian. Office: Stanford U Bldg One Stanford CA 94305

MAHONEY, ANNE RANKIN, sociology educator, writer; b. Meadville, Pa., Sept. 7, 1937; d. William Taylor and Ellen Ardena (Jackson) Rankin; m. Barry Paul Mahoney, Nov. 27, 1965; children: Katherine Ailene, Michael Andrew. BA in Sociology, Kent State U., 1959; MS in Applied Comm., U. Denver, 1989; MA in Sociology, Northwestern U., 1961; PhD in Sociology, Columbia U., 1970. Rsch. dir. Manhattan Bail Vera Inst. Justice, N.Y.C., 1961-63; lectr. Bklyn. Coll., 1964-65; rsch. asst. Russell Sage Found., N.Y.C., 1965-66; lectr. Hunter Coll., N.Y.C., 1966-67; asst. prof. social sci. N.Y. Med. Coll., N.Y.C., 1970-72; rsch. assoc. NYU Law Sch., N.Y.C., 1972-73; asst. prof. dept. sociology U. Denver, 1973-80, assoc. prof. dept. sociology, 1980-87, prof. dept. sociology, dir. women's studies, 1992-95, prof. sociology, 1987—; mem. Nat. Adv. Com. for Study of Juvenile Detention, Washington, 1976; peer review com. NIMH-Ctr. for Studies of Crime and Delinquency, Washington, 1976-78; elected faculty rep. U. Denver Bd. Trustees Faculty and Ednl. Affairs Com., 1987-90. Author: Juvenile Justice in Context, 1987, Exploring Florida, 1992; contbr. poetry and articles to publs. Mem. Colo. Commn. for Ch. and Families, Denver, 1980-81; mem. summer inst. Soc. for Rsch. in Child Behavior, Cornell, N.Y., 1984; participant UN 4th Internat. Conf. on Women, Beijing, 1995. Recipient Engleman Creative Writing award, 1959, Writers award Denver Women's Press Club, 1984; Russel Sage fellow in law and soc. Russell Sage Found., 1963-64. Mem. Am. Sociol. Assn., Authors Guild, Nat. Coun. Family Rels., Sociologists for Women in Soc., Soc. for Applied Sociology, Groves Conf. on Marriage and Family.

MAHONEY, CATHERINE ANN, artist, educator; b. Macon, Mo., Nov. 18, 1948; d. Joe H. and Berniece Joyce (Garnett) Dickson; m. Michael W. Mahoney, July 19, 1969; children: Karin Lynn Mahoney Broeker, Ryan Michael. BS in Edn. with honors, N.E. Mo. State U., Kirksville, 1969. Mo. state life cert. for teaching art. Elem./secondary art instr. Bucklin (Mo.) R-I Schs., 1970-74; pvt. art instr. Groom (Tex.) Artist's Assn., 1974-75; substitute tchr. Gasconade R-I Schs., Hermann, Mo., 1977-89; pvt. art instr. Colorful Brushes Studio, Hermann, Mo., 1987-96; elem./secondary art instr. Crosspoint Christian Schs., Union, Mo., 1994—; pres. City of Hermann Arts Coun., 1983-87, membership chmn., 1980-82; dir. Summertime Childrn's Watercolor Workshops, Colorful Brushes, Hermann, 1987-96. One-woman shows at N.E. Mo. State U., Kirksville, 1969, Capitol City Art Guild, Jefferson City, Mo., 1983, Kolbe Gallery of Art, Hermann, 1984, Colorful Brushes Studio, Hermann, 1987-94; designer Sister Cities Emblem City of Hermann/Arolsen, Germany, 1989. Pres. Hermann Parent-Tchr. Orgn., 1985-87; organist, pianist, tchr. Hermann Cath. and Bapt. Chs., 1977-96; leader 4-H, Girl and Boy Scouts, Hermann, 1982-95. Named Outstanding Young Woman of Yr., Hermann Jaycees, 1984, 1st Pl. Mo. Artists Collection, Mo. Pub. Svc., Sedalia, Mo., 1992, 3d Pl. and Purchase prize Watercolor USA, Springfield (Mo.) Art Mus., 1995. Mem. Nat. Watercolor Soc. (assoc., included Nat. Art Show 1995), Okla. Watercolor Assn. (assoc., included Art Show 1989), St. Louis Artist Guild (mem. art sect., Honorable Mention 1993), Watercolor USA Honor Soc. (hon., Art Show award 1995). Home: 1058 Old Stonehill Hermann MO 65041 Office: Colorful Brushes Studio 126 E 4th St Hermann MO 65041

MAHONEY, JOËLLE KATHERINE, astrological consultant, communications educator; b. Amiens, France, Jan. 6, 1948; came to U.S., 1953; d. Louis James and Regine (LeClercq) Dennis; m. John William Christopher Mahoney, Aug. 14, 1971. AA, Boro Manhattan C.C., 1971; BA, Adelphi U., 1982; MS student, Hofstra U., 1989—. Profl. cert. in astrology; cert. master practitioner neurolinguistic programming. Tri-lingual translator N.A. Bogdan Co., N.Y.C., 1967-71; practicing astrologer Long Island, N.Y., 1971-74; founding pres. Astrological Rsch. Centre and Tng. Inst. Ltd., Mineola, N.Y., 1974-84; internat. astrological cons. Brewster, N.Y., 1984—. Author: Concept I, II and III, 1974, In Search of Time, 1989. Vol. fund raiser Americares, New Canaan, Conn., 1991—, Silver Hill Hosp., New Canaan, 1992—. Mem. Astrologers Guild Am. (pres. 1980-83), Congress of Astrological Orgns. (v.p. 1981-84). Home: 5 Fair Meadow Dr Brewster NY 10509-9814

MAHONEY, MARGARET ELLERBE, foundation executive; b. Nashville, Oct. 24, 1924; d. Charles Hallam and Leslie Nelson (Savage) M.; BA magna cum laude, Vanderbilt U., 1946; LHD (hon.), Meharry Med. Coll., 1977, U. Fla., 1980, Med. Coll. Pa., 1982, Williams Coll., 1983, Smith Coll., 1985, Beaver Coll., 1985, Brandeis U., 1989, Marymount Coll., 1990, Rush U., 1993, SUNY, Bklyn., 1994, N.Y. Med. Coll., 1995. Fgn. affairs officer State Dept., Washington, 1946-53; exec. assoc., assoc. sec. Carnegie Corp., N.Y.C., 1953-72; v.p. Robert Wood Johnson Found., Princeton, N.J., 1972-80; pres. Commonwealth Fund, N.Y.C., 1980-94; pres. MEM Assocs., Inc., N.Y.C., 1995—. Contbr. articles to profl. jours. Trustee John D. and Catherine T. Mac Arthur Found., 1985—, Dole Found., 1984—, Smith Coll., 1988-93, Columbia U., 1991—, Goucher Coll., 1995—; vis. fellow Sch. Architecture and Urban Planning, Princeton U., 1973-80; bd. dirs. Council on Found., 1982-88; mem. N.Y.C. Commn. on the Yr. 2000, 1985-87, MIT Corp., 1984-89; bd. govs. Am. Stock Exchange, 1987-92; adv. bd. Office of the Chief Med. Examiner, N.Y.C., 1987—, Barnard Coll, Inst. Med. Research, 1986-92; vice chmn. N.Y.C Mayor's Com. for Pub./Pvt. Partnerships, 1990-93; bd. dirs. Alliance for Aging Rsch., 1987—, Overseas Devel. Coun., 1988—, Nat. Found. Center for Disease Control and Prevention, Inc., 1994—; mem. vestry Parish of Trinity Ch., 1982-89, 91-95; active Atlantic Fellowships Selection Com., 1994—. Recipient Frank H. Lahey Meml. award, 1984, Women's Forum award, 1989, Walsh McDermott award, 1992, Disting. Grantmaker award Coun. Founds., 1993, Edward R. Loveland award Am. Coll. Physicians, 1994, Special Recognition award AAMC, 1994, Merit medal Lotos Club, 1994, Terrance Keenan Leadership award in Health Philanthrophy, Grantmakers in Health, 1995. Mem. AAAS, Inst. Medicine of NAS, Am. Acad. Arts and Scis., Am. Philos. Soc., Coun. Fgn. Rels., Fin. Women's Assn. N.Y., N.Y. Acad. Medicine (vice chmn. bd. govs.), N.Y. Acad. Scis., Alpha Omega Alpha. Office: MEM Assocs Inc 521 Fifth Ave Ste 2010 New York NY 10175

MAHONEY, MARGARET ELLIS, executive assistant; b. Detroit, Mar. 17, 1929; d. Seth Wiley and Mildred Elizabeth (Hill) Ellis; m. Stephen Bedell Smith, Mar. 15, 1956 (div. Oct. 1962); 1 child, Laura Elizabeth; m. Patrick John Mahoney, Sept. 1, 1972 (dec.). BA, Butler U., 1953. Copywriter Hook Drugs Inc., Indpls., 1953; continuity dir. Sta. WXLW, Indpls., 1954-57; ptnr. Steve Smith and Assocs. Advt., Indpls., 1956-62; account mgr. Sive Advt., Cin., 1963-64, Associated Advt., Cin., 1964-65; copywriter SupeRX Drugs Inc., Cin., 1965-72; promotion writer U.S. News and World Report, Washington, 1974; asst. mgr. advt. Drug Fair, Alexandria, Va., 1975-82; dir. advt. Cosmetic and Fragrance Concepts Inc., Beltsville, Md., 1982-89; cons. Woodbridge, Va., 1989-94; asst. to real estate agt. Carmel, Ind., 1994—. Vestrywoman St. Matthews Episcopal Ch., Cin., 1969-71; hosp. chmn. Sleepy Hollow Citizens Assn., Falls Church, Va., 1973; vol. resident assoc. program Smithsonian Instn., Washington, 1989-94; chmn. membership and pub. rels. Friends Chinn Park Regional Libr., Woodbridge, Va., 1991-94; vol. Indpls. Art Ctr. Mem. Potomac Valley Aquarium Soc. (past treas., past sec., editor jour.), Am. Cichlid Assn. (nat. pub. rels. chair 1985-90), Delta Delta Delta. Republican. Home: 9850 Greentree Dr Carmel IN 46032-9099

MAHONEY, MARY DZURKO, educator, counselor; b. McKeesport, Pa., Apr. 5, 1946; d. William Thomas and Anne Cecelia (Basarab) Dzurko; m. Thomas Francis Mahoney; 1 child, David. BA in Eng. Lit., U. Pitts., 1968; MA in Teaching in Elem. Edn., George Washington U., 1969; MS in Applied Behavioral Counseling, Johns Hopkins U., 1993. Tchr. Seven Locks Elem. Sch., Bethesda, Md., 1970-73, Tuckerman Elem. Sch., Potomac, Md., 1973-78, Stedwick Elem. Sch., Gaithersburg, Md., 1976-78; sub. tchr. Barnesville (Md.) Sch., 1985-86; home instr. Montgomery County Pub. Schs., Rockville, Md., 1984—; instr. writing Montgomery Coll., 1990-91. Active PTA, Poolesville, Md., 1990—; counselor Women's Commn., 1984-88; sr. counselor GUIDE Youth Svcs. Mem. Woman's Club Upper Montgomery County (sec. 1986, scholarship com. 1988), Phi Delta Gamma (historian 1974-75, newsletter editor 1975-76). Democrat. Roman Catholic.

MAHONEY, PATRICIA, software engineer; b. Pitts., Dec. 26, 1957; d. John Francis and Lillian Rosemary (Peck) Mahoney; 1 child, Mark Benjamin. BS, Towson State U., 1980; postgrad., U. Md., 1980-83, Johns Hopkins U., 1993—. Computer programmer FBI, Washington, 1984-88; software engr. Quality Systems, Inc., Tysons Corner, Va., 1988-89; sr. software engr. Martin Marietta Corp., Washington, 1989-95; sr. engr. BDM Corp., 1995—. Vol. Big Bros. and Big Sisters, Balt., 1982. Recipient Md. State Senatorial scholarship, 1981. Mem. Assn. for Computing Machinery, Nat. Student Speech and Hearing Assn., Omicron Delta Kappa (Student Leader of Yr. 1981). Republican. Roman Catholic. Home: 9610 Sparrow Ct Ellicott City MD 21042-1773

MAHONEY, ROSEMARY, writer; b. Boston, Jan. 28, 1961; d. John Peter and Nona Mary (Rohan) M. BA, Harvard Coll., 1983; MA, Johns Hopkins U., 1985. Instr. writing Johns Hopkins U., Balt., 1985-86. Author: The Early Arrival of Dreams, 1990 (N.Y. Times Notable Book 1990), Whoredom in Kimmage, 1993 (N.Y. Times Notable Book 1993). Recipient Henfield award Henfield Found., 1985, Whiting Writer's award Mrs. Giles Whiting Found., 1994. Office: 14E 1060 Park Ave New York NY 10128

MAHONEY, SALLY, academic administrator. Pres. Mount Mary Coll., Milw. Office: Mount Mary Coll Office of Pres Milwaukee WI 53222-4597*

MAHONY, RHONA, writer; b. Boston, Oct. 31, 1957; d. David T. and Deborah P. (Paradise) M.; m. Jeremy I Bulow. BA, Brown U., 1979; JD, Harvard U., 1984. Staff atty. Legal Assistance Found. of Chgo., 1984-86; vis. scholar Stanford (Calif) U. Law Sch., 1995-96. Author: Kidding Ourselves: Breadwinning, Babies & Bargaining Power, 1995.

MAHONY, SHEILA A., cable television executive; b. Yonkers, N.Y., Jan. 30, 1942; d. Paul Ambrose and Grace (Sullivan) M.; m. Charles A. Riggs, July 7, 1983; stepchildren: Charles Riggs, Julia Riggs. BA, Newton Coll. Sacred Heart, Mass., 1963; JD, Fordham U., 1967. Asst. corp. counsel Law Dept. City of N.Y., N.Y.C., 1967-72; regional dir. Cable TV Info. Ctr., The Urban Inst., Washington, 1972-74, gen. counsel, 1974-75, exec. dir., 1976-77; exec. dir. Carnegie Commn. on Future of Pub. Broadcasting, N.Y.C., 1977-79; v.p. govt. rels. Cablevision Systems Corp., Woodbury, N.Y., 1980-95, sr. v.p. comm. and pub. affairs, 1995—, dir., 1988—; exec. dir. Carnegie Commn. onf Future of Pub. Broadcasting, 1977-79; exec. dir. Cable TV Info. Ctr. of Urban Inst. Author: Keeping PACE With the New Television, 1979. Dir. C-SPAN, Washington, 1990—, Found. for Minority Interests in Media, N.Y.C., 1992—; asst. corp. counsel City of N.Y. Mem. Cable TV Pub. Affairs Assn. (dir. 1994—). Office: Cablevision Systems Corp 1 Media Crossways Woodbury NY 11797

MAHOSKY, NANCY LYNNE, secondary education educator; b. Pitts., Oct. 5, 1951; d. Alfred Charles and Eva Marie (Bruni) Melani; m. Henry John Mahosky, Jr., July 25, 1987. BS, Indiana U. Pa., 1973; MS, Duquesne U., 1977. Cert. tchr., Pa. Tchr. math. and computer sci. Blackhawk Sch. Dist., Beaver Falls, Pa., 1973—. NSF grantee, 1991. Mem. AAUW. Home: 1904 17th St Beaver Falls PA 15010 Office: Blackhawk HS 500 Blackhawk Rd Beaver Falls PA 15010

MAHRENHOLTZ, DAYLA DIANNE, elementary school principal; b. Glendale, Calif., Apr. 12, 1957; d. Preston Paul Buby and Evangeline Ruth (Sickler) B.; m. Laurence J. Mahrenholtz, Nov. 21, 1987 (div. Feb. 1993). AA, El Camino Jr. Coll., Torrance, Calif., 1975-77; BA, Calif. State U., Carson, 1979; MA, Calif. State U., L.A., 1990; EdD, U. LaVerne, Calif., 1996. Cert. edn. adminstr., Calif. Teller Ban of Am., Lawndale, Calif., 1977-79; tchr. Whittier (Calif.) City Sch. Dist., 1980-88, tchr., mentor, 1988-92; prin. Los Nietos Sch. Dist., Whittier, Calif., 1992—. Mem. AAUW, Calif. Assn. Bilingual Edn., Assn. Calif. Adminstrs., Computer Users in Edn., Whittier Area Sch. Adminstrs. (program chair 1993—). Democrat. Office: Aeolian Sch 11600 Aeolian St Whittier CA 90606-3306

MAI, ELIZABETH HARDY, lawyer; b. Ithaca, N.Y., Nov. 7, 1948; d. William Frederick and Barbara Lee (Morrell) M.; m. Edward John Gobrecht III, May 19, 1990. BA in Am. Studies, Cornell U., 1970; JD, Dickinson Sch. Law, 1975. Bar: Pa. 1975, U.S. Dist. Ct. (mid. dist.) Pa. 1976. Atty. Keystone Legal Svcs., Inc., State Coll., Pa., 1975-76; asst. atty. gen. Pa. Dept. Commerce, Harrisburg, Pa., 1976-77; chief counsel Pa. Dept. Commerce, Harrisburg, 1978; assoc. Wolf, Block, Schorr and Solis-Cohen, Phila., 1979-83, ptnr., 1986—; v.p., gen. counsel EQK Ptnrs., Bala Cynwyd, Pa., 1983-86; chair environ. dept. Wolf, Block, Schorr and Solis-Cohen; chair Pa. state govt. affairs Internat. Coun. Shopping Ctrs., 1988-93; founding dir., mem. Comml. Real Estate Women, Phila.; bd. dels. Nat. Network Comml. Real Estate Women; adj. prof. Villanova (Pa.) U. Sch. Law, 1986—. Active Cornell U. Real Estate Coun., 1990—. Mem. ABA, Am. Coll. Real Estate Lawyers, Pa. Bar Assn., Phila. Bar Assn. Office: Wolf Block Schorr and Solis-Cohen 15th & Chestnut Sts 12th Fl Philadelphia PA 19102

MAIBENCO, HELEN CRAIG, anatomist, educator; b. New Deer, Aberdeenshire, Scotland, June 9, 1917; came to U.S., 1917; d. Benjamin C. and Mary (Brown) Craig; children: Thomas Allen, Douglas Craig. BS, Wheaton (Ill.) Coll., 1948; MS, DePaul U., 1950; PhD, U. Ill., Chgo., 1956. Asst. prof., assoc. prof., then prof. U. Ill., Chgo., 1956-73; prof. Rush U., Chgo., 1973-86, prof. emeritus, 1993—; anatomist dept. anatomy, dept. rehab. medicine Rush-Presbyn.-St. Luke's Med. Ctr., Chgo., 1986—, rsch. cons., 1973—; prof. emeritus Rush-U. Chgo., 1986—; cons. on grant application NIH, Bethesda, Md. Contbr. articles to profl. jours. Mem. AAAS, Endocrine Soc., Am. Assn. Anatomists, Sigma Xi. Republican. Presbyterian. Home: 1324 S Main St Wheaton IL 60187-6480

MAICKI, G. CAROL, former state senator, consultant; b. Holden, Mass., July 16, 1936; d. John Arne and Mary Emily (Bumpus) Mannisto; m. Henry F. Maicki, May 4, 1957; children: Henry III, Matthew, Scott, Julia, Mary. BA, U. Mich., 1978. Exec. dir. Sweetwater County Task Force/Sexual Assualt, Rocksprings, Wyo., 1978-81; program mgr. Family Violence/Sexual Assault, Cheyenne, Wyo., 1981-85; coord. S.D. Coalition Against Domestic Violence and Sexual Assault, Black Hawk, 1985-90; state senator S.D. Legislature, Pierre, 1990-92; cons. Black Hawk, 1990-94, Nat. Coalition Against Domestic Violence, 1987; speaker Nat. Coalition Against Sexual Assault, Portland, Oreg., 1987, Rutger Ctr. for Women in Politics, San Diego, 1991; mem. planning com. Office for Victims of Crime, U.S. Justice, Phoenix, 1989; expert witness state and fed. cts., 1990-96. Author: (manuals) Operating Standards, 1984, Rules and Regulations, 1986, Shelter Procedures, 1987, Administrative Procedures, 1995, Responders to Rope, 1996. Com. mem. Health and Human Svc. State Legislature, Pierre, 1990-92, local govt., 1990-92; commn. mem. local govt. study commn., Pierre, 1990-92; bd. dirs. Crisis Intervention Svcs., 1991—; apptd. def. adv. com. on women in svcs. Sec. of Def., 1995—; apptd. exec. com. def. adv. com. on women in the svcs., 1996—. Recipient award Gov. Wyo., 1985, Spirit of Peace award Women Against Violence, Rapid City, 1993, U.S. Dept. of Justice award, 1994, fellowship Share Our Strength, 1996—, Equity award S.D. chpt. AAUW, 1996. Mem. S.D. Alliance for Mentally Ill, Rapid City Womens Network, S.D. Advocacy Network for Women, Lions (Black Hawk), Women Against Violence. Democrat. Home: PO Box 375 Black Hawk SD 57718-0375

MAIDEN, EVA WENKART, psychotherapist, school psychologist; b. Vienna, Austria, Apr. 8, 1935; d. Simon I. and Antonia (Taubes) Wenkart; m. Henry George Maiden, Aug. 26, 1956 (div. 1977); children: Peter David, Benjamin Paul; m. Martin Leonard Primack, Jan. 1, 1989. BA, Antioch U., 1957; MA, San Francisco State U., 1967. Cert. sch. psychologist, Calif.; lic. marriage, family and child counselor, Calif. Sch. psychologist Ravenswood Schs., East Palo Atlo, Calif., 1967-69; tchr., sch. counselor Richmond (Ind.) Schs., 1969-70; sch. psychologist Yellow Springs (Ohio) Schs., 1970-72, Alum Rock Schs., San Jose, Calif., 1973-85; founder, psychotherapist Midpeninsula Mental Health Svcs., Palo Alto, 1976-91; psychotherapist Palo Alto, 1976—; instr. psychology Cen. State U., Wilberforce, Ohio, 1971; cons. psychologist Children's Hosp., Dayton, Ohio, 1972; counselor DeAnza Coll. Re-entry Program, Cupertino, Calif., 1987. Chair for consciousness raising NOW, Palo Alto, 77-82; group leader women's support group Jewish Comty. Ctr., Palo Alto, 1983-89; v.p. bd. dirs. Tikvah network for Holocaust survivors, San Francisco, 1992—. Fellow Am. Orthopsychiat. Assn.; mem. Calif. Assn. Marriage and Family Therapists, Calif. Assn. Sch. Psychologists. Office: 550 California Ave Palo Alto CA 94306

MAIDLOW-KRAMER, DOLORES MARY, retired federal agency executive; b. Westphalia, Mich., Apr. 19, 1934; d. Joseph Ludwig and Ida Veronica (Spitzley) Fox; m. Donald Eugene Maidlow, July 25, 1953 (dec.); children: Thomas O., Randolph E., Fredric P., Nicholas D., Geoffrey J., Sarah E.; m. Roy Joseph Kramer, Oct. 13, 1993. Postal clk. U.S. Postal Svc., 1962-77; supr. U.S. Postal Svc., Okemos, Mich., 1977-80; postmaster U.S. Postal Svc., Howell, Mich., 1980-92. Bd. dirs. Livingston County United Way, Howell, 1985-92, sec., 1987, treas., 1989, v.p., 1990, pres., 1991; bd. dirs. United Way Mich., 1987-92; pres. Forest View Citizens Assn., 1990—. Mem. Nat. Assn. Postmasters (area dir. 1982-84), Nat. Mus. Women in Arts, Smithsonian Instn. Home: 2806 Forest Rd Lansing MI 48910-3783 Office: US Postal Svc 325 S Michigan Ave Howell MI 48843-9998

MAIER, DIANA ELIZABETH, epidemiologist, photographer; b. Irvington, N.J., Nov. 11, 1957; d. Erich Joseph and Hildegard (Hennemann) M.; married. BS, Rutgers U., 1979; M in Pub. Health, UCLA, 1981. Registered med. technologist; cert. in healthcare quality. Immunohematology North Jersey Blood Ctr., East Orange, 1979-80; hematology technologist Santa Monica (Calif.) Med. Ctr., 1980-81; community liaison team coord. immunization program N.Y.C. Dept. Health, 1981; epidemiologist St. Joseph's Hosp. and Med. Ctr., Paterson, N.J., 1982-88, supr. epidemiology and infection control, 1988-91; project coord. Mountain Plains Regional AIDS Edn. Tng. Ctr., Denver, 1991-93; dir. epidemiology and quality improvement The Health Care Initiative, Inc., Denver, 1993-95; dir. rsch. and epidemiology Primera Healthcare, LLC, Denver, 1995—; mem. AIDS adv. com. licensure reform project N.J. State Dept. Health, Trenton, 1986-88; developer, speaker AIDS roving symposia, Lawrenceville, N.J., 1989-91; expert cons. Community Health Care, Daycare and Emergency Svcs., 1985-91; speaker, writer, presenter sci. paper on measles First Internat. Conf. Hosp. Infection Soc., London, 1987. Guest commentator on AIDS and HIV Infection Paterson Teen Scene, 1990. Authored legislation regarding Allied Health Edn., N.J., 1988-91; team walker, vol. Walkathon, March of Dimes, Sussex County/Bergen County, N.J., 1988-91, fundraiser, Fairfield, N.J., 1990; expert cons. assembly and senate N.J. State Pub. Health Coun., Trenton, 1988-91. Mem. APHA, Nat. Assn. Quality Assurance Profls., Assn. Health Svc. Rsch., Assn. Practitioners in Infection Control and Epidemiology, Inc., Colo. Healthcare Outcomes and Utilization Rsch. Coalition (founder 1993), Phi Beta Kappa, Beta Beta Beta. Home: 14330 W 5th Ave Golden CO 80401-5226 Office: Primera Healthcare LLC 600 Grant St Ste 700 Denver CO 80203-3524

MAIER, DONNA JANE-ELLEN, history educator; b. St. Louis, Feb. 20, 1948; d. A. Russell and Mary Virginia Maier; m. Stephen J. Rapp, Jan. 3, 1981; children: Alexander John, Stephanie Jane-Ellen. BA, Coll. of Wooster, 1969; MA, Northwestern U., 1972, PhD, 1975. Asst. prof. U. Tex. at Dallas, Richardson, 1975-78; asst. prof. history U. No. Iowa, Cedar Falls, 1978-81, assoc. prof., 1981-86, prof., 1986—; cons. Scott, Foresman Pub., Glenview, Ill., 1975-94; editl. cons. Children's Press, 1975-76, Macmillan Pubs., 1989-90, Haper-Collins Pubs., 1994. Co-author: History and Life, 1976, 4th edit., 1990; author: Priests and Power, 1983; co-editor African Economic History, 1992—; contbr. articles to profl. jours., essays to books. Mem. Iowa Dem. Cen. Com., 1982-90, chmn. budget com., 1986-90; chmn. 3d Congl. Dist. Cen. Com., 1986-88. Fulbright-Hays fellow, Ghana, 1972,

Arab Republic Egypt, 1987; fellow Am. Philos. Soc., London, 1978. Mem. Am. Hist. Assn., African Studies Assn., AAUW (fellow Ghana 1973), Quota Club. Home: 219 Highland Blvd Waterloo IA 50703-4229 Office: U No Iowa Dept History Cedar Falls IA 50614

MAIMBOURG, RITA BARTNIK, lawyer; b. Erie, Pa., Oct. 29, 1956. BA magna cum laude, U. Pitts., 1978; JD, Case Western Res. U., 1981. Bar: Ohio 1981. Of counsel Arter & Hadden, Cleve. Notes editor Case Western Res. U. Law Rev., 1980-81. Mem. Ohio State Bar Assn., Cleve. Bar Assn., Order of Coif. Office: Arter & Hadden 1100 Huntington Bldg 925 Euclid Ave Cleveland OH 44115-1475*

MAIN, BETTY JO, management analyst; b. Hatch, N.Mex., May 22, 1939; d. Truman Oliver and Madeline Kate (Bennett) Hickerson; m. Andrew Allan Burich, June 21, 1958 (div. Sept. 1977); children: Cari Lynn, Andrew Allan Jr.; m. Ralph Monroe Main, Apr. 21, 1979; stepchildren: Michael, Randall, Kelly. AA in Liberal Arts, Marymount Coll., 1988; BS in Bus. & Mgmt., U. Redlands, 1993, MBA, 1996. Escrow officer Palos Verdes Escrow, San Pedro, Calif., 1975-80; sec. City of L.A., San Pedro, 1980-85, wharfinger, 1985-87, mgmt. aide, 1987-89, mgmt. analyst II, 1989—. Mem. City of L.A. Tutoring Program, City of L.A. Spkrs. Bur. Mem. AAUW, Marymount Coll. Alumni, U. Redland Alumni, Alfred North Whitehead Leadership Soc., Emblem Club (L.A.). Episcopalian. Home: 2238 W Paseo Del Mar San Pedro CA 90732-4521 Office: City of LA 425 S Palos Verdes St San Pedro CA 90731-3309

MAIN, EDNA (JUNE) DEWEY, education educator; b. Hyannis, Mass., Sept. 1, 1940; d. Seth Bradford and Edna Wilhelmina (Wright) Dewey; m. Donald John Main, Sept. 9, 1961 (div. Dec., 1989); children: Alison Teresa Main Ronzon, Susan Christine Main Leddy, Steven Donald Main. Degree in Merchandising, Tobe-Coburn Sch., 1960; BA in Edn., U. North Fla., 1974, MA in Edn., 1979, M. Adminstrn. and Supervision, 1983; PhD in Curriculum and Instrn.,U. Fla., 1990. Asst. buyer Abraham & Straus, Bklyn., 1960-61; asst. mdse. mgr. Interstate Dept. Stores, N.Y.C., 1962-63; tchr. Holiday Hill Elem. Sch., Jacksonville, Fla., 1974-86; mem. adv. coun. Coll. Edn., U. North Fla., 1982—, instr. summer sci. inst., 1984-92—, prof., 1990-92; assoc. prof. Jacksonville U., 1992—, also coord. masters program in integrated learning and ednl. tech.; instr. U. Fla., 1987-90. Co-author: Developing Critical Thinking Through Science, 1990. Rep. United Way, 1981-86; tchr. rep., chpt. leader White House Young Astronaut Program, 1984-85; team leader NSF Shells Elem. Sci. Project. Mem. ASCD, Nat. Sci. Tchrs. Assn. (sci. tchrs. achievement recognition award 1983), Coun. Elem. Sci. Internat., Fla. Assn. Sci. Tchrs., Phi Kappa Phi, Phi Delta Kappa, Delta Kappa Gamma, Kappa Delta Pi. Republican. Episcopalian. Office: Jacksonville U 2800 University Blvd N Jacksonville FL 32211-3321

MAIN, LAURA LEE, critical care nurse; b. New Bern, N.C., Aug. 26, 1963; d. Charles Pittman Humphrey and Vicki Susan (Lee) Wood; m. Guy Walter Long, Sr., May 8, 1982 (div. June 1990); children: Guy Walter, Jr., Joshua Brandon; m. Jeffrey Michael Main, July 3, 1993. AAS, Craven C.C., New Bern, 1989. ACLS instr., PALS instr., NALS, EMT, RN, BLS, BTLS, CEN, TNCC. Charge nurse Craven Regional Med. Ctr., New Bern, 1989-94; staff nurse emergency dept. Coastal Govt. Svcs., Durham, N.C., 1991-95; charge nurse Naval Hosp Cherry Point, 1991-95; nurse emergency dept. Yale-New Haven Hosp., 1995—; with emergency dept. Naval Hosp., Groton, Conn., 1995—. Mem. AACN, ENA, Am. Trauma Soc. Democrat. Home: 252 Niantic River Rd Waterford CT 06385

MAINARDI, CAROL MARGREITHER, artist, framer, bookbinder; b. Hackensack, N.J., Apr. 19, 1967; d. Alan René and Arlene Carol (Clark) Margreither; m. Christopher Louis Mainardi, Apr. 21, 1990; children: Robin Clark, Samantha Rose. BFA in Printmaking, William Paterson Coll., Wayne, N.J., 1990. Owner Prints and Books, Wayne, 1987-90, Pompton Plains, N.J., 1987—; conservation libr. intern N.Y. Bot. Garden, Bronx, 1992-93. Bd. dirs. Salute to Women in the Arts, 1991—, newsletter editor, 1991-94, pres., 1994—. Recipient Excellence in Mixed Media award Salute to Women in the Arts, Old Church Cultural Ctr., 1993. Presbyterian. Home and Office: 14 White Birch Ave Pompton Plains NJ 07444-1659

MAINWARING-HEALEY, PEPPER, horse trainer; b. Wollaston, Mass., May 13, 1923; d. Herbert James and Marion Jessie (Imrie) Mainwaring; m. A.D. Healey, June 23, 1950; children: Eric, Robin. BS, Simmons Coll., 1948. Advanced lic. riding instr., Mass. Head of riding Camps and Riding Ctrs., N.E. U.S., N.Y., 1942-50, Foxhollow Sch., Lennox, Mass., 1948-50; owner, dir. High Hickory Dressage Farms, Framingham, Mass., 1953—, Langdon, N.H.; trainer horses and riders for dressage and eventing, Langdon, N.H., 1986—; dir. Farm Bur. Fedn., Ashland, Mass., 1989—. Author: You and Your Pony, 1972; contbr. articles to profl. jours. Mem. U.S. Dressage Fedn., N.Am. Sheep Dog Soc., N.E. Border Collie Club (sec.-treas. 1960-80), N.E. Welsh Pony Soc. (hon. life). Address: High Hickory Dressage Farms RR 5 Framingham MA 01701 also: High Hickory Dressage Farms Langdon NH 03602

MAIOCCHI, CHRISTINE, lawyer; b. N.Y.C., Dec. 24, 1949; d. George and Andreina (Toneatto) M.; m. John Charles Kerecz, Aug. 16, 1980; children: Charles George, Joan Christine. BA in Polit. Sci., Fordham U., 1971, MA in Polit. Sci., 1971, JD, 1974; postgrad., NYU, 1977—. Bar: N.Y. 1975, U.S. Dist. Ct. (so. and ea. dists.), N.Y. 1975, U.S. Ct. Appeals (2nd cir) 1975. Law clk. to magistrate U.S. Dist. Ct. (so. dist.) N.Y., N.Y.C., 1973-74; atty. corp. legal dept. The Home Ins. Co., N.Y.C., 1974-76; asst. house counsel corp. legal dept. Allied Maintenance Corp., N.Y.C., 1976; atty. corp. legal dept. Getty Oil Co., N.Y.C., 1976-77; v.p., mgr. real estate Paine, Webber, Jackson & Curtis, Inc., N.Y.C., 1977-81; real estate mgr. GK Techs., Inc., Greenwich, Conn., 1981-85; real estate mgr., sr. atty. MCI Telecom. Corp., Rye Brook, N.Y., 1985-93; real estate and legal cons. Wallace Law Registry, 1994-96; sr. assoc. counsel Met. Transp. Authority, 1996—. Bd. dirs. League Women Voters, Dobbs Ferry, N.Y., 1988; co-pres. The Home/Sch. Assn., Immaculate Conception Sch., Irvington, N.Y. Mem. ABA, Nat. Assn. Corp. Real Estate Execs. (pres. 1983-84, treas. 1985-86, bd. dirs. 1986), Indsl. Devel. Rsch. Coun. (program v.p. 1985, Profl. award 1987), N.Y. Bar Assn., Women's Bar Assn. Manhattan, The Corp. Bar (sec. real estate divsn. 1987-89, chmn. 1990-92), Home Sch. Assn. Immaculate Conception Sch. (co-pres.), Jr. League Club, Dobbs Ferry Women's Club (program dir. 1981-92, 94—, publicity dir. 1992-94). Home and Office: 84 Clinton Ave Dobbs Ferry NY 10522-3004

MAISEL, MARGARET ROSE MEYER, lawyer; b. Manila, Philippines, Dec. 5, 1937; came to U.S., 1952; d. Paul Emil and Conchita (De La Riva) Meyer; m. Donald F. Maisel, Dec. 31, 1956; children: Vicky Colemere, Leslie Otero, Kristi Langford. BA, St. Mary's U., 1965, JD, 1971. Bar: Tex. 1971, U.S. Dist. Ct. (we. dist.) Tex. 1973. Atty., shareholder Tinsman-Houser, San Antonio, 1971-84, 85—; chmn. Tex in indsl. accident bd. State of Tex., 1984-85. Mem., adv. bd. Santa Rosa Health Care, San Antonio, 1993-94; bd. trustees St. mary's Univ., San Antonio, 1988-89; chmn. Santa Rosa Health Care Found., San Antonio, 1994—. Recipient Outstanding Law Alumnus St. Mary's U., 1989; named Outstanding Lawyers Bexar County Womens Bar. Fellow Tex. Bar Found., San Antonio Bar Found. (bd. dirs.); mem. San Antonio Trial Lawyers (bd. dirs.), Tex. Trial Lawyers (bd. dirs.). Roman Catholic. Home: 1402 Fortune Hill San Antonio TX 78258-3201 Office: Tinsman Houser Inc 700 N Saint Marys St San Antonio TX 78205-3501

MAITLAND, ALANA MAE, academic administrator; b. Buffalo, Nov. 16, 1946; d. Frank Marshall and Dorothy B. (Spaulding) Fuller; m. Norman Gean Maitland Sr., May 3, 1969; children: Jennifer, Christine, Norm Jr., Heather. BA in Sociology, Houghton Coll., 1968; MA in Mgmt., Cen. Wesleyan Coll., 1994. Cert. social worker. Social worker Allegany County, Belmont, N.Y., 1968-69; case worker Health and Rehabilitative Svcs., Bartow, 1974-78; tchr. 1st Congl., North Collins, N.Y., 1980-82, Blossom Garden, Collins, N.Y., 1982-85; social worker S.C. Dept. Social Svc., Greenville, 1987-90; coord. Sch. Dist. Greenville County, Greenville, 1990—; mem. adv. bd. Living with Young Families in Edn., Greenville, 1991—. Mem. bd. Kids Helping Kids; bd. mem. S.C. Parents Anonymous; mem. Gov.'s Immunization Campaign. Mem. S.C. Sch. Social Work Assn., So. Early Childhood Assn. Home: 23 Riverwood Cir Greenville SC 29617-1558 Office: Sch Dist Greenville County 206 Wilkins St Greenville SC 29605-3972

MAITLAND, CAROLYN PRISCILLA, art educator; b. N.Y.C., Dec. 19, 1931; d. Eldon Sylvanus and Anne Caroline (Humphrey) Swann; m. Leo Cecil Maitland, Oct. 1955 (dec. Jan. 1992); children: Leo Eldon, Tracy Vincent, Anne Lydia. BFA, Syracuse U., 1953; MFA, Columbia U., 1955, EdD in Art Edn., 1978. Fine arts tchr. Theodore Roosevelt H.S., Bronx, N.Y., 1961-86; asst. prof. secondary art edn. Lehman Coll., CUNY, Bronx, 1986-89; adj. instr. fine art Kean Coll., Union, N.J., 1990-92; adj. prof. African studies N.Y. Tech. Coll., Bklyn., 1989-95; adj. prof. African Am. art Montclair (N.J.) State U., 1992—; nat. pres. Nat. Conf. of Artists, 1991-94, v.p., 1988-91. Ford scholar Nat. Fellowship Fund, 1975-77, Martin Luther King scholar NYU, 1971-72. Episcopalian. Home: 160 Henry St Brooklyn NY 11201-2564

MAJCEN, SISTER SUSAN MARY, principal; b. Sheboygan, Wis., Sept. 12, 1947. BA, DePaul U., 1978; MS, Duquesne U., 1983. Tchr. St. Nicholas, Pitts., 1980-83; prin. St. Joseph the Worker, Gary, Ind., 1983-87, St. John the Evangelist, Greenfield, Wis., 1987-92; St. Basil, Chgo., 1992—. Mem. ASCD, Nat. Cath. Edn. Assn., Pax Christi.

MAJOR, CAROLYN LEDFORD, counselor; b. Hopkinsville, Ky., Nov. 6, 1962; d. Robert Howard and Martha Virginia (Aldridge) Ledford; m. James Kent Major, May 15, 1982; children: Ella Ashley, Madison Edward. BS, Murray (Ky.) State U., 1983, MS, 1985. Cert. tchr. K-12 phys. edn., history, elem. counselor. Elem. phys. edn. tchr. Christian County Bd. of Edn., Hopkinsville, Ky., 1984-91, elem. guidance counselor, 1991—. Mem. Am. Assn. Sch. Counselors, Ky. Assn. Sch. Adminstrs., Alpha Omicron Pi. Baptist. Home: 2421 Kings Chapel Rd Cadiz KY 42211-9737 Office: Ind Hills Elem Sch 313 Blane Hopkinsville KY 42211

MAJOR, MARY JO, dance school artistic director; b. Joliet, Ill., Dec. 5, 1955; d. George Francis and Lucille Mae (Ballun) Schmidberger; m. Perry Rex Major, June 9, 1979. AA, Joliet Jr. Coll., 1976; BA, Lewis U., 1978; MS, Ill. State U., 1983; postgrad., No. Ill. U., Nat. Lewis U. and Gov.'s State U. Cert. tchr., Ill. Tchr., softball coach St. Rose Grade Sch., Wilmington, Ill., 1977-78; tchr., coach volleyball, basketball, softball Reed Custer High Sch., Braidwood, Ill., 1978-79; pvt. tutor, 1979; tchr. Coal City (Ill.) Middle Sc, 1980—, basketball coach, 1980-84; owner, dir., choreographer Major Sch. Dance, Inc., Coal City, 1984—; owner Technique Boutique, 1991; founder Major Motion Dancers, 1984—; aerobics instr. Wilmington Park Dist.,1977-82, Coal City Shape Shoppe, 1980-82; cheerleading sponsor Joliet Jr. Coll., 1976-77, aerobics instr., 1980-81; pvt. dance instr., Coal City, 1981; dancer, choreographer Coal City Bi-Centennial Celebration, 1981, Coal City Community Celebration, 1982; founder Major Motion Dancers, 1984-95; tchr., Russia, 1990; dancer, choreographer various performances for ch. and civic orgns.; televised half-time performance and tour Citrus Bowl. Commd. to choreograph and appear in video prodn.: Jacinta, Not an Ordinary Love, The Patty Waszak Show A Bit of Branson, 1995-96. Mem. Arts Coun. Co-op. Recipient Proclamation of Achievement award Dance Olympus, Chgo., 1986, 87, 88, 89, 90, 91, 92, 93, 94, 95, 96, Best Choreographer award 1990, Merit award Tremaine Dance Conv., 1991-92; named Best Actress, Joliet Kiwanis, 1989, Best Musician, 1990. Mem. NEA, Ill. Edn. Assn., Coal City Cmty. Unit Edn. Assn. Office: Major Sch Dance Inc 545 E 1st St Coal City IL 60416-1635

MAJORS, NELDA FAYE, physical therapist; b. Houston, Aug. 3, 1938; d. Columbus Edward and Mary (Mills) M. Cert. in Phys. Therapy, Hermann Sch. Phys. Therapy, Houston, 1960; BS, U. Houston, 1963. Lic. phys. therapist, Tex. Staff therapist Tex. Med. Ctr. Hermann Hosp., Houston, 1960-61; phys. therapist Chelsea Orthopedic Clinic, Houston, 1961-63; dir. phys. therapy Meml. Hosp. Southwest, Houston, 1963-75; owner, pres. Nelda Majors, Inc., Houston, 1975—; mem. profl. adv. bd. Logos Home Health Agy., Houston, 1985-86; adv. dir. 1st Northwestern Bank, Houston. Active Meml. Dr. Meth. Ch., Houston, 1983—; ptnr. Houston Proud Ptnr., 1986—; founder, pres. Instnl. Safety Advs. Inc., 1994—; bd. dirs. Texans for the Improvement of Long Term Care Facilities, 1995—. Named All Am. Softball Pitcher, Amateur Softball Assn., 1964, All Regional and All-State Pitcher, Tex. Amateur Softball Assn., 1954-70; named to Houston Amateur Softball Assn. Softball Hall of Fame, 1994. Mem. Am. Phys. Therapy Assn. (pvt. practice sect.), Tex. Phys. Therapy Assn., U. Houston Alumni Assn., E. Cullen Soc. (U. Houston), N.W. Crossing Optimist Club (Houston), charter mem., bd. dirs.), River Oaks Rotary (Houston), Phi Kappa Phi. Republican. Club: U. Houston Cougar.

MAJUMDAR, PUSPITA, nutritionist; b. Calcutta, India; came to U.S., 1985; d. Late Surendra Chandra and Sushama Bala (Bhowal) Pal; m. Barun Kanti Majumdao, May 25, 1984. BE, Burdwan (India) U., 1984; MSc in Biol. Sci., U. Calcutta, India, 1980; MS in Food and Nutrition, Tex. Tech. U., 1988. Registered dietician, Calif. Assoc. instr. Surendranath Vidyaniketan, India, 1981-85; rsch. asst. Tex. Tech U., Lubbock, 1987-88; nutrition cons. VP Discount Health Food, North Hollywood, Calif., 1988-89; nutrition counselor Calif. State U., Northridge, 1990; asst. to dietition Northridge Hosp., 1991; nutritionist Watts Health Found., L.A., 1993—; cons. Health Fair Expo, L.A., 1992; participant Sweet Success, Irvine, Calif., 1994, Calif. Dietetic Assn., L.A., 1995. Author: (newsletter) Watts Up!, 1994. Tex. Tech. U. scholar, 1986-88. Mem. Am. Dietetic Assn. Home: 350 S Oakland Ave # 106 Pasadena CA 91101

MAJZOUB, MONA KATHRYNE, lawyer; b. Memphis, June 19, 1949; d. A. Joseph and Mary Majzoub. BA, U. Mich., 1970, MA, 1972; JD, U. Detroit, 1976. Bar: Mich. 1977, U.S. Dist. Ct. (ea. dist.) Mich. 1977, U.S. Supreme Ct. 1988. Sr. prin. Kitch, Drutchas, Wagner & Kenney, P.C., Detroit, 1977—. Bd. dirs. Saratoga Community Hosp., Detroit, 1986—, Family Svcs. Detroit and Wayne County, 1988—. Mem. ABA, State Bar Mich. (tort law review com.), Detroit Bar Assn., Women Lawyers Assn. of Mich., Am. Arab Bar Assn. (treas. 1982-86, pres. 1986-94), Am. Hosp. Assn., Mich. Soc. of Hosp. Attys., Nat. Assn. of Women Lawyers, Assn. of Def. Trial Counsel, Inc., Assn. Trial Lawyers of Am., Mich. Def. Trial Counsel, Leadership Detroit XVI. Office: Kitch Drutchas Wagner et al 1 Woodward Ave Fl 10 Detroit MI 48226-3422

MAKAR, LINDY CHARLOTTE, corporate executive, motivational speaker, former commercial model; b. Ft. Worth, Oct. 18, 1949; d. Charles Kimbrough Jr. and Lydia Joe (Sachse) Cates; m. James Makar, Jr., June 30, 1986; children: Jennifer, Tony, Mike. AA, Okaloosa-Walton Jr. Coll., Niceville, Fla., 1970; student, U. West Fla., 1970; MBA in Exec. Mgmt. Psychology, California U., L.A. Corp. sec. Ft. Worth, 1977-86; founder, pres. Profl. Models Am., 1986—; creator Motivation in Motion, 1968-91; cover model Noxema, 1970; judge various model and talent competitions and pageants; dir. pub. rels. LinStar Entertainment, Inc. Author: (with others) Dallas Models Guide, 1991; contbg. writer Ft. Worth Star-Telegram; one-person shows include paintings, 1976-77. Amb. Dwight D. Eisenhower Found., Spokane, Wash., 1990; fellow Habitat for Humanity, Americus, Ga., 1991; mem. USA Film Festival, 1991—; bd. dirs. Dallas/Ft. Worth Film Commn., Dallas, 1991; mem. event bd. Harris Meth. Hosp. Hurst, Euless and Bedford, Tex., 1987-91, com. chmn., 1990, chmn. 1991; mem. Models Against Drug Abuse, 1987—; co-prodr. Miss Dallas USA and Miss Dallas Teen USA. Named Miss N.W. Fla., Miss USA and Miss Universe Sys., 1968-69, Miss Ft. Walton Beach, Miss Am. Sys., 1968-70, Maid of Cotton Rep., Fla., 1969-70, Mrs. Dallas-Ft. Worth, Mrs. Am. Sys., 1985, Woman of Yr., Ft. Worth Star-Telegram, 1989-90; winner nat. awards Profl. Photographers Am., 1988-91. Mem. Internat. Photographers Orgn. (life), Am. Med. Assn. Aux., Nat. Audubon Soc., Ft. Worth Symphony, Tarrant County Med. Soc., Sundance Inst.

MAKARA, CAROL PATTIE, education educator, consultant; b. Norwich, Conn., Feb. 27, 1943; d. Howard G. and Ruth R. Robinson; m. Benjamin Makara, Feb. 19, 1966; children: Cheryl A., John J. AS, Three Rivers Community-Tech. Coll., 1988; BS, Cen. Conn. State U., 1965; MA, U. Conn., 1967. Cert. tchr., Conn. Tchr. Ledyard (Conn.) Bd. of Edn., 1965-66, Preston (Conn.) Bd. of Edn., 1974—; continuing edn. unit mgr. Preston (Conn,) Pub. Schs., 1993—; computer analyst Clinton (Conn.) plant Stanley Bostitch, summers 1987-92; evening instr. Three Rivers Cmty. Tech. Coll., 1989—; evening mgr. AutoCad Tng. Ctr., 1990-95; coop. mentor tchr. Dept. Edn., Conn., 1988—; advisor Conn. Educators' Computer Assn., 1992—; tchr. assessor The Begining Educator Support and Tng. Program, Conn. State Dept. Edn., 1995—. Author: (with others) Pedagogical Guide: Strategies for Improving Instruction, 1992. Active Fellowship Program for Disting. Tchrs., 1987-94. Fellow Conn. Bus. and Industry Assn.; mem. NEA, Conn. Edn. Assn. Home: 89 Mathewson Mill Rd Ledyard CT 06339-1114 Office: Preston Plains Sch 1 Route 164 Preston CT 06365-8818

MAKER, CAROL JUNE, gifted and talented educator; b. Caneyville, Ky., Aug. 7, 1948; d. Arnold David and Bernice (Smith) Shartzer. BS, Western Ky. U., 1970; MS, So. Ill. U., 1971; PhD, U. Va., 1978. Cert. elem. edn. tchr. Tchr. Caneyville (Ky.) Pub. Schs., 1970; tchr. of gifted Edwardsville (Ill.) Pub. Sch., 1971; regional supr. Ill. Office Edn., Springfield, 1971-74; adminstrv. intern U.S. Office Edn., Washington, 1974-75; grad. instr. U. Va., Charlottesville, 1976-77, off-campus instr., 1977-78; asst. prof. U. N.Mex., Albuquerque, 1978-81; asst. prof. U. Ariz., Tucson, 1981-83, assoc. prof., 1983-96, prof., 1996—; keynote spkr. World Coun. for Gifted, Oporto, Portugal, 1986, Sydney, Australia, 1989, Victorian Assn for the Gifted, Melbourne, 1996. Author: Teaching Models in Education of Gifted, 1982, 2d edit., 1995, Curriculum Development for the Gifted, 1982, Curriculum Development and Teaching Strategies for Gifted Learners, 2d edit., 1996; co-author: Intellectual Giftedness in Disabled Persons, 1985, Nurturing Giftedness in Young Children, 1996; editor: (book series) Critical Issues in Education of Gifted, Vol. I, 1986, Vol. II, 1989, Vol. III, 1994; mem. editl. bd. Jour. for Edn. of Gifted, 1977—, Gifted Edn. Internat., 1985—. Mem. H.S. task force Tucson (Ariz.) Unified Sch. Dist., 1983, 85; mem. task force gifted concerns Ariz. State Bd. Edn., Phoenix, 1985-87; mem. adv. bd. Satori Sch., Tucson, 1986—; bd. dirs. Arts Genesis, Inc., Tucson, 1994—. Recipient Fulbright scholarship Universidad de las Ams., Mexico City, 1987, funding for rsch. U.S. Dept. Edn., Office of Bilingual Edn., 1987-89, 93—, U.S. Dept. Edn., Javits Gifted Edn. Program, 1993—. Mem. Nat. Assn. for Gifted (bd. dirs., sec. 1972-89), Ariz. Assn. for Gifted and Talented (bd. dirs., sec. 1981-87), World Coun. for Gifted and Talented (com. chair 1986-93), Coun. for Exceptional Children (com. chair 1975-94). Democrat. Home: 503 E 2nd St Tucson AZ 85705 Office: Univ Ariz Dept Special Edn & Rehab Tucson AZ 85721

MAKER, JANET ANNE, author, lecturer; b. Woburn, Mass., Feb. 13, 1942; d. George Walter and Margaret Anna (Kopasz); children: Thomas Walter, Jane McKinley. BA, UCLA, 1963; MS, Columbia U., 1967; PhD, U. So. Calif., 1978. Prof. L.A. Trade Tech. Coll., 1991—. Author: Get It All Together, 1979, Interpretive Reading Comprehension, 1984, Keys to a Powerful Vocabulary, Level I, 1981, 88, 94, Level II, 1983, 90, 94, Keys to College Success, 1980, 85, 90, College Reading, Book 1, 1984, 88, 91, 96, Book 2, 1982, 86, 89, 92, 96, Book 3, 1985, Academic Reading with Active Critical Thinking, 1995. Home and Office: 925 Malcolm Ave Los Angeles CA 90024-3113

MAKIN, ANN ELISE, writer, photographer, copy editor; b. Munich, Bavaria, Germany, Aug. 2, 1961; came to the U.S., 1983; d. Lorenz and Elisabeth (Hanfstingl) Schlickenrieder; m. Inder Raj Singh Makin, Sept. 21, 1994. MA in Anthropology, U. Tex., 1986, MA in Photojournalism, 1993. Freelance print and photo various German and Am. publs., 1981—; freelance radio Bayerischer Rundfunk, Munich, 1986—; assoc. editor Munich (German) Kath. Kirchenz, 1986-88; project editor Harcourt Brace Coll. Pubs., Fort Worth, 1993-95; freelance editor, 1995—; ptnr. Insight Features, San Antonio, 1994—. Tex. Photog. Soc., 1992; pub. (newsletter) Talent Exch., 1994. Martin Emmett Walter fellow U. Tex., Austin, 1991. Mem. Women in Comm., Internat. Cath. Union of the Press (Best of Your Country award 1992). Home: 7024 24th Ave NE Seattle WA 98115

MAKKAY, MAUREEN ANN, broadcast executive; b. Chgo.; d. John Paul and Bernice Ann (Williams) Monaghan; m. Albert Makkay, Oct. 20, 1962; children: Allison, Albert Jr., Colleen. BA, U. R.I., 1974. Cert. secondary sch. tchr., Mass. Adminstr. Ednl. Records Bur., Wellesley, Mass., 1979-81; local sales mgr. Sta. WKZE, Orleans, Mass., 1981-83; nat. sales mgr. Sta. WKFM, Syracuse, N.Y., 1983-85; pres. Sta. WPXC-FM, Hyannis, Mass., 1987—; v.p. Sta. WRZE, Nantucket, Mass., Sta. WCIB-FM, Falmouth, Mass. Pres. Cape and Islands unit Am. Cancer Soc., 1988-91, bd. dirs., 1989-95; mem. pers. bd. Town of Barnstable, Mass., 1989-94, chmn., 1990-91; bd. dirs. Cape Cod Alcoholism Intervention and Rehab., Inc., 1995—. Mem. Bus. and Profl. Women Cape Cod (bd. dirs. 1989—), Am. Women in Radio and TV, Nat. Assn. Broadcasters. Office: Sta WPXC-FM Radio 154 Barnstable Rd Hyannis MA 02601-2930

MAKOW, TRACY ELLEN, lawyer; b. Newark, Nov. 2, 1961. BA, Brandeis U., 1983; JD, George Washington U., 1988. Bar: N.J. 1988, U.S. Dist. Ct. N.J. 1988, N.Y. 1990, D.C. 1990, U.S. Dist. Ct. (so. and ea. dists.) N.Y. 1990. Ptnr. Anderson Kill Olick & Oshinsky, P.C., N.Y.C. Contbr. articles to law rev. Mem. Assn. of Bar of City of N.Y. Office: Anderson Kill Olick & Oshinsky PC 1251 Ave of the Americas New York NY 10020-1182*

MAKOWSKI, MICHELE RENEE, accountant; b. Detroit, June 1, 1961; d. Stewart Wilfred Barry and Sophie Mary Babiasz; m. Mark Joseph Makowski, Oct. 15, 1994. BBA, Western Mich. U., 1983. Acctg. supr. The Gap Stores, Inc., San Bruno, Calif., 1983-85, IKON Fin. Systems, San Mateo, Calif., 1985-86; controller Western Devel. Group, San Francisco, 1986-92, Lettergraphics/Detroit, Inc., 1993—. Mem. Inst. Cert. Mgmt. Accts. (cert.). Home: 2107 Hollywood Grosse Pointe Woods MI 48236 Office: Lettergraphics/Detroit Inc 2000 Porter St Detroit MI 48216

MAKOWSKY, VERONICA ANN, educator; b. New Haven, Nov. 29, 1954; d. John S. and Olga Veronica (Popylisen) M.; m. Jeffrey C. Gross, June 30, 1978; children: Joshua Jeffrey, Zachary Alexander. BA, Conn. Coll., 1976; MA, Princeton U., 1978, PhD, 1981. Asst. prof. Am. lit. Middlebury (Vt.) Coll., 1981-85; asst. prof. English La. State U., Baton Rouge, 1985-89, assoc. prof.,1989-93; prof. English U. Conn., 1993—. Author: Caroline Gordon: A Biography, 1989, Susan Glaspell's Century of American Women, 1993; editor Henry Adams (R.P. Blackmur), 1980, Studies in Henry James (Blackmur), 1983; assoc. editor Henry James Rev., 1988-89, acting editor, 1989-90. Fellow Nat. Endowment for Humanitities, 1984-85, Newberry Library, 1985. Mem. MLA, Soc. for the Study of Southern Culture, Phi Beta Kappa. Office: Dept of English U-25 U Conn Storrs Mansfield CT 06269

MAKRI, NANCY, chemistry educator; b. Athens, Greece, Sept. 5, 1962; came to the U.S., 1985; d. John and Vallie (Tsakona) M.; m. Martin Gruebele, July 9, 1992; 1 child, Alexander Makris Gruebele. BS, U. Athens, 1985; PhD, U. Calif., Berkeley, 1989. Teaching asst. U. Calif., Berkeley, 1985-87; rsch. asst. U. Calif., 1986-89; jr. fellow Harvard U., Cambridge, Mass., 1989-91; asst. prof. U. Ill., Urbana, 1991—. Recipient Beckman Young Investigator award Arnold & Mabel Beckman Found., 1993, Ann. medal Internat. Acad. Quantum Molecular Sci., 1995; named NSF Young Investigator, 1993; Packard fellow for sci. and engring. David and Lucille Packard Found., 1993, Sloan Rsch. fellow Alfred Sloan Found., 1994, Cottrell scholar Rsch. Corp., 1994. Home: 2208 Wyld Dr Urbana IL 61801-6753 Office: U Ill at Urbana Dept Chem 505 S Mathews Ave Urbana IL 61801-3617

MAKUPSON, AMYRE PORTER, television station executive; b. River Rouge, Mich., Sept. 30, 1947; d. Rudolph Hannibal and Amyre Ann (Porche) Porter; m. Walter H. Makupson, Nov. 1, 1975; children: Rudolph Porter, Amyre Nisi. BA, Fisk U., 1970; MA, Am. U., Washington, 1972. Asst. dir. news Sta. WGPR-TV, Detroit, 1975-76; dir. pub. rels. Mich. Health Maintenance Orgn., Detroit, 1974-76, Kirwood Gen. Hosp., Detroit, 1976-77; mgr. pub. affairs, news anchor Sta. WKBD-TV, Southfield, Mich., 1977—, Children's Miracle Network Telethon, 1989—. Mem. adv. com. Mich. Arthritis Found., Co-Ette Club, Inc., Met. Detroit Teen Conf. Coalition, Cystic Fibrosis Soc.; mem. adv. com., bd. dirs. Alzheimers Assn.; mem. exec. com. March of Dimes; pres. bd. dirs. Detroit Wheelchair Athletic Assn.; bd. dirs. Providence Hosp. Found., Sickle Cell Assn., Kids In Need of Direction, Drop-out Prevention Collaborative, Merrill Palmer Inst. Recipient Emmy award for best commentary NATAS, 1993, 12 Emmy nominations NATAS, Editorial Best Feature award AP, Media award UPI, Oakland County Bar Assn., TV Documentary award, Detroit Press Club, numerous svc. awards including Arthritis Found. Mich., Mich. Mchts. Assn., DAV, Jr. Achievement, City of Detroit, Salvation Army, Spirit award City of Detroit, Spirit award City of Pontiac, Golden Heritage award Little Rock Bapt. Ch., 1993; named Media Person of the Yr. So. Christian Leadership Conf., 1994,

Humanitarian of the Yr. March of Dimes, 1995. Mem. Pub. Rels. Soc. Am., Am. Women in Radio and TV (Outstanding Achievement award 1981, Outstanding Woman in TV Top Mgmt. 1993, Mentor award 1993), Women in Communications, Nat. Acad. TV Arts and Scis., Detroit Press Club, Ad-Craft. Roman Catholic. Office: 26955 W 11 Mile Rd Southfield MI 48034-2292

MALACHOWSKI, ANN MARY, elementary art educator; b. Chelsea, Mass., May 13, 1948; d. Bronislaw Paul and Stephanie (Mikolajewski) M. BS in Art Edn., Mass. Coll. Art, 1970; MEd, Lesley Coll., 1990; Cert. Fine Arts Dir., Fitchburg State Coll., 1990. Cert. art tchr., art supr., elem. edn. tchr. Art specialist, coord. Norwood (Mass.) Pub. Schs., 1970—; adj. faculty Fitchburg (Mass.) State Coll., 1991-95; focus group mem. Mass. Curriculum Frameworks for Arts, 1994; mem. sch. coun. J.P. Oldham Sch., Norwood, 1993-95; conf. presenter N.E. Art Edn. Bi-annual Conf., 1991; presenter Nat. Art Edn. Conv., 1994, 95. Recipient Horace Mann grant Mass. Dept. Edn., 1989. Mem. Mass. Art Edn. Assn. (coun. 1991—, conf. presenter 1990, 94, Mass. Art Educator of Yr. 1994-95), Mass. Dirs. of Art Edn. (pres. 1994-96), Art Allstate (steering com. 1991-94), Polish Falcons of Am. (dist. sec. 1988—), Delta Kappa Gamma (corr. sec. Theta chpt. 1992-94).

MALAN, JANICE ELAINE, music educator, publisher and record producer; b. Fort Scott, Kans., Oct. 11, 1951; d. Harry Leland and Betty Faye (Flora) Sellers; m. Steven Paul Malan, Aug. 12, 1977; children: Jennifer Renee, Denise Nicole, Beau Christopher. AA, Fort Scott Coll., 1971; BA in Music Edn., Pittsburg State U., 1973, MusM, 1991. Cert. music tchr., Kans., Mo. Band and vocal tchr. Liberal, Mo., 1973-74; band dir. Fort Scott, 1974-76; music tchr. Wheaton, Mo., 1989-91; vocal music tchr. Unified Sch. Dist. 504, Oswego, Kans., 1992—; mem. adv. bd. fine arts camp Pittsburg State U.; workshop leader for orchestra and band. Composer gospel, country and popular songs; conductor S.E. Kans. String Orchestra. Founder Fort Scott Cmty. Symphony, 1974; mem., performer Pittsburg State and Cmty. Symphony; conductor Mid Am. Youth Symphony, 1976. Mem. Kappa Delta Pi. Home: 504 Hobson Pl Pittsburg KS 66762-6319 Office: USD 504 323 Commercial St Oswego KS 67356-1605

MALATESTA, ROSALIE ELINOR, accountant, owner bookkeeping company; b. San Francisco, Feb. 10, 1938; d. Albert Angelo and Alba (Botto) M.; m. Otto Henry Saltenberger, May 16, 1959 (div. Sept. 26, 1977). AA in Acctg., Am. River Coll., 1974; postgrad., Sacramento State U., 1974-76. Staff acct. D.E. Pomerantz & Co., CPA, San Francisco, 1956-63, 66-67; cost acct. Roberts Constrn. Co., San Mateo, Calif., 1963-67; staff acct. Goldsmith, Exline & Seidman, CPAs, San Mateo, Calif., 1968-72; tax examiner Franchise Tax Bd. State of Calif., Sacramento, 1976; staff acct. Phil A. Baender, Acctg. Corp., Danville, Calif., 1976-80; owner Profl. Bookkeeping Systems, Alamo, Calif., 1980—. Pres. Pacifica (Calif.) Police Wives Assn., 1969-71, Vallemar Women's Club, Pacifica, 1966-68; treas. San Ramon Valley Congl. Ch., Danville, 1978-80. Mem. Profl. Bookkeepers Assn. (sec. 1993-95), Inst. Mgmt. Accts. (manuscript chmn. 1984-86), Am. Inst. Profl. Bookkeepers, Diablo Network (treas. 1994—), Diablo Valley C. of C., Meadow Creek Homeowner's Assn. (treas. 1995—). Republican. Roman Catholic. Office: Profl Bookkeeping Systems 3237 Danville Blvd Alamo CA 94507-1913

MALAYERY, NASRIN, educator, consultant; b. Tehran, Iran, Jan. 27, 1943; U.S. citizen, 1990; d. Mahmoud Malayery and Ghamar Narjis Ki-a. BA with spl. honors in history, George Washington U., 1964; EdM in Edn. and Social Studies, Boston U., 1967, EdM in Media and Tech., 1977, EdD in Media Tech., 1986. Editor in-house mgmt. jour. Oil Consortium, Employee Comm., Tehran, 1970-74; mgr. documents and publs. Iran-UNESCO Adult Literacy Program, Tehran, 1974-76; instr., instrnl. designer Shiraz (Iran) U. Med. Sch., 1977-81; ednl. cons. WHO, Alexandria, Egypt, 1981-87; sr. ednl. cons. Digital Equipment Corp., Littleton, Mass., 1987—. Mem. Internat. Soc. for Performance Improvement, Nat. Mus. of Women in the Arts (assoc.), Phi Beta Kappa. Home: 88 Tower Hill Rd Osterville MA 02655

MALCOLM, NANCY LEE, accountant, tax preparer; b. Elmira, N.Y., Feb. 15, 1948; d. John E. and Lillian L. (Moore) Miller; m. Raymond F. Malcolm, May 25, 1972 (div. Nov. 1980); m. Larus Gunnarsson, Nov. 22, 1984. BS in Acctg., BS in Bus. Fin., Fla. Southern Coll., 1983. Enrolled agt. IRS. Acct., tax preparer Wilson & Assocs., Stuart, Fla., 1983-84, Malcolm & Assocs., Stuart and Lake Worth, Fla., 1984—. Mem. NAFE, Nat. Assn. Tax Preparers, Nat. Soc. Tax Practioners. Office: Malcolm & Assocs 6149 Lake Worth Rd Lake Worth FL 33463 also: 10 SE Central Pkwy # 305 Stuart FL 34994

MALDONADO-BEAR, RITA MARINITA, economist, educator; b. Vega Alta, P.R., June 14, 1938; d. Victor and Marina (Davila) Maldonado; m. Larry Alan Bear, Mar. 29, 1975. BA, Auburn U., 1960; PhD, NYU, 1969. With Min. Wage Bd. & Econ. Devel. Adminstrn., Govt. of P.R., 1960-64; assoc. prof. fin. U. P.R., 1969-70; asst. prof. econs. Manhattan Coll., 1970-72; assoc. prof. econs. Bklyn. Coll., 1972-75; vis. assoc. prof. fin. Stanford (Calif.) Grad. Bus. Sch., 1973-74; assoc. prof. fin. and econs. Grad. div. Stern Sch. Bus. NYU, 1975-81, prof., 1981—, acting dir. markets, ethics and law, 1993-94; cons. Morgan Guaranty Trust Co., N.Y.C., 1972-77, Bank of Am., N.Y.C., 1982-84, Res. City Bankers, N.Y.C., 1978-87, Swedish Inst. Mgmt., Stockholm, 1982-91, Empresas Master of P.R., 1985-90; bd. dirs. Medallion Funding Corp., 1985-87; apptd. adv. bd. dirs. equity and diversity in ednl. environs. Mid. States Commn. on Higher Edn., 1991—; trustee Securities Industry Assn., N.Y. Dist. Econ. Edn. Found., 1994—; chairperson NSF, Nat. Vis. Com. Curriculum Devel. Project Networked Fin. Simulation, 1995—. Author: Role of the Financial Sector in the Economic Development of Puerto Rico, 1970; co-Author: Free Markets, Finance, Ethics, And Law, 1994; contbr. articles to profl. jours. Trustee Bd. Edn., Twp. of Mahwah, N.J., 1991-92. P.R. Econ. Devel. Adminstrn. fellow, 1960-65; Marcus Nadler fellow, NYU, 1966-67, Phillip Lods Dissertation fellow, 1967-68. Mem. Am. Econs. Assn., Am. Fin. Assn., Metro. Econ. Assn. N.Y., Assn. for Social Econs. (trustee exec. coun. 1994-96). Home: 95 Tam O Shanter Dr Mahwah NJ 07430-1526 Office: Mgmt Edn Ctr 44 W 4th St Ste 9-190 New York NY 10012-1126

MALEK, MARLENE ANNE, advocate, cultural organization, foundation executive; b. Oakland, Calif., June 22, 1939; d. William Alexander and Yolanda Katherine (Stella) McArthur; m. Frederic Vincent Malek, Aug. 5, 1961; children: Frederic William, Michelle Anne. attended Armstrong U., 1959, Marymount U., 1979. Women's bd. Am. Heart Assn., 1973—. Bd. dirs. Fed. Rep. Women, Washington, 1972-74; bd. dirs., mem. exec. com. Marymount U., Arlington, Va., 1974—; mem. cmty. bd. and nat. com. for the performing arts Kennedy Ctr. Cmty. Bd., Kennedy Ctr., 1991—, mem. nat. com.; chmn. Eisenhower Meml. Found., Washington, 1972-74; mem. adv. bd. Second Genesis Drug Rehab. Program, Bethesda, Md., 1983—; mem. nat. adv. bd. Susan G. Komen Breast Cancer Found., Dallas, 1992—; founding mem. Arena Stage Guild, Washington; bd. dirs. Nat. Mus. Women in Arts, 1987; presdl. appointment to Nat. Cancer Adv. Bd., 1991—; mem. bd. overseers Duke U. Cancer Ctr. Mem. Nat. Symphony Orch. Assn. (bd. dirs.). Episcopalian. Avocations: cross country skiing, mountain and cross country biking.

MALES-MADRID, SANDRA KAY, medical facility administrator; b. South Gate, Calif., Aug. 1, 1942; d. Albert Odus and Evelyn Louise (Corbett) Males; m. James O. Spurbeck, Apr. 15, 1963 (div. Nov. 1967); m. Miguel Madrid Jr., Feb. 9, 1980; stepchildren: Priscilla, Betty, Dru, Rachel. BA, U. Redlands, Calif., 1987; MHA, Chapman U., 1993. Payroll clk. Lever Bros. Co., Los Angeles, 1961-69; med. asst. William Stafford, M.D., Fullerton, Calif., 1969-71; mgr. office David H. Armstrong, M.D., Inc., Fullerton, 1971-79; mgr. office Med. Ctr. for Women, Fullerton, 1977-79, adminstr., 1986—; owner Sandy's Discount Boutique, Hemet, Sun City, Calif., 1979-83; asst. adminstr. Fullerton Cardiovascular Med. Group, 1983-86; cons., tchr. Riverside (Calif.) Community Coll., 1984-86; bd. dirs. No. Orange County Regional Occupational Ctr., Anaheim, Calif., 1985—. Vol. Riverside Rape Crisis Ctr., 1984-87. Mem. DAR. Republican. Club: Fullerton. Lodge: Soroptimist (Sun City) (sec. 1982-83, Women Helping Women award 1985). Office: Fullerton Cardiovascular Med Group 2720 N Harbor Blvd Ste 210 Fullerton CA 92635-2626

MALEY, PATRICIA ANN, preservation planner; b. Wilmington, Del., Dec. 25, 1955; d. James Alfred and Frances Louise (Fenimore) M.; m. Scott A. Stone, Dec. 7, 1991. AA, Cecil C.C., 1973; BA, U. Del., 1975, MA, 1981. Cert. planner: cert. secondary tchr., Del. Analyst econ. devel. City of Wilmington, 1977-78, evaluation specialist, 1978-80, planner II mayor's office, 1980-86, cons. preservation, 1986-87; dir. Belle Meade Mansion, Nashville, 1987-88; dir. planning, devel. Children's Bur. of Del., Wilmington, 1988; prin. preservation planner Environ. Mgmt. Ctr., Brandywine Conservancy, Chadds Ford, Pa., 1988-92; planning cons., 1992-95; design review and preservation commn. coord. Wilmington Dept. Planning, 1995—; cons. cultural resources M.A.A.R. Inc., Newark, Del., 1987, ITC Cons., Wilmington, 1985-86. Contbg. photographer America's City Halls, 1984; author numerous Nat. Register nominations, 1980-86; 88—. Pres., founder Haynes Park Civic Assn., Wilmington, 1977-80; photographer Biden U.S. Senate Campaign, New Castle County, Del., 1984; sec. parish coun. Our Lady Fatima Roman Cath. Ch., 1985-86, choir dir., 1983-87; mem. com. on design & renovation of worship spaces Diocese of Wilmington, also mem. com. on music; bd. dirs. Del. Children's Theatre; music dir. St. Elizabeth Ann Seton parish, Bear, Del., 1988—. U. Del. fellow, 1976-77. Mem. Nat. Trust Hist. Preservation, Am. Inst. Cert. Planners, Am. Planning Assn., Nat. Pastoral Musicians Assn., Del. Soc. Architects, Del. Archeol. Soc., Del. Hist. Soc., Pi Sigma Alpha. Democrat. Office: City of Wilmington Dept Planning 800 French St 7th Fl Wilmington DE 19801

MALIN, JO ELLEN, college administrator; b. St. Louis, Sept. 25, 1942; d. Louis and Bernice (Lasky) M.; children: David Malin-Roodman, Sarah Malin-Roodman. BA, Washington U., St. Louis, 1964; MA, Ind. U., 1968; PhD, SUNY, Binghamton, 1995. Pub. rels. coord. Broome County chpt. ARC, Binghamton, N.Y., 1979-80; asst. to med. dir. So. Tier Women's Svcs., Binghamton, 1980-84; dir. pub. rels. and devel. Good Shepherd-Fairview Home, Binghamton, 1983-86; asst. to vice provost for undergrad. studies SUNY, Binghamton, 1996—, project dir. ednl. talent search Sch. Edn. and Human Devel., 1987—; field reader Upward Bound Proposal Competition, U.S. Dept. Edn., 1995; presenter in field. Recipient Woman of Achievement award Broome County Status of Women Coun., 1995, Mary McLeod Bethune Edn. award Broome County Urban League, 1992. Mem. Nat. Coun. Ednl. Opportunity Assn. (founder Women's Network, editl. bd. jour.), Assn. for Equality and Excellence in Edn. (bd. dirs., Pres.'s award 1991-92), N.Y. State Fin. Aid Adminstrs. Assn. Office: Binghamton U PO Box 6000 Binghamton NY 13902-6000

MALINA, JUDITH, actress, director, producer, writer; b. Kiel, Germany, June 4, 1926; came to U.S., 1945; d. Max and Rosel (Zamora) M.; m. Julian Beck, Oct. 30, 1948 (dec.); m. Hanon Reznikov, May 6, 1988; children—Garrick Maxwell, Isha Manna. Graduate, Dramatic Workshop, New Sch. Social Research, 1945-47. adj. prof. Columbia U. Founder, producer, actress, dir. The Living Theatre, 1947—; dir., actress: The Thirteenth God, Childish Jokes, Ladies Voices, He Who Says Yes and He Who Says No, The Dialogue of the Mannequin and the Young Man, 1951, Man Is Man, 1962, Mysteries and Smaller Pieces, 1964, Antigone, 1965, Paradise Now, 1968, The Legacy of Cain (including Seven Meditations on Political Sadomasochism), 1970-77, Strike Support Oratorium, 1974, Six Public Acts, The Money Tower, 1975, Prometheus, 1978, Masse Mensch, 1980, The Living Theatre Retrospectacle, 1986, The Zero Method, 1991; dir.: Doctor Faustus Lights the Lights, 1951, Desire Trapped by the Tail, Faustina, Sweeney Agonistes, The Heroes, Ubu the King, 1952, The Age of Anxiety, The Spook Sonata, Orpheus, 1954, The Connection, 1959, In the Jungle of Cities, 1960, The Apple, 1961, The Mountain Giants 1962, The Brig, 1963, The Maids, Frankenstein, 1965, The Archeology of Sleep, 1983, Kassandra, 1987, Us, 1987, VKTMS, 1988, I and I, 1989, German Requiem, 1990, Not in My Name, 1994; actress: The Idiot King, 1954, Tonight We Improvise, Phedre, The Young Disciple, 1955, Many Loves, The Cave at Machpelah, 1959, Women of Trachis, 1960, The Yellow Methuselah, 1982, Poland/1931, 1988, Anarchia, 1993; appeared in films: Flaming Creatures, 1962, Amore, Amore, 1966, Wheel of Ashes, 1967, Le Compromise, 1968, Etre Libre, 1968, Paradise Now, 1969, Dog Day Afternoon, 1974, Signals Through the Flames, 1983, Radio Days, 1986, China Girl, 1987, Lost Paradise, 1988, Enemies, A Love Story, 1989, Awakenings, 1990, The Addams Family, 1991, Household Saints, 1993; author: Paradise Now, 1971, The Enormous Despair, 1972, The Legacy of Cain (3 pilot projects), 1973, Seven Meditations on Political Sadomasochism, 1977, Living Means Theater, 1978, Theatre Diaries: Brazil and Bologna, 1978, Poems of a Wandering Jewess, 1983, The Diaries of Judith Malina 1947-57, 1984; translator: Antigone (B. Brecht), 1990. Vice chmn. U.S. Com. for Justice to Latin Am. Polit. Prisoners, 1973-74; sponsor Am. Friends of Brazil, 1973; mem. exec. coun. War Resisters League. Recipient Lola D'Annunzio award, 1959, Page One award Newspaper Guild, 1960, Obie awards, 1960, 1964, 1969, 1975, 87, 89, Grand Prix de Theatre des Nations, 1961, Paris Critics Circle medallion, 1961, Prix de l'Universite Paris, 1961, New Eng. Theatre Conf. award, 1962, Olympio prize Italy, 1967, 9th Centennial medal U. Bologna, Italy, 1988; named Humanist of the Yr., 1984; Guggenheim fellow, 1985. Office: Writers & Artists Agency 19 W 44th St Ste 100 New York NY 10036

MALINOWSKI, MARYA, child development specialist, consultant, dancer; b. Willimantic, Conn., Oct. 29, 1957; d. Zenon Stanley and Shirley (Nathanson) M. BA in History, Conn. Coll., 1978; MA in Dance and Movement Therapy, UCLA, 1986; MA Early Childhood Spl. Edn., Calif. State U., 1991. Program dir. Calif. Pediat. and Family Svcs., Azusa, 1988—, Spl. Children's Ctr., Pasadena, Calif., 1988—; child devel. coord. family recovery program Calif. State U., L.A., 1990-94, infant dept. specialist high risk infant project, 1994—; lead tchr., dance movement therapist, Atwater Park Ctr., L.A., 1982-89; cons. Children's Inst. Internat., L.A., 1994-96; presenter, trainer in field. Mem. Nat. Assn. Edn. Young Children, Infant Devel. Assn., Assn. for Suprvsn. and Curriculum Devel. Office: Calif Pediat and Family Svcs 326 E Foothill Pl Azusa CA 91702

MALINOWSKI, PATRICIA A., community college educator; b. Buffalo, N.Y., Jan. 19, 1950; d. Raymond J. and Emily M. (Ferek) Cybulski; m. Leonard T. Malinowski, July 12, 1975; children: Adam, Christopher. BA, SUNY, Fredonia, 1971; MEd, Bowling Green State U., 1972. Asst. prof. devel. studies Finger Lakes C.C., Canandaigua, N.Y., 1987-92, assoc. prof., 1992-96, prof. devel. studies, 1996—, chairperson devel. studies dept., 1991—. Editor: Rsch. and Teaching in Devel. Edn., 1990—, (monographs) Perspectives on Teaching in Development Edn., 1992, 93, Issues in Assessment, 1993, 94; contbr. articles to profl. jours. Mem. sch. bd. St. Mary's Sch., Canandaigua, 1993—, sec. parent's adv. com., 1994-95; mem. program com. Literacy Vols., Canandaigua, 1994—. Mem. N.Y. Coll. Learning Skills (v.p., sec., conf. chair 1987—), NADE (Outstanding Publ. award 1995), N.Y. State Reading Assn., Nat. C.C. Chair Acad. (editl. bd. 1992—), Internat. Reading Assn. (editl. bd. 1994—), Nat. Coun. Tchrs. English. Office: Finger Lakes CC 4355 Lake Shore Dr Canandaigua NY 14424

MALKIEL, NANCY WEISS, college dean, history educator; b. Newark, Feb. 14, 1944; d. William and Ruth Sylvia (Puder) W.; m. Burton G Malkiel, July 31, 1988. BA summa cum laude, Smith Coll., 1965; MA, Harvard U., 1966, PhD, 1970. Asst. prof. history Princeton (N.J.) U., 1969-75, assoc. prof., 1975-82, prof., 1982—, master Dean Mathey Coll., 1982-86, dean of coll., 1987—. Author (as Nancy J. Weiss): Charles Francis Murphy, 1858-1924: Respectability and Responsibility in Tammany Politics, 1968, (with others) Blacks in America: Bibliographical Essays, 1971, The National Urban League, 1910-1940, 1974, Farewell to the Party of Lincoln: Black Politics in the Age of FDR, 1983 (Berkshire Conf. of Women Historians prize 1984), Whitney M. Young Jr., and the Struggle for Civil Rights, 1989. Trustee Smith Coll., Northampton, Mass., 1984-94, Woodrow Wilson Nat. Fellowship Found., 1975—. Fellow Woodrow Wilson Found., 1965, Charles Warren Ctr. for Studies in Am. History, 1976-77, Radcliffe Inst., 1976-77, Ctr. for Advanced Study in Behavioral Scis., 1986-87. Mem. Am. Hist. Assn., Orgn. Am. Historians (chmn. status women hist. profession 1972-75), So. Hist. Assn., Phi Beta Kappa. Democrat. Jewish. Office: Princeton U Office Dean Of College Princeton NJ 08544

MALKIEWICZ, ELIZABETH MARY, art director; b. Buffalo, Mar. 26, 1943; d. Frank Joseph and Jennie (Ferner) Tomaselli; m. Thaddeus F. Malkiewicz, June 13, 1975 (dec. Oct. 1995); children: Allen, June. Student, IBM Computer Ctr., Buffalo, 1962-64; A in Comm. Art, Bryant & Stratton Bus. Inst., Buffalo, 1987. With creativity ctr. Ingram Micro D, Buffalo, 1987-88; art dir. Langston Hughes Ctr., Buffalo, 1988-89; art dir., designer Adventures Mktg., Buffalo, 1988-89; exec. dir. to executrix Sisti Art Gallery, Buffalo, 1990-94; pres., art instr. Elizabeth's Creative Svcs., Buffalo, 1995—. Group shows include Bryant & Stratton Bus. Inst., Buffalo, 1985-87, Big Orbit Gallery, Buffalo, 1987-95, Lewiston Italian Art Ctr., 1988-89, Buffalo Soc. Artists, 1989-91, Perimeter Gallery, Buffalo, 1990-96, Carnegie Art Ctr, 1993-96, John Yergers Studio & Gallery, Buffalo, 1994—, Fine Line Gallery, Buffalo, 1995-96, Benjamins Art Gallery, Buffalo, 1996, Buffalo Hist. Soc. Photo Show, 1996; author The Personnal Planner. Exec. asst. to dir. Ashford Hollow Arts Found., Buffalo, 1974-94, asst. after sch. art program, 1989, cons.; active Alzheimer's Assn., 1995—. Mem. Carnegie Art Inst. Democrat. Roman Catholic. Home and Office: 43 Essex St Buffalo NY 14213

MALLARY, GERTRUDE ROBINSON, civic worker; b. Springfield, Mass., Aug. 19, 1902; d. George Edward and Jennie (Slater) Robinson; m. R. DeWitt Mallary, Sept. 15, 1923; children: R. DeWitt, Richard Walker; student, Bennett Coll., 1921-22, U. Conn., 1941-42; LLD (hon.), U. Vt., 1996. Co-owner, ptnr. Mallary Farm, Bradford, Vt., 1936-93; mem. Vt. Ho. of Reps., 1953-56, sec. agr. com., 1953, mem. appropriations com., 1955; mem. Vt. Senate, 1957-58, mem. appropriations com., clk. pub. health com., vice chmn. edn. com. Pres., Jr. League, Springfield, 1931-33; trustee Wesson Meml. Hosp., Springfield, 1937-42, chmn. nursing services, 1939-42; chmn. Springfield Council Social Agys., 1938-40; mem. Mass. Commn. Pub. Safety, 1941-42; pres. Vt. Holstein Club, 1951-53; mem. Vt. Bd. Recreation, 1959-65; trustee Fairlee (Vt.) Public Library, 1953-84, Asa Bloomer Found., 1963-71, Justin Smith Morrill Found., 1964-71, pres., 1968-71; chmn. Fairlee Bicentennial Com., 1974-77. Recipient Theresa R. Brungardt award, 1979, co-recipient with husband Master Breeders award Vt. Holstein Assn., 1979, Master Breeders award New Eng. Holstein Assn., 1969, Disting. Svc. award, 1989. Mem. Vt. Hist. Soc. (hon.), Bradford Hist. Soc. (pres. 1965-69), Fairlee Hist. Socs., Am. Antiquarian Soc. Editor New Eng. Holstein Bull., 1947-50. Address: Mallary Farm RR1 Box 620 Bradford VT 05033

MALLERY, ANNE LOUISE, elementary education educator, consultant; b. Myersdale, Pa., June 14, 1934; d. Samuel Addison and Ruth Elizabeth (Meehan) M.; m. Richard Gwen Jones, Mar. 9, 1953 (div. 1974); children: Valerie Anne, Joseph Samuel, Richard Alan (dec.). BS in Edn., Calif. U., Pa., 1970, MEd, 1972; EdD, Pa. State U., 1980. From proficiency coord. to prof. elem. edn. Millersville (Pa.) U., 1980—; asst. to pres. for planning MobileVision Tech., Inc., Coral Gables, Fla., 1990—; editor Innovative Learning Strategy, Nat. Publ., 1989—; cons. East Brunswick Pub. Schs., 1995; cons. Pequea Valley H.S., Lancaster, Pa., 1985, Cambridge Adult Edn. Co., 1987, Conawago Elem. Sch., York, Pa., 1991; co-dir. NEH grant, 1993-94. Co-author The Secret Cave Multimodal Reading Program; contbr. numerous articles to profl. jours. Judge Intelligencer Reg. Spelling Bee, Lancaster, 1990,91. Mem. Assn. Pa. State Coll. and U. Faculty, Internat. Reading Assn., Lancaster Lebanon Reading Assn., Assn. Tchr. Educators, Am. Assn. Colls. Tchr. Edn., Am. Reading Forum. Republican. Presbyterian. Home: 24 Strawberry Ln Lancaster PA 17602-1639 Office: Millersville Univ Stayer Education Ctr Millersville PA 17551

MALLETT, HELENE GETTLER, elementary education educator; b. Goshen, N.Y., Aug. 20, 1937; d. John and Anna Gettler; m. Richard David Mallett, July 29, 1967; 1 child, Anna Alma. BS in Fgn. Svc., Georgetown U., 1959; MA, SUNY, Stonybrook, 1989. Supr. Fulbright Program/Europe Inst. Internat. Edn., N.Y.C., 1961-65; editor Am. Assn. Fund Raising Coun., N.Y.C., 1965-67; coord. adult ED/ESL programs BOCES 3, Deer Park, N.Y., 1973-85; tchr. UFSD #3 and UFSD #4, Huntington, N.Y., 1967—; trustee Eastwood Sch., Oyster Bay, N.Y., 1977-83; alumni interviewer, Georgetown U., Washington, 1989—. Mem. ASCD, Nat. Coun. for the Social Studies, N.Y. State United Tchrs. (com. 100), Chemist Club. Home: 79 Little Neck Rd Centerport NY 11721-1615

MALLETTE, PHYLLIS SPENCER COOPER, medical/surgical nurse; b. Chestertown, Md., Nov. 18, 1944; d. Charles P. and Elma (Brown) Spencer; children: Winsor A. Cooper, III and Elma Cooper Henderson; m. Arthur E. Mallette, June 5, 1982. ASN, Rutgers U., 1965; BSN cum laude, Trenton State Coll., 1978. Cert. critical care, IV therapy, acute respiratory care, OSHA regulations, advanced coronary care, med. office mgmt., case mgmt., utilization rev.; RN, Md., N.J., Pa. Nurse delivery room St. Francis Med. Ctr., Trenton, N.J., 1971-73; nurse ICU Delaware Valley Med. Ctr., Langhorne, Pa., 1973-74; coord. nights Robert Wood Johnson U. Hosp., New Brunswick, N.J., 1974-75; occupational health RN Warner-Lambert/Parke-Davis Co., Morris Plains, N.J., 1977-79; sr. profl. rep. hosp., coord. sales tng. Merck Human Health Svcs. Divsn., Phila., 1979-89; co-coord. 400 trainee field force expansion Merck Sharp & Dohme, Denver, 1989; clin. nurse Johns Hopkins Hosp., Balt., 1989-90; office mgr. Arthur E. Mallette, M.D., Pikesville, Md., 1990-94; quality mgmt. specialist United Health Care, Inc., Balt., 1994—; med. cons. N.J. Pub. TV, Trenton, 1974. Mem. Sigma Theta Tau. Democrat. Methodist. Home: 10 Dodworth Ct Apt 303 Timonium MD 21093-2033 Office: United Health Care Inc 814 Light St Baltimore MD 21230-3945

MALLEY, FRANCES, health facility administrator, counselor; b. N.Y.C., Aug. 31, 1936; d. Frederick Peal and Theresa Jandersits; m. Denis Malley, June 30, 1962 (div. Jan. 1987); children: Donna, Scott. BS, Fordham U., 1963; MA, Hunter Coll., 1970; attended, Rutgers Sch. Alcohol Studies, 1982, 89, Ackerman Inst. Family Therapy, Calif. Coast U. Cert addictions counselor, alcohol and drug counselor, Pa., adminstrn. and supervision, N.J. Counselor in trng. Recovery unit Perth Amboy (N.J.) Gen. Hosp., 1981-82; family edn. counselor Princeton House Treatment Facility, 1982-84; family edn. counselor, primary therapist Passaic Addiction Rehabilitative Treatment Svcs. Facility, 1984-85; counselor, clin. supr., program dir. Cath. Charities Agy., N.J., 1985-92; exec. dir. Berks Counseling Ctr., Reading, Pa., 1992—; adj. prof. Essex C.C., 1986-87, Cedar Crest Coll., 1990—; mem. Mayor's com. on drug abuse, Edison, N.J., 1978-82, N.J. task force on women and alcohol, 1982-88; chair Profl. adv. coun. on alcohol and drug abuse, 1990-92; bd. dirs. Lehigh Valley Addiction Treatment Svcs. Active coun. World Affairs; v.p. N.J. League Women Voters, Edison, 1969-73; bd. dirs. Edison Bd. Edn., 1973-80. Mem. AAUW, Nat. Assn. Alcohol and Drug Abuse Counselors, Pa. Assn. Alcohol and Drug Abuse Counselors.

MALLISON, CAROL SUE, human services administrator; b. N.Y.C., July 10, 1952; d. Glenn Stanley and Carolyn Murray (Weddell) M. AAS, SUNY Farmingdale, 1972; BA in Psychology, SUNY Oswego, 1974. Dir. tng., asst. dir., dir. Farnham Youth Devel. Ctr., Oswego, 1975-77; dep. dir., case worker Cmty. Action Planning Coun., Watertown, N.Y., 1977-79; law asst. Legal Svcs. Ctrl. N.Y., Watertown, 1979-82; mgr. sect. and housing Econ. Opportunity Corp, Ithaca, N.Y., 1982-85; mgr. rental, dep. dir. Ithaca Neighborhood Housing Svcs., 1985-95; exec. dir. McGraw House, 1996—; ombudsperson Village of Lansing, N.Y., 1989—; com. mem. City of Ithaca, 1990—; sec. Landlords Assn. Tompkins County, N.Y., 1990—; mem. Homeless Task Force, Ithaca, 1989—. Vol. mediator Cmty. Dispute and Resolution Ctr., Ithaca, 1995—; co-coord. New Fields of Fun Playground com., Newfield, N.Y., 1992—; vol. staff N.Y. Yearly Meeting, Silver Bay, 1984—. Mem. Bus. and Profl. Women's Club (sec. 1994—), Women's Motorcycle Found. (vol.). Democrat. Mem. Soc. of Friends. Home: 137 Bank St Newfield NY 14867 Office: 200 McGraw House Ithaca NY 14850

MALLO, MAUREEN ELIZABETH, elementary education educator; b. Niagara Falls, N.Y., June 18, 1949; d. Joseph Peter and Lorraine Elizabeth (Kenneth) M.; m. Matthew Joel Singer, Feb. 7, 1981; children: Jacob, Joseph, Elizabeth. BA, Nazareth Coll. of Rochester, N.Y., 1971, MSE, 1978. Cert. tchr. N-8 Wis.; Am. Montessori cert.; Internat. Elem. Montessori cert. Tchr. Trinity Montessori Sch., Rochester, 1971-76, MacDowell Montessori Sch., Milw., 1977-82, Littleham Primary-Infant Sch., Eng., summer 1980, Greenfield Montessori Sch., Milw., 1985-90, Grand Ave. Mid. Sch., Milw., 1991-92, MacDowell Montessori Sch., Milw., 1992—. Troop leader Girl Scouts U.S. Mem. Wis. Edn. Assn. Coun., Milw. Tchr. Assn., PTO, N.Am. Montessori Tchr. Assn. Home: 250 N 50th St Milwaukee WI 53208-3630 Office: 1711 W Highland Ave Milwaukee WI 53233-1166

MALLORY, GLORIA GRIFFIN, educational consultant; b. Alhambra, Calif., May 30, 1938; d. Robert Wiley and Anna (Marcotrigiano) Griffin; m. Robert Glenn Mallory, May 1, 1971; 1 child, Jeremy Griffin. BFA, U.

N.Mex., 1960, MA, 1965, PhD, 1972. Tchr. Coronado (Calif.) H.S., 1960-62, Jefferson Jr. H.S., Albuquerque, 1962-63; grad. asst. U. N.Mex., Albuquerque, 1963-65, Northwestern U., Evanston, Ill., 1965-66; tchr. St. Michal's H.S., Santa Fe, 1966-67; cons. Albuquerque Pub. Sch., 1967-68; instr. U. N.Mex., 1968-71; sr. rsch. assoc. Child Devel. Program, Albuquerque, 1971-72; sr. rsch. assoc. Albuquerque Urban Obs., 1972-76, dir., 1976-81; cons. Albuquerque Pub. Schs., 1981-82; headmistress Manzano Day Sch., Albuquerque, 1983-93; interim headmistress Good Shepherd Episcopal Sch., Dallas, 1994-95; cons. The Edn. Group, Dallas, 1995—. Pres. YWCA, Albuquerque, 1982-83; chmn. United Way of Ctrl. N.Mex., Albuquerque, 1985; pres. Albuquerque Cmty. Fedn., 1988-91, Alumni Assn. U. N.Mex., 1990-91. Recipient Outstanding Vol. award United Way, 1985, Lobo award U. N.Mex. Mortar Bd. Alumni, 1994. Mem. Elem. Sch. Heads Assn. (assoc.), Jr. League Albuquerque (sustainer). Democrat. Episcopalian. Home: PO Box 1500 Corrales NM 87048 Office: The Edn Group 5952 Royal Ln Ste 203 Dallas TX 75230

MALLOY, KATHLEEN SHARON, lawyer; b. Evergreen Park, Ill., Apr. 7, 1948; d. Clarence Edmund and Ruth Elizabeth (Petrini) M.; m. Randall Kleinman, Aug. 5, 1978; children: Brighid, Ellena, Grant. BA in Psychology, St. Louis U., 1970; JD, Loyola U., Chgo., 1976. Bar: Ill. 1976, Calif. 1977. CPCU; assoc. in reinsurance. Account exec. Complete Equity Mkts., Wheeling, Ill., 1970-76, corp. counsel, 1976-80, v.p., gen. counsel, 1980-83, exec. v.p., gen. counsel, 1983, chief oper. officer, gen. counsel, 1984-85, vice chmn. bd., gen. counsel, 1986-90; founding ptnr. firm Malloy & Kleinman, P.C., Des Plaines, Ill., 1985—. Vol. atty. legal aid orgns., Calif., 1976-79; dir. Keep Des Plaines Beautiful, Inc., 1990-92. Mem. ABA, Calif. State Bar Assn., Mensa, Women's Bar Assn., Nat. Legal Aid and Defender Assn. (ex-officio mem. ins. com. 1986-94), Am. Soc. Chartered Property Casualty Underwriters. Office: Malloy & Kleinman PC 640 Pearson St Ste 206 Des Plaines IL 60016-4624

MALLOY, SANDRA MIRIAM, information specialist; b. Pitts., Sept. 22, 1953; d. David Leonard and Frances (Hershkowitz) M.; m. William Edward O'Brien, June 22, 1992. BA, UCLA, 1975; MLS, U. So. Calif., 1976. Asst. reference libr. Health Scis. Libr. Tex. Tech U., Lubbock, 1978-79, El Paso Pub. Libr., Tex., 1979-81; reference libr. Health Scis. Libr. U. Calif., Davis, 1981, reference libr. Shields Libr., 1982; rsch. dir. Am. Internat. Data Search, Sacramento, 1983, Info. on Demand, Berkeley, Calif., 1983-87; western region mktg. rep. ORBIT Search Svc., Mac Lean, Va., 1987-89; sr. info. specialist Business Wire, San Fransisco, 1989—. Contbr. articles to profl. jours., also East Bay Express newspaper, 1988—. Mem. Nat. Orgn. Women, Spl. Librs. Assn., Phi Beta Kappa. Office: Business Wire 44 Montgomery 39th Floor San Francisco CA 94104

MALM, RITA H., securities executive; d. George Peter and Helen Marie (Woodward) Pellegrini; student Packard Jr. Coll., 1950-52, N.Y. Inst. Fin., 1954, Wagner Coll., 1955; m. Robert J. Malm, Apr. 19, 1970. Sales asst. Dean Witter & Co., N.Y.C., 1959-63, asst. v.p., compliance dir., 1969-74; v.p., dir. Securities Ind. Assocs., N.Y.C., 1969-72; chief exec. officer Muriel Siebert & Co., Inc., N.Y.C., 1981-83; pres., founder Madison-Chapin Assocs., N.Y.C., 1984-89; pres. Hayward Malm Securities, Ltd., 1989-93; pres., founder Concord Stuart, Inc., 1993—; art mktg. cons. Author: Dying On Wall Street, 1996. Mem. NAFE (bd. dirs), Am. Cancer Soc. (bd. dirs. Jupiter/Tequesta chpt. 1992-95), Profl. Women's Network (founder Palm Beach and Martin Counties 1991), Women's Bond Club N.Y. (dir., v.p., program chmn., pres. 1980-82), Cornell U. Club Ea. Fla. (bd. dirs. 1992—). Office: 1061 E Indiantown Rd Ste 410 Jupiter FL 33477

MALMBERG, AMANDA KAYE, corporate auditor; b. Ariz., Mar. 2, 1971; d. J. Paul and Robyn L. (Tegge) M. BSBA in Acctg. and Mktg., Trinity U., 1993. CPA, Minn., CMA, Minn. Internal auditor 3M, St. Paul, 1993-95, advanced internal auditor, 1995, sr. auditor, 1996—; cons. Jr. Achievement, Minn., 1994—. Vol. 2d Harvest Food Bank, St. Paul, 1994-95. Mem. Inst. Mgmt. Accts. Presbyterian. Office: 3M Bldg 224-5N-11 3M Center Saint Paul MN 55144

MALME, JANE HAMLETT, lawyer, educator, researcher; b. N.Y.C., Dec. 2, 1934; d. Robert T. and Minnie (Means) Hamlett; m. Charles I. Maime, June 17, 1961; children: Robert H., Karen I. AB, Brown U., 1956; cert., U. Kobenhavn, Copenhagen, Denmark, 1959; JD, Northeastern U., 1977. Bar: Mass., 1977. Counsel Mass. Tax Commn., Boston, 1978-79; chief bur. local assessment Mass. Dept. Revenue, Boston, 1978-90; owner Mcpl. Mgmt. and Taxation Cons. Svcs., Hingham, Mass., 1990—; fellow Lincoln Inst. Land Policy, Inc., Cambridge, Mass., 1993—; faculty Lincoln Inst. Land Policy, Inc., Cambridge, 1989—; cons. state, provincial coun. Internat. Assn. Assessing Officers Chgo., 1990—; advisor property tax OECD, Paris, 1993—; advisor property tax USAID, Russia, 1995-96, Korea Tax Inst., 1995-96. Co-author: (with Joan Youngman) Internat. Survey of Taxes on Land and Buildings, 1994; contbr. articles to tax jours., papers for Lincoln Inst. of Land Policy, Inc., 1991—. Mem. Dem. Town Com., Hingham, 1990-96; trustee Old Ship Ch., Hingham, 1992—; treas. Betty Taymor Scholarship Fund, Boston, 1992—; pres. Network for Women in Politics and Govt., McCormick Inst., Boston, 1992-94. Mem. Internat Assn. Assessing Officers (founder, state and prov. adminstrv. sec., Presidential citation 1983), Mass. Assn. Assessing Officers (hon. lifetime), Mass. Bar Assn., Womens Bar Assn., Nat. Assn. Tax Adminstrs. (chair property tax sect. 1988). Unitarian Universalist. Office: Lincoln Inst Land Policy 113 Brattle St Cambridge MA 02138-3407

MALONE, PERRILLAH ATKINSON (PAT MALONE), retired state official; b. Montgomery, Ala., Mar. 17, 1922; d. Odolph Edgar and Myrtle (Fondren) Atkinson. BS, Oglethorpe U., 1956; MAT, Emory U., 1962. Asst. editor, then acting editor Emory U., 1958-64; asst. project officer Ga. Dept. Pub. Health, Atlanta, 1965-68; asst. project dir. Ga. Ednl. Improvement Coun., 1968-69, assoc. dir., 1970-71; dir. career svcs. State Scholarship Commn., Atlanta, 1971-74; rev. coord. Div. Phys. Health, Ga. Dept. Human Resources, Atlanta, 1974-79; project dir. So. Regional Edn. Bd., 1979-81; specialist Div. Family and Children Svcs., Atlanta, 1982-91, ret., 1991; mem. Gov.'s Commn. on Nursing Edn. and Nursing Practice, 1972-75, Aging Svcs. Task Force, Atlanta Regional Commn., 1985-95; book reviewer Atlanta Jour.-Constn., 1962-79. Recipient Recognition award Ga. Nursing Assn., 1976, Korsell award Ga. League for Nursing, 1974, Alumni Honor award Emory U., 1964. Mem. APHA, Ga. Gerontology Soc. (editor GGS Newsletter 1988-92, Lewis Newmark award 1991). Methodist. Home: 1146 Oxford Rd NE Atlanta GA 30306-2608

MALONEY, CAROLYN BOSHER, congresswoman; b. Feb. 19, 1948; d. R.G. and Christine (Clegg) Bosher; m. C.H.W. Maloney, 1976; children: Christina, Virginia. Student, Greensboro Coll., New Sch. for Social Rsch., N.Y., U. Dijon, Paris. Former mem. N.Y. State Assembly Housing Com., N.Y.C Council dist. 8; mem. 103rd Congress from 14th N.Y. dist., Washington, 1993—, mem. banking and fin. svcs. com. capital markets, securities and govt. sponsored enterprise, mem. fin. instns. and consumer credit com., mem. govt. reform and oversight com. govt. mgmt., info. and tech., mem. joint economic com. Past chmn. Common Cause; active Assn. for a Better N.Y., Manahattan Women's Polit. Caucus. Mem. NAACP, Nat. Orgn. Women, Hadassah. Home: 49 E 92nd St Apt 1A New York NY 10128-1326 Office: US Ho of Reps 1504 Longworth Washington DC 20515*

MALONEY, CAROLYN SCOTT (LYNN MALONEY), marketing professional; b. Clinton, Mass., Aug. 22, 1950; d. Harry Thomas and Veronica Scott (O'Donnell) Maedler; m. Wm. J. Maloney, Jan. 11, 1975. BS, State Coll. Worcester, 1972. Adminstr. Astra Pharmaceutical, Worcester, Mass., 1974-77; sales coord. Tracor Analytic, Elk Grove, Ill., 1977-81; sr. exec. asst. A.C. Nielsen Co., Northbrook, Ill., 1981-94; adminstrv. asst. Altair Corp., Lincolnshire, Ill., 1994-95, Marquette Venture Ptnrs., Deerfield, Ill., 1995—. Mem. Great Lakes Yacht Club, Bay Shore Yacht Club (newsletter editor 1988-90). Republican. Roman Catholic. Home: 144 Mockingbird Ln Wheeling IL 60090-3940 Office: Altair Corp 350 Barclay Blvd Lincolnshire IL 60069-3606

MALONEY, CHERYL ANN, author, photographer, theologian, entrepreneur; b. St. Paul, Aug. 30, 1949; d. Arlie Chester and Mary Dawn (Holm) M. AA, U. Minn., 1969, BA in Speech and Theatre, 1972; MA in Theology/Spirituality, Coll. St. Catherine, St. Paul, 1989, MA cert. in Pastoral Ministry, 1990; postgrad., Calif. Inst. Integral Studies, 1994—. Dir. Women's Network, Mpls., 1975-76; dir. cultural arts City of Bloomington, Minn., 1977-78; community organizer Mpls. Crime Prevention Program, 1979-80; bus. adminstr. Al's Auto Crushing, Inc., Mpls., 1980-81; rsch. assoc. St. Paul Ramsey Med. Ctr., 1981-83; adjustor Dependable Auto Appraisal, Inc., Bloomington, 1983; dir. mktg. and devel. Health Recovery Center, Mpls., 1983-85; cons. Autowoman, Inc., Mpls., 1985—; mktg. rep. Dashe and Thomson, Mpls., 1987-89; dir. sales and mktg. Fredrickson Communications, Mpls., 1989-91; freelance photographer, Mpls., 1971—; quality cons., 1991-94; ofcl. photographer Internat. Women's Ecumenical Decade Chs. Solidarity Women, 1993; speaker U. Bethlehem, Israel, 1993; tchr. Holy Childhood H.S., Jamaica, 1992; presenter M.R.A. Internat. 50th Anniversary Conf., Caux, Switzerland, 1996; dir. devel. Sisters of Holy Family, editor Family of Friends Newsletter; participant World Media Forum; co-coord. Women's Spirituality Workshop Series Sisters of Holy Family, 1996-97. Author: Housing Resource Book for Minneapolis, 1974, Women's Network Directory, 1976; photographer: Goodwill Designer Showcase Magazine, 1975. State Dem. del., St. Paul, 1976; coach and youth leader Unity South Ch., Bloomington, 1967-93; coach Ind. Ch., Mpls., 1984-92; chaplain U. St. Thomas, St. Paul, 1989-92, chair women and religion com.; outreach min., outreach min. Unity of Valley, Minn., 1990-93; U.S. rep. Gov. Gen.'s Conf., Jamaica, 1992; lay consociate Sisters St. Joseph, 1992, appt. peace and justice commn. and comm. adv. bd., 1993-95; presenter Reaching Beyond Borders, San Diego, 1996; chair 125th Anniversary Celebration Sisters of the Holy Family, 1997; presenter Internat. Youth Leadership Conf., Brazil, Uruguay, Argentina, 1993, coord., Caux, Switzerland, 1996. Recipient Celtic Studies award Coll. St. Catherine, St. Paul, 1988; honoree Hamnline U., St. Paul, 1993; Great Lakes Region scholar, 1986. Mem. AAUW, Mpls. Women's Rotary (bd. dirs. 1990-94), Minn. Coun. for Quality (editor newsletter 1993-94, Sales and Mktg. Execs. Am., Theol. Insights Prog. Coll. St. Catherine, M.R.A. Internat. (nat. team planners for M.R.A. N.Am. and S.Am. activities), Self-Employed Womens Club (co-dir., 1992-94), Le Group, Nat. Fedn. Ind. Bus. Home: 5501 E Queen Ave S Minneapolis MN 55410-2532 Office: Sisters of the Holy Family Dir of Devel 159 Washington Blvd Fremont CA 94539-0324

MALONEY, IRENE RYAN, artist, art educator; b. L.A., Feb. 26, 1946; d. John Louis and Irene Ercelle (Brannen) Ryan; m. Patrick Edward Maloney, Jan.15, 1972; children: Ryan, Brannen. BA in Art, Marymount/Loyola Marymount U., 1968; MFA, U. Ill., 1990. Art instr. Middleton Sch., Skokie, Ill., 1975-77, Libertyville (Ill.) H.S., 1977-79; drawing instr. U. Ill., Chgo., 1989; art instr. Montay Coll., Chgo., 1991-95; adj. instr. painting U. Wis. Parkside, Kenosha, Fall 1993, Ray Coll. Design Woodfield, Schaumburg, Ill., Fall 1995; art fair chairperson Montay Coll., Chgo., 1992; jurur Scholastic Art award, Lake City, Ill., 1985, 87, Gruen Gallery, Chgo., Millenium Gallery, Libertyville, Ill.; tchg. asst. U. Ill., chgo., 1989; one person exhbn. St. Xavier U., 1995. One person exhbn. Saint Xavier U., 1995.

MALONEY, LINDA MITCHELL, editor, religion educator; b. Houston, Apr. 10, 1939; d. David Bruce and Alta Marguerite (Chevrier) Mitchell. AB, St. Louis U., 1965, PhD, 1968, MA, 1983; M.I.B.S., U. S.C., 1981; ThD, U. Tübingen, Fed. Republic Germany, 1990. Asst. prof. New Testament Franciscan Sch. Theology, Berkeley, Calif., 1989-92, assoc. prof., 1992-95; acad. editor The Liturgical Press, Collegeville, Minn., 1995—. Author: The Captain from Connecticut, 1986, All That God Had Done with Them, 1991. Postdoctoral fellow Smithsonian Inst., 1969-70. Mem. Soc. Bibl. Lit., Cath. Bibl. Assn., Cath. Theol. Soc. Am., Am. Hist. Assn., Coordinating Com. on Women in the Hist. Profession, Am. Acad. Religion, Appalachian Mountain Club (Boston). Episcopalian. Office: The Liturgical Press Saint Johns Abbey Collegeville MN 56321

MALONEY, MARSHA ANN, health facility administrator; b. Kankakee, Ill., June 26, 1953; d. Vern K. and Marie L. (Sheehan) Van Der Karr; m. Matthew S. Maloney, Feb. 21, 1973. BA, Vanderbilt U., 1974. Lic. property/casualty ins. agt. Tenn., Miss. Property and casualty underwriter INA, Tenn., 1974-76; property and casualty ins. agt., office mgr. Robinson, Miller Inc., Tenn., 1976; sr. property and casualty ins. agt. Wirt, Yerger Ins. Agy., 1987-86; adminstr. Flagler Med., West Palm Beach, Fla., 1994—. Republican. Roman Catholic. Office: Flagler Med Assn 2801 N Flagler Dr West Palm Beach FL 33407

MALONEY, SHARON SUE, job-site coordinator; b. Parkersburg, W.Va., Aug. 5, 1943; d. Levin J. and Florence E. (Dye) Fordyce; m. Don Maloney Jr., Oct. 27, 1961; children: Don III, Chad Alan. Student, W.Va. State U. Job-site coord. Wood County Bd. Edn., Parkersburg, 1978—. Mem. Parkersburg City Coun., 1993—. Recipient Women of Excellence award Altrusa, 1991; named Outstanding Citizen W.Va., Gov. Gaston Caperton, 1992, Citizen of Yr., Fraternal Order of Police, 1991. Mem. Order Ea. Star (past officer), Ladies Oriental Shrine, White Shrine Jerusalem. Democrat. Methodist. Home and Office: 913 33rd St Parkersburg WV 26101

MALONEY, THERESE ADELE, insurance company executive; b. Quincy, Mass., Sept. 15, 1929; d. James Henry and F. Adele (Powers) M. BA in Econs., Coll. St. Elizabeth, Convent Station, N.J., 1951; AMP, Harvard U. Bus. Sch., 1981. CPCU. With Liberty Mut. Ins. Co., Boston, 1951-94, asst. v.p., asst. mgr. nat. risks, 1974-77, v.p., asst. mgr. nat. risks, 1977-79, v.p., mgr. nat. risks, 1979-86, sr. v.p. underwriting mktg. and adminstrn. 1986-87, exec. v.p. underwriting, policy decision, 1987-94, also bd. dirs.; pres. and bd. dirs. subs. Liberty Mut. (Bermuda) Ltd., 1981-94, LEXCO Ltd.; bd. dirs., dep. chmn. Liberty Mut. (U.K.) Ltd., London; bd. dirs. Liberty Mut. Ins. Co., Liberty Mut. Fire Ins. Co., Liberty Mut. Life Assurance Co., Liberty Fin. Cos.; mem. faculty Inst. Inst., Northeastern U., Boston, 1969-74; mem. adv. bd., risk mgmt. studies Ins. Inst. Am., 1977-83; mem. adv. coun. Suffolk U. Sch. Mgmt., 1984-96; mem. adv. coun. to program in internat. bus. rels. Fletcher Sch. Law and Diplomacy, 1985-94; cons. Exec. Svd. Corp., 1994—. Mem. Soc. CPCUs (past pres. Boston chpt.), Univ. Club, Boston Club.

MALOOF-MCCORMICK, RENÉE VERONICA, artist; b. N.Y.C., Mar. 25, 1926; d. Joseph J. and Afdokia (Gabriel) Maloof; m. Charles Joseph McCormick; children: Renée, Barbara, Kevin, Trisha, Charles Michael. Student, Drake Bus. Sch., 1946, Art Students League, N.Y.C., 1984, Arts Ctr. No. N.J.; studied with, Richard Poussette-Dart, Leo Manso, Bruce Dorfman, Roberto de Lamonica, Robert Beauchamp. Sec. Met. Life Ins. Co., N.Y.C., 1946-49; acting dir. Art Ctr. of N.J., New Milford, 1989-90; tchr. art St. Cecilia's, Englewood, N.J., 1990-91; tchr. religion New Milford, N.J., 1980-89; organizer art exhibits Art Ctr. N.J., 1985-89. One person shows include Broadway Gallery, Paterson, N.J., 1989, Ridgewood, N.J., 1990, Piermont (N.Y.) Fine Arts Gallery, 1995; exhibited in group shows Ridgewood Art Assn., 1983, Little Firehouse Theater Gallery, N.J., 1984, Interch. Ctr., N.Y.C., 1986, Bergen Mus. Art and Sci., N.J., 1985, 87, Saddle River Cultural Ctr., N.J., 1986, 87, 88, Summerfest Art Ctr. N.J., 1993, Unitarian Soc., Ridgewood, 1993, Ringwood (N.J.) Art Assn., 1993, Paterson Mus., 1993, others. Recipient awards Ringwood Art Assn., 1988, 93, Hudson County Artists Guild, 1984, Oil Pastel Assn., 1983; merit scholar Art Students League, 1983. Mem. Artists for Mental Health, Art Ctr. No. N.J. (bd. dirs.), Salute to Women in the Arts (past bd. dirs., awards 1985, 88), The Artists Circle, Watercolor Affiliates of N.J. Home: 1119 Warren St New Milford NJ 07646 Studio: Mill House 100 Cooper Mill Cooper St Bergenfield NJ 07621

MALOUF-CUNDY, PAMELA BONNIE, visual arts editor; b. Reseda, Calif., July 9, 1956; d. Jubert George and Marguerite I. (Llido) Malouf. AA in Cinema with honors, Valley Community Coll., 1976. Asst. film editor various film studios including Paramount, 20th Fox, CBS MTM, and others, 1976-80; post prodn. coordinator, supr. David Gerber Co., Culver City, Calif., 1981-82; post prodn. coordinator Paramount TV, Los Angeles, 1982-84; sole proprietor Trailers, Etc., North Hollywood, Calif., 1984-85; film and video editor Paramount Pictures, L.A., 1985-86; film editor Universal Studios, Universal City, Calif., 1987-89; film, video editor New World TV, L.A., 1991-92; associate dir. Tri-Star TV, Studio City, Calif., 1992-93; film and video editor various studios, Studio City, 1993—; owner, mgr. Choice Editing Systems, Northridge, Calif., 1993—. Film and video editor: (TV shows) A Year in the Life, MacGyver, Call to Glory, The Making of Shogun, Nightingales, Mission Impossible, Murder C.O.D., I'll Take Romance, Get a Life, A Fire in the Dark, The Fifth Corner, The Edge, others (movies) Search for Grace, Eyes of Terror, Then There Was One, Sweet Bird of Youth, Without You I'm Nothing, All in the Family, Rockford Files, Is There Life Out There?, Thrill; asst. film editor: (movies) King of Gypsies, Star Wars, others. Mem. Internat. Alliance of Theatrical Stage Employees and Moving Picture Machine Operators of U.S. and Can., Tri-Network (pres. 1979-80), Acad. Magical Arts, Inc., Am. Cinema Editors, Acad. TV Arts and Scis., Dir.'s Guild of Am. Democrat. Roman Catholic.

MALPEDE, KAREN, playwright, humanities educator; b. Wichita Falls, Tex., June 29, 1945; d. Joseph James Malpede and Doris Jane (Liebshutz) Isgrig; m. George M. Bartenieff, Oct. 4, 1993; 1 child, Carrie Sophia. BS with honors, U. Wis., 1967; MFA, Columbia U., 1971. Asst. prof. drama dept. Tisch Sch. of the Arts, N.Y.C., 1983-86; vis. prof. Smith Coll., Northampton, Mass.; co-founder, artistic dir. Theater Three Collaborative, Inc., N.Y.C., 1995—; playwright Theater for the New City, N.Y.C., 1987-94; resident playwright New Cycle Theater, Bklyn., 1976-84. Author: (play) The Beekeeper's Daughter, 1994, Kassandra, 1992, Better People, 1990, Us, 1987, (book) A Monster Has Stolen the Sun and Other Plays, 1987. Recipient Nat. McKnight Playwright's grant, 1994-95; Goddard fellow, 1994, Art Matters fellow, 1991. Mem. PEN (Am. ctr., woman's com. 1985-87), Dramatists Guild, Ctr. on Violence and Human Survival. Office: Tisch Sch of Arts 721 Broadway 3rd Fl New York NY 10003

MALSON, VERNA LEE, special education educator; b. Buffalo, Wyo., Mar. 29, 1937; d. Guy James and Vera Pearl (Curtis) Mayer; m. Jack Lee Malson, Apr. 20, 1955; children: Daniel Lee, Thomas James, Mark David, Scott Allen. BA in Elem. Edn. and Spl. Edn. magna cum laude, Met. State Coll., Denver, 1975; MA in Learning Disabilities, U. No. Colo., 1977. Cert. tchr., Colo. Tchr.-aide Wyo. State Tng. Sch., Lander, 1967-69; spl. edn. tchr. Bennett Sch. 29J, Colo., 1975-79, chmn. health, sci., social studies, 1977-79; spl. edn. tchr. Deer Trail Sch., Colo., 1979—, chmn. careers, gifted and talented, 1979-87, spl. edn./preschool tchr. 1992—; course cons. Regis Coll., Denver, 1990; mem. spl. edn. parent adv. com. East Central Bd. Coop. Ednl. Services, Limon, Colo. Colo. scholar Met. State Coll., 1974; Colo. Dept. Edn. grantee, 1979, 81; recipient Cert. of Achievement, Met. State Coll., 1993. Mem. Council Exceptional Children, Bennett Tchrs. Club (treas. 1977-79), Kappa Delta Pi. Republican. Presbyterian. Avocations: coin collecting; reading; sports. Home: PO Box 403 Deer Trail CO 80105-0403 Office: Deer Trail Pub Schs PO Box 26J Deer Trail CO 80105-0026

MALTZ, BRENDA MARIE, artist, nurse; b. Sacramento, Aug. 3, 1962; d. Robert Allen and Beverly Jean (Vaughn) Nelson; m. Charles Floyd Crawley, Oct. 1, 1982 (div. June 1986); 1 child, Krista; m. Ben Ray Maltz, Nov. 5, 1988; children: Kevin, John. Diploma in Nursing, Bapt. Sys. Sch. Nursing, Little Rock, 1982. RN, Wash. RN Bapt. Med. Ctr., Little Rock, 1982-83; RN emergency rm. Rogers (Ark.) Meml. Hosp., 1983-85; flight nurse Aero Med Express, Rogers, 1985-88; RN emergency rm. Health Scis. Ctr. U. Colo., Denver, 1988-89; RN emergency rm. Swedish Med. Ctr., Englewood, Colo., 1989-90; artist KB Maltz Sculpture Studio, Shelton, Wash., 1992—. Commd. bronze sculpture, 1995, 96. Mem. health curriculum bd. Coeur d'Alene (Idaho) Sch. Dist., 1991-92; bd. dirs. Shelton Art Commn., 1995—, Mason Gen. Hosp. Art Commn., Shelton, 1992—. Recipient 1st place award Internat. Doll Makers Assn., 1991, Best and the Brightest Show award Scottsdale (Ariz.) Artist Sch., 1994. Mem. Christians in the Visual Arts, Peninsula Art Assn. (bd. dirs. 1993—, Best of Show award 1995), Internat. Sculpture Soc. Baptist. Home: E 90 Arellem Rd Union WA 98592 Office: KB Maltz Sculpture Studio PO Box 1867 Shelton WA 98584

MALUNIS, ELENA BERGONZI, management and marketing executive; b. Vernasca, Italy, Nov. 13, 1940; d. Angelo and Mary (Dadomo) Bergonzi; m. Gary Paul Malunis, Oct. 26, 1968. BA, Hunter Coll., 1963; postgrad., NYU, 1963-68, U. Pa./Pa. State U., 1984-88. Various sales and mktg. mgmt. positions IBM Corp.; mgr. S/36 product line mgmt. mktg. and sales IBM Corp., White Plains, N.Y., 1984-88; mgr. segment mgmt. applications solution line of bus. IBM Corp., Valhalla, N.Y., 1988-91; mgr. decisions support sys. IBM Corp., Purchase, N.Y., 1991-93; mgr. software mktg. ops. IBM Corp., White Plains, 1993-94; program dir. mktg. ops. software group IBM Corp., Somers, N.Y., 1994-95, dir. ops. personal sys. product divsn., 1996—. Mem. Found. for Tarrytown (N.Y.) Schs., 1995-96, Sleepy Hollow Tax Payers Assn., North Tarrytown, 1990, Archtl. Rev. Bd., Village of North Tarrytown, 1991-94, St. Cabrini Nursing Home Aux., 1994-96, pres. Downing Wood Assn., Irvington, N.Y., 1984-86. Mem. Phi Beta Kappa, Pi Mu Epsilon. Home: 25 Hemlock Dr North Tarrytown NY 10591

MALVILLE, NANCY JEAN, anthropologist; b. Ft. Collins, Colo., July 24, 1937; d. Philip Grant and Florence Rebekah (Eyre) Koontz; m. John McKim Malville, Mar. 26, 1960; children: Katherine Malville Shipan, Leslie Malville Ellwood. BA, Coll. Wooster, 1959; MA, U. Colo., 1971, U. Colo., 1982; PhD, U. Colo., 1987. Rsch. assoc. dept. anthropology U. Colo., Boulder, 1988—. Contbr. rsch. articles to profl. jours. Office: U Colo Dept Anthropology Campus Box 233 Boulder CO 80309-0233

MAMARY, ANNE JENNIFER MANBECK, philosophy educator, women's studies educator, writer; b. Hempstead, N.Y., Nov. 2, 1964; d. Albert Mamary and Janet Jane Bright Manbeck. AB, Bryn Mawr (Pa.) Coll., 1986; PhD, SUNY, Binghamton, 1995. House mgr., counselor Clear Visions for Women, Binghamton, N.Y., 1987-89; tchg. asst. SUNY, Binghamton, 1989-91, instr., 1991-93; instr. Broome C.C., Binghamton, 1992-94; vis. asst. prof. SUNY, Cortland, 1994-95, St. Lawrence U., Canton, N.Y., 1995—. Co-editor: (anthology) Cultural Activisms: Poetic Voices, Political Voices, 1997; asst. book review editor: Hypatia: Jour. Feminist Philosophy, 1989-91; contbr. articles to profl. jours., chpt. to book. Intern, asst. editor Peace and Freedom, Women's Internat. League for Peace and Freedom, Phila., 1985; crisis line counselor Rape and Abuse Crisis Ctr., Binghamton, N.Y., 1986-89; coord. diversity project Girl Scouts Am., Indian Hills, Binghamton, N.Y.; vol. breast cancer program Health Dept., Broome County, N.Y., 1992-95; mem. Welfare Watch, Canton, N.Y., 1996—. Mem. Am. Philosoph. Assn., Nat. Women's Studies Assn., Soc. Ancient Greek Philosophy, Soc. Women in Philosophy. Office: St Lawrence U Philosophy Dept Canton NY 13617

MAMLOK, URSULA, composer, educator; b. Berlin, Feb. 1, 1928; d. John and Dorothy Lewis; m. Dwight G. Mamlok, Nov. 27, 1947. Student, Mannes Coll. Music, 1942-45; MusB, Manhattan Sch. Music, 1955, MusM, 1958. Mem. faculty dept. music NYU, 1967-74, CUNY, 1971-74; prof. composition Manhattan Sch. Music, N.Y.C., 1974—. Composer: numerous works including Variations and Interludes for 4 percussionists, 1973, Sextet, 1977, Festive Sounds, 1978, When Summer Sang, 1980, piano trio Panta rhei, 1981, 5 recital pieces for young pianists, 1983, From My Garden for solo viola or solo violin, 1983, Concertino for wind quintet, Strings and percussion, 1984, Der Andreas Garten for voice, flute and harp, 1986, Alariana for recorder, clarinet, bassoon, violin and cello, 1986, 3 Bagatelles for harpsichord, 1987, 5 Bagatelles for clarinet, violin, cello, 1988, Rhapsody for clarinet, viola, piano Inward Journey for Piano, 1989, Sonata for violin and piano, 1989, Music for flute, violin, cello, 1990, Girasol, a sextet for flute, violin, viola, cello and piano, 1991, Constellations for orch., 1993, Polarities for flute, violin, cello, piano, 1995. Recipient Serge Koussevitzky Found. commn., 1988, Walter Hinrichsen award Acad. Inst. Arts and Letters, 1989, commn. San Francisco Symphony, 1990; Nat. Endowment Arts grantee, 1974, Am. Inst. Acad. Arts and Letters grantee, 1981, 89, Martha Baird Rockefeller grantee, 1982; John Simon Gugenheim fellow, 1995. Mem. Am. Composers Alliance (dir., Opus One Rec. award 1987), Am. Soc. Univ. Composers, Am. Women Composers, N.Y. Women Composers, Internat. League Women Composers, Music Theory Soc. N.Y., Am. Music Ctr., Internat. Soc Contemporary Music (bd. dirs.), Fromm Found. Commn., Am. Guild Organists Com. Address: 315 E 86th St New York NY 10028-4714

MAMPRE, VIRGINIA ELIZABETH, communications executive; b. Chgo., Sept. 12, 1949; d. Albert Leon and Virginia S. (Joboul) M. BA with honors, U. Iowa, 1971; Masters degree, Ind. U., 1972; spl. cert., Harvard U., 1981. Cert. tchr. Harris Intern WTTW-TV Sta., Chgo., 1972, asst. dir., 1972-73; prod. and dir. WSIU/WUSI-TV Sta., Carbondale, Ill., 1973-74; instr. So. Ill. U., Carbondale, 1972-77; prog. and prod. mgr. WSIU/WUSI-TV, Carbondale, 1974-77; prog. dir. KUHT-TV Sta., Houston, 1977-83; pres. Victory Media, Inc., Houston, 1984-89, Mampre Media Internat., Houston, 1984—; pres. A.I.C.B.; cons. Corp. for Pub. Broadcasting, Washington,

1981-83; chmn. AWRT/YCOC Houston Metro Area, 1983-85, pres., 1983—, nat. v.p., 1985-90; adv. coun. PBS, Washington, 1981-83; bd. and programming chmn. So. Edn. Comms., Columbia, S.C., 1978-83; bd. dirs. TVPC; program bd. EEN. Contbg. author/editor to mags. including Focus, 1989, News & Views, 1987-88, In the Black, 1984-93; creator: (report card campaign) Multi-media, U.S., 1985—; exec. prodr. TV spls., pub. affairs and info., 1977-83 (awards 1978-91). Pres. bd. dirs. Houston Fin. Coun., 1983—; pres. Child Abuse Prevention Coun., Houston, 1984—; bd. dirs. Child Abuse Prevention Network, 1990—; officer bd. dirs. Crime Stoppers Houston, 1984—; chmn. exhbns. Mayor's 1st Hearing, Children and Youth, Houston, 1985-88; founder, bd. dirs. Friends of WSIU-TV, 1974-77; chmn. Evening Guild St. John the Divine, St. Kevork/ACYO Nat. sports fair, 1990; rep. for Houston 2d World Conf. on Mayors, Japan, 1989; exec. bd. nat. com. to prevent child abuse, 1990—; bd. dirs. Houston Read Com., 1995—; mem. nat. faculty Ctr. for Children's Issues, 1995—. Fellow W.K. Kellogg Found., Battle Creek, Mich., 1987-90; recipient award for Excellence Pres. Pvt. Sector, White House, Washington, 1987, Ohio State U., Columbus, 1983, Feddersen award for excellence in Pub. TV Ind. U., Bloomington, 1981, Heritage award Child Abuse Prevention Coun., 1990, Dona J. Stone Founders award Nat. Assn. for Prevention of Child Abuse, 1990; named among Outstanding Women Vols. for community, civic and profl. contbns., Fedn. Houston Profl. Women, 1989; finalist Woman on the Move, 1987, Rising Star, 1987. Mem. Am. Women in Radio and TV (nat. v.p. 1986-90, award 1987, pres. Houston chpt. 1990, bd. dirs. 1985—), Houston Fed. Profl. Women (pres., del. 1986-93, chmn. 1994), Nat. Assn. Ednl. Broadcasters (presenter nat. conv. 1975-76), Tex. Lyceum (v.p., bd. dirs. 1990—), Dephians, Nat. Assn. for Programming TV Execs., Fedn. Houston Profl. Women Ednl. Found. (bd. dirs. 1994—), Ctr. for Bus. Women's Devel. (bd. dirs. 1993-94). Republican. Episcopalian. Office: Mampre Media Internat 5123 Del Monte Dr Houston TX 77056-4316

MAMUT, MARY CATHERINE, retired entrepreneur; b. Calabria, Italy, Oct. 17, 1923; came to U.S., 1928; d. Carmelo Charles and Caterina (Tripodi) Cogliandro; m. Michael Matthew Mamut, May 15, 1954; children: Anthony Carl, Charles Terrance. Student, Stenotype Comml. Coll., 1946-50. Sec. to pres. Thomas Goodfellow, Inc., Detroit, 1942-50; asst. to v.p. R.G. Moeller Co., Detroit, 1951-52; sec. to pres. United Steel Supply Co., Detroit, 1952-54; sec. to libr. Farmington (Mich.) Schs., 1962-68; real estate agt., 1969; owner, mgr. Crystal Fair, Birmingham, Mich., 1969-88; ret. Crystal Fair, Mich.; tchr. Stenotype Comml. Coll., Detroit, 1952-54. Vol. Henry Ford Mus., Dearborn, Mich., 1989-90, Greenfield Village, 1989-90, West Bloomfield Libr., 1993-95. Recipient World Lifetime Achievement award Am. Biog. Inst. U.S.A., 1993. Mem. Am. Bus. Women's Assn., Birmingham-Bloomfield C. of C., Profl. Secs. Internat, NAFE. Roman Catholic. Home: 7423 Coach Ln West Bloomfield MI 48322-4022

MAÑAS, RITA, educational administrator; b. Newark, N.J., Dec. 6, 1951; d. John and Sofia Mañas. BA, Kean Coll., 1974; MA, Seton Hall U., 1977; PhD, Rutgers U., 1990. Cert. tchr. K-12, N.J. Ednl. counselor Aspira Inc. of N.J., Newark, 1974-75; student devel. specialist ednl. opportunity program Seton Hall U., South Orange, N.J., 1975-88; asst. dir. ednl. opportunity fund program Fairleigh Dickinson U., Madison, N.J., 1988-89; dir. office of minority edn. William Paterson Coll., Wayne, N.J., 1990-95; asst. prof. dept. modern langs. Coll. N.J., 1995-96; dir. ednl. opportunity fund program Centenary Coll., Hackettstown, N.J., 1996—; adj. instr. Ctr. for African Am. Studies, English dept. Seton Hall U., South Orange, 1978-79, modern langs. dept., 1981-82, 85-91, 91-93; adj. instr. fgn. langs. dept. Bergen C.C., Paramus, N.J., 1990; adj. instr. langs. and cultures dept. William Paterson Coll., Wayne, N.J., 1991, 95. Bd. dirs. North End Nursery, Newark, 1993-94; mem. adv. bd. Sch. and Comty. Organized to Promote Edn. Program (S.C.O.P.E.), Paterson, N.J., 1993-95. Recipient Achievement award P.R. Inst. of Seton Hall U., 1977, Svc. award Black Student Assn. of William Paterson Coll., 1991, 92, Orgn. of Latin Am. Students of William Paterson Coll., 1991, 93, Tri State Disting. Alumni award Tri-State Consortium of Opportunity Programs in Higher Edn., 1993. Mem. MLA (del. 1993-95, P.R. Lit. and Culture com. 1995—), Am. Assn. Tchrs. of Spanish and Portuguese, N.E. MLA, Mid. Atlantic Coun. Latin Am. Studies, N.J. Ednl. Opportunity Fund Profl. Assn. (20th anniv. conf. planning com. 1989, Svc. award 1989, 93), Hispanic Women's Task Force (Svc. award 1991), Hispanic Assn. Higher Edn.

MANASC, VIVIAN, architect, consultant; b. Bucharest, Romania, May 19, 1956; d. Bercu and Bianca (Smetterling) M.; m. William A. Dushenski, Feb. 25, 1984; children: Peter Gabriel, Lawrence Alexander. BS in Architecture, McGill U., Montreal, Que., Can., 1977, BArch, 1979; MBA, U. Alta., Edmonton, 1982. Architectural insp. Transport Can., Edmonton, 1977-79; project architect Bell Spotowski Architects, Edmonton, 1980-82; asst. dir. design constrn. Edmonton Pub. Schs., 1982-84; mgr., prin. Ferguson, Simek, Clark Architects Ltd., Edmonton, 1985-88; mng. dir. FSC Groves Hodgson Manasc Architects Ltd., Edmonton, 1988—. Contbr. articles to profl. jours. and confs. Sect. chair, co-chair innovative practice group in arch. United Way Edmonton; advisor YWCA, Edmonton, 1980-82; mentor RAIC Syllabus Program, Edmonton, 1982-88; bd. dirs. Design Workshop, Edmonton, 1983. Scholar McGill U., 1974. Mem. Royal Archtl. Inst. Can. (past chmn. architecture for healthcare com., assoc. regional dir.), Alta. Assn. Archs., Manitoba Assn. Archs., B.C. Assn. Archs., Saskatchewan Assn. Archs., Coun. Edn. Facility Planners, Nat. Coun. Jewish Women (past pres. Edmonton sect.), Jewish Fedn. Edmonton (v.p. planning). Office: FSC Groves Hodgson Manasc, 10417 Saskatchewan Dr, Edmonton, AB Canada T6E 4R8

MANASIAN, KATHLEEN MARY, small business owner; b. Detroit, Apr. 13, 1948; d. William Lee and Winifred E. (Hunter) Reeves; m. Ronald Lee Manasian, Nov. 17, 1967; children: Ted James, Jennifer Rebecca. BS, Wayne State U., 1970; EMT, Madonna Coll., 1980; M. Psychology Hypnotherapy, Columbia Pacific U., San Rafael, Calif., 1981, PhD in Psychology, 1985. Paramedic Am-Care, Detroit, 1980-82; dir.medic Thin Sight, Farmington, Mich., 1982-85; author/writer West Graphics, San Francisco, 1984-85; dir., CEO Applied Possibilities, Southfield, Mich., 1985—; cons. GM, Warren, Mich., 1986, Absopure, Canton, Mich., 1985. Author: Thin Sight, 1982; contbr. articles to profl. jours. State advisor U.S. Congl. Adv. Bd., Mich., 1985, 86. Mem. Am. Assn. Profl. Hypnotherapists. Republican. Roman Catholic. Home and Office: 22205 Tulane Farmington Hills MI 48336

MANASSE, ARLYNN H., pediatric nurse practitioner; b. Aurora, Ill., Apr. 10, 1947; d. Oliver J. and Arlene M. (Lehman) Hem; m. Henri R. Manasse Jr., Aug. 9, 1969; children: Bryan, Sheralynn. BSN, U. Ill., Chgo., 1969, MPH, 1989; pediatric nurse practitioner cert., Rush-Presbyn.-St. Luke's Ctr., 1971. Pub. health nurse, pediatric nurse practitioner, acting dir. Infant Welfare Soc., Chgo., 1969-72; pediatric nurse practitioner Mpls. Health Dept., 1972-74; pub. health nurse, pediatric nurse practitioner LaGrange (Ill.) Cmty. Nurse and Svc. Assn., 1978-88; pediatric nurse practitioner Bethel Wholistic Health Ctr., Chgo., 1991-93, Circle Family Care, Chgo., 1994—; adj. nursing faculty U. Ill., Chgo., 1994—; regional health adv. bd. Cmty. and Econ. Devel. Assn., Head Start, Chgo., 1978-88. Active, mem. of choir Western Springs (Ill.) Bapt. Ch., 1976—; bd. dirs., officer Westside Holistic Family Svcs., Chgo., 1990—. Fellow Nat. Assn. Pediatric Nurse Assocs. and Practitioners; mem. ANA, Ill. Nurses Assn., Am. Pub. Health Assn., Ill. Pub. Health Assn.

MANCHER, RHODA ROSS, federal agency administrator, strategic planner; b. N.Y.C., Sept. 28, 1935; d. Joseph and Hannah (Karpf) Ross; m. Melvin Mancher, May 27, 1962 (dec.); children: Amy Meg, James Marc. B.S. in Physics, Columbia U., 1960; M.S. in Ops. Research, George Washington U., 1978. Cons. pvt. practice, Bethesda, Md., 1994—; staff FEA, Washington, 1974-77; dir. info. systems devel. div. The White House, Washington, 1977-79; dir. office systems devel. Social Security Adminstrn., Balt., 1979-80; dep. asst. atty. gen. Office Info. Tech., Dept. Justice, Washington, 1980-84; assoc. dir. info. resources mgmt. Dept. Navy, Washington, 1985-87; dir. Office Info. Tech. VA, Washington, 1987-94; pres. H.W.&W., Inc., 1994—; mem. ad hoc com. on recommendations to merge chem. and biol. info. systems Nat. Cancer Inst., Washington; chmn. permanent com. on info. tech. Iternat. Criminal Police Orgn. (INTERPOL); mem. curriculum com. USDA, adv. bd. computer system security and privacy U.S. Govt.; internat. tech. com. AFCEA. Contbr. articles to profl. publs. Recipient Assoc. Commr.'s citation Social Security Adminstrn., 1980, managerial excellence award Interagy. Com. on ADP, 1983; Meritorious award Sr. Exec. Svc., 1982, 83, 85, 87, 88, 91-93, Presdl. Rank of Meritorious Exec., 1990. Mem. Am. Fedn. Info. Processing Socs. (nat. info. issues panel).

MANCHESTER, CAROL ANN FRESHWATER, psychologist; b. Coshocton, Ohio, Sept. 30, 1942; d. James M. and Kathleen C. (Call) Freshwater; m. Crosby Manchester, Mar. 16, 1963 (dec. 1973). BS, Ohio State U., 1963, MS, 1973, PhD, 1977. Diplomate Internat. Soc. Psychotherapy and Behavioral Medicine, Am. Bd. Forensic Examiners. Elem. counselor Columbus (Ohio) Pub. Schs., 1973-79; counselor Regional Alcoholism & Tng. Ctr., Columbus, 1977-79; therapist Beechwold Clinic, Columbus, 1977-80; counselor Gifted and Talented Program, Columbus, 1979-81; dir. Freshwater Mental Health Clinic, Columbus, 1982—; asst. clin. prof. Coll. Medicine Ohio State U., 1990-95; instr. psychology Urbana Coll., Columbus, 1977-79; dir. Freshwater Clinic, Columbus, 1983—; bd. dirs. Ecole Francaise, Columbus, 1985—; cons. Columbus Cmty. Hosp., 1988—, Mt. Carmel Med. Ctr., Park Med. Ctr., Columbus, 1990—; presenter in field. Author: Affective Model The Gifted and Talented Handbook for Columbus Public Schools, 1981. Active Gov.'s Task Force on Child Abuse, Columbus. Recipient Disting. Svc. award Ohio Counselor's Assn., Valley Forge Freedom award. Mem. ACLU, AOA, Am. Acad. Cert. Neurotherapists (v.p. 1993, 94, diplomate, exec. bd. dirs.), Am. Acad. Neurobrainwave Therapists (v.p.), Soc. of Neuronal Regulation (v.p.), Nat. Soc. Clin. Hypnosis, Meninger Soc., Internat. Soc. Post Traumatic Stress, Internat. Soc. Multiple Personality Disorder, Assn. Applied Psychophysiology and Biofeedback, Ohio Psychol. Assn., Delta Omicron, Tau Beta Sigma. Office: Freshwater Clinic 6065 Glick Rd Ste C Powell OH 43065-9604

MANCINI, ELAINE CAROL, public relations executive; b. Chgo., Sept. 21, 1953; d. Edward A. and Adeline (Renella) M.; m. Alan G. Morrice, Aug. 14, 1974; children: Zachary, Fiona. BA, U. Ill., 1975; MA, NYU, 1977, PhD, 1981. Dir. Film Archive and Film Libr. Svcs., N.Y.C., 1980-86; asst. prof. Sch. Visual Arts St. John's U., CUNY, S.I., N.Y., 1980-86; account exec. Ruder Finn & Rotman, N.Y.C., 1985-86; sr. v.p. GCI Group subs. Grey Advt., N.Y.C., 1986-92; assoc. ptnr. Strategy XXI Group, N.Y.C., 1993-95; sr. v.p., dir. econ. devel. Makovsky & Co., 1996—; bd. dirs. Internat. Bus. Network of Greater N.Y., 1996—. Author: The Free Years of the Italian Film Industry, 1985, Luchino Visconti: A Guide to References and Resources, 1986, D.W. Griffith and The Biograph Company, 1986. Recipient Golden World award Internat. Pub. Rels. Assn., 1992; Fulbright teaching grantee U. Bologna, Italy, 1983. Mem. Internat. Bus. Network Greater N.Y. (bd. dirs. 1996). Office: 575 Lexington Ave 15th Fl New York NY 10022

MANCINI, MARY CATHERINE, cardiothoracic surgeon, researcher; b. Scranton, Pa., Dec. 15, 1953; d. Peter Louis and Ferminia Teresa (Massi) M. BS in Chemistry, U. Pitts., 1974, MD, 1978; postgrad. in Anatomy and Cellular Biolog, La. State U. Med. Ctr., 1994—. Diplomate Am. Bd. Surgery (speciality cert. critical care medicine), Am. Bd. Thoracic Surgery. Intern in surgery U. Pitts., 1978-79, resident in surgery, 1979-87; fellow pediatric cardiac surgery Mayo Clinic, 1987-88; asst. prof. surgery, dir. cardiothoracic transplantation Med. Coll. Ohio, Toledo, 1988-91; assoc. prof. surgery, dir. cardiothoracic transplantation La. State U. Med. Ctr., Shreveport, 1991—. Author: Operative Techniques for Medical Students, 1983; contbr. articles to profl. jours. Rsch. grantee Am. Heart Assn., 1988; recipient Pres. award Internat. Soc. Heart Transplantation, 1983, Charles C. Moore Tchg. award U. Pitts., 1985, Internat. Woman of Yr. award Internat. Biog. Inst., Eng., 1992-93, Internat. Order of Merit award, 1995, Nina S. Braunwald Career Devel. award Thoracic Surgery Found. Fellow ACS, Am. Coll. Chest Physicians, Internat. Coll. Surgeons (councillor 1991—); mem. Assn. Women Surgeons, Rotary (gift of life program 1991). Roman Catholic. Office: La State U Med Ctr 1501 Kings Hwy Shreveport LA 71103-4228

MANCO-MARTIN, DONNA, principal; b. Pitts., May 6, 1949; d. Arthur and Audrey (North) Manco; m. Paul J. Martin. BS, Slippery Rock U., 1971; MA in Counseling, Duquesne U., 1989, MA in Adminstrn., 1996. Tchr. St. Leo Sch., Pitts., 1972-90; prin. St. Robert Bellarmine Sch., East McKeesport, Pa., 1992—; pvt. children's counselor, Pa., 1989—. Mem. ASCD, Nat. Cath. Edn. Assn., Phi Delta. Roman Catholic.

MANCUSO, CAROLINA ANNA, educator, writer; b. Utica, N.Y., Jan. 28, 1947. Student, Marymount Coll., 1964-66; BA in English/Theatre, Utica Coll./Syracuse U., 1968; MA in English Edn., NYU, 1992, postgrad., 1992—. Comms. asst. Munson-Williams-Proctor Inst., Utica, 1968-72; rsch. cons. The New Sch. of Utica, 1975-79; exec. dir. Children's Theatre for Arts and Humanities, Utica, 1977-78; freelance writer Utica and N.Y.C., 1977—; instr. Bklyn. Coll., 1991; writer-in-residence Eugene Lang Coll./New Sch. for Social Rsch., N.Y.C., 1990-94; instr. writing, cons., faculty mentor NYU, N.Y.C., 1991-96; core faculty MST program New Sch. for Social Rsch., 1994—; writing cons. and workshop dir., N.Y.C., 1991—; performer, dir., writer various studios and theatres, N.Y.C., 1979-83; lectr. Fulbright program Multinat. Inst. Am. Studies, NYU, 1994, 95. Contbr. short fiction to 4 anthologies, 1988, 90, 91, 93, to Amelia, 1991, to Ikon, 1989; contbr. essays and articles to jours. Recipient 1st pl. for short fiction Reed Smith Fiction award, 1988. Mem. AAUW, Internat. Fedn. for Teaching of English, Nat. Coun. Tchrs. English, Phi Delta Kappa. Office: New Sch for Social Rsch Tchr Edn 68 Fifth Ave New York NY 10011

MANDABACH, CARYN, television producer; m. Paul Mandabach; children: Marisa, Jon. Pres. Carsey-Werner Co., Studio City, Calif., 1987—. Prodr.: The Cosby Show, Roseanne, A Different World, Grace Under Fire, Cybill, Third Rock from the Sun. Bd. dirs. The Center Theatre Group, The Curtis Sch., AFI Third Decade Coun. Recipient Emmy for The Cosby Show, Humanitas award, People's Choice award, Peabody award. Office: care CBS/MTM Studios 4024 Radford Ave Studio City CA 91604-2101

MANDEL, CAROLA PANERAI (MRS. LEON MANDEL), foundation trustee; b. Havana, Cuba; d. Camilo and Elvira (Bertini) Panerai; ed. pvt. schs., Havana and Europe; m. Leon Mandel, Apr. 9, 1938. Mem. women's bd. Northwestern Meml. Hosp., Chgo. Trustee Carola and Leon Mandel Fund Loyola U., Chgo. Life mem. Chgo. Hist. Soc., Guild of Chgo. Hist. Soc., Smithsonian Assos., Nat. Skeet Shooting Assn. Frequently named among Ten Best Dressed Women in U.S.; chevalier Confrerie des Chevaliers du Tastevin. Capt. All-Am. Women's Skeet Team, 1952, 53, 54, 55, 56; only woman to win a men's nat. championship, 20 gauge, 1954, also high average in world over men, 1956, in 12 gauge with 99.4 per cent; European women's live bird shooting championship, Venice, Italy, 1957, Porto, Portugal, 1961; European woman's target championship, Torino, Italy, 1958; woman's world champion live-bird shooting, Sevilla, Spain, 1959, Am. Contract Bridge League Life Master, 1987. Named to Nat. Skeet Shooting Assn. Hall of Fame, 1970; inducted in U.S. Pigeon shooting Fedn. Hall of Fame, 1992. Mem. Soc. Four Arts. Club: Everglades (Palm Beach, Fla.), The Beach. Home: 324 Barton Ave Palm Beach FL 33480-6116

MANDEL, KARYL LYNN, accountant; b. Chgo., Dec. 14, 1935; d. Isador J. and Eve (Gellar) Karzen; m. Fredric H. Mandel, Sept. 29, 1956; children: David Scott, Douglas Jay, Jennifer Ann. Student, U. Mich., 1954-56, Roosevelt U., 1956-57; AA summa cum laude, Oakton Community Coll., 1979. CPA, Ill. Pres. Excel Transp. Service Co., Elk Grove, Ill., 1958-78; tax mgr. Chunowitz, Teitelbaum & Baerson, CPA's, Northbrook, Ill., 1981-83, tax ptnr., 1984—; sec-treas. Lednam, Inc., Coffee Break, Inc.; mem. acctg. curriculum adv. bd. Oakton Community Coll., Des Plaines, Ill., 1987—. Contbg. author: Ill. CPA's News Jour. Recipient State of Israel Solidarity award, 1976. Mem. AICPA, Am. Soc. Women CPA, Women's Am. ORT (pres. Chgo. region 1972-74, v.p. midwest dist. 1975-76, nat. endowment com., nat investment adv. com.), Ill. CPA Soc. (chmn. estate and gift tax com. 1987-89, legis. contact com. 1981-82, pres. North Shore chpt., award for Excellence in Acctg. Edn., Bd. dirs. 1989-91), Chgo. Soc. Women CPA, Chgo. Estate Planning Coun., Nat. Assn. Women Bus. Owners, Lake County Estate Planning, Coun., Greater North Shore Estate Planning Coun. Office: 401 Huehl Rd Northbrook IL 60062-2300

MANDEL, LESLIE ANN, investment advisor, fundraiser, business owner, author; b. Washington, July 29, 1945; d. Seymour and Marjorie Syble Mandel. BA in Art History, U. Minn., 1967; cert., N.Y. Sch. Interior Design, 1969. Cert. Brailled Libr. Congress. Pres. Leslie Mandel Enterprises, Inc., N.Y.C., 1972—; sr. v.p. Maximum Entertainment Network, L.A. and N.Y.C., 1988-90; pres. Rich List Co., 1989—; pres., CEO Mandel Airplane Funding and Leasing Corp., N.Y.C., Hong Kong, China and Mongolia, 1990—; CEO Mandel-Khan Inc., Ulaanbaatar, Mongolia, 1994—; fin. advisor Osmed, Inc., Mpls., 1986—, Devine Comm./Allen & Co., N.Y., Del., Utah, N.Mex., N.Y. WUWV, Utah KBER, WKTC-AM-FM, 1984—, Am. Kefir Corp., N.Y.C., 1983—, Shore Group (Internat., Guyana), Flight Internat., 1991—; owner The Rich List Co., 150 internat. catalogs, mags. and fundraising lists; joint venture Mongolian Ind. Broadcasting Channel, Ulaanbaatar, 1995; pres., owner Mandel Airplane Funding and Leasing Corp.; rep. Israeli govt. IAI Satellite, China, Romania, Costa Rica, Mongolia, Amos Satellite Network, China, 1992—; advisor rep. Gt. Wall Corp., Long March Corp., China, 1992—, Chinese Silk, 1993—, Am. Oil Refinery, 1993—; cons. Exclusive Miat Airlines, Mongolia; purchasing agt. Peoples Republic of China-Aircraft; advisor Aeropostalis, Mex., 1994-95; photographer; lectr. UN Internat. Direct Mail; lectr. Explorers Club, Mongolia. Photographer: Vogue, 1978, Fortune mag.; braille transcriber: The Prophet (Kalil Gibran), 1967, Getting Ready for Battle (R. Prawe Jhabuala), 1967; exec. prodr. film: Hospital Audiences, 1975 (Cannes award 1976); author: Hungry at the Watering Hole, Gardiners Island, 1636-1990, 1989, Expedition: In the Steps of Ghengis Kahn, 1994; advisor Port Libertè Ptnrs., 1988-94; contbr. articles to profl. jours. Fin. advisor Correctional Assn., Osborn Soc., 1977—; founder, treas. Prisoners Family Transportation and Assistance Fund, N.Y., 1972-77; judge Emmy awards of Acad. TV Arts and Scis., N.Y.C., 1970; bd. dirs. Prisoners Assn., 1990; chmn. U.S.A. com. Violeta B. de Chamarro for Pres. of Nicaragua Campaign. Recipient Inst. for the Creative and Performing Arts fellowship, N.Y.C., 1966, Appreciation cert. Presdl. Inaugural Com., Washington, 1981. Fellow N.Y. Women in Real Estate, Explorers Club (lectr. on Mongolia, fin. com.); mem. Com. on Am. and Internat. Fgn. Affairs, Lawyers Com. on Internat. Human Rels., Bus. Exec. Nat. Security, Venture Capital Breakfast Club, The Coffee Club House, Sigma Delta Tau, Sigma Epsilon Sigma. Democrat. Home: 4 E 81st St New York NY 10028-0235 Office: Mandel-Khan Inc c/o Boldbaatar Mandel Khan, PO Box 97, Ulaanbaatar 210648, Mongolia also: Leslie Mandel Enterprises PO Box 294 Wainscott NY 11975

MANDELBAUM, DOROTHY ROSENTHAL, psychologist, educator; b. N.Y.C., May 18, 1935; d. Benjamin Daniel and Rachael (Osofsky) Rosenthal; m. Seymour Jacob Mandelbaum, Aug. 19, 1956; children: David Gideon, Judah Michael, Betsy Daniella. AB cum laude, Hunter Coll., 1956; PhD, Bryn Mawr Coll., 1975. Lic. clin. psychologist, Pa. Tchr., Valley Road Sch., Princeton, N.J., 1956-59; instr. ednl. psychology dept. Temple U., Phila., 1970; asst. prof. dept. edn. Rutgers U., Camden, N.J., 1974-80, assoc. prof., 1980—, dir. women's studies, 1981-86, chair edn. dept., 1986-91, pres. faculty senate, 1990-91. Author: Work, Marriage and Motherhood: The Career Persistence of Female Physicians, 1981; contbr. articles on psychology of women and med. edn. to profl. publs. Dir. Am. Liver Found., 1991-93. AAUW predoctoral fellow, 1973-74. Mem. AAUP, APA. Home: 2290 N 53rd St Philadelphia PA 19131 Office: Rutgers U Camden NJ 08102

MANDELBAUM, JEAN, director, educator; b. N.Y.C., May 19, 1934; d. Nathan Frank and Ann (Rubee) Isaacson; m. Bernard David Mandelbaum, March 25, 1956; children: Eric, Carl Steven. BA, U. Mich., Ann Arbor, 1955; MS, Bank Street Coll. of Edn., N.Y.C., 1959; PhD, N.Y.U., N.Y.C., 1978. Tchr. Marble Hill Nursery Sch., N.Y.C., 1957-60; music, movement specialist Horace Mann Sch. for N. Years, N.Y.C., 1968-73; ednl. cons. N.Y. State Dept. of Edn., Albany, N.Y., 1976-80; instr., asst. prof. The City Coll., N.Y.C., 1973-81; adj. faculty Bank Street Coll. of Edn., N.Y.C., 1986—; dir. All Souls Sch., N.Y.C., 1981—; validator and mentor Nat. Acad. of Early Childhood Programs, Washington, 1986—; bd. dirs. Ind. Schs. Admissions Assn. of Greater N.Y., N.Y. State Assn. for the Edn. of Young Children; adv. bd. N.Y.C. UN Children's Fund, N.Y.C., 1992-95. Home: 55 E End Ave New York NY 10028 Office: All Souls Sch 1157 Lexington Ave New York NY 10021

MANDELCORN, REVA SCHLESSINGER, international marketing manager; b. Erie, Pa., Sept. 9, 1965; d. G. Gustav and Ina (Swade) Schlessinger; m. Howard M. Mandelcorn, June 3, 1990; 1 child: Ethan Samuel Mandelcorn. BA in Econs., Brandeis U., 1987; MBA in Internat. Mktg., McGill U., 1991. Ops. mgr. Emerson Investment Mgmt., Inc., Boston, 1987-89; product mktg. mgr. Elin Computer Resources, Inc., Montreal, Que., Can., 1991-92; mktg. mgr. Mass. Office of Bus. Devel., Boston, 1992-94; internat. mktg. mgr., Mass. office of bus. devel. Commonwealth of Mass., Boston, 1994—. Chmn. Boston chpt. Brandeis U. Alumni Admissions Coun., Waltham, Mass., 1995—, chmn. Montreal chpt., 1990-92. Office: Mass Office Bus Devel 21st Fl 1 Ashburton Pl Boston MA 02108

MANDELL, ARLENE LINDA, writing and communications educator; b. Bklyn., Feb. 19, 1941; d. George and Esther Kostick; m. Lawrence W. Mandell, May 23, 1982; children by previous marriage: Bruce R. Rosenblum, Tracey B. Grimaldi. BA magna cum laude, William Paterson Coll., 1973; MA Columbia U., 1989. Newspaper reporter Suburban Trends, Riverdale, N.J., 1972-73; writer Good Housekeeping mag., N.Y.C., 1976-78; account exec. Carl Byoir & Assocs., N.Y.C., 1978-86; v.p. Porter/Novelli, N.Y.C., 1986-88; adj. prof. composition, lit., poetry, women's studies William Paterson Coll., Wayne, N.J., 1989—. Contbr. articles to profl. jours. and newspapers, poetry to N.Y. Times and poetry jours. Recipient 1st place women's interest writing N.J. Press Assn., 1973; named John W. Stahr Writer of Yr., Carl Byoir & Assocs., N.Y.C., 1981. Mem. N.J. Coll. English Assn.

MANDELL, HELENE TEIBLOOM, education educator; b. Chgo., June 6, 1950; d. Severyn and Geraldine (Erenberg) Teibloom; m. Alex Johnson, Mar. 3, 1990; children from previous marriage: Torrey T. Mandell, Jonathan W. Mandell. BS with honors, U. Wis., 1972; MA in Tchg. Polit. Sci. cum laude, U. San Diego, 1977; EdD, U. So. Calif., L.A., 1994. Calif. std. elem. credential; Calif. std. secondary credential; cert. adult edn. Calif. C.C.; Wis. std. tchg. credential. Tchr. Orchard Ridge Middle Sch., Madison, 1972-74; instr. adult edn. Calif. C.C., San Diego, 1974-75; tchr. St. Columba Sch., San Diego, 1975-76; thcr., chairperson math. dept. St. James Acad., Solana Beach, Calif., 1976-85; v.p., cons. Math Power, Del Mar, Calif., 1985-92; dir. clin. experiences/instr. Nat. U., Sch. Edn. and Human Svcs., San Diego, 1989-92, asst. prof., coord. crosscultural lang. & acad. devel., 1992—; instr., cons. Best Prep Test Preparation, Del Mar, 1985-92; adj. instr. U. Calif. Ext., San Diego, Irvine, Riverside, 1985-92, Webster U., San Diego, 1988-90, Nat. U. Sch. Edn. and Human Svcs., Vista, Calif., 1988-89; spkr. edn. programs Grossmont C.C., Southwestern C.C., Mira Costa Coll., 1990-91; mem. Calif. Commn. on Tchr. Credentialing Caltf. Basic Edn. Skills Test Validity Study Taskforce, 1990, Calif. State Dept. Edn. Program Quality Integration Rev. Team, 1992, Calif. Commn. on Tchr. Credentialing Program Evaluation Team, Azusa Pacific U., 1994; presenter in field. Co-author: I Can Do Algebra, 1986. Mem. ASCD, AAUW, Calif. Coun. Tchr. Educators, State Calif. Assn. Tchr. Educators. Office: Nat Univ Sch Edn & Human Svcs 4025 Camino Del Rio S San Diego CA 92108-4107

MANDELL, SARA, religious studies educator; b. N.Y.C., May 11, 1938; d. George and Beatrice (Ross) Sindel; m. Leon Mandell, Apr. 23, 1971; stepchildren: Paul Bradford Mandell, David Mandell. BA in Latin, NYU, 1964, MA in Latin, 1965, PhD in Classics, 1969. Asst. prof. classics Emory U., Atlanta, 1969-72; vis. asst. prof. classics U. South Fla., Tampa, 1985-86, asst. prof. classics, 1986-91, assoc. prof. classics, 1991, assoc. prof. religious studies, 1991-94, prof. religious studies, 1994—; page turner for organist Virgil Fox, The Riverside Ch., N.Y.C., 1958-64. Primary author: (with D.N. Freedman) The Relationship Between Herodotus' History and Primary History, 1993; contbr. chpt. to Approaches to Ancient Judaism, 1993, Approaches to Ancient Judaism, 1995, Was There Ever a Talmud of Caesarea?; contbr. articles to Cath. Bibl. Quar., Harvard Theol. Rev., The Second Century, Jour. Ritual Studies, Ancient World, others. Recipient Honorable Mention, Westinghouse Sci. Talent Contest, 1956, State of Fla LUTE award, 1991, Fla. Tchg. Incentive Program award, 1994, 95, Founders Day award NYU, 1969. Mem. Cath. Bibl. Assn., Soc. Bibl. Lit., Am. Schs. Oriental Rsch. (v.p., program chair Southeastern region 1992-93, pres. 1993-94), Am. Oriental Soc., Am. Acad. Religion, Classical Assn. Middle West and South, United Faculty of Fla. (pres. U. South Fla. chpt.). Home: 514 Riverhills Dr

Temple Terrace FL 33617 Office: U South Fla Religious Studies CPR 107 Tampa FL 33620-5550

MANDERS, SUSAN KAY, artist; b. Burbank, Calif., Dec. 29, 1948; d. Gus H. and Erika (Stadelbauer) M.; m. Allan D. Yasnyi, Dec. 18, 1992; children: Brian Mallut. Attended, U. Guadalajara, 1969; BA, Calif. State U., 1971; postgrad., Otis Parsons, L.A., 1985, Royal Coll. of the Arts, London, 1987; grad., Silicon Digital Arts. Owner, dir., tchr. The Art Experience Sch. and Gallery, Studio City, Calif., 1978—; cons. in field. One-woman shows include La Logia, Studio City, Calif., 1991, Il Mito, Studio City, 1991, Bamboo, Sherman Oaks, Calif., 1991—, L.A. Art Installations, 1990, 92, Fed. Bldg., L.A., 1993, Art Experience, Studio City, 1993, Emerson's Gallery, Sherman Oaks, 1994, Raphael's, Beverly Hills, Calif., 1994; group shows include Beverly Hills Affair in the Gardens, 1984, 94, Otis Parsons, L.A., 1987, Hilderbrand Galleries, New Orleans, 1993, Studio City Art Festival, 1994, Parents Found., New Haven, Conn., 1994, Project Studio 8, San Francisco, 1994, Bistango Studio-Gallery, Irvine, Calif., 1994—, Montserrat Gallery, N.Y.C., 1995; creator, publ. prints Iron Jane Collections, 1994, Children's Hosp. Docent UCLA; active Tuesday's Child, Pillars of Hope Project San Fernando Valley County Fair, 1995. Mem. L.A. Art Assn., Beverley Hills Art Assn., Nat. Mus. Women in the Arts, L.A. County Mus. of Art, Dada, L.A., Mus. Contemporary Art Coun. Office: The Art Experience 11830 Ventura Blvd Studio City CA 91604-2617

MANDEVILLE, LOUISE ELAINE, psychiatric nurse; b. Martinez, Calif., Jan. 1, 1936; d. Ernest Emilio and Rose Delores (Tarantino) Baroni; m. Robert Jex Mandeville, Nov. 23, 1956; 1 child, Ralph D. Diploma, St. Mary's Coll. Nursing, San Francisco, 1956; AA, Diablo Valley Coll., 1981; BSN, Holy Name Coll., 1985. RN; cert. psychiat., mental health nurse. Psychiat. staff nurse Herrick Meml. Hosp., Berkeley, Calif., 1956-60, Martinez (Calif.) VA Med. Ctr., 1965-90; chief day treatment ctr. VA Northern Calif. Health Care Sys., Martinez, 1990—; staff devel. com. Martinez VA Med. Ctr., 1966-68, nurse profl. standards bd., 1980-84; adv. bd. Martinez VA, 1992—. Mem. Am. Psychiat. Nurses Assn., Sigma Theta Tau. Democrat. Roman Catholic. Home: 222 Amigo Rd Danville CA 94526 Office: VA Northern Calif Health Care Sys 1111 Haven St Martinez CA 94553

MANDLER, SUSAN RUTH, dance company administrator; b. Kew Gardens, N.Y., Feb. 11, 1949; d. Ernest and Clea (Reisner) M.; m. Robert Morgan Barnett, July 30, 1982. B.S., Boston U., 1971. Mgr. Pilobolus, Inc., Washington, Conn., mgr., 1977—. Address: PO Box 166 Washington Depot CT 06794-0388

MANDRAVELIS, PATRICIA JEAN, healthcare administrator; b. Hanover, N.H., May 7, 1938; d. William J. and Ruth E. (Darling) Bartis; m. Anthony M. Mandravelis, Nov. 8, 1959; children: Michael A., Tracy J. Diploma in nursing, Nashua (N.H.) Meml. Hosp. Sch. Nursing; BS in Psychology, Sociology, New Eng. Coll.; MBA, N.H. Coll., 1989. Cert. nursing adminstr., advanced nursing adminstr. Staff nurse Nashua Meml. Hosp. (name now So. N.H. Regional Med. Ctr.), 1959-60, obstet. nurse, 1962-65, charge nurse, 1969-71, supr., 1971-76, assoc. dir. nursing, 1976-81, dir. nursing, 1981-83, asst. exec. dir. nursing, 1983-87, v.p. nursing, 1987-91; v.p. ops., chief operating officer Nashua Meml. Hosp., 1991-95; v.p. cmty. health and wellness S. N.H. Regional Med. Ctr., Nashua, 1995—. Contbr. articles to profl. jours. Bd. dirs. deNicola Women's Ctr., Nashua, 1987-95, Nashua Vis. Nurse Program, 1986-88; v.p. Nashua chpt. ARC, 1985-87; bd. dirs. Home Health Hosp., 1988-94, chmn. bd., 1991-93, vice chmn. bd., 1993-94; mem. citizens adv. bd. W.R. Grace, 1989—. Mem. Am. Coll. Healthcare Execs., Nat. League of Nursing, Am. Nurses Assn., Am. Orgn. Nurse Execs., N.H. Nurses Assn., N.H. Orgn. Nurse Execs., Sigma Theta Tau. Office: So NH Regional Med Ctr 8 Prospect St Nashua NH 03060-3925

MANDRELL, BARBARA ANN, singer, entertainer; b. Houston, Dec. 25, 1948; d. Irby Matthew and Mary Ellen (McGill) M.; m. Kenneth Lee Dudney, May 28, 1967; children: Kenneth Matthew, Jaime Nicole, Nathaniel. Grad. high sch. Country music singer and entertainer, 1959—, performed throughout U.S. and in various fgn. countries; mem., Grand Ole Opry, Nashville, 1972—; star TV series Barbara Mandrell and the Mandrell Sisters, 1980-82, Barbara Mandrell: Get to the Heart, 1987; albums include Midnight Oil, Treat Him Right, He Set My Life To Music, This Time I Almost Made It, This is Barbara Mandrell, Midnight Angel, Barbara Mandrell's Greatest Hits, Christmas at Our House, 1987, Morning Sun, 1990, Greatest Country Hits, 1990, Standing Room Only, 1993. Author (with George Vecsey): Get To the Heart: My Story, 1990. Named Miss Oceanside, Calif., 1965; Named Most Promising Female Singer, Acad. Country and Western Music, 1971; Female Vocalist of Yr., 1978; Female Vocalist of Yr., Music City News Cover Awards, 1979; Female Vocalist of Yr., Country Music Assn., 1979; Entertainer of Yr., 1980, 81; People's Choice awards (6), 1982-84. Mem. Musicians Union, Screen Actors Guild, AFTRA, Country Music Assn. (v.p.). Mem. Order Eastern Star. Home: PO Box 620 Hendersonville TN 37077-0620 Office: Creative Artists Agy 3310 W End Ave Fl 5 Nashville TN 37203-1083*

MANEKER, DEANNA MARIE, advertising executive; b. Albany, N.Y., Dec. 13, 1938; d. Marion K. and Florence R. (Krell) Colle; m. Morton Maneker, Sept. 15, 1957 (div. Feb., 1981); children: Meryl C., Amy J., Marion Kenneth. AB, Barnard Coll., 1960. Dir. circulation Westchester Mag., Mamaroneck, N.Y., 1971-73; pub. Change Mag., New Rochelle, N.Y., 1973-78; gen. mgr. Ctr. for Direct Mktg., Westport, Conn., 1978-81; sr. v.p. The Stenrich Group, Glen Allen, Va., 1981-88, exec. v.p., 1988-94; COO Martin Direct (formerly The Stenrich Group), Glen Allen, Va., 1994-96, exec. v.p. applied info. mgmt. divsn., 1995—. Home: 206 Tamarack Rd Richmond VA 23229-7039 Office: The Martin Agency 4413 Cox Rd Glen Allen VA 23060

MANFORD, BARBARA ANN, contralto; b. St. Augustine, Fla., Nov. 13, 1929; d. William Floyd and Margaret (Kemper) Manford; Mus.B. in Voice, Fla. State U., 1951, Mus.M., 1970; studied with L. Palazzini, A. Strano, Japelli, E. Nikolaidi, E. Joseph. Appearances in Europe, performing major roles in 12 leading opera houses, 1951-68, with condrs. including Alfredo Strano, Felice Cilario, Robert Shaw, Arnold Gamson, Giuseppe Patané, Ottavio Ziino, also numerous concerts and recitals in Paris and throughout Italy and Belgium; performed in world premiere Fugitives (C. Floyd), Fla. State U., Tallahassee, 1950; chosen by Gian Carlo Menotti for leading role in world premiere The Leper, Fla. State U., 1970; numerous radio, TV, and concert appearances, U.S., 1968—; artist-in-residence, assoc. prof. voice Ball State U., Muncie, Ind., 1970-90; numerous recs. Semi-finalist vocal contest, Parma, Italy, 1964; winner contest, Lonigo, Italy, 1965. Mem. Nat. Assn. Tchrs. Singing, Chgo. Artists Assn., Am. Tchrs. Nat. Assn., Sigma Alpha Iota, Pi Kappa Lambda. Christian Scientist. Home: 405 S Morrison Rd Apt 106 Muncie IN 47304-4015

MANGAN, ELIZABETH UNGER, librarian; b. Cleve., Mar. 18, 1945; d. Frederick William and Mary Vincetta (Branson) Unger; m. Harold Francis Mangan, May 9, 1970 (div. 1975). BA, Coll. Wooster, 1967; MLS, U. Pitts., 1968. Spl. recruit Lib. of Congress, Washington, 1968-69, map cataloger geography and map divsn., 1969-74, head data preparation and files maintenance geography and map divsn., 1974—; Mem. stds. working group Fed. Geographic Data Com., Washington, 1992—. Author: MARC Conversion Manual: Maps, 1984; co-author: Content Standard for Digital Geo-Spatial Metadata, 1994 (Cert. Appreciation USDI 1994); editor: Map Cataloging Manual, 1991; contbr. article to profl. jour. Mem. ALA, Map and Geography Roundtable. Office: Lib of Congress Geography and Map Divsn Washington DC 20540-4652

MANGAN, PATRICIA ANN PRITCHETT, research statistician; b. Hammond, Ind., Feb. 4, 1953; d. Edward Clayton and Helen Josephine (Mills) Pritchett; m. William Paul Mangan, Aug. 30, 1980; 1 child, Ryan Christopher. BS in Maths. and Stats., Purdue U., 1975, MS in Applied Stats., 1977. Tobacco devel. statistician R.J. Reynolds Tobacco Co., Winston-Salem, N.C., 1978-82, R&D statistician, 1982-86, sr. R&D statistician, 1986-90, sr. staff R&D statistician, 1990-93; dir. software devel. ARJAY Equipment Corp., Winston-Salem, N.C., 1993—; cons. Lab. for Application of Remote Sensing, West Lafayette, Ind., 1976-77; statis. engr. Corning Glass Works, Harrodsburg, Ky., 1977. Editor Jour. of Sensory Studies, 1992—; contbr. articles to sci. jours. Rep. United Way, Winston-Salem, 1985. Recipient G.R. DiMarco award, 1990, Excalibur award for Outstanding Performance, 1991, 93. Mem. Am. Statis. Assn., Wash. Statis. Assn., Purdue Alumni Assn. Office: RJ Reynolds PO Box 1487 Winston Salem NC 27102-1487

MANGANO, SANDRA DOLCE, school administrator; b. Silver Creek, N.Y., Sept. 20, 1942; d. Russell F. and Sarah H. (Scalice) Dolce; m. Richard A. Mangano, Apr. 24, 1965; children: Amy, Kathryn. BS, Daemen Coll., 1964; MS, SUNY, Fredonia, 1968; EdD, Temple U., 1985. Cert. elem. and secondary edn., Pa. Tchr. North Penn Sch. Dist., Lansdale, Pa., 1971-88, asst. prin., 1994, supr. gifted, ESL, multicultural edn., dir. strategic planning, 1996—; lectr. Gwynned (Pa.) Mercy Coll., 1976—; sr. trainer, cons REACH Ctr., Seattle, 1993—. Active Dem. Party, Montgomery County, Pa., 1971—. Named Gifted Tchr. of Yr., State of Pa., 1987. Mem. NAFE, ASCD, NAME. Roman Catholic. Home: 924 Sturgis Ln Lower Gwynedd PA 19002 Office: North Penn Sch Dist 401 E Hancock Lansdale PA 19446

MANGER, CAROL, manufacturing executive; b. Perth Amboy, N.J., Jan. 24, 1962; d. Joseph John and Jeanette Manger. BA in biology, Douglas Coll., 1984; MBA, Monmouth U., 1990. Report coord. Amerada Hess Corp., Woodbridge, N.J., 1984-89, price coord., 1990-91, sales coord., 1991—. Avocations: world travel, cultural events, stamp collecting, coin collecting., crafts. Home: 635 Barron Ave Woodbridge NJ 07095 Office: Amerada Hess Corp 1 Hess Plz Woodbridge NJ 07095

MANGIAMELI, PATRICIA ANN, payroll and personnel administrator, minister; b. Omaha, Mar. 7, 1956; d. Joseph Alfred and Irene (Costanzo) M. BTh, Evangel Christian U. Am., Monroe, La., 1995. Ordained minister, Souls Outreach Ministerial Assn. Acct. C.T.S. Co., Commerce, Calif., 1977-82, Pro Express, Commerce, Calif., 1982-85; payroll/personnel adminstr. L.S.C., Pico Rivera, Calif., 1985—. Composer (songs) Soon You'll Hear the Trumpet, 1988, Jesus, Mighty Jesus, 1990, Yet I Will Praise Him, 1993. Praise and Worship leader, One Way Family Ministries, Powney, Calif., 1986-89, v.p./treas., bd. dirs. Praise Hymn Ministries, Bellflower, Calif., 1989—. Participant in Battle of the Bands, Hollywood Bowl Battle of the Bands Assn., Calif., 1976.

MANGO-HURDMAN, CHRISTINA ROSE, psychiatric art therapist; b. Garden City, N.Y., May 13, 1962; d. Camillo Andrew and Dorothy Mae (Harrison) Mango; Keith Hurdman, Sept. 11, 1993; 1 child, Clarissa Rose Hurdman. BFA summa cum laude, Coll. of New Rochelle, 1984; MA, NYU, 1987. Registered art therapist; cert. structural family therapy tng.; cert. psycho-edn. multi family therapy tng. Art therapist Bronx Mcpl. Hosp. Ctr., 1984-88; art therapist, clin. supr. Fordham-Tremont Cmty. Mental Health Ctr., Bronx, 1988—; art therapy fieldworker Bronx State Hosp., 1984, art therapy intern Bronx Children's Hosp., 1985, Saint Lukes Hosp., N.Y.C., 1986. Contbr. articles to profl. jours. Mem. N.Y. Art Therapy Assn., No. N.J. Art Therapists Assn., Am. Art Therapy Assn. Home: 11 Turnure St Bergenfield NJ 07621-2035

MANHART, MARCIA Y(OCKEY), art museum director; b. Wichita, Kans., Jan. 14, 1943; d. Everett W. and Ruth C. (Correll) Yockey; children: Caroline Manhart Sanderson, Emily Alexandrea Morrison. BA in Art, U. Tulsa, 1965, MA in Ceramics, 1971. Dir. edn. Philbrook Art Ctr., Tulsa, 1972-77, exec. v.p., asst. dir., 1977-83, acting dir., 1983-84; exec. dir. Philbrook Mus. Art (formerly Philbrook Art Ctr.), Tulsa, 1984—; instr. Philbrook Art Ctr. Mus. Sch., Tulsa, 1963-72; gallery dir. Alexandre Hogue Gallery, Tulsa U., 1967-69; NEH Challenge Grant panelist, 1991, presenter to AAM Conv., 1991; MAAA Craft Fellowship panelist, 1988, 93, NEA Craft Fellowship panelist, 1990; curator nat. touring exhibit Nature's Forms/Nature's Forces: The Art of Alexandre Hogue, 1984-85; co-curator internat. exhbn.: The Eloquent Object, 1987-90; curator Sanford and Diane Besser Collection exhbn., 1992. Vis. com. Smithsonian Instn./Renwick Gallery, Washington, 1986; cultural negotiator Gov. George Nigh's World Trade Mission (Okla.), China., 1985; com. mem. State Art Coll. of Okla., 1985—; mem. Assocs. of Hillcrest Med. Ctr., 1983-88, exec. com., 1985-88; com. mem. Neighborhood Housing Services, 1985-87; mem. Mapleridge Hist. Dist. Assn., 1982—; steering com. Harwelden Isnt. for Aesthetic Edn., 1983; com. mem. River Parks Authority, 1976; mem. Jr. League of Tulsa Inc., 1974-78; adv. panel mem. Nat. Craft Planning Project, NEA, Washington, 1978-81; craft adv. panel mem. Okla. Arts and Humanities Council, 1974-76; juror numerous art festivals, competitions, programs; reviewer Inst. Mus. Services, Washington, 1985, 88, 92; auditor Symposium on Language & Scholarship of Modern Crafts, NEA and NEH, Washington, 1981; nominator MacArthur Fellows Program, 1988. Recipient Harwelden award for Individual Contbrn. in the Arts, 1989, Gov.'s award State of Okla., 1992. Mem. Assn. Am. Mus., Assn. Art Mus. Dirs., Art Mus. Assn. Am., Mountain Plains Assn. Mus., Am. Craft Coun., Okla. Mus. Assn., Rotary. Office: Philbrook Mus Art PO Box 52510 Tulsa OK 74152-0510

MANHEIM, MARGARET DONOVAN, educational association administrator; b. Boston, Sept. 4, 1946; d. George Henry and Margaret Mary (Gilligan) Donovan; m. Marvin Lee Manheim, July 20, 1974; children: Susannah Leigh, Marisa Kara. BA, Boston U., 1969; MEd, Boston State Coll., 1971. Cert. tchr. English, history, social studies, Mass. Homebound tchr. Somerville (Mass.) Pub. Schs., 1971-73, English tchr., 1973-75; program dir. Rochelle Lee Fund, Chgo., 1996—; mem. Evanston Sch. Dist. 202 Cmty. Task Force, 1995—. Bd. dirs. Invest Evanston, 1994—; mem. parents' coun. Shady Hill Sch., Cambridge, Mass., 1981-83; mem. parents' assn. North Shore Country Day Sch., Winnetka, Ill., 1984-86, v.p., 19877-88; v.p. PTA, King Lab. Sch., Evanston, Ill., 1990-91; sec. PTA Coun., Evanston/Skokie County ot PTAs, 1991-92, pres., 1992-94; v.p. Dist. 202 Parent/Tchr./Student Assn., Evanston Twp. H.S., 1994—, mem. curriculum forum, 1994—, writer sch.-based health clinic com., 1994—; mem. curriculum adv. coun. Sch. Dist. 65, Evanston, 1992-94; co-founder, co-chair, sec. Mothers Against Gangs, Evanston, 1992—; founder HIV Edn. Task Force, PTA Coun., Evanston, 1992—; observer Dist. 65 Sch. Bd., LWV, 1992—; bd. dirs. Youth Orgns. Umbrella, Evanston, 1993—; mem. violence prevention curriculum task force Ill. Coun. for Prevention of Violence, Chgo., 1994—; bd. dirs. Evanston Symphony Orch., 1987-92. Recipient State PTA HIV Edn. award Ill. PTA, 1993. Mem. North End Mothers Club. Democrat. Roman Catholic. Home: 2855 Sheridan Pl Evanston IL 60201-1725 Office: Rochelle Lee Fund 5153 N Clark St Chicago IL 60645

MANIERSTON, SUSAN ELAINE, educational administrator; b. Quincy, Ill., Sept. 16, 1948; d. Warren William and Lillian Charlene (Ingles) Huddleston; m. Michael Manierston, Mar. 10, 1979; children: Jonahtan, Geoffrey. BA, U. Ill., 1970, MA, 1974; MA, Ea. Mich. U., 1995. Tchr. Urbana (Ill.) Pub. Schs., 1970-71, Brookfield (Ill.) Dist. 95, 1971-76; Uniserv dir. Ill. Ednl. Assn., Elgin, 1976-80; Uniserv dir. Mich. Ednl. Assn., Lansing, 1980-84, from rsch. dir. to Uniserv dir., 1984—; cons. Mich. Dept. Edn., Lansing, 1990. Precinct del. Mich. Dem. Party, Livingston County, 1995—. Recipient pay equity award NEA, 1993, pres.'s award Profl. Staff Orgn., 1995. Mem. NOW, Mich. Sch. Bus. Ofcls. Home: 1986 Clover Ridge Dr Howell MI 48843

MANION, KAY DAUREEN, newspaper executive; b. St. Francis, Kans., Feb. 7, 1943; d. Edward William and Martha Dankenbring; children: Todd, Jon, Bandel. AS in Mktg. and Art, Western Nebr. C.C., 1990; postgrad., Colby (Kans.) C.C., 1992-94, Ft. Hays (Kans.) State Coll., 1995—. Various banking positions Kans. and Nebr., 1960-73; mgr. Alliance (Nebr.) Area C. of C., 1974-79; bridal cons., dept. mgr. Hatch Drug, Alliance, 1980-85; bridal cons. Herbergers, Scotts Bluff, 1986-88; salesperson, script writer Sta. KIMB, Kimball, 1989-90; med. records analyst Dunn Med. Equipment and Svcs., Inc., Colby, 1990-93; graphic designer Quad County Star, Oakley, Kans., 1993-95; news asst., advt. sales rep. Sherman County Star, Goodland, Kans., 1995—; freelance creative designer, 1988—; dir. tng. H.S. Distributive Edn. Clubs Am., Alliance, 1980-85, CETA, Alliance, 1976-79. Bd. dirs., sec. Alliance Cmty. Improvement Com., Alliance, 1974-79; mem. Oakley Tourism Com., 1994-96. Named Businesswoman of Yr. Alliance Area C. of C., 1978; recipient Disting. Svc. award Jaycees, Alliance, 1979. Mem. Am. Legion Aux., Elks Ladies' Aux., Phi Theta Kappa. Republican. Methodist. Home: 515 E 5th Apt 305 PO Box 429 Goodland KS 69935 Office: Sherman County Star 1015 Main PO Box 599 Goodland KS 69935

MANIS, LAURA GLANCE, retired psychology educator; b. Chgo., May 25, 1924; d. Nathan Glance and Minnie Walters; m. Jerome G. Manis, May 31, 1949; children: Robert, Lisa Neela. BEd, Chgo. State U., 1945; MA, Western Mich. U., 1965. Elem. sch. tchr. City Chgo., 1945-47; aptitude, personality assessor Johnson O'Conner Human Engring. Co., Chgo., 1947-49; pers. dir. Dr.'s Hosp., N.Y.C., 1949-52; counselor Climax (Mich.) H.S., 1965-66; psychol. counseling assoc. prof. Western Mich. U., Kalamazoo, 1966-83, assoc. prof. emerita, 1983—; co-founder, dir. Women's Ctr., Western Mich. U., 1975-83, developer of women's studies, chair, 1979-73. Author: (manual) Woman Power, 1977, Assertion Training, 1983, Training for Alzheimer's Group Leaders, 1984; contbr. articles to profl. jours. pres. League Women Voters, Kalamazoo, 1964-66; v.p. ACLU, Kalamazoo, 1978-82; chair Hawaii State Legis. Co. AARP, Honolulu, 1994-95; pres. bd. dirs. Alzheimer's Assn. Hawaii, Honolulu, 1988-90; apptd. to State Health Planning Commn., Honolulu, 1995—; bd. mem. Planned Parenthood, 1978-82. Recipient Women Pioneer award Mich. Women Lawyer's Assn., Detroit, 1978, Women of Yr. award Commn. on Status of Women, Kalamazoo, 1980, Outstanding Sr. Vol. award Gov. First Lady Awards, Honolulu, 1993, Outstanding Alumna of Yr. Western Mich. U., 1995. Mem. Hawaiian Women in Sci. (bd. dirs. 1982—), AARP (state legis. com. chair 1995), Honolulu Acad. Art.

MANKILLER, WILMA PEARL, tribal leader; b. Stilwell, Okla., Nov. 18, 1945; d. Charley and Clara Irene (Sitton) M.; m. Hector N. Olaya, Nov. 13, 1963 (div. 1975); children: Felicia Marie Olaya, Gina Irene Olaya; m. Charlie Soap, Oct. 13, 1986. Student, Skyline Coll., San Bruno Coll., 1973, San Francisco State Coll., 1973-75; BA in Social Sci., Flaming Rainbow Coll., 1977; postgrad., U. Ark., 1979. Cmty. devel. dir. Cherokee Nation, Tahlequah, Okla., 1977-83, dep. chief, 1983-85, prin. chief, 1985-87; pres. Inter-Tribal Coun. Okla.; mem. exec. bd. Coun. Energy Resource Tribes; bd. dirs. Okla. Indsl. Devel. Commn. Author: Mankiller: A Chief and Her People, 1993. Bd. dirs. Okla. Acad. for State Goals, 1985—. Recipient Donna Nigh First Lady award Okla. Commn. for Status of Women, 1985, Am. Leadership award Harvard U., 1986; inducted Okla. Women's Hall of Fame, 1986. Mem. Nat. Tribal Chmn. Assn., Nat. Congress Am. Indians, Cherokee County Dem. Women's Club. Home: PO Box 308 Park Hill OK 74451 Office: Cherokee Prin Chief PO Box 948 Tahlequah OK 74465-0948

MANLEY, AUDREY FORBES, medical administrator, physician; b. Jackson, Miss., Mar. 25, 1934; d. Jesse Lee and Ora Lee (Buckhalter) Forbes; m. Albert Edward Manley, Apr. 3, 1970. A.B. with honors (tuition scholar), Spelman Coll., Atlanta, 1955; M.D. (Jesse Smith Noyes Found. scholar), Meharry Med. Coll., 1959; MPH, Johns Hopkins U.-USPHS traineeship, 1987; LHD (hon.), Tougaloo (Miss.) Coll., 1990, Meharry Med. Coll., Nashville, 1991; LLD (hon.), Spelman Coll., 1991. Diplomate: Am. Bd. Pediatrics. Intern St. Mary Mercy Hosp., Gary, Ind., 1960; from jr. to chief resident in pediatrics Cook County Children's Hosp., Chgo., 1960-62; NIH fellow neonatology U. Ill. Rsch. and Ednl. Hosp., Chgo., 1963-65; staff pediatrician Chgo. Bd. Health, 1963-66; practice medicine specializing in pediatrics Chgo., 1963-66; assoc. Lawndale Neighborhood Health Ctr. North, 1966-67; asst. med. dir., 1967-69; asst. prof. Chgo. Med. Coll., 1966-67; instr. Pritzker Sch. Medicine, U. Chgo., 1967-69; asst. dir. ambulatory pediatrics, asst. dir. pediatrics Mt. Zion Hosp. and Med. Center, San Francisco, 1969-70; med. cons. Spelman Coll., 1970-71, med. dir. family planning program, chmn. health careers adv. com., 1972-76; med. dir. Grady Meml. Hosp. Family Planning Clinic, 1972-76; with Health Services Adminstrs., Dept. Health and Human Services, 1976—; commd. officer USPHS, 1976—; chief genetic diseases services br. Office Maternal and Child Health, Bur. Community Health Services, Rockville, Md., 1976-81; acting assoc. adminstr. clin. affairs Office of Adminstr. Health Resources and Services Adminstrn., 1981-83, chief med. officer, dep. assoc. adminstr. planning, evaluation and legis., 1983-85; sabbatical leave USPHS Johns Hopkins Sch. Hygiene and Pub. Health, 1986-87; dir. Nat. Health Service Corps.; asst. surgeon gen., 1988; dep. asst. Sec. for Health USPHS/HHS, 1989-93, acting asst. Sec. Health, 1993, dep. asst. Sec. Health/intergovtl. affairs, 1993-94; dep. surgeon gen., acting dep. asst. sec. for minority health USPHS, 1994-95; acting surgeon gen., 1995—; mem. U.S. del. UNICEF, 1990-94. Author numerous articles, reports in field. Trustee Spelman Coll., 1966-70. Recipient Meritorious Svc. award USPHS, 1981, Mary McLeod Bethune award Nat Coun. Negro Women, 1979, Dr. John P. McGovern Ann. Lectureship award Am. Sch. Health Assn., Disting. Alumni award Meharry Med. Coll., 1989, Spelman Coll. 108 Founder's Day Convocation, 1989, Disting. Svc. medal USPHS, 1992, Hildrus A. Poindexter award OSG/PHS, 1993, numerous other svc. and achievement awards. Fellow Am. Acad. Pediatrics; mem. Nat. Inst. Medicine of Nat. Acad. Sci., Nat. Med. Assn., APHA, AAUW, AAAS, Spelman Coll. Alumnae Assn., Meharry Alumni Assn., Operation Crossroads Africa Alumni Assn., Delta Sigma Theta (hon.). Home: 2807 18th St NW Washington DC 20009-2205 Office: 200 Independence Ave SW Washington DC 20201-0004

MANLEY, BARBARA LEE DEAN, occupational health nurse, hospital administrator, safety and health consultant; b. Washington, Nov. 5, 1946; d. Robert L. Dean and Mary L. (Jenkins) Dean Smallwood. BS, St. Mary-of-the-Woods, Terre Haute, Ind., 1973; MA, Central Mich. U., 1981. Cert. occupl. health nurse specialist. Indsl. nurse Ford Motor Co., Indpls., 1973-80; employee health nurse Starplex, Inc., Washington, 1981-84, Doctor's Hosp., Lanham, Md., 1984-85; regional occupational health nurse coordinator Naval Hosp., Long Beach, Calif., 1985-88; project mgr. East Coast Health Care Network, Inc., San Francisco, 1980-84; occupl. health nurse cons. HHS, Washington, 1980-84; occupational health and safety cons., mgr. FPE Group, Torrence, Calif., 1988-91; safety and loss control mgr. Assn. Calif. Hosp. Dists., Sacramento, 1991-93, v.p. loss control svcs., 1993-96; exec. dir. Quantum Inst., Sacramento, 1996—; part-time lectr. Compton (Calif.) Coll., 1986. Vol. ARC, Ft. Lewis, Wash., 1974-76, Ft. Harrison, Ind., 1978-80; counselor Crisis Hot-Line, Laurel, Md., 1981-83, Laurel Boy's and Girls Club, 1981-84. Recipient Navy's Meritorious Civilian Svc. Medal, 1989, Women of Excellence award Long Beach Press-Telegram Newspaper Guild, 1990, LCM Profl. of Yr. Acad. Loss Control Mgmt., 1995. Fellow Acad. Ambulatory Nursing Adminstrs. (Honor plaque 1981); mem. SCVAOHN (chair govt. affairs 1994—), Assn. Exec. Females, Am. Nurses Assn., Nat. Safety Mgmt. Soc. (2d v.p. 1992-96, 1st v.p. 1996—), Am. Assn. Occupational Health Nurses, Assn. Occupl. Healthcare Profls. (sec. 1986-88, conf. chairperson 1988, Outstanding Nurse of Yr. 1987), Fed. Safety and Health Council, Cen. Mich. U. Alumni Assn. (sec. 1985-88), Chi Eta Phi (regional bd. dirs. 1978-81). Presbyterian. Avocations: reading; crocheting; traveling; music. Office: Assn Calif Hosp Dists 2260 Park Towne Cir # Cl Sacramento CA 95825-0402

MANLEY, GERTRUDE ELLA, librarian, media specialist; b. Phila., Dec. 29, 1930; d. William Eugene and Anna G. (Price) Lomas; m. Harley E. Manley, Jr., July 20, 1957; children: Marc Alan, Karen Sue Manley Thornton, Gail Ann Manley Rivera. BRE, Shelton Coll., 1955; MSEd, Queens Coll., 1958, MS in Libr. Edn., 1958; postgrad., various. Libr. tchr. Plainedge (N.Y.) Sch. Dist., 1955-60; libr. dir. Huntington (N.Y.) Christian Sch., 1968-70; libr./media specialist Connetquot Ctrl. Sch. Dist. of Islip, Bohemia, N.Y., 1970—. Editor: Manley Family Newsletter, 1983—; contbr. articles to profl. jours. Mem. nursery sch. bd. New Life Community Ch. Nursery Sch., Sayville, N.Y., 1985-89; adminstr. pre-sch. story time program, E.J. Bosti Sch., Bohemia, 1972—, sign lang. instr., 1988—, Huffine award chairperson, 1985—, spell bee judge, 1984—, arranger speakers program, 1988—, kindergarten screening participant, 1988—, numerous in-house site-base planning and mgmt. coms., 1990-93. Mem. N.Y. State Ret. Tchrs. Assn. (life), N.Y. State United Tchrs., Western Suffolk Ret. Tchrs. Assn. (life), Connetquot Tchrs. Assn. (chmn. scholarship com.1978-93), Connetquot Ret. Tchrs. Assn. (rec. and corr. sec. 1993—). Baptist/Reformed Ch. of Am. Home: 171 Nathan Dr Bohemia NY 11716-1319 Office: Connetquot Ctrl Sch Dist Islip 780 Ocean Ave Bohemia NY 11716-3631

MANLEY, NANCY JANE, environmental engineer; b. Ft. Smith, Ark., Sept. 13, 1951; d. Eugene Hailey and Mary Adele (Chave) M. BSE, Purdue U., 1974; MSE, U. Wash., 1976; postgrad., U. Minn., 1976-77; grad., Air Command and Staff Coll., 1984, Exec. Leadership Devel. Program Dept. Def., 1988. Lic. profl. engr., Ga. Sanitary engr. Minn. Dept. Health, Mpls., 1976-77; sanitary engr. water supply EPA, Chgo., 1977; leader primacy unit water supply EPA, Atlanta, 1977-79, leader tech. assistance team, 1979-82; chief environ. and contract planning, project mgr. Grand Bay Range design USAF, Moody AFB, Ga., 1982-84; dep. base civil engr. USAF, Carswell

AFB, Tex., 1984-86, Scott AFB, Ill., 1986-89; mem. tech. adv. com. Scott AFB master plan study USAF, Belleville, Ill., 1986-89; dep. base civil engr. USAF, Robins AFB, Ga., 1989-91, acting chief engr., 1990-91, chief pollution prevention divsn., dir. environ. mgmt., 1991-93; chief engr. divsn. 78 Civil Engr. Group, Robins AFB, Ga., 1993—; mem. Fla. Tech. Adv. Com. for Injection Wells, Tallahassee, 1980-82, Nat. Implementation Team for Underground Injection Control Program, Washington, 1979-82, tech. panel Nat. Groundwater Protection Strategy Hearings, 1981; judge Internat. Sci. and Engring. Fair, 1986. Active various ch. support activities, 1969-74; sec. Perry Area Hist. Soc., 1991-93; vol. Meals-on-Wheels, Girl Scouts U.S., others, various locations, 1982—; founder, crisis intervention counselor Midwest Alliance, West Lafayette, Ind., 1970-74; active St. Louis Math. and Sci. Network Day, 1989, Adopt-a-Sch. Program, Lebanon, Ill., 1987-89; scientist by mail Boston Mus. Sci., 1989—. Recipient Presdl. Point of Light award USAF, 1991, Disting. Govt. Svc. award Dallas/Ft. Worth Fed. Exec. Bd., 1986, Lady of the Black Knights award 19th Air Refueling Wing, 1991. Mem. NSPE (v.p. local chpt. 1994-95, pres.-elect local chpt. 1995-96, pres. 1996—), ASCE, Soc. Women Engrs. (regional mem.-at-large rep. 1990-93, sr. mem. local officers 1979-82, 84-86), Am. Women in Sci., Soc. Am. Mil. Engrs. (local membership and contingency coms.), Internat. Platform Assn. Office: 78 CEG/CEC Robins AFB GA 31098-1864

MANLEY, PAULA ELIZABETH, accountant, fast food chain official; b. Chgo., Dec. 6, 1953; d. James Peter and Elizabeth Young (McQuattie) Bellas; m. Rob Lon Manley, Dec. 22, 1973. B Gen. Studies, Chaminade U., Honolulu, 1980; cert. in acctg., U. Miami, 1986, M Profl. Acctg., 1988. CPA, Fla. Fin. analayst Koster Cruises, Miami, Fla., 1982-89; contr. People's Computers, Charleston, S.C., 1989-91; gen. and adminstrv. contr. Burger King Corp., Miami, 1991-92, region contr., 1992-95, corp. asset mgr., 1995—. Ombudsman Navy Wives, Miami, 1992-93. With USN, 1973-80. Mem. AICPA, Fla. Inst. CPA's. Democrat. Greek Orthodox. Office: Burger King Corp 17777 Old Cutler Rd Miami FL 33157

MANLY, CAROL ANN, speech pathologist; b. Canton, Ohio, Nov. 21; d. William George and Florence L. (Parrish) M.; m. William Merget, Sept. 19, 1992; children: William, John. MA, U. Cin., 1970; PhD, NYU, 1988. Instr. U. Cin. Med. Ctr., 1970-72; asst. dir. Goldwater Hosp. NYU, 1972-83; pvt. practice N.Y.C., 1983—; cons. Mary Manning Walsh Home, N.Y.C., 1974-85, Beth Israel Med. Ctr.-North Divsn., N.Y.C., 1983—; adj. asst. prof. NYU, 1989-90, C.W. Post campus L.I. U., Brookville, 1990—. Author: (with others) Current Therapy in Physiatry, 1984, Communication Disorders of the Older Adult: A Practical Handbook for Health Care Professionals, 1993; contbr. articles to profl. jours. Mem. N.Y. Acad. Scis., Am. Speech-Lang.-Hearing Assn., N.Y. State Speech-Lang.-Hearing Assn., N.Y. Neuropsychology Group, NOW. Office: 360 E 65th St Ste 21D New York NY 10021-6726

MANN, EMILY BETSY, writer, artistic director, theater and film director; b. Boston, Apr. 12, 1952; d. Arthur and Sylvia (Blut) M.; 1 child, Nicholas Isaac Bamman. BA, Harvard U., 1974; MFA, U. Minn., 1976. Resident dir. Guthrie Theater, Mpls., 1976-79; dir. BAM Theater Co., Bklyn., 1980-81; freelance writer, dir. N.Y.C., 1981-90; artistic dir. McCarter Theater Ctr. for the Performing Arts, Princeton, N.J., 1990—; cons. N.Y. Theatre Workshop, 1987. Author: (plays) Annulla, An Autobiography, Still Life (6 Obie awards 1981, Fringe First award 1985), Execution of Justice (Helen Hayes award, Bay Area Theatre Critics Circle award, HBO/USA award, Playwriting award Women's Com. Dramtists Guild for Dramatizing Issues of Conscience 1986), Greensboro: A Requiem; co-author: (with Ntozake Shange) (musical) Betsey Brown; (screenplays) Naked, Fanny Kelly, The Winnie Mandela Story, The Greensboro Massacre; dir. Hedda Gabbler, A Doll House, Annulla, Still Life (Obie award), Execution of Justice (Guthrie and Broadway), Betsey Brown, The Glass Menagerie, Three Sisters, Cat on a Hot Tin Roof, Twilight: L.A., 1992 (L.A. NAACP award for best dir.), The Perfectionist, The Matchmaker: adaptor, dir. Miss Julie, Having Our Say (Tony nomination-direction of a play 1995, Dramatist Guild's Hull Warriner award), Greensboro, A Requiem; translator: Nights and Days (Pierre Laville), 1985; pub. in New Plays U.S.A. 1, New Plays 3, American Plays and the Vietnam War, The Ten Best Plays of 1986, Out Front. Recipient BUSH fellowship, 1975-76, Rosamond Gilder award New Drama Forum Assn., 1983, NEA Assocs. grant, 1984, Guggenheim fellowship, 1985, McKnight fellowship, 1985, CAPS award, 1985, NEA Playwrights fellowship, 1986. Mem. Soc. Stage Dirs. and Choreographers, Theatre Comms. Group (v.p.), New Dramatists, PEN, Writers' Guild, Dramatists' Guild, Phi Beta Kappa.

MANN, JOAN ELLONA, artist, editor; b. Seattle, Aug. 21, 1931; d. Henry Hughes and Jeanetta Maurine (Baker)) Jacobsen; m. Hugh Mann, Sept. 2, 1955 (div. Aug. 1981); children: Susan, Kristi, Steven, Nancy, Roy. BA in Journalism, U. Wash., 1953, BFA in Sculpture, 1970, MFA in Sculpture, 1985. Reporter East Side Jour., Kirkland, Wash., 1953-55; med. editor Virginia Mason Med. Ctr., Seattle, 1965-69; info. specialist Continuing Edn. News Svc. U. Wash., Seattle, 1969-73; editor Seattle Arts Commn., 1973-77; pub. info. officer King County Arts Commn., Seattle, 1973-90; owner, mgr. Joan Mann, Editor, Seattle. Sculptures include multi-media floor sculpture Trident, Ship of Fools, 1988 (award); shows include U. Wash. Henry Gallery, 1971; group shows include Roscoe Louie Gallery, Seattle, 1975, Univ. Unitarian Gallery, 1978, U. Wash. Henry Gallery, 1987, U. Wash. Meany Hall, 1987, SJW Studios, Seattle, 1988, Seattle Ctr. Opera House, 1988, PNAC, Bellevue, 1988, Ctr. for Contemporary Art, Seattle, 1989. Precinct del. Wash. Dem. Com., Seattle, 1992. Recipient 2d and 3d place ann. awards Wash. Press Women, 1971, 1st prize Ctr. for Contemporary Art, 1989; travel grantee Goethe Inst., Berlin, 1988. Mem. Women in Comm. (Nat. Clarion award 1974), Allied Arts Seattle (adv. bd. 1990—), Seattle Art Mus. Roman Catholic. Office: 1100 University St Seattle WA 98101

MANN, JULIE ANNE, business educator; b. Owensboro, Ky., July 2, 1959; d. Walter Sherwood and Barbara Nell (Higgs) McGehee; m. Terry Glen Mann, Apr. 22, 1988; children: Kelsey Rae, Dylan Tyler. BS in Bus. Edn., Brescia Coll., 1981; MS in Bus. Edn., Western Ky. U., 1991. Sec. trust dept. Citizens State Bank, Owensboro, 1981-83; adminstrv. asst. Green River Steel Corp., Owensboro, 1983-87; office mgr. Constance Revlett Law Offices, Calhoun, Ky., 1987-91; instr. bus. Owensboro H.S., Ky., 1991-95; computer keyboarding instr. Owensboro Mid. Sch., Ky., 1995—; mem. Ky. Task Force on Bus. Edn., Frankfort, 1992—. Mem. Nat. Bus. Edn. Assn., So. Bus. Edn. Assn., Ky. Bus. Edn. Assn. (bd. dirs. 1993-95), Ky. Edn. Assn., Ky. Mid. Sch. Assn., Delta Pi Epsilon. Democrat. Methodist. Home: PO Box 402 Calhoun KY 42327-0402

MANN, KAREN, consultant, educator; b. Kansas City, Mo., Oct. 9, 1942; d. Charles and Letha (Anderson) M. BA, U. Calif.-Santa Barbara, 1964; MPA, Golden Gate U., 1975, PhD, 1994. Cert. lay minister Order of Buddhist Contemplatives. Tchr. Sisters of Immaculate Heart, Los Angeles, 1964-68; group counselor San Francisco and Marin County Probation Depts., parole agt. Calif. Dept. Corrections, Sacramento and San Francisco, 1970-86; researcher and cons. Non-profit Orgnl. Devel., 1986—, Computer Applications for Persons with Disabilities, 1986—; adj. faculty Grad. Theol. Union, Berkeley, 1984—; Compuserve Disabilities Forum, 1988—; forum adminstr.; mem. faculty Golden Gate U., 1990. Co-author: Prison Overcrowding, 1979; Community Corrections: A Plan for California, 1980; sec., bd. dirs. Spirit Rock Meditation Ctr. Active Fellowship of Reconciliation, N.Y., 1970—; co-founder Network Ctr. for Study of Ministry, San Francisco, 1982; pres. San Francisco Network Ministries, 1980-82; mem. Disabled Children's Computer Resource Group, 1988—, Springwater Ctr. for Meditative Inquiry and Retreats, 1986—; emotional support counselor Marin AIDS Project, 1992—. Office: PO Box 377 Lagunitas CA 94938-0377

MANN, LINDA MARIE, elementary school educator; b. Pitts., July 11, 1949; d. Howard Robert and Matilda Elizabeth (Baumann) M. BA in Edn., Syracuse U., 1972; MS in Instructional Systems Tech., Ind.U., 1975; post-grad. studies Edn.-related, SUNY, Oswego, Plattsburgh, Albany, 1991-92. Cert. tchr. lifetime (N-6), libr. media specialist (K-12), English (7-12) permanent, N.Y. Secondary English tchr. Liverpool (N.Y.) Ctrl. Schs., 1972-74, media specialist, 1975-91, elem. tchr. vertical team grades 3-4-5, 1992, elem. tchr., 1992—; edn. cons., mem. educators' adv. bd. Ste Marie Mus., Liverpool, 1976-92; tour guide, guest speaker Hist. Assn. Greater Liverpool, 1989-92. Tchr., tchr. trainer, supt. Sunday sch., chairperson curriculum com., coord. ref. libr. Greater Love in Christ Ch., Syracuse, N.Y., 1985-92. Mem. ASCD, Internat. Reading Assn., Tchrs. Applying Whole Lang., Ctrl. N.Y. Coun. Social Studies, Delta Kappa Gamma. Office: Liverpool Ctrl Sch 800 4th St Liverpool NY 13088-4455

MANN, MARYLEN, adult services institute director; b. St. Louis, Mar. 13, 1937; d. Morris and Ruth (Sobel) Lipkind; (widowed); children: Robert Gordon, John Douglas. BA in Philosophy, Washington U., St. Louis, 1957; MA in Edn., Washington U., 1959. Tchr. St. Louis Pub. Schs., 1961-62; supr. student tchrs. dept. edn. Washington U., 1969, rsch. instr. Med. Sch., 1984—; instr. edn. U. Mo., St. Louis, 1972-74, dir. Older Adult Service and Info. System, fellow Ctr. Metro Studies, lctr. Dept. Edn., 1983-84; instr. curriculum devel. Webster U., St. Louis, 1977-78; dir. various programs CEMREL Inc., St. Louis, 1974-82; exec. dir. OASIS Inst. Barnes-Jewish Hosp., St. Louis, 1984—; bd. dirs. Gerontology Concentration Adv. Com., Washington U., 1987-90; mem. nat. coun. George Warren Brown Sch. Social Work, Washington U., 1987—; trustee Fontbonne Coll., 1989-93. Contbr. articles to profl. jours. Bd. dirs. Jewish Ctr. Aged, 1984-87, 94—, St. Louis Psychoanalytic Inst., 1983-91, 95—, Arts and Edn. Coun. St. Louis, 1981-87, 88—, mem. exec. com., 1986, v.p. bd. dirs., 1986, chair program com., 1986, chmn. membership com., 1989-92, v.p., 1991, co-chair awards com., 1993-94, mem. alllocations and membership coms., 1993-94; mem. Gov.'s Adv. Coun. Aging, Mo. exec. com., 1984-86, Gov.'s Task Force Alternative Care Elderly, 1982, Clayton (Mo.) Sch. Bd., 1970-84, pres., 1979-81, v.p., 1976, sec., 1975; mem. pres.'s coun. The Repertory Theatre St. Louis, 1988—, bd. dirs., 1989-95; mem. cmty. adv. bd. Jr. League St. Louis, 1990—; bd. dirs. St. Louis Regional Commerce and Growth Assn., 1990-94, Internat. Women's Forum, 1992—, Square One Found., 1992-94; bd. govs., v.p. Fair St. Louis, 1991—; mem. adv. coun. St. Louis chpt. Alzheimer's Assn., 1992—; mem. chancellor's adv. panel St. Louis C.C., 1992—; mem. adv. bd. nonprofit mgmt. and leadership program U. Mo.-St. Louis, 1994—; bd. dirs. Parents as Tchrs. Nat. Ctr., 1994—; mem. exec. bd. Women of Achievement, 1995—; del. White House Conf. Aging, 1995. Recipient numerous grants on care of the elderly, Creativity award Adult Edn. Coun., 1979, Spl. Leadership award YWCA, 1985, Bronze medal award U.S. Surgeon Gen., 1988, Community award of merit Jewish Ctr. for Aged of Greater St. Louis, 1991, Cmty. Svc. award St. Louis chpt. Am. Jewish Com., 1992, Woman That Makes A Difference award Internat. Women's Forum, 1992; named Woman of Yr. City of Clayton, 1981, Woman of Achievement St. Louis Globe Democrat, 1980. Mem. Am. Assn. Internat. Aging, Gerontol. Soc. Am., Nat. Coun. Aging Inc., Am. Soc. Aging, Nat. Soc. Fund Raising Execs., Women's Forum Mo. Home: 900 Audubon Dr Saint Louis MO 63105-2932 Office: OASIS Inst 7710 Carondelet Ave Ste 125 Saint Louis MO 63105-3319

MANN, NANCY LOUISE (NANCY LOUISE ROBBINS), entrepreneur; b. Chillicothe, Ohio, May 6, 1925; d. Everett Chaney and Pauline Elizabeth R.; m. Kenneth Douglas Mann, June 19, 1949 (div. June 1979); children: Bryan Wilkinson, Laura Elizabeth. BA in Math., UCLA, 1948, MA in Math., 1949, PhD in Biostatistics, 1965. Sr. scientist Rocketdyne Div. of Rockwell Internat., Canoga Park, Calif., 1962-75; mem. tech. staff Rockwell Sci. Ctr., Thousand Oaks, Calif., 1975-78; rsch. prof. UCLA Biomath., L.A., 1978-87; pres., CEO, owner Quality Enhancement Seminars, Inc., L.A., 1982—; pres., CEO Quality and Productivity, Inc., L.A., 1987—; curriculum adv. UCLA Ext. Dept. of Bus. and Mgmt., L.A., 1991—; mem. com. on Nat. Statistics, Nat. Acad. Scis., Washington, 1978-82; mem adv. bd. to supt. U.S. Naval Posgrad. Sch., Monterey, Calif., 1979-82. Co-author: Methods for Analysis of Reliability and Life Data, 1974; author: Keys to Excellence, 1985, The Story of the Deming Philosophy, 2d edit., 1987, 3d edit., 1989; contbr. articles to profl. jours. Recipient award IEEE Reliability Soc., 1982, ASQC Reliability Divsn., 1986. Fellow Am. Statis. Assn. (v.p. 1982-84); mem. Internat. Statis. Inst. Office: Quality and Productivity Inc 1081 Westwood Blvd # 217 Los Angeles CA 90024-2911

MANN, TRUE SANDLIN, psychologist, consultant; b. Longview, Tex., Aug. 4, 1934; d. Bob Murphy and Stella True (Williams) Sandlin; m. Jack Matthewson Mann, Sept. 4, 1954 (div. Dec. 1989); children: Jack Matthewson Jr., Bob Sandlin, Daniel Williams, Nathaniel Currier. BS, Stephen F. Austin State U., Nacogdoches, Tex., 1973, MA, 1977; PhD, East Tex. State U., 1982. Lic. psychologist, Tex., Ark. Instr. Stephen F. Austin State U., 1975-76, vis. asst. prof. psychology, 1986-87; instr. East Tex. State U., Commerce, 1980-81; postdoctoral fellow Southwestern Med. Sch., Dallas, 1982-83; pvt. practice, Longview, Tex., 1983-92; psychologist dept. family practice U. Tex. Health Sci. Ctr., Tyler, 1990-92; dir. psychol. svcs. St. Michael's Hosp., Texarkana, Tex., 1992-93; cons. psychologist, Longview, 1993—; weekly newspaper columnist HARBUS, Cambridge Mass., 1959-60; cons. Made-Rite Co., Longview, 1989—. Mem. candidate com. Assoc. Reps. Tex., Austin, 1990—; bd. dirs. Mental Health Assn. Tex., 1977-82, 84-92, Longview Symphony, 1995, Longview Mus. of Art, 1995; mem. Leadership Tex., 1988—. Mem. APA, Tex. Psychol. Assn. Episcopalian. Home: 1309 Inverness St Longview TX 75601-3548 Office: 1203 Montclair St Longview TX 75601-3565

MANNEL, BARBARA J., physician; b. Neptune, N.J., Apr. 1, 1958; d. William Morgan and Leah Jane Mannel. BA in English, U. Va., Charlottesville, 1980; MD, Vanderbilt U., 1993. Adminsrv. asst. Ga. Mil. Coll., Ft. Gordon, 1980-83; spl. edn. tchr. Reading Success, Augusta, Ga., 1980-85; spl. edn. tutor Augusta, 1984-87; resident in psychiatry Alton Ochsner Med. Found., New Orleans, 1993-96, chief resident in psychiatry, 1996—. Mem. AMA, Am. Psychiat. Assn., La. Psychiat. Med. Assn., Phi Beta Kappa. Office: Ochsner Clinic Psychiatry Dept 1514 Jefferson Hwy New Orleans LA 70121

MANNER, JENNIFER FOUSE, social worker; b. Balt., June 15, 1964; d. Richard Erb and Patricia Ann (Matthews) Fouse; m. David Bruce Manner, Aug. 16, 1986. BA in Psychology, Hop Coll., 1986; MS in Social Adminstrn., Case Western Reserve U., 1988. Lic. ind. social worker, Ohio; cert. chem. dependency counselor. Counselor Women in Transition, Grand Haven, Mich., 1986; adolescent continuing care counselor Lakeland Inst. Lorain (Ohio) Cmty. Hosp., 1988-90; dir. Laurelwood Counseling Ctr., Mayfield Heights, Ohio, 1990-93; ind. social worker, chem. dependency counselor Elyria, Ohio, 1993—; lectr. in field. Youth fellowship leader St. Andrew's Presbyn. Ch., Olmsted Falls, Ohio, 1987-89; vol. counselor Christ Ch. Indian Reservation, Canton, Ohio, 1990. Mem. NASW, Psi Chi. Democrat. Presbyterian. Home: 6641 Myrtle Hill Rd Valley City OH 44280 Office: Psychiat & Psychol Svcs 412 E River St Elyria OH 44035

MANNERS, RUTH ANN, writer; b. Keene, Ohio, Aug. 6, 1919; d. George Frank and Eva Barbara (Bissantz) Bauer; m. David X. Manners, Feb. 22, 1945; children: Paul, Jonathan, Michael, Timothy. BA, Randolph-Macon Woman's Coll., 1941; student, Art Students League, N.Y.C., 1941-43. V.p. David X. Manners Co. Inc., Norwalk, Conn., 1966-82. Author: Today's Woman Prize Kitchens, 1964, Today's Woman Sewing Simplified, 1965, (with William Manners) The Quick and Easy Vegetarian Cookbook, 1978 (Tastemaker award for cookbook excellence 1979), The New Quick and Easy Vegetarian Cookbook, 1993. Office: David X Manners Co Inc 4 Landmark Sq Stamford CT 06880

MANNES, ELENA SABIN, film and television producer, director; b. N.Y.C., Dec. 3, 1943; d. Leopold Damrosch and Evelyn (Sabin) M. BA, Smith Coll., 1965; MA, Johns Hopkins U., 1967. Researcher Pub. Broadcast Lab. Nat. Ednl. TV, N.Y.C., 1968-70; writer Sta. WPIX-TV, N.Y.C., 1970-73; assignment editor Sta. ABC-TV, N.Y.C., 1973-76; producer, writer Sta. WCBS-TV, N.Y.C., 1976-80; producer CBS News, N.Y.C., 1980-87, Pub. Affairs TV/Bill Moyers PBS Documentaries, N.Y.C., 1987-90; ind. documentary dir. and producer, 1987—. Recipient Emmy award NATAS, 1984, 85, 87, 90, 94, 96, Peabody award, 1985, Cine Golden Eagle award, 1988, 90, 93, 94, 95, Robert F. Kennedy journalism award, 1989, DGA awards, 1987, 90. Mem. Writers Guild Am., Dirs. Guild Am., Am. Film Inst. (dir. Workshop for Women).

MANNING, BLANCHE M., federal judge; b. 1934. BEd, Chgo. Tchrs. Coll., 1961; JD, John Marshall Law Sch., 1967; MA, Roosevelt Univ., 1972; LLM, Univ. of Va. Law Sch., 1992. Asst. states atty. State's Atty.'s Office (no. dist.) Ill., 1968-73; supervisory trial atty. U.S. EEOC, Chgo., 1973-77; gen. atty. United Airlines, Chgo., 1977-78; asst. U.S. atty. U.S. Dist. Ct. (no. dist.) Ill., 1978-79; assoc. judge Cir. Ct. of Cook County, 1979-86, circuit judge, 1986-87; appellate court judge Ct. of Review Ill. Appellate Ct., 1987-94; district judge U.S. Dist. Ct. (no. dist.) Ill., Chgo., 1994—; tchr. A. O. Sexton Elem. Sch. James Wadsworth Elem. Sch., Wendell Phillips H.S. Adult Program, Morgan Park H.S. Summer Sch. Program, South Shore H.S. Summer Sch. Program, Carver H.S. Adult Edn. Program; lectr. Malcolm X C.C., 1970-71; adj. prof. NCBL C.C. of Law, 1978-79, DePaul Univ. Law Sch., 1992-94; tchg. team mem. Trial Advocacy Workshop, Harvard Law Sch., U. Chgo. Law Sch., 1991-94; chmn. Com. on Recent Devels. in Evidence, Ill. Judicial Conf., 1991; faculty mem. New Judges Seminar, Ill. Judicial Conf.; past faculty mem. Profl. Devel. Seminar for New Assoc. Judges, Cook County Cir. Ct.; mem. bd. dirs., trained intervenor Lawyers' Assistance Program, Inc.; mem. adv. coun. Lawyer's Asst. Program, Roosevelt U. Trustee Sherwood Music Conservatory Bd. Mem. Cook County Bar Assn. (second v-p 1974), Nat. Bar Assn., Nat. Judicial Coun., Ill. Judicial Coun. (treas. 1982-85, chmn. 1988, chmn. judiciary com. 1992), Ill. Judges Assn., Women's Bar Assn. of Ill., Nat. Assn. of Women Lawyers, Ill. State Bar Assn. (bd. dirs. Lawyers Assistance Program Inc.), Am. Bar Assn. (fellow 1991), Chgo. Bar Assn. (bd. dirs. Lawyers Assistance Program Inc.), Nat. Assn. of Women Judges, Appellate Lawyers Assn. (hon.); John Marshall Law Sch. Alumni Assn. (bd. dirs.), Chgo. State Univ. Alumni Assn. (bd. dirs.). Office: US Dist Ct 2156 US Courthouse 219 S Dearborn St Chicago IL 60604-1706

MANNING, CATHERINE MARIE, health care administrator; b. Bradford, Pa., Nov. 10, 1938; d. James Joseph and Mary Magdalen (Chohrach) M. BS in Elem. Edn., Villa Maria Coll., Erie, Pa., 1966; MEd, Gannon U., Erie, 1971; MA in Theology, Boston Coll., 1981. Joined Sisters of St. Joseph, Roman Cath. Ch., 1956. Tchr. Erie Diocesan Sch. Sys., Erie, 1956-66; piano instr. Villa Maria Conservatory, Erie, 1957-58; prin. Erie Diocesan Sch. Sys., 1966-73; dir. admissions Villa Maria Coll., Erie, 1973-76; med. social svc. caseworker St. Vincent Health Ctr., Erie, 1976-79; sociology and psychology instr. Marian Ct. Bus. Coll., Swampscott, Mass., 1981-82; acad. dean Marymount Internat. Sch., Rome, Italy, 1982-85; v.p. St. Vincent Health Ctr., Erie, 1985-91, pres., 1991-96; pres., CEO St. Vincent Health Sys., 1996—; trustee St. Mary's Home of Erie, 1985-95; bd. dirs. Cath. Charities of Erie Diocese, 1991, St. Vincent Health Ctr.; mem. bd. visitors Behrend Sch. Bus., Pa. State U. Bd. dirs. United Way of Erie County, 1994—. Mem. AAUW, Am. Coll. Healthcare Execs., Erie Art Mus., Pax Christi USA. Democrat. Roman Catholic. Home: 2816 Burgundy Dr Erie PA 16506-5260

MANNING, DAWN E., cosmetics company executive; b. Akron, Ohio, Mar. 2, 1958; d. John Barrett and Janet Elaine (Kirk) Bittinger; m. Michael Wayne Manning; stepchildren: Jon Michael, Shelby Arica. BBA in Mktg., U. Iowa, 1981. Mktg. rep. Xerox Corp., Des Moines, 1981-82; promotional coord. Parfums Stern Inc., N.Y.C., 1983-85; regional account mgr. Jean Marc Sinan, N.Y.C., 1985-86; account exec. Sanofi Beauty Products, N.Y.C., 1986-89; real estate broker Perry & Butler Realty, Denver, 1991-92; bus. mgr. CosFrance Sisley Inc., N.Y.C., 1993—; jr. ptnr. SynTec Partnership, LLC, N.J., 1995-96. Named Woman of the Week, Cable Network Channel 23, N.Y., 1996, one of 2000 Notable Am. Women, Am. Biographical Inst., 1996. Mem. NAFE, Fin. Women's Assn. n.Y. Republican. Presbyterian. Home: 2 Meadow Lake Dr Mahwah NJ 07430

MANNING, DIANE LOUISE, behavioral health administrator; b. Norwich, Conn., Feb. 25, 1958; d. Edward Hoxie and Loretta (Topping) Manning. AB, Coll. of the Holy Cross, Worcester, Mass., 1980; MBA, U. Conn., 1982. Cert. mental health adminstr. Dir. planning and evaluation United Svcs., Inc., Dayville, Conn., 1983-89, dir. adminstrv. svcs., 1989-93, dep. dir., 1993-95, exec. v.p., 1995—; cons. Conn. Cmty. Provicer Assn., Rocky Hill, Conn., 1989-95. Dir. liturgical music St. Mary Parish, Jewett City, Conn., 1990-96; treas. Griswold (Conn.) Players, 1993-96. Assn. of Mental Health Adminstrs. (pres. Tri-state chpt. 1993), NAFE, Griswold Players Cmty. Chorus. Roman Catholic. Home: 40 William Dr Jewett City CT 06351 Office: United Svcs Inc PO Box 839 1007 N Main St Dayville CT 06241

MANNING, JOAN ELIZABETH, health association administrator; b. Davenport, Iowa, July 7, 1953; d. George John and Eugenie Joan (Thomas) Stolze; m. Michael Anthony Manning, July 30, 1977. BA, U. No. Iowa, 1975; MPH, U. Minn., 1990. Traveling collegiate sec. Alpha Delta Pi Nat. Sorority, Atlanta, 1975-76; recreational therapist Americana Healthcare Ctr., Mason City, Iowa, 1976-81; communication coord. Area Agy. on Aging, Mason City, 1981-83; exec. dir. United Way Cerro Gordo County, Mason City, 1983-85, Health Fair of the Midlands, Omaha, 1985-87; dir. health services ARC, Omaha, 1987-90, chief ops. officer, 1990-95; CEO ARC, 1995—; vis. rsch. prof. Niels Bohr Inst., Denmark, 1995-96. Bd. dirs. YMCA of U.S.A., Chgo., 1981-83, Mason City YMCA, 1980-84, Mason City Parks and Recreation Bd., 1983-85, Camp Fire Coun., 1989—, Potters Therapy House, 1989—; mem. spl. adv. bd. Cerro Gordo County Human Svcs. Bd., 1983-85; mem. spl. activities com. Omaha Wellness Coun. of Midlands, 1986-89; chmn. wider opportunity task force Great Plains (Nebr.) Girl Scouts U.S., 1986-89; bd. dirs. Omaha South YMCA; mem. Jr. League of Omaha. Mem. U. Minn. Alumnae Assn., Suburban Rotary, Alpha Delta Pi. Republican. Roman Catholic. Office: ARC 3838 Dewey Ave Omaha NE 68105-1148

MANNING, MARTHA MARY, writer, psychologist; b. Chgo., Aug. 18, 1952; d. John Eugene and Mary Louise M.; m. Brian J. Depenbrock, Oct. 20, 1973; 1 child, Keara. BA with honors, U. Md., College Park, 1974; MA, Cath. Univ. Am., 1978, PhD, 1981. Postdoc. fellow McLean Hosp./Harvard Med. Sch., Boston, 1981-83; asst. prof. George Mason Univ., Fairfax, Va., 1983-88; pvt. practice Alexandria, Va., 1994-96; psychology instr., 1989-93. Author: A Season of Mercy, 1985, Undercurrents: A Life Beneath the Surface, 1995, Chasing Grace, 1996; columnist, Salt of the Earth, 1993—; contbr. to popular mags. including Mirabella, New Woman, Ladies' Home Jour., Glamour, U.S. Cath., N.Y. Times Book Review, Family Therapy Networker, Washington Post. Recipient Merit award Associated Ch. Press, 1994, 96, Best Mag. Column Cath. Press Assn., 1995. Mem. APA (Patient Advocacy award 1996). Office: Arielle Eckstut James Levine Comm Inc care FWI 330 7th Ave 14th Fl New York NY 10001*

MANNING, SHERRY FISCHER, college president emerita, business executive; b. Washington, Apr. 28, 1943; d. Fred W. and Eleanor A. (Mertz) Fischer; BA cum laude, Western Md. Coll., 1965, LHD, 1979; MA, William and Mary Coll., 1967; PhD, U. Colo. 1973; m. Charles W. Manning, Dec. 23, 1966; children: Shannon Marie, Charles Fischer, Kelly Eleanor. Mktg. rep., systems engr. IBM, 1967-71; staff assoc. Nat. Ctr. for Higher Edn. Mgmt. Systems, 1971-72; exec. asst. to exec. dir. Nat. Commn. of the Financing of Postsecondary Edn., 1972-73; adj. prof. U. Colo., 1973-74; asst. prof. U. Kans., 1975-77; cons. to pres. for acad. planning Universidade Fed. de Ceara, 1976-77; exec. v.p. Colo. Women's Coll., 1977-78, pres., 1978-81, pres. emerita, 1981—; chief exec. officer John Madden Co., Englewood, Colo., 1982-87, bd. dirs., 1984—; founder SIGMAN Communications, Inc., Edn. Comm. Consortice, Inc., 1988—; bd dirs. Solar Energy Rsch. Inst., 1987-90, Regis Coll., 1987-91, Univ. So. Colo. Found., 1987-91, United Bank Svcs. Co., 1978-81, Imperial Am. Energy Inc., Adopt-A-School 1979-82, Denver Symphony 1979-82, Colo. Council on Econ. Edn., 1984-87, Colo. Assn. Commerce and Industry Edn. Found., 1984-87, Colo. Assn. Commerce and Industry, 1985—; Recipient DAR Outstanding Citizen award, 1961, Faculty Devel. award U. Kans., 1976, Soroptimists Women Helping Women award, 1980. Mem. Nat. Assn. Christians & Jews, Nat. Women's Coalition, Women's Forum, Zonta, Altrusa., Com. of 200 Club, Newcomen Soc. of U.S., Sports Hall of Fame Western Md. Coll., Phi Beta Kappa, Denver Met. Club. Republican, Presbyterian. Host community affairs program, KHOW Radio, 1979-80; contbr. articles in field. Office: PO Box 4584 Charleston WV 25364-4584

MANNING, SYLVIA, English studies educator; b. Montreal, Que., Can., Dec. 2, 1943; came to U.S., 1967; d. Bruno and Lea Bank; m. Peter J. Manning, Aug. 20, 1967; children—Bruce David, Jason Maurice. B.A., McGill U., 1963; M.A., Yale U., 1964, Ph.D. in English, 1967. Asst. prof. English Calif. State U.-Hayward, 1967-71, assoc. prof., 1971-75, assoc. dean, 1972-75; assoc. prof. U. So. Calif., 1975-94, prof., assoc. dir. Ctr. for Humanities, 1975-77, assoc. dir. Ctr. for Humanities, 1975-77, chmn. freshman writing, 1977-80, chmn. dept. English, 1980-83, vice provost, exec.

v.p., 1984-94; prof. English U. Ill., 1994—, v.p. for acad. affairs, prof. English, 1994—. Author: Dickens as Satirist, 1971; Hard Times: An Annotated Bibliography, 1984. Contbr. essays to mags. Woodrow Wilson fellow, 1963-64, 66-67. Mem. MLA, Dickens Soc. Office: U of Ill 377 Henry Adm Bldg 506 S Wright St Urbana IL 61801-3614

MANNING, VESTA FORTSON, foreign language educator, humanities educator; b. Henderson, N.C., Dec. 4, 1949; d. Richard deYarman Manning and Vesta Fortson (Wester) Hughes. BS, Grand Valley State Coll., 1977; MA, U. Ariz., 1980; postgrad., U. Fla., 1987. Libr., dir. internat. exchange program Costa Rica Acad., San Jose, 1973-76; instr., dir. fgn. langs. Grand Rapids (Mich.) Pub. Schs., 1976-79; instr. fgn. langs. Catalina Foothills Sch. Dist., Tucson, 1979-81; tchg. asst., paleographer U. Ariz., Tucson, 1981-85; rsch. asst. U. Fla., Gainesville, 1985-87; instr. history Am. Sch. Found., Mexico City, 1988-89; instr. fgn. langs. Eaton-Johnson Mid. Sch., Henderson, N.C., 1989-90; program head, instr. fgn. langs. and humanities Vance-Granville C.C., Henderson, N.C., 1990—; mem. adv. bd. So. Conf. on Lang. Tchg., Valdosta, Ga., 1993—; spkr. in field. Mem. adv. bd. Human Rels. Commn., Oxford, N.C., 1992-93; dir. tng. Amigos de las Americas, Tucson chpt., 1983-84; sec.-treas. Ptnrs. of Americas, Tucson, 1981-82. Recipient Tinker Field Rsch. grant U. Ariz., 1986. Mem. Am. Hist. Assn., Fgn. Lang. Assn. N.C., Am. Coun. on Tchg. of Fgn. Langs., Orgn. Am. Historians, Am. Assn. Tchrs. of Spanish and Portuguese, Phi Alpha Theta (sec.-treas. 1983-84, pres. 1984-85), Sigma Delta Mu (sponsor 1996). Episcopalian. Home: 108 E Front St Oxford NC 27565 Office: Vance Granville CC PO Box 917 Henderson NC 27536

MANSEAU, MELISSA MARIE, infosystems specialist; b. Exeter, N.H., Mar. 24, 1962; d. Stuart Wayne and Dorothy Edith (Follis) Cady; m. Gerald Vincent Manseau; children: Lindsay Marie, Megan Elise. AS in Electronic Engrng. Tech., N.H. Tech. Inst., Concord, 1982; BS in Computer Sci., U. So. Maine, 1988. Assoc. system technician Nat. Semiconductor Corp., Inc. (formerly Fairchild Semiconductor), South Portland, Maine, 1982-83, system technician, 1983-85, sr. system technician, 1985, assoc. computer system engr., 1985-88, software engr., 1988—; sr. software engr., 1993; sr. analyst Konica Quality Photo East, Scarborough, Maine, 1994; engr. Systems Consulting Co., Portland, Maine, 1994—. Mem. IEEE, IEEE Computer Soc. (chmn. 1987-91). Congregationalist. Home: 10 Pinecrest Dr Hollis Center ME 04042-9763

MANSELL, JOYCE MARILYN, special education educator; b. Minot, N.D., Dec. 17, 1934; d. Einar Axel and Gladys Ellen (Wall) Alm; m. Dudley J. Mansell, Oct. 31, 1954; children: Michael, Debra Mansell Richards. BS, U. Houston, 1968; MEd, Sam Houston State U., 1980. Cert. provisional elem. tchr. 1-8, provisional mentally retarded tchr., provisional lang. and/or learning disabilities tchr., profl. elem. tchr. gen. 1-8, profl. reading specialist. 1st grade tchr. Johnson Elem. Sch., 1968-72, 2nd grade tchr., 1972-76, 3rd grade tchr., 1976-77; spl. edn. tchr. mentally retarded/learning disabled Meml. Parkway Jr. H.S., 1982-86, Waller Mid. Sch., 1986-90; spl. edn. tchr. mentally retarded Royal Mid. Sch., Tex., 1990-95, Royal H.S., 1995-96; ret., 1996; tchr. Am. sign lang. for retarded students Holy Three and One Luth. Ch. of Deaf. Lutheran. Home: 2155 Paso Rello Dr Houston TX 77077-5622

MANSFIELD, KAREN LEE, lawyer; b. Chgo., Mar. 17, 1942; d. Ralph and Hilda (Blum) Mansfield; children: Nicole Rafaela, Lori Michele. BA in Polit. Sci., Roosevelt U., 1963; JD, DePaul U., 1971; student U. Chgo., 1959-60. Bar: Ill. 1972, U.S. Dist. Ct. (no. dist.) Ill. 1972. Legis. intern Ill. State Senate, Springfield, 1966-67; tchr. Chgo. Pub. Schs., 1967-70; atty. CNA Ins., Chgo., 1971-73; law clk. Ill. Apellate Ct., Chgo., 1973-75; sr. trial atty. U.S. Dept. Labor, Chgo., 1975—, mentor Adopt-a-Sch. Program, 1992-95. Contbr. articles to profl. jours. Vol. Big Sister, 1975-81; bd. dirs. Altgeld Nursery Sch., 1963-66, Ill. div. UN Assn., 1966-72, Hull House Jane Addams Ctr., 1977-82, Broadway Children's Ctr., 1986-90, Acorn Family Entertainment, 1993-95; mem. Oak Park Farmers' Market Commn., 1996—; rsch. asst. Citizens for Gov. Otto Kerner, Chgo., 1964; com. mem. Ill. Commn. on Status of Women, Chgo., 1964-70; del. Nat. Conf. on Status of Women, 1968; candidate for del. Ill. Constl. Conv., 1969. Mem. Chgo. Council Lawyers, Women's Bar Assn. Ill., Lawyer Pilots Bar Assn., Fed. Bar Assn. Unitarian. Clubs: Friends of Gamelan (performer), 99's Internat. Orgn. Women Pilots (legis. chmn. Chgo. area chpt. 1983-86, legis. chmn. North Cen. sect. 1986-88, legis. award 1983, 85). Home: 204 S Taylor Ave Oak Park IL 60302-3307 Office: US Dept Labor Office Solicitor 230 S Dearborn St Fl 8 Chicago IL 60604-1505

MANSFIELD, LOIS EDNA, mathematics educator, researcher; b. Portland, Maine, Jan. 2, 1941; d. R. Carleton and Mary (Bowdish) M. BS, U. Mich., 1962; MS, U. Utah, 1966, PhD, 1969. Vis. asst. prof. computer sci. Purdue U., 1969-70; asst. prof. computer sci. U. Kans., Lawrence, 1970-74, assoc. prof., 1974-78; assoc. prof. math. N.C. State U., Raleigh, 1978-79; assoc. prof. applied math. U. Va., Charlottesville, 1979-83, prof., 1983—; mem. adv. panel computer sci. NSF, 1975-78; cons., vis. scientist Inst. Computer Applications in Sci. and Engring., Hampton, Va., 1976-78. Contbr. articles to profl. jours. Grantee NSF and DOE. Mem. Am. Math. Soc., Soc. Indsl. and Applied Math. (mem. editorial bd. Jour. Sci. Statis. Computing, 1979-88), Assn. Computing Machinery (bd. dirs. SIGNUM 1980-83). Office: U Va Dept Applied Math Thornton Hall Charlottesville VA 22903

MANSMANN, CAROL LOS, federal judge, law educator; b. Pittsburgh, Pa., Aug. 7, 1942; d. Walter Joseph and Regina Mary (Pilarski) Los; m. J. Jerome Mansmann, June 27, 1970; children: Casey, Megan, Patrick. B.A., J.D., Duquesne U., 1964, 67; LL.D., Seton Hill Coll., Greensburg, Pa., 1985; PhD (hon.), La Roche Coll., 1990; LLD (hon.), Widener U., 1994. Asst. dist. atty. Allegheny County, Pitts., 1968-72; assoc. McVerry Baxter & Mansmann, Pitts., 1973-79; assoc. prof. law Duquesne U., Pitts., 1973-82; judge west dist. U.S. Dist. Ct. Pa., Pitts., 1982-85; judge U.S. Ct. Appeals (3rd cir.), Phila., 1985—; Mem. Pa. Criminal Procedural Rules Com., 1972-77; spl. asst. atty. gen. Commonwealth of Pa., 1974-79; co-adminstr. Local Criminal Rules Reorg. Project, 1978-79; chair 2 Bar Assn. CLE programs, 1982; bd. govs. Pa. Bar Inst., Harrisburg, 1984-90; mem. 3d Cir. jud. coun., 1985—; adj. prof. law U. Pitts., 1987—; mem. U.S. Jud. Conf. on adminstrn. of magistarte-judge sys., 1990—;. Mem. bd. consultors Villanova U. Law Sch., 1985-91; trustee Duquesne U., 1987—, Sewickley Acad., 1988-91. Recipient St. Thomas More award, Pitts., 1983, Phila., 1984, Ann. Dinner award Duquesne U. Law Alumni Assn., 1986, Faculty Alumni award Duquesne U., 1987. Mem. ABA, Nat. Assn. Women Judges, Pa. Bar Assn., Fed. Judges Assn., Am. Judicature Soc., Allegheny County Bar Assn. (gov., bd. govs. 1982-85), Phi Alpha Delta. Republican. Roman Catholic. Office: US Ct Appeals 1036 US Courthouse Pittsburgh PA 15219*

MANSOOR, LORETTA JULIA, retired medical/surgical nurse; b. Walnut Grove, Minn., Oct. 28, 1924; d. Oscar Ramie and Irma Mary (Verlinde) Callewart; m. Raja Audi Mansoor, (div.); 1 child, Mary Ann. Diploma, Presentation Sch. of Nursing-McKennan Unit, Sioux Falls, S.D., 1946. RN, Minn. Head nurse Veteran's Hosp., Hot Springs, S.D., 1946-48; pvt. duty nurse various pvt. hosps., Mpls., 1949-50; asst. head nurse St. Mary's Hosp., Mpls., 1951-59; charge nurse Tracy (Minn.) Hosp., 1953-54, Renville County Hosp., Olivia, Minn.; charge nurse, team leader, staff nurse med. and surgical Redwood Mcpl. Hosp., Redwood Falls, Minn., 1962-94; ret., 1994. Hospice vol.; active in cmty. orgns. Cadet nurse, U.S. Army, 1943-46. Roman Catholic. Home: 407 E Wyoming St Redwood Falls MN 56283-2123

MANSOUR, FATEN SPIRONOUS, interior designer, multimedia computer designer, realtor; b. Amman, Jordan, May 8, 1958; came to U.S., 1981; d. Spironous Mansour and Margret Mousa Nijmeh; 1 child, Lara. AS in Bus. Adminstrn., Wasifia Coll., Amman, 1977; AS in Computer Sci., Sec. Bus. Adminstrn., West Valley Coll., 1988; BS in Interior Design, Art, Photography, San Jose State U., 1992, M in Physiology, 1994. Cert. notary pub. Tchr. French Rawdat Al-Sa'adeh, Amman, 1976-78; office mgr. of Min. of Transp. Queen Alia Internat. Airport, Amman, 1977-88; coord. banquets and weddings Marquee Club and Café, San Jose, Calif., 1988-93; interior designer, realtor, multi-media computer designer Esquisite, San Jose, 1992—, desktop pub., 1992—. Prodr. Arab Am. TV, L.A., 1990—. Active Arab Am. Anti-Discrimination Com. Home: PO Box 10355 San Jose CA 95157-1355 Office: Esquisite PO Box 10355 San Jose CA 95157-1355

MANTEL, WENDY LUISE, advertising firm executive; b. Indpls., Jan. 21, 1954; d. Thomas David and Flo Mary (Foreman) M.; m. Daniel Victor Garbowit, June 5, 1988. BA magna cum laude, Amerst Coll., 1976; MA, Columbia U., 1977. Asst. editor Am. Cancer Soc., N.Y.C., 1977-78; copy writer Springer-Verlag, Inc., N.Y.C., 1978-80; sr. med. writer Instructional Techniques, Manhasset, N.Y., 1980-83; account exec. William Douglas McAdams, N.Y.C., 1983-84; account supr. Sudler and Hennessey, N.Y.C., 1984-87, v.p., 1987—, now sr. v.p. Mem. Pharm. Advt. Council, Amherst Alumni Admissions Com. Office: Sudler & Hennessey Inc 1633 Broadway New York NY 10019-6708*

MANTHE, CORA DE MUNCK, real estate and investment company executive; b. Alton, Iowa, Oct. 10, 1928; d. Cornelius John and Bessie Bell (Miller) De Munck; m. Carl Robert Manthe, Apr. 5, 1952 (dec. Dec. 1987); children: Barry Paul, David Glenn. BA in Econs., U. Iowa, 1950; posgrad., U. Wis., Madison and Oshkosh; grad., Realtors Inst., 1972, 73, 74,75. Cert. residential appraiser. Rsch. analyst Dept. Def., Washington, 1951-52; social work investigator Dane County, Madison, 1960-62; civic hostess Welcome Wagon, Beaver Dam, Wis., 1963-70; real estate broker "C" Manthe Realty, Ltd., Beaver Dam, 1979—, property mgr., investment mgr., pres., treas., 1982—. Deacon Grace Presbyn. Ch., 1974-77, elder, 1979-82, ruling elder, 1989-92; staff worker Kohl Senate Campaign, 1994. Mem. AAUW (life), Internat. Platform Assn., Beaver Dam C. of C., U. Iowa Alumni Assn. (life), Optimist Internat. (life). Home and Office: 404 Declark St Beaver Dam WI 53916-1714

MANTHEI, DAWN REBECCA, food scientist; b. La Crosse, Wis., July 12, 1970; d. Dennis Lee and Barbara Marie (Gerndt) M.; m. Vernon H. Manter, Oct. 22, 1994. BS in Food Sci., U. Wis., 1992. Product devel. intern Wis. Dairies, Sauk City, 1991; food technolgist intern Henri's Food Products, Inc., Milw., 1992; food technologist Aunt Nellie's Farm Kitchens, Clyman, Wis., 1993—; mem. Sensory Evaluation Team U. Wis., Madison, 1992. Mem. Inst. Food Technologists, Nature Conservancy, U. Wis. Alumni Club. Lutheran. Office: Aunt Nellie's Farm Kitchens 640 Caughlin Rd Clyman WI 53016

MANTYLA, KAREN, sales executive; b. Bronx, N.Y., Dec. 31, 1944; d. Milton and Sylvia (Diamond) Fischer; m. John A Mantyla, May 30, 1970 (div. 1980); 1 child, Michael Alan. Student, Rockland Community Coll., Suffern, N.Y., 1962, NYU, 1967, Mercer U., 1981. Mktg. coordinator Credit Bur., Inc., Miami, Fla., 1973-79; dist. mgr. The Research Inst. Am., N.Y.C., 1979-80, regional dir., 1980-85, field sales mgr., 1985-86, nat. sales mgr., 1986-87; dir. mktg. TempsAmerica, N.Y.C., 1987-88; nat. accounts mgr. The Rsch. Inst. Am., N.Y.C., 1989; v.p. sales Bur. Bus. Practice/Paramount Comm., Inc., Waterford, Conn., 1989-93; pres. Quiet Power, Inc., Washington, 1993—. Author: Consultative Sales Power, 1995. Mem. ASTD, Sales and Mktg. Execs. (past bd. dirs. N.Y. chpt., v.p. Ft. Lauderdale chpt. 1979), U.S. Distance Learning Assn., Nat. Assn. Women Bus. Owners, U.S. C. of C., Women Entrepreneurs. Home: 5449 Grove Ridge Way Rockville MD 20852-4648 Office: Quiet Power Inc 655 15th St NW Ste 300 Washington DC 20005-5701

MANTZELL, BETTY LOU, school health administrator; b. Brookville, Pa., Oct. 16, 1938; d. Elmer William and Wilda Mae (Enterline) M. Diploma, Ind. (Pa.) Hosp. Sch. Nursing, 1959; BSN, Case Western Res. U., 1969, MA, 1978; cert. supr. ednl. adminstrn., Cleve. State U., 1983; cert. supr., John Carroll U., 1989. RN, Ohio, Pa. Oper. rm. nurse Univ. Hosps. of Cleve., 1963-69; sch. nurse various locations Cleve. Pub. Schs., 1969-85, coord. sch. nurses, 1976-85, acting asst. supr. health svcs., 1985-86, supr. health svcs., 1986—; mem. adv. com. to baccalaureate nursing program Cleve. Stae U.; prevention of blindness adv. com. Cleve. Sight Ctr.; active All Kids County Consortium Cleve. Dept. Pub. Health; mem. sch. health com. Acad. Medicine Cleve.; Frances Payne Bolton Sch. Nursing, mem. alumni assn.; clin. instr. cmty. health nursing Case We. Res. U., Cleve., 1988-90, women's connection; mem. coun. econ. opportunities Greater Cleve.; mem. adv. com. Headstart Health Svcs. Mem. Am. Sch. Health Assn., Nat. Assn. Sch. Nurses, Ohio Assn. Sch. Nurses, Northeastern Ohio Assn. Sch. Nurses, Ohio Assn. Secondary Sch. Adminstrs., Cleve. Coun. Adminstrs. and Suprs., Cleve. Med. Libr. Assn. Office: Jane Addams Bus Careers Ctr Office Health Svcs Rm 206 2373 E 30th St Cleveland OH 44115

MANUEL, MELISSA MARIE, pediatrics nurse, consultant; b. Nashville, Mar. 1, 1962; d. Francis Albert and Gerri S. (diBenedetto) Puyau; m. James William Manuel, Aug. 4, 1995. BSN, U. Ala., 1984. Cert. critical care nurse, 1991. Staff nurse PICU Ochsner Hospl, New Orleans, 1989, flight nurse, 1989-92; pediat. cardiology nurse clinician, 1992-93, pediat. cardiothoracic nurse clinician, 1994; staff nurse pediat. emergency room U. Miss., Jackson, 1994-96, pediat. nephrology nurse clinician, 1996—; staff nurse Burn Ctr. Vanderbilt U. Hosp., 1984-85, pediat. stepdown, 1985-86, PICU, 1986-88, NICU Woman's Hosp., Baton Rouge, La., 1986. Mem. Am. Assn. Critical Care Nurses, AHA. Roman Catholic. Office: U of Miss Med Ctr 2500 N State St Jackson MS 39216-4505

MANUEL, VIVIAN, public relations company executive; b. Queens County, N.Y., May 6, 1941; d. George Thomas and Vivian (Anderson) M. BA, Wells Coll., Aurora, N.Y., 1963; MA, U. Wyo-Laramie, 1965. Mgmt. analyst Dept. Navy, 1966-68; account supr. Gen. Electric Co., N.Y.C., 1968-72, corp. rep. bus. and fin., 1972-76; dir. corp. comm. Standard Brands Co., N.Y.C., 1976-78; pvt. cons., N.Y.C., 1978-80; pres. V M Comm. Inc., N.Y.C., 1980—. Mem. com. Girls Club N.Y., 1983-84; trustee Wells Coll., 1983-90; mem. adv. bd. Glenholme Sch., 1991-92. Mem. AAUW, N.Y. Women in Comm. (bd. v.p. 1983-85, chair Matrix awards 1985), Women Execs. in Pub. Rels. (bd. dirs. 1985-88), Women's Econ. Roundtable, Friend N.Y.C. Commn. on Status of Women. Office: V M Comm Inc 501 E 79th St New York NY 10021-0735

MANUTI, ANNABELLE THERESA, advertising agency financial executive; b. Bklyn., Sept. 11, 1928; d. Decio Dan and Anna Michelle (Vanacore) Assorto; m. John Thomas Manuti, Dec. 31, 1958. Student, Hunter Coll., 1950, postgrad. in real estate sch. Continuing Edn., 1980-82. Lic. real estate broker, N.Y. Statis. auditor Am. Fore Ins. Group, N.Y.C., 1950-55; bookkeeper Picard Advt., N.Y.C., 1955-60; supr. dept. acctg. Moquel Williams & Saylor Advt., N.Y.C., 1960-65; comptroller's asst. Frolich Advt., N.Y.C., 1965-70; supr. accounts payable Miller Advt., N.Y.C., 1970-80; v.p. fin. Jaffe Communications, N.Y.C., 1980-90; free-lance, 1990—. Roman Catholic.

MANWILL, DIANE RACHEL, counselor; b. Palo Alto, Calif., Sept. 14, 1959; d. Harry and Geraldine Ann (Caliri) Copelan; m. Walter Blair Manwill, Aug. 4, 1979; 1 child, Rachel Anna. BS summa cum laude, U. Md., 1987; MEd, Boston U., 1989. Lic. ind. adoption svcs. investigator; lic. profl. clin. counselor, N.Mex.; cert. mediator. Mental health counselor U. Cambridge (Eng.) Counseling Clinic, 1988-89; program dir. IV Jud Dist Casa Program, Boise, Idaho, 1990-92; substance abuse instr. Boise Sch. Dist., 1990-91; coll. lectr. Chapman U., Cannon AFB, N.Mex., 1992-94; exec. dir. IX Jud. Dist. Family & Children's Ct. Svcs., Clovis, N.Mex., 1992—, counselor, play therapist, 1994—; pvt. divorce mediator Clovis, 1994—; cons., clin. supr. Oasis-Child's Safe House, Clovis, 1992-93; clin. supr. Youth Opportunities Unltd., Clovis, 1994-95. Co-author: Idaho State Gal Standards, 1992; author: (workbook) Custody Education Workshop Manual, 1994. Mem. Families in Need Svcs. Team, Clovis, 1994—, Custody Visit Guidelines Com., Clovis, 1995—; pres. bd. Idaho Case Assn., Boise, 1990-91; legis. liaison for children's issues Gali Casa, Boise, 1992; treas. bd. Cmty. Ptnrs., Inc., 1994—. Recipient Cambridge internships Boston U., 1988, Liberty Bell awards 4th Dist. Bar Assn., Boise, 1992, 9th Dist. Bar Assn., Clovis, N.Mex., 1994. Mem. ACA, Assn. Family and Conciliation Cts., Am. Mental Health Counselors Assn., Phi Kappa Phi. Democrat. Home: 2801 Bratton St Columbia SC 29205

MANZARI, LAURA LYNN, law educator; b. N.Y.C., Jan. 4, 1959; d. Charles John and Rose Marie (Lepik) Slepetis. BA, Queen's Coll., 1979, MLS, 1986; JD, St. John's U., 1982. Bar: N.Y. 1983. Claim atty. Allstate Ins. Co., Lake Success, N.Y., 1984-85; law libr. Parker Chapin Flattau & Klimpl, N.Y.C., 1985; libr. Pace U., N.Y.C., 1987-89; assoc. prof. L.I. U., Greenvale, 1989—. Mem. ALA, Greater N.Y. Assn. Coll. and Rsch. Librs., Nassau County Libr. Assn. Office: LI U B Davis Schwartz Meml Libr Greenvale NY 11548

MAPLE, MARILYN JEAN, educational media coordinator; b. Turtle Creek, Pa., Jan. 16, 1931; d. Harry Chester and Agnes (Dobbie) Kelley; B.A., U. Fla., 1972, M.A., 1975, Ph.D., 1985; 1 dau., Sandra Maple. Journalist various newspapers, including Mountain Eagle, Jasper, Ala., Boise (Idaho) Statesman, Daytona Beach (Fla.) Jour., Lorain (Ohio) Jour.; account exec. Frederides & Co., N.Y.C.; producer hist. films Fla. State Mus., Gainesville, 1967-69; writer, dir., producer med. and sci. films and TV prodns. for six medically related colls. U. Fla., Gainesville, 1969—; pres. Media Modes, Inc., Gainesville. Recipient Blakslee award, 1969, spl. award, 1979, Monsour Lectureship award, 1979. Mem. Health Edn. Media Assn. (dir., awards, 1977, 79), Phi Delta Kappa, Kappa Tau Alpha. Author: On the Wings of a Butterfly; columnist: Health Care Edn. mag.; contbr. Fla. Hist. Quar. Home: 1927 NW 7th Ln Gainesville FL 32603-1103 Office: U Fla PO Box 16J Gainesville FL 32602-0016

MAPLE, OPAL LUCILLE, school psychologist; b. Canton, Ill., Nov. 15, 1935; d. Dwight Willard and Eileen Beatrice (Cadwalader) Beaty; m. Gilbert Roy Maple, June 30, 1967 (dec. 1985). BA, Wheaton (Ill.) Coll., 1958; MS, We. Ill. U., 1962. Cert. sch. psychologist, Ill. Tchr. Community Dist. #5, Cuba, Ill., 1958-60, Community Dist. #66, Canton, Ill., 1960-61; asst. dean women Moody Bible Inst., Chgo., 1961-64; sch. psychologist intern Chgo. Pub. Schs., 1964-65; sch. psychologist Peoria (Ill.) pub. schs., 1965-69, Waukegan (Ill.) pub. schs., 1969-81, Knox-Warren Spl. Edn., Galesburg, Ill., 1986—. Co-author pre-sch. test, 1975. Deaconess, treas. Antioch Evang. Free Ch., 1971-81; deaconess, fin. sec. Bethel Bapt. Ch., Galesburg, 1982—. Mem. Cen. Ill. Sch. Psychologists Assn. (pres. 1967-68), Ill. Psychol. Assn. (sec. 1977-79), DAR, Knox County Genealogical Soc., Nat. Assn. Sch. Psychologists, Ill. Sch. Psychologists Assn. Republican. Baptist.

MAPLES, MARY FRANCES (FRAN MAPLES), program director; b. Iraan, Tex., Oct. 2, 1943; d. Robert Hugh and Vernice Lura (Lyles) M. BA in French, U. North Tex., 1966; MA in French, U. Tex., 1972. Tchr. French Richardson (Tex.) Ind. Sch. Dist., 1966-84; tchr. French Richland C.C., Dallas, 1980-83, bldg. coord., 1983-85; coord. fgn. langs. Richardson Ind. Sch. Dist., 1984—. Vol. Am. Cancer Soc., Dallas, 1996. Fgn. Lang. Assistance Program grantee U.S. Dept. Edn., 1992-95, 94-96. Mem. ASCD, Am. Coun. Teaching Fgn. Langs., Nat. Assn. Dist. Suprs. Fgn. Langs., Am. Assn. Tchrs. French (pres. & v.p. North Tex. chpt. 1978-82), Southwest Conf. Lang. Teaching, Tex. ASCD, Tex. Assn. Lang. Supervision (pres. 1995—), Tex. Fgn. Lang. Assn. (pres. 1988-89, advt. mgr. 1985-87), Metroplex Fgn. Langs. Suprs., Delta Kappa Gamma (music chmn. 1993—), Alpha Delta Pi Richardson Alumnae (v.p. 1991—). Republican. Methodist. Office: Richardson Ind Sch Dist 707 E Arapaho Rd Richardson TX 75081

MAPLES, MONICA L., legislative staff member. Student, U. S.D., 1983-86. Legis. asst. to Senator Thomas A. Daschle, 1987-89, rsch. dir. to Senator John D. Rockefeller IV, 1989-90; rsch. dir. Dem. Nat. Campaign Com., 1991-93, polit. dir., 1993; chief of staff Dem. Caucus, 1993—. Office: Rep Vic Fazio D-Calif 2113 Rayburn House Office Bldg Washington DC 20515

MAPSTONE, KIMBERLY I., psychotherapist; b. Pitts., Apr. 24, 1958; d. Ralph M. and Irma S. (Sutton) M. Student, Allegheny County C.C., Pitts.; M in Human Svcs. summa cum lauda, Lincoln U., 1995. Clk. stenographer II, clk. stenographer I Referee's Office, Unemployment Compensation Bd. Rev., Commonwealth of Pa., Pitts., 1977-91; counselor Creative Living Ctr., Pitts., 1991-96; pvt. practice, 1996—; bd. dirs. Visions of Healing, Ctr. Creative Living, Pitts., 1993—; presenter workshops and seminars Overeaters Anonymous, 1983—, Women United in Recovery, Inc., 1986—, Wilkinsburg Family Cmty. Fun Festival, 1991, Allegheny County C.C., 1991, Life-Work Ctr., 1992, Women United in Recovery, Inc., 1992; vol. hotline counselor Pitts. Action Against Rape, 1987-88. Mem. Women's Bus. Network, Pi Gamma Mu. Home: 2327 Buena Vista St Pittsburgh PA 15218-2232

MAPULA, OLGA MARCELA, communications executive; b. Williams, Ariz., Jan. 30, 1938; d. Raul P. Arreola and Olga C. (Espinoza) Moskal; m. Robert M. Mapula (div. Sept. 1991); children: Melissa (dec.), Robert, Jaime. BA, Tex. Western Coll., 1958; MA, U. Tex., El Paso, 1973. Field rep. Social Security Adminstrn., El Paso, 1961-72; lectr., supr. student tchg. U. Tex., El Paso, 1973-75; program evaluator Bilingual Consortium, Anthony, Tex., 1974-76; mgr., mktg. and promotions KXCR, El Paso, 1983-85; owner The Comm. Group, El Paso, 1986-96; pres., owner Tech. & Comm. Gateway, Inc. (formerly The Comm. Group), El Paso, 1996—. Author: The Employer's Guide to Hiring Requirements & Sanctions, 1987, A Comparative Study of Teacher Receptivity Toward Bilingual/Bicultural Education, 1973; co-author; The Complete Twin Plant Guide, 1987-91, Latinos and Political Coalitions, 1992. Bd. dirs. Greater El Paso C. of C., 1987-88; trustee Providence Meml. Hosp., El Paso, 1993-95, Paso del Norte Health Found., El Paso, 1995—; appointed to Tex. Bd. Examiners of Psychologists, 1993-94; elected rep. El Paso C.C., 1986—; adv. bd. MADD, 1986—. Recipient Women of Enterprise award Avon and SBA, Adelante award Hispanic Mag. and Nations Bank, 1994; named Bus. Woman of Yr., U.S. Hispanic Chamber, 1994. Fellow Nat. Hispana Leadership Inst.; mem. El Paso Hispanic C. of C. (bd. dirs. 1994—), El Paso 8(a) Assn. (bd. dirs. 1994—), Hispanic Leadership Inst. Democrat. Roman Catholic. Office: Tech and Comm Gateway Inc 4141 Pinnacle Ste 201 El Paso TX 79902

MARAFIOTI, KAYALYN A., lawyer; b. Rochester, N.Y., 1954. AB cum laude, Harvard U., 1976; JD, NYU, 1979. Bar: N.Y. 1980. Ptnr. Skadden, Arps, Slate, Meagher & Flom, N.Y.C. Note and comment editor NYU Jour. Internat. Law and Politics, 1978-79. Office: Skadden Arps Slate Meagher & Flom 919 3rd Ave New York NY 10022*

MARALDO, ANGELA MARIE, project engineer; b. Grosse Pointe, Mich., Sept. 26, 1966; d. Mario Victor and Judith Ann (Raether) M. BSCE, Mich. Tech. U., 1989. Registered profl. engr. Mich. Project engr. City of Monroe (Mich.), 1989—. Mem. site selection com. Monroe County Habitat for Humanity. Mem. ASCE, Mich. Soc. Profl. Engrs. Office: City of Monroe 120 E 1st Monroe MI 48161

MARANO, BARBARA STASKAUSKAS, computer educator; b. Waterbury, Conn., Sept. 10, 1962; d. Albert Everett and Patricia Mae (Bergin) Staskauskas; m. Clifford Douglas Marano, Aug. 5, 1995. BS in Edn., U. Conn., 1983; MLS, So. Conn. State U., 1989. Cert. tchr., Conn. Tchr. Regional Sch. Dist. #15, Middlebury, Conn., 1984—. Republican. Roman Catholic. Home: 49 Danna Marie Dr Waterbury CT 06708 Office: Meml Middle Sch PO Box 903 Middlebury CT 06762

MARAVICH, MARY LOUISE, realtor; b. Fort Knox, Ky., Jan. 4, 1951; d. John and Bonnie (Balandzic) M. AA in Office Adminstrn., U. Nev., Las Vegas, 1970; BA in Sociology and Psychology, U. So. Calif., 1972; grad. Realtors Inst. Cert. residential specialist. Adminstrv. asst. dept. history U. So. Calif., L.A., 1972-73; asst. pers. supr. Corral Coin Co., Las Vegas, 1973-80; realtor, Americana Group div. Better Homes and Gardens, Las Vegas, 1980-85, Jack Matthews and Co., 1985-93, Realty Execs., Las Vegas, 1993—. Mem. Nev. Assn. Realtors (cert. realtors inst.), Las Vegas Bd. Realtors, Nat. Assn. Realtors, Women's Council of Realtors, Am. Bus. Women's Assn., NAFE, Million Dollar Club, Pres.'s Club. Office: Realty Execs 1903 S Jones Blvd # 100 Las Vegas NV 89102-1260

MARAZITA, ELEANOR MARIE HARMON, secondary education educator; b. Madison County, Ind., Oct. 25, 1933; d. William Houston Harmon and Martha Belle (Savage) Hinds; m. Philip Marazita; children: Mary Louise, Frank, Dominic, Vincent, Elizabeth Faye, Candice Marie, Daniel William. BS in Home Econs., Ctrl. Mich. U., 1955; MA in Human Ecology, Mich. State U., 1971. Cert. vocat. home econs. tchr., K-Jr. Coll., cert. speech correction tchr. Tchr. adult edn. Mt. Pleasant, Mich., 1956; substitute tchr. North Branch (Mich.) Schs., 1961-64; tchr. Pied Piper Cooperative Nursery Sch., Lansing, Mich., 1964-69, Lansing C.C., 1971-81, Grand Ledge (Mich.) H.S., 1969—; debate coach, forensic coach, student congress advisor Grand Ledge H.S.; Mich. tchr. del. World Conf. Tchg. Profls., 1985; adv. mem. Mich. Tchr. Competency Testing Program, 1992. Bd. dirs. Greater Lansing chpt. U.N., 1995—; vol. St. Lawrence Mental Health Hosp., 1972-73, Listening Ear Crisis Intervention Ctr., 1973-77, Capital City Convalescent Home, 1969-73; chmn. study com. Delta Twp. Libr., 1969-73, Jr. League, 1969—; interviewer Youth for Understanding, 1978-83; active exch.

student orientation program Mich. State U., 1977, exch. trips, 1979-82; mem. adv. bd. Mich. League Human Svcs., 1988-91, Eaton County Extension Svcs., 1988-91, Mich. Women's Assembly, 1986-91; mem. Friends of Waverly Libr.; participant 3rd Congress Educators Caucus, 1986-92; 4-H leader, 1950-65. Recipient State Tchr. Multicultural award, 1989, UN Global Educator award, 1991, State Tchr. Maureen Wyatt feminist award, 1996. Mem. NEA, Mich. Edn. Assn. (mem. polit. action exec. bd. 1986—, v.p. women's caucus 1986-93, Liz Siddell State Internat. Cultures award 1992), Internat. Platform Assn., Circumnavigators Club (travel around world in one trip 1993), Century Club (travel in 100 countries outside U.S. 1994), Mich. Speech Coaches Assn. (scholarship com. 1984—), Mich. Assn. Speech Coaches, Delta Kappa Gamma (co-chairperson State World Fellowship 1993-95, chpt. Women of Distinction award 1993), Phi Delta Kappa (Tchr. of Yr. Mich. State U. 1992). Home: 214 Farmstead Ln Lansing MI 48917-3015

MARBELL, PAMELA MARTINE, tax director; b. Kansas City, Mo., Dec. 30, 1960; d. Lawrence R. and Carol J. (Burke) M.; life ptnr. Judith M. Soenvur, June 15, 1985; children: Brett, Erik. BS, Calif. State U., 1984. Tax dir., v.p. Downey Savs. and Loan, Newport Beach, Calif., 1987—. Office: Downey Savs 3501 Jamboree Newport Beach CA 92660

MARBERRY, SARA O'DAFFER, writer, public relations consultant; b. Hammond, Ind., Nov. 17, 1959; d. Phares Glenn and Harriet Joanne (Gove) O'Daffer; m. Richard Joe Marberry, Feb. 25, 1984; 1 child, Wesley Phares. BS in Speech, Northwestern U., Evanston, Ill., 1981. Coord. comm. The Merchandise Mart, Chgo., 1981-83; editor Contract Mag., N.Y.C., 1984-90; cons., writer S.M. Comm., Matawan, N.J., 1990-95, Evanston, Ill., 1995—. Author: Color in the Office, 1992; co-author: Power of Color, 1995; editor: (books) Innovations in Healthcare, 1995, Healthcare Design, 1995, (jour.) Jour. Healthcare Design, 1990-96. Bd. dirs. The Ctr. for Health Design, Martinez, Calif., 1988-95, Interior Design for Legis./N.Y., N.Y.C., 1990-92; mem. media adv. bd. Inst. Bus. Designers, Chgo., 1992. Mem. Internat. Interior Design Assn. (affil.), Northwestern U. Alumni Club. Methodist. Office: Sara Marberry Comm 1830 Sherman Ave Ste 304 Evanston IL 60201

MARBLE, MELINDA SMITH, writer, editor; b. Ponca City, Okla., June 17, 1960; d. Monte Gene and Dorothy Worthington Smith; m. Sanford Marble. BA with high hons., spl. hons. English, U. Tex., 1984. Mktg. Data Base Publs., Austin, Tex., 1986-87; assoc. editor Austin Area Bus. Women Directory, 1987-88; asst. pub. Travelers' Times, Austin, 1988-89; assoc. editor Tex. Bar Jour., Austin, 1989-95; freelance editor, Austin, 1989-95, novelist, freelance journalist, Morristown, N.J., 1995—. Contbr. articles to newspapers and profl. jours. Recipient Gold Quill award of merit Internat. Assn. Bus. Communicators, 1993, Gold Quill Excellence award for First Person Articles, 1995; Best of Austin 4 Color Mag. award, 1993, 2 awards of merit, 1995, Presdl. Citation, State Bar of Tex., 1993, Nat. Assn. Govt. Communicators award of Honor 4 Color Mag., 1994, Best of Austin Feature Writing award, 1995, Best of Austin Advocacy Writing award, 1995.

MARCALI, JEAN GREGORY, chemist; b. Jermyn, Pa., May 29, 1926; d. John Robert and Anna Marie Gregory; student U. Pa., 1948-52, U. Del., 1971-72; m. Kalman Marcali, Oct. 6, 1956; children: Coleman, Frederick. Microanalyst E. I. du Pont de Nemours & Co., Deepwater, N.J., 1943-60, tech. info. analyst, Jackson Lab., Deepwater, N.J. also Wilmington, Del., 1960-67, sr. adviser tech. info., Wilmington, 1967-70, supr. tech. info., 1970-82, 85-89, supr. adminstrv. svcs., 1982-85, cons., 1989-92, ret., 1992. Sec., Alfred I. DuPont Elem. PTA, 1971, pres., 1972; pres. PTA of Brandywine Sch. Dist., 1973; mem. Wilmington Dist. Republican Com., 1976—. Mem. Am. Chem. Soc. (treas. div. chem. info. 1976-81, chmn.-elect 1981, chmn. 1982, 83, div. councilor 1983-90), Am. Chem. Soc. (com. on chem. abstracts svc. 1983-85, 87-93, mem. joint bd.-coun. com. on chem. abstracts svc. 1994—). Lutheran. Clubs: Order Eastern Star, Du Pont Country. Home: 312 Waycross Rd Wilmington DE 19803-2950

MARCASIANO, MARY JANE, fashion designer; b. N.J., Sept. 23, 1955. Grad., Parsons Sch. Design, 1978. Designer under own label, 1979—. Recipient Cartier Stargazer award, 1981, Wool Knit award, 1983, DuPont award for most promising designer, 1984, Cutty Sark award for most promising men's wear designer, 1984. Office: Mary Jane Marcasiano Inc 138 Spring St New York NY 10012-3854*

MARCEAU, YVONNE, ballroom dancer. Ballet dancer Ballet West; ptnr. with Pierre Dulaine, 1976; founder, artistic dir. Am. Ballroom Theatre, N.Y.C., 1984—; guest tchr. Sch. Am. Ballet, N.Y.C.; tchr. ballroom dancing Juilliard Sch. Appearances include The Smithsonian Inst., JFK Ctr. for Performing Arts, N.Y. State Theater, N.Y.C., Sadlers Wells, London, (Broadway and London show) Grand Hotel, 1989-92; toured with Pierre Dulaine and Am. Ballroom Theatre worldwide. Recipient Brit. Theatrical Arts Championships 4 times, Spl. Astaire award, Dance Educator awards, Outstanding Achievement in Dance award Nat. Coun. Dance Am., 1992, Dance Mag. award, 1993. Office: Am Ballroom Theatre 129 W 27th St No 705 New York NY 10001*

MARCEL, ALICE NANCY, fine arts designer; b. Bronx, N.Y., Dec. 17, 1944; d. Alphonse Michael and Winifred Cecelia (Rogers) Marcel; m. Dietmar Gunther Trick, Mar. 1, 1969 (div. Aug. 1994); children: Kelly Colleen, Kristin Ingrid. BFA in Painting, Hunter Coll., 1966. Illustrator Appleton-Century-Crofts, N.Y.C., 1967-69; freelance artist inflatable toys Ideal Toy Corp., Hollis, N.Y., 1972, 74, 76, designer vinyl products, 1969-71, creative mgr. dolls, 1980-82; creative mgr. girls' toys Pac Toys, Farmingdale, N.Y., 1983-84; art dir. Tara Toy Corp., Hauppauge, N.Y., 1989-92; operator, mgr. The Painted Cottage Gift Shop, East Moriches, N.Y., 1987-90; freelance artist, illustrator East Moriches, N.Y., 1995-96. Designer vinyl doll collectibles, Shirley Temple costumes, 1980-83; sculptor, painter Mixed Media 2D and 3D, 1994-95. Mem. Nat. Soc. Painters in Casein and Acrylic, Moriches Bay Hist. Soc., South Bay Art Assn., Guild Hall. Roman Catholic. Home and Studio: PO Box 210 East Moriches NY 11940

MARCH, CATHLEEN CASE, elementary education educator; b. Port Jervis, N.Y., Dec. 8, 1942; d. Fred Baker Case and Elizabeth (Mayes) Allen; children: Elizabeth, Brian, Matthew, Mindy. BS, U. Pa., 1963; MS, SUNY, Buffalo, 1979, postgrad., 1996. Cert. K-12 tchr., N.Y. 1st grade tchr. Anna Merritt Sch., Lockport, N.Y., 1964-65; kindergarted tchr. Dewitt Clinton Sch., Lockport, N.Y., 1966-69; asst. librarian Lockport Pub. Libr., 1970-72; reading tchr. Starpoint Ctrl. Sch., Lockport, 1975-78, Medina (N.Y.) Ctrl. Schs., 1979—; adj. prof. Canisius Coll., Buffalo, 1992-96. Editor: Niagara Frontier Reading Coun., 1991-96. Named Educator of Excellence N.Y. State English Coun., 1994. Mem. Internat. Reading Assn., Internat. Whole Lang. Umbrella, N.Y. State Reading Assn. (Svc. to Reading award 1996). Home: 6801 Lilac Dr Apt A Lockport NY 14094-6824

MARCH, JACQUELINE FRONT, retired chemist; b. Wheeling, W.Va.; m. A.W. March (dec.); children: Wayne Front, Gail March Cohen. BS, Case Western Res. U., 1937, MA, 1939; postgrad. U. Chgo., U. Pitts. (1942-45), Ohio State U. Clin. chemist, Mt. Sinai Hosp., Cleve.; med. rsch. chemist U. Chgo.; rsch. analyst Koppers Co., also info. scientist Union Carbide Corp., Carnegie-Mellon U., Pitts.; propr. March Med. Rsch. Lab., etiology of diabetes, Dayton, Ohio; guest scientist Kettering Found., Yellow Springs, Ohio; Dayton Found. fellow Miami Valley Hosp. Rsch. Inst.; chemistry faculty U. Dayton, computer/chem. info. scientist Rsch. Inst. U. Dayton; on-base prin. investigator Air Force Info. Ctr. Wright-Patterson AFB, 1969-79; chem. info. specialist Nat. Inst. Occupl. Safety and Health, Cin., 1979-90; propr. JFM Cons., Ft. Myers, Fla., 1990-93; ret., 1993; designer info. sys., spkr. in field. Contbr. articles to profl. publs. Active Retired & Sr. Vol. Program Lee County Sch. Dist., 1992-93, Lee County Hosp. Med. Libr., Rutenberg County Libr., Wyeth Gastrointestinal fellow med. rsch. U. Chgo., 1940-42. Mem. AAUP (exec. bd. 1978-79), Am. Soc. Info. Sci. (treas. South Ohio chpt. 1973-75), Am. Chem. Soc. (emeritus, Fla. chpt., pres. Dayton 1977), Dayton Engrng. Soc. (hon.), Soc. Advancement Materials & Process Engrng. (Fla. chpt., pres. Midwest chpt. 1977-78), Dayton Affiliated Tech. Socs. (Outstanding Scientist and Engr. award 1978), Sigma Xi (emeritus, Fla. chpt., pres. Cin. fed. environ. chpt. 1986-87). Home: 1301 SW 10th Ave F-203 Delray Beach FL 33444-1280

MARCH, KAREN SUE (EARON), critical care nurse, medical surgical nurse, educator; b. Lock Haven, Pa., Oct. 2, 1962; d. Darl Joseph and Patricia Ann (Frye) Earon; m. Bradley Eugene March, Jan. 23, 1988; 1 child, Zachary McDowell. BSN, Indiana U. of Pa., 1984; MSN with distinction, Gannon U., 1993. RN, Pa.; CCRN, CS- ANCC, ACLS, BLS; cert. ACLS instr. Staff nurse med.-surg. York (Pa.) Hosp., 1984-85, staff nurse SICU, 1985-88; critical care float pool Geisinger Med. Ctr., Danville, Pa., 1988-89; staff nurse ICU, relief nursing supr. Bradford (Pa.) Regional Med. Ctr., 1989-91, critical care nurse mgr., 1991-93, per diem staff nurse ICU, 1993—, relief nursing supr., 1993-94; asst. prof. nursing U. Pitts., Bradford, 1993—; ednl. cons., Bradford, 1994—; rschr. presentations Mellen Conf., Cleve., 1993, U. Mass. Sigma Theta Tau Rsch. conf., 1995. Vol. Ptnrs. in Edn., Bradford Regional Med. Ctr./Derrick City (Pa.) Sch., 1994, Am. Heart Assn. Dear Neighbor Campaign, 1995, Nat. Kidney Found. of N.W. Pa., 1996; patron Bradford Creative and Performing Arts, 1994. Mem. AACN, Bradford Twp. Lioness Club (bd. dirs. 1996-97), Sigma Theta Tau. Home: 529 South Ave Bradford PA 16701-3974 Office: U Pitts Bradford 300 Campus Dr Bradford PA 16701-2812

MARCH, KATHLEEN PATRICIA, federal judge; b. May 18, 1949; married; 2 children. BA, Colo. Coll., 1971; JD, Yale U., 1974. Bar: N.Y. 1975, Calif. 1978. Law clk. to hon. judge Thomas J. Griesa U.S. Dist. Ct. (so. dist.) N.Y., 1974-75; assoc. Cahill, Gordon & Reindel, N.Y.C., 1975-77; asst. U.S. atty. criminal div. Office of U.S. Atty. Cen. Dist. Calif., L.A., 1978-82; assoc. Adams, Duque & Hazeltine, L.A., 1982-85; ptnr. Demetriou, Del Guercio & Lovejoy, L.A., 1985-88; judge U.S. Bankruptcy Ct. Cen. Dist. Calif., L.A., Calif., 1988—. Bd. editors Yale U. Law Jour. Mem. ABA, Fed. Bar Assn., L.A. County Bar Assn., Women Lawyers Assn., , Nat. Assn. Women Judges, Phi Beta Kappa. Office: Roybal Fed Ct Bldg 255 E Temple St Ste 1460 Los Angeles CA 90012-3334*

MARCH, MARION D., writer, astrologer, consultant; b. Nürnberg, Germany, Feb. 10, 1923; came to the U.S., 1941; d. Franz and Grete Dispeker; m. Nico D. March, Sept. 1, 1948; children: Michele, Nico F. Diploma, Ecole de Commerce, Lausanne; attended, Columbia U. Cons. astrologer L.A., 1970—; founder, pres., tchr. Aquarius Workshops, L.A., 1975—; internat. lectr. in field, 1976—; chmn. bd. dirs., convention dir. United Astrology Congress, 1986, 89, 92; co-founder, mem. bd. dirs. Assn. for Astrological Networking; cons. in astrology to psychology profls. Author: (books) (with Joan McEvers) The Only Way To... Learn Astrology, 1981-94 (6 vol. series), Astrology: Old Theme, New Thoughts, 1984; editor (mag.) ASPECTS, 1976-93; contbr. numerous articles to jours. in field. Recipient Regulus award for edn. United Astology Congress, 1989, for community svc., 1992, PAI Annual award Profl. Astrologers, Inc., 1990, Syotisha Ratna award Syotish Samsthan of Bombay, India, 1986, Robert Carl Jansky Astrology Leadership award, 1994. Mem. Nat. Coun. for Geocosmic Rsch. (mem. adv. bd.), Internat. Soc. Astrological Rsch., Profl. Astrologers Inc., Astrological Assn. Great Britain. Office: care Publisher ACS PO Box 34487 San Diego CA 92163-4487

MARCHAND, NANCY, actress; b. Buffalo, June 19, 1928; d. Raymond L. and Marjorie F. M.; m. Paul Sparer, July 7, 1951; children: David, Kathryn, Rachel. BFA, Carnegie Inst. Tech., 1949. Vol. actress Actors studio, N.Y.C.; TV appearances include A Touch of the Poet, Marty, Of Famous Memory, Cheers, Coach, Night Court; series regular on TV show Lou Grant, 1977-82 (Emmy award 1978, 1980, 1981, 1982); theater: performed at Circle in the Sq., N.Y.C., L.A. Music Center, Lincoln Center, N.Y.C., Am. Shakespeare Festival, Goodman Theater, Chgo., Ahmanson Theatre, Los Angeles; appeared on Broadway in And Miss Reardon Drinks a Little, After the Rain, Miss Isobel, Three Bags Full, Mornings at Seven, 40 Carats, Octette Bridge Club; off-Broadway plays: Children, Sister Mary Ignatius, The Balcony (Obie award 1959), Cocktail Hour (Obie Award 1989), The End of the Day, 1992, White Liars and Black Comedy, 1993; films include Bachelor Party, 1957, Ladybug, Ladybug, 1963, Me, Natalie, 1969, Tell Me That You Love Me Junie Moon, 1969, The Hospital, 1971, The Bostonians, 1984, From the Hip, 1987, Naked Gun, 1988, Brain Doners, 1991, Jefferson in Paris, 1994, Sabrina, 1995; TV films include Some Kind of Miracle, North and South Book II. Recipient Drama Desk award, Outstanding Ensemble Performances, 1979.

MARCHETTA, ANN ELLEN, critical care nurse; b. New London, Wis., Feb. 21, 1949; d. Marlyn Martin and Luella Margarite (Koehler) Wendt; m. Nicholas Carl Marchetta, July 27, 1968; children: Antionette, Elizabeth, Jessica. BSN magna cum laude, U. Wis., Oshkosh, Wis., 1992; postgrad., U. Wis., 1994—. Staff nurse St. Michael Hosp., Stevens Point, Wis., 1968; charge nurse Bethany Nursing Home, Waupaca, Wis., 1969-78; staff nurse Alpha Home Care, Waupaca, 1984-86; nurse med.-surg. ICU, Riverside Med. Ctr., Waupaca, 1978—; with Am. Home Care, Appleton, Wis., 1995. Pub. speaking on advanced med. directives, Waupaca, 1994-95. Recipient Nurse of the Yr., Riverside Med. Ctr., 1989, Peggy Spees award U. Wis. Oshkosh, 1991, Outstanding Sr., U. Wis. Oshkosh, 1992. Mem. Sigma Theta Tau. Republican. Lutheran. Home: E1599 Murray Ln Waupaca WI 54981-9184 Office: Riverside Med Ctr 800 Riverside Dr Waupaca WI 54981-1943

MARCHINI, CLAUDIA CILLONIZ, artist; b. Lima, Peru, Feb. 3, 1959; came to U.S., 1983; d. Alberto Peschiera and Matilde Spiers (Toledo) Cilloniz; m. Carlos Edwards, Nov. 14, 1983; 1 child, Renzo. BFA, Memphis Coll. Art, 1987; MFA, U. Tex., San Antonio, 1989. Part-time mgr. Lung Clinic, Grants Pass, Oreg. One woman shows at Foyer Auditorium and Gallery, U. Tex., San Antonio, 1990, GPHS Libr. Gallery, Oreg., 1991, Instituto Cultural Peruano Norteamericano, Lima, 1992, 93, Rogue Gallery, Medford, Oreg., 1992, Portland (Oreg.) State U., 1994, Firehouse Gallery, Grants Pass, Oreg., 1995, D.O.T. N.W., Portland, 1995, Galeria Cecilia Gonzalez, Lima, 1996, Gallery at Stevenson Union, SOSC, Ashland, 1996; group exhbns. include Instituto Cultural Peruano Norteamericano, 1988, 110 Broadway, San Antonio, 1988, Mexic-Arte, Austin, Tex., 1988, Bank One, San Antonio, 1989, Rolling Oaks Mall, San Antonio, 1989, Art League Gallery, Beaumont, Tex., 1990, U. Toronto, Can., 1990, Art Gallery at Lower Columbia Coll., 1991, Newport (Oreg.) Visual Arts Ctr., 1991, 92, Grants Pass Mus., 1991, 92, 93, Rogue Gallery, 1991, 92, 95, Stonington Gallery, Seattle, 1992, 93, Wiseman Gallery, Grants Pass, 1993, Paris Gibson Sq. Mus. of Art, Great Falls, Mont., 1993, Ctr. Contemporary Art, Seattle, 1993, Pulliam Deffengaugh Gallery, Portland, 1994, Ctr. for Visual Arts, Oakland, Calif., 1994, Washington State Convention and Trade Ctr., 1995, D.O.T. Northwest, 1995, Graven Images Gallery, Ashland, Oreg., 1995, Portland Mus. of Art, 1995, So. Oreg. Art Exhbn., Grants Pass, 1996; represented in various pvt. collections. Mem. Nat. Mus. Women in the Arts, Grants Pass Mus. of Art, Ctr. on Contemporary Art, Greenpeace, World Wildlife Fund, Arts Coun. So. Oreg., U.S. Squash Racquet Assn. Office: Lung Clinic 874 NE 7th St Grants Pass OR 97526

MARCHIONE, SHARYN LEE, computer scientist; b. Schenectady, Oct. 1, 1947; d. Albert Jr. and Estelle Mabelle (Christiansen) O'Brien; m. Joseph Michael Marchione, May 4, 1972; 1 child, Heather E. AS in Engring., Hudson Valley Community Coll., Troy, N.Y., 1967; BS in Computer Sci., Skidmore Coll., 1987; MBA, Coll. of St. Rose, Albany, N.Y., 1993. Computer programmer info. systems GE, Schenectady, 1967-72, 78-81, shift leader CAD-CAM systems, 1981-84, advanced techniques specialist, 1984-88, mgr. end user computing decision support ops., 1988-95; mgr. info. systems Westinghouse, 1995—; chmn. windows spl. interest group Westinghouse, Schenectady, 1990-95, mgr. info. sys., 1995—; mem. adv. coun. Software Pub. Co., 1991. Vol. Rep. Town Supr. Campaign, Halfmoon, N.Y., 1987-91, Concerned for Hungry, Schenectady, 1988—; cons. Schenectady Econ. Devel. Coun., 1991—, Cobleskill Coll., SUNY, 1991—.

MARCINEK, MARGARET ANN, nursing educator; b. Uniontown, Pa., Sept. 29, 1948; d. Joseph Hugh and Evelyn (Bailey) Boyle; m. Bernard Francis Marcinek, Aug. 11, 1973; 1 dau., Cara Ann. R.N., Uniontown Hosp., 1969; B.S. in Nursing, Pa. State U., 1970; M.S.N., U. Md., 1973; Ed.D., W.Va. U., 1983. Staff nurse Presbyn. U., Pitts., 1970-71; instr. nursing W.Va. U., Morgantown, 1973-77, asst. prof., 1977-80, assoc. prof., 1980-83; assoc. prof. California U. of Pa., 1983-87, prof., 1987—, dept. chmn., 1985—. Contbg. author: Critical Care Nursing. Contbr. articles to profl. jours. Mem. adv. coun. In Home Health, Inc.; mem. adv. coun. Albert Gallatin VNA. Mem. Am. Nurses Assn., Am. Assn. Critical Care Nurses, Nat. League for Nurses, Sigma Theta Tau, Phi Kappa Phi.

MARCINKO, JACQUELINE MICHELE, social worker; b. Cleve., Oct. 11, 1965; d. Frank and Dorrine Ann (Barber) Turk; m. John Michael Marcinko, Nov. 21, 1992; 1 child, Elizabeth Dorrine. BA, U. Dayton, 1987; MSW, U. Ga., 1994. Lic. master's social worker, Ga. Cottage supr. Village of St. Joseph, Atlanta, 1987-90, therapist, 1994-95; trainer, server Peasant Restaurants, Atlanta, 1990-92; case mgr. Dekalb Co., Atlanta, 1992; intern Laurel Heights Hosp., Atlanta, 1993-94; pres., treas. North Ga. Childcare Assn., 1988-89. Vol. RCIA, AIDS ministry, baptism prep., liturgy coord., Cathedral of Christ the King, Atlanta, 1988—; vol. Summer Olympics, Atlanta, 1996. Mem. NASW, Phi Alpha Theta. Democrat. Roman Catholic.

MARCOCCIA, ROSE MARIE, accountant; b. Bridgeport, Conn., Nov. 17, 1970; d. Mario and Pasqualina (Paola) M. BA in Acctg., Sacred Heart U., Fairfield, Conn., 1992. CPA, Conn.; cert. notary public, Conn. Teller Lafayette Bank & Trust, Bridgeport, Conn., 1988-90; jr. acct. Hobert H. Summers, Norwalk, Conn., 1991-92; sr. acct. Hope & Hernandez, Bridgeport, 1992—. Mem. AICPA, Inst. Mgmt. Accts., Conn. Soc. CPAs. Home: 645 Westfield Ave Bridgeport CT 06606

MARCOLIS, LILLIAN, political activist; b. Chgo., July 19, 1919; d. Hyman and Pauline (Chain) Marcus; m. Irving Margolis, Jan. 28, 1940 (dec. Mar. 1986); children: Marleen, Harvey, Ronald; m. Trevor Gelick, July 2, 1989. BA, 1940. Tchr., libr. Irving Park Sch., Chgo.; developer, fund-raiser Urban Gateways, Chgo.; tchr., coord. Hanson Park and Schubert Elem. Schs., Chgo. Mem. Nat. Coun. Jewish Women. Democrat. Jewish. Home: 1771 Mission Hills Rd Northbrook IL 60062

MARCOUX, JULIA A., midwife; b. St. Helens, England, Aug. 7, 1928; d. Robert Patrick and Margaret Mary Theresa (White) Ashall; m. Albert Marcoux, Apr. 23, 1955; children: Stephen, Ann Marie, Richard, Michael, Maureen, Patrick, Margaret, Julie. Diploma, Withington Hosp., Manchester, England, 1950; grad., Cowley Hill Hosp., St. Helens, England, 1952; BS in Pub. Adminstrn., St. Joseph's Coll. RN, Conn.; lic. midwife, Conn. Nurse, labor, delivery rm. and nursery Day Kimbal Hosp., Putnam, Conn.; sch. nurse Marianapolis Prep. Sch., Thompson, Conn.; occupational nurse U.S. Post Office, Hartford, Conn.; pvt. duty and gerontology nurse Conn. Contbr. articles to profl. jours. Named Internat. Cath. Family of Yr., 1982.

MARCUCCIO, PHYLLIS ROSE, association executive, editor; b. Hackensack, N.J., Aug. 25, 1933; d. Filippo and Rose (Henry) M. AB, Bucknell U., 1955; MA, George Washington U., 1976. Trainee Time, Inc., 1956-57; art prodn. for mags. of Med. Econs., Inc., 1958-60; mem. staff Nat. Sci. Tchrs. Assn., Washington, 1961—; assoc. editor Sci. and Children, 1963-65, editor, 1965-95, dir. divsn. elem. edn., 1974-78, dir. div. program devel. and continuing edn., 1978-83, pub., 1993—; dir. publs. Nat. Sci. Tchrs. Assn., 1983—, assoc. exec. dir., 1990—; pub. Dragonfly, 1996—; lectr., cons. in field. Author, photographer, illustrator numerous articles; co-author: Investigation in Ecology, 1972; editor: Science Fun, 1977, 2d edit., 94; illustrator: Selected Readings for Students of English as a Second Language, 1966; compiler: Opportunities for Summer Studies in Elementary Science, 1968, 2d edit., 1969. Apptd. commr. Rockville (Md.) Housing Authority, 1981-91, chairperson, 1984-86; bd. dirs. Nat. Sci Resource Ctr., Nat. Acad. Sci., 1986—, Hands on Sci. Outreach, Inc., 1988—. Recipient Citizenship medal DAR, 1951; hon. life mem. Ohio Council Elem. Sch. Sci., 1974. Life mem. Nat. Sci. Tchrs. Assn.; mem. Council Elem. Sci. Internat. (Internat. award outstanding contbns. sci. edn. 1971, 72, 86, 94), Am. Nature Study Soc., Soil Conservation Soc. Am., Nat. Free Lance Photographers Assn., Photog. Soc. Am., Nat. Wildlife Fedn., Nat. Audubon Soc., Nat. Geog. Soc., Wilderness Soc., AAAS, Washington Edn. Press Assn. (treas. 1966-67, pres. 1975-76), Ednl. Press Assn. Am. (regional dir. 1969-71, sec. 1979—, Disting. Achievement award 1969, 71-74, 76, 77, 80, 88, 93, 95, Eleanor Fishburn award 1978), Sci. Teaching Assn. N.Y. (Outstanding Service to Sci. Edn. award 1987), Nat. Assn. Industry Edn. Coop. (bd. dirs. 1980-86), Pocono Environ. Edn. Ctr. (bd. dirs. 1989—), Nat. Press Club, Theta Alpha Phi, Phi Delta Gamma, Phi Delta Kappa., Sigma Delta Chi. Home: 406 S Horners Ln Rockville MD 20850-1556 Office: Nat Sci Tchrs Assn 1840 Wilson Blvd Arlington VA 22201-3000

MARCUM, DEANNA BOWLING, library administrator; b. Salem, Ind., Aug. 5, 1946; d. Anderson and Ruby (Mobley) Bowling; m. Thomas P. Marcum, June 13, 1974; 1 child, Ursula. BA, U. Ill., 1967; MA, So. Ill. U., 1969; MLS, U. Ky., 1971; PhD, U. Md., 1991. Tchr. Deland-Weldon (Ill.) High Sch., 1967-68; instr. English U. Ky., Lexington, 1969-70, cataloging librarian, 1970-73, asst. to dir., 1973-74; asst. dir. pub. svcs. Joint U. Librs., Nashville, 1974-77; mgmt. tng. specialist Assn. Rsch. Librs., Washington, 1977-80; sr. cons. Info. Systems Cons., Inc., Washington, 1980-81; v.p. Coun. on Libr. Resources, Washington, 1981-89; dean Sch. Libr. and Info. Sch. Cath. U., Washington, 1989-92; dir. pub. svcs. and collections mgmt. Libr. of Congress, Washington, 1993-95; pres. Coun. on Libr. Resources, Washington, 1995—; adv. bd. So. Edn. Found., Atlanta, 1986-91; chmn. grants com. Coun. on Libr. resources, Washington, 1990-94. Author: Good Books in a Country Home, 1993; co-author: (with Richard Boss) The Library Catalog, 1980, On-Line Acquisitions Systems, 1981; contbr. articles to profl. jours. Pres., Commn. on Preservation and Access, 1995—. Mem. ALA, Am. Studies Assn., Orgn. Am. Historians, Am. Antiquarian Soc. (adv. bd. 1989—), Beta Phi Mu, Phi Kappa Phi. Home: 3315 Wake Dr Kensington MD 20895 Office: Coun on Libr Resources 1400 16th St NW Ste 715 Washington DC 20036-2217

MARCUS, ADRIANNE STUHL, writer; b. Everett, Mass., Mar. 7, 1935; d. George Zachariah and Edith Delores (Cohen) Stuhl; m. Warren M. Marcus (div. 1981); children: Stacey Ann, Shelby Alice, Sarah Naomi; m. Ian Holroyde Wilson. AB, San Francisco State U., 1955, MA, 1961. Poet, 1955—; tchr. Coll. of Marin, 1965-79; food columnist San Francisco Chronicle, 1985-87; writer, 1968—. Author: The Moon is a Marrying Eye, 1969, The Chocolate Bible, 1975; co-author: Carrion House World of Gifts, 1980. Fellow Ossabaw, 1982, Yaddo Corp., 1985, Va. Ctr. for the Creative Arts, 1993-95. Mem. Overseas Press Club, PEN, Internat. Food Journalists and Writers, Acad. Am. Poets. Democrat. Hebrew. Home and Office: 79 Twin Oaks San Rafael CA 94901

MARCUS, ANDREA CANDACE SILLS, nurse, lawyer; b. Brookline, Mass., Nov. 23, 1947; d. Benjamin and Mary Natalie (Rogers) Sills; m. Lawrence I. Marcus, Aug. 9, 1974; children: David, Anthony, Rebecca. Grad. with honors, Norwalk Hosp. Sch. Nursing, 1973; BSN, U. Miami, Coral Gables, Fla., 1985, MSN, 1987; JD, Sch. of Law, U. Miami, 1991. Bar: Fla., U.S. Dist. Ct. (so. dist.) Fla.; clin. nurse specialist oncology nurse/adult health; RN, Fla.; RN, Conn. Head nurse, mem. psychotherapeutic team Hall-Brooke Hosp., Westport, Conn., 1973-75; founder, bd. dirs. Hospice of Boca Raton, 1978-81; staff RN oncology Boca Raton (Fla.) Community Hosp., 1983-84, psychiat. nurse liaison, 1984-89; patient care coord. Hospice by the Sea, Boca Raton, 1973-75; law clk. Legal Aid Soc. of Palm Beach County, 1989-91, atty., 1991-93; asst. counsel Interim Svcs. Inc., Ft. Lauderdale, Fla., 1993-95; assoc. atty. Krathen & Roselli, 1995-96; atty. Gary, Williams, Parenti, Lewis & McManus, Fort Pierce, Fla., 1996—. Coeditor OnCare, 1987-88. Mem. ambs. program U. Miami; bd. dirs. Estancia Homeowners Assn.; treas. Palm Beach County Med.Soc. Aux., Diabetes Assn. Palm Beach County; mem. svc. & rehab. com., steering com. Am. Cancer Soc.; mem. psychosocial support team Boca Raton Cmty. Hosp. Mem. ABA, ATLA, ANA, Fla. Nurses Assn., Acad. Fla. Trial Lawyers, Am. Assn. Corp. Counsel, Nat. Health Lawyers Assn., Am. Bd. Forensic Examiners, Am. Assn. Nurse Attys., Am. Soc. Law, Medicine and Ethics, Internat. Nurses Cancer Care, Am. Inn Ct. (Spellman chpt.), Oncol. Nurses Soc., Nurses Alliance Prevention Nuc. War, Health & Law Soc., St. Lucie Hist. Soc., U. Miami Alumni Club, Sigma Theta Tau, Phi Alpha Delta. Home: 6913 Corto Cir Boca Raton FL 33433-2730 Office: 320 S Indian River Dr Fort Pierce FL 34948-3390

MARCUS, CLAIRE, artist; b. Cambridge, Mass., Feb. 7, 1945; d. Isadore Cohen and Judith (Daum) Satenstein; m. Ira Marcus, Feb. 12, 1967. Student, Vesper George Sch. Art, Boston, 1962-63, Mus. Fine Arts, Boston, 1967-79. Exhibited in shows including All New Eng./Cape Cod Art Assn., 1995, 96, Printmakers of Cape Cod Past and Present, 1996, MGNE Monoprint/Monotype Celebration, 1996; in collections including AT&T,

Prime Computer in Mass., also pvt. collections. Founding bd. dirs. Arts/Wayland, Mass., 1980. Recipient 1st place award Lighthouse Gallery, 1993. Mem. Weston Arts and Crafts Assn. (bd. dirs. 1976-86, coord.), Cape Cod Art Assn. (1st prize for graphics 1995, 2d prizes for graphics 1995), Monotype Guild New Eng., Printmakers Cape Code, Ceramic League Palm Beaches, Cap Cod Potters, Soc. Cape Cod Craftesmen.

MARCUS, EILEEN, public relations and advertising executive; b. Naples, Italy, June 11, 1946; came to U.S., 1947; d. Isaac and Mina (Cyplowicz) Einik; m. Zvi Marcus, May 24, 1974; children: Neely, Kerren. BS in Journalism, U. Fla., 1967. Acct. exec. EV Clay Assocs., Miami, Fla., 1972-74; account exec., pub. relations dir. Hume Smith Mickleberry Advt. Co., Miami, 1974-77; dir. publs. Fla. Internat. U., Miami, 1977-81; dir. mktg. Northshore Hosp., Miami, 1981-85; ptnr. Mktg. Mix, Inc., Miami, 1985-88; sr. v.p., gen. mgr. Burson-Marsteller, Miami, 1988-96; exec. v.p. Zynyx Mktg. Comms. Inc., Miami, 1996—. Mem. South Fla. Hosp. Assn. (pres. 1985-86), South Fla. Advt. Fedn. (Gold, Silver and Bronze Addy awards 1988). Office: Zynyx Mktg Comms Inc 407 Lincoln Rd Fl 3 Miami Beach FL 33139

MARCUS, H. LOUISE, educator, writer; b. Chgo., Apr. 10, 1928; d. Philip and Dora G. (Abraham) Moshel; m. Bernard Louis Marcus, Mar. 29, 1948; children: Bonnie Gail Marcus Graybill, Donald Lawrence, Leonard Michael, Sally Marcus Rodeman. AA, Wright Jr. Coll., Chgo., 1947; BA, U. Calif., Santa Barbara, 1967. Tchr. Temple B'nai B'rith, Santa Barbara, 1965-72; tutor handicapped Santa Barbara Adult Edn., 1991-94; aide Hollister Sch., Goleta, Calif., 1996—. Writer short stories. Program chmn. Orgn. for Rehab. Tng., 1990-93; pres. Hadassah, 1970-71. Mem. LWV, B'nai B'rith Sisterhood, Elderhostel. Democrat. Jewish.

MARCUS, JANET CAROL, cytotechnologist; b. N.Y.C., Mar. 15, 1941; d. David and Adele (Rosenberg) M. BS, Fairleigh Dickinson U., 1963. Cytotechnologist Good Samaritan Hosp., Suffern, N.Y., 1966-70; cytotechnology supr. Newark (N.J.) Beth Israel Med. Ctr., 1970-76; chief cytotechnologist Gyn Cytology and Pathology Assocs. merged Bio Reference Lab., Englewood, N.J., 1976-94; rsch. cytotechnologist Neurmed. Systems, Inc., Suffern, N.Y., 1994—; guest lectr. U. of Medicine and Dentistry of N.J., Newark, 1980-85. Mem. N.J. Assn. Cytology (pres. 1983-85), N.J. Assn. of Cytology, Greater N.Y. Assn. of Cytotechnologists, Delaware Valley Soc. of Cytology, Am. Soc. of Clin. Pathologists (assoc. mem., cert. cytotechnology, specialist in cytotechnology), Am. Soc. of Cytopathology (assoc.), Am. Soc. for Cytotech. Home: 162 Jefferson Ave River Edge NJ 07661 Office: Neuromedical Systems Inc Ste 102 2 Executive Blvd Suffern NY 10901

MARCUS, KAREN MELISSA, foreign language educator; b. Vancouver, B.C., Feb. 28, 1956; came to the U.S., 1962; d. Marvin Marcus and Arlen Ingrid (Sahlman) Bishop; m. Jorge Esteban Mezei, Jan. 7, 1984 (div. Mar. 1987). BA in French, BA in Polit. Sci., U. Calif., Santa Barbara, 1978, MA in Polit. Sci., 1981; MA in French, Stanford U., 1984, PhD in French, 1990. Lectr. in French Stanford (Calif.) U., 1989-90; asst. prof. French No. Ariz. U., Flagstaff, 1990-96, assoc. prof. French, 1996—; cons. Houghton Mifflin, 1993, Grand Canyon (Ariz.) Natural History Soc., 1994. Vol., letter writer Amnesty Internat. Urgent Action Network, 1991-95; vol. No. Ariz. Aids Outreach Orgn., Flagstaff, 1994—. Recipient medal for outstanding achievement in French, Alliance Francaise, Santa Barbara, 1978; named Scholarship Exch. Student, U. Geneva, Switzerland, 1979-80; doctoral fellow Stanford (Calif.) U., 1981-85. Mem. MLA, Am. Assn. Tchrs. French, Am. Coun. on the Tchg. Fgn. Langs., Am. Literary Translators Assn., Women in French, Coordination Internat. des Chercheurs Sur Les Litteratures Maghrebines, Phi Beta Kappa, Pi Delta Phi, Alpha Lambda Delta. Democrat. Jewish. Office: No Ariz Univ Modern Lang Dept Box 6004 Flagstaff AZ 86011

MARCUS, MARIA LENHOFF, lawyer, law educator; b. Vienna, Austria, June 23, 1933; came to U.S., 1938, naturalized, 1944; d. Arthur and Clara (Gruber) Lenhoff; m. Norman Marcus, Dec. 23, 1956; children: Valerie, Nicole, Eric. BA, Oberlin Coll., 1954; JD, Yale Law Sch., 1957. Bar: N.Y. 1961, U.S. Dist. Ct. (so. and ea. dists.) N.Y. 1962, U.S. Ct. Appeals (2d cir.) 1962, U.S. Supreme Ct. 1964. Assoc. counsel NAACP, N.Y.C., 1961-67; asst. atty. gen. N.Y. State, N.Y.C., 1967-78; chief litigation bur. Atty. Gen. N.Y. State, 1976-78; adj. assoc. prof., Law Sch. NYU, 1976-78; assoc. prof. law Fordham Law Sch., N.Y.C., 1978-86, prof. law, 1986—; arbitrator Nat. Assn. Securities Dealers; chair subcom. interrogatories U.S. Dist. Ct. (so. dist.) N.Y., 1983-85. Contbr. articles to profl. jours. Fellow N.Y. Bar Found.; mem. Assn. Bar City of N.Y. (v.p. 1995-96, exec. com. 1976-80, com. audit 1988-95, labor com. 1981-84, judiciary com. 1975-76, chmn. civil rights com. 1972-75), N.Y. State Bar Assn. (exec. com. 1979-81, ho. dels. 1978-81, com. constitution and by-laws 1984-93). Office: Fordham Law Sch 140 W 62d St New York NY 10023

MARCUS, PHYLLIS SCARCELL, elementary school educator; b. Olean, N.Y., Feb. 26, 1936; d. Mark and Ethel (Statham) Scarcell; m. Richard Marcus, Aug. 23, 1958; 1 child, Kristi. BS, Mansfield U., 1957; postgrad., St. Bonaventure U., 1958-61. 1st grade tchr. Olean (N.Y.) Schs., 1957—. Author: Hector Duck Stories, 1988, Why Johnny Can Read, (coloring book) Johnny Applesead Revisits Olean, 1989; contbr. articles to Instructor mag. Sunday sch. tchr. Christ United Meth. Ch., dir. cherub choir, 1957—; vol. My Brother's Keeper - Quilts for the Homeless. Recipient Spl. Mission award United Meth. Women, 1993. Mem. NEA, Olean Tchrs. Assn., Enchanted Mountain Country Dancers, The Twin Tier Twisters Line Dancing Clubs, Kappa Delta Phi. Home: 1012 King St Olean NY 14760-3034

MARCUS, ROBIN FRANCES AVERBUCK, nursing administrator; b. Oakland, Calif., May 21, 1964; d. Nathan Earl and Maxine Joan (Katz) Averbuck; m. Irving Charles Marcus, June 3, 1990; children: Ariel Halie, Maxwell Eli. BA in Sociology, U. Calif.-San Diego, 1985; BSN, U. San Francisco, 1988; student, Laney Jr. Coll., Oakland, Calif., 1982-89. RN, Tex., Calif. Teaching asst. U. San Francisco, 1987-88, Laney Coll., Oakland, Calif., 1986-89; staff nurse bone marrow transplant unit Pacific Presbyn. Med. Ctr., San Francisco, 1989-91; IV nurse, vis. nurse VNA of Sonoma & Marin County, Santa Rosa, Calif., 1991; dir. nursing Personal Homecare of Calif., Santa Rosa, 1991, Critical Care Sys., Santa Rosa, 1991-93, Critical Care Am., Monterey, Calif., 1993-94; clin. ops. dir. Caremark, San Antonio, 1994-95; dir. intervention and compliance programs Caremark, Northbrook, Ill., 1995—; case mgr. HIV case mgmt., Santa Rosa, 1992-93. Mem. Intravenous Nurses Soc., Oncology Nursing Soc., U. San Francisco Alumni Assn., U. Calif.-San Diego Alumni Assn., Sigma Theta Tau. Jewish. Home: 1172 Wade St Highland Park IL 60035 Office: Caremark 2211 Sanders Rd Northbrook IL 60062

MARCUS, RUTH BARCAN, philosopher, educator, writer, lecturer; b. N.Y.C.; d. Samuel and Rose (Post) Barcan; divorced; children: James Spencer, Peter Webb, Katherine Hollister, Elizabeth Post. BA, NYU, 1941; MA, Yale U., 1942, PhD, 1946; LHD (hon.), U. Ill., 1995. Rsch. assoc. in anthropology Inst. for Human Relations, Yale U., New Haven, Conn., 1945-47; AAUW fellow, 1947-48; vis. prof. (intermittently) Northwestern U., 1950-57, Guggenheim fellow, 1953-54; asst. prof., assoc. prof. Roosevelt U., 1957-63; NSF fellow, 1963-64; prof. philosophy U. Ill. at Chgo., 1964-70, head philosophy dept., 1963-69; fellow U. Ill. Center for Advanced Study, 1968-69; prof. philosophy Northwestern U., 1970-73; Reuben Post Halleck prof. philosophy Yale U., 1973-93; sr. rsch. scholar, 1994—; fellow Ctr. Advanced Study in Behavioral Sci., Stanford, Calif., 1979; vis. fellow Inst. Advanced Study, U. Edinburgh, 1983, Wolfson Coll., Oxford U., 1985, 86; vis. fellow Clare Hall, Cambridge U., 1988, lifetime mem. common room, 1989—; past or present mem. adv. coms. Princeton U., MIT, Calif. Inst. Tech., Cornell U. Humanities Ctr., Columbia U., UCLA, others. Author: Modalities, 1993; editor: The Logical Enterprise, 1975, Logic Methodology and Philosophy of Science VII, 1986; mem. editorial bd. Past or Present Metaphilosophy, Monist, Philos. Studies, Signs, Jour. Symbolic Logic, The Philosophers Annual; editor, contbr. to profl. jours. and books. Recipient Machette prize for contbn. to profession; Medal, College de France, 1986; Mellon sr. fellow Nat. Humanities Ctr., 1992-93; vis. disting. prof. U. Calif., Irvine, 1994; fellow Conn. Acad. Arts & Scis. Fellow Am. Acad. Arts and Scis.; mem. Coun. on Philos. Studies (pres. 1988—), Assn. for Symbolic Logic (past exec. coun., exec. com. 1973-83, v.p. 1980-82, coun. 1980-85, pres. 1982-84), Am. Philos. Assn. (past sec., treas., nat. bd. dirs. 1967-83, pres. ctrl. divsn. 1975-78, chmn. nat. bd. officers 1977-85), Philosophy of Sci. Assn., Inst. Internat. Philosophie (past exec. com., v.p. 1983-86, pres. 1990-93, hon. pres. 1994—), Fedn. Internat. Philosophy (exec. com., steering com. 1985—), Elizabethan Club (v.p. 1989, pres. 1989-90), Phi Beta Kappa (professorial lectr. 1993).

MARCY, JEANNINE KOONCE, educational administrator; b. Lake City, S.C., Dec. 22, 1935; d. Alton Earle Sr. and Bernice Eva (Gerrald) K.; m. Shawn Jeannine Marcy Suarez, Vanessa Anne Marcy Berrios. BA, Winthrop Coll., 1957; MS, Barry Coll., 1976. Tchr. Florence (S.C.) County Schs., 1957-59, Kershaw County Schs., Camden, S.C., 1959-61; tchr., dept. chmn. Dade County Pub. Schs., Miami, Fla., 1961-82, asst. prin., 1982-86, coord. personnel staffing, 1986-89, dir. cert., 1989-92, pers. adminstr., 1993—; mem. collective bargaining team Dade County Pub. Schs., 1983-84, trainer tchr. assessment devel. systems, 1983-85, trainer master tchr. program, 1984-85; panelist nat. conv. Assn. Supervision and Curriculum Devel., Altanta, 1980; presenter in field. Campaign worker Bob Graham for Gov., Miami, 1980's, Janet Reno for State Dist. Atty., Miami, 1980's. Mem. Dade County Sch. Adminstrn. Assn., Kappa Delta Pi (pres. 1978-80), Alpha Delta Kappa (hist. 1989—), Phi Delta Kappa. Democrat. Episcopalian. Home: 4740 NW 102nd Ave # 208 Miami FL 33178-2231 Office: Dade County Pub Schs 1500 Biscayne Blvd Ste 129 Miami FL 33132-1421

MARDER, CAROL, advertising specialist and premium firm executive; b. Bklyn., Sept. 20, 1941; d. Simon and Sylvia (Rothstein) Cohen; m. Edwin Marder, Apr. 15, 1961; children: Elisa, Steven Alan, Susan. Prin. owner Boys Ego Retail Clothing, Englishtown, N.J., 1974-76; pres. Motivators, Inc., Old Bridge, N.J., 1976-83, Inkwell Promotions Corp., Morganville, N.J., 1983—; cons. Specialty Advt. of N.Y., 1988—. Recipient citation Monmouth County Bd. Recreation Commrs., Lincroft, N.J., 1987. Mem. East Flatbush League Retarded Children (bd. dirs. 1965-69), Marlboro Chpt. Retarded Children (founder, pres. 1969-71, 73-74, bd. dirs. 1971-76), Marlboro Jewish Ctr. Sisterhood (bd. dirs. 1971-73), N.J. Women in Bus., Middlesex County C. of C., Western Monmouth C. of C. Democrat. Jewish. Office: Inkwell Promotions 1210 Campus Dr Morganville NJ 07751-1262

MARDER, NORMA, writer; b. Bethlehem, Pa., June 8, 1934; d. Max Rajeck and Gertrude Oppenheim Mintz; m. Herbert Marder, Nov. 4, 1956; children: Michael, Yuri. BA, Brandeis U., 1956; postgrad., Manhattan Sch. Music, 1956-59. Singer, voice tchr. Champaign, Ill., 1965-90, freelance editor, 1989-93, writer, 1980—; music dir. Depot Theater, Urbana, Ill., 1968-76; asst. dir. Red. Herring Fiction Workshop, Urbana, 1985-95; co-dir. New Verbal Workshop, Champaign, 1970-80. Author: An Eye for Dark Places, 1993; contbr. stories and essays in literary journals. Bd. dirs. Amasong Chorus, Urbana, 1994—, Monhegan (Maine) Libr., 1992—, Monhegan Mus., 1990—, Arts Coun. Champaign County, 1983-85. Spl. assistance grantee Ill. Arts Coun., Chgo., 1985; Lit. fellow Ill. Arts Coun., 1991.

MARDIS, LINDA KEISER, educator, consultant, author; b. New Haven, Jan. 9, 1937; d. Donald Eskil and Elizabeth Marie Hallsten; m. Gordon Delbert Craig, June 29, 1957 (dec. Jan. 1963); m. Harry Robert Keiser, June 11, 1964 (div.); children: Harry Rudolph, Robert Hungerford; m. Arthur Lowell Mardis, Dec. 29, 1990. BA, Mount Holyoke Coll., 1957; MA, Yale U., 1958. Chmn. Dept. Foreign Langs. Walter Johnson High Sch., Bethesda, Md., 1960-65; music dir. Geneva United Presbyn. Ch., Rockville, Md., 1966-79; assoc. dir. ICM Tng. Seminars, Balt., 1979-85; Reiki master Archedigm, Inc., Olney, Md., 1982—, pres., founder, 1985—; v.p. Archedigm Pubs., 1985—; founder, dir. The Archedigm Collection, 1990—; workshop, retreat leader, 1959—; bd. dirs. Well-Springs Found., Madison, Wis., 1980-88; cons. LIND Inst., San Francisco, 1988—. Author: Conscious Listening, 1986, Light Search, 1987, Teaching Guided Imagery & Music, 1989, Program 33: A New Guided Imagery & Music Program and a New Programming Concept, 1996 (taped music series) Creativity I, II and III, Grieving, Expanded Awareness, Changing Patterns, 1984-88, Mythic Experience, 1984, Capriccio, 1996, Relax With the Classics, vol. 5, 7, 8, 1996. Deacon Christ Congregational Ch, Silver Spring, Md., 1981-84. Fellow Inst. Music and Imagery (bd. dirs. 1981-88, assoc. exec.-dir. 1986-89); mem. Soc. Noetic Scis., Assn. Music and Imagery, The Reiki Alliance, U. Holistic Healers Assn., Internat. Assn. Healthcare Practitioners, Associated Bodyworkers and Massage Profls., Mt. Holyoke Coll. Alumnae Assn. (bd. dirs. 1978-83). Republican. Home: 17247 Sandy Knoll Dr Olney MD 20832-2036 Office: Archedigm Inc PO Box 1109 Olney MD 20830-1109

MARECEK, JEANNE ANN, psychologist, educator; b. Berwyn, Ill., May 28, 1946; d. Frank J. and Josephine (Serio) M. BS, Loyola U., Chgo., 1968; MS, Yale U., 1971, PhD, 1973. From asst. prof. to prof. psychology Swarthmore (Pa.) Coll., 1972—, chmn. dept., 1986-91, 94-95; Fulbright sr. lectr., Sri Lanka, 1988. Co-author: Making a Difference: Psychology and the Construction of Gender; contbr. numerous articles to profl. jours. and chpts. to books. Bd. dirs. Women in Transition, Phila., 1980-86; vice patron Nest, Hendala, Sri Lanka, 1995—; bd. dirs. Women's Therapy Ctr., Phila. Various fed. research grants. Mem. APA, Ea. Psychol. Assn., Assn. for Asian Studies, Am. Inst. Sri Lanka Studies (sec. 1994-95). Office: Swarthmore Coll Dept Psychology 500 College Ave Swarthmore PA 19081

MAREE, WENDY, painter, sculptor; b. Windsor, Eng., Feb. 10, 1938. Student, Windsor & Maidenhead Coll., 1959; studied with Vasco Lazzlo, London, 1959-62. Exhibited in group shows at Windsor Arts Festival, San Bernardino (Calif.) Mus.; one-woman shows include Lake Arrowhead (Calif.) Libr., 1989, Amnesty Internat., Washington, 1990, Phyllis Morris Gallery, Many Horses Gallery, L.A., 1990, Nelson Rockefeller, Palm Springs, Calif., 1992, 94, Stewart Gallery, Rancho Palos Verdes, Calif., Petropavlovsk (Russia) Cultural Mus., Kamchatka, Russia, 1993, Coyle-Coyle Gallery, Blue Jay, Calif., 1995, La Quinta Sculpture Park, Calif., 1995, Avante-Garde Gallery, Palm Springs, 1996, Avante-Garden Gallery, La Jolla, Calif., 1996, Avante Garde Gallery, La Jolla, 1996, others; represented in pvt. collections His Royal Highness Prince Faisal, Saudi Arabia, Gena Rowlands, L.A., John Cassavetes, L.A., Nicky Blairs, L.A., Guilford Glazer, Beverly Hills, Calif., June Allyson, Ojai, Calif., Amnesty Internat., Washington. Recipient award San Bernardino County Mus., 1988, Gov. Kamchatka of Russia, 1993. Mem. Artist Guild of Lake Arrowhead. Address: 246 Saturmino Dr Palm Springs CA 92262

MARENCO, GENEVIEVE ELIZABETH, financial planning analyst; b. Bethpage, N.Y., July 5, 1964; d. Lawrence George and Genevieve Theresa (Tagliaferri) Gundlach; m. John Andrew Marenco, Sept. 9, 1990. BBA in Banking and Fin., Hofstra U., 1986; MBA in Corp. Fin., Bernard M. Baruch Coll., 1990; postgrad., U. Nev. Mgr. Cidapeg, Inc., Deer Park, N.Y., 1982-90; mgmt. trainee Morgan Guaranty Trust Co., N.Y.C., 1986-87; loan specialist Fin. Funding Nev., Las Vegas, 1992-93; fin. planning analyst Texaco Inc., Las Vegas, 1993—. Mem. Inst. Mgmt. Accts., Nev. Cogeneration Assocs. (rec. sec. 1994—). Office: Texaco Cogeneration Ops 420 N Nellis Blvd # A3-117 Las Vegas NV 89110

MARESH, ALICE MARCELLA, retired educational administrator; b. Chgo., Sept. 17, 1922; d. Joseph Anton and Barbara Magdalene (Slad) M. BEd, Chgo. Tchrs. Coll., 1944; MEd, Loyola U., Chgo., 1962. Chemist Best Foods, Inc., Chgo., 1944-54; tchr. Chgo. Bd. Edn., 1954-65, counselor, 1965-67, asst. prin., 1967-69, prin., 1969-93; retired, 1993. Recipient Outstanding and Dedicated Svc. award Puerto Rican Congress, 1975, Those Who Excel award Ill. Bd. Edn., 1978, Whitman award for excellence in ednl. mgmt. Whitman Acad., Chgo., 1990, Outstanding Svc. to Edn. in Chgo. award Nat. Coun. Negro Women, 1992. Mem. Chgo. Prins. Assn., Chgo. Area Reading Assn., Aquin Guild (Dedicated Svc. award 1976), Delta Kappa Gamma (pres. 1976-78), Phi Delta Kappa, Pi Lambda Theta (sec. 1995—). Democrat. Roman Catholic. Home: 3850 W Bryn Mawr Ave #308 Chicago IL 60659-3135

MARGED, JUDITH MICHELE, middle school educator; b. Phila., Nov. 27, 1954; d. Bernard A. and Norma Marged. Student, Drexel U., 1972-73; AA in Biology, Broward Community Coll., Ft. Lauderdale, Fla., 1975; BA in Biology, Fla. Atlantic U., 1977, BA in Exceptional Edn., 1980, MEd in Counseling, 1984; EdD in Early and Middle Childhood, Nova U., 1991. Cert. tchr., Fla. Tchr. Coral Springs (Fla.) Mid. Sch., 1979-80, Am. Acad., Wilton Manors, Fla., 1980-83, Ramblewood Mid. Sch., Coral Springs, 1984—; creator programs for mid. sch. students. Author: A Program to Increase the Knowledge of Middle School Students in Sexual Education and Substance Abuse Prevention, An Alternative Education Program to Create Successful Learning for the Middle School Child At-Risk. Mem. NSTA, AACD, ASCD, Am. Sch. Counselors Assn., Nat. Assn. Sch. Psychologists, Fla. Assn. Sch. Psychologists, Fla. Assn. Sci. Tchrs., Fla. Assn. Counseling and Devel., Am. Sch. Health Assn., Fla. Sch. Health Assn., Phi Delta Kappa. Democrat. Jewish. Home: 9107 NW 83rd St Tamarac FL 33321-1509 Office: Ramblewood Mid Sch 8505 W Atlantic Blvd Pompano Beach FL 33071-7456

MARGELEFSKY, LAURA JEANNE, hospital marketing professional; b. Toledo, Sept. 30, 1962; d. David John and Shirley Janet (McComas) Anaple; m. Gregory Scott Crosby, Aug. 20, 1984 (div. May 1988); m. Michael Peter Margelefsky, May 29, 1993; children: Evan, Eric, Ross. BBA, U. Toledo, 1984, MBA, 1992. Mktg. analyst Riverside Hosp., Toledo, 1984-85, mktg. svcs. coord., 1985-86; dir. mktg. and pub. rels. Lakeside Hosp., Kansas City, Mo., 1987; corp. dir. mktg. U. Health Scis., Kansas City, Mo., 1987-88; asst. dir. pub. rels. St. Luke's Hosp., Maumee, Ohio, 1988-89, physician svcs. coord., 1989—; adj. prof. Bowling Green (Ohio) State U., 1992-93. Tournament chmn. Jamie Farr Kroger Classic, Toledo, 1996. Mem. Am. Coll. Healthcare Execs., Ohio Soc. for Physician Svcs. (founder, pres. 1994-96), Women in Comms. (regional v.p. 1994—, pres. Toledo chpt. 1992-93). Jewish. Home: 5319 Westcroft Dr Sylvania OH 43560 Office: St Luke's Hosp 5901 Monclova Rd Maumee OH 43537

MARGESSON, MAXINE EDGE, professor; b. Cordele, Ga., Aug. 29, 1933; d. Bryant Peak and Maxie (Grantham) Edge; m. Burland Drake Margesson, June 24, 1956; children: Anda Margesson Foxwell, Risa Margesson Carpenter. BS, Bob Jones U., 1958; MEd, SUNY, Buffalo, 1971; EdD, Western Mich. U., 1983. Elem. tchr. Cheektowaga (N.Y.) Cen. Sch. Dist., 1965-72; elem. prin. Grand Rapids (Mich.) Bapt. Acad., 1972-85; reading rsch. Wake Forest U., Winston-Salem, N.C., 1987-90; prof. Piedmont Bible Coll., Winston-Salem, 1985-90; reading specialist Randolph (N.Y.) Ctrl. Sch. Dist., 1990—; bd. dirs. Salem Day Sch., Winston-Salem. Mem. Forsyth County Coalition for Literacy Com. Mem. Assn. for Supervision and Curriculum Devel., Assn. Christian Schs. Internat. Republican. Baptist. Office: Randolph Ctrl Sch Randolph NY 14772

MARGIOTTA, MARY-LOU ANN, software engineer; b. Waterbury, Conn., June 14, 1956; d. Rocco Donato and Louise Antoinette (Carosella) M. AS in Gen. Edn., Mattatuck Community Coll., Waterbury, 1982; BS in Bus. Mgmt., Teikyo Post U., 1983; MS in Computer Sci., Rensselaer Polytech. Inst., 1989. Programmer analyst Travelers Ins. Co., Hartford, Conn., 1985-87; sr. programmer analyst Conn. Bank and Trust Co., East Hartford, Conn., 1987-88; programmer analyst Ingersoll-Rand Corp., Torrington, Conn., 1990-91; sr. programmer analyst Orion Capital Cos. Inc., Farmington, Conn., 1991-92; pres., prin. A.M. Consultants, New Britain, Conn., 1992-95; project leader Travelers Ins. Co., Hartford, 1995—; pres. C++ Spl. Interest Group; bd. dirs. Conn. Object Oriented Users Group. Mem. social action com. St. Helena's Parish, West Hartford, Conn., 1988-95; advisor Jr. Achievement, Waterbury, 1981-83; tutor Traveler's Ins. Co. Tutorial Program, West Hartford, 1986-87; trainer CPR, ARC, Hartford, 1986-87. Clayborn Pell grantee Post Coll., 1982-83, State of Conn. grantee, 1982-83; recipient Citation, Jr. Achievement, 1982; Bd. Trustees scholar Post Coll., 1982-83. Mem. IEEE, Assn. for Systems Mgmt., Assn. Computing Machinery, Toastmasters Internat., Tau Alpha, Beta Gamma. Roman Catholic. Home: 210 Brittany Farms Rd Ste E New Britain CT 06053-1282

MARGO, KATHERINE LANE, physician; b. Buffalo, June 3, 1952; d. Warren Wilson and Virginia (Penney) Lane; m. Geoffrey Myles Margo, Apr. 20, 1980; 1 child, Benjamin; stepchildren: Jenny, Judy. BA, Swarthmore Coll., 1974; MD, SUNY Health Sci. Ctr., Syracuse, 1978. Resident physician St. Joseph's Hosp., Syracuse, 1979-82; attending physician Health Svcs. Assn., Syracuse, 1982-90, asst. med. dir. for quality assurance, 1985-90; asst. prof. family medicine SUNY-HSC at Syracuse, 1990-94; residency faculty Harrisburg (Pa.) Hosp., 1994—; med. dir. Harrisburg Family Practice Ctr., 1996—. Contbr. articles to profl. jours. Bd. of trustees Pt. Choice, Syracuse, 1993-94, Planned Parenthood, Syracuse, 1984-94, Friends of Chamber Music, Syracuse, 1985-94. Mem. Soc. Tchrs. of Family Medicine, Am. Acad. of Family Practitioners (v.p. Syracuse chpt.), Am. Acad. Ortho. Medicine. Home: 4705 Maple Shade Dr Harrisburg PA 17110-3217

MARGOLIN, DEBORAH SUSAN, performance artist, educator, writer; b. N.Y.C., Sept. 8, 1953; d. Harold and Elaine Marjorie (Rose) M.; m. Neal Ira Kirschner, Sept. 3, 1990; children: Bennett Alexander, Molly Cara. BA cum laude, NYU, 1975. Founding mem. Split Britches Theater Co., N.Y.C., 1980—, solo performance artist, 1985—; workshop creator, instr. creative writing Interart Theater, N.Y.C., 1988—; instr. performance composition NYU, N.Y.C., 1994—; artist-in-residence Hampshire Coll., Amherst, Mass., 1989, U. Hawaii, Oahu, 1992. Playwright, 1980—; author: More Monologues for Women, 1996, Out of Character, 1996, Split Britches: Feminist Performance, 1996. Bd. govs. N.Y. Found. for Arts, 1993—. Univ. honors scholar NYU, 1975; performance art fellow N.Y. Found. for Arts, 1990-91. Home: 106 Woodland Rd Montvale NJ 07645

MARGOLIN, JEAN SPIELBERG, artist; b. N.Y.C., Oct. 12, 1926; d. Jack and Ida (Grossman) Spielberg and Bess Liebowitz Spielberg (stepmother); m. Paul Margolin, May 19, 1946 (dec. Mar. 1989). Student, Ind. U., 1951-55, Skowhegan Sch. Painting/Sculp., 1954. tchr. painting and drawing Ind. U., Bloomington, 1954-55; curator group show Pace U. Gallery, N.Y.C., 1984. Paintings exhibited John Herron Art Mus., Indpls., 1952-55, J.B. Speed Art Mus., Louisville, 1953, Cin. Mus. Art, 1955, L.A. County Mus. Art, 1956, A.C.A. Gallery, N.Y.C., 1959-60, Pa. Acad. Fine Arts, Phila., 1962, Heckscher Mus., Huntington, N.Y., 1964, Skowhegan Benefit Exbhn., Nat. Arts Club, N.Y.C., 1974, Arthouse, Storrs, Conn., 1979, Landmark Gallery, N.Y.C., 1980-82, Pace U. Gallery, N.Y.C., 1980, 84, The Artists Choice Mus., Alex Rosenberg Gallery, N.Y.C., 1983; paintings exhibited by appointment only, N.Y.C., 1985—. Recipient 1st prize purchase award for painting Skowhegan Sch. Painting and Sculpture, 1954, scholar, 1954. Home: Apt 12S 4 Washington Sq Village New York NY 10012

MARGOLIS, SYLVIA GANZ, retired secondary education educator; b. Norfolk, Va., Aug. 6, 1910; d. Morris Louis and Pauline (Buch) Margolius; m. Irving H. Ganz, Feb. 23, 1941 (dec. Sept. 1969); 1 child, Marshall Louis; m. Morris D. Margolis, Mar. 30, 1974 (dec. May 1977). AB, Coll. William and Mary, 1932; postgrad., UCLA, Calif. State U., Fresno, U. Calif., Long Beach, Sorbonne, Paris. Cert. tchr., Calif., Va. English tchr. YWCA, Richmond, Va., 1937-40; substitute tchr. Am. Dependents' Schs., Germany, 1946-49; tchr. Fresno City Schs., 1951-53, Kern County Schs., Richland, Calif., 1953-66, L.A. Unified Sch. Dist., 1966-76; mem. State Com., Sacramento, 1964-65; del. Nat. Edn. Assn. to World Conf. of Educators, West Berlin, 1975; lectr. numerous orgns. Bd. mem. YWCA, Bay City, Mich., 1943-46; chair United Nations Day, Bakersfield, Calif., 1960; bd. mem. Jewish Fedn. Coun. L.A., 1968-74; vol. tchr. at local C.C., Northridge, Calif., 1980-81; mem. com. Judaic studies at Coll. William and Mary, Williamsburg, Va., 1983-87. Recipient cert. appreciation Girl Scout Coun., Johnstown, Pa., 1942; Fed. Dept. Edn. grantee Univ. Pitts., 1962. Mem. AAUW (edn. rep. 1978-80, San Fernando Valley br. bd. mem. 1979-84, del. to UN Conf. on Women in Copenhagen 1980), Anti-Defamation League, Hadassah (bd. mem. 1978-85), Bridges for Peace (Am.), Coll. William and Mary Alumni Assn. (mem. com. on Judaic studies 1980s), B'nai Brith Women, Phi Kappa Phi, Tau Kappa Alpha. Democrat. Jewish. Home: 18627 Victory Blvd Reseda CA 91335-6442

MARGULIES, JULIANNA, actress; b. N.Y.C.. Student, Sarah Lawrence Coll. Actress (film) Out for Justice, 1991, (TV) Murder, She Wrote, Law and Order, Homicide, Philly Heat, ER, 1994— (Emmy award for supporting actress Drama, 1995, Golden Globe award nominee, SAG award nominee), (theater) The Substance of Fire, At Home, Fefu and Her Friends, Living Expenses, Dan Drift, and Book of Names. Office: care Cari Ross 335 N Maple Dr Ste 254 Beverly Hills CA 90210*

MARGULIES, LYNNE ELAINE, artist, educator; b. San Fernando, Calif., Feb. 28, 1957; d. Bernard and Mary Elizabeth (Richards) M.; m. James Edward Childers. BFA, Acad. Art Coll., 1995. Ind. film editor L.A., 1980-

84; producer, co-owner Joe Lynne Prodns., San Francisco, 1984-89, Fleet St. Pictures, San Francisco, 1989-91; tchr. Acad. Art Coll., San Francisco, 1995—. Prodr., dir. video documentary I'm From Hollywood, 1989. Home: 128 Ridge Rd Fairfax CA 94930

MARGULIES-EISNER, TONI, academic administrator; b. Bklyn., June 21, 1944; d. Samuel A. and Lillian (Meyer) Margulies; m. Jerry Eisner, Jan. 21, 1973; children: Miriam, Beckah. BS in Edn., SUNY, New Paltz, 1965; MA in Spl. Edn., Columbia U., 1968; EdD in Counseling, U. Miami, Coral Gables, Fla., 1972. Tchr. N.Y.C. Pub. Schs., 1965-68; asst. dean student affairs Fla. Atlantic U. Dade Ctr., Miami Beach, Fla., 1970-72; program officer project devel. divsn. Dade County Cmty. Rels. Bd., Miami, Fla., 1972-73; asst. dir. cultural and human interaction ctr. Fla. Internat. U., Miami, 1973-78, dir. ctrs. and insts., univ. outreach and svcs., 1978-80, dir. grant contracts and personnel sch. edn., 1980-84, dir. office of equal opportunity programs, 1984-92, asst. v.p. office of equal opportunity programs, 1992—; mem. chair Dade County Equal Opportunity Bd., Miami, 1976—; diversity trainer U.S. IRS, Ft. Lauderdale, Fla., 1990; expert witness legal firms within Fla., 1993—. Founding mem. Feminist Alternative, Miami, 1991—. Awarded Toni Eisner Day Metro Dade County gov., Miami, 1987. Office: Equal Opportunity Programs Fla Internat U University Park Miami FL 33199

MARGULIS, LYNN (LYNN ALEXANDER), biologist; b. Chgo., Mar. 5, 1938; d. Morris and Leone (Wise) Alexander; m. Carl Sagan, June 16, 1957; m. Thomas N. Margulis, Jan. 18, 1967; children: Dorion Sagan, Jeremy Sagan, Zachary Margulis, Jennifer Margulis. A.B., U. Chgo., 1957; A.M., U. Wis., 1960; Ph.D., U. Calif., Berkeley, 1965. Mem. faculty Boston U., 1966-88, asst. prof. biology, 1967-71, assoc. prof., 1971-77, prof., 1977-88, Univ. prof., 1986-88; Disting. Univ. prof. U. Mass., Amherst, 1988—; Sherman Fairchild Disting. scholar Calif. Inst. Tech., 1976-77; vis. prof. dept. microbiology U. Autónoma de Barcelona, Spain, 1986, 88; Disting. univ. prof. U. Mass. Author: Origin of Eukaryotic Cells, 1970, Symbiosis in Cell Evolution, 1981, 2d edit., 1993, Early Life, 1982, (with K.V. Schwartz) Five Kingdoms, 1982, 2nd edit., 1988, (with Dorion Sagan) Microcosmos, 1986, (with Dorion Sagan) Origins of Sex, 1986, (with Dorion Sagan), Garden of Microbial Delights, 1988, 2d edit. 1993, (with Dorion Sagan) Biospheres From Earth To Space, 1988, (with Dorion Sagan) Mystery Dance: On the Evolution of Human Sexuality, 1991, (with René Fester) Symbiosis as a Source of Evolutionary Innovation, 1991, (with Lorraine Olendzenski) Environmental Evolution: The effect of the origin and evolution of life on planet Earth, 1992, (with L. Olendezski and H. McKhann) Glossary of Protoctista, 1993; editor:(with René Fester), Global Ecology, 1989, (with others) Handbook of Protoctista, 1990, (with René Fester) Symbiosis as a Source of Evolutionary Innovation: Speciation and Morphogenesis, 1991, What Happens to Trash and Garbage: An Introduction to the Carbon Cycle, 1993, (with Dorion Sagan) What is Life?, 1995; prodr. videos of live microorganisms; contbr. chpts. to books, articles to profl. jours. Guggenheim fellow, 1979. Fellow AAAS; mem. NAS, Soc. Evolutionary Protistology (co-founder). Office: U Mass Biology Dept Morrill Science Ctr Amherst MA 01003

MARIA, DOROTHY CAROLINE, optometrist; b. Salisbury, Md., Jan. 11, 1966; d. Ross Lamonte and Gail Louise (Schmidt) Whealton; m. John Joseph Maria, May 15, 1988. BA, Western Md. Coll., 1988; OD, So. Coll. Optometry, 1992. Lic. optometrist, Tenn., Ohio, Tex; cert. in treatment and mgmt. of ocular disease. Optometrist, asst. chief staff U.S. Army Blanchfield Army Cmty. Hosp., Ft. Campbell, Ky., 1992-95; Clarksville (Tenn.) ctr. dir. Vision Am./Omega, 1995; ind. OD Clarksville, 1995—. Capt. U.S. Army, 1992-95. Decorated Army Achievement medal U.S. Army, 1995. Mem. Am. Optometry Assn., Tenn. Optometry Assn., Armed Forces Optometry Soc., Phi Beta Kappa, Sigma Beta Kappa.

MARICICH, SUZANNE A., advertising, marketing executive; b. New Haven, Sept. 11, 1941; d. Harold Paul and Edwina Ayotte; m. Tom J. Maricich; chldren: Mark, Janet, David. BA, Albertus Magnus Coll., 1963; MA, Moorhead State U., 1971. Mgr. pub. rels. Children's Village Family Svc., Fargo, N.D., 1971-73; dir. pub. rels. Southeast Mental Health and Retardation Ctr., Moorhead, Minn., 1973-75, St. Mary Med. Ctr., Long Beach, Calif., 1976-79, Hoag Meml. Presbyn. Hosp., Newport Beach, Calif., 1979-86; pres. Suzanne Maricich & Assocs., Seal Beach, Calif., 1986—. Account exec. mag. and direct mail campaign, Arthro-Ease, 1987 (Helios award 1988). Recipient Gold Quill award, Internat. Assn. Bus. Communicators, 1986. Mem. Healthcare Pub. Rels. and Mktg. Assn. (bd. dirs. 1987—), Pub. Rels. Soc. Am. (bd.dirs. hosp. sect. 1987—), Orange County Advt. Fedn. (numerous awards). Office: Suzanne Maricich & Assocs 829 Ocean Ave Ste A Seal Beach CA 90740-6604*

MARIE, LINDA, artist, photographer; b. Cheverly, Md., Nov. 8, 1960; d. Thomas Grason Jr. and Rosalinda (Wepf) McWilliams; 1 child, Ann Marie. AA with honors, Cecil C.C., North East, Md., 1991. One-woman shows include Franklin Hall Arts Ctr., Chesapeake City, Md., 1993, Humanities and Arts Gallery-Essex (Md.) C.C., 1993, Widner Art Mus., Chester, Pa., 1996; group exhbns. include Del. Ctr. Contemporary Art, Wilmington, 1991, Md. Fedn. Art, Annapolis, 1991-93, Acad. of Arts, Easton, Md., 1992, Elkton (Md.) Arts Ctr., 1990-92, Md. Gallery East, Havre de Grace, 1992, Chautaqua (N.Y.) Inst., 1992, Washington Project for Arts, 1992, Ward-Nasse Gallery, N.Y.C., 1994, Sinclair C.C., Dayton, Ohio, 1994, AAAS, Washington, 1994-95, ACP, College Park, Md., 1994, B.A.I., Barcelona, Spain, 1996; represented in permanent collections at AAAS, Cecil C.C. Mem. Del. Ctr. Contemporary Arts, Md. Fedn. Art, Cecil County Arts Coun., Alpha Alpha Theta. Home and Studio: 6 Walnut St North East MD 21901

MARIK, KAREN L., manufacturing company executive; b. St. Louis, Sept. 26, 1967; d. Thomas Richard and Donna Jean M. BSBA, U. Mo., 1989. Mgmt. trainee Caterpillar Inc., Peoria, Ill., 1989-90, inventory rsch. analyst inventory mgmt., 1990-92, tng. analyst human resources, 1992-93, graphic artist, pub. affairs asst., 1992-95; mktg. coord. City of Coral Springs, Fla., 1995; graphics prodn. specialist Maritz Mktg. Rsch. Inc., Fenton, Mo., 1996—. Editor: Caterpillar Manifold Newsletter. Coord. United Way Campaign, 1994; bus. cons. Jr. Achievement of Ill., Peoria, 1991, 92; youth counselor Woodland Bapt. Ch., Peoria, 1990. Recipient O'Connor-Carey Bus. award Stephens Coll., 1987. Me. U. Mo. Alumni Assn., Pub. Relations Soc. of Am. Office: Maritz Marketing Research Inc 1297 N Highway Dr Fenton MO 63099

MARINELLI, ADA SANTI, retired government official, real estate broker; b. Borgo a Mozzano, Italy, July 27, 1942; came to U.S., 1953; d. Attilio and Maria Josephine (Biondi) Santi; m. Rudolph Marinelli, July 12, 1964; children: Gina Marie Basile, Marisa Bianca Marinelli Harper. Student, Rivier Coll., 1962-63, George Washington U., 1963; AA with high honors, Prince Georges Community Coll., 1980. Sec. U.S. Post Office, Washington, 1963-70; administrv. sec. U.S. Postal Service, Washington, 1970-80, real estate specialist trainee, 1980-82, realty mgmt. and acquisition analyst, 1982-84; real estate specialist Washington, 1984—; realty mgmt. specialist U.S. Postal Service, Washington, 1989-92; ret., 1992; assoc. broker Century 21 Advantage, Camp Springs, Md., 1992—; assoc. broker Larry Eul Realty, Inc., Camp Springs, 1977-83, Alvin Turner Real Estate Upper Marlboro, Md., 1988-92. Recipient spl. achievement award U.S. Postal Svc., 1987, meritorious award U.S. Postal Svc., 1991. Mem. Fed. Real Property Assn., Alumnae Assn. Rivier Coll., Orsogna Club (pres. Washington, 1975-76). Democrat. Roman Catholic. Home: 7006 Sheffield Dr Temple Hills MD 20748-4149 Office: 6320 Allentown Rd Temple Hills MD 20748-2609

MARINELLI, LYNN M., county official; b. Akron, Ohio, Aug. 4, 1962; d. Michael and Christine (Golonka) Madden; divorced; 1 child, Jessica. BA in English, Daemen Coll., 1985. Pub. rels. coord. Bison Baseball Inc., Buffalo, 1985-86; exec. asst. to Assemblyman William B. Hoyt N.Y. State Assembly, Buffalo, 1986-92; exec. dir. Erie County Commn. on Status of Women, Buffalo, 1992—; chair Erie County Coalition Against Family Violence, 1992-95; co-chair domestic violence com. Multidisciplinary Coordinating Coun., 1992—; mem. adv. bd. Dept. Social Svcs., Erie County, 1992—. Sec. dem. com. Town of Tonawanda, 1991—; active Dem. Jud. Adv. Com. Erie County, 1990—, Reapportionment Com., Erie County, 1991, Ct. Care Project, 1992—, Compass House, Erie County, 1993—, Women for Downtown, 1993—, Citizens Com. on Rape and Sex Assault, 1993—, Leadership Buffalo, 1994, United Way Family Support and Safety, 1994—. Recipient Disting. Svc. award Coalition Against Family Violence, 1992; named Young Careerist, Bus. and Profl. Women, 1991; named to 40 Under Forty list, Bus. First, 1993. Roman Catholic. Office: Erie County Commission on Women 95 Franklin St Rm 1655 Buffalo NY 14202-3904

MARING, MARY MUEHLEN, lawyer; b. Devils Lake, N.D., July 27, 1951; d. Joseph Edward and Charlotte Rose (Schorr) Muehlen; m. David Scott Maring, Aug. 30, 1975; 1 son, Christopher David. B.A. in Polit. Sci. summa cum laude, Moorhead State U., 1972; J.D., U. N.D., 1975. Bar: Minn., N.D. Law clk. Hon. Bruce Stone, Mpls., 1975-76; assoc. Stefanson, Landberg & Alm, Ltd., Moorhead, Minn., 1976-82, Ohnstad, Twichell, Breitling, Rosenvold, Wanner, Nelson, Neugebauer & Maring, P.C., West Fargo, N.D., 1982—; assoc. justice N.D. State Supreme Ct.; women's bd. mem. 1st Nat. Bank, Fargo, 1977-82; career day speaker Moorhead Rotarians, 1980-83. Contbr. note to legal rev.: note editor, N.D. Law Rev., 1975. Mem. ABA (del. ann. conv. young lawyers sect. 1981), Minn. State Bar Assn. (pres. young lawyers sect. 1981-82, bd. govs. 1982-83), Minn. Women Lawyers, N.D. State Bar Assn., Minn. Trial Lawyers, Clay County Bar Assn. (v.p. 1983-84). Roman Catholic. Clubs: Fargo Country, Southgate Racquetball. Office: State Capitol Judicial Wing 1st Fl 600 E Bird Ave Bismarck ND 58505-0530*

MARING, NORMA ANN, military academy administrator; b. Humboldt, Kans., Oct. 1, 1933; d. Edward Simon and Anna Agnes (Friederich) Breiner; m. L. Keith Maring, Dec. 27, 1951 (dec. July 1988); children: Stan, Steve, Scot, Ron. Grad. high sch., Chanute, Kans. Cert. swimming pool operator. Instr. dance, water safety courses Wentworth Mil. Acad., Lexington, Mo., 1968-91, alumni dir., 1979—; operator Chanute Mcpl. Swimming Pool, 1956—; water safety trainer ARC, Kans., Mo., 1969-1996. Bd. dirs., chmn. water safety Neosho County unit ARC, Chanute, 1965-85; pres. Lexington PTA, 1960-64, Lafayette County PTA, 1965-70; active Wentworth-Lexington Cmty. Coun., 1991—. Recipient Disting. Svc. award Nat. ARC, 1982, Employee of the Month, Outstanding Pub. Rels., City of Chanute, 1993, Pub. Cmty. Svc. award, 1993; named 1st hon. alumnus Wentworth Mil. Acad. Alumni Assn., 1992; coll. scholarship in her name given by PTA Coun., Chanute, 1982. Mem. Kans. Swimming Pool Assn., Kans. PTA (hon. life), Wentworth Mil. Acad. Alumni Assn. (sec. coun. 1986—, named 1st hon. mem. 1992), Gen. Fed. Women's Clubs (pres. Lexington 1970-72), Lexington Garden Club (v.p. 1969-70), Am. Contract Bridge League. Roman Catholic. Home: 1622 South St Lexington MO 64067-1432 Office: Wentworth Mil Acad 18th and Washington Sts Lexington MO 64067

MARINI, ELIZABETH ANN, civilian military executive; b. Dubuque, Iowa, Feb. 8, 1940; d. Cletus Nicholas and Catherine Margaret (Blasen) Freiburger; m. John J. Marini, Jan. 12, 1980. BA, Carinal Stritch Coll., 1962; MPA, George Washington U., 1982. Claims examiner Social Security Adminstrn., Chgo., 1962-64; supply systems analyst Navy Electronic Supply Office, Great Lakes, Ill., 1964-67; investment rep. Investors Planning Corp. Am., N.Y.C., 1967; supply systems analyst Naval Electronic Systems Command, Washington, 1968-76, head Saudi naval expansion program, 1976-80, head def. security assistance office internat. program, 1979-80; chief East Asia/Latin Am. divsn. Office of Sec. of Def. Def. Security Assistance Agy., Washington, 1980-84; chief East Asia Pacific divsn. Office of the Sec. of Def., DSAA, Washington, 1984-90; chief arms coop. and policy analysis divsn. Office of the Sec. of Def., Def. Tech. Security Adminstrn., Washington, 1990—. Tchr. religion classes Blessed Sacrament Ch., Alexandria, Va., 1972-73. Mem. Kappa Gamma Pi, Pi Alpha Alpha. Roman Catholic. Office: Def Tech Security Adminstrn 400 Army Navy Dr Arlington VA 22202-2884

MARINO, JOANNE MARIE, psychotherapist, consultant; b. Greenwich, Conn., Feb. 15, 1951; d. Frank Dominic and Matilda (Salvatore) M. B.A., U. Conn., 1973, M.A. in Ednl. Psychology/Rehab. Counseling, 1975. Cert. profl. counselor, Conn.; nat. cert. counselor, cert. clin. mental health counselor. Counselor Ea. Ct. Drug Action Program, Inc., Willimantic Conn., 1974-77; sr. counselor Liberation Programs, Inc., Stamford, Conn., 1977-79, program dir. 1980-83, quality assurance coordinator, 1982-83; gen. practice psychotherapy, cons. counseling and vocat. assessment, 1983-92; clin. coord. Guideline Info. & Referral Phone Line, 1992—. Mem. Am. Counseling Assn., Conn. Counseling, Assn., Ct. Mental Health Counseling Assn., Am. Mental Health Counselors Assn., Assn. Gay, Lesbian and Bisexual Issues in Counseling. Avocations: films, traveling, sports, gardening, reading. Office: The Learning Exch 21 Strickland Rd Cos Cob CT 06807-2727

MARINO, PAMELA ANNE, health sciences administrator; b. Milford, Conn., Feb. 28, 1951; d. Angelo and Christine M. BA in Biology with honors, U. Conn., 1973; PhD in Biomed. Scis., U. Conn., Farmington, 1986. Rsch. assoc., lab. supr. Yale Med. Sch., New Haven, 1973-80; from postdoctoral fellow to sr. staff fellow Nat. Cancer Inst., Bethesda, Md., 1986-93; sr. staff fellow FDA, Bethesda, Md., 1993-94; program dir. Nat. Inst. Gen. Med. Scis., Bethesda, Md., 1994—; chair Minority Opportunities Rsch. divsn. Cmtys. Nat. Inst. Gen. Med. Sci., Bethesda, 1995—. Contbr. articles to profl. jours. Tchr. NIH Sci. Alliance with Pub. Schs., Rockville, Md., 1994—. Conn. State scholar, 1969-73; U. Conn. fellow, 1980-86, Nat. Cancer Soc. fellow, 1986-90; recipient Performance award NIGMS, 1994. Mem. Am. Soc. Biol. Chemists and Molecular Biologists (assoc.), Women in Cancer Rsch. (co-chair mentoring com. 1995-96, chair database com.), Fedn. Am. Socs. Exptl. Biology. Home: Apt 201 17128 King James Way Gaithersburg MD 20877-2219 Office: Nat Inst Gen Med Scis 45 Center Dr Bethesda MD 20892

MARINO, SHEILA BURRIS, education educator; b. Knoxville, Nov. 24, 1947; d. David Paul and Lucille Cora (Maupin) Burris; m. Louis John Marino, Dec. 19, 1969; children: Sheila Noelle, Heather Michelle. BS, U. Tenn., 1969, MS, 1971, EdD, 1976; postgrad., W.Va. U., Europe. Elem./ early childhood tchr. Knoxville City Schs., 1969-71; cooperating tchr. U. Tenn., Knoxville, 1969-71; dir. early childhood edn./tchr. Glenville (W.Va.) State Coll., 1971-72, Colo. Women's Coll., Denver, 1972-73; asst. prof. edn. Lander U., Greenwood, S.C., 1973-75; instr., spl. asst. coordinator of elem./ early childhood edn. U. Tenn., 1975-76; prof. edn., dir. clin. experiences, asst. dean Sch. Edn. Lander U., 1976-95, dean sch. edn., 1993-94; cons. in field; dir. Creative Activities Prog. for Children, Lander U., 1979—; mem. W.Va. Gov.'s Early Childhood Adv. Bd., 1971-72, Gov.'s Team of Higher Edn. Profls. on Comprehensive Plan for S.C. Early Childhood Edn., 1982; moderator Presbytery of Southeast, 1995—. Contbr. articles to profl. jours.; author: International Children's Literature, 1989. Bd. dirs. Greenwood Lit. Coun., v.p., 1990, pres., 1991; bd. dirs. St. Nicholas Speech and Hearing Ctr., Greenwood, pres., 1992; bd. dirs. Old Ninety-Six coun. Girl Scouts U.S.A., 1987-92; vol. March of Dimes Program, Greenwood, 1987. Mem. AAUW (pres. 1990—), AAUP, SNEA (state advisor 1981-88), S.C. Student Edn. Assn., Piedmont Assn. Children and Adults with Learning Disabilities (pres. 1986—, exec. bd.), Learning Disabilities Assn. S.C. (pres. 1990-94), S.C. Edn. Assn., S. C. Assn. for Children Under Six, So. Assn. for Children under Six, S.C. Assn. Tchr. Educators, Piedmont Reading Coun. (v.p. 1985-86, 90-91, pres. 1986-88, 91-92), S.C. Coun. Internat. Reading Assn. (exec. bd. 1986-88, 91—), Delta Kappa Gamma (pres. Epsilon chpt. 1984-88, 92-94, mem. exec. bd.), Pi Lambda Theta, Kappa Delta Pi (pres. U. Tenn. chpt. 1974-75), Phi Delta Kappa (v.p. 1988-90, pres. Lander U. chpt. 1990-91, 94—). Democrat. Presbyterian. Home: 103 Essex Ct Greenwood SC 29649-9561 Office: Lander U Stanley Avenue Greenwood SC 29649

MARINOFF, ISABELLA BLUMENSTOCK, English educator; b. Brussels, Dec. 28, 1946; came to U.S., 1948; d. Abraham Samuel and Ela Blumenstock; m. Philip Sherman Marinoff, July 23, 1972 (dec. Apr. 1993); children: Sarah, Rebecca. BA summa cum laude, Barnard Coll., 1967; MA, Yale U., 1968, PhD, 1980. Cert. English tchr. grades 7-12, N.Y. Lectr. Marymount Manhattan Coll., N.Y.C., 1979-80, Hunter Coll., N.Y.C., 1984-85, Bklyn. Coll., N.Y.C., 1988-91; asst. to coord. acad. devel. and planning Touro Coll., N.Y.C., 1991-95; English tchr. Hebrew Acad. Nassau County, Uniondale, N.Y., 1995—; adj. asst. prof. Kingsborough C.C., N.Y.C., 1990-94; presenter in field. Contbr. articles to profl. jours. Fellow Woodrow Wilson Found., 1967, NDEA Title IV fellow Yale U., 1968. Mem. MLA.

MARION, GAIL ELAINE, reference librarian; b. Bloomington, Ill., May 31, 1952; d. Ralph Herbert and Norma Mae (Crump) Nyberg; m. David Louis Marion, May 13, 1972 (div. Apr. 1983). AA in Liberal Arts, Fla. Jr. Coll., 1976; BA in U.S. History, U. North Fla., 1978; MS in Libr. and Info. Sci., Fla. State U., 1985. Law libr., legal rschr. Mathews Osborne et al, Jacksonville, Fla., 1979-82; reference libr. City of Jacksonville-Pub. Librs., 1982—. With U.S. Army, 1970-72, maj. U.S. Army Res., 1978—, with Fla. Army N.G., 1974-78. Named to Outstanding Young Women of Am., 1985; N.G. Officers Assn. scholar, 1980. Mem. ALA, WAC Vets. Assn., Adj. Gen. Regimental Corps, Res. Officers Assn., Fla. Libr. Assn., Fla. Paleontol. Soc., Jacksonville Gem and Mineral Soc. Republican. Methodist. Home: 3200 Hartley Rd Apt 70 Jacksonville FL 32257-6719 Office: Jacksonville Pub Librs 122 N Ocean St Jacksonville FL 32202-3314

MARION, MARJORIE ANNE, English educator; b. Winterset, Iowa, May 6, 1935; d. Virgil Arthur and Marilyn Ruth (Sandy) Hammon; m. Robert H. Marion, Dec. 20, 1964; 1 dau., Kathryn Ruth. BA, Colo. Coll., 1958; MA, Purdue U., 1969; postgrad., Inst. Mgmt. Lifelong Edn. Harvard U., 1981. Chairperson English dept. Lincoln-Way High Sch., New Lenox, Ill., 1964-68; dir. pub. rels. Coll. St. Francis, Joliet, Ill., 1968-70, chairperson English dept., 1971-75, chairperson div. humanities and fine arts, 1975-79, coord. instructional devel., 1979-80, dir. continuing edn., 1980-84, acting v.p. for acad. affairs, 1984-85, dean of faculty, 1985-89, assoc. prof. English, 1989—; dir. Freshman Core Program, 1993-95; dir. Writing Ctr., 1996; mem. vis. team North Cen. Assn., Joliet & Lockport, Ill, 1975-79; lectr. at ednl. workshops and insts.; TV and radio appearances regarding lifelong edn., Chgo., St. Louis, Albuquerque, Pheonix, 1982-85. Drama critic Joliet Herald News, 1970-82. Recipient Pres.'s award Coll. St. Francis, 1975. Mem. Am. Assn. Higher Edn., Nat. Coun. Tchrs. of English. Roman Catholic.

MARISOL (MARISOL ESCOBAR), sculptor; b. Paris. Ed., Ecole des Beaux-Arts, Paris, 1949, Art Students League, N.Y.C., 1950, New Sch. for Social Research, 1951-54, Hans Hofmann Sch., N.Y.C., 1951-54; DFA (hon.), Moore Coll. Arts, Phila., 1969, R.I. Sch. Design, 1986, SUNY, Buffalo, 1992. One-woman shows include Leo Castelli Gallery, 1958, Stable Gallery, 1962, 64, Sidney Janis Gallery, N.Y.C., 1966, 67, 73, 75, 81, 84, 89, Hanover Gallery, London, 1967, Moore Coll. Art, Phila., 1970, Worcester (Mass.) Art Mus., 1971, N.Y. Cultural Center, 1973, Columbus (Ohio) Gallery of Fine Arts, 1974, Makler Gallery, Phila., 1982, Boca Raton Mus. Art, Fla., 1988, Galerie Tokoro, Tokyo, 1989, Hasagawa Gallery, Tokyo, 1989, Nat. Portrait Gallery, Washington, 1991, Marlborough Gallery, 1995, Hakone Open Air Mus., Kanagawa, Japan, 1995, Mus. Modern Art, Shiga, Japan, 1995, Iwai City Art Mus., Fukushima, Japan, 1995, Kagoshima City (Japan) Mus. Art, 1995, numerous others; exhibited in group shows including Painting of a Decade, Tate Gallery, London, 1964, New Realism, Municipal Mus., The Hague, 1964, Carnegie Internat., Pitts., 1964, Art of the U.S.A., 1670-1966, Whitney Mus. Am. Art, N.Y.C., 1966, American Sculpture of the Sixties, Mus. of Art, Los Angeles, 1967, Biennale, Venice, 1968, Art Inst. Chgo., 1968, Boymans-van Beuningen Mus., Rotterdam, The Netherlands, 1968, Inst. Contemporary Art, London, 1968, Fondation Maeght, Paris, 1970, Hirshhorn Mus. and Sculpture Garden, 1984, Nat. Portrait Gallery, Washington, 1987, Heckscher Mus., Huntington, N.Y., 1987, Whitney Mus. at Philip Morris, N.Y.C., 1988, Rose Art Mus., Waltham, Mass., 1990, Nat. Portrait Gallery, London, 1993; represented in permanent collections at Mus. Modern Art, N.Y.C., Whitney Mus. Am. Art, Albright-Knox Gallery, Buffalo, Hakone Open Air Mus., Tokyo, Nat. Portrait Gallery, Washington, Harry N. Abrams Collection, N.Y.C., Yale U. Art Gallery, Art Inst. Chgo., Met. Mus., N.Y.C., numerous others; pub. installation Am. Mcht. Mariner's Meml., Promenade Battery Pk. Pier A., Port of N.Y., N.Y.C. Mem. Am. Acad. and Inst. Arts and Letters (v.p. art 1984-87). Address: Marlborough Gallery 40 W 57th St New York NY 10019-4001

MARJERRISON, MARY KATHRYN, artist, educator; b. Ellensburg, Wash., Nov. 14, 1951; d. Charles Ray and Dora Mary (Beach) Haight; m. Robert Matthew Marjerrison, Oct. 4, 1986; children: Amanda Clarke, Autumn, Jessica, Heidi Clarke. AA, Wenatchee Valley Coll., 1976; BA, Ctrl. Wash. U., 1979, MA, 1982. Orthodontic asst. Gary Miller, DMD, Vancouver, Wash., 1971-74; instr. early childhood edn. Ctr. Wash. U., Ellensburg, 1979-80; first grade tchr. Selah (Wash.) Pub. Schs., 1980-82; tchr. grades 3 and 4 Ellensburg (Wash.) Schs., 1982-87, tchr. talented and gifted, 1987-96, tchr. middle sch. art, 1996—; adj. prof. Ctrl. Wash. U., 1980-90; artist, bus. owner Lookout Mtn. Studios, Ellensburg, 1994—. curriculum writer Wash. State Office for Supt. Pub. Instrn., 1983-85, 96; chair regional Gifted Task Force, Yakima, Wash., 1991-93, mem., 1989-96. Mem. ASCD, Wash. Assn. Edn. Talented & Gifted (state bd. dirs. 1993-95), Phi Delta Kappa.

MARK, LILLIAN GEE, private parochial school administrator; b. Berkeley, Calif., Mar. 18, 1932; d. Pon Gordon and Sun Kum (Wong) Gee; m. Richard Muin Mark, June 20, 1954; children: Dean, Kim, Faye, Glenn, Lynne. AB in Psychology, U. Calif., Berkeley, 1954; MS in Christian Sch. Adminstrn., Pensacola Coll., 1987. Founder, prin. Alpha Beacon Christian Sch., San Carlos, Calif., 1976—; chief exec. officer Alpha Beacon Christian Ministries. Author: Handbook for Parents and Students, 1983, How to Encourage Your Staff. Mem. Christian Ministries, Assn. Christian Schs. Internat., Internat. Fellowship Christian Sch. Adminstrs. Republican. Avocations: tennis, swimming, piano, Bible study. Home: 384 Montserrat Dr Redwood City CA 94065 Office: Alpha Beacon Christian Ministries 750 Dartmouth Ave San Carlos CA 94070-1709

MARK, MARSHA YVONNE ISMAILOFF, artistic director; b. Bridgeport, Conn., Mar. 15, 1938; d. Nicholas and Louba (Foullon) Ismailoff; m. Robert Louis Mark, June 25, 1960; children: Robert, William, Staci. Ballet tng. with, George Balanchine, 1946-50, George Volodine, 1945-60, 65-69; student, Skidmore Coll., 1978-80, Vaganova Method Sch., Minsk, USSR, 1983, U. of the Arts, 1990. Founder Marsha Imailoff Mark Sch. of Ballet, Newtown, Conn., 1969—; artistic dir. Com. for Ballet Miniatures, Newtown, Conn., 1974—, Malenkee Ballet Repertoire Co., Newtown, Conn., 1980—; v.p. Cmty. Arts Project Ext., Newtown, 1987-91; artistic dir. Danbury (Conn.) Music Ctr., 1989; instr. for neurologically impaired Ripton Sch., Shelton, Conn., 1992; choreographed section of Nutcracker Ballet for Special Children; toured Russia with Malenkee Ballet Repertoire Co. Choreographer including original works: Mademoiselle Angot, 1974, Circus, 1975, Haydn Concerto, 1976, Evening at the Zoo, 1977, Match Girl, 1978, The Four Seasons, 1979, Malenkee Waltz, 1980, Magic Key, 1981, Midsummer Night's Dream, 1982, Macbeth A Witches Haunt, 1983, Etudes, 1984, Toy Boutique, Etudes, 1985, Under the Sea, 1986, Nutcracker, 1987, 88, 89, 90, 91, 92, 93, 94, 95, Mere, Mere, Mere, 1988, Ellis Island Memoirs, 1991, Moonlight Etudes, 1992, Echoes of Soft Thunder, 1995; premiered in Baku USSR. Hostess for artists from Russia, translator UN Hostess Com., N.Y.C., 1988; Russian translator Friends of Music, Newtown, 1990, Sacred Heart U., Fairfield, Conn., 1994. Home: 57 Mount Pleasant Rd Newtown CT 06470-1530

MARKEE, KATHERINE MADIGAN, librarian, educator; b. Cleve., Feb. 24, 1931; d. Arthur Alexis and Margaret Elizabeth (Madigan) M. AB, Trinity Coll., Washington, 1953; MA, Columbia U., 1962; MLS, Case Western Res. U., 1968. Employment mgr., br. store tng. supr. The May Co., Cleve., 1965-67; assoc. prof. libr. sci., data bases libr. Purdue U. Libr., West Lafayette, Ind., 1968—. Contbr. articles to profl. jours. Mem. ALA, AAUP, Spl. Librs. Assn., Ind. Online Users Group, Sigma Xi (Rsch. Support award 1986). Office: Purdue U Libr West Lafayette IN 47907-1530

MARKGRAF, ROSEMARIE, real estate broker; b. Grantsburg, Wis., Oct. 31, 1934; d. Helen Elizabeth Pribil. BS, U. Wis., 1957, MS, 1958. Cert. educator;. Tchr. High Schs., Wis., Conn, 1958-61; office mgr. Robert S. Palmer, Middletown, Conn., 1962-64; edn. adv. Girl Scouts U.S.A., N.Y.C., 1964-66; community relation assoc. Motion Picture Assn. Am., N.Y., 1967-69; mgr. The Chateau Inn, Stamford, N.Y., 1970-78; real estate salesman Atkins Realty, Ltd., Bklyn., 1979-80; real estate broker, prin. The Markgraf Group, Ltd., Bklyn., 1980—; cons. Real Estate Counseling Group Conn., Storrs, 1963-91; pres. Tuff Transport, Inc., 1977—; adj. prof. Real Estate Inst., 1995-96. Mem. Real Estate Bd. N.Y., Steuben Soc., C. of C. Roman Catholic. Home: 60 Remsen St Brooklyn NY 11201-3453 Office: The Markgraf Group Ltd 144 Montague St Brooklyn NY 11201-3505

MARKHAM, CAROLE PILLSBURY, medical-surgical nurse educator; b. Beaumont, Tex., Aug. 18, 1951; d. Walter Earl and Leatrice Joy (Wall) P.; divorced; children: Ryan Vance, Reed Taylor. AS, Tyler Jr. Coll., 1972; diploma of nursing, Tex. Ea. Sch. of Nursing, 1973; BSN, U. Tex., Tyler, 1993. RN, Tex. Charge nurse, staff nurse Meth. Hosp., Houston, 1973-79; mem. staff emergency dept. Baylor U. Med. Ctr., Dallas, 1979-80; heart catheter nurse Schumpert Med. Ctr., Shreveport, La., 1989-91; mem. staff emergency dept. Mother Frances Hosp., Tyler, Tex., 1992-93, med.- surg. nurse educator, 1993—; staff devel. educator, 1995—; chair Nurse Oncology Edn. Program, 1994. Charter mem. La. Child Passenger Safety, Shreveport, 1983-87; sustainor Jr. League of Shreveport. Mem. AAUW, ANA, Tex. Nurse Assn. (dist. 19), Emergency Nurse Assn., Sigma Theta Tau. Presbyterian. Home: 4920 Pine Knoll St Tyler TX 75703-2624 Office: Trinity Mother Frances Health Sys 800 E Dawson St Tyler TX 75701-2036

MARKHAM, SISTER M(ARIA) CLARE, chemistry educator, educational director; b. New Haven, Aug. 12, 1919; d. James J. and Agnes V. Markham. BA in Chemistry, St. Joseph Coll., West Hartford, Conn., 1940, DHL, 1989; PhD in Chemistry, Cath. U. Am., 1952. Instr. Sacred Heart High Sch., Waterbury, Conn., 1945-49; prof. chemistry St. Joseph Coll., West Hartford, 1952—, chair sci. div., 1960-70, dean grad. div., 1980-87, asst. to pres., acad. affairs, 1987-91, dir. instl. rsch., 1992-95, prof. chemistry emerita, 1996—; experimentation chair Sisters of Mercy, West Hartford, 1969-73, councilor, 1969-77. Editor: (sci. series) Elementary Science & Living in Today's World, 1965; contbr. articles to profl. jours. Under sec. of energy Office of Policy and Mgmt. of Conn., Hartford, 1977-79. Fellow Sci. Faculty, Trondheim, Norway, 1967, U. Calif., Berkeley, 1967-68; recipient Travel award Madras India, Consulting Scientist, U.S. Fgn. Currency Program, 1975-77, Hon. degree Humane Letters, St. Joseph Coll., 1990, Excellence in Equity award, AAUW, 1992. Mem. AAAS, Am. Chem. Soc. (nat. councilor 1968, 80, chmn. Conn. valley sect. 1974, 77), Conn. Acad. Sci. and Engring. (founding, chair nominating com. 1973, chair tech. bd. on energy prodn. and conservation 1995-96), Sigma Xi (pres. 1992-93). Democrat. Roman Catholic. Home and Office: Saint Joseph College 1678 Asylum Ave West Hartford CT 06117-2764

MARKLE, CHERI VIRGINIA CUMMINS, nurse; b. N.Y.C., Nov. 22, 1936; d. Brainard Lyle and Mildred (Schwab) Cummins; m. John Markle, Aug. 26, 1961 (dec. 1962); 1 child, Kellianne. RN, Ind. State U. and Union Hosp., 1959; BS in Rehab. Edn., Wright State U., 1975; BSN, Capital U., 1987; postgrad. in nursing adminstrn., Wright State U., 1987-89; MS, Calif. Coll. Health Sci. Administration, 1994; postgrad., Columbia Pacific U., 1996—. Cert. clin. hypnotherapist Nat. Guild Hypnotherapists. Coordinator Dayton (Ohio) Children's Psychiat. Hosp., 1962-75; dir. nursing Stillwater Health Ctr., Dayton, 1975-76; rehab. cons. Fairborn, Ohio, 1976-91; sr. supr. VA, Dayton, 1977-85, nurse coord. alcohol rehab., 1985-86; DON Odd Fellows, Springfield, Ohio, 1987-88, Miami Christel Manor, Miamisburg, Ohio, 1988—; DON, rehab. cons. NMS Tng. Sys., Dayton, 1989-91; psychiat. unit nurse VA Med. Ctr., N.Y. Rheab., 1991, mem. com. women vets., 1991-93; advisor Calif. Coll. Health Sci. Newspaper columnist Golden Times, Clark County. Bd. dirs. Temple Universal Judaism. 1st lt. USAF, 1959-61; advisor Calif. Coll. Health Sci. Mem. ANA (cert. adminstrn. 1983, cert. gerontology 1984), NAFE, AAUW, Nat. Rehab. Nursing Soc., Nurse Mgrs. Assembly, Gerontol. Nurse Assembly, Rehab. Soc., Nat. Guild Hypnotherapists, Internat. Assn. Counselors and Therapists, Wright State U. Alumni Assn., Am. Legion, Women's City Club N.Y., Gilbert & Sullivan Soc., Internat. Consortium Parse Scholars, Alpha Sigma Alpha, Sigma Theta Tau. Democrat. Jewish. Office: VA Med Ctr 423 E 23rd St New York NY 10010-5050

MARKOVICH, PATRICIA, economist; b. Oakland, Calif.; d. Patrick Joseph and Helen Emily (Prydz) Markovich; BA in Econs., MS in Econs., U. Calif.-Berkeley; postgrad. (Lilly Found. grantee) Stanford U., (NSF grantee) Oreg. Grad. Rsch. Ctr.; children: Michael Sean Treece, Bryan Jeffry Treece, Tiffany Helene Treece. Cert. Emergency Mgmt. Planner. pub. rels. Pettler Advt., Inc.; pvt. practice polit. and econs. cons.; aide to majority whip Oreg. Ho. of Reps.; lectr., instr., various Calif. instns., Chemeketa (Oreg.) Coll., Portland (Oreg.) State U.; commr. City of Oakland (Calif.), 1970-74; chairperson, bd. dirs. Cable Sta. KCOM; mem. gen. plan commn. City of Piedmont, Calif.; mem. Oakland Mus. Archives of Calif. Artists. Mem. Internat. Soc. Philos. Enquiry, Mensa (officer San Francisco region), Bay Area Artists Assn. (coord., founding mem.), Berkeley Art Ctr. Assn., San Francisco Arts Commn. File, Calif. Index for Contemporary Arts, Pro Arts, YLEM: Artists Using Sci. and Tech., NAFE, No. Calif. Pub. Ednl. and Govt. Access Cable TV Com. (founding), Triple Nine Soc., Nat. Coord. Coun. Emergency Mgmt., Am. Econs. Assn., Allied Social Scis. Assn., N.Y. Acad. Scis.

MARKOWITZ, PHYLLIS FRANCES, mental health services administrator, psychologist; b. Malden, Mass., Sept. 2, 1931; d. Abraham and Rose (Kaplan) Kalishman: children: Gary Keith, Carol Diane Donnelly. AB, Harvard U., 1972, EdM, 1974; EdD, Boston U., 1987. Lic. psychologist; lic., cert. social worker, Mass.; cert. sch. psychologist, secondary English and social studies tchr., Mass. Rsch. asst. Boston Coll., Newton, Mass., 1971-73; social worker Combined Jewish Philanthropies, Boston, 1973-74; instr. Harvard U., Cambridge, Mass., 1974-75, counselor, 1974-79; supr. Dept. Social Svcs., Newton and Marlborough, Mass., 1979 88; area dir. case mgmt. and tng., 1988-94, area coord. medically-mentally ill, 1988—, chair consumer/family empowerment project, 1992—; area dir. Svcs. Integration, 1994-95; project dir. Sup. Employment Svcs., 1994-95; area dir. Clin. Svcs., 1995—; area Ams. with Disabilities coord. Dept. Mental Health, Boston, 1995—; instr. human devel. U. Mass., Boston, 1990—. Grantee Radcliffe Inst., 1972; recipient Rsch. scholar award Boston U., 1981-82. Mem. APA, Mass. Psychol. Assn. Office: Dept Mental Health 20 Vining St Boston MA 02115-6115

MARKOWSKA, ALICJA LIDIA, neuroscientist, researcher; b. Warsaw, Poland, Aug. 22, 1948; came to U.S., 1986; d. Marian Boleslaw and Eugenia Krystyna (Wodzynska) Pawlak; m. Janusz Jozef Markowski, Oct. 23, 1971; children: Marta Agnieszka, Michal Jacek. BA, MSc, Warsaw U., 1971; PhD, Nencki Inst., Warsaw, 1979. Postdoctoral fellow Nencki Inst., 1979-81, asst. prof., 1981-86; assoc. rschr. Johns Hopkins U., Balt., 1987-91, rsch. scientist, 1991-92, prin. rsch. sci., prof., 1992-94, head of neuromnemonic lab., 1994—; vis. fellow Czechoslovak Acad. Sci., Prague, 1981; rschr., lectr. U. Bergen, Norway, 1983; vis. faculty Johns Hopkins U., 1986-87; cons. Sigma Tau & Otsuka Co., Italy, Japan, 1990-92. Reviewer Neurobiology of Aging, 1992—, Behavioral Brain Rsch., 1992—' contbr. chpts. to Preoperative Events, 1989, Prospective on Cognitive Neuroscience, 1990, Encyclopedia of Memory, 1992, Neuropsychology of Memory, 1992, Methods in Behavioral Pharmacology, 1993. Grantee Nat. Inst. Age, 1993—, NSF, 1990-93, NIH, 1992—. Mem. AAAS, Soc. for Neuroscience, Internat. Brain Rsch., N.Y. Acad. Sci. Home: 1301 Kingsbury Rd Owings Mills MD 21117-1343 Office: Johns Hopkins U 34th Charles St Baltimore MD 21218

MARKS, ANN THRASHER, secondary and special education educator; b. Palo Alto, Calif., Feb. 2, 1946; d. J. Fred and Elizabeth (Chastain) Thrasher; m. Robert E. Marks, July 26, 1980; children: Bobby, Keith, Jared, Beth, Katie. BS, U. So. Miss., 1968; MA, U. Ala., Tuscaloosa, 1970, EdS, 1973. Tchr. Jefferson County Bd. Edn., Birmingham, Ala., 1968-70, Homewood (Ala.) Bd. Edn., 1970-71, Ctr. for Devel. and Learning Disorders, Birmingham, 1971-72; ednl. specialist Child Devel. Ctr., Mobile, Ala., 1972-73; ednl. specialist Albert P. Brewer Devel. Ctr., Mobile, 1973, coord. insvc. tng., 1973-76, dir. edn. and tng., 1976-80; tchr. home econs. and spl. edn. Tuscaloosa County Bd. Edn., Tuscaloosa, 1980-95; ret., 1995; ind. rep. Excel Telecoms., 1995—. Mem. Kappa Delta Pi. Home: 2008 Antietam Ave Tuscaloosa AL 35406-1729 Office: Excel Telecoms PO Box 650582 Dallas TX 75265-0582

MARKS, CAROL PAGE, nurse; b. Jackson, Miss., Dec. 13, 1961; d. Simon Seelig and Rose (Walley) M. BSN, U. Miss., 1983. RN., Miss.; cert. BLS, ACLS. Staff nurse U. Miss. Med. Ctr., 1983; commd. officer USN, 1984, advanced through grades to lt., 1987; staff nurse US Naval Hosp., Groton, Conn., 1984-87, Bethesda, Md., 1987-89; resigned, 1989; travel nurse, 1989-92; staff nurse surg. ICU, Tulane U. Hosp. and Clinic, New Orleans, 1992-93; staff nurse post anesthesia care unit Touro Infirmary, New Orleans, 1993-94; staff nurse CCU, VA Med. Ctr., New Orleans, 1994—. Mem. AACN, Sigma Theta Tau, Pi Beta Phi. Republican. Roman Catholic.

MARKS, FLORENCE CARLIN ELLIOTT, nursing informaticist; b. Louisville, Ky., Oct. 15, 1928; d. David Carlin and Anna Marie (Lance) Elliott; m. George Edward Marks, Mar. 18, 1961; children: Mary Ellen Marks Fox, Ruth Ann, Charles Douglas. BS in Chemistry, Zoology, U. Cin., 1949; BSN, U. Minn., 1953, M of Nursing Adminstrn., 1956. RN, Minn. From staff nurse to asst. head nurse U. Minn. Hosps., Mpls., 1953-54; staff nurse Marseilisbog Hosp., Aarhaus, Denmark, 1954-55; nursing supr. U. Minn. Hosps., Mpls., 1956-61, spl. asst. to dir. of nursing svc., 1962; rsch. asst. Hill Family Found. Nursing Rsch. Project, Mpls., 1966-69; writer U. Minn. Sch. of Nursing, Mpls., 1976; cons. U. Minn. Sch. of Nursing, 1976, 1978; nursing program specialist Hennepin County Med. Ctr., Mpls., 1978-84, nursing info. systems dir., cons., 1987—; nursing utilization system coord. U. Minn. Hosps., Mpls., 1984-87; cons. Creative Nursing Mgmt., 1992—; speaker, lectr. various nursing confs. in U.S. Contbr. articles to profl. publs., chpts. to profl. books, posters, abstracts; co-author: (with Joan Williams) (TV series) TLC, 1953 (McCall's award 1954); editor: Tomorrow's Nurse, 1960-62; Minn. Nursing Accent (commemorative issue 60th anniversary) May, 1965. Prin. flutist St. Anthony Civic Orch., 1975—, bd. dirs., 1988-92, adminstrv. bd. Hennepin Ave. United Meth. Ch., 1974-77, tchr., 1966-83 intermittently, cmty. outreach ministry, chair adv. com., 1992-95; mem. U. Minn. Sch. Nursing Densford Recognition Com., 1992-96; troop leader Mpls. coun. Girl Scouts USA, 1971-85, bd. dirs., 1977-79, svc. unit mgr., 1973-77; den leader Cub Scouts Webelo den, Viking coun. Boy Scouts Am., 1977-79; v.p. Wilshire Park PTSA, 1975-76, pres., 1976-77. Recipient Thanks Badge Greater Mpls. Girl Scout Coun. Mem. Minn. Nurses Assn. (various coms., bd. dirs. 1959-61), Minn. League for Nursing, Minn. Heart Assn. (profl. edn. com. 1959-61), Nursing Info. Discussion Group (chmn. Twin City program com. 1985-91, 95—), U. Minn. Sch. Nursing Alumni Assn. (bd. dirs. 1963-67, pres. 1965-66), Mortar Bd., Zeta Tau Alpha, Tau Beta Sigma, Sigma Theta Tau (bd. dirs. Zeta chpt. 1969-73, 89-91, pres. 1972-73, heritage com. 1990). Home: 3424 Silver Lake Rd NE Minneapolis MN 55418-1605

MARKS, JENNIFER, surveyor, consultant; b. Quontico, Va., Nov. 4, 1961; d. Anthony Michael and Ellen Mary (Regan) M.; m. Paul Francisco Muniz, July 7, 1990; 1 child, Alexander Philip Muniz. BA in Geology, Boston U., 1983. Registered land surveyor, Conn., Mass. ROD person, drafter R.F. Sarko & Assocs., Madison, Wis., 1983-84; crew chief Flaherty Giavara Assocs., New Haven, 1984-85, Des Lauriers & Assocs., Stoughton, Mass., 1985-87; br. mgr. Des Lauriers & Assocs., Sturbridge, Mass., 1987-89; crew chief, survey coord. Associated Surveys, Branford, Conn., 1989-92; dept. mgr. Barakos-Landino Design Group, Hamden, Conn., 1992—. Bd. dirs. Hotchkiss Grove Shore Dist., Branford, 1996. Mem. Am. Congress Surveying & Mapping, Conn. Assn. Land Surveyrs (dir. New Haven 1995—), Mass. Assn. Land Surveyors & Civil Engrs., South Ctrl. Conn. Proprietors Coun. Home: 12 Fourth Ave Branford CT 06405 Office: Barakos-Landino Design Group 2911 Dixwell Ave Hamden CT 06518

MARKS, JOAN FLORENCE, social worker; b. N.Y.C., Apr. 1, 1945; d. Alfred and Ellen Josephine (Strauss) Kallos; m. Stephen Roy Marks, June 13, 1965; children: Peter Jay, Andrew Eric. BA, Clark U., 1965; MSW, Simmons Coll., 1968. Diplomate in social work; lic. clin. social worker; ACSW. Rehab. social worker Ea. Maine Med. Ctr., Bangor, 1974-75; outpatient clinician Cmty. Health and Counseling Ctr., Bangor, 1975-78; staff counselor U. Maine, Orono, 1978-79; lic. ind. practice social worker Turning Point, Bangor, 1978—; co-dir. Axis Cons. and Tng., Austin, Tex., 1995—; clin. cons. Families and Children Together, Bangor, 1995—, Good Samaritan Agy., Bangor, 1995—, Maine Child Welfare Tng. Inst., Augusta, 1995—. Co-founder steering com. Rape Crisis Ctr., Bangor, 1972-77; mem. steering com. Spruce Run Women's Shelter, Bangor, 1977-85; vol. Maine Won't Discriminate, Bangor, 1994-95. Mem. NASW, Acad. Cert. Social Workers, Group Explorations Inst., Acad. Family Mediators. Home: 21 Grove St Orono ME 04473 Office: Axis Cons and Tng Ste One 96 Harlow St Bangor ME 04401

MARKS, KAREN ANNETTE SPEECE (KAREN A. SPEECE), management consultant; b. Novato, Calif., Nov. 17, 1956; d. Robert G. and Irene B. (Erickson) Speece; m. John (Pixley) Marks, Nov. 23, 1985; children: Allison, Jordan. BA, U. No. Iowa, 1978; MS, San Francisco State U., 1984. Editor Americas Beh. Rsch. Corp., San Francisco, 1979-81; orgn. devel. cons. Levi Strauss & Co., San Francisco, 1981-84; sr. orgn. devel. cons. Mervyns, Hayward, Calif., 1985-87, dist. pers. mgr., 1987-89; mgmt. cons., prin. self-employed Novato, Calif., 1989—; sch. adminstr. Good Shepherd Luth. Sch., Novato, Calif., 1996-97. Editor: (book) Handbook for Women Scholars, 1980. Pres. sch. bd. Good Shepherd Sch., Novato, 1992-95. Mem. Bay Area Orgn. Devel. Democrat. Lutheran. Home and Office: 200 Adams St Novato CA 94947

MARKS, LILLIAN SHAPIRO, secretarial studies educator, author; b. Bklyn., Mar. 16, 1907; d. Hayman and Celia (Merowitz) Shapiro; m. Joseph Marks, Feb. 21, 1932; children: Daniel, Sheila Blake, Jonathan. BS, NYU, 1928. High sch. tchr., N.Y.C., 1929-30; tchr. Evalina de Rothschild Sch., Jerusalem, Palestine, 1930-31; social worker United Jewish Aid, Bklyn., 1931-32; tchr. Richmond Hill High Sch., 1932-40, Andrew Jackson High Sch., Cambria Heights, N.Y., 1940-71; mem. faculty New Sch. Social Rsch., N.Y.C., 1977-87; staff Vassar Summer Inst., 1946; vol. tchr. English Israel schs., 1987—. Am. editor: Teeline, A System of Fast Writing, 1970; author: College Teeline, 1977, College Teeline Self-Taught, 1983, Touch Typing Made Simple, 1985; contbr. articles to profl jours. Mem. Am. Fedn. Tchrs. Democrat. Home and Office: 11716 Park Ln S Kew Gardens NY 11418-1021

MARKS, LINDA BEATRICE, land surveyor; b. Trenton, N.J., Jan. 15, 1959; d. Wallace Bertram Marks and Mary Sue Schultz. AAS in Civil Engring. Tech., Mercer County C.C., 1979, surveying tech. cert., 1983. Lic. profl. land surveyor, N.J., Pa. Engring. technician Van Note-Harvey Assn., Princeton, N.J., 1979-85; survey technician Goldenbaum Assocs., Lambertville, N.J., 1985-86; project mgr. Robert Buda Assocs., Lawrenceville, N.J., 1986-89; v.p., surveyor, co-owner Land Map, Inc., Hamilton Square, N.J., 1989—. Mem. Nat. Soc. Profl. Surveyors, Profl. Land Surveyors of N.J. (sec., dir. 1987-96). Office: Land Map Inc 3694 Nottingham Way Hamilton Square NJ 08690

MARKS, LISA DIANE, fashion marketing executive; b. L.A., Nov. 10, 1961; d. Robert Benjamin and Jacqueline (Stern) M. BS in Bus. Adminstrn., Marketing, C.S. Dominguez Hills, Carson, Calif., 1989; AA in Fashion Design, Fashion Inst. Design & Merchandising, L.A., 1981; attended, Ariz. State U., Tempe, 1979-80, El Camino C.C., Torrance, Calif., 1985-87. Graphic designer Artwear, Manhattan Beach, Calif., 1981-82; asst. fashion designer Yves Daniel Paris, 1982-84; fashion designer First Glance, L.A., 1984-86; coord. retail devel., mktg. comms. L.A. Gear, Santa Monica, Calif., 1989-94; dir. retail mktg. Skechers U.S.A., Inc., Manhattan Beach, Calif., 1994—. Democrat. Jewish. Home: 44 10th Ct Hermosa Beach CA 90254 Office: Sketchers USA Inc 228 Manhattan Beach Blvd Manhattan Beach CA 90266

MARKS, MARTHA ALFORD, author; b. Oxford, Miss., July 27, 1946; d. Truman and Margaret Alford; m. Bernard L. Marks, Jan. 27, 1968. BA, Centenary Coll., 1968; MA, Northwestern U., 1972, PhD, 1978. Tchr. Notre Dame High Sch. for Boys, Niles, Ill., 1969-74; teaching asst. Northwestern U., Evanston, Ill., 1974-78, lectr., lang. coord., 1978-83; asst. prof. Kalamazoo (Mich.) Coll., 1983-85; writer Riverwoods, Ill., 1985—; cons. WGBH Edn. Found., Boston, 1988-91, Am. Coun. on the Tchg. of Fgn. Langs., 1981-92, Ednl. Testing Svcs., 1988-90, Peace Corps., 1993. Co-author: Destinos: An Introduction to Spanish, 1991, Al corriente, 1989, 93, Que tal?, 1986, 90; author: (workbook) Al corriente, 1989, 93; contbr. articles to profl. jours. Mem. Lake County (Ill.) Bd., Forest Preserve Commn., 1992—, Lake County Conservation Alliance; vice chmn. Friends of Ryerson Conservation Area Bd.; co-founder, pres. Rep Am., Reps. for Environ. Protection. Home: 2940 Cherokee Ln Riverwoods IL 60015-1609 Office: County Bd Office County Bldg Rm 1001 18 N County St Waukegan IL 60085-4304

MARKS, SARA MARIE, military officer; b. Jackson, Miss., Dec. 16, 1960; d. Simon S. and Rose Marks. BSN, U. Miss., 1983; MA in Orgnl. Mgmt., U. Phoenix, 1993; MSN, U. San Diego, 1996. Cert. ACLS instr., PALS instr., BLS instr. Commd. ensign USN, 1983, advanced through grades to lt. comdr., 1993; staff nurse Naval Hosp., Beaufort, S.C., 1983-86, Portsmouth, Va., 1986-88; asst. charge nurse labor and delivery, staff nurse emergency rm. Naval Hosp., Okinawa, Japan, 1988-90; instr., acad. advisor Naval Sch. Health Scis., San Diego, 1991-93; instr. U. San Diego, 1994-95; dept. head family practice and pediat. clinics Naval Hosp., Lemoore, Calif., 1996—, dept. head health promotions, health edn. & home health. Recipient scholarship Matt Miller Meml., 1978, Navy Achievement medal, 1988, Navy Commendation medal, 1993. Mem. Emergency Nurses Assn., Grad. Nursing Student Assn. (program chair 1994-95), Sigma Theta Tau. Office: Naval Hosp Lemoore 930 Franklin Ave Lemoore CA 93246

MARKS, SUSAN MARIE, speech/language pathologist; b. Milw., Jan. 28, 1943; d. Albert T. and Marie P. (Hanson) New; m. Dennis P. Marks, Sept. 3, 1966. BS, U. Wis., 1965, MS, 1966. Cert. clin. competence Am. Speech Lang. Hearing Assn. Speech pathologist DeForest (Wis.) Pub. Schs., 1966, Newport News (Va.) Pub. Schs., 1967, Riverside Hosp. Rehab. Hosp., Newport News, 1967-70; mgr. Speech & Hearing Ctr. Children's Hosp. Wis., Milw., 1970—; mem. adv. coun. Marquette U. Coll. Comm., Milw., 1993-96. Contbr. articles to profl. jours. Chair Coun. on Speech Pathology and Audiology, Dept. Regulatory Licensing, Madison, 1990-96. Fellow Am. Speech Lang. Hearing Assn. (legis. coun. 1986—); mem. Wis. Speech and Hearing Assn. (pres. 1987-88, outstanding svc. award 1990), Nat. Stuttering Project. Roman Catholic. Office: Childrens Hosp Wis PO Box 1997 MS 785 Milwaukee WI 53201

MARKS, VICTORIA, artistic director, choreographer; b. New Jersey, Feb. 6, 1956. Victoria Marks Performing Co., 1985-93; dir. choreography program London Contemporary Dance Sch., 1992-95; asst. prof. fac. World Arts and Cultures UCLA, 1995—. Choreographer for various films, including Candoco; stage works duets, solos, quartet Dancing to Music.,. Fulbright fellow; grantee Nat. Endowment for Arts, N.Y. State Coun. on Arts, N.Y. Found. for Arts, London Arts Bd., Brit. Arts Coun. fulbright fellow, 1987-88, grantee NEA, 1995—. Office: UCLA Dept World Arts and Cultures 124 Dance Bldg Los Angeles CA 90095

MARKWOOD, SANDRA REINSEL, human services administrator; b. Washington, Aug. 27, 1955; d. Francis Eugene and Delores Jean (Horning) Reinsel-Kahn; m. James Scott Markwood, Aug. 4, 1984; children: Christopher Scott, Anne Meredith. BA with distinction, U. Va., 1977, M in Urban and Environ. Planning, 1979. Sr. rsch. asst. Nat. League of Cities, Washington, 1979-80; rsch. assoc./ project dir. Nat. Assn. Counties, Washington, 1980-84; asst. to county exec. Albemarle County, Charlottesville, Va., 1984-86; sr. rsch. assoc./ project dir. Nat. Assn. Counties, Washington, 1986—; exec. sec. Nat. Assn. County Aging Programs, Washington, 1986—; co-staff dir. Local Collaboration for Children and Youth; com. co-chair Generations United, Washington, 1988-90; intergovtl. liaison Nat. Hwy. Traffic Safety Adminstrn., Washington, 1989-91; chair Aging Needs Assessment Com., Charlottesville, 1985-86. Author: (handbook) Local Officials Guide to Urban Recreation, 1980, (guide) Building Support for Traffic Safety Programs, 1991; co-author: (guide) Graying of Suburbia, 1988; editor: Counties and Volunteers, Partners in Service, 1992-95; co-author: Counties Care for Kids: Programs That Work. Vol. tchr. St. Louis Cath. Sch., Alexandria, Va., 1980-83, St. Rita's Cath. Sch., Alexandria, 1987-89; vol. Jr. Friends of Campaign Ctr., Alexandria; coord. Sister Cities Exch. Program, Charlottesville, 1985. Recipient Cert. of Appreciation, Nat. Hwy. Traffic Safety Adminstrn., 1991. Mem. Women's Transp. Seminar, Smithsonian Assocs., Generations United. Roman. Catholic. Home: 3106 Lot A Russell Rd Alexandria VA 22305-1742

MARLAR, JANET CUMMINGS, public relations officer; b. Burnsville, Miss., Dec. 22, 1942; d. James E. and Juanita (Hale) Cummings; m. David C. Linton, May 21, 1961 (div. 1984); 1 child, Jeffory Mark, m. Thomas Gilbert Cupples, Mar. 5, 1984 (div. 1990); m. Fredrick Marlar, Nov. 19, 1994. Student, NE Miss. Jr. Coll., 1960-61, Memphis State U., 1975-76, Sheffield Tech. Ctr., Memphis, 1984-85. Property owner, Burnsville, 1974—, Glen, Miss., 1993—; mem. bus. adv. com. Sheffield Tech. Ctr., 1987—; with community svcs. St. Francis Hosp., 1989—; exec. bd. Internat. Heritage Commn., Memphis, 1987-92; pub. rels. officer Interant. Heritage Ethnic Festival, Memphis. Co-editor Internat. Heritage Bull./Newsletter. Vol. Memphis Brooks Mus. Art, 1980—; mem. exec. com., pub. info. officer Bldg. Bridges for A Better Memphis, 1985—; pres. Eagle Watch Assn.; founder Janet C. Cupples Citizenship awards, Memphis City Inter-City Sch., 1975, Student Leadership award, Memphis City Schs.; founder, chair women's com. on crime, City of Memphis, 1985—, chair Heritage-City of Memphis, chair internat. heritage program, 1987, 88—, Ethnic Outreach Neighborfest, 1988; hon. mem. city council, 1987; donor, exec. com. Women of Achievement, Inc., Memphis, 1986; mem. speakers bur. United Way of Greater Memphis, Friends of Shelby County Library, 1986—, YWCA; chair ethnic outreach com. Neighborfest, Memphis, 1987, chairperson exec. com. 1988; amb. Memphis Internat. Heritage Commn., 1988; youth mentor Memphis Youth Leadership Devel. Inst.; internat. coord. Neighborfest '88; chairperson Internat. Heritage City of Memphis, 1987, Ethnic Outreach Neighborfest, 1988. Contbr. articles to newspapers. Mem. community coun. Memphis City Schs., Memphis Cablevision Edn. Task Force; appointed col. aide de camp to staff of Gov. Ned McWherter of Tenn., 1988; sec. Shelby County Dem. Women, 1991; sec. safety com. St. Francis Hosp., 1992; participant Vol. Miss. Food Network Distbn. For Disabled Persons, 1996. Recipient 10 certs. of recognition Memphis City Council, 1986-89, Outstanding Service to Pub. Edn. award, 1986, merit award City of Memphis, 1987; named Outstanding Female Participant, Neighborhood, Inc., 1987; named Woman of Achievement 1988; honored by Pres. George Bush as Outstanding Vol., 1989; featured one of top 1000 Vols. in Mid-South, 1989; Svc. award Cummings Sch., 1993; apptd. Hon. Memphis City Councilwoman, 1995-96; recipient Royal award HRH Prince Kevin, 1996. Mem. NAFE, NOW (2d v.p. Memphis chpt. 1987, del. nat. conf. 1987, 2d v.p.), Network Profl. Women's Orgn., NCCJ, Rep. Career Women, Memphis Peace and Justice Ctr., Women's Polit. Caucus Tenn., Nat. Children's Cancer Soc. (friend 1995-96). Methodist. Avocations: community service, writing, teaching.

MARLEAU, DIANE, Canadian government official; b. Kirkland Lake, Ont., Can., June 21, 1943; d. Jean-Paul and Yvonne (Desjardins) LeBel; m. Paul C. Marleau, Aug. 3, 1963; children: Brigitte, Donald, Stéphane. Student, U. Ottawa, Ont., 1960-63; BA in Econs., Laurentian U., Sudbury, Ont., 1976. With Donald Jean Acctg. Svcs., Sudbury, 1971-75; receiver mgr. Thorne Riddell, Sudbury, 1975-76; treas. No. Regional Residential Treatment Program for Women, Sudbury, 1976-80, Com. for the Industry and Labour Adjustment Program, Sudbury, 1983; mem. transition team Ont. Premier's Office, Toronto, 1985; firm adminstr. Collins Barrow-Maheu Noiseux, Sudbury, 1985-88; M.P. from Sudbury House of Commons, Ottawa, 1988—; minister of health for Can., 1993-96; min. of public works Canada, 1996; councilor Regional Municipality of Sudbury, 1980-85, chair fin. com., 1981; alderman City of Sudbury, 1980-85; mem. No. Devel. Coun., Sudbury, 1986-88; vice chair Nat. Liberal Standing Com. on Policy, 1989; chair Ont. Liberal Caucus, 1990; apptd. nat. exec. Liberal Party Can., 1990, assoc. critic Govt. Ops., 1990, Dep. Opposition Whip, 1991, assoc. critic Fin., 1992; vice chair standing com. fin., 1992. Chmn. fund-raising Canadian Cancer Soc., Sudbury, 1987-88; co-chmn. Laurentian Hosp. Cancer Care Svcs. fund-raising campaign, Sudbury, 1988; chair bd. govs. Cambrian Coll., 1987-88, bd. govs., 1983-88; mem. Sudbury and Dist. Health Unit Bd., 1981-82; mem. fin. com., bd. dirs. Laurentian Hosp., 1981-85; chair Can. Games for the Physically Disabled, 1983; apptd. Ont. Adv. Coun. Women's Issues, 1984. Mem. Sudbury Bus. and Profl. Women Club. (named Woman of the Day 1989). Office: Public Works & Gov't Serv, 18A1 Place du Portage Phs III11 Laurier, Hull, PQ Canada K1A 0S5 also: 36 Elgin St, Sudbury, ON Canada P3C 5B4*

MARLER, ADDIE KAREN, elementary school educator; b. Dothan, Ala., Nov. 5, 1950; d. James Luther and Beulah Lee (Clenney) Savell; m. Thomas Franklin Marler, June 15, 1967; children: Jeffery, Jamie, Pamela. AA, Pasco Hernado C.C., 1981; BA, St. Leo Coll., 1985, postgrad. 6th and 7th grade lang. arts tchr. Moore Mickens Mid. Sch., Dade City, Fla., 1985-86, 7th grade gifted class tchr., 1985-86; developmental kindergarten tchr. Pasco

Elem. Sch., Dade City, 1986-88, tchr. 6th grade self-contained class, 1988-89, 1st grade tchr., 1989-90, 1st/2d grade tchr., 1990-91, primary house K-2d grade tchr., 1991-93, intermediate house 3d-5th grade tchr., 1993-94, ESOL resource tchr., 1994—; migrant lead tchr. Pasco Elem. Sch., 1990-92, ESL tchr., 1994-95, ESOL resource tchr., 1994-96; dist. curriculum writer Pasco County Schs., 1991-93; ednl. cons., 1990—. Mem. adv. bd. Fla. League of Tchrs./Fla. Dept. Edn.; mem. Heritage Arts Assn., Dade City. Named 20th Anniversary Ambassador, Edn. Ctr. N.C., 1993-94. Mem. Fla. Assn. Childhood Edn., Alpha Delta Kappa (historian, scholarship chmn. 1990-93 Alpha Phi chpt.). Republican. Baptist. Office: Pasco Elem 37350 Florida Ave Dade City FL 33525-4041

MARLETT, JUDITH ANN, nutritional sciences educatr, researcher; b. Toledo. BS, Miami U., Oxford, Ohio, 1965; PhD, U. Minn., 1972; postgrad., Harvard U., 1973-74. Registered dietitian. Therapeutic and metabolic unit dietitian VA Hosp., Mpls., 1966-67; spl. instr. in nutrition Simmons Coll., Boston, 1973-74; asst. prof. U. Wis., Madison, 1975-80, assoc. prof. dept. nutritional scis., 1981-84, prof. dept. nutritional scis., 1984—; cons. U.S. AID, Leyte, Philippines, 1983; acting dir. dietetic program dept. Nutritional Scis. U. Wis., 1977-78, dir., 1985-89; cons. grain, drug and food cos., 1985—, adv. bd. U. Ariz. Clin. Cancer Ctr., 1987-95; sci. bd. advisors Am. Health Found., 1988—; reviewer NIH, 1982—. Mem. editl. bd. Jour. Sci. of Food and Agrl., 1989—, Jour. Food Composition and Analysis, 1994—; contbr. articles to profl. jours. Mem. AAAS, NIH (Diabetes and Digestive and Kidney Disease spl. grant rev. com. 1992-96), Am. Inst. Nutrition, Am. Dietetic Assn., Am. Soc. Clin. Nutrition, Inst. Food Technologists, Am. Assn. Cereal Chemists. Office: U Wis Dept Nutritional Sci 1415 Linden Dr Madison WI 53706-1527

MARLIN, PENNY ZINN, foundation executive; b. N.Y.C., Feb. 4, 1942; d. Charles A. and Miriam H. (Braunstein) Zinn; m. Robert Earl Marlin, June 21, 1964; children: Charles, Adam. BA, U. Miami, Fla., 1962, MA, 1967. Math. tchr. North Miami (Fla.) H.S., 1962-66; pres. The Pub. Eye, Miami, 1976-81; devel. coord. The Players Theatre, Miami, 1980-82; asst. dir. Found. Jewish Philanthropies, Miami, 1982-85, dir., 1987-94; dir. Jewish Cmty. Found., Hollywood, Fla., 1986-87, Found. Jewish Fedn. of Palm Beach, Palm Beach, Fla., 1994—; chair Endowment Profl. Inst., Ft. Lauderdale, Fla., 1995—. Vice chair Dade County Housing and Urban Devel. Bd., 1978-80; pres. Family Counseling Svc. Greater Miami, 1985-86. Mem. LWV (v.p.), Nat. Soc. Fund Raising Execs., Planned Giving Coun. Palm Beach, Nat. Com. Planned Giving. Office: Jewish Fedn Palm Beach County 4601 Community Dr West Palm Beach FL 33417

MARLING, KARAL ANN, art history and social sciences educator; b. Rochester, N.Y., Nov. 5, 1943; d. Raymond J. and Marjorie (Karal) M. PhD, Bryn Mawr Coll., 1971. Prof. art history and Am. studies U. Minn., Mpls., 1977—. Author: Federal Art in Cleveland, 1933-1943: An Exhibition, 1974, Wall-to-Wall America: A Cultural History of Post-Office Murals in the Great Depression, 1982, The Colossus of the Roads: Myth and Symbol along the American Highway, 1984, Tom Benton and His Drawings: A Biographical Essay and a Collection of His Sketches, Studies, and Mural Cartoons, 1985, Frederick C. Knight (1898-1979), 1987, George Washington Slept Here: Colonial Revivals and American Culture, 1876-1986, 1988, Looking Back: A Perspective on the 1913 Inaugural Exhibition, 1988, Blue Ribbon: A Social and Pictorial History of the Minnesota State Fair, 1990, (with John Wetenhall) Iwo Jima: Monuments, Memories, and the American Hero, 1991, Edward Hopper, 1992, As Seen on T.V.: The Visual Culture of Everyday Life in the 1950's, 1994, Going Home with Elvis, 1995; editor (with Jessica H. Foy) The Arts and the American Home, 1890-1930, 1994; contbr. essays to exhbn. catalogs. Recipient Minn. Humanities Commn. award 1986, Minn. Book award History, 1994, Robert C. Smith award Decorative Arts Soc., 1994. Office: 1920 S 1st St Ste 1301 Minneapolis MN 55454

MARLOW, AUDREY SWANSON, artist, designer; b. N.Y.C.; d. Sven and Rita (Porter) Swanson; student (scholarships) Art Students League, 1950-55; spl. courses SUNY (Stony Brook), L'Alliance Française m. Roy Marlow, Nov. 30, 1968. With Cohn-Hall-Marx Textile Studio, 1961-65, R.S. Assocs. Textile Studio, 1965-73; freelance designer, illustrator Prince Matchabelli, Lester Harrison Agy., J. Walter Thompson Agy., 1957-78; portrait and fine artist, Wading River, N.Y., 1973—; instr. Phoenix Sch. Design (N.Y.C.); illustrator children's books: Breads of Many Lands and 4H Club Bakes Bread, 1966, Anna Smith Strong and the Setauket Spy Ring, 1991, Timothy and the Acrobat, 1992; exhibits include: Nat. Arts Club, NAD, Parish Art Mus., South Hampton, N.Y., Guild Hall, East Hampton, N.Y., Portraits Inc., Lincoln Ctr., Chung-Cheng Art Gallery, St. John's U., Mystic (Conn.) Art Assn., Harbour Gallery, St. Thomas, V.I., Palais Rameau, Lisle, France, 1988, Sumner Mus., Washington, 1992, East End Arts & Humanities Coun., L.I., N.Y., 1996; one-person shows: Salmagundi Club, 1982, Rockefeller Gallery, N.Y.C., 1992; portrait commns. include: Millicent Fenwick, Harrison J. Goldin, Thomas R. Bayles, Mons. John Fagan, others. Trustee, Middle Island Public Library, 1972-76. Recipient John W. Alexander medal, 1976, award Council on Arts, 1978, award of excellence Cork Gallery, Lincoln Center, 1982; Grumbacher Bronze medal, 1983; Grumbacher Silver medal 1986; Best in Show award N.Y. Arts Council, 1986, Suburban Art League, 1993, Excellence award Town of Oyster Bay, 1995. Mem. Pastel Soc. Am. (award 1977, 80, 90), Am. Artists Profl. League (2 1st prize awards), Hudson Valley Art Assn. (award), Knickerbocker Artists (2 awards), Catharine Lorillard Wolfe Art Club (award 1982), Salmagundi Club (5 awards), Nat. League Am. Pen Women (Gold award, Gold medal of Honor, Best in Show 1990). Works represented at NYU, Longwood Pub. Libr., Sr. Citizen's Complex, Newark, St. Theresa of the Child Jesus Convent, L.I., pvt. collections. Home: 147 Northside Rd Wading River NY 11792-1112

MARLOW, JUDITH ANN, English and French educator; b. Washington, Apr. 22, 1952; d. Spencer Marcus and Evelyn Lucia (Pearson) M.; children: Tim, Chris, Anna. BA in French, Wake Forest U., 1974; MAT in French, English as 2d Lang., Sch. for Internat. Tng., Brattleboro, Vt., 1981. French tchr. Ursuline Acad. H.S., Bethesda, Md., 1974-76; English tchr. Open Sch. voor Vrouwen, Alkmaar, Holland, 1981-82; French tchr., English/French lang. cons. Andrew Lewis Jr. H.S., Salem, Va., 1982-83; English tchr. Ecole Inlingua, Geneva, 1984-86, Acad. Langs. and Comm., Fribourg, Switzerland, 1986-88; French tchr. Centre Ave. Blanc AGECAS, Geneva, 1989-91; English tchr., coord. Am. English dept. Cours Industriels de Genève, Geneva, 1986-91; edn. liaison Refugee Resettlement and Immigration Svcs., Roanoke, Va., 1991-92; English as second lang. tchr. Roanoke City Schs., 1992—; Odyssey of the Mind coach Salem City Schs., 1994, 95. Exec. bd. PTA, Salem, 1993. Mem. NEA. Quaker. Home: 825 Illinois Ave Salem VA 24153-5347

MARMER, ELLEN LUCILLE, pediatrician; b. Bronx, N.Y., June 29, 1939; d. Benjamin and Diane (Goldstein) M.; m. Harold O. Shapiro, June 5, 1960; children: Cheri, Brenda. BS in Chemistry, U. Ala., 1960; MD, U. Ala., Birmingham, 1964. Cert. Nat. Bd. Med. Examiners; diplomate Am. Bd. Sports Medicine, Bd. Pediatrics, Bd. Qualified and Eligible Pediatric Cardiology, Bd. cert. sports medicine. Intern Upstate Med. Ctr., Syracuse, N.Y., 1964-65, resident, 1965-66; fellow in pediatric cardiology Columbia Presbyn. Med. Ctr.-Babies Hosp., N.Y.C., 1967-69; pvt. practice Hartford, Vernon, Conn., 1969—; examining pediatrician child devel. program Columbia Presbyn. Med. Ctr.-Babies Hosp., N.Y.C., 1967, instr. pediatrics, 1967-69; dir. pediatric cardiology clinic St. Francis Hosp., Hartford, 1970-80; asst. state med. examiner, Tolland County, Conn., 1974-79; sports physician Rockville (Conn.) High Sch., 1976—; advisor Cardiac Rehab. com., Rockville, 1984-90; mem. bd. examiners Am. Bd. Sports Medicine, 1991—, chmn. credentials com., 1991—. Mem. Vernon Town Coun., 1985-89; bd. dirs. Child Guidance Clinic, Manchester, Conn., 1970—; life mem. Tolland County chpt. Hadassah, v.p., 1969-70, pres., 1970-72, bd. dirs., 1973-74; mem. B'nai Israel Congregation and Sisterhood, Vernon, 1969—, chmn. youth commn., 1970-72. Recipient Outstanding Svc. award Indian Valley YMCA, 1985. Fellow Am. Acad. Pediatrics, Am. Coll. Cardiology, Am. Coll. Sports Medicine (bd. examiners 1991—, chmn. credentials com. 1991—); mem. Conn. Med. Soc., Am. Heart Assn. (mem. coun. cardiovascular disease in young 1969—, chmn. elect New Eng. regional heart com. 1990-91), Conn. Heart Assn. (bd. dirs. 1974-75, 83-84, pres. 1986-88), Heart Assn. Greater Hartford (bd. dirs. 1970-89, mem. exec. com. 1972-73, 79-84, pres. 1982-84), Tolland County Med. Assn. (sec. 1971-72), Vis. Nurse and Community Care Tolland County, LWV (state program chairperson Vernon chpt. 1971-73). Democrat. Jewish. Office: 520 Hartford Tpke Vernon Rockville CT 06066-5037

MAROHN, ANN ELIZABETH, health information professional; b. Grand Rapids, Mich., Feb. 26, 1946; d. Luther Alfonse and Mary Inez (Pinkstaff) M. BS, Ind. U., 1968; MS, SUNY, Buffalo, 1978. Asst. med. record dir. Highland Park (Mich.) Gen. Hosp., 1968-70; asst. dir. med. record svcs. Meml. Hosp., Elmhurst, Ill., 1970-73; dir. med. record tech. program Alfred (N.Y.) State Coll., 1974-76; mem. faculty med. record adminstrn. dept. Lincoln Coll., Melbourne, Australia, 1977-78, Kean Coll., Union, N.J., 1984-85, Med. U. S.C., Charleston, 1985-87; mem. faculty health record dept. Ferris State Coll., Big Rapids, Mich., 1979-80; dir. health info. mgmt. Armstrong State Coll., Savannah, Ga., 1980-84; dir. med. record dept. Tucson Gen. Hosp., 1988-89, N.D. State Hosp., Jamestown, 1990-92; cons. Prospective Payment Specialists, Tucson, 1992-93; health info. mgr. Sierra Med. Ctr., El Paso, Tex., 1993-94; dir. health info. mgmt. program Southern U., Shreveport, La., 1994—; cons. Oglethorpe Ctr., Savannah, 1983-84. Columnist Australian Med. Record Jour., 1981-87, Communique, 1981-84, Palmetto Breeze, 1985-87, Progress Notes, 1984-85. Recipient disting. mem. award Ga. Med. Record Assn., 1984. Mem. NAFE, Am. Health Info. Mgmt. Assn., Ariz. Health Info. Mgmt. Assn. (program chmn. 1988-89, sec. 1989—), Tex. Health Info. Mgmt. Assn. (dist. III v.p.), La. Health Info. Mgmt. Assn., N.W. La. Health Info. Mgmt. Assn., Assembly on Edn. Episcopalian. Home: 215 Sand Beach Blvd 1205 Shreveport LA 71105

MARONEY, JANE P., state legislator; b. Boston, July 29, 1923; d. John Henry and Mary (Boland) Perkins; m. John Walker Maroney, July 7, 1956; children: Jane Maroney El Dahr, John Walker Jr. Student, Radcliffe Coll., 1940-41; studnet, Katharine Gibbs Sch., 1941-42; LHD (hon.), Golden Beacon Coll., 1995. Elected official Del. Gen. Assembly, Dover, 1978—. Chmn. Del. Family Law Commn., 1990—, Health and Human Devel. Com., 1984—; moderator, panelist Pub. Policy Conf., annually; bd. dirs. YWCA, New Castle County, (J.Thompson Brown award 1992), Child Care Connection, Coord. Coun. Children with Disabilities, chmn. 1990-91; mem. adv. bd. Rockwood Mus., Del. Hospice, Girl Scouts Del., Del. Internat. Yr. of Family, March of Dimes, Coalition for Literacy, Inst. Human Behavior; past mem. Jr. League Wilmington. Named 1 of 10 Best Rep. Legislators of Yr. Pres. Reagan, 1985; recipient Outstanding Svc. to Children award Acad. Pediatrics, Disting. Svc. award Del. Bar Assn., Alfred R. Shands Disting. Svc. award, 1992, Order of Merit award U. Del., 1993, J. Donaldson Brown Disting. Svcs. award Children and Family Svcs. Del. to Dr. & Rep. Maroney, 1992; named to Women's Hall of Fame, Del., 1996. Roman Catholic. Home: 4605 Concord Pike Wilmington DE 19803-1406 Office: Del House of Reps PO Box 1901 Dover DE 19903-1901

MARONI, ALICE C., federal official; b. Washington, D.C., Oct. 8, 1953; d. Yves and Frances (Tower) M. BA magna cum laude, Mount Holyoke Coll., 1975; attended, Williams Coll., 1974; MA, Tufts U., 1978; grad., Nat. War Coll., 1988-89. Internat. risk analyst Rockwell Internat., 1979-80; specialist in nat. defense Congl. Rsch. Svc., Libr. of Congress, 1980-90; prof. staff mem. House com. on armed svcs., 1990-93; prin. dep. undersec. of defense Dept. of Defense, Washington, 1993—. Contbr. article to profl. publs.

MARONI, DONNA FAROLINO, biologist, researcher; b. Buffalo, Feb. 27, 1938; d. Enrico Victor and Eleanor (Redlinska) Farolino; m. Gustavo Primo Maroni, Dec. 16, 1974. BS, U. Wis., 1960, PhD, 1969. Project assoc. U. Wis., Madison, 1960-63, 68-74; Alexander von Humboldt fellow Inst. Genetics U. Cologne, Fed. Republic Germany, 1974-75; Hargitt fellow Duke U., Durham, N.C., 1975-76, rsch. assoc., 1976-83, rsch. assoc. prof., 1983-87; sr. program specialist N.C. Biotech. Ctr., Research Triangle Park, 1987-88, dir. sci. programs div., 1988-92, v.p. for sci. programs, 1992-94, ret., 1995; mem. adv. com. MICROMED at Bowman Gray Sch. Medicine, Winston-Salem, N.C., 1988—, Minority Sci. Improvement Alliance for Instrn. and Rsch. in Biotech. Ala. A & M U., Normal, 1990-91. Contbr. over 20 articles and revs. to profl. jours. Grantee NSF, 1977-79, NIH, 1979-82, 79-83, 82-87. Mem. Am. Soc. Cell Biology, Genetics Soc. Am., N.C. Acad. Sci., Inc. (bd. dirs. 1983-86), Sigma Xi (mem. exec. com. Duke U. chpt. 1989-90).

MAROON, MICKEY, clinical social worker; b. Flint, Mich., July 20, 1948; d. Harold Clifford and Dorothy Ruth (Fuller) McDaniel; m. Michael Martin Maroon, Aug. 22, 1970. BA, Bradley U., 1970; MSW, Denver U., 1975. Lic. clin. social worker, Colo.; bd. cert. diplomate. Social worker Ill. Dept. Children and Family Svcs., Peoria, Ill., 1970-73; clin. social worker Adams County Social Svcs., Westminster, Colo., 1975-77, Bethesda Hosp., Denver, 1977-84; pvt. practice Denver, 1979—; clin. cons. Human Svcs., Inc., Denver, 1988-91; vol. faculty Health Sci. Ctr. U. Colo., Denver, 1987—; chair attending social work staff West Pines Hosp., Wheat Ridge, Colo., 1988-89. Mem. NASW (pres. Colo. chpt. 1994—), Colo. Soc. Clin. Social Work (Denver chpt. pres. 1992, state pres. 1993).

MAROT, LOLA, accountant; b. Providence, Oct. 6; d. Frank and Iola (Lombardi) Ansuini; m. Joseph Marot (div. 1973); 1 child, David Joseph. B.A. with distinction, U. R.I., 1973; postgrad. Bryant Coll. Bookkeeper, Diamond Paper Box Co., Providence, 1958-69; export sales adminstr. Brite Industries, Providence, 1973-77; property services asst. Met. Property and Liability Ins. Co., Warwick, R.I., 1977-79, buyer, 1979-83, sr. buyer, 1983-86, supr. printing adminstrn., 1986-87, expense control adminstr., 1987-88; accountant Dept of Adminstrn. State of R.I. Divsn. Ctrl. Svcs., 1992—. Mem. Univ. Soc. Providence (pres. 1978). Office: 1 Capitol Hl Providence RI 02908-5803

MAROTTA, SUSAN M., lawyer; b. N.Y.C., Feb. 8, 1963. BS, Cornell U., 1985; JD, Fordham U., 1989. Bar: N.Y. 1990, U.S. Dist. Ct. (so. and ea. dists.) N.Y. 1990. Ptnr. Anderson Kill Olick & Oshinsky, N.Y.C. Editor-in-chief: Fordham Moot Ct. Bd. Mem. ABA, N.Y. State Bar Assn., Nassau County Bar Assn., Bar of City of N.Y. (sec. com. on state legislation 1992-94). Office: Anderson Kill Olick & Oshinsky 1251 Ave of the Americas New York NY 10020-1182*

MARQUARDT, CHRISTEL ELISABETH, lawyer; b. Chgo., Aug. 26, 1935; d. Herman Albert and Christine Marie (Geringer) Trolenberg; children: Eric, Philip, Andrew, Joel. BS in Edn., Mo. Western Coll., 1970; JD with honors, Washburn U., 1974. Bar: Kans. 1974, Mo. 1992, U.S. Dist. Ct. Kans. 1974, U.S. Dist. Ct. (we. dist.) Mo. 1992. Tchr. St. John's Ch., Tigerton, Wis., 1955-56; pers. asst. Columbia Records, L.A., 1958-59; ptnr. Cosgrove, Webb & Oman, Topeka, 1974-86, Palmer & Marquardt, Topeka, 1986-91, Levy and Craig P.C., Overland Park, Kans., 1991-94; sr. ptnr. Marquardt and Assocs., L.L.C., Fairway, Kans., 1994—; judge Kans. Ct. Appeals, 1995—; mem. atty. bd. discipline Kans. Supreme Ct., 1984-86. Mem. editorial adv. bd. Kans. Lawyers Weekly, 1992—; contbr. articles to legal jours. Bd. dirs. Topeka Symphony, 1983-92, Arts and Humanities Assn. Johnson County, 1992—, Brown Found., 1988-90; hearing examiner Human Rels. Com., Topeka, 1974-76; local advisor Boy Scouts Am., 1973-74; bd. dirs., mem. nominating com. YWCA, Topeka, 1979-81; bd. govs. Washburn U. Law Sch., 1987—, v.p., 1994-95; mem. dist. bd. adjudication Mo. Synod Luth. Ch., Kans., 1982-88. Names Woman of Yr., Mayor, City of Topeka, 1982; Obee scholar Washburn U., 1972-74. Fellow Am. Bar Found., Kans. Bar Found. (trustee 1987-89); mem. ABA (labor law, family and litigation sects., mem. ho. dels. 1988—, state del. 1995—, specilization com. 1987-93, chmn. 1989-93, lawyer referral com. 1993—, bar svcs. and activities, 1995—), Kans. Bar Assn. (sec., treas. 1981-82, 83-85, v.p. 1985-86, pres. 1987-88, bd. dirs.), Kans. Trial Lawyers Assn. (bd. govs. 1982-86, lectr.), Topeka Bar Assn., Am. Bus. Women's Assn. (lectr., corr. sec. 1983-84, pres. career chpt. 1986-87, named one of Top 10 Bus. Women of Yr., 1985). Home: 3408 Alanceda Dr Topeka KS 66614 Office: 4330 Shawnee Mission Pky Fairway KS 66205-2522

MARQUARDT, KATHLEEN PATRICIA, professional society administrator; b. Kalispell, Mont., June 6, 1944; d. Dean King and Lorraine Camille (Buckmaster) Marquardt; m. William Wewer, Dec. 6, 1987; children: Shane Elizabeth, Montana Quinn. Purser, Pan Am. World Airways, Washington, 1968-75; info. specialist Capital Systems Group, Kensington, Md., 1979-81; dir. pub. affairs Subscription TV Assn., Washington, 1981-83, exec. dir., 1983-86; pres. Internat. Policy Studies Orgn., 1983-90; pres., designer Elizabeth Quinn Couture; lectr. in field. Chmn. bd. Friends of Freedom, 1982-90, Putting People First, 1990—, Mont. Matters, 1996—; v.p. Am. Policy Ctr., 1996—; treas. Mont. Tax Reduction Movement. Author: Animal Scam-The Beastly Abuse of Human Rights, 1993, (national newpaper column) From the Trenches; contbr. articles to syndicated newspapers and mags.; host Grass Roots radio. Recipient Citizen Achievement award Ctr. fo Def. Free Enterprise, 1992, Gold Medal award Pa. State Fish and Game Protective Assn., 1993. Mem. Outdoor Writers Assn. Am. Home: 533 5th Ave Helena MT 59601-4359 Office: Putting People First 21 N Last Chance Gulch Helena MT 59601

MARQUARDT, MARY MEYERS, critical care nurse, educator; b. Austin, Tex., Mar. 9, 1959; d. Joseph Louis and Gladys Therese (New) Meyers; m. Michael Paul Marquardt, Feb. 23, 1985; children: Patricia Marie, Stephen Michael. BSN cum laude, Incarnate Word Coll., San Antonio, 1981; postgrad., Tex. Women's U., 1994—. CCRN, RN, Tex.; cert. ACLS instr., pediatric advanced life support instr. Staff nurse, charge nurse Scott and White Meml. Hosp., Temple, Tex., 1982-83; staff nurse, charge nurse Olin E. Teague Vets. Ctr., Temple, Tex., 1983-87, head nurse geriatric/rehab. unit, 1987-88, critical care coord., 1988-89; staff devel./edn. coord. Nan Travis Meml. Hosp., Jacksonville, Tex., 1989-90; staff nurse critical care St. Joseph's Health Ctr., Bryan, Tex., 1991—, quality assessment analyst, 1994; instr. nursing students Blinn C.C., Bryan, 1994—; critical care lectr., Bryan/College Station, Tex., 1991—. Co-author: Pocket Guide to Critical Care Assessment, 1989, 2d edit., 1994; contbg. author: Principles and Practices of Adult Health Nursing, 1989, Health Assessment, 4th edit., 1989. Mem. AACN (pres.-elect Lond Star chpt. 1994-95, pres. Lone Star chpt. 1995-96), ANA, Tex. Nurses Assn., Alpha Chi. Methodist. Office: Blinn CC ADN Program 1905 S Texas Ave Bryan TX 77802-1832

MARQUIS, HARRIET HILL, social worker; b. Rocky Mount, N.C., Sept. 4, 1938; d. Robert Foster and Anne Ruth (Daughtry) Hill; m. James Ralph Marquis, Apr. 23, 1967; children: Margaret Anne, Karen Lee. BA in English, Meredith Coll., 1960; MA in English, Seton Hall U., 1971; PhD in English, Drew U., 1984; MSW, NYU, 1987. Diplomate Am. Bd. Social Workers. Tchr. English S.C. Pub. Schs., 1960-61, Peace Corps, Sierra Leone, West Africa, 1963-65; psychotherapist Child Guidance & Family Svc. Ctr., Orange, N.J., 1987; staff clinician Esther Dutton Counseling Ctr., Morristown, N.J., 1987-90; psychotherapist Ctr. Evaluation & Psychotherapy, Morristown, N.J., 1990-93; clin. social worker pvt. practice, Madison, N.J., 1990—; adj. prof. English Fairleigh Dickenson U., Madison, 1983-85; speaker in field. Fellow N.J. Assn. Clin. Social Workers; mem. NASW, Nat. Fedn. of Socs. for Clin. Social Work (nat. membership com. psychoanalysis in clin. social work), N.J. Soc. Study of Multiple Personality and Dissociative Disorders, Internat. Conf. Advancement of Pvt. Practice Clin. Social Work, Grad. Coun. Psychoanalytic Psychotherapists. Democrat. Methodist. Office: Clin Psychotherapy Assocs Madison NJ 07940

MARR, PHEBE ANN, historian, educator; b. Mt. Vernon, N.Y., Sept. 21, 1931; d. John Joseph and Lillian Victoria (Henningsen) Marr. B.A., Barnard Coll., 1953; Ph.D., Harvard U., 1967. Research assoc. ARAMCO, Dhahran, Saudi Arabia, 1960-62; dir. middle east program Fgn. Service Inst., 1963-66; research fellow Middle East Ctr., Harvard U., Cambridge, Mass., 1968-70; asst. prof. Stanislaus State Coll., Turlock, Calif., 1970-71, assoc. prof., 1971-74; assoc. prof. history U. Tenn., Knoxville, 1974-85, chmn. Asian Studies Program, 1977-79; sr. fellow Nat. Def. U., Washington, 1985—; cons. ARAMCO, 1979-83. Harvard U. traveling fellow, 1956; mem. Coun. Fgn. Rels. Author: The Modern History of Iraq, 1985; co-editor: Riding the Tiger: Middle East Challenge After the Cold War, 1993; contbr. articles to profl. jours. Mem. Middle East Inst. (bd. govs.), Middle East Studies Assn. Home: 2902 18th St NW Washington DC 20009-2954 Office: Nat Def U 4th & P Sts SW Fort McNair DC 20319

MARRA, MARY MOLLENHOFF, secondary education educator; b. Phoenix, May 7, 1948; d. Herbert Harold and Hazel Roselle (Doty) Mollenhoff; m. Ronald Eldon Marra, Aug. 6, 1977; children: Nicholas Eldon, Allison Mary. BS, U. So. Calif., 1970, MS, 1971, adminstrv. credential, 1975. Tchg. and adminstrv. credential, Calif. Tchr. history Torrance (Calif.) Unified Sch. Dist., 1970—. Tchr. rep. Bert M. Lynn Mid. Sch. PTA, Torrance, 1986—; girls sports rep. West H.S. Booster Club, Torrance, 1994—. Recipient hon. svc. award Bert M. Lynn Mid. Sch. PTA, 1987. Mem. NEA, Calif. Tchrs. Assn., Calif. League Mid. Schs., Calif. Elem. Edn. Assn., Calif. Social Studies Edn. Assn., Torrance Tchrs. Assn., Kappa Kappa Gamma. Democrat. Home: 21821 Barbara St Torrance CA 90503 Office: Bert M Lynn Mid Sch 5038 Halison St Torrance CA 90503

MARRELLA, MARIA PIA, artist, graphic designer, illustrator; b. Jersey City, N.J., Dec. 11, 1954; d. Louis Frank and Regina R. (DeStefano) M.; m. Allen Elliot Galant, July 1988; 1 child, Leah Michaela. BA in Art, Art Edn., Marymount Coll., 1976; MFA with honors, Parsons Sch. Design, 1980. Cert. tchr., N.Y. Freelance graphic designer, art dir. various ednl. publ. cos., N.Y.C., 1980—. One-woman shows include Prince St. Gallery, N.Y.C., 1987-96; illustrator: Seven Kisses in a Row, 1983, My Cousin Charlie, 1984, Man and the Sea Monster, 1990. Recipient fellowship Va. Ctr. for Creative Arts, 1983, Merit award in ednl. pub. N.Y. Bookbinders Guild, 1986, fellowship N.Y. State Coun. on Arts, 1995-96.

MARRERO, MARITZA, municipal official; b. Tampa, Fla., Sept. 25, 1956; d. Arnulfo and Petra (Robledo) M.; m. Nelson Carlo, Aug. 14, 1993. BA, Northeastern Ill. U., 1978; MPA, Ill. Inst. Tech., 1994. Pers. staffing specialist U.S. Dept. Housing and Urban Devel., Chgo., 1978-84; dir. pers. Dept. Housing, Chgo., 1984-85, dep. for fin. and adminstrn., 1984-89; first dep. commr. Dept. Pers., Chgo., 1989-95; dir. Mayor's Office of Employment and Tng., Chgo., 1995—; bd. dirs. U.S. Conf. of Mayors, Washington. Bd. dirs. Latino Inst., Chgo., 1989-95, pres. 1992-93; bd. dirs. sec. Latin Am. Mus. Art, Chgo.; bd. dirs. Girl Scouts Am., Chgo., Personal PAC, Chgo. Roman Catholic. Office: Mayor's Office Employment and Tng 510 N Peshtigo Ct 2A Chicago IL 60611

MARRIOT, SALIMA SILER, state legislator, social work educator; b. Batl., Dec. 5, 1940; d. Jesse James and Cordie Susie (Ayers) Silver; m. David Small Mariott, Sept. 24, 1964 (div. 1972); children: Terrez Siler, Patrice Kenyatta. BS, Morgan State Coll., 1964; M in Social Work, U. Md., 1972; D in Social Work, Howard U., 1988. Tchr. Balt. City Pub. Sch., 1964-65; social worker N.Y.C. Social Svcs., 1965-67, Balt. City Social Svcs., 1968-72; instr., asst. prof. Morgan State U., Balt., 1972-96; mem. Md. Ho. of Dels., 1990—; chair Park Heights Devel. Corp., Balt., 1976-92, Nat. Black Women's Health Project, 1993-94. Co-editor: U.S. Policy Toward Southern Africa, 1984. Cons. Balt. City Head Start, 1985-94; del. Dem. Conv., Atlanta, 1988; active Md. Dem. Ctrl. Com., 1988-90; sec. Nat. Rainbow Coalition; exec. bd. Nat. Black Caucus of State Legislators; vice chmn. Md. Legis. Black Caucus. Flemming fellow, 1995. Mem. Delta Sigma Theta. Office: Md House of Dels 4515 Homer Ave Baltimore MD 21215-6302

MARRIOTT, CHRISTINE LEIGH, auditor; b. Corning, N.Y., Oct. 8, 1961; d. Jack Frederick and Beatrice Ruby (Johnson) M. BS, Elmira Coll., 1991. Fin. analyst Corning Inc., from 1986, now internal auditor. Mem. Inst. Mgmt. Accts. (cert., dir. employment Corning 1994, dir. cert. mgmt. acct. programs 1995), Inst. Internal Auditors. Republican. Office: Corning Inc 1 Riverfront Plz Corning NY 14831

MARRIOTT, MARCIA ANN, human resources administrator, educator, consultant; b. Rochester, N.Y., Mar. 21, 1947; d. Coyne and Alice (Schepler) M.; children: Brian, Jonathan. AA, Monroe C.C., Rochester, 1967; BS, SUNY, Brockport, 1970, MA, 1975; PhD, S.W. U., La., 1985. Program adminstr. N.Y. Dept. of Labor, N.Y.C., 1970-75; employment mgr. Rochester Gen. Hosp., 1975-77, salary adminstr., 1982—; dir. wage and salary dept. Gannett Newspapers, Rochester, 1977-80; compensation and benefits adminstr. Sybron Corp., Rochester, 1980-82; instr. N.Y. State Sch. Indsl. Rels., Cornell U., N.Y.C., 1976-79; assoc. prof. Rochester Inst. Tech., 1978—, Monroe C.C., 1981—, dir. career adv. coun., 1989—; cons. in field; dir. Rochester Presbyn. Home, 1987-91, 96—; dir. area hosp. coun. Kidney Svc. Ctrs., Rochester, 1988-91. Author: (pamphlets) Guideline for Writing Job Descriptions, 1983, Redesigning the Performance Appraisal, 1996, Skill Based Job Descriptions for Sterile Processing Technicians: A Total Quality Approach, 1994, (manual) Career Planning Manual, 1985, (booklet) Guideline for Writing Criteria-Based Job Descriptions, 1988, Skill-based Job Descriptions: A Quality Approach, 1994, Redesigning the Performance Appraisal Process, 1996. Campaign mgr. Carter Campaign Commn., Rochester, 1975; mem. coun. Messiah Luth. Ch., Rochester, 1991-94. Davenport-Hatch Found. grantee, 1973, Wegman Found. grantee, 1975. Mem. Am. Compensation Assn., Single Adopted Parents Group (pres. 1988-93). Office: Rochester Gen Hosp 1425 Portland Ave Rochester NY 14621-3001

MARRON, DARLENE LORRAINE, real estate development executive, financial and marketing consultant; b. Auburn, N.Y., July 20, 1946; d. William Chester and Elizabeth Barbara (Gervaise) Kulakowski; m. Edward W. Marron, Jr., Apr. 28, 1973. BS cum laude, Rider U., 1968; MBA, NYU, 1970. Lic. securities broker. Dir. mktg. Am. Airlines, N.Y.C., 1970-79; asst. v.p. Merrill Lynch, N.Y.C., 1979-83; v.p. Kidder, Peabody & Co., N.Y.C., 1983-86; owner, principal, Marron Cos., Upper Saddle River, N.J., 1986—, Marron Bros. Realty Corp., 1990—; fin. and mktg. cons. to real estate devel. industry. Avocations: pianist, flutist, skiing, fly fishing. Home: 9 Normandy Ct Ho Ho Kus NJ 07423-1217 Office: Marron Cos 118 State Rt 17 U Saddle Riv NJ 07458-2313

MARRS, SHARON CARTER, librarian; b. Andover, Va., May 7, 1943; d. Wallace Ralph and Dorothy (Stout) Carter; m. Glenn Robert Marrs, July 3, 1965. BS, East Tenn. State U., 1965; MLS, U. Pitts., 1974, postgrad., 1983—. Cert. libr. sci. and English, Pa. Tchr. English grades 8 and 10 Powell Valley H.S., Big Stone Gap, Va., 1964-65; libr. Coeburn (Va.) Elem., 1967-68, tchr. grade 2, 1968; libr. Wise (Va.) Elem., 1968-69; tchr. English grade 7 Christiansburg (Va.) Elem. Sch., 1969-70, libr., 1970-71; libr. Myrtle, Vernridge and Kelton Schs., Pitts., 1972—; apptd. to serve on Microcomputer in the Media Ctr. Award com., Am. Assn. Sch. Librs.; presenter workshops in field. Inventor games for children on use of card catalog, the Dewey Decimal System, various ref. books. Mem. ALA, Pa. State Libr. Assn. (mem. tech. com.), Internat. Assn. Sch. Librarianship, Beta Phi Mu. Home: 620 Broughton Rd Bethel Park PA 15102-3775

MARS, VIRGINIA CRETELLA, volunteer; b. New Haven; d. Albert William and Josephine Vera (Nutile) Cretella; m. Forrest E. Mars Jr., Oct. 20, 1955 (div. Jan. 1990); children: Victoria B., Valerie A., Pamela D., Marijke E. BA, Vassar Coll., 1951. Cert. tchr. mem. adv. coun. Music Educators Nat. Conf., 1996—. Mem. Nat. Symphony Orch. Bd., Washington, chmn. exec. com., 1980-83, pres., 1983-87; mem. Smithsonian Women's Com., Washington, 1988—; trustee The Potomac Sch. Bd., McLean, Va., The Langley Sch., McLean, Vassar Coll. Bd., Poughkeepsie, N.Y., 1987—; bd. dirs. Wildlife Preservation Trust Internat., 1990—; chmn. Campaign for Vassar; mem. Cathedral chpt. bd. dirs. Washington Nat. Cathedral, 1994—. Mem. Vassar Club Washington, Cosmos Club, Chevy Chase Club, Sulgrave Club. Republican. Episcopalian. Home: 702 Belgrove Rd Mc Lean VA 22101-1836

MARSDEN, HERCI IVANA, classical ballet artistic director; b. Omis-Split, Croatia, Dec. 2, 1937; came to U.S., 1958; d. Ante and Magda (Smith) Munitic; m. Myles Marsden, Aug. 10, 1957 (div. 1976); children—Ana, Richard, Mark; m. Dujko Radovnikovic, Aug. 27, 1977; 1 child, Dujko. Student, Internat. Ballet Sch., 1955. Mem. corps de ballet Nat. Theatre, Split, 1954-58; founder Braecrest Sch. Ballet, Lincoln, R.I., 1958—; founder State Ballet of R.I., Lincoln, 1960—, artistic dir., 1976—; artistic dir. U. R.I. Classical Ballet, Kingston, 1966—, lectr., 1966—. Office: Brae Crest School of Ballet 52 Sherman Ave Lincoln RI 02865

MARSDEN, MARILYN WEBER, airline executive, consultant; b. N.Y.C., Oct. 27, 1944; d. Martin Jack and Naomi Ruth (Sternberg) Weber; m. Charles Joseph Marsden, Nov. 12, 1988; stepchildren: Anne, George. BA, American U., 1966; MA, New Sch. Social Rsch., 1981. Cert. tchr., N.Y. Elem. sch. tchr. N.Y.C. and Chevy Chase, Md., 1966-70; flight attendant, purser Pan Am. World Airways, Inc., N.Y.C., 1970-72, coord. community action programs, 1972-75, mgr. crew staffing, 1975-76, mgr. mgmt. devel., 1976-78, dir. mgmt. resources, 1978-81, mgr. charter mktg., planning and analysis, 1981-84, dir. contract adminstrn., 1984-91; cons. N.Y.C., 1992—. Aux. police officer, Mounted Div., N.Y.C. Police Dept., 1973-75; organizer Viet Nam Orphan Escort Program, Pearl S. Buck Found., 1974. Recipient Citation of Merit, Nat. Multiple Sclerosis Soc., 1973, Outstanding Achievement award N.Y. Interline Club, 1973. Mem. Nat. Bus. Aircraft Assn. Jewish. Home: 880 Fifth Ave New York NY 10021-4951

MARSDEN, PAULINE MARGARET, electrical engineer; b. Chorley, Eng., Feb. 14, 1950; d. John Colin and Dorothy Margaret (Malley) M.; m. Stephen Kendrick Pierce (div. 1989). AA, Highline C. C., 1972; AS, N. Seattle C. C., 1981; BA, U. Wash., 1983, BSc elec. engring., 1995. Adminstrn. asst. U. Wash., Seattle, 1985-90, sec., 1990-95; elec. engr. FAA, Renton, Wash., 1995—. Fellow Eta Kappa Nu Assoc; mem. IEEE. Anglican.

MARSEE, SUSANNE IRENE, lyric mezzo-soprano; b. San Diego, Nov. 26, 1941; d. Warren Jefferson and Irene Rose (Wills) Dowell; m. Mark J. Weinstein, May, 1987; 1 child, Zachary. Student, Santa Monica City Coll., 1961; BA in History, UCLA, 1964. Mem. voice faculty Am. Mus. and Dramatic Acad., N.Y.C., 1994—; assoc. prof. La State U. Appeared with numerous U.S. opera cos., 1970—, including N.Y.C. Opera, San Francisco Opera, Boston Opera, Houston Grand Opera; appeared with fgn. cos., festivals, Mexico City Bellas Artes, 1973, 78, Canary Islands Co., 1976, Opera Metropolitana, Caracas, Venezuela, 1977, Spoleto (Italy) Festival, 1977, Aix en Provence Festival, France, 1977, Calgary, Alta., Can., 1986; recorded Tales of Hoffman, ABC/Dunhill Records; TV appearances include Live from Lincoln Center, Turk in Italy, Cenerentola, 1980, Live from Wolftrap, Roberto Devereux's Rigoletto, 1988, A Little Night Music, 1990, Marriage of Figaro, 1991, (PBS TV) Rachel, La Cubana; recs. and CDs Anna Bolena with Ramey, Scotto, Roberto Devereux with Beverly Sills, Roberto Devereux with Monserat Caballé, Tales of Hoffmann with Beverly Sills, Rigoletto with Quilico and Carreras; videotape Roberto Devereux with Beverly Sills. Recipient 2d place award Met. Opera Regional Auditions, 1968, San Francisco Opera Regional Auditions 1968; named winner Liederkranz Club Contest, 1970; Gladys Turk Found. grantee, 1968-69; Corbett Found. grantee, 1969-73; Martha Baird Rockefeller grantee, 1969-70, 71-72. Mem. AFTRA, Am. Guild Mus. Artists (past bd. dirs.), Nat. Assn. Tchrs. of Singing (bd. dirs. for N.Y.). Democrat.

MARSH, CLARE TEITGEN, retired school psychologist; b. Manitowoc, Wis., July 7, 1934; d. Clarence Emil and Dorothy (Napiezinski) Teitgen; m. Robert Irving Marsh, Jan. 30, 1955; children: David, Wendy Marsh Tootle, Julie Marsh Domino, Laura Marsh Beltrame. MS in Ednl. Psychology, U. Wis., Milw., 1968. Sch. psychologist Milw. Pub. Schs., 1975-76; lead psychologist West Allis (Wis.)-West Milw. Pub. Schs., 1968-95; sch. psychologist Wauwatosa (Wis.) Pub. Schs., 1987; instr. Milw. Sch. Engring., 1989-90, Alverno Coll., 1990-91. NDEA fellow, 1966-68. Mem. Internat. Sch. Psychologists Assn., Nat. Assn. Sch. Psychologists (del.), Suburban Assn. Sch. Psychologists (pres. 1976-77, 86-87), Wis. Assn. Sch. Psychologists (pres. 1990-91, chmn. membership com. 1980-84, sec. 1985-89, chmn. conv. 1987), Wis. Fedn. Pupil Svcs., Phi Kappa Phi, Pi Lambda Theta (pres.), Kappa Delta Pi, Phi Delta Kappa, Sigma Tau Delta, Alpha Chi Omega. Home: 14140 W Honey Ln New Berlin WI 53151-2442

MARSH, JOAN KNIGHT, educational film, video and computer software company executive, publisher children's books; b. Butler, Mo., Apr. 8, 1934; d. E. Lyle and Ruth (Hopkins) Knight; m. Alan Reid Marsh, Sept. 27, 1958; children: Alan Reid, Clayton Knight. BA, Tex. Tech. U., 1956. Owner, pres. MarshMedia, Kansas City, Mo., 1969—. Bd. dirs., Crittenton Ctr., Kansas City, 1983-88, Mark Twain Pla. Bank, 1981-89; mem. council Family Study Ctr., U. Mo., Kansas City, 1983-89, Children's Relief Assn. Mercy Hosp., Kansas City, 1984—, pres. 1989-91; pres. Friends of Childrens' Mercy Hosp., 1996—. Gamma Phi Beta. Republican. Presbyterian. Club: Jr. League (sustaining chmn. 1982-84). Avocation: Egyptology, filmology.

MARSH, MERRILYN DELANO, sculptor, painter; b. Larchmont, N.Y., Dec. 26, 1923; d. Merrill Potter and Hazel (Holmes) Delano; m. George Estabrook Marsh, Sept. 18, 1954; children: Merrill Delano, George Estabrook Jr., Robert Houston. Diploma, Sch. of Mus. of Fine Arts, Boston, 1947; postgrad., Acad. Grande Chaumière, Paris, 1947-48. Art tchr. Choate Sch., Brookline, Mass., 1948, 49, Brookline Cmty. Ctr., Brookline, 1948, 49; pvt. art tchr. Newton, Mass., 1948-49; comml. sculptor for display and mfg. cos., 1948-55; sculpture tchr. De Cordova Mus., Lincoln, Mass., 1950-54; juror for numerous art exhbns., New Eng. area, 1954-55, 72-74. Commd. 7 reliefs for Sch. for Environ., Levine Sci. Ctr., Duke U., Durham, N.C., 1994, bronze statue for cloister garden St. Andrew's Episcopal Ch., Wellesley, Mass., 1995, other pvt. commissions. Mrs. David Hunt Sculpture scholar; recipient Katherine Thayer Hobson award Pen and Brush Soc., 1991, Best in Show award Juliani Gallery, 1991. Mem. Copley Soc. Boston (Copley master, Maria Maravigna award 1988, 1st prize in sculpture and large works 1994, other awards, 1983, 89), New Eng. Sculptors Assn. (bd. dirs. 1986, award 1988), Wellesley Soc. Artists (awards 1985, 87, 89, 91, 92, 95, bd. dirs. 1970, 88—), Cambridge Art Assn. (awards 1993, 94). Republican. Episcopalian.

MARSH, NANCY JUDITH, oncology nurse; b. Jacksonville, Fla., Jan. 11, 1948; d. William Austin and Virginia Marie (Colby) M. BA in Home Econs. Edn., Fontbonne Coll., 1970; ADN, Ga. State U., 1978, MS in Adult Health and Oncology, 1993. Staff nurse Crawford Long Meml. Hosp., Atlanta, 1978-79, St. Joseph Hosp., St. Paul, 1979-80; staff nurse clinician II St. Joseph Health Ctr., Kansas City, Mo., 1980-91; staff nurse Haven House-AIDS Hospice, Atlanta, 1992—; clin. nurse specialist West Paces Med. Ctr., 1993-94; IV home infusionist Midtowne Home Infusion, Atlanta, 1994—. Scholar Am. Cancer Soc., 1990. Mem. Oncology Nursing Soc. (oncology cert. nurse, historian UC chpt. 1980-91), Sigma Theta Tau (rec. sec. Epsilon Alpha chpt.). Democrat. Roman Catholic.

MARSH, ROBERTA REYNOLDS, elementary education educator, consultant; b. Kokomo, Ind., June 2, 1939; d. Elwood Bert and Mildred Bell (Wolford) Reynolds; m. Ronald Dean Marsh Sr., Apr. 5, 1958; children: Ronald Jr., Bryan William, Joel Allen. BEd, Ind. U., Kokomo, 1970; MEd, Ind. U., Bloomington, 1971. Cert. tchr., spl. edn. tchr., Ind., Ariz. Tchr. spl. edn. Kokomo Ctr. Schs., 1970-77; tchr. spl. edn. Tempe (Ariz.) Elem. Dist. #3, 1978-86, tchr. civics, geography, English/lit., 1986—. Local dir. Spl. Olympics, Kokomo, 1974-77, Tempe Assn. Retarded Citizens, 1978-88; den mother Boy Scouts Am., Kokomo, 1967-73; leader 4-H Club, Kokomo, 1974-77. Recipient Excellence in Edn. award Tempe Diablo, 1991. Mem. Coun. for Exceptional Children (state pres. 1986-87, Tempe chpt. pres. 1994-95, Outstanding Leader 1985, Outstanding Regular Tchr. of Yr. Tempe coun.), Internat. Reading Assn., Assn. for Children with Learning Disabilities, Ind. U. Alumni Assn., Alpha Delta Kappa (corr. sec. 1986-88, Theta pres. 1990-92). Democrat. Home: 4113 E Emelita Cir Mesa AZ 85206-5109 Office: Hudson Sch 1325 E Malibu Dr Tempe AZ 85282-5742

MARSH, TERI ELLEN, defense attorney; b. Bklyn., June 12, 1950; d. Memoir Ray and Greta (Berk) M.; m. David Ackerman, June 17, 1973 (div. Aug. 1979). BA, SUNY, Buffalo, 1972, MA, 1975, PhD, 1979; JD, NYU Sch. Law, 1992. Prof. U. Calif. San Diego, La Jolla, 1979-82, Ohio Wesleyan, Delaware, 1983-84, Wake Forest U., Winston-Salem, N.C., 1984-88; law clk. Lawyers for Children, N.Y.C., 1990, NYU Family Def. Clinic, N.Y.C., 1991-92; atty., policy asst. NOW Legal Def. and Edn. Fund, Washington, 1994; writer, researcher Clinton/Gore Presdl. Campaign, Manhattan, N.Y., 1992; juv. def. atty. D.C. Superior Ct., Washington, 1992—, D.C. Sch. of Law, Washington, 1992-95; dir. D.C. Youth Ct. Divsn. Program, 1995—; educator/cons. RFK Meml. Found., Washington, atty./cons., D.C. Sch. Law; cons. Ctr. Law and Social Policy, 1994. Cons./editor: Law Review/Pre-Trial Detention in Washington, D.C.; contbr. articles to profl. jours. Campaign writer, researcher, Clinton Presdl. Campaign, 1992; steering com. Women's Studies Program, Wake Forest U., N.C., 1984-88; del. Travis County Dem. Conv., Austin, 1981; vol. Battered Women's Shelter, Austin, 1981, 86-88. Grantee Root-Tilden, NYU Sch. Law, 1990, 91, PFW Charitable Trust, Wake Forest U., 1987, Mellon Found., Ohio Wesleyan U., 1983, Archie Found., Wake Forest U., 1986. Mem. Am. Philol. Assn. (paenlist 1978—), Classical Assn. Midwestern States (panelist 1987-90), ABA, Pa. Bar, Phi Beta Kappa. Democrat. Home: 3133 Connecticut Ave NW Washington DC 20008 Office: DC Superior Court Bldg B 409 E St NW Washington DC 20005

MARSHAK, HILARY WALLACH, psychotherapist, owner; b. N.Y.C., May 27, 1950; d. Irving Isaac and Suni (Fox) Wallach; m. Harvey Marshak, Jan. 1, 1981; children: Emily Fox, Jacob Randall. BA, U. Conn., Storrs, 1973; MSW, N.Y.U., 1992; cert., Inst. for Study of Culture, and Ethnicity, N.Y.C., 1994. Cert. social worker, N.Y. Tchr. English Glastonbury (Conn.) High Sch., 1973, U. Autonoma de Guerrero, Acapulco, Mexico, 1974; adminstrv. asst. 4M Pub. Svcs. Corp., N.Y.C., 1975, bus. mgr.; exec. v.p. Vitalmedia Enterprises Inc., N.Y.C., 1977-87, pres., chief exec. officer, 1987—; psychotherapist Fifth Ave. Ctr. Counseling and Psychotherapy, N.Y.C., 1992-95; pvt. practice N.Y.C., 1992—; mktg. cons. Frana Ltd., London, 1988-89. Editor: Before the Bar, 1978-80, Guide to Higher Edn., 1980; reviewer vol 32, The Jour. of Sex Rsch. Founder Women's Radical Caucus, U. Conn., 1970; broadcaster Sta. WHUS; bd. dirs. N.Y. Theater Ballet, 1990—, Am. AIDS Assn., 1992—; mem. writers coun. Writers in Performance series Manhattan Theater Club. Recipient 2nd Place Flowers Ulster County Agrl. Fair, New Paltz, N.Y., 1987, 1st Place Herbs, 1988. Mem. NASW, Am. AIDS Assn. (bd. dirs. 1992—), Soc. for Sci. Study of Sex, Sex Edn. and Info. Coun. of U.S., Nat. Coun. Family Rels. Jewish. Home and Office: 95 Horatio St Apt 629 New York NY 10014-1533

MARSHALL, BELINDA SMITH, finance executive; b. Garland, Tex., Sept. 1, 1966; d. William Howard and Ruth Marie (Block) Smith; m. William Wesley Marshall, Apr. 16, 1994. BBA in Acctg., MIS, Baylor U., 1988. CPA, Tex. Staff auditor Ernst & Young, Dallas, 1988-89, sr. auditor, 1989-90; internal auditor AMR Corp., Dallas, 1990-92, fin. analyst, 1992-93, sr. fin. analyst, 1993-95, mgr. finance, 1995—. Vol. Time for Dallas, 1993, 500 Inc., Dallas, 1989.

MARSHALL, CAK (CATHERINE ELAINE MARSHALL), music educator, composer; b. Nashville, Nov. 24, 1943; d. Dean Byron and Petula Iris (Bodie) M. BS in Music Edn., Ind. U. Pa., 1965; cert., Hamline U., 1981, 82, 83, Memphis State U., 1985; MME, Duquesne U., 1992. Nat. registered music educator, 1993; vocal music tchr., Pa. Tchr. music Mars (Pa.) Area Sch. Dist., 1965-66; music specialist Fox Chapel (Pa.) Area Sch. Dist., 1966—; Orff specialist Chatham Coll. Fine Arts Camp, Pitts., 1977-91; instrn. rep. elem. curriculum Dist. I, Pitts., 1986-92; arts curriculum project Pa. Dept. Edn., 1988. Author: (plays) The Rainbow Recorder, 1988, The Gift Disk Dilemma, 1989; composer, author: (play) Pittsburgh-The City with a Smile on Her Face, 1986, (holiday musical) The Dove That Could Not Fly, 1986, (book) Seasons in Song, 1987, (play) The Search for Happiness, 1990; composer: What Color Was the Baby, 1990, Kaia, 1990, Sing Praises To His Name, 1990, Go In Peace, 1990, Sing Unto The Lord, 1990, I Love America, 1992. Actor North Star Players, Pitts., 1975-80; soloist Landmark Bapt. Ch., Penn Hills, Pa., 1981-86, Bible Bapt. Ch., 1987; performer Pitts. Camerata, 1977-89; group leader Pitts Reocrder Soc., 1985-86; soloist Grace Bapt. Ch., Monroeville, 1991—. Mem. NEA, Am. ORFF-Schulwerk Assn., Pitts. Golden Triangle Chpt. (pres. 1985—), Music Educators Nat. Confl., Pa. Music Educators Assn. (elem. jour. 1986—), Am. Recorder Assn., Pi Kappa Lambda. Baptist. Home: 1707 Kirk Dr Verona PA 15147-3917 Office: O'Hara Elem Sch 115 Cabin Ln Pittsburgh PA 15238-2500

MARSHALL, CAROL JOYCE, clinical research data coordinator; b. Mt. Holly, N.J., July 29, 1967; d. Oliver Jr. and Ruby Jean (Bennefield-Smith) M. BA in Biol. Scis., Rutgers U., 1985-89. Transplant-procurement coord. Nat. Disease Rsch. Interchange, Phila., 1989-90, supr. procurement dept., 1990-91, rsch. mgr., 1991-92; clin. rsch. data coord. U.S. Biosci., West Conshohocken, Pa., 1992-93, Corning Besselaar, Princeton, N.J., 1993—. Home: 2211 Durham Ct Mount Laurel NJ 08054-4224 Office: Corning Besselaar 210 Carnegie Ctr Princeton NJ 08540-6233

MARSHALL, CAROL SYDNEY, labor market analyst, employment counselor; b. N.Y.C., Nov. 21, 1930; d. Charles Herbert and Tillie (Muriel) Helman; m. Bogdan Branislav Denitch, 1952 (div. 1954); m. Charles Marshall, Oct. 9, 1954 (div. Aug. 1973); children: Katrina, Peter Morgan Helman, Bonnie Sophia Brija, Athena. Student, Antioch Coll., 1948-50, Hunter Coll., 1953-61, U. Mo., 1967-68; AB in Geography & Urban Planning with honors & distinction, San Diego State U., 1971, postgrad., 1972-73. Copy person, cub reporter Chgo. Sun-Times, 1949-50; adminstrv. asst. Hudson Guild Child Care Ctr., N.Y.C., 1951-54; rsch. asst. City of Antioch Planning Dept., Calif., 1971-72; planning aide San Diego County Planning Dept., 1972-73; labor market analyst Labor Market Info. Divsn. Calif. Employment Devel. Dept., San Francisco, 1973-94; employment rep. Job Svc. Calif. Employment Devel. Dept., San Francisco, 1994—; speaker, panelist on labor mkt. issues, 1985-94; labor mkt. rsch. cons. San Francisco Pvt. Industry Coun., 1986-94, San Mateo Pvt. Industry Coun., 1986-91, Alameda County Econ. Devel. Adv. Bd., 1991-94; mem. profl. working group Health Occupations Study Nat. Ctr. for Rsch. in Vocat. Edn., Berkeley, Calif., 1989-91; mem. adv. bd. Dept. Health Info. Tech. City Coll. San Francisco, 1992-94. Contbr. articles to profl. jours. Mem. Young Peoples Socialist League, N.Y.C., 1947-54, nat. sec., 1953-54; mem. Young Socialists, N.Y.C., 1954-62; organizer, co-founder San Diego State U. Child Care Ctr., 1971. Mem. Ctr. for Sci. in the Pub. Interest, Pub. Citizens Health Rsch. Group, East Bay Bicycle Coalition, San Francisco Bicycle Coalition. Jewish. Office: Calif Employment Devel Dept Job Svc 801 Turk St San Francisco CA 94102

MARSHALL, CAROLYN ANN M., church official, consultant; b. Springfield, Ill., July 18, 1935; d. Hayward Thomas and Isabelle Bernice (Hayer) McMurray; m. John Alan Marshall, July 14, 1956 (dec. Sept. 1990); children: Margaret Marshall Bushman, Cynthia Marshall Kyrouac, Clinton, Carol. Student, De Pauw U., 1952-54; BSBA, Drake U., 1956; D of Pub. Svc. (hon.), De Pauw U., 1983; LHD (hon.), U. Indpls., 1990. Corp. sec. Marshall Studios, Inc., Veedersburg, Ind., 1956-89, exec. cons., 1989-93; sec. Gen. Conf., lay leader South Ind. conf. United Meth. Ch., 1988—; Carolyn M. Marshall chair in women studies Bennett Coll., Greensboro, N.C., 1988; fin. cons. Lucille Raines Residence, Inpls., 1977—. Pres. Fountain Ctrl. Band Boosters, Veedersburg, 1975-77; del. Gen. Conf., United Meth. Ch., 1980, 84, 88, 92, 96, pres. women's divsn. gen. bd. global ministries, 1984-88; bd. dirs. Franklin (Ind.) United Meth. Ch. Home: 204 N Newlin St Veedersburg IN 47987-1358

MARSHALL, CHRISTINE LEE, community executive; b. Lansing, Mich., Oct. 30, 1956; d. Willis Walter and Mary Jane (Beatty) M.; m. David Wright Bowman; children: Charlotte Sofia, Karina Jane. BS, No. Mich. U., 1979; postgrad., Boston U., 1980. Co-hose, prodr. P.M. Mag.-WJIM-TV, Lansing, 1980-82; prodr. internat. programming Scandinavian Broadcasting Sys., Oslo, 1983-89; dir. cable, satellite TV and tech. dept. U. Wis., Milw., 1990—. Freelance film and video prodr./dir. SRS Info. Film/Video, Oslo, London, 1989-96. Senator Acad. Staff Senate, U. Wis., Milw., 1993. Recipient 1st place film award Scandinavian Film and Video, 1990, 2d place, 1988, 1st place film award U.S. Indusl. Film and Video, 1988, Nat. Prod. award P.M. Mag., 1982. Mem. NOW, ASPRO Union. Office: Univ of Wisconsin PO Box 413 Milwaukee WI 53217

MARSHALL, CONSUELO BLAND, federal judge; b. Knoxville, Tenn., Sept. 28, 1936; d. Clyde Theodore and Annie (Brown) Arnold; m. George Edward Marshall, Aug. 30, 1959; children: Michael Edward, Laurie Ann. A.A., Los Angeles City Coll., 1956; B.A., Howard U., 1958, LL.B., 1961. Bar: Calif. 1962. Dep. atty. City of L.A., 1962-67; assoc. Cochran & Atkins, L.A., 1968-70; commr. L.A. Superior Ct., 1971-76; judge Inglewood Mcpl. Ct., 1976-77, L.A. Superior Ct., 1977-80, U.S. Dist. Ct. Central Dist. Calif., L.A., 1980—; lectr. U.S. Information Agy. in Yugoslavia, Greece and Italy, 1984, in Nigeria and Ghana, 1991, in Ghana, 1992. Contbr. articles to profl. jours.; notes editor Law Jour. Howard U. Mem. adv. bd. Richstone Child Abuse Center. Recipient Judicial Excellence award Criminal Ct. Bar Assn., 1992; research fellow Howard U. Law Sch., 1959-60;. Mem. State Bar Calif., Calif. Women Lawyers Assn., Calif. Assn. Black Lawyers, Calif. Judges Assn., Black Women Lawyers Assn., Los Angeles County Bar Assn., Nat. Assn. Women Judges, NAACP, Urban League, Beta Phi Sigma. Office: US Dist Ct 312 N Spring St Los Angeles CA 90012-4701*

MARSHALL, ELLEN RUTH, lawyer; b. N.Y.C., Apr. 23, 1949; d. Louis and Faith (Gladstone) M. AB, Yale U., 1971; JD, Harvard U., 1974. Bar: Calif. 1975, D.C. 1981, N.Y. 1989. Assoc. McKenna & Fitting, Los Angeles, 1975-80; ptnr. McKenna, Conner & Cuneo, Los Angeles and Orange County, Calif., 1980-88, Morrison & Foerster, Orange County, Calif., 1988—. Mem. ABA (bus. law sect., savs. inst. com., asset securitization com., tax sect., employee benefits com.), Orange County Bar Assn. Club: Center (Costa Mesa, Calif.). Office: Morrison & Foerster 19900 Macarthur Blvd Irvine CA 92612

MARSHALL, JANE PRETZER, newspaper editor; b. Chase County, Kans.; married; 2 children. BS in Home Econs. and Journalism, Kans. State U., 1967; student, Tex. A&M, U. Mo., Tex. Christian U., Brite Divinity Sch. Asst. editor dept. agr. info. Tex. Agrl. Ext. Sta. Tex. A&M U., College Station, 1967-70; staff writer Gazette-Telegraph, Colorado Springs, Colo., 1970-72; editor corporate publ. Colorado Interstate, Colorado Springs, 1972-75; co-editor The Pampa (Tex.) News, 1975-78; exec. features editor Ft. Worth Star-Telegram, 1978-84; features editor Denver Post, 1984-88, Houston Chronicle, 1988—. Recipient 1st place for feature writing Tex. AP Mng. Editors Assn., 1978. Mem. Am. Assn. Sunday and Features Editors (bd. dirs., founding chairperson Features First), Women's Found. Health Edn. and Rsch. (bd. dirs.), Journalism and Women Symposium (1st pres.). Office: Houston Chronicle 801 Texas St Houston TX 77002-2906*

MARSHALL, JULIE W. GREGOVICH, engineering executive; b. Pasadena, Calif., Mar. 3, 1953; d. Gibson Marr and Anna Grace (Peterson) Wolfe; m. Michael Roy Gregovich Dec. 18, 1976 (div. June 1994); children: Christianna, Kerry Leigh; m. Robert Brandon Marshall, Aug. 6, 1994. BA magna cum laude, Randolph-Macon Woman's Coll., 1975; MBA, Pepperdine U., 1983. cert. tchr. K-12, Calif. Test engr. Westinghouse Hanford, Richland, Wash., 1975-76; startup engr. Bechtel Power Corp., Norwalk, Calif., 1976-77; test engr. Wash. Pub. Power, Richland, 1978-80; from mgr. to v.p. Sun Tech. Svcs., Mission Viejo, Calif., 1983-93; cons. Mission Energy Co., Irvine, Calif., 1993-94; owner, CEO, pres. Key Employee Svcs., Inc., Key Largo, Fla., 1994—. contbr. article to jour. Named Young Career Woman of the Yr. Wash. Pub. Power Supply System, 1979. Mem. Am. Nuc. Soc. (mem. bd. trustees pub. edn. program 1992—), Phi Beta Kappa.

MARSHALL, LINDA LANTOW, pediatrics nurse; b. Tulsa, Dec. 13, 1949; d. Lawrence Lee and Lena Mae (Ross) Lantow; m. David Panke Hartson, Aug. 25, 1970 (div. 1982); children: Michael David, Jonathan Lee; m. Roger Nathan Marshall, Dec. 11, 1985; 1 child, Sarabeth Megan. A, U. Okla., 1970; BSN, U. Tulsa, 1983. Cert. pediatric nurse. Pediats. nurse Youthcare, Claremore, Okla., 1983-85, 87—; staff nurse ICU Doctors Hosp., Tulsa, 1985-87. Bd. dirs. PTA Barnard, tulsa, 1993-95; leader Brownie troop Girl Scouts U.S., Tulsa, 1994-95, leader jr. scouts, 1995—. Mem. Sigma Theta Tau. Home: 2628 E 22nd St Tulsa OK 74114-3123 Office: Youth Care of Rogers County 525 E Blue Starr Dr Claremore OK 74017-4401

MARSHALL, MARGARET HILARY, lawyer; b. Newcastle, Natal, South Africa, Sept. 1, 1944; came to U.S., 1968; d. Bernard Charles and Hilary A.D. (Anderton) M; m. Samuel Shapiro, Dec. 14, 1968 (div. Apr. 1982); m. Anthony Lewis, Sept. 23, 1984. BA, Witwatersrand U., Johannesburg, 1966; MEd, Harvard U., 1969; JD, Yale U., 1976; LHD (hon.), Regis Coll., 1993. Bar: Mass. 1977, U.S. Dist. Ct. Mass., U.S. Dist. Ct. N.H., U.S. Dist. Ct. D.C., U.S. Dist. Ct. (ea. dist.) Mich., U.S. Tax Ct., U.S. Ct. Appeals (1st, 11th and D.C. cirs.), U.S. Supreme Ct. Assoc. Csaplar & Bok, Boston, 1976-83, ptnr., 1983-89; ptnr. Choate, Hall & Stewart, Boston, 1989-92; v.p., gen. counsel Harvard U., Cambridge, Mass., 1992—; mem. jud. nominating coun., 1987-90, 92; chairperson ct. rules subcom. Alternative Dispute Resolution Working Group, 1985-87; mem. fed. appts. commn., 1993; mem. adv. com. Supreme Judicial Ct., 1989-92, mem. gender equality com., 1989-94; mem. civil justice adv. group U.S. Dist. Ct. Mass., 1991-93; spl. counsel Jud. Conduct Commn., 1988-92; trustee Mass. Continuing Legal Edn., Inc., 1990-92. Trustee Africa News, Africa Fund, Regis Coll., 1993-95; bd. dirs. Internat. Design Conf., Aspen, 1986-92, Boston Mcpl. Res. Bur., 1990—, Supreme Judicial Ct. Hist. Soc., 1990-94, sec., 1990-94. Fellow Am. Bar Found. (Mass. state chair); mem. Boston Bar Assn. (treas. 1988-89, v.p. 1989-90, pres.-elect 1990-91, pres. 1991-92), Internat. Women's Forum, Mass. Women's Forum, Boston Club, Phi Beta Kappa (hon.). Home: 8 Lowell St Cambridge MA 02138-4726 Office: Harvard U Massachusetts Hall Cambridge MA 02138

MARSHALL, MARY JONES, civic worker; b. Billings, Mont.; d. Leroy Nathaniel and Janet (Currie) Dailey; m. Harvey Bradley Jones, Nov. 15, 1952 (dec. 1989); children: Dailey, Janet Currie, Ellis Bradley; m. Boyd T. Marshall, June 27, 1990. Student, Carleton Coll., 1943-44, U. Mont., 1944-46, UCLA, 1959. Owner Mary Jones Interiors. Founder, treas. Jr. Art Council, L.A. County Mus., 1953-55, v.p., 1955-56; mem. costume council Pasadena (Calif.) Philharm.; co-founder Art Rental Gallery, 1953, chmn. art and architecture tour, 1955; founding mem., sec. Art Alliance, Pasadena Art Mus., 1955-56; benefit chmn. Pasadena Girls Club, 1959, bd. dirs., 1958-60; chmn. L.A. Tennis Patron's Assn. Benefit, 1965; sustaining Jr. League Pasadena; mem. docent council L.A. County Mus.; mem. costume council L.A. County Mus. Art., program chmn. 20th Century Greatest Designers; mem. blue ribbon com. L.A. Music Ctr.; benefit chmn. Venice com. Internat. Fund for Monuments, 1971; bd. dirs. Art Ctr. 100, Pasadena, 1988—; pres. The Pres.'s L.A. Children's Bur., 1989; co-chmn. benefit Harvard Coll. Scholarship Fund, 1974, steering com. benefit, 1987, Otis Art Inst., 1975, 90th Anniversary of Children's Bureau of L.A., 1994; mem. Harvard-Radcliffe scholarship dinner com., 1985; mem. adv. bd. Estelle Doheny Eye Found., 1976, chmn. benefit, 1980; adv. bd. Loyola U. Sch. Fine Arts, L.A., Art Ctr. Sch. Design, Pasadena, Calif., 1987—; patron chmn. Benefit Achievement Rewards for Coll. Scientists, 1988; chmn. com. Sch. Am. Ballet Benefit, 1988, N.Y.C.; bd. dirs. Founders Music Ctr., L.A., 1977-81; mem. nat. adv. council Sch. Am. Ballet, N.Y.C., nat. co-chmn. gala, 1980; adv. council on fine arts Loyola-Marymount U.; mem. L.A. Olympic Com., 1984, The Colleagues; founding mem. Mus. Contemporary Art, 1986; chmn. The Pres.'s Benefit L.A. Children's Bur., 1990; exec. com. L.A. Alive for L.A. Music Ctr., 1992; mem. exec. com. Children's Bur. of L.A. Found., 1992; chmn. award dinner Phoenix House, 1994, 96; bd. dirs. Andrews Sch. Gerontology, U. So. Calif., 1996—, Leakey Found., 1996—; bd. regents Children's Hosp. L.A., 1996—. Mem. Am. Parkinson Disease Assn. (steering com. 1991), Valley Hunt Club (Pasadena), Calif. Club (L.A.), Kappa Alpha Theta. Home: 10375 Wilshire Blvd Apt 8B Los Angeles CA 90024-4728

MARSHALL, MARYANN CHORBA, office administrator; b. Scranton, Pa., Apr. 18, 1952; d. Edward M. and Mildred (Polc) Chorba; m. Daniel V. Marshall III. BA, Emmanuel Coll., 1974. Personal, social sec. Jordan Embassy Mil. Office, Washington, 1974-76; exec. asst, office mgr. Jordan Embassy Info. Bur., Washington, 1976-81; asst. to pres. Nat. Press Club, Washington, 1982-91; adminstr. Harvard Bus. Sch. Club, Washington, 1995—. Mem. League Rep. Women. Republican. Roman Catholic. Home: 331 North Pitt St Alexandria VA 22314 Office: 1010 Vermont Ave NW Ste 301 Washington DC 20005-4902

MARSHALL, NANCY, psychotherapist; b. Orange, Calif., Dec. 16, 1944; d. Philip and Blanche (Archer) Shetenhelm; 1 child, Elizabeth. BA in Fine Arts, Va. Commonwealth U., 1966; MA in Counseling Psychology, Kutztown (Pa.) U., 1994. Advt. designer, film animator J.C. Prodns., N.Y.C., 1967-86; counselor Northampton County Children and Youth, Easton, Pa., 1987-93; psychotherapist Kidspeace, Allentown, Pa., 1993; program coord. Rape Crisis Ctr., Belvidere, N.J., 1993-95; mgr. sexual assault treatment program coord. Vis. Nurses Assn. Domestic Abuse, Lehigh and Allentown, Pa., 1995—; pvt. practice, Easton, 1986—. Vol. tchr. Easton Area Boys and Girls Club, Northampton County Juvenile Probation, 1988—. Mem. N.J. Network for Treatment of Sexual Offenders, Eyem Movement Desensitation and Reprocessing Network. Home: 49 N Delaware Dr Easton PA 18042 Office: VNA Lehigh 1710 Union Blvd Allentown PA 18103

MARSHALL, NANCY HAIG, library administrator; b. Stamford, Conn., Nov. 3, 1932; d. Harry Percival and Dorothy Charlotte (Price) Haig; m. William Hubert Marshall, Dec. 28, 1953; children—Bruce Davis, Gregg Price, Lisa Reynolds, Jeanine Haig. B.A., Ohio Wesleyan U., 1953; M.A.L.S., U. Wis., 1972. Dir. Wis. Inter Libr. Svcs., Madison, 1972-79; Reference librarian U. Wis., Madison, 1972, assoc. dir. univ. libraries, 1979-86; dean univ. librs. Coll. William and Mary, Williamsburg, Va., 1986—; mem. adv. com. Copyright Office, Washington, 1978-82; dir. USBE, Inc., Washington, 1983-86; trustee OCLC, Inc., Dublin, Ohio, 1982-88. Contbr. articles to profl. jours. Mem. ALA (coun. 1980-88, 90-93), Wis. Libr. Assn. (Libr. of the Yr. award 1982), Va. Libr. Assn., Beta Phi Mu. Office: Coll William and Mary E G Swem Libr Williamsburg VA 23185

MARSHALL, NATHALIE, artist, writer, educator; b. Pitts., Nov. 10, 1932; d. Clifford Benjamin and Clarice (Stille) Marshall; m. Robert Alfred Van Buren, May 1, 1952 (div. June 1965); children: Christine Van Buren Popovic, Clifford Marshall Van Buren, Jennifer Van Buren Lake; m. David Arthur Nadel, Dec. 30, 1976 (div. Oct. 1995). AFA, Silvermine Coll. Art, New Canaan, Conn., 1967; BFA, U. Miami, Coral Gables, 1977, MA, 1982, PhD in English and Fine Art, 1982. Instr. humanities Miami Ednl. Consortium, Miami Shores, Fla., 1977-79, Barry U., Miami Shores, 1979-81, U. Miami, Coral Gables, 1977-81; sr. lectr. Nova U., Ft. Lauderdale, Fla., 1981-84, assoc. prof. humanities, 1985-86; prof. art, chair dept. art. Old Coll., Reno, Nev., 1986-88; chief artist Rockefeller U., N.Y.C., 1973-75; asst. registrar Lowe Art Mus., Coral Gables, 1976-78; co-founder, dir. The Bakehouse Art Complex, Miami, 1984-86; advisor, bd. mem. NAH YAH EE (Indian children's art exhibits), Weimar, Calif., 1984—; mem. adv. bd. New World Sch. Arts, Miami, 1985-86. One-woman shows include Silvermine Coll. Art, New Canaan, Conn., 1968, Ingber Gallery, Greenwich, 1969, Capricorn Gallery, N.Y.C., 1969, Pierson Coll. at Yale U., New Haven, 1970, The Art Barn, Greenwich, 1972, Art Unltd., N.Y.C., 1973, Benevy Gallery, N.Y.C., 1974, Richter Libr., U. Miami, 1985, Nova U., Ft. Lauderdale, 1985, Ward Nasse Gallery, N.Y.C., 1985, Old Coll., Reno, 1986, Washoe County Libr., Reno, 1987, Sabal Palms Gallery, Gulfport, Fla., 1992, Ambiance Gallery, St. Petersburg, 1995, 96, Gulfport Libr., 1996; group shows include: Capricorn Gallery, N.Y.C., 1968, Ingber Gallery, Greenwich, 1968, Compass Gallery, N.Y.C., 1970, Optimums Gallery, Westport, Conn., 1970, Finch Coll. Mus., N.Y.C., 1971, Town Hall Art Gallery, Stamford, Conn., 1973, 74, Jewish Community Ctr., Miami Beach, 1981, Continuum Gallery, Miami Beach, 1982, South Fla. Art Inst., Hollywood, Fla., 1984, Met. Mus., Coral Gables, Fla., 1985, Ward Nasse Gallery, N.Y.C., 1985, Brunnier Mus., Iowa State U., Ames, 1986, Nat. Mus. of Women in The Arts Libr., Washington, 1987, 89, U.S. Art in Embassies Program, 1987-88, UN World Conf. Women, Nairobi, 1987, Raymond James Invitational, St. Petersburg, Fla., 1989-92, Arts Ctr., St. Petersburg, 1990, 91, 92, Global Gallery, Tampa, Fla., 1990, 91, Sabal Palms Gallery, Gulfport, Fla., 1992, No. Nat. Nicolet Coll., Rhineland, Wis., 1992, Internat. Biennale, Bordeaux, France, 1993, Salon de Vieux Colombier, Paris, 1993, Synchronicity Space, N.Y.C., 1993, Women's 1st Internat. Biennal of Women Artists, Stockholm, 1994-95 (gold medal), Tampa Arts Forum, Fla., 1995, 96, Salon Internat. des Seigneurs de l'Art, Aix-en-Provence, France, 1995 (silver medal), World's Women Online Internet Installation Ariz. State U. 1995-96, UN 4th Conf. on Women, Beijing, 1995-96, Artemisa Gallery, Chgo., 1995-96; author, artist: Vibrations on Revelations, 1973, The Firebird, 1982, Homage to John Donne's Holy Sonnets 10 & 13, 1987, Tidepool, 1995; numerous artist books, 1968—; author: Be Organized for College, 1980; artist: (children's book) The Desert: What Lives There?, 1972; editor, designer: Court Theaters of Europe, 1982; writer, dir. T.V. programs Moutain Mandala: Autumn, Mountain Mandala: Winter, The Unexpected, 1992; contbr. poems to poetry mags., articles to profl. jours. Recipient Sponsor's award for Painting Greenwich Art Soc., 1967; Steven Buffton Meml. award Am. Bus. Women's Assn., 1980; grantee Poets & Writers, 1993; one of 300 global artists in Internat. Hope and Optimism Portfolio, Oxford. Mem. MLA, Coll. Art Assn., Nat. Women's Studies Assn., Women's Caucus for Art (nat. adv. bd. 1983-88, pres. Miami chpt. 1984-86, southeast regional v.p. 1986). Address: 5444 1/2 30th Ave S # 5C Gulfport FL 33707-5207

MARSHALL, NAVARRE, retired secondary education educator; b. Stockton, Calif., Oct. 31, 1916; d. Winfield Scott and Elizabeth (Brophy) Baggett; m. Robert Frank Marshall, Aug. 10, 1947; 1 child, Roberta Navarre Marshall. BA, San Francisco State U., 1937; postgrad., U. Calif., Berkeley, 1945-47, U. Calif., Santa Cruz, 1970-72. Cert. elem.-jr. high tchr. Tchr. Pittsburg (Calif.) Sch. Dist., 1937-40, Martinez (Calif.) Sch. Dist., 1941-49, Pajaro Valley Sch. Dist., Watsonville, Calif., 1958-76; ret., 1976. Sec., sponsor Watsonville Friends of the Libr.; mem. Pajaro Valley Arts Coun., 1994, Pajaro Valley Hist. Assn. Mem. AAUW (sec. 1963-64, pres. Watsonville br. 1992-93, sec. 1994-95, publicity chair 1995—), Calif. Tchrs. Assn., Order Ea. Star, Delta Kappa Gamma (charter pres. 1961-62), Libr. of Congress (nat. mem. 1995), Internat. Zeta Epsilon (charter pres. 1961-62, chpt. pres. 1986-88, scholarship chair 1984-86, 88-90, Woman Making History award 1994). Democrat.

MARSHALL, PATRICIA HILL, resource educator; b. Louisville, Jan. 1, 1947; d. George Abraham and Lena Eleanor (Feiock) Hill; m. James Thomas Marshall, Jr., Aug. 31, 1968; 1 child, Elizabeth Aynsley. BS, Western Ky. U., 1972, MS, 1976; postgrad., U. Louisville. Tchr. bus. edn. Western H.S., Louisville, 1970-89, coord. tech. preparation, 1990-93; resource tchr. for sch. restructuring Jefferson County Pub. Schs., Louisville, 1994—. Recipient Kudo award Western H.S., 1985, Disting. Educator award Tandy Corp., 1988, Excel award for teaching excellence Jefferson County Pub. Schs. and WHAS-TV, 1996. Mem. Ky. Assn. Supervision and Curriculum Devel. (past pres.), Execs. Club, Phi Delta Kappa, Delta Gamma Gamma, Phi Delta Theta. Democrat. Office: Gheens Profl Acad 4425 Preston Hwy Louisville KY 40213-2033

MARSHALL, (C.) PENNY, actress, director; b. N.Y.C., Oct. 15, 1943; d. Anthony W. and Marjorie Irene (Ward) M.; m. Michael Henry (div.); 1 child, Tracy Lee; m. Robert Reiner, Apr. 10, 1971 (div. 1979). Student, U. N.Mex., 1961-64. Appeared on numerous television shows, including The Odd Couple, 1972-74, Friends and Lovers (co-star), 1974, Let's Switch, 1974, Wives (pilot), 1975, Chico and the Man, 1975, Mary Tyler Moore, 1975, Heaven Help Us, 1975, Saturday Night Live, 1975-77, Happy Days, 1975, Battle of Network Stars (ABC special), 1976, Barry Manilow special, 1976, The Tonight Show, 1976-77, Dinah, 1976-77, Mike Douglas Show, 1975-77, Merv Griffin Show, 1976-77, Blansky's Beauties, 1977, Network Battle of the Sexes, 1977, Laverne and Shirley (co-star), 1976-83; TV films More Than Friends, 1978, Love Thy Neighbor, 1984, Challenge of a Lifetime, 1985, The Odd Couple: Together Again, 1993; appeared in motion pictures How Sweet It Is, 1967, The Savage Seven, 1968, The Grasshopper, 1970, 1941, 1979, Movers and Shakers, 1985, She's Having a Baby, 1988, The Hard Way, 1991, Hocus Pocus, 1993, Get Shorty, 1995; dir. films: Jumpin' Jack Flash, 1986, Big, 1988, Awakenings, 1990, A League of Their Own, 1992, Renaissance Man, 1994, The Preacher's Wife, 1996; co-exec. prodr. TV series A League of Their Own, 1993 (also dir. pilot); prodr. Getting Away With Murder, 1995. Office: care CAA/Todd Smith 9830 Wilshire Blvd Beverly Hills CA 90212-1804*

MARSHALL, ROBERTA NAVARRE, middle school educator; b. Martinez, Calif., Sept. 26, 1949; d. Robert Frank and Navarre (Baggett) M. BS, Calif. Polytech. State U., 1971; MS in voc. edn., Calif. State U., 1981. Cert. secondary educator, Calif. Consumer-homemaking tchr. Hanford (Calif.) H.S., 1972-73, Eagle Mountain (Calif.) H.S., 1974-79, Solano Jr. H.S., Vallejo, Calif., 1980—; competitive recognition events coord. FHA-HERO Region 3, 1991-95; workshop presenter. Middle grades curriculum task force Calif. Dept. Edn., Sacramento, 1987-88. Recipient home econs. curriculum grants, 1985-86, 89-90; named Tchr. of Yr. Elks Lodge, 1988-89. Mem. Calif. Tchrs. Assn., Home Econs. Tchrs. Assn. Calif. (v.p. 1991-93), Am. Assn. Univ. Women, Am. Voc. Assn., Am. Assn. Family & Consumer Scis., Future Homemakers of Am. (adv. 1972), Home Econs. Related Occupations. Home: 5038 Brittany Dr Fairfield CA 94585 Office: Solano Jr H S 1025 Corcoran St Vallejo CA 94589

MARSHALL, SHEILA HERMES, lawyer; b. N.Y.C., Jan. 17, 1934; d. Paul Milton and Julia Angela (Meagher) Hermes; m. James Josiah Marshall, Sept. 30, 1967; 1 child, James J.H. BA, St. John's U., N.Y.C., 1959; JD, NYU, 1963. Bar: N.Y. 1964, U.S. Ct. Appeals (2d, 3d, 5th and D.C. cirs.), U.S. Supreme Ct. 1970. Assoc. LeBoeuf, Lamb, Greene & MacRae, N.Y.C., 1963-72, ptnr., 1973—; specialist in field. Mem. ABA, N.Y. State Bar Assn., Assn. of Bar of City of N.Y. Republican. Home: 1035 Park Ave New York NY 10028-0912 Office: LeBoeuf Lamb Greene & MacRae 125 W 55th St New York NY 10019-5369

MARSHALL, SUSAN ELIZABETH, lawyer; b. Sherman, Tex., Nov. 11, 1944; d. Arnold J. Korpi and Lily Hivala; m. J. C. Douglas Marshall, Sept. 1, 1967; children: Laura E., Andrew J. MusB, Mich. State U., 1965; MA, U. Pa., 1968; JD, Franklin Pierce Law Ctr., 1980. Bar: N.H., U.S. Dist. Ct. N.H. Grad. tchg. fellow U. Pa., Phila., 1966-68; spl. collections technician Dartmouth Coll., Baker Libr., Hanover, N.H., 1970-71; legis. bill drafter Ofice of Legis. Svcs., Concord, N.H., 1980-82, legis. atty., 1982-85, sr. atty., 1985, dep. dir., 1985-89, dep. dir., chief legal officer, 1989—; workshop faculty mem. ABA/Cen. and Ea. European Law Initiative, Washington, 1995. Mem. Concord Chorale, Inc., 1975—; co-dir. Early Music Concord, 1985-89. Fulbright scholar U.S. Govt., 1965-66. Mem. N.H. Bar Assn. (past mem. pub. info. com., quality of life com., mem. publs. com., bd. editors N.H. Bar Jour. 1994—). Home: St Paul's Sch 325 Pleasant St Concord NH 03301 Office: Office of Legis Svcs Rm 109 107 N Main St Concord NH 03301

MARSHALL, SUSAN LOCKWOOD, civic worker; b. Orange, N.J., Dec. 2, 1939; d. Richard Douglas and Helen Lockwood (Stratford) Nelson; BE, Wheelock Coll., 1961; m. William Pendleton Marshall, Aug. 20, 1960; children: Jill, James. Vol., Newton-Wellesley (Mass.) Hosp., 1962-63, New Eyes for the Needy, Inc., 1963-64, amblyopia screening program, Short Hills, N.J., 1969-71; bd. dirs. Jr. League of Oranges and Short Hills, Inc., 1967-69, 70-72, corr. sec., 1970-72; fund raising vol. Children's Aid and Adoption Soc. N.J., 1969-73, dir., 1970-73, asst. sec., 1970-72, 1st v.p., 1972-73; bd. dirs. Jr. League Stamford-Norwalk (Conn.), 1974-78, asst. treas., 1976-77, treas., 1977-78; bd. dirs. Program One to One, Inc., 1975-76, also treas.; vol. Voluntary Action Ctr. 1975-76; bd. dirs. Episcopal Churchwomen of St. Luke's Parish, 1974-75, 76-81, 2d v.p., 1976-77, asst. treas., 1977-78, treas., 1978-80, pres., 1980-81; bd. dirs. Lockwood Mathews Mansion Mus., 1979-88, 89-95, vol., 1979—, treas., 1979-88, 89-95, v.p., 1983-88; mem. council Darien Sch. Parent Bd., 1978-83, recording sec. 1981-83; bd. dirs. Middlesex Jr. High Parents Assn., 1979-83, treas., 1982-83; mem. The Vol. Ctr., 1984—; mem. vol. mgmt. assistance program adv. comm. Darien Chpt. Am. Field Service, 1984-87; Darien H.S. Parents Assn., 1982-85, chmn., 1984-85; bd. dirs. Darien United Way, 1984-95, asst. treas., 1988-95, treas. 1995—. Address: 358 Hollow Tree Ridge Rd Darien CT 06820-3218

MARSHALL, VIRGINIA MARY, secondary education educator, media specialist; b. Medford, Mass., Nov. 2, 1940; d. Frederick Edward and Louise Angela (Lombardi) Gordinier; m. Dana Philip Marshall, Apr. 17, 1970; children: Jennifer Susanne, Kristin Terese Justyne Marshall. BS in Secondary Edn. cum laude, Salem (Mass.) State Coll., 1962; MS in Secondary Edn., Boston State Coll., 1967; MS in Edn. Libr. Media, Bridgewater State Coll., Mass., 1992. Cert. secondary tchr. and libr. media specialist, Mass. Tchr. English Somerville (Mass.) Sch. System, 1962-73; tchr. jr. high Blessed Sarament Sch., Walpole, Mass., 1983—, sch. libr. media sepcialist, 1991—; literary cons. Koller Enterprises, 1971; pres. Glass Castle, 1974-83, Ginny's Pincushion, 1983-87. Named Outstanding Young Educator, Somerville Jaycees, 1970, Am. Yearbook Outstanding Advisor, 1970, 71. Mem. NEA, Mass. Sch. Libr. Media Assn., Nat. Coun. English Tchrs. Home: 17 Country Club Dr Walpole MA 02081

MARSHMAN-JOHNSON, KENYA LATRICE, secretary; b. Washington, July 5, 1973; d. William McKinley and Joan (Carter) Marshman; m. Wiley Johnson, Apr. 21, 1995; 1 child, Kai DeAndré. BA in Bus., George Washington U., 1994. Sr. sec. internat. svc. George Washington U., Washington, 1993-94; adminstrv. asst. Acad. for Ednl. Devel., Washington, 1994-95; sec. Columbia Hosp. for Women, Washington, 1995-96; exec. sec. Delmarva Found. Med. Care, Inc., Washington, 1996—. Mem. Nat. Home Bus. Assn., Nat. Coun. Negro Women, Inc. Baptist. Home: 3703 Dunlap St Temple Hills MD 20748-4222 Office: Delmarva Found Med Care Inc Ste 507 1000 Thomas Jefferson St NW Washington DC 20007

MARSTON, BETSY PILAT, newspaper editor; b. N.Y.C., July 6, 1940; d. Oliver and Alice (Riddle) Pilat; m. Ed Marston; children: Wendy, David. BA, U. Del., 1962; MS, Columbia U., 1963. Producer WNET-TV, N.Y.C., 1967-74; host KVNF Pub. Radio, Paonia, Colo., 1995-96. Democrat. Home: Box 279 Paonia CO 81428 Office: High Country News 119 Grand Ave Paonia CO 81428

MARTEAU, KIMBERLY K., federal agency administrator; b. L.A., Feb. 22, 1959; d. Donald S. Mart and Roberta Blank; m. John B. Emerson, Sept. 15, 1990. BA magna cum laude, UCLA, 1981; JD, U. Calif., Hastings, 1984. Practicing atty. Tuttle & Taylor, 1986-88; mem. nat. adv. staff Dukakis for Pres. Com., 1988; dir. internat. devel. and distbn. Patchett-Kaufman Entertainment, 1989-90; mgmt. assoc. Sony Pictures Entertainment, 1990-92; v.p. Motion Pictures, Savoy Pictures, Entertainment, 1992-93; dir. office of pub. liaison U.S. Info. Agy., 1993—. Editor Hastings Law Review, 1984-85. Grantee Edn. Abroad Program, 1979; fellow Rotary Club, 1984-85. Office: Public Liaison US Info Agy 301 4th St SW Rm 602 Washington DC 20547-0009

MARTEL, EVA LEONA, accountant; b. Bristol, Conn., Feb. 14, 1945; d. Samuel L. and Irene A. (Beaulieu) Martel. BS in Acctg., N.H. Coll., 1986; MBA, Plymouth State Coll., 1990. Cert. mgmt. acct.; cert. continuing edn. educator. Accts. payable Elliot Hosp., Manchester, N.H., 1971-79; bookkeeper Elliot Hosp., Manchester, 1979-84, dir. acctg., 1984-94; portfolio mgr. Optima Health Inc., Manchester, N.H., 1994—; adj. faculty N.H. Coll., 1991—; speaker Daniel Webster coun. Boy Scouts Am., Manchester, 1988; panel mem. ednl. seminar, 1993. Treas. N.H. Indian Cun., 1980-84; vol. United Way, Manchester, 1988—, accountexec., 1990, 91; mem. adv. coun. health care adminstrn. N.H. Coll., 1990, faculty advisor weekend program, 1990-91; vol. N.H. Heart Assn., 1990-92; bd. dirs. N.H. chpt. Am. Cancer Soc., 1991—; road race com. Elliot Hosp. Mem. NAFE, Hosp. Fin. Mgmt. Assn., Speaker's Bur. (smoke free com., recycling com. 1991), IMA, Healthcare Fin. Mgmt. Assn. Roman Catholic. Home: RR 4 11 Medford Farms Goffstown NH 03045-9804

MARTELL, DENISE MILLS, lay worker; b. Newberry, S.C., Apr. 8, 1965; d. Wyman Harman and Evangeline (Berry) Mills; m. Marty Martell, FEb. 29, 1992. Grad., Newberry High Sch., 1983. Tchr. Vacation Bible Sch., Newberry, 1984-95, Sun. Sch., Newberry, 1989-92; dir. Bapt. Young Women, Newberry, 1989-92; sec. Sunday Sch. Bapt. Ch., Newberry, S.C., 1993-95, Sun. Sch. tchr. 1-3 grades, 1995-96; tchr. mission trips, various locations, 1987-89; tchr. Mission Friends, Newberry, 1987-96, mem. choir, 1986—, mem. Newberry Cmty. choir, 1992-95, tchr. children's choir, 1993-95; leader Weekday Bible Club, 1990-92, missionary to Bolivia, South Am., 1996. Active March of Dimes Walk Am., Am. Diabetes Assn. Bike-a-thon. Home: 8769 Monticelle Rd Columbia SC 29203-9708 Office: Shakespeare E and F Newberry SC 29108

MARTENS, HELEN EILEEN, elementary school educator; b. Atkinson, Nebr., Jan. 13, 1926; d. Robert McKinley and Minnie Viola (Alfs) M. BS, Dana Coll., 1971; postgrad., U. Nebr., 1971-94, Wayne (Nebr.) U., 1971-94. Cert. tchr., Nebr. Rural sch. tchr. Dist. 231, Atkinson, Nebr., 1943-44, Dist. 77, Atkinson, Nebr., 1944-45, Dist. 119, Atkinson, Nebr., 1945-47; tchr. Emmet (Nebr.) Pub. Sch., 1947-59, O'Neill (Nebr.) Pub. Sch., 1959-96; mgr. Saddle Horn Ranch for Youth. Mem. Holt County 4-H Coun., 1986-90, leader, 1946—; mem. youth edn. com. Holt County Cancer Soc., 1976-94; activity sec. Dr. Boots and Saddle Club, Holt County, 1969-95; demonstration tchr. Nebr. Tchrs. Help Mobile. Recipient Good Neighbor citation Knights of Aksarben, 1986, Amb. award O'Neill C. of C., 1986, Tchr. of Yr. World Herald Newspaper, 1986, Outstanding Elem. Tchr. Nebr. Rural Cmty. Schs., 1994; named Grand Marshall O'Neill St. Patrick's Parade, 1986. Mem. NEA, Nebr. Edn. Assn., O'Neill Edn. (sec., v.p., pres. 1960-94), Order Eastern Star, Alpha Delta Kappa, Delta Kappa Gamma (sec., v.p. 1959-94). Republican. Methodist. Home: HC 69 Box 41 Atkinson NE 68713-9615

MARTENS, PATRICIA FRANCES, adult education educator; b. St. Louis, Nov. 27, 1943; d. John William and Mary Ruth (Bolds) Martens; m. George Joseph Miller, Aug. 7, 1965 (div.); children: Nicolette, George Jr., Jeffrey. BS in Psychology, So. Ill. U., 1975; MA in Counseling, St. Louis U., 1990, PhD in Psychol. Founds., 1996. Cert. sexuality educator. Primary, intermediate tchr. St. Hedwig Sch., St. Louis, 1961-66; jr. high tchr. Assumption Sch., St. Louis, 1976-81; tchr. trainer grad. students Paul VI Cathechetical Inst., St. Louis, 1986-88; nat. tchr. trainer St. Louis, 1989—; cons. Archdiocese L.A., Archdiocese St. Louis, Nat. Coun. Cath. Bishops, 1991; del. Nat. Cath. Ednl. Del. to Russia and Lithuania, 1993; frequent spkr. and presenter at schs., parishes ednl. confs., nat. and internat. religious edn. mtgs.; TV appearances on ABC and CTNA; nat. ednl. cons. Tabor Pub. Author: (videos) In God's Image: Make and Female, 1989, God Doesn't Make Junk, 1989 (Cath. Audio Visual Educators award 1991), (books) Parent to Parent, 1989, Sex Is Not A Four-Letter Word!, 1994. Recipient Award Cath. Press Assn., 1995. Mem. AACD, Nat. Cath. Educators Assn., Am. Assn. Sex Educators, Counselors, Therapists, Assn. for Religious Values in Counseling, Am. Sch. Counselor Assn., Am. Coll. Personnel Assn., Soc. for Sci. Study of Sex, Pi Lambda Theta. Home and Office: 8061 Daytona Dr Apt 1E Saint Louis MO 63105-2549

MARTESLO, DEBRA LEE, elementary school educator; b. Pottsville, Pa., May 15, 1949; d. Albert John and Eldora Harvene (Fidler) Seaman; m. George Marteslo; children: Alexis, Amanda, Dustin. BS in Art Edn., Kutztown U., 1972. Elem. art tchr. Blue Mountain Sch. Dist., Orwigsburg, Pa., 1978—, artist-in-residence coord., 1987—; pilot team mem. Pa. Dept. Edn. Arts Assessment Project, 1993-94; cons., workshop presenter I.U. # 29, Minersville, Pa., 1994-95; conf. presenter Pa. Art Edn. Assn., 1995. Mem. adv. bd. Schuylkill County Coun. for the Arts, Pottsville, Pa., 1994—. Recipient grant awards Pa. Coun. on the Arts, 1987, 88, 89, 90, 91, 92, 94, 95, Gift of Time award Am. Family Inst., 1991, 92, 96, Excellence in Edn. award Time Warner, 1993. Mem. NEA, Nat. Art Edn. Assn., Pa. Coalition for Arts in Edn., Schuylkill Ballet Theatre. Republican. Roman Catholic. Home: 58 Deerfield Dr Pottsville PA 17901 Office: Blue Mountain East Elem Reddale Rd Orwigsburg PA 17961

MARTIKAINEN, A(UNE) HELEN, retired health education specialist; b. Harrison, Maine, May 11, 1916; d. Sylvester and Emma (Heikkinen) M.; AB, Bates Coll., 1939, DSc (hon.), 1957, Smith Coll., 1969; MPH, Yale, 1941; DSc, Harvard U., 1964. Health edn. sec. Hartford Tb and Public Health Assn., 1941-42; cons. USPHS, 1942-49; chief health edn. WHO, Geneva, 1949-74; chair internat. affairs N.C. div. AAUW, 1986-94. Trustee Bridgton Acad., North Bridgton, Maine; mem. N.C. Women's Forum, 1984—; bd. dirs. N.C. Ctr. of Laws Affecting Women, Inc.; bd. dirs. West Triangle chpt. UNA-USA; mem. program com. and health and social svcs. coms. Carol Woods Retirement Cmty. Recipient Delta Omega award Yale U.; Nat. Adminstrv. award Am. Acad. Phys. Edn.; Bates Key award; Internat. Service award, France, 1953; Prentiss medal, 1956; spl. medal, certificate for internat. health edn. service Nat. Acad. Medicine for France, 1959; Profl. award Soc. Pub. Health Educators, 1963, Benjamin Elijah Mays award Bates Coll. Alumni Assn., 1989. Fellow APHA (chmn. health edn. sect., Excellence award 1969); mem. AAUW, LWV (Chapel Hill, N.C. br. 1987—), Women's Internat. League for Peace and Freedom, U.S. Soc. Pub. Health Educators, Internat. Union Health Edn. (Parisot medal, tech. adviser), Acad. Phys. Edn. (assoc.), N.C. Coun. Women's Orgns. (mem. coun. assembly 1988-92, Women of Distinction award 1989), Phi Beta Kappa. Home: 3113 Carol Woods 750 Weaver Dairy Rd Chapel Hill NC 27514

MARTIN, ALOISE MARIE BRITTEN, school nurse; b. Groom, Tex., Jan. 25, 1939; d. Harry Francis and Mary Veronica (Drerup) Britten; m. Chester Bruce Martin Jr., Oct. 14, 1960; children: Kenneth, Joe, Larry, Robert. AA, Amarillo Coll., 1959; diploma in nursing, St. Anthony's Hosp., 1960. RN, Tex. Head nurse Highland Gen. Hosp., Pampa, Tex., 1960-61, 64-71, pvt. duty nurse, 1961-64, insvc. dir., 1970-71; sch. nurse White Deer (Tex.) Ind. Sch. Dist., 1971—; office nurse Porviance Clinic, Pampa, summers 1971-84; med. chmn. Carson County Cancer Bd., Panhandle, Tex., 1990—. Mem. Nat. Assn. Sch. Nurses, Tex. Assn. Sch. Nurses, Region XVI Nurses Assn. Republican. Roman Catholic. Home: PO Box 158 White Deer TX 79097-0158

MARTIN, ANN MATTHEWS, writer; b. Princeton, N.J., Aug. 12, 1955; d. Henry R. and Edith Aiken (Matthews) M. BA cum laude, Smith Coll., 1977. Elem. sch. tchr. Plumfield Sch., Noroton, Conn., 1977-78; editorial asst. Simon & Schuster, N.Y.C., 1978-80; copywriter Teenage Book Club, Scholastic Books, Inc., N.Y.C., 1980-81; assoc. editor Scholastic Books, Inc., N.Y.C., 1981-83, editor, 1983; sr. editor Bantam Books, N.Y.C., 1983-85; free lance writer, editor, N.Y.C., 1985—. Author: (novels) Bummer Summer, 1983, Just You and Me, 1983, Inside Out, 1984, Stage Fright, 1984, Me and Katie (the Pest), 1985, With You and Without You, 1986, Missing Since

Monday, 1986, Just a Summer Romance, 1987, Slam Book, 1987, Yours Turly, Shirley, 1988, Ten Kids, No Pets, 1988, Fancy Dance in Feather Town, 1988, Ma and Pa Dracula, 1989, Moving Day in Feather Town, 1989, Eleven Kids, One Summer, 1991, Rachel Parker, Kindergarten Show-Off, 1992, (novels in series) The Baby-sitters Club, Baby-sitters Little Sister, Baby-sitters Club Mysteries, The Kids in Ms. Colman's Class. Mem. PEN, Authors Guild, Soc. Children's Book Writers and Illustrators. Democrat. Office: care Scholastic Inc 555 Broadway New York NY 10012-3919

MARTIN, ANNA LOU, secondary education educator, small business owner; b. Trenton, Mo., Aug. 24, 1931; d. James Oscar Mack and Naomi Lee (Paramore) Elledge; m. George Alfred Smith, May 20, 1951 (div. Aug. 1975); children: Leanna Smith Eversmeyer, Linda Kay Smith Crowe, Steven Smith; m. Richard Earl Martin, Nov. 19, 1977. BS in Edn., N.E. Mo. State U., 1962, MA, 1969; DEd, U. Ark., 1978. Cert. secondary tchr., Mo., Ariz., adult edn. tchr., Ariz. Tchr. Mo. Rural Schs., Spickard and Chula, 1950-52, Kidder, Galt and Laredo, 1962-69; group counselor Mo. Tng. Sch. for Girls, Chillicothe, 1969-72; exec. dir. Benton County Youth Svc. Bur., Bentonville, Ark., 1976-77, Info. and Referral of United Way, Ft. Worth, 1978; guidance cons. ACTION-Peace Corps, Washington, 1980-82; owner Realm Line and An-Di's Cuties, Laredo, Mo. and Yuma, Ariz., 1982-86; literacy coord./exec. dir. Yuma County Libr./Yuma Reading Coun., 1986-93; owner Nana's Treasure Trunk, Yuma, 1993-95; ret., 1995; regional rep. Ariz. Adult Edn. Consortium, Phoenix, 1989-91; sec. Ariz. State Literacy Assn., Phoenix, 1988-89; treas. Yuma County Coordinating Coun., 1989-90; mem. adv. bd. Yuma Reading Coun., 1994-95. Author: A Study of First Offender Community College Programs with Focus on the Transfer to Four Year Colleges, 1978; editor News and Cues newsletter, 1987-90, Main St. News newsletter, 1995—. Rec. sec. Zonta Club Yuma, 1989-90, pres., 1991-92; legis. chmn. Dem. Club Yuma, 1995; East County co-chair campaign United Way of Yuma County, 1995. Recipient Citizen of Yr. award KC, Yuma, 1993. Mem. Order of Ea. Star, Potpourri Artists, Phi Delta Kappa, Beta Sigma Phi (pres., treas. 1979-95, Woman of Yr. 1995). Democrat. Mem. Disciples of Christ.

MARTIN, BARBARA JEAN, elementary school principal; b. Mt. Vernon, Tex., May 17, 1940. BA, Fisk U., Nashville, 1961; MEd, U. Ill., Chgo., 1979, PhD, 1992. Cert. tchr. kindergarten to 3rd grade, type 75 adminstr., Ill. Tchr. Chgo. Pub. Schs., 1969-93, prin., 1993—. Mem. Nat. Alliance Black Sch. Educators, Delta Kappa Gamma (sec. 1992—), Pi Lambda Theta, Alpha Kappa Alpha. Home: 825 E Drexel Sq Chicago IL 60615-3705 Office: O W Holmes Sch 955 W Garfield Blvd Chicago IL 60621-2240

MARTIN, BARBARA JEAN, elementary education educator; b. St. Louis, May 20, 1949; d. Robert Clarke and Ruth Eloise (Baseler) M. BS in Elem. Edn., N.E. Mo. State U., 1971; MA in Elem. Edn., Maryville U., 1991. Classroom instr. Hazelwood (Mo.) Sch. Dist., 1971—; mem. curriculum revision com., Hazelwood Sch. Dist., 1974-94, profl. devel. Com., 1992-94, steering com. 1993-94; advisor/cons. Hazelwood Sch. Dist. Early Childhood Parents and Staff, 1985—. Mem. chmn. PTA, Russell Sch., 1989—; tchr., musician Bermuda Bible Hall Ch., St. Louis, 1965—; asst. dir., sec., musician, tchr. Hickory Cove Bible Camp, Hickory, N.C., 1975—. Recipient Disting. Vol. award Christian Camping Internat., 1986; recipient Robert D. Elsea scholarship St. Louis Cooperating Sch. Dist., St. Louis County, 1989. Mem. Assn. for Edn. of Young Children (pres. seminar 1994), Christian Educators Assn., Sigma Alpha Iota (pres. 1978-81, v.p. 1976-78, scholarship chmn. 1981—, Sword of Honor 1981, Rose of Honor 1996). Home: 18 Buckeye Dr Ferguson MO 63135-1515 Office: Russell Sch 7350 Howdershell Rd Hazelwood MO 63042-1306

MARTIN, BARBARA JEAN, guidance counselor, secondary education educator; b. Princeton, Ill., Nov. 26, 1946; d. James E. and Dorothy L. (Cluff) Richmond; m. Thomas P. Martin. BS in Math. and Chemistry, Ill. State U., 1968, MS in Guidance and Counseling, 1970; student in type 75 adminstrn., Governors State U., 1985, MS in Drug and Alcohol Counseling, 1991. Nat. bd. cert. counselor. Counselor, tchr. Rich Ctrl. H.S., Olympia Fields, Ill., 1968-70; counselor Rich Ctrl. H.S., Olympia Fields, 1970-88; tchr. Rich South H.S., Richton Park, Ill., 1988-89; counselor, tchr. Rich Ctrl. H.S., 1989—. Home: 931 Shetland Dr Frankfort IL 60423-9767

MARTIN, BETTY CAROLYN, library director; b. Louisville, Nov. 2, 1933; d. Earl Francis and Marie Dorothy (Baertich) Snyder; m. Charles Frank Martin, Aug. 18, 1956. BS, Ind. U., 1956, MLS, 1982. Sch. libr. Decatur Twp. Schs., Indpls., 1955-57; tchr. Indpls. Schs., 1957-58; libr., libr. dir. Vigo County Pub. Libr., Terre Haute, Ind., 1958—; exec. bd. Ind. State Libr. Adv. Coun., Indpls., 1989-94. Contbr. articles to profl. jours. Bd. dirs. State Student Assistance Commn., Indpls., 1991—, United Way Wabash County, Terre Haute, 1989-95, Alliance for Growth and Progress, sec., 1989; bd. dirs. LWC, pres., 1980; bd. dirs. Pres. Adv. Bd. St. Mary of Woods Coll., Salvation Army, pres., 1990-92; sec. bd. dirs. Work Force Devel. Commn. Western Ind., Terre Haute, 1990—. Recipient Louise Maxwell award SLIS-IU Alumni Assn., Bloomington, Ind., 1991; named Outstanding Woman of COmmunity, Bus. & Profl. Womens Club, Terre Haute, 1990. Mem. ALA, Ind. Libr. Fedn. (bd. dirs., pres. 1989-90, Assn. Leadership award 1990), Ind. U. Libr. Sch. Alumni (pres. 1992-94), C.of C. (Terre award 1989). Democrat. Roman Catholic. Home: 5351 N 13th St Terre Haute IN 47805-1613 Office: Vigo County Public Lib 1 Library Sq Terre Haute IN 47807-3609

MARTIN, BETTY S., minister, retired educator; b. Milw., Mar. 19, 1919; d. John Raymond and Lillian Alberta (Goldthorp) Schoonmaker; m. Ralph Wilson Martin, June 30, 1951; children: Janet (Mrs. Will Cummings), E. Paul. BA cum laude, Lawrence U., 1941; MA, Northwestern U., 1946; M Divinity, Garrett-Evang. Theol. Sem., 1951. Cert. secondary math. tchr. Wis., Pa.; ordained minister United Meth. Ch. Secondary math. tchr. Lake Mills (Wis.) Schs., 1942-44, Milw. Pub. Schs., 1944-46, New Castle (Pa.) Schs., 1959-87; guidance counselor West Bend (Wis.) Sch., 1946-49; min. United Meth. Conf., West Pittsburg, Pa., 1974-76; organist United Meth. Ch., Ellwood City, Pa., 1979—; tutor, Ellwood City, 1972-74, Beaver Falls, 1975-77; dist. dir. children's work United Meth. Ch., Brocton, N.Y., 1957-58; tchr. math. class Adult Literacy, Beaver, Pa., 1988-89; instr., trainer, assoc. state coord. 55 Alive/Mature Driving program AARP, 1990—. Contbr. articles, poems to profl. publs. Host Am. Field Svc., 1969-70, numerous educators, 1972-94; dir. jr. choirs, handbell choir with various Meth. Chs.; vol. Very Spl. Persons, 1970's; bd. dirs. Am. Heart Assn., 1987-89; freedom writer Amnesty Internat., 1990—; dist. dir. spiritual life United Meth. Women's Soc., Grove City Dist., Pa., 1960-63; tng. dir. CONTACT, Lawrence and Beaver Counties, 1977—; sec.-treas. Am. Field Svc., 1970, pres., 1971; sec. Beaver Valley Cmty. Concerts, Beaver Falls, 1982—. Recipient Alumni Disting. Svc. award Lawrence U., 1974, Gov.'s Hwy. Safety award for older Pennsylvanians, Pa. Dept. Transp., 1994; grantee NSF, 1969. Mem. AAUW (Educator of Yr. 1988, Ednl. Found. Named Gift award 1994, chmn. elem. and secondary edn. com. 1960, 61, treas. 1980, 81, chmn. internat. rels. 1992), LWV (editor 1988, 89, corr. sec. 1994-95), Outlook Soc. (sec. 1990-91), Pi Lambda Theta. Home: 1813 7th St PT Beaver Falls PA 15010

MARTIN, CAROL JACQUELYN, educator, artist; b. Ft. Worth, Tex., Oct. 6, 1943; d. John Warren and Dorothy Lorene (Coffman) Edwards; m. Boe Willis Martin, Oct. 6, 1940; children: Stephanie Diane, Scott Andrew. BA summa cum laude, U. N. Tex., 1965; MA, U. Tex., El Paso, 1967. Tchr. Edgemere Elem. Sch., El Paso, Tex., 1965-66, Fulmore Jr. H.S., Austin, 1966-67, Monnig Jr. H.S., Ft. Worth, 1967-68, Paschal H.S., Ft. Worth, 1968-69; instr. Tarrant County Jr. Coll., Ft. Worth, 1968-69, 71-72; press sec. U.S. Sen. Gaylord Nelson, Washington, 1969-71; instr. Eastfield C.C., Dallas, 1981, Richland C.C. Dist., 1982. Editor The Avesta Mag., 1964-65; exhibited in group shows at City of Richardson's Cottonwood Park, 1970-86, Students of Ann Cushing Gantz, 1973-85, Art About Town, 1979, 80, shows by Tarrant County and Dallas County art assns. Active Dallas Symphony Orch. League, Easter Seal Soc., Dallas Hist. Soc., Women's Bd. of the Dallas Opera, Dallas Arboretum and Garden Club, Dallas County Heritage Soc. Mem. Internat. Platform Assn., Mortar Bd., Alpha Chi, Sigma Tau Delta, Kappa Delta Pi, Delta Gamma. Democrat. Methodist. Address: 4435 Arcady Ave Dallas TX 75205-3604

MARTIN, CATHERINE ELIZABETH, anthropology educator; b. N.Y.C., Feb. 14, 1943; d. Walter Charles and Ruth (Crucet) Strodt; children: Kai Stuart, Armin Wade. BA, Reed Coll., 1965; MA, UCLA, 1967, PhD, 1971. Cert. C.C. tchr., Ariz., Calif. From asst. to full prof. anthropology Calif. State U., L.A., 1970-96, coord. women's studies, 1979-88, acting dir. acad. advisement, 1992-93, dir. Can. studies, 1991, advisement coord., 1996; assoc. faculty Mohave C.C., Kingman, Ariz., 1996—. Contbr. chpts. to books and poetry to profl. publs. Cubmaster, den mother Boy Scouts Am., L.A. and Pasadena, 1982-85; leader Tiger Cubs, Boy Scouts Am., 1983. Recipient Outstanding Tiger Cub Leader award Boy Scouts Am., L.A., 1983, Cub Scout Growth award Boy Scouts Am., L.A., 1984. Fellow Soc. Applied Anthropology; mem. Am. Anthropol. Assn., Southwestern Anthropol. Assn.

MARTIN, CHERI CHRISTIAN, health services administrator; b. Nashville, Mar. 9, 1956; d. Jesse Thomas and Eloise (McClain) Christian; m. George A. Martin, June 25, 1977 (div. May 1995); children: Matthew Alexander, Kristin Leigh. BS in Family Resources and Consumer Scis., U. Wis., 1977; cert. healthcare mgmt., U. St. Thomas, 1991. Asst. buyer Dayton Hudson, Mpls., 1978-79, assoc. buyer, 1979-81; instr. Nat. Coll., Mpls., 1981-82; mgr. store Connco Shoes, Inc., Mpls, 1982-83; patient svcs. rep. Group Health, Inc., Mpls., 1984-89, dental mgr., 1989-94, regional mgr., 1994—; cert. facilitator the Seven Habits of Highly Effective People, 1996. Cert. facilitator (seminar) The Seven Habits of Highly Effective People, 1996. Mem. Minn./Dakota Assn. Patient Reps. (v.p. 1989-90), U. Wis. Alumni Assn., Group Health Social Club Mpls. (pres. 1987-89).

MARTIN, DEBORAH ANN, intensive care nurse, educator; b. Chester, Pa., June 4, 1957; d. Clarence Hayden and Freida Florence (Hubacher) Williams; m. Gary Gene Martin, Aug. 14, 1982; children: Sean, Jeremy, Kyle. BSN, U. Del., 1979; MSN, U. Ctrl. Ark., 1994. RN, Ark.; cert. ACLS. Staff RN renal transplant and surg. ICU Hosp. U. Pa., Phila., 1979-81; staff RN burn treatment ctr., charge nurse ICU relief Crozer-Chester Med. Ctr., Upland, Pa., 1981-83; staff RN ICU, ICU clin. educator Bapt. Med. Ctr., Jacksonville, Fla., 1983-85; staff nurse ICU Med. Pers. Pool and Staff Builders, Tampa, Fla., 1985-88; staff RN ICU Berwick (Pa.) Hosp., 1988-89; staff RN ICU, spl. recovery, relief cardiac/diabetes educator, instr. dysrhythmia and pacemaker instr. St. Edward's Mercy Med. Ctr., Ft. Smith, Ark., 1990—; part-time faculty Westark C.C., Ft. Smith, 1996—. Mem. AACN, Sigma Theta Tau. Home and Office: 7515 Bear Hollow Rd Fort Smith AR 72916-7408

MARTIN, DIANE MARIE, lawyer; b. Utica, N.Y., Oct. 14, 1962; d. Fred Edward and Jane Ann (Williams) M. BA cum laude, Siena Coll., 1984; JD, Syracuse U., 1990. Asst. corp. counsel City of Rome, N.Y., 1991-92, corp. counsel, 1992—; instr. Mohawk Valley Law Enforcement Acad., Utica, 1994—. Bd. dirs. Salvation Army, 1994—. Mem. ABA, N.Y. State Bar Assn., Oneida County Bar Assn. (bd. dirs. 1995—), Rome Bar Assn. (bd. dirs. 1994-95). Office: City of Rome City Hall on the Mall Rome NY 13440

MARTIN, DIANNE LESLIE, artist, educator; b. Boston, Apr. 8, 1940; d. James Donald and Ina (Mac Lerie) M.; m. William Paul Kennedy, June 15, 1961 (div. June 1978). BFA in Painting, RISD, 1965; MA in Painting, U. Iowa, 1968. Head art dept. Spence Sch., N.Y.C., 1971-95; represented by Markel/Sears Works on Paper, N.Y.C., 1991—; reader advanced placement art portfolios Ednl. Testing Svc., Princeton, N.J., 1993-95. One woman exhbns. include Noho Gallery, N.Y.C., 1981, 82, 85, Leonarda Di Mauro Gallery, N.Y.C., 1984, 87; group exhbns. include Brooklyn (N.Y.) Mus., 1975, Women in the Arts Found., N.Y.C., 1978, Salgamundi Club, N.Y.C., 1979, Bjorn Lindgren Gallery, N.Y.C., 1982, Ethel Putterman Gallery, Orleans, Mass., 1982, 83, Queens (N.Y.) Mus., 1985, Newmark Gallery, N.Y.C., 1989, Mus. of the Nat. Arts Found., N.Y.C., 1989, Ceres Gallery, N.Y.C., 1990, Citicorp Ctr., Long Island City, N.Y., 1992; represented in permanent collections David Rockefeller Jr., Pfizer, Inc., Pepsico, J.C. Penney, Inc., Southeast Bank, Manhattan Musicians Union. Resident fellow Va. Ctr. Creative Arts Sweetbrier Coll. , 1995.

MARTIN, EDYTHE LOUVIERE, business educator; b. Breaux Bridge, La., Dec. 30, 1940; d. James Ivy and Volna Mary (Landry) L.; m. James Henry Martin, Aug. 23, 1969; 1 child, Lois Elizabeth. BS in Bus. Edn., U. Southwestern La., 1972; MEd in Supervision, La. State U., 1977, Specialist Degree in Ednl. Adminstrn., 1988, postgrad studies in Ednl. Adminstrn., 1989—. Geol. sec. Sohio Petroleum Co., Lafayette, La., 1960-67, Bintliff Oil & Gas Co., Lafayette, 1967-69; bus. tchr. Cottonport (La.) H.S., 1972-74; bus. instr. Acadian Tech. Coll., Crowley, La., 1975—; team leader, mem. accrediting teams So. Assn. Colls. and Schs., 1978—, chmn. of steering com. for Acadian Tech. evaluation, 1991; speaker, presenter at meetings and seminars of educators. Publicity chairperson Miss Eunice (La.) Pageant, 1981-88; chairperson Eunice Lady of Yr. award, 1982; organizer chairperson, St. Jude Children's Hosp., Fund Raiser, Memphis, Eunice, 1985-91; PTC sec. St. Edmund Sch., Eunice, 1982-84; vol. March of Dimes, 1995-96. Mem. Office Occupations Assn., La. Vocat. Assn. Inc., La. Vocat. Assn. (trade and indsl. divsn.). Democrat Roman Catholic. Home: 750 Viola St Eunice LA 70535-4340 Office: Acadian Tech Coll 1933 W Hutchinson Ave Crowley LA 70526-3215

MARTIN, GLADYS CHRISTINE, housing executive; b. Arlington, Tex., Aug. 24, 1948; d. Grady Taylor and Bessie Marie (Parker) Pointer; m. Arthur Ray Martin, Nov. 18, 1968; children: Kriste, Arthur II, Kandace, Maribeth. Student, Tarrant County Jr. Coll. Exec. dir. Housing Authority/City of Cooper, Tex., 1991—. Recipient award Girl Scouts Am. Recipient award Girl Scouts U.S., 1991. Mem. NAACP, Nat. Assn. Housing Ofcls., Pub. Housing Dirs. Assn., Tex. Housing Assn. (bd. dirs.), S.W. Nat. Orgn. Housing Ofcls. (vice chair commn., S.W. Media award 1994), N.E. Tex. Housing Assn., Lamar County Housing Assn. (v.p. 1994-95), Delta County Ext. Agy. (bd. dirs. 1995-96). Home: 1870 Graham St Paris TX 75432

MARTIN, GRACE BURGDORF, creative writing educator; b. Buffalo, N.Y., Mar. 4, 1916; d. Paul Max and Grace Victoria (Claven) Burgdorf; m. Edwin Russel Martin, Aug. 1, 1936; children: Bonnie Jean, Hope Elizabeth. BA in Drama and Speech, SUNY, Buffalo, 1967, postgrad., 1968. Cert. tchr. grades 7-12, N.Y. adv. bd. citizen emeritus Niagara C.C., Sanborn, N.Y., 1983-84; adv. bd. Unitarian Fellowship, Chautauqua, N.Y., 1995-96. Author: Postcard From Armageddon, 1986, Magic Ain't Nothin' But a Pair o'Big Sleeves, 1988, Grannies: 101, 1992. Mem. Internat. Ctr. for Women Playwrights, Just Buffalo Writer's Ctr. Democrat. Unitarian-Universalist.

MARTIN, HELEN ELIZABETH, secondary mathematics and science educator; b. West Chester, Pa., Feb. 19, 1945; d. Thomas Edwin and Elizabeth Temple (Walker) M.; BA, The King's Coll., Briarcliff Manor, N.Y., 1967; MEd, West Chester U., 1970; postgrad. Goethe Inst., Freiberg, Fed. Republic Germany, 1979, Oxford U., 1979. Tchr. math. and sci. Unionville (Pa.) High Sch., 1967—; adj. prof. W. Chester (Pa.) U., 1989—; mem. Carnegie Forum on Edn. and the Economy. Mem. Pa. Rep. State Com., 1982-90, Rep. Com. of Chester County, 1984-94. Named Alumna of the Yr. The King's Coll., 1987; recipient State Presdl. award, 1989, Frank G. Brewer Civil Air Patrol Meml. Aerospace award, 1989, Outstanding Achievement award U.S. Dept. Commerce, 1993; Bus. Week/Challenger Seven fellow, 1991. Fellow Am. Sci. Affiliation; mem. AAAS (founding dir.), Nat. Bd. Profl. Teaching Standards (founding dir.), Satellite Educators Assn. (pres. 1987—), Nat. Sci. Tchrs. Assn., Nat. Council Tchrs. Math., History Sci. Soc., Nat. Sci. Tchrs. Assn. (internat. lectr. 1987), Assn. for Sci. Edn. in U.K. (internat. lectr. 1987). Home: PO Box 605 Unionville PA 19375-0605 Office: Unionville HS 750 Unionville Rd Kennett Square PA 19348

MARTIN, HELENE GETTER, university administrator; b. Boston, May 24, 1940; d. Seymour Samuel and Doris Viola (Taylor) Getter; children: Lauren Renee, Susannah Taylor. AB in English Lit. with distinction, Wheaton Coll., 1962; MS, Columbia U., 1964; postgrad., U. Calif., Berkeley, 1981. Caseworker, cons. Mass. Dept. Mental Health, Milton, 1965-78; program analyst dept. nursing Ambulatory Care Ctr., U. Calif., San Francisco, 1980-81; cons. mental health, mem. faculty Boston Coll. Legal Assistance Bur., Waltham, Mass., 1978-80; mktg. assoc. Vesper Hosps., San Leandro, Calif., 1981-83; dir. resource devel. Am. Acad. Ophthalmology, San Francisco, 1983-85; mgr. membership devel. The Mus. Soc., San Francisco, 1986-89; dir. devel. and alumni rels. Sch. Social Work Columbia U., N.Y.C., 1989-93; sr. devel. officer, dir. campaign L.I. U., Bklyn., 1993—; case worker Mass. Dept. of Mental Health, 1965-78; programs dir. Mass. Mental Health Assn., 1978-80. Co-founder Marin Parents and Community Together, Marin County, Calif., 1987; bd. dirs., mem. exec. com. Oxfam-Am., Boston, 1973-79; mem. Com. to Aid East Pakistan, Cambridge, Mass., 1970; chairperson Emergency Relief Fund-Bangladesh, Newton, Mass., 1972, Ad-Hoc Com. to Remove Asbestos, Newton, 1978; mem. Dem. City Com., Newton, 1978; chairperson welfare com. LWV, Newton, 1970. Mem. Nat. Soc. Fund Raising Execs. (Golden Gate chpt., bd. dirs 1989, chairperson Nat. Philanthrophy Day awards com. 1989). Home: 263 W End Ave Apt 3G New York NY 10023-2621 Office: Gilda's Club 195 W Houston St New York NY 10014

MARTIN, JANE EVERETTE, financial company executive; b. Hopewell, Va., Jan. 14, 1943; d. Robert Thornton and Myrtle Iola (Dale) Tuggle; m. Thomas Joy Martin, June 27, 1964 (div. Mar. 1970); children: Michael Joy, David Thomas. Student, William and Mary Coll., 1961-63. Sales asst. Merrill Lynch, Palo Alto, Calif., 1976-77; mem. staff broker's trading desk E.F. Hutton, Palo Alto, 1977-81, asst. v.p., 1981-87; pres. Jane Martin Assocs., Palo Alto, 1987-94, Shooting Star Pictures, Palo Alto, 1993—; exec. dir. Managed Futures Assn., Palo Alto, 1991—; bd. dirs. Frederick Gilbert & Assocs., Redwood City, Calif. Office: Managed Futures Assn 471 Emerson St Palo Alto CA 94301

MARTIN, JEAN ANN, school administrator, educational diagnostician; b. Omaha, June 27, 1942; d. Clarid Fee and Frances Catherine (Dugan) McNeil; m. Robert William Martin, Dec. 28, 1968. BS, Pa. State U., 1963; MEd, U. Del., 1968. Cert. English tchr., Pa., N.Y., Del., reading specialist, Va., N.Y., Del., secondary prin., reading supr., dir. of instrn., Del. Tchr. English Neshaminy Sch. Dist., Langhorn, Pa., 1963-65; tchr. English and reading Unionville (Pa.) Sch. Dist., 1965-68; tchr. reading Jamesville-DeWitt (N.Y.) Sch. Dist., 1968-69, South Colonie Sch. Dist., Albany, N.Y., 1969-70; tchr. English Bethlehem Cen. Sch. Dist., Delmar, N.Y., 1970-71, Smyrna (Del.) Sch. Dist., 1971-73; reading specialist, tchr. English Delmar Sch. Dist., 1973-88; reading specialist Accomack (Va.) County Schs., 1988-93; sch. adminstr., diagnostician Silver Lake Ctr., Middletown, Del., 1994—. Past pres. Lioness, Delmar. Mem. ASCD, Del. ASCD, Va. Reading Assn. (bd. dirs. 1989-93, editorial adv. bd. Reading in Va. 1990-92), Ea. Shore Reading Coun. Va. (pres. 1989-91), Sussex County Orgn. for Reading Excellence (pres. 1980-81), Diamond State Reading Assn. (pres. 1985-86), Del. Assn. Sch. Adminstrs., Internat. Reading Assn., Coun. for Exceptional Children, Cedar Shores Condominium Assn. (sec.), Lions Club (Onancock, Va.), Alpha Delta Kappa (past pres. Theta chpt. and Del.). Home: 33 E 6th St New Castle DE 19720-5087 Office: Silver Lake Ctr PO Box 423 493 E Main St Middletown DE 19709

MARTIN, JOAN FRIEDMAN, lawyer; b. Washington, Apr. 15, 1941; d. Maurice Harold and Gertrude (Sanders) Friedman; m. Jackson W.T. Kennedy, Dec. 15, 1962 (div. 1983); children: Elizabeth, Richard, Alexandra; m. William R. Martin, Jan. 29, 1988. AB, Mt. Holyoke Coll., 1961; JD, Georgetown U., 1983. Bar: Va. 1983, U.S. Dist. Ct. (ea. and we. dists.) Va. 1983, U.S. Ct. Appeals (4th cir.) 1983, U.S. Bankruptcy Ct. (ea. dist.) Va. 1987, U.S. Supreme Ct. 1988. Assoc. Williams, Worrell, Kelly, Greer & Frank P.C., Norfolk, Va., 1983-88; ptnr. Williams, Kelly & Greer, P.C. (formerly, Williams, Worrell, Kelly, Greer & Frank P.C.), Norfolk, 1988—. Bd. dirs. YWCA, Norfolk, 1985-86, Tidewater Coun. Am. Heart Assn., 1987-89, Feldman Chamber Music Soc., 1989—. Mem. ABA, Va. Bar Assn., Norfolk-Portsmouth Bar Assn. Republican. Office: Williams Kelly & Greer 600 Crestar Bank Bldg Norfolk VA 23510

MARTIN, JUDY BRACKIN HEREFORD, higher education administrator; b. York, Ala., May 25, 1943; d. Julian Byron and Willie Lee (Aiken) B.; m. Roy Nichols Hereford, Jr., Apr. 1, 1962 (dec. Mar. 1988); children: Leanne, Roy Nichols III, Rachel, Samantha; m. John Lawrence Martin Sr., Nov. 23, 1988. BA, Judson Coll., 1964. Co-owner, ptnr. Hereford Haven Farms, Faunsdale, Ala., 1962-93; ptnr. The Mustard Seed, Demopolis, Ala., 1974-76; ptnr., sales mgr. Hereford & Assocs. Auction Co., Faunsdale, Ala., 1967-91; alumnae dir., dir. admissions Judson Coll., Marion, Ala., 1988-90, asst. to pres., 1990-94, interim v.p. for instnl. advancement, 1996—; exec. sec.-treas. Ala. Women's Hall of Fame, Judson Coll., Marion, 1991—; exec. dir. Ala. Rural Heritage Found., Thomaston, 1991-95. Officer Marengo County Red. Cross, 1987-88; mem. Marengo County Hist. Soc., Econ. Devel. Assn. Ala., 1991—; com. mem. Marengo Dem. Exec. Com.; bd. dirs. Dept. Human Resources, Marengo County, 1987-95, Marengo County Farmers Fedn. Bd., 1985-95; mem. So. Arts Fedn. Adv. Coun., 1994-95; mem. steering com. Leadership Marengo, 1994; chmn. bd. Faunsdale United Meth. Ch., 1989-91. Mem. Blackbelt Tourism Coun. (bd. dirs. 1991), Judson Coll. Alumnae Assn. (treas. 1992-96). Methodist.

MARTIN, JUDY CAROL, guidance counselor; b. Cynthiana, Ky., Jan. 14, 1949; d. Norman Edward and Thelma (Henson) Taylor; m. Jerry Lee Martin, Nov. 22, 1970; children: Carol Ann, Connie Lee. Grad. in home econs., Georgetown Coll., 1972; MEd, Georgetown U., 1976; Rank I Cert., Xavier U., 1979, Cert. Guidance Counselor, 1993. Home econs. tchr. Williamstown (Ky.) Jr. H.S., 1971-72, home econs., math., sci. tchr. North Ky. Treatment Ctr., Crittenden, 1972-81; spl. edn. tchr. Grant County Mid. Sch., Dry Ridge, Ky., 1988-93, counselor, 1993—; psychology educator Maysville C.C., Cynthiana, Ky., 1992—; mem. com. OSHA, Crittenden, 1974-81; tchr.-mem. site-based Decision Making, Dry Ridge, 1992-94; chmn. Drug Awareness Program, Dry Ridge, 1993. Pianist Marcus Bapt. Ch., 1982—, Sunday sch. tchr., 1972—, mem. choir, 1972—.

MARTIN, JULIE ANN, parochial school biology educator; b. Cin., Apr. 8, 1970; d. Robert John and Karen Rae (Terrill) M. BS in Biology, Denison U., 1992; postgrad., Earlham Coll., 1993. Biology tchr. Saint Mark's Sch., Southborough, Mass., 1992—; faculty rep. sr. disciplinary com. St. Mark's Sch., Southboro, Mass., 1994-95, dorm head, 1993—, varsity girl's soccer and basketball coach, 1992—, athletic coun., 1993—, head student assistance team residential curriculum review com., faculty rep. bd. trustees. Mem. Nat. Soccer Coaches Assn. of Am. Home and Office: St Marks Sch 25 Marlboro Rd Southborough MA 01772-1207

MARTIN, JUNE JOHNSON CALDWELL, journalist; b. Toledo, Oct. 6; d. John Franklin and Eunice Imogene (Fish) Johnson; m. Erskine Caldwell, Dec. 21, 1942 (div. Dec. 1955); 1 child, Jay Erskine; m. Keith Martin, May 5, 1966. AA, Phoenix Jr. Coll., 1939-41; BA, U. Ariz., 1941-43, 53-59; student Ariz. State U., 1939, 40. Free-lance writer, 1944—; columnist Ariz. Daily Star, 1956-59; editor Ariz. Alumnus mag., Tucson, 1959-70; book reviewer, columnist Ariz. Daily Star, Tucson, 1970-94; ind. book reviewer and audio tape columnist, Tucson, 1994—; panelist, co-producer TV news show Tucson Press Club, 1954-55, pres., 1958; co-founder Ariz. Daily Star Ann. Book & Author Event. Contbg. author: Rocky Mountain Cities, 1949; contbr. articles to World Book Ency., and various mags. Mem. Tucson CD Com., 1961; vol. campaigns of Samuel Goddard, U.S. Rep. Morris Udall, U.S. ambassador and Ariz. gov. Raul Castro. Recipient award Nat. Headliners Club, 1959, Ariz. Press Club award, 1957-59, 96, Am. Alumni Council, 1966, 70. Mem. Nat. Book Critics Circle, Jr. League of Tucson, Tucson Urban League, PEN U.S.A. West, Planned Parenthood of So. Ariz., Pi Beta Phi. Democrat. Methodist. Club: Tucson Press. Home: Desert Foothills Sta PO Box 65388 Tucson AZ 85728

MARTIN, KATHLEEN ANNE, information management consultant; b. Rochester, N.Y., Aug. 19, 1942; d. Edwin Wilkins and Hilda Ellen (Hartell) Martin; BA, Marygrove Coll., Detroit, 1964; MA in Libr. Sci. (Josenhans scholar 1965), U. Mich., 1965; advanced online tng. cert. Nat. Libr. Medicine, 1979; m. Oliver Kalman Peterdy, Oct. 15, 1971 (div. 1981); children: Elizabeth, Matthew. Libr. Detroit Pub. Libr., 1964-66; bibliographer, then asst. tech. svcs. libr. Edward G. Miner Med. Libr., U. Rochester, 1969-72; libr. lab. indsl. medicine Eastman Kodak Co., Rochester, 1966-69, libr. health, safety and human factors lab., 1972-78, tech. info. analyst, 1978-84, health and environment lab., 1978-86, Info Edge, 1987—; libr. Monroe Devel. Ctr., 1987-90, Park Ridge Hosp., 1990—. Mem. AAUW (treas. Rochester br. 1979-80), Spl. Librs. Assn., Med. Libr. Assn., N.Y. Libr. Assn. Home: 332 Gnage Ln Rochester NY 14612-3200

MARTIN, KATHRYN A., academic administrator. Dean Sch. Fine and Performing Arts Wayne State U., Detroit; chancellor U Minn, Duluth, 1995—. Office: University of Minnesota-Duluth Office of the Chancellor Admin Bldng 10 University Dr Duluth MN 55812-2496*

MARTIN, LAURA BELLE, real estate and farm land manager, retired educator; b. Jackson County, Minn., Nov. 3, 1915; d. Eugene Wellington and Mary Christina (Hanson) M. BS, Mankato State U., 1968. Tchr. rural schs., Renville County, Minn., 1937-41, 45-50, Wabasso (Minn.) Pub. Sch., 1963-81; pres. Renville Farms and Feed Lots, 1982—. Pres. Wabasso (Minn.) Edn. Assn., 1974-75, publicity chmn., 1968-74; sec. Hist. Renville Preservation Com., 1978—; publicity chmn. Town and Country Boosters, Renville, 1982-83. Mem. Genealogy Soc. Renville County, Am. Legion Aux. Democrat. Lutheran. Home and Office: 334 NW 1201 Holden MO 64040-9804

MARTIN, LAURIE STEWART, art educator; b. Oakland, Calif., Jan. 20, 1947; d. Varick Dey Jr. and Prudence Stewart (White) M. BS, Moore Coll. of Art, 1986; MEd, Beaver Coll., U. Pa., 1992. Hotel asst., store mgr. Internat. Student's Info. Svc., Paris, 1967; art tchr. Phila. Bd. Edn., 1969—; tchr. World Harvest Mission, Uganda, Africa, 1983-84; part-time prof. Moore Coll. Art, Phila., 1991—, dir. summer program, 1994. Recipient Woman of Yr. award Women in the Arts Coun., 1991, Tchr. of Excellence award Phila. Fedn. Tchrs., Beneficial Savs. Bank, 1993-94, grant AIA, 1985, grant State of Pa., 1980. Home: 907 Edge Hill Rd Glenside PA 19038 Office: JS Jenks Germantown and Southampton Philadelphia PA 19118

MARTIN, LISA DEMET, lawyer; b. Pa., 1959. BA with honors, Wellesley Coll., 1980; JD, U. Pa., 1984. Bar: Mo. 1984. Ptnr. Bryan Cave LLP, St. Louis. Durant scholar Wellesley Coll. Mem. Phi Beta Kappa. Office: Bryan Cave LLP 211 N Broadway One Metropolitan Sq Saint Louis MO 63102*

MARTIN, LIZBETH LEE, researcher; b. Fort Worth, Tex., Sept. 23, 1965; d. David Lee and Maxine Marie (Monson) M. BA in Econs., U. Wash., 1987; MS in Agrl. Econs., U. Idaho, 1993; postgrad., Purdue U., 1993—. English tchr., agrl. coord. U.S. Peace Corps, Trang, Thailand, 1987-90; food program specialist USDA-Food and Nutrition Svc., Trenton, N.J., 1990-91; rsch. asst. U. Idaho, Moscow, 1991-93; campus recruiter Purdue U.-Dept. Internat. Programs, West Lafayette, Ind., 1993-95; rsch. asst. Purdue U.-Dept. Agrl. Econs., West Lafayette, 1993—. Mem. AAUW, Am. Assn. Agrl. Economists, Nat. Peace Corps Assn., Hoosier Area Returned Vols. (membership coord.). Democrat. Home: 914 N 21st St Apt 3 Lafayette IN 47904 Office: Purdue Univ Dept Agrl Econs Krannert Bldg West Lafayette IN 47906

MARTIN, LORNA CAMPBELL, secondary education educator; b. Ridgewood, N.J., June 28, 1967; d. Robert F. and Pearl Campbell; m. Michael Glenn Martin, July 8, 1995. BA in English, Wake Forest U., 1989. Cert. tchr., 1991. Tchr. English, soccer coach, yearbook advisor Moore County Schs., Southern Pines, N.C., 1991—. Mem. N.C. English Tchrs. Assn., Nat. Soccer Coaches Assn. Presbyterian. Home: 114 Heather Ln Southern Pines NC 28387 Office: Pinecrest HS PO Box 1259 Southern Pines NC 28388

MARTIN, LORRAINE B., humanities educator; b. Utica, N.Y., Aug. 18, 1940; d. Walter G. and Laura (Bochenek) Bolanowski; m. Charles A. Martin; children: Denise M. Stringer, Tracy M. Weinrich. Student, SUNY, Albany, 1958-60, postgrad.; BA in English and Edn. magna cum laude, Utica Coll. of Syracuse U., 1977; MS in Edn. and Reading, SUNY, Cortland, 1979, CAS in Edn. Adminstrn., 1984; postgrad., Syracuse U., 1990—, SUNY, Albany, 1992—. Cert. elem. tchr., secondary tchr., sch. adminstr. and supr., sch. dist. adminstr., reading specialist, N.Y. Tchr. Poland (N.Y.) Cen. Sch., 1972-80, reading specialist, 1980-84; instr. reading Utica Coll. of Syracuse U., summer 1982-84; adminstr. spl. edn. and chpt. 1 remedial program Little Falls (N.Y.) City Sch. Dist., 1984-85; adminstr. adult and continuing edn. Madison-Oneida Bd. Coop. Ednl. Svcs., Verona, N.Y., 1985-86; dir. gen. programs Herkimer (N.Y.) Bd. Coop. Ednl. Svcs., 1986-88; assoc. prof. English, children's lit., reading, freshman seminar, and honors program Herkimer County Community Coll., Herkimer, 1988—; ednl. cons., 1979—; pvt. cons. for reading and writing, 1980—; participant SUNY brainstorming session on underprepared students, 1993; trainer tchr. performance evaluation program N.Y. State Dept. Edn., Herkimer, 1984, facilitator effective schs. program, 1986-88; cons. Two-Yr. Coll. Devel. Ctr. SUNY, 1985-89, tchr. trainer for the Writing Process; developer summer reading, writing and study skills course for Bridge program. Author: The Bridge Program—Easing the Transition from High School to College, 1990; editorial bd. Research and Teaching in Developmental Education; contbr. to Teaching Writing to Adults Tips for Teachers: An Idea Swap, 1989; textbook reviewer for pubs., 1993—. Vol. arts and crafts fair HCCC Found.; active Myasthenia Gravis Found., 1988—, Muscular Dystrophy Assn., 1989—, Thyroid Found. of Am., 1988—; advisor Network for Coll. Re-Entry Adults; mem. Profl. Devel. Com., Acad. Computer Com. Recipient Leader Silver award for volunteerism 4-H Coop. Extension, Utica, 1980; HCCC Found. grantee, Writing grantee Readers's Digest. Mem. Internat. Reading Assn., N.Y. State Reading Assn., Assn. Supervision and Curriculum Devel., Nat. Coun. Tchrs. English, Conf. on Coll. Composition and Communication, N.Y. Coll. Learning Skills Assn., N.Y. State Assn. Two-Yr. Colls., Inc., Phi Kappa Phi, Alpha Lambda Sigma. Home: 7099 Crooked Brook Rd Utica NY 13502-7203 Office: Herkimer County Comm Coll SUNY Reservoir Rd Herkimer NY 13350-1545

MARTIN, LUAN, accountant, payroll and timekeeping supervisor; b. Dimmitt, Tex., Dec. 9, 1952; d. Walter Johnnie and Nellie Beth (Connell) Martin; 1 child, Dani D'Ann. Grad., Amarillo Jr. Coll., 1986. Credit mgr. Castro County Credit Bur., Dimmitt, 1978-79; parts mgr. Case Power and Equipment, Dimmitt, 1979-82; bookkeeper Dimmitt Agri Industries, Inc., 1982; personnel dir. Deaf Smith Gen. Hosp., Hereford, Tex., 1983-84; payroll acct. Mason & Hanger-Silas Mason Co., Inc., Amarillo, Tex., 1984—; owner, pres. Dugan Mgmt., Amarillo, 1987-94. Vol. local sch.; spkr. in behalf of blood, bone marrow and organ donations. Mem. Toastmasters Internat. (Pantex Lunch Bunch chpt.). Methodist. Office: Mason Hanger Silas Mason Co PO Box 30020 Amarillo TX 79177-0001

MARTIN, LUCY Z., public relations executive; b. Alton, Ill., July 8, 1941; d. Fred and Lucille J. M. BA, Northwestern U., 1963. Adminstrv. asst., copywriter Batz-Hodgson-Neuwoehner, Inc., St. Louis, 1963-64; news reporter, Midwest fashion editor Fairchild Publs., St. Louis, 1964-66; account exec. Milici Advt. Agy., Honolulu, 1967; publs. dir. Barnes Med. Ctr., St. Louis, 1968-69; communications cons. Fleishman-Hillard, St. Louis, 1970-74; communications cons., chief exec. officer, pres. Lucy Z. Martin & Assocs., Portland, Oreg., 1974—; spkr. Healthcare Assn. Hawaii, Honolulu, 1993, Oreg. Assn. Healthcare, 1992, Healthcare Fin. Mgmt. Assn., 1993, Healthcare Communicators Oreg., 1994, Pub. Rels. Soc. Am., Columbia River chpt., 1996. Featured in Entrepreneurial Woman mag.; contbr. articles to profl. jours. Chmn. women's adv. com. Reed Coll., Portland, 1977-79; mem. Oreg. Commn. for Women, 1984-87; bd. dirs. Ronald McDonald House Oreg., 1986, Oreg. Sch. Arts and Crafts, 1989—, Northwestern U. Alumni Coun., 1992—; chmn. bd. Good Samaritan Hosp. Assocs., 1991-94; mem. pub. policy com. YMCA, 1993-95; mem. adv. bd. Jr. League, 1994—. Recipient MacEachern Citation Acad. Hosp. Pub. Relations, 1978, Rosey awards Portland Advt. Fedn., 1979, Achievement award Soc. Tech. Communications, 1982, Disting. Tech. Communication award, 1982, Exceptional Achievement award Council for Advancement and Support Edn., 1983, Monsoon award Internat. Graphics, Inc., 1984; named Woman of Achievement Daily Jour. Commerce, 1980. Mem. Pub. Rels. Soc. Am. (pres. Columbia River chpt. 1984, chmn. bd. 1980-84, Oreg. del. 1984-86, judicial panel N. Pacific dist 1985-86, exec. bd. health care sect. 1986-87, mem. Counselors Acad., Spotlight awards 1985, 86, 87, 88, nat. exec. com. 1987-91), Portland Pub. Rels. Roundtable (chmn. 1985, bd. dirs. 1983-85), Assn. Western Hosps. (editorial adv. bd. 1984-85), Best of West awards 1978, 80, 83, 87), Oreg. Hosp. Pub. Relations Orgn. (pres. 1981, chmn. bd. 1982, bd. dirs. 1992-93), Acad. Health Service Mktg., Am. Hosp. Assn., Am. Mktg. Assn. (Oreg. chpt. bd. dirs. 1992-93), Am. Soc. Hosp. Mktg. & Pub. Relations, Healthcare Communicators Oreg. (conf. keynote speaker 1994), Internat. Assn. Bus. Communicators (18 awards 1981-87), Oreg. Assn. Hosps. (keynote speaker for trustee, 1991, speaker, 1993, bd. dirs. 1992-93), Oreg. Press Women, Nat. and Oreg. Soc. Healthcare Planning and Mktg., Women in Comms. (Matrix award 1977), Bus. Social Responsibility, Inst. for Managerial and Profl. Women (bd. dirs. 1992-94). Office: 1881 SW Edgewood Rd Portland OR 97201-2235

MARTIN, MARGARET GATELY, elementary education educator; b. Teaneck, N.J., July 24, 1928; d. Martin F. and Grace (Hammell) Gately; m. Phillips H. Martin, June 27, 1953 (div. 1977); children: Paul H., Patrick W., Thomas P. BA, Hunter Coll., 1950, MA, 1953. Cert. elem. tchr., N.Y. Tchr. Pub. Sch. # 5, Queens, N.Y., 1950-53, Wappingers Cen. Sch., Wappingers Falls, N.Y., 1953-55, Jamestown (N.Y.) Pub. Schs., 1977-95; ret., 1996; tchr. S.S. Peter and Paul Sunday Sch., Jamestown, 1977-95; citizen amb. to Russia, 1995. mem. NEA, AAUW (pres. 1980-82, 92-94, Edn. Found. Program award 1985), Jamestown Tchrs. Assn. (membership chair 1976-78, sec. 1982-84), Jamestown Inter Club Coun. (pres. 1984-86, v.p. 1995-96, Woman of Yr. 1991), Green Thumb Garden Club (pres. 1986-88, 96—, v.p. 1991-93, 95-96), Delta Kappa Gamma (membership chair 1991-94, corr. sec. 1988-90, v.p. 1994—). Republican. Roman Catholic. Home: 130 Ellis Ave Jamestown NY 14701-6218 Office: Lincoln Sch 301 Front St Jamestown NY 14701-6242

MARTIN, MARILYN JOAN, library director; b. Golden Meadow, La., Jan. 17, 1940; d. Marion Francis Mobley and Audrey Virna (Goza) Sapaugh; m. James Reginald Martin, Dec. 16, 1958; children: James Michael, Linda Jill Michaels. BA in History, U. Wash., 1975, MLS, 1976; MA in Pub. History, U. Ark., 1992; PhD in Libr. Sci., Tex. Woman's U., 1993. Cataloger, reference libr. St. Martin's Coll., Lacey, Wash., 1976-78; asst. reference libr. Pacific Luth. U., Tacoma, 1978-85; serials libr. Henderson State U., Arkadelphia, Ark., 1985-86, collection devel. libr., 1987-88, dir. learning resources, 1989-95; dean libr. svcs. Rowan Coll. of N.J., Glassboro, 1995—. Contbr. articles to profl. jours. Bd. dirs. N.J. Acad. Libr. Network; mem. exec. com. Tri-state Coll. Libr. Mem. ALA (rsch. com. 1993—, stds. com. 1994—), Assn. Coll. and Rsch. Librs. Republican. Office: Library Rowan Coll of NJ Glassboro NJ 08028-1701

MARTIN, MARSHA PYLE, federal agency administrator; married; 2 children. BA, Tex. Woman's U.; MS, Tex. A&M U. Sr. officer Fed. Intermediate Credit Bank Tex., 1970-94; apptd. chmn. Farm Credit Adminstrn. Bd., 1994—; bd. dirs. Farm Credit Sys. Ins. Corp. Office: Farm Credit Adminstrn 1501 Farm Credit Dr Mc Lean VA 22102-5090*

MARTIN, MARY, secondary education educator; b. Detroit, Mich., May 17, 1954; d. Enos and Sara (Evans) M. AS, Highland Park C.C., 1975; BA, Wayne State U., 1975, MA in Teaching, 1981; postgrad., So. Calif. Sch. Ministry, Detroit, 1992—. Dietary aide Allan Dee Nursing Home, Detroit, 1972; dietary aide Harper Hosp., Detroit, 1973, 74, nurse aide, 1974-75, respiratory technician, 1975-80; respiratory technician Dr.'s Hosp., Detroit, 1980; head cook, supr. Focus Hope, Detroit, 1981; substitute tchr. Detroit Bd. Edn., 1984-90, tchr. adult edn., 1990-93, tchr., 1993—; interim advisor student coun. Wayne State U., Detroit, 1985. Sunday sch. teaching trainer People's Missionary Bapt. Ch., Detroit, 1986, del., 1984-87, mem. All Aid, 1984-87, mem. choir, 1984, usher, 1984; precinct del. 13th Congl. Dist., 1986-88, 90-92, model, 1985. Recipient Spirit of Detroit award Detroit City Coun., 1993, Spl. Congl. cert. Hon. Barbara Rose Collins, 1994, Proclamation, Wayne County Commr. George Cushingberry, 1994. Mem. Nat. Sociol. Honor Soc. Democrat.

MARTIN, MARY COATES, genealogist, writer, volunteer; b. Gloucester County, N.J.; d. Raymond and Emily (Johnson) Coates; m. Lawrence O. Kupillas (dec.); m. Clyde Davis Martin (dec.); 1 child, William Raymond. Contbg. editor Md. & Del. Genealogist, St. Michaels, Md., 1985—. Author: The House of John Johnson (1731-1802) Salem County, N.J. and His Descendants, 1979, Fifty Year History of Daughters of Colonial Wars in the State of New York, 1980, 350 Years of American Ancestors: 38 Families: 1630-1989, 1989, Colonial Families: Martin and Bell Families and Their Kin: 1657-1992, Clifton--Coates Kinfolk and 316 Allied Families, 1995. Pres. Washington Hdqrs. Assn., 1970-73, bd. dirs., 1962—; Centennial pres. Sorosis, Inc., 1966-68; bd. dirs. Soldiers Sailors Airmen's Club, N.Y.C., 1976-81, Yorkville Youth Coun., N.Y.C., 1954-60; co-chmn. Colonial Ball, N.Y.C., 1965-67; rec. sec. Parents League of N.Y., Inc., 1954-57; mem. com. Internat. Debutante Ball, N.Y.C., 1977-81; mem. Am. Flag Inst., N.Y.C., 1963-72. Mem. Hereditary Order of Descendants of Colonial Govs. (gov. gen. 1981-83), Nat. Soc. Colonial Dames of Seventeenth Century (N.Y. State pres. 1977-79, parlimentarian 1979-81), Nat. Soc. Daus. of Colonial Wars (N.Y. State pres. 1977-80), Nat. Soc. DAR (regent 1962-65, pres. roundtable 1964-65, N.Y. State chaplain 1968-71, parliamentarian 1980-83, nat. platform com. 1970-76, certificate of award 1971, nat. vice chmn. lineage rsch. com. 1977-80, geneal. com. 1980-83), Nat. Soc. New Eng. Women (dir. gen. 1972-77, nat. vice chmn. helping hand disbursing fund 1968-71), Order of Crown of Charlemagne U.S.A. (corr. sec. gen. 1985-88, 3rd v.p. 1988-89, 2nd v.p. 1989-91), Nat. Soc. Children Am. Revolution, Nicasius de Sille Soc. (pres. 1960-62), Order Ams. of Armorial Ancestry (1st v.p. gen. 1985-88, councillor gen. 1988—), Nat. Gavel Soc., Nat. Soc. Magna Carta Dames, Descendants of Soc. of Colonial Clergy, Huguenot Soc. Am., Descendants of a Knight of Most Noble Order Garter, Nat. Soc. Daus. Am. Colonists, Nat. Soc. U.S. Daus. 1812, Order of Descendants of Colonial Physicians and Chirurgiens, Plantagenet Soc., Vt. Soc. Colonial Dames, Del. Geneal. Soc., Huguenot Hist. Soc., DuBois Family Assn. (1st v.p.), Cumberland County N.J. Hist. Soc., Gloucester County N.J. Hist. Soc., Md. Hist. Soc., Hist. Soc. Del., Salem County N.J. Hist. Soc., Woodstown-Pilesgrove N.J. Hist. Soc., Hereditary Order First Families of Mass., Inc. Home: Hague Towers # 1815 330 W Brambleton Ave Norfolk VA 23510-1307

MARTIN, MARY EVELYN, advertising, marketing and business writing consultant; b. Lexington, Ky.; d. George Clarke and Georgann Elizabeth (Bovis) M. BA magna cum laude, Lindenwood Coll., 1980; MA with honors, U. Ky., 1991. Asst. to pres. The Hamlets, Ltd/Park Place Country Homes, Louisville, 1984-85; advt. designer, copywriter Park Place Country Homes, Anchorage, Ky., 1985-86; creative dir. of advt., mktg., v.p., treas. Park Place Country Homes/Park Place Properties, Anchorage, Ky., 1986—; founder, pres. Good Help Cons. Svcs., Louisville and Lexington, Maison Marche Advt. & Promotions, Louisville, 1989; instr. dept. English U. Ky., 1989-91; adj. prof. composition U. Louisville, 1991-96; vis. lectr. lit. Bellarmine Coll., Louisville, 1992; adj. prof. humanities Ind. U. S.E., 1991-95; prof. arts and humanities McKendree Coll., Louisville, 1993-96. Editor: (poetry mag.) The Griffin, 1979-80; contbr. series to mag., 1996. Mem. People for the Am. Way, Greenpeace. Recipient Spahmer creative writing award, 1979; Haggin fellow U. Ky., 1987; grantee U. Louisville, 1992-95. Mem. Am. Film Inst., Nat. Assn. Home Builders (affiliate), Internat. Platform Assn., Ky. Film Artists Coalition. Democrat. Home: PO Box 23282 Anchorage KY 40223-0282 Office: Park Place Country Homes PO Box 23226 Anchorage KY 40223-0226

MARTIN, MARY LOIS, nursing director, critical care nurse; b. Greensburg, Ky., June 19, 1954; d. John Will and Nellie Gertrude (Akin) M.; 1 child, Amanda. ADN, Midway (Ky.) Coll., 1974. RN, Ky.; CCRN; cert. BLS, ACLS and pediatric advanced life support provider and instr., affiliate faculty ACLS, Am. Heart Assn. Med. surg. staff nurse Ctrl. Bapt. Hosp., Lexington, Ky., 1974-75, 76-77; med. surg. staff nurse Taylor County Hosp., Campbellsville, Ky., 1975-76, house shift supr., 1978-79, staff nurs ICU and med.- surg. unit, 1979-84, emergency room ICU coord., 1984-89, ICU nursing dir., 1989-90, 92—, ICU, emergency rm. nursing dir., 1991-92. Mem. AACN, Greater Louisville chpt. AACN. Democrat. Baptist. Home: 101 Churchill Dr Campbellsville KY 42718-2129 Office: Taylor County Hosp 1700 Old Lebanon Rd Campbellsville KY 42718-9662

MARTIN, MARY WOLF, newspaper editor; b. Corwith, Iowa, Nov. 6, 1930; d. Henry Herbert and Mabel M. (Keeney) Wolf; m. Charles William Martin, Oct. 16, 1950; children: Stephen C., Neal J., Sally Martin Kindell. Grad. high sch., Weyauwega, Wis. Corr. Britt (Iowa) News Tribune, 1946-47; staff writer Wheaton (Ill.) Daily Jour., 1963-65; reporter, photographer Rhinelander (Wis.) Daily News, 1967-69, news editor, 1969-74, mng. editor, 1974-76; mng. editor Neenah-Menasha Northwestern, Neenah, 1976-80; editor Oshkosh Northwestern, 1980-94. Pres. Fox Valley Press Club, Oshkosh, 1982; bd. dirs. Goodwill Industries N.E. Wis., Menasha, 1978-86, Rape Crisis Ctr., Oshkosh, 1981-85, Fox Valley Arts Alliance, Appleton, Wis., 1980-85, Fox Valley Cmty. Tech. Coll., Oshkosh, 1986-92; trustee Paine Art Ctr. Arboretum, Oshkosh, 1990-93. Named Woman of Yr., Bus. and Profl. Women, Rhinelander, 1975, Vol. of Yr., Sexual Abuse Svcs., Oshkosh, 1989. Mem. Wis. Assoc. Press Mng. Editors (pres. Milw. 1985-86), Nat. Assoc. Press Mng. Editors, Am. Soc. Newspaper Editors, Media-Law Com. Wis. Bar Assn. Roman Catholic. Home: 898 County Road Q Pelican Lake WI 54463-9537

MARTIN, MARY-ANNE, art gallery owner; b. Hoboken, N.J., Apr. 26, 1943; d. Thomas Philipp and Ruth (Kelley) M.; m. Henry S. Berman, June 9, 1963 (div. 1976); 1 child, Julia Berman. Student, Smith Coll., 1961-63; BA, Barnard Coll., 1965; MA, NYU, 1967. Head dept. painting Sotheby Parke Bernet, N.Y.C., 1971-78; sr. v.p. Sotheby's, N.Y.C., 1978-82; pres. Mary-Anne Martin, Fine Art, N.Y.C., 1982—; founder Latin Am. dept. Sotheby's, 1977. Mem. Art Dealers Assn. Am. (v.p., bd. dirs.). Office: 23 E 73rd St New York NY 10021-3522

MARTIN, MELISSA CAROL, radiological physicist; b. Muskogee, Okla., Feb. 7, 1951; d. Carl Leroy and Helen Shirley (Hicks) Paden; m. Donald Ray Martin, Feb. 14, 1970; 1 child, Christina Gail. BS, Okla. State U., 1971; MS, UCLA, 1975. Cert. radiol. physicist, Am. Bd. Radiology, radiation oncology, Am. Bd. Med. Physics. Asst. radiation physicist Hosp. of the Good Samaritan, L.A., 1975-80; radiol. physicist Meml. Med. Ctr., Long Beach, Calif., 1980-83, St. Joseph Hosp., Orange, Calif., 1983-92, Therapy Physics, Inc., Bellflower, Calif., 1993—; cons. in field. Editor: (book) Current Regulatory Issues in Medical Physics, 1992. Fund raising campaign div. mgr. YMCA, Torrance, Calif., 1988-92; dir. AWANA Youth Club-Guards Group, Manhattan Beach, Calif., 1984—. Named Dir. of Symposium, Am. Coll. Med. Physics, 1992. Fellow Am. Coll. Med. Physics (chancellor western region 1992-95); mem. Am. Assn. Physicists in Medicine (profl. coun. 1990-95), Am. Coll. Radiology (econs. com. 1992-95), Calif. Med. Physics Soc. (treas. 1991-95), Am. Soc. for Therapeutic Radiology and Oncology, Health Physics Soc. (pres. So. Calif. chpt. 1992-93), Am. Brachytherapy Soc. Baptist. Home: 507 Susana Ave Redondo Beach CA 90277-3953 Office: Therapy Physics Inc 9156 Rose St Bellflower CA 90706-6420

MARTIN, NANCY KAY, education educator; b. San Antonio, June 21, 1954. BA, Sam Houston State U., 1977, MEd, 1980; EdD, Tex. Tech U., 1988. Cert. sch. counselor, Tex.; cert. secondary sch. tchr., Tex. Tchr. English Amanda Burks Elem. Sch., Cotulla, Tex., 1977-78; tchr. English and speech Uvalde (Tex.) Jr. H.S., 1978-82; asst. prof. edn. Southea. La. U., Hammond, 1989-93; asst. prof. U. Tex., San Antonio, 1993—. Contbr. articles to profl. jours. Mem. Am. Ednl. Rsch. Assn., S.W. Ednl. Rsch. Assn. (bd. dirs. 1995—). Presbyterian. Office: Univ Tex Divsn Edn San Antonio TX 78249

MARTIN, PAULA K., management consultant; b. Lawrenceville, Ill., Nov. 5, 1951; d. David M. and Patsy Ann (Roper) M.; m. Joel Weinstein, Nov. 9, 1981. BA, Empire State Coll., 1975; MS, Colo. State U., 1981. Office mgr. Albany (N.Y.) County Mental Health, 1975-76; mgr. adminstrn. group ins. PIA, Glenmont, N.Y., 1976-78; assoc. dir. Am. Cyanamid Co., Princeton, N.J., 1981-89; pres. Renaissance Edn. Svc., Flemington, N.J., 1989—. Author: The Buck Stops Here, 1995, Leading Project Management into the 21st Century, 1995. Recipient Tribute to Women in Industry award YWCA, 1988. Mem. Vis. Nurses of Delaware Valley (bd. dirs. v.p. 1992—). Office: Renaissance Ednl Svcs 120 Amwell Rd Flemington NJ 08822

MARTIN, REBECCA FAITH, special education educator; b. Union, W.Va., July 2; m. Marc Edwin Martin, Mar. 25, 1988; 1 child, Katherine Elizabeth. BA in Elem. Edn., W.Va. Wesleyan Coll., 1986, postgrad.; postgrad., Shenando U., James Madison U., U. Va. Cert. elem. tchr., spl. edn. tchr., W.Va. Spl. edn. tchr. Lewis County Pub. Schs., Westen, W.Va., 1987, Upshur County Pub. Schs., Buckhannon, W.Va., 1987-89, Federick County Pub. Schs., Winchester, Va., 1989—. Mem., activist Nat. Assn. Polit. Action Com., Winchester, 1995-96; freshman parent band rep. Sherando H.S. Band Boosters, 1993-94. Mem. AAUW, NEA, Va. Edn. Assn., Frederick County Edn. Assn., Tchrs. as Readers, Shenandoah Valley Reading Coun., Shenando H.S. Parent Tchr. Orgn. (membership chair band boosters 1995-96). Office: Indian Hollow Elem 1548 N Hayfield Rd Winchester VA 22603

MARTIN, REBECCA REIST, librarian; b. Princeton, N.J., Mar. 2, 1952; d. Benjamin A. and Harriet (Nold) Reist; 1 child, Benjamin R. BA, U. Calif., Santa Cruz, 1973; MA, San Jose State U., 1975; DPA, U. So. Calif., 1992. Med. libr. VA Med. Ctr., San Francisco, 1975-77, chief libr. svc., 1977-81; head biology libr. U. Calif., Berkeley, 1981-85; assoc. libr. dir. San Jose (Calif.) State U., 1985-90; dean of librs. U. Vt., Burlington, 1990—. Author: Libraries and the Changing Face of Academia, 1994; contbr. articles to profl. jours., chpts. in books. Mem. Libr. Commn. San Jose, 1989-90. Mem. ALA, New England Libr. Assn., Am. Soc. Pub. Adminstrn., Am. Assn. Coll. and Rsch. Librs., Libr. Adminstrn. and Mgmt. Assn. (bd. dirs. 1987-89), NELINET (bd. dirs. 1995—). Office: U Vt Bailey/Howe Libr Burlington VT 05405

MARTIN, RETHA JANE, lawyer; b. Bloomington, Ind., Mar. 8, 1955; d. Delbert Eugene and Beverly June (Carr) M.; m. Robert Ralph Van Alstine, Dec. 26, 1986. BS, Taylor U., 1977; JD, Ind. U., 1980. Assoc. Alexander & Zaleva, Chgo., 1980-83; legal counsel Kimberly Clark Corp., Neenah, Wis., 1983-86; sr. counsel Kimberly Clark Corp., Roswell, Ga., 1986-88; v.p., sr. counsel Whirlpool Corp., Benton Harbor, Mich., 1988—. Sponsor, advisor Project Together, Benton Harbor, Mich., 1993-94. Mem. Internat. Trademark Assn. (bd. dirs. 1993—). Home: 4232 Ridge Rd Stevensville MI 49127-9370 Office: Whirlpool Properties Inc 400 Riverview Dr Ste 420 Benton Harbor MI 49022-5016*

MARTIN, ROSE KOCSIS, law librarian; b. Kiralyrev, Hungary, Aug. 25, 1928; came to U.S., 1949, naturalized, 1954; d. Ferenc and Zsuzsanna (Nehai Szabo) Kocsis; m. Donald L. Martin, Aug. 23, 1961; 1 child, Virginia Kim. Student Seton Hall U., 1960-61; BBA, Kensington U., Glendale, Calif., 1968-69; cert. Cath. U. Am. 1981, George Washington U., 1982. Documents libr. Seton Hall U., South Orange, N.J., 1958-61; mem. office staff Dept. Def., Washington, 1962-63, Dept. Agr., Washington, 1963-67; info. specialist law Office Adminstrv. Law Judges, Dept. Labor, Washington, 1976—. Active Rep. Club, Great Falls, Va., 1986—. Recipient Meritorious award Dept. Agr., 1966, Outstanding award Dept. Labor, 1977, Honorable Svc. to the Nation award Dept. Labor, 1988, Spl. Achievement award, 1990. Mem. Am. Assn. Law Libraries, NAFE, Nat. Mus. Women in Arts, Internat. Platform Assn., Great Falls Woman's Club, River Bend Golf and Country Club. Roman Catholic. Avocations: travel, tennis, reading, swimming, cooking. Home: PO Box 651 Middleburg VA 22117-0651

MARTIN, SUSAN ANN, educator; b. Rahway, N.J., June 15, 1950; d. Frederick Edward and Doris Bertha (Heid) Schmidt; m. Chester B. Martin, Nov. 25, 1980; children: Julie Virginia, Stacie Diane. BA, Wittenberg U., 1972; MA, Marietta Coll., 1982. Tchr. Belpre (Ohio) City Schs., Ohio; yearbook advisor Stone Sch., Belpre, 1995. Mem. Belpre Edn. Assn. (v.p. 1993-94), DKG (hon.). Home: 833 Third St Marietta OH 45750

MARTIN, SUSAN KATHERINE, librarian; b. Cambridge, Eng., Nov. 14, 1942; came to U.S., 1950, naturalized, 1961; d. Egon and Jolan (Schonfeld) Orowan; m. David S. Martin, June 30, 1962. BA with honors, Tufts U., 1963; MS, Simmons Coll., 1965; PhD, U. Calif., Berkeley, 1983. Intern libr. Harvard U., Cambridge, Mass., 1963-65, systems libr., 1965-73; head systems office gen. libr. U. Calif., Berkeley, 1973-79; dir. Milton S. Eisenhower Libr. Johns Hopkins U., Balt., 1979-88, exec. dir. Nat. Commn. on Libraries and Info. Sci., 1988-90; univ. libr. Georgetown U., Washington, 1990—; mem. libr. adv. com. Princeton (N.J.) U., 1987-95; mem. vis. com. Harvard U. Libr., 1987-93, 94—; bd. overseers for univ. libr. Tufts U., 1986—; mem. libr. adv. com. Hong Kong U. Sci. Tech., 1988-95; mem. acad. libr. adv. group U. Md. Sch. Librs. and Info. Sci., 1994-96; cons. to various librs. and info. cos., 1975—; mem. adv. bd. ERIC, 1990-92, History Assocs., Inc., 1990-92. Author: Library Networks; Libraries in Partnership, 1986-87; editor; Jour. Libr. Automation, 1972-77; mem. editorial bd. Advanced Tech./Librs., 1973-93, Jour. Libr. Adminstrn., 1986—, Libr. Hi-Tech., 1989-93, Jour. Acad. Librarianship, 1994—; contbr. articles to profl. jours. Trustee Phila. Area Libr. Network, 1980-81; bd. dirs. Universal Serials and

Book Exch., 1981-82, v.p., 1983, pres., 1984; trustee Capital Consortium, 1992-95; mem. bd. Potomac Internet, 1995-96. Recipient Simmons Coll. Disting. Alumni award, 1977; Council on Library Resources fellow, 1973. Mem. ALA (coun. 1988-92, structure revision TF, 1995—), Internat. Fedn. Libr. Assns. Commn. on Access to Info. and Freedom of Expression, Rsch. Librs. Group (gov., exec. com. 1985-87), Libr. and Info. Tech. Assn. (pres. 1978-79), Assn. Rsch. Librs., Libr. of Congress (optical disk pilot project adv. com. 1985-89), Coalition for Networked Info. (leader working group 1990-92), Assn. Coll. and Rsch. Librs. (pres. 1994-95), Internat. Fedn. Libr. Assns. (com. mem. 1995—), Cosmos Club (libr. com. 1989-96), Grolier Club, Phi Beta Kappa. Home: 4709 Blagden Ter NW Washington DC 20011-3719 Office: Georgetown U Lauinger Libr Washington DC 20057

MARTIN, SUSAN TAYLOR, newspaper editor; b. N.Y.C., Aug. 3, 1949; d. Lewis Randolph and Carolyn Emmons (Douthat) Taylor; m. James Addison Martin Jr., Nov. 15, 1975; 1 child, Steven Randolph. BA in Polit. Sci., Duke U., 1971. Reporter Ft. Myers (Fla.) News Press, 1972-75, Tampa (Fla.) Tribune, 1975-77, Associated Press, Detroit, 1977-78; bur. chief Detroit News, 1978-81; asst. city editor Orlando (Fla.) Sentinel, 1981-82; exec. bus. editor St. Petersburg (Fla.) Times, 1982-86, city editor, 1986-87, nat. corr., 1987-91, asst. mng. editor, 1991-93, dep. mng. editor, 1993—. Trustee Poynter Fund, St. Petersburg, 1992—. Recipient Non-Deadline Reporting award Soc. Profl. Journalists, 1990, Investigative Reporting award, 1991, Feature, Depth Reporting award Fla. Soc. Newspaper Editors, 1990, Depth Reporting award, 1991. Mem. Suncoast Figure Skating Club. Democrat. Episcopalian. Home: 1312 51st Ave NE Saint Petersburg FL 33703-3209 Office: St Petersburg Times 490 1st Ave S Saint Petersburg FL 33731

MARTIN, TANYA LEIGH, psychologist; b. Redlands, Calif., Dec. 2, 1960; d. Raymond F. Martin and Shawna L. (Eastwood) Farmer. BA, Calif. State U., San Bernardino, 1984; PhD, U. S.C., 1991. Lic. psychologist, Calif. Post doctoral fellow Harbor-UCLA Med. Ctr., Torrance, Calif., 1991-92; psychologist Hathaway Children's Svc., Sylmar, Calif., 1992—. Mem. APA. Office: Hathaway Childrens Services PO Box 923670 Sylmar CA 91392

MARTIN, ULRIKE BALK, laboratory analyst; b. Kelheim, Germany, Oct. 28, 1965; d. Gunther Anton and Elfriede Babette (Eiser) Balk; m. Kent Daniel Martin, May 1, 1988. BS summa cum laude, Stephen F. Austin State U., Nacogdoches, Tex., 1992; MS, 1994. Lab. analyst Eastman Chem. Co., Longview, Tex., 1994—. Author: An Analysis of Heavy Metals on Forest Stream Ecosystems Receiving Run Off from an Oil Field, 1992. Mem. Tex. Acad. Sci., Sigma Xi. Home: 3019 B Tryon Rd Longview TX 75605

MARTIN, WILLIE PAULINE, elementary school educator, illustrator; b. Pendleton, Tex., May 27, 1920; d. Lester B. and Stella (Smith) M.; m. Charles M., June 23, 1946; 1 child, Charles Jr. BS, Middle Tenn. State U., Murfreesboro, 1944; MS, U. Tenn., 1965; postgrad., U. Ga., 1980. Cert. tchr., Tenn., Tex., Ga. Elem. tchr. Bd. Edn., Sparta, Tenn., 1940-44; home econs. tchr. Bd. Edn., Salado, Tex., 1944-46; rsch. technician Oak Ridge (Tenn.) Nat. Lab., 1946-50; art, gen. sci. tchr. Bd. Edn., State of Tenn., 1965-69; art, reading, elem. tchr. Bd. Edn., State of Ga., 1970-83; elem. tchr. Bd. Edn., Augusta, Ga., 1984-86; tchr. aerospace edn. workshop Middle Tenn. State U., 1969; spkr. in field. Contbr. articles in field to profl. jours. Exhibitor Oak Ridge (Tenn.) Festival. Mem. Nat. Art Edn. Assn. (del. conv. Washington 1989, Balt. 1994), Ga. Art Edn. Assn. (del. state conv., dist. pres. 1974, del. conv. Savannah 1986, Augusta 1993, del. state conv. Athens 1994), Tenn. Edn. Assn. Methodist. Home: 1406 Flowing Wells Rd Augusta GA 30909-9767

MARTINAC, PAULA, writer, editor; b. Pitts., July 30, 1954; d. Robert W. and Dorothy (Kalinoski) M.; life ptnr. Katie Hogan. BA, Chatham Coll., 1976; MA, Coll. William and Mary, 1979. Asst. curator W.Va. State Mus., Charleston, 1979-82; prodn. editor Prentice-Hall, Inc., Englewood Cliffs, N.J., 1982-85; prodn. dir. The Feminist Press at CUNY, N.Y.C., 1985-94; freelance writer N.Y.C., 1994—. Author: Out of Time, 1990 (Lambda Lit. award 1990), Home Movies, 1993, (biography) k.d. lang, 1996; editor: (anthology) The One You Call Sister, 1989; mem. editl. bd.: (mag.) Conditions, 1990-92; mem. editl. collective: (newspaper) Womanews, 1982-85. Curator In Our Own Write reading series Lesbian and Gay Cmty. Svcs. Ctr., N.Y.C., 1988-90, bd. dirs., 1990-95, co-chair, bd. dirs., 1992-94; panelist Cultural Coun. Found., N.Y.C., 1991. Grantee Puffin Found., 1990. Mem. PEN Am. Ctr., Editl. Freelancers Assn., Phi Beta Kappa. Democrat.

MARTIN-BOWEN, (CAROLE) LINDSEY, freelance writer; b. Kansas City, Kans., Aug. 4, 1949; d. Lawrence Richard and V. Marie (Schaffer) Pickett; m. Frederick E. Nicholson, July 3, 1971 (div. 1977); 1 child, Aaron Frederick; m. Edwin L. Martin, June 18, 1980 (div. 1987); 1 child, Ki Elise; m. Michael L. Bowen, Dec. 23, 1988. BA in English Lit., U. Mo., Kansas City, 1972, MA in English and Creative Writing, 1988, postgrad., 1991-94; postgrad., U. Mo. Kansas City Sch. Law, Kansas City, 1995—. Tech. editor Office Hearings and Appeals, U.S. Dept. Interior, Washington, 1976-77; reporter, photographer Louisville Times, 1982-83; reporter, features editor Sun Newspapers, Overland Park, Kans., 1983-84; assoc. editor Modern Jeweler, Overland Park and N.Y.C., 1984-85; writer Coll. Blvd. News, Overland Park, 1985-89, KC View, Kansas City, Mo., 1988-89; editor Number One, Kansas City, Mo., 1986-88, cons., 1988-89; copywriter Sta KXEO/KWWR Radio, Mexico, Mo., 1989; editorial asst. New Letters, 1985—; features writer, columnist The Squire, Prairie Village, Kans., 1990-95; instr. English U. Mo., Kansas City, 1986-88, Johnson County C.C., 1988-95; tchr. English and fiction Longview C.C., 1988-95; instr. writing and mass comm. Webster U., 1990—; instr. world lit., Am. lit., women in lit., creative writing Penn Valley C.C., 1993—, faculty sponsor The Penn; owner, writer Paladin Freelance Writing Svc., Kansas City, 1988—; prodn. editor Nat. Paralegal Reporter, 1992-95, editor 1994—; staff writer, editor Nat. Fedn. Paralegal Assns., Inc. books and pubs.; writing contest judge New Letters, 1987—. Author: (novel) The Dark Horse Waits in Boulder, 1985, (poetry) Waiting for the Wake-Up Call, 1990, Second Touch, 1990, (fiction) Cicada Grove and Other Stories, 1992; contbr. poems, book revs., features, cartoon artwork, and photographs to numerous publs. including New Letters, Lip Service and Contemporary Lit. Criticism. Campaigner McGovern for Pres. Campaign, Kansas City, 1971-72. Regents scholar, 1967; GAF fellow, 1986. Mem. U. Mo.-Kansas City Alumni Assn. (media com. 1983-84), Phi Kappa Phi. Roman Catholic. Home: 7109 Pennsylvania Ave Kansas City MO 64114-1316 Office: Nat Paralegal Reporter Hdqs. 32 W Bridlespur Ter. Kansas City MO 64114

MARTINE, ANDREA SCHULTZ, secondary school educator; b. Washington, Aug. 24, 1945; d. George Norman and Grace Lois (DiBetetto) S.; m. Leonard Francis Martine, June 10, 1967 (div. Apr. 1978). BS, Duquesne U., 1967, MA, 1970; postgrad., U. Pitts., 1970—. Cert. English tchr., prin., Pa. English tchr. Allderdice H.S., Pitts., 1967—, chair English dept., 1970-90, facilitator Ctrs. for Advanced Studies, 1990—, advanced placement coord., 1995—; day care dir. Tot Town Day Care Ctr., Pitts., 1978-82; instr. English dept. Allegheny C.C., Pitts., 1982—; advanced placement English cons. Coll. Bd., Phila., 1986—. Contbr. chpts. to books; author curriculum in field. Vol. Mercy Hosp., Pitts., 1985-87; vol. various elections Rep. Party, Pitts., 1980—. Howard Heinz fellow, 1990-94, Harper Collins fellow, 1991; finalist Pa. Tchr. of the Yr., 1992. Mem. AAUW, Conf. Coll. Composition and Comm., Nat. Coun. Tchrs. English, Pa. Coun. Tchrs. English, Duquesne U. Alumni Assn. (bd. dirs. 1970-78, v.p. 1972-76), Tchr. of Yr. Orgn., Internat. Poetry Forum (mem. adv. bd. 1978—), Nat. Assn. Gifted Children, Alpha Delta Kappa (pres. Pa. Iota chpt. 1994-96). Roman Catholic. Home: 634 Crystal Dr Pittsburgh PA 15228-2527 Office: Allderdice HS 2409 Shady Ave Pittsburgh PA 15217

MARTINEAU, JANET I., journalist, critic; b. Jackson, Mich., Sept. 4, 1945; d. James V. and K. Lucille (Astling) M. AA, Jackson C.C., 1964; BA, Mich. State U., 1967. From copy editor to arts/entertainment editor The Saginaw (Mich.) News, 1967—. Appearances on all local radio/TV stas. on talk shows, interviews, trivia series; speaker in field. Vol. Big Sisters/Little Sisters, Saginaw, 1975—, Spl. Olympics, Saginaw, 1990, Habitat for Humanity, Saginaw, 1995, Jr. Achievement, Saginaw, 1975-77. Recipient Media Lifetime Achievement award Concerned Citizens for the Arts in Mich., Detroit, 1994. Mem. Am. Bus. Women's Assn. (rec. sec. 1967-75), Zonta, Saginaw Valley Press Club (newsletter 1975-93). Office: The Saginaw News 203 S Washington Saginaw MI 48607

MARTINEAU, JULIE PEPERONE, social worker; b. Kilgore, Tex., Oct. 31, 1956; d. Angelo Gerad and Jane Margaret (Reppel) Peperone; m. Russell Joseph Martineau, Dec. 30, 1950; children: Adria Helen, Brittany Jane. AA, Marymount Palos Verdes Coll., Calif., 1976; BA, Calif. State U., Long Beach, 1979. Staff cons. United Way of L.A., 1979-83; group mgr. United Way of the Tex. Gulf Coast, Houston, 1983; dir. community devel. Tri-County Mental Health and Mental Retardation Svcs., Conroe, Tex., 1984-87; exec. dir. Montgomery County Com. on Aging, Conroe, 1987—; chmn. South Montgomery County Healthier Cmty. Forum, Conroe, 1996—; chmn. Project CARE Monitoring Coun., Conroe, 1989—; mem. long term care task force Tex. Health and Human Svcs. Commn., Austin, 1993-95; mem. aging programs adv. coun. Houston-Galveston Area Coun., 1987—; mem. aging and disabled adv. coun. Dept. Human Svcs., Houston, 1993—. Bd. dirs. Conroe Regional Med. Ctr., 1993—, United Way of Montgomery County, Conroe, 1984-87; congl. del. 1995 White House Conf. on Aging; chmn. Leadership Montgomery County, 1996—, South Montgomery County Cmty. Health Forum, The Woodlands, 1996—; v.p. Bluebonnet chpt. Nat. Charity League. Named Oustanding Woman of Yr., YWCA of Montgomery County, 1990, recipient awards. Mem. John Ben Shepherd Leadership Forum, Leadership Conroe, Area Agy. on Aging Execs. Network, South Montgomery C. of C. (chmn. bd. 1992-93), LWV of Montgomery County (pres. 1990-92, v.p. 1995—). Roman Catholic. Office: Montgomery County Com Aging 2015 N Frazier Conroe TX 77301

MARTINELLI, ROSEMARY, public relations executive; b. Pitts., May 13, 1957. BA summa cum laude, Duquesne U., 1979, MA summa cum laude, 1988. News dir., reporter Sta. WDUQ-FM, Pitts., 1977-78; news and pub. affairs producer Sta. KDKA-AM/WPNT-FM, Pitts., 1978-80; news assignment mgr. and consumer producer WPXI-TV, Pitts., 1980-83, creative dir., publicist, 1983-85; dir. spl. events and publicity Gimbels, Pitts., 1985-86; mgr. community rels. Columbia Gas of Pa., Pitts., 1987—. Mem. corp. com., in-kind svcs. com. Pitts. Ballet Theatre, 1988—; mem. Assocs. Civic Light Opera, Pitts., Pitts. Conv. and Visitors Bur., 1987—, Destination Greater Pitts. Attraction Assn.; mem. tribute to women corp. support com. YWCA, Pitts.; mem. mktg. comm. com. Housing Opportunites, Inc.; mem. Points of Light Found. Pilot Program, Pitts.; mem. fundraising com. Western Pa. Leukemia Soc.; mem. women and heart disease task force Western Pa. Heart Assn.; mem. mktg. communications com. Points of Light Founds., Pitts.; bd. advisors New Options program Calif. U. of Pa.; chair person Golden Quill awards for Journalistic Excellence, 1993—; chair corp. contbns. roundtable Grantmakers of Western Pa. Recipient Nat. Community Rels. Report Bellringer award, 1990, Committment to Safety of Children award Pa. Chiefs Police, 1990, Eleanor Polis Capone award for creative writing excellence, Tribute to Women award in comm. YWCA Pitts., 1992, Scripps Howard award for journalistic excellence. Mem. NAFE, Women in Communications (profl. advisor 1987-88, v.p. programming 1990-91, v.p. mktg. 1991-92, v.p publicity 1992-93, Matrix award 1989, 91), Pub. Rels. Soc. Am. (publicity, pub. svc. coms.), Soc. Profl. Journalists (Golden Quill award 1984), Am. Women in Radio and TV (bd. dirs. 1991—), Pitts. C. of C. (publicity com. celebrating women in sports com. 1987-91, publicity chmn. 1989), Women's Press Club Pitts., Exec. Women's Coun. Pitts., Pitts. Radio and TV Club, Press Club Western Pa., Phi Kappa Phi, Kappa Tau Alpha, Omicron Delta Kappa. Office: Columbia Gas of Penn 650 Washington Rd Pittsburgh PA 15228-2702

MARTINEZ, BONNIE YVONNE, retired social services worker; b. Billings, Mont., Apr. 16, 1925; d. John Aaron and Dorothy Vernon (Best) Lewis; m. Antonio Avalos Martinez, Jan. 6, 1950 (div. Nov. 1974); children: Karla Dababneh, Yvette A., Anthony K., Robin M., Dana M., Lance M., Maria B. Van Haren. Grad. in Cosmetology, Edison Tech., 1950; student, Rocky Mountain Coll., 1970. Clk. Prudential Ins., L.A., 1967-68; crime/traffic auditor L.A. Police Dept., 1968-70; clk. Dept. Motor Vehicles, L.A., 1970-71; comty. action social worker Billings, 1971-74; eligibility technician San Diego County Welfare, 1974-76, Yellowstone County Welfare, Billings, 1976-91. House rep. State of Mont., Helena, 1994—. Mem. Hispanics and Friends Phyllis Wheatley (pres. 1971). Republican. Pentecostal. Home: 769 Fallow Ln Billings MT 59102

MARTINEZ, CELIA, community relations director, resource development administrator; b. San Antonio, Tex.; d. Antonio and Celestina (Sauceda) Acuna; m. John Albert Martinez, Apr. 18, 1965; children: Keith, Denise. AS, St. Philips Coll., San Antonio, 1986; BAAS, Southwest Tex. U., San Marcos, 1988. Asst. vol. coord. San Antonio State Sch., 1988-95, cmty. rels. svc. coord., 1993-95; resource devel. officer Camino Real State MHMR, San Antonio; mem. selected media rels. Pope John Paul II visit to San Antonio, 1987; apptd. com. mem. Gov's. Vol. Conf., Austin, 1991; mem. adv. bd. Highways and Hedges, San Antonio, 1993-95; mem. bd. dirs. Dirs. of Vols. in Agys., San Antonio, 1990-95. vol. registration AAU/USA Jr. Olympics, San Antonio, 1989; vol. media rels. U.S. Olympic Festival, San Antonio, 1993. Reicpient Vol. award San Antonio Sch. Vol. Coun., 1979. Home: 116 Bonnell San Antonio TX 78223 Office: Camino Real State Operated MHMR Cmty Svcs 1201 Austin Hwy Ste 116 San Antonio TX 78209

MARTINEZ, DEBRA LYNN, hotel owner; b. Wood River, Ill., Oct. 19, 1954; d. Glenn Keith and Ruth Ann (Holt) Pyle; m. Robert Alvarez Martinez, June 30, 1989 (div. Dec. 1995); 1 child, Richard Phillip. Portrait cons. Olan Mills, Lawton, Okla., 1980-82; apt. mgr. S-L Properties, Lawton, Okla., 1982-84; club mgr. Rainbow Club, Lawton, 1984-86, Helen's Club, Lawton, 1986-88; waitress Rise N Shine, Lawton, 1988-92; hotel owner Duncan, Okla., 1992—; cosmetologist His-Her Affair, St. Charles, Mo., 1979-80; advt. coord. Nat. Truck Sch., St. Louis, 1978-79. Police dispatcher City of St. Roberts, Mo., 1974-75, City of Waynesville, Mo., 1973-74; bd. dirs. Crisis Intervention, Duncan, 1995. Republican. Home and Office: 708 W Oak Duncan OK 73533

MARTINEZ, DENISE KAY, academic program assistant director; b. Beaver Dam, Wis., July 6, 1957; d. Donald Duane and Marjorie Jean (Kovalaske) Dolgner; m. Curtis Ascension Martinez, Oct. 9, 1982; children: Desiree, Brock, Mitchell. BA in Psychology, U. Wis., Platteville, 1978; MSE in Counseling, U. Wis., Oshkosh, 1992. Adj. instr. psychology Ripon (Wis.) Coll., 1986-93, asst. dir. student support svcs., 1994—; vol. coord. St. Agnes Hosp., Fond Dulac, Wis., 1992-93, EAP counselor, 1993—. Choir dir. Our Lady of The Lake Cath. Ch., Green Lake, Wis., 1989-94; mental health cons. Quad County Critical Incident Stress Debreifing Team, 1993—; co-pres. Murray Park Elem. Sch., Ripon, 1993—. Mem. ACA, Am. Colls. Midwest (concerned women coun. 1994—), Wis. Assn. Counseling and Devel., Wis. Assn. Ednl. Opportunity Program Pers., Midwest Assn. Ednl. Opportunity Program Pers. Home: N6929 County Rd PP Ripon WI 54971 Office: Ripon Coll Student Support Svcs 300 Seward St Ripon WI 54971

MARTINEZ, GAYLE FRANCES, protective services official; b. Joplin, Mo., June 25, 1954; d. Jackie Ray Jackson and Shirley Joann (Williams) Jackson Hulett; m. Randy Louis Brown (div. Sept. 1974); 1 child, Randy Louis Brown II; m. Alan John Dwinells, July 15, 1975 (div. Sept. 1977); children: Christopher Ray Dwinells. AA, Longview Coll., 1979; indsl. drafting cert., Marin County Adult Sch., 1984; BA, Sacramento State Coll., 1989. Cert. peace officer. Computer operator JC Penney, Kans., 1977-81; air cargo specialist USAF, 1980-92; ins. agent Prudential, Richmond, Calif., 1983-85; peace officer Calif. State Prison, Vacaville, 1985—; trainer Calif. Dept. Corrections, Vacaville, 1989—. Author: Whispers in the Wind. Mem. Calif. Correctional Peace Officers Assn. Democrat. Assembly of God. Home: 599 Greenwood Dr Vacaville CA 95687

MARTINEZ, HERMINIA S., economist, banker; b. Havana, Cuba; came to U.S., 1960, naturalized, 1972; d. Carlos and Amelia (Santana) Martinez Sanchez; m. Mario Aguilar, 1982; children: Mario Aguilar, Carlos Aguilar; BA in Econs. cum laude, Am. U., 1965; MS in Fgn. Svc. (Univ. fellow), MS in Econs., Georgetown U., 1967, PhD in Econs., 1969; postgrad. Nat. U. Mex. Instr. econs. George Mason Coll., U. Va., Fairfax, 1967-68; researcher World Bank, 1967-69, indsl. economist, industrialization div., 1969-71, loan officer, Central Am., 1971-79, loan officer, economist, Mex., 1973-74, Venezuela and Ecuador, 1973-77, sr. loan officer in charge of Panama and Dominican Republic, Washington, 1977-81, sr. loan officer for Middle East and North Africa, 1981-84, sr. loan officer for Western Africa region, 1985-87, sr. economist Africa Region, 1988-91, prin. ops. officer Africa region, 1991—. Mid-Career fellow Princeton U., 1988-89. Mem. Am. Econ. Assn., Soc. Internat. Devel., Brookings Inst. Latin Am. Study Group. Roman Catholic. Contbg. author: The Economic Growth of Colombia: Problems and Prospects, 1973, Central American Financial Integration, 1975. Home: 5145 Yuma St NW Washington DC 20016-4336 Office: World Bank 1818 H St NW Washington DC 20433

MARTINEZ, IDA CAMACHO, city official; b. Port Isabel, Tex., Oct. 6, 1960; d. Jose R. and Elva (Ochoa) Camacho; m. Enrique V. Martinez, July 27, 1979; children: Adrian E., E. Alicia, Noah E., I. Raquel, Adelaida. BBA, U. Houston, 1986. CPA, Tex. Sec. Panhandle Ea., Houston, 1981-86, from acct. to sr. acct., 1986-91; chief acct. H & H Foods, Mercedes, Tex., 1992-93; dir. fin. City of San Benito, Tex., 1993—; treas. Firemen's Relief and Retirement, San Benito, 1993—; mgr. Indsl. Devel. Authority, San Benito, 1993—. Mem. AICPA, Govt. Fin. Officers Assn., Tex. Soc. CPA's. Office: City of San Benito 485 N San Houston San Benito TX 78586

MARTINEZ, KARIN JEAN, journalist; b. Malone, N.Y., Apr. 29, 1969; d. John Henry and Patricia Jean (Lamica) Horner; m. Ralph Kennedy Martinez, May 16, 1993. BA, SUNY, Plattsburgh, 1990. Journalist U.S. Army 101st Abn. Divsn., Fort Campbell, Ky., 1992, leisure editor, 1993-95, news editor, 1995-96; journalist, editor U.S. Army Joint Task Force, Soto Cano, Honduras, 1992-93; pub. affairs non-commd. officer in charge U.S. Army 19th TAACOM, Camp Henry, Korea, 1996—. Recipient Joint Svc. Achievement award U.S. Army, 1993, Humanitarian award, 1993, Army Achievement award, 1994, 95, Army Commendation award, 1995. Mem. Assn. of the U.S. Army.

MARTINEZ, LINDA MARIA, lawyer; b. Mo., 1954. BA, U. Mo., Columbia, 1976; JD, Washington U., 1982. Bar: Mo. 1982. With Profl. Svc. Rev. Orgns., 1976-79; ptnr. Bryan Cave LLP, St. Louis, 1982—. Office: Bryan Cave LLP 211 N Broadway One Metropolitan Sq Saint Louis MO 63102*

MARTINEZ, MARIA DOLORES, pediatrician; b. Cifuentes, Cuba, Mar. 16, 1959; d. Demetrio and Alba Silvia (Perez) M.; m. James David Marple, Apr. 25, 1992. MD, U. Navarra, Pamplona, Spain, 1984. Med. diplomate. Resident in pediatrics Moses Cone Hosp., Greensboro, N.C., 1986-89; pvt. practice Charlotte, N.C., 1989-93, Mooresville, N.C., 1993—; with Univ. Med. Hosp., Tucson. Mem. AMA, Am. Acad. Pediatrics, N.C. Med. Soc., Mecklenburg County Med. Soc. Republican. Roman Catholic. Office: Univ Med Hosp 1501 Campbell Ave Tucson AZ 85741

MARTINEZ, PATRICIA ANN, middle school educator, administrator; b. Phoenix, Oct. 12, 1963; d. Jack Leon and Eleanor Jean (Gripman) McMullen; m. Gerald Marc Martinez, Aug. 11, 1984. BA, Calif. State U., 1986, MA magna cum laude, 1994. Cert. tchr. Calif. Tchr. St. Athanasius Elem. Sch., Long Beach, Calif., 1987-93; vice prin. St. Athanasius Elem. Sch., Long Beach, 1990-93; lang. arts specialist Washington Mid. Schs., Long Beach, 1993—; mentor tchr. St. Athanasius Elem. Sch., Long Beach, 1988-90, mem. restructuring team, family leader Site-Based Decision Making Com. Mem. ACLU, Greenpeace, 1988—. Mem. ASCD, NEA, AAUW, Nat. Cath. Edn. Assn., Internat. Reading Assn., Internat. Platform Assn., Tchrs. Assn. Long Beach, Calif. Tchrs. Assn., Kappa Delta Pi, Phi Kappa Phi. Democrat. Lutheran. Home: 3601 Gardenia Ave Long Beach CA 90807-4303 Office: Washington Mid Sch 1450 Cedar Ave Long Beach CA 90813-1705

MARTÍNEZ-VERGNE, TERESITA, history educator; b. San Juan, P.R., Oct. 11, 1955; d. Gonzalo Alberto Martí-Lázaro and Tesoro Vergne -Texidor; 1 child, Irene Toro-Martínez. Student, Georgetown U., 1973-75; BA, Emory U., 1977; MA, U. Tex., 1979, PhD, 1985. Asst. instr. history U. Tex., Austin, 1984; asst. prof. history Colgate U., Hamilton, N.Y., 1985-87; asst. prof. history U. Puerto Rico, San Juan, 1988-91, assoc. prof. history, 1991; asst. prof. history Macalester Coll., St. Paul, Minn., 1991-93; assoc. prof. history Macalester Coll., St. Paul, 1994—; panel evaluator planning com., Ford Found., Washington, 1994-95; mem. affirmative action oversight com. Colgate U., 1987; activities and audio visual coms., history dept., curriculum and admissions coms. grad. program in history, U. Puerto Rico, 1988, rules and procedure com. grad. program in history U. Puerto Rico; rep. to com. for univ. support of the commn. to celebrate 5th Centennary Discovery of Am. and Puerto Rico, 1988-90; coord. grad. program in history U. Puerto Rico, 1988, mem. rules and program com. dept. history, 1989-91; mem. com. to evaluate goals of the faculty of Edn., 1989; mem. Latin Am. Studies Program com., Macalester Coll., 1991—, com. on affirmative action, 1993—, Women's Studies Search, 1993-95; faculty rep. from Macalester in 4 coll. consortium for study-abroad program at Pontifica U. Catolica Madre y Maestra, Santiago, Dominican Republic, 1993—; mem. of many panels and conductor and presenter of seminars and workshops on Latin Am. history and related subjects. Author: (book) Capitalism in Colonial Puerto Rico, 1992; contbr. numerous articles to profl. jours. Recipient Fulbright scholarship, 1986, NEH summer inst. participantation, 1989; named fellow Ford Found., 1992-93; grantee Dora Bonham Fund, 1978, Ford Found., 1987, Knight Fund, 1991, Wallace Faculty Devel. Program, 1994 and others. Mem. Am. Hist. Assn., Conf. on Latin Am. History, Assn. Carribean Historians (exec. com. 1991-92, sec.-treas. 1992-95), Latin Am. Studies Assn., Assn. Puerto Rican Historians. Home: 436 Ashland Ave Apt #1 Saint Paul MN 55102 Office: Macalester Coll History Dept 1600 Grand Ave Saint Paul MN 55105

MARTINO, CHERYL DERBY, insurance company executive; b. Paterson, N.J., Jan. 19, 1946; d. Elles Mayo and Sarah Emma (Steele) D.; m. Leonard D. Martino, Nov. 4, 1995. BA, Elmira Coll., 1967; MBA, NYU, 1982. Tchr. Ramsey (N.J.) High Sch., 1967-70; contbns. analyst Met. Life Ins. Co., N.Y.C., 1970-83, fin. writer investments dept., 1983-93, asst. sec., 1994—. Bd. trustees United Meth. Ch. of Waldwick, N.J., v.p., 1989-91, pres., 1992-93. Fellow Life Mgmt. Inst. (bd. dirs. Greater N.Y. chpt. 1984-91, pres. 1986, edn. coun. 1990-93), Life Mgmt. Inst. Edn. Coun. (nat. adminstrv. com. chmn. 1990-92, mktg. subcom. 1985-93), Nat. Orchestral Assn. (bd. dirs. 1990-92); mem. Elmira Coll. Alumni Club N.J. (exec. bd. 1982-87). Methodist. Office: Met Life 1 Madison Ave New York NY 10010-3603

MARTINSON, IDA MARIE, nursing educator, nurse, physiologist; b. Mentor, Minn., Nov. 8, 1936; d. Oscar and Marvel (Nelson) Sather; m. Paul Varo Martinson, Mar. 31, 1962; children—Anna Marie, Peter. Diploma, St. Luke's Hosp. Sch. Nursing, 1957; B.S., U. Minn., 1960, M.N.A., 1962; Ph.D., U. Ill., Chgo., 1972. Instr. Coll. St. Scholastica and St. Luke's Sch. Nursing, 1957-58, Thornton Jr. Coll., 1967-69; lab. asst. U. Ill. at Med. Ctr., 1970-72; lectr. dept. physiology U. Minn., St. Paul, 1972-82; asst. prof. Sch. Nursing U. Minn., 1972-74, assoc. prof. rsch., 1974-77, prof., dir. rsch., 1977-82; prof. dept. family health care U. Calif., San Francisco, 1982—, chmn. dept., 1982-90; vis. rsch. prof. Nat. Taiwan U., Def. Med. Ctr., 1981; vis. prof. nursing Sun Yat-Sen U. Med. Scis., Guang Zhou, Republic of China, Ewha Women's U., Seoul, Korea; vis. prof. nursing Frances Payne Bolton Sch. Nursing, Case Western Res. U., Cleve., 1994—; chair, prof. dept. health scis. Hong Kong Poly. U., 1996—. Author: Mathematics for the Health Science Student, 1977; editor: Home Care for the Dying Child, 1976, Women in Stress, 1979, Women in Health and Illness, 1986, The Child and Family Facing Life Threatening Illness, 1987, Family Nursing, 1989, Home Health Care Nursing, 1989; contbr. chpts. to books, articles to profl. jours. Active Am. Cancer Soc. Recipient Book of Yr. award Am. Jour. Nursing, 1977, 80, 87, 90, Children's Hospice Internat. award, 1988, Humanitarian award for pediatric nursing, 1993; Fulbright fellow, 1991. Mem. ANA, Coun. Nurse Rschrs., Am. Acad. Nursing, Inst. Medicine, Sigma Xi, Sigma Theta Tau. Lutheran. Office: U Calif Family Health Care Nursing San Francisco CA 94143-0606

MARTINSON, RITA R., state legislator; b. Gloster, Miss., Sept. 11, 1937; d. D.M. and Beulah (LeDoux) Randall; m. William K. Martinson Sr., Aug. 2, 1958; children: Ginny Martinson Vampran, Karen Martinson McKie, W.K. Jr., Allen. BA in Polit. Sci., Millsaps Coll., 1991. Mem. Miss. Ho. of Reps., 1992—. Mem. Madison County Rep. Exec. Com., 1988-91; active Madison Arboretum, 1992—. Mem. Madison County C. of C. (Outstanding Citizen 1992), City of Madison C. of C., Madison County Rep. Women's

Club, Ridgeland/Northpark Lions Club (past v.p. 1990-91), Ofcl. Miss. Women's Club (pres.), Rep. Elected Ofcls. Club (sec.). Roman Catholic. Home: 1472 Highway 51 Madison MS 39110-9095 Office: Miss State Ho of Reps PO Box 1018 Jackson MS 39215-1018

MARTINSON-SILUK, CAROL LINDA, elementary school educator; b. Mpls., Minn., June 30, 1946; d. Gerhard and Karolyn Ericka (Skalnik) Hanson; m. Oct. 18, 1975 (div. Aug. 1992); children: Melissa, Natalie; m. Dennis L. Siluk, Aug. 13, 1993. BA, Luther Coll., 1968. Cert. elem. tchr. Elem. tchr. St. Paul Fedn. of Tchrs., 1968-95; bldg. steward St. Paul Fedn. Tchrs., 1979-96, chair profl. policies com., 1991-96, social com., 1990-95. Mem. exec. bd. W.E.L.C.A., St. Paul, 1991-93, pres., 1992-93; soloist, music dir. Sunday Sch., 1983-93. Mem. Fedn. of Tchrs. (exec. bd. 1991-96). Home: 6727 Gretchen Ct N Oakdale MN 55128-3132

MARTONE, JEANETTE RACHELE, artist; b. Mineola, N.Y., June 5, 1956; d. John and Mildred Cecilia (Loehr) M. BFA, SUNY, Purchase, 1978. One woman shows include Ariel Gallery, N.Y.C., 1990, La Mantia Gallery, Northport, N.Y., 1994-96, Inter-Media Arts Ctr., Huntington, N.Y., 1996, Inter-Media Arts Ctr., Huntington, N.Y., 1996; exhibited in group shows from 1980 to 1996 including Harbor Gallery, Cold Spring Harbor, 1980, Huntington Coun. Arts, 1986, Pindar Gallery, N.Y.C., 1987, Mills Pond House, Smithtown, N.Y., 1987, Suffolk County Exec. Offices, Hauppage, N.Y., 1988, La Mantia Gallery, Northport, N.Y., 1990, Nassau County Office Cultural Affairs, 1991, Ward-Nasse. Gallery, N.Y.C., 1991, Monsterrat Gallery, N.Y.C., 1991, Priscilla Redfield Roe Gallery, Bellport, N.Y., 1991, L.I. U., Brookville, 1992, Northport B.J. Spoke Gallery, Huntington, N.Y., 1992, Fischetti Gallery, N.Y., 1992, Artists Space, N.Y.C., 1992, N.Y. Botanical Gardens, Bronx, N.Y., 1993, Visions Gallery, Albany, L.I. U., Brookville, N.Y., 1994, Goodman Gallery, Southampton, N.Y., 1994, B.J. Spoke Gallery, Huntington, N.Y., 1994-95, Islip Art Mus., East Islip, N.Y., 1994, L.I. MacArthur Airport, Ronkonkoma, N.Y., 1995. Recipient Award of Excellence Gold medal Art League of Nassau County, 1993, Best in Show award Nat. League Am. PEN Women Artists, 1990, 92, Windsor and Newton award for oil Arts Coun. East Islip, N.Y., 1989, award of excellence Art League of Nassau County, 1987, 88, many best in shows including 1st Ann. Juried Art Exhibit, Brookhaven Arts and Humanities Coun., Farmingville, N.Y., 1996, Supervisor's award Bablylon Citizens Coun. Arts Juried Exhbn., 1994, Bob Jones Glad Hand Press award Stamford Art Assn., 1995, Faber Biren Nat. Color award Stamford Art Assn., 1995. Mem. Catherine Lorillard Wolfe Art Club (Frank B. and Mary Anderson Cassidy Meml. award 1992, Award for Oil 1987), Allied Artists of Am. (John Young Hunter Meml. award 1993, Antonio Cerino Meml. award 1990), Hudson valley Art Assn., Knickerbock Artists of Am., Nat. Art League. Home: 47 Summerfield Ct Deer Park NY 11729-5642

MARTORANA, BARBARA JOAN, secondary education educator; b. N.Y.C., Oct. 18, 1942; d. Samuel and Joan Renee (Costello) M. BA, St. John's U., Jamaica, N.Y., 1970, MS in English Edn., 1972; advanced cert. computers in edn., L.I. U., 1988, profl. diploma in edn. adminstrn., 1990. Cert. sch. dist. adminstr., sch. adminstr. and supr., tchr. English grades 7-12, N.Y. Exec. sec. Am. Petroleum Inst., N.Y.C., 1960-65; exec. asst. to v.p. Goldring, Inc., N.Y.C., 1965-67; exec. asst. Rsch. Inst. for Cath. Edn., N.Y.C., 1967-69; English tchr. St. Martin of Tours Sch., Amityville, N.Y., 1970-77, Oceanside (N.Y.) Jr. H.S., 1977-78, Freeport (N.Y.) H.S., 1979—; rec. sec. Freeport (N.Y.) Tchr. Ctr. Policy Bd., 1986-89; co-chair Middle States Steering Com., Freeport, 1988-90; chair Freeport (N.Y.) H.S. Shared Decision Team, 1992-93; workshop facilitator L.I. Writing Project, Garden City, N.Y., 1993—, co-leader Summer Insts. Co-author: (textbooks) Writing Competency Practice, 1980, Writing Competency Practice-Revised and Expanded, 1989. With Seaford (N.Y.) Rep. Club, 1975—. Mem. ASCD, Nat. Coun. Tchrs. English (conf. on English edn.), N.Y. State English Coun., L.I. Writing Project. Office: Freeport HS 50 S Brookside Ave Freeport NY 11520-3144

MARTS, TERRI LOUISE, management executive; b. Wilkinsburg, Pa., June 8, 1958; d. Robert Jackson and Margaret Elaine (Frescura) Gebrosky; m. Norman Vincent Marts, Sept. 27, 1980. BS in Bus. Adminstrn., U. Pitts., 1980; MBA, Robert Morris Coll., 1985. Clk. Westinghouse Electric Corp., Pitts., 1977-79, pers. rep., 1980-81, adminstr., 1985-89; quality engr. Westinghouse Energy Systems, Pitts., 1989-91, mgr. employee svcs., 1991-93; asst. dir. human resources Westinghouse Corp. Hdqs., Pitts., 1993-95; mng. dir. Westinghouse Source W, Pitts., 1995—; faculty mem. Human Resource Planning Soc., N.Y.C., 1992-95; nat. spkr. Am. Soc. Quality Control, 1985-90. Bd. dirs. Jr. Achievement, Pitts., 1995-96. Recipient Am. Legion award, 1970. Mem. Quality Network (sponsorship com. 1992-95), Women in Comm. Home: 5974 Kemerer Hollow Rd Export PA 15632 Office: Westinghouse Electric Corp 11 Stanwix St Pittsburgh PA 15222

MARUGG-WOLFE, MARJORIE, career counselor; b. Roswell, N.Mex., Dec. 16, 1933; d. Adley Grady and Annie Lee (Thrasher) Ford; m. Alfred F. Marugg, Oct. 11, 1958 (dec. 1990); children: Mikki Michele Marugg Bates, Tami Laris; m. John R. Wolfe II, May 16, 1992; stepchildren: John R. III, Barbara Wolfe Hill, Bev Wolfe Featherston. BS in Home Econs., U. Ark., 1957, EdS in Vocat. Edn., 1982, EdD, 1993; MS in Home Econs., U. Md., 1966. Social editor Rogers (Ark.) Daily News, 1951-54; banquet, catering mgr. Miss Hullings' Cafeteria, St. Louis, 1958-60; home econs. tchr. Steger Jr. High Sch., Webster Groves, Mo., 1960-61; info. specialist Fgn. Agrl. Svc. USDA, Washington, 1966-67; salesperson Routh Robbins Realtors, Oxon Hill, Md., 1968-75; rsch. assoc. vocat. edn. U. Ark., Fayetteville, 1978-80; developer, coord. displaced homemaker program N.W. Vo Tech, Springdale, Ark., 1980-89; program specialist tng. and career devel. Econ. Opportunity Agy. JTPA, Springdale, 1990-92; dir. project self determination Econ. Opportunity Agy. JTPA, Fayetteville, Rogers, 1992-93; dir., chair, developer Benton County Single Parent Program, Rogers, 1984-96, project developer, 1996—; project developer non-traditional opportunities Econ. Opportunities Ag/Vo Tech, Fayetteville, 1986-92; project developer child care tng. VoTech/JTPA, 1985-87. Contbr. articles to profl. jours. Treas., vice chair Ark. Single Parent Com., Little Rock, Fayetteville, 1994-96; past pres. Benton County United Cmty. Svcs., 1989; past pres., organizer Rogers High Sch. Orch. Parents, 1979; regional rep. dist. VI Displaced Homemakers Network, 1986-88. Grantee Rockefeller Found., 1991-92. Mem. Mother to Mother Ministries (bd. dirs., nominating chair 1995-96), Altrusa (hon. mem. Fayetteville club, past v.p., sec., treas. Rogers club 1982-88), Phi Upsilon Omicron (past pres., sec. 1962-96), Phi Delta Kappa, Omicron Nu. Republican. Home: 8782 S Park Rd Rogers AR 72756

MARUMOTO, BARBARA CHIZUKO, state legislator; b. San Francisco, July 21, 1939; d. Takeo and Kathleen (Tsuchiya) Okamoto; B.A., U. Hawaii, 1971; student U. Calif., 1957-60, UCLA, 1957; children—Marshall, Jay, Wendy, Megan. Legis. aide, researcher, Honolulu, 1972-78; mem. Hawaii Ho. of Reps., 1978—, minority floor leader, 1981; elected del. to Constl. Conv., 1978; real estate agt., 1979—. Mem. exec. bd. Hist. Hawaii Found.; bd. dirs. Pacific council Girl Scouts U.S.A.; active Rep. Party, Common Cause, LWV, PTA, Ripon Soc. Clubs: Honolulu, Jr. League Honolulu. Contbr. various news columns to publs. Office: State Office Tower 235 S Beretania St Rm 1305 Honolulu HI 96813*

MARUOKA, JO ANN ELIZABETH, information systems manager; b. Monrovia, Calif., Jan. 1, 1945; d. John Constantine and Pearl (Macovei) Gotsinas; m. Lester Hideo Maruoka, Nov. 8, 1973 (div. Aug. 1992); stepchildren: Les Scott Kaleohano, Lee Stuart Keola. BA with honors, UCLA, 1966; MBA, U. Hawaii, 1971. Office mgr. and asst. R. Wenkam, Photographer, Honolulu, 1966-69; computer mgmt. intern and sys. analyst Army Computer Sys. Command, Honolulu, 1969-78; reservations mgr. Hale Koa Hotel, Honolulu, 1978-79; equal employment opportunity specialist U.S. Army Pacific Hdqs., Honolulu, 1979-80, computer specialist, 1980-87, supervisory info. sys. mgr., chief plans and programs, 1987—; bd. dirs. High Performance Computing and Comm. Coun., Tiverton, R.I.; pacific v.p. Fedn. Govt. Info. Processing Couns., Washington, 1992-95. Mem. Nat. and Hawaii Women's Polit. Caucus, Honolulu, 1987—; advisor Fed. Women's Coun. Hawaii, Honolulu, 1977—. Recipient EEO Excellence award Sec. of Army, 1989, Pacific Fed. Mgr. award Honolulu-Pacific Fed. Exec. Bd., 1990, Info. Resources Mgmt. award Interagy. Com. on Info. Resources Mgmt., 1991, Lead Dog Leadership award Fedn. Govt. Info. Processing Couns., 1993; named One of Fed. 100 (Execs.) of Yr., Fed. Computer Week, 1996. Mem. NAFE, Nat. Women's Polit. Caucus, AAUW, LWV, Armed Forces Comm.-Electronics Assn. (Hawaii chpt., Internat. award for Info. Resources Mgmt. Excellence 1992), Assn. U.S. Army (Pacific Fed. Mgr. award 1990), Federally Employed Women (advisor Aloha and Rainbow chpts. 1977—), Army Signal Corps Regimental Assn., Hawaii Intergovt. Info. Processing Coun. (pres. 1988-89, svc. award 1989). Democrat. Office: APIM-PR US Army Pacific Hdqrs Fort Shafter HI 96858

MARUSHIGE-KNOPP, YUKA, food scientist; b. Kyoto, Japan, Feb. 15, 1964; came to U.S., 1964; d. Keiji and Yasuko (Nakamura) Marushige; m. Thomas Karl Knopp, Dec. 16, 1989. BS in Human Nutrition, Ohio State U., 1986, MS in Food Sci., 1987. Assoc. project leader product R&D Ross Products divsn. Abbott Labs., Columbus, Ohio, 1987-89, project leader product R&D, 1989-90, clin. rsch. monitor med. nutritional rsch., 1990-92, project leader divsn. quality assurance, 1992-95, project leader Abbott quality assurance, 1995—. Contbr. articles to profl. jours. Univ. fellow Ohio State U., 1986-87. Mem. Inst. Food Technologists, Ohio Valley Inst. Food Technologists, Kappa Omicron Nu, Zeta Tau Kappa. Office: Ross Products Divsn Abbott Labs 625 Cleveland Ave Columbus OH 43215

MARVEL, WANDA FAYE, home health clinical consultant; b. Price, Utah, Nov. 10, 1951; d. Albert Jr. and Hazel A. Marvel; m. John M. Robinsin Jr. ADN, Westark Community Coll., 1978; BSN, U. Mo., 1986, MSN, 1993. Cardiac nurse Bapt. Med. Ctr., Little Rock, 1978-79; ICU staff nurse Ellis Fischel Cancer Ctr., Columbia, Mo., 1982-84; staff nurse emergency svc., med. ICU U. Mo., Columbia, 1984-87; head nurse surgery dept. Ellis Fischel Cancer Ctr., Columbia, 1987-89; rsch. asst. U. Mo., Columbia, 1988-89; asst. dir. Columbia Regional Hosp. Home Health, 1990-92; area v.p. HealthCor, Inc., Dallas, 1993-94, clin. cons., 1995—; guest lectr. Columbia Coll. RN Completion, 1989; clin. instr. Cen. Meth. Coll., Fayette, Mo., 1987; bd. dirs. Carpe Diem Hospice, Inc. Vol. Hospice Cen. Mo., Columbia, 1990; bd. dirs. Hospice Found., Columbia, 1990-91; mem. risk mgmt. advisory com. City of Columbia, 1996—. Recipient Grad. Nurse Assn. scholarship U. Mo., 1989, Nursing Fund scholarship, 1989, Superior Grad. Achievement award, 1990. Mem. AAUW, ANA, Grad. Nurses Assn. (pres. 1988-89), Oncology Nurses Soc., Emergency Nurses Assn. (chmn. govtl. 1988), Sigma Theta Tau.

MARVET, JODI RAE, prosecutor; b. Highland Park, Ill., Jan. 21, 1962; d. Robert Boris and Corinne Jean (Hoffman) Mattes; m. Larry Elliot Marvet, Dec. 23, 1990; 1 child, Claire Rose. BA in English, U. Fla., 1984, JD, 1987. Bar: Fla. 1988. Assoc. Mattlin & McClosky, Boca Raton, Fla., 1988-91; asst. gen. counsel State of Fla. Dept. Banking and Fin., Ft. Lauderdale, 1991-92; asst. atty. gen. State of Fla. Dept. Legal Affairs, Hollywood, 1992—. Mem. Sierra Club (group chair Broward Group 1992-94), Phi Beta Kappa. Democrat. Jewish. Home: 5561 SW 7th St Plantation FL 33317 Office: Fla Office Atty Gen 110 SE 6th St Fort Lauderdale FL 33301

MARVIN, URSULA BAILEY, geologist; b. Bradford, Vt., Aug. 20, 1921; d. Harold Leslie and Alice Miranda (Bartlett) Bailey; m. Lloyd Burton Chaisson, June 28, 1944 (div. 1951); m. Thomas Crockett Marvin, Apr. 1, 1952. BA, Tufts Coll., 1943; MA, Harvard/Radcliffe Coll., 1946; PhD, Harvard U., 1969. Rsch. asst. dept. geology U. Chgo., 1947-50; mineralogist Union Carbide Corp., N.Y.C., 1952-58; instr. dept. geology Tufts U., Medford, Mass., 1958-61; geologist, sr. staff Smithsonian Astrophys. Obs., Cambridge, Mass., 1961—, fed. womens program coord., 1974-77; vis. prof. dept. geology Ariz. State U., Tempe, 1978; lectr. geology Harvard U., 1974-92; trustee Tufts U., 1975—, U. Space Rsch. Assn., Columbia Md., 1979-84, chair 1982-83. Author: Continental Drift, 1973; contbr. chpt.: Astronomy from Space, 1983, The Planets, 1985; assoc. editor Earth in Space, Am. Geophys. Union, 1988-90; contbr. articles to profl. jours. Mem. Lunar and Planetary Sci. Coun., Houston, 1987-91; chair antarctic meteorite working group Lunar and Planetary Inst., Houston, 1993—. Recipient Antarctic Svc. medal NSF, 1983, Group Achievement award NASA, 1984, Sustained Superior Achievement award SAO, 1988; Asteroid Marvin named in her honor Minor Planet Bur. of Internat. Astron. Union, 1991, Marvin Nunatak (mountain peak rising through the Antarctic ice sheet) named in her honor U.S. Bd. on Geog. Names, 1992. Fellow AAAS, Meteoritical Soc. (pres. 1975-76), Geol. Soc. Am. (History of Geology award 1986); mem. Assn. Women in Sci., Am. Geophys. Union, History of Earth Scis. Soc. (pres. 1991), Internat. Commn. on History Geol. Scis. (sec.-gen. 1989-96), Sigma Xi (pres. Harvard-Radcliffe chpt.1971-72). Office: Harvard-Smithsonian Ctr for Astrophysics 60 Garden St Cambridge MA 02138-1516

MARX, KARI ANN, accountant; b. Long Branch, N.J., Nov. 22, 1969; d. Donald Arthur and Brenda June (Luca) Stine; m. Douglas Todd Marx, May 28, 1995. BBA, U. Miami, 1991; MBA, U. Del., 1993. CPA, Pa. Acctg. clk. City of Tamarac, Fla., 1986-90; dir. advisement U. Del. Bus. Sch., Newark, 1991-93; semi-sr. acct., U. Del. recruiter Arthur Andersen LLP, Phila., 1993-96; recruiter Arthur Andersen LLP, Ft. Lauderdale, Fla., 1996—. Mem. AICPA, U. Miami Alumni Club (activities com. 1993—). Home: 9734 NW 7th Circle Plantation FL 33324 Office: Arthur Andersen 100 NE 3d Ave Ste 700 Fort Lauderdale FL 22201

MARX, KATHRYN, photographer, author; b. N.Y.C., June 4, 1950; d. Arthur and Emilie (Hyman) M. Freelance journalist, photographer N.Y. Newsday, N.Y. Daily News, Village Voice, Soho News, 1974-82, Infinito Mag., Italy, 1986; photographer Photo-Reporter, Paris, 1986, Editions Paris-Musées, 1992. Photography exhbns. include Le Grand Palais, Paris, 1991, U.S. Embassy, Brussels, 1990, Carnavalet Mus., Paris, 1992, N.Y. Pub. Libr., 1992, Mus. Modern Art, Paris, 1994, exhbn. of mobiles Galerie Monde de L'Art, 1996; author: Photography for the Art Market, 1988, Right Brain/Left Brain Photography, 1994; collaborator (with author Michael S. Lasky) The Complete Junkfood Book, 1974-76; contbr. articles to profl. jours. Rape crisis counselor St. Vincents Hosp., N.Y.C., 1981-83; active ACLU, N.Y.C., 1974-76; mem. Plan Internat. Foster Program, R.I., 1992—. Grantee Acad. Am. Poets, 1982, Eastman Kodak Co., Paris, N.Y., 1992-96, Fuji Film France, Paris, 1991-94, Sernam Corp., Paris, 1992-97. Mem. Author's Guild, Author's League of Am. Democrat. Home: 61 Jane St New York NY 10014-5107 Office: 77 rue Notre Dame Des Champs, 75006 Paris France

MARX, SHARON ROSE, health facility administrator; b. Ferndale, Mich., Dec. 11, 1951; d. William Bernard and Evelyn Grace (Culbert) M. Student, U. Mich., 1970-72; BSN, U. Tex., Galveston, 1975; MS, U. Colo., Denver, 1984. RNC, cert. ob/gyn. nurse practitioner. Staff nurse John Sealy Hosp., Galveston, 1975, Harper Grace Hosp., Detroit, 1975-77, Hutzel Hosp., Detroit, 1977-79; office nurse Sellers & Sanders Clinic, New Orleans, 1979-82; clin. mgr. Rocky Mountain Hosp., Denver, 1982-83; clin. nurse specialist William Beaumont Hosp., Royal Oak, Mich., 1985-89; dir. maternal, child health Botsford Gen. Hosp., Farmington Hills, Mich., 1989-92; dir. women's and children's svcs. McLaren Regional Med. Ctr., Flint, Mich., 1992—; rsch. coord. maternal child health demonstration project Mich. Dept. Pub. Health, Royal Oak, 1985. Bd. dirs. March of Dimes, Flint, 1993—, Children's Wish Fund, Flint, 1992—; mem. task force on children Flint Focus Coun./Focus on Children, 1994. March of Dimes ednl. grantee, 1993. Mem. Mich. Orgn. Nurse Execs., Perinatal Assn. of Mich. (bd. dirs. 1985-86), Assn. Women's Health, Obstetric and Neonatal Nursing (membership coord. Mich. sect. 1993-95, chpt. coord. Detroit 1986-88). Home: 6036 W Dodge Rd Clio MI 48420-8508 Office: McLaren Regional Med Ctr 401 S Ballenger Hwy Flint MI 48532-3638

MARZELL, LILLI KOENIGSBERG, artist, educator; b. Irvington, N.J., Sept. 15, 1916; d. Soloman and Augusta (Ring) Koenigsberg; m. Robert Paul Marzell, Dec. 17, 1939 (div. Nov. 1989); children: Madeline Sue Marzell Loder, Jane Ellen Marzell. Art degree, Bklyn. Art Mus., 1955. Instr. No. N.J. Art Ctr., Tenafly, 1975-85, Art Cultural Ctr., Demerest, N.J., 1985-89, Lauderhill (Fla.) Vets. Art Instrn., 1990-93; dir. Paramus (N.J.) Art Workshop, 1979—; instr., artist-in-residence N.J. Coun. on Arts, Trenton, 1983-85; adj. prof. Ramapo (N.J.) Coll., 1987-89; jurist Teen Art Festivals, Hudson and Middlesex Counties, N.J., 1983-86, Coconut Creek (Fla.) Guild, 1993; artist-in-residence Merrit Meml. Elem. Sch., Mattwah, N.J., 1985. One-woman shows Fairleigh Dickenson U., Teaneck, N.J., 1962, Silvermine Artist's Guild, New Canaan, Conn., 1967, Bergen Cmty. Mus., 1973, Ft. Lee Hist. Mus., Palisades, N.J., 1991, Dover Gallery, Boca Raton, Fla., 1993, Broward C.C., Coconut Creek, Fla., 1995, numerous others; exhibited in group shows U. Alaska, 1974, Meridian (Miss.) Mus., 1975, George Washington Carver Mus., Tuskagee Inst., Ala., 1976, U. Ga., Athens, 1977, Mint Mus. Art, Charlotte, N.C., 1978, U. Ky., Paducah, 1979, U. N.C., Charlotte, 1980, Temple U., Phila., 1980, Purdue U., West Lafayette, Ind., 1980, Fla. A&M U., Tallahassee, 1982, SUNY, Alfred, 1982, Norton Mus., Palm Beach, Fla., 1985, Broward Art Guild, 1991-93, Boca Mus., 1992, Art Inst. Ft. Lauderdale, 1993, numerous others; represented in permanent collections N.J. Coun. Arts, Trenton Mus., Bergen Cmty. Mus., also corp., orgn. and libr. collections. Recipient numerous awards for art, 1955—, including 1st prize Fairlawn Art Assn., 1961, 2d prize Montclair Art Mus., 1962, 1st prize silver medal Les Semaines Internat., Cannes, France, 1969, Marion Haldenstein Meml. prize Nat. Assn. Women Artists, 1971, purchase award AT&T, 1982, hon. mention and purchase award Norton Mus. Art, 1992, Best in Show award Broward Art Guild, 1995, hon. mention Fla. Pastel Assn., 1995; fellow, grantee MacDowell Fellowship Colony, 1972. Mem. Broward Art Guild (instr. 1989—, 14 awards 1990—), Boca Mus. Art Profl. Artists Guild (jurist 1990—, 2d prize 1992), Ft. Lauderdale Pastel Assn. (3 awards 1993—). Home and Studio: 1110 NW 69th Ter Margate FL 33063

MARZETTI, LORETTA A., government agency executive, policy analyst; b. N.Y., Mar. 13, 1943; d. Lawrence Arthur and Josephine (Palazzo) M.; m. Gerald Oren Miller, July 12, 1986. AB in Sociology, Cath. U. Am., 1965. Chief info. svcs. br., OARM EPA, Washington, 1985-88, dir. comm., analysis and budget divsn. Office Solid Waste, 1988-95, dir. comms., info., resources mgt. divsn. Office Solid Waste, 1995-96; ret., 1996. Home: 3088 S Woodrow St Arlington VA 22206-2115

MASCHERONI, ELEANOR EARLE, investment company executive; b. Boston, June 6, 1955; d. Ralph II and Eleanor Forbes (Owens) Earle; m. Mark Mascheroni, May 30, 1981; children: Olivia Forbes, Isabella Starbuck, Rex Owens. AB, Brown U., 1977. Dept. adminstr. Sotheby Parke Benet, N.Y.C., 1978-79; asst. dir. devel. Inst. Architecture and Urban Studies, N.Y.C., 1979-81; assoc. in pub. rels. Prudential Securities Inc., N.Y.C., 1981-84, asst. v.p. pub. rels., 1984-86, assoc. v.p. pub. rels., 1986-87, v.p., mgr. pub. rels., 1987-89, lst v.p., dir. pub. rels., 1989-91, 91-95; v.p. pub. rels. Scudder, Stevens & Clark, N.Y.C., 1991—, prin., 1996—. bd. govs. St. Timothy's Sch., Stevenson, Md., 19877-94. Democrat. Episcopalian.

MASHBURN, SYLVIA ANITA SMITH, public relations specialist; b. McRae, Ga., Mar. 28, 1964; d. Alexander Peterson and Sylvia Ann (Hartman) Smith; m. Thomas Matthew Mashburn, May 18, 1991; 1 child, Melissa Anne. BA, Vanderbilt U., Nashville, 1986; MA, Ga. State U., 1994. Cert. assoc. pub. mgr., Ga. Staff asst. U.S. Info. Agy., Washington, 1986-88; newspaper reporter The Courier-Herald, Dublin, Ga., 1989; pub, rels., info. specialist Ga. Dept. Transp., Atlanta, 1989-93, sr. pub. rels., info. specialist, 1993—. Vol. DeKalb Amb., Decatur, Ga., 1992—. Recipient Better Newspaper Contest award Ga. Press Assn., 1993, 94, 1st pl. award, 1995, Publ. Excellence award Ga. Milepost, 1991, 93. Mem. Pub. Rels. Soc. Am., Ga. Soc. Cert. Pub. Mgrs. Methodist. Office: Ga Dept Transportation Public Affairs Office 2 Capitol Sq SW Atlanta GA 30334-9003

MASHIN, JACQUELINE ANN COOK, medical sciences consultant; b. Chgo., May 11, 1941; d. William Hermann and Ann (Smidt) Cook; m. Fredric John Mashin, June 7, 1970; children: Joseph Glenn, Alison Robin. BS, U. Md., 1984. Cert. realtor. Adminstrv. asst. CIA, Washington, 1963-66; asst. to mng. dir. Aerospace Edn. Found., Washington, 1966-74; exec. asst. to asst exec. dir. Air Force Assn., Washington, 1974-79; v.p., ptnrship. owner Discount Linen Store, Silver Spring, Md., 1979-81; asst. regional polit. dir. Office of Pres.-elect, Washington, 1980-81; confidential asst. to dir. Office of Personnel Mgmt. (US), Washington, 1981-83; spl. asst. to dep. dir. Office of Mgmt. and Budget, Washington, 1983-86; dir. internat. communications and spl. asst. to commr. Dept. of the Interior, Washington, 1986-89, cons., 1989-93; with Washington Hosp. Ctr., 1993—. Pres. Layhill Civic Assn., Silver Spring, Md., 1980; state chmn. Md.'s Reagan Youth Delegation, Annapolis, Md., 1980; state treas., office mgr. Reagan-Bush State Hdqrs. of Md., Silver Spring, 1980; mem. Women's Com. Nat. Symphony Orch. Mem. Air Force Assn. (life), Aux. Salvation Army (life), Am. League Lobbyists, Internat. Platform Assn., U.S. Capital Hist. Soc., Women's Nat. Rep. Club (N.Y.C.), Indian Springs Country Club. Republican. Home and Office: 2429 White Horse Ln Silver Spring MD 20906-2243

MASI, MARY ELIZABETH ANDREWS, assistant editor; b. Cambridge, Minn., Sept. 23, 1968; d. Edwin and Ruth Edith Andrews; m. Thomas Allen Masi, Oct. 10, 1993. BA, Ambassador U., 1991; MA, St. Cloud State U., 1993. Coll. writing instr. St. Cloud (Minn.) State U., 1991-93; asst. editor John Wiley and Sons, Inc., N.Y.C., 1994—. Author profl. publs. Mem. Priests for Equality, Dearborn, Mich., 1994, Feminist Majority, Arlington, Va., 1995, Nat. Parks and Conservation. Grantee St. Cloud State U., 1992, recipient Coard Meml. scholarship 1992. Mem. NOW. Home: 9031 Fort Hamilton Pkwy #1G Brooklyn NY 11209 Office: John Wiley & Sons Inc 605 Third Ave New York NY 10158

MASKALL, MARTHA JOSEPHINE, executive recruiter, publisher; b. Kearny, N.J., Mar. 30, 1945; d. Charles Edgar and Mathilda (Comba) M. BA in Biology, Stanford U., 1966; MA, Duke U., 1969. Cert. data processor, 1979. Data base adminstr. Armco Steel, Ashland, Ky., 1972-74; project mgr. Rand Info. Systems, San Francisco, 1974-78; sales rep. Datacom ADR, San Francisco, 1980-81; systems engr. Four-Phase Systems, Sacramento, Calif., 1981-83; exec. recruiter Sacramento, 1983—; owner Attitude Works Pub., Fair Oaks, Calif., 1990—. Author: The Attitude Treasury: 101 Inspiring Quotations, 1990, The Athena Treasury: 101 Inspiring Quotations by Women, 1993. NDEA fellow, 1966-68. Mem. Data Processing Mgmt. Assn. (program dir. 1980, 82, sec. 1983), Sierra Club, Nat. Assn. Profl. Saleswomen (pres. 1992), Bus. and Profl. Women, Optimists, Toastmasters (v.p. 1985, pres. 1986, div. gov. 1987, speakers bur. 1988, Disting. Toastmaster award 1989). Democrat. Home: 8456 Hidden Valley Cir Fair Oaks CA 95628-6121 Office: Marty Maskall & Assoc PO Box 1765 Fair Oaks CA 95628-1765

MASLAND, LYNNE S., university official; b. Boston, Nov. 18, 1940; d. Keith Arnold and Camilla (Puleston) Shangraw; m. Edwin Grant Masland, Sept. 19, 1960 (div. 1975); children: Mary Conklin, Molly Allison; m. Steven Alan Mayo, July 1, 1995. Student, Mt. Holyoke Coll., South Hadley, Mass., 1958-60; BA, U. Calif., Riverside, 1970; MA, U. Calif., 1971; PhD, U. B.C., Vancouver, Can., 1994. Asst. pub. rels. dir. Inter-Am. U., San German, P.R., 1963-64; asst. to dir. elem. edn. Govt. of Am. Samoa, Pago Pago, 1966-68; project dir., cons. Wash. Commn. for Humanities, Seattle, 1976-80; exec. editor N.W. Happenings Mag., Greenbank, Wash., 1980-84; media specialist Western Wash. U., Bellingham, 1984-88; dir. pub. info. Western Wash. U., 1988—; asst. prof. Fairhaven Coll., 1995—; cons. William O. Douglas Inst., Seattle, 1984, Whatcom Mus. History and Art, Bellingham, 1977; instr. U. Nebr., Omaha, 1972-86, Western Wash. U., 1972-86. Editor: The Human Touch: Folklore of the Northwest Corner, 1979, Proceedings: The Art in Living, 1980, Reports to the Mayor on the State of the Arts in Bellingham, 1980-81; contbr. numerous articles to profl. jours. Pres. LWV, Whatcom County, Bellingham, 1977-79; bd. dirs. N.W. Concert Assn., 1981-83, Wash. State Folklife Coun., 1985-90; docent Nat. Gallery, Washington, 1969; bd. dirs. Sta. KZAZ, nat. pub. radio, Bellingham, 1992-93. Univ. grad. fellow U. B.C., 1990-94. Mem. Am. Comparative Lit. Assn., Nat. Assn. Presswomen, Wash. Press Assn. (pres. 4th Corner chpt. 1987-88, Superior Performance award 1986), Can. Comparative Lit. Assn., Internat. Comparative Lit. Assn., Philological Assn. of Pacific Coast, Coun. for Advancement and Support Edn. (Case Dist. VIII Gold award for Media Rels.), Rotary (bd. dirs. 1992-94). Episcopalian. Office: Western Wash U High St Bellingham WA 98225

MASLANSKY, CAROL JEANNE, toxicologist; b. N.Y.C., Mar. 3, 1949; d. Paul Jeremiah and Jeanne Marie (Filiatrault) Lane; m. Steven Paul Maslansky, May 28, 1973. BA, SUNY, 1971; PhD, N.Y. Med. Coll., 1983. Diplomate Am. Bd. Toxicology; cert. gen. toxicology. Asst. entomologist N.Y. State Dept. Health, White Plains, 1973-74; sr. biologist Am. Health Found., Valhalla, N.Y., 1974-76; rsch. fellow N.Y. Med. Coll., Valhalla, 1977-83, Albert Einstein Coll. Medicine, Bronx, N.Y., 1983; copr. toxicologist Texaco, Inc., Beacon, N.Y., 1984-85; prin. GeoEnviron. Cons., Inc., White Plains, N.Y., 1982—; lectr. in entomology Westchester County Parks and Preserves, 1973—, lectr. toxicology and hazardous materials, 1985—. Author: Air Monitoring Instrumentation, 1993, (with others) Training for

Hazardous Materials Team Members, 1991 (manual, video) The Poison Control Response to Chemical Emergencies, 1993. Mem. Harrison (N.Y.) Vol. Ambulance Corps., 1986-91, Westchester County (N.Y.) Hazardous Materials Response Team, 1987—. Monsanto Fund Fellowship in Toxicology, 1988-90; grad. fellowship N.Y. Med. Coll., 1977-83. Mem. AAAS, Nat. Environ. Health Assn., N.Y. Acad. Sci., Am. Coll. Toxicology, Am. Indsl. Hygiene Assn., Environ. Mutagen Soc.

MASLIN, JANET, film critic; b. N.Y.C., Aug. 12, 1949; d. Paul and Lucille (Becker) M.; m. Benjamin Cheever; children: John, Andrew. BA in Math., U. Rochester, 1970. Film and music critic The Boston Phoenix, 1972-76; film critic Newsweek, N.Y.C., 1976-77; dep. film critic The N.Y. Times, N.Y.C., 1977-93, chief film critic, 1993—. Office: The NY Times 229 W 43rd St New York NY 10036-3913*

MASON, AIMEE HUNNICUTT ROMBERGER, retired philosophy and humanities educator; b. Atlanta, Nov. 3, 1918; d. Edwin William and Aimee Greenleaf (Hunnicutt) Romberger; m. Samuel Venable Mason, Aug. 16, 1941 (dec. 1988); children: Olivia Elizabeth (Mrs. Mason Butcher), Christopher Leeds. BA, Conn. Coll., 1940; postgrad. Emory U., 1946-48; MA, U. Fla., 1979, PhD, 1980, MA, Stetson U., 1968. Jr. exec. merchandising G. Fox & Co., Hartford, Conn., 1940-41; air traffic contr. CAA, Atlanta, 1942; ptnr. Coronado Concrete Products, New Smyrna Beach, Fla., 1953-81; adj. faculty Valencia Jr. Coll., Orlando, Fla., 1969; instr. philosophy and humanities Seminole Community Coll., Sanford, 1969, ret. Area cons. ARC, 1947-50; del. Nat. Red Cross, Washington, 1949; founding mem. St. Joseph Hosp. Aux., Atlanta, 1950-53; v.p., treas. New Smyrna Beach PTA 1955-60; bd. dirs. Atlanta Symphony Orch., Fla. Symphony Orch., 1954-59; mem. Code Enforcement Bd., Edgewater, Fla., 1992-94. Lt. USCGR, 1943-46. Recipient award in graphics Nat. Assn. Women Artists, 1939, 41. Mem. AAUP, AAUW (founding mem. New Smyrna Beach, exec. bd. 1984-85, chmn. scholarship com. 1984-87, coll./univ. liaison 1987-91, citizen's code enforcement bd. Edgewater 1992-94), DAV, Am. Philos. Assn., Fla. Philos. Assn. (exec. coun. 1978-79), Collegium Phenomenologicum, Soc. Existential and Phenomenological Philosophy, Soc. Phenomenology in Human Scis., Merleau-Ponty Circle, Fla. Assn. Community Colls. Home: 511 N Riverside Dr Edgewater FL 32132-1631

MASON, BARBARA E. SUGGS, educator; b. Champaign, Ill., July 9, 1952; d. Raymond Eugene and Hester Barbara (Nelson) Suggs; m. Frederick A. Mason, May 7, 1988. B of Music Edn., Northwestern U., 1974; MS in Music Edn., U. Ill., 1976, M of Music, 1985. Cert. music tchr. K-12, supervisory endorsement, voice performance and lit., Ill. Gen. music specialist Oak Park (Ill.) Sch. Dist. 97, 1976-82; tchr. for the gifted performing arts unit Champaign Community Schs., 1985-86; choral dir. Evanston (Ill.) Twp. H.S., 1986-87, dist. curriculum leader for gen. music, 1990-95; coord. for mid. level edn. Oak Park Sch. Dist. 97, 1995—; adj. instr. Elmhurst Coll., 1990-95; curriculum cons. Office of Cath. Edn. Black History Com., Chgo., 1992—; acad. task team mem. Quigley Preparatory Sem., Chgo, 1993; curriculum cons., presenter Dept. of Mus. Edn., Art Inst. of Chgo., 1992; chmn. dist. comprehensive arts grant com. Dist. 97, Oak Park, 1992—. Bd. dirs. Oak Park and River Forest Children's Chorus, 1991-95; mem. arts fund com. Oak Park Area Arts Coun., 1993-95. Grad. coll. fellowship U. Ill., 1984-85; recipient Award of Merit Those Who Excel Program Ill. State Bd. of Edn., 1993. Mem. NEA, ASCD, Nat. Middle Sch. Assn., Music Educators Nat. Conf., Ill. Alliance for Arts Edn. (svc. award selection com. 1993), In-and-About Chgo. Music Educators Club, Mu Phi Epsilon, Phi Delta Kappa. Roman Catholic. Office: Oak Park Sch Dist 97 970 Madison St Oak Park IL 60302-4430

MASON, BETTY G(WENDOLYN) HOPKINS, school system administrator; b. Tulsa, Mar. 3, 1928; d. Stacy Ervin and Carrie (McGlory) Hopkins; 1 child, Trena Janell Milliner Combs. BA, Bishop Coll., Marshall, Tex., 1949; MEd, Calif. State U., Haywood, 1974; EdD, U. Okla., 1986. Tchr. pub. schs., Kansas City, Mo., 1963-69; asst. Title I schs. Berkeley (Calif.) Unified Schs., 1970-71, asst. prin., 1971-72, dir. elem. edn., 1974-79; prin. Le Conte Elem. Sch., Berkeley, 1972-74; dir. high schs. Oklahoma City Pub. Schs., 1979-82, asst. supt., 1982-88; supt. of schs. Gary (Ind.) Pub. Schs., 1988-90; ednl. cons. Oklahoma City Pub. Schs., 1990-91, asst. supt., 1991-92, supt. of schs., 1992-95, ret., 1995; mem. exec. bd. supt.'s initiative Nat. Urban League, N.Y.C., 1988-90. Mem. exec. bd. YWCA, Gary, 1988-90, N.W. Ind. chpt. Urban League, Gary, 1988—. Recipient Citizen of Yr. award Omega Phi Psi, 1985, Outstanding Woman in Edn. award Okla. Commn. in Edn., 1987, Youth Svc. award City and Mayor of Gary, 1988, Outstanding Educator award Ind. U. Dons, 1989; Disting. Educator's award, 1993, Silver Beaver award Boy Scouts Am., 1995, Woman of Yr. award Girl Scouts, 1995. Mem. Am. Assn. Sch. Adminstrs., Nat. Assn. Black Educators, NW Ind. Supts. Coun., Phi Delta, Phi Delta Kappa (chpt. basileus, edn. chmn., soror of yr. 1996), Alpha Kappa Alpha. Home: 2217 NW 119th St Oklahoma City OK 73120-7815

MASON, BOBBIE ANN, novelist, short story writer; b. Mayfield, Ky., May 1, 1940; d. Wilburn A. and Christianna (Lee) M.; m. Roger B. Rawlings, April 12, 1969. BA, U. Ky., 1962; MA, SUNY, Binghamton, 1966; PhD, U. Conn., 1972. Asst. prof. English Mansfield (Pa.) State Coll., 1972-79. Author: Nabokov's Garden, 1974, The Girl Sleuth: A Feminist Guide to the Bobbsey Twins, Nancy Drew and Their Sisters, 1976, 2d edit., 1995, Shiloh and Other Stories, 1976 (Ernest Hemingway award Nat. Book Critic's Circle award nominee, Am. Book award nominee, PEN Faulkner award nominee), In Country, 1985, Spence + Lila, 1988, Love Life, 1989, Feather Crowns, 1993 (Nat. Book Critic's Circle award nominee, So. Book award); comtbr. regularly to the New Yorker, 1980—; contbr. fiction to the Atlantic, Redbook, Paris Rev., Mother Jones, Harpers, N.Am. Rev., Va. Quar. Rev., Story, Ploughshares, So. Rev., Crazyhorse; contbr. works Best American Short Stories, 1981, The Pushcart Prize; Best of the Small Presses, 1983, Best American Short Stories, 1983. Recipient O. Henry Anthology awards, 1986, 88; grantee Pa. Arts Coun., 1983, 89, Nat. Endowment Arts, 1983, Am. Acad. and Inst. Arts and Letters, 1984; Guggenheim fellow, 1984. Office: Internat Creative Mgmt 40 W 57th St New York NY 10019

MASON, CHARLOTTE, advertising executive; b. Detroit; d. David and Mariam (Cooper) Yamshon; m. Harvey Stuart Magitz, Aug. 29, 1964 (div. July 1972); children: Robin Melinda, Kevin Reid. Lic. real estate and ins. Ill., 1984. Legal sec. Bell & Howell, Lincolnwood, Ill., 1978-79; regional mgr. Tobin & Kreitman, Chgo., 1979-84; ins. agt. Metropolitan Ins. Co., N.Y.C., 1984-86; sales exec. Columbia Communications, N.Y.C., 1987-88; dist. mgr. Arbonne Internat., Calif., 1990-92; pres. CM Promotions, Prospects Heights, Ill., 1992—. Vol. Pasteur Sch., Detroit, 1971, Channel 56, Detroit, 1967. Democrat. Jewish.

MASON, DEBORAH, entrepreneur; b. Columbus, Ohio, Oct. 10, 1951; d. Neil E. and Georgia M. (Hargan) M. BFA in Comml. Art Design, Art Therapy, Columbus Coll. Art & Design, 1974. Registered art therapist; cert. profl. child care worker; cert. in RET, PET, RBT, family relations, awareness through movement, parent to parent; cert. instr. N.G. Bur. Art therapist St. Ann's Hosp., Columbus, 1973-76; cmty. rels./edn. and tng. specialist Franklin County 648 Bd., Columbus, 1976-79; trainer Bank One Columbus N.A., 1981-83; coord. Ctrl. Ohio ADMS Women's Set-Aside Funds, 1987-90; exec. dir. Inst. for Human Awareness, Inc., 1979—; adminstr. Bus. Against Substance Abuse Coalition, 1990—; cons. ABA, AMA, Am. Hosp. Assn., NIMH, Nat. Inst. Drug Abuse, N.Am. Rockwell, Nationwide Ins., Compuserve, Inc., others, 1979—; instr. Ohio State U., Columbus, 1989—; trainer Robert Stutman & Assocs., Inc., Dedham, Mass., 1994—; adv. bd. Franklin U., Columbus, 1994—. Founder: The Working Partners Program: Substance-Free Workplace Consultation Program for Small Businesses, 1993 (Trademark award 1996), Psycho-Social Drama: A Training and Education Process, 1976 (trademark 1980); dir.: (videotape) The Ohio State University Drug and Alcohol Prevention Education Tape, 1989 (FIPSE grantee 1989); contbr. articles to profl. jours. Founder Bus. Against Substance Abuse (BASA) Coalition, 1990; bd. comm. chmn. Ctrl. Ohio Red Ribbon Com., Columbus,1991-94; founder Bus. to Bus. Spkrs. Bur., Columbus, 1990. Recipient Ms Executive award Columbus Dispatch Newspaper, 1980, Gov.'s Spl. Recognition award State of Ohio, 1990, Award of Achievement, Franklin County Drug-Free Schs. Consortium, 1993, Extra Mile award Franklin County ADAMH Bd., 1995; named to Outstanding Young Women of Am., 1984; grantee Yassenoff Found., 1979, Columbus Found., 1979, Ohio Dept. Health, 1980. Mem.Inst. for a Drug-Free Workplace, Cmty. Anti-Drug Coalitions Assn. (CADCA). Home: 178 Homestead Dr Pickerington OH 43147 Office: BASA Coalition 700 Bryden Rd 3d Fl Columbus OH 43215

MASON, ELIZABETH ABRUZESE, management and corporate reputation consultant; b. Richmond, Va., Oct. 20, 1960; d. Thomas Joseph and Judith Ann (Toler) Abruzese; m. Richard Gary Mason, May 22, 1983. BS in Mass Communications, Va. Commonwealth U., 1984. Account exec. Pezzano and Co., N.Y.C., 1985-86; account supr. Levine Huntley Schmidt & Beaver, N.Y.C., 1986-87, assoc. dir. strategic svcs., 1989, v.p., assoc. dir. new bus., 1989-90, v.p., dir. new bus., 1990-91; sr. v.p., dir. bus. devel. Levine, Huntley, Vick and Beaver, N.Y.C., 1991; advt. mgr. Trans World Airlines, N.Y.C., 1987-88; pres. Friedman & Benjamin Advt., N.Y.C., 1992-93; mng. dir. Newton, Lao, Leonard & Locke, Inc., N.Y.C., 1993—. Bd. dirs. Sch. Mass. Comms., Va. Commonwealth U., 1996—. Recipient Va. Commonwealth U. Leadership and Svc. award, 1984, Va. Commonwealth U. Alumni award, 1991. Mem. Am. Mktg. Assn. (Gold Effie award 1987, Effie judge 1991, 92, 95, 96, chair Effie award 1992, 93, 94), Advt. Club N.Y., Advt. Women N.Y. (chair Addy award 1991-92, chair judging com. Addy awards 1990-91, co-chair career issues 1992-93), Turnabout Mgmt. Assn. Home: 921 Hudson St Hoboken NJ 07030-5101 Office: Newton Lao Leonard & Locke 921 Hudson St Hoboken NJ 07030-5101

MASON, JANET, magazine editor, journalist; b. Montclair, N.J., Aug. 11, 1930; d. Mayne Seguine and Rachel (Entorf) Mason. BA, Smith Coll., 1952; MA, Stanford U., 1955. Asst. feature editor, Omnibus TV-Radio Workshop of the Ford Found., N.Y.C., 1955-57; reporter Life Mag., N.Y.C., 1957-58; prodr./dir. KQED-TV, San Francisco, 1958-61; reporter to assoc. editor Life Mag., 1961-64, contbg. editor, 1964—. Co-author: A Long Way Up, a Biography of Jill Kinmont, 1965; contbr. to The Other Side of the Mountain, 1967; contbr. articles to Life Mag. for more than 30 yrs. Trustee INTERALP, Princeton, N.J., 1968-75; bd. counselors Smith Coll., 1964-69. Recipient ann. award of merit Mental Health Assn. Am., 1980. Mem. Presbyn. Meml. Iris Gardens (trustee 1993—), Smith Coll. Club. Office: Life Magazine Rockefeller Ctr Time & Life Bldg New York NY 10020

MASON, JOHANNA HENDRIKA ANNEKE, retired secondary education educator; b. Indramajoe, Indonesia, Feb. 17, 1932; came to U.S., 1957; d. Johannes Simon and Hendrika Jacoba (De Vroedt) Vermeulen; m. Alfred Bob Markholt, Feb., 1958 (div. Dec. 1966); children: Bob, Anneke, Joe Ralph, Lee Markholt; m. Rollin Mason, 1968 (div. 1978). French lang. diploma with top honors, Paris Alliance Française, 1952; BA in Philosophy summa cum laude, U. Puget Sound, 1976, MA in Comparative Lit., 1979, BA in Edn., 1988. Cert. pub. sch. tchr. 4-12. Adminstrv. asst. to pres. N.V. Nutricia, Zoetermeer, The Netherlands, 1953-57; pvt. sec. Grad. Sch. Bus. Harvard U., Cambridge, Mass., 1957; adminstrv. asst., lectr. humanities divsn. U. Puget Sound, Tacoma, 1966-88; tchr. English and French h.s. and mid. sch. Tacoma, 1988-94; mem. pres. staff orgn. U. Puget Sound, Tacoma, 1978-80, budget task force, 1981-86, sec. Phi Kappa Phi chpt., 1970-77, pres. Phi Kappa Phi chpt., 1970-73. Author: (poetry compilation) Journey, 1981, A Handfull of Bubbles, 1981, Echoes, Mirrors, Reflections, 1983; contbr. poetry to lit. mags. Mem. city's task force on hate crimes, Tacoma, 1992, translator, 1974-90; spkr. Unitarian Universalist Assn., Tacoma, 1994-95; mem. Tacoma Art Mus. Mem. NOW, So. Poverty Law Ctr., Phi Kappa Phi (nat. com. on comms. 1991-94).

MASON, JUDITH ANN, freelance writer; b. Newark, Dec. 27, 1945; d. Richard Algie and Mary Ann (Beneck) M. Diploma in legal sci., Spencerian Bus. Coll., 1965; BA, Northeastern Ill. U., 1984. Legal sec. Harney B. Stover, Atty., Milw., 1967-69, Robert P. O'Meara, Atty., Waukegan, Ill., 1969-70; sec. to pres. First Midwest Bank, Waukegan, 1970-72, asst. cashier, 1972-76; legal sec. Eugene M. Snarski, Atty., Waukegan, 1976-81; adminstrv. aide Lake County Forest Preserve Dist., Libertyville, Ill., 1981-89; freelance writer Tucson, 1989—; legal sec., asst. Jeffrey H. Greenberg, Atty.; office mgr. Greenberg & Assocs., Tucson, 1989—; travel rep. Antioch (Ill.) Travel Agy., 1980-89, Advance Travel Agy., Zion, Ill., 1980-89; pub. speaker for various orgns., Lake County, Ill., 1984-89. Author: Why I Remember Yesterday, 1979, Haggadah (play), 1982; editor poetry column: Bank Man Magazine, 1972-75; contbg. article writer Compendum Mag. Tchr. Confraternity Christian Doctrine St. Patrick's Ch., Wadsworth, Ill., 1980-85; lector, eucharistic min. Prince of Peace Ch., Lake Villa, Ill., 1980-89; hospice vol. St. Therese Hosp., Waukegan, 1984; speech writer Grace Mary Stern lt. gubernatorial campaign, Lake County, 1984; voter registrar County of Lake Ill., 1986-89; cons. pub. rels. Lake County Cir. Ct. Judge campaign, 1988, Presdl. Campaign Paul Simon; co-chmn., organizer Women's Exhibit, Evergreen Air Show, 1993. Recipient Brian F. Shehanhan Creative Writing award Am. Inst. Banking, 1972, 1st Place pub. speaking, 1974. Mem. AAUW (pub. rels. chair 1986, pres. Chain O'Lakes br. 1988-89, Ill. Pub. Info. award 1987, pub. rels. chair Tucson br. 1991-92), NAFE, Northeastern Ill. U. Alumni Assn., Soc. Southwestern Authors, Pi Rho Zeta (pres. 1964-65). Democrat. Roman Catholic.

MASON, LESA ANN, art history educator; b. Brighton, Mass., Sept. 4, 1959; d. Joseph Butler and Carol Cilley M. BA, Rosemont Coll., 1981; MA, Temple U., 1985; PhD, Ind. U., 1991. Tchng. replacement DePauw U., Greencastle, Ind., 1985-87, 90-91; rsch. asst. Ind. U., Bloomington, Ind.; art mgr. Kunst-Station Sank & Peter, Cologne, Germany, 1987—; intern Wallraf-Richartz-Mus., Cologne, 1987-90; prof. The Savannah Coll. of Art and Design, Ga., 1991—; cons./translator Wallraf-Richartz-Mus., Cologne, 1991—; U.S. cons. Kunst-Station Sankt & Peter, 1991—; Joseph Bevys symposium spkr. Ea. Carolina U., 1995. Curator: (exhibition catalogue) Deepening Concerns and New Impulses, 1992, Impulses from Cologne, 1993; author: Indiana Collects DePauw University, 1991; translator: Beuys on Christ, 1989. Samuel H. Kress fellow Ind. U., Bloomington, 1986-87, Albert Coomb & Barnes Found., Merion, Pa., 1976-79; grantee NEH, 1985-89, L'Aquila U., Italy, 1982, 84. Mem. Am. Kennel Club. Catholic. Home: PO Box 97 Tybee Island GA 31328-0097 Office: Savannah Coll Art & Design 201 W Charlton Savannah GA 31402-3146

MASON, LUCILE GERTRUDE, fundraiser, consultant; b. Montclair, N.J., Aug. 1, 1925; d. Mayne Seguine and Rachel (Entorf) M. AB, Smith Coll., 1947; MA, NYU, 1968, 76. Editor ABC, N.Y.C., 1947-51; asst. casting dir. Compton Advt., Inc., N.Y.C., 1951-55, dir. and head casting, 1955-65; conf. mgr. Camp Fire Girls, Inc., N.Y.C., 1965-66; exec. dir. Assn. of Jr. Leagues of Am. Inc., N.Y.C., 1966-68; dir. div. pub. affairs Girl Scouts U.S.A., N.Y.C., 1969-71; dir. pub. rels. YWCA of City of N.Y., 1971-73; dir. community rels. and devel. Girl Scout Coun. of Greater N.Y., N.Y.C., 1973-76; dir. devel. Montclair Kimberley Acad., Montclair, N.J., 1976-78, Ethical Culture Schs., N.Y.C. and Riverdale, N.Y., 1978-80; pres. Lucile Mason & Assocs., Montclair, 1980-83; devel. officer founds. Fairleigh Dickinson U., Rutherford, N.J., 1983-85; dir. devel. Whole Theatre, Inc., Montclair, 1985-86, YMWCA of Newark & Vicinity, 1986-88; v.p. adminstrn. and fin. devel. Inst. Religion and Health, N.Y.C., 1988-90; dir. corp. and found. rels. Upsala Coll., East Orange, N.J., 1990-91; pres. Lucile Mason & Assocs., Montclair, 1991—. Vol. bd. counselors Smith Coll., 1964-74, chmn. theatre com., mem. exec. com., 1969-74; trustee Citizens Com. Presby Meml. Iris Gardens of Montclair, 1992—; trustee Friends of Barnet, 1994-95; v.p. Neighborhood Ctr., Inc., Montclair, 1987-95; mem. fund devel. com. Girl Scout Coun. Greater Essex County, 1986-92. Mem. Am. Women in Radio and TV (pres. N.Y.C. chpt. 1955-56), Community Agys. Pub. Rels. Assn. (membership chmn. 1973-76), Nat. Soc. Fund Raising Execs. (bd. dirs. N.J. chpt 1983-86, mem. awards com. 1994, co-chair awards com. N.J. Conf. on Philanthropy 1995), Pub. Rels. Soc. Am., Smith Coll. Club of Montclair (bd. dirs. 1986-90). Home and Office: 142 N Mountain Ave Montclair NJ 07042-2350

MASON, MARILYN GELL, library administrator, writer, consultant; b. Chickasha, Okla., Aug. 23, 1944; d. Emmett D. and Dorothy (O'Bar) Killebrew; m. Carl L. Gell, Dec. 29 1965 (div. Oct. 1978); 1 son, Charles E.; m. Robert M. Mason, July 17, 1981. B.A., U. Dallas, 1966; M.L.S., N. Tex. State U., Denton, 1968; M.P.A., Harvard U., 1978. Libr. N.J. State Libr., Trenton, 1968-69; head dept. Arlington County Pub. Libr., Va., 1969-73; chief libr. program Metro Washington Coun. Govts., 1973-77; dir. White House Conf. on Librs. and Info. Svcs., Washington, 1979-80; exec. v.p. Metrics Rsch. Corp., Atlanta, 1981-82; dir. Atlanta-Fulton Pub. Libr., Atlanta, 1982-86, Cleve. Pub. Libr., 1986—; trustee Online Computer Library Ctr., 1984—; Evalene Parsons Jackson lectr. div. librarianship Emory U., 1981. Author: The Federal Role in Library and Information Services, 1983; editor: Survey of Library Automation in the Washington Area, 1977; project dir.: book Information for the 1980's, 1980. Bd. visitors Sch. Info. Studies, Syracuse U., 1981-85, Sch. of Libr. and Info. Sci. , U. Tenn.-Knoxville, 1983-85; trustee Coun. on Libr. Resources, Atlant, 1992—. Recipient Disting. Alumna award N. Tex. State U., 1979. Mem. ALA (mem. council 1986—), Am. Assn. Info. Sci., Ohio Library Assn., D.C. Library Assn. (pres. 1976-77). Home: 12427 Fairhill Rd Cleveland OH 44120-1015 Office: Cleve Pub Libr 325 Superior Ave E Cleveland OH 44114-1205

MASON, MARSHA, actress, director, writer; b. St. Louis; d. James and Jacqueline M.; m. Gary Campbell, 1965 (div.); m. Neil Simon, Oct. 25, 1973 (div.). Grad., Webster (Mo.) Coll. Performances include cast Broadway and nat. tour Cactus Flower, 1968; other stage appearances include The Deer Park, 1967, The Indian Wants the Bronx, 1968, Happy Birthday, Wanda June, 1970, Private Lives, 1971, You Can't Take It With You, 1972, Cyrano de Bergerac, 1972, A Doll's House, 1972, The Crucible, 1972, The Good Doctor, 1973, King Richard III, 1974, The Heiress, 1975, Mary Stuart, 1982, Amazing Grace, 1995, Night of the Iguana, 1996; one-woman show off-Broadway, The Big Love, Perry St. Theatre, 1988, Lake No Bottom, Second Stage, 1990, Escape From Happiness, With the Naked Angels, 1994; film appearances include Blume in Love, 1973, Cinderella Liberty, 1973 (recipient Golden Globe award 1974, Acad. award nominee), Audrey Rose, 1977, The Goodbye Girl, 1977 (recipient Golden Globe award 1978, Acad. award nominee), The Cheap Detective, 1978, Promises in the Dark, 1979, Chapter Two, 1979 (Acad. award nominee), Only When I Laugh, 1981 (Acad. award nominee), Max Dugan Returns, 1982, Heartbreak Ridge, 1986, Stella, 1988, Drop Dead Fred, 1990, I Love Trouble, 1994; TV appearances include PBS series Cyrano de Bergerac, 1974, The Good Doctor, 1978, Lois Gibbs and the Love Canal, 1981, Surviving, 1985, Trapped in Silence, 1986, The Clinic, 1987, Dinner At Eight, 1989, The Image, 1990, Broken Trust, 1994, series Sibs, 1991; dir. (plays) Juno's Swans, 1987, Heaven Can Wait; dir. ABC Afternoon Spl. Little Miss Perfect, 1988. Office: care Internat Creative Mgmt 8942 Wilshire Blvd Beverly Hills CA 90211-1934

MASON, NANCY TOLMAN, state agency director; b. Buxton, Maine, Mar. 14, 1933; d. Ansel Robert and Kate Douglas (Libby) M. Grad., Bryant Coll., Providence, R.I., 1952; BA, U. Mass., Boston, 1977; postgrad., Inst. Governmental Services, Boston, 1985, The Auditor's Inst., 1988. Asst. to chief justice Mass. Superior Ct., Boston, 1964-68; community liaison Action for Boston Community Devel., Boston, 1968-73; mgmt. cons. East Boston Community Devel. Assn., Boston, 1973-78; asst. dir. Mass. Office of Deafness, Boston, 1978-86; dir. of contracts Mass. Rehab. Commn., Boston, 1986—; cons. Jos. A Ryan Assocs., Boston and Orleans, Mass., 1981-86, Radio Sta. WFCC, Chatham, Mass., 1987-91. Author: Bromley-Heath Security Patrols, 1974, Reorganization of East Boston Community Development Corporation, 1976, How to Start Your Own Small Business, 1981. Bd. dirs. Deaf-Blind Contact Ctr., Boston, 1988-91; vol. Am. Cancer Soc., Winchester, Mass., 1986-93, Tax Equity Alliance Mass., 1994. Recipient Good Citizen award DAR, 1950, Community Svc. award Northeastern U., 1986, Gov.'s citation for outstanding performance, 1993; named to Outstanding Young Women of Am., 1965. Mem. NOW, NAFE, Mass. State Assn. Deaf, MRC Statewide Cen. Office Dirs. (chair 1995—). Democrat. Episcopalian. Office: Mass Rehab Commn 27-43 Wormwood St Boston MA 02210

MASON, SARA SMITH, managed healthcare consultant; b. Rochester, N.Y.; d. Harry F. and Louise S. (Sullivan) Smith; m. Larry S. Mason, Oct. 14, 1972. BA, Lewis and Clark Coll., Portland, Oreg., MA in Tchg.; MBA, U. Oreg., 1987. Dir. N.W. area Intracorp., Portland, 1979-90; dir. ops. Western region Ptnrs. In Exec. Solutions, Irvine, Calif., 1990-91; asst. v.p. group and casualty svcs. ETHIX Nat., Portland, Oreg., 1992-94; managed care product mgr. Fireman's Fund Ins. Cos., Portland, 1994-95; exec. v.p. Cyber Metrix, Beaverton, Oreg., 1995—. Mem. med. subcom. Worker's Compensation, Salem, Oreg., 1987. Mem. Oreg. Exec. MBA Alumni Bd. (bd. dirs.), Nat. Assn. Rehab. Profl. in Pvt. Sector, Portland City Club (bus. labor com. 1990-91). Office: Firemans Fund Ins Cos 101 SW Main St Ste 710 Portland OR 97204-3215

MASSA, BARBARA K., corporate communications specialist; b. July 28, 1950. BA, W.Va. U., MBA. Joined First Union Corp., 1973—, credit adminstr., comml. lending office, sr. corp. lending officer, v.p. investor rels., 1983-86, sr. v.p. corp. comm./investor rels., 1986-89, dir. cmty. reinvestment, 1989—; past pres. Women Execs. of Charlotte, The Bank Investor Rels. Assn., YWCA of the Ctrl. Carolinas. Office: First Union Corp 201 S Tryon St Charlotte NC 28288-0570

MASSEY, W(ILMET) ANNETTE, nurse, former educator; b. Big Chimney, W.Va., June 30, 1920; d. Robert Lee and Twila Augusta (Pringle) M.; student Morris Harvey Coll., 1938-39; diploma, Phila. Gen. Hosp. Sch. Nursing, 1943; BS in Edn., U. Pa., 1948; MSN, Yale U., 1959. Nurse cadet instr. U.S. Cadet Nurse Corps, Huntington (W.Va.) Meml. Hosp., 1943-45; nurse instr. St. Mary's Sch. Nursing, Huntington, 1948-51; WHO nurse cons. Govt. Ceylon, 1951-55; staff nurse instr. VA Hosp., Ft. Thomas, Ky., 1955-57; asst. prof. nursing Brigham Young U., Provo, Utah, 1959-61; assoc. prof. nursing W.Va. U., Morgantown, 1961-83, chmn. dept. psychiat. nursing, 1968-72, ret.; cons. Appalachian Regional Hosp., Beckley, W.Va., W.Va. Dept. Mental Health, Charleston, Valley Community Mental Health Center, Kingwood, W.Va.; group leader med.-nursing group to India, Expt. Internat. Living, Brattleboro, Vt., 1965. Mem. Appalachian Trail, Morgantown Hospice, Rep. Nat. Com., Drummond Chapel United Meth. Ch., United Meth. Women, health adv. com. Coun. Mins., ARC, Nat. Coun. Sr. Citizens, Monongalians Srs., Rails to Trail, W.Va. Highlands Conservancy, W.Va. Citizens Action, Cooper's Rock Found. NIMH grantee, 1964-75. Mem. ANA, League Nursing, Am. Orthopsychiat. Assn., Internat. Transactional Analysis Assn., Am. Counseling Assn. (dir. 1981-82, v.p. 1982), Am. Soc. Profl. and Exec. Women, Environ. Def. Fund, Nat. Parks and Conservation Assn., Nat. Trust for Hist. Preservation, Tarrytown Group, Nat. Registry Psychiat. Nurse Specialists (edn. and resources com.), Internat. Acad. Cancer Counselors and Cons., Nat. Alliance Family Life, Inc. (founding), AAUP, Nat. Hist. Soc., Hastings Ctr., Nat. Wildlife Fedn., Smithsonian Assos., Phila. Gen. Hosp. Sch. Nursing Alumni, U. Pa., Yale U., W.Va. U. Sch. Nursing (hon.) Alumni Assns., 20/20 Vision Winterthur Guild, Empower Am., Pub. Citizen, Friends of the Earth, W.Va. Pub. Theatre, Am. Rivers, Project Vote Smart, W.Va. Rivers Coalition, World Learning, Wash. Nat. Cathedral, So. Property Law Ctr., Am. Red Cross, Am. Farmland Trust, Sierra Club, Lakeview Resort Club, Appalachian Trail, Sigma Theta Tau. Clubs: Alpine Lake Recreation Cmty.(Terra Alta, W.Va.), Penn (N.Y.C.). Home: 432 Western Ave Morgantown WV 26505-2135

MASSIE, ANN MACLEAN, law educator; b. South Bend, Ind., Sept. 17, 1943; d. John Allan and Gladys Sherill (Wilkie) MacLean; m. Kent Belmore Massie, Aug. 25, 1973; children: Allan Barksdale, Laura Sherrill. BA, Duke U., 1966; MA in English, U. Mich., 1967; JD, U. Va., 1971. Bar: Ga. 1971. Assoc. Alston, Miller & Gaines, Atlanta, 1971-73, Long and Aldridge, Atlanta, 1974-76; staff atty. regional office FTC, Atlanta, 1973-74; law clk. to Hon. J. Harvie Wilkinson III U.S. Ct. Appeals (4th cir.), Charlottesville, Va., 1984-85; adj. prof. law Washington & Lee U., Lexington, Va., 1985-88, asst. prof. law, 1988-93; assoc. prof. law Washington & Lee U., Lexington, 1993—. Contbr. articles to law jours. Deacon Waynesboro (Va.) Presbyn. Ch., 1986-88; bd. dirs., v.p. Hosp. Aux., Waynesboro, 1986-88; elder Lexington Presbyn. Ch., 1995—. Named Prof. of Yr., Women Law Students Orgn., 1993. Mem. Am. Soc. Law, Medicine and Ethics, Hastings Ctr., Choice in Dying. Home: PO Box 1076 Lexington VA 24450-1076 Office: Washington and Lee U Sch of Law Lexington VA 24450

MASSIE, ANNE ADAMS ROBERTSON, artist; b. Lynchburg, Va., May 30, 1931; d. Douglas Alexander and Annie Scott (Harris) Robertson; m. William McKinnon Massie, Apr. 30, 1960; children: Anne Harris, William McKinnon, Jr. Grad., St. Mary's Coll., Raleigh, N.C., 1950; BA in English, Randolph Macon Woman's Coll., 1952. Tchr. English E.C. Glass High Sch., Lynchburg, 1955-60. Bd. dirs. Lynchburg Hist. Found., 1968-81, 91-95, pres., 1978-81; bd. dirs. Lynchburg Fine Arts Ctr., 1992—; trustee Va.

Episcopal Sch., Lynchburg, 1983-89. Mem. Am. Watercolor Soc. (signature, Dolphin fellow 1993, Gold medal Honor 1993), Nat. Watercolor Soc. (signature, Artist's Mag. award), Nat. League Am. Pen Women (pres. 1987, Best in Show 1994), Knickerbocker Artists (signature, Silver medal Watercolor 1993), Watercolor USA Honor Soc., Watercolor West (signature), Catharine Lorrilard Wolfe Art Club (signature), Southern Watercolor Soc (signature), Va. Watercolor Soc. (artist mem., Best in Show 1992, chmn. exhbns. 1986, pres. 1995-96), Colonial Dames Am. (chmn. 1987-90), Hillside Garden Club (pres. 1974-76), Jr. League (editor 1953-72), Lynchburg Art Club (bd. dirs. 1995—, chmn. 1981-84), Antiquarian Club. Episcopalian. Home: 3204 Rivermont Ave Lynchburg VA 24503-2028

MASSIE, LORNA SCOTT, artist; b. Milw., Dec. 27, 1938; d. Fitzhugh and Eileen (Schlesinger) Scott; m. Kim Massie, July 10, 1965; children: Miranda, Luke. Student, Smith Coll., 1957-59; BA, U. Calif., Berkeley, 1961. Exhibited in group shows at Hudson Valley (N.Y.) Art Assn., 1981 (award 1981), Berkshire Mus., Pittsfield, Mass., 1981-82, Audubon Artist, Nat. Arts Club, N.Y.C., 1981, 83-85, Salmagundi Club, N.Y.C., 1983, 94 (Cert. of Merit award 1994), Allied Artists of Am., Nat. Arts Club, N.Y.C., 1988, 93 (Helen Open Oehler award for Graphics 1988, Nicholas Reale Meml. award for Graphics 1993), Knickerbocker Artists, N.Y.C., 1989, 90, 91, 93 (Philip Isenberg award for Graphics and Drawing 1991), Print Club of Albany, Schenectady (N.Y.) Mus., 1992, 95 (Cert. of Achievement award 1992, 95). Recipient First prize in Graphics, Barrett House, Dutchess County Art Assn., 1985. Home and Office: 452 Whitfield Rd Accord NY 12404

MASSON, GAYL ANGELA, airline pilot; b. L.A., Feb. 5, 1951; d. Jack Watson and Margaret Jean (Evans) M.; 1 child, Athena. BFA, U. So. Calif., 1970, MA, 1972, MPA, 1975, PhD, 1976. Lic. airline transport, seaplane, glider pilot, flight instr., flight engr. Pilot Antelope Valley Land Investment Co., Century City, Calif., 1972; ROTC flight instr. Claire Walters Flight Acad., Santa Monica, Calif., 1973; flight instr. Golden West Airways, Santa Monica, 1974; co-pilot Express Airways, LaMoore Naval Air Sta., Calif., 1975-76; charter pilot, instr. Shaw Airmotive, Orange County Airport, Calif., 1976; flight engr. Am. Airlines, Dallas, 1976-79, co-pilot, 1979-86, capt., 1986—; accident prevention counselor FAA, 1993—. Contbr. articles to profl. publs. Participant Powder Puff Derby, Angel Derby, Pacific Air Race and others. First woman type-rated on Boeing 747, also type-rated on DC-10, DC-9, Boeing 767, Boeing 757, Airbus-310. Mem. Airline Pilots Assn., Internat. Soc. Women Airline Pilots (charter), Ninety-Nines (past v.p. Smo Bay chpt.), Aerospace Med. Assn., Aerospace Human Factors Assn.

MASSOUD, SAMIA LAMIE, mathematics educator, computer systems analyst; b. Cairo, Egypt, July 1, 1959; d. Lamie and Lyla F. (Saad) M.; m. Erian A. Baskharone, Sept. 24, 1978; children: Richie, Bobby. BS, U. Garunis, Cairo, 1978; MS, U. Cin., 1980; PhD, Tex. A&M U., 1989. Cert. tchr., Ariz. Math. instr. U. Cin., 1979-80, Ariz. State U., Tempe, 1980-82; math. and computer sci. instr. Maricopa County Coll., Phoenix, 1982-85; systems analyst Tex. A&M U., College Station, 1987—, math. instr., 1992—; computer cons. Garrett Turbine Engine Co., Phoenix, 1984-85; presenter Conf. on Innovation, Phoenix, Coll., 1985, Am. Assn. Adult and Continuing Edn. Conf., Hollywood, Fla., 1986, Computer Literacy in Community, Tex. A&M U., 1990. Author: (software package) Steps in Solving Word Problems, 1983, (textbook) Calculus with Maple, 1994, Calculus with Mathematica, 1995; asst. editor: Computer Assisted Instruction, 1985, Lifelong Learning, 1986; contbr. articles to profl. jours. Instrnl. design coord. Maricopa County Coll. Dist., Phoenix, 1983. Grantee Funds for Improvement of Postsecondary Edn., 1984, Dist. Edn. and Devel. Projects, 1985. Mem. Am. Math. Soc., Assn. Computing Machinery, Acad. Computer Assn. Office: Tex A&M U Computing Info Sys College Station TX 77843

MASSURA, EILEEN KATHLEEN, family therapist; b. Chgo., July 25, 1925; d. John William and Loretta (Feil) Stratemeier; m. Edmund Karamanski, July 24, 1948 (dec.); children: John, Kathleen; m. Alfred Massura, Aug. 30, 1963; children: Michael, Kathryn, Mark. BS in Nursing, DePaul U., 1963; MS in Nursing, St. Xavier Coll., 1971. RN; cert. family therapist. Dir. nurses Franklin Blvd. Hosp., Chgo., 1958-62; adminstr. Mich. Ave Hosp., Chgo., 1962-64; instr. St. Xavier Coll., Chgo., 1972-74, Joliet (Ill.) Jr. Coll., 1972-81; family therapist Oak Lawn (Ill.) Family Svc., 1978-88; prof. nursing Govs. State U., University Park, Ill., 1981-89; family therapist McCarthy & Assocs., Oak Lawn, 1982-93, Massura & Assocs., Oak Lawn, 1994—; preceptor to grads. St. Xavier Coll., 1980-90, Govs. State U., 1980-89; co-leader Clin. Study Med./Surg. Nursing, Moscow, 1984; presenter Am. Nursing Rev., Ala., Fla., Va., Pa., Tex., Md., 1985-86. Leader Campfire Girls, Oak Lawn, 1964-74; co-leader Orient/Am. Med./Surg. Nursing, 1987; mem. Marist Women's Bd., Chgo., 1978-82, Bro. Rice Women's Bd., Chgo., 1969-72; Luth. Family Svc. Bd. Day Care for Srs., 1988-89. Grantee HEW, 1969-71; named Disting. Nurse Alumnae, St. Xavier Coll., 1985; named Nursing Prof. of Yr., Govs. State U., 1983. Mem. Am. Nurses Assn. (nominating com. 1982-87), Ill. Nurses Assn. (program com. 1980-84), Am. Assn. Marital and Family Therapists, Cath. Order Foresters, Sigma Theta Tau (v.p. 1971-75). Roman Catholic. Office: 5660 W 95th St Oak Lawn IL 60453-2380

MASSY, PATRICIA GRAHAM BIBBS (MRS. RICHARD OUTRAM MASSY), social worker, author; b. Newbury, Eng., Mar. 21, 1918; came to U.S., 1963, naturalized, 1969; d. Oswald Graham and Dorothy (French) Bibbs; m. Richard Outram Massy, July 22, 1944 (dec. Aug. 1986); children: Patricia Lynn Massy Holmes, Julie Suzanne, Shaun Adele Massy Brink. BA, U. B.C., 1941, MSW, 1962. With B.C. Welfare Field Svc., Vancouver, Kamloops, Abbottsford, 1942-44; social worker Brandon Welfare Dept., Man., Can., 1945; with Children's Aid Soc., Vancouver, 1948-62; supr. Dept. Pub. Social Svc., L.A., 1963-70, staff devel. specialist-mgmt., 1970-77; lectr. colls. and seminars; lectr. Rogue Coll., Grants Pass, 1990; author, publisher: A Study Guide for a Course in Miracles, 1984; One, 1985. Mem. AAUW (treas. 1970), Nat. Assn. Social Workers, Alpha Phi. Mem. Unity Ch. Home: 18936 Upper Cow Creek Rd Azalea OR 97410-9730

MAST, KANDE WHITE, artist; b. St. Louis, Mar. 10, 1950; d. Elliott Maxwell and Mary (Barritt) W. Student, U. Mo., 1968-70, Longview Community Coll., Kansas City, Mo., 1970-71. Free-lance artist Albany, N.Y., 1973-74, Kansas City, 1974—; dir., tchr. Studio Kande, Sch. Fine Arts, Kansas City, 1983-86; founder, exec. dir. Art Ctr. Kansas City, 1986-90. Pres., bd. dirs. Advocates for Children, Inc., 1996—; vol. Ozanam Home for Boys, Kansas City, 1987—, mem. adv. bd., 1991—. Mem. Nat. Mus. Women in the Arts, Greater Kansas City Art Assn. Home and Office: 10243 Cedarbrooke Ln Kansas City MO 64131-4209

MASTERMAN, MARGUERITE A. (MEG MASTERMAN), private school educator; b. Charlotte, N.C., Jan. 31, 1958; d. William Augustus and Gloria Jean (Surtman) Masterman; m. Harry Scott Scruggs, Mar. 14, 1989. BA in Art, U. N.C., Wilmington, 1987; student, U. N.C., Charlotte, 1989. Cert. tchr., N.C. Chief cartographer Champion Map Corp., Charlotte, 1980-85; graphic artist McKim & Creed, Wilmington, N.C., 1987-88; tchr. art, head dept. fine arts Charlotte Country Day Sch., 1990—. Author/artist Signet (Queens Coll. Publ.), 1977, 78. Chair Lakeview Homeowners Assn., Charlotte, 1994. World Affairs Coun. grantee, 1994. Mem. Nat. Art Edn. Assn., Sigma Upsilon. Democrat. Roman Catholic. Home: 9705 Myrtle Lynn Ct Charlotte NC 28213-3732 Office: Charlotte Country Day Sch 1440 Carmel Rd Charlotte NC 28226-5012

MASTERS, ELAINE, educator, writer; b. Kansas City, Kans., Oct. 6, 1932; d. David Shepherd and Stella Frances (Ragan) M.; m. Donald Ramon Masters, Apr. 27, 1951; children: David, Vicki, Jennifer, Kevin. BS in Edn. with honors, U. Mo., Kansas City, 1968. Cert. tchr., Mo., Va. Tchr. grade 4 Am. Sch., Manila, 1956-57; tchr. grade 5 Escuela Gloria Felix, Caracas, Venezuela, Venezuela, 1960-62; tchr. grade 6 Okinawa Christian Sch., Urasoe, 1968-70; tchr. grade 5 Flint Hill Elem. Sch., Vienna, Va., 1970-73; tchr. Bible Inst. Hawaii, Honolulu, 1991-92; dir. Christian edn. St. Thomas United Meth. Ch., 1983-84; tchr. children's ministries Salvation Army, Kaneohe, Hawaii, 1992-94; evangelist, Hong Kong, Malaysia, Nigeria, Thailand, Russia; seminar leader on Bible and Christian living, Hong Kong, Malaysia, Nigeria, Thailand; advisor Pentecostal Assemblies of Tribes, Chiang Mai, Thailand, 1991—; lectr. Christian Writers Workshop, 1993—. Author: Ali and the Ghost Tiger, 1967, Teach Us To Pray, 1970, Day Camp and Day Care Handbook, 1989; contbr. articles to mags. and newspapers; inventor cricket transposer tool for musicians. Mem. spkrs. bur. Alzheimer's Assn., Honolulu, 1991—. Mem. Women's Aglow Fellowship Internat., Nat. Writers Club, Soc. Children's Book Writers and Illustrators (regional advisor State of Hawaii 1996—). Home: 2355 Ala Wa Blvd Apt 502 Honolulu HI 96815-1809

MASTERSON, LINDA HISTEN, medical company executive; b. N.Y.C., May 21, 1951; d. George and Dorothy (Postler) Riddell; m. Robert P. Masterson, March 6, 1982; m. William J. Histen, May 24, 1971 (div. 1979). BS in med. tech., U. R.I., 1973; MS in microbiology, U. Md., 1977; student, Wharton U. Pa., Phila., 1988. Med. technologist various hosps., 1972-78; microbiology specialist Gen. Diagnostics, Warner-Lambert, Morris Plains, N.J., 1978-80; from tech. sales rep. to dir. internat. mktg. Micro-Scan, Baxter Internat., Sacramento, 1980-87; dir. mktg. Ortho Diagnostics, Johnson & Johnson, Raritan, N.J., 1987-89; sr. v.p. mktg/sales GenProbe, San Diego, 1989-92; v.p. mktg./sales Bio Star, Boulder, Colo., 1992-93; exec. v.p. Cholestech Inc., Hayward, Calif., 1994—; bd. dirs. U.S. Alcohol Testing of Am., Inc., Rancho Cucamonga, Calif. Tribute to women in industry Young Women's Christian Assn., N.J., 1989. Mem. Biomedical Mktg. Assn., Med. Mktg. Assn., Phi Kappa Phi. Office: Cholestech Inc 5347 Investment Blvd Hayward CA 94541-9999

MASTERSON, MARY STUART, actress; b. N.Y.C., June 29, 1966; d. Peter and Carlin Glynn Masterson. Theatre appearances include Alice in Wonderland, 1982, Been Taken, 1985, The Lucky Spot, 1987, Lily Dale, 1987; TV movies include Love Lives On, 1985, City in Fear, 1980, Lily Dale, 1996; films: The Stepford Wives, 1975, Heaven Help Us, 1984, At Close Range, 1985, My Little Girl, 1986, Gardens of Stone, 1987, Some Kind of Wonderful, 1987, Mr. North, 1988, Chances Are, 1989, Immediate Family, 1989, Funny About Love, 1990, Fried Green Tomatoes, 1991, Married To It, 1993, Benny and Joon, 1993, Bad Girls, 1994, Radioland Murders, 1994, Heaven's Prisoners, 1996, Bed of Roses, 1996. Office: Creative Artists Agency 9830 Wilshire Blvd Beverly Hills CA 90212*

MASTERSON, PATRICIA O'MALLEY, publications editor, writer; b. Worcester, Mass., May 15, 1952; d. Paul Francis and Dorothy M. (O'Malley) M. BFA, Emerson Coll., 1974; MA, Goddard Coll., 1980. Reporter, photographer Patriot Newspaper, Webster, Mass., 1975-78; pub. relations dir. Mt. Pleasant Hosp., Lynn, Mass., 1980-84; pubs. editor Ocean Spray Cranberries, Inc., Plymouth, Mass., 1984-89; mktg. comms. coord. Groundwater Tech., Norwood, Mass., 1989-93; pres. O'Malley Masterson Comm., Belmont, Mass., 1993—; freelance writer newspaper and mag. articles, 1974—. Mem. adv. bd. Ad. Com. mag.; contbr. numerous articles to newspapers, mags.; stringer Hanover (Mass.) Mariner Newspaper, 1987-91. Bd. dirs. YWCA, Cambridge, Mass., 1982-86; elected Nat. Alumni Assn., Emerson Coll., 1994—, chair student rels. com.; judge Coop. Info. Fair, 1992; mem. publicity com. Healthworks, United Way, 1987; pres. Softball Leagues, Abington, Mass., 1991-92; vol. Rosie's Homeless Shelter, Boston, 1987-93. Recipient Amy England award YWCA, 1986, Green Eyeshade award Internat. Assn. Bus. Communicators, 1987, Yankee Ingenuity award Internat. Assn. Bus. Communicators, 1991, Employee Pub. 2d Place award Cooperative Info. Fair, 1987, 88, Membership Mag. award Cooperative Info. Fair, 1988; named One of Outstanding Young Women in Am. Jaycees, 1983, MVP Northeast Regional Women's Softball Championship, 1995. Mem. Internat. Assn. Bus. Communicators (ann. internat. conf. planning bd. 1993-94, accredited 1993—, mem. accreditation bd. 1995—), South Shore Ad Club (publicity com., newsletter com., 9th Wave award 1987, 89, 92, judge 9th Wave awards 1994), Coop. Communicators Assn. (1st pl. employee publ. award 1987, 3rd pl. mag. award 1989, participant Boston to N.Y. AIDS bicycle ride). Home: 1690 Centre St West Roxbury MA 02132-2305

MASTERTON, PAULINE MERBITZ, writer, publisher; b. Chgo., Oct. 20, 1931; d. Arnold Gustav and Helen Elizabeth (Scherbarth) Merbitz; m. R. Bruce Masterton, Jan. 5, 1951; children: Christopher E., Alexander S., Benjamin A. BEd, Chgo. State U., 1953; MEd, U. Chgo., 1958; PhD, Fla. State U., 1981. Cert. tchr., Ill., Ind., N.C., Tenn., Fla. Elem. tchr. Chgo. Pub. Schs., 1953, Valparaiso (Ind.) City Schs., 1956-59, Durham (N.C.) City Schs., 1960-63, Metro Nashville Schs., 1964-67; edn. cons. Fla. State U., Tallahassee, 1968-70; assoc. for tchr. edn. State of Fla., Tallahassee, 1970-76, assoc. for policy analysis, 1976-87; editor, columnist Snap Mag., Tallahassee, 1989-91; editor, freelance author Multiverse Press and other publs., 1989—; cons. for evaluation Nat. Assn. Retarded Citizens, Tallahassee and Washington, 1977-80; cons. for planning Nat. Telecom. Inst. Adminstrn., Washington, 1979-80; bd. dirs., coord. Fla. Coun. on Tchr. Aides, Tallahassee, 1981-83; bd. dirs., pres. World Future Soc., Tallahassee, 1978-88. Author, editor (poetry books) Multiverse Press, 1991—; author, editor Snap Mag., 1989-91, Panarama Mag., 1993; contbr. articles to profl. jours. Bd. dirs., pres. Tallahassee Futures Group, 1981-83; coord., leadership com. Fla. Endowment for Humanities, Tallahassee, 1982; bd. dirs., pres. Unitarian Universalist Ch. Tallahassee, 1986-87. Recipient Media for Tchrs. grant 3-M Co., 1964, Edn. Policy fellowship George Washington U., 1979, numerous poetry awards, 1988-95. Mem. Tallahassee Writers Assn. (v.p. 1987-88, pres. 1989-90, at-large bd. 1994-96).

MASTNY-FOX, CATHERINE LOUISE, administrator, consultant; b. New Rochelle, N.Y., June 4, 1939; d. Louis Francis and Catherine Marie (Haage) Kacmarynski; m. Vojtech Mastny, July 25, 1964 (div. Oct. 1987); m. Richard K. Fox, Oct. 10, 1993; children: Catherine Paula (dec.), John Adalbert (dec.), Elizabeth Louise. BA magna cum laude, Coll. New Rochelle, 1961; MA, Columbia U., 1963, PhD, 1968. Lectr. in history various colls., N.Y. and Calif., 1968-71; researcher, writer H. W. Wilson Co., N.Y.C., 1971-81; contbg. editor Columbia U. Press, N.Y.C., 1972-74; v.p., exec. dir. Internat. Mgmt. and Devel. Inst., Washington, 1978-84, exec. dir., spl. asst. to chmn., 1986-91; v.p. Meridian House Internat., Washington, 1984-85; dir. corp. devel. Washington Music Ensemble, 1991—, also bd. dirs.; cons. in field; panelist NEH, Washington, 1983; internat. advisor Global Nomads, Washington, 1990—. Contbg. author: The American Book of Days, 1978, World Authors, 1970-1971, 1980; contbg. editor: Columbia Ency., 3d edit., 1975. Fulbright Found. grantee, 1961-62; fellow Woodrow Wilson Found., 1962-63, Walter L. Dorn, 1963-64, Konrad Adenauer fellow, 1965-66. Democrat. Roman Catholic. Home: 5102 Wyoming Rd Bethesda MD 20816-2267

MASTON, KAREN KAY, lawyer; b. Kansas City, Mo., Apr. 16, 1956. BS magna cum laude, U. Mo., 1978; JD, U. Tex., 1986. Bar: Tex. 1986. Ptnr. Baker & Botts L.L.P., Houston. Mem. State Bar Tex., Houston Bar Assn., Phi Delta Phi, Kappa Delta Pi, Phi Eta Sigma. Office: Baker & Botts LLP 1 Shell Plz 910 Louisiana Houston TX 77002*

MASTRANGELO, BOBBI, artist, educator; b. Youngstown, Ohio, May 16, 1937; d. Herman Louis and Martha Bertha (Krause) Betschen; m. Alfred Anthony Mastrangelo, Dec. 20, 1958; children: Michael, Peter, Ann Marie. BS cum laude, SUNY, Buffalo, 1959. One-woman shows include Port Washington (N.Y.) Libr. Gallery, 1987, East End Arts Coun., Riverhead, N.Y., 1991, Suffolk County Water Auth., Oakdale, N.Y., 1993—, N.Y. Hall of Sci., Corona, 1994, Mus. Pub. Works, Balt., 1996; group shows include N.Y. Acad. Sci., N.Y.C., 1991, Del. Bello Gallery, Toronto, Ont., Can., 1991-92, Adelphi U., Garden City, N.Y., 1992, Staller Ctr. for Arts, Stony Brook, N.Y., 1992, Emerson Gallery, Hamilton Coll., Clinton, N.Y., 1995; represented in permanent collections Balt. Pub. Works Mus., Heckscher Mus., Huntington, N.Y., Islip (N.Y.) Mus., N.Y.C. Fire Mus., Nat. Assn. Women Artists Permanent Collection, Jane Voorhees A. Zimmerli Art Mus., Rutgers U., others. Founder Com. for Litter Elimination and Neatness, 1986, chairperson, 1986-88. Grantee N.Y. Found. for Arts, 1992, 94; Paul Harris fellow Rotary Internat., 1996; recipient Disting. Alumni award Maryvale H.S., 1994. Mem. Nat. Assn. Women Artists (Eva Helman award 1992), Nat. Mus. Women in Arts, Guild Hall Artists, Arts and Sci. Collaboration, Smithtown Twp. Arts Coun. Home: 21 Princess Tree Ct Port Jefferson NY 11777-1741

MASTRANTONIO, MARY ELIZABETH, actress; b. Lombard, Ill., Nov. 17, 1958; d. Frank A. and Mary D. (Pagone) M. Student, U. Ill., 1976-78. Actress: (stage prodns.) Copperfield, 1981, Oh, Brother, 1981, Amadeus, 1982, Sunday in the Park with George, 1983, The Human Comedy, 1984, Henry V, 1984, Measure for Measure, 1985, The Knife, 1987, Twelfth Night, (feature films) Scarface, 1983, The Color of Money, 1986 (Acad. award nomination 1986), The January Man, 1989, The Abyss, 1989, Fools of Fortune, 1990, Class Action, 1991, Robin Hood: Prince of Thieves, 1991, Consenting Adults, 1992, White Sands, 1992, Three Wishes, 1995; (TV movie) Mussolini: The Untold Story, 1985, Two Bits, 1995. Office: Internat Creative Mgmt 8942 Wilshire Blvd Beverly Hills CA 90211-1934*

MASTROIANNI, CAROLYN ANN, artist; b. Evansville, Ind., Nov. 21, 1945; d. Walter Louis and Loretta Anna (Mertz) Stegeman; m. Joseph Robert Mastroanni, Dec. 21, 1968; children: Catherine Ann, Michael Robert. BS, S.D. State U., 1968; MA, No. Ill. U., 1994. Art, math. educator Rockford (Ill.) Sch. Dist., 1968-69; art educator Freeport (Ill.) Sch. Dist., 1969-72; dir. Freeport Art Mus., 1987; salesperson Chpt. One Books, Freeport, 199-95; art instr. Highland C.C., Freeport, 1996. Bd. dirs. Freeport Cmty. Pub. Sch. Fund, 1983-96. Mem. Freeport Shakespeare Soc. Lutheran.

MATALIN, MARY, political consultant; d. Steven and Eileen Matalin; m. Artie Arnold (div.); m. James Carville, Nov. 25, 1993. Grad., Western Ill. Univ.; student, Hofstra Univ. With the Rep. Nat. Com., since the early 80's; polit. dir. George Bush's 1992 re-election campaign. Co-host, CNBC talk show Equal Time, 1993—; author: (with James Carville) All's Fair, 1994. *

MATAN, LILLIAN KATHLEEN, educator, designer; b. Boston, Aug. 18, 1937; d. George Francis and Lillian May (Herbert) Archambault; m. Joseph A. Matan, Aug. 6, 1960; children: Maria, Meg, Tony, Elizabeth, Joan, Molly. BS, Seton Hall Coll., 1960; MA, San Francisco State U., 1984; postgrad. studies, U. San Francisco. Tchr. St. Jone de Chantal, Bethesda, Md., 1956-60; tchr. home econs. Surrottsville (Md.) H.S., 1960-61; tchr., head home econs. dept. Bruswick (Md.) H.S., 1972-73; designer Dudley Kelley and Assocs., San Francisco, Calif., 1976-84; designer (prin.) K. Matan Antiques and Interiors, Ross, Calif., 1985-87; designer Charles Lester Assocs., San Francisco, 1987-88; dean of students St. Rose Acad., San Francisco, 1988-90; dir., asst. devel. The Branson Sch., Ross, Calif., 1990-92; prin. St. Anselm Sch., San Anselmo, Calif., 1993-94; adminstrv. head Ring Mt. Day Sch., Tiburon, Calif., 1995—; ednl. cons. Head Start, Frederick County, Md., 1972-73. Pres. Cath. Charities, Marin County, Calif.; mem. Ecumenical Assn. for Housing, Marin County. Mem. KM (dame), ASCD, Am. Assn. Interior Design (cert. interior designer Calif.), Am. Assn. Family and Consumer Scis., Serra Club, Phi Delta Kappa. Democrat. Roman Catholic. Home: PO Box 1140 Ross CA 94957 Office: Ring Mountain Day Sch 215A Blackfield Dr Tiburon CA 94920

MATAPENE-STAGGS, PENNY LYNNE, dialysis nurse; b. Ft. Sill, Okla., Mar. 29, 1962; d. Megal and Betty Louise (Fortune) Matapene; m. James Brian Staggs, Apr. 6, 1991. AS, Seminole Jr. Coll., 1982; BS, East Ctrl. U., 1985. RN, CNN, Okla. Staff nurse med.-surg. S.W. Med. Ctr., Oklahoma City, 1985-87, asst. patient care mgr., 1987-88; staff nurse continuous ambulatory peritoneal dialysis Bapt. Med. Ctr., Oklahoma City, 1988-93, team leader continuous ambulatory peritoneal dialysis, 19926, clin. career advancement program level I, 1994-95, clin. career advancement program level III, 1995—. Vol. nurse Bapt. Med. Ctr. Free Clinic, 1994—. Mem. Am. Nephrology Nurses Assn. Democrat. Baptist. Home: 20921 Silver St Harrah OK 73045-9736 Office: Bapt Med Ctr 3435 NW 56th St Ste 600 Oklahoma City OK 73112-4934

MATASAR, ANN B., former dean, business and political science educator; b. N.Y.C., June 27, 1940; d. Harry and Tillie (Simon) Bergman; m. Robert Matasar, June 9, 1962; children—Seth Gideon, Toby Rachel. AB, Vassar Coll., 1962; MA, Columbia U., 1964, PhD, 1968; M of Mgmt. in Fin., Northwestern U., 1977. Assoc. prof. Mundelein Coll., Chgo., 1965-78; prof., dir. Ctr. for Bus. and Econ. Elmhurst Coll., Elmhurst, Ill., 1978-84; dean Roosevelt U., Chgo., 1984-92; prof. Internat. Bus. and Fin. Walter E. Heller Coll. Bus. Adminstrn. Roosevelt U., 1992—; dir. Corp. Responsibility Group, Chgo., 1978-84; chmn. long range planning Ill. Bar Assn., 1982-83; mem. edn. com. Ill. Commn. on the Status of Women, 1978-81. Author: Corporate PACS and Federal Campaign Financing Laws: Use or Abuse of Power?, 1986; (with others) Research Guide to Women's Studies, 1974. Contbr. articles to profl. jours. Dem. candidate 1st legis. dist. Ill. State Senate, no. suburbs Chgo., 1972; mem. Dem. exec. com. New Trier Twp., Ill., 1972-76; rsch. dir., acad. advisor Congressman Abner Mikva, Ill., 1974-76; bd. dirs. Ctr. Ethics and Corp. Policy, 1985-90. Named Chgo. Woman of Achievement Mayor of Chgo., 1978. Fellow AAUW (trustee ednl. found. 1992—, v.p. fin.); mem. Am. Polit. Sci. Assn., Midwest Bus. Adminstrn. Assn., Acad. Mgmt., Women's Caucus for Polit. Sci. (pres. 1980-81), John Howard Assn. (bd. dirs. 1986-90), Am. Assembly of Coll. Schs. of Bus. (bd. dirs. 1989-92, chair com. on diversity in mgmt. edn. 1991-92), North Ctrl. Assn. (commr. 1994—), Beta Gamma Sigma. Democrat. Jewish. Office: Roosevelt U Coll Bus Adminstrn Dept Fin 430 S Michigan Ave Chicago IL 60605-1301

MATASEJE, VERONICA JULIA, sales executive; b. St. Ann's, Ontario, Can., Apr. 5, 1949; came to U.S., 1985; d. John and Anna Veronica M. Grad. H.S., Smithville, Can. Clk. typist, typesetter Crown Life Ins. Co., Toronto, Can., 1966-70; typesetter Toronto Life/Calendar Mag., 1970-71; typesetter, exec. sec. Cerebrus Prodns. Ltd., Toronto, 1971-74; pres. Veron Prodns. Ltd., Toronto, 1975-81, Acclaim Records Inc., Toronto, 1981-88; pvt. health care provider Las Vegas, Nev., 1989-94; retail sales mgr. Top Cats, Las Vegas, Nev., 1994—. Campaign vol. Dist. Atty., Las Vegas, 1994; vol. pilot Angel Planes, Las Vegas, 1989. Home: 4326 Caliente St Las Vegas NV 89119-5801 Office: Top Cats PO Box 61173 Las Vegas NV 89160-1173

MATASOVIC, MARILYN ESTELLE, business executive; b. Chgo., Jan. 7, 1946; d. John Lewis and Stella (Butkauskas) M. Student, U. Colo. Sch. Bus., 1963-69. Owner, pres. UTE Trail Ranch, Ridgway, Colo., 1967—; pres. MEM Equipment Co., Mokena, Ill., 1979—; sec./treas. Marlin Corp., Ridgway, 1991—, v.p., sec.-treas., 1991—; sec.-treas. Linmar Corp., Mokena, 1991-93, pres., 1994—; ptnr. Universal Welding Supply Co., New Lenox, Ill., 1964-90; v.p. OXO Welding Equipment Co, Inc., New Lenox, 1964-90; ptnr. Universal Internat., Mokena, Ill., 1990—; ind. travel agt. Ideal Travel Concepts, Mokena, Ill., 1994—. Co-editor newsletters. U.S. rep. World Hereford Conf., 1964, 68, 76, 80, 84, 96. Mem. Am. Hereford Aux. (charter, bd. dirs. 1989-94, historian 1990-92, v.p. 1992, pres.-elect 1993, pres. 1994), Am. Hereford Assn., Am. Hereford Women (charter, pres. 1994, bd. dirs. 1994—), Am. Agri-Women, Colo. Hereford Aux., Ill. Hereford Aux. (v.p. 1969-70), U. Colo. Alumni Assn., Ill. Agri-Women, Las Vegas Social Register.

MATEJ, ELAINE DIANE, critical care nurse; b. Berea, Ohio, Dec. 19, 1951; d. Joseph J. and Helen M. Elek; m. Jonathan R. Matej, June 1, 1996; children by previous marriage: Jennifer, Rachel, Derek. Diploma in nursing, Fairview Hosp., Cleve., 1981; BSN, Ursuline Coll., 1992. RN, Ohio; cert. CCRN; cert. BCLS. ICU staff nurse Cleve. Clinic, 1981—; cons. Wm. McCarter, Esq., Concord, Ohio, 1992—. Vol. Kirtland (Ohio) Elem. Sch., 1989—. With U.S. Army Res., 1990—. Mem. AACN, Res. Officers Assn., Assn. Mil. Surgeons U.S., Sigma Theta Tau (bd. dirs. Iota Psi chpt. 1993-95). Republican. Home: PO Box 26 Chesterland OH 44026-0026

MATER, MAUD E., federal agency administrator, lawyer. BA in English, Case Western Reserve U., 1969, JD, 1972. Asst. gen. counsel Fed. Home Loan Mortgage Corp., 1976-78, assoc. gen. counsel, 1978-79, dep. gen. counsel, 1979-81, v.p., dep. gen. counsel, 1981-84, sr. v.p., gen. counsel, sec., 1984—. Mem. ABA, Fed. Bar Assn., Ohio Bar Assn., D.C. Bar Assn., Washington Met. Corp. Counsels Assn. (dir., sec.). Office: Fed Home Loan Mortgage Corp 8200 Jones Branch Dr Mc Lean VA 22102-3107*

MATERA, FRANCES LORINE, elementary educator; b. Eustis, Nebr., June 28, 1926; d. Frank Daniel and Marie Mathilda (Hess) Daiss; m. Daniel Matera, Dec. 27, 1973; children: Richard William Post, Mary Jane Post Craig. BS in Edn., Concordia Tchrs. Coll., Seward, Nebr., 1956; MEd, U. Oreg., 1963; Luth. tchrs. diploma, Concordia Tchrs. Coll., Seward, 1947. Elementary tchr. Our Savior's Luth. Ch., Colorado Springs, Colo., 1954-57; tchr. 5th grade Monterey (Calif.) Pub. Schs., 1957-59; tchr. 1st grade Roseburg (Oreg.) Schs., 1959-60; tchr. several schs. Palm Springs (Calif.) Unified Sch. Dist., 1960-73; tchr. 3rd grade Vista del Monte Sch., Palm

Springs, Calif., 1973-93; ret., 1993. Named Tchr. of the Yr., Palm Springs Unified Schs. Mem. Kappa Kappa Iota (chpt. and state pres.).

MATERIA, KATHLEEN PATRICIA AYLING, nurse; b. Jersey City, Nov. 7, 1954; d. Donald Anthony and Muriel Cecilia (Joyce) Ayling; m. Francis Peter Materia, June 5, 1983; children: Christopher Michael, Donna Nicole. BS in Nursing, Fairleigh Dickinson U., 1976. RN. Critical care nurse Palisades Gen. Hosp., North Bergen, N.J., 1976-87, grad. nurse, 1976-77; nurse CCU, North Hudson Hosp., Weehawken, N.J., 1977-78. Mem. Alpha Sigma Tau. Democrat. Roman Catholic. Avocations: bowling, dancing.

MATES, SUSAN ONTHANK, medical educator, physician, writer, violinist; b. Oakland, Calif., Aug. 8, 1950; d. Benson and Lois (Onthank) M.; m. Joseph Harold Friedman, Dec. 10, 1978; children: Rebecca, Deborah, William. Student, Juilliard Sch. Music, 1967-69; BA magna cum laude with distinction, Yale Coll., 1972; MD, Albert Einstein Coll. Medicine, 1976. Cert. Am. Bd. Internal Medicine, Nat. Bd. Med. Examiners. Intern Boston City Hosp., 1976-77; fellow in gen. medicine Coll. of Physicians and Surgeons-Columbia U., N.Y.C., 1977-78; resident/fellow in infectious diseases Montefiore Hosp., Bronx, 1978-82; asst. prof. medicine Brown U., Providence, 1982-85, asst. prof. biochemistry, 1985-86, clin. assoc. prof. medicine, 1993—; staff mem., former dir. R.I. State Tuberculosis Ctr. R.I. Dept. Health, Providence, 1986—; cons. tuberculosis program R.I. Dept. Health, Providence, 1987—; judge short story contest Providence Jour., 1994; contbg. editor Pushcart Prize, Pushcart Press, 1995, 96. Author: (fiction) The Good Doctor, 1994 (Iowa Short Fiction award 1994); contbr. stories to revs. and jours. (Pushcart prize 1990, John Simmons Short Fiction award). Founding mem. Barrington Ednl. Com., 1993. Recipient Recognition award for young scholars AAUW, 1985, Clin. Investigator award NIH, 1984, R.I. Found. award, 1983; McDowell Colony fellow, 1995, Yaddo fellow, 1996. Mem. Am. Med. Women's Assn., Poets and Writers, Alpha Omega Alpha. Home: 52 Bluff Rd Barrington RI 02806 Office: R I State TB Clinic 877 Chalkstone Ave Providence RI 02908

MATESICH, SISTER MARY ANDREW, college president; b. Zanesville, Ohio, May 5, 1939. BA, Ohio Dominican Coll., 1962; MS, U. Calif., Berkeley, 1963, PhD in Chemistry, 1966. Asst. prof. chemistry Ohio Dominican Coll., Columbus, 1965-70, assoc. prof., from 1970, chmn. dept., 1965-73, acad. dean, 1973-78, pres., 1978—. Petroleum Research Fund grantee Ohio Dominican Coll., 1965-68; NSF grantee Case Western Res. U. and Ohio Dominican Coll., 1969-72. Mem. Council Ind. Colls. (bd. dirs. 1985—), Nat. Assn. Ind. Colls. and Univs. (bd. dirs. 1986—), Assn. Ind. Colls. and Univs. Ohio (chmn. 1984-86). Office: Ohio Dominican Coll Office of the President 1216 Sunbury Rd Columbus OH 43219-2099

MATEUS, LOIS, manufacturing executive; b. 1946. Grad., U. Ky., 1968. Asst. mgr. advt. Begley Drug, 1969-70; staff writer Commonwealth of Ky., 1970-72; dir. pub. rels. Ky. Dem. Party, 1973-75; exec. dir. Hist. Events Celebration Commn., 1976; free-lance writer, 1977-79; press sec., various other adminstrv. positions Gov. John Y. Brown of Ky., 1979-82; sr. v.p. corp. communications and corp. svcs. Brown-Forman Corp., Louisville, 1982—. Office: Brown-Forman Corp 850 Dixie Hwy Louisville KY 40210-1038*

MATHAI-DAVIS, PREMA ANNA, association executive; b. Thiruvalla, Kerala, India, Oct. 28, 1950; came to U.S., 1974; d. Stephen and Susy (Kovoor) Mathai; m. Wallace Mathai-Davis, Oct. 15, 1978; children: Stephen, Lisa, Tara. BS, Delhi U., 1970, MS, 1972; EdD, Harvard U., 1979. Family and child care specialist Grail Internat., New Delhi, 1972-73; instr. Samoa Coll., Western Samoa, 1973-74; project dir., rsch. assoc. Grad. Sch. Edn. Harvard U., Cambridge, Mass., 1978-79; dir. Gerontology Ctr. Mt. Sinai-Hunter Coll., N.Y.C., 1979-81; dir. S.I. social svc. programs Cmty. Svc. Soc., N.Y.C., 1981-85; pres., CEO Cmty. Agy. for Sr. Citizens, Inc., S.I., 1985-90; commr. City of N.Y. Dept. Aging, 1990-94; nat. exec. dir. YWCA of U.S., N.Y.C., 1994—; bd. dirs. Health Sys. Agy. of N.Y.C., 1990-94; vis. lectr. Sch. Social Sci. Bhopal U., India, 1972-73; mem. adv. coun. N.Y. State Assembly Com. on Aging; chair policy com. N.Y. State Assn. of Area Agencies on Aging; vis. fellow New Sch. Social Rsch.. Bd. dirs. Met. Transp. Authority State of N.Y., N.Y.C., 1991-95. Recipient Staten Island Borough medallion, 1995, numerous other awards; named Woman of Yr., Ms. mag., 1995. Fellow N.Y. Acad. Medicine; mem. Asian Am. Forum of N.Y. (bd. dirs.), Women's Forum. Episcopalian. Office: YWCA of the USA 726 Broadway New York NY 10003-9511

MATHAY, MARY FRANCES, marketing executive; b. Youngstown, Ohio, July 26, 1944; d. Howard E. and Mary C. (Siple) M.; m. Thomas Stone Withgott, Dec. 20, 1969 (div. June 1973). BA in English Lit. and Composition, Queens Coll., 1967; grad. in bus., Katharine Gibbs Sch., 1968. Corp. mktg. mgr., assoc. Odell Assocs., Inc., Charlotte, N.C., 1973-90; dir. pub. rels. and spl. events Charlotte (N.C.)-Mecklenburg Arts and Sci. Coun., 1990-92; pres. Mathay Comm., Inc., Charlotte, 1992—; speakers bur. chmn. Hospice at Charlotte, Inc., 1980-83; pub. rels. and advt. dir. "Chemical People" program PBS, Charlotte, 1983-84. Author: Legacy of Architecture, 1988; editor: Mint Mus. Antiques Show Mag., 1980, editorial advisor Crier, 1987-92; producer Charlotte's Web, 1977. Bd. dirs. Jr. League of Charlotte, Inc., 1978-79, mem. 1968—; bd. dirs. ECO, Inc., Charlotte, 1979-86, Queens Coll. Alumni, Charlotte, 1984-87, Learning How, Inc., Charlotte, 1988-91; bd. dirs. on adolescent pregnancy Mecklenburg County Coun., 1986-88; vol. tchr. ABLE Cen. Piedmont C.C., 1987-90; comm. com. vol. Am. Cancer Soc., 1994—, Charlotte-Mecklenburg Edn. Found., 1992-94, Charlotte-Mecklenburg Sr. Ctrs., 1994—. Mem. Pub. Rels. Soc. Am. (bd. dirs. 1989—, pres. 1995), Charlotte Pub. Rels. Soc. (bd. dirs. 1986-89, 92-93), Olde Providence Racquet Club, Tower Club. Republican. Presbyterian.

MATHENY, RUTH ANN, editor; b. Fargo, N.D., Jan. 17, 1918; d. Jasper Gordon and Mary Elizabeth (Carey) Wheelock; m. Charles Edward Matheny, Oct. 24, 1960. B.E., Mankato State Coll., 1938; M.A., U. Minn., 1955; postgrad., Universidad Autonoma de Guadalajara, Mex., summer 1956, Georgetown U., summer, 1960. Tchr. in U.S. and S.Am., 1938-61; asso. editor Charles E. Merrill Pub. Co., Columbus, Ohio, 1963-66; tchr. Confraternity Christian Doctrine, Washington Court House, Ohio, 1969-70; assoc. editor Jr. Cath. Messenger, Dayton, Ohio, 1966-68; editor Witness Intermediate, Dayton, 1968-70; editor in chief, assoc. pub. Today's Cath. Tchr., Dayton, 1970—; editor in chief Catechist, Dayton, 1976-89, Ednl. Dealer, Dayton, 1976-80; v.p. Peter Li, Inc., Dayton, 1980—. Editorial collaborator: Dimensions of Personality series, 1969—; co-author: At Ease in the Classroom; author: Why a Catholic School?, Scripture Stories for Today: Why Religious Education?. Mem. Bd. Friends Ormond Beach Library. Mem. Nat. League Am. Pen Women, Nat. Coun. Cath. Women, Cath. Press Assn., Nat. Cath. Ednl. Assn., 3d Order St. Francis (eucharistic minister 1990—). Home: 26 Reynolds Ave Ormond Beach FL 32174-7143 Office: Peter Li Inc 330 Progress Rd Dayton OH 45449-2322

MATHER, ELIZABETH VIVIAN, health care executive; b. Richmond, Ind., Sept. 19, 1941; d. Willie Samuel and Lillie Mae (Harper) Fuqua; m. Roland Donald Mather, Dec. 26, 1966. BS, Maryville (Tenn.) Coll., 1963; postgrad., Columbia U., 1965-66. Tchr. Richmond Community Schs., 1963-67, Indpls. Pub. Schs., 1967-68; systems analyst Ind. Blue Cross Blue Shield, Indpls., 1968-71, Ind. Nat. Bank, Indpls., 1971; med. cons. Ind. State Dept. Pub. Welfare, Indpls., 1971-78, cons. supr., 1978-86; systems analyst Ky. Blue Cross Blue Shield, Louisville, 1988-89; contracts specialist Humana Corp., Louisville, 1989—. Active Rep. Cen. Com. Montgomery County, Crawfordsville, 1976-86, Centenary Meth. Ch., adminstrv. bd., 1990. Mem. DAR (treas. 1963-66, sec. 1978-86). Home: 6106 Partridge Pl Floyds Knob IN 47119 Office: Humana Corp 500 W Main St Louisville KY 40201-1438

MATHER, STEPHANIE J., lawyer; b. Kansas City, Mo., Dec. 5, 1952; d. Edward Wayne and H. June (Kunkel) M.; m. Miles Christopher Zimmerman, Sept. 23, 1988. BA magna cum laude, Okla. City U., 1975, JD with honors, 1980. Lawyer Pierce, Couch, Hendrickson, Johnston & Baysinger, Okla. City, Okla., 1980-88, Manchester, Hiltgen & Healy, P.C., Okla. City, 1989-90; sr. staff counsel Nat. Am. Ins. Co., Chandler, Okla., 1990—; asst. v.p. Lagere & Walkingstick Ins. Agy., Inc., Chandler, Okla., 1993—. Co-chair Lincoln County Dem. Party, 1991-92, 95—; v.p. Lincoln County Dem. Women, 1992-95, pres., 1995—; bd. dirs. Lincoln County Partnership for Chidlren, 1994—, Gateway to Prevention and Recovery, 1996—. Mem. Okla. Bar Assn. (editor, bd. editors 1992—), Lincoln County Bar Assn. (mem. libr. bd. 1990—), Lincoln County Profl. Women, Alpha Phi. Democrat. Home: PO Box 246 Chandler OK 74834-0246 Office: Nat Am Ins Co PO Box 9 Chandler OK 74834-0009

MATHERS, MARGARET, charitable agency consultant, political activist; b. Ada, Okla., Feb. 16, 1929; d. Robert Lee and Josiephine Margaret (Reed) Erwin; m. Coleman F. Moss, Sept. 1956 (div. 1966); children: Carol Lee Doria, Marilyn Frances; m. Boyd Leroy Mathers, Apr. 10, 1967. BS in Music, Tex. U., 1950. Svc. rep. Gen. Tel. Co., Santa Monica, Calif., 1955-58; tchr. pvt. sch., Santa Monica, 1958-60; computer program and data analyst System Devel. Corp., Santa Monica, 1961-66; computer programmer Inst. Def. Analyses, Arlington, Va., 1966-70; typist, transcriber, Edgewater, Md., 1971-80; sec. People Assisting the Homeless, 1992-94, bd. dirs., 1985-95; asst. dir. San Juan Cath. Charities, Farmington, N.Mex., 1993—; sec. Cmty. Network Coun., 1992-94, treas. 1994—; pres. San Juan Coun. Cmty. Agys., 1986-87, treas., 1987-89, 92—, sec., 1989-90; pres. Davidsonville-Mayo Health Assn., Edgewater, 1973-76, 77-80; cons. in field, 1983—. Chmn. county Libertarian Party of N.Mex., San Juan County, 1985, sec. ctrl. com., 1988-92, mem. ctrl. com., 1988—; asst. sec. Our Lady of Perpetual Help, Parish Coun., Edgewater, 1979-82, Parish Coun. Sacred Heart, Farmington, 1987, sec., 1988-90, mem. social justice com., 1992; mem. adv. bd. San Juan County DNA Legal Aid, 1992, sec., 1993; sec. River Club Community Assn., Edgewater, 1975-82; mem. selection com. Habitat for Humanity, 1990; mem. San Juan County Task Force on Housing, 1991, Task Force on Transp., 1991; sec. Com. Preserve 2d Amendment Rights, 1994. Mem. Informed Citizens Alliance, Secular Franciscan Order. Roman Catholic. Avocations: nature study, birdwatching, reading, music, Indian studies. Office: San Juan Cath Charities 119 W Broadway Farmington NM 87401-6419

MATHES, CARYN G., broadcast executive; b. Terre Haute, Ind., Jan. 10, 1955; d. Robert Nathaniel and Carcelia James (Rudy) M; m. Charles David Stanley, Oct. 18, 1975 (div. June 1980), m. Phillip James Lesky, Jan. 9, 1993. BS in Print Journalism, Ind. State U., 1976. News anchor, reporter Sta. WTHI-TV, Terre Haute, 1974-78, Sta. WCKY-AM, Cin., 1978-80, Sta. WJR-AM, Detroit, 1980-82; news dir. Sta. WDET-FM, Detroit, 1982-84, gen. mgr., 1984—. Sec. Mich. Corp. for Pub. Broadcasting, 1986—; pres. Mich. Pub. Radio Network. Recipient Minority Achievement award Detroit YMCA, 1986. Baptist. Office: Sta WDET-FM 4600 Cass Ave Fl 1 Detroit MI 48201-3400*

MATHES, DOROTHY JEAN HOLDEN, occupational therapist; b. Paterson, N.J., Mar. 13, 1953; d. Cornelius Fred and Dorothy Johanna (Ferguson) Holden; m. Clayton Derald Mathes, May 26, 1973 (div. Dec. 1984); children: Christy, Carl, Chuck, Chad; m. Elie Youssef Hajjar, Oct. 4, 1989. BS in Occupational Therapy, Tex. Woman's U., Denton, Tex., 1988; MA in Occupational Therapy, Tex. Woman's U., 1995. Lic. occupational therapist, Tex.; cert. pediatric occupational therapist. Occupational therapy cons. Lakes Regional -SOCS, ECI, 1988—. Mem. Am. Occupational Therapy Assn., Tex. Occupational Therapy Assn. Home: 2608 Woodhaven St Denton TX 76201-1340 Office: Lakes Regional SOCS-ECI 3969 Teasley Lane Denton TX 76205

MATHESON, LINDA, retired clinical social worker; b. Martna, Estonia, Dec. 29, 1918; came to U.S., 1962, naturalized, 1969; d. Endrek and Leena Endrekson; m. Charles McLaren Matheson, Feb. 5, 1955. Diploma, Inst. for Social Scis., Tallinn, Estonia, 1944; MS, Columbia U., 1966; D in Social Work, Columbia U., 1974. Diplomate clin. social work. Social work officer UN Rehab. and Resettlement Assn., Germany, 1946-48; social worker Victorian Mental Hygiene, Australia, 1955-62; rsch. assoc., social work project dir. Arthritis Midway Ho., N.Y.C., 1966-68; rschr. Columbia Presbyn. Med. Center, N.Y.C., 1971-75; field instr. Columbia U. Sch. Social Work, 1977-79, Columbia Presbyn. Med. Ctr., NYU Sch. Social Work, 1989-90; ret., 1992. Family Found. fellow, 1966, 89-90; NIMH grantee, 1969-72. Mem. Nat. Assn. Social Workers, Nat. Wildlife Fedn., Center for Study of Presidency, Smithsonian Assn., English Speaking Union, Alliance Francaise, Columbia U. Alumni Assn., Internat. Platform Assn., Met. Mus. of N.Y. Lutheran. Home: 30-95 29th St Astoria NY 11102-2735

MATHEWS, ANNE JONES, consultant, library educator and administrator; b. Phila.; d. Edmond Fulton and Anne Ruth (Reichner) Jones; m. Frank Samuel Mathews, June 16, 1951; children: Lisa Anne Mathews-Bingham, David Morgan, Lynne Elizabeth Bietenhader-Mathews, Alison Fulton Sawyer. AB, Wheaton Coll., 1949; MA, U. Denver, 1965, PhD, 1977. Mem. field staff Intervarsity Christian Fellowship, Chgo., 1949-51; interviewer supr. Colo. Market Rsch. Svcs., Denver, 1952-64; reference libr. Oreg. State U., Corvallis, 1965-67; program dir. Ctrl. Colo. Libr. Sys., Denver, 1969-70; inst. dir. U.S. Office of Edn., Inst. Grant, 1979; dir. pub. rels. Grad. Sch. Librarianship and Info. Mgmt. U. Denver, 1970-76, dir. continuing edn., 1977-80, assoc. prof., 1977-79, prof., 1979-85; dir. Office Libr. Programs, Office Ednl. Rsch., Improvement U.S. Dept. Edn., Washington, 1986-91; dir. Nat. Libr. Edn., Washington, 1992-94; cons. Acad. Ednl. Devel., Washington, 1994—; vis. lectr. Simmons Coll. Sch. Libr. Sci., Boston, 1977; cons. USIA, 1984-85, mem. book and libr. adv. com., 1981-91; faculty assoc. Danforth Found., 1974-84; speaker in field; mem. secondary sch. curriculum com. Jefferson County Pub. Schs., Colo., 1976-78; mem. adv. com. Golden H.S., 1973-77; mem. adv. coun. White House Conf. on Librs. and Info. Svcs., 1991; del. Internat. Fedn. Libr. Assn., 1984-93. Author, editor 6 books; contbr. articles to profl. jours., numerous chpts. to books. Mem. rural librs. and humanities program Colo. planning and resource bd. NEH, 1982-83; bd. mgrs. Friends Found. of Denver Pub. Libr., 1976-82; pres. Faculty Women's Club, Colo. Sch. Mines, 1963-64. Mem. ALA (visionary leaders com. 1987-89, coun. mem. 1979-83, com on accreditation 1984-85, orientation com. 1974-77, 83-84, pub. rels. com.), Am. Soc. Info. Sci. (pub. rels. chmn. 1971), Mountain Plains Libr. Assn. (profl. devel. com. 1979-80, pub. rels. and publs. com. 1973-75, continuing edn. com. 1973-76), Colo. Libr. Assn. (pres. 1974, bd. dirs. 1973-75, continuing edn. com. 1976-80), Assn. Libr. & Info. Sci. Edn. (communication com. 1978-80, program com. 1977-78), Cosmos Club (Washington). Home: 492 Mount Evans Rd Golden CO 80401-9626

MATHEWS, BARBARA EDITH, gynecologist; b. Santa Barbara, Calif., Oct. 5, 1946; d. Joseph Chesley and Pearl (Cieri) Mathews; AB, U. Calif., 1969; MD, Tufts U., 1972. Diplomate Am. Bd. Ob-Gyn. Intern, Cottage Hosp., Santa Barbara, 1972-73, Santa Barbara Gen. Hosp., 1972-73; resident in ob-gyn Beth Israel Hosp., Boston, 1973-77; clin. fellow in ob-gyn Harvard U., 1973-76, instr., 1976-77; gynecologist Sansum Med. Clinic, Santa Barbara, 1977—; faculty mem. ann. postgrad. course Harvard Med. Sch.; bd. dirs. Sansum Med. Clinic, vice chmn. bd. dirs., 1994-96; dir. ann. postgrad course UCLA Med. Sch. Bd. dirs. Meml. Rehab. Found., Santa Barbara, Channel City Club, Santa Barbara, Music Acad. of the West, Santa Barbara, St. Francis Med. Ctr., Santa Barbara; mem. citizen's continuing edn. adv. council Santa Barbara C.C.; moderator Santa Barbara Cottage Hosp. Cmty. Health Forum. Fellow ACS, Am. Coll. Ob-gyn.; mem. AMA, Am. Soc. Colposcopy and Cervical Pathology (dir. 1982-84), Harvard U. Alumni Assn., Tri-counties Obstet. and Gynecol. Soc. (pres. 1981-82), Phi Beta Kappa. Clubs: Birnam Wood Golf (Santa Barbara). Author: (with L. Burke) Colposcopy in Clinical Practice, 1977; contbg. author Manual of Ambulatory Surgery, 1982. Home: 2105 Anacapa St Santa Barbara CA 93105-3503 Office: 317 W Pueblo St Santa Barbara CA 93105-4355

MATHEWS, JESSICA TUCHMAN, policy researcher, columnist; b. N.Y.C., July 4, 1946; d. Lester Reginald and Barbara (Wertheim) Tuchman; m. Colin D. Mathews, Feb. 25, 1978; children: Oliver Max Tuchman, Jordan Henry Morgenthau; stepchildren: Zachary Chase, Hilary Dustin. AB magna cum laude, Radcliffe Coll., 1967; PhD, Calif. Inst. Tech., 1973. Congrl. sci. fellow AAAS, 1973-74; profl. staff mem. Ho. Interior Com. on Energy and Environment, Washington, 1974-75; dir. issues and rsch. Udall Presdl. campaign, 1975-76; dir. Office of Global Issues NSC staff, Washington, 1977-79; mem. editorial bd. The Washington Post, 1980-82; v.p., dir. rsch. The World Resources Inst., Washington, 1982-92; dep. to undersec. for global affairs U.S. Dept. State, Washington, 1993; sr. fellow Coun. on Fgn. Rels., Washington, 1993—; columnist Washington Post, 1991—; mem. numerous adv. panels Office Tech. Assessment, NAS, AAAS, EPA; bd. dirs. Population Ref. Bur., Washington, 1988-93; adv. com. Air Products Corp. Bd. dirs., Joyce Found., Chgo., 1984-91, Inter-Am. Dialogue, 1991—, Radcliffe Coll., 1992—, Carnegie Endowment for Internat. Peace, Washington, 1992—, Rockefeller Bros Fund, N.Y.C., 1992—, Brookings Instn., Washington, 1995—, Surface Transportation Policy Project. Named Disting. fellow Aspen Inst. Mem. Coun. Fgn. Rels., Fedn. Am. Scientists (bd. dirs. 1985-87, 88-92, trilateral commn.), Inst. for Internat. Econs. (adv. com.). Democrat. Jewish. Office: Council on Fgn Relations 2400 N St NW Washington DC 20037-1153

MATHEWS, JOAN HELENE, pediatrician; b. Manchester, N.H., Feb. 3, 1940; d. John Barnaby and Helen A. Wlodkoski; m. Ernest Stephen Mathews, June 1, 1965; 3 children. BS, U. N.H., 1961; MD, Columbia U., 1965. Diplomate Am. Bd. Pediatrics. Med. intern Roosevelt Hosp., N.Y.C., 1965-66; pediatric resident Babies Hops. Columbia Presbyn. Med. Ctr., N.Y.C., 1966-68, pediatric endocrine fellow Babies Hosp., 1968-70; instr. clin. pediat. Columbia U. Coll. Physicians and Surgeons, N.Y.C., 1973-77; asst. prof. pediat. Cornell U. Med. Coll., N.Y.C., 1977-81; clin. instr. pediat. Harvard Med. Sch., Boston, 1985—; clin. assoc. children's svc. Mass. Gen. Hosp., Boston, 1985—. Fellow Am. Acad. Pediat.; mem. Phi Beta Kappa. Office: 777 Concord Ave Cambridge MA 02138-1053

MATHEWS, LINDA MCVEIGH, newspaper editor; b. Redlands, Calif., Mar. 14, 1946; d. Glenard Ralph and Edith Lorene (Humphrey) McVeigh; m. Thomas Jay Mathews, June 15, 1967; children—Joseph, Peter, Katherine. B.A., Radcliffe Coll., 1967; J.D., Harvard U., 1972. Gen. assignment reporter Los Angeles Times, 1967-69, Supreme Ct. corr., 1972-76, corr., Hong Kong, 1977-79, China corr., Peking, 1979-80, op-ed page editor, 1980-81, dep. nat. editor, 1981-84, dep. fgn. editor, 1985-88, editorial writer, 1988-89, editor L.A. Times mag., 1989-92; sr. producer ABC News, 1992-93; nat. editor N.Y. Times, 1993—; corr. Wall St. Jour., Hong Kong, 1976-77; lectr.; freelance writer. Author: (with others) Journey Into China, 1982; One Billion: A China Chronicle, 1983. Mem. Women's Legal Def. Fund, 1972-76; co-founder, pres. Hong Kong Montessori Sch., 1977-79; bd. dirs. Ctr. for Childhood. Mem. Fgn. Corrs. Club Hong Kong. Office: NY Times 229 W 43rd St New York NY 10036-3913

MATHEWS, MARY KATHRYN, government official; b. Washington, Apr. 20, 1948; d. T. Odon (dec.) and Kathryn (Augustine) M. Student, Pa. State U., 1966-68; BBA, Am. U., 1970, MBA, 1975. Personnel mgmt. specialist, coordinator coll. recruitment program, GSA, Washington, 1971-75, adminstrv. officer, 1975-78; personnel mgmt. specialist Office of Personnel Mgmt., Washington, 1978; employee devel. specialist Office Sec. Transp., Washington, 1978-80, dep. chief departmental services and spl. programs div., 1980-81; asst. dir. adminstrv. div. Farm Credit Adminstrn., Washington, 1981-84; dir. adminstrv. div. Farm Credit Adminstrn., McLean, Va., 1984-86; chief adminstrv. services div. Farm Credit Adminstrn., McLean, 1987-88; dep. staff dir. for mgmt. U.S. Commn. Civil Rights, Washington, 1988-90, asst. staff dir. for mgmt., 1990-91, asst. staff dir. for congl. affairs, 1991-94, staff dir., 1994—; chief spl. programs staff and homebound handicapped employment program GSA, Washington, 1973-74; mem. task force Presdl. mgmt. intern program U.S. Office Pers. Mgmt., Washington, 1977-78; coord. mgmt. devel. program for women Office Sec. Transp., Washington, 1979-81. Vol. mentor, speaker Alexandria Commn. on Women. Mem. Exec. Women in Govt. (treas. 1993-94, v.p. 1994-95, pres. 1995-96, bd. dirs.), Small Agy. Coun. (exec. com. 1990-91, 94—, chmn. micro agy. group 1990-91), Nat. Trust Hist. Preservation, Nat. Assn. Mus. Women in Arts (charter), Delta Gamma (rush advisor 1971-73, pres. bd. dirs. local chpt. house corp. 1972-73). Home: 405 S Royal St Alexandria VA 22314-3717 Office: US Commn on Civil Rights 624 9th St NW Washington DC 20001-5303

MATHEWS, SUSAN MCKIERNAN, health care executive; b. N.Y.C., May 28, 1946; d. Thomas Joseph and Eileen Ann (Looschen) McK.; m. Robert Emmett Mathews, June 17, 1967 (div.); children: Colin Robert, Brendan Robert, Devin Robert, Kiernan Robert. Diploma in nursing, St. Francis Sch. Nursing, 1966; BS in Health Adminstrn., St. Joseph's Coll., 1979; MS in Pub. Svc. Adminstrn., Russell Sage Coll., 1983; PhD in Health Adminstrn., Columbia Pacific U., 1985. RN, N.Y. Utilization rev. analyst N.Y. State Office Mental Retardation & Devel. Disabilities, Albany, 1980-83; with Empire Blue Cross & Blue Shield, Albany, 1983-86, dir. instl. utilization rev., cons. in field, 1986-88; pres., COO Corp. Health Dimensions, Troy, N.Y., 1988—; spkr. in field. Mem. bus. adv. bd. SUNY Coll., New Paltz; grad. Capital Leadership, 1990; mem. pres. coun. Sage Colls., 1994. Recipient Excellence in Mgmt. Pvt. Sector award, 1992. Mem. Med. Group Mgmt. Assn., Albany Colonie Regional C. of C. (chmn. 1996), Rensselaer County C. of C. (Woman of Achievement award 1994), The 50 Group. Roman Catholic. Office: Corp Health Dimensions 500 Federal St Ste 601 Troy NY 12180-2832

MATHEWS, WILMA KENDRICK, public relations executive; b. Danville, Va., Dec. 23, 1945; d. Clarence Blanchard and Tina Collins (Powell) Kendrick; AA, Stratford Coll., 1966, BA, 1970; student East Carolina U., 1966-67, U. Md., European div., 1967-68, Guilford Coll., 1978-80. Asst. editor The Commonwealth Mag., Richmond, Va., 1970-72; news editor The Comml. Appeal, Danville, Va., 1972-73; pub. rels. mgr. Danville C. of C., 1973-74; publs. officer Bowman Gray Bapt. Hosp. Med. Ctr., Winston-Salem, N.C., 1974-78; sr. pub. rels. specialist Western Electric, 1978-82; mgr. pub. rels. AT&T Internat., Basking Ridge, N.J., 1982-84; media rels. mgr. AT&T Network Systems, 1985-87, mgr. pub. rels. field support, 1987-90, pub. rels. adv. dir., 1990-93, cons., 1993—; dir. pub. rels. Ariz. State U., 1995—; sr. pub. rels. adv. N.C. Epilepsy Info. Svc., 1979-80. Co-author: On Deadline: Managing Media Relations, 1985, 94; Inside Organizational Communications, 2d edit., 1985, Marketing Communications, 1987; Mem. Danville Bicentennial Commn., 1972-74; bd. dirs. Nat. Tobacco-Textile Mus., 1973-74; mem. Danville City Beautiful Com., 1973-74, Maplewood Cultural Commn., 1986-87. Fellow Internat. Assn. Bus. Communicators (dir. 1978-81, pres. N.C. chpt. 1977, 78, dir. Found. 1984-87, chmn. Found. 1987-90, accreditation bd. 1983-89, 94—, bd. chmn. 1990-91), Pub. Rels. Soc. Am. (dir. Valley of Sun chpt. 1996—); mem. Danville Hist. Soc. (dir. 1973-74), N.C. Zool. Soc., Smithsonian Instn., Internat. TV Assn. (sec. N.C. chpt. 1979-80), Internat. Pub. Rels. Assn., Coun. for Communications Mgmt. (bd. dirs. 1987-89), Friends of Maplewood Libr. (pres. 1985-86), Ahwatukee Foothills C. of C. (bd. dirs. 1994—, vice chair 1996—), Stratford Coll. Alumni Assn., Internat. Order Job's Daus. Republican. Baptist. Home: 14836 S Foxtail Ln Phoenix AZ 85048-4335 Office: Ariz State U Box 871002 Tempe AZ 85287

MATHIAS, ALICE IRENE, health plan company executive; b. N.Y.C., Mar 2, 1949; d. Murray and Charlotte (Kottle) M. B.S. in Math., Western New Eng. Coll., 1972. Programmer, Carnation Co., Los Angeles, 1973-78; programmer/analyst Cedars-Sinai Med. Ctr., Los Angeles, 1978-79, Union Bank, Los Angeles, 1979-81; group leader Kaiser Found. Health Plan, Pasadena, Calif., 1981—. Mem. Nat. Assn. Female Execs., Am. Mgmt. Assn., Kaiser Mgmt. Assn., Kaiser Women in Mgmt., Los Angeles County Mus. Art (sponsor), Smithsonian Inst., KCET Pub. TV, Choice In Dying, U.S. Holocaust Meml. Mus. (charter mem.), Caithness Collectors Club, Statue of Liberty Ellis Island Found. Home: 4210 Via Arbolada Apt 311 Los Angeles CA 90042-5124 Office: Kaiser Found Health Plan Info Svcs Dept 393 E Walnut St Pasadena CA 91188-0001

MATHIAS, BETTY JANE, communications and community affairs consultant, writer, editor, lecturer; b. East Ely, Nev., Oct. 22, 1923; d. Royal F. and Dollie B. (Bowman) M.; student Merritt Bus. Sch., 1941, 42, San Francisco State U., 1941-42; 1 child, Dena. Asst. publicity dir. Oakland (Calif.) Area War Chest and Community Chest, 1943-46; pub. rels. Am. Legion, Oakland, 1946-47; asst. to pub. rels. dir. Cen. Bank of Oakland, 1947-49; pub. rels. dir. East Bay chpt. of Nat. Safety Council, 1949-51; propr., mgr. Mathias Pub. Rels. Agy., Oakland, 1951-60; gen. assignment reporter and teen news editor Daily Rev., Hayward, Calif., 1960-62; freelance pub. rels. and writing, Oakland, 1962-66, 67-69; dir. corp. communications Systech Fin. Corp., Walnut Creek, Calif., 1969-71; v.p. corp. communications Consol. Capital companies, Oakland, 1972-79, v.p. community affairs, Emeryville, Calif., 1981-84, v.p. spl. projects, 1984-85; v.p., dir. Consol. Capital Realty Svcs., Inc., Oakland, 1973-77; v.p., dir. Centennial Adv. Corp., Oakland, 1976-77; communications cons., 1979—; cons. Mountainair Realty, Cameron Park, Calif., 1986-87; pub. rels. coord. Tuolumne County

Visitors Bur., 1989-90; lectr. in field; bd. dirs. Oakland YWCA, 1944-45, ARC, Oakland, So. Alameda County chpt., 1967-69, Family Ctr., Children's Hosp. Med. Ctr. No. Calif., 1982-85, March of Dimes, 1983-85, Equestrian Ctr. of Walnut Creek, Calif., 1983-84, also sec.; adult and publs. adv. Internat. Order of the Rainbow for Girls, 1953-78; communications arts adv. com. Ohlone (Calif.) Coll., 1979-85, chmn., 1982-84; mem. adv. bd. dept. mass communications Calif. State U.-Hayward, 1985; pres. San Francisco Bay Area chpt. Nat. Reyes Syndrome Found., 1981-86; vol. staff Columbia Actors' Repertory, Columbia, Calif., 1986-87, 89; mem. exec. bd., editor newsletter Tuolumne County Dem. Club, 1987; publicity chmn. 4th of July celebration Tuolumne County C. of C., 1988; vol. children's dept. Tuolumne County Pub. Libr., 1993—; vol. Annual Cmty. Christmas Eve Dinner, Sonora, Calif., 1990—; mem. adv. com. Ride Away Ctr. for Therapeutic Riding for the Handicapped, 1995—. Recipient Grand Cross of Color award Internat. Order of Rainbow for Girls, 1955. Order Eastern Star (worthy matron 1952, publicity chmn. Calif. state 1955), Northeastern Nev. Hist. Soc. Editor East Bay Mag., 1966-67, TIA Traveler, 1969, Concepts, 1979-83. Home: 20575 Gopher Dr Sonora CA 95370-9034

MATHIAS, MARGARET GROSSMAN, manufacturing company executive, leasing company executive; b. Detroit, June 26, 1928; d. D. Ray and Lila May (Skinner) Grossman; children: Deborah, Robert, Lesley, Jennifer, Mary. BA, Mt. Holyoke Coll., 1949; cert., Am. Acad. Art, 1951. Artist and co-mgr. Mary Chase Marionettes, N.Y.C., 1951-54; exec. v.p. Star Five Corp., Elkhart, 1975-88, pres., treas., chmn. bd., 1985-90; sec., chmn. bd. L & J Press Corp., Elkhart, Ind., 1985-91, also chmn. bd. dirs.; chmn. MAGCo Inc., Elkhart, 1986—; pres. Tech Products, Inc., Elkhart, 1992—. Mem. fin. com. United Fund, Elkhart, 1960-64, parents adv. bd. Furman U., Greenville, S.C., 1978-83, art adv. bd. Mount Holyoke Coll., South Hadley, Mass., 1982—; pres. Tri Kappa Service Orgn., Elkhart, 1965-66; trustee Stanley Clark Sch., South Bend, Ind., 1977-87. Recipient Lawson Top Sculpture Purchase award Midwest Mus. Am. Art, 1990. Mem. Elkhart C. of C. Republican. Clubs: Elcona Country (Elkhart), Woman's Athletic (Chgo.), Thursday (Elkhart) (pres. 1976). Home and Office: 1077 Greenleaf Blvd Apt 209 Elkhart IN 46514-3563

MATHIAS, MARY WOODWARD, social worker, psychotherapist; b. N.Y.C., Aug. 29, 1937; d. David Bernard and Ida Erwin Mathias; life ptnr. Mary A. Ide; children: Susan Erwin Houriet, David Mathias Houriet. BA, Wellesley Coll., 1959; MA, NYU, 1961; MSW, Boston U., 1990. Lic. ind. clin. social worker, Mass. Clin. social worker Indochinese Psychiatry Clinic, Boston, 1991—; pvt. practice in psychotherapy Boston, 1994—; lectr. and trainer Harvard Program in Refugee Trauma Project in Croatia, Cambridge, Mass., 1996—. Mem. NASW (co-chair internat. social welfare com. 1994—), Soc. Family Therapy and Rsch. (bd. dirs. 1993—, Rsch. Recognition award 1994). Office: Indochinese Psychiatry Clinic Deaconess Hosp 1 Autumn St Boston MA 02215

MATHIEU, HELEN M., state legislator; b. Newport, R.I., May 8, 1940; m. Roger E. Mathieu, 1964. Grad., Salve Regina Coll. Mem. R.I. State Senate, dist. 46. Mem. Kappa Gamma Pi. Democrat. Roman Catholic. Home: 160 Lawrence Dr Portsmouth RI 02871-4063 Office: R I State Senate State Capital Providence RI 02903

MATHIEU-HARRIS, MICHELE SUZANNE, association executive; b. Chgo., Mar. 24, 1950; d. Joseph Edward Mathieu and Mary Ellen (Knapp) Fisher; m. Robert Steven Harris, May 1, 1988. Student DePaul U., 1971, 74-76, Regents Coll., Albany, N.Y., 1987—; Roosevelt U., 1995—. Broadcast coord. Grey-North Advt., Chgo., 1967-71; head drama dept. Patricia Stevens Coll., Chgo., 1972; instr. beginning acting Ted Liss Sch. of Performing Arts, Chgo., 1973-75; project coord. grants and contracts Am. Dietetic Assn., Chgo., 1974-81, adminstr. govt. affairs, 1981-86, mgr. licensure communications, 1986-90, adminstr. nutrition svcs. payment systems, 1990-94, team leader, health care fin. team, 1994—; grant proposal cons. various performance arts, Chgo., 1978—; med. reporter, writer various internat. clients, 1994—; PC cons., Chgo., 1994—. Editor Legis. Newsletter, 1981-86; contbg. editor Nutrition Forum, 1986, Courier, 1987—; contbr. articles to profl. jours., mags., newspapers. Treas. Am. Dietetic Assn. polit. action com., Washington, 1981-86. Ill. Arts Coun. grantee, 1981; recipient award Excellence in Govt. Rels. Am. Soc. Assn. Execs., 1989, gen. mgnt. certificate program, 1992. Mem. Am. Soc. Assn. Execs.. Roman Catholic. Avocations: reading, fitness walking. Office: Am Dietetic Assn 216 W Jackson Blvd Chicago IL 60606-6909

MATHIS, KAREN MCHUGH, artist; b. Alma, Mich., June 13, 1945; d. James Edward and Nelda Ellen (Grubaugh) McHugh; m. John Prentiss Mathis, May 31, 1966; children: Lisa Lynne Mathis Kirkpatrick, Andy Prentiss. BS, So. Meth. U., 1965; BA, George Washington U., 1979. Cert. secondary tchr., Washington. Mem. gen. staff for spl. events Nat. Gallery Art, Washington, 1985-88. One-woman shows Landon Gallery, Landen Sch., Bethesda, Md., 1989, 93, Town Ctr. Gallery, Rockville, Md., 1990, Met. Meml. United Meth. Ch., Washington, 1990, Grenleaf Gallery, Nags Head, N.C., 1994, Yellow Barn Gallery, Glen Echo, Md., 1996; exhibited in group shows Art League, Alexandria, Va., 1988, 91, 94, 95, 96, Rockville Art League, 1988, 90, Montgomery County Watercolor Assn., Bethesda, 1990, Albany (Ga.) Mus. Art, 1991, Mansion Art Gallery, Rockville, 1993, George Mason U., 1994, James Madison U., Fairfax, Va., 1995, Gwinnett Fine Arts Ctr., Duluth, Ga.a, 1996, Howard Mandville Gallery, Kirkland, Wash., 1996; represented by Verandah Art Gaallery, Bridgetown, Barbados, Greenleaf Gallery, Lawrence Gallery, Alexandria. Docent chmn. Jr. League Washington, 1985, designer spl. exhibit project, 1986. Mem. Art League Washington, Ga. Watercolor Assn., N.W. Watercolor Assn., Potomac Valley Watercolor Assn. Democrat. Methodist. Home and Studio: 9400 Turnberry Dr Potomac MD 20854

MATHIS, LOIS RENO, retired elementary education educator; b. Vinson, Okla., June 10, 1915; d. William Dodson and Trudie Frances (Brady) Reno; m. Harold Fletcher Mathis, June 6, 1942 (dec.); children: Robert F., Betty Mathis Sproule. BS, Southwestern Okla. U., 1939; MA, U. Pitts., 1945; PhD, Ohio State U., 1965. Cert. elem. tchr.; cert. elem. supr. Tchr. Okla. Pub. Schs., Tea Cross, 1936-39, Tipton, 1939-42; tchr. Ohio County Schs., Wheeling, W.Va., 1944-45, Norman (Okla.) Pub. Schs., 1951-52, Kent (Ohio) State U., 1954-60, Ohio State U., Columbus, 1961-62, Columbus (Ohio) Pub. Schs., 1967-80; ret., 1980; ednl. cons. in field, 1965—. Mem. Women's Round Table, Columbus, 1986-88; mem. data collection com. 100 Good Schs., Columbus, 1982-84. Mem. AAUW (pres. 1986-88), Ohio State Univ. Women's Club, Phi Delta Gamma (pres. 1980-82), Pi Lambda Theta, Alpha Delta Kappa, Kappa Delta Pi (counselor 1976—, alumni counselor exec. coun. internat. 1990-92, Honor Key 1991). Democrat. Baptist. Home: 2905 Halstead Rd Columbus OH 43221-2917

MATHIS, MARSHA DEBRA, software company executive; b. Detroit, Dec. 22, 1953; d. Marshall Junior and Anita Willene (Biggers) M. BS, Fla. State U., 1978; MBA, Miss. Coll., 1982. With telecommunications dept. Fla. State Dept. Safety, Tallahassee, 1973-76; asst. to chmn. Tallahassee Savs. and Loan Assn., 1976-78; sales engr. Prehler, Inc., Jackson, Miss., 1978-82; mktg. mgr. Norand Corp., Arlington, Tex., 1982-87; v.p. mktg. and sales Profl. Datasolutions, Inc., Irving, Tex., 1987-88; v.p. mktg. and sales, ptnr. Target Systems, Inc., Irving, 1988-89, also bd. dirs.; v.p. mktg. Profl. Datasolutions, Inc., Temple, Tex., 1990—. Contbr. articles to industry trade jours. Advisor Am. Diabetes Assn., Jackson, 1983—. Mem. Internat. Platform Assn., Nat. Adv. Group, Nat. Assn. Convenience Stores (Industry Task Force 1987-88). Republican. Roman Catholic. Home: 325 Old York Rd Irving TX 75063-4247 Office: Profl Datasolutions Inc 3407 S 31st St Temple TX 76502-1921

MATHIS, MELISSA LYNNE, documentary producer, journalist; b. Dayton, Ohio, Jan. 11, 1963; d. Dallas Kent and Judith Louise (Huffman) M. BS in Internat. Studies, L.Am. History, U. N.C., 1986. Rschr. investigative unit Washington Post, 1987-89; rschr. "Other People's Money" Frontline/PBS, Washington, 1989-90; prodr. "Perspectives on Peace" Close Up Found./U.S. Inst. Peace, Washington, 1991; assoc. prodr. "Citizen Stories" Close Up Found./Smithsonian Instn., Washington, 1989-92; prodr. Washington Jour., C-Span, Washington, 1992-95; prodr. "A Third Choice" New River Media/PBS, Washington, 1995—; judge RFK Journalism Awards, Washington, 1995. Mem. World Affairs Coun., Washington, 1995—, Nat. Mus. of Women in the Arts, Washington, 1995—. Home: Ste 28 1615 Kenyon St NW Washington DC 20010

MATHIS, SAMANTHA, actress; b. N.Y.C., 1971. Films include: The Bulldance, Pump Up the Volume, This is My Life, Super Mario Bros., The Music of Chance, The Thing Called Love, Little Women, Jack and Sarah, How to Make an American Quilt, The American President, Broken Arrow, (voice) FernGully...The Last Rainforest; TV series: Knightwatch, Cold Sassy Tree to My Daughter, 83 Hours 'Til Dawn; TV pilot Aaron's Way. Office: care SAG 5757 Wilshire Blvd Los Angeles CA 90036*

MATHIS, SHARON BELL, author, elementary educator, librarian; b. Atlantic City, Feb. 26, 1937; d. John Willie and Alice Mary (Frazier) Bell; m. Leroy F. Mathis, July 11, 1957 (div. Jan. 1979); children: Sherie, Stacy, Stephanie. B.A., Morgan State Coll., 1958; M.L.S., Catholic U. Am., 1975. Interviewer Children's Hosp. of D.C., Washington, 1958-59; tchr. Holy Redeemer Elementary Sch., Washington, 1959-65, Charles Hart Jr. High Sch., Washington, 1965-72; spl. edn. tchr. Stuart Jr. High Sch., Washington, 1972-74; librarian Benning Elementary Sch., Washington, 1975-76; librarian Friendship Ednl. Center, 1976-95, ret., 1995; writer-in-charge children's lit. div. D.C. Black Writers Workshop; writer-in-residence Howard U., 1972-73. Author: Brooklyn Story, 1970, Sidewalk Story, 1971 (Council on Interracial Books for Children award 1970), Teacup Full of Roses, 1972 (Outstanding Book of Yr. award New York Times 1972), Ray Charles, 1973 (Coretta Scott King award 1974), Listen for the Fig Tree, 1974, The Hundred Penny Box, 1975 (Boston Globe-Horn Book Honor book 1975, Newberry Honor Book 1976), Cartwheels, 1977, Red Dog Blue Fly: Football Poems, 1991 (Children's Book of Yr. award Bank St. Coll. 1992), Red Dog Blue Fly: An American Bookseller (Pick of the List 1995). Mem. bd. advisers lawyers com. D.C. Commn. on Arts, 1972. Nominated Books for Brotherhood list NCCJ, 1970; recipient D.C. Assn. Sch. Librs. award 1976, Arts and Humanities award Archdiocese of Washington Black Secretariat, 1978; Weekly Reader Book Club fellow Bread Loaf Writers Conf., 1970, MacDowell Colony fellow, 1978. Roman Catholic.

MATHISEN-REID, RHODA SHARON, international communications consultant; b. Portland, Oreg., June 25, 1942; d. Daniel and Mildred Elizabeth Annette (Peterson) Hager; m. James Albert Mathisen, July 17, 1964 (div. 1977); m. James A. Reid Sr., Jan. 1, 1991. BA in Edn., Music, Bible Coll., Mich., 1964. Community Rels. officer Gary-Wheaton Bank, Wheaton, Ill., 1971-75; br. mgr. Stivers Temporary Personnel, Chgo., 1975-79; v.p. sales Exec. Technique, Chgo., 1980-83; prin. Mathisen Assocs., Clarendon Hills, Ill., 1983—; presenter seminars; featured speaker Women in Mgmt. Oak Brook Chpt., 1988; cons. Haggai Inst., Atlanta; adv. mem. Nat. Bd. Success Group, 1986. Pres. chancel choir Christ Ch. of Oak Brook, 1985-87, chmn. 1st Profl. Women's Seminar, 1995; mem., 1992—, bd. dirs. Career Devel. Inst., Oak Brook, 1992; judge Mrs. Ill., USI Pageant, 1994. Mem. NAFE, Bus. and Profl. Women (charter mem. Woodfield chpt.), Execs. Club Oak Brook, Assn. Commerce and Industry (named Ambassador of Month N.W. suburban chpt. 1979), Oak Brook Assn. Commerce and Industry (mem. membership com.), Women Entrepreneurs of DuPage County (membership chmn., featured speaker Jan. 1988), Art Inst. Chgo., Willowbrook/Burr Ridge C. of C. Republican. Office: Mathisen Assocs 17 Lake Shore Dr Clarendon Hills IL 60514-2221

MATHISON, BETH, not-for-profit association executive; b. Statesville, N.C., July 4, 1956; d. Daniel Harold Young and Alice Virginia (Newton) Golden; m. Ronald Bruce Mathison, June 9, 1979; children: Blair, Ben. BS, U. Ga., 1978; MEd, West Ga. Coll., 1980. Cert. tchr., Ga. Tchr. Bartow County Schs., Cartersville, Ga., 1978-80, Cartersville City Schs., 1980-82; from adult literacy tchr. to CEO Peach program Bartow County Schs., 1984—; bd. dirs. BREAK, Cartersville, 1996. Sch. bd. Cartersville City Schs., 1992—. Recipient administrator award Ga. Adult Literacy Assn., 1991. Mem. Bus. and Profl. Women, Women's Coun. of Chamber, Non Profit Resource Ctr., Cartersville Svc. League. Home: 234 Parkview Dr Cartersville GA 30120 Office: PEACH Early Intervention Program 105 N Bartow St Cartersville GA 30120

MATHUR, RUPA AJWANI, former state official, risk management consultant; b. Khairpur, Sind, India, Nov. 2, 1939; came to U.S., 1980; d. Menghraj Lalchand and Giani Ajwani; m. Ramesh Saran Mathur, Mar. 2, 1967; children: Sanjay Saran, Seema. BA with honors, Bombay U., 1962, LLB, 1965. CPCU. Lawyer High Ct., Bombay; with GM, U.K., Lindus & Horton, U.K.; welfare staff Brit. High Commn., Africa, 1977-78; English tchr. Thailand, 1978-80; ins. specialist, analyst Met. Transit Authority, Houston, 1980-83; ins. analyst Coastal Corp., Houston, 1983-84; dir. ins. and employee benefits Houston Ind. Sch. Dist., 1984-88; dir. risk mgmt. and benefits Harris County, Houston, 1988-94; dir. State Risk Mgmt., Austin, 1994—; pres. Rupa Mathur & Assocs.; bd. dirs. Surplus Line; owner Health Environ. and Risk Mgmt. Co. (HER Inc.); team leader risk mgmt. del. People to People, Ea. Europe and Russia, 1993, China, 1994; instr. CPCU and accredited advisor ins. courses U. Houston Sch. Inst. Mktg. and Fin., 1985-88; speaker in field. Author: Managing Occupational Injury Costs, 1993; contbr. articles to profl. jours. Chmn. Multi Cultural Soc., Ft. Bend County, Tex., 1992, Indian Cmty.-Equal Opportunity, Houston, 1990; bd. dirs. Children at Risk, Ft. Bend Sch. Dist., 1990, mem. task force Multi Culture Ctr., 1993; co-founder Internat. Gourmet Club, 1976; sec.-treas. Internat. Ladies Club, 1976; tchr. English, YMCA, Thailand, 1976; founder Indian Am. Orgn. for Equal Opportunity; bd. dirs. India Culture Ctr., 1993-94, Surplus Lines Stamping. Recipient Honor award Tex. Safety Assn., 1993, Woman on the Move award Houston Post and KPRC/Channel 2, 1993. Mem. Profl. Women in Govt., Risk and Ins. Mgrs. Soc. (com.), Pub. Risk and Ins. Mgmt. Assn. (past pres. Tex. chpt., mem. internat. com.), World Safety Orgn. (cert. safety exec., appreciation award 1991, Concerned Safety Profl. award 1993), CPCU's (edn. com.), State and Local Govt. Benefits Assn., Nat. Safety Coun. (safety awards), Profl. Devel. Inst. (past officer), Internat. Hospitality Coun. (bd. dirs.), People to People Orgn. (Austin chpt.). Home: 3400 Pace Bend Rd Spicewood TX 78669

MATIAS, PATRICIA TREJO, secondary education educator; b. Havana, Cuba; came to U.S., 1967; d. Juan Mario and Maria (Rexach) Trejo; m. Miguel Matias, Mar. 20, 1972; children: Michael George, Mark Patrick. BA in French/Spanish, Ga. Coll., 1973; MAT in Spanish Edn., Ga. State U., 1985, EdS in Fgn. Lang. Edn., 1991. Cert. Spanish tchr., Ga. Spanish lead tchr. Wheeler High Sch., Marietta, Ga., 1980—; mem. adv. bd. So. Conf. Lang. Teaching, Ga., 1987—; part-time instr. Kennesaw State Coll., 1991—. VIP guest svc. goodwill amb. Olympics Games Com., Atlanta, 1995—. Mem. AAUW, ASCD, Am. Assn. Tchrs. Spanish and Portuguese, Profl. Assn. Ga. Educators, Fgn. Lang. Assn. Ga., Kappa Delta Pi, Sigma Delta Pi (hon.). Office: Wheeler High Sch 375 Holt Rd Marietta GA 30068-3560

MATILE, MADELON ELIZABETH, secondary education educator; b. Youngstown, Ohio, Feb. 9, 1940; d. Oscar William and Alice Elizabeth (Laflin) Mitchell; m. Robert William Matile, July 13, 1963; children: David Robert, Elizabeth Ann, Michael William. BS in Edn., Bowling Green (Ohio) State U., 1962; MEd, U. Toledo, Ohio, 1987; postgrad, U. Toledo, 1988—. Tchr. Youngstown (Ohio) City Schs., 1962-63; tchr. Sylvania (Ohio) City Schs., 1963-69, LD tutor, 1978-82, tchr., 1982—, GRADS coord., 1991—; facilitator Sylvania City Schs., 1985-90. Mem. Jr. League, Toledo, 1972—, sec. exec. com., 1978-80; v.p. exec. com. Crittenton Svcs., Toledo, 1978-84, 88-94; mem. bd. dirs., v.p., sec. Parents Helping Parents, Toledo, 1989—. Mem. AAUW (exec. com. 1969-74), Toledo Home Econs. Assn., Phi Upsilon Omicron.

MATISOFF, SUSAN, cultural research organization administrator. Dir. Ctr. East-Asian Studies, Stanford U., Calif. Office: Stanford Univ/Ctr E Asian Stud Asian Lang Dept Bldg 250 300 Lasuen St Stanford CA 94305-8311*

MATJASKO, M. JANE, anesthesiologist, educator; b. Harrison Twp., Pa., 1942. MD, Med. Coll. Pa., 1968. Diplomate Am. Bd. Anesthesiology (bd. dirs.). Resident in anesthesiology Md. Hosp., Balt., 1968-72; prof., chmn. anesthesiology U. Md., Balt.; appt. U. Md. Hosp., Balt. Mem. Am. Soc. Anesthesiologists, Assn. Univ. Anesthesiologists. Office: U Md Hosp Dept Anesthesiology 22 S Greene St Baltimore MD 21201-1544*

MATLIN, MARLEE, actress; b. Morton Grove, Ill., Aug. 24, 1965; m. Kevin Grandalski, Aug. 29, 1993. Attended William Rainey Harper Coll. Appeared in films Children of a Lesser God (Acad. award for best actress), 1986, Walker, 1987, Linguini Incident, 1990, The Player, 1992, Hear No Evli, 1993; TV film: Bridge to Silence, 1989, Against Her Will: The Carrie Buck Sotry, 1994; TV series: Reasonable Doubts, 1991-93; guest of Picket Fences, 1993 (Emmy nomination, Guest Actress-Drama Series, 1994), Seinfeld, 1993 (Emmy nomination Guest Actress-Comedy Series, 1994). Recipient Golden Globe award Hollywood Fgn. Press Assn., 1987, named Best Actress. Office: care ICM 8942 Wilshire Blvd Beverly Hills CA 90211-1934*

MATLOW, BARBARA ALICE, mathematics educator; b. Chgo., Jan. 3, 1934; d. Barnett and Sylvia (Sigel) Bender; m. Sheldon Leo Matlow, June 22, 1958; children: Jaron Baker, Mitchell Aaron, Rosalind Beth Matlow Taylor. BA in Liberal Arts, U. Chgo., 1952, MA in Edn., 1958; MA in Math., San Jose State U., 1972. Std. elem. teaching credential, std. secondary teaching credential, Calif.; cert. crosscultural lang. acquisition and devel. Math. tchr. Roosevelt Sch., Dolton, Ill., 1957-58, Lincoln Sch., Evanston, Ill., 1958-59, Sylvandale Sch., San Jose, Calif., 1966—; mentor tchr. Franklin-McKinley Sch. Dist., San Jose, 1986. Mem. NEA, Nat. Coun. Tchrs. Math, Calif. Math. Coun., Calif. Tchrs. Assn., Franklin-McKinley Edn. Assn. (dir., rep., v.p.), Santa Clara Valley Math. Assn., Phi Kappa Phi. Office: Sylvandale Sch 653 Sylvandale Ave San Jose CA 95111-1414

MATLOW, LINDA MONIQUE, photographic agency executive, publishing executive; b. Chgo., July 24, 1955; d. Charles and Milly Matlow. Grad. high sch., Chgo.; student, Sch. Modern Photography, N.Y.C., 1977-79. Promotions and pub. relations staff Jaydee Enterprises, Chgo., 1971-73; mgr. First Venture, Inc., Chgo., 1973-77; photographer, pub. relations staff Bands & Mags., Chgo., 1977—; photographer, writer, editor Pix Internat., Chgo., 1982—; pub. variety of monthly mags. on disk including Retro, ARTchive, Cre-8, Event; photo editor Beat. Chgo. Sounds; bur. chief Praire Sun; electronic pub. and image design Internet Pub. Contbr. photographs to publs. including N.Y. Times, Chgo. Tribune, Boston Globe, Harper's Bazaar, Redbook. Vol. telethon Variety Club of Chgo., 1986, Spl. Childrens' Charities, Little City Found., Chgo. Acad. for the Arts. Named Rock Photographer Night Rock newspaper, Chgo., 1980, 81, one of Chgo.'s Most Successful and Eligible Bachelorettes Today's Chgo. Woman mag., 1989; recipient Hon. mention Internat. Photographer Mag., 1990, winner B&W Print of Ray Charles, 1991; finalist Photographers Forum B&W Print, 1991. Mem. Nat. Press Photographers Assn., NARAS, Internat. Freelance Photographers Orgn., Chgo. Women in Pub., Chgo. Area Internet Soc. Roman Catholic.

MATON, ANTHEA, education consultant; b. Burnley, Lancashire, England, Feb. 1, 1944; d. William Douglas Newton-Dawson and Beatrice Joan (Simpson) Bateman; m. K.F. Edward Asprey, Nov. 13, 1965 (div. 1978); children: George William Edward, Mariana Alexandra Beatrice; m. Paul Nicholas Maton, Mar. 23, 1978; 1 child, Petra Beatrice Suzanne. Tchg. cert., higher diploma, tchg. diploma; postgrad., U. Okla. Clin. instr. radiotherapy Hammersmith Hosp., London, 1970-75; prin. sch. radiotherapy Royal Free Hosp., London, 1977-80, acting supt., 1979-80; head of careers Putney High Sch. for Girls, London, 1981-83; head of physics St. Andrews Episc. High Sch., Bethesda, Md., 1984-88; vis. fellow Am. Assn. Physics Tchrs., 1988-89; nat. coord. project scope, sequence, and coordination Nat. Sci. Tchrs. Assn., 1989-91; exec. dir. Edn. Commections, Oklahoma City, 1991—, dir. exhbn. on art and physics, 1994—; vis. faculty physics Western Wash. U., 1995; vis. faculty Okla. Sch. Sci. and Math. 1995—; organizer U.S.-Soviet H.S. Physics Student Exch. and Visit, 1989; conducted numerous workshops on sci. curriculum reform and assessment reform, 1987—; faculty USA Physics Olympiad Team, 1986, 89; physics tchr. St. Andrews Episc. H.S., 1984-88, Putney H.S. for Girls, 1980-83, tchr. med. ethics, 1982-83; tchr. physics, anatomy and physiology, radiobiology Royal Free Hosp., 1977-80, contemporary physics edn. project, 1989—. Lead author Prentice Hall Sci., 1993; contbr. articles to profl. jours. Mem. Nat. Mus. Women Arts (charter), Women's Philharm. (charter); apptd. to scientific adv. bd. OMNIPLEX Sci. Mus., Okla. City; cons. Sta. WGBH, Boston, Smithsonian, Am. Mus. of Moving Image, UCLA, Del. Edn. Dept., Ark. Project Advise, Newcastle (Del.) Sch. Dist. Named one of Today's Leaders Okla. Edn. Equity Roundtable, 1992. Mem. NAFE, ASCD, AAUW (pub. policy chair 1995-96), NOW (coord. metro chpt. 1992-95, treas. Okla. state chpt. 1993-95), Nat. Sci. Tchrs. Assn., Am. Assn. Physics Tchrs., N.Y. Acad. Scis., Assn. for Sci. Edn., Soc. Radiographers U.K., Soc. Radiographers Radiotherapy. Home and Office: 1804 Dorchester Dr Oklahoma City OK 73120-4706

MATORIN, SUSAN, social work administrator, educator; b. Boston, Jan. 9, 1943; d. Mervyn Donald and Eleanor (Marinoff) M.; m. Richard Charles Friedman, Nov. 24, 1978; 1 child, Jeremiah Simon. AB, Vassar Coll., 1964; postgrad., Columbia Sch. Social Work, 1966. Cert. social worker, N.Y. Chief social work Washington Heights Cmty. Svc., N.Y. State Psychiat. Inst., 1966-78; chief ambulatory social work in psychiatry Presbyn. Hosp., Columbia Med. Ctr., N.Y., 1978-81; dir. social work Payne Whitney Clinic of N.Y. Hosp., Cornell, 1981—; mem. adv. coun., 2d vice chair Columbia U. Sch. of Social Work, 1994—; adj. assoc. prof. Columbia Sch. Social Work, 1977—; bd. trustees Selig Ednl. Inst. Jewish Bd. Family Svcs., N.Y.; spkr. in field. Contbr. articles to profl. jours. and books. Recipient Disting. Svc. award Columbia U., 1989. Fellow Am. Orthopsychiatry Assn.; mem. NASW (Met. chpt. licensing task force, bd. dirs.), Acad. Cert. Social Workers, Soc. for Social Work Adminstrs. in Health Care (N.Y. chpt. program co-chair 1994—, nominated Social Work Dir. of Yr. 1995). Democrat. Jewish. Home: 27 W 86th St Apt 9C New York City NY 10024 Office: Payne Whitney Clinic 525 E 68th St New York NY 10021

MATSA, LOULA ZACHAROULA, social services administrator; b. Piraeus, Greece, Apr. 16, 1935; came to U.S., 1952, naturalized 1962; d. Eleftherios Georgiou and Ourania E. (Fraguiskopoulou) Papoulias; student Pierce Coll., Athens, Greece, 1948-52; BA, Rockford Coll., 1953; MA, U. Chgo., 1955; m. Ilco S. Matsa, Nov. 27, 1953; 1 child, Aristotle Ricky. Diplomate clin. social worker. Marital counselor Family Soc. Cambridge, Mass., 1955-56; chief unit II, social service Queen's (N.Y.) Children's Psychiat. Ctr., 1961-74; dir. social services, supr.-coord. family care program Hudson River Psychiat. Ctr., Poughkeepsie, N.Y., 1974-91; supr. social work Harlem Valley Psychiat. Ctr., Wingdale, N.Y., 1991-93; supr. social work Hudson River Psychiat. Ctr., 1993—; field instr. Adelphi, Albany and Fordham univs., 1969—. Fulbright Exch. student, 1952-53; Talcott scholar, 1953-55. Mem. NASW, Internat. Platform Assn., Internat. Coun. on Social Welfare, Acad. Cert. Social Workers, Assn. Cert. Social Workers, Bd. Certified Clin. Social Workers, N.Y. Certified Social Workers, Pub. Employees Fedn., Pierce Coll. Alumni Assn. Democrat. Greek Orthodox. Contbr. articles to profl. jours.; instrumental in state policy changes in treatment and court representation of emotionally disturbed and mentally ill. Office: Hudson River Psychiat Ctr Branch B Poughkeepsie NY 12601

MATSON, VIRGINIA MAE FREEBERG (MRS. EDWARD J. MATSON), retired special education educator, author; b. Chgo., Aug. 25, 1914; d. Axel George and Mae (Dalrymple) Freeberg; m. Edward John Matson, Oct. 18, 1941; children: Karin (Mrs. Donald H. Skadden), Sara M. Drake, Edward Robert, Laurence D., David O. BA, U. Ky., 1934; MA, Northwestern U., 1941. Spl. edn. tchr. area high schs., Chgo., 1934-42, Ridge Farm, 1944-45; tchr. high schs. Lake County (Ill.) Pub. Schs., 1956-59; founder Grove Sch., Lake Forest, Ill., 1958-87, ret., 1987; instr. evening sch. Carthage Coll., 1965-66. Author: Shadow on the Lost Rock, 1958, Saul, the King, 1968, Abba Father, 1970 (Friends Lit. Fiction award 1972), Buried Alive, 1970, A School for Peter, 1974, A Home for Peter, 1983, Letters to Lauren, A History of the Methodist Campgrounds, Des Plaines, 1985; contbr. many articles to profl. pubs. Mem. Friends of Lit. Dem. Recipient Humanitarian award Ill. Med. Soc. Aux. Home: 4133 Mockingbird Ln Suffolk VA 23434-7186

MATSUI, DOROTHY NOBUKO, elementary education educator; b. Honolulu, Jan. 9, 1954; d. Katsura and Tamiko (Sakai) M. Student, U. Hawaii, Honolulu, 1972-76, postgrad., 1982; BEd, U. Alaska, Anchorage, 1979, MEd in Spl. Edn., 1986. Clerical asst. U. Hawaii Manoa Disbursing

Office, Anchorage, 1974-76; passenger service agt. Japan Air Lines, Anchorage, 1980; bilingual tutor Anchorage Sch. Dist., 1980, elem. sch. tchr., 1980—; facilitator for juvenile justice courses Anchorage Sch. Dist., Anchorage Police Dept., Alaska Pacific U., 1992-93; mem. adv. bd. Anchorage Law-Related Edn. Advancement Project. Vol. Providence Hosp., Anchorage, 1986, Humana Hosp., Anchorage, 1984, Spl. Olympics, Anchorage, 1981, Municipality Anchorage, 1978, Easter Seal Soc. Hawaii, 1975. Mem. NAFE, NEA, Alaska Edn. Assn., Smithsonian Nat. Assoc. Program, Nat. Space Soc., Smithsonian Air and Space Assn., World Aerospace Edn. Orgn., Internat. Platform Assn., Nat. Trust for Hist. Preservation, Nat. Audubon Soc., Planetary Soc., Cousteau Soc., Alaska Coun. for the Social Studies, Alaska Coun. Tchrs. Math., World Inst. Achievment, U.S. Olympic Soc., Women's Inner Circle Achievement, U. Alaska Alumni Assn., World Wildlife Fund, Japanese-Am. Nat. Mus., Alpha Delta Kappa (treas. Alpha chpt. 1988-92, corr. sec. 1993-96, sgt. at arms 1996—). Office: Anchorage Sch Dist 7001 Cranberry St Anchorage AK 99502-7145

MATSUMURA, DONNA SHIGEKO, secondary education English educator; b. Cleve., Oct. 24, 1950; d. Isamu J. and Alice Kivoko (Okamura) M. BS in Edn., Ohio State U., 1972. Tchr., coach Columbus (Ohio) Pub. Schs., 1972-78; coach jr. varsity women's volleyball Ohio State U., Columbus, 1977-78, athletic tutor, 1974-78; dir. ice skating Nat. Youth Sports Program, Columbus, 1974-78; tchr. Dallas Pub. Schs., 1978—, coach, 1982-83, 89—, dir. drill team, 1989—, staff devel. assoc., 1993-95; English co-chair textbook com. Dallas Pub. Schs., 1991-92; McDougal Littel panel mem., 1992; offcl. USA Track and Field, Tex., 1992—. Mem. Nat. Staff Devel. Coun. Presbyterian. Office: WH Adamson H S 201 E 9th St Dallas TX 75203-2229

MATSUMURA, MOLLEEN, educational organization executive; b. Riverside, Calif., May 1, 1948; d. Leston and Sarah Lee (Rightman) Stark; m. Kenneth Naoyuki Matsumura; 1 child, Miriam Ellen. BA, U. Calif., Berkeley, 1970. Sr. editor, dir. Alin Found., Berkeley, 1981—; network project dir. Nat. Ctr. for Sci. Edn., El Cerrito, Calif., 1993—. Editl. assoc. Free Inquiry mag., Buffalo, 1989-95, assoc. editor, 1995—, Missing Link newsletter, 1995; editor: Voices for Evolution, 1995; co-author: Japan's Economy in World Perspective, 1983, Sex in China, 1991, Mother-to-be: Pregnancy and Birth for Women with Disabilities, 1991; contbr. numerous articles to profl. jours. Bd. dirs. Coun. for Secular Humanism, Buffalo, 1996—; nat. adv. coun. mem. Ams. United for Separation of Ch. and State, Washington, 1992—; mem. Feminists for Free Expression. Recipient Disting. Svc. award Coun. for Secular Humanism, 1993. Mem. AAUW, ACLU, Soc. for Sci. Study of Sex. Office: National Center for Science Education PO Box 9477 Berkeley CA 94709

MATTERSON, JOAN MCDEVITT, physical therapist; b. Bryn Mawr, Pa., Feb. 24, 1949; d. William J. and Wanda Jean (Edwards) McD.; children: Brian, Jennie, Kira. BS in Biology, St. Joseph's U., Phila., 1973; cert. in phys. therapy, U. Pa., 1974. Assoc. pharmacologist, researcher immunology and arthritis Progressive Phys. Therapy, P.A., Wilmington, Del., 1976-93, pediatric phys. therapist, 1974-81, pres., 1976-95; rehab. dir. Achievement Rehab.; phys. therapist Liberty Home Health, 1995—; rehab. dir. Office of Joan Matterson, 1995—, Integrated Health Svcs.- Kent, Smyrna, Del., 1996—; lectr. in field of low level laser therapy. Dep. gov. Am. Biog. Rsch. Inst.; mem. adv. bd. Internat. Biographical Rsch. Inst., Cambridge, England. Mem. Am. Soc. Laser Medicine and Surgery, Internat. Platform Assn., Am. Phys. Therapy Assn., Am. Acad. Pain (assoc.), Inst. Noetic Sci., Am. Bd. Forensic Examiners.

MATTESON, BARBARA ANN VANCE, secondary education educator; b. Ft. Collins, Colo., Mar. 1, 1940; d. Wilford Walton and Louise (Hinchliffe) Vance; m. David Russell Matteson, Apr. 9, 1961 (dec. Oct. 12, 1988); 1 child, Deborah Jean. BA, U. No. Colo., 1965; postgrad., U. Colo., 1967-78, Colo. State U., 1967-78, U. Wyo., 1978—. Tchr. reading and lang. arts Westminster (Colo.) H.S., 1968-78; tchr. reading and lang. arts Natrona County H.S., Casper, Wyo., 1978—, chmn. dept. lang. arts, 1981 87; tchr. Natrona Acad., 1994—; coord. secondary lang. arts Natrona County Sch. Dist. 1, 1992-95, writing assessment facilitator, 1992-93. Named Outstanding Educator, Natrona County Sch. Dist. 1, 1990. Mem. ASCD, Nat. Coun. Tchrs. English, Wyo. ASCD, Delta Kappa Gamma. Home: 2700 Belmont Rd Casper WY 82604 Office: Natrona County HS 930 S Elm St Casper WY 82601

MATTHAEUS, RENATE G., high school principal; b. Dresden, Saxony, Germany, Aug. 18, 1942; d. Gerhard R. and Gerda (Kemter) M. BA, DePaul U., 1964; MS, No. Ill. U., 1974, CAS, 1977; doctoral studies, Loyola U., 1991. Cert. adminstr., supt. Statistician Jewel Cos., Melrose Pk., Ill., 1964-66; tchr. German Larsen & Ellis Jr. & Elgin (Ills.) Sr. High Sch., 1966-74; asst. prin. Abbott Jr. High Sch., Elgin, 1974-82; prin. Canton Mid. Sch., Elgin, 1982-88, Larkin High Sch., Elgin, 1988—. Team mem. Jayne Shover Easter Seal Ctr. Telethon, Elgin, 1991, team capt. Telethon, 1992-95; team leader Elgin Symphony Sustaining Fund Drive, Elgin, 1991. Recipient Women of Achievement award Women in Mgmt., 1988, YWCA Harriett Gifford award in Edn., 1993. Mem. Ill. Prins. Assn. (Region VIII legis. chair 1991—, program chair 1989-91, mem. chair 1986-89), Assn. Elgin Sch. Adminstrs. (sec., v.p., pres. 1975 77), Rotary Club (bd. dirs. Elgin chpt. 1991—, community svc. chair 1991-92, new project com. chair 1990-91, vocat. svc. chair 1992-93, sec. 1993-94, pres.-elect 1994, pres. 1995—). Lutheran. Office: Larkin High Sch 1475 Larkin Ave Elgin IL 60123-5173

MATTHES, BETSY DURKIN, lyricist, actress; b. Ft. Benning, Ga., Mar. 11, 1942; d. Edwin Joseph and Marjorie (Flynn) Ostberg; m. Gerald Stephen Rutter Matthes, Aug. 22, 1965 (div.); children—Peter, Charlton; m. Jack Cordrey Cortner, May 21, 1993. Grad. Am. Theatre Wing, 1961; BA summa cum laude in Internat. Studies, Women's Studies Marymount Manhattan Coll., 1996. Pres. Peter's Pride Pub. Appeared in various TV commls.; appeared in plays including: Cactus Flower (Broadway), Mary Mary (nat. co.); appeared in day-time series Dark Shadows, Hidden Faces; lyricist Love Express, Love is Holdin' On, Slip Into Somethin' Comfortable, Pleasure Man, Let's Go Another Round, Chocolate Shake, Someone Just For Me, I Was Made for You, Not In the Same Way, Do You Love Him, Crazy In Love, Right Before My Eyes, She's Gonna Love Ya to Death, Come Out Fightin, My Favorite Bedtime Story, Forever is Not For Everyone. Gerard scholar, Curian scholar. Mem. Actors Equity Assn., Screen Actors Guild, AFTRA, ASCAP, NOW, NAFE, Women's Commn. Refugee Women and Children, Alpha Chi, Omicron Delta Kappa. Democrat. Home and Office: Apt #15A 65 Central Park West New York NY 10023

MATTHEW, LYN, sales and marketing executive consultant, educator; b. Long Beach, Calif., Dec. 15, 1936; d. Harold G. and Beatrice (Hunt) M.; m. Wayne Thomas Castleberry, Aug. 12, 1961 (div. Jan. 1976); children: Melanie, Cheryl, Nicole, Matthew. BS, U. Calif.-Davis, 1958; MA, Ariz. State U., 1979. Cert. hotel sales exec., 1988, meeting profl. Pres., Davlyn Cons. Found., Scottsdale, Ariz., 1979-82; cons., vis. prof. The Art Bus., Scottsdale, 1982—; pres., dir. sales and mktg. Embassy Stes., Scottsdale, 1987—, bd. trustees Hotel Sales and Mktg. Assn. Internat. Found., 1988—, chmn., 1991-93, mem. exec. com., 1993—; vis. prof. Maricopa C.C., Phoenix, 1979—, Ariz. State U., Tempe, 1980-83; cons. Women's Caucus for Art, Phoenix, 1983-88. Bd. dirs. Rossom House and Heritage Square Found., Phoenix, 1987-88. Author: The Business Aspects of Art, Book I, 1979, Book II, 1979; Marketing Strategies for the Creative Artist, 1985. Mem. Women Image Now (Achievement and Contbn. in Visual Arts award 1983), Women in Higher Edn., Nat. Women's Caucus for Art (v.p. 1981-83), Ariz. Women's Caucus for Art (pres. 1980-82, hon. advisor 1986-87), Ariz. Vocat. Edn. Assn. (sec. 1978-80), Ariz. Visionary Artists (treas. 1987-89), Hotel Sales and Mktg. Assn. Internat. (pres. Great Phoenix chpt. 1988-89, regional dir. 1989-90, bd. dirs. 1985-90), CHSE (profl. designation tng. chair), Meeting Planners Internat. (v.p. Ariz. Sunbelt chpt. 1989-91, pres. 1991-92, Supplier of Yr. award 1988, CMP certification trainer), Soc. Govt. Meeting Planners (charter bd. dirs. 1987, Sam Gilmer award 1992, nat. conf. co-chmn. 1993-94), Ariz. Visionary Artists (treas. 1987-88), Ariz. Acad. Performing Arts (v.p. bd. dirs. 1987-88, pres. 1988-89).

MATTHEWS, BETTY PARKER, special education educator; b. Port Arthur, Tex., Dec. 9, 1929; d. Clarence G. and Florence (Sudduth) Parker; m. Paul A. Matthews, Mar. 25, 1955; children: Michael A., Scott P., Lisa M. Alexander. BS, La. Coll., 1975; MEd, Northwestern U., 1981. Specialist in edn. La., 1984; cert. elem. tchr., mentally retarded, learning disabled, ednl. cons., generic mild/moderate, assessment tchr., ednl. diagnostician, child search coord., La. 3d grade tchr. Rapides Parish Sch. Bd., Alexandria, La., 1975-76, tchr. spl. edn., 1976-81, assessment tchr., 1981-93; ednl. diagnostician Rapides Parish Sch. Bd., Alexandria, 1993—; ednl. cons. Briarwood Psychiatric Hosp., Alexandria, La., 1986-93, Crossroads Psychiat. Hosp., Alexandria, 1993-96; adj. prof. La. State U., Alexandria, 1990—. Dir. children's Bible study 1st Bapt. Ch., Pineville, La., 1985—. Mem. La. Ednl. Diagnosticians Assn. (regional rep. 1987-88, treas. 1988-90, Pres.'s Svc. award 1990-91, La. Assessment Tchr. of Yr. 1993), Coun. Exceptional Children, Reading Coun., Alpha Delta Kappa, Phi Delta Kappa, Epsilon Sigma Alpha (state pres., regional sec.). Home: 3050 Rigolette Rd Pineville LA 71360-7219

MATTHEWS, DANE DIKEMAN, urban planner; b. Memphis, Dec. 19, 1950; d. Neil Jude and Virginia Ann (Turnbull) Dikeman; m. John Wesley Matthews, Dec. 28, 1971. BA with distinction, U. Okla., 1972, M of Regional and City Planning, 1974. Planner Hudgins, Thompson & Ball, Inc., Tulsa, 1975-76; econ. devel. planner Tulsa Metro. Area Planning Commn., 1976-77; planner II Tulsa Met. Area Planning Commn., 1977-80; prin. regional planner Indian Nations Coun. Govts., Tulsa, 1980—. Project dir. Kendall-Whittier Neighborhood Master Plan, 1992. Bd. dirs. Met. Tulsa Urban League, 1993-95, Parkside Cmty. Mental Health Ctr., Tulsa, 1986—; bd. dirs., chair house com. Arts and Humanities Coun., Tulsa, 1991—; div. chair Tulsa Area United Way, 1988—. Recipient Spl. Recognition award Downtown Tulsa Unltd., 1988. Mem. Am. Inst. Cert. Planners (cert.), Am. Planning Assn. (Okla. chpt. pres. 1988-89, Master Plan award 1992, Outstanding Profl. Planner 1991), Phi Beta Kappa. Democrat. Episcopalian. Office: INCOG 201 W 5th St Ste 600 Tulsa OK 74103-4278

MATTHEWS, ELIZABETH WOODFIN, law librarian, law educator; b. Ashland, Va., July 30, 1927; d. Edwin Clifton and Elizabeth Frances (Luck) Woodfin; m. Sidney E. Matthews, Dec. 20, 1947; 1 child, Sarah Elizabeth Matthews Wiley. BA, Randolph-Macon Coll., 1948, LLD (hon.), 1989; MS in Libr. Sci., U. Ill., 1952; PhD, So. Ill. U., 1972; LLD, Randolph-Macon Coll., 1989. Cert. law libr., med. libr., med. libr. III. Libr. Ohio State U., Columbus, 1952-59; libr., instr. U. Ill., Urbana, 1962-63, lectr. Grad. Sch. Libr. Sci., 1964; libr., instr. Morris Libr. So. Ill. U., Carbondale, 1964-67, classroom instr. Coll. Edn., 1967-70, med. libr., asst. prof. Morris Libr., 1972-74, law libr., asst. prof., 1974-79, law libr., assoc. prof., 1979-85, law libr., prof., 1985-92, prof. emerita, 1992—. Author: Access Points to Law Libraries, 1984, 17th Century English Law Reports, 1986, Law Library Reference Shelf, 1988, 2d edit., 1992, 3d edit., 1996, Pages and Missing Pages, 1983, 2d edit., 1989, Lincoln as a Lawyer: An Annotated Bibliography, 1991. Mem. AAUW (pres. 1976-78, corp. rep. 1978-88), Am. Assn. Law Librs., Mid Am. Assn. Law Librs., Beta Phi Mu, Phi Kappa Phi. Methodist. Home: 811 S Skyline Dr Carbondale IL 62901-2405 Office: So Ill U Law Libr Carbondale IL 62901

MATTHEWS, ESTHER ELIZABETH, education educator, consultant; b. Princeton, Mass., June 20, 1918; d. Ralph Edgar and Julia Ellen (Cronin) M. BS in Edn., Worcester State Coll., 1940; EdM, Harvard U., 1943, EdD, 1960. Tchr. various Mass. schs., 1942-47; guidance dir. Holden (Mass.) Pub. Schs., 1947-53, Wareham (Mass.) Pub. Schs., 1954-57; counselor Newton (Mass.) High Sch., 1957-60, head counselor, 1960-66; assoc. prof. edn. U. Oreg., 1966-70, prof. edn., 1970-80, prof. emerita, 1980—; vis. prof. U. Toronto, Ont., Can., summer 1971; lectr. on edn. Harvard U., 1963-66; cons. in field; lectr. various colls. and univs. Author book chpts.; contbr. numerous articles to profl. jours. and papers to conf. proc. Mem. ACD (Recognition for Contbn. to Promote Human Rights 1987), World Future Soc., Nat. Vocat. Guidance Assn. (pres. 1974-75, chair nat. com. 1966-67, sec. 1967-68, bd. trustees 1968-71, editl. bd. Vocat. Guidance Quar. 1966-68), Oreg. Pers. and Guidance Assn. (Leona Tyler award 1973, Disting. Svc. award 1979), Oreg. Career Devel. Assn. (Disting. Svc. award 1987, Esther E. Matthews Ann. award for outstanding contbn. to career devel. in Oreg. established in her honor 1993). Home: 832 Lariat Dr Eugene OR 97401-6438

MATTHEWS, GLENNA CHRISTINE, historian; b. L.A., Nov. 7, 1938; d. Glen Leslie and Alberta Marie (Nicolais) Ingles; m. James Duncan Matthews (div. Jan. 1978); children: Karen, David. BA, San Jose State U., 1969; MA, Stanford U., 1971, PhD, 1977. Assoc. prof. history Okla. State U., 1978-85. Author: Just a Housewife, 1987, The Rise of Public Woman, 1992; co-author: Running as a Woman, 1993. Recipient The Sierra prize Western Assn. Women Historians. Mem. Am. Hist. Assn., Orgn. Am. Historians.

MATTHEWS, HEATHER MARIE, women's shelter administrator, educator; b. Dowagiac, Mich., Dec. 18, 1969; d. Wilburt Ray and Deborah Sue (Heeter) Tetzlaff; m. Martin A. Matthews, Dec. 31, 1994. BS in Psychology, St. Mary-of-Woods Coll., Ind., 1992. Adv. Coun. on Domestic Abuse, Terre Haute, Ind., 1992; case mgr. YWCA Women's Shelter, South Bend, Ind., 1992-95, shelter supr., 1995—; field instr. St. Mary's Coll., South Bend, 1995—; mem. Stewart Mckinney Homeless Assistance Task Force, South Bend, 1995—. Contbr. poems to lit. mag. Spkr. YWCA, South Bend, 1995. Mem. Nat. Coalition Against Domestic Violence, Ind. Coalition Against Domestic Violence, Internat. Thespian Soc. Democrat. Roman Catholic. Home: 634 S Ironwood Dr South Bend IN 46615 Office: YWCA Shelter for Battered Women 802 N Lafayette Blvd South Bend IN 46601

MATTHEWS, ROWENA GREEN, biological chemistry educator; b. Cambridge, Eng., Aug. 20, 1938 (father Am. citizen); d. David E. and Doris (Cribb) Green; m. Larry Stanford Matthews, June 18, 1960; children: Brian Stanford, Keith David. BA, Radcliffe Coll., 1960; PhD, U. Mich., 1969. Instr. U. S.C., Columbia, 1964-65; postdoctoral fellow U. Mich., Ann Arbor, 1970-75, asst. prof., 1975-81, assoc. prof. biol. chemistry, 1981-86, prof. 1986—, assoc. chmn., 1988-92, G. Robert Greenberg disting. prof., 1995—, chair biophysics rsch. divsn., 1996—; mem. phys. biochemistry study sect. NIH, 1982-86; mem. adv. coun. Nat. Inst. Gen. Med. Scis., NIH, 1991-94; adv. bd. NATO, 1994-96. mem. editorial adv. bd. Biochem. Jour., 1984-92, Arch. Biochemistry, Biophysics, 1992—, Biochemistry, 1993—, Jour. Bacteriology, 1995—. Contbr. articles to profl. jours. Recipient Faculty Recognition award U. Mich., 1984, Merit award Nat. Inst. Gen. Med. Scis., 1991; NIH grantee, 1978—; NSF grantee, 1992—. Mem. AAAS, Am. Soc. Biochem. and Molecular Biol. (program chair 1995, chair human resources 1996—), Am. Chem. Soc. (program chmn. biochemistry div. 1985, sec. biochemistry div. 1990-92, chair 1994—), Phi Beta Kappa, Sigma Xi. Avocations: bicycling, snorkeling, cross country skiing, cooking, gardening. Home: 1609 S University Ave Ann Arbor MI 48104-2620 Office: U Mich Biophysics Rsch Divsn 4024 Chemistry 930 N University Ave Ann Arbor MI 48109-1055

MATTHEWS, VALERIE JO, development company executive; b. Omaha, June 6, 1947; d. Blaine Leroy and Betty Rae (Peterson) Rish; m. L. D. Matthews (div. 1975); children: Amy Lynne, Timothy Bryan. Grad. high sch., Omaha, 1965. Acct. various firms, Fremont, Nebr., 1967-78; sales assoc. Sunrise Home, Lincoln, Nebr., 1979-81, Lamb Realty, Thousand Oaks, Calif., 1981-82; rep. and mgr. sales Centex Homes, Oklahoma City, 1982-85; div. pres. Oklahoma City and Denver, 1985-87; with Lamb Realty, Thousand Oaks, Calif., 1988; dir. constrn. and land C.R. Wood Devel. Inc., Thousand Oaks, 1987-91; pres. C.R. Wood Devel., Inc., Thousand Oaks, 1991-92, Rish Homes, Inc., Meridian, Idaho, 1992—; owner Sunrise Realty, Meridian, Idaho, 1993—; pres. Learning Dynamics, Meridian, Idaho, 1994—; pvt. practice tax and fin. cons. Vol. YMCA, Fremont, 1972, Vols. in Arts, Oklahoma City, 1985, Make-A-Wish-Found.; active Boys Scouts Am., F.O.P. Mem. Calif. Assn. Realtors, Nat. Assn. Home Builders, Bldg. Industry Assn.

MATTHEWS, WYHOMME S., music educator, college administrator; b. Battle Creek, Mich., July 22, 1948; d. Woodrow R. and LouLease (Graham) Sellers; m. Edward L. Matthews, Apr. 29, 1972; children: Channing DuVall, Triston Curran, Landon Edward, Brandon Graham. AA, Kellogg C.C., 1968; MusB, Mich. State U., 1970, MA, 1972, MusM, 1972. Cert. elem. and secondary tchr., Mich. Tchr., vocal music dir. Benton Harbor (Mich.) Pub. Schs., 1971-72, dir. vocal music, 1972; dir. edn. head start program Burlington (N.J.) County, 1972-73; pvt. music tchr., 1973-89; tchr. Southeastern Jr. H.S., 1986-87, W.K. Kellogg Jr. H.S., 1987-89; chair visual and performing arts dept. Kellogg C.C., Battle Creek, Mich., 1989—; 1972; part-time instr. Kellogg C.C., 1973-89, dir. Eclectic Chorale, 1994—, dir., organizer Kellogg C.C. Eclectic Chorale Sacred Cultural Festival, 1979—, judge various contests; presenter in field. Pres. Dudley Elem. Sch., 1981-85; active Battle Creek Pub. Schs. PTA, Pennfield Pub. Schs. PTA, Mt. Zion African Meth. Episc. Ch. Mich. State U. fellow, 1971; recipient Outstanding Cmty. Svc. award, 1975. Mem. Mich. Music Tchr. Assn., Nat. Music Tchrs. Assn., Battle Creek Music Tchrs. Assn., Battle Creek Morning Music Club (bd. dirs.), Nat. Leadership Acad., Battle Creek Cmty. Concert Assn. Home: 466 Alton Ave Battle Creek MI 49017-3212 Office: Kellogg CC 450 North Ave Battle Creek MI 49017-3397

MATTHIAS, CHERYL ANNE, counselor, psychotherapist; b. Oelwein, Iowa, June 23, 1943; d. Soren Peter Hartvig and Vermelia Genetha (Christiansen) Sorensen; m. Robert Lee Matthias, Aug. 7, 1965; children: Tanya Kristine, Brock David. BA in Phys. Edn., Wartburg Coll., 1965; MS, U. Wis., 1977. High sch. counselor Manitowoc (Wis.) Pub. Schs., 1977-80, dept. head, 1980-94; psychotherapist Lakeshore Mental Health, Manitowoc, Wis., 1994—. Mem. Nixonette Rep. Party Nat. Conf., Miami. Mem. Wis. Sch. Couns. (pres., past. pres., mem. bd.), East Ctrl. Wis. Counselors Assn. (pres., past. pres., pres. elect.), Sunrise Manitowoc Optimist (pres. 1994-95), Phi Delta Kappa. Lutheran. Home: 230 Harvest Ct Manitowoc WI 54220

MATTHIAS, REBECCA C., social services administrator. Pres., COO Mothers Work, Inc., Phila. Office: Mothers Work Inc 1309 Noble St Philadelphia PA 19123*

MATTIE, JEANNE MARIE, public relations and communications consultant; b. Sendai, Japan, Aug. 4, 1950; came to U.S., 1952; d. John D. and Edna H. M.; m. Donald J. Patrican, June 14, 1986; 1 child, Julian M. Patrican. BA, U. Del., 1970. Co-founder Cyrk, Inc., Gloucester, Mass., 1975-80; pres. Mattie Assocs., Inc., Boston and Rockport, Mass., 1980—. Office: Mattie Assocs Inc 178 South St Rockport MA 01966-2301

MATTILA, MARY JO KALSEM, elementary and art educator; b. Canton, Ill., Oct. 26, 1944; d. Joseph Nelson and Bernice Nora (Milbauer) Kalsem; m. John Peter Mattila, Jan. 27, 1968. BS in Art, U. Wis., 1966; student, Ohio State U., 1972, Drake U., 1981; MS in Ednl. Adminstrn., Iowa State U., 1988. Cert. tchr., prin., supr., adminstr., art tchr., secondary tchr., Iowa. Tchr. 2d grade McHenry (Ill.) Pub. Schs., 1966-67, Wisconsin Hts. Schs., Black Earth, Wis., 1967-69; substitute tchr. Columbus (Ohio) City Schs., 1969-70; elem. art tchr. Southwestern City Schs., Columbus, 1972-73; adminstrv. intern Ames, Iowa, 1984-86; lead tchr. at Roosevelt Sch. Ames Cmty. Schs., 1986-87, art vertical curriculum chair, 1983-89, art educator, elem. and spl. edn., 1973—. Author articles. Active LWV, Ames, 1982—; fundraiser Altrusa, Ames, 1992—. Recipient Very Spl. Svc. award for Disting. Svc. in Very Spl. Arts, Gov. of Iowa, 1984. Mem. ASCD, NEA, Nat. Assn. Elem. Sch. Prins., Nat. Art Edn. Assn. Home: 2822 Duff Ave Ames IA 50010-4710 Office: Ames Cmty Schs 120 S Kellogg Ave Ames IA 50010-6719

MATTLEMAN, MARCIENE SCHREIBER, organization executive; b. Phila., Jan. 26, 1930; d. Abner and Miriam (Lamm) Schreiber; m. Herman Mattleman, June 25, 1950; children: Ellen Mattleman Kaplan, Jon, Barbara. BS in Edn., Temple U., 1951, MEd in Elem. Edn., 1962, EdD, 1967. Tchr. elem. schs. Cheltenham (Pa.) Twp., 1951-53; reading tutor Lower Merion (Pa.) Twp. Schs., 1957-59; lectr., instr. English edn. Temple U., Phila., 1962-67, asst. prof., 1967-69, assoc. prof., 1969-72, prof., 1973-84; exec. dir. Phila. Mayor's Commn. on Literacy, 1984-88; founder, exec. dir. Phila. Futures, 1989—. Author: 101 Activities for Teaching Reading, 1973, (with Herman Mattleman) Expanding Language Skills, 1981. Trustee C.C. Phila., 1985—; trustee Free Libr. Phila., 1987—, chmn. bd. trustees, 1993—; bd. dirs. Pub. Interest Law Ctr. Phila., 1986—; mem. Phila. Mayor's Commn. on Literacy, 1992—, mem. adv. bd. Nat. Inst. for Literacy, 1995—. Recipient Humanitarian award Am. Jewish Com., 1985, B'nai B'rith Educators, 1987, literacy award Keystone State Reading Assn., 1986, leadership honoree Luth. Settlement House, 1988, cert. of recognition Phila. Coun. Adminstrv. Women in Edn., 1988, humanities award Jewish Chaplaincy Svc., 1989, ann. award Phila. Com. on City Policy, 1991, Clarence Farmer award Phila. Commn. on Human Rels., 1991, alumni award Temple U. Coll. Edn., 1991, Gimbel award Med. Coll. Pa., 1993, ednl. leadership award Phila. United Negro Coll. Fund, 1994, gold medal Phila. Pub. Rels. Assn., 1995; named One of 1000 Women for '90s, Mirabella mag., 1994; named to Alumni Hall of Fame, Overbrook H.S., 1994. Democrat. Jewish. Office: Phila Futures 230 S Broad St 7th Fl Philadelphia PA 19102

MATTSON, CAROL LINNETTE, social services administrator; b. Frederic, Wis., Oct. 3, 1946; d. Clarence Waldemar and Lucille Anna Mathilda (Bengtson) Hedlund; m. Wesley Harlan Mattson, June 24, 1967; 1 child, Aaron Ray. BS, U. Wis., Menomonie, 1968. Home econs. tchr. Luck (Wis.) High Sch., 1968-72; clk. Daniels Twp., Siren, Wis., 1973-75; family living instr. Wis. Indianhead Tech. Inst., New Richmond, 1974-77; aging program dir. Polk County, Balsam Lake, Wis., 1977—; sec., bd. dirs. Polk County Transp. for the Disabled and Elderly, Inc., Balsam Lake, 1978—; sec., mem. com. Long Term Support Com., Balsam Lake, 1985-90. Mem. Wis. Assn. Nutrition Dirs., Wis. Assn. Aging Unit Dirs. Lutheran. Office: Polk County Aging Programs PO Box 605 Balsam Lake WI 54810-0605

MATTSON, JOY LOUISE, oncological nurse; b. Moline, Ill., Feb. 1, 1956; d. Norman O. and Jeannette (Squier) M.; m. Duncan F. Crannell, Sept. 9, 1988. BA magna cum laude, Bates Coll., 1977; MTS, Harvard U., 1982; BSN magna cum laude, Rutgers U., Newark, 1988; MLS, Rutgers U., 1993. RN, N.J. Staff nurse oncology Muhlenberg Reg. Med. Ctr., Plainfield, N.J., 1987-88; staff nurse St. Lawrence Rehab. Ctr., Lawrenceville, N.J., 1988-89; clin. rsch. asst. G.H. Besselaar Assocs., Princeton, N.J., 1990-91; med. writer Convatec, Skillman, N.J., 1991-92, G.H. Besselaar Assocs., Princeton, N.J., 1992-94; clin. safety assoc. Pfizer Inc., N.Y.C., 1994—. Mem. Phi Beta Kappa. Home: 5 Tudor City Pl Apt 508 New York NY 10017

MATTULAT, S. DIANE, bank executive. Sr. v.p. tax Calif. Fed. Bank, L.A. Office: Calif Fed Bank 5700 Wilshire Blvd Ste 243 Los Angeles CA 90036*

MATULEF, GIZELLE TERESE, secondary education educator; b. Budapest, Jan. 17, 1945; came to the U.S., 1948; d. Louis and Gizelle Beke; m. Gary Matulef, Mar. 21, 1975; 1 child, Margaret. AA in Bus., Phoenix (Ariz.) Coll., 1964; BS in Edn., No. Ariz. U., 1966; MA, Ind. U., 1970, PhD in Comparative Lit., 1983. Cert. secondary teaching credential, Calif., C.C. instr. credential, Calif. Bus. instr. Drake Bus. Coll., N.Y.C., 1973, Cerro Coso Coll., Ridgecrest, Calif., 1973-74; English and bus. instr. Sawyer Bus. Coll., Westwood, Calif., 1974-75; bus. instr. Sierra Sands Adult Sch., Ridgecrest, 1975-82; Indian edn. dir. Sierra Sands Unifed Sch. Dist., Ridgecrest, 1980-82; sch. improvement program dir. Murray Jr. High Sch., Ridgecrest, 1982-89; English and econs. instr. Trona (Calif.) High Sch., 1989-92; tng. dir. High Desert Experience Unlimited Career Counseling, Ridgecrest, 1991-92; substitute tchr. Sierra Sands Unified Sch. Dist., Ridgecrest, 1993-96; archives asst. Albert Michelson Mus., Naval Weapons Ctr., China Lake, Calif., 1976-77, editorial asst. Tech. Info. Dept., 1977-78. Contbr. articles to profl. jours. Active PTA, Ridgecrest Schs., 1983-93, Music Parents Assn., Ridgecrest, 1985-93. Recipient fellowship Ind. U., Bloomington, 1966-69. Mem. AAUW (pres. China Lake/Ridgecrest br. 1992-96), NEA. Home: PO Box 1041 Ridgecrest CA 93556-1041

MATUSOW, NAOMI C., state legislator; b. Nashville, Oct. 31, 1938; m. Gene R. Matusow; children: Gary, Jason. BA cum laude, Vanderbilt U.; MA in Counseling and Guidance, NYU; JD, Pace U. Bar: N.Y. 1981. Editl. asst. Golden Press; tchr. math. N.Y.C. pub. schs., guidance counselor; pvt. practice as lawyer Armonk, 1981-90, White Plains, 1990—; mem. N.Y. State Assembly, 1992—, mem. various coms. Past mem. Dem. State Com., Westchester County Dem. Exec. Com., North Castle Dem. Com.; assoc. Westchester Land Trust; bd. dirs. Family Svc. Westchester; chair Hudson River Valley Task Force. Mem. NOW, Nat. Women's Polit. Caucus, N.Y. State Women's Bar Assn., Westchester County Bar Assn., Westchester Assn.

Women Bus. Owners. Office: NY State Assembly State Capitol Albany NY 12224 also: 125-131 Main St Mount Kisco NY 10549

MATUSZAK, ALICE JEAN BOYER, pharmacy educator; b. Newark, Ohio, June 22, 1935; d. James Emery and Elizabeth Hawthorne (Irvine) Boyer; m. Charles Alan Matuszak, Aug. 27, 1955; children: Matthew, James. BS summa cum laude, Ohio State U., 1958, MS, 1959; postgrad., U. Wis., 1959-60; PhD, U. Kans., 1963. Registered pharmacist, Ohio, Calif. Apprentice pharmacist Arensberg Pharmacy, Newark, 1953-58; rsch. asst. Ohio State U., Columbus, 1958, lab. asst., 1958-59; rsch. asst. U. Wis., Madison, 1959-60, U. Kans., Lawrence, 1960-63; asst. prof. U. of the Pacific, Stockton, Calif., 1963-67, assoc. prof., 1971-78, prof., 1978—; vis. fgn. prof. Kobe-Gakuin U., Japan, 1992. Contbr. articles to profl. jours. Recipient Disting. Alumna award Ohio State U. Coll. Pharmacy, 1994; NIH grantee, 1965-66. Fellow Am. Pharm. Assn. (chmn. basic scis. 1990); mem. Am. Assn. Colls. of Pharmacy (chmn. chemistry sect. 1979-80, bd. dirs. 1993-95), Am. Inst. History of Pharmacy (exec. coun. 1984-88, 90-92, 92-95, chmn. contributed papers 1990-92, pres.-elect 1995—), Cert. of Commendation 1990), Am. Chem. Soc., Internat. Fedn. Pharmacy, Acad. Pharm. Rsch. Sci. (pres. 1993-94), Coun. Sci. Soc. Pres., U.S. Adopted Names Coun. U.S. Pharmacopeial Conv., Sigma Xi, Rho Chi, Phi Kappa Phi, Kappa Epsilon (Unicorn award, award of merit 1995), Lambda Kappa Sigma, Delta Zeta. Democrat. Episcopalian. Home: 1130 W Mariposa Ave Stockton CA 95204-3021 Office: U of the Pacific Sch of Pharmacy Stockton CA 95211

MAU, C. S. See SALERNO, CHERIE ANN

MAU, MARY LOU, elementary education educator; b. State Center, Iowa, Sept. 2, 1944; d. Thomas Robert and Pauline Geraldine (Schulz) Borton; m. Alvin H. Mau, June 7, 1975; children: Rachelle, Janice. AA, Marshalltown C.C., 1963; BA, Buena Vista Coll., 1969. Cert. elem. tchr. 1st grade tchr. Maple Valley Sch., Mapleton, Iowa, 1969-82, Chpt. I tchr., 1982—, reading recovery tchr., 1993—; mem. Chpt. I Adv. Bd., Sioux City, Iowa, 1992—; mem., sec. Chpt. I/Chpt. II Com., Mapleton, 1991—; mem. Prin. Selection Com., Mapleton, 1991-92. Mem. circle St. Paul Luth. Ch., Ida Grove, Iowa, 1980—, Sunday sch. tchr., 1985-90, 93; leader Girl Scouts, Ida Grove, 1984-92. Mem. Internat. Reading Assn., Iowa Edn. Assn., Iowa Reading Assn., Quint County Reading, Maple Valley Edn. Assn. Home: 100 King St Ida Grove IA 51445-1032 Office: Maple Valley Sch Mapleton IA 51034

MAUGHAN, SUSAN IRENE, school psychologist, therapist; b. Youngstown, Ohio, Dec. 19, 1951; d. James Frances and Lorna Maxine (Leichter) Rogers; m. James William Maughan, Aug. 24, 1973; children: James Jr., Erin E.; 2 adopted children: Melissa E., Rebecca M. BS in Education, Kent State U., 1974, MS in Sch. Psychology, 1979, EdS, 1981; cert. drug/alcohol abuse couselor, Cadwalder Behavior Inst., Houston, 1987. Cert. tchg. educable mentally retarded; learning disabilities; behavior disorders; phys. edn.; child study certification; lic. psychol. assoc.; marriage and family therapist, Tex.; lic. chem. dependency counselor. Tchr. spl. edn. Warren Sch. Dist., Ohio, 1978-79; grad. asst., recreation for handicapped Kent State U., Ohio, 1979-80; intern, sch. psychologist Windham Sch. Dist., Ohio, 1980-81; assoc. sch. psychologist Friendswood Sch. Dist., Tex., 1981-85; psychol. assoc. Ruscelli Clinic, Webster, Tex., 1985-92; assoc. sch. psychologist Santa Fe Sch. Dist., Tex., 1992—; coord. Spl. Transitional Edn. Program Santa Fe Sch. Dist., 1992-94, coord. Student Support Svcs., 1994—, instr. crisis prevention, 1994—; spkr. state Tex. Counsel Adminstrs. Spl. Edn. meeting. Democrat. Roman Catholic. Home: 1206 Pineywoods Dr Friendswood TX 77546 Office: Santa Fe Sch Dist PO Box 370 Santa Fe TX 77510

MAUK, AMY MARGARET, purchasing agent; b. Lubbock, Tex., Mar. 1, 1963; d. Clarence Delmar and Anna Mary (Ripper) House; m. Bryan Keith Mauk, June 9, 1984; children: Ashley Denise, Brittney Elise. BBA, Baylor U., 1986. Office mgr. Roming & Porter Engrs., Temple, Tex., 1986-90; dir. mgmt. svcs. City of Belton, Tex., 1990-94; purchasing agt. City of Temple, Tex., 1994—. Loaned exec. United Way, Temple, 1992-94, bd. dirs., 1994—; mem. Leadership Temple, 1995-96. Mem. Nat. Inst. Govt. Purchasing, Tex. Purchasing Mgmt. Assn., Ctrl. Tex. USTI Software Group (v.p. 1990-94), Nat. Assn. Purchsing Mgrs. Republican. Baptist. Home: 1019 Westgate I Rd Eddy TX 76524 Office: City of Temple 2 N Main Ste 302 Temple TX 76501

MAUKE, LEAH RACHEL, counselor; b. Newport, R.I., Aug. 29, 1924; d. Louis and Annie (Price) Louison; m. Otto Russell Mauke, June 18, 1950. BSBA, Boston U., 1946, MBA, 1948. Teaching fellow Boston U., 1946-48; head advt. dept. Endicott Coll., Beverly, Mass., 1948-66; guidance counselor Vineland (N.J.) Sr. High Sch., 1966-69; guidance counselor Black Horse Pike Regional Sch. Dist., Blackwood, N.J., 1969-86, ret., 1986. Vol. ARC, Vero Beach, Fla., 1988—. Boston U. fellow 1946. Mem. AAUW (life, pres. North Shore br. 1955-59, state fellowship chmn. 1957-58), NEA, N.J. Edn. Assn., Camden County Pers. and Guidance Assn. (sec. 1972). Home: 2119 E Lakeview Dr Sebastian FL 32958-8519

MAUL, MARGARET ELEANOR, financial planner; b. Fresno, Calif., Aug. 2, 1943. BBA magna cum laude, Calif. State U., Fresno, 1979; attended, U. Pa., 1991, 92, 94. CFP. Sr. acct. exec. Merrill Lynch, 1979-84; sr. v.p. investments Prudential Securities, Nev., 1984—; created Maul Fin. within Prudential Securities, 1994, chmn.'s coun., 1985—, equity coun.; spkr. fin. issues; leader fin. seminars. Guest, expert Sta. KVBC-TV News, Las Vegas; contbg. writer Fin. Planning on Wall St.; host Focus on Finance News 3 FM, Las Vegas. Bd. dirs. San Joaquin Valley Health Consortium, 1982; mem., corp. patron, corp. coun. Fresno Art Mus., 1993—; mem. fund raising com. Mus. Soc. Fresno Met. Mus., 1990-92; mem. steering com. Leon S. Peters Bldg. Campaign Calif. State U., 1986-94; mem. St. Regis Assn., 1995. Named Woman of Yr. by Fresno Bus. and Profl. Women. Mem. Inst. CFPs, Internat. Assn. Fin. Planning. Office: Prudential Securities 3763 Howard Hughes Pky Ste 330 Las Vegas NV 89109-0939

MAULDIN, JEAN ANN, controller; b. Ft. Chaffee, Ark., Oct. 12, 1957; d. Lawrence Ray and Antoinette Marie (Tusa) Mitchell; 1 child, Michele L. Carter. BBA in Acctg., U. Ctrl. Ark., 1979, MBA, 1985. Cost acct. FMC Automotive Svc. Divsn., Conway, Ark., 1979-82, mgr. cost acctg., 1982-85, divsnl. fin. analyst, 1985, plant contr., 1985-86, divsn. contr., 1986-88; mgr. cost acctg. Columbian Chems. Co., Atlanta, 1988-90, dir. field acctg., 1990-92, No. Am. contr., 1992-93, corporate controller, 1993-94; v.p., CFO Accuride Corp., Henderson, Ky., 1995—. Recipient Young Career Woman award Bus. and Profl. Women, 1986. Mem. Inst. Mgmt. Accts. (cert., v.p. adminstrn. 1993-94). Republican. Roman Catholic.

MAUN, MARY ELLEN, computer consultant; b. N.Y.C., Dec. 18, 1951; d. Emmet Joseph and Mary Alice (McMahon) M. BA, CUNY, 1977, MBA, 1988. Sales rep. N.Y. Telephone Co., N.Y.C., 1970-76, comml. rep., 1977-83, programmer, 1984-86; systems analyst Telesector Resources Group, N.Y.C., 1987-89, sr. systems analyst, 1990-95; pres. Sleepy Hollow Techs., Inc., North Tarrytown, N.Y., 1995—. Corp. chmn. United Way of Tri-State Area, N.Y.C., 1985; recreation activities vol. Pioneers Am., N.Y.C., 1982—; active Sleepy Hollow Hist. Soc. Recipient Outstanding Community Service award, Calvary Hosp., Bronx, N.Y., 1984. Mem. N.Y. Health and Racquet Club, Road Runners. Democrat. Home: 3 Farrington Ave Tarrytown NY 10591 Office: Sleepy Hollow Techs Inc 3 Farrington Ave Tarrytown NY 10591

MAUNDER, JILL ELLEN, consulting executive; b. Hartford, Conn., Oct. 9, 1955; d. David Kenneth and Rhoda Betty (Gofberg) Grossman; m. Richard Lawrence Maunder, Oct. 20, 1984. BA in Social Svcs., U. N.H., 1977. Cons. Robert Kleven & Co., Lexington, Mass., 1979-83; human resources rep. Comml. Union Assurance Co., Boston, 1983-84; sr. human resources rep. Gen Rad, Inc., Concord, Mass., 1984-89; dir. human resources Bull Worldwide Info. Sys., Billerica, Mass., 1989-92, Thomson Fin. Svcs., Boston, 1992-93; v.p. cons. Strategic Outsourcing, Inc., Wellesley, Mass., 1993-96; pres., prin. Outsourcing Solutions, Inc., Newton, Mass., 1996—; speaker in field. Mem. Northeast Human Resources Assn. Office: Outsourcing Solutions Inc 1185 Washington St Ste 200 Newton MA 02165

MAUNSBACH, KAY BENEDICTA, financial analyst, consultant, real estate developer; b. N.Y.C., Apr. 25, 1933; d. Eric and Katherine M. BA, Hunter Coll., 1961; postgrad., NYU, 1961-64. CLU. Jr. fin. analyst Vilas and Hickey, N.Y.C., 1960-62; v.p. investment services Shearson Loeb, Rhoades and Co. Inc., N.Y.C., 1962-73; v.p., dir. corp. communications Manhattan Life Ins. Co., N.Y.C., 1974-80; pres. Atrium Group Ltd., 1979-92; gen. ptnr. Prospero Properties, 1982—; gen. ptnr. Prospero Properties II, 1982-89; pres. Atrium Holding Corp., 1982—, Prospero Property II of N.Y., 1985-89, Pegasus Asset Mgmt. Corp., 1985—; v.p. Eaton St. Assn. Fla., 1986-91, Oceanview Owners Inc., 1990—, Shadowood Group, Riverview Assocs. Trustee Art Festival of Continents, Key West, Fla., 1988; commr. Cultural Affairs Commn. of Key West; bd. dirs. Founders Soc. Fellow Fin. Analysts Fedn.; mem. Life Advertisers Assn., Nat. Assn. Bus. Economists, Pub. Relations Council, Am. Council Life Ins., Internat. Assn. Bus. Communicators, Fin. Communications Soc., Pub. Affairs Council, Women's Econ. Roundtable, Life Ins. Council N.Y., N.Y. Soc. Security Analysts, Chartered Life Underwriters, Life Underwriters Assn. N.Y., N.Y. Bd. Realtors, N.Y. Bus. Communicators, World Futurists Soc., N.Y. Soc. Security Analysts.

MAUNUS, EILEEN SUSAN, lawyer; b. Phila., June 18, 1958; d. Alan Jacob and Loretta Paula (Trachtenberg) M. BA, Temple U., 1979, JD, 1982. Bar: Pa. 1982, U.S. Supreme Ct. 1986, U.S. Dist. Ct. (ea. and mid. dists.) Pa. Law clk. Phila. Common Pleas Ct., 1982-83; asst. counsel Pa. Liquor Control Bd., Harrisburg, 1983-89, dep. chief counsel, 1989-96; chief adminstrv. law judge Pa. Bar Inst., 1996—; lectr. on Pa. Alcohol Beverage Practice, 1987, 96. Contbr. articles to profl. jours. Mem. ABA (vice-chair alcohol beverage practice com. 1993—, editor The Bar 1993—), Dauphin County Bar Assn. Office: Office of Adminstrv Law Judge Brandywine Plaza 2221 Paxton Ch Rd Harrisburg PA 17110-9661

MAUPIN, ELIZABETH THATCHER, theater critic; b. Cleve., Oct. 21, 1951; d. Addison and Margaret (Thatcher) M. BA in English, Wellesley (Mass.) Coll., 1973; M in Journalism, U. Calif., Berkeley, 1976. Editorial asst. Houghton-Mifflin Co., Boston, 1973-74; intern Washington bureau McClatchy Newspapers, 1975; reporter, movie critic Times-Standard, Eureka, Calif., 1976-78; theater and movie critic Chronicle-Telegram, Elyria, Ohio, 1978-79; movie and restaurant critic Ledger-Star, Norfolk, Va., 1979-82; feature writer Va.-Pilot and Ledger-Star, Norfolk, 1982-83; sr. theater critic Orlando (Fla.) Sentinel, 1983—. Fellow Nat. Arts Journalism program Columbia U., 1995—. Fellow Nat. Critics Inst.; mem. Am. Theatre Critics Assn. (exec. com. 1993—). Office: Orlando Sentinel 633 N Orange Ave Orlando FL 32801-1300

MAURER, ADAH ELECTRA, psychologist; b. Chgo., Oct. 26, 1905; d. Frank Ulysses and Mary Louise (Meng) Bass; m. Harry Andrew Maurer, June 14, 1937 (div. 1947); children: Douglas, Helen. BS, U. Wis., 1927; MA, U. Chgo., 1957; PhD, Union Inst., 1976. Lic. sch. psychologist, Calif. Tchr. pub. schs. Chgo., 1927-61; psychologist pub. schs. Calif., 1962-71; pvt. practice marriage, family and child counselor Berkeley, Calif., 1965-75; organizer, chief exec. officer End Violence Against the Next Generation, Inc., Berkeley, 1972—; lectr. U. Calif., Davis, 1965-68; bd. dirs. Nat. Ctr. for Study Cpl. Punishment & Alternatives in Schs. Temple U., Phila.; liaison People Opposed to Paddling Students, Houston, 1981—; v.p. Nat. Coalition to Abolish Cpl. Punishment in Schs., Columbus, Ohio, 1987—; cons. Calif. State Dept. Social Svcs., 1988. Author: Paddles Away, 1981, 1001 Alternatives, 1984, (with others) The Bible and the Rod, 1983, Think Twice, 1985; editor: (newsletter) The Last? Resort, 1972—; contbr. numerous articles to profl. jours. Sponsor End Phys. Punishment of Children Worldwide. Recipient Disting. Humanitarian award Calif. State Psychol. Assn., Presdl. award Nat. Assn. Sch. Psychologists, 1988, Donna Stone award Nat. Commn. for Prevention of Child Abuse, 1988, commendation Giraffe Project, 1988, award in recognition of pioneering efforts in banning corporal punishment in nation's schs. Nat. Coalition to Abolish Corporal Punishment in Schs., Achievement award Child, Youth and Family Svcs. Am. Psychol. Assn., 1994. Fellow Am. Psychol. Assn. (Lifetime Career Achievement award 1995); mem. Hemlock Soc. Home and Office: 977 Keeler Ave Berkeley CA 94708-1440

MAURER, BEVERLY BENNETT, school administrator; b. Bklyn., Aug. 23, 1940; d. David and Minnie (Dolen) Bennett; m. Harold M. Maurer, June 12, 1960; children: Ann Maurer Rosenbach, Wendy Maurer Rausch. BA, Bklyn. Coll., 1960, postgrad., 1961; postgrad., U. Richmond, 1980-90, Va. Commonwealth U., 1980-90. Cert. tchr., N.Y., Va. Math. tchr. Col. David Marcus Jr. High Sch., Bklyn., 1960-61, Pomona (N.Y.) Jr. High Sch., 1967-68; math. tchr. Hebrew day sch. Rudlin Torah Acad., Richmond, Va., 1969-80, asst. prin., 1980-86, prin., 1986-89; dir. edn. Jewish Community Day Sch. Ctrl. Va., Richmond, 1990-93; ednl. cons., 1993—; propr. East Coast Antiques. Developed talented and gifted program, pre-admission program for children at Med. Coll. Va., 1982. Bd. dirs. Jewish Comty. Ctr., Richmond, 1980s; bd. dirs. Aux. to Med. Coll. Va., Richmond, 1980s, Aux. to U. Nebr. Med. Ctr., 1994—, Uta Hallee, 1994—. Recipient Master Tchr. award Rudlin Torah Acad., 1983. Mem. Jewish Community Day Sch. Network, Anti-Defamation League, Jewish Women's Club. Republican.

MAURER, ELEANOR JOHNSON, oil company executive; b. Milan, Mo., Jan. 23, 1914; d. Harvey Clifton and Bertha Delaney (Wilkerson) M.; m. Darwin T. Maurer, Aug. 5, 1968 (dec. 1978); 1 child, Jacqueline Eleanor. Student, Stephens Coll., Columbia, Mo., 1930-31, Southwestern State U., Weatherford, Okla., 1932, Draughons Bus. Coll., Oklahoma City, 1933. Sec. Kirkpatrick Oil Co., Oklahoma City, 1951-66, asst. to pres., 1966-80, chief exec. officer, 1980-93, cons., 1993-95; cons. J. Kirkpatrick, 1995—. Treasl. Oklahoma City Community Found.; bd. dirs. Kirkpatrick Found., Okla. Sch. Sci. and Math. Found. Named Corp. Woman of Yr. Jour. Record Newspaper/Okla. City Woman's Forum, 1984, one of Ladies in the News Okla. Hospitality Club, 1992; recipient Trustees' award Omniplex Sci. Mus., Oklahoma City, 1988. Mem. English Speaking Union U.S. (Oklahoma City chpt.), Rotary. Republican. Mem. Christian Ch. Home: 7900 Lakehurst Dr Oklahoma City OK 73120-4324 Office: Kirkpatrick Oil Co PO Box 268822 Oklahoma City OK 73126

MAURER, JANE KATHRENE, school principal; b. Oakland, Calif., Feb. 28, 1945; d. Eben Matthew and Ida Mae Riordan; m. Richard Eugene Maurer, Apr. 22, 1972; children: Christopher Bryson, Jennifer Marie. Student, N.E. Mo. U., Kirksville, 1962-65; BA in Elem.Edn., Incarnate Word Coll., San Antonio, 1971; MEd in Adult Edn., Lincoln U., Jefferson City, Mo., 1977. Tchr. 4th and 5th grades St. GEorge Sch., Hermann, Mo., 1964-66; tchr. 1st and 2d grades Immaculate Conception Sch., Macon, Mo., 1970; jr. h.s. tchr. St. Dismas Sch., Florissant, Mo., 1970-71; jr. h.s. tchr. St. Peters Sch., Jefferson City, 1971-74, tchr. 4th grade, 1976-77; Chpt. I reading tchr. Columbia (Mo.) Cath. Sch., 1980-81; tchr. 4th and 5th grade remedial reading Cole R-2/St. Thomas (Mo.) Bldg., 1981-87; prin. Holy Family Sch., Freeburg, Mo., 1987—; chair sch. evaluation team Diocese of Jefferson City, 1991, 92, 95, 96, mem. standards for success com., 1993-94. Vol. Show Me State Games, Columbia, 1989-93; pres. Mid-Mo. Swim Conf., Jefferson City, 1985-86; active St. Peters Ch., Jefferson City, 1971—. Named Outstanding Young Educator, Jefferson City Jaycees, 1977. Mem. ASCD, Nat. Cath. Edn. Assn. Roman Catholic. Office: Holy Family Sch PO Box 156 Hwy 63 South Freeburg MO 65035

MAURICE, CYNTHIA M., artist, illustrator, educator; d. Juste and Nan Maurice; m. Richard Garrett, June 30, 1938; children: Elizabeth, Margaret. BFA in Painting, Boston U., 1963, MFA in Painting, 1965; MFA in Illustration, Sch. Visual Arts, N.Y.C., 1989. Lectr. U. Portland, Gorham, Maine, 1965-66, Middlesex C.C., Bedford, Mass., 1979-87; lectr., artist-in-residence U. Sudbury, Sudbury, Ont., Can., 1966-67; tchr. H.B. Beal Tech. Sch., London, Ont., Can., 1967-69; assoc. prof. Art Inst. Boston, 1995—. One-woman shows include Chapel Gallery, Newton, Mass., 1985, Helen Bumpus Gallery, Duxbury, Mass., 1985, South Shore Art Gallery, Hingham, Mass., 1991; group shows include Danforth Mus., 1981, Newton (Mass.) Art Ctr., 1982, 93, Francesca Anderson Gallery, Boston, 1985, 86, 93, 95, Starr Gallery, Newton, 1986, 91, Nat. Arts Club, N.Y.C., 1988, 93, Washington Sq. Gallery, N.Y.C., 1989, 91, Bromfield Gallery, Boston, 1995; illustrations published in various mags. including Am. Jour. Nursing, Boston Globe, Chronicle Higher Edn., Nat. Law Jour., N.Y. Times, Washington Post. Resident fellow Cummington (Mass.) Cmty.-Arts, 1976, Ossabaw (Ga.) Island Project, 1979, Edna St. Vincent Millay Art Colony, 1982; recipient Bush-Brown award Helen Bumpus Gallery, 1985, Sieffert award Nat. Arts Club, 1989. Studio: 1 Fitchburg St C323 Somerville MA 02143

MAU-SHIMIZU, PATRICIA ANN, lawyer; b. Honolulu, Jan. 17, 1953; d. Herbert G.K. and Leilani (Yuen) Mau; 1 child, Melissa Rose. B.S., U. San Francisco, 1975; J.D., Golden Gate U., 1979. Bar: Hawaii 1979. Law clk. State Supreme Ct., Honolulu, 1979-80; atty. Bendet, Fidell & Sakai, Honolulu, 1980-81; legis. atty. Honolulu City Council, 1981-83; legi. atty. House Majority Staff Office, Honolulu, 1983-84, dir., 1984-93, chief clk. Hawaii Ho. of Reps., 1993—. Mem. Hawaii Bar Assn., Hawaii Women Lawyers, Jr. League Hawaii. Democrat. Roman Catholic. Home: 7187 Hawaii Kai Dr Honolulu HI 96825-3115 Office: State House Reps 415 S Beretania St Rm 027 Honolulu HI 96813

MAUST, MELODY S., newspaper editor; b. Washington, Dec. 22, 1965; d. Dwight Allen and Wanda (Stoll) M. AA, Vincennes U., 1985. Staff writer Washington (Ind.) Times-Herald, 1985-89, editor, 1989—. Mem. Washington Rotary (bull. editor). Republican. Mem. Mennonite Ch. Home: Rt 1 Box 128 Montgomery IN 47558 Office: Washington Times-Herald 102 E Van Trees St Washington IN 47501

MAVRINAC, EMILY GREGOR, private school educator; b. Waterville, Me., Aug. 29, 1962; d. Albert Anthony and Marilyn (Sweeney) M. BA cum laude, Harvard U., 1985, student education, 1991. Tchr. grade 1 S.A.D. #49, Fairfield, Me., 1985-86; tchr. grades 3-5 West Street Sch., Fairfield, Me., 1986-87; tchr. grade 2 Bernard Zell Anshe Emet Day Sch., Chgo., 1987-90, tchr. grade 1, 1991—; Tutor Cambrini Green Tutoring Ctr., Chgo., 1994—. Vol., head group 570 Amnesty Internat., Chgo., 1989-95; mem. Ill. Coalition Against Death Penalty, Chgo., 1995—. Summer fellow NEH, 1989, 93. Democrat. Roman Catholic. Office: Bernard Zell Anshe Emet Sch 3760 N Pine Grove Chicago IL 60013

MAX, CLAIRE ELLEN, physicist; b. Boston, Sept. 29, 1946; d. Louis William and Pearl (Bernstein) M.; m. Jonathan Arons, Dec. 22, 1974; l child, Samuel. AB, Harvard U., 1968; PhD, Princeton U., 1972. Postdoctoral researcher U. Calif., Berkeley, 1972-74; physicist Lawrence Livermore (Calif.) Nat. Lab., 1974—; dir. Livermore br. Inst. Geophysics and Planetary Physics, 1984-93; mem. Math.-Sci. Network Mills Coll., Oakland, Calif.; mem. com. on fusion hybrid reactors NRC, 1986, mem. com. on internat. security and arms control NAS, 1986-89, mem. com. on phys. sci., math. and applications NRC, 1991-94, mem. policy and computational astrophys. panels, astron. and astgrophys. survey NRC, 1989-91. Editor: Particle Acceleration Mechanisms in Astrophysics, 1979; contbr. numerous articles to sci. jours. Fellow AAAS, Am. Phys. Soc. (exec. com. div. plasma physics 1977, 81-82); mem. Am. Astron. Soc. (exec. com. div. high energy astrophysics 1975-76), Am. Geophys. Union, Internat. Astron. Union, Phi Beta Kappa, Sigma Xi. Office: Lawrence Livermore Nat Lab PO Box 808 7000 East Ave L-413 Livermore CA 94550-9900

MAXCY, JOAN GORMAN, artist; b. Washington, Nov. 20, 1948; d. Samuel and Rhoda (Wolman) Gorman; m. Phil. Jr. Maxcy; children: Jana, Lena. Student, U. Charleston, 1966, Montgomery Coll., Takoma Park, Md., 1967-69, Md. Sch. Art and Design, 1970. Artist Kennedy Ctr. Imagination Celebration, Dallas, 1990-92; artist-in-residence Art Vanguard Sch., Dallas, 1990-93, Navarro Arts Coun., Corsicanna, Tex., 1991, Young Audiences, Dallas, 1992-94; condr. workshops Office Cultural Affairs, Dallas, 1990-93, Dallas Ind. Sch. Dist., 1988-93; juror City of Dallas, 1992. One person shows include So. Meth. U., Dallas, 1988, White Horse Gallery, Dallas, 1990, Dallas Arts Acad., 1991, Carver Cultural Ctr., San Antonio, Tex., 1993, Millenium, Dallas, 1994; exhibited in group shows V Brooks Gallery, Dallas, 1989, New Age Space, Miami, Fla., 1988, 89, Maj. Artery in the Quadrangle, Dallas, 1995, Adkins-Hoover Gallery, Dallas, 1995. Grantee Marcus Found., 1992, Edmund J. Kahn Found., 1992, Dallas Office of Cultural Affairs, 1993. Mem. Nat. Mus. Women in Arts. Home and Studio: 219 E Woodin Blvd Dallas TX 75216

MAXEY, PAULINE EVANS, postal service manager; b. Pendergrass, Ga., Apr. 15, 1943; d. Paul R. and Vivian O. (Nabors) Evans; divorced; children: Richard S., Mitchell A., Regina P. Student, U. Ga., Athens, 1981, Christian Coll. Ga., 1981; supr. cert., Gainesville (Ga.) Coll., 1990, student, 1991-92. Clk., carrier U.S. Postal Svc., Winterville, Ga., 1975-83; officer in charge U.S. Postal Svc., Mansfield, Ga., 1981-82; part-time flexible clk. U.S. Postal Svc., Lawrenceville, Ga., 1983-84, fill-in supr., 1984-86; distbn. clk. U.S. Postal Svc., Lawrenceville, 1984-85, window clk., 1985-86, window clk. trainer, 1986; supt. window svc. U.S. Postal Svc., Gainesville, 1986-92; officer in charge U.S. Postal Svc., Lexington, Ga., 1992-93; customer svc. supr. U.S. Postal Svc., Athens, Ga., 1993—, Alps Postal Store, Athens, 1996—. Tchr. Comty. Ch., Athens and Winterville, 1967-85; counselor Bible Camp, Waycross, Ga., 1967. Mem. Nat. Assn. Postal Suprs. (sec. treas. 1989-96, treas. 1996), Internat. Soc. of Poets, Concerned Women for Am., Billion Souls for Christ. Home: 155 McAlpin Dr Winterville GA 30683

MAXFIELD, ANNE M., sales executive; b. Cin., Apr. 18, 1961; d. Howard B. and Nancy C. (O'Connell) M.; m. William Eugene Lege. BA, No. Ky. U., 1994; cert., Inst. Orgn. Mgmt., 1990, Salesability, 1991. Supr. St. Elizabeth Med. Ctr., Covington, Ky., 1979-86; v.p. No. Ky. C. of C., Covington, 1986-90; account rep. Olsten STaffing Svcs., Florence, Ky., 1990—; bd. dirs. New Perceptions, Inc., Edgewood, Ky., 1990-96, chair nominating com., 1992. Advocacy mgr. Wood Hudson Cancer Rsch., Newport, Ky., 1988-90; chmn. small bus. sect. Cin. United Way, 1990; cmty. chair Fine Arts Fund, 1990-94; vol. AIDS Vols. of No. Ky., 1996—; mem. devel. com. Villa Madonna Acad., 1995—. Mem. Nat. Assn. Temp. Svcs., Ky. Assn. Temp. Svcs., No. Ky. C. of C. (chmn. bus. svcs. com.). Democrat. Office: Olsten Staffing Svcs 5 Spiral Dr Florence KY 41042-1395

MAXFIELD, MARY CONSTANCE, management consultant; b. Washington, Mar. 16, 1949; d. Orville Eldred and Rose Mary (Stiarwalt) Maxfield; m. Robert Charles Kneip, III, Aug. 21, 1971 (div. Apr. 1981); 1 child, Stephanie Alexandra; m. Richard Howard Cowles, May 16, 1981 (dec.); m. Phillip Walker, July 25, 1985 (div. June 1991). BA in History and Spanish, Va. Tech., 1970; MS in Occupl. Tech. U. Houston, 1996. Clk.-typist HEW, Social Security Adminstrn., New Orleans, 1971-72, svc. rep., 1972-73; mgmt. analyst Office Comptroller of Currency, Treasury Dept., Washington, 1974-77; dir. mgmt. analysis divsn. U.S. Customs, New Orleans, 1978-80, mgmt. analyst, Houston, 1980-81, program analyst, 1981-82, chief data processing br., 1982-83, chief mgmt. analysis br., 1983-85; pres. Constance Walker Assocs., Inc., 1985-91, Maxfield Productivity Cons., Inc., 1991—; co-founder Supplier Registry. Author: MBO Handbook, 1979, Professional Problem Solving, 1985, The Productivity Ascent, 1987, Participative Problem Solving: A Guide for Work Teams, 1988; (with others) Program Management Handbook, 1983, Introduction to Employee Involvement, 1985, Team Approach to Problem Solving, 1991, Quality School Facilitator Training, 1992, Gender Awareness Training, 1992, Interpersonal Communications Skills, 1992, Introduction to Total Quality Schools, 1992, Tex. Leadership Ctr. DuPont LDP Tng., TQM Module, 1993, Introduction to ISO 9000, 1993, Total Quality Management, 1993, Benchmarking, 1994, Effective Facilitation Skills, 1995, Strengthening Team Development, 1995, Internal Auditing to ISO 9000 Standards, 1995, Personnel Management in Food Service, 1995, Successfully Leading Change, 1996, Leading Change Through Site-Based Teams, 1996; contbr. numerous articles to profl. jours. Mem. Friends of Stehlin Found., 1982-88, Friends of the Cabildo, 1978-80. Named Customs Woman of Yr., U.S. Customs, 1979, recipient Outstanding Performance award, 1979, 80, 81, 82, 83, 84, 85; named Fed. Exec. Bd. Woman of Yr., 1979; recipient Outstanding Service award Office of Sec. of Treasury, 1976, Key to City, New Orleans, 1990; Cora Bell Wesley scholar, UDC, 1969. Mem. DAR, Am. Soc. for Quality Control, Assn. for Quality and Participation, Treasury Hist. Assn., Daus. Rep. of Tex., Daus. 1812. UDC, Va. Tech. Alumni Assn., Austin Old 300 (founding mem.), Delta Zeta. Episcopalian. Home and Office: Maxfield Productivity Cons Inc 8007 Liberty Elm Ct Spring TX 77379-6125

MAXFIELD, SANDI, secondary education educator; b. Des Moines, Feb. 20, 1971; d. John and Judy (Hansen) M. BA, Grandview Coll., 1993. Cert. 7-12 lang. arts, English, reading tchr., Iowa. 7th grade English tchr. Fort Madison (Iowa) Schs., 1993—; team leader, student coun. advisor, McREL mem. Fort Madison Jr. High, 1994—. Mem. ASCD, Ft. Madison Edn. Assn. (bldg. rep.), Iowa Assn. Middle Level Educators. Office: Fort Madison Jr HS 18th & Ave G Fort Madison IA 52627

MAXSON, LINDA ELLEN, biologist, educator; b. N.Y.C., Apr. 24, 1943; d. Albert and Ruth (Rosenfeld) Resnick; m. Richard Dey Maxson, June 13, 1964; 1 child, Kevin. BS in Zoology, San Diego State U., 1964, MA in Biology, 1966; PhD in Genetics, U. Calif. and San Diego State U., 1973. Instr. biology San Diego State U., 1966-68; tchr. gen. sci. San Diego Unified Sch. Dist., 1968-69; instr. biochemistry U. Calif., Berkeley, 1974; asst. prof. zoology, dept. genetics and devel. U. Ill., Urbana-Champaign, 1974-76, asst. prof. dept. genetics, devel. and ecology, ethology & evolution, 1976-79, assoc. prof., 1979-84, prof., 1984-87, prof. ecology, ethology and evolution, 1987-88; prof., head dept. biology Pa. State U., State College, 1988-94; assoc. vice-chancellor acad. affairs/dean undergrad. acad. affairs, prof. ecology and evolutionary biology U. Tenn., Knoxville, 1995—; exec. officer biology programs Sch. Life Scis., U. Ill., 1981-86, assoc. dir. acad. affairs, 1984-86, dir. campus honors program, 1985-88; vis. prof. ecology and evolutionary biology U. Calif., Irvine, 1988; mem. adv. panel rsch. tng. groups behavioral biol. scis. NSF, 1990-94. Author: Genetics: A Human Perspective, 3d edit., 1992; edtl. bd. Molecular Biology Evolution, Amphibia/Reptilia; exec. editor Biochem. Sys. & Ecology, 1993—; contbr. numerous articles to scientific jours. Recipient Disting. Alumni award San Diego State U., 1989, Disting. Herpetologist award Herpetologists' League, 1993. Fellow AAAS (disting. herpetologist award 1993); mem. Am. Men and Women in Sci., Am. Genetics Assn. (coun. 1994—), Soc. for Study of Amphibians and Reptiles (pres. 1991), Internat. Herpetol. Com., Soc. Study Evolution, Soc. Systematic Biology, Soc. Molecular Biology and Evolution (sec. 1992-95, treas. 1992-94), Am. Soc. Ichthyologists and Herpetologists, Am. Soc. Zoologists, Herpetologists League, Soc. Europea Herpetologica, European Soc. Evolutionary Biology. Home: 409 Boxwood Sq Knoxville TN 37919 Office: U Tenn 505 Andy Holt Twr Knoxville TN 37996-0154

MAXWELL, AIMEE REBECCA, lawyer; b. Atlanta, Feb. 5, 1961; d. Elmer and Joyce Lynn (Shoaf) M. AB, U. Ga., 1982; MEd, Ga. State U., 1983, JD, 1987. Bar: Ga. Atty. pvt. practice, Atlanta, 1987-90, Decatur, Ga., 1990-91; staff atty. Ga. Indigent Def. Coun., Atlanta, 1991-92, divsn. dir., 1992—. Author: Georgia Jurisprudence, 1996. Mem. Nat. Assn. Criminal Defense Lawyers, Ga. Assn. Criminal Defense Lawyers (pres. 1996—), State Bar Ga. (young lawyers sect., high sch. mock trial com., criminal law com.), Atlanta Bar Assn. (criminal law sect., chair 1993-94). Home: 703 E Paces Ferry Rd Atlanta GA 30305 Office: Ga Indigent Def Coun 985 Ponce de Leon Ave Atlanta GA 30306

MAXWELL, AUDREY L., academic administrator; b. Wilmington, Del., Sept. 2, 1957; d. Richard Lee and Dorothy Jean (Bass) M.; children: Curtis Maxwell Frey, Emily Rose Frey. BS in Edn. with honors, U. Del., 1979; postgrad., Del. Tech. and Community Coll., 1984-85; MBA, Widener U., 1991. Cert. tchr., Del., 1980. Tchr. New Castle County Sch. Dist., Wilmington, Del., 1979-81; pvt. practice as editor New Castle, Del., 1981-83; asst. office mgr. VVM, Inc., Claymont, Del., 1983-86; mktg. coord. Enterprise Pub., Inc., Wilmington, 1986-88; supr. of edn. Alfred I. duPont Inst., Wilmington, 1988-90, asst. to rsch. dir., 1990-91, asst. dir. rsch., 1991—; cons. Enterprise Pub., Inc., Wilmington, Del., 1988-89. Editor: The Golden Mailbox, 1988; prodn. editor: Capitalism for Kids, 1987 (Phila. Book Show award 1987); asst. editor First State Woman, 1988-91; tech. reviewer Pediatric References, 1990—; contbr. articles to profl. jours. Vol. Girl Scouts Am., Claymont, Del., 1990—; tchr. St. Paul's United Meth. Ch., Wilmington, Del., 1981—. Mem. NAFE, Nat. Fedn. Bus. and Profl. Women (pres. 1991-92, sec. 1987-89, Young Careerist award 1989), Am. Coll. Healthcare Execs., Kappa Delta Pi. Republican. Methodist. Office: Alfred I duPont Inst PO Box 269 Wilmington DE 19899-0269

MAXWELL, BARBARA SUE, consultant, educator; b. Bklyn., Feb. 22, 1950; d. Vincent and Esther Alice (Hansen) M. BA in Math Edn., Rider Coll., 1972; postgrad., Montclair State U., 1973. Cert. secondary tchr., N.J. Math tchr. Westwood (N.J.) H.S., 1973-80; programmer Prudential Ins. Co., Roseland, N.J., 1980-81; programmer, analyst Grand Union, Paramus, N.J., 1981-82; cons. Five Techs., Montvale, N.J., 1987-90; project mgr. Info. Sci., Inc., Montvale, 1982-84, cons., project mgr., 1987-90; pres. B. Maxwell Assoc., Inc., Westwood, N.J., 1990—; guest spkr. Info. Sci., Best of Am., Computer Assocs. B.A.C. Contbr. articles to profl. jours. Mem. Westwood Heritage Soc. Mem. NAFE, APA (v.p. N.J. chpt. 1996), Human Resource Sys. Profls., N.J. Info., Am. Payroll Assn. Republican. Lutheran.

MAXWELL, CARLA LENA, dancer, choreographer, educator; b. Glendale, Calif., Oct. 25, 1945; d. Robert and Victoria (Carbone) M. Student, Bennington Coll., 1963-64; B.S., Juilliard Sch. Music, 1967. Mem. Jose Limón Dance Co., N.Y.C., 1965; prin. dancer Jose Limón Dance Co., 1969—, acting artistic dir., 1977-78, artistic dir., 1978—; lectr., tchr. in field. Soloist, Louis Falco Dance Co., 1967-71, Harkness Festival at N.Y.C. Delacorte Theater, from 1964, artist-in-residence, Gettysburg Coll., 1970, Luther Coll., Decorah, Iowa, 1971, U. Idaho, 1973, guest tchr., performer, Centre Internat. de la Danse, Vichy, France, 1976; choreographer: Function, 1970, Improvisations on a Dream, 1970, A Suite of Psalms, 1973, Homage to José Linón, Place Spirit, 1975, Aadvark Brothers; Schwartz and Columbo Present Please Don't Stone The Clowns, 1975, Blue Warrier, 1975, Sonata, 1980, Keeping Stil, Mountain, 1987; featured in Carlota, Dances For Isadora, La Malinche, Comedy, The Moor's Pavane, The Winged, There Is A Time, The Shakers, Brandenburg Concerto No. 4, Trnaslucence, Caviar, Missa Brevis, Day on Earth, Two Ecstatic Themes, A Choreographic Offering, The Exiles, Sacred Conversations; toured East and West Africa, 1969. N.Y. State Cultural Council grantee, 1971; recipient Dance Mag. award, 1995. Home: 7 Great Jones St New York NY 10012-1135 Office: Jose Limon Dance Ctr 611 Broadway Fl 9 New York NY 10012-2617*

MAXWELL, CYNTHIA NEAGLE, mitigation professional; b. Charlotte, N.C., July 15, 1953; d. Emmett Orr and Nettie Prue (McCaslin) Neagle; m. L.A. Waggoner III, Apr. 30, 1977 (div. Aug. 1987); 1 child, Margaret "Rett" Emma Waggoner; m. Kirby Ben Maxwell, June 19, 1991; stepchildren: Rachel Meredith, Jennifer Lauren Maxwell. BA in Psychology, U. N.C., 1975. Health care techician II, asst. recreational therapist Gaston-Lincoln Area Mental Health, Gastonia, N.C., 1975-77; social worker I Mecklenburg County Mental Health Svcs., Charlotte, N.C., 1978; vol. svcs. coord. Mecklenburg County Mental Health Svcs., Charlotte, 1978-79, dir. community rels., 1979-81; exec. dir. Heart Soc. Gaston County, Inc., Gastonia, N.C., 1983-85; product rep. Perma-Bound, Jacksonville, Fla., 1984-86; dist. adminstr. Guardian Ad Litem Program, Gastonia, N.C., 1985-91; v.p., food products exec. Maxwell Assocs., 1991—; criminal law mitigation expert; jury selection specialist. Author: Volunteer Manual, 1979; author, editor: Gaston County Bar Assn., 1993. bd. dirs., chmn., exec. com., personnel com., search com., pub. rels. com., sec., program com., fin. com., by laws com., Gaston-Lincoln Area Mental Health, Mental retardation and Substance Abuse Program, 1978-87; search com., by laws com., rep., pres. bd. dirs., 1983-87; co-chair, chair, exec. by laws chair, Jr. League Gaston County, N.C., 1980-91; CPR instr. Gaston County Red Cross, 1985—; mem. devel. chair. Civitans, 1986-90; mem. planning and zoning bd., Belmont, N.C., 1994-95; dir. Alliance Healthier Babies. Named Vol. of Yr. Gaston County C. of C., 1982, Gaston County Mental Health Assn., 1983; N.C. Col. of Yr. N.C. Coun. of Community Mental health Programs, 1983. Mem. Gaston County C. of C., United Meth. Women, Humane Soc. Gaston County, Gaston County Commn. of Family. Democrat. Methodist.

MAXWELL, DIANA KATHLEEN, early childhood education educator; b. Seminole, Okla., Dec. 16, 1949; d. William Hunter and ImoJean (Mahurin) Rivers; m. Clarence Estel Maxwell, Jly 3, 1969; children: Amanda Hunter, Alexandra Jane. BS, U. Md., 1972; M of Secondary Edn., Boston U., 1974; PhD, U. Md., 1980. Cert. tchr., counselor, Tex. Tchr. Child Garden Presch., Adelphi, Md., 1969-71; tchr., dir. PREP Edn. Ctr., Heidelberg, Germany, 1972-74; tchr. N.E. Ind. Schs. Larkspur, San Antonio, 1974-77, 89-90, Headstart, Boyds, Md., 1978; dir., founder First Bapt. Child Devel. Ctr., Bryan, Tex., 1982-84; instr. English lang. Yonsei Med. Ctr., Seoul, Republic of Korea, 1985-87; asst. prof. Incarnate Word Coll., San Antonio, 1987-89; tchr. kindergarten Fairfax County Pub. Schs., Kings Park, Va., 1990-94; tchr. Encino Park, San Antonio, Tex., 1994-95; lectr. U. Tex., San Antonio, 1995—; cons. Sugar N'Spice Child Devel. Ctr., Kilgore, Tex., 1980-90; bd. dirs. Metro Area Assn. for Childhood Edn. Internat., 1991-93. Author: (book revs.) Childhood Education, 1979, 80, 92. Block chairperson March of Dimes, 1991, 92, 93, Am. Heart Assn., Fairfax, Fa., 1991, 92, Am. Diabetes Assn., Fairfax, 1992; judge speaking com. Burke Optomists, 1992, 931 judge writing competition N.E. Ind. Sch. Dist., 1996; sec. Cole H.S. Cougar Club, Ft. Sam Houston, San Antonio, 1996-97; Bible tchr. 1st Bapt. Ch., Alexandria, Va., 1992-94; tchr. kindergarten Trinity Bapt. Ch., San Antonio, 1995—. Named one of Outstanding Young Women of Am., 1983; Md. fellow State of Md., 1978, 79; grantee San Antonio, 1990, Springfield, 1991. Mem. ASCD, Internat. Reading Assn., Assn. Profl. Tchr. Educators, Edn. Internat., Assn. for Childhood Edn. Internat. (v.p., pres.-elect), Tex. Assn. Childhood Edn., Bexar County and Surrounding Areas Assn. Childhood Edn. Home: 106 Artillery Post Rd San Antonio TX 78234 Office: U Tex Divsn Edn 6900 North Loop 1604 San Antonio TX 78249-0616

MAXWELL, DOROTHEA BOST ANDREWS, civic worker; b. Greenville, Ill., Apr. 20, 1911; d. Samuel Washington and Viola Maud (Bost) Andrews; m. Richard Wesley Maxwell, June 1, 1935; children: Andrea Judith Maxwell Platz, Anne Dorothea Maxwell Walsh. BA with honors, diploma in piano, Greenville Coll., 1933; MusM, Northwestern U., 1937. Cert. prinary and secondary tchr., music tchr., Mo. Dir. sch. music Spring Arbor (Mich.) Jr. Coll., 1933-34; tutor orthopedic handicapped children St. Louis Pub. Schs., 1950-56. Pres. Women's Assn., 2d Presbyn. Ch., St. Louis, 1956-58; tour guide Mo. Bot. Garden, St. Louis, 1975-87; pres. The Wednesday Club St. Louis, 1983-85, archivist, 1985-92; guide tours of distinction St. Louis Symphony Soc., 1980-85. Mem. Clan Maxwell Soc. U.S.A., Mo. Hist. Soc., St. Louis Genealogy Soc., Nat. Soc. DAR (Jefferson chpt. St. Louis), Piano Club St. Louis, Washington U. Faculty women's Club, Mu Phi Epsilon. Republican. Presbyterian. Home: 901 S Skinker Blvd Saint Louis MO 63105-3242

MAXWELL, FLORENCE HINSHAW, civic worker; b. Nora, Ind., July 14, 1914; d. Asa Benton and Gertrude (Randall) Hinshaw; BA cum laude, Butler U., 1935; m. John Williamson Maxwell, June 5, 1936; children: Marilyn Maxwell Grissom, William Douglas. Coord., bd. dirs. Sight Conservation and Aid to Blind, 1962-73, nat. chmn., 1969-73; active various fund drives; chmn. jamboree, hostess coms. North Cen. High Sch., 1959, 64; Girl Scouts U.S., 1937-38, 54-56; mus. chmn. Sr. Girl Scout Regional Coun., 1956-57; scorekeeper Little League, 1955-57; bd. dirs. Nora Sch. Parents' Club, 1958-59, Eastwood Jr. High Sch. Triangle Club, 1959-62, Ind. State Symphony Soc. Women's Com., 1965-67, 76-79, Symphoguide chmn., 1976-79; vision screening Indpls. innercity pub. sch. kindergartens, pre-schs., 1962-69, also Headstart, 1967—; asst. Glaucoma screening clinics Gen. Hosp., Glendale Shopping Ctr., City County Bldg., Am. Legion Nat. Hdqrs., Ind. Health Assn. Conf., 1962-73; chmn. sight conservation and aid to blind Nat. Delta Gamma Found., Indpls., Columbus, Ohio, 1969-73; mem. telethon team Butler U. Fund, 1964; symphoguide hostess Internat. Conf. on Cities, 1971, Nat. League of Cities, 1972; mem. health adv. com. Headstart, 1976—, sec., 1980—, mem. social svcs. com., 1987—, coord. vision rescreening and referrals, assessment team of compliance steering com., 1978-79, 84, 86, 87, 88, 91, 92 (appreciation award 1983); founder People of Vision Aux., 1981, bd. dirs., 1981—, v.p., 1990-92, mem. coordinate vision and glaucoma screenings and office svcs.; initiated vision screening and eye safety education at Jameson Camp for Children:, 1987; trainer vision screening, 1988—. Recipient Key to City of Indpls., 1972, Those Spl. People award Women in Communication, 1980, Jefferson award for disting. pub. svc. Indpls. Star, 1991, Cmty. Action Head Start Outstanding Vol. award, 1996. Mem. Nat. Soc. to Prevent Blindness (now Prevent Blindness Am.), Ind. Audubon Soc., Ind. Hist. Soc., Ind. Soc. to Prevent Blindness (now Prevent Blindness Ind., dir. 1962—, exec. com. 1971—, v.p. 1983-86, sec., 1971-83, asst. sec.-treas., 1987-92), Ind. del. to nat. 3-yr. program planning conf. 1985, internal analysis task force for svcs. 1987, Sight Saving award 1974, life hon. v.p. 1983—), Jameson Camp Auxiliary, Ind. State Symphony Soc. Women's Com. (vol. Indpls. symphony orch.'s discovery concerts, vol. Indpls. noon-time concerts, vol. Yuletide coffee concerts), People of Vision, Delta Gamma (chpt. golden anniversary celebration decade and communication chmn. 1975, treas. Alpha Tau house corp. 1975-78, nat. chmn. Parent Club Study Com. 1976-77, instr. province leadership seminar workshop 1989, Cable award 1969, Outstanding Alumna award 1973, Svc. Recognition award 1977, Shield award 1981, scholarship honoree 1981, Stellar award 1986, Oxford award, 1992). Republican. Address: 1502 E 80th St Indianapolis IN 46240-2706

MAXWELL, JANE, cable television executive. Sr. v.p. and dir. spl. events CNN, Atlanta. Office: CNN 100 International Blvd PO Box 105366 Atlanta GA 30348-5366*

MAXWELL, MELISSA FAYE, business owner; b. Pensacola, Fla., Sept. 19, 1939; d. James Crawford and Zadie Magdalene (Wise) Maxwell. Grad. high sch. Founder, owner Carburetor World, Inc., Miami, Fla., 1973—. Author: Gas Mileage for the Serious Tinkerer, 1982; patents and blueprints twenty known carburetors claiming 50-200 MPGs; inventor in field of carburetors. Benefactor various youth orgns., 1976—; mem. coun. Carburetor World Rehab. for Troubled Youths, Miami, 1976-80.

MAXWELL, PATRICIA ANNE, writer; b. Winn Parish, La., Mar. 9, 1942; d. John Henry and Daisy Annette (Durbin) Ponder; m. Jerry Ronald Maxwell, Aug. 1, 1957; children: Jerry Ronald Jr., Richard Dale, Delinda Anne, Katherine Leigh. GED, 1960. Author (as Patricia Maxwell): Secret of Mirror House, 1970, Stranger At Plantation Inn, 1971, The Bewitching Grace, 1974, Notorious Angel, 1977, Night of the Candles, 1978, numerous others; (as Elizabeth Trehearne): Storm At Midnight, 1973; (as Patricia Ponder); Haven of Fear, 1977, Murder For Charity, 1977; (as Maxine Patrick): The Abducted Heart, 1979, numerous others; (as Jennifer Blake): Love's Wild Desire, 1977, Golden Fancy, 1980, Embrace and Conquer, 1981, Royal Seduction, 1983, others. Recipient Hist. Romance Author of Yr. award Romantic Times Mag., 1985; inducted into Romance Hall of Fame, 1995. Mem. Nat. League Am. Penwomen, Romance Writers of Am. (charter, Golden Treasure award 1987), Novelists, Inc. Home: PO Box 9218 Quitman LA 71268-9218

MAXWELL, RUTH ELAINE, artist, interior designer, decorative painter; b. Cleve., Oct. 7, 1934; d. Norman Lee and Katherine Ellen (Hamilton) Brown; m. Clarence LeRoy Maxwell, June 25, 1955; children: Lisa Maxwell Callahan, Lynne Maxwell Quinn, Laura Maxwell Jochem, James. BFA, Ohio State U., 1956, teaching cert., 1956. Cert. elem. sch. tchr., Ohio. Tchr. Hilliard (Ohio) Elem. Sch., 1956-58; comptr. Callahan Family Golf Ctr., Hilliard, 1989—. Pres. Capa Colleagues, Ohio Theatre, Columbus, 1986; pres., governing bd. Theatre Shop, 1988, buyer, 1995—; vol. Columbus Assn. Performing Arts Colleagues, 1981—; mem. Hilliard Arts Coun., 1989-91; vocalist Damenchor of Columbus Maennerchor, 1975—, treas., 1979-81, fin. sec., 1991-94; sec. Canterbury Unit of Columbus Symphony Orch. Women's Assn., 1993-94, treas., 1995-96, project chairperson, 1996—, v.p., 1996—; mem. Women's Guild of Opera, Columbus, 1994—. Mem. Gamma Alpha Chi (hon., sec. Ohio State U. chpt. 1954), Gamma Phi Beta. Republican.

MAXWELL-BROGDON, FLORENCE MORENCY, school administrator, educational adviser; b. Spring Park, Minn., Nov. 11, 1929; d. William Frederick and Florence Ruth (LaBrie) Maxwell; m. John Carl Brogdon, Mar. 13, 1957; children: Carole Alexandra, Cecily Ann, Daphne Diana. B.A., Calif. State U., L.A., 1955; MS, U. So. Calif., 1957; postgrad. Columbia Pacific U., San Rafael, Calif., 1982-86. Cert. tchr., Calif. Dir. Rodeo Sch., L.A., 1961-64; lectr. Media Features, Culver City, Calif., 1964—; dir. La Playa Sch., Culver City, 1968-75; founding dir. Venture Sch., Culver City, 1974—, also chmn. bd.; bd. dirs., v.p. Parent Coop. Preschools, Baie d'Urfe Que., Can., 1964—; del. to Ednl. Symposium, Moscow-St. Petersburg, 1992, U.S./China Joint Conf. on Edn., Beijing, 1992, Internat. Confedn. of Prins., Geneva, 1993, Internat. Conf., Berlin, 1994. Author: Let Me Tell You, 1973; Wet'n Squishy, 1973; Balancing Act, 1977; (as Morency Maxwell) Framed in Silver, 1985; (column) What Parents Want to Know, 1961—; editor: Calif. Preschooler, 1961-74; contbr. articles to profl. jours. Treas. Democrat Congl. Primary, Culver City, 1972. Mem. Calif. Council Parent Schs. (bd. dirs. 1961-74), Parent Coop. Preschools Internat. (advisor 1975—), Pen Ctr. USA West, Mystery Writers of Am. (affiliate), Internat. Platform Assn., Nat. Assn. Secondary Sch. Prins., Libertarian. Home: 10814 Molony Rd Culver City CA 90230-5451 Office: Venture Sch 5333 Sepulveda Blvd Culver City CA 90230-5233

MAY, AVIVA RABINOWITZ, music educator, linguist, musician; b. Tel Aviv; naturalized, 1958; d. Samuel and Paula Pessia (Gordon) Rabinowitz; (divorced); children: Chelley Mosoff, Alan May, Risa McPherson, Ellanna May/Gassman. AA Oakton Community Coll., 1977; BA in Piano Pedagogy, Northeastern Ill. U., 1978. Folksinger, educator, musician Aviva May Studio/Piano and Guitar, 1948—; Sunday sch. dir. Canton (Ohio) Synagogue, 1952-54; nursery sch. tchr. Allentown (Pa.) Jewish Community Ctr., 1954-56; Hebrew, music tchr. Brith Shalom Community Ctr., Bethlehem, Pa., 1954-62; Hebrew tchr. Beth Hillel Congregation, Wilmette, Ill., 1964-83, Beth Emet Congregation, Evanston, Ill., 1964-83; tchr. B'nai Mitzva, 1973; tchr., music dir. McCormick Health Ctrs., Chgo., 1978-79, Cove Sch. Perceptually Handicapped Children, Chgo., 1978-79; prof. Hebrew and Yiddish, Spertus Coll. Judaica, Chgo., 1980-89; Hebrew tchr. Anshe Emet Day Sch, 1989—, West Suburban Temple Har Zion, Oak Park, Ill, 1993—; music studio tchr. Cosmopolitan Sch., Chgo., 1992—; tchr. continuing edn. Northeastern Ill. U., 1978-80, Niles Twp. Jewish Congregation, 1993—, also Jewish Community Ctrs.; with Office Spl. Investigations, Dept. Justice, Washington; music dir. Temple Emanuel Rosenwald Sch. Composer classical music for piano, choral work, folk songs; developer 8-hour system for learning piano or guitar; contbr. articles to profl. jours. Recipient Magen David Adom Pub. Service award, 1973; grantee Ill. State, 1975-79, Ill. Congressman Woody Bowman, 1978-79. Mem. Music Tchrs. Nat. Assn. (co-founder), North Shore Music Tchrs. Assn. (charter mem., sec.), Ill. Music Tchrs. Assn., Organ and Piano Tchrs. Assn., Am. Coll. Musicians, Ill. Assn. Learning Disabilities, Sherwood Sch. Music, Friends of Holocaust Survivers, Nat. Yiddish Book Exchange, Nat. Ctr. for Jewish Films, Chgo. Jewish Hist. Soc., Oakton Community Coll. Alumni Assn., Northeastern Ill. U. Alumni Assn. Democrat. Office: Aviva May Studio 410 S Michigan Ave Ste 527 Chicago IL 60605-1401

MAY, DIANE MARIE, protective services official; b. Andrew AFB, Md., Nov. 4, 1959; d. Robert Henry and Joann (McKenzie) Shimer; m. Walter K. May II, June 29, 1985; children: Robert Kenneth, Kristina Marie. AA in Nursing, Allegeny C.C., Cumberland, Md., 1983; BS in Fire Sci. Mgmt., U. Md., 1990; MEd, Frostburg (Md.) State U., 1992. RN, Md.; cert. EMT instr. Emergency med. technician Tri-Towns Rescue Squad, Westerport, Md., 1976-82, cardiac rescue technician, 1982-85; nursing asst. Frostburg Village (Md.) Nursing Home, 1978-79, Heartland Nursing Home, Keyser, W. Va., 1979-80, Frostburg (Md.) Hosp., 1980-81; security officer Westvaco, Luke, Md., 1981-88, tng. instr., 1988-94, security and property conservation supr., 1994—; RN Potomac Valley Hosp., Keyser, W. Va., 1982-84; instr. Am. Heart Assn., instr. trainer, Balt., 1977—; instr. Md. Fire and Rescue Inst., College Park, 1985—, mem. EMT med. adv. coun., Grantsville, Md., 1985. Leader Daisy Girl Scouts, Cumberland, md., 1995—; firefighter Luke (Md.) Vol. Fire Dept., 1984—; cardiac rescue tech. LaVale Vol. Rescue Squad, tng. officer cardiac rescue tech., 1987-95; emergency med. tech. Tri-Towns Vol. Rescue Squad, capt., bd. dirs., 1977-87; coach Pee Wee Girls Dapper Don League, Cumberland, Md., 1995. Named Luke (Md.) Firefighter of the Yr. Luke Vol. Fire Dept., 1987, Md. State Firefighter fo the Yr., Md. State Fireman Assn., 1987, Outstanding Individual Emergency Med. Tech. W. Va. Competition, 1993. Mem. Am. Soc. Indsl. Security, Bus. Profl. Women, Chesapeake Soc. Fire Svc. Inst. Office: Westvaco 300 Pratt St Westernport MD 21540

MAY, ELAINE, actress, theatre and film director; b. Phila., Apr. 21, 1932; d. Jack Berlin; m. Marvin May (div.); 1 child, Jeannie Berlin; m. Sheldon Harnick, Mar. 25, 1962 (div. May 1963). Ed. high sch., studied Stanislavsky method of acting withMarie Ouspenskaya. Stage and radio appearances as child actor; performed with Playwright's Theatre, in student performance Miss Julie, U. Chgo.; appeared with improvisational theatre group in night club The Compass, Chgo., 1954-1957, (with Mike Nichols) appeared N.Y. supper clubs, Village Vanguard, Blue Angel, also night clubs other cities; TV debut on Jack Paar Show, 1957; also appeared in Omnibus, 1958, Dinah Shore Show, Perry Como Show, Laugh Line, Laugh-In, TV spls.; comedy albums include Improvisations to Music, An Evening with Mike Nichols and Elaine May, Mike Nichols and Elaine May Examine Doctors; weekly appearance NBC radio show Nightline; appeared (with Mike Nichols) NBC radio show, N.Y. Town Hall, 1959, An Evening with Mike Nichols and Elaine May, Golden Theatre, N.Y.C., 1960-61; theater appearances include The Office, N.Y.C., 1966, Who's Afraid of Virginia Woolf?, Long Wharf Theatre, New Haven, Conn., 1980; dir. plays The Third Ear, N.Y.C., 1964, The Goodbye People, Berkshire Theatre Festival, Stockbridge, Mass., 1971, various plays at Goodman Theatre, Chgo., 1983; dir., author screenplay, actress film A New Leaf, 1972; dir. films The Heartbreak Kid, 1973, Mikey and Nicky, 1976 (writer, dir. remake 1985), Ishtar, 1987 (also writer); appeared in films Luv, 1967, California Suite, 1978 (Acad. award Best Supporting Actress 1978), In The Spirit, 1990; co-author screenplay Heaven Can Wait, 1978, Birdcage, 1996; author plays A Matter of Position, 1962, Not Enough Rope, 1962, Adaptation, 1969, Hot Line, 1983, Better Part of Valor, 1983, Mr. Gogol and Mr. Preen, 1991, (one act) Death Defying Acts, 1995; stage revue: (with Mike Nichols) Telephone, 1984; co-recipient (with Mike Nichols) Grammy award for comedy performance, Nat. Acad. Recording Arts & Scis., 1961. Office: care Julian Schlossberg Castle Hill Productions 1414 Ave of the Americas New York NY 10019*

MAY, GITA, French language and literature educator; b. Brussels, Sept. 16, 1929; came to U.S., 1947, naturalized, 1950; d. Albert and Blima (Sieradska) Jochimek; m. Irving May, Dec. 21, 1947. BA magna cum laude, CUNY-Hunter Coll., 1953; MA, Columbia U., 1954, PhD, 1957. Lectr. French CUNY-Hunter Coll., 1953-56; instr. Columbia U., 1956-58, asst. prof., 1958-61, assoc. prof., 1961-68, prof., 1968—, chmn., 1983-93, mem. senate, 1979-83, 86-88, chmn. Seminar on 18th Century Culture, 1986-89; lecture tour English univs., 1965. Author: Dederot et Baudelaire, critiques d'art, 1957, De Jean-Jacques Rousseau à Madame Roland: essai sur la sensibilité préromantique et révolutionaire, 1964, Madame Roland and the Age of Revolution, 1970 (Van Amringe Disting. Book award), Stendhal and the Age of Napoleon, 1977; co-editor: Diderot Studies III, 1961; mem. editl. bd. 18th Century Studies, 1975-78, French Rev., 1975-86, Romanic Rev., 1959—; contbg. editor: Deuvres completes de Diderot, 1984, 95; gen. editor: The Age of Revolution and Romanticism: Interdisciplinary Studies, 1990—; contbr. articles and revs. to profl. jours. Decorated chevalier and officier Ordre des Palmes Acad.; recipient award Am. Coun. Learned Socs., 1961, award for outstanding achievement CUNY-Hunter Coll., 1963; Fulbright rsch. grantee, 1964-65; Guggenheim fellow, 1964-65, NEH fellow, 1971-72. Mem. AAUP, MLA (del. assembly 1973-75, mem. com. rsch. activities 1975-78, mem. exec. coun. 1980-83), Am. Assn. Tchrs. of French, Am. Soc. 18th Century Studies (pres. 1985-86, 2nd v.p. 1983-84, 1st v.p. 1984-85), Soc. Française d'Etude du Dix-Huitième Siècle, Soc. Diderot, Am. Soc. French Acad. Palms, Phi Beta Kappa. Home: 404 W 116th St New York NY 10027-7202

MAY, LORI ANN, critical care nurse; b. Waterloo, Iowa, July 5, 1961; d. Donald Andrew and Karen Kay (Kelley) Peterson; m. Stewart Keith May, Jan. 1, 1989; children: Alex, Benjamin, Daniel. Diploma, Allen Sch. of Nursing, 1984. RN, Tex., Wis., Iowa; cert. BLS instr., pediat. life support instr., trauma nurse core curriculum, mobile intensive care nurse. Intern in critical care Scott & White Hosp., Temple, Tex., 1984, staff/charge nurse, preceptor in pediatric intensive care and emergency room, 1984-89; staff nurse emergency room Allen Meml. Hosp., Waterloo, Iowa, 1989-90; charge/staff nurse intensive care, emergency room and cardiac rehab., flight nurse Covenant Med. Ctr., Waterloo, 1990—; emergency med. technician Scott & White Hosp., 1985; advisor Jesup (Iowa) Ambulance, 1990—; cons. report and profl. coms., Coventant Hosp., Waterloo, 1994; tchr. in field. Supporter, mem. Waterloo Cmty. Playhouse, 1991—; supporter Jesup Pub. Libr., 1994, Pub. TV, Johnson, Iowa, 1994—. Mem. AACN (CCRN), Nat. Flight Nurses Assn., Emergency Nurses Assn. Republican. Methodist. Home: 428 S Holgate Rd Waterloo IA 50703-9348

MAY, MARGRETHE, allied health educator; b. Tucson, Ariz., Oct. 6, 1943; d. Robert A. and Margrethe (Holm) M. BS in Human Biology, U. Mich., 1970, MS in Anatomy, 1986. Cert. surg. technologist. Surg. technologist Hartford (Conn.) Hosp., 1965-68, U. Mich. Hosps., Ann Arbor, 1968-70; asst. operating room supr. U. Ariz. Med. Ctr., Tucson, 1971-72; coord. operating room tech. program Pima Coll., Tucson, 1971-76; prof., coord. surg. tech. and surg. first asst. programs Delta Coll., University Center, Mich., 1978—; commr. Comm. on Accreditation of Allied Health Ednl. Programs, Chgo., 1994—, Coun. Accreditation and Unit Recognition, 1994-96. Editor: Core Curriculum for Surgical Technology, 3d edit., 1990, Core Curriculum for Surgical First Assisting, 1993; contbr. articles to profl. jours. Mem. Assn. Surg. Technologists (bd. dirs. 1987-89, pres.-elect 1989-90, pres. 1990-91, on-site visitor program accreditation 1974—, chmn. exam writing com. 1981, liaison coun. on cert. co-chmn. 1977, chmn. 1978, sec.-treas. 1979, chmn. accreditation review com for edn. in surg. tech. 1994—), Am. Soc. Law, Medicine and Ethics, Mich. Assn. Allied Health Professions (sec. 1994—), Nat. Network Health Career Programs in Two-Year Colls. Home: 2506 Abbott Rd Apt P-2 Midland MI 48642-4876 Office: Delta Coll Allied Health Divsn University Center MI 48710

MAY, NORMA BUTLER, reading educator; b. Cairo, Ill., Sept. 6, 1940; d. John William and Irene Virginia (Cartwright) Butler; m. Willie L. May, July 4, 1964; children: Kristian, Karen. AS, Vincennes U., 1960; BS, Ind. State U., 1961, MS, 1966. Kindergarten tchr. Sch. Dist. 130, Blue Island, Ill., 1961-70; subs. tchr. Chgo. Bd. Edn., 1974-76; reading specialist Evanston Twp. H.S., Ill., 1976—. Recipient internat. teaching award Delores Kohl Found., 1994. Mem. NEA, ASCD, Nat. Coun. Tchrs. English, AAUW (presenter Title I IASA statewide conf. 1995), NAACP, Internat. Reading Assn., Ill. Edn. Assn., Jack & Jill of Am., U. Ill. Mothers Assn. (2d v.p. 1992-93, pres. 1993-94). Methodist. Home: 8333 S Dorchester Ave Chicago IL 60619-6401 Office: Evanston Twp HS 1600 Dodge Ave Evanston IL 60201-3449

MAY, PHYLLIS JEAN, financial executive; b. Flint, Mich., May 31, 1932; d. Bert A. and Alice C. (Rushton) Irvine; m. John May, Apr. 24, 1971. Grad. Dorsey Sch. Bus., 1957; cert. Internat. Corr. Schs., 1959, Nat. Tax Inst., 1978; MBA, Mich. U., 1970. Registered real estate agt; lic. life, auto and home ins. agent. Office mgr. Comml. Constrn. Co., Flint, 1962-68; bus. mgr. new and used car dealership, Flint, 1968-70; contr. various corps., Flint, 1970-75; fiscal dir. Rubicon Odyssey Inc., Detroit, 1976-87, Wayne County Treas.'s Office, 1987-93; exec. fin. office Grosse Pointe Meml. Ch., 1993—; acad. cons. acctg. Detroit Inst. Commerce, 1980-81; pres. small bus. specializing in adminstrv. cons. and acctg., 1982—; supr. mobile svc. sta., upholstery and home improvement businesses; owner retail bus. Pieces and Things. Pres. PTA Westwood Heights Schs., 1972; vol. Fedn. of Blind, 1974-76, Probate Ct., 1974-76; mem. citizens adv. bd. Northville Regional Psychiat. Hosp., 1988, sec. 1989-90. Recipient Meritorious Svc. award Genesee County for Youth, 1976, Excellent Performance and High Achievement award Odyssey Inc., 1981. Mem. NAFE (bd. dirs.), Am. Bus. Women's Assn. (treas. 1981, rec. sec. 1982, v.p. 1982-83, Woman of Yr. 1982), Womens Assn. Dearborn Orch. Soc., Dearborn Community Art Ctr., Mich. Mental Health Assn., Internat. Platform Assn., Guild of Carillonneurs in N.Am., Pi Omicron (officer 1984-85). Baptist.

MAYBIN, PATRICIA JANE, retired army officer, mass media writer, photographer; b. Birmingham, Ala., Dec. 29, 1927; d. Robert Henry and Rose (Milligan) M. BA in Journalism, La. State U., 1950, MA in Journalism, 1951, BA in Speech, 1980; PhD in Pub. Adminstrn., Kennedy Western U., 1992. Commd. 2d lt. U.S. Army, 1955, advanced through grades to lt. col., 1975, ret., 1977. Contbr. numerous stories to mags. and newspapers including Morning Advocate, The Baton Rouge Register Mag., Pelican Mag., Family Mag., Jack and Jill, Woman's Da. Swimming instr. YMCA, ARC; active United Fund Drive, Salvation Army, Food for the Hungry. Decorated Bronze Star, Meritorious Svc. medal with one oak leaf cluster, Nat. Def. Svc. medal, Vietnam Svc. medal with four stars, Vietnam Campaign medal with 60 device, Vietnam Cross of Gallantry with palm; recipient Key to City of Anniston, Ala., Key to City of Baton Rouge. Mem. NAFE, VFW, Ret. Officers Assn., Tex. Press Women, La. Press Women (state publicity chairperson 1954), Nat. Fedn. Press Women, Press Club Ala., Nat. Soc. Arts and Letters (mem. San Antonio chpt.), Am. Legion. Home: 119 Pike San Antonio TX 78209

MAYDEN, BARBARA MENDEL, lawyer; b. Chattanooga, Sept. 18, 1951; d. Eugene Lester Mendel and Blanche (Krugman) Rosenberg; m. Martin Ted Mayden, Sept. 14, 1986. AB, Ind. U., 1973; JD, U. Ga., 1976. Bar: Ga. 1976, N.Y. 1980. Assoc. King & Spalding, Atlanta, 1976-79, Willkie Farr & Gallagher, N.Y.C., 1980, Morgan Lewis & Bockius, N.Y.C., 1980-82, White & Case, N.Y.C., 1982-89; spl. counsel Skadden, Arps, Slate, Meagher & Flom, N.Y.C., 1989-95; lectr. Vanderbilt U. Sch. Law, Nashville, 1995—. Mem. U. Ga. Bd. Visitors, Athens, 1986-89. Fellow Am. Bar Found. (life); mem. ABA (chairperson young lawyers div. 1985-86, house of dels. 1986—, commr. commn. on women 1987-91, commr. commn. opportunities for minorities in profession 1986-87, chmn. assembly resolutions com. 1990-91, select com. of the house 1989-91, membership com of the house 1991-92, bd. govs. 1991-94, chair bd. govs. ops. com., exec. com. 1993-94, mem. task force long range fin. planning 1993—), Nat. Assn. Bond Lawyers (bd. dirs. 1985-86), Bond Attys.' Workshop (chmn. 1986), N.Y. State Bar Assn. (mem. ho. of dels. 1993—), Assn. of Bar of City of N.Y. (internat. human rights com. 1986-89, 2d century com. 1986-90, com. women in the profession, 1989-92), N.Y. County Lawyers Assn. (com. spl. projects, chair com. rels with other bars). Democrat. Jewish. Home: 4414 Herbert Pl Nashville TN 37215 Office: Vanderbilt U Sch Law Nashville TN 37245

MAYDEN, DEBRA ANN, music educator; b. Paoli, Ind., Oct. 29, 1962; d. Donald Lee and Charlotte Ann (James) M. BS, Ball State U., 1985; MS, Ind. U., 1988. Tchr. music Tell City (Ind.) - Troy Twp. Sch. Corp., 1985-96; ch. organist St. Pius Ch., Troy, Ind., 1990. Music Honors award scholar Ball State U., 1981. Office: Newman Elem Sch 821 10th St Tell City IN 47586-2117

MAYER, ELIZABETH BILLMIRE, educational administrator; B.Ed., Nat. Coll. Edn., Evanston, Ill., 1953; M.A. in Liberal Studies, Wesleyan U., 1979. Teaching asst. Hull House, Chgo., 1950-51; teaching scholar Nat. Coll. Edn. Demonstration Sch., 1952-53; pre-sch. tchr. St. Matthew's Sch., Pacific Palisades, Calif., 1959-63, tchr. 2d grade, 1963-67; librarian Chandler Sch., Pasadena, Calif., 1971-72, tchr. 4th grade, 1972-80, curriculum coordinator 1st-8th grades, 1979-80; tchr. 4th-6th grades Inst. for Experimentation in Tchr. Edn., SUNY-Cortland, 1980; asst. prof. edn. SUNY-Cortland, 1980-82; founder, headmistress The Mayer Sch., Ithaca, N.Y., 1982-92, Ariz. State U., Tempe, 1992—, Coll. Edn., 1992-94, faculty liaison Acad. Affairs, 1994—. Mem. Nat. Council Tchrs. Math., Nat. Council Tchrs. English, Nat. Sci. Tchrs. Assn., Rotary Internat. (mem. bd. dirs. 1994-96), Phi Delta Kappa (officer 1980-81, 92-96), Mem. Leadership America, class of 1995. Office: Ariz State U MS 3N21 Box 870101 Tempe AZ 85287

MAYER, KAY MAGNOR, writer; b. Chgo.; d. Frank J. and Harriet (Schnell) Magnor; m. Kenneth W. Mayer, May 2, 1943; children: Michael J., Patricia A., Mark T. Student Northwestern U., 1938-43. News reporter Tampa Times, 1943; advt. copywriter Marshall Field & Co., Chgo., Earle Ludgin & Co., Chgo., Henri, Hurst & McDonald, Chgo., 1944-58; spl. editor, writer Scott, Foresman & Co., Glenview, Ill., 1966-71; freelance writer Ariz. Hwys., Southwest Art, Am. Artist, Am. Way, Columbia, 1971—. Recipient Press Women's awards, 1983, 84, 85, 89, 92, 93. Mem. Nat. Fedn. Press Women, Ariz. Press Women, Nat. Council Social Studies, Western History Assn., Soc. Southwestern Authors (dir. 1981-83), The Writers. Home: 1855 Tanglewood Dr Apt C Glenview IL 60025-1629

MAYER, KRISTINE I., mental health professional; b. Tulsa, Okla., Dec. 11, 1959; d. Harry W. and Eleanor M. (Westphal) Meeker; m. Heinz C. Mayer, Jan. 18, 1986 (div. 1995); children: Justin, Forrest. BA in journalism, Okla. State Univ., 1987; MS in counseling psych., Northeastern State Univ., 1991. Mental health counselor Mayer Counseling Svcs., Inc., Tulsa, 1991-96; mental health profl. State of Okla. Dept. Human Svc., 1996—; lectr., cons. in field. Mem. pub. svc. adv. com. DHS; bd. dirs. Mary K. Oxley Nature Ctr. Assn., 1994—. Mem. Am. Counseling Assn., Internat. Assn. Marriage & Family Therapists, Assn. for Adult Devel. & Aging, Assn. Specialists in Group Work, Psi Chi. Office: P O Box 35653 Tulsa OK 74153-0653

MAYER, LAURA LOUISE PIKE, small business owner; b. El Paso, Tex., Nov. 24, 1958; d. Edward A. and Phyllis L. (Hancock) Pike. Legal sec. cert., Pensacola (Fla.) Jr. Coll., 1977, student, 1995; student, Oxnard Coll., 1989, Rota (Spain) C.C., 1982. Sec. U. West Fla., Pensacola, 1977-81; adminstrv. asst. U.S. Naval Activities, Rota, 1982-85; sec., stenographer Exxon Co. USA, 1985-86; adminstrv. asst. Oxnard Coll., 1987-89; night club mgr. Dock, Inc., Pensacola Beach, Fla., 1989-91; mgr. McGuire's Mgmt. Group, Pensacola Beach, Fla., 1991; car sales cons. KeyFord, Pensacola, 1993-95; owner Unique Painting & Cleaning, Inc., Gulf Breeze, Fla., 1993—; sec. Manpower, Pensacola, 1980-82. Home: 2201 Scenic Hwy Unit C-6 Pensacola FL 32503

MAYER, MARGERY WEIL, publishing executive; b. Beaufort, S.C., Feb. 11, 1952; d. Warren Burke Weil and Elise Jean (Schiff) Rubel; m. Theodore Van Huysen Mayer, Dec. 28, 1975; children: Lily, Henry. BA, Middlebury Coll., 1974; MS, MIT, 1976. Planning analyst Digital Equipment Corp., Maynard, Mass., 1976-77; editor-in-chief sch. pub. sect. Holt, Rinehart & Winston, N.Y.C., 1977-87; pres. Ginn div. Silver, Burdett & Ginn, Needham, Mass., 1987-90; exec. v.p. Scholastic Inc., N.Y.C., 1990—. Editor Sloan Mgmt. Rev., 1975-76. Trustee program Read With Me, Dedham, Mass., 1989; mem. rev. panel U.S. Dept. Edn. Sch. Recognition Program. Mem. Phi Beta Kappa. Office: Scholastic Inc 555 Broadway New York NY 10012-3919*

MAYER, MARILYN GOODER, steel company executive; b. Chgo.; d. Seth MacDonald and Jean (McMullen) Gooder; m. William Anthony Mayer, Nov. 14, 1959; children—William Anthony Jr., Robert MacDonald. grad. Career Inst. Chgo., 1941; student Lake Forest Coll., Ill., 1942. Adminstrv. asst. Needham, Louis & Brorby, Chgo., 1949-53; v.p. RMB Corp., Chgo., 1963-71, Mayer Motors, Ft. Lauderdale, Fla., 1965-74, Gooder-Henrichsen, Chicago Heights, Ill., 1975—; dir. Barnett Bank, West Palm Beach, Fla. Trustee Gulf Stream (Fla.) Sch., St. Andrew's Sch., Boca Raton, Fla.; bd. dirs. Bethesda Hosp. Assn., Boynton Beach, Fla., pres. 1981-82; bd. dirs. Gulf Stream Civic Assn. Mem. Soc. Four Arts. Republican. Episcopalian. Clubs: Little, Gulf Stream Bath and Tennis. Avocation: travel. Home: 2925 Polo Dr Delray Beach FL 33483-7331

MAYER, PATRICIA JAYNE, financial officer, management accountant; b. Chgo., Apr. 27, 1950; d. Arthur and Ruth (Greenberger) Hersh; m. William A. Mayer Jr., Apr. 30, 1971. AA, Diablo Valley Coll., 1970; BSBA, Calif. State U., Hayward, 1975. Cert. mgmt. acct. Staff acct., auditor Elmer Fox Westheimer and Co., Oakland, Calif., 1976; supervising auditor Auditor's Office County of Alameda, Oakland, 1976-78; asst. acctg. mgr. CBS Retail Stores doing bus. as Pacific Stereo, Emeryville, Calif., 1978-79; contr. Oakland Unified Sch. Dist., 1979-84; v.p. fin., CFO YMCA, San Francisco, 1984-96; v.p. fin. customer segments Charles Schwab & Co., San Francisco, 1996—; instr. acctg. to staff YMCA, San Francisco, 1984-96, CBS Retail Stores, 1978-79. Draft counselor Mt. Diablo Peace Ctr., Walnut Creek, Calif., 1970-72; dep. registrar of voters Contra Costa County Registrar's Office, Martinez, Calif., 1972-77. Mem. Fin. Execs. Inst. (bd. dirs. San Francisco chpt.), Inst. Mgmt. Accts. (pres.-elect Diablo Valley chpt. 1995—, pres. 1995-96), Dalmatian Club No. Calif., Dalmation Club Am. Democrat. Jewish. Office: Charles Schwab & Co 101 Montgomery st San Francisco CA 94104

MAYER, PATRICIA LYNN SORCI, mental health nurse, educator; b. Chgo., July 22, 1942; d. Ben and Adonia (Grenier) Sorci; 1 child, Christopher David Mayer. AGS with high honors, Pima Community Coll., Tucson, 1983; BSN with honors, U. Ariz., 1986, MS in Nursing, 1987. RN, Ariz.; cert. addictions counselor, chem. dependency therapist; lic. pvt. pilot. Nurse educator Tucson. Contbr. articles to profl. jours. Mem. Nat. Nurses Soc. on Addictions, Phi Kappa Phi, Sigma Theta Tau, Pi Lambda Theta, Golden Key.

MAYERSOHN, NETTIE, state legislator; m. Ronald Mayersohn; children: Jeffrey, Lee. BA, Queens Coll., 1978. Exec. dir. N.Y. State Crime Victims Bd.; mem. N.Y. State Assembly, 1982—, chairperson assembly ho. ops. com. and subcom. elderly crime victims, mem. legis. women's caucus, mem. various coms.; dist. leader 27th N.Y. State Assembly Dist.-Part A, 1972—. Past mem. Cmty. Bd. # 8, former chairperson youth com.; past chairperson Pomonok Cmty. Ctr.; founder, organizer Pomonok Neighborhood Ctr., Inc.; active Electchester Jewish Ctr., Israel Ctr. of Hillcrest Manor; N.Y. state del. Internat. Women's Conf., 1977; bd. dirs. Harry Van Arsdale, Jr. Meml. Assn. Recipient Builders of Brotherhood award Nat. Conf. Christians and Jews, 1977, Legislator of Yr. award N.Y. State chpt. NOW, 1989. Mem. Stevenson Regular Dem. Club, Inc. (exec. mem.), Alpha Sigma Lambda. Home: 67-11 Parsons Blvd Flushing NY 11365-2961 Office: NY State Assembly State Capitol Albany NY 12224

MAYERSON, SANDRA ELAINE, lawyer; b. Dayton, Ohio, Feb. 8, 1952; d. Manuel David and Florence Louise (Tepper) M.; m. Scott Burns, May 29, 1977 (div. Oct. 1978); 1 child, Katy Joy. BA cum laude, Yale U., 1973; JD, Northwestern U., 1976. Bar: Ill. 1976, U.S. Ct. Appeals (7th cir.) 1976, U.S. Dist. Ct. (no. dist.) Ill. 1977, U.S. Dist. Ct. Md. 1989, U.S. Ct. Appeals (5th cir.) 1994. Assoc. gen. counsel JMB Realty Corp., Chgo., 1979-80; assoc. Chatz, Sugarman, Abrams et al, Chgo., 1980-81; ptnr. Pollack, Mayerson & Berman, Chgo., 1981-83; dep. gen. counsel AM Internat., Inc., Chgo., 1983-85; ptnr. Kirkland & Ellis, Chgo., 1985-87; ptnr., chmn. bankruptcy group Kelley Drye & Warren, N.Y.C., 1987-93; ptnr., chmn. N.Y. bankruptcy group McDermott, Will & Emery, N.Y.C., 1993—; examiner Interco chpt. II, 1991. Bd. dirs. Jr. Med. Rsch. Inst. coun. Michael Reese Hosp., Chgo., 1981-86; mem. met. div. Jewish Guild for Blind, 1990-92; mem. nat. legal afffairs com. Anti-Defamation League, 1990—. Fellow Branford Coll., Yale U., 1993—. Mem. ABA (bus. bankruptcy com. 1976—, sec. 1990-93, chair avoiding powers subcom. 1993—), Ill. State Bar Assn. (governing council corp. and securities sect. 1983-86), Chgo. Bar Assn. (current events chmn. corp. sect. 1980-81), 7th Cir. Bar Assn. Democrat. Jewish. Clubs: Yale (N.Y.C.), Metropolitan (Chgo.). Office: McDermott Will & Emery 1211 Avenue Of The Americas New York NY 10036

MAYES, ILA LAVERNE, minister; b. Eldorado, Okla., Dec. 23, 1934; d. Thomas Floyd and Irene Elizabeth (Buchanan) Jordan; m. Forrest Clay Mayes, July 2, 1954; children: Barbara, Marian, Cynthia, Janice. BA, U. Tex., 1973; MSW, U. Mich., 1976; MDiv, Austin Presbyn. Sem., 1986. Ordained to ministry Presbyn. Ch. (U.S.A.), 1986; cert. social worker. Pastor First Presbyn. Ch., Childress, Tex., 1986—; med./social worker Childress Regional Med. Ctr., Tex., 1996—; mem. Austin Sem. Alumni Bd., 1991-94, Synod of the Sun Evangelism Com., Denton, 1990-93, Transition Coordinating Agy., 1991—. Chmn. ARC, Childress, 1990; bd. dirs. Am. Cancer Soc., Childress, 1988-89. Mem. AAUW, Mortarboard, Rotary Internat., Alpha Chi, Alpha Lambda Delta. Home: 309 Avenue B SE Childress TX 79201-5429 Office: First Presbyn Ch 311 Commerce St Childress TX 79201-4525 also: Childress Regional Med Ctr Hwy 83 N Childress TX 79201

MAYES, MAUREEN DAVIDICA, physician, educator; b. Phila., Oct. 16, 1945; d. David M. and Marguerite Cecilia (Fineran) M.; m. Charles William Houser, Dec. 18, 1976; children: David Steven, Edward Charles. BA, Coll. Notre Dame, 1967; MD, Ea. Va. Med. Sch., 1976; MA in Pub. Health, U. Mich., Ann Arbor, 1994. Resident in internal medicine Cleve. Clinic Found., 1977-79, fellow in rheumatology, 1979-81; asst. prof. medicine W.Va. U., Morgantown, 1981-85; asst. prof. medicine Wayne State U., Detroit, 1985-90, assoc. prof. medicine, 1990—; dir. scleroderma unit Wayne State U., Detroit, 1991—. Contbr. articles to profl. jours. Pres. bd. United Scleroderma Found., 1988-89, mem. med. adv. bd., 1995—; bd. trustees Mich. chpt. Arthritis Found. Robert Wood Johnson scholarship EVMS, 1972, NIH fellow, 1993-94, NIAMS Sr. Rsch. fellowship, 1994; recipient Lower award Cleve. Clinic Found., 1981. Fellow Am. Coll. Rheumatology (mem. ctrl. region coun. 1995—), Am. Coll. Physicians; mem. Am. Fedn. Clin. Rsch., Mich. Rheumatism Soc. Office: Wayne State U Hutzel Hosp 4707 Saint Antoine St Detroit MI 48201-1427

MAYFIELD, LORI JAYNE, marketing professional; b. Newport Beach, Calif., Sept. 11, 1955; d. John Vincent and Marilyn Jane (Huish) M. Student Linn-Benton Community Coll., 1973-75, N.W. Coll., 1975-76; AA in Gen. Edn. Saddleback Community Coll., 1993. Gen. ins. cert. Ins. Inst. Am. Cashier Auto Club So. Calif., Anaheim, 1977-80; ins. clk., sec., Fullerton, 1980-81, ins. rep., 1981, field coord., Costa Mesa, Calif., 1981-86; auto. club sales rep., 1986-88; pres. LJM Enterprises; customer svc. rep. Roadway Express, Irvine, Calif., 1989-93; ins. processor Prudential Ins., Laguna Hills, Calif., 1993-95, mktg. asst. specialist, 1995—. Recipient Outstanding Citizenship award YMCA, Santa Ana, Calif., 1984. Mem. NAFE. Office: Prudential Fin Svcs 24036 Avenida De La Carlota # 570 Laguna Hills CA 92653-3121

MAYFIELD, ROBIN S., surgeon, researcher; b. Pitts., Nov. 28, 1957; d. Lamont and Patricia Anne (Flaherty) S.; m. Chancey C. Mayfield; 1 child, Zoe Bryson Mayfield. BA, Swarthmore Coll., 1980; MD, Harvard U., 1990. Intern U. Calif., San Francisco, 1990-91, resident gen. surgery, 1991-93; rsch. fellow Mass. Gen. Hosp., Boston, 1993—. Resident scholar Am. Coll. Surgeons, 1994. Office: Mass Gen Hosp TBRC 149 13th St Boston MA 02129-2060

MAYGINNES, BARBARA ANN, coatings company executive; b. Portland, Oreg., Mar. 20, 1945; d. John Wesley and Marion Josephine (Hill) Clausen; children: Shamaz, Hukam, Mardana. BA, Lindenwood Coll. for Women, 1968; MA, Portland State U., 1972. Owner Shamaz Trading Co., Ukiah, Calif., 1974-77; mgr. small bus. dept. Ernst & Ernst, Portland, 1977-78; CFO All Heart Lumber Co., Ukiah, 1978-83; CFO, CEO Performance Coatings Inc., Ukiah, 1983—, chmn. bd. dirs., 1992—; bd. dirs. West Co., Mendocino County Health Clinic; CEO, chmn. bd. dirs. Dusky Rose & Assoc. Pres. Rare Conifer Found., Ukiah, 1994—. Mem. Nat. Paint and Coatings Assn., Golden State Paint and Coatings Assn., Ukiah C. of C. (mem. econ. devel. com. 1993-94), Women in Coatings (Leadership award 1994), Leadership Mendocino. Office: Performance Coatings Inc 360 Lake Mendocino Dr Ukiah CA 95482-9432

MAYNARD, JOAN, education educator; b. Louisa, Ky., Oct. 18, 1932; d. Macon Scott and Jeanette (Thompson) Chambers; m. Frank Maynard Jr., June 15, 1951 (dec. Oct. 1988); children: Mark Steven, Julia Beth Maynard McFann, Robert Blake. BA, Wittenberg U., 1977; MEd, Wright State U., 1980, Wright State U., 1984. Tchr., reading specialist Mechanicsburg (Ohio) Exempted Village Schs., 1976—; pres. TOTT Publs. Inc., Bellbrook, Ohio, 1988—; rep. Career Edn., Mechanicsburg, 1981-88, mem. Thompson Grant Com., Mechanicsburg, 1987-88. Author: Mud Puddles, 1988, Mud Pies, 1989. Vol. Mechanicsburg Schs. Levy, 1980, 82, 88, Congl. Race, Campaign County, Ohio, 1982, 84, 86; cons. Urbana U., Ohio, 1988-90, 91, 92, 93; tutor Laubach Lit. Action, Urbana, 1989-90, 91-93, 94. Recipient Thompson grant, 1982, 88, 92. Mem. AAUW (edn. chmn. Champaign County chpt. 1988-89, treas. 1989-90), Internat. Reading Assn., Champaign County Reading Coun. (treas. 1990-91), Midwestern Assembly Lit. Young People (treas. 1989-93), Kappa Delta Pi. Home: 1546 Parkview Rd Mechanicsburg OH 43044-9779 Office: Exempted Village Schs 60 High St Mechanicsburg OH 43044-1003

MAYNARD, NANCY GRAY, biological oceanographer; b. Middleboro, Mass., Apr. 18, 1941; d. Thomas LaSalle and Clara (Gray) M.; m. Conrad Dennis Gebelein, Jan., 1969 (div. 1977); 1 child, Jennifer Lynn. BS, Mary Washington Coll., 1963; MS, U. Miami (Fla.), 1968, PhD, 1974. Rsch. assoc. Bermuda Biol. Sta., Ferry Reach, 1972-75; rsch. fellow Lamont-Doherty Geol. Obs. Columbia U. (CLIMAP), 1972-75; post-doctoral fellow Div. Engring., Applied Physics Harvard U., Cambridge, Mass., 1975-76; field coord. environ. studies Alaska Outer Continental Shelf Office U.S. Dept. Interior, Anchorage, 1976-78; with oil spills sci. support Nat. Oceanic and Atmospheric Adminstrn., Alaska and S.E. U.S., 1978-81; policy analyst Exec. Office Pres. U.S. Office Sci. and Technology Policy, Washington, 1982-83; fellow Dept. of Commerce Sci. and Tech., 1982-83; staff dir. Bd. Ocean Sci. and Policy NAS, Washington, 1983-85; resident rsch. assoc. Nat. Rsch. Coun. Scripps Instn. Oceanography and Jet Propulsion Lab NASA, 1985-87; br. head Oceans and Ice Br. Goddard Space Flight Ctr. NASA, Greenbelt, Md., 1987-88, assoc. chief rsch. Lab. for Oceans, 1988-89; asst. dir. for environment Exec. Office of Pres. Office Sci. and Tech. Policy, Washington, 1989-93; dep. dir. sci. div. NASA Mission to Planet Earth HQ, Washington, 1993—. Contbr. numerous articles profl. jours. Recipient Pub. Svc. Commendation USCG, 1979. Mem. AAAS, Assn. Women in Sci., The Oceanography Soc., Am. Geophys. Union, Women's Aquatic Network (bd. dirs.), Corp. Bermuda Biol. Sta. Rsch. Office: NASA Mission Planet Earth Sci Divsn 300 E St NW Washington DC 20546-0001

MAYNARD, VIRGINIA MADDEN, charitable organization executive; b. New London, Conn., Jan. 29, 1924; d. Raymond and Edna Sarah (Madden) Maynard; B.S., U. Conn., 1945; postgrad. Am. Inst. Banking, 1964-66, Cornell U., 1975. With Nat. City Bank (now Citibank), N.Y.C., 1954-79, asst. cashier, 1965-69, asst. v.p., 1969-74, v.p. internat. banking group, 1974-76, comptroller's div., 1976-79; v.p. First Women's Bank, N.Y.C., 1979-80; Internat. Fedn. Univ. Women rep. UN, 1982—. Trustee fellowships endowment fund AAUW Ednl. Found., Washington, 1977-80, Va. Gildersleeve Internat. Fund Univ. Women, Inc. (pres., 1987-93, dir. 1994—). Mem. AAUW (fin. chmn. N.Y.C. br. 1976-79, bylaws chmn. 1979-83, adminstr. Meml. Fund 1983-92, dir., 1992-94, 96—, Woman of Achievement 1976). Republican. Congregationalist. Home: 601 E 20th St New York NY 10010-7622

MAYO, ELISSA ADELE, criminalist; b. Camp Pendleton, Calif., Sept. 30, 1963; d. Ashton Stokes Jr. and Emma Louise (Wilkerson) M. BS in Biology, U. Calif., Irvine, 1986. Sr. criminalist Calif. Dept. Justice, Riverside, 1990—. Office: Calif Dept Justice Crime Lab 1500 Castellano Rd Riverside CA 91720

MAYO, JOAN BRADLEY, microbiologist, healthcare administrator; b. Ada, Okla., Oct. 24, 1942; d. Samuel S. and Norene (Parker) Bradley; m. Harry D. Mayo III, Sept. 30, 1967. BA, Drake U., 1964; MS in Microbiology, NYU, 1978; MBA in Mgmt., Fairleigh Dickinson U., 1989. RN. Technologist clin. labs. St. John's Episc. Hosp., Bklyn., 1964-66; supr. Med. Tech. Sch. Bklyn.-Cumberland Med. Ctr., 1966-71; clin. instr., technologist SUNY Downstate Med. Ctr., Bklyn., 1970-73; supr. bacteriology lab. Meml. Sloan-Kettering Cancer Ctr., N.Y.C., 1973-82, mgr. microbiology labs., 1982-87; dir. infection control svc. N.Y.C. Health and Hosp. Corp./Harlem Hosp. Ctr., 1987-95; mgr. infection control dept. Atlantic Health System/The Mountainside Hosp., Montclair, N.J., 1995—; mem. com. for prevention of bloodborne diseases N.Y.C. Health and Hosp. Corp., 1990-95. Contbr. articles to profl. publs. Active Friends of Harlem Hosp., 1988—, North Bergen (N.J.) Action Group, 1987—. Mem. Am. Soc. Microbiology, Am. Pub. Health Assn., Assn. Practitioners in Infection Control, Delta Mu Delta, Alpha Kappa Alpha. Home: 7855 Boulevard E North Bergen NJ 07047-5938 Office: The Mountainside Hosp Bay and Highland Aves Montclair NJ 07047

MAYO, KATHLEEN OWENS, librarian; b. Miami Beach, Fla., May 23, 1948; d. Edwin Shepherd and Theodora Winifred (Jones) Morris; m. Harold Anthony Mayo, June 30, 1972; children: Giuliana Nora, Adam Anthony. BS in Art Edn., Fla. State U., 1970, MS in Libr. Sci., 1971. Sch. libr. Funston & Hamilton Schs., Moultrie, Ga., 1971-72; libr. asst. Fla. State U., Tallahassee, 1972-73; libr. dir. Fla. State Hosp., Chattahoochee, 1973-78; libr. cons. State Libr. Fla., Tallahassee, 1978-89; head spl. svcs. Lee County Libr. Sys., Fort Myers, Fla., 1989—. Editor Health Info at Your Library, 1987; (newsletter) Keystone Tech. Bull. Librs., 1979-89; co-editor: ADA Library Kit, 1994. Mem. rape task force/trauma ctr. Fort Myers, 1990—; bd. dirs. Meals on Wheels Lee County, Fort Myers, 1993—, Assn. Provider Orgns., Fort Myers, 1991-94. Recipient Citizen of Yr. award SW Fla. Unit NASW, 1996. Mem. NOW, ALA, Assn. Specialized & Cooperative Libr. Agys. (bd. dirs. 1979-81, Exceptional Svc. award 1991), ADA Assembly Health Care Librs. (chair 1983-84, 93-95), Pub. Libr. Assn. Bookmobile Svcs (chair 1994-95), Fla. Libr. Assn. Democrat. Unitarian Universalist. Office: Lee County Libr Sys 2050 Lee St Fort Myers FL 33901

MAYO, TERRY LYNN, psychiatric home health nurse; b. Washington, July 27, 1959; d. Charles Edward and June Loving (Christian) Hutcheson; m. Donald Ray Mayo, Oct. 21, 1989. AS, Eastern Ky. U., Richmond, 1981; RN, Jewish Hosp. Sch. Nursing, Cin., 1984; BS in Nursing, U. Cin., 1988; MSN, Xavier U., Cin., 1995. RN; cert. psychiat. mental health nursing Am. Nurses Credential Ctr., nursing continuing edn. and staff devel. Supr. Rollman Psychiat. Inst., Cin., 1984-86; staff nurse Bethesda Hosp., Cin., 1986-88; charge nurse Emerson North Hosp., Cin., 1988-90; nurse instr. Franciscan Health Sys., Cin., 1990-94, psychiat. home health nurse Pro

Health Home Nursing Svcs., 1994-96; total quality mgmt. facilitator Franciscan Health Sys., 1993—; program mgr. mental health svcs. Am. Nursing Care, Milford, Ohio, 1996—. Mem. Sigma Theta Tau (program com.). Home: 2387 Adams Rd Cincinnati OH 45231-2824 Office: Am Nursing Care Ste C 300 Techne Center Dr Milford OH 45150

MAYRON, MELANIE, actress, writer; b. Phila., Oct. 20, 1952. Ed., Am. Acad. Dramatic Arts, N.Y.C. Writer Tribeca Prodns. Appearences include (films) Harry and Tonto, 1974, Car Wash, 1976, The Great Smokey Road Block, 1976, Gable and Lombard, 1976, Girl Friends, 1978 (British Acad. award nomination), You Light Up My Life, 1977, Heart Beeps, 1981, Missing, 1982, Sticky Fingers (also co-writer, co-producer), 1988, Checking Out, 1989, My Blue Heaven, 1990, Drop Zone, 1994; (TV movies) Hustling, 1975, The New Love Boat, 1977, Katie: Portrait of a Centerfold, 1978, The Best Little Girl in the World, 1981, Will There Really Be a Morning?, 1983; (TV miniseries) Wallenberg: A Hero's Story, 1985, Playing for Time, 1980, The Boss's Wife, 1986, Other Women's Children, 1993, Ordeal in the Arctic, 1993; (TV series) thirtysomething (Emmy award for best supporting actress in a drama series, 1989), dir. 2 episodes; dir.: Tribeca, 1993, Freaky Friday, 1995, The Baby-Sitters Club, 1995; author (anthology): Stepping Back. *

MAYS, GLENDA SUE, retired education educator; b. Freer, Tex., July 18, 1938; d. Archie Richard and Helen Hildred (Morgan) Cox; m. Dewey William Mays, Sept. 7, 1963; children: Rose Marie, Teresa Sue, Frank Dewey. BS, Tex. Tech. U., 1959, MA, 1961; PhD, North Tex. State U., 1969. Cert. tchr., supr., prin. Tchr. Lubbock (Tex.) Pub. Schs., 1959-61, Amarillo (Tex.) Pub. Schs., 1961-62, Austin (Tex.) Pub. Schs., 1962-63; curriculum intern/rsch. asst., elem. coord. U. Tex. at Austin, Hurst, Tex., 1963-65; asst. prof. McMurry U., Abilene, Tex., 1965-67; assoc. prof. Dallas Bapt. U., 1968-71; reading resource tchr., dept. chair Ft. Worth (Tex.) Ind. Sch. Dist., 1971-74, reading specialist, 1974-82, instructional specialist, 1982-95, ret., 1995; spkr. lang. acquisition and reading 7th World Congress in Reading, Hamburg, Germany, 1978. Advisor/writer (English textbook): McDouglas Littel Language, 1985-86; writer: Bilingual Stories for Ft. Worth Ind. Sch. Dist., 1979-80. Patron Kimbell Mus. Art, Ft. Worth, 1994—; mem. Nat. Cancer Soc., Ft. Worth, 1980—. Fulbright-Hays scholar, Kenya, Africa, 1970; grantee in fgn. langs. Nat. Endowment Arts U. Ark., 1987, Ft. Worth Ind. Sch. Dist. Study grantee U. London, 1978. Fellow ASCD, NEA, Tex. State Tchrs. Assn., Ft. Worth Edn. Assn., Internat. Reading Assn. (hostess 1st Tex. breakfast 1969), Nat. Geog. Soc., Smithsonian Instn., Libr. of Congress, Ft. Worth Reading Assn., Nat. Coun. for Social Studies spkr. social studies symposium N.Y.C. 1970, Tex. Elem. Prins. and Suprs. Assn. (sec. 1971-72). Home: 1225 Clara St Fort Worth TX 76110-1009

MAYS, JANICE ANN, lawyer; b. Waycross, Ga., Nov. 21, 1951; d. William H. and Jean (Bagley) M. AB (hon.), Wesleyan Coll., Macon, Ga., 1973; JD, U. Ga., 1975; LLM in Taxation, U. Georgetown, 1980. Bar: Ga. 1976. Tax counsel com. on ways and means U.S. Ho. Reps., Washington, 1975-88, chief tax counsel com. on ways and means, staff dir. subcom. select revenue measures, 1988-93, chief counsel, staff dir. com. on ways and means, 1993-95, minority chief counsel, staff dir. com. on ways and means, 1995—. Mem. Tax Coalition (past chair). Office: Ways & Means Com 1106 Longworth Office Bldg Washington DC 20515

MAYSILLES, ELIZABETH, speech communication professional, educator; b. Sleepy Creek, W.Va.; d. Evers and Rose (Scott) M. AB, W.Va. U.; MA, Hunter Coll., 1963; PhD, NYU, 1980. Announcer Radio Sta. WAJR, Morgantown, W.Va.; broadcaster Radio Sta. WGHF-FM, Rural Radio Network, N.Y.C.; group leader GMAC, N.Y.C.; instr. NYU, N.Y.C.; adj. prof. speech communication Pace U., N.Y.C., 1978—; exec. adminstr. Am.-Scottish Found., N.Y.C., 1980-90; adminstrv. asst. Brit. Schs. and Univs. Found., Inc.; cons. to hosps. and acctg., 1971—; lectr. seminars in field, travel Eng. and Scotland. Counselor Help Line, N.Y.C., 1971-75. Recipient Disting. Svc. award NYU Grad. Orgn., 1970, 71. Mem. Internat. Platform Assn. (bd. govs. 1980—), N.Y. Acad. Scis., Speech Comm. Assn., Ctr. for Study of Presidency, English-Speaking Union, Caledonian Club N.Y. Home: 155 E 77th St Apt 6-f New York NY 10021-1944 Office: Pace U 41 Pace Plz New York NY 10038-1502

MAZA-BORKLAND, ELENA MICAELA, artist, martial arts educator; b. Havana, Cuba, Sept. 29, 1947; came to US, 1961; d. Aquiles and Olga (Caturla) de la Maza; m. Herbert Kennington Borkland, Nov. 28, 1975. Student, Catholic U., 1967-69, U. Md., 1973-74, The Corcoran Sch. Art, 1991-92. Draftswoman Cohen & Haft Archs., Silver Spring, Md., 1969-72; draftswoman, designer Beachem, Richardson & Williamson, Vienna, Va., 1973-74, Lee-Thorpe Consulting Engrs., Chevy Chase, Md., 1974-75, Cobb & del Castillo, Ltd., Rockville, Md., 1976-91; owner, instr. Olney T'ai Chi, Sandy Spring, Md., 1991-96; instr. t'ai chi Shaolin Martial Arts Acad., Rockville, Md., 1990—, The Aspen Hill Club, Silver Spring, Md., 1994; curator Dover Art League, 1995. Co-author: (screenplay) Free Tibet, 1995; one-woman shows include Parish Gallery, Washington, 1994, Dover Art League, 1996. Mem. Casa Cuba, 1994. Individual artist grantee Arts Coun. Montgomery County, 1994; placed First advanced t'ai chi form US Nat. Kuoshu Championships, 1992. Mem. The Black Bean Coalition, Womens Caucus for Art Greater Washington (treas, exhbn. chmn. 1992-95, exhbn. organizer 1994, pres. 1996—), Dover Art League, Rehoboth Art League. Home: 16806 Excaliber Way Sandy Spring MD 20860 Office: Olney T'ai Chi 16806 Excaliber Way Sandy Spring MD 20860

MAZEAU, ZOE ANN, speech pathologist; b. Mineola, N.Y., July 18, 1948; d. Jeremiah and Naima Viola (Persson) M.; m. Grant Joseph Holland, Apr. 22, 1982 (div. Apr. 1995); children: Christopher Erik Majors, Richard Joseph Holland, Jeremiah Mark Holland. BS, SUNY, 1972; M in Speech Pathology, L.I. U., 1976, MBA, 1984. Supervisor, speech therapist Staten Island Devel. Ctr., N.Y.C., 1972-77; assoc. exec. dir. United Cerebral Palsy Assn., N.Y.C., 1977-87; speech pathologist Rose Med. Ctr., Denver, 1996; co-owner, artist Mural Makers of Colo., Englewood, 1995—; cons. Consumer Adv. Bd., Staten Island, 1972-80; action com. United Cerebral Palsy Assn., 1981-87, chair grievance com., 1982-87. Recipient appreciation award Cherry Creek (Colo.) Schs. PTO, 1993. Mem. Am. Speech, Lang. & Hearing Assn., Denver Art Students League, Valley Country Club. Republican. Roman Catholic.

MAZUR, STELLA MARY, former organization administrator; b. Lowell, Mass.; d. Stanley and Katherine (Cichowicz) M.; BS in Edn., U. Mass., Lowell; student ARC Mgmt. Tng. Sch., 1962, Nat. Tng. Lab. for Applied Behavioral Sci., 1963. USO club dir., Windsor Locks, Conn., 1942; gen. field rep. ARC, 1944, mgr., Waltham, Mass., 1944-79. Spl. assignment State Dept. USIA Graphic Arts Cultural Exchange Program, Eastern Europe, Poland, 1965. Mem. pres. cir. U. Mass., Lowell, also mem. centennial planning com. Recipient Waltham Rotary Club spl. citation, 1952; Waltham Community 25 Year Service award, 1969; Recognition award Waltham chpt. ARC, 1971; Outstanding Woman, Waltham News Tribune, 1974; Woman of Today, Waltham Bus. and Profl. Women's Club, 1976; Outstanding Service award ARC New Eng., 1979; Disting. Alum,ni award Coll. Edn. U. Mass., Lowell, 1956, U. Mass., 1979. Mem. Internat. Platform Assn., ARC Retiree Assn., Am. Assn. Ret. Persons, Smithsonian Assos., Lowell U. Alumni Assn. (hon. life). Seton Guild Lowell, Lowell Hist. Soc., Lowell Mus. Corp. Clubs: Vesper Country (Tyngsboro, Mass.); Longmeadow Golf, Country. Author, pub.: Roots and Heritage of Polish People in Lowell, 1976. Home: 170 Andover St Lowell MA 01852-2360

MAZURKIEWICZ, CYNTHIA HALL, geriatrics nurse, administrator; b. Loudoun County, Va., Aug. 31, 1949; d. Otto Gibson and Esther Margaret (Poston) Hall; m. Edward John Mazurkiewicz, Nov. 28, 1970; 1 child, Gibson Edward. Diploma, Alexandria Hosp. Sch. Nursing, 1971. RN, Va.; cert. gerontol. nurse; cert. dir. nursing adminstrn. Charge nurse Loudon Long Term Care Ctr., Leesburg, Va., head nurse, asst. dir. nursing; dir. nursing Oak Springs of Warrenton. Mem. No. Va. Dirs. Nursing Assn. for Long Term Care, Va. Dirs. Nursing Assn. for Long Term Care (chmn. legis. com., pres. 1994—), No. Va. Alzheimer's Assn. (pub. policy com.). Home: 158 Meadows Ln NE Leesburg VA 22075-4445

MAZZAFERRI, KATHERINE AQUINO, lawyer, bar association executive; b. Phila., May 14, 1947; d. Joseph William and Rose (Aquino) M.; m. William Fox Bryan, May 5, 1984 (separated); 1 child, Josefa Mazzaferri Bryan; 1 stepchild, Patricia M. Bryan. BA, NYU, 1969; JD, George Washington U., 1972. Bar: D.C., 1972. Trial atty. EEOC, Washington, 1972-75; dir. litigation LWV Edn. Fund, Washington, 1975-78; dep. asst. dir. for advt. practices FTC, Washington, 1978-80, asst. dir. for product liability, 1980-82, asst. dir. for advt. practices, 1982; exec. dir., v.p. pub. svcs. activities corp. D.C. Bar, Washington, 1982—; bd. dir. regulatory analysis project U.S. Regulatory Coun.; mediator D.C. Mediation Svc., 1982; vis. instr. Antioch Law Sch., Washington, 1985; mem. Bd. of Women's Bar Assn. Found., 1990-93; mem. FBA Meml. Found., 1991—. Recipient Superior Service award FTC, 1979. Mem. ABA (rep. of the homeless project steering com. 1988-90), D.C. Bar , Womens Legal Def. (pres. 1972-73, bd. dirs. 1971-75, 76-79), FBA Meml. Found. Home: 5832 Lenox Rd Bethesda MD 20817-6070 Office: DC Bar 1250 H St NW Fl 6 Washington DC 20005-3952

MAZZARELLA, ROSEMARY LOUISE, business administration executive; b. Phila., Aug. 20, 1959; d. Samuel Charles and Rosemarie Claire Mazzarella. BA, La Salle U., 1985, MS in Orgnl. Devel. & Mgmt., 1991. Materials mgmt. exec. Sun Refining & Mktg. Co., Phila., 1979-91; purchasing asst. Children's Seashore House, Phila., 1992-94; adminstr. FMC Corp., Phila., 1994—. Vol. Child Abuse Prevention Com. Greater Phila., 1992, Walnut Street Theatre, Phila., 1992; vol. tutor Ctr. for Literacy, Phila., 1992. Mem. Assn. Behavior Analysis (sustaining), Alpha Epsilon.

MAZZOCCO, ELIZABETH HUNT DAVIS, foreign language educator; b. Chapel Hill, N.C., Feb. 11, 1958; d. Bertran E. and Betty Hunt (Seeger) Davis; m. Angelo Mazzocco, Oct. 7, 1990. BA summa cum laude, East Tex. State U., Commerce, 1980; MA, Bryn Mawr (Pa.) Coll., 1983, PhD, 1988. Acting undergrad. chair dept. Italian U. Pa., Phila., 1988-89; vis. asst. prof. Spanish and Italian Mt. Holyoke Coll., South Hadley, Mass., 1989-90; asst. prof. French/Italian U. Mass., Amherst, 1990—; dir. Five Coll. Fgn. Lang. Resource Ctr. Five Colls. Inc., Amherst, 1990—; bd. dirs. Nat. Assn. Self-Instrnl. Lang. Programs, 1992—. Editor: Learning to See, Learning to Learn, 1991; book reviewer Italica, 1991, Renaissance Quar., 1995, Modern Philology, 1996, Rivista di Studi Italiani, 1996, Mediaevalia et Humanistica, 1996; editor in chief Nat. Assn. Self-Instrnl. Lang. Programs Jour., 1994—, Mountain Interstate Foreign Lang. Jour., 1993—. Fulbright fellow in Italian Fulbright Found., Italy, 1986-87; grantee Charles E. Culpeper Found., 1994—, Booth-Ferris Found., 1993-95, Dept. Edn., 1995—. Mem. MLA, Renaissance Soc. Am., Am. Assn. Tchrs. italian, Medieval Acad., Dante Soc. Am., Nemla. Home: 7 Cedar Ridge Estates South Hadley MA 01075 Office: Dept French & Italian U Mass Herter Hall Amherst MA 01003

MC AFEE, MARILYN, ambassador; b. Portsmouth, N.H., Jan. 23, 1940; m. Joel William Febel. BA in History with honors, U. Pa., 1961; MA, Johns Hopkins U., 1962. Joined Fgn. Svc., Washington, 1968; served with U.S. Embassy, Guatemala, 1969-70, Nicaragua, 1970-72, Iran, 1972-77; served with Fgn. Svc., Dept. State, Washington, 1977-80; served with U.S. Embassy, Costa Rica, 1980-83, Venezuela, 1983-86, Chile, 1986-89; dep. chief of mission U.S. Embassy, Bolivia, 1989-92; amb. U.S. Embassy, Guatemala City, Guatemala, 1993-96; career min., 1996—. Ford Found. fellow; recipient 4 Meritorious Honor awards, 1 Superior Honor award, 1 Presdl. Meritorious Svc. award. Mem. Army Navy Country Club, Marsh Landing Country CLub. Office: Am Embassy Guatamala APO AA 34024-5000

MCALHANY, TONI ANNE, lawyer; b. Decatur, Ind., May 1, 1951; d. Robert Keith and Evelyn L. (Fisher) McA. BA, Ind. U., 1973; JD, Valparaiso U., 1976. Bar: Mich. 1976, Ind. 1982, Ill. 1986, U.S. Dist. Ct. (no. dist.) Ind. 1989. Asst. prosecutor Ottawa County Prosecutor's Office, Grand Haven, Mich., 1976-81; assoc. Hann, Doss & Persinger, Holland, Mich., 1981-82, Romero & Thonert, Auburn, Ind., 1982-85; ptnr. Dahlgren & McAlhany, Berwyn, Ill., 1985-88, Colbeck, McAlhany & Stewart, Angola, Ind. & Coldwater, Mich., 1988—; atty. Angola (Ind.) Housing Authority, 1989—. Bd. dirs. Child and Family Svcs., Ft. Wayne, Ind., 1983, Fillmore Ctr., Berwyn, 1986-88, Altrusa, Coldwater, 1989-92. Mem. ATLA, State Bar Mich., State Bar Ind., State Bar Ill., Branch County Bar Assn., Steuben County Bar Assn. Office: McAlhany & Stewart 215 W Maumee Angola IN 46703

MCALINDON, MARY NAOMI, nursing administrator; b. Ebensburg, Pa., Oct. 16, 1935; d. S. David and Genevieve (Little) Solomon; m. James Daniel McAlindon, Nov. 23, 1961; children: Robert, Donald, James, Peter, M. Catherine. BSN, Georgetown U., 1957; MA, U. Mich., 1979; EdD, Wayne State U., 1992. RN, Mich. Staff nurse Georgetown U. Hosp., Washington, 1957-59; instr. St. Joseph Hosp., Flint, 1959-62; clin. instr. Mott. C.C., Flint, 1980-81; asst. DON McLaren Hosp., Flint, 1980-89, adminstrv. asst., 1989-92, asst. v.p., 1992-95; clin. informatics mgr. McLaren Health Care Corp., Flint, 1995—. Mem. bd. trustees United Way Genesee County, Flint, 1988-95. Mem. ANA (exec. com. 1991-93), Am. Med. Informatics Assn. (chair nursing group 1993-94), Mich. Nursing Informatics Network (charter), Vis. Nurses Assn. (pres., bd. dirs. 1988-90), Dist. Nurses Assn. (prfes. 1993-96), Nursing Honor Soc. U. Mich. (pres. 1996—). Office: McLaren Health Care Corp 401 S Ballenger Hwy Flint MI 48532-3638

MCALLISTER, NANCY HARDACRE, music academy administrator; b. Highland Park, Ill., Feb. 24, 1940; d. Milton Joseph Jr. and Virginia Letitia (Engels) Hardacre; m. Claude Huntley McAllister, Sept. 5, 1970. MusB, B Music Edn., Oberlin Coll., 1962; MA, U. N.C., 1967, M Music Edn., 1968. Cert. in music edn., violin performance, composition. Organist, choir dir. St. Mark's Episcopal Ch., Barrington, Ill., 1957-58; orch. dir. Adrian (Mich.) Pub. Schs., 1964-66, Luther Coll., Decorah, Iowa, 1966-67; orch. dir., tchr. New Hanover Pub. Schs., Wilmington, N.C., 1964-87; dir., owner Wilmington Acad. Music, 1987—; grad. asst. U. N.C., Chapel Hill, 1962-66; violinist Columbus (Ohio) Symphony Orch., 1961-62, Acad. Music Chamber Trio, Wilmington, 1987—; concertmaster Wilmington Symphony Orch., 1987-92; condr. Acad. Music Orch., 1987-96, Cape Fear Symphony Orch., 1996—. Composer: Sonata in A Major for violin and piano, 1961, Suite for Horn and Strings, 1961 (2d place Priz de Rome 1965). Mem. Am. String Tchrs. Assn. (sec. 1987-91), Music Educators Nat. Conv., Nat. Sch. Orch. Assn., Wilmington C. of C., P.E.O. Episcopalian. Office: Wilmington Acad Music 1635 Wellington Ave Wilmington NC 28401-7758

MCANALLY, JOHNNIE SUE, library director; b. Decatur, Ala., June 13, 1945; d. Ruth Whitt Gurley; m. David R. McAnally, Mar. 17, 1967; 1 child, Jon David. BS, Auburn (Ala.) U., 1966; MA, U. North Ala., 1975, Cert. in Supervision, 1989. Tchr. Morgan County Schs., Decatur, 1967-72, libr. media specialist, 1967-92, dir. libr. media svcs., 1992—. Recipient Exemplary Sch. Libr. Svc. award Ala. State Dept. Edn., 1990, Exceptional Svc. award Lib. and Media Profls., 1992. Mem. Ala. Libr. Assn., Ala. Instructional Media Assn. (Carrie C. Robinson award 1987, Lois E. Henderson award 1994), DAR (chaplain 1988—), Decatur Bus. and Profl. Women, Phi Delta Kappa. Baptist. Office: Morgan County Schools 1325 Point Mallard Pky Decatur AL 35601-6542

MCANALLY, MICHELLE RENÉE, reporter; b. Vicksburg, Miss., Nov. 17, 1969; d. William H. and Carol Ann (Larner) McA.; m. Michael Joseph Coody, May 20, 1995. BS in Journalism, Miss. U. for Women, 1992; BA in Anthropology, Miss. State U., 1995. Program dir. WMUW Coll. Radio, Columbus, Miss., 1989-90; news anchor Northland Cable News, Starkville, Miss., 1991-94; lab. asst. Cobb Inst. Archeology, Starkville, Miss., 1994-95; staff writer Vicksburg (Miss.) Evening Post, 1995—; vol. archeol. dig.Archeol. Assessments, Inc., Little Rock, 1995. Loaned exec. United Way of West Ctrl. Miss., Vicksburg, 1995; vol. Good Sheperd Cmty. Ctr., Vicksburg, Miss., 1995. Mem. NOW (pub. rels. officer 1995). Democrat. Home: 358 Marian Ln Vicksburg MS 39180

MCANDREW, URSULA K., former pediatrics nurse; b. Pottsville, Pa., Aug. 2, 1955; d. John and U. Ursula (Paulosky) Balnanosis; m. Joseph F. McAndrew, Nov. 26, 1977; children: John, James, Jana, Joseph, Jeffrey. BSN cum laude, Coll. Misericordia, 1977. Float staff nurse Hershey Med. Ctr., Pa. State U.; charge nurse Childrens Care Ctr., Hummelstown, Pa. Mem. Sigma Theta Tau.

MCANIFF, NORA P., publishing executive. BA, CUNY. Pub. People Weekly, N.Y.C., 1994—. Office: People Magazine Time Inc Rockfeller Ctr New York NY 10020-1393

MC ANULTY, MARY CATHERINE CRAMER (MRS. CHARLES GILBERT MC ANULTY), retired principal, educator; b. Braddock, Pa., June 26, 1908; d. Albert R. and Sara (Kelly) Cramer; AB, Fla. So. Coll., 1929; MA, Tchrs. Coll. Columbia, 1937; postgrad. Fla. State U., 1946-50; m. Charles Gilbert McAnulty, Dec. 25, 1937. Elem. tchr. Lake Ann Sch., Lake Garfield, Fla., 1930-31, elem. prin., 1932-34; prin. South Winter Haven Elem. Sch., Winter Haven, Fla., 1935-55; adminstrv. asst. to supervising prin. Winter Haven Area Schs., 1956-60; prin. Fred Garner Elem. Sch., Winter Haven, 1961-68, Lake Alfred Elem. Sch., 1969-70. Asst. chmn. vols., asst. tng. chmn., local chpt. ARC, 1967-68, 2d v.p., also chmn. vols., 1969-70, bd. mem. 12 yrs., chmn. service to mil. families, 1970-71, chmn. coll. youth, 1971-72; treas. Imperial Harbours Condominium, 1980-82, pres., 1984; v.p. Beymer United Methodist Women, 1973-75, pres., 1976-77; lay del. ann. conf. Meth. Ch., 1978, 79, 89-91; pres. Lake Region Extension Homemaker's Club, 1974, 75; bd. dirs. Winter Haven Hosp. Aux., rec. sec., 1985-86, corr. sec., 1986-88; co-chmn. Residents Coun., 1992, 93, 94, 96, Lake Howard Heights, sec., 1995. Mem. Am. Assn. Supervision and Curriculum Devel., Internat. Reading Assn. (pres., Polk County chpts.), NEA, Nat. Ret. Tchrs. Assn., Fla. Edn. Assn. (dir. dept. elem. sch. prins. 1965-67), Polk County Elem. Prins. Assn. (sec.), LWV (local dir. 1962), AAUW (local br. chmn. status women com. 1963), DAR (chpt. treas. 1967-68, historian 1969-70, regent 1970-72, state chmn. jr. Am. citizens 1972—, dir. dist. VI 1973-74, parliamentarian 1986-94), Fla. So. Coll. Alumni Assn. (sec.), Internat. Platform Assn., P.E.O. (chpt. treas. 1970-74, 80-89, chaplain 1976, 77, chpt. pres. 1978-79), Ch. Women United (v.p. 1977-93, chmn. adminstrn. bd. 1980-81), Pi Gamma Mu, Delta Kappa Gamma (State Achievement award 1964, Fla. pres. 1962-63, chpt. parliamentarian 1968-73, 87-94, pres., state v.p., treas., expansion chmn.). Methodist (choir mem., chmn. comm. edn. 1959-60, supt. study program 1969-70, organist 1970-77, pres. Wesley fellowship class 1972-73, chmn. adminstrv. bd. 1980, 81, 83-85 trustee 1983-88, hon. trustee 1989—, pres. bd. trustees 1987-88, lay leader 1985, 86, fin. com., worship com., staff Parish com 1989-91, organ com., 1987-93). Clubs: Pilot (charter, pres. 1954-55, 61-62), Poinsettia Garden (pres. 1984-85). Lodge: Order Eastern Star (fin. chair 1987-89), Winter Haven Woman's (edn. chmn. 1967-68, v.p. 1983-84, pres. 1984-85, parliamentarian 1986-94, dist. 9 parliamentarian 1988-90). Home: 650 N Lake Howard Dr Apt 4B Winter Haven FL 33881-3133

MCARDLE, LOIS WOOD, artist, educator; b. Jamestown, N.Y., July 26, 1933; d. Charles Edward and Marguerite Regina (Murray) McArdle; m. James Lombard Pettee, Aug. 6, 1977; children: Jane Hasson, David, Jonathan, Marguerite McArdle-Pettee, Catherine McArdle-Pettee. BA, U. Kans., 1955; MFA, George Washington U., 1966. Lectr. Corcoran Sch. Art, Washington, 1966-68; asst. divsn. chair for art, assoc. prof. No. Va. C.C., Annandale, 1968-78; assoc. prof. Art Inst. Boston, 1979-86; chair visual arts The Madeira Sch., McLean, Va., 1988—; vis. prof. Georgetown U., Washington, summer 1973; adj. prof. Mass. Coll. Art, Boston, 1978-80; advanced placement reader Coll. Bd., Princeton, N.J., 1994—; master tchr. The Madeira Sch., 1991-95; vis. artist No. Va. C.C., 1984; cons. Accrediting Commn. of Nat. Home Study Coun., 1972. Author: Portrait Drawing, 1984; editor: Hilda Thorpe, 1989; illustrator: Visual Aids, 1967; commd. by U.S. Army Divsn. of Mil. History; solo exhbn. include Franz Bader Gallery, Washington, No. Va. C.C., Annandale, Habitat, Boston, Georgetown U., Washington, Jane Haslem Gallery, Washington; Mahler Gallery, Washington; group exbhns. include Boca Raton (Fla.) Mus., Jane Haslem Gallery, Washington, DeCordova Mus., Lincoln, Mass., Clark Gallery, Lincoln, Mass., Alexandria (Va.) Athenaeum, Smithsonian Instn., Washington; permanent public collections include DeCordova Mus., Touche Ross, Inc., Coopers & Lybrand, Inc., George Washington U., No. Va. C.C., U.S. Army. Chmn. bd. Sign of Jonah, Washington, 1972-74. Mem. Delta Phi Delta, Phi Beta Kappa. Democrat.

MCARDLE, MOLLY ANN, health foundation administrator; b. Ft. Wayne, Ind., Aug. 1, 1959; d. James Edward and Agnes Therese (Parker) McA.; m. Paul James Walker, Oct. 27, 1983 (dec. Oct. 1993); children: Elizabeth Hannah, Dylan James. Vol. rural edn. agr. U.S. Peace Corps, Belize, 1983-84; corp. account exec. Air France Internat., Abu Dhabi, United Arab Emirates, 1985-86; account exec. Caldwell Van Riper, Ft. Wayne, 1986-88; dir. devel. and mktg. Ft. Wayne Mus. Art, 1988-90; exec. dir. St. Joseph Health Found., Ft. Wayne, 1990-93, Deaconess Found., Evansville, Ind., 1993—; mem. adv. bd., yoga instr. Awareness Ctr., Evansville, Ind., 1994—. Mem. steering com. Ft. Wayne Fundraisers, 1988-92; pres.-elect Leadership Evansville, 1995—, grad. exec. series; bd. dirs. Found. for Comty. Health, Evansville, 1996—, Washington Ave. Clinic, Evansville, 1996—; grad. Leadership Ft. Wayne, 1994—. Mem. Nat. Soc. Fundraising Execs. (cert. fundraising exec.), Assn. Healthcare Philanthropy (chmn. region VI 1995—), Network Evansville Women. Office: Deaconess Hosp Found 600 Mary St Evansville IN 47747

MCARTHUR, JOAN D., state official; b. Sauk County, Wis.; d. Lawrence A. and Grace (Thering) Dederich; m. John F. McArthur, Nov. 16, 1957; children: Morgan J., Laura Grace. BS, U. Wis., 1957, MS, 1960. Cert. tchr.; cert. speech pathologist, flight instr., instrument instr.; cert. pub. mgr. Speech pathologist in pvt. practice Baraboo, Wis., 1961-78; chief flight and instrument instr. Chaplin Aviation Inc., Baraboo, 1976-79; commr. Wis. Transp. Commn., Madison, 1979-83; CEO JDMCO, Baraboo, 1985-89; govt. adminstr. dept. workforce devel. State of Wis., Madison, 1989—; cons. McArthur Assocs., Baraboo, 1983-85. Chmn. Wis. Transp. Commn., Madison, 1979-83; adv. bd. U. Wis. Cert. Pub. Mgrs., Madison, 1993-96; bd. supr. Sauk County Bd., Baraboo, 1986-92; mem. Baraboo Bd. Edn., 1963-79. Recipient Appreciation award Delta Nu Alpha, 1982, Wis. Aviation Assn., 1983. Mem. Am. Acad. Cert. Pub. Mgrs. (del. 1993-96), Wis. Soc. Cert. Pub. Mgrs. (charter pres. 1993-96), Wis. Counties Assn., Wis. Sch. Bd. Assn., Aircraft Owners and Pilots Assn., Am. Speech Hearing and Lang. Assn.

MCATEE, PATRICIA ANNE ROONEY, medical educator; b. Denver, Apr. 20, 1931; d. Jerry F. and Edna E. (Hansen) Rooney; m. Darrell McAtee, Sept. 4, 1954; 1 son, Kevin Paul. BS, Loretto Heights Coll., 1953; MS, U. Colo., 1961; PhD, Union of Univs., 1976. Supr. St. Anthony Hosp., Denver, 1952-55; pub. health nurse, edn. dir. Tri-County Health Dept., Colo., 1956-58; adminstr. sch. health program Littleton (Colo.) Pub. Schs., 1958-60; asst. prof. community health, acad. adminstr. continuing edn. U. Colo., 1968-70; project dir. Western Interstate Commn. for Higher Edn., 1972-74; asst. prof. pediatrics, project co-dir. Sch. Medicine U. Colo., 1975—; mem. profl. svcs. staff Mead Johnson & Co., 1981—; cons. Colo. Safety Coun.; treas. Vista Nueva Assocs. Editor: Pediatric Nursing, 1975-77. Chmn. bd. dirs. Found. for Urban and Neighborhood Devel.; mem. Arapahoe Health Planning Coun. Mem. NAS, APHA, Inst. Medicine, Nat. Bd. Pediatric Nurse Practitioners and Assocs. (pres.), Nat. Assn. Pediatric Nurse Practitioners (v.p.), Am. Acad. Polit. and Social Scientist, Nat. League Nursing, Western Soc. Rsch., Am. Sch. Health Assn., Sigma Theta Tau. Home: 877 E Panama Dr Littleton CO 80121-2531 Office: 4200 E 9th Ave Box C-219 Denver CO 80262

MCATEER, DEBORAH GRACE, travel executive; b. N.Y.C., Nov. 3, 1950; d. Edward John and Ann Marie (Cassidy) McAteer; m. William A. Helms, Feb. 5, 1948 (div. 1993); children: Elizabeth Grace, Kathleen Marie, Margaret Ann. Student, Montgomery Coll., 1969, Am. U., 1972. Sec. Polinger Co., Chevy Chase, Md., 1969-72, Loews Hotels, Washington, 1972-73; adminstr. asst. Am. Gas Assn., Arlington, Va., 1973-75; mgr. Birch Jermain Horton Bittner, Washington, 1975-77; asst. mgr. Travel Services, McLean, Va., 1977-79; founder, pres. Travel Temps, Washington, Atlanta, Phila., Miami and Ft. Lauderdale, Fla., 1979—; pres. Diversified Communications, Atlanta, 1990—; tchr. Ga. State U., Atlanta, 1996; tchr. Montgomery Coll., Rockville, Md., 1980-84, Ga. State U., 1996. Mem. Christ Child Soc., Washington, 1975—. Mem. Internat. Travel Soc. (pres. 1983-84), Am. Soc. Travel Agts., Pacific Area Travel Assn., Inst. Cert. Travel Cons. (cert., life mem.), Nat. Assn. Women Bus. Owners (chair membership com. 1983-84), Women Bus. Owners Atlanta (bd. dirs. 1991—, pres. 1994), Women's Commerce Club, PROST (v.p. 1991), Atlanta Women in Travel. Republican. Roman Catholic. Home: 7390 Twin Branch Rd NE Atlanta GA 30328-1771 Office: Travel Temps 7390 Twin Branch Rd NE Atlanta GA 30328-1771

MCAULAY, JESSIE ANN, counseling administrator; b. Cosala, Sinaloa, Mex., Sept. 26, 1957; came to U.S., 1969; d. Manuel Arturo and Mary (Celaya) Robles; m. Douglas Everett McAulay, Aug. 11, 1979; children: Audrey, Shannon. BA, U. St. Thomas, Houston, Tex., 1979; MEd, U. Tex. El Paso, 1993. Cert. tchr., counselor, trauma resolution therapy, Tex. Lab. technologist Childrens Hosp., Houston, 1980-83, Cmty. Hosp., Boulder, Colo., 1983-85; health coord. Health Dept., Boulder, Colo., 1985-90; sch. counselor Socorro Ind. Sch. Dist., El Paso, Tex., 1990—. Chairperson Juvenile Court Counsel Com., El Paso, Tex., 1995. Mem. Chi Sigma Ita Nat. Honor Counseling Assn. Home: 1504 Charles Owens El Paso TX 79936-5209 Office: SISD 205 Buford Rd El Paso TX 79927

MCAULIFFE, BEVERLY LOUISE, school system administrator, principal; b. Louisville; d. William George and Mary Elizabeth (Ahearn) McA.; m. Ronald Paul Bisig, Jan. 28, 1984; 1 child, Abigail. BA, Brescia Coll., 1966; MA, U. Louisville, 1976; postgrad., Spalding U., 1994—. Cert. secondary ed. Tchr. Louisville Cath. Schs., 1968-72; prin. Resurrection Elem. Sch., Louisville, 1972-76; tchr. St. Xavier H.S., Louisville, 1976-77; prin. St. Agnes Elem. Sch., Louisville, 1977-83, Holy Rosary Secondary Sch., Louisville, 1983-90; asst. prin. Assumption H.S., Louisville, 1990—. Mem. tchr. edn. com. Bellarmine Coll., Louisville, 1980—; choral dir. Carousels, Louisville, 1974-80, St. Ignatius Choir, Louisville, 1973-83. Mem. Ky. Ednl. Leadership Inst., Commonwealth Inst. for Instrnl. Leaders, Nat. Assn. Secondary Sch. Prins. (prin. assessor 1994), Leadership Louisville. Roman Catholic. Office: Assumption HS 2170 Tyler Ln Louisville KY 40205-2950

MCAULIFFE, CATRINA, advertising executive. Sr. v.p., acct. planning dir. Goldberg Moser O'Neill, San Francisco. Office: Goldberg Moser O'Neill 77 Maiden Ln San Francisco CA 94108*

MCBAIN, NAN, accountant. ABA, Kellogg Cmty. Coll., 1968; BBA, Western Mich. Univ., 1983, MBA, 1989. Controller Family and Children's Svc., Battle Creek, Mich., 1976-86, Kellogg Cmty. Coll., Battle Creek, 1986—; bus. instr. Kellogg Cmty. Coll., 1990—. Mem. Inst. Mgmt. Accts. (nat. dir.). Office: Kellogg CC 450 North Ave Battle Creek MI 49017

MCBEAN, SHARON ELIZABETH, church administrator; b. Chgo., July 15, 1937; d. Archibald Lewis Jr. and Mary Elizabeth (Rees) McBean; children: Debra Sue Sanders, Catherine Leigh Sanders Ferguson. BA cum laude, La Roche Coll., 1977; MS in Edn., Duquesne U., 1978. Cert. ch. bus. adminstr. Adminstrv. asst. 1st Presbyn. Ch., Santa Barbara, Calif., 1988-89, bus. mgr., 1989—; deacon 1st Presbyn. Ch., Santa Barbara, 1987-89. Mem. bd. mgrs. Valle Verde Retirement Comty., chair health svcs. com. Mem. Presbyn. Ch. Bus. Adminstrn. Assn., Nat. Assn. Ch. Bus. Adminstrs.

MCBEE, MARY LOUISE, state legislator, former academic administrator; b. Strawberry Plains, Tenn., June 15, 1924; d. John Wallace and Nina Aileen (Umbarger) McB. BS, East Tenn. State U., 1946; MA, Columbia U., 1951; PhD, Ohio State U., 1961. Tchr. East Tenn. State U., Johnson City, 1947-51; asst. dean of women, 1952-56, 57-60, dean of women, 1961-63; dean of women U. Ga., Athens, 1963-67; world campus afloat adminstr., 1966-67, assoc. dean of students, 1967-72, dean of students, 1972-74, asst. v.p. acad. affairs, 1974-76, assoc. v.p. acad. affairs, 1976-86, v.p. acad. affairs, 1986-88; now mem. Ga. Gen. Assembly; bd. dirs. Ga. Nat. Bank, Athens, 1989—. Author: College Responsibility for Values, 1980; co-author: The American Woman: Who Will She Be?, 1974, Essays, 1979,, 2d edit. 1981. Bd. dirs. Salvation Army, Athens, 1978—, United Way, Athens. Fulbright scholar, The Netherlands, 1956-57. Mem. Athens C. of C. (bd. dirs.). Democrat. Methodist. Home: 145 Pine Valley Pl Athens GA 30606-4031 Office: GA House of Reps State Capitol Atlanta GA 30334

MCBEE, SUSANNA BARNES, journalist; b. Santa Fe, Mar. 28, 1935; d. Jess Stephen and Sybil Elizabeth (Barnes) McBee; m. Paul H. Recer, July 2, 1983. AB, U. So. Calif., 1956; MA, U. Chgo., 1962. Staff writer Washington Post, 1957-65, 73-74, 77-79, asst. nat. editor, 1974-77; asst. sec. for public affairs HEW, 1979; articles editor Washingtonian mag., 1980-81; assoc. editor U.S. News & World Report, 1981-86; news editor Washington Bur. of Hearst Newspapers, 1987-89, asst. bur. chief, 1990—; Washington corr. Life mag., 1965-69; Washington editor McCall's mag., 1970-72. Bd. dirs. Washington Press Club Found., 1992-95. Recipient Penney-Missouri mag. award, 1969, Hall of Fame award, Soc. Profl. Journalists 1996; Sigma Delta Chi Pub. Svc. award, 1969. Mem. Nat. Press Club, Cosmos Club. Home: 5190 Watson St NW Washington DC 20016-5329 Office: 1701 Pennsylvania Ave NW Washington DC 20006-5805

MCBRATNEY-STAPLETON, DEBORAH DIANE, museum director; b. Kansas City, Kans., Nov. 24, 1954; d. Thomas Carey and Mary Catherine (Koonse) McBratney; m. Earl L. Stapleton, Apr. 11, 1981 (dec. Apr. 1993). BA in Museology and Sociology, Anderson U., 1976; postgrad. Arts Adminstrn. Summer Inst., Sangamon State U., 1982; MA in Exec. Devel., Ball State U., 1990. Exec. dir. Anderson (Ind.) Fine Arts Found., Inc., 1980—; grants rev. adv. panelist Ind. Arts Commn., 1984-87, 96; 2d v.p. in charge of devel. statewide profl. workshops Assn. Ind. Mus., 1991-93; mem. co-chair pers. evaluation com. Small Mus. Adminstrs. of Am. Assn. Mus., 1995—; chair legis. com. Midwest Mus. Conf., 8 midwestern states, 1995—; co-curator exhbns. including The Art of Indiana Sports, 1995, 96, 19th Century American Arts, 1995; curator exhbn. Native American Traditions--Art and Artifacts, 1993; team leader children's hands-on exhbn. Fresh, 1985-96. Commr. Mayor's Arts and Culture Commn., Anderson, 1995—; mayoral appointee White River Devel. Commn., Anderson, 1987-93; mem. Indian Trails Festival steering com., image coun. C. of C., Anderson, 1987-93; mem. grants rev. panel, bd. dirs. Conv. Bur., Madison Co., 1982-84, 85-89, 90-92. Mem. Nat. Soc. Arts and Letters (1st v.p. 1992-94, competition chair 1995-96), Rotary Internat. Office: Anderson Fine Arts Found 226 W 8th St Anderson IN 46016

MCBRAYER, LAURA JEAN H., school media specialist; b. Bremen, Ga., July 11, 1944; d. Robert Byron Holloman and Ruth Mildred (McGukin) McLaughlin; m. Dennis Durrett McBrayer; children: Keith, Dana, Scott, Leah. BA in English, West Ga. Coll., 1966, MEd, 1977, M in Media, 1982. Cert. media tchr., secondary English tchr., Ga. English tchr. Bremen (Ga.) H.S., 1966-72, Villa Rica (Ga.) H.S., 1974-75, Ctrl. H.S., Carrollton, Ga., 1975-78; libr., English tchr. Mt. Zion (Ga.) H.S., 1979-80; media specialist West Haralson Jr. H.S., Tallapoosa, Ga., 1980-86, Bremen H.S./Sewell Mid. Sch., Bremen, 1986—. Mem., past sec. West Ga. Regional Libr. Bd., 1988—; sec. Warren P. Sewell LIbr. Bd., Bremen, 1989—, Haralson County Libr. Bd., 1988—; mem. choir First Bapt. Ch., Bremen, 1987-92; mem. centennial com. Dem. Party, Haralson County, 1989—. Mem. ALA, Ga. Libr. Media Assn., Ga. Libr. Assn., Ga. Assn. for Instrnl. Tech., Phi Delta Kappa (Tchr. of Yr. 1977). Home: 623 Laurel St Bremen GA 30110-2129 Office: Sewell Mid-Bremen HS Media Ctr 504 Laurel St Bremen GA 30110-2128

MCBREEN, MAURA ANN, lawyer; b. N.Y.C., Aug. 18, 1953; d. Peter J. and Frances S. (McVeigh) McB. AB, Smith Coll., 1975; JD, Harvard U., 1978. Bar: Ill. 1978. Ptnr. Kirkland & Ellis, Chgo., 1978-86, Isham, Lincoln & Beale (merged with Reuben & Proctor), Chgo., 1986-88, Baker & McKenzie, Chgo., 1988—. Mem. ABA, Chgo. Bar Assn., Midwest Pension Conf. Office: Baker & McKenzie 1 Prudential Pla 130 E Randolph Dr Chicago IL 60601*

MCBRIDE, ANGELA BARRON, nursing educator; b. Balt., Jan. 16, 1941; d. John Stanley and Mary C. (Szcpepanska) Barron; m. William Leon McBride, June 12, 1965; children: Catherine, Kara. BS in Nursing, Georgetown U., 1962; LHD (hon.), 1993; MS in Nursing, Yale U., 1964; PhD, Purdue U., 1978; D of Pub. Svc. (hon.), U. Cin., 1983; LLD (hon.), Ea. Ky. U., 1991; DSc(hon.), Med. Coll. of Ohio, 1995. Asst. prof., rsch. asst. inst. Yale U., New Haven, 1964-73; assoc. prof., chairperson Ind. U. Sch. Nursing, Indpls., 1978-81, 80-84, prof., 1981-92, disting. prof., 1992—; assoc. dean rsch. Ind. U. Sch. Nursing, 1985-91, interim dean, 1991-92, univ. dean, 1992—. Author: The Growth and Development of Mothers, 1973, Living with Contradictions, A Married Feminist, 1976, How to Enjoy A Good Life With Your Teenager, 1987; editor: Psychiatric-Mental Health Nursing: Integrating the Behavioral and Biological Sciences, 1996 (Best Book award 1996). Recipient Disting. Alumna award Yale U., Disting. Alumna award Purdue U., Univ. Medallion, U. San Francisco, 1993; Kellog nat. fellow; Am. Nurses Found. scholar. Fellow APA (nursing and health psychology award divsn. 38 1995), Am. Acad. Nursing (past pres.), Nat. Acads. Practice; mem. Midwest Nursing Rsch. Soc. (Disting. Rsch. award 1985), Soc. for Rsch. in Child Devel., Inst. of Medicine, Nat. Acad. Scis., Sigma Theta Tau Internat. (past pres., mentor award 1993). Office: Ind U Sch Nursing 1111 Middle Dr Indianapolis IN 46202-5107

MCBRIDE, BEVERLY JEAN, lawyer; b. Greenville, Ohio, Apr. 5, 1941; d. Kenneth Birt and Glenna Louise (Ashman) Whited; m. Benjamin Gary McBride, Nov. 28, 1964; children: John David, Elizabeth Ann. BA magna cum laude, Wittenberg U., 1963; JD cum laude, U. Toledo, 1966. Bar: Ohio 1966. Intern Ohio Gov.'s Office, Columbus, 1962; asst. dean of women U. Toledo, 1963-65; assoc. Title Guarantee and Trust Co., Toledo, 1966-69; spl. counsel Ohio Atty. Gen.'s Office, Toledo, 1975; assoc. Cobourn, Smith, Rohrbacher and Gibson, Toledo, 1969-76; vice counsel, gen. counsel, sec. The Andersons, Maumee, Ohio, 1976—. Exec. trustee, bd. dirs. Wittenberg U., Springfield, Ohio, 1980-93; trustee Anderson Found., Maumee, 1981-93; mem. Ohio Supreme Ct. Task Force on Gender Fairness, 1991-94; chmn. Sylvania Twp. Zoning Commn., Ohio, 1970-80; candidate for judge, Sylvania Mcpl. Ct., 1975; trustee Goodwill Industries, Toledo, 1976-82, Sylvania Community Svcs. Ctr., 1976-78, Toledo-Lucas County Port Authority, 1992—, vice chair St. Vincent Med. Ctr., 1992—, vice chair; founder Sylvania YWCA Program, 1973; active membership drives Toledo Mus. Art, 1977-87. Recipient Toledo Women in Industry award YWCA, 1979, Outstanding Alumnus award Wittenberg U., 1981. Fellow Am. Bar Found.; mem. ABA, AAUW, Ohio Bar Assn. Toledo Bar Assn. (pres., treas., chmn., sec. various coms.), Toledo Women Attys. Forum (exec. com. 1978-82), Pres. Club (U. Toledo, exec. com.). Home: 5274 Cambrian Rd Toledo OH 43623-2626 Office: The Andersons 480 W Dussel Dr Maumee OH 43537-1639

MCBRIDE, CAROL LYNNE, adult education educator; b. Sterling, Colo., Oct. 21, 1939; d. Virgil C. and Mildred (Haynes) Koenig; m. Lyle Charles McBride, Apr. 9, 1961 (div. 1979); children: Tracy Lynne McBride Smillie, Kelley Shannon McBride. BA, Colo. State U., 1961; MA, Colo. State U. , 1976. English tchr. Re 1 Valley Sch. Dist., Sterling, 1963-70; GED tchr. Northeastern Jr. Coll., Sterling, 1970-72, study skills coord., 1972-74, coord. adult basic edn., 1974—; mem. adv. bd. Cmty. Edn., Sterling, 1980—, Self Sufficiency, Sterling, 1991—, Adult Reentry, Sterling, 1992—, Family Ctr., Sterling, 1993—. Mem. Logan County Hosp. Aux., Sterling, 1963-72. Recipient Spl. award GED Alumni Assn., 1990. Mem. Am. Assn. for Adult and Continuing Edn., Colo. Assn. for Adult and Continuing Edn. (Coll. and Univ. Educator of Yr. 1984-85), Mountain Plains Adult Edn. Assn. Home: 610 Oleander Way Sterling CO 80751-4714 Office: Northeastern Jr Coll 100 College Dr Sterling CO 80751-2344

MCBRIDE, JOYCE BROWNING, accountant; b. Ga., May 28, 1927; d. Eph and Zula (Harden) Browning; grad. So. Bus. U., 1947; children: Jan Burge, Gary McBride, Kandie Van Affelen. Asst. controller Hampton Court Knits, Los Angeles, 1967-78; owner, mgr. McBride & Assocs. Bookkeeping Service, 1978—. Address: 2925 Tyler Ct Simi Valley CA 93063-1742

MCBRIDE, KERRY RAE, elementary education educator; b. Winchester, Va., Aug. 30, 1960; d. Rhea Jean and Zellene (Marston) Kirk; m. James Warren McBride, June 22, 1985 (div. June 1988). Student, Ind. U., 1978-80; BS in Elem. Edn., Evangel Coll., Springfield, Mo., 1982. Cert. elem. edn., middle sch. math. and social studies tchr. 1st and 2nd grade tchr. Calvary Christian Sch., Elkhart, Ind., 1982-85; lab. technician Whitehall Labs., Elkhart, 1986-91; substitute tchr. Elkhart (Ind.) Cmty. Schs., 1991-93; middle sch. math. tchr., math. dept. chair St. Thomas Sch., Elkhart, 1993—; sponsor Student Govt., Elkhart, 1994—; mem. Student Tchr. Assistance Team, Elkhart, 1994—; girls athletic dir. youth activity com. St. Thomas Sch., Elkhart, 1994—. Mem. planning com. Women's Ministries, Calvary Assembly of God, Elkhart. Mem. Assembly of God Ch. Office: St Thomas Sch 1331 N Main St Elkhart IN 46514-3226

MCBRIDE, MARTINA, vocalist; b. Medicine Lodge, Kans., July 29, 1966; d. Darryl Schiff; m. John McBride, 1988. Vocalist Schiffters, 1975-86, assorted bands, Wichita, Kans.; represented by RCA Records, 1991—; backup singer Garth Brooks, 1992-93; European tour, 1994. Albums include The Time Has Come, 1992, The Way That I Am, 1993, Wild Angels, 1995; TV appearances include Baywatch, General Hospital, 1994. Office: RCA Nashville One Music Circle N Nashville TN 37203-4310*

MCBRIDE, SANDRA TEAGUE, critical care nurse; b. Corinth, Miss., Sept. 13, 1958; d. Clarence R. and Alice (Ingram) T. AAS, Shelby State Community Coll., 1983; BSN, U. North Ala., 1987. RN, Miss., Tenn. Nurse supr. Alcorn County Care, Inc., Corinth, Miss., 1985-87; staff nurse Bolivar (Tenn.) Community Hosp., 1988-90; staff nurse West Tenn. High Security Facility Tenn. Dept. of Corrections, Ripley, 1990-91; staff nurse U.S. Med. Ctr. for Fed. Prisoners, Springfield, Mo., 1991-92, Western Mental Health Inst., Bolivar, 1992—.

MCBRIDE, TERRI RENEÉ, elementary education educator; b. Laurel, Ms., Mar. 23, 1968; d. Jimmy Ray and Karen Sue (Wheeler) Hill; m. Gregory Allison McBride, Sept. 21, 1961; children: Zachary Tate, Blake Evans, Brady Wilson. BS in elem. edn., U. Southern Miss., 1989, MS, 1991. Tchr. Jones County Sch. System, Ellisville, Miss., 1989—; owner Top of the Class, Laurel, 1991—; grant writer Jones Cmty. Schs., Ellisville, 1989—. Recipient J award Jones Cmty. Jr. Coll., Ellisville, Miss., 1987; reading grant Assn. Academic, 1994, Assn. Excellence, 1993, 94. Mem. Internat. Reading Assn., Assn. Supervision and Curriculum Devel., Miss. Assn. Educators Assn., Assn. Excellence in Edn. Republican. Baptist. Home: PO Box 312 Sandersville MS 39477-0312 Office: Sandersville Elem Sch PO Drawer E Sandersville MS 39477

MCBROOM, APRIL THEOLINA, elementary education educator; b. Guymon, Tex., Apr. 15, 1965; d. Homer Chester and Carrol Iona (Reust) Bursell; m. Casey Carl McBroom, Aug. 29, 1988. BS in Recreation, West Tex. State U., 1988; BS in Interdisciplinary Studies, West Tex. A&M U., 1993. Cert. elem. tchr., Tex. Instr. water aerobics Shape-Up Canyon, Tex., 1987-88; substitute tchr. Nueces Canyon Consol. Ind. Sch. Dist., Camp Wood, Tex., 1989, Happy (Tex.) Ind. Sch. Dist., 1989-90; proof operator 1st State Bank, Happy, 1990-91; fabric clk., cashier Wal-Mart, Canyon, 1991-92; tchr. English, girl's coach Dimmit (Tex.) Mid. Sch., 1993; tchr. sci. and social studies Happy Elem. Sch., 1993—; pool mgr. City of Tulia, Tex., summer 1991. Troop leader Girl Scouts U.S.A., Happy, 1990-91; mem. hospitality com., youth adv. coun., missions com. Happy United Meth. Ch., 1995—. Mem. Assn. Tex. Profl. Educators. Republican. Home: PO Box 171 705 NW 4th St Happy TX 79042 Office: Happy Elem Sch 400 NW 3d St Happy TX 79042

MCBROOM, DIANE CRAUN, accountant, horse trainer; b. Gettysburg, Pa., Jan. 2, 1962; d. Edward Kenneth and Suzanne (Catchings) Craun; m. Stephen Cushing, June 3, 1993; children: Emily, Michael Ross. AAS, Piedmont Va. C.C., 1983; BA in Environ. Sci. with distinction, U. Va., 1985, MS in Taxation with distinction, 1990. CPA, Va., Md.; notary public, Va. Rsch. asst. U. Va. Hosp., Charlottesville, 1980-86; instr. The Miller Sch. of Albemarle, Charlottesville, 1986-88; adj. prof. U. Va., Charlottesville, 1987-90; tax assoc. Deloitte & Touche, N.Y.C., 1990-91, Coopers & Lybrand, Roanoke, Va., 1991-92; acct. Owl Hollow Farm, Floyd, Va., 1992—; horse trainer Owl Hollow Farm, Floyd, 1980—. Asst. editor: (instrnl. book) Lotus 1-2-3, 1987. Leader Jr. Achievement, Roanoke, 1991-92; exec. dir. Boy Scouts Am., Charlottesville, 1986-90. Edmund P. Berkely scholar Commonwealth of Va., 1982. Mem. AICPA, Va. Soc. CPAs, U.S. Equestrian Team, U.S. Combined Tng. Assn., U.S. Dressage Fedn., Am. Horse Shows Assn. Republican. Episcopalian. Home and Office: Owl Hollow Farm RR 4 Box 212 Floyd VA 24091-9117

MCBROOM, NANCY LEE, insurance executive; b. Tulsa, Nov. 7, 1925; d. Lee Webster and Dora Irene (Londigan) Adams; m. Robert B. McBroom, Jan. 22, 1945 (dec. Aug. 1969); children: Dacia Adams, Rene McBroom, Robert McBroom. Student, John Brown U., 1941-42, Little Rock Bus. Coll., 1941-42. Profl. horse trainer, judge, breeder N.C., Va. and Calif., 1955-75; owner Stombock's West, Inc., Del Mar, Calif., 1968-74; agt. Mut. Omaha Ins. Co., San Diego, 1978-84; owner, broker McBroom Ins. Svcs., San Diego, 1984—; dir. Dependent's Riding Program, USMC, Camp LeJeune, N.C., 1963-66. Author: Handbook for Riding Instructors, 1963. Mem. com. Civitan Fund Raiser for Spl. Olympics, 1986. Mem. Nat. Assn. Securities Dealers, Rancho Bernardo C. of C. (com. 1986). Republican. Lodge: Soroptomist Internat. (mem. com. Women Helping Women 1985-86). Home: 12093 Caminito Campana San Diego CA 92128-2061 Office: McBroom Ins Svcs 16776 Bernardo Ctr Dr Ste 203 San Diego CA 92128-2534

MCBURNEY, ELIZABETH INNES, physician, educator; b. Lake Charles, La., Dec. 24, 1944; d. Theodore John and Martha (Caldwell) Innes; divorced, 1980; children: Leanne Marie, Susan Eleanor. BS, U. Southwestern La., 1965; MD, La. State U., 1969. Diplomate Am. Bd. Internal Medicine, Am. Bd. Dermatology. Intern Pensacola (Fla.) Edn. Program, 1969-70; resident in internal medicine Boston U. and Carney Hosps., 1970-72; resident in dermatology Charity Hosp., New Orleans, 1972-74; staff physician Ochsner Hosp., New Orleans, 1974-80; assoc. head of dermatology Ochsner Clinic, New Orleans, 1974-80; clin. asst. prof. Sch. Medicine La. State U., New Orleans, 1976-79, clin. assoc. prof., 1979-90, clin. prof., 1990—; clin. asst. prof. Sch. Medicine Tulane U., New Orleans, 1976-88, clin. assoc. prof., 1988-91, clin. prof., 1991—; mem. staff Northshore Regional Med. Ctr., Slidell, La., 1985—, Slidell Meml. Hosp., 1988—, chmn. CME courses, 1988—; regional dir. Mycosis Fungoides Study Group, Balt., 1974-94. Author: (with others) Dermatologic Laser Surgery, 1990; contbr. articles to profl. jours. Bd. dirs. Slidell Art Coun., 1988—, Camp Fire, New Orleans, 1979-83, Cancer Assn. New Orleans, 1978-83; juror Art in Pub. Places, Slidell, 1989. Fellow ACP; mem. Am. Soc. Dermatologic Surgery (treas. 1991-94, bd. dirs. 1988-91, pres. elect 1995-96, pres. 1996—), Am. Acad. Dermatology (bd. dirs. 1994—), Am. Bd. Laser Medicine & Surgery (bd. dirs. 1991-96), La. Dermatologic Soc. (pres. 1989-90), St. Tammary Med. Soc. (pres. 1988), Phi Kappa Phi, Alpha Omega Alpha. Office: 1051 Gause Blvd Ste 460 Slidell LA 70458-2950

MCCABE, LINDA MICHELLE, accountant; b. Fort Dix, N.J., Aug. 30, 1951; d. Leon Tillman and June Campbell (Brown) Stewart; m. Roger Leo McKenzie, Nov. 16, 1969 (div. 1977); 1 child, Michelle Lynn; m. John Joseph McCabe, May 7, 1979. BS, U. Md., 1992. CPA, Md. Customer svc. rep. Forman Bros. Inc., Washington, 1981-84, credit mgr., 1984-87, acctg. supr., 1987-91, controller, 1991—. Mem. Md. Assn. CPAs, AICPA, NAFE, U. Md. U. Coll. Alumni Assn., ALpha Sigma Lambda, Phi Kappa Phi. Democrat. Lutheran. Home: 7891 Mayfield Ave Elkridge MD 21227

MCCABE, MARY WILLIAMSON, computer systems analyst; b. Memphis, Aug. 8, 1934; d. Edwin Lacey and Mary Maxine (Maners) Williamson; m. Henry Arthur McCabe, Sept. 22, 1973; stepchildren: Patrick, Anne, Kevin, Cathleen, John. BA, Rhodes Coll., 1956. Math. tchr. Bolton (Tenn.) High Sch., 1956-57; programmer/analyst Mallory AF Sta., Memphis, 1957-61; sr. systems specialist computer dept. GE, Huntsville, Ala., 1961-66; sr. systems specialist Honeywell Info. Systems, Phoenix, 1966-78, Honeywell Bull, Mpls., 1979-88; pres. McCabe & Assocs., Inc., Minnetonka, Minn., 1990-91, v.p. 1992. Vol. Am. Cancer Soc., Minnetonka, 1980-91. Mem. Alpha Omicron Pi (v.p. Kappa Omicron chpt. 1955-56). Republican. Episcopalian. Home: 7967 E Via Costa Scottsdale AZ 85258-2821

MCCABE, MONICA JANE, oncological nurse; b. Anaheim, Calif.; d. Thurman Huston and Marcia Diane (Gandy) Walker; m. Roger Alan McCabe, July 27, 1985; children: Justin Robert, Sarah Jane. Assoc. Nursing, N.Mex. State U., Alamogordo, 1993. RN, N.Mex., Ariz. Med.-surg. nurse Meml. Med. Ctr., Las Cruces, N.Mex., 1993-94; oncology nurse Dr. Bishnu Rauth, Las Cruces, 1994-95; oncology and bone marrow transplant nurse Univ. Med. Ctr., Tucson, 1995—, mem. reengring. core team, 1996; nurse clinician Nat. Med. Care Homecare, Tucson, 1995-96; computer cons. Meml. Med. Ctr., Las Cruces, 1994. Mem. ANA, Ariz. Nursing Assn., N.Mex. Nurses Assn., Oncology Nursing Soc., So. Ariz. Oncology Nursing Soc. Republican. Home: PO Box 91198 Tucson AZ 85752

MCCAFFERTY, BARBARA JEAN (BJ MCCAFFERTY), sales executive; b. Lincoln, Nebr., Dec. 6, 1940; d. Russell Rowley and Ruth Alice (Williams) Wightman; m. Eriks Zeltins, Dec. 29, 1962 (div. Oct. 1976); 1 child, Brian K. Zeltins; m. Charles F. McCafferty Jr., Oct. 3, 1981 (div. July 1986). BS magna cum laude, Del. Valley Coll. Sci. and Agri., Doylestown, Pa., 1984; student, Drexel U., 1958-61. Dept. mgr. Strawbridge & Clothier, Neshaminy, Pa., 1968-73; asst. buyer Strawbridge & Clothier, Phila., 1973-76; office adminstr. Am. Protein Products, Croydon, Pa., 1976-78; tech. librarian Honeywell Power Sources Ctr., Horsham, Pa., 1978-85; sales dir. Colonial Life and Accident Ins., Wayne, Pa., 1985-86; adminstrn. mgr. Mobi Systems, Inc., Ft. Washington, Pa., 1986-88; spl. rep. Universal Mktg. Corp., Southampton, Pa., 1988-89; ind. contractor McCafferty Ins. Svcs., Doylestown, Pa., 1989—. Mem. alumni recruitment connection Delaware Valley Coll. Sci. and Agr. Mem. NAFE, Nat. Assn. Profl. Saleswomen, Options, Inc., Franklin Mint Collectors Soc., Optomists, Shawnee-at-Highpoint Racquet Club (Chalfont, Pa.). Republican. Presbyterian. Home: 224 Hastings Ct Doylestown PA 18901-2506

MCCAFFERTY, MARGO KEIRSEY, artist, educator; b. Portland, Oreg., July 2, 1952; d. Chester Alonzo and Olive Marie (Thomas) K.; 1 child, Ursula Vernon. BA, Willamette U., 1974, Western Oreg. State Coll., 1984; MFA, Ariz. State U., 1990. Instr. Matty's English Coll., Oppama, Japan, 1976-77; pub. art registrar/conservation coord. Oreg. Arts Commn., Salem, 1991-93; lectr. Western Oreg. State Coll., Monmouth, 1994-95; project coord. Oreg. Arts Commn., 1992-95; instr. Salem Art Commn., 1994, Chemeketa C.C., Salem, 1994; grant review panelist Nat. Mus. Am. Art Smithsonian Instn., Washington, 1992; art selection com. Oreg. State Fair, Salem, 1993; critic Arts Oregon mag., 1993-94. Exhbns. include Phoenix Visual Arts Ctr., 1986, Harry Wood Gallery, Tempe, Ariz., 1987, Joseph Sanchez Gallery, Scottsdale, Ariz., 1987, Ariz. Mus. for Youth, Mesa, 1988, Jefferson (Oreg.) Gallery, 1990, Western Oreg. State Coll., 1995, Artspace Gallery, Bay City, Oreg., 1995, Flatlanders Gallery, Blissfield, Mich., 1995, Sunburd Gallery, Bend, Oreg., 1996, Mich. Gallery, Detroit, 1996, Northwest Print Coun. Gallery, Portland, 1996. Vol. instr. 4-H, Mill City, Oreg., 1994. Mem. Northwest Print Coun., Phi Kappa Phi. Democrat.

MCCAFFREY, CARLYN SUNDBERG, lawyer; b. N.Y.C., Jan. 7, 1942; d. Carl Andrew Lawrence and Evelyn (Back) Sundberg; m. John P. McCaffrey, May 24, 1967; children: John C., Patrick, Jennifer, Kathleen. Student, Barnard Coll., 196.; AB in Econs., George Washington U., 1963; LLB cum laude, NYU, 1967, LLM in Taxation, 1970. Bar: N.Y. 1974. Law clk. to presiding justice Calif. Supreme Ct., 1967-68; teaching fellow law NYU, N.Y.C., 1968-70, asst. prof. law, 1970-74; assoc. Weil, Gotshal & Manges, N.Y.C., 1974-80, ptnr., 1980—; prof. in residence Rubin Hall NYU, 1971-75; adj. prof. law NYU, 1975—, U. Miami, 1979-81; lectr. in field. Contbr. articles to profl. jours. Mem. ABA (chmn. generation-skipping transfer tax 1979-81, 93—, real property probate and trust law sect.), N.Y. State Bar Assn. (exec. com. tax sect. 1979-80, chmn. estate and gift tax com. 1976-78, 95—, life ins. com. 1983-85, trusts and estates sect.), Assn. of Bar of City of N.Y. (matrimonial law com., chmn. tax subcom. 1984-86, ACTEC (bd. regents 1992—, mem. exec. com. 1995—). Home: 38 Sidney Pl Brooklyn NY 11201-4607 Office: Weil Gotshal & Manges 767 Fifth Ave New York NY 10153

MCCAFFREY, JUDITH ELIZABETH, lawyer; b. Providence, Apr. 26, 1944; d. Charles V. and Isadore Frances (Langford) McC.; m. Martin D. Minsker, Dec. 31, 1969 (div. May 1981); children: Ethan Hart Minsker, Natasha Langford Minsker. BA, Tufts U., 1966; JD, Boston U., 1970. Bar: Mass. 1970, D.C. 1972, Fla. 1991. Assoc. Sullivan & Worcester, Washington, 1970-76; atty. FDIC, Washington, 1976-78; assoc. Dechert, Price & Rhoads, Washington, 1978-82, McKenna, Conner & Cuneo, Washington, 1982-83; gen. counsel, corp. sec. Perpetual Savs. Bank, FSB, Alexandria, Va., 1983-91; ptnr. Powell, Goldstein, Frazer & Murphy, Washington, 1991-92, McCaffrey & Raimi, P.A., 1992—. Contbr. articles to profl. jours. Mem. edn. com. Bd. Trade, Washington, 1986-92. Mem. ABA (chairperson subcom. thrift instns. 1985-90), Fed. Bar Assn. (exec. com., banking law com. 1985-91), D.C. Bar Assn. (bd. govs. 1981-85), Women's Bar Assn. (pres. 1980-81), Zonta Club of Naples (dir. 1994—). Episcopalian. Home: PO Box

2081 Naples FL 33939-2081 Office: McCaffrey & Raimi PA Ste 206-A 5811 Pelican Bay Blvd Naples FL 33963

MCCAIN, BETTY LANDON RAY (MRS. JOHN LEWIS MCCAIN), political party official, civic leader; b. Faison, N.C., Feb. 23, 1931; d. Horace Truman and Mary Howell (Perrett) Ray; student St. Marys Jr. Coll., 1948-50; AB in Music, U. N.C., Chapel Hill, 1952; MA, in Music Columbia U., 1953; m. John Lewis McCain, Nov. 19, 1955; children: Paul Pressly III, Mary Eloise. Courier, European tour guide Ednl. Travel Assocs., Plainfield, N.J., 1952-54; asst. dir. YWCA, U. N.C., Chapel Hill, 1953-55; chmn. N.C. Democratic Exec. Com., 1976-79 (1st woman); mem. Dem. Nat. Com., 1971-72, 76-79, 80-85, chmn. sustaining fund, N.C., 1981, 88-91, mem. com. on Presdl. nominations (Hunt Commn.), 1981-82, mem. rules com., 1982-85, mem. cabinet Gov. James B. Hunt, Jr., sec. dept. cultural resources 1993—; mem. Winograd Commn., 1977-78; pres. Dem. Women of N.C., 1971-72, dist. dir., 1969-72; pres. Wilson County Dem. Women, 1966-67; precinct chmn., 1972-76; del. Dem. Nat. Conv., 1972, 88; mem. Dem. Mid-term Confs., 1974, 78, mem. judicial council Dem. Nat. Com., 1985-89; dir. Carolina Tel. & Tel. Co. (now Sprint), 1981— (1st woman). Sunday sch. tchr. First Presbyn. Ch., Wilson, 1970-71, 86-88, 90-92, mem. chancel choir, 1985—, deacon, 1986-92, elder, 1992-95, chmn. fin. com., 1990-91; treas. Wilson on the Move, 1990-92; mem. Council on State Goals and Policy, 1970-72, Gov.'s Task Force on Child Advocacy, 1969-71, Wilson Human Relations Commn., 1975-78, chmn. Wilson-Greene Morehead scholarship com., 1986-89; mem. career and personal counseling service adv. bd. St. Andrews Coll.; charter mem. Wilson Edn. Devel. Council; active Arts Council of Wilson, Inc., N.C. Art Soc., N.C. Lit. and Hist. Assn.; regional v.p., bd. dirs. N.C. Mental Health Assn.; pres., bd. dirs., legis. chmn. Wilson County Mental Health Assn.; bd. dirs. U. N.C. Ctr. Pub. TV, 1993—, Country Doctor Mus., 1968-93, Wilson United Fund; bd. govs. U. N.C., 1975-81, personnel and tenure com., 1985-91, chmn. budgets and fin. com. 1991-93; bd. regents Barium Springs Home for Children; bd. dirs., pres. N.C. Mus. History Assocs., 1982-83, membership chair, 1987-88; co-chmn. Com. to Elect Jim Hunt Gov., 1976, 80, co-chmn. senatorial campaign, 1984; mem. N.C. Adv. Budget Com., 1981-85 (1st woman); chmn. State Employees Combined Campaign N.C., 1993; bd. visitors Peace Coll., Wake Forest U. Sch. Law, U. N.C., Chapel Hill; co-chmn. fund drive Wilson Community Theatre; state bd. dirs. N.C., Am. Lung Assn., 1985-88; bd. dirs. Roanoke Island Commn. 1994—, USS/NC Battleship Commn., 1993—. Recipient state awards N.C. Heart Assn., 1967, Easter Seal Soc., 1967, Community Service award Downtown Bus. Assocs., 1977, award N.C. Jaycees, 1979, 85, Women in Govt. award N.C. and U.S. Jaycettes, 1985, Flora Mac Donald Scottish Heritage award, 1995, Carpathian award N.C. Equity, 1995; named to Order of Old Well and Valkyries, U. N.C., 1952; named Dem. Woman of Yr., N.C., 1976, Disting. Alumna U. N.C., Chapel Hill, 1993. Mem. U. N.C. Chapel Hill Alumni Assn. (dir.), St. Marys Alumni Assn. (regional v.p.), AMA Aux. (dir., nat. vol. health services chmn., aux. liaison rep. AMA Council on Mental Health, aux. rep. Council on Vol. Health Orgns.), N.C. (pres., dir., parliamentarian) med. auxs., UDC (historian John W. Dunham chpt.), DAR, N.C. Found. for Nursing (bd. dirs. 1989-92), N.C. Agency Pub. Telecoms.(bd. dirs. 1993—), Info. Resources Mgmt. Commn. N.C. (bd. dirs. 1993—), N.C. Symphony (bd. dirs. 1993—), N.C. Soc. Internal Medicine Aux. (pres., bd. dirs. N.C. Equity), N.C. Sch. Arts (bd. trustees 1993—), Pi Beta Phi. The Book Club (pres.), Little Book Club , Wilson Country Club. Contbg. editor History of N.C. Med. Soc. Home: 1134 Woodland Dr Wilson NC 27893-2122

MCCAIN, CLAUDIA, music educator; b. Streator, Ill., June 29, 1947; d. Lowell E. and Lisa Forney; m. James W. McCain; children: James K., Chad O. BS in Edn., Ea. Ill. U., 1969; MA, Western Ill. U., 1979; EdD, U. Ill., 1993. Cert. piano tchr. Vocal music dir. Donovan (Ill.) Cmty. Schs., 1969-71; pvt. practice as piano tchr. LaHarpe, Quincy, Ill., 1972-89; assoc. prof. music, dir. music bus. and piano pedagogy Western Ill. U., Macomb, 1988—; mem. adv. bd. D.H. Baldwin Fellowships, Loveland, Ohio, 1994-95; presented numerous workshops, seminars, and clinics, 1992—. Contbr. articles to profl. jours. Mem. Nat Assn. Music Merchants Affiliated Music Bus. Instns. (pres. 1994-96, v.p. 1991-94), Music and Enterntainment Industry Educators Assn. (treas. 1993—), Music Tchrs. Nat. Assn., Nat. Guild Piano Tchrs. Office: Western Ill U Dept Music Macomb IL 61455

MCCAIN, SHARON TEAGUE, learning specialist; b. Birmingham, Ala., Oct. 21, 1941; d. Claxton Harles and Rebeckah Almeda (Young) Teague; m. Douglas Owens McCain, June 12, 1964; children: Matthew, Michael, Melissa, Marc, Jeanette. BA English/Speech, U. Montevallo, 1964; MS Adminstrn./Supervision Curriculum, Nova U., 1975. Tchr. Five Points (Ala.) High Sch., 1964-65, Okeechobee (Fla.) High Sch., 1965-68, Vero Beach (Fla.) High Sch., 1968—. Author: Poems of the Heart, 1982. Lay minister United Meth. Ch., Vero Beach, 1985—. Named to Outstanding Young Women of Am., 1978. Mem. Nat. Coun. Tchrs. English, Fla. Coun. Tchrs. English, Delta Kappa Gamma (pres. 1980-82). Democrat. Methodist. Home: 1585 28th Ave Vero Beach FL 32960-3279 Office: Vero Beach High Sch 1707 16th St Vero Beach FL 32960-3626

MCCAIRNS, REGINA CARFAGNO, pharmaceutical executive; b. Phila., Dec. 23, 1951; d. Carmen Augustus and Regina Mary (Yost) Carfagno; m. Robert Gray McCairns Jr., Nov. 6, 1982. BS, Marymount Manhattan Coll., 1973; MS, Villanova U., 1976; cert. bus., U. Pa., 1982. Rsch. asst. Temple U. Med. Coll., Phila., 1975-77; mfg. supr. William H. Rorer, Ft. Washington, Pa., 1977-79; mgmt. trainee, tech. asst. SmithKline & French Labs., Phila., 1979-80, shift leader antibiotics, 1980-81, validation team mem., 1984-87, validation coord., 1987; mgr. validation svcs. SmithKline Beecham, Phila., 1987-96; quality assurance investigator pharm. tech. SmithKline Beecham, King of Prussia, Pa., 1996—. Trustee Country Day Sch. of the Sacred Heart, 1993—. Mem. Parenteral Drug Assn. (bd. dirs. 1985-92, chmn. spring program 1988, 90, chmn. tng. com. 1986-88, chmn. nat. program com. 1990-93), Jefferson Med. Coll. Faculty Wives Club (v.p. 1988-90, program chmn., 1988-90, pres.-elect 1990-92, pres. 1992-94). Democrat. Roman Catholic. Office: SmithKline Beecham R&D 709 Swedeland Rd King Of Prussia PA 19406-0939

MCCALEB, SARA WOODWARD, entrepreneur; b. Nassawaddox, Va., Feb. 6, 1966; d. E. Philip and Majorie Ellen (Loving) McC.; 1 child, Michael Philip McCaleb LaBlanc. BFA, U. Pa., 1989, MFA, 1991. Owner, pres. New Ravenna, Inc., Exmore, Va., 1991—. Bd. dirs. Waves, Belle Haven, Va., 1994—. Recipient New Bus. award Nat. Assoc. of Female Exec. Home: Box 265 Belle Haven VA 23306 Office: New Ravenna 2619 Lankford Hwy Exmore VA 23350

MCCALL, DOROTHY KAY, social worker, psychotherapist; b. Houston, July 18, 1948; d. Sherwood Pelton Jr. and Kathryn Rose (Gassen) McC. BA, Calif. State U., Fullerton, 1973; MS in Edn., U. Kans., 1978; PhD, U. Pitts., 1989. Lic. social worker. Counselor/intern Ctr. for Behavioral Devel., Overland Park, Kans., 1976-77; rehab. counselor Niagra Frontier Voc. Rehab. Ctr., Buffalo, 1978-79; counselor/instr. dept. motor vehicles Driving While Impaired Program N.Y. State, 1979-80; alcoholism counselor Bry Lin Hosp., Buffalo, 1979-81; instr. sch. social work U. Pitts., 1984, 91; alcohol drug counselor The Whale's Tale, Pitts., 1984-86; sole practice drug and alcohol therapy Pitts., 1986—; faculty Chem. People Inst., Pitts., 1987-89; guest lectr. sch. social work U. Pitts., 1982-87, 89; educator, trainer Community Mental Health Ctr., W.Va., 1986-87, Tenn., 1986; tchr. Tri-Community Sch. System, Western Pa., 1984-87; cons. Battered Women's Shelter, Buffalo, 1980, Buffalo Youth and Alcoholism Abuse program, 1980; lectr. in field. Mem. Spl. Adv. Com. on Addiction, 1981-83; bd. dirs. Chem. People, Task Force Adv. Com., 1984-86; bd. dirs. Drug Connection Hot Line, 1984-86; mem. Coalition of Addictive Diseases, 1984—; co-founder Greater Pitts. Adult Children of Alcoholics Network, 1984; mem. adv. bd. Chem. Awareness Referral and Evaluation System Duquesne U., 1988-93. Recipient Outstanding Achievement award Greater Pitts. Adult Children of Alcoholics Network, 1987, Disting. Svc. award Pa. Assn. for Children of Alcoholics, 1993; Nat. Inst. Alcohol Abuse tng. grantee, 1981; U. Pitts. fellow, 1983. Mem. NASW, Pa. Assn. for Children of Alcoholics (bd. dirs. 1987—, v.p. 1990-94, Disting. Svc. award 1993), Employee Assistance Profls.. Assn. Inc., Am. Soc. for Clin. Hypnosis, Nat. Assn. for Children of Alcoholics, Inst. for Noetic Scis., Internat. Soc. for Study of Subtle Energies and Energy Medicine. Democrat. Office: 673 Washington Rd Pittsburgh PA 15228-1917

MCCALL, LOUISE HARRUP, artist; b. Oklahoma City, July 8, 1925; d. Paul Louis and Lucile (Martin) Harrup; m. Robert Theodore McCall, July 20, 1945; children: Linda Louise, Catherine Anne. Student, Okla. State U., 1943-44, U. N.Mex., 1944-45, Art Inst., 1946; pvt. study, N.Y., 1955-65. Freelance artist Chgo., 1946-48, Tarrytown, N.Y., 1949-53, Chappaqua, N.Y., 1953-67, 68-71, London, 1967, Paradise Valley, Ariz., 1971—; owner McCall Studios, Inc., Paradise Valley, 1986—. Murals executed (with husband) Air and Space Mus., Washington, 1975-76, Johnson Space Ctr., Houston, 1978, Disney Epcot Ctr., L.A., 1983. Designed, with husband, windows of Valley Presbyn. Chapel, Scottsdale; paintings in private collection of H.R.H. Prince Fahd Bin Salman and H.R.H. Prince Sultan Bin Salman of Saudi Arabia. Fundraiser Crisis Nursery, Phoenix, 1984, Ariz. Hist. Soc., Phoenix, 1986, Scottsdale Cultural Ctr. 1990-92, Phoenix Art Mus., 1993-94, Scottsdale Art. Sch., 1996, 1994 Art Show O'Brien's Gallery, 1995 Art Show Peoria Sch. Dist.; ann. fund raiser Hospice Phoenix, 1983-92. Winner 1st Prize, State of Tex., 1943, 1st Prize, Jr. League Artists No. Westchester and N.Y., 1961; honored by Glendale C.C. Mem. NASA Permanent Art Collection, Nat. Mus. Women in the Arts, Jr. League of Phoenix. Republican. Presbyterian. Home and Office: 4816 E Moonlight Way Paradise Valley AZ 85253

MCCALLA, SANDRA ANN, principal; b. Shreveport, La., Nov. 6, 1939; d. Earl Gray and Dorothy Edna (Adams) McC. BS, Northwestern La. State U., 1960; MA, U. No. Colo., 1968; EdD, Tex. A&M U., 1987. With Caddo Parish Sch. Bd., Shreveport, 1960-88; asst. prin. Capt. Shreve H.S., 1977-79, prin., 1979-88, 94—; dir., dean divsn. edn. Northwestern State U., Natchitoches, La., 1988-94; instr. math. La. State U., 1979-81. Named Educator of Yr. Shreveport Times-Caddo Tchrs. Assn., 1966, La. H.S. Prin. of Yr., 1985, 87; recipient Excellence in Edn. award Capt. Shreve H.S., 1982-83; Danforth fellow, 1982-83. Mem. adv. bd. Sta. KDAQ Pub. Radio, 1985-89. Mem. Shreveport Women's Commn., 1983-89. Mem. Nat. Assn. Secondary Sch. Prins., La. Assn. Prins. (Prin. of Yr. 1985), La. Assn. Sch. Execs. (Disting. Svc. award 1983), Times-Caddo Educators Assn. (Educator of Yr. 1984), Rotary Internat., Phi Delta Kappa, Kappa Delta Pi. Democrat.

MC CANDLESS, ANNA LOOMIS, university official; b. Aspinwall, Pa., July 21, 1897; d. George Wilberforce and Estella (Loomis) McC.; BS, Carnegie-Mellon U., 1919. Pres. Vis. Nurses Assn. of Allegheny County, 1955-57; mem. vis. com. Margaret Morrison Carnegie Coll., 1962-66; v.p. Alumni Fedn. Carnegie Inst. Tech., 1963-66. Trustee Carnegie-Mellon U., 1966—. Mem. AAUW. Clubs: Coll., Univ., Twentieth Century (pres. 1956-58) (Pitts.); Appalachian Mountain. Home: Park Plaza Apts Craig St Pittsburgh PA 15213

MCCANDLESS, BARBARA J., auditor; b. Cottonwood Falls, Kans., Oct. 25, 1931; d. Arch G. and Grace (Kittle) McCandless; m. Allyn O. Lockner, 1969. BS, Kans. State U., 1953; MS, Cornell U., 1959; postgrad. U. Minn., 1962-66, U. Calif., Berkeley, 1971-72. Cert. family and consumer scientist; enrolled agt. IRS. Home demonstration agt. Kans. State U., 1953-57; teaching asst. Cornell U., 1957-58, asst. extension home economist in marketing, 1958-59; consumer mktg. specialist, asst. prof. Oreg. State U., 1959-62; instr. home econs. U. Minn., 1962-63, research asst. agrl. econs., 1963-66; asst. prof. U. R.I., 1966-67; assoc. prof. family econs., mgmt., housing, equipment dept. head S.D. State U., 1967-73; asst. to sec. Dept. Commerce and Consumer Affairs, S.D., 1973-79, tax cons., 1980-91, revenue auditor, 1991—. Mem. Nat. Council Occupational Licensing, dir., 1973-75, v.p., 1975-79. Mem. Am. Agrl. Econs. Assn., Am. Assn. Family and Consumer Scis., Am. Coun. Consumer Interests, Assn. Govt. Accts., Inst. Internal Auditors, Nat. Coun. on Family Rels., LWV, Kans. State U. Alumni Assn., Pi Gamma Mu. Research on profl. and occupational licensing bds. Address: 2114 SW Potomac Dr Topeka KS 66611-1445

MCCANDLESS, CARLA JEAN, rehabilitation nurse, consultant, corporate trainer; b. Galveston, Tex., Mar. 20, 1956; d. Dana Lee and Joan Adell (Miller) Inbody; m. David McCandless III, Aug. 24, 1982. BSN, U. Tex., 1989. CRRN, CCM. Shift supr. Healthcare Rehab. Ctr., Austin, Tex., 1989-91; cons.-in-charge Crawford & Co., Austin, 1991-95; tng. specialist Crawford & Co., Atlanta, 1995—; presenter workshop: Walking Wounded, Mild TBI, 1994. Chairperson Austin Case Mgmt. Assn., 1992-93, Healthcare Rehab. Ctr., 1990. Mem. Assn. Rehab. Nurses, Tex. Head Injury Assn., Tex. Nurses Assn. (newsletter editor 1990-91). Home: 4509 Wedewer Way Woodstock GA 30188 Office: Crawford & Co 5620 Glenridge Dr NE Atlanta GA 30342

MCCANDLESS, CAROLYN KELLER, human resources specialist; b. Patuxent River, Md., June 6, 1945; d. Stevens Henry and Betty Jane (Bethune) Keller; m. Stephen Porter McCandless, Apr. 22, 1972; children: Peter Keller, Deborah Marion. BA, Stanford U., 1967; MBA, Harvard U., 1969. Fin. analyst Time Inc., N.Y.C., 1969-72, mgr. budgets and fin. analysis, 1972-78, asst. sec., dir. internal adminstrn., 1978-85, v.p., dir. employee benefits, 1985-90; v.p human resources and adminstrn. Time Warner, Inc., N.Y.C., 1990—; bd. dirs. LifeRe Corp. Republican. Mem. Unitarian Ch. Office: Time Warner Inc 1271 Avenue Of The Americas New York NY 10020

MCCANDLESS, J(ANE) BARDARAH, retired religion educator; b. Dayton, Ohio, Apr. 16, 1925; d. J(ohn) Bard and Sarah Catharine (Shuey) McC. BA, Oberlin Coll., 1951; MRE, Bibl. Sem., N.Y.C., 1953; PhD, U. Pitts., 1968. Dir. Christian edn. Wallace Meml. United Presbyn. Ch., Pitts., 1953-54, Beverly Heights United Presbyn. Ch., Mt. Lebanon, Pa., 1956-61; instr. religion Westminster Coll., New Wilmington, Pa., 1961-65, asst. prof., 1965-71, assoc. prof., 1971-83, prof. religion, 1983-94, prof. emeritus, 1994—, chair dept. religion and philosophy, 1988-92; leader Christian edn. workshops Presbytery of Shenango, Presbyn. Ch. (U.S.A.), 1961—, Synod of Trinity, 1972, 76. Author: An Untainted Saint...Ain't, 1978; contbr. articles to profl. jours., Harper's Ency. Religious Edn. Mem. session New Wilmington Presbyn. Ch., 1977-79. Mack grantee Westminster Coll., 1962-63, Faculty rsch. grantee, 1972, 78, 90. Mem. Religious Edn. Assn., Assn. Profs. and Researchers in Religious Edn. (mem. exec. com. 1978-80), Soc. for Sci. Study Religion, Phi Beta Kappa, Pi Lambda Theta.

MCCANDLESS, SANDRA RAVICH, lawyer; b. Revere, Mass., Sept. 5, 1948; d. Merrill Earl and Goldie (Clayman) Ravich; m. Ross Erwin McCandless; 1 child, Phyra. BA, Radcliffe Coll., 1970; JD, Georgetown U., Washington, 1973. Bar: Calif. 1973, U.S. Ct. Appeals (1st and 7th cirs.) 1974, U.S. Ct. Appeals (6th and 9th cirs.) 1975, U.S. Dist. Ct. (no. dist.) Calif. 1976, U.S. Dist. Ct. (ea. dist.) Calif. 1978. Law clk. NLRB, Washington, 1971-73, atty. appellate ct. br., 1973-75; assoc. Pillsbury, Madison & Sutro, San Francisco, 1975-79; from assoc. to ptnr. Graham & James, San Francisco, 1979-93; atty. Sonnenschein, Nath & Rosenthal, San Francisco, 1993—; mem. faculty Nat. Inst. Appellate Advocacy, San Francisco. Mem. ABA, Bar Assn. San Francisco, San Francisco Barrister Club (co-chair com. on labor law 1979-82). Office: Sonnenschein Nath & Rosenthal 685 Market St Fl 10 San Francisco CA 94105-4200

MC CANN, CECILE NELKEN, writer; b. New Orleans; d. Abraham and Leona (Reiman) Nelken; children: Dorothy Collins, Cecile Isaacs, Annette Arnold, Denise Bachman, Albert Hews III. Student, Vassar Coll., Tulane U.; BA, San Jose State Coll., 1963, MA, 1964; postgrad., U. Calif.-Berkeley, 1966-67; hon. doctorate, San Francisco Art Inst., 1989. Tool designer Convair Corp., New Orleans, 1942-45; archtl. draftsman, various companies New Orleans and Clinton, Iowa, 1945-47, 51-53; owner, operator ceramics studio Clinton, 1953-58; instr. San Jose State Coll., 1964-65, Calif. State U., Hayward, 1964-65, Chabot Coll., Hayward, 1966-69, Laney Coll., 1967-70, San Francisco State U., 1977-78; founder, editor, pub. Artweek mag., Oakland, Calif., 1970-89; freelance writer, art advisor Kensington, Calif., 1989—; cons. Nat. Endowment Arts, 1974-78, fellow in art criticism, 1976; panelist numerous confs. and workshops. Contbr. to profl. publs.; one-woman shows at, Davenport Mus. Art, Robert North Galleries, Chgo., Crocker Art Mus., Sacramento, Calif., Calif. Coll. Arts and Crafts, Oakland, others; exhibited in group shows at, DeYoung Mus., San Francisco, Everson Mus. Art, Syracuse, N.Y., Oakland Mus., Pasadena Mus., Los Angeles County Mus. Art, others; represented in permanent collections, San Jose State Coll., Mills Coll., Coll. Holy Names, City of San Francisco, State of Calif., others. Bd. dirs. Rene and Veronica di Rosa Found. Recipient Vesta award Woman's Bldg. mag., L.A., 1988, Honor award Art Table, 1988, Media award Bay Area Visual Arts Coalition, 1989, Achievement award Art Table, 1992. Mem. Art Table, Internat. Assn. Art Critics, Coll. Art Assn., Soc. Encouragement Contemporary Art. Office: 244 Colgate Ave Kensington CA 94708-1122

MCCANN, COLLEEN MARY, public affairs specialist, lobbyist; b. Phila., June 28, 1964; d. John Francis and Agnetta Marie (McLaughlin) McC. BA, Rutgers U., 1986. Staff asst. subcom. on commerce, transp. and tourism U.S. Congress, Washington, 1986; staff asst., legis. coord. U.S. Rep. Jim Florio, Washington, 1986-88; legis. asst. U.S. Rep. Jim Florio, 1988-89; policy analyst Gov.-elect Jim Florio's Transition Team, 1989-91; legis. liaison Dept. of State, Trenton, N.J., 1990-93; dir. state govtl. affairs MWW/Strategic Comms., Trenton, 1993-96; dir. govtl. affairs and comm. NJ Am. Water Co., Trenton, 1996—. Active N.J. Women's Polit. Caucus, 1990—; mem. govt. affairs alumni com. Rutgers U., trustee, 1994—. Democrat. Roman Catholic. Home: 45 Quarry St Lambertville NJ 08530-1104 Office: 46 W Lafayette St Trenton NJ 08608-2011

MC CANN, FRANCES VERONICA, physiologist, educator; b. Manchester, Conn., Jan. 15, 1927; d. John Joseph and Grace E. (Tuttle) Mc C.; m. Elden J. Murray, Sept. 20, 1962 (dec. Nov. 1975). AB with distinction and honors, U. Conn., 1952, PhD, 1959; MS, U. Ill., 1954; MA (hon.), Dartmouth Coll., 1973. Investigator Marine Biol. Lab., Woods Hole, Mass., 1952-62; instr. physiology Dartmouth Med. Sch., Hanover, N.H., 1959-61, asst. prof., 1961-67, assoc. prof., 1967-73, prof., 1973—; adj. prof. biol. scis. Dartmouth Coll., 1974—; mem., cons. physiology study sect. NIH, 1973-77, mem. biomed. rsch. devel. com., 1978-82, chmn, 1979; cons. Hayer Inst., 1979—; cons. staff Hitchcock Hosp., Hanover, 1980—, sr. staff rsch. Norris Catton Cancer Ctr., 1980—; mem. NRC, 1982-86; chmn. Symposium on Comparative Physiology of the Heart, 1968. Editor: Comparative Physiology of the Heart: Current Trends, 1965; contbr. numerous articles to profl. jours. Trustee Lebanon Coll., 1970-73, Montshire Mus. Sic., Hanover, 1975—, Hanover Health Coun., 1976, Lebanon Coll., 1978—; incorporator Howe Libr., 1975—; active LWV, 1980—, Conservation Coun., 1983—, Hist. Soc., 1975—, N.H. Lakes Assoc., 1992—; pres. Armington Lake Assn., 1991—. Nat. Heart Inst. fellow, 1959; NIH rsch. grantee, 1959—, Nat. Heart Inst., 1960, N.H. Heart Assn., 1964-65, Vt. Heart Assn., 1966—. Mem. AAAS, Am. Assn. Advancement of Lab. Animal Care, Am. Physiol. Soc., Soc. Gen. Physiologists, Biophys. Soc., Am. Heart Assn. (coun. basic sci., exec. coun. Dallas chpt. 1982-86), Soc. Neurosci. Marine Biol. Lab., LWV, Sigma Xi, Phi Kappa Phi. Office: Dartmouth Med Sch Lebanon NH 03756

MCCANN, JEAN FRIEDRICHS, artist, educator; b. N.Y.C., Dec. 6, 1937; d. Herbert Joseph and Catherine Brady (Ward) Friedrichs; m. William Joseph McCann, May 14, 1960; children: Kevin, Brian, Maureen McCann Breslin, William, James, Denis Gerard, Kathleen. Student, Caton-Rose Inst. Fine Arts, 1955-57; AAS, SUNY, Farmingdale, 1959; BS, SUNY-Empire State Coll., Binghamton, 1986; MA summa cum laude, Marywood Coll., 1987, MFA in Art summa cum laude, 1989; completed Kellogg Leadership Progam, Sch. Mgmt., SUNY, Binghamton, 1992; PhD, Nova Coll., 1995. Dir. ArtSpace Gallery, Owego, N.Y., 1992-94; substitute art tchr. Owego-Apalachin Sch. Dist., Owego, 1968-88; tutor, evaluator SUNY-Empire State Coll., 1987—; v.p. bd. dirs. Tioga County Coun. on Arts, 1990-91, pres., 1992-95; demonstrator for various schs., ednl. TV and county museums. One woman shows include IBM, Owego, 1972, Tioga County Hist. Soc. Mus., Owego, 1975, Nat. Hist. Ct. House, 1982, Visual Arts Ctr., Scranton, Pa., 1989-90, ArtSpace Gallery, 1991, MacDonald Art Gallery of Coll. Misericordia, Dallas, Pa., 1992, Plaza Gallery, Binghamton, 1992, Artist Guild Gallery, Binghamton, 1993, Wilson Gallery, Johnson City, N.Y., 1994; exhibited in numerous group shows, including IBM, Owego, 1970, Roberson Ctr., Binghamton, 1972, Arnot Art Mus., Elmira, 1974, 89, 92, Nat. Exhibits at Arena, Binghamton, 1974-76, Riise Gallery, St. Thomas, 1975-78, Penninos Gallery, Burlington Vt., 1975-77, Visual Arts Ctr., Scranton, Pa., 1987, Grand Concourse Gallery, Albany, N.Y., 1987, Tioga County Hist. Soc. Mus., 1990, ArtSpace Gallery, 1990, Contemporary Gallery, Scranton, 1992, 96; art represented in numerous pvt. collections including those of Pres. George Bush, Congressman Matt McHugh, Senator Tom Libous, also pub. collections. Bd. dirs. Birthright of Owego, 1993—. Recipient N.Y. State Artisans award, 1982, Nat. Strathmore Silver award, 1989, 1st pl. in Graphic Arts award Jericho Arts Coun., 1994. Mem. Nat. mus. Women in Arts (charter), Kappa Pi (pres. Zeta Omicron chpt. 1987-89, life). Home: 23 Paige St Owego NY 13827-1617

MCCANN, LOUISE MARY, paralegal; b. Bklyn., Apr. 12, 1949; d. James Joseph and Edith Dorothea (Wubbe) McC. AAS, Elizabeth Seton Coll., 1967; BS, N.Y. Inst. Tech., 1981; paralegal cert., Adelphi U., 1987. Cert. ind. adjustor, motor vehicle and casualty, N.Y. Adminstrv. asst. J.P. Stevens & Co., Inc., N.Y.C., 1969-86; legal asst. Congdon, Flaherty, O'Callaghan, Reid, Donlon, Travis & Fishlinger, Garden City, N.Y., 1986—. Capt. tng. divsn. Aux. Police Force, N.Y.C. Police Dept., 1975-92; trooper Boots & Saddles Civil War Re-enactment Unit, 10th N.Y. Cavalry Co.; contbg. sponsor U.S. Equestrian Team, Gladstone, N.J., 1980. Master sgt. USAR. Decorated Meritorious Svc. medal, Nat. Def. Svc. medal, Army Achievement medal, Army Commendation medal, Armed Forces Res. medal. Mem. Nassau Suffolk (L.I.) Horseman's Assn. (dir.). Republican. Roman Catholic. Home: 305 Main St Roslyn NY 11576-2114 Office: 377 Oak St Garden City NY 11530

MCCANN, MARY CHERI, medical technologist, horse breeder and trainer; b. Pensacola, Fla., July 29, 1956; d. Joseph Maxwell and Cora Marie (Underwood) McC.; m. Robert Lee Spencer, July 20, 1977 (div. Nov. 1983). AA, Pensacola Jr. Coll., 1975; student, U. Md., 1977-78; BS in Biology, Troy State U., 1979; postgrad., U. Fla., 1979. Med. technologist Cape Fear Valley Med. Ctr., Fayetteville, N.C., 1981-85, Doctors Diagnostic Ctr., Fayetteville, 1985-86; sales rep. Waddell & Reed, Fayetteville, 1985-86; med. technologist Roche Biomed. Lab., Burlington, N.C., 1986-87; lab. mgr. Cumberland Hosp., Fayetteville, 1987-89, Naval Hosp., Pensacola, 1989-90, chemistry supr., 1990-96, night shift supr., 1996—. With U.S. Army, 1976-77. Mem. NAFE, Am. Soc. Clin. Pathologists (registrant), Am. Quarter Horse Assn., Japan Karate Assn., Pinto Horse Assn. Am. Republican. Avocations: horses, karate, guns, oil painting. Home: 300 Dogwood Dr Pensacola FL 32505-5323 Office: Naval Hosp Pensacola Lab US Hwy 98 Pensacola FL 32512

MCCANN, PAULA GIROUARD, school system administrator; b. Boston, Feb. 17, 1952; d. Paul Charles and Marjorie Rose (Follen) G.; m. Francis Paul McCann, July 6, 1975. BA magna cum laude, Boston Coll., 1973; MA, U. Mass., 1980; postgrad., Bridgewater State Coll., 1990, U. Mass., 1995—. Cert. prin., Eng. tchr., sch. libr. From English tchr. to h.s. vice prin. Milton (Mass.) Pub. Schs., 1973—; mem. tech. adv. com. Milton Pub. Schs., 1991—, computer study com., 1989-91, chair profl. improvement com., 1977-90. Grantee Mass. Edn. Tech., 1989. Mem. NEA, ASCD, Mass. Computer Using Educators, Milton Educators Assn., Mass. Tchrs. Assn., Delta Kappa Gamma. Office: Milton Pub Schs Brook Rd at Central Ave Milton MA 02186

MCCARGAR, ELEANOR BARKER, painter; b. Presque Isle, Maine, Aug. 30, 1913; d. Roy Morrill and Lucy Ellen (Hayward) Barker; m. John Albert McCargar, Feb. 18, 1974; children: Margaret, Lucy, Mary. Cert. elem. sch. tchg., Aroostook State Normal Sch., Presque Isle, 1933; student, Acadia U., 1935-36; B of Sociology, Colby Coll., 1937; postgrad., Harvard U., 1939, Cambridge Sch. Art, 1939; studied portrait painting with Kenneth Washburn, Thomas Leighton, Marion Ridelstein, Jean Henry, 1957-67. Ltd. svc. credential in fine and applied arts and related techs. Calif. C.C. Tchr. sci. and geography Limestone (Maine) Jr. H.S., 1937-41; ins. claim adjuster Liberty Mut. Ins. Co., Boston, 1941-42, Portland, Maine, 1943; ARC hosp. worker 20th Gen. Army Hosp., Ledo, Assam, India, 1944-45; portrait painter Burlingame and Apple Vly., Calif., 1982—. Commns. include more than 650 portraits. Recipient M. Grumbacher Inc. Merit award of outstanding contbn. to arts, 1977; named Univ. of Maine Disting. Alumnus in Arts, 1981.

MCCARRA, MARYANN, editor; b. Bronx, N.Y., Oct. 21, 1967; d. Michael Francis and Nellie Patricia (Walsh) M. BA in English and world literature, Manhattan Coll., Bronx, 1985-89. Selector Saks Fifth Ave., Yonkers, N.Y., 1986; telemarketing sales Harris Publ. Co., White Plains, N.Y., 1986; asst. to exhibits mgr. Alan R. Liss, Pub., N.Y.C., 1987; editl. asst. Garland Publ.

Co., N.Y.C., 1988; adminstrv. asst. Churchill Livingstone Co., N.Y.C., 1989; adj. instr. English La Guardia C.C.-CUNY, Queens, N.Y., 1989; asst. editor Plenum Publ. Corp., N.Y.C., 1990—. Independent. Roman Catholic. Home: 1304 Midland Ave Apt A64 Yonkers NY 10704 Office: Plenum Publ Corp 233 Spring St 5th Fl New York NY 10013-1578

MCCARROLL, KATHLEEN ANN, radiologist, educator; b. Lincoln, Nebr., July 7, 1948; d. James Richard and Ruth B. (Wagenknecht) McC.; m. Steven Mark Beerbohm, July 10, 1977 (div. 1991); 1 child, Palmer Brooke. BS, Wayne State U., 1974; MD, Mich. State U., 1978. Diplomate Am. Bd. Radiology. Intern/resident in diagnostic radiology William Beaumont Hosp., Royal Oak, Mich., 1978-82, fellow in computed tomography and ultrasound, 1983; radiologist, dir. radiologic edn. Detroit Receiving Hosp., 1984—, vice-chief dept. radiology, 1988-96, chief dept. radiology, 1996—; pres.-elect med. staff Detroit Receiving Hosp., 1992-94, pres., 1994-96; mem. admissions com. Wayne State U. Coll. Medicine, Detroit, 1991—; trustee Detroit Med. Ctr., 1996—; officer bd. dirs. Dr. L. Reynolds Assoc., P.C., Detroit, 1991-94, 96—; presenter profl. confs.; assoc. prof. radiology Wayne State U. Sch. Medicine, Detroit, 1995—. Editor: Critical Care Clinics, 1992; mem. editorial bd. Emergency Radiology; contbr. articles to profl. publs. Mem. AMA, Am. Coll. Radiology (Mich. chpt. sec. 1995—), Radiol. Soc. N.Am., Assn. Univ. Radiologists, Am. Roentgen Ray Soc., Am. Soc. Emergency Radiologists (bd. dirs. 1996—), Mich. State Med. Soc., Wayne/Oakland County Med. Soc., Phi Beta Kappa. Office: Detroit Receiving Hosp 3L-8 4201 Saint Antoine St Detroit MI 48201-2153

MCCARTER, LINDA MARY, computer programmer; b. Dallas, July 23, 1951; d. Richard Ferguson and Florence Ann (Bzdafka) Jossel; m. Robert Franklin McCarter Jr., June 10, 1978; children: Robert Franklin III, Brian Edward. Cert., Network Bus. Sys., Anchorage, 1991; AS, Anchorage C.C., 1990; BA, U. Alaska, 1995. Cert. network engr. Novell. Aide computer lab. U. Alaska, Anchorage, 1986-89; analyst programmer III State of Alaska, Anchorage, 1989-95, analyst programmer IV, 1995—; cons. Alaska State Troopers, Anchorage. Scorekeeper Knik Little League, Eagle River, Alaska, 1988—. Sgt. USAF, 1976-82. Mem. Novell Users Group, U. Alaska Alumni Assn., Beta Gamma Sigma. Home: 23046 Live Alder Chugiak AK 99567 Office: State of Alaska 3601 C St Dept Epidemiology Anchorage AK 99507

MCCARTHY, BETTIE S., public relations executive; b. Washington, June 26, 1948. BA in History, Duke U., 1970; MBA in Fin., George Washington U., 1986. Sr. assoc. pub. affairs Borden, 1974-76; mgr. govt. rels. Borden Inc., 1976-79; mgr. pub. rels. Rexnord, Inc., 1980-87; pres. Bettie McCarthy & Assocs., Washington, 1987—; legis. analyst Grocery Mfrs. of Am. Mem. Women in Govt. Rels. (founder 1975, v.p. 1977, pres. 1978), Pub. Affairs Coun. Office: 733 15th St NW Ste 700 Washington DC 20005-2112*

MCCARTHY, CAROL POPE, public relations specialist; b. Bklyn., Nov. 21, 1950; d. Albert and Elsie Frieda (Salzmann) Pope; m. Thomas Joseph McCarthy, Apr. 8, 1968 (dec. 1993); children: Frank Michael McCarthy, Christina McCarthy Baumann. BA summa cum laude, Fairleigh Dickinson U., 1986, postgrad., 1996—. Newspaper editor, reporter The Leader, Lyndhurst, N.J., 1986-88; newspaper editor The Observer, Kearny, N.J., 1988-91; editor, pub. rels. coord. Freshness Cleaning Co., Lyndhurst, 1989—; copy editor The Star-Ledger, Newark, N.J., 1991-94; pub. rels. coord. CSI, Ramsey, N.J., 1994-95; asst. to novelist J.J.B. Pub., Haledon, N.J., 1992—. Mem. VFW (hon.), Telephone Pioneers Am. (hon.). Home: 602 Skyline Dr Haledon NJ 07508

MCCARTHY, DENISE EILEEN, clinical psychologist; b. Syracuse, N.Y., Jan. 25, 1941; d. Raymond Dennis McCarthy and Elizabeth Dorne MacBrearty. BS, Cornell U., 1962; MA, Syracuse U., 1969; postgrad., SUNY, Albany, 1977-83; D in Clin. Psychology, Antioch/New Eng. Grad. Sch., Keene, N.H., 1988; postgrad., The Beck Inst., Bala Cynwyd, Pa., 1994-95. Lic. psychologist, N.Y. Home econ. Monroe County Extension Svc., Rochester, N.Y., 1962-65; team leader, sr. counselor N.Y. State Dept. Labor, Albany, Syracuse, 1966-73; rehab. counselor N.Y. State Office Vocat. Rehab., Albany, 1973-80; dir. community support systems Schenectady Shared Svs., 1981-82; masters level psychologist O.D. Heck Devel. Ctr., Schenectady, 1982-83, A.I.M., Saratoga Springs, N.Y., 1983-84; staff counselor Siena Coll., Loudonville, N.Y., 1985; asst. psychologist Capital Dist. Psychiat. Ctr., Cairo, N.Y., 1985-88, assoc. psychologist, 1988-93; pvt. practice Albany, 1990—; co-founder Ctr. for Cognitive Therapy of the Capital Dist. Bd. dirs. Dominion House, Schenectady, 1981-82. Mem. Am. Psychol. Assn., N.Y. State Psychol. Assn., Psychologists of Northeastern N.Y., Nat. Registry Health Svc. Providers. Office: Ctr Cognitive Therapy One Pinnacle Pl Ste 217 Albany NY 12203-3439

MCCARTHY, GAIL HUDSON, photographer; b. Rochester, N.Y., Aug. 27, 1938; d. Howard Henry and Joyce Hannah Hudson; m. John William McCarthy II, May 8, 1982; children: Matthew, Elizabeth. AS, Elmira Coll., 1958; AAS with honors, Rochester Inst. Tech., 1975. Freelance fine arts photographer White Salmon, Wash.; staff photographer U. Pa. Scheie Eye Inst., 1976-77, 86; owner Garfunkel Gallery, Rochester, N.Y., 1978-79. Prin. works exhibited in local shows nationwide. Mem. Columbia Gorge Regional Arts Assn. (bd. dirs.). Home: PO Box 993 White Salmon WA 98672 Office: Columbia Art Gallery 207 2d St Hood River OR 97031

MCCARTHY, HEIDI MARIE, accountant; b. Helena, Mont., Sept. 29, 1970; d. Robert D. and Ellen Marie (Norsby) Miller; m. Steven Gerard McCarthy, June 13, 1992. BBA, Gonzaga U., 1993. Fin. acct. Hewlett-Packard, Boise, Idaho, 1993—. Vol. YMCA Capital Campaign, Boise, 1993, Take Our Daus. to Work, Boise, 1996; chmn. United Way Day of Caring, Boise, 1995. Mem. Inst. Managerial Accts. Roman Catholic. Home: 1295 N Mirror Creek Pl Meridian ID 83642

MCCARTHY, KAREN MARIE, sales promotion executive; b. Rochester, N.Y., June 29, 1960; d. Anthony Vincent and Dolores (Stokes) Lombard; m. Craig Steven McCarthy. BA, St. Bonaventure, 1982. Program coordinator Muscular Dystrophy Assn., White Plains, N.Y., 1982-83; promotion adminstr. Don Jagoda Assoc., Syosset, N.Y., 1983-85; acct. supr. Ventura Assocs., N.Y.C., 1985-87; v.p. Wesco Group, N.Y.C., 1987-88; pres. Little & King Co., Inc., Amityville, N.Y., 1988—. Mem. NAFE, Promotion Mktg. Assn. Am., Direct Mktg. Assn., Premium Merchandising Club. Office: Little & King Co Inc 140 Broadway Amityville NY 11701

MCCARTHY, KAREN P., congresswoman, former state representative; b. Mass., Mar. 18, 1947. BS in English, Biology, U. Kans., 1969, MBA, 1985; MEd in English, U. Mo., Kansas City, 1976. Tchr. Shawnee Mission (Kans.) South High Sch., 1969-75, The Sunset Hill (Kans.) Sch., ., 1975-76; mem. Mo. House of Reps., Jefferson City, Mo., 1977-94; cons. govt. affairs Marion Labs., Kansas City, Mo., 1986-93; congresswoman, Mo. 5th Dist. U.S. Congress, Washington, D.C., 1995—; rsch. analyst pub. fin. dept. Stearn Bros. & Co., 1984-85, Kansas City, Mo.; rsch. analyst Midwest Rsch. Inst., econs. and mgmt. scis. dept., Kansas City, 1985-86. Del. Dem. Nat. Conv., 1992, Dem. Nat. Party Conf., 1982, Dem. Nat. Policy Com. Policy Commn., 1985-86. Recipient Outstanding Young Woman Am. award, 1977, Outstanding Woman Mo. award Phi Chi Theta, Woman of Achievement award Mid-Continent Coun. Girl Scouts U.S., 1983, 87, Annie Baxter Leadership award, 1993; named Conservation Legislator of Yr., Conservation Fed. Mo., 1987. Fellow Inst. of Politics; mem. Nat. Inst. of Politics; mem. Nat. Conf. on State Legis. (del. on trade and econ. devel. to Fed. Republic of Germany, Bulgaria, Japan, France and Italy, mem. energy com. 1978-84, fed. taxation, trade and econ. devel. com. 1986, chmn. fed. budget and taxation com. 1987, vice chmn. state fed. assembly 1988, pres.-elect 1993, pres. 1994), Nat. Dem. Inst. for Internat. Affairs (instr. No. Ireland 1988, Baltic Republics 1992, Hungary 1993). Office: US House Reps House Office Bldg 1232 Longworth Washington DC 20515-2505

MCCARTHY, KAREN VICTORIA, state administrator; b. Dubuque, Iowa, Nov. 3, 1960; d. Floyd Victor and Janet Louise (Groh) Efferding. BBA in Fin., U. Iowa, 1982; MAEd in Counseling, Loras Coll., 1987; postgrad., Drake U., 1995—. Nat. cert. counselor; cert. family devel. specialist. Data analyst Dun & Bradstreet, Dubuque, 1983; tax preparer H&R Block, Dubuque, 1983-89; control ctr. mgr. YM/YWCA of Dubuque, 1984-86; career counselor N.E. Iowa Cmty. Coll., Peosta, Iowa, 1987-91; career counselor Operation: New View, Dubuque, 1989-91, family devel. and self sufficiency program mgr., 1991-93; family devel. and self sufficiency program mgr. State of Iowa, Des Moines, 1993—; cons. Ill. Cmty. Action Assn., Ill., 1995; mem. chair Project Self-Sufficiency Task Force, 1991-93. Sr. tutor, tutor trainer, Laubach Lit. Coun., Dubuque, 1985-93, bd. dirs., exec. com., chair family sect. Nature Com. Habitat for Humanity, Dubuque, 1991-93; bd. dirs. YWCA of Dubuque, 1977-79, pres. 1984, sec. 1990-93, chair pers. com. 1991-93, exec. dir. search com. 1991. Mem. ACA, Nat. Career Devel. Assn., Nat. Employment Counselors Assn., Family Resource Coalition. Office: Iowa Dept of Human Rights Lucas State Office Bldg Des Moines IA 50319

MC CARTHY, KATHRYN A., physicist; b. Lawrence, Mass., Aug. 7, 1924; d. Joseph Augustine and Catherine (Barrett) McCarthy. A.B., Tufts U., 1945, M.S., 1946; Ph.D., Radcliffe Coll., 1957; D.Sc. (hon.), Coll. Holy Cross, 1978; D.H.L. (hon.), Merrimack Coll., 1981. Instr. physics Tufts U., 1946-53, asst. prof., 1953-59, assoc. prof., 1959-62, prof., 1962-95, emerita, 1995—, dean Grad. Sch., 1969-74, provost, sr. v.p., 1973-79; research fellow in metallurgy Harvard, 1957-59, vis. scholar, 1979-80; research assoc. Baird Assocs., 1947-49, 51, Boston U. Optical Research Lab., summer 1952; assoc. research engr. U. Mich., summer 1957-58; dir. Mass. Electric Co., State Mut. Assurance Co. Trustee Southeastern Mass. U., 1972-74, Merrimack Coll., 1974-83, Coll. Holy Cross, 1980—; corporator Lawrence Meml. Hosp., 1975—, dir., 1978—, chmn., 1991. Fellow Optical Soc. Am., Am. Phys. Soc.; mem. Soc. Women Engrs. (sr.), Phi Beta Kappa, Sigma Xi. Roman Catholic. Home: 1580 Massachusetts Ave Apt 5D Cambridge MA 02138-2926 Office: Tufts U Dept Physics 4 Colby St Medford MA 02155-6013

MCCARTHY, MARIE GERALDINE, program director, coordinator, educator; b. San Francisco, Nov. 7, 1940; d. Emmett Francis and Marie Delores (Costello) McC.; children: Peter, Robert, Todd Brockman. BA, Lone Mountain Coll., 1962; MA, Dominican Coll., San Rafael, Calif., 1972. Gen. secondary credential; cert. cmty. coll. chief adminstrv. officer, supr., history, basic edn., spl. edn., profl. edn. educator, counselor. Coord., counselor Work Incentive Program, Employment Devel. Dept., Marin County, Calif., 1970-72; coord., instr. Neighborhood Youth Corps Program, Marin County, Calif., 1972-74; coord. Marin City Project Area Com., Marin County, Calif., 1978-79; coord. basic skills program Coll. of Marin, Kentfield, Calif., 1973-79, edn. cons., 1980-83, pres. acad. senate, 1993—, coord. Disabled Students Program, 1984—; faculty advisor Challenged Students Club, Coll. of Marin, Kentfield, 1983—, exec. coun. United Profs. of Marin, Local 1610, 1984-92, mem. staff devel. com., 1986-88, event coord. ann. student fundraiser for students with disabilities, 1985—, dist. psychol. disabilities task force, 1994—, dist. councilmem. Faculty Assn. Calif. C.C.s, 1994—, dist. budget com., 1994—, dist. master planning com., 1994—, mem. crisis intervention team, 1990—, editor DSPS Forum, 1995—; exec. com. Statewide Acad. Senate, 1995-96. Author: How To Learn To Study: Bridging the Study Skills Gap, 1982, The Faculty Handbook on Disabilities, 1993. Bd. dirs., v.p. CENTERFORCE, 1992—; bd. dirs. Marin Coalition, Marin Athletic Found., 1992—, Marin Ctr. for Ind. Living, 1994—, EXODUS, 1992—, sec.; past v.p. Bay Faculty Assn.; founder Youth Helping Homeless, 1990—; mem. Alliance for the Mentally Ill., 1994—, JERICHO, 1994—; founding bd. dirs. INSPIRIT, 1984—. Recipient Spl. Achievement award Calif. Youth Soccer Assn., 1980, Marin County Mother of Yr. award, 1984, Spl. Recognition awards The Indoor Sports Club for Physically Handicapped, 1984, 88-90, 92-93, Mom Makes the Difference honoree Carter Hawley Hale Stores, Inc., 1994, Cert. of Recognition, Marin Human Rights Commn., 1994, Hayward award, 1995, Buckelew Partnership award, 1995, Disting. Faculty award Com. Alumni Assn., 1995. Mem. AAUW, Calif. Assn. Postsecondary Educators for the Disabled, Faculty Assn. Calif. C.C.'s, Amnesty Internat. Platform Assoc.,, AHEAD, Commonwealth Club Calif., U.S. Soccer Fedn. Home: 6004 Shelter Bay Ave Mill Valley CA 94941-3040 Office: Coll of Marin College Ave Kentfield CA 94904

MCCARTHY, MARY ANN, counselor, educator; b. Barstow, Calif., Jan. 16, 1954; d. Thomas Edward and Helen C. (Krutell) McC. BA in Psychology, San Francisco State U., 1975; MS in Counseling, Calif. State U., Fullerton, 1995. Cert. pupil pers. svcs., 1995. Br. mgr., asst. v.p. Great American First Savings, Orange County, Calif., 1981-88, dist. mgr., v.p., 1988-90; dir. re-entry ctr. Saddleback Coll., Mission Viejo, Calif., 1995; intern coord. Orange Coast Coll., Costa Mesa, Calif., 1995—; assoc. prof. Saddleback Coll., Mission Viejo, Calif., 1996—. Vol. Beverly Manor Convalescent Hosp., Laguna Hills, Calif., 1989-94, Mission Viejo Animal Shelter, 1996—; big sister Big Brothers/Big Sisters Am., Mission Viejo, 1980-83; mem scholarship & ednl. coms. Saddleback Valley C. of C., Laguna Hills, 1982-86; spkr. local schs. Saddleback Valley Vol. Network, Mission Viejo, 1982-86. Recipient Outstanding Young Woman Am. award, 1983; named Saddleback Valley Young Careerist, Bus. & Profl. Women, 1983. Mem. AAUW (past pres., editor, scholarship chair, pub. info. officer, sec. 1996-97), Am. Counseling Assn., Am. Coll. Counseling Assn., Calif. C.C. Counselor Assn., Calif. Assn. Counseling & Devel. Home: 5 Martinique Laguna Niguel CA 92677 Office: Orange Coast Coll 2701 Fairview Rd Costa Mesa CA 92626

MCCARTHY, MARY FRANCES, hospital foundation administrator; b. Washington, Apr. 16, 1937; d. Joseph Francis and Frances (Oddi) McGowan; m. Charles M. Sappenfield, Dec. 14, 1963 (div. June 1990); children: Charles Ross, Sarah Kathleen; m. Daniel Fendrick McCarthy, Jr., Aug. 25, 1990. BA, Trinity Coll., Washington, 1958; cert. in bus. adminstrn., Harvard U.-Radcliffe Coll., 1959; MA, Ball State U., Muncie, Ind., 1984. Systems engr. IBM, Cambridge, Mass., 1959-61; editorial asst. Kiplinger Washington Editors, 1961-63; feature writer pub. info. dept. Ball State U., 1984-85, coll. editor Coll. Bus., 1985-86, coord. alumni and devel., 1986-88, dir. major gift clubs and donor rels., 1988-90; dir. devel. Sweet Briar (Va.) Coll., 1990-91; adminstr. St. Mary's Hosp. and Med. Ctr. Found., Grand Junction, Colo., 1991—. Editor: A History of Maxon Corporation, 1986, Managing Change, 1986, Indiana's Investment Banker, 1987; assoc. editor Mid-Am. Jour. Bus., 1985-86. Participant Leadership Lynchburg, 1990, Jr. League; mem. Sr. Companions Bd., Grand Junction, 1992—; mem. Mesa County Healthy Communities Steering Com., 1992—; mem. Mesa County Health Assessment, 1994—; mem. bd. Sta. KRMJ TV Channel 18, 1995—; regional dir. region, 1996—. Recipient Golden Broom award Muncie Clean City, 1989; svc. of distinction award Ball State U. Coll. Bus., 1990. Mem. Coun. for Advancement and Support of Edn., Assn. of Healthcare Philanthropy (regional 9 cabinet 1992—), Nat. Soc. Fundraising Execs. (cert., Colo. chpt. bd. dirs. 1994—). Republican.

MCCARTHY, PATRICE ANN, lawyer; b. New Haven, Jan. 23, 1957; d. Robert Edmund and Faith Arline (Augur) McC.; m. Donald Allen Kirshbaum, Oct. 25, 1986; children: Lynn Anne, Sara. BA, Mt. Holyoke Coll., 1978; JD, U. Conn., 1981. Bar: Conn. 1981, U.S. Dist. Ct. Conn. 1981. Staff assoc. Conn. Conf. Municipalities, New Haven, 1981-83; legal counsel Conn. Assn. Bds. Edn., Hartford, 1983-88, gen. counsel, assoc. exec. dir. for govt. rels., 1988-91; dep. dir., gen. counsel, 1991—. Editor: Conn. Manual Bd. Policy Regulations and By-laws, 1987; contbr. articles to profl. jours. Mem. ABA, Nat. Sch. Bds. Assn. Coun. Sch. Attys. (bd. dirs. 1990-94), Am. Soc. Pub. Adminstrn. (coun. 1988—), Nat. Orgn. for Legal Problems in Edn., Conn. Bar Assn., Conn. Sch. Attys. Coun. (pres. 1988-89), Conn. Pub. Employers Labor Rels. Assn. (bd. dirs. 1985-88), Mt. Holyoke Club (v.p. 1986-88, pres. 1990-94). Office: Conn Assn Bds Edn 81 Wolcott Hill Rd Hartford CT 06109

MCCARTHY, SHARON SWEENEY, special education educator; b. Blue Island, Ill., Aug. 6, 1960; d. James J. and Lucy (Lee) Sweeney. BS, Ill. State U., 1983; MEd, Loyola U., Chgo., 1989. Cert. spl. edn. tchr., Ill. Asst. prin. Lt. Joseph P. Kennedy Sch., Palos Park, Ill.; spl. edn. tchr. Dist. #102 L.A.D.S.E., Brookfield, Ill. Mem. Assn. Supervision and Curriculum Devel.

MCCARTNEY, CATHERINE ELLEN, educational psychology educator; b. Mankato, Minn.; d. Bernard John and Charlotte Ann (Cope) Venn; m. Timothy James McCartney, June 25, 1983. BS, Mankato State U., 1979; MS, St. Cloud (Minn.) State U., 1986; PhD, U. Idaho, 1989. Secondary tchr. Turtle Mountain Cmty. Sch., Turtle Mountain Indian Reservation, Belcourt, N.D., 1979-84; grad. asst. U. Idaho, Moscow, 1987-88; asst. prof. ednl. psychology Bemidji (Minn.) State U., 1989-92, assoc. prof., 1992-96, prof., 1996—. Author: (monograph) Social Systems, Girls and Self-Esteem, 1995. Mem. NOW, AAUW, Am. Ednl. Rsch. Assn., Assn. Tchr. Educators. Democrat. Office: Bemidji State U 1500 Birchmont Dr NE Bemidji MN 56601

MCCARTNEY, KAREN ANN, secondary education educator; b. Oklahoma City, Okla., Aug. 1, 1940; d. Joel Okle and Helen Pauline (Holmes) Keeter; m. Thomas Richard McCartney, Nov. 24, 1961; 1 child, Patrick. BA, U. Tulsa, 1961; MEd, Northeastern State U., 1989. Math. tchr. Cleveland Jr. H.S., Tulsa, Okla., 1961-66; math. tchr., chair math. dept. Edison H.S., Tulsa, 1966-94. Home: 5530 S Hudson Pl Tulsa OK 74135-7518

MCCARTNEY, MARY JANE, utilities/energy executive. Sr. v.p. gas ops. Consol. Edison Co. of N.Y., Inc., N.Y.C., 1994—. Office: Consol Edison Co of NY Inc 4 Irving Pl Rm 1640 New York NY 10003*

MCCARTNEY, RHODA HUXSOL, farm manager; b. Floyd County, Iowa, June 30, 1928; d. Julius Franklin and Ruth Ada (Carney) Huxsol; m. Ralph Farnham McCartney, June 25, 1950; children: Ralph, Julia, David. AA, Frances Shimer, 1948; BA, U. Iowa, 1950. Mng. dir. McCartney-Huxsol Farms, Charles City, Iowa, 1969—; prin. trustee J.F. Huxsol Trusts, Charles City, Iowa, 1984—. Pres. Nat. 19th Amendment Soc., Charles City, 1991—; mem. Terace Hill Commn., Des Moines, 1988-94; bd. dirs. Iowa Children and Family Svcs., Des Moines, 1963-68; mem. Iowa. Arts Coun., Des Moines, 1974-78. Mem. AAUW, Iowa LWV, PEO. Congregationalist. Home: 1828 Cedar View Dr Charles City IA 50616-9129 Office: McCartney-Huxsol Farms 117 N Jackson St Charles City IA 50616-2002

MCCARTY, DEBORAH OWNBY, city commissioner, lawyer; b. Houston, Aug. 28, 1952; d. John Edward and Patricia Ann (Turriff) Ownby; m. John Rea Myer, June 24, 1992; children: John Ownby, Peter Turriff. BA, Southwestern U., 1973; postgrad. in theology, Emory U., 1973-74; internat. bus. fellow, London (Eng.) Bus. Sch., 1983; LHD (hon.), Southwestern U., 1990; JD, Ga. State U., 1992. Bar: Ga., 1992; Ga. real estate lic. 1986; completed program for sr. execs. J.F.K. Sch. Govt., Cambridge, Mass., 1982. City council mem. City of Atlanta, 1978-93, commr. parks, recreation and cultural affairs, 1993—; chair housing code commn., City of Atlanta, 1978-79, chair city utilities, human resources, and council com., pres. pro tempore, 1982, mem. fin. com., 1984-92, chair zoning and exec. coms.; steering com. human devel. 1983, policy com. transp. and comm., steering com. energy and the environment, 1992-93, Nat. League of Cities; transp. com. 1983, environment com. 1992-93, Ga. Mcpl. Assn.; elected mem., sec. Met. Atlanta Olympic Game Authority, 1991-93; adj. faculty Candler Sch. Theology, Emory U., 1984-91; law clk. Long, Aldridge and Norman, Atlanta, 1989-91, Trotter, Smith and Jacobs, Atlanta, 1990-91; bd. dirs. C.O.T. Devel. Corp., Loveland, Colo.; assoc. dir. Grant Park Neighborhood Housing Svcs., Atlanta, 1976-77. Presdl. elector State of Ga., 1992; co-chair Clinton for Pres., Ga. primary, 1992; charter mem., founder Grant Park/SAND Fed. Credit Union, 1976; mem. City-Wide League of Neighborhoods, 1976-84; mem. Atlanta Women's Network, 1980-90; mem. 1994 Superbowl Host Com.; V.I.S.T.A. vol., Atlanta, 1975-76; bd. mem. Ga. State U., 1989-91, chair, 1992. Recipient Outstanding Alumni award Southwest U., 1983, "Other Voices" Theater award 1982, Leadership Atlanta award 1980; selected Woman of Achievement, Capitol City Bus. and Profl. Women, Atlanta, 1978, Outstanding Woman Student, Ga. Assn. Women Lawyers-Ga. State U., 192, one of Ten Outstanding Young People of Atlanta, 1979; HUD fellow, 1982; bd. dirs. USA Mobile Indoor Track & Field Championships, Atlanta Botanical Garden, P.A.T.H., Piedmont Park Conservancy, Park Pride Atlanta. Mem. ABA, Nat. Recreation and Parks Assn., Am. Public Works Assn., Ga. Assn. Dem. Women, Ga. Recreation and Parks Assn., Assn. Women Law Students Ga. State U., Assn. to Revive Grant Park (founding mem.), Ctrl. Presbyn. Ch., Delta Theta Phi. Home: 1280 Beechwood Hills Ct NW Atlanta GA 30327 Office: City of Atlanta Parks & Recreation, Ste 8 675 Ponce de Leon Ave NE Atlanta GA 30308-1807

MCCARTY, LORRAINE CHAMBERS, painter, educator; b. Detroit, Aug. 17, 1920. Student, Detroit Art Acad., 1938, Stephens Coll., 1940, Wayne State U., 1942; studied with, Glen Michaels, Emil Weddidge, Robert Wilbert. Mem. faculty Flint (Mich.) Inst. Arts, 1970—, Grosse Point (Mich.) War Meml., 1972—; pvt. tchr. art Royal Oak, Mich.; mem. faculty Muskegon (Mich.) Inst. Arts, 1978—, Flint Inst. Arts, 1978—; artist in residence Stephens Coll., Columbia, Mo., 1981; advisor, designer Internat. Women's Air & Space Mus., Ohio, 1986, Okla., juror, critic in field, lectr.in field; ofcl. artist USAF, 1981; instr. Birmingham Bloomfield (Mich.) Art Assn., Islanders of St. Loud-Workshop Retreats in No. Mich., Paint Creek Ctr. for Arts, Rochester, Mich., Mt. Clemens Ctr. for Arts, Mich., Flint Inst. Arts,, Muskegon Mus. of Art, Jessee Besser Mus., Alpena, Ella Sharpe Mus., Jackson, Mich, Ctr. for Creative Studies, Detroit, others; cons. Greenfield Village Mus., 1991; mentor U. Mich., 1992. Numerous one woman shows including Midland Arts Coun., 1978, Dayton Art Inst., 1978, Flint Inst. Arts, 1980, Nat. Acad. Arts and Letters, 1980, Stephens Coll., 1981; numerous group shows including Women '71, DeKalb, Ill., Butler Mus. Am. Art, Youngstown, Ohio, Detroit Inst. Arts, 1980, Ohio Arts Coun. Nat. Traveling Show, 1982; represented in permanent collections including Smithsonian Nat. Air and Space Mus., Muskegon Mus. Art, Butler Mus. Am. Art, Dow Chem. Co., Midland, Mich., No. Ill. U., DeKalb, K Mart Internat. Hdqrs., Troy, Mich., Capital City Airport, Lansing, R.L. Polk Co., Detroit, Bohn Copper and Brass, Southfield, Mich., Jug Pilots P047s, N.Y.C.; commns. include murals for Gen. Dynamics Landsystems 1 Mich., Alpena Light & Power Co., art works for Lear Siegler Seating Co., Mich., 4 H Hdqrs., Washington, Trusswall Internat., Mich., R.L Polk Co., Mich., Capitol City Airport, Mich., Gerald Behaylo, Mich.; producer TV series The Artist in You; inventor, designer Artist's Eye: Visual Aid for Artists. Mem. exec. com. Oakland County Cultural Coun. Recipient numerous awards including Purchase prize Butler Mus. Am. Art, 1969, Grand Jury award 16th Ann. Mid-Mich., Best Painting by a Woman award Detroit Inst. Arts, 1971, Disting. Alumnae award Stephens Coll., 1982, 1st place award Nat. Fedn. Local Cable Programmers, 1984; recipient grant Lester Hereward Cooke Found., 1984, creative artist, Mich. Coun. Arts, 1983, master to apprentice, Mich. Coun. Arts, 1983, artists consultancy, Mich. Coun. Arts, 1983, OIP Project, Savannah, Ga., 1965, 67, 72. Mem. Detroit Soc. Women Painters and Sculptors, All Women Transcontinental Air Race Assn., Mich. Watercolor Soc., Artists Equity Assn., Mich. Acad. Arts Sci. Letters. Home: 1112 Pinehurst Ave Royal Oak MI 48073-3370

MCCASLAND, KATHRYN ANN, counselor, special education educator; b. Ithaca, N.Y., Oct. 13, 1960; d. Joseph Howard and Cary Elizabeth (Bayne) Kenrick; m. Scott Eugene McCasland; children: Anthony Padilla, David. BA, No. Ariz. U., 1987, MA in Edn., 1994. Tchr. Yarnell (Ariz) Sch. Dist., 1987-88, Bering Strait Sch. Dist., St. Michael, Alaska, 1988-91; spl. edn. tchr. Bering Strait Sch. Dist., Unalakleet, Alaska, 1991-95; counselor Bering Strait Sch. Dist., White Mountain, Alaska, 1995—. Area dir. Spl. Olympics, Unalakleet, 1991-95; peer helper advisor Bering Strait Sch. Dist., Unalakleet, 1992-95; site rep. Nat. Edn. Assn., Unalakleet, 1991-95. Grantee Southeast Regional Resources, 1991-94. Mem. Nat. Counselor Assn., Alaska Counselor Assn. Republican. Lutheran. Home: 602 Oceanview Ln Golovin AK 07002 Office: Bering Strait Sch Dist Golovin AK 99762

MCCASLIN, F. CATHERINE, consulting sociologist; b. Chattanooga, Feb. 21, 1947; d. John Jacob and Elizabeth Dorothy (Johnson) McC. AB, Hollins Coll., Roanoke, Va., 1969; MA, Ga. State U., 1972; PhD, UCLA, 1979. Assoc. dir. Ga. Narcotics Treatment Program, Atlanta, 1972-73; research assoc., dir. research Health Care Delivery Services, Inc., Los Angeles, 1974-76; sr. survey analyst Kaiser Found. Health Plan, Los Angeles, 1978-80; program officer The Robert Wood Johnson Found., Princeton, 1980-84; faculty U. Pa. Sch. Medicine, Phila., 1984-86; ptnr. Schuhmacher & McCaslin Assocs., Phila., 1986—; exec. dir. The H.F. Lenfest Found., Pottstown, Pa., 1988-89; dir. rsch. Beaufort (S.C.) County Sch. Dist., 1992—; adj. faculty sociology U. S.C., Beaufort, 1992—; mem. adv. bd. Nat. Childhood Asthma Project, NHBLI, Washington, 1982-84; adv. com. mem. Statewide Adolescent Pregnancy, New Brunswick, 1981-84; trainee NIH, 1973-79; cons. in field. Mem. editorial bd. Jour. Health & Social Behavior, 1988—; editor Med. Sociology newsletter, 1984—; contbr. articles to profl. jours. Fellow NIMH, 1975; grantee Spl. Action Office for Drug Abuse Prevention, 1972, Robert Wood Johnson Found., 1984. Mem. Am. Sociol.

Assn. (nat. council med. sociology sect. 1984—). Am. Pub. Health Assn., Sociologists for Women in Soc. Democrat. Episcopalian. Home: Mossy Oaks Rd Ste K-1 Beaufort SC 29902 Office: Beaufort County Sch Dist 1300 King St Beaufort SC 29902-4936

MCCASLIN, TERESA EVE, human resources executive; b. Jersey City, Nov. 22, 1949; d. Felix F. and Ann E. (Golaszewski) Hrynkiewicz; m. Thomas W. McCaslin, Jan. 22, 1972 (div.). BA, Marymount Coll., 1971; MBA, L.I. U., 1981. Adminstrv. officer Civil Service Commn., Fed. Republic Germany, 1972-76; personnel dir. Oceanroutes, Inc., Palo Alto, Calif., 1976-78; mgr., coll. relations Continental Grain Co., N.Y.C., 1978-79, corp. personnel mgr., 1979-81, dir. productivity, internal cons., 1981-84; dir., human resources Grow Group, Inc., N.Y.C., 1984-85, v.p. human resources, 1985-86, v.p. adminstrn., 1986-89; corporate v.p. human resources Avery Dennison Corp., Pasadena, Calif., 1989-94, Monsanto Co., St. Louis, 1994—; adv. bd. St Johns Mercy Med. Ctr., Goodwill Industries of Mo., St. Louis U. Internat. Sch. Bus. Bd. advisers St. John's Mercy Med. Ctr., Goodwill Industries of Mo., St. Louis U. Grad. Sch. Internat. Bus. Mem. Am. Mgmt. Assn., Human Resources Coun. Roman Catholic. Office: Monsanto Co 800 N Lindbergh Blvd Saint Louis MO 63167

MCCAUGHEY ROSS, ELIZABETH P. (BETSY MCCAUGHEY), state official; b. Oct. 20, 1948; d. Albert Peterkin; m. Thomas McCaughey, 1972 (div. 1994); children: Amanda, Caroline, Diana. BA, Vassar Coll., 1970; MA, Columbia Univ., 1972, PhD, 1976. Public policy expert Manhattan Inst., N.Y.C.; lt. gov. State of N.Y., 1995—; instr. Vassar Coll., 1979, Columbia Univ., 1980-84; chmn. Governor's Medicaid Task Force, 1994. Author: From Loyalist to Founding Father, 1980, Government By Choice, 1987; also articles including an article in The New Republic (Nat. Mag. award for Pub. Policy 1995). Recipient Bancroft Dissertation award, Richard B. Morris prize; Woodrow Wilson fellow, Herbert H. Lehman fellow, Honorary Vassar fellow, John Jay fellow, Post Doctoral Rsch. fellow NEH, 1984, John Molin fellow Manhattan Inst., 1993, sr. fellow Ctr. Study of the Presidency. Republican. Office: Office of Lt Governor Executive Chamber State Capitol Rm 326 Albany NY 12224*

MCCAULEY, FLOYCE REID, psychiatrist; b. Braddock, Pa., Dec. 30, 1933; d. John Mitchel and Irene (Garner) Reid; m. James Calvin McCauley, July 15, 1955; children: James Stanley, Lori Ellen. BS in Nursing, U. Pitts., 1956; D.O., Coll. Osteopathic Medicine, Phila., 1972. Bd. eligible in child and adult psychiatry. Intern Suburban Gen. Hosp., Norristown, Pa., 1972-73; resident in adult psychiatry Phila. State Hosp. and Phila. Mental Health Clinic, 1973-75; fellow Med. Coll. of Pa. and Ea. Pa. Psychiat. Inst., Phila., 1975-78; Chief child psychiatry inpatient unit Med. Coll. Pa., Phila., 1978-80; med. dir. Carson ValleySch., Flourtown, Pa., 1980-82; dir. outpatient psychiat. clinic Osteopathic Med. Ctr. Phila., 1980-86; staff psychiatrist Kent Gen. Hosp., Dover, Del., 1986-89; psychiat. cons. Del. Guidance Svcs. for Children, Dover, 1986-91; clin. dir. children's unit HCA Rockford Ctr., Newark, 1991-93; with Kid's Peace Nat. Hosp. for Kids in Crisis, 1993-95, Pa. Found., Sellersville, 1995—; mem. Mental Health Code Rev. Com. for Del., 1991; inducted into the Chapel of Four Chaplains, Phila., 1983; psychiat. cons. Seaford (Del.) Br. of New Eng. Fellowship for Rehab., 1991-93, Cath. Charities Day Treatment Program for 3-6 Yr. Olds, Dover, Del., 1990—; cons. Del. Guidance Day Treatment Program, 1990—; staff psychiatrist Kids Peace Nat. Hosp. for Kids in Crisis, 1993-95, Penn Found., 1995—. Mem. Mayor's Com. for Mental Health, Phila., 1983. Mem. Am. Osteopathic Assn., Am. Coll. Neuropsychiatrists, Am. Psychiat. Assn., Am. Acad. Child Psychiatrists (Del. br.). Democrat. Methodist.

MCCAULEY, JANE REYNOLDS, journalist; b. Wilmington, Del., Oct. 22, 1947; d. John Thomas and Helen (Campbell) McC. BA, Guilford Coll., 1969. Rchr. Nat. Geographic Soc., Washington, 1970-75, writer, 1975-80, writer, editor, 1980-90. Author of numerous children's books; co-author adult and travel chpts. Mem. Children's Book Soc. of Am., Washington Ind. Writers, Am. Quilters' Soc.

MCCHESNEY, S. ELAINE, lawyer; b. Bowling Green, Ky., Sept. 14, 1954; d. Kelsey H. McChesney and Lorraine (Carter) Durey; m. Paul Boylan; children: Michael, Jessica, Andrew. AB summa cum laude, Western Ky. U., 1975; JD, Harvard U., 1978. With Bingham Dana & Gould, Boston, 1978—, ptnr., 1985—; chair joint MBA/BBA bar com. on jud. appts., 1988-89, 90-91; trial practice advisor moot ct. exercises Harvard Law Sch.; moot ct. judge Harvard Law Sch., Boston U., Suffolk U. Bd. editors Mass. Lawyer's Weekly, 1987-88; panelist, speaker in field; contbr. articles to profl. jours. Treas., bd. dirs. St. Paul's Nursery Sch., Dedham, Mass., 1990-95; parent rep. Charles River Sch., Dover, Mass., vol. numerous coms.; vol. Am. Heart Found., March of Dimes; vol. street canvassing on zoning issues. Mem. ABA (labor law sect. subcom. individual rights in the workplace 1982—, comml. banking or fin. transactions litigation 1982), Mass. Bar Assn., Boston Bar Assn. (coun. 1994—, law sch. liaison com. 1984-85, IOLTA com., co-chair ann. mtg.), Women's Bar Assn. (editor calendar 1988-92). Office: Bingham Dana & Gould 150 Federal St Boston MA 02110-1745

MCCLAIN, JONI LYNN, medical examiner; b. Oklahoma City, May 9, 1957; d. John Norman and Mary Ann (Johnson) McC. BS in Chemistry, Cen. State U., Edmond, Okla., 1979; MD, U. Okla., 1983. Resident pathology U. Okla., 1983-87; fellow forensic pathology Ind. U., 1987-88; dep. med. examiner Office of the Armed Forces Med. Examiner, Washington, 1988-92; med. examiner Southwestern Inst. Forensic Scis., Dallas, 1992—. Med. examiner Nat. Disaster Med. System (D-MORT Team VI), Rockville, Md., 1992—. Recipient joint svc. achievement medal Dept. Def., 1991, joint svc. commendation medal, 1992, def. meritorious svc. medal, 1992. Fellow Am. Acad. Forensic Scis.; mem. Nat. Assn. Med. Examiners (bd. dirs. 1993—). Office: SW Inst Forensic Scis PO Box 35728 Dallas TX 75235-0728

MCCLAIN, JUDITH ELAINE, school counselor; b. Hillsboro, Tex., Dec. 15, 1946; d. Larry and Mary Jane (Hensley) Watson; m. Randall Scott McClain, Mar. 3, 1971; 1 child, Richard Andrew. B in Music Edn., Baylor U., 1970, MEd, 1975. Music tchr. spl. edn. Waco ISD, Tex., 1969-75; resource tchr. spl. edn. Moody ISD, Tex., 1976-78, Midway ISD, Hewitt, Tex., 1978-93; sch. counselor for h.s. Lorena ISD, Tex., 1993—. Bd. dirs. Arthritis Found., Waco, 1992-94. Mem. Tex. Counseling Assn., Heart of Tex. Counseling Assn., Alpha Delta Kappa. Baptist. Home: 120 Linden Ln Hewitt TX 76643 Office: Lorena HS PO Box 97 Lorena TX 76655

MCCLAIN, KATRINA, basketball player; b. Charleston, S.C.. Student, Ga. State U., 1987. Basketball player USA Women's Nat. Team; mem. U.S. Women's Olympic Basketball Team, 1988, 92; mem. 1994 World Championship Team. Office: USA Basketball 5465 Mark Dabling Blvd Colorado Springs CO 80918-3842

MCCLAIN, SYLVIA NANCY, voice educator, classical vocalist; b. Worthington, Minn., July 16, 1943; d. Walter Deming and Naomi Leona (Deters) Grimm.; m. Joseph T. McClain (div. Feb. 4, 1994); children: Raimund, Hermine. MusB with honors, Ind. U., 1966, MusM with honors, 1969; D of Musical Arts with commendation, U. Tex., Austin, 1989. Apprentice artist Santa Fe (N.Mex.) Opera, 1968-69; performing singer various concert and opera venues, Germany, 1970-78; asst. prof. music Howard Payne U., Brownwood, Tex., 1992, 94; asst. prof. voice dept. fine arts Southwestern U., Georgetown, Tex., 1986-91; assoc prof., chair voice dept. sch. music Hardin-Simmons U., Abilene, Tex., 1992—. Performer: (recitals) Portraits of Women in Songs of. Vol. cons. Leadership of Edn. in Arts Professions, Austin, 1990-92; co-founder, Austin Lyric Opera, 1983-92. Fulbright scholar, Stadtliche Hochschule für Musik, Stuttgart, Germany, 1969-70. Mem. NOW, AAUW, Nat. Assn. Tchrs. of Singing, Phi Kappa Lambda, Mu Phi Epsilon. Democrat. Methodist. Home: 457 Merchant Abilene TX 79603

MCCLAIN-OWNS, JUANITA, library director; m. Danny Owes; children: Thaddeus Davis, Danielle. BS in English, Ala. State U.; MEd in Libr. Ednl. Media, Atlanta U., MS in Libr. and Info. Sci. Libr. Ill. Ctrl. Coll., Peoria, Southside Elem. Sch., Selma, Ala., Macon County Pub. Sch. Sys., Tuskegee, ala.; reference libr. Macon County-Tuskegee Pub. Libr., Montgomery, Ala., 1989, head Coliseum Blvd. br., 1989-94, asst. dir., 1994, dir., 1994. Mem. sesquicentennial history com. Macon County; mem. bd. ushers, matrons, mem. edn. com. Mt. Gillard Missionary Bapt. Ch. Ala. Pub. Libr. Svc. scholar, 1983; fellow Sch. Libr. and Info. Scis., Atlanta U. Office: 245 High St PO Box 1950 Montgomery AL 36102-1950

MCCLANAHAN, CONNIE DEA, pastoral minister; b. Detroit, Mar. 1, 1948; d. Manford Bryce and Dorothy Maxine (Keely) McC. BA, Marygrove Coll., 1969; MRE, Seattle U., 1978; D Ministry, St. Mary Sem. and U., Balt., 1988. Cert. in spiritual direction, youth ministry, advanced catechist. Campus minister Flint (Mich.) Newman Ctr., 1970-80; coord. religious edn. Blessed Sacrament Ch., Burton, Mich., 1981-84; pastoral assoc. Good Shepherd Cath. Ch., Montrose, Mich., 1984-90; pastor Sacred Heart Ch., Flint, 1990—; music min. New Light Prayer Cmty., Flint, 1979—; co-chaplain Dukette Cath. Sch., Flint, 1991—; ind. spiritual dir., 1988—; rep. Diocesan Regional Adult Edn., 1993-96; mem. Nat., State and Lansing Diocese Catholic Campus Ministry Assns., 1970-80; mem. campus ministry task force Interfaith Metro. Agy. for Planning, 1974-76; mem. Lansing Diocesan Liturgical Commn., 1977-80; mem. Flint Cath. Urban Ministry, 1977-80, 90—, co-chair, 1992-94; mem. Flint Cath. Healing Prayer Team, 1977-84; coord. nat. study week Cath. Campus Ministry Assn., 1978; mem. steering com. All-Mich. cath. Charismatic Com. on Lay Ministry, 1984-86; convener Diocesan Lay Ministry Com. on Cert./Continuing Edn./Spirituality, 1985-86; mem. Diocesan Com. to Update Catechist Formation Handbook, 1989-91; mem. Diocesan All Family Conf. Steering Com., 1990—; mem. Lansing Diocese svc. com. of Cath. Charismatic Renewal, 1979-85, 95—. Mem. Assn. Cath. Lay Ministers (co-chair Region III 1986-87), Profl. Pastoral Ministers Assn. (co-chair 1988-90). Roman Catholic. Office: Sacred Heart Ch 719 E Moore St Flint MI 48505-3905

MCCLANAHAN, PATSY HITT, women's health nurse practitioner; b. Pasadena, Tex., Sept. 17, 1954; d. Clifton Lee and Doris Allene (Edwards) Hitt; m. George Terrell McClanahan, Nov. 26, 1980; children: Terry Lee, Jennifer Allene. BSN, N.E. La. U., 1976; Ob/gyn. Nurse Practitioner Cert., U. Tex., Dallas, 1987; MSN, Northwestern State U., 1990. Lic. RN/advanced nurse practitioner, ob-gyn. sonography, NAACOG. Nurse dir. Columbia (La.) State Sch., 1976-77; staff nurse Caldwell Meml. Hosp., Columbia, La., 1977-79; instr. N.E. La. U., Monroe, 1979; staff nurse Schumpert Med. Ctr., Shreveport, La., 1979; dir. nurses Citizens Med. Ctr., Columbia, La., 1980-84; pub. health nurse III Caldwell Parish Health Unit, Columbia, La., 1984-88; nurse II E.A. Conway Hosp., Monroe, La., 1988; regional pub. specialist Regional Pub. Health, Monroe, La., 1988-89; instr. dept. ob/gyn La. State U. Med. Ctr., Monroe, La., 1989—. Dir. youth Music Fellowship Bapt. Ch., Columbia, 1990-92; youth Sunday sch. tchr. Fellowship Bapt. Ch., 1995-96, softball coach Caldwell Parish Dixie Youth, Columbia, 1989-90. Mem. ANA, La. Nurse Practitioners (N.E. regional rep. 1990-95, prescriptive task force 1992-94, treas. 1995—), Assn. Women's Health, Obstet. and Neonatal Nurses, Am. Inst. Ultrasound Medicine, Am. Acad. Nurse Practitioners (State award for Excellence 1991), Am. Acad. Nurse Practitioners (state rep. 1995), La. Coalition for Maternal and Infant Health, Sigma Theta Tau. Democrat. Baptist. Home: 1780 Blankston Rd Monroe LA 71202 Office: La State U Med Ctr E A Conway Divsn 4864 Jackson St Monroe LA 71202-6400

MCCLANAHAN, RUE (EDDI-RUE MC CLANAHAN), actress; b. Healdton, Okla.; d. William Edwin and Dreda Rheua-Nell (Medaris) McC.; m. 1st, Tom Bish, 1958; 1 child, Mark Thomas Bish; m. 2nd, Norman Hartweg; m. 3rd, Peter DeMaio; m. 4th, Gus Fisher, 1976; m. 5th, Tom Keel, 1984 (div. 1985). B.A. cum laude, U. Tulsa, 1956. Appearances include (theatre) Erie (Pa.) Playhouse, 1957-58, Harvey (London); (Broadway) Jimmy Shine, 1968-69, Sticks and Bones, 1972, California Suite, 1977, After-Play, 1995; (TV appearances) L.A., 1959-664, N.Y.C., 1964-73; (TV series) Maude, 1973-78, Apple Pie, 1978, Mama's Family, 1982-84, Golden Girls, 1985-92, Golden Palace, 1992-93; (TV movies) Having Babies III, 1978, Sgt. Matlowch vs. the U.S. Air Force, 1978, Rainbow, 1978, Topper, 1979, The Great American Traffic Jam, 1980, Word of Honor, 1981, The Day the Bubble Burst, 1982, The Little Match Girl, 1987, Liberace, 1988, Take My Daughters Please, 1988, Let Me Hear You Whisper, 1988, To the Heroes, 1989, After the Shock, 1990, Children of the Bride, 1990, To My Daughter, 1990, The Dreamer of Oz, 1990, Baby of the Bride, 1991, Mother of the Bride, 1993, Danielle Steele's Message from Nam, 1993, Burning Passion: The Margaret Mitchell Story, 1994; (films) The People Next Door, 1970, They Might Be Giants, 1971, The Pursuit of Happiness, 1971, Modern Love, 1990, (mini-series) Innocent Victims, 1995. Recipient Obie award for leading off-Broadway role in Who's Happy Now, 1970; Emmy award Best Actress in a comedy, 1987; named Woman of Yr., Pasadena Playhouse, 1986; Spl. scholar Pasadena (Calif.) Playhouse, 1959, Phi Beta Gamma scholar, 1955. Mem. Actors Studio, Actors Equity Assn., AFTRA, Screen Actors Guild. Office: Agy for Performing Arts 9000 W Sunset Blvd Ste 1200 Los Angeles CA 90069-5812*

MCCLARON, LOUISIANNA CLARDY, retired secondary school educator; b. Clarksville, Tenn., Dec. 12, 1929; d. Abe and Chinaster (Simpson) Clardy; m. Joe Thomas McClaron, July 17, 1965. BS, Tenn. State U., 1952; MA, Ohio State U., 1956; EdS, Tenn. State U., 1977; PhD, Vanderbilt U., 1981. Cert. secondary tchr., sch. adminstr., supr., Tenn. Tchr. Madison County Bd. Edn., Normal, Ala., 1952-58, Metro Nashville Bd. Edn., 1958-94; ret., 1994; presenter workshops in field. Mem. NEA, Tenn. Edn. Assn., Metro Nashville Edn. Assn. (exec. bd., dist. dir.), Tenn. Bus. Edn. Assn., Nat. Bus. Edn. assn., Am. Vocat. Assn., Delta Pi Epsilon (former v.p. Omega chpt., now pres.), Alpha Kappa Alpha, Alpha Delta Omega Chpt. Found. (housing treas.).

MCCLEAN, MARTHA LOUISE, retail executive; b. Memphis, Mar. 26, 1956; d. James Porter Jr. and Juanita Louise (Blanchard) McC.; 1 child, James Luis Luengas. BBA, Fla. Internat. U., 1980. Adminstrv. asst. Burger King Corp., Miami, 1975-81; pers. mgr. Cen. Bank and Trust, Miami, 1981-83; dir. pers. Holiday Inn, Inc., Miami, 1983-84; various retail positions, 1984-90; retail mgr. J.C. Penney Co., Inc., Miami, 1991—. Mem. bd. dirs. Miami Master Chorale, 1995—; mem. Cultural Coun., Miami, 1991—, DAR, Miami, 1983; dean leader Boy Scouts Am., Miami, 1994—. Republican. United Methodist. Home: 11513 SW 90 Terr Miami FL 33176 Office: JC Penney Co Inc 20505 S Dixie Hwy Miami FL 33189

MCCLEARY, BERYL NOWLIN, civic worker, travel agency executive; b. Ft. Worth, Feb. 22, 1929; d. Henry Bryant and Phyllis (Tenney) Nowlin; m. Henry Glenn McCleary, May 29, 1950; children: Laura Gail, Glenn Nowlin, Neil Ray, Paul Tenney. BS in Zoology, Tex. Tech U., 1950. Owner, mgr. Beryl McCleary Travels, Chicago, 1975-81, Denver, 1981-84. Treas. Kappa Alpha Theta Ednl. Found., Tex. Christian U., Ft. Worth, 1958-61; pres. study club Jr. Woman's Club, Ft. Worth, 1959-60; pres. Symphony League, Ft. Worth, 1961-62; v.p., dir. Ft. Worth Symphony Orch. Assn. Inc., 1961; treas. Jr. Pro-Am Tarrant County, 1961-62; corr. sec. Ft. Worth Children's Mus. Guild, 1961; sec. Tarrant County (Tex.) Democratic Exec. Com., 1956-62; pres. guild, bd. dirs. Maadi Community Ch., Cairo, 1964-66; mem. women's bd. Lincoln Park Zool. Soc., Chgo, 1976-81; mem. Episcopal Ch. Women's Diocesan Bd., Chgo., 1976-79; pres., charter mem. Rainbow Investment Club, London, 1970-71, travel dir. Over the Hill Gang Ski Team Internat., Denver, 1982-84. Mem. AAAS, DAR, Geol. Geophys. Aux., Service Club Chgo., Jr. League Denver, Denver Symphony Guild, Central City Opera Guild, Houston Symphony League, Alpha Epsilon Delta, Kappa Alpha Theta (charter mem. Gamma Phi chpt. 1953). Home: 232 Warrenton Dr Houston TX 77024-6226

MCCLELLAN, ANN ELAINE, elementary education educator; b. Canton, Ohio, July 12, 1953; d. Roy Allen and Margaret Ann (Jones) McClellan; children: David, Sarah, Adam. BS, Miami U., Oxford, Ohio, 1975. Cert. tchr., Ohio. Chpt. I reading tchr. Bolivar (Ohio) Elem. Sch., 1975-79; tchr. remedial reading and 1st grade Clyde Miller Sch., Aurora, Colo., 1983; flight attendant United Airlines, Chgo., 1979-94; tchr. 1st grade St. Paul's Sch., North Canton, Ohio, 1994—. Substitute Sunday sch. tchr. Faith Meth. Ch., North Canton, 1994. Mem. Alpha Lambda Delta. Republican. Methodist. Home: 2185 Beechmoor Dr NW North Canton OH 44720-5853

MCCLELLAND, EMMA L., state legislator; b. Springfield, Mo., Feb. 26, 1940; m. Alan McClelland; children: Mike, Karen. BA, U. Mo., 1962. Dir. field office, corp. divsn. Mo. Sec. of State, St. Louis; committeewoman Gravis Township; mem. St. Louis County Rep. Cent. Com., Mo. Rep. State Com.; mem. Mo. State Ho. Rep., 1991—, mem. appropriations, edn., budget, and mcpl. corps. coms. Bd. dirs. Epworth Children's Home, Family Support Network; elder Webster Groves Presbyn. Ch. Recipient Silver Svc. award Nat. Soc. Autistic Children, Outstanding Svc. award Am. Assn. Mental Deficiency, Spl. Leadership award for govt. YWCA of St. Louis. Mem. Webster Groves C. of C., Pi Lambda Theta. Republican. Presbyterian. Home: 455 Pasadena Ave Webster Grove MO 63119-3126 Office: Mo Ho of Reps State Capitol Building Jefferson City MO 65101-1556

MCCLELLAND, HELEN, music educator; b. Chgo., Dec. 5, 1951; d. Leon Leroy and Willie Jo (Darnell) McC.; (div. Sept. 1981); 1 child, Tasha Renee. Diploma in arts, Kennedy-King Coll., 1971; cert. in voice, Sherwood Music Coll., 1971-73; BS, Chgo. State U., 1975, MA in Adminstrn., 1983; D in Adminstrn. and Supervision, U. Calif., 1993. Tchr. Faulkner Sch., Chgo., 1975-78; tchr. music Harvey (Ill.) Pub. Sch. Dist. 152, 1978—; dir. music Pleasant Green Missionary Bapt. Ch., Chgo., 1971—; mem. sch. bd. New World Christian Acad., Chgo., 1988—; bd.d irs. South Shore Drill Team, Chgo. Author: operetta So You Want to Be a Star, 1987. Cmty. worker People United to Save Humanity, Chgo., 1973, Harold Washington Orgn., Chgo., 1987; cmty. educator Chgo. Planned Parenthood, 1988; cmty. counselor Lincoln Cmty. Ctr., Chgo., 1975; mem. sch. bd. Dist. 160, 1994. Named Tchr. of the Yr., Faulkner Sch., 1976. Mem. Ill. Edn. Assn., NEA, Harvey Edn. Assn., Tennis Club, Traveling Club, Phi Delta Kappa, Pi Lambda Theta. Democrat. Baptist. Home: 18029 Ravisloe Ter Country Club Hills IL 60478-5169

MCCLELLAND, KAMILLA KURODA, news reporter, proofreader, book agent; b. Bozeman, Mont., June 16, 1964; d. Yasumasa and Alice (Kassis) Kuroda; m. Craig Alexander McClelland, June 25, 1989. BA in Asian Studies, U. Calif., Berkeley, 1987; MS in Print News, U. Ill., Champaign-Urbana, 1989. Legis. aide Hawaii State Ho. of Reps., Honolulu, 1987; grad. asst. U. Ill. Dept. Journalism, Champaign, 1987-89; asst. op-ed editor The Daily Illini, Champaign, 1988-89; reporter AP, Seattle, 1989, Tacoma News Tribune, 1989-90; bus. news reporter The Olympian, Olympia, Wash., 1990—; proofreader Minerva Rsch., Inc., Honolulu, 1982—. Vol. Am.-Arab Anti Disc Com., Berkeley, Calif., 1984-87, Capital City Marathon, Olympia, 1993-95, Olympia Symphony, 1996, Black Hills Triathalon, 1993—; active Japanese Am. Citizens League, Honolulu, also Berkeley, 1983-89. Recipient Recognition awards for newswriting Gannett, 1991, 92, 95, 1st Pl., Best of Gannett award for bus. and consumer reporting, 1994, Well Done Bus. Reporting Gannett award, 1995, 2nd place business and consumersGarnnett award, 1995. Mem. Asian Am. Journalists Assn. Office: The Olympian PO Box 407 Olympia WA 98507-0407

MCCLENAHAN, MARY TYLER FREEMAN, civic and community volunteer; b. Richmond, Va., Apr. 6, 1917; d. Douglas Southall and Inez Virginia (Goddin) Freeman; m. Leslie Cheek Jr., June 3, 1939 (dec. Dec. 1992); children: Leslie III, Richard Warfield, Elizabeth Cheek Morgan; m. John Lorimer, Aug. 14, 1993. AB, Vassar Coll., 1937; LHD (hon.), St. Paul's Coll., 1977, Washington and Lee U., 1983, Va. Commonwealth U., 1993, Hollins Coll., 1993; HHD (hon.), U. Richmond, 1985. Author: (religious booklet) Death, The Key to Life, 1982, (hist. booklet, with Alonzo T. Dill) A Visit to Stratford and the Story of the Lees, 1986; (biographical booklet) Douglas Southall Freeman: Reflections By His Daughter, His Research Associates and a Historian, 1986; contbr. articles to mags. Active Robert E. Lee Meml. Assn., Stratford, Va., 1964-95, hon. dir., 1995—; dame, bd. govs. Order of Hosp. St. John, N.Y.C., 1984—; bd. dirs. Maymont Found., 1982—, Va. Cmty. Devel. Corp., 1989—, Trees for Richmond, 1991—, Caucus for Future Ctrl. Va., 1992—, (hon.) Va. League Planned Parenthood (Outstanding Svc. award), 1952—; bd. dirs., exec. com. Richmond Renaissance, 1982-96; former bd. dirs., chair, mem. adv. bd. Coun. Am.'s First Freedom; trustee Va. Union U., Richmond, 1985—, Va. Hist. Soc. (hon.), Black History Mus. and Cultural Ctr. of Va., Hist. Richmond Found.; chair, founder Richmond Better Housing Coalition, 1989—; vice chair Conserve Va., mem. pres.'s coun. So. Environ. Law Ctr.; adv. bd. ARC, 1992—, Christian Children's Fund, 1993-95; adv. com. Girl Scouts U.S., Va; mem. nat. com. Jefferson Poplar Forest Fund. Recipient Mary Mason Anderson Williams Preservation award Assn. Preservation Va. Antiquities, 1977, Barbara Ransome Andrews disting. vol. award Jr. League Richmond, 1982, Fair Housing award Housing Opportunities Made Equal, 1983, Brotherhood award Nat. Conf. Christians and Jews, 1983, Human Rels. award, 1984, Ten Outstanding Women award YWCA-Richmond, 1986, Sallie Wilson Peake Meml. award Housing Opportunities Made Equal, 1987, Charlotte J. Washington cmty. svc, award Richmond Urban League, 1988, Archtl. medal Am. Inst. Architects, 1991, Liberty Bell award Richmond Bar Assn., 1991, Faith in Action award Va. Coun. Churches, 1992, Outstanding Citizen award Civitan Club, 1992, Hope award Nat. Multiple Sclerosis, 1994; named Richmonder of Yr. STYLE mag., 1990, Va. Women Hall Fame Va. Coun. on Status Women, 1991. Mem., founder, chair (hon.) Richmond Urban Forum; mem. Women's Club of Richmond, Cosmopolitan Club, The Acorn Club of Phila., Hroswitha Club, James River Garden Club, Va. Writer's Club, Richmond First Club (Good Govt. award, 1987), Omicron Delta Kappa, Phi Beta Kappa. Democrat. Episcopalian. Home: 4703 Pocahontas Ave Richmond VA 23226

MCCLENDON, MAXINE, artist; b. Leesville, La., Oct. 21, 1931; d. Alfred Harry and Clara (Jackson) McMillan; student Tex. U., 1948-50, Tex. Woman's U., 1950-51, Pan Am. U., 1963-64; m. Edward Edson Nichols, Mar. 28, 1967; children—Patricia Ann, Joan Terri, Christopher, Jennifer. Instr. McAllen Internat. Mus., 1987-90, in studio, Mission, Tex., 1990—. One-woman shows include: Art Mus. S. Tex., Corpus Christi, 1971, McAllen (Tex.) Internat. Mus., 1976, Amarillo (Tex.) Art Center, 1982, U. Tex., Pan American, 1994; group shows in Wichita, Kans., 1972, Marietta, Ohio, 1975, Dallas, 1977; represented in permanent collections: Mus. Internat. Folk Art, Santa Fe, Ark. Mus. Fine Art, Little Rock, McAllen Internat. Mus., Lauren Rogers Mus., Laurel, Miss.; commns. include: Caterpillar Corp., Peoria, Ill., Union Bank Switzerland, N.Y.C., Crocker Bank, Los Angeles, Tarleton U., Tex., Hyatt Regency, Ft. Worth Forbes Inc., San Francisco, First Savs. & Loan, Shreveport, La., Continental Plaza, Ft. Worth. curator Mexican folk art McAllen Internat. s., 1974-80. Recipient judges award 4th Nat. Marietta, 1975, numerous others. Mem. World Crafts Council, Am. Crafts Council (Tex. rep. 1976-80), Tex. Designer/Craftsmen (pres. 1973-74). Christian Scientist. Home and Studio: 2018 Sharyland St Mission TX 78572

MCCLENDON, SARAH NEWCOMB, news service executive, writer; b. Tyler, Tex., July 8, 1910; d. Sidney Smith and Annie Rebecca (Bonner) McClendon; 1 child, Sally Newcomb Mac Donald. Grad., Tyler Jr. Coll., U. Mo. Mem. staff Tyler Courier-Times and Tyler Morning Telegraph, 1931-39; reporter Beaumont (Tex.) Enterprise; Washington corr. Phila. Daily News, 1944; founder McClendon News Svc., Washington, 1946—; talk show host Ind. Broadcasters Network; lectr. Faneuil Hall, Boston, Poor Richard's Club, Phila., Cobo Hall, Detroit, Chautauqua Instn., N.Y., Comstock Club, Sacremento; adv. to Senior Beacon; v.p. Nat. Press Club. Author: My Eight Presidents, 1978 (1st prize); contbr. articles to mags. including Esquire, Penthouse, Diplomat; TV appearances include Merv Griffin Show, Tomorrow, Inside the White House, PBS, NBC Meet the Press, KUP Show, NBC Today Show, C-Span, CNN, Fox Morning News, Late Night with David Letterman, Michael Jackson Show (L.A. radio). Mem. VA Adv. Bd. on Women Vets, def. adv. com. Women in the Svcs.; army advisor, mem. task force Women in the Army Policy Rev.; bd. dir. Sam Rayburn Libr., In Our Own Way, So. Poverty Relief Orgn. Served with WAC. Recipient Woman of Achievement award Tex. Press Women, 1978, 2d prize Nat. Fedn. Press Women, 1979, Headliner award Women in Comm., 1st Pres. award for Journalism in Washington, Nat. Fedn. Press Women, Pub. Rels. award Am. Legion, Bob Considine award, 1990, Am. Woman award Women's Rsch. Edn. Inst., 1991. Mem. DAR (Nat. Constn. award 1990), U. Mo. Alumni Assn. (chpt. pres.), Women in Comm. (Margaret Caskey award), Am. Legion (post comdr.), Nat. Woman's Party (v.p.), Nat. Coun., Soc. Profl. Journalists (Hall of Fame Washington chpt.), Nat. Press Club (v.p.), Am. Newspaper Women's Club (pres.), Capitol Hill First Friday Club (pres.). Club: Capitol Hill First Friday (pres.).

MCCLENNEN, MIRIAM J., former state official; b. Seattle, Sept. 16, 1923; d. Phillip and Frieda (Golub) Jacobs; m. Louis McClennen, Apr. 25, 1969; stepchildren: Peter Adams, James C.A., Helen, Persis, Crane, Emery. BA,

U. Wash., 1945; MBA, Northwestern U., 1947. Exec. trainee Marshall Field & Co., Chgo., 1945-47; asst. buyer Frederick & Nelson (subs. of Marshall Field), Seattle, 1947-49; buyer Frederick & Nelson (subs. of Marshall Field), 1949-57; fashion coordinator, buyer Levy Bros., Burlingame/San Mateo, Calif., 1957-63; buyer Goldwaters, Phoenix, 1963-67; adminstrv. asst. to pres. Ariz. State Senate, Phoenix, 1973-76; dir. publs. Office of Sec. of State, Phoenix, 1976-87; chairwoman legis. subcom. adminstrv. procedure Ariz. State Legislature, Phoenix, 1984-85. Original compiler, codifier, editor publ. Ariz. Adminstrv. Code, 1973-87, Ariz. Adminstrv. Register, 1976-87. Bd. dirs., mem. Phoenix Art Mus. League, 1972-90; mem. exec. bd. Phoenix Symphony Guild, 1969-88; bd. dirs., sec. Combined Met. Phoenix Arts and Scis., 1974-90, mem. adv. bd., 1990-95; bd. dirs. Phoenix Art Coun., 1973-78, Master Apprentice Programs, 1980-83; bd. dirs., mem. exec. com. Heard Mus., 1982-88, 90—, chmn. publs. com., 1982-88, chmn. exhibit and edn. com., 1990-93; mem. adv. bd. Ariz. State Hist. Records, 1987-90, Ariz. Commn. on Arts, 1989-96, Phoenix Art Mus., 1966—, dir.'s circle, 1988—; bd. dirs. Arizonans for Cultural Devel., 1996—. Recipient Disting. Svc. award Atty. Gen. Ariz., 1987, Outstanding Svc. to People, Ariz. State Senate, 1987, Nat. Assn. Secs. of State award, 1987. Mem. English Speaking Union, Nat. Soc. Arts and Letters, Charter 100 (bd. dirs. 1981-85), Phoenix County Club, Ariz. Club, Eastward Ho! Country Club (Chatham, Mass.). Home: 5311 N La Plaza Cir Phoenix AZ 85012-1415 Address: 2267 Orleans Rd Chatham MA 02633

MCCLINTOCK, JESSICA, fashion designer; b. Frenchville, Maine, June 19, 1930; d. Rene Gagnon and Verna Hedrich; m. Frank Staples (dec. 1964); 1 child Scott. BA, San Jose State U., 1963. Elem. sch. tchr. Marblehead, Mass., 1966-68, Long Island, N.Y., 1968, Sunnyvale, Calif., 1964-65, 68-69; fashion designer Jessica McClintock, Inc., San Francisco, 1969—. Active donor, AIDS and Homeless programs; scholarship sponsor Fashion Inst. Design and Merchandising. Recipient Merit award Design, 1989, Dallas Fashion award, 1988, Tommy award, 1986, Pres. Appreciation award, 1986, Best Interior Store Design, 1986, Calif. Designer award, 1985, Earnie award, 1981, numerous others. Mem. Coun. Fashion Designers of Am., Fashion Inst. Design & Merchandising (adv. bd. 1979—), San Francisco Fashion Industry (pres. 1976-78, bd. dirs. 1989). Office: Jessica McClintock Inc 1400 16th St San Francisco CA 94103-5110

MCCLINTOCK, SANDRA JANISE, writer, editor; b. Connersville, Ind., July 28, 1938; d. Owen Dale and Mary Janis (Tierney) M.; m. Harvey Miles Garrison, Jr., Aug. 1, 1959 (div. 1967); children: Heidi, Katherine, H. Miles III; m. Joseph Lloyd Fagen, May 15, 1969; 1 child, Adam Joseph. BA, Drake U., 1960; postgrad., Calif. State U., Fullerton, 1966-67; cert., Am. Grad. U., 1987. Lic. gen. contractor. Coord. copy desk Time Mag., N.Y.C., 1960-62; mem. graphics prodn. staff Times-Mirror Co., L.A., 1962-64; mgr. prodn. Miller Freeman Publs., Long Beach, Calif., 1964-68; supr. Design Svc., Anaheim, Calif., 1968-73; prin. Fagen Graphics, Long Beach, 1973-77, Palomar Publs., Ranchita, Calif., 1977-84; cons. Cons. & Designers, Anaheim, 1984-87; mgr. publs. Tracor Flight Systems, Inc., Santa Ana, Calif., 1987-88; coord. publs. Rockwell Internat. Corp., Anaheim, 1988-92; dir. comms. Terra Christa Comms., Tucson, 1992-93; tech. writer CH2M Hill, Santa Ana, Calif., 1993—; cons. Aerotest, Inc., Mojave, Calif., 1986, Voice Telecom Corp., Laguna Beach, Calif., 1986. Editor: Psychopharmacology, 1984, Joseph of Aramathea, 1982, Who is Who at the Earth Summit, 1992; guest editor Interface Age mag., 1976; contbg. editor Rockwell News in U.S. and Can., 1988. Bd. dirs. Vol. Fire Dept., Ranchita, 1979; fund raiser Dem. candidate Calif. Assembly, Orange county, 1964. Mem. NAFE, Nat. Mgmt. Assn., So. Calif. Astrological Network, Amnesty Internat. Mem. Religious Sci. Ch. Home: 2607 Solana Way # 7 Laguna Beach CA 92651-3957

MCCLINTON, JOANN, state legislator; m. Emory McClinton; 3 children. Grad., Washington High Sch. State rep., mem. children & youth, human rels., aging, state planning, cmty. affairs coms. Ga. House of Reps., Atlanta, 1992—. Democrat. Office: Ga House of Reps State Capitol SE Atlanta GA 30334*

MCCLOUD, PATRICIA CAROLYN KAISER, nurse educator; b. Dayton, Aug. 23, 1945; d. Leonard George and Dorothy Carolyn Louise (Klawuhn) K.; divorced; children: Scott William, Aaron Leonard, Brook Elizabeth Dorothy. Student, Washtenaw C.C., 1967; diploma magna cum laude, Mercy Sch. Nursing, 1969; BSN, U. Mich., 1975, MS, 1977. Staff nurse dept. obstet. St. Joseph Mercy Hosp., Ann Arbor, Mich., 1970-75, staff and evening charge nurse dept. obstet., 1975; from tchg. asst. to asst. prof. parent child nursing U. Mich., Ann Arbor, 1975-81; instr. dept. nursing Washtenaw C.C., Ann Arbor, 1988-90; lectr. divsn. acute, critical-long term care programs U. Mich. Sch. Nursing, Ann Arbor, 1991-92, lectr., course coord. divsn. acute, critical-long term care, 1992—; camp nurse Interlochen Ctr. for the Arts, summer, 1993-94; adj. faculty Concordia Coll., Ann Arbor, 1991-94; instr., cons. Nursing Edn. Consortium, Ann Arbor, 1994-95; instr. nursing Eastern Mich. U., Ypsilanti, Mich., summer, 1977; presenter in field. Contbr. articles to profl. jours. Co-chair benefit auction acquisitions com. Greenhills Sch., 1991—; choir coord. Ann Arbor Youth Chorale, 1992; choral mgr., bd. dirs. Boychoir of Ann Arbor, 1989-91, events coord., 1990-91; vol. March of Dimes, 1991, Arthritis Found., 1994, Martin Luther King Jr. Sch., 1984-93; mgr. Summer Youth League Baseball, 1983-93; founder, block capt. Neighborhood Watch, 1982-94; co-leader Girl Scouts Am., 1992-93; pres. Ann Arbor Suzuki Inst., 1984-85, bd. dirs., 1982-84, dir. ann. workshop, 1984-85, chair fundraising com., 1982-83; choral asst., substitute tchr., Law Montessori Sch., 1988-89; dir. religious edn. St. Lukes Episcopal Ch., coord. vol. svcs., health fair com., 1989. Shirley C. Titus scholar U. Mich.; recipient Faculty Rsch. Publ. award U. Mich. Mem. U. Musical Soc. (cheers and encore, choral union, festival chorus 1984—). Episcopalian. Office: Univ Mich Sch Nursing 2177 Sch Nursing Bldg 400 N Ingalls St Ann Arbor MI 48109

MCCLUNG, CHRISTINA, instructional design company executive; b. Newark, Jan. 19, 1948; d. Fred and Maria (Dallinger) Palensar; m. Ken McClung, Mar. 21, 1975. BA, Kean Coll., 1970; MS, Seton Hall U., 1973; EdD, U. So. Calif., L.A., 1976. Team leader Chatham (N.J.) Twp. Sch., 1970-74; instrnl. designer Tratec Inc., L.A., 1976-78; prof. Lehman Coll., Bronx, N.Y., 1978-80; sr. ptnr. Instrnl. Design Group, Morristown, N.J., 1981—. Mem. ASTD, Internat. Soc. Performance Instrn. (track chair 1994-96), Soc. Alt. Learning Techniques. Office: Instrnl Design Group 144 Speedwell Ave Morristown NJ 07960

MCCLUNG, GINGER LEE, interior designer; b. Ft. Worth, Nov. 18, 1947; d. Carlos B. and Anna Beatrice (Smith) Mathews; m. Richard William McClung, July 15, 1978; 1 child, John Patrick. BFA, U. Tex., Arlington, 1973. Registered interior designer, Tex. Interior designer S & A Restaurants, Dallas, 1973-78, S.A.G.A., Seattle, 1979; interior designer, asst. scenic designer Peter Wolf Concepts, Dallas, 1979-84; sr. interior designer Club Desing Inc., Dallas, 1984-90; sr. interior designer, computer mgr. Media Five, Honolulu, 1991; fine artist, restaurant designer McClung Studio, Rockwall, Tex., 1992-94; design dir. Feizy Import & Export Co., Dallas, 1995—; interior designer S.A.G.A., Seattle, 1979; party designer Mayor's Internat. Ball, Dallas, 1984, P.A.W.S. Ball, Dallas, 1984; interior designer/project mgr. Bankers Club, Miami, Fla., 1990, Frito Lay Learning Ctr., Plano, Tex., 1984; interior designer Rafters, Portland, Oreg., 1977; dir. renovation Club Corp. Internat., Inc., Dallas, 1985,90. Bd. dirs. Assn. Hawaii Artists, Honolulu, 1992. Mem. Internat. Interior Design Assn., Color Mktg. Group. Office: Feizy Import & Export Co 1949 Stemmons Fwy Dallas TX 75207

MCCLURE, ANN CRAWFORD, lawyer; b. Cin., Sept. 5, 1953; d. William Edward and Patricia Ann (Jewett) Crawford; m. David R. McClure, Nov. 12, 1983; children: Kinsey Tristen, Scott Crawford. BFA magna cum laude, Tex. Christian U., 1974; JD, U. Houston, 1979. Bd. cert. in family law and civil appellate law Tex. Bd. Legal Specialization. Assoc. Piro and Lilly, Houston, 1979-83; pvt. practice El Paso, Tex., 1983-92; ptnr. McClure and McClure, El Paso, 1992-94; justice Eighth Ct. of Appeals, El Paso, 1995—; former mem. Tex. Bd. Law Examiners, Bd. Disciplinary Appeals; mem. Family Law Specialization Exam Com., 1989-93. Contbr. numerous articles to profl. jours.; past editor The Family Law Forum; contbg. editor: Texas Family Law Service; mem. Tex. Family Law Practice Manual editl. com., 1982-93. Mem. State Bar Tex. (dir. Family Law Coun. 1987-91, treas. family law sect. 1993-94, sec. family law sect. 1994-95, vice chair family law sect. 1995-96, chair-elect family law sect. 1996—, treas. appellate & advocacy sect. coun. 1996—), Tex. Acad. Family Law Specialists (past dir.). Democrat. Presbyterian.

MCCLURE, NANCY LYNNE, charitable organization executive; b. Clearfield, Pa., Sept. 23, 1965; d. Charles John McClure and Ruthann (Raleigh) Wighaman. BA in Psychology and Comm., Westminster Coll., New Wilmington, Pa., 1987. County crime reporter Progressive Pub. Co., Clearfield, 1987-88; field mgr. Am. Heart Assn., Clearfield, 1988-89; exec. dir. Clearfield Area United Way, 1989—; Mem. Pa. Small United Ways Task Force, 1991-93; mem. planning com. United Way Pa. Staff Leadership Conf., 1992; mem. N.E. regional coun. United Way Am., 1995-96. Pub. info. officer Clearfield County Emergency Mgmt., 1988—; vol. Big Bros. and Big Sisters, 1993—. Scholar Nat. Acad. Voluntarism, 1990; scholar United Way Pa., 1992, Al Rojohn Meml. scholar, 1994. Mem. AAUW, Rotary (bull. editor Clearfield 1990—, bd. dirs. 1992-94). Republican. Presbyterian. Office: Clearfield Area United Way 121 E Market St Clearfield PA 16830

MCCLURE, VERONICA ANN, elementary education educator; b. Muskogee, Okla., Mar. 3, 1952; d. Raymond Frederick and Veronica Alexina (Gillis) McGee; m. Gary Jerome McClure Sr., Dec. 26, 1971; children: Gary J., Bruce, Jeremy. BS in Edn., Northeastern State U., 1976, MEd in Counseling, 1978. Sch. counselor Cherokee Elem., Tahlequah, Okla., 1978-82; tchr. Greenwood Elem., Tahlequah, 1982-92; tchr., chairperson lang. arts dept. Ctrl. Elem., Tahlequah, 1993—; SOS sch. counselor Tahlequah Jr. H.S., 1996; Gesell test adminstr. Tahlequah (Okla.) Pub. Schs., 1980-94; educator Indian edn. J.O.M. Summer Sch., Tahlequah, 1987-94. Aide to Edn. grantee Elks Lodge, Tahlequah, 1991-94. Mem. NEA, Okla. Edn. Assn., Internat. Reading Assn. Home: PO Box 432 Tahlequah OK 74465-0432

MCCLURE-BIBBY, MARY ANNE, former state legislator; b. Milbank, S.D., Apr. 21, 1939; d. Charles Cornelius and Mary Lucille (Whittom) Burges; m. D.J. McClure, Nov. 17, 1963 (dec. Apr. 1990); 1 child, Kelly Joanne Kyro; m. John E. Bibby, May 1, 1993. BA magna cum laude, U. S.D., 1961; postgrad., U. Manchester, Eng., 1961-62; M of Pub. Adminstrn., Syracuse (N.Y.) U., 1980. Staff asst. U.S. Senator Francis Case, Washington, 1959-61; sec. to lt. gov. State of S.D., Pierre, 1963, with budget office, 1964; exec. sec. to pres. Frontier Airlines, Denver, 1963-64; tchr. Pub. High Schs., Pierre and Redfield, S.D., 1965-66, 68-70; mem. S.D. State Senate, Pierre, 1975-89, pres. pro tem, 1979-89, vice chmn. coun. of state govts., 1987, chmn. coun. of state govts., 1988; spl. asst. to Pres. Bush for intergovernmental affairs, 1989-92; exec. dir. S.D. Bush-Quayle Campaign, 1992. Vice chmn. sch. bd. Redfield Ind. Sch. Dist., 1970-74. Fulbright scholar, 1961-62, Bush Leadership fellow, 1977-80. Mem. Phi Beta Kappa. Republican. Congregationalist. Home: 817 8th Ave Brookings SD 57006-1315

MCCLURG, PATRICIA A., minister; b. Bay City, Tex., Mar. 14, 1939; d. T.H. and Margaret (Smith) McC. BA, Austin Coll., 1961; M in Christian Edn., Presbyn. Sch. of Christian Edn., 1963; BD, Austin Presbyn. Theol. Sem., 1967; postgrad., So. Meth. U., 1971-73; DD (hon.), Austin Coll., 1978. Dir. Christian edn. 2d Presbyn. Ch., Newport News, Va., 1963-65; asst. pastor Westminster Presbyn. Ch., Beaumont, Tex., 1967-71; assoc. pastor 1st Presbyn. Ch., Pasadena, Tex., 1969-71; assoc. exec. Synod of Red River, Denton, Tex., 1973-75; dir. gen. assembly mission bd. Presbyn. Ch., Atlanta, 1975-86; assoc. exec. for mission The Presbytery of Elizabeth, Plainfield, N.J., 1986-91; exec. Presbyter of New Castle, Newark, Del., 1992—; pres. Nat. Coun. Chs. of Christ in the U.S.A., N.Y.C., 1988-89, v.p., 1985-87; del., budget com. chmn. World Coun. Chs. Assembly, Vancouver, Can., 1985; sect. leader World Coun. Chs. Mission and Evang. Confs., Melbourne, Australia, 1980. Contbr. articles to prof. jours. Mem. chs. spl. commn. on South Africa, N.Y.C., 1985—, Anti-Pollution Campaign, Pasadena, 1970. Recipient Disting. Alumni award Austin Coll., 1979. Democrat. Presbyterian. Lodge: Rotary. *

MCCLUSKEY, LOIS THORNHILL, photographer; b. Boston, Apr. 7, 1945; d. Fred S. and Mary (Evans) T.; BA, Middlebury Coll., 1966; postgrad. U. St. Thomas, Houston, 1967-69; MA, NYU, 1971; cert. in graphic design U. Calif.-Santa Cruz, 1983; m. Edward J. McCluskey, Feb. 14, 1981. Research technician dept. virology Baylor Sch. Medicine, Houston, 1966-68; with Kelly Girls, Palo Alto, 1971-72; slide curator dept. art Stanford (Calif.) U., 1972-80; founder, pres. Stanford Design Assocs., Palo Alto, 1981—; cons. copy and museum photography; designer, producer custom lecture slides. Mem. Smithsonian Assos. Home: 895 Northampton Dr Palo Alto CA 94303-3434 Office: PO Box 60451 Palo Alto CA 94306-0451

MCCLYMONDS, JEAN ELLEN, marketing professional; b. Richmond, Calif.; d. Rollin John Lepley and Doris Ellen Baughman; m. Gareth Lynn McClymonds, Sept. 18, 1981. BS in Edn., U. Calif., Berkeley, 1970; M Bus. Communications, San Jose State U., 1987. Adminstr. sales Dohrmann Div. Envirotech, Santa Clara, Calif., 1970-74; supr. order processing Molectron Corp., Sunnyvale, Calif., 1974-79; mgr. mktg. svcs. Gould-Biomation, Santa Clara, 1979-84; dir. corp. communications Madic Corp., Santa Clara, 1984-86; dir. mktg. nat. accounts Skyway Freight Systems, Inc., Watsonville, Calif., 1986-89; pres. Just Mktg., Scotts Valley, Calif., 1989—; pub. speaker various local orgns., 1984—. Contbr. articles industry jours., 1986—. Mem. Am. Trucking Assn. (dir.-at-large 1996, outstanding achievement award 1996), Bus. Profl. Advt. Assn., Nat. Assn. Quality Control, Peninsula Mktg. Assn., Coun. Logistics Mgmt., San Jose Women in Bus. Republican. Office: 5524 Scotts Valley Dr Ste 21 Scotts Valley CA 95066-3464

MCCOLLUM, BETTY, state legislator; b. July 12, 1954; m. Douglas McCollum; 2 children. BS in Edn., Coll. St. Catherine. Retail store mgr. Minn.; mem. Minn. Ho. Reps., 1992—, mem. edn. com., environ. and natural resources com., mem. gen. legis. com., vet. affairs and elections com., mem. transportation and transit com., asst. majority leader, chair Legis. Commn. on Econ. Status of Women. Mem. St. Croix Valley Coun. Girl Scouts, Greater East Side Boy Scouts. Democrat. Home: 2668 4th Ave E North Saint Paul MN 55109-3116 Office: Minn Ho of Reps State Office Bldg 100 Constitution Ave Rm 501 Saint Paul MN 55155-1606

MCCOLLUM, JEAN HUBBLE, medical assistant; b. Peoria, Ill., Oct. 21, 1934; d. Claude Ambrose and Josephine Mildred (Beiter) Hubble; m. Everett Monroe Patton, Sept. 4, 1960 (div. Jan. 1969); 1 child, Linda Joanne; m. James Ward McCollum, Jan. 2, 1971; 1 child, Steven Ward. Student, Bradley U., Ill. Cen. Coll. Stenographer Caterpillar Tractor Co., Peoria, 1952-53, supr. stenographer pool, 1953-55, adminstrv. sec., treas., 1955-60, sec., asst. dept. mgr., 1969-71; med. staff sec. Proctor Cmty. Hosp., Peoria, 1978-82; med. asst. Drs. Taylor, Fox and Morgan, Peoria, 1982-84; freelance med. asst. Meth. Hosp. and numerous physicians, Peoria, 1984-89; office mgr. Dr. Danehower, McLelland and Stone, Peoria, 1989—. Vol. tutor Northmoor Sch., Peoria, 1974-78; bd. dirs., mem. exec. com., com. chmn. Planned Parenthood, Peoria, 1990-92. Recipient Outstanding Performance award Proctor Hosp., 1981, also various awards for svc. to schs., ch. and hosps. for mentally ill. Mem. Nat. Wildlife Fedn., Mensa Internat. (publs. officer, editor 1987-89), Mothers League (treas. 1977), Willow Knolls Country Club (social com. 1989-90), Nature Conservancy, World Wildlife Fund, Forest Park Found., Jacques Cousteau Soc., Wilderness Soc. Methodist. Home: 228 W Pine Hill Ln Peoria IL 61614-3256

MCCOMB, KARLA JOANN, educational curriculum and instruction administrator, consultant; b. Tacoma, July 23, 1937; d. John Frank and Lorraine Beatrice (Winters) Bohac; m. Russell Marshall McComb, Nov. 27, 1959 (div.); children: Marsha McComb Hayes, Kathleen McComb Bridge. Cert. instr. French, U. Paris, 1958; BA, Calif. State U.-Sacramento, 1960; MS, Nova U., 1984. Cert. secondary tchr., Nev. Tchr. French and music Sacramento Waldorf Sch., 1960-62; tchr. French, Red Bluff High Sch., 1967-68; tchr. French and music Pocatello (Idaho) Schs., 1969-71; tchr., chairperson dept. Clark County Sch. Dist., 1971-76; curriculum cons. social sci., fgn. lang., profl. growth, Las Vegas, 1976-84; cons. staff devel. and profl. growth, 1984-91, dir. staff devel., multicultural edn. and substance abuse edn., 1991-93, dir. multicultural edn., substance abuse edn., 1993—; cons. Taft Inst. Govt., Salt Lake City, 1977—, Tchr. Inservice, Follett Pub. Co., 1980-81; author: A Cultural Celebration, 1980, Project MCE: Multicultural Education in the Clark County School District, 1992; editor The Nevada Holocaust Curriculum, 1987. Coordinator Nev. Close-Up Program, 1980-88. Mem. Sacramento Symphony Orch., 1954-66, Nev. Humanities Com., Nev. commn. Holocaust; pres., bd. dirs. Ctr. Ind. Living, 1995—; v.p. Nev. Assn. Handicapped, 1994—; bd. dirs. Love All People Youth Group, supt. Love All People Sch., 1983—, producer staff devel. films, 1986—; v.p., bd. dirs. Nev. Assn. Handicapped, pres., bd. dirs. Ctr. Ind. Living. Mem. Clark County Fgn. Lang. Tchrs. Assn. (pres.), Nat. Council Social Studies, Social Studies Suprs. Assn., Nev. Fgn. Lang. Tchrs. Assn. (pres., Outstanding Humanities Nevadan 1994), AAUW, Phi Theta Kappa, Mu Phi Epsilon, Alpha Delta Kappa, Phi Delta Kappa. Democrat. Clubs: Vegas Valley Dog Obedience (pres.), Jackpot Obedience Assn. (pres.). Home: 409 N Lamb Blvd # A Las Vegas NV 89110-3370 Office: 601 N 9th St Las Vegas NV 89101-2505

MCCONE, JACQUELINE PATRICIA, real estate executive; b. Bridgeport, Conn., Oct. 4, 1953; d. Thomas Pershing and Irene Virginia (Good) McCone; m. R. Alan Doan, May 2, 1992. BS in Edn., North Tex. State U., 1974, MEd, 1976. Lic. real estate broker, Tex. Reservation salesperson Delta Air Lines, Dallas, 1978-84; loan officer Great Am. Funding, Dallas, 1984-86; sr. cons. Ferguson & Co., Dallas, 1986-87; regulatory examiner Fed. Home Loan Bank, Dallas, 1987-88; asst. v.p. LSunbelt Savs., Dallas, 1988-89; pres. MD & Assocs., Inc., Dallas, 1990—. Sec. fin. coun. St. Monica Ch., Dallas, 1992—. Mem. Greater Dallas Assn. Realtors. Roman Catholic. Office: MD & Associates Inc Ste 245 17311 Dallas Pky Dallas TX 75248

MCCONNELL, BARBARA ANN ROGERS, accounting manager; b. Pelzer, S.C., July 27, 1939; d. Walter Herbert and Genav (Garrett) Rogers; 1 child, William D. Jr.; m. William Dendy McConnell, Aug. 24, 1957. AAS, Greenville Tech. Coll., 1973; B of Gen. Studies magna cum laude, U. S.C., 1975, MBA, 1986. CPA, N.C. Gen. acct. J. P. Stevens & Co., Greenville, S.C., 1975-77; acctg. mgr. Reliance Electric Co., Greenville, S.C., 1977-81; fin. analyst Digital Equip. Corp., Greenville, S.C., 1981-83, cost acct., 1983-86, planning analyst, 1986-88, planning mgr., 1988-92; dir. cost acctg. London Internat. U.S. Holdings, Inc., 1993-94; fin. mgr. Motorola, Inc., Lawrenceville, Ga., 1994—. Mem. AAUW (coalition bds. and commns. 1981), Nat. Assn. Accts., Order of Ea. Star (worthy matron 1978), Am. Legion (pres. 1977).

MCCONNELL, CELESTE ANDREA, English educator; b. Bklyn., July 25, 1952; d. Carmelo Vincent and Dolores Ruth (Quinn) Pernicone; m. Herbert David Friedman, Dec. 22, 1973 (div. Mar. 1981); 1 child, Eric Brian; m. Frank DeMay McConnell, Oct. 5, 1985. AA, Pierce C.C., 1973; BA, U. Calif., 1982, MA, 1985. Page, adminstrv. asst. CBS TV, L.A., 1972-77; writing coach, instr. U. Calif., Santa Barbara, 1983-88; English instr. Santa Barbara City Coll., 1995—. Mem. Mobile Home Rent Stabilization Bd., Lompoc, Calif., 1993—; pres. Lompoc Valley NOW, 1991-93. Roman Catholic. Home: 501 South R St Lompoc CA 93436

MCCONNELL, JUDITH LEE MILLER, social services administrator; b. Longview, Wash., Oct. 14, 1942; d. Wilbert Wayne and Virginia Lee (Wagner) Doble; m. Alan William Miller, Oct. 14, 1961 (div. May 1979); children: Scott, Susan, Brian; m. Conrad Peter McConnell, Jan. 4, 1992. BS in Social Scis., Western Oreg. State Coll., 1979; MPA, Harvard U., 1984. Com. asst. Oreg. Ho. of Reps., Salem, 1973-79; govt. liaison officer Ctrl. Lincoln Pub. Utility Dist., Newport, Oreg., 1980-84; program coord. light dept. City of Seattle, 1985-86, pub. info. officer water dept., 1986-92; exec. dir. Seattle Cmty. Youth at Risk, 1992—. Chmn. Polk County (Oreg.) Dem. Com., 1969-71; del. Dem. Nat. Conv., 1972; vice chmn. Dem. Com. Oreg., 1975-76; mem. Monmouth (Oreg.) City Coun., 1975-79; bd. dirs. Polk Adolescent Day Treatment Ctr., Dallas, Oreg., 1981-83. Mem. AAUW, Harvard-Radcliffe Club. Home: 5644 36th Ave SW Seattle WA 98126

MCCONNELL, LORELEI CATHERINE, library director; b. Port Jefferson, N.Y., Dec. 5, 1938; d. Alvin and Mary (McConnell) Philibert; m. Thomas McConnell, Jan. 20, 1962; children: Catherine, Michael. BA, Drew U., 1960; MLS, Rutgers U., 1963. Reference libr. Irvington (N.J.) Pub. Libr., 1963-90, dir., 1990—; founder Irvington Literacy Program, 1986, dir., 1986-90. Mem. ALA, N.J. Libr. Assn. (mem. exec. bd. 1990-93, N.J. Libr. of Yr. 1993-94), Irvington (N.J.) C. of C. (exec. bd. 1992—, Civic award 1996), Internat. Primal Assn., Beta Phi Mu. Home: 563 Park St Montclair NJ 07043-2027 Office: Irvington Pub Libr Civic Sq Irvington NJ 07111

MCCONNELL, PATRICIA ANN, health facility administrator; b. Bklyn., Feb. 28; d. Philip P. and Dagney C. (Petersen) Powers; m. Alexander McConnell, Jan. 15; children: Francis X., Robert M., Bonnie J., Douglas P. AAS in Nursing, Milw. Area Tech. Coll., Milw., 1978; student, U. Wis., 1980; BA, Nat. Lewis U., 1989. RN, Ill., Ind., Wis., Inc.; registered profl. nurse; cert. case mgr.; cert. pain mgr.; cert. ins. rehab. specialist; cert. occupational hearing conservationalist. Nurse, oncology dept. St. Luke's Hosp., Milw., 1976-79; supr. employee health dept. Harnisfeger P&H, Cudahy, Wis., 1979-82; staff nurse employee health dept. 1st Wis. Nat. Bank, Milw., 1982-83; med. svcs. cons. Crawford Risk Mgmt. Svcs., Schaumburg, Ill., 1983-86; case mgmt. specialist Nat. Rehab. Cons., Westmont, Ill., 1986-87; pres., dir. Mid-State Health and Rehab., Westmont, 1987—; bd. dirs. Women in Workers Compnsation of Ill., vice chmn. 1993-94, sponsor chair 1994-95. Founding mem. Rape Recovery Project Hot Line, vol. support group, Chgo., 1989—, bd. dirs. 1990—; active Ill. Coalition Against Sexual Assault, 1990; vol. literacy tutor World Relief Orgn. and Literacy Vols. Am., 1990—; den mother Cubs, Boy Scouts of Am., 1966-68; health and safety svcs. instr. ARC, 1993-94; religion instr. St. Helena Cath. Ch., Greendale, Wis. 1973-75. Mem. LWV, Am. Assn. Occupational Health Nurses Group (treas. 1990-91, pres. 1992-93), Assn. Rehab. Nurses, Am. Acad. Pain Mgmt. (clin. assoc. 1991—), Assn. Vocat. Rehabilitationists in Ill., Women in Workers Compensation of Ill. (mem. bd. 1993-96), Oak Brook Assn. Commerce and Industry (small bus. com. 1989-90), Dolton Regional Hosp. Aux. (charter, nominating com., publicity chair 1965), Women in Mgmt. (hospitality chair). Roman Catholic. Home: 821 Oakwood Dr Westmont IL 60559-1035 Office: 504A E Ogden Ave Ste 249 Westmont IL 60559-1228

MCCONNELL, PATRICIA LYNN, vocational consultant; b. Denver, Feb. 20, 1956; d. James Donald and Joyce Clemence (Wortman) McC.; m. Roger Tribble, 1989. BS, U. No. Colo., 1979. Mental health worker Arapahoe Mental Health Ctr., Littleton, Colo., 1977-79; work adjustment cons. recycling ctr. City of El Cerrito (Calif.), 1980-83; job developer, ind. contractor with Dept. of Rehab., Pleasant Hill, Calif., San Pablo, Vallejo, Calif., 1983-87; vocat. rehab. cons. Guitterez & Co., Oakland, Calif., 1987-89; owner, vocat. cons. JobPerfect, Berkeley, Calif., 1989—; owner, fundraiser Community Svcs. Mktg., Oakland; workshop leader Calif. Dept. of Rehab., Pleasant Hill, 1983-87, San Pablo, 1989. Author: (workbook) Job Search for the Disabled, 1985, JobPerfect Job Search manual Datebook and Organizer, 1995; dir., producer (video) JobPerfect, 1992, How To Improve Your Communication and Interview Skills, 1994, JobPerfect Job Search, 1995, Legacies, 1995; creator, producer (cable show) A Good Book to Live In, 1996, Homecare, 1996. Mem., fundraiser No. Calif. Recyclers Assn., Berkeley, 1982-87, Calif. Marine Mammal Ctr., Marine Headlands, Calif., 1987-90, Bay Area Cmty. Svcs., 1993—. Recipient Dance award Englewood High Sch., Colo., 1974, Appreciation award Regional Occupational Program, San Pablo, 1989. Mem. Calif. Assn. for Rehab. Profls., Nat. Rehab. Assn. (bd. dirs. 1983-85). Office: JobPerfect at BFTI 2236 Derby St Berkeley CA 94705-1018

MCCOOK, KATHLEEN DE LA PEÑA, university educator; b. Chgo.; d. Frank Eugene and Margaret L. (de la Peña) McEntee; m. Philip G. Heim, Mar. 20, 1972 (div.); 1 child, Margaret Marie; m. William Woodrow Lee McCook, Oct. 12, 1991; stepchildren: Cecilia, Billie Jean, Nicole. B.A., U. Ill.; M.A., Marquette U., U. Chgo.; Ph.D., U. Wis.-Madison. Reference librarian Elmhurst Coll. Library, Ill., 1971-72; dir. pub. services Rosary Coll. Library, River Forest, Ill., 1972-76; lectr. U. Wis., Madison, 1976-78; asst. prof. library sci. U. Ill., Urbana, 1978-83; dean, prof. La. State U. Sch. Library and Info. Sci., Baton Rouge, 1983-90; dean grad. sch. La. State U., 1990-92; dir. Sch. Libr. and Info. Sci. U. South Fla., 1993—. Author: (with L. Estabrook) Career Profiles, 1983, (with William E. Moen) Occupational Entry, 1989, Adult Services, 1990, (with Gary O. Rolstad) Developing Readers' Advisory Services, 1993, Toward a Just and Productive Soc., 1994; contbr. essays to books, articles to profl. jours. Chmn. Equal Rights Amendment Task Force, Ill., 1977-79; mem. Eugene McCarthy campaign, U.

Ill., Chgo., 1968; mem. La. Gov.'s Commn. for Women, 1985-88; bd. dirs. La. Endowment for Humanities, 1991-92. Recipient Disting. Alumnus award U. Wis., 1991; Bradshaw scholar Tex. Woman's Univ., 1994. Mem. ALA (com. chmn. 1980—, editor RQ jour. 1982-88, Pub. Librs. Jour. 1989-90, Am. Librs. adv. com. 1994-96, Equality award 1987, Adult Svc. award 1991), Assn. for Libr. and Info. Sci. Edn. (com. chmn. 1981—, pres. 1987-88), Fla. Libr. Assn. (bd. dirs. 1995—, Transformer award 1996), Tampa Bay Libr. Consortium (bd. dirs. 1994—), Women Libr. Workers, Ill. Libr. Assn. (treas. 1981-83), Beta Phi Mu. Democrat. Roman Catholic. Office: U South Fla Sch Libr and Info Sci 4202 E Fowler Ave CIS 1040 Tampa FL 33620-9951

MCCORD, GLORIA DAWN HARMON, music educator, choral director, organist; b. Jacksonville, Fla., June 14, 1949; d. Earl H. and C. Grace (Lupo) Harmon; m. Mark L. McCord, Sr., Aug. 7, 1971; children: M. Lance, Ian H. BMus in Edn., Fla. State U.; MMus in Choral Conducting, La. State U.; postgrad., U. New Orleans, U. Ga. Cert. tchr., Ga. Classroom music tchr. Nassau County (Fla.) Bd. Edn., 1971, Orange County (Fla.) Bd. Edn., 1971-74; choral dir., gen. music tchr. Fulton County (Ga.) Bd. Edn., 1974-75; dir. music Aldersgate United Meth. Ch., Slidell, La., 1978-86; tchr. for gifted and talented in music St. Tammany Parish Schs., La., 1988-91; asst. prof. arts and scis. Brenau U., Gainesville, Ga., 1991—; registrar, pub. rels. dir., choral dir. Firespark Summer Sch. for Students Gifted in Arts, 1992—; organist Riverside Mil. Acad., 1994—; presenter, adjudicator North Gwinnett Piano club, 1992, North Gwinnett Federated Festival, 1993, 95, 96, Ga. Music Educators Edn. Piano Festival, 1993; choir dir. Ga. Music Educators Dist. IX Honor Choir, 1993, others; series dir. radio broacast Panorama; adjudicator West Gwinnett Fed. Piano, 1995. Interim organist 1st United Meth. Chancel Choir, 1993, other positions; evaluator United Meth. Ch.; sec. Gainesville H.S. Band Boosters, Gainesville H.S. PTA, 1992-94. Recipient Lake Como (Orange county, Fla.) NEA Tchr. of the Yr., 1973. Mem. Am. Choral Dirs. Assn., United Meth. Am. Guild of Organists, Music Educators Nat. Assn (seminar facilitator 1993), Music Tchrs. Nat. Assn., Ga. Music Tchrs. Assn., Ga. Music Educators, Sigma Alpha Iota. Office: Brenau Univ 1 Centennial Cir Gainesville GA 30501-3668

MCCORD, JACQUELIN SALVATTO, secondary education educator, consultant; b. Meherrin, Va., Apr. 5, 1947; d. Alfred Allen and Naomi Miller Salvatto; m. Joseph Andre McCord, Mar. 29, 1972; children: Tesha Joy, Tovah Andrea. BS, Fordham U., 1971; D of Naprapathy, Chgo. Nat. Coll. Naprapathy, 1986; postgrad., Spertus Coll., 1994—. Bd. cert. naprapath. Founder, dir. Messiah Bapt. Day Camp, Yonkers, N.Y., 1980; tchr. Yonkers (N.Y.) Pub. Schs., 1980-81; sec. ATLA-Religion Indexes, Chgo., 1981-87; naprapathic physician Naprapathic Assocs., Chgo., 1987-91; tchr. DuSable H.S., Chgo., 1989—; program coord. Math./Sci. Literacy Program, Chgo., 1993; cons. Sch. Improvement Network, Chgo., 1993—; curriculum writer Med.-Tech. Program, Chgo. (Ill.) Pub. Sch., 1994; presenter in field. Author: (children's storybook) When We Get Straight, 1994. Membership chairperson YWCA Bd. Dirs., Yonkers, 1979-80; usher First Bapt. Ch. Chgo., Ill., 1981—; troop leader Girl Scouts Am., Chgo., 1982-86; mem. 1st Congl. Dist. Women's Task Force, Chgo., 1982-85. Named to Outstanding Young Women in Am., 1979. Mem. Nat. Coun. for Social Studies, Ill. Coun. for Social Studies Tchrs., Phi Delta Kappa, Delta Sigma Theta. Baptist. Office: T Joy Andrea Pub PO Box 167054 Chicago IL 60616-7054

MCCORD, JEAN ELLEN, secondary art educator, coach; b. Ilion, N.Y., Oct. 20, 1952; d. Harold Shepard and Marian Alice (Bernier) Shepard; m. Colin McCord, May 10, 1977 (div. Sept. 1993). AA, Mohawk Valley C.C., Utica, N.Y., 1972; BA, SUNY, New Paltz, 1975, postgrad., 1976-77. Cert. art educator, N.Y. Jr. kindergarten tchr. Norfolk (Va.) Naval Base, 1978-79; jr. kindergarten and art tchr. Sunnybrook Day Sch., Virginia Beach, Va., 1979-81; tchr. art Fisher Elem. Sch., Mohawk, N.y., 1982-84, Mechanicstown Sch., Middletown, N.Y., 1984-88, Middletown (N.Y.) Start Ctr., 1986-87, tchr. synergetic edn., Middletown Tchr. Ctr., 1986-87; pvt. portfolio tutor Middletown, 1989-91; tchr. art Middletown Elem. Summer Sch., 1989—, Middletown H.S., 1987—; sec. of policy and exec. bds. Middletown Tchr. Ctr., 1988-91, chmn. policy and exec. bds., 1991-92; mem. Bicentennial of Edn. com.; advisor NAt. Art Honor Soc., 1989—; coord. After Sch. Program for Youth at Risk, 1995—, tchr., 1992-94. Actress, vocalist, designer in regional theatre, 1993-94; artistic designer sch. plays and Creative Theatre Group; writer, dir. for local cabarets and charities; local muralist and portraitist, 1990—. County svc. coord. Orange County Youth-In-Govt. (adv. 1988—), Goshen, N.Y., 1991-93; Odyssey of the Mind Coach, 1984-92;. Named for outstanding set design Times Herald Record, 1994; honored by Bd. Edn. Outstanding Educator, 1992. Episcopalian. Home: 638 Route 211 E Middletown NY 10940-1718 Office: Middletown City Schs Wisner Ave Middletown NY 10940

MCCORMACK, GRACE LYNETTE, civil engineering technician; b. Dallas, Nov. 2; d. Audley and Janice Meredith (Metcalf) McC. Tech. degree, Durham's Coll., 1958; grad. in civil engring., El Centro Coll., 1972; grad. in advanced surveying, Eastfield, 1975. Cert. sr. engr. technician. Contract design technician various engring firms, Dallas, 1958-70; sr. design engr. technician City of Dallas Survey Div., 1970-80, street light div., 1980-95, ret. 1995. Mem. Unity Ch. Avocations: numerology, astrology, metaphysics, Egyptian-Arabian horses, lighting and designing black and white portrait photography. Home: 1428 Meadowbrook Ln Irving TX 75061-4435

MCCORMACK, MARY BEATRICE (BEE MCCORMACK), retired food manufacturing executive; b. Albany, Ga., Aug. 21, 1925; d. Robert Emmet and Anna Louise (Keller) McC. BA, Ga. Coll., 1946. Dir. personnel Bobs Candies, Inc., Albany, 1946-61; v.p. Bob's Candies, Inc., Albany, 1961-94; ret., 1994. Pres. Albany Symphony, 1972-74; co-chmn. capital funds campaign Albany Mus., 1981-82, sec., 1990-93; chmn. arts devel. dir. Albany Arts Coun., 1984; mem. Ga. Bus. Com. for the Arts, 1989-93, Albany Local Devel. Commn., 1986-93; bd. dirs. Mt. Zion Civil Rights Mus., 1996—. Recipient Pro Deum et Juventatum medal Roman Cath. Diocese of Savannah, Ga., 1970, Alumni Achievement award Ga. Coll., Milledgeville, 1983; co-recipient Albany Woman of Yr. award, 1978. Mem. Nat. Confectioners Assn. (dir., v.p. 1979-84, Candy Mfr. Yr. 1981), Profit-sharing Council Am. (dir. 1975-81), Profit Sharing Research Fedn. (dir. 1978-81), Albany C. of C. (dir. 1982-85). Roman Catholic. Office: Bobs Candies Inc PO Box 3170 1505 W Oakridge Dr Albany GA 31707-5308

MCCORMACK, MELISSA LEIGH, pediatric resident; b. Melrose, Mass., Nov. 16, 1963; d. Leonard Raymond and Carol Ann (Danahy) McC. BA, Coll. of the Holy Cross, Worcester, Mass., 1985; PhD, Brown U., 1992, MD, 1995. Rsch. asst. Dana Farber Cancer Inst., Boston, 1985-87; postdoctoral fellow U. Calif. San Diego, La Jolla, 1992-93. Mem. Physicians for Social Responsibility, Providence, 1989-92. Travel grantee Am. Paralysis Assn., 1991. Mem. AAAS, AMA, Am. Acad. Pediats., Soc. Neurosci., Internat. Brain Rsch. Orgn., Am. Med. Women's Assn., Sigma Xi, Phi Beta Kappa, Pi Mu Epsilon. Home: 1639 Rodman St Philadelphia PA 11946 Office: Children's Hosp of Phila Dept Pediats Philadelphia PA 19104

MCCORMACK, PATRICIA SEGER, independent press service editor, journalist; b. Pitts., June 11, 1927; d. Arthur John and Anne Irene (McCaffrey) Seger; m. Donald P. McCormack, Apr. 28, 1951; 1 son, Christopher Paul. B.A., U. Pitts., 1949; certificate, A.P. Inst. Seminar, 1967. News editor weekly newspapers Mt. Lebanon, Pa., 1950-52; med. editor Pitts. Sun Telegraph, 1952-57; med. sci. editor INS, N.Y.C., 1958-59; columnist, family, health and edn. editor UPI, 1959-84, sr. editor, 1987-90. Mem. Boy of Year selection com. Boys Clubs Am., 1966; mem. Coty Fashion award jury, 1965-72, nat. selection com. Century III Leader Scholarship Competition Nat. Assn. Secondary Sch. Prins., 1986. Recipient Biennial Media award Family Service Assn. Am., 1965, Freedom Found. medal; 1st place Sci. Writing award Am. Dental Assn., 1976; Nat. Media award United Negro Coll. Fund, 1977; John Swett award for disting. educating reporting Calif. Edn. Assn., 1981. Mem. AAAS, Nat. Assn. Sci. Writers (life), Edn. Writers Assn., Women's Forum Inc. (N.Y.C.), Nat. Fedn. Press Women (Comm. Achievement medal 1993), Conn. Press Club (v.p., Communicator of Achievement 1993), Conn. Women's Forum. Home and Office: PO Box 3539 Westport CT 06880-8539

MCCORMICK, ALMA HEFLIN, writer, retired educator, psychologist; b. Winona, Mo., Sept. 2, 1910; d. Irvin Elgin and Nora Edith (Kelley) Heflin; m. Archie Thomas Edward McCormick, July 14, 1942 (dec.); children: Thomas James, Kelly Jean. BA, Ea. Wash. Coll., 1936, EdM, 1949; PhD, Clayton U., 1977. Originator dept. severely mentally retarded Tri-City Public Schs., Richland, Wash., 1953, Parkland, Wash., 1955; co-founder, dir. Adastra Sch. for Gifted Children, Seattle, 1957-64; author profl. publs., novels; contbr. articles to various publs., 1937—. Mem. Am. Psychol. Assn., OX 5 Aviation Pioneers, Kappa Delta Pi. Republican. Roman Catholic. Editor: Cub Flyer, Western Story Mag., Wild West Weekly; assoc. editor: Mexico City Daily News (English sect. of Novedades). One of the first Am. woman test pilot's, 1942. Home and Office: 11437 Chimayo Rd Apple Valley CA 92308-7754

MCCORMICK, DALE, state legislator; b. Jan. 17, 1947. BA, U. Iowa, 1970. Mem. Maine State Senate from 18th dist, 1991—. Home: 22 Mayflower Rd Hallowell ME 04347 Address: 1250 Turner St Auburn ME 04210-6436

MCCORMICK, DONNA LYNN, social worker; b. Austin, Minn., Aug. 13, 1944; d. Raymond Alois and Grace Eleanor (Hayes) Schrom; m. James Michael McCormick, Jan. 15, 1972. BA in Psychology, Coll. St. Catherine, 1966. Caseworker Phila. County Bd. Pub. Assistance, 1968-70; sr. social worker San Francisco Dept. Social Svcs., 1986—. Mem. AAUW, Coll. St. Catherine Alumnae Assn., Emily's List Nat. Trust Hist. Preservation, Nat. Mus. Women in Arts, Met. Opera Assn. Democrat. Home: 168 17th Ave San Francisco CA 94121 Office: San Francisco Dept Social Svcs PO Box 7988 San Francisco CA 94120

MCCORMICK, ELAINE ALICE, former nurse, fundraising executive; b. Jersey City, Nov. 19, 1943; d. Johannes and Anni (Gantenberg) Kratz; m. Thomas A. McCormick, Oct. 1, 1966; 1 child, Thomas John. Diploma, Mt. Sinai Sch. Nursing, 1964; BA summa cum laude, Georgian Ct. Coll., 1982. RN, N.Y., N.J. Staff nurse Holy Name Hosp., Teaneck, N.J., 1964-65, 69-70; office nurse Drs. Higdon, Beaugard and Fox, Teaneck, 1965-67; indsl. nurse Dun & Bradstreet, Inc., N.Y.C., 1967-69; camp nurse, ski area dir. Camp Arrowhead, Cmty. YMCA, Marlboro, N.J., 1974-78; adminstrv. asst. DeJesse Advt., Woodbrige, N.J., 1982-83; staff writer Georgian Ct. Coll., Lakewood, N.J., 1983-84, dir. pub. rels., 1984-92, asst. v.p. for coll. advancement, 1992-94; v.p. for coll. advancement Georgian Ct. Coll., Lakewood, 1994—; cons. in field. Mem. adv. bd. Ret. Sr. Vol. Program Ocean County, Toms River, N.J., 1987-94, mem. bd. advisors, 1994—; mem. adv. coun. Eldermed Scan Ocean County; mem., chairwoman, bd. advisors, mem. exec. bd. Sr. Citizen Activities Network Monmouth County; mem. Mercy Higher Edn. Colloquium, Monmouth Ocean Devel. Coun., Nat. Bd. Med. Coll. Pa., 1995—. Mem. Am. Mgmt. Assn., Nat. Soc. Fundraising Execs., West Monmouth C. of C., Sigma Tau Delta. Republican. Roman Catholic. Home: 9 Pamela St Marlboro NJ 07746-1621 Office: Georgian Ct Coll 900 Lakewood Ave Lakewood NJ 08701-2600 also: 4452 NE Ocean Blvd Jensen Beach FL 34957-4373

MCCORMICK, MARIE CLARE, pediatrician, educator; b. Haverhill, Mass., Jan. 7, 1946; d. Richard John and Clare Bernadine (Keleher) McC.; m. Robert Jay Blendon, Dec. 30, 1977. BA magna cum laude, Emmanuel Coll., 1967; MD, Johns Hopkins Medical Sch., 1971; ScD, Johns Hopkins, 1978; MA, Harvard, 1991. Diplomate Am. Bd. Pediatrics. Pediatric resident, fellow Johns Hopkins Hosp., Balt., 1971-75; rsch. fellow Johns Hopkins Hosp., 1972-75; asst. prof. U. Ill. Schs. Medicine & Pub. Health, Chgo., 1975-76; pediatrics instr. Johns Hopkins Medical Sch., Balt., 1976-78; asst. prof. healthcare orgn. Johns Hopkins Sch. Hygiene & Pub. Health, 1978-81; asst. prof. pediatrics U. Pa., Phila., 1981-86, assoc. prof. pediatrics, 1986-87; assoc. prof. pediatrics Harvard Medical Sch., Boston, 1987-91; prof., chair. maternal & child health Harvard Sch. Pub. Health, 1992—; prof. pediatrics . Harvard Medical Sch., 1992—; adj. assoc. prof. pediatrics U. Pa., 1987-92; active attending physician, Johns Hopkins Hosp., 1976-81, asst. physician Children's Hosp. Phila., 1981-84, assoc. physician, 1984-86, sr. physician, 1986-87, assoc. pediatrician Brigham & Women's Hosp., 1987, 88—; vis. prof. Wash. U., St. Louis, 1993; editorial bds. Health Svcs. Rsch., 1985-94, Pediatrics in Review, 1986-91, Pediatrics, 1993—; adv. coun. Ctr. Perinatal & Family Health Brigham & Women;s Hosp., 1991—; cons. to numerous coms., orgns. and bds. Contbr. articles to profl. jours. Adv. The David and Lucile Packard Found., 1993-95; bd. dirs. Family Planning Coun. S.E. Pa., 1984-87; chair com. child health Mayor's Commn. Phila., 1982-83. Named Henry Strong Denison scholar Johns Hopkins Sch. Medicine, 1971, Leonard Davis inst. Health Econs. fellow U. Pa. 1984, First Sumner and Esther Feldberg prof. maternal and child health, 1996; recipient Johns Hopkins U. Soc. Scholars award, 1995, Ambulatory Pediat. Assn. Rsch. award, 1996. Fellow Am. Acad. Pediatrics; mem. AAAS, Ambulatory Pediatrics Assn. (Rsch. award 1996), Soc. Pediatric Rsch. (sr.), Am. Pediatric soc., Am. Pub. Health Assn., Internat. Epidemiological Assn., Assn. Health Svcs. Rsch., Eastern Soc. Pediatric Rsch., Soc. Pediatric Epidemiologic Rsch., Assn. Tchrs. Maternal and Child Health, Mass. Med. Soc., Norfolk Dist. Med. Soc., Mass. Pub. Health Assn., Johns Hopkins U. Soc. Scholars. Office: Harvard Sch Pub Health 677 Huntington Ave Boston MA 02115-6028

MCCORMICK, MAUREEN OLIVEA, computer systems programmer; b. Toledo, Mar. 24, 1956; d. Richard Ernest and Rita Maureen (Pratt) McC. BS in Elem. Edn., Kent State U., 1978, MA Reading Specialization, 1980. Reading instr. Elyria City Schs., Elyria, Ohio, 1978-79; tchr. Wellington Village Schs., Wellington, Ohio, 1979-80; devel. edn. instr. Lorain County Community Coll., Elyria, 1980-83; computer programmer analyst Navy Fin. Ctr., Cleve., 1981-86, Naval Mil. Personnel Command, Arlington, Va., 1986; computer systems analyst Marine Corps Cen. Design & Programming Activity/MCDEC, Quantico, Va., 1986-87; computer systems programmer Navy Fin. Ctr., Cleve., 1987-91, Def. Fin. and Acctg Svc.-Cleve. Ctr., 1991-92, Def. Info. Tech. Svc. Orgn.-Cleve. Ctr., Cleve., 1992-93; supervisory computer specialist Def. Fin. & Acctg. Svc.-Fin. Sys. Activity, Cleve., 1993—. Mem. Am. Soc. Mil. Compts., TransAtlantic Brides & Parents Assn. Home: 153 Burns Rd Elyria OH 44035-1510 Office: DFAS-FSA-CL 1240 E 9th St Cleveland OH 44199-2001

MCCOWN, GLORIA BOOHER, school system administrator; b. Dallas, Apr. 5, 1945; d. George T. and Lillian (Martine) Booher; m. James R. McCown, July 22, 1962 (dec. May 1994); children: Kelley Lynn, William Scott. BS, Houston Bapt. U., 1976; MEd, U. North Tex., 1983, EdD, 1992. Tchr. Fort Bend Ind. Sch. Dist., Stafford, Tex., 1976-78; tchr. Lancaster (Tex.) Ind. Sch. Dist., 1978-83, prin., 1983-87, dir. curriculum, 1987-88, asst. supt. instrn., 1988-91; dir. elem. edn. Keller (Tex.) Ind. Sch. Dist., 1992—. Author: Site Based Management The Role Of The Central Office, 1992. Life mem. Lancaster Coun. PTA, 1987—. Named Prin. of Yr., U. North Tex., 1987. Mem. ASCD, Tex. ASCD, Tex. Elem. Sch. Prins., Tex. Assn. Sch. Adminstrs., Internat. Reading Assn., Phi Delta Kappa. Office: Keller Ind Sch Dist 304 Lorine St Keller TX 76248-3435

MCCOWN, JUDITH KAPLAN, advertising executive; b. Memphis, Dec. 2, 1943; d. Solomon and Marianne (Uditsky) Kaplan; m. Murray Harwood McCown,Aug. 7, 1964 (div. 1991); children: Murray Harwood Jr., Melissa Hope. BS, Memphis State U., 1967. With Tenn. Dept. Human Services, Memphis, 1967-73; sec. Country Day Sch., Memphis, 1974-80; ptnr., account exec. Tri-Mark of Greater Memphis, 1980-81; account exec. Rodney Baber & Co., Memphis, 1981—. Bd. dirs. Arthritis Found. Memphis Chpt., 1986—, Alumni Assn. U. Memphis, Memphis chpt. Direct Mktg. Assn.; co-chmn. Silent Auction Memphis Concert Ballet Luncheon. Mem. Memphis Advt. Fedn. (bd. dirs., chmn. advt. review com., named Vol. of Yr. 1989), Am. Advt. Fedn. (mem. nat. advt. standards com., rev. coord., LARP coord. 7th dist., exec. com. local advtg. review network), Nat. Assn. Female Execs., Nat. Council Jewish Women, Memphis State U. Journalism Alumni (bd. dirs.). Jewish. Lodges: B'Nai Brith Women, Temple Israel Sisterhood.

MCCOY, CAROL P., psychologist, training executive; b. Bronxville, N.Y., June 14, 1948; d. Rawley Deering and Jane (Wiske) McC.; m. Lanny Gordon Foster, Nov. 29, 1975 (div. 1985). BA, Conn. Coll., 1970; MS in Psychology, Rutgers U., 1974, PhD in Psychology, 1980. Adj. instr. psychology Rutgers U., New Brunswick, N.J., 1974-75; faculty chair dept. social sci. Misericordia Hosp. Sch. Nursing, Bronx, N.Y., 1976-79; tng. and devel. cons. Chase Manhattan Bank N.A., N.Y.C., 1980-85, tng. mgr. internat. consumer banking div., 1985-88, tng. mgr. individual banking, 1988-91; dir. corp. tng. UNUM Life Ins. Co. Am., Portland, Maine, 1991—. Author: Managing a Small HRD Department, 1993. Mem. Am. Soc. Tng. and Devel., Am. Psychol. Assn. Home: 11 Johnson Rd Falmouth ME 04105-1408 Office: UNUM Life Ins Co Am 2211 Congress St Portland ME 04122-0002

MCCOY, CATHERINE COLLINS, lawyer; b. Greensboro, N.C., Nov. 5, 1947. BA, Manhattanville Coll., 1969; JD, Am. U., Washington, 1977. Bar: D.C. 1978. Atty. SEC, Washington, 1977-86, assoc. dir. legal divsn. corp. fin., 1984-86; dep. exec. dir., gen. counsel Nat. Commn. on Fraudulent Fin. Reporting, 1986-87; ptnr. Arnold & Porter, Washington; mem. legal adv. bd. Nat. Assn. Securities Dealers, 1993—. Office: Arnold & Porter Thurman Arnold Bldg 555 Twelfth St NW Washington DC 20004-1202*

MCCOY, DONNA LEE, elementary education educator; b. Columbus, Ohio, Dec. 12, 1960; d. Arthur Lee and Anna Margaret (Keefer) King; m. Russell Dean McCoy, Sept. 15, 1990. BS in Elem. Edn., W.Va. State Coll., 1990. Cert. tchr., W.Va. 1st grade tchr. Parsons (W.Va.) Elem. Sch., 1990-95, extended yr. tchr. kindergarten-3d grade, summer 1991-95; core mem. Outcome Driven Devel. Model, Parsons Elem. , Tucker County Bd. of Edn., 1990-95. Recipient Exemplary Tchg. Techniques award RESA VII, 1994. Mem. AAUW, NEA, W.Va. Edn. Assn., Tucker County Edn. Assn.

MCCOY, DOROTHY ELOISE, writer, educator; b. Houston, Sept. 4, 1916; d. Robert Major and Evie Letha (Grimes) Morgan; m. Roy McCoy, May 22, 1942; children: Roy Jr., Robert Nicholas (dec.). B., Rice U., 1938; M., Tex. A&I U., 1968; postgrad., Ind. U., 1971, U. Calif., Berkeley, 1972, U. Calif., Santa Cruz, 1977. Cert. secondary tchr. BA Corpus Christi (Tex.) Independent Schs., 1958-84, MA, 1985; freelance writer Corpus Christi, 1987—; co-owner United Iron and Machine Works, Corpus Christi, 1946-82; freelance lectr.; master tchr. Nat. Coun. Tchrs. English, 1971, Nat. Humanities Faculty, Concord Mass., 1977-78; mem. steering com. Edn. Summit, Corpus Christi, 1990-91, mem. summit update, 1991. Author: A Teacher Talks Back, 1990, Let's Restructure the Schools, 1992; contbr. articles and columns to profl. jours. Sr. advisor to U.S. Congress, Washington, 1982-85; trustee Corpus Christi Librs., 1987-90; mem. Corpus Christi Mus.; mem. Friends Corpus Christi Librs., chmn. publicity com., 1988; participant Walk to Emmaus Group, 1990, UPDATE, U. Tex., 1978-92; cons. Libr. Bd. Democracy competition Am. 2000; sec. adminstrv. bd. First United Meth. Ch., 1992-93. Recipient Teacher of Yr. Paul Caplan Humanitarian award, 1981, Advanced Senior Option Program award, 1968. Mem. AAUW, LWV, Phi Beta Kappa. Home and Office: 612 Chamberlain St Corpus Christi TX 78404-2605

MCCOY, ELIZABETH MILLS, French educator; b. Leesburg, Va., Nov. 4, 1942; d. Esker and Oma Mae (Herrell) Mills; m. Marshall P. Howard Griffith, June 20, 1964 (div. 1985); children: Mark Stephen, Laura Michelle, Seth Julian, Karen Elizabeth; m. Francis Maurice McCoy Jr., Nov. 8, 1986; children: Elizabeth Frazier, James Ramsey. BA, U. Md., 1964; postgrad., Old Dominion U. Cert. secondary French tchr., Md., Va. French tchr. Montgomery County Pub. Schs., Rockville, Md., 1964-69, Norfolk (Va.) City Pub. Schs., 1990—; mem. mentor team Norfolk Pub. Schs., 1993—, SMART team, 1993—. Vol., project coord. Operation Smile Internat., Norfolk, 1993—, team mem., 1994—. Scholar-in-resident U. Va., 1992. Mem. Edn. Assn. Norfolk (legis. chair 1992—), Va. Edn. Assn. (resolutions com. 1994), NEA. Home: 720 Reasor Dr Virginia Beach VA 23464-2426 Office: Norfolk Pub Schs 1111 Park Ave Norfolk VA 23504-3619

MC COY, LEE BERARD, paint company executive; b. Ipswich, Mass., July 27, 1925; d. Damase Joseph and Robena Myrtle (Bruce) B.; student U. Ala., Mobile, 1958-60; m. Walter Vincent de Paul McCoy, Sept. 27, 1943; children: Bernadette, Raymond, Joan, Richard. Owner, Lee's Letter Shop, Hicksville, L.I., N.Y., 1950-56; mgr. sales adminstrn. Basila Mfg. Co., Mobile, Ala., 1957-61; promotion mgr., buyer Mobile Paint Co., Inc., Theodore, Ala., 1961—. Curator, Shepard Meml. Libr., 1972—; bd. dirs. Monterey Tour House, Mobile, 1972-78, Old Dauphin Way Assn., 1977-79, Friends of Mus., Mobile, 1978—, Miss Wheelchair Ala., 1980—; del. Civic Roundtable, 1977-78, bd. dirs., 1980-81, 1st v.p., 1980-81, pres., 1981-82; pres.'s Com. Employment of Handicapped, 1981—; chmn. Mobile, Nat. Yr. Disabled Persons, 1982; chmn. Mobile, Internat. Decade Disabled Persons, 1983—; mem. Nat. Project Adv. Bd., 1983—, Nat. Community Adv. Bd., 1983—, World Com. for Decade of Disabled Persons, 1983—; v.p. Bristol Sister City Soc.; active Mobile Area Retarded Citizens, Am. Heart Assn.; mem. City of Mobile Cultural Enrichment Task Force, 1985—, Mobile United Recreation and Culture Com.; dir. Culture Mobile, 1986—; v.p., bd. dirs. Joe Jefferson Players, 1986; co-chmn. Brit. Faire, 1983; chmn. Mobile Expo, 1990, Culture & Recreation Com. Mobile United, 1989, steering com., 1990. Recipient Honor award Civic Roundtable, 1979, 80; Service award Women's Com. of Spain Rehab. Center, State of Ala., 1980; award Nat. Orgn. on Disability, 1983, Gayfer's Outstanding Career Woman award, 1988; Golden Rule award, 1991. Mem. Spectromatic Assos., Nat. Paint Distbrs., Hist. Preservation Soc., Color Mktg. Group, English Speaking Union (v.p., pres. 1992, 94, 95, 96), U.S. C. of C. (chmn. local cultural enrichment task force 1986), Toastmasters (pres. 1995-96), The Nat. Mus. of Women of the Arts, Washington (charter), Internat. Platform Assn. Methodist. Republican. Clubs: Quota (charter mem. Mobile chpt., dir. 1977—, pres. 1978-80, chmn. numerous coms., recipient Service award Dist. 8, 1979, Internat. award for serving club objectives, 1980, editor Care-Gram, Weekly newsletter for nursing homes 1980—), Bienville; writer 10 books; lectr., worldwide traveler. Home: 1553 Monterey Pl Mobile AL 36604-1227 Office: 4775 Hamilton Blvd Theodore AL 36582-8523

MCCOY, LISA JO, special education educator; b. Bluefield, W.Va., Feb. 27, 1959; d. Joseph Clark and Elizabeth Ann (Yost) McC. BS, Radford U., 1982; MEd summa cum laude, East Tenn. State U., 1994. Cert. tchr., Va. Tchr., dept. head, tennis, basketball and volleyball coach Pound (Va.) H.S., 1982-94; tchr. E.B. Stanley Mid. Sch., Abingdon, Va., 1994—; tchr. jr. varsity tennis/volleyball Abingdon (Va.) H.S., 1995—, 8th grade volleyball and basketball coach, 1995—; coach jr. varsity volleyball, 8th grade volleygball, tennis Abingdon High and Mid. Sch. Coord. Spl. Olympics Wise County, Va., 1987-90. Mem. NEA, Va. Edn. Assn., Washington County Edn. Assn. Presbyterian.

MC COY, LOIS CLARK, emergency services professional, retired county official, magazine editor; b. New Haven, Oct. 1, 1920; d. William Patrick and Lois Rosilla (Dailey) Clark; m. Herbert Irving McCoy, Oct. 17, 1943; children: Whitney, Kevin, Marianne, Tori, Debra, Sally, Daniel. BS, Skidmore Coll., 1942; student Nat. Search and Rescue Sch., 1974. Asst. buyer R.H. Macy & Co., N.Y.C., 1942-44, assoc. buyer, 1944-48; instr. Mountain Medicine & Survival, U. Calif. at San Diego, 1973-74; cons. editor Search & Rescue Mag., 1975; cons. editor, Rescue Mag., 1988—; editor Press On Newsletter, 1992—. coord. San Diego Mountain Rescue Team, La Jolla, Calif., 1973-75; exec. sec. Nat. Assn. for Search and Rescue, Inc., Nashville and La Jolla, 1975-80, comptr., 1980-82; disaster officer San Diego County, 1980-86, Santa Barbara County, 1986-91, ret. Contbr. editor Rescue Mag., 1989—, editor-in-chief Response! mag., 1982-86; editor Press On! Electronic mag., 1994—; mem. adv. bd. Hazard Montly, 1991—; cons. law enforcement div.; Calif. Office Emergency Svcs., 1976-77; pres. San Diego Com. for Los Angeles Philharmonic Orch., 1957-58. Bd. dirs. Search and Rescue of the Californias, 1976-77, Nat. Assn. for Search and Rescue, Inc., 1980-87, pres., 1985-87, trustee, 1987-90, mem. Calif. OES strategic com., 1992—; pres., CEO Nat. Inst. For Urban Search & Rescue, 1989—; mem. Gov.'s Task Force on Earthquakes, 1981-82, Earthquake Preparedness Task Force, Seismic Safety Commn., 1982-85. Recipient Hal Foss award for outstanding service to search and rescue, 1982. Mem. IEEE, Armed Forces Comm. and Electronics Assoc., Nat. Assn. for Search & Rescue (life, Svc. award 1985), San Diego Mountain Rescue Team (hon. life), Santa Barbara Amateur Radio Club. Episcopalian. Author: Search and Rescue Glossary, 1974; contbr. to profl. jours. Office: PO Box 91648 Santa Barbara CA 93190-1648

MCCOY, MARILYN, university official; b. Providence, Mar. 18, 1948; d. James Francis and Eleanor (Regan) McC.; m. Charles R. Thomas, Jan. 28, 1983. BA in Econs., Smith Coll., 1970; M in Pub. Policy, U. Mich., 1972. Dir. Nat. Ctr. for Higher Edn. Mgmt. Systems, Boulder, Colo., 1972-80; dir.

planning and policy devel. U. Colo., Boulder, 1981-85; v.p. adminstrn. and planning Northwestern U., Evanston, Ill., 1985—; bd. dirs. Pegasus Funds. Co-author: Financing Higher Education in the Fifty States, 1976, 3d edit., 1982. Bd. dirs. Evanston Hosp., 1988—, Met. Family Svcs., Chgo., 1988—, Mather Found., 1995—. Mem. Am. Assn. for Higher Edn., Soc. for Coll. and Univ. Planning (pres., v.p., sec., bd. dirs. 1980—), Assn. for Instnl. Rsch. (pres., v.p., exec. com., publs. bd. 1978-87), Chgo. Network (chmn. 1992-93), Chgo. Econ. Club. Home: 1100 N Lake Shore Dr Chicago IL 60611-1053 Office: Northwestern U 633 Clark St Evanston IL 60208-0001

MCCOY, MAUREEN, novelist, writing educator; b. Des Moines, Dec. 18, 1949; d. John Robert and Frances Ellen (Sullivan) McC. BA, U. Denver, 1972; MFA, U. Iowa, 1983. Writing fellow Fine Arts Work Ctr., Provincetown, Mass., 1983-85; freelance writer Provincetown, 1985-87; Albert Schweitzer fellow in humanities SUNY, Albany, 1987; assoc. prof. English Cornell U., Ithaca, N.Y., 1989—, dir. creative writing program, 1994—; mem. Creative Coun. for Arts, Ithaca, 1994—. Author: Walking After Midnight, 1985, Summertime, 1987, Divining Blood, 1992. Recipient James Michener award Copernicus Found., 1984; Albert Schweitzer fellow, 1987-89, APPEL fellow, 1995; Hawthornden residency Hawthornden Castle Internat. Writer's Retreat, Scotland, 1996, Helene Wurlitzer Found. residency, 1996. Mem. Assoc. Writers Program, Am. Conf. Irish Studies. Office: Cornell U English Dept GS 250 Ithaca NY 14853

MCCOY, PATRICIA KATHLEEN, writer, poet, educator; b. Gallipolis, Ohio, May 21, 1959; d. William E. and Eva Leah (Robinson) McC.; m. Robert Louis Medve, Aug. 10, 1991. BA summa cum laude, Georgetown (Ky.) Coll., 1981; MA, U. Mo., 1982, PhD in Modern Lit., 1991. Rsch. asst. to Dr. Richard Hocks U. Mo., Columbia, 1989, writing lab tutor, 1987-90, grad. tchr. dept. English, 1982-89; legal asst. Harry D. Boul, Atty. at Law, Columbia, 1989-91; adj. faculty English divsn. Adirondack C.C., Queensbury, N.Y., 1995—; Writing Ctr. tutor Adirondack C.C., Queensbury, 1996—; rsch. analyst Scarsdale (N.Y.) Cmty. Bapt. Ch., 1993; guest poet, lectr. U. Mo., Columbia, 1986-91; workshop leader Mo. Writing Festival, 1984, 87; co-coord. Pub. Libr. Poetry Series, Columbia, 1985-86. Co-editor: (lit. mag.) Inscape, 1980, Midlands, 1984; poetry advisor: (lit. mag.) Mo. Rev., 1982-84; dir. Tennessee Williams' 27 Wagons Full of Cotton, Columbia Entertainment Co., 1989; actor and stage mgr. dramas and musicals Columbia Entertainment Co., Maplewood Barn Community Theatre, Georgetown Coll., Rio Grande U., Ohio, 1978-90; radio announcer Sta. WJEH/WYPC, 1979, 80, Sta. WGTC, Ky., 1978-79; intern reporter The Georgetown News & Times, 1979; features editor The Georgetonian, 1978-80; author numerous poems; contbr. articles to profl. jours. Former deacon, sec., tchr., mem. choir Scarsdale Cmty. Bapt. Ch. Recipient semifinalist award poetry competition The Nation, 1992, 3d pl. Nat. Libr. of Poetry, 1992; fellow in creative writing U. Mo., 1981-82. Mem. MLA, Nat. Coun. Tchrs. English, Acad. Am. Poets, Assoc. Writing Programs, World Poetry Soc., Sierra Club, Sigma Tau Delta. Democrat. Baptist. Home: 25 Sunset Dr Queensbury NY 12804

MCCOY, VERA, lawyer; b. Phila., May 26, 1957; d. Simon and Lela McCoy; 1 child, Alonzo. BA, Rutgers U., Camden, N.J., 1979, JD, 1095; tchr. cert., Glassboro (N.J.) State Coll., 1983. Bar: N.J. Caseworker Senator Bill Bradley, Maple Shade, N.J., 1979-81; head tchr., owner Real McCoy Day Care Ctr., Marlton, N.J., 1983-95; pvt. practice, Wenonah, N.J., 1996—. Treas. Womens Major League, 1994—. Home: 110 Linden Ave Wenonah NJ 08090 Office: 1800 Davis St Ste 201 Camden NJ 08104

MCCRACKEN, CARON FRANCIS, computer company executive, consultant; b. Detroit, Jan. 12, 1951; d. William Joseph and Constance Irene (Kramer) McC. AS, Mott C.C., 1971; BS, Ctrl. Mich. U., 1973; MA, U. Mich., 1978; postgrad., Wayne State U., 1979-81, 93—. Tchr. Elkton, Pigeon, Bayport (Mich.) High Sch., 1973-74, Davison (Mich.) Jr. High Sch., 1974-75; instr. Mott C.C., Flint, Mich., 1974-78; planning and rsch. specialist Flint Police Dept., 1977-79; campus coord., programmer Systems & Computer Tech. Corp., Detroit, 1981-82, acad. specialist, 1982-83, mgr. acad. computing systems, 1983-84, mgr. adminstrv. computing systems, 1984-85; communications analyst Fruehauf Corp., Detroit, 1985-86, sr. comms. analyst, 1986-87; account cons. US Sprint Communications Co., Detroit, 1987-89; account mgr. US Sprint Communications Corp., Detroit, 1989-90; sr. mgr. Technology Specialists, Inc., Phila., 1990-91; sr. tech. cons. Digital Mgmt. Group, Detroit, 1991-92; sr. assoc. info. tech. practice, tech. delivery svcs. Coopers & Lybrand, Detroit, 1992—; adv. bd. CONTEL Bus. Networks, Atlanta, 1987. Contbr. articles to profl. jours. Vol. charitable and homeless orgns., including COTS - Coalition on Temporary Shelter, Core Cities, Paint the Town; vol. computer project Wayne State U., 1993-95; vol. tech. advisor on 1992 elections project City of Detroit; vol. St. Joseph's Mercy Hosp., Pontiac, Mich., 1995; bd. dirs. Bloomfield Hills Condominium Assn., 1996—. Mem. Data Processing Mgmt. Assn., Assn. Computing Machinery, Detroit Inst. Arts, Alumni Assn. U. Mich., Alumni Assn. Wayne State U., Smithsonian Instn. (assoc.), Adventure Cycling Assn. (Missoula, Mont.). Home: 100 W Hickory Grove H4 Bloomfield Hills MI 48304-2169 Office: Coopers & Lybrand 400 Renaissance Ctr Detroit MI 48243-1507

MCCRACKEN, DONNA DEE, accounting manager; b. Saint Louis Park, Minn., July 18, 1962; d. Wayne Melville and Beverly Dawn Soule; m. Anthony Dominick Simone, June 25, 1983 (Jan. 1, 1986); m. John Riley McCracken, Sept. 19, 1992. AA in Mktg., Red Rocks, Lakewood, Colo., 1982, AA in Mgmt., 1982; BS in Acctg. cum laude, W. Internat. U., Phoenix, 1990, MBA, 1996. Owner The Spa Doctor, Winter Park, Colo., 1983-87; firm adminstr. Laventhal & Horwath, Phoenix, 1987-88; adminstr. and acctg. mgr. TRW, Phoenix, 1988-90; dist. controller Anacomp, Phoenix, 1990-93; acctg. mgr. FHP Health Care, Phoenix, 1993—. Sec., treas. 3301 E. Earll Homeowners, Phoenix, 1989-92. Mem. Inst. Mgmt. Accts. (dir. employment 1993-94, dir. mem. 1995-96, v.p. adminstrn. and fin. 1996—), Healthcare Fin. Mgmt. Assn. (com. mem. 1995-96), Greater Phoenix Ariz. Health Underwriters (edn. com. 1996—). Home: 4588 West Dublin St Chandler AZ 85226

MCCRACKEN, INA, business executive; b. Highland Park, Mich., Oct. 7, 1939; d. James Howard and Lodaskia (Smoot) Smith; children: Michalene, Colet, Paulet, Pauleta. BA, Mich. State U., 1961, MEd, 1980; Edn. Specialist cert., Wayne State U., 1982, EdD, 1994. Cert. tchr., adminstr., supt., Mich. Pres. Career Mgmt. Systems, Inc., Detroit; instr. Highland Park Bd. Edn. Bus. trainer Detroit Self-Employment Project. Mem. Minority Bus. Inc. (corr. sec.), Nat. Alliance of Black Sch. Educators, Wayne State U. Coll. Edn. Alumni (chmn. bd. govs.), Phi Delta Kappa. Office: PO Box 04721 Detroit MI 48204-0721

MCCRACKEN, LINDA, librarian, commercial artist; b. Rochester, N.Y., Apr. 13, 1948; d. Frederick Hugh Craig and Shirley Betty (Shacter) Bickford; m. Alan Cheah, June 13, 1972 (div. 1978); m. Bruce E. McCracken, Sept. 23, 1978 (div. 1985); 1 child, Karen Elizabeth. BA in History, SUNY-Geneseo, 1970, MLS, 1970. Reference libr. Northeastern U., Boston, 1971-72; asst. libr. Burlington Pub. Libr., Mass., 1972-74; rsch. asst. Data Resources, Inc., Lexington, Mass., 1974-76; comml. artist McCracken's, Wolfeboro, N.H., 1973-91; asst. libr. N.H. Vocat.-Tech. Coll., Manchester, 1985-87; libr. N.H. Hosp., Concord, 1987-91. Participant paintings Horseheads Mall Art Show (3rd place award 1968); graphic artist Rare Coin Rev. mag., 1983; layout artist: Market Media Guide, 1979; market rschr. Delahaye Group, Newington, N.H., 1993-94; author Burlington Times-Union, 1973, Pleasant News, 1987-88. Treas. Village Players, Wolfeboro, 1982-83; pub. rels. com. Gov.'s Arts Coun., Wolfeboro, 1982. Mem. State Employees Assn. N.H., Mensa. Avocations: skiing, gardening, singing, acting, hiking. Home: 44 Pine Hill Rd Wolfeboro NH 03894-4330 Office: NH Hosp Dorothy M Breene Meml Libr 105 Pleasant St Concord NH 03301-3852

MCCRACKEN, PEGGY JANE, reporter; b. Flomot, Tex., Jan. 31, 1935; d. Robert Houston and Sallie Ann (Matthews) Gunn; m. Leon V. McCracken, Apr. 18, 1951; children: David Leon McCracken, Peggy Lynn Goddard. Cashier CIT, Pecos, Tex., 1953-56; sec. Hwy. Dept. State of Tex., Pecos, 1958-59; sec. West Park Bapt. Ch., Pecos, 1961-71; reporter/mng. editor Pecos Enterprise, 1972-78, reporter/editl. page editor, reporter web page dir., 1988—; news dir. Sta. KIUN-AM, Pecos, 1978-87; freelance writer Pecos, 1978-88. Media rels. Emergency Mgmt., Pecos, 1993—. Baptist. Home: 1804 S Park St Pecos TX 79772 Office: Pecos Enterprise 324 S Cedar St Pecos TX 79772-3211

MCCRADY, CHRISTINE SEKULA, lawyer; b. New Kensington, Pa., Aug. 9, 1967; d. Raymond Francis and L. Kathleen (Clifford) Sekula; m. Thomas Jamison McCrady, Sept. 3, 1994. BA in English, U. Va., 1989; JD, Duquesne U., 1992. Bar: Pa. 1992. Law clk. to Hon. James Kelly Commonwealth Ct. of Pa., Greensburg, Pa., 1992-95; pvt. practice Arnold, Pa., 1995—. Mem. Pa. Bar Assn., Allegheny County Bar Assn., Westmoreland County Bar Assn. Home: 3955 Bigelow Blvd # 517 Pittsburgh PA 15213 Office: Profl Bldg 1706 5th Ave Arnold PA 15068

MCCRAE, LINDA REED, secondary education educator; b. Reading, Pa., May 27, 1945; d. Charles Abner and Marian Elizabeth (Stauffer) Reed; m. Richard Dean McCrae, June 28, 1970; children: Sean Christoph, Patrick Michael Richard Reed. BA cum laude, Albright Coll., 1967; MED, Kutztown U., 1969. Permanent tchr. cert., Pa. Tchr. German, Latin and English Muhlenberg Sch. Dist., Laureldale, Pa., 1967—; instr. German, Reading Area C.C., 1971-72; instr. edn. methodology Albright Coll., Reading, 1975-76; mem. adj. faculty dept. German, Alvernia Coll., Reading, 1995; co-advisor Acad. Challenge, Laureldale, 1986—; mem. Wyomissing (Pa.) Sch. Dist. Strategic Planning. Author: Latina Vivit: A Guide to Lively Latin Classes, 1986, 95. Mem. NEA, Am. Assn. Tchrs. Fgn. Langs., Am. Assn. Tchrs. German, Am. Classical League, Pa. Edn. Assn., Muhlenberg Edn. Assn., Phi Delta Sigma, Delta Phi Alpha. Democrat. Lutheran. Office: Muhlenberg Sch Dist 800 Bellevue Ave Laureldale PA 19605

MCCRAMER-WOJDYLO, MICKI, operating room nurse; b. Lock Haven, Pa., Nov. 6, 1947; d. Eugene E. and Katherine A. (Frey) McCramer; m. Peter Wojdylo, Aug. 4, 1984; children: A. Michael, Kevin J., Lucas P. Nursing diploma, St. Joseph Hosp., Elmira, N.Y., 1968; BS in Health Edn., U. Vt., 1980. RN, N.Y., Fla., Vt.; cert. K-12 sch. nurse and health edn., Vt., N.Y. Health care analyst Blue Cross/Blue Shield, Syracuse, N.Y., 1985-87; charge nurse/staff nurse oper. rm. Comty. Gen. Hosp., Syracuse, 1987-88; staff nurse oper. rm. Rochester (N.Y.) Gen. Hosp., 1988-90; team leader vascular and thoracic svc. oper. rm. Highland Hosp., Rochester, 1990-93; procedure rm. nurse Rochester Park Med. Group, 1993—. Mem. AAUW, NOW, DAR (mem. and regent Irondequot chpt. 1993). Home: 374 Mendon Rd Pittsford NY 14534 Office: Ste 106 990 South Ave Rochester NY 14620

MCCRARY, EUGENIA LESTER (MRS. DENNIS DAUGHTRY MCCRARY), civic worker, writer; b. Annapolis, Md., Mar. 23, 1929; d. John Campbell and Eugenia (Potts) Lester; m. John Campbell Howard, July 15, 1955 (dec. Sept. 1965); m. Dennis Daughtry McCrary, June 28, 1969; 1 child, Dennis Campbell. AB cum laude, Radcliffe Coll.-Harvard U., 1950; MA, Johns Hopkins U., 1952; postgrad., Harvard U., 1953, Pa. State U., 1953-54, Drew U., 1957-58, Inst. Study of USSR, Munich, 1964. Grad. asst. dept. Romance langs. Pa. State U., 1953-54; tchr. dept. math. The Brearley Sch., N.Y.C., 1954-57; dir. Sch. Langs., Inc., Summit, N.J., 1958-69; trustee Sch. Langs., Inc., Summit, 1960-69. Co-author: Nom de Plume: Eugenia Campbell Lester, (with Allegra Branson) Frontiers Aflame, 1987. Dist. dir. Ea. Pa. and N.J. auditions Met. Opera Nat. Coun., N.Y.C., 1960-66, dist. dir. publicity, 1966-67, nat. vice chmn. publicity, 1967-71, nat. chmn. public rels., 1972-75, hon. nat. chmn. pub. rels., 1976—; bd. govs., chmn. Van Cortlandt House Mus., 1985-90. Mem. Nat. Soc. Colonial Dames Am. (bd. mgrs. N.Y. 1985-90), Met. Opera Nat. Coun., Soc. Mayflower Desc. (former bd. dirs. N.Y. soc., chmn. house com. 1986-89), Soc. Daus. Holland Dames (bd. dirs. 1982-87, 3d directress gen. 1987-92, directress gen. 1992-96), L'Eglise du St.-Esprit (vestry 1985-88, sr. warden 1988-90), Huguenot Soc. Am. (governing coun. 1984-90, asst. treas. 1990-91, sec. 1991-95, 2d v.p. 1995—), Colonial Dames Am., Daus. of Cin., Colony Club (bd. govs. 1988-96). Republican. Episcopalian. Home: 24 Central Park S New York NY 10019-1632

MCCRARY, SHARON HASH, medical and surgical nurse; b. Manassas, Va., Nov. 6, 1960; d. Fred and Ilene (Walker) Hash; m. Walter Larry McCrary, July 20, 1979. ADN, Polk Community Coll., Winter Haven, Fla., 1986. Nurse Hardee Meml. Hosp., Wauchula, Fla.; gen. nurse Erlanger Med. Ctr., Chattanooga, trauma stepdown nurse; med.-surg. nurse Fla. Hosp., Wauchula.

MCCRAVEN, EVA STEWART MAPES, health service administrator; b. L.A., Sept. 26, 1936; d. Paul Melvin and Wilma Zech (Ziegler) Stewart; m. Carl Clarke McCraven, Mar. 18, 1978; children: David Anthony, Lawrence James, Maria Lynn Mapes. ABS magna cum laude, Calif. State U., Northridge, 1974, MS, Cambridge Grad. Sch. Psychology, 1987; PhD, 1991. Dir. spl. projects Pacoima Meml. Hosp., 1969-71, dir. health edn., 1971-74; asst. exec. dir., v.p., Hillview Community Mental Health Center, Lakeview Terrace, Calif., 1974—, supr. for all clin. depts; past dir. dept. consultation and edn. Hillview Ctr., developer, mgr. long-term residential program, 1986-90; former program mgr. Crisis Residential Program, Transitional Residential Program and Day Treatment Program for mentally ill offenders, dir. mentally ill offenders svcs.; former program dir. Valley Homeless Shelter Mental Health Counseling Program; dir. Integrated Services Agy., Hillview Mental Health Ctr., Inc., 1993—; Former pres. San Fernando Valley Coordinating Coun. Area Assn., Sunland-Jujunga Coordinating Coun.; bd. dirs. N.E. Valley Health Corp., 1970-73, Golden State Community Mental Health Ctr., 1970-73. Recipient Resolution of Commendation award State of Calif., 1988, Commendation award, 1988, Spl. Mayor's plaque, 1988, Commendation awards for community svcs. City of L.A., 1989, County of L.A., 1989, Calif. State Assembly, 1989, Calif. State Senate, 1989, award Sunland-Tujunga Police Support Coun., 1989, Woman of Achievement award Sunland-Tujunga BPW, 1990. Mem. Assn. Mental Health Adminstrs., Am. Pub. Health Assn., Valley Univ. Women, Health Services Adminstrn. Alumni Assn. (former v.p.), Sunland-Tujunga Bus. and Profl. Women, LWV. Office: Hillview Community Mental Health Ctr 11500 Eldridge Ave San Fernando CA 91342-6523

MCCRAW, DENISE A., secondary education educator; b. Oconomowoc, Wis., Aug. 1, 1970; d. Edward J. and Barbara A. (Risberg) McC. AA&S, U. Wis. Waukesha, 1990; BS, Carroll Coll., 1993. Cert. tchr. 1-6 elem. edn., 6-9 sci., Wis. Tchr. 9th grade Catholic Meml. H.S., Waukesha, Wis., 1993—; asst. fencing coach Cath. Meml. H.S., Waukesha, 1988—. Roman Catholic. Office: Cath Meml HS 601 E College Ave Waukesha WI 53186

MC CRAY, EVELINA WILLIAMS, librarian, researcher; b. Plaquemine, La., Sept. 1, 1932; d. Turner and Beatrice (Gordon) Williams II; m. John Samuel McCray, Apr. 7, 1955; 1 child, Johnetta McCray Russ. BA, So. U., Baton Rouge, 1954; MS in Library Sci., La. State U., 1962. Librarian, Iberville High Sch., Plaquemine, 1954-70, Plaquemine Jr. High, 1970-75; proofreader short stories, poems Associated Writers Guild, Atlanta, 1982-86; library cons. Evaluation Capitol High Sch., 1964, Iberville Parish Educators Workshop, 1980, Tchrs. Core/Iberville Parish, 1980-81. Contbr. poetry New Am. Poetry Anthology, 1988, The Golden Treasury of Great Poems, 1988, Acres of Diamonds A Collection of Poetry, The Power and the Glory, A Collection of Poetry, Favorite Poems Southern Poetry Association, 1996. Vol. service Allen J. Nadler Library, Plaquemine, 1980-82; librarian Local Day Care Ctr., Plaquemine, 1978-79; mem. adv. bd. Iberville parish Project Independence, 1992—. Mem. ALA, La. Library Assn., Nat. Ret. Tchrs. Assn., La. Ret. Tchrs. Assn. (cons. ann. workshops 1986—, state appointee to informative and protective svcs. com. 1988-92), Iberville Ret. Tchrs. Assn. (info. and protective services dir. 1981—), Internat. Soc. Poets, So. Poetry Assn. (asst. coll. State Arts Mus. Miss., Blue Ribbon award 1989, SPA's Finest award 1992). Democrat. Baptist. Home: PO Box Q Plaquemine LA 70765-0220

MCCRAY, NIKKI, basketball player; b. Collierville, Tenn.. Basketball player USA Women's Nat. Team. Office: USA Basketball 5465 Mark Dabling Blvd Colorado Springs CO 80918-3842

MCCREADY, DOROTHY JANE, post-anesthesia nurse; b. Alexandria, La., July 26, 1948; d. Robert Bruce Jr. and Dorothy Louise (Frisch) Wallace; m. Edward Benjamin Scheps, Sept. 14, 1968 (div. 1989); 1 child, Mary Louise Scheps; m. Walter Stephen McCready, Jan. 9, 1991. BA in English, Parsons Coll., 1970, BSN, William Carey Coll., 1975. Cert. post anesthesia nurse, ACLS. Staff nurse surg. ICU So. Bapt. Hosp., New Orleans, 1975-77; staff nurse ICU Our Lady of Lourdes, Lafayette, La., 1978, 82-90, head nurse post anesthesia care unit, 1990-92, staff nurse post anesthesia care unit, 1992—. Mem. Am. Soc. Post Anesthesia Nurses, La. Assn. Post Anesthesia Nurses, Atchafalaya Assn. Post Anesthesia Nurses (founder, pres. 1994). Republican. Methodist. Home: 101 Bocage Cir Lafayette LA 70503-4354 Office: Our Lady of Lourdes 611 St Landry Lafayette LA 70502

MCCRIMMON, BARBARA SMITH, writer, librarian; b. Anoka, Minn., May 3, 1918; d. Webster Roy and Jessie (Sargeant) Smith; m. James McNab McCrimmon, June 10, 1939; children—Kevin Mor, John Marshall. B.A., U. Minn., 1939; M.S.L.S., U. Ill., 1961; Ph.D., Fla. State U., 1973. Asst. librarian Ill. State Nat. Hist. Survey, Champaign, Ill., 1961-62; research assoc. Bur. Community Planning, U. Ill., Champaign, 1962-63; librarian Ill. Water Survey, Champaign, 1964-65; librarian Am. Meteorol. Soc., Boston, 1965-67; editorial asst. Jour. Library History, Tallahassee, 1967-69, 73-74; adj. asst. prof. Sch. Library Sci., Fla. State U., Tallahassee, 1976-77. Author: Power, Politics and Print, 1981, Richard Garnett: The Scholar as Librarian, 1989; editor: American Library Philosophy, 1975; contbr. articles to profl. jours. Mem. ALA, Pvt. Libraries Assn., Beta Phi Mu, Manuscript Soc. Democrat.

MCCUE, JANET MARIE, accountant; b. Waltham, Mass., May 8, 1969; d. Joseph Peter and Jeanette Marie (Hines) Cloherty; m. Steven Mark McCue, July 9, 1994. BS in Fin. summa cum laude, Bentley Coll., 1991, M in Accountancy with high distinction, 1995. CPA, Mass. Fin. mgmt. trainee Raytheon Co., Lexington, Mass., 1991-93; budget and planning analyst Raytheon Co., Lexington, 1993-95, budget and planning overhead supr., 1995—. Mem. Beta Gamma Sigma. Republican. Roman Catholic. Home: 26 Arbor Dr Shrewsbury MA 01545

MCCUE, JUDITH W., lawyer; b. Phila., Apr. 7, 1948; d. Emanuel Leo and Rebecca (Raffel) Weiss; m. Howard M. McCue III, Apr. 3, 1971; children: Howard, Leigh. BA cum laude, U. Pa., 1969; JD, Harvard U., 1972. Bar: Ill. 1972, U.S. Tax Ct. 1984. Ptnr. McDermott, Will & Emery, Chgo., 1995—; dir. Schawk, Inc., Des Plaines, Ill.; pres. Chgo. Estate Planning Coun. Trustee The Orchestral Assn., 1995—. Fellow Am. Coll. Trust and Estate Counsel (com. chair 1991-94, regent 1993—); mem. Chgo. Bar Assn. (chmn. probate practice com. 1984-85, chmn. fed. estate and gift tax divsn. fed. tax com. 1988-89). Office: McDermott Will & Emery 227 W Monroe St Chicago IL 60606-5096

MCCUE, MARY MADELINE, public relations executive; b. Long Branch, N.J., Aug. 25, 1947; d. Alfred Raymond and Margaret Ann (Egan) McC. BS, Boston U., 1969. Copywriter, co-dir. pub. info. Foster Parents Plan (now PLAN Internat.), N.Y.C., 1969-72; dir. pub. info. Office Neighborhood Govt., City of N.Y., 1972-73; account exec. Burson Marstellar, N.Y.C., 1973-75; v.p., sr. v.p. Burson Marstellar, Washington, 1991—; with editl. svcs. dept. Hill and Knowlton, N.Y.C., 1975-78; from dir. corporate info. to v.p. First Boston (now CS First Boston), N.Y.C., 1978-84; dir. Office Pub. Affairs, SEC, Washington, 1984-91. Mem. Nat. Investor Rels. Inst., D.C. Bar (sect. corporate and securities law), Women in Housing and Fin. Republican. Home: 305 11th St SE Washington DC 20003-2104 Office: Burson Marsteller 1801 K St NW Ste 1000L Washington DC 20006-1201

MCCULLOCH, LISA MICHELLE, job consultant; b. St. Louis, Aug. 20, 1970; d. Paul E. Jr. and Sharon Cecilia (O'Brien) Rhodes. AA, St. Louis C.C., 1991; BA magna cum laude, U. Mo., 1993; MA, Webster U., 1996. Server Denny's Restaurant, Fenton, Mo., 1989—; job cons. Life Skills Found., St. Louis, 1995—; counseling practicum Comtrea Cmty. Treatment, Jefferson County, Mo., 1995-96. Mem. Am. Counseling Assn., Psi Chi Nat. Honor Soc. Home: 10090 Sakura Dr Apt 35 Saint Louis MO 63128 Office: Life Skills Found 10176 Corporate Sq Dr Ste 100 Saint Louis MO 63143

MCCULLOCH, RACHEL, economics researcher, educator; b. Bklyn., June 26, 1942; d. Henry and Rose (Offen) Preiss; m. Gary Edward Chamberlain; children: Laura Meressa, Neil Dudley. BA, U. Pa., 1962; MA in Teaching, U. Chgo., 1965, MA, 1971, PhD, 1973; student, MIT, 1966-67. Economist Cabinet Task Force on Oil Import Control, Washington, 1969; instr., then asst. prof. Grad. Sch. Bus. U. Chgo., 1971-73; asst. prof., then assoc. prof. econs. Harvard U., Cambridge, Mass., 1973-79; assoc. prof., then prof. econs. U. Wis., Madison, 1979-87; prof. Brandeis U., Waltham, Mass., 1987—, Rosen Family prof., 1989—, dir. Lemberg Program in Internat. Econs. and Fin., 1990-91, dir. PhD program Grad. Sch. Internat. Econs. and Fin., 1994—; mem. Pres.'s Commn. on Indsl. Competitiveness, 1983-84; mem. adv. coun. Office Tech. Assessment U.S. Congress, 1979-88; cons. World Bank, Washington, 1984-86; mem. com. on internat. rels. studies with People's Republic of China, 1984-91; rsch. assoc. Nat. Bur. Econ. Rsch., Cambridge, 1985-93; mem. adv. com. Inst. for Internat. Econs., Washington, 1987—; faculty Advanced Mgmt. Network, La Jolla, Calif., 1985-92; mem. com. examiners econs. test Grad. Record Exam. Ednl. Testing Svc., 1990-96, chair, 1992-96; mem. discipline adv. com. for Fulbright scholar awards in econs. Coun. Internat. Exch. Scholars, 1991-93, chair, 1992-93; cons. Global Economy Project, Edn. Film Ctr., 1993-94; mem. study group on pvt. capital flows to developing and transitional economies Coun. Fgn. Rels., 1995—. Author: Research and Development as a Determinant of U.S. International Competitiveness, 1978; contbr. articles to profl. jours. and books. Grantee NSF, 1975-79, Hoover Inst., 1984-85, German Marshall Fund of U.S., 1985, Ford Found., 1985-88, U.S. Dept. Edn., 1990-91. Mem. Am. Econ. Assn. (dir. summer program for minority students 1983-84), Internat. Trade and Fin. Assn. (bd. dirs. 1993-95), New England Women Economists Assn. Home: 10 Frost Rd Lexington MA 02173-1904 Office: Brandeis U Dept Econs Waltham MA 02254

MCCULLOCH, TERRI, secondary school educator; b. Salt Lake City, Sept. 18, 1957; d. Hilton Clair and Ranae (Brown) McCulloch; m. John Carl Stoughton, July 28, 1989. BS, Weber State U., Ogden, Utah, 1979; MBA, Utah State U., 1987, adminstr. and supervisory endorsement, 1993. Night mgr. Dee's, Ogden, 1973-78; with Smith's Food King, Clearfield, Utah, 1978-89; smoking cessation instr. Humana Hosp., Layton, Utah, 1987-91; tchr. Ogden Sch. Dist., 1979-95, secondary math. specialist, 1992—; asst. prin. Ogden Sch. Dist., Ogden, 1995—; workshop presenter Utah Bd. Edn., Ogden, 1979—. Bd. dirs. Cath. Cmty. Svcs., 1987-89, Utah Election Law Task Force, 1989-92; mem. Atty. Gen.'s Cmty. AGREE Team. Named Tchr. of the Yr., Ogden Sch. Dist., 1988-89, Woman of the Yr., YWCA, Ogden, 1986, Focus on Excellence award, Ogden Sch. Dist., 1988, Golden Apple award, 1988. Mem. ASCD, Tchr. Acad. for Math., AAUW, Utah LWV (state pres. 1989-92, dir. resource devel. 1990-92), Weber County LWV (local pres. 1985-89, treas. 1993—), Delta Kappa Gamma, Phi Delta Kappa. Democrat. Mem. LDS Ch. Home: 1369 Orchard Ave Ogden UT 84404-5853 Office: Ben Lomond HS 800 Scot's Way Ogden UT 84404

MCCULLOUGH, BETH V., pharmacist, educator; b. Harrison, Ark., May 15, 1953; d. A. G. and Willene L. (McLain) McC.; m. David Mark Pearson, Oct. 25, 1980; children: Colin McCullough-Pearson, Emily McCullough-Pearson. BS in Edn. cum laude, Southwest Mo. State U., 1976; BS in pharmacy, U. Mo., 1981. Registered Pharmacist, Mo. Chief pharmacist Mt. Vernon Park Pharmacy, Springfield, Mo., 1981-89; dir. pharmacy Foster Health Care Group, Springfield, 1989—; long term care pharmacy cons. Foster Health Care Group, Springfield, 1981-83. Mem. NOW, Springfield, 1982—, assoc. mem. Animal Shelter League of the Ozarks, Nixa, Mo. Mem. Southwest Mo. Humane Soc., Mo. Equine Coun., Mo. Pharmacy Assn., Long Term Care Acad. Home: Rt 1 Fordland MO 65652 Office: Foster Health Care Group 426 S Jefferson St Springfield MO 65806

MCCULLOUGH, JULIE KIDD, elementary education educator; b. Navasota, Tex., Nov. 9, 1958; d. George B. and Lois A. (Dollins) Kidd; m. David A. McCullough, May 13, 1978; children: Joshua, Adam, Matthew. AA, Hill Jr. Coll., 1978; AS, Trinity Valley C.C., 1991; BS, U. Tex., Tyler, 1994. Cert. elem. edn. educator, Tex. Printer's asst. Hill Printing, Hillsboro, Tex., 1977-78; pharmacist asst. C&S Pharmacy, Hillsboro, Tex., 1978-79; sec. P&S Hosp., Pittsburg, Tex., 1979-80; owner Kustom Kommercial, Phoenix, 1982-85; sec. Super 1, Tyler, Tex., 1989-92, TVCC, Athens, Tex., 1989-91; elem. educator Chandler (Tex.) Elem. Sch.,

1993—. Den leader Pack 342, Chandler, 1992-95. Home: PO Box 1017 Chandler TX 75758 Office: 615 N Broad Chandler TX 75758

MCCULLOUGH, KATHLEEN ERIN, public relations account executive; b. Silver Spring, Md., Jan. 27, 1971; d. Maxwell Blair and Marion (Ladue) McC. BA in Comm., Trinity U., 1992. Asst. acct. exec. Read-Poland Assocs., Washington, 1992-94; pub. rels. assoc. Commtek Comm., Vienna, Va., 1994-95; acct. exec. Stanton Comm., Washington, 1995—. Mem. Women in Comms. (chair pub. rels. com. 1995-96, v.p. student affairs 1996—). Office: Stanton Comms 1700 K Street NW Ste 502 Washington DC 20006

MCCULLOUGH, KATHRYN T. BAKER, social worker, utility commissioner; b. Trenton, Tenn., Jan. 5, 1925; d. John Andrew and Alma Lou (Wharey) Taylor; m. John R. Baker, Sept. 30, 1972 (dec. Oct. 1981); m. T.C. McCullough, May 14, 1988. BS, U. Tenn., 1945, MSW, 1954; postgrad., U. Chgo., 1950, Vanderbilt U., 1950-51. Lic. social worker, Tenn.; emeritus diplomate in clin. social work Am. Bd. Examiners. Home demonstration agt., agrl. extension svc. U. Tenn., Hardeman County, 1946-49; Dyer County, 1949-50; dir. med. social work dept. Le Bonheur Children's Hosp., Memphis, 1954-57; chief clin. social worker clinic mentally retarded children U. Tenn. Dept. Pediatrics, Memphis, 1957-59; clin. social worker Children's Med. Ctr., Tulsa, 1959-60; dir. med. social work dept. Coll. of Medicine U. Tenn., Memphis, 1960-69; dir. community svcs. regional med. program Coll. of Medicine, 1969-76; dir. regional clinic program Child Devel. Ctr. Coll. of Medicine, 1976-85; mem. faculty Coll. of Medicine, Coll. of Social Work U. Tenn., Memphis, 1960-85; social worker admissions rev. bd. Arlington Devel. Ctr., Memphis, 1976—. Author 14 books. Active Gibson County Fedn. Dem. Women, 1987—; commr. Dist. I, Gibson Utility Dist., 1990—. Fellow Am. Assn. Mental Retardation (life); mem. NASW, AAUP, Acad. Cert. Social Workers, Tenn. Conf. on Social Welfare, Sigma Kappa Alumni. Mem. Ch. of Christ. Home: 627 Riverside Yorkville Rd Trenton TN 38382-9513

MCCULLY, EMILY ARNOLD, illustrator, writer; b. Galesburg, Ill., 1939; d. Wade E. and Kathryn (Maher) Arnold; m. George E. McCully, 1961 (div. 1975); children: Nathaniel, Tad. BA, Brown U., 1961; MA, Columbia U., 1964. Author: How's Your Vacuum Cleaner Working? O'Henry Collection, 1977, A Craving, 1982, (novel) Picnic, 1984 (Christopher award), First Snow, 1985, (novel) Life Drawing, 1986, The Show Must Go On, 1987, School, 1987, You Lucky Duck!, 1988, New Baby, 1988, The Grandma Mix-up, 1988, The Christmas Gift, 1988, Zaza's Big Break, 1989, Grandma's at the Lake, 1990, The Evil Spell, 1990, Speak Up, Blanche!, 1991, Mirette on the Highwire, 1992 (Caldecott medal 1992), Grandma's at Bat, 1993, The Amazing Felix, 1993, My Real Family, 1994, Crossing The New Bridge, 1994, Little Kit, or: The Industrious Flea Circus Girl, 1995, The Pirate Queen, 1995; illustrator: Sea Beach Express, 1966, The Seventeenth Street Gang, 1966, Rex, 1967, Luigi of the Streets, 1967, That Mean Man, 1968, Gooney, 1968, Journey From Peppermint Street, 1968 (Nat. Book award 1969), The Mouse and the Elephant, 1969, The Fisherman, 1969, Tales from the Rue Brocca, 1969, Here I Am, 1969, Twin Spell, 1969, Hobo Toad and the Motorcycle Gang, 1970, Slip! Slop! Gobble!, 1970, Friday Night is Papa Night, 1970, Maxie, 1970, Steffie and Me, 1970, The Cat and the Parrot, 1970, Gertrude's Pocket, 1970, Go and Hush the Baby, 1971, Finders Keepers, 1971, Ma n Da La, 1971 (Bklyn. Mus. award 1976, N.Y. Pub. Libr. award 1976), Hurray for Captain Jane!, 1971, Michael Is Brave, 1971, Finding Out With Your Senses, 1971, Henry's Pennies, 1972, Jane's Blanket, 1972, Grandpa's Long Red Underwear, 1972, Girls Can Too!, 1972, The Boyhood of Grace Jones, 1972, Black Is Brown Is Tan, 1973, Isabelle the Itch, 1973, When Violet Died, 1973, That New Boy, 1973, How To Eat Fried Worms, 1973, Jenny's Revenge, 1974, Her Majesty, Grace Jones, 1974, Tree House Town, 1974, I Want Mama, 1974, Amanda, the Panda and the Redhead, 1975, The Bed Book, 1976, My Street's A Morning Cool Street, 1976, Professor Coconut and the Thief, 1977, Martha's Mad Dog, 1977, That's Mine, 1977, Where Wild Willie, 1978, No Help At All, 1978, Partners, 1978, The Twenty-Elephant Restaurant, 1978, What I Did Last Summer, 1978, The Highest Hit, 1978, I and Spraggy, 1978, Edward Troy and the Witch Cat, 1978, My Island Grandma, 1979, Whatever Happened to Beverly Bigler's Birthday?, 1979, Last Look, 1979, Ookie-Spooky, 1979, The Black Dog Who Went Into the Woods, 1980, How I Found Myself at the Fair, 1980, How We Got Our First Cat, 1980, Oliver and Allison's Week, 1980, Pajama Walking, 1981, The April Fool, 1981, I Dance in My Red Pajamas, 1982, The Halloween Candy Mystery, 1982, Go and Mush the Baby, 1982, Mitzi and the Terrible Tyrannosaurus Rex, 1983, Best Friend Insurance, 1983, Mail-Order Wings, 1984, Gertrude's Pocket, 1984, Fifth Grade Magic, 1984, The Ghastly Glasses, 1985, Fourth of July, 1985, The Explorer of Barkham Street, 1985, Wheels, 1986, Lulu and the Witch Baby, 1986, Richard and the Vratch, 1987, Molly, 1987, Molly Goes Hiking, 1987, Jam Day, 1987, The Boston Coffee Party, 1988, The Take-Along Dog, 1989, Selene Goes Home, 1989, The Magic Mean Machine, 1989, It Always Happens to Leona, 1989, The Grandpa Days, 1989, Dinah's Mad, Bad Wishes, 1989, Stepbrother Sabotage, 1990, Lulu Goes to Witch School, 1990, The Evil Spell, 1990, The Day Chubby Became Charles, 1990, The Christmas Present Mystery, 1990, Sky Guys to White Cat, 1991, Meatball, 1991, Leona and Ike, 1991, The Butterfly Birthday, 1991, Yankee Doodle Drumsticks, 1992, One Very Best Valentine's Day, 1992, Meet the Lincoln Lions Band, 1992, Jingle Bells Jam, 1992, In My Tent, 1992, Anne Flies the Birthday Bike, 1993, Amzat and His Brothers, 1993, The Ballot Box Battle, 1996, The Bobbin Girl, 1996. *

MCCULLY, RUTH ALIDA, elementary education educator; b. Port Huron, Mich., Feb. 13, 1933; d. Leon Eugene Lounsberry and Rachel Elizabeth (DeSerano) Lounsberry-Maser; m. Donald Cecil McCully, Feb. 8, 1952; children: Stephen Donald, Robert Leon, Julie Ann. BS, Ea. Mich. U., 1976, MA, 1980. Asst. children's librarian Monroe County Library, Mich., 1962-64; dir. Weekday Nursery Sch., Youngstown, Ohio, 1964-71; dir. children's programs Lake-in-the-Woods, Ypsilanti, Mich., 1974-76; tchr. 1st grade Dundee Community Schs., Mich., 1976-88; tchr. young fives Dundee Community Schs., 1988-90; tchr. 1st grade, 1990—. Lay speaker Ann Arbor Dist., United Meth. Ch., 1979—, dir., 1990-92; chmn. Dundee Community Caring and Sharing, 1982—; sec. Monroe County Food Bank, 1983—, Dundee Interfaith Coun., 1984—, Dundee Area Against Substance Abuse, 1984-88; sec. bd. dirs. Habitat for Humanity, Monroe County, 1995—. Named Woman of Yr., United Meth. Women, Dundee United Meth. Ch., 1983, United Meth. Ann Arbor Dist. Coun. on Ministries; recipient cert. of Commendation Village of Dundee, 1993, State of Mich., 1994, J.C. Penney Gold Rule award for outstanding vol. svc., 1995. Mem. NEA, Nat. Assn. Edn. Young Children, The Whole Lang. Umbrella, Mich. Edn. Assn., Mich. Reading Assn., Mich. Assn. Edn. Young Children, Monroe County Edn. Assn., Monroe County Tchrs. Elem. Lit. and Lang., Dundee Sch. Employees Club (sec. 1985-86), Phi Delta Kappa. Avocations: playing piano/guitar, needlework, sketching/painting, gardening, reading. Home: 510 E Monroe St Dundee MI 48131-1310

MCCUNE, MARY JOAN HUXLEY, microbiology educator; b. Lewistown, Mont., Jan. 14, 1932; d. Thomas Leonard and Anna Dorothy (Hardie) Huxley; m. Ronald William McCune, June 7, 1965; children: Anna Orpha, Heather Jean. BS, Mont. State Coll., 1953; MS, Wash. State U., 1955; PhD, Purdue U., 1965. Rsch. technician VA Hosp., Oakland, Calif., 1956-59; bacteriologist U.S. Naval Radiol. Def. Lab., San Francisco, 1959-61; teaching assoc. Purdue U., West Lafayette, Ind., 1961-65, vis. asst. prof., 1965-66; asst. prof. Occidental Coll., L.A., 1966-69; asst. rsch. bacteriologist II U. Calif., L.A., 1969-70; affiliate asst. prof. Idaho State U., Pocatello, Idaho, 1970-80, from asst. prof. to prof. microbiology, 1980—; instr. U. Calif., Davis, 1964. Contbr. articles to profl. jours. Pres. AK chpt. PEO, Pocatello, 1988-89; chair faculty senate Idaho State U., 1994-95. David Ross fellow Purdue U., 1964. Mem. AAAS, N.Y. Acad. Sci., Idaho Acad. Sci. (trustee 1989-95, v.p. 1992-93, pres. 1993-94), Am. Soc. for Microbiology (v.p. Intermountain br. 1988-89, pres. 1989-90), Idaho Edn. Alliance for Sci. (bd. dirs.), Sigma Xi, Sigma Delta Epsilon. Presbyterian. Home: 30 Colgate St Pocatello ID 83201-3459 Office: Idaho State U Dept Biol Scis Pocatello ID 83209

MCCURDY, GISELA ANN, physician; b. Breslau, Germany, Aug. 10, 1917; came to U.S., 1951; d. Ernst and Elizabeth (Schimpff) Wohl; m. Frank C. McCurdy, Aug. 22, 1959 (dec. July 1986); 1 child, Carole Ann. BS, U. Perugia, Italy, 1939; MD, U. Graz, Austria, 1951. Rotating intern Chgo. Meml. Hosp., 1952-53; pathology resident Michael Reese Hosp., Chgo., 1953-54; internal medicine resident Belmont Hosp., Chgo., 1954-55; staff physician Mcpl. Tuberculosis Sanitarium, Chgo., 1955-58, sr. staff physician, 1958-65; dir. employees health Mt. Sinai Hosp., Chgo., 1965-70; staff physician Neighborhood Health Clinic, Chgo., 1970-72; pvt. practice Chgo., 1972-75; student health physician Cir. Campus U. Ill., Chgo., 1975-82. Mem. AMA, NOW, Planned Parenthood.

MCCUSKER, SISTER JOAN, parochial school educator, music educator; b. Bklyn., Dec. 11, 1957; d. James Francis and Edna Joan (deNicola) McC. BM in Mus. Edn., Marywood Coll., 1979; MM in Mus. Edn., Ithaca Coll., 1990; postgrad., Eastman Sch. Music. Cert. tchr., Pa., N.Y. Organist, choir dir. Holy Trinity Parish, Glen Burnie, Md., 1979-80; music tchr. St. Charles Borromeo, Arlington, Va., 1979-80, Most Precious Blood Sch., Balt., 1979-80, Nativity Sch., Scranton, Pa., 1980-81, St. Ephrem Sch., Bklyn., 1983-89, Notre Dame Elem. Sch., East Stroudsburg, Pa., 1989-90, St. Rose Elem. Sch./Sacred Heart H.S., Carbondale, Pa., 1990-93; music edn. instr. Marywood Coll., Scranton, 1992-93; music tchr. St. Joseph-by-the-Sea H.S., S.I., 1993—; mem. Music Edn. Nat. Conf., 1983. Composer (sacred/vocal) Mass in D, 1980, Let Me Be Your Reed, 1983, The Word of Life, 1983, With One Voice, 1994. Mem. Nat. Cath. Educators Assn., Nat. Pastoral Musicians Assn., Pa. Music Edn. Assn., Kappa Gamma Pi (St. Catherine medal for Nat. Achievement 1978). Home: 327 Warrington Dr Rochester NY 14618

MCCUSKER, MARY LAURETTA, library science educator; b. Sillery, Que., Can., Jan. 18, 1919; came to U.S., 1938, naturalized, 1942; d. Albert James and Laura (Cleary) McC. B.A., Western Md. Coll., 1942; M.S.L.S., Columbia U., 1952, D.L.S., 1963. Joined Order of Preachers, Roman Catholic Ch., 1961; librarian Annapolis (Md.) High Sch., 1942-44, McDonogh Mil. Sch., 1944-47; asst. prof. Iowa State Tchrs. Coll. (now No. Iowa U.), Cedar Falls, 1948-59; vis. prof. library sci. U. Minn., Mpls., summers, 1958-59; assoc. prof. Sch. Library Sci. Rosary Coll., 1963-67, dir., prof. Grad. Sch., 1967-81, prof. emeritus, rsch. assoc., 1981-94, dean grad. sch., 1969-81, prof. emeritus, 1994—. Contbr. articles to profl. jours. Continuing Edn. grantee World Book Ency., 1994. Mem. ALA, Assn. Libr. and Info. Sci. Edn., Nat. Cath. Libr. Assn. (pres. No. Ill. chpt. 1987-89, chair acad. sect. No. Ill. chpt. 1992—, v.p. pres.-elect 1995—), Ill. Libr. Assn., Ill. Sch. Libr. Media Assn. (chair awards com. 1990-91, 94-95, co-chair cert. and stds. com. 1995—), Chgo. Libr. Club, Sch. Libr. Assn. Office: Rosary Coll Grad Sch Library and Info Sci 7900 Division St River Forest IL 60305-1066

MCCUTCHAN, JUDITH KATHERINE, special education educator; b. Evansville, Ind., Oct. 12, 1941; d. Herbert Adelbert and Frances (Neblung) Grunow; m. Neil Jason McCutchan, Feb. 17, 1962; 1 child, Allen Neil. BS, U. N.D., 1979, MEd, 1986, PhD, 1992. Cert. spl. edn. tchr., elem. tchr. Tchr. substitute Grand Forks (N.D.) Pub. Schs., 1979-85, 95-96; grad. tchg. asst. U. N.D., Grand Forks, 1985-88; lectr. Mayville (N.D.) State U., 1988-89; tchr. spl. edn. Minot (N.D.) Pub. Schs., 1989-90, Upper Valley Spl. Edn. Unit, Grafton, N.D., 1991-95, Polk County Pub. Schs., Winter Haven, Fla., 1996—; rsch. asst. Bur. Ednl. Rsch. U. N.D., Grand Forks, 1986-87. Bd. dirs., sec./treas. Greater Grand Forks Emergency Food Cupboard, 1978-85. Mem. NEA, ASCD, Fla. Edn. Assn., Polk County Edn. Assn., Order Ea. Star (Worthy Matron 1992-93). Methodist. Home: 1740 Terry Cir NE Winter Haven FL 33881

MCDADE, LINNA SPRINGER, retired academic program administrator; b. Lincoln, Ill., May 18, 1932; d. Clifford Harry and Lois Mae (Lovett) S.; m. Wesley Dale McDade, June 13, 1951; children: Kimberly Rachel, Chance Linnea, Wesley Dale Jr., Bryan Anthony, Darby Erin. Student, Northwestern U., 1950; AB with honors, U. Ill., 1971. Cert. tchr., Ill. Substitute tchr. Sch. Dist. 116, Urbana, Ill., 1972-74; mng. editor Am. Sociol. Rev., Am. Sociol. Assn., Urbana, 1977-80; asst. to head dept. sociology U. Ill., Urbana, 1980-90; ret., 1990; grants coord. The Reading Group, Urbana, Ill., 1995-96. Chorus mem. Ill. Opera Theatre, 1979-82; pres. Evening Etude Music Club, 1958-60; dir. children's choir 1st Presbyn. Ch., Urbana, 1977, deacon, 1985—, elder, 1989—; co-pres. Washington Sch. PTA, Urbana, 1963-64; bd. dirs. Frances Nelson Health Ctr., Champaign, Ill., 1989-93; vol. fundraising coord. New Hope Jobs, Champaign, 1994—; bd. dirs. Adoption Studies Inst., Washington, 1995-96. Recipient " So Proudly We Hail" Community Svc. award The Exch. Club Urbana, 1990. Mem. Phi Alpha Theta. Home: 2433 County Road 1225 N Saint Joseph IL 61873-9727

MCDANELD, MARLA MICHELE, counselor; b. Centralia, Ill., Aug. 21, 1960; d. David Lee and Rosanna C. (West) Perkins; m. Mickey Ray McDaneld, June 21, 1986; 1 child, DyLan Lee. AA, Kaskakia Coll., 1980; BS in Edn., Ea. Ill. U., 1982, MS in Edn., 1993, Ed specialist, 1996. Cert. sch. counselor, Ill. Behavior disorders tchr. Centralia City Schs. Jr. High, 1982-84, Centralia H.S., 1984-85, Nashville (Ill.) Mid. Sch., 1985-86; tchr., English and spl. edn. Salem (Ill.) Cmty. H.S., 1986-93, crisis supr., 1993-94, sch. counselor, 1994—. sponsor Peer Helpers, Salem, 1993-94. Mem. ACA, Ill. Counseling Assn., Ill. Sch. Counselors Assn., Am. Sch. Counseling Assn., Okaw Valley Counseling Assn. Home: 5823 McDaneld Rd Kell IL 62853 Office: Salem Cmty High Sch 1200 North Broadway Salem IL 62881

MCDANIEL, GERALDINE HOWELL, geriatrics rehabilitation nursing consultant; b. Como, N.C., Feb. 21, 1943; d. Jarvis Littleton and Nell Carson (Daughtley) Howell; m. Paul G. McDaniel; children: Christopher Louis Winstead, Kimberley Ann Winstead. Student, Old Dominion U., 1961-62; diploma, RN, Norfolk (Va.) Gen. Hosp. Sch., 1964. RN, Va.; cert. nurse adminstr. ANA; cert. rehab. RN Am. Rehab. Assn. Office nurse ob-gyn. Dr. A.R. Garnett, Norfolk, Va., 1964; staff nurse Radford (Va.) Cmty. Hosp., 1965-66, Med. Coll. Va., Richmond, 1965; student health nurse Union Coll., Schenectady, N.Y., 1966-69; DON Confederate Home for Women, Richmond, 1975-80; clin. coord. Catawba (Va.) Hosp. Mental/Geriatric, 1981-86; DON Friendship Manor, Roanoke, Va., 1986-89, Avanté of Roanoke, Va., 1989-92, Va. Vets. Care Ctr., Roanoke, 1992-94; rehab. nurse cons. Mariner Rehab., Chapel Hill, N.C., 1994—; mem. Task Force to Study How Regulations Affect Patient Outcomes in Long Term Care, Roanoke, 1994; state coord. for parish nursing Va. Bapt. Women's Missionary Union. Sunday sch. tchr., com. chairperson, mission trips to Argentina, Mexico, Peru First Bapt. Ch., Roanoke, 1987—. Mem. ANA (cert. nurse adminstr.), Am. Rehab. Assn. (cert. rehab. RN), Assn. Rehab. Nurses, Va. Bapt. Nurses Fellowship (sec., treas., area rep. 1993—), Noble Dirs. Nurses S.W. Va., Va. Nurses Assn., Va. Dirs. Nurses Long Term Care (past dist. rep.). Baptist.

MCDANIEL, GRACIE SWAIN, nursing administrator; b. Hernando, Miss., Nov. 5, 1958; d. Edgar Ernest and Margarite Jane (Calvert) Swain; m. David Kenneth McDaniel, July 28, 1978; children: Bethany, Patrick. ADN, N.W. C.C., 1979; postgrad., Miss. State U., 1991-93. RN, Tenn., Miss., Ala., Ga., La. Staff nurse LeBonheur Children's Med. Ctr., Memphis, 1979-84, North Panola Regional Hosp., Sardis, Miss., 1984-90; home health nurse Miss. Dept. Health, 1990—; instr. N.W. C.C., Senatobia, Miss., 1991-94; DON, Dixie Home Care, Batesville, Miss., 1994—. Mem. ANA, Miss. Nurses Assn. Democrat. Baptist. Home: 117 S Pocahontas St Sardis MS 38666-1624 Office: Dixie Home Care PO Box 686 Batesville MS 38606

MCDANIEL, JANIE LEA, musician, educator; b. Greeley, Colo., July 31, 1942; d. Ernest Trafford and Beatrice (Gray) Soper; m. James E. McKedy, Aug. 25, 1965 (div. 1981); children: Shelley B. McKedy, Kelley Anne McKedy; m. Douglas D. McDaniel, Sept. 22, 1995. BS with honors, U. No. Colo., 1964; MST, Portland State U., 1970. Tchr's. Cert. Wash., Oreg., Colo. Tchr. Crowley County Sch. Dist., Ordway, Colo., 1964-65, Kelso (Wash.) Sch. Dist., 1965-68, Clark County Christian Sch., Vancouver, Wash., 1968-69; tchr. Washington State Sch. Blind, Vancouver, Wash., 1970-82, music dir., 1982—; music resource person Evergreen Sch. Dist.; music tchr. Riverview Elem. Sch., Vancouver, Wash., 1992-94; musical dir. Parangello Players, Vancouver, Wash., 1989-91. Author: The Tadoma Method, 1970, Oratory During the Baroque Period, 1970. Vol. Clark County Election Bd., Columbia Arts Ctr., Vancouver, Wash., 1969—, 1981—, Old Slocum House Theater, Vancouver, Wash., 1987—; mem. Arts and Entertainment Com., Vancouver, Wash., 1991, Vancouver Piano Class, Chamber Singers, Songspinners, Brahms Singers, 1982-87; ch. organist; mem. Fairway Village Singers, dir., 1990-95; with New Orleans Jazz and Heritage Festival, 1996—. Recipient Honors scholarship Ottawa U., 1960, Academic scholarship, U. No. Colo., Greeley, Colo., 1960, Colo. State U., Fort Collins, Colo., 1960. Mem. Am. Edn. Assn., Washington Edn. Assn., Vancouver Edn. Assn., Am. Fedn. for Blind, Beta Sigma Phi, Epsilon Chi, Sigma Alpha. Republican. Home: 4720 Lennox Blvd New Orleans LA 70131

MCDANIEL, KAREN JEAN, university library administrator; b. Newark, Nov. 16, 1950; d. Alphonso Cornell Cotton Jr. and Maude Jean (Smoot) Cotton Bledsoe; m. Rodney McDaniel Sr., Aug. 25, 1971; children: Rodney Jr., Kimberly Renee, Jason Bradley. BSBA, Berea Coll., 1973; MS in Libr. Sci., U. Ky., 1975, postgrad., 1977-78; postgrad., Ky. State U., 1979-83, Ea. Ky. U., 1983. Asst. libr., instr. reference studies Paul G. Blazer Libr.-Ky. State U., Frankfort, 1975-79, asst. libr., instr. cataloging, 1980-83, head cataloging and classification, 1983; program coord. libr. svcs. Ky. Dept. Pub. Advocacy, Frankfort, 1983-85, libr. sr., 1985-87, program coord. state publs., 1987-89; dir. libr. svcs. Paul G. Blazer Libr.-Ky. State U., Frankfort, 1989—; bd. dirs. Solinet; mem. adv. bd. African Am. Ednl. Archives Initiative, Wayne State U.; mem. faculty adv. bd. Ctr. of Excellence for Study of Ky. African Ams.; mem. subcom. on target groups Ky./White House Conf. on Libr. and Info. Svcs. II, chair, 1990-91. Mem. State of Ky. Textbook Commn., 1993—; mem. Nat. Coun. Negro Women; adult membership Girl Scouts Am., 1987—, asst. troop leader, 1991-93; active Frankfort H.S. PTA, 1994—, Hearn Elem. Sch. PTA, 1983-94, Elkhorn Mid. Sch. PTA, 1991—, Friends of Paul Sawyer Libr.; active St. John AME Ch.; mem. bd. Frankfort YMCA, 1995—. Mem. ALA, AAUP, NAACP, Assn. Coll. and Rsch. Librs., Black Caucus of ALA (affirmative action com.), Southeastern Libr. Assn. (planning and devel. com. 1991—, preservation round table 1993—), Land Grant and Tuskegee Libr. Dir.'s Assn. (editor Libline 1993—, vice-chair, chair 1994—), State Assisted Acad. Libr. Coun. Ky. (sec. 1991-92, sec. 1992-93), Ky. Libr. Assn. (sec. acad. sect. 1990-91), Ky. Coun. Archives, Ky. Assn. Blacks in Higher Edn., Alpha Delta Kappa, Delta Sigma Theta. Democrat. African Methodist Episcopalian. Home: 147 Northwood Rd Frankfort KY 40601-1477 Office: Ky State U Paul G Blazer Libr Frankfort KY 40601

MCDANIEL, MYRA ATWELL, lawyer, former state official; b. Phila., Dec. 13, 1932; d. Eva Lucinda (Yores) Atwell; m. Reuben Roosevelt McDaniel Jr., Feb. 20, 1955; children: Diane Lorraine, Reuben Roosevelt III. BA, U. Pa., 1954; JD, U. Tex., 1975; LLD, Huston-Tillotson Coll., 1984, Jarvis Christian Coll., 1986. Bar: Tex. 1975, U.S. Dist. Ct. (we. dist.) Tex. 1977, U.S. Dist. Ct. (so. and no. dists.) Tex. 1978, U.S. Ct. Appeals (5th cir.) 1978, U.S. Supreme Ct. 1978, U.S. Dist. Ct. (ea. dist.) Tex. 1979. Asst atty. gen. State of Tex., Austin, 1975-81, chief taxation div., 1979-81, gen. counsel to gov., 1983-84, sec. of state, 1984-87; asst. gen. counsel Tex. R.R. Commn., Austin, 1981-82; gen. counsel Wilson Cos., San Antonio and Midland, Tex., 1982; assoc. Bickerstaff, Heath & Smiley, Austin, 1984, ptnr., 1987-96; mng. ptnr. Bickerstaff, Heath, Smiley, Pollan, Kener & McDaniel, Austin, 1996—; mem. asset. mgmt. adv. com. State Treasury, Austin, 1984-86; mem. legal affairs com. Criminal Justice Policy Coun., Austin, 1984-8, Inter-State Oil Compact, Oklahoma City, 1984-86; bd. dirs. Austin Cons. Group, 1983-86; mem. Jud. Efficiency Coun., Austin, 1995-96; lectr. in field. Contbr. articles to profl. jours., chpts. to books. Del. Tex. Conf. on Librs. and Info. Sci., Austin, 1978, White House Conf. on Librs. and Info. Scis., Washington, 1979; mem. Libr. Svcs. and Constrn. Act Adv. Coun., 1980-84, chmn., 1983-84; mem. long range plan task force Brackenridge Hosp., Austin, 1981; clk. vestry bd. St. James Episcopal Ch., Austin, 1981-83, 89-90; bd. visitors U. Tex. Law Sch., 1983-87, cice chmn., 1983-85; bd. dirs. Friends of Ronald McDonald House Ctrl. Tex., Women's Advocacy, Inc., Capital Area Rehab. Ctr.; trustee Episcopal Found. Tex., 1986-89, St. Edward's U., Austin, 1986—, chmn. acad. com., 1988—; chmn. divsn. capital area campaign United Way, 1986; active nat. adv. bd. Leadership Am.; trustee Episcopal Sem. S.W., 1990-96, Assn. Governing Bds. Univs. and Colls., Leadership Edn. Arts Program, 1995—. Recipient Tribute to 28 Black Women award Concepts Unltd., 1983; Focus on women honoree Serwa Yetu chpt. Mt. Olive grand chpt. Order of Eastern Star, 1979, Woman of Yr. Longview Metro C. of C., 1985, Woman of Yr. Austin chpt. Internat. Tng. in Communication, 1985, Citizen of Yr. Epsilon Iona chpt. Omega Psi Phi. Master Inns of Ct.; mem. ABA, Am. Bar Found., Tex. Bar Found. (trustee 1986-89), Travis County Bar Assn., Travis County Women Lawyers' Assn., Austin Black Lawyers Assn., State Bar Tex. (chmn. Profl. Efficiency & Econ. Rsch. subcom. 1976-84), Golden Key Nat. Honor Soc., Longhorn Assocs. for Excellence in Women's Athletes (adv. coun. 1988—), Order of Coif (hon. mem.), Omicron Delta Kappa, Delta Phi Alpha. Democrat. Home: 3910 Knollwood Dr Austin TX 78731-2915 Office: Bickerstaff Heath Et Al 1700 Forst Bank Plz 816 N Congress Ave Austin TX 78701-2443

MCDANIEL, OLA JO PETERSON, social worker, educator; b. Hot Springs, Ark., Sept. 17, 1951; d. Milton Paul and Ella Floyd (Dickerson) Peterson; m. Daniel Tillman McDaniel, June 11, 1994; 1 child, Cadra Peterson. B Music Edn., Henderson State Coll., Arkadelphia, Ark., 1973; MA in Edn., Lindenwood Colls., St. Charles, Mo., 1983, cert. in Social Studies, 1977. Cert. tchr., Mo., Ark. Mem. faculty Sch. Dist. St. Charles, 1974-84; adj. faculty Garland County C.C., Hot Springs, 1988-90; social worker Ark. Dept. Human Svcs., Hot Springs, 1990-94; substitute tchr. Hot Springs Sch. Dist., 1994-95; tutor St. Michael's Sch., Hot Springs, 1995—; cons. scholarships Hot Springs Music Club, 1988; const. student performance Garland County C.C., Hot Springs, 1988. Author, contbr. (learning activities) 3 R's for the Gifted: Reading, Writing, Research, 1982. Vol. Hot Springs Mayorial Campaign, 1993, Dem. Gubernatorial campaign, Hot Springs, 1990; hon. mem. Nat. Steering Com. to Reelect the Pres., Washington, 1995; mem. Dem. Nat. Com., Washington, 1995. Recipient Certs. of Appreciation, St. Chrysostom's Am. Episcopal Ch., Hot Springs, 1990, Nat. Mus. Am. Indian, Washington, 1995, award Alpha Chi. Mem. AAUW, Nat. Mus. Am. Indian, Nat.Mus. Women in Arts, Mid-Am. Sci. Mus., Henderson Alumni Assn., Lindenwood Alumni Assn. Democrat. Roman Catholic. Home: 102 Woodberry Ave Hot Springs AR 71913

MCDANIEL, SUE POWELL, cultural organization administrator; b. Jefferson City, Mo., Mar. 13, 1946; d. Ernest Gayle and Ruth Angeline (Raithel) Powell; m. Walter Lee Zimmerman, Aug. 14, 1966 (div. 1980); m. Olin Cleve McDaniel, June 23, 1985. BS in Edn., U. Mo., 1968, MEd in Edn., 1977, EdS, 1980, PhD, 1985. Cert. tchr., Mo. Tchr. Jefferson City Pub. Schs., 1968-80; fiscal assoc. Mo. Coordinating Bd. for Higher Edn., Jefferson City, 1980-90; exec. dir. Mo. Women's Coun., Jefferson City, 1990—. Co-author: Missouri Women Today, 1993, Status of the Women, 1994. Mem. Zonta Internat., Lincoln Women in Devel. (pres. 1993—). Office: Mo Women's Coun PO Box 1684 Jefferson City MO 65102-1684

MCDANIEL, THELMA LOUISE, drama/theater educator; b. Staten Island, N.Y., Sept. 20, 1923; d. Carlous Lee Richardson and Maria Elena (Fasulo) Geddes; m. Fred R. McDaniel, Aug. 26, 1946; children: Susan McDaniel Hill, Jamie Ruth Hodges. BFA, U. Iowa, 1946; MA, Ea. Mich. U., 1964. Prof. comm. and theatre arts Ea. Mich. U., Ypsilanti, 1961-86, prof. emerita, 1986—. Newsletter editor Nat. Assn. for Nat. Drama Therapy, 1988-90; author numerous scripts for story theatre and adaptations of plays for the young. Mem. Social and Environ. Concerns Group, Naples. Named Creative Drama Leader of the Yr. award Am. Assn. Theatre in Edn., 1990, Cert. of Merit, Ea. Mich. U. Mem. Naples Woman's Club (homelife chair 1992-96, drama chair 1996—), Naples Theatre Guild (publicity chair 1995-96). Democrat. Unitarian Universalist.

MCDANIELS, PEGGY ELLEN, special education educator; b. Pulaski, Va., Jan. 4, 1945; d. James H. and Gladys M. (Hurd) Fisher; m. Robert A. McDaniels, Feb. 17, 1973; children: Dawn Marie, Robert C. A Gen. Studies, Schoolcraft Coll., 1976; BA, Ea. Mich. U., 1980, MA, 1985. Cert. adminstr. Woodcock Johnson Psychoednl. Battery (Orton-Gillingham Tng). Payroll sec. Otto's Painting and Drywall, West Bloomfield, Mich., 1964-75; office mgr., closing sec. Bing Constrn. Co., West Bloomfield, 1964-75; substitute tchr. Wayne-Westland Schs., Westland, Mich., 1980-83, Farmington (Mich.) Schs., 1980-83; tchr. spl. edn. Romulus (Mich.) Community Schs., 1983-85, Cros-Lex Schs., Croswell, Mich., 1985-87, Pointe Tremble Elem. Sch., Algonac, Mich., 1987—; organizer, recorder Tchr. Assistance Team, Algonac, 1991—. Mem. Coun. Exceptional Children, Learning Disability Assn. (treas. 1988-90), Mich. Assn. Learning Disability Edn., ASCD. Home: 2406 Military St # 1 Port Huron MI 48060-6665

MCDARIS, WENDY CLAIRE, curator, educator, graphic designer; b. Tulsa, Okla., Feb. 7, 1951; d. Oliver Gordon and Rita Claire (Gay) Oldham; m. Robert Lester McDaris, Nov. 2, 1977 (dec. June 1991); children: Glynnis Claire, Blaise Rory. BA in English Lit., Washington U., St. Louis, 1972; MFA, U. Memphis, 1990. Dir., prin. McDaris Exhibit Group, Memphis, 1990—; asst. prof. art, art history U. Memphis, 1990—; vis. prof. art, arts adminstrn. U. Miss., Oxford, 1995-96; bd. dirs. Art Today-Contemporary Art Acquisition Group for Memphis Brooks Mus. Art, Memphis, 1995—; cons. special projects Memphis Coll. Art, 1995—. Author, co-editor: Elvis & Marilyn: 2X Immortal, 1994; co-author, co-designer: Educators Guide: Danzig 1939, 1988 (1st prize Tenn. Assn. Mus. 1988); design cons.: Images of Power: Bacinese Paintings Made for Gregory Bateson and Margaret Mead, 1995; curator: (exhibition) Elvis & Marilyn; 2X Immortal, 1994; designer, conceptual author: Muddy Waters: Big Blues, Small World. Judge Memphis Theatre Awards, 1986-88, Master of Fine Arts Exhibition, U. Miss., Oxford, 1995; curatorial advisor Tenn. State Mus. Bicentennial Adv. Panel, Nashville, 1995—. Mem. Am. Assn. Mus., Coll. Art Assn., Assn. Independent Historians of Art, Soc. of Arts, Religion, Culture, Nat. Assn. Mus. Exhibitors, Kappa Kappa Gamma. Home and Office: McDaris Exhibit Group 3576 Spottswood Ave Memphis TN 38111-5819

MCDARRAH, GLORIA SCHOFFEL, editor, author; b. Bronx, N.Y., June 22, 1932; d. Louis and Rose Schoffel; m. Fred W. McDarrah, Nov. 5, 1960; children: Timothy, Patrick. BA in French, Pa. State U., 1953; MA in French, NYU, 1966. Editorial asst. Crowell-Collier, N.Y.C., 1957-59; exec. asst. to pub. Time Inc., N.Y.C., 1959-61; libr., tchr. N.Y.C. Pub. Schs. and St. Luke's Sch., 1972-76; exec. asst. to pres. Capital Cities Communications Inc., N.Y.C., 1972-76; analyst N.Y.C. Landmarks Preservation Commn., 1976-79; project editor Grosset & Dunlap Inc., N.Y.C., 1979-80; sr. editor Prentice Hall trade div. Simon & Schuster Inc., N.Y.C., 1980-88; pres. McDarrah Media Assocs., N.Y.C., 1988—. Author: Frommer's Guide to Virginia, 1992, 2d edit., 1994-95, Frommer's Atlantic City and Cape May, 1984, 4th edit., 1991, 5th edit., 1993-95, The Artist's World, 2d edit., 1988; co-author: Museums in New York, 5th edit., 1990, Photography Marketplace, 1975 (book rev. sect.), The Beat Generation: Glory Days in Greenwich Village, 1996; co-editor Exec. Desk Diary Saturday Rev., 1962-64; contbg. editor quar. Dollarwise Traveler, Fodor's Cancun, Cozumel, Yucatan Peninsula, Fodor's Arizona; editor book rev. The Picture Profl., 1990—; book columnist Manhattan Spirit, 1989—; book reviewer Pub.'s Weekly, 1994—.

MCDAVID, SARA JUNE, librarian; b. Atlanta, Dec. 21, 1945; d. William Harvey and June (Threadgill) McRae; m. Michael Wright McDavid, Mar. 23, 1971. BA, Mercer U., 1967; MLS, Emory U., 1969. Head librarian Fernbank Sci. Ctr., Atlanta, 1969-77; dir. rsch. libr. Fed. Res. Bank of Atlanta, 1977-81; mgr. mem. services SOLINET, Atlanta, 1981-82; media specialist Parkview High Sch., Atlanta, 1982-84; ptnr. Interncontinental Travel, Atlanta, 1984-85; librarian Wesleyan Day Sch., Atlanta, 1985-86; mgr. info. svcs. Internat. Assn. Fin. Planning, Atlanta, 1986-90; dir. rsch. Korn Ferry Internat., Atlanta, 1990-95; rschr. Lamalie Amrop Internat., Atlanta, 1995—; bd. dirs. Southeastern Library Network, Atlanta, 1977-80, vice chmn. bd., 1979-80. Contbr. articles to profl. jours. Pres., mem. exec. com. Atlanta Humane Soc., 1985-86, bd. dirs. aux., 1978-90. Mem. Ga. Library Assn. (v.p. 1981-83), Spl. Libraries Assn. Home: 1535 Knob Hill Dr NE Atlanta GA 30329-3206 Office: Lamalie Amrop Internat 191 Peachtree St Ste 800 Atlanta GA 30303-1747

MCDERMOTT, JUDITH RIVA, financial analyst; b. Jamestown, N.Y., July 27, 1948; d. Leo and Carol (Himes) Sade; m. John Michael McDermott, June 10, 1972; children: Andrew Michael, Stephen Leo. BA in History, Hiram (Ohio) Coll., 1970; MBA in Fin., Loyola Coll., Balt., 1982. Fin. analyst Jos. A. Bank Clothiers, Hampstead, Md., 1983-88, acct., 1988-90; fin. analyst Computer Scis. Corp., Lanham, Md., 1990-92, sr. fin. analyst, 1992-95, sr. program control adminstrv. officer, 1995—. Bd. dirs., treas. Unitarian Universalist Congregation of Columbia, Md., 1990-92. Unitarian. Home: 6307 Golden Hook Columbia MD 21044

MCDERMOTT, KATHLEEN E., retail executive. Exec. v.p., gen. counsel Am. Stores, Salt Lake City. Office: American Stores Company 709 E South Temple Salt Lake City UT 84102*

MCDERMOTT, LISA ANN, pharmacist; b. Buffalo, Jan. 24, 1966; d. Paul Joseph and Jean Ann (Tomczak) McD. BS in Pharmacy, U. Tex., 1991; student, U. Tex., Dallas, 1996—. Registered pharmacist, Tex. Staff pharmacist Parkland Health and Hosp. Sys., Dallas, 1991-92, pharmacy resident, 1992-93, pharmacy coord., 1993-96; pharmacy preceptor U. Tex. Coll. Pharmacy, Dallas, 1991—; instr. Richland C.C., Dallas, 1994—. Contbr. articles to profl. jours. Violinist, New Philharm. Orch., Irving, Tex., 1994—. Recipient Lilly Achievement award Eli Lilly Co., 1991; Endowed Presdl. scholar U. Tex., 1990. Mem. Am. Soc. Health-Sys. Pharmacists, Tex. Soc. Health-Sys. Pharmacists, North Ctrl. Tex. Soc. Health-Sys. Pharmacists, Am. Soc. for Parenteral and Enteral Nutrition. Home: 4018 Esters Rd # 1065 Irving TX 75038

MCDERMOTT, LUCINDA MARY, minister, teacher, philosopher, poet, author; b. Lynwood, Calif., June 3, 1947; d. R. Harry and Cathrine Jaynne (Redmond) Boand. BA, U. So. Calif., L.A., 1969; MS, Calif. State U., Long Beach, 1975; PhD, Saybrook Inst., San Francisco, 1978. Pres. Environ. Health Systems, Newport Beach, Calif., 1976-90, Forerunner Publs., Newport Beach, 1985—; founder, pres. Life-Skills Learning Ctr., Newport Beach, 1985—; founder, dir. Newport Beach Ecumenical Ctr., 1993—; pres. Tri Delta Mgmt.; pres. The Boand Family Found. Author: Bridges to Another Place, 1972, Honor Thy Self, Vol. I and II, 1973, Hello-My-Love-Good Bye, 1973, Life-Skills for Adults, 1982, Au Courants, 1983, Life-Skills for Children, 1984, Myrika-An Autobiographical Novel, 1989, White Knights and Shining Halos: Beyond Pair Bonding, 1996. Mem. APA, Truthsayer Minstrels (founder, dir. 1996—), Alpha Kappa Delta, Kappa Kappa Gamma.

MCDERMOTT, MARY ANN, former dean, nursing educator. Dean Niehoff Sch. Nursing Loyola U., Chgo., prof. cmty. health, 1996—. Office: Loyola Univ Chicago Niehoff Sch Nursing 6525 N Sheridan Rd Chicago IL 60626*

MCDERMOTT, MOLLY, lay minister; b. Cloquet, Minn., Aug. 19, 1932; d. Harry W. McD.; children: Elizabeth Sanders Hellenbrand, Sarah Sanders, Mary Sanders Day, Margaret Kathleen Sanders Lorfeld. Student, Oreg. State Coll., 1951, U. Minn., Duluth, 1953. Claims specialist Cuna Mut. Ins. Soc., Madison, Wis., 1975—; propr. Molly's Garden. Storyteller, ventriloquist St. Bernard's Parish, liturgical environ. com. Mem. Perennial Soc., Toastmasters, The Rose Soc. (storyteller, ventriloquist). Roman Catholic. Home: 1724 Parmenter St Middleton WI 53562-3153

MCDERMOTT, PATRICE, policy analyst; b. Denver, June 4, 1950; d. Thomas James and Elinor Jeanne (Goettelman) McD.; m. Glenn Alan Harper, June 11, 1971. BA cum laude, Fla. State U., 1972; MA in Polit. Sci., Brown U., 1974; M Libr. and Info. Mgmt., Emory U., 1986; PhD in Polit. Sci., U. Ariz., 1982. Co-owner, mgr. Harper's Flowers, Inc., Atlanta, 1976-84; archives technician Jimmy Carter Presdl. Libr., Atlanta, 1984-86; asst. dir. Office for Intellectual Freedom ALA, Chgo., 1986-88; asst. prof. Sch. Libr. and Info. Studies Clark Atlanta U., 1988-90; archives specialist, life cycle coord. Nat. Archives and Records Adminstrn., Washington, 1990-93; info. policy analyst OMB Watch, Washington, 1994—; adj. asst. prof. dept. polit. sci. Clark Atlanta U., 1989-90; adj. asst. prof. women's studies program Georgetown U., Washington, 1991—; spkr., presenter in field; convenor panel Conf. Women and the Constitution: A bicentennial Perspective, 1988; manuscript reviewer Women & Politics. Editor Govt. Info. Insider, 1994—; contbr. articles, revs. to profl. publs. Mem. women's studies adv. bd. Georgetown U., 1991—. NDSL fellow, 1973-74, tchg. fellow U. Ariz., 1974-75. Mem. Am. Soc. Access Profls., Telecomms. Policy Roundtable, Am. Polit. Sci. Assn., Women's Caucus for Polit. Sci., Pub. Access Working Group (chair 1994—), Working Group Against Info. Redlining (chair 1994—). Office: OMB Watch 1742 Connecticut Ave NW Washington DC 20009

MCDERMOTT, PATRICIA ANN, nursing administrator; b. Bklyn., July 10, 1943; d. John J. and Lillian E. (Sweeney) Skelly; m. Joseph Kevin McDermott, Oct. 5, 1963; children: Colleen Mary, John Joseph. Diploma, Kings County Hosp. Ctr. Sch. Nursing, Bklyn., 1963; BS in Health Care Adminstrn., St. Francis Coll., Bklyn., 1979. Staff nurse Kings County Hosp., Bklyn., 1963-66, head nurse outpatient dept., 1966-74; evening supr. Park Nursing Home, Rockaway Park, N.Y., 1974-83; day supr. Hyde Park Nursing Home, Staatsburg, N.Y., 1984-85, DON, 1985—; nurse aide evaluator PRI assessor, MDS, coord. N.Y. State. Active local Girl Scouts U.S.A., 1971-78, Boy Scouts Am., 1978-82, Stella Maris Parents Club, 1978-82, St. Francis de Sales Altar and Rosary Soc., 1970-83, St. Francis de Sales Little League, 1978-80, also softball coach, 1974-77. Republican. Roman Catholic. Avocations: knitting; crocheting; roller skating; bowling; oil painting. Home: 286A Shadblow Ln Clinton Corners NY 12514 Office: Hyde Park Nursing Home RR 9 Staatsburg NY 12580

MCDERMOTT, RENÉE R(ASSLER), lawyer; b. Danville, Pa., Sept. 26, 1950; d. Carl A. and Rose (Gaupp) Rassler; m. James A. McDermott, Jan. 1, 1986. BA, U. So. Fla., 1970, MA, 1972; JD, Ind. U., 1978. Bar: Ind. 1978, U.S. Dist. Ct. (so. and no. dists.) Ind. 1978, U.S. Dist. Ct. Ariz. 1984, U.S. Ct. Appeals (7th cir.) 1979, U.S. Ct. Appeals (9th cir.) 1985. Law clk. to presiding judge U.S. Dist. Ct. (no. dist.) Ind., Ft. Wayne, 1978-80; assoc. Barnes & Thornburg, Indpls., 1980-84, ptnr., 1985-93; pvt. practice Nashville, Ind., 1994—; county atty. County of Brown, Ind., 1994—. Editor in chief Ind. U. Law Jour., 1977-78. Bd. visitors Ind. U. Law Sch., Bloomington, 1979—; bd. dirs. Environ. Quality Control Inc., Indpls. Named one of Outstanding Young Women Am., 1986. Fellow Ind. Bar Found., Am. Bar Found. (life); mem. ABA (bus. sect. coun. 1995—, chmn. environ. controls com. 1991-95, liaison to standing com. on environ. law bus. law sect.), Ind. State Bar Assn. (chmn. young lawyers sect. 1985-86, chmn. environ. law sect. 1989-91), Bar Assn. 7th Fed. Cir., Ind. Mfrs. Assn. (environ. affairs com.), Order of Coif. Home and Office: 1008 W McLary Rd Nashville IN 47448-9176

MCDERMOTT, SUSAN JEAN CASSI, fundraising and development consultant; b. Astoria, N.Y., Mar. 1, 1953; d. Walter George and Jean Louise (Krivicich) Cassi; m. Michael I. McDermott, Apr. 13, 1980; children: Ian Walter, Marielle Leigh. AA in Liberal Arts and Spanish, Nassau Community Coll., Garden City, N.Y., 1973; BA in Speech and Communications, SUNY, Oneonta, 1975; postgrad. bus. law and stats., Hofstra U. With advt. sales dept. N.Y. Daily News, N.Y.C., 1975-78, mgr. circulation dept., 1978-82; sales rep. Radio Relay, Hicksville, N.Y., 1983; with circulation ops. dept. USA Today, Bayside, N.Y., 1983-85; exec. dir. AHHS Neighborhood Press Coalition, Rockaway, N.Y., 1985-86; dir. devel. Threshold Svcs. Inc., Kensington, Md., 1989-94; founder, pres. S&M Devel. Resources, Silver Spring, Md., 1994—. Contbg. editor Newspix mag., 1982. Adv. com. Montgomery County Pub. TV Network; mem. cmty. adv. com. Visions Montgomery County, Md., 1993-94, bd. dirs., 1995; mem., bd. dirs. Silver Spring Cmty. Visions Homeless Project, 1994—. Mem. Silver Spring C. of C. (bd. dirs. 1993-96). Democrat. Roman Catholic. Home: 9009 2nd Ave Silver Spring MD 20910-2158 Office: S&M Devel Resources 9009 2nd Ave Silver Spring MD 20910-2158

MCDEVITT, SHEILA MARIE, lawyer, energy company executive; b. St. Petersburg, Fla., Jan. 15, 1947; d. Frank Davis and Marie (Barfield) McD. AA, St. Petersburg Jr. Coll., 1966; BA in Govt., Fla. State U., 1968, JD, 1978. Bar: Fla. 1978. Research asst. Fla. Legis. Reference Bur., Tallahassee, 1968-69; adminstr., research assoc. Constitution Revision Commn. Ga. Gen. Assembly, Atlanta, 1969-70; adminstrv. asst., analyst Fla. State Sen., Tallahassee, Tampa, 1970-79; assoc. McClain, Walkley & Stuart, P.A., Tampa, Seminole, Fla., 1979-81; govtl. affairs counsel Tampa Electric Co., 1981-82, corp. counsel, 1982-86; sr. corp. counsel Teco Energy, Inc., Tampa, 1986-89, asst. v.p., 1989-92; v.p., asst. gen. counsel, 1992—; mem. Worker's Compensation Adv. Council Fla. Dept. Labor, Tallahassee, 1984-86. Bd. dirs. Vol. Ctr. Hillsborough County, Tampa, 1984-85; chmn., trustee Tampa Lowry Park Zoo Soc., 1986-94, also legal advisor; bd. dirs. Hillsborough County Easter Seal Soc., 1994-95; mem. Fla. Rep. Exec. Com., Tallahassee, 1974-75, Hillsborough County Rep. Exec. Com., 1974-75; mem. transition team for Fla. Gov. Bob Martinez, 1986-87; mem. Fed. Jud. Adv. Commn., 1989-93. Mem ABA, Fla. Energy Bar Assn., Fla. Bar (vice chmn., then chmn. energy law com. 1984-87, jud. nominating procedures com. 1986-91, jud. adminstrn. selection and tenure com. 1991-93), Hillsborough County Bar Assn. (chmn. law week com. 1990, corp. counsel com. 1986-87, internat. law com. 1994-95), Am. Corp. Counsel Assn. (bd. dirs. Ctrl. Fla. chpt. 1986-87), Tampa Club, Tiger Bay Club, Tampa Yacht and Country Club. Roman Catholic. Office: TECO Energy Inc PO Box 111 702 N Franklin St Tampa FL 33602

MCDONALD, ALICE COIG, state education official; b. Chalmette, La., Sept. 26, 1940; d. Olas Casimere and Genevieve Louise (Heck) Coig; m. Glenn McDonald, July 16, 1967; 1 child, Michel. B.S., Loyola U., New Orleans, 1962; M.Ed., Loyola U., 1966; cert. rank I sch. adminstrn., Spalding Coll., 1975. Tchr. St. Bernard Pub. Schs., Chalmette, La., 1962-67; counselor, instructional coordinator Jefferson County Schs., Louisville, 1967-77; ednl. adviser Jefferson County Govt., Louisville, 1977-78; chief exec. asst. Office of Mayor, Louisville, 1978-80; dep. supt. pub. instrn. Ky. Dept. Edn., Frankfort, 1980-83, supt. pub. instrn., 1984-88; bd. dirs., com. mem. Ky. Coun. on Higher Edn., 1984-88, Ky. Juvenile Justice com., 1984-88, Ky. Ednl. TV Authority, 1984-88, So. Regional Coun. Ednl. Improvement, 1984-88. Mem. Pres.'s Adv. Com. on Women, 1978-80; active Dem. Nat. Conv., 1972, 76, 80, 84; pres. Dem. Woman's Club Ky., 1974-76, mem. exec. com., 1977-88; bd. dirs. Ky. Found. for Blind; exec. dir. Ky. Govtl. Svcs. Ctr., 1996—. Mem. NEA, Coun. Chief State Sch. Officers, Women in Sch. Adminstrn., Ky. Edn. Assn., River City Bus. and Profl. Women. Home: 6501 Gunpowder Ln Prospect KY 40059-9334 Office: 4th Fl W Acad Bldg Ky State Univ Frankfort KY 40601

MCDONALD, ANNE ARDEN, artist, photographer; b. London, Mar. 15, 1966; came to U.S., 1967; d. John Hutcheson McDonald and Nancy Hilmers (Peck) Landt. Studied with, William Parker, 1986, 87; BA in Art with honors, Wesleyan U., 1988; postgrad., R.I. Sch. Design, 1988. lectr. Camera Club N.Y., N.Y.C., 1993, Iisalmen (Finland) Kamera Festival, 1993, The Moor, Amsterdam, 1994, Bratislava (Slovakia) Month of Photography, 1995, Houston Ctr. of Photography, 1996; artist-in-residence The Millay Colony, Austerlitz, N.Y., 1994; Orgn. of Ind. Artists rep. anniversary show, 1991; presenter and spkr. Spazi Fine Art, Housatonic, Mass., 1992, Soros Found., Tallinn, Estonia, 1993, Pyramid Fine Arts, Rochester, N.Y., 1994. One-person shows include Zilkha Gallery, Middletown, Conn., 1988, Soho Photo Gallery, N.Y.C., 1990, Colorstone Exhbn. Space, N.Y.C., 1991, Spazi Fine Art, Housatonic, Mass., 1992, Coker Coll., Hartsville, S.C., 1993, In Focus Gallerie, Cologne, Germany, 1993, 96, Atlanta Photography Gallery, 1994, Alma (Mich.) Coll., 1994, Gallerie 3.14, Laon, France, 1996, Tel Aviv Mus., 1996, Books and Co., N.Y.C., 1996; exhibited in group shows Rayco Phot Ctr., San Francisco, 1991, Azido Arts, San Francisco, 1992, Images Gallery, Cin., 1993, Paul Cava Gallery, Phila., 1994, Schrattenberg Castle, Schiefling, Austria, 1995, Mus. Applied Arts, Budapest, Hungary, 1995, S.E. Mus. Photography, Daytona Beach, Fla., 1996; represented in collections Houston Mus. Fine Art, Bklyn. Mus., Detroit Art Inst., Bibliotheque Nat.; commns. include Tiny Mythic Theatre Co., N.Y.C., 1989, album cover for Freedy Johnston's Can You Fly?, 1992, book cover for Gerard Neval's Aurelia/Sylvie, 1993, poster for French dance co. Chrisiane Blaise, 1996; works published in N.Y. Newsday, Cen. Pk. Mag., Photo Rev. Mag., also catalogs; editor: (mag.) Blink, 1995-96; contbr. articles to mags. Organizer Photo Salon Group, Bklyn., 1995-96. Recipient Best in Show, Robin Rule Gallery, 1995, Best in Show, Images Gallery, 1992; finalist Ruttenberg Found., Friends of Photography, 1993; grantee Marie Walsh Sharpe Found., 1994; Savannah Coll. Art and Design scholar for summer art study, London and Paris, 1984. Mem. Houston Mus. Fine Art, Detroit Art Inst., Bklyn. Mus., Bibliotheque Nat. (Paris), Leo Steinberg. Home: # 5C 247 Water St Brooklyn NY 11201

MCDONALD, ANNE B., state legislator; b. Syracuse, N.Y.. BS, LeMoyne Coll.; MS, Syracuse U. Mem. Commn. on Aging, Stamford, Conn., 1969-76, chair, 1972-76; mem. State Adv. Coun. on Aging, 1977-80; mem. Bd. of Edn., Stamford, 1980-87, pres., 1984-85; chmn. Housing Authority, Stamford, 1988-90; state rep. Conn. House of Reps., Hartford, 1991—. Democrat. Home: 53 Courtland Hill St Stamford CT 06906-2306 Office: Conn House Reps Legislative Bldg Capitol Ave Hartford CT 06106*

MCDONALD, AUDRA ANN, actress. BFA in Voice, Juilliard Sch., 1993; attended, Sch. Arts., Calif. Stage appearances include (regional) Man of La Mancha, Evita, The Wiz, A Chorus Line, Grease, Anything Goes, The Real Inspector Hound, Master Class (L.A. Ovation award for Best Featured Actress in a Play, 1996), (Broadway) The Secret Garden, Carousel (Tony award for Best Featured Actress in a Musical, 1994, Antoinette Perry award for Featured Actress in a Musical 1994), Master Class (Tony award nominee for Best Featured Actress in a Play, 1996); (film appearance) Seven Servants, (TV) Bill Cosby pilot, 1996; concert performances include S'Wonderful, Some Enchanted Evening, Christa Ludwig and James Levine Recital, Revelation in Courthouse Park, Requiem Canticles. Recipient Theatre World award, 1994, Outer Critics Circle for Outstanding Actress in a Musical, 1994, Drama Desk award for Best Supporting Actress in a Musical, 1994. Office: care Linda Jacobs—Writers & Artists Agy 19 W 44th St Ste 1000 New York NY 10036*

MC DONALD, BARBARA ANN, psychotherapist; b. Mpls., July 15, 1932; d. John and Georgia Elizabeth (Baker) Rubenzer; B.A., U. Minn., 1954; M.S.W., U. Denver, 1977; m. Lawrence R. McDonald, July 27, 1957 (dec. Sept. 1993); children—John, Mary Elizabeth. Diplomate Am. Bd. Social Work; lic. psychotherapist. Day care cons. Minn. Dept. Public Welfare, St. Paul, 1954-59; social worker Community Info. Center, Mpls., 1959-60; exec. dir. Social Synergistics Co., Littleton, Colo., 1970—; cons. to community orgns., Indian tribes. Family therapist , 1979—. Bd. dirs. Vol. Bur. Sun Cities, Ariz., 1988, 89, 90. Named 1 of 8 Women of Yr. and featured on TV spl. Ladies Home Jour., 1974; Clairol scholar, 1974; Am. Bus. Women's Assn. scholar, 1974; Alpha Gamma Delta scholar, 1974. Mem. Minn. Pre-Sch. Edn. Assn. (hon. life), AAUW, Nat. Assn. Social Workers, Ariz. Assn. Social Workers, Assn. Clin. Social Workers, Am. Bus. Women's Assn., U. Minn. Alumni Club (sun cities chpt.), Alpha Gamma Delta (Disting. Citizen award 1975). Club: Altrusa (hon.). Author: Selected References on the Group Day Care of Pre-School Children, 1956; Helping Families Grow: Specialized Psychotherapy with Hearing Impaired Children and Their Families, 1984. Office: 13720 W Franciscan Dr Sun City West AZ 85375-5219

MCDONALD, CAROLYN ANN, dance educator, choreographer; b. Blytheville, Ark., Aug. 27, 1963; d. Travis Eugene and Barbara Jean (Myers) McD. BA in Dance, U. Calif., Irvine, 1987; postgrad., U. Iowa, 1995—. Instr. dance Kirkwood C.C., Cedar Rapids, Iowa, 1987-90; choreographer Kirkwood C.C., Cedar Rapids, 1987—, artistic dir., 1990-96, 1996—; Choreographer Colorguard dance ensemble Wash. H.S., Cedar Rapids, 1996—; instr. dance Coe Coll., Cedar Rapids, 1989—; owner, pres. McDonald Arts Ctr., Marion, Iowa, 1988—; choreographer Washington H.S. Color Guard, Cedar Rapids, 1996—; cons. Jane Boyd Cmty. House, Cedar Rapids, 1993-94; choreographer, color guard dance ensemble Washington H.S., Cedar Rapids, 1996—. Office: 105 Southview Dr Marion IA 52302-3055

MCDONALD, GABRIELLE ANNE KIRK, lawyer, former federal judge; b. St. Paul, Apr. 12, 1942; d. James G. and Frances R. Kirk; m. Mark T. McDonald; children: Michael, Stacy. LLB, Howard U., 1966. Bar: Tex. 1966. Staff atty. NAACP Legal Def. and Ednl. Fund, N.Y.C., 1966-69; ptnr. McDonald & McDonald, Houston, 1969-79; judge U.S. Dist. Ct., Houston, 1979-88; ptnr. Matthews Branscomb, Austin, Tex., 1988—; judge World Ct.-Internat. War Crime Tribunal, Hague, The Netherlands, 1995—; asst. prof. Tex. So. U., Houston, 1970, adj. prof., 1975-77; lectr. U. Tex., Houston, 1977-78; active UN Gen. Assembly War Crime Tribunal, 1993. Bd. dirs. Community Service Option Program; bd. dirs. Alley Theatre, Houston, Nat. Coalition of 100 Black Women, ARC; trustee Howard U., from 1983; bd. vistors Thurgood Marshall Sch. Law, Houston. Mem. ABA, Nat. Bar Assn., Houston Bar Assn., Houston Lawyers Assn., Black Women Lawyers Assn. Democrat. Congregationalist. *

MCDONALD, GAIL CLEMENTS, government official; b. Ft. Worth, Tex., Mar. 9, 1944; d. Eugene and Cornelia (Nagle) Clements; m. William C. Scott, Aug. 26, 1967 (div. 1976); 1 child, Jill Miriah Scott; m. Danny Lee McDonald, Aug. 6, 1982. BA, Tex. Christian U., Ft. Worth, 1966, MA, 1967. Instr. social sci. Cooke County Jr. Coll., Gainesville, Tex., 1967-69, Langston (Okla.) U., 1969, Tulsa Jr. Coll., 1977-79; instr. humanities Okla. State U., Stillwater, 1971-74; adminstrv. asst. edn. and cultural affairs Gov. David L. Boren, Oklahoma City, 1975-78; legis. aide Sen. David L. Boren, Tulsa, 1979; state assoc. Inst. for Ednl. Leadership, George Washington U., Washington, 1979-81; exec. asst. Commr. Norma H. Eagleton, Okla. Corp. Commr., Oklahoma City, 1990-95; commr. ICC, Washington, 1990—, vice chmn., 1993, chmn, 1993-95; adminstr. St. Lawrence Seaway Devel. Corp. U.S. Dept. Transp., Wahsington, 1995—. Bd. dirs. Okla. Sci. & Arts Found., 1975-83; exec. com. Frontiers of Sci. Found., 1976-80; fundraiser Washington chpt. Spl. Olympics. Named Woman of Yr., Women's Transp. Seminar, 1991. Mem. Nat. Assn. Regulatory Commrs. (transp. com.), Exec. Women in Govt., Conservation Round Table (chmn. 1990), Transp. Table Washington, Toastmasters (pres. 1988), Phi Alpha Theta. Democrat. Episcopalian. Office: US Dept Transp St Lawrence Seaway Devel Co 400 7th St SW Ste 5424 Washington DC 20590

MCDONALD, IRIS MARIE, real estate sales associate, interior designer; b. Manhattan, N.Y., Sept. 11, 1963; d. Mary Emma (Voyles) McDonald. Grad. h.s., North Miami Beach. Real estate sec. and interior designer Gulfstream, Plantation, Fla., 1987-89; real estate salesperson Brookman-Fels, Pembroke Pines, Fla., 1989-94, Lennar Homes, Fort Lauderdale, Fla., 1994—. Republican. Home: 11431 NW 18th St Plantation FL 33323

MCDONALD, JACQUELYN MILLIGAN, parent and family studies educator; b. New Brunswick, N.J., July 28, 1935; d. John P. and Emma (Mark) Milligan; m. Neil Vanden Dorpel; five children. BA, Cornell U., 1957; MA, NYU, 1971; MEd, Columbia U., 1992, EdD, 1993. Cert. in behavior modification, N.J.; cert. tchr. grades K-8, N.J.; cert. family life educator. Instr. Montclair (N.J.) State Coll., 1982-93, Edison C.C., Naples, Fla., 1994—; mem. steering com. Fla. Gulf Coast U. Family Ctr.; parent vol. tng. project coord. Montclair Pub. Schs., 1984-86; coord. Collier County IDEAS for Parenting, Inc., Naples, 1993—. Chairperson Interfaith Neighbors Juvenile Delinquency Prevention, N.Y.C., 1960-68; support family Healing the Children, 1970-90; founder The Parent Ctr., Montclair, 1983, Essex County N.J. Fair Housing Coun., 1990. Mem. Pre-Sch. Interagy. Couns., Family Svc. Planning Team, Raven and Serpent Hon. Soc. (pres. 1956). Psi Chi, Kappa Detla Pi. Home: 27075 Kindlewood Ln Bonita Springs FL 33923-4370

MCDONALD, JOANNE, human resources company executive; b. San Diego, June 10, 1947; d. Paul and Dolores (Paganucci) McD. BA, U. Md., 1970. High tech. exec. ENSCO Inc., Springfield, Va., 1981—, v.p. adminstrn. and human resources, 1992—; bd. dirs. ENSCO, Inc., Springfield, Va. Office: ENSCO Inc 5400 Port Royal Rd Springfield VA 22151-2301

MCDONALD, LESLEY SCOTT, clinical nurse specialist; b. Toronto, Jan. 29, 1946; d. Louis Johnstone and Frances Elizabeth (Pruder) McD.; m. Richard Eldon Jacobson, May 26, 1984. Grad. in nursing, Health Scis. Ctr., Winnipeg, Man., Can., 1969; BA, U. Winnipeg, 1974; MS, Johns Hopkins U., 1984. RN, Md., Wis., Ill., Tenn.; cert. neurosci. RN, ANCC. Neuro nurse clinician, staff nurse Johns Hopkins Hosp., Balt., 1974-83; neuro clin. nurse specialist Madison (Wis.) Gen., 1983-84, St. Anthony Med. Ctr., Rockford, Ill., 1984-90, Nashville Meml., 1990-94; neuro charge nurse Vanderbilt-Stallworth, Nashville, 1994—; lectr. No. Ill. U. Sch. Nursing, Rockford, 1989-90, Austin Peay State U. Sch. Nursing, Clarksville, Tenn., 1991-94. Mem. AACN, Am. Assn. Neurosci. Nurses (Madison chpt. pres. 1983-84, Rockford chpt. pres. 1986-90). Home: 147 Flat Rock Rd Lebanon TN 37090-9217

MCDONALD, MARIANNE, classicist; b. Chgo., Jan. 2, 1937; d. Eugene Francis and Inez (Riddle) McD.; children: Eugene, Conrad, Bryan, Bridget, Kirstie (dec.), Hiroshi. BA magna cum laude, Bryn Mawr Coll., 1958; MA, U. Chgo., 1960; PhD, U. Calif., Irvine, 1975, doctorate (hon.) Am. Coll. Greece, 1988, hon. diploma Am. Archaeological Assn. Teaching asst. classics

U. Calif., Irvine, 1974, D Litt (hon.) U. Athens, Greece, 1994, U. Dublin, 1994. instr. Greek, Latin and English, mythology, modern cinema, 1975-79, founder, rsch. fellow Thesaurus Linguae Graecae Project, 1975—; bd. dir. Centrum. Bd. dirs. Am. Coll. of Greece, 1981-90, Scripps Hosp., 1981; Am. Sch. Classical Studies, 1986—; mem. bd. overseers U. Calif. San Diego, 1985—; nat. bd. advisors Am. Biog. Inst., 1982—; pres. Soc. for the Preservation of the Greek Heritage, 1990—; founder Hajime Mori Chair for Japanese Studies, U. Calif., San Diego, 1985, McDonald Ctr. for Alcohol and Substance Abuse, 1984, Thesaurus Linguarum Hiberniae, 1991—; vis. prof. U. Dublin, 1990—; adj. prof. theatre U. Calif., San Diego, 1990, prof. theatre and classics, 1994. Recipient Ellen Browning Scripps Humanitarian award, 1975; Disting. Svc. award U. Calif.-Irvine, 1982, Irvine medal, 1987, 3rd Prize Midwest Poetry Ctr. Contest, 1987; named one of the Community Leaders Am., 1979-80, Philanthropist of Yr., 1985, Headliner San Diego Press Club, 1985, Philanthropist of Yr. Honorary Nat. Conf. Christians and Jews, 1986, Woman of Distinction Salvation Army, 1986, Eleventh Woman Living Legacy, 1986, Woman of Yr. AHEPA, 1988, San Diego Woman of Distinction, 1990, Woman of Yr. AXIOS, 1991; recipient Bravissimo gold medal San Diego Opera, 1990, Gold Medal Soc. Internationalization of Greek Lang., 1990, Athens medal, 1991, Piraeus medal, 1991, award Desmoi, 1992, award Hellenic Assn of Univ. Women, 1992, Academy of Achievement award AHEPA, 1992, Woman of Delphi award European Cultural Ctr. Delphi, 1992, Civis Universitatis award U. Calif. San Diego, 1993, Hypatia award Hellenic U. Women, 1993, Am.-Ireland Fund Heritage award, 1994, Contribution to Greek Letters award Aristotle U. Thessaloniki, 1994, Mirabella Mag. Readers Choice One of 1000 Women for the Nineties, 1994, Order of the Phoenix, Greece, 1994, citations from U.S. Congress and Calif. Senate, Alexander the Gt. award Hellenic Cultural Soc., 1995, made hon. citizen of Delphi and gold medal of the Amphiktuonon, Delphi, Greece, 1995, award European Cultural Ctr. of Delphi, 1995, Women Who Mean Bus. award for Fine Arts San Diego Bus. Jour., 1995. Vol. of Decade Women's International Ctr., 1994, 96. Mem. MLA, AAUP, Am. Philol. Assn., Soc. for the Preservation of the Greek Heritage (pres.), Libr. of Am., Am. Classical League, Philol. Assn. Pacific Coast, Am. Comparative Lit. Assn., Modern and Classical Lang. Assn. So. Calif., Hellenic Soc., Calif. Fgn. Lang. Tchrs. Assn., Internat. Platform Assn., Greek Language Found., Royal Irish Acad., Greece's Order of the Phoenix (commdr. 1994), KPBS Producers Club, Hellenic Univ. Club (bd. dir.). Author: Terms for Happiness in Euripides, 1978, Semilemmatized Concordances to Euripides' Alcestis, 1977, Cyclops, Andromache, Medea, 1978, Heraclidae, Hippolytus, 1979, Hecuba, 1984, Hercules Furens, 1984, Electra, 1984, Ion, 1985, Trojan Women, 1988, Iphigenia in Taurus, 1988, Euripides in Cinema: The Heart Made Visible, 1983; translator: The Cost of Kindness and Other Fabulous Tales (Shinichi Hoshi), 1986, (chpt.) Views of Clytemnestra, Ancient and Modern, 1990, Classics and Cinema, 1990, Modern Critical Theory and Classical Literature, 1994, A Challenge to Democracy, 1994, Ancient Sun/Modern Light: Greek Drama on the Modern Stage, 1990, Star Myths: Tales of the Constellations, 1996; contbr. numerous articles to profl. jours. Avocations: karate, harp (medieval), skiing, diving. Home: PO Box 929 Rancho Santa Fe CA 92067-0929 Office: U Calif at San Diego Dept Theatre La Jolla CA 92093

MCDONALD, MARY M., lawyer; b. 1944. BA, D'Youville Coll., 1966; JD, Fordham U., 1969. Bar: N.Y. 1969. Counsel corp. staff Merck & Co., v.p., gen. counsel, 1991—, now sr. v.p., gen counsel. Office: Merck & Co PO Box 100 Whitehouse Station NJ 08889-0100*

MC DONALD, MEG, public relations executive; b. Santa Monica, Calif., Oct. 11, 1948. Dir. radio & TV svcs. Fran Hynds Pub. Rels., 1969-75; owner, CEO Mc Donald Media Svcs., 1975—. Recipient Buccaneer award PIRATES, 1980, 82, Prisms award Pub. Rels. Soc. Am., 1981, Pro awards Publicity Clubs. of L.A. Mem. Pub. Rels. Soc. Am. (sec. 1985), Radio & TV News Assn. of So. Calif. (mem. bd. dirs. 1973-88), Publicity Club of L.A. (pres. 1979-80), L.A. Advtg. Women (v.p. 1984-85), Pub. Interest Radio & TV Ednl. Soc. (PIRATES) (mem. bd. dirs.), Radio & TV News Assn. Office: Mc Donald Media Svcs. 11076 Fruitland Dr Studio City CA 91604-3541

MCDONALD, MYRTLE LUCILLE, lawyer; b. Hamilton County, Tex., June 29, 1941; d. William Eugene and Leta Lucille (Oxley) Davis; m. James Lee McDonald, Mar. 4, 1967; children: Lara Liane, Joshua Davis. BBA, Tex. Tech. U., 1970, JD, 1972. Bar: Tex. 1973. Asst. criminal dist. atty. Lubbock County, Tex., 1973-76; assoc. J.R. Blumrosen, Lubbock, 1976-80; ptnr. Blumrosen & McDonald, Lubbock, 1980-89; ptnr., shareholder Jones, Flygare, Galey, Brown & Wharton, Lubbock, 1989—; panel trustee U.S. Bankruptcy Ct., no. dist., Tex., 1982—; mem. bankruptcy adv. comm. State Bar of Tex., Austin, 1987—, mem. dist. 16A grievance com., Lubbock, 1993—. Dir. Lubbock Day Care Assn., Lubbock Rape Crisis Ctr., 1987—. Mem. W. Tex. Bankruptcy Bar Assn. (pres. 1987-88), Exec. Forum, Altrusa Internat., Lubbock Dawners. Office: Jones, Flygare, Galey, Brown & Wharton 1600 Civic Center Plz Lubbock TX 79401

MCDONALD, PATRICIA ANNE, professional society executive; b. Detroit, Mar. 16, 1947; d. William and Esther Carpenter (Rodger) McD. Student, Eastern Mich. U., 1965-68, Wayne State U., 1970-71, U. Mich., 1983. Cert. social worker, Mich. Caseworker State Mich., Detroit, 1968-69; counselor City Detroit Health Dept., 1970-75; psychotherapist The Life Ctr., Ferndale, Mich., 1975-79; field rep. Nat. Multiple Sclerosis Soc., Southfield, Mich., 1979-80, dir. svcs., 1980-83, exec. dir., 1983—; bd. dirs. Mariners Inn, Detroit, Housing Alternatives Inc., Lansing, Mich., 1984-89; svc. cons. Nat. Multiple Sclerosis Soc., N.Y.C., 1981-82, others. Coun. mem. Judson Ctr., Royal Oak, Mich., 1991—. Recipient The Americans with Disabilities Act award, Washington, 1990. Mem. Coun. Exec. Officers (sec. 1988-89). Roman Catholic. Office: Nat Multiple Sclerosis Soc 26111 Evergreen Rd Ste 100 Southfield MI 48076-4481

MCDONALD, PATRICIA HAMILTON, insurance agency administrator, real estate broker; b. Raleigh, N.C., Sept. 15, 1952; d. Marvin Stancil Hamilton and Josephine (Blake) Rummage; m. Thomas Wayne McDonald, Jan. 22,1972; children: Wendi Dannette, Thomas Wayne. Diploma, Inst. of Ins., Phila., 1987. Cert. in gen. ins., agy. mgmt.; cert. profl. ins. woman; real estate broker. Sr. comml. lines account rep. Tomlinson Insurors, Fayetteville, N.C., 1970-76, Wachovia Ins. Agy., Fayetteville, 1976-78; agy. mgr., sec.-treas. Ins. Svc. Ctr., Fayetteville, 1978-91, Assoc. Ins. Agy. of Fayetteville, Inc., 1991—; instr. continuing edn. N.C. Dept. Ins., Raleigh, 1990-91; agts. adv. coun. Seibels Bruce Ins. Co., 1991-92, 94—; ins. agts. pre-licensing instr., CPCU instr. Fayetteville Tech. C.C., 1993, 94. Bd. dirs. Fayetteville Tech. Community Coll., 1990—. Recipient State award Cystic Fibrosis Found., 1988. Mem. Ind. Ins. Agts. (assoc., bd. dirs. 1989—), Fayetteville Assn. Ins. Profls. (pres. 1989—, chmn. edn. 1987-89, chmn. pub. rels. 1988, Ins. Woman of Yr. 1989), N.C. Assn. Ins. Women (chmn. edn. 1990, Edn. award 1989, Gen. Excellence award 1991, 92, state treas. 1992-93), Nat. Assn. Ins. Women (dec. 1985—), Ind. Ins. Agts. N.C. (trainer 1986—), Home Builders Assn. Fayetteville (Life Spike award), N.C. Foresters Assn., N.C. Grange, Hope Mills Kiwanis Club (treas. 1994—, bd. dirs. 1994—), Kiwanis Internat., Hope Mills Assn. Ins. Profls. (edn. chmn. 1992-93, long-range planning chmn. 1992-93), Fayetteville Area C. of C. Republican. Baptist. Office: Assoc Ins Agy Fayetteville 2547 Ravenhill Dr Ste 101 Fayetteville NC 28303-5461

MCDONALD, PEGGY ANN STIMMEL, retired automobile company official; b. Darbyville, Ohio, Aug. 25, 1931; d. Wilbur Smith and Bernice Edna (Hott) Stimmel; missionary diploma with honor Moody Bible Inst., 1952; B.A. cum laude in Econs. (scholar), Ohio Wesleyan U., 1965; M.B.A. with distinction, Xavier U., 1977; m. George R. Stich, Mar. 7, 1953 (dec.); 1 son, Mark Stephen (dec.); m. Joseph F. McDonald, Jr., Feb. 1, 1986. . Missionary in S. Am., Evang. Alliance Mission, 1956-61; cost acct. Western Electric Co., 1965-66; acctg. mgr. Ohio Wesleyan U., 1966-73; fin. specialist NCR Corp., 1973-74, systems analyst, 1974-75, supr. inventory planning, 1975, mgr. material planning and purchasing control, 1976-78; materials mgr. U.S. Elec. Motors Co., 1978; with Gen. Motors Corp., 1978-92, shift supt. materials, Lakewood, Ga., 1979-80, gen. ops. supr. material data base mgmt. Central Office, Warren, Mich., 1980, dir. material mgmt. GM Truck and Bus. div., Balt., 1980-91; dir. edn. & tng. GM Truck and Bus, Linden, N.J., 1991-92; ret., 1992. vis. lectr. Inst. Internat. Trade, Jiao Tong U., Shanghai, China, 1985, Inst. Econs. and Fgn. Trade, Tianjin, China, 1986-87; part time instr. Towson (Md.) State U., 1986-87. Capt. USCG. Mem. Am. Prodn. and Inventory Control Soc., Am. Soc. Women Accts., AAUW, Balt. Exec. Women's Network, Balt. Council on Fgn. Relations, Presbyterian. Avocation: sailing. Home: 455 N Alt 19 S Apt 182 Palm Harbor FL 34683-5931

MCDONALD, PENNY S(UE), educational administrator; b. Portland, Oreg., May 1, 1946; d. Norman James and Edna (Kaufmann) McD. BA, Oreg. State U., 1968, MEd, 1974; EdD, Portland State U./U. Oreg., 1981, Harvard U., summer 1987. Tchr. English, Fleming Jr. High Sch., Los Angeles, 1968-69; tchr. lang. arts and social studies Highland View Jr. High Sch., Corvallis, Oreg., 1970-72; tchr. English, dir. student activities Crescent Valley High Sch., Corvallis, 1973-78; grad. asst. Portland State U., Oreg., 1978-80; evaluation intern N.W. Regional Edn. Lab., Portland, 1980; Nat. Inst. Edn. assoc., edn. policy fellow Nat. Commn. on Excellence in Edn., Washington, 1981-83; prin. Inza R. Wood Middle Sch., West Linn Sch. Dist., Wilsonville, Oreg., 1983-88; adminstr. in residence for ednl. adminstrn. Lewis & Clark Coll., Portland, 1988-91; prin. Adams Hillside Alternative Elem., Eugene (Oreg.) Sch. Dist., 1991—; cons. Oreg. Dept. Edn., 1980-81; sr. counselor Oreg. Assn. Student Councils Camps, 1976-78, 80; adj. prof. ednl. adminstrn. Lewis & Clark Coll., 1987-88, 95-96. Coord., com., adminstr. Oreg. Mentorship Program, 1986-87. Named to Outstanding Young Woman Am., U.S. Jaycees; AFL-CIO scholar Oreg. State U., Corvallis, 1964; Univ. scholar Oreg. State U., 1965-68; nat. Alpha Delta Pi scholar Oreg. State U., 1967-68; Delta Kappa Gamma scholar Portland State U./U. Oreg. 1979-81. Mem. Nat. Assn. Student Councils, Oreg. Assn. Activities Advisors (chmn. 1976-77, bd. dirs. 1977-78), Oreg. Assn. Student Councils, Confedn. Oreg. Sch. Adminstrs. (curriculum commn. 1985-86, asst. chmn., sec. 1986-87, chmn. 1987-88, ex-officio mem. exec. bd. 1987-88), Nat. Assn. Secondary Sch. Prins., N.W. Women in Ednl. Adminstrn. (Oreg. bd. dirs., chairperson 1993-94), Delta Kappa Gamma (chpt. rec. sec.), Phi Delta Kappa. Democrat. Office: Adams Trad Hillside Elem Sch 950 W 22nd Ave Eugene OR 97405-2119

MCDONALD, ROSA NELL, federal research and budgets manager; b. Boley, Okla., Feb. 12, 1953; d. James and Beatrice Irene (Hayes) McD. BS, Calif. State U., Long Beach, 1975; MBA, Calif. State U., Dominquez Hills, 1980 also postgrad; BS computer information systems, Chapman Coll, 1988. Acct., The Aerospace Corp., El Segundo, Calif., 1976-77; analytical accountant, 1977-79, budget analyst, 1979-81, sr. budget analyst, 1981-84, budget adminstr., 1984-86, mgr. indirect budgets, 1986-91, head budgets and pricing dept., 1991-95, dir. budgets, pricing & fin. planning, 1996—. Vol., Youth Motivation Task Force, El Segundo, 1980—, Holiday Project, El Segundo, 1984, 85. Recipient Adminstrn. Group Achievement award The Aerospace Corp., 1985, Robert Herndon Image award, 1988; named Woman of Yr, Aerospace Corp., 1987, NAACP Legal Def. Fund Woman of Achievement, 1988. Mem. NAFE, Am. Bus. Woman's Assn., Beta Gamma Sigma. Democrat. Avocations: dancing; aerobics; reading; contests. Office: 2350 E El Segundo Blvd # M1 400 El Segundo CA 90245-4609

MCDONALD, SALLY J., lawyer; b. West Lafayette, Ind., Feb. 15, 1964; d. Homer C. and Esteleen M. (Bowman) McD.; m. Richard M. Levin, Oct. 16, 1993. BS, Ind. U., 1986; JD, Duke U., 1990. Bar: Ill. 1990. Assoc. Bell, Boyd & Lloyd, Chgo., 1990-92, Rudnick & Wolfe, Chgo., 1992—. Contbr. chpt. to book. Personnel bd. Gtr. Chgo. Food Depository, Chgo., 1995—. Mem. Chgo. Bar Assn. (chair elect. Young Lawyers sect. 1995-96, Maurice Weigle award 1994).

MCDONALD, SUSAN F., business executive, county official; b. Rockford, Ill., Jan. 18, 1961; d. John Augustus and Jeanne (Reitsch) Floberg; m. Robert Arthur McDonald, June 19, 1981; children: Molly Jeanne, Amanda Elizabeth. AAS in Bus. Mgmt., Colo. Mountain Coll., Glenwood Springs, 1981. Teller, bookkeeper Alpine Bank, Glenwood Springs, 1981-82; teller Macktown State Bank, Rockford, 1982-83; treas., mgr., owner Roscoe (Ill.) Movie House, 1984-94; sales cons. Lou Bachroot, Inc., Rockford, 1992-93; mem. bd. suprs. Winnebago County Bd., Rockford, 1992—; exec. v.p., owner Corp. Svc. Alliance, Machesney Park, Ill., 1993-95; leasing and fleet mgr. Budweiser Motors, Inc., Beloit, Wis., 1994-95; bus. mgr. Finley Oldsmobile GMC, South Beloit, Ill., 1995—. Pres. Roscoe Bus. Assn., 1990, 91, v.p., 189; chair, founder Roscoe Beautification Assn., 1991; mem. county bd. dirs. Winnebago County, 1992—, vice chmn. econ. devel. com., 1993—; chmn. econ. devel. environ. com. Winnebago County Bd., 1994—; commr. Winnebago County Forest Preserve, Rockford, 1992—; co-founder, bd. dirs. Very Important Pregnancy, Rockford Meml. Hosp.; bd. dirs. Family Advocate Aux., Rockford, 1987-88; bd. dirs. U. Ill. Extension Svc./Winnebago County, 1994—. Nominated Video Retailer of Yr., Am. Video Assn., 1989, Leadership award, Stateline YWCA, 1989. Republican. Methodist. Office: Finley Oldsmobile GMC 1790 Gardner St South Beloit IL 61080

MCDONALD, WYLENE BOOTH, former nurse, pharmaceutical sales professional; b. Kinston, N.C., Sept. 29, 1956; d. Wiley Truett and Hilda Grey (Brinson) Booth; m. Robert H. McDonald; stepchildren: Stephanie Lynn, Robin Leigh. BSN, Barton Coll., 1979; MSN, East Carolina U., 1984. Pub. health nurse Sampson Co. Health Dept., Clinton, N.C., 1979-81; pub. health coord. New Hanover Co. Health Dept., Wilmington, N.C., 1981-83; med. ctr. liaison Cape Fear Valley Med. Ctr., Fayetteville, N.C., 1984-85; profl. sales rep. Merck, Human Health Div., West Point, Pa., 1985-88; hosp. specialist sales rep. Human Health divsn. Merck, West Point, Pa., 1988-90, sr. prostate health specialist rep., 1990-94; exec. cardiovascular specialist Human Health divsn. Merck, West Point, Pa., ž, 1995—; speaker Coastal Area Perinatal Assn., 1983, Career Week, U. N.C. Sch. Bus., Wilmington, 1987, 88, 89, 93. Fundraiser March of DImes, Fayetteville, 1987, Wilmington, 1991, Am. Heart Assn., Wilmington, 1991-93. Named one of Outstanding Young Women of Am., 1981. Mem. ANA, AAUW, N.C. Nurses Assn., N.C. Pub. Health Assn., Sigma Theta Tau. Home and Office: 108 Seapath Estate Wrightsville Beach NC 28480-1964

MCDONALD-MUNOZ, VALESKA ROSANNA, educator; b. San Juan, P.R., Mar. 13, 1965; d. Richard Francis and Mercedes (Guadalupe) McD.; m. Efrain Juan Munoz, Dec. 26, 1993. BS in Spl. Edn., Syracuse U., 1988, MS in Spl. Edn., 1992; MEd in Ednl. Adminstrn. and Leadership, U. San Diego, 1995—. Faculty asst. intern Syracuse (N.Y.) U., 1988; asst. to dir. program devel. Hutchings Psychiatric Ctr. Dept. Edn./Tng., Syracuse, 1988; summer housmother adolscent girls Girls Ranch, Inc., Scottsdale, Ariz., 1988; asst. to dirs. program devel. The Syracuse Ctr., 1989; master tchr. LeMoyne Coll., Syracuse, 1990, Syracuse U., 1990; translator, bilingual assessor/specialist Omondoga Judicial System, Syracuse, 1991; instr. leadning disabilities assn. CCNY, Syracuse, 1989-92; tutor fgn. lang. and acad. Syracuse, 1988-92; educator bilingual spl. edn. Syracuse City Sch. Dist., 1988-92, Escondido (Calif.) Union High Sch. Dist., 1992-96; interlude tchr., transition team mem. Arlington (Va.) Pub. Sch. Dist., 1996—; chair San Pasqual H.s. site based com., 1995-96. Grad. fellow U. San Diego, 1993; Barbizon Modeling Agy. Collegiate scholar, 1983-84, Syracuse U. Dept. Rehab. Undergrad. scholar, 1986, Syracuse U. Internat. Study Abroad scholar, 1987. Mem. ASCD. Roman Catholic. Home: 1400 S Joyce St # 726 Arlington VA 22202 Office: Arlington Pub Sch Dist 4901 Chesterfield Rd Arlington VA 22206

MCDONALD-WEST, SANDI M., headmaster, consultant; b. Lowell, Mass., May 8, 1930; d. Walter Allan and Celina Louise (Lalime) MacLean; m. Thomas D. McDonald, Sept. 8, 1951 (div.); children: Todd F. McDonald, Brooke McDonald Killian, Ned M. McDonald, Reid A. McDonald, Heather McDonald Acker. BA, DePauw U., 1951; MA, Fairleigh Dickinson U., 1966; MEd, North Tex. State U., 1980. Cert. in Montessori teaching. Tchr., adminstr. Hudson (Ohio) Montessori Sch., 1966-68, Berea (Ohio) Montessori Sch., 1968-70, Creative Learning Ctr., Dallas, 1970-71; tchr., head of lower sch. The Selwyn Sch., Denton, Tex., 1971-83; tchr., headmaster Cimarron Sch., Enid, Okla., 1983-87; cons. Corpus Christi (Tex.) Montessori Sch., 1987-89, Azlann-Eren Horn Montessori Sch., Denton, 1989-95, Highland Meadow Montessori Acad., Southlake, Tex., 1994—; ednl. dir., pres. Southwestern Montessori Tchg. Ctr., Inc., Denton, 1974—; adj. prof. North Tex. State U., Denton, 1979-80; cons., lectr. Am. Montessori Soc., N.Y.C., 1970—, Japanese Montessori Soc., 1978—, also pub. and pvt. schs., 1972—; chair commn. for accreditation Montessori Accreditation Coun. Tchr. Edn., Denton, 1991—. Developer various Montessori materials; contbr. articles to profl. jours. Mem. Am. Montessori Soc., No. Ohio Montessori Assn. (pres. 1968-70), Assn. Montessori Internat., N.Am. Montessori Tchrs. Assn., Wheat Capital Assn. for Children Under Six (pres. 1986-87), LWV. Mem. Am. Montessori Soc., No. Ohio Montessori Assn. (pres. 1968-70), Assn. Montessori Internat., N.Am. Montessori Tchrs. Assn., Wheat Capital Assn. for Children Under Six (pres. 1986-87), LWV, Concerned Scientists. Home: 2005 Marshall Rd Denton TX 76207-3316

MCDONIEL, JUDY ANN, elementary education educator; b. Detroit, May 23, 1943; d. Chester Dewey and Violet Myrtle (Pettit) Sims; m. Jimmie Vaughn McDoniel, Dec. 20, 1964; children: Randall, Jennifer, Chester. BS, David Lipscomb U., Nashville, 1965; MEd, Tex. Woman's U., Denton, 1996. Cert. elm. edn.; cert. in mid-mgmt. Tchr. 2nd grade Harding Acad., Memphis, 1966-68; tchr. 3rd grade Mobile (Ala.) Christian, 1968-69; leader Weight Watchers, Bossier City, La., 1982-90; tchr. adult edn. and 5th grade Bossier Parrish Sch. Sys., Bossier City, 1988-90; tchr. 6th grade Hurst Euless Bedford Ind. Sch. Dist., Bedford, Tex., 1991—. Named Honor Young Mother of Am., Mothers' of Am., Bossier City, 1981. Mem. ASCD, Tex. Sci. Tchrs. Assn., Classrm. Tchrs. Assn. Tex., Delta Kappa Gamma. Mem. Ch. of Christ.

MC DONNELL, LORETTA WADE, lawyer; b. San Francisco, May 31, 1940; d. John H. and Helen M. (Tinney) Wade; m. John L. McDonnell, Jr., Apr. 27, 1963 (div.); children: Elizabeth, John L. III, Thomas. BA, San Francisco Coll. for Women, 1962; MA, Stanford U., 1963; grad. Coro Pub. Affairs Tng. Program for Women, 1976; JD Golden Gate U., 1989. Bar: Calif. 1990. High sch. tchr. East Side Union High Sch. Dist., San Jose, Calif., 1962-63; project coordinator Inter Agency Collaboration Effort, Oakland, Calif., 1977; legal asst. Pacific Gas and Electric Co., 1980-89, coord., 1989—. Bd. dirs. Carden Redwood Sch., 1975-77, St. Paul's Sch., 1974-75; budget panelist United Way of Bay Area, 1975-77; community v.p. Jr. League, 1976-77, nat. conv. del., 1976; bd. dirs. Alameda County Vol. Bur., 1973-74; chmn. speakers panel Focus on Am. Women, 1973-74. Mem. Jr. League of Oakland-East Bay, Inc., Stanford Alumni. Democrat. Roman Catholic. Clubs: Stanford San Francisco Luncheon, Commonwealth. Assoc. editor The Antiphon, 1971-74.

MCDONNELL, MARY A., sales and marketing executive; b. Paterson, N.J., July 11, 1959; d. Peter J. and Eugenia M. (Grish) McDonnell. BA in Chemistry, Rutgers U., 1981; MBA in Mktg. and Fin., Columbia U., 1985. Devel. chemist Nat. Starch and Chem. Co., Bridgewater, N.J., 1981-83; chemist, chem-met mgmt. program GE, Worthington, Ohio, 1985-86, applications engr., 1986-87, mktg. mgr., 1987-88; U.K. sales mgr. GE, London, 1988-91; regional sales mgr. GE, Saddle Brook, N.J., 1991-93; product mgr. Tempo Tech. Corp., Somerset, N.J., 1993-95, dir., sales, 1995-96, v.p., sales & mktg., 1996—. Mem. NAFE, Soc. Petroleum Engrs., Polycrystalline Products Assn., Concrete Sawing and Drilling Assn. Home: 235 Bloomfield St Unit 1 Hoboken NJ 07030 Office: Tempo Technology Corp 500 Apgar Dr Somerset NJ 08873

MCDONNELL, MARY THERESA, travel service executive; b. N.Y.C., Nov. 9, 1949; d. John J. and Mary B. (Lunney) McD.; m. Robert T. Barber, Oct. 7, 1989. Mgr. Kramer Travel Agy., White Plains, N.Y., 1967-79; owner, mgr. New Trends Travel, Rye, N.Y., 1979-90; mgr. Honey Travel Inc., Rye, N.Y., 1990—. Office: Honey Travel Inc 11 Elm Pl Rye NY 10580-2918

MCDONNELL, MARYANN MARGARET, medical marketing executive; b. Detroit, Aug. 26, 1947; d. Patrick J. and Margaret Ann (Novallo) McD.; children: Anais Kathryn Alexander, Colin Michael McDonnell. BS, Wayne State U., 1970. Consumer protection specialist FTC, Washington, 1970-73; fin. analyst Price Commn., Washington, 1972-73; co-founder Full Circle Process & Xenium, Los Gatos, Calif., 1973-77; asst. adminstr. Arts In the Image of Man, Fair Oaks, Calif., 1981-83; adminstr. Mariposa Waldorf Sch., Cedar Ridge, Calif., 1983-84; pres. Counseling Endevors, Grass Valley, Calif., 1984-86; v.p. Sr. Vision Inst., Carmichael, Calif., 1986-88; pres. Empire Health Mktg., Grass Valley, 1988 , Elder Sight Inst., Grass Valley, 1988—; exec. Cell Tech, Klammath Falls, Oreg., 1994—. Founder, chairperson Los Gatos (Calif.) Waldorf Sch. Assn., 1977; mem. Mariposa Waldorf Sch. Bd. Trustees, Cedar Ridge, 1984; founding mem. Gia Sophia, Nevada City, Calif., 1987. Mem. Orthopedic Edn. Alliance (pres. 1992—), Earth Spirit (bd. dirs. 1996). Democrat. Home: 16611 Alexandra Way Grass Valley CA 95949-7353

MCDONNELL, ROSEMARY CYNTHIA, social services administrator; b. Washington, July 31, 1969; d. Joseph Patrick and Judith Ann (Bruscino) McD. BS, Bradley U., Peoria, Ill., 1991; postgrad., Ill. Ctrl. Coll., 1993. Qualified mental retardation profl. Team leader Community Workshop and Tng. Ctr., Peoria, 1989-92; polit. sci. intern City of Peoria, 1991; undergrad. teaching asst. Bradley U., Peoria, 1991; family support coord. Tazewell County Resource Ctr., Pekin, Ill., 1992-93, early intervention asst., 1993-94; spl. populations programmer Pekin Pk. Dist. Recreation Office, 1994—. Asst. coach Spl. Olympics, Peoria, 1992. Olive B. White scholar Bradley U., 1990. Mem. NOW, Pi Gamma Mu, Phi Alpha Theta. Roman Catholic. Home: PO Box 363 Pekin IL 61555-0363

MCDONOUGH, BRIDGET ANN, music theatre company director; b. Milw., June 19, 1956; d. James and Lois (Hunzinger) McD.; m. Gregory Paul Opelka, Sept. 20, 1986. BS, Northwestern U., 1978. Bus. mgr. Organic Theater Co., Chgo., 1979-80; mng. dir., founder Light Opera Works, Evanston, Ill., 1980—; U.S. rep. European Congress Musical Theatre, 1995. Founder, mem. Chgo. Music Alliance, 1984—, pres., 1995-96; mem. Ill. Arts Alliance. Recipient Women on the Move award Evanston YWCA, 1991. Mem. Evanston C. of C. (bd. dirs.), Rotary. Office: Light Opera Works 927 Noyes St Evanston IL 60201-2705

MCDONOUGH, KAYE (KATHRYN SUSAN MCDONOUGH), poet, playwright; b. Pitts., Aug. 8, 1943; d. Edward Arthur and Lucille Marie (Bechman) M.; life ptnr. Gregory Nuncio Corso; 1 child, Nile Joseph Corso. Student, Vassar Coll., 1961-63, Boston U., 1964-65; BA, U. Calif., Berkeley, 1967. Author: (book/play) Zelda: Frontier Life in America, 1978; contbr. poems to City Lights Rev., 1994, City Lights Jour., 1978, City Lights Anthology, 1974, The Stiffest of the Corpse, 1989, Exquisite Corpse, 1985, Cafe Society, 1978, Umbra, over 50 other publs.; poetry readings at San Francisco 1st Ann. Poetry Festival, 1976, Polyphonix Franco-Am. Poetry Festival, Paris, 1979, Shakespeare & Co., Paris, 1979, Santa Cruz Poetry Festival, 1982, Poetry Ctr. San Francisco State Coll., 1984, Cody's Bookstore, Berkeley, Calif., 1992, over 100 other benefits and readings; play performed at St. Clement's Theatre, N.Y.C., 1978, 79, U. Cambridge, New Zealand, 1979, The Glass Factory, Salt Lake City, 1980. Poet Big Mountain Navajo/Hopi Support Com. Benefit, San Francisco, 1981, Anti-Nuclear Proposition 15 Benefit, San Francisco, Internat. Women's Day Benefit, San Francisco, El Salvador Benefit, San Francisco. Home: 236 Santa Fe Ave Hamden CT 06517

MCDONOUGH, MAMIE, public relations executive; b. Plainfield, N.J., Mar. 24, 1952; d. Peter J. and Elizabeth (Driscoll) McD. BA, Elmira Coll., 1974; DFA (hon.), Pratt Inst., 1990. Protocol asst. U.S. Dept. State, Washington, 1974-75; staff asst. Office of U.S. V.P., Washington, 1975-77; dir. info. service Rep. Nat. Com., Washington, 1977-79; pres. Festive Occasions, Inc., Washington, 1979-81; staff asst. Office of Dep. Chief of Staff The White House, Washington, 1981-82; sr. ptnr. Britt-McDonough Assocs., Washington, 1982-86; owner The McDonough Group, Washington and N.Y.C., 1986—; Co-author, developer Student/Corp. Jr. Bd. Dirs. Program, 1984. Admissions rep. Washington area Elmira Coll., 1975-76; bd. dirs. Jr. League Washington, 1977-90, Camp Fire Boys and Girls, Washington area, 1985-90; mem. fin. com. various Rep. congl. campaigns, 1979—; corp. bd. Vanderbilt Mus., 1985-90. Recipient Outstanding Service award Camp Fire Council, 1986. Roman Catholic. Office: 157 E 75th St Apt 1W New York NY 10021-3279

MCDORMAND, FRANCES, actress; b. Ill., 1957. Student, Yale U. Sch. Drama. Stage appearances include Awake and Sing!, N.Y.C., 1984, Painting Churches, N.Y.C., 1984, The Three Sisters, Mpls., 1985, N.J., 1991, All My Sons, New Haven, 1986, A Streetcar Named Desire, N.Y.C., 1988, Moon for the Misbegotten, 1992, Sisters Rosensweig, N.Y.C., 1993, The Swan, N.Y.C., 1993; TV appearances include The Twilight Zone, The Equalizer, Spencer:

For Hire, Hill Street Blues, (series) Legwork, 1986-87, (TV movies) Scandal Sheet, 1985, Vengeance: The Story of Tony Cimo, 1986, Crazy In Love, 1992; film appearances include Blood Simple, 1984, Crime Wave, 1986, Raising Arizona, 1987, Mississippi Burning, 1988, Chattahoochee, 1990, Darkman, 1990, Miller's Crossing, 1990, Hidden Agenda, 1990, The Butcher's Wife, 1991, Passed Away, 1992, Short Cuts, 1993, Beyond Rangoon, 1995, Fargo, 1996, Lone Star, 1996. Office: William Morris Agy 1325 Avenue Of The Americas New York NY 10019-4702*

MCDOUGALL, JACQUELYN MARIE HORAN, therapist; b. Wenatchee, Wash., Sept. 24, 1924; d. John Rankin and Helen Frampton (Vandivort) Horan; m. Robert Duncan McDougall, Jan. 24, 1947 (div. July 1976); children: Douglas, Stuart, Scott. BA, Wash. State U., 1946. Lic. therapist, Wash.; cert. nat. addiction counselor II. Pres. oper. bd. Ctr. for Alcohol/Drug Treatment, Wenatchee, 1983-85; sec. Wash. State Coun. on Alcoholism, 1988-89, supr. out-patient svcs., 1989-90; case mgmt. counselor Lakeside Treatment Ctr., East Wenatchee, Wash., 1991-92; ret., 1994. Treas. Allied Arts, Wenatchee, 1984; pres. Rep. Women, Wash., 1969-70.

MCDOUGALL, SUSAN, financial services executive; b. Pitts., Dec. 21, 1961; d. Robert James and Barbara (Hicks) McD.; m. Kirk Thomas Dackow, Sept. 24, 1988; 1 child, Christopher Thomas. Student, Am. Univ., 1982; BS, Carnegie Mellon U., 1983; MBA, U. Pitts., 1986. Lobbying asst. Bayh, Tabbert and Capehart, Washington, 1982; legal asst. Agent Orange plaintiffs' mgmt. com. Henderson and Goldberg, N.Y.C., Pitts., 1983-85, bus. analyst. corp. staff, 1986-88; market devel. rep. Specialities dept. Mobay Corp., Pitts., 1988-89; asst. product dir. mktg. planning The Nat. Assn. Securities Dealers, Inc., Washington, 1990; product dir. Nat. Assn. of Securities Dealers, Inc., Washington, 1991-92; dir. trading and market svcs. The NASDAQ Stock Mkt., Inc., Washington, 1992—. Office: NASDAQ Stock Market Inc 1735 K St NW Washington DC 20006-1516

MCDOWELL, ELIZABETH MARY, retired pathology educator; b. Kew Gardens, Surrey, Eng., Mar. 30, 1940; came to U.S., 1971; d. Arthur and Peggy (Bryant) McD. B Vet. Medicine, Royal Vet. Coll., London, 1963; BA, Cambridge U., 1968, PhD, 1971. Gen. practice vet. medicine, 1964-66; Nuffield Found. tng. scholar Cambridge (Eng.) U., 1966-71; instr. dept. pathology U. Md., Balt., 1971-73, asst. prof., 1973-76, assoc. prof., 1976-80, prof., 1980-96, ret., 1996. Co-author: Biopsy Pathology of the Bronchi, 1987; editor: Lung Carcinomas, 1987; contbr. over 120 articles to sci. jours., chpts. to books. Rsch. grantee NIH, 1979-92. Fellow Royal Coll. Vet. Surgeons Gt. Britain and Ireland. Home: 606 W 37th St Baltimore MD 21211

MCDOWELL, JENNIFER, sociologist, composer, playwright, publisher; b. Albuquerque; d. Willard A. and Margaret Frances (Garrison) McD.; m. Milton Loventhal, July 2, 1973. BA, U. Calif., 1957; MA, San Diego State U., 1958; postgrad., Sorbonne, Paris, 1959; MLS, U. Calif., 1963; PhD, U. Oreg., 1973. Tchr. English Abraham Lincoln High Sch., San Jose, Calif., 1960-61; free-lance editor Soviet field, Berkeley, Calif., 1961-63; rsch. asst. sociology U. Oreg., Eugene, 1964-66; editor, pub. Merlin Papers, San Jose, 1969—, Merlin Press, San Jose, 1973—; rsch. cons. sociology San Jose, 1973—; music pub. Lipstick and Toy Balloons Pub. Co., San Jose, 1978—; composer Paramount Pictures, 1982-88; tchr. writing workshops; poetry readings, 1969-73; co-producer radio show lit. and culture Sta. KALX, Berkeley, 1971-72. Author: (with Milton Loventhal) Black Politics: A Study and Annotated Bibliography of the Mississippi Freedom Democratic Party, 1971 (featured at Smithsonian Inst. Spl. Event 1992), Contemporary Women Poets, 1977, Ronnie Goose Rhymes for Grown-Ups, 1984; co-author: (plays off-off Broadway) Betsy and Phyllis, 1986, Mack the Knife Your Friendly Dentist, 1986, The Estrogen Party To End War, 1986, The Oatmeal Party Comes To Order, 1986, (plays) Betsy Meets the Wacky Iraqui, 1991, Bella and Phyllis, 1994; contbr. poems, plays, essays, articles, short stories, and book revs. to lit. mags., news mags. and anthologies; rschr. women's autobiog. writings, contemporary writing in poetry, Soviet studies, civil rights movement, and George Orwell, 1962—; writer: (songs) Money Makes a Woman Free, 1976, 3 songs featured in Parade of Am. Music; co-creator mus. comedy Russia's Secret Plot To Take Back Alaska, 1988. Recipient 8 awards Am. Song Festival, 1976-79, Bill Casey Award in Letters, 1980; doctoral fellow AAUW, 1971-73; grantee Calif. Arts Coun., 1976-77. Mem. Am. Sociol. Assn., Soc. Sci. Study of Religion, Poetry Orgn. for Women, Dramatists Guild, Phi Beta Kappa, Sigma Alpha Iota, Beta Phi Mu, Kappa Kappa Gamma. Democrat. Office: care Merlin Press PO Box 5602 San Jose CA 95150-5602

MCDOWELL, JO ANN C., college president; b. Apr. 23, 1943. AA in Liberal Arts, Independence (Kans.) Community Coll., 1969; BS in Psychology, Pittsburg (Kans.) State U., 1976, MS in Psychology, 1981, EdS in Edn. with honors, 1982; PhD in Edn., Kans. State U., 1984. Dir. pub. rels. and govtl. affairs Union Gas System Inc., Independence, 1967-79; dir. Students and Coll. Devel. Independence Community Coll., 1979-83, dean student pers. svcs., 1983-85, interim dean instrn., 1987-88, v.p., 1985-88, pres., 1988—; adj. prof. Pittsburg State U., 1976—, lectr. psychology, 1983—; mem. Kans. Bd. regents, 1991—; prin. speaker Nat. Inst. Leadership Devel., Omaha, 1990. Presenter, host TV and radio program Sta. KODE TV, 1979, (weekly program) Sta. KGGF Radio, 1979—; columnist 5 weekly newspaper, 1980-89; author: The Self-Perceived Effectiveness of Kansas CETA Programs Operated in Kansas from 1976 through 1981, 1984, A Collection of Papers on Self-Study and Institutional Improvement, 1989. Exec. dir. Independence Community Coll. Found., 1979-88; grad. Leadership Independence, 1988; del. Dem. Nat. conv., 1988; trustee Mid-Am. Inc., 1989—; mem. Independence Arts. Coun., S.E. Kans. Film Commn., St. Francis Xavier Cath. Ch.; bd. dirs. Mercy Hosp. Found., 1989—, States for Scholars Found., Georgetown U., 1989—. Named Woman of Yr. Independence, 1989, Exec. of Yr. Independence, 1988, Outstanding Young Kansan Independence Jaycees 1978. Mem. Nat. Assn. Women Deans, Adminstrs., and Counselros, Am. Assn. Women Community and Jr. Colls., Kans. Assn. Community Colls., S.E. Kans. Higher Edn. Consortium Coun. Pres. (chmn. 1990-91, vice chmn. 1989), North Cen. Assn. Colls. and Schs. (evaluator 1985—, team chmn. 1988—, commr.-at-large 1988—, bd. dirs. 1985-87), Kans. C. of C. and Industry (com. polit. action and pub. affairs 1983—), Independence C. of C. (com. govtl. affairs 1979—, v.p. 1982-86, bd. dirs. 1980-86), Kans. State U. Alumni Assn., Pittsburg State U. Alumni Assn. (Outstanding Young Alumna 1983). Office: Prince William Sound CC Office of the President Valdez AK 99686*

MCDOWELL, KAREN ANN, lawyer; b. Ruston, La., Oct. 4, 1945; d. Paul and Opal Elizabeth (Davis) Bauer; m. Gary Lee McDowell, Dec. 22, 1979. BA, N.E. La. U., 1967; JD, U. Mich., 1971; diploma, John Robert Powers Sch., Chgo., 1976, Nat. Inst. Trial Advocacy, 1990. Bar: Ill. 1973, Colo. 1977, U.S. Dist. Ct. (so. dist.) Ill. 1973, U.S. Dist. Ct. Colo. 1977. Reference libr. assoc. Ill. State Library, Springfield, 1972-73; asst. atty. gen. State of Ill., Springfield, 1973-75; pvt. practice Boulder, Colo., 1978-79, Denver, 1979—. Mem. So. Poverty Law Ctr. Mem. ABA, DAR, Am. Assn. Retired Persons, Amnesty Internat., Colo. Bar Assn. (com. alcohol and related problems), Denver Bar Assn., Colo. Women's Bar Assn. (editor newsletter 1982-84), Colo. Soc. Study Multiple Personality and Dissociation, Colo. Hist. Soc., Survivors United Network (legal coord. 1992-93), Survivors United Network Profls. (exec. com. 1992), Internat. Platform Assn., Mensa (local sect. Ann Arbor, Mich. 1968), Colonial Dames, Nat. Soc. Magna Carta Dames, Phi Alpha Theta, Sigma Tau Delta, Alpha Lambda Delta. Office: 428 E 11th Ave Ste 100 Denver CO 80203-3207

MCDOWELL, LINDA GOETTE, special education educator; b. Camden, S.C., Dec. 4, 1955; d. Robert Lewis and Emily Townsend (Smith) Goette; m. Scott Dixon McDowell, June 11, 1977; children: Erin Eileen, Sean Devin, Scott Dylan, Kaitlin Kara. BA Elem. Edn., Covenant Coll., 1977; MEd, U. Tenn., 1980; PhD Spl. Edn., U. So. Miss., 1995. Cert. elem. tchr. K-8, spl. edn. K-12. Spl. edn. tchr. Walker County Schs., Lafayette, Ga., 1977-79; kindergarten tchr. Chattanooga Christian Sch., 1981; French tchr. Korea Christian Acad., Taejon, Korea, 1981-83; spl. edn. tchr. Peoria (Ill.) Pub. Schs., 1987, West Aurora Pub. Schs., Aurora, Ill., 1987-89, Hattiesburg (Miss.) Pub. Schs., 1989-93; instr. U. So. Miss., 1993—; cons. spl. projects Hattiesburg Pub. Schs., 1993-95; cons. Inst. for Disabilities Study, Hattiesburg, 1994—, supt. student tchrs., 1994-95, grant coord. Inst. for Disability Studies, 1995-96; presenter at conf. Tchr. First Presbyn. Ch., Hattiesburg, 1993-96. Grantee Miss. Coun. for Exceptional Children, Jackson, 1994-95, Care Consistency Found., Meridian, 1993-94; rsch. grantee U. So. Miss., 1993. Mem. Am. Coun. on Rural Spl. Edn., Coun. for Exceptional Children, Assn. for Retarded Citizens (bd. dirs. 1994-96), Phi Delta Kappa (v.p. 1996—). Home: 33 Sailfish Cir Hattiesburg MS 39402 Office: Univ So Miss PO Box 5163 Hattiesburg MS 39406

MCDOWELL, SHERRIE LORRAINE, secondary education educator; b. Manchester, Ky., Apr. 20, 1948; d. Alonzo and Madge Loudean (Christensen) Garrison; m. Gary Lynn McDowell, July 11, 1970; 1 child, Marc Ryan. BA, U. No. Colo., 1970; MA, Lesley Coll., 1989; postgrad., U. Wyo. Cert. tchr., Wyo. Tchr. English St. Mary's Cath. Sch., Cheyenne, Wyo., 1971-72; instr. homebound program Laramie County Sch. Dist., Cheyenne, 1978-84; English instr. Cen. High Sch., Cheyenne, 1984—; Wyo. coach Nat. Tournament of Acad. Excellence, 1988-90. Mem. NEA (Assembly rep. 1993-96, cadre trainer state level women's leadership tng. program 1995-96), AAUW (sec. 1975-77), Wyo. Edn. Assn. (co-chair profl. standards and practices commn. 1995—), Nat. Coun. Tchrs. English, Cheyenne Tchrs. Edn. Assn. (edn. assn. del. 1992—, chair instrnl. issues 1995, co-chair pub. rels. 1988-90, editor ACCENTS 1988-90, sec. 1995—), Wyo. Assn. Tchrs. English (presenter), Wyo. Chautauqua Soc. (pres. 1985-86, bd. dirs. 1984-85), Delta Kappa Gamma (state scholarship chair 1989-90, pres. chpt. 1988-90). Home: 100 Grandview Ct Cheyenne WY 82009-4912 Office: Ctrl High Sch 5500 Education Dr Cheyenne WY 82009-4008

MCDUFFIE, ADELINA FERRARO, pediatrics nurse; b. N.Y.C., Mar. 16, 1958; d. Thomas Joseph and Justine Rita (Condello) Ferraro; m. Ernest Paul McDuffie, Sept. 21, 1991. BSN, Georgetown U., 1980; MS, U. Mich., 1984. Staff nurse Concord (N.H.) Hosp., 1980; ICU staff nurse Boston Children's Hosp., 1981-82, staff nurse, 1984-85; nursing cons. Children's Ctr. U. Mich., Ann Arbor, 1982-83, tchr. asst. Sch. Nursing, 1983-84; pediatric clin. instr. Cleve. Clinic Found., 1985-87; clin. nurse specialist Rainbow Babies & Children's Hosp., Cleve., 1987-89; GI/nutrition clin. specialist Children's Hosp. of The King's Daus., Norfolk, Va., 1989—. Contbr. articles to profl. publs. Grantee U.S. Dept. HHS, 1982-84. Mem. ANA, Am. Soc. Parenteral and Enteral Nutrition (cert. nutrition support nurse), Pediatric Gastroenterology and Nutrition Nurses. Office: Children's Hosp of King's Daus 601 Childrens Ln Norfolk VA 23507-1910

MCEACHERN, SUSAN MARY, database analyst; b. Royal Oak, Mich., May 3, 1960; d. Donald Keith and Lois Jean (Robison) McE.; m. James Paul Corbett, Jan. 8, 1983 (div. 1995). BS, Mich. State U., 1982; MBA, New Mex. State U., 1985. From acct. adminstr. trainee to acct. adminstr. IBM, El Paso, Tex., 1985-89; customer support rep. IBM, Southfield, Mich., 1989-90; sr. adminstrv. specialist IBM, Southfield, 1991-92, adv. customer support rep., 1992-93; fin. analyst IBM, Boulder, Colo., 1993-95, database adminstr., analyst, 1995—; cons. Integrated Sys. Solutions Co., Dallas, 1990-93. Author: Treasury of Poetry, 1992. Vol. supr. Easter Seals, Southfield Mich., El Paso, Tex., 1978-88, Crisis Pregnancy, Las Cruces, New Mex., 1982-86, Multiple Sclerosis, Mich., 1983, Longmont (Colo.) Vol. Assn., 1994. Recipient Photography award Mich. State Fair, 1991, 92. Mem. IBM PC Club, Creative Designs (pres. 1994—, Nat. Sci. and Engring. vol. rep. 1994). Home: PO Box 6043 Longmont CO 80501-2008

MCELHENY, ANNA CONNER, family therapist; b. St. Petersburg, Fla., Nov. 14, 1967; d. Ann Conner Davis; m. Carl William McElheny, Jan. 8, 1994. BS in Polit. Sci., Charleston So. U., 1990; MEd in Clin. Counseling, Citadel, 1993. Social worker Dept. Social Svcs., Charleston, S.C., 1990-93; guidance counselor Vance County Schs., Henderson, N.C., 1994-95; family therapist Area Mental Health, Henderson, N.C., 1995—; coord., creator PAL to pal Vol. program, Henderson, 1994—; mem. Vance Against Substance Abuse, 1994-95, Task Force Sch. Violence, 1994-95. Vol. Friends Youth Program, Henderson, 1994-95. Mem. Youth Svcs. Adv. Coun. Democrat. Home: 912 S Chestnut St Henderson NC 27536 Office: Area Mental Health 303 S Garnett St Henderson NC 27536

MCELHINNEY, SUSAN KAY (KATE MCELHINNEY), legal assistant; b. Greeley, Colo., May 20, 1947; d. Glenn Eugene and Maxine (Filkins) McE. Student, U. N.C., 1965-67, U. Kans., 1969, U. Colo., 1971-72, 80. Adminstrv. sec. Colo. Pub. Defender, Denver, 1970-74; clk. Colo. Dist. Ct., Boulder, 1974-80; legal asst., office mgr. Law Office Ben Echeverria, San Marcos, Calif., 1986—. Mem. black tie fund raising com. Palomar Community Coll., 1991-92. Democrat. Office: Law Offices Ben Echeverria 1557-B Grand Ave San Marcos CA 92069-2461

MCELROY, ABBY LUCILLE WOLMAN, financial consultant; b. Washington, Oct. 16, 1957; d. M. Gordon and Elaine (Mielke) Wolman; m. Peter J. McElroy, Mar. 15, 1986; children: Abel Hurst, Leo Frederick. BA, St. Lawrence U., 1979; MS, Ind. U., 1981. Fin. cons. Smith Barney, Westport, Conn., 1986—. London Group Study Exch. grantee Rotary Internat., 1989. Office: Smith Barney 1 Village Sq Westport CT 06880-3211

MCELROY, JACQUELYN MERCEDES, secondary school educator, artist; b. Savannah, Ga., Apr. 11, 1951; d. George Washington Wise and Nelida Blanca (Romano) Hug; m. Jackie Gibson, Nov. 1969 (div. Apr. 1972); children: Christopher Gibson, Michael Gibson; m. Carl McElroy, June 19, 1972 (div. Sept. 1987); children: David, Matthew. BFA, U. Tex., Tyler, 1987; MEd, East Tex. State U., 1991. Cert. art instr., Tex. Tchr. Como (Tex.)-Pickton Ind. Sch. Dist., 1987—. Mem. Cmty. Players, Inc., Sulphur Springs, Tex., 1988—, pres., 1995, 96; mem. Hopkins County Hist. Soc., Sulpher Springs, 1988-93. Mem. Tex. Assn. Sch. Art, Kappa Delta Pi. Office: Como-Pickton Ind Sch Dist PO Box 18 Como TX 75431

MCELROY, JANICE HELEN, government agency executive; b. Topeka, Kans., Dec. 12, 1937; d. Rudolph Ralph and Josephine Elizabeth (Kern) Jilka; m. James Douglas McElroy, June 25, 1967; children: Helen Elizabeth, Bryan Douglas. BS cum laude, Colo. Coll., Colorado Springs, 1960; MAT, Johns Hopkins U., 1964; PhD, U.S. Internat. U., San Diego, 1970. Biology tchr. Roland Park Country Day Sch., Balt., 1962-63, Edmundston H.S., Balt., 1964; chmn. dept. sci. Bishop's Sch., La Jolla, Calif., 1964-69; instr. Somerset County C.C., Somerville, N.J., 1973-75; instr. Cedar Crest Coll., Allentown, Pa., 1976-82, dir. re-entry program, 1979-82; exec. dir. Resource Devel. Svcs., Allentown, Pa., 1982-86; dir. planning and devel. Montgomery County C.C., Blue, Pa., 1986-88; exec. dir. Pa. Commn. for Women, Harrisburg, 1988-95; editor, pub. Womansword, Allentown, 1996—. Research dir./editor: Our Hidden Heritage: Pennsylvania Women in History, 1983; contbr. articles to profl. jours. Mem. Women's Adv. Bd. Task Force, Lehigh County, Pa., 1981-82, Nat. Child Care Adv. Coun.; chair Gov.'s Conf. on Responses to Workforce 2000, 1990; lay corp. mem. Pa. Blue Shield, 1992; alt. del. Dem. Nat. Conv., 1992; elder, trustee, commr. Presbyn. Ch.; bd. dirs. Women's Polit. Network Pa., 1988—, pres., 1996—; bd. dirs. Coalition Adult Literacy, 1989-95; NGO del. UN Fourth World Conf. Women, Beijing, 1995; founder Leadership Devel. Inst. for Women in State Govt., 1993. Fulbright scholar, 1960; Ford Found. fellow, 1963; NSF fellow, 1965. Mem. AAUW (pres. Pa. divsn. 1984-88, nat. bd. dirs. 1989-93), Nat. Assn. Commns. for Women (nat. bd. dirs. 1991-93), LWV, Delta Epsilon, Phi Beta Kappa, Alpha Lambda Delta, Kappa Kappa Gamma. Home: 2826 Crest Ave N Allentown PA 18104-6106 Office: Womansword 3140-B Tilghman St #263 Allentown PA 18104

MCELROY, JILL MARIE, financial specialist; b. Richland, Wash., Mar. 18, 1965; d. Jack Lawrence and Carol Cecil (Bambino) McE.; children: Ryan C., Justin C. BBA, Wash. State U., 1996. Cert. travel agt. Travel agt. Kennewick (Wash.) Travel, 1984-87; sr. fin. asst. Battelle N.W., Richland, 1987—; aerobics instr. Gold's Gym, Kennewick, 1996—. Scholar Inst. Mgmt. Accts., 1995. Mem. Inst. Mgmt. Accts. (dir. ednl. seminars 1995-96, dir. scholarships 1996—), Tri-Cities Amateur Hockey Assn. (cert. coach), Phi Theta Kappa. Roman Catholic. Home: 613 Newcomer Richland WA 99352

MCELROY, JUNE PATRICIA, sales consultant; b. Atlantic City, Sept. 26, 1929; d. Edmund N. and Dorothy R. (McDowell) Ricchezza; m. David Waycott Carson, Apr. 8, 1947 (div. 1954); m. Ottavio Gelmi, Dec. 16, 1954 (div. 1964); 1 child, Alessandra; m. Robert Joseph McElroy, Oct. 16, 1970 (dec. May 1974). Student Temple U., 1947-48, Inst. linguistics, Georgetown U., 1951-53. Mem. staff Am. consulate gen., Milan, Italy, 1954; legis. asst. U.S. Senate, Washington, 1956; social sec. to ambassador of Finland, Washington, 1958; legis. asst. to congressman, Washington, 1960-65; sr. assoc. Gillmore M. Perry Co., Washington, 1965-76; sales exec./cons. furniture industry, Hilton Head, S.C., 1985-87; ptnr. Mfrs. Representatives Internat., 1987—. Mem. Georgetown U. Alumni Assn., John Carroll Soc. Republican. Roman Catholic. Club: Army Navy (Washington). Home: 4000 Cathedral Ave NW 208B Washington DC 20016-5249

MCELVEEN, PATTI EILEEN, accountant, payroll and computer specialist; b. Sumter, S.C., Mar. 16, 1961; d. Francis Brainard and Mildred Edna (Evans) Watford; m. Mitchell R. McElveen, Aug. 30, 1995. Student, Sumter (S.C.) Area Tech., 1990—, Ctrl. Carolina Tech. Coll. (previously Sumter Area Tech.), 1992-94. Sec. McIntosh Mech., Manning, S.C., 1984-85, Glen Mfg., Sumter, 1985; office mgr. Hose & Equipment Indsl. Maintenance, Sumter, 1985-89; with sales Chromate Indsl. Sales, Sumter, 1989; sec. Associated Psychotherapists Chromate Indsl. Sales, 1989-90; records inventory clk. Laidlaw Environ. Svcs. Inc., Pinewood, S.C., 1990-91, purchasing asst., 1991, payroll clk., 1991-92, computer supr., 1991-92; office mgr., bookkeeper Whitaker's Inc. of Sumter, S.C., 1992; sec. People's Resources, Sumter, S.C., 1993-94; traffic coord. Cadco, Inc., Florence, S.C., 1994; sec. People's Resources at Ga. Pacific, Alcolu, S.C., 1994; payroll coord. Ga.-Pacific Corp., 1994-95, office mgr., 1996—. Sec.-treas. Brewington Presbyn. Ch., 1990—; sec.-treas. Watford Family Reunion, 1990—; v.p. Evans Family Reunion, 1993-94, pres., 1994-95. Office: Ga Pacific PO Box 267 Alcolu SC 29001-0267

MCELYEA, JACQUELYN SUZANNE, accountant, real estate consultant; b. Dallas, July 19, 1958; d. Owen Clyde and Mary Lou (Cockerill) Harvey; m. James E. McElyea, June 14, 1983. BBS, Tex. A&M U., 1980. CPA, Tex. Acctg. mgr. Oxford Tex. Devel., Dallas, 1980-81; staff to dir. Price Waterhouse, Dallas, 1981—; bd. dirs. Nat. Assn. Corp. Real Estate, Dallas. Co-author: Real Estate Accounting Reporting, 1995. Bd. dirs. Am. Diabetes Assn., Dallas, 1996-97. Mem. AICPA, Nat. Assn. Real Estate Cos., Tex. Soc. CPAs. Presbyterian. Office: Price Waterhouse 2001 Ross Ave Dallas TX 75201

MCENTIRE, REBA N., country singer; b. McAlester, Okla., Mar. 28, 1955; d. Clark Vincent and Jacqueline (Smith) McE.; m. Narvel Blackstock, 1989; 1 child, Shelby Steven McEntire Blackstock. Student elem. edn., music, Southeastern State U., Durant, Okla., 1976. Rec. artist Mercury Records, 1978-83, MCA Records, 1984—. Albums include Whoever's in New England (Gold award), 1986, What Am I Gonna Do About You (Gold award), 1987, Greatest Hits (Gold award, Platinum award, U.S., Can.), 1987, Merry Christmas To You, 1987, The Last One To Know (Gold award), 1988, Reba (Gold award 1988), Sweet 16 (Gold award 1989, U.S.), Rumor Has It (Gold award 1991, Platinum award 1992, Double Platinum 1992), Reba Live (Gold award 1990, Gold award 1991, Platinum award 1991), For My Broken Heart, 1991, Forever in Your Eyes, 1992, It's Your Call, 1992, Read My Mind, 1994, Starting Over, 1995, Reba compilation video (Gold award, Platinum award 1992); author: (with Tom Carter) Reba: My Story, 1994; actress: (miniseries) Buffalo Girls, 1995. Spokesperson Middle Tenn. United Way, 1988, Nat. and State 4-H Alumni, Bob Hope's Hope for a Drug Free Am.; Nat. spokesperson Am. Lung Assn., 1990-91. Recipient numerous awards in Country music including Disting. Alumni award Southeastern State U., Female vocalist award Country Music Assn., 1984, 85, 86, 87, Grammy award for Best Country Vocal Performance, 1987, 2 Grammy nominations, 1994, Grammy award, Best Country Vocal Collaboration for "Does He Love You" with Linda Davis, 1994, Entertainer of Yr. award Country Radio Awards, 1994, Female Vocalist award, 1994; named Entertainer of Yr., Country Music Assn., 1986, Female Vocalist of Yr. Acad. Country Music, 1984, 85, 86, 87, 92, Top Female Vocalist, 1991, Am. Music award favorite female country singer, 1988, 90, 91, 92, 93, Am. Music award, 1989, 90, 91, 92, Best Album, 1991, Favorite Female Vocalist, 1994, Favorite Female Vocalist, Peoples Choice Award, 1992, Favorite Female Country Vocalist, 1992, 93, Favorite Female Vocalist, TNN Viewer's Choice Awards, 1993, Favorite Female Country Artist, Billboard, 1994, Favorite Country Album award Am. Music Awards, 1995, Favorite Female Country Vocalist award Am. Music Awards, 1995, Favorite Female Vocalist award People's Choice Awards, 1995, Top Female Vocalist of Yr. award Acad. Country Music, 1995, Entertainer of Yr. award Acad. Country Music, 1995, Favorite Female Vocalist award TNN Viewer's Choice Awards, 1995. Mem. Country Music Assn., Acad. Country Music, Nat. Acad. Rec. Arts and Scis., Grand Ol' Opry, AFTRA, Nashville Songwriters Assn. Inc. *

MCEUEN, MELISSA ANN, American history educator; b. Princeton, Ky., Mar. 19, 1961; d. James Bruce and Peggy Sue McEuen. BA magna cum laude, Georgetown Coll., 1983; MA, La. State U., 1986, PhD, 1991. Teaching asst. La. State U., Baton Rouge, 1984-90; asst. prof. history Georgetown (Ky.) Coll., 1991-95, Transylvania U., Lexington, Ky., 1995—; curator Concern for Worthy & Effective Citizens photography exhibit, 1991-92. T. Harry Williams fellow La. State U., 1990-91. Mem. Am. Studies Assn., Am. Hist. Assn., Orgn. Am. Historians, So. Hist. Assn. (mem. com. 1995-96), Sigma Kappa. Office: Transylvania U 300 N Broadway Lexington KY 40508

MCEVOY, GRACE ELIZABETH, photographer; b. Patterson, N.J., Nov. 18, 1961; d. Charles Joseph and Mary Hayes (Lyons) McEvoy-French; m. Eugene Anthony Cusimano, Nov. 25, 1989. BS in Media Arts, U. S.C., 1986. Photographer McKissick Mus., Columbia, S.C., 1983-86; freelance photographer, Austin, Tex., 1986-89; photographer Austin History Ctr., 1989—; mem. peer panel Austin Arts Commn., 1993, chmn. adv. panel, 1994—; judge Tex. Media Awards, Austin, 1994—; bd. dirs. Diverse Arts; cons. Austin, 1996—. Photographer, rschr. Art in Pub. Places, Austin, 1993; photographer Progressive rts Collective, Austin, 1992-94. Recipient svc. award Austin Parks and Recreation Dept., 1994, Mayor of Austin, 1994, 95, Progressive Arts Collective, 1994. Mem. Tex. Photog. Soc., Tex. Fine Arts Assn. Democrat. Office: Austin History Ctr 810 Guadalupe St Austin TX 78701

MCEVOY, NAN TUCKER, publishing company executive; b. San Mateo, Calif., July 15, 1919; d. Nion R. and Phyllis (de Young) Tucker; m. Dennis McEvoy, 1948 (div.); 1 child, Nion Tucker McEvoy. Student, Georgetown U., 1975. Newspaper reporter San Francisco Chronicle, 1944-46, N.Y. Herald Tribune, N.Y.C., 1946-47, Washington Post, 1947-48; rep. in pub. rels. John Homes, Inc., Washington, 1959-60; spl. asst. to dir. U.S. Peace Corps, Washington, 1961-64; mem. U.S. delegation UNESCO, Washington, 1964-65; dir. Population Coun., Washington, 1965-70; co-founder, dep. dir. Preterm, Inc., Washington, 1970-74; former chmn. bd. Chronicle Pub. Co., San Francisco, 1975-95, dir. emeritus, 1995—. Mem. nat. bd. dirs. Smithsonian Instn., Washington, 1994—; mem. Brookings coun. Brookings Instn., Washington, 1994—; commr. Nat. Mus. Art, Washington; mem. U. Calif. San Francisco Found., 1993—; formerly arbitrator Am. Arbitration Assn., Washington. Named Woman of Yr., Washingtonian Mag., 1973. Mem. Am. Art Forum, Burlingame Country Club, The River Club, Commonwealth Club of Calif., World Affairs Coun., Villa Taverna. Office: 655 Montgomery St Ste 1430 San Francisco CA 94111*

MCEVOY, SHARLENE ANN, business law educator; b. Derby, Conn., July 6, 1950; d. Peter Henry Jr. and Madaline Elizabeth (McCabe) McE. BA magna cum laude, Albertus Magnus Coll., 1972; JD, U. Conn., West Hartford, 1975; MA, Trinity Coll., Hartford, 1980, UCLA, 1982; PhD, UCLA, 1985. Bar: Conn., 1975. Pvt. practice Derby, 1984—; asst. prof. bus. law Fairfield (Conn.) U. Sch. Bus., 1986—; adj. prof. bus. law, polit. sci. Albertus Magnus Coll., New Haven, Conn., 1978-80, U. Conn., Stamford, 1984-86; acting chmn. polit. sci. dept. Albertus Magnus Coll., 1980; assoc. prof. law Fairfield U., 1992—; Chmn. Women's Resource Ctr., Fairfield U., 1989-91. Staff editor Jour. Legal Studies Edn., 1989-94; reviewer Am. Bus. Law Assn. jour., 1988—, staff editor, 1995—; sr. articles editor N.E. Jour. of Legal Studies in Bus., 1995-96. Mem. Derby Tercentennial Commn., 1973-74; bd. dirs. Valley Transit Dist., Derby, 1975-77, Justice of Peace, City of Derby, 1975-83; alt. mem. Parks and Recreation Commn., Woodbury, 1995—; mem., treas. Woodbury Dem. Town Com., 1995-96, corr. sec. 1996—. Recipient Best Paper award N.E. Regional Bus. Law Assn., 1990, Best Paper award Tri-State Regional Bus. Law Assn., 1991; Fairfield U. Sch. Bus. rsch. grantee 1989, 91, 92, Fairfield U. rsch. grantee, 1994. Mem. ABA,

Conn. Bar Assn., Acad. Legal Studies in Bus. (coord. SINISTRAL spl. interest group 1977—). Democrat. Roman Catholic. Office: 198 Emmett Ave Derby CT 06418-1258

MCEWEN, INGER THEORIN, English as second language tutor and consultant; b. Goteborg, Sweden, July 22, 1935; came to U.S., 1955; m. William C. McEwen; children: Karin, Erik. BA, Peabody at Vanderbilt U., 1973, MLS, 1976. Cert. tchr. ESL, N.H. Libr. Scales Elem. Sch., Brentwood, Tenn., 1977-82; reference libr. Dartmouth Coll., Hanover, N.H., 1982-85; media supr. Hartford (Vt.) Sch. Dist.; edn. asst. SAU 22, Hanover, 1985-86, ESL tutor, 1992—; cons. White River Elem. Sch., White River Junction, Vt. Actuve Ch. of Christ at Dartmouth Coll., Hanover. Mem. No. New Eng. TESOL, Beta Phi Mu.

MCFADDEN, CHERYL ELLEN, health care professional; b. Wilkinsburg, Pa., Jan. 24, 1955; d. Robert John and Lois Evelyn (Butler) Worbois; m. Danny Earl McFadden, Aug. 2, 1980; children: Robert Dean, James Michael. Diploma in practical nursing, Westmoreland County C.C., Youngwood, Pa., 1978; BSN, N.W. Okla. State U., 1989; MS, U. Okla., 1996. RN, Okla.; cert. ACLS instr., Okla. Staff nurse Montifiore Hosp., Pitts., 1978-79, Enid (Okla.) Meml. Hosp., 1979-86; staff nurse critical care unit Mercy Health Ctr., Oklahoma City, 1986-89; nurse, edn. coord. N.W. Area Health Edn. Ctr., Enid, 1989-90; nurse, dir. insvc. Enid Regional Meml. Hosp., 1990-92; relief nurse ICU, house supr. Bass Meml. Bapt. Hosp., Enid, 1992—; instr. nursing N.W. Okla. State U., Alva, 1992-95; mem. trauma systems planning coalition Okla. State Dept. Health, Oklahoma City, 1994, trauma systems regional adv. coun., 1994; health care finder Found. Health Fedn. Svcs., Tricare Svc. Ctr., Vance AFB, Enid, Okla., 1995—. Co-author grants Teen Pregnancy Prevention Project, 1990, N.W. Area Health Edn. Ctr. Continuation Grant, 1990. Phone bank personnel Gary Maxey for Sit. #40 Ho. of Reps., Enid, 1990, John McPhail for Dist. Judge, Enid, 1994. Mem. Okla. Nurses Assn. (chairperson govt. activities 1991-92, bd. dirs. 1990-92, nurse of day Okla. State Legislature 1990, 92), Alpha Epsilon Lambda (Delta chpt.), Sigma Theta Tau (Beta Delta chpt.). Democrat. Baptist. Home: 2109 N Meadowbrook Dr Enid OK 73701-2568 Office: Found Health Fed Svcs Tricare Svc Ctr Vance AFB Enid OK 73705

MCFADDEN, MARY JOSEPHINE, fashion industry executive; b. N.Y.C., Oct. 1, 1938; d. Alexander Bloomfield and Mary Josephine (Cutting) McF.; m. Philip Harari; 1 child, Justine. Ed., Sorbonne, Paris, France, Traphagen Sch. Design, 1957, Columbia, 1959-62; DFA, Internat. Fine Arts Coll., 1984. Pub. relations dir. Christian Dior, N.Y.C., 1962-64; merchandising editor Vogue South Africa, 1964-65, editor, 1965-69; polit. and travel columnist Rand (South Africa) Daily Mail, 1965-68; founder sculptural workshop Vukutu, Rhodesia, 1968-70; spl. projects editor Vogue U.S.A., 1973; pres. Mary McFadden, Inc., N.Y.C., 1976—; ptnr. MMcF Collection by Mary McFadden, 1991—; bd. dirs., advisor Sch. Design and Merchandising Kent State U., Eugene O'Neill Meml. Theatre Ctr.; mem. profl. com. Cooper-Hewitt Mus., Smithsonian Inst., Nat. Mus. of Design. Fashion and jewelry designer, 1973—. Advisor Nat. Endowment for Arts. Recipient Am. Fashion Critics award-Coty award, 1976, 78, 79, Audemars Piguet Fashion award, 1976, Rex award, 1977, award More Coll. Art, 1977, Pa. Gov.'s award, 1977, Roscoe award, 1978, Pres.'s Fellows award RISD, 1979, Neiman-Marcus award of excellence, 1979, Design Excellence award Pratt Inst., 1993, award N.Y. Landmarks Conservancy, 1994, NU Breed Fashion award, 1996, Marymount Coll. Fashion award, 1996; named to Fashion Hall of Fame, 1979; fellow RISD. Mem. Fashion Group, Coun. Fashion Designers Am. (pres., past bd. dirs.). Office: Mary McFadden Inc 240 W 35th St Fl 17 New York NY 10001-2506

MCFADDIN, JEAN ELEANOR, executive; b. Lufkin, Tex., July 13, 1942; d. Ora Lance and Eleanor (Clark) McF. AA, Stephen's Coll., 1962; BFA, U. Tex., 1964, MFA, 1966. Assoc. dir. Mummers Theatre, Okla., 1967-70; artistic dir. Liquid Theatre, N.Y.C., Paris and London, 1971, Dubuffets "Coucou Bazaar", N.Y.C., Paris and London, 1972; producer, dir. Phila. Greater Arts Coun., 1973; artistic dir. NEA Projects, N.Y.C. and Washington, 1974; dir. nat. tour promotion Am. Shekespeare Commn., Stratford, Conn., 1975; project dir. N.Y.C. Bicentennial COmmn., 1976; group v.p. promotions & events Macy's East, N.Y.C., 1977—. Bd. dirs. Race Against Time, Calif. 1992-96, Cystic Fibrosis Found., N.Y., 1984-96; mem. com. NY95 & NY96, N.Y.C., 1995, 96, UN 50th Anniversary, N.Y.C., 1995. Recipient Emmy awards (5) Nat. Acad. TV, Arts and Scis., 1984-94, N.Y. Cmtys. Mayor's Humanitarian award, 1985, Mary T. Norton Congrl. award United Way, N.Y./N.J., 1993; named Outstanding Vol. Cystic Fibrosis Found., N.Y., 1986. Mem. Nat. Music Found. (bd. dirs. 1992-96). Home: 185 W End Ave New York NY 10023

MCFADIN, HELEN LOZETTA, retired elementary education educator; b. Tucumcari, N.Mex., Sept. 7, 1923; d. Henry J. and LaRue Altha (Ford) Stockton; m. John Reece McFadin, July 3, 1946; 1 child, Janice Lynn McFadin Koenig. AB in Edn./Psychology, Highlands U., Las Vegas, N.Mex., 1956; MA in Teaching, N.Mex. State U., 1968; postgrad., U. N.D., 1965, St. Leo's Coll., St. Leo, Fla., 1970. Cert. tchr., K-12 reading/psychology specialist, N.Mex. Tchr. 1st and 2d grades Grant County Schs., Bayard, N.Mex., 1943-44; tchr. 4th grade Durango (Colo.) Pub. Schs., 1946-48; tchr. 2d grade Artesia Pub. Schs., Loco Hills, N.Mex., 1955; tchr. 3d grade Alamogordo (N.Mex.) Pub. Schs., 1957-66, h.s. reading specialist, 1966-72, elem. reading specialist, 1972-77, tchr. 4th grade, 1977-82, reading tchr. 7th grade, dept. chair, 1982-87; ret. N.Mex. State U., Alamogordo, 1987, instr. edn., 1987-90; organizer reading labs. h.s., elem. schs., Alamogordo, 1966-77, designer programs and curriculum, 1957-89; presenter/cons. in field; cons. Mary Kay Cosmetics. Contbr. articles to profl. jours. Local and dist. judge spelling bees and sci. fairs Alamogordo Pub. Schs., 1987—. Recipient Literacy award Otero County Reading Coun., 1986; inducted in Women's Hall of Fame, Alamogordo Women's Clubs, 1989. Mem. Am. Bus. Women's Assn. (pres. 1986-87, Woman of the Yr. 1988), C. of C., NEA (del. 1957-87, Dedicated Svc. award 1987), N.Mex. Edn. Assn., Internat. Reading Assn. (mem. Spl. League of the Honored 1985, pres. 1975-76), N.Mex. Reading Assn. (bd. dirs. 1988-94, del. to 1st Russian reading conf. 1992, Dedicated Svc. award 1994), Beta Sigma Phi, Kappa Kappa Iota (Disting. Educator Emeritus Cert. of Merit 1988). Republican. Baptist. Home: 2364 Union Ave Alamogordo NM 88310-3848

MCFARLAND, DEBORAH YOUNG, accountant; b. Burlingame, Calif., July 31, 1958; d. Thomas Suey and Lucille Ann (Ho) Young; m. David Alan McFarland, Aug. 9, 1956. BS, U. Calif., Berkeley, 1980. CPA, Calif.; Cert. Info. Systems Auditor, Info. Systems Auditors. Fin. analyst Ampex Corp., Redwood City, Calif., 1980-81, internal auditor, 1981-83; staff auditor Arthur Young and Co., San Jose, Calif., 1983-87; acctg. mgr. Western area Digital Equipment Corp., Santa Clara, Calif., 1987-88; sr. mgr. ISA Ernst and Young, San Jose, 1988-93; internal audit supr. Apple Computer, Cupertino, Calif., 1993-95, fin. sys. mgr., 1995-96; with Price Waterhouse, San Jose, 1996—. Contbr. papers to profl. publs. Mem. AICPA, Info. Sys. Audit and Control (programs dir. 1990), Cal. Bus. Alumni, Phi Beta Kappa (treas. 1980—). Home: 1550 Kennewick Dr Sunnyvale CA 94087

MCFARLAND, JANE ELIZABETH, librarian; b. Athens, Tenn., June 22, 1937; d. John Homer and Martha Virginia (Large) McFarland. AB, Smith Coll., 1959; M in Divinity, Yale U., 1963; MS in LS, U. N.C., 1971. Tchr. hist. and religion Northfield Schs., Mass., 1961-62; head librarian reference and circulation Yale Divinity Library, New Haven, Conn., 1963-71; head librarian Bradford (Mass.) Coll., 1972-77; reference librarian U. Tenn., Chattanooga, Tenn., 1977-80; head librarian reference dept Chattanooga-Hamilton County Bicentennial Library, Tenn., 1980-86, acting dir., 1986, dir., 1986—. Mem. Chattanooga Library Assn., Tenn. Library Assn., Southeastern Library Assn., Am. Library Assn., Phi Beta Kappa (treas. 1987, 88). Democrat. Roman Catholic. Home: 1701 Estrellita Cir Chattanooga TN 37421-5754 Office: Chattanooga-Hamilton County Libr 1001 Broad St Chattanooga TN 37402-2620

MCFARLAND, JANET CHAPIN, consulting company executive; b. New Castle, Pa., Jan. 5, 1962; d. Robert Chapin McFarland and Dorothy Jean (Heade) Jost; m. Steven Mitchell Walters, July 30, 1994. BS in Imaging Sci. and Engring., Rochester Inst. Tech., 1985; MBA in Innovation Mgmt. and Mktg., Syracuse U., 1990. Rsch. engr. Shipley Co., Inc., Newton, Mass., 1985-88; mktg. cons. Syracuse (N.Y.) U. Sch. Mgmt., 1988-90; market rsch. coop. AT&T Consumer Comms. Svcs., Basking Ridge, N.J., summer 1989; tech. analyst DynCorp Meridian, Alexandria, Va., 1991-93; dir. studies and analysis Tech. Strategies & Alliances, Burke, Va., 1993-94; pres. ArBar, Inc., Alexandria, Va., 1994—; presenter in field. Mem. Internat. Soc. Optical Engrs., Soc. Mfg. Engrs. (chpt. chair 1995), Beta Gamma Sigma, Alpha Mu Alpha. Office: ArBar Inc 312 S Washington St Ste 5B Alexandria VA 22314

MCFARLAND, KAY ELEANOR, state supreme court chief justice; b. Coffeyville, Kans., July 20, 1935; d. Kenneth W. and Margaret E. (Thrall) McF. BA magna cum laude, Washburn U., Topeka, 1957, JD, 1964. Bar: Kans. 1964. Sole practice Topeka, 1964-71; probate and juvenile judge Shawnee County, Topeka, 1971-73; dist. judge Topeka, 1973-77; assoc. justice Kans. Supreme Ct., 1977-95, chief justice, 1995—. Mem. Kans. Bar Assn. Office: Kans Supreme Ct Kans Jud Ctr 301 W 10th St Topeka KS 66612

MCFARLAND, KAY FLOWERS, medical educator; b. Daytona Beach, Fla., Jan. 27, 1942; d. Ernest Clyde and Sarah Elizabeth (Holder) Flowers; m. Dee Edward McFarland, Aug. 18, 1963; children: Grace, Joy, Eric, Sarah. BS, Wake Forest Coll., 1963; MD, Bowman Gray Sch. Medicine, 1966. Diplomate Am. Bd. Internal Medicine, Endocrinology, Geriatrics. Intern N.C. Bapt. Hosp., Winston-Salem; resident medicine Cleve. Clinic; fellow endocrinology Med. Coll. Ga., Augusta, from instr. to asst. prof. medicine, 1971-77; assoc. prof. to prof. ob-gyn. Sch. Medicine U. S.C., Columbia, 1977-86, prof. medicine Sch. Medicine, 1986—, assoc. dean continuing edn. Sch. Medicine, 1986-91. Contbr. chpts. to books and articles to profl. jours. Fellow ACP, ACE; mem. Am. Diabetes Assn. (Profl. award 1975, Woman of Valor award 1996). Office: USC Sch Medicine Ste 506 Two Medical Park Columbia SC 29203

MCFARLAND, LYNNE VERNICE, pharmaceutical executive; b. San Antonio, Tex., June 3, 1953; d. Earle Clifford and Avis Marie (Jones) Olson; m. Marcus Joseph McFarland, July 27, 1975. BS in Microbiology, Portland State U., 1975, MS, 1980; PhD in Epidemiology, U. Wash., 1988. Pub. Health Cert. Rsch. asst. U. Oreg. Health Sci. Ctr., Portland, 1977-79, lab. supr., 1980-82; intern Wash. State Pub. Health Labs, Seattle, 1983; teaching asst. Dept. Epidemiology U. Wash., Seattle, 1984, rsch. asst., 1984-88, postdoctoral researcher Dept. Med. Chemistry, 1988, lectr. Dept. Med. Chemistry, 1988, rsch. asst. prof., 1991—; dir. scientific affairs Biocodex, Inc., Seattle, 1988—; reviewer McGraw-Hill Book Co., N.Y.C., 1982; editorial reviewer Ob-Gyn, L.A., 1989—, Jour. of Infect Diseases, 1991, 95—, Vet. Adminstrn., 1991; also review for gastroenterology, 1990, clin. infectious diseases, 1995—. Reviewer Gastroenterology; contbr. articles to profl. jours. Lobbyist environ. issues Wash. State Biotech. Assn., Seattle, 1990; vol. Literacy Plus, Seattle, 1990. Recipient Poncin scholarshp, Seafirst Bank, Seattle, 1985-88. Mem. Am. Soc. Microbiology, Soc. for Epidemiol. Rsch., Soc. Microbiol. Ecology and Diseases, Wash. Assn. of Epidemiology. Office: Biocodex Inc 1910 Fairview Ave E Ste 208 Seattle WA 98102-3620

MCFARLAND, MARY A., elementary and secondary school educator, administrator; b. St. Louis, Nov. 12, 1937; d. Allen and Maryann (Crawford) Mabry; m. Gerald McFarland, May 30, 1959. BS in Elem. Edn., S.E. Mo. State U., 1959; MA in Secondary Edn., Washington U., St. Louis, 1965; PhD in Curriculum and Instrn., St. Louis U., 1977. Cert. tchr. elem., secondary, supt., Mo. Elem. tchr. Berkeley Sch. Dist., St. Louis, 1959-64; secondary tchr. Parkway Sch. Dist., St. Louis, 1965-75, social studies coord. K-12, 1975—, dir. staff devel., 1984—; adj. prof. Maryville U., St. Louis, 1990—; cons. pvt. practice, Chesterfield, Mo. Co-author: (text series) The World Around Us, 1990, 3d rev. edit., 1995; contbr. articles to profl. jours. Nat. faculty Nat. Issues Forum, Dayton, Ohio. Mem. ASCD, Social Sci. Edn. Consortium, Nat. Coun. for Social Studies (pres. 1989-90), Mo. Coun. for Social Studies (pres. 1980-81). Democrat. Methodist. Office: Parkway Schs Dist Instrnl Svcs 12657 Fee Fee Rd Saint Louis MO 63146-3855

MCFARLAND, SHIRLEY ANN, women's health nurse; b. Greensburg, Pa., Sept. 25, 1935; d. Charles Thomas and Hettie Jane (Kunkle) Brown; m. Marion Luther McFarland, July 5, 1958; children: Shirley Marie McKinney, David Eugene, Kevin Paul. Diploma in Nursing, Johnstown (Pa.) Meml. Hosp., 1956; BS, U. Kans., 1976; MSN, Wayne State U., 1985. Cert. nurse practitioner; RN, Pa., Mich. Operating rm. staff nurse Conemaugh Valley Meml. Hosp., Johnstown, 1956, chg. nurse, 1957-58; staff nurse, clin. instr. Torrence State Hosp., Blairsville, Pa., 1956-57; instr. classroom and clinic Clarinda (Iowa) C.C., 1960-62; head nurse Standish (Mich.) Cmty. Hosp., 1971-82; insvc. dir. Geriatric Village, West Branch, Mich., 1982-83; instr. classroom and clinic Kirtland C.C., Roscommon, Mich., 1982-83; nurse practitioner Dist. Health Dept. #2, West Branch, 1988-94, Primary Care Practice, West Branch, 1985—. Contbg. author: Protocols for Cervical Cancer, 1995. Precinct del. Rep. Party, Rose City, 1984; singer Ogeman Players. Named Woman of the Yr., Bus. and Profl. Women, 1987. Mem. Mich. Nurses Assn. (Outstanding Nurse in Advanced Practice 1992), Sigma Theta Tau. Reformed Presbyterian. Home: 1841 N Ogemaw Trail West Branch MI 48661 Office: Primary Care Practice 2331 Progress St West Branch MI 48661-9384

MCFARLAND-ESPOSITO, CARLA RAE, nursing executive; b. Cin., July 20, 1957; d. Jay Crawford McFarland and Stella (Herndon) O'Donnell; m. S. Esposito; 1 child, Jayson Vincenzo Esposito. BSN, Ea. Ky. U., 1979. RN, Calif.; cert. pub. health nurse. Charge nurse St. Elizabeth Med. Ctr., Covington, Ky., 1980-82; traveling nurse various cities, 1983-86; nurse recruiter Med. Recruiters of Am., Culver City, Calif., 1987; nurse recruiter, liaison nurse, br. mgr. traveling nurse program NSI Svcs., Inc., Beverly Hills, Calif., 1987-90; dir. traveling nurse network, dir. nursing acute care Associated Health Profls. Inc., Culver City, 1990-91; dir. traveling profls., dir. bus. devel. NSI Svcs., Inc., Beverly Hills, 1991-92; clin. dir. ultra care and med. surg. units Westside Hosp., L.A., 1992-94, dir. utilization rev. and discharge planning, 1994-96, mem. case mgmt. team, 1992-96; dir. utilization rev. and discharge planning Thompson Meml. Med. Ctr., Burbank, Calif., 1996—; mem. utilization rev. com. Associated Physicians of St. John's, 1994. Vol. pediatric assessments, immunizations Oscar Romera Clinic., L.A., 1991—. Mem. NAFE, AACN, Assn. Nurse Execs., Networking Orgn., Case Mgmt. Soc. Am. Home: 411 Whitegate Rd Thousand Oaks CA 91320 Office: Thompson Meml Med Ctr 466 E Olive Ave Burbank CA 91501-4419

MCFARLANE, BETH LUCETTA TROESTER, former mayor; b. Osterdock, Iowa, Mar. 9, 1918; d. Francis Charles and Ella Carrie (Moser) Troester; M. George Evert McFarlane, June 20, 1943 (dec. May 1972); children: Douglas, Steven (dec.), Susan, George. BA in Edn., U. No. Iowa, 1962, MA in Edn., 1971. Cert. tchr. Tchr. rural and elem. schs., Iowa, 1936-50, 55-56; elem. tchr. Oelwein Cmty. Schs., Iowa, 1956-64, jr. high reading tchr., 1964-71, reading specialist, 1971-83; mayor of Oelwein, 1982-89; evaluator North Cen. Accreditation Assn. for Ednl. Programs; mem. planning team for confs. for Iowa Cities, N.E. Iowa, 1985; v.p. N.E. Iowa Regional Council for Econ. Devel., 1986-89; mem. Area Econ. Devel. Com. N.E. Iowa, 1985, Legis. Interim Study Com. on Rural Econ. Devel., 1987-88; mem. policy com. Iowa League Municipalities, 1987-88; bd. dirs. Oelwein Indsl. Devel. Corp., 1982-91, Oelwein Betterment Corp., 1982-94. V.p. Fayette County Tourism Council, 1987-88; Iowa State Steering Com. on Road Use Tax Financing, 1988-89; chmn. bd. govs. Oelwein Community Ctr, 1990-94; chmn. Reorganized LDS Ch. Bldg. and Fin. Com., 1980—, Dist. Ch. Fin. Com., 1992—, Dist. Ch. Revolving Loan Com., 1982—. Named Iowa Reading Tchr. of Yr., Internat. Reading Assn. Iowa, 1978; recipient Outstanding Contbrn. to Reading Council Activities award Internat. Reading Assn. N.E. Iowa, 1978, State of Iowa's Gov.s' Leadership award, 1988. Mem. N.E. Iowa Reading Council (pres. 1975-77), MacDowell Music and Arts Orgn. (pres. 1978-80), Oelwein Bus. and Profl. Women (Woman of Yr. 1983), Oelwein Area Ret. Sch. Pers. (pres. 1994-96), Oelwein Area C. of C. (bd. dirs. 1986-89, Humanitarian award 1987), Delta Kappa Gamma (pres. 1980-82). Republican. Mem. Reorganized Ch. of Jesus Christ of Latter Day Saints. Avocations: hiking, refinishing antiques, gardening, jogging, creative sewing. Home: 512 7th Ave NE Oelwein IA 50662-1326

MC FARLANE, KAREN ELIZABETH, concert artists manager; b. St. Louis, Jan. 2, 1942; d. Nicholas and Bonita Margaret (Fults) Walz; m. Ralph Leo McFarlane, Nov. 30, 1968 (div.); children: Sarah Louise.; m. Walter Holtkamp, June 19, 1982. B.Mus.Ed. (Presser Music Found. scholar), Lindenwood Coll., 1964. Public sch. music tchr. St. Louis County, 1964-66; music asst. Riverside Ch., N.Y.C., 1966-70; dir. music St. Mark's Episc. Ch., San Marcos, Tex., 1971-73, Park Ave. Christian Ch., N.Y.C., 1974-81; also pres. Murtagh/McFarlane Artists, Inc., Cleve., 1976-88; pres. Karen McFarlane Artists, Cleve., 1989—. Mem. Am. Guild Organists, Nat. Assn. Performing Arts Mgrs. and Agts., Inc., Internat. Soc. Performing Arts Adminstrn. Republican. Presbyterian. Office: 12429 Cedar Rd Ste 29 Cleveland OH 44106-3172

MCFARLIN, DIANE H., newspaper editor; b. Lake Wales, Fla., July 10, 1954; d. Ruffie Denton Hooten and Anna Loraine (Peeples) Huff; m. Henry Briggs McFarlin, Aug. 28, 1976 (div. 1993). BS, U. Fla., 1976. Reporter Sarasota (Fla.) Jour., 1976-77, asst. news editor, 1977-78, city editor, 1978-82; asst. mng. editor Sarasota (Fla.) Herald Tribune, 1983-84, mng. editor, 1985-87; exec. editor Gainesville (Fla.) Sun, 1987-90, Sarasota Herald-Tribune, 1990—; mem. adv. bd. U. Fla. Coll. Journalism and Comm., 1987—. Mem. accrediting coun. Edn. in Journalism and Mass Comms., 1994—. Mem. Am. Soc. Newspaper Editors (com. chair 1992, 94, bd. dirs. 1994—), Fla. Soc. Newspaper Editors (sec.-treas. 1993, v.p. 1994, pres. 1995). Office: Sarasota Herald-Tribune PO Box 1719 Sarasota FL 34230

MC FATE, PATRICIA ANN, scientist, education, foundation executive; b. Detroit, Mar. 19, 1936; d. John Earle and Mary Louise (Bliss) McF.; m. Sidney Norman Graybeal, Sept. 10, 1988. B.A. (Alumni scholar), Mich. State U., 1954; M.A., Northwestern U., 1956, Ph.D., 1965; M.A. (hon.), U. Pa., 1977. Assoc. prof. English, asst. dean liberal arts and scis. U. Ill., Chgo., 1967-74; assoc. prof. English, assoc. vice chancellor acad. affairs U. Ill., 1974-75; assoc. prof. folklore Faculty Arts and Scis., U. Pa., Phila., 1975-81; prof. tech. and soc. Coll. Engring. and Applied Sci., 1975-81, vice provost, 1975-78; dep. chmn. Nat. Endowment for Humanities, Washington, 1978-81; exec. v.p. Am.-Scandinavian Found., N.Y.C., 1981-82, pres., 1982-88; sr. scientist Sci. Applications Internat. Corp., Mc Lean, Va., 1988—, program dir. Ctr. for Nat. Security Negotiations, 1988—; cons. UN, 1994-95; vis. assoc. prof. dept. medicine Rush U., Chgo., 1970-85; bd. dirs. CoreStates Bank, N.A., CoreStates Fin. Corp. Author: The Writings of James Stephens, 1979, Uncollected Prose of James Stephens, 1983; exec. producer Northern Stars, 1985, Diego Rivera: I Paint What I See, 1989; contbr. articles in fields of sci. policy and lit. to various jours. Mem. sci. and policy adv. com. Arms Control and Disarmament Agy., 1995—; bd. dirs. Raoul Wallenberg Com. of U.S., Swedish Coun. Am., Santa Fe Stages. Decorated officer Order of Leopold II Belgium, comdr. Order Icelandic Falcon, comdr. Royal Order of Polar Star (Sweden), comdr. Order of Lion (Finland), comdr. Royal Norwegian Order Merit, Knight 1st class Royal Order Dannebrog (Denmark); U. Ill. Grad. Coll. faculty fellow, 1968; Swedish Bicentennial Fund grantee, 1981. Fellow N.Y. Acad. Scis.; mem. AAAS (chmn. com. on sci., engring. and pub. policy 1984-87, com. on sci. and internat. security 1976-79, 88-93), Coun. on Fgn. Rels., Acad. Scis. Phila. (founding mem., corr. sec. 1977-79), N.Y. Sci. Policy Assn., Am. Women for Internat. Understanding, Cosmpolitan Club (Phila.), Theta Alpha Phi, Omega Beta Pi, Delta Delta Delta.

MCFAUL, PATRICIA LOUISE, editor; b. Jersey City, June 28, 1947; d. James Leo and Ethel Louise (Shea) McF.; 1 child, Jennifer Jeanne. Student Nassau Community Coll., 1969-70. Pub. info. officer L.I. Cath. Newspaper, Hempstead, N.Y., 1967-68, researcher, 1968-70, staff writer, 1970-73, copy editor, 1973-78, layout and copy editor, 1978—, advt. layout editor, 1989—; readership surveyor, Rockville Centre, N.Y., 1971, 75; mem., com. chmn. Diocesan Family Life Bd., Rockville Centre, 1978-82. Researcher: Mission to Latin America, 1976. Pres. Florence A. Smith Sch. PTA, Oceanside, N.Y., 1982-84, Oceanside High Sch. Marching Band Parents Assn., 1987-89; chmn. talented and gifted com. Oceanside Council PTAs, 1984-85; elem. tchr. aide, 1985—; mem., sec.-treas. L.I. Interfaith Council, Rockville Centre, 1977-80; band dir. search com. Oceanside Sch. Dist., 1988, art and music dir. search com., 1989. Recipient Citation, Diocese of Rockville Centre, 1984, 88. Mem. Cath. Press Assn. (U.S. and Can. citations 1985; mem. research com. 1975-80, mem., chmn. credentials and inspectors of elections com. 1976—, 1st place award design 1978, 86, citations 1980-85). Democrat. Roman Catholic. Avocations: flying, classical music. Home: 37 Rodney Pl Rockville Centre NY 11570-5823 Office: The LI Catholic 99 N Village Ave Rockville Centre NY 11570-4607

MCGARITY, MARGARET DEE, federal judge; b. 1948. BA, Emory U., 1969; JD, U. Wis., 1974. Bar: Wis. 1974. Pvt. practice, 1974-87; bankruptcy judge U.S. Dist. Ct. (ea. dist.) Wis., 1987—; lectr. on marital property, bankruptcy and family law Fed. Judicial Ctr., Nat. Conf. Bankruptcy Judges, State Bar Wis., Nat. Child Support Enforcement Assn., others. Co-author: Marital Property Law in Wisconsin, 2d edit. 1986, Collier Family Law and the Bankruptcy Code, 1991. Mem. Nat. Conf. Bankruptcy Judges, State Bar Wis. Office: 160 US Courthouse 517 E Wisconsin Ave Milwaukee WI 53202*

MCGARRY, CARMEN RACINE, historian, artist; b. Plattsburgh, N.Y., Dec. 15, 1941; d. Allyre Joseph and Annette Cecile (Roy) Racine; sep.; children: Suzanne, John Jr., Annette, Patrick. BA, Coll. St. Rose, 1962. Tchg. cert. Ill.; lic. real estate broker, Ill.; cert. interior designer, Ill. Tchr. Chgo. Bd. Edn., 1962-69; comptr., mgr., broker K&G Bldg. Mgmt., Chgo., 1969-90; rsch. asst. U. Chgo., 1985-89. Designer and creator stained glass windows St. Anne's Shrine, Isle La Motte, Vt., 1995. Mem. Women's History Coalition, Broward County, Ft. Lauderdale, Fla., 1993—; com. mem. County Health Fair, Broward County, 1994—; bd. mem. Hillsboro Lighthouse Com., 1994—; co-chair adv. coun. Area Agy. on Aging, Ft. Lauderdale, 1996—; mem. nominating com. for women's hall of fame Broward County, 1996; advocate for srs. on transp. Disadvantaged Coord. Bd. Broward County. Mem. ASID, Stained Glass Assn. Am., Women's League Hillsboro (bd. mem. 1993—), Broward County Hist. Commn., Palm Beach Hist. Soc., Hillsboro Beach Hist. Commn. (founder, pres.), Deerfield Beach Hist. Soc., Deerfield Beach Rotary (dir. 1996—). Home: 1073 Hillsboro Mile Hillsboro Beach FL 33062

MCGARRY, MARCIA LANGSTON, community service coordinator; b. Washington, Dec. 9, 1941; d. Emil Sylvester and Bernice B. (Bland) Busey. BS, Morgan State U., 1964. Cert. tchr., law enforecment officer, Fla. Payroll clk., jr. acct. U.S. Dept. Labor, Washington, 1964-65; English tchr., Taiwan, 1968-70; tchr. Monroe County Sch. Bd., Key West, Fla., 1971-81; exec. dir. Monroe Assn. Retarded Citizens, Key West, 1977-79; dep. sheriff Monroe County Sheriff's Dept., Key West, 1979-83, 1986-90; probation/parole officer Fla. State Dept. Corrections, Key West, 1983-91; law enforcement instr. Fla. Keys C.C., 1983-91; cmty. svc. coord. City of Bradenton, 1991—; mem. rev. bd. City of Bradenton Police Dept., 1996—, mem. cmty. rels. com. 1996. Active local polit. campaigns; co-founder day schs. for under-privileged children; former mem. Big Bros./Big Sisters Am., mem. com. 1985-86, former bd. dir., Spouse Abuse, former bd. dirs.; bd. dirs. Adv. Coun. Orange-Ridge Elem., 1991-93; bd. dirs. mayor's com., chmn. task force Drug Free Communities, 1991-94, bd. dirs. 1996—; bd. dirs. Human Rels. Commn., 1991-93, Drug Free Schs. and Cmty. Adv. Coun., 1991—; former mem. adv. coun. Byrd Edn. Found., Sweet Adelines Internat., 1992-94, commr. 12th Jud. Nominating Commn. 1992—, cons., facilitator Cultural Diversity Conflict Resolution Workshops, Manatee County High Schs. and Bradenton Police Dept.; attendance avd. com. Bayshore High, 1993, multicultural com., 1994, former rep. Women's Forum; former dir. Choir, Lutheran Ch.; founding mem. Comprehensive Neighborhood Support Network; mem. adv. bd. Manatee County Sheriff's Dept., 1994—. Recipient Appreciation cert. Lions Club, 1978, 79, Career Week award Harris Elem. Sch., 1981, Glynn Archer Elem. Sch., 1989, Trainers award Probation/Parole Acad., 1987, cert. of acknowledgement for cmty. svc. AAUW, 1995, Vol. Army for the War on Drugs. Mem. NAFE, Fla. Police Benevolent Assn., Fla. Women in Govt. (mem. Manatee County chpt.), Ecumanical Luth. Ch. of Am. (elected consultation con. Fla. Synod 1989), Key West Profls., Luth. Ch. Women, Delta Sigma Theta (v.p. 1990-91, corr. sec. 1993-95). Office: City of Bradenton Caller Svc 25015 Bradenton FL 34206

MCGARRY, MARTHA E., lawyer; b. Boston, 1951. BA cum laude, Middlebury Coll., 1973; JD, Fordham U., 1977. Bar: N.Y. Ptnr. Skadden, Arps, Slate, Meagher & Flom, N.Y.C. Office: Skadden Arps Slate Meagher & Flom 919 3rd Ave New York NY 10022*

MCGARRY, RANI GOYAL, social studies educator; b. Chgo., Jan. 18, 1966; d. Raghbir Chand and Diane Mary (Procissi) Goyal; m. James Robert McGarry, Mar. 26, 1994. BA in History, James Madison U., 1990. Lic. tchr., Va. 7th grade tchr. social studies Sidney Lanier Intermediate, Fairfax, Va., 1991-93; 9th and 11th grade tchr. Oakton (Va.) H.S., 1993—; volleyball coach Paul VI H.S., Fairfax, 1992—, track coach, 1992, 96, Oakton H.S., 1993-95, block scheduling chair, 1995—; team leader Sidney Lanier, Fairfax, Va., 1991-93; world studies team leader Oakton H.S., 1994-96. Mem. AAUW. Home: 14433 Gringsby Ct Centreville VA 20120-3222 Office: Oakton High Sch 2900 Sutton Rd Vienna VA 22181

MCGARVEY, VIRGINIA CLAIRE LANCASTER, volunteer; b. Erie, Pa., Feb. 10, 1934; d. Walter Joseph and Clara Marguerite (Johannesen) Lancaster; m. Raymond Leroy McGarvey, Sept. 3, 1955; children: Keith Thomas, Emy Sue, Stephen Bruce. Cert., Thiel Coll., 1954; BS in Bus. Edn., U. Ill., 1957. Sec. P.A. Meyer & Sons, Erie, 1952, Thiel Coll., Greenville, 1953-55; sec. coord. placement office U. Ill., Champaign, 1955-59; tchr. adult edn. Champaign Sch. Dist., 1957-58; dir. Sarah A. Reed Retirement Ctr., Erie, 1972—, chmn., 1980-83, endowment treas., 1984-96; dir. Meadow Brook Dairy Co., Erie, 1975-91; treas. Erie County Hist. Soc., 1989-94, dir., 1989-96; dir. Country Fair, Inc., Erie, 1975—. Mem. Harborcreek (Pa.) Zoning Bd., 1990—; chmn., supt. Wesley United Meth. Ch. Christian Edn., 1960-84, chmn. adminstrv. bd., 1986-95; commr. Greater Erie Bicentennial Commn., 1994-95. Recipient Edward C. Doll Cmty. Svc. award, 1994. Mem. AAUW (pres. 1970-72, Woman of Yr. 1981), Greater Erie Young Men's Christian Assn. (dir. 1981—, pres. elect 1991-93, chmn. 1993-96, Woman of Yr. 1987). Republican. Home and Office: 5191 Jordan Rd Erie PA 16510-4617

MCGARY, BETTY WINSTEAD, minister, counselor, individual, marriage, and family therapist; b. Louisville, June 21, 1936; d. Philip Miller and Mary Jo (Winstead) McG.; married, 1960 (div. 1979); children: Thomas Edward, Mary Alyson, Andrew Philip Pearce. BS, Samford U., 1958; MA, So. Bapt. Theol. Sem., 1961; EdD, U. Louisville, 1988. Ordained to ministry Bapt. Ch., 1986; cert. secondary tchr., Ky., Ga.; lic. profl. counselor, marriage and family therapist, Tex. Min. to youth Broadway Bapt. Ch., Louisville, 1958-60; learning disability and behavior disorders specialist Jefferson County Schs., Muscogee Schs., Cobb County Schs., Louisville, Columbus, Ga., Atlanta, 1964-88; min. to adults South Main Bapt. Ch., Houston, 1986-90; assoc. pastor Calder Bapt. Ch., Beaumont, Tex., 1991—; marriage enrichment cons. Pastoral Inst., Columbus, 1973-76; co-founder and coord. Ctr. for Women in Ministry, Louisville, 1983-86, exec. bd. dirs., 1983-90; cons. Tex. Christian Life Commn., Ft. Worth, 1989-93; co-therapist pvt. practice, Houston, 1989—. Author: (with others) The New Has Come, 1988, A Costly Obedience: Sermons by Women of Steadfast Spirit, 1994; co-editor nat. newsletter Folio: A Newsletter for Southern Bapt. Women in Ministry, 1983-86. Vice-chairperson exec. bd. dirs. handicapped Boy Scouts Am., Houston, 1986-90; mem. leadership coun. Triangle Interfaith Project, Beaumont, 1995—. Recipient citation for Disting. Svc. So. Bapt. Theol. Sem., 1984, Dean's citation Outstanding Achievement U. Louisville, 1988. Mem. The Alliance of Baptists (exec. bd. dirs. 1988-90, v.p. 1990-91), So. Bapt. Women in Ministry (pres. 1988-90, treas. 1995-96), Bapt. Gen. Conv. of Tex. (exec. bd. dirs.), Leadership Beaumont. Home: 2107 Bartlett St Houston TX 77098-5305 Office: Calder Bapt Ch 1005 N 11th St Beaumont TX 77702-1204

MCGARY, RITA ROSE, social worker; b. Frenchville, Me., Sept. 18, 1927; d. Joseph N. and Lula (Labbe) Babin; m. Lawrence E. McGary; children: Philip, Robert, Kathleen. BA in Sociology, Rivier Coll., 1949; MEd, U. Va., 1978; MSW, U. Nev., 1994. Lic. social worker, Nev., nat. cert. counselor, clin. mental health counselor. Tchr. Fort Kent (Me.) H.S., 1949-51; dir., tchr. Nursery Sch., Palembang, Indonesia, 1954-56; tchr. Am. Sch., Asunción, 1963-66; tchr. for homebound Fairfax County Pub. Schs., Fairfax, Va., 1971-74, presenter workshop, cons., case mgr., vis. tchr., 1980-92, sch. social worker, conflict mediator, 1990-92; case mgr. Washoe County Sch. Dist., Reno, 1994—; mediator Fairfax County Family Ct., Fairfax, Va.,1 991-92; case mgr., program coord. Family Resource Ctr., Reno, 1996; social work intern Nev. State Prison, Nev. Women's State Prison, 1993, VA Med. Ctr. and Vet. Ctr., Reno, Nev., 1994, 1994; presenter in field; adj. prof. U. Nev., Reno. Contbr. article to profl. jour. Election worker Dem. Party, Va., 1984; sch. rep. Hisp. Multidisciplinary Team Child Protective Svcs., Fairfax, Va., 1990-92; coord. V.A. Day of Svc. for Homeless, 1994; field exec. Girl Scout Coun. Nation's Capital, Washington, 1975-79. Recipient Excellence in Edn. Dept. of Cmty. Action, Fairfax, Va., 1991. Mem. AAUW, NASW (chair com. sch. social work), NOW, Sch. Social Work Assn. Am., So. Poverty Law Ctr., People for Am. Way, Phi Kappa Phi. Home: 1539 Foster Dr Reno NV 89509

MCGAUGHY, SANDRA LEE, speech pathologist, assistant principal; b. Aledo, Ill., Nov. 12, 1944; d. Harold R. and Bernice F. (Stegall) Esp; m. Michael L. McGaughy, Dec. 24, 1978; 1 child, Eric. A in Gen. Studies, Parkland Jr. Coll., 1971; BS, Western Ill. U., 1974, MA, 1975, Edn. Specialist Cert., 1988. Cert. edn. adminstr., speech pathologist, learning disabilities tchr. Speech pathologist, coord. gifted programs Winola Sch. Dist., Viola, Ill., 1977-86; speech pathologist, asst. elem. prin. Aledo (Ill.) Sch. Dist., 1986—; speech pathologist Mercer County Hosp. and Mercer County Homecare, Aledo, 1994—. Lay youth min., Sunday sch. supt. Calvary Luth. Ch., New Windsor, Ill., 1984—; bd. dirs. Friends of New Windsor Pub. Libr., 1985—. Mem. Am. Speech and Hearing Assn., Nat. Storytelling Assn., Riverbend Storytelling Guild (pres., treas. 1989—), Ill. State Profl. Affairs (chmn.), Phi Delta Kappa, Delta Kappa Gamma (pres. 1992-94). Home: 209 N Fifth Ave New Windsor IL 61465 Office: Aledo CUSD # 201 801 SW Ninth St Aledo IL 61231

MCGAVIC, JUDY L., coal company official; b. Evansville, Ind., June 29, 1944; d. M. Galen and Helen L. (Sims) Barclay; m. Ronald R. McGavic, Aug. 22, 1962; 1 child, Michael D. Student, Ky. Wesleyan Coll., 1965-66, Murray (Ky.) State U., 1968, U. Ky., 1969; B of Liberal Arts, U. Evansville, 1994. Mine clk. Peabody Coal Co., Centertown, Ky., 1973-78, chief mine clk., 1978-81, sr. mine clk., 1981-86, panel technician, 1986, sr. coord. employee rels., 1987-88, employee rels. rep., 1988-92; sr. employee rels. rep. Peabody Coal Co., Lynnville, Ind., 1993-95. Peabody Coal Co. campaign chmn. United Way, 1992, 93, also chmn. blood drive. Mem. NAFE. Home: 7600 Edgedale Dr Newburgh IN 47630-3062

MCGEADY, KATHLEEN BIRMINGHAM, grant administrator; b. Oceanside, N.Y., Aug. 27, 1949; d. James Joseph and Doris Martha (Fraser) Birmingham; m. Dennis J. McGeady, June 14, 1970; children: Kelly, Lauren. Student, Mercer County Community Coll., Mercer County Vocat. Tech. Sch, 1976-77. Office asst. Madison Square Garden, N.Y.C., 1967-69, PICA, N.Y.C., 1969-70; exec. sec. Pubs. Distbg. Corp., N.Y.C., 1970-74; program mgr. Princeton U.; mem. animal care com. Princeton U., 1974-90; grant adminstr. Law Sch. Admission Coun., Newtown, Pa., 1990—. Vol. libr. Plainsboro Free Pub. Libr., 1982-86; co-dir. Plainsboro Founders Day, 1982-87; co-coord. bicycling portion Liberty to Liberty Triathlon, Plainsboro, 1983-86; founder, dir. Bookworm Five Mile Race, Plainsboro, 1984-85; elected councilman Plainsboro Town Coun., 1986-89, chmn., 1988-89; mem. Plainsboro-Cranbury Juvenile Conf. Com., 1988-95, chmn., 1992-95; vice chmn. Plainsboro Dem. Mcpl. Com., 1990-92, 94—; v.p. Plainsboro Dem. Club, 1991-92; bd. dirs. Teen League Softball, 1993-95. Home: 50 Linden Ln Plainsboro NJ 08536-2521

MCGEADY, SISTER MARY ROSE, religious organization administrator, psychologist; b. Hazelton, Pa., June 28, 1928; d. Joseph James and Catherine Cecilia (Mundie) McG. BA in Sociology, Emmanuel Coll., 1955; MA in Clin. Psychology, Fordham U., 1961; DHL (hon.), St. John's U., Queens, N.Y., 1982, Coll. New Rochelle, N.Y., 1991, Fordham U., 1991, Niagara U., 1991, Coll. St. Rose, Albany, N.Y., 1991, DePaul U., 1991. Joined Daus. of Charity St. Vincent De Paul, Roman Cath. Ch., 1946. Dir. Astor Home Clinics, Rhinebeck, N.Y., 1961-66; exec. dir. Nazareth Child Care Ctr., Boston, 1966-71; dir. mental health Cath. Charities Bklyn., 1971-79, assoc. exec. dir., 1987-90; dir. Kennedy Child Study Ctr., N.Y.C., 1979-81; provincial supr. Daus. of Charity St. Vincent DePaul, Albany, 1981-87; pres., chief exec. officer Covenant House, N.Y.C., 1990—; bd. dirs. Cardinal Cooke Health Care Ctr., N.Y.C., Meninger Found., Kans., St. Michael's Coll., Vt., Ctr. for Human Devel., Washington. Author: Catholic Special Education, 1979. Mem. N.Y. State Mental Health Svcs. Coun., Albany, 1983-90, N.Y. State Mental Health Planning Coun., Albany, 1986-91, Cath. Charities USA, 1966—. Recipient svc. award N.Y.C. Dept. Mental Health, 1988, Encouragement award Cath. U. Am., 1991. Home: 75 Lewis Ave Brooklyn NY 11206-7015 Office: Covenant House 346 W 17th St New York NY 10011-5002

MCGEE, BARBARA, publishing executive; b. N.Y.C., Feb. 24, 1949; d. Adolph and Lena (Bicocchi) Marzoli; m. John McGee, June 6, 1970; 1 child, Brian. BS, Douglass Coll., New Brunswick, N.J., 1971; postgrad., Chubb Inst., Summit, N.J., 1983, Montclair (N.J.) State Coll.; cert., Small Bus. Assn., 1983. Subscription acctg. mgr. Newsweek, Inc., Livingston, N.J., 1979-81; mgr. order processing Newsweek, Inc., Mountain Lakes, N.J., 1981-90, dir. order processing svcs., 1991—. Mem. NAFE, Assn. for Work Process Improvement, Fulfillment Mgrs. Assn., Data Entry Mgrs. Assn., Computer Entry Sys. Users Assn., Recognition Equipment Inc., User Assn., Douglass Coll. Alumni Assn. Office: 333 Route 46 Mountain Lakes NJ 07046-1720

MCGEE, CAROL A., reading educator; b. Huntsville, Ala., Aug. 4, 1942. BS, U. North Ala., 1964; MEd, Mid. Tenn. State U., 1976; postgrad., Tex. A&M U., 1992. Cert. tchr. Tenn., Ala., S.C., Tex. Tchr. Tuscaloosa (Ala.) County Schs., 1962-63, Cartagena Colombia/Am. Sch., S.Am., 1963-64, Franklin County Schs., Russellville, Ala., 1964-67, Decatur (Ala.) City Schs., 1967-71, Rutherford County Schs., Murfreesboro, Tenn., 1971-79, Charleston (S.C.) County Schs., 1979-82, Windham Prison Schs., Huntsville, Tex., 1982-88, Conroe (Tex.) Pub. Schs., 1988—; bd. dirs. SHARC, Huntsville. Author two books in field; contbr. articles to profl. jours. Campaign chmn. Sch. Bd. Candidate, Walker County, Tex., 1988, 91, 94; mem. Walker County Hy. Commn., Huntsville, 1990—; adult leader Boy Scouts of Am., Walker County, 1982—; state reading adv. com. Tex. Edn. Agy., Austin, 1985-86. Mem. Sam Houston Area Reading Coun. (pres. 1987-88, bd. dirs. 1985—), Tex. State Tchrs. Assn. (bldg. rep. 1988-90). Republican. Baptist. Home: 660 Elkins Lk Huntsville TX 77340-7316 Office: Peet Jr HS Travis Jr HS 400 SW Dr Conroe TX 77305

MCGEE, DOROTHY HORTON, writer, historian; b. West Point, N.Y., Nov. 30, 1913; d. Hugh Henry and Dorothy (Brown) McG.; ed. Sch. of St. Mary, 1920-21, Green Vale Sch., 1921-28, Brearley Sch., 1928-29, Fermata Sch., 1929-31. Asst. historian Inc. Village of Roslyn (N.Y.), 1950-58; historian Inc. Village of Matinecock, 1966—. Author: Skipper Sandra, 1950; Sally Townsend, Patriot, 1952; The Boarding School Mystery, 1953; Famous Signers of the Declaration, 1955; Alexander Hamilton-New Yorker, 1957; Herbert Hoover: Engineer, Humanitarian, Statesman, 1959, rev. edit., 1965; The Pearl Pendant Mystery, 1960; Framers of the Constitution, 1968; author booklets, articles hist. and sailing subjects. Chmn., Oyster Bay Am. Bicentennial Revolution Commn., 1971—; historian Town of Oyster Bay, 1982—; mem. Nassau County Am. Revolution Bicentennial Commn.; hon. dir. The Friends of Raynham Hall, Inc.; treas. Family Welfare Assn. Nassau County, Inc., 1956-58; dir. Family Service Assn. Nassau County, 1958-69. Recipient Cert. of award for outstanding contbn. children's lit. N.Y. State Assn. Elem. Sch. Prins., 1959; award Nat. Soc. Children of Am. Revolution, 1960; award N.Y. Assn. Supervision and Curriculum Devel., 1961; hist. award Town of Oyster Bay, 1963; Cert. Theodore Roosevelt Assn., 1976. Fellow Soc. Am. Historians; mem. Soc. Preservation L.I. Antiquities (hon. dir.), Nat. Trust Hist. Preservation, N.Y. Geneal. and Biol. Soc. (dir., trustee), Oyster Bay Hist. Soc. (hon., pres. 1971-75, chmn. 1975-79, trustee), Theodore Roosevelt Assn. (trustee), Townsend Soc. Am. (trustee). Republican. Address: PO Box 142 Locust Valley NY 11560-0142

MCGEE, JANE MARIE, retired educator; b. Paducah, Ky., Nov. 3, 1926; d. William Penn and Mary Virginia (Martin) Roberts; m. Hugh Donald McGee, Oct. 11, 1946; children: Catherine Jane McGee Bacon, Nancy Ann McGee McManus. BS in Elem. Edn., Murray State U., 1948; cert. in gifted edn., Nat. Coll. Edn., 1976. Tchr. Hazel (Ky.) Pub. Schs., 1948-49, Pittsford (Mich.) Pub. Schs., 1949-50, Leal Elem. Sch., Urbana, Ill., 1950-53, Cleveland Elem. Sch., Skokie, Ill., 1953-57; pvt. tutor, pre-sch. tchr., 1953-61; tchr. Woodland Park Elem. Sch., Deerfield, Ill., 1968-83; ret., 1983; beauty and skin care cons. Mary Kay Cosmetics, Gunnison, Colo., 1984—. Soprano Western State Coll. and Cmty. Chorus, Gunnison, 1986—, European concert tour, 1990. Mem. AAUW, Top o' the World Garden Club (sec. 1984—, winner first place at numerous garden club shows). Republican. Baptist. Home: 206 N Colorado St Gunnison CO 81230-2104

MCGEE, LYNNE KALAVSKY, principal; b. Jersey City, N.J., July 25, 1949; d. Michael V. and Ann (Fedowitz) K.; m. Thomas Robert, Aug. 12, 1972; children: Todd Michael, Ryan Thomas. BS, St. Francis Coll., Loretto, Pa., 1971; MEd, Seton Hall U., 1972; EDS, Fla. Atlantic U., 1978, EdD, 1986. Cert. tchr., Fla., Ill., prin., Fla. Asst. prin. for curriculum, math instr. Palm Beach County (Fla.) Bd. Edn., 1980-82, asst. prin. for student svcs., 1982-86, asst. prin. for adminstrn., 1986-91; prin. Belle Glade (Fla.) Elem. Sch., 1991-94, New Horizons Elem. Sch., Wellington, Fla., 1994—; adj. prof. grad. Nova U., 1991—. Mem. Assn. Supervision and Curriculum Devel., Phi Kappa Phi. Office: New Horizons Elem Sch 13900 Greenbriar Blvd Wellington FL 33414-7718

MCGEE, MARY ALICE, health science research administrator; b. Winston-Salem, N.C., Oct. 14, 1950; d. C.L. Jr. and Mary Hilda (Shelton) McG. AB, Meredith Coll., 1972. Tchr. Augusta (Ga.) Schs., 1972-73; specialist grants Med. Sch. Brown U., Providence, R.I., 1974-76; profl. basketball player, 1975-76; dir. research adminstn. Med. Sch. Brown U., Providence, 1976-94; tchr., coach Providence Country Day Sch., East Providence, R.I., 1995—. Bd. dirs. Sojourner House, Providence, 1983—, v.p., 1986, 91, treas. 1987-89. Mem. Soc. Rsch. Adminstrs., Nat. Coun. U. Rsch. Adminstrs., R.I. Assn. Women in Edn. Home: 121 Plain St Rehoboth MA 02769-2540 Office: Providence Country Day Sch 2117 Pawtucket Ave East Providence RI 02914-1724

MCGEE, MYRA B., personnel coordinator; b. Beaufort, S.C., Nov. 16, 1957; d. Paul E. and Betty (Bishop) Underwood; m. Daniel Lee McGee, July 3, 1993; children: Jeffrey Paul Blanton, Daniel Eugene Blanton, Alicia Joann McGee. BA, U. S.C. Spartanburg, 1979; postgrad., Webster U. Tchr. Dist. II Schs., Spartanburg, S.C., 1982; asst. dir. pub. rels. Converse Coll., Spartanburg, S.C., 1986; mgr. Waldenbooks, Spartanburg, S.C., 1986-87; exec. asst. Spartburg Personnel Agy., 1988-89; purchasing asst. Spartanburg Steel, 1989-92; customer svc. Hoechst Celanese, Spartanburg, 1992-93; personnel coord. Senior Power Svcs., Lyman, S.C., 1996—; dir. S.C. Telco Credit Union, Greenville, S.C., 1996. Editor (newsletter) Spartanburg Steel "Press Lines", 1989-92 (Gold Star merit 1990, 92), Local #291 "Your Local News", 1994-96. Recipient Brenlin Merit award The Brenlin Group, 1992. Mem. Smithsonian Inst. Baptist.

MCGEE, PATRICIA K., state legislator; m. Mike McGee, 1960; foster children: Ann, Carol, Norma. AA, Alfred State Coll. Asst. to the dean Jamestown C.C., Cattaraugus, N.Y.; mem. N.Y. State Assembly, vice chmn. minority joint conf. com., ranking minority mem. assembly higher edn. com., assembly intern com., ranking minority mem. assembly transportation com., mem. assembly standing com. on environ. conservation and higher edn. com., appointed asst. minority wip.; mem. legis. commn. on Hazardous and Toxic Waste and Rural Resources Commn.; rep. task force mem. on Econ. Devel. and the Future of SUNY; guest speaker Chautauqua Inst. Mem. 219 Liaison Com., Farm Bur., Portville Parent Tchr Assn., Cattaraugus County Tourist Bur. Mem. Am. Legis. Exchange Coun., Nat. Conf. State of State Legis., Nat. Order of Women Legis., N.Y. State Fire Safety Consortium, VFW, Am. Legion, Disabled Am. Vets. Home: 20 Green St Franklinville NY 14737-1045 Office: NY State Assembly State Capitol Albany NY 12224

MCGEE, VIVIENNE LYDIA, biologist, nutritionist; b. Yonkers, N.Y., July 27, 1959; d. Valerio Anthony and Susan J. (Frasca) Pasqua; m. James R. McGee Jr.; children: James R. III, Tobin Patrick, Lydia Marie. BS, Herbert H. Lehman U., 1982; MS in Biology concentration in nutrition, U. Bridgeport, 1988. Sr. nutritionist, office mgr. Chiropractic Office, Bronx, N.Y., 1980-82; mgr., nutritionist Boston Park Pla. Health Club, 1982-84, The Exercise Rm., Roslyn Heights, N.Y., 1984-86; pvt. practice Rye, N.Y., 1989—; cons. HRH Body and Mind, Scotts Corners, N.Y., 1986—. Mem. Am. Dietetic Assn., Am. Chiropratic Assn. Coun. on Nutrition, Ctr. for Sci. in Pub. Interest. Home and Office: 277 Locust Ave Rye NY 10580

MCGERVEY, TERESA ANN, technology information specialist; b. Pitts., Sept. 27, 1964; d. Walter James and Janet Sarah (Donehue) McG. BS in Geology, Calif. U. Pa., 1986, MS in Earth Sci., 1988. Phys. sci. technician U.S. Geol. Survey, Reston, Va., 1989-90; editor, indexer Am. Geol. Inst., Alexandria, Va., 1990-91; cartographer Def. Mapping Agy., Reston, 1991-93; tech. info. specialist Nat. Tech. Info. Svc., Springfield, Va., 1993—; intern Dept. Mineral Scis., Smithsonian Instn., summers 1985, 1986.

MCGHEE, CARLA, basketball player; b. Mar. 6, 1968. Degree in Sports Mgmt. with honors, U. Tenn. Basketball player USA Women's Nat. Team. Office: USA Basketball 5465 Mark Dabling Blvd Colorado Springs CO 80918-3842

MCGHEE, JENNIE SUE, art educator, artist; b. Norfolk, Va., June 4, 1971; d. Richard Louis and Susanne Marie (Barker) McG. Cert. of completion, Art Instrns. Sch., Mpls., 1989; BFA, Old Dominion U., 1994; postgrad., Savannah Coll. Art and Design. Floral designer House of Flowers/Farm Fresh, Virginia Beach, Va., 1990-95; substitute tchr. Virginia Beach Schs., 1995, Sherwood Forest Elem. Sch., Norfolk, 1995—; vis. artist Taylor Elem. Sch., Norfolk, 1995; art tchr. Georgetown Primary Sch., summer 1994, Rena B. Wright Primary Sch., Va., summer 1995. Exhibited in Arts on the River, Savannah, Ga., 1996, Allive Art Studio, Norfolk. Exhibited in group show at Stockley Gardens Arts Festival, 1992, 93. Home: 5209 Lowery Downs Virginia Beach VA 23464

MCGIBBON, PHYLLIS ISABEL, artist, educator; b. Madison, Wis., Jan. 9, 1961; d. Henry and G. Louise McGibbon. BFA, U. Wis., 1983, MFA, 1988. Luther Gregg Sullivan vis. artist Wesleyan U., Middletown, Conn., 1989-91; asst. prof. art Pomona Coll., Claremont, Calif., 1991-94, Wellesley (Mass.) Coll., 1994—; artist residency Bemis Ctr. for Contemporary Art, Omaha, 1995. Artist: solo installations include Davison Art Ctr., Middletown, Conn., 1990, Clarke Coll., Dubuque, Iowa, 1990, Orange County Ctr. for Contemporary Art, Santa Ana, Calif., 1992, Sushi Performance and Visual Art, Inc., San Diego, 1994, Davis Mus. and Cultural Ctr., Wellesley, 1996. Recipient award Elizabeth Greenshields Found., Montreal, Can., 1991, visual arts fellowship Western States Arts Fedn. (NEA), Santa Fe, N.Mex. 1992, fellowship Kala Inst., Berkeley, Calif., 1992-93, award Art Matters, Inc., N.Y.C., 1994, Individual Artist fellowship NEA, 1995. Mem. Coll. Art Assn., Women's Caucus for Art, Am. Print Alliance. Office: Wellesley Coll Dept of Art Jewett Arts Ctr Wellesley MA 02181

MCGILL, GRACE ANITA, occupational health nurse; b. Lawrence, Mass., Mar. 8, 1943; d. Joseph John and Tina Mary (Sicurella) Tabacco; m. Howard L. McGill, Jr., Feb. 28, 1965; children: Cynthia, Deborah, David. RN, Mass. Gen. Hosp., 1963; BS, Lesley Coll., 1987; MS in Mgmt., Lesley Grad. Sch., 1990. Cert. occupl. health nurse Am. Bd. Occupl. Health Nurses, Inc. Nurse Phillips Acad., Andover, Mass., 1963-65, 97th Gen. Hosp., Frankfurt, Germany, 1966, Highsmith-Rainey Hosp., Fayetteville, N.C., 1968, Lawrence (Mass.) Gen. Hosp., 1969-78, Baldpate Psychiat. Hosp., Georgetown, Mass., 1978-79; nursing staff St. Joseph's Hosp., Lowell, Mass., 1980-81; head nurse St. Joseph's Hosp., Lowell, 1981-83; occupl. health nurse Wang Labs., Inc., Lowell, 1983-87, corp. safety specialist, 1987-90; health svcs. adminstr. Loral Infrared and Imaging Sys., Inc., Lexington, Mass., 1990-93; supr. health svcs. Osram Sylvania, Inc., Danvers, Mass., 1993-95; occupl. health nurse Occupl. Health Strategies, Inc., Chelmsford, Mass., 1995—; contract instr. Sch. Pub. Health, Harvard U.; contract adminstr. occupl. health programs at Hewlett-Packard-Chelmsford, OHS, Inc., Madbury, N.H.; treas. Am. Bd. Occupational Health Nurses, 1996—. Mem. NAFE, Am. Assn. Occupl. Health Nurses, Am. Soc. Safety Engrs., Mass. Gen. Hosp. Nurses Alumnae Assn., Lesley Coll. Alumnae. Episcopalian. Home: 81 Lancaster Dr Tewksbury MA 01876-1322

MCGILL, JENNIFER HOUSER, non-profit association administrator; b. Abingdon, Va., Mar. 3, 1957; d. Mason L. and Margaret Jane (Powers) H.; m. James B. McGill, July 15, 1978; children: Melissa Diane, Mark James. AA, Va. Highlands C.C., Abingdon, 1978; BA, U. S.C., 1980. Reporter, editor Sumter (S.C.) Daily ITEM, 1980-81; assoc. editor Sandlapper Mag., Columbia, S.C., 1981-82; membership editor Assn. for Edn. in Journalism/Mass Comm., Columbia, 1982-83, adminstrv. asst., 1984-85, exec. dir., 1985—; mem. nat. steering com. Journalist-in-Space Project, Columbia, 1985-86. Mem. Lioness Club (3d v.p. 1990-91, 2d v.p. 1991-92). Office: Assn Schs Journalism & Mass Comm Univ SC Columbia SC 29208-0251

MCGILLICUDDY, JOAN MARIE, psychotherapist, consultant; b. Chgo., June 23, 1952; d. James Neal and Muriel (Joy) McG. BA, U. Ariz., 1974, MS, 1976; PhD, Walden U., 1996. Cert. nat. counselor. Counselor ACTION, Tucson, 1976; counselor, clin. supr. Behavioral Health Agy. Cen. Ariz., Casa Grande, 1976-81; instr. psychology Cen. Ariz. Coll., Casa Grande, 1978-83; therapist, co-dir. Helping Assocs., Inc., Casa Grande, 1982—, v.p., sec., 1982—; cert. instr. Silva Method Mind Devel., Tucson, 1986—. Mem. Mayor's Com. for Handicapped, Casa Grande, 1989-90, Human Svcs. Planning, Casa Grande, 1985-95. Named Outstanding Am. Lectr. Silva Midn Internat., 1988-96. Mem. ACA. Office: Helping Assocs Inc 1901 N Trekell Rd Casa Grande AZ 85222-1706

MCGILLIS, KELLY, actress; b. Newport, Calif., July 9, 1957; m. Fred Tillman, Dec. 31, 1988; 3 children. Student, Pacific Conservatory of Performing Arts, Juilliard Sch. Music. Actress: (feature films) Reuben, Reuben, 1983, Witness, 1985, Top Gun, 1986, Made in Heaven, 1987, Promised Land, 1988, The House on Carroll Street, 1988, The Accused, 1988, Winter People, 1989, The Babe, 1992, North, 1994; (TV films) Sweet Revenge, 1984, Private Sessions, 1985, Grand Isle (also prod.), 1991, Bonds of Love, 1993, In the Best of Families: Marriage, Pride and Madness, 1994; (stage) Hedda Gabler, Roundabout Theatre Company, 1994. *

MCGILLIVRAY, KAREN, elementary school educator; b. Richland, Oreg., Aug. 24, 1936; d. Kenneth Melton and Catharina (Sass) McG. BS in Edn. cum laude, Ea. Oreg. State Coll., 1958; MRE, Pacific Sch. Religion, 1963. Cert. tchr., Oreg. 4th grade tchr. Salem (Oreg.)-Keizer Pub. Schs.; ret., 1995. Contbr. articles, stories to ednl. mags. U.S. Govt. grantee. Mem. NEA (rep. assembly), NEA-Ret. Oreg. (state officer), Oreg. Edn. Assn. (rep. assembly), Oreg. Ret. Educators Assn. (officer), Salem Edn. Assn. (officer), Delta Kappa Gamma (officer), Phi Delta Kappa (officer). Methodist. Home: 325 SW Cedarwood Ave McMinnville OR 97128

MCGINLEY, ANN MAUREEN, health insurance executive; b. Hazleton, Pa., Mar. 7, 1957; d. James J. and Eileen M. (Meyers) McG. BA in English and Journalism, Bloomsburg U., 1973. Inside sales reps. Raub Supply Co., Allentown, 1973-80; sales rep. Bared Jewelers, V.I., 1978-79; casino operator SunLine Cruises, N.Y.C., 1983; auditor Aetna, Allentown, 1983-85, trainer, 1985-88, network mgr., 1993—; cons. Wetlands Conservancy, Allentown, 1995, Key Club, Parkland H.S., Allentown. Rep. Demos for Republications/Vote!, 1994-95; tour guide East Coast Tours, Easton, Pa., 1990—; mem. exec. bd. Capital Campaign, St. Joseph's, Orefield, Pa., 1995-96. Mem. NAFE, Kiwanis (bd. dirs. 1990—, Kiwanian of Yr. 1992, bd. dirs. 1990—). Democrat. Roman Catholic. Home: 1913 W Livingston St Allentown PA 18104

MCGINLEY, SUZANNE, environmental and civil engineer; b. Jamaica Queens, N.Y., Aug. 24, 1964; d. John Joseph and Bobbie Sue (Herron) McG. BSCE, SUNY, Buffalo, 1986; MS in Environ. Engring., U. Tenn., 1996. Registered profl. engr., N.Y., Ala., Ky., Tenn. Civil engr. Nelson & Pope Engrs., Melville, N.Y., 1986-91; environ. engr. Advanced Scis. Inc., Oak Ridge, Tenn., 1992-94; project mgr., engr., lead engr. Geraghty & Miller, Inc., Oak Ridge, 1994-95. Mem. ASCE (tech. rep. WATTec com. 1996—), NSPE. Home: 507 Cross Creek Rd Apt A Knoxville TN 37923-6419

MCGINN, CHERIE M., secondary education educator; b. Oil City, Pa., Feb. 5, 1949; d. Rendall Baxter and Helen Joyce (Kunselman) Agnew; 1 child from previous marriage, Joshua Edward; m. Stephen James McGinn, Jan. 1, 1983; 1 child, Kathleen Erin. BS Clarion State Coll., 1971. Cert. secondary tchr., Md. Grad. asst. Clarion State Coll., Pa., 1971-72; tchr. Montgomery County Pub. Schs., 1972—; chairperson Montgomery Blair

H.S., Silver Spring, Md., 1994—; cons. curriculum, Upper Marlboro, Md., 19; panelist Odyssey 1984, Excellence in Edn., Md. Humanities Coun., Balt., 1984. Vol. reader grant proposal Coun. for Basic Edn., fellow, 1983.91. NEH, Washington, 1984—. NEH fellow, 1989, 92, 95. Mem. Nat. Coun. for Social Studies, U.S. Capitol Hist. Soc., Assn. Supervision and Curriculum Devel., Md. Social Studies Assn., Montgomery County Social Studies Coun., NEA, Md. State Tchrs. Assn., Montgomery County Educators Assn. Democrat. Mem. Unitarian Ch. Home: 14228 Rutherford Rd Upper Marlboro MD 20774-8564 Office: Montgomery Blair HS 313 Wayne Ave Silver Spring MD 20910

MCGINN, LORETTA, food service administrator; b. S.I., N.Y., May 23, 1934; d. Francis Aloysious and Maryan (Russell) Byrne; m. Thomas A. McGinn, Jan. 21, 1956 (dec. Nov. 1991); children: Thomas A.J., Consuelo, Marianne Byrne, Julia Gaetano, Laura. BA, Coll. S.I., 1979; MSW, Rutgers U., 1989. Sec. S.I. (N.Y.) Hosp., 1975-82; office mgr. Cmty. Svc. Soc. N.Y., N.Y.C., 1982-85; exec. dir. N.Y. RSVP/SERVE, N.Y.C., 1985-90; exec. dir. Meals in Wheels, S.I., 1990-93, pres., CEO, 1993—. Bd. dirs. S.I. Cares, 1993-96; officer S.I. Interagy. Coun., 1984-90; sec., treas., v.p., pres. S.I. United Way, 1985—. Mem. AAUW, NAFE, Nat. Assn. Fundraising Execs., Nat. Assn. Meal Programs, Rotary. Roman Catholic. Office: Meals on Wheels 304 Port Richmond Ave Staten Island NY 10302

MCGINN, MARY JOVITA, lawyer, insurance company executive; b. St. Louis, Apr. 9, 1947; d. Martin J. and Janet (Hogan) McG.; m. Bernard H. Shapiro, Sept. 6, 1971; children: Sara, Colleen, Molly, Daniel. BA, Rosary Coll., River Forest, Ill., 1967; JD, St. Louis U., 1970. Bar: Mo. 1970, Ill. 1971. Atty. tax div. U.S. Dept. Justice, Washington, 1970-73; atty. Allstate Ins. Co., Northbrook, Ill., 1973—; v.p., asst. gen. counsel Allstate Ins. Co., 1980—. Mem. ABA, Am. Coll. Investment Counsel, Assn. Life Ins. Counsel. Roman Catholic. Home: 155 N Buckley Rd Barrington IL 60010-2607 Office: Allstate Ins Co 3075 Sanders Rd Ste G5A Northbrook IL 60062

MCGINN, MARY LYN, real estate company executive; b. New Orleans, Aug. 12, 1949; d. Dan Creedon and Millicent Virginia (White) Midgett; m. Walter Lee McGinn, Mar. 14, 1985. BA, La. State U., 1970, MA, 1972; PhD, U. So. Miss., 1976; MBA, Loyola Coll., 1990. Cert. comml.-investment mem., cert. property mgr., master appraiser. Dir., prof. Dillard U., New Orleans, 1972-76, Loyola U., New Orleans, 1976-80; sr. v.p. Equity Investment Svcs., Inc., New Orleans, 1980-84; pres. Mgmt. Svcs. Group, Inc., New Orleans, 1984-85, Assoc. Investment Svcs. Inc., New Orleans, 1985-87, Northshore Property Mgmt., Inc., New Orleans, 1985-87; asst. v.p. USF&G Realty, Balt., 1987-89, v.p., 1989-90; exec. mng. dir. Galbreath Co., 1990—; cons. colls. and univs., 1976—. Bd. dirs. Pitts. Zoo, Salvation Army, Jr. Achievement. Mem. Nat. Assn. Corporate Real Estate Execs., Bldg. Owners and Mgrs. Assn., Comml.-Investment Council, Nat. Assn. Master Appraisers. Office: Galbreath Co 600 Grant St Pittsburgh PA 15219-2702

MCGINNESS, PAULA RENÉE, customer service administrator, business owner; b. Jamestown, N.Y., Dec. 30, 1943; d. Paul Rudolph and Clara Ann (Magnone) Peterson; m. Ronald C. McGinness, Jan. 28, 1967; children: Heather Anne, Holly Alicia. BA, Ind. U. Pa., 1966; M of Libr. and Info. Sci., U. Pitts., 1970. Tchr. United Sch. Dist., Armagh, Pa., 1966-67; counselor Youth Devel. Ctr., Cresson, Pa., 1967-68; claims rep. Liberty Mutual Ins. Co., Pitts., 1968-70; libr. asst. Hunt Libr., Carnegie Mellon U., Pitts., 1970; libr. Chester County Libr., Exton, Pa., 1977-85; customer svcs. adminstr., owner Software Innovations Inc., Elverson, Pa., 1985—. Co-author: A Programmed Manual for Searching, 1972. Mem. AAUW (pres. West Chester Br. 1993-94, Outstanding Woman 1994), Soc. Pa. Archaeology (bd. dirs. 1994-96), Exton PC Users, Brandywine Bicycle Club (v.p. 1980). Democrat. Presbyterian. Home and Office: Software Innovations Inc 135 New Road Elverson PA 19520

MCGINNIS, JACQUELINE JEAN, financial accountant; b. Media, Pa., July 20, 1968; d. Robert Edward and Jean Alberta (Hoch) Wehner. AS in Acctg., Delaware County C.C., 1991; BS in Acctg., Widener U., 1994. Payroll clk. SCT, Malvern, Pa., 1988-89; payroll tax acct. SmithKline Beecham, Phila., 1989-92, fixed asset acct., 1993-94; fin acct. SmithKline Beecham, Exton, Pa., 1994-95, Pfizer Inc., Exton, Pa., 1995—. Home: 280 Bridgewater Rd A-18 Brookhaven PA 19015 Office: Pfizer Inc 812 Springdale Dr Exton PA 19341

MCGINNIS, JOÁN ADELL, secondary school educator; b. Erie, Pa., Jan. 20, 1932; d. Roy Hamilton and Sara Zelma (Gorman) Sjöberg; m. Richard H. Edwards, Aug. 6, 1954 (div. 1965); m. George William McGinnis, Dec. 29, 1966 (dec. Apr. 1994). BA, St. Lawrence U., Canton, N.Y., 1953. Cert. tchr., Calif. Spl. proxies Sun Life Assurance Co., Montreal, 1952-53; pvt. sec. Detroit Trust, 1953-54; sec. Meth. Ch., Lancaster, Calif., 1964—; tchr. Sunny Hills H.S., Fullerton, Calif., 1966—; contr. Mission Viejo (Calif.) Sheet Metal, 1980-81; dept. sec. Fgn. Lang. Dept. Sunny Hills H.S., 1966-80, dept. chair, 1987-89; internat. baccalaureate examiner in Spanish, 1991—, French, 1992—; advanced placement examiner in Spanish, 1990—. Mem. Am. Assn. Tchrs. Spanish and Portuguese, Modern Classical Lang. Assn. Calif., Fgn. Lang. Assn. Orange County (Exptl. Tchr. of Orange County award 1994), Am. Women's Orgn. Republican. Home: 26382 Estanciero Dr Mission Viejo CA 92691-5401 Office: Sunny Hills HS 1801 W Warburton Way Fullerton CA 92633-2235

MCGINNIS, MARY LOUISE, counselor, legal assistant; b. Tampa, Fla., July 1, 1957; d. Harold Glen and Peggy Joyce (Hawley) McG.. AA in Education, Hillsborough Cmty. Coll., 1979; BA in Psychology, U. So. Fla., 1991, MA in Counselor Edn., 1995. Cert. legal assistant. Legal asst., mental health counselor intern Sessums & Mason PA, Tampa, 1987—; pvt. practice, 1996—; adj. instr. Hillsborough Cmty. Coll., Tampa, 1992—. Bd. chmn. Bd. of Social Ministry, Holy Trinity Luth. Ch., 1991-92. Mem. Nat. Assn. of Legal Assts., Am. Counseling Assn., Fla. Adlerian Soc., Hillsborough County Bar Assn., Tampa Bay Assn. for Marriage & Family Therapy (exec. com.), Phi Kappa Phi, Pi Gamma Mu, Psi Chi, Golden Key. Lutheran. Office: Sessums & Mason PA 307 S Magnolia Ave Tampa FL 33606 also: 1304 DeSoto Ave #200 Tampa FL 33606

MCGINNITY, MAUREEN ANNELL, lawyer; b. Monroe, Wis., Apr. 6, 1956; d. James Arthur and Marie Beatrice (Novak) McG.; m. Richard W. Ziervogel, July 17, 1982; 1 child, Brigitte Kathleen. BS, U. Wis., Milw., 1977; JD, U. Wis., 1982. Bar: Wis. 1982, U.S. Dist. Ct. (ea. and we. dists.) Wis. 1982, U.S. Ct. Appeals (7th cir.) 1989, U.S. Ct. Appeals (1st cir.) 1991, U.S. Tax Ct. 1995, U.S. Supreme Ct. 1991. Assoc. Foley & Lardner, Milw., 1982-91, ptnr., 1991—; mem. Wis. Supreme Ct. Planning and Policy Adv. Com., Madison, 1991-94; adv. bd. Domestic Violence Legal Clinic, Milw., 1991—. Treas. Waukesha (Wis.) Food Pantry, 1988-94; trustee Boys & Girls Club Greater Milw., 1991—; bd. dirs. Task Force on Battered Women & Children, Inc., 1994—. Recipient Outstanding Svc. award Legal Action Wis., Milw., 1984, 93 Outstanding Fundraising awards Boys & Girls Club Greater Milw., 1987-92, Cert. Recognition, Common Coun. Task Force on Sexual Assault & Domestic Violence, Milw., 1991, Cert. Appreciation, Wis. Equal Justice Task Force, Madison, 1991, Cmty. Svc. award Wis. Law Found., 1995. Mem. ABA, State Bar Wis. (bd. govs. 1992-96, Pro Bono award 1990, chair 1993-94), Assn. for Women Lawyers (various offices, pres. 1992-93), Milw. Young Lawyers Assn. (bd. dirs. 1987-92, pres. 1990-91, Pres.' award 1991), Profl. Dimensions. Office: Foley & Lardner 777 E Wisconsin Ave Milwaukee WI 53202-5302

MCGINTY-POTEET, DEBRA, banker; b. Hanford, Calif., 1956; married; 3 children. BA, UCLA; MA, Calif. State U., Long Beach. With mut. fund group Security Pacific Nat. Bank (merged with Bank Am. 1992), L.A., 1986-92; sr. v.p., mgr. mut. funds investment mgmt. svcs. group Bank Am. NT&SA, L.A., 1992—. Mem. Investment Co. Inst. (rsch. com., shareholder cmms. com., dir. mktg. com.).

MCGIVERN, DIANE, nursing educator. PhD, NYU, 1972. RN. Head divsn. nursing NYU, N.Y.C. Fellow AAN. Office: New York Univ Hosp Rm 429 50 W 4th St New York NY 10012

MCGLYNN, BETTY HOAG, art historian; b. Deer Lodge, Mont., Apr. 28, 1914; d. Arthur James and Elizabeth Tangye (Davey) Lochrie; m. Paul Sterling Hoag, Dec. 28, 1936 (div. 1967); children: Peter Lochrie Hoag, Jane Hoag Brown, Robert Doane Hoag; m. Thomas Arnold McGlynn, July 28, 1973. BA, Stanford U., 1936; MA, U. So. Calif., 1967. Cert. secondary tchr., Calif. Rsch. dir. So. Calif. Archives of Am. Art, L.A., 1964-67, Carmel (Calif.) Mus. Art, 1967-69; dir. Triton Mus. Art, Santa Clara, Calif., 1970; archivist, libr. San Mateo County (Calif.) Hist. Soc. Mus., 1972-74; cons. Monterey Peninsula Mus. Art, Calif., 1964—; tchr. art extension Monterey Peninsula Coll., Calif., 1970, San Jose City Coll., 1971; lectr. in field. Author: The World of Mary DeNeale Morgan, 1970, Carmel Art Association: A History, 1987; contbg. author: Plein Air Painters of California, The North, 1986, Orchid Art and The Orchid Isle, 1982, Hawaiian Island Artists and Friends of the Arts, 1989; editor, author of jours. La Peninsula, 1971-75, Noticias, 1983-88, 95; author of booklets; contbr. articles to profl. jours. Appraiser art work City of Carmel, 1967, City of Monterey, 1981; mem. Friends of Harrison Meml. Libr., Carmel, Friends of Sunset Found., Carmel, Pacific Grove Art Ctr., Monterey Bay Aquarium. Mem. Butte (Mont.) Arts Chateau, Carmel Art Assn. (hon.), Carmel Heritage Soc., Carmel Found., Carmel Residents Assn., Chinese Hist. Soc., Monterey History and Art Assn. (art cons.), Monterey Peninsula Mus. Art (acquisitions bd.), Monterey County Geneal. Soc., Gallatin County Hist. Soc. (Mont.), Stanford Alumni Assn., Robinson Jeffers Tor House Found. (art cons.), Hawaiian Hist. Soc., Mont. Hist. Soc., Nat. Mus. of Women in Arts, The Westerners, P.E.O., Book Club of Calif. Republican. Home and Office: PO Box 7189 Carmel CA 93921-7189

MCGLYNN, VIRGINIA DAVIS, small business owner, councilwoman; b. Reading, Mass., Apr. 10, 1924; d. Louis and Priscilla (Twombly) Davis; widow; children: Jean, Beverly, Louise, John, Annie, Elizabeth, Virginia, Katherine. AA, Colby Jr. Coll., New London, N.H., 1943; degree in art, Vesper George Sch. Art, Boston, 1948. Sales rep. McGlynn Studio, Beverly, Mass., 1968-73; owner, mgr. Abbott Yarn Shoppe, Beverly, 1973—; mem. Beverly City Council, 1994—; adult edn. tchr., Beverly, Salem, Lynn, Peabody, Mass. Author: (handbooks) Finishing Illustrated, 1980, Simple Knit and Crochet Patterns, 1984, Knitting Illustrated, 1990. Mem. coun. Sea Path, Beverly, 1995—; mem. leadership com. Cmty. Oriented Policing; mem. Elem. Sch. Facilities Com. With USMC, 1944-46. Republican. Roman Catholic. Home: 111 Corning St Beverly MA 01915 Office: 160 Cabot St Beverly MA 01915

MCGONIGAL, SHIRLEY JOAN O'HEY, secondary education educator; b. Phila., Aug. 13, 1920; d. Joseph Matthew and Alice Agnes (Smith) O'Hey; m. Edward Stephen McGonigal, Oct. 30, 1948; children: Alice, Stephen, Richard, Nancy Lynn, Michelle, Barry Joseph. BA, Coll. of Chestnut Hill, 1942, postgrad., 1943-44; postgrad., Community Coll. Mays Landing, N.J., 1955-56, Community Coll. Mays Landing, N.J., 1983-84. Libr. Pa. Dept. of Agr., Wynnemore, 1943-45; tchr. grade sch. Barren Hill, Pa., 1945-46, Mays Landing, 1962-83; tchr. English Oakcrest High Sch., Mays Landing, 1984—; tchr. Literacy Vols. of Am., Atlantic County, N.J., 1983—. Mem. exec. com. Betty Bacharach Rehab. Ctr., Ventnor, N.J.; sec. adv. bd. Children's Seashore Hosp., Ventnor, N.J.; chairperson Atlantic Cultural and Hist. Com., Northfield, N.J. Recipient Cert. of Appreciation, Family Svc. Assn., Svc. award Oakcrest High Bd. of Edn., 1967-82, Cert. of Appreciation, Rutgers U., Svc. Plaque, County Cultural and Hist. Com., 1988-90. Mem. AAUW, Nat. Edn. Soc. (life), Navy League of U.S., Delta Kappa Gamma (fellow, scholarship com. 1979). Republican. Roman Catholic. Home and Office: Box 539 221 Lenape Ave Mays Landing NJ 08330-1843

MCGOVERN, DIANNE, legal administrator; b. Pitts., Feb. 26, 1948; d. John David and Mary Elizabeth (Shirk) McG. BA, Millsaps Coll., Jackson, Miss., 1970; MS in Mgmt., Baker U., 1992. Docket clk. Popham Law Firm, Kansas City, Mo., 1972-78, paralegal, 1978-81, legal adminstr., 1981—. Bd. dirs. Kansas City Zoo Docents, 1994-96. Mem. ABA (assoc.), Assn. Legal Adminstrs. (asst. regional v.p. 1991), Kansas City Assn. Legal Adminstrs. (pres., bd. dirs. 1987-90). Democrat. Roman Catholic. Home: 4425 Jarboe St Apt 10 Kansas City MO 64111-3555 Office: The Popham Law Firm PC 922 Walnut St Kansas City MO 64106-1809

MCGOVERN, MARGARET, advertising executive. Sr. v.p., asst. creative dir. Arnold, Fortuna, Lawner & Cabot, Boston. Office: Arnold Fortuna Lawner & Cabot 101 Arch St Boston MA 02110*

MCGOWAN, ELLEN ELIZABETH, communications specialist; b. Humboldt, Tenn., Sept. 24, 1949; d. Robert W. and Ellen (Fossey) McG.; children: Laura Smith, Rachel Smith. BS in Edn., Memphis State U., 1969, MA in Comm., 1981; MA in English, U. Memphis, 1995. Cert. tchr., Tenn. Dir. cmty. rels. Seratobia (Miss.) Cmty. Hosp., 1981-84; group mgr. human resources Goldsmiths, Inc., Memphis, 1984-88; dir. tng. comm. Catherine's Inc., Memphis, 1988-91, Virginia Specialty Stores, Newport News, Va., 1991-92; sr. instrnl. design specialist FedEx, Memphis, 1992-95, sr. comm. specialist, 1995—. Mem. Women in Comm., Thomas Hardy Soc., Brontë Soc., Phi Kappa Phi. Home: 50 Hicks Rd Oakland TN 38060 Office: FedEx 3003 Airways Blvd Ste 1102 Memphis TN 38131

MCGOWAN, SISTER MARY KENAN, retired alumni affairs director; b. Albany, N.Y., Sept. 2, 1933; d. Francis Joseph and Irene Helen (Moreau) McG. BA in math., Coll. St. Rose, 1968; MA in theology, St. Michael's Coll., 1976. Elem. sch. tchr. Albany Diocese, Albany, Troy, Ilion, Waterford, N.Y., 1954-63; math. tchr. Cath. Cen. H.S., Troy, N.Y., 1963-96, alumni dir., 1979-96. Democrat. Roman Catholic. Home: PO Box 234 Grafton NY 12082-0234 Office: St John Francis Church Owen Rd Grafton NY 12082

MCGOWAN, MARY STRAYER, art dealer; b. N.Y.C., Feb. 3, 1995; d. Paul Johnston and Sarah (Kollock) Strayer; m. Duncan S. McGowen (July 2, 1967 (dec. Mar. 1991); children: Molly Strayer McGowan, Abigail Strayer McGowan. BA, Conn. Coll., 1965. History and geography tchr. Waltham (Mass.) Schs., 1965-67; asst. dir. Summer Program in Humanities, New London, Conn., 1966-68; supr. cmty. action program VISTA, Frederick, Md., 1967-69; self-employed jeweler Concord, N.H., 1970-80; pres. McGowen Fine Art, Concord, 1981—; originator, cons. Craf. Exhibited in group shows at New Eng. Coll., Henniker, N.H., 1975-77, Sunapee (N.H.) Crafts Fair, 1973-79, Rhinebeck (N.Y.) Crafts Fair, 1979-80, Parsonage Gallery, Durham, N.H., 1980. Mem. founding bd. dirs. N.H. Feminist Health Ctr., Concord, 1976-77; mem. plan devel. com. United Health Sys. Agy., 1978-79; mem., chair N.H. Coun. for Humanities, 1977-79; mem. arts selection com. N.H. Commn. on Arts, 1980; bd. dirs. Downtown Concord Inc., 1990-92; incorporator Canterbury Shaker Village, 1990-93, trustee, 1993—. Mem. League of N.H. Craftsmen (bd. dirs. 1988-91). Office: McGowan Fine Art 11 Tahanto St Concord NH 03301

MCGOWAN-GIVENS, BETTIE KAY, anthropologist, educator; b. Ripley, Miss., Nov. 16, 1948; d. H. Herman and Jewell Francis (Lockhart) Givens; m. Thomas J. Campbell, Aug. 25, 1964 (dec. Aug. 1972); children: Thomas Stephen Campbell, Patrick Joseph Campbell; m. Blair Jude McGowan, Dec. 23, 1975; children: Kathleen Grace, Daniel Charles, Michael Diego. Degree in fine arts, Ctr. for Creative Study, Detroit, 1976; BS in Psychology and Sociology, U. Mich., Dearborn, 1976; MA in Anthropology, Wayne State U., 1985, PhD in Anthropology, 1994. Dep. dir., registered lobbyist, dir. Mich. Citizens Lobby, Southfield, 1973-84; prof. anthropology U. Toledo, Ohio, 1988-96, Wayne State U., Detroit, 1995—. Monthly columnist: Indian World Publ., 1995—; contbr. articles to profl. publs.; appeared on radio and TV shows, 1974—. Creator nat. scholarship Irish Am. Unity Found., Washington, 1995-96; mem. Mich. women's com. Task Force on Friends of the Ct., 1979-80; founding mem. 1st Step Domestic Violence Shelter, 1978-80; counselor victims of sexual assault D.A.R.E. (Downriver Anti-Rape Effort), 1978-81; vol. United Farm Workers Union, Detroit, 1974-78. Mem. AAUW (Outstanding Woman Downriver chpt. 1996), NOW (del. 4th world conf. Beijing 1995, Woman of Achievement 1992), Am. Indian Health and Family Svcs. (bd. dirs. 1994—), Am. Anthropologists, Am. Indian Svcs. (vol. 1995—), Irish Am. Unity Conf., Grosse Ile (Mich.) Dem. Club (historian 1994—). Democrat. Home: 22241 Miami Grosse Ile MI 48138

MCGRADY, CORINNE YOUNG, design company executive; b. N.Y.C., May 6, 1938; d. Albert I. and Reda (Bromberg) Young; m. Michael Robinson McGrady; children: Sean, Siobhan, Liam. Student, Bard Coll., Annandale-on-Hudson, N.Y., 1960, Harvard U., 1968-69. Founder, pres. Corinne McGrady Designs; designer Corinneware (joint venture of Corinne McGrady Designs and Boston Warehouse Trading Corp. 1990), East Northport, N.Y., 1970—. Acrylic works exhibited in group shows at Mus. Contemporary Crafts, N.Y.C., 1969-70, Smithsonian Instn., 1970-71, Pompidou Ctr., Paris, 1971, Mus. Sci. and Industry, 1970; sculpture exhibited at Guild Hall Show, Southampton, N.Y., 1968, Hecksher Mus., 1968. Vice pres. Woman's Internat. League for Peace and Freedom, Huntington, N.Y., 1971. Recipient Design Rev. award Indsl. Design, 1969, 70; Instant Supergraphic Indsl. Design Rev. award, 1971. Patentee cookbook stand. Home and Office: PO Box 27 Lilliwaup WA 98555-0027

MCGRAIL, JEANE KATHRYN, artist, educator, poet, curator; b. Mpls., May 1, 1947; d. Robert Vern and Mary Virginia (Kees) McGrail. BS, U. Wis.-River Falls, 1970; MFA, Cranbrook Acad. Art, 1972; postgrad. Sch. of Art Inst. of Chgo., 1985, Ill. Inst. Tech., 1993. Group exhbns. include Saginaw Art Mus., Mich., 1972, Met. Mus. Art, Miami, Fla., 1974, Lowe Mus. Art, Coral Gables, Fla., 1974, 76, Miller Galleries, Coconut Grove, Fla., 1978, 80, Cicchinelli Gallery, N.Y.C., 1980-82, Harper Coll., 1984, Contemporary Art Ctr. Arlington, Arlington Heights, Ill., 1984, 85, 86, 94, Evanston Art Ctr., 1985, South Shore Cultural Ctr., Chgo., 1990, N.A.M.E. Gallery, 1990, Artemisia Gallery, Chgo., 1991, 92, 93, 94, North Lakeside Art Ctr., Chgo., 1991, 94, 95, Ceres Gallery, N.Y.C., 1992, Harper Coll., Ill., 1993, Environ. Concerns, Chgo., 1993, North Pk. Coll., Chgo., 1993, Franklin Square Gallery, Chgo., 1994, 95, 96, Space 900 Gallery, Chgo., 1994, 95, 96, Chuck Levitan Gallery, N.Y.C., 1995, Riverwest Art Ctr., Milw., 1995, Artworks Gallery, Oak Park, Ill., 1995, 96, Nat. Mus. Women in the Arts, Washington, 1996; represented in permanent collections at U. Chgo., Mus. Photography, Chgo., Miami-Dade Pub. Libr., U. Wis.-River Falls, MacGregor Found., Printmakers Workshop, N.Y.C., others; solo exhbns. include Gallery at the Commons, Chgo., 1982, Truman Coll. Gallery, Chgo., 1991, C.G. Jung Inst., Evanston, Ill., 1992, Carlson Tower Gallery, Chgo., 1994; pub. "Mosaic", 1992; contbr. publs. to profl. jours. Art curriculum specialist, presenter on portfolios Ill. Art Edn. Assn. Conf., 1992, art cons. for inner child healing. Cranbrook Acad. Art scholar, 1971; CAAP grantee Dept. Cultural Affairs City Chgo., 1992; recipient Poster Competition award Vizcaya Mus., 1974; Print award Auction WPBT, 1979. Mem. Coll. Art Assn., Chgo. Women's Caucus for Art (bd. dirs. 1992-95, sec.), Chgo. Artists Coalition. Democrat. Home: 1S035 Euclid Ave Oakbrook Terrace IL 60181-3437 Studio: 1040 West Huron St LL#5 Chicago IL 60622

MCGRATH, ANNA FIELDS, librarian; b. Westfield, Maine, July 4, 1932; d. Fred Elber and Nancy Phyllis (Tarbell) Fields; m. Bernard McGrath (div.); children: Timothy, Maureen, Patricia, Colleen, Rebecca. BA, U. Maine, Presque Isle, 1976; MEd, U. So. Maine, 1979; MLS, U. R.I., 1982. Libr. U. Maine, Presque Isle, 1976-86, assoc. libr. dir., 1986-89, interim libr. dir., 1989-92, dir., 1992-94, spl. coll. libr., 1994—. Editor: County: Land of Promise, 1989. Mem. Friends of Aroostook County Hist. Ctr. at Libr., U. Maine-Presque Isle. Mem. ALA, Maine Libr. Assn., Friends of Arrostook County Hist. Ctr. at Libr. U. Maine-Presque Isle, Inst. Noetic Scis., Am. Mensa. Office: U Maine Libr 181 Main St Presque Isle ME 04769-2888

MCGRATH, CHRYSTYNE MARY, retail clothing store owner; b. New Haven, Dec. 16, 1968; d. Walter Gerard and Geraldine Mary (Ward) Pieper; m. David Vincent McGrath, Aug. 10, 1991. Student, Stone Acad., 1988-89, U. New Haven, 1990-91. Sales rep. Exclusively Children's, Guilford, Conn., 1984—; front desk clk. Marriott, Trumbull, Conn., 1988-89, Waters Edge, Westbrook, Conn., 1989-90; asst. mgr. Brooks-Hirsh, Hamden, Conn., 1990-91; owner Chrystyne's (formerly Exclusively Jrs.), Guilford, 1991-96, Exclusively Children's and Chrystyne's, Guilford, 1995—. Mem. Nat. Assn. Women Bus. Owners, Guilford C. of C. (bd. dirs.). Roman Catholic. Home: 1451 West St Guilford CT 06437 Office: Exclusively Children's 1250 Boston Post Rd Guilford CT 06437-2452

MCGRATH, JOAN, religious organization executive; m. Jack McGrath; 3 children. Pres. Nat. Coun. Cath. Women, Washington, 1995. Former chmn. nominating com., site coord. Leadership Inst., sec., 1st v.p. Nat. Coun. Cath. Women, also spkr., workshop presenter; social ministry and vol. coord. Ch. Ch., White Bear Lake, Minn. Recipient Gov.'s vol. award for RESPITE, Archdiocesan Svc. award, Papal Pro Ecclesia et Pontifice medal. Office: Nat Coun Cath Women 1275 K St NW Ste 975 Washington DC 20005

MCGRATH, JUDITH, broadcast executive; b. Scranton, PA, 1952. Former fashion copywriter Mademoiselle; now pres. MTV, New York, NY. Office: MTV 1515 Broadway New York NY 10036*

MCGRATH, KATHRYN BRADLEY, lawyer; b. Norfolk, Va., Sept. 2, 1944; d. James Pierce and Kathryn (Hoyle) Bradley; children: Ian M., James D. AB, Mt. Holyoke Coll., 1966; JD, Georgetown U., 1969. Ptnr. Gardner, Carton & Douglas, Washington, 1979-83; dir. div. investment mgmt. SEC, Washington, 1983-90; ptnr. Morgan, Lewis & Bockius, LLP, Washington, 1990—. Named Disting. Exec. Pres. Reagan, 1987. Mem. Fed. Bar Assn. (exec. council securities law com.). Office: Morgan Lewis & Bockius LLP 1800 M St NW Washington DC 20036-5802

MCGRATH, MARY HELENA, plastic surgeon, educator; b. N.Y.C., Apr. 12, 1945; d. Vincent J. and Mary M. (Manning) McG.; m. Richard H. Simon, Apr. 11, 1970; children: Margaret E. Simon, Richard M. Simon. BA, Coll. New Rochelle, 1966; MD, St. Louis U., 1970; MPH, George Washington U., 1994. Lic. surgeon, D.C. Resident in surg. pathology U. Colo. Med. Ctr., Denver, 1970-71, intern in gen. surgery, 1971-72, resident in gen. surgery, 1971-75, chief resident in gen. surgery, 1975-76; resident in plastic and reconstructive surgery Yale U. Sch. Medicine, New Haven, Conn., 1976-77; chief resident plastic and reconstructive surgery Yale U. Sch. Medicine, New Haven, 1977-78; fellow in hand surgery U. Conn.-Yale U., New Haven, 1978; instr. in surgery divsn. plastic and reconstructive surgery Yale U. Sch. Medicine, New Haven, 1977-78, asst. prof. plastic surgery, 1978-80; attending in plastic and reconstructive surgery Yale-New Haven Hosp., 1978-80, Columbia-Presbyn. Hosp., N.Y.C., 1980-84, George Washington U. Med. Ctr., Washington, 1984—, Children's Nat. Med. Ctr., Washington, 1985—; asst. prof. plastic surgery Columbia U., N.Y.C., 1980-84; assoc. prof. plastic surgery Sch. Medicine, George Washington U., Washington, 1984-87, prof. plastic surgery, 1987—; attending physician VA Hosp., West Haven, Conn., 1978-80; attending in surgery Hosp. Albert Schweitzer, Deschapelles, Haiti, 1980; co-investigator Charles W. Ohse Fund, Yale U. Sch. Medicine, 1979; prin. investigator various rsch. grants, 1979-89; historian, bd. dirs. Am. Bd. Plastic Surgery, 1991-95; guest examiner certifying exam., 1986-88, 95-96; specialist site visitor Residency Rev. Com. for Plastic Surgery, 1985, 87, 91, 94; presenter in field; cons. in field; senator med. faculty senate George Washington U., bd. govs. Med. Faculty Assocs. Co-editor: (with M.L. Turner) Dermatology for Plastic Surgeons, 1993; assoc. editor: The Jour. of Hand Surgery, 1984-89, Plastic and Reconstructive Surgery, 1989-95, chmn. nominating com., 1994—; contbr. book chpts.: Problems in General Surgery, 1985, Human and Ethical Issues in the Surgical Care of Patients with Life-Threatening Disease, 1986, Problems in Aesthetic Surgery, Biological Causes and Clinical Solutions, 1986; guest reviewer numerous jours.; contbr. articles, abstracts to profl. jours. Fellow ACS (bd. govs. 1995—, chmn. adv. coun. for plastic surgery 1995—); mem. AAAS, AMA, Am. Surg. Assn., Am. Assn. Hand Surgery (exec. sec. 1988-90, rsch. grants com. 1983-86, chmn. edn. com. 1983-88, 1st prize ann. resident contest 1978, numerous other c ms., D.C. chpt. program ann. meeting chmn. 1992, v.p. 1993-94, pres. 1994—), Am. Assn. Plastic Surgeons (pub. info. com. 1988-89, James Barrett Brown com. 1990-92, rsch. and edn. com. 1992-95), Am. Burn Assn., Am. Soc. for Aesthetic Plastic Surgery (FDA implant task force 1990—, pub. edn. com. 1991-92, sci. rsch. com. 1990—), Am. Soc. Maxillofacial Surgeons, Am. Soc. Plastic and Reconstructive Surgery (chmn. ethics com. 1985-87, chmn. device/tech. evaluation com. 1993-94, bd. dirs. 1994—, mem. edn. found. bd. dirs. 1985-96, treas. 1989-92, v.p. 1992-93, pres.-elect 1993-94, pres. 1994-95), Am. Soc. Reconstructive Microsurgery (mem. edn. com. 1992-94), Am. Soc. Surgery of Hand (chmn. 1987 ann. residents' and fellows conf. 1986-87, mem. rsch. com. 1988-90), Assn. Acad. Chmn. Plastic Surgery (mem. prerequesite tng. com. 1990-92, mem. com. aesthetic surgery tng. 1992—), Assn. Acad. Surgery, D.C. Met. Area Soc. Plastic and Reconstructive Surgeons, Internat. Soc.

Reconstructive Surgery, Met. D.C. Soc. Surgery Hand, N.Y. Surg. Soc., Northeastern Soc. Plastic Surgeons (chmn. sci. program com. 1991, chmn. fin. com. 1992-93, treas. 1993—), Plastic Surgery Rsch. Coun. (chmn. 1990), Surg. Biology Club III, The Wound Healing Soc., Washington Acad. Surgery, Washington Med. and Surg. Soc. Office: George Washington U # 6B-422 2150 Pennsylvania Ave NW Washington DC 20037-2396

MCGRATH, SYLVIA WALLACE, historian, educator; b. Montpelier, Vt., Feb. 27, 1937; d. George John and Martha Eloise (Cooper) Wallace; m. W. Thomas McGrath, June 11, 1966; children: Sandra Jean, Charles George. BA, Mich. State U., East Lansing, 1959; MA, Radcliffe Coll., Cambridge, 1960; PhD, U. Wis., Madison, 1966. Tchr. Falmouth (Mass.) Pub. Schs., 1960-61, M. County Day Sch., C. Madera, Calif., 1961-62; asst. prof. history Stephen F. Austin State U., Nacogdoches, Tex., 1968-73, assoc. prof. history, 1973-87, prof. history, 1987—; Regents' prof. Stephen F. Austin State U., Nacogdoches, 1994-95. Author: (book) Charles Kenneth Leith, Scientific Advisor, 1971; book reviewer: various jours. including Jour. of Am. History, Jour. So. History, Forest and Conservation History, Southwestern Hist. Quarterly, East Tex. Hist. Jour., Environ. History Review, ISIS, Science Books and Films, Legacies, various jours; contbr. chpts. to books, articles to encylopedias. Mem. Orgn. Am. Historians, Tex. Assn. Coll. Tchrs. (regional v.p. 1992-93), So. Hist. Assn., History Sci. Soc., Soc. History of Tech., Forest History Soc. Presbyterian. Home: 216 N Mound St Nacogdoches TX 75961 Office: Stephen F Austin State U Box 13013 SFA Nacogdoches TX 75962

MCGRATTAN, MARY K., state legislator; b. N.Y.C.. RN, St. Catherine's Hosp. Sch. of Nursing. Mem. town coun. Town of Ledyard, Conn., 1977-83, mayor, 1983-91; pres. Conn. Conf. of Municipalities, 1990-91; mem. Conn. Ho. of Reps., Hartford, 1993—. Mem. Ledyard Dem. Town Com. Address: 13 Lynn Dr Ledyard CT 06339 Office: Conn Ho of Reps State Capitol Hartford CT 06106

MCGRAW, LAVINIA MORGAN, former retail company executive; b. Detroit, Feb. 26, 1924; d. Will Curtis and Margaret Coulter (Oliphant) McG. AB, Radcliffe Coll., 1945. Mem. Phi Beta Kappa. Home: 2501 Calvert St NW Washington DC 20008-2620

MCGREEVY, MARY, retired psychology educator; b. Kansas City, Kans., Nov. 10, 1935; d. Donald and Emmy Lou (Neubert) McG.; m. Phillip Rosenbaum (dec.); children: David, Steve, Mariya, Chay, Allyn, Jacob, Dora. BA in English with honors, Vassar Coll., 1957; postgrad., New Sch. for Social Rsch., NYU, 1958-59, Columbia U., 1959-60, U. P.R., 1963-65, U. Mo., 1965-68, U. Kans.; PhD, U. Calif., Berkeley, 1969. Formerly exec. Doubleday & Co., N.Y.C., 1957-60; chief libr. San Juan Sch., P.R., 1962-63; NIMH drug rschr. Russell Sage Found., Clinico de los Addictos, Rio Piedras, P.R., 1963-65; psychiat. rschr. U. P.R. Med. Sch., 1963-65; psychiat. researcher U. Kans., Lawrence, 1966-68; rsch. assoc. Ednl. Rsch., 1968-69; assoc. prof. U. Calif., Berkeley, 1969-68; disting. prof., ret., 1969; yacht owner Encore; lectr. in field. Author: (poetry) To a Sailor, 1989, Dreams and Illusions, 1993, Coastings, 1996, also articles, poems, book revs. Founder, exec. dir. Dora Achenbach McGreevy Poetry Found., Inc.; active Fla. Atlantic U. Found., 1993—; vol. Broward County Hist. Commn., Friends of the Libr., Ft. Lauderdale and Main Broward County Librs., 1969—; mem. Am. Friends of Bodleian Libr., Oxford, Eng., Frances Loeb Lehman Art Gallery, Vassar Coll., Ctr. de las Artes, Miami, Fla., Friends of Modern Mus. Art, Friends of the Guggenheim, Friends of Met. Mus. Art, Nelson-Atkins Mus. Art, Friends of U. Mo. Libr., Johnson County Mental Health Assn., Ft. Lauderdale Philharm. Soc., St. Anthony's Cath. Women's Club, Women's Rsch. inst., Nova Southea. U., Davie, Fla. Recipient Cert. for Svc. Broward County Hist. Commn., 1994, Nat. Women's History Project award, 1995; Sproul fellow, Bancroft Libr. fellow, Russell Sage Found. fellow; postdoctoral grantee U. Calif. Mem. AAUW (corr. sec. 1991-95, bd. dirs. 1991—, honoree Ednl. Found. Fund 1993, Jeanne Faiks meml. scholarship fund com. 1992—, chairperson cultural events 1995—, Women of History awards), Pres.'s Coun., Broward Women's History Coalition (bd. dirs. 1991—, archivist, mem. ad hoc com.), Am. Philos. Assn., Women in Psychology, Union of Concerned Scientists, South Fla. Poetry Inst. (yearly poetry anthology 1991—), Poets of the Palm Beaches (yearly poetry anthology 1992, 93—, 1st prize free verse ann. contest), Mo. Sociol. Assn., Fla. Philosophy Assn. (spkr. 1991, 93, chairperson self in philosophy 1994), Vassar Alumni Assn. (class historian), Oxfam Am., Pem-Hill Alumni Assn., Sierra Club (newspaper reporter, mem. environ. com., archivist 1993-95, co-chairperson beach clean-up 1993), Secular Humanists (bd. dirs. 1992—, program chairperson 1995—), Fla. Women's Consortium, Vassar Club Kansas City, Vassar Alumni Assn. N.Y. Home: PO Box 900 Fort Lauderdale FL 33302-0900

MCGREGOR, DEBORAH KUHN, history and women's studies educator; b. South Hadley, Mass., June 29, 1944; d. Manford and Mary (Reagan) Kuhn; m. Robert Kuhn, Oct. 9, 1982; children: Molly Meyersohn, Leaf, Blue, Janna, Bran. BA, U. Wis., 1966, MA, 1968; PhD, SUNY, Binghamton, 1986. Asst. prof. history U. Utah, Salt Lake City, 1985-86, So. Ill. U. Sch. Medicine, Springfield, 1987-90; asst. prof. history and women's studies U. Ill., Springfield, 1990—. Author: Sexual Surgery and the Origins of Gynecology: J. Marion Sims, His Hospital and His Patients, 1989. Mem. Orgn. Am. Historians, Am. Assn. for History Medicine. Office: U Ill Dept History Springfield IL 62794

MC GRORY, MARY, columnist; b. Boston, 1918; d. Edward Patrick and Mary (Jacobs) McGrory. A.B., Emmanuel Coll. Reporter Boston Herald Traveler, 1942-47; book reviewer Washington Star, 1947-54, feature writer for nat. staff, 1954-81; now syndicated columnist The Washington Post, Universal Press Syndicate. Recipient George Polk Meml. award; Pulitzer prize for commentary, 1975. Office: Washington Post 1150 15th St NW Washington DC 20071-0001*

MCGRORY, MARY KATHLEEN, retired non-profit organization executive; b. N.Y.C., Mar. 22, 1933; d. Patrick Joseph and Mary Kate (Gilvary) McG. BA, Pace U., 1957; MA, U. Notre Dame, 1962; PhD, Columbia U., 1969; DHL, Albertus Magnus Coll., 1984; LLD, Briarwood Coll., 1990; DHL, Trinity Coll., 1991. Prof. English Western Conn. State U., Danbury, 1969-78; dean of arts and scis. Eastern Conn. State U., Willimantic, 1978-80, v.p. for acad. affairs, 1981-85; pres. Hartford Coll. for Women, Conn., 1985-91; sr. fellow U. Va. Commonwealth Ctr., Charlottesville, 1991-92; exec. dir. Soc. Values in Higher Edn./Georgetown U., Washington, 1992-96; ret., 1996; pres. MKM Assocs., Holland, Ma., 1983—. Author: Yeats, Joyce & Beckett, 1975. Bd. dirs. Hartford Hosp., 1985-93; chmn. bd. govs. Greater Hartford Consortium Higher Edn., 1989-90. Fcls Found. fellow, 1966-67, NEH summer fellow, 1975; Ludwig Vogelstein Found. travel grantee, 1973. Mem. New Eng. Jr. Community and Tech. Coll. Coun. (v.p. 1988-91), Am. Assn. Higher Edn., Med. Acad. of Am., Greater Hartford C. of C. (bd. dirs. 1989-91), Hartford Club (bd. dirs. 1988-91). Home: Apt 809 1727 Massachusetts Ave NW Washington DC 20036-2153

MCGUCKIN, WENDY MICHELLE BLASSINGAME, accounting specialist; b. Guymon, Okla., June 11, 1966; d. Ronald Clifford Blassingame and Evelyn Marie (Maddox) Martin; m. Randall Mack McGuckin, Sept. 11, 1993. BS, U. Okla., 1989. Tchr. Norman (Okla.) Pub. Schs., 1989-90; pub. rels. coord. Hatfield and Bell, Inc., Norman, 1990-91; fin. cons. Sun Fin. Group, Oklahoma City, 1991; acctg. specialist U. Okla., Norman, 1991—; co-owner Wildfire Horse Ranch, EnviroPin; chair awards com. U. Okla. Staff Senate. Environ. activist, Oklahoma City, 1990; vol. Okla. Equine Hosp., 1994. Mem. NAFE, Okla. Equestrian Trail Riders Assn. Office: Univ Okla 620 Elm Ave Norman OK 73069-8801

MCGUE, CHRISTIE, federal official; b. Colombus, Ohio, Feb. 1, 1949; m. Robert Calt, Nov. 13, 1992. Sr. mgmt. analyst Nuclear Regulatory Comm., Washington, 1973-76; asst. sec., asst. dir. Office of Elec. Power Regulations, asst. dir. Office of Hydropower Licensing Fed. Energy Regulatory Comm., Washington, 1977-85; with Dept. Interior, Washington, 1986-88; dep. exec. dir. Fed. Energy Regulatory Commn., Washington, 1990-93, exec. dir., CFO, 1994—. Office: Fed Energy Regulatory Commn 888 1st St NE Rm 11-J Washington DC 20002-4232

MC GUFFEY, WENDY SUE, special education educator, consultant; b. Albany, N.Y., Mar. 17, 1968; d. Verne C. and Barbara M. (Mc Elheney) Mc G. BS, Coll. of St. Rose, 1990, MS in Edn., 1992. Cert. tchr., N.Y., permanent in elem. edn., spl. edn., reading. Master tchr. Ctr. for the Disabled, Albany, N.Y., 1990—; cons. on Mobiltiy Opportunities Via Edn., 1993—, presenter, 1993—. Recipient 2nd degree Reiki cert., 1992-93. Mem. Coun. for Exceptional Children. Home: 22 Lombard St Schenectady NY 12304 Office: Ctr for Disabled 314 S Manning Blvd Albany NY 12208

MCGUIRE, CAMILLE HALL, elementary education educator; b. Wayne County, Miss., Mar. 2, 1949; d. Howard Edward Sr. and Margaret Louise (Cochran) Hall; m. Richard Jay McGuire Sr., Mar. 17, 1972; 1 child, Richard Jay Jr. BS, U. Mobile, 1971; MEd, U. South Ala., 1978. Cert. early childhood edn. 1st grade tchr. Holloway Elem. Sch., Mobile, Ala., 1971-75, Orchard Elem. Sch., Mobile, 1976-87; v.p., buyer Pestop Exterminator Inc., Mobile, 1987-91; 2nd grade tchr. O'Rourke Elem. Sch., Mobile, 1991—; pvt. tutor, Mobile, 1978—; 1st and 2nd grade chairperson Orchard and O'Rourke Schs., mobile, 1978—; supr. tchr.-trainer coll. students, 1973-86; chairperson So. Accreditation for Pub. Schs., 1979, 94; leader constant profl. growth through workshops, 1971-94. Mem. Mobile Opera Guild, 1986-91; mem. adult choir Hilcrest Bapt.Ch., 1971—, dir. children's choir, 1983—. Named Outstanding Reading Tchr. Metro Mobile Reading Coun., 1985-86. Mem. ASCD, Ashley Estates Garden Club (achievement task force 1995), Assn. Univ. Women. Office: Pauline O'Rourke Elem 1975 LeRoy Stevens Rd Mobile AL 36695

MCGUIRE, CAROLE BAKER, legislative staff member; b. Seattle, Dec. 26, 1951. BA, Western Wash. U., 1974. Budget aide Sen. Warren Magnuson, 1974-76; legis. analyst, 1976-81, legis. and budget analyst, 1981-85; dir. appropriations activities Budget Com., 1985—. Office: Com Budget 621 Senate Dirksen Office Bldg Washington DC 20510*

MC GUIRE, DOROTHY HACKETT, actress; b. Omaha, June 14, 1916; d. Thomas Johnston and Isabel (Flaherty) McG.; m. John Swope, July 18, 1943 (dec.); children: Topo Swope, Mark Swope. Student, Pine Manor Jr. Coll., 1936-38. Stage debut in A Kiss for Cinderella, Omaha, 1933; played stock in Deertrees, Maine; N.Y.C. debut as understudy in Stop-Over, 1938; played role of Emily in Our town, on Broadway, 1938; toured with My Dear Children, 1939; starred in Claudia, 1941; toured in USO prodn. Dear Ruth, Europe, 1945, USO prodn. Tonight at 8:30, 1947, Summer and Smoke, 1950; appeared in Broadway prodn. Legend of Lovers, 1951, Joan at the Stake, 1954, Winesburg, Ohio, 1958, The Night of the Iguana, 1976, Cause Celebre, 1979; film appearances include: Claudia, 1943, A Tree Grows in Brooklyn, 1945, The Enchanted Cottage, 1945, Claudia and David, 1946, The Spiral Staircase, 1946, Gentlemen's Agreement, 1947, Mr. 880, Invitation, 1952, Make Haste to Live, 1954, Three Coins in the Fountain, 1954, Trial, 1955, Friendly Persuasion, 1956, Old Yeller, 1957, This Earth is Mine, 1959, A Summer Place, 1959, The Remarkable Mr. Penny Pincher, The Swiss Family Robinson, 1960, The Dark at the Top of the Stairs, 1960, Susan Slade, 1961, Summer Magic, 1962, The Greatest Story Ever Told, 1965, Flight of the Doves, 1971; film appearances include (voice only) Jonathan Livingston Seagull, 1973; appeared in: TV movie She Waits, 1971, TV prodn Am. Playhouse: I Never Sang For My Father, 1988; radio serial Big Sister, 1937; Juliette in: Romeo and Juliette; Ophelia in Hamlet, 1951; TV appearances include U.S. Steel Hour, 1954, Lux Video Theatre, 1954, Climax, 1954, 56, Play House 90, Another Part of the Forest, 1972, The Runaways, 1975, The Philadelphia Story, 1954, Rich Man Poor Man, 1970, Little Women, 1978, The Incredible Journey of Doctor Meg Laurel, Ghost Dancing, 1983, Love Boat, 1984. Recipient N.Y. Drama Critics Circle award, 1941; named Best Actress by Nat. Bd. Rev., 1955. Mem. Screen Actors Guild, Actors Equity Assn., AFTRA. Office: Raymond J Gertz Acctg Corp 10351 Santa Monica Blvd Los Angeles CA 90025-6908

MCGUIRE, MARY JO, state legislator; b. 1956. BA in Bus. Adminstrn., Coll. of St. Catherine; JD, Hamline U.; postgrad., Harvard U., 1995—. Mem. Minn. Ho. of Reps., 1988-94, mem. judiciary com., judiciary fin. divsn., vice chair local govt. and met. affairs; mem. labor and mgmt. rels. com. Democrat. Home: 1529 Iowa Ave W Saint Paul MN 55108-2128 Office: Minn Ho of Reps State Ho Office Bldg Saint Paul MN 55155*

MCGUIRE, PATRICIA A., lawyer, academic administrator; b. Phila., Nov. 13, 1952; d. Edward J. and Mary R. McGuire. BA cum laude, Trinity Coll., 1974; JD, Georgetown U., 1977. Bar: Pa. 1977, D.C. Ct. Appeals 1979. Program dir. Georgetown U. St. Law Clinic, Washington, 1977-82; asst. dean for devel. and external affairs Georgetown U. Law Ctr., Washington, 1982-89; pres. Trinity Coll., Washington, 1989—; adj. prof. law Georgetown U., 1977-82, Georgetown Law Ctr., 1987—; commr. Mid. States Commn. on Higher Edn., 1991—; bd. dirs. Acacia Group. Editor: Street Law Mock Trial Manual, 1984; contbr. articles to profl. jours. Trustee Trinity Coll., 1986—; bd. dirs. Assn. Cath. Colls. and Univs., 1991—, Eugene and Agnes Meyer Found.; mem. adv. bd. Merion Mercy Acad. and Sisters of Mercy, 1990—; bd. dirs. Nat. Assn. Ind. Colls. and Univs.; mem. commn. govt. rels. Am. Coun. Edn. Recipient Daytime Emmy, TV Acad., N.Y.C., 1979-80. Mem. ABA, Assn. Am. Law Schs. (instl. advancement 1985—), Coun. for the Advancement and Support of Edn., Trinity Coll. Alumnae Assn. (pres. 1986-89). Democrat. Roman Catholic. Office: Trinity Coll Office of the President 125 Michigan Ave NE Washington DC 20017-1094

MCGUIRE, ROSEMARY D., lawyer; b. St. Louis, Apr. 2, 1960; d. James J. and Rosemary (Dunn) McG. BA, Benedictine Coll., 1982; JD, St. Louis U., 1985. Bar: Mo. 1985, Ill. 1986, U.S. Dist. Ct. (so. dist.) Ill. 1987, U.S. Ct. Appeals (7th cir.) 1994. Law clk. Mo. Ct. Appeals, St. Louis, 1985-86; assoc. Carr, Korein, Kunin et. al., East St. Louis, Ill., 1986-87, Brennan, Cates & Constance, Belleville, Ill., 1987—. Mem. Am. Trial Lawyers Assn., Ill. State Bar Assn., Mo. State Bar Assn., various mcpl. bar assns. Office: Brennan Cates & Constance 10 Executive Woods Ct Ste A Belleville IL 62226

MCGUIRE, SANDRA LYNN, nursing educator; b. Flint, Mich., Jan. 28, 1947; d. Donald Armstrong and Mary Lue (Harvey) Johnson; m. Joseph L. McGuire, Mar. 6, 1976; children: Matthew, Kelly, Kerry. BS in Nursing, U. Mich., 1969, MPH, 1973, EdD, 1988. Staff nurse Univ. Hosp., Ann Arbor, Mich., 1969; pub. health nurse Wayne County Health Dept., Eloise, Mich., 1969-72; instr. Madonna Coll., Livonia, Mich., 1973; pub. health coord. Plymouth Ctr. for Human Devel., Northville, Mich., 1974-75; asst. prof. cmty. health nursing U. Mich., Ann Arbor, 1975-83; asst. prof. U. Tenn., Knoxville, 1983-88, assoc. prof., 1990—; dir. Kids Are Tomorrow's Srs. Program, 1988—; resource person Gov.'s Com. Unification of Mental Health Services in Mich.; speaker profl. assns. and workshops; bd. dirs. Ctr. Understanding Aging, 1987-93, v.p. 1995—. Author: (with S. Clemen-Stone and D. Eigsti) Comprehensive Family and Community Health Nursing, 1981, 4th edit. 1995. Bd. dirs. Mich. chpt. ARC, 1980-83, Knoxville chpt., 1984-85; founder Knoxville Intergenerational Network, 1989. USPHS fellow, 1972-73, Robert Woodruff fellow, 1996—. Mem. APHA, ANA, Tenn. Nurses Assn., Nat. League Nursing, Tenn. League Nursing, Tenn. Pub. Health Assn., (chmn. mental health sect. 1976) Mich. Pub. Health Assn. (dir., co-chmn. residential services com. 1976-79, chmn. health services 1979-82), Nat. Coun. on Aging, Ctr. for Understanding Aging (v.p., 1994-95), Plymouth (chmn. residential services com. 1975-77) Tenn. Assn. Retarded Citizens, So. Nursing Rsch. Soc., Sigma Theta Tau, Pi Lambda Theta, Phi Kappa Phi. Home: 11008 Crosswind Dr Knoxville TN 37922-4011 Office: 1200 Volunteer Blvd Knoxville TN 37916-3806

MCGUIRL, MARLENE DANA CALLIS, law librarian, educator; b. Hammond, Ind., Mar. 22, 1938; d. Daniel David and Helen Elizabeth (Baludis) Callis; m. James Franklin McGuirl, Apr. 24, 1965. AB, Ind. U., 1959; JD, DePaul U., 1963; MALS, Rosary Coll., 1965; LL.M., George Washington U., 1978, postgrad. Harvard U., 1985. Bar: Ill. 1963, Ind. 1964, D.C. 1972. Asst., DePaul Coll. of Law Libr., 1961-62, asst. law libr., 1962-65; ref. law librarian Boston Coll. Sch. Law, 1965-66; libr. dir. D.C. Bar Library, 1966-70; asst. chief Am.-Brit. Law Div. Libr. of Congress, Washington, 1970, chief, 1970-90, environ. cons., 1990—; counsel Cooter & Gell, 1992-93; adminstr. Washington Met. Transit Authority, 1994—; libr. cons. Nat. Clearinghouse on Poverty Law, OEO, Washington, 1967-69, Northwestern U. Nat. Inst. Edn. in Law and Poverty, 1969, D.C. Office of Corp. Counsel, 1969-70; instr. law librarianship Grad. Sch. of U.S. Dept. of Agr., 1968-72; lectr. legal lit. Cath. U., 1972; adj. asst. prof., 1973-91; lectr. environ. law George Washington U., 1979—; judge Nat. and Internat. Law Moot Ct. Competition, 1976-78, 90—; pres. Hamburger Heaven, Inc., Palm Beach, Fla., 1981-91, L'Image de Marlene Ltd., 1986-92, Clinique de Beauté Inc., 1987-92, Heads & Hands Inc., 1987-92, Horizon Design & Mfg. Co., Inc., 1987—; dir. Stoneridge Farm Inc., Gt. Falls, Va., 1984—. Contbr. articles to profl. jours. Mem. Georgetown Citizens Assn.; trustee D.C. Law Students in Ct.; del. Ind. Democratic Conv., 1964. Recipient Meritorious Svc. award Libr. of Congress, 1974, letter of commendation Dir. of Pers., 1976, cert. of appreciation, 1981-84. Mem. ABA (facilities law libr. Congress com. 1976-89), Fed. Bar Assn. (chpt. council 1972-76), Ill. Bar Assn., Women's Bar Assn. (pres. 1972-73, exec. bd. 1973-77, Outstanding Contbn. to Human Rights award 1975), D.C. Bar Assn., Am. Bar Found., Nat. Assn. Women Lawyers, Am. Assn. Law Libraries, (exec. bd. 1973-77), Law Librarians Soc. of Washington (pres. 1971-73), Exec. Women in Govt. Home: 3416 P St NW Washington DC 20007-2705

MCHALE, CAROL ANN, secondary education educator; b. Detroit, Feb. 19, 1944; d. Joseph Frank and Stella Julia (Duch) Gasperut; m. Dennis Paul McHale, Nov. 29, 1974; children: Robert, Matthew. AB, U. Detroit, 1966; M in Gen. Secondary Edn., Wayne State U., 1969. Cert. specialist in gen. secondary edn., Mich. Tchr. English Shrine High Sch., Royal Oak, Mich., 1966-86, Birmingham (Mich.) Bro. Rice High Sch., 1986-88, Shrine Acad., Royal Oak, Mich., 1988—. Roman Catholic.

MCHALE, MAUREEN THERESA, student affairs administrator; b. L.A., May 6, 1967; d. Thomas and Annette (Smith) McH. BA in Psychology, UCLA, 1989, MA in Higher Edn., 1992, postgrad., 1992—. Cert. coll. counselor. Program coord. UCLA Ext., 1990-94; tchg. asst. UCLA Grad. Sch. Edn., 1993—; student affairs officer UCLA Summer Sessions, 1993—; presenter in field. Welcoming call com. UCLA Alumni Assn., 1992—, alumni scholar com. 1995—; grad. student rep. UCLA Student Conduct Com., 1994-95; student rep. UCLA Grad. Sch. Edn., 1993-94; vol. Santa Monica (Calif.) Aids Project, 1996—. Recipient Rsch./Conf. Travel grant UCLA, 1994. Mem. AAUW, Am. Ednl. Rsch. Assn. (presenter), Assn. for Study of Higher Edn. (presenter), Am. Assn. for Higher Edn., UCLA Assn. of Acad. Women, Delta Delta Delta (chpt. devel. adv. 1996—). Home: 556 Via de la Paz Pacific Palisades CA 90272 Office: UCLA Box 951418 Los Angeles CA 90095-1418

MCHENRY, IRENE ELIZABETH, psychologist, consultant; b. York, Pa., Jan. 24, 1946; d. Ira Ricketts and Lois Elaine (Fine) McHenry; 1 child, Michael McHenry Koehler. BA cum laude, Susquehanna U., 1967; MS magna cum laude, Bucknell U., 1979; PhD, The Fielding Inst., Santa Barbara, Calif., 1996. Cert. sch. psychologist, Pa.; lic. psychologist, Pa.; cert. instr. elem. edn. and English, Pa. Founding head Delaware Valley Friends Sch., Bryn Mawr, Pa., Greenwood Friends Sch., Millville, Pa.; founding coord. dance group The Moving Co., Bloomsburg, Pa.; psychologist Clin. Assocs. West, Radnor, Pa.; learning team cons. The Wharton Sch., U. Pa.; cons. to ind. schs. Editor-in-chief Systems--Centered Theory and Practice, 1996; editor newsletter Friends Coun. Reflections on Edn., 1995-96; writer poetry; contbr. articles to profl. jours. Mem. adv. bd. Delaware Valley Friends Sch., 1994-96; mem. program com. Friends Coun. on Edn.; bd. dirs. Gladwyne (Pa.) Montessori Sch.), 1995-96. Mem. APA, C.G. Jung Soc. of Phila., Nat. Assn. Sch. Psychologists, Orton Dyslexia Soc. (bd. dirs. Phila. br.). Quaker and Buddhist. Office: Clin Assocs West 252 Radnor-Chester Rd Radnor PA 19087

MCHENRY, PATRICIA ROSE, state agency administrator; b. Burbank, Calif., Mar. 24, 1950; d. Clarence U. and Neota Etta (Common) Benton. BA with distinction, U. N.Mex., 1977. Office mgr. S.W. Cable TV, Espanola, N.Mex., 1978-79; exec. asst. Baha'i' Internat. Ctr., Haifa, Israel, 1980-83; exec. mgmt. analyst N.Mex. Dept. Fin. and Adminstrn., Santa Fe, 1979, exec. budget analyst, 1983-85; sr. fiscal analyst N.Mex. Legis. Fin. Com., Santa Fe, 1985-88; dep. dir. adminstrv. svcs. divsn. N.Mex. Dept. Corrections, Santa Fe, 1988-89; adminstr. data processing N.Mex. Human Svc. Dept., Santa Fe, 1990-92; dep. dir. property control divsn. N.Mex. Gen. Svc. Dept., Santa Fe, 1992—. V.p. Mil. Hist. Found. N.Mex. Mem. Baha'i' Faith. Office: NMex Gen Svc Dept Property Control Divsn 1100 S Saint Francis Dr Santa Fe NM 87505-4147

MCHUGH, BARBARA ELAINE, adapted physical education educator, consultant; b. Washington, Oct. 11, 1947; d. Loughlin Francis and Barbara Huntington (Whitman) McH.; 1 child, Angela Jean. BA, Oberlin Coll., 1969; MA, UCLA, 1973; PhD, Tex. Woman's U., 1995. Sch. bus. driver Laidlaw Transit, San Francisco, 1973-88; instr. Coll. of Marin, Kentfield, Calif., 1981-85, Chabot Coll., Hayward, Calif., 1981-91; instr. City Coll. San Francisco, 1987-91, San Francisco State U., 1987-91; cons. Wise County Spl. Edn. Coop., Decatur, Tex., 1992-95; adj. instr. Tex. Christian U., Ft. Worth, 1992; asst. prof. adapted phys. edn. Sonoma State U., Rohnert Park, Calif., 1995—; cons. Children's Movement Ctr., San Francisco, 1987-91; cons. on orientation and mobility Bluebonnet Coop., Weatherford, Tex., 1992-94, Denton Spl. Edn. Coop., Sanger, Tex., 1993-94. Contbr. articles to profl. jours. Bd. dirs. United Cerebral Palsy North Bay, Petaluma, Calif., 1995—. Scholar Assn. for Retarded Citizens, Denton, Tex., 1992. Mem. AAHPERD, Assn. Edn. and Rehab. Blind and Visually Impaired, Calif. Assn. Health, Phys. Edn., Recreation and Dance, Phi Beta Kappa (scholar No. Calif. chpt. 1989), Phi Kappa Phi. Democrat. Office: Sonoma State U 1801 E Cotati Ave Rohnert Park CA 94928

MCHUGH, BETSY BALDWIN, sociologist, educator, journalist, business owner; b. Concord, N.H., 1928; d. Walter Killenbeck and Eliza Alice (Hunt) Slater; m. Michael Joseph McHugh, Dec. 19, 1954; children: Betsy, Michael. MusB in Vocal Music, Syracuse (N.Y.) U., 1954; grad. student, Cornell U. Tchr. pub. schs. Juneau, Alaska, 1966-85; owner, founder Cashè Pub. Co., Tampa, Fla., and Juneau, 1986—, Nikish Ki Lodges and Youth Camps subsidiaries Baldwin Enterprises. Named one of Alaska's Outstanding Educators, Gov. Alaska Woman's Commn., 1985, Uno of Yr., 1993, 94, Internat. Una of Yr., 1993, 94, one of 2000 Most Notable Women, 1994, Better Profl. WOmen, 1993, 94. Mem. Can. Nat. Libr., Nat. Press Club, Bus. Assn. N.Y. State, Libr. of Congress, Can. Bus., D.C. C. of C., Mex. C. of C., Sigma Delta Chi. Office: Cashé Pub Co PO Box 22031 Juneau AK 99801

MCHUGH, CARIL DREYFUSS, art dealer, gallery director, consultant; b. New Haven, Conn.; d. Irving and Gertrude (Lax) Eisenstein; m. Barney Dreyfuss II (div.); children: Caryn, Barney III (Terry), Andrew, Evan; m. James Marshall McHugh Jr., Dec. 31, 1976. BA, Smith Coll.; MA, Am. U. Libr. archivist, mem. staff art rental Washington Gallery of Modern Art, 1963-67; asst. to curator of prints and drawings Nat. Mus. Am. Art, Washington, 1967-69; dir. Studio Gallery, Washington, 1970-75; dir., ptnr. Parsons-Dreyfuss Gallery, N.Y.C., 1976-80; dir. Frank Marino Gallery, N.Y.C., 1981, Humphrey Fine Art, N.Y.C., 1988-90, Gregory Gallery, N.Y.C., 1995—; art cons., writer, N.Y.C., 1982-95; arranger exhbns. Nat. Mus. Am. Art, Washington, 1968, 69, USIA, Washington, 1976, Automation House, N.Y.C., 1983. Contbr. essays to catalogs, articles to profl. mags. Bd. dirs. Women's Nat. Dem. Club, Washington, 1972-76, Friends of the Corcoran, Washington, 1972-76, Smith Club of Washington, 1974-76; Sophia Smith Assoc. Smith Coll., Northampton, Mass., 1985, 90, 95. Home: 241 Central Park W Apt 9C New York NY 10024

MCILVAIN, FRANCES H., artist, art educator, art gallery director; b. Newark, May 11, 1925; d. Frank Earl Haines and Edith Lewis Braddock; m. Douglas Lee McIlvain, Feb. 7, 1948; children: Bonnie W. Werse, James Douglas. BFA, Temple U., 1946, BS in Edn., 1947; postgrad., Phil. Mus. of Art, 1950, Tyler Sch. of Art, Rome, 1973. Art tchr. Rancocas Valley Regional High Sch., Mt. Holly, N.J., 1947-53; staff artist Halsted and Van Vechten, Red Bank, N.J., 1953-63; art tchr. Tinton Falls (N.J.) Schs., 1963-83; pres. N.J. Watercolor Soc., 1992-94; v.p. Guild of Creative Art, Shrewsbury, N.J., 1983—. One woman shows include Guild of Creative Art, Shrewsbury, 1995, Georgian Ct. Coll., Lakewood, N.J., 1995. Mem. Am. Watercolor Soc., Friends of Arts and Scis., Garden State Watercolor Soc., Phila. Watercolor Club (assoc.), Longboat Key Art Ctr. (vol.), Art Alliance (vol.). Home: 40 Whitman Dr Red Bank NJ 07701

MCILWAIN, CLARA EVANS, agricultural economist, consultant; b. Jacksonville, Fla., Apr. 5, 1919; d. Waymon and Jerusha Lee (Dickson) Evans; m. Ivy McIlwain, May 15, 1942 (dec. 1987); children: Ronald E., Carol A. McIlwain Edwards, Marilyn E. McIlwain Ross, Ivy J. McIlwain Lindsay. BS, U. D.C., 1939; M Agrl. Econs., U. Fla., 1972. Notary pub., Va.; lic. life and health ins. agt., Md., Va., D.C. Statis. asst. Hist. and Statis. Analysis Div., Washington, 1962-67; statistician Econ Devel. Div. USDA, Washington, 1967-70, 72, agrl. economist, 1972-74; program analyst Office Equal Opportunity, USDA, Washington, 1974-79; staff writer Sci. Weekly, Chevy Chase, Md., 1988-89; ins. agt. A.L. Williams, Primerica, Camp Springs, Md., 1990—; workshop coord. Author: Steps to Eloquence, 1989; contbr. to profl. publs. Coord., instr. Youth Leadership and Speechcraft, Toastmasters Internat., Washington area, 1972-78; tchr., bd. dirs. Sat. Tutorial Enrichment Program, Arlington, Va., 1988-89; mem. network Christian women, mem. women's fellowship com. Christ Fellowship Ministries. Rockefeller Found. scholar, 1970-72. Mem. Toastmasters Internat. (past pres. Potomac Club, Gavel award 1976, Able Toastmaster award 1978), Am. Assn. Notaries, So. Assn. Agrl. Economists, Nat. Assn. Agrl. Econs., Internat. Platform Assn. Office: Evans Unlimited 8350 Greensboro Dr Mc Lean VA 22102-3533

MCILWAIN, NADINE, principal; b. Canton, Ohio, July 29, 1943; d. Willie J. and Mabel W. (White) Williams; m. Albert H. McIlwain, Aug. 20, 1966 (dec. June 1989); children: Jeaneen J., Floyd R. BA, Malone Coll., 1970; MA, U. Akron, 1978; MEd, Ashland U., 1990. Cert. tchr. social studies, sociology. Lab. asst. Canton City Health Dept., 1962-65; telephone operator Ohio Bell Telephone Co., 1965-71; svc. cons. Ohio Bell Telephone Co., Akron, 1970-71; tchr. Canton City Schs., 1971-90, curriculum specialist, 1985-90; prin. Alliance (Ohio) City Schs., 1990—. Chair Stark Met. Housing Authority, Canton, 1992—; v.p. Alliance Symphony Assn., 1991—; mem. Canton City Coun., 1985-86; bd. dirs. Canton Players Guild; mem. minority outreach com. Canton Cultural Ctr.; life mem. Alliance br. NAACP; active Am. Cancer Soc., Canton Urban League, Alliance Area Farmworkers Housing Assn., Alliance Project Hope. Recipient Black History award Stark County African-Am. History Month Com., 1975, Polit. award Nat. Black Women's Leadership Caucus, 1981, Liberty Bell award Stark County chpt. ABA, 1989, Achievement award Alliance br. NAACP, 1993, Nat. Educator award Milken Family Found., 1993, Ohio Humanitarian award for Edn. State of Ohio of Adminstrv. Svcs. Civil Rights Divsin. and Martin Luther King Jr. Holiday Commn., 1994; named Woman of Yr., Canton Negro Oldtimers Athletic Assn., 1982, Woman of Yr., Am. Bus. Women's Assn., 1983. Mem. NEA, Nat. Alliance of Black Sch. Educators, Nat. Sociol. Hon. Soc., Ohio Mid. Sch. Assn., Ohio Coun. for Social Studies (exec. bd. dirs.), Ohio Edn. Assn. (Doris L. Allen minority caucus), Canton Profl. Educators Assn., Leila Green Alliance of Black Sch. Educators, Stark County African-Am. Fedn., Delta Sigma Theta. Home: 586 Briarcliff Ave Alliance OH 44601-2120 Office: Alliance City Schs 311 S Union Ave Alliance OH 44601-2663

MCINERNEY, ELLEN EUSTIS, finance company executive; b. Bayshore, N.Y., Feb. 22, 1946; d. John Joseph Sr. and Ellen Eustis (Pugh) McI. AAS, Marjorie Webster Coll., 1966; postgrad., NYU, 1967-68. Pers. mgr. The Slick Corp., N.Y.C., 1968-70; supr. employment Am. Express Travlers Cheque, N.Y.C., 1970-72; mgr. human resources Gulf & Western Industries, Inc., N.Y.C., 1972-74; dir. staffing The N.Y. Times Co., N.Y.C., 1974-78; sr. v.p. Daniel A. Silverstein Assoc., Inc., N.Y.C., 1979-84; ptnr. Claveloux, McCaffrey, McInerney & Co., Green Farms, Conn., 1984—; COO Wentworth USA, Inc., Auckland, New Zealand, 1995—; ptnr., bd. dirs. OSIRIS Group, LP, N.Y.C., 1995—; CEO WARP Group, LLC, N.Y.C., 1996—; pres., COO, bd. dirs. Global Securitization, Inc., Parlin, N.J., 1994-96; bd. dirs. Blumberg Investments, N.Y.C.; lectr., cons. death and living dying, 1989—. Adv. bd. cons. Recovery Ctr., Monticello, N.Y., 1995—. Mem. Nurse healers profl. assoc., Inc., Shanti Nilaya, Internat. Health Rsch. Network. Democrat. Tibetan Buddhist. Home and Office: PO Box 38 John George Rd Grahamsville NY 12740

MCINNIS, HELEN LOUISE, publishing company executive; b. Fall River, Mass.; d. Hugh Michael and Louise Patricia (Waldron) McI. B.A., Merrimack Coll., 1967; M.A., Duquesne U., 1969. Asst. editor Holt, Rinehart & Winston, N.Y.C., 1971-73; editor D. Van Nostrand Co., N.Y.C., 1972-75; sr. v.p., dir. coll. dept. Scribner Book Cos., Inc., N.Y.C., 1976-91; asst. v.p., exec. editor Macmillan Pub. Co., 1985-91; v.p., editl. dir. acad./trade Oxford U. Press, N.Y.C., 1991—. Editor, author: Viewpoints: American Cities, 1972. Mem. Assn. Am. Pubs. (chmn. com. higher edn. div. 1980-82, exec. bd. 1982-84). Democrat. Roman Catholic. Home: 253 W 72nd St Apt 1505 New York NY 10023-2708 Office: Oxford U Press 200 Madison Ave New York NY 10016-3903

MCINTIRE, MELINDA I., public relations executive; b. Seattle. BA in Psychology, Duke U. Rsch. asst. Bus. Rsch. Assocs.; paralegal Burns & Fox Attys. at Law; news asst. WTVD-TV; mgr., writer Dunwoody Crier; news prodn. asst., assoc prodr. CNN, TBS, 1987-88; awards coord. TBS, 1988-89; unit publicist TNT, Turner Broadcasting, 1989-90; mgr. pub. rels., nat. assignment desk CNN, 1990—. Office: Turner Broadcasting System Inc 1 CNN Ctr PO Box 105366 Atlanta GA 30348*

MCINTOSH, CAROLYN MEADE, retired educational administrator; b. Waynesburg, Ky., Oct. 21, 1928; d. Clarence Hobert and Sarah Letitia (Bentley) Meade; m. Edgar G. McIntosh, Aug. 21, 1948; children: Wayne, Jeanne, Penny, Jimmi, Carol. BS, Miami U., Oxford, Ohio, 1962; MEd, Xavier U., Cin., 1966. Elem. tchr. Ohio, 1961-79; prin. New Richmond (Ohio) Sch. Dist., 1980-91; ret., 1991; tchr. Clermont County Adult Edn. Program, 1970-95, Clermont County dir.of Headstrart 1971-72, Clearmont County Rep. to Ohio elem. adminstr., 1985-87, Pres. Clermont and Brown County adminstr., 1988-89. Editor Ret. Tchrs. Newsletter. Pres. New Richmond Bd. Edn.; v.p. U.S. Grant Vocat. Sch. Bd. Edn.; mem. Clermont County Excellence in Edn. Com.; mem. edn. adv. com. Clermont Coll.; mem. adv. bd. Bethany Children's Home; mem. Clermont 2001 Com.; mem. Rep. Ctrl. Com. of Clermont County. Recipient New Richmond Adminstr. of the Yr. award City of New Richmond, 1989. Mem. AAUW, ASCD, NAESP, Nat. Sch. Bd. Assn., Ohio Sch. Bd. Assn., Ohio Assn. Elem. Sch. Adminstrs. (all county legis. liaison), Ohio County Ret. Tchrs. Assn., Clermont County Ret. Tchrs. Assn. (pres.), Order Eastern Star, Phi Delta Kappa, Delta Kappa Gamma (pres. chpt.). Baptist.

MCINTOSH, CECILIA ANN, biochemist, educator; b. Dayton, Ohio, Apr. 30, 1956; d. Russell Edward McIntosh and Geraldine Rita (Cochran) Slemp; m. Kevin Smith Schweiker, May 28, 1978 (div. Mar. 1989); children: Katrina Lynn McIntosh Schweiker, Rebecca Sue McIntosh Schweiker. BA in Biology cum laude, U. South Fla., 1977, MA in Botany, 1981, PhD in Biology, 1990. Rsch. assoc. U. South Fla., Tampa, 1981-86, teaching/rsch. asst. dept. biology, 1986-90; postdoctoral fellow dept. biochemistry U. Idaho, Moscow, 1990-93; asst. prof. dept. biol. scis. East Tenn. State U., Johnson City, 1993—; adj. asst. prof. dept. biochemistry Quillen Coll. Medicine, East Tenn. State U., Johnson City, 1995—; sci. mentor U. So. Fla. Ctr. for Excellence, Tampa, 1984-90; rsch. forum judge Coll. Medicine Rsch. Forum, East Tenn. State U., Johnson City, 1994—. Author: (rev. articles) The Molecular Biology of Mitrochondria, 1995, Biotechnology of Medicinal and Aromatic Plants, 1991; contbr. rsch. articles to profl. jours. including Plant Physiology, Archives of Biochemistry & Biophysics. Sci. fair judge East Tenn. Regional Sci. Fair, Johnson City, 1994—. Strenghthening program grantee USDA, 1994-95, Seed grantee, 1995-97; rsch. devel. grantee East Tenn. State U. Rsch. Devel. Coun., 1994-96. Mem. Am. Assn. Women in Sci., Am. Soc. Plant Physiologists, Phytochem. Soc. N.Am., Sigma Xi (sci. fair workshop coord. Appalachian chpt. 1995—, dissertation award 1991). Office: East Tenn State U Dept Biol Scis Box 70 703 Johnson City TN 37614-0703

MCINTOSH, DAWN MARIE, administrative assistant; b. New London, Conn., Aug. 26, 1970; d. Traviss Collier Jr. and Marilyn Antone (Letzelter) McI. Student, Schenectady (N.Y.) County C.C., 1988-91. Sec., receptionist Kelly Temporary Svcs., Schenectady, 1988-91; adminstrv. sec. Unitech Corp., Schenectady, 1991-92; adminstrv. asst. N.Y. State Senate, Albany, 1993-95; adminstrv. assoc. Hanys Ins. Co., Albany, 1995—. Roman Catholic.

MCINTOSH, ELAINE VIRGINIA, nutrition educator; b. Webster, S.D., Jan. 30, 1924; d. Louis James and Cora Boletta (Bakke) Nelson; m. Thomas Henry McIntosh, Aug. 28, 1955; children: James George, Ronald Thomas, Charles Nelson. BA magna cum laude, Augustana Coll., Sioux Falls, S.D., 1945; MA, U. S.D., 1949; PhD, Iowa State U., 1954. Registered dietitian. Instr., asst. prof. Sioux Falls Coll., 1945-48; instr. Iowa State U., Ames, 1949-53, rsch. assoc., 1955-62; postdoctoral rsch. assoc. U. Ill., Urbana, 1954-55; asst. prof. human biology U. Wis., Green Bay, 1968-72, assoc. prof., 1972-85, prof., 1985-90, emeritus prof., 1990—, writer, cons., 1990—, chmn. human biology dept., 1975-80, asst. to vice chancellor, asst. to chancellor, 1974-76. Author 2 books including American Food Habits in Historical Perspective, 1995; contbr. numerous articles on bacterial metabolism, meat biochemistry and nutrition edn. to profl. jours. Fellow USPHS, 1948-49. Mem. Am. Dietetic Assn., Inst. Food Technologists, Wis. Dietetics Assn., Wis. Nutrition Coun. (pres. 1974-75), Sigma Xi. Office: U Wis - Green Bay ES 301 Human Biology 2420 Nicolet Dr Green Bay WI 54311-7001

MCINTOSH, ROBERTA EADS, retired social worker; b. Milw., Oct. 1, 1936; d. Robert Howard and Carlene (Rosboro) Eads; m. James Stuart Cameron McIntosh, Sept. 19, 1959; children: Ronald Stuart, Ian Robert, Peter Cameron. BA, Bucknell U., 1958; MS in Social Adminstrn., Case Western Reserve U., 1977. Lic. social worker, Ohio, Fla. Foster care caseworker Monroe County Child Welfare, Rochester, N.Y., 1958-63; group home counselor Betterway, Inc., Elyria, Ohio, 1974-75; group program coord. Elyria YWCA, 1975; caseworker, group home supr. Lorain County Children's Svcs., Elyria, 1977-83; treatment counselor Glenbeigh Adolescent Hosp., Cleve., 1984-86; youth dir. Washington Ave. Christian Ch., Elyria, 1984-85; outreach counselor Spouse Abuse Shelter Religious Community Svcs., Clearwater, Fla., 1986-93; pvt. practice Dunedin, Fla., 1993—; expert witness in domestic violence. Bd. pres. Elyria YWCA, 1972-75; sec., pres. Community Coordinated Child Care, Lorain County, 1970-72. Named Friend of Guidance Guidance Counselors Assn., 1982, Woman of Interest Elyria YWCA & City of Elyria, 1985. Mem. NASW, Acad. Cert. Social Workers, Fla. Coalition Against Domestic Violence (v.p. bd. 1993-94), Nat. Coalition Against Domestic Violence, Leadership Pinellas, Deaf Svc. Ctr. (bd. dirs. 1991-94), Victim Rights Coalition Pinellas County (v.p. bd. 1992-93), Fla. Network Victim Witness Svcs., Ctrl. Christian Ch. Christian Womens Fellowship (pres. 1988-90), Delta Zeta. Democrat. Home: 1501 Pleasant Grove Dr Dunedin FL 34698-2341 Office: PO Box 32 Dunedin FL 34697-0032

MCINTOSH, RUTH LYNNE, maternal, pediatric nurse; b. Mexico City, Mar. 8, 1956; came to the U.S., 1956; d. John Baldwin and Cordelia Genevieve (Hartshorn) McI. Student, LeTourneau U., 1975-78; BSN cum laude, U. Tex., Arlington, 1980, postgrad., 1981; postgrad., Our Lady of the Lake U., 1991. RN, Tex., Calif. Staff nurse newborn nursery Grim-Smith Hosp., Kirksville, Mo., 1980; staff nurse ICU Grim-Smith Hosp., Kirksville, 1981; staff nurse med.-surg. Intercommunity Hosp., Arlington, Tex., 1981-82; staff nurse post partum unit David Grant USAF Med. Ctr., Travis AFB, Calif., 1982; staff nurse combined obstet. unit George AFB Hosp., Victorville, Calif., 1986; asst. dept. nursing edn. Wilford Hall USAF Med. Ctr., Lackland AFB, Tex., 1987; cons. mil. med. care Concerned Ams. for Mil. Improvements, Pompano, Fla., 1988—; mem., RN cons. Fibromyalgia Support Group, San Antonio, 1991—, Chronic Pain Support Group, San Antonio, 1992—; demo artist All Night Media Rubber Stamps, San Raphael, Calif.; instr. (2) craft classes Lackland AFB Skills Devel. Ctr., Northside Ind. Sch. Dist. Adult Cmty. Edn. Mem. Calvary Ch., Santa Ana, Calif., 1980—; RN, vol. ARC, Travis AFB and Lackland AFB, 1984, 87-92; mem. air transportable hosp. team 831st Combat Support Group, George AFB, Calif., 1986. 1st lt. USAF, 1982-91. Mem. Soc. Ret. Air Force Nurses (outreach com. 1987-88), Endometriosis Assn., Air Force Assn. (life), Am. Legion, Disabled Am. Vets., Sigma Theta Tau. Republican. Baptist. Home: 7407 Micron Dr San Antonio TX 78251-2103

MCINTOSH, TERRIE TUCKETT, lawyer; b. Ft. Lewis, Wash., July 20, 1944; d. Robert LeRoy and Elda (Perry) Tuckett; m. Clifton Dennis McIntosh, Oct. 13, 1969; children: Alison, John. BA, U. Utah, 1967; MA, U. Ill., 1970; JD, Harvard U., 1978. Bar: N.Y. 1979, Utah 1980. Assoc. Hughes, Hubbard & Reed, N.Y.C., 1978-79; assoc. Fabian & Clendenin, Salt Lake City, 1979-84, shareholder, 1984-86; staff atty. Questar Corp., Salt Lake City, 1986-88, sr. atty., 1988-92, sr. corp. counsel, 1992—; instr. philosophy Douglass Coll. Rutgers U., New Brunswick, N.J., 1971-72; mem. adv. com. civil procedure Utah Supreme Ct., Salt Lake City, 1987—; mem. jud. nominating com. 5th Cir. Ct., Salt Lake City, 1986-88. Mem. Utah State Bar (ethics and discipline screening panel 1989—, co-chair law related edn. com. 1985-86), Women Lawyers of Utah (chair exec. com. 1986-87), Harvard Alumni Assn. Utah (bd. dirs. 1987—), Phi Beta Kappa, Phi Kappa Phi. Office: Questar Corp PO Box 45433 180 E 1st South St Salt Lake City UT 84145

MCINTURFF, JOHANNA ROBINSON, special education educator; b. South Charleston, W.Va., Dec. 13, 1952; d. Donald Hill and Doris Ruth (Hanna) Robinson; m. George Franklyn McInturff IV, Apr. 13, 1978; children: Dylan, Ryan, Mia. BA in Psychology, Concord Coll., 1973; MA in Spl. Edn., U. W.Va., 1978; EdD, Nova Southeastern U., 1995. Tchr. of mentally impaired Summers County Schs., Hinton, W.Va., 1974-76, tchr. of learning disabled, 1976-82; learning disabilities tchr. Mercer County Schs., Princeton, W.Va., 1982—; prof. Concord Coll., Athens, W.Va., 1993—; ednl. specialist IBM Corp., Atlanta, 1994; pres. Faculty Senate, Athens, 1992—; sec. Sch. Adv. Coun., Athens, 1992-94. Grantee W.Va. Edn. Fund, 1990, 92, 94. Mem. Coun. for Exceptional Children, Assn. for Children with Learning Disabilities. Home: PO Box 525 Athens WV 24712-0525

MCINTYRE, ANITA GRACE JORDAN, lawyer; b. Louisville, Ky., Jan. 29, 1947; d. Blakely Gordan and Shirley Evans (Grubbs) Jordan; m. Kenneth James McIntyre, Oct. 11, 1969; children: Abigail, Jordan Kenneth. BA, Smith Coll., 1969; JD, U. Detroit, 1975. Bar: Mich. 1975, U.S. Dist. Ct. (ea. dist.) Mich. 1975, U.S. Dist. Ct. (we. dist.) Mich. 1979, U.S. Ct. Appeals (6th cir.) 1979. Ptnr. Rollins White & Rollins, Detroit, 1975-79; vis. assoc. prof. Detroit Coll. Law, 1979-81; assoc. Tyler & Canham, Detroit, 1981-82; prin. Anita G. McIntyre, P.C., Grosse Pointe, Mich., 1982-87, 91—; of counsel Nederlander Dodge & Rollins, Detroit, 1987-90; assoc. Damm & Smith, P.C., Detroit, 1990-91. Editor, author (case notes) U. Detroit Jour. Urban Law, 1975; contrbr. articles to profl. jours. Sec. Berry Subdivsn. Assn., Detroit, 1975-77; pres. Smith Coll. Club Detroit, 1982-86; mem. parents bd. U. Liggett Sch., Grosse Pointe, Mich., 1991-95. Mem. State Bar Mich., Detroit Bar Assn. (family law, debtor-creditor sect. 1980-95), Wayne County (Mich.) Probate Bar Assn., Wayne County Juvenile Trial Lawyers Assn. Episcopalian. Office: 15324 Mack Ave Grosse Pointe Park MI 48224

MCINTYRE, MILDRED JEAN, clinical psychologist, writer, neuroscientist; b. Boston; d. William James and Theodora Grace (Jackson-McCullough) McI. BA, Swarthmore Coll., 1965; MA, Clark U., 1972, PhD, 1975. Lic. psychologist, Mass., Alaska, Hawaii. Ford Found. fellow, 1972, 73. Mem. APA, Internat. Neuropsychol. Soc., Cognitive Neurosci. Soc. Office: PO Box 990124 Boston MA 02199-0124

MCINTYRE-IVY, JOAN CAROL, data processing executive; b. Portchester, N.Y., Mar. 1, 1939; d. John Henry and Molly Elizabeth (Gates) Daugherty; m. Stanley Donald McIntyre, Aug. 24, 1957 (div. Jan. 1986); children: Michael Stanley, David John, Sharon Lynne; m. James Morrow Ivy IV, June 1, 1988. Student, Northwestern U., 1956-57, U. Ill., 1957-58. Assoc. editor Writer's Digest, Cin., 1966-68; instr. creative writing U. Ala.-Huntsville, 1975; editor Strode Pubs., Huntsville, 1974-75; paralegal Smith, Huckaby & Graves (now Bradley, Arant, Rose & White), Huntsville, 1976-82; exec. v.p. Micro Craft, Inc., Huntsville, 1982-85, pres., 1985-89, chief exec. officer, chmn. bd., 1989—, also dir. and co-owner. Author numerous computer-operating mans. for law office software, 1978-88; co-author: Alabama and Federal Complaint Forms, 1979; Alabama and Federal Motion and Order Forms, 1980; also numerous articles, short stories, poems, 1955-88. Editor: Alabama Law for the Layman, 1975. Bd. dirs. Huntsville Lit. Soc., 1976-77. Hon. scholar Medill Sch. Journalism, Northwestern U., 1956. Republican. Methodist. Office: Micro Craft Inc 6703 Odyssey Dr NW Ste 102 Huntsville AL 35806-3301

MCIVER, BEVERLY JEAN, art educator, artist; b. Greensboro, N.C., Dec. 14, 1962; d. Ethel Mae (McMaster) McI. BA, N.C. Ctrl. U., 1987; MFA, Pa. State U., 1992. Asst. prof. art Duke U., Durham, N.C., 1995—; artist-in-residence Vt. Studio Ctr., 1992, Atlantic Ctr. for Arts, 1992, 94, Headlands Ctr. for Arts, Sausalito, Calif., 1995; adj. lectr. N.C. Ctrl. U., Durham, 1992-95; adminstrv. facilitator N.C. Arts Coun., 1994—, panelist, 1995—; juror in field. One woman shows include Durham Art Guild, 1991, Paul Robeson Cultural Ctr., Pa. State U., 1992, Bivins Gallery, Duke U., 1993, 96, Formal Gallery, Pa. State U., 1994, Tyndall Galleries, Durham, N.C., 1994, Glaxo Inc., Research Triangle Park, N.C., 1995, Western Carolina U., Cullowhee, N.C., 1996; group shows include Appalachian State U., Boone, N.C., 1990, Zoller Gallery, Pa. State U., 1990, The Cotton Exch. Gallery, 1993, The Greensboro Artist League, 1993, Sunshine Cultural Ctr., Raleigh, N.C., 1993, Green Hill Ctr. for N.C. Art, Greensboro, 1994, N.C. State U., 1994, Fayetteville (N.C.) Mus., 1994, 95, Stedman Art Gallery Rutgers U., 1994, Duke U. Mus. Art, 1994, Wilson (N.C.) Art Ctr., 1995, Durham Art Guild, 1995, Tyndall Galleries, 1996, Soho 20 Gallery, N.Y.C., 1996, many others. Fellow Pa. State U., 1989, Visual Artist fellow N.C. Arts Coun., 1994; grantee Durham Arts Coun., 1994; ednl. scholar St. James Bapt. Ch., 1990, Headlands Ctr. for Arts, 1995. Mem. Coll. Arts Assn., Durham Art Guild (bd. dirs. 1993), City Gallery (bd. dirs. 1993). Baptist. Office: Duke U Art and Art History Dept Durham NC 27702

MCKAY, ALICE VITALICH, academic administrator; b. Seattle, Sept. 6, 1947; d. Jack S. and Phyllis (Bourne) Vitalich; m. Larry W. McKay, Aug. 14, 1973 (div. Jan. 1983). BA, Wash. State U., 1969; MEd, U. Nev., Las Vegas, 1975; EdD, U. Nev., Reno, 1986. High sch. tchr. Clark County Sch. Dist., Las Vegas, 1972-77, specialist women's sports, 1977-80, high sch. counselor, 1980-84, high sch. asst. prin., 1984-95; dir. Project Lead U. Nev., Reno, 1995—; pres. Lotus Profit, Inc., Las Vegas, 1985-86; dir. Nev. Project Lead. Sec. exec. bd. Gang Alternatives Partnership, 1993—. Mem. Am. Assn. Counseling and Devel. (committee on women 1985—), Nev. State Counseling and Devel. (pres. 1985-86), Nat. Assn. Female Execs., AAUW, Phi Delta Kappa (exec. bd. 1980-82). Office: U Nev Coll Edn Reno NV 89557-0217

MCKAY, APRILLE COOKE, prosecutor; b. Buffalo, Oct. 29, 1965; d. Jon Anson Cooke and Melody Marsh McCormick; m. Timothy Alexander McKay; children: Isabel Cooke, Jordan John. BA, U. Va., 1987; JD, U. Chgo., 1990. Bar: Ill. 1990, Mich. 1996. Law clk., then assoc. Levin & Funkhouser, Ltd., Chgo., 1989-91; asst. state's atty. Kane County States Atty. Office, Geneva, Ill., 1991-95. Editor The Legal Forum, U. Chgo. Law Sch., 1989-90. Bd. dirs. Ill. Family Support Enforcement Assn., Springfield, 1993-94. Mem. New Eng. Hist. and Geneal. Assn. Democrat. Unitarian. Home: 1409 Granger Ave Ann Arbor MI 48104

MCKAY, LAURA L., banker, consultant; b. Watonga, Okla., Mar. 3, 1947; d. Frank Bradford and Elizabeth Jane (Smith) Drew; m. Cecil O. McKay, Sept. 20, 1969; 1 child, Leslie. BSBA, Oreg. State U., 1969. New br. research U.S. Bank, Portland, Oreg., 1969-80; cash mgmt. officer U.S. Bank, Portland, 1980-82, asst. v.p., 1982-87, v.p., 1987-94; founder, cons. LLM Cons., Milw., 1994—. Chmn. Budget Com., North Clackamas Sch. Dist., 1982-84. Mem. Nat. Corp. Cash Mgrs. Assn., Nat. Assn. Bank Women (chmn. Oreg. group 1979-80), Portland Cash Mgrs. Assn., Portland C. of C. Republican. Office: LLM Cons 5686 SE Viewcrest Dr Portland OR 97267-4146

MCKAY, MIMI, pediatric nurse, psychiatric nurse; b. Louisville, June 7, 1954; d. Charles Henry and Helen Dorothy (Palla) McK. BSN, Ind. U., New Albany, 1986; MSN, IUPUI, Indpls., 1992. RN, Ky.; cert. RNC-mental health, psychiat. nursing. Charge nurse Kosair Children's Hosp., Louisville, 1988-94; clin. nurse specialist child/adolescent psychiat. Alliant Health System/Kosair Children's Hosp., Louisville, 1994—; adolescent group psychotherapist Bingham Child Guidance Ctr., Louisville, 1994—; lectr. Ind. U. Southeast; course leader psychiat. mental health nursing; pvt. practice cons., psychotherapy.

MCKAY, RENEE, artist; b. Montreal, Que., Can.; came to U.S., 1946, naturalized, 1954; d. Frederick Garvin and Mildred Gladys (Higgins) Smith; m. Kenneth Gardiner McKay, July 25, 1942; children: Margaret Craig, Kenneth Gardiner. BA, McGill U., 1941. Tchr. art Peck Sch., Morristown, N.J., 1955-56; one woman shows: Pen and Brush Club, N.Y.C., 1957, Cosmopolitan Club, N.Y.C., 1958; group shows include: Weyhe Gallery, N.Y.C., 1978, Newark Mus., 1955, 59, Montclair (N.J.) Mus., 1955-58, Nat. Assn. Women Artists, Nat. Acad. Galleries, 1954-78, N.Y. World's Fair, 1964-65, Audubon Artists, N.Y.C., 1955-62, 74-79, N.Y. Soc. Women Artists, 1979-80, Provincetown (Mass.) Art Assn. and Mus., 1975-79; traveling shows in France, Belgium, Italy, Scotland, Can., Japan; represented in permanent collections: Slater Meml. Mus., Norwich, Conn., Norfolk (Va.) Mus., Butler Inst. Am. Art, Youngstown, Ohio, Lydia Drake Library, Pembroke, Mass., many pvt. collections. Recipient Jane Peterson prize in oils Nat. Assn. Women Artists, 1954, Famous Artists Sch. prize in watercolor, 1959, Grumbacher Artists Watercolor award, 1970; Solo award Pen and Brush, 1957; Sadie-Max Tesser award in watercolor Audubon Artists, 1975, Peterson prize in oils, 1980; Michael Engel prize Nat. Soc. Painters in Casein and Acrylic, 1983. Mem. Nat. Assn. Women Artists (2d v.p. 1969-70, adv. bd. 1974-76), Audubon Artists (pres. 1979, dir. oils 1986-88), Artist Equity (dir. 1977-79, v.p. 1979-81), N.Y. Soc. Women Artists, Pen and Brush, Nat. Soc. Painters in Casein and Acrylic M.J. Kaplan prize 1984, Nat. Arts Club, Provincetown Art Assn. and Mus., Key West Art Assn. Club: Cosmopolitan. Home: 5 Carolina Meadows # 206 Chapel Hill NC 27514-8522

MCKECHNIE, MARGARET A., public relations professional; b. Niagara Falls, N.Y., Jan. 7, 1944; d. Donald and Margaret Frances (Hayes) McK. BS in Journalism cum laude, Ohio U., 1966. Pub. rels. asst. The 1st Nat. Bank Cin., 1966-69; assoc. dir. prodn. Computer Image Corp., Denver, 1969-75; comm. mgr. United Bank Denver, 1976-85; dir. corp. comm. Norwesr Bank Colo. (formerly United Banks Colo., Inc.), Denver, 1986—. Mem. Pub. Rels. Soc. Am. (Accredited Pub. Rels., bd. dirs. Colo. chpt. 1980-92, pres. 1991, assembly del. 1994—), Women Comm. (bd. dirs. 1976-80, v.p. fin.). Office: Norwest Bank Colorado 1740 Broadway Denver CO 80274-8705

MCKEE, BARBARA JEFFCOTT, consultant; b. Madison, Wis., Jan. 21, 1948; d. William Francis and Florence Ann (Jeffcott) McK.; m. Richard Arthur Rocha, Oct. 1, 1988. BBA, U. Wis., 1968; M in Mgmt., Northwestern U., 1981. CPA, Ill., Calif., Wis.; cert. internal auditor. Auditor Peat, Marwick, Mitchell & Co., Chgo., 1968-78; cons. Esmark, Inc., Chgo., 1978-79; audit mgr. Deloitte Haskins & Sells, Chgo., 1979-84, controller, 1984-85; v.p. Safeway Stores, Inc., Oakland, Calif., 1985-90; co-founder Achievers Internat., Oakland, Calif., 1990—. Mem. AICPA, Inst. Internal Auditors. Office: Achievers Internat 5255 Pinecrest Dr Oakland CA 94605-3812

MCKEE, DENISE ARLENE, neonatal intensive care nurse; b. Gary, Ind., June 24, 1956; d. Billy D. Warren and Charlotte I. (Hellyer) Buckley; m. Phillip W. McKee, Sept. 24, 1977; children: Mathew, Melissa. LPN, Ind. Vocat. Tech. Coll., 1977; ADN, SUNY, 1988; BSN, Ind. U., 1993. Staff nurse ICU Porter Meml. Hosp., Valparaiso, Ind., 1977-80; staff nurse med.-surg. unit St. Mary's Hosp., Hobart, Ind., 1980-82; sch. nurse Cerebral Palsy Ctr., Hobart, Ind., 1985-88, 89-92; staff nurse Miller Merry Manor, Hobart, 1989; staff nurse neonatal ICU Porter Meml. Hosp., 1993—. Mem. health and welfare com. Trinity United Meth. Ch., Hobart, 1994. Mem. Sigma Theta Tau. Methodist. Home: 315 W 8th Pl Hobart IN 46342-5127

MCKEE, ELSIE ANNE, history educator, writer; b. Luebo, Kasai, Zaire, Feb. 14, 1951; came to U.S.; d. Charles Theodore and Anne Candlish (Shepherd) McK. BA with high honors, Hendrix Coll., 1973; diploma in theology, Cambridge U., Eng., 1974; PhD summa cum laude, Princeton Theol. Sem., 1982. Asst. prof. ch. history Andover Newton Theol. Sem., Newton Ctr., Mass., 1982-88; assoc. prof. Andover, Mass., 1988-92; Archibald Alexander assoc. prof. Princeton Theol. Sem., N.J., 1992-94, Archibald Alexander prof. history of worship, 1994—; mem. H. H. Meeter Ctr. Gov. Bd. Calvin Coll. and Sem., Grand Rapids, Mich., 1988-92; vis. prof. Faculte de Theologie Reformee au Kasai, Zaire, 1995. Author: John Calvin on the Diaconate and Liturgical Almsgiving, 1984, Elders and the Plural Ministry: The Role of Exegetical History in Illuminating John

Calvin's Theology, 1988, Diakonia: In the Classical Reformed Tradition and Today, 1989, German translation, 1995, Reforming Popular Piety in Sixteenth-Century Strasbourg: Katharina Schütz Zell and Her Hymnbook, 1994; co-editor: (with B. Armstrong) Probing the Reformed Tradition: Historical Studies in Honor of Edward A. Dowey, Jr., 1989; mem. editl. coun. Sixteenth Century Jour., 1990—, Studies in Reformed Theology and History, 1991—; contbr. articles to profl. jours., chpts. to books. Recipient Deutsche Akademische Austauschdienst grant for German lang. study, 1978, Fulbright award, 1979-81, Rsch. and Travel grant Am. Philosoph. Soc., 1984, Am. Coun. of Learned Socs. fellowship, 1986-87, Faculty Devel. Travel grant Lilly Found., 1989. Mem. Am. Soc. Ch. History, N.Am. Acad. of Liturgy, Scholars of Early Modern Europe, Calvin Studies Soc. (v.p. 1993-95, pres. 1995—), Soc. for Reformation Rsch., Soc. Liturgica. Democrat. Presbyterian. Office: Princeton Theol Sem 64 Mercer St Princeton NJ 08540

MCKEE, KATHRYN DIAN GRANT, human resources consultant; b. L.A., Sept. 12, 1937; d. Clifford William and Amelia Rosalia (Shacher) G.; m. Paul Eugene McKee, June 17, 1961; children: Scott Alexander, Grant Christopher. BA, U. Calif., Santa Barbara, 1959; grad. Sch. Mgmt. Exec. Program, UCLA, 1979. Cert. compensation and benefits. Mgr. Mattel, Inc., Hawthorne, Calif., 1963-74; dir. Twentieth Century Fox Film Corp., L.A., 1975-80; sr. v.p. 1st Interstate Bank, Ltd., L.A., 1980-93; sr. v.p. and human resources dir. Am.'s Standard Chartered Bank, 1993-95; pres. Human Resources Consortia, Santa Ana, Calif., 1995—; dir. Accordia benefits of Southern Calif., 1991—, mem. exec. com. H.R. div. of Am. Bankers Assn., 1991-93; bd. dirs. Bank Certification Inst. Am. Bankers Assn., 1992-94; treas. Pers. Accreditation Inst., 1983-86, pres., 1986. Contbr. articles to profl. jours. Pres. GEM Theatre Guild, Garden Grove, Calif., 1984-86; bd. dirs. Vis. Nurses Assn., L.A., 1984-88; bd. dirs. SHRM, 1986-92, treas., 1989, vice-chmn., 1990, chmn., 1991, pres. SHRM Found., 1994, 95; bd. dirs. Laguna Playhouse, 1996—. Recipient Sr. Honor Key award U. Calif., Santa Barbara, 1959, named Outstanding Sr. Woman, 1959; recipient William Winter award Am. Compensation Assn., 1986, Excellence award L.A. Pers. Indsl. Rels. Assn., 1990, Profl. Excellence award SHRM, 1994. Mem. Internat. Assn. Pers. Women (various offices, past nat. pres., Mem. of Yr. 1986), Orgn. Women Execs. Office: Human Resources Consortia 2700 N Main St Ste 800 Santa Ana CA 92705-6636

MCKEE, MARGARET CRILE, pulmonary medicine and critical care physician; b. Cleve., Jan. 12, 1945; d. Richard List and Florence Mae (Johnson) McK. BA, Coll. Wooster, 1967; M in Regional Planning, Cornell U., 1971; MD, SUNY, Stony Brook, 1976. Diplomate Am. Bd. Internal Medicine, Pulmonary Medicine and Critical Care. Social planner Model Cities, Binghamton, N.Y., 1970-71; resident internal medicine Harlem Hosp., N.Y.C., 1976-79; physician Health Ins. Plan, Bedford-Williamsburg, N.Y., 1979-80; pulmonary fellow Columbia Presbyn. Med. Ctr., N.Y.C., 1980-82; chief of medicine Phoenix Indian Med. Ctr., 1983-92; pvt. practice Ariz. Med. Clinic, Sun City, Ariz., 1992—. Mem. Am. Coll. Chest Physicians, Am. Thoracic Soc., Soc. of Critical Care Medicine, Union of Concerned Scientists, Sierra Club. Methodist. Office: Ariz Med Clinic 13640 N Plaza Del Rio Blvd Peoria AZ 85381-4848

MCKEE, MARGARET JEAN, federal agency executive; b. New Haven, June 20, 1929; d. Waldo McCutcheon and Elizabeth (Thayer) McKee; A.B., Vassar Coll., 1951. Staff asst. United Rep. Fin. Com., N.Y.C., 1952; staff asst. N.Y. Rep. State Com., N.Y.C., 1953-55; staff asst. Crusade for Freedom (name later changed to Radio Free Europe Fund), N.Y.C., 1955-57; researcher Stricker & Henning Research Assocs., Inc., N.Y.C., 1957-59; exec. sec. New Yorkers for Nixon (name later changed to N.Y. State Ind. Citizens for Nixon Lodge), N.Y.C., 1959-60; asst. to Raymond Moley, polit. columnist, N.Y.C., 1961; asst. campaign com. Louis J. Lefkowitz for Mayor, N.Y.C., 1961; research programmer, treas. Consensus, Inc., N.Y.C., 1962-67; spl. asst. to U.S. Senator Jacob K. Javits, N.Y., 1967-73, adminstrv. asst., 1973-75; dep. adminstr. Am. Revolution Bicentennial Adminstrn., 1976, acting adminstr., 1976-77; chief of staff Perry B. Duryea (minority leader) N.Y. State Assembly, 1978; public affairs cons., 1979-80; dir. govt. relations Gen. Mills Restaurant Group, Inc., 1980-83; exec. dir. Fed. Mediation and Conciliation Service, 1983-86; mem. Fed. Labor Rels. Authority, 1986-89, chmn., 1989-94; mem. Nat. Partnership Coun., 1993-94; bd. dirs. Interam. Life Ins. Co., 1979-86, UNNC, Inc., 1992— (treas.). Mem. N.Y. State Bingo Control Commn., 1965-72, U.S. Adv. Commn. on Public Diplomacy, 1979-82; mem. Nat. Partnership Coun., 1993—; pres. Bklyn. Heights Slope Young Rep. Club, 1955-56; co-chmn. Bklyn. Citizens for Eisenhower-Nixon, 1956; chmn. 2d Jud. Dist. Assn. N.Y. State Young Rep. Clubs, Inc., 1957-58, vice-chmn., mem. bd. govs., 1958-60, v.p., 1960-62; pres., 1962-64; mem. exec. com. Fedn. Women's Rep. Clubs N.Y. State, Inc., 1960-64, mem. council, 1964-70; mem. exec. com. N.Y. Rep. State Com. 1962-64; co-chmn. spl. assts. Rockefeller for Pres. Nat. Campaign com., N.Y.C., 1964; co-dir. N.Y. Rep. State Campaign Com., 1964; asst. campaign mgr. Kenneth B. Keating for Judge Ct. Appeals, N.Y., 1965; dir. scheduling Gov. Rockefeller campaign, 1966, Sen. Charles E. Goodell campaign, 1970; dir. scheduling and speakers' bur. N.Y. Com. to Re-elect the Pres., 1972; dir. planning and strategy, Conn. Reagan-Bush campaign, Hartford, 1980; mem. annual fund adv. com. Vassar Coll., 1992-96. Mem. bd. govs. Women's Nat. Rep. Club, N.Y.C., 1963-66. Mem. Jr. League of Bklyn. (past (dir.), Exec. Women in Govt. (chmn. 1986), Nat. Women's Edn. Fund (mem. bd.), Am. Newspaper Women's Club, Nat. Soc. Colonial Dames Am. Episcopalian. Club: Vassar (past dir., Bklyn.). Home: 532 S Brooksvale Rd Cheshire CT 06410

MCKEE, MARY ELIZABETH, producer; b. Syracuse, N.Y., Feb. 14, 1949; d. Anthony Henry and Mary (Robards) Krystosik; m. Peter S. Fama, June 27, 1970 (div. Mar. 1973); 1 child, Kiralie Fama; m. Michael R. McKee, Feb. 15, 1975 (Oct. 1978); 1 child, Quinn. BFA, Fla. Internat. U., Miami, 1974; MFA, Memphis State U., 1977. Copywriter announcer Sta. WREC/WZXR Radio, Memphis, 1978-79; creative dir. Cit Neifert & Assoc. Advt., Memphis, 1979-82; promotion dir. Sta. WGNX-TV, Atlanta, 1982-86; program mgr. Sta. WVEU-TV, Atlanta, 1986-90; v.p., sta. mgr. Sta. WHSP-TV, Vineland, N.J., 1990-95; v.p. V Boxes Worldwide, Phila., 1995—, V Box Prodns., Atlantic City, 1995—; adj. prof. Glassboro State U., 1990—. Actor in field (Top 10 Memphis Mag. 1979). Vol. Com. to Feed the Hungry, Atlanta, 1988, Tenn. Talking Libr., Memphis, 1982; mem. Greenpeace, 1987—; mem. adv. coun. SES, Easter Seal Soc. N.J. Recipient Merit award Tenn. Talking Libr., 1982; named Best TV Comml. Memphis Advt. Club, 1982; Hair scholar Fla. Internat. U., 1973. Mem. AFTRA, Nat. Assn. Broadcasters, Am. Women in Radio and TV (publicity chmn. 1985-86), Nat. Assn. TV Program Execs., N.J. Broadcasters Assn. (TV chair 1995—), Broadcast Cable Fin. Mgmt. Assn., Chelsea Neighborhood Assn. (exec. bd.), Rotary. Democrat. Roman Catholic. Home: 55 S Dover Ave Atlantic City NJ 08401-5912 Office: 5918 Hammond Ave Philadelphia PA 19120

MCKEE, PENELOPE MELNA, library director; b. New Liskeard, Ont., Can., Dec. 31, 1938; d. Melvin Hugh and Violet Mary (Hooton) Olimer; m. Arthur Donald McKee, Mar. 5, 1960 (div. 1985); children: Suzanne, Carolyn, Stephen. BA with honors, U. Toronto, Can., 1960, BLS, 1961, MLS, 1980; diploma, Coll. Applied Arts and Tech., 1976. Cert. mcpl. mgr., Ont. Mcpl. Mgmt. Devel. Bd. Fine arts libr. North York Pub. Libr., Ont., Can., 1961-63, reference libr., 1969-74; reference libr. Toronto Montessori Schs., Thornhill, Ont., 1974-76; cons. Grolier Pub., Toronto, 1976; libr. supr. Toronto Pub. Libr., 1977-80; dir. Aurora Pub. Libr., Ont., Can., 1980-86, Peterborough Pub. Libr., Ont., Can., 1986-90, Edmonton Pub. Libr., Alta., Can., 1990—; adj. assoc. prof. U. Alta., Edmonton, 1992—; cons. Edmonton Cath. Sch. Bd., 1992. Contbr. articles to profl. jours. Vice chmn. Project Hostel, Aurora, 1986-89; bd. dirs. Friends of Trent Severn Waterway, Peterborough, 1990; active Edmonton Centennial Celebrations Com., 1992. Russell scholar U. Toronto, 1956. Mem. Canadian Libr. Assn., Ontario Libr. Assn. (pres.), Libr. Assn. Alta., Alta. Pub. Libr. Dirs. Coun. (chair), Rotary Club of Downtown Edmonton (pub. rels. chmn. IVT Woman of Vision 1995, ABI Woman of Yr. 1995). Office: Edmonton Pub Libr, 7 Sir Winston Churchill Sq, Edmonton, AB Canada T5J 2V4

MCKEEL, LILLIAN PHILLIPS, education educator; b. Rocky Mount, N.C., Aug. 23, 1932; d. Ellis Elma and Lillian Bonner (Archbell) Phillips; m. James Thomas McKeel Jr., July 23, 1955; children: Sarah Lillian McKeel Youngblood, Mary Kathleen McKeel Welch. BA, U. N.C., 1954; MEd, Pa. State U., 1977, DEd, 1993. Tchr. State Coll. (Pa.) Area Schs., 1964-90; instr. Pa. State U., University Park, 1990-93; asst. prof. Shippensburg (Pa.) U., 1993-94; mem. of panel NSTA Book Rev. Panel/Outstanding Sci. Tradebooks for Children, Washington, 1992; faculty sponsor Shippensburg U. Sch. Study Coun., 1993-95. Contbr. articles to profl. jours. Recipient Presdl. award for Excellence in Sci. and Math. Tchng., NSF, Washington, 1990; finalist Tchr. of Yr. program Pa. Dept. Edn., Harrisburg, 1992, cert. Recognition, Hon. Robert Casey/Gov., Harrisburg, Pa., 1991; named Achieving Women of Penn State, Pa. State U., 1993. Mem. Nat. Sci. Tchrs. Assn., Soc. Presdl. Awardees, Assn. Edn. Tchrs. in Sci., Coun. Elem. Sci. Internat., Phi Delta Kappa (Disting. Svc. award 1992), Pi Lambda Theta, Phi Kappa Phi. Office: Shippensburg U 1871 Old Main Dr Shippensburg PA 17257-2200

MCKEEVER, MARY ALICE, science educator; b. Midland, Tex., June 8, 1957; d. Carl Daniel and Velmo Ann (Brummett) McK.; 1 child, Cody Zane. BS, Baylor U., 1980. Cert. tchr. specialities, English, life sci., earth sci. Tchr. sci. and math. Arlington (Tex.) Ind. Sch. Dist., 1980-82; all-level spl. edn. tchr. Hill Sch. Ft. Worth, Tex., 1982-84; tchr. 7th grade sci. Leander (Tex.) Jr. High, 1984—; com. mem. Dist.-wide Ednl. Improvement Com., Leander, 1992-94; sci. dept. head Leander Ind. Sch. Dist., 1993—; presenter Horizons Conf., 1994, Continuous Improvement Conf., 1995, 96. Contbr.: (video) Video Journal of Education, 1993; author poems. Campaign worker Doggett for Congress, Austin, 1984. Grantee GTE, 1992. Mem. ASCD, Tex. Outdoor Edn. Assn., PTA, Nat. Sci. Tchrs. Assn., Nat. Sci. Edn. Leadership Assn. Democrat. Home: 9817 Circle Dr # 331 Austin TX 78736 Office: Leander Jr High Sch 501 S Hwy 183N Leander TX 78641

MCKEITHEN, SUSAN CABOT, bank executive; m. m. R. Malloy McKeithen; 1 child, Veronica. BA in Humanities and Social Scis., Jacksonville U., 1973; postgrad., U. South Fla., Tampa, Queens Coll., Charlotte, N.C. Mgr. Jacksonville (Fla.) Br. Fed. Res. Bank of Atlanta, 1973-77; mgr. Barnett Banks of Fla., Inc., Atlanta, 1978-81; product mgr. Barnett Banks of Fla., Inc., Jacksonville, 1977-78; v.p. NationsBank of Fla., N.A., Tampa, 1981-90; sr. v.p. NationsBank of N.C., N.A., Charlotte, 1990-91; dir. AMRESCO Instl., Inc., Charlotte, 1991-94; sr. v.p. NationsBank N.A., Charlotte, 1994—. Vice chmn. N.C. Dance Theatre, Charlotte, 1994-95, chmn., 1995-96; mem. Charlotte Convs. and Visitors' Bur. Citizens Adv. Com., 1993, Friends of the Opera, Charlotte, Com. of 300 Tampa Bay Performing Arts Ctr.; food chmn. Zoofari, Tampa, 1988, 89; membership chmn. Lowry Pk. Zoo Aux. Bd., 1989, 90; countryside coord. Upper Pinellas Assn. Retarded Citizens, Tampa. Home: 228 Perrin Pl Charlotte NC 28207 Office: NC Dance Theatre 800 N College St Charlotte NC 28202

MCKELLAR, CAROLYN PERKINS, educational administrator; b. Memphis, Sept. 24, 1945; d. Robert Sidney Perkins and Edna (Luster) Lanning; children: Alice Anne Jacobs, Robert Clifton. BS, Miss. U. for Women, 1967; MS, Miss. State U., Starkville, 1969; EdD, U. Memphis, 1977. Lic. tchr., Tenn., Miss. Dir. of ednl. resources dept. family medicine U. Tenn., Memphis, 1981-84, assoc. dir., chief of edn. Boling Ctr. Devel. Disabilities, 1984—, asst. prof. pediats. Ctr. for Health Scis., 1994—, assoc. prof. allied health Ctr. for Health Scis., 1994—; cons., author, editor on grants dept. family medicine U. Tenn., Memphis, 1979. Asst. editor: (book) Patient Education in the Primary Care Setting, 1980; author numerous funded grants and articles. Mem. region IX adv. com. Tenn.'s Dept. Mental Health/Mental Retardation, Nashville, 1986—; vol. host. (syndicated radio show) Book Talk, Memphis/Shelby County Libr. Sta. WYPL, Memphis, 1989—; govtl. appointee Interagy. Coord. Coun., Nashville, 1996; mem. Mid-South ARC, pres., 1995—. Mem. Children and Youth Coun. (exec. bd. 1987—), Phi Kappa Phi (life), Kappa Delta Pi (sec. 1992—, pres. Lambda Gamma chpt. 1988). Home: 8010 Neshoba Rd Germantown TN 38138-3028 Office: U Tenn Boling Ctr Devel Disabil 711 Jefferson Memphis TN 38105

MCKELVY, NIKKI KAY, nurse; b. Honolulu, May 16, 1956; d. Donald and Virginia Katherine (Davis) McK.; m. David Stuart Murry, Dec. 9, 1978 (dec. 1992); children: Ryan Cobb, Caleb Murry. AA, Saddleback Coll., 1989; BSN, Dominican Coll., 1994. RN. Customer svc. clk. United Parcel Svc., Little Rock, 1974-78; resident/extern Vets. Hosp., Montrose, N.Y., 1993-94; staff nurse Harrison (Ark.) Nursing Ctr., 1995—. Recipient Student Leadership award Dominican Coll., Orangeberg, N.Y., 1994. Fellow Sigma Theta Tau; mem. Nursing Assn. Dominican Coll. (v.p. 1994—). Democrat. Roman Catholic. Home: Rt 7 Box 243-2C Harrison AR 72601

MCKENNA, FAY ANN, electrical manufacturing company executive; b. Bennington, Vt., Jan. 7, 1944; d. George Francis and Barbara Mae (Youngangel) Hoag; m. James Dennis McKenna, Sept. 3, 1963 (div. 1983); children: Russell (dec.), Laura, James, Sean, Michael. Student, Mercy Coll. Key punch operator N.Y. State Taxation and Fin. Dept., Albany, 1960-61; receptionist Trine Mfg./Square D Co., Bronx, 1972-76; clk. Square D Co., Bronx, 1976-78, exec. sec., 1978-79, personnel mgr., 1979-86; mgr. mktg. adminstrn. Trine Products Corp., 1986-89, adminstrv. mgr., 1989-92; prin. Bookkeeping & Tax Preparation Svc., 1976—; full charge bookkeeper Absolute Coatings Inc., New Rochelle, N.Y., 1994—. Mfg. Fund raiser YMCA, Bronx, 1979—; mem. Community Bd. #9, Bronx, 1984—. Recipient Svc. to Youth award YMCA, 1985. Mem. Adminstrv. Mgmt. Soc. Republican. Roman Catholic. Avocations: physical fitness, reading, interior decorating. Home and Office: 4100-20 Hutchinson River Pky E Bronx NY 10475

MCKENNA, JEANETTE ANN, archaeologist; b. N.Y.C., Aug. 6, 1953; d. Edward Patrick and Ann Jeanette (O'Brien) McKenna; children: Stephanie Jane, Daniel Glen Edward. AA in Phys. Edn., Mount San Antonio Jr. Coll., 1974; BA in Anthropology, Calif. State U., Fullerton, 1977, MA in Anthropology, 1982; postgrad., Ariz. State U., 1981-84, U. Calif., Riverside, 1991-92. Field archaeologist Archaeol. Rsch., Inc., Costa Mesa, Calif., 1976-79; rsch. asst. Calif. State U., 1979; lab. dir. Environ. Rsch. Archaeologists, L.A., 1978-79; staff archaeologist Ariz. State U., Tempe, 1979-82; rsch. archaeologist Soil Systems, Inc., Phoenix, 1982-84, Sci. Resource Surveys, Huntington Beach, Calif., 1984-87; co-owner, prin. Hatheway & McKenna, Mission Viejo, Calif., 1987-89; owner, prin. McKenna et al., Whittier, Calif., 1989—. Contbr. numerous articles to profl. jours. and reports. Bd. dirs. Whittier Conservancy, 1987—, interim treas., 1994, pres., 1994-95. Mem. Soc. Profl. Archaeologists (bd. dirs. 1993—), Archaeol. Inst. Am., Am. Soc. Conservation Archaeology, Am. Mus. Natural History, Soc. Am. Anthropology, Ariz. Archaeol. Coun., Ariz. Hist. Found., Calif. Hist. Soc., Nat. Arbor Day Found., Nat. Parks and Conservation Assn., Nat. Trust for Historic Preservation, Soc. Calif. Archaeology, Soc. Hist. Archaeology, S.W. Mus. Assn., Wilderness Soc., Whittier Conservancy, Southwestern Anthrop. Assn., Gene Autry Western Heritage Mus. Assn., Nature Conservancy, Smithsonian Assocs., Sierra Club, otehrs. Democrat. Roman Catholic. Home: 6008 Friends Ave Whittier CA 90601 Office: McKenna et al 6008 Friends Ave Whittier CA 90601

MCKENNA, KATHARINE LOUISE, artist, art gallery administrator; b. Berkeley, Calif., May 22, 1956; d. Malcolm Carnegie and Priscilla (Coffey) McK. BA in Am. Studies-Anthropology cum laude, Wesleyan U., Middletown, Conn., 1979; M Indsl. Design, Pratt Inst., 1984; student painting with Nicholas Buhalis, N.Y.C., 1989-92; student, Kingston (N.Y.) Sch. Art, 1989-92. Mus. asst. Mus. No. Ariz., Flagstaff, 1977-80; design asst. Ralph Appelbaum Assocs., N.Y.C., 1980-81; designer Albert Woods Design Assocs., N.Y.C., 1986-87; design cons. devel. div. Citicorp Inc., N.Y.C., 1988-89, IBM Citicorp Enterprise Br., Inc., N.Y.C., 1989-90; graphical user interface design cons. Market Focus Techs., N.Y.C., 1990-91, KLM Cons., N.Y.C., 1991-94; owner, dir. Coffey Gallery, Kingston, 1994—; mem. adv. bd. Unison Arts Ctr., New Paltz, N.Y., 1994—. Co-author: Hopis, Tewas and the American Road, 1983, 2d edit., 1986; exhibited in group shows Livingston Strauss Gallery, N.Y.C., Park West Gallery, Kingston, Warwick (N.Y.) Gallery, Woodstock (N.Y.) Artists Assn., Ezra and Cecile Zilkha Gallery, Wesleyan U., Unison Arts and Learning Ctr., New Paltz; represented in permanent collections Unison Arts Ctr., and pvt. collections. Mem. Arts Soc. Kingston (pres. 1995—), Woodstock Artists Assn. Office: Coffey Gallery 37 N Front St Kingston NY 12401

MCKENNA, KATHLEEN KWASNIK, artist; b. Detroit, Nov. 6, 1946; d. John J. and Eleanor H. (Ciosek) K.; m. Frank J. McKenna, Jr., Mar. 16, 1968. Cert., Cooper Sch. Art, Cleve., 1973; student, Art Students' League, N.Y.C., 1972, 74. Instr. portrait painting Baycrafters, Bay Village, Ohio, 1976-79; self-employed painter, 1972—. One-person shows include Ctrl. Nat. Bank, Cleve., 1975, Women's City Club Gallery, Cleve., 1979, Kennedy Ctr. Art Gallery, Hiram, Ohio, 1980, Chime Art Gallery, Summit, N.J., 1985, Bolton Art Gallery, Cleve., 1986, 91, Lakeland C.C. Gallery, Kirtland, Ohio, 1996; group shows include Butler Inst. Am. Art, 1981, 89, 91, 93, Mansfield (Ohio) Art Ctr., 1990, Circle Gallery, N.Y.C., 1978, Canton (Ohio) Art Inst., 1990, others. Recipient Pres.'s award Am. Artists Profl. League, 1993, other awards. Mem. New Orgn. for the Visual Arts, Catharine Lorillard Wolfe Art Club (Pastel Soc. plaque 1989, Mae Berlind Bach award 1983, Cert. of Merit 1981), Allied Artists Am. (assoc.; Gold medal of Honor 1989). Roman Catholic. Studio: 15914 Chadbourne Rd Shaker Heights OH 44120

MCKENNA, MARGARET ANNE, college president; b. R.I., June 3, 1945; d. Joseph John and Mary (Burns) McK.; children: Michael Aaron McKenna Miller, David Christopher McKenna Miller. BA in Sociology, Emmanuel Coll., 1967; postgrad., Boston Coll. Law Sch., 1968; JD, So. Meth. U., 1971; LLD (hon.), U. Upsala, N.J., 1978, Fitchburg (Mass.) State Coll., 1979, Regis Coll., 1982; D Community Affairs, U. R.I., 1979. Bar: Tex. 1971, D.C. 1973. Atty. Dept. Justice, Washington, 1971-73; exec. dir. Internat. Assn. Ofcl. Human Rights Agys., Washington, 1973-74; mgmt. cons. Dept. Treasury, Washington, 1975-76; dep. counsel to Pres. White House, Washington, 1976-79; dep. undersec. Dept. Edn., Washington, 1979-81; dir. Mary Ingraham Bunting Inst., Radcliffe Coll., Cambridge, Mass., 1981-85; v.p. program planning Radcliffe Coll., Cambridge, 1982-85; pres. Lesley Coll., Cambridge, 1985—; bd. dirs. Stride Rite Corp., Cambridge, Best Products Co., Inc., Richmond, Va., Consolidated Natural Gas Co., Pitts., Coun. of Ind. Colls., Washington. Chair higher edn. task force Clinton Transition, 1992-93; chair edn. task force Mayor Thomas Menino Transition Com., 1994. Recipient Outstanding Contribution award Civil Rights Leadership Conf., 1978; named Woman of Yr. Women's Equity Action League, 1979, Outstanding Woman of Yr. Big Sister Assn., 1986. Democrat. Office: Lesley Coll Office of the President 29 Everett St Cambridge MA 02138-2790*

MCKENNA, MARY PATRICIA, educational and human resources management consultant, performance technologist; b. N.Y.C.; d. Frank and Delia (Hannon) McK. BA in Edn., Seat of Wisdom Coll., 1967; MA in Sociology, Fordham U., 1971, MS in Guidance and Counseling, 1974, PhD in Counseling and Per. Svcs., 1979. Cert. in edn. and counseling, N.Y. Grad. asst. Fordham U., N.Y.C., 1973-75; with psychol. and career counseling dept. St. Francis Coll., Bklyn., 1976-83; adminstr. tng. & human resource devel. Coopers and Lybrand, N.Y.C., 1984-86; acad. dean The Berkeley Coll., N.Y.C., 1986-87; internal ednl. cons. Nat. Continuing Edn. Div. Price Waterhouse, N.Y.C., 1988-90; mgr. CPE Planning and Devel. N.Y. State Soc. CPAs, 1991-92; mgr. career and profl. devel. Deloitte & Touche, N.Y.C., 1993—. Author: Mid-Life Career Choices. Mem. APA, ACA, Nat. Soc. for Performance and Instrn., Nat. Career Devel. Assn., Phi Delta Kappa.

MCKENNA, NINA SCHLOESSER, lawyer; b. Topeka, Kans., June 18, 1955; d. Harvey Leopold and Patricia (Turk) Schloesser; m. Douglas Charles McKenna, Dec. 5, 1981; children: Sean, Nicholas, Dylan. BA cum laude, Williams Coll., 1977; JD, U. Kans. Law Sch., 1981. Bar: Kans. 1981, Mo. 1983. Atty. Alder, Nelson & McKenna, Overland Park, Kans., 1981-83; gen. counsel Oppenheimer Industries, Kansas City, Mo., 1983-85; regional counsel dist. 4 Nat. Assn. Securities Dealers, Inc., Kansas City, Mo., 1985—; securities adv. bd. Mo. Sec. State, Jefferson City, 1991-94. Office: NASD 120 W 12th St Ste 900 Kansas City MO 64105

MCKENNEE, ARDEN NORMA, art educator, retired, consultant; b. N.Y.C.; d. Archibald McKennee and Norma (Bischof) Kirkley. BA, U. Minn., 1953. Exec. sec. John & Mable Ringling Mus. of Art, Sarasota, Fla., 1964-79, mus. edn. programmer, 1980-94; ret., 1994. Mem. Very Spl. Arts Adv. Bd. for Sarasota County, 1988-94. Mem. Nat. Art Edn. Assn., Delta Gamma Alumni Assn.

MCKENNEY, BETSY RUSSELL, artist; b. Petersburg, Va., June 29, 1949; d. Frank Dargan Jr. McK. and Betty (Russell) Steele. BFA, Va. Commonwealth U., 1972; MFA, Radford U., 1994. Mktg. mgr. T.M.W. Industries, Troutville, Va., 1980-83; mktg. dir., gen. mgr. Azalia Mall, Richmond, Va., 1987-91, Tirangle Mall, Raleigh, N.C., 1991; instr. art Radford (Va.) U., 1992-94, Govs. Sch. for Arts, Norfolk, Va., 1994-95, Va. Commonwealth U., Richmond, 1994—. One-woman show Radford U. Galleries, 1993; group shows include Artspace Gallery, 1991, Anderson Gallery, 1995. Treas. ARC, Roanoke, Va., 1984-86. Teaching fellow Radford U., 1992-94. Mem. Phi Kappa Phi. Presbyterian.

MCKENNEY, GLADYS HOLDEMAN, educational consultant, artist; b. Jackson, Mich., Jan. 5, 1928; d. Walter Ray and Florence Hester (Barthel) Holdeman; m. Robert Dorion McKenney, June 10, 1950; children: Wayne Brian, Cathleen Renee (dec.), Michael Brent, Marcia Lynn, Linda Denise. BA in Psychology, Mich. State U., 1949; MEd in Guidance, Wayne State U., 1963, EdD, 1979. Permanent tchg. cert. Mich. State Bd. Edn. H.S. English tchr. Beaverton (Mich.) Pub. Schs., 1950-51; H.S. social studies tchr. Rochester (Mich.) Schs., 1965-83; pres. McKenney Ednl. Cons., Rochester, 1982—, ind. and family counseling, 1983-87, creator, spkr. Women's History Project, 1984—. Author, actress (one-woman play) Our Fabulous Foremothers--A Celebration, 1984, (audio tape) Votes for Women, 1990; sculpture, artist, mus. exhibitor. Pres. North Oakland NOW, Rochester, 1979-80. Chataqua Presenter grantee Mich. Humanitites Coun., 1992-96. Mem. AAUW (Rochester ednl. found. chair 1995-96), LWV, Mich. Assn. Ret. Sch. Pers., Mich. Women's Studies Assn., Storyteller's Guild.

MCKENNEY, IRENE JUNE, business manager, former educator; b. Hutchinson, Kans., June 8, 1930; d. William Paul and Ethel Ida (Laabs) Radtke; widowed, Feb. 1985; children: Judy Floy, Kent Floy, Timothy Floy, Jane Floy, Paul Floy; m. 2d, June 30, 1990. Std. elem. tchg. cert., Wartburg Coll., 1950; BS, Westmore Coll., 1963; MS, N.D. State U., 1970, Drake U., 1979. Cert. elem. tchr., Iowa, Minn.; cert. secondary tchr., Iowa. Tchr. 1st grade pub. sch. Emmetsburg, Iowa, 1950-52, LeSuer, Minn., 1952-53, Olivia, Minn., 1953-54; substitute tchr. pub. sch. LeMars and Osage, Iowa, 1960-75; secondary tchr. Carroll (Iowa) H.S., 1975-90; psychologist Des Moines Area C.C., Carroll, 1980-83; bus. mgr. N.W. Iowa Radiology, P.C., Storm Lake, Iowa, 1990—; instr. Parent Effectiveness, Iowa, 1972-75, Tchr. Effectiveness, Carroll, 1976-78. Pres. Iowa Luth. Pastor's Wives, Des Moines, 1974-76; bd. dirs. Ingham Okoboji Luth. Bible Camp, 1992—. Mem. AAUW, Profl. Assn. Health Care Mgrs. (cert., bus. mgr. 1990—). Republican. Lutheran. Home: PO Box 901 1700 W 5th St Storm Lake IA 50588-0901

MCKENNY, COLLIN GRAD, banker; b. Seattle, July 29, 1944; d. Edward Paul and Betty B. (Collins) Grad; m. Jon W. McKenny, June 15, 1975 (div. June 1982); m. Spencer Frank Ison, Dec. 31, 1985. BA, U. Wash., Seattle, 1966; MBA, Seattle U., 1969; grad., Pacific Coast Banking Sch., 1979. From mgmt. trainee to v.p. Peoples Nat. Bank, Seattle, 1966-85; sr. v.p. Barclays Bank of Calif., San Francisco, 1985-88, Star Banc Corp., Cin., 1988—. Treas. Salvation Army, Federal Way, Wash., 1981-83; bd. dirs. Boys and Girls Clubs, Seattle, 1982-85; mem. risk adv. bds. Visa USA and Visa International. Mem. Am. Bankers Assn. (bd. dirs. bancard exec. com., chmn. ann. conf. 1989—, chmn. bankcard schools 1990-94), Cin. Bus. Incubator (chmn.), Bankers Club, Chi Omega. Office: Star Banc Corp 311 Elm St PO Box 956 Cincinnati OH 45201-0956

MCKENZIE, DIANA LYNNE, information technology executive; b. Indpls., Oct. 6, 1964; d. Donald Raymond and Marian Sue (Cheaney) Seib; m. Paul Michael McKenzie, June 4, 1988; children: Paul Aaron Geza, Evan Nicholas Medvegy. BS, Purdue U., 1986. From med. sys. analyst to mgr. regulatory affairs Lilly & Co., Indpls., 1987—. Office: Eli Lilly & Co Lilly Corp Ctr Indianapolis IN 46285

MCKENZIE, KAY BRANCH, public relations executive; b. Atlanta, Feb. 12, 1936; d. William Harllee and Katherine (Hunter) Branch; m. Harold Cantrell McKenzie, Jr., Apr. 11, 1958; children: Ansley, Katherine, Harold Cantrell III. Student, Sweet Briar Coll., 1955, Emory U., 1956-57. Account exec. Hill and Knowlton Inc., Atlanta, 1979-80, account supr./dir. S.E. govt.

rels., 1981-83; ptnr. McKenzie, Gordon & Potter, Atlanta, 1983-85; pres. McKenzie & Assocs. Inc., Atlanta, 1986-89; sr. v.p. Manning Selvage & Lee, Atlanta, 1989-93; v.p. comm. and creative svcs. 1996 Atlanta Paralympic Games, 1993-96. Mem. Commn. on Future of South, 1974; co-chmn. John Lewis for Congress, Atlanta, 1986; bd. dirs. Bedford Pines Day Care Ctrs., Atlanta, 1987-92, Ga. Clean and Beautiful, 1987-88, Ga. Fund for Edn., 1987-92; regional bd. dirs. Inst. Internat. Edn., 1987-93. Fellow Internat. Bus. Fellows (bd. dirs. 1983-85, 92-93, v.p. 1986-88); mem. Pub. Rels. Soc. Am., Ga. C. of C. (bd. dirs. 1983—), Leadership Atlanta. Democrat. Episcopalian. Home: 172 Huntington Rd NE Atlanta GA 30309-1504 Office: 1201 W Peachtree St NW Ste 2500 Atlanta GA 30309-3400

MCKENZIE, LORENE LANDS, marriage and family counselor, educator; b. Arab, Ala., Mar. 3, 1932; d. Alver Lee and Maggie Jane (Nixon) Lands; m. Jesse E. McKenzie, Nov. 22, 1947; children: Barbara Hemrick, Dennis, Rayford J., Debbie Argo, Dianne Morgan. BA in Psychology, West Ga. Coll., 1977, MEd, 1980, postgrad., 1982. Clergy counselor Mt. Pleasant Bapt. Ch., Carrollton, Ga., 1964-84; tchr. Bremen (Ga.) High Sch., 1980-81, Spemedial-Bowdon H.S., 1981-82, Heritage Pvt. Sch., Newman, Ga., 1982-83; pvt. practice counselor in field; indsl. supr. Sewell Mfg. Co., Bremen, Ga., 1970-72, mental health counselor, Carrrollton, 1978. Chaperoned tour group pen-pals to Eng.; mem. Rep. campaign, Carrollton, 1980; speaker, Bible lectr. to women's groups. Home and Office: 218 Perry St Carrollton GA 30117-2423

MCKENZIE, MARY BETH, artist; b. Cleve.; d. William Jennings and Mary Elizabeth (McCray) McK.; m. Tony Mysak, May 8, 1974; children: Zsuzsa McKenzie Mysak, Maria McKenzie Mysak. Student, Mus. Fine Arts, Boston, 1964-65, Cooper Sch. Art, Cleve., 1965-67; diploma, Nat. Acad. Design, N.Y.C., 1974. Painting instr. Nat. Acad. Design, N.Y.C., 1981—. Author: A Painterly Approach, 1987; contbr. articles to profl. jours.; one-woman shows include Nat. Arts Club, N.Y.C., 1976, FAR Gallery, N.Y.C., 1980, Perin and Sharpe Gallery, New Canaan, Conn., 1981, Frank Caro Gallery, N.Y.C., 1988-89, Joseph Keiffer Gallery, N.Y.C., 1991; exhibited in group shows at Sindin Gallery, N.Y.C., 1985-86; permanent collections include Met. Mus. Art, N.Y.C., The Butler Mus. Am. Art, Mus. City of N.Y., NAD, Art Student's League of N.Y. Recipient Nat. Scholastic award Mus. Fine Arts, Boston, numerous awards including Thomas B. Clark prize and the Isaac N. Maynard prize Nat. Acad. Design, Greenshields Found. grantee, Stacey Found. grantee. Mem. Nat. Acad. Design, Pastel Soc. Am. (Best In Show, Award of Exceptional Merit, Exhbn. Com. award), Allied Artists Am. (Gold medal, The Jane Peterson award, Grumbacher Cash award, Silver medal), Audubon Artists (Pastel Soc. Am. award). Home: 525 W 45th St New York NY 10036-3405

MCKENZIE, SUSAN SMITH, business writer; b. N.Y.C., Dec. 30, 1964; d. John Brewster and Ida (Hawa) Smith. BA in English, Tex. A&M U., 1986; MA in Journalism, Ind. U., 1988. Parachutist and broadcast journalist 1st Special Ops. Command, Ft. Bragg, N.C., 1989-91; media rels. journalist U.S. Army Parachute Team - Golden Knights, Ft. Bragg, N.C., 1991-92; TV reporter Sta. WLTX-TV, Columbia, S.C., 1992; bus. writer The Herald, Rock Hill, S.C., 1992-94; plant comms. specialist Brunswick Nuclear Plant Carolina Power & Light, Southport, 1994—. With U.S. Army, 1988-92, Panama, Persian Gulf. Recipient South Korean Jump Wings Republic of Korea Spl. Warfare Ctr., 1989. Mem. Women in Communications, Inc., Nat. Press Photographers Assn. Presbyterian. Home: 3917 Mayfield Ct Wilmington NC 28412-0965 Office: Carolina Power & Light PO Box 10429 Southport NC 28461-0429

MCKENZIE-ANDERSON, RITA LYNN, psychologist; b. Boston, Nov. 25, 1952; d. Wallace Andrew and Angelina Rita (Bagnoli) McK; m. Brien Anderson, Oct. 22, 1994. BA, Framingham State Coll., 1974; MEd, Northeastern U., 1975; PhD, Temple U., 1983. Lic. psychologist, Mass. Pvt. practice Fairfield, Conn., 1984-86; psychologist Johnson Life Ctr., Springfield, Mass., 1986-87, dir. outpatient therapy, 1987-88; pvt. practice Springfield, 1988—; investigator Springfield Juvenile Ct., 1989—; adj. faculty Holyoke (Mass.) Community Coll., 1989-90, Springfield Tech. Community Coll., 1989-90; dir. day treatment DuBois Day Treatment Ctr., Stamford, Conn., 1982-86; cons. psychologist Community Care Mental Health Ctr., Springfield, 1989—, Spofford Hall Treatment Ctr., Ludlow, Mass., 1991-92. Trustee Northampton (Mass.) State Hosp., 1989-93; mem. organizing com. Week of Young Child, Springfield, 1988-93; bd. dirs. Stop Abuse Against Kids. Mem. Women Bus. Owners Alliance, Zonta Internat. Office: 380 Union St Ste 14 West Springfield MA 01089-4123

MCKENZIE-MITIKU, KATHY E., auditor; b. Sanford, N.C., June 21, 1963; d. Leo Sr. and Doris Edna (McIver) McKenzie; m. Fassil M. Mitiku, Sept. 17, 1988; children: Theodros, Solomon George-Edward. BA, Duke U., 1985; student, Harvard U., 1985; MPA, U. Tex., 1987. Legis. aide to rep. Al Price Tex. State Legislature, 1987; eligibility specialist Dept. Social Svcs. Guilford County, 1987; budget and evaln. analyst City of Winston-Salem (N.C.), 1988-92, dir. internal audit, 1992—; Spkr. Nat. Assn. Black Accts., Winston-Salem, 1996; adv. Smart Start Ednl. Program, 1996. Budget dir. Hawley House, 1988-92; bd. dirs. Bethlehem Cmty. Ctr., 1988-89. Mem. Twin City Civitan Club (sec. 1989-91), Internat. City/County Mgmt. Assn., Inst. Internal Auditors, Inst. Mgmt. Accts. Baptist. Office: City of Winston-Salem 225 W 5th St #110 Winston Salem NC 27102

MCKEOWN, MARY ELIZABETH, educational administrator, medical office manager; d. Raymond Edmund and Alice (Fitzgerald) McNamara; BS, U. Chgo., 1946; MS, DePaul U., 1953; m. James Edward McKeown, Aug. 6, 1955. Supr. high sch. dept. Am. Sch., 1948-68, prin., 1968—, trustee, 1975—, v.p., 1979, exec. v.p., 1992—. Mem. ASCD, LWV, Nat. Assn. Secondary Sch. Prins., North Cen. Assn. Colls. and Schs. (exec. bd. 1990-93). Assn., Nat. Home Study Coun. (chairperson rsch. and edn. com. 1988-93). Author study guides for algebra, geometry and calculus. Home: 5120 Deblin Ln Oak Lawn IL 60453 Office: 2200 E 170th St Lansing IL 60438

MCKEOWN, REBECCA J., principal; b. Wayne, Okla., Apr. 4, 1937; d. William S. and Ila Rebekah (Mitchell) Lackey; m. Loren Ferris, Apr. 5, 1958; children: Michael, Thomas, Nancy, David. BS, Okla. State U., 1966; MEd, U. Okla., 1976. Cert. elem. tchr., elem. prin. 6th grade tchr. Ponca City (Okla.) Pub. Schs., 1966-67; 1st and 6th grade tchr. Peru Elem. Sch., Auburn, Nebr., 1967-69; 4th grade tchr. Woodland Hills Sch., Lawton, Okla., 1971-76; asst. prin. Douglass Learning Ctr., Lawton, Okla., 1976-78; prin. Lincoln Elem. Sch., Lawton, Okla., 1978-84, Hugh Bish Elem., Lawton, Okla., 1984—. Recipient Disting. Achievement award Lawton Bd. Edn., 1992, Adminstr. of Yr. award Lawton Area Reading Coun., 1993, Arts Adminstr. of Yr. award Okla. Alliance for Arts, 1993, Nat. Blue Ribbon Sch. Recognition award 1993-94, D.A.R.E. Adminstrn. award Lawton Police Dept., 1993. Mem. ASCD, Okla. Reading Coun., Okla. ASCD, Lawton Area Reading Coun., Elem. Prins. Assn. (pres. 1986-87). Democrat. Methodist. Home: 6 SW 71st St Lawton OK 73505-6615 Office: Lawton Pub Schs 751 NW Fort Sill Blvd Lawton OK 73507-5421

MCKERROW, AMANDA, ballet dancer; b. Albuquerque; d. Alan and Constance McKerrow; m. John Gardner. Student, Met. Acad. Ballet, Bethesda, Md., Washington Sch. Ballet. With Washington Ballet Co., 1980-82; with Am. Ballet Theatre, N.Y.C., 1982—, soloist, from 1983, prin. dancer, 1987—. Toured Europe with Washington Ballet; danced in Margot Fonteyn Gala at Metropolitan Opera House; featured in Pavlova Tribute film, also many guest appearances; leading roles in Ballet Imperial, La Bayadere, Manon, Birthday Offering, Dim Lustre, Donizetti Variations, Giselle, Graduation Ball, The Leaves Are Fading, Nine Sinatra Songs, The Nutcracker, Pillar of Fire, Requiem, Romeo and Juliet, The Sleeping Beauty, Les Sylphides, Push Comes to Shove, Symphony Concertante, Symphonic Variations, Theme and Variations, Stravinsky Violin Concerto, Swan Lake, Triad, Duets, Etudes, Coppelia, Voluntaries and Rodeo; created leading role in Bruch Violin Concerto No. 1, Some Assembly Required and Agnus De Mille's The Other. Recipient N.Y. Woman award for dance, 1991; co-winner gold prize for women Moscow Internat. Ballet Competition, 1981. Office: Am Ballet Theatre 890 Broadway New York NY 10003-1211

MCKIE, CAROLIN LAVERN, elementary education educator; b. Hollywood, Fla., Jan. 22, 1955; d. Roman Scott, Jr. and Tryphena (Pratt) Childs; m. Sheldon Oliver McKie, Dec. 8, 1973 (div. Jan. 14, 1981); 1 child, Christopher Noel. AA, Compton (Calif.) C.C., 1979; BS, U. So. Calif., 1982; MA, Calif. State U. Dominguez Hill, Carson, 1990. Pre-sch. tchr. Child Care Ctr. Compton C.C., 1978-79; tchr. Compton Coll., 1979-80; tchr. PACE Head Start, L.A., 1980-82, Urban League - Head Start, L.A., 1982-83, L.A. Unified Sch. Dist., 1984—; UCLA leadership conf./multiple subject instructorship, lang. devel. specialist; active UCLA math. and scis. projects, 1991-94; mem. Calif. Lit. Project, Calif. State U. Dominguez Hills, 1990; coord. Track C Miramonte Sch., L.A., 1988-90; sch.-based mgmt. Miramonte Sch., L.A. Unified Sch. Dist., 1989-91. Mem. Double Rock Bapt. Ch., mass choir, treas. 1993—, v.p. community outreach 1994—, asst. dir. 1995—; mem. Ch. of God of Prophecy, dir. Vacation Bible Sch., 1976-77, Sunday Sch. clk., treas. 1976-77, children's ch. dir. 1974-76. CTIP grantee L.A. Unified Sch. Dist., 1988; Toyota grantee Toyota Found., L.A., 1993; Title VII grantee OBEMLA, Washington, 1994-97. Mem. HUMIFA (v.p. 1994—). Home: 212 W Regent St #17 Inglewood CA 90301 Office: Miramonte Elem Sch 1400 E 68th St Los Angeles CA 90001

MCKILLIP, PATRICIA CLAIRE, operatic soloist; b. Milw., Apr. 28; d. Lester J. and Ruth J. (Lohneis) McK.; m. Mark Richard McKillip, June 16, 1990. BA in English-Drama, Creative Writing, Lit., Alverno Coll., 1980; MusB in Applied Music, Alverno Coll., Milw., 1981; postgrad., Wis. Conservatory of Mus., 1981-82, U. Wis., Milw., 1982, The Juilliard Sch., 1982-84, Am. Acad. Dramatic Arts, 1983-84, Adelphi U., 1984; MS in Fine Arts Edn., U. Wis., Milw., 1996, MS in English-Creative Writing and Lit., 1997. Soloist Amadeus Opera Co.; instr. vocal music seminars various high schs., N.Y.; co-founder, co-dir. The Masque Consort, N.Y.C., 1990-91, exec. v.p., 1991; v.p., co-founder Creative Learning Assocs.; instr. Cardinal Stritch Coll., Milw., 1994—. Performed with numerous opera cos. including The Florentine Opera Co., Music Under the Stars Prodns., Milw. Opera Co., Westchester Lyric Opera Co., Profl. Opera Workshop at Lincoln Ctr., Met. Opera Co., N.Y. Grand Opera Co., Monteverdi Opera Guild Prodns., Republic Opera Co., La Puma Opera Co., and other chamber, theater and folk groups; puppeteer, costumer, designer Puppet Art Troupe; performed in over 50 mus. shows and prodns., 6 solo recitals, also medieval concerts, choruses, orchestras, oratorio; 42 other recitals. Exec. v.p. Masque Consort, a multi-media theatrical orgn. Music dept. scholar Alverno U. Mem. AFTRA, SAG, Nat. Assn. Music Tchrs., Music Educators Nat. Conf. (treas.), Internat. Platform Assn., Wis. Fedn. Music Clubs, Music Clubs Am., Am. Guild Mus. Artists, Q'ahal-Liturgical Music Soc., Delta Omicron (v.p., chaplain, warden Gamma Gamma chpt., WMA State and Regional Vocal award 1978, Star of Delta Omicron award 1980, 40 music medals from state and dist. WSMA), Alpha Sigma Tau. Democrat. Roman Catholic. Home: 4860 S 69th St Greenfield WI 53220-4452

MCKINLESS, KATHY JEAN, accountant; b. Augusta, Ga., June 15, 1954; d. Jack M. and Jean K. (Norby) VanderWood; m. Darryl P. Calderon, Mar. 17, 1979 (dec. June 1988); children: Christopher, Jackie; m. Richard T. McKinless, July 1, 1989; children: Ashley, Thomas. BS in Acctg., U. S.C., 1975, MBA, 1978. CPA, D.C. Acct. Clarkson, Harden & Gantt, Columbia, 1975-79; sr. acct. KPMG Peat Marwick, Washington, 1979-80, mgr., 1980-86, ptnr., 1986—; spkr. Mortgage Bankers Assn., Fin. Mgrs. Soc., Nat. Assn. Coll. and Univ. Bus. Officers, Fed. Fin. Insts. Exam. Coun., Diocesan Fiscal Mgrs. Mem. governance com., treas., pres. bd. dirs. Nations Capital coun. Girl Scouts U.S., 1985—; mem. fin. com. Cath. Charities, U.S.A. Mem. AICPAs, D.C. Inst. CPAs. Office: KPMG Peat Marwick 2001 M St NW Washington DC 20036-3310

MCKINLEY, CATHERINE ELIZABETH, writer, editor; b. Boston, Apr. 25, 1967; d. Donald Sellers and Elizabeth (Wilson) McK. Student, U. West Indies, Mona, Jamaica, 1987-88; BA, Sarah Lawrence Coll., 1989; postgrad. Africana Studies, Cornell U., 1989-91. Editorial asst. The Feminist Press of CUNY, N.Y.C., 1991-92; assoc. Marie Brown Assocs., Literary Svcs., N.Y.C., 1992-94; editor pvt. practice, N.Y.C., 1994-96; writing instr. Eugene Lang Coll. New Sch. for Social Rsch., N.Y.C., 1995—; coord. PEN writers fund coord., PEN open book com. PEN Am., 1996—. Editor: Afrekete: An Anthology of Black Lesbian Writing, 1995; author: Sisters: A Reunion Story, in The Adoption Reader, 1995, chpt. in Black Women in Am., 1993. Recipient Andre Lorde Emerging Writer award Andre Lorde Estate, 1995; MacDowell Colony for Arts resident, 1996; N.Y. Found. for Arts fiction grantee, 1996. Mem. Black Women in Publishing. Home: 291 13th St Brooklyn NY 11215 Office: Charlotte Sheedy Lit Agy 65 Bleeker St New York NY 10012

MCKINLEY, ELLEN BACON, priest; b. Milw., June 9, 1929; d. Edward Alsted and Lorraine Goodrich (Graham) Bacon; m. Richard Smallbrook McKinley, III, June 16, 1951 (div. Oct. 1977); children: Richard IV, Ellen Graham, David Todd, Edward Bacon. BA cum laude, Bryn Mawr Coll., 1951; MDiv Yale U., 1976; STM, Gen. Theol. Sem., N.Y.C., 1979; PhD, Union Theol. Sem., N.Y.C., 1988. Ordained to ministry Episcopal Ch. as deacon, 1980, as priest, 1981. Intern St. Francis Ch., Stamford, Conn., 1976-77; pastoral asst. St. Paul's Ch., Riverside, Conn., 1979-80, curate, 1980-81; priest assoc. St. Saviour's Ch., Old Greenwich, Conn., 1982-90; asst. St. Christopher's Ch., Chatham, Mass., 1987-88, interim asst., Trinity Ch., Princeton, N.J., 1990-91; priest assoc. All Saints Ch., Princeton, 1992—, interim rector, 1993; mem. major chpt. Trinity Cathedral, Trenton, 1992-96. Mem. Episcopal Election Com., Diocese of Conn., 1986-87, Com. on Human Sexuality, 1987-90; Com. on Donations and Bequests Diocese of Conn., 1987-90; sec., Greewich Com. on Drugs, 1970-71; bd. dirs. Greenwich YWCA, 1971-72. Mem. Episcopal Women's Caucus, Colonial Dames Am., Jr. League. Clubs: Sulgrave.

MCKINLEY, (JENNIFER CAROLYN) ROBIN, writer; b. Warren, Ohio, Nov. 16, 1952; d. William and Jeanne Carolyn (Turrell) McK; m. Peter Dickinson, Jan. 3, 1992. Student, Dickinson Coll., 1970-72; BA, Bowdoin Coll., 1975, PhD (hon.), 1986. Editor, transcriber Ward and Paul, Washington, 1972-73; rsch. asst. Rsch. Assocs., Brunswick, Maine, 1976-77; tchr., counselor pvt. secondary sch., Natick, Maine, 1978-79; edit. asst. Little, Brown & Co., Boston, 1979-81; barn mgr. horse farm Holliston, Mass., 1981-82; clerk Books of Wonder, N.Y.C., 1983—; freelance reader, copy and line editor, 1983—. Author: Beauty: A Retelling of the Story of Beauty and the Beast, 1978 (Horn book Honor list citation 1978), The Door in the Hedge, 1981, The Blue Sword, 1982 (Best Young adult books citation ALA 1982, Newbery Honor citation 1983), The Hero and the Crown, 1984 (Horn book honor list citation 1985, John Newbery medal 1985), The Outlaws of Sherwood, 1988, Rowan, 1992, My Father is in the Navy, 1992, Deerskin, 1993 (Best Young Adult Books citation ALA 1993, Best Adult Books for Young Adults citation ALA 1993), A Knot in the Grain and Other Stories, 1994, The Sea King's Son, 1994; contbr.: Elsewhere Vol. II, 1982, Vol. III, 1984, Faery, 1985, Writers for Children, 1988; editor, contbr.: Imaginary Lands, 1985 (World Fantasy award Best Anthology 1986); adapter: Jungle Book Tales, 1985, Black Beauty, 1986, The Light Princess, 1988. Address: Bramdean Lodge, Bramdean, Alresford, Hants SO24 0JN, England*

MCKINLEY BALFOUR, STEPHANIE ANN, learning resources director, librarian; b. Galesburg, Ill., Mar. 27, 1948; d. William Chester and Virginia Ann (Clugsten) McKinley; m. James Robert Miller, Mar. 2, 1968 (div. Mar. 1978); 1 child, Christopher Antonin Miller; m. David Alan Balfour, Nov. 23, 1991. BA in Speech, Drama, Western Ill. U., 1970; MLS, Drexel U., 1974. Cert. tchr., Ill., media specialist, Ill. Libr. William McKinley Elem. Sch., Phila., 1971-76, Regional Jr. H.S., Amherst, Mass., 1976-77, Garfield Elem. Sch., Monmouth, Ill., 1977-79; dir. learning resources Spoon River Valley Sch. Dist., London Mills, Ill., 1979-95; dir. librs. Spoon River Valley Sch. Dist./Avon Sch. Dist., Ill., 1995—; dir. summer reading program Avon (Ill.) Pub. Libr., 1980-95. Leader 4-H, Avon, 1983-92; vol. EMT Galesburg Hosp. Ambulance Svc., Galesburg/Avon, 1978—; dir. religious edn. Avon Federated Ch., 1984—. Named Outstanding Young Educator by Monmouth Jaycees, 1979. Mem. Am. Found. Vision Awareness Ill. Affiliate (pres.), Nat. Edn. Assn., Ill. Edn. Assn., Ill. Sch. Libr. Media Assn., Phi Delta Kappa, Gamma Lambda-Delta Kappa Gamma Soc. Internat. (pres. 1992-94, 1st v.p. 1990-92, recording sec. 1988-92). Republican. Mem. United Ch. of Christ. Home: RR2 274 Funcheon Ct Avon IL 61415 Office: Spoon River Valley Sch Dist RR 1 London Mills IL 61544-9801

MCKINNEY, BETSY, state legislator; b. Bangor, Maine, Mar. 24, 1939. BS, Bentley Coll., 1972. Accountant N.H.; mem. N.H. Ho. Rep., mem. budget com., 1977-81, 87-88, mem. regulated revenues com.; del. N.H. Constl. Conv., 1984. Treas. Friends of the Libr., 1988—; chmn. Old Home Day, 1990, treas., 1978—; chmn. Rockingham County Exec. Com., 1991-92; mem. Londonderry Charter Commn., 1995; mem. Libr. Bldg. Com., 1995-96; treas. N.H. OWLs, 1994—. Recipient Citizen of the Yr. award City of Londonderry, 1987. Mem. Londonderry C. of C. (treas. 1980-88). Republican. Roman Catholic. Home and Office: 120 Litchfield Rd Londonderry NH 03053-7407

MCKINNEY, BRENDA JANE, mathematics educator; b. Longview, Tex., Sept. 15, 1948; d. Billy Joe and Betty Jane (Smith) Cabbiness; m. Ronald Lester McKinney, Sept. 10, 1966; children: Kit, Jeff. BS in Math., Stephen F. Austin U., MS in Math. Tchr. math. Forest Park Jr. High Sch., Longview, Tex., 1973-76, Longview High Sch., 1976-79, 85—, Spring Hill High Sch., Longview, 1979-85. Mem. NEA, Nat. Coun. Tchrs. Math., Tex. State Tchrs. Assn., Tex. Coun. Tchrs. Math., East Tex. Coun. Tchrs. Math., Deep East Tex. A&M Mothers Club. Home: RR 2 Box 260 Longview TX 75605-9637 Office: Longview High Sch 201 E Tomlinson Pky Longview TX 75601

MCKINNEY, BRENDA KAY, nursing educator; b. Bakerfield, Calif., Sept. 25, 1962; d. Jerry and Linda Sue (Perkins) Murray; m. Carl Dewayne McKinney, Aug. 8, 1980. Diploma, Black River Vo-Tech., Pocahontas, Ark., 1987; ASN, Park Coll., 1994. RN, Ark., Mo.; cert. ACLS. Nursing instr. Black River Tech. Coll., Pocahontas, 1990—. Home: 6062 Hwy 67 N Corning AR 72422-9762

MCKINNEY, CAROLYN JEAN, lawyer; b. Holly Springs, Miss., Sept. 28, 1956; d. Walter H. and Elizabeth (Lawrence) McK. BA in History and Polit. Sci., Rust Coll., Holly Springs, 1977; JD, Harvard U., 1980. Bar: Tex. 1980, U.S. Dist. Ct. (no., ea., so. and we. dists.) Tex. 1980, Ill. 1995. Atty. Gulf Oil Corp., Houston, 1980-84; sr. atty. ARCO, Dallas, 1984-90; atty. Amoco Corp., Houston, 1990-94, 1996—, Chgo., 1994-96; vis. prof., mentor black exec. exch. program Nat. Urban League, 1985—; mem. adv. bd. Nat. Soc. Black Engrs., 1987—. Vol. Meals on Wheels program Vis. Nurse's Assn., 1985, Kid Care, 1992; participant Miss. Gov.'s Leadership Conf. on Youth, 1988. Recipient Outstanding Alumni award Nat. Assn. for Equal Opportunity in Higher Edn., 1989. Mem. ABA. Office: Amoco Corp 501 Westlake Park Blvd Houston TX 77079

MCKINNEY, CYNTHIA ANN, congresswoman; b. Mar. 17, 1955; d. Billy and Leola McKinney; 1 child, Coy Grandison, Jr. B, U. So. Calif.; postgrad., Ga. State U., U. Wis.; Tufts U. Former instr. Clark Atlanta U., Atlanta Met. Coll.; former mem. Ga. Ho. of Reps.; mem. 103rd Congress from 11th Ga. dist., 1993—, mem. banking and fin. svcs. com. housing and cmty. devel., mem. internat. rels. com. internat. ops. and human rights; instr. Agnes Scott Coll. Diplomatic fellow Spellman Coll. Home: 765 Shorter Ter NW Atlanta GA 30318-7140 Office: US Ho of Reps 124 Cannon Washington DC 20515*

MCKINNEY, ELIZABETH ANNE, government purchasing professional; b. Austin, Tex., Mar. 28, 1962; d. Richard Raymond Sr. and Frances Hester (Coleman) Blair; m. Richard Allen McKinney Jr., Sept. 25, 1993. Student, Averett Coll., 1994—. Clk. typist Fairfax County Govt. Purchasing, Fairfax, Va., 1986-87, jr./asst. buyer, 1987-89, buyer I-contract adminstr., 1989-93, buyer II-contract adminstr., 1993—; adv. mem. regional coop. svc. team Dept. Fire and Rescue, Washington, 1995—; mem Met. Washington Coun. Govts. Purchasing Officers Com., 1994—. Mem. Nat. Inst. Govtl. Purchasing (cert. profl. pub. buyer, sec. Met. Washington chpt. 1993-94, treas. 1994-95, v.p. 1995-96), Internat. Coalition for Procurement Stds. Episcopal.

MCKINNEY, JANE-ALLEN, artist and educator; b. Owensboro, Ky., Jan. 8, 1952; d. William Holland and Jane Wilhoit (Moore) McK. BA, Scarritt Coll., Nashville, 1974; MA, Vanderbilt U., 1977; MFA, Memphis Coll. of Art, 1993. Grad. asst. dept. art Peabody Coll. for Tchrs., Vanderbilt U., Nashville, 1975-76; tchr. Smyrna (Tenn.) Comprehensive Vocat. Ctr., 1977-78; pres., bd. dirs. Jane Allen Flighton Artworks Inc., Nashville, 1978—; jeweler Wright's Jewelry Store, Clarksville, Tenn., 1982; tchr. art Belmont U., Nashville, 1984-88, Met. Centennial Park Art Ctr., Nashville, 1988-91, Cheekwood Mus. of Art, Nashville, 1990-94, Nossi Coll. of Art, Nashville, 1991-94, Western Ky. U., Bowling Green, 1991-94; ednl. cons. fine art Nossi Coll. Art, Nashville, 1993—; artist for Women of Achievement awards, sculptures and jewelry YWCA, Nashville, 1992—; artist for Bus. Award Sculpture, C. of C., Nashville, 1990. One and two person shows include Cheekwood Mus. Art, 1981, 93, Owensboro Mus. Fine Art, 1992, Western Ky. U., 1992-94, Belmont U., 1984, others; exhbns. include Watkins Art Inst., Nashville, 1991, Western Ky. U., 1992, Parthenon, Nashville, 1992, Owensboro Mus. Art, 1993, Tenn. Performing Arts Ctr., 1995; invitational and juried exhibits include Sculptors of Mid. Tenn. Arts in the Airport, Nashville, 1996, Nat. Coun. on the Edn. of Ceramics Arts, Rochester, N.Y., 1996, Ceramic Exhibn. Tenn. State U., 1996, and numerous others; represented in permanent collections including City of Chattanooga's Visitors Ctr., IBM, Bapt. Hosp., Nations Bank of Tenn., Mass. Pub. Libr., First Am. Bank Corp., and numerous others. Adv. bd. Belmont U., Nashville, 1984—, Nossi Coll. Art, 1993—; mem edn. com. Nat. Mus. of Women in the Arts, Tenn., 1992—; artist for fundraising sculpture Arthritis Found., Nashville, 1989-90; vol. singer VA Hosp., Nashville, 1989—; bd. dirs. Visual Arts Alliance Nashville, 1996; vol. soloist Vet.'s Hosp., 1991-96; artist for ann. fundraiser YWCA, 1993-96. Recipient Best Tchr. award Nossi Coll. Art, 1992-93; grantee City of Chattanooga Welcome Ctr., 1993, Memphis Arts Festival Spl. Projects, 1994. Mem. AAUW, Assn. of Visual Artists, Soc. of N.Am. Goldsmiths, Visual Artists Alliance of Nashville, Nat. Art Edn. Assn., Internat. Sculpture Ctr., Nat. Coun. on Edn. of the Ceramic Arts, Tenn. Assn. of Craft Artists, Coll. Art Assn. Home: PO Box 120454 Nashville TN 37212-0454

MCKINNEY, KATHRYN BROCK, professional fundraiser, consultant; b. Wichita Falls, Tex., Oct. 4, 1959; d. Earl S. and Mary E. (Kelley) Brock; m. Donald K. McKinney, Apr. 4, 1986; 1 child, Justin S. Tubbs. BS in Psychology with honor, Midwestern State U., Wichit Falls, 1980; grad. plaanned giving cert. program, U. Wis., 1993. Exec. dir. Big Bros. and Sisters Wichita County, Inc., Wichita Falls, 1982-89; program coord., asst. exec. dir. Rolling Medows Retirement Cmty., 1989-91; coord. capital campaign First Step, Inc., 1991; regional dir. Am. Heart Assn., Wichita Falls, 1991-92; mgr. capital campaign Boys and Girls Clubs Wichita Falls, 1992; dir. devel. Wichita Gen. Hosp., Wichita Falls, 1993—; chmn. bd. North Tex. Ctr. for Nonprofit Mgmt., Wichita Falls, 1994—; condr. numerous seminars, workshops and tng. sessions for nonprofit orgns. and vol. groups on fund rising and nonprofit mgmt., 1987—; spkr. in field. Bd. dirs. Wichita Falls Mayor's Commn. on Status of Women, 1983-89, Interfaith Ministries, Wichita Falls, 1995—; v.p. United Way Greater Wichita Falls, 1995—. Recipient Founder's awrd Wichita Falls Maternity Cottage, 1988. Mem. Nat. Soc. Fund Raising Profls. (pres. 1993—), Assn. Healthcare Philanthropy (cert., cabinet region V 1995—, legis. chmn. 1996, Outstanding Newcomer aaward 1994), Met. Bus. and Profl. Women (legis. chmn. 1988-90, Young Careerist award 1988, 90). Mem. Assembly of God. Home: Three Archway Ct Wichita Falls TX 76310 Office: Wichita Gen Hosp 1600 8th St Wichita Falls TX 76301

MCKINNEY, VENORA WARE, librarian; b. Meridian, Okla., June 16, 1937. BA, Langston U., 1959; MLS, U. Ill., 1965. Librarian Milw. Pub. Library, 1962-68, br. librarian, 1979-83, dep. city librarian, 1983—; librarian Peoria Pub. Schs., Ill., 1969, Milw. Pub. Schs., 1972-79; adj. faculty U. Wis., Milw.; mem. Wis. Govs. Coun. on Libr. Devel., 1983-92; bd. dirs. V.E. Carter Child Devel. Group. Bd. dirs. Milw. Repertory Theatre; coun. adv. Sch. Libr. and Info. Sci., U. Wis., Madison, 1992-96. Nat. Forum for Black Pub. Adminstrs. fellow Exec. Leadership Inst., George Mason U. Mem. ALA Black Caucus, Wis. Libr. Assn. (v.p. 1994, pres. 1995—, bd. dirs. 1996), Wis. Libr. Assn. Found., Wis. Black Librs. Network, ALA Pub. Libr. Assn., Links, Delta Sigma Theta. Baptist. Office: Milw Pub Libr 814 W Wisconsin Ave Milwaukee WI 53233-2309

MCKINNEY-KELLER, MARGARET FRANCES, retired special education educator; b. Houston, Mo., Nov. 25, 1929; d. George Weimer and Thelma May (Davis) Van Pelt; m. Roy Calvin McKinney Sr., Nov. 11, 1947 (dec. Feb. 1990); children: Deanna Kay Little, Roy Calvin Jr.; m. Clarence Elmore

Keller, June 8, 1991; 1 child, Dennis Lee Keller. BS with honors, Bradley U., 1963, MA in Counselor Edn., 1968, postgrad., 1992; postgrad., U. Ill., 1993—, Aurora Coll., Ill. Ctrl. Coll. In real estate Peoria, Ill., 1951-57; tchr. Oak Ridge Sch., Willow Springs, Mo., 1947-48, pvt. kindergarten, Washington, Ill., 1957-59, Dist. 50 Schs., Washington, Ill., 1959-67; tchr. socially maladjusted Washington Twp. Spl. Edn. Coop., 1967-70; tchr. behavior disordered Tazewell-Mason Counties Spl. Edn., Washington, Ill., 1970-78; resource tchr. Dist. 50 Schs., Washington, 1978-94; ret., 1994. Cons. moderator Active Parenting Group, Washington, 1972—; adv. bd. to establish Tazewell County Health Dept., 1960s; pres. gov. bd. Faith Luth. Day Care Ctr., Washington, 1970—, Washington Sr. Citizens, 1982-91; coach Spl. Olympics, Washington, 1979—; pres. Faith Luth. Ch. Coun., Washington, 1985-86; laity v.p. No. Conf. Evang. Luth. Ch. Am., Ctrl. Ill., 1986-92; vol. Proctor Hosp., 1994—. Mem. AAUW, Washington Bus. and Profl. Women (pres. 1979-80, 88-89, dist. 9 dir. 1995-96), Am. Legion Aux., German-Am. Soc., Alpha Delta Kappa (state office, ctrl. region). Home: 603 Sherwood Park Rd Washington IL 61571-1828

MCKINNEY-LUDD, SARAH LYDELLE, middle school education, librarian; b. Feb. 29, 1948. BA, U. Md., 1973; MA, Cen. Mich. U., 1975; MA in Legal Studies, Antioch Sch. Law, Washington, 1982; postgrad., Sch. Edn. George Washington U., 1989—. Cert. advanced profl. tchr. grades 5 through 12, Md., cert. adminstr. Tchr. of learning disabled Azores (Portugal) Elem. Sch., 1974-76; tchr. English Spaulding Jr. High Sch., Forestville, Md., 1976-82, Prince George's Cmty. Coll., 1982-84, Benjamin Tasker Sch., Bowie, Md., 1982-85, Crossland Night Sch., Temple Hills, Md., 1984-85, Thomas Pullen Mid. Sch., Landover, Md., 1985-87, Kettering (Md.) Mid. Sch., 1985-88, Kenmoor Mid. Sch., Landover, 1988-91; tchr. English, libr. Drew Freeman Mid. Sch.(formerly Francis Scott Key Mid. Sch.), District Heights, Md., 1991—; chairperson multicultural com., chairperson sch. based mgmt. Francis Scott Key Mid. Sch., 1992—; reader Jarvis Grants, U.S. Dept. Edn., 1990—. Contbr. articles to various publs. Mem. Md. State Tchr.'s Legis. Com., 1987-90; chairperson Profl. Rights and Responsibility, 1978-81; active Prince George's Com. on Acad. Achievement, Prince George's Com. Women's Fair Steering Com., Md. State Hosp. Bd., Prince George's County affiliate United Black Fund, area speakers bur.; programs chairperson, sec. Project Safe Sts.-2000, 1989; pres. Bowie Therapeutic Nursery; judge ACT-SO NAACP, Washington, 1989—; mem. exec. bd. Prince George's County chpt., 1984-89; active polit. campaigns; bd. dirs. Landover Ednl. Athletic Recreational Non-Profit Found. of Washington Redskins. Mem. Md. State Tchrs. Assn. (editor Women's Caucus), Sigma Gamma Rho (Community Activist award 1992). Home: 4411 Cape Cod Cir Bowie MD 20720-3582 Office: Drew Freeman Mid Sch 5100 Silver Hill Rd Suitland MD 20746

MCKINNIE, NANCY ELLIOTT, banker; b. Jackson, Miss., Feb. 28, 1952; d. Morelle A. and Elaine (Heard) Elliott; m. William D. McKinnie, May 18, 1974. BA in English Lit., Memphis State U., 1974, MBA in Fin., 1980. Office mgr. Group Ins. Analysts, Memphis, 1972-75; pension adminstr. Conn. Gen. Life, Memphis, 1975-77; trust officer 1st Tenn. Bank, Memphis, 1977-79, v.p. trust sales, 1979-82, v.p., mgr. corp. trust sales, 1982-86, v.p. cash mgmt., 1986-87; pres. 1st Tenn. Bank, Bartlett, 1987-92; sr. v.p. 1st Tenn. Bank, Memphis, 1992—. Trustee, past pres. U. Memphis Found., 1978-96; sec./treas., charter mem. U. Memphis Women's Leadership Coun., 1996—; past pres. Civitan Club, Bartlett, Exch. Club, Bartlett. Mem. Leadership Memphis (grad.). Unitarian.

MCKNIGHT, ELIZABETH CONWAY, conservation organization executive, educator; b. Proctor, Vt., May 27, 1945; d. John Thomas and Phyllis Irene (Creaser) Conway; m. James Brian McKnight, June 6, 1964 (div. 1983). BS with honors, Northeastern U., 1975; cert., Doscher Sch. Photography, Woodstock, Vt., 1976; MA in Environ. Affairs, Clark U., 1978. Reporter AP, Boston, 1974-75; tchr. journalism and environ. sci. Lawrence Acad., Groton, Mass., 1975-78; publs. mgr. Zellars-Williams, Inc., Lakeland, Fla., 1978-79; photographer, writer E.C. McKnight, Burlington, Vt., 1979-81; communications and mktg. mgr. Dufresne-Henry, Inc., North Springfield, Vt., 1981-82; gen. mgr. Assoc. Cons., Inc., Londonderry, Vt., 1982-85; dir. ops. Group Design Architects, Rutland, Vt., 1986-90; co-leader Rio Roosevelt Expedition, 1991-92, Livingstone's Last Journeys Expedition, 1993; founder, dir. New Century Conservation Trust Inc., 1991—; freelance photographer, writer. Co-prodr. (documentaries for PBS' New Explorers): The River of Doubt, 1992, In the Footsteps of Dr. Livingstone, 1993; prodr. and host: (interactive television series) Living Classroom. Chairwoman citizens adv. com. Rutland County (Vt.) Solid Waste Dist., 1989-90; mem. Rutland Mayor's Com. on Volvo Site Selection, 1989; cons. Rutland Partnership, 1988-90, interim dir., mem. exec. com., 1989-90; bd. dirs. Merrymeeting AIDS Support Svcs., 1991-95; mem. Brunswick planning bd., 1995—; mem. Brunswick Zoning Devel. Task Force, 1995-96; co-chmn., mem. bd. dirs. New Century Conservation Trust. Recipient Theodore Roosevelt Disting. Svc. medal Theodore Roosevelt Assn., 1992. Fellow Explorers Club, Royal Geog. Soc.; mem. Soc. Profl. Journalists, Soc. Woman Geographers (Outstanding Achievement award 1996), Women's Environ. and Devel. Orgn., Worldwide Network. Home: PO Box 125 Harpswell ME 04079

MCKNIGHT, LYNDA KEITH, music educator, opera singer; b. Pasadena, Tex., Oct. 25, 1960; d. David Box and Suzann (Prim) Keith; m. Cleavy Louis McKnight, Dec. 16, 1995. BM, Baylor U., 1982; MM, artist diploma, U. Cin., 1985. Prin. artist Met. Opera, N.Y.C., 1991-92; asst. prof. voice Baylor U., Waco, Tex., 1993—. Performances include L'Amour des Trois Oranges, 1988, Don Giovanni, 1988, Ariadne auf Naxos, 1989, The Merry Widow, 1990, La Sonnambula, 1991, Idomeneo, 1991, Parsifal, 1992, The Ghosts of Versailles, 1992, La Boheme, 1992, Faust, 1993. Winner Nat. Winner Met. Opera Auditions, 1988, Nat. Fedn. Music Clubs Competition, 1989, WGN/Ill. Opera Guild Nat. Competition, 1989; recipient Singer of Yr. award Shreveport Opera Competition, 1994. Mem. AAUW, Am. Guild Musical Artists, Nat. Assn. Tchrs. Singing (Steber award 1989, Singer of Yr. Texoma Region 1994, winner artist auditions regional competition 1995). Democrat. Baptist. Home: 602 Indian Springs Dr Waco TX 76708

MCKOWEN, DOROTHY KEETON, librarian; b. Bonne Terre, Mo., Oct. 5, 1948; d. John Richard and Dorothy (Spoonhour) Keeton; m. Paul Edwin McKowen, Dec. 19, 1970; children: Richard James, Mark David. BS, Pacific Christian Coll., 1970; MLS, U. So. Calif., 1973; MA in English, Purdue U., 1985, postgrad., 1991—. Libr.-specialist Doheny Libr., U. So. Calif., L.A., 1973-74; asst. libr. Pacific Christian Coll., 1974-78; serials cataloger Purdue Univ. Librs., 1978-88; head children's and young adult svcs. Kokomo-Howard County Pub. Libr. (Ind.), 1988-89, coord. children's and tech. svcs., 1989-91; cataloger, network libr. Ind. Coop. Libr. Svcs. Authority, 1991—; vice chairperson Christian Edn. Com., Brady Lane Ch. of Christ, 1986-87, chairperson, 1987-88, pianist, 1978—, adult Sunday Sch. tchr., 1989—, choir dir., 1990—, organist, 1992—; bd. dirs. Good Shepherd Learning Ctr., 1990—, vice-chairperson, 1991-92, chairperson, 1992-94; bd. dirs. Purdue Christian Campus House, 1985-90, v.p., 1986-88, pres., 1988-90. Mem. ALA, Modern Lang. Assn., Soc. Early Americanists, Assn. for Libr. Collections and Tech. Svcs. (bd. dirs. 1986-90, 95—, vice chairperson, chairperson elect coun. of regional groups 1986-88, chairperson 1988-90, conf. program com. 1986-88, internat. rels. com. 1986-88, micropub. com., 1986-87, subject analysis com., subcom. to rev. Dewey 621.38, 1987, membership com. 1988-90, libr. resources and tech. svcs. editorial bd. 1988-90, planning and rsch. com. 1988-90, planning com. 1990-91, program initiatives com. 1991-93, chairperson 1991-93, orgn. and bylaws com. 1991-92), Ind. Libr. Fedn. (vice chmn. tech. svcs. div. 1983-84, chmn. 1984-85), Ohio Valley Group Tech. Svcs. Librs. (vice chmn. 1984-85, chmn. 1985-86). Republican. Home: 7625 Summit Ln Lafayette IN 47905-9729 Office: INCOLSA 6202 Morenci Trail Indianapolis IN 46268-2536

MCKOWN, MARTHA, minister, writer; b. Dixie, Ky., May 29, 1933; d. John William and Dora Ellen (Melton) Powell; m. Leslie Henry McKown, June 22, 1957; children: Karen Marie McKown Lee, Liana Jane McKown Hicks. AB in English, Evansville Coll., 1955; M of Religious Edn., Boston U., 1957; MDiv, Christian Theol. Sem., 1978. Ordained to ministry Meth. Ch., 1959. Dir. ch. edn. Maple St. Congl. Ch., Danvers, Mass., 1957-58, Temple United Meth. Ch., Terre Haute, Ind., 1973-75; pastor East Park United Meth. Ch., Indpls., 1979-80; assoc. pastor Trinity United Meth. Ch., Evansville, Ind., 1980-82; pastor Faith United Meth. Ch., Princeton, Ind., 1982-85, St. Paul United Meth. Ch., Poseyville, Ind., 1985-89. Author: Palm Sunday Parade, 1995; contbr. articles to various pubs. Pastoral counselor Pike County (Ind.) Hospice, 1993-96. Mem. Ohio Valley Writers Guild, Tri-State Geneal. Soc., Woman's Club, Brownin Club (pres. 1996—), So. Ind. Conf. United Meth. Ch. Democrat. Home and office: 4890 N Pack Ln Petersburg IN 47567

MCKUIN-AULT, CYNTHIA ANN, special education educator; b. Morrilton, Ark., Jan. 3, 1966; d. Bobby George and Carol Ann (Smith) McK.; m. Marty E. Ault, Sept. 3, 1994. BS in Edn., U. Ctrl. Ark., 1989. Cert. tchr. spl. edn., Ark. Tchr. Mulberry (Ark.) Sch. Dist., 1989-91, Rivendell Psychiat. Hosp., Benton, Ark., 1990, Sheridan (Ark.) Pub. Schs., 1991—; founder first alt. sch. for elem. age Sheridan Intermediate, 1994; cons. in field. Mem. Ark. Childhood Assn. Office: Sheridan Intermediate Sch 1101 Skyline Dr Sheridan AR 72150-9184

MCLACHLIN, BEVERLEY, supreme court judge; b. Pincher Creek, Alta., Can., Sept. 7, 1943; m. Roderick McLachlin (dec. 1988); 1 child, Angus; m. Frank E. McArdle, 1992. B.A., U. Alta., MA in Philosophy, LLB, LLD (hon.), 1990; LLD (hon.), U. B.C., 1990, U. Toronto, 1995. Bar: Alta. 1969, B.C. 1971. Assoc. Wood, Moir, Hyde and Ross, Edmonton, Alta., Can., 1969-71, Thomas, Herdy, Mitchell & Co., Fort St. John, B.C., Can., 1971-72, Bull, Housser and Tupper, Vancouver, B.C., 1972-75; lectr., assoc. prof., prof. with tenure U. B.C., 1974-81; appointed to County Ct., Vancouver, 1981; justice Supreme Ct. of B.C., 1981-85, B.C. Ct. of Appeal, 1985-88; chief justice Supreme Ct. of B.C., 1988; justice Supreme Ct. Can., Ottawa, Ont., 1989—. Co-author: B.C. Supreme Court Practice, B.C. Court Forums, Canadian Law of Arch. and Engring.; mem. editorial adv. bd. Family Law Restatement Project, 1987-88, Civil Jury Instruction, 1988; contbr. numerous articles to profl. jours. Office: Supreme Ct Bldg, Wellington St, Ottawa, ON Canada K1A 0J1

MCLAIN, JANICE DARLENE, newspaper foundation administrator; b. Ottumwa, Iowa, Dec. 20, 1943; d. Arthur George and Daisy (Thompson) Sells; m. Richard L. McLain, July 4, 1964; 1 child, Christopher. BS in Journalism, Iowa State U., 1967. Asst. women's editor La Crosse (Wis.) Tribune, 1967-69, feature editor, 1969-74; with rsch. and pub. rels. depts. La Crosse Econ. Devel., 1975; pres., pub. Gazette Newspapers, La Crosse, 1976-79; with sales and pub. rels. depts. Wilson Learning, Sydney, Australia, 1980-81; news editor Minn. Suburban Newspapers, Mpls., 1986-87; rsch. asst. Custom Rsch., Mpls., 1988-89; gen. mgr., editor Format mag., Mpls., 1989-92; exec. dir. Minn. Newspaper Found., Mpls., 1992—. Bd. dirs. Minn. Parenting Assn., 1994—. Recipient Ad Fed Paul Foss award, 1992; named Outstanding Young Alumnus, Iowa State U., 1975, Woman of Achievement, Wis. Press Woman, 1979, numerous journalism awards. Mem. Women in Comms., Soc. Profl. Journalists. Home: 4125 Upland Ln N Minneapolis MN 55446-2636 Office: Minn Newspaper Found 12 S 6th St #1116 Minneapolis MN 55402

MCLAIN, PEGGY ANNE, healthcare company official, nurse epidemiologist; b. Charleston, S.C., Oct. 15, 1935; d. John Woodrow and St. Clare Anne (McIndoe) Sneed; widow; children: Teresa Anne, James Roland, Christopher, Stephen, John. Grad., McLeod Infirmary Sch. Nursing, 1957; BS magna cum laude, Lander Coll., 1987; MA, U. Ga., 1990. RN, S.C.; cert. nurse epidemiologist, S.C.; cert. ACLS, CPR instr., S.C., Ga. Charge nurse labor and delivery room Tuomey Hosp., Sumter, S.C., 1957-59; oper. room nurse St. Louis State Hosp., 1959; ob-gyn. nurse St. Mary's Hosp., East Orange, N.J., 1960; charge nurse med.-surg. unit St. Francis Xavier Hosp., Charleston, 1970; nurse epidemiologist, guest instr. epidemology Med. U. S.C. Hosp., Charleston, 1971-76; primary and ICU nurse, nurse epidemiologist Hilton Head (S.C.) Hosp., 1976-81; dir. nurses, nurse epidemiologist Hilton Head Nursing Ctr., 1981-85; weekend supr. Gilbert Health Clinic, U. Ga., Athens, 1987-90; field home health nurse The Nursing Registry, Inc., Hilton Head, 1989-92, nursing and pub. rels. coord., 1992-93, primary nurse, mgr. cmty. rels., 1993; regional cmty. rels. mgr. CareOne, Bluffton, S.C., 1989—, sr. primary nurse; cons. nurse, epidemiologist Charleston County Hosp., Charleston VA Hosp., Carolina Nursing Home, Charleston, McClennan Banks Hosp., Charleston; mem. adv. bd. Beaufort Tech. Coll.; instr. home health Tech. Coll. Low County, Beaufort-Jasper Career Ednl. Ctr., S.C. Divsn. on Aging, Hilton Head H.S., Wade Hampton H.S. Grad. Leadership Hilton Head, 1995; bd. dirs. Am. Heart Assn.; working mem. Hilton Head Island Cmty. Playhouse; capt. Am. Cancer Soc. Mem. ANA, AAUW, S.C. Nurses Assn. (polit. action com. 1993—, del. dist. 10), Nat. Home Health Nurses Assn., S.C. Health Care Assn. (regional rep.), S.C. Nurses in Long Term Care Assn. for Practitioners in Infection Control, Low County Coun. Nurses in Long Term Care, Hilton Head Art League, Beaufort Art League, Hilton Head Island C. of C. (govt. affairs com. 1993—, amb.), Women's Assn. Hilton Head, Profl. Women's Club Hilton Head Island (sunshine chmn.), Kiwanis (pres. Low County, Blue Key, Mu Rho Sigma, Alpha Kappa Gamma. Roman Catholic.

MCLAMB, PEGGY JOYCE, school counselor; b. Bladenboro, N.C., July 16, 1957; d. Claudie Robert and Gertie Lee (Bryan) Brisson; 1 child, Betty Faith Thompson. BS in Edn., Pembroke State U., 1985; MEd, Campbell U., 1986. Lic. counselor N.C. Counselor Bladen County Schs., Elizabethtown, N.C., 1986—; testing coord. Bladen Lakes Sch., Elizabethtown, 1990—; parent involvement coord. Plain View Sch., Tar Heel, N.C., 1990—. Jr. advisor SADD, Dublin, N.C., 1988, Beta Club, 1989. Mem. Southeastern Counselor Assn., Alpha Chi.

MCLANE, BOBBIE JONES, retired government official, genealogist, publisher; b. Hot Springs, Ark., Feb. 19, 1927; d. Julian Everette and Eula (Deaton) Jones; m. Gerald Bert McLane, Aug. 14, 1954 (dec. 1994). Chief clk. Army and Navy Hosp., Hot Springs, 1950-52; adminstrv. asst. Wis. Mil. Dist., Milw., 1952-54; exec. sec. to postmaster U.S. Postal Svc., Hot Springs, 1954-70, supr. employment svcs., 1970-74, dir. employee and labor rels., 1974-80; acting postmaster U.S. Postal Svc., Arkadelphia, Ark., 1978; dir. employee and labor rels. U.S. Postal Svc., Ft. Smith, Ark., 1980-86; ret., 1986. Compiler, author pub. Ark. Ancestors, 72 titles, 1962; editor The Record, 1966—. Organizer, charter mem. Garland County Hist. Soc., Hot Springs, 1960—; bd. dirs., chmn. Ark. History Commn., 1966-80, 90—; charter mem., bd. dirs. Community Players Hot Springs, 1949-55. Recipient award for contbns. to hist. and geneal. rsch. Am. Assn. State and Local History, 1967, Bicentennial award Postmaster Gen. U.S. Postal Svc., 1976; named One of 100 Ark. Women of Achievement, Ark. Press Women, 1980; Am. Assn. State and Local History fellow Vanderbilt U., 1967. Mem. Profl. Genealogists Ark. (bd. dirs. 1988—), Ark. Geneal. Soc. (charter, bd. dirs. 1960—, past pres.). Democrat. Episcopalian. Home and Office: 222 McMahan St Hot Springs National Park AR 71913-6243

MCLANE, CAROLYN SUE, elementary education educator; b. Charleston, W.Va., Mar. 27, 1951; d. Clyde Lee Landfried and Thelma Maxine (Nelson) Ramsey; m. Kenneth Wayne Hall, Sept. 11, 1970 (div. May 1981); m. Timothy Wayne McLane, Aug. 8, 1981; 1 child, Joshua. BS in Elem. Edn., W.Va. State Coll., 1981; MA, U. W.Va., 1991. Classroom aide Jackson County Bd. Edn., Ripley, W.Va., 1972-80, tchr., 1981—; ednl. cons. Jackson County Bd. Edn., 1991—, textbook com. 1993—; ednl. cons., W.Va. Dept. of Edn., 1991—; local sch. improvement coun., Kenna, W.Va., 1992—; mem. selection com. W.Va. STEP, Charleston, 1994. Grantee W.Va. Dept. of Edn., 1993; recipient Jackson County Tchr. of the Yr., 1994. Mem. NEA, Jackson County Tchrs. Assn., W.Va. Edn. Assn. Republican. Baptist. Office: Kenna Elem Sch PO Box 127 Kenna WV 25248-0127

MCLAREN, KAREN LYNN, advertising executive; b. Flint, Mich., Feb. 14, 1955; d. Max W. and Barbara J. (Cole) Hoeffgen; m. Michael L. McLaren, June 18, 1974. AA, Mott Community Coll., Flint, 1976; BA, Mich. State U., 1978. Writer Sta. WGMZ-FM, Flint, 1979-84; writer, producer Tracy-Stephens Advt., Flint, 1984-87; pres. McLaren Advt., Troy, Mich., 1987—. Contbr. articles to profl. jours. Mem. centennial com. Wolverine region ARC, 1981, pub. rels. com., 1981-84; vol. coord., pub. rels. tour guide Whaley Hist. Ho., Flint, 1980-91; home designer, tour guide Romeo (Mich.) Hist. Home Tour, 1992; mem. Nat. Trust for Hist. Preservation, 1991-95; com. chair Crim Festival of Races, Flint, 1992, 93, 94, 95; active Sta. WFUM-Pub. TV, Flint, 1980-91; panelist career fair Modona U., Livonia, Mich., 1994, 95, 96. Recipient 3 awards, 2 Nat. Health Care Mktg. Competition awards, Women's Adv. Club Detroit Pres.'s award, 1994. Mem. NAFE, Women's Advt. Club Detroit (scholar chmn. 1988-88, bd. dirs. 1989, 92-93, chmn. scholarship fundraiser 1991, co-chmn. career fair 1989, 90, 92, career fair panelist 1993, v.p. 1990, pres. 1991, amb. 1992, chmn. woman of yr. award 1994-96, by-laws chmn. 1994), Women's Econ. Club Detroit (workplace of tomorrow com. 1996, program com. 1996). Office: 3001 W Big Beaver Ste 306 Troy MI 48084

MCLAREN, SUSAN SMITH, therapist, healing touch practitioner, instructor; b. Plymouth Meeting, Pa., Jan. 21, 1941; d. Robertson Fobes and Jane (Leiper) Smith; m. Michael Eric McLaren (div. 1993). BA, Mount Holyoke Coll., 1962; cert. orthoptic technician, Bellevue Hosp., N.Y.C., 1963; MS, Villanova U., 1994. Cert. counselor Nat. Bd. Cert. Counselors, Inc. Orthoptist Bascom Palmer Eye Inst., Miami, Fla., 1963-69; lab. technician Pvt. Pathology Practice, Sydney, N.S.W., Australia, 1970-78, 81-87, Nambour, Queensland, 1970-78, 81-87; asst. renal medicine Mater Hosp., Sydney, 1978-81; hospice vol. Hospice of Watauga County, Boone, N.C., 1988-91; cert. practitioner, instr. Colo. Ctr. for Healing Touch (now Healing Touch Internat., Inc.), 1991—; Reiki therapist Spirit Releasement Therapy, Kimberton, Pa., 1995—; adv. Camphill Village, Kimberton, 1993—, Cmty. Supported Agr., Kimberton, 1994—. Editl. bd. mem. Aspen Publ., Inc., Gaithersburg, Md., 1994—; contbr. articles to profl. jours. Mem. ACA, Am. Holistic Nurses' Assn., Nat. Hospice Orgn., Nat. Fedn. Spiritual Healers, Australian Spiritual Healers Assn., Inst. Noetic Scis.

MCLARNON, MARY FRANCES, neurologist; b. Montreal, Que., Canada, May 13, 1944; came to U.S., 1969; d. John Francis and Patricia Jessica (Dore) McL.; m. Malcolm Weiner, Dec. 21, 1975; m. Lawrence Zingesser, Oct. 12, 1982; children: Andrea, Eliza. BS, McGill U., 1965, MD, 1969. Intern St. Vincent's Hosp., N.Y.C., 1969-70; fellow seizure unit Boston Children's Hosp., 1970-71; resident in neurology Albert Einstein Coll. Medicine, Bronx, N.Y., 1971-73; resident in radiology N.Y. Hosp.-Cornell Med. Ctr., N.Y.C., 1973-76; pvt. practice.

MCLAUGHLIN, ANN, public policy, communications executive; b. Newark, Nov. 16, 1941; d. Edward Joseph and Marie (Koellhoffer) Lauenstein; m. John McLaughlin, 1975 (div. 1992). Student, U. London, 1961-62; B.A., Marymount Coll., 1963; postgrad., Wharton Sch., 1987. Supr. network comml. schedule ABC, N.Y.C., 1963-66; dir. alumnae relations Marymount Coll., Tarrytown, N.Y., 1966-69; account exec. Myers-Infoplan Internat. Inc., N.Y.C., 1969-71; dir. communications Presdl. Election Com., Washington, 1971-72; asst. to chmn. and press sec. Presdl. Inaugural Com., Washington, 1972-73; dir. Office of Pub. Affairs, EPA, Washington, 1973-74; govt. relations and communications exec. Union Carbide Corp., N.Y.C. and Washington, 1974-77; pub. affairs, issues mgmt. counseling McLaughlin & Co., 1977-81; asst. sec. for pub. affairs Dept. Treasury, Washington, 1981-84; under sec. Dept. of Interior, Washington, 1984-87; cons. Ctr. Strategic and Internat. Studies, Washington, 1987; sec. of labor Dept. of Labor, Washington, 1987-89; vis. fellow The Urban Inst., 1989-92; pres., CEO New Am. Schs. Devel. Corp., 1992-93; chmn. Pres.'s Commn. Aviation Security and Terrorism, 1989-90; mem. Am. Coun. on Capital Formation, 1976-78; mem. environ. edn. task force HEW, 1976-77; mem. Def. Adv. Com. of Women in the Svcs., 1973-74; bd. dirs. GM, Union Camp Corp., Kellogg Co., Nordstrom Co., Host Marriott Corp., Vulcan Materials Co., AMR Corp., Fannie Mae, Potomac Electric Power Co., Pub. Agenda Found.; vice-chmn., trustee Aspen Inst.; pres. Fed. City Coun., 1990-95. Mem. bd. overseers Wharton Sch. U. Pa.; bd. dirs. Charles A. Dana Found., The Conservation Fund; trustee Urban Inst., 1989—. Mem.•Cosmos Club, Met. Club, Econ. Club, F St. Club. Republican. Roman Catholic.

MCLAUGHLIN, DEBORAH ANN, public relations and marketing executive; b. Hoisington, Kans., Nov. 12, 1952; d. Kenneth Theodore and Mildred Marie (Steiner) Siebert; m. Donald Raymond McLaughlin, July 17, 1976; 1 child, Kalla Dawn. AS, Barton County Coll., Great Bend, Kans., 1972; BS, Kans. State U., 1975. News editor Great Bend Tribune, 1975-76; deposition indexer Turner & Boisseau, Great Bend, 1976-77; feature editor Mid-Kans. Ruralist, Hoisington, 1977-78; copywriter, audio-editor Advt. Assocs., Great Bend, 1978-79; photographer, sales mgr. Clay Ward Color Portraits, Great Bend, 1979-80; news editor, photographer St. John (Kans.) News, 1980-83; freelance writer, photographer Great Bend, 1984-85; pres., owner McLaughlin Pub. Rels. Agy., Great Bend, 1985-87; owner Cen. Kans. Sunrise mag., Great Bend, 1987-88, Creative Mktg. Svcs., Great Bend, 1988—; dir. pub. info. Unified Sch. Dist. 428, Great Bend, 1991-93. Editor Ellinwood Leader, 1995—; contbr. articles and photographs to various publs. Mem. Coalition for Prevention Child Abuse, Great Bend, 1986-87; mem. 75th anniversary com. Kansas State U. Coll. Journalism and Mass Communications, Manhattan, 1986. Mem. Kans. State U. Alumni Assn. Roman Catholic. Home and Office: 381 Grove Ter Great Bend KS 67530-9710

MCLAUGHLIN, HELEN E., writer; b. Denver, June 27, 1920; d. Elpha Elmer and Grace Ruth (Reddock) Bailey; m. Burl William McLaughlin, July 9, 1947; children: Becky Beryl, Kathleen Jean, Patricia Nanette, William Bailey. BA, Colorado Coll., 1942. Cert. in sociology, elem. edn. tchg. Hostess Continental Airlines, Denver, 1943-45; stewardess United Airlines, Denver, 1946-47; substitute tchr. various sch. systems, 1966-91. Author: (aviation books) Walking on Air, 1986, Footsteps In The Sky, 1994. Vol./United Clipped Wings, Spl. Olympics, New Haven, Conn., 1995, Mpls., 1991. Mem. United Airlines Clipped Wings Assn. of Stewardesses and Flt. Attendants, Continental Golden Penguins, Rock Island Army Wives Club, AAUW, World Airline Hist. Soc. Republican. Presbyterian. Home: 7125 106th Ave Coal Valley IL 61240

MCLAUGHLIN, JOAN B., literature and writing educator, writer; b. New Orleans, Aug. 22, 1945; d. Norvell Clark and Velma Agnes (Boudreaux) Bobbitt; m. John J. McLaughlin, Apr. 15, 1978; 1 child, Susanna. BA, Nicholls State U., 1968; MA, La. State U., 1970; PhD, U. Tex., 1975. Tchg. asst. La. State U., New Orleans, 1968-70; tchg. asst., asst. instr. U. Tex., Austin, 1970-75; asst. prof. Clemson (S.C.) U., 1975-82, assoc. prof., 1982-87; ind. edn. cons., workshop leader, writer, 1987—. Contbr. articles to profl. jours. Mem. MLA.

MCLAUGHLIN, LINDA LEE HODGE, federal judge; b. 1942. BA, Stanford U., 1963; LLB, U. Calif., Berkeley, 1966. With Keatinge & Sterling, L.A., 1966-70, Richards, Martin & McLaughlin, Beverly Hills and Newport Beach, Calif., 1970-73, Bergland, Martin & McLaughlin, Newport Beach, 1973-76, Bergland & McLaughlin, Costa Mesa, Calif., 1976-80; judge North Orange County Mcpl. Ct., Fullerton, Calif., 1980-82, Orange County Superior Ct., Santa Ana, Calif., 1982-92, U.S. Dist. Ct. (ctrl. dist.) Calif., Santa Ana, 1992—; mem. adv. com. jud. forms Jud. Coun., 1978—, mem. adv. com. gender bias in cts., 1987-90. Active Edgewood Sch. Parents Assn., Cate Sch. Parents Aux.; mem. governing bd. Victim-Witness Assistance Program Orange County. Mem. Nat. Assn. Women Judges, Calif. State Bar Assn. (mem. com. profl. ethics 1976-80, disciplinary referee dist. 8 1978-80), Calif. Women Lawyers (gov. dist. 8 1978-80), Calif. Judges Assn. (chair civil law and procedure com. 1985-86), Orange County Bar Assn. (mem. com. adminstrn. justice 1975-78, client rels. com. 1978-80, com. jud. appointments 1979-80), Orange County Women Lawyers, Boalt Hall Alumni Assn., Stanford U. Alumni Assn., Cap and Gown Hon. Soc. *

MCLAUGHLIN, MARGARET BROWN, educator, writer; b. Miami Beach, Fla., Aug. 24, 1926; d. J. Clifford and Grace Lindsey (DuPre) Brown; m. Francis Edward McLaughlin, Oct. 30, 1982 (dec.). BA cum laude, U. Miami, 1946; MA, Duke U., 1949; PhD, Tulane U., 1976. Instr., lectr. in English, U. Miami, Coral Gables, Fla., 1946-47, 56-61, 73-91; English tchr. Narimasu Am. Sch., Tokyo, 1963-65; asst. prof. Manchester Coll., North Manchester, Ind., 1965-67; instr. Miami-Dade Community Coll., 1977, 81; prodr. Dade County Cable TV series Caribbean Writers and Their Art, 1991; prodr., host cable tv series Haiti Cherie, 1993-94; dir. writing workshop for fgn. students U. Miami Sch. Medicine, 1991, 92. Contbr. articles to popular mags. and newspapers; contbr. play reviews to Internet pub. Trustee Mus. Sci., Miami, 1977-78. Mem. MLA, Am. Lit. Assn. (Henry Adams Soc.), Egyptology and Asian Civilizations Soc. Miami (bd. dirs., pres. 1976-78, 83-85). Home and Office: 1621 S Bayshore Dr Miami FL 33133-4201

MCLAUGHLIN, MARGUERITE P., state senator, logging company executive; b. Matchwood, Mich., Oct. 15, 1928; d. Harvey Martin and Luella Margaret (Livingston) Miller; m. George Bruce McLaughlin, 1947; children:

Pamela, Bruce Jr., Cynthia. Owner, operator contract logging firm, Orofino, Idaho; mem. Idaho Ho. of Reps., 1978-80; mem. Idaho Senate, 6th term., asst. Dem. leader, 1990, 91, 92, 93; chair Democrat Caucus, 1995—. mem. Senate Fin. Com., 1987—, Gov.'s Adv. Coun. Workers Compensation, 1990—, State of Idaho Endowment Fund Investment Bd., 1991—, legis. coun., 1989-94, State of Idaho Job Tng. Coun., 1989—. Trustee Joint Sch. Dist. 171, 1976-80; pres. Orofino Celebration, Inc. Democrat. Roman Catholic. Office: Idaho State Senate State Capital Boise ID 83720*

MCLAUGHLIN, MARY RITTLING, magazine editor; b. Buffalo; d. Joseph and Irene (Meyer) Rittling; m. Charles Edward McLaughlin, June 21, 1962 (div. June 1981) children—Daniel (dec.), Maud Rosie. BA, Manhattanville Coll., 1956. Reporter Buffalo Evening News, 1956-58; copywriter Harper's Bazaar, N.Y.C., 1959-61; editor McCall's Mag., N.Y.C., 1973-79; mng. editor Working Mother Mag., N.Y.C., 1979-85; exec. editor Working Mother Mag., 1985—. Mem. Am. Soc. Mag. Editors, Women's Media Group. Office: Working Mother Mag 230 Park Ave New York NY 10169-0005

MCLAUGHLIN, SANDRA MURRAY, elementary education educator; b. Millen, Ga., Jan. 20, 1945; d. Alton L. and Marguerite J. (Chandler) Murray; m. Bruce D. McLaughlin, June 6, 1980. BS, Ga. So. U., 1968; MEd, U. S.C., Aiken, 1978. Cert. tchr. Tchr. Richmond County Bd. Edn., Augusta, Ga., 1968-70, Aiken County Bd. Edn., Langley, S.C., 1970-80, Washington Twp. Bd. of Edn., Sewell, N.J., 1981—; grade level lead tchr. Washington Twp. Bd. Edn., Sewell, 1989-91, 93-94, mem. affirmative action com., 1994—. State cabinet mem. Gideons Internat., N.J., 1989-90. Mem. NEA, N.J. Edn. Assn., Washington Twp. Edn. Assn. Republican. Methodist. Home: 304 Snowy Owl Ct Sewell NJ 08080-3404 Office: Birches Sch Westminster Blvd Turnersville NJ 08012

MCLAUGHLIN, SHARON GAIL, principal, small business owner; b. Little Rock, Jan. 2, 1946; d. William Harry and Marion Virginia (Johnson) Fowler; m. Elbert Leroy Anderson, Apr. 3, 1969 (div. 1975); 1 child, William Eric; m. James Jerry McLaughlin, Nov. 22, 1986. BA, Baker U., Baldwin City, Kans., 1968; MA, U. Mo., Kansas City, 1976, postgrad., 1996—; EdS, U. Cen. Ark., 1987. Tchr. Kansas City (Mo.) Sch. Dist., 1968-77; dir. recruiting Lincoln U., Jefferson City, Mo., 1977-78; tchr., dept. chmn. Magnet Sch., Kansas City, 1978-79; asst. prin. Pulaski County Sch. Dist., Little Rock, 1979-87; prin. Little Rock Sch. Dist., 1987-91; owner L Image Ltd, Little Rock, 1989—; tchr. broadcast journalism, tv prodn., theatre arts Dallas Ind. Sch. Dist., 1991—; speaker Clinto-Gore Campaign; cons. in field. Producer/dir.: Take: Teen, Bridging the Gap, 1980—; author prog. for women, Prisms, 1980, prog. for youth, Kaleidescope III, 1980. Mem. nat. bd. ethics Mrs. Am. Pageant Sys., 1991; Tex. state chair rsch. and status women of African descent AME Ch., 1992—; mem. workshops/seminars Performing Arts in Worship. Named Outstanding Black Arkansan, Women in Motion, 1988, Outstanding Educator, Ark. PTA, 1988, Mrs. Ark. Am., 1990-91. Mem. NAACP, Nat. Assn. Black Sch. Educators, Student Adminstrs. Assn. (prog. chmn. 1986-87), Nat. Assn. Sec. Sch. Prins., Internat. Platform Assn., Smithsonian Assocs., Urban League of Mo.-Ark., Top Ladies of Distinction (Dallas chpt.), Alpha Kappa Alpha, Phi Delta Kappa. Democrat. Home: SMU Box 754699 Dallas TX 75275

MCLAUGHLIN, SUZETTE NINA LINDSAY, artist, educator; b. Gulfport, Miss., Dec. 12, 1957; d. William Earl and Sarah Elizabeth (Hoffman) Lindsay; m. robert Lawson Johns, June 18, 1982 (div. Oct. 1990); m. Kent Douglas McLaughlin, Nov. 3, 1995. BS, Pa. State U., 1980; MFA, La. State U., 1990. Montessori cert. tchr. Tchr. of hearing impaired Orleans Parish Pub. Schs., New Orleans, 1980-84; tchr. kindergarten Children's House Montessori, New Orleans, 1984-87; tchr. ceramics Tulane U., New Orleans, 1992, Haystack Mt. Sch. of Crafts, Deer isle, Maine, 1995; artist-in-residence Penland (N.C.) Sch. of Crafts, 1990-93; studio potter Bakersville, N.C., 1990—; curator Balt. Clayworks, 1995. Recipient award for functional art Richmond (Va.) Craft and Design Sch., 1993, Best of Show, Strictly Functional Pottery Nat., Lancaster, Pa., 1993, hon. mention, 1994, 95; Emerging Artist grantee N.C. Art Coun., 1996. Mem. So. Highland Handicraft Guild, Am. Craft Coun., Nat. Coun. for Edn. of Ceramic Art. Democrat. Presbyterian. Home: Rte 1 Box 164A Bakersville NC 28705

MCLAUGHLIN-HAUSCH, DOROTHY JOAN, song writer; b. Trenton, N.J., Apr. 24, 1933; d. Daniel Francis and Dorothy Theresa (Lyons) McLaughlin; m. Reid Arthur Hausch, June 8, 1979. Libr. N.J. State Police, Trenton, 1967-80; pers. mgr. Vanderbilt U., Nashville, 1980-86; songwriter Tree Internat., Nashville, 1986—. Lyracist 36 gospel songs; contbr. articles to Muse Mag. Mem. NOW. Wiccan.

MCLAURIN, MARTHA REGINA, parking service company executive; b. Raleigh, N.C., Feb. 17, 1948; d. William Lentis and Martha Catherine (Hester) McL. BA, Meth. Coll., 1970. Pres., chief fin. officer McLaurin Parking Co., Inc., Raleigh, 1970—; dir. Brancy Banking & Trust Co. Br., Cary, N.C., 1980—. Pres. bd. dirs. Raleigh Mchts. Bur., 1988-89; mem. Cary Town Coun., 1987-95; chmn. Wake County Planning Bd., 1983-86. Named Outstanding Bus. Alumnus Meth. Coll., 1985, Cary's Outstanding Woman Cary Jaycettes, 1984. Mem. Nat. Parking Assn. (bd. dirs. 1979—, pres. 1989-90, chmn. 1990-92), Parking Industry Inst. (bd. dirs. 1987-89, 92-94, chmn. 1995-96). Office: McLaurin Parking Co Inc PO Box 781 Raleigh NC 27602-0781

MCLEAN, HELEN CANDIS, writer, publisher, professional speaker; b. Yorkton, Sask., Feb. 27, 1949; m. J. Ross McLean; children: Stuart, Steven. BA in English Lit., U. Sask., 1970, MA in English Lit., 1977. Psychiat. social worker Sask. Dept. Social Svcs., 1970-71; free-lancer CBC Radio, 1975-76, weekly theatre reviewer Calgary Eye Opener program, 1976-77, news reporter, 1979; writer, prodr. Creative Assocs., 1976-77; tchr. journalism U. Calgary, Alta., 1976-77; news reporter Sta. CHQR Radio, 1977-79, The Albertan, 1979-80; free-lance writer, 1980-90; pres., CEO Hummingbird Press, Calgary, 1987—. Author: Mother Love is Solar Powered...That Would Account for What Happens to Me at Night and on Rainy Days, 1987, Surviving a Nuclear Powered Family, 1992; contbr. articles to Calgary Mag., Alta. Report, Western Prodr., Parent's Mag., Great Expectations, The Compleat Mother. Recipient Nat. Dan McArthur award for Outstanding Work in Documentary Field; various scholarships. Office: 324 Silver Crest Dr NW, Calgary, AB Canada T3B 2Y2

MCLEAN, HULDA HOOVER, volunteer, conservationist, naturalist, artist; b. Palo Alto, Calif., Aug. 18, 1906; d. Theodore Jesse and Mildred (Brooke) Hoover; m. Charles Alexander McLean (dec. 1981); children: Charles Alexander, Allan Hoover, Robertson Brooke. BA, Stanford U., 1927. Rancher Santa Cruz County, Calif., 1943-85; v.p. Waddell Creek Assn., Davenport, Calif., 1985—; vol. mgr. Waddell Creek Ranger Sta., Davenport, 1993—. Author: Uncle Bert, 1975, Huala's World, 1848-1884, 1989, Tidedrift Shells of Monterey Bay, 1995, The Herbert Hoover Family, 1996. Pres. Calif. Coun. Youth, Sacramento, 1961-65; mem. Santa Cruz County Bd. Suprs., 1956-63, foreman county grand jury, 1980-81; vol. Calif. Dept. Parks and Recreation, 1975-96; conservation chmn. Native Daus. of Golden West, 1990-96. Recipient Superiot Achievement award Calif. Dept. Parks and Recreation, 1996. Mem. DAR (conservation chmn. 1985—, Conservation award 1990), LWV (pres. Calif . 1941-43), AAUW, Am. Pen Women, Soroptimists Internat., Santa Cruz Bus. and Profl. Women (Woman of Yr. Santa Cruz County 1982), Santa Cruz Art League. Home: 512 Walnut Ave Santa Cruz CA 95060-3636

MCLEAN-WAINWRIGHT, PAMELA LYNNE, educational consultant, college educator, counselor, program developer, clinical therapist; b. Rockville Centre, N.Y., Oct. 25, 1948; d. George Clifford Sr. and Violet Maude (Jones) McLean; m. Joseph Charles Everest Wainwright Jr., Jan. 20, 1982; children: Joseph Charles Everest III, Evan Clifford Jerome. BS, NYU, 1973; MEd, Fordham U., 1974; MSW, Adelphi U., 1986. Qualified clin. social worker. Tchr. Martin Deporres Day Care Ctr., Bklyn., 1973-77; dir. student pers. svcs. Ujamaa Acad., Hempstead, N.Y., 1977-78; coord. Hempstead, 1978; ednl. opportunity counselor SUNY, Farmingdale, 1978-79; assoc. prof. student pers. svcs. Nassau C.C., Garden City, N.Y., 1979-93; with counseling/advisement for health occupations program Ctrl. Fla. C.C., Ocala, N.Y., 1991-95; social work assoc. dept. home care U. Fla./Shands Hosp., Gainesville, 1995—; founder, program dir. Adult Individualized Multi-Svc. Program, Garden City, 1985—. mem. L.I. Coalition for Full Employment; mem. citizens adv. coun. Nassau Tech. Ctr., Women-on-Job Task Force, Port Washington, N.Y.; mem. adv. bd. Region 2 Displaced Homemakers Network; bd. dirs. Children's Greenhouse Inc., 1987-89, mem. founding com., 1980-81; civil rights adv., 1963—; mem. adv. bd. L.I. Cares, Hempstead, 1986-90; pres., CEO Faith-Builders Ministries; coord. Black male coll. explorers program Inverness/Fla. A&M U. Recipient Women's History Month citation Nassau County, N.Y., 1988, honoree in edn. Women-on-Job Task Force, 1989, Alumni Achievement award Fordham U. Grad. Sch. Edn., 1994. Mem. Assn. Black Psychologists, Assn. Black Women in Higher Edn. (bd. dirs.), Nat. Assn. Black Coll. Alumni, Nat. Assn. Female Execs., Women's Faculty Assn. Nassau Community Coll. (pres. 1986-88), L.I. Women's Council for Equal Edn. Employment and Tng.

MCLEER, LAUREEN DOROTHY, marketing professional; b. N.Y.C., Feb. 5, 1955; d. William Myers and Una Lee (Massey) McL. BS, Columbia U., 1977; MBA, U. London, 1981. RN, N.Y.; state registered nurse Eng., Wales. Staff nurse NYU Med. Ctr., N.Y.C., 1977-78; charge nurse Scripps Clinic and Rsch. Found., La Jolla, Calif., 1979-80; clin. rschr. Ayerst Labs., N.Y.C., 1982-83; sales rep. Pfizer, Inc., N.Y.C., 1983-87, Cahners Pub. Co., N.Y.C., 1988-89; dir. bus. devel. Pro Clinica, N.Y.C., 1990-91; account supr. Salthouse Torre Norton, Inc., Rutherford, N.J., 1992-93; dir. bus. devel. Med. & Tech. Rsch. Assocs., Inc., Wellesley, Mass., 1993-94; dir. clin. and regulatory rsch. Biometric Rsch. Inst., Inc., Arlington, Va., 1993-94; mem. com. for healthcare issues and legislation United Hosp. Fund., N.Y.C., 1992-94. Chmn. Help Our Neighbors Eat Yr. 'Round, N.Y.C., 1987-89; trustee Murray Hill Com., N.Y.C., 1988-90; bd. dirs. East Midtown Svcs. for Older People, 1987-94; vol. nurse Whitman Walker Clinic, 1995—. Mem. Pharm. Advt. Coun., Healthcare Bus. Women's Assn., Drug Info. Assn., Biotech. Industry Orgn. Regulatory Affairs Profls. Home: 15604 Marathon Cir Apt 301 Gaithersburg MD 20878 also: Mansion Farm Courthouse Point Rd Chesapeake City MD 21915 Office: BRI Internat Ste 300 1300 N 17th St Arlington VA 22209-3801

MCLENNAN, BERNICE CLAIRE, human resources professional; b. Malden, Mass., Dec. 26, 1936; d. Ralph Cyril Worth and Alice Seaman (Hunter) Worth Barrett; m. Hubert Earle McLennan, Oct. 28, 1961; 1 child, Cynthia Alice. Student, Moody Bible Inst., 1958, Salem State Coll., 1988, Bentley Coll., 1989. Youth dir. Faith Evangelical Ch., Melrose, Mass., 1971-77; adminstrv. asst. Boston Redevel. Authority, 1977-85, adminstr. coord., 1985-87, asst. sec. to the authority, 1981—, dir. human resources, 1988-95, asst. dir., 1995—; moderator Faith Evangelical Ch., Melrose, 1985-88, Christian edn. chair, 1973-76. Sec. Melrose (Mass.) Sch. Com., 1983-85; vol. Boston (Mass.) Youth Campaign, 1989, 90. Mem. Internat. Pers. Mgmt. Assn., Assn. Affirmative Action Profls. Home: 31 Botolph St Melrose MA 02176-1126 Office: Boston Redevel Authority City Hall One City Hall Sq Boston MA 02201

MCLENNAN, EMILY LOUISE, designer, art educator; b. Rochester, N.Y., Oct. 23, 1943; d. Walter W. and Betty Jane (Crandell) Murphy; m. Charles Grant McLennan, Apr. 29, 1969; children: Ann Boughton, Katherine. BFA, Ohio Wesleyan U., Delaware, 1966; student, Basel Design Sch., Switzerland, 1967-69. Graphic design faculty Cooper Union Sch. Art and Architecture, N.Y.C., 1970-71; fine arts faculty Briarcliff (N.Y.) Coll., 1976-77; painting and drawing faculty Purchase (N.Y.) Coll. SUNY, 1984-88, 92-94; vis. artist The Katonah (N.Y.) Mus., 1975-85; asst. dean Sch. Visual Arts Purchase Coll. SUNY, 1987-92. Exhibited in group shows at The Mus. of Contemporary Crafts, N.Y., 1975, The Katonah (N.Y.) Mus., 1975, 78, 85, The Bronx (N.Y.) Mus., 1987; exhibited in solo show PS1 L.I. City N.Y.C., 1980; designer: Interior Design Mag., 1995. Recipient Editor's award for lighting Editor's from Interior Design Mag., Contract Design, Elle Decor, Metropolis, Home Accents Today, ID and Interiors, 1995. Home: 2504 Manitou Island White Bear Lake MN 55110 Office: 212 Third Ave N Minneapolis MN 55401

MCLEOD, CAROLYN LOUISE, artist; b. Palo Alto, Calif., Sept. 26, 1946; d. Daniel James McLeod and Virginia Eleanor Eckland; m. William Eversly Bailey, Nov. 19, 1965 (div. 1969); 1 child, William Dwain; m. Thomas William Walker, Aug. 27, 1977 (div. 1986); m. Peter John Johnson, Dec. 31, 1987. AA in Art with honors, Foothill Coll., 1972; postgrad., Sonoma State U., 1973-74; BA in Art with honors, San Jose State U., 1976, postgrad., 1976-77; postgrad., Truckee Meadows C.C., 1975—. Sec. Stanford (Calif.) U., 1982-87, U.S. Geol. Survey, Menlo Park, Calif., 1988-92. One-woman shows include Hollister (Calif.) City Hall, 1993, The Elegant Touch, Hollister, 1994, King St. Gallery, Carson City, Nev., 1995; exhibited in group shows at Gilroy (Calif.) Art Show, 1990 (2d place oils), San. Benito County Arts Commn. Open Studio, 1991-92, 94, Pacific Art League Palo Alto, 1991 (2d place oils), 93-94, Lodi (Calif.) Art Ctr., 1993-94, Galivan Coll. Libr., Gilroy, 1993 (2 Hon. Mention awards), 94, Garlic Festival Store and Gallery, Gilroy, 1994 (Hon. Mention award), Santa Clara County Fair, 1994, Sacramento Fine Arts Ctr., Carmichael, Calif., 1994 (Excellence award), Wilbur D. May Mus., Reno, 1994, King St. Gallery, Carson city, 1994 (3d place award), 95 (1st place award), 96 (3d place award), Carl Cherry Ctr. for Arts, Carmel, Calif., 1994, Plaza Hotel Conservatory, Las Vegas, Nev., 1995, Poudre Valley Art League, Lincoln Ctr., Ft. Collins, Colo., 1995, River Gallery, Reno, 1995 (Best of Show, Hon. Mention), Nat. Assn. Women Artists, N.Y.C., 1995-96, Odette's Restaurant, Reno, 1995, Nev. State Fair, Reno, 1995, 96 (Hon. Mention award 1995, Judge's Merit award 1996), Nev. Mus. Art at MountainGate, Reno, 1995 (1st place award), Nat. Mus. Women Arts, Washington, 1996, China World Trade Ctr., Beijing, 1995, King St. Gallery, Carson City, 1996 (1st place and 3d place awards), River Gallery, Reno, 1996 (1st place award). Dean's scholar San Jose State U., 1976. Mem. AAUW, Nat. Assn. Women Artists (juried exhibiting mem.), Nev. Artists Assn. (newsletter editor 1994—), Nat. Mus. Womenin Arts, Gavilan Hills Art Assn. (sec., newsletter editor 1994, Outstanding Effort award 1994), Sierra Arts Found., Nev. Mus. Art, Mendocino Art Ctr. Home and Studio: 2512 Plumas St Reno NV 89509

MCLIN, ELVA BELL, archivist; b. Norcatur, Kans., June 5, 1917; d. James Shirley and Ruth Inez (Diefendorf) Bell; m. Paul Edward McLin Sr., Oct. 18, 1940; children: Jan Ellen Bexhoeft, Paul Jr., Carl Whitfield, Sheila roberts. BA, BS in Edn., Emporia (Kans.) State U., 1940; MA, U. Ala., 1962; PhD, Peabody of Vanderbilt, 1971. Tchr. U.S. Army Dependent Schs.; historian, pub. info. officer U.S. Army Ordnance; tchr. Brooke Hill Sch. for Girls, Birmingham, Ala., 1962-64; prof. English Athens (Ala.) State Coll., 1965-87, archivist, 1987—. Author plays including Woman Grown, 1940, Zelda, 1974; author: History of Athens College 1921-1991, 1991, revised edition, 1994, (biographies) Bell-Shirley Family History, 1989, Mollie!, 1992, Madame Childs, 1993. Named Disting. Alumnus, Emporia State U., 1991; named Outstanding Tchr., Athens State Alumni Assn., 1987, Tchr. of the Yr., Phi Mu, 1972, 80. Mem. AAUW, Nat. Soc. DAR, Coll. English Assn. (officer) Shakespeare Assn., Sigma Tau Delta, Phi Mu. Democrat. Episcopalian. Home: 210 S Beaty St Athens AL 35611-2606 Office: Archives Athens State Coll Athens AL 35611

MCLIN, RHINE LANA, state legislator, funeral service executive, educator; b. Dayton, Ohio, Oct. 3, 1948; d. C. Josef, Jr., and Bernice (Cottman) McL. B.A. in Sociology, Parsons Coll., 1969; M.Ed., Xavier U., Cin., 1972; postgrad. in law U. Dayton, 1974-76, AA in Mortuary Sci., Cin. Coll., 1988. Lic. funeral dir.; cert. tchr., Ohio. Tchr. Dayton Bd. Edn., 1970-72; divorce counselor Domestic Relations Ct., Dayton, 1972-73; law clk. Montgomery Common Pleas Ct., Dayton, 1973-74; v.p., dir., embalmer McLin Funeral Homes, Dayton, 1972—; instr. Central State U., Wilberforce, Ohio, 1982—; mem. Ohio Ho. of Reps., 1988-94; state senator Ohio State Senate, 1994—. com. mem. Human Svcs. and Aging Com., Agrl. Com., Hwys. and Transp. Com., Energy, Natural Resources and Environ. Com. Mem. Democratic Voters League, Dayton, Dem. Nat. Com.; mem. inspection com. V.C. Correctional Instn. Mem. Nat. Funeral Dirs. Assn., Ohio Funeral Dirs. Assn., Montgomery County Hist. Soc., NAACP (life), Nat. Council Negro Women (life), Delta Sigma Theta. Home: 1130 Germantown St Dayton OH 45408-1465 Office: Ohio State Senate State House Columbus OH 43215

MCMAHAN, SUSAN EVON, travel agency executive; b. McMinnville, Oreg., Apr. 9, 1962; d. James Donald and Delores Ann (Miller) McM. BA, Linfield Coll., 1984. Jr. acct. J. Ormiston, Beaverton, Oreg., 1985; analyst, mgr. ops. Rosenbluth Travel Agy Inc, Portland, Oreg., 1988-93; Rosenbluth Internat. account leader IVI/Bus. Travel Internat. at Nike, Beaverton, Oreg., 1993—; cons. Evergreen Internat. Aviation, McMinnville, Oreg., 1989. Fellow DAR; mem. Internat. Air Transport Assn., Airline Reporting Corp., Nat. Assn. Female Execs., Bus. Oreg. Women in Travel, Linfield Coll. Alumni Assn., Phi Sigma Sigma (scholarship chmn. 1983-84). Republican. Roman Catholic. Office: Nike One Bowerman Dr Beaverton OR 97005-0979

MCMAHON, ANITA SUE, women's health nurse; b. Elgin, Ill., Dec. 11, 1940; d. Herman Henry and Neva Imogene (Lusted) Mass; m. Daniel D. McMahon, Aug. 20, 1960; children: Daniel, Patrick, Christine, Joseph, Susanne. AAS with high honors, Elgin C.C., 1983; BS, St. Francis Coll., Joliet, Ill., 1992; student, Alverno Coll., Milw. Cert. inpatient obstet. nurse; cert. childbirth educator. Nurse preceptor, staff nurse med.-surg. Sherman Hosp., Elgin, 1983-90, ob-gyn. nurse, 1990—, childbirth instr., 1991—, charge nurse, 1992—, obstet. leadership coun., 1995—. Creator, editor quar. Nurse's Notes. Home: 617 Hawthorne Ct Carpentersville IL 60110-1970

MCMAHON, CATHERINE DRISCOLL, lawyer; b. Mineola, N.Y., Apr. 28, 1950; d. Matthew Joseph and Elizabeth (Driscoll) McM.; m. Gregory Arthur McGrath, Sept. 10, 1977 (div. 1991); children: Elizabeth Driscoll, Kerry Margaret, Michael Riley. BA, Simmons Coll., 1972; JD, Boston Coll., 1975; postgrad., Suffolk U., 1972-73; LL.M., NYU, 1980. Bar: N.Y. 1976, D.C. 1979, U.S. Supreme Ct. 1980, U.S. Tax Ct., 1991. Tax atty. asst. Exxon Corp., N.Y.C., 1975-76, asst. tax atty., 1976-77, sr. tax atty., 1979-81; tax atty. Exxon Internat. Co., N.Y.C., 1977-79, sr. tax counsel, Florham Park, N.J., 1990-92; sr. tax counsel Exxon Co., U.S.A., Houston, 1992—; tax mgr. Exxon Rsch. & Engring. Co., Florham Park, 1981-90. Bd. dirs. S.E. Morris chpt. ARC, Madison, N.J., 1983. Recipient TWIN award YMCA, Plainfield/Westfield, N.J., 1983. Mem. ABA, N.Y. State Bar Assn., D.C. Bar Assn. Roman Catholic. Office: Exxon Co USA 800 Bell St Houston TX 77002-7426

MCMAHON, COLLEEN, judge; b. Columbus, Ohio, July 18, 1951; d. John Patrick and Patricia Paterson (McDanel) McM.; m. Frank V. Sica, May 16, 1981; children: Moira Catherine, Patrick McMahon, Brian Vincent. BA summa cum laude, Ohio State U., 1973; JD cum laude, Harvard U., 1976. Bar: N.Y. 1977, U.S. Dist. Ct. (so. and ea. dists.) N.Y. 1977, U.S. Ct. Appeals (2d cir.) 1978, U.S. Supreme Ct. 1980, U.S. Ct. Appeals (5th cir.) 1985, D.C. 1985. Spl. asst. U.S. mission to the UN, N.Y.C., 1979-80; assoc. Paul, Weiss, Rifkind, Wharton & Garrison, N.Y.C., 1976-79, 80-84, ptnr., 1984-95; judge N.Y. Ct. Claims, N.Y.C., 1995—; acting justice N.Y. Supreme Ct., 1995—; bd. dirs., gen. counsel Danceworks, Inc., N.Y.C., 1977-81; mem. Coun. N.Y. Law Assocs., 1977-81; chair The Jury Project, N.Y. Office Ct. Adminstrn., 1993-94. Bd. dirs. Vol. Lawyers for the Arts, N.Y.C., 1979-83, Dance Theater Workshop, 1978-83; vice chancellor Episcopal Diocese of N.Y., 1992-95. Mem. ABA, Assn. of Bar of City of N.Y. (mem. coun. on jud. adminstrn. 1983-89, chmn. com. on state cts. of superior jurisdiction 1983-86, com. on women profession 1989-95, chmn. 1992-95), Am. Law Inst., Am. Judicature Soc., Westchester County Bar Assn., N.Y. State Bar Assn. (mem. ho. of dels. 1986-89), Fed. Bar Coun. Republican. Episcopalian. Office: Chamber 1146 111 Center St New York NY 10013

MCMAHON, DEBRA BRYLAWSKI, management consultant; b. Washington, Jan. 1, 1956; d. E. Fulton Brylawski and Laura (Carizzoni) Brylawski Miller; m. Neil M. McMahon, Oct. 2, 1982; children: Alexa Lauren, Brendan Patrick, Morgan Lane. BA, Northwestern U., 1976; MBA, Kellogg Grad. Sch. Mgmt., 1977. Asst. brand mgr. Gen. Mills Inc., Mpls., 1977-80; mgr. new products and corp. devel. William Wrigley Jr. Co., Chgo., 1980-84; v.p., C.I.E. practice, head of Washington office Mercer Mgmt. Cons., Washington, 1984—. Contbr. articles to profl. jours. Mem. Beta Gamma Sigma. Republican. Roman Catholic. Office: Mercer Mgmt Cons 2300 N St NW Washington DC 20037-1122

MCMAHON, JANET MANKIEWICH, critical care nurse; b. Rockville Centre, N.Y., Apr. 23, 1957; d. Matthew J. and Lois May (Johns) Mankiewich; m. Michael T. McMahon, July 12, 1985; children: Shannon and Sandy (twins), Patrick. BSN, Adelphi U., 1980. RN, N.Y., Va.; cert. BLS instr., ACLS. Nurse St. Francis Hosp., Roslyn, N.Y.; charge nurse L.I. Jewish Hillside Med. Ctr., New Hyde Park, N.Y., Alexandria (Va.) Hosp., Mary Washington Hosp., Fredricksberg, Va., Mt. Vernon (Va.) Hosp., George Washington U. Hosp., Washington; nurse Potomac Hosp., Woodbridge, Va. Mem. AACCN.

MCMAHON, MARIA DRISCOLL, artist; b. Sayre, Pa., Jan. 8, 1959; d. Thomas James and Betty Jane (Taylor) Driscoll; m. Hugh Michael McMahon, May 27, 1978; children: Ian Thomas, Lea Shea. BS in Art Edn. summa cum laude, U. Pa. Kutztown, 1988; MA in Studio Art, Marywood Coll., 1993. Cert. art tchr., N.Y. Tchr. art Horseheads (N.Y.) Ctrl. Sch. Dist., 1989-94; artist Ithaca, N.Y., 1993—; lectr. Allentown (Pa.) Art Mus., 1987. One-person shows include Three River Reading Series, Corning, N.Y., 1996; exhibited in group shows at Bradford County Regional Exhbn., 1995, State of Art Gallery, Ithaca, 1993—, Susquehanna Regional Art Exhbn., 1994, Merit award, 1994, N.Y. State Fair, 1993, State of the Art Gallery, 1996, George Waters Gallery, Elmirea Coll., N.Y., 1996; author: (poem) Steele Meml. Libr. Poetry Festival, Elmira, N.Y., 1980, Merit award, 1980. Vol. Schrader Creek Assn., Bradford County, Pa., 1993—. Mem. NYSUT, Cmty. Arts Partnership of Tompkins County. Democrat. Home and Office: 4 Main St Lockwood NY 14859

MCMAHON, MARIA O'NEIL, social work educator; b. Hartford, Conn., Jan. 2, 1937; d. John Joseph and Margaret (Galvin) O'Neil; m. Dennis Richard McMahon, June 10, 1988; stepchildren: Lezlie, Nora, Kelly, Stacie, Michael. BA, St. Joseph Coll., West Hartford, Conn., 1958; MSW, Cath. U. Am., 1964, D. Social Work, 1978. Supr., child and family therapist Highland Heights Residential Treatment Ctr., New Haven, 1964-71; chair dept. sociolgy and social work St. Joseph Coll., 1971-84; prof. E. Carolina U., Greenville, N.C., 1985—, dean Sch. Social Work, 1985-91; cons. to various univs., 1970—; trainer Conn. Dept. Social Svcs., 1982-84, N.C. Dept. Social Svcs., 1987-89. Author: The General Method of Social Work Practice, 1984, 2d edit., 1990, 3d edit., 1996, Advanced Generalist Practice, With An International Perspective, 1994; editor report in field; contbr. articles, book revs. to profl. publs. Commr. Nat. Coun. Social Work Edn., Alexandria, Va., 1983-85; chair bd. dirs. Ea. N.C. Poverty Com., 1987—, Cath. Social Ministries of Archdiocese of Raleigh (N.C.), 1989-92. Recipient Outstanding Educator award AAUW, 1981, Disting. Alumnae award, Cath. U. of Am., 1994. Mem. Nat. Assn. Social Workers (Outstanding Social Worker of Yr., Conn. chpt. 1981), Acad. Cert. Social Workers, Am. Correctional Assn., Nat. Assn. Women Deans, Nat. Coun. Social Work Edn. Democrat. Roman Catholic. Office: E Carolina U Sch Social Work Ragsdale Hall Greenville NC 27858

MCMAHON, STEPHANIE MARIE, oncological nurse; b. Pitts., Oct. 16, 1952; d. Harvey L. and Marie (Sekelik) Corba; m. Mark E. McMahon, Mar. 20, 1981; children: William, Brian. ADN, C.C. Allegheny County, Pitts., 1974; lic. funeral dir., Pitts. Inst. Mortuary Sci., 1977; BSN, Pa. State U., 1993; postgrad., U. Pitts., 1994—. RN, Pa.; cert. oncology nurse specialist, Pa. Staff nurse Allegheny Gen. Hosp., Pitts., 1974-76; funeral dir. Harvey L. Corba Funeral Home, Pitts., 1977-78; staff nurse Presbyn. U. Hosp., Pitts., 1979-82; office nurse Drs. Ellis and Dameshek, Pitts., 1981-88; nurse mgr. outpatient oncology clinic VA Hosp., Pitts., 1988-96; clin. support specialist Amgen, 1996—; vis. staff nurse Interim Health Care, Pitts., 1992—; intravenous team staff nurse Presbyn. U. Hosp., Pitts., 1984-93; group leader Teen Fresh Start Program, Am. Cancer Soc., Pitts., 1994. Concessions mgr. Crafton Little Cougars, Pitts., 1989-94. Mem. Oncology Nurse Soc. (ambulatory care spl. interest group 1994, elected dir.-at-large Pitts. chpt. 1996-98). Home and Office: 44 Belvidere St Pittsburgh PA 15205-2819

MCMANAMA, TRUDY E., psychologist, educator; b. Pitts., Mar. 30, 1945; d. Francis J. and Mary Margaret (McDonough) Figura; m. Patick J. McManama, Nov. 25, 1967 (div. 1977); 1 child, Steven Patrick. BS, Mansfield U., 1967; MS, So. Conn. U., 1973, postgrad., 1974; postgrad., Harvard U., 1988. Cert. sch. psychologist. Tchr. New Milford Schs., Conn., 1967-69, Shepaug Valley H.S., Washington Depot, Conn., 1969-72; tng. cons. Danbury Area Unified Social Svcs., Conn., 1971-72; psychologist Bd. Coop. Svcs., Poughkeepsie, N.Y., 1974-75; psychologist Berrien County Ind. Sch. Dist., Berrien Springs, Mich., 1975—, sec., 1995—; cons. Stanley Clark Sch.,

South Bend, Ind., 1981-88; adj. prof. Ind. U., South Bend, 1979—; instr. St. Joseph Hosp., South Bend, 1985-87; elected trustee South Bend Sch. Corp., 1987-90, pres. 1989. Vol. Internat. Spl. Olympics, 1987; pres., Neighborhood Watch Program, South Bend, 1982-83; hospice vol., South Bend; bd. dirs. Child Abuse and Neglect Coordination Orgn., South Bend, 1986-92; mem. Selective Svc. Bd., 1989—; mem. Handicapped Camping Bd., 1986-89; mem. Dem. Precinct Com., South Bend, 1980-82; del. Ind. Dem. State Conv., 1984; co-chair Carnival for The Arts, 1991-92; chair polit. action Mich. Edn. Assn. Berrien County, 1993—, SNAP negotiator, 1994-95. Berrien County Task Force grantee, 1979, Adj. fellow, 1995. Mem. Assn. Supervision and Curriculum Devel., NASP, NEA (assembly del. 1995—), Panhillenic Assn. Democrat. Roman Catholic. Avocations: jogging, reading, cross country skiing, international travel. Home: 2725 Erskine Blvd South Bend IN 46614-1201 Office: Berrien County Intermediate Sch Dist 711 Saint Joseph Ave Berrien Springs MI 49103-1602

MCMANIGAL, SHIRLEY ANN, university dean; b. Deering, Mo., May 4, 1938; d. Jadie C. and Willie B. (Groves) Naile. BS, Ark. State U., 1971; MS, U. Okla., 1976, PhD, 1979. Lic. med. technologist, clin. lab. dir. Med. technologist, 1958-75; chair dept. med. tech. U. So. Miss., Hattiesburg, 1979-83; chair dept. med. tech. Tex. Tech U. Health Scis. Ctr., Lubbock, 1983-87, dean Sch. Allied Health, 1987—; gov.'s appointee to statewide health coord. coun., 1994—. Leadership Tex., 1992; Lt. Alumnae Regl. dir., 1994—. Recipient Citation, State of Tex., 1988; named Woman of Yr., AAUW, Tex. div., 1990, Woman of Excellence in Edn. YWCA, Lubbock, 1990. Mem. AAUW (bd. dirs. Tex. 1990-94), Am. Coun. on Edn./Nat. Identification Program (steering com. for Tex.), Clin. Lab. Mgmt. Assn. (chair edn. com. 1989, 91), Am. Soc. Med. Tech., Nat. Assn. Women in Edn., So. Assn. Allied Health Deans at Acad. Health Ctrs., S.W. Assn. Clin. Microbiology, Tex. Soc. Allied Health Professions (pres. 1990-91), Tex. Soc. Med. Tech. (Educator of Yr. 1990), Alpha Eta, Phi Beta Delta. Home: 5003 94th St Lubbock TX 79424-4839 Office: Tex Tech U Sch Allied Health Dept Scis Ctr Lubbock TX 79430

MCMANN, EDITH MAY, performing and visual artist; b. Totowa, N.J., Mar. 26, 1929; d. Henry and Lena (Ulmer) Brozek; m. Frank Richard McMann, May 25, 1957; children: Robert, Stephen. BPS in Dance and Visual Arts, SUNY, 1984; MS in Studio Art, Coll. of New Rochelle, 1989. Performing artist Nat. Ballet of Cuba, Havana, 1948-50; performing artist ballet N.Y.C. Ballet, 1950-57; visual artist N.Y.C., 1969—. Exhbns. include Mamaroneck Artists Guild Gallery, 1990-96, Beaux Arts Exhibits, 1991-94, Manhattanville Coll., 1991, Gutman Gallery, 1990, 89, Coll. Ctr. Gallery, Coll. of New Rochelle, 1989-94, SUNY, 1979, Art Students League, 1977, New Rochelle Libr., 1976, Greenburgh Libr., 1976, Westchester Art Workshop, 1976, Town Ctr. Gallery, Mamaroneck, 1993-96, Westbeth Gallery, N.Y.C., 1994, Hammond Mus., Salem, 1994, N.Y.C. Ballet, Lincoln Ctr., 1993, Fine Arts Gallery, Westchester Cmty. Coll., Valhalla, N.Y., 1992, many others. Recipient Cert. of Merit U.S. Senator-N. Spano, 1989, U.S. State Assemblyman-R. Brodsky, 1989, Letter of Appreciation U.S. Senator Pat Moynihan, 1989, Letter of Congratulations U.S. Congressman -B. Gilman, 1989. Mem. Allied Artist of Am., Hudson River Contemporary Artists, Nat. Mus. for Women in ARt, Silvermine Guild of Artists, Scarsdale Art Soc., Mamaroneck Artists Guild (bd. dirs. assoc. rep. 1990-91, receiving com. 1992). Home: 10 Burkewood Rd Hartsdale NY 10530

MCMANUS, MARY HAIRSTON, English language educator; b. Danville, Va., Nov. 23; d. Benjamin and Essie (Walton) Hairston; m. Booker Taliaferro McManus, June 27; children: Philip, Kenneth. BA, Va. State U., Petersburg, MA; PhD, U. Md. Cert. in English lang. and lit. edn. Instr. English Va. State U., Petersburg, 1965-70; lectr. English European div. U. Md., Berlin, 1972-73; instr. English Fayetteville (N.C.) State U., 1975-78; instr. ESOL Venice (Ill.)-Lincoln Tech. Ctr., 1978-83; lectr. English Anne Arundel C.C., Arnold, Md., 1983-84; asst. prof. English Bowie (Md.) State U., 1984—, dir. honors program, 1993—; cons. Anne Arundel County Govt., Glen Burnie, Md., 1983-84, Prince George's County Govt., Upper Marlboro, Md., 1985-86; mem. adv. bd. Collegiate Press, Alta Loma, Calif., 1992—. Recipient Outstanding Educator award Prince George's County Fire Dept., 1988; NEH fellow, 1991. Mem. MLA, Nat. Coun. Tchrs. English, Coll. Lang. Assn., CHUMS Inc. (pres. 1995—), Middle Atlantic Writers Assn., Kiwanis, Alpha Kappa Alpha, Sigma Tau Delta. Democrat. Home: 432 Lakeland Rd N Severna Park MD 21146-2420 Office: Bowie State U 14000 Jericho Park Rd Bowie MD 20715-3318

MCMASTER, BELLE MILLER, religious organization administrator; b. Atlanta, May 24, 1932; d. Patrick Dwight and Lila (Bonner) Miller; m. George R. McMaster, June 19, 1953; children: Lisa McMaster Stork, George Neel, Patrick Miller. BA, Agnes Scott Coll., 1953; MA, U. Louisville, 1970, PhD, 1974. Assoc. corp. witness Presbyn. Ch. USA, Atlanta, 1974-77, dir. corp. witness, 1977-81, dir. div. corp. and social mission, 1981-87; dir. social justice and peacemaking unit Presbyn. Ch. USA, Louisville, Ky., 1987-93; acting dir. program women in theology and ministry Candler Sch. Theology Emory U., 1993-96; dir. advanced studies Candler Sch. Theology Emory U., 1995—; 1993-96; vice moderator chs. commn. internat. affairs World Coun. Chs., 1984-91; chair commn. internat. affairs Nat. Coun. Chs., N.Y.C., 1986-89, v.p., 1990-95, chair ch. world svc. and witness unit com., 1990-95; bd. dirs. Ecumenical Devel. Corp. U.S.A., 1992—, Prison Ministries with Women, 1995—. Author: Witnessing to the Kingdom, 1982, book columnist "What I Have Been Reading" in Church and Society Magazine, 1993—; contbr. articles to profl. jours. Pres. League of Women Voters, Greenville, S.C., 1963-64; bd. dirs. Interfaith Housing, Atlanta, 1975-81. Danforth fellow, 1969-74. Mem. MLA, Acad. Am. Religion, Soc. for Values in Higher Edn., Phi Beta Kappa. Office: Emory U Candler Sch Theology Atlanta GA 30322

MCMATH, ELIZABETH MOORE, graphic artist; b. Iredell, Tex., Feb. 20, 1930; d. Fred William and Elizabeth Carol (Smith) Moore; m. Charles Wallis McMath, Jan. 16, 1978 (dec. Dec. 1990); children: Charles Wallis, John Seals. BA, BS in Advt. Design, Tex. Woman's U., Denton, 1951; grad. gemologist, Gemol. Inst. Am., L.A., 1977. Layout artist Leonard's Dept. Store, Ft. Worth, Tex., 1951-52; artist/bookkeeper Bud Biggs Studio, Dallas, 1953; sec./artist Squire Haskins Studio, Dallas, 1953-54; artist/art dir. Dowdell-Merrill, Inc., Dallas, 1954-58; owner/artist Moore Co., Dallas, 1958-90. Mem. Stemmons Corridor Bus. Assn., Dallas, 1988-89. Mem. Dallas/Ft. Worth Soc. Visual Comm. (founder), Tex. Woman's U. Nat. Alumnae Assn., Greater North Tex. Orchid Soc. (treas. 1987), Daylily Growers of Dallas (sec. 1989-90, 1st v.p. and program chmn. 1992), Internat. Bulb Soc., Native Plant Soc. Tex. (publicity chmn. Trinity Forks chpt. 1991-96). Presbyterian. Home: PO Box 1068 Denton TX 76202-1068

MCMAUGH, CONNIE LYNN, federal agency administrator; b. Sheboygan, Wis., Feb. 20, 1951; d. Bernard James and June (Kober) Ertel; m. Earl Vincent McMaugh, Aug. 11, 1984; children: Marco A. Mireles, Christopher J. McMaugh. BA, U. Wis., 1973; grad., NYU, 1991; student, Inter Am. Def. Coll., 1990-91. Bilingual tech. Def. Intelligence Agy., Madrid, 1973-79; intelligence analyst Def. Intelligence Agy., Washington, 1979-83, intelligence officer, 1983-85, intelligence opers. officer, 1985-95, fed. women's program mgr., 1991-94, congressional liaison officer, 1995, fgn. disclosure officer, 1995—; mem. Dept. Def. Sr. Profl. Women.; sole propr. Angel Faces Doll Studio, Falls Church, Va., 1995—. Mem. Falls Church Commn. for Women, 1993-94. Lutheran. Office: Def Intelligence Agy Pentagon Arlington VA 20340-2552

MCMEEKIN, DOROTHY, botany, plant pathology educator; b. Boston, Feb. 24, 1932; d. Thomas LeRoy and Vera (Crockatt) McM. BA, Wilson Coll., 1953; MA, Wellesley Coll., 1955; PhD, Cornell U., 1959. Asst. prof. Upsala Coll., East Orange, N.J., 1959-64, Bowling Green State U., Ohio, 1964-66; prof. natural sci. Mich. State U., East Lansing, 1966-89, prof. botany, plant pathology, 1989—. Author: Diego Rivera: Science and Creativity, 1985; contbr. articles to profl. jours. Mem. Am. Phytopath. Soc., Mycol. Soc. Am., Soc. Econ. Bot., Mich. Bot. Soc. (bd. dirs. 1985—), Mich. Women's Studies Assn., Sigma Xi, Phi Kappa Phi. Home: 1055 Marigold Ave East Lansing MI 48823-5128 Office: Mich State U Dept Botany-Plant Pathology 335 N Kedzie Hall East Lansing MI 48824-1031

MCMENAMIN, HELEN MARIE FORAN, home health care, pediatric, maternal nurse; b. Buffalo, May 21, 1943; d. John Michael and Helen Marie (McCarty) Foran; m. John Patrick McMenamin, Aug. 21, 1965; children: Maureen Regina, Kathleen Noelle, Terence Michael, Amy Colleen, Shannon Rosemary, Barry Patrick. BSN, Niagara U., 1965; cert. instr. natural family planning, St. Margaret's Hosp., Boston, 1983. RN N.Y., N.H., Maine, D.C., Va., Md., Pa. Instr. perinatal, neonatal nursing Mercy Hosp. Sch. of Nursing, Portland, Maine, 1981-83; staff/charge nurse neonatal intensive care unit Georgetown Univ. Hosp., Washington, D.C., 1984-93; staff nurse neonatal ICU, renal unit, home care case mgr. Children's Hosp. Nat. Med. Ctr., Washington, 1986-93; educator infant APNEA/CPR, Fairfax Hosp. Infant APNEA Program, Fairfax, Va., 1988-89; pediatric and maternal-child case mgr. Vis. Nurse Assn. No. Va., Arlington, 1992; staff nurse pediatric emergency room Mercy Hosp., Balt., 1992-93; case mgr. maternal-child pediatrics, high-risk neonatal home care Bay Area Health Care, Balt., 1993-95; mgr. maternal-child/neonatal and pediatric program 1st Am. Home Care, Hanover, Pa., 1994-95; pvt. duty pediatric home care Mount Washington Pediatric Hosp., Balt., 1995; coord. high risk maternal-child & pediatric program Future Health Corp., Timonium, Md., 1995—; organizer, co-dir. health clinics Cathedral Elem. Sch., Portland, Maine, 1981-83. Block capt. Am. Cancer Assn., Springfield, Va., 1986-90; mem. Healthy Mothers/Health Babies and Teen Pregnancy Coalition York County. Mem. Nat. Assn. Neonatal Nurses, Nat. Assn. Pro-Life Nurses (bd. dirs. of Pa.), Nat. Assn. Pediatric Nurses. Roman Catholic. Home: RR 1 Box 1456 Brodbecks PA 17329-9603

MCMICHAEL, JEANE CASEY, real estate corporation executive; b. Clarksville, Ind., May 7, 1938; d. Emmett Ward and Carrie Evelyn (Leonard) Casey; m. Norman Kenneth Wenzler, Sept. 12, 1956 (div. 1968); m. Wilburn Arnold McMichael, June 20, 1978. Student Ind. U. Extension Ctr., Bellermine Coll., 1972-73, Ind. U. S.E., 1973—, Kentuckiana Metroversity, 1981—; Grad. Realtors Inst., Ind. U., 1982; grad. Leadership Tng., Clark County, Ind.; lic. real estate broker, Ind., Ky.; master Grad. Realtors Inst., Cert. Residential Specialist, Cert. Real Estate Broker, Leadership Tng. Grad. Owner, pres. McMichael Real Estate, Inc., Jeffersonville, 1979-88, 90-96; mgr., owner Buzz Bauer Realtors, Clark County, 1989-91; mng. broker Parks & Weisberg Realtors, Jeffersonville, Ind., 1989-91; instr. pre-license real estate Ivy Tech. State Coll., 1995-96, real estate Tng. Concepts, Inc. Pres. of congregation St. Mark's United Ch. of Christ, 1996, pres., Mr. and Mrs. Class, chmn., fin. trustee and bus. adv., chmn. devel. com., 1993, 94; chmn. bd. trustees, Brooklawn Youth Svcs., 1988-94, chmn. 1994-95; chmn. social com. Rep. party Clark County (Ind.); v.p. Floyd County Habitat for Humanity, 1991, 94/95. Recipient cert. of appreciation Nat. Ctr. Citizen Involvement, 1983; award Contact Kentuckiana Teleminnistries, 1978. Mem. Nat. Assn. Realtors (nat. dir. 1989—), Ind. Assn. Realtors (state dir. 1987—, quick start speaker 1989-91), Nat. Women's Council Realtors (state pres., chmn. coms., state rec. sec., 1984, state pres. 1985-86, Nat. Achievement award 1982, 83, 84, 85, 86, 87, 88, 89, 90, nat. gov. Ind. 1987, v.p. region III 1988, Ind. Honor Realtor award 1982—), Women's Council of Realtors (speaker 1990-94, Mem. of Yr. 1988), Ky. Real Estate Exchange, So. Ind. Bd. Realtors (program chmn. 1986-87, bd. dirs., pres., 1988—, Realtor of Yr. 1985, instr. success series, 1989-92, Snyder Svc. award 1987, Omega Tau Rho award 1988, Excellence in Edn. award 1989), Ind. Assn. Realtors (state dir. 1985—, bd. govs., instr./trainer, speaker 1989-94, chair bd. govs. 1991), Toastmasters (pres. Steamboat chpt.), Psi Iota Xi. Office: McMichael Real Estate Inc 1402 Blackiston Mill Rd Jeffersonville IN 47129-1227 Address: 23 Arctic Springs Rd Jeffersonville IN 47130

MCMICHEN, HARRIET FARMER, training analyst; b. Charlotte, N.C., Aug. 26, 1954; d. Ralph Nuckols and Ethel Florence (Scism) Farmer; m. Douglas Ford Adams, May 3, 1979 (div. May 1983); 1 child, Mary Healey Adams; m. Jephory Franklin McMichen, Oct. 30, 1989; 1 child, Schaula April. BA in Psychology, Queens Coll., Charlotte, N.C., 1977. Founder, owner Executaries, Charlotte, 1983-87; English, music and computer tchr. Marish Bros. Sch., Pago Pago, Samoa, 1988-89; co-owner Heart of the Orient (Thailand Co. Ltd.), Bangkok and Atlanta, 1989-92; sr. tng. analyst Bianco Hopkins & Assocs., Atlanta, 1996—. Chmn. fundraising com. Fulton County Magnet Program for Performing Arts, Atlanta, 1995-96; mem. tech. com. Alpharetta (Ga.) Elem. Sch., 1995-96. Mem. ASTD. Republican. Home: 7134 Surrey Point Alpharetta GA 30201

MCMILLAN, ADELL, educational administrator, retired; b. Portland, Oreg., June 22, 1933; d. John and Eunice A. (Hoyt) McM. AB in Social Sci., Whitman Coll., 1955; MS in Recreation Mgmt., U. Oreg., 1963. Program dir. Erb Meml. Union, U. Oreg., Eugen, 1955-68; program cons. Willard Straight Hall, Cornell U., Ithaca, N.Y., 1966-67; assoc. dir. Erb Meml. Union, U. Oreg., Eugene, 1968-75; dir. Erb Meml. Union, U. Oreg., 1975-91, dir. emeritus, 1992—. Editor, co-author: College Unions: Seventy-Five Years, 1989; interviewer, editor oral history interviews, 1978, 92, 93, 94, 96. Bd. dirs. United Way, Lane County, Oreg., 1976-83, 87—, pres., 1982-83, 88-90; commr. Eugene City Planning Commn., 1992—; mem. Hist. Rev. Bd., 1992—; mem. Tree Commn., 1992-93; bd. dirs., treas., 1994-95, Eugene Opera Co., 1992—. Named Woman of Yr. Lane County Coun. Orgns., Eugene, Oreg., 1985. Mem. Assn. Coll. Unions-Internat. (v.p. 1977-80, pres. 1981-82, Butts-Whiting award 1987, hon. 1992), Zonta Club of Eugene, Zonta Internat. (pres. 1984-86, dist. treas. 1990-92, 92-94), Emerald Valley Women's Golf Club (pres. 1995). Democrat. Episcopalian. Office: 55 W 39th Ave Eugene OR 97405-3344

MCMILLAN, JULIA A., pediatrician; b. Pinehurst, N.C., July 10, 1946. MD, SUNY, Syracuse, 1976. Intern SUNY Upstate Med. Ctr., Syracuse, 1976-77, resident in pediatrics, 1977-78, 79-80, fellow in infectious diseases, 1979-81; mem. staff Johns Hopkins U. Hosp., Balt.; assoc. prof. Johns Hopkins U., Balt. Mem. ASM, IDSA, Am. Acad. Pediatrics. OFfice: Johns Hopkins Hosp Dept Pediatrics 600 N Wolfe St Baltimore MD 21287-3224

MCMILLAN, SHEILA DON, lawyer; b. Pageland, S.C., Jan. 30, 1953; d. Elliott Foster and Minnie Parker (Blakeney) McM. BA, Winthrop U., 1973; MEd, U. N.C., 1975; JD, U. S.C., 1979. Bar: S.C. 1979. Educator Charlotte (N.C.)-Mecklenburg Schs., 1973-76; law clk. Chambers Stein Ferguson & Becton, Charlotte, 1977, U.S. Atty.'s Office, Columbia, S.C., 1978; from staff atty. to mng. atty. Palmetto Legal Svcs., Lexington, 1979-80; staff atty. Senate Rsch., Columbia, 1981-84; atty., dir. S.C. Sen. Gen. Com., Joint Election Law Com., Columbia, 1984-90, S.C. Senate Fish, Game & Forestry Com., Columbia, 1991-96; atty. S.C. Sen. Rsch., Columbia, 1996—. Bd. dirs. Boys and Girls Clubs of Midlands; fin. com. chmn. bd. trustees Winthrop U.; bd. dirs. ARC. Mem. S.C. Black Lawyers Assn. (former pres.), Columbia Lawyers Assn. (former v.p.), Alpha Kappa Alpha (past local pres.). Presbyn. Office: SC Senate Rsch Senate Office Bldg 301 Gressette Columbia SC 29201

MCMILLAN, TERRY L., writer, educator; b. Port Huron, Mich., Oct. 18, 1951; d. Edward McMillan and Madeline Washington Tillman; 1 child, Solomon Welch. BA in Journalism, U. Calif., Berkeley, 1979; MFA, Columbia Univ., N.Y.C., 1979. Instr. U. Wyoming, Laramie, 1987-90; prof. U. Ariz., Tucson, 1990-92. Author: Mama, 1987, Disappearing Acts, 1989, Waiting to Exhale, 1992, How StellaGot Her Groove Back, 1996, (with Nawal El Saadawi) Ergo! the Bumbershoot Literary Magazine (vol. 8 no. 1), 1993; editor: Breaking Ice: An Anthropology of Contemporary African-American Fiction, 1990; screenwriter (with Ron Bass) (movie) Waiting to Exhale, 1995. Recipient National Endowment for the Arts fellowship, 1988. Office: care Free at Last PO Box 2408 Danville CA 94526-7408 also: care Molly Friedrich Aaron Priest Literary Agency 708 Third Ave 23rd Fl New York NY 10017

MCMILLEN, ELIZABETH CASHIN, artist; b. Chgo.; d. James Blaine and Hortense (Fears) Cashin; m. John Stephen Jerabek; 1 child, Michael N. Student, Western Coll. for Women, 1961-63; BA, Bard Coll., 1965. coord. com. and juror Spectra I, sponsor state exhbn. women artists Westbrook Coll., Portland, Maine, 1979; dir. Hancock County Auditorium Art Gallery, Ellsworth, Maine, 1984, 85. rin. works include sculpture Ahimsa Gallery, Maine, 1976; exhibited at Frick Gallery, Belfast, Maine, 1993, 94, Maine Coast Artists Juried Show, Rockport, 1994, Portland Children's Mus., 1995, Lakes Gallery, Sebago, Maine, 1995; one-person shows include Area Gallery, Portland, 1994, Frick Gallery, Belfast, Maine, 1995; two persons show Maine Coast Artists, Rockport, 1996. Dem. chair Town of Lamoine, Maine, 1984-85, 86-87, 88-89; legislation coord. Amnesty Internat., Ellsworth, 1991—. Democrat. Episcopalian.

MCMILLER, ANITA WILLIAMS, army officer, transportation professional, educator; b. Chgo., Dec. 23, 1946; d. Chester Leon and Marion Claudette (Martin) Williams; m. Robert Melvin McMiller, July 29, 1967 (div. 1980). BS in Edn., No. Ill. U., 1968; MBA, Fla. Inst. Tech., 1979; M of Mil. Arts and Sci., U.S. Army Command & Gen. Staff Coll., 1990; postgrad., U.S. Army War Coll., Carlisle, Pa., 1993-94. Social worker Cook County, Chgo., 1968-69; recruiter analyst, dir. pers. State of Ill., Chgo., 1969-75; commd. 1st lt. U.S. Army, 1975, advanced through grades to col., 1996; platoon leader, motor officer, exec. officer 155th Transp. Co., Ft. Eustis, Va. and Okinawa, Japan, 1976-78; S-1 pers. and adminstrn. officer 38th Transp. Bn., Ft. Eustis, 1978-79; installation transp. officer, fin. mgr. 3d Armor Div., Hanau, Germany, 1979-82, transp. co. comdr., 1982-83; transp. plans officer Mil. Traffic Mgmt. Command, Falls Church, Va., 1983-85; tour with Sea Land Corp., Menlo Park, N.J., 1985-86; dep. comdr., ops. officer Bremerhaven (Germany) Terminal, 1986-89; logistics staff officer The Pentagon, Washington, 1990-91; comdr. 1320th Port Battalion U.K. Terminal, Felixstowe, Great Britain, 1991-93; dep. legis. asst. to Chmn. Joint Chiefs of Staff, The Pentagon, Washington, 1994—; instr. Ctrl. Tex. Coll., Hanau, Germany, 1981-83, Phillips Bus. Coll., Alexandria, Va., 1983-84, City Colls. Chgo., 1987-89. Editor: Rocks, Inc. Pictoral Album, 1996; contbr. articles to profl. jours. Child adv., foster mother Army Cmty. Svc., Hanau, 1980-83; tutor Parent-Tchr. Club Hanau Schs., 1981-83; vol. Vis. Nurses Assn. No. Va., 1983-85; coord., English tutor Adopt-a-Sch. Project, Washington, 1983-85; treas. Bremerhaven Girl Scouts Coun., 1987-89, mem. ARC, Big Sisters. Mem. Nat. Def. Transp. Assn., World Affairs Coun., Assn. U.S. Army, Fedn. Bus. Profl. Women, Club: Rocks, Inc., Am. Legion, British Legion, Alpha Kappa Alpha. Home: PO Box 46344 Washington DC 20050-6344 Office: Office of Chmn Joint Chiefs of Staff The Pentagon Washington DC 20318

MCMILLIN, KATHRYN WILLIAMS, middle school educator, coach; b. Detroit, Feb. 25, 1956; d. Raymond Henry and Edith Kelly (Bundy) Williams; m. Bruce Daniels Cutler, July 23, 1983 (div. July 1989); m. James Clark McMillin, July 10, 1993. AA, Normandale C.C., Bloomington, Minn., 1976; BS in Edn., U. Tenn., 1978, MS in Edn., 1980. Cert. tchr., Tenn. Volleyball ofcl. Tenn. Secondary Sch. Athletics, Knoxville, 1978-80; gymnastics instr. Westside YMCA, Knoxville, 1979-81; volleyball staff coach Bob Bertucci's Lady Vol. Corp., Knoxville, 1985; driver edn. instr. Webb Sch., Knoxville, 1981-87, intramural sports dir., 1987—, head coach, 1981—, phys. edn. tchr., 1981—, United Way coord., 1989—, Webb Fest coord., 1993-94, field day coord., 1987—; field trip coord. Webb Day Camp, Knoxville, summers 1990-91, dir. girls day camp, summer 1992; dir. WebbFit for Life Club, 1994—. Player U.S. Volleyball Assn., Knoxville, 1977-90, volleyball ofcl., 1977-90. Mem. AAHPERD, Tenn. Athletic Coaches Assn., Nat. Fedn. Intercollegiate Coaches Assn., Tenn. Secondary Schs. Athletic Assn., Tenn. Volleyball Coaches Assn., Tenn. Assn. for Health, Phys. Edn., Recreation, and Dance. Home: 11301 Berryhill Dr Knoxville TN 37931-2802 Office: Webb Sch of Knoxville 9800 Webb School Ln Knoxville TN 37923-3307

MCMINN, CYNTHIA ANNE, elementary school principal; b. Tachikawa Air Base, Japan, Sept. 10, 1951; m. Robert Clark McMinn, Sr., Feb. 23, 1990 (dec.). BS, U. So. Miss., Hattiesburg, 1972; MEd, Miss. U. for Women, Columbus, 1980; EdD, Miss. State U., 1990. Cert. tchr., adminstr. Tchr. Biloxi (Miss.) Pub. Schs., 1971-75, Monroe County Schs., Key West, Fla., 1975-77; ednl. advisor officer USAF, Point Arena, Calif., 1977-79, Columbus (Miss.) Pub. Schs., 1979-88; grad. teaching and rsch. asst. Miss. State U., 1988-90; asst. prin. Starkville (Miss.) Pub. Schs., 1990-92; prin. Columbus Pub. Schs., 1992—; mem. adv. bd. Miss. Ednl. Leadership Inst. for Women, Miss. State Dept. Edn., Jackson, 1994-95. Mem. ASCD, NAESP, Nat. Staff Devel. Coun., Mid-South Ednl. Rsch. Assn., Miss. Coun. Pub. Schs. (chmn. com. of elem. prin. 1993-95), Miss. Assn. Sch. Adminstrs., Phi Delta Kappa. Home: 2141 Old Highway 82 E Starkville MS 39759-8510 Office: Cook Elem Sch 2217 7th St North Columbus MS 39701

MCMINN, VIRGINIA ANN, human resources consulting company executive; b. Champaign, Ill., Apr. 7, 1948; d. Richard Henry and Esther Lucille (Ellis) Taylor; m. Michael Lee McMinn, Dec. 29, 1973. BA in Teaching of English, U. Ill., 1969; MS in Indsl. Rels., Loyola U., Chgo., 1985. Pers. sec. Solo Cup Co., Urbana, Ill., 1972-74; pers. asst. Rust-Oleum Corp., Evanston, Ill., 1974-75, asst. pers. mgr., 1974-80; mgr. employee rels. Rust-Oleum Corp., Vernon Hills, Ill., 1980-81, mgr. human resources, 1981-84; dir. human resources Field Container Corp., Elk Grove Village, Ill., 1984-87; regional mgr. human resources Hartford Ins. Corp., Chgo., 1987-90; owner, pres. McMinn & Assocs., Ltd., Palatine, Ill., 1988—; founder S.W. Human Resources Group, Chandler, Ariz., 1995; instr. bus. and mgmt. divsn. Trinity Coll., Deerfield, Ill., 1984-85; instr. bus. and social scis. Harper Coll., Palatine, Ill., 1990-93; bd. dirs. Nierman's Hard-To-Find Sizes Shoes, Chgo.; spkr. on legal issues, terminations, employment at will, career planning, job search, and human resources function to area colls., industry and profl. and women's groups. Bd. dirs. Ill. Crossroads coun. Girls Scouts USA, Elk Grove, 1988-92; mem. Ill. Com. to Implement Clean Indoor Air Act, Chgo., 1990-91; past mem. adv. bd. Coll. of Lake County, 1982-84. Mem. Soc. for Human Resource Mgmt., Nat. Network Sales Profls. (program chmn. 1990-93), Women in Mgmt. (chpt. Leadership award corp. category, past pres.), Palatine C. of C., Rotary Club Palatine. Office: 1423 Michele Dr Palatine IL 60067-5656

MCMONIGAL, MEG JOSEPHINE, urban planner; b. St. Paul, Dec. 31, 1958; d. William Edward and Elizabeth Ann (Schwartz) McM. BA in Geography, U. Wis., 1982, MS in Urban and Regional Planning, 1985; postgrad., U. St. Thomas. Planning intern City of St. Paul, 1984-85; assoc. planner City of Apple Valley, Minn., 1986-93; city planner City of Northfield, Minn., 1993-95; sr. planner McCombs Frank Roos Assocs., Plymouth, Minn., 1995—. Bd. dirs., writer, vol. East Calhoun News, Mpls., 1989-93. Mem. Am. Planning Assn. (profl. devel. officer Minn. chpt. 1993—), Am. Inst. Cert. Planners, Minn. Assn. Urban Mgmt. Assts., Women's Transp. Seminar, Sensible Land Use Coalition. Home: 3448 Hennepin Ave S Minneapolis MN 55408 Office: McCombs Frank Roos Assocs 15050 23d Ave N Plymouth MN 55447

MCMORRIES, MELISSA ELIOT, lawyer; b. Bethesda, Md., Nov. 18, 1952; d. Edwin Eliot and Cynthia Lowe (Read) McM.; m. Jonathan Daniel Simmons, June 23, 1990. AB cum laude, Duke U., 1973; JD cum laude, Wake Forest U., 1982. Bar: N.C. 1982, Ga. 1990. Data svcs. officer Wachovia Svcs., Inc., Winston-Salem, N.C., 1975-79; atty. R.J. Reynolds Industries, Winston-Salem, N.C., 1982-85; asst. counsel RJR Nabisco, Inc., Winston-Salem, N.C., 1985-87; assoc. counsel RJR Nabisco, Inc., Atlanta, 1987-89, counsel, 1989; v.p., gen. counsel The Regina Co., Atlanta, 1989-95, Enercon Environmenta Sys., 1995—. Exec. editor Wake Forest Law Rev., 1981-82. Bd. dirs. Winston-Salem Coun. on Status of Women, 1983-87, pres. 1987; bd. dirs. law alumni coun. Wake Forest U., 1988-93, Metro. Atlanta Coun. on Alcohol and Drugs, 1993—. Mem. ABA, Ga. Bar Assn., Atlanta Bar Assn., Am. Corp. Counsel Assn., Phi Alpha Delta. Democrat. Episcopalian. *

MCMORROW, MARGARET MARY (PEG MCMORROW), retired educator; b. N.Y.C., Dec. 18, 1924; d. Patrick Joseph and Ellen Veronica (Quinn) McIntyre; m. Joseph Patrick McMorrow, Oct. 12, 1948; children: Linda Karen, Robert Michael (dec.), Patrice Ann, Jane Ellen. BS, Queens Coll., 1946; MS in Edn., Hofstra U., 1959. Space controller Am. Airlines Co., N.Y.C., 1946-48; bus. rep. N.Y. Telephone Co., N.Y.C., 1948-52; tchr. Elwood Sch. Dist, Huntington, N.Y., 1965-89, ret., 1989. Fellow Elwood Tchrs. Assn., L.I. Scribes, N.Y. State United Tchrs., Mensa; mem. Elwood Ret. Tchrs. Assn., Alpha Lambda Omicron. Roman Catholic.

MCMORROW, MARY ANN G., judge; b. Chgo., Jan. 16, 1930; m. Emmett J. McMorrow, May 5, 1962; 1 dau., Mary Ann. Student Rosary Coll., 1948-50; J.D., Loyola U., 1953. Bar: Ill. 1953, U.S. Dist. Ct. (no. dist.) Ill. 1960, U.S. Supreme Ct. 1976. Atty. Riordan & Linklater Law Offices, Chgo., 1954-56; asst. state's atty. Cook County, Chgo., 1956-63; sole practice, Chgo., 1963-76; judge of Cir. Ct. Cook County, 1976-85, Ill. Appellate Ct., 1985-92, Supreme Ct. Ill., 1992—. Contbr. articles to profl. jours. Faculty adv. Nat. Jud. Coll., U. Nev., 1984. Mem. Chgo. Bar Assn., Ill. State Bar Assn., Women's Bar Assn. of Ill. (pres. 1975-76, bd. dirs. 1970-78), Am. Judicature Soc., Northwestern U. Assocs., Ill. Judges Assn., Nat. Assn. Women Judges, Advocates Soc., Cath. Lawyers Guild (bd. dirs. 1980—), Northwest Suburban Bar Assn., West Suburban Bar Assn., Loyola Law Alumni Assn. (bd. govs. 1985—), Ill. Judges Assn. (bd. dirs.), Cath. Lawyers Guild (v.p.), The Law Club of the City of Chgo., Inns of Ct. Office: Supreme Ct of Ill 160 N La Salle St Chicago IL 60601-3103

MCMULLIN, JOYCE ANNE, general contractor; b. Tulsa, Jan. 6, 1952; d. Junior Lawrence Patrick and Carol Anne (Morris) McM.; m. David Lawrence Tupper, Jan. 1, 1980 (div. May 1982). BFA, Calif. Coll. Arts and Crafts, 1973. Interior designer Design Assocs., Oakland, Calif., 1974; interior designer, sales rep. Sullivan's Interiors, Berkeley, Calif., 1975; supr. bldg. maintenance Clausen House, Inc., Oakland, 1975-82; owner New Life Renovation, Lafayette, Calif., 1981—. Contbr. articles to mags., newspapers. Mem. Contra Costa Coun., Nat. Trust Historic Preservation. Mem. AAUW, Am. Plywood Assn., We. Regional Builders Assn., NAFE, Bus. and Profl. Women, Contra Costa County Women's Network, Self-Employed Tradeswomen (sec. 1984), Contra Costa Coun., Leads Club.

MCMULLIN, RUTH RONEY, publishing company executive, management fellow; b. N.Y.C., Feb. 9, 1942; d. Richard Thomas and Virginia (Goodwin) Roney; m. Thomas Ryan McMullin, Apr. 27, 1968; 1 child, David Patrick. BA, Conn. Coll., 1963; M Pub. and Pvt. Mgmt., Yale U., 1979. Market rschr. Aviation Week Mag., McGraw-Hill Co., N.Y.C., 1962-64; assoc. editor, bus. mgr. Doubleday & Co., N.Y.C., 1964-66; mgr. Natural History Press, 1967-70; v.p., treas. Weston (Conn.) Woods, Inc., 1970-71; staff assoc. GE, Fairfield, Conn., 1979-82; mng. fin. analyst GECC Transp., Stamford, Conn., 1982-84; credit analyst corp. fin. dept. GECC, Stamford, Conn., 1984-85; sr. v.p. GECC Capital Markets Group, Inc., N.Y.C., 1985-87; exec. v.p., COO John Wiley & Sons, N.Y.C., 1987-89, pres., CEO, 1989-90; pres., CEO Harvard Bus. Sch. Pub. Corp., Boston, 1991-94; mem. chmn.'s com., acting CEO UNR Industries Inc., Chgo., 1991-92, also bd. dirs.; mgmt. fellow, vis. prof. Sch. Mgmt. Yale U., New Haven, 1994-95; now bus. cons.; bd. dirs. Bausch & Lomb, Rochester, N.Y., UNR Industries Inc., Chgo., Middlesex (Conn.) Mut. Assurance, Fleet Financial, 1992-94; vis. prof. Sch. Mgmt., Yale U., New Haven, 1994-95. Mem. dean's adv. bd. Sch. Mgmt. Yale U.; bd. dirs. Yale U. Alumni fund, 1986-92, Yale U. Press, Math. Scis. Edn. Bd., 1990-93. Mem. N.Y. Yacht Club, Stamford Yacht Club. Home: 274 Beacon St Boston MA 02116-1230

MCMURTRY, FLORENCE JEAN, educational administrator; b. Schenectady, N.Y., Feb. 1, 1947; d. Louis Frederick Jr. and Eleanore Jean (Noyes) McM. BA in Edn. with honors, Simmons Coll., 1969; MEd, U. Vt., 1975; grad. cert. advanced studies in mgmt., Radcliffe Coll., 1993. Elem. tchr. Pittsford, N.Y., 1969-70; reading specialist Lincoln, Vt., 1971-73, Pembroke, Mass., 1976; grad. teaching asst U. Vt., 1975; elem tchr. Chatham, Mass., 1977-80; with Arthur D. Little, Cambridge, Mass., 1981-82; exec. sec. Meredith & Grew, Inc., Boston, 1982—; v.p. alumnae fund Simmons Coll., Boston, 1994-96. Bd. mgrs. Jr. League Boston, 1990-92, v.p. pres., 1992, 93, chair endowments, 1993-94; chair Boston Pub. Libr. com., 1987-90; pres., v.p., rec. sec., ednl. loan fund chmn. Boston chpt. Philanthropic Ednl. Orgn., Des Moines, 1983—. Recipient Vol. Recognition award Jr. League Boston, 1989. Mem. The Coll. Club (pres. 1994—), PEO.

MCNABB, DARCY LAFOUNTAIN, medical management company executive; b. Middletown, N.J., Aug. 27, 1955; d. Donald Mark LaFountain and Suzanne (Gilman) LaFountain Westergard; m. Leland Monte McNabb, July 4, 1981 (div. Feb. 1989); 1 child, Leland Monte Jr. BBA in Internat. Fin. cum laude, U. Miami, 1977. Real estate agent, Grad. Realtor's Inst. Market rsch. asst. Burger King Corp., Miami, Fla., 1975-77; regional mktg. supr. Burger King Corp., Huntington Beach, Calif., 1977-78; mgr., restaurant planning Holiday Inns, Inc., Memphis, 1978-79, mgr., nat. promotions, 1979-83; dir., lodging and travel planning Holiday Corp., Memphis, 1983-86; affiliate broker The Hobson Co., Realtors, Memphis, 1986-88, Crye Leike, Memphis, 1988-92; v.p. comm. and planning Medshares Mgmt. Group, Inc., Memphis, 1991—. Active Friends Pink Palace Mus., Memphis, 1987-91, Family Link/Runaway, Memphis, 1980-88; chmn. Foster Care Rev. Bd., Memphis, 1988—; bd. dirs. Bethany House, Memphis, 1989—, pres., 1995; pres., bd. dirs. Am. Cancer Soc., 1994—; mktg. com. Health Industry Coun., 1994-95. Named Profl. Vol. of Yr., Friends of Pink Palace Mus., Memphis, 1989, 93, U.S. Masters Swimming All-Am., 1993, 94; grad. Leadership Memphis, 1995; named Cmty. Hero for Olympic Torch Relay, 1996. Mem. Le Bonheur Club, Memphis Runners Track Club. Republican. Episcopalian. Home: 1948 Harbert Ave Memphis TN 38104-5216 Office: Medshares Mgmt Group Inc 2714 Union Avenue Ext Memphis TN 38112-4415

MCNAIRN, PEGGI JEAN, speech pathologist, educator; b. Dallas, Sept. 22, 1954; d. Glenn Alton Harmon and Anna Eugenia (McVay) Hicks; m. Kerry Glen McNairn, Jan. 27, 1979; children: Micah Jay, Nathan Corey. BS in Speech Pathology, Tex. Christian U., 1977, MS in Communications Pathology, 1978; PhD in Ednl. Adminstrn., Kennedy Western U., 1991. Cert. speech pathologist, mid mgmt. Staff speech pathologist, asst. dir. infant program Easter Seal Soc. for Crippled Children and Adults Tarrant County, Ft. Worth, 1978-80; staff speech pathologist, spl. edn. tchr. Sherrod Elem. Sch. Arlington (Tex.) Ind. Sch. Dist., 1981-84, secondary speech/lang. specialist, early childhood assessment staff Spl. Services dept., 1984-89; owner, dir. Speech Assocs., 1989-92; mem. state forms com. Arlington (Tex.) Ind. Sch. Dist., 1985-86, chairperson assessment com., 1986-87; cons. augmentative communication Prentke Romich Co., 1992—; adj. prof., clin. supr. Tex. Christian U., Ft. Worth, 1978-79; clin. speech pathologist North Tex. Home Health Assn., Ft. Worth, 1980-92. Author: Quick Tech Activities for Literacy, 1993, Readable, Repeatable Stories and Activities, 1994, Quick Tech Magic: Music-Based Literacy Activities, 1996. Chairperson United Cerebral Palsy Toy Lending Libr., 1989-90; sunday sch. tchr. 1st United Meth. Ch., Arlington, 1982-87; mem. South Arlington Homeowners Assn., Arlington, 1985-87; 3rd v.p. Bebensee Elem. PTA. Recipient Outstanding Svc. to Handicapped Am. Biog. Inst., 1989; Cert. of Achievement John Hopkins U. for computing to assist persons with disabilities, 1991. Mem. Internat. U.S. Tex. Socs. for Augmentative and Alternate Comm. (sec. Tex. branch), Neurodevelopmental Assn., Assn. for Curriculum and Supervision, Am. Speech and Hearing Assn., Tex. Speech-Lang.-Hearing Assn., Tex. Speech and Hearing Assn. (task force mem for augmentative comm.) Teaching Tex. Tots Consortium, Tex. Christian U. Speech and Hearing Alumni Assn., Kappa Delta Pi, Alpha Lambda Delta. Democrat. Home and Office: 215 Spanish Moss Dr Arlington TX 76018-1540

MCNAMARA, ANN DOWD, medical technologist; b. Detroit, Oct. 17, 1924; d. Frank Raymond and Frances Mae (Ayling) Sullivan; m. Thomas Stephen Dowd, Apr. 23, 1949 (dec. 1980); children—Cynthia Dowd Restuccia, Kevin Thomas Dowd; m. Robert A. McNamara, June 15, 1985. BS Wayne State Univ., 1947. Med. technologist Woman's Hosp. (now Hutzel Hosp.), Detroit, 1946-52, St. James Clin. Lab., Detroit, 1960-62; supr. histopathology lab. Hutzel Hosp., Detroit, 1962-72, Mt. Carmel Mercy Hosp., 1972-87, ret. 1987. docent Domino's Ctr. Architecture & Design, Ann Arbor, Mich. 1988. Mem. Am. Soc. Clin. Pathologists, Am. Soc. Med. Technology, Mich. Soc. Med. Technology, Nat. Soc. Histotechnology, Mich. Soc. Histotechnologists, Wayne State U. Alumni Assn., Smithsonian Assos., Detroit Inst. Arts Founders Soc. Home: 29231 Oak Point Dr Farmington Hills MI 48331-2774 Office: 6071 W Outer Dr Detroit MI 48235-2624

MCNAMARA, ANNE H., lawyer, corporate executive; b. Shanghai, Republic of China, Oct. 18, 1947; came to U.S. 1949; d. John M. and Marion P. (Murphy) H.; m. Martin B. McNamara, Jan. 15, 1977. AB, Vassar Coll., 1969; JD, Cornell U., 1973. Bar: N.Y. 1973, Tex. 1981. Assoc. Shea, Gould, Climenko & Casey, N.Y.C., 1972-76; from asst. corp. sec. to corp. sec. Am. Airlines, Inc., Dallas, 1976-88, v.p. pers. resources, 1988; sr. v.p., gen. counsel Am. Airlines (AMR Corp.), Dallas, 1988—; bd. dirs. Louisville Gas & Electric Co., LG&E Energy Corp. Office: Am Airlines Inc Mail Drop 5618 PO Box 619616 Dallas/Ft Worth Airp TX 75261

MCNAMARA, BRENDA NORMA, secondary education educator; b. Blackpool, Lancashire, Eng., Aug. 8, 1945; came to U.S., 1946; d. Milford Hampson and Nola (Welsby) Jones; m. Michael James McNamara, July 19, 1969. BA in History, Calif. State U., Long Beach, 1967; postgrad., Calif. State U., various campuses, 1967—. Cert. secondary tchr. and lang. devel. specialist, Calif. Tchr. history West High Sch., Torrance, Calif., 1968—, dept. chair, 1989—; cons. in field. Co-author: World History, 1988. Western Internat. Studies Consortium grantee, 1988. Mem. Calif. Tchrs. Assn., Calif. Coun. for Social Studies, Torrance Tchrs. Assn. (bd. dirs. 1992—), South Bay Coun. for Social Studies, Nat. Tchrs. Assn., Nat. Coun. for Social Studies. Office: West High Sch 20401 Victor St Torrance CA 90503-2255

MCNAMARA, PAULA RUTH WAGNER, therapeutic recreation programs director; b. St. Louis, Feb. 23, 1925; d. Paul Brooks and Leah Ruth (Dick) Wagner; m. Raymond Edmund McNamara, May 28, 1949; children: Carol Rae, Marla Ann, Cynthia Ruth, Erin Marie, Brian Francis. BFA, Sch. of Art Inst., 1948; MA, W. Va. Grad. Coll., 1988. Cert. therapeutic recreation specialist. Supr. leisure edn. W. Va. Rehabilitaion Ctr., Institute, 1970-91; exec. dir. W. Va. Therapeutic Recreation Assn., Institute, 1992—; rep. Nat. Therapeutic Recreation Assn., Arlington, Va., 1984—. Amb. Friendship Force, 1993—; conf. del. Partners of the Americas, Washington, 1991. Mem. Nat. Therapeutic Recreation Assn., Am. Therapeutic Recreation Assn., W.Va. Therapeutic Recreation Assn. (sec. 1991). Office: WVa Therapeutic Recreation Assn PO Box 554 Institute WV 25112-0554

MCNAMARA, THERESA MARIE, development officer; b. Bryn Mawr, Pa., Mar. 3, 1961; d. John Gerald and Kathleen Mary (Brophy) McN. BA, St. Norbert Coll., DePere, Wis., 1983. Field rep. Am. Cancer Soc., Omaha, 1983-84; fundraising/pub. rels. field rep. Am. Cancer Soc., Berwyn, Ill., 1984-85; dir. alumni programs Loyola U., Chgo., 1985-86, dir. law sch. devel., 1986-90; dir. ann. giving Loyola Marymount U., L.A., 1990-93; dir. devel. Sch. Bus. Adminstrn. U. So. Calif., L.A., 1993—; lectr. in field. Mem. Coun. for Advancement and Support of Edn., Active 20-30 Internat. (pres. 1994-95, 1st v.p. 1995-96, Mem. of the Yr. 1994-95). Democrat. Roman Catholic. Home: 414 Second St Apt 345 Hermosa Beach CA 90254 Office: Univ of So Calif Sch Bus Adminstrn HOH 200 Los Angeles CA 90089-1421

MCNAMARA, WANDA G., state legislator; b. Bristol, S.D., Sept. 4, 1944; widowed; 4 children. Student, No. State Coll., Aberdeen, S.D., 1962-65. Bus. cons. N.H.; mem. N.H. State Ho. Reps., 1996—, mem. children, youth and juvenile justice com. Mem. Chesterfield Sch. Bd., 1985-88, chair, 1987-88. Republican. Protestant. Office: NH Ho of Reps State Capitol Concord NH 03301 Home: 101 Streeterhill West Chesterfield NH 03466*

MCNAMARA-RAISCH, M. EILEEN, marketing professional; b. Abington, Pa.; d. Edward J. and Mary L. (Perozze) McNamara; m. Thomas R. Raisch; children: Meghan, Michael. BA, LaSalle U., 1973; postgrad., Temple U., 1978, Dartmouth U., 1990, Tufts U., 1993. Bus. rschr. Bell of Pa., 1974-78; market rschr. AT&T, Parsippany, N.J., 1978-81; div. mgr., dist. mgr. consumer svcs. AT&T, Basking Ridge, N.J., 1981-85, 87-88; dir. consumer lab. AT&T, Basking Ridge, 1988-89, mktg. dir. new bus. devel., 1989-91; transponder svcs. dir. satellite svcs. AT&T, Bedminster, N.J., 1991-93; mktg. dir. bus. comms. AT&T, Bedminster, 1993-94; pres., CEO AT&T Tridom, Marietta, Ga., 1994—. Mem. Electronic Industry Assn. (adv. com. 1987-89), Am. Mktg. Assn., Soc. Satellite Profls. Internat., Soc. Internat. Bus. Fellows, Cobb Chamber Chmn.'s Club, Atlanta C. of C. (internat. divsn.). Home: 4356 Highborne Dr Marietta GA 30066-2429 Office: AT&T Tridom 835 Franklin Ct Marietta GA 30067-8946

MCNAMEE, SISTER CATHERINE, educational association executive; b. Troy, N.Y., Nov. 13, 1931; d. Thomas Ignatius McNamee and Kathryn McNamee Marois. B.A., Coll. of St. Rose, 1953, D.H.L. (hon.), 1975; M.Ed., Boston Coll., 1955, M.A., 1958; Ph.D., U. Madrid, 1967. Grad. asst. Boston Coll., 1954-55; asst. registrar Boston Coll. (Grad. Sch.), 1955-57; acad. v.p. Coll. St. Rose, Albany, N.Y., 1968-75; dir. liberal arts Thomas Edison Coll., Trenton, 1975-76; pres. Trinity Coll., Burlington, Vt., 1976-79, Coll. St. Catherine, St. Paul, 1979-84; dean Dexter Hanley Coll., U. Scranton, Pa., 1984-86; pres. Nat. Cath. Ednl. Assn., Washington, 1986-96; now. sr. scholar Inst. Christian Social Thought and Mgmt., St. Paul, Minn., 1996—. Bd. dirs. Am. Forum, Boston Coll., Internat. Cath. Child Bur. Spanish Govt. grantee, 1965-67; OAS grantee, 1967-68; Fulbright grantee, 1972-73. Mem. Inter-Am. Confedn. Cath. Edn., Internat. Orgn. Cath. Edn., Coun. for Am. Pvt. Edn., Internat. Fedn. Cath. Univs., Delta Epsilon Sigma. Roman Catholic. Office: Inst Christian Social Thought and Mgmt U St Thomas MCN 6001 2115 Summit Ave Ste 100 Saint Paul MN 55105*

MCNAMEE, LOUISE, advertising agency executive; m. Tom M. Attended, Mary Baldwin Coll., Va. With rsch. dept. Kelly Nason; exec. v.p., dir. mktg. and rsch. Della Femina, Travisano & Ptnrs., Inc. (now Della Famina McNamee, Inc.), N.Y.C., 1979-84, ptnr., 1982—, acting pres., from 1984, past pres., chief operating officer, chief exec. officer, 1992-93; now ptnr., pres. Messner, Vetere, Berger, McNamee, Schmetterer, Euro RSCG, N.Y.C., 1993—. Named Advt. Woman of Yr., Advt. Women of N.Y., 1988. Office: Messner, Vetere, Berger, McNamee, Schmetterer, Euro RSCG 350 Hudson St New York NY 10014-4504*

MCNANAMY, EVE WEEKS, clinical psychologist, marriage therapist; b. N.Y.C., Feb. 14, 1933. BEd, U. Miami, 1957, MEd, 1958, PhD in Clin. Psychology, 1966. Lic. clin. psychologist and marriage and family therapist, Fla. Practicum in counseling and psychotherapy dept. medicine U. Miami, Fla., 1959-60; psycho. counselor Lighthouse for the Blind, Miami, 1960-61; clin. intern Jackson Meml. Hosp., Miami, 1961-62; psychol. counselor Bascom-Palmer Eye Inst., Miami, 1962-64; staff psychologist Long Term Illness Project, Miami, 1964-65; clin. psychologist Jackson Meml. Hosp., Miami, 1965-66; comty. programs dir. Mental Health Assn., Miami, 1965-67; psychologist Children's Psychiat. Ctr., Miami, 1967-68, Maxine Baker Mental Health Clinic, Miami, 1966-69; pvt. practice as psychologist Miami, 1968—; mem. med. staff Health South Larkin Hosp., Health South Dr.'s Hosp., Harborview Hosp., Grant Ctr. Deering Hosp., Former Homestead Air Force Base Hosp., Charter Hosp. Miami, South Miami Hosp., Miami Children's Hosp. Miami, Bapt. Hosp. Mem. advocate program AAUW, Miami; active Big Sisters of Miami, Ednl. Guidance Svc., Inc., Jr. League Miami, Miami Palmetto Sr. H.S. Feeder Sys., Protestant Social Svcs. Seagull Orientation, Rec. for Blind and Dyslexic, Miami, South Dade Mental Health Found., Women's Alcoholic Edn. Ctr. Recipient Presdl. award for svc. to Com. of Total Employment, 1967, Haddassah Myrtle Wreath award for outstanding comty. svc. in mental health field, 1965, Comty. Headliner's award Women in Comms., 1983, Women of Yr. award Am. Cancer Soc., 1989, Trailblazer's award Women's Com. of One Hundred, 1992, Women of Yr. award Comty. Coalition for Women's History, 1992; grantee Fla. Coun. Tng. and Rsch. in Mental Health, 1957-63; scholar U. Miami, 1957-66; Marsdon Found. fellow for outstanding student in psychology, 1958-62. Fellow Internat. Coun. Sex Edn. and Parenthood, Am. Orthopsychiat. Assn.; mem. APA, Am. Assn. for Marriage and Family Therapy, Am. Soc. Adolescent Psychiatry, Nat. Vocat. Rehab. Assn., Coun. for Exceptional Children, Southeastern Psychol. Assn., Fla. Soc. Clin. Hypnosis, South Fla. Vocat. Rehab. Assn., Dade County Psychol. Assn., South Dade C. of C., Greater South Miami C. of C., Zonta Club Coral Gables. Office: Ste 208 7400 N Kendall Dr Miami FL 33156

MCNARY, SUE TUSHINGHAM, artist; b. Collingswood, N.J., Dec. 9, 1942; d. Herbert Wallis and Marty Louise (Brown) Tushingham; m. William Francis McNary III, Apr. 5, 1962 (dec. 1982); children: William Wallis, Glenn Michael. AA, Columbia Coll., 1961; student, Mich. State U., 1968-69. Gallery owner Hotel del Coronado, Calif., 1984—; commd. cover artist Childrens Home Soc. of Calif., San Diego, 1991, Kennedy Pub., Coronado, 1988, 95; commd. mural artist Village Elem. Sch., Coronado, 1992, San Diego Visitor and Conv. Bur., 1993; commd. artist USN, Coronado, 1993-94, Hotel del Coronado, 1995, Portal Pub. Co., 1991, Sunset Mktg. Pub., 1992, Bentley Ho. Pub., 1995; v.p., bd. dirs. Delta, Coronado, 1993-95. juried exhibitor N.Y. Art Expo, N.Y.C., 1989-92. Mem. San Diego Visitor and Conv. Bur., San Diego, 1985—; artist Childrens Sch. Found., 1988—; bd. dirs. San Diego County Art Coun., San Diego, 1984-88, San Diego Art Inst., 1975-79. Mem. Coronado Rotary Club, The Charter 100, Coronado Investment Club (v.p.), Connections, Del Mar Turf Club. Methodist. Home: 151 Carob Way Coronado CA 92118 Office: Sue Tushingham McNary Art Gallery Hotel del Coronado Coronado CA 92118

MCNEAR, BARBARA BAXTER, financial communications executive, consultant; b. Chgo., Oct. 9, 1939; d. Carl Henden and Alice Gertrude (Parrish) Baxter; m. Robert Erskine McNear, Apr. 13, 1968 (div. 1981); 1 child, Amanda Baxter; m. Glenn Philip Eisen, June 7, 1987. B.S. in Journalism, Northwestern U., 1961. Editorial asst. Scott Foresman & Co., Chgo., 1961; pub. rels. dir. Market Facts Inc., Chgo., 1961-63; account supr. Philip Lesly Co., Chgo., 1963-68, 69; account exec. Burson-Marsteller, Chgo., 1968; dir. communications CNA Fin. Corp., Chgo., 1969-74; dir. pub. rels. Gould Inc., Chgo., 1974; v.p. Harris Bank, Chgo., 1974-80, Fireman's Fund Ins. Co., San Francisco, 1980-83; sr. v.p. First Chgo. Corp., 1983-86; v.p. communications Xerox Fin. Svcs., Inc., Stamford, Conn., 1987-93; mgr. shareholder comm. Xerox Corp., Stamford, 1993—. Mem. Pub. Rels. Soc. Am., Fairfield County Pub. Rels. Assn., Nat. Investor Rels. Inst. (pres. Chgo. chpt. 1974-75, bd. dirs. Chgo. chpt.), Cliffdwellers, Princeton Club. Episcopalian. Home: 23 Telva Rd Wilton CT 06897-3733 Office: Xerox Corp 800 Long Ridge Rd Stamford CT 06902-1227

MCNEELY, JUANITA, artist; b. St. Louis; d. Robert Hunt and Alta B. (Green) McN.; m. Jeremy Lebensohn, Mar., 1982. BFA, Washington U. St. Louis, 1959; MFA, So. Ill. U., 1964. Prof. figure drawing So. Ill. U., Carbondale, 1962-64; prof. drawing Chgo. Art Inst., 1964-65; prof. drawing and painting Western Ill. U., Macomb, 1965-67; prof. painting Suffolk (N.Y.) Coll., 1969-82; artist, 1959—, art tchr., 1962—; part-time tchr. painting Parsons Sch. Art, N.Y.C., NYU; artist-judge art exhbn. White House, Washington, 1994; art judge, spkr. Very Spl. Arts, Washington, 1990-96. One-person shows include Elaine Benson Gallery, N.Y.C., 1994; represented in print and painting collections Nat. Mus. Art, Taipei, Taiwan, Palacio de Las Bellas Artes, Mexico City, Oakleigh Collection, Boston, and others; represented in galleries Evelyn Amis Gallery, Can., 1980-84, Soho 20 Gallery, N.Y.C., 1980-82, Prince St. Gallery, N.Y.C., 1970-80. Studio: 463 West St New York NY 10014

MCNEELY, PATRICIA MORSE, educator, poet, writer; b. Galveston, Tex., Apr. 2, 1923; d. Bleecker Lansing Sr. and Annie Maud (Pillow) Morse; m. Chalmers Rankin McNeely, Mar. 22, 1949 (div. Aug. 1959); children: David Lansing, Timothy Ann McNeely Caldwell, Patricia Grace MdNeely Dragon, Abigail Rankin. BS in Edn., U. Tex., 1972; MA in Ednl. Psychology & Spl. Edn., U. Tex., San Antonio, 1978, MA in Ednl. Psychology-Counseling, 1981. Cert. tchr., Tex.; lic. profl. counselor. Sec./adminstrv. sec. various cos., Galveston & Austin, Tex., 1960-70; police stenographer Austin Police Dept., 1970-74; spl. edn. tchr. N.E. Ind. Sch. Dist., San Antonio, 1974-76, S.W. Ind. Sch. Dist., San Antonio, 1978-81; vocat. adjustment coord. East Ctrl. Ind. Sch. Dist., San Antonio, 1981-82; counselor, tchr. Stockdale (Tex.) Ind. Sch. Dist., 1982-84; clinic sec. Humana Hosp., Dallas, 1985-87; tchr. history Dallas Ind. Sch. Dist., Dallas, 1987—; assn. rep. Hill Mid. Sch., Dallas, 1988-89, E.B. Comstock Mid. Sch., Dallas, 1991—. Author: (poetry) Texas City, 1947, A Gift of Love, 1978, Words of Praise: Treasury of Religious and Inspirational Poetry, 1987, Love's Greatest Treasures, 1989, The Key, 1991, Between the Raindrops, 1995 (3d prize 1995); contbr. articles to newspapers and co. publs. V.p. zone, sec., libr., various coms. Parents Without Ptnrs., Inc., Austin, 1965-72, internat. com. for writing leadership tng. program, 1968. Recipient Bernice Milburn Moore scholarship award U. Tex. Austin Alumni Assn., 1972. Mem. NEA, Tex. State Tchrs., Classroom Tchrs. of Dallas (del. to Tex. State Tchrs. Assn. 1978-81, 91-95). Episcopalian. Office: Dallas Ind Sch Dist EB Comstock Mid Sch Dallas TX 75208

MCNEES, PAT (PATRICIA ANN MCNEES), writer, editor; b. Riverside, Calif., Jan. 30, 1940; d. Glenn Harold and Eleanor Maxine (McCoskrie) McN.; m. Anthony V. Mancini, Apr. 22, 1967 (div. 1978), 1 child, Romana Mancini. BA, UCLA, 1961, postgrad., 1961-63. Instr. English Stanford U., Palo Alto, Calif., 1962-63; assoc. editor Harper & Row, N.Y.C., 1963-66; editor Fawcett Publishers, N.Y.C., 1966-70; ind. writer and editor N.Y.C., Washington, 1970—; cons. clients include World Bank, UN, 1987—, Young Pres.'s Orgn. Author: Dancing: A Guide to the Capital Area, 1987, An American Biography: An Industrialist Remembers the 20th Century, 1995, editor: (anthologies) Contemporary Latin American Short Stories, 1974, Dying: A Book of Comfort, 1996; contbr. articles to mags. including New York Mag., Washington Post. Mem. Am. Soc. Journalists and Authors, Authors Guild, PEN, Nat. Assn. Sci. Writers.

MC NEESE, WILMA WALLACE, social worker; b. Chgo., Apr. 30, 1946; d. Nettie Fletcher Wallace; student Wilson City Coll., 1964-66; B.A., So. Ill. U., 1969; M.S.W., Loyola U., Chgo., 1976; m. Mose D. McNeese, Dec. 27, 1969; children—Derrick, Christina. Program coordinator Intensive Tng. and Employment Program, East St. Louis, Ill., 1970-71; methods and procedures adviser Ill. Dept. Pub. Aid, Chgo., 1972-73; social work intern Robbins (Ill.) Presch. Center, 1974; with U.S. Probation Office, Chgo., 1975; officer U.S. Pretrial Services Agy., Chgo., 1976-87; chief U.S. pretrial services officer for western dist. Pa., 1987—; fieldwork instr. Aurora Coll., 1981, Chgo. State U., 1981-82; grad. fieldwork instr. U. Ill. Sch. of Social Work, 1986; mem. bd. trustees The Wesley Inst. Inc., 1993—. Recipient Community Service award Village of Robbins, 1975; advanced tng. cert. Fed. Jud. Ctr. Mem. Nat. Assn. Social Workers, Acad. Cert. Social Workers, Nat. Assn. Pretrial Svcs. Agencies, Greater Pitts. Commn. for Women. Baptist. Home: 833 Chalmers Pl Pittsburgh PA 15243-1967 Office: 1000 Liberty Ave Ste 822 Pittsburgh PA 15222-4003

MCNEIL, DEBORAH LYNN, artist, art educator; b. Rome, Ga., June 5, 1955; d. E. Daniel and Gloria Claire (Davis) McN.; children: Davis McNeil Moore, Jason, Rebecca Bedingfield. BFA, West Ga. Coll., 1993, BA in art edn., 1993. Art instr., 1993—. One women shows include Cashin Hall, 1993, Manget Brannen Art Gallery, 1993; exhibited in group shows at Gallery 118, 1993. Scout leader Boy Scout Am. Troop 92, Welcome, Ga., 1989—; sec. NHS Band Orgn., Newnan, Ga., 1994—; instr. C.O.P.E. Training, 1991—. Mem. Newnan Coweta Art Assn., Nat. Art Edn. Assn., Omicron Delta Kappa, Phi Kappa Phi., Order of Arrow. Office: Deborah L McNeil Artist 1504 Welcome Rd Newnan GA 30263

MCNEILL, JOAN REAGIN, volunteer consultant; b. Atlanta, July 8, 1936; d. Arthur Edward and Annie May (Busby) Reagin; m. Thomas Pinckney McNeill, Sr., Aug. 3, 1957; childen: Thomas Pinckney, Clyde Reagin. Student, U. Louisville, 1955-57; BA, U. Tenn., Chattanooga, 1976. Founding pres. Family and Children's Svcs. Assocs., Chattanooga, 1987-88; bd. dirs. Chattanooga Symphony and Opera Assn., 1984-88, pres., 1984-87; pres. Chattanooga Ballet Assn., 1986-88; bd. dirs. U. Chattanooga Found., 1986-89; mem. vol. coun. bd. dirs. Am. Symphony Orch. League, Washington, 1986—; pres.-elect, 1992-93, pres., 1993-95. Recipient Outstanding Svc. award U. Tenn., Chattanooga, 1988. Mem. U. Tenn. Chattanooga Alumni Assn. (pres. 1985-86), Golden Key, Sigma Kappa Found. (trustee 1992—, sec. 1993-94, pres. 1994—, Colby award for volunteerism 1990). Republican. Episcopalian. Office: 7457 Preston Cir Chattanooga TN 37421-1839

MCNEILL, MARY KATHRYN MORGAN, librarian; b. Greenville, S.C., Feb. 22, 1958; d. Harvey Eugene and Mary Anna (Walser) Morgan; m. George Terrence McNeill, May 17, 1980; 1 child, Terrence Morgan. BS, Winthrop Coll., 1980; MLS, Emory U., 1985. Media specialist Thurston Elem. Sch., Thomaston, Ga., 1980-85; asst. libr. Oxford (Ga.) Coll. Libr. Emory U., 1985-88, dir., 1988—. Sunday Sch. tchr. Thomaston United Methodist Ch., 1981. Mem. ALA, Assn. Coll. and Rsch. Librs., Libr. Adminstrn. and Mgmt. Assn., Southeastern Libr. Assn., Ga. Libr. Assn., Delta Kappa Gamma (sec. chpt. 1992-96, pres. chpt. 1996—). Home: 3303 Sams Way Conyers GA 30208-2250 Office: Emory U Oxford Coll Libr PO Box 1448 Oxford GA 30267-1448

MCNEILL, MAXINE CURRIE, county official; b. Rockingham, N.C., Oct. 17, 1934; d. Daniel Franklin and Lollie Mae (Davis) Currie; m. James Albert McNeill, May 5, 1956; children: James C., David A., Jon S., Ellen F. BSN, Wingate Coll., 1986; MPH, U. N.C., 1991. Cert. nurse practitioner; cert. in ambulatory health care Nat. Cert. Corp. Dir. nursing svc. Hamlet, N.C., 1967-69; sch. nurse Rockingham, N.C., 1970-72; dir. Richmond County Home Health Agy., Rockingham, 1972-74; pub. health nurse Scotland County Health Dept., Laurinburg, N.C., 1974-75, nurse practitioner, 1975-79; nurse practitioner Laurinburg Surg. Clinic, 1979-80; nursing supr. Scotland Count Health Dept., Laurinburg, 1980-82, Richmond County

Health Dept., Rockingham, N.C., 1982-88, local health dir. Montgomery County Health Dept., Troy, N.C., 1988-92; nurse practitioner Richmond OBGYN, Rockingham, N.C., 1992-93, Bladen County Health Dept., 1993-95; dir. daily ops. St. Joseph Home Health Agy., Troy, N.C., 1995—; staff nurse, relief supr. Richmond Meml. Hosp., Rockingham, N.C., 1955-67; mem. Maternal-Health Liason Com., 1990-91, N.C. State Pers. Liason Com., 1990-91. Mem. ANA, N.C. Nurses Assn. (disting. achievement award dist. V 1986), N.C. Pub. Health Assn. (dist. 12), N.C. Assn. Local Health Dirs., N.C. Dist. V Perinatal Assn., Kiwanis, Sigma Theta Tau. Democrat. Presbyterian. Home: 5080 Woodrun-on-Tillery Mount Gilead NC 27306

MCNELIS, ALICE MURRAY, physical therapist, educator; b. Berkeley, Calif., Oct. 26, 1965; d. James Edward and Patricia (Bronson) Murray; m. Brian John McNelis, June 22, 1991. BS cum laude, U. Calif., Santa Barbara, 1987; MS, Duke U., 1989. Lic. phys. therapist, Calif. Phys. therapist Duke U. Med. Ctr., Durham, N.C., 1989-90, Children's Hosp. Oakland, Calif., 1990-92, Interim Healthcare, Santa Clara, Calif., 1992-93; ind. contractor phys. therapist Cmty. Assn. for Rehab., Santa Clara and Palo Alto, Calif., 1993—; per diem phys. therapist Lucille Salter Packard Childrens Hosp., Palo Alto, 1993—; part-time instr. De Anza C.C., Cupertino, Calif., 1994—; per diem phys. therapist Stanford Home Care, Palo Alto, 1996—; guest lectr. Samuel Merritt Phys. Therapy Sch., Oakland, 1991, Stanford U., Palo Alto, 1994, 96; presenter for career panel U. Calif., Santa Clara U., 1992, 93, 95. Mem. AAUW, Am. Phys. Therapy Assn. Democrat. Presbyterian. Home: 2398 Kenwood Ave San Jose CA 95128

MCNICHOL, JANE EILEEN, artist; b. Phila., May 19, 1952; d. Francis Joseph and Mary (Somens) McN.; m. James David Conboy, May 28, 1988. BA, Temple U., 1974. Bus. mgr. Richard Gluckman, Architect, N.Y.C., 1991-94; ops. controller Petersburg Press, N.Y.C., 1991-94; asst. dir. Judson Art Warehouse, N.Y.C., 1988-89; sales mgr. Continental Auto Parts, Havertown, Pa.; mem. exhbn. com. Art Initiatives, N.Y.C. One woman shows include Michaelian & Kohlberg, N.Y.C., 1995, Benjamin Cardoza Law Sch. Gallery, 1996; exhibited in group shows at Painted Bride Art Ctr., Phila., 1982, Phila. Mus. Art, 1982, The Art Salon, Third Street Gallery, Phila., 1982, Triangle Gallery, Washington, 1983, Phila. Coll. Art, 1984, Nat. Arts Club, N.Y.C., 1990, Cooperstown (N.Y.) Art Assn., 1991, Phila. Sketch Club, 1992, Art Ctr. No. N.J., New Milford, 1992, Art Initiatives, Gallery 148, N.Y.C., 1992, Tyler Gallery, Temple U., Phila., 1993, Bridgewater Lustberg Gallery, N.Y.C., 1994, Art Initiatives, N.Y.C., 1994; represented in permanent collections Reader's Digest, Pleasantville, N.Y., Morgan, Lewis & Bockius, N.Y.C., Cave Cross Advt., Ardmore, Pa.; represented in pvt. collections. Pres. Concerned Residents East 11th St., N.Y.C., 1994-95. MacDowell Colony fellow, 1985; recipient Anna Hyatt Huntington Bronze medal Nat. Arts Club, 1989. Democrat. Home: 534 E 11th St # 26 New York NY 10009 Studio: 155 Hope St Brooklyn NY 11211

MCNIERNEY, LISA MARIE, critical care nurse; b. Lackawanna, N.Y., Dec. 22, 1958; d. Gerald Francis and Marie Frances (Carlin) Buck; divorced; children: Melissa, William, Brooke, Corey, Cameron, Brittany. ADN, Trocaire Coll., 1979. Nurse Sheehan Meml. Hosp., Buffalo, 1979-80, Erie County Med. Ctr., Buffalo, 1980-81, 94—; charge nurse night shift, cardio thoracic unit Erie County Med. Ctr., Buffalo, Ill., 1981-93; nurse St. Francis Hosp., Evanston, 1981-93; asst. head nurse cardiothoracic unit Erie County Med. Ctr., 1996—. Mem. N.Y. State Nurses Assn. (local and state chpts.). Home: 29 Miriam Ave Blasdell NY 14219-1210

MCNULLY, LYNNETTE LARKIN, elementary education educator; b. Iowa City, Iowa, Jan. 22, 1966; d. Ernest F. and Karen (Schaeferle) Larkin; m. William S. McNully, May 14, 1988. BA in English, U. Okla., 1987; MEd in Early Childhood Edn., East Tex. State U., 1994. Cert. tchr., Tex. Prekindergarten and kindergarten tchr. Dallas Pub. Schs., 1989—; founding mem. site-based mgmt. coun. Arlington Park Sch., 1994—. Vol. North Texas Irish Festival, Dallas, 1992, On the Wing Again, Ferris, Tex., 1993—. Named Tchr. of Yr., Arlington Park Sch., Dallas, 1992; Write, Right! grantee Dallas Jr. League, 1993. Mem. Nat. Assn. for Edn. of Young Children, Assn. for Childhood Edn. Internat., Dallas Quilters Guild, PTA (exec. bd. 1993—), Phi Beta Kappa.

MCNULTY, NANCY G(ILLESPIE), management consultant, business writer, editor; b. Greenville, Pa., May 1, 1919; d. Stanley A. and Bess (Anthony) Gillespie; m. Arthur P. McNulty, July 16, 1942 (dec. 1961); 1 child, Terence. BA, Thiel Coll., 1940; MA, NYU, 1948. Industry analyst Equity Corp., 1940-42; writer, researcher Time Inc., N.Y.C., 1942-45; internal cons., 1957-68; founder, dir. Internat. Survey of Mgmt. Edn., N.Y.C., 1968—; cons. Chase Bank World Info. Svc., Japan Soc., Am. Mgmt. Assn., Inst. for Advancement of Economy, Austria, The Conf. Bd., UN Dept. of Tech. Coop. for Devel., N.Y. State Commn. on Edn., Time Inc.; editor, writer, cons. mgmt. edn., 1968—; lectr. St. Thomas U. Writer, editor: Training Managers-The International Guide, 1969, Management Education Programs-The World's Best, 1980, The International Directory of Executive Education, 1985; contbr. numerous articles to Am. and internat. jours. Ford Found. scholar, 1968, 78. Fellow Internat. Acad. Mgmt. (hon.); mem. European Found. Mgmt. Devel., Internat. Found. Action Learning in the USA (founder, diir.), Acad. Mgt., Yale Club of N.Y.C. Episcopalian. Home and Office: K-104 Pennswood Village Newtown PA 18940

MCNULTY, ROBERTA JO, educational administrator; b. Cin., July 17, 1945; d. Edward Norman and Ruth Marcella (Glass) Stuebing; children: Meredith Corinne, Brian Edward, Stephen Barrett. BS in Edn., U. Cin., 1967; MA in Edn., Coll. of Mount St. Joseph, 1989; PhD in Ednl. Adminstrn. and Supervision, Bowling Green State U., 1993. Elem. tchr. St. Mary Sch., Urbana, Ohio, 1968; elem. tchr. Urbana (Ohio) City Schs., 1968-70, middle sch. tchr., 1970-71; off-campus liaison Mt. St. Joseph Coll., 1987-89; adj. faculty Bowling Green State U., 1990—; gen. edn. supr., testing 540 coord. curriculum devel. and implementation Fulton County Ednl. Svc. Ctr., Wauseon, Ohio, 1992—; Lamaza instr. Scioto Meml. Illustrated Lamaze Edn., Portsmouth, Ohio, 1983-84, Tiffin (Ohio) Childbirth Edn. Assn., 1984-87; edn. symposium com. chair Project Discovery, 1995—; proficiency test rev. com. Ohio Dept. Edn., 1993-94. Grad. editor Am. Secondary Edn., 1989-92. Mem. sch. bd. St. Mary Sch., Urbana, 1971-75; mem. parent adv. com. Wheelersburg (Ohio) Local Schs., 1978-84; mem. parents coun. U. Evansville, 1990-93; exec. dir. Am. Cancer Soc., Tiffin, Ohio, 1985; treas. Parents' Boosters Club, Portsmouth YMCA, 1979-84; chmn. Y-wives com. Tiffin-Cmty. YMCA, 1984-87; mem. Archbold (Ohio) Teen Issues Adv. Com., 1995—. Recipient Doctoral fellowship Bowling Green State U., 1989-92, Svc. Appreciation award Cub Scouts, 1990-92. Mem. ASCD, Ednl. Leadership Assn., N.W. Ohio Assn. for Supervision and Curriculum Devel., Ohio Sch. Suprs. Assn., Ohio Coun. Tchrs. English Language Arts, Assn. Tchr. Educators, Ohio Assn. Tchr. Educators (nat. del.), Phi Delta Kappa. Office: Fulton County Ednl Svc Ctr 602 S Shoop Ave Wauseon OH 43567-1712

MCNULTY, SHARON ANN, counseling administrator; b. Elmhurst, N.Y., July 2, 1968. BS, U. Scranton, 1990; MEd, U. Del., 1992. Grad. asst. career planning & placement office U. Del., Newark, 1990-92; asst. dir. St. Peter's Coll., Jersey City, N.J., 1992—. Mem. ACA, Am. Coll. Pers. Assn., N.J. Coll. Pers. Assn., Psi Chi, Alpha Sigma Nu, Delta Tau Kappa, Pi Gamma Mu. Roman Catholic. Office: St Peters Coll Counseling Ctr 2641 Kennedy Blvd Jersey City NJ 07306

MCNUTT, KRISTEN WALLWORK, consumer affairs executive; b. Nashville, Nov. 17, 1941; d. Gerald M. and Lee Wallwork; m. David McNutt, Sept. 13, 1969. BA in Chemistry, Duke U., 1963; MS in Nutrition, Columbia U., 1965; PhD in Biochemistry, Vanderbilt U., 1970; JD, DePaul U., 1984. Bar: N.Y. 1984, D.C. 1984. Exec. dir. Nat. Nutrition Consortium, Washington, 1979-81; asst. prof. pub. health U. Ill., Chgo., 1981-83; assoc. dir. Good Housekeeping Inst., N.Y.C., 1982-85; v.p. consumer affairs Kraft Inc., Glenview, Ill., 1985-87; pres. Consumer Choices Inc., Winfield, Ill., 1988—. Author: Nutrition and Food Choices, 1979; editor: Sugars in Nutrition, 1975, Consumer Mags. Digest, 1989—. Bd. dirs. Better Bus. Bur., Chgo. and No. Ill., 1986-88; FDA Food Adv. Com., 1992-94. Mem. N.Y. Bar Assn., D.C. Bar Assn., Fedn. Am. Socs. Exptl. Biology (Congl. Sci. fellow), Soc. for Nutrition Edn. (pres. 1983-84), Am. Inst. Nutrition, Am. Dietetics Assn. Home and Office: Consumer Choices Inc 28W176 Belleau Dr Winfield IL 60190

MCNUTT, MARCIA KEMPER, geophysicist; b. Mpls., Minn., Feb. 19, 1952; widowed, 1988; 3 children. BA, Colorado Coll., 1973; PhD, Scripps Inst. Oceanography, 1978. Geophysicist US Geol. Survey, 1979-82; asst. prof. geophysics MIT, 1982-86, assoc. prof., 1986-89, prof., 1989—, Griswold prof., 1991—; pres. tectonophysics sect. AGU, 1994—; mem. com. on criteria for fed. support of rsch. & devel., 1995—. Mem. Am. Geophys. Union (Macelevane award 1988). Office: MIT Dept Earth Atmospheric & Planetary Sci 77 Massachusetts Ave Cambridge MA 02139-3594

MCPARTLAND, PATRICIA ANN, health educator; b. Passaic, N.J.; d. Daniel and Josephine McP. BA, U. Mo., 1971; MCRP, Ohio State U., 1975, MS in Preventive Medicine, 1975; EdD in Higher and Adult Edn., Columbia U., 1988. Cert. holistic, aromatherapy and hypnotherapy. Sr. health planner Merrimack Valley HSA, Lawrence, Mass., 1977-79; planning cons./adminstr. Children's Hosp., Boston, 1979-80; exec. dir. Southeastern Mass. Area Health Edn. Ctr., Marion, Mass., 1980—; v.p. New Bedford (Mass.) Cmty. Health Ctr., 1993-94; chmn. edn. and tng. com. Health and Human Svc. Coalition, 1988-89; vis. lectr. Bridgewater State Coll.; lectr. in field. Editorial bd. Jour. Healthcare Edn. and Tng., 1989-93; author: Promoting Health in the Workplace, 1991; contbr. articles to profl. jours. Vol. speaker March of Dimes Found., Wareham, Mass., 1992-93; coll.-wide vocat. Cape Cod C.C., Hyannis, Mass., 1989—; planning adv. 2nd Internat. Symposium, Pasco, Wash., 1992; v.p. New Bedford chpt. Am. Cancer Soc., 1985-90. Recipient award Excellence in Continuing Edn. Nat. AHEC Ctr. Dirs. Assn., 1994, 95, 96, Sec.'s awards for Outstanding Progam in Community Health, Nat. Cancer Inst., Washington, 1990. Mem. Am. Pub. Health Assn., Inst. for Disease Prevention (steering com. 1982—), Southeastern Mass Health Planning (bd. dirs., sec., 1982-87), Nat. Planning Conf. (mem. com. 1984-85, 86-87). Home: PO Box 491 Marion MA 02738-0491 Office: Southeastern Mass AHEC PO Box 280 2 Spring St Marion MA 02738

MCPETERS, SHARON JENISE, artist, writer; b. San Bernardino, Calif., Oct. 17, 1951; d. Cecil L. and Mary I. (Tanner) McP.; 1 child, Angela M. Benders. BA in Journalism and English, U. So. Calif., 1981. Proofreader Ventura (Calif.) Coll., 1979. Painter: My Professors, 1993, Interpretations, 1994, The Thoughts of Socrates, 1995, Self Portrait, 1995.

MCPHAIL, JOANN WINSTEAD, writer, producer, publisher, art dealer, owner; b. Trenton, Fla., Feb. 17, 1941; d. William Emerson and Donna Mae (Crawford) Winstead; m. James Michael McPhail, June 15, 1963; children: Angela C. McPhail Morris, Dana Denise, Whitney Gold McPhail Casso. Student, Fla. So. Coll., 1959-60, St. John's River Jr. Coll., Palatka, Fla., 1960-61, Houston (Tex.) C.C. With Jim Walter Corp., Houston, 1961-62; receptionist, land lease sec. Oil and Gas Property Mgmt. Inc., Houston, 1962-63; sec. to mng. atty. State Farm Ins. Co., Houston, 1963-64; saleswoman, decorator Oneil-Anderson, Houston, 1973; sec. Law Offices of Ed Christensen, Houston, 1980-82; advt. mgr. Egalitarian Houston (Tex.) C.C. Systems, 1981; fashion display artist, 1985-86; entrepreneur, writer, art agt., playwright Golden Galleries, Houston, 1990—; owner, property mgr. APT Investments, 1994—; lyricist, producer, publisher Anna Gold Classics, 1995—, writer, publisher of song lyrics and music, 1996—. Freelance writer, photographer: Elegance of Needlepoint, 1970, S.W. Art Mag., A Touch of Greatness, 1973, Sweet 70's Anthology, The Budding of Tomorrow, 1974; columnist, photographer: Egalitarian: The Name Game, Design Your Wall Covering, Student Profile, 1981, National Library of Poetry, Fireworks, 1995; contbr. poetry various publs.; playwright, 1993—; prodr. religious drama The Missing Crown, KYND-AM, World Wide Christian Radio, KCBI-FM, and other radio stations, 1995—. Vol. PTO bd. Sharptown Middle Sch.; active ch. leadership activities. Mem. NAFE, ASCAP, Houston World Affairs Coun. Methodist. Home: 2608 Stanford St Houston TX 77006-2928

MCPHERSON, DEBRA S., nurse anesthetist; b. N.C., Sept. 9, 1961; d. Jerry Wayne and Patsy Ruth (Wagner) Simmons. AS, Southeastern C.C., 1982, Durham Tech. Coll., 1992; BSN, U. N.C., 1992; postgrad., Duke U., 1993, U. N.C., Greensboro, 1995—. RN, N.C., S.C.; ACLS instr., BCLS instr., PALS. Charge nurse Loris (S.C.) Cmty. Hosp., 1982-84; staff nurse Columbus County Health Dept., Whiteville, N.C., 1984-86; advanced staff nurse Duke U. Med. Ctr., Durham, N.C., 1986—; instr. ACLS, BCLS, Duke U., 1986—, Am. Heart Assn., Chapel Hill, N.C., 1990-92. Recipient Scholars award N.C. Legislature, 1990, 91, 92, 94, 95, Excellence in Nursing award N.C. Legislature, 1992. Fellow ANA, N.C. Nurses Assn., Sigma Theta Tau; mem. AACN, Am. Assn. for Nurse Anesthetists, N.C. Assn. Nurse Anesthetists. Home: 14 Little Springs Ln Durham NC 27707-3619 Office: Raleigh Sch Nurse Anesthesia 200 H Blue Ridge Rd Raleigh NC 27607

MCPHERSON, GAIL, advertising and real estate executive; b. Fort Worth; d. Garland and Daphne McP. Student U. Tex.-Austin; BA, MS, CUNY. Advt. sales exec. Harper's Bazaar mag., N.Y.C., 1974-76; sr. v.p., fashion mktg. dir. L'Officiel/USA mag., N.Y.C., 1976-80; fashion mgr. Town and Country mag., N.Y.C., 1980-82; v.p. advt. and mktg. Ultra mag., Tex. and N.Y.C., 1982-84; fragrance, jewelry and automotive mgr. M. Mag., N.Y.C., 1984-85; sr. real estate sales exec. Fredric M. Reed & Co., Inc., N.Y.C., 1985-88; AT&T security system rep. Home-Watch Inc., Amarillo, Tex.,1989-92; sales rep. Universal Comm., Dallas, 1992-94; acct. exec. Corporate Mktg., Inc., Dallas, 1994—. Sponsor Southampton Hosp. Benefit Com., N.Y.; mem. jr. com. Mannes Sch. Music, N.Y.C., Henry St. Settlement, N.Y.C. Mem. Fashion Group N.Y., Advt. Women N.Y., Real Estate Bd. N.Y., U. Tex. Alumni Assn. of N.Y. (v.p.), Amarillo C. of C. (Comm. com.). Republican. Presbyterian. Clubs: Corviglia (St. Moritz, Switzerland), Doubles, El Morocco (mem. jr. com. 1976-77), Le Club (N.Y.C.). Home: 10812 Stone Canyon Rd Apt 3143 Dallas TX 75230-4312 Office: 12200 Ford Rd Dallas TX 75234

MCPHERSON, MARY PATTERSON, academic administrator; b. Abington, Pa., May 14, 1935; d. John B. and Marjorie Hoffman (Higgins) McP. A.B., Smith Coll., 1957, LL.D., 1981; M.A., U. Del., 1960; Ph.D., Bryn Mawr Coll., 1969; LL.D. (hon.), Juniata Coll., 1975, Smith Coll., 1981, Princeton U., 1984, U. Rochester, 1984, U. Pa., 1985; Litt.D. (hon.), Haverford Coll., 1980; L.H.D. (hon.), Lafayette Coll., 1982, U. Pa., 1985; LHD (hon.), Med. Coll. Pa., 1985. Instr. philosophy U. Del., 1959-61; asst., fellow and lectr. dept. philosophy Bryn Mawr Coll., 1961-63, asst. dean, 1964-69, assoc. dean, 1969-70; dean Bryn Mawr Coll. (Undergrad. Coll.), 1970-78, assoc. prof., from 1970; acting pres. Bryn Mawr Coll., 1976-77, pres., 1978—; bd. dirs. Provident Nat. Bank of Phila., Bell Telephone Co. Pa., Dayton Hudson Corp.; mem. commn. on women in higher edn. Am. Council on Edn., bd. dirs., 1979-82. Bd. dirs. Agnes Irwin Sch., 1971—; bd. dirs. Shipley Sch., 1972—, Phillips Exeter Acad., 1973-76, Wilson Coll., 1976-79, Greater Phila. Movement, 1973-77, Internat. House of Phila., 1974-76, Josiah Macy, Jr. Found., 1977—, Carnegie Found. for Advancement Teaching, 1978-86, Univ. Mus., Phila., 1977-79, University City Sci. Center, 1979-85, Brookings Inst., 1984—, Phila. Contributionship, 1985—, Carnegie Corp. N.Y., 1985—, Nat. Humanities Ctr., 1986—, Amherst Coll., 1986—. Mem. Soc. for Ancient Greek Philosophy, Am. Philos. Soc. Clubs: Fullerton, Cosmopolitan. Office: Bryn Mawr Coll Office of the President 101 N Merion Ave Bryn Mawr PA 19010-2899*

MCPHERSON, VANZETTA PENN, federal judge; b. Montgomery, Ala., May 26, 1947; d. Luther Lincoln and Sadie Lee (Gardner) P.; m. Winston D. Durant, Aug. 17, 1968 (div. Apr. 1979); 1 child, Raegan Winston; m. Thomas McPherson Jr., Nov. 16, 1985. BS in Speech Pathology, Howard U., Washington, 1969; MA in Speech Pathology, Columbia U., 1971, JD, 1974. Bar: N.Y. 1975, Ala. 1976, U.S. Dist. Ct. (so. dist.) N.Y. 1975, U.S. Dist. Ct. (mid. dist.) Ala. 1980, U.S. Ct. Appeals (2d cir.) 1975, U.S. Ct. Appeals (11th cir.) 1981, U.S. Supreme Ct. Assoc. Hughes, Hubbard & Reed, N.Y.C., 1974-75; asst. atty. gen. Ala. Atty. Gen. Office, Montgomery, 1975-78; pvt. practice Montgomery, 1978-92; magistrate judge U.S. Dist. Ct. (mid. dist.) Ala., Montgomery, 1992—; co-owner Roots & Wings, A Cultural Bookplace, Montgomery, 1989—. Dir. Ala. Shakespeare Festival, Montgomery, 1987—; chmn. trustees Dexter Ave. King Meml. Bapt. Ch., Montgomery, 1988; chmn. Leadership Montgomery; bd. mem. Lighthouse Counseling Ctr., Montgomery, 1981-84, Montgomery County Pub. Libr., 1989-90; v.p. Lanier High Sch. Parent Tchr. Student Assn., Montgomery, 1990-91. Recipient cert. Ala. Jud. Coll.; named Woman of Achievement Montgomery Advertiser, 1989, Boss of Yr. Montgomery Assn. Legal Secs., 1992, Woman of Yr. Gamma Phi Delta, Montgomery, 1992, Citizen of Yr. Delta Sigma Theta, Montgomery, 1992. Mem. ABA (law office design award 1985), Nat. Bar Assn., Ala. State Bar Assn. (chmn. family law sect. 1989-90), N.Y. State Bar Assn., Montgomery Inn of Cts. (master bencher 1992—), Ala. Black Lawyers Assn. (pres. 1979-80). Office: US Dist Ct Mid Dist Ala PO Box 1629 15 Lee St Montgomery AL 36102

MCQUARRIE, BEATRICE SUE, assistant bank treasurer; b. Lancaster, N.H., June 17, 1956; d. Elliott A. and Elaine G. (Enman) Keinson; m. Kevin F. McQuarrie; children: Bernard J., Michael F. AS, Fisher Jr. Coll., 1980; BGen Studies cum laude, U. N.H., Durham, 1984; postgrad., U. Md., 1992-94. CPA, CMA, Md. Acct. Sch. Adminstrn. Unit 36, Whitefield, N.H., 1980-82; sch. bus. adminstr. Sch. Adminstrn. Unit 58, Groveton, N.H., 1982-86; pvt. practice fin. cons. Whitefield, 1986-91; acct. Village at Maplewood, Bethlehem, N.H., 1988-90; adj. faculty mem. Berlin (N.H.) Vocat. Tech. Coll., 1990-91; asst. treas. Bank of Glen Burnie, Md., 1991—. Vol. IRS, Whitefield, 1991; active Four Seasons Elem. Sch. PTA, Gambrills, Md., 1991—, Arundel H.S. Booster Club, Gambrills, 1992—, Four Season Cmty. Assn., Gambrills, 1991—; active Gambrills Odenton Recreation Coun., 1992—. With U.S. Army, 1974-77. Mem. Inst. Mgmt. Accts. (cert.), Md. Assn. CPAs, Am. Legion. Office: Bank of Glen Burnie 106 Padfield Blvd Glen Burnie MD 21061

MCQUEEN, ONELLIA JOY, medical, surgical and oncology nurse; b. Big Springs, Ala., Nov. 29, 1937; d. Lula Cornelia Bonner; m. James L. McQueen, Nov. 29, 1986; children: Joe, Marie, Paula, Anthony, Katherine. ADN, Okla. State U. Tech. Inst., 1971; student, Cen. State U. Cert. oncology and med. surg. nurse. Mem. planning com. Am. Cancer Soc., Oklahoma City; speaker on oncology cert. Okla. Meml. Hosp. Vol. Oklahoma City Bomb Recovery Ctr. for ARC. Mem. ANA, Okla. Nurses Assn., Oncology Nurse Assn.

MCQUEEN, REBECCA HODGES, health care executive, consultant; b. Dothan, Ala., July 20, 1954; d. Edward Grey and Shirley Louise (Varner) Hodges; m. David Raymond McQueen, Mar. 5, 1982; children: Matthew David, Owen Grey. BS, Emory U., 1976, MPH, 1979. Research assoc. North Cen. Ga. Health Systems Agy., Inc., Atlanta, 1979-80; assoc. dir. Health Services Analysis, Inc., Atlanta, 1980-82; med. group adminstr. Southeastern Health Services, Inc./Prucare, Atlanta, 1982-84; sr. v.p., COO SouthCare Med. Alliance, Atlanta, 1985-93; pres., CEO, PROMINA N.W. Health Network, Atlanta, 1993-96; sr. v.p. managed care PROMINA Health Sys., Atlanta, 1996—; cons. North Cen. Ga. Health Systems Agy., 1980-81, Region 4 HHS, Atlanta, 1980-82, instr. Applied Stats., Washington, 1980-82; mem. Health Data com. and Health Cost subcom. Atlanta Healthcare Alliance, 1985—; cons. Atlanta Com. for the Olympic Games, 1992. Contbr. articles to profl. jours. Adviser to med. support panel Atlanta Com. for Olympic Games; mem. Morningside/Lenox Park Civic Assn., Friends of Atlanta-Fulton Pub. Libr., Atlanta Bot. Garden, Planned Parenthood-Atlanta, Ga. Coun. on Child Abuse, Atlanta Wellness Coun. Recipient rsch. award Nat. Conf. on High Blood Pressure Control, 1981; nominee Woman of Achievement award YWCA. Mem. APHA (women's caucus com., presenter 1980, 81), ACLU, NOW, Am. Coll. Healthcare Execs. (diplomate), Women Healthcare Execs., Am. Managed Care and Rev. Orgn. (presenter nat. conf. 1989), Am. Assn. Preferred Provider Orgns., Delta Omega, Delta Delta Delta. Democrat. Methodist. Office: PROMINA Health Sys-Managed Care 2000 S Park Pl Atlanta GA 30339

MCQUERN, MARCIA ALICE, newspaper publishing executive; b. Riverside, Calif., Sept. 3, 1942; d. Arthur Carlyle and Dorothy Louise (Krupke) Knopf; m. Lynn Morris McQuern, June 7, 1969. BA in Polit. Sci., U. Calif., Santa Barbara, 1964; MS in Journalism, Northwestern U., 1966. Reporter The Press-Enterprise, Riverside, 1966-72, city editor, 1972-74, capitol corrs., 1975-78, dep. mng. editor news, 1984-85, mng. editor news, 1985-87, exec. editor, 1988-94, pres., 1992—; editor, publisher, 1994—; asst. metro editor The Sacramento Bee, 1974-75; editor state and polit. news The San Diego Union, 1978-79, city editor, 1979-84; juror Pulitzer Prize in Journalism, 1982, 83, 92, 93. Mem. editorial bd. Calif. Lawyer mag., San Francisco, 1983-88. Bd. advisors U. Calif.-Berkeley Grad. Sch. Journalism, 1991-96, U. Calif.-Riverside Grad. Sch. Mgmt., 1994—. Recipient Journalism award Calif. State Bar Assn., 1967, Sweepstakes award Twin Counties Press Club, Riverside and San Bernardino, 1972, Athena award YWCA, 1994. Mem. Am. Soc. Newspaper Editors (bd. dirs. 1992—), Calif. Soc. Newspaper Editors (bd. 1988-95), Calif. Newspaper Pubs. Assn. (bd. dirs. 1992—), Calif. Press Assn. (bd. dirs. 1996—), Soc. Profl. Journalists, U. Calif.-Santa Barbara Alumni Assn. (bd. dirs. 1983-89). Home: 5717 Bedford Dr Riverside CA 92506-3404 Office: Press-Enterprise Co 3512 14th St Riverside CA 92501-3814

MCQUIDDY, LORETTA ASHER, entrepreneur; b. L.A., Nov. 13, 1946; d. Peter Gabriel Incao; widowed; children: John Bruner, Jeff Bruner. Student, Scottsdale Jr. Coll. Salesperson Bruner Wholesale Co., Phoenix, 1959-75; co-owner Bambino Boutique, Scottsdale, Ariz., 1976-79, Visions of Sugarplums, Scottsdale, Ariz., 1981-86; owner Cherubini Ltd., Scottsdale, Ariz., 1986—; bd. dirs. Visual Merchandising, Borgata of Scottsdale, sec., treas. Mem. Scottsdale C. of C. Republican.

MCQUINN, NANCY KATHLEEN, retail business owner, horticulture educator; b. Seattle, May 18, 1945; d. Alex Jerome and Ruth Adeline (Jackson) McQ.; children: Anya Ruth Rubin-McQuinn, Iliana Rose Rubin. BA in Anthropology, U. Wash., 1967; BS in Horticulture, Colo. State U., 1979; MA in Bus. Mgmt., Ctrl. Mich. U., 1976. Cert. water quality specialist. Prodn. supr. Johnson & Johnson, Sherman, Tex., 1976-77; plant dept. mgr. Pier 1 Imports, Ft. Collins, Colo., 1977-79; horticulturist Simpson Timber Co., Arcata, Calif., 1979-86; mgr. Multi-Pure Drinking Water Systems, Arcata, 1990—; owner Just For Kids, Arcata, 1992—. Mediator Humboldt Mediation Group, Arcata, 1990—; bd. dirs. Equinox Sch., Arcata, 1995—. Capt. USAF, 1968-76, Turkey. Mem. Humboldt Bot. Gardens Found. (charter mem.). Office: Just For Kids 5000 Valley West Blvd Arcata CA 95521

MCRAE, KAREN K., state legislator; b. Detroit, Feb. 19, 1944; m. Gossett W. McRae; 2 children. BSL, Georgetown U., 1965. Mem. N.H. Ho. of Reps.; vice chmn. sci., tech. and energy com. Active Goffstown Conservation Com., 1972—, chmn., 1975-79. Mem. Georgetown U. Alumni Assn. (class rep. 1970—). Home: 469 Black Brook Rd Goffstown NH 03045-2931 Office: NH Ho of Reps 107 N Main St Rm 105 Concord NH 03301*

MCRAE, MARION ELEANOR, critical care nurse; b. Kingston, Ont., Can., Sept. 19, 1960; d. James Malcolm and Madeline Eleanor (MacNamara) McR. BSN, Queen's U., Kingston, 1982; MSN, U. Toronto, 1989. RN, Calif., CCRN; cert. BCLS, ACLS, PALS. Staff nurse thoracic surgery Toronto (Can.) Gen. Hosp., 1982-83, staff nurse cardiovascular ICU, 1983-85; nurse clinician critical care St. Michael's Hosp., Toronto, 1985-87; external critical care clin. tchr. Ryerson Poly. Inst., Toronto, 1986-87; staff nurse cardiovascular ICU The Toronto Hosp.-Toronto Gen. Divsn., 1987-89; clin. nurse specialist cardiac surgery The Toronto Hosp., 1989-90; clin. nurse II cardiothoracic ICU UCLA Med. Ctr., 1990-92, clin. nurse III cardiothoracic ICU, 1992—; mem. critical care nursing adv. bd. George Brown Coll., Toronto, 1987-88. Contbr. articles to profl. nursing jours. Reicpient Open Master's fellowship U. Toronto, 1987-88, M. Keyes brusary Toronto Gen. Hosp., 1988-89, Nursing fellowship Heart and Stroke Found. Ont., 1988-89, Outstanding Svc. award UCLA Med. Ctr., 1994, Cardiothoracic ICU Nurse of Yr. award UCLA, 1995. Mem. AACN, Am. Heart Assn. Coun. on Cardiovascular Nursing. Home: 1400 Midvale Ave Apt 210 Los Angeles CA 90024-5498 Office: UCLA Med Ctr Cardiothoracic ICU 10833 Le Conte Ave Los Angeles CA 90095

MCREE, CELIA, composer; b. Memphis; d. John Louis and Leta Gwendolyn (Phillips) McR. Student, Phila. Coll. Art (U. of Arts), 1976-77, Herbert Berghof Studio, 1989, Playwrights Horizon Theater, 1989; cert. with distinction, Nat. Acad. Paralegal Studies, Christian Bros. U., 1992. Pres. Mother Records, Memphis, 1984—, You Should Meet My Mother (publishing), Memphis, 1984—, Wild Thing Music, Memphis, 1987—, Mother

Prodns., Memphis, 1986—; producer, host Indian Talk, WEVL-FM90, Memphis, 1992-95; pres. Dancing Heart Pictures, Memphis, 1996—. Artist, group and solo exhbns. including Eads Gallery, Grover Cleveland Arts Inst., Phila. Mus. Natural History; screenwriter, film scoring; singer, writer (nat. album) including Celia McRee/Back From Under, 1985 (ASCAP Spl. Pop award 1985-86, 86-87, Archives of Modern Music NY.), Celia McRee/Passion, 1994; composer, arranger, producer, pub. background and feature music ABC Network, Cable TV and Radio. Entertainer Vets. Bedside Network, N.Y.C., 1981. Recipient cert. of scholarly distinction Nat. Acad. for Paralegal Studies, 1992, cert. of appreciation United Music Heritage, 1990, spl. pop award ASCAP, 1982-84, 87-93, 95-96, 96-97, Henrietta Hickman Morgan writing award DAR; named Female Pop Songwriter and Female Pop Vocalist of Yr., Entertainer Indi-Assn., 1994, Female Vocalist and Female Entertainer of Yr., 1995; named Most Popular Female Entertainer, Indi-Assn., 1996. Mem. AFTRA, ASCAP, NARAS, Broadcast Music Inc. (pub. mem.), N.Y. Acad. Sci., Assn. Am. Indian Affairs, Nat. Mus. of the Am. Indian (charter), Environ. Def. Fund, Animal Legal Def. Fund, Greenpeace, Humane Soc. U.S., Mensa, Memphis Kennel Club. Office: Mother Prodns 5159 Wheelis Dr # 110 Memphis TN 38117-4519

MC REYNOLDS, MARY BARBARA, retired secondary school educator, community volunteer; b. Los Angeles, Feb. 18, 1930; d. Clyde C. and Dorothy (Slaten) McCulloh; m. Zachariah A. McReynolds, Feb. 9, 1952 (dec.); children: Gregg Clyde, Barbara, Zachariah A.; m. John Richard Street, May 7, 1994. BA, U. N.Mex., 1951, MA, 1972, Edn. Specialist, 1975, postgrad., 1981—. Dept. sec. USAF Intelligence, Wiesbaden, W. Ger., 1953-54; tchr. Annandale (Va.) Elem. Sch., 1962-65, supr. adult edn., 1965-66; tchr. Albuquerque High Sch., 1968-77, 79-91, social studies curriculum dir., 1973-75; instr. U. N.Mex., Albuquerque, 1975-76, acad. decathlon coach Albuquerque High Sch., 1986-91; evaluator N. Central Assn., 1970-81, dir. Cultural Awareness Workshop, 1976, 79; coord. Sex Equality, 1979, 80. Bd. dirs. Greater U. N.Mex. Fund, 1978-79, 79-80, fund raiser, 1976-81, pres. club, 1977-80; campaign mgr. state senatorial campaign, 1976; exec. sec. Civic Assn., 1958-60; sponsor Black Student Union, 1978-80; sponsor Boys and Girls State, 1968-75; rep. Am. Fedn. Tchrs., 1982-91; sponsor Close-Up, 1987—; precinct chmn. Democratic Party, Albuquerque, 1985-86; mem. exec. bd. Albuquerque Rehab. Ctr., 1993—; vol. Cancer Soc., KKM; mem. fin. and pub. rels. coms. RCI Bd. Indian research and tuition edn. grantee, 1971; grantee U. N.Mex., 1975-76, others. Mem. Assn. Supervision and Curriculum Devel., Nat. Social Studies Council, N.Mex. Social Studies Council, Phi Kappa Phi, Phi Delta Kappa, Pi Alpha Theta, Kappa Kappa Gamma. Democrat. Episcopalian. Clubs: N.Mex. Democratic Women, Air Force Officers Wives, Kappa Kappa Gamma Alumni (pres. 1991-93, chmn. ways and means com. 1994, Outstanding Alumna award 1994, nat. conv. del. 1996). Condr. research in field. Home: 749 Tramway Ln NE Albuquerque NM 87122-1601

MCREYNOLDS, MARY MAUREEN, municipal environmental administrator, consultant; b. Tacoma, July 15, 1940; d. Andrew Harley and Mary Leone (McGuire) Sims; m. Gerald Aaron McReynolds, Dec. 10, 1964. Student Coll. Puget Sound, 1957-59; BA, U. Oreg., 1961; PhD, U. Chgo., 1966; postgrad. San Diego State U., 1973-75. NIH postdoctoral fellow U. Tex., Austin, 1966-68, mem. adj. faculty, 1980-82, mem. biohazards com., 1981—; research assoc. Stanford U., Calif., 1968-71; chemist assoc. Syva Co., Palo Alto, Calif., 1972; environ. specialist County of San Diego, Calif., 1973-75; dept. head City of Austin, 1976-84, chief environ. officer, 1984-85, utility environ. mgr., 1985-92, mgr. environ. and regulatory support, 1992—; dir. Ctr. for Environ. Rsch., 1992—; part-time mem. faculty Austin Community Coll., 1993—; cons. ecologist Mirassou Vineyards, San Jose, Calif., 1969-72; lectr. Wright Inst., Berkeley, Calif., 1971-72; instr. San Diego State U., 1974-75. Editor Dist. 56 newsletter, 1989-90; contbr. articles to profl. publs. Mem. Austin-Satillo Sister City Assn., 1980—; U.S.-Mexico Sister Cities del., 1983-85; sponsor, chaperone Tex.-South Australia Youth Exchange, 1986; active Leadership Austin, 1987-88; mem. Austin-Adelaide Sister City Com., 1986—, chmn., 1989-91, sec., 1992-96; bd. dirs. Internat. Hospitality Coun. of Austin, 1989-96. USPHS tng. grantee U. Chgo., 1961-64; univ. fellow U. Chgo., 1961-66. Mem. NAFE, AAAS, Water Environment Fedn. (v.p. local chpt. 1988-89, pres.-elect 1989-90, pres. 1990-91, sect. rep. 1991-94), Am. Planning Assn., Am. Inst. Cert. Planners (cert.), Assn. Environ. Profls., Am. Water Resources Assn., Tex. Assn. Met. Sewage Agys. (sec. 1994, v.p. 1995, pres. 1996), Austin Soc. Pub. Adminstrn., Zeta Tau Alpha. Lodges: Soroptimists (dir. Soroptimist Manor 1978-80, 83-85, v.p. chpt. 1983-85, pres. chpt. 1985-87, chpt. dir. 1987-88, rep. youth citizenship award com. 1986-88, chmn. South Cen. region UN com. 1988-90, rep. youth forum com. 1990-92), Toastmasters (club pres. 1981, 88, area gov. 1981-82, div. lt. gov. 1982-83, Able Toastmaster award 1983, Dist. 56 Table Topics award 1986, Disting. Toastmaster award 1987, Outstanding Toastmaster Dist. 56 no. divsn. 1987, Able Toastmaster Bronze award 1990, Able Toastmaster Silver award 1993). Avocations: gourmet food and wine. Office: City of Austin PO Box 1088 Austin TX 78767-8865

MCREYNOLDS, PAMELA KAY, controller; b. Knoxville, Tenn., July 19, 1953; d. Harold Edward and Betty Jane (Badgett) McR. BS, U. Tenn., 1975; MBA, Berry Coll., 1979. Acct. Ala. Kraft Co., Mahrt, 1975; corp. acct. Ga. Kraft Co., Rome, 1979-81, ops. acctg. supr., 1981-86, fin. acctg. mgr., 1987-88; mgr. MIS Holliston Mills, Inc., Kingsport, Tenn., 1988-90, controller, 1991-92; contr. Elo TouchSys., Inc., Oak Ridge, Tenn., 1992-96, dir. fin., 1996—; mem. adv. bd. S.I. Users Group, Boston, 1983-88; seminar leader. Republican. Baptist. Office: Elo Touch Sys Inc 105 Randolph Rd Oak Ridge TN 37830-5028

MCSHAY, YVONNE MANGRAM AL'MEDIA, English educator, consultant; b. Jacksonville, Fla., Dec. 2, 1944; d. Demous Wesley and Georgia Mae (Brown) Mangram; m. Aubrey McShay, Aug. 12, 1976 (div.); 1 child, Juli Von; 1 child, Lisa Ann Henderson. BS, Edward Waters Coll., 1963; MS, Ind. U., 1973. Asst. dir. Planned Parenthood, South Bend, Ind., 1971-72; dist. mgr. Avon Cosmetics, Cinn., 1972-74; tchr. English Polk County Schs., Lakeland, Fla., 1974-92; prof. English Polk C.C., Winter Haven, Fla., 1992—; owner, dir. Polm Yvonne's Ednl. Techniques, Lakeland. Author (booklet) Rainbow, 1982. Participant Leadership Lakeland VIII, 1990; mem., 1st v.p. NAACP, Lakeland, 1990; organizer, pres. North Lakeland Friends of Libr., 1990-92. Mem. AAUW (v.p. 1989-90, Woman of Yr. 1991), Am. Assn. Women in C.C. (1st v.p.-elect 1996—), Phi Delta Kappa. Home: 202 Pinehurst St Lakeland FL 33805 Office: Polk CC 999 Ave H NE Winter Haven FL 33881

MCSHIRLEY, SUSAN RUTH, gift industry executive, consultant; b. Glendale, Calif., July 31, 1945; d. Robert Claude and Lillian Dora (Mable) McS. BS, U. Calif.-Berkeley, 1967. Nat. sales dir. McShirley Products, Glendale, Calif., 1967-71, Viade Products, Camarillo, Calif., 1972-80; pres. SRM Press, Inc., L.A., 1980—; nat. sales cons. Warner Bros. Records, Burbank, Calif., 1985. Author: Racquetball: Where to Play, USA, 1978; patentee picture pen; creator novelty trademarks including The Pig Pen, The Road Hog, DFZ/Drug Free Zone, Tobacco Free Zone, Protect Our Planet. Mem. Calif. Alumni Assn., Alpha Omicron Pi. Avocations: travel, photography, tennis, foreign languages. Home: 15947 Temecula St Pacific Palisades CA 90272-4239 Office: SRM Press Inc 4216 Glencoe Ave Marina Del Rey CA 90292

MCSORLEY, RITA ELIZABETH, adult education educator; b. Baraboo, Wis., Feb. 13, 1947; d. Charles Gervase and Bertie Ellen (Baker) Collins; m. William David McSorley III, June 6, 1967; children: William David IV, Kathryn Rita, Stephen Charles, Matthew Thomas. B Liberal Studies, Mary Washington Coll., Fredericksburg, Va., 1988; MEd, U. Va., Charlottesville, 1994. Adult edn. instr. Waipahu (Hawaii) Cmty. Sch. for Adults, 1989-91, literacy coord., 1990-91; dir. religious edn. Marine Meml. Chapel, Quantico, Va., 1992-94; adult edn. instr. Prince William County Schs., Quantico, 1992-93; coord. computer assisted lang. learning project Literacy Coun. No. Va., Falls Church, 1995—. Mem. sch. bd. Quantico Dependent Schs., 1980-82; vol. Boy Scouts Am., Quantico and Pearl City, Hawaii, 1985—. Mem. AAUW, TESOL, Washington Area TESOL, U. Va. Alumni Assn. Roman Catholic. Office: Literacy Coun No Va 2855 Annandale Rd Falls Church VA 22042

MCSPADDEN, LETTIE, political science educator; b. Battle Creek, Mich., Apr. 9, 1937; d. John Dean and Isma Doolie (Sullivan) McSpadden; m. Manfred Wilhelm Wenner, Apr. 3, 1962; children: Eric Alexis, Adrian Edward. AB, U. Chgo., 1959; MA, U. Calif., Berkeley, 1962; PhD, U. Wis., 1972. Fgn. svc. officer Dept. State, Washington, 1961-63; rsch. assoc. Dept. HEW, Washington, 1965-67; asst. prof. polit. sci. U. Ill., Chgo., 1972-79, assoc. prof. polit. sci., 1979-88; prof. and chair dept. polit. sci. No. Ill. U., De Kalb, 1988-94, prof. dept. polit. sci., 1994—. Author: One Environment Under Law, 1976, The Environmental Decade in Court, 1982, United States Energy and Environmental Interest Groups, 1990. Mem. Am. Polit. Sci. Assn., Midwest Polit. Sci. Assn., Law and Society Assn., Pub. Policy Assn., Audubon Soc., Sierra Club. Democrat. Home: 3112 Fairway Oaks Dr De Kalb IL 60115-4925 Office: No Ill U Dept Polit Sci De Kalb IL 60115

MCSTEEN, MARTHA ABERNATHY, organization executive; b. Iowa Park, Tex., May 25, 1923; d. King Peyton and Iva Mae (Dawson) Abernathy; m. George Steven McSteen, Oct. 13, 1943 (dec. Jan. 1945); m. Marshall Parks, Apr. 6, 1991. BA, Rice U., 1944; MA, U. Okla., 1972; JD (hon.), Austin Coll., 1985. Claims rep., supr. and dist. mgr. Social Security Adminstrn., Dallas, 1947-65, regional commr., 1976-83; acting commr. Social Security Adminstrn., Washington, 1983-86; regional adminstr. Medicare, Denver and Dallas, 1965-76; cons. Nat. Com. To Preserve Social Security and Medicare, Washington, 1987-89, pres., 1989—; U.S. rep. to Internat. Social Security Assn., 1985, 86. Bd. dirs. Alliance Rsch. in Aging, Nat. Children's Eye Found., Internat. Fedn. Aging; bd. advisors Internat. Ctr. Rsch. and Tng. for Programs on Aging, Setting Priorities for Retirement Yrs. Found., Washington, 1991—, Prevention of Blindness Found., Washington, 1993—, Claude and Mildred Pepper Found. Recipient Commr.'s citation Social Security Adminstrn., 1961, 66, 71, Disting. Svc. award HEW, 1979, Presdl. Meritorious Exec. award, 1980, Nat. Pub. Svc. award Am. Soc. for Pub. Adminstrn., 1986, Presdl. Disting. Exec. award, 1987; fellow Social Security Adminstrn., 1968-69. Office: Nat Com Preserve Soc Sec & Medicare 2000 K St NW Ste 800 Washington DC 20006-1809

MCSWEENEY, FRANCES KAYE, psychology educator; b. Rochester, N.Y., Feb. 6, 1948; d. Edward William and Elsie Winifred (Kingston) McS. BA, Smith Coll., 1969; MA, Harvard U., 1972, PhD, 1974. Lectr. McMaster U., Hamilton, Ont., Can., 1973-74; asst. prof. Wash. State U., Pullman, 1974-79, assoc. prof., 1979-83, prof. psychology, 1983—, chmn. dept. psychology, 1986-94; cons. in field. Contbr. articles to profl. jours. Woodrow Wilson fellow, Sloan Fellow, 1968-69; NSF fellow, 1970-72; NIMH fellow, 1973. Fellow Am. Psychol. Assn., Am. Psychol. Soc.; mem. Western Psychol. Assn., Psychonomic Soc., Assn. Behavior Analysis, Phi Kappa Phi, Phi Beta Kappa, Sigma Xi. Home: SW 860 Alcora Pullman WA 99163 Office: Wash State U Dept Psychology Pullman WA 99164-4820

MCVAY, MARY FRANCES, portfolio manager; b. Washington, Sept. 17, 1955; d. Joseph J. and Stella F. (Walejko) McVay; m. Theodore R. Rosenberg, Sept. 21, 1991. BS in Acctg., Va. Tech., 1978, MBA, 1981. CPA; CFA. Auditor CIA, Washington, 1975-83; sr. cons. Booz, Allen & Hamilton, Arlington, Va., 1983-85; portfolio mgr. Burney Mgmt. Co., Falls Church, Va., 1985—. Mem. Inst. Mgmt. Accts. (dir. newsletter 1992—, v.p. adminstrn. 1993—, dir. program roster 1994—), Assn. Investment, Mgmt. and Rsch. Office: Burney Mgmt Co 123 Rowell Ct Falls Church VA 22046-3126

MCVEIGH-PETTIGREW, SHARON CHRISTINE, communications consultant; b. San Francisco, Feb. 6, 1949; d. Martin Allen and Frances (Roddy) McVeigh; m. John Wallace Pettigrew, Mar. 27, 1971; children: Benjamin Thomas, Margaret Mary. B.A. with honors, U. Calif.-Berkeley, 1971; diploma of edn. Monash U., Australia, 1975; M.B.A., Golden Gate U., 1985. Tchr., adminstr. Victorian Edn. Dept., Victoria, Australia, 1972-79; supr. Network Control Ctr., GTE Sprint Communications, Burlingame, Calif., 1979-81, mgr. customer assistance, 1981-84, mgr. state legis. ops., 1984-85, dir. revenue programs, 1986-87; communications cons. Flores, Pettigrew & Co., San Mateo, Calif., 1987-89; mgr. telemarketing Apple Computer, Inc., Cupertino, Calif., 1989-94; prin. The Call Ctr. Group, San Mateo, Calif., 1995—; telecomm. cons. PPG Svcs., 1994—; telecomm. spkr. Dept. Consumer Affairs, Sacramento, 1984. Panelist Wash. Gov.'s Citizens Council, 1984; founding mem. Maroondah Women's Shelter, Victoria, 1978; organizer nat. conf. Bus. Women and the Polit. Process, New Orleans, 1986; mem. sch. bd. Boronia Tech. Sch., Victoria, 1979. Recipient Tchr. Spl. Responsibilities award Victoria Edn. Dept., 1979. Mem. Women in Telecommunications (panel moderator San Francisco 1984), Am. Mgmt. Assn., Peninsula Profl. Women's Network, Am. Telemktg. Assn. (bd. dirs. 1992), Women's Econ. Action League. Democrat. Roman Catholic.

MCVEY, DIANE ELAINE, accountant; b. Wilmington, Del., Apr. 20, 1953; d. C. Granville and Margaret M. (Lindell) McV. AA in Acctg., Goldey Beacom Coll. (Del.), 1973, BS in Acctg., 1980; MBA in Mgmt., Fairleigh Dickinson U., 1985. Acct. Audio Visual Arts, Wilmington, 1973; cost acct. FMC Corp., Kennett Sq., Pa., 1973-75; asst. acct. NVF Corp., Kennett Sq., 1978-80; staff analyst GPU Nuclear, Parsippany, N.J., 1980-93; staff acct., 1993—; owner, Demac Cons., Dover, N.J., 1988—. Elder First Presbyn. Ch., Rockaway, N.J., 1986—, session mem., 1988-91; commr. to bd. adjustment, Dover, N.J., 1994—. With U.S. Army, 1975-78. Mem. Assn. MBA Execs. Republican. Presbyterian.

MCVICKER, MARCIA ANN, investment research; b. Altoona, Pa., Jan. 11, 1955; d. Eugene Robbins and Mildred (Cook) McV.; children: William G., Marc R. BS in Bus. and Music, Towson (Md.) State U., 1987; postgrad., Johns Hopkins U., 1994—. Lic. series 7 Nat. Assn. Securities Dealers. Sales asst. Alex. Brown & Sons, Balt., 1982-85; equity rschr. T. Rowe Price Assocs., Balt., 1987—. Bd. dirs. Canticle Singers, Balt., 1993—. Mem. AAUW (co-chmn. pub. policy 1995—), Exec. Women's Network. Republican. Lutheran. Office: T Rowe Price Assocs 100 E Pratt St Baltimore MD 21202

MCVICKER, MARY ELLEN HARSHBARGER, museum director, art history educator; b. Mexico, Mo., May 5, 1951; d. Don Milton and Harriet Pauline (Mossholder) Harshbarger; m. Wiley Ray McVicker, June 2, 1973; children: Laura Elizabeth, Todd Michael. BA with honors, U. Mo., 1973, MA, 1975, PhD, Columbia, Mo., 1989. Instr. Columbia U., Mo., 1977-78, Cen. Meth. Coll., Fayette, Mo., 1978-85, mus. dir., 1980-85; project dir. Mo. Com. for Humanities, Fayette, 1981-85, Mo. Dept. Natural Resources Office Hist. Preservation, 1978-85; owner, Memories of Mo. & Tour Tyme, Inc., 1986—; prof. history Kemper Mil. Coll., 1993—. Author: History Book, 1984. V.p. Friends Hist. Boonville, Mo., 1982-87, pres., 1989-90; bd. dirs. Mus. Assocs. Mo. U., Columbia, 1981-83, Mo. Meth. Hist. Soc., Fayette, 1981-84; chmn. Bicentennial Celebration Methodism, Boonville, Mo., 1984; pres. Arts & Sci. Alumni, U. Mo., 1992—; bd. dirs. Mo. Humanities Coun., 1993—. Mem. Mo. Alliance for Hist. Preservation (charter), AAUW (treas. 1977-79), Am. Assn. Museums, Centralia Hist. Soc. (project dir. 1978), Mus. Assocs. United Meth. Ch. (charter, bd. dir. 1981-83), Phi Beta Kappa, Mortar Bd. Democrat. Clubs: Women's (treas. 1977-79), United Meth. Women's Group (charter mem.). Avocations: collecting antiques, gardening, family farming, singing, travelling. Home: 22151 Highway 98 Boonville MO 65233 Office: Tour Tyme PO Box 72 Columbia MO 65205

MCWETHY, PATRICIA JOAN, educational association administrator; b. Chgo., Feb. 27, 1946; d. Frank E. and Emma (Kuehne) McW.; m. H. Frank Eden; children: Kristin Beth, Justin Nicholas. BA, Northwestern U., 1968; MA, U. Minn., 1970; MBA, George Washington U., 1981. Geog. analyst CIA, McLean, Va., 1970-71; research asst. NSF, Washington, 1972-74, spl. asst. to dir., 1975; assoc. program dir. human geography and regional sci. program NSF, 1976-79; exec. dir. Assn. Am. Geographers, Washington, 1979-84, Nat. Assn. Biology Tchrs., Reston, Va., 1984-95, Nat. Sci. Edn. Leadership Assn., Arlington, Va., 1995—; prin. investigator NSF grant on biotech. equipment ednl. resource partnership, 1989-93, NSF funded internat. symposium on "Basic Biol. Concepts: What Should the World's Children Know?", 1992-94; co-prin. investigator NSF grant, 1995—; mem. chmn.'s adv. com. Nat. Com. Sci. Stds. & Assessment, 1992—; mem. Commn. for Biology Edn., Internat. Union Biol. Sci., 1988—; mem. exec. com. Alliance for Environ. Edn., 1987-90, chmn. program com., 1990; condr. seminars in field; lectr. in field. Author monograph and papers in field; editor handbook. NSF grantee, 1989-93, 95—; NSF fellow, 1968-69; recipient Outstanding Performance award, NSF, 1973. Mem. Am. Soc. Assn. Execs., Phi Beta Kappa. Office: PO Box 5556 Arlington VA 22205

MCWHIRTER, GLENNA SUZANNE (NICKIE MCWHIRTER), newspaper columnist; b. Peoria, Ill., June 28, 1929; d. Alfred Leon and Garnet Lorene (Short) Sotier; m. Edward Ford McWhirter (div.); children: Suzanne McWhirter Orlicki, Charles Edward, James Richard. BS in English Lang. and Lit., U. Mich., postgrad., 1960-63. Editl. asst. McGraw-Hill Pub. Co., Detroit, 1951-54; staff writer Detroit Free Press, Inc., Detroit, 1963-88; columnist Detroit News Inc., Detroit, 1988—; advt. copy writer Campbell-Ewald Co., Detroit, 1967-68. Author: Pea Soup, 1984. Winner 1st Place Commentary award UPI, Mich., 1979; 1st Place Columns AP, Mich., 1978, 81; 1st Place Columns Detroit Press Club Found., Mich., 1978; Disting. Service award State of Mich., 1985. Mem. Women in Comm. (Headliner award 1978), Alpha Gamma Delta. Home: 88 Meadow Ln Grosse Pointe MI 48236-3803

MCWHORTER, KATHLEEN THOMPSON, reading and writing educator; b. Buffalo, Oct. 10, 1944; d. Harry and Ruth Elizabeth (Berry) Thompson. BA, SUNY, Buffalo, 1965, EdM, 1968, EdD, 1974. Reading specialist West Seneca (N.Y.) Pub. Schs., 1965-68; instr. SUNY, Buffalo, 1968-71; prof. Niagara County C.C., Sanborn, N.Y., 1971—; cons. Carborundum Corp., Niagara Falls, N.Y., 1974, Jefferson Edn. Ctr., Buffalo, 1970. Author: Efficient and Flexible Reading, 1996, College Study and Thinking Skills, 1995, The Writer's Express, 1993, Guide to College Reading, 1993, Academic Reading, 1994, College Reading and Study Skills, 1995, The Writer's Compass, 1995; contbr. to profl. jours. Mem. Internat. Reading Assn., Nat. Coun. Tchrs. English, Coll. Reading Assn., N.Y. State Learning Skills Assn., New Eng. Reading Assn., Nat. Assn. Devel. Educators, Coll. Reading and Learning Assn., Textbook Authors Assn. Office: Niagara County CC 3111 Saunders Settlement Rd Sanborn NY 14132-9487

MCWHORTER, RUTH ALICE, counselor, marriage and family therapist; b. Norfolk, Va., May 14, 1946; d. Lester Arthur and Mabel Winifred (Hopwood) Gorman; m. Dean Gundersen, Dec. 27, 1967 (div. Oct. 1971); m. R. Dale Lawhorn, Jan. 6, 1972 (div. Nov. 1979); m. Brent Wilson McWhorter, Aug. 16, 1986; stepchildren: Daniel Chastin, Kenley Reid, Scott Jason. BA in Edn., Ariz. State U., 1970, M of Counseling Psychology, 1979. Cert. profl. counselor, Ariz., cert. marriage and family therapist, Ariz. Tchr. lang. arts Globe (Ariz.) Mid. Sch., 1969-72; tchr. English Isaac Jr. High Sch., Phoenix, Ariz., 1973-74; real estate salesperson Ben Brooks & Assocs., Phoenix, 1975-76, Century 21 Metro, Phoenix, 1976-77; overnight counselor The New Found., Phoenix, 1978-80; family therapist Youth Svc. Bur., Phoenix, 1980-81; owner, corp. officer, profl. counselor/marriage & family Family Devel. Resources (now Family Psychology Assocs.), Phoenix, 1981—; cons., vol. counselor Deseret Industries, Phoenix, 1992-96. Bd. dirs. Westside Mental Health Svcs., Phoenix, 1982-87; vol. facilitator Ariz. Multiple Sclerosis Soc., Phoenix, 1988. Mem. ACA, Internat. Assn. Marriage and Family Therapists, Am. Assn. Marriage and Family Therapists, Am. Mental Health Counselors Assn., Ariz. Counselors Assn., Ariz. Mental Health Counselors Assn. (sec.-treas. ctrl. chpt. 1982, sec. ctrl. chpt. 1995), Am. Assn. Christian Counselors, Assn. Mormon Counselors and Psychotherapists (sec.-treas. 1990—). Office: Family Devel Resources PC PO Box 55291 Phoenix AZ 85078-5291

MCWILLIAMS, CHRIS PATER ELISSA, elementary school educator; b. Cin., Oct. 23, 1937; d. Ray C. and Mary Loretta (Collins) Pater; m. Nabeel David Elissa, Aug. 15, 1964 (dec. Aug. 1975); children: Sue Renee, Ramsey Nabeel; m. Jim Bill McWilliams, Apr. 14, 1977 (dec. Sept. 1993). BA, Our Lady of Cin. Coll., 1959; MEd, Xavier U., 1965. Cert. tchr. elem., social studies, environ. edn., Tex. Elem. tchr. Cin. Parochial Schs., 1960-64, Champaign County Schs., Urbana, Ohio, 1968; tchr. social studies St. Mary's Elem. Sch., Urbana, 1968-73; tchr. Granbury (Tex.) Ind. Sch. Dist., 1981—; instr. Tarleton State U., Stephenville, Tex., 1989-90. Contbr. (text) Texas: Yesterday, Today and Tomorrow, 1988; music editor (newspaper) Jerusalem Star, 1966. Me. Hood Gen. Hosp. Aux., 1978—; chmn. Hood County Blood Drive, Granbury, 1978-82. Recipient scholarship Our Lady of Cin. Coll., 1955, Betty Crocker Homemaker award, Gen. Mills, 1955. Mem. Nat. Coun. Social Studies, Tex. Alliance for Geog. Edn., Phi Delta Kappa, Delta Kappa Gamma (pres. Lambda Pi chpt. 1988-90, 96—). Roman Catholic. Home: 249 Northwood Ter Granbury TX 76049-5709

MCWILLIAMS, MARGARET ANN, home economics educator, author; b. Osage, Iowa, May 26, 1929; d. Alvin Randall and Mildred Irene (Lane) Edgar; children: Roger, Kathleen. BS, Iowa State U., 1951, MS, 1953; PhD, Oreg. State U., 1968. Registered dietitian. Asst. prof. home econs. Calif. State U., L.A., 1961-66, assoc. prof., 1966-68, prof., 1968-92, prof. emeritus, 1992—, chmn. dept., 1968-76; pres. Plycon Press, 1978—. Author: Food Fundamentals, 1966, 6th edit., 1995, Nutrition for the Growing Years, 1967, 5th edit., 1993, Experimental Foods Laboratory Manual, 1977, 4th edit., 1994, (with L. Kotschevar) Understanding Food, 1969, Illustrated Guide to Food Preparation, 1970, 7th edit., 1995, (with L. Davis) Food for You, 1971, 2d edit., 1976, The Meatless Cookbook, 1973, (with F. Stare) Living Nutrition, 1973, 4th edit., 1984, Nutrition for Good Health, 1974, 2d edit., 1982, (with H. Paine) Modern Food Preservation, Fundamentals of Meal Management, 1978, 2d edit., 1993, Foods: Experimental Perspectives, 1989, 2d edit., 1993. Chmn. bd. Beach Cities Symphony, 1991-94. Recipient Alumni Centennial award Iowa State U., 1971, Profl. Achievement award, 1977; Phi Upsilon Omicron Nat. Founders fellow, 1964, Home Economist in Bus. Nat. Found. fellow, 1967; Outstanding Prof. award Calif. State U., 1976. Mem. Am. Dietetic Assn., Inst. Food Technologists, Phi Kappa Phi, Phi Upsilon Omicron, Omicron Nu, Iota Sigma Pi, Sigma Delta Epsilon, Sigma Alpha Iota. Home: PO Box 220 Redondo Beach CA 90277-0220

MCWILLIAMS, MARY ANN, school administrator; b. Shreveport, La., July 5, 1944; d. Joseph Vivian and Helen Claire (McKinney) McW. BS, Northwestern State U., 1966; MEd, U. North Tex., 1989. Cert. composite sci., Tex., adminstrn. cert. Tchr. biology Willapa Valley Schs., Menlo, Wash., 1966-67; med. technologist Meth. Hosp., Houston, 1967-68; tchr. biology Caddo Parish Schs., Shreveport, 1968-74, 77-79; advt. account exec. Sta. KCOZ Radio, Shreveport, 1979-80; coord. tng./documentation Tri-State Computer Svcs., Shreveport, 1980-83; tchr. biology, team leader Plano (Tex.) Ind. Sch. Dist., 1983-94, environ. studies coord., coord. for environ. outdoor sch. camp program, 1994—, coord. for environ. outdoor sch. camp program, 1994—; dir. Holifield Sci. Learning Ctr., Plano, 1994—; chmn. ednl. improvement coun. Plano Ind. Sch. Dist., 1990-94; tchr. trainer Jason V Project, Dallas, 1993-94; dir. Environ. Studies Camp, Plano, 1994—. Mem. Dallas Mus. of Art, 1987—; bd. dirs. Camp Classen, Oklahoma City YMCA, 1996. Named Jane Goodall Environ Educator of Yr., Jane Goodall Inst. and Boreal Labs., Dallas, 1993, one of Outstanding Young Women of Am., 1980. Mem. ASCD, NEA, Nat. Sci. Tchrs. Assn., Sci. Tchrs. of Tex., Jane Goodall Inst. Roots and Shoots. Roman Catholic. Office: Plano Ind Sch Sys 2700 W 15th St Plano TX 75075-7524

MEAD, BEVERLY MIRIUM ANDERSON, author, educator; b. St. Paul, May 29, 1925; d. Martin and Anna Mae (Oshanyk) Anderson; m. Jerome Morton Nemiro, Feb. 10, 1951 (div. May 1975); children: Guy Samuel, Lee Anna, Dee Martin; m. William Isaac Mead, Aug. 8, 1992. Student Reed Coll., 1943-44; BA, U. Colo., 1947; postgrad., U. Denver. Tchr., Seattle Pub. Schs., 1945-46; fashion coord., dir. Denver Dry Goods Co., 1948-51; fashion model, Denver, 1951-58, 78—; fashion dir. Denver Market Week Assn., 1952-53; free-lance writer, Denver, 1958—; moderator TV program Your Preschool Child, Denver, 1955-56; instr. writing and communications U. Colo. Denver Ctr., 1970—, U. Calif., San Diego, 1976-78, Met. State Coll., 1985; dir. pub. relations Fairmont Hotel, Denver, 1979-80; free lance fashion and TV model; author, co-author: The Complete Book of High Altitude Baking, 1961, Colorado a la Carte, 1963, Colorado a la Carte, Series II, 1966, (with Donna Hamilton) The High Altitude Cookbook, 1969, The Busy People's Cookbook, 1971 (Better Homes and Gardens Book Club selection 1971), Where to Eat in Colorado, 1967, Lunch Box Cookbook, 1965, Complete Book of High Altitude Baking, 1961, (under name Beverly Anderson) Single After 50, 1978, The New High Altitude Cookbook, 1980. Co-founder, pres. Jr. Symphony Guild, Denver, 1959-60; active Friends of Denver Libr., Opera Colo. Recipient Top Hand award Colo. Authors' League, 1969, 72, 79-82, 100 Best Best Books of Yr. award N.Y. Times, 1969, 71; named one of Colo.'s Women of Yr., Denver Post, 1964. Mem. Am. Soc. Journalists and Authors, Colo. Authors League (dir. 1969-79), Authors Guild, Authors League Am., Friends Denver Library, Rotary, Kappa Alpha Theta. Address: 23 Polo Club Dr Denver CO 80209-3309

MEAD, HARRIET COUNCIL, librarian, author; b. Franklin, Va., Jan. 11; d. Hutson and Ollie (Whitley) Council; m. Berne Matthews Mead, Jr., Dec. 2, 1940; children—William Whitley, Charles Council. BA, Coll. William and Mary, 1935; postgrad. Fla. State U., 1958-62, Rollins Coll., 1966, 70, 84. County libr. Carroll County, Hillsville, Va., 1935-36; city libr. Suffolk City Schs., Va., 1936-41; libr., media specialist Orange County Schs., Orlando, Fla., 1961-80. Author: The Irrepressible Saint, 1983, A Family Legacy, 1987, Stained Glass in Cathedral Church of St. Luke, 1994. Contbr. article to mag. Mem. Fla. Hist. Soc., Friends of Libr., Orange County Media Specialists (pres. Greater Orlando 1968-69), Nat. Soc. Colonial Dames, Jr. League of Greater Orlando, Orange County Ret. Educators. Democrat. Episcopalian. Avocation: watercolor painting. Home: 500 E Marks St Orlando FL 32803-3922

MEAD, PHILOMENA, mental health nurse; b. Yonkers, N.Y., June 23, 1934; d. Alfonso F. and Jennie (Saltarelli) D'Amato; m. Kenneth Mead, Nov. 10, 1956; children: Scott Kenneth, Jeanne Bette. RN, St. Vincents Hosp., Bridgeport, Conn., 1955; BS in Psychology, Sacred Heart U., 1980; cert. in nursing mgmt., Fairfield U., 1988. Cert. psychiat. mental health nurse, nursing specialist, nat. chem. dependency nurse, CPR. Day supr.-relief, night supr. Hall Brooke Hosp., Westport, Conn., 1956-58, day supr., asst. dir. nurses, 1958-66, evening supr.-relief, 1967-68, team nurse, 1974-83, coord. nursing care, 1983-86, adminstrv. coord., 1986-87, nursing care coord. substance abuse treatment unit, 1987-91; charge evening nurse Carolton Hosp., Fairfield, Conn., 1971-73; nurse psychiat. emergency rm. and brief treatment unit West Haven (Conn.) VA, 1991—, mem. staff psychiat. emergency rm., 1995—. Roman Catholic. Home: 67 Adams Rd Fairfield CT 06430-3018

MEAD, PRISCILLA, state legislator; m. John L. Mead; children: John, Willian, Neel, Sarah. Student, Ohio State U. Councilwoman Upper Arlington, Ohio, 1982-90, mayor, 1986-90; mem. Ohio Ho. of Reps. Mem. Franklin County Child Abuse and Neglect Found., Coun. for Ethics and Econs. Recipient Svc. award Northwest Kiwanis, Woman of Yr. award Upper Arlington Rotary, Citizen of Yr. award U.S. C. of C. Mem. LWV, Upper Arlington Edn. Found., Jr. League Columbus, Upper Arlington C. of C., Delta Gamma. Republican. Home: 2281 Brixton Rd Columbus OH 43221-3117 Office: Ohio Ho of Reps State House Columbus OH 43215*

MEAD, TERRY EILEEN, clinic administrator, consultant; b. Portland, Oreg., Mar. 14, 1950; d. Everett L. and Jean (Nonken) Richardson; divorced; 1 child, Sean Knute Wade Adcock. AA summa cum laude, Seattle U., 1972; postgrad., U. Wash., 1971. Project mgr. Assoc. Univ. Physician, Seattle, 1971-74; pathology supr. Swedish Hosp., Seattle, 1974-77; svcs. supr. Transamerica, Seattle, 1977-78; various mgmt. positions Providence Hosp., Seattle, 1978-83; CEO Mead's Med. Mgmt. Cons. Firm, Chiloquin, Oreg., 1980—; adminstr. Evergreen Surg. Ctr., Kirkland, Wash., 1983-86; bus. mgr. Ketchikan (Alaska) Gen. Hosp., 1986—; instr. U. Alaska, Ketchikan, 1990; adminstr. Bethel (Alaska) Family Clinic, 1994—; CEO Southeast Oreg. Rural Health Network, 1996—, Mead's Med. Mgmt., 1980—; mead's med. mgmt., CEO. 1980—, sec. S.E. adv. bd. U. Alaska, Ketchikan, 1987-94; cons. to hosps. and physicians, Wash., Alaska, 1980—; mgr. Practice Mgmt. Cons., Seattle, 1982-83. Mem. City Charter Rev. Com., Ketchikan, 1990-94; High Sch. Facilities Com. Ketchikan, 1990; S.E. dir. search com. U. Alaska, Ketchikan, 1990; treas. Calvary Bible Ch., Ketchikan, 1989-91; bd. dirs. S.E. Alaska Symphony, 1992-94, Jr. Achievement, 1992-93; chmn. fin. com. City of Bethel, 1994-96. Mem. Rotary Internat. Home: PO Box 1287 Chiloquin OR 97624-1287 Office: PO Box 379 Chiloquin OR 97624-2580

MEADE, DOROTHY WINIFRED, retired educational administrator; b. N.Y.C., Jan. 26, 1935; d. Percival and Fraulien Franklin; m. Gerald H. Meade (div. 1987); 1 child, Myrla E. BA in Am. History, Queens Coll., Flushing, N.Y., 1970; MA in Corrective Reading, Bklyn. Coll., 1975; BA in Religious Edn., United Christian Coll., Bklyn., 1980; postgrad., Bklyn. Coll., 1984. Tchr. social studies cluster Pub. Sch. 137, Bklyn., 1979-83, curriculum coord. Follow Through Program, 1984-88, adminstrv. intern, 1983-84; staff developer social studies Cen. Sch. Dist. 23, Bklyn., 1988-89, dist. coord. Project Child, 1989-91; mem. faculty Coll. of New Rochelle, Bklyn., 1994; mem. coop. bd. dirs. 1053 E 13th St., Bklyn. Former mem. Ch. of the Master; participant in Crossroads Africa, 1958; nursery worker Bklyn. Tabernacle, 1986-95, mem. sr. choir, 1992, mam. prayer band, 1995. Mem. African Christian Tchrs., N.Y. Pub. Sch. Early Childhood Edn., N.Y. Geography Inst. Pentecostal. Home: 1053 E 13th St Brooklyn NY 11230-4252

MEADE, MELINDA SUE, geographer, educator; b. N.Y.C., Nov. 2, 1945; d. Melville J. and Katherine Meade. BA, Hofstra U., 1966; MA, Mich. State U., 1970; PhD, U. Hawaii, 1974. Rsch. assoc. Internat. Ctr. Med. Rsch. U. Calif., Kuala Lumpur, Malaysia, 1972-74; asst. prof. UCLA, 1974-76, U. Ga., Athens, 1976-78; asst. prof., assoc. prof., prof. U. N.C., Chapel Hill, 1978—; vol. Peace Corps, Thailand, 1966-68. Author: Medical Geography, 1988. Mem. AAAS (steering com. 1984-87), Assn. Am. Geographers (councillor 1984-87), Assn. Asian Studies (councillor 1981-84), Med. Geography Splty. (sect. chair, councillor 1977-92). Democrat. Office: Univ NC Dept Geography Chapel Hill NC 27599-3220

MEADE, NANCY, accounting educator; children: Theodore, Lisa Lanman. BA in Math., Marshall U., Huntington, W.Va., 1966; M.Accountancy, Va. Poly. Inst. and State U., 1986, PhD in Acctg., 1990. CPA, Va. Asst. prof. acctg. U. Louisville, 1992-95, Radford (Va.) U., 1995—. Contbr. articles to profl. jours. Mem. AICPAs, Inst. Mgmt. Accts., Am. Acctg. Assn.

MEADERS, NOBUKO YOSHIZAWA, therapist, psychoanalyst; b. Kobe, Hyogo-ken, Japan, Mar. 2, 1942; d. Shigenobu and Ayako (Takahashi) Tsuchiya; m. Wilson E. Meaders, Apr. 2, 1976 (div. Apr. 1985); m. Takeshi Yoshizawa, June 15, 1989. AA, Seiwa Coll., Nishinomiya, Japan, 1965, Warren Wilson Coll., Swannanoa, N.C., 1967; BA, So. Meth. U., Dallas, 1969; MS in Social Work, U. Tex., Arlington, 1971; cert. psychotherapy-psychoanalysis, Postgrad. Ctr. Mental Health, N.Y.C., 1977, cert. in supervision psychotherapeutic processes, 1979. Cert. social worker, N.Y.; diplomate Am. Bd. Examiners in Clin. Social Work. Psychiat. social worker Killgore Children's Psychiat. Hosp., Amarillo, Tex., 1971-73, Jewish Child Care Assn., Childville div., N.Y.C., 1973-74; supr. social work, social work dept. Bellevue Hosp., N.Y.C., 1974-76; asst. dir. tng. Postgrad. Ctr. Mental Health, N.Y.C., 1979-82, assoc. supr., 1979-82, supr., 1982-85, sr. supr., 1985—, tng. analyst, 1989—; pvt. practice psychotherapy and psychoanalysis N.Y.C., 1976—; clin. cons. Pace U. Personal Devel. Ctr., N.Y.C., 1987—; mem. adv. bd. Japanese-Am. Cons. Ctr., N.Y.C., 1983—. Fellow N.Y. Soc. Clin. Social Work Psychotherapists; mem. NASW, Acad. Cert. Social Workers.

MEADLOCK, NANCY B., computer graphics company executive; b. 1938; married. BSMA, Athens Coll., 1969. With Intergraph Corp., 1969—, v.p. for adminstrn., now exec. v.p., dir. Office: Intergraph Corp 1 Madison Industrial Park Huntsville AL 35894-0001*

MEADOR, RITA CROWDER, special education educator; b. Tampa, Fla., Jan. 19, 1951; d. Reggie Ray and Bonnie M. (Walton) Crowder; m. Edward Ferrell Meador, June 28, 1974. BA, Anderson Coll., 1972; MA, Tenn. Tech. U., 1978. Sec. English dept. Anderson (Ind.) Coll., 1969-72; sec. Willard Walton's Sassafras Products, Lafayette, Tenn., 1972-73; tchr. spl. edn. Macon County Bd. Edn., Lafayette, Tenn., 1973-94, supr. spl. edn., 1994—; adv. bd. Head Start, Lafayette, 1994-96; organizer, mem. Macon County Vocat. Group, Lafayette, 1994-95; organizer Westside Schs. Ann. Fall Festival, Easter Egg Hunt, Jr. Beta Club, Miss Westside Pagaent, Tournament of Lemons, Lafayette, 1974-94. Fundraiser Girl Scouts Heart Fund, Cancer Soc., Lafayette; mem. Cmty. Chorus, Lafayette, 1986-91, Home Demonstration Club, Lafayette. Named Spl. Edn. Tchr. of Yr. Upper Cumberland Coun. Exceptional Children Cookeville, Tenn., 1990. Mem. NEA, Tenn. Edn. Assn., Macon County Edn. Assn. (treas. 1973—), Delta Kappa Gamma (pres. 1982—), Beta Sigma Phi. Independent. Home: 5047 Long Creek Rd Lafayette TN 37083 Office: Macon County Bd Edn 501 College St Lafayette TN 37083

MEADOW, LYNNE (CAROLYN MEADOW), theatrical producer and director; b. New Haven, Nov. 12, 1946; d. Frank and Virginia R. Meadow. BA cum laude, Bryn Mawr Coll., 1968; postgrad., Yale U., 1968-70. Dir. Theatre Communications Group, 1978-80; adj. prof. SUNY, Stony Brook, 1975-76, Yale U., Circle in the Sq., 1977-78, 89-91, NYU, 1977-80; theatre and music/theatre panelist Nat. Endowment for Arts, 1977-88; artistic advisor Fund for New Am. Plays, 1988-90. Artistic dir. Manhattan Theatre Club, N.Y.C., 1972—; guest dir. Nat. Playwrights Conf., Eugene O'Neill Theatre Ctr., 1975-77, Phoenix Theatre, 1976; dir. Ashes for Manhattan Theatre Club and N.Y. Shakespeare Festival, 1977; prodr. off-Broadway shows Ain't Misbehavin', 1978, Crimes of the Heart, 1981, Miss Firecracker Contest, 1984, Frankie and Johnny, 1987, Eastern Standard, 1988, Lisbon Traviata, 1989, Lips Together, Teeth Apart, 1991, Four Dogs and a Bone, 1993, Love! Valour! Compassion!, 1994; dir. Principia Scritoriae, 1986, Woman in Mind, 1988 (Drama Desk award), Eleemosynary, 1989, Absent Friends, 1991; dir. Broadway prodn. A Small Family Business, 1992, The Loman Family Picnic, 1993, Nine Armenians, 1996; co-prodr. off-Broadway and Broadway show Mass Appeal, 1981. Recipient Citation of Merit Nat. Coun. Women, 1976, Outer Circle Critics award 1977, Drama Desk award, 1977, Obie award for Ashes, 1977, Margo Jones award for Continued Encouragement New Playwrights, 1981, Critics Circle award Outstanding Revival on or off Broadway for Loot, 1986, Lucille Lortel award for Outstanding Achievement, 1987, Spl. Drama Desk award, 1989, N.Y. Drama Critics Circle award Best Fgn. Play for Aristocrats, 1989, Torch of Hope award, 1989, Manhattan Mag. award, 1994, Lee Reynolds award League Profl. Theatre Women, 1994; named Northwood Inst. Disting. Woman of Yr., 1990, Person of Yr., Nat. Theatre Conf., 1992. Office: Manhattan Theatre Club 453 W 16th St Fl 2 New York NY 10011-5835

MEADOWS, JENNIFER ELIZABETH, retired editor, tattoo artist; b. Texarkana, Tex., Jan. 20, 1947; d. Walter Edward and Martha Elizabeth (McCoy) Willis; m. Joe R. Matthews (div.); 1 child, Chris; m. Rich Meadows. AA, Cottey Coll., 1965; BS, U. Tex., Arlington, 1978. Actuarial asst. S.W. Life Ins. Co., Dallas; proofreader Royal Bus. Forms, Arlington, Tex.; substitute tchr. Arlington (Tex.) Ind. Sch. Dist.; reporter The Dallas Morning News, 1980-83, asst. editor, 1983-86, editor, 1986-94; columnist The Dallas Morning News, 1980-94. Vol. The Dallas Opera; tng. coord. Kairos Found., 1990—. Office: 904 W Pioneer Pky Arlington TX 76013-6330

MEADOWS, LOIS ANNETTE, elementary education educator; b. Harrisville, W.Va., Jan. 12, 1948; d. Orvle Adam and Una Pauline (Slocum) Ingram; m. David Alan Meadows, June 15, 1969; children: Lynecia Ann, Eric Justin. BA, Glenville State Coll., 1969; MA, W.Va. U., 1980. Cert. music, elem. edn., reading, W.Va. Tchr. grade six Acad. Park-Portsmouth (Va.) City Schs., 1969-73; elem. substitute Wood County Schs., Parkersburg, W.Va., 1973-77; real estate agt. Nestor Realty, Parkersburg, 1974-77; tchr. grade five/music Emerson Elem. Wood County Schs., Parkersburg, W.Va., 1977-78, tchr. grade three, 1978—; edn. cons. World Book, Parkersburg, 1986—; mentor tchr.-trainer Wood County Schs., parkersburg, 1990—; W.Va. S.T.E.P. Test com./trainer W.Va. Dept. Edn., Charleston, 1994—, mem. writing assessment com., 1994—; grant writer and speaker in field; mem. W.Va. Dept. Edn. State Writing Manual Com., 1996—. Author: (reading projects) Operation Blackout, 1986-94 (grant 1994), The Reading Room, 1988 (grant 1990), Storytime at the Mall, 1986— (grant 1994, 95). Life mem. Emerson PTA, Parkersburg, 1977—; Sunday Sch. tchr. North Parkersburg Bapt. Ch., 1976—, children's choir dir., 1976-88; fund raiser local charities, Parkersburg. Women of Excellence and Leadership Timely Honored award, W. Va. State Reading Tchr. of Yr., 1988, Finalist W. Va. State Tchr. of Yr., W.VA. Dept. Edn., 1993, Wood County Tchr. of Yr., 1993, Ashland Oil Golden Apple Achiever award, 1995, Wood Co. PTA Outstanding Educator of Yr. award, 1995-96, award for ann. contbrs. and project work Emerson PTA. Mem. W.Va. Reading Assn. (pres. 1993-94, mem. chmn. 1994—), Internat. Reading Assn., Wood County Reading Coun. (past pres. 1986-88, 90-92, Am. Fedn. Tchrs., Delta Kappa Gamma. Republican. Home: 102 Jo Mar Dr Parkersburg WV 26101 Office: Wood County Schs Emerson Elem 1605 36th St Parkersburg WV 26104

MEADOWS, MARY BETH, speech language pathologist; b. Erie, Pa., Oct. 16, 1956; d. Charles E. and Joan M. (Carney) McCallion; m. Daniel P. Meadows, June 15, 1985; children: D.J., John. BA in Edn., U. Fla., 1978; MA in Speech Communication, Auburn U., 1980. Lic. speech lang. pathologist, Ga. Speech lang. pathologist Coweta County Schs., Newnan, Ga., 1980-81, Ctr. for Speech and Lang. Therapy, Carrollton, Ga., 1981-84, Bremen (Ga.) City Schs., 1984-86; dir. Speech Therapy Assocs., Carrollton, 1986—, Comprehensive Ednl. Svcs., Carrollton, 1990—; clin. instr. West Ga. Coll., Carrollton, 1983—. Mem. Carroll County Coun. on Child Abuse (bd. dirs. 1993—), Am. Speech Lang. Hearing Assn., Ga. Speech Lang. Hearing Assn. (various chairs 1984—, Vol. award 1993), Carrollton Jr. Womens Club (com. chairs 1982-91, Clubwomen award 1990), Carroll County C. of C. (chair cmty. leadership com. 1993-95, bd. dirs. 1996—), Sertoma (v.p. Carroll C ounty club 1994—). Office: Comprehensive Ednl Svcs 806 Dixie St Carrollton GA 30117-4416

MEADOWS, PATRICIA BLACHLY, art curator, civic worker; b. Amarillo, Tex., Nov. 12, 1938; d. William Douglas and Irene Bond Blachly; m. Curtis Washington Meadows, Jr., June 10, 1961; children: Michael Lee, John Morgan. BA in English and History, U. Tex., 1960. Program dir. Ex-Students Assn., Austin, Tex., 1960-61; co-founder, dir. Dallas Visual Art Ctr., 1981-86, curator, 1987—, founder The Collectors, 1988—; exhbn. dir. Tex. bd. Nat. Mus. Women in Arts, Washington, 1986-91; mem. acquisition com. Dallas Mus. Art, 1988-92; chmn. adv. bd. Oaks Bank and Trust, 1993—; juror numerous exhibits, Dallas and Tex.; speaker on arts subjects; cons. city, state and nat. projects concerning arts; bd. dirs., mem. exec. com. Uptown Pub. Improvement Dist., 1993-96; chmn. bd. dirs. State-Thomas TIF Zone # 1, 1994—. Author: (art catalogues) Critic's Choice, 1983—, Texas Women, 1989-90, Texas: reflections, rituals, 1991; organizer exhbns. Presenting Nine, D-Art Visual Art Ctr., 1984, Mosaics, 1991—, Senses Beyond Sight, 1992-93. Bd. dirs. Mid-Am. Arts Alliance, Kansas City, Mo., 1989-93, Tex. Bd. Commerce, Austin, 1991-93, Women's Issues Network, Dallas, 1994—; bd. dirs. Dallas Summit, 1989-95, pres., 1993-94; mem. Charter 100, 1993—, Dallas Assembly, 1993—, Leadership Tex., 1987; co-founder, mem. steering com. Emergency Artists Support League, Dallas, 1992—; mem. originating task force Dallas Coalition for Arts, 1984; also others. Recipient Dedication to Arts award Tex. Fine Arts Assn., 1984, Assn. Artists and Craftsmen, 1984, Southwestern Watercolor Soc., 1985, Flora award Dallas Civic Garden Ctr., 1987, James K. Wilson award TACA, 1988, Maura award Women's Ctr. Dallas, 1991, Disting. Woman award Northwood U., 1993, Excellence in the Arts award Dallas Hist. Soc., 1993. Mem. Tex. Assn. Mus., Tex. Sculpture Assn. (originating task force), Arts Dist. Mgmt. Assn. (bd. dirs., exec. com. 1984-92, Artists Square design com. 1988-90), Artists and Craftsmen Assn. (pres. bd. dirs. 1982-83), Dallas Woman's Club. Presbyterian. Office: 2707 State St Dallas TX 75204-2634

MEAGHER, JOAN CECELIA, elementary education educator; b. Balt., June 6, 1948; d. Joseph Alfred Morris and Florence Cecelia (Geyton) Treece; m. Bernard Francis Meagher, Sept. 6, 1969; 1 child, Thomas Francis. BS, Towson State U., 1970, MEd, 1974; MS, Johns Hopkins U., 1983. Cert. elem. tchr., reading specialist, Md. Classroom tchr. Baltimore County Pub. Schs., Balt., 1970-92, reading specialist, 1992—. Mem. State of Md. Internat. Reading Assn. Coun., Balt. County Coun. Internat. Reading Assn. (pres. 1989-91).

MEAGHER, SANDRA KREBS, artist; b. N.Y.C., Dec. 18, 1936; d. Oswald Armand and Ella Katherine (Coleman) Krebs; m. John Forsyth Meagher, Oct. 15, 1966. BA, Smith Coll., Northampton, Mass., 1958. Author, artist: (book of drawings and poetry) NORA, 1991. Vice chmn. bd. dirs. Stoneleigh-Burnham Sch., Northampton, 1984-87. Recipient fellowship Va. Ctr. for the Creative Arts, Mt. San Angelo, Va., 1993. Mem. Art/Place Gallery (pres. 1993), Silvermine Guild of Artists, Rowayton Arts Ctr., Art Students League (life).

MEAGHER, SHARON MARY, philosophy educator; b. New Haven, Mar. 2, 1960; d. Richard Francis and Joan Alice (Hartley) M. BA, Boston Coll., 1982; PhD, SUNY Stony Brook, 1991. Grad. asst. SUNY, Stony Brook, 1983-89; asst. prof. U. Scranton, Pa., 1989-95; assoc. prof. U. Scranton, 1995—. Contbr. chpts. to books. Dir. Habitat for Humanity, Scranton, 1991-94; pres. bd. dirs. Mulberry Ctrl. Neighborhood Devel. Corp., Scranton, 1994—. Recipient Rotary Grad. fellowship Rotary Internat., 1987-88, Univ. Teaching award SUNY Stony Brook, 1989; grantee NEH, 1992, 94; named vis. scholar U. Calif. Santa Cruz, 1996. Mem. MLA, Am. Philos. Assn., Internat. Assn. Philosophy & Literature, Soc. for Women & Philosophy, Soc. for the Study of Narrative Literature. Office: Philosophy Dept Univ Scranton Scranton PA 18510-4507

MEAHL, BARBARA, occupational health nurse; b. N.Y.C., Aug. 15, 1938; d. Raymond G. and Alice (Duncan) Reynolds; m. Robert P. Meahl, Oct. 29, 1988; children: Susan, Mark, Ruth. Diploma in Nursing, Presbyn. Hosp., Phila., 1959; BS, St. Joseph's Coll., Windham, Maine, 1986. Cert. occupl. health nurse, CCM. Staff nurse various hosps. N.J./Pa., 1959-74; staff nurse AMP Inc., Harrisburg, Pa., 1974-75; mgr. safety and health Carlisle (Pa.) Corp., 1975-86; chief nurse Naval Shipyard, Phila., 1986-89; DON Concorde Inc., Phila., 1990-95; cons. Barbara Meahl & Assoc., Springfield, Pa., 1995—; dir., vice chmn. Am. Bd. Occupational Health Nurses, Inc., Palos Hills, Ill., 1988-92; lectr. in field. Mem./chair Cumberland County Drug and Alcohol Comm., Carlisle, Pa., 1986-88; instr. ARC, 1976—; ordained elder Presbyn. Ch., Springfield, Pa., 1987. Mem. Am. Assn. Occupl. Health Nurses, Pa. Assn. Occupl. Health Nurses (v.p. 1985-86, Outstanding Occupl. Health Nurse 1984), Delaware Valley Assn. Occupl. Health Nurses (v.p. 1987-88, sec. 1994—).

MEAL, LARIE, chemistry educator, researcher, consultant; b. Cin., June 15, 1939; d. George Lawrence Meal and Dorothy Louise (Heileman) Fitzpatrick. BS in Chemistry, U. Cin., 1961, PhD in Chemistry, 1966. Rsch. chemist U.S. Indsl. Chems., Cin., 1966-67; instr. chemistry U. Cin., 1968-69, asst. prof., 1969-75, assoc. prof., 1975-90, prof., 1990—, researcher, 1980—; cons. in field. Contbr. articles to sci. jours. Mem. AAAS, N.Y. Acad. Scis., Am. Chem. Soc., Internat. Assn. Arson Investigators, NOW, Planned Parenthood, Iota Sigma Pi. Democrat. Home: 2231 Slane Ave Norwood OH 45212-3615 Office: U Cin 2220 Victory Pky Cincinnati OH 45206-2822

MEALER, LYNDA REAM, physical education educator; b. Lima, Ohio, Sept. 19, 1946; d. Don A. and Sue (Pringle) Duncan; m. Ben T. Mealer, Aug. 29, 1970; children: Thomas Lee, Theresa Lynn. AA, LaSalle U., Chgo., 1976; BS, La. State U., 1983, 1992. Office mgr. M. Quick Ins., Glenmora, La., 1975-77; ind. bus. owner Glenmora (La.) Exxon, 1977-82; kindergarten tchr. Glenmora (La.) Elem. Sch., 1986-87; 4th grade tchr., 1983-86, 92-94; 6th grade tchr. Forest Hill (La.) Acad., 1989-90; 4th grade tchr. Glenmora (La.) Elem. Sch., 1992-94; phys. edn. tchr., 1994—; intervention strategist Drug Free Schs., Rapides Parish, La., 1994-95; crisis intervention Team Glenmora (La.) Elem. Sch., 1994-95. Author: (poem) Who's Who in Poetry, 1993, Vengeance is Mine, 1988. Sec., pres. Glenmora (La.) Garden Club, 1974-87; sec., pres., legis. chair Bus. and Profl. Women, Glenmora, La., 1981-91. Recipient Student Svc. award Student Govt. Assn., La. State U. 1983, Lifetime mem. Gamma Beta Phi, La. State U., 1983, Scholarship award Sm. Assn. Women, Alexandria, La., 1992, Lifetime/charter mem. Golden Key Hon. Soc., Baton Rouge, La., 1992. Mem. NEA, La. Assn. Educators, Rapides Fedn. Tchrs. Home: PO Box 72 806 Hwy 165 S Glenmora LA 71433 Office: Glenmora Elementary School PO Box 1188 Glenmora LA 71433-1188

MEALING, ISABEL THORPE, retired social worker; b. Townsend, Ga., Oct. 4, 1907; d. Elisha McDonald and Maude (Davis) Thorpe; student Ga. State Tchrs. Coll., 1924-26; A.B., Randolph-Macon Woman's Coll., 1928; M.S.W., Tulane U., 1943; postgrad. U. Va., 1929; m. John Pace Mealing, Jr., Aug. 15, 1929 (div. Dec. 1939); children—Elisha Thorpe, Margaret Mae (Mrs. Wayne Frederick Orlowski). H.S. English tchr., Blacksburg, Va., 1928-29; visitor, Fulton County Dept. Pub. Welfare, Atlanta, 1937-38; dir. McIntosh County Dept. Pub. Welfare, Darien, Ga., 1938-40; child welfare cons. State of Ga., Atlanta, 1941-44; social worker ARC, Lawson Gen. Hosp., Atlanta, 1944-45; asst. field dir. Lawson Gen. Hosp., and Sta. Hosp., Ft. Benning, Ga., 1945-46; chief social work service VA Regional Office, Ft. Jackson, S.C., 1947-48; pub. welfare officer Dept. Army, Japan, 1949-51; sr. social worker Valley Forge Army Hosp., 1951; chief social work service VA Hosp., Richmond, Va., 1951-52, VA Center, Wadsworth, Kans., 1952-68, Dublin, Ga., 1968-77; ret., 1977; Peace Corps vol., Morocco, 1978-80. Author of 2 books. Mem. Social Planning Council, Leavenworth, Kans., 1952-68, v.p., 1955-56, 67-68, pres., 1956-57; bd. dirs. ARC, Leavenworth, 1960-68; bd. govs. United Fund, Leavenworth, 1967-68; bd. dirs. YWCA, Leavenworth, 1962-68, pres., 1964; chmn. welfare com. Mayor's Adv. Com., Leavenworth, 1968; mem. organizational bd. Leavenworth Community Action Program, 1966; adviser Explorer Scouts Am., 1972; bd. dirs. Dublin Mental Health Assn., v.p., 1971-72, pres., 1972-74; pres. Mental Health Assn. Leavenworth, 1964, Darien United Meth. Women, 1987; mem. Midway Mus. Bd., 1982-84; sec. Dorcas Soc., 1986—; treas. Lanier of Glyn UDC, 1986-88; vol. Welcome Ctr., Darien, 1987; active Stroll thru History, 1987. Recipient various certs., awards, commendations. Mem. Nat. Assn. Social Workers (exec. bd. Mo., Kans. chpt. 1954-56, pres. cen. Ga. chpt. 1970-71, del. to assembly 1971), Am. Assn. Med. Social Workers (pres. Mo.-Kans. chpt. 1954-55), Internat. Soc. Poets, Nat., Internat., Ga. (nominating com. 1945) confs. on social welfare, Hist. Soc. McIntosh County (v.p. 1982-84), Daughters Am. Colonists (regent St. Johns Parish 1982-84, state chmn. vets. affairs), St. Andrew's DAR, United Daughters of the Confedercy, DAR (time keeper 1987-88), Colonial Dames 17th Century (treas. Golden Isles chpt. 1982-84), Magna Charta Dames (regent St. John's Parish 1982-84, state com. on accreditation 1984-86, vice regent St. Andrews 1982-84, registrar 1984-96), Dublin Community Resource Forum (pres. 1971-73), First Families of Ga., First Families of S.C., Clan Donald, Dorcas Sewing Soc. Club: Dublin Pilot (charter). Address: PO Box 1118 Darien GA 31305-1118

MEARA, ANNE, actress, playwright, writer; b. Bklyn., Sept. 20; d. Edward Joseph and Mary (Dempsey) M.; m. Gerald Stiller, Sept. 14, 1954; children: Amy, Benjamin. Student, Herbert Berghoff Studio, 1953-54. Apprentice in summer stock, Southold, L.I. and Woodstock, N.Y., 1950-53; off-Broadway appearances include A Month in the Country, 1954, Maedchen in Uniform, 1955 (Show Bus. off-Broadway award), Ulysses in Nightown, 1958, The House of Blue Leaves, 1970; Broadway plays: Spookhouse, 1983, Bosoms and Neglect, 1986, Shakespeare Co., Two Gentlemen of Verona, Cen. Park, N.Y.C., 1957, Romeo and Juliet, 1988, Eastern Standard, 1989, Anna Christie, 1993 (Tony nomination Best Supporting Actress), After-Play, 1995; film appearances include The Out-of-Towners, 1968, Lovers and Other Strangers, 1969, The Boys From Brazil, 1978, Fame, 1979, Nasty Habits (with husband Jerry Stiller), 1976, An Open Window, 1990, Mia, 1990, Awakenings, 1991, Reality Bites, 1994; comedy act, 1963—; appearances Happy Medium and Medium Rare, Chgo., 1960-61, Village Gate, Phase Two and Blue Angel, N.Y.C., 1963, The Establishment, London, 1963; syndicated TV series Take Five With Stiller and Meara, 1977-78; numerous appearances on TV game and talk shows, also spls. and variety shows; rec. numerous comml. for TV and radio (co-recipient Vocie of Imagery award Advt. Bur. N.Y.); star TV series Kate McShane, 1975; other TV appearances Archie Bunker's Place, 1979, The Sunset Gang, The Detective, 1990, Avenue Z Afternoon, 1991, Alf, 1986, Murphy Brown, 1994; writer, actress TV movie The Other Woman, 1983 (co-recipient Writer's Guild Outstanding Achievement award 1983), Alf, To Make Up to Break Up, The Stiller and Meara Pilot; author: (play) After-Play, 1994; video host (with Jerry Stiller) So You Want to Be an Actor?. Recipient Outer Critic's Cir. Playwriting award for "After-Play", 1995.

MEARS, RONA ROBBINS, lawyer; b. Stillwater, Minn., Oct. 3, 1938; d. Glaydon Donaldson and Lois Lorane (Hoehne) Robbins; m. John Ashley Mears, Aug. 20, 1960; children: John LaMonte, Matthew Von. BS, U. Minn., 1960; MBA, JD, So. Meth. U., 1982. Bar: Tex. 1992. Bus. adminstr. 1st Unitarian Ch., Dallas, 1973-77; assoc. atty. Haynes and Boone, Dallas, 1982-89, ptnr., internat. sect., 1989—; adv. bd. S.W. Inst. Dispute Resolution, Dallas, 1990—. Co-editor: International Loan Workouts and Bankruptcies, 1989; contbr. articles to profl. jours. Mem. U.S. Delegation, NAFTA Adv. Com. on Pvt. Comml. Disputes, 1994—. Rsch. fellow Southwestern Legal Found., Dallas, 1986—; recipient 1st prize INSOL Internat. Article Competition, 1989. Mem. ABA (sec. internat. sect. 1994—), Tex. Bar Found., State Bar Tex. (chmn. internat. sect. 1993-94), Tex.-Mex. Bar Assn. (co-vice chair 1994-95, co-chair 1995—), Dallas Bar Assn. (chmn. internat. sect. 1984-86), Internat. Bar Assn. (mem. com. on creditors rights, coord. internat. insolvency coop. project 1988-91), U.S.-Mex. C. of C. (bd. dirs. S.W. chpt. 1987—). Democrat. Office: Haynes and Boone LLP 3100 Nations Bank Plz 901 Main St Dallas TX 75202-3707

MEASURES, SUSAN PRATER, reading educator; b. Des Moines, Apr. 20, 1943; d. Richard and Gretchen (Gerhardt) Prater; m. Richard Lloyd Measures, Jan. 10, 1975. BA, U. Ariz., 1965; MA, Calif. Lutheran U., 1983. Classroom tchr. Garden Grove (Calif.) Sch. Dist., 1965-71, Hueneme Sch. Dist., Port Hueneme, Calif., 1971-89; reading specialist Hueneme Sch. Dist., 1989—; newsletter editor Glenbard West H.S. Class of 1961, Glen Ellyn, Ill., 1988—. Mem. Ventura County Reading Assn. (bd. dirs. 1983—, pres. 1993-94), Somis Town & Country Club (pres. 1981, 83, 84, 90). Home: 6455 La Cumbre Rd Somis CA 93066-9721 Office: Richard Bard Sch 622 E Pleasant Valley Rd Port Hueneme CA 93041-2638

MEBANE, BARBARA MARGOT, service company executive, studio owner; b. Sylacauga, Ala., July 21, 1947; d. Audrey Dixon and Mary Ellen (Yaikow) Baxley; m. James Lewis Mebane, Dec. 31, 1971; 1 child, Cieson Brooke. Student Brookhaven Coll., Dallas. Line performer J. Taylor Dance Co., Miami, Fla., 1964-65; sales mgr. Dixie Readers Svc., Jackson, Miss., 1965-67; regional sales mgr. Robertson Products Co., Texarkana, Tex., 1967-75; owner, pres. Telco Sales, Svc. and Supply, Dallas, 1976—; owner The Dance Factory, ATS Svcs., Lewisville, Tex., Dancers Workshop, Lewisville; mem. Dance Masters, Miami, 1975—; mgmt. specialist SBA; choreographer music videos for pay/cable TV, 1985, cabarette shows coll. and H.S. musicals; founder, dir. The Dance Factory, Lewisville, Tes.; owner, tchr. Dancers Workshop, 1992—; contract cons. for self-employed women; pub. speaker in field. Author: Paper on Positive Thinking, 1983. Sponsor St. Jude's Rsch. Hosp., Memphis, Cancer Rsch. Ctr., Dallas; active Cancer Rsch. Found.; sponsor Nat. Kidney Found., Dallas. Named Bus. Woman of the Yr., Gov. Anne Richards, Tex., 1994. Mem. Nat. Fedn. Ind. Businesses, Internat. Register of Profiles Cambridge, Eng., Female and Minority Owned Bus. League, PDTA (Dallas Dance Coun.), TITAS, Female Exec. Club N.Y.C. Avocations: working with children, teaching dance, writing. Home: 3701 Twin Oaks Ct Lewisville TX 75028-1244 Office: Dancers Workshop 502 S Old Orchard #150 Lewisville TX 75067

MECHLEM, DAPHNE JO, vocational school educator; b. Cin., Oct. 20, 1946; d. Louis Edward Griffith and Esther Eileen (Calvert) Griffith-Schultz; m. James T. Mechlem, Nov. 18, 1967 (div. June 1983); 1 chld, Louis Henry. BS summa cum laude, U. Cin., 1982, MS, 1983, MEd, 1984. Cert. vocat. and adult dir., supr., cosmetology instr., real estate agt. Stylist, mgr. Fashion Flair Styling, Cin., 1965-70, Anne Wolfe Coiffures, Cin., 1970-71; salon owner Curls by Daphne, Cin., 1971-77; tchr. Great Oaks Joint Vocat. Sch. Dist., Cin., 1976-83, adminstrv. intern, 1983; probation officer Hamilton County Juvenile Ct., Cin., 1983—; tchr. Great Oaks Joint Vocat. Sch. Dist., Cin., 1983—; spkr., presenter workshops in field. Author: Critical Issues in Campus Policing, 1983; lectr: workshops, seminars and classes. Sec.-treas. Cin. Fashion Guild. Mem. ASCD, Nat. Cosmetology Assn., Criminal Justice Assn., Am. Vocat. Assn., Ohio Vocat. Assn., Ohio Vocat. Cosmetology Tchrs. Assn. (2d v.p., continuing edn. adminstr.). Home: 5776 Pleasant Hill Rd Milford OH 45150-2301

MEDALIE, SUSAN DIANE, management consultant; b. Boston, Oct. 7, 1941; d. Samuel and Matilda (Bortman) Abrams; m. Richard James Medalie, June 5, 1960; children: Samuel David, Daniel Alexander. BA, Sarah Lawrence Coll., 1960; MA, George Washington U., 1962, Cert. Pubs. Spec., 1977; JD, Am. U., 1986. Bar: Pa., 1987, D.C., 1987. Pres. Medalie Cons., Washington, 1980—; dep. dir. U.S. Holocaust Meml. Coun., Washington, 1980-82; assoc. pub. Campaigns & Elections, Washington, 1983-84; legis. analyst Subcom./House Energy and Commerce, Washington, 1985; ea. regional dir. Josephson Found. for Adv. Ethics, L.A., 1986-88; asst. dean for external affairs George Washington U. Nat. Law Ctr., Washington, 1988-90; exec. dir. Internat. Soc. Global Health Policy, Washington and Paris, 1990-93; pvt. practice law Washington, 1993—; cons. Kettering Found., Washington, 1986; corp. liaison First Hosp. Corp., Norfolk, Va., 1986-88; assoc. producer and cons. Prof. Arthur Miller's "Headlines on Trial" (NBC), N.Y.C., 1987-91. Editor/pub.: Getting There mag., 1977-80; sr. editor: Am. Univ. Law Rev., Washington, 1984-86. Nat. dep. fin. dir. Edward M. Kennedy for Pres. Com., Washington, 1979-80; cons. Lt. Gov. Davis for Senate, Va., 1982; co-chair Patricia Roberts Harris for Mayor, Washington, 1982. Mem. Sarah Lawrence Alumnae Assn. (mem. coun. 1980-83), Florence Crittenton Home (bd. dirs. exec. com. 1980-83), ABA, DC Bar. Office: Medalie Cons 1901 Pennsylvania Ave NW Washington DC 20006-3405

MEDD, MARJORIE MURRAY, volunteer, educational consultant; b. Pitts., June 23, 1942; d. Joseph Francis Murray and Florence Juliet Domergue; m. William Lowell Medd, July 13, 1942; children: Catherine, Donald, Michael. BS in Edn., Tufts U., 1964; cert. in phys. edn., Bouvé Boston Sch., 1964. Co-chair phys. edn. dept. Mt. Ida Jr. Coll., Newton, Mass., 1964-65; instr. phys. edn. dept. U. Rochester, N.Y., 1965-69; vice-chair tchr. study group Nat. Assn. of State Bds. of Edn., 1991, mem. higher edn. study group, 1994; co-chair task force on yr.-round edn. Dept. of Edn., 1993-94; chair Initial Tchr. Cert. Pilot Project, 1993-94; vice-chair Results-Based Initial Tchr. Cert. Exec. Com., 1994; mem. Bowdoin Coll. Program Approval Visitation Team, 1994, 96, Westbrook Coll. Program Approval Visitation Team, 1991; mem. exec. com. Coalition for Excellence in Edn., 1995—; bd. dirs. Maine Math. and Sci. Alliance, Maine LEADership Consortium; spkr., presenter numerous ednl. panels. Mem., chair sch. bd. Oxford Hills Sch. Bd., South Paris, Maine, 1977-87, Maine State Bd. Edn., Augusta, 1987—, chair, 1992-94, 95-96; chair task force learning results Goals 2000 Panel, 1993-96; mem. Jobs for Maine's Grads. Bd., 1988—, Gov.'s Coun. on Phys. Fitness and Sports, 1993-94, Gov.'s Task Force on Sch. Funding, 1993-94; corporator Stephens Meml. Hosp., 1987—; mem. Tufts Alumni Admissions Program, 1992—; bd. dirs., mem. fin. com. New Eng. Assn. Schs. and Colls., 1995—; vice chair exec. bd., chair adminstrv. and fin. com. N.E. and Islands Regional Ednl. Lab. at Brown U., 1996—. Recipient Coalition for Excellence in Edn. Recognition award, 1994, Layperson award Maine Assn. Phys. Health, Edn., Recreation and Dance, 1993; selected as one of 25 Nat. State Bd. Edn. mems. to participate in March for Remembrance in Poland, 1994. Mem. AAUW, Oxford Hills C. of C. (chair edn. com. 1990-96), Norway/South Paris Kiwanis Club. Roman Catholic. Office: Maine State Bd Edn Dept Edn State House St 23 Augusta ME 04334

MEDEROS, CAROLINA LUISA, transportation policy consultant; b. Rochester, Minn., July 1, 1947; d. Luis O. and Carolina (del Valle) M. BA, Vanderbilt U., 1969; MA, U. Chgo., 1971. Adminstrv. asst. Lt. Gov. of Ill., Chgo., 1972; sr. research assoc. U. Chgo., 1972; project mgr., cons. Urban Dynamics, Inner City Fund and Community Programs Inc., Chgo., 1972-73; legis. asst. to Senate pres. Ill. State Senate, Chgo. and Springfield, 1973-76; program analyst Dept. Transp., Washington, 1976-79, chief, trans. assistance programs div., 1979-81, dir. programs and evaluation, 1981-88, chairwoman, sec.'s safety rev. task force, 1985-88; deputy asst. sec. for safety Dept. Transp., 1988-89; cons. Patton Boggs LLP, Washington, 1990—. Recipient award for Meritorious Achievement, Sec. Transp. 1980, Superior Achievement award U.S. Dept. Transp., 1981, Sec.'s Gold Medal Award for Outstanding Achievement, 1986, Presdl. Rank award, 1987. Mem. Womens Transp. Seminar, Coun. for Excellence in Govt. Home: 2723 O St NW Washington DC 20007-3128 Office: Patton Boggs LLP 2550 M St NW Washington DC 20037-1301

MEDICUS, HILDEGARD JULIE, retired dentist, orthodontist, educator; b. Frankfurt, Germany, July 25, 1928; came to U.S., 1961, naturalized, 1995; d. Gustav and Elizabeth Berta (Neunhoeffer) Schmelz; m. Heinrich Adolf Medicus, June 15, 1961. DMD, U. Marburg, W. Germany, 1953; orthodontics diploma, U. Düsseldorf, W. Germany, 1957. lic. dentist, N.Y. Postdoctoral fellow dental sch. U. Zürich, Zürich, Switzerland, 1957; postdoctoral fellow U. Liège, Belgium, 1958; postdoctoral fellow Forsyth Dental Ctr., Boston, 1959, orthodontics rsch. affiliate, 1963-74; sch. dentist Pub. Sch. System, Zürich, 1975-76; dental hygiene instructor Hudson Valley Community Coll., Troy, N.Y., 1976-77; pvt. practice Troy, N.Y., 1977-89. Active Hudson Mohawk Swiss Soc. Mem. AAUW, ADA, European Orthodontic Soc., German Orthodontic Soc. Presbyterian. Home: 1 The Knoll Troy NY 12180

MEDIN, JULIA ADELE, mathematics educator, researcher; b. Dayton, Ohio, Jan. 16, 1929; d. Caroline (Feinberg) Levitt; m. A. Louis Medin, Dec. 24, 1950; children: Douglas, David, Thomas, Linda. BS in Maths. Edn., Ohio State U., 1951; MA in Higher Edn., George Washington U., 1977; PhD in Counseling and Edn., Am. U., 1985. Cert. tchr., Fla., Md. Rsch. engr. Sun Oil Co., Marcus Hook, Pa., 1951-53; tchr. maths. Montgomery County Pub. Schs., Rockville, Md., 1973-88; asst. prof. maths. U. Ctrl. Fla., Orlando, 1988-90, sr. ednl. technologist Inst. for Simulation and Tng., 1990—; mem. adv. steering com. U.S. Dept. Edn. Title II, Washington, 1985-89; sr. math educator, rschr. Inst. for Simulation and Tng., Orlando, 1988—; judge NII Nar. Awards. Author: Loc. of Cont. and Test Anxiety of Mar. Math. Studies, 1985; contbg. author: Math for 14 & 17 Yr. Olds, 1987; editor: Simulation Technology for Education; contbr. articles to profl. jours. Dem. committewoman Town of Monroeville, Pa., 1962; religious sch. dir. Beth Tikva Religious Sch., Rockville, 1971; cons. Monroeville Mental Health, 1960. Mem. Nat. Coun. Tchrs. Math., Math. Assn. Am. (task force on minorities in math.), Women in Math. in Edn., Nat. Coalition for Tech. in Edn. and Tng., Phi Delta Kappa, Kappa Delta Pi. Home: 714 Bear Creek Cir Casselberry FL 32708-3857 Office: U Ctrl Fla Inst for Simulation and Tng 3280 Progress Dr Orlando FL 32826-3229

MEDINA, KATHRYN BACH, book editor; b. Plainfield, N.J.; d. F. Earl and Elizabeth E. Bach; m. Standish F. Medina Jr.; 1 child, Nathaniel Forde. BA, Smith Coll.; MA, NYU. Various editorial positions Doubleday Pub. Co., Inc., N.Y.C., 1965-85; exec. editor, v.p. Random House, N.Y.C., 1985—; assoc. fellow Jonathan Edwards Coll., Yale U., New Haven, 1982—; fellow Bunting Inst., 1994-95; cons., 1995-96. Editor books by James Atlas, Peter Benchley, Amy Bloom, Elizabeth Berg, Anita Brookner, Ethan Canin, Robert Coles, Agnes deMille, Henry Louis Gates, Jr., Mary Gordon, David Halberstam, Kathryn Harrison, Tracy Kidder, Bobbie Ann Mason, James A. Michener, Anna Quindlen, Nancy Reagan, James Reston, William Safire, Maggie Scarf, Christopher Tilghman, Alice WalkerDaniel Yergin, others.

MEDLEY, NANCY MAY, nurse; b. Knoxville, Oct. 8, 1948; d. Donald Raymond and Josephine Ruth (Blakley) M. AA, Riverside City Coll., 1970. RN, Calif. Staff nurse in medicine Riverside Gen. Hosp., Calif., 1970-71; staff nurse neonatal unit Kaiser Permanente Hosp., Hollywood, Calif., 1971-72; critical care nurse neuro unit Harbor-UCLA Hosp., Torrance, 1972-78, head nurse CCU, 1978—, temp. head nurse Neurosurg. ICU, 1988-90; head nurse surg. ICU and cardiothoracic units Harbor UCLA Med. Ctr., Torrance, 1992-94. Mem. AACN, Am. Heart Assn. Republican. Presbyterian. Home: 636 Manhattan Ave Apt C Hermosa Beach CA 90254-4529 Office: Harbor-UCLA Hosp 1000 W Carson St Torrance CA 90502-2004

MEDVEDOW, PHYLLIS KRONICK, service executive; b. New Haven, Feb. 18, 1931; d. Louis Barnard and Anna Helen (Skolnick) Kronick; m. Leon A. Medvedow, June 29, 1952; children: Jill Susan, Elisabeth Jane. BS, U. Conn., 1952; cert. advanced mgmt., Yale U., 1988. Exec. v.p. Congress Printers, Inc., New Haven, 1977-81; adminstrv. aide Conn. Gen. Assembly, Hartford, 1979-80; cons. community affairs Yale New Haven Hosp., 1982-83, pub. affairs specialist, 1983-85; asst. dir. community and govt. rels. Yale U., New Haven, 1985-87, assoc. dir. community and govt. rels., 1987-88, dir. community and govt. rels., 1988—; hosp. rep. Conn. Organ and Tissue Donor Coalition, New Haven, 1985—, Coalition on Financing Health Care for the Poor, New Haven, 1987—. Bd. dirs. Anti-Defamation League, New Haven, 1972-81; trustee, sec., chmn. metro unit Am. Cancer Soc., Woodbridge, Conn., 1955-74; v.p. New Haven Bd. Edn., 1970-74; mem. distbn. com. New Haven Found., 1973-79, United Way, Greater New Haven, 1988—; mem. cmty. rels. com. Greater New Haven Jewish Fedn., 1972—; mem. exec. com. Shubert Performing Arts Ctr., 1994—. Mem. Jewish Fedn. Bus. and Profl. Womens Group (bd. dirs. New Haven chpt. 1986-88), Nat. Coun. Jewish Women (publicity chair 1984), Urban League of Greater New Haven (bd. dirs. and 2nd vice chair 1991-95), C. of C. Greater New Haven (govtl. affairs com.), New Haven Lions (1st Woman, 1988—). Democrat.

MEEHAN, JANET LOUISE, secondary school educator, coach; b. North Tarrytown, N.Y., Aug. 16, 1941; d. John Joseph and Louise Theresa (Cancro) M. BA in Math., Good Counsel Coll., 1965; postgrad., NYU, 1967; MA, U. Notre Dame, 1970. Joined Sisters of Divine Compassion, Roman Cath. Ch., 1960; cert. tchr., N.Y. Math. and art tchr. Preston H.S., Bronx, N.Y., 1965-67; math. and art tchr. J.F. Kennedy H.S., Somers, N.Y., 1967-82, tchr., art dept. chair, 1967—, head coach spring track, 1969—, head coach cross-country, 1977—, head coach indoor track, 1978—; coord. indoor track and field N.Y. State Pub. H.S.'s Athletic Assn. Sect. I, Westchester, Putnam, Rockland, and Dutchess Counties, 1981—. Named Coach of Yr., Gannet Westchester Newspapers, 1977, 81, 82, 85, 86, 91, 92. Mem. Nat. Art Educators Assn., Nat. Cath. Educators Assn., Nat. Fedn. Coaches and Ofcls., N.Y. State Art Tchrs. Assn., Westchester Coaches and Ofcls. Assn. (sec. 1977-86). Office: JF Kennedy Cath HS 54 Route 138 Somers NY 10589-2711

MEEHAN, JENNIFER BENNETT, psychiatric social worker; b. Stamford, Conn., May 31, 1967; d. Jonathan Michael Bennett and Barbara Iris (London) Kaufman; m. Christopher Meehan, Sept. 30, 1995. BA in Comm., Coll. New Rochelle, N.Y., 1989; MSW, Fordham U., 1994. Psychiat. social worker Dept. Children & Families, State of Conn., Bridgeport, Conn., 1994—; mem. support staff Project Return - Group Home for Young Women, Westport, Conn., 1995—; clin. social worker Family and Children's Agy., Norwalk, Conn., 1996—. Participant/contbr. Gay Men's Health Crisis, N.Y.C., 1992; mem. Bridgeport Child Advocacy Coalition, 1995. Mem. NASW, NOW. Democrat. Office: State of Conn Dept Children and Families 3885 Main St Bridgeport CT 06606

MEEHAN, LINDA VANN, nurse; b. Norfolk, Va., Oct. 26, 1951; d. Charles Brinkley and Shirley Vann (Gwynn) Campbell; m. Carlos Robert Cardoza, July 3, 1970 (div. 1983); children: Carlos Brinkley, Autumn Ann; m. Albert William Meehan, Mar. 15, 1986. Cert., Cen. Sch. Practical Nursing, Norfolk, 1980; ADN, Norfolk State U., 1991. RN, Va. Nurse med./surg. and telemetry unit Leigh Meml. Hosp., Norfolk, 1980-86; nursing asst. pediatric and psychiatric units James Paton Meml. Hosp., Gander, New Foundland, 1986-88; nurse Patient First, Virginia Beach, Va., 1986-94; dir. med. support Patient First Johns Hopkins Pavilion, Lutherville, Md., 1994—. Den mother Cub Scouts Am., Norfolk, 1980-82; troop leader Brownies U.S., Norfolk, 1982-83; sec. Boys/Girld Clubs Can., Gander, 1987-87, v.p. 1986-87; vol. YWCA Battered Wives and Children Shelter, Norfolk, 1985-86, Gander Women's Ctr., 1986-88, Am. Heart Assn., Norfolk, 1983-85, speaker, 1983-84. Roman Catholic. Home: 2211 Fox Hunt Ln Lutherville MD 21093-4732

MEEHAN, NANCY CATHERINE, choreographer, dancer; b. San Francisco, Mar. 20, 1931; d. Thomas Francis and Mildred (Hathaway) M.; m. Anthony Nicholas Candido, Dec. 9, 1967. B.A., U. Calif.-Berkeley, 1952. With Ann Halprin-Welland Lathrop Dance Co., San Francisco, 1953-56; leading soloist Erick Hawkins Dance Co., 1961-70; choreographer, dancer Nancy Meehan Dance Co., N.Y.C., 1970—; faculty Ann Halprin Welland Lathrop Dance Co. Sch., 1954-56, Erick Hawkins Dance Sch., 1963-70, Hunter Coll., 1968-69; tchr., performer Am. Dance Festival, 1973-76, 81-82; artist-in-residence/guest tchr. various univs. and colls. Choreography includes: Live Dragon, 1972; Split Rock, 1974; Grapes and Stones, 1975; Ptarmigan Wall, 1977; White Wave, 1978; Seven Women, 1980; Dreams of Leaves, 1982; Swift Garden, 1983; Cloud ... Roots, 1984; Guest to Star, 1985, Guest to Star Part II, 1986, Into the Summer, 1987, Coastal Traces, 1988, Switchback, 1988, Switchback Part II, 1989, 9 Leaf Window, 1990, Beginnings, 1991, Moments and Regard, 1992, The Other Side, 1993, Record of an Ocean Cliff, 1994, Crossings in a Mountain Dream, 1995, Glacier Track, 1996; others. Address: Nancy Meehan Dance Co 463 West St Apt A1111 New York NY 10014-2040

MEEHAN, PATRICIA MARIE, statistician; b. Newport News, Va., June 19, 1963; d. James Patrick and Eileen Theresa (Breen) M.; m. Terence Rikio Oi, June 28, 1986; children: Curran, Bryna. BA in Psychology, Boston U., 1986; MA in Statistics, Harvard U., 1988, PhD in Statistics, 1993. Sr. statistician Frontier Sci. Tech. Rsch. Found., Inc., Brookline, Mass., 1993; Contbr. articles to profl. jours. Fellow AAUW (fellowship (1990-91); mem. Am. Statis. Assn., Assn. Women in Sci. Home: 30 Overbrook Dr Wellesley MA 02181 Office: Frontier Science Tech 303 Boylston St Brookline MA 02146

MEEHAN, SANDRA GOTHAM, advertising executive, communications consultant; b. Tokyo, June 9, 1948; d. Fred C. and Evelyn (Dirr) Gotham; m. James P. Jenkins, June 15, 1970 (div. 1989); m. Dayton T. Carr, Dec. 27, 1986 (div. 1989); m. Michael J. Meehan, Jan. 16, 1992. Student, Stanford-in-France, Tours, 1968-69; BA, Stanford U., 1970, MA, 1971. Account exec. Young & Rubicam Inc., N.Y.C., 1972-78, account supr., 1978-80; pres., Gotham Prodns., N.Y.C., 1980-82; v.p., mgmt. supr. Ogilvy & Mather, 1982-85; v.p. Steuben Glass, N.Y.C., 1985-88; sr. v.p. Siegel & Gale, N.Y.C., 1988-92; prin. Gotham Meehan Ptnrs., N.Y.C., 1992—; cons. Congl. coms., FDA, FTC for exec. program Am. Assn. Advt. Agys., Washington, 1978-80; cons. Ctr. Arctic Studies Sorbonne, Paris, in U.S. and Can., 1980-82; seminar dir. N.Y. chpt. Women in Bus., N.Y.C., 1983-84. Writer and editor 4-part TV documentary script Invit! The Universal Cry of the Eskimo People, 1981. Writer speeches for Georgetown Ctr. Strategic and Internat. Studies, also newsletter for Am. Assn. Advt. Agys. Bd. dirs. Rensselaerville (N.Y.) Inst., trustee; fund raiser Stanford U., N.Y.C., promotion coord. of benefits and advt. Medic Alert, N.Y.C., 1983-84; mem. exec. com. Youth Counseling League, N.Y.C., 1984. Mem. Writers Guild Am., Young Profls. Group of Fgn. Policy Assn. (organizing chmn. 1980-81), N.Y. Women in Communications, Stanford Club. Home: 220 E 73rd St New York NY 10021-4319 Office: Gotham Meehan Ptnrs 220 E 73rd St Ste 5G New York NY 10021-4319

MEEK, AMY GERTRUDE, retired elementary education educator; b. Frostburg, Md., Jan. 3, 1928; d. Arthur Stewart and Amy Laura (Brain) M. BS, Frostburg State U., 1950; MEd, U. Md., 1956; postgrad., Columbia U., 1964, Am. U., 1968-70. Cert. tchr., Md. Tchr. elem. sch. Prince Georges County Schs., Bradbury Heights, Md., 1950-51; tchr. elem. sch. Allegany County Schs., Cumberland, Md., 1951-60, Frostburg, 1960-84; now ret. Author: (with others) Stir Into Flame, 1991; contbr. articles to hist. publs. Mem. Frostburg Hosp. Aux., 1987-91; bd. dirs. Frostburg Hist. Mus., 1988, 95—, Coun. of Allegheniess, 1991, sec., 1993; sec. Braddock Estates Civic Assn., Frostburg, 1988; mem. com. Frostburg Libr., 1989; tchr. Ch. Conf. Schs. Missions, 1970; vol. tutor, 1986-92; pres. Ch. Women United, Frostburg, 1989-95; trustee Frostburg United Meth. Ch.; mem. endowment fund com. Balt. Conf. United Meth. Ch., 1992—; pres. Cumberland-Hagerstown dist. United Meth. Women, 1985-89, chmn. fin. interpretation Balt. Conf., 1990-94. Mem. AAUW (pres. 1993-95, treas. Md. divsn. 1974, Woman of Yr. award Frostburg br. 1980, New Frostburg Libr. Bldg. Com. 1994). Republican.

MEEK, CARRIE P., congresswoman; 3 children. BS, Fla. A&M U., 1946, MS, U. Mich., 1948. Mem. Fla. Senate from Dist. 36, 1982-1992. Mem. 103rd-104th Congress from 17th Fla. dist., 1993—. Democrat. Office: US Ho of Reps 404 Cannon House Office Bldg Washington DC 20515*

MEEK, VIOLET IMHOF, dean; b. Geneva, Ill., June 12, 1939; d. John and Violet (Krepel) Imhof; m. Devon W. Meek, Aug. 21, 1965 (dec. 1988); children: Brian, Karen; m. Don M. Dell, Jan. 4, 1992. BA summa cum laude, St. Olaf Coll., 1960; MS, U. Ill., 1962, PhD in Chemistry, 1964. Instr. chemistry Mount Holyoke Coll., South Hadley, Mass., 1964-65; asst. prof. to prof. Ohio Wesleyan U., Delaware, Ohio, 1965-84, dean for ednl. svcs., 1980-84; dir. annual programs Coun. Ind. Colls., Washington, 1984-86; assoc. dir. sponsored programs devel. Rsch. Found. Ohio State U., Columbus, 1986-91; dean, dir. Ohio State U., Lima, 1992—; vis. dean U. Calif., Berkeley, 1982, Stanford U., Palo Alto, Calif., 1982, reviewer GTE Sci. and Tech. Program, Princeton, N.J., 1986-92, Goldwater Nat. Fellowships, Princeton, 1990-96. Co-author: Experimental General Chemistry, 1984; contbr. articles to profl. jours. Bd. dirs. Luth. Campus Ministries, Columbia, 1988-91, Luth. Social Svcs., 1988-91, Americorn Bank, Lima, 1992—, Lima Symphony Orch., 1993—, Art Space, Lima, 1993—, Allen Lima Leadership, 1993—, Am. House, 1992—, Lima Vets. Meml. Civic Ctr. Found., 1992—; chmn. synodical coms. Evang. Luth. Ch. Am., Columbus, 1982; bd. trustees Trinity Luth. Sem., Columbus, 1996—; chmn. Allen County C. of C., 1995—. Recipient Woodrow Wilson Fellowship, 1960. Mem. Nat. Coun. Rsch. Adminstrs. (named Outstanding New Profl. midwest region 1990), Am. Assn. Higher Edn., Phi Beta Kappa. Home: 209 W Beechwold Blvd Columbus OH 43214-2012 Office: Ohio State U 4240 Campus Dr Lima OH 45804-3576

MEEKER GREEN, HEATHER JEANNE, educational administrator; b. Mass., Apr. 14, 1968; d. Stafford Daniel Meeker and Louise Ann Richmond; m. Sande Rishava Green, Aug. 20, 1994. BA in Hispanic Studies, Conn. Coll., 1990; MA in Liberal Studies, Simmons Coll., 1995. From tng. coord. to facilitator Conflict Mgmt., Inc., Cambridge, Mass., 1990-96; policy assoc. Recruiting New Tchrs., Inc., Belmont, Mass., 1996—. Vol., bd. dirs. Mass. Choice, Boston, 1992—. Mem. NAFE, AAUW, Nat. Coun. Rsch. on Women and Girls, Mass. Nat. Abortion and Reproductive Rights Action League, World Music, WGBH. Democrat. Office: Recruiting New Tchrs Inc 385 Concord Ave Belmont MA 02178

MEEKS, CAROL JEAN, educator; b. Columbus, Ohio, Mar. 9, 1946; d. Clarence Eugene and Clara Johanna (Schwartz) B.; m. Joseph Meeks, Aug. 17, 1968 (div. 1981); 1 child, Catherine Rachael. BS, Ohio State U., Mex., 1968; MS, Ohio State U., 1969, PhD, 1972. Rsch. asst., assoc. Ohio State U., Columbus, 1968-71; internship Columbus Area C. of C., Ohio, 1970; lectr. Ohio State U., Columbus, 1970, 72; asst. prof. U. Mass., Amherst, 1972-74; asst. prof. Cornell U., Ithaca, N.Y., 1974-78, assoc. prof., 1978-80; legis. fellow Senate Com. Banking, 1984; supr. economist, head housing section USDA, Washington, 1980-85; assoc. prof. housing and consumer econs. U. Ga., Athens, 1985-90, prof., 1990—, head housing and consumer econs., 1992—; rsch. fellow Nat. Inst. for Consumer Rsch., Oslo, Norway, 1982; cons. Yale U., 1976-77, HUD, Cambridge, Mass., 1978, MIT Ctr. for Real Estate Devel. Ford Found. Project on Housing Policy; del. N.E. Ctr. for Rural Devel. Housing Policy Conf. Reviewer Home Econ. Rsch. Jour., 1987—, ACCI conf., 1987—; contbr. articles to profl. mags. Mem. panel town of Amherst Landlord Tenant Bd.; bd. dirs. Am. Coun. Consumer Interests; mem. adv. coun. HUD Nat. Mfg. Housing, 1978-80, 91-93; chair Housing Mfg. Inst. Consensus Commn. on Fed. Standards. Recipient Young Profl. award Ohio State U., 1979, Lender award AAFCS, 1996; named one of Outstanding Young Women of Am., 1979; Columbus Womens Chpt. Nat. Assn. Real Estate Bds. scholar, Gen. Foods fellow, 1971-72, HEW grantee, 1978, travel grantee NSF bldg. rsch. bd., AID grantee, USDA Challenge grant, 1995—. Mem. Am. Assn. Housing Educators (newsletter editor 1976-79, pres. 1983-84), Nat. Inst. Bldg. Sci. (bd. sec. 1984, 85, 89—, bd. dirs. 1981-83, 85, 87-93, features commn.), Am. Real Estate and Urban Econs. Assn., Internat. Assn. Housing Sci., Com. on Status of Women in Econs., Nat. Assn. Home Builders (Smart House contract 1989), Epsilon Sigma Phi, Omicron Nu, Kappa Omicron Nu (v.p. of programs 1995-96), others. Office: U Ga 215 Dawson Hall Athens GA 30602-3622

MEEKS, DONNA LEE, educational administrator; b. Amesbury, Mass., July 22, 1956; d. John C. and Kathleen A. (Savage) M.; m. Kevin R. Hall, May 14, 1990; 1 child, Clifford L. B, Wesleyan U., 1979; MEd, NYU, 1983; MSW, Hunter Coll., 1988. Lic. social worker, N.Y. Dir. publicity Kitchen Ctr. for Video, N.Y.C., 1980-82, dir. devel., 1982-84; dir. devel. Theatre by the Sea, Portsmouth, N.H., 1984-86; edn. assoc. Citizens' Com. for Children of N.Y., Inc., N.Y.C., 1988—. Mem. NASW, Kappa Delta Phi. Democrat. Home: 312A 15th St Brooklyn NY 11215-5006 Office: Citizens Com Children NY 105 E 22nd St New York NY 10010-5413

MEELHEIM, HELEN DIANE, nursing administrator; b. Charleston, W.Va., Mar. 25, 1952; d. Richard Young and Dolores (Frick) M. BS in Nursing, U. N.C., 1974; MS in Nursing, East Carolina U., 1982; JD, U. N.C., 1992. Bar N.C. 1995. Charge nurse Pitt County Health Dept., Greenville, N.C., 1974-77; nursing adminstr. East Carolina U. Sch. of Med., Greenville, N.C., 1978-89, clin. instr., 1986-92; cons. Eastern Area Health Edn. Ctr., Greenville and Fayetteville, 1989-92; staff emergency room U. N.C. Hosps., Chapel Hill, 1989-92; dir. fin. ops., human resources N.C. Bd. Med. Examiners, 1992—. Maj. Army Nurse Corps, USAR, Oper. Desert Storm/Shield, 1990-91. Mem. ANA (cert. family nurse practitioner, 1987—), Am. Acad. Nurse Practitioners, Nat. Health Lawyers Assn., N.C. Soc. Health Care Attys, Sigma Theta Tau. Episcopalian. Avocation: painting.

Home: 4622 Pine Trace Dr Raleigh NC 27613-3316 Office: NC Bd Med Examiners PO Box 20007 Raleigh NC 27619

MEER, AMEENA BIBI, editor, journalist, writer; b. Boston, May 29, 1964; d. Syed Ahmed and Arshiya Bibi (Rauf) M.; m. Andrew Dominic Douglas, May 10, 1992 (div. Oct. 1994); 1 child, Sasha Iman Douglas; m. James Nathaniel Nares, Oct. 19, 1996; 1 child, Zarina Elizabeth Nares. BA, U. Calif., Santa Cruz, 1985. Adminstrv. and editorial asst. Harper's Mag., N.Y.C., 1985-86; mng. editor East Village Eye, N.Y.C., 1986-87; copy editor, book editor PAPER Mag., N.Y.C., 1989-91; mng. editor BOMB Mag., N.Y.C., 1988-92; contbg. writer India Mag., New Delhi, 1987-89, Times of India, New Delhi, 1987-89. Author: (short stories) Indian-Am. mag., 1991, (novel) Bombay Talkie, 1994; contbr. articles to various mags. Selection com. Asian-Am. Film Festival, N.Y.C., 1991, 92; caseworker Sakhi for Women, N.Y.C., 1991—; Salman Rushdie defense Pen-Am. Ctr., N.Y.C., 1989. Mem. Nat. Writers Union, Asia Soc. Democrat. Muslim.

MEFFERT, LINDA BREWSTER, restaurant franchise holding company executive; b. New Orleans, May 2, 1967; d. Clarence Burke and Terry (Pappas) Brewster; m. Gregory John Meffert, Mar. 21, 1992. BBA cum laude, Loyola U., New Orleans, 1988, MBA, 1992. Prodn. mgr. Margie Darnell, Ltd., Metairie, La., 1986-90; gen. mgr. Loubat Equipment Co., Inc., New Orleans, 1990-92; CFO, Lundy Enterprises, Inc., New Orleans, 1992—. Mem. NOW (treas. Greater New Orleans chpt. 1995-96). Home: 3901 Tolmas Dr Metairie LA 70002

MEFFERT, MARCELLA ANN (MARCY MEFFERT), freelance writer; b. Milw., June 10, 1934; d. John George and Margaret (Stankiewicz) Czarnecki; m. Roland M. Meffert, June 12, 1954; children: Jeffrey, Lisa, Sarah, Gregory, Douglas. Student, Marquette U., 1952-53, San Antonio Coll., 1983-84, U. New Orleans, 1990-92. Humor columnist Citizen News, San Antonio, 1974-76; staff writer Northwest Light, San Antonio, 1976-78; staff writer, columnist San Antonio Light, 1978-81; assoc. producer Sta. WOAI Radio, San Antonio, 1981-83; with pub. rels. Sunshine Sch. for Deaf, San Antonio, 1983-84; rsch. editor Heloise, 1983—. Contbr. articles to newspapers, mags. and other publs., 1983—. Vol., bd. dirs. Sta. WRBH for the Blind, New Orleans, 1985-92; mem. Leon Valley City Coun., 1994—. Mem. Women in Communications, Inc., Tex. Press Women, Press Clubs in San Antonio, Press Clubs in New Orleans, La. Press Women, Profl. Journalism Soc. Home and Office: 6532 Adair Dr San Antonio TX 78238

MEGAHY, DIANE ALAIRE, physician; b. Des Moines, Iowa, Oct. 12, 1943; d. Edwin Dare and Georgiana Lee (Butcher) Raygor; m. Mohamed H. Saleh Megahy, Sept. 20, 1969; children: Hassan, Hamed, Hala, Heba. MD, U. Alexandria, Egypt, 1981. Diplomate Am. Bd. Family Practice. Intern Univ. Hosps., Alexandria, Egypt, 1982-83; resident Siu Family Practice, Belleville, Ill., 1987-90; physician St. Joseph's Hosp., Highland, Ill., 1988—. Fellow Am. Assn. Family Practice; mem. AMA, AAUW. Home: 812 S Virginia Belleville IL 62220 Office: 415 S Main St Columbia IL 62236

MEGGINSON, ELIZABETH R., legislative director, federal and state government lawyer; b. Clarksdale, Miss., Oct. 27, 1947; d. Mitford Ray and Cleo Ruth (Faggard) M.; m. Mark W. Menezes; children: Paige Jennings, Marisa Menezes. BM, La. State U., 1969, MM, 1970, JD, 1977. Pvt. practice, 1977-78; counsel natural resources com. La. Ho. Reps., 1978-81, legis. svc. coord. comml. regulation divsn., 1981-84; asst. atty. gen. environ. enforcement divsn. La. Dept. Justice, 1984-88; asst. sec. for office legal affairs and enforcement La. Dept. Environ. Quality, 1988-89; adminstrv. asst. to Rep. W.J. Billy Tauzin, Washington, 1989-90; staff dir. counsel sub-com. om coast guard and navigation Ho. Com. on Merchant Marine and Fisheries, Washington, 1990—; now chief coun. to State Com. Mem. Phi Kappa Phi. Office: 1324 Longworth House Office Bldg Washington DC 20515*

MEGLEY, SHEILA, university president; b. Binghampton, N.Y., Feb. 16, 1938; d. John Edward and Ann (Feely) M.; BA in Math., Philosophy, and Edn., Rosary Coll., River Forest, Ill., 1961; MA in Theology, St. Xavier Coll., Chgo., 1968; MA in English Lit, U. Chgo., 1970; PhD, U. Nebr., 1974; MS in Fin. Mgmt., Acctg., Salve Regina U., 1989. Tchr. math. Holy Child H.S., Waukegan, Ill., 1961-64, Immaculate Heart of Mary H.S., Westchester, Ill., 1964-65; resident hall dir., instr. math. St. Xavier Coll., Chgo., 1965-69; instr. English, U. Nebr., 1970-74; prof. English, acad. dean, dean students Salve Regina U., 1974-76, v.p., acad. dean, dean students, 1976-80, v.p. instrn. and curriculum, acad. dean, 1980-85, provost, v.p. instrn. and curriculum, 1985-88, exec. v.p., provost, 1988-92; pres. Regis Coll., Weston, Mass., 1992—; chmn. exec. com. Mercy Higher Edn. Colloquim, 1977-83; mem. secretariat Nat. Assn. Ind. Colls. and Univs., mem. com. on pub. rels., 1994—; mem. exec. com. Neylan Commn., Assn. Cath. Colls. and Univs., Mass. Campus Compact; mem. Sisters St. Joseph Coll. Consortium, 1996—. Chmn. R.I. Equal Ednl. Opportunity Task Force, 1974-76; mem. R.I. Com. Humanities, 1980-87; trustee Trinity Rep Theater, Providence; mem. adv. com. City of Newport, R.I., 1989-93, Western Land Trust, 1993—; trustee Cardinal Spellman Philatelic Mus., 1992—; trustee, mem. acad. affairs Com. St. Xavier U., Chgo., 1995—; mem. Weston Land trust; mem. Jubilee 2000 com. Archdiocese of Boston, 1996—. Mem. AAUW, Am. Assn. Coll. Deans, Assn. Ind. Colls. and Univs. Mass., Women Pres. Group Mass., Erie Soc. (Ireland). Office: Regis Coll Weston MA 02193-1571

MEHRING, MARGARET, filmmaker, retired educator; b. Millbank, S.D., Sept. 3, 1925; d. Robert Dunbrack and Bernice (Case) Jones; m. William Samuel Mehring, June 21, 1947 (dec. June 1958); 1 child, William Dunbrack. BA, Lawrence Coll., 1947; MS in Edn., U. So. Calif., 1972, PhD in Cinema, 1978. Writer, dir., prodr. Mehring Prodns., L.A., 1953—; mem. faculty U. So. Calif. Sch. Cinema and TV, L.A., 1959-91, dir. filmic writing program, 1978-91, dir. emerita, 1991—. Author: The Screenplay, 1989; writer, dir., prodr. numerous ednl., documentary and indsl. tng. films for Employers Ins. Wausau, 1955, 57, 59-62, Golden State Ins. Co., 1964, Techno Electric Mfg. Co., 1965, Calif. Dept. Social Welfare, 1967, Andersen Windowall Corp., 1969, Golden State Mut. Life Ins. Co., 1983; writer, dir. ednl. films for MLA, U. So. Calif., 1959-60, John Tracy Clinic, 1961-62, Calif. Dept. Social Welfare, 1963-64, Am. Assn. Ret. Persons and Nat. Ret. Tchrs. Assn., 1965-67, Profl. Rsch., Inc., 1968, Acad. Comm. Facility, UCLA, 1969, ednl. sound film strips dept. daytime programs ans spl. projects UCLA Ext., 1971, San Diego County Dept. Edn., 1972, Iran film series Instrnl. Media Ctr., Mich. State U., 1975-77; writer films Who's Behind the Wheel, Part 1, 1966, Part II, 1967, Mayday, Mayday, 1970, The Man, Part I, 1972, Part II, 1973, How To Manage your resources-Safety, Part I, 1973, Part II, 1974 (all for USAF), Immunity-The Power To Resist a Disease, 1970. Pres. El Moro Dem. Club, Los Osos, Calif., 1994-95; bd. dirs. Ctrl. Coast Women's Polit. Com., San Luis Obispo, Calif., 1995-96; vol. Global Vols.-Poland, 1995, Oglala Lakota Coll., Pine Ridge Indian Reservation, Kyle, S.D., 1995. Mem. Univ. Film and Video Assn., Script Coalition for Industry, Profls. and Tchrs., Delta Kappa Alpha (assoc.). Home and Office: PO Box 6171 Los Osos CA 93412

MEHTA, MARY BAILEY, pediatric cardiologist; b. San Augustine, Tex., Jan. 7, 1961; d. Doyle Esco and Mary Landon (Gatling) Bailey; m. David Kishor Mehta, June 8, 1985; 1 child, Erin Elizabeth. BA, Austin Coll., 1983; MD, U. Tex., 1987. Resident in pediatrics Tulane U., 1988-91; fellow U. Miami/Jackson Meml. Hosp., 1991-94; pediat. cardiologist Pediatrix Med. Group, Ft. Lauderdale, Fla., 1994—. Recipient Best Presentation Pediat. Rsch. award U. Miami Dept. Pediats., 1994. Mem. AMA, Am. Acad. Cardiology, Am. Acad. Pediats., Broward County Med. Assn. (mem. child and adolescent com. 1992—, mem. pub. rels. com. 1992—). Episcopal. Office: Pediatrix Med Group 3990 Sheridan St Ste 207 Hollywood FL 33021

MEI, DOLORES MARIE, research administrator; b. Ludlow, Mass., Sept. 3, 1955; d. Paul John and Pauline Lavoie M.; m. Jack Irwin, June 28, 1981 (div. Feb. 1988); 1 child, Robert Aaron. AB in Psychology cum laude with honors, Smith Coll., 1977; MA, Columbia U., 1979, M of Philosophy, 1980, PhD, 1981. Rsch. assoc. Columbia U., Henry Krumb Sch. Mines, N.Y.C., 1981-82; mem. staff Office Ednl. Rsch., Bklyn., 1982-83, evaluation mgr., 1983—; ind. cons. N.Y. Zool. Soc., Bronx, 1980-82, 86—. Recipient Nat. Rsch. Svc. award Nat. Inst. Mental Health, 1979-80. Democrat. Roman Catholic. Home: 138 71st St Apt 1F Brooklyn NY 11209-1149 Office: Divsn Assessment and Accountability 110 Livingston St Rm 740 Brooklyn NY 11201-5065

MEIER, DIANE JONES, lawyer; b. Huron, S.D., Jan. 20, 1951; d. Daryl D. and Delila D. (Waldner) Jones; m. Kenneth J. Meier, Dec. 31, 1972. AB, U. S.D., 1972; JD, Syracuse U., 1976. Bar: Tex. 1976, Okla. 1978, Wis. 1986. Atty. Williams & Meier, Houston, 1976-77; pvt. practice Houston, 1977; title ins. underwriter, abstractor Southwest Title & Trust Co., Oklahoma City, 1978-81; assoc. Linn & Helms, Oklahoma City, 1981-85; staff atty. Wis. Ct. of Appeals, Milw., 1986—. Local officer Women's Equity Action League, Houston, 1976-77; bd. dirs., pres. Women's Resource Ctr., Norman, Okla., 1979-83. Mem. ABA, Milw. Bar Assn. Assn. Women Lawyers (treas.), Bus. and Profl. Women Milw. (bd. dirs., pres. 1990-92), Wis. Fedn. Bus. and Profl. Womens Clubs (chair com. 1993-95). Home: 2648 N Summit Ave Milwaukee WI 53211 Office: Wis Ct Appeals 633 West Wisconsin Ave # 1400 Milwaukee WI 53203

MEIER, ENGE, preschool educator; b. N.Y.C., Jan. 17; d. Rudolf and Kate (Furstenow) Pietschyck; children: Kenneth Randolph, Philip Alan. BBA, Western States U., 1987, MBA, 1989. Tchr. nursery sch. Neu Ulm, Fed. Republic Germany, 1963-64; sec. Brewster (N.Y.) Mid. Sch., 1969-72; teaching asst. Brewster Elem. Sch., 1972-73; office asst. Bd. Coop. Edn., Yorktown Heights, N.Y., 1973-76; sec. Am. Can. Co., Greenwich, Conn., 1976-77, adminstrv. sec., 1977-79, exec. sec., 1979-84; adminstrv. asst. U. Tex., Austin, 1984-85, 88-90, adminstrv. assoc., 1985-86, sr. adminstrv. associ., 1986-88; exec. asst. DTM Corp., Austin, 1990; funds asst. mgr. Tex. Assn. Sch. Bds., Austin, 1991-92; nursery sch. tchr. Westlake Presbyn. Sch., Austin, 1992-95; tchr. Grace Covenant Christian Sch., 1995—. Docent LBJ Libr. and Mus., Austin, 1984—; mem. Women's Polit. Caucus, 1988—; bd. dirs. Leadership, Edn. and Devel., 1991. Mem. Women in Mgmt., Bus. and Profl. Women (pres. 1989, bd. dirs. Austin chpt. 1987—), Women's C. of C. Presbyterian. Office: Westlake Hills Presbyn Presch 7127 Bee Caves Rd Austin TX 78746-4102

MEIER, JEANNETTE PATRICIA, lawyer; b. Chgo., May 15, 1947; d. Edward Daniel and Darlene Phyllis (White) M. BA, Northwestern U., 1969, JD, 1972. Bar: Colo. 1972, Calif. 1974, Tex. 1987. Assoc. Holland & Hart, Denver, 1972-73; asst. gen. counsel Boothe Computer Corp., San Francisco, 1974-76; asst. gen. counsel Pertec Computer, L.A., 1976-81, v.p., gen. counsel, 1981-82; assoc. counsel Wickes Cos., Santa Monica, Calif., 1982-84; v.p., gen. counsel Informatics Gen., Woodland Hills, Calif., 1984-85; sr. v.p., gen. counsel Sterling Software (acquired Informatics Gen.), Dallas, 1985-93, exec. v.p., gen. counsel, 1993-96, exec. v.p., CFO, gen. counsel, 1996—; exec. v.p., CFO and gen. counsel Sterling Commerce Inc., 1996—. Office: Sterling Software Inc 8080 N Central Expy Ste 1100 Dallas TX 75206-1807

MEIER, NANCY JO, nursing consultant; b. Sidney, Nebr., Dec. 15, 1951; d. Donald William and Clara Jo (Miller) M. BA, Midland Luth. Coll., 1974; diploma in Nursing, Immanual Hosp. Sch. Nursing, Omaha, 1974; MS in Nursing Edn., Tex. Women's U., 1978. RN, Tex. Staff nurse St. Lukes Episcopal Hosp./Tex. Heart Inst., Houston, 1974-75, Park Plaza Hosp., Houston, 1976; clin. nursing specialist Houston Thoracic and Cardiovascular Assn., 1977-78; instr. clin. nursing Cedar Sinai Med. Ctr., Los Angeles, 1978-79; dir. dept. nursing edn. Los Angeles New Hosp., 1979-80; ind. cons. nursing edn. Los Angeles, 1980-81; systems support specialist IVAC Corp., San Diego, 1981-83; med. specialist, advt. account exec. Kenneth C. Smith & Assocs., La Jolla, Calif., 1983-87; ind. nursing cons. San Diego, 1987—; cons. nursing edn. Nat. Med. Enterprises, Saudi Arabia, 1980-81, Nursing Services Internat., Los Angeles, 1980, Grossmont Hosp., San Diego, 1985; instr. cardiac life support Los Angeles chpt. Am. Heart Assn., 1978-84; lectr. in field. Organist United Meth. Ch., Sidney, 1967-69, Immanual Sch. Nursing, 1971-74, Meml. Luth. Ch., Houston, 1977-78; bd. dirs. Bluffs of Fox Run Homeowners Assn., San Diego, 1984-85, pres., 1985-86. Mem. Am. Nurses Assn., Am. Assn. Operating Room Nurses, Med. Mktg. Assn., Sigma Theta Tau. Republican. Lutheran. Home and Office: 2963 Old Bridgeport Way San Diego CA 92111-7724

MEIKLEJOHN, (LORRAINE) MINDY JUNE, political organizer, realtor; b. Staunton, Colo., June 9, 1929; d. Edward H. and Erna E. (Schwabe) Mindrup; m. Alvin J. Meiklejohn, Apr. 25, 1953; children: Pamela, Shelley, Bruce, Scott. Student Ill. Bus. Coll., 1948, Red Rocks C.C., 1980-81. Pvt. sec. Ill. Liquor Commn., 1948-51, David M. Wilson, Ill. Sec. of State's Office, 1951-52; flight attendant Continental Airlines, 1952-53, pvt. sec. to mgr. flight svcs. office, 1953-54; organizational dir. Colo. Rep. Party, Denver, 1981-85, mem. Cen. Com., 1987—; campaign coord. Hank Brown's Exploratory Campaign for Gov., 1985, mgr. Hank Brown for Congress, 1985-86; dep. campaign dir. Steve Schuck for Gov., 1985-86; vice chmn. 2d Congl. Cen. Com. Colo.; active campaigns; del., alt. to various, county, state, dist. and nat. assemblies and convs.; Colo. chmn. Citizens for Am., 1987-96; realtor, sales assoc. Metro Brokers, Inc.; mem. polit. action com. Jefferson County Bd. Realtors. Apptd. trustee Harry S. Truman Scholarship Found., 1991; mem. Jefferson County Hist. Commn., Colo., 1974-82, pres., 1979; vol. Jefferson County Legal Aid Soc., 1970-74; vice chmn. Jefferson County Rep. Party, 1977-81, exec. com., 1987; vice chmn. Colo. State Rep. Party, 1981-85; chmn. Rep. Nat. Pilot Project on Volunteerism, 1981; mem. adv. coun. U.S. Peace Corps, 1982-84; sect. chmn. Jefferson County United Way Fund Drive; mem. exec. bd. Colo. Fedn. Rep. Women; pres. Operation Shelter, Inc., 1983—; bd. dirs. Scientific and Cultural Facilities dist. 1989-94, Jefferson County chpt. Am. Cancer Soc., 1987-91, Jefferson Found., 1991—, Rocky Mountain Butterfly Consortium, 1996—. Mem. Jefferson County Women's Rep. (edn. chmn. 1987-91). Lutheran. Home: 7540 Kline Dr Arvada CO 80005-3732

MEIL, KATE, sculptor; b. N.Y.C., June 15, 1925; d. Jacob and Becky (Lichtman) Meil; 1 child, Maria Rebecca Black. BBA in Acctg., CCNY, 1949. Acct. chem., printing, garment, machine and tool, film and car industries, 1943-91. Sculptor: Mein Kind, 1976, Determined to Be, 1977, Inner Mirror, 1979, Zeyda, 1980, Meydele, 1985, Remembering, 1987, Single Parent, 1988, Survivors, 1989, Einstein, 1991, We Too Have Dreams, 1992, Alone Together, 1995. Leader Hudson Ave Area Residents Assn., Edgewater, 1973; participant Can. Nat. Exhibit, 1989, Cork Gallery, N.Y.C., 1994. Recipient Red and Blue ribbons 3d Ann. N.J. Woodcarving and Wildlife Art Show, 1987, 3d Pl. ribbon Bergen County Dept. Parks, 1991, 92, 2nd Place Bergen County Dept. Parks, 1994, 95, 2nd Place natural relief, 3rd Place painted relief No. Jersey Woodcarvers, 1995, 3rd place Ringwood State Manor Exhibit of Salute to Women in the Arts, 1992. Mem. Salute to Women in Arts, Whittle Ones, Ethical Culture Soc., Palisades Nature Assn. Avocations: chess; theater; folk dancing.

MEILAN, CELIA, food products executive; b. Bklyn., Jan. 21, 1920; d. Ventura Lorenzo and Susana (Prego) M. Student, CCNY, 1943-46. Codes and ciphers translator security divsn. U.S. Censorship Office, N.Y.C., 1942-46; sec., treas. Albumina Supply Co., N.Y.C., 1946-55; co-founder, co-owner, sec., treas., fin. officer Internat. Proteins Corp., Fairfield, N.J., 1955-86, exec. v.p., 1986-92, pres., 1992-94, chair emeritus, bd. dirs., 1994—; bd. dirs. Pesquera Taboquilla, Panama City, Republic of Panama, 1969—, Inversiones Pesqueras S.A., Brit. V.I.; v.p., bd. dirs. Atlantic Shippers of Tex. Inc., Port Arthur, 1989, Atlantic Shippers Inc., Morehead City, N.C., Empacadora Nacional S.A., Panama City, Republic of Panama; exec. v.p., bd. dirs. Fairfield Fishing Co., Liberia, Internat. Proteins Chile S.A., Santiago. Named One of Top 50 Women Bus. Owners, Working Woman mag. and Nat. Found. Women Bus. Owners, 1994, 95. Mem. Nat. Found. Women Bus. Owners, Spanish Benevolent Soc. (bd. dirs. 1955-62). Avocations: travel, hand crafts, backgammon, puzzles. Office: 204 Passaic Ave Fairfield NJ 07004-3503

MEINER, SUE ELLEN THOMPSON, gerontologist, nursing educator and researcher; b. Ironton, Mo., Oct. 24, 1943; d. Louis Raymond and Verna Mae (Goggin) Thompson; m. Robert Edward Meiner, Mar. 5, 1971; children: Diane Thompson Bubb, Suzanne Elaine. AAS, Meramec C.C., 1970; BSN, St. Louis U., 1978, MSN, 1983; EdD, So. Ill. U., Edwardsville, 1991. RN, Mo.; cert. med./surg. clinician; cert. gerontol. nurse practitioner; cert. clin. specialist in gerontol. nursing. Staff RN St. Joseph's Hosp., St. Charles, Mo., 1976-78; nursing supr. Bethesda Gen. Hosp., St. Louis, 1975-76, 71-74; adult med. dir. Family Care Ctr.-Carondelet, St. Louis, 1978-79; program dir., lectr. Webster Coll./Bethesda Hosp., Webster Groves, Mo., 1979-82; diabetes clin. specialist Washington U. Sch. Medicine, St. Louis, 1982; chmn. dept. nursing, asst. prof. St. Louis C.C., 1983-88, Barnes Hosp. Sch. Nursing, 1988-89; instr. U. Mo., St. Louis, 1989; assoc. prof. St. Charles County C.C., St. Peters, Mo., 1990-92, Deaconess Coll. of Nursing, 1991-93; patient care mgr. Deaconess Hosp., St. Louis, 1993-94; assoc. prof. Jewish Hosp. Coll. of Nursing and Allied Health, 1994-96; gerontol. nurse, instr. Wash. U. Sch. Med., St. Louis, 1996—; nat. dir. edn. Nat. Assn. Practical Nurse Edn. and Svc., Inc., St. Louis, 1984-86; mem. task force St. Louis Met. Hosp. Assn., 1987-88; mem. adv. com. Bd. Edn. Sch. Nursing, St. Louis, 1986-90; project dir. NIH Grant Washington U., St. Louis, 1996—. Contbr. articles to profl. jours. and books. Chmn. bd. dirs. Creve Coeur Fire Protection Dist. Mo., 1984-89; vice chmn. Bd. Cen. St. Louis County Emergency Dispatch Svc., 1985-87; asst. leader Girl Scouts U.S., St. Louis, 1975; treas. Older Women's League, St. Louis, 1992-93. Recipient Woman of Worth award Gateway chpt. Older Women's League, 1993. Mem. ANA, Am. Nurses Found., Nat. League for Nursing, Am. Soc. of Aging, Mid-Am. Congress on Aging, Creve Coeur C. of C., Order Ea. Star (chaplain 1970), Jobs Daus. (guardian 1979-80), Sigma Theta Tau (fin. chmn. 1984, archivist 1985-87), Sigma Phi Omega (pres. 1990-91), Kappa Delta Pi. Home and Office: 700 Wren Path Ct Ballwin MO 63021-4794

MEINERS, GINNY, clinical psychologist, nurse consultant; b. St. Louis; d. Robert and Mary Meiners. BA in Psychology, U. Mo., 1977, MEd in Counseling, 1994; PhD in Clinical Psychology, St. Louis C.C., 1988. Dir., nurse cons. Weight Loss Clinics, St. Louis, 1981-87; sr. adminstr. Mid-East Area Agy., St. Louis, 1987-88; owner Profl. Weight Cons., St. Louis, 1988-93; nurse instr., cons. Gen. Protestant Children's Home, St. Louis, 1993—; clinical psychologist, nurse consultant Insights Psychol. Svcs., St. Louis, 1994—; spkr. in field. Active Volvo Nat. Tennis Team. Mem. ACA, Am. Assn. Christian Counselors, Mo. Nurses Assn., Assn. for Spiritual, Ethical and Religious Values, St. Louis Track Club, Phi Kappa Phi, Chi Sigma Iota. Office: Insights Psychol Svcs 777 S New Ballas Rd Creve Coeur MO 63141

MEINERT, LYNLEY SHERYL, clinical neuropsychologist; b. Battle Creek, Mich., Nov. 30, 1964; d. Lewis Sanford and Janis Gayle (Palmiter) M.; m. Mark Alan Ebeling, July 14, 1990. BA, Mich. State U., 1986; MA, Calif. Sch. Profl. Psychology, 1988, PhD, 1990. Lic. psychologist, Ill., Mo., Tex. Psychol. trainee St. Mary's Rehab. Care, Enid, Okla., 1990-91; cert. psychologist in pvt. practice Lubbock, Tex., 1991; neuropsychologist Community Rehab. Svcs., Scottsdale, Ariz., 1991-93, Ctr. Comprehensive Svcs., Carbondale, Ill., 1994—. Mem. APA, Internat. Neuropsychol. Assn., Nat. Acad. Neuropsychology, Phi Beta Kappa, Psi Chi, Phi Kappa Phi. Office: Ctr For Comprehensive Svs 306 W Mill St Carbondale IL 62901

MEINHARD, HERMINE LYNN, poet, educator; b. Newark, June 29, 1947; d. Rosalie B. Meinhard. Student, St. Hilton's Coll., Oxford, Eng., summer 1968; BA in English with high honors, Douglass Coll., 1969; MFA in Poetry, Sarah Lawrence Coll., 1991. Poetry instr. N.Y. City Ballet Poetry Project, 1991-94; poetry tchr. Prospect Heights H.S., Bklyn., 1992-94, Pub. Sch. 76, N.Y.C., 1993-94; poetry workshop tchr. The Writer's Voice of the West Side YMCA, N.Y.C., 1994—; poetry readings: Cornelia St. Cafe, N.Y.C., 1995, Barrow St. Series at Greenwich House, N.Y.C., 1995, N.Y.U., Dixon Pl., N.Y.C., 1995. Contbr. poetry to lit. jours. including: One Meadway, Sonora Rev., The Prose Poem: An Internat. Jour., Willow Springs, Kalliope, So to Speak, Poetry New York, 1991—. Recipient Sue Saniel Elkind Poetry award Kalliope: A Jour. of Women's Art, Jacksonville, Fla., 1993; named fellow Va. Ctr. for the Creative Arts, Sweet Briar, Va., 1996; nominated for Pushcart prize Pushcart Press, 1996-97. Mem. Associated Writing Programs, Phi Beta Kappa. Home and Office: 1574 First Ave Apt 102 New York NY 10028

MEIS, NANCY RUTH, marketing and development executive; b. Iowa City, Aug. 6, 1952; d. Donald J. and Theresa (Dee) M.; m. Paul L. Wenske, Oct. 14, 1978; children: Alexis Meis Wenske, Christopher Meis Wenske. BA, Clarke Coll., 1974; MBA, U. Okla., 1981. Cultural program supr. City of Dubuque, Iowa., 1974-76; community services dir. State Arts Council of Okla., Oklahoma City, 1976-78, program dir., 1978-79; mgr. Cimarron Circuit Opera Co., Norman, Okla., 1979-82, bd. dirs., 1982-86; account exec. Bell System, Kansas City, Mo., 1982; mgr. spl. svcs. Children Internat., Kansas City, 1983-86; dir. mktg. and fund raising, 1986-87, dir. devel., 1987-88, v.p. devel., 1988-90; dir. mktg. and consulting svcs, Unimedia div. Universal Press Syndicate, Kansas City, 1990-95; dir. mktg. Universal New Media divsn. Universal Press Syndicate, 1996—; cons., copywriter; speaker in field. Co-founder Girls to Women.

MEISNER, JUDITH ANNE, clinical social worker, marital and sex therapist, psychotherapist; b. Dayton, Ohio, Mar. 20, 1931; d. Lowell DeWight and Mary Elizabeth (Anderson) Richardson; m. S. Clair Varner, 1953 (div. 1964); m. Carl E. Meisner, Dec. 31, 1970; children: Christopher, Cynthia, Deborah, Catherine; stepchildren: Janet, Elizabeth, Barbara. BA, Oberlin Coll., 1952; MSW, Fla. State U., 1970; PhD, Inst. Advanced Study Human Sexuality, 1987. Cert. Acad. Cert. Social Workers; bd. cert. diplomate; lic. clin. social worker; lic. marriage and family therapist; diplomate Am. Bd. Sexology, Am. Coll. Sexologists, clin. supr. Am. Bd. Sexology. Psychiat. aide Inst. Living, Hartford, Conn., 1952-53; caseworker, supr. Div. Family Svcs., Dept. Health and Rehabilitative Svcs., St. Petersburg, Fla., 1964-66, 66-68; dir. standing com. on health and rehabilitative svcs. Fla. Ho. Reps. , Fla. State Legis., Tallahassee, 1970-72; adj. prof. grad. sch. social work Fla. State U., Tallahassee, 1972-73; family life cons. Family Counseling Ctr., St. Petersburg, 1973-75; coord. Teenage Info. Program for Students Pinellas County Sch. Bd., St. Petersburg, 1975-78, coord. Citizen's Task Force on Edn. for Family Living, 1978-80; psychotherapist Counseling & Cons. Svcs., St. Petersburg, 1975—; profl. adv. bd. Nat. Found. March of Dimes Pinellas chpt., Clearwater, Fla., 1976-85, Parents Without Ptnrs. chpt. 186, St. Petersburg, 1973—; mem. Family Life Edn. Coun. Pinellas County Sch. Bd., Clearwater, 1980-85. Bd. dirs. Neighborly Sr. Svcs., Clearwater, 1974-85, pres., bd. dirs., 1982, 83; bd. dirs. Marriage and Family Counseling of Pinellas County, Inc., 1993—. Fellow Am. Acad. Clin. Sexologists (life); mem. NASW, Am. Assn. for Marriage and Family Therapists (clin.), Pinellas Assn. for Marriage and Family Therapists (clin.), Am. Assn. Sex. Educators, Counselors and Therapists (life, cert. sex educator, sex therapist), Soc. for the Sci. Study of Sex, Fla. Soc. Clin. Social Workers, Soc. of Neuro-Linguistic Programming (cert. master practitioner), Harry Benjamin Internat. Gender Dysphoria Assn., Fla. Soc. of Clin. Hypnosis. Home: 7 Marina Ter Treasure Island FL 33706

MEISNER, MARY JO, editor; b. Chgo., Dec. 24, 1951; d. Robert Joseph and Mary Elizabeth (Casey) M.; 1 child, Thomas Joseph Gradel. BS in Journalism, U. Ill., 1974, MS in Journalism, 1976. Copy editor Wilmington (Del.) News Jour., 1975-76, labor and bus. reporter, 1975-79; labor and gen. assignment reporter Phila. Daily News, 1979, city editor, 1979-83, met. editor, 1983-85; PM city editor San Jose (Calif.) Mercury News, 1985-86, met. editor, 1986-87; city editor The Washington Post, 1987-90; mng. editor The Ft. Worth Star-Telegram, 1991-93; editor and v.p. The Milw. Jour., 1993-95; editor, sr. v.p The Milw. Jour. Sentinel, 1995—. Mem. AP Mng. Editors (bd. dirs. 1992-95), Am. Soc. Newspaper Editors, Internat. Press Inst. (bd. dirs. 1994—, Pulitzer prize juror 1994, 96). Office: The Milw Jour Sentinel 333 W State St Milwaukee WI 53201-0371*

MEISSNER, ALICE MARTHA, real estate broker; b. Bklyn., June 30, 1926; d. Karl Frederick and Marta Alexandria (Kaipiainen) Nilsson; m. Charles Joseph Meissner, Mar. 31, 1952; children: Gregory, Christopher, Melissa. Diploma, Adelphi Coll., 1946; BS cum laude, Adelphi U., 1949; postgrad., NYU, 1950-51. RN, N.Y.; registered real estate broker, Fla. V.p. North Manor Constrn., Great Neck, N.Y., 1955-58; vol. ARC, Bradenton, Fla., 1960-66; owner, founder Meissner Real Estate, Bradenton, 1969—. Mem. AAUW, Nat. Assn. Realtors, Fla. Assn. Realtors, Manatee County Bd. Realtors, Manatee County Art League, Epsilon Sigma Alpha (v.p. 1970, pres. 1979). Presbyterian. Home: 500 Palma Sola Blvd Bradenton FL 34209-3226 Office: Meissner Real Estate 4411 60th St W Bradenton FL 34210-2731

MEISSNER, DORIS, federal commissioner; b. Nov. 3, 1941; d. Fred and Hertha H. (Tromp) Borst; m. Charles F. Meissner, June 8, 1963; children: Christine M., Andrew D. BA, U. Wis., 1963, MA, 1969. Asst. dir. student fin. aid U. Wis., 1964-68; exec. dir. Nat. Women's Polit. Caucus, 1971-73; asst. dir. office policy and planning U.S. Dept. Justice, 1975, exec. dir. cabinet com. illegal aliens, 1976, dep. assoc. atty. gen., 1977-80, acting commr. immigration and naturalization svc., 1981, exec. assoc. commr. immigration and naturalization svc., 1982-86; sr. assoc., dir. immigration policy project The Carnegie Endowment for Internat. Peace, 1986-93; commr. immigration and naturalization svc., 1993; adv. coun. U.S./Mex. project Overseas Devel. Coun., 1981-86; trustee Refugee Policy Group, 1987-93; adv. bd. Program for Rsch. on Immigration Policy Rand Corp./Urban inst., 1988-92; cons. panel to comptroller gen. GAO, 1989-93; with Coun. Fgn. Rels., 1990—, Washington Office Latin Am., 1989-93. White Ho. fellow, 1973-74. Mem. Nat. Women's Polit. Caucus (nat. adv. bd. 1976—), White House Fellows Alumni Assn. and Found. (sec., exec. com. 1979-82, Assn. Governing Bds. Colls. and Univs. (panel higher edn. issues 1990-92), Phi Kappa Phi, Mortar Board, Alpha Chi Omega. Office: Dept Justice Immigration & Naturalization Svc 425 I St NW Rm 7100 Washington DC 20536

MEISSNER, DOROTHY THERESA, reading specialist; b. Jersey City, N.J., Apr. 20, 1932; d. John and Mary (Garofalo) Biondo; m. Carl Frederick Meissner; children: Kathleen Ann, Mary Gretl. BA summa cum laude, Jersey City State Coll., 1970, MA summa cum laude, 1974. Cert. tchr. of reading, reading specialist, supr. and adminstr. Metallographer Engelhard Industries, Newark, N.J., 1953-61; 2nd grade tchr. Rutherford (N.J.) Bd. Edn., 1970-74, 4th grade tchr., 1974, reading specialist, 1974-94, 94—; instr. Fairleigh Dickinson U., Rutherford, 1977; spl. edn. steering com. Kearny (N.J.) Pub. Schs., 1968-69; G&T adv. coun. Rutherford Pub. Schs., 1978-79; v.p. Union Fin. Chain, Rutherford, 1985-89, pres., 1989-92; adj. prof. reading dept. Jersey City State Coll. Contbr. articles to profl. jours.; designer sculpture; artist charcoal drawing (hon. mention 1987). Lector Roman Cath. Ch., Kearny, 1988—; coord. William Carlos Williams Project, Rutherford, 1984. Recipient Gov.'s Tchr.'s Recognition State of N.J., 1987; seminar grantee N.J. Coun. for Humanities, 1995. Mem. Internat. Reading Assn. (program chair 1992-93, v.p. 1994-95, pres. 1995—, rec. sec. North Jersey coun. 1996—), Women's Coll. Club, Phi Delta Kappa, Kappa Delta Pi. Home: PO Box 355 Kearny NJ 07032-0355

MEISTAS, MARY THERESE, endocrinologist, diabetes researcher; b. Grand Rapids, Mich., July 22, 1949; d. Frank Peter and Anne Therese (Karsokas) M. MD, U. Mich., 1975. Diplomate Am. Bd. Internal Medicine, Am. Bd. Endocrinology. Intern, then resident in internal medicine Cleve. Clinic Hosp., 1975-78, endocrinology fellow, 1978-79; fellow in pediatric endocrinology Johns Hopkins Hosp., Balt., 1979-81; diabetes researcher Joslin Diabetes Ctr., Boston, 1981-86; assoc. in medicine Brigham and Women's Hosp., Boston, 1981-86; asst. in medicine, diabetes researcher Mass. Gen. Hosp., Boston, 1986-92; staff endocrinologist Emerson Hosp., Concord, Mass., 1989—. Mem. ACP, Am. Diabetes Assn., Am. Fedn. Clin. Research, Endocrine Soc. Office: Emerson Hosp 747 Main St Ste 111 Concord MA 01742-3302

MEISTER, DORIS POWERS, investment management executive; b. Ames, Iowa, Sept. 12, 1954; d. James Phillip and Doris (Goess) P.; m. Gilbert Meister Jr., Oct. 18, 1980. AB, Smith Coll., 1976; MBA, U. Chgo., 1979. Mgr. currency Harris Trust & Savs. Bank, Chgo., 1976-78; sr. engagement mgr. McKinsey & Co. Inc., N.Y.C., London, 1979-84; dir., dept. head portfolio strategies dept., adminstrv. mgr. fixed income rsch. group C S First Boston, N.Y.C., 1984-90; exec. v.p., COO Christie, Manson & Woods Internat. Inc., N.Y.C., 1990-94; mng. dir. Copley Real Estate Advisors, Boston, 1994—. Bd. dirs. Arts Connection, 1990, Am. Women's Econ. Devel. Corp., 1994. Named one of "Top 40 under 40" Execs., Crain's N.Y., 1992. Mem. Fin. Women's Assn., Com. of 200, Women's Forum. Episcopalian. Office: Copley Real Estate Advisors 399 Boylston St Boston MA 02116-3305

MEISTER, ELYSE S., reading specialist; b. Bklyn., May 23, 1944; d. Irving and Syd (Kushner) Spitz; m. Myron S. Meister, Aug. 15, 1965; children: Lynn Mueller, Jill Kimmel, Adrienne. BA, Bklyn. Coll., 1966; MA, Montclair State Coll., 1986. Cert. adminstr., supr., reading specialist. Elem. tchr. East Orange (N.J.) Sch. Dist., 1979-85; reading tchr. West Orange (N.J.) Sch. Dist., 1985-94; instr. reading Kean Coll., Union, N.J., 1994—, cons. Estelle Finkel Assocs., Livingston, N.J., 1994—. Mem. LWV (bd. dirs.), ASCD, Phi Kappa Phi.

MEITIN, DEBORAH DORSKY, health care executive; b. Cleve., July 25, 1951; d. Irving and Rosalind (Lewis) D.; m. Samuel R. Meitin, Dec. 6, 1987. BS, Mich. State U., 1973; M Health Adminstrn., Ohio State U., 1981. Cert. med. technologist. Med. technologist U. Hosps., Cleve., 1974-79; adminstrv. dir. surgery and anesthesiology Cleve. Met. Gen. Hosp., 1981-86; sr. cons. Ernst & Whinney, Chgo., 1986-87; sr. v.p. Diversified Health Search, Maitland, Fla., 1988-89; pres. Health Search Cons., Altamonte Springs, Fla., 1989-91; pres. Greater Fla. Devel. Co., Altamonte Springs, 1988—; sr. cons. Ernst & Young, Orlando, 1991-92, mgr., 1992-94; sys. analyst Fla. Hosp., Orlando, 1995—. Mem. bd. profl. women's group Jewish Fedn., Chgo., 1986-87; mem. coms. Jewish Cmty. Ctr., Chgo., 1986-87, Orlando, Fla., 1990—, v.p., 1991-94; bd. dirs. Michael Reese Hosp.-Jr. Med. Rsch. Coun., Chgo., 1986-87, Temple Israel, Orlando, 1989—. Fellow Am. Coll. Healthcare Execs.; mem. Ctrl. Fla. Healthcare Exec. Group (pres. 1995-96), Ohio State U. Grad. Program in Health Adminstrn. Alumni Assn. (bd. dirs. 1982-84), Phi Kappa Phi, Beta Beta Beta. Democrat. Home: 268 Buttercup Clr Altamonte Springs FL 32714-5844 Office: 601 E Rollins St Orlando FL 32803-1248

MEITNER, PAMELA, lawyer, educator; b. Phila., Aug. 23, 1950; d. Alfred Victor Meitner and Claire Jane (Carroll) Harmer; m. William Bruce Larson, Sept. 13, 1980; 1 child, William Bruce, Jr. BS in chem. engring., Drexel U., 1973; JD, Del. Law Sch., 1977. Bar: Del. 1977, U.S. Dist. Ct. Del. 1977, U.S. Patent and Trademark Office 1977. Engr. DuPont Co., Deepwater, N.J., 1973-77; lawyer DuPont Co., Wilmington, Del., 1977; prof. Del. Law Sch., Wilmington, 1985—. Commr. State Emergency Response Com., Dover, Del., 1986-90. Mem. Del. Bar Assn. Club: DuPont Country (Wilmington) (bd. govs. 1984-85). Home: 211 Welwyn Rd Wilmington DE 19803-2951 Office: DuPont Co Legal Dept 1007 Market St Wilmington DE 19898

MEIUSI, RHONDI SUE, ophthalmologist; b. St. Paul, Minn., Oct. 9, 1961; d. Allen Keith and Carol Delores (Sandlund) Larson; m. Daniel Walter Meiusi, Sept. 9, 1989; children: Elizabeth Mairi, Katrin Ruth, Anna Grace. BS, Oral Roberts Univ., 1983; MD, Mayo Medical Sch., 1987. Diplomate Am. Bd. Ophthalmology. Residency Univ. Minn., Mpls., 1991; gen. ophthalmologist Edina (Minn.) Eye Clinic, P.A., 1992—; Med. Grand Mission Ophthalmology Mission Cajabamba, Ecuador, 1987, Kissy United Meth. Ch. Eye Clinic, Sierra Leone, West Africa, 1987, Med. Grand Mission Ophthalmology Mission Monterey, Mexico, 1988. Author (book chpt.): Ophthalmology Clinics of N.Am., 1989; contbr. articles to profl. jours. Recipient The Harry Plotke award Univ. Minn., 1990; rsch. fellow, 1988. Mem. Minn. Acad. Ophthalmology, Hennepin County Medical Soc., Christian Medical Dental Soc., Alpha Epsilon Iota (Honor award 1989). Office: Edina Eye Clinic P A 3939 West 50th St # 200 Edina MN 55424

MELAMED, CAROL DRESCHER, lawyer; b. N.Y.C., July 12, 1946; d. Raymond A. and Ruth W. (Schwartz) Drescher; children: Stephanie Weisman, Deborah Weisman; m. Arthur Douglas Melamed, May 26, 1983; children: Kathryn, Elizabeth. AB, Brown U., 1967; MAT, Harvard U., 1969; JD, Catholic U. Am., 1974. Bar: Md. 1974, D.C. 1975, U.S. Ct. Appeals, (D.C. cir.) 1975, U.S. Dist. Ct. D.C. 1981, U.S. Supreme Ct. 1982. Tchr. English, Wellesley High Sch., Mass., 1968-69; law clk. U.S. Ct. Appeals, (D.C. cir.), Washington, 1974-75; assoc. Wilmer, Cutler & Pickering, Washington, 1975-79; dir. govt. affairs, assoc. counsel, The Washington Post, 1979-95, v.p. govt. affairs, 1995— . Mem. Phi Beta Kappa. Office: The Washington Post 1150 15th St NW Washington DC 20071-0001

MELANSON, ANNE M., advertising agency executive. Former sr. v.p. Ted Bates Advt., N.Y.C.; sr. v.p., dir. human resources Backer Spielvogel Bates Worldwide, Inc., N.Y.C.; now exec. v.p., dir. human resources and ops. Bates Worldwide, Inc., N.Y.C. Office: Bates Worldwide 405 Lexington Ave New York NY 10174*

MELANSON, SUSAN C., property manager; b. Boston, May 6, 1946; d. Arthur Wood and Marion (Saunders) Chapman; m. Arthur S. Melanson. AA, Colby-Sawyer Coll., 1966; BA, Hiram Coll., 1970. Founder, pres. Gem Island Software, Reading, Mass., 1985-90; dir. Gem Island Software, Carlisle, Mass., 1990-93; property mgr. Finard & Co., Burlington, Mass., 1993—; co-owner Washington Kennel; breeder, trainer, racer Siberian and Alaskan huskies. Class historian Wellesley High Class, 1964; leader, bd. dirs. Camp Fire, Reading, Antiquarian Soc., Reading, 1990-93; mem. steering com., officer Reading 350th Celebration, 1989-94. Mem. Soc. Property Mgmt. Profls., Omicron Beta. Office: Finard & Co 1 Monument Sq Ste 200 Portland ME 04101

MELBY, MARIA WESTY, artist, educator; b. Schenectady, N.Y., Feb. 15, 1934; d. Willem F. and Mary (Andrews) Westendorp; 2 children. BFA, U. Colo., 1956; MFA, U. Wash., 1958. Cert. tchr., Colo. Elem. multicultural bilingual art specialist Colorado Springs (Colo.) Sch. Dist. #11, 1977-81, jr. h.s. art tchr., 1982-87; acad. art tchr. Dept. of Corrections, Cañon City, Colo., 1987-90; prof. art Regis U., Denver, Cañon City, 1990-94; art tchr. Sange de Cristo Arts & Conf. Ctr., Pueblo, Colo., 1995-96. Author, illustrator 4 books of drawings & poems; contbr.: Ethnic Autonomy, 1978; exhbns. include Colo. State Fair, Colorado Springs Fine Arts Ctr., Pueblo Art Guild Gallery, Staircase 22, Pueblo, Sharon's Gallery, Colorado Springs, Bus. Art Ctr., Manitou Springs; illustrator 7 children's books; artist info. displays USDA Forest Svc., Pueblo, 1994-95. Artist, voter registrar King's Movement Equality Now, Nacogdoches, Tex., 1968-71. Recipient Purchase award Utah State Inst. Art, 1964, Outstanding Young Woman U.S. award, 1969, Best of Show award Colorado Springs Art Guild, 1994, 8 art ribbons. Mem. Friends El Pueblo Mus., Bus. Art Ctr., Native Am. Women's Assn., Phi Beta Kappa. Unitarian.

MELCHER, TRINI URTUZUASTEGUI, accounting educator; b. Somerton, Ariz., Dec. 1, 1931; d. Francisco Juan and Dolores (Barraza) Urtuzuastegui; m. Arlyn Melcher, Aug. 3, 1957 (div. Feb. 1972); children: Teresa Dolores, Michael Francis, Jocelyn Marie. BS, Ariz. State U., 1954; MBA, Kent State U., 1964; PhD, Ariz. State U., 1977. Acct. CPA firm, L.A., 1954-56; instr. L.A. Sch. Dist., 1956-58, Dolton (Ill.) Sch. Dist., 1958-61; asst. prof. Kent (Ohio) State U., 1962-72; prof. Calif. State U., Fullerton, 1976-89; founding faculty mem. Calif. State U., San Marcos, 1990—. Author: Intermediate Accounting Study Guide, 1984. Treas. Community Devel. Coun., Santa Ana, 1985-88, chmn. bd., 1989; mem. com. U.S. Dept. Labor, 1989—. Named Outstanding Educator, League of United Latin Am. Citizens, Stanton, Calif., 1987, Mex. Am. Women's Nat. Assn., Irvine, Calif., 1987; recipient Outstanding Faculty award Calif. State U. Sch. Bus., 1983, Pub. Svc. award Am. Soc. Women CPAs, San Antonio, 1989; Affirmative Action grantee, 1990. Mem. AICPA (editorial bd. The Woman CPA), Am. Acctg. Assn., Calif. Soc. CPAs (Merit award 1991), Hispanic CPAs. Home: 2024 Sequioa St San Marcoa CA 92069 Office: Calif State U San Marcos CA 92096-0001

MELCHERT, SANDRA ANN, science educator, researcher; b. Chgo., July 7, 1954; d. Clifford Colburn and Germania Erna (Muenzer) De La Monte Heverly de Heverly; m. David J. Holmes, Jan. 15, 1995; children: Yolanda, Heather, Amethyst, Erika. BSBA, Ea. Wash. U., 1986; MA, MS, Ea. Washington U., 1990; PhD, U. Idaho, 1993. Cert. elem. and secondary tchr., Wash. Tchr. Wilson Creek (Wash.) Pub. Schs., 1986; tchr. 6th grade Moses Lake (Wash.) Sch., 1986-89; teaching asst. Ea. Wash. U., Cheney, 1989-90; sci. and maths. tchr. Spokane (Wash.) Pub. Schs., 1990; project coord., inst. sci. U. Idaho, Moscow, 1990-93; asst. prof. sci. edn. U. S.D., Vermillion, 1993-96, Messiah Coll., Grantham, Pa., 1996—; reviewer sch. sci. and math. U. Mo., 1993—; reviewer nat. sci. stds. Fund for Improvement and Rsch. Sci. Tng., U.S. Dept. Edn., 1992-96; grant reviewer NSF, 1996. Author and editor: Topically Relevant Approaches for Increasing Learning in Science-Biological/Physical/Earth Sciences, series 1992-94; author and editor video tape series; contbr. articles to profl. jours. Mem. steering com. Vermillion Water Festival, 1993-96, rep. Civic Coun., Vermillion, 1994-6, promoter, supporter cultural arts First Nighter, Vermillon, 1994-96; vol. Vermillion Beautification Com., 1993-96. Recipient ASCD Outstanding Dissertation award, 1994; CHEM Nat. fellow, 1994—. Fellow Am. Meterol. Soc. (reviewer nat. sci. stds. 1991—); mem. AAAS, AAUW, NSTA, Nat. Assn. Rsch. in Sci. Tchg., Nat. com. for Study Options for Rural Sci. Edn., Assn. for Edn. Tchrs. in Sci., Sch. Sci. and Math. Assn. (membership com. 1994—), Kappa Delta Pi, Phi Delta Kappa (sec. Wilkes chpt. 1996—). Home: 418 Clemens Dr Dillsburg PA 17019 Office: Messiah Coll Ste 308 College of Edn Grantham PA 17027

MELCHIORRE, CAROLYN, intermediate school educator; b. Whitestone, N.Y., Dec. 20, 1969; d. Guerino and Marian (Migliorato) M. BS in Edn., St. John's U., 1991; MEd, U. Va., 1992. Diagnostician McGuffey Reading Ctr., Charlottesville, Va., 1991-92; clinician McGuffey Reading Ctr., Charlottesville, 1991-92, rsch. asst., 1992; tchr. N.Y.C. Bd. Edn., 1992—; data entry cons. Rocky Mountain River Expedns., Denver, 1989-90; U.S. del. to China, Citizen Ambassador Program, Spokane, 1994. Mem. ASCD, Internat. Reading Assn., Sigma Tau Delta (treas. 1990), Kappa Delta Pi. Office: Woodside Intermediate Sch 46-02 47th Ave Woodside NY 11377-6123

MELCONIAN, LINDA JEAN, state senator, lawyer; b. Springfield, Mass.; d. George and Virginia Elaine (Noble) Melconian. B.A., Mt. Holyoke Coll., 1970; M.A., George Washington U., 1976, J.D., 1978. Bar: Mass. Chief legis. asst. to Ho. of Reps. Speaker Thomas P. O'Neill, Jr., U.S. Congress, Washington, 1971-80; pros. atty. Hampden County Dist. Atty., Springfield, Mass., 1981-82; state senator Mass. Gen. Ct., Boston, 1983—; instr. Western New Eng. Coll., Springfield, 1978-82; Our Lady of the Elms Coll., Springfield, 1982-83. Chmn., Heart Fund Ball, Western Mass., 1983; incorporator Springfield Coll., 1982—; ex officio trustee Ella T. Grasso Found., Conn., 1982—; active Democratic State Com., Mass., 1983, Hampden County Dems. Recipient Appreciation award Vietnam Vets. of Greater Springfield, 1983; Equal Edn. for All Children award Bilingual Parents of Springfield, 1983; Appreciation award Vets.-Hampden County Council, 1984. Mem. Hampden County Bar Assn. Home: 257 Fort Pleasant Ave Springfield MA 01108-1521 Office: Mass State Senate Rm 213-b Boston MA 02133

MELESIO, KATHRYN MARY, oncological nurse, educator; b. Binghamton, N.Y., June 20, 1961; d. Frank Conrad and Mary Anne (Stazinski) Dombroski; m. James. W. Vandyke, Nov. 5, 1982 (div. Nov. 1986); 1 child, Jason; m. Faustino Soto Melesio, Apr. 25, 1987; children: Benjamin, Faustino, Andrew. RN, Ill.; cert. trauma nurse specialist, RN intravenous therapy, pediatric advanced life support, oncology cert. nurse, ACLS, RN cert. Nurse Kimberly Nurses, Long Beach, Calif., 1982-85; nurse oncology St. Therese Med. Ctr., Waukegan, Ill., 1985-86, Am. Internat., Zion, Ill., 1986-89; nurse oncology N.W. Community Hosp., Arlington Heights, Ill., 1989-90, cons. clin. nursing, 1990—; staff nurse Manpower Agy., Waukegan, Ill., 1992-95; clin. instr. McHenry C.C., Crystal Lake, Ill., 1993-96; instr. Harper Coll., Palatine, Ill., 1995—. Mem. AACN, Nat. Intravenous Nurses Soc., Ill. Intravenous Nurses Soc. (spkr. in field, pres.-elect 1995-96, pres. 1996—), Ill. Coalition Nursing Orgns. Roman Catholic. Office: NW Community Hosp 800 W Central Rd Arlington Heights IL 60005-2349

MELHISER, MYRNA RUTH, secondary education educator; b. Owensboro, Ky., Mar. 20, 1937; d. John Robert and Annie Laurie (Nicholson) Gregory; m. Robert Harold Melhiser, July 17, 1964 (wid.); 1 child, Amy Ruth. BA English, Ky. Wesleyan Coll., 1958; MA English, Western Ky. U., 1971. Cert. tchr. English, Ky. Tchr. of English Owensboro High Sch., 1958-59; tchr. music and English Daviess County Jr. High, Owensboro, 1959-62; tchr. of English Daviess County High Sch., Owensboro, 1962—, head English dept., 1983-93; organist, dir. of choirs, various chs. in Owensboro, 1954-88; interim organist First Bapt. Ch., Owensboro, 1994-95; cluster leader under KERA, Daviess County High. Pres. Owensboro Concert Assn., 1984-89, 95-96. Mem. Delta Kappa Gamma. Republican. Baptist. Home: 4520 Taylor Dr Owensboro KY 42303-1853

MELICH, DORIS S., public service worker; b. Salt Lake City, Apr. 8, 1913; d. Edward Harrison and Marie Cushing Snyder; m. Mitchell Melich, June 3, 1935; children: Tanya Marie Melich Silverman, Michael E., Nancy Lynne, Robert Allen. BA in Western History, U. Utah, 1934. Mem. Nat. Commn. Arthritis and Related Musculoskeltal Diseases, 1974-76, Nat. Arthritis Adv. Bd., 1977-84, 86-90; Utah del. Nat. Ho. of Dels. Arthritis Found., 1982-87; pres. Utah Arthritis Found. Bd., 1975-78, v.p., 1968-69, 73-74; Utah rep. Arthritis Found. Govt. Affairs, 1983—. Leader, founder 1st Girl Scouts Lone Troop U.S., Moab, Utah, 1947, regional selections com., 1958-67; active Utah Ballet Guild, Salt Lake Art Ctr., Utah Arts Coun., 1988—, Utah State Rep. Women, YWCA; trustee emeritus Arthritus Found. Recipient Pyramid award Nat. Arthritis Found., 1986, Utah Girl Scouts Regional award, 1987, Thanks Badge, 1963, Merit Honor award U. Utah Emeritus Club, 1978, Minute Man award Utah N.G., 1985; named to Nat. Women's Wall of Fame, Seneca Falls, N.Y., 1993. Mem. AAUW, Nat. Assistance League of Salt Lake City (charter mem.), Utah Women's Forum, Order Ea. Star, Alpha Delta Pi, Beta Sigma Phi (sponsor). Home: 900 Donner Way Apt 708 Salt Lake City UT 84108-2112

MELLBLOM, BARBARA LYNN, artist; b. Havre, Mont., Oct. 4, 1946; d. Howard Milton and Vanelda Elaine (Novak) M. Illustrator Volt Tech., Anaheim, Calif., 1965-70; art dir. Subia Graphics, Phoenix, 1970-80; owner Wildflower pottery, Kalispell, Mont., 1980-89, Mellblom Studios, Kalispell, 1990—; instr. Glacier Inst., Kalispell, 1993-96; bd. dirs. Hockaday Ctr. for Arts, Kalispell, Mont. Watercolor Soc.; artist-in-residence Glacier Park, Mont., 1991-94. Artist: (ltd. edit. prints) numerous images of landscapes, botanicals and wildlife. Fire marshall, investigator, Flathead Co. Fire, Kalispell, 1985-91. Recipient People's Choice awards Mont. Watercolor Soc., 1992, 94, 95. Mem. Kalispell C. of C., Rotary. Republican. Lutheran. Office: Mellblom Studios 136 1st Ave E Kalispell MT 59901

MELLERT, LUCIE ANNE, writer; b. Charleston, W.Va., June 6, 1932; d. Wilbur Conant and Grace Martin (Taylor) Frame; m. William Jennings Mellert, March 15, 1957; 1 child, James Floyd Kelly III. Student, Mason Coll. of Music Fine Arts, Charleston, 1937-49, W.Va. U., Morgantown, 1950-51. Pub. rels. exec., asst. treas., office mgr. J. H. Milam, Inc., Dunbar, W.Va., 1959-71; pub. rels. exec., office mgr. Hallcraft, Inc., Dunbar, 1972-74; office mgr. Kanawha Stone Co. Inc., Nitro, W.Va., 1975-78; freelance writer Dunbar, 1978—, Charleston, W.Va., 1978—. Beautification commr. City of Dunbar, 1969-72; activity coordinator, program dir. Dunbar Bicentennial Com., 1971; coordinator Dunbar City wide Beautification and Improvement Com., 1969-72. Mem. Nat. Fedn. Press Women, Pioneer Women's (past pres.), Women of Moose. Methodist. Home: 1604 Virginia St E Charleston WV 25311

MELLI, MARYGOLD SHIRE, law educator; b. Rhinelander, Wis., Feb. 8, 1926; d. Osborne and May (Bonnie) Shire; m. Joseph Alexander Melli, Apr. 8, 1950; children: Joseph, Sarah Bonnie, Sylvia Anne, James Alexander. BA, U. Wis., 1947, LLB, 1950. Bar: Wis. 1950. Dir. children's code revision Wis. Legis. Coun., Madison, 1950-53; exec. dir. Wis. Jud. Coun., Madison, 1955-59; asst. prof. law U. Wis., Madison, 1961-66, assoc. prof., 1966-67, prof., 1967-84; Voss-Bascom prof. U. Wis., 1985-93, emerita, 1993—; assoc. dean U. Wis., 1970-72, rsch. affiliate Inst. for Rsch. on Poverty, 1980—; mem. spl. rev. bd. Dept. Health and Social Svcs., State of Wis., Madison, 1973—. Author: (pamphlet) The Legal Status of Women in Wisconsin, 1977, (book) Wisconsin Juvenile Court Practice, 1978, rev. edit., 1983, (with others) Child Support & Alimony, 1988, The Case for Transracial Adoption, 1994; contbr. articles to profl. jours. Bd. dirs. Am. Humane Assn., 1985-95. Named one of five Outstanding Young Women in Wis., Jaycees, 1961; rsch. grantee NSF, 1983; recipient award for Outstanding Contbn. to Advancement of Women in State Bar of Wis., award for Lifelong Contbn. to Advancement of Women in the Legal Prof., 1994. Fellow Am. Acad. Matrimonial Lawyers (exec. editor jour. 1985-90); mem. Am. Law Inst. (reporter, cons. project on law of family dissolution), Internat. Soc. Family Law (v.p.), Wis. State Bar Assn. (reporter family law sect.), Nat. Conf. Bar Examiners (chmn. bd. mgrs. 1989). Democrat. Roman Catholic. Home: 2904 Waunona Way Madison WI 53713-2238 Office: U Wis Law Sch Madison WI 53706

MELLON, JOAN ANN, educator; b. Massena, N.Y., Nov. 29, 1932; d. Leo Herbert and Irene (Tyo) French; m. Donald Emmett Mellon, Aug. 24, 1963. B.A., Coll. St. Rose, 1954; M.Ed., St. Lawrence U., 1956; M.Ed., Tchrs. Coll. Columbia U. 1972, Ed.D., 1985. Tchr. math. Copenhagen Sch. Dist., N.Y., 1954-57, Massena Sch. Dist., N.Y., 1957-62; supr. student tchrs. SUNY-Albany, 1962-63; asst. prof. math SUNY-Potsdam, 1963-67; tchr. math. Long Beach Sch. Dist. (N.Y.), 1967-70; chmn. math. dept. Edgemont Sch. Dist., Scarsdale, N.Y., 1971—; instr. inservice course for elem. tchrs. SUNY-Potsdam, 1965; instr. Inst. for Jr. High Sch. Tchrs., 1966; vis. com. Middle States Assn., 1973, 76, 79. Vice grand regent Cath. Daus. Am., Norwood, N.Y., 1959, grand regent, 1960; treas. St. Lawrence Deanery of Council Cath. Women, Ogdensburg, N.Y., 1958; chmn. Jr. Cath. Daus., Norwood, 1964. Mem. Assn. Math. Tchrs. N.Y. State (exec. council 1977-78), N.Y. Assn. Math. suprs. (v.p. 1978-79), Nat. Council Tchrs. Math., Math. Assn. Am., Edgemont Tchrs. Assn. (pres.), Delta Kappa Gamma. Republican. Roman Catholic. Home: 8 Woodhaven Dr New City NY 10956-4417 Office: Edgemont High Sch White Oak Ln Scarsdale NY 10583-1712

MELLON, NANCY SCOTT, arts therapist; b. Syracuse, N.Y., Apr. 25, 1941; d. Sydney Walter and Helen Claire (Dann) Stringer. BA, Wellesley Coll., 1962; MA in Lit., CCNY, 1972; MA in Expressive Therapy, Lesley Coll., Cambridge, Mass., 1993. Cert. secondary sch. tchr., N.Y. Tchr. high sch. English, Conn., 1962-75; Waldorf educator children/adults, 1977—; dir. Story Arts, Cambridge, Mass., 1982-90; intern expressive therapy Harvard Cmty. Health Plan/New Eng. Meml. Hosp., Boston, 1991-93; dir. Hearthrose Therapy Through the Arts, Carlisle, Mass., 1993—; faculty Sch. Storytelling Emerson Coll., Sussex, U.K., 1992—; ednl. advisor tchrs., schs. 1982—; co-leader symposia Emerson Coll., 1992—; conf. presenter. Author: Storytelling and the Art of Imagination, 1992; poetry in various publs. Mem. League of New Eng. Storytellers.

MELLOR, ANNE K., English literature educator; b. Albany, N.Y., July 15, 1941; d. Austin John Tidaback and Dorothy Jane (Grannis) Gannett; m. Ronald John Mellor, June 6, 1969; 1 child, Blake. BA summa cum laude, Brown U., 1963; PhD, Columbia U., 1968. Asst. prof. Stanford (Calif.) U., 1966-73, assoc. prof., 1873-80, prof., 1980-86, Watkins U. prof., 1983-85; prof. UCLA, 1986—; cons. BBC, London, 1993, Melvin Bragg's South Bank Show, London, 1994, Discovery Channel, Washington, 1995. Author: 12 books including Blake's Human Form Divine, 1974, English Romantic Irony, 1980, Mary Shelley, 1986, Romanticism and Gender, 1993; mem. editl. bd. NC-C, ERR, NCL, Women's Studies. Recipient fellowship J.S. Guggenheim Found., 1972-73, 83-84, NEH, 1977-78, Am. Coun. for Learned Socs., 1983-84. Mem. MLA (adv. bd. publs. 1994-97, adv. bd. conf. on romanticism 1995-98). Home: 2620 Mandeville Canyon Los Angeles CA 90049

MELMAN, JOY, civic volunteer; b. St. Louis, Jan. 15, 1927; d. Simon Monroe and Esther Marion (Friedman) Werner; m. Albert Morris Melman, June 5, 1949; children: Robin Melman Feder, Kenneth, Mark. Student, Washington U., St. Louis, 1943; BS in Speech and Hearing, Emerson Coll., 1948. Cert. tchr., Mo. Tchr. Cen. Inst. for Deaf, St. Louis, 1948-50; bd. dirs. Temple Israel, St. Louis, 1974-80, Dance St. Louis, 1976—, Arts and Edn. Coun., St. Louis, 1977-90, Nat. Coun. Jewish Women, St. Louis, 1980-91, Gifted Resource Coun., St. Louis, 1983-88, KWMU Pub. Radio, St. Louis, 1980-84, bd. dirs. Jewish Community Ctrs. Assn., St. Louis, 1980-90, treas., 1986-88; v.p. St. Louis Symphony Women's Assn., 1975; adv. coun. KETC-TV pub. broadcasting, St. Louis, 1978—. Chmn. Camelot fund raiser Arts and Edn. Coun., St. Louis, 1972, 77; dir. fund raising auction PBS, 1978; adminstrv. chmn. St. Louis Bicentennial, 1974-76; Mo. chmn. Nat. Advs. for Arts, Washington, 1975-77; dir. fund raising auction PBS, 1978; chmn. Jewish Book Festival, Jewish Community Ctrs. Assn., St. Louis, 1980; couturier sale chmn. Nat. Coun. Jewish Women, St. Louis, 1982, v.p. fund raising, 1984-86; chmn. 3,000 vols. Nat. Sr. Olympics, 1987, 89; vol. chmn. vols. Jewish Hosp. Assocs., 1991; chmn. Phantom of Opera fund raiser Nat. Coun. Jewish Women, 1993; chmn. fundraiser featuring Thomas Keneally, Nat. Coun. Jewish Women, 1994; co-chair Street of Dreams Fundraiser Jewish Hosp., 1995. Named Woman of Achievement for Cmty. Svcs., St. Louis Globe-Democrat, 1984. Home: 10933 Rondelay Dr Saint Louis MO 63141-7757

MELNICK, ALICE JEAN (AJ MELNICK), counselor; b. St. Louis, Dec. 25, 1931; d. Nathan and Henrietta (Hausfater) Fisher; BJ, U. Tex., Austin, 1952; MEd, U. North Tex., 1974; m. Harold Melnick, May 24, 1953; children: Susan, Vikki, Patrice. Lic. profl. counselor. Reporter, San Antonio

Light, 1952-53; instr. journalism project Upward Bound, So. Meth. U., Dallas, 1967-71; instr. writing El Centro Dallas County Community Coll., Dallas, part time 1972-74; instr. human devel. Richland Community Coll., Dallas, part-time 1974-79; tchr. English, journalism and psychology Dallas Ind. Sch. Dist., 1969-81; counselor Ursuline Acad., 1981-94; part-time instr. human devel. Sante Fe C.C. Freelance photographer. Mem. Am. Counseling Assn., N.Mex. Counseling Assn., Assn. Humanistic Edn., Dallas Sports Car Club. Jewish. Home: 101 Monte Alto Rd Santa Fe NM 87505-8865

MELNICK, VIJAYA LAKSHMI, biology educator, research center director; b. Kerala, India; came to U.S., 1959; m. Daniel Melnick, June 28, 1963; 1 child, Anil D. BS, Madras Agriculture Coll., India, 1959; MS, U. Wis., 1961, PhD, 1964, postgrad., 1964-66. Asst. prof. dept. biology Fed. City Coll., Washington, 1970-74; assoc. prof. dept. biology U. D.C., Washington, 1974-77, prof. biology, 1977—; dir. Ctr. for Applied Rsch. and Urban Policy, Washington, 1992—; sr. staff assoc. Internat. Ctr. Inter-Disciplinary Studies in Immunology Georgetown U. Med. Sch., 1978-85, assoc. dir. tech. transfer, edn. and community outreach Ctr. Inter-Disciplinary Studies in Immunology, 1985—; sr. rsch. scholar Ctr. for Applied Rsch. and Urban Policy, Washington, 1984-85; spl. asst. policy and bioethics Nat. Inst. Aging/NIH, Bethesda, Md., 1980-82; vis. prof., rsch. participant Carnegie program Oak Ridge Grad. Sch. Biomed. Sci., U. Tenn., 1974-78; vis. scientist Biology and Medicine Inst., Lawrence Livermore Labs., U. Calif., 1972-73; invited del. cell biologist to People's Republic of China, 1990, to Initiave on Edn. Sci. & Tech. to Republic South Africa, 1995; mem. health edn. adv. com. Internat. Med. Svc. for Health, Washington; mem. Nestle Infant Formula Audit Commn., 1981-91; mem. Mayor's Adv. Bd. on Infant and Maternal Health, 1987—; del. 1st Asian-Pacific Orgn. for Cell Biology Congress, Shanghai, 1990; mem. nat. coun. on rsch. in child welfare Child Welfare League Am., Inc., 1992—; mem. adv. coun. D.C. family policy seminar Georgetown U. Grad. Pub. Policy Program, 1993—; mem. adv. com. tng. program for postdoctoral program in devel. immunology Internat. Ctr. Interdisciplinary Studies in Immunology, Georgetown U. Med. Ctr., 1993—; mem. steering com. Nat. Consortium for African Am. Children, Nat. Commn. to Prevent Infant Mortality, 1993—; host scientist Science in American Life exhibition Nat. Mus. Am. Hist. The Smithsonian Inst., 1994—. Invited del. initiative on edn., sci., and tech. to Republic of South Africa, 1995. Recipient Outstanding Svc. award March of Dimes, 1987; postdoctoral fellow U. Wis. Med. Sch., 1964-66. Mem. APHA, AAAS, Am. Soc. Cell Biology, Assn. for Women in Sci., Am. Polit. Sci. Assn., Nat. Assn. Minority Med. Educators (legis. com. 1977—), Nat. Assn. for Equal Opportunities in Higher Edn. (sci. and tech. adv. com. 1982), N.Y. Acad. Sci., Sigma Xi, Sigma Delta Epsilon. Office: U DC Ctr Applied Rsch 4200 Connecticut Ave NW Washington DC 20008-1174

MELNIKOFF, SARAH ANN, gem importer, jewelry designer; b. Chgo., Feb. 12, 1936; d. Harry E. and Marie Louise (Straub) Caylor; m. Casimir Adam Jestadt, Feb. 27, 1959 (div. Sept. 1972); 1 child, Christina Marie Jestadt-Russo; m. Sol Melnikoff, July 31, 1981. Student Gemol. Inst. Am., 1968-69, Am. Acad. Art, Chgo., 1952-56, Art Inst. Chgo., 1953, Mundelein Coll., Chgo., 1953-54. Pres., Casmira Gem, Inc., Chgo., 1963—; comml. artist, Chgo., 1957-78; owner Acorn Antiques and Uniques, Chgo. U.S. del. Internat. Colored Gemstone Dealers Assn., W.Ger., 1985; lectr., cons. in field. Mem. Chgo. Salesman's Alliance, MINK Inc., Women's Jewelry Assn., Am. Gem Trade Assn. (nat. sec. 1982-86, 88—, dir. 1988-92), Chgo. Jewelers Assn. (bd. dirs. 1994-96), Women's Jewelry Assn., Inc., Am. Horse Show Assn., Am. Saddlebred Horse Show Assn., Mid-Am. Horse Show Assn. (dir. 1980-83). Republican. Roman Catholic. Avocation: horses, antiques.

MELONE, JANIS, furniture designer; b. Bridgeport, Conn., June 21, 1955; d. Dominic and Marie (Roberts) M.; m. Lane Aubrey duPont, Sept. 8, 1979; children: Stefaan Rene, Julian Melone. Art degree, Paier Sch. Art, Hamden, Conn., 1978. Illustrator N.Y.C., 1978-83; illustrator, designer Westport, Conn., 1983-88; designer furniture Santora Melone, New Haven, 1988—. Designer: (catalog) Catalog Design Projects by The World's Leading Designer's, 1995. Recipient Best Furniture design Internat. Contemporary Furniture Fair, N.Y.C., 1993, Design 100 award Met. Home Mag., 1994. Office: Santora Melone 85 Willow St New Haven CT 06511

MELOY, SYBIL PISKUR, lawyer; b. Chgo., Dec. 1, 1939; d. Michael M. and Laura (Stevenson) Piskur; children: William S., Bradley M. BS in Chemistry with honors, U. Ill., 1961; JD, Chgo. Kent Coll. Law, 1965. Bar: Ill. 1965, Fla. 1985, D.C. 1995, U.S. Dist. Ct. (no. dist.) Ill. 1965, U.S. Supreme Ct. 1972, U.S. Ct. Appeals (fed. cir.) 1983, U.S. Dist. Ct. (so. dist.) Fla. 1985, D.C. 1995. Patent chemist, patent atty., sr. atty., internat. counsel G.D. Searle & Co., Skokie, Ill., 1961-72; regional counsel Abbott Labs., North Chicago, Ill., 1972-78; pvt.practice, Arlington Heights, Ill., 1978-79; asst. gen. counsel Alberto Culver Co., Melrose Park, Ill., 1979-83; corp. counsel Key Pharms., Inc., Miami, Fla., 1983-86; assoc. Ruden, Barnett McCloskey, Smith, Schuster and Russell, Pa., 1987-89, ptnr., 1990-91; ptnr. Foley & Lardner, Miami, Washington 1991—; adj. prof. Univ. of Miami Sch. of Law, 1986—. Recipient Abbott Presdl. award, 1977; Bur. Nat. Affairs prize, 1965; Law Rev. prize for best article. Mem. ABA, Chgo. Bar Assn. (chmn. and vice chmn. internat. and fgn. law com.), Am. Patent Law Assn., Am. Chem. Soc., Licencing Execs. Soc., Phi Beta Kappa, Phi Kappa Phi. Patentee oral contraceptive, 1965; contbr. article on fertility control and abortion laws, book rev. on arbitration to law revs. Home: 1915 Brickell Ave Apt 1108C Miami FL 33129-1736 also: 1676 32nd St NW Washington DC 20007-2960 Office: Foley & Lardner 3000 K St NW Washington DC 20007-5109

MELSON, ELOISE ANN, computer programmer analyst; b. South Bend, Ind., July 16, 1943; d. William Corley and Neteth Estelle (Nash) M. BA in Psychology, Rice U., 1965; MA in Psychology, Emory U., 1968; MPA, Pa. State U., 1980. Cert. data processor. Rsch. asst. Coop. Edn. Rsch. Labs., Inc., Chgo., 1968-69; vocat. evaluator Goodwill Industries, Chgo., 1969-70; instr./rsch. asst. Marywood Sch. of Social Work, Scranton, Pa., 1970-72; aging specialist Dept. of Aging Commonwealth of Pa., Harrisburg, 1973-85; computer programmer analyst Navy Inventory Control Point, USN, Mechanicsburg, Pa., 1985-95, Fleet Material Support Office, Mechanicsburg, Pa., 1996—; facilitator for process action teams Navy Inventory Control Point, 1993-94. Author (packets) The Elderly in Pennsylvania, 1994-95. Democrat. Unitarian. Home: 21 N 31st St Harrisburg PA 17111 Office: FMSO Code 9722 PO Box 2020 5450 Carlisle Pike Mechanicsburg PA 17055

MELSTED, MARCELLA H., retired administrative assistant, civic worker; b. Mayville, N.D., Mar. 3, 1922; d. Hans Morris and Betsy (Stenerson) Hanson; m. Alvin K. Melsted, June 6, 1965 (dec. June 1994). BS in Commerce, U. N.D., 1946, postgrad. Sec. Off. Sci. R&D, Washington, 1943-45; adminstrv. asst. Am. Embassy (Marshall Plan), Oslo, 1948-50, Paris, 1950-52; adminstrv. asst. N.D. Geol. Soc., Grand Forks, 1953-65. Co-editor: Memories of Homemakers, 1988. Pres. Borg Home Auxiliary, 1984—; apptd. cons. rep. State Plumbing Bd.; chmn. needlepointing dining room chairs N.D. Gov.'s mansion; parliamentarian N.D. Extension Homemakers, Women of Evang. Luth. Ch. Am., v.p., bd. dirs., 1985-91; mem. N.D. Humanities Coun., 1985-91; bd. dirs. Friends of N.D. Mus.; mem. Quad County Cmty. Action Bd., 1995—. Mem. AAUW (parliamentarian N.D. State divsn., 2 fellowships, author branch history, state pres. 1962-64, nat. membership com. 1964-66), N.D. State Fedn. Garden Clubs (state pres., life, tree chmn. nat. bd., state treas. 1991—), Four Seasons Garden Club (sec.-treas. 1987—), Homemakers Clubs (various coms.), China Painters Guild (various coms.). Democrat. Home: 7862 127th Ave NE Edinburg ND 58227-9604

MELTEBEKE, RENETTE, career counselor; b. Portland, Oreg., Apr. 20, 1948; d. Rene and Gretchen (Hartwig) M. BS in Sociology, Portland State U., 1970; MA in Counseling Psychology, Lewis and Clark Coll., 1985. Lic. profl. counselor, Oreg.; nat. cert. counselor. Secondary tchr. Portland Pub. Schs., 1970-80; project coord. Multi-Wash CETA, Hillsboro, Oreg., 1980-81; coop. edn. specialist Portland C.C., 1981-91; pvt. practice career counseling, owner Career Guidance Specialists, Lake Oswego, Oreg., 1988—; mem. adj. faculty Marylhurst (Oreg.) Coll., 1989-93, Portland State U., 1994—; assoc. Drake Beam Morin Inc., Portland, 1993—; career cons. Occupational Health Svcs. Corp., 1994—, Career Devel. Svcs., 1990—, Life Dimensions, Inc., 1994—. Author video Work in America, 1981. Pres. Citizens for Quality Living, Sherwood, Oreg., 1989; mem. Leadership Roundtable on Sustainability for Sherwood, 1994-95. Mem. ASTD, Assn. for Psychol. Type, Nat. Career Devel. Assn., Oreg. Career Devel. Assn. (pres. 1990), Assn. for Quality Participation, Assn. for Humanistic Psychology, Willamette Writers. Home: 890 SE Merryman St Sherwood OR 97140-9746 Office: Career Guidance Specialists 15800 Boones Ferry Rd # C104 Lake Oswego OR 97035-3456

MELTON, ELAINE WALLACE, small business owner; b. Rock Hill, S.C., June 14, 1948; d. David Dewitt Wallace and Myrtle Mae (Johnson) Threatt; m. John H. Melton, July 21, 1966 (div. 1979); children: John David, Rodney Dwayne. BS in Bus. Mgmt., Wingate Coll., 1987. Sec. Monroe (N.C.) City Schs., 1969-73; supr. Comar Mfg., Monroe, 1974-78; with Mut. Industries, Monroe, 1978—; owner, operator Melton's Acctg., Secretarial and Tax Svc., Monroe, 1978—. Walk coord. March of Dimes, Monroe, 1988—. Recipient Spl. Svcs. award March of Dimes, 1988—. Mem. Am. Inst. Profl. Bookkeepers, Federated Tax Svc., NAFE, Am. Soc. for Notary Pub., Monroe Bus. Assn. Home: PO Box 1272 Monroe NC 28111-1272

MELTON, JUNE MARIE, nursing educator; b. St. Louis, Oct. 16, 1927; d. Thomas Jasper and Alice Marie (Sloas) Hayes; m. Malcolm Adrian Essen, July 12, 1947 (dec. July 1978); children: Alison, William, Terrence, Mark, Cathleen, Melodie; m. Denver A. Melton, Sept. 6, 1989 (dec.). Grad., Jewish Hosp. Sch. Nursing, 1948; student, U. Mo., Lincoln U., U. Colo., Stephens Coll., U. S.W. RN, Mo.; nurse ARC. Instr. home nursing U. Mo., Columbia, 1948-49; acting dir. nurses, 1957-68; supr. instr., obstet. supr. Charles E. Still Hosp., Jefferson City, Mo.; supr. nurse ICU, primary nurse St. Mary's Health Ctr., Jefferson City; health dir. Algoa Correctional Instn., Jefferson City, 1979-83; home health vis. nurse A&M Home Health, Jefferson City, 1983—; mem. adv. bd. A&M Home Nursing, Jefferson City; instr. GED Lincoln U., Jefferson City; participant study of premature baby nursing U. Colo., 1964. Vol., instr. home nursing ARC, Belle-Rolla, Mo.; missionary to Togo, West Africa from mission bd. Mo. Synod, Luth. Ch., 1996—. Mem. U.S. Nurse Corps. Democrat. Lutheran. Home: 1753 Roberts St Holts Summit MO 65043 Office: A&M Home Health 1411 Southwest Blvd Jefferson City MO 65101-1503

MELTON, LYNDA GAYLE, reading specialist, educational diagnostician; b. Gatesville, Tex., Mar. 11, 1943; d. Dee and Myrtle (Dunlap) White; divorced; children: Melanie Gayle, William Matthew. BS, U. Tex., 1964; MA, U. North Tex., 1979, PhD, 1983, postgrad., 1993, 94; postgrad., Tex. Womans U., 1983. Cert. elem. tchr., spl. edn. tchr., supervision, spl. edn. supr., learning disabilities tchr., orthpedically handicapped tchr., reading specialist, Tex., adminstrs., ednl. diagnostician. Tchr. 2d and 4th grades, spl. edn. tchr. Irving (Tex.) Ind. Sch. Dist., 1964-79, tchr., 1982-83; 4th grade tchr. Northwest Ind. Sch. Dist., Justin, Tex., 1980-81; asst. prin. Grapevine-Colleyville Ind. Sch. Dist., Tex., 1983-87; tchr. reading improvement Carrollton (Tex.)-Farmers Branch Ind. Sch. Dist., 1988-89; cons. lang. arts Edn. Svc. Ctr. Region 10, Richardson, Tex., 1989-91; pvt. practice diagnostic reading and ednl. diagnostician Trophy Club, Tex., 1991—; reading clinician N.Tex. State U., Denton, 1980; instr. spl. edn. U. Tex., Dallas, 1983, U Tex., Arlington, 1988; vis. prof. Tex. Women's U., Denton, 1983, 84, 87-88. Contbr. Reading Rsch. Revisited, also revs. to Case Mgmt. Monthly Confs., Scottish Rite Hosp. and profl. jours. Mem. ASCD, Internat. Reading Assn. (North Tex. coun.), Learning Disabilities, Orton Disability Soc., Coun. for Exceptional Children, Phi Delta Kappa. Home: 30 Sonora Dr Trophy Club TX 76262 Office: 30 Sonora Trophy Club TX 76262

MELTON, MARIE FRANCES, university dean; b. Bayshore, N.Y.; d. Edward Kilgallon and Anne (Mohan) M. BS in Edn., St. John's U., Jamaica, N.Y., 1960, MS in Edn., 1975; MLS, Pratt Inst., Bklyn., 1961; EDD, St. John's U., Jamaica, N.Y., 1981. Dir. media ctr. Mater Christi High Sch., Astoria, N.Y., 1961-72; libr. sci. libr. St. John's U., Jamaica, N.Y., 1972-76, asst. dir., 1976-83, dir. Univ. Libr., 1983-89, dean Univ. Libr., 1989—. Mem., officer St. John's Prep Bd. of Trustees, Astoria, N.Y., 1980—, Holy Cross High Sch., Flushing, N.Y., 1979-89; chair Sunnyside Hist. Com., Sunnyside, N.Y., 1988-91. Mem. Am. Libr. Assn., Cath. Libr. Assn., N.Y. Libr. Assn., Council Nat. Libr. & Info. Assns. Roman Catholic. Office: St Johns Univ 8000 Utopia Pkwy Jamaica NY 11439

MELTON, MELINDA WALLACE, archaeologist, laboratory director; b. Wisconsin Rapids, Wis., Mar. 27, 1966; d. Mike Wallace and Peggy Kay (O'Brien) Maley; m. Japhy Arlo Melton, Feb. 20, 1993; children: Anna J'Nevelyn, Kathryn Allison. BA in Anthropology, U. Tex., El Paso, 1991. Archaeologist, lab. dir. Human Systems Rsch., Ft. Bliss, El Paso, Tex., 1991-94; lab dir. Archaeol. Rsch., Inc., El Paso, 1995, Ctr. de Investigationes Arqueologicas, El Paso, 1996—. Author: (monograph) (with others) Along the River's Edge, 1996. Mem. NOW, ACLU. Home: 415 W Redd Rd 6A El Paso TX 79932 Office: Ctr Investigaciones Arqeol 140 N Stevens Ste 202 El Paso TX 79905

MELTON, PATRICIA ANN, cardiovascular nurse; b. Roanoke Rapids, N.C., Sept. 14, 1936; d. Dewey Paul and Bessie Mae (Thompson) Todd; m. Q. L. Melton, Aug. 19, 1970; children: Kenneth, Cindy, Patty, Debbie, Reginia, Shannon, Quinton. Lic. vocat. nurse, Pasadena Vocat. Sch. Nursing, 1976; student, Coll. of the Mainland, 1986-89; RN, ADN, Galveston Coll. Nursing, 1989; postgrad., U. Tex., 1992—. Nurses aid, lic. vocat. nurse Pasadena (Tex.) Bayshore Hosp., 1975-78; lic. vocat. nurse UpJohn Health Svcs., Pasadena, 1978-83; lic. vocat. staff nurse Jefferson Davis Hosp., Houston, 1981-83, King Fahad Nat. Guard Hosp., Riydh, Saudi Arabia, 1983-86; lic. vocat. staff nurse cardiothoracic care unit U. Tex. Med. Br., John Sealy Hosp., 1988-89, RN staff nurse cardiothoracic care unit, 1989; RN staff nurse, nurse clinician IV in cardio ICU recovery St. Luke's Episcopal Hosp., Houston Med. Ctr., 1989; vol. to pre-natal and post-natal care nurses and drs., Saudi Arabia, 1983. Recognition for vol. svcs. Saudi Arabia N.G. and Hosp. Corp. Am., 1983. Mem. AACN (historian Galveston chpt. 1991-92, head membership com. 1992-93, mem. Houston chpt.), Tex. Student Nurses Assn. (officer 1986-89), Assn. of Nurses Endorsing Transplantation, Phi Theta Kappa, Phi Beta Lambda. Baptist.

MELTZER, E. ALYNE, educator, social worker, volunteer; b. Jersey City, May 16, 1934; d. Abraham Samuel and Fannie Ruth (Nydick) M. BA, Mich. State U., 1956. Acctg. clerk Louis Marx Co. Inc., N.Y.C., 1957-60; tchr. social studies Haverstraw H.S., N.Y., 1960-61; tchr. Sachem Ctrl. Sch. dist., Farmingville, N.Y., 1961-63, East Paterson Sch. Dist., N.J., 1964-65; case worker dept. social svc. Human Resource Adminstrn., N.Y.C., 1966-89. Policy advisor Senator Roy Goodman Adv. Com., Albany, 1987-90; social action facilitator N.C.J.W. N.Y. sect. Coun. Sr. Ctr., 1995; active Yorkville Civic Coun., 1988-93, Temple Shaaray Tefila. Recipient Sabra Soc. Plaque award State of Israel New Leadership Divsn., N.Y.C., 1979, Prime Min. Club Plaque award State of Israel Bonds, 1986-87, 96, Pin award, 1986-87, 90, 94-96. Mem. AAUW, Nat. Coun. Jewish Women (life N.Y. and Rockland County sects., bd. dirs. N.Y. sect. 1991—, sec. state and sect. 1990-93, mem. pub. affairs com. 1990—, co-chairperson Hunger Program Sunday Family Soup Kitchen 1991-93, chairperson Roosevelt Island Svcs. 1993—, mem. Israel affairs com. sect. 1991-96, Israel roundtable 1996—, participant nat. conv. 1987, 93, 96, N.E. dist. conv. 1988, Albany Inst. 1987, 88, 91, 93, Washington Inst. 1987, 89, 92, Israel Summit V 1988, Washington Mission 1991, Outstanding Vol. award 1973-74, 90-91, Donor award 1987-93, 96), Internat. Coun. Jewish Women (participant Jerusalem seminar 1991), Mich. State U. Alumni Orgn. (life, sec. N.Y. chpt. 1959-60), Am. Jewish Com., Assn. Ref. Zionists Am., Jewish Geneol. Soc., Hadassah (life), Women's League for Israel (life).

MELTZER, SUSAN DEE, retired utilities educator; b. Dayton, Ohio, July 25, 1945; d. Ralph Norman and Marian (Gurevitz) Kopelove; m. Steven Ira Lyons, Dec. 17, 1967 (div. Dec. 1971); m. Edward Meltzer Jr., June 3, 1990. BS in Elem. Edn., U. So. Calif., 1967, MS in Elem. Edn., 1968. Tchr. Santa Monica/Malibu (Calif.) Unified Sch. Dist., 1968-76, curriculum asst., 1976-79; prin. Pt. Dume ELEA.SM/M Unified Sch Dist., Malibu, 1979-80, Ctr. St. Sch., El Segundo, Calif., 1980-81; co-dir. investor svcs. program mgmt. Minoco So. Corp., L.A., 1981-82; mgr. edn. programs Met. Water Dist. So. Calif., L.A., 1983-95; mem. water edn. adv. bd. Dept. Water Resources, Sacramento, 1983-95; cons. in field. Editor: (newsletter) Splash, 1985-95, The Wave, 1989-95. Vol. Cedars Sinai Hosp., L.A., 1980-90; bd. dirs. Women's Guild, L.A., 1980-85, Jewish Family Svc. Santa Monica, 1986-90; mem. Civic Angels, L.A., 1991-92; mem. art. mus. coun. L.A. County Mus. Art, 1996—. Mem. L.A. City/County Energy & Environ. Edn. Assn., Hillcrest Country Club, Phi Delta Kappa. Jewish. Home: 2222 Avenue Of The Stars Los Angeles CA 90067-5655

MELVILLE, CATHY LOUISE, human resources specialist; b. Johnstown, Pa., May 8; d. Charles Richard and Doris Louise (Fritz) Galbraith; m. Roger Daniel Melville, Nov. 27, 1976; 1 child, Melissa Lynn. Mail clk. Johnstown (Pa.) Bank and Trust Co., 1972-73, steno-clk., sec., 1973-81; human resources clk. BT Fin. Corp., Johnstown, 1982-94, human resources officer, 1994—. Treas. West Fairfield Cemetery Assn., 1980—; reader Johnstown Radio Reader, 1993—; asst. troop leader Girl Scouts U.S., Fairfield, 1994—; asst. treas. Laurel Valley Band Parents, 1996—; elder, ch. auditor local Presbyn. ch., Sunday sch. tchr., various coms. Mem. Order Eastern Star. Presbyterian. Home: RD 1 Box 197-1 New Florence PA 15944

MELVIN, MARGARET, nurse, consultant; b. Thomasville, Ga., July 13, 1927; d. Robert and Lorene Elizabeth (Barrett) M. BS in Nursing Edn., Duke U., 1953. Cert. Occupational Health Cons. Head nurse Duke U. Med. Ctr., Durham, N.C., 1947-54; charge nurse med. clinic U. Mich. Med. Ctr., Ann Arbor, 1955-59; occupational health nurse State Farm Ins. Co., Jacksonville, Fl., 1960-65; dir. ins. edn. Baptist Hosp. Med. Ctr., Jacksonville, 1965-68; various positions Wausau Ins. Co., Orlando, Fla., 1968-80; sr. cert. occupational health cons. Wausau Ins. Co., Orlando, 1980—; lectr. various hosps. and orgns. Developed, created nat. teaching program for back problems, 1976, program for emergency care industry, 1974. Am. Cancer Soc. grantee, 1968. Mem. ANA, Am. Assn. Occupational Health Nurses, Fla. State Assn. Occupational Health Nurses (chmn. 1982, conf. sec. 1980-84), Am. Bd Occupational Health Nurses. Republican. Home: 610 Cranes Way Apt 301 Altamonte Springs FL 32701-7781

MELZER, ALICE, artist, educator; b. Queens, N.Y., July 29, 1950. BA, SUNY, Old Westbury, 1973; MS in Art Edn., Pratt Inst., 1975. Permanent cert. K-12 art edn., N.Y. Tchr. art Brentwood (N.Y.) Pub. Schs., 1980-81, Lindenhurst (N.Y.) Pub. Schs., 1987-88; tchr. photography and woodworking Riverdale Country Sch., Bronx, N.Y., 1985-87; instr. art continuing edn. program Hofstra U., Hempstead, N.Y., 1993—, Bklyn. Coll., CUNY, 1996—; instr. art edn. program Freeport (N.Y.) Arts Coun., 1994; instr. fine art and crafts Homestead Home for Aged, Queens, 1973, 92d Street YM-YWHA, Bklyn., 1973, Bedford Avenue YM-YWHA, Bklyn., 1974, Stein Sr. Ctr., N.Y.C., 1978-79. One-woman shows SUNY Old Westbury, Oyster Bay, 1973, Amityville (N.Y.) Pub. Libr., 1973-74, South Shore Paddle Ball Club, Oceanside, N.Y., 1983, West Hills Day Camp, Huntington, N.Y., 1989, Uniondale (N.Y.) Pub. Libr., 1994-95; exhibited in group shows Pratt Inst., Bklyn., 1973, Clinton Hill Artists, Bklyn., 1975, Salmagundi Club, N.Y.C., 1977-78, Valsamis Gallery, Bklyn., 1979, Dey Mansion, N.J., 1980, Pub. Image Gallery, N.Y.C., 1983, 85, Henry Hicks Gallery, Ltd., Bklyn., 1984, A.I.R. Gallery, N.Y.C., 1991, Nassau County, Rockville Centre, N.Y., 1992, Planting Fields Arboretum, Old Westbury, 1992; murals executed in fitness center, nightclub and pvt. homes; contbr. poems to Forever and a Day, 1996. Mem. L.I. Arts Coun., 1994—. Recipient award for involvement L.I. chpt. Am. Soc. Mag. Photographers, 1989, award of excellence in photography Photographer's Forum mag. Mem. Coll. Art Assn.

MENAKER, SHIRLEY ANN LASCH, psychology educator, academic administrator; b. Jersey City, July 22, 1935; d. Frederick Carl and Mary Elizabeth (Thrall) Lasch; m. Michael Menaker, June 4, 1955; children: Ellen Margaret, Nicholas. BA in English Lit., Swarthmore Coll., 1956; MA, Boston U., 1961, PhD in Clin. Psychology, 1965. Adminstrv. asst. N.J. State Fedn. Dist. Bds. Edn., Trenton, 1956-59; trainee clin. psychology Mass. Mental Health Ctr., Boston, 1960-61; intern clin. psychology Thom Guidance Clinic for Children, Boston, 1961-62; research assoc. ednl. psychology U. Tex.-Austin, 1964-67, asst. prof. ednl. psychology, 1967-70. assoc. prof., 1970-79, assoc. dean grad. sch., 1975-77, psychology cons. Research and Devel. Ctr. for Tchr. Edn., 1965-67, faculty investigator, 1967-74; assoc. prof. counseling psychology U. Oreg., Eugene, 1979-85, prof., 1985-87 , assoc. dean grad. sch., 1979-84, acting dean grad. sch., 1980-81, 82-83, dean grad sch., 1984-87; assoc. provost for acad. support, prof. gen. faculty, U. Va., Charlottesville, 1987—. Bd. dirs. Nat. Grad. Record Exam. Bd. and Policy Council-Test of English as Fgn. Lang., Ednl. Testing Services, 1984-88. Contbr. articles to profl. jours. NIMH fellow, 1963-64. Office: U Va Adminstrn Madison Hall Charlottesville VA 22906-9014

MENARD, EDITH, English language educator, artist, poet, actress; b. Washington, Dec. 5, 1919; d. Willis Monroe and Edith Berncenia (Gill) M. BS summa cum laude, Miner Tchrs. Coll., Washington, 1940; MA in English, Howard U., 1942; postgrad., NYU, 1944-46; MA in Teaching English, Columbia U., 1952; postgrad. in edn., George Washington U., 1966-79, 89-92, doctoral candidate, 1992—. Instr. English and speech Howard U., Washington, 1946-53; high sch. tchr. English D.C. Pub. Schs., Washington, 1953-73; chmn. dept. English Woodrow Wilson High Sch., Washington, 1972-73; adj. asst. prof. English fundamentals U. D.C., 1988-90; founder, dir. Miss Menard's Exclusive English Tutorial Svc., 1991—; substitute tchr. D.C. and Montgomery County (Md.) pub. schs. Contbr. articles and poetry to various publs., including At Day's End, 1994. Reader poetry to civic orgns.; vol. Washington Nat. Cathedral Assn., 1993—. Recipient Golden Poet award World of Poetry, 1988, Silver Poet award, 1989, Editor's Choice award The Nat. Libr. of Poetry, 1994; Julius Rosenwald fellow Yale U., 1943-44. Mem. Internat. Soc. Poets (Disting. mem. 1995, Merit award 1995), Smithsonian Assocs. Episcopalian. Home: Ste 916 6101 16th St NW Washington DC 20011-1766

MENDELSOHN, NAOMI, biomedical pharmaceutical consultant. BA, NYU; MA, Boston U.; PhD, CUNY, 1975. Fellow Meml. Sloan-Kettering Cancer Ctr., N.Y.C., 1975-78; asst. prof. Mt. Sinai Med. Ctr., N.Y.C., 1978-82; assoc. sci. dir. Sterling Drug, Inc. Internat., N.Y.C., 1982-91; dir. product devel. Innapharma, Inc., 1992-96; adjunct asst. prof. Mt. Sinai Med. Ctr., 1982—. NSF fellow, 1969, NIH fellow 1975-78. Mem. AAAS, Am. Chem. Soc., Am. Soc. Hematology, Fedn. Am. Socs. Exptl. Biology (edn1. affairs com. 1989—), Am. Heart Assn., N.Y. Acad. Scis. (women sci. com., planning com. 1983-85), Drug Info. Assn., Fgn. Policy Assn., Licensing Exec. Soc. Office: 322 W 57th St New York NY 10019-3701

MENDELSON, SUSAN GAIL, school counselor; b. Cleve., Jan. 7, 1949; d. Edward J. and Corinne (Deutsch) Coen; m. S. Robert Mendelson, June 25, 1972. BA, Carleton Coll., 1971; MEd, U. Pitts., 1974, MSW, 1983. Cert. secondary sch. guidance. Tchr. psychology Cleveland Heights H.S., Cleve., 1971-72, Penn Hills H.S., Pitts., 1972-86; sch. counselor Peters Twp. H.S., McMurray, Pa., 1986—; alumni admissions rep. Carleton Coll., 1971—. Co-author: Social Networks and Mental Health, 1985. Named Pa. H.S. Counselor of Yr., 1996; Univ. scholar U. Pitts., 1984. Mem. Nat. Assn. for Coll. Admission Counseling, Pa. Sch. Counselors Assn. (mem. sch./coll. rels. com., Pa. Counselor of Yr. 1996), Pa. Assn. Secondary Sch. and Coll. Admission Counselors, Washington Greene County Counselors Assn. (sec., past pres.). Office: Peters Twp H S 264 E McMurray Rd McMurray PA 15317

MENDER, MONA SIEGLER, writer, music educator; b. Jersey City, May 24, 1926; d. George and Freda (Steierman) Siegler; m. Irving M. Mender, Aug. 25, 1946; children: Donald Matthew, Judith J. BA, Mt. Holyoke Coll., 1947. Instr. piano and music theory, Fair Lawn, N.J., 1947-75; state edn. chmn. N.J. Symphony Orch., Newark, 1980-82, state chmn. bd. regents, 1983-84, bd. dirs., 1983-91. Author: Music Manuscript Preparation: A Concise Guide, 1991. Recipient Women's Network commendation Sen. Bill Bradley, 1984. Mem. Mountain Ridge Country Club (West Caldwell, N.J.), Plantation Golf and Country Club (Venice, Fla.).

MENDEZ, C. BEATRIZ, obstetrician, gynecologist; b. Guatemala, Apr. 21, 1952; d. Jose and Olga (Sobalvarro) M.; m. Mark Parshall, Dec. 12, 1986. BS in Biology and Psychology, Pa. State U., 1974; MD, Milton Hershey Coll. Medicine, 1979. Diplomate Am. Bd. Ob-gyn. Resident in ob-gyn. George Washington U., Washington, 1979-83; pvt. practice Santa Fe, 1985-95, Locum Tenens, 1996—; vol. physician Women's Health Svcs., Santa Fe, 1995—; chair perinatal com. St. Vincent's Hosp., Santa Fe, 1986-89, quality assurance mem., 1986—, chief ob-gyn., 1992-94; bd. dirs. Milton S. Hershey Coll. Medicine, Hershey, Pa., 1977-82. Vol. Women's Health Svcs., Santa Fe, 1985—. With USPHS, 1983-85. Mosby scholar Mosby-Hersey Med. Sch., Hershey, 1979. Fellow Am. Coll. Ob-Gyn. (Continuing Med. Edn.

award 1986—); mem. AMA (Physician Recognition award 1986—), Am. Assn. Gynecol. Laparascopists, Internat. Soc. Gynecol. Endoscopy, Am. Fertility Soc., Am. Soc. Colposcopy and Cervical Pathology, N.Mex. Med. Soc., Santa Fe Med. Soc., Residents Assn. George Washington U. (co-founder 1981-83). Democrat.

MENDEZ, OLGA A., state legislator; b. Mayaguez, P.R.. BA, U. P.R.; MEd, Columbia U., 1960; PhD in Ednl. Psychology, Yeshiva U., N.Y.C., 1975. Previously assoc. prof. SUNY-Stony Brook, research psychologist Albert Einstein Coll. Med., N.Y.C., dep. commr. N.Y.C. Agy. for Child Devel.; mem. from dist. 28 N.Y. Senate, 1978—; del. Dem. Nat. Conv., 1980, leadership position, 1984—, sec. minority conf., 1992—, chairperson conf. Home: 1215 5th Ave Apt 15D New York NY 10029-5211 Office: N Y State Senate State Capitol Rm 420 Albany NY 12224*

MENDIOLA, ANNA MARIA G., mathematics educator; b. Laredo, Tex., Dec. 21, 1948; d. Alberto and Aurora (Benavides) Gonzalez; m. Alfonso Mendiola Jr., Aug. 11, 1973; children: Alfonso, Alberto. AA, Laredo C.C., Tex., 1967; BA, Tex. Woman's U., 1969, MS, 1974. Tchr. math. Laredo Ind. Sch. Dist., 1969-81; math instr. Laredo C.C., 1981—, organizer Jaime Escalante program, 1991-92; tech. prep. com. mem., 1991-92; ednl. coun., sec. Christen Mid. Campus, 1992-94; mem. site based campus com. Martin H.S., 1994—; vis. instr. St. Augustine Sch., Laredo, 1987-88; evaluator So. Assn., Corpus Christi, 1981, So. Assn. Colls. and Schs., United H.S., 1991; juror Higher Edn. Coord. Bd. Report, San Antonio, 1989; mem. quality improvement coun. Laredo C.C., 1993-94, mem. instrn. coun.; participant SC3 Calculus Reform Inst., NSF, 1996. Producer slide promo, Mathematics at LCC, 1983. V.p., bd. dirs. Our Lady of Guadalupe Sch., Laredo, 1988-91; sec. Laredo C.C. Faculty Senate, 1986-87, v.p., 1995-96, pres., 1996—; active Boy Scouts Am., 1985-86. Recipient Teaching Excellence award NISOD, 1993. Mem. AAUW (pres. 1979-81, v.p. 1987-89, scholarship chair 1993-94, membership chair 1994—), Am. Math. Assn. Two-Yr. Colls., Math. Assn. Am., Tex. State Tchrs. Assn., Tex. C.C. Tchrs. Assn., Tex. Woman's U. Alumnae Assn., Blessed Sacrament Altar Soc., Tex. Assn. Ch. Higher Edn., Delta Kappa Gamma (membership chair 1993—). Democrat. Roman Catholic. Office: Laredo CC West End Washington St Laredo TX 78040

MENDIUS, PATRICIA DODD WINTER, editor, educator, writer; b. Davenport, Iowa, July 9, 1924; d. Otho Edward and Helen Rose (Dodd) Winter; m. John Richard Mendius, June 19, 1947; children: Richard, Catherine M. Graber, Louise, Karen M. Chooljian. BA cum laude, UCLA, 1946; MA cum laude, U. N.Mex., 1966. Cert. secondary edn. tchr., Calif., N.Mex. English teaching asst. UCLA, 1946-47; English tchr. Marlborough Sch. for Girls, L.A., 1947-50, Aztec (N.Mex.) High Sch., 1953-55, Farmington (N.Mex.) High Sch., 1955-63; chair English dept. Los Alamos (N.Mex.) High Sch., 1963-86; sr. technical writer, editor Los Alamos Nat. Lab., 1987—; adj. prof. English, U. N.Mex., Los Alamos, 1970-72, Albuquerque, 1982-85; English cons. S.W. Regional Coll. Bd., Austin, Tex., 1975—; writer, editor, cons. advanced placement English test devel. com. Nat. Coll. Bd., 1982-86, reader, 1982-86, project equality cons., 1985-88; book selection cons. Scholastic mag., 1980-82. Author: Preparing for the Advanced Placement English Exams, 1975; editor Los Alamos Arts Coun. bull., 1986-91. Chair Los Alamos Art in Pub. Places Bd., 1987-92; chair adv. bd. trustees U. N.Mex., Los Alamos, 1987-93; pres. Los Alamos Concert Assn., 1972-73, 95—; chair Los Alamos Mesa Pub. Libr. Bd., 1990-94, chair endowment com., 1995—. Mem. Soc. Tech. Communicators, AAUW (pres. 1961-63, state bd. dirs. 1959-63, Los Alamos coordinating coun. 1992-93, pres. 1993-94), DAR, Order Ea. Star, Mortar Bd., Phi Beta Kappa (pres. Los Alamos chpt. 1969-72, v.p. 1996-97), Phi Kappa Phi, Delta Kappa Gamma, Gamma Phi Beta. Home: 124 Rover Blvd Los Alamos NM 87544-3634 Office: Los Alamos Nat Lab Diamond Dr Los Alamos NM 87544

MENDONCA, ROSE MARY, secondary school educator; b. Lowell, Mass., Oct. 17, 1971; d. Anacleto and Nizalda (Silva) M. BA in English, U. Mass., 1993, BA in Spanish, 1993, MEd, 1994. Cert. English tchr., ESL tchr., Mass. Rsch. asst., site coord. TEAMS Project, Amherst, Mass., 1993; ESL grade 6 & 8 tchr. Holyoke-Lynch (Mass.) Middle Sch., 1994-95; lang. arts tchr. grade 7 Benjamin Banneker Acad., Bklyn., 1995—; tchg. asst. U. Mass. Sch. Edn., 1993-95; faculty advisor Comet Coffee Shop, Bklyn., 1995—; editor-in-chief Sch. Parent Newsletter, Bklyn., 1995—; pres. Lighthouse Learning, Woodhaven, N.Y., 1995—. Commonwealth scholar, 1989, 93. Mem. Phi Beta Kappa. Office: Benjamin Banneker Acad 77 Clinton Ave Brooklyn NY 11238

MENDOZA, JOANN AUDILET, nurse; b. Beaumont, Tex., Sept. 15, 1943; d. Jack Ernest and Ottie (Craig) Audilet; m. M.A. Mendoza, June 2, 1971; children: Danny Russell Myers, Shawna Laurene Rosco. BSN magna cum laude, Lamar U., Beaumont, 1989. RN, Tex.; CEN; cert. ACLS, advanced burn life support, BTLS instr.-coord., instr. truama nurses core course, PALS instr.-coord., emergency nurse pediatric course coord., ACLS course dir. Vocat. nurse Stat Care Inc., Beaumont; lic. vocat. nurse Jefferson County Jail Infirmary, Beaumont, Bapt. Hosp., Beaumont; emergency rm. charge nurse Columbia Beaumont Med. Ctr., Beaumont; Mem. Coun. Workplace Issues Dist. and State. Mem. ANA, Tex. Nurses Assn. (pres. Dist. 12), Lamar U. Student Nurse Assn. (sec.), Internat. Honor Soc. Nurses, Emergency Nurses Assn., Sigma Theta Tau (program com.), Phi Kappa Phi. Baptist. Home: RR 5 Box 23 Beaumont TX 77713-9673 Office: Beaumont Regional Med Ctr 3680 College St Beaumont TX 77701-4616

MENDOZA, RUTH, art educator; b. San Antonio, Nov. 17, 1941; d. Rudy Aleman and Lucy (Lopez) Hernandez. BS, Howard Payne U., 1965; M of Liberal Arts, So. Meth. U., Dallas, 1981. Cert. tchr., Tex. Tchr. Woodsboro (Tex.) Ind. Sch. Dist., 1966-69, Corpus Christi (Tex.) Ind. Sch. Dist., 1970-73, Grand Prairie (Tex.) Ind. Sch. Dist., 1974—; cons. State Textbook Com., Grand Prairie, 1988. Mem. com. First Bapt. Ladies Ministry, Grand Prairie, 1992-95; translator The Master's Builders, Grand Prairie, 1990—. Recipient Hon. Life membership Tex. Congress of Parents and Tchrs., 1979. Mem. AAUW, Nat. Mus. Women in Arts, Tex. PTA, Dallas Mus. Art.

MENES, PAULINE H., state legislator; b. N.Y.C., July 16, 1924; d. Arthur B. and Hannah H. Herskowitz; m. Melvin Menes, Sept. 1, 1946; children: Sandra Jill Menes Ashe, Robin Joy Menes Elvord, Bambi Lynn Menes Gavin. BA in Bus. Econs. and Geography, Hunter Coll., N.Y.C., 1945. Economist Quartermaster Gen. Office, Washington, 1945-47; geographer Army Map Service, Washington, 1949-50; chief clk. Prince George's County Election Bd., Upper Marlboro, Md., 1963; substitute tchr. Prince George's County H.S.s, Md., 1965-66; mem. Md. Ho. of Dels., Annapolis, 1966—, mem. judiciary com., 1979—, mem. com. on rules and exec. nominations, 1979-94, 95—, chmn. spl. com. on drug and alcohol abuse, 1986—, chmn. Prince George's County del., 1993-95, parliamentarian, 1995—. Mem. Md. Arts Coun., Balt., 1968-95, Md. Commn. on Aging, Balt., 1975-95; bd. dirs. Prisoner's Aid Assn., Balt., 1971-94. Recipient Internat. Task Force award Women's Yr., 1977; named to Hall of Fame Hunter Coll. Alumni Assn., 1986, Women's Hall of Fame Prince George County, 1989. Mem. NOW, Nat. Conf. State Legislators (com. on drugs and alcohol 1987), Md. NOW (Ann London Scott Meml. award for legis. excellence 1976), Nat. Order Women Legislators (pres. 1979-80), Women's Polit. Caucus, Bus. and Profl. Women. Home: 3517 Marlbrough Way College Park MD 20740-3925 Office: Md Ho of Reps Rm 210 Lowe State Office Bldg Annapolis MD 21401

MENFI, DEBBIE, advertising executive. Sr. v.p. media dir. Deutsch Inc., N.Y.C. Office: Deutsch/Dworin 215 Park Ave S New York NY 10003-1603*

MENGES, PAMELA ANN, aerospace engineer, consultant; b. Northport, Mich.; d. Raymond Alfred and Margaret Carolyn (St. Amand) M. BS in Biomathematics, Thomas More Coll., 1985; PhD in Aerospace Engring., Union Inst., Cin., 1995. Teaching asst. in physics Am. U. Paris, 1982-83; intern sci. writing Behringer-Crawford, Covington, Ky., 1984; specialist overseas prodn. GE, Evendale, Ohio, 1984; dir. project svcs., rsch. engineer, mgr. intern ops. Ray A. Menges and Assocs. (formerly RAM Assocs. Inc.), Cin., 1984-92; pres., CEO Elysium Sys., Inc. (formerly Menges Consulting, Inc.), Cin., 1992—; postdoctoral rsch. asso. nonproliferation/internat. security NIS-8, Los Alamos (N.Mex.) Nat. Lab., mem, 1995—; prin. investigator/project mgr. Nat. Air Intelligence Ctr., Wright-Patterson AFB, Ohio, 1996—. Mem. AIAA (flight testing tech. com. assoc.), Am. Def. Preparedness Assn., Am. Phys. Soc., Exptl. Aircraft Assn. Office: Elysium Sys Inc PO Box 395 Los Alamos NM 87544-0395

MENIO, DIANE AMELIA, elderly rights advocate; b. Bethlehem, Pa., July 12, 1955; d. Peter and Sylvia Marie (Kincade) M.; m. Mark Joseph Garvin, Aug. 26, 1989; 1 child, Madi Elizabeth Garvin. BA, Kutztown U., 1977; MS, St. Joseph's U., 1994. Coord. aftercare Northampton County Mental Health, Bethlehem, Pa., 1977-85; cmty. svcs. coord. Nat. Multiple Sclerosis Soc., Phila., 1986-89; from asst. dir. to exec. dir. Coalition of Advocates for the Rights of the Infirm Elderly, Phila., 1989—. Democrat. Office: CARIE 1315 Walnut St Ste 1000 Philadelphia PA 19107

MENKEN, JANE AVA, demographer, educator; b. Phila., Nov. 29, 1939; d. Isaac Nathan and Rose Ida (Sarvetnick) Golubitsky; m. Matthew Menken, 1960 (div. 1985); children: Kenneth Lloyd, Kathryn Lee; m. Richard Jessor, Nov. 13, 1992. A.B., U. Pa., 1960; M.S., Harvard U., 1962; Ph.D., Princeton U., 1975. Asst. in biostats. Harvard U. Sch. Pub. Health, Boston, 1962-64; math. statistician NIMH, Bethesda, Md., 1964-66; research assoc. dept. biostats., Columbia U., N.Y.C., 1966-69; mem. research staff Office of Population Research Princeton U., N.J., 1969-71, 75-87, asst. dir., 1978-86, assoc. dir., 1986-87, prof. sociology, 1980-82, prof. sociology and pub. affairs, 1982-87; prof. sociology and demography U. Pa., Phila., 1987—, UPS Found. prof. social scis., 1987—, dir. Population Studies Ctr., 1989-95; mem. social scis. and population study sect., NIH, Bethesda, Md., 1978-82, chmn., 1980-82, population adv. com. Rockefeller Found., N.Y.C., 1981-93, com. on population and demography, NAS, Washington, 1978-83, com. on population, 1983-85, com. nat. stats., 1983-89, com. on AIDS research, 1987-94, co-chair panel data and rsch. priorities for arresting AIDS in sub-Saharan Africa, 1994—, Commn. on Behavioral and Social Scis. and Edn., 1991—, sci. adv. com., Demographic and Health Surveys, Columbia, Md., 1985-90, Nat. Adv. Child Health and Human Devel. Council, 1988-91; cons. Internat. Centre for Diarrhoeal Disease Research, Bangladesh, Dhaka, 1984—. Author: (with Mindel C. Sheps) Mathematical Models of Conception and Birth, 1973; editor: (with Henri Leridon) Natural Fertility, 1979, (with Frank Furstenberg, Jr. and Richard Lincoln) Teenage Sexuality, Pregnancy and Childbearing, 1981, World Population and U.S. Policy: The Choices Ahead, 1986; contbr. articles to profl. jours. Bd. dirs. Alan Guttmacher Inst., N.Y.C., 1981-90, 93—. Nat. Merit scholar, 1957; John Simon Guggenheim Found. fellow, 1992-93, Ctr. for Advanced Study in Behavioral Scis. fellow, 1995-96. Fellow AAAS, Am. Statis. Assn.; mem. NAS, Am. Acad. Arts and Scis., Population Assn. Am. (Mindel Sheps award 1982, pres. 1985), Am. Pub. Health Assn. (Mortimer Spiegelman award 1975, program devel. bd. 1984-87), Am. Sociol. Assn., Soc. for Study of Social Biology, Internat. Union for Sci. Study of Population (coun. 1989—), Sociol. Research Assn. (exec. com. 1991—). Office: U Pa Population Studies Ctr 3718 Locust Walk Philadelphia PA 19104-6298

MENNA, CHRISTINE ANN, public relations executive; b. Johnstown, Pa., Dec. 4, 1955; d. Joseph and Cecilia (Wojnaroski) Pisczek; m. Thomas Menna, Oct. 20, 1984; 1 child, Elizabeth. BA in Journalism, U. Pitts., 1977. Copywriter, account exec. Accent-Midstate Advt., Johnstown, Pa., 1977-85; mgr. corporate comm. Crown Am. Realty Trust, Johnstown, 1985—, dir. corp. comm., 1995—; pub. rels. cons. Johnstown Chiefs, 1990—. Mem. adv. bd. Salvation Army, Johnstown, 1989—; bd. dirs. United Way, Johnstown, 1993—. Mem. Nat. Orgn. Underwater Instrs. (open water I diver), Internat. Coun. Shopping Ctrs. Office: Crown Am Realty Trust Pasquerilla Plz Johnstown PA 15901

MENNES, MARIE MABEL, elementary education educator, artist; b. Miami, Fla., June 9, 1959; d. Elmer J. and Marie S. (Scollin) Frischholz; m. John J. Mennes, Mar. 19, 1988; 1 child, Douglas. BFA, Barry U., 1982; MS in Art Edn., Fla. Internat. U., 1986, EdS, 1992. Cert. K-12 art tchr., ednl. leadership, Fla. Tchr. art Dade County Pub. Schs., Miami, 1983—; adj. prof. art edn. Barry U., Miami, 1989-93, 96; curriculum trainer Very Spl. Arts, Ohio, 1995; elem. art edn. curriculum cons. SRA/McGraw-Hill, Washington, 1996, contbg. writer, Ohio, 1996. Exhibited in group shows Valencia C.C., Orlando, Fla., 1995 (purchase award), Amos Eno Gallery, N.Y.C., 1995, Bianca Lanza Gallery, Miami Beach, Fla., 1995, Galeria Mesa, Ariz., 1995 (Body of Work award 1995), Ft. Lauderdale Mus. Art, 1992, 96. Motivator grantee Magnet Ednl. Choice Assn., 1995. Mem. Nat. Art Edn. Assn., Fla. Art Edn. Assn. (Elem. Art Educator of Yr. award 1995), Dade Art Educators Assn. (treas. 1990-94). Democrat. Roman Catholic. Office: Charles R Drew Elem Sch 1775 NW 60th St Miami FL 33142

MENNINGER, ROSEMARY JEANETTA, art educator, writer; b. N.Y.C., Feb. 2, 1948; d. Karl Augustus and Jeanetta (Lyle) M. BA, Washburn U., 1983, BFA, 1984. Cert. tchr., Kans. Rsch. specialist, grant writer Navajo Tribe Navajo Community Coll., Many Farms, Ariz., 1969, 71; adminstrv. asst., counselor San Francisco Drug Treatment Program, 1972-73; exec. dir. Inst. Applied Ecology, San Francisco, 1973-80; coord. Calif. Community Gardening program Gov.'s Office State of Calif., Sacramento, 1976-80; editor Whole Earth Catalogs and CoEvolution Quar., Sausilito, Calif., 1973-80; editor, rsch. specialist Dept. Agr. Scis. Colo. State U., Ft. Collins, 1981-82; instr. Mulvane Art Ctr., Topeka, 1982-86, 90—; art tchr. Topeka Pub. Schs., 1985—. Author: Community Gardening in California, 1977; editor: (newspaper) California Green, 1977 80; contbr. articles to profl. jours. Mem. San Francisco Parks and Recreation Open Space Commn., 1975-78; mem. master plan task force Calif. State Fair, Sacramento, 1978-80; commr. Gov.'s Commn. on Children and Families, Topeka, 1988-89; bd. dirs. The Villages, Inc., 1989—. Democrat. Presbyterian. Home: 1819 SW Westwood Cir Topeka KS 66604-3269

MENTLIK, GAIL, filmmaker; b. Toronto, Dec. 30, 1960; d. Joseph Abraham and Hilda Fanny (Rosenthal) M. BA, Ryerson U., 1989; MA, SUNY, Buffalo, 1997. Freelance film editor Toronto, 1990-92; filmmaking instr. SUNY, Buffalo, 1992-94, Rochester (N.Y.) Inst. Tech., 1994-95; film/video programmer Hallwalls Contemporary Arts Ctr., Buffalo, 1996—; on-air prodr., co-host Sta. CKLN 88.1 FM, Toronto, 1990-92. Filmmaker: Glimpses of My Mother, 1992, Migraine, 1990. Mem. Canadian Filmmakers Distbn. Ctr. (bd. dirs., treas. 1991-93), Squeaky Wheel. Home: 557 Richmond Ave # 3 Buffalo NY 14222 Office: Hallwalls Contemporary Arts Ctr 2495 Main St Ste 425 Buffalo NY 14214

MENTON, TANYA LIA, lawyer, educator; b. Chgo., Sept. 13, 1964; d. Joseph Bernard and Rosalind Marie (Macey) M. BA magna cum laude, Northwestern U., 1986, JD, 1989. Bar: Calif. 1989, N.Y. 1993. Atty. O'Melveny and Myers, L.A., 1989-91, Townley and Updike, N.Y.C., 1991-96; gen. atty. Capital Cities/ABC, N.Y.C., 1996—; adj. prof. Mercy Coll., Dobbs Ferry, N.Y., 1993—; lectr. on sexual harassment various orgns. including Def. Rsch. Inst. programs, N.Y.C., 1995-96. Editor: (legal publ.) California Employment Law Letter, 1989-91. Nat. Harry S. Truman scholar, 1982-86. Mem. ABA, Calif. Bar Assn. (labor and employment sect.), N.Y. State Bar Assn. (labor and employment sect.). Democrat. Home: # 17P 301 E 79th St New York NY 10021 Office: Capital Cities/ABC 77 W 66th St New York NY 10023

MENTZER, MERLEEN MAE, adult education educator; b. Kingsley, Iowa, July 25, 1920; d. John David and Maggie Marie (Simonsen) Moritz; m. Lee Arnold Mentzer, June 1, 1944. Student Westman Coll., 1939, Wayne State U., Nebr., 1942, Bemidji State U., 1950, Mankato Coll., 1978, U. Minn.-St. Paul, 1979. Lic. health and life ins., Minn. Tchr., Kingsley, Iowa, 1938-41; owner, mgr. Mentzer's Sundries, Hackensack, Minn., 1946-76, House of Mentzers, Pine River, Minn., 1974-77; instr. Hennepin Tech., Eden Prairie, Minn., 1978—; owner, mgr. Cass Co. Minn. Real Estate, 1993—; mem. score evaluation bd. Small Bus. Assn. Loans, 1993—; sales rep. in annuity and insurance investment; counselor Sr. Citizen Orgn. Ret. Execs.-Via of Mpls. C. of C. Coord. motivational program (with others) Five Steps to the Best Years of Your Life, 1991, Five Steps to Success, Attitudes Are Everything. Mem. Mpls. C. of C., Hackensack C. of C., (v.p. 1970-76), Northern Lights Federated Woman's Club (pres. 1958-59). Republican. Lutheran. Avocations: dancing, bowling, reading, theatre, seminars. Home and Office: 6781 Tartan Curve Eden Prairie MN 55346-3354

MENZA, CLAUDIA MARCELLA, literary agent; b. N.Y.C., June 11, 1947; d. John Gaetano and Antonina (di Lorenzo) M.; m. James R. Forker, May 29, 1971 (div. 1980); m. Charles Anthony Frye, Dec. 16, 1989 (dec. Oct. 1994). BA, Oberlin Coll., 1969. Asst. editor Evergreen Rev., N.Y.C., 1969-73; gen. editor, prodn. mgr. Grove Press, Inc., N.Y.C., 1973-83; sr. editor Art Dir. News, N.Y.C., 1983-85; pres. Claudia Menza Lit. Agy., N.Y.C., 1983—; cons. Riverrun Press, N.Y.C., 1983—; guest lectr. Tex. A&M U., Prairie View, Tex., 1986, NYU, N.Y.C., 1986, 87; cons., panelist Nat. Civil Rights Mus. Conf. "The Power of the Word", Memphis, 1995. Author: (book of poetry) Cage of Wild Cries, 1990, (book of poetry and monologues) The Lunatics Ball, 1994; contbr. author: (anthology) The Dream Book: An Anthology of Writing by Italian-American Women, 1985 (Am. Book award 1985). Working mem. Congress of Racial Equality, Hempstead, N.Y., 1961, Student Nonviolent Coord. Com., Oberlin, Ohio, 1965, Students for Dem. Soc., Oberlin, 1965, The West Village Com., N.Y.C., 1980. Mem. PEN, Italian-Am. Writers Assn., Assn. Authors Reps. Office: Claudia Menza Lit Agy Rm 807 1170 Broadway New York NY 10001

MERCER, DEBRA OWENS, principal; b. Pensacola, Fla., Dec. 25, 1952; d. E.M. Owens; m. Harry Mercer, May 3, 1975; 1 child, Catherine. AS, Pensacola Jr. Coll., 1972; BM, William Carey Coll., Hattiesburg, Miss., 1974, MM, 1979; student, We. Ky. U., Bowling Green, 1986, U. Louisville, 1987. Cert. tchr., adminstr., Ky. Tchr. Hattiesburg Schs., 1974-80, Jefferson County Pub. Schs., Louisville, 1981-89; counselor Kenton County Schs., Taylor Mill, Ky., 1989-93; asst. prin. Beechwood Ind. Schs., Ft. Mitchell, Ky., 1993-95; prin. Eminence H.S., Ft. Mitchell, Ky., 1995—; assessment coord.; presenter in field. Recipient Outstanding Staff award Jefferson County Pub. Schs., 1988. Mem. Nat. Assn. Secondary Sch. Prins., Ky. Assn. Sch. Adminstrs., Ky. Assn. Secondary Sch. Prins., Ky. Assn. Assessment Coords. Democrat. Episcopalian. Office: Beechwood HS 54 Beechwood Rd Covington KY 41017-2716

MERCER, LAURA A., public relations executive; b. St. Petersburg, Fla., July 8, 1959. BA in Journalism, U. N.C., 1980. Reporter Wilmington (N.C.) Star News, 1980-84; staff writer Barclays American, Charlotte, N.C., 1984-88; acct. exec. Price/McNabb, Charlotte, 1988-89, sr. acct. exec., 1989-92, account supr., v.p., 1990-92, sr. v.p., dir. pub. rels., 1992—. Mem. Pub. Rels. Soc. Am., U. N.C. Journalism Sch. Found. Office: Price/McNabb Corp 100 N Tryon St Charlotte NC 28202*

MERCER, MARGARET TEELE, medical andfilm industry marketing executive; b. Bronxville, N.Y., Sept. 10, 1962; d. William Earl Jr. and Judith (Forster) M.; m. Robert Mitchell Fromcheck, May 23, 1993. BS, U. Colo., 1985. Assoc. product mgr. Prescription Products divsn. Fisons Pharms., Denver, 1988-92; mktg. mgr. HealthScan Products, Cedar Grove, N.J., 1992-93; account exec. Sandler Comm., N.Y.C., 1993-94; mktg. dir. Proctor Cos., Littleton, Colo., 1995—. Youth leader Calvary Ch., Denver, 1988-91. Mem. NAFE, Healthcare Bus. Assn. Home: 2 Rose Clover Littleton CO 80127-2220

MERCHANT, CAROL BROOKS, stockbroker; b. Granville, N.Y., July 18, 1942; d. Maynard T. and Dorothy E. (Roberts) Brooks; m. James E. West; children: James E. Jr., Brett R.; m.Alfred M. Merchant, May 4, 1985; 1 stepchild, Alfred J. AS, Endicott Coll., Beverly, Mass., 1962. V.p., co-founder TV Data, Inc., Glens Falls, N.Y., 1969-78; stockbroker E. F. Hutton, Glens Falls, 1981-87; stockbroker Shearson Lehman Hutton, Glens Falls, Saratoga Springs, N.Y., 1987-90; stockbroker Paine Webber, Glens Falls, 1990—. Bd. trustees Presbyn. Ch., Glens Falls, 1979-81; bd. dirs., pres. Glens Falls Home, 1990—; bd. dirs., co-chair Adirondack chpt. ARC, Glens Falls, 1991—; bd. dirs. Chapman Mus., 1995—. Republican. Presbyterian. Home: 51 Horicon Ave Glens Falls NY 12801 Office: PaineWebber 1 Broad St Plaza Glens Falls NY 12801

MERCHANT, NATALIE, musician, singer, popular; b. Jamestown, N.Y., Oct. 26, 1963; d. Tony and Ann Merchant. Lead singer band 10,000 Maniacs, 1981-1993; solo artist, 1993—. Albums with 10,000 Maniacs include Human Conflict Number Five, 1982, Secrets of the I Ching, 1983, The Wishing Chair, 1986, In My Tribe, 1987, Blind Man's Zoo, 1989, Hope Chest, 1990, Our Time in Eden, 1992, 10,000 Maniacs MTV Unplugged, 1993; solo album Tigerlilly, 1995. Office: Elektra Records 75 Rockefeller Plz New York NY 10019*

MERCHEY, RUTH ANN, artist, designer; b. Bell, Calif., Feb. 26, 1947; d. Charles Wesley and Esther (Rogers) Lester; m. Morton Donald Merchey, Aug. 19, 1971 (div. Sept. 1991); children: Jason Aaron, Kelly Leigh. BA, Woodbury U., L.A., 1971; postgrad., UCLA, 1972-73. Designer Regal Rugs, Inc., Beverly Hills, Calif., 1968-75; designer, artist Ruth Merchey Designs, Downey, Calif., 1975-90; artist, builder Ruth Merchey Designs, Big Bear City, Calif., 1990—; owner R&S Designs, Downey, 1980-91. Author: (play) 12 Steps for 12 and Under, 1988 (spl. recognition award 1989); exhibited in group shows L.A. County Fair, 1978 (Best of Show), Valley Art Guild, Encino, Calif., 1989, 90 (1st place 1989, Best of Show award 1990), Costa Mesa Art Guild, 1991, San Bernardino County Art Mus., Redlands, Calif., 1991. Fundraiser L.A. County Med. Assn. Aux., Downey, 1975-80, City of Hope, Downey; officer Downey Elem. Sch., Downey Mid. Sch., Downey High Sch., 1979—; chmn. election campaign Downey Unified Sch. Bd., 196-88; cons., vol. S.E. Coun. on Alcohol Abuse, Downey, 1986-89, Polonaise Ball, Beverly Hills, Calif., 1985—. Recipient hon. award City of Hope, 1976, 80, 84. Mem. Redlands Art Assn., Taos Art Assn., Fine Arts Inst., Bear Valley Art Assn. Republican.

MERCHLEWITZ, ANN ELIZABETH, lawyer; b. Decatur, Ill., Oct. 31, 1958; d. Thomas Lee and Joyce Ann (Hofman) Burford; m. Mark Anthony Merchlewitz, Aug. 20, 1983; children: Daniel Thomas, Emily Ann, Frank John. BA summa cum laude, Ill. Coll., Jacksonville, 1980; JD, U. Notre Dame Law Sch., Notre Dame, 1983; MA, Saint Mary's U. Minn., Winona, 1996. Staff atty. Southern Minn. Reg. Legal Svcs., Winona, Minn., 1983-84; asst. county atty. Winona County Attys. Ofc., 1984-92; spec. counsel to pres. Saint Mary's Coll. of Minn., 1992-96, v.p., gen. counsel, 1996—; mem. Physician Recruitment Task Force, Winona, 1994—, Task Force on Violence Against Women, 1996—; facilitator Winona Bus. Edn. Partnership, Winona, 1994—. Chairperson Winona Area Cath. Schs. Bd., Winona, 1992-94; v.p. Winona County Hist. Soc., 1994-96; chair, bd. dirs. Cath. Charities, Diocese of Winona, 1993—; bd. dirs. Paul Watkins Meml. Meth. Home, Winona, 1996—. Recipient Outstanding Woman of Law and Govt. Winona YWCA, 1989. Mem. Winona County Bar Assn., (v.p. 1994), Minn. Planned Giving Coun., Nat. Assn. of Coll. and Univ. Attorneys, Phi Beta Kappa. Roman Catholic. Office: St Marys U of Minn 700 Terrace Hts # 30 Winona MN 55987

MERCOUN, DAWN DENISE, manufacturing company executive; b. Passaic, N.J., June 1, 1950; d. William S. and Irene F. (Micci) M. BS in Bus. Mgmt., Fairleigh Dickinson U., 1978. Personnel payroll coordinator Bentex Mills, Inc., East Rutherford, N.J., 1969-72; employment mgr. Inwood Knitting Mills, Clifton, N.J., 1972-75; gen. mgr. Consol. Advance, Inc., Passaic, 1975-76; v.p. human resources Gemini Industries, Inc., Clifton, 1976—; v.p., bd. dirs. Contact Morris-Passaic. Mem. Soc. for Human Resource Mgmt., Am. Compensation Assn., Internat. Found. Employee Benefits, Earthwatch Rsch. Team, IMA Mgmt. Assn. (bd. dirs., trustee 1996—), Daus. of the Nile (Maalas Temple No. 20, elective officer 1993-96, queen 1996—). Republican. Office: 179 Entin Rd Clifton NJ 07014-1424

MEREDITH, ALICE FOLEY, publisher, consultant; b. Roslindale, Mass., Jan. 1, 1941; d. Francis Gerard and Alice Elizabeth (Hayes) Foley; m. Ellis Edson Meredith; children: Candace Marie Rodal, Scott Corcoran; stepchildren: Shane Meredith Snowdon, Scott Emery, Kent Williamson. Grad., Boston Sch. Bus. Edn., 1960. Exec. sec., adminstrv. asst. various firms, 1960-68; asst. to pres. Am. Apparel Mfrs. Assn., Arlington, Va., 1968-77; pres. ACS Assocs., Bethesda, Md., 1972—; pres., treas. Newsletters, Inc., Bethesda, 1986—, also bd. dirs.; pres., treas. Food Execs. Internat. Found., Bethesda, 1988—, also bd. dirs.; asst. treas. Am. Apparel Polit. Action Com., Fairfax, Va., 1973-78; treas. Orgn. Mgmt., Inc., Washington, 1973—, also bd. dirs.; pres. Polit. Action, Inc., Fairfax, 1976-89; treas. Allied Realty Corp., Bethesda, 1978-85. Gen. mgr., treas. Apparel Polit. Edn. Com., Fairfax, 1976-78. Roman Catholic.

MEREDITH, KAREN ANN, accountant, financial executive; b. San Antonio, Sept. 30, 1954; d. Carroll J. and Doris J. (Calvin) Keller; m. William F. Meredith, July 6, 1974; children: Brian, Matthew. BBA in Acctg., U. North Tex., 1979. CPA, Tex.; CFP. Sr. acct. Deloitte Haskins & Sells, Dallas, 1979-82; CFO, sr. v.p. Commerce Savs. Assn., Dallas, 1982-86; exec. dir., chmn. bd. Am. Assn. Boomers, Irving, Tex., 1989-95; mng. ptnr. Meredith & Assocs., Irving, 1986—. Author various ednl. programs, 1991. Bd. dirs. Generations Found., N.Y.C., 1992. Recipient Fin. Edn. and Awareness award H.D. Vest Fin. Svcs., 1990. Mem. AICPA, Tex. Soc. CPAs (mem. Dallas chpt.), Internat. Assn. CFPs. Office: Meredith & Assocs 2621 W Airport Fwy Ste 101 Irving TX 75062-6069

MERGENOVICH, SHIRLEY ANN, educator; b. Clinchco, Va., July 13, 1938; d. Floyd Fuller and Cara Mae (Deel) Fuller; m. Carl Mullins (div. 1963); children: Roger Dean, Rex Dale; m. Peter Mergenovich, May 1, 1971 (dec.). AA, Community Coll. St. Louis, 1973; BA in History summa cum laude, Maryville Coll., St. Louis, 1975; MEd in Adminstrn., U. Mo., 1980; cert. in small bus. mgmt., C.C. St. Louis, 1989. Cert. lifetime secondary prin. and tchr. Sales Libson Shops, St. Louis, 1960-61; inventory control and customer svc. Precision Auto Components Co., St. Louis, 1961-64; exec.sec. Precision Auto/TRW, St. Louis, 1964-65; city clk. City of Ballwin (Mo.), 1965-66; exec. dir. Charter Rev. Commn., St. Louis County, Mo., 1966-67; adminstrv. asst. Planning Dir. of St. Louis County, 1968-69; asst. econ. researcher Reg. Ind. Devel. Co., Clayton, Mo., 1969-70; tchr. Eastern history and culture N.W. R-1 Sch. Dist., House Springs, Mo., 1975-90; founder/dir. adult edn. prog. Jefferson Coll. R-1 Schs., House Springs, 1985-86; founder, prin. cons. Performance Builders, St. Louis, 1989; mem. adj. faculty C.C. St. Louis, Webster U., Maryville U., St. Louis; dir. adult continuing edn. Jefferson Coll., 1985-86; part-time mgmt. cons., 1970-79; designer, facilitator numerous tng. programs; designer, implementor pilot study for tchrs. on tchg. and learning styles in pub. schs. Author: A Statistical Summary of Vocational Technical Programs in St. Louis Metro Area, 1970; co-author: Analysis and Projection of Manpower Requirements in St. Louis Metro Area, 1970, Discipline Handbook, 1978; contbr. articles to profl. jours. Tchr. Sunday sch. Ballwin Bapt. Ch.; active Mentoring Women in Transition, Working with Execs. and Mgrs. Out of Work. Named Woman Entrepreneur, Small Bus. Adminstrn., 1989, others; Fulbrightscholar Korea on quality exch. tchr. program, 1982. Mem. NEA, ASTD (bd. dirs., v.p. 1984-88, editor/pub. Torch newsletter 1984-88), Am. Soc. Quality Control, Mo. Cmty. Edn. Assn. (bd. dirs. 1979-81), St. Louis Woman's Commerce Assn. (mem. gov.'s adv. coun. on vocat. edn. 1968-70), N.W. St. Louis Hons. Assn., Woman Entrepreneurial Alumnae Assn.

MERIDITH, SANDRA LEE, administrator; b. Waco, Tex., July 13, 1943; d. Bobby Wendell and Elizabeth A. (Hudson) S.; m. Frederick VanCleve Meridith, Aug. 19, 1963 (div. 1971); children: Alice Chalista Meridith Freeman, Emily Elizabeth Meridith Henderson. BS, U. North Tex., 1965; MS, Baylor U., 1976; cert. mid-mgmt., East Tex. State U., 1982. Cert. mid-mgmt., supr., spl. edn. supr., early childhood mentally retarded, kindergarten, elem. Elem. tchr. Terrell (Tex.) Ind. Sch. Dist., 1965-66; kindergarten tchr. Waco (Tex.) Ind. Sch. Dist., 1973-75; elem. tchr. Plano (Tex.) Ind. Sch. Dist., 1975-78, curriculum specialist, 1978-80, elem. prin., 1980-82, elem. pers. dir., 1982-85, dir. elem. adminstr., 1985-90, exec. dir. elem. adminstr., 1990—. Bd. dirs. Plano Sports Authority, Jr. League, Plano, 1988-90, Am. Liver Found., Dallas, 1989-91, By Invitation Only, Dallas, 1986-94. Mem. Plano Metro Rotary Club (bd. dirs.), Tex. Assn. Elem. Prins., Phi Delta Kappa, Alpha Delta Kappa, Delta Kappa Gamma. Methodist. Home: 812 Oakway Ct Richardson TX 75081-5115 Office: Plano Ind Sch Dist Plano TX 75075

MERINI, RAFIKA, foreign language and literature and women's studies educator; b. Fès, Morocco; came to U.S., 1972; d. Mohamed and Fatima (Chraibi) M. BA in English cum laude, U. Utah, 1978, MA in Romance Langs. and Lits., 1981; postgrad., U. Wash., 1980-82; cert. in translation, SUNY, Binghamton, 1988, PhD in Comparative Lit., 1992. Teaching asst. U. Utah, Salt Lake City, 1978-80, U. Wash., Seattle, 1980-82; adminstrv. asst., tchr. French, interpreter The Lang. Sch., Seattle, 1982-83; lectr. Pacific Luth. U., Tacoma, Wash., 1983; instr. Fort Steilacoom C.C. (now Pierre C.C.), 1983-85; teaching asst. dept. romance langs. SUNY, Binghamton, 1985-87, teaching asst. women's studies dept., 1988, teaching asst. comparative lit. dept., 1986-88; vis. instr. Union Coll., Schenectady, N.Y., 1988-89; vis. instr. dept. fgn. langs. and lits. Skidmore Coll., Saratoga Springs, N.Y., 1989-90; assoc. prof. dept. fgn. langs. State U. Coll., Buffalo, 1990—; coord. Women's Studies Interdisciplinary unit State U. Coll., Buffalo, 1993—, adviser French Club, 1990-93; mem. French Circle, Buffalo, 1990—. Contbr. articles to profl. pubs.; presenter at seminars, workshops, confs. Grantee Nat. Defense Student Award. Mem. MLA, Nat. Women's Studies Assn., Am. Assn. Tchrs. French, Conseil Internat. d'Etudes Francophones, Pi Delta Phi, Soc. Hon. Française, Kappa Theta (hon.). Home: PO Box 1063 Buffalo NY 14213-7063 Office: State Univ Coll-Buffalo Dept Fgn Langs 1300 Elmwood Ave Buffalo NY 14222-1095

MERITT, YVONNE EDELL, public health nurse; b. Enid, Okla., Apr. 28, 1954; d. Raymon Alfred and Jewell Frances (Lancaster/Turner) Haymaker; m. Kay Lee Meritt, Aug. 31, 1973; children: Kristen, Nickolas (dec.). Diploma, St. Anthony's Hosp., 1976; BSN, So. Nazarene U., 1994. Cert. cmty. health nurse, ANA. Staff nurse Bapt. Med. Ctr., Oklahoma City, 1976-78; supr. Bethany (Okla.) Gen. Hosp., 1978-85; staff nurse South Cmty. Hosp., Oklahoma City, 1986-88, Mercy Med. Ctr., Oklahoma City, 1985-88; pub. health nurse Canadian County Health Dept., Yukon, Okla., 1988-94; dist. nursing supr. Okla. Dept. Health, Oklahoma City, 1994—; mem. adv. bd. Canadian Valley Vocat. Tech., El Reno, Okla., 1990, Okla. State U. Extension, El Reno, 1992. Mem. Nat. Assn. Pediat. Nurse Assocs. and Practitioners (cert. pediat. nurse), Okla. Nurses Assn. (nominating com. 1994), Okla. Grange (state sec. 1993—), St. Anthony's Sch. Nursing Alumni Assn. (treas. 1993-95, dir. 1995—). Roman Catholic. Home: Rt 1 Box 254-D Union City OK 73090 Office: Okla Dept Health PO Box 53551 1000 NE 10th St Oklahoma City OK 73152

MERK, ELIZABETH THOLE, sales representative; b. Salt Lake City, July 29, 1950; d. John Bernard and Emily Josephine T.; 1 child, William Lance Ulich; m. J. Eliot Merk, July 26, 1996. BA, U. Hawaii, Hilo, 1984, paralegal cert. cum laude, 1989; postgrad.in bus. adminstrn., U. Hawaii, Manoa, 1985-86. Lic. ins. agt. Hawaii. Regional rep. Lightolier, Inc., Salt Lake City, 1978-80; group sales rep. FHP/Utah, Salt Lake City, 1980-81; health net rep. Blue Cross Corp., L.A., 1981-82; v.p. fin. Bus. Support Systems, Hilo, 1983-89; rep. Prudential Ins. and Fin. Svcs., Honolulu, 1989—; registered rep. Pruco Securities Corp. subs. Ins. & Fin. Svcs., 1989—. Docent Lyman House, 1984-85, L.A. County Mus. of Art, 1980-81, S.L.C. Art Mus., 1970-80; bd. dirs. YWCA, Hawaii Island, 1980-91, 1st v.p., 1988. Recipient Nat. Quality award 1991, 92, 93, 94, Nat. Sales Achievement award 1992, 93; named YWCA Vol. of Yr., 1991. Fellow Life Underwriters Tng. Coun.; mem. AAUW (fundraiser chair Kona chpt. 1992, bd. dirs. Hilo chpt. 1987-89, comty. area rep. 1989), Am. Bus. Women's Assn. (past pres. Nani O Hilo chpt. 1995-96, mem. chair 1996-97, cmty. svc. chair 1993-95, membership chair 1996—, audit com. chair Kanoelani chpt. 1992, program chair Hilo chpt. 1985, expansion com. Hilo Lehua chpt. 1985, Steven Bufton grantee 1985, ways and means com. 1984, memberships chair Lehua chpt. 1983), Nat. Assn. Life Underwriters (legis. rep. West Hawaii 1989—), Million Dollar Round Table (qualifying mem. 1992, 93, 94, 95). Roman Catholic.

MERKLE, HELEN LOUISE, chef; b. Carrington, N.D., May 23, 1950; d. Orville F. and Lillian M. (Argue) M. BS, N.D. State U., 1972. Asst. dir. food mgmt. Stouffer's Atlanta Inn, Atlanta, 1972-74; dir. food mgmt. Stouffer's Indpls. Inn, 1974-78; adminstrv. dir. food mgmt. Stouffer's Riverfront Towers, St. Louis, 1978-80; food mgmt. cons. Fraser Mgmt., Westlake, Ohio, 1980-83; exec. chef Marriott Hotel, Cleve., 1983-89; exec. chef Snavely Mgmt. Svcs, 1989-95, Catering Chef Westfield Cos., 1995—. Recipient First Place award for soups Taste of Indpls., 1976. Mem. NAFE, Am. Culinary Fedn., Am. Culinary Fedn. (cert. exec. chef, sec. Cleve. chpt. 1989-92, Pres.'s award 1992, treas. 1993, 94, first v.p. 1995, 96, named Chpt. Chef of the Yr., 1993). Democrat. Lutheran. Home: 4137 W 160th St Cleveland OH 44135-4349 Office: Westfield Cos PO Box 5001 One Park Cir Westfield Center OH 44251-5001

MERLING, STEPHANIE CAROLINE, speech and language pathologist; b. Whiteville, N.C., June 2, 1948; d. Ellis Garland and Lois Jayne (Rice) Osborne; m. Paul David Merling, Oct. 18, 1969; children: Paul David, Jr., Jeremy Daniel. BS Speech-Lang. Pathology/Audiology, Andrews U., 1988; MA in Speech-Lang. Pathology, We. Mich. U., 1989. Adminstrv. sec. Andrews U., Berrien Springs, Mich., 1982-89; speech-lang. pathologist Dowagiac (Mich.) Union Schs., 1989-92, South Bend (Ind.) Comm. Sch. Corp., 1993—. Pottery registrar and vol. Madaba Plains Archaeol. Inst., Andrews U., excavations in Amman, Jordan, 1984, 91, 93, 96. Recipient Nat. AMBUCS scholarship Am. Businessmen's Assn., 1988, 89, Nat. Collegiate Speech and Hearing Pathology award U.S. Achievement Acad., 1988, Computer-based Telecom. in Elem. Classroom grant Ind. Dept. Edn., 1995. Mem. Am. Speech-Lang.-Hearing Assn. (cert.), Ind. Speech-Lang.-Hearing Assn. Home: 2036 N US Highway 31 Niles MI 49120-1162 Office: South Bend Community Sch 635 S Main St South Bend IN 46601-2223

MERLIS, ANNETTE FAYE, artist; b. Omaha, Nebr., Sept. 20, 1925; d. Isadore and Gertrude (Gold) Forbes; m. Sidney Merlis, Aug. 11, 1946; children: Gale B. Tauberer, Michael H., Laurence M. BS in Journalism, Creighton U., 1947; postgrad., New Sch. Group exhbns. include: Roads Gallery, N.Y.C., 1975, Parrish Art Mus., Southampton, N.Y., 1976, Northport Galleries, N.Y., 1980, Gallery Three, Sayville, N.Y., 1986, Anthony Giordano Gallery, Oakdale, N.Y., 1988, Elaine Benson Gallery, Bridgehampton, N.Y., 1990, Islip (N.Y.) Art Mus., 1993, 95, various others; solo exhbts. include: Mallette Gallery, Garden City, N.Y., 1974, Northport Galleries, 1984, Port Washington (N.Y.) Libr., 1996; represented in permanent collection Islip (N.Y.) Art Mus.

MERMELSTEIN, ISABEL MAE ROSENBERG, senior citizen consultant; b. Houston, Aug. 20, 1934; d. Joe Hyman and Sylvia (Lincove) Rosenberg; m. Robert Jay Mermelstein, Sept. 6, 1953 (div. July 1975); children: William, Linda, Jody. Student U. Ariz., 1952, Mich. State U., 1974, Lansing (Mich.) C.C., 1975. Exec. dir. Shiawassee County YWCA, Owosso, Mich., 1975-78; real estate developer F&S Devel. Corp., Lansing, Mich., 1978-79, Corum Devel. Corp., Houston, 1979-81; adminstrv. fin. planner, sr. citizen cons. Investec Asset Mgmt. Group, Inc.; owner Ins. Filing Svcs. Sr. Citizens, 1985-96; guardian VA, 1990—. Author: For You! I Killed the Chicken, 1972. Mem. Older Women's League, Houston, 1st Ecumenical Council of Lansing, Nat. Mus. Women in Arts, Judaica Mus., Houston, Mus. Fine Arts, Houston, Mus. Natural Sci., Houston; docent Holocaust Mus., Houston; mem. African-Jewish Dialogue Group, Houston. Recipient State of Mich. Flag, 1972, Key to City, City of Lansing, 1972-73. Mem. Nat. Assn. Claims Assistance Profls., Internat. Women's Pilot Orgn. (The 99's), Jewish Geneal. Soc., Internat. Directorate Disting. Leadership. Republican. Jewish. Lodges: Zonta, Licoma, B'nai B'rith, Hadassah, Nat. Fedn. Temple Sisterhoods. Flew All Women's Transcontinental Air Race (Powder Puff Derby), 1972, 73. Avocations: flying, gourmet cooking, needlepoint, knitting, snow skiing. Home: 4030 Newshire Dr Houston TX 77025-3921

MERNALYN, actress, writer, producer; b. Detroit, July 23; d. Irwin and Myldred (Kolb) Hamburger. GPA with highest honors, Northwood of Mich. Profl. internat. model, freelance fashion cons.; creator, producer for pvt. Clubs Art Deco Fashion Shows; former fashion commentator Radio Luxembourg; nat. spokesperson GM; internat. spokesperson Jaguar; concierge L'Ermitage Hotel Group; customer cons. Tiffany & Co., Beverly Hills; pub. rels. Bunny Playboy Club Internat.; radio personality various USA stas.; creator, pres. PillowTalk Ltd., U.K. and U.S. Producer, writer, narrator nationally syndicated radio shows In a Word Mood, BabyTalk, The Children's Corner, FlashBack, The Veneration Generation, Today's Woman, Movie Moments; recurring role ABC-TV primetime sitcom New World Television, others; frequent guest nat. TV and radio talkshows; author: My Book, two volumes Philosophy/Humanity, contbg. author poetry anthology to profl. journals; dir. creator, instr. of Improving Quality of Humanity and Personal Certitude Classes; Shakespearean lead actress The Globe Theatre, American debut, A Yorkshire Tragedy, Much Ado About Nothing, Twelfth Night, Taming of the Shrew, Man of La Mancha, and many others. Active Am. Lung Assn., Friends of Animals. Named the Most Perfect Girl, Miss Budweiser Anheuser-Busch, Miss Internat. MG Brit. Leyland Eng.-USA. Mem. Screen Actors Guild, Am. Film Inst., Museum of the City of New York, Los Angeles County Museum of Art, Northwood of Mich. Alumni Assn., Art Deco Soc. N.Y. and L.A., Smithsonian.

MERRICK, BEVERLY CHILDERS, journalism, communications educator; b. Troy, Kans., Nov. 20, 1944; d. Horace Buchanan Merrick and Vola Yolantha (Clausen) Maul; m. John Douglas Childers, July 10, 1963; children: John Kevin, Pamela Christine, Jessica Faye. BA in Journalism with honors, Marshall U., 1980, BA in English with honors, 1980, M Journalism, 1982; M Creative Writing, Ohio U., 1986, cert. in Women's Studies, 1984, PhD in Comm. with honors, 1989. Reporter, photographer Ashland (Ky.) Daily Ind., 1981; tchr., instr. Albuquerque Pub. Schs., 1986-89; gen. assignment reporter, photographer Rio Rancho (N.Mex.) Observer, 1986; editor, rsch. cons. Ins. Pub. Law, Sch. of Law U. N.Mex., Albuquerque, 1990; asst. prof. Ga. So. U., Statesboro, 1991-94; assoc. prof. dept. mass comm. U. S.D., Vermillion, 1994-95; asst. prof. dept. journalism and mass comm. N. Mex. State U., Las Cruces, 1995—; part-time tchr., tchg. assoc. Ohio U., Athens, 1981-84; part-time copy editor Albuquerque Tribune, 1991; vis. prof. East Carolina U., Greenville, N.C., 1989-90; adj. prof. Embry-Riddle U., Kirtland AFB, N.Mex., 1989, 91; organizer diversity conf., 1st amendment conf. Ga. So. U.; mem. session MIT, 1989. Author: (poetry) Navigating the Platte, 1986, Pearls for the Casting, 1987, Closing the Gate, 1993; contbr. poems to profl. publs., jours. and chpts. to books. Pub. rels. liaison Nat. Convention Bus. and Profl. Women, Albuquerque, 1988; pres. Albuquerque Bus. and Profl. Women, 1986-87, Rio Rancho Civic Assn., 1987-89, So. Ohio Improvement League, 1973-76; pres. bd. dirs. Pine Creek Conservancy Dist., 1976-83. Named Outstanding Citizen, N.Mex. Legislature, Truly Fine Citizen of Ohio, Ohio Gen. Assembly, 1973, Outstanding Homemaker of Ohio, Gov. of Ohio, 1974; grantee Reader's Digest, 1980, 83; John Houk Meml. grantee W.Va. Women's Conf., 1982; fellow Nat. Women's Studies Inst., Lilly Found., 1983, Freedom Forum Ethics, 1995, Am. Newspaper Inst., 1996; E.W. Scripps scholar, 1984; recipient Silver Clover award 4-H, Writing award Aviation/Space Writers Assn., 1981, 1st place open rsch competition Nat. Assn. Women's Dean's, Adminstrs. and Counselors, 1990; rsch. grantee N.Mex. State U., 1996. Mem. Soc. Profl. Journalists, Assn. for Edn. in Journalism and Mass Comm. (mem. nat. convention com. 1993-94, vice head mag. divsn. 1995-96, head mag. divsn., 1996-97), N.Mex. State Poetry Soc. (pres. 1987-89), Sigma Tau Delta. Office: N Mex State U Dept 3J Box 30001 Las Cruces NM 88003-8001

MERRICK, DOROTHY SUSAN, interior designer; b. N.Y.C.. BA, Skidmore Coll.; MA, Adelphi U. Owner, pres. Dorothy Merrick Interiors Ltd., Sands Point, N.Y., 1968—. Project published in Newsday, N.Y. Times, House Mag. Recipient Gold Archi award Nassau/Suffolk AIA, 1986. Mem. Internat. Interior Designers Assn., Am. Soc. Interior Designers, Allied Bd. of Trade, Knickerbocker Yacht Club.

MERRILL, JEAN FAIRBANKS, writer; b. Rochester, N.Y., Jan. 27, 1923; d. Earl Dwight and Elsie (Fairbanks) M. B.A., Allegheny Coll., 1944; M.A., Wellesley Coll., 1945. Feature editor Scholastic Mags., 1947-50; editor Lit. Cavalcade, 1956-57; publs. div. Bank St. Coll. Edn., 1964-65. Children's books include Henry, the Hand-Painted Mouse, 1951, The Woover, 1952, Boxes, 1953, The Tree House of Jimmy Domino, 1955, The Travels of Marco, 1956, A Song for Gar, 1957, The Very Nice Things, 1959, Blue's Broken Heart, 1960, Shan's Lucky Knife (Jr. Lit. Guild selection), Emily Emerson's Moon, 1960 (Jr. Lit. Guild selection), The Superlative Horse (Jr. Lit. Guild selection), 1961 (Lewis Carroll Shelf award 1963), Tell About the Cowbarn, Daddy, 1963, The Pushcart War (Lewis Carroll Shelf award), 1964 (Boys Club Am. Jr. Book award), High, Wide & Handsome, 1964 (Jr. Lit. Guild selection), The Elephant Who Liked to Smash Small Cars, 1967, Red Riding, 1968, The Black Sheep, 1969, Here I Come—Ready or Not!, 1970, Mary, Come Running, 1970, How Many Kids are Hiding on My Block?, 1970, Please, Don't Eat My Cabin, 1971, The Toothpaste Millionaire (Dorothy Canfield Fisher Meml. award 1975-76), 1972 (Sequoyah award 1977), The Second Greatest Clown in the World, 1972, The Jackpot, 1972, The Bumper Sticker Book, 1973, Maria's House, 1974, The Girl Who Loved Caterpillars, 1992; poetry books edited include A Few Flies and I, 1969; libretto for chamber opera Mary Come Running, 1983. Fulbright fellow India, 1952-53. Mem. N. Am. Mycol. Assn., Authors League, Vt. Arts. Coun., War Resisters League, Vt. Inst. Natural Sci., Dramatists Guild, Vt. Nat. Resources Coun., Vt. League Writers, Soc. Children's Book Writers, Fulbright Assn., Sierra Club, Audobon Soc., Phi Beta Kappa.

MERRILL, JUDITH ROBIN, artist; b. Ann Arbor, Mich., Mar. 9, 1924; d. Charles Jerome and Cornelia Charlotte (Boutell) M.; m. Paul W. Pencke, Jan. 30, 1943 (div. 1965); children: Michael D., Laura C., Liza, William B. Student, Conservatory Art, Ft. Lauderdale, Fla., 1938-41, Am. Acad. Art, Chgo., 1941-42, Moore Coll. Art, Phila., 1976, 77,78. Office mgr. R.H. Bolster, MD, Paoli, Pa., 1963-68; head order dept., staff artist Betsy Ross Co., Paoli, 1968-76; office mgr. M.P. Erdman, AIA, Haverford, Pa., 1980-91; charter mem. Port Deposit (Md.) Arts Coun., 1994-95; judge Nat. Vets. Art Festival, Coatesville, Pa., 1995; assoc. mem. Women's Art Mus., Washington. One-person shows at Lippincott Gallery, Phoenixville, Pa., 1990, Artworks, Kennett Square, Pa., 1990, Montgomery Sch., Chester Springs, Pa., 1991, Cecil County Arts Coun., Elkton, Md., 1992, North St. Studio, Elkton, 1993, Picture Show, Havre de Grace, Md., 1994; exhibited in group shows at Sketch Club, Phila., Woodmere Art Mus., Chestnut Hill, Pa., Am. Coll., Bryn Mawr, Pa., Brandywine Nursing Sch. Invitational, Coatesville, Pa., Poldi Hirsch Meml. Nat. Show, Havre De Grace, Md., Pa. State, Delaware Campus, Media, Pa., Immaculata Coll. Ann. Art Show, Frazer, Pa., Chester County Invitational Show, West Chester, Pa., Phila. Country Club, Gladwyne, Pa., Norbertine Abbey Spring Show, Paoli, Pa., Yellow Springs Ann. Art Show, Chester Springs, Pa., Cassatt Mansion Ann. Art Show, Berwyn, Pa., Birchrun Gallery, Birchrunville, Pa., The Studio, Swarthmore, Pa., Cabrini Coll. Invitational Show, Radnor, Pa., Moore Coll. Art, Phila., Fleisher Gallery, Miami Beach, Fla. Mem. Cecil County Arts Coun., 1992-95, Del. Art Mus., 1995, Woodmere Art Mus., 1991-95. Recipient 2nd prize oils Impressions XII Am. Coll., Bryn Mawr, Pa., 1993, Best in Show award St. Citizens Show, Elkton, Md., 1993, 1st and 2nd prizes Chestertown (Md.) Art League, 1995, 2nd prize oils 5th Nat. Juried Exhbn., Havre de Grace, Md., 1995, 2nd prize Chester County Art Assn. spring show, 1994, 95, Best in Show award Md., You are Beautiful, 1993. Mem. Chester County Art Assn., Woodmere Art Mus., Cecil County Arts Coun., Coun. Del. Artists. Home: 594 Liberty Grove Rd Port Deposit MD 21904

MERRILL, MARTHA, instructional media educator; b. Anniston, Ala., Apr. 21, 1946; d. Walter James and Polly (McCarty) M. BA, Birmingham-So. Coll., 1968; MS, Jacksonville (Ala.) State U., 1974; PhD, U. Pitts., 1979. Social worker Tuscaloosa (Ala.) County Dept. Human Resources, 1968-71, Calhoun County Dept. Human Resources, Anniston, Ala., 1971-73; social scis./bus. libr. Jacksonville State U., 1974-86, prof. instrnl. media, 1987—. Mem. Friends of Libr. bd. Anniston-Calhoun County Pub. Libr., 1984—. Recipient Ala./SIRS Intellectual Freedom award, Intellectual Freedom Com., Ala. Libr. Assn., 1992. Mem. ALA (exec. bd., Intellectual Freedom Round Table 1987-93), Ala. Libr. Assn. (pres. 1990-91, Disting. Svc. award 1995), Ala. Assn. Coll. and Rsch. Librs. (pres. 1989-90), Southeastern Libr. Assn. (chair intellectual freedom com. 1986-88, chair resolutions com. 1990-92). Office: Jacksonville State U Dept Ednl Resources Coll Edn Jacksonville AL 36265

MERRIM, LOUISE MEYEROWITZ, artist, actress; b. N.Y.C.; d. Leo and Jeanette (Harris) Meyerowitz; m. Lewis Jay Merrim, June 27, 1948; children: Stephanie, Andrea Merrim Goff (dec.). BFA, Pratt Inst., 1947; MFA, Columbia U., 1951; postgrad., Post Coll., 1971-72, New Sch., 1977-78. Art tchr. pub. schs., N.Y.C., 1947-51, Port Washington, N.Y., 1970-83. One-woman shows include Plandome Gallery, L.I., Isis Gallery, N.Y., San Diego art Inst., Pan Pacific Hotel, San Diego; exhibited in group shows at Nassau County Fine Arts Mus. (Bronze award), Heckscher Mus., Nat. Acad., Nat. Assn. Women Artists (Medal of Honor, Charlotte Whinston award), Audubon Artists (Stephen Hirsch Meml. award), Cork Gallery, Warner Comm. Gallery, L.I. Art Tchrs. (two awards of excellence), L.I. Art Tchrs. Award Winners Show, Pt. Washington Libr. Invitational, Glen Cove (2d prize), Manhasset Art Assn. (best in show, five 1st prizes), San Diego Art Inst., La Jolla Art Assn. (hon. mention), Hank Baum Gallery, San Francisco, Tarbox Gallery, Clark Gallery, Knowles Gallery, San Diego, Henry Chastain Gallery, Scottsdale, San Diego Mus. of Art (Gold award); appeared in numerous prodns. including Fiddler on the Roof, Barefoot in the Park, N.Y., Anything Goes, The Musical Comedy Murders of 1940, Anastasia (Drama award),Fiddler on the Roof, The Music Man, What's Wrong With this Picture?, Marvin's Room, San Diego; dir. Under Milkwood; dir., appeared in Spoon River Anthology. Mem. Nat. Assn. Women Artists, N.Y. Soc. of Women Artists, Contemporary Artists Guild of N.Y., Audubon Artist (N.Y.), San Diego Art Inst., Artists Guild of San Diego Art Mus. (pres. 1993), Artists Equity, Actors Alliance. Home: 3330 Caminito Vasto La Jolla CA 92037-2929

MERRIS, DONNA ROSE, lawyer; b. Bluffs, Ill., Nov. 25, 1939; d. Donald Doyle and Helen Louise (Frohwitter) M.; 1 child, Laura Katherine Merris Huffman. BS in Edn., Ill. State U., 1961; MMus, Northwestern U., 1965; JD, Bklyn. Law Sch., 1987. Bar: N.Y. 1989, N.J. 1989. Dir. instrumental music Lanark (Ill.) Pub. Schs., 1961-64, Winchester (Ill.) H.S., 1965-66; dir. music edn. Malden (Mass.) Pub. Schs., 1966-74; instr. music Mannes Coll. Music, N.Y.C., 1974-80; exec. dir. Bklyn. Music Sch., 1977-85; spl. asst. U.S. Atty. U.S. Dist. Ct. (so. dist.) N.Y., N.Y.C., 1988-90; asst. gen. counsel Office of the Comptroller, N.Y.C., 1990-94; gen. counsel Mayor's Office of Contracts, N.Y.C., 1994—; adv. bd. Bklyn. Music Sch., 1986—; trustee Nat. Guild Cmty. Schs. of the Arts, N.Y.C., 1993—. Mem. Assn. Bar City of N.Y. Home: 255 West End Ave #13A New York NY 10023

MERRITT, DEBORAH FOOTE, state legislator, vocational coordinator; b. Peterborough, N.H., June 19, 1961; d. William Lewis and Mary Elizabeth (Moore) Foote. BA in Sociology, Bowdoin Coll., 1983; MPA, U. N.H., 1994. Tchr. math. Buckley Sch., Sherman Oaks, Calif., 1983-84, Chaminade Coll. Prep. Sch., Canoga Park, Calif., 1984-85; saleswoman Smith Barney, L.A., 1985-87, B.R. Stickle & Co., Chgo., 1987; trader Harris Trust, Chgo., 1988-90; bus. mgr. Merritt Chiropractic, Durham, N.H., 1990-94; state rep. N.H. Gen. Ct., Concord, 1993—; marketer Devel. Svcs. of Stafford County, Dover, 1994; residential counselor Our House, Dover, 1994; vocat. coord. Riverbend Cmty. Mental Health, Concord, N.H., 1995—. Bd. dirs. Our House, 1993-94, counselor, 1994—; adv. bd. health & human svcs. dist. coun. Inst. Disability. Mem. NOW, N.H. Women's Lobby, Gt. Concord C. of C., Planned Parenthood No. New Eng., Women's Legis. Lobby (vice chair Strafford County del. 1994—). Democrat. Home: 20 Cedar Point Rd Durham NH 03824-3305 Office: Riverbend Cmty Mental Health PO Box 2032 Concord NH 03302

MERRITT, HELEN HENRY, retired art educator, ceramic sculptor; b. Norfolk, Va., June 15, 1920; d. John Crockett and Mabel Deborah (Richards) Henry; m. James Willis Merritt, Jan. 22, 1946; 1 child, Deborah Branan Merritt Aldrich. BA, Colby Coll., 1942; MA, Rockford Coll., 1956; MFA, No. Ill. U., 1962; postgrad., Tokyo U. Fine Arts, Cambridge (Eng.) U. Sec. U.S. Naval Hosp., Norfolk, 1942-46; art tchr. DeKalb (Ill.) Schs., 1956-57; instr. art history No. Ill. U., DeKalb, 1964, asst. prof., 1965-71, assoc. prof., 1972-79, prof., 1980-90; ceramic sculptor, DeKalb, 1952—. Author: Guiding Free Expression in Children's Art, 1964, Modern Japanese Woodblock Prints, 1990, Guide to Modern Japanese Woodblock Prints, 1992; contbr. articles to profl. jours. Founding mem. Gurler Heritage Assn., DeKalb, 1978-92; community activist DeKalb Pond, Fisk Block Group, 1989—. Home: 419 Garden Rd De Kalb IL 60115-2384

MERRITT, JUDY M., academic administrator. Pres. Jefferson State Community Coll., Birmingham, Ala. Office: Jefferson State Community Coll Office of the Pres 2601 Carson Rd Birmingham AL 35215-3098*

MERRITT, NANCY-JO, lawyer; b. Phoenix, Sept. 24, 1942; d. Robert Nelson Meeker and Violet Adele Gibson; children: Sidney Kathryn, Kurt, Douglas. BA, Ariz. State U., 1964, MA, 1974, JD, 1978. Bar: Ariz. 1978, U.S. Dist. Ct. Ariz. 1978, U.S. Ct. Appeals (9th cir.) 1984. Assoc. Erlichman, Fagerberg & Margrave, Phoenix, 1978-79, Pearlstein & Margrave, Phoenix, 1979-81, Corwin & Merritt, P.C., Phoenix, 1982-87; with Nancy-Jo Merritt & Assocs., P.C., Phoenix, 1987-88; shareholder Bryan Cave, Phoenix, 1988—. Author: Understanding Immigration Law, 1993; contbr. articles to profl. jours. Active Ariz. Coalition for Immigration Representation, Phoenix, 1988—. Fellow Ariz. Bar Found.; mem. ABA, Am. Immigration

Lawyers Assn. (chairperson Ariz. chpt. 1985-87, several coms., Pro Bono award), Am. Immigration Law Found. (trustee), Ariz. Bar Assn. (immigration sect.), Nucleus Club. Democrat. Office: Bryan Cave 2800 N Central Ave Fl 21 Phoenix AZ 85004-1007

MERRITT, SUSAN MARY, computer science educator, university dean; b. New London, Conn., July 28, 1946; d. Nelson Alfred and Mary (Cory) M. BA summa cum laude, Cath. U. Am., 1968; MS, NYU, 1969, PhD, 1982; Cert., Inst. for Edn. Mgmt., Harvard U., 1985. Joined Sisters of Divine Compassion, 1975; permanent cert. tchr., N.Y. Systems programmer Digital Equipment Corp., Maynard, Mass., 1969-70; tchr. Good Counsel Acad. High Sch., White Plains, N.Y., 1970-75; adj. instr. computer sci. Pace U., 1972-78; asst. prof. Pace U., White Plains, 1978-82, assoc. prof., 1982-85, prof., 1985—, chmn. dept., 1981-83, dean Sch. Computer Sci., 1983—; mem. gen. coun. Sisters Divine Compassion, 1988-92. Contbr. articles to profl. jours. Recipient Cert. of Appreciation IEEE, 1990. Mem. Assn. for Computing Machinery (edn. bd. 1988—), Phi Beta Kappa, Sigma Xi. Roman Catholic. Office: Pace U 1 Martine Ave White Plains NY 10606

MERRY, CAROL LEE, communications professional; b. Marietta, Ohio, Jan. 21, 1957; d. David R. and Mary E. Merry. BA in Journalism, Ohio State U., 1979. Mktg. dir. Phil Fry Enterprizes, New Concord, Ohio, 1979-83; mktg. coord. Cardinal Lodging Group, Columbus, Ohio, 1983-84, mktg. svcs. mgr., 1984-86, mktg. svcs. dir., 1986-88, sales and mktg. dir., 1988-90; mktg. dir. Cardinal Apt. Mgmt. Group, Columbus, 1990-93; corp. mktg./comm. dir. Cardinal Realty Svcs., Columbus, 1993-96; comm. and shareholder dir. Cardinal Realty Svcs., Inc., Reynoldsburg, Ohio, 1996—. Mem. Pub. Rels. Soc. Am. (chair cmty. svc. com. 1996). Office: Cardinal Realty Svcs Inc 6954 Americana Pky Reynoldsburg OH 43068

MERSEREAU, LORI MICHELLE, lawyer; b. Cin., Aug. 12, 1963; d. Leo and Sonya Ingrid (Rosenfeld) Roos; m. Richard Charles Mersereau, Nov. 20, 1988. BS, U. Calif., Davis, 1985; JD, U. So. Calif., 1989; LLM, Univ. of Pacific, 1992. Bar: Calif. 1989, U.S. Dist. Ct. (ea. dist.) Calif., U.S. Ct. Appeals (9th cir.), U.S. Tax Ct. Assoc. tax and corp. div. Weintraub, Genshlea, Hardy, Erich and Brown, Sacramento, 1989-90; pvt. practice Fair Oaks, Calif., 1990-91; atty. office of dist. counsel U.S. Dept. Treasury, Sacramento, 1991—; spl. asst. to U.S. atty. East and North Dists. Calif., Sacramento, 1994—; lectr. in tax law and internat. tax law U. Calif. Davis Law Sch. Sr. assoc. U. So. Calif. Law Rev., 1988-89; sr. editor Harvard Jour. Law and Pub. Policy, 1988. Bd. dirs. Protection and Advocacy, Inc., Sacramento, 1987-93; vol. atty. Vol. Legal Svcs., Sacramento, 1989—; chair fundraising Hadassah, Sacramento, 1990-91. Mem. Order of Coif, Phi Kappa Phi, Phi Alpha Delta. Republican. Jewish.

MERSEREAU, NANCY LEONA, journalist, editor; b. Green Bay, Wis., Jan. 25, 1934; d. Wilfred Joseph and Leona Josephine (Rondeau) Baye; m. John Wilfrid Mersereau, Dec. 27, 1958; children: Mark, Thomas. BA, Coll. of St. Scholastica, Duluth, Minn., 1956; student, U. Wis., Green Bay, 1969. Lifetime teacher's license, Wis. Tchr. Antico (Wis.) Sch. Dist., 1956-59, El Paso Sch. Dist., 1960-62, Pulaski (Wis.) Sch. Dist., 1969-70; journalist, editor Port Publications, Port Washington, Wis., 1971—. Author numerous newspaper articles, 1972—. Pres. Hanau (Germany) Officers News Club, 1963-64; pres., bd. dirs. United Way, Port Washington, 1970s; bd. dirs. Ozaukee Unit ARC, Port Washington, 1995—; pres., bd. dirs. Fish Day, Inc., Port Washington, 1971—. Recipient Leadership award Girl Scouts Am., Hanau, 1965. Mem. Nat. Newspaper Assn. (com. mem., state chmn.), Wis. Newspaper Assn. (bd. dirs., 1st woman pres. 1992-93, asst. sec. Found. 1995—). Roman Catholic. Home: 219 Summit Dr Port Washington WI 53074

MERSKEY-ZEGER, MARIE GERTRUDE FINE, retired librarian; b. Kimberley, South Africa, Oct. 10, 1914; came to U.S., 1960, naturalized, 1965; d. Herman and Annie Myra (Wigoder) Fine; m. Clarence Merskey, Oct. 8, 1939 (dec. 1982); children: Hilary Pamela Merskey Nathe, Susan Heather Merskey Sinistore, Joan Margaret Merskey Schneiderman; m. Jack I. Zeger, July 15, 1984. Grad. Underwood Bus. Sch., Cape Town, South Africa, 1934; BA, U. Cape Town, 1958, diploma librarianship, 1960. Sec. to Chief Rabbi Israel Abrahams, South Africa, 1945-49, Jewish Sheltered Employment Council, 1954-56; reference librarian New Rochelle Pub. Library, 1960-63; research librarian Consumers Union, Mt. Vernon, 1963-66; asst. readers services, head union catalog Westchester Library System, 1966-69, trustee, 1989-93, v.p., 1991; dir. Harrison (N.Y.) Pub. Library and West Harrison Br., 1969-84; acting dir. Mamaroneck (N.Y.) Free Library, 1987-88, also trustee, 1988-93. Pub. edn. officer USCG Aux. Flotilla 63. Author: History of the Harrison Libraries, 1980; editor: (cookbook) On Harrison's Table, 1976; Harrison Highlights and Anecdotes, 1989. Bd. dirs. Shore Acres Point Corp., Mamaroneck, 1985-89; program dir. Friends of the Mamaroneck Libr., N.Y., 1993—. Recipient Brotherhood award B'nai B'rith, 1974; named Woman of Yr., Harrison, 1984. Mem. ALA, Westchester Library Assn., N.Y. Library Assn. (adult edn. com. for continuing edn. 1971-75, adult services com. 1973-75, vice chmn., 1975, exec. bd. 1981-82), Pub. Library Dirs. Assn. (tech. services com. chmn. Westchester County 1971, exec. bd. 1974-75, vice chmn. 1975), Clubs: YMCA, Charles Dawson History Ctr. (bd. dirs., founder), Rye Womans Club. Contbr. articles to local newspapers. Home: 316 S Barry Ave Mamaroneck NY 10543-4201

MERSMANN, PATTI JAN, librarian; b. Fort Sill, Okla., May 2, 1951; d. Arthur Jack Wiggins and Georgia Mae (Montgomery) Aldridge; children: Aaron Joseph, Adam Thomas. BS in Elem. Edn., U. Kans., 1973; MLS, Emporia State U., 1993. Dept. head reference and Interlibrary loan Ctrl. Kans. Libr. System, Great Bend, 1993-95; dir. libr. info. tech. Kans. State Libr., Topeka, 1995—; presenter/workshop leader in field. Recipient Snowbird Leadership Inst. award, 1996. Mem. AAUW, ALA, Kans. Libr. Assn. (Presdl. award for New Profl. 1996), Mountain Plains Libr. Assn., Beta Phi Mu. Office: Kansas State Libr 300 SW 10th St 343N Topeka KS 66612

MERTZ, ANNE MORRIS, writer, freelance journalist; b. Indpls., Sept. 29, 1913; d. Theodore Hatfield and Lisette Susanna (Krauss) Morris; m. Walter Day Mertz, June 29, 1937; children: Suzanne Day Mertz Flanagan, Elizabeth Morris Mertz O'Brien, Walter Day, Jr., Theodore Morris. BA cum laude, Randolph-Macon Woman's Coll., 1935; cert. tchr., U. Pa., 1935. Newspaper reporter, columnist Wayne (Pa.) Suburban, 1928-31, Main Line Times, Ardmore, Pa., 1928-31; tchr. ch. sch. Germantown Unitarian Ch., Phila., 1935-40; tchr. Yeadon (Pa.) Sch. Dist., 1935-40; religious edn. dir. Unitarian Ch., Wilmington, Del., 1949-51; mus. guide Hagley Mus., Wilmington, 1964-76; travel lectr., 1965-96. Author: (booklets) History of Delaware Colonial Dames Headquarters, 1990, History of Delaware Mayflower Society, 1993, (book) Morris Migration, 1996; contbr. articles to several jours., newspapers and mags. Active pres.'s adv. bd. Wilmington Trust of Fla., Stuart, 1990-92; bd. dirs. Wilmington Music Sch., 1952-73, Family Svcs. Del.; spkr., dir. United Fund Planning Com., Wilmington, 1957-65, pres. Travelers Aid Soc., Wilmington, 1954-56; pres. Randolph-Macon Woman's Coll. Alumnae of No. Del., 1949-51, 65-68; nat. v.p. Randolph-Macon Woman's Coll., Lynchburg, Va., 1961-63; vol. mus. guide Winterthur Mus., Wilmington, 1956-60; hon. bd. mem. Family and Children's Svcs., Del. Mem. AAUW (life mem., chair trustees, 1st v.p. Wilmington br. 1970-75, Scholarship-Grant named for her 1940—), Nat. League Am. PEN Women, Del. Mayflower Soc. (state gov. 1990-93, Gold medal), Del. Hist. Soc., Del. Colonial Dames, Del. Geneal. Soc. Home: 726 Loveville Rd # 904 Hockessin DE 19707-1515

MERUVIA, MARY ALETHA LUNDY, rehabilitation manager; b. Phila., Oct. 26, 1965; d. Earl Lowry and Ouida Elizabeth (Whinery) Lundy. AA, Meridian (Miss.) Jr. Coll., 1985; BS, U. Southern Miss., 1987; MEd, Miss. State U., 1989. Cert. rehab. counselor. Dir. rehab. svcs. Miss. Band of Choctaw Indians, Phila., 1988—; teaching asst. Miss. State U., Starkville, 1989. Meridian Jr. Coll. scholar, 1983-85. Mem. Nat. Rehab. Assn. Home: 427 Columbus Ave Philadelphia MS 39350 Office: Choctaw Vocat Rehab Choctaw Br PO Box 6010 Philadelphia MS 39350-6010

MESA, YOLANDA DEL CARMEN, artist; b. Medellin, Colombia, Dec. 14, 1953; came to U.S., 1983; d. John and Lucia (Hoyos) M.; m. Nicholas George Sperakis, Feb. 1, 1984; 1 child, Constanza. Student, Art Inst., Medellin, Colombia, 1972-75, San Fernando Sch. Fine Arts, Madrid, Spain, 1976-77, Pratt Graphic Ctr., 1983-84, Art Students League N.Y., 1982-83. Tchr. graphic design Svc. of Nat. Apprenticeship, 1976-77, Art Inst., Medellin, 1979-81, U. de Los Andes, Santafe de Bogota, Colombia, 1990, 93. One-woman shows include Museo de Antioquia, Medellin, 1976, Ctrl. Libr. Gallery, Medellin, 1979, La Mancha Blanca Gallery, Cali, Colombia, 1980, Galerie Taub, Phila., 1983, Gal A.R.T. Gallery, Bogota, Colombia, 1985, Aura Gallery, Mexico City, 1985, Mus. Contemporary Hispanic Art, N.Y.C., 1986, Die Alte Reithalie, Stuttgart, Germany, 1986, Galeria Gasa Negret, Bogota, 1987, Galerie Leopold, Hamburg, Germany, 1988, Volksbank, Weinheim, Germany, 1989, Museo Rayo, Valle, Colombia, 1991, Galeria Gartner/Torres, Santa Fe de Bogota, Colombia, 1992, 93, others; group shows include Museo de la Universidad de Antioquia, Medellin, 1977, Partes Gallery, Medellin, 1980, Nat. Exhbn. Art, Medellin, 1981-87, Mus. Contemporary At, Bogota, 1982, 84, Chronocide Gallery, N.Y.C., 1986, La Jeune Peinture, Paris, 1987, Galeria El Museo, Bogota, 1989, Art Forms Gallery, Redbank, N.J., 1990, Maximillian Gallery, N.Y.C., 1990, Sindin Gallery, N.Y.C., 1993, Museo de Arte Moderno De Cartagena, Colombia, 1993, others.

MESCHAN, RACHEL FARRER (MRS. ISADORE MESCHAN), obstetrics and gynecology educator; b. Sydney, Australia, May 21, 1915; came to U.S., 1946, naturalized, 1950; d. John H. and Gertrude (Powell) Farrer; m. Isadore Meschan, Sept. 3, 1943; children: David Farrer-Meschan, Jane Meschan Foy, Rosalind Meschan Weir, Joyce Meschan Lawrence. MB, BS, U. Melbourne (Australia), 1940; MD, Wake Forest U., 1957. Intern Royal Melbourne Hosp., 1942; resident Women's Hosp., Melbourne, 1942-43, Bowman-Gray Sch. Medicine, Wake Forest U., Winston-Salem, N.C., 1957-73, asst. clin. prof. dept. ob-gyn, 1973—; also marriage counselor. Co-author (with I. Meschan): Atlas of Radiographic Anatomy, 1951, rev., 1959; Roentgen Signs in Clinical Diagnosis, 1956; Synopsis of Roentgen Signs, 1962; Roentgen Signs in Clinical Practice, 1966; Radiographic Positioning and Related Anatomy, 1968; Analysis of Roentgen Signs in General Radiology, 1973; Roentgen Signs in Diagnostic Imaging, Vol. III, 1986, Vol. IV, 1987. Home: 305 Weatherfield Ln Kernersville NC 27284-8337

MESCHKE, DEBRA JOANN, polymer chemist; b. Elyria, Ohio, Oct. 22, 1952; d. Loren Willis and JoAnne Elizabeth (Meyer) M. BS, U. Cin., 1974; MS, Case Western Res. U., 1976, PhD, 1979. Sr. chemist Union Carbide Corp., South Charleston, W.Va., 1979-82, project scientist, 1982-85, chair research and devel. Exempt Women's Group, 1980-81, chair research and devel. Ctr. Safety Team, 1981-82, coordinator Polymer Methods Course, 1982-83; project scientist Union Carbide Corp., Tarrytown, N.Y., 1985-86; sr. prin. research chemist Air Products and Chems. Inc., Allentown, Pa., 1986-88, chmn. waste disposal com., 1986-88; rsch. scientist Union Carbide Corp., South Charleston, W.Va., 1988-95, sr. rsch. scientist, 1995—. Author chpts. in textbooks; patentee in field. Bd. dirs. Overbrook Home Owners Assn., Macungie, Pa., 1987. Case Western Res. U. grad. fellow, 1974-79. Mem. AAAS, Am. Chem. Soc. (Polymer div.), Iota Sigma Pi. Home: 2022 Parkwood Rd Charleston WV 25314-2244

MESCHTER, JAYNE ANN, elementary school educator; b. Temple, Tex., Oct. 10, 1942; d. Robert Preston and Jaynelle Virginia (Askew) Reynolds; m. Charles A. Meschter, Dec. 26, 1964; 1 child, Jennifer Ann Meschter Parker. BS, Tex. Tech. U., 1966; MA, Chapman U., 1991. Cert. Calif. Tchg. Credential Commn., 1990. Substitute tchr. Killeen (Tex.) Sch. Dist., 1972-73, Victor Christian Sch., Victorville, Calif., 1976-79; substitute tchr. Victor Elem. Dist., Victorville, Calif., 1980-87, classroom tchr., 1988—. Site coord. Am. Heart Assn., Victorville, 1995. Recipient ednl. grant Rotary Internat., 1992, 93, 94. Mem. NEA, ASCD, Internat. Reading Assn., Calif. Tchrs. Assn., Calif. Reading Assn., Mountain Desert Reading Assn., Victor Elem. Tchrs. Assn. Home: 16350 Villa Dr Victorville CA 92392

MESLANG, SUSAN WALKER, educational administrator; b. Norfolk, Va., Sept. 15, 1947; d. Stanley Clay and Sybil Bruce (Moore) Walker: m. Curtis Allen Meslang, Nov. 6, 1976. BS in Edn., Old Dominion U., 1973, MS in Spl. Edn., 1986. Cert. tchr., Va. Child devel. specialist Norfolk Pub. Sch., 1973-77, tchr. spl. edn., 1979-82; tchr. spl. edn. San Diego Pub. Schs., 1977-79; ednl. evaluator Va. Ctr. Psychiatry, Portsmouth, 1983-84; instr. child study, spl. edn. Norfolk, 1990—; dir. CHANCE Program, Norfolk, 1983—; dir. rsch. & grants devel. Darden Coll. Edn. Old Dominion U., 1989—; cons. Eastern Va. Ctr. Children & Youths, Norfolk, 1993—, Cmty. Mental Health Ctr., Portsmouth, Va., 1993—. Bd. dirs. Va. Zool. Soc., Norfolk, 1990—, Va. Opera Assn., Norfolk, 1995—; mem. Norfolk Democratic com., 1995—, Children's Hosp. King's Downtown Cir., 1994—; dir. Va. Assistive Tech. Southeast Va. Dept. Rhabilitative Svcs., Norfolk, 1992—. Recipient Honor award Norfolk Commn. Persons with Disabilities, 1993, Commendation Va. House, 1994. Mem. Assn. Persons Supported Employment, Regional Grants Collaboration Group, Norfolk Pub. Schs. Spl. Edn. Adv. Com., Hampton Rds. Coalition Persons with Phys. & Sensory Disabilities. Democrat. Methodist. Office: Old Dominion U Coll Edn 4607 Hampton Blvd Norfolk VA 23529

MESNEY, DOROTHY TAYLOR (HEDI MUNRO), mezzo-soprano, pianist, composer, comedienne, educator; b. Bklyn., Sept. 15, 1916; d. Franklin and Kathryn Munro Taylor; diploma Berkeley Inst., 1934; m. Peter Michael Mesney, Oct. 15, 1942; children: Douglas, Kathryn, Barbara. BA, Sarah Lawrence Coll., 1938; MA in Journalism, Columbia U., 1939, postgrad. Juilliard Sch. of Music, 1963-71, Manhattan Sch. Music, 1971-73. Mezzo-soprano, operetta, mus. comedy, concert and oratorio; ch. soloist, N.Y.C., 1956—; debuts include: N.Y. Cultural Center, 1971, Carnegie Recital Hall, 1974; leading roles with local opera and Gilbert and Sullivan groups, (as Hedi Munro singing comedienne), various nightclubs and cabarets including Trocadero, Don't Tell Mama, Dangerfield's Adams Apple, Sullivan Street Theatre, Broadway Baby, Danny's Skylight Rm., 55 Grove St.; appeared on Joe Franklin TV Show, Joey Adams Radio Show; dir. a capella vocal quintet The Notebles; rec. artist Folkways Records, Musicanza Records; dir. American Experience ensemble, also An Elizabethan Encounter, Renaissance Revels; tchr. piano and singing, Douglaston, N.Y., 1958—, also tchr. "Introduction to Music Classes" for pre-schoolers, tchr. of condr. James Conlon and clarinetist Jon Manasse and singer, songwriter Steve Stavola; founder, dir. children's series Concerts for Children, Community Ch. Concert Series; soloist Community Ch. Douglaston, N.Y.; founder Introduction to Music for Preschoolers; performer early Am. music for mus., hist. socs., schs., colls.; performer Renaissance music N.Y. State Renaissance Festival, 15 yrs.; 2c authority on Am. and Renaissance music; composer hymns, songs, instrumental quartets and trios, ballads, also songs for children; recordings for Folkways-Smithsonian, Musicanza Records. Com. chmn. PTA, Douglaston, 1952-55; den mother Greater N.Y. council Cub Scouts Am., 1953-56; Brownie leader Greater N.Y. council Girl Scouts U.S.A.; bd. dirs. Community Concerts Assn. of Great Neck, N.Y. Mem. ASCAP (songwriter), AFTRA, Nat. Piano Tchrs. Guild, Nat. Fedn. Music Clubs (N.Y. chpt.), Met. Opera Guild, Tuesday Morning Music Club (pres. 1979-81), Manhattan Assn. Cabaret Artists. Democrat. Congregationalist.

MESROBIAN, ARPENA SACHAKLIAN, publisher, editor, consultant; b. Boston; d. Aaron Harry and Eliza (Der Melkonian) Sachaklian; m. William John Mesrobian, June 22, 1940; children: William Stephen, Marian Elizabeth (Mrs. Bruce MacCurdy). Student, Armenian Coll. of Beirut, Lebanon, 1937-38; A.A., Univ. Coll., Syracuse (N.Y.) U., 1959, B.A. magna cum laude, 1971; MSsc, Syracuse U., 1993. Editor Syracuse U. Press, 1955-58, exec. editor, 1958-61, asst. dir., 1961-65, acting dir., 1965-66, editor, 1968-85, assoc. dir., 1968-75, dir., 1975-85, 87-88, dir. emeritus, 1985; dir. workshop on univ. press. pub. U. Malaysia, Kuala Lumpur, 1985; cons. Empire State Coll. Book rev. editor: Armenian Rev., 1967-75; mem. publs. bd. Courier, 1970-94; mem. adv. bd. Armenian Rev., 1981-83; contbr. numerous articles, revs. to profl. jours. Pres. Syracuse chpt. Armenian Relief Soc., 1972-74; sponsor Armenian Assembly, Washington, 1975; mem. mktg. task force Office of Spl. Edn., Dept. Edn., 1979-84, Adminstrn. of Developmental Disabilities, HHS; mem. publs. panel Nat. Endowment for Humanities, Washington; bd. dirs. Syracuse Girls Club, 1982-87; pres. trustees St. John the Bapt. Armenian Apostolic Ch. and Cmty. Ctr., 1991-95. Named Post-Standard Woman of Achievement, 1980; recipient Chancellor's award for disting. service Syracuse U., 1985; Nat. award U.S. sect. World Edn. Fellowship, 1986; N.Y. State Humanities scholar. Mem. Women in Communications, Soc. Armenian Studies (adminstrv. council 1976-78, 85-87, sec. 1978, 85-87), Syracuse U. Library Assocs. (v.p. 1983-88), Am. Univ. Press Services (dir. 1976-77), Armenian Lit. Soc., Armenian Community Center, Assn. Am. Univ. Presses (v.p. 1976-77), UN Assn. (bd. dirs. 1983-88, v.p. 1985), Phi Kappa Phi, Alpha Sigma Lambda. Mem. Armenian Apostolic Ch. (trustee). Club: Zonta of Syracuse (pres. 1979-80, 1st v.p. 1985-86, dist. historian Dist. 2 Zonta Internat. 1993). Home: 4851 Pembridge Cir Syracuse NY 13215-1023

MESSER, ANGELA, systems development executive; b. Hartlepool, Eng., Dec. 29, 1960; came to U.S., 1991; d. Andrew and Marguerite Thornton (Bruce) M.; Richard John Burdett, Aug. 16, 1986 (div. 1988); m. Gregory Gene Weinman, Feb. 24, 1994. BS with honors in Computation, U. Manchester, Eng., 1983. Computer programmer Brit. Steel Corp., Redcar, Eng., 1979-80; analyst programmer Internat. Computers Ltd., Bracknell, Eng., 1983-85; systems analyst Visa Internat., London, 1985-88, supr. systems devel., 1988-91; project mgr. Visa Internat., San Mateo, Calif., 1991-92; bus. mgr. Visa Internat., San Mateo, 1992-94, dir., 1994-95, dept. head systems devel., 1995—. Mem. NAFE, Mensa. Home: 2100 Coronet Blvd Belmont CA 94002 Office: Visa Internat 900 Metro Center Blvd Foster City CA 94404

MESSER, SHARON KAY, nurse; b. Farmington, N.Mex., Jan. 27, 1958; d. Royce Elwood and Alma Jean (Peters) M.; divorced; 1 child, Keifer. AAS in Nursing, C.C. Denver, 1996; postgrad., Metro State Coll., 1996—. Retail salesperson Unique Boutique, Denver, 1992—; tchr.'s aide C.C. Denver, 1993—; nurse intern Denver Gen., 1995—; grad. nurse Denver Gen. Hosp. Bd. dirs. Warren Village, Denver, 1995, 96. Named one of Women to Watch 1995, LWV, 1995; Father Woody scholar Continental, 1994, 95, Colo. scholar C.C. Denver, 1994, 95, 96; recipient Pres.'s Svc. award CCD, 1996; scholarship Asst. League of Denver, 1995-96. Mem. AAUW (assoc.), Adhoc (treas. 1995—).

MESSERLE, JUDITH ROSE, medical librarian, public relations director; b. Litchfield, Ill., Jan. 16, 1943; d. Richard Douglas and Nelrose B. (Davis) Wilcox; m. Darrell Wayne Messerle, Apr. 26, 1968; children: Kurt Norman, Katherine Lynn. BA in Zoology, So. Ill. U., 1966; MLS, U. Ill., 1967. Cert. med. libr. Libr., St. Joseph's Sch. Nursing, Alton, Ill., 1967-71, dir. med. info. ctr., 1971-76, dir. info. services, 1976-79, dir. ednl. resources and community relations, St. Joseph's Hosp., Alton, Ill., 1979-84; dir. Med. Ctr. Libr., St. Louis U., 1985-88; libr. Francis A. Countway Libr. for the Harvard Med. Sch. and Boston Med. Libr., 1989—; instr. Lewis and Clark Coll., 1975; cons. 1973—; instr. Med. Library Assn. Bd. dirs. Family Services and Vis. Nurses Assn., Alton, 1976-79. Mem. Med. Library Assn. (dir. 1981-84, pres. 1986-87, task force for knowledge and skills, 1988-92, Legis. task force 1986-90, nom. com. 1996, search com. for exec. dir. 1979), Ill. State Libr. Adv. Com., Midwest Health Sci. Libr. Network (dir. health sci. council), St. Louis Med. Librs., Hosp. Pub. Relations Soc. of St. Louis, Nat. Libr. Medicine (biomed. libr. rev. com. 1988-92), AMA (com. on allied health edn. and accreditation 1991-94), Assn. Acad. Health Sci. Libr. Dirs. (pres. 1993, joint legis. task force 1992—, editorial bd. for ann. stats. 1989-94, Region 8 Adv. Bd. 1992-93), Am. Med. Informatics Assn. (planning com. 1990, publications com. 1994-96, annual mtg. com. 1996—), OCLC (spl. libr. adv. com. 1994—). Office: Countway Libr of Medicine 10 Shattuck St Boston MA 02115-6011

MESSINA, ROSALBA M., foundation administrator; b. Bklyn., Mar. 16, 1961. AS in Acctg., Nassau Cmty. Coll., 1986. Asst. mgr. The Gap Stores, Valley Stream, N.Y., 1977-81; acctg. mgr. Franklin United Life Ins., Garden City, N.Y., 1981-84; v.p. finance Fred Smith Co., N.Y., 1984-94; dir. finance Lesbian & Gay Cmty. Svcs. Ctr., Inc., N.Y., 1994—. Mem. NOW (chair lesbian rights task force 1991-93), Phi Theta Kappa. Democrat. Office: Lesbian/Gay Cmty Svcs Ctr Inc 208 W 13th St New York NY 10011

MESSING, CAROL SUE, communications educator; b. Bronx, N.Y.; d. Isidore and Esther Florence (Burtoff) Weinberg; m. Sheldon H. Messing; children: Lauren, Robyn. BA, Bklyn. Coll., 1967, MA, 1970. Tchr. N.Y.C. Bd. Edn., 1967-72; prof. lang. arts Northwood U., Midland, Mich., 1973-93, prof., 1993—; owner Job Match, Midland, 1983-85, cons. Mich. Credit Union League, Saginaw, 1984-87, Nat. Hotel & Restaurant, Midland, 1985-89, Univ. Coll. program, Continuing Edn. program, Northwood U., 1986—, Dow Chem. Employee's Credit Union, 1988—. Author: (anthology) Symbiosis, 1985, rev. edit., 1987, Controlling Communication, 1987, rev. edit., 1993, Creating Effective Team Presentations, 1995; co-author: PRIMIS, 1993. Mem. LWV, Nat Coun. Tchrs. English, Kappa Delta Pi, Delta Mu Delta (advisor). Office: Northwood U 3225 Cook Rd Midland MI 48640-2311

MESSNER, ANN, artist, sculptor; b. N.Y.C., Sept. 16, 1952; d. Robert Messner and Lynn (Hamby) Norris; 1 child, Ben Moennig. Student, West Surrey Coll. of Art, Eng., 1971; BFA, Pratt Inst., 1972. Postdoctoral fellow Sch. of Art Bath (Eng.) Coll. Higher Edn., 1995; represented by Tim Greathouse Gallery, N.Y.C., 1984-87, Joe Fawbush Gallery, N.Y.C., 1988-95; tchr. sculpture Pratt Inst., 1993-96, Princeton U., 1994, U. of Arts, Phila., 1993, Md. Inst., 1996; lectr. RISD, Bennington (Vt.) Coll., Cranbrook Acad. Arts, others. Sculpture commd. by Pub. Art Fund, 1986. Sculpture fellow Nat. Endowment Arts, 1987, N.Y. Found. for Arts, 1987, 89, Henry Moore Found., 1995, John Simon Guggenheim Found., 1996.

MESTRES, JEAN L. See SULC, JEAN LUENA

METCALF, CRYSTA JANINE, business and industrial anthropologist; b. San Gabriel, Calif., June 19, 1966; d. Ronna Jean Metcalf; 1 child, Brittany Jacqueline; life ptnr., Tami Sioux. BA in Anthropology, U. South Fla., 1988; MA in Anthropology, Wayne State U., 1991, postgrad., 1991—. Rsch. asst. urban, labor and met. affairs Wayne State U., Detroit, 1989, teaching asst. cultural anthropology and bus. anthropology, 1990-93, part-time faculty, 1991; adj. prof. anthropology Eckerd Coll., St. Petersburg, Fla., 1994—; vis. prof. anthropology Eckerd Coll., St. Petersburg, 1995—; adj. prof. anthropology U. South Fla., 1994-95; orgnl. and cultural cons. various orgns., Detroit, 1990-91; vol. spkr. on anthropology in elem. sch. edn. Detroit City Schs., 1991; field rschr. in human issues in info. tech. implementation Wizdom Sys., Inc., 1993-95. Sr. researcher and author papers and orgnl. briefs. Mem. Nat. Assn. Practice Anthropology (governing coun. 1992), Soc. Applied Anthropology, Soc. Anthropology of Work, Am. Anthropol. Assn., Nat. Assn. Student Anthropology. Office: Eckerd Coll PEL 4200 54th Ave S Saint Petersburg FL 33711

METCALF, LAURIE, actress; b. Edwardsville, Ill., June 15, 1955; 1 child, Zoe. Student, Ill. State U. Off-Broadway appearances: Balm in Gilead (debut, Theatre World award), 1984; stage appearances: Who's Afraid of Virginia Woolf?, 1982, Coyote Ugly, 1985, Bodies Rest, and Motion, 1986, Educating Rita, 1987 (Joseph Jefferson award best performance by principal actress in a play), Little Egypt, 1987, Killers, 1988, My Thing of Love, 1995; films: Desperately Seeking Susan, 1984, Making Mr. Right, 1987, Stars and Bars, 1988, The Appointments of Dennis Jennings, 1988, Candy Mountain, 1988, Miles from Home, 1988, Uncle Buck, 1989, Internal Affairs, 1989, Pacific Heights, 1990, Frankie and Johnny, 1991, JFK, 1991, Mistress, 1992, A Dangerous Woman, 1993, Blink, 1994, The Secret Life of Houses, 1994, Leaving Las Vegas, 1995, Dear God, 1996, (voice) Toy Story, 1995; TV series: Saturday Night Live, 1981, Roseanne, 1988— (Emmy award, Outstanding Supporting Actress in a Comedy Series, 1993, 94); TV appearances: The Equalizer, 1986, The Execution of Raymond Graham, 1985. Address: care ICM 8942 Wilshire Blvd Beverly Hills CA 90211*

METCALF, LYNNETTE CAROL, naval officer, journalist, educator, gemologist; b. Van Nuys, Calif., June 22, 1955; d. William Edward and Carol Annette (Keith) M.; m. Scott Edward Hruska, May 16, 1987. BA in Comm. and Media, Our Lady of Lake, 1978; MA in Human Rels., U. Okla., 1980; MA in Mktg. Webster U., 1986; cert. diamond grading, gem identification and colored stone grading Gemology Inst. Am., 1991, diploma, grad. gemologist, 1992. Enlisted USAF, 1973, advanced through grades to sgt., 1975; intelligence analyst, Taiwan, Italy and Tex., 1973-76; historian, journalist, San Antonio, 1976-78; commd. officer USN, 1978, advanced through ranks to lt. comdr., 1988; pub. rels. officer, Rep. of Panama, 1979-81; mgr. system program, London, 1981-82; ops. plans/tng., McMurdo Sta., Antarctica, 1982-84; exec. officer transient pers. unit Naval Tng. Ctr., Great Lakes, Ill., 1984-86, comdg. officer transient pers. unit, 1986-87; asst. prof. naval sci. U. Notre Dame NROTC, 1987-89; nat. curriculum, 1987-89; staff comm. plans U.S. Naval Forces Japan, 1989-91, network transp. officer pers. support activity Japan, 1991-92, Far East, 1992-93, adminstrv. mgr., automated Data processing and mgmt. rev. dir. pers. support activity, 1992-93; ret., 1993; freelance writer, desktop pub.; anchorwoman USN-TV CONTACT, 1986-87; adj. prof. Far East divsn. Chapman U., 1990-93; founder Profl. Gemological Cons., Japan, 1991, Far East Fed. Sales Group, Inc., 1993; founder. Profl. Gemol. Svc., Japan 1992, Far East Trading Co., Dolphin Comms., 1993, Desk Top Publishing, 1993. Author: Winter's Summer, 1983, A Walter Mitty Romance, 1995, Retired List, 1996; editor Naval Station Anchorline, 1979-81, WOPN Caryatides, 1985-86, Lollipop Landing Lantern; contbr. articles to profl. jours. Sec. San Vito Dei Normanni theatre group, Italy, 1975-76; coord. Magic Box Theater, Zion, Ill., 1984-86; dir. Too Bashful for Broadway variety show, Naval Tng. Ctr., 1986-87; treas. Yokosuka Little Theatre Group, 1990-91. Mem. Women Officers' Prof. Network (communications chair 1985-86, programs chair 1986-87), Am. Legion, Disabled Am. Vets., Ret. Officers Assn., Romance Writers of Am., Internat. Soc. Appraisers, Corp. Sponsor Tokyo Internat. Players, JHF Theater Soc. (co-founder 1990-93), McMurdo Club, Soc. of South Pole, Gemological Inst. Am. Alumni. Avocations: gardening, gemology, research, snorkeling, theatre. Home: 9120 Mint Ave Frankston TX 75763

METHVIN, MILDRED E., judge; b. Alexandria, La., Oct. 24, 1952; d. DeWitt T. Jr. and Lallah Hill (Cunningham) M.; m. James T. McManus, Jan. 2, 1988; children: Michael James, Connor Hill; stepchildren: Christine Lynn, Matthew Robert, John Thomas. BA in Philosophy, Newcomb Coll., Tulane Univ., 1974; student, Tulane Univ. Law Sch., 1973-74; JD, Georgetown Univ. Law Ctr., 1976. Bar: La. 1977, D.C. 1977. Staff asst. to U.S. Rep. Gillis Long La., 1974-77; assoc. Gist, Methvin & Trimble, Alexandria, La., 1977-78; asst. U.S. atty. U.S. Dist. Ct. (we. dist.) La., Shreveport, 1979-81; staff atty. Dept. of Interior, Charleston, W. Va., 1981-83; magistrate judge U.S. Dist. Ct. (we. dist.) La., Lafayette, 1983—. Mem. La. Bar Assn., Nat. Assn. Women Judges, Fed. Magistrate Judges Assn., Am. Inn of Ct. Acadiana (pres. 1995-96). Office: 705 Jefferson St Rm 707 Lafayette LA 70501-6090*

METTEE-MCCUTCHON, ILA, army officer; b. Mobile, May 1, 1945; d. John Martin and Anna Ruth (Cleveland) Mettee; BS, Auburn (Ala.) U., 1967, MS, 1969; grad. various army schs.; m. John Robert McCutchon, Oct. 13, 1974; 1 child, Erin Tempest. Research psychologist VA Hosp., Tuskegee, Ala., 1967-69; clin. psychologist U. Ala. Med. Center, Birmingham, 1969-71; commd. 1st lt. U.S. Army, 1971, advanced through grades to col., 1992; OIC, Alcohol and Drug Abuse Rehab. Ctr., Presidio, San Francisco, 1971-73; strategic intelligence officer 8th Psychol. Bn., 1973-75; tactical intelligence officer, ops. officer, co. comdr. 525th MI Brigade (Airborne), Ft. Bragg, N.C., 1976-79; project officer Command, Control, Comms. and Intelligence Directorate, Combined Arms Combat Devel. Activity, Ft. Leavenworth, Kans., 1979-82; student Command and Gen. Staff Coll., 1982-83; ops. officer Army Spl. Security Group, Washington, 1983-86; Def. Lang. Inst. Presidio of Monterey, 1986-87; chief U.S. So. command Joint Intelligence Ctr., Republic of Panama, 1987-89; comdr. 741st M.I. Bn., Ft. Meade, Md., 1989-91; U.S. Army War Coll., 1991-92; strategic intelligence officer Internat. Military Staff NATO, Brussels, Belgium, 1992-94; comdr. Presidio of Monterey and Ft. Ord, Calif., 1994—. Decorated Army Commendation medal (3), Meritorious Svc. medal (4), Defense Meritorious Svc. medal (1), Army Achievement award (2), Def. Superior Svc. medal (1). Mem. NAFE, Assn. U.S. Army. Mem. Alumni Assn. U.S. Army War Coll., Women's Army Corps Found., Women in NATO. Home: 7 Bayonet Dr Seaside CA 93955-6339 Office: Presidio of Monterey ATZP-GC Monterey CA 93944

METZ, MARILYN JOYCE, bank executive; b. Denver, Colo., Nov. 10, 1949; d. James C. and Lois M. (Roach) M.; m. Jack W. Calabrese, Apr. 15, 1977 (div. 1981); m. Frank C. Margowski, Oct. 13, 1986 (div.). Student, Colo. State U., 1968-72; diploma, Colo. Grad. Sch. Banking, 1983. With First Interstate Bank Denver, 1972-83; v.p., mgr. United Banks Colo., Denver, 1983-88; v.p., area mgr. First Interstate Bank Oreg., Portland, 1988-89; v.p., dist. mgr. 5 brs. 1st Interstate Bank Wash., Seattle, 1989-91; v.p., dist. mgr. 11 brs. 1st Interstate Bank, Bellevue, Wash., 1991—. Bd. dirs., Met. Child Dental Care Assn., 1985-87. Mem. Nat. Assn. Bank Women (state pres. Colo. 1986-87), Cherry Creek Commerce Assn., Seattle C. of C., Pres. Club Seattle. Republican. Office: First Interstate Bank Bellevue Fin Ctr 225 108th Ave NE Bellevue WA 98004-5705

METZ, MARY SEAWELL, university dean, retired college president; b. Rockhill, S.C., May 7, 1937; d. Columbus Jackson and Mary (Dunlap) Seawell; m. F. Eugene Metz, Dec. 21, 1957; 1 dau., Mary Eugena. BA summa cum laude in French and English, Furman U., 1958; postgrad., Institut Phonetique, Paris, 1962-63, Sorbonne, Paris, 1962-63; PhD magna cum laude in French, La. State U., 1966; HHD (hon.), Furman U., 1984; LLD (hon.), Chapman Coll., 1985; DLT (hon.), Converse Coll., 1988. Instr. French La. State U., 1965-66, asst. prof., 1966-67, 1968-72, assoc. prof., 1972-76, dir. elem. and intermediate French programs, 1966-74, spl. asst. to chancellor, 1974-75, asst. to chancellor, 1975-76; prof. French Hood Coll., Frederick, Md., 1976-81, provost, dean acad. affairs, 1976-81; pres. Mills Coll., Oakland, Calif., 1981-90; dean of extension U. Calif., Berkeley, 1991—; vis. asst. prof. U. Calif.-Berkeley, 1967-68; mem. commn. on leadership devel. Am. Coun. on Edn., 1981-90, adv. coun. Stanford Rsch. Inst., 1985-90, adv. coun. Grad. Sch. Bus., Stanford U.; assoc. Gannett Ctr. for Media Studies, 1985—; bd. dirs. PG&E, Pacific Telesis, PacTel & PacBell, Union Bank, Longs Drug Stores, S.H. Cowell Found. Author: Reflets du monde francais, 1971, 78, Cahier d'exercices: Reflets du monde francais, 1972, 78, (with Helstrom) Le Francais a decouvrir, 1972, 78, Le Francais a vivre, 1972, 78, Cahier d'exercices: Le Francais a vivre, 1972, 78; standardized tests; mem. editorial bd.: Liberal Edn., 1982—. Trustee Am. Conservatory Theater. NDEA fellow, 1960-62,, 1963-64; Fulbright fellow, 1962-63; Am. Council Edn. fellow, 1974-75. Mem. Western Coll. Assn. (v.p. 1982-84, pres. 1984-86), Assn. Ind. Calif. Colls. and Univs. (exec. com. 1982-90), Nat. Assn. Ind. Colls. and Univs. (govt. rels. adv. coun. 1982-85), So. Conf. Lang. Teaching (chmn. 1976-77), World Affairs Coun. No. Calif. (bd. dirs. 1984-93), Bus.-Higher Edn. Forum, Women's Forum West, Women's Coll. Coalition (exec. com. 1984-88), Phi Kappa Phi, Phi Beta Kappa. Address: PO Box 686 Stinson Beach CA 94970-0686

METZER, PATRICIA ANN, lawyer; b. Phila., Mar. 10, 1941; d. Freeman Weeks and Evelyn (Heap) M.; m. Karl Hormann, June 30, 1980. BA with distinction, U. Pa., 1963, LLB cum laude, 1966. Bar: Mass. 1966, D.C. 1972, U.S. Tax Ct. 1988. Assoc., then ptnr. Mintz, Levin, Cohn, Glovsky and Popeo, Boston, 1966-75; assoc. tax legis. counsel U.S. Treasury Dept., Washington, 1975-78; shareholder, dir. Goulston & Storrs, P.C., Boston, 1978—; lectr. program continuing legal edn. Boston Coll. Law Sch., Chestnut Hill, Mass., spring 1974; mem. adv. com. NYU Inst. Fed. Taxation, N.Y.C., 1981-87; mem. practitioner liaison com. Mass. Dept. Revenue, 1985-90; spkr. in field. Author: Federal Income Taxation of Individuals, 1984; mem. adv. bd. Corp. Tax and Bus. Planning Review, 1996—; mem. editl. bd. Am. Jour. Tax Policy, 1995—; contbr. articles to profl. jours., chpts. to books. Bd. mgrs. Barrington Ct. Condominium, Cambridge, Mass., 1985-86; bd. dirs. University Road Parking Assn., Cambridge, 1988—; trustee Social Law Libr., Boston, 1989-93. Mem. ABA (tax sect., chmn. subcom. allocations and distbns. partnership com. 1978-82, vice chmn. legis. 1991-93, chmn. 1993-95, com. govt. submissions, vice liaison 1993-94, liaison 1994-95, North Atlantic region, co-liaison 1995-96, N.E. region, regional liaison meetings com., mem. coun. 1996—), Mass. Bar Assn., Boston Bar Assn., (coun. 1987-89, chmn. tax sect. 1989-91), Fed. Bar Assn. (coun. on taxation, chmn. corp. taxation com. 1977-81, chmn. com. partnership taxation 1981-87), Boston Estate Planning Coun. (exec. com. 1975, 79-82), Am. Coll. Tax Counsel. Office: Goulston & Storrs PC 400 Atlantic Ave Boston MA 02110-3333

METZGER, CAROLYN DIBBLE, accountant, educator; b. South Bend, Ind., May 27, 1924; d. Harry Hurlburt and Mae Floretta (Parker) Dibble; m. Franklin Dale Metzger, Aug. 17, 1946; children: Lawrence, Bruce, Douglas. BS in Acctg. with honors, Ind. U., South Bend, 1972, MS in Bus. Adminstrn., 1975. CPA, Ind. Ptnr. Metzger and Co. CPAs, South Bend, 1972-84; mng. ptnr. Metzger and Mancini CPAs, South Bend, 1984-93; adj. prof. Ind. U., South Bend, 1975-90. Treas. St. Joseph County Rep. Party, 1973-79, co-auditor candidate, 1973, 77; mem. exec. coun. audit com. Ind. U., Bloomington, 1978-88; mem. alumni bd. dirs. Ind. U., South Bend, 1974-81, orgn. com., 1973, founding pres., 1974, rep. to alumni assn., exec. coun., 1975-81, chancellor's com. on curriculum priorities, 1975; bd. dirs., sec., vice chmn. Michiana Community Hosp., 1977-80, 90-93; vol. speaker Women in Bus., 1975-91; guest tour guide Spl. Olympics, Chgo., 1987, numerous others; mem. Hoosiers for Higher Edn., 1992—. Recipient Athena award South Bend C. of C., 1992, Alumni award Ind. U., 1993. Mem. AICPA (mem. exam, tax forms and sml. bus. coms., Pub. Svc. award 1989), Ind. CPA Soc. (mem. ethics com., bd. dirs., Pub. Svc. award 1989), Am. Women's Soc. CPAs (nat. bd. dirs. 1979-81, charter pres. local chpt. 1982), Nat. Assn. Accts. (pres. 1978-79, bd. dirs.), Order of the Eastern Star. Presbyterian. Home and Office: Metzger and Mancini CPAs PO Box 4143 South Bend IN 46634-4143

METZGER, DIANE HAMILL, paralegal, poet; b. Phila., July 23, 1949; d. David Alexander Sr. and Eunice (Shelton) Hamill; 1 child, Jason. AA in Bus. Adminstrn. magna cum laude, Northampton Coll., 1980; BA in Polit. Sci. magna cum laude, Bloomsburg U., 1987; paralegal cert., Pa. State U., 1988; MA in Humanities, Calif. State U., Dominguez Hills, 1995. Statistician Am. Viscose div. FMC Corp., Phila., 1967-72; research asst. Temple U., Phila., 1972-73; freelance writer, 1964—, paralegal, 1989—. Author: (poems) Coralline Ornaments, 1980; lyricist: Come Now, Shepherds, 1979, Sleep Now, My Baby, 1986, History in Verse, 1995; poetry pub. in numerous mags., publs. including Phila. Poets, The Grit, The Long Islander, Inside/Out, Working Parents, South Coast Poetry Jour., Pearl (featured poet 1989), ANIMA: A Jour. of Human Experience, Collages and Bricolages. Recipient numerous awards for poetry including 2d place award Phila. Writers Conf., 1969, 1st prize PEN Writing Awards, 1985, 2d prize Carver Prize Essay Competition, 1986; also Citation for Outstanding Achievement Pa. Ho. of Reps., 1988, Citation for Outstanding Achievement Pa. Senate, 1988, Honorable Mention award Writers Digest Nat. Writing Competition, 1994. Mem. Am. Humanist Assn., Mensa, Nat. Wildlife Found.

METZGER, KATHERINE H., state legislator; b. Middletown, Ohio, Nov. 5, 1923; m. J. Hayes Metzger; 5 children. BS, Ohio State U., 1945; MA, St. Bonaventure, 1974. Mem. N.H. Ho. of Reps.; mem. corrections and criminal justice coms. Chmn. exec. com. Southwest Regional Planning Com.; chmn. Conservation Commn. Home: Lower Troy Rd Fitzwilliam NH 03447 Office: NH Ho of Reps Speakers Office House Rm 312 Concord NH 03301*

METZGER, KATHLEEN ANN, computer systems specialist; b. Orchard Park, N.Y., Aug. 4, 1949; d. Charles Milton and Anna Irene (Matwijow) Wetherby; m. Robert George Metzger, Aug. 29, 1970 (div. June 1988). BS in Edn. cum laude, SUNY Coll., Buffalo, 1970; postgrad., SUNY, Fredonia, 1975. Cert. secondary tchr. Math. tchr. Crestwood High Sch., Mantua, Ohio, 1970-71; sec., bookkeeper Maple Bay Marina, Lakewood, N.Y., 1972; math., bus. tchr. Falconer (N.Y.) High Sch., 1972-76; bookkeeper Darling Jewelers, Lakewood, 1977-78; computer operator Ethan Allen Inc., Jamestown, N.Y., 1978-79, So. Tier Bldg. Trades, Jamestown, 1979; program analyst TRW Bearings Div., Inc., Jamestown, 1980-82, Fla. Power Corp., St. Petersburg, 1982—. Campaign advisor United Way, St. Petersburg, 1985; Beachfest vol. Suncoast Children's Dream Fund, 1988-92; vol. Christmas Toy Shop. Mem. Data Processing Mgmt. Assn. (sec.), St. Petersburg Second Time Arounders Marching Band Color Guard, Kappa Delta Pi. Republican. Roman Catholic. Home: 8701 Blind Pass Rd Apt 110 Saint Petersburg FL 33706-1463 Office: Fla Power Corp 3201 34th St S Saint Petersburg FL 33711-3828

METZGER, LOIS, writer; b. N.Y.C., Dec. 22, 1955; d. David and Ilse (Stern) M.; m. Tony Hiss, Feb. 22, 1986; 1 child, Jacob. BA in English, BA in Psychology, SUNY, Buffalo, 1976; MA, Johns Hopkins U., 1978. Author: Barry's Sister, 1992 (Best Books award Parents Mag. 1992), Ellen's Case, 1995. Mem. Authors Guild. Home and Office: 22 E 8th St Apt 3A New York NY 10003

METZNER, BARBARA STONE, university counselor; b. St. Louis, June 9, 1940; d. Wendell Phillips and Lois Custer (Rake) Metzner. AB, Ind. U., 1962, MS, 1964, EdD, 1983; BA, Purdue U., 1979. Asst. dean students U. Ill., Urbana, 1964-68; undergrad. advisor UCLA, 1968-69; asst. dean students Ohio State U., 1969-72; student affairs officer San Diego State U., 1972-76; sr. counselor Ind. U. - Purdue U., Indpls., 1976—; supr. Ednl. Testing Svc., Indpls., 1980-90; cons. editorial bd. Nat. Acad. Advising Assn., Manhattan, Kans., 1987-93; adj. prof. Ind. U., 1987—; mgr. Info. Svcs., Ind. U.-Purdue U., 1989-91. Contbr. articles to profl. jours. Mem. Marion County Precinct Election Bd., 1980—; exec. com. Ind. Allied Health Assn., 1983-84; VIP escort Pan Am. Games, 1987. Spencer Found. grantee, 1985. Mem. APA, Am. Edn. Rsch. Assn., Nat. Acad. Advising Assn., Assn. Instl. Rsch., Assn. Study Higher Edn., Kappa Alpha Theta (vol. charity benefits 1980—). Office: IUPUI 620 Union Dr Unit 242 Indianapolis IN 46202-5130

MEUTER, MARIA COOLMAN, lawyer; b. New Albany, Ind., July 17, 1915; d. William Edmund and Hundley Love (Wells) Coolman; m. Walter Frederick Meuter, Jan. 9, 1942; children: Stephen, Craig Frederick. Student, New Albany Bus. Coll., 1933; LLB, Jefferson Sch. Law, 1939; JD, U. Louisville, 1971. Bar: Ky. 1939, U.S. Ct. Internat. Trade, 1980. Clk. Fed. Land Bank of Louisville, 1933-41; exec. dir. Louisville Bar Assn., 1952-70; trial judge County Ct., Jefferson County, Louisville, 1962-70; assoc. dir. Law Alumni Affairs, U. Louisville, 1970—; exec. dir. Continuing Legal Edn., U. Louisville, 1978-83; pvt. practice, Louisville, 1970—; life trustee Law Alumni Found. Vice pres. Beechmont Civic Club, Louisville, 1987-91. Named Disting. Alumnae, U. Louisville Sch. Law, 1976, Ky. col., 1968, Master of Steamboat Flotilla of Jefferson County, 1968. Mem. Ky. Bar Assn. (rec. sec. ho. of dels. 1964-68), Louisville Bar Assn., Jefferson County Women Lawyers (pres.), Nat. Assn. Bar Execs. (rec. sec. 1969-70), DAR (com. chmn. John Marshall chpt. 1991), Daus. Am. Colonists, Colonial Dames, Law Alumni Assn. U. Louisville (treas., sec. 1970-75), South Park Country Club. Republican. Episcopalian. Home: 1313 Marret Pl Louisville KY 40215-2368 also: 2855 Gulf Shore Blvd N Naples FL 33940-4339

MEWHORT, MARTHA MCGONIGLE, history educator; b. West Reading, Pa., Apr. 15, 1940; d. Walter Raymond and Gertrude Leora (Kempf) McG.; m. Donald Milton Mewhort, Aug. 10, 1963; children: Donald, Kerry, Julie. AB, Duke U., 1962; MA, U. Toledo, 1982. Cert. tchr., Braille transcriber. Elem. educator Durham (N.C.) City Schs., 1963-65; tchr. visually handicapped Toledo (Ohio) Pub. Schs., 1970-74; adj. instr. liberal studies U. Toledo, 1982-84; adj. prof., continuing edn. adminstr. Lourdes Coll., Sylvania, Ohio, 1984-88, prof. history, 1988—; dir. women's studies Lourdes Coll., Sylvania, 1982-86, coord. Divsn. Arts & Humanities, 1981-86, chairperson history dept., 1988-96. Contbg. author: (book) In Search of Our Past, Vols. 3 and 4, 1992, 94. Mem. Duke U. Alumni Assn., 1962—, U. Toledo Alumni Assn., 1982—, Duke U. Women's Studies Assn., 1986—; coll. rep. Women Alive! Coalition, 1992-96; mem. YMCA Met. Bd., 1994—; bd. dirs., founding group Wellness Cmty., 1994—. Milestones award nominee YWCA, 1996. Mem. Maumee Valley Hist. Soc. (v.p. bd. dirs. 1990-95). Home: 436 Pine Valley Rd Holland OH 43528 Office: Lourdes Coll 6832 Convent Blvd Sylvania OH 43560-2853

MEYER, ALICE VIRGINIA, state official; b. N.Y.C., Mar. 15, 1921; d. Martin G. and Marguerite Helene (Houzé) Kliemand; m. Theodore Harry Meyer, June 28, 1947; children: Robert Charles, John Edward. BA, Barnard Coll., 1941; MA, Columbia U., 1942. Tchr. pub. schs. Elmont, N.Y., 1942-43; tchr. Fairlawn (N.J.) High Sch., 1943-47; office mgr., sales rep. N.Y.C., 1948-55; substitute tchr. Pub. Schs., Easton, Conn., 1965-72; state rep., asst. minority leader Conn. State Legislature, Hartford, 1976-93; mem. Ct. Bd. of Govs. for Higher Edn., 1993—, vice-chair. Mem. bd. trustees Discovery Mus., 1980—, United Way Regional Youth Substance Abuse Project, Bridgeport, 1983-93; bd. dirs. 3030 Park, 1993—, Fairfield County Lit. Coalition, Bridgeport, 1988-94; vice chmn. Easton Rep. Town Com., 1970-78; mem. strategic planning com. Town of Easton, 1993—; vice-chmn. ct. adv. coun. on intergovtl. rels., 1988—; mem. Conn. Commn. on Quality Edn., 1992-93; supporter of Conn. Small Towns, 1988; mem. lt. gov.'s commn. on mandate reduction, 1995; sec. Easton Fire Sch. Scholarship Fund, 1980—. Named Legislator of Yr. Conn. Libr. Assn., 1985; Guardian Small Bus. grantee Nat. Fedn. Ind. Bus., 1987; honoree Fairfield YWCA Salute to Women, 1988; named grant to AAUW Fellowship Fund, Bridgeport Br., 1970, Conn. State AAUW, 1974. Mem. AAUW (past local pres. 1976, bd. dirs. 1982), LWV, Bus. and Profl. Women, Nat. Order Women Legislators (regional dir. 1987—, past pres. Conn. chpt.). Congregationalist. Home: 18 Lantern Hill Rd Easton CT 06612-2218

MEYER, ANDREA PEROUTKA, small business owner; b. Prague, Czechoslovakia, Nov. 29, 1963; came to U.S. 1970; d. George and Alena Peroutka; m. Dana Charles Meyer, Oct. 16, 1983. BA in Liberal Arts, U. Tex., 1985, M in Libr. of Info. Sci., 1986. Libr. IBM, Austin, Tex., 1985-86; rsch. specialist Career Track Seminars, Boulder, Colo., 1986-88; founder, pres. Working Knowledge, Boulder, 1988—; project mgr. Interesting Orgns. Database for MIT, 1995—; cons. The Tom Peters Group, Palo Alto, Calif., 1989—. Author: (workbooks) Stress Management Strategies, 1987, How to Give Presentations, 1988; co-author: (audio tape) How to Set Up a Corporate Library, 1989; co-editor Briefing Book for Inventing the Organizations of the 21st Century, 1995—; assoc. editor Inside Decisions, 1995—; contbr. chpt. to book. Recipient Ray C. Janeway scholarship, Tex. Libr. Assn., 1985, Philip Morris scholarship, 1981-85. Mem. Planning Forum (v.p. comm., bd. dirs. Denver chpt.), Product Devel. and Mgmt. Assn. (newsletter editor), Toastmasters, Mensa (chmn. scholarship com.), Pres.'s Assn., European Consortium of Info. Cons., Phi Beta Kappa. Home and Office: 515 Forest Ave Boulder CO 80304-2550

MEYER, ANN JANE, human development educator; b. N.Y.C., Mar 11, 1942; s. Louis John and Theresa M. B.A., U. Mich., 1964; M.A., U. Calif.-Berkeley, 1967, Ph.D., 1971. Asst. prof. dept. human devel. Calif. State U.-Hayward, 1972-77, assoc. prof., 1977-84, prof., chmn. dept., 1984—. Mem. Am. Psychol. Assn., Western Psychol. Assn., Am. Soc. Aging. Office: Dept Human Devel Calif State U Hayward CA 94542

MEYER, BARBARA ANN, tax specialist; b. Indpls., Mar. 20, 1924; d. Horace Wright and Sibyl Conklin (Lindley) Townsend; m. Robert James Scott, Dec. 15, 1941 (dec. 1949); children: Sue Meyer Suppiger, Randolph David, Steven James; m. Fred J. Meyer, Jan. 3, 1950; 1 child, Johanna Laura Meyer-Mitchell. Student, U. Md., 1958-60, Big Bend C.C., 1965-69. Cert. enrolled agent, U.S. Treasury, 1980. Owner, mgr. Meyer Tax Svc., Coulee Dam, Wash., 1969-94, cons., 1994—; enrolled agent emeritus; income tax tchr. Big Bend C.C., Coulee Dam, 1975-80. Contbr. articles to newspapers. Chair svc. to mil. families ARC, Ephrata, Wash., 1941—, Roosevelt History Month, Grand Coulee, 1995-96; bd. chmn. Pub. Hosp. Dist. #6, Grand Coulee, 1990-94. Mem. Nat. Assn. Enrolled Agents, Wash. State Soc. Enrolled Agents (v.p. 1984—, bd. dirs. 1985-88), Am. Cancer Soc. (bd. dirs. 1995—), Calif. Soc. Enrolled Agents (affiliate), Grand Coulee C. of C. (life, hon., pres. 1979-80), Grand Coulee Yacht Club (life, hon.), Grand Coulee Dam Rotary (pres. 1992-93). Democrat. Home: 201 Columbia Ave Coulee Dam WA 99116-1401 Office: Meyer Tax Svc 102 Stevens Coulee Dam WA 99116

MEYER, BETTY JANE, former librarian; b. Indpls., July 20, 1918; d. Herbert and Gertrude (Sanders) M.; B.A., Ball State Tchrs. Coll., 1940; B.S. in L.S., Western Res. U., 1945. Student asst. Muncie Public Library (Ind.), 1936-40; library asst. Ohio State U. Library, Columbus, 1940-42, cataloger, 1945-46, asst. circulation librarian, 1946-51, acting circulation librarian, 1951-52, adminstrv. asst. to dir. libraries, 1952-57, acting asso. reference librarian, 1957-58, cataloger in charge serials, 1958-65, head serial div. catalog dept., 1965-68, head acquisition dept., 1968-71, asst. dir. libraries, tech. services, 1971-76, acting dir. libraries, 1976-77, asst. dir. libraries, tech. services, 1977-83, instr. library adminstrn., 1958-63, asst. prof., 1963-67, asso. prof., 1967-75, prof., 1975-83, prof. emeritus, 1983—; library asst. Grandview Heights Public Library, Columbus, 1942-44; student asst. Case Inst. Tech., Cleve., 1944-45; mem. Ohio Coll. Library Center Adv. Com. on Cataloging, 1971-76, mem. adv. com. on serials, 1971-76, mem. adv. com. on tech. processes, 1971-76; mem. Inter-Univ. Library Council, Tech. Services Group, 1971-83; mem. bd. trustees Columbus Area Library and Info. Council Ohio, 1980-83. Ohio State U. grantee, 1975-76. Mem. ALA, Assn. Coll. and Research Libraries, AAUP, Ohio Library Assn. (nominating com. 1978-81), Ohioana Library Assn., Ohio Valley Group Tech. Services Librarians, No. Ohio Tech. Services Librarians, Franklin County Library Assn., Acad. Library Assn. Ohio, PEO, Beta Phi Mu, Delta Kappa Gamma. Club: Assn. Faculty and Profl. Women Ohio State U. Home: 970 High St Apt H2 Worthington OH 43085-4061

MEYER, BILLIE JEAN, special education educator; b. Kansas City, Mo., July 27, 1943; d. Charles William and Dorothy Ellen (Alt) Emerson; m. Kenneth Lee Morris, Aug. 24, 1963 (div. Oct. 1985); 1 child, Darla Michelle Morris Stewart; m. Gordon Frederick Meyer, June 1, 1986 (dec. May 1994); stepchildren: Ardith Helmer, Susan Stanford, Gary, Geneace, Patti Draughon, Shari Mohr. BS in Edn., Northeastern State U., 1965, M in Tchg., 1968. Cert. tchr., Okla.; cert. visually impaired, Braille. Substitute tchr. Muskogee (Okla.) Pub. Schs., 1965; elem. tchr. Okla. Sch. for the Blind, Muskogee, 1965-67, elem. tchr., computer tchr., 1969—; adj. lectr. Northeastern State U., Tahlequah, summers 1990-92, 94, 95-96; on-site team mem. Nat. Accreditation Coun., 1987; mem. com. revision cert. stds., State of Okla., 1982. Author: A Sequential Math Program for Beginning Abacus Students, 1979. Mem. Assn. of Edn. and Rehab. of the Blind and Visually Impaired, Okla. Assn. of Edn. Rehab. of the Blind and Visually Impaired (pres.-elect 1985-86, pres. 1986-87, sec. 1993-96), Computer Using Educators, Epsilon Sigma Alpha (state pres. 1981-82, Girl of Yr. 1971). Office: Okla Sch for the Blind 3300 Gibson St Muskogee OK 74403-2811

MEYER, CAROL FRANCES, pediatrician, allergist; b. Berea, Ky., June 2, 1936; d. Harvey Kessler and Jessie Irene (Hamm) Meyer; m. Daniel Baker Cox, June 5, 1955 (div. Apr. 1962). AA, U. Fla., 1955; BA, Duke U., 1957; MD, Med. Coll. Ga., 1967. Diplomate Am. Bd. Pediatrics, Am. Bd. Allergy and Immunology. Intern in pediatrics Med. Coll. Ga., Augusta, 1967-68; resident in pediatrics Gorgas Hosp., Canal Zone, 1968-69; fellow in pediatric respiratory disease Med. Coll. Ga., 1969-71, instr. pediat., 1971-72; med. officer pediatrics Canal Zone Govt., 1972-79; med. officer pediatrics Dept. of Army, Panama, 1979-82, med. officer allergy, 1982-89, physician in charge allergy clinic, 1984-89; asst. prof. pediatrics and medicine Med. Coll. Ga., Augusta, 1990—; mem. Bd. of Canal Zone Merit System Examiners, 1976-79. Contbr. articles to profl. jours. Mem. First Bapt. Ch. Orch., 1992—; founding mem., violoncello Curundu Chamber Ensemble, 1979-89. Recipient U.S. Army Exceptional Performance awards, 1985, 86, 89, Merck award Med. Coll. Ga.,, 1967; U. Fla. J. Hillis Miller scholar, 1954. Mem. AAAS, Am. Coll. Rheumatology, Allergy and Immunology Soc. Ga., Hispanic-Am. Allergy and Immunology Assn., Ga. Pediatric Soc., Pan Am. Med. Assn., Soc. Leukocyte Biology, Am. Coll. Allergy, Asthma and Immunology, Am. Acad. Allergy, Asthma and Immunology, Am. Acad. Pediat., Am. Med. Women's Assn., Panama Canal Soc. Fla., Ga. Ornithol. Soc., Ga. Thoracic Soc., Am. Lung Assn. (Ga. East Ctrl. br. exec. bd.), Am. Assn. Ret. Persons, Nature Conservancy, Royal Soc. for Preservation Birds, Nat. Assn. Ret. Fed. Employees, Nat. Audubon Soc., Panama Audubon Soc., Willow Run Homeowner's Soc. (pres.), Alpha Omega Alpha. Office: Med Coll Ga BG 232 1120 15th St Augusta GA 30912

MEYER, CATHERINE ELEANORE MARY, artist, educator; b. Milw., Aug. 17, 1917; d. Aloysius and Elinore (Matt) Grosspietsch; divorced; children: Marc Jan, Gregory George. Degree in fine and comml. art, Layton Sch. Art, Milw., 1030. Freelance painter Milw., 1940; advt. artist Cramer-Grasselt Co., Milw., 1941-43; watercolor artist Milw. Wire and Frame Co., Milw., 1943-47; layout and color artist Nazarene Pub., Kansas City, Mo., 1947-74; art tchr. Kansas City Juvenile Divsn., 1974-75; freelance artist signs and illustrations Mountain View, Ark., 1975—; art tchr. Mountain View, 1988—. Works exhibited in 4 one-person shows, collections, Stargap Gallery, Little Rock and Fayetteville, Ark., one-woman show Stargap Bballery, 1996; contbr. pen and ink drawing for newspaper, 1994—; author: (cartoon book) Cartooning with Cathe, 1995, (poetry) Tomorrow Never Knows, 1995. Sec., treas. Stone County Rep. Party, 1982, 94, 96. Mem. Mid-South Watercolors (signature mem.). Republican. Christian.

MEYER, DIANNE SCOTT WILSON, secondary school educator, librarian; b. Austin, Tex., Nov. 28, 1941; d. Herbert Cook and Velma Estelle (Scott) Wilson; m. George Edward Hopper, Jr., Apr. 11, 1963 (div. Mar., 1983); children: David Scott, Daniel Wilson; m. James Raymond Meyer, June 21, 1984; step children: Karen Ray, Sheila Kay, Jayme Caroline. BA, Baylor U., 1962; MLA, Houston Bapt. U., 1991; postgrad., U. St. Thomas,

1988, Sam Houston State U., 1973, 79-81, 94, U. Houston, 1979-83, 84-88. Cert. tchr. secondary schs. (provisional) Tex., cert. libr. Tex. Tchr. 7th and 8th grades history and lang. arts La Marque (Tex.) Jr. H.S., 1962-64; tchr. English II and IV Lincoln H.S., La Marque, 1966-67; 7th and 8th grades history and lang. arts Tom Browne Jr. H.S., Corpus Christi, Tex., 1967-68; tchr. English II Tioga (La.) H.S., 1969; tchr. 8th grade lang. arts Anson Ward Sch., Anson, Tex., 1969-72; tchr. English II and IV Cypress Fairbanks H.S., Houston, 1972-81; journalism tchr. yearbook and newspaper Westchester H.S., Houston, 1981-83; tchr. study skills 9th gr. Cypress Creek H.S., Houston, 1983-87, tchr. English I, II and IV, 1988—, tchr. humanities 10th gr., 1992-93; leader Gt. Books Found., 1990-96; presenter in field. Sponsor lit. mag. Equinox of Cy Fair H.S., 1973-76. Grassroots organizer Harris County Dems., Houston, 1978-79; mem. steering com. John Hill Gubernatorial Campaign, Houston, 1978-79; pres. Cy-Fair Edn. Assn., 1978-79; vol. KUHT-TV (PBS sta.), Houston, 1975—; pres. Band Aides Parent-Boosters of Jersey Village H.S. Band, 1981; organizing hostess Marching Bands of Am. Competition, C.F.I.S.D., 1981. Named Cypress Fairbanks H.S. Tchr. of Yr., Houston, 1975, 78, Cypress Fairbanks Ind. Sch. Dist. Tchr. of Yr. 1978; NEH Common Ground grantee: U. Houston, 1992. Mem. ALA, NEA (del. 1976), Young Adult Libr. Assn., Tex. Libr. Assn., N. Harris County Coun. Tchrs. of English, Tex. Coun. Tchrs. of English (nominating com. 1991), Nat. Coun. Tchrs. of English, Tex. State Tchrs. Assn. (del. state and nat. 1975-79, pres. Houston 1978-79, mem. steering com. 1962-95), Delta Kappa Gamma Internat. (charter mem. Kappa Alpha chpt.), Kappa Alpha Theta (charter mem. Epsilon Epsilon chpt.), Baylor Ex-Students Assn. (life alumnae mem.). Democrat. Baptist. Office: Cypress Creek HS 9815 Grant Rd Houston TX 77070-4599

MEYER, FRANCES MARGARET ANTHONY, elementary and secondary school educator, health education specialist; b. Stella, Va., Nov. 15, 1947; d. Arthur Abner Jr. and Emmie Adeline (Murray) Anthony; m. Stephen Leroy Meyer, Aug. 2, 1975. BS, Longwood Coll., 1970; MS, Va. Commonwealth U., 1982, PhD, 1996. Cert. tchr., Va. Health, phys. edn., and dance tchr. Fredericksburg (Va.) City Pub. Schs., 1970-89; AIDS edn. coord. Va. Dept. Edn., Richmond, 1989-90, health edn. specialist, 1990-94, comprehensive sch. health program specialist, 1994—. Author: (with others) Elementary Physical Education: Growing through Movement--A Curriculum Guide, 1982; health editor Va. Jour., 1994—; contbr. articles to profl. jours. Mem. pub. edn. coun., comprehensive sch. health edn. team Va. affiliate, Am. Cancer Soc., Richmond, 1990—; dir. Va. Children's Dance Festival, Hist. Fredericksburg Found., Inc., 1981—; vol. ARC, Fredericksburg, 1976-84. Mem. AAUW (com. 1989-90), ASCD, NEA, AAPHERD (past v.p., chmn. divsn. 1970—, mem. Nat. Mid. Sch. Assn., So. Dist. Honor award 1995), Va. Edn. Assn., Va. Mid. Sch. Assn., Va. Alliance for Arts Edn., Internat. Coun. for Health, Phys. Edn., Recreation, Sport and Dance (internat. commns. for health edn. and commn. for dance and dance edn.), Va. Health Promotion and Edn. Coun. (bd. dirs. 1990—), Soc. State Dirs. Health, Phys. Edn. and Recreation (legis. affairs com. 1994—), Longwood Coll. Alumni Coun. (bd. dirs. 1987-90), Nat. Network for Youth Svcs. (rev. panel, adv. bd. 1994—), Am. Coll. Health Assn. (curriculum and tng. rev. panel 1992-94), Va. Alliance for Arts Edn. (adv. bd. 1980-83, 89-90, 95—), Va. Assn. for Health, Phys. Edn., Recreation and Dance (past pres., various coms. 1970—, Tchr. of Yr. 1983), Delta Kappa Gamma (pres. Beta Eta chpt. 1988-90), Nat. Dance Assn. (bd. dirs. 1996—). Baptist.

MEYER, GOLDYE W., psychologist, educator; b. Wilkes Barre, Pa., Feb. 6, 1927; d. Harry Samuel Weisberger and Jennie Iskowitz; div.; children: Jodie, Howard, Natlee. BS, Wilkes U., Wilkes Barre, 1962; MS, Temple U., Phila., 1964; PhD, U. Conn., Storrs, 1975. Day camp dir. JCC, Wilkes Barre, 1962-64; chemistry instr. Wilkes U., Wilkes Barre, 1962-64, U. Bridgeport, Conn., 1964-65; prof. sec. edn. U. Bridgeport, 1966-74, assoc. prof. counseling and human resources, 1974-78, prof. counseling and human resources, 1978-91; owner pvt. cons. firm, Bridgeport, 1977-90; pvt. psychotherapy practice Fairfield, Conn., 1975—; internat. bioenergetic analysis trainer Switzerland, Israel, 1981—; trainer bioenergetic analysis Conn. Bioenergetic Soc., Conn., 1980-83; adj. prof. Nova U., Ft. Lauderdale, Fla., 1991-93; doctoral adv., acad. supr. Columbia-Pacific U., San Rafael, Calif., 1992—; adj. prof., doctoral adv. The Union Inst., Cin., 1994—; dir. Fairfield (Conn.) Orgnl. Cons., 1977-90, Brooklawn Family Ctr., Fairfield, 1985—; mem. human resources adv. bd. U. Bridgeport, 1986-90; mem. bd. edn. adv. bd. Bridgeport Schs., 1984-87; leader AIDS caregiver support group The Yale New Haven Hosp., 1992—. Contbr. articles to jours, chpts. to books. Co-chair Fairfield Citizens for Edn. Recipient Doctoral Rsch. Grant U. Conn., 1974, Multicultural Rsch. Grant U. Bridgeport, 1980. Mem. ACLU, NOW, APA, Am. Acad. Psychotherapists, Nat. Substance Abuse Counselors, Conn. Coun. for Substance Abuse Counselors, Mass. Soc. for Bioenergetic Analysis (chair ethics com. 1993—), Sierra Club, Appalachian Club. Hebrew. Home: 615 Brooklawn Ave Fairfield CT 06430

MEYER, HELEN (MRS. ABRAHAM J. MEYER), retired editorial consultant; b. Bklyn., Dec. 4, 1907; d. Bertolen and Esther (Greenfield) Honig; m. Abraham J. Meyer, Sept. 1, 1929; children—Adele Meyer Brodkin, Robert L. Grad. pub. schs. With Popular Sci., McCall's mag., 1921-22; pres., dir. Dell Pub. Co., Inc., N.Y.C., 1923-57, Dell Distbg., Inc., from 1957, Dell Internat., Inc., from 1957; pres. Dell Pub. Co., Inc., Montville Warehousing Co., Inc.; chmn. bd. Noble & Noble Pubs., Inc.; v.p. Dellprint, Inc., Dunellen, N.J.; pres. Dial Press.; later editorial cons. Doubleday & Co., N.Y.C.; cons. Fgn. Rights, N.Y.C. Bd. dirs. United Cerebral Palsy. Named to Pub.'s Hall of Fame, 1986. Mem. Assn. Am. Pubs. (dir.). Home: 1 Claridge Dr Apt 608 Verona NJ 07044-3054

MEYER, KAREN SUE, lawyer; b. St. Louis, June 24, 1946; d. Ferdinand Clark and Grace David (Toomey) M. BA, Duke Univ., 1968; MEd, U. Mo., St. Louis, 1972; JD, Wash. U., St. Louis, 1980. Bar: Mo. 1980. Social worker City of Richmond, Va., 1968-70; pers. analyst St. Louis County Govt., 1970-77; field atty. Nat. Labor Rels. Bd., St. Louis, 1980-82; staff atty. U.S. Dept. of Vet. Affairs, St. Louis, 1982-83, asst. dist. counsel, 1983-88; litigation atty. U.S. Dept. of Vet. Affairs, Washington, 1988-90; dist. counsel U.S. Dept. of Vet. Affairs, Bay Pines, Fla., 1990-95; regional counsel (Fla., P.R., V.I.) U.S. Dept. of Vet. Affairs, Bay Pines, 1995—; various task forces U.S. Dept. of Vet. Affairs, 1992—. Mem. Fed. Bar Assn., Mo. Bar Assn. Office: Regional Counsel Office VA Med Ctr 10,000 Bay Pines Blvd Bay Pines FL 33504

MEYER, KATHLEEN MARIE, English educator; b. St. Louis, Oct. 29, 1944; d. Richard Henry and Leonora (Moser) Bailey; m. Thomas A. Meyer, Dec. 26, 1966; children: Richard, Amy, Mindy, Heidi. BA, Webster Coll., Webster Groves, Mo., 1966; MA, Fla. Atlantic U., 1981; postgrad., No. Ill. U., 1982—. Cert. secondary tchr., Mo., Ill. Tchr. English Notre Dame High Sch., St. Louis, 1966-67; tchr. English, chmn. dept. Rosary High Sch., Aurora, Ill., 1981-91; instr. English DeKalb Coll., Decatur, Ga., 1992—; mem. adv. bd. Univ. High Sch.; mem. joint enrollment coun. DeKalb Coll. Mem. ASCD, Nat. Coun. Tchrs. English.

MEYER, LESLEY ANNE, nurse recruiter, nursing administrator; b. Beaufort, S.C., Nov. 8, 1944; d. Andrew M. and Helen Margaret (Mark) Olesak; m. Gary B. Glick, DDS, July 1983; 1 child Gregory Andrew Meyer. Diploma in nursing, L.A. County-U. So. Calif. Med. Ctr., 1965; BSN magna cum laude, Pepperdine U., 1979. RN, CAlif., N.J.; cert. in nursing adminstrn. Charge nurse Kaiser Found. Hosp., San Diego, 1976-81, nurse recruiter, 1981-83; N.E. recruitment cons. So. Calif. region Kaiser Permanente Med. Group, Pasadena, 1983-86; mgr. nurse recruitment and retention Morristown (N.J.) Meml. Hosp., 1986-96; employment svcs. mgr. Mountainside (N.J.) Hosp./Atlantic Health Sys., 1996—; shared governance coordinating coun. facilitator; speaker to local and nat. groups. Contbr. articles to profl. jours. Mem. ANA, N.J. State Nurses Assn., Nat. Assn. Healthcare Recruitment, N.J. Assn. Hosp. Recruiters (2d v.p., corr. sec. 1988-90), Morristown Bus. Edn. Adv. Coun. Home: 3 Fern Ct Flanders NJ 07836-9140

MEYER, LYNN NIX, lawyer; b. Vinita, Okla., Aug. 10, 1948; d. William Armour and Joan Ross Nix; m. Lee Gordon Meyer; children: Veronica, Victoria, David. BA, Baldwin Wallace Coll., 1978; JD, Case Western Res. U., 1981. Bar: Ky. 1982, Colo. 1984. Paralegal Texaco Devel., Austin, Tex., 1976-77; legal asst. Alcan Aluminum, Cleve., 1977-79; assoc. Wyatt, Tarrant & Combs, Lexington, Ky., 1982-83; ptnr. Meyer, Meyer & Assocs., P.C., Denver, 1984-95; in private practice, 95—; pres. Cherokee Fuel Systems, Inc.; v.p., gen. counsel Carbon Fuels Corp., Denver. Mem. ABA, Am. Trial Lawyers Assn., Colo. Bar Assn., Ky. Bar Assn., Arapahoe County Bar Assn. Republican. Home: 10487 E Ida Ave Englewood CO 80111-3746 Office: Carbon Fuels Corp 5105 Dtc Pky Ste 317 Englewood CO 80111-2600*

MEYER, MARA ELLICE, special education educator, consultant; b. Chgo., Oct. 28, 1952; d. David and Harriett (Lazar) Einhorn; m. Leonard X. Meyer, July 20, 1986; children: Hayley Rebecca, David Joseph. BS in Speech and Hearing Sci., U. Ill., 1974, MS in Speech Pathology, 1975, ABD in Pub. Policy Analysis, 1990—. Cert. speech and lang. pathologist, spl. edn. tchr., reading tchr. Speech and lang. pathologist Macon-Piatt Spl. Edn. Dist., Decatur, Ill., 1975-76; speech and lang. pathologist, reading specialist, learning disabilities coord. Community Consolidated Sch. Dist. # 59, Arlington Heights, Ill., 1976-87; test cons. Psychol. Corp., San Antonio, 1987-89; adj. prof. Nat.-Lewis U., Evanston, Ill., 1985-87; ednl. cons. Am. Guidance Svc., Circle Pines, Minn., 1989-94; pvt. practice ednl. cons. Deerfield, Ill., 1994—; project dir. Riverside Pub. Co., Chgo., 1993-94; mem. adv. coun. to Headstart, Dept. Human Svsc., City of Chgo., 1990—; cons. Spl. Edn. Dist. of Lake County, 1995—. Area coord. Dem. Party, Lake County, Ill., 1978—; pres. Park West Condo Assn., Lake County, 1983-88. Mem. NEA, ASCD, Am. Speech-Lang. and Hearing Assn., Internat. Reading Assn., Coun. on Exceptional Children. Home: 1540 Central Ave Deerfield IL 60015-3963

MEYER, MARION M., editorial consultant; b. Sheboygan, Wis., July 14, 1923; d. Herman O. and Viola A. (Hoch) M. BA, Lakeland Coll., 1950; MA, NYU, 1957. Payroll clk. Am. Chair Co., Sheboygan, 1941-46; tchr. English and religion, dir. athletics Am. Sch. for Girls, Baghdad, Iraq, 1950-56; mem. edn. and publ. staff United Ch. Bd. for Homeland Ministries, United Ch. Press/Pilgrim Press, 1958-64, sr. editor, 1965-88, ret., 1988; cons. to individuals and orgns. on editorial matters and copyrights. Editor Penney Retirement Cmty. Newsletter, 1990—; contbr. articles to various publs.; writer hymns Look to God, Be Radiant, 1989, Be Still, 1990, Come, God, Creator, 1992, Something New! (extended work), 1993, Our Home is PRC, 1996. Incorporating mem. Contact Phila., Inc., 1972, bd. dirs., 1972-75, v.p., chmn. com. to organize community adv. bd., chmn. auditing com., editor newsletter, 1972-74, pres., 1974-75, assoc. mem., 1977—; mem. ofcl. bd. Old First Reformed Ch., Phila., 1984-89; deacon United Ch. Christ, 1984—, Mid.-East Com. of Pa. SE Conf. United Ch. Christ, 1986-88. Honored as role model United Ch. of Christ, 1982, 85. Mem. AAUW, NOW, Nat. Mus. Women in the Arts (charter mem.), Nat. Trust for Hist. Preservation. Home: PO Box 656 Penney Farms FL 32079-0656

MEYER, MARY-LOUISE, art gallery executive; b. Boston, Feb. 21, 1922; d. Alonzo Jay and Louise (Whitledge) Shadman; m. Norman Meyer, Aug. 9, 1941; children: Wendy C., Bruce R., Harold Alton, Marilee, Laurel. BA, Wellesley Coll., 1943; MS, Wheelock Coll., 1965. Head tchr. Page Sch., Wellesley Coll., Mass., 1955-60; instr. early childhood edn. Pine Manor Coll., Brookline, Mass., 1960-65; chaplain/counselor Charles St. Jail, Boston, 1974-79; Christian Sci. practitioner, Wellesley, Mass., 1974—; owner Alpha Gallery, Boston, 1972-87; cons. Living & Learning Centers, Boston, 1966-69; 2d reader Christian Sci. Ch., 1979-82. Contbr. articles to profl. jours. Overseer Sturbridge Village, 1981—, trustee, 1986; visitor Am. Decorative Arts dept. Mus. Fine Arts, Boston, 1973—; chmn. Wellesley Voters Rights Com., 1983-84; state organizer Ednl. Channel 2 Group, Boston, 1960; co-founder Boston Assn. for Childbirth Edn., 1950; overseer Strawberry Banke Living Mus., 1987; trustee Maine Coast Artists, Rockport, Maine, 1991, v.p. Friends of Montpelier (Knox Mansion-Thomaston), 1994-96, pres. 1996—; trustee Bay Chamber Concerts, Rockport, 1990; bd. dirs. Down East Singers, 1996. Mem. Mus. Trustees Assn., Farnsworth Mus., Waldoboro Hist. Soc., Soc. for Pres. New Eng. Antiquities (mem. Maine coun.), Wellesley Coll. Club.

MEYER, PAULETTE ANN, history educator; b. Newport, Oreg., Feb. 20, 1945; d. Paul Merrill and Shirley (Cooper) Billbe; m. Richard John Meyer, Jan. 9, 1965; children: Erika Meyer, Rodrick Meyer. AB in History, Stanford (Calif.) U., 1966, AM in Edn., 1967; postgrad., U. Minn., 1992. Cert. secondary tchr., Calif. Instr. world history U. Minn., Mpls., 1992; instr. European intellectual history S.W. State U., Marshall, Minn., 1994, lectr. history of biology, world history Humboldt State U., Arcata, Calif., 1995—. Action chair LWV, Humboldt; bd. suprs. Recreational Trails Com., Humboldt. Fellowship U. Minn., 1989; Nat. Merit scholar. Mem. Western Assn. of Women Historians (sem. presenter 1995), Columbia History of Science Group (seminar presenter 1996). United Methodist. Home: 581 Redmond Rd Eureka CA 95503

MEYER, PEARL, executive compensation consultant; b. N.Y.C.; d. Allen Charles and Rose (Goldberg) Weissman; m. Ira A. Meyer. BA cum laude, NYU, postgrad. Statis. specialist, exec. comp. div. Gen. Foods Corp., White Plains, N.Y.; exec. v.p. and cons. Handy Assocs., Inc., N.Y.C.; founder, pres. Pearl Meyer & Ptnrs., N.Y.C., 1989—; lectr. on exec. compensation at confs. and seminars. Contbr. numerous articles to profl. jours. Recipient Entrepreneurial Woman award Women Bus. Owners N.Y., 1983. Mem. Am. Mgmt. Assn., Am. Compensation Assn., Soc. for Human Resources Mgmt. (cert. accredited pers. diplomate), Women's Econ. Roundtable, Pers. Accreditation Inst., Women's Forum, Sedgewood Club, Atrium Club, Sky Club, Phi Beta Kappa, Pi Mu Epsilon, Kappa Pi Sigma. Clubs: Sedgewood, Bd. Rm., Atrium, Sky. Office: Pearl Meyer & Partners Inc 300 Park Ave 21st Fl New York NY 10022-7402*

MEYER, PUCCI, newspaper editor; b. N.Y.C., Sept. 1, 1944; d. Charles Albert and Lollo (Offer) M.; m. Thomas M. Arma, Sept. 16, 1979. BA, U. Wis., 1966. Asst. editor Look mag., N.Y.C., 1970-71; editorial asst. Look mag., Paris, 1967-69; reporter Newsday, Garden City, L.I., N.Y., 1971-73; style editor N.Y. Daily News Sunday Mag., N.Y.C., 1974-76, assoc. editor, 1977-82, editor, 1983-86; sr. editor Prodigy, White Plains, N.Y., 1987; spl. projects editor N.Y. Post, N.Y.C., 1988-89, style editor, 1990-92, food editor, 1992-93, assoc. features editor, 1993—, travel editor, 1994—. Contbr. articles to various nat. mags. Recipient Pulitzer prize as mem. Newsday investigative team that wrote articles and book The Heroin Trail, 1973. Office: NY Post 1211 6th Ave New York NY 10036

MEYER, RACHEL ABIJAH, foundation director, artist, theorist, poet; b. Job's Corners, Pa., Aug. 18, 1963; d. Jacob Owen and Velma Ruth (Foreman) M.; children: Andrew Carson, Peter Franklin. Student, Lebanon Valley Coll., 1982-84. Restaurant owner Purcy's Place, Ono, Pa., 1985-87; restaurant mgr. King's Table Buffet, Citrus Heights, Calif., 1987-89; product finalizer TransWorld Enterprises, Blaine, Wash., 1989-91; dir., support svcs. adminstr. Tacticar Found., Sacramento, 1991—; tchr. Tacticar Inst., 1995; chair Conirems, Sacramento, 1996—. Author: Year of the Unicorn, 1994. Home and Office: 2052 Janice Ave Sacramento CA 95821-1519

MEYER, SANDRA W(ASSERSTEIN), bank executive, management consultant; b. N.J., Aug. 20, 1937; children—Jenifer Anne Schweitzer, Samantha Boughton Schweitzer. Student, U. Mich.; B.A. cum laude, Syracuse U., 1957; postgrad., London Sch. Econs., 1958. Advt. account exec. London Press Exchange, 1959-63; product mgr. Beecham Products Inc., Clifton, N.J., 1963-66; with Gen. Foods Co., White Plains, N.J., 1966-76; mktg. mgr. coffee div. Gen. Foods Co., 1973-74, dir. corp. mktg. planning, 1975-76; with Am. Express Co., N.Y.C., 1976-84; pres. communications div. Am. Express Co., 1980-84; mng. dir. Russell Reynolds Assocs., N.Y.C., 1985-89; sr. corp. officer corp. affairs Citicorp, N.Y.C., 1989-93; sr. partner Clark & Weinstock, N.Y.C., 1993—. Trustee Met. Opera Guild, East Hampton Guild Hall; mng. dir. Met. Opera Assn.; bd. dirs. St. Luke's Orch. Office: Clark & Weinstock 52 Vanderbilt Ave New York NY 10017-3808

MEYER, SUSAN MOON, speech language pathologist, educator; b. Hazleton, Pa., Mar. 8, 1949; d. Robert A. and Jane W. (Walters) Moon; m. John C. Meyer Jr., Feb. 16, 1989; children: Chris, Scott. BS, Pa. State U., 1971, MS, 1972; PhD, Temple U., 1983. Cert. tchr., Pa. Speech-lang. pathologist, instr. Elmira (N.Y.) Coll., 1973-74; speech-lang. pathologist Arnot-Ogden Hosp., Elmira, 1973-74; supr. Sacred Heart Hosp. Speech and Hearing Ctr., Allentown, Pa., 1974-75; speech-lang. pathology instr. Kutztown (Pa.) U., 1975-78, asst. prof., 1978-82, assoc. prof., 1982-85, prof., 1985—; owner Speech and Lang. Svcs., Allentown, 1975-87; cons. Vis. Nurses Assn., Allentown, 1975-85, Home Care, Allentown, 1975-85. Mem. Am. Speech-Lang.-Hearing Assn. (cert., councilor 1986-89, Continuing Edn. award 1982, 85, 88, 91, 93, 94, 95, 96), Pa. Speech-Lang.-Hearing Assn. (cert., v.p. profl. preparation 1985-89, Appreciation award 1987, 88, 89), Northeastern Speech and Hearing Assn. Pa. (pres. 1984-86, Outstanding Dedication award 1985), Coun. Suprs. Speech-Lang. Pathology and Audiology. Office: Kutztown U Dept Speech-Lang Kutztown PA 19530

MEYER, SUSAN THERESA, business and training industry consultant; b. Ames, Iowa, Mar. 29, 1950; d. Robert William Keirs and Jeanne Marion (Thomas) Kaufer; m. John Allen Meyer, Dec. 18, 1972; children: Katherine Jeanne, Robert John. BS cum laude, U. Wis., 1972; MBA, Ea. Mich. U., 1982. Cert. spl. edn. tchr., Wis., Va. Spl. edn. tchr. Prince George (Va.) Pub. Schs., 1972-73; acct. DEMPUBCO Printing Co., Colorado Springs, Colo., 1973-74; adminstr., dir. EEO Dept. of Army, Frankfurt, Fed. Rep. of Germany, 1974-77; program coordinator Wake Up La., New Orleans, 1977-78; buyer Ford Motor Co., Dearborn, Mich., 1978-81; fgn. procurement specialist Ford Motor Co., Dearborn, 1981-85; pres. Mgmt. Recruiters of No. Del., Wilmington, 1985-91, The Obermeyer Group Ltd., Fort Collins, Colo., 1991—; dir. Small Bus. and Internat. Devel. Ctr., Ft. Collins, Colo., 1993-94; adj. prof. mktg. U. No. Colo., 1991—, Colo. State U., 1992—; cons. Fed. Women's Program, Frankfurt, 1974-77. Adv. bd. Women's Devel. Coun./Women Bus. Owners, Ft. Collins, 1993—, Ft. Collins Chamber Bus. Assistance Ctr., Ft. Collins, 1992—; mem. adv. bd. Comty. Involvement for Bank One, Ft. Collins, 1993—. Mem. Wilmington Women in Bus., Nat. Assn. Female Execs. Republican. Roman Catholic. Home: 6465 Hidden Springs Rd Fort Collins CO 80526-6511 Office: The Obermeyer Group Ltd PO Box 270711 Fort Collins CO 80527-0711

MEYER, WENDY BETH, artist, educator; b. Rahway, N.J., June 19, 1962; d. Arnold F. Meyer and Carole M. (Fried) Wolfe. BA, Emory U., 1984. Art dir. The Wave/New Times, Miami, Fla., 1987-88, Emmons Advt., Ft. Lauderdale, Fla., 1988-93; creative dir., prin. In You Wendo Design, West Palm Beach, Fla., 1992—; adj. faculty Palm Beach C.C., Lake Worth, Fla., 1995—; curriculum com. Palm Beach C.C., Lake Worth, 1992-93; steering com. Very Spl. Arts, Palm Beach County, 1995—, artist/instr., 1995, 96; co-chair Design Electronica, Ft. Lauderdale, 1992-93. Designer: (newsletter) CMYK, 1992 (Gold award of Design Excellence, How Internat. Ann. Design award), 1996 PRINT Regional Design Ann., 1996—, (advt. publ.) Everything is Permitted, 1993 (Best of Show/Best of Print Addy award 1994), (digital painting) Kool Kat, 1995 (Fractal Design Art Expo finalist, 1995; designer various graphic arts publs. Active Hurricane Andrew Relief Effort, West Palm Beach. Mem. Electronic Design Assn. (sec. 1991-93), AIGA, Graphic Artist Guild, Ad Club of the Palmbeaches, ISC. Office: In You Wendo Design 5636 Souchak Dr West Palm Beach FL 33413

MEYERROSE, SARAH LOUISE, bank holding company executive; b. Jefferson City, Mo., Nov. 26, 1955; d. William J. and Mary L. (Fricke) Wollenburg; m. Michael J. Meyerrose, Aug. 18, 1978. BA, Vanderbilt U., 1978, MBA, 1987. Chartered fin. analyst. Corp. fin. asst. Commerce Union Corp., Nashville, 1978-80, money market sales rep., 1980-82; asst. treas. First Tenn. Nat. Corp., Memphis, 1982-84, v.p., treas., 1984-88, v.p. sr. fin. officer, 1988-90; sr. v.p. fin. & adminstrn. First Tenn. Nat. Corp., 1990-93; exec. v.p. retail, mortgage, trust First Tenn. Bank, N.A., Johnson City, 1993-95; pres. First Tenn. Bank, N.A., Kingsport, 1996—; guest lectr. Vanderbilt U., 1987; instr. Am. Inst. Banking, Memphis, 1985, Tenn. Bankers Assn., Nashville, 1987, 88, 89. Chair Johnson City Symphony Orch., 1994-95; bd. dirs. United Way, Kingsport Tomorrow, Girls, Inc., YMCA, Salvation Army. Mem. Fin. Analysts Fedn., Kingsport C. of C. (bd. dirs.), Econs. Club Memphis. Office: First Tenn Bank NA 235 E Center St Kingsport TN 37662

MEYERS, AMY REAGLE, executive search consultant; b. N.Y.C., Jan. 14, 1961; d. Charles Marshall Reagle and Nancy Smith Clapp; m. Stephen C. Meyers, May 12, 1990; children: Edward, Lucy. BA, Coll. William and Mary, 1983. Cons. Russell Reynolds Assocs., Inc., Boston, 1987-92; exec. search cons. Boston, 1992—. Pres. Jr. League of Boston, 1996—; bd. dirs. Shelter, Inc., Cambridge, Mass., 1994—. Republican. Christian Scientist. Home and Office: 51 E Concord St Boston MA 02118

MEYERS, ANN ELIZABETH, sports broadcaster; b. San Diego, Mar. 26, 1955; d. Robert Eugene and Patricia Ann (Burke); m. Donald Scott Drysdale, Nov. 1, 1986; children: Donald Scott Jr., Darren John, Drew Ann. G-rad., UCLA, 1978. Profl. basketball player N.J. Gems, 1979-80; profl. basketball player Ind. Pacers NBA, 1979; sports broadcaster Ind. Pacers, 1979-80; sportscaster men's basketball U. Hawaii, Honolulu, 1981-82; sportscaster men's and women's basketball UCLA, 1982-84, 89—; sportscaster volleyball, basketball, softball, tennis ESPN, 1981—; sportscaster Olympic Games ABC, L.A., 1984; sportscaster volleyball, softball, tennis, basketball, soccer Sportsvision, 1985-87; sportscaster volleyball, basketball, softball Prime Ticket, 1985—; sportscaster CBS-TV, 1991—; sportscaster Goodwill Games, WTBS, 1986, 90. Winner Silver medal Montreal Olympics, 1976, Gold medal Pan Am. Games, 1975, Silver medal, 1979, All-Am. UCLA, 1975, 76, 77, 78; 1st woman named to Hall of Fame UCLA, 1987; named to Women's Sports Hall of Fame, 1987, Orange County Sports Hall of Fame, 1985, Calif. H.S. Hall of Fame, 1990, Basketball Hall of Fame, 1993, Nat. H.S. Hall of Fame, 1995, NBC Hoop It Up, 1995, Cath. Youth Org. Hall of Fame, 1996. Office: care Lampros and Roberts 16615 Lark Ave # 101 Los Gatos CA 95030-2439

MEYERS, ANNE ROTH, real estate consultant; b. Cambridge, Mass., Aug. 19, 1946; d. Wilfred and Norma (Miller) Roth; m. Allan R. Meyers, Apr. 6, 1968; children: David, Jonathan. BA, Skidmore Coll., 1968; MBA, Boston U., 1981. Rsch. mgr. Boston U., 1974-77; project mgr., bus. mgr. Mass. Port Authority, Boston, 1977-83; assoc. dir. Health Effects Inst., Cambridge, Mass., 1983-84; dep. dir. devel. Mass. Port Authority, Boston, 1984-95; prin. Anne Meyers Assocs., Brookline, Mass., 1995—; founder, steering com. New Eng. Women in Real Estate, Boston, 1981-84; chair Urban Land Inst.-Boston Dist. Coun., Washington, 1994—. Mem. Boston Harbor Assn., The Waterfront Ctr., Women's Transp. Ctr. Office: Anne Meyers Assocs 109 Columbia St Brookline MA 02146

MEYERS, CHRISTINE LAINE, marketing and media executive, consultant; b. Detroit, Mar. 7, 1949; d. Ernest Robert and Eva Elizabeth (Laine) M.; 1 child, Kathryn Laine; m. Oliver S. Moore III, May 12, 1990. BA, U. Mich., 1968. Editor, indsl. relations Diesel div. Gen. Motors Corp., Detroit, 1968; nat. advt. mgr. J.L. Hudson Co., Detroit, 1969-76, mgr. internal sales promotion, 1972-73, dir. pub., 1973-76; nat. advt. mgr. Pontiac Motor div., Mich., 1976-78; pres., owner Laine Meyers Mktg. Cos., Inc., Troy, Mich., 1978—; dir. Internat. Inst. Met. Detroit, Inc. Contbr. articles to profl. publs. Mem. bus. adv. council Cen. Mich. U., 1977-79; mem. pub. adv. com. on jud. candidates Oakland County Bar Assn.; mem. adv. bd. Birmingham Community Hosp., bd. dirs. YMCA, Mich., 1992—; Named Mich. Ad Woman of Yr., 1976, one of Top 10 Working Women Glamour mag., 1978, one of 100 Best and Brightest Advt. Age, 1987, one of Mich.'s top 25 female bus. owners Nat. Assn. Women Bus. Owners, One of Top 10 Women Owned Bus., Mich., 1994; recipient Vanguard award Women in Communications, 1986. Mem. Internat. Assn. Bus. Communicators, Adcraft Club, Women's Advt. Club (1st v.p. 1975), Women's Econ. Club (pres. 1976-77), Internat. Women's Forum Mich. (pres. 1986—), Internat. Inst. of Detroit (bd. dirs. 1986-89), Detroit C. of C., Troy C. of C., Mortar Board, Quill and Scroll, Pub. Relations Com. Women for United Found., Founders Soc. Detroit Inst. Arts, Fashion Group, Pub. Relations Soc. Am., First Soc. Detroit (exec. com. 1970-71), Kappa Tau Alpha. Home: 1780 Kensington Rd Bloomfield Hills MI 48304-2428 Office: Laine Meyers Marketing Companies Inc 3645 Crooks Rd Troy MI 48084-1642

MEYERS, DIANA LEE, public relations and fundraising consultant; b. Bremerton, Wash., July 27, 1937; d. Albert Earl and Evelyn Francis (Baldauf) Clark. BA in English and History, U. Calif., Santa Barbara, 1960. Office mgr. Alfred Millard Hist. Research, Santa Barbara, 1959-64; adminstrv. asst. Puritan Cos., Santa Barbara, 1964-75; ops. officer MacElhenny/Levy Real Estate, Santa Barbara, 1975-76; pub. rels. and devel. officer Cancer Found. Santa Barbara, 1976-84; owner Diana L. Meyers Consulting Svcs., Santa Barbara, 1984—. Contbr. articles to profl. jours. Assoc.

Compton Internat. Fundraising, Ltd., 1996. Mem. AAUW (named gift award 1981), Nat. Soc. Fund Raising Execs. (Profl. Fundraiser of Yr. 1993), Santa Barbara Assocs., Santa Barbara C. of C. (Recognition award 1989), Santa Barbara Advt. Club (Silver medal award 1987), Univ. Club, U. Calif. Santa Barbara Alumni Assn., U. Calif. Santa Barbara Affiliatus, Bus. and Industry Assocs., Channel City Club. Republican. Unitarian. Office: Ste 10 928 Carpinteria St Santa Barbara CA 93103

MEYERS, DOROTHY, education consultant, writer; b. Chgo., Jan. 9, 1927; d. Gilbert and Harriet (Levitt) King; m. William J. Meyers, Oct. 9, 1947; children: Lynn, Jeanne. BA, U. Chgo., 1945, MA, 1961, postgrad.; postgrad. Columbia U., New Sch. Social Rsch., Northwestern U. Instr. sr. adults, Chgo. Bd. and/City Colls. Chgo., 1961-78; coord. pub. affairs forum and health maintenance program City Colls. Chgo.-Jewish Community Ctrs., Chgo., 1975-78; lectr. adult program City Colls. Chgo., 1984; tchr. Dade County Adult Edn. Program, Miami, Fla., 1983-85; discussion leader Brandeis U. Adult Edn., 1985-86; cons., lectr. in field. Contbr. articles to profl. jours. Chmn. legis. PTA; discussion leader Great Decisions, 1984-86; chmn. civic assembly Citizens Sch. Com.; v.p. community rels. Womens Fedn. and Jewish United Fund; discussion leader LWV, Gt. Decisions, Fgn. Policy Assn.; program chmn. Jewish Community Ctrs., 1966-67, mem. sr. adult com.; bd. dirs. coun. Jewish Elderly, Open U.; mem. art and edn. com. Chgo. Mayor's Com. for Sr. Citizens and Handicapped; mem. com. on media Met. Coun. on Aging; active Bon Secour's Villa Maria Hosp.; founder Mt. Sinai Hosp., Miami Beach; sponsor Miami Heart Inst.; active Royal Notable Alzheimer Care Unit-Douglas Home Miami; com. mem. March of Dimes; amb. Project Newborn U. Miami Pre Natal Unit. Recipient Prima Donna award Men's Opera Guild-Fla., 1995, Miami Children's Hosp. honor, 1996. Mem. ASA, Gerontol. Assn., Nat. Coun. Aging, Nat. Coun. Jewish Women, Women's Auxiliary Jewish Community Ctr., Chgo. Met. Sr. Forum (media com.), Coun. Women Chgo. Real Estate Bd., Women in Communications, Chgo. Real Estate Bd., Nat. Assn. Real Estate Bds., Cultural Ctr. (Miami, Fla.), Mus. Art Ft. Lauderdale, Miami Internat. Press Club, Gastrointestinal Rsch. Found., Brandeis U., Art Inst. Chgo., Mus. Contemporary Art (life), Mus. Art Boca Raton, Brandeis Women's Auxiliary, Circumnavigator Club (Chgo. and Fla. chpts.). Office: 77 W Washington St Chicago IL 60602-2801

MEYERS, ELLEN ANNE, state agency administrator; b. Balt., Feb. 4, 1958; d. Michael Carroll and Barbara Ellen (Seifert) M. Bachelor's degree, Lawrence U., 1980; Master's degree, Columbia Coll., 1987. Instr. Chgo. Access Corp., 1987-88, Comty. Film Workshop, Chgo., 1988; exec. dir. Women in the Dirs. Chair, Chgo., 1986-87; dir. grants and spl. projects Ctr. for New TV, Chgo., 1988-91; cons. Retirement Rsch. Found., Chgo., 1991-92; strategist Citizens for O'Malley, Chgo., 1992; liaison for lesbian and gay issues Cook County State's Attorney, Chgo., 1992—; chair State's Atty.'s Task Force on Lesbian and Gay Issues and Criminal Justice Sys., 1994—. Prodr.: (videos) Just Keep Going, 1987 (Gold Plaque Chicago Internat. Film Festival 1988, Cert. of Merit Suffolk County Film Festival 1988, Bronze Seal Internat. Arts Festival London), One Day You Hear, 1991 (Bronze Plaque Columbus Internat. Film Festival). Bd. dirs., founder Ill. Fedn. for Human Rights, Chgo., 1992—, Ill. Fedn. for Human Rights Pac, Chgo., 1993—; vol. Open Hand Chgo., 1991—. Media arts fellow Nat. Endowment Arts, 1988. Home: 1969 W Winona Chicago IL 60640 Office: Cook County State's Atty Comty Svcs Unit 406 Daley Ctr Chicago IL 60602

MEYERS, FERN BRAKKE, retired elementary school educator, campground owner; b. Pilot Mound, Minn., Mar. 18, 1920; d. John T. and Hulda Christina (Marburger) Brakke; m. Millard Richard Meyers, Aug. 15, 1943; children: Judith Altobell, Nancy Bechtold, Randall M. Meyers, John R. Meyers, Deidre Meyers Wagener. AS, Winona State Coll., 1940; BS, Mankato State U., 1963, postgrad., 1964-80. Elem. tchr. Douglas (Minn.) Rural Dist., 1940-42, #42 & 2 Steele County, Owatonna, Minn., 1942-44, Warsaw (Minn.) Rural Sch., 1948-50, Waterville (Minn.) Ind. Sch. Dist., 1956-88; mgr., co-owner Camp Maiden Rock, Morristown, Minn., 1972-96; pres. Waterville Edn. Assn., 1985-87, rep. Cannon Valley Uniserv Assn., Faribault, Minn., 1984-88. Editor Peace Notes, 1994-95. County del. Democratic Farmer-Labor Party, Rice County, 1980, 84, 88, vol. tax aide AARP, Faribault, 1992-95; lay mem. del. state conf. Meth. Ch., St. Cloud, 1980-92. Mem. Women's Soc. Christian Svc. (pres. 1991-96), Ret. Educators Minn., Morristown Hist. Soc. (v.p. 1994-96), Faribault C. of C. Office: Camp Maiden Rock Box 326 Maiden Rock Ln Morristown MN 55052

MEYERS, JAN, former congresswoman; b. Lincoln, Nebr., July 20, 1928; m. Louis Meyers; children: Valerie, Philip. A.A. in Fine Arts, William Woods Coll., 1948; B.A. in Communications (hon.), U. Nebr.-Lincoln, 1951; LittD, William Woods Coll., 1986; LLD (hon.), Baker U., 1993. Mem. Overland Park (Kans.) City Coun., 1967-72; pres. Overland (Kans.) Park City Council; mem. Kans. Senate, 1972-84, chmn. pub. health and welfare com., local govt. com.; mem. 99th-103rd Congresses from 3rd Kans. Dist., 1985-96, mem. com. internat. rels., chmn. sml. bus. com., mem. com. on econ. and ednl. opportunities. 3rd Dist. co-chmn. Bob Dole for U.S. Senate, 1968; chmn. Johnson County Bob Bennett For Gov., 1974; mem. Johnson County Cmty. Coll. Found.; bd. dirs. Johnson County Mental Health Assn. Recipient Outstanding Elected Ofcl. of Yr. award Assn. Cmty. Mental Health Ctrs. Kans., Woman of Achievement Matrix award Women in Communications, Disting. Service award Bus. and Profl. Women Kansas City, William Woods Alumna award of distinction, Cmty. Svc. award Jr. League Kansas City, 1st Disting. Legislator award Kans. Assn. C.C.s, Outstanding Svc. award Kans. Library Assn., United Community Services, Kans. Pub. Health Assn., award Gov.'s Conf. Child Abuse and Neglect, Outstanding Legislator award Kans. Action for Children, Friend award Nat. Assn. County Park and Recreation Ofcls., 1987, Disting. Alumna award, 1991, numerous others. Mem. LWV (past pres. Shawnee Mission). Methodist. Office: US Ho of Reps 2303 Rayburn Bldg Ofc Washington DC 20515-0005*

MEYERS, JUDITH ANN, education educator; b. Scranton, Pa., Aug. 5, 1946; d. Paul Meyers and Elaine Jenkins; m. Stuart M. Olinsky, July 10, 1977; children: Seth, Noah. BA with honors, Rutgers U., 1969; MA in Early Childhood Edn., Kean Coll., 1973. Cert. tchr. early childhood K-8, N.J., Pa. Tchr. Tchr.'s Corp., Newark, 1970-71; head tchr. Arlington Ave. Presch., East Orange, N.J., 1972-75, ednl. dir., 1976-78, exec. dir., 1979-81; program developer for early childhood program, instr. early childhood Williamsport (Pa.) Area C.C./Penn Tech., 1987-89; community mem. curriculum rev. com. Penn Tech. C.C., Williamsport, 1990-91; parent mem. West Branch. Sch., tchr. selection com., 1991-93, tchr. evaluation com., 1991-93, curriculum devel. com., 1993. Author, program developer early childhood edn. courses. Chmn. Victorian Williamsport Preservation Com., 1993-94; bd. dirs. Community Theatre, Williamsport, 1993-94. Home: 150 Selkirk Rd Williamsport PA 17701-1869

MEYERS, KAREN DIANE, lawyer, educator, corporate officer; b. Cin., July 8, 1956; d. Willard Paul and Camille Jeannette (Schutte) M.; m. William J. Jones, Mar. 27, 1982. BA summa cum laude, Thomas More Coll., 1974; MBA, MEd, Xavier U., 1978; JD, U. Ky., Covington, 1978. Bar: Ohio 1978, Ky. 1978; CLU; CPCU. Clk. to mgr. Baldwin Co., Cin., 1970-78; adj. prof. bus. Thomas More Coll., Crestview Hill, Ky., 1978—; asst. sec., asst. v.p., sr. counsel The Ohio Life Ins. Co., Hamilton, 1978-91; prin. KD Meyers & Assocs., 1991; v.p. Benefit Designs, Inc., 1991—. Bd. dirs. ARC, Hamilton, 1978-83, vol., 1978—; bd. dirs. YWCA, Hamilton, 1985-91; v.p. Benefit Designs Inc., 1991—. Gardner Found. fellow, 1968-71; recipient Ind. Progress award Bus. & Profl. Women, 1990. Fellow Life Mgmt. Inst. Atlanta; mem. ABA, Soc. Chartered Property Casualty Underwriters (instr. 1987—), Cin. Bar Assn., Butler County Bar Assn., Ohio Bar Assn., Ky. Bar Assn. Roman Catholic. Home: 7903 Hickory Hill Dr Cincinnati OH 45241-1363

MEYERS, LINDA LEE, health, physical education, and recreation educator; b. Williamstown, W.Va., Aug. 26, 1939; d. Robert and Elizabeth Mary (Duvall) Mayo; m. Charles Otto Meyrs, July 27, 1975. BA, Glenville State Coll., 1961; MS, Ind. U., 1970; postgrad., U. Va., 1973. Jr. high tchr. Hamilton Jr. H.S., Parkersburg, W.Va., 1961-70; prof. health, phys. edn., recreation Va. Western C.C., Roanoke, 1970-75, W.Va. U., Parkersburg, 1978—; adv. bd. mem. Women Sports Edn., Slippery Rock, Pa., 1992—. Mem. WVAHPERD (chair coll. sports 1994-95, chair women sports 1994-96), AAUW, AAHPERD, NOW, Nat. Girls & Women in Sport (coord. 1993-95), Assn. Health & Edn. Democrat. Roman Catholic. Home: 610 4th St Williamstown WV 26187 Office: WVa U Rt 5 Box 167-A Parkersburg WV 26101

MEYERS, LYNN BETTY, architect; b. Chgo., Dec. 2, 1952; d. William J. and Dorothy (King) M.; m. Dana Terp, May 17, 1975; children: Sophia, Rachel. Student, Royal Acad. Architecture, Copenhagen, Denmark, 1971; BArch, Washington U., St. Louis, 1974, MArch, 1977. Registered architect, Ill., Fla. Architect Holabird & Root Architects, Chgo., 1973, 76, Jay Alpert Architects, Woodbridge, Conn., 1976, City of Chgo. Bur. Architects, 1978-80; sole practice architecture Chgo., 1980-82; prin., architect Terp Meyers Architects, Chgo., 1982—; real estate salesman, Ill., 1991, Fla.; v.p. Paradise Grove Devel. Corp., 1991—. Exhbns. include: Centre George Pompidou, Paris, 1978, Fifth Internat. Congress Union Internat. Des Femmes Architects, Seattle, 1979, Frumkin Struve Gallery, Chgo., 1981, Art. Inst. Chgo., 1983, Inst. Francais d'Architecture, Paris, 1983, Mus. Sci. and Industry, Chgo., 1985, Hyde Park Art Ctr., 1990, 91, Chgo. Architecture and Design Art Inst. 1923-1993, 1993; pub. in profl. jours. including Progressive Architecture, Modo Design, Inland Architect, 1984, Chgo. Archtl. Jour., 1983, L.A. Architect; work featured in various archtl. books; exhibited 150 Yrs. of Chgo. Architecture, Mus. Sci. and Industry, Chgo., 1985, Chgo. Women in Architecture - Progress and Evolution, Chgo. Hist. Soc., 1974-84. Recipient Progressive Architecture mag. award, 1980, citation Archtl. Design, 1980. Mem. AIA (task force com. for 1992 World's Fair, 1st place award L.A. Real Problems Competition 1986, Art By Architects award 1989, Art award 1990), Union Internat. Des Femmes Architects, Chgo. Women in Architecture (v.p. 1980-81, Allied Arts award 1974), Young Chgo. Architects. Office: Terp Meyers Architects 919 N Michigan Ave Chicago IL 60611-1601

MEYERS, MARY ANN, writer, college administrator; b. Sodus, N.Y., Sept. 30, 1937; d. Harold Galpin and Clarice Mildred (Daniel) Dye; m. John Matthew Meyers, Aug. 22, 1959; children: Andrew Christopher, Anne Kathryn. BA magna cum laude, Syracuse U., 1959; MA, U. Pa., 1965, PhD, 1976. Editorial asst. Ladies' Home Jour., Phila., 1959-62; editor, asst. dir. news bur. U. Pa., Phila., 1962-65, asst. to pres., 1973-75, univ. sec., lectr. Am. civilization, 1980-90; contbg. writer The Pennsylvania Gazette, Phila., 1965—; dir. coll. rels., editor Haverford Horizons, lectr. in religion Haverford (Pa.) Coll., 1977-80; pres. The Annenberg Found., St. Davids, Pa., 1990-92; v.p. for external affairs Moore Coll. Art and Design, Phila., 1995—. Author: A New World Jerusalem, 1983; contbg. author: Death in America, 1975, Gladly Learn, Gladly Teach, 1978, Coping with Serious Illness, 1980, Religion in American Life, 1987; contbr. articles to profl. jours. Judge recognition program Coun. for Advancement and Support Edn., Washington, 1977-78, chair creative editing and writing workshop, 1978; mem. Picker Found. Program on Human Qualities in Medicine, N.Y.C. and Phila., 1980-83; del. Phila.-Leningrad Sister Cities Project, 1986; trustee U. Pa. Press, 1985—, vice chmn. U. Pa., 250th Anniversary Commn., 1987-90, mem. steering com. of bd. trustees, U. Pa., Annenberg Sch. for Communication, 1990-92, mem. adv. bd. U. Pa., Annenberg Ctr. for the Performing Arts, 1990—; mem. bd. overseers, U. Pa., Sch. Arts and Scis., 1990—; mem. steering com. of bd. trustees Annenberg Ctr. for Communication, U. So. Calif., L.A., 1990-92, The Annenberg Washington Program in Communications Policy Studies of Northwestern U., Washington, 1990-92; trustee Am. Acad. Polit. and Social Sci., 1992—, World Affairs Coun. Phila., 1990-95; dir. Diagnostic and Rehab. Ctr., Phila., 1993—. Recipient Excellence award Women in Communications, Inc., 1973-74, award for pub. affairs reporting Newsweek/Coun. for Advancement and Support Edn., 1977, Silver medal Coun. for Advancement and Support Edn., 1986. Mem. Cosmopolitan Club, Sunday Breakfast Club, Phi Beta Kappa (mem. steering com. Delaware Valley chpt. 1995—). Roman Catholic. Home: 217 Gypsy Ln Wynnewood PA 19096-1112

MEYERS, NANCY JANE, screenwriter, producer; b. Phila., Dec. 8, 1949; d. Irving H. and Patricia (Lemisch) M. BA, Am. U., Washington, 1971. Co-writer, prodr.: (films) Private Benjamin (Acad. award nominee, Writers Guild award 1980), Irreconcilable Differences, 1984, Baby Boom, 1987, Father of the Bride, 1991, I Love Trouble, 1994, Father of the Bride Part II, 1995. Mem. ASCAP, Acad. Motion Picture Arts and Scis., Writers Guild Am. West. Office: Starr & Co 350 Park Ave Flr 9 New York NY 10022

MEYERS, PAMELA SUE, lawyer; b. Lakewood, N.J., June 13, 1951; d. Morris Leon and Isabel (Leibowitz) M.; m. Gerald Stephen Greenberg, Aug. 24, 1975; children: David Stuart Greenberg, Allison Brooke Greenberg. AB with distinction, Cornell U., 1973; JD cum laude, Harvard U., 1976. Bar: N.Y. 1977, Ohio 1990. Assoc. Stroock & Stroock & Lavan, N.Y.C., 1976-80; staff v.p., asst. gen. counsel Am. Premier Underwriters, Inc., Cin., 1980—. Mem. Am. Soc. Corp. Secs. (membership chmn. 1990-91, adv. com. 1991—), Cin. Bar Assn., Greater Cin. Women Lawyers Assn., Harvard Club of Cin. (bd. dirs. 1993—), Phi Beta Kappa. Jewish. Home: 3633 Carpenters Creek Dr Cincinnati OH 45241-3824 Office: Am Premier Underwriters 1 E 4th St Cincinnati OH 45202-3717

MEYERSON, BARBARA TOBIAS, elementary school educator; b. Rockville Centre, N.Y., May 17, 1928; d. Sol and Hermine (Sternberg) Tobias; m. Daniel Meyerson, Sept. 4, 1962; children: George D., Barbara Meyerson Ayers. BEd, SUNY, New Paltz, 1948; postgrad., NYU, Hofstra U. Tchr. kindergarten Dix Hills (N.Y.) pub. schs., Hicksville (N.Y.) pub. schs., Valley Stream (N.Y.) pub. schs.; tchr. 6th grade Flushing (N.Y.) Bd. Edn. Dist. commr. Boy Scouts Am., mem. tng. staff, organizer new units; founder, sec. Repertory Theatre, Rio Rancho, N.Mex.; sec. Italian Am. Assn., Rio Rancho; vol. Rio Rancho City Hall Pub. Offices. Mem. ACE, VFW (jr. v.p.), United Fedn. Tchrs. Home: 6127 Cottontail Rd NE Rio Rancho NM 87124-1545

MEYR, SHARI LOUISE, computer consultant; b. San Diego, Dec. 6, 1951; d. Herchell M. and Etta Louise (Bass) Knight; m. William Earl Groom, Oct. 22, 1977 (div. Sept. 1989), Herbert Carl Meyr Jr., Feb. 23, 1990. AS in Fire Scis., San Diego Mesa Coll., 1976. T.O.S.S. specialist Spectrum Scis. & Software, Mountain Home AFB, 1989-94; computer cons., Internet webmaster ComputerLand of Boise, 1995—; equestrian instr. Summerwind Ctr., Mountain Home, Idaho, 1979-91; Chow Chow breeder Meyr Kennels, Mountain Home, 1990—; multimedia P.C. cons., CEO Access to Answers, Mountain Home, 1990—; seasonal zoo keeper Soco Gardens Zoo, Maggie Valley, N.C., 1995. Mem. U.S. Ski Assn. (competition lic., alpine ofcl. profl. coach, master's alpine racer 1991—), Gorilla Found., Summerwind Riding Club (founder, pres. 1981-89), Mountain Home Ski Club (founder, bd. dirs. 1991—), Bogus Basin Ski Club, Sun Valley Ski Club, Amateur Trapshooting Assn. (life), Mountain Home Internet Users Group (founder, dir. 1995—), Mensa. Home: 570 E 16th N Mountain Home ID 83647-1717

MEYSENBURG, MARY ANN, principal; b. L.A., Sept. 16, 1939; d. Clarence Henry and Mildred Ethel (McGee) Augustine; m. John Harold Meysenburg, June 17, 1967; children: Peter Augustine, Amy Bernadette. BA magna cum laude, U. So. Calif., 1960; MA Pvt. Sch. Adminstrn. magna cum laude, U. San Francisco, 1995. Cert. elem. tchr., Calif. Auditor, escrow officer Union Bank, L.A., 1962-64; v.p., escro mgr. Bank of Downey, Calif., 1964-66; cons., tchr. Santa Ana (Calif.) Coll. Bus., 1964-66; elem. tchr. St. Bruno's Sch., Whittier, Calif., 1966-70, Pasadena (Calif.) Unified Sch. Dist., 1971-84, Holy Angels Sch., Arcadia, Calif., 1985-89; vice prin., computer coord. Our Mother of Good Counsel, L.A., 1989-93; prin. St. Stephen Martyr, Monterey Park, Calif., 1993—; master catechist religious edn. L.A. Archdiocese, 1988—. Author: History of the Arms Control and Disarmament Organization, 1976; organizer, editor newsletter Cath. Com. for Girl Scouts and Campfire. Eucharistic min. Our Mother of Good Counsel, 1989-95; sec. of senatus Legion of Mary, 1980-85; counselor Boy Scouts Am., 1985—; mem. Cath. com. for Girl Scouts U.S.A. and Campfire, vice chmn. acad. affairs L.A. Archdiocese, 1985-90. Recipient Pius X medal L.A. Archdiocese, 1979, St. Elizabeth Ann Seton award Cath. Com. for Girl Scouts, 1988, St. Anne medal Cath. Com. for Girl Scouts, 1989, Bronze Pelican award Cath. Com. for Boy Scouts, 1989; grantee Milken Family Found., 1989, 92. Mem. Phi Beta Kappa, Phi Delta Kappa (historian 1991-92, founds. rep. 1992-93, treas. 1993-94, 1st v.p. 1994-95, pres. 1995-96), Phi Kappa Phi. Home: 6725 Brentmead Ave Arcadia CA 91007 Office: 119 S Ramona Ave Monterey Park CA 91754-2802

M'GONIGLE, BARBARA JOSEPHINE, secondary education educator; b. Bayonne, N.J., Sept. 1, 1946; d. Michael and Rose (Delimat) Giordano; m. William George M'Gonigle, Nov. 28, 1987. BA, Montclair State U., 1968, MA, 1974; MS, Iona Coll., 1986. Tchr. high sch. math. Dumont (N.J.) Bd. Edn., 1968—; adj. educator math. dept. Montclair (N.J.) State Coll., 1982-83, edn. dept., 1991—; trainer, mentor Weight Watchers, Paramus, N.J., 1989-91; presenter internat. conf. on critical thinking ASCD Conv., 1995. Choir mem. St. Joseph's Ch., East Rutherford, N.J., 1991—. Recipient Outstanding Educator award Cornell U., 1990, Gov.'s award for Outstanding Teaching, 1994. Mem. NEA, Bergen County Edn. Assn., Dumont Edn. Assn., Nat. Coun. Tchrs. Math., N.J. Edn. Assn., Assn. Math. Tchrs. N.J., Phi Kappa Phi. Office: Dumont High Sch 101 New Milford Ave Dumont NJ 07628-2913

MIALL, ELIZABETH NEAL, nurse, case manager; b. Brevard, N.C., Aug. 22, 1957; d. William Bert and Alma (Crawford) Neal; m. John Patrick Miall, Jr., Dec. 19, 1985; 1 child, Allison Crawford. BSN, U. N.C., Greensboro, 1979. RN: N.C., S.C.; cert. case mgr., occupl. health nurse. Staff nurse neonatal unit Meml. Mission Hosp., Asheville, N.C., 1979; staff nurse ob-gyn. Transylvania Cmty. Hosp., Brevard, N.C., 1979-80; employee health nurse City of Asheville, 1980-84, Sybron Corp., Arden, N.C., 1984-85; employee health coord. Square D Corp., Asheville, 1985-88; nursing mgr. St. Joseph's Health designs, Asheville, 1988-91; rehab. cons. Am. Eagle Rehab., Asheville, 1991-93; pres., CEO Tordec, Inc., Asheville, 1994—; pub. health nurse II, Buncombe County, Asheville, 1994-95; case mgr. CRA Managed Care, Asheville, 1995—; preceptor grad. nursing program U. N.C., Chapel Hill, 1991; mem. safety svcs. bd. ARC, Ashville, instr. advanced first aid and CPR, 1981-91. Mem. candidate rev. bd. Asheville Fire Dept., 1984. Mem. Rehab. and Ins. Profls., Western N.C. Occpl. Health Nurse Assn. (bd. dirs. 1988-92, treas. 1985-88), N.C. Occupl. Health Nurses Assn. (spkrs. bur., rsch. com. 1988-91). Republican. Methodist. Home: 18 Northwood Rd Asheville NC 28804-2845 Office: Thordec Inc PO Box 8727 Asheville NC 28814 also: CRA Managed Care 401 Executive Plz Asheville NC 28801

MIASKIEWICZ, THERESA ELIZABETH, secondary education educator; b. Salem, Mass., Aug. 29, 1933; d. Chester and Anastasia (Zmijewski) M. BA, Emmanuel Coll., Boston, 1954. Cert. tchr., Mass.; lic. real estate broker, Mass. Tchr. fgn. lang. dept. Salem Sch. Dept., 1954-94; head tchr. Salem High Sch., 1954-94; ret., 1994; vol. Salem Hosp., 1979-88, Salem Hosp. Aux., 1980—; playground instr. City of Salem summers, 1951-54; mem. vis. com. New Eng. Assn. Secondary Schs. and Colls., Salem Sch. Com., 1996—, Mass. Assn. Sch. Coms., 1996—; active Salem Sch. Com., 1996—. Vol. Salem Hosp., 1979-88, House of Seven Gables, Salem, summers, 1987-89; active North Shore Med. Ctr. Aux.; mem. com. Salem Sch., 1996. Mem. Am. Assn. Ret. Persons (NRTA divsn.), Ret. State, County and Mcpl. Employees Assn., Nat. Ret. Tchrs. Assn., New Eng. Assn. Secondary Schs. and Colls., Mass. Ret. Tchrs. Assn., Mass. Fedn. Polish Women's Clubs (v.p. 1988-89, regional chmn. scholarship com.), Mass. Assn. Scg. Coms., Polish Bus. and Profl. Women's Club Greater Boston (past corr. sec., chmn. scholarship com.,pres. 1988-89).

MICCIO, G. KRISTIAN, law educator; b. N.Y.C., Dec. 14, 1951; d. Guy Joseph and Lucille (D'Andrea) M.; m. Peri L. Rainbow, June 18, 1993. BA, Marymount Coll., Tarrytown, N.Y., 1973; MA, SUNY, Albany, 1975; JD, Antioch U., Washington, 1985; postgrad., Columbia U. Bar: N.Y. 1986, U.S. Dist. Ct. (so. and ea. dists.) N.Y., 1986, U.S. Ct. Appeals (2d cir.) 1986, U.S. Supreme Ct. 1989. Asst. dist. atty. Bronx (N.Y.) Dist. Atty.'s, 1985-87; prof. law CUNY, Queens, 1987-91; adj. prof. law CUNY, N.Y.C., 1990-92; adj. prof. N.Y. Law Sch., 1990-93; clin. prof. Albany (N.Y.) Law Sch., Albany, N.Y., 1993-96; sr. rsch. assoc., dir. project for domestic violence studies Ctr. for Women in Govt., Rockefeller Inst., U. N.Y., Albany, 1996—; prof. law and pub. policy U. N.Y., Albany, 1996—; lectr. in field. Contbr. articles to profl. and law jours. Founding dir., atty.-in-charge Ctr. for Battered Women's Legal Svcs., N.Y.C., 1988-93; pres. bd. Coalition of Battered Women's Advs., N.Y.C., 1989—; bd. dirs. Prisoners Legal Svcs., N.Y.C., 1990-93, N.Y.C. Adv. Bd. for N.Y. Police Dept. on Gay and Lesbian Affairs, 1991-93; chair domestic violence com. N.Y.C. Commn. on Status of Women, 1992-93, mayoral appointee, 1992-93; faculty mem. N.Y. State Jud. Inst. Recipient Susan B. Anthony award NOW, 1991, Atty. of Yr. award Kings County D.A.'s Office, 1993, Making Waves award NOW Albany Chpt., 1996; named Outstanding Lawyer of the Yr. on Behalf of Women and Children of the City of New York, CUNY Law Sch. at Queens Coll., 1991. Mem. N.Y. Bar Assn. (task force on family law 1993—), N.Y. County Lawyers Assn (Outstanding Pub. Svc. award 1991, Pro-Bono award 1992), Assn. of Bar of City of N.Y. (Pub. Interest Lawyer award 1993). Office: Albany Law Sch 80 New Scotland Ave Albany NY 12208

MICCO, TAMMY LYNN, elementary education educator; b. New Castle, Pa., Sept. 14, 1970; d. Harry Anthony and Georgia Ann (Padula) M. BS in Psychology, U. Pitts., 1992, MA in Elem. Edn., 1993, cert. in children's lit. Tutor student athletes U. Pitts., 1991—; intern Falk Lab. Sch., U. Pitts., 1992-93; technology facilitator Seneca Valley Sch. Dist./Evans City (Pa.) Elem. Sch., 1993—; mem. tech. adv. bd. Seneca Valley Sch. Dist., Harmony, Pa., 1993—; in-svc. dir.Evans City Elem. Sch., 1994—. Vol. Office of Disabled Student Svcs., U. Pitts., 1989-93; tchr.'s asst. Frick Internat. Acad., Pitts., 1991-92, girls' softball coach, 1995—. Mem. Pa. State Edn. Assn., Pa. Sci. Tchrs. Assn., Three Rivers Reading Coun., Kappa Delta Pi, Psi Chi. Democrat. Roman Catholic. Office: Evans City Elem Sch 345 W Main St Evans City PA 16033-1235

MICELI, CATHERINE MARIE, artist, educator; b. Syracuse, N.Y., Nov. 19, 1959; d. William John and Patricia Lee Madigan; m. Joseph S. Miceli; four children. AS in Graphic Design, Onondoga C.C., Syracuse, 1992. Art dir., sole proprietor Heart of the Art Co., Syracuse, 1986—; art tchr. OCM BOCES, Liverpool, N.Y., 1993—; visual arts chairperson Met. Sch. for the Arts, Syracuse, 1995—. Exhbns. include Carousel Ctr., Syracuse, N.Y., 1992, Gallery 320, Syracuse, 1995, Agora Gallery, Soho, N.Y.C., 1995, Courage Collection, Golden Valley, Minn., 1996. With USNR, 1995—. Scholar Amicita Inc., Syracuse, 1978. Mem. Camillus Art Guild, Confraternity of Christian Mothers (chairperson, Mother of Yr. 1994), Phi Delta Kappa. Roman Catholic. Office: Heart of the Art Co 210 Morton St Syracuse NY 13204

MICH, CONNIE RITA, mental health nurse, educator; b. Nebr., Feb. 5, 1926; d. Henry B. and Anna (Stratman) Redel; m. Richard Mich. BSN, Alverno Coll.; postgrad., Marquette U.; MSN, Cath. U. Am. Asst. clin. dir. in-patient svcs. Fond du Lac (Wis.) County Health Ctr., 1974-78; head nurse, program coord. acute psychiat. unit St. Agnes Hosp., Fond du Lac, 1979-83; mental health clinician Immanuel Med. Ctr., Omaha, 1984-89; instr., clin. supr., asst. prof. psychiat. mental health Coll. St. Mary, Omaha, 1989-93; med. programs dir. Inst. Computer Sci. Ltd., 1989—; program dir. med. programs Gateway Coll., Omaha, 1995; chairperson Examining Coun. on RNs; writer items State Bd. Test Pool Exam.; pres. Milw. Coun. Cath. Nurses; vice chairperson Wis. Conf. Group Psychiat. Nursing Practice. Mem. Sigma Theta Tau, Pi Gamma Mu.

MICHAEL, CAROLINE MARSHALL, religious organization administrator; b. Bangor, Maine, Oct. 30, 1923; d. Walter S. and Hazel Elizabeth (Day) Marshall; m. Forrest L. Michael, Sept. 10, 1947; children: Janet Elizabeth, David Gregory. BS, Aurora U., 1946; MS in Edn., U. So. Maine, 1974. Cert. travel agent. Instr. Aurora (Ill.) U., 1945-49, U. Maine, Farmington, 1969-77; travel agt. Day's Travel, Waterville, Maine, 1979-81; dir. women's ministries Advent Christian Denomination, Charlotte, N.C., 1981-92. Author, editor: Advent Christian Witness, 1981-92; editor newsletter for AAUW, 1974-75; author, editor numerous seminars. Mem. Rep. Women's Club, Farmington, 1970-80; violinist Symphony and Civic Orchs., Bangor and Farmington, Maine, Aurora, and Alliance, Ohio, 1940-80; mem. N.Am. Women's Track of AD2000 & Beyond, 1992-95; mem. steering com. Praying Women, 1994—. Recipient Violin Playing award Rubinoff, 1940; scholar Husson Coll., 1941-42, Aurora U., 1942-46. Mem. Nat. Assn. Evangs. (chmn. women's commn. 1989-92, mem. exec. com. 1993-96). Home: 10402 Meadow Hollow Dr Charlotte NC 28227-5431

MICHAEL, DOROTHY ANN, nurse, naval officer; b. Lancaster, Pa., Sept. 20, 1950; d. Richard Linus and Mary Ruth (Hahn) Michael.; m. Juan Roberto Morales, July 15, 1995. Diploma, R.N., Montgomery Hosp. Sch.

Nursing, Norristown, Pa., 1971; BSN, George Mason U., 1980; MSN, U. Tex. Health Sci. Ctr., 1985. Commd. ensign USN, 1970, advanced through grades to capt. Nurse Corps, 1994; staff nurse Nat. Naval Med. Ctr., Bethesda, Md., 1971-73; charge nurse Naval Hosp., Guantanamo Bay, Cuba, 1973-74, Naval Regional Med. Ctr., Phila., 1974-76, Naval Hosp., Keflavik, Iceland, 1977, Naval Hosp., Bethesda, 1980-84, sr. nurse, asst. officer-in-charge Br. Med. Clinic, Naval Weapons Ctr., China Lake, Calif., 1986-89; coord. quality assurance Naval Hosp., Oakland, Calif., 1989-92, assoc. dir. inpatient nursing, 1992-93; divsn. officer USNS Mercy, Persian Gulf, 1990-91, assoc. dir. surg. nursing, 1993-95; dir. nursing svc. Naval Hosp., Great Lakes, Ill., 1995—; splty. advisor to dir. Navy Nurse Corp., Navy Med. Command, Washington, 1983-84. V.p. Deepwood Homeowners Assn., Reston, Va., 1978-82; advisor, com. mem. Reston Found., 1979. Recipient R.W. Bjorklund Mgmt. Innovator award Kern County, Calif., 1988, Comdr.'s Award for Outstanding Professionalism in Pub. Health Support, 1988. Mem. Vietnam Vets Am., Vets. Fgn. Wars, Orgn. Nurse Execs., Am. Nurses Assn. (cert. nursing adminstrn.), Am. Legion, Sigma Theta Tau. Roman Catholic. Home: 421 Flanders Ln Grayslake IL 60030

MICHAEL, KAREN MARTHA, retired personnel coordinator; b. Virginia, Minn., Oct. 10, 1938; d. George Alfred Kakela and Fannie Martha (Viitala) Kakela-Jyring; m. Richard Wayne Michael, June 27, 1964; 1 child, Laura Jane Michael Exner. BA, Mich. State U., 1960. City planner City of Mpls., 1960-66; rec. sec. City Coun. Eden Prairie, Minn., 1981-86, personnel coord., 1986-94; ret., 1994; exec. sec. Minn. Planning Assn., 1966-70. pres. Mpls. Coun. of Camp Fire, 1983; Minnetonka Area Investors, 1987-94; Salolampi Found. Mpls., 1984-. Mem. AAUW (pres. Minnetonka br. 1979-81), LWV (bd. dirs. 1965-70), Eden Prairie Women's Network (bd. dirs. 1984), Sun Lakes Scandinavian Club (v.p. 1995-96, pres. 1996—), Alpha Delta Pi (life). Home: 25024 S Desert Trail Ct Sun Lakes AZ 85248-7610 also: 7805 Lake Leander Rd Britt MN 55710

MICHAEL, MARTHA GALLAGHER, special education and art educator; b. Columbus, Ohio, Oct. 9, 1955; d. Clarence Mankopf and Mary Curtis (Garvin) Gallagher; m. Kevin H. Michael, June 23, 1979; children: Guthrie Gallagher, Chelsea Hackett, Georgia Carvin. BFA, Capital U., 1978; MA in Art Edn., Ohio State U., 1981, PhD in Spl. Edn., 1990. Cert. tchr. multiply handicapped, orthopedically and other handicaps, Ohio; phys. and other health impaired, Minn. Grad. rsch. assoc. Ohio State U., Columbus, 1984-86; project dir. Ohio Developmental Disabilities Planning Coun. Edn. Grant, Columbus, 1989-90; tech. assistance program asst. Helen Keller Nat. Ctr.-Tech. Assistance Ctr., Columbus, 1986-91; project coord., data coord. Ctr. for Spl. Needs Populations, Columbus, 1989-91; tchr. Columbus Pub. Schs., 1991-95; acting dir. Gt. Lakes Area Regional Ctr., Columbus, summer 1993, cons. for deaf-blind edn., 1994-95; tchr. Mpls. Pub. Schs., 1995—; cons. U. Dayton, 1994-95; mem. Ohio Edn. Task Force, Columbus, 1990-92; evaluator Ill. Edn. Dept., Chgo., 1985; profl. jeweler/metalsmith, oil painter and children's book illustrator. Co-author: (monograph) Interagency Collaboration/Helen Keller Center, 1992; contbr. articles to profl. jours.; editor of newsletters Ohio Interest Group for Individuals with Deaf-Blindness-Great Lakes Area Regional Ctr. for Deaf-Blind Edn., 1990-92, 92-95. Co-founder, charter mem. Ohio Interest Group for Individuals with Deaf-Blindness, Columbus, 1991-95. Mem. NEA, Nat. Mus. Women in Arts, Coun. Exceptional Children. Home: 5320 Culver Rd Minneapolis MN 55422

MICHAEL, MARY AMELIA FURTADO, retired educator, freelance writer; m. Eugene G. Michael; children: David, Douglas, Gregory. BA, Albertus Magnus Coll.; MS, U. Bridgeport, 1975; CAS, Fairfield U., 1982. Cert. secondary sch. sci. tchr., ednl. adminstr. Housemaster, sci. tchr. Fairfield (Conn.) Pub. Schs., adminstrv. housemaster, sci. tchr., sci. dept. coord., 1992, retired, 1992; freelance fin. rsch. and investment writer and cons., 1994—. Author: The Art and Science of Cooking, 1996; contbr. articles to profl. jours. Mem. Discovery Mus., Conn. Arts & Sci. Mus. Mem. AAUW, LWV, Conn. Assn. Suprs. and Curriculum, Fairfield Sch. Adminstrs. Assn., Retired Educators of Fairfield, Fairfield Hist. Soc. Home: 942 Valley Rd Fairfield CT 06432-1671

MICHAEL, PHYLLIS CALLENDER, composer; b. nr. Berwick, Pa., Dec. 24, 1908; d. Bruce Miles and Emma (Harvey) Callender; grad. Bloomsburg Coll., 1928; B. Mus., U. Extension Conservatory, Chgo., 1953; m. Arthur L. Michael, Aug. 21, 1933; children: Robert Bruce, Keith Winton. Elem. tchr. Berwick Schs., 1928-33; substitute tchr. Shickshinny and Northwest Area, Pa., 1954-66; tchr. Northwest Area High Sch., 1966-71; gen. tchr. piano, organ, theory and voice, 1943-89; hymnwriter, poet, author, composer, 1943—. Recipient first place in Nat. Favorite Hymns contest for Take Thou My Hand, 1953, Cert. of Merit for disting. service to composition outstanding hymns, 1967, and others. Adv. mem. MBLS. Mem. Nat. Ret. Tchrs. Assn., Internat. Platform Assn., Nat. Soc. Lit. and the Arts, Hymn Soc. Am. Author: Poems for Mothers, 1963, Poems From My Heart, 1964, Beside Still Waters, 1970, Fun to Do Showers, 1971, Bridal Shower Ideas, 1972, Is My Head on Straight, 1976, This Is Christmas, 1985, Quotes, 1986, Hi, Lord!, 1987, Bright Tomorrows, 1989, Home Sweet Home, 1991, Reach for the Rose, 1992, God Promised, 1992, Why Me Lord, 1993, Golden Gems, 1994, Mountains, Molehills, and Mustard Seed, 1995, Surely Goodness and Mercy, 1995, Some Golden Daybreak, 1995, When Petals Fall, 1996; contbr. songs, articles, poems to books, hymn-books, booklets, mags. and other national and international publications. Address: Berwick Retirement Village II 901 E 16th St Rm 725 Berwick PA 18603-2440

MICHAEL, SANDRA DALE, reproductive endocrinology educator, researcher; b. Sacramento, Calif., Jan. 23, 1945; d. Gordon G. and Ruby F. (Johnson) M.; m. Dennis P. Murr, Aug. 12, 1967 (div. 1974). BA, Calif. State Coll., Sonoma, 1967; PhD, U. Calif., Davis, 1970. NIH predoctoral fellow U. Calif., Davis, 1967-70, NIH postdoctoral fellow, 1970-73, asst. rsch. geneticist, 1973-74; asst. prof. SUNY, Binghamton, 1974-81, assoc. prof., 1981-88, prof. reproductive endocrinology, 1988—, dept. chair, 1992—; adj. prof. dept. ob-gyn. SUNY Health Scis. Ctr., Syracuse; mem. NIH Reproductive Endocrinology Study Sect., 1991-95—; cons., presenter in field; grant reviewer NIH, NSF, USDA and others. Contbr. articles to profl. jours. Vice chair Tri Cities Opera Guild, Binghamton, 1987-90, chair, 1990-92; mem. Harpur Forum, Binghamton, 1987—, SUNY Found., Binghamton, 1990-96. Fulbright Sr. scholar Czech Republic, 1994; grantee NIMH, 1976-79, Nat. Cancer Inst., 1977-80, 83-87, Nat. Inst. Environ. Health Scis., 1979-80, NSF, 1981-83, NIH, 1987—. Mem. Endocrine Soc., Soc. for the Study of Reprodn., Soc. for Study of Fertility, Am. Soc. for Immunology of Reprodn., Women in Endocrinology (sec.-treas. 1992-95), Soc. for Exptl. Biology and Medicine, N.Y. Acad. Sci., Sigma Xi. Office: State Univ of NY Dept Biol Scis Binghamton NY 13902

MICHAEL, SUSAN DALE, speech/language pathologist; b. Oak Hill, Ohio, Feb. 23, 1953; d. Delbert Dale and Wylodine (Leach) Armstrong; m. Stephen Dana Michael, Aug. 17, 1974; children: Aaron, Adam, Ethan, Seth. BS in Speech and Hearing Scis. cum laude, Ohio U., 1975; MS in Ednl. Adminstrn., U. Dayton, 1992. Cert. speech, lang. pathologist, k-12 ednl. handicapped speech/hearing specialist; cert. supr., elem. prin., secndary prin., asst. supt., Ohio. Tchr. of learning disabilities/behavioral disorder students Marion County Schs., Moral, Ohio, 1975-76; speech/lang. pathologist East Seals, Kenton, Ohio, summer 1977, Jackson County Mental Retardation Bd., Jackson, Ohio, 1978-79, Oak Hill (Ohio) Union Local Schs., 1990—; part-time speech/lang. pathologist Oak Hill Cmty. Med. Ctr., 1985-94. Oak Hill Acad. Boosters officer, 1989—. Mem. NEA, Ohio Edn. Assn., Dist. Tchr.'s Assn., Ohio Speech/Hearing Assn., Jr. Federated Women's Club (officer 1981—), Optimist Club (officer), Oak View Parent Tchr. Club (officer 1980—). Republican. Methodist. Home: 112 E Cross St Oak Hill OH 45656-1246

MICHAELS, CINDY WHITFILL (CYNTHIA G. MICHAELS), educational consultant; b. Plainview, Tex., Aug. 31, 1951; d. Glenn Tierce and Ruby Jewell (Nichols) Whitfill; m. Terre Joe Michaels, July 16, 1977. BS, W. Tex. State U., 1972; MS, U. Tex., Dallas, 1976; postgrad. cert., E. Tex. State U., 1982. Registered profl. ednl. diagnostician, Tex.; cert. supr. (gen. and spl. edn.), elem. edn. tchr., K-8 English tchr., spl. edn. tchr. (generic and mental retardation), Tex. Gen. and spl. edn. tchr. Plano (Tex.) Ind. Sch. Dist., 1972-76; dependents' sch. tchr. U.S. Dept. Def., Office of Overseas Edn., Schweinfurt, West Germany, 1976-77; asst. dir. edn. dept. spl. edn. Univ. Affiliated Ctr., U. Tex., Dallas, 1977-80; asst. to acting dir. edn., dept. pediatrics, Southwestern Med. Sch. Univ. Affiliated Ctr., U. Tex. Health Sci. Ctr., Dallas, 1980-82; dir. Collin County Spl. Edn. Coop., Wylie, Tex., 1982-89; dir. spl. svcs. Terrell (Tex.) Ind. Sch. Dist., 1989-92; cons. for at-risk svcs. instrnl. svcs. dept. Region 10 Edn. Svc. Ctr., Richardson, Tex., 1992-93, cons. for staff devel., 1993-95; cons. Title I Svcs., 1995-96; ind. rep. Am. Communications Network, 1995—; owner Strategic Out-Source Svcs., Garland, Tex., 1996—; self-employed ednl. cons. Strategic Outsource Svcs., 1996—; regional cons. presenter and speaker Region 10 Adminstrs. Spl. Edn., Dallas, 1982-92; state conf. presenter and speaker Tex. Assn. Bus. Sch. Bds., Houston, 1991, Tex. Edn. Agy., Austin, 1992, grant reveiwer, 1984; cons. S.W. regional tng. program educators U. So. Miss., 1992-93; regional coord. H.S. mock trial competition State Bar Tex., 1993; regional liaison Tex. Elem. Mentor Network, 1993-96; state presenter Tex. Vocat. Educators Conf., 1994. Active Dance-A-Thon for United Cerebral Palsy, Dallas, 1986; area marcher March of Dimes, Dallas, 1990, Park Cities Walkathon for Multiple Sclerosis, 1994, 95. Grantee Job Tng. & Partnership Act, 1991, Carl Perkins Vocat. Program, 1991, Tex. Edn. Agy., 1990, 91, 92; named Outstanding Young Woman in Am., Outstanding Young Women in Am., 1981. Mem. AAUW, Assn. Compensatory Educators of Tex. (state conf. com. 1996), Tex. Assn. for Improvement of Reading, Tex. Assn. Sect. 504 Coords. and Hearing Officers, Nat. Coun. Adminstrs. Spl. Edn., Coun. Exceptional Children (chpt. pres. 1973-74), Tex. Assn. Supervision & Curriculum Devel. (mem. leadership team Project Pathways 1992-93), Tex. Coun. Adminstrs. Spl. Edn. (region 10 chairperson 1985-87, state conf. presenter 1989, 92), Tex. Ednl. Diagnosticians Assn. (Dal-Metro v.p., state conf. program chair 1982-83, state conf. presenter 1983), Internat. Reading Assn., Nat. Assn. Supervision and Curriculum Devel., Alpha Delta Pi (Richardson alumnae, philanthropy chair 1988, v.p. 1989, 90, 91, v.p./sec. 1993-94, v.p. 1994-95, 95-96). Home and Office: 2613 Oak Point Dr Garland TX 75044-7809 also: 232 Broadmoor Alto NM 88312

MICHAELS, ELISE MARIE See GILLEM, ELISE MARIE

MICHAELS, JENNIFER ALMAN, lawyer; b. N.Y.C., Mar. 1, 1948; d. David I. and Emily (Arnow) Alman; 1 child, Abigail Elizabeth. BA, Douglas Coll., 1969; JD, Cardozo Sch. of Law, 1990. Ptnr. Alman & Michaels, Highland Park, N.J., 1990—. Author, composer: (record) Music for 2's and 3's, 1981; producer, writer: (film) Critical Decisions in Medicine, 1983. Mem. ABA, Middlesex County Bar Assn., N.J. State Bar Assn., Am. Trial Lawyers Assn., Phi Kappa Phi. Office: Alman and Michaels 611 S Park Ave Highland Park NJ 08904-2928

MICHAELS, MARION CECELIA, writer, editor, news syndicate executive; b. Black River Falls, Wis.; d. Leonard N. and Estelle O. (Payne) Doud; m. Charles Webb (div.); children: Charles, David, Robert; m. Mark J. Michaels (div.); 1 child, Merry A. Student, MIT, 1962-64, U. Wis., 1971-76; BS in Bus. Edn., U. Wis., 1978, MS in Spl. Edn., 1981. Mgr., instr. bus. program Blackwell Job Corps Ctr., 1987-89; mgr. Michaels Secretarial Svc., Black River Falls, Wis., 1979-83; columnist, editor Michaels News, Black River Falls, 1983—, pres., 1989—. Columnist: Single Parenting, 1983-94, Parenting Plus, 1990—; editor, contbr. (column) Surviving Single, 1990-95, To Read or Not, Report From Planet Earth, 1989—, Travel Tidbits, 1991—, Surviving Sane, 1995—. Chmn. Brockway Community Orgn., 1969-71; chair, counselor Brockway Youth Group, 1970-72; chmn. labor com. Dem. Platform Com., Wis., 1975-76; candidate State Assembly, 1978, 82. Mem. Bus. Edn. Honor Soc., Edn. Hon. Soc. Office: Michaels News RR 5 Box 367 Black River Falls WI 54615-9160

MICHAK, HELEN BARBARA, educator, nurse; b. Cleve., July 31; d. Andrew and Mary (Patrick) M. Diploma Cleve. City Hosp. Sch. Nursing, 1947; BA, Miami U., Oxford, Ohio, 1951; MA, Case Western Res. U., 1960. Staff nurse Cleve. City Hosp., 1947-48; pub. health nurse Cleve. Div. Health, 1951-52; instr. Cleve. City Hosp. Sch. Nursing, 1952-56; supr. nursing Cuyahoga County Hosp., Cleve., 1956-58; pub. information dir. N.E. Ohio Am. Heart Assn., Cleve., 1960-64; dir. spl. events Higbee Co., Cleve., 1964-66; exec. dir. Cleve. Area League for Nursing, 1966-72; dir. continuing edn. nurses, adj. assoc. prof. Cleve. State U., 1972-86; asst. regional cons. Ohio Bd. Nursing, 1991—. Trustee N.E. Ohio Regional Med. Program, 1970-73; mem. adv. com. Dept. Nursing Cuyahoga C.C., 1967-87; mem. long term care com. Met. Health Planning Corp., 1974-76, plan devel. com. 1977; mem. policy bd. Ctr. Health Data N.E. Ohio, 1972-73; mem. Rep. Assembly and Health Planning and Devel. Commn., Welfare Fedn. Cleve., 1967-72, Cleve. Cmty. Health Network, 1972-73, United Appeal Films and Speakers Bur., 1967-73; mem. adv. com. Ohio Fedn. Lic. Practical Nurses, 1970-73; mem. tech. adv. com. No. Ohio Lung Assn., 1967-74, 90-93; mem. Ohio Commn. on Nursing, 1971-74; mem. citizens com. nursing homes Fedn. Community Planning, 1973-77; mem. com. on home health services Met. Health Planning Corp., 1973-75; mem. profl. adv. com. on home care Fairview Gen. Hosp., 1987-91. Mem. Nat. League Nursing (mem. com. 1970-72), Am. Nurses Assn. (accreditation visitor 1977-78, 83-88) Ohio Nurses Assn., (com. continuing edn. 1974-79, 82-87, 89-92, chmn. 1984-86), Greater Cleve. (joint practice com. 1973-74, Greater Cleve. Nurses Assn. (trustee 1975-76) , Cleve. Area Citizens League for Nursing (trustee 1976-79, v.p. 1988-90), Zeta Tau Alpha, Sigma Theta Tau. Home and Office: 4686 Oakridge Dr North Royalton OH 44133

MICHALAK, JANET CAROL, reading education educator; b. Buffalo, Mar. 22, 1949; d. Theodore and Thelma Ruth (Roesch) Vukovic; m. Gerald Paul Michalak, June 19, 1971; children: Nathan, Justin. BS in Edn., SUNY Coll. at Buffalo, Buffalo, 1970; MS in Edn., SUNY, Buffalo, 1971, EdD, 1981. Cert. tchr. nursery, kindergarten, grades 1-6, reading tchr., English tchr. grades 7-12, N.Y. Reading tchr. Tonawanda (N.Y.) Sch. System, 1971-80; instr. Niagara County C.C., Sanborn, N.Y., 1980-82, asst. prof., 1982-85, assoc. prof., 1985-91, prof., 1991—; adj. lectr. SUNY, Buffalo, 1990-91. Recipient Pres.'s award for Excellence in Teaching, Niagara County C.C., 1990, Nat. Inst. for Staff & Orgnl. Devel. Excellence award, 1991, SUNY Chancellor's award for Excellence in Teaching, 1991. Mem. Coll. Reading Assn., Internat. Reading Assn., N.Y. Coll. Learning Skills Assn., Niagara Frontier Reading Coun. (bd. dirs. 1986-88). Republican. Presbyterian. Home: 184 Montbleu Dr Getzville NY 14068-1329 Office: Niagara County CC 3111 Saunders Settlement Rd Sanborn NY 14132-9487

MICHALIK, LYNNETTE MARIE BERNADETTE, secondary education educator, artist; b. Garden City, Mich., Jan. 23, 1958; d. Stanley Joseph and Delia Marie (Testani) M.; m. Karl. W Staffeld, Feb. 18, 1994. BA in Classical Archaeology, U. Mich., 1980; K-12 tchr. cert. in art, Ea. Mich. U., 1990, BFA in Sculpture, 1991. Day planner WhiffleTree Restaurant, Ann Arbor, Mich., 1980-81; proofreader, with inventory dept. Kux Mfg. Co., Detroit, 1981-85; advt. asst. Book Inventory Sys., Inc., Ann Arbor, 1985-88; window display designer, clk. Crystal Collector Shop, Plymouth, Mich., 1988-90; fact-resistance skill tchr. U. Mich. Med. Sch., Ann Arbor, 1990; tchr. art and basic skills Hugs & Kisses Presch., Plymouth, 1991-92; tchr. art Father Gabriel Richard H.S., Ann Arbor, 1992—. One-woman show Ea. Mich. U. Libr., 1989. Co-founder Friends of New Dimensions, Ann Arbor, 1983-86; fundraiser Stas. WUOM and WCBN, U. Mich., 1984-86; co-leader Ann Arbor Moonlodge, 1995—. Grantee U. Mich., 1976-80. Mem. NOW, Women's Caucus for Arts, Nat. Audubon Soc., Arbor Day Found., Detroit Inst. Arts, Nat. Parks and Conservation Assn. Home: 622 S Main St Chelsea MI 48118

MICHALS, LEE MARIE, retired travel agency executive; b. Chgo., June 6, 1939; d. Harry Joseph and Anna Marie (Monaco) Perzan; children: Debora Ann, Dana Lee, Jami. BA, Wright Coll., 1959. Cert. travel specialist and cons., destination specialist. Internat. travel sec. E.F. MacDonald Travel, Palo Alto, Calif., 1963-69; pres. Travel Experience, Santa Clara, Calif., 1973-88; ptnr. Cruise Connection, Mountain View, Calif., 1983-85; travel specialist Allways Travel, Sunnyvale, Calif., 1992—; former stars rep. Hertz, Ritz Carlton, Marriott Hotels, various airlines and tour cos. Mem. Am. Soc. Travel Agts., Inst. Cert. Travel Agts., Bay Area Travel Assn., Pacific Area Travel Agts., San Jose Women in Travel (organizing pres. 1971, 1st v.p. 1989). Office: Allways Travel 139 S Murphy Ave Sunnyvale CA 94086-6113

MICHALSKI, CAROL ANN, medical, surgical and psychiatric nurse, writer, poet; b. Balt., Feb. 21, 1955; d. John B. Rassa and Genevieve J. Ryncewicz; m. Martin Joseph Michalski, June 21, 1976; children: Matthew, Nathan. RN, Grand View Hosp., Sellersville, Pa., 1976; BS in Health Care Adminstrn., Pacific Western U., 1986, PhD in Religious Studies/Ministry, 1987. RN; ordained to ministry Christian Ch., 1983. Staff nurse Md. Gen. Hosp., Balt., 1974-75, Union Meml. Hosp., Balt., 1975-77; head nurse Levindale Chronic Hosp., Balt., 1977-79; charge staff nurse Franklin Sq. Hosp. Ctr., Balt., 1979—, pain mgmt. liaison, 1993—; head procedure com. Levindale Chronic Hosp., Balt., 1978-79; min. Faith Seed Ministries, Balt., 1983—; Bible Coll. adminstr. L.W. Christian Ctr., Balt., 1987-89. Author: Don't Blame God-Making Sense Out of Tragedy and Suffering, 1995; contbr. articles and poetry to profl. jours. and anthologies. Asst. youth activities Ridgeleigh Cmty. Assn., Balt., 1980; block capt. Woodcroft Civic Assn., Balt.; coord. Churchville Christian Sch., 1993-94; Christian Home Educator's Network group coord. Teen Boys Group, 1995—. Recipient Nursing Achievement award Johnston Sch.-Union Meml. Hosp., 1984, Ministry Recognition Certs. Gospel Tabernacle Balt., 1990, 91, poetry awards. Mem. Md. League Nursing, Nat. Author's Registry, Internat. Soc. Poets.

MICHALSKI, JEANNE ANN, human resources professional; b. Tampa, Fla., Nov. 7, 1958; d. Enrique and Mary Ellen (Bandi) Escarraz; m. Michael John Michalski, Nov. 24, 1984. BA in Psychology, U. South Fla., 1979, MA in Indsl. Psychology, 1983, PhD in Indsl. Psychology, 1990. Human resource coord. GTE Data Svcs., Tampa, 1984-86, mgmt. cons., 1986-87, mgr. human resource planning, employment office, 1987-88, mgr. human resource, 1988-89; mgr. testing and performance mgmt. GTE Telephone Ops., Irving, Tex., 1989-90, mgr. continuity planning and performance mgmt., 1990-94; asst. v.p. human resources planning Burlington No., Fort Worth, 1994-95; asst. v.p. staffing and devel. Burlington No. Santa Fe, Fort Worth, 1995—; cons. Herb Meyer Assocs./TECO, Tampa, 1983-84, Mail Prescriptions, Tampa, 1989-90. Campaign worker Dem. state legislator election, St. Petersburg, Fla., 1980; mem. Polit. Action Com., Irving, 1989-90. Grad. fellowship scholar U. South Fla., 1979. Mem. APA, Soc. for Indsl./Orgnl. Psychologists, Dallas/Ft. Worth Indsl. Orgn. Psychologist Group, Human Resource Planning Soc. Roman Catholic. Home: 505 Woodland Trl Keller TX 76248-2634 Office: Burlington No 3000 Continental Plz Fort Worth TX 76161

MICHAUD, NORMA ALICE PALMER, real estate investor, paralegal; b. Concord, N.H., May 6, 1946; d. Leon Charles and Goldie May (Maxfield) Palmer (both dec.); m. Bob Michaud, July 21, 1973; 1 child, Derrick Charles. AAS in Bus. Mgmt., Mississippi County C.C., 1994; student, State Tech., Memphis, 1994—. With United Life & Accident Ins. Co., Concord, N.H., 1965-68, 71-74; data processor Blue Cross/Blue Shield, Concord, 1968-71; adminstr. fed. agy. U.S. Govt., 1976-92; house renovator, real estate owner Blytheville, Ark., 1988—; dep. cir. clk., 1994; with Daniel Law Firm, 1994-95. Mem. NAFE, Nat. Wildlife Assn., Nat. Geog. Soc., Bus. Profls. Am. (chpt. v.p. 1994), Phi Theta Kappa. Methodist.

MICHEL, HARRIET R., association executive; b. Pitts., July 5, 1942; d. John and Vida (Fish) Richardson; m. Yves Michel, Apr. 13, 1968; children: Christopher, Gregory. BA, Juniata Coll., 1965; LHD (hon.), Baruch Coll., 1990. Dir. spl. projects Nat. Scholarship Svcs. & Fund for Negro Students, N.Y.C., 1971; asst. to Mayor Lindsay City of N.Y. for Anti-Drug Efforts, 1971-72; exec. dir. N.Y. Found., 1972-77; dir. Cmty. Youth Employment Program U.S. Dept. Labor, Washington, 1977-79; established Women Against Crime Found. John Jay Coll., N.Y.C., 1980-81; cons. U.S. Dept. Housing & Urban Devel., Washington, 1982; pres., CEO N.Y. Urban League, 1983-88; pres. Nat. Minority Supplier Develop. Coun., N.Y.C., 1988—; bd. dirs. Ctr. for Advance Purchasing Studies, Phoenix, Maxima Corp., Balt., N.Y.C. Partnership; mem. nat. adv. coun. U.S. SBA, Washington, 1993—; lectr., cons. in field; U.S. rep. Ditchley Found. Confs., London. Vice chair N.Y.C. Charter Revision Commn., 1986-91; bd. dirs. African Am. Inst., N.Y.C., 1985—, Citizens Com. of N.Y., 1984—, Juniata Coll., Huntington, Pa., 1989—, Trans Africa Forum, Washington, 1988—. Recipient 1st Non-Profit Leadership award new Sch. Social Rsch., 1988, Women on the Move award Anti-Defamation League of B'nai B'rith, 1990, Appreciation award Pres. Commn. Minority Bus. Devel., 1992, Bus. Advocate award Mayor of N.Y.C., 1993, Black Entrepreneurial award Wall St. Jour., 1994, others; named one of 50 Outstanding Internat. Bus. and Profl. Women by Dollars and Sense Mag., 1987. Mem. Assn. Black Found. Execs. (founder), Coun. on Founds. (bd. dirs.). Office: Nat Minority Supplier Devel Coun 15 W 39th St Fl 9 New York NY 10018-3806

MICHEL, MARY ANN KEDZUF, nursing educator; b. Evergreen Park, Ill., June 1, 1939; d. John Roman and Mary (Bassar) Kedzuf; m. Jean Paul Michel, 1974. Diploma in nursing, Little Company of Mary Hosp., Evergreen Park, 1960; BS in Nursing, Loyola U., Chgo., 1964; MS, No. Ill. U., 1968, EdD, 1971. Staff nurse Little Co. of Mary Hosp., 1960-64; instr. Little Co. of Mary Hosp. (Sch. Nursing), 1964-67, No. Ill. U., DeKalb, 1968-69; asst. prof. No. Ill. U., 1969-71; chmn. dept. nursing U. Nev., Las Vegas, 1971-73; prof. nursing U. Nev., 1975—, dean Coll. Health Scis., 1973-90; pres. PERC, Inc.; mgmt. cons., 1993—; mgmt. cons. Nev. Donor Network, 1993; mem. So. Nev. Health Manpower Task Force, 1975; mem. manpower com. Plan Devel. Commn., Clark County Health Sys. Agy., 1977-79, mem. governing body, 1981-86; mem. Nev. Health Coordinating Coun., Western Inst. Nursing, 1971-85; mem. coordinating com. assembly instnl. adminstrs. dept. allied health edn. and accreditation AMA, 1983-88, mem. bd. advisors So. Nev. Vocat. Tech. Ctr., 1976-80; sec.-treas. Nev. Donor Network, 1988-89, bd. dirs., 1986-90, chmn. bd., 1988-90. Contbr. articles to profl. jours. Trustee Desert Spring Hosp., Las Vegas, 1976-85; bd. dirs. Nathan Adelson Hospice, 1982-88, Bridge Counseling Assocs., 1982, Everywoman's Ctr., 1984-86; chmn. Nev. Commn. on Nursing Edn., 1972-73, Nursing Articulation Com., 1972-73, Yr. of Nurse Com., 1978; moderator Invitational Conf. Continuing Edn., Am. Soc. Allied Health Professions, 1978; active Nev. Donor Network, Donor Organ Recovery Svc., Transplant Recipient Internat. Orgn., S.W. Eye Bank, S.W. Tissue Bank. Named Outstanding Alumnus, Loyola U., 1983; NIMH fellow, 1967-68. Fellow Am. Soc. Allied Health Professions, 1991, (chmn. nat. resolutions com. 1981-84, treas. 1988-90, sec's. award com. 1982-83, 92-93, nat. by-laws com. 1985, conv. chmn. 1987); mem. AAUP, Am. Nurses Assn., Nev. Nurses Assn. (dir. 1975-77, treas. 1977-79, conv. chmn. 1978), So. Nev. Area Health Edn. Coun., Western Health Deans (co-organizer 1985, chair, 1988-90), Nat. League Nursing, Nev. Heart Assn., So. Nev. Mem. Hosps. (mem. nursing recruitment com. 1981-83, mem. nursing practice com. 1983-85), Las Vegas C. of C. (named Woman of Yr. Edn.) 1988, Slovak Catholic Sokols, Phi Kappa Phi (chpt. sec. 1981-83, pres.-elect 1983, pres. 1984, v.p. Western region 1989-95, editl. bd. jour. Nat. Forum 1989-93), Alpha Beta Gamma (hon.), Sigma Theta Tau, Zeta Kappa. Office: U Nev Las Vegas 4505 S Maryland Pky Las Vegas NV 89154-9900

MICHEL, PETRA, publishing executive, physicist; b. Hilkerode, Germany, June 29, 1955; d. Gunther Johannes and Margareta Amalia (Forster) Wagner; 1 child, Neris Anika. MS, Rheinische-Ludwig U., Bonn, Germany, 1980. Mgr. Siemens AG, Munich, 1980-82, sr. mgr., 1982-85, dir., dept. head, 1985-93; sr. publ. editor Bluestar Comm., Woodside, Calif., 1993-95, pres. and CEO, 1995—; adj. prof. Tech. U., Munich, 1986-93, U. Passau, Germany, 1988-92; co-founder, translator, editor Aquamarin Verlag, Grafing, Germany, 1981—; co-owner P&P Lichtsatz GmbH, Grafing, 1988—; chmn. numerous confs. Co-author: The Synthesis Approach to Digital System Design, 1992; contbr. numerous articles to profl. publs.; patentee in field. Mem. IEEE (sr.), Internat. Fedn. of Info. Processing, German Physicists Assn., Info. Technology Assn.

MICHELFELDER, ELLEN HADEN, hospital administrative executive; b. Richmond, Va., Dec. 8, 1945; d. William H. III and Dorothy (Fowler) Miller; m. Joerg R. Michelfelder, June 10, 1972. BS, Longwood Coll., 1967; MBA, Pepperdine U., 1982. Tchr. Jefferson High Sch., Alexandria, Va., 1967-69, Stuttgart (Germany) High Sch., 1969-73; adminstrv. asst. Sanwa Bank, San Francisco, 1973-74; asst. v.p. Security Pacific Nat. Bank, San Francisco, 1974-78; dir. human resources Nat. Semiconductor, Santa Clara, Calif., 1978-82; exec. dir. human resources Atari Inc., Sunnyvale, Calif., 1983-84; dir. human resources Fujitsu Am., Inc., San Jose, Calif., 1985; exec. v.p. Bank of Calif., San Francisco, 1985-92; v.p. human resources & support svcs. Lucile Packard Children's Hosp. at Stanford, Palo Alto, Calif., 1993—; bd. dirs., pres. Alumnae Resources, San Francisco, 1990—. Vol. Am. Cancer Soc., San Francisco, 1991-92. Mem. City Club San Francisco. *

MICHELI, PAULA JEAN, special education educator; b. Elko, Nev., June 15, 1967; d. Louie Gino and Carol Mary (Boner) M. AA, Coll. So. Idaho, 1987; BA in Edn., U. Nev., Reno, 1993. Cert. tchr., Nev. Supr. lifeguard City of Wells, 1986—; aqua instr., lifeguard YWCA, Reno, 1989-93; security guard Lawlor Event Ctr., Reno, 1990-93, Event Svcs., Reno, 1990-93; spl. edn. tchr. Elko (Nev.) Sch. Dist., 1994—. Swimming and safety instr. ARC, Elko, 1983—, mem. disaster svcs. team, 1994—, health and safety com., 1995—; ASCD 1995—; counselor Boy Scouts Am. Recipient 10-Yr. Svc. award ARC, 1993, 3d pl. award Walking Assn., 1994.

MICHELINI, SYLVIA HAMILTON, auditor; b. Decatur, Ala., May 16, 1946; d. George Borum and Dorothy Rose (Swatzell) Hamilton; m. H. Stewart Michelini, June 4, 1964; children: Stewart Anthony, Cynthia Leigh. BSBA summa cum laude, U. Ala., Huntsville, 1987. CPA, Ala.; cert. govt. fin. mgr. Acct. Ray McCay, CPA, Huntsville, 1987-88; auditor Def. Contract Audit Agy., Huntsville, 1989-92; auditor-office of inspector general George C. Marshall Space Flight, Center, Ala., 1992—. Mem. exec. bd. Decatur City PTA, 1976-78; pres., v.p. Elem. Sch. PTA, Decatur, 1977-79; leader Girl Scouts U.S. and Cub Scouts, Decatur, 1972-77; active local ARC, 1973-77. Mem. AAUW (chpt. treas. 1988-90), Nat. Assn. Accts. (dir. community svc. 1987-88, v.p. adminstrn. and fin. 1988-89, pres. 1989-90, nat. com. on ethics 1990-91), Am. Inst. CPAs, Am. Soc. Women Accts. (chpt. treas. 1989-90, dir. chpt. devel. 1989-90), Assn. Govt. Accts. (sec. 1992-93, chmn. pub. rels. 1993-94), Ala. Soc. CPAs (profl. ethics com. 1993-94), Inst. Internal Auditors (dir. awards and recongnition 1996-97), Inst. Mgmt. Accts. (v.p. communications, dir. program book 1991—, Dixie coun. dir. newsletters 1992-93, dir. ednl. programs 1992-93, 93-94, nat. com. ethics, 1990—), Ala. Soc. CPAs (govtl. acctg. and auditing com. 1994—), Inst. Mgmt. Accts. (nat. bd. dirs. 1994—), Phi Kappa Phi. Baptist. Home: 2801 Sylvia Dr SE Decatur AL 35603-9381 Office: NASA Office Inspector Gen M-DI Marshall Space Flight Ctr Huntsville AL 35812

MICHELMAN, KATE, advocate; married; 3 daughters. Dir. Planned Parenthood, Harrisburg, Pa., 1980-85; pres. Nat. Abortion and Reproductive Rights Action League, Washington, 1985—. Spkr. in field. Named one of 100 Most Powerful Elites in the Nation's Capitol Washingtonian Mag., named a fellow of John F. Kennedy Sch. Govt.'s Inst. of Politics Harvard U., 1994. Office: Nat Abortion Rights Action League 1156 15th St NW Ste 700 Washington DC 20005-1704*

MICHELS, KRISTIN CARA, special education educator; b. Roswell, N.Mex., Sept. 23, 1966; d. Gary Antone and Barbara Eleanor (Steen) M. BS in Edn., N.Mex. State U.; postgrad., Pacific Lutheran U., Tacoma, 1996—. Elem. and spl. edn. lic. Behavior disorder tchr. grades K-6 Las Cruces (N.Mex.) Pub. Sch., 1989-90; spl. day class tchr. Moreno Valley (Calif.) Unified Schs., 1990-91; spl. edn. tchr. Roswell (N.Mex.) Pub. Schs., 1991-96. Home: 2001 S Sunset A201 Roswell NM 88201

MICHELSEN, ANNE CHRISTINA, artist; b. Salem, Ohio, Feb. 24, 1969; d. Harold Wyman and Nancy Lee (Royce) Martin; m. Daniel Edward Michelsen, June 6, 1993; 1 child, Isaac Neil. BA, St. Olaf Coll., 1991. Freelance artist and illustrator, 1989—; illustrator dept. biology No. Mich. U., Marquette, 1991-94; mem. Perspective 17 Gallery, Marquette, 1994-95; tchr. Liberty Children's Art Project, Negaunee, Mich., 1996—. Exhibited in group shows Nat. League Am. Penwomen, 1992, N.Mex. Art League, 1994, Lafayette (La.) Art Gallery, 1994, Nicolet Area Tech. Coll., Rhinelander, Wis., 1994; illustrator Jour. Crustacean Biology, 1993, 94. Nat. Merit scholar St. Olaf Coll., 1987; recipient Best of Mixed Media award Lake Superior Art Assn., Glacier Glide Art Show, 1996. Mem. Nat. Mus. Women in the ARts, Lake Superior Art Assn. (Duane Deloach Premier award 1994), Phi Beta Kappa. Home and Office: 334 Iron St #1 Negaunee MI 49866

MICHELSON, GAIL IDA, lawyer; b. N.Y.C., Sept. 19, 1952; d. Max and Virginia (Seames) M. BA, Columbia U., 1984; JD, W.Va. U., 1993. Bar: W.Va. 1993, U.S. Dist. Ct. (so. dist.) W.Va. Assoc. Kopelman & Assocs., Charleston, W.Va., 1994; asst. atty. gen. Atty. Gen. State of W.Va., Charleston, 1995—. Actor: (soap operas) Another World, Guiding Light, All My Children, 1976-79; contbr. articles W.Va. Quar. Dir./staff Am. Theatre of Actors, N.Y.C., 1985-90. Mem. ABA, W.Va. Bar Assn., W.Va. Trial Lawyers Assn., ACLU. Home: 300 Park Ave Charleston WV 25302 Office: Atty Gen State of W Va Capitol Complex Charleston WV 25305

MICHELSON, LILLIAN, motion picture researcher; b. Manhattan, N.Y., June 21, 1928; d. Louis and Dora (Keller) Farber; m. Harold Michelson, Dec. 14, 1947; children: Alan Bruce, Eric Neil, Dennis Paul. Vol. Goldwyn Libr., Hollywood, Calif., 1961-69; owner Former Goldwyn Rsch. Libr., Hollywood, Calif., 1969—; ind. location scout, 1973—. Bd. dirs Beverlywood After Care Ctr., L.A., 1988—; mem. Friends of L.A. Pub. Libr. Office: care Dreamworks SKG 100 Universal Plz Lakeside Bldg #601 Universal City CA 91608

MICHETTI, SUSAN JANE, media relations director, video producer, communications consultant; b. Kenosha, Wis., Dec. 20, 1948. BA cum laude, U. Wis., 1981; Cert. A, B, C for real estate law, appraisal and mktg., Gateway Tech. Inst., Kenosha, 1979; postgrad., Carthage Coll., Kenosha, 1984. Pub. rels. and media dir. Big Bros./Big Sisters of Kenosha County, Wis., 1978-79; newspaper editor U. Wis., Parkside, 1979-81; news reporter, newscaster Sta. WRJN Radio, Racine, Wis., 1982-84; pub. info. specialist, graphic designer Kenosha Unified Sch. Dist., 1983-84; book editorial and prodn. coord. Scott, Foresman and Co., Glenview, Ill., 1985-88; instr. profl. devel. U. Wis., Parkside, 1988-89; fin. svcs./pub. rels. editor Phillips Pub., 1986-95; propr. Michetti Multi-Media Assocs., Kenosha, 1981—; cons. in field. Contbr. articles to profl. jours. Media cons. Friends of Peter Barca for State Legislature, Kenosha, 1985-92; art fair asst. Friends of Kenosha Pub. Mus., 1986-92; mem. program devel. com. Racine Hist. Soc. and Pub. Mus., 1984-85. Scholar, Kenosha Found., 1979-81, Kenneth L. Greenquist, 1980, Vilas, 1968-71, Ida D. Altemus, 1969-70. Mem. NAFE, Am. Soc. Profl. and Exec. Women, Internat. Soc. Unified Sci. Home and Office: Michetti Multi-Media Assocs PO Box 54 Kenosha WI 53141-0054

MICHNA, ANDREA STEPHANIE, real estate agent and developer; b. Chgo., Nov. 4, 1948; d. Andrew Stephen and Ann Barbara (Ciesla) M. Student, Northwestern U., 1984-86. Travel cons. Internat. Sporting Travel, Chgo., 1975-77; office mgr., legal asst. Law Office of J.A. Rosin, Chgo., 1977-83; asst. to pres. Mt. Sinai Hosp., Chgo., 1983-85; exec. v.p. real estate Continental Fin., Ltd., Northbrook, Ill., 1985—. Office: Continental Financial Ltd 555 Skokie Blvd Ste 285 Northbrook IL 60062-2833

MICHNEY, KAREN MARIE, secondary education educator; b. Cleve., Aug. 9, 1965; d. Robert Joseph and Kathleen Karen (Lewicki) M. BA in Elem. Edn. summa cum laude, Wilmington Coll., 1987; MA in Religious Studies, John Carroll U., 1989. Cert. tchr., Ohio; joined as lay co-mem. Congregation of St. Joseph, Roman Cath. Ch., 1995. Co-instr. acad. resources, then substitute instr. Wilmington (Ohio) Coll., 1983-87; grad. asst. dept. religious studies John Carroll U., University Heights, Ohio, 1987-89, rsch. asst., 1989; tchr. theology Trinity H.S., Garfield Heights, Ohio, 1989-91; tchr. theology St. Joseph Acad., Cleve., 1991—, dir. at risk spl. edn. program, 1996—, retreat dir., 1989-95, facilitator adult edn., 1993, dept. chmn., 1994—. Contbr. articles to religious publs. Mem. AAUW, Nat. Cath. Educators Assn., Nat. Assembly Religious Women, Ohio Assn. Women in Edn., Ctr. for Women and Religion, Women's Ordination Conf., Futurechurch (outreach com. Cleve.), Phi Beta Kappa. Democrat. Office: 3430 Rocky River Dr Cleveland OH 44111

MICK, MARGARET ANNE, communications executive; b. Phila., Apr. 24, 1947; d. Charles Philip and Helen Margaret (Amig) Maurer; m. Donald Kenneth Mick, Sept. 8, 1979. BS with honors, Pa. State U., 1969; MA, NYU, 1972. Assoc. producer Visual Edn. Corp., Princeton, N.J., 1972-73; program devel. specialist AEtna Life & Casualty, Hartford, Conn., 1973-78; sr. program devel. specialist AEtna Life & Casualty, Hartford, 1978-81, mgr. audiovisual communications, 1981-82, dir. audiovisual and mktg. communications, 1982-84, dir. mktg. communications, 1984-86, dir. bus. devel., 1986-88, asst. v.p. customized communications, 1988—; juror EFLA Am. Film Festival, Hartford, 1977-79. Writer, dir., producer TV films including (ednl.) PAC-Man in the Money Works. Mem. Info. Film Producers Am. (chmn. 1981, treas. 1982, Conn. Valley Chpt.), Internat. TV Assn. (chmn. 1983), Hartford Women's Network, Mature Market Inst., Bus. and Profl. Advt. Assn. Republican. Home: 483 Coloniel Rd Guilford CT 06437

MICKIEWICZ, ELLEN PROPPER, political science educator; b. Hartford, Conn., Nov. 6, 1938; d. George K. and Rebecca (Adler) Propper; m. Denis Mickiewicz, June 2, 1963; 1 son, Cyril. B.A., Wellesley Coll., 1960; M.A., Yale U., 1961, Ph.D., 1965. Lectr. dept. polit. sci. Yale U., 1965-67; asst. prof. dept. polit. sci. Mich. State U., East Lansing, 1967-69; assoc. prof. Mich. State U., 1969-73, prof., 1973-80; prof. dept. polit. sci. Emory U., Atlanta, 1980-88; dean Grad. Sch. Arts and Scis. Emory U., 1980-85, Alben W. Barkley prof. polit. sci., 1988-93; James R. Shepley prof. pub. policy, prof. polit. sci. Duke U., Durham, N.C., 1994—, dir. DeWitt Wallace Ctr. for Comm. and Journalism Terry Sanford Inst. Pub. Policy, 1994—; vis. prof. Kathryn W. David Chair Wellesley Coll., 1978; vis. com. dept. Slavic lang. and lit. Harvard U., 1978-85, vice chmn. vis. com. Russian Rsch. Ctr., Harvard U., 1986-92; mem. subcom. on comms. and society Am. Coun. Learned Socs./Soviet Acad. Scis., 1986-90; mem. com. on internat. security studies, Am. Acad. Arts and Scis., 1988-90; fellow The Carter Ctr., 1985—, dir. Commn. on Radio and TV Policy; mem. area adv. com. for Ea. Europe and USSR, Coun. for Internat. Exch. Of Scholars, 1987-90; mem. acad. adv. coun. The Kennan Inst. for Advanced Russian Studies, 1989-93; mem. bd. overseers Internat. Press Ctr., Moscow, 1995; dir., commr. Commn. Radio and TV Policy, 1990. Author: Soviet Political Schools, 1967, Media and the Russian Public, 1981, Split Signals: Television and Politics in the Soviet Union, 1988 (Electronic Book of Yr. award Nat. Assn. Broadcasters and Broadcast Edn. Assn. 1988); co-author: Television and Elections, 1992, Television/Radio News and Minorities, 1994; editor: Soviet Union Jour., 1980-90; co-editor: International Security and Arms Control, 1986, The Soviet Calculus of Nuclear War, 1986; editor, contbr.: Handbook of Soviet Social Science Data, 1973; mem. editl. bd. Jour. Politics, 1985-88, Harvard Internat. Jour. Press/Politics, 1995—, Polit. Comms., 1996—. Founder, 1st chmn. bd. dirs. Opera Guild of Greater Lansing, Inc., 1972-74. Recipient Outstanding Svc. to Promote Dem. Media in Russia award Journalists Union of Russia, 1994; Ford Found. Fgn. Area Tng. fellow, 1962-65, Guggenheim fellow, 1973-74; Sigma Xi grantee, 1972-74, John and Mary R. Markle Found. grantee, 1984-88, 94-96, 95—, Ford Found. grantee, 1985, 88-91, 92—, Rockefeller Found. grantee, 1985-87, W. Alton Jones Found. grantee, 1987-88, Eurasia Found. grantee, 1993-94, Carnegie Corp. of N.Y. grantee, 1996—. Mem. Am. Assn. for Advancement Slavic Studies (bd. dirs. 1978-81, mem. awards com., mem. endowment com. 1984-86, pres. 1987-88), Am. Polit. Sci. Assn.,Internat. Studies Assn. (v.p. N.Am. 1983-84), Dante Soc. Am., So. Conf. Slavic Studies (exec. com. 1983-84), Counc. Fgn. Rels. Office: Duke U Sanford Inst Pub Policy PO Box 90241 Durham NC 27708-0241

MICKLE, KATHRYN ALMA, security company executive; b. Pittsfield, Mass., May 17, 1946; d. Frederick Louis and Bertha Laura (Webster) Wick; m. William Joseph Mickle III, May 11, 1968; children: William J. IV, Deborah Sharon. Cert. in nursing Cooley Dickinson Hosp., Northampton, Mass., 1967. Charge nurse Berkshire Med. Ctr., Pittsfield, 1967-75; intensive and coronary care nurse, 1975-81; nursing cons. Springside Nursing Home, Pittsfield, 1974-76; owner New Eng. Security, Pittsfield, 1978—. Stage mgr. Doo Wah Days Variety Show, 1988-96. Active Western Mass. coun. Girl Scouts U.S., 1975—, Citizen's Against Child Abuse, 1988-96; dir., tchr. Dalton Vacation Bible Sch., Mass., 1979-83; vice chmn. bd. Berkshire County Christian Sch., 1984-86, bd. chmn., 1986-88, bd. dirs., 1982-88; chmn. pub. rels. exec. com. Billy Graham Crusade, Pittsfield area, 1982; Dalton coord. Silvio O. Conte Re-election Campaign, 1984; deaconess Congregationalist Ch., 1989-91, 94-96; lay preacher, 1995-96. Recipient numerous sales awards Dynamark Inc., 1980—, Franchise Adv. Coun., 1994-96, Internat. Franchise award, 1987, Appreciation award Dalton Vacation Bible Sch., 1983, John Walsh award Nat. Ctr. Missing and Exploited Children, Dynamark, 1992, David Shapiro award, 1993. Fellow Cen. Berkshire C. of C. (Outstanding Vol. award 1991, 93-94, bd. dirs. 1992-96, chair home show com. 1990-94, mem. exec. com. 1993—, vice chair 1993-95, chair edn. coun. 1993-94, chair-elect 1994-95, chair bd. 1995-96), Cooley Dickinson Alumni Assn., Pittsfield Bus. and Profl. Women, Exch. Club (child abuse prevention chmn., bd. dirs. Pittsfield club 1992-96). Avocations: reading, gardening, camping. Home: 72 Braeburn Rd Dalton MA 01226-1019 Office: New England Dynamark Security 397 North St Pittsfield MA 01201-4603

MICKLITSCH, CHRISTINE NOCCHI, health care administrator; b. Hazleton, Pa., Oct. 23, 1949; d. Nicholas Edmund and Matilda Nocchi; m. Wayne D. Micklitsch, May 20, 1972; children: Sarah N., Emily M. BS, Pa. State U., State College, 1971; MBA, Boston U., 1979. Blood bank med. technologist The Deaconess Hosp., Boston, 1971-73; sr. blood bank med. technologist Tufts New Eng. Med. Ctr., Boston, 1973-76, environ. svcs. coord., 1976-78; adminstrv. resident Joslin Diabetes Found., Boston, 1978-79; sr. analyst Analysis, Mgmt. & Planning, Inc., Cambridge, Mass., 1979-80; adminstrv. dir. Hahnemann Family Health Ctr., Worcester, Mass., 1980-84; exec. dir. Swampscott (Mass.) Treatment & Trauma Ctr., 1984-85; dir. practice mgmt., instr. U. Mass. Med. Ctr., Worcester, 1985-91; dir. adminstrv. svcs. The Fallon Clinic, Worcester, 1991-94; mgr. physician network devel. The Fallon healthcare Sys., Worcester, 1994—. Incorporator, pres. Newton (Mass.) Highlands Cmty. Devel. Corp., 1981-82; treas. Patriot's Trail coun. Girl Scouts U.S., Newton, 1993—; Christian edn. instr. Newton Highlands Congl. Ch., 1987-94. Kellogg fellow Ctr. for Rsch. in Ambulatory Health Care Adminstrn., Denver, 1979; grantee in grad. tng. in family medicine HHS, U. Mass. Med. Sch., Worcester, 1989. Fellow Am. Coll. Med. Practice Execs. (state coll. forum rep. 1989—, ea. sect. coll. forum rep. 1993—); mem. Am. Coll. Med. Practice Execs. (mem. chair 1995-96), Mass. Med. Group Mgmt. Assn. (pres. 1987-89, newsletter editor 1984—), Boston U. Health Care Mgmt. Program Alumni Assn., Alpha Omicron Pi (parlimentarian Epsilon Alpha chpt. 1969-70). Home: 320 Lake Ave Newton MA 02161-1212 Office: Fallon Healthcare Sys Chestnut Pl 10 Chestnut St Worcester MA 01608-2804

MICKLOS-MAISEY, JANET M., state agency administrator, human services director; b. Jacksonville, Fla., July 24, 1947; d. Thomas Anthony and Yolanda Mae (Murphy) Micklos; married; children: Shawn E. Satterthwaite, Ryan W. Satterthwaite; m. Terry Mercer Maisey, May 28, 1988. BA, U. No. Colo., 1969; MA disting. grad., Webster U., 1985; grad., N.H. Part-Time Police Acad., 1995. Phys. edn. tchr. Terrell Wells Middle Sch., San Antonio, 1969-70; fitness instr./gymnastic coach Victor Valley Community Coll., Apple Valley, Calif., 1977-79; dir. phys. dept. Victor Valley YMCA, Victorville, Calif., 1978-79; secretarial support joint U.S. mil. mission aid to Turkey Ankara, Turkey, 1981-82; secretarial support U.S. Logistics Group, Ankara, 1982-83; pub. edn. dir. Alamo Area Rape Crisis Ctr., San Antonio, 1986-88; admissions coord. Horizon Hosp., San Antonio, 1988; psychiat. counselor Portsmouth Pavilion, Portsmouth, N.H., 1988-89; dir. human svcs. Rockingham County (N.H.) Dept. of Corrections, Brentwood, 1989—. Mem. adv. task force N.H. Coun. Chs., 1992; mem. gov.'s coun. on volunteerism, Seacoast, 1990-93; chmn. outreach commn. 1st United Meth. Ch., Portsmouth, 1990-93; mem. task force on victim restitution Rockingham County, 1992—; spl. dep. Rockingham County Sheriff's Dept.; police officer Newfields Police Dept. Mem. AAUW, Am. Correctional Assn., Am. Jail Assn., Rockingham County Law Enforcement Officers Assn., N.H. Police Assn., Boston Seaman's Friend Soc. Methodist. Office: Rockingham County Dept Corrections 99 North Rd Brentwood NH 03833-6617

MIDDENDORF, ALICE CARTER, volunteer; b. Balt., Dec. 7, 1940; d. John William and Alice Temple (Carter) M. BA, Wellesley Coll., 1963, Oxford U., England, 1972. Librarian Boston Athenaeum Libr., 1963-66; editor Houghton Mifflin Co., Boston, 1966-69; bd. dirs. Balt. Zool. Soc., 1976; cons. Nat. Zoo, Washington, 1976-77, G. Ward & Assocs., Ridgefield, Conn., 1976-79; from bd. dirs. to bd. govs. Nat. Aquarium in Balt., 1976-88, sec. bd. govs., 1987-88, chmn. animal policy com., 1982-88; bd. dirs. Total Health Care (merger Constant Care Med. Ctr. and West Balt. Constant Health Ctr.), Balt., 1981—, sec. bd. dirs., 1990-93; mem. adv. bd. Nat. Aquarium in Balt., 1989-94, bd. govs., 1994—, sec. bd. govs., 1995-96; bd. dirs. Constant Care Med. Ctr., Balt.; bd. dirs. Park Heights Street Acad., Balt., sec., 1988-90; pres. Fulmar Corp., Cayman Islands, Brit. West Indies, 1991—; pres., chmn. bd. dirs. Lystra Hill Farms, Inc., Goleta, Calif. Recipient Pres.'s Citation, Pres. City Coun. Balt., 1974, 76, Award of Appreciation, Mayor of Balt., 1981. Mem. Am. Assn. Zool. Parks and Aquariums. Home and Office: 1301 Hillside Rd Stevenson MD 21153 Office: Lystra Hill Farms Inc Rte 1 PO Box 237-A Goleta CA 93117

MIDDLEBROOK, DIANE WOOD, English language educator; b. Pocatello, Idaho, Apr. 16, 1939; d. Thomas Isaac and Helen Loretta (Downey) Wood; m. Jonathan Middlebrook, June 15, 1963 (div. 1972); 1 child, Leah Wood Middlebrook; m. Carl Djerassi, June 21, 1985. BA, U. Wash., 1961; MA, Yale U., 1962, PhD, 1968. Asst. prof. Stanford (Calif.) U., 1966-73, assoc. prof., 1973-83, prof., 1983—, D, dir. Ctr. for Rsch. on Women, 1977-79. Author: Walt Whitman and Wallace Stevens, 1974, Worlds into Words: Understanding Modern Poems, 1980, Anne Sexton, A Biography, 1991, (poems) Gin Considered as a Demon, 1983; editor: Coming to Light: American Women Poets in the Twentieth Century, 1985. Founding trustee Djerassi Resident Artists Program, Woodside, Calif., 1980-83, chair, 1994; trustee San Francisco Art Inst., 1993. Ind. study fellow NEH, 1982-83, Bunting Inst. fellow Radcliffe Coll., 1982-83, Guggenheim Found. fellow, 1988-89, Rockefeller Study Ctr. fellow, 1990; recipient Yale Prize for Poetry; finalist Nat. Book award, 1991. Mem. MLA. Home: 1101 Green St Apt 1501 San Francisco CA 94109-2016 Office: Stanford U Dept English Stanford CA 94305-2087

MIDDLEBROOKS, PHYLLIS, preschool educator, poet; b. N.Y.C., Jan. 6, 1940; d. Joseph Goodhue and Mildred Ann (Curran) Weatherly; divorced; 1 child, Benje. BS in Comms./Film, Temple U., 1973, MEd in Media, 1985, MA in English/Creative Writing, 1987. Diplomate Assn. Montessori Internationale; cert. tchr., Pa. Coord. audio visual svc. Children's Hosp. of Phila., 1974-90; tchr. ESL Forestry U., Beijing, China, 1989-90; preschool Montessori tchr. Sch. Dist. of Phila., 1968-71, 91—. Author: Shadow Blue, 1988; editor mags. 6ix, 1991—, The World, 1992-93. Dean's scholar Temple U., 1985-87; Pa. Coun. on the Arts poetry fellow, 1989. Mem. NOW. Home: 44 W Washington Ln Philadelphia PA 19144-2602

MIDDLEMAN, ROSE RUTH, public health physician; b. Pitts., Apr. 14, 1911; d. David and Fanny Rachel (Opachevsky) M.; m. Leo Silverblatt; children: Norma Silverblatt Caplan, Howard W., Alan M. BS, U. Pitts., 1932, MD, 1934, MPH, 1961. Lic. Ohio, Pa. Intern Sewickley (Pa.) Valley Hosp., 1934-35; pvt. practice Youngstown, Ohio, 1936-42, Pitts., 1943-59; clinician Allegheny County Health Dept., Pitts., asst. dir. bur. maternal and child health, 1962-64, dir. bur. maternal and child health, 1964-68; med. coord. Planned Parenthood of Pitts., 1968-70, med. dir., 1970-76; ret., 1976; bd. dirs. adv. bd. Pub. Sch. Program for Unwed Mothers, Pitts., 1969-72; adv. com. for Sch. for Cert. Nurse Assts., W. Palm Beach, Fla., 1988-96. V.p. Abortion Justice Assn., Pitts., 1969-73. Mem. AMA, ACLU, LWV (bd. dirs. 1995-97), Retired Physicians Club (W. Palm Beach). Democrat. Jewish. Home: 4 Greenway Village N # 108 Royal Palm Beach FL 33411

MIDDLETON, ALYSSA MONIQUE, athletic administrator, marketing professional; b. Danville, Ky., June 25, 1970; d. Gene Philip and Tommye Lynn (Brackett) M. BS in Advt./Mktg., U. Ky., 1993; MS in Athletic Adminstrn., W.Va. U., 1994. Staff asst. U.K. Athletics Dept., Lexington, Ky., 1989-93; asst. dir. mktg. promotions and licensing U. Ky., Lexington, 1994—. Bd. dirs., sec. Citizen's for Sports Equity, Lexington, 1994—; com. mem. Women's Sports Found., Lexington, 1991—; big sister Big Bros./Big Sisters, Lexington, 1995. Office: U Ky Athletics Dept Euclid Ave Meml Coliseum Lexington KY 40506

MIDDLETON, CHARLENE, retired medical and surgical nurse, educator; b. Ennis, Tex., Sept. 13, 1922; d. Charles Silvester and Harriet Eugenia (Ford) M. Diploma, Scott and White Hosp., Temple, Tex., 1945; AA, Temple Jr. Coll., 1947; BA, U. Tex., Austin, 1956. Nurse coord., ambulatory care svcs. Naval Regional Med. Ctr., Long Beach, Calif.; instr. nursing arts Scott and White Hosp., evening supr.; now ret. Lt. comdr. U.S. Navy, 1957-77. Mem. Scott and White Alumni Assn. (past pres. Dist. 7).

MIDDLETON, LINDA JEAN GREATHOUSE, lawyer; b. Poplar Bluff, Mo., Sept. 22, 1950; d. Casper Scott and Anna Garnelle (Qualls) Greathouse; m. Roy L. Middleton, Sept. 27, 1969. BS cum laude, Ark. State U., 1972; JD, Baylor U., 1974. Bar: Tex., 1974; CPCU, CLU. Asst. v.p., asst. sec., atty. Equitable Gen. Ins. Co., Ft. Worth, 1977-81; gen. counsel, corp. sec. Chilton Corp., Dallas, 1981-83; asst. corp. sec., sr. atty., mgr. pub. affairs Fina Oil and Chem., Dallas, 1983-85; sec. Parliamentarian, Dallas, 1985—. Sec. Homeowners Assn., Dallas, 1981—. Mem. Tex. Bar Assn., Dallas Bar Assn. Baptist. Office: Fina Inc 8350 N Ctrl Expwy PO Box 2159 Dallas TX 75221

MIDDLETON, MARY, secondary education educator; b. Lackawana, N.Y., Nov. 13, 1942; d. Arthur Jordan and Kathryn (Sternburg) M. BS in Edn., Ohio State U., 1965; postgrad., Akron U., 1970, Cleve. State U., 1981-84. Profl. cert. in edn. Tchr. Columbus (Ohio) Schs., 1966-68, Brooklyn (Ohio) Schs., 1968—; co-dir. C.A.R.E. (Chem. Abuse Reduced through Edn.), Brooklyn (Ohio) City, 1986—, English dept. chair, acad. team advisor Brooklyn (Ohio) Schs., 1987—; mem. dimensions of learning task force Bklyn. Schs., Advisor: English hon. 1990—. Contbr. articles to profl. jours. Campaign worker North Olmsted (Ohio) Dem. club, 1988, 92, 96; recreation dir. Country Club Condominiums, 1992—. Recipient N.E. Ohio Writing Project fellowship Martha Holden Jennings, Cleve. State U., 1985. Mem. ASCD, NEA, AAUW, Ohio Edn. Assn., Brooklyn (Ohio) Edn. Assn. (sec.), Ohio Coun. Tchrs. English and Lang. Arts, Cinnamon Woods Condominiums Assn. (bd. dirs.), Re-elect the Pres. Com., Ohio State U. Alumni Assn., Phi Mu. Methodist. Home: 7127 Bayberry Cir North Olmsted OH 44070-4765 Office: Brooklyn City Schs 9200 Biddulph Rd Brooklyn OH 44144-2614

MIDDLETON-DOWNING, LAURA, psychiatric social worker; b. Edinburg, Ind., Apr. 20, 1935; d. John Thomas Jr. and Rowene Elizabeth (Baker) Middleton; m. George Charles Downing, 1974 (div. 1986). BA in English Lit., U. Colo., 1966, MFA, 1969, BA in Psychology, 1988; MSW, U. Denver, 1992; Doctor of Clin. Hypnotherapy, Am. Inst. Hypnotherapy, 1995. Cert. clin. hypnotherapist, Calif.; cert. past-life therapist, Colo. Profl. artist Silver Plume and Boulder, Colo., 1965—; profl. photographer Silver Plume, 1975-87; art tchr. U. Colo., Boulder and Longmont, 1971-73; mem. survey crew Bur. of Land Mgmt., Empire, Colo., 1984-85; pvt. practice psychiat. social worker Boulder, 1992—; med. social worker Good Samaritan Health Agy., Boulder, 1993—; pvt. practice clin. hypnotherapy Boulder, 1995—, pvt. practice past-life therapist, 1995—. Author, photographer Frontiers, Vol. IV, No. 1, 1979; works exhibited in 10 one-woman shows, 1969-88; numerous group exhbns. Trustee Town of Silver Plume, Colo., 1975-84; co-founder, pres. Alma Holm Rogers Nat. Orgn. Women, Clear Creek County, 1975-82; mem. Ctrl. Mountain Coun., Clear Creek County, 1980; bd. dirs. Clear Creek Day Sch., Idaho Springs, Colo., 1981-82; chairperson Mary Ellen Barnes Cmty. Ctr. Project, Silver Plume, 1983; vol. Rape Crisis Team, Boulder, 1989-90, Child & Family Advocacy Program, Boulder, 1992-96; adv. bd. mem. Good Samaritan Agy., Boulder, 1993-96; caring minister vol. First Congl. Ch., Boulder, 1995-96. Recipient Juried Exhbn. Merit award Colo. Women in the Arts, 1979; Women's Incentive scholar U. Colo., Boulder, 1989; Grad. Sch. Social Work scholar U. Denver, 1991; Colo. Grad. grantee U. Denver, 1992. Mem. NASW, DAR, Colo. Advs. for Responsible Mental Health Svcs., Eye Movement Desensitization Reprocessing Network, Assn. for Past-Life Rsch. and Therapies, Inc. (Colo. group leader), Psi Chi. Office: PO Box 2312 Boulder CO 80306

MIDLER, BETTE, singer, entertainer, actress; b. Honolulu, Dec. 1, 1945; m. Martin von Haselberg, 1984; 1 child, Sophie. Student, U. Hawaii, 1 year. Debut as actress film Hawaii, 1965; mem. cast Fiddler on the Roof, N.Y.C., 1966-69, Salvation, N.Y.C., 1970, Tommy, Seattle Opera Co., 1971; night-club concert performer on tour, U.S., from 1972; appearance Palace Theatre, N.Y.C., 1973, Radio City Music Hall, 1993; TV appearances include The Tonight Show, Bette Midler: Old Red Hair is Back, 1978, Gypsy, 1993 (Golden Globe award best actress in a mini-series or movie made for television 1994, Emmy nomination, Lead Actress - Special, 1994), Seinfeld, 1995; appeared Clams on The Half-Shell Revue, N.Y.C., 1975; recs. include The Divine Miss M, 1972, Bette Midler, 1973, Broken Blossom, 1977, Live at Last, 1977, The Rose, 1979, Thighs and Whispers, 1979, Songs for the New Depression, 1979, Divine Madness, 1980, No Frills, 1984, Mud Will Be Flung Tonight, 1985, Beaches (soundtrack), 1989, Some People's Lives, 1990; motion picture appearances include Hawaii, 1966, The Rose, 1979 (Academy award nomination best actress 1979), Divine Madness, 1980, Jinxed, 1982, Down and Out in Beverly Hills, 1986, Ruthless People, 1986, Outrageous Fortune, 1987, Oliver and Company (voice), 1988, Big Business, 1988, Beaches, 1988, Stella, 1990, Scenes From a Mall, 1991, For the Boys, 1991 (Academy award nomination best actress 1991), Hocus Pocus, 1993; appeared in cable TV (HBO) prodn. Bette Midler's Mondo Beyondo, 1988; author: A View From A Broad, 1980, The Saga of Baby Divine, 1983. Recipient After Dark Ruby award, 1973; Grammy awards, 1973, 1990; spl. Tony award, 1973; Emmy award for NBC Spl., Ol' Red Hair is Back, 1978; 2 Golden Globe awards for The Rose, 1979, Golden Globe award for The Boys, 1991; Emmy award The Tonight Show appearance, 1992. Office: care Atlantic Records 75 Rockefeller Plz New York NY 10019-6908*

MIDORI (MIDORI GOTO), classical violinist; b. Osaka, Japan, Oct. 25, 1971. Attended, Juilliard Sch. Music; grad., Profl. Childrens Sch., 1990. Performer worldwide, 1981—. Recordings on Philips, Sony Classical, Columbia Masterworks; performed with N.Y. Philharmonic Orch., Boston Symphony Orch.; worldwide performances include Berlin, Chgo., Cleve., Phila., Montreal, London; recordings include Encore, Live at Carnegie Hall. Named Best Artist of Yr. by Japanese Govt., 1988; recipient Dorothy B. Chandler Performing Arts award, L.A. Music Ctr., 1989, Crystal award Ashani Shimbun Newspaper contbn. arts, Suntory award, 1994. Office: Sony Classical Sony Music Entertainment Inc 550 Madison Ave New York NY 10022-3211*

MIEDEMA, BARBARA J., public relations executive; b. Pontiac, Mich., July 25, 1958; d. Donald H. and Jere B. (Flory) B.; m. Ronald C. Miedema, 1981; children: Matthew Charles, Mallory Elizabeth. BA, Mich. State U., 1980. APRP in 1992. Pub. Marion County Publs., Pella, Iowa, 1980-85; v.p. pub. rels. Fla. Sugar Cane League, Clewiston, 1986-91; mgr. pub. rels. Sugar Cane Growers Coop. of Fla., Belle Glade, Fla., 1991—. Dir. Clewiston Sugar Festival Com., 1987-89; South Fla. Water Mgmt. Dist. Agrl. Advisory Com. (bd. mem. 1993—); Ag Inst. Fla. (bd. mem. 1991—, v.p. 1991-93). Mem. Fla. Pub. Rels. Assn., Clewiston C. of C. (dir. 1987-89), Palm Beaches C. of C. (dir. 1995—), Coop. Communicators Assn., Women in Communication. Office: Sugar Cane Growers Coop Fla PO Box 666 Belle Glade FL 33430

MIEL, VICKY ANN, municipal government executive; b. South Bend, Ind., June 20, 1951; d. Lawrence Paul Miel and Virginia Ann (Yeagley) Hernandez. BS, Ariz. State U., 1985. Word processing coordinator City of Phoenix, 1977-78, word processing adminstr., 1978-83, chief dep. city clk., 1983-88, city clk. dir., 1988—; assoc. prof. Phoenix Community Coll., 1982-83, Mesa (Ariz.) Community Coll., 1983; speaker in field, Boston, Santa Fe, Los Angeles, N.Y.C. and St. Paul, 1980—. Author: Phoenix Document Request Form, 1985, Developing Successful Systems Users, 1986. Judge Future Bus. Leaders Am. at Ariz. State U., Tempe, 1984; bd. dirs. Fire and Life Safety League, Phoenix, 1984. Recipient Gold Plaque, Word Processing Systems Mag., Mpls., 1980, Green Light Productivity award City of Phoenix, 1981, Honor Soc. Achievement award Internat. Word Processing Assn., 1981, 1st Ann. Grand Prize Records Mgmt. Internat. Inst. Mcpl. Clks., 1990, Olsten Award for Excellence in Records Mgmt., 1991, Tech. Award of Excellence, 1995. Mem. Assn. Info. Systems Profls. (internat. dir. 1982-84), Internat. Inst. Mcpl. Clks. (cert., Tech. award of excellence 1995, 2nd v.p. 1996—), Am. Records Mgrs. Assn., Assn. Image Mgmt., Am. Soc. Pub. Adminstrs., Am. Mgmt. Assn. Office: City of Phoenix 200 W Washington St Ste 1500 Phoenix AZ 85003-1611

MIERKE, KATHRYN LORNA, art therapist; b. Ann Arbor, Mich., Nov. 28, 1961; d. Harvey Oliver Jr. and Lorna Mary (Hall) M. BA, Cornell Coll., Mt. Vernon, Iowa, 1984; BFA, Cleve. Inst. Art, 1988; MA in Art Therapy, Ursuline Coll., Pepper Pike, Ohio, 1995. Ordained deacon Ch. of the Covenant, 1989. Various positions, 1987-90; ind. mfr.'s rep. Nat. Safety Assn., 1990-93; activity dir. Alzheimer's patients Parkland Centre Nursing Home, Beachwood, Ohio, 1995; activity asst. Parkland Centre Nursing Facility, Beachwood, 1995-96; asst. dir. activities, art therapist Alvarado Convalescent and Rehab. Hosp., San Diego, 1996—. Mem. Am. Art Therapy Assn., Buckeye Art Therapy Assn. Presbyterian. Home: 3506 Collier Ave San Diego CA 92116-1901

MIESSE, MARY ELIZABETH (BETH MIESSE), special education educator; b. Amarillo, Tex. BA, BS, MEd in Guidance and Counseling, MA, West Tex. State U., Canyon, 1952, MBA, 1960; M in Pers. Svc., U. Colo., Boulder, 1954. Cert. in spl. edn. supr., spl. edn. counselor, ednl. diagnostician, spl. edn. (lang. and/or learning disabled, mentally retarded) tchr., profl. counselor, profl. tchr., supt., prin., Tex. With various bus. firms and radio stas., 1940-47; prof. Amarillo Coll., 1947-63; tchr. pvt. and pub. schs., also TV work, 1963-78; spl. edn. cons., 1978—; freelance writer-prodr. in radio/TV, 1978—. Former editor Tex. Jr. Coll. Tchrs. Assn. Mag. Pioneered in ednl. TV in West Tex.; recipient various lit. awards, awards in ednl. TV. Mem. AAUP, AAUW, APA, ASCAP, NEA, Nat. Fedn. State Poetry Socs., Poetry Soc. Tex., Tex. State Tchrs. Assn., Bus. Profl. Womens Club, Am. Bus. Women's Assn. (named one of Top Ten Women of Yr.), North Plains Assn. for Children with Learning Disabilities, Panhandle Profl. Writers, ASCA Writers, High Plains Poetry Soc., Inspirational Writers, Alive!, Cowboy Poets Assn., Toastmistress Internat. Home and Office: PO Box 3133 Valle De Oro TX 79010-3133

MIGALA, LUCYNA JOZEFA, broadcast journalist, arts administrator, radio station executive; b. Krakow, Poland, May 22, 1944; d. Joseph and Estelle (Suwala) M.; came to U.S., 1947, naturalized, 1955; student Loyola U., Chgo., 1962-63, Chicago Conservatory of Music, 1963-70; BS in Journalism, Northwestern U., 1966. Radio announcer, producer sta. WOPA, Oak Park, Ill., 1963-66; writer, reporter, producer NBC news, Chgo., 1966-69, 1969-71, producer NBC local news, Washington, 1969; producer, coord. NBC network news, Cleve., 1971-78, field producer, Chgo., 1978-79; v.p. Migala Communications Corp., 1979—; program and news dir., on-air personality Sta. WCEV, Cicero, Ill., 1979—; lectr. City Colls. Chgo., 1981, Morton Coll., 1988. Columnist Free Press, Chgo., 1984-87. Founder, artistic dir., gen. mgr. Lira Ensemble (formerly The Lira Singers), Chgo., 1965—, Artist-in-Residence, Loyola U. Chgo.; mem., chmn. various cultural coms. Polish Am. Congress, 1970-80; bd. dirs. Nationalities Svcs. Ctr., Cleve., 1973-78; bd. dirs., v.p. Cicero-Berwyn Fine Arts Coun., Cicero, Ill.; mem. City Arts I and II panels Chgo. Office of Fine Arts, 1986-89, 94; v.p. Chgo. chpt. Kosciuszko Found., 1983-86; bd. dirs. Polish Women's Alliance Am., 1983-87, Ill. Humanities Coun., 1983-89, mem. exec. com., 1986-87; bd. dirs. Ill. Arts Alliance, 1989-92; founder, gen. chmn. Midwest Chopin Piano Competition (now Chgo. Chopin Competition), 1984-86; founding mem. ethnic and folk arts panel Ill. Arts Coun., 1984-87, 92-94. Recipient AP Broadcasters award, 1973, Emmy award NATAS, 1974, Cultural Achievement award Am. Coun. for Polish Culture, 1990, Award of Merit Advocates Soc. Polish Am. Attys., 1991, Human Rels. Media award City of Chgo., 1992, Outstanding Achievement in Polish Culture award Minister of Fgn. Affairs, Rep. of Poland, 1994; Washington Journalism Ctr. fellow, spring 1969. Mem. Soc. Profl. Journalists. Office: Sta WCEV 5356 W Belmont Ave Chicago IL 60641-4103 also: The Lira Ensemble 6525 N Sheridan Rd # SKY 905 Chicago IL 60626

MIGDAL, RUTH AIZUSS, sculptor, educator; b. Chgo., Aug. 17, 1932; d. Joseph and Anna (Smith) Aizuss; m. Norman Bernard Migdal, June 20, 1954 (div. Oct. 1967); children: Allison, James; life ptnr. James Allison Brown. BFA, Sch. of Art. Inst. of Chgo., 1954; MFA, U. Ill., 1958. Art tchr. grades 2-8 Sunset Ridge Sch., Northfield, Ill., 1958-60; art instr. Columbia Coll., Chgo., 1967-68; lectr. U. Ill., Chgo., 1968-69; asst. prof. Malcolm X Coll., Chgo., 1969-81, Loop Coll. (now Harold Washington Coll.), Chgo., 1981-84; from assoc. prof. to prof. Harold Washington Coll., Chgo., 1984-96, prof. emeritus, 1996—; emeritus bd. dirs. Victory Garden Theater, Chgo.; artist sculptor Virginia Lust Gallery, N.Y.C., U. Ill., Springfield, 1995; vis. artist lectr. U. Mont., Missoula, 1988, Soc. of Arts, Religion and Contemporary Culture, N.Y.C., 1996. One-person shows include U. P.R., San Juan, 1956, Tacoma (Wash.) Mus., 1964, Veridian Gallery, N.Y.C., 1978, Elaine Starkman Gallery, N.Y.C., 1986, Virginia Lust Gallery, N.Y.C., 1992, exhibited in group shows Am. Gallery, N.Y.C., 1962, Tacoma Mus., 1964, Springfield Art Assn., 1979, Viridian Gallery, N.Y.C., 1985, Albright Knox Gallery, Bronx, 1985, Elaine Starkman Gallery, N.Y.C., 1985, Rockford Art Mus., 1986, Wolf Gallery, Townsend, Wash., 1991, U. Ill., Springfield, 1995Contbr. art revs. and articles to radio and publs. Recipient William Bartel prize Art Inst. Chgo., 1961, Pauline Palmer prize Art Inst. Chgo., 1973; Arts Coun. grantee Ill. Arts Coun., 1981, Spl. Assistance grantee, Ill. Arts Coun., 1995. Mem. Chgo. Artist's Coalition (founding mem., 1st chairperson 1974-75), Coll. Art Assn., Internat. Sculpture Ctr., Women's Caucus for Art, Arts Club Chgo. Home: 2238 N Geneva Ter Chicago IL 60614

MIGNERON, KATHY ANN, secondary education English educator; b. St. Louis, Apr. 9, 1950; d. Norman George and Flora Ann (Sprick) Kuhn; m. William C. Migneron Jr., Aug. 13, 1971; 1 child, Christopher. BA in English, Fontbonne Coll., St. Louis, 1972; MLS, Emporia (Kans.) State U., 1984. Cert. secondary edn. educator in lang. arts/composition, Mo., Kans., libr. media, Kans. Tchr. English St. Roch's Sch., St. Louis, 1972-74, Blue Valley North High Sch., Overland Park, Kans., 1985—. Elder, bd. elders Grace Covenant Presbyn. Ch., Overland Park, 1991-93. Recipient Robert G. Graef award Fontbonne Coll., 1972, Kans. Excellence in Edn. award Kans. State Bd. Edn., 1991. Mem. NEA, Nat. Coun. Tchrs. English. Presbyterian. Home: 9607 W 116th Ter Overland Park KS 66210-2805

MIGUEL DESOUSA, LINDA J., critical care nurse, nursing educator; b. Honolulu, Dec. 6, 1946; d. Gregory and Irene N. (Calasa) Furtado; children: Joseph H. Miguel Jr., Brett A. Miguel. ADN, Maui Community Coll., Kahului, Hawaii, 1980; BSN, U. Hawaii, 1987, MS, 1990. RN, Hawaii. Charge nurse ICU-CCU Maui Meml. Hosp., Wailuku; nursing instr. Maui Community Coll., Kahului; unit supr.-coronary care Straub Clinic and Hosp., Honolulu; nursing instr. Kapiolani Community Coll., Honolulu; edn. dir. Waianae Health Acad.; researcher in field. Contbr. articles to profl. jours. Outer Island Students Spl. Nursing scholar, 1988-90, Rsch. scholarship, 1989. Mem. AACN, Hawaii Nurses Assn., Hawaii Soc. for Cardiovascular and Pulmonary Rehab., Assn. Am. Women in C. C.s, Sigma Theta Tau. Home: 98-402 Koauka Loop #1202 Aiea HI 96701

MIILLER, SUSAN DIANE, artist; b. N.Y.C., June 10, 1953; d. Elwood Charles and Alyce Mary (Gebhardt) Knapp; m. Denis Miiller, May 22, 1982. MA, Queens Coll., 1980; BFA, SUNY, 1988; MFA, U. North Tex., 1992. Palynologist Phillips Petroleum Co., Bartleville, Okla., 1980-85; scenic designer Forestburgh (N.Y.) Playhouse, 1989; rsch. asst. Lamont-Doherty Geol. Observatory, Palisades, N.Y., 1990; adj. prof. Tex. Christian U., Ft. Worth, 1992-94; lectr. U. Tex., Dallas, 1995—; lectr. U. Tex., Dallas, 1995-96; treas. mem. 500X Gallery, Dallas, 1991-92. One-woman shows include Western Tex. Coll., 1993, Brazos Gallery, Richland Coll., 1993, Women & Their Work Gallery, 1995 (Gallery Artists Series award 1995), A.I.R. Gallery, 1996. Recipient 4th Nat. Biennial Exhbns., Grand Purchase award, 1991, Mus. Abilene award, 1992, Lubbock Art Festival Merit award, 1992, 2d pl. award Matrix Gallery, 1995, Hon. Mention award 3d Biennial Gulf of Mex. Exhbn., 1995, 1st place award Soho Gallery, 1996. Mem. Tex. Fin Arts Assn., Dallas Mus. Art, Coll. Art Assn., Dallas Visual Art Ctr., Art Initiatives. Home: 449 Harris St # J102 Coppell TX 75019-3224 Studio: 3309 Elm St # 3E Dallas TX 75226-1637

MIKE, DEBORAH DENISE, systems engineering and software consultant; b. Norfolk, Va., Oct. 19, 1959; d. William A. and Mophecia (Cook) Brickhouse. BA in Math., U. Va., 1981; postgrad., Johns Hopkins U., 1982-83; MS in Computer Systems Mgmt., U. Md., 1994. Primary systems engr. GTE Govt. Systems Corp., Rockville, Md., 1984-85, Vienna, Va., 1985-87; computer analyst Info. Systems and Networks Corp., Arlington, Va., 1987-88; realtor Mount Vernon Realty, Chevy Chase, Md., 1988-89; primary systems engr. Grumman Corp., McLean, Va., 1988-91, J.G. Van Dyke & Assocs., Alexandria, Va., 1991-93; systems engr. Pulse Engring., Inc., Beltsville, Md., 1993-94; sr. systems software quality assurance engr. Unisys at NASA, Greenbelt, Md., 1995-96; owner DDM Cons., Designs by Debbie. Active Smithsonian Resident Assoc. Program, 1988; mem. Friends of the Kennedy Ctr. Mem. NAFE (bd. dirs. Reston chpt. 1986), Nat. Assn. Realtors, Md. Assn. Realtors, Montgomery County Bd. Realtors, N.Y. Inst. Photography, U. Va. Alumni Assn., U. Va. Club Washington.

MIKEL, BRENDA JO, elementary education educator; b. Story City, Iowa, Apr. 23, 1961; d. Willis Fredric Butler and Mary Jane (Goodrich) Heishman; m. Douglas Wayne Mikel, Dec. 30, 1988; children: Brandon Jon, Ashley Marie. BA in Elem. Edn., U. No. Iowa, Cedar Falls, 1991, BA in Early Childhood Edn., 1991. Resident treatment worker Woodward (Iowa) State Hosp. Sch., 1979-83, tchrs. asst., 1983-85; tchrs. asst. Dallas Center (Iowa)-Grimes Sch., 1986-88; peer advisor U. No. Iowa, Cedar Falls, 1988-90; substitute tchr. Grinnell (Iowa)-Newburg Schs., 1991-92, kindergarten tchr., 1992—. Vol. Hospice Grinnell, 1991. Mem. Internat. Reading Assn., Nat. Edn. Young Children. Lutheran. Home: 843 330th Ave Grinnell IA 50112-8332 Office: Davis Elem Sch 818 Hamilton Ave Grinnell IA 50112-2411

MIKEL, SARAH ANN, librarian; b. Bklyn., Aug. 29, 1947; d. Robert H. and Sarah A. (Saver) Whalen; m. John R. Mikel, Oct. 21, 1977; 1 dau., Katherine Ann. B.A., U. Miami, 1969; M.A., U. Fla., 1971; M.A.L.S., Rosary Coll., River Forest, Ill., 1973. Editorial researcher Field Ednl. Enterprises, Chgo., 1971-72; librarian Purdue U., West Lafayette, Ind., 1973-75, U.S. Army Corps of Engrs., Rock Island, Ill., 1975-76, chief librarian, Washington, 1976-87, major command librarian, 1987-91; libr. dir. Nat. Def. Libr., Washington, 1991—; chmn. FEDLINK Users Group, 1980-83; mem. exec. adv. coun. FEDLINK, 1988-90; program chmn. Fed. Interagy. Field Librs. Workshop, 1983-84; mem. com. Fed. Libr. and Info. Ctr., 1992-95; mem. mil. edn. coordinating com. Libr. Group. Mem. Spl. Libr. Assn. (chmn. mil. librs. 1978-79), Army Libr. Inst. (chmn. 1988, 94, Army dep. functional chiefs rep. 1992-94). Home: 3343 Reservoir Rd NW Washington DC 20007-2312 Office: Nat Def Univ Ft Leslie J McNair 4th & P St SW Washington DC 20319

MIKIEWICZ, ANNA DANIELLA, marketing and sales representative; b. Chgo., Dec. 22, 1960; d. Zdislaw and Lucy (Magnusewska) K. BS in Mktg., Elmhurst Coll., 1982; postgrad. Triton Coll. Asst. to Midwestern regional mgr. Meister Pub. Co., Chgo., 1983; sales rep. First Impression, Elk Grove, Ill., 1984; mktg. and customer svcs. rep. Airco Ind. Gases, Broadview and Carol Stream, Ill., 1985, Yamazen USA, Inc., Schaumburg, Ill., 1985-88; nat. sales and mktg. coord. Kitamura Machinery U.S.A. Inc., 1988-95; mktg. mgr. Beth Lee Boutique, 1995—. Named Chgo. Polish Queen Polish Am. Culture Club, 1983-84; nominated White House Fellowship Program. Mem. NAFE. Republican. Roman Catholic.

MIKOSZ, JERI ANN, counselor; b. North Tonawanda, N.Y., Oct. 17, 1952; d. Gerald G. and Hazel R. (Durnell) Burkett; m. Ben Mikosz, Oct. 21, 1972; children: Gregory, Brian. BA in Interdisciplinary Social Scis., SUNY/AB, 1991; MS in Counselor Edn., Canisius Coll., 1995. Cert. sch. counselor, 1995. Rsch. asst. WNY Geriat. Edn. Ctr., SUNY/AB, Buffalo, 1991; adminstrv. asst., HIV counselor SUNY/AB, Buffalo, 1991-94; rehab. counselor DeGraff Adult Day Care, North Tonawanda, 1995; counselor AIDS Cmty. Svcs., Buffalo, 1995—; counselor, educator Hospice Buffalo, N.Y., 1995—; trainer Regional AIDS Interfaith Network, Buffalo, 1995—. Author: (tng. manuals) Rape Manual for Anti-Rape Task Force, 1993, AIDS Manual for AIDS Coalition, 1994. Rec. sec. St. Christopher's Parish Coun., 1994; vol. counselor Ptnrs. in Healing, Tonawanda, 1994—. Recipient Excellence in Volunteerism award DADC, North Tonawanda, 1995. Mem. ACA, Western N.Y. AIDS Network, Am. Rehab., Counselors Assn. Democrat. Roman Catholic. Home: 990 Thomas Fox Drive East North Tonawanda NY 14120 Office: AIDS Cmty Svcs 121 W Tupper St Buffalo NY 14201

MIKULSKI, BARBARA ANN, senator; b. Balt., July 20, 1936; d. William and Christine (Kutz) M. BA, Mt. St. Agnes Coll., 1958; MSW, U. Md., 1965; LLD (hon.), Goucher Coll., 1973, Hood Coll., 1978, Bowie State U., 1989, Morgan State U., 1990, U. Mass., 1991; DHL (hon.), Pratt Inst., 1974. Tchr. Vista Tng. Ctr. Mount St. Mary's Sem., Balt.; social worker Balt. Dept. Social Services, 1961-63, 66-70; mem. Balt. City Council, 1971-76, 95th-99th Congresses from 3d Md. Dist., 1977-87; U.S. senator from Md., 1987—, sec. Dem. Conf. 104th Congress; adj. prof. Loyola Coll., 1972-76. Bd. visitors U.S. Naval Acad. Recipient Nat. Citizen of Yr. award Buffalo Am.-Polit. Eagle, 1973, Woman of Yr. Bus. & Profl. Women's Club Assn., 1973, Outstanding Alumnus U. Md. Sch. Social Work, 1973, Govt. Social Responsibility award, 1991. Mem. LWV. *

MIKUS, ELEANORE ANN, artist; b. Detroit, July 25, 1927; d. Joseph and Bertha (Englot) M.; m. Richard Burns, July 6, 1949 (div. 1963); children: Richard, Hillary, Gabrielle. Student, Mich. State U., 1946-49, U. Mex., summer 1948; B.F.A., U. Denver, 1957, M.A., 1967; postgrad., Art Students League, 1958, NYU, 1959-60. Asst. prof. Cornell U., Ithaca, N.Y., 1979-80, assoc. prof., 1980-92, prof. art, 1992-94, prof. emerita, 1994—; asst. prof. art Monmouth Coll., West Long Branch, N.J., 1966-70, prof. Cornell, Rome, 1989; vis. lectr. painting Cooper Union, N.Y.C., 1970-72, Central Sch. Art and Design, London, 1973-77, Harrow (Eng.) Coll. Tech. and Art, 1975-76. Exhibited in 14 one-person shows at, Pace Gallery, N.Y.C. and O.K. Harris Gallery, N.Y.C., Baskett Gallery, Cin., 1982, 84, 85; represented in permanent collections including, Mus. Modern Art, N.Y.C., Whitney Mus., N.Y.C., Los Angeles County Mus., Cin. Mus., Birmingham (Ala.) Mus. Art, Indpls. Mus. Art, Nat. Gallery Art, Washington, Victoria and Albert Mus., London, Library of Congress, Washington; subject of book Eleanore Mikus, Shadows of the Real (by Robert Hobbs and Judith Bernstock), 1991. Guggenheim fellow, 1966-67; Tamarind fellow, summer 1968; MacDowell fellow, summer 1969; grantee Cornell U., 1988. Mem. AAUP. Home: PO Box 6586 Ithaca NY 14851-6586 Office: Cornell U Dept Art Tjaden Hall Ithaca NY 14853

MILANOVICH, NORMA JOANNE, occupational educator, training company executive; b. Littlefork, Minn., June 4, 1945; d. Lyle Albert and Loretta (Leona) Drake; m. Rudolph William Milanovich, Mar. 18, 1943; 1 child, Rudolph William Jr. BS in Home Econs., U. Wis., Stout, 1968; MA in Curriculum and Instrn., U. Houston, 1973, EdD in Curriculum and Program Devel., 1982. Instr. human svcs. dept. U. Houston, 1971-75; dir. videos project U. N.Mex., Albuquerque, 1976-78, dir. vocat. edn. equity ctr., 1978-88, asst. prof. tech. occupational edn., 1982-88, coord. occupational vocat. edn. programs, 1983-88, dir. consortium rsch. and devel. in occupational edn., 1984-88; pres. The Alpha Connecting Tng. Corp., Albuquerque, 1988—; adj. instr. Cen. Tng. Acad., Dept. Energy, Wackenhut; mem. faculty U. Phoenix; mem. adj. faculty So. Ill. U., Lesley Coll., Boston. Author: Model Equitable Behavior in the Classroom, 1983, Handbook for Vocational-Technical Certification in New Mexico, 1985, We, The Arcturians, 1990, Sacred Journey to Atlantis, 1991, The Light Shall Set You Free, 1996, A Vision for Kansas: Systems of Measures and Standards of Performance, 1992, Workplace Skills: The Employability Factor, 1993; editor: Choosing What's Best for You, 1982, A Handbook for Handling Conflict in the Classroom, 1983, Starting Out. . .A Job Finding Handbook for Teen Parents, Going to Work. . .Job Rights for Teens; author, editor: Majestic Raise newsletter, 1996, Celestial Voices newsletter, 1991-96. Bd. dirs. Albuquerque Single Parent Occupational Scholarship Program, 1984-86; del. Youth for Understanding Internat. Program, 1985-90; mem. adv. bd. Southwestern Indian Poly. Inst., 1984-88; com. mem. Region VI Consumer Exch. Com., 1982-84; ednl. lectures, tng., tour dir. internat. study toursto Japan, Austria, Korea, India, Nepal, Mex., Eng., Greece, Egypt, Australia, New Zealand, Fed. Republic Germany, Israel, Guatemala, Peru, Bolivia, Chile, Easter Island, Tibet, China, Hong Kong, Turkey, Italy, Russia, Ukraine, Sweden, Norway, 1984-95. Grantee N.Mex. Dept. Edn., 1976-78, 78-86, 83-86, HEW, 1979, 80, 81, 83, 84, 85, 86, 87, JTPA Strategic Mktg. Plan. Mem. ASTD, Am. Vocat. Assn., Vocat. Edn. Equity Coun., Nat. Coalition for Sex Equity Edn., Am. Home Econs. Assn., Inst. Noetic Scis., N.Mex. Home Econs. Assn., N.Mex. Vocat. Edn. Assn., N.Mex. Adv. Coun. on Vocat. Edn., Greater Albuquerque C. of C., NAFE, Phi Delta Kappa, Phi Upsilon Omicron, Phi Theta Kappa. Democrat. Roman Catholic.

MILBRATH, MARY MERRILL LEMKE, quality assurance professional; b. Evanston, Ill., Aug. 13, 1940; d. William Frederick and Martha Merrill (Slagel) Lemke; m. Gene McCoy Milbrath, Aug. 22, 1964; children: Elizabeth Ann, Sarah Toril Jeanne. BA in Biology, Albion Coll., 1962; MS in Plant Pathology, U. Ariz., 1966. Microbiologist Abbott Labs., North Chicago, Ill., 1962; toxicologist U. Ariz., Tucson, 1965-67; toxicologist U. Ill., Urbana, 1976-77, entomologist, 1978; plant pathologist State of Oreg., Salem, 1979, chemist, 1980-82; quality auditor Siltec Corp., Salem, 1983-84, quality control supr., 1985-91, quality auditing mgr., 1992—, implementor ISO 9002, 1994, implementor ISO Environ. Standard, 1996—; Active Ill. Emergency Svcs.toxic sub task force U. Ill., Urbana, 1978; mem. Responsible Corp. Citizens Com., Salem, 1989—. Mem. citizens adv. com. Sch. Bd., Urbana, 1976-78; campaigner Oreg. 5th Dist. Race, Salem, 1984, Oreg. Nat. Abortion Rights Assn. League, Salem, 1986; bd. dirs. Tribute to Outstanding Women, YWCA, 1994, Tribute to Women, 1992, 93, 95; vol. Tree Giving, 1991, 92. NDEA fellow U.S. Dept. Def., 1962. Mem. AAUW (chmn. interest group), Am. Soc. for Quality Control (cert. quality auditor exam writing com. 1993, 95, 96), Willamette U. House Corp. (treas. 1982-85, v.p. 1991—), Delta Gamma (treas. Salem Alumnae chpt. 1981-85, pres. Salem Alumnae chpt. 1987-89, scholarship advisor Willamette U. chpt. 1986-90). Office: Siltec Corp 1351 Tandem Ave NE Salem OR 97303-4105

MILDVAN, DONNA, infectious diseases physician; b. Phila., June 20, 1942; d. Carl David and Gertrude M.; m. Rolf Dirk Hamann; 1 child, Gabriella Kay. AB magna cum laude, Bryn Mawr Coll., 1963; MD, Johns Hopkins U., 1967. Diplomate Am. Bd. Internal Medicine and Infectious Diseases. Intern, resident Mt. Sinai Hosp., N.Y.C., 1967-70, fellow, infectious diseases, 1970-72; asst., assoc. prof. clin. medicine Mt. Sinai Sch. Medicine, N.Y.C., 1972-87; prof. clinical medicine Dept. Medicine, Mt. Sinai Sch. Medicine, N.Y.C., 1987-88, prof. medicine, 1988-94; physician-in-charge infectious diseases Beth Israel Med. Ctr., N.Y.C., 1972-79, chief, div. infectious diseases, 1980—; prof. medicine Albert Einstein Coll. of Medicine, N.Y.C., 1994—; mem. AIDS charter rev. com., NIH/Nat. Inst. Allergy and Infectious Diseases, Bethesda, 1987—; cons. FDA, Rockville, 1987—, Ctrs. for Disease Control, Atlanta, 1985-86; among first to describe AIDS, "Pre-AIDS", AIDS Dementia, 1982, among first to study AZT, 1986; Keynote speaker, II Internat. Conf. on AIDS, Paris, 1986 and other achievements in field; Sophie Jones Meml. lectr. in infectious diseases U. Mich. Hosps., 1984. Contbr. numerous articles to profl. jours; co-editor two books, several book chpts. and abstracts on infectious diseases and AIDS. Grantee N.Y. State AIDS Inst., 1986-87; Henry Strong Denison scholar Johns Hopkins U. Sch. Medicine, 1967; recipient Woman of Achievement award AAUW, 1987; contract for antiviral therapy in AIDS, Nat. Cancer Inst./Nat. Inst. Allergy and Infectious Diseases, 1985-86, subcontract Nat. Inst. Allergy and Infectious Diseases, ACTU, 1987—. Fellow Infectious Diseases Soc. Am.; mem. Am. Soc. Microbiology, AAAS, Harvey Soc., Internat. AIDS Soc. Democrat. Jewish. Office: Beth Israel Med Ctr 1st Ave New York NY 10003-7903

MILES, CHARLENE, small business owner; b. Pine City, Ark., Dec. 4, 1928; d. Albert and Katherine (Coakes) Banks; m. James Dixon Jr., Jan. 5, 1947 (div. 1955); children: James Walter II, Shirley; m. Joe Miles, Apr. 21, 1955 (dec.); 1 child, Donell. AA, Shorter Coll., Little Rock, Ark., 1946; cert., Buffalo (N.Y.) Beauty Coll., 1960. Lic. cosmetologist. Technician Posner Beauty Products, N.Y.C., 1960-63; instr. Peter Piccolo Beauty Sch., Buffalo, 1974-75; founder, pres. Charlene's Unisex Salon of N.Y., Detroit, 1975—; judge Student Cosmetology Assn., Buffalo, 1980—; founder, advisor Charlene Katherine Nat. Hair Network; advisor, cons. Waiting 2 Exhale Salon Inc. Pres. Profls. Against Drugs, Detroit, 1988—; corp. dir. Op. Push, Chgo., 1987—; mem. St. John Bapt. Ch., St. James Bapt. Ch. Named Pres. of Yr. CUS Bd. Dirs., 1984. Mem. Nat. Hairdressers Assn., Pacesetters (outstanding service award 1984), Mary B. Tolbert Assn., Beverly Area Planning Assn., Coalition of 100 Women. Democrat. Home: PO Box 7518 Bloomfield Hills MI 48302-7518 Office: Charlenes Unisex Salon NY 433 Fifth Ave New York NY 10016-2207

MILES, CYNTHIA LYNN, theatrical costume designer, consultant; b. Tucson, June 18, 1954; d. Bob D. Davis and Ella Kathleen (Kay) Clements; m. Ronald E. Anderson, May 1980 (div. July 1981); m. Charles D. Miles, Apr. 25, 1982; children: Wesley Clements, Travis Nichols. BA, U. N.Mex., 1977. Propr. Cindy's Couture et Costume, Lenexa, Kans., 1988—; tour mgr./stage mgr. Honolulu Theatre for Youth, 1991, program specialist, 1991-92; freelance costume designer Honolulu, 1991-93; stitcher The Mo. Repertory Theatre, Kansas City, 1994-96; costume designer Opera House Theatre Co., Wilmington, N.C., 1987-89, Tapestry Theatre Co., Wilmington, 1989-91, Honolulu Theatre for Youth, 1991-92, Diamond Head Theatre, Honolulu, 1992, Manoa Valley Theatre, Honolulu, 1991-93; costume mgr. Opera House Theatre Co., 1987-89, Manoa Valley Theatre, 1992-93; costume asst. Diamond Head Theatre, Honolulu Theatre for Youth, asst. props mgr., 1991, state mgr./tour mgr., 1991, program specialist, 1991-92; stitcher Mo.

Repertory Theatre, Kansas City, 1994-95, dresser, 1995; design cons. in field. costume designer for plays My Fair Lady, Company, One Flew Over the Cuckoo's Nest, Camelot, South Pacific, Harvey, A Streetcar Named Desire, Mister Roberts, Brigadoon, Last of the Red Hot Lovers, Hello Dolly, Steel Magnolias, Kiss Me Kate, Opera House Theatre Co., Corn is Green, Lion in Winter, Importance of Being Earnest, Tapestry Theatre Co., Wuthering Heights, Hoggard High Sch., N.C., The Garden, James Burke Prodns., N.C., Fool for Love, Triad Prodns., N.C., 1987-90, Murder at Howard Johnson's, Sweeney Todd (Po'Okela award for Costume Excellence, State of Hawaii 1992), Beyond Therapy, Manoa Valley Theatre, Spoon River Anthology (Po'Okela award for Best Overall Prodn. of a Play, State of Hawaii), Revenge of The Space Pandas, Honolulu Theatre for Youth, 1991-93, The Deputy, The Dickens Faire, Julius Caeser, Mo. Repertory Theatre, 1994, The Dickens Faire, Christmas Carol, Two Gentlemen of Verona, 1995; asst. to designer Into The Woods, Leader of The Pack, Big River, Manoa Valley Theatre, 1991-93; stitcher Dancing at Lughnasa, Christmas Carol, Whispers in The Mind, Mo. Repertory Theatre, 1994, Imaginary Invalid, 1995, (film), Kansas City, 1995, (ballet) The Nutcracker, State Ballet of Mo., Kansas City, 1995. Democrat. Episcopalian. Home: 569 Oder Ave Staten Island NY 10304

MILES, JEANNE PATTERSON, artist; b. Balt.; d. Walter and Edna (Webb) M.; m. Frank Curlee, Dec. 31, 1935 (dec.); m. Johannes Schiefer, Feb. 11, 1939 (div.); 1 child, Joanna. BFA, George Washington U.; postgrad., Philips Meml. Gallery Sch., Atelier Gromaire, Grand Chaumiere, Paris. One-woman shows include Betty Parsons Gallery, N.Y.C., 1945, 52, 55, 56, 59, 77, 82, Grand Central Moderns, N.Y.C., 1968, Wesbeth Galleries, N.Y.C., 1972; group shows include N.Y. Rome Found., 1957, Walker Art Gallery, Mpls., 1954, Corcoran Biennial, Yale U. Mus., 1957, Chateau Gagnes, France, 1938, Whitney Mus., 1963, Nat. Fedn. Am. Art, 1963, Mus. Modern Art, 1966, Riverside Mus., N.Y.C., 1964, Guggeheim Mus., 1965-66, Geodok Am. Women Show, Hamburg and Berlin, 1972, Springfield (Mass.) Art Mus., 1975, Hunterton Art Center, Clinton, N.J., 1975, Betty Parsons Gallery, 1977, 82, Sid Deutch, 1978, 79, Marlyn Pearl Gallery, N.Y.C., 1986, 88, Bronx Mus. Art, 1986, George Washington, 1989, 55 Mercer St, N.Y.C., 1989, Marlyn Pearl Gallery, N.Y.C., 1991, Anita Shapalsky Gallery, N.Y.C., 1994, Shapalsky Gallery, 1993; represented in permanent collections NYU, Santa Barbara (Calif.) Mus., Muson Proctor Mus., Utica, N.Y., Rutgers Coll., U. Ariz., Guggenheim Mus., Cin. and Newark museums, White Art Mus., N.Y. State U. at Purchase, Cornell U., Ecumenical Inst., Garrison, N.Y., Graymoor, Garrison, Springfield Art Mus., Weatherspoon Art Mus., U. N.C., Wichita (Kans.) Mus., Mus. of Wichita, Mus. of St. Mary's (Md.) Coll., L.A. County Mus., Alexander Mus., La., also pvt. collections, N.Y.C. and France; traveling exhibits; poster and cover for catalogues, 1987-92; video tape showing of exhibits on cable TV, N.Y.C., 1989. Charles C. Ladd painting scholar Tahiti, 1938, 56, traveling scholar France, 1937-48; grantee Am. Inst. Arts and Letters, 1968, Mark Rothko Found., 1970-73, Pelham von Stoeffler Art Fund, 1974; invited residency (award) to Yaddo Art Colony, Saratoga Springs, N.Y., 50s and 60s, MacDowell Colony, N.H. Mem. Abstract Artists Am., George Washington U. Alumni Assn. (Disting. Achievement award 1987).

MILES, JOAN FOWLE, journalist, writer; b. Woburn, Mass., Aug. 5, 1921; d. Donald Adams and Ethel Adelaide (Wallace) Fowle; m. Stephen Lewis Miles, Sept. 8, 1945; children: Joanna Miles Griffith, Deborah Allen Miles. BA, Mt. Holyoke Coll., 1943. Copy clk. NBC, N.Y.C., 1943-44; editl. asst. Robert St. John, N.Y.C., 1944-45; cmty. rels. cons. Lahey Clinic, Burlington, Mass., 1978—; dir. student art project Lahey Hitchcock Med. Ctr., Burlington, 1983—; profl. svcs. chair Eliot Cmty. Human Svcs., Lexington, Mass., 1988—; mem. legis. action com. Coop. Met. Ministries, Newton, Mass., 1994—. Author: Burlington--The Growth Years, 1990; editorial writer Burlington Times Union, 1964-68. Mem. sch. bldg. need and sites com. Town of Burlington, 1964-68; me. Burlington Sch. Com., 1968-86; founder, pres. Burlington Cmty. Scholarship Found./Dollars for Scholars, 1988—. Named Outstanding Citizen, Town of Burlington, 1976; Joan F. MIles Libr. named in her honor Burlington Sch. Com., 1986. Democrat.

MILES, LAVEDA ANN, advertising executive; b. Greenville, S.C. Nov. 21, 1945; d. Grady Lewis and Edna Sylvia (Mahaffey) Bruce; m. Charles Thomas Miles, Nov. 10, 1974; 1 child, Joshua Bruce. A in Bus. Adminstrn., North Greenville Jr. Coll. Traffic mgr. WFBC-TV, Greenville, S.C., 1968-74; pub. svc. dir., traffic mgr. WTCG-TV, Atlanta, 1974-75; traffic mgr. Henderson Advt. Co., Greenville, 1975-77, broadcast coord., 1977-79, dir. broadcast bus., 1979-82, dir. broadcast bus., v.p., 1982-89, bus. mgr. creative dept., 1989-91, dir. creative svcs., 1991-93, sr. v.p., 1993—. Named one of 100 Best and Brightest Women for 1988 Ad Age and Advt. Women of N.Y. Mem. Advt. Fedn. of Greenville (sec. 1979-81, Leadership S.C. Class 1994-95). Democrat. Baptist.

MILES, MARYLYN ELIZABETH, assistant principle elementary school; b. Fort Worth, Oct. 19, 1953; d. Grant and Lois (Fretwell) Ellison; children: Earl, Harith, Aleah. BS, N. Tex. State U., 1976; MS, Tex. Christian U., 1986; postgrad studies in Edn., Nova U., 1994—. Cert. tchr. early childhood, mid mgmt., gifted edn. tech., Tex. Elementary sch. tchr. Fort Worth Ind. Sch. Dist., 1976-86, instrnl. specialist, 1986-89; asst. prin. Luella Merrett Elem. Sch., Fort Worth, Tex., 1989—; dir. City Univ., Fort Worth, Tex., 1996—. Founder Heath Federated Women's Orgn., Fort Worth, 1967, Higland Hills Comty. Orgn., Fort Worth, 1987; youth dir. Univ. Ch., Fort Worth, 1989-94; dir. Citizens Concerned about Children, 1992-94. Named Most Outstanding Educator, Stop Six Citizens Group, Fort Worth, 1991, Mother of Yr., Forest Hill Ch., Fort Worth, 1992. Mem. Forum Fort Worth, Phi Delta Kappa. Office: Luella Merrett Elem Sch 7325 Kermit Ave Fort Worth TX 76116-9434

MILES-KIRK, KIMBERLY KAY, educational administrator; b. Beaver, Okla., Aug. 9, 1956; d. Robert Lee and Doralee Annetta (Holman) Miles; children: Michelle Lee, Jason Royce. BS, U. Ctrl. Okla., 1982, MS, 1989; PhD, Okla. State U., 1994. Sci. instr. Mayfield Jr. H.S., Oklahoma City, 1983-84, Putnam City H.S., Oklahoma City, 1984-85; sci. instr. Putnam City North H.S., Oklahoma City, 1985-91, gifted and talented supr., 1991-92; career edn. supr. Edmond (Okla.) Pub. Schs., 1992-94; coord. Sch.-to-Wk. Moore/Norman Consortium, 1994—, facilitator, 1994—; facultator Edmond Pub. Schs., 1992-94. Author: (curriculum manual) Youth At Risk/Earth at Risk, 1992. Adv. bd. Francis Tuttle Vo-Tech., Oklahoma City, 1994-95. Mem. ASCD, NEA, Edmond C. of C. (Excellence in Edn. mem. 1992-94), Okla. Environ. Edn. Assn., Am. Vocat. Assn., Okla. Vocat. Assn. (guidance divsn. 1994, new and related svcs. divsn. 1994, instructional materials divsn. 1994), Women in Ednl. Adminstrn. Home: 13109 Brooke Ave Edmond OK 73013-5114 Office: Moore/Norman Area Vo-Tech 4701 12th Ave NW Norman OK 73069-8308

MILES-LAGRANGE, VICKI LYNN, federal judge; b. Oklahoma City, Sept. 30, 1953; d. Charles and Mary (Greenard) Miles. BA, Vassar Coll., 1974; LLB, Howard U., 1977. Congl. aide Speaker of the Ho., Rep. Carl Albert, 1974-76; formerly grad. fellow, trial atty. U.S. Dept. Justice, 1979-82; mem. Okla. Senate from Dist. 48, 1987-93; U.S. atty. U.S. Dept. of Justice, Oklahoma City, Okla., 1993-94; judge U.S. Dist. Ct. (we. dist.) Okla., Oklahoma City, 1994—. Democrat. Baptist.

MILEWSKI, BARBARA ANNE, pediatrics nurse, neonatal intensive care nurse; b. Chgo., Sept. 11, 1934; d. Anthony and LaVerne (Sepp) Witt; m. Leonard A. Milewski, Feb. 23, 1952; children: Pamela, Robert, Diane, Timothy. ADN, Harper Coll., Palatine, Ill, 1982; BS, Northern Ill. U., 1992; postgrad., North Park Coll. RN, Ill.; cert. CPR instr. Staff nurse Northwest Community Hosp., Arlington Heights, Ill., Resurrection Hosp., Chgo.; nurse neonatal ICU Children's Meml. Hosp., Chgo.; day care cons. Cook County Dept. Pub. Health; CPR instr. Stewart Oxygen Svcs., Chgo.; instr., organizer parenting and well baby classes and clinics; vol. Children's Meml. Hosp.; health coord. CEDA Head Start; cons. day care Cook County Dept. Pub. Health. Vol. first aid instr. Boy Scouts Am.; CPR instr. Harper Coll., Children's Meml. Hosp.; dir. Albany Park Cmty. Ctr. Head Start, Chgo.; day care cons. Cook County Dept. Pub. Health. Mem. Am. Mortar Bd., Sigma Theta Tau.

MILICEVIC, JELENA, health science specialist; b. Skopje, Macedonia, Yugoslavia, Jan. 1, 1939; came to U.S., 1972; d. Miladin and Hedy (Hem) M.; m. Ernst Anzbock, Dec. 14, 1959 (div. 1971); children: Harald, Evelyn; m. Ranko Caric, Nov. 3, 1973 (div. 1980); 1 child, Peter. Student, Molloy Coll., 1979-81, L.I. U., 1981-82, Rockland C.C., 1985, Vt. Coll., 1985-86, Orange County C.C., 1988, Empire State Coll., 1990—. Ordained to ministry Universal Spiritualist Assn. U.S.A., 1985; lic., real estate agt., N.Y.; registered and cert. reflexologist, N.Y. Owner Walter's Bake Shop, 1973-79; nurse's aide Hillside Manor, 1980; clerical worker Molloy Coll., 1980-81, L.I. U., 1981-82; chiropractor asst. Steven R. Siegel D.C., 1982; owner Linden Motel, 1983; lectr. on Shiatsu and reflexology New Age Ctr., 1985-86; v.p., min. Universal Ctr. New Age Consciousness, Inc., Milford, Pa., 1985—; with Abatelli Realty, 1988; gen. agt. Intern Cons. Exchange, San Diego, Calif., 1986; spa and skincare therapist, 1993. Mem. Am. Message Therapy Assn., Alliance of Message Therapists, Inc., Universal Spiritualist Assn., N.Y. State Soc. Med. Massage Therapists, Internat. Platform Assn., Assoc. Bodywork and Massage Profls., Carmel Art Assn. Home: 25930 Colt Ln Carmel Valley CA 95924 Office: 15-71 208th St Bayside NY 11360

MILIO, VANESSA R., community outreach director; b. Balt., Jan. 30, 1970; d. Frank R. and Frances A. (Welker) M. BFA in Printmaking, U. Hartford, 1991; MFA in Bookmaking, Univ. of Arts, 1993. Coord., instr. West Indian Found., Hartford, Conn., 1991; resident artist United Communities of South Phila., 1991-93, Fleisher Art Meml., Phila., 1993, Henry St. Settlement, N.Y.C., 1993; art specialist/recreation Menorah Homes Hosp., Bklyn., 1993-94; ctr. dir. YMCA of Greater N.Y.-West Side, N.Y.C., 1994—. Author: Fostering Hope, 1993. Active So. Poverty Law Ctr., 1991—, Children's Def. Fund, 1993—, Nature Conservancy, 1994—. Recipient Brandywine Printshop award Univ. of Arts, 1993. Democrat. Office: West Side YMCA 5 W 63d St New York NY 10023

MILITELLO, ROBERTA JAN, artist, illustrator, designer; b. L.I., N.Y., July 28, 1959; d. William S. and Hilde (Lauterbach) M.; m. Thomas Schiel, Sept. 12, 1987 (div.); 1 child, Tara Schiel. BFA magna cum laude, SUNY, Albany, 1981. Freelance artist N.Y., 1981-91; instr. painting and drawing Cmty. Sch., Munich, 1991-93, BMW, Munich, 1991-93; freelance illustrator N.Y., 1993—. One-woman shows include Univ. Art Gallery, Albany, 1980; exhibited in group shows at Schenectady Mus., 1980, Limner Gallery, East Village, N.Y., 1988, Pasing (Germany) Culture Ctr., 1990, Gasteig Culture Ctr., Munich, 1990, Blutenburg Castle, Munich, 1991, Leppert & Schiel, Rastatt, Germany, 1992, Women's Rights Nat. Hist. Pk., Seneca Falls, N.Y., 1993-94. Recipient Exhbn. grant City of Munich, 1990, grant Philip Morris Performance Series, 1990, grant Art in Architecture, Germany, 1990. Mem. Woodstock Art Assn. (bd. dirs. 1981-87), German Artist Union.

MILKIE, LINDA LOUISE, mental health services professional; b. Decatur, Ill., May 27, 1947; d. Clifford Jess and Pearl I. (Curtis) Langenfeld; m. Donald Yelverton, June 1965 (div. Feb. 1971); 1 child, Jim Allen; m. Robert C. Janes, Feb. 1977 (div. Feb. 1986); 1 child, Paul Bryan; m. Thomas Theodore Milkie, May 3, 1986. BS in Orgnl. Behavior, U. San Francisco, 1989; MS in Marriage, Family, Child Counseling, Calif. State U., Fullerton, 1994. Registered to practice therapy towards licensure, Va. Human resources mgr. Northrop Corp., Hawthorne, Calif., 1975-87, Silicon Sys., Inc., Tustin, Calif., 1987-89, McDonnell Douglas Corp., Huntington Beach, Calif., 1989-91; family therapist Family Svcs. Assn., Irvine, Calif., 1992-93, No. Va. Family Svc., Dale City, 1995—; cons. Aurora Flight Sci., Manassas, Va., 1994. Mem. Nat. Alliance for Mentally Ill, Arlington, Va., 1995. Mem. ACA, APA, Am. Assn. Marriage and Family Therapy. Republican. Office: No Va Family Svc 14377 Hereford Rd Dale City VA 22193

MILKMAN, BEVERLY L., federal agency administrator; b. Ft. Pierce, Fla., Jan. 9, 1945; d. Robert George and Annette (Leatherwood) Lyford; m. Raymond H. Milkman, Feb. 27, 1972; 1 child, Katherine. BA magna cum laude, U. Ariz., 1967; MLA with honors, Johns Hopkins U., 1972; MA, George Washington U., 1978. Rsch. analyst Peat, Marwick, Mitchell & Co., 1967-69, program analyst, 1970-72, spl. asst. to dep. sec., 1972-74, spl. asst. to asst. sec., 1974-80, dir. office tech. assistance, 1980-81, dir. office of planning, tech. assistance, rsch. and evaluation, 1981-86, dep. dir. grant programs, 1986-88; exec. dir. Com. for Purchase from People Who are Blind or Severely Disabled, 1988—. Assoc. editor Economic Development Quarterly; contbr. articles to profl. publs. Office: Com Purchase from People Who Are Blind or Severely Disabled 1735 Jefferson Davis Hwy Arlington VA 22202-3401

MILKMAN, MARIANNE FRIEDENTHAL, retired city planner; b. Berlin, May 13, 1931; came to U.S., 1957; d. Ernst Leopold and Margarethe (Goldschmidt) Friedenthal; m. Roger Dawson Milkman, Oct. 18, 1958; children: Ruth, Louise, Janet, Paul. BA, Cambridge (Eng.) U., 1952, MA, 1956; teaching diploma, London U., 1953. Tchr. biology Milham Ford High Sch., Oxford, Eng., 1953-57; teaching fellow, rsch. asst. U. Mich., Ann Arbor, 1957-59; sci. dir. Children's Sch. Sci., Woods Hole, Mass., 1971-72; planning technician dept. planning and program devel. City of Iowa City, 1975-76, planner I, 1976-79, assoc. planner, 1979-85, coord. comty. devel., 1986-96; ret., 1996. Bikeways chmn. Project Green, Iowa City, 1968-75. State scholar Cambridge U. and London U., 1949-53, Fulbright travelling scholar U. Mich., 1957; fellow English Speaking Union, 1957-58. Mem. Am. Planning Assn. (sec.-treas. Iowa chpt. 1982-84, v.p. 1984-86, pres. 1986-88, chmn. univ. rels. com. 1987-91, President's award 1988), Nat. Assn. Housing and Redevel. Ofcls., Nat. Community Devel. Assn. Jewish. Home: 12 Fairview Knoll NE Iowa City IA 52240-9147

MILLANE, LYNN, town official; b. Buffalo, N.Y. Oct. 14, 1928; d. Robert P. Schermerhorn and Justine A. (Ross) m. J. Vaughan Millane, Jr.; Aug. 16, 1952 children: Maureen, Michele, John, Mark, Kathleen. EdB, U. Buffalo, 1949, EdM, in Health Education 1951. Mem. Amherst Town Bd., 1982—, dep. town supr., 1990—, supr., 1996—; pres., E. J. Meyer Hosp. Jr. Bd., 1962-64; pres. Aux. to Erie County Bar Assn., 1966-68; pres. Women's Com. of Buffalo Philharm. Orch., 1976-78, v.p. adminstrn., 1975-76, v.p. pub. affairs, 1974-75, chmn. adv. bd., 1979-82; v.p. Buffalo Philharm. Orch. Soc., Inc., 1976-78, mem. coun., trustee, 1979-87, bd. overseers, 1987-92; dir. 8th judicial dist. N.Y. State Assn. of Large Towns, 1989-90, 90-91; bd. dirs. oper. bd. Millard Fillmore Suburban Hosp., 1992-2001; 1st v.p. Fans for 17, 1980-82; 1st. v.p. Friends of Baird Hall, SUNY-Buffalo, 1980-82; exec. bd. mem. Longview Protestant Home for Children, 1979-85, 2d v.p., 1982-85; bd. dirs. ARC, Town of Amherst br., 1982-91, by-laws com., 1981, 84, chmn. sr. concerns com., 1982-91, liaison code of ethics com., 1987-89; bd. dirs. Amherst Symphony Orch. Assn., 1981-87, roster chmn., 1982-84, nominating chmn., 1985-86, vice-chmn. 50th anniversary com. 1994—; nat. music com. Women's Assn. for Symphony Orchs. in Am. and Can., 1977-79; coun. mem. Am. Symphony Orch. League; sec. Amherst Sr. Citizen's Adv. Bd., 1980-81, liaison from Amherst Town Bd., 1982—; founder, liaison 1st adult day svcs. adv. bd. Town of Amherst, 1988; liaison to ad hoc cable TV com., 1992—, liaison to Amherst C. of C., 1993—, mem. 1st records mgmt. adv. bd., liaison ethics bd. Town of Amherst, 1994—, dep. supr. 1990—; liaison to the Alternate Fuel and Clean Cities Com., 1994-96; dir.-at-large community adv. coun. SUNY-Buffalo, 1981-91; co-assoc. chmn. maj. gift div. capital campaign Daemen Coll., 1983-84; co-chmn. Women United Against Drugs Campaign, 1970-72; founding mem. Lunch and Issues, Amherst, 1981—; mem. edn. com. Network in Aging of Western N.Y., Inc., 1982-89, bd. dirs., 1982-89, housing com., 1987-89; bd. dirs. Amherst Elderly Transp. Corp., 1982—; committeeman dist. Town of Amherst Republican Com.; treas. Town and Country Rep. Club, 1980-81; mem. nominating com. Fedn. Rep. Women's Clubs Erie County, 1980; exec. bd. mem. Women's Exec. Coun. of Erie County Rep. Com., 1969-71; dir. Amherst Rep. Women's Club, 1963-65; delegate N.Y. State Govs. Conf. on Aging, 1995, White House Conf. on Aging, 1995, named mem. aging svcs. adv. com. N.Y. State Office of the Aging Gov. George Pataki, 1996. Named Homemaker of Yr., Family Circle Mag., 1969; Woman of Substance, 20th Century Rep. Women, 1983; Woman of Yr., Buffalo Philharm. Orch. Soc., Inc., 1982; Outstanding Woman in Community Svc., SUNY-Buffalo, 1985; recipient Good Neighbor award Courier Express, 1978; Merit award Buffalo Philharm. Orch., 1978; award Fedn. Rep. Women's Clubs Erie County, 1982; Disting. Svc. award Town of Amherst Sr. Ctr., 1985; Susan B. Anthony award Interclub Coun. of Western N.Y., 1991, Community Svc. award Amherst Rep. Com., 1991, D.A.R.E. award Town of Amherst Police Dept., 1994, Disting. Svc. award Amherst Adult Day Care and Vis. Nurses Assn., 1994. Mem. Amherst C. of C. (VIP dinner com. 1984), LWV, SUNY-Buffalo Alumni Assn. (life, presdl. advisor 1977-79), Zonta (pres. Amherst chpt. 1986-88, Zontian of Yr. 1992), Pi Lambda Theta (hon.). Office: 5583 Main St Buffalo NY 14221-5409

MILLAR, DORINE MARIE AGNES, real estate agent, artist; b. Pos, Td'ad, West Indies, Apr. 20, 1924; d. Victor and Elsie (Dumoret) Sellier. Lic. real estate agt., Fla. Artist Millar Agencies Inc., Ft. Lauderdale, Fla., 1964—; real estate agt. Ft. Lauderdale, Fla., 1970—. Recipient 1st pl. award Hollywood Art Guild Ann. Mem. Show, 1993, 2d pla. prize Palm Beach Water Color Soc., 1990, 3rd pl. prize Coral Springs Art Guild, 1990. Mem. Gold Coast Watercolor Soc., Palm Beach Watercolor Soc., Fla. Watercolor Soc., Broward Art Guild.

MILLENDER-MCDONALD, JUANITA, congresswoman, former school system administrator; b. Birmingham, Ala., Sept. 7, 1938; d. Shelly and Everlina (Dortch) M.; m. James McDonald III, July 26, 1955; children: Valeria, Angela, Sherryll, Michael, Roderick. BS, U. Redlands, Calif., 1980; MS in Edn., Calif. State U., L.A., 1986; postgrad., U. So. Calif. Manuscript editor Calif. State Dept. Edn., Sacramento; dir. gender equity programs L.A. Unified Sch. Dist.; mem. 104th Congress from 37th Calif. dist. U.S. Ho. of Reps., Washington, 1996—. City councilwoman, Carson; bd. dirs. S.C.L.C. Pvt. Industry Coun. Policy Bd., West Basin Mcpl. Water Dist., Cities Legis. League (vice chmn.; mem. Nat. Women's Polit. Caucus; mem. adv. bd. Comparative Ethnic Tng. U. So. Calif.; founder, exec. dir. Young Advocates So. Calif. Mem. NEA, Nat. Assn. Minority Polit. Women, NAFE, Nat. Fedn. Bus. and Profl. Women, Assn. Calif. Sch. Adminstrs., Am. Mgmt. Assn., Nat. Coun. Jewish Women, Carson C. of C., Phi Delta Kappa. Office: US House of Reps 419 Cannon Washington DC 20515*

MILLER, ADELE ENGELBRECHT, educational administrator; b. Jersey City, July 31, 1946; d. John Fred and Dorathea Kathryn (Kamm) Engelbrecht; m. William A. Miller, Jr., Dec. 21, 1981. BS in Bus. Edn., Fairleigh Dickinson U., 1968, MBA magna cum laude, 1974; cert. in pub. sch. adminstrn. and supervision, Jersey City State Coll., 1976. Bus. tchr. Jersey City Bd. Edn., 1967—, coord. coop. bus. edn. programs, 1973—, acting v.p., 1985-86, prin. of summer sch., 1986, chmn. dept., 1996—; adj. instr. St. Peter's Coll., 1974-75; curriculum cons. Cittone Bus. Sch., 1981-82; mem. adv. coun. Dickinson H.S., 1973—, chmn., 1978-80; organizer, bd. dirs. Frances Nadel and Cooke-Connolly-Coffey-Witt Faculty Meml. Scholarships, 1978—; trustee Dickinson H.S. Parents Coun., 1985-88. Co-author: New Jersey Cooperative Business Education Coordinators Resource Manual, 1984; author coop. bus. edn. study course Jersey City Pub. Schs., 1980, 84. Mem. Citizens Adv. Coun. to Mayor of Jersey City, 1968-71; organizer, dir. Jersey City Youth Week, 1970-72; chmn. juv. conf. com. Hudson County Juv. Ct., 1978—; v.p., sec., trustee, chmn. dinner-musicale Jersey City Coll.-Comty. Orch., 1979-88; Explorer Scouting adv. bd. Hudson-Hamilton coun. Boy Scouts Am., 1985-88; trustee YWCA of Hudson County, 1988—. Recipient Dickinson High Sch. Key Club Tchr. of Yr. award 1971, Merrill-Lynch Outstanding Performance in Edn. award, 1995; named Educator of Yr. Dickinson High Sch. Parents Coun., 1987, 88. Mem. NEA, N.J. Edn. Assn., Jersey City Edn. Assn. (bldg. dir.), N.J. Coop. Bus. Edn. Coords. Assn. (pres., v.p., sec., treas. 1991-92, Coop. Edn. Coord. of Yr.), N.J. Bus. Edn. Assn., Vocat. Edn. Assn. N.J., N.J. Fedn. Women's Clubs, Jersey City Woman's Club (scholarship chmn., adviser Jr. Women's Club), AAUW (edn. chmn., sec. N.J. divsn., del. to White House briefing on edn., women's issues, arms control, dist. coord., chmn. nominations, historian), Coll. Club Jersey City (pres., v.p., sec.), Jersey City Rotary Club (dir., Interact club adviser, program chmn.), Phi Delta Kappa. Home: 91 Sherman Pl Jersey City NJ 07307-3729 Office: Dickinson H S 2 Palisade Ave Jersey City NJ 07306-1202

MILLER, ALICE ANN, state utilities executive; b. Des Moines, June 8, 1955; d. Edwin and Ethel (Kjaer) Barker; m. Mark Miller, Nov. 25, 1977; children: Eric, Katherine (Katie). BA in Edn., U. Iowa, Iowa City, 1974, MA in English, 1976; MBA, SUNY, Albany, 1991. Rsch. asst. N.Y. Dept. Pub. Svc., Albany, 1981-82, utility rates analyst, 1982-85, utility ops. examiner, 1985-90, chief utility rates analyst, 1990—. Mem. Phi Beta Kappa, Beta Gamma Sigma. Office: Dept Pub. Svc Albany NY 12223

MILLER, BARBARA ANN, operations analyst; b. Long Branch, N.J., June 10, 1956; d. Donald R. and Mary Ann (Topper) M. BSIM, U. Akron, 1979. Bookkeeper, dispatcher Am. Auto Assn., Akron, 1975-79; asst. mgr. K-Mart Corp., Troy, Mich., 1979-81; owner, operator Miller Residential Cleaning Svc., Akron, 1981-83; sys. analyst, programmer Roadway Express, Akron, 1983-91; ptnr. stained glass studio Kresler Enter., Akron, 1991—; sr. ops. analyst, sys. analyst Roadway Express, Akron, 1991—. Vol. emergency support hotline Comty. Support Svcs., Akron, 1992-94. Home: 45 Iuka Ave Akron OH 44310-1036

MILLER, BARBARA JEAN, nephrology home care nurse; b. Viroqua, Wis., June 27, 1961; d. Alan Wayne and Sharon Joan (Phillips) Bennett; m. Leonard Ralf Miller, May 5, 1984; children: Kari Elizabeth, Ronald Alan. BSN, Viterbo Coll., La Crosse, 1983. RN, Mich.; cert. nephrology nurse; cert. peritoneal dialysis nurse. Nursing asst. Bethany St. Joseph Health Care Ctr, La Crosse, 1978-81; staff and charge nurse Butterworth Hosp., Grand Rapids, Mich., 1983-84; hemodialysis charge nurse St. Mary's Health Svcs., Grand Rapids, 1984-90, peritoneal dialysis nurse, 1990—; speaker, educator in field. Bd. dirs., health chair Sparta (Mich.) Presch., 1992-94. Mem. Am. Nephrology Nurses Assn., Nat. Kidney Found. (coun. nephrology nurses 1991—). Republican. Roman Catholic. Office: St Mary's Health Svcs Nephrology Home Care 200 Jefferson SE Grand Rapids MI 49503

MILLER, BARBARA KAYE, lawyer; b. Omaha, Aug. 21, 1964; d. Carl Reuben and Sandra Jean (Matthews) Wright; m. Julius Anthony Miller, May 4, 1991. BA, U. Iowa, 1987, JD, 1990. Bar: Ohio 1990, U.S. Dist. Ct. (no. dist.) Ohio 1991. Assoc. Fuller & Henry, Toledo, Ohio, 1990-92; law clk. to Hon. John W. Potter U.S. Dist. Ct. (no. dist.) Ohio, Toledo, 1992-93; asst. prosecutor Lucas County Prosecutor's Office, Toledo, 1994-96; ptnr. Wise People Mgmt., Toledo, 1994—, Ryan, Wise, Miller & Dorner, Toledo, 1995—; adj. prof. Lourdes Coll., Sylvania, Ohio, 1994—. Bd. dirs. Toledo Ballet Assn., 1992-94, Hospice, Toledo, 1992-94. Martin Luther King scholar, 1987; named to Profl. Women in Christ, 1992. Mem. ABA, Lucas County Bar Assn., Toledo Bar Assn. (mem. grievance com. 1994—), Thurgood Marshall Law Assn. (v.p. 1993-94), Lawyers Roundtable of Toledo (mem. steering com., recruiting program com. 1994—). Office: Wise People Mgmt Ste 333 151 N Michigan St Toledo OH 43624 also: Ryan Wise Miller Dorner Ste 333 151 N Michigan St Toledo OH 43624

MILLER, BARBARA STALLCUP, development consultant; b. Montague, Calif., Sept. 4, 1919; d. Joseph Nathaniel and Maybelle (Needham) Stallcup; m. Leland F. Miller, May 16, 1946; children: Paula Kay, Susan Lee, Daniel Joseph, Alison Jean. B.A., U. Oreg., 1942. Women's editor Eugene (Oreg.) Daily News, 1941-43; law clk. to J. Everett Barr, Yreka, Calif., 1943-45; mgr. Yreka C. of C., 1945-46; Northwest supr. Louis Harris and Assocs., Portland, Oreg., 1959-62; dir. pub. relations and fund raising Columbia River council Girl Scouts U.S.A., 1962-67; pvt. practice pub. relations cons., Portland, 1967-72; adviser of student publs., asst. prof. communications U. Portland, 1967-72, dir. pub. relations and info., asst. prof. communications, 1972-78, dir. devel., 1978-79, exec. dir. devel., 1979-83; assoc. dir. St. Vincent Med. Found., 1983-88; dir. planned giving Good Samaritan Found., 1988-95; planned giving cons., 1995—. Pres. bd. dirs. Vols. of Am. of Oreg., Inc., 1980-84, pres. regional adv. bd., 1982-84; chmn. bd. dirs. S.E. Mental Health Network, 1984-88; nat. bd. dirs. Vols. of Am., Inc., 1984-96; pres., bd. dirs. Vol. Bur. Greater Portland, 1991-93; mem. U. Oreg. Journalism Advancement Coun., 1991—; named Oasis Sr. Role Model, 1992. Recipient Presdl. Citation, Oreg. Communicators Assn., 1973, Matrix award, 1976, 80, Miltner award U. Portland, 1977, Communicator of Achievement award Oreg. Press Women, 1992, Willamette Valley Devel. Officers award, 1992 (Barbara Stallcup Miller Profl. Achievement award, 1992), Mem. Nat. Soc. Fundraising Execs., Nat. Planned Giving Coun, Women in Comm. (NW regional v.p. 1973-75, Offbeat award 1988), Nat. Fedn. Press Women, Oreg. Press Women (dist. dir.), Pub. Rels. Soc. Am. (dir. local chpt., Marsh award 1989), Oreg. Fedn. Womens Clubs (communications chmn. 1978-80), Alpha Xi Delta (found. trustee, editor 1988-95). Unitarian. Clubs: Portland Zenith (pres. 1975-76, 81-82). Contbr. articles to profl. jours. Home and Office: 1706 Boca Ratan Dr Lake Oswego OR 97034-1624

MILLER, BEATRICE DIAMOND, anthropologist; b. N.Y.C., May 29, 1919; d. Benjamin and Fannie (Haims) Diamond; m. Robert James Miller, Nov. 6, 1943 (dec. Apr. 1994); children: Karla, Erik, Terin. AB, U. Mich., 1948; PhD, U. Wash., 1958. Vis. asst. prof. Beloit (Wis.) Coll., 1961-62, 69-70; vis. asst. prof. U. Wis., Madison, 1973-74, 78, hon. fellow, 1978-93. Co-editor: Anthropology of Tibet and the Himalaya, 1992. Fellow Am. Anthropol. Assn., Asian Studies Assn., Soc. for Applied Anthropology; mem. AAUW (co-chair programs, 1993-94, 95-96). Home: 1347 S Country Club Dr Camano Island WA 98292

MILLER, BETTY BROWN, freelance writer; b. Altus, Ark., Dec. 21, 1926; d. Carlos William and Arlie Gertrude (Sublett) Brown; m. Robert Wiley Miller, Nov. 15, 1953; children: Janet Ruth, Stephen Wiley. BS Okla. State U., 1949; MS, U. Tulsa, 1953; postgrad., Am. U., 1966-68. Tchr. LeFlore (Okla.) High Sch., 1947-48, Osage Indian Reservation High Sch., Hominy, Okla., 1948-50, Jenks (Okla.) High Sch., 1950-51; instr. Sch. Bus., U. Tulsa, 1950-51; tchr. Tulsa public schs., 1951-54; instr. Burdette Coll., Boston, 1954-55; reporter Bethesda-Chevy Chase Tribune, Montgomery County, Md., 1970-73; freelance writer, contbr. newspapers and mags., 1973—. V.p. Kenwood Park (Md.) Citizens Assn., 1960; mem. Ft. Sumner Citizens Assn., editor newsletter, 1969; mem. Md. State PTA, editorial coord. leadership conf., 1973-74; founder and chmn. Montgomery County Forum for Edn., 1970-75; trustee Friends Valley Forge Nat. Hist. Park; bd. dirs. Friends Curtis Inst. Music; mem. The Nat. Mus. Women in the Arts, The Musical Fund Soc. Phila.; bd. trustee, adv. Help the Aged. Mem. Nat. Soc. Arts and Letters (past editor mag., bd. dir. pub. rels., past nat. corr. sec.), Nat. League Am. Pen Women (budget chmn., past nat. treas.) PEO, Montgomery County Press Assn., Internat. Platform Assn., The Nat. Gravel Soc., Melba T. Croft Music Club, Capital Speakers Club of Washington (past pres.), Adventures Unltd. (chmn. Washington chpt.), U.D.C., Soc. Descs. of Washington's Army at Valley Forge (nat. comdr. in chief, past insp. gen.), DAR, Huguenot Soc. Pa. (v.p. 1989—, pres. 1993-95, past bd. dirs.), Washington Club, Sedgeley Club (pres. 1985-88, Phila.), The Acorn Club, Phila. Republican. Address: PO Box 573 Valley Forge PA 19481-0573

MILLER, BEVERLY WHITE, academic administrator; b. Willoughby, Ohio; d. Joseph Martin and Marguerite Sarah (Storer) White; m. Lynn Martin Miller, Oct. 11, 1945 (dec. 1986); children: Michaela Ann, Craig Martin, Todd Daniel, Cass Timothy, Simone Agnes. AB, Western Res. U., 1945; MA, Mich. State U., 1957; PhD, U. Toledo, 1967; LHD (hon.), Coll. St. Benedict, St. Joseph, Minn., 1979; LLD (hon.), U. Toledo, 1988. Chem. and biol. researcher, 1945-57; tchr. schs. in Mich., also Mercy Sch. Nursing, St. Lawrence Hosp., Lansing, Mich., 1957-58; mem. chemistry and biology faculty Mary Manse Coll., Toledo, 1958-71; dean grad. div. Mary Manse Coll., 1968-71, exec. v.p., 1968-71; acad. dean Salve Regina Coll., Newport, R.I., 1971-74; pres. Coll. St. Benedict, St. Joseph, Minn., 1974-79, Western New Eng. Coll., Springfield, Mass., 1980—; cons. U.S. Office Edn., 1980; mem. Pvt. Industry Count./Regional Employment Bd., exec. com., 1982-94; cons. in field. Author papers in field. Corporator Mercy Hosp., Springfield, Mass. Recipient President's citation St. John's U., 1979; also various service awards. Mem. AAAS, Am. Assn. Higher Edn., Assn. Cath. Colls. and Univs. (exec. bd.), Internat. Assn. Sci. Edn., Nat. Assn. Ind. Colls. and Univs. (govt. rels. adv. com., bd. dirs. 1990-93, exec. com. 1991-93, treas. 1992-93), Nat. Assn. Biology Tchrs., Assn. Ind. Colls. and Univs. of Mass. (exec. com. 1981—, vice chmn. 1985-86, chmn. 1986-87), Nat. Assn. Rsch. Sci. Teaching, Springfield C. of C. (bd. dirs.), Am. Assn. Univ. Adminstrs. (bd. dirs. 1989-92), Delta Kappa Gamma, Sigma Delta Epsilon. Office: Western New Eng Coll Office of the President 1215 Wilbraham Rd Springfield MA 01119-2654

MILLER, BONNIE SEWELL, marketing professional; b. Junction City, Ky., July 24, 1932; d. William Andrew and Lillian Irene (McCowan) Sewell; m. William Gustave Tournade Jr., Nov. 5, 1950 (div. 1974); children: Bonnie Sue Tournade Zaner, William Gustave III, Sharon Irene Tournade Leach; m. Bruce George Miller, Nov. 15, 1981. BA, U. South Fla., 1968, MA, 1973. Cert. tchr., Fla. Chair dept. English Tampa (Fla.) Cath. High Sch., 1972-78; tchr. Clearwater (Fla.) High Sch., 1978-80; mgr. prodn. svcs. Paradyne Corp., Largo, Fla., 1980-83; freelance writer, cons. Tampa, 1983-84; mgr. product documentation PPS, Inc., Largo, 1984-86; mgr. mktg. communications PPS, Inc., 1986-87; writer Nixdorf Computer Corp., Tampa, 1988-89; mktg. dir. Suncoast Schs. Fed. Credit Union, Tampa, 1989—; instr. English, Hillsborough C.C., Tampa, 1975-87; adj. instr. profl. writing U. South Fla., 1993; cons. bus. writing Coronet Instrnl. Media Writing Project, Tampa, 1976, Nat. Mgmt. Assn., Tampa, 1981-87. Contbr. tech. articles to various publs. Bd. dirs. SERVE, Tampa, Sing Parent Displaced Homemakers Group; legis. chair Tampa PTA, 1965; judge speech contest Am. Legion, Tampa, 1976; vol. North Tampa Vol. Libr., 1988. NEH fellow, 1975. Mem. NAFE, Internat. Assn. Bus. Communicators, Soc. Tech. Communicators, Am. Assn. Bus. Women, Internat. Platform Assn., Toastmasters Internat., Kappa Delta Pi. Democrat. Baptist. Home: 4014 Hudson Ter Tampa FL 33624-5349 Office: Suncoast Schs Fed Credit Union 6801 E Hillsborough Ave Tampa FL 33610-4110

MILLER, CANDICE S., state official; b. May 7, 1954; m. Donald G. Miller; 1 child, Wendy Nicole. Student, Macomb County C.C., Northwood Inst. Sec., treas. D.B. Snider, Inc., 1972-79; trustee Harrison Twp., 1979-80, supr., 1980-92; treas. Macomb County, 1992-95; sec. of state State of Mich., Lansing, 1995—; chair Mich. State Safety Commn., 1995—; mem. M-59 Task Force Strategy Com. Mem. community coun. Selfridge Air Nat. Guard Base. Mem. Boat Town Assn., Ctrl. Macomb C. of C., Harrison Twp. Indsl. Corridor. Office: Treasury Building 430 W Allegan, 1st Fl Lansing MI 48918-9900

MILLER, CAROL LYNN, librarian; b. Kingsville, Tex., Mar. 31, 1961; d. Walter Edward Jr. and Emma Lee (Nelson) M. BS in Early Childhood Edn., So. Nazerene U., 1985; M in Early Childhood Edn., Ala. A & M U., 1987; MLS, U. Ala., 1993. Office worker Salvation Army, Huntsville, 1979-83; libr. Madison (Ala.) Branch Library, 1985; sub. tchr. Huntsville (Ala) City and Madison County Sch. System, 1986-87; br. head Madison Br. Libr., 1987-92, Madison Square Mall Br. Libr., Huntsville, 1992—. Mem. Asbury Meth. Ch., Upbeat Vol. Program. Mem. ALA. Office: Huntsville Madison City Library Madison Square M 5901 University Dr Huntsville AL 35806-2506

MILLER, CAROLINE, editor-in-chief. Exec. editor Variety mag., N.Y.C., 1989-92; editor-in-chief Lear's mag., N.Y.C., 1992-94, Seventeen mag., N.Y.C., 1994—. Office: Seventeen 850 3rd Ave New York NY 10022-6222*

MILLER, CAROLYN JEAN, county official; b. Cuba, N.Y., Oct. 16, 1947; d. Kenneth E. and Ruth J. (Van Fleet) Miller. BA, SUNY, Fredonia, 1969, MS, 1973. English tchr. Little Valley (N.Y.) Ctrl. Sch., 1969-72; legal sec. Allegany County Pub. Defender's Office, Wellsville, N.Y., 1973-83; confidential sec. Allegany County Ct. Judge, Belmont, N.Y., 1983-90; chief clk. III Allegany County Cts., Belmont, N.Y., 1990—. Mem., past pres. So. Tier Libr. Sys., Corning, N.Y., 1983—; mem., sec./treas. Scio (N.Y.) Pub. Libr., 1976—; bd. dirs. Allegany Area Found., 1992—. Mem. AAUW (past pres. Wellsville br.), 20-20 Investments. Home: 4449 W Sciota St Scio NY 14880 Office: Allegany County Cts Court St Belmont NY 14813

MILLER, CATHERINE ANN, secondary education educator; b. Hampton, Va., Nov. 18, 1953; d. Alfred and Marjorie Mae (Leverett) Becker; m. James Arthur Miller, Aug. 4, 1972; children: Stephanie, Timothy, Amy. BS in Edn., U. Tex., 1987. Tchr. Austin (Tex.) Ind. Sch. Dist., 1987-95, Lake Travis Ind. Sch. Dist., Austin, 1995—. Mem. Nat. Assn. Social Studies. Roman Catholic. Home: 13165 Fieldstone Loop Austin TX 78737 also: 3322 RR 620 South Austin TX 78734

MILLER, CECELIA SMITH, chemist; b. Tyron, N.C., Apr. 3, 1965; d. Thad Lewis Jr. and Johnnie Lucille (Staley) Smith; m. Ronnie Edward Miller, Apr. 16, 1988; children: Joshua Edward, Jaylin. BA in Chemistry, Converse Coll., 1987. Lab. technician Groce Labs., Greer, S.C., 1988; quality assurance technician Baxter Pharmaseal, Spartanburg, S.C., 1988-89; lab. dir. CAPSCO, Inc., Greenville, S.C., 1989, quality assurance mgr., 1989—. Mem. Am. Soc. Quality Control, S.C. Lab. Mgmt. Soc. Democrat. Baptist. Home: 3017 Southfield St Inman SC 29349-9190 Office: CAPSCO Inc 1101 W Blue Ridge Dr Greenville SC 29609-3350

MILLER, CHERYL DEANN, women's basketball coach, broadcaster; b. Riverside, Calif., Jan. 3, 1964. BA in Broadcast Journalism, U. So. Calif. Basketball player Jr. Nat. Team, 1981, U.S. Nat. Team, 1982, U.S. Olympics, 1984; commentator ABC Sports; head coach women's basketball U. So. Calif., 1993—; commentator TNT Sports, Atlanta, 1996; player JC Penney All-Am. Team Five, U. So. Calif. Women's Basketball Team, World Championship Team, 1983. Recipient Sports Illustrated Player of Yr., 1986, Naismith Player of Yr. award, Kodak All-Am. award, more than 1,140 trophies and 125 plaques including Nat. Sports Festival, 1981, Pan Am. Games, 1983, FIBA World Championship, Goodwill Games, gold medal 1984 Olympic Games; elected to Naismith Basketball Hall of Fame, 1995. *

MILLER, CHRISTINE MARIE, marketing executive; b. Williamsport, Pa., Dec. 7, 1950; d. Frederick James and Mary (Wurster) M.; m. Robert M. Ancell, Mar. 30, 1985. BA, U. Kans., 1972; MA, Northwestern U., 1978, PhD, 1982. Pub. rels. asst. Bedford County Commr., Bedford, Pa., 1972-73; teaching asst. Northwestern U., Evanston, Ill., 1977-80; asst. prof. U. Ala., Tuscaloosa, 1980-82; Loyola U., New Orleans, 1982-85; vis. prof. Ind. U. Sch. Journalism, Bloomington, 1985-86; mktg. dir. Nat. Inst. Fitness & Sport, Indpls., 1986-88; program dir. Nat. Entrepreneurship Acad., Bloomington, 1986-88; mgmt. assoc. community and media rels. Subaru-Isuzu Automotive, Inc., Lafayette, Ind., 1988-91; dir. pub. rels. Giddings & Lewis, Fond Du Lac, Wis., 1991-93; v.p. comm. and enrollment mgmt. Milton Hershey (Pa.) Sch., 1993-94, dir. adminstrn., 1994-95; mktg. comms. mgr. MCI Govt. Markets, McLean, Va., 1995—. Co-author: The Biographical Dictionary of World War II General and Flag Officer ; contbr. articles to profl. jours. Bd. dirs. Indpls. Entrepreneurship Acad., 1988-91, Area IV Agy., Greater Lafayette Mus. Art, 1989-91. With USN, 1973-77, comdr. USNR, 1977—. Mem. Pub. Rels. Soc. Am., Naval Order of the U.S., Naval Res. Assn., Res. Officers Assn. Presbyterian. Home: 7406 Salford Ct Alexandria VA 22315 Office: MCI Govt Markets 6th Fl 8200 Greensboro Ave Mc Lean VA 22102

MILLER, CHRISTINE ODELL COOK, judge; b. Oakland, Calif., Aug. 26, 1944; d. Leo Marshall II and Carolyn Odell Cook; m. Dennis F. Miller. AB in Polit. Sci., Stanford Univ., 1966; JD, Univ. of Utah, 1969. Cert. gemologist. Law clk. to chief judge U.S. Court of Appeals, 10th circuit, Salt Lake City; trial atty. Dept. of Justice Honors Program, Foreign Litigation Unit, Ct. of Claims Sect. of Civil Div., 1970-72; team leader atty. FTC, 1972-74; with Hogan & Hartson, D.C., 1974-76; spl. counsel Pension Benefit Guaranty Corp., 1976-80; dep. gen. counsel U.S. Railway Assn., 1980-82; with Shack & Kimball, D.C., 1980-82; judge U.S. Ct. of Fed. Claims, D.C., 1982—. Mem. D.C. Bar Assn., Calif. State Bar, Univ. Club (bd. govs.). Office: US Court of Federal Claims 717 Madison Pl NW Ste 709 Washington DC 20005-1011

MILLER, CHRISTINE TALLEY, physical education educator; b. Wilmington, Del., Sept. 11, 1959; d. Willard Radley and Anna Rose (Oddo) Talley; m. Jeffrey Lynch Miller, Nov. 14, 1987; children: Radley Edward, Rebecca Anna. BS in Phys. Edn., U. Del., 1981, MS in Phys. Edn., 1984. Cert. phys. edn. tchr., Del. Phys. edn. tchr. Pilot Sch. Inc., Wilmington, 1981-85; EKG technician Med. Ctr. Del., Newark, 1978-88; phys. edn. tchr. Red Clay Consol. Sch. Dist., Wilmington, 1985—; mem. stds. revision com. Del. Dept. Pub. Instrn., 1991; mem. stds. rev. com. Red Clay Consol. Sch. Dist., 1993-94, curriculum revision com., 1988-92; coach spl. olympics, 1985-88. Contbg. author: A Legacy of Delaware Women, 1987. Jump Rope for Heart coord. Am. Heart Assn., Newark, 1994—; mem. Gov.'s Coun. for Lifestyles and Fitness, State of Del., 1991-93. Recipient Gov.'s Cup award for outstanding phys. edn. program Gov. Mike Castle, Del., 1991. Mem. AAHPERD, Del. Assn. for Health, Phys. Edn., Recreation and Dance (sec. 1981-86, v.p. health, Outstanding Phys. Edn. Tchr. of Yr. 1986). Home: 1206 Arundel Dr Wilmington DE 19808-2137

MILLER, CYNTHIA ANN, publisher; b. Roanoke, Va., Feb. 8, 1951; d. Elisha J. and Margaret Lee (Flora) M.; m. Frank A. Leonard, Sept. 24, 1977 (div. Apr. 1980). BA in History, Va. Poly. Inst. and State U., 1973; MA in History, Duke U., 1975. Rschr., editor Va. State Libr., Richmond, 1974-77; editor Pelican Pub. Co., Gretna, La., 1978, U. S.C. Press, Columbia, 1979-82; exec. editor Wesleyan U. Press, Middletown, Conn., 1982-84; mktg. mgr. Cath. U. Press, Washington, 1984-87, Brookings Instn., Washington, 1987-89; editor-in-chief Univ. Press of Kans., Lawrence, 1989-95; dir. U. Pitts. Press, 1995—; AAUP/USIA del. Moscow Internat. Book Fair, 1987. Editor, compiler: The Virginia General Assembly, 1976. Mem. LWV (bd. dirs. 1986-87, 82-85), Women in Scholarly Publishing (pres. 1985-86), Women's Nat. Book Assn. (bd. dirs. 1987-89, named to 70 Who've Made a Difference 1987). Office: U Pitts Press 127 N Bellefield St Pittsburgh PA 15260

MILLER, DARCY M., publishing executive; b. Glen Ridge, N.J., June 17, 1953; d. Paul Richardson and Susan (Alling) Miller; m. James R. Donaldson III, Feb. 6, 1988 (div.); 1 child, Zoe Alling; m. James R. Moffa. Co-founder, assoc. pub. Mus. Mag., N.Y.C., 1979-83; pub. Crop Protection Chemicals Reference, N.Y.C., 1983-85; assoc. pub. Chief Exec. Mag., N.Y.C., 1986-87, pub., 1987-89, exec. v.p., 1989-96; pub. Stagebill, N.Y.C., 1996—. Mem. ASCAP, Advt. Women of N.Y. Democrat. Episcopalian. Office: Stagebill 144 E 44th St New York NY 10017

MILLER, DAWN MARIE, meteorologist, product marketing specialist; b. Hartford, Conn., Sept. 17, 1963; d. Eugene E. Miller and Audrey E. (Flagg) Laurel; m. Dennis James Miller, Sept. 9, 1989; children: Zackarey, Amanda. BS in Meteorology, SUNY, Oneonta, 1985. Customer support specialist WSI Corp., Bedford, Mass., 1985-87; in media (TV) mktg. WSI Corp., Billerica, Mass., 1987-91, media (TV) and industry mktg. rep., 1991-92, mktg. communications specialist, 1992-93, product mktg. specialist-data svcs., 1993—. Mem. Oneonta Alumni Assn., Nat. Arbor Day Found., Nat. Audubon Soc., The Am. Horticultural Soc., The Nature Conservancy, Am. Meteorol. Soc. Republican. Episcopalian. Home: 37 Wren St Litchfield NH 03052-2540 Office: WSI Corp 4 Federal St Billerica MA 01821-3569

MILLER, DEBORAH JEAN, computer training and document consultant; b. Elmhurst, Ill., Oct. 2, 1951; d. Thomas Francis and Ruthe Conn (Johnston) M. BFA, Ill. Wesleyan U., 1973; MA, Northwestern U., 1974. Pres. Miller & Assocs., Evanston, Ill., 1980—. Mem. AAUW, NOW, Internat. Interactive Comm. Soc., Soc. Tech. Comm., Ind. Writers Chgo. (bd. dirs. 1985-86), Chgo. Coun. Fgn. Rels., Internat. Soc. Performance and Instrn. (Chgo. chpt.), Northwestern U. Alumni Assn. Office: 814 Mulford St Evanston IL 60202-3331

MILLER, DIANA J., circuit court clerk; b. Terre Haute, Ind., Jan. 18, 1952; d. Robert J. and Virginia H. (Hampsten) Dix; m. Keith W. Miller, July 23, 1975. BA in Liberal Arts, U. Wis., Eau Claire, 1974; attended, Chippewa Valley Tech. Coll., Eau Claire, 1988-90. Media clerk Eau Claire Area Schs., 1975-89; clerk of court Eau Claire County, 1989—; pres. Eau Claire Support Staff Union, 1983-88; sec. Area Labor Coun., Eau Claire, 1981-86; v.p. Wis. Fedn. Tchrs., 1983-88; exec. bd. dirs. Boston Refuge House, Eau Claire, 1991—. Editor: (newsletter) Eau Claire Dem. Party, 1983-88, Wis. Clerks of Circuit Court, 1993—; author: (jour.) The Court Manager, 1996. Mem. exec. bd. Eau Claire County Dem. Party, 1983-88; pol. action coord. Eau Claire Support Union, 1980-89. Mem. AAUW, Nat. Assn. for Ct. Mgmt., Wis. Clerks of Cir. Ct. Assn. (legis. com. 1989—). Democrat. Home: 144 S Victory St Fall Creek WI 54742 Office: Eau Claire County Cir Cts 721 Oxford Ave Eau Claire WI 54703

MILLER, DIANE DORIS, executive search consultant; b. Sacramento, Calif., Jan. 18, 1954; d. George Campbell and Doris Lucille (Benninger) M. BA, U. Pacific, 1976, Golden Gate U., 1985, MBA, 1987. Mgr., A.G. Spanos, Sacramento, 1977-81, Lee Sammis, Sacramento, 1981-83; v.p. Consol. Capital, San Francisco, 1983-86; ptnr. Wilcox, Bertoux and Miller, Sacramento, 1986—. Bd. dirs. Sacramento Symphony En Corps, 1982-84, Sacramento Ballet, 1983-84, 86-92, Sacramento Symphony Assn., 1988-92, Oakland Ballet, Calif., 1984-85, Sacramento Symphony Found., 1994—, Sacramento Reg. Found., 1996—; mem. adv. bd. Golden Gate U., 1995—. Named Vol. of Yr., Junior League, 1983, Bus. Vol. in the Arts, Sacramento C. of C., 1989. Mem. U. Pacific Alumni Assn. (bd. dirs. 1978-85). Republican. Avocations: ballet, water sports.

MILLER, DIANE FAYE, art education educator, business owner; b. Wauseon, Ohio, Dec. 10, 1966; d. Richard Lee and Twila Fern (Bontrager) Beck; m. Wendell Eugene Miller, June 29, 1991. BS in Art Edn., Grace Coll., Winona Lake, Ind., 1989. Gen. edn., art edn. tchr. New Horizons Ministries, Marion, Ind., 1989-90; art edn., ceramics tchr. Warsaw (Ind.) Cmty. H.S., 1990-94; sponsor Art Club, Warsaw Cmty. H.S., 1992-94, chairperson Student Asst. Program, 1992-94; coord. Tri Kappa H.S. Art Show, Warsaw, 1992-94; speaker Fellowship of Christian Athletes, Warsaw, 1992, 93. Mem. Nat. Art Edn. Assn., Warsaw Cmty. Edn. Assn. Republican. Mennonite.

MILLER, DIANE WILMARTH, human resources director; b. Clarinda, Iowa, Mar. 12, 1940; d. Donald and Floy Pauline (Madden) W.; m. Robert Nolen Miller, Aug. 21, 1965; children: Robert Wilmarth, Anne Elizabeth. AA, Colo. Women's Coll., 1960; BBA, U. Iowa, 1962; MA, U. No. Colo., 1994. Cert. tchr., Colo.; vocat. credential, Colo.; cert. sr. profl. in human resources. Sec.-counselor U. S.C., Myrtle Beach AFB, 1968-69; instr. U. S.C., Conway, 1967-69; tchr. bus. Poudre Sch. Dist. R-1, Ft. Collins, Colo., 1970-71; travel cons. United Bank Travel Svc., Greeley, Colo., 1972-74; dir. human resources Aims Community Coll., Greeley, 1984—; instr. part-time Aims Community Coll., Greeley, 1972—. Active 1st Congl. Ch., Greeley. Mem. Coll. Univ. Pers. Assn., Coll. Univ. Pers. Assn. Colo., No. Colo. Human Resources Assn., Soc. Human Resource Mgmt., Philanthropic Ednl. Orgn. (pres. 1988-89), Women's Panhellenic Assn. (pres. 1983-84), Scroll and Fan Club (pres. 1985-86), WTK Club, Questers. Home: 3530 Wagon Trail Pl Greeley CO 80634-3405 Office: Aims Cmty Coll 5401 20th St PO Box 69 Greeley CO 80634-3002

MILLER, DOROTHY ANNE SMITH, retired cytogenetics educator; b. N.Y.C., Oct. 20, 1931; d. John Philip and Anna Elizabeth (Hellberg) Smith; m. Orlando Jack Miller, July 10, 1954; children: Richard L., Cynthia K., Karen A. BA in Chemistry magna cum laude, Wilson Coll., Chambersburg, Pa., 1952; PhD in Biochemistry, Yale U., 1957. Rsch. assoc. dept. ob-gyn Columbia U., N.Y.C., 1964-72, from rsch. assoc. to asst. prof. dept. human genetics-devel., 1973-85; prof. depts. molecular biology and genetics and pathology Wayne State U., Detroit, 1985-94, prof. dept. pathology, 1985-96, prof. Ctr. for Molecular Medicine and Genetics, 1994-96; vis. scientist clin. and population cytogenetics unit Med. Rsch. Coun., Edinburgh, Scotland, 1983-84; vis. prof. dept. genetics and molecular biology U. la Sapienza, Rome, 1988; vis. disting. fellow La Trobe U., Melbourne, Australia, 1992. Contbr. numerous articles to sci. jours. Grantee March of Dimes Birth Defects Found., 1974-93, NSF, 1983-84. Mem. Am. Soc. Human Genetics, Genetics Soc. Am., Genetics Soc. Australia, Phi Beta Kappa. Presbyterian. Home: 1915 Stonycroft Ln Bloomfield Hills MI 48304-2339 Office: Wayne State U 540 E Canfield St Detroit MI 48201-1928

MILLER, DOROTHY ELOISE, education educator; b. Ft. Pierce, Fla., Apr. 13, 1944; d. Robert Foy and Aline (Mahon) Wilkes. BS in Edn., Bloomsburg U., 1966, MEd, 1969; MLA, Johns Hopkins U., 1978; EdD, Columbia U., 1991. Tchr. Cen. Dauphin East High Sch., Harrisburg, Pa., 1966-68, Aberdeen (Md.) High Sch., 1968-69; asst. dean of coll., prof. Harford C. C., Bel Air, Md., 1969—; owner Ideas by Design, 1995—; mem. accreditation team Mid. States Commn., 1995, 96. Editor: Renewing the American Community Colleges, 1984; contbr. articles to profl. jours. Pres. Harlan Sq. Condominium Assn., Bel Air, 1982, 90—, Md. internat. divsn. St. Petersburg Sister State Com., 1993—; edn. liaison AAUW, Harford County, Md., 1982-92; cen. com. mem. Rep. Party, Harford County, 1974-78; crusade co-chair Am. Cancer Soc., Harford County, 1976-78; mem. faculty adv. com. Md. Higher Edn. Commn., 1993—; mem. people's adv. coun. Harford County Coun., 1994—. Recipient Nat. Tchg. Excellence award Nat. Inst. for Staff and Orgn. Devel., U. Tex.-Austin, 1992. Charter mem. Nat. Mus. Women in the Arts. Republican. Methodist. Office: Harford Community Coll 401 Thomas Run Rd Bel Air MD 21015-1627

MILLER, EILEEN RENEE, counselor; b. Flushing, N.Y., Aug. 28, 1951; d. Edward and Alice Miller; m. Gary Martin Russell. BA, Syracuse U., 1972, MS, 1975. Cert. employee assistance profl., master addiction counselor, nat. cert. addiction counselor II, substance abuse counselor, cert. alcohol counselor. Dir. residence hall Syracuse (N.Y.) U., 1975-76; counselor Liverpool (N.Y.) Schs., 1976-83, Family Svc. Assocs., Liverpool, 1985—, Confidential Assistance Svcs., Liverpool, 1986—; supr. employee assistance program OCM Bd. Coop. Ednl. Svcs., Syracuse, 1984—; presenter in field; chmn. Upstate N.Y. Student and Employee Assistance Program Edn. Network, Syracuse, 1987—. Bd. dirs. Rape Crisis Ctr., Syracuse, 1982-85; com. mem. City-County Drug Commn., Syracuse, 1991—. Recipient award of appreciation Upstate N.Y. Employee Assistance Program Edn. Network, 1993; grantee OSHA, 1984-86, OASAS, 1985-88. Mem. ACA, NASW, N.Y. State Assn. Counseling and Devel., Employee Assistance Program Assn., NYFAC, Mental Health Assn. Office: Confidential Assistance Svc 129 Sun Harbor Dr Liverpool NY 13088

MILLER, ELAINE WILSON, computer consultant; b. Ft. Worth, Sept. 16, 1944; d. Phillip Loren and Artie Inez (Neel) Wilson; m. Robert J. Copeland, Aug. 17, 1963 (div. 1983); children: Karen Kay Prince, Donna Lynn Copeland-Nay; m. Jared N. Miller Jr., Dec. 12, 1993. BS in Bus., Info. Systems, U. Colo., Denver, 1984. Sec. Hartford Life Ins. Co., Dallas, 1964-66, St. George's Episcopal Ch., Dallas, 1976-77; technician data processing Manville Corp., Denver, 1980-81, assoc. analyst, 1984-85, analyst data processing, 1985-94; fin. technician 1st Interstate Bank, Denver, 1982-84; computer cons. Miller Cons., Lakewood, Colo., 1994—; bus. process analyst US WEST Comm., Inc., Denver, 1994—; dir. Denver SAS Users Group, 1994—. Chmn. precinct Rep. Party Tex., Dallas, 1970-76. Recipient Silver Spark award Camp Fire Girls, Denver, 1982. Mem. Home Based Bus. Connection, Data Processing Mgmt. Assn. (v.p. publicity 1986-88, 90-91, sec. 1989-90, asst. editor newsletter 1985-86, v.p. newsletter 1991-94, Individual Performance award 1991, exec. v.p. 1994-95, pres. 1995-96), Jaycee-Ettes (hon. lifetime), Grand Prairie (Tex.) C. of C. (Newcomer of Yr. 1971), St. Paul's Ultreya Club (lay leader 1987-88). Episcopalian. Office: US West Comm 1801 California St Rm 2810 Denver CO 80202-2658

MILLER, ELIZABETH ELLEN, guidance counselor; b. New Brunswick, N.J., Nov. 18, 1946; d. James and Elizabeth (Pfeiffer) Madarasz; m. Glen Miller, Oct. 10, 1970; 1 child, Glen James-Martin Miller. BA, Newark State Coll., 1969; MA, Kean Coll. of N.J., 1977. Cert. student personnel svcs. adminstr., elem. tchr., N.J. Tchr. Edison (N.J.) Twp. Bd. Edn., 1969-70, Brick (N.J.) Bd. of Edn., 1970-84; guidance counselor Lacey Twp. (N.J.) Bd. Edn., 1984—. Active Boy Scouts of Am., Community Against Substance Abuse. Fellow NEA, Am. Sch. Counselor Assn., Am. Counselor Assn., N.J. Edn. Assn., Ocean County Edn. Assn., Lacey Twp. Edn. Assn. (rep. 1984—); mem. N.J. Counselors Assn., N.J. Sch. Counselors Assn. (v.p. 1987—, mem. exec. bd., County Counselor of Yr. 1993), Ocean County Pers. and Guidance Assn. (mem. exec. bd., trustee 1985—, County Counselor of Yr. 1993). Roman Catholic. Home: 629 Huckleberry Ln Toms River NJ 08753-4582 Office: Lanoka Harbor Elem Sch PO Box 186 Lanoka Harbor NJ 08734-0186

MILLER, ELLEN, advertising executive. Pres. health care mktg. svcs. DraftDirect Worldwide, Chgo. Office: DraftDirect Worldwide 142 E Ontario Chicago IL 60611-2818*

MILLER, ELLEN S., marketing communications executive; b. Indpls., June 28, 1954; d. Harold Edward and Lilian (Gantner) M. BA, DePauw U., 1976; postgrad., Sch. Visual Arts, N.Y.C., 1981-82. Editorial asst. Daisy mag., N.Y.C., 1976-77; asst. dept. mgr., Christmas hiring mgr. Bloomingdale's, N.Y.C., 1978; sales rep. Rosenthal USA Ltd., N.Y.C., 1979, mktg. asst., 1980-81, dir. mktg. comms., 1982-90; mgr. consumer mktg. Creamer Dickson Basford, Providence, 1990, v.p., 1991-94; prin. E.S. Miller Comm., Providence, 1994—; instr. Learning Connection. Editor Community Prep. Sch. newsletter, 1993. Trustee Cmty. Prep Sch., Providence, 1993—. Recipient Bell Ringer award New Eng. Pub. Club, 1992, 93, Iris award N.J. chpt. Internat. Assn. Bus. Communicators, 1993, Silver Quill award Dist. I, 1993. Mem. Pub. Rels. Soc. Am., Nat. Tabletop Assn. (com. chair 1989), Internat. Tabletop Awards (bd. dirs. 1989). Republican. Presbyterian.

MILLER, EMILIE F., former state senator; b. Chgo., Aug. 11, 1936; d. Bruno C. and Etta M. (Senese) Feiza; m. Dean E. Miller; children: Desireé M., Edward C. BS in Bus. Adminstrn., Drake U., 1958. Asst. buyer Jordan Marsh Co., Boston, 1958-60, Carson, Pirie, Scott & Co., Chgo., 1960-62; dept. mgr., asst. buyer Woodward & Lothrop, Washington, 1962-64; state labor coord. Robb Davis Daliles Joint Campaign; legis. aide Senator Adelard Brandt, Va., 1980-83; fin. dir. Saslaw for Congress, 1984; legis. cons. Va. Fedn. Bus. Profl. Women, 1986-87; senator Va. Gen. Assembly, Richmond, 1988-92; apptd. by Gov. Wilder to bd. dirs. Innovative Tech. Authority, 1992, Ctr. for Innovative Tech., 1992; cons., 1992—; mem. Edn. and Health com., Gen. Laws com., Local Gov. com., Rehab. and Social Scis. com.; bus. tng. seminars Moscow, Nizhny Novgorod, Russia, 1993, Novgorod, St. Petersburg, 1995; cons. in field. Guest editorial writer No. Va. Sun, 1981; host, producer weekly TV program, Channel 61. Mem. State Ctrl. Com. Dem. Party Va., Richmond, 1974-92, Fairfax County Dem. Com., 1968—, Presdl. Inaugural Com., 1977, 1992 Dem. Nat. Platform Com., Va. mem. on temp. coms., Dem. Adv. Com. Robb-Spong Commn., 1978-79; founder, chmn. Va. Assoc. Dem. County and City Chmn., 1976-80, Fairfax County Dem. Com., 1976-80; security supr. 1980 Dem. Nat. Conv.; v.p. Va. Fedn. Dem. Women, 1992—; bd. dirs. Stop Child Abuse Now, 1988, Ctr. Innovative Tech., 1992-94, Ct. Apptd. Spl. Advs., 1993—; mem. nat. alumni bd. J.A. Achievement, BRAVO adv. com. for the first Gov.'s Awards for Arts in Va., 1979-80; lay tchr. St. Ambrose Cath. Ch., 1963-80; del. to White House Conf. on Children, 1970; chmn. Va. Coalition for Mentally Disturbed, 1992-94. Recipient Disting. Grad. award Jr. Achievement, 1973, Woman of Achievement award Fairfax (Va.) Bd. Suprs. and Fairfax County Commn. for Women, 1982, Cmty. Svc. award Friends of Victims Assistance Network, 1988, Founders award Fairfax County Coun. of Arts, 1989, Mental Health Assn. of Northern Va. Warren Stambaugh award, 1991, Ann. Svc. award Va. Assn. for Marriage and Family Therapy, 1991, Psychology Soc. of Washington Cmty. Svc. award, 1993. Mem. NOW, Nat. Mus. Women in the Arts, Va. Assn. Female Execs. (mem. adv. bd., bd. dirs., v.p. 1992—), Va. Assn. Cmty. Svc. Bds. (chmn. 1980-82), North Va. Assn. Cmty. Bds. (chmn. 1978-79), Fairfax County Coun. Arts (v.p. 1980—, mem. exec. com. internat. children's festival, Founders award 1989), Fairfax County C. of C. (mem. legis. com.), Greater Merrifield Bus. and Profl. Assn., Mental Health Assn. No.Va. (bd. dirs.), Ctrl. Fairfax C. of C., Falls Church C. of C., Bus. and Profl. Women's Fedn. Va., Mantua Citizen's Assn. (mem. exec. bd.), Tower Club (Fairfax), Bus. and Profl. Women's Club (pres. Falls Church chpt. 1994-96, Woman of Yr. award 1990), Women's Nat. Dem. Club (past v.p., mem. bd. govs.), Downtown Club (Richmond), Phi Gamma Nu. Roman Catholic. Home: 8701 Duvall St Fairfax VA 22031-2711

MILLER, FRANCES SUZANNE, historic site curator; b. Defiance, Ohio, Apr. 17, 1950; d. Francis Bernard Johnson and Nellie Frances (Holder) Culp; m. James A. Batdorf, Aug. 7, 1970 (div. Aug. 1979); 1 child, Jennifer Christine Batdorf; m. Rodney Lyle Miller, Aug. 8, 1982 (div. Apr. 1987). BS in History/Museology, The Defiance Coll., 1990; AS in Bus. Mgmt., N.W. Tech. Coll., 1986. With accts. receivable dept. Ohio Art Co., Bryan, Ohio, 1984-87; leasing agent Williams Met. Housing Authority, Bryan, 1987-91; curator, property mgr. James A. Garfield Nat. Historic Site, Mentor, Ohio, 1991—. Mem. AAUW (pres. 1993-95, treas. 1995-97), Nat. Trust Hist. Preservation, Ohio Mus. Assn., Ohio Assn. Host. Socs. and Mus., Cleve. Restoration Soc., Phi Alpha Theta. Office: James A Garfield Nat Historic Site 8095 Mentor Ave Mentor OH 44060-5753

MILLER, FRANCIE LORADITCH, college recruiter; b. Avilton, Md., Apr. 18, 1937; d. John William and Agnes Wilda (Broadwater) Loraditch; m. George Aloys Miller, Feb. 27, 1965; children: Peter Raymond, Sandra Patricia. Student, Kent State U., 1955-57; BA in English, Calif. State U., Dominguez Hills, 1978, Ma in English, 1980. Flight attendent Western Airlines, L.A., 1957-65; lectr. English Calif. State U., Carson, 1980-82, asst. coord. learning assistance ctr., 1979-84, asst. dir. univ. outreach svcs., 1984—; dir. advisement & transfer svcs. Marymount Coll., Palos Verdes, Calif., 1996. Editor Campus Staff Newsletter, 1992—. Mem. edn. com. Palos Verdes (Calif.) C. of C., 1994—; vol. Olympic Games, L.A., 1984; campus rep. Statewide Alumni Coun., Sacramento, 1982-84; participant Civic Chorale, Torrance, Calif., 1993—; apptd. statewide campus adv. com. Project Assist, 1996. Acad. scholar Kent State U., 1955. Mem. Calif. Intersegmental Articulation Coun. (newsletter editor 1993—, vice chair 1995—), Western Assn. Coll. Admission Counselors, South Coast Higher Ednl. Coun., Phi Kappa Phi (chpt. pres. 1992—, mem. nat. comm. com. 1996). Republican. Roman Catholic. Office: Calif State U Dominguez Hills 1000 E Victoria St Carson CA 90747-0001

MILLER, FRANCINE KOSLOW, art history educator, art critic; b. Boston, Apr. 26, 1951; d. Myer and Lillian (Witten) Koslow; m. Mark Jay Miller, Oct. 6, 1991; 1 child, Rebecca. BA, Brandeis U., 1973; MA, U. Calif., Berkeley, 1976; PhD, Boston U., 1981. Asst. editor Worldwide Books, Allston, Mass., 1975-76; prof. art history McGill U., Montreal, Que., Can., 1981-83; guest curator De Cordova Mus., Lincoln, Mass., 1983-84; asst. prof. art history Pine Manor Coll., Chestnut Hill, Mass., 1984-86; prof. art history Mass. Coll. Art, Boston, 1986—. Author: Gaudier-Brzeska par Ezra Pound, 1992, (catalogs) Henry David Thoreau as a Source for Artistic Inspiration, 1984, David Brody Selected Works, 1995; contbg. writer, reviewer Artforum, 1988—; feature writer Print Collectors Newsletter, 1988—. Mem. Internat. Assn. of Art Critics, Phi Beta Kappa. Democrat. Jewish. Home and Office: 9 Woodhaven Dr Andover MA 01810

MILLER, GAY DAVIS, lawyer; b. Florence, Ariz., Dec. 20, 1947; d. Franklin Theodore and Mary (Belshaw) Davis; m. John Donald Miller, May 15, 1971; 1 child, Katherine Alexandra. BA, U. Colo., 1969; JD, Am. U., 1975. Bar: D.C. 1975. Atty., spl. asst. to gen. counsel, sr. counsel corp. affairs Inter Am. Devel. Bank, Washington, 1975-78, 83—; atty. Intelsat, Washington, 1978-80. Articles editor Am. U. Law Rev., 1974-75. Bd. dirs. Hist. Mt. Pleasant, Inc., Washington, 1985-86, Washington Bridle Trails Assn., 1992—. Mem. ABA, Am. Soc. Internat. Law, Inter Am. Bar Assn., Women's Bar Assn. Office: Inter Am Devel Bank 1300 New York Ave NW Washington DC 20577-0001

MILLER, GENEVIEVE, retired medical historian; b. Butler, Pa., Oct. 15, 1914; d. Charles Russell and Genevieve (Wolford) M. AB, Goucher Coll., 1935; MA, Johns Hopkins U., 1939; PhD, Cornell U., 1955. Asst. in history of medicine Johns Hopkins Inst. of History of Medicine, Balt., 1943-44, instr., 1945-48, rsch. assoc., 1979-94; asst. prof. history of medicine Sch. Medicine, Case Western Res. U., Cleve., 1953-67, assoc. prof., 1967-79, assoc. prof. emeritus, 1979—; research assoc. in med. history Cleve. Med. Library Assn., 1953-62, curator Howard Dittrick Mus. of Hist. Medicine, 1962-67, dir. Howard Dittrick Mus. Hist. Medicine, 1967-79. Author: William Beaumont's Formative Years: Two Early Notebooks 1811-1821, 1946; The Adoption of Inoculation for Smallpox in England and France (William H. Welch medal Am. Assn. for History of Medicine 1962), 1957; Bibliography of the History of Medicine of the U.S. and Canada, 1939-1960, 1964; Bibliography of the Writings of Henry E. Sigerist, 1966; Letters of Edward Jenner and Other Documents Concerning the Early History of Vaccination, 1983; assoc. editor Bull. of History of Medicine, 1944-48, acting editor, 1948, mem. adv. editorial bd. 1960-92; mem. bd. editors Jour. of History of Medicine and Allied Scis., 1948-65; editor Bull. of Cleve. Med. Library, 1954-72; editor newsletter Am. Assn. for History of Medicine, 1986-96; contbr. articles in field to profl. jours. Am. Council Learned Socs. fellow, 1948-50; Dean Van Meter fellow, 1953-54. Alumna trustee Goucher Coll., Balt., 1966-69; trustee Judson Retirement Cmty., Cleve., 1993—. Hon. fellow Cleve. Med. Library Assn.; mem. Am. Assn. for History of Medicine (pres. 1978-80, mem. council 1960-63), Am. Hist. Assn., Internat. Soc. for History of Medicine, Soc. Archtl. Historians, Phi Beta Kappa; corr. mem. fgn. socs. for history of medicine. Democrat. Home and Office: Judson Manor 1890 E 107th St Apt 816 Cleveland OH 44106-2245

MILLER, GEORGIA ELLEN, business owner; b. Seattle; d. George Rynd Sr. and Mary Edith (Martin) M. BE, UCLA, 1934, MEd, 1956. Tchr. Punahou Sch., Honolulu, 1948-74; owner Miller's Bus. Svcs., Honolulu, 1975—. Bd. dirs. Waikiki Improvement Assn., Honolulu, 1980—, Waikiki Cmty. Ctr., Honolulu, 1992-95; pres. Waikiki Residents Assn., Honolulu, 1978—; sec. Waikiki Neighborhood Bd., 1980-86, v.p., 1990—, acting chair, 1992-93; county chmn. Oahu (Hawaii) Rep. Party, 1976; founding mem. Waikiki Neighbook Bd., officer; lobbyist Waikiki Residents Assn. Recipinet Kilohana award for Outstanding Vol. Svc. Gov. Coyetano, 1996. Mem. Bus. and Profl. Women (pres. 1973, legis. chair 1980, 88, state lobbyist 1988—), AAUW, Alpha Chi Omega, Pi Lambda Theta. Mem. United Ch. of Christ. Home: 2415 Ala Wai Blvd Apt 1603 Honolulu HI 96815-3409 Office: Millers Bus Svcs 1720 Ala Moana Blvd Apt B4C Honolulu HI 96815-1347

MILLER, GERRI, magazine editor, writer; b. Bklyn., Mar. 2, 1954; d. Norman and Isobel (Rand) M. BA, SUNY, Binghamton, 1976. Assoc. editor Sixteen Mag., N.Y.C., 1977-80; editor, then exec. editor Sterling/Macfadden, N.Y.C., 1981—. Office: Metal Edge TV Picture Life Sterling/Macfadden 233 Park Ave S New York NY 10003-1606

MILLER, HARRIET SANDERS, art center director; b. N.Y.C., Apr. 18, 1926; d. Herman and Dorothy (Silbert) S.; m. Milton H. Miller, June 27, 1948; children—Bruce, Jeffrey, Marcie. B.A., Ind. U., 1947; M.A., Columbia U., 1949; M.S., U. Wis., 1962, M.F.A., 1967. Dir. art sch. Madison Art Ctr., Wis., 1963-72; acting dir. Center for Continuing Edn., Vancouver, B.C., 1975-76; mem. fine arts faculty Douglas Coll., Vancouver, 1972-78; exec. dir. Palos Verdes Arts Center, Calif., 1978-84; dir. Junior Arts Center, Los Angeles, 1984—; one woman exhibits at Gallery 7, Vancouver, 1978, Gallery 1, Toronto, Ont., 1977, Linda Farris Gallery, Seattle, 1975, Galerie Allen, Vancouver, 1973. Mem. Calif. Art Edn. Assn., Museum Educators of So. Calif., Arts and Humanities Symposium. Office: Junior Arts Ctr 4814 Hollywood Blvd Los Angeles CA 90027-5302

MILLER, HEATHER ELYSE, occupational therapist; b. N.Y.C., Dec. 30, 1966; d. Ken and Vera Miller. BS, Boston U., 1988; MS, Ohio State U., 1996. Registered occupl. therapist, AOTCB. Staff therapist Rehab. Ctr. of Fairfield County, Bridgeport, Conn., 1989-91; sr. staff Rehab. Ctr. of Fairfield County, Bridgeport, 1991-92, pediat. supr., 1992-93; staff therapist Allied Therapy Assocs., Dublin, Ohio, 1993-96; staff therapist pre-sch. program Madison County Schs., 1996—. Editor (newsletter) OT/PT Update, 1996; author (newsletter) Sensory Integration SIS Newsletter. Mem. Am. Occupl. Therapy Assn., Ohio Occupl. Therapy Assn., Phi Kappa Phi, Phi Theta Epsilon (v.p. 1987-88).

MILLER, IRIS ANN, landscape architect, urban designer, educator; b. Pitts., Jan. 6, 1938; d. Bernard and Sadye (Topel) Ress; m. Lawrence Alan Miller, Jan. 24, 1959; children: Bradley Stuart, Richard Lyle, Stefan Ress. BS cum laude, U. Pitts., 1959, MEd in Secondary Edn., 1961; postgrad. in psychology and counseling, U. Md., 1962-68; MArch, Cath. U. Am., 1979. Tchr. various pub. and pvt. schs., Pitts., Monroeville, Pa., Montgomery County, Md., 1959-61, 63-64; free lance landscape design Washington, 1965-81; architecture design and research O'Neil and Manion Architects, Bethesda, Md., 1979, 81; architecture design and drawing Frank Schlesinger Architects/Planners, Washington, 1979-80; prin. Iris Miller Urbanism and Landscape Design, 1982—; cons. architecture design Washington, 1982—; vis. lectr. Cath. U. Am., Washington, 1983-86, vis. asst. prof., 1987-93, adj. asst. prof., 1993—, dir. landscape and architecture studies, 1986-89, dir. landscape studies, 1990—; urban design cons. Techworld, Washington, 1984-86; devel. dir. Tech. 2000 Mus., 1985-86; dir., presenter lectr. series resident assoc. program Smithsonian Instn., Washington, 1982, 83, 85, 87, 89; dir., founder 7th, 8th and 9th Sts. Group Streetscape project, Washington, 1986—, others; founder Charrette urgan design seminar, Washington, Dallas, Alexandria, Va., St. Louis and Cleve., 1982-89; initiator, participant Sarasota (Fla.) Regional Urban Design Assistance R/UDAT team, 1983, seminar Nat. Gallery Art, Washington, 1984, Nat. Arboretum, 1988, symposia Cath. U. Am., 1987—; apptd. mem. D.C. Downtown Partnership Streetscape subcom., 1989-91, D.C. Interactive Downtown Task Force Streetscape and Traffic subcom., 1996; founder, co-dir. symposium. Libr. of Congress, 1995; dir. symposium D.C. Interagy. Task Force on Streetscape and Signage, 1995; dir., mem. steering com. numerous confs. in field; invited participant Congress for New Urbanism, 1994—; program spkr. U.S. Embassy Amman, Jordan, 1992, U. Va., 1993, Ecole Nationale Superieure du Paysage/Versailles, France, 1993, U. Osaka, Japan, 1993, 95, 96, Tokyo Inst. Tech. U., 1993, SUNY, Buffalo, 1994, U. Colo., Denver, 1994, Inst. on City Design, St. Louis, 1994, Tongji U., Shanghai, China, 1995, Beijing U., China, 1995; jury critic Cath. U. Am., 1980-94, U. Puerto Rice, U. Va., 1993; instr. ceramics, Bethesda, Md., 1975-76. Author, co-editor: (book) Urban Design: Visions and Reflections, 1991, Capital Visions: Reflections on a Decade of Urban Design Charrettes and a Look Ahead, 1995, (map and text) Visions of Washington: Composite Plan of Urban Interventions, 1991; contbr. articles to profl. jours.; curator, author exhbn. and catalogue on Washington Maps Sumner Sch. Mus., 1987, 92, U. Md., 1993, Embassy of France, 1993, SUNY Buffalo, 1994, U. Calif., Berkeley, 1994, U. Toronto, Can., 1995; curator, author exhbn. ACSA Ann. Meeting, Montreal, 1994; co-curator, author exhbn. and catalogue Octagon Mus., 1987; project dir., curator Paris-Washington Exhbn., 1987—; recent residential landscape projects include Kahn Residence, Arlington, Va., 1993-94, Marks Residence, Silver Spring, Md., 1993, Nesse, Lewis Residence, Silver Spring, 1992, Friedman Residence, Washington, 1992, Drysdale Hershon Residence, Washington, 1991, Miller Residence, Washington, 1990—, Sexton Residcne, Kenwood, Chevy Chase, Md., 1990, 95, Romano Residence, Fairfax Station, Va., 1989, Mushinski Residence, Bethesda, Md., 1989, 8th St. Mall Washington, 1987-88, Mishkin, Jennis Residence, Bethesda, 1988, Cramer Residence, Bethesda, 1988; recent home design and renovations include Sexton Residence, Chevy Chase, 1994, Miller Jayapal Residence, San Francisco, 1993, Marks Residence, Silver Spring, 1993, Miller Residence, 1991, Washington, Mishkin Jennis Residence, Bethesda, 1988. Co-chmn. stamp com. Bicentennial Washington, 1987-90; founding mem. Washington Network, 1986-89; mem. adv. panel L'Enfant Forum, Washington, 1987-90, Hist. Georgetown Found., 1989—; trustee John J. Sexton Fund for Local Govt. Studies, Sch. Pub. Affairs, U. Md., College Park, 1983—; dir., founder Pub.-Pvt. Partnership and Univ. Scholarship Outreach Inner-City H.S. Program, Cath. U. Am., Washington Pub. Schs., 1985—; dir., founder Intern Exch. Program Landscape Architecture France-U.S.A., Cath. U. Am., U. Va., Friends of Vieilles Maisons Francaises, 1991—; dir., co-founder Intern Exch. Program Landscape Architecture China-U.S.A., Cath. U. Am., Tongji U., Shanghai, 1995—, Osaka U., Japan, 1996—; historic landscape com. U.S./Internat. Coun. on Monuments and Sites, 1990—; active Cultural Alliance Greater Washington, Nat. Trust Historic Preservation, Ikebana Internat., His. Soc. Washington, Nat. Mus. for Bldg. Arts; alumni coun. Sch. Architecture and Planning, Cath. U. Am., 1986—. Travel rsch. grantee Cath. U. Am., 1978, 79, Rsch. grantee Govt. France, 1985; grantee NEA (2), 1982, grantee D.C. Commn. on Arts, 1991, 92; recipient Program Devel. award Cath. U. Am., 1978. Mem. AIA (assoc., nat., regional and urban design exhbn. and panel, chmn. edn. subcom. 1987—, chmn., founder data base on design edn. and urban design, chmn. edn. conf. 1983, chmn. newsletter 1993, edn. com. D.C. chpt. 1981-83, Charrette co-chmn., program devel. award 1982), Assn. Collegiate Schs. Architecture (spkr. N.E. region conf. 1989, spkr. ann. meeting 1991-92, chmn. panel 1989—, chair Collegiate Exhbn. for Excellence in Urban Design 1990—, author conf. procs. 1991-93, Citation for Urban Design 1993, 95), Am. Soc. Landscape Architects (Potomac chpt. strategic planning com. 1994-95), Am. Planning Assn., U.S.-Internat. Cun. on Monuments and Sites (program spkr. 1987, 92, 93, hist. landscapes com.), Friends Vieilles Maisons Francaises (program spkr. 1987, 92), Friends of Vieilles Maisons Francaises, Alpha Epsilon Phi (pres. D.C. alumni 1965-67). Home: 3820 52nd St NW Washington DC 20016-1924 Office: 914 11th St NW Washington DC 20001-4408

MILLER, JACQUELINE WINSLOW, library director; b. N.Y.C., Apr. 15, 1935; d. Lynward Roosevelt and Sarah Ellen (Grevious) W.; 1 child, Percy Scott. BA, Morgan State Coll., 1957; MLS, Pratt Inst., 1960; grad. profl. seminar, U. Md., 1973. Cert. profl. librarian. With Bklyn. Pub. Libr., 1957-68; head extension svcs. New Rochelle (N.Y.) Pub. Libr., 1969-70; br. adminstr. Grinton Will Yonkers (N.Y.) Pub. Libr., 1970-75; dir. Yonkers Pub. Libr., 1975-96; mem. adj. faculty grad. libr. studies Queens Coll., CUNY, 1989, 90. Mem. commr.'s com. Statewide Libr. Devel., Albany, N.Y., 1980; mem. N.Y. Gov.'s Commn. on Librs., 190, 91; bd. dirs. Community Planning Coun., Yonkers, N.Y., 1987; mem. Yonkers Black Women's Polit. Caucus, 1987; pres. bd. Literacy Vols. of Westchester County, 1991-92; mem. fair practices com. LWV, 1996—. Recipient Yonkers Citizen award Ch. of Our Saviour, 1980, 2d Ann. Mae Morgan Robinson award Yonkers chpt. Westchester Black Women's Polit. Caucus, 1992, 3d Ann. Equality Day award City of Yonkers, 1992, African-Am. Heritage 1st award YWCA, 1994; named Outstanding Profl. Woman Nat. Assn. Negro Bus. and Profl. Women's Clubs Inc., 1981. Mem. ALA (councilor 1987-91), N.Y. State Libr. Assn., Pub. Libr. Dirs. Assn. (exec. bd.), N.Y. State Pub. Libr. Dirs. Assn., Westchester Libr. Assn., Yonkers C. of C. (bd. dirs. 1992-95), Rotary (Yonkers chpt.).

MILLER, JANEL HOWELL, psychologist; b. Boone, N.C., May 18, 1947; d. John Estle and Grace Louise (Hemberger) Howell; BA, DePauw U., 1969; postgrad. Rice U., 1969; MA, U. Houston, 1972; PhD, Tex. A&M U., 1979; m. C. Rick Miller, Nov. 24, 1968; children: Kimberly, Brian, Audrey, Rachel. Asso. sch. psychologist Houston Ind. Sch. Dist., 1971-74; research psychologist VA Hosp., Houston, 1972; asso. sch. psychologist Clear Creek Ind. Sch. Dist., Tex., 1974-76; instr. psychology, counseling psychology intern Tex. A. and M. U., 1976-77; clin. psychology intern VA Hosp., Houston, 1977-78; coordinator psychol. services Clear Creek Ind. Sch. Dist., 1978-81, assoc. dir. psychol. services, 1981-82; pvt. practice, Houston, 1982—; faculty U. Houston-Clear Lake, 1984—; adolescent suicide cons., 1984—. DePauw U. Alumni scholar, 1965-69; NIMH fellow U. Houston, 1970-71; lic. clin. psychologist, sch. psychologist, Tex. Mem. APA, Tex. Psychol. Assn., Houston Psychol. Assn. (media rep. 1984-85), Am. Assn. Marriage and Family Therapists, Tex. Assn. Marriage and Family Therapists, Houston Assn. Marriage and Family Therapists, Soc. for Personality Assessment. Home: 806 Walbrook Dr Houston TX 77062-4030 Office: Southpoint Psychol Svcs 11550 Fuqua St Ste 450 Houston TX 77034-4537

MILLER, JEAN PATRICIA SALMON, art educator; b. Little Falls, Minn., Sept. 28, 1920; d. Albert Michael and Wilma (Kaestner) Salmon; m. George Fricke Miller, Sept. 8, 1951 (dec. Apr. 1991); children: Victoria Jean, George Laurids. BS, St. Cloud State Tchrs. Coll., 1942; MS, U. Wis., Whitewater, 1976. Lic. cert. secondary English, art, Wis. Tchr. elem. and secondary art Pub. Schs. Sauk Center, Minn., 1943; tchr. secondary art Bd. Edn., Idaho, 1945; tchr. elem. and secondary art Elkhorn (Wis.) Area Schs., 1950-78; tchr. art adult edn. Kenosha Tech. Coll., Elkhorn, Wis., 1969; cooperating tchr., supr. art majors in edn. U. Wis., Whitewater, 1970-77; coord. Art Train Project, Madison. Represented in permanent collections Irwin L. Young Auditorium, Fern Young Ter., U. Wis., Whitewater. Sec. Walworth County Needs of Children and Youth, Williams Bay, Wis., 1956-57; co-chair, sponsor Senate Bill 161-art requirement for h.s. grad., 1988-89. Recipient Grand award painting Walworth County Fair, 1970, 3rd award painting Geneva Lake Art Assn., Lake Geneva, Wis., Acrylic Painting First award Badlants Art Assn., 1994. Mem. Nat. Art Edn. Assn., Wis. Women in the Arts, Wis. Art Edn. Assn., Wis. Regional Artists Assn. (co-chair Wis. regional art program 1992, 93, corr. sec. 1992—), Walworth County Art Assn. (bd. dirs. 1979-94, pres. 1986-87), Alpha Delta Kappa (pres. Theta chpt. Wis. 1968-70). Home and Office: 671 24th St W Apt 8 Dickinson ND 58601

MILLER, JEANETTE ALLISON, educator; b. Oklahoma City, Okla., Sept. 1, 1964; d. Jimmie Mack and Charlotte Annette (Mosley) Rogers; m. Glen Dean Miller, Oct. 20, 1990; children: Taylor Dean, Jordan Ian. BS, Ctrl. State U., 1986; MS, Okla. State U., 1995. Instr. cosmetology Tri County Tech., Bartlesville, Okla., 1987—. Author: Basic Facialist, 1989, Facial Specialty, 1990. Recipient Bartlesville Golden Apple award Bartlesviles C. of C., 1995. Mem. Am. Vocat. Assn., Nat. Cosmetology Assn., Okla. Vocat. Assn. (sec./treas. trade & indsl. edn. 1987-94, pres.- elect 1994—), Okla. Cosmetology Assn., Iota Lambda Sigma. Baptist. Office: Tri County Tech 6101 SE Nowata Rd Bartlesville OK 74006

MILLER, JEANNE-MARIE ANDERSON (MRS. NATHAN J. MILLER), English language educator, academic administrator; b. Washington, Feb. 18, 1937; d. William and Agnes Catherine (Johns) Anderson m. Nathan John Miller, Oct. 2, 1960. BA, Howard U., 1959, MA, 1963, PhD, 1976. Instr. dept. English Howard U., Washington, 1963-76, asst. prof., 1976-79, assoc. prof., 1979-92, prof., 1992—, also asst. dir. Inst. Arts and Humanities, 1973-75, asst. acad. planning, office v.p. for acad. affairs, 1976-90; cons. Am. Studies Assn., 1972-75, Silver Burdett Pub. Co., Nat. Endowment for Humanities, 1978—; adv. bd. D.C. Libr. for Arts, 1973—, John Oliver Killens Writers Guild, 1975—, Afro-Am. Theatre, Balt., 1975—. Editor, Black Theatre Bull., 1977-86; Realism to Ritual: Form and Style in Black Theatre, 1983; assoc. editor Theatre Jour., 1980-81; contbr. articles to profl. jours. Mem. Washington Performing Arts Soc., 1971—, Friends of Sta. WETA-TV, 1971—, Mus. African Art, 1971—, Arena Stage Assos., 1972—, Washington Opera Guild, 1982—, Wolf Trap Assocs., 1982—, Drama League N.Y., 1995—. Ford Found. fellow, 1970-72, So. Fellowships Fund fellow, 1973-74; Howard U. rsch. grantee, 1975-76, 94-95, 96-97, ACLS grantee, 1978-79, NEH grantee, 1981-84. Mem. AAUP, ACLU, MLA, Nat. Coun. Tchrs. English, Coll. English Assn., Am. Studies Assn., Assn. for Theatre in Higher Edn., D.C. LWV, Common Cause, Am. Acad. Polit. and Social Sci., Coll. Lang. Assn., Am. Assn. Higher Edn., Nat. Assn. Women Deans, Adminstrs. and Counselors, Friends of Kennedy Ctr. for Performing Arts, Pi Lambda Theta. Democrat. Episcopalian. Home: 504 24th St NE Washington DC 20002-4818

MILLER, JO CAROLYN DENDY, family and marriage counselor, educator; b. Gorman, Tex., Sept. 16, 1942; d. Leonard Lee and Vera Vertie (Robison) Dendy; m. Douglas Terry Barnes, June 1, 1963 (div. June 1975); children: Douglas Alan, Bradley Jason; m. Walton Sansom Miller, Sept. 19, 1982. BA, Tarleton State U., 1964; MEd, U. North State, 1977; PhD, Tex. Women's U., 1993. Tchr., Mineral Wells (Tex.) High Sch., 1964-65, Weatherford (Tex.) Middle Sch., 1969-74; counselor, instr. psychology Tarrant County Jr. Coll., Hurst, Tex., 1977-82; pvt. practice family and marriage counseling, Dallas, 1982—. Author: (with Velma Walker, Jeannene Ward) Becoming: A Human Relations Workbook, 1981. Mem. ACA, Tex. State Bd. Examiners Profl. Counselors, Tex. State Bd. Marriage and Family Therapists, Tex. Counseling Assn., Am. Mental Health Counselors Assn., North Ctrl. Tex. Counseling Assn., Dallas Symphony Orch. League, Nat. Coun. Family Rels., Tex. Mental Health Counselors Assn., Internat. Assn. for Marriage & Family Counselors. Methodist. Office: Counseling & Consulting of North Dallas 8222 Douglas Ave Ste 777 Dallas TX 75225-5938

MILLER, JOANNE LOUISE, middle school educator; b. Milton, Mass., Apr. 4, 1944; d. Joseph Louis and Marion Theresa (Saulnier) Fasci; m. William Frederick Miller, Dec. 4, 1962; 1 child, Robert Joseph. BS, U. Oreg., 1972, MS in Curriculum and Instrn., 1973; EdD, Brigham Young U., 1980; postgrad., Oreg. State U., 1995. Lic. counselor, tchr., adminstr., Oreg. Tchr. South Lane Sch. Dist., Cottage Grove, Oreg., 1973—, lang. arts div. chairperson, 1975-78, 89-90, reading coord., 1978-79, 7th grade block chairperson, 1982-92, mid. sch. talented and gifted coord., 1992-93, counselor, 1991-93; mem. Oreg. State Assessment Content Panel Reading, Salem, 1987-88; mem. Oreg. Lang Arts Curriculum Devel. Com., Salem, 1985-87; del. to Citizen Amb. Program of People to People Internat. 1st U.S.-Russia Joint Conf. on Edn., Moscow, 1994. Vol. Am. Cancer Soc., Am. Diabetes Assn., 1990—. Mem. ACA, NEA, Internat. Reading Assn., Am. Sch. Counselor Assn., Oreg. Counseling Assn., Oreg. Edn. Assn., South Lane Edn. Assn., Oreg. Reading Assn., Delta Kappa Gamma, Alpha Rho State (v.p. 1995—). Democrat. Roman Catholic. Home: 85515 Appletree Dr Eugene OR 97405-9738 Office: Lincoln Mid Sch 1565 S 4th St Cottage Grove OR 97424-2955

MILLER, JUDITH ANN, elementary education educator; b. Chgo., Dec. 16, 1956; d. Clarence William and Jean E. Miller; children: Carey Michael, Rachael Marie. BA, Nat. Coll. Edn., 1978. Cert. tchr., Ill. Buyer, mgr. Learning Village Store, Chgo., 1977-80; adminstrv. and tech. cons. Chatham Bus. Assn., Chgo., 1980-81; adminstrv. asst. Chatham-Avalon Local Devel. Corp., Chgo., 1981-82; dir. Devel. Inst., Chgo., 1983-85; sub-tchr. Chgo. Bd. Edn., 1985-87; cadre tchr. John J. Pershing Magnet Sch., Chgo., 1987-88;

tchr. Charles N. Holden Sch., Chgo., 1988—; master tchr. Columbia Coll. Sci. Inst., Chgo., 1992—. V.p. parent aux. bd. Link Unltd., Chgo., 1992-94. Mem. Chgo. Tchrs. Union, Ill. Fedn. Tchrs., Alpha Kappa Alpha. Roman Catholic. Office: Charles N Holden Sch 1104 W 31st St Chicago IL 60608-5602

MILLER, KAREN LYNN, clinical social worker; b. Trenton, Mo., Mar. 3, 1956; d. Arthur Leon and JoAnn (Ellis) Sawyer; m. Stuart W. Miller, May 31, 1975; children: Matthew A., and Michael A. AA, Longview C.C., Lees Summit, Mo., 1992; BSW, Ctrl. Mo. State U., 1994; postgrad. in social work, U. Kans., 1994—. Accts. payable clk. Panhandle Ea. Pipeline, Kansas City, Mo., 1975-81; hairdresser The Hairdresser, Independence, Mo., 1984-87; self employed hairdresser Independence, 1987-93, 94-95; case mgr. intern Hope House, Independence, 1994; clin. social worker, intern Heart Am. Family Svcs., Kansas City, 1994—, Western Mo. Mental Health Ctr., Kansas City, 1989—; vol. hotline Hope House Battered Women's Shelter, Independence, 1989—; mem. adv. bd. home econs. dept. Independence Schs., 1990—. Vol. Juvenile Family Ct., Kansas City; sec. Assn. S.W. Students Ctrl. Mo. State U., 1992-93. Mem. Nat. Assn. S.W., Phi Alpha (sec. 1994—), Phi Theta Kappa. Home: 4815 S Kendall Dr Independence MO 64055-5344

MILLER, KAREN MARIE, county commissioner; b. Gary, Ind., Aug. 20, 1952; d. Donald Dean and Geraldine Joan (Inderski) Childress; m. Ronald Russell Miller, July 30, 1972 (div. July 1980); 1 child, Russell Dean (dec. Dec. 1975). Grad. H.S., Memphis, Mo. Lic. real estate broker Mo. Real Estate Commn. Counter staff Hi-Ho Drive Inn, Kirksville, Mo., 1971-72; bookkeeper Feese Automotive, Kirksville, 1972-74; waitress Gaspers Restaurant, Kingdom City, Mo., 1974-76; office mgr. Wulff Bros. Masonry, Columbia, Mo., 1976-79; lounge mgr. Holiday Inn West, Columbia, 1979-82; restauranteur The Establishment, Columbia, 1982-93; commr. Boone County, Columbia, 1993—; pres. Columbia/Mid-Mo. Restaurant Assn., 1984; state dir. Mo. Restaurant Assn., Kansas City, 1985-92. Author (weekly column) Boone County Jour., 1993—. Dir. Columbia (Mo.) Quaterback Club, 1985-89, Cedar Creek Therapeutic Riding Ctr., Columbia, 1992-93; mem. Boone County Muleskinners/Ctrl. Com., Columbia, 1992—, Nat. Dem. County Ofcl., Columbia, 1993—. Named Restauranteur of Yr., Columbia/Mid-Mo. Chpt. Restaurant Assn., 1985, Democrat of the Month, Boone County Muleskinners, Columbia, 1991. Mem. Nat. Assn. Counties (nat. dir. 1995—), Mo. Commn. on Intergovtl. Coop. (appointee 1995—), Mo. Assn. Counties (state dir. 1995—), County Commrs. Assn. State of Mo., Balloon Fedn. Am., Elks. Roman Catholic. Home: 2700 Northridge Columbia MO 65202-2140 Office: Boone County Commn 801 East Walnut Rm #245 Columbia MO 65201-4890

MILLER, KATHRYN ANN JUDKINS, counselor educator, research consultant; b. San Antonio, Tex., Dec. 23, 1964; d. Kennard Francis and Ethelyn Beth (Miller) Judkins. BA, U. Tex., San Antonio, 1985; MS, St. Mary's U., San Antonio, 1989, PhD, 1995. Lic. profl. counselor, 1994, counselor supr., 1995. Test editor The Psychological Corp., San Antonio, 1986-89; instrnl. devel. Eagle Tech., San Antonio, 1989-90; career counselor St. Mary's U., San Antonio, 1994-95; counselor Bexar County Women's Ctr., San Antonio, 1991-95; counselor, cons. Kathryn Miller, PhD & Assocs., 1995—; instr. St. Philip's Coll., San Antonio, San Antonio Coll., U. Tex., San Antonio, 1990—; asst. prof. S.W. Tex. State U., 1996—. Mem. ACA, Tex. Counseling Assn., Assn. for Counselor Edn. and Supervision, Tex. Assn. for Counselor Edn. and Supervision, Tex. Jr. Coll. Tchrs. Assn. Home: 10866 Lake Path San Antonio TX 78217

MILLER, KIM ANN, mental health nurse; b. North Tonawanda, N.Y., Oct. 23, 1957; d. John Walter and Helen May (Hartman) Jakopac; children: Katherine Rose Miller. ASN, Clarion U. Pa., 1990, BSN, 1993. RN, Pa.; cert. mental health nursing ANCC. Mental health nurse child-adolescent unit Clarion (Pa.) Psychiat. Ctr., 1990-91, St. Vincent Health Ctr., Erie, Pa., 1991-93, Braddock (Pa.) Med. Ctr., 1993-95; staff nurse Ctr. for Treatment of Addictive Disorders and acute psychiat. unit. VA Med. Ctr., Pitts., 1995—. Co-author: Potential for General Systems, 1993. Mem. Hillcrest United Presbyn. Ch., Monroeville, Pa., 1994; participant Crop Walk For Second Harrest Greater Pitts. Cmty. Food Bank. Mem. Phi Eta Sigma, Phi Theta Kappa, Sigma Theta Tau. Democrat. Presbyterian. Home: Apt D-6 3952 Monroeville Blvd Monroeville PA 15146-2419 Office: VA Med Ctr Highland Dr Pittsburgh PA 15206

MILLER, KUBY SUSIE, dance and modeling school owner; b. Romal, Italy, May 14, 1954; d. Stephen and Josette (Jorma) Kuby; m. Lyle G. Miller, Nov. 14, 1988. Grad. high sch., Madison, Wis. Dancer Royal Ballet, London, 1964-70; model Lynette Berit, Paris, 1967-69; dancer Ballet Repertoire, N.Y.C., 1970-75, Southeast Dancing Co., N.Y.C., 1975-76, Bulter Jazz Co., Salt Lake City, 1976-77, Music Ctr., Salt Lake City, 1977-78, Utah Ballet Co., Salt Lake City, 1979-85; model Channel Runway, Paris, 1986-87; dancer Musical Theater Fine Arts, Salt Lake City, 1988-89, TCG Theatre Group, 1993-94, Accop Arts USA, 1994—. Bd. dirs. Mus. Theaters, Salt Lake City, 1988-89, Ballet Dept., Salt Lake City, 1989-90, Susie's Dancing Co., Salt Lake City, 1990—, Susie's Modeling Co., Salt Lake City, 1990-92; mem. Back Stage West, 1994-96, Top Model, 1996, Wake Adoption, North Falmouth, 1991, Nat. Abortion Rights Action League, Salt Lake City, 1990, Nat. Wildlife Fedn., Salt Lake City, 1991. Mem. Theatre Critics (honor 1991), N.Y. Theatre. Home and Office: 273 East 2100 South Salt Lake City UT 84115

MILLER, LAURA ANN, linguistic anthropologist, educator; b. L.A., Dec. 15, 1953; d. Walter Eugene Carlos Valdez-Miller; m. Roland John Erwin, 1988. BA, U. Calif., Santa Barbara, 1977; MA, UCLA, 1983, PhD, 1988. Cert. (life) community coll. instr., Calif. Sr. English instr. Teijin Ednl. Systems Co., Osaka, Japan, 1978-81; teaching asst. UCLA, 1983-84, teaching fellow, 1986-87; asst. prof. Phila. Coll. Textiles and Sci., 1990-93; vis. asst. prof. U. Pa., Phila., 1993-95; asst. prof. Loyola U., Chgo., 1995—; lectr. Calif. State U., Dominiquez Hills, 1983-85, El Camino Community Coll., Torrance, Calif., 1986, U. Pa., Phila., summers 1989, 90, 91, 92; vis. asst. prof. Temple U., Phila., 1990; project coord. Nat. Fgn. Lang. Ctr., Johns Hopkins U., Washington, 1989-92; Japanese instr. GE Aerospace, Moorestown, N.J., 1989, 91; Japan program cons. West Chester (Pa.) U., 1989; rsch. analyst ZEMI Corp., L.A., 1986; lang. analyst Japan Conv. Svcs., Tokyo, 1985; vis. faculty U. Pa., 1993-94. Editor: Jour. Asian Culture, 1984, assoc. editor, 1987; asst. editor: The American Asian Review, 1992-93, assoc. editor, 1993—; contbr. articles to profl. jours. Chair Act 101 Acad. Achievement Program, Phila., 1990-92; mem. Greater Phila. Internat. Network, 1990. Grantee Dept. Edn., 1972-73, UCLA, 1985; Nat. Resource fellow Dept. Edn., 1982-83, UCLA-Japan Exch. Program fellow, 1986-87. Fellow Am. Anthrop. Assn.; mem. Internat. Pragmatics Assn., Assn. for Asian Studies, Assn. for Japanese Bus. Studies, Soc. for Applied Anthropology, Soc. for Linguistic Anthropology. Home: 1544 W Estes Chicago IL 60626 Office: Loyola U Chgo Dept Sociology/Anthropology 6525 Sheridan Rd Chicago IL 60626

MILLER, LENORE, labor union official; b. Union City, N.J., Mar. 10, 1932; d. Louis and Lillian (Bergen) Shapiro; m. Louis Miller, Dec. 25, 1952; 1 child, Jessica. BA, Rutgers U., 1952; postgrad., Purdue U., 1952-56, New Sch. Social Research, 1957. Sec., asst. to pres. Panel of Ams.; sec., asst. to pres. Retail, Wholesale & Dept. Store Union, AFL-CIO, CLC, N.Y.C., 1958-78, v.p., 1978-80, sec.-treas., 1980-86, pres., 1986—; vice chair civil rights com. AFL-CIO, 1990-95, chair occupl. safety and health com., 1996—; exec. bd. AFL-CIO Indsl. Union Dept., Washington, 1980-82, AFL-CIO Food & Beverage Trades Dept., Washington, 1980—, Maritime Trades Dept., 1986; v.p. Transp. Trades Dept. AFL-CIO, 1992—; vice-chmn. Nat. Trade Union Coun. for Human Rights, N.Y.C., 1980—; mem. Nat. BD. Workers Def. League, N.Y.C., 1980—, Pres. Commn. Tariff & Trade, 1994—; mem. com. Am. Trade Union Coun. for Histadrut & Afro-Asian Inst., N.Y.C., 1980—; chmn. RWDSU Welfare and Pension Plan, 1986—. Bd. dirs. A. Philip Randolph Inst. Fund, 1988; chair Cen. Labor Rehab. Coun. N.Y., Grand Marshall Labor Day Parade; charter trustee Rutgers U., 1988-94; pres. Jewish Labor Com., 1989—; mem. platform com. Dem. Nat. Conv., del. 1992, 96; mem. Dem. Nat. Com., 1993—; mem. Pres. Commn. on Family and Med. Leave, 1993-96. Named to Acad. of Women Achievers YWCA, 1987. Mem. AFL-CIO (v.p. 1987—, mem. exec. coun.), Douglass Soc. Office: Retail Wholesale & Dept Store Union AFL-CIO CLC 30 E 29th St Fl 4 New York NY 10016-7925

MILLER, LILLIE M., nursing educator; b. Atlanta, Nov. 16, 1937; d. George W. and Lillie M. (Reese) McDaniel; m. Harold G. Miller, June 30, 1962; children: Daren K., Lisa K. Diploma in nursing, Jewish Hosp. of Cin., 1959; BSN, U. Cin., 1961; MEd, Temple U., 1970; MSN, Villanova U., 1987. RN, Pa.; cert. sch. nurse, cert. clin. specialist in med.-surg. nursing ANCC. Instr. sch. nursing Jewish Hosp. Cin., 1959-62; instr. Phila. Gen. Hosp. Sch. Nursing, 1962-67; sch. nurse Norristown (Pa.) Area Sch. Dist., 1967-70; nursing instr. Villanova U., Villanova, Pa., 1988; asst. prof. Montgomery County C.C., Blue Bell, Pa., 1983-93, assoc. prof, 1993—; advisor Student Nurses Assn. Pa. Recipient Pi Tau Delta scholarship, Chapel of Four Chaplains. Mem. ANA, Nat. League for Nursing, Pa. League for Nursing, Jewish Hosp. Alumni Assn., Temple U. Alumni Assn., Villanova U. Alumni Assn., Sigma Theta Tau.

MILLER, LINDA ELLEN, museum administrator, education expert; b. Paterson, N.J., Aug. 31, 1947; d. Edward E. and Flora M. (Christen) Douglas; m. Philip R. Miller, Sept. 19, 1970; 1 child, Douglas Scott. BA in Human Resource Mgmt., Upsala Coll., 1983; MS in Mus. Leadership and Edn., Bank St. Coll. Edn., 1992. Curator of edn. Old Barracks, Trenton, N.J., 1989-92; educator Kaleidoscope Kids Program N.J. State Mus., Trenton, 1992-93; curator edn. Clinton (N.J.) Hist. Mus., 1993-95; curator, adminstr. Vernon Twp. (N.J.) Hist. Mus., 1995—. Mem. Am. Assn. Mus. (nat. edn. com.), Mus. Edn. Roundtable, N.J. Assn. Mus., League of Hist. Socs. of N.J. (chmn. edn. com., trustee 1994—), N.J. Studies Acad. Alliance (steering com. 1993-94). Home: 517 Retreat Dr Highland Lakes NJ 07422 Office: Vernon Twp Hist Soc Vernon Twp Mcpl Complex Church St Vernon NJ 07462

MILLER, LINDA LOU, association executive, communications specialist; b. Pottsville, Pa., Feb. 5, 1955; d. Cletus Isaac and Erma Ruth (Brown) M.; m. William Joseph Murray Jr., July 23, 1989; 1 stepchild, Nathan Andrew. BA, Shippensburg (Pa.) U., 1977. Copywriter, media buyer Williams & Assocs., Harrisburg, Pa., 1977-78; dir. communications Pa. Newspaper Pub.'s Assn., Harrisburg, 1978-82; dir. alumni affairs Shippensburg U. Pa., 1982-85; exec. v.p. Pa. Soc. Assn. Execs., Harrisburg, 1985-90; dir. communications The Milton Hershey (Pa.) Sch., 1990—. Sec. Kimberley Meadows Civic Assn., Mechanicsburg, Pa., 1990; adv. coun. Shippensburg U, 1990; pers. chair Chapel Hill United Ch. of Christ, 1992-94, ops. commn., 1992—; mem. Milton Hershey Postage Stamp Celebration Com., 1995. Mem. NAFE, Pa. Soc. Assn. Execs., Ctrl. Pa. Assn. Profl. Women, Coun. for Advancement and Support of Edn., Am. Soc. Assn. Execs. (bd. dirs. 1989, cert.), Conf. Assn. Soc. Execs. (pres. 1988-89), Allied Socs. Coun. (chmn. 1988-89), Exec. Club of Ctrl. Pa. (bd. dirs. 1988-90), Rotary Club. Home: 27 Conway Dr Mechanicsburg PA 17055-6136 Office: The Milton Hershey Sch Rt 322 And Homestead Ln Hershey PA 17033

MILLER, LISA ELLEN, university development director; b. Cleve., Jan. 21, 1964; d. William Fleek and Ellen Reeder M.; 1 child, Morgan Ellen. BS in Econs., Ohio State U., 1989. Rsch. assoc. Ohio State U., Columbus, 1992-95, dir. devel. rsch., 1995—; rsch. cons. Nature Conservancy, Columbus, Ohio, 1996. Vol. Counsel for Urban Peace and Justice, Granville, Ohio, 1993-95. Mem. Assn. Profl. Rechrs. for Advancement, Ohio Prospect Rsch. Network (v.p. 1996—). Methodist. Office: Ohio State U Univ Devel 2400 Olentangy Rd Rm 114 Columbus OH 43210

MILLER, LIZ RODRIGUEZ, public library system director, librarian; b. Tucson, Feb. 22, 1954; d. Tony S. Martinez and Maria (Corral) Rodriguez; m. Marc Alan Miller, Nov. 5, 1972; children: Andrea Eve, Matthew Luke, Meredith C. BA in Spanish, U. Ariz., 1976, MLS, 1978. Unit mgr. S. Tuscon Libr., 1978-80; activities coord. community cable com. City of Tuscon, 1980; info./reference mgr. Tuscon Pub. Libr., 1981-84, agy. mgr., 1984-85, regional mgr., 1985-87, asst. dir. pub. svcs., 1987-89; dep. exec. dir. divsn. ALA Libr. Adminstrn. & Mgmt. Assn., Chgo., 1990; dep. dir. Tuscon Pima Libr., 1990-91, libr. dir., 1991—. Co-editor: Great Library Propotion Ideas V, 1990; contbr. articles to profl. jours. Mem. adv. bd. libr. power grant Tuscon Unified Sch. Dist., 1992—; bd. dirs. Tuscon area Literacy Coalition, 1992—; active Hispanic Profl. Action Com., 1992—. Mem. ALA (mem. pres. program com. 1987, mem. nominating com. 1991-93), REFORMA (chair elections com. 1983-84, 85, chair conf. program 1987, pres. 1987-88), Am. Soc. Pub. Adminstrn., Libr. Adminstrn. and Mgmt. Assn. (mem. cultural diversity com. 1991-92, chair 1992-93, mem. nominating com. 1992-93), Pub. Libr. Assn. (mem. Pub. Libr. Assn.-Libr. Adminstrn. and Mgmt. Assn. cert. com. 1991-92, chair 1992-93, chair Allie Beth Martin Award com. 1987-88, mem. 1989), Ariz. State Libr. Assn. (chair svcs. to Spanish-speaking Roundtable 1980-82, pres. pub. libr. divsn. 1984-85, chair ann. conf. 1986), U. Ariz. Hispanic Alumni Assn., Beta Phi Mu. Office: Tucson Pima Library PO Box 27470 101 N Stone Ave Tucson AZ 85726-7470*

MILLER, LOANN M., marketing consultant; b. Dickinson, ND, Aug. 23, 1961; d. Wallace Frank and Judith Yvonne (Hutmacher) Roshau; m. Mark Anthony Charchenko, Aug. 15, 1980 (dec. May 1990); children: Aften, Cameron, Celeste; m. Michael David Miller, May 24, 1991; 1 child, Michael Jr. Degree in secretarial arts, Dickinson State U., 1980. Exec. dir. Dickinson Conv. and Visitor's Bur., 1988-91; dir. comms. Garrison Diversion Conservancy Dist., Carrington, N.D., 1991-92; v.p. programs Bismarck(N.D.)-Mandan C. of C., 1992; asst. v.p. mktg., ops. Farmers & Merchants Bank, Beach, N.D., 1992-95; mktg., planning coord. St. Joseph's Hosp. and Health Ctr., Dickinson, 1995—.

MILLER, LORRAINE, business owner. BA in History, U. Utah. Lab. technician U. Utah Med. Ctr., 1972-75; pres. Cactus & Tropicals, Inc., Salt Lake City, 1975—; mem. adv. bd. Utah Securities Commn., 1994; panelist Am. Arbitration Assn., 1991; pres., bd. dirs. Phoenix Inst., 1986-87. Vol. VISTA, 1966-69; mem. Gov.'s Task Force Entrepreneurism, 1988, Gov.'s Task Force Work Force Devel., 1994; mentor Women's Network Entrepreneurial Tng., Small Bus. Adminstrn., 1990; mem. adv. bd. Utah Dem. Health Care Task Force, 1991, Women's Bus. Devel. Office State of Utah, 1990-92; employer Supportive Employment for the Handicapped, 1990-92. Recipient Pathfinder award Salt Lake C. of C., 1986, Women of Achievement award YWCA, 1992; named Nat. Small Bus. Person of Yr. by U.S. Small Bus. Adminstrn., 1994. Mem. Nat. Assn. Women's Bus. Owners (pres. Salt Lake chpt. 1992), Utah Assn. Women's Bus. Owners (pres. 1992, 1st v.p. 1991, bd. dirs. 1985, 89-90, named Woman Bus. Owner of Yr. 1987), Wasatch Cactus & Succulent Soc. (co-founder). Office: Cactus & Tropicals of Utah 2735 S 20th St E Salt Lake City UT 84109

MILLER, LOUISE DEAN, writer, retired journalist; b. Lubbock, Tex., Dec. 10, 1921; d. Arlie David and Ludie Lee (Hart) Dean; m. Mickey Lester Miller, Aug. 30, 1946; children: Linda Miller Kelly, Lee Miller Parks, Lynne Miller Carson. BA in Journalism, Tex. Woman's U., 1943, BS in Journalism, 1943. Gen. reporter Vernon (Tex.) Daily Record, 1943-4; feature gen. reporter Tinker AFB Paper, Oklahoma City, 1944-46; women's editor Albuquerque Tribune, 1946-48; writer Albuquerque Pub. Schs., 1967-68; program dir. Young Women's Christian Assn., Albuquerque, 1970-72; newspaper columnist Albuquerque Jour., 1972-87. Author, editor: The Book of Windows, 1990; co-author, editor: Administration of Secondary Athletics, 1991. Sec.-treas. El Vado (N.Mex.) Cabin Owners Assn., 1977-95. Mem. AAUW (pres. 1964-66, sec. N.Mex. div. 1989-93), Soc. Profl. Journalists, Women in Comms. (Albuquerque chpt. pres. 1968-70). Democrat. Methodist. Home: 1201 Richmond Dr NE Albuquerque NM 87106-2023

MILLER, LYNDA LOU, school system administrator; b. Lansing, Mich., Sept. 18, 1946; d. Charles F. and Jane E. Howald; m. Monte R. Miller, Aug. 11, 1968; children: Shawn A., Kourtney A. BS in Edn., Emporia State U., 1968, MS in Edn., 1987, administration cert., 1994. Art tchr. Jardine Jr. H.S., Topeka, Kans., 1968-72, Jardine Mid. Sch., Topeka, 1981-84; counselor Topeka Pub. Sch. Fgn. Studies Program, 1984 (summer); art tchr., dept. chair Topeka West H.S., 1985-94; co-chair North Ctrl. Outcomes Based Accreditation Team, 1991-96; curriculum coord. Highland Park H.S., Topeka, 1994—; tennis coach Topeka West High Sch., 1985-87; presenter numerous confs. Author: (with T. Steinlage and M. Printz) Cultural Cobblestones: Teaching Cultural Diversity, 1994; contbr. articles to profl. jours. Bd. trustees Emporia State U. Alumni. Recipient Kans. Regional Scholastic Congl. award, 1993; named Topeka Tchr. of Yr., 1990, Disting. Secondary Tchr. of Yr., 1990. Mem. ASCD, Nat. Art Edn. Assn., Kans. Art Edn. Assn., Kans. Bus. Edn. Assn., Emporia State U. Alumni Assn. (Topeka chpt.), Topeka Art Guild, Phi Delta Kappa. Office: Highland Park High Sch 2424 SE California Ave Topeka KS 66605-1760

MILLER, LYNNE MARIE, environmental company executive; b. N.Y.C., Aug. 4, 1951; d. David Jr. and Evelyn (Gulbransen) M. AB, Wellesley Coll., 1973; MS, Rutgers U., 1976. Analyst Franklin Inst., Phila., 1976-78; dir. hazardous waste div. Clement Assocs., Washington, 1978-81; pres. Risk Sci. Internat., Washington, 1981-86, Environ. Strategies Corp., Vienna, Va., 1986—, Environ. Strategies Ltd., London, 1986—. Editor: Insurance Claims for Environmental Damages, 1989, editor-in-chief Environ. Claims Jour.; contbr. chpts. to books. Named Ins. Woman of Yr. Assn. Profl. Ins. Women, 1983. Mem. AAAS, Am. Cons. Engrs. Coun., N.Y. Acad. Sci., Washington Wellesley Club, Wellesley Bus. Leadership Coun. Office: Environ Strategies Corp 11911 Freedom Dr Ste 900 Reston VA 22090-5602

MILLER, M. JOY, financial planner, real estate broker; b. Enid, Okla., Dec. 29, 1934; d. H. Lee and M.E. Madge (Hatfield) Miller; m. Richard L.D. Berlemann, July 21, 1957 (div. Nov. 1974); children: Richard Louis, Randolph Lee. BSBA, N.Mex. State U., 1956. Cert. fin. planner; grad. Realtors Inst. Tchr. of bus. and mathematics Alamogordo (N.Mex.), Las Cruces (N. Mex.) and Omaha Pub. Schs., 1956-63; tchr., dir. Evelyn Wood Reading Dynamics Southern N.Mex. Inst., 1967-68; registered rep. Westamerica Fin. Corp., Denver, 1968-76; gen. agt. Security Benefit Life, Topeka, 1969—, Delta Life & Annuity, Memphis, 1969—; registered rep. Am. Growth Fund Sponsors, Inc., Denver, 1976—; pres., broker Fin. Design Corp. R.E., Las Cruces, 1977—; official goodwill ambassador of U.S. Treasury, U.S. Savs. Bond Div., Washington, 1968-70. Contbr. articles to profl. jours. Vice pres. Dona Ana County Fedn. Rep. Women. Recipient Top Sales Person award Investment Trust and Assurance, 1976-77. Fellow Life Underwriting Tng. Coun.; mem. Nat. Assn. Realtors, Nat. Assn. Life Underwriters, Internat. Bd. CFP's, Internat. Assn. Registered Fin. Planners, S.W. N.Mex. Assn. Life Underwriters (treas. 1990-91, pres.-elect 1991-92, pres. 1992-93), Las Cruces City Alumnae Panhellenic, Altrusa, Order Ea. Star, Delta Zeta Alumnae. Presbyterian. Home: 1304 Wolf Trl Las Cruces NM 88001-2357 Office: Fin Design Corp PO Box 577 Las Cruces NM 88004-0577

MILLER, MARCIA E., legislative counselor. BA, Miami U., 1977; MA, Johns Hopkins U., 1981. With internat. trade divsn. Am. Textile Mfrs. Inst.; internat. economist Wilmer, Cutler & Pickering, 1985-87; profl. staff mem. Senate Com. on Fin., 1987-93, chief internat. trade counsellor, 1993-95, minority chief internat. trade counsellor, 1995—. Office: Com on Fin 203 Senate Hart Office Bldg Washington DC 20510

MILLER, MARGARET ALISON, chief state academic officer; b. L.A., Dec. 17, 1944; d. Richard Crump and Virginia Margaret (Dudley) M.; m. Spencer Hall, Aug. 21, 1967 (div. 1977); 1 child, Justin Robinson; m. Alan Blair Howard, Oct. 7, 1990. BA, UCLA, 1966; postgrad., Stanford U., 1966-67; PhD, U. Va., 1971. English instr. U. Va., Charlottesville, 1971-72; prof. English U. Mass., North Dartmouth, 1972-86, co-dir. women's studies program, 1981-83, asst. to dean arts and scis., 1983-85, asst. to pres., 1985-86; acad. affairs coord. State Coun. Higher Edn. for Va., Richmond, 1986-87, assoc. dir. for acad. affairs, 1987—; cons. Coun. Rectors, Budapest, 1993, Minn. State U. System, Mpls., 1992, U.S. Dept. Edn., Washington, 1990-94, S.C. Higher Edn. Commn., 1989-90, Edn. Commn. States, Denver, 1994. Contbr. articles to profl. jours. Mem. Am. Assn. Higher Edn. (leadership coun.), Am. Coun. on Edn. (exec. com. identification program in Va. 1988—, participant nat. identification program's 41st nat. forum for women leaders in higher edn. 1989). Home: 2176 Lindsay Rd Gordonsville VA 22942-1620 Office: State Coun Higher Edn 101 N 14th St Fl 9 Richmond VA 23219-3684

MILLER, MARGARET JOANNE, pediatrics nurse; b. Rolette, N.D., Apr. 12, 1939; d. William J. and Nora (Slaubaugh) Graber; m. Ervin S. Miller, June 16, 1962; children: Charlene, Angela, Lisa. ASN, Vincennes U., 1960; student, St. Mary's-of-the-Woods Coll., Terre Haute, Ind., 1986-87, Ind. U., South Bend, 1989, Regents Coll., 1995-96. RN, Ind., Tex. Head nurse St. Joseph Mem. Hosp., Kokomo, Ind., 1975-77; asst. dir. Mennonite Mutul Aid, 1982 84; staff nurse Meml. Hosp., South Bend, Ind., 1984-87, asst. head nurse, 1987-89, asst. unit dir., 1989-91; unit dir. for pediatrics Med. Ctr. Hosp., Odessa, Tex., 1992—. Mem. Soc Pediatric Nurses. Home: 3411 Rocky Lane Rd Odessa TX 79762-5046

MILLER, MARILYN ANN, lawyer, mediator; m. Stephen A. Westlake; children: Eleanor, Michael Yeomans. BSEd, Syracuse U., 1967, MS in Counseling, 1968, postgrad., 1988—; JD cum laude, N.Y. Law Sch., 1979. Bar: N.Y. 1980, U.S. Dist. Ct. (so. dist.) N.Y. 1980. Counselor Plainfield (N.J.) H.S., 1968-76; student law clk. to Hon. Gerard L. Goettel, U.S. Dist. Ct. for So. Dist. N.Y., 1979; atty. U.S. Dept. Transp., 1979-80; pvt. practice Syracuse, N.Y., 1985-88; dir. career svcs. Coll. of Law Syracuse U., 1988-94, cons. alternative dispute resolution course, 1991—; pvt. practice law, mediator Syracuse, N.Y., 1994—; adj. prof. family mediation SUNY, Oswego, 1994—; speaker, presenter seminars Cayuga County Dispute Resolution Ctr.; acting justice Village of Fayetteville, 1993-96. Vol. mediator New Justice Svcs., Syracuse, 1989-94, Child Find Am., 1992—. Mem. N.Y. State Bar Assn., Onondaga County Bar Assn. (founder, co-chmn. alternative dispute resolution com. 1991—), Am. Arbitration Assn. (panel divorce arbitrators), Acad. Family Mediators, N.Y. State Coun. on Divorce Mediation. Home: Redfield Ave Fayetteville NY 13066 Office: 1221 E Genesee St Syracuse NY 13210-1913

MILLER, MARILYN LEA, library science educator. AA, Graceland Coll., 1950; BS in English, U. Kans., 1952; AMLS, U. Mich., 1959, PhD of Librarianship and Higher Edn., 1976. Bldg.-level sch. libr. Wellsville (Kans.) High Sch., 1952-54; tchr.-libr. Arthur Capper Jr. High Sch., Topeka, Kans., 1954-56; head libr. Topeka High Sch., 1956-62; sch. libr. cons. State of Kans. Dept. of Pub. Instrn., 1962-67; from asst. to assoc. prof. Sch. Librarianship Western Mich. U., Kalamazoo, 1967-77; assoc. prof. libr. sci. U. N.C., Chapel Hill, 1977-87; prof., chair dept. libr. and info. studies U. N.C., Greensboro, 1987-95, prof. emeritus, 1996—; vis. faculty Kans. State Tchrs., Emporia, 1960, 63, 64, 66, U. Minn., Mpls., 1971, U. Manitoba, Winnipeg, Can., 1971; vis. prof. Appalachian State U., Boone, N.C., 1987; mem. adv. bd. sch. libr. media program Nat. Ctr. for Ednl. Stats., 1989, mem. user rev. panel, 1990; chair assoc. dean search com. Sch. Edn., 1988, coord. Piedmont young writers conf., 1989-94, chair race and gender com., 1990-93, SACS planning and evaluation com., 1990, 91, learning resources ctr. adv. com., 1991-93; hearing panel for honor code U. N.C. Greensboro, 1988-91, assn. women faculty and administrv. staff, 1987—, faculty coun., 1987—, univ. libr. com., 1987-88, com. faculty devel. in race and gender scholarship, 1990-92; lectr. and cons. numerous confs., seminars in field. Mem. editorial bd. The Emergency Librarian, 1981 , Collection Building: Studies in the Development and Effective Use of Library Resources, 1978—; contbr. numerous chpts. to books, and articles to profl. jours., procs. and revs. Selected as one of four children's libr. specialists to visit Russian sch. and pub. librs., book pubs., Moscow, Leningrad, Tashkent, 1979; hon. del. White House Conf. on Libr. and Info. Svcs., Washington, 1991; head del. Romanian Summer Inst. on Librarianship in U.S., 1991; citizen amb. People to People Internat. Program, People's Republic of China, 1992, Russian and Poland, 1992, Russia, 1994, Barcelona, 1995. Recipient Freedom Found. medal, 1962, Disting. Svc. to Sch. Librs. award Kans. Assn. Sch. Librs., 1982, Disting. Svc. award Graceland Coll., 1992, Disting. Alumnus award Sch. Libr. and Info. Studies, U. Mich., 1988; Delta Kappa Gamma scholar, 1972. Mem. ALA (chair rsch. com., exec. dir. 1994, pres. 1992-93, adv. com. Nat. Ctr. Ednl. Stats. 1984, standing com. libr. edn. 1987-91, chair 1989-90, chair Chgo. conf. resolutions 1972, awards com. 1971-72, chair 1973-75, resolutions com. 1976-78, yearbook adv. com. 1988-90, Disting. Svc. award Am. Assn. Sch. Librs. 1993, other coms.), Am. Assn. Sch. Librs. (nominating com. 1980, pub. com. 1981-82, v.p.-pres.-elect 1985-86, chair search com. exec. dir. 1985, pres. 1986-87), Assn. for Ednl. Comms. and Tech., Assn. for Libr. and Info. Sci. Edn., Assn. of Libr. Svc. to Children (bd. dirs. 1976-81, pres. 1979-80, rsch. com. 1982-85, chair 1984-85, chair nominating com. 1984, other coms.), N.C. Libr. Assn. (edn. libr. com. 1978-80, 82-86, exec. bd. status of women roundtable 1989—), N.C. Assn. Sch. Librs., Southeastern Libr. Assn. (chair libr. educators sect. 1990-92), So. Assn. of Colls. and Schs. (mem. accreditation team 1988).

MILLER, MARTHA J., author, bank officer; b. Springfield, Ill., Dec. 21, 1947; d. Carl Edward and Geraldine (Drum) Thompson; m. Phillip Dale Miller, May 3, 1971 (div. Jan. 1989); children: Phillip Duane, Andrew Ryan. AA, Lincoln Land Coll., 1984; BA, U. Ill., 1996. Supr. data and check processing Bank One (formerly Marine Bank of Springfield, Ill.), 1973—. Contbr. stories and revs. to profl. publs.; performed various readings, Springfield area; produced plays MAPS Theater; writer monthly column The SALO Newsletter. Bd. dirs. Ill. Writers, Inc., 1994-96. Recipient Lincoln Libr. Writer of Yr. award, 1995; named Best Writer in Springfield, Ill. Times Readers poll, 1995. Office: Bank One Springfield 909 E Adams Springfield IL 62701

MILLER, MARY HELEN, retired public administrator; b. Smiths Grove, Ky., June 30, 1936; d. Walter Frank and Lottie Belle (Russell) Huddleston; m. George Ward Wilson, Sept. 12, 1958 (div. Sept. 1973); children: Ward Glenn, Amy Elizabeth Huddleston; m. Francis Guion Miller Jr., June 6, 1981. BA, Western Ky. U., 1958. Tchr. Fayette County Schs., Lexington, Ky., 1958-60, Seneca High Sch., Louisville, 1960-63, Shelby County High Sch., Shelbyville, Ky., 1963-69; rsch. analyst Legis. Rsch. Com., Frankfort, Ky., 1973-79, asst. dir., 1979-83, 90-91; chief exec. asst. Office Gov., Frankfort, 1983-87, 93-95, legis. liaison, 1991-93; cabinet sec. Natural Resources and Environ. Protection Cabinet, Frankfort, 1987-88; sales assoc. W. Wagner, Jr. Comml. Real Estate, Louisville, 1989-91; ret., 1996. Author: (constl. revision) Citizens Guide To/Perspective, 1978, (booklet) A Look at Kentucky General Assembly, 1979, A Guide to Education Reform, 1990, (handbook) Gubernatorial Transition in Kentucky, 1991. Active Leadership Ky. Alumni, Frankfort, 1986, Waterfront Devel. Corp. Bd., Louisville, 1986-87, Greater Louis Partnership Econ. Devel., 1988-92, Shelbyville 2000 Found. Bd., 1991-92; mem., sec. Regional Airport Authorty Bd., Louisville, 1986-89; pres. Shelby County Cmty. Theatre Bd., Shelbyville, 1989-90; active Ky. Long Term Policy Bd., 1992—, chair, 1995; active Ky. Hist. Properties Commn., 1995—; chair Shelby County Cmty. Found., 1995; active Ky. Applachian Commn., 1995-96. Mem. Pendennis Club, Jefferson Club. Democrat. Episcopalian. Home: 1116 Main St Shelbyville KY 40065-1420

MILLER, MARY HOTCHKISS, lay worker; b. Washington, Dec. 4, 1936; d. Neil and Esther LeMoyne (Helfer) H.; m. Ronald Homer Miller, May 20, 1961; 1 child, Timothy Ronald. BA, Western Md. Coll., 1958; MRE, Union Theol. Sem, 1960; Cert., Windham House, N.Y.C., 1960. Dir. Christian Edn. Bruton Parish ch., Williamsburg, Va., 1960-61; dir. Christian Edn. (part-time) All Saints Episcopal Ch., Bklyn., 1961-62; adminstrv. and program asst., Christian Social Rels. Dept., Exec. Coun. Episcopal Ch. U.S.A. Episcopal Ch. Ctr., N.Y.C., 1967-72; nat. treas., chmn. Episcopal Peace Fellowship, Washington, N.Y.C., 1972-85; exec. sec. Episcopal Peace Fellowship, Washington, 1989—; bd. dirs., exec. com. Nat. Campaign for Peace Tax Fund, Washington, 1989—; bd. dirs., consultative coun. Nat. Interreligious Svc. Bd. for COs, Washington, 1989—. Contbr. articles to Witness mag. and jours., newsletters in field; editl. bd. ISSUES of Gen. Convs. of the Episcopal Ch., 1973-91; designer ch. vestments and banners. Democrat. Office: PO Box 28156 Washington DC 20038-8156

MILLER, MILDRED, opera singer, recitalist; b. Cleve.; d. William and Elsa (Friedhofer) Mueller; m. Wesley W. Posvar, Apr. 30, 1950; children: Wesley, Margot Marina, Lisa Christina. MusB, Cleve. Inst. Music, 1946; hon. doctorate, Cleve. Ins. Music, 1983; artists' diploma, New England Conservatory Music, 1948, hon. doctorate, 1966; MusD (hon.), Bowling Green State U., 1960; hon. doctorate, Washington and Jefferson U., 1988. Founder, pres., artistic dir. Opera Theater of Pitts., 1978—; mem. music faculty Carnegie-Mellon U., 1996. Operatic debut in Peter Grimes, Tanglewood, 1946; appeared N.E. Opera Theater, Stuttgart State Theater, Germany, 1949-50, Glyndebourne Opera, Edinburgh Festival; debut as Cherubino in Figaro, Met. Opera, 1951; 23 consecutive seasons Met. Opera; radio debut Bell Telephone Hour; TV debut Voice of Firestone, 1952; appeared in films including Merry Wives of Windsor (filmed in Vienna), 1964; Vienna State Opera debut, 1963, appearances with San Francisco, Chgo. Lyric, Cin. Zoo, San Antonio, Berlin, Munich, Frankfurt, Pasadena, Ft. Worth, Kansas City, Pitts., Tulsa and St. Paul operas. Bd. dirs. Gateway to Music. Recipient Frank Huntington Beebe award for study abroad, 1949, 50, Grand Prix du Disque, 1965, Outstanding Achievements in Music award Boston C. of C., 1959, Ohioana Career medal, 1985, Outstanding Achievement in Opera award, Slippery Rock U., 1985, YWCA Ann. Tribute to Women award, 1989, Keystone Salute award Pa. Fedn. Music Clubs, 1994; named one of outstanding women of Pitts., Pitts. Press-Pitts. Post-Gazette, 1968, Person of Yr. in Music, Pitts. Jaycees, 1980. Mem. Nat. Soc. Arts and Letters (pres. 1989-90, Gold medal 1984), Disting. Daus. Pa. (pres. 1991-93), Tuesday Mus. Club, Phi Beta Kappa, Phi Delta Gamma, Sigma Alpha Iota. Office: PO Box 110108 Pittsburgh PA 15232-0608*

MILLER, MONICA JEANNE, public relations administrator; b. Laramie, Wyo., Mar. 18, 1948; d. R. Walt and Margaret Louise (Carroll) M.; m. Stephen Lee Spellman, June 3, 1973 (div. Aug. 1980); 1 child, Andrew M. French. BS cum laude in Journalism, U. Wyo., 1971. cert. food safety Nat. Restaurant Assn. Press officer Min. of Agr., Botswana, 1971-73; cmty. rels. officer Colo. Civil Rights Commn., Denver, 1973-80; chief info. officer Colo. Dept. Personnel, Denver, 1980-83, Colo. Divsn. Parks and Recreation, Denver, 1986-88; pub. rels. mgr. Unicover Corp., Cheyenne, Wyo., 1989-91, Taco John's Internat., Inc., Cheyenne, Wyo., 1991—; cons. The Promethean Corp., Denver, 1983-85. Author: (with others) Sexual Harassment in Public Employment, 1983. Dir. Children's Heritage Montessori Sch., Cheyenne, 1993-95, Wyo. Higher Edn. Assistance Authority, 1996—. Mem. ARC (High Plains chpt. dir. 1996—), Soc. Profl. Journalists, Pub. Rels. Soc. Am., Greater Cheyenne C. of C. (vice chair 1995—), Rotary (dir. 1996—). Democrat. Home: 6840 Bomar Dr Cheyenne WY 82009 Office: Taco John's Internat, Inc 808 W 20th St Cheyenne WY 82001

MILLER, NANCY A., nursing administrator; b. Lehighton, Pa., Apr. 6, 1942; d. Calvin Erck and Mabel Rosetta (Burkett) Geiger; children: Michael Todd Miller, Nicole Ann Miller. Diploma, St. Luke's Sch. Nursing, Bethlehem, Pa., 1962. RN, Pa. Staff nurse Vis. Nurse Assn., Stroudsburg, 1981-89; dir. community health svcs. Home Health Schs., Stroudsburg, Pa.; adminstr. Home Care Affiliates, Stroudsburg; DON Stroud Manor, East Stroudsburg, Pa., 1989-91, Brookmont Health Care Ctr. Inc., Effort, Pa., 1991—. Office: Brookmont Health Care Ctr Box 50 Effort PA 18330

MILLER, NANCY ELLEN, computer consultant; b. Detroit, Aug. 30, 1956; d. George Jacob and Charlotte M. (Bobroff) M. BS in Computer and Comm. Sci., U. Mich., 1978; MS in Computer Sci., U. Wis., 1981. Product engr. Ford Motor Co., Dearborn, Mich., 1977; computer programmer Unique Bus. Systems, Inc., Southfield, Mich., 1978; tchg. asst. computer sci. dept. U. Wis., Madison, 1978-82; computer scientist Lister Hill Nat. Ctr. for Biomed Comm., Nat. Libr. Medicine NIH, Bethesda, Md., 1984-88; knowledge engr. Carnegie Group, Inc., Dearborn, 1989; computer cons. West Bloomfield, Mich., 1993—. Mem. Nat. Abortion and Reproductive Rights Action League, Washington, 1984—, Nat. Women's Polit. Caucus, 1984—, Jewish Fedn. Met. Detroit, 1991—. Recipient Jour. of Am. Soc. for Info. Sci. Best Paper award, 1988. Mem. IEEE Computer Soc., Assn. for Computing Machinery (sec. S.E. Mich. spl. interest group on artificial intelligence 1993-94), Am. Assn. for Artificial Intelligence and Spl. Interest Groups in Mfg. and Bus., Assn. for Logic Programming, U. Wis. Alumni Club (life), U. Mich. Alumni Club (life). Democrat. Jewish. Home and Office: 6220 Village Park Dr #104 West Bloomfield MI 48322

MILLER, NANCY SUZANNE, artist, educator; b. Springfield, Mass., Nov. 8, 1946; d. Harry J. and Helen G. (Golden) Corwin; m. Daniel B. Morgan, May 26, 1983; children: Jillian Morgan, Bradley Morgan. BA, Barnard Coll., 1969; postgrad., NYU, 1972-74; MFA, CCNY, 1996. Temporary Per Diem lic. N.Y.C. Bd. Edn. Part-time tchr. N.Y.C. Bd. Edn., 1986—; tchr. Dist. Coun. 1707, 1993-95; acting dir. adult edn. tutoring program Stanley Isaacs Ctr., N.Y.C., 1992-93, mem. adv. com., 1992—. One-person shows include Ingrid Cusson Gallery, N.Y.C., 1989, Fire Island (N.Y.) Pines Gallery, 1990, Z Gallery, N.Y.C., 1991, New World Gallery, Boston, 1992, R.M. Bradley & Co., Boston, 1994, Mulberry Gallery, N.Y.C., 1995, Aquasource Gallery, N.Y.C., 1995; exhibited in group shows at Daniel Gallery, Ft. Lauderdale, Fla., 1988, Soha Open Studio Show, N.Y.C., 1988, Whitehall Gallery, Palm Springs, Calif., 1989, Peabody Gallery, Boston, 1989, AIR Gallery, N.Y.C., 1989, Tallahassee Gallery, 1990, Valerie Miller Gallery, Palm Springs, 1990, 91, Gallery Gaudi, Watermill, N.Y., 1991, Z Gallery, N.Y.C., 1992, C.W. Post Coll., 1993, Soha Art Gallery, 1993, New England Fine Arts Inst., Boston, 1993, Benton Gallery, Southampton, N.Y., 1993, Zimerlee Mus., Rutgers U., N.J., 1993, Viva Galeria, N.Y.C., 1994; represented in permanent collections Bankers Trust Co., N.Y., Morgan Stanley, Bryan Cave McPheeters & McRoberts, N.Y., Cellular One, Boston, Citibank, N.Y., Daiwa Am. Securities, N.Y., Equitable, N.Y., Gen. Instruments, N.Y., John Hancock, Boston, IBM, N.Y., Irving Trust, N.Y., others. Vol. fund raiser Pub. Sch. 87, 1990-92, vol. art tchr., 1995-96; dir. spring soccer Am. Youth Soccer Orgn., 1995. Mem. Barnard Bus. and Profl. Women. Democrat. Jewish. Home: 527 W 110th St Apt New York NY 10025

MILLER, NAOMI, art historian; b. N.Y.C., Feb. 28, 1928; d. Nathan and Hannah M. B.S., CCNY, 1948; M.A., Columbia U., 1950, NYU, 1960; Ph.D., NYU, 1966. Asst. prof. art history R.I. Sch. Design, 1963-64; asst. prof. U. Calif.-Berkeley, 1969-70; asst. to assoc. prof. Boston U., 1964—, prof. art history, 1981—; vis. prof. U. B.C., Vancouver, 1967, Hebrew U., Jerusalem, 1980, U. Padua, 1990; vis. scholar I Tatti, 1984-85. Author: French Renaissance Fountains, 1977, Heavenly Caves, 1982, Renaissance Bologna, 1989; co-author: Fons Sapientiae: Garden Fountains in Illustrated Books, 16th-18th Centuries, 1977, Boston Architecture 1975-90, 1990; book rev. editor: Jour. Soc. Archtl. Historians, 1975-81, editor, 1981-84; articles, catalogues. Jr. fellow NEH, 1972-73; sr. fellow Dumbarton Oaks, 1976-77, 83-89; vis. sr. fellow Ctr. for Advanced Study in Visual Arts, 1988, 95. Mem. Coll. Art Assn., Soc. Archtl. Historians, Renaissance Soc. Office: 725 Commonwealth Ave Boston MA 02215-1401

MILLER, NICOLE JACQUELINE, fashion designer; b. Ft. Worth, Tex., Mar. 20, 1951; d. Grier Bovey and Jacqueline (Mahieu) M. BFA, RISD, 1973; cert. de coursspeciale, École de la Chambre Syndicale de la Couture Parisienne, Paris, 1971. Asst. designer Clovis Ruffin, N.Y.C., 1974; designer Raincheetahs, N.Y.C., 1974-75, P.J. Walsh, N.Y.C., 1975-82, Nicole Miller, N.Y.C., 1982—; mem. Sports Commn. of N.Y., Commn. of Status of Women; bd. trustees R.I. Sch. of Design. Bd. dirs. Smith's Food and Drug. Recipient Dallas Fashion award, 1991, Earnie award for children's wear, Michael award for fashion. Mem. Fashion Group, Fashion Roundtable, Coun. of Fashion Designers of Am., N.Y. Athletic Club. Office: 525 7th Ave Fl 20 New York NY 10018-4901*

MILLER, PAMELA, performing company executive. BA, U. Wis.; MA, Columbia U.; JD, Case Western Res. U. Former asst. dean acad. affairs Coll. Letters and Sci. U. Wis.; former trust officer Cleve. Trust Co.; exec. dir. Madison Festival of the Lakes, 1984-88; gen. mgr. Miami (Fla.) City Ballet, 1988—. Office: Miami City Ballet 905 Lincoln Rd Miami FL 33139-2601

MILLER, PAMELA GUNDERSEN, city official; b. Cambridge, Mass., Sept. 7, 1938; d. Sven M. and Harriet Adams Gundersen; A.B. magna cum laude, Smith Coll., 1960; m. Ralph E. Miller, July 7, 1962; children—Alexander, Erik, Karen. Feature writer Congressional Quar., Washington, 1962-65; dir. cable TV franchizing Storer Broadcasting Co., Louisville, Bowling Green, Lexington, and Covington, Ky., 1978-80, 81-82; mem. 4th Dist. Lexington, Fayette County Urban Council, 1973-77, councilwoman-at-large, 1982-93, vice-mayor, 1984-86, 89-93, mayor, 1993—; dep. commr. Ky. Dept. Local Govt., Frankfort, 1980-81; pres. Pam Miller, Inc., 1984—, Community Ventures Corp., 1985—. Mem. Fayette County Bd. Health, 1975-77, Downtown Devel. Commn., 1975-77; alt. del. Dem. Nat. Conv., 1976; bd. dirs. YMCA, Lexington, 1975-77, 85-90, Fund for the Arts, 1984-93, Council of Arts, 1978-80, Sister Cities, 1978-80; treas. Prichard Com. for Acad. Excellence, 1983—. Named Woman of Achievement YWCA, 1984, Outstanding Woman of Blue Grass, AAUW, 1984. Mem. LWV (dir. 1970-73), Profl. Women's Forum, NOW, Land and Nature Trust of the Bluegrass. Home: 140 Cherokee Park Lexington KY 40503-1304 Office: 200 E Main St Lexington KY 40507-1315

MILLER, PAMELA LYNN, sales director; b. Elmhurst, Ill., Sept. 14, 1958; d. Gilbert Jack and Joan Leona (Friedberg) Mintz; m. Arthur Neal Miller, Mar. 5, 1994. BS, Ariz. State U., 1980. Virologist Automated Pathology, Inc., Phoenix, Ariz., 1980-81; territory mgr. MetPath Lab., Inc. (Corning, Inc.), Phoenix, Ariz., 1981-91; regional sales dir. Lab. Corp. of Am., Phoenix, 1991—; advisor med. home project Acad. Pediat., Phoenix, 1995. Vol. Phoenix Children's Cancer Ctr., 1990—.

MILLER, PATRICIA ANN, adult education educator; b. Mich., Dec. 19, 1933; d. Bernard James and Veronica Loretta (Hominga) M.; m. Mar. 2, 1957 (div. 1981); children: Sharon, Paula, Philip Jr., Douglas. BA, Mich. State U., 1955. Tchr. Perry (Mich.) Pub. Schs., 1955-56, Glen Lake (Mich.) Cmty. Schs., 1956-57, various pub. schs., Mich., 1957-61, Traverse City (Mich.) Pub. Schs., 1963; salesperson Theta's Real Estate, Traverse City, 1977-88, 93—, Century 21 Real Estate, Traverse City, 1988-90; tchr. Montessori Children's Ctr., Traverse City, 1984; instr./facilitator adult edn. Enterprise Learning Lab., Kingsley/Traverse City, 1986-94, Traverse Bay area, Traverse Bay area, 1994; instr./facilitator Pvt. Ind. Coun., summer 1991-94, 95—; pvt. tutor Grand Traverse, 1986-94; bus. ptnr. FitzMiller Learning Ctr., 1992; mem. learning ctr. task force Northwestern (Mich.) Coll., Traverse City, 1994, 95; lectr., condr. workshops in field. Contbr. articles to profl. jours. Mem. League of Women Voters, Traverse City, 1984; vol. Women's Resource Ctr., Traverse, 1983; ambassador Nat. Cherry Festival, Traverse City, 1984. Recipient Cert. of Appreciation, Traverse Bay Intermediate Schs., 1985, award for work in field of improving adult literacy Traverse City Area Pub. Schs. Bd. Ed., 1991-92; named Region 7 Tchr. of Yr., Mich. Dept. Edn., 1990. Mem. Mich. Reading Assn. (named Mich. Adult Edn. Tchr. of Yr. 1991), Mich. Lit. Coun., Northwestern Mich. Reading Assn. (hon.), Alpha Xi Delta. Office: Enterprise Learning Lab 1707 E Front St Traverse City MI 49686-3016 also: PO Box 4231 Traverse City MI 49685-4231

MILLER, PATRICIA G., lawyer; b. Northfield, Vt., Nov. 20, 1933. BS, U. Colo., 1957; JD, U. Pitts., 1976. Bar: Phila. 1976. Ptnr. Reed Smith Shaw & McClay, Pitts. Office: Reed Smith Shaw & McClay James H Reed Bldg 435 6th Ave Pittsburgh PA 15219-1809

MILLER, PATRICIA LOUISE, state legislator, nurse; b. Bellefontaine, Ohio, July 4, 1936; d. Richard William and Rachel Orpha (Williams) Miller; m. Kenneth Orlan Miller, July 3, 1960; children: Tamara Sue, Matthew Ivan. RN, Meth. Hosp. Sch. Nursing-Indpls., 1957; BS, Ind. U., 1960. Office nurse A.D. Dennison, MD, 1960-61; staff nurse Meth. Hosp., Indpls., 1959, Community Hosp., Indpls., 1958; representative, State of Ind., Dist. 50, Indpls., 1982-83, senator, State of Ind., Dist. 32, Indpls., 1983—, mem. edn. com., 1984-90, health welfare and aging com. 1983-90, labor and pension com. 1983-94, legis. apportionment and elections coms., chmn. interim study com. pub. health and mental health Ind. Gen. Assembly, 1986; chair Senate Environ. Affairs, 1990-92, Health and Environ. Affairs, 1992—; mem. election com., 1992—; mem. budget subcom. Senate Fin. Com., 1995— . Mem. Bd. Edn., Met. Sch. Dist. Warren Twp., 1974-82, pres., 1979-80, 80-81; mem. Warren Twp. Citizens Screening Com. for Sch. Bd. Candidates, 1972-74, 84, Met. Zoning Bd. Appeals, Div. I, appointed mem. City-County Council, 1972-76; bd. dirs. Central Ind. Council on Aging, Indpls., 1977-80; mem. State Bd. of Voc. and Tech. Edn., 1978-82, sec., 1980-82; mem. Gov.'s Select Adv. Commn. for Primary and Secondary Edn., 1983; precinct committeeman Republican Party, 1968-74, ward vice chmn., 1975-78, ward chmn., 1978-85, twp. chmn., 1985-87; vice chmn. Marion County Rep., 1986—; del. Rep. State Conv., 1968, 74, 76, 80, 84, 86, 88, 90, 92, 94, sgt. at arms, 1982, mem. platform com., 1984, 88, 90, 92, co-chmn. Ind. Rep. Platform Com., 1992; del. Rep. Nat. Conv., 1984, alternate del., 1988, Rep. Presdl. Elector Alternate, 1992; active various polit. campaigns; bd. dirs. PTA, 1967-81; pres. Grassy Creek PTA, 1971-72; state del. Ind. PTA, 1978; mem. child care adv. com. Walker Career Center, 1976-80, others; bd. dirs. Ch. Fedn. Greater Indpls., 1979-82, Christian Justice Center, Inc., 1983-85, Gideon Internat. Aux., 1977—; mem. United Meth. Bd. Missions Aux. of Indpls., 1974-80, v.p., 1974-76; bd. dirs. Lucille Raines Residence, Inc., 1977-80; exec. com. S. Ind. Conf. United Meth. Women, 1977-80, lay del. S. Ind. Conf. United Meth. Ch., 1977—, fin. and adminstrn. com., 1979-88, planning and research com., 1980-88, co-chmn. law adv. com., chmn. health and welfare, conf. council ministries, also mem. task force, bd. ordained ministry, also panel, chmn. com. on dist. superintendency, dist. council on ministries; sec. Indpls. S.E. Dist. Council on Ministries, 1977-78, pres., 1982; chmn. council on ministries Cumberland United Meth. Ch., 1969-76; chmn. stewardship com. Old Bethel United Meth. Ch., 1982-85, fin. com., 1982-85, adminstrv. bd., mem. council on ministries, 1981-85; co-chair Evangelism Com., 1994—; jurisdictional del. United Meth. Ch., 1988, 92; alternate del. United Meth. Ch. Gen. Conf., 1988, delegate, 1992; mem. health and human svcs. com. Midwest Legis. Conf., 1995. Recipient Phi Lambda Theta Honor for outstanding contbr. in field of edn., 1976; Woman of the Year, Cumberland Bus. and Profl. Women, 1979; Ind. Voc. Assn. citation award, 1984, others. Mem. Indpls. Dist. Dental Soc. Women's Aux., Ind. Dental Assn. Women's Aux., Am. Dental Assn. Women's Aux., Council State Govt. (intergovtl. affairs com.), Nat. Conf. State Legislatures (health com. vice chmn. 1994—), Warren Twp. Rep. Franklin Rep., Lawrence Rep., Center Twp. Rep., Fall Creek Valley Rep., Marion County Council Rep. Women, Ind. Women's Rep., Indpls. Women's Rep., Ind. Fedn. Rep. Women, Nat. Fedn. Rep. Women, Beech Grove Rep., Perry Twp. Rep. Home: 1041 Muessing Rd Indianapolis IN 46239-9614

MILLER, PATRICIA ORSINO, federal agency administrator; b. Utica, N.Y., Feb. 12, 1948; d. Patrick F. and Rose Marie (Fanelli) Orsino; m. James John Miller, Nov. 12, 1977; children: Alexandra, Victoria. BS, Syracuse U., 1970, MS, 1972. Cert. in counseling and guidance, N.Y. Counselor, field support analyst N.Y. State Dept. Labor, Albany, 1972-77; pub. info. officer NIH, Bethesda, Md., 1978-88; pub. affairs officer Def. Logistics Agy., Battle Creek, Mich., 1988; dep. dir. pub. affairs Def. Logistics Agy., Alexandria, Va., 1989-96; Founder InterCom, Kalamazoo, 1988. Editor: A Century of Piety Hill, 1971. Mem. St. Mary's Home and Sch. Assn., 1987—. Recipient Mercury award Nat. Media Conf., N.Y.C., 1987, Blue Pencil award Nat. Assn. Govt. Communicators, Washington, 1984, award of merit, award of achievement Soc. for Tech. Comm., Washington, 1982, 83, 85, 87, 88. Mem. Women in Comm. (pres. D.C. chpt. 1980-81, bd. dirs. 1978-82), Mortar and Pestle Soc. (charter). Roman Catholic.

MILLER, PEGGY MCLAREN, management educator; b. Tomahawk, Wis., Jan. 12, 1931; d. Cecil Glenn and Gladys Lucille (Bame) McLaren; m. Richard Irwin Miller, June 25, 1955; children: Joan Marie, Diane Lee, Janine Louise. BS, Iowa State U., 1953; MA, Am. U., 1959; MBA, Rochester Inst. Tech., 1979; PhD, Ohio U., 1987. Instr. Beirut Coll. for Women, 1953-55, U. Ky., Lexington, 1964-66, S.W. Tex. State U., San Marcos, 1981-84; home economist Borden Co., N.Y.C., 1955-58; cons. Consumer Cons., Chgo., Springfield, Ill., 1972-77; sr. mktg. rep. N.Y. State Dept. Agr., Rochester, 1978-79; asst. prof., coord. bus. and mgmt. Keuka Coll., Keuka Park, N.Y., 1979-81; lectr. mgmt. Ohio U., Athens, 1984—. Co-editor: Fifty States Cookbook, 1977; contbr. articles to profl. jours. Mem. Soc. for Advancement of Mgmt. (advisor campus chpt.), Mortar Bd., Phi Kappa Phi. Home: 17 Briarwood Dr Athens OH 45701-1302 Office: Ohio U Copeland Hall Athens OH 45701

MILLER, PENELOPE ANN, actress; b. Jan. 13, 1964; d. Mark and Beatrice (Ammidown) M. Studies with Herbert Berghof. Appeared in (plays) The People From Work, 1984, Biloxi Blues, 1984-85, Moonchildren, Our Town (Tony Award nom.), (TV shows) The Guiding Light, 1984, As the World Turns, 1984, The Popcorn Kid, (films) Adventures in Babysitting, 1987, Biloxi Blues, 1988, Big Top Pee-Wee, 1988, Miles From Home, 1988, Dead-Bang, 1989, Downtown, 1990, The Freshman, 1990, Kindergarten Cop, 1990, Awakenings, 1990, Other People's Money, 1991, Year of the Comet, 1992, The Gun in Betty Lou's Handbag, 1992, Chaplin, 1992, Carlito's Way, 1993 (Golden Globe nom.), The Shadow, 1994. Mem. Actors' Equity Assn., AFTRA. *

MILLER, PHOEBE AMELIA, marketing professional; b. Jan. 13, 1948; d. William Prescott and Elizabeth Helen (Lucker) M.. BA in Math., U. Wis., 1970; postgrad., Stanford U., 1973, Golden Gate U., 1975-76. Engr. Bechtel, San Francisco, 1972-77; asst. mgr. Rand Info. Systems, San Francisco, 1977-79; sr. mktg. rep. Computer Sci. Corp., San Francisco, 1979-81; mgr. distbr. sales COGNOS Corp., Walnut Creek, Calif., 1981-86; owner, mgr. P.A. Miller & Assocs., San Francisco, 1986—. Office: PA Miller & Assocs 1750 Montgomery St San Francisco CA 94111-1003

MILLER, RACHEL JOANNA, public relations executive; b. Pitts., Nov. 27, 1971; d. Raymond Joseph and Judith Anne (McDonald) M. BA, Westminster Coll., 1993. From intern to sr. account exec. assoc. Burson-Marsteller, Pitts., 1993-96, assoc. knowledge ctr. liaison, 1996—; mem. selection com. Golden Quill Awards, Pitts., 1993-96. Mem. Pub. Rels. Soc. Am. (newsletter editor 1995-96), Jr. Achievement We. Pa. (vol., corp. liaison 1995—), Omicron Delta Kappa. Lutheran. Home: 529 Hamilton Rd Pittsburgh PA 15205 Office: Burson-Marsteller One Gateway Ctr 20th Fl Pittsburgh PA 15222

MILLER, RITA ANNETTE, elementary education educator; b. Sallisaw, Okla., Nov. 6, 1960; d. Leonard Boyd and Bonnie LaRue (Anderson) Toney; m. Gary Joe Fears, May 24, 1980 (div. Sept. 1989); m. Gregory James Miller, Aug. 10, 1991; 1 child, Katie Nicole Miller. BS in Edn., Northeastern State U., 1983, MS in Edn., 1988; diploma, Acad. of Mil. Sci., 1987. Tchr. Coweta (Okla.) Pub. Schs., 1985-91, McAlester (Okla.) Pub. Schs., 1991—; tchr. cons. Okla. State Dept. Edn., Oklahoma City, 1994—, Aerospace Acad., Norman, Okla., 1991—, Okla. Alliance of Geographic Edn., Norman, 1992—. Capt. Air Force ANG, 1984—. Lit. Study Unit grantee McAlester Pub. Sch. Found., 1993. Mem. NEA, Okla. Assn. Edn., Okla. Aerospace Educators Assn., Okla. Sci. Tchrs. Assn., Epsilon Sigma Alpha Beta Alpha (treas. 1991-94). Democrat. Presbyterian. Home: 1200 E Delaware Ave McAlester OK 74501-6006

MILLER, ROBERTA SELWYN, communications director; b. Bklyn., Aug. 15; d. Phillip Gordon and Lillian (Blumin) Selwyn; m. Stuart Miller, Sept. 3, 1956 (div. May 1977); children: Eric, Nancy Miller Cook, Leslie. Student, Bennington (Vt.) Coll., 1953-56; BS, Barry U., 1981. Lic. real estate broker, Fla. Owner Fabulous Finds, Miami, Fla., 1975-85; real estate brokerage Deco Dr. Realty, Miami Beach, Fla., 1985-90; dir. corp. comms. Interaxx Network, Inc., Miami, Fla., 1990—; owner Image Inc., Miami, 1975-85. Pres. Chopin Found., Miami, 1988.

MILLER, ROSEMARY MARGARET, accountant; b. Jersey City, Jan. 3, 1935; d. Joseph John and Marguerite (Delatush) Corbin; m. James Noyes Orton, 1956 (div. 1977); m. Julian Allen Miller, Oct. 14, 1978 (dec. 1993); children: Alexandria Lynn Hayes, Jennifer Ann Orton Cole. Student Barnard Coll., 1953-54, Rutgers U., Newark, 1954-56, Howard U., 1962-63, No. Va. Community Coll., 1976-83; AA, Thomas A. Edison State Coll., 1981; BS in Acctg., U. Md., 1987; cert. H & R Block, 1981; cert. tax profl. Am. Inst. Tax Studies. Bookkeeper Gen. Electronics, Inc., Washington, 1970-73; cost acct. Radiation Systems, Inc., Sterling, Va., 1973-80; acct. Bilsom Internat., Inc., Reston, Va., 1980-83; sales mgr. Bay Country Homes, Inc., Fruitland, Md., 1984; sr. staff acct. Snow, Powell & Meade, Salisbury, Md., 1985-86; acct. Meadows Hydraulics, Inc., Fruitland, Md., 1987-88; acct. Porter & Powell CPAs, Salisbury, 1988-93; owner, prin. RCOM Cons., acctg., bookeeping, taxes, Princess Anne, Md. Mem. Accreditation Council for Accountancy (accredited 1981), Nat. Soc. Public Accts., Inst. Mgmt. Accts., Nat. Soc. Tax Profls. (cert. tax profl. 1994). Democrat. Lutheran. Address: care Allen 6249 N 78th St Apt 17 Scottsdale AZ 85250-4775

MILLER, SALLY LIPLES, English language teacher; b. Scranton, Pa., July 24, 1954; d. Paul J. and G. Leila (Harris) Liples; m. Walter J. Miller, Jr., Nov. 12, 1976; children: Kathleen, Suzanne. BA in Psychology/Comm. Arts, Marywood Coll., 1976; MEd Curriculum and Instrn., U. Va., 1994. Cert. tchr., Va. Substitute tchr. Scranton (Pa.) Sch. Dist., 1978; grade 7-8 English/U.S. history Holy Cross Regional Sch., Lynchburg, Va., 1979-81; tchr. English Roanoke (Va.) Cath. Sch., 1987—; drama dir. Roanoke Cath. Sch. Leader Girl Scouts U.S., Roanoke, 1987—; Sunday Sch. tchr. St. Andrew's Ch., Roanoke, 1982-92, vacat. Bible sch. tchr., 1984-88, bd. dirs. Christian Formation com., 1983-87. Edn. grantee Dow Jones Newspaper Inst., Va. Commonwealth U., 1990; recipient Outstanding OMer, Odyssey of the Mind, Vinton, Va., 1994. Mem. Jour. Edn. Assn., Nat. Coun. Tchrs. of English, Va. Assn. Journalism (bd. dirs. 1991-96), Diocesan Master Curriculum Coun., Kappa Gamma Pi. Republican. Roman Catholic. Home: 8311 Willow Ridge Rd Roanoke VA 24019-1814 Office: Roanoke Cath Sch 621 N Jefferson St Roanoke VA 24016-1401

MILLER, SANDRA LEE, nurse, administrator; b. Woodbury, N.J., Dec. 4, 1947; d. John Michael Uher and Erma Grace Hayes Bone; m. Gary Dan Miller, Aug. 16, 1969; children: Stephanie Ann, Laura Lee. Diploma, Helene Fuld Sch. Nursing, 1969; BA, Nat. Louis U., 1989, MS, 1991. RN, N.J. Charge nurse Potomac Hosp., Woodbridge, Va., 1972-75, emergency room staff nurse, 1975-87; clin. coord. Kaiser Permanente, Woodbridge, Va., 1989-95; regional med. advice mgr. Kaiser Permanente, Fair Oaks, Va., 1995—; bd. dirs. Am. Heart, Prince William County. Mem. APHA. Home: 15701 Buck Ln Dumfries VA 22026

MILLER, SANDRA PERRY, middle school educator; b. Nashville, Aug. 3, 1951; d. James Ralph and Pauline (Williams) Perry; m. William Kerley Miller, June 22, 1974. BS, David Lipscomb U., 1973; MEd, Tenn. State U., 1983, cert. in spl. edn., reading splty., 1986. Cert. tchr., Tenn. Tchr. Clyde Riggs Elem. Sch., Portland, Tenn., 1973-86; tchr. social studies Portland Mid. Sch., 1986—; adv. bd. tech. and comm. in edn. Sumner County Sch. Bd., Gallatin, Tenn., 1990—; co-dir., cons. Tenn. Students-at-Risk, Nashville, 1991—; assoc. edn. cons. Edn. Fgn. Inst. Cultural Exch., 1991-92; fellow World History Inst., Princeton (N.J.) U., 1992—; awards com. Tenn. Dept. Edn., Nashville, 1992; U.S. edn. amb. E.F. Ednl. Tours, Eng., France, Germany, Belgium, Holland, 1991; ednl. cons. HoughtonMifflin Co., Boston; apptd. Tenn. Mini-Grants award com., Tenn. 21st Century Tech. Com.; mem. Tenn. Textbook Com., 1995, Think-Tank on 21st Century Edn., Tenn. and Milliken Nat. Educator Found.; apptd. to Gov.'s Task Force Commn. on 21st Schs., Gov.'s Task Force for Anti-Drug and Alcohol Abuse Among Teens; mem. nat. com. for instnl. tech. devel. Milken Family Found. Nat. Edn. Conf., 1996; apptd. to Instrnl. Tech. Devel.-Project Strand, 1996 Milken Family Found., Nat. Edn. Conf. Author curriculum materials; presenter creative crafts segment local TV sta., 1990-93; producer, dir. documentary on edn. PBS, Corona, Calif., 1990. Performer Nashville Symphony Orch., 1970-73; leader Sumner County 4-H Club, 1976-86; mem. Woodrow Wilson Nat. Fellowship Found. on Am. History, Princeton U., 1994; nat. com. Instructional Tech. Devel. Project Strand of the 1996 Milken Family Found. Nat. Edn. Conf., L.A., 1996. Recipient Excellence in Teaching award U. Tenn., 1991-92, 92-93, award for Outstanding Teaching in Humanities Tenn. Humanities Coun., 1994; named Tchr. of Yr. Upper Cumberland dist. Tenn. Dept. Edn., 1991-92, 92-93, Mid. Tenn. Educator of Yr. Tenn. Assn. Mid. Schs., 1991, Tenn. Tchr. of Yr. Tenn. Dept. Edn., 1992, Nat. Educator of Yr. Milken Family Found., 1992; recipient grant Tenn. Dept. Edn. for Devel. of Model Drop Out Prevention Program, 1996. Mem. NEA, ASCD, Sumner County Edn. Assn. (sch. rep. 1973—, Disting. Tchr. of Yr. 1992), Tenn. Edn. Assn. (rep. 1973—), Nat. Geographic Tenn. Alliance (rep. 1990—, grantee 1990), Tenn. Humanities Coun. (rep. 1990—), Nat. Coun. Social Studies. Baptist. Office: Portland Mid Sch 922 S Broadway Portland TN 37148-1624

MILLER, SANDRA RITCHIE, artist, art therapist; b. Downers Grove, Ill., Aug. 15, 1940; d. Joseph Edgar and Ruby Irene (McAllister) Ritchie; m. David Martin Miller, Dec. 13, 1968; 1 child, Ritchie Wayne. Student, Cambridge (Eng.) U., 1975-76, U. Minn., 1971; AA in Art, Glendale Coll., 1979; BS in Psychology, Ariz. State U., 1982. Adminstrv. asst. Rand Corp., Santa Monica, Calif., 1959, System Devel. Corp., Santa Monica, Calif., 1965-69; art tchr. Wheelersburg, Ohio, 1983-85; artist, 1970—; art person, therapist Oak Meadow Nursing Home, Alexandria, Va., 1987—, Woodbine Nursing Home, Alexandria, Va., 1992—; bd. dirs., v.p. Gallery West, Alexandria. One-woman shows Gallery West, Alexandria, Va., 1992, 93, 95, 96, Hamilton Gallery, Alexandria, 1991, Yarrow Gallery, Oundle, Eng., 1996; exhbns. include Women's Internat. League for Peace and Freedom Calendar, 1983, Nat. Mus. of Women in Arts archives, 1994—, Mus. Contemporary Art, Washington, 1996, Internat. Artists' Support Group, 1996. Vol. USAF Family Svcs., Duluth, Minn., 1970-72, RAF Alconbury, Eng., 1972-75, Friends of the Earth, San Francisco, 1980-81, Child Assault Prevention Program, Portsmouth, Ohio, 1983-85; bd. dirs. Art League/Torpedo Factory, Alexandria, 1989-91, Belle Haven on the Green, Alexandria, 1988-92, pres. 1991-92. Mem. Ward Nasse Gallery, Knickerbocker Artists, Washington Project for the Arts, Mus. Contemporary Art. Democrat. Home: 1810 Duffield Ln Alexandria VA 22307 Office: Sandi Ritchie Miller Studio 1810 Duffield Ln Alexandria VA 22307

MILLER, SHANNON, Olympic athlete; b. Rollo, Mo., Mar. 10, 1977. Silver medalist, All-Around Competition Barcelona Olympic Games, 1992, Silver medalist, Balance Beam, 1992, Bronze medalist, Uneven Bars, 1992; Gold medalist all-around competition Birmingham Great World Championships, Britain, 1993, Brisbane Austrlia World Championships, St. Petersburg, Russia, 1994. Bronze medalist in floor exercise, Olympics, 1992; World Champion Gold medalist in all around, 1993, 94, in uneven bars and fl. exercise, 1993, in balance beam, 1994; Gold medal Team competition Atlanta Olympics, 1996, gold medal balance beam, 1996; recipient Up & Coming award Women's Sports Found., 1991, Steve Reeves Fitness award Downtown Athletic Club, 1992, Comeback award Nuprin, 1992, Dial award, 1994; named Athlete of Yr. USA Gymnastics Congress, 1994. Christian Scientist. Address: US Olympic Committee 1750 E Boulder St Colorado Springs CO 80909-5724

MILLER, SHERRIE LYNN, artist; b. Quinton, Va., June 14, 1973; d. Eddie Roger and Cynthia Louise (Davis) M. BFA, Va. Commonwealth U., 1995. Picture framer Reflections, Mechanicsville, Va., 1995; photog. finisher Richmond (Va.) Camera, 1995—. One-woman shows include Va. Commonwealth U., 1995. Dean's scholar Va. Commonwealth U., 1991-95. Mem. Va. Mus. Fine Arts, Golden Key, Phi Kappa Phi, Phi Eta Sigma.

MILLER, SUSAN ANN, school system administrator; b. Cleve., Nov. 24, 1947; d. Earl Wilbur and Marie Coletta (Hendershot) M. BS in Edn., Kent State U., 1969; MEd, Cleve. State U., 1975; PhD, Kent State U., 1993. Cert. supt.; cert. elem. prin., cert. elem. supervisor; cert. Learning Disabled/Behavior Disabled tchr.; cert. tchr. grades 1-8; cert. sch. counselor; lic. counselor. Tchr., guidance counselor, interim prin. North Royalton City Schs., Ohio, 1969-84; dir. elem. and spl. edn., acting supt., asst. supt. Cuyahoga County Bd. Edn., Valley View, Ohio, 1984—. Contbr. articles to profl. jours. Recipient grant Latchkey Program, State Dept. Edn. Mem. ASCD, Coun. Exceptional Children, Phi Delta Kappa. Home: 14508 Cross Creek Ln Cleveland OH 44133-4811 Office: Department Education 5700 W Canal Rd Valley View OH 44125-3326

MILLER, SUSAN ROBERTA, special education educator; b. Bayonne, N.J., Aug. 3, 1958; d. Robert and Frieda Elizabeth (Weiwoda) M. BS in Edn., SUNY at Geneso, 1980; MS in Edn., Trenton State Coll., 1985. Cert. tchr. of mentally and physically handicapped, N.J., Pa. Spl. educator The Midland Sch., North Branch, N.J., 1981-85; learning support educator Bethlehem (Pa.) Area Sch. Dist., 1988—; instructional support team mem. Bethlehem Area Sch. Dist., 1990—. Author: (pamphlet) Behavior Management at Home, 1986. First aid, CPR instr. ARC, Bethlehem, 1982—; adult trainer Great Valley Girl Scout Coun., Allentown, Pa., 1983—. Recipient The Great Valley award Great Valley Girl Scout Coun., 1991. Mem. Coun. for Exceptional Children, Am. Camping Assn. (stds. visitor 1980—). Office: Lincoln Elem Sch 1810 Renwick St Bethlehem PA 18017-6177

MILLER, SUZANNE MARIE, law librarian, educator; b. Sioux Falls, S.D., Feb. 25, 1954; d. John Gordon and Dorothy Margaret (Sabatka) M.; 1 child, Altinay Marie. B.A. in English, U. S.D., 1975; M.A. in Library Sci., U. Denver, 1976; postgrad. in polit. sci. U. LaVerne, 1980, postgrad. in law, 1984. Librarian II, U. S.D. Sch. of Law, Vermillion, 1977-78; law libr. U. LaVerne, Calif., 1978-85, instr. in law, 1980-85; asst. libr. tech. svcs. McGeorge Sch. Law, 1985—, prof. advanced legal rsch., 1994—. Co-author (with Elizabeth J. Pokorny) U.S. Government Documents: A Practical Guide for Library Assistants in Academic and Public Libraries, 1988; contbr. chpt. to book, articles to profl. jours. Recipient Am. Jurisprudence award Bancroft Whitney Pub. Co., 1983. Mem. Am. Assn. Law Librs., So. Calif. Assn. Law Librs. (arrangements com. 1981-82), Innovacq Users Group (chairperson, 1986-88), No. Calif. Assn. Law Librs. (mem. program com., inst. 1988), Western Pacific Assn. Law Librs. (sec. 1990-94, pres. elect 1994-95, pres. 1995-96). Roman Catholic. Home: 4030 Jeffrey Ave Sacramento CA 95820-2551 Office: McGeorge Sch Law Library Univ of the Pacific 3200 Fifth Ave Sacramento CA 95817

MILLER, TAMARA DEDRA, psychologist; b. Cleve., Jan. 13, 1961; d. Taswill Taylor and Ethel (Midgett) M.; stepd. Gwendolyn (Hicks) M. BA in Psychology, Wittenberg U., 1982; D in Psychology, Wright State U., 1987. Lic. clin. psychologist, Ohio. Chief psychol. svc. USAF, Altus, Okla., 1987-89; chief psychol. testing USAF, Dayton, Ohio, 1989-92; dir. PTSD program Dept. VA, Dayton, 1992—; clin. prof. Wright State U., Dayton, 1992—; cons. Jackson County Youth, Altus, 1987-89, Ctr. for Retardation, Altus, 1987-89; adj. prof. Ctrl. State U., Wilberforce, 1991—; mem. panel Women's Fed. Program, Dayton, 1991; clin. advisor Les Femmes Concerned Citizens for Cancer, Dayton, 1992—. Consulting editor: Professional Psychology: Research and Practice, 1994. Capt. USAF, 1986-89. Mem. Nat. Coun. Negro Women Inc., VA Psychologists, Delta Sigma Theta. Home: 5670 Olive Tree Dr Dayton OH 45426-1313 Office: Dept VA Affairs Med Ctr 4100 E 3rd St Dayton OH 45403-2244

MILLER, THERESA ANN, management consultant; b. St. Charles, Mo., Apr. 1, 1945; d. Ford Emmett Wilkins and Alice Mary (Faerber) Wilkins Burrow. Cert. secretarial, N.E. Mo. State Tchrs. Coll., 1964; AA, St. Louis Community Coll., 1976; BSBA, Lindenwood Coll., 1983, MBA, 1990; MBA Cert. Internat. Bus., 1991. With McDonnell Douglas Aerospace-East, St. Louis, 1985—, supr. master files dept., 1984—, sect. mgr. office svcs., 1987—, auditor self-governance audit program, 1991—, sr. analyst command media, 1993-95, sr. analyst, investigations/corp. human resource, 1995—. Mem. NAFE, Nat. Notary Assn., Lindenwood Coll. Alumni Club (past pres. St. Charles chpt.), Mgmt. Club McDonnell Douglas Aerospace. Roman Catholic. Home: 15618 Coventry Farm Dr Chesterfield MO 63017-7386

MILLER, VEL, artist; b. Nekoosa, Wis., Jan. 22, 1936; d. Clarence Alvin Krause and Celia Mae (Houston) Clark; m. Warren Eugene Miller, Apr. 30, 1955; children: Jennifer, Andre, Matthew, Stuart. Student, Valley Coll., Art League L.A. Exhbns. include Stamford (Tex.) Art Found., Haley Libr., Midland, Tex., Peppertree Ranch, Santa Ynez, Calif., Trappings of Am. West, Flagstaff, Ariz., Mountain Oyster Club, Tucson, Cowboy Classic, Phoenix, Cowboy Gathering, Paso Robles, Phoenix, Cattlemans Show, San Luis Obispo, Calif.; represented in permanent collections at Home Savings and Loan L.A., Glendale (Ariz.) Coll., Cavalry Mus., Samore, France; also pvt. collections. Recipient Best of Show award San Fernando Valley Art Club, San Gabriel Art Assn., Death Valley Invitational Show, numerous others. Mem. Am. Woman Artist (founder), Oil Painters Am.

MILLER, WENDY, artist; b. N.Y.C., May 3, 1955; d. Robert George and Bernice Fox (Rosenberg) M.; m. George Beckwith, Oct. 15, 1989; 1 child, Noah Miller Beckwith. BA in Philosophy, Wesleyan U., Middletown, Conn., 1977; attended, Corcoran Sch. of Art, Washington D.C., 1979-81. Solo exhbns. include Dru Arstark Gallery, N.Y., 1995-96, Painting Ctr., 1996; group exhbns. include: Geoffrey Young Gallery, Great Barrington, Mass., 1994, Dru Arstark Gallery, N.Y., 1995, 450 Broadway Gallery, N.Y., 1995, The WorkSpace, N.Y., 1995. Recipient Residency fellow Yaddo, Saratoga Springs, N.Y., 1994.

MILLER, WENDY LYNN, art therapist, sculptor, consultant, educator; b. Waterville, Me., May 21, 1950; d. Howard Avery and Gisele (Baroukel) M.; 1 child, Eliana Frey Miller. BA, Simmons Coll., 1972; MA, San Francisco State U., 1978; PhD, Union Inst., 1992. Cert. expressive therapist; registered art therapist. Artist in residence Thunderseed Aftercare, San Francisco, 1978-82; pvt. practice Bethesda, Md., 1988—; co-founder Create Therapy Inst., Bethesda, Md., 1994—; lectr. San Francisco State U., 1984-88; adj. faculty JFK U., Orinda, Calif., 1984-88, Calif. Inst. Integral Studies, San Francisco, 1990—; dir. Beyond Boundaries, Bethesda, Md., 1988-93; trainer Calif. Arts Coun., San Francisco, 1984-85. One-woman show So. Exposure Gallery, San Francisco, 1985; contbr. articles to profl. jours. Mem. Am. Art Therapy Assn., Potomac Art Therapy Assn., Internat. Expressive Arts Therapy Assn. (founding mem., co-chair governance com. 1994—). Democrat. Jewish. Office: Create Therapy Inst 4905 Del Ray Ave #301 Bethesda MD 20814

MILLER, WILMA HILDRUTH, education educator; b. Dixon, Ill., Mar. 8, 1936; d. William Alexander and Ruth Karin (Hanson) M. BS in Edn., No. Ill. U., DeKalb, 1958, MS in Edn., 1961; DEd, U. Ariz., 1967. Cert. reading specialist. Elem. tchr. Dist. 170, Dixon, Ill., 1958-63, Dist. 1, Tucson, Ariz., 1963-64; asst. prof. edn. Wis. State U., Whitewater, 1965-68; assoc. prof. edn. Ill. State U., Normal, 1968-72, prof., 1972—. Author: Diagnosing and Correcting Reading Difficulties in Children, 1988, Reading Comprehension, 1990, Complete Reading Disabilities Handbook, 1993, Alternative Assessment Techniques in Reading and Writing, 1995, others; contbr. 200 articles to profl. jours. Altar Guild, usher, greeter, communion asst. Our Saviour Luth. Ch., Normal, 1990—. Mem. Internat. Reading Assn. (parent and reading com. 1972-74, editl. adv. bd. 1995—, Outstanding Dissertation award 1968), Mid-State Reading Coun. (editl. adv. bd. 1991—), Alpha Upsilon Alpha (advisor Reading chpt. 1993—), Pi Lambda Theta, Kappa Delta Pi, Phi Delta Kappa. Home: 302 N Coolidge St Normal IL 61761-2435 Office: Ill State U 5910 SED Normal IL 61761

MILLER, YVONNE BOND, state senator, educator; b. Edenton, N.C.; d. John and Pency Bond. BS, Va. State Coll., Petersburg, 1956; postgrad., Va. State Coll., Norfolk, 1966; MA, Columbia U., 1962; PhD, U. Pitts., 1973; postgrad., CCNY, 1976. Tchr. Norfolk Pub. Schs., 1956-68; asst. prof. Norfolk State U., 1968-71, assoc. prof., 1971-74, prof., 1974-88, head dept. early childhood/elem. edn., 1984-87; mem. Va. Ho. Dels., Richmond, 1984-87, mem. edn. com., health, welfare and instns. com., militia and police com., 1983-87; mem. Va. Senate, Richmond, 1987—; now mem. commerce and labor com., gen. laws com., transp. com., rehab. and social svcs. com. Va. Senate, now chair rehab. and social svcs. com., mem. rules com.; Va. Dems. vice chair; mem. Nat. Dem. Com.; cons. to chs., parent orgns. and community groups. Commr. Ea. Va. Med. Authority; adv. bd. Va. Div. Children; active C.H. Mason Meml. Ch. of God in Christ. 1st black woman to be elected to Va. Legislature, 1983, 1st black woman to be elected to Va. Senate, 1987. Mem. Nat. Alliance Black Sch. Educators (bd. dirs.), Va. Assn. for Early Childhood Edn., Nat. Assn. Dem. Chairs, Zeta Phi Beta (past officer). Office: 960 Norchester Ave Norfolk VA 23504-4038 also: Norfolk State U 2401 Corprew Ave Norfolk VA 23504-3907 also: Va Senate Gen Assembly Bldg Rm 365 Richmond VA 23219

MILLER, ZOYA DICKINS (MRS. HILLIARD EVE MILLER, JR.), civic worker; b. Washington, July 15, 1923; d. Randolph and Zoya Pavlovna (Klementinovska) Dickins; m. Hilliard Eve Miller, Jr., Dec. 6, 1943; children: Jeffrey Arnot, Hilliard Eve III. Grad. Stuart Sch. Costume Design, Washington, 1942; student Sophie Newcomb Coll., 1944, New Eng. Conservatory Music, 1946, Colo. Coll., 1965; grad. Internat. Sch. Reading, 1969. Instr. Stuart Summer Sch. Costume Design, Washington, 1942; fashion coord. Julius Garfinckel, Washington, 1942-43; fashion coord., cons. Mademoiselle mag., 1942-44; star TV show Cowbelle Kitchen, 1957-58, Flair for Living, 1958-59; model mags. and comml. films, also nat. comml. recs., 1956—; dir. devel. Webb-Waring Inst. for Biomedical Rsch., Denver, 1973—. Contbr. articles, lectures on health care systems and fund raising. Mem. exec. com., bd. dirs. El Paso County chpt. Am. Lung Assn., Colo., 1954-63; mem. exec. com. Am. Lung Assn. Colo., 1965-84, bd. dirs. 1965-87, chmn. radio and TV coun., 1963-70, mem. med. affairs com., 1965-70, pres., 1965-66, procurer found. funds, 1965-70; developer nat. radio ednl. prodns. for internat. use Am. Lung Assn., 1963-70, coord. statewide pulmonary screening programs Colo., other states, 1965-72; chmn. benefit fund raising El Paso County Cancer Soc., 1963; co-founder, coord. Colorado Springs Debutante Ball, 1967—; coord. Nat. Gov.'s Conf. Ball, 1969; mem. exec. com. Colo. Gov.'s Comprehensive Health Planning Coun., 1967-74, chmn., 1971-72; chmn. Colo. Chronic Care Com., 1969-73, chmn. fund raising, 1970-72, chmn. spl. com. congl. studies on nat. health bills, 1971-73; mem. Colo.-Wyo. Regional Med. Program Adv. Coun., 1969-73; mem. Colo. Med. Found. Consumers Adv. Coun., 1972-78; mem. decorative arts com. Colorado Springs Fine Arts Ctr., 1972-75; founder, state coord. Nov. Noel Pediatrics Benefit Am. Lung Assn., 1973-87; founder, state pres. Newborn Hope, Inc., 1987—; mem. adv. bd. Wagon Wheel Girl Scouts, 1991—, Cmty. in Schs., 1995—. Zoya Dickins Miller Vol. of Yr. award established Am. Lung Assn. of Colo., 1979; recipient James J. Waring award Colo. Conf. on Respiratory Disease Workers, 1963, Nat. Pub. Rels. award Am. Lung Assn., 1979, Gold Double Bar Cross award, 1980, 83, Jefferson award Am. Inst. Pub. Svc., 1991, Thousand Points of Light award The White House, 1992, Recognition award So. Colo. Women's C. of C., 1994, Silver Spur Community award Pikes Peak Range Riders, 1994, Silver Bell award Assistance League Colorado Springs, 1996; named Humanitarian of Yr., Am. Lung Assn. of Colo., 1987, One of 50 Most Influential Women in Colorado Springs by Gazette Telegraph Newspaper, 1990, One of 6 Leading Ladies Colo. Homes & Lifestyles Mag., 1991. Lic. pvt. pilot. Mem. Colo. Assn. Fund Raisers, Denver Round Table for Planned Giving, Nat. Soc. Fund Raising Execs., Nat. Cowbell Assn. (El Paso county pres. 1954, TV chmn., chmn. nat. Father of Yr. contest Colo. 1956-57), Broadmoor Garden Club. Home: 74 W Cheyenne Mountain Blvd Colorado Springs CO 80906-4336

MILLER CALANDRA, LINDA MARGUERITA, pediatrics nurse; b. Lansdale, Pa., June 7, 1957; d. Clarence P. and Ruth E. (Priester) Miller; m. Robert T. Calandra Jr.; 1 child, Lindsey. BSN, U. Del., 1979; MSN, U. Pa., 1986. Lic. nurse, Pa.; PNP, ANA; cert. otorhinolaryngology nurse Nat. Certifying Bd. Otorhinolaryngology and Head-Neck Nurses. Assoc. nurse Children's Hosp. Phila., 1979-80, primary surg. nurse, 1980-82, clin. nurse specialist in pediat. otorhinolaryngology, 1983-86, PNP in otorhinolaryngology, 1986—; mem. Nat. Cert. Bd. of Otorhinolaryngology, Head and Neck Nurses, 1991—; clin. preceptor Sch. Nursing, U. Pa., 1992—; presenter Neonatal Nursing Conf., Boston, 1988, Nat. Nurse Practitioner Debate, Balt., 1992, U. Pa., 1993, various profl. assn. confs. Mem. editl. adv. bd. ADVANCE for Nurse Practitioners, 1993—; contbr. articles to profl. jours. Mem. Nat. Assn. Pediat. Nurse Assocs. and Practitioners, Soc. Ear, Nose and Throat Advances in Children (mem. com. on coms. 1993-95, mem. liaison com. 1993-95), Soc. Otorhinolaryngology and Head and Neck Nurses (co-chairperson edn. com. 1993—), Am. Soc. Pediat. Otorhinolaryngology Nurses (mem. study group), Pa. Acad. Otorhinolaryngology, Sigma Theta Tau. Home: 2120 Jenkintown Rd Glenside PA 19038-5314 Office: Childrens Hosp Pa 34th And Civic Center Blvd Philadelphia PA 19104-4343

MILLER DAVIS, MARY-AGNES, social worker; b. Montgomery, Ala., Jan. 21; d. George Joseph and Mollie (Ingersoll) M.; m. Edward Davis, Sept. 20, 1941. BA, Wayne State U., 1944; MSW, U. Mich., 1970. Lic. social worker, Mich. Social caseworker Cath. Family Ctr., Detroit, 1946-48; foster homes worker Juvenile Ct., Detroit, 1953-57; youth svc. bur. League of Cath. Women, Detroit, 1957-59; mayor's community action for youth com. worker City of Detroit, 1963; instr. urban sociology Madonna Coll., Livonia, Mich., 1968; pers. cons. Edward Davis Motor Sales, Detroit, 1963-70; exec. cons. Edward Davis Assocs., Inc., Detroit, 1975—; founder Co-Ette Club, Inc., Detroit, 1941—, Met. Detroit Teen Conf. Coalition, Detroit, 1983—; program chair Wayne State U.-Merrill Palmer Inst., Detroit, 1976—. Editor Girl Friends, Inc. Mag., 1960-62; contbr. numerous articles to profl. publs. Life mem. NAACP, League of Cath. Women; charter mem. Meadowbrook Summer Music Festival, com. of Oakland (Mich.) U.; adv. bd. Women for the Detroit Symphony Orch.; mem./patron Founder's Soc. the Detroit Inst. of Arts; bd. dirs., other offices ARC, Detroit, 1974—; mem. The Detroit Hist. Soc., Heart of Gold Coun., Women for United Found. (named to Heart of Gold coun. 1968), Friends of the Detroit Libr., Mich. Opera Theatre; mem. nat. hon. com./nat. vol. week United Cmty. Svc. and Nat. Vol. Ctr., Washington, 1990—; former bd. dirs. United Community Svcs. Women's Com., Campfire Girls, LWV, Neighborhood Svcs. Orgn., Cath. Interracial Coun. and others. Recipient Nat. Community Leadership award Nat. Coun. Women of U.S., Inc., 1984, Am. Human Resources award Am. Bicentennial Rsch. Inst., 1976, Heart of Gold award United Way, 1968, Nat. Leadership award United Negro Coll. Fund, 1963, Recognition award Westin Hotel, 1991, Top Ladies of Distinction award, 1994; named One of Mich. Outstanding Women City of Detroit, 1976, Heart of Gold 25th Anniversary honoree United Way Southeastern Mich., 1992; Vassar Summer Seminar scholar NCCJ, 1953, Notre Dame Summer Seminar scholar, 1960. Mem. NASW, ARC (bd. dirs. 1973—), Nat. Conf. of Social Work, The Cons. Club of Detroit (adv. bd. edn. com.), Detroit Econ. Club (mem. adv. com.). Home: 2020 Chicago Blvd Detroit MI 48206-1783

MILLER-GIRSON, EILEEN BONNIE, insurance underwriter; b. Chgo., Nov. 22, 1953; d. Sol and Evelyn (Brenner) Miller; m. David Jay Girson, June 12, 1977. AA, Kendall Coll., Evanston, Ill., 1973; BA, MacMurray Coll., Jacksonville, Ill., 1975; MEd, Nat. Coll. Edn., Evanston, 1976. Cert. profl. ins. woman; assoc. in underwriting. Tchr. Evanston Sch. Dist. 65, 1975-76; lawyers profl. liability underwriter Shand Morahan Co., Evanston, 1977-78; personal lines underwriter Farmers Ins. Group, Aurora, Ill., 1978-80; comml. lines underwriter Hanover Ins. Co., Chgo., 1980-81; workers compensation underwriter EBI Cos., Chgo., 1981-83; package underwriter CNA Ins., Chgo., 1983-84, dentists profl. liability underwriter, 1984-86; casualty underwriter Hartford Ins. Co., Chgo., 1986-87; sr. comml. accounts underwriting specialist Home Ins. Co., Chgo., 1987-95; sr. underwriter First State Mgmt. Group, 1995—. Ill. Edn. Assn. scholar, 1975-76. Mem. Ins. Distaff Exec. Assn., The Saints, Cinema Chgo. Home: 511 Leclaire Ave Wilmette IL 60091-2062 Office: First State Mgmt Group 303 W Madison Ste 1000 Chicago IL 60606

MILLER-PERRIN, CINDY LOU, psychology educator; b. McKeesport, Pa., Feb. 26, 1962; d. Emerson and Helen Francis (Beck) M.; m. Robin D. Perrin, Aug. 3, 1985; children: Jacob, Madison. BA, Pepperdine Univ., 1983; MS, Washington State Univ., 1987, PhD, 1991. Psychology intern Univ. Wash., Seattle, 1990-91, postdoctoral fellow, 1991-92; asst. prof. Pepperdine Univ., Malibu, Calif., 1992-96, assoc. prof., 1996—. Author: Preventing Child Sexual Abuse: Sharing..., 1992, Family Violence Across the Lifespan, 1996; contbr. articles to profl. jours. Senator Grad. & Profl. Student Assn. Washington State U., 1988-89; guardian ad ligem Whitman County, Wash., 1987-89. Mem. Am. Psychological Assn., Western Psychological Assn., Internat. Soc. Prevention of Child Abuse Neglect, Am. Profl. Soc. on the Abuse of Children, Sigma Xi, Psi Chi (faculty adv. 1992—). Office: Pepperdine Univ Social Sci Div Malibu CA 90263

MILLER-VIDETICH, EVA JOHANNA, secondary school educator; b. Darmstadt, Germany, Dec. 31, 1953; d. Ronald J. and Johanna Rosa (Linke) Miller; m. Joe Charles Videtich, Feb. 20, 1988; children: Lindy, John. BA, Grand Valley State Coll., 1976; postgrad., Western Mich. U. Lic. practical counselor. German tchr. Northview Pub. Schs., Grand Rapids, Mich., 1977—; ESL tchr. Sparta (Mich.) Migrant Program, 1985; gifted-talented tchr. Grand Rapids Pub. Sch., 1980-82; adult edn. tchr. Northview Pub. Sch., 1982. Trustee Kent City (Mich.) Sch. Bd., 1994, pres., 1995. Recipient Outstanding Tchr. award U. Chgo., 1984, Hope Coll., 1994; Lifetouch grantee, 1994. Mem. AATG, MCA, WMCA. Roman Catholic.

MILLESON, VICKIE JO, elementary education educator; b. Cumberland, Md., Oct. 27, 1948; d. William H. Jr. and Helen C. Ansel; m. William J. Milleson, June 20, 1970; children: Julie, Jill, Joe. BA in Elem. Edn., Shepherd Coll., Shepherdstown, W.Va., 1970. Cert. elem. tchr., social studies tchr., W.Va. Tchr. 4th grade Ft. Ashby (W.Va.) Elem. Sch., 1970-72; substitute tchr. Hampshire County (W.Va.) Schs., 1978-87; tchr. 6th grade John J. Cornwell Elem. Sch., Levels, W.Va., 1987-88, Romney (W.Va.) Elem. Sch., 1988—; mem. staff devel. coun. Hampshire County Schs., Romney, 1994—. Mem. NEA, W.Va. Edn. Assn., Hampshire County Edn. Assn. Presbyterian. Home: PO Box 162 Springfield WV 26763-0162

MILLETT, KATE (KATHERINE MURRAY MILLETT), political activist, sculptor, artist, writer; b. St. Paul, Sept. 14, 1934; m. Fumio Yoshimura, 1965. BA magna cum laude, U. Minn., 1956; postgrad. with 1st class honors, St. Hilda's Coll. Oxford, Eng., 1956-58; PhD with distinction, Columbia U., 1970. Instr. English U. N.C. at Greensboro, 1958; file clk. N.Y.C., kindergarten tchr., 1960-61; sculptor, Tokyo, 1961-63; tchr. Barnard Coll., 1964-70; tchr. English Bryn Mawr (Pa.) Coll., 1970; disting. vis. prof. Sacramento State Coll., 1972-73; founder Women's Art Colony Farm, Poughkeepsie, N.Y. Author: Sexual Politics, 1970, The Prostitution Papers, 1973, Flying, 1974, Sita, 1977, The Basement, 1979, Going to Iran, 1982, The Loony Bin Trip, 1990, The Politics of Cruelty, 1994, A.D., 1995; coprodr., co-dir. film Three Lives, 1970; one-woman shows Minami Gallery, Tokyo, Judson Gallery, N.Y.C., 1967, Noho Gallery, N.Y.C., 1976, 79, 80, 82, 84, 86, 93, Women's Bldg., L.A., 1977; drawings Andre Wanters Gallery, Berlin, 1980, Courtland Jessup Gallery, Provincetown, Mass., 1991, 92, 93, 94, 95. Mem. Congress of Racial Equality; chmn. edn. com. NOW, 1966; active supporter gay and women's liberation groups, also mental patients liberation and political prisoners. Mem. Phi Beta Kappa. Office: 295 Bowery New York NY 10003-7104

MILLIGAN, SISTER MARY, theology educator, religious consultant; b. Los Angeles, Jan. 23, 1935; d. Bernard Joseph and Carolyn (Krebs) M. BA, Marymount Coll., 1956; Dr. de l'Univ., U. Paris, 1959; MA in Theology, St. Mary's Coll., Notre Dame, Ind., 1966; STD, Gregorian U., 1975; D. honoris causa, Marymount U., 1988. Tchr. Cours Marymount, Neuilly, France, 1956-59; asst. prof. Marymount Coll., Los Angeles, 1959-67; gen. councillor Religious of Sacred Heart of Mary, Rome, 1969-75, gen. superior, 1980-85; asst. prof. Loyola Marymount U., Los Angeles, 1977-78, provost, 1986-90, prof., 1990—, dean liberal arts, 1992—; pres. bd. dirs. St. John's Sem., Camarillo, Calif., 1986-89; mem. exec. com. Internat. Union Superiors Gen., Rome, 1983-85; mem. planning bd. spiritual renewal program Loyola Marymount U., Los Angeles, 1976-78. Author: That They May Have Life, 1975; compiler analytical index Ways of Peace, 1986; contbr. articles to profl. jours. Vis. scholar Grad. Theol. Union, Berkeley, 1986. Mem. Calif. Women in Higher Edn., Coll. Theology Soc., Cath. Biblical Assn. Democrat. Roman Catholic. Office: Loyola Marymount U 7900 Loyola Blvd Los Angeles CA 90045-8319

MILLIGAN, MARY BETH, marketing professional, communications executive; b. Sidney, Ohio, Sept. 10, 1955; d. Patrick Henry and Carol Anne (Benson) M.; m. Charles Martin Sheaffer, Jr., Sept. 9, 1978; children: Caitlin Margaret, Hannah Clare. BA, Macalester Coll., 1977. Editor Conklin Co., Mpls., 1977-78; project mgr., v.p. Mktg. Decisions, Inc., Mpls., 1979-82; mktg. planner Hazelden Found., Center City, Minn., 1982-89, mgr. new market devel., 1990-91; mng. dir., European subs. Hazelden Found., Cork, Ireland, 1989-90; exec. dir. Graywolf Press, St. Paul, 1991-93; dir. mktg. devel. and comm. Vinland Ctr., Loretto, Minn., 1994—; cons. editor Devine Multi-Media, St. Paul, 1993-94; publ. cons. Utne Reader, Mpls., 1994; group facilitator Minn. Early Learning Design, Mpls., 1987-88, Cath. Charities, St. Paul, 1978-85. Co-author: Today's Gift, 1985. Panelist Minn. State Arts Bd. Prose Fellowship Rev. Panel, St. Paul, 1995-96; judge Ramsey Internat. Fine Arts Ctr., Mpls., 1996; steering com. family partnership campaign Greater Mpls. Girl Scouts Coun., 1994; founder, chair Little Flowers Montessori PTA, 1992-94; Co-chair com. mem. I love to read math Hale Elem., 1994, mgmt. curriculum com. parent chair 1993-94. Mem. Minn. Citizens for the Arts (membership com. 1991—). Home: 4820 12th Ave S Minneapolis MN 55417 Office: Vinland Ctr PO Box 308 Lake Independence Loretto MN 55357

MILLIGAN, NONA VERNICE, retired elementary educator, pianist; b. Triadelphia, Ohio, Apr. 13, 1916; d. Harry Milton Nelson and Goldie Edna (Loughman) Nelson-Lipp; m. Dana Clifton Milligan, May 27, 1951. BS in Edn., Ohio U., 1941. Cert. elem., history, English, biology, and music tchr., Ohio. Tchr., prin. Muskingum County, Ohio, 1936-39, tchr. grades 5 and 6, 1939-43; tchr. grade 5 Zanesville (Ohio) Pub. Schs., 1943-51; pvt. tchr. music Zanesville, 1939-53, Takoma Park, Md., 1959-70; ret., 1970; pianist accompanying chorus Lewisdale Sch., Md., 1976-81. Chief judge voting Prince George's County Bd. Elections, 1968-74; substitute ch. organist, Zanesville and Columbus, Ohio, Silver Spring, Md., 1952-70; vol. Lifeline at Washington Adventist Hosp., Takoma Park, mem. staff, 1984-93; v.p. Christian Women's Fellowship Shepard Park Christian Ch., 1988-92, svc. chmn. Shepherd Park Ch., 1992-94, svc. dir., 1996—; deaconess Shepherd Park Ch., 1966-90, mem. ch. bd., 1966-90, vice chmn., 1986-88; capital area study dir., 1968-70. Mem. Takoma Park Women's Club (1st v.p. 1974-76, pres. 1976-78, parliamentarian 1992-94, asst. rec. sec. 1996—), D.C. Fedn. Women's Club (2d v.p. 1978-80, 1st v.p. 1980-82, 92-96, pres. 1982-84, parliamentarian 1992-94), Conf. 7 States (chmn. S.E. region 1986, v.p. S.E. region 1990-92), Ky. Col., Sligo Creek Club (program chmn. 1960-64, sec. 1970), Women's City Club of Washington (pres. 1990-92, 92-94, 96—), Columbia Arts Club (1st v.p. 1996—).

MILLIMAKI, CLAUDIA RAE, alcohol and drug counselor; b. Peoria, Ill., May 15, 1946; d. Erwin Roy and Lois Marie (Amick) Arnold; m. James Alan Millimaki, Apr. 15, 1977 (div. June 1989); children: Lloyd Edward, James Alan II. Degree, Calif. Assn. Alcoholism & Drug Abuse Counselors, Sonoma State U., 1989. Counselor Alternatives, Napa, Calif., Woman Alive, Napa; counselor Napa County Drinker Driver program St. Helena Hosp., Deer Park, Calif.; counselor Napa County Jail, Deer Park; mem. joint commn. Commn. on Status of Women, Napa, 1995; mem. Napa Valley Domestic Violence Prevention Coun. Author: (workbook) Domestic Violence. Home: 1415 Earl St Napa CA 94559 Office: Woman Alive/Alternatives Ste 204 1100 Lincoln Ave Napa CA 94558

MILLMAN, JODE SUSAN, lawyer; b. Poughkeepsie, N.Y., Dec. 28, 1954; d. Samuel Keith and Ellin Sadenberg (Bainder) M.; m. Michael James Harris, June 20, 1982; children: Maxwell, Benjamin. BA, Syracuse U., 1976, JD, 1979. Bar: N.Y. 1980, U.S. Dist. Ct. (so. and ea. dists.) N.Y. 1982, U.S. Supreme Ct. 1983. Asst. corp. counsel City of Poughkeepsie, 1979-81; assoc. Law Office of Lou Lewis, Poughkeepsie, 1981-85; pvt. practice Poughkeepsie, 1985—; staff counsel City of Poughkeepsie Office of Property Devel., 1990—; gen. mgr. WCZX-Communicatons Corp. Contbg. author: Kaminstein Legislative History of the Copyright Law, 1979. Pres. Dutchess County (N.Y.) Vis. Bur., 1980-82; bd. dirs. Poughkeepsie Ballet Theater, 1982, Jewish Comty. Ctr., 1988; mem. assigned counsel program Dutchess County Family Ct., 1985—; trustee Greater Poughkeepsie Libr. Dist., 1991-94, Poughkeepsie Day Sch., 1995—. Mem. ABA, N.Y. State Bar Assn., Dutchess County Bar Assn. (chmn. pub. rels. 1991—), Mid-Hudson Women's Bar Assn., Poughkeepsie Area C. of C. (econ. devel. com. 1994—). Democrat. Jewish. Office: 97-99 Cannon St Poughkeepsie NY 12601-3140

MILLS, CAROL DEE, special education educator; b. Ottawa, Ill., Dec. 23, 1954; d. Robert E. and Barbara Jean (Dunavan) M. AA, Lincoln Coll., 1974; BA, BS, Ea. Ill. U., 1976. Cert. tchr. elem. and spl. edn.; cert. tchr. types 3 and 10. Tchr. spl. edn. Streator (Ill.) Elem. Sch. 44, 1977—; mem. computer com. Streator Elem. Sch. 44, 1990—, mem. health and discipline com., 1992—, mem. spl. edn. com., 1994—. Author/editor (newsletter) Turnrow Times, 1992-93. Bd. dirs. Ottawa (Ill.) Campfire Girls, 1977-83; deacon 1st Congl. Ch., Ottawa, 1982-85. Recipient Ill. Horse & Pony Breeder High Point Champion award, 1995, Ill. Walking Horse Assn. High Point Plantation Champion award, 1995, Ill. Walking Horse Assn. Res. Versatility Champion award, 1995. Mem. PEO, Ill. Horse and Pony Breeder's Assn. (Hi-Point champion 1989, Hi-Point rex. champion 1990—), Ill. Walking Horse Assn. (bd. dirs., Hi-Point Plantation 2-gait In State/Out of State award 1989), Tenn. Walking Horse Breeder's and Exhibitors Assn. Republican. Office: Myrtel Kimes Sch 1207 Reading Streator IL 61364

MILLS, CAROL JANE, secondary education educator; b. Yakima, Wash., Feb. 23, 1946; d. Stanley Lionel and Mildred Davis (Shaw) Quinn; m. Donald Dwane Mills, July 12, 1969; children: Michael Robert, Jason Tyler. BA in History/Edn., Wash. State U., 1968; postgrad., schs. in Oreg. and Wash., 1980-92; MEd, Heritage Coll., Toppenish, Wash., 1994. Cert. tchr. K-12, Wash. Tchr. Northshore Sch. Dist., Bothell, Wash., 1968-69; substitute tchr. various locations, 1970-78; tchr. Volusia County Schs., DeLand, Fla., 1978-79; tchr. social studies Yakima Sch. Dist., 1979—; mem. h.s. standards com. Yakima Sch. Dist., 1985—; participant Wash. State-Hyogo (Japan) Social Studies Tchr. Exch., Kobe, 1992. Mem. stewardship/fin. com. Westpark United Meth. Ch., Yakima, 1991—; del. to county conv. Rep. Party, Yakima, 1992. Mem. Nat. Coun. for Social Studies, Wash. State Coun. for Social Studies (secondary rep. 1994—), Delta Delta Delta (dist. pres. 1978-81). Office: Eisenhower HS 702 S 40th Ave Yakima WA 98908-3331

MILLS, CAROL MARGARET, business consultant, public relations consultant; b. Salt Lake City, Aug. 31, 1943; d. Samuel Lawrence and Beth (Neilson) M.; BS magna cum laude, U. Utah, 1965. With W.S. Hatch Co., Woods Cross, Utah, 1965-87, corp. sec., 1970-87, traffic mgr., 1969-87, dir. publicity, 1974-87; cons. various orgns., 1988—; dir. Hatch Service Corp., 1972-87, Nat. Tank Truck Carriers, Inc., Washington, 1977-88; bd. dirs. Intermountain Tariff Bur. Inc., 1978-88, chmn., 1981-82, 1986-87; bd. dirs. Mountainwest Venture Group. Fund raiser March of Dimes, Am. Cancer Soc., Am. Heart Assn.; active senatorial campaign, 1976, gubernatorial campaign, 1984, 88, congl. campaign, 1990, 92, 94, vice chair voting dist., 1988-90, congressional campaign, 1994; chmn. 1990-92, chmn. party caucus legis. dist.; witness transp. com. Utah State Legislature, 1984, 85; apptd. by gov. to bd. trustees Utah Tech. Fin. Corp., 1986—, corp. sec., mem. exec. com., 1988—; mem. expdn. to Antarctica, 1996, Titanic '96 expdn. Recipient svc. awards W. S. Hatch Co., 1971, 80; mem. Pioneer Theatre Guild, 1985—; V.I.P. capt. Easter Seal Telethon, 1989, 90, recipient Outstanding Vol. Svc. award Easter Seal Soc. Utah, 1989, 90. Mem. Nat. Tank Truck Carriers Transp. Club Salt Lake City, Am. Trucking Assn. (pub. rels. coun.), Utah Motor Transport Assn. (dir. 1982-88), Internat. Platform Assn., Beta Gamma Sigma, Phi Kappa Phi, Phi Chi Theta. Home and Office: 77 Edgecombe Dr Salt Lake City UT 84103-2219

MILLS, CELESTE LOUISE, hypnotherapist, professional magician; b. L.A., May 16, 1952; d. Emery John and Helen Louise (Bradbury) W.; m. Robert Richardson Feigel, Apr. 11, 1971 (div. 1973); m. Peter Alexander Mills, June 12, 1991. (div. 1992). BBA, Western State U., Doniphan, Mo., 1987; PhD in Religion, Universal Life Ch. Univ., 1987; grad., Hypnotism Tng. Inst., Glendale, Calif., 1990. Cert. hypnotherapist. Credit mgr. accounts receivable Gensler-Lee Diamonds, Santa Barbara, Calif., 1973-74, Terry Hinge and Hardware, Van Nuys, Calif., 1975-78; credit mgr., fin. analyst Peanut Butter Fashions, Chatsworth, Calif., 1978-82; personal mgr. Charter Mgmt. Co., Beverly Hills, Calif., 1982-83; co-owner, v.p. Noreen Jenney Communicates, Beverly Hills, 1983-85; corp. credit mgr., fin. analyst Cen. Diagnostic Lab., Tarzana, Calif., 1985-89; credit mgr., fin. analyst Metwest Clin. Lab., Inc., Tarzana, Calif., 1989-90; pvt. practice, 1990—; cons. Results Now, Inc., Tarzana, 1986-87. Prodr., host (TV) Brainstorm, 1993—. Media spokesperson Am. Cancer Soc., 1990—. Mem. NAFE, NOW, Nat. Humane Ednl. Found., Credit Mgrs. Assn. Trade Groups (bd. govs. 1988-89), Nat. Clin. Lab. Trade Group (chmn. 1988-89), Med. and Surg. Suppliers Trade Group (vice chmn. 1988-89, chmn. 1989-90), Soc. Am. Magicians, Acad. Magical Arts, Internat. Brotherhood of Magicians, Assn. Advanced Ethical Hypnosis, Am. Coun. Hypnotist Examiners.

MILLS, DOROTHY ALLEN, investor; b. New Brunswick, N.J., Dec. 14, 1920; d. James R. and Bertha Lovilla (Porter) Allen; m. George M. Mills, Apr. 21, 1945; children: Dianne, Adele, Dorothy L. BA, Douglass Coll., New Brunswick, N.J., 1943. Investment reviewer Cen. Hanover Bank, N.Y.C., 1943-44; asst. to dir. of admissions and sec. undergrad. yrs. Douglass Coll., New Brunswick, 1944-45; sec., regional dir. O.P.A., Ventura, Calif., 1945-46; corp. sec. George M. Mills Inc., Highland Park, N.J., 1946-75; pvt. investor N. Brunswick, N.J., 1975—. Sr. v.p. Children Am. Revolution, N.J., 1965; active alumni com. Douglass Coll., 1990—. Recipient Douglass Alumni award, 1992. Mem. AAUW, New Brunswick Hist. Soc., DAR, English Speaking Union, Rutgers Alumni Faculty Club, Princeton-Douglass Alumni Club, N. Brunswick Women's Club, Auxiliary Robert Wood Johnson Hosp. and Med. Sch. Republican. Mem. Dutch Reformed Ch. Home: 1054 Hoover Dr New Brunswick NJ 08902

MILLS, ELIZABETH JENNINGS, art educator; b. Baton Rouge, La., Feb. 19, 1947; d. Robert Bernard Jennings and Virginia Adelia (Lobdell) Jennings; m. Wilmer Riddle Mills Dec. 28, 1967; children: Wilmer Hastings, Evelyn Kate, Virginia Young, John Jennings. BA in Art and English, La. State Univ., 1969. Agrl. missionary to Brazil S.Am. Presbyn. Ch. in U.S., La., 1972-80; weaving demonstrator ch. and civic groups, St. Francisville, La., 1983—; guest lectr. James Madison U., Harrisonburg, Va., 1995. Exhbns. include Zeigler Mus., Jennings, La., 1993, La. State U., 1995, Cabaret Theater, 1995, La. Arts and Science Ctr. Mus., 1996. Mem., officer, tchr. The Plains Presbyn. Ch., Zachary, La., 1980—; mem., officer Study Clubs/Book Clubs, Baton Rouge and Zachary, 1982—; vol. Baton Rouge Symphony, 1987-90; tour guide Plantation Homes St. Francisville Pilgrimage, West Feliciana, La., 1985—. Mem. Assoc. Women in the Arts (sec. 1991-93), Artist Guild of West Feliciana (bd. dirs. 1992—), The Weaving Group. Home: 22552 Old Scenic Hwy 964 Zachary LA 70791

MILLS, ELIZABETH SHOWN, genealogical editor; b. Cleve., Dec. 29, 1944; d. Floyd Finley Shown and Elizabeth Thulmar (Jeffcoat) Carver; m. Gary Bernard Mills, Apr. 15, 1963; children: Clayton Bernard, Donna Rachal, Daniel Garland. BA, U. Ala., 1980. Cert. genealogist. Profl. geneal., writer, 1972-86; editor Nat. Geneal. Soc., Arlington, Va., 1987—; faculty Samford U. Inst. of Genealogy and Hist. Rsch., Birmingham, Ala., 1980-96, trustee Assn. for Promotion of Scholarship in Genealogy, N.Y., 1984-90, contract dir., cons. U. Ala., 1985-92, faculty Nat. Inst. of Geneal. Rsch., 1989-96. Contbr. articles to profl. jours. Mem. adv. bd. Assn. for Preservation of Historic Natchitoches, La., 1972-80, bd. mem. Friends of La. State Archives, Baton Rouge, 1976-77, Tuscaloosa (Ala.) Preservation Soc., 1984-85, chair Hist. Records Task Force Ala. State Archives, Montgomery, 1984-85; trustee Nat. Bd. Certification Genealogists, 1984-89, v.p., 1989-94, pres., 1994—. Named Outstanding Young Women of Am. Jaycees, Gadsden, 1976, Outstanding Alumna award U. Ala. New Coll., Tuscaloosa, 1990. Fellow Am. Soc. of Geneal. (sec. 1992-95, v.p. 1995—), Nat. Geneal. Soc., Utah Geneal. Assn.; mem. Assn. of Profl. Geneal. (smallwood Svc. award, 1989),. Republican. Roman Catholic. Home: 1732 Ridgedale Dr Tuscaloosa AL 35406-1942 Office: Nat Geneal Soc 4527 17th St N Arlington VA 22207-2399

MILLS, GLORIA ADAMS, environmental service company executive; b. Chgo., Mar. 1, 1940; d. Edward Charles and Olive Margaret (McCarty) Adams; m. Peter Mills, Dec. 29, 1962 (div. July 1986). BA, Rosary Coll., River Forest, Ill., 1962, MALS, 1970; MBA, U. Chgo., 1976. Lit. chemist UOP, Inc., Des Plaines, Ill., 1962-70, supr. patent libr., 1970-77, mktg. engr., 1977-81, mgr. project devel., 1981-83; v.p. mktg. Ogden Projects, Inc., Fairfield, N.J., 1983-87, sr. v.p. mktg., 1987-89, exec. v.p. mktg., 1989-94; exec. v.p. bus. devel., 1994—; mem. indsl. adv. bd. So. Ill. U. Coll. Engring. and Tech., Carbondale, 1985-90. Contbr. articles to profl. jours. Mem. ASME (solid waste processing div.), Am. Chem. Soc., Air and Waste Mgmt. Assn. Office: Ogden Projects Inc 40 Lane Rd Fairfield NJ 07004-1012

MILLS, INGA-BRITTA, artist; b. Eskilstuna, Sweden, Sept. 14, 1925; came to U.S., 1954; d. Gerhard Valdemar and Märta Kristina (Söderberg) Stenhäll; m. Mogens Schiött, June, 1950 (div. 1952); m. Victor Moore Mills, June 6, 1956; children: Karl-Olof, Victoria Inga Kristina. Attended, U. Gothenburg, Sweden, 1946-48; BA, MA, Montclair State Coll., 1979; postgrad., Temple U., 1980-82. Sec. to port dir. Port Authority, Gothenburg, Sweden, 1952-54; adminstrv. asst. UN, N.Y.C., 1954-55. One-person shows include Montclair Pub. Libr., 1977, UN Food and Agr. Orgn., Rome, 1979, Libr. Arts Ctr., Newport, N.H., 1984, Ariel Gallery, Soho, N.Y.C., 1986, Stamford Mus. and Nature Ctr., 1989, Burnham Libr., Bridgewater, Conn., 1991, Westover Sch., Middlebury, Conn., 1993, Roxbury Libr., 1995, Gallery AE, Gothenburg, Sweden, 1995, Conn. Housing Fin. Authority, Rockyhill; exhibited in group shows including Am. Women's Assn. of Rome, 1982, Marian Graves Mugar Gallery, Colby-Sawyer Coll., New London, N.H., 1984, Artworks Gallery, Hartford, Conn., 1986, Greene Gallery, Guilford, Conn., 1989, The Discovery Mus., Bridgeport, Conn., 1990, Silvermine Galleries, New Canaan, Conn., 1990, Ward-Nasse Gallery, Soho, 1991, 92, Internat. Juried Print Exhibit, Somers, N.Y., 1992, Grand Prix Fine Art de Paris, 1993, Stamford Hist. Soc., 1993, Montserrat Gallery, Soho, 1994, Internat. Print Biennial, Cracow, Poland, 1994, Trenton (N.J.) State Coll., 1995, New Haven Paint and Clay Club, 1995, Conn. Women Artists, New Britain Mus. Am. Art, 1995; represented in collections Conning & Co., N.Y.C., New Haven Paint and Clay Club, Somerstown Gallery, Somers; represented in pvt. collections, U.S., Europe, Japan, and Australia. Recipient Marjorie Frances Meml. award Stamford (Conn.) Mus. and Nature Ctr., 1990, Faber-Birren Color award Stamford Art Assn., 1990. Mem. Wash. Art Assn. (mem. exhbn. com. 1992—, bd. trustees 1995—). Democrat.

MILLS, JENNIFER LYNN, technical support analyst; b. Albuquerque, Sept. 12, 1962; d. Kenneth Dean and Jean Ellen (Easley) M. A of Tech. Arts and Computer Info. Svcs., Edmonds C.C., Lynnwood, Wash., 1989. Tech. support analyst Revelation Technologies, Inc., Bellevue, Wash., 1992-94; contract cons. CJ Enterprises, Los Alamos, N.Mex., 1994; tech. support analyst Lovelace Biomedical Rsch. Inst., Albuquerque, 1995, Inhalation Toxicology Rsch. Inst., Albuquerque, 1995, BASIS Internat., Ltd., Albuquerque, 1995—. Mem. Sigma Chi, Alpha Alpha Tau. Office: BASIS Internat Ltd 5901 Jefferson NE Albuquerque NM 87109

MILLS, KATHLEEN CLAIRE, anthropology and mathematics educator; b. Pitts., Dec. 27, 1948; d. Clair I. and Ruth (McDowell) Wilson; m. William G. Mills, May 27, 1978; 1 child, David Lee. AS, Kilgore Coll., 1968; BS, Met. State Coll., Denver, 1982; MA in Secondary Edn., U. Colo., 1987, MA in Anthropology, 1989. Mem. staff U.S. Geol. Survey, Denver, 1980-82; computer application specialist Petroleum Info., Englewood, Colo., 1982-83; entry level geologist La. Land and Exploration, Denver, 1983-86; prof. anthropology and math. C.C. of Aurora, 1987—, GED coord., 1996—; prof. anthropology Red Rocks C.C., 1994—; excavation supr. Caesarea Maritima, Israel, 1989—. Drafter U.S. Oil and Gas Map, 1981. Mem. Am. Schs. Oriental Rsch., Denver Natural History Mus., Archaeol. Inst. Am. Colo. Archaeol. Soc., Nat. Geog. Soc. Home: 7946 E Mexico Ave Denver CO 80231-5687 Office: Community Coll Aurora 16000 E Centretech Pky Aurora CO 80011-9057

MILLS, KATHRYN, publishing manager; b. Nyack, N.Y., July 14, 1955; d. Charles Wright and Ruth (Harper) M.; m. Michael Moore, Aug. 25, 1984; 1 child, Eric Mills Moore. BS in Polit. Econs., Hampshire Coll., 1976. Facilitator housing and svcs. Mission Hill Planning Commn., Boston, 1978-81; editl. asst. trade and reference divsn. Houghton Mifflin Co., Boston, 1982-85, permissions editor sch. divsn., 1985-87, supr. permissions sch. divsn., 1987-90, asst. mgr. contracts, trade and reference divsn., 1990-92, mgr. contracts, trade and reference divsn., 1992—. Bd. dirs. Assn. for Pub. Transp., Cambridge, Mass., 1978-79. Mem. NOW, Audubon Soc., Pub. Citizen. Office: Houghton Mifflin Co 222 Berkeley St Boston MA 01226

MILLS, LETHA ELAINE, physician, educator; b. Norwalk, Conn., Nov. 14, 1952; d. Clifford Wheeler and Letha Lucille (Jones) M.; m. Lloyd Herbert Maurer, Sept. 1, 1984; children: Adam, Jason, Stephen. BA, U. Pa., 1974; MD, Dartmouth U., 1977. Diplomate Am. Bd. Internal Medicine, Am. Bd. Hematology, Am. Bd. Oncology. Internal medicine intern Dartmouth-Hitchcock Med. Ctr., Hanover, N.H., 1977-78, internal medicine resident, 1978-80, hematology fellow, 1981-83; hematology fellow U. Wash., 1980-81; with Lawy-Hitchcock Clinic, Lebanon, N.H., 1986—; asst. prof. medicine Dartmouth Med. Sch., Hanover, N.H., 1983-91, assoc. prof. medicine, 1991—; med. advisor N.H. Breast Cancer Coalition, 1994—; mem. Gov.'s Adv. Panel on Cancer and Chronic Diseases, Concord, N.H., 1996—. Contbr. articles to profl. jours. Mem. Am. Soc. Hematology, Am. Soc. Clin. Oncology, Am. Fedn. Clin. Rsch. (mem. bone marrow transplant com. cancer and leukemia group B), Phi Beta Kappa, Alpha Omega Alpha. Democrat. Home: 286 Maple Hill Rd Norwich VT 05055 Office: Dartmouth-Hitchcock Med Ctr Lebanon NH 03756

MILLS, LINDA S., public relations executive; b. San Antonio, June 26, 1951; d. Frank M. and Betty A. (Young) M. BA, St. Mary's U., 1971. Asst. dir. Paseo Del Rio Assn., San Antonio, 1971-74; mktg. officer Frost Nat. Bank, San Antonio, 1974-79; account exec. Fleishman-Hillard Inc., St. Louis, 1979-81, v.p., sr. ptnr., 1981-85, exec. v.p., sr. ptnr., 1985—, dir. corp. planning, 1986—; bd. dirs. Fleishman-Hillard U.K. Ltd., London, Fleishman-Hillard France, Paris. Mem. adv. bd. St. John's Mercy Med. Ctr. Mem. Pub. Relations Soc. Am., Noonday Club. Office: Fleishman Hillard Inc 200 N Broadway Saint Louis MO 63102-2730

MILLS, LOIS JEAN, company executive, former legislative aide, former education educator; b. Chgo., Oct. 20, 1939; d. Martin J. and Annabelle M. (Hrabik) Rademacher; m. Frederick V. Mills, Dec. 1, 1974; children: Todd, Susan, Randal, Merre, Mollie, Michael, Mark (dec.). BS in Edn., Ill. State U., Normal, 1962, MS in Edn., 1969. Lectr. elem. curriculum Ill. State U., 1973-90; in-svc. advisor for elem., gifted, critical thinking and study skills, coop. learning Title I State Bd. Edn., Springfield, Ill., 1969-90; elem. tchr., supr. Metcalf Lab. Sch. Ill. State U., 1962-72; legis. aide to Asst. Majority Leader Senator John Maitland, Jr., Ill. Gen. Assembly, 1990-95; pres., ptnr. Mills Design Assocs., 1996—; mem. state rep. Dan Rutherford's house task force for statute repeal, 1995—, adv. roundtable, 1995—, legis. task force for cmty. residential svcs. deaf adults, 1995—; campaign coord. Asst. Majority Leader Senator John Maitland Jr., 1995—; county campaign coord. for Ill. Comptroller Loleta Didrickson, 1994—. Contbr. articles to profl. jours. Pres. Leadership Ill., 1994—, pres.-elect, 1993-94; past pres. governing bd. Lake Bloomington Assn., v.p., 1993-94, pres., 1994-95; mem. mgmt. com. McLean County 21st Century commn., 1991-92, vice chair cmty. rels., 1991-92; commr. McLean County Regional Planning commn., vice chair 1994-95; charter bd. govs. Ill. Lincoln Excellence in Pub. Svc. Series, 1994—, other civic activities; mem. Ill. steering com. Beijing-UN Women's Conf. One Yr. Later, 1996. Recipient Exemplary Tchr. awards Ill. State U. Student Elem. Edn. Bd., Women of Distinction award YWCA of McLean County. Mem. NAFE, Ill. State U. Alumni Assn. (bd. dirs. 1982—, nat. pres. 1992-94, past nat. pres. 1994—), McLean County Rep. Women's Club (v.p. 1986, pres. 1987, past pres. 1988), Ill. Rep. Committeewoman's Roundtable, Ill. Fedn. Rep. Women, Nat. Fedn. Rep. Women, Internat. Platform Assn. Home: K-162 Lake Bloomington RR 2 Box 60A Hudson IL 61748-9414

MILLS, MARGIE BATLEY, home health care executive; b. Gloster, Miss., Apr. 13, 1939; d. Charlie James and Celia Dee (Pettis) Batley; m. Robert Jackson Mills, Nov. 26, 1958; children: David Glen, Angela Denise Mills Dobson, Joel Vincent. Diploma, Mobile Gen. Hosp. Sch. Nursing, 1961; BS, St. Joseph's Coll., 1985. Assoc. dir. nurses D.W. McMillan Hosp., Brewton, Ala., 1961-63; head nurse burn unit Mobile (Ala.) Gen. Hosp., 1963-65, instr. Sch. Nursing, 1965-67; dir. nurses Twin Oaks Nursing Home, Mobile, 1968-70; field nurse Bur. Crippled Children, Panama City, Fla., 1970-72; dir. nurses Mary and Joseph Home of Elderly, New Orleans, 1972-73; Medicare coord. Eastwood Hosp., El Paso, Tex., 1973-76; dir. nurses ABC Home Health of Jacksonville, Fla., 1976-77; pres., COO, owner First Am. Home Care (formerly ABC Home Health Svcs., Inc.), Brunswick, Ga., 1977—. Author: Homebound, 1994. Pres. Glynn County Crisis Ctr., 1989; bd. dirs. Brunswick unit Am. Cancer Soc., 1991-92, pres., 1995—; bd. dirs. Am. Heart Assn., 1991-92, Salvation Army, 1994; bd. dirs. Brunswick United Way, 1992, pres. 1993-94; cmty. svc. chair Brunswick Kiwanis, 1991-92, pres., 1994; mem. vocat. adv. bd. Brunswick Coll., 1992; 2d v.p. United Way of Glynn, 1992. Recipient Top Ten Bus. Women of Yr. nomination Am. Bus. Womens Assn., 1996. Mem. ANA, Nat. League Nursing, Am. Fedn. Home Health (pres. 1987-91), Ga. Assn. Home Health (pres. 1980-82, 86-88). Methodist. Home: 2660 Frederica Rd Saint Simons Island GA 31522-1917 Office: First Am Home Care 3528 Darien Hwy Brunswick GA 31525

MILLS, MIRIAM KOSINER, social sciences educator; b. Leipzig, Germany, May 22, 1938; d. Robert and Freida (Leipziger) Kosiner. BA in Philosophy, CUNY, 1964; PA, NYU, 1969, PhD in Pub. Adminstrn., 1978. Asst. prof. N.J. Inst. Tech. Sch. Indsl. Mgmt., Newark, 1975-83, assoc. prof., 1983-88, prof., 1988—; Disting. prof. N.J. Inst. Tech., Newark, 1992; grad. faculty Rutgers U., Newark, 1986—; vis. scholar U. Ill., Urbana, 1984-85; dir. manpower and labor rels. Jersey Med. Ctr., Jersey City, 1972-75; dir. pers. Jewish Home and Hosp. for Aged, N.Y.C., 1965-72; cons. in field; founder Miriam K. Mills Rsch. Ctr. for Super-Optimizing Analysis and Developing Nations, 1992. Author, co-author: Multi-Criteria Methods for Alternative Dispute Resolution: With Microcomputer Software Applications, 1990, The Penny Diary: Countering Illness, 1991, Developing Nations and Super-Optimum Policy Analysis, 1992, Professional Developments in Policy Studies, 1992; editor, co-editor: Conflict Resolution and Public Policy, 1990, Alternative Dispute Resolution in the Public Sector, 1991, Systematic Analysis in Dispute Resolution, 1991, Health Insurance and Public Policy: Risk, Allocation and Equity, 1992, Publica Administration in China, 1993, Public Policy in China, 1993; sponsor Encyclopedia of Policy Studies, 1993, Treatise of Policy Studies and Developing Nations, multi-vol. 1994, Super-Optimizing Methods and Processes, 1994; contbr. articles to jours. Bd. dirs. Am. Cancer Soc., Ill., 1990; mem. exec. bd. Upjohn Home Health Svcs., Newark, 1988-91; bd. govs. Palisades (N.J.) Gen. Hosp., 1983-85; mem. exec. com. Coun. State Govts. Recipient Thomas R. Dye award for policy studies svc., 1992. Mem. Am. Soc. Pub. Adminstrn., Am. Hosp. Assn., Internat. Polit. Sci. Assn., Indsl. Rels. Rsch. Assn., Soc. Profls. in Dispute Resolution, Evaluation Soc. & Evaluation Network, Policy Studies Orgn. (coun. mem. 1991). Democrat. Jewish. Home: 711 Ashton Ln S Champaign IL 61820-7304 Office: NJ Inst Tech Martin Luther King Dr Newark NJ 07102

MILLS, NANCY STEWART, chemistry educator; b. Osceola, Nebr., Mar. 31, 1950; d. Robert Lees and Margaret Eva (Stewart) M.; m. Mark Alan

Hurd, Aug. 20, 1977; children: Caroline Margaret Mills Hurd, William Clark Mills Hurd. BA, Grinnell Coll., 1972; PhD, U. Ariz., 1976. Asst. prof. Carleton Coll., Northfield, Minn., 1977-79; asst. prof. Trinity U., San Antonio, 1979-83, assoc. prof., 1983-89, prof., 1979—, chmn. chemistry dept., 1990-93; mem. dept. rev. team Bowdoin Coll., Brunswick, Maine, 1986, Macalester Coll., St. Paul, 1989, Albion Coll., 1991, Hamilton Coll., 1996; mem. Coun. on Undergrad. Rsch., 1991—, chair chemistry divsn., 1996—. Contbr. articles to profl. jours. Grantee NSF, Welch Found., Petroleum Rsch. Fund, Rsch. Corp., 1977—; Camille and Henry Dreyfus Found. scholar, 1994; recipient Outstanding Teaching and Campus Leadership award Sears Roebuck Found., 1990, Z.T. Scott Fellowship for outstanding teaching Trinity U., 1992. Mem. AAUP, Sigma Xi. Home: 137 Alta Ave San Antonio TX 78209-4508 Office: Trinity U 715 Stadium Dr San Antonio TX 78212-7200

MILLS, PATRICIA JAGENTOWICZ, political philosophy educator, writer; b. Newark, Mar. 18, 1944; d. Alexander A. and Louise A. (Breunig) Jagentowicz; 1 child, Holland Mills. BA, Rutgers U., 1973; MA, SUNY, Stony Brook, 1975; PhD, York U., Toronto, Ont., Can., 1984. Lectr. U. Toronto, 1984-85, vis. scholar, 1985-86, asst. prof. philosophy, 1986-88; asst. prof. polit. theory U. Mass., Amherst, 1988-91, assoc. prof. polit. theory, 1991—; lectr. philosophy dept. Smith Coll., spring 1992; manuscript referee Social Scis. and Humanities Rsch. Coun. Can., 1985-86, 87-88, 91-92, Polity: Jour. of Northeastern Polit. Sci. Assn., 1990, 91; invited spkr. NEH seminar, Mt. Holyoke Coll., 1992, U. Pitts., 1993, Coll. Holy Cross, 1991, New Sch. for Social Rsch., 1990. Author: Woman, Nature, and Psyche, 1987; editor: Feminist Interpretations of G.W.F. Hegel, 1996; author, contbr.: (book chpts.) The Sexism of Social and Political Theory: Women and Reproduction from Plato to Nietzsche, 1979, Ethnicity in a Technological Age, 1988, Taking Our Time: Feminist Perspectives on Temporality, 1989, Renewing the Earth: The Promise of Social Ecology, 1990, The Future of Continental Philosophy and the Politics of Difference, 1991, Ecological Feminist Philosophies, 1996; contbr. articles to profl. jours. Dir. Drop-In Ctr., Newark, 1972-73; mem. N.J. Abortion Project, 1971-73; mem. Fortune Soc., N.J., 1972; grassroots organizer against the war in Vietnam, N.J., 1970-71; grassroots organizer women's movement, N.J. and N.Y., 1971-73. Postdoctoral fellow Social Scis. and Humanities Rsch. Coun. Can., 1983-85; scholar York U., 1975; faculty grantee for tchg. U. Mass., 1991-92. Mem. Am. Philos. Assn. (conf. presenter 1995 meeting), Soc. for Phenomenology and Existential Philosophy (presenter conf. papers 1988, 91, 92), Hegel Soc. Am., Soc. for Women in Philosophy, Nat. Women's Studies Assn. Office: U Mass Thompson Hall Dept Polit Sci Amherst MA 01003

MILLS, SANDRA SUE, accountant; b. Neosho, Mo., Oct. 31, 1954; d. Theodore John and Nora Mozelle (Sharp) Sandlin; m. Bryce Mahlon Toler, Mar. 20, 1976 (div. Dec. 1986); 1 child, Bradley John Toler; m. John Davis Mills, Jan. 1, 1988. BS in Bus. Adminstrn., Mo. So. State U., 1976; MBA, S.W. Mo. State U., 1991. Accounts payable mgr. Sunbeam Outdoor Products, Neosho, Mo., 1980-81, staff acct., 1981-85, acctg. mgr., 1985-88, asst. contr., 1988-95, contr., 1995—. Mem. Neosho Area Bus. and Industry Found., 1995-96. Named to Outstanding Young Women of Am., 1988. Mem. Inst. Cert. Mgmt. Accts. (bd. dirs.), Kiwanis Internat. (treas.). Office: Sunbeam Outdoor Products 4101 Howard Bush Dr Neosho MO 64850

MILLS, SHIRLEY SANDLIN, administrator; b. L.A., June 11, 1937; d. Lyle Lauriston and Vera Mae (Hallmark) Sandlin; m. Roger Lee Smith, Feb. 1, 1955 (div. Feb. 1962); children: Sheryl Lee Durham Bartlett English, Roger Sandlin; m. William Allen Mills, Aug. 4, 1965 (div. Oct. 1986); children: Cynthia Sue, William Foster. BA in Psychology, Calif. State U., L.A., 1965; MA in Ednl. Psychology, Calif. State U., Long Beach, 1975; PhD in Edn., UCLA, 1996. Tchr., counselor L.A. Unified Sch. Dist., 1965-74; intern sch. psychologist Garden Grove (Calif.) Unified Sch. Dist., 1975-76; sch. psychologist Little Lake (Calif.) City Sch. Dist., 1976-79; dist. psychologist San Gabriel (Calif.) Sch. Dist., 1979-83, asst. supt., 1983-86; adminstrv. dir. Corona (Calif.) - Norco Unified Sch. Dist., 1986-87, asst. supt. edn. svcs., 1987-90, asst. supt. curriculum, 1990-93, asst. supt. pupil personnel svcs., 1993-95, asst. supt. testing, evaluation and quality control, 1995—; mem. adv. bd. Family Svcs. Assn., West San Gabriel, Calif., 1984-86; cons. human resources Robert Cash & Assocs., Long Beach, 1973-78. Author: Human Resources Development, 1977. Pres. women's divsn. San Gabriel C. of C., 1986; mem. The Thursday Group, Riverside, Calif., 1992-94m World Affairs Coun., Riverside, 1986-94; commr. Riverside County Commn. Status of Women, 1993-94. Mem. AAUW (exec. bd. 1989-93), ASCD, So. Counties Women in Ednl. Mgmt., Assn. Calif. Sch. Adminstrs. (exec. bd. 1983-86), Soroptimists Internat., Pi Lambda Theta. Home: 1549 Paseo Grande Corona CA 91720-3704 Office: Corono-Norco Unified Schs 2820 Clark Ave Norco CA 91760-1903

MILLS, STEPHANIE ELLEN, writer; b. Berkeley, Calif., Sept. 11, 1948; d. Robert C. and Edith (Garrison) M.; m. Philip Thiel (div. 1990). BA, Mills Coll., 1969. Campus organizer Planned Parenthood, Alameda, San Francisco, Calif., 1969-70; also Oakland, Calif., 1969-70; editor in chief Earth Times, San Francisco, 1970; story editor Earth, San Francisco, 1971; conference facilitator Mills Coll., Oakland, 1973-74; writer family planning program Emory Univ., Atlanta, 1974; dir. outings program Friends of the Earth, San Francisco, 1975-76, dir. membership devel., 1976-78; fellow Found. for Nat. Progress, San Francisco, 1978-80; from asst. editor to editor CoEvolution Quar., Sausalito, Calif., 1980-82; editor in chief, rsch. dir. Calif. Tomorrow, San Francisco, 1982-83; dir. devel. World Coll. West, San Rafael, Calif., 1983-84; freelance writer, lectr., 1984—; v.p. Earth First! Found., 1986-89; pres. No. Mich. Environ. Action Coun., 1987-88; mem. planning com. Great Lakes Bioregional Congress, 1991; pres. bd. dirs. Oryana Natural Foods Coop., 1992-93; mem. adv. coun. Earth Island Inst., Alliance for Paving Moratorium, Northwoods Wilderness Recovery. Author: In Service of the Wild: Restoring and Reinhabiting Damaged Land, 1995; editor, contbr. Whatever Happened to Ecology?, 1989, In Praise of Nature, 1990; corr. Wild Earth; editor-in-chief Not Man Apart newsletter from Friends of the Earth, 1978; editl. adv. E; contbr. articles to popular mags. Bd. dirs. Planned Parenthood Fedn. Am., 1970-76. Recipient award Mademoiselle, 1969, Friends of UN Environ. Program, 1987; grantee Point Found., 1972, IRA-HITI Found., 1992; resident Blue Mountain Ctr., 1983, 86. Office: care Katinka Matson Brockman Inc 5 East 59th St New York NY 10022*

MILLS, SYLVIA ANNE, educator; b. Carlsbad, N. Mex., June 24, 1943; d. Charles William and Tommie Kate (Mayes) Campbell; m. Sidney Lane Mills, Jul. 26, 1964; children: Marquesa, Kim, Kris. BA, McMurry U., 1964. Cert. elem. tchr. Tchr. Albuquerque (N. Mex.) Pub. Sch., 1964-68, 1975—; tech. coord. Albuquerque Pub. Sch. Zuni Magnet Sch., 1987—. Sec. 1 Meth. Kids Nursery and Presch., Albuquerque, 1994-95, bd. dirs. 1995—. Named N. Mex. IBM Tchr. of the Year IBM, 1990, Christa McAuliffe fellow for N. Mex., U.S. Dept. of Edn., 1990, Outstanding Educator award Milken Family Found., N. Mex. Bd. of Edn., 1994. Mem. Nat. Edn. Assn., Internat. Soc. for Tech. in Edn., Phi Delta Kappa. Republican. Methodist. Home: 2820 California NE Albuquerque NM 87110 Office: Zuni Elem Magnet Sch 6300 Claremont NE Albuquerque NM 87110

MILLSAPS, ELLEN MCNUTT, English language educator; b. Sheffield, Ala., Feb. 10, 1947; d. Ershell Jerome and Annie Inez (Quillen) McNutt; m. Douglas Edward Millsaps, Nov. 27, 1971; 1 child, Stephen Edward. BA, Miss. Coll., 1969; MA, U. Tenn., 1972, PhD, 1976. Teaching asst. U. Tenn., Knoxville, 1970-71, 75-76; assoc. prof. English, dept. head Walters State Community Coll., Morristown, Tenn., 1971-79; prof. English, dir. writing across curriculum Carson-Newman Coll., Jefferson City, Tenn., 1979—; cons. on writing Omicron Nu, 1989, Tenn. Network Foxfire Tchrs., 1992. Contbr. essays to profl. jours. Fellow NDEA, 1969-72, John C. Hodges fellow U. Tenn., 1975; rsch. grantee Appalachian Coll. Found., 1993, Appalachian Coll. Assn., 1995. Mem. South Atlantic MLA, Nat. Coun. Tchrs. English, Conf. on Coll. Composition and Comm., Soc. for Study So. Lit., Assn. Profl. Writing Cons., Alpha Chi (region v.p. 1992.-4, region pres. 1994-96), Sigma Tau Delta, Kappa Delta Pi, Delta Omicron, Alpha Lambda Delta. Baptist. Home: 7604 Sagefield Dr Knoxville TN 37920-9223 Office: Carson-Newman Coll PO Box 71957 Jefferson City TN 37760-7001

MILLSTEIN, ELIZABETH TOROP, training director; b. Phila., Mar. 23, 1961; d. William Torop and Nancy Torop Bloomfield; m. Cary David Millstein, Apr. 8, 1989; children: Rachel, Adam. BA in Music/Philosophy, Wellesley Coll., 1983; cert. tng. specialist, Georgetown U., 1995. Asst. v.p. Town and Country Mortgage, Fairfax, Va., 1984-85; v.p. Merich Brokers, Alexandria, Va., 1985-86, Wye Mortgage Corp., Lutherville, Md., 1986-89, Greater Atlantic Savs. Bank, Rockville, Md., 1989-90; asst. v.p. 1st Nat. Mortgage Corp., Glen-Burnie, Md., 1990-93; sr. tng. analyst Fannie Mae, Washington, 1993-94, dir. tng. and devel., 1994—. Mem. ASTD, Profl. Soc. for Sales and Mktg. Tng. Office: Fannie Mae 4000 Wisconsin Ave NW Washington DC 20016

MILMAN, DORIS HOPE, pediatrics educator, psychiatrist; b. N.Y.C., Nov. 17, 1917; d. Barnet S. and Rose (Smoleroff) Milman; m. Nathan Kreeger, June 15, 1941; 1 child, Elizabeth Kreeger Goldman. BA, Barnard Coll., 1938; MD, NYU, 1942. Diplomate Am. Bd. Pediats.; lic. physician, N.Y. Intern Jewish Hosp., Bklyn., 1942-43, resident, 1944-46, fellow in pediat., 1946-47; postgrad. extern in psychiatry Bellevue Hosp., N.Y.C., 1947-49; attending pediat. psychiatrist Jewish Hosp., Bklyn., 1950-56; asst. prof. pediat. Health Sci. Ctr. at Bklyn. SUNY, 1956-67, assoc. prof., 1967-73, prof., 1973-93, prof. emeritus, 1993—, acting chmn. dept. pediat., 1973-75, 82; pvt. practice child and adolescent psychiatry, Bklyn., 1950-90; vis. prof. Ben Gurion U. of the Negev, Beersheva, Israel, 1977. Mem. adv. bd. N.Y. Assn. for the Learning Disabled, N.Y.C., 1975-80. Recipient Disting. Alumna award Barnard Coll., 1986, Solomon R. Berson Achievement award NYU Sch. Medicine, 1991; Grace Potter Rice fellow Barnard Coll., 1938-39. Fellow Am. Acad. Pediat. (emeritus), Am. Psychiat. Assn. (life); mem. AAAS, Am. Orthopsychiat. Assn. (life), Am. Pediat. Soc. (emeritus), N.Y. Pediat. Soc. (emeritus). Home: 126 Westminster Rd Brooklyn NY 11218-3444 Office: Health Sci Ctr at Bklyn SUNY Box 49 450 Lenox Rd Brooklyn NY 11203-2020

MILNER, MARY DETTMAN, elementary education educator; b. Gonzales, Tex., Aug. 28, 1949; d. Henry Roland and Roberta (Meneley) Dettman; m. James D. Milner, Aug. 29, 1969; 1 child, Deborah Carleton. BS in Elem. Edn., U. Tex., Austin, 1970, MEd in Curriculum and Instrn., 1974. Cert. elem. tchr., Tex. Tchr. Burnet (Tex.) Consolidated Sch. Dist., 1970-72, Lufkin (Tex.) Ind. Sch. Dist., 1972-73, Austin Ind. Sch. Dist., 1974-80; tchr., 1st grade team leader Ft. Bend Ind. Sch. Dist., Sugar Land, Tex., 1985—; tchr. trainer N.J. Writing Project in Tex., Spring, 1993—. Chair family life com. First Meth. Ch., Sugar Land, 1983-86, mem.-at-large coun. on ministries, 1987. Mem. Nat. Coun. Tchrs. English, Internat. Reading. Assn., West Houston Area Coun. Tchrs. English (bd. dirs. 1994—), Daughters of the Republic of Tex. (3d v.p. 1993—). Methodist. Office: Ariz Fleming Elem Sch 14850 Bissonnet Houston TX 77083

MILOSH, MILANA M., personnel company executive; b. Sewickley, Pa., Aug. 11, 1954; d. Samuel Milanovich and Veda Yorkich; m. Larry Milosh, June 20, 1982; children: Samantha, Helen, George, Lawrence. BA, Ohio Wesleyan U., Delaware, 1976. Acct. rep. The Timken Co., Atlanta, Ga., 1976-77; dist. mgr. Norrell Co., Atlanta, Ga., 1977-82; v.p., gen. mgr. Alzed Enterprises Ltd., Pitts., 1982-93; regional dir. Olsten Staffing Svcs., Pitts., 1993-95, area v.p., 1995—. Mem. strategic planning com. Ctr. Area Sch. Dist., Pa., 1996. Mem. Soc. Human Resources Mgrs., Nat. Assn. Temporary Svcs., Pitts. Pers. Assn., Ctr. Area PTA, St. Elijah Mothers Club (bd. dirs.). Home: 128 Radcliffe Dr Aliquippa PA 15001 Office: Olsten Staffing Svcs Robinson Plz 3 Ste 130 Pittsburgh PA 15205

MILOY, LEATHA FAYE, university program director; b. Marlin, Tex., Mar. 12, 1936; d. J. D. and Leola Hazel (Rhudy) Hill; m. John Miloy, June 20, 1960; children: Tyler Hill, David Reed, Nancy Lee. BA, Sam Houston State U., 1957; MS, Tex. A&M U., 1967, PhD, 1978. Dir. pub. affairs Gulf Univs. Rsch. Corp., College Station, Tex., 1966-69; asst. dir. Ctr. for Marine Resources Tex. A&M U., College Station, 1974-76, dir. edn. svcs., 1974-78; dir. info. and spl. svcs. Tex. Woman's U., Denton, 1978-79; asst. v.p. univ. advancement S.W. Tex. State U., San Marcos, 1979-83, asst. to pres., 1983-84, v.p. student and instl. rels., 1984-90, v.p. univ. advancement, 1990-93, dir. capital campaign, 1993—; vis. lectr. humanities and sea U. Va., 1972-73; cons. Office Tech. Assessment, Washington, 1976-86, Tex. A&M U., Galveston, 1979-82, Bemidji State U., Glassboro State Coll., 1984; mem. Task Force on Edn. and Pub. Interest, 1987-88. Editor: The Ocean From Space, 1969; author, editor Sea Grant 70's, 1970-79 (Sea Grant award 1973-74); contbr. articles to profl. jours. Ad hoc mem. Marine Resources Coun. Tex., Austin, 1971-72, Tex. Energy Adv. Coun., 19174-75; chmn. United Way, Bryan, Tex., 1976; com. mem. various local elections, 1974-78. NSF grantee, 1970-78; recipient Marine Resources Info. award NSF, 1969-71, Tex. Energy Info. award Gov.'s Office, 1974-75, Tex. Water Info. award Dept. Interior, 1977-79. Mem. Nat. Soc. Fundraising Execs., Coun. for the Advancement and Support Edn. (bd. dirs. 1979-81), Coun. Student Svcs. (v.p. Tex. 1988-90). Home: PO Box 712 Buchanan Dam TX 78609-0712 Office: SW Tex State U 601 University Dr San Marcos TX 78666-4684

MILTNER, REBECCA SUZANNE, women's health nurse, pediatrics nurse; b. Memphis, May 1, 1958; d. V. Patrick and Peggy Sue (Lamb) Ellis; m. Kristopher F. Miltner, June 19, 1982; children: Mary Frances, Kathleen Elizabeth, Daniel Patrick. BSN summa cum laude, Med. Coll. Ga., 1982; MS in Nursing, U. Wis., 1990; postgrad., U. Md., Balt., 1996—. Army officer ICU nursery U.S. Army Corps, El Paso, Tex.; staff nurse obstetrics Ft. Atkinson (Wis.) Meml. Hosp.; staff nurse labor and delivery Sinai Samaritan Med. Ctr., Milw., U. Kans. Med. Ctr., Kansas City, Kans., 1992; staff nurse neonatal ICU Humana Hosp., Overland Park, Kans., 1991-92; maternal-child clin. nurse specialist Ga. Bapt. Med. Ctr., Atlanta, 1992, L&D/perinatal nurse mgr., 1992-96. Capt. U.S. Army, 1982-88. Mem. AWHONN (cert., coord. Atlanta chpt. 1995-96), Sigma Theta Tau.

MILTON, CORINNE HOLM, art history educator; b. Nogales, Ariz., Oct. 16, 1928; d. Walter and Louise (Oates) Holm; m. Lee B. Milton, July 17, 1950 (dec. Oct. 1986); children: Bruce, Marina, Alan, Stuart. BA in Polit. Sci., U. Ariz., 1951, MLS, 1982; tchg. cert., U. N.Mex., 1973. Cert. secondary sch. tchr., Ariz., C.C. tchr., Ariz., Calif. Real estate sales agt. Walter Holm & Co., 1951-67; French and history tchr. Dept. State Overseas Schs., Washington, 1968-76; Sci. Tran Sci. Translating Co., Santa Barbara, Calif., 1976-78; libr. City of Nogales, 1982-83, City of Tucson, 1990-93; lectr. U. Ariz. Extension, Tucson, 1984—; Spanish instr. Pima Coll., Tucson, 1990-93; mem. Ariz.-Sonora Gov.'s Commn., Phoenix, 1993—; evaluator Ariz. Coun. for Humanities. Author, abstracter ABC Clio Press, 1976-78. Mem. Ariz. Opera Guild, 1989-96; bd. dirs. Hilltop Gallery, Nogales, 1989—; hostess, translator Tuscon Internat. Vis. Coun., 1994-96; lectr. on art history to cmty. schs. and retirement homes, Tucson, 1989—. Mem. UN Coun., Tucson Mus. Art (docent 1989—), Sunbelt World Trade Assn., Pimeria Alta Hist. Soc., Sierra Club. Democrat. Episcopalian. Home: 6981 E Jagged Canyon Pl Tucson AZ 85750

MINANOV, DEBORAH ANN, clinical nurse specialist, educator; b. Kingston, R.I., Feb. 15, 1965; d. Paul Joseph and Margaret Gail (Smith) Scheele; m. Kristijan George Minanov. BSN, U. N.C., Greensboro, 1987; MSN, U. N.C., Chapel Hill, 1994. RN, Ga. Staff nurse U. N.C. Hosp., Chapel Hill, 1987-94; nursing instr. Emory U., Atlanta, 1995—; clin. nurse specialist Dekalb Med. Ctr., Decatur, Ga., 1994—. Editor newsletter Atlanta Area Assn. Critical Care Nursing, 1994—. Mem. AACN, Sigma Theta Tau. Roman Catholic. Home: 3448-B North Druid Hills Decatur GA 30033 Office: Dekalb Med Ctr 2701 North Decatur Rd Decatur GA 30033

MINARIK, ELSE HOLMELUND (BIGART MINARIK), author; b. Aarhus, Denmark, Sept. 13, 1920; d. Kaj Marius and Helga Holmelund; m. Walter Minarik, July 14, 1940 (dec.); 1 child, Brooke Ellen; m. Homer Bigart, Oct. 3, 1970 (dec.). BA, Queens Coll., 1942. Tchr. 1st grade, art Commack (N.Y.) Pub. Schs., 1950-54. Author children's books: Little Bear, 1957, Father Bear Comes Home, 1959, Little Bear's Friend, 1960, Little Bear's Visit, 1961, No Fighting, No Biting, 1958, Cat and Dog, 1960, The Winds That Come From Far Away, 1960, The Little Giant Girl and the Elf Boy, 1963, A Kiss for Little Bear, 1968, What If, 1987, Percy and the Five Houses, 1988, It's Spring, 1989, The Little Girl and the Dragon, 1991, Am I Beautiful, 1992. Mem. PEN Club. Home: 31 Gebig Rd Nottingham NH 03290

MINASIAN, SUSAN R., lawyer; b. N.Y.C., Feb. 28, 1948; d. Arthur S. and Rhoda R. (Magid) Feldman; m. Michael Bruce Roff, Oct. 13, 1973 (div. Mar. 1986); m. Paul Ryan Minasian, Mar. 25, 1989; children: Rachel, Jackson. BA, Pitzer Coll., Claremont, Calif., 1970; JD, Lincoln U., 1976. Bar: Calif. 1976. Lawyer Wells Fargo Bank, San Jose, Calif., 1976-78; pvt. practice Quincy, Calif., 1978-80; lawyer Chevron USA, San Francisco, 1980-83; county counsel Plumas County, Quincy, 1983-85; asst. county counsel Sonoma County, Santa Rosa, Calif., 1985-87; county counsel Butte County, Oroville, Calif., 1987—. Democrat. Jewish. Office: Butte County 25 County Center Dr Oroville CA 95926

MINAULT, GAIL, history educator; b. Mpls., Mar. 25, 1939; d. Paul Adrien and Martha (McKim) M.; m. Thomas Graham, May 13, 1967 (div. 1973); 1 child, Mark Emlen (dec.); m. Leon W. Ellsworth, Apr. 11, 1992; children; Laila Minault, Alex Ellsworth. BA, Smith Coll., Northampton, Mass., 1961; MA, U. Pa., 1966, PhD, 1972. Trainee U.S. Info. Agy., Washington, 1961-62; jr. officer U.S. Info. Svc., Beirut, Lebanon, 1962-63; asst. cultural affairs officer U.S. Info. Svc., Dacca, East Pakistan, 1963-64; asst. prof. U. Tex., Austin, 1972-79, assoc. prof., 1980-95, prof., 1996—. Author: The Khilafat Movement: Religious Symbolism and Plitical Mobilization Among Indian Muslims, 1982; editor: The Extended Family: Women's Politicla Participation in India and Pakistan, 1981, Abul Kalam Azad: An Intellectual and Religious Biography, 1988; translator: Voices of Silence, 1986. Nat. Humanities Ctr. fellow, 1987-88, Social Sci. Rsch. Coun. fellow, 1993, NEH, 1994-95. Mem. Assn. for Asian Studies, Berkshire Conf. Women Historians, Am. Inst. Pakistan Studies (sec. 1994-96). Democrat. Office: U Tex Dept History Austin TX 78751

MINDES, GAYLE DEAN, education educator; b. Kansas City, Mo., Feb. 11, 1942; d. Elton Burnett and Juanita Maxine (Mangold) Taylor; BS, U. Kans., 1964; MS, U. Wis., 1965; EdD, Loyola U., Chgo., 1979; m. Marvin William Mindes, June 20, 1969 (dec.); 1 son, Jonathan Seth. Tchr. pub. schs., Newburgh, N.Y., 1965-67; spl. educator Ill. Dept. Mental Health, Chgo., 1967-69; spl. edn. supr. Evanston (Ill.) Dist. 65 Schs., 1969-74; lectr. Northeastern Ill. U., Chgo., 1974, Loyola U., Chgo., 1974-76, Coll. St. Francis, Joliet, Ill., 1976-79, North Park Coll., Chgo., 1978; cons. Chgo. Head Start, 1978-79; asst. prof. edn. Oklahoma City U., 1979-80; vis. asst. prof., rsch. assoc. Roosevelt U. Coll. Edn., Chgo., 1983-87, prof., dir. R&D, dir. tchr. edn., dir. early childhood, dir. grad. edn. ctr., Roosevelt U. Coll., Albert A. Robin campus, 1993; prof. sch. edn. De Paul U., 1993—, assoc. dean sch. edn., 1996—; chair Roosevelt U. Senate, 1986-89; co-chair ILAEYC Bldg. Bridges; cons. Ill. Resource Ctr., Arts Coun. Oklahoma City, Indian Affairs Commn., 1979-80, Bensenville Pub. Schs., Lincolnwood (Ill.) Pub. Schs., Chgo. Pub. Schs., Atwood Sch. Dist, Chgo. Assn. Retarded Citizens, Nat. Assn. Tech. Tng. Schs., Ill. State Bd. Edn., Itasca Pub. Schs., Decatur Pub. Schs., Robin Scholarship Found., 1982—, Rasho Media, Ill. Facilities Fund for Childcare; alt. rep. faculty coun. Sch. Edn. DePaul U., mem. faculty adv. com. to univ. plan. and info. tech., also mem. panel on grievances, 1995—, mem. comprehensive pers. devel. com., 1995—; mem. tng. sub-com. adv. Ill. Dept. Children & Family Svcs., 1993-95; mem. panel of advisers comprehensive pers. devel. sys. Ill. State Bd. Edn., 1995—; mentor, cons. to partnerships project tng. early intervention svcs. U. Ill., Champaign; early childhood panelist Ill. Initiative for Articulation between Ill. Bd. Higher Edn. and Ill. Cmty. Coll. Bd.; education panelist for Early Childhood Assessment System. Assoc. editor Ill. Sch. R & D; Ill. Div. Early Childhood Edn. Adv. Com. to Ill. Bd. Edn.; co-chair early childhood panelist for early childhood assessment system, Bansenville Pub. Schs.; meditor: Depaul U. Sch. Edn. Newsletter. Co-author: Planning a Theme Based Curriculum for 4's or 5's, 1993, Assessing Young Children, 1996; assoc. editor Jour. Rsch. in Childhood Edn., 1996—; contbr. articles to profl. jours. Bd. dirs. North Side Family Day Care, 1981; northside affiliates Mus. Contemporary Art, 1991-96; trustee Roosevelt U., 1987-93; mem. edn. adv. com. Okla. Dept. Edn., 1979-80; mem. adv. bd. bilingual early childhood program Oakton Community Coll.; mem. adv. bd. early childhood tech. assistance project Chgo. Pub. Schs., Lake View Mental Health, 1986-90; mem. planning com. Lake View Citizens Coun. Day Care Ctr., 1978-79, local planning coun. Ill. Dept. Child and Family Svcs., childcare block grant tng. sub. com.; co-chair Ill. Assn. for Edn. Young Children Building Bridges Project; chmn. teen com. Florence G. Heller JCC, membership com.; mem. adv. bd. Harold Washington Coll. Child Devel., regional tech. assistance grant LICA; mem. parents com. Francis W. Parker Sch. Cerebral Palsy Assn. scholar, 1965; U. Wis. fellow in mental retardation, 1964-65; U. Kans. scholar, 1960. Fellow Am. Orthopsychiat. Assn.; mem. AAUP, ASCD, AAUW, Assn. Children with Learning Disabilities, Nat. Assn. for Edn. Young Children (tchr. edn. bd. 1990—), Am. Ednl. Rsch. Assn., Coun. for Exceptional Children, Ill. Coun. for Exceptional Children (mem. multicultural affairs com. divsn. early childhood), Ill. Assn. for Edn. Young Children, Coun. for Adminstrs. Spl. Edn., Am. Assn. U. Women, Coun. on Children with Behavioral Disorders, Soc. for Rsch. in Child Devel., Foun. for Excellence in Teaching (selection com. Golden Apple 1989-94), Alpha Sigma Nu, Phi Delta Kappa, Pi Lambda Theta. Office: DePaul Univ Sch Of Edn Chicago IL 60614

MINDLIN, PAULA ROSALIE, reading educator; b. N.Y.C., Nov. 27, 1944; d. Simon S. and Sylvia (Naroff) Bernstein; m. Alfred Carl Mindlin, Aug. 14, 1965; 1 child, Spencer Douglas. BA in Edn., Bklyn. Coll., 1965; MS in Edn., Queens Coll., 1970, Specialist Sch. Adminstrn, 1973. Tchr. Dist. 16 Pub. Sch., Bklyn., 1965-68; reading tchr. Dist. 29 Pub. Sch. and Dist. 16, Bklyn., 1968-85; instr. insvc. courses Cmty. Sch. Dist. 29, Queens Village, N.Y., 1984-93; reading coord. Reading/Comms. Arts Program Cmty. Sch. Dist. 29, Queens, N.Y., 1985-90; dir. reading Cmty. Sch. Dist. 29, Queens Village, N.Y., 1990-94;, 1993-95; adj. lectr. York Coll., 1989; dir. chpt. 1 program U.S. Sec. Edn., 1993 (Nat. Recognition award). Recipient Educator of Yr. award Qeensboro Coun. Reading. Mem. ASCD, Internat. Reading Assn., Nassau Reading Coun., Queensboro Reading Coun. (pres. 1994-96, Educator of Yr. award 1994), Phi Delta Kappa. Office: Dist 29 Queens 1 Cross Island Plz Rosedale NY 11422-1484

MINE, HILARY ANNE, telecommunications company executive, consultant; b. Portland, Oreg., Aug. 21, 1961; d. Lewis Stuart Keizer and Ann Christina (Kelly) Mine. BA in Econs., Reed Coll., 1983; MBA in Bus. Analysis, San Francisco State U., 1990. Analyst Berkeley Roundtable on Internat. Economy, U. Calif., Berkeley, 1984-85, program mgr. Engring. Sys. Rsch. Ctr., 1985-88; project mgr., computer cons. San Francisco State U., 1988-89; bus. planning analyst Chips and Techs., Inc., 1989-90; rsch. dir. info. techs. Frost & Sullivan, 1990-92; prin. Info. Techs. Cons., 1992-94; dir. global cons. No. Bus. Info./Datapro, 1994-96; sr. v.p. Probe Rsch., Inc., Folsom, Calif., 1996—. Tutor St. John's Tutoring Ctr., 1988; asst. edn. coord. Planned Parenthood, 1990-91. Mem. IEEE, NAFE. Office: Probe Rsch Inc Ste 7-170 9580 Oak Avenue Pky Folsom CA 95630

MINEAR, ALANA WILFONG, alumni affairs director; b. Elkins, W.Va., Aug. 25, 1947; d. Dewey Lyle and Gail Ruth (Ours) Wilfong; m. Larry Wayne Minear, May 26, 1973 (dec. Oct. 1993); 1 child, Stacey Elizabeth. BA, Fairmont (W.Va.) State Coll., 1970; postgrad., Davis & Elkins Coll., W.Va.; MA, W.Va. U., 1996. Lic. social worker, W.Va. Alcoholism and drug abuse counselor Appalachian Mental Health Ctr., Elkins, W.Va., 1970-73; teller Union Fed. Savs. & Loan, Elkins, W.Va., 1973-75; salesperson Fletcher Real Estate, Elkins, W.Va., 1975-79; dir. Tucker County Sr. Citizens Program, Elkins, 1980-86; adminstr., dir. alumni rels. Davis & Elkins Coll., Elkins, 1986—; visual-artist-in-residence Tucker County Visual Artist Program. Pres. Tucker County Planning Commn., Parsons, W.Va., 1982-86; v.p. St. George Med. Clinic Bd., St. George, 1982-86; mem. Randolph County Bi-Centennial Com., Elkins, 1989-90; mem. Elkins state adv. coun. Pub. Transp., Charleston, W.Va., 1984-86; bd. dirs. Am. Heart Assn., 1991—; mem. Woman's Club; campaign chmn., bd. dir. United Way; bd. dirs. Elkins Main St.; bd. dir., chair Adult Christian Edn. Named Pub. Employee of the Yr., C. of C. Tucker County, 1985, Outstanding Leader, Adminstrn. on Aging, 1985. Mem. Nat. Soc. Fund Raising Execs., Coun. for Advancement and Support of Edn., Randolph County C. of C. Republican. Baptist. Home: 115 Westview Dr Elkins WV 26241-3246 Office: Davis & Elkins Coll 100 Campus Dr Elkins WV 26241-3971

MINEHAN, CATHY ELIZABETH, banker; b. Jersey City, Feb. 15, 1947; d. Harry Manford Jones and Rita Jane (Decora) Jones Leary; m. Gerald Paul Minehan, July 18, 1970; children: Melissa Jane, Brian Patrick. BA, U. Rochester, 1968; MBA, NYU, 1977. Various positions to sr. v.p. Fed. Reserve Bank N.Y., N.Y.C., 1968-91; chief operating officer Fed. Reserve Bank Boston, 1991-94, pres., 1994—; cons. IMF, Washington, 1990-91; bd. dirs. Boston Mcpl. Rsch. Bur., Park St. Corp., The New Eng. Coun.; mem.

Gov.'s Coun. Econ. Growth and Tech. Mem. Mass. Women's Forum, Boston, 1991—; trustee Bentley Coll., 1992—; trustee coun. U. Rochester, 1993—. Mem. Pub. Securities Assn. (ex officio, govt. ops. com. 1986-91), Beta Gamma Sigma. Democrat. Roman Catholic. Home: 416 Commonwealth Ave Boston MA 02215 Office: Fed Reserve Bank Boston 600 Atlantic Ave Boston MA 02210-2211

MINEHART, JEAN BESSE, tax accountant; b. Cleve., Nov. 8, 1937; d. Ralph Moore and Augusta (Mitchell) Besse; m. Ralph Conrad Minehart, Aug. 28, 1959; children: Patricia Minehart Miron, Deborah, Elizabeth, Stephen. BA, Mass. Wellesley Coll., 1959; MEd, U. Va., 1971. Rsch. assoc. Age Ctr. of New Eng., Boston, 1959-61; substitute tchr. Charlottesville (Va.) Sch. System, 1976-81; tax acct. H&R Block, Charlottesville, 1982-94, Huey & Bjorn, Charlottesville, 1994—. Past pres. Ephitha Village Housing for the Deaf, Charlottesville, 1984-87; bd. dirs. Tues. Evening Concert Series, Charlottesville, 1990-94; sec., bd. dirs. Family Svc., Inc., Charlottesville, 1987-91; elder Westminster Presbyn. Ch., 1979-81, 94-96. Mem. LWV (v.p., treas. 1991-95) Blue Ridge Wellesley Club (pres. Charlottesvillechpt. 1989-91). Home: 1714 Yorktown Dr Charlottesville VA 22901-3034 Office: Huey & Bjorn 408 E Market St Apt 207B Charlottesville VA 22902-5252

MINER, CAROL BURKE, sales exective; b. N.Y.C., Oct. 7, 1939; d. James E. and Dorothy F. Burke. BS, Cortland Coll., 1961; MS, Hofstra U., 1967. Cert. paralegal N.Y. State Bar Assn.; cert. playground safety inspector Nat. Recreation and Parks Assn. Pres. Park, Playground and Recreation Inc., Port Jeff Station, N.Y., 1982—. Office: PPRP Inc 21 Beach Ave Port Jefferson Station NY 11776

MINER, GENEVIEVE FITCH, retired social worker, poet; b. Lake Bluff, Ill., Jan. 19, 1906; d. Henry Martin and Eleonore (Post) M. BA, Wellesley Coll., 1927; DJ, Rutgers U., 1932; MSW, U. Chgo., 1938. Social worker United Charities, Chgo.; asst. prof. U. Minn., Mpls.; supr. Family and Children's Agy., Akron, Ohio; assoc. prof. La. State U. Sch. Social Work, Baton Rouge, Ohio, until 1976; ret., 1976. Author: Libations, 1933; contbr. poetry to anthology. Home: 1014 Keystone Ln Clemson SC 29631

MINER, JACQUELINE, political consultant; b. Mt. Vernon, N.Y., Dec. 10, 1936; d. Ralph E. and Agnes (McGee) Mariani; B.A., Coll. St. Rose, 1971, M.A., 1974; m. Roger J. Miner, Aug. 11, 1975; children: Laurence, Ronald Carmichael, Ralph Carmichael, Mark. Ind. polit. cons., Hudson, N.Y.; instr. history and polit. sci. SUNY, Hudson, 1974-79. Rep. county committeewoman, 1958-76; vice chmn. N.Y. State Ronald Reagan campaign, 1980; candidate for Rep. nomination for U.S. Senate, 1982; co-chair N.Y. state steering com. George Bush for Pres. campaign, 1986-88; vice chmn. N.Y. State Rep. Com., 1991-93; del. Rep. Convention, 1992; chmn. Coll. Consortium for Internat. Studies; mem. White House Outreach Working Group on Central Am.; co-chmn. N.Y. State Reagan Roundup Campaign, 1984-86; mem. nat. steering com. Fund for Am.'s Future, 2d cir. Hist. Com. Mem. U.S. Supreme Ct. Hist. Soc., P.E.O. Address: 1 Merlin's Way Camelot Heights Hudson NY 12534

MINER, JANET MAE, special education educator; b. Evergreen Park, Ill., Nov. 15, 1951; d. William John Sr. and Adele Clara (Wilk) M. BA in Elem. Edn., Augustana Coll., 1973; MS in Spl. Edn., Western Ill. U., 1982. 1st, 4th and 6th grade tchr. Crete (Ill.)-Monee Sch. Dist., 1973-79; tchr., dept. chair Edison Jr. H.S. Macomb (Ill.) Sch. Dist., 1980-91; tchr., facilitator Becker Mid. Sch. Clark County Sch. Dist., Las Vegas, Nev., 1991—; presenter workshops dept. continuing edn. Western Ill. U., Macomb, 1990-91, mem. NCATE team to evaluate tchr. edn. programs, 1992. Bd. dirs. Ill. br. Orton Dyslexia Soc., Macomb, 1989-92, Nev. Alliance of Dyslexics, Las Vegas, 1992—; v.p. ch. coun. Trinity Luth. Ch., Macomb, 1981-91; ;mem. com. ADA Law Com.-Town Accessibility, Macomb, 1992; chair Pace com. Macomb Edn. Assn., 1988. Recipient Hon. Mention Outstanding Tchr. aware Phi Delta Kappa 1991. Mem. Nev. Alliance Dyslexics (bd. dirs. 1992—), Coun. for Exceptional Children. Office: Becker Mid Sch 9151 Pinewood Hills Dr Las Vegas NV 89134

MINER, MARY ELIZABETH HUBERT, secondary school educator; b. Provident City, Tex., Mar. 25, 1921; d. Fred Edward and Charlotte Alice (Haynes) Hubert; m. Daniel Bowen Miner, Jan. 29, 1945 (dec. Aug. 1979); children: Charlotte Martelia Miner Williams, Daniel Bowen Jr., Mary Elizabeth Miner Martinez, Joseph Frederick, William McKinley. BA, Rice U., 1942; postgrad., U. Houston, East Tenn. State U., 1959, U. Tenn., 1961. Cert. tchr. math., English, French, history, Tex., 8th grade, math., English, French, Am. history grades 9-12. Math. tchr. Crosby (Tex.) H.S., 1942-43; office mgr. Uvalde Rock Asphalt, Houston, 1943-44; tchr. math., English, health Rogersville (Tenn.) H.S., 1947-49, 55-78; tchr. math., English, French Ch. Hill. (Tenn.) H.S., 1949-51, 53-55; tchr. 8th grade Rogersville (Tenn.) City Schs., 1951-53; tchr. math. Cherokee Comprehensive H.S., Rogersville, 1978-84; chmn. math. and sci. planning com., Hawkins County, Tenn., 1977-79; pvt. tutor, Rogersville. Tchr. ladies Bible class Rogersville United Meth. Ch., 1952—, mem. choir, 1979—, sec., 1967-94, sec. adminstr. bd. dirs.; blood donor ARC, Rogersville, 1974-75. Lt. Women's Corps USNR, 1944-47. Recipient Apple award Sta. WKGB, 1956. Mem. NEA (life), Tenn. Edn. Assn. (life), Rogersville Bus. and Profl. Women (pres. 1953-55, treas. 1948-53), Am. Legion Aux. (pres.), Delta Kappa Gamma (Alpha Iota chpt. pres.). Republican.

MINISTER, KRISTINA, speech communication educator; b. Dayton, Ohio, Aug. 27, 1934; d. Roy J. and Margaret (Chatterton) Arndt; m. Edward Minister, Mar. 1959 (div. 1972); children: Matthew, Margaret; m. Hal W. Howard, Sept. 10, 1977 (dec. Sept. 1993). BFA, Ohio U., 1958; MA, Columbia U., 1962; PhD, Northwestern U., 1977. Instr. speech St. John's U., Bklyn., 1962-65, Bowdoin Coll., Brunswick, Maine, 1969-71; asst. prof. speech communication U. Ariz., Tucson, 1974-77, Calif. State U., Northridge, 1978-79; vis. asst. prof. communication Ariz. State U., Tempe, 1979-82; oral historian Oral History Ctr., Inc., Phoenix, 1982-89; prof. comm. Midway (Ky.) Coll., 1989—; cons. oral history to bus., families, mus. and schs., 1982-89. Author: Oral History: The Privilege You Inherit, 1985; contbr. scholarly essays to various publs. Actor Cmty. Profl. Theatre. Mem. Women in Comm., Inc., Speech Comm. Assn., Oral History Assn., Am. Folklore Soc. Democrat. Unitarian Universalist. Office: Midway Coll 512 E Stephens St Midway KY 40347-1112

MINK, GWENDOLYN, political science educator; b. Chgo., Mar. 6, 1952; d. John Francis and Patsy (Takemoto) M. BA, U. Calif., Berkeley, 1974; PhD in Govt., Cornell U., 1982. Asst. prof. politics U. Calif., Santa Cruz, 1981-86; assoc. prof. politics U. Calif., 1986-94, prof. politics, 1994—; chair com. on the status of women U. Calif., Santa Cruz, 1987-94. Author: Old Labor and New Immigrants in American Political Development, 1986, The Wages of Motherhood, 1995; co-editor Reader's Companion to US Women's History, 1997; editl. bd. Dilemmas in Democracy Series, 1993—. Co-chair Women's Com. of 100, Washington, 1995—; coord. Nat. Conf. on Welfare Reform, Washington, 1993. Gender Roles grant Rockefeller Found., 1989. Mem. Am. Polit. Sci. Assn. (exec. coun. 1991-93, Victoria Schuck book award 1996), Am. Hist. Assn. Office: U Calif Santa Cruz Merrill Faculty Svcs Santa Cruz CA 95062

MINK, MAXINE MOCK, real estate executive; b. Lakeland, Fla., Jan. 17, 1938; d. Idus Frank and Elizabeth (Warren) Mock; student Fla. So. Coll.; children: Lance Granger, Justin Chandler. With Union Fin. Co., Lakeland, Fla., 1956-62; ptnr./owner S & S Ent. & Arrow Lake Mobile Home Pk., Lakeland, 1957-66; head bookkeeper Seaboard Fin., Lakeland, 1964-68; ptnr. Custom Chem., Inc., Lakeland, 1968-75, Don Emilio Perfumers, Newport Beach, Calif., 1978-79; owner Maxine Mink Public Relations, Newport Beach, 1978-83; fine homes and relocation specialist Merrill Lynch Realty, Newport Beach, 1985-90, Tarbell Realtors, Newport Beach, 1990-93, Prudential Calif. Realty, Newport Beach, 1993-95, Grubb & Ellis Real Estate, 1996—. Bd. dirs. Guild of Lakeland Symphony Orch., 1972-75; mem. Lakeland Gen. Hosp. Aux., 1974-76, Mus. Modern Art. Mem. NAFE, Newport Beach C. of C., Hoag Hosp. Aux., Orange County Music Center Guild. Republican. Clubs: Balboa Bay, Sherman Library and Gardens, The 552. Office: PO Box 1262 Newport Beach CA 92659-0262

MINK, PATSY TAKEMOTO, congresswoman; b. Paia, Maui, Hawaii, Dec. 6, 1927; d. Suematsu and Mitama (Tateyama) Takemoto; m. John Francis Mink, Jan. 27, 1951; 1 child, Gwendolyn. Student, Wilson Coll., 1946, U. Nebr., 1947; BA, U. Hawaii, 1948; LLD, U. Chgo., 1951; DHL (hon.), Chaminade Coll., 1975, Syracuse U., 1976, Whitman Coll., 1981. Bar: Hawaii. Pvt. practice Honolulu, 1953-65; lectr. U. Hawaii, 1952-56, 59-62, 79-80; atty. Territorial Ho. of Reps., 1955; mem. Hawaii Ho. of Reps., 1956-58, Ter. Hawaii Senate, 1958-59, Hawaii State Senate, 1962-64, 89th-94th Congresses from 2nd Hawaii dist., 101st-104th Congresses from 2d dist. Hawaii, 1989—; mem. econ. and ednl. opportunity com., mem. budget com.; mem. U.S. del. to UN Law of Sea, 1975-76, Internat. Woman's Yr., 1975, UN Environ. Program, 1977, Internat. Whaling Commn., 1977; asst. sec. of state U.S. Dept. State, 1977-78. Charter pres. Young Dem. Club Oahu, 1954-56, Ter. Hawaii Young Dems., 1956-58; del. Dem. Nat. Conv., 1960, 72, 80; nat. v.p. Young Dem. Clubs Am., 1957-59; v.p. Ams. for Dem. Action, 1974-76, nat. pres., 1978-81; mem. nat. adv. com. White House Conf. on Families, 1979-80; mem. nat. adv. com. Federally Employed Women. Recipient Leadership for Freedom award Roosevelt Coll., Chgo., 1968, Alii award 4-H Clubs Hawaii, 1969, Nisei of Biennium award, Freedom award Honolulu chpt. NAACP, 1971, Disting. Humanitarian award YWCA, St. Louis, 1972, Creative Leadership in Women's Rights award NEA, 1977, Human Rights award Am. Fedn. Tchrs., 1975, Feminist of Yr. award Feminist Majority Found., 1991, Margaret Brent award ABA, 1992. Office: US Ho of Reps 2135 Rayburn HOB Washington DC 20515*

MINKER, KAREN ANN, occupational health nurse; b. Phila., July 16, 1947; d. William and Isabella (O'Neill) Henry; m. Wayne Ronald Minker, Oct. 3, 1968; children: Lisa, Todd. Diploma in Nursing, Coatesville (Pa.) Hosp., 1968. RN; cert. emergency nurse, COHN, CCM, BLS, ACLS. Med./surg. staff nurse Coatesville Hosp., 1968-69, Ft. Walton Beach (Fla.) Hosp., 1969-70; med./surg. staff nurse Chester County Hosp., West Chester, Pa., 1970-73, emergency rm. nurse, 1974-87; occupl. health nurse Peco Energy Co., Coatesville, 1987—. Leader Girl Scouts U.S., West Bradford, 1982-87. Mem. Am. Occupl. Health Nurse Assn., pa. Occupl. Health Nurse Assn., Delaware Valley Occupl. Health Nurse Assn. (treas. 1995—). Presbyterian. Office: Peco Energy Co 175 N Caln Rd Coatesville PA 19320-2309

MINKOFF, ALICE SYDNEY, interior designer; b. Washington, Jan. 29, 1948; d. Lawrence and Ellen (Altman) Glassman; children: Adam Pollin, Shane Pollin, Jacob, Sam. Student, U. Md. Owner Fredrick, Miley & Assocs., Inc., 1983—; interior designer for homebuilders, 1975-82; interior designer high end residential homes, 1980—. Vol. Food and Friends, Washington, 1991—; chair Heartstrings, Washington, 1990—; active AIDS awareness. Mem. NOW, ACLU, Nat. Trust Hist. Preservation, Nature Conservancy. Home: PO Box 1003 Amagansett NY 11930 Office: Matches at Miley 300 D St SW Ste 440 Washington DC 20024

MINKOFF, EVELYN WEINSTEIN, volunteer; b. Madison, Wis., Nov. 23, 1925; d. Max and Freida (Blachman) Weinstein; m. Ben Minkoff, Oct. 20, 1946 (dec. Oct. 1984); children: David Ira, Joel Stewart, Fredlyn Sue, Marc J. Student, U. Wis., 1943-46. Bd. dirs. Coun. Jewish Fedns., exec. com., 1995—; pres. Madison Jewish Cmty. Coun., 1992-94, Disting. Svc. award, 1995; profl. vol. Op. Headstart, Nat. Kidney Found. Recipient Golda Meir award State of Israel Bonds, 1990. Mem. Hadassah (life, past pres. local, past pres. Great Lakes region). Democrat.

MINKOFF, JILL S., management consultant executive; b. Kansas City, Mo., July 12, 1953; d. Julius Burt and Eloise Joy (Shlensky) Minkoff; m. Barry Charles Goldman, Jan. 30, 1982 (div. Nov. 1995); children: Joshua Scott, Elise Lynn. Certificat D'Assiduite, Université de Grenoble (France), 1968; BA, Pomona Coll., 1974. Mktg. rep. IBM, Riverside, Calif., 1974-77, San Francisco, 1978-79; dir. store systems Neiman Marcus, Dallas, 1979-81; dir. end-user computing services. Marion Labs., Kansas City, Mo., 1982-89, dir. info. systems data and techs., 1989—; dir. corp. info. systems Marion Merrell Dow Inc., 1989-91; dir. Bus. Process Improvement, 1992-93; pres. Visions Connections, Inc., Kans., 1993—. bd. dirs. Creative Courseware. Sch. pres. ARC, Kansas City, Mo., 1966-67; v.p. chpt. B'nai B'rith Girls, Kansas City, 1968-69. Mem. Silicon Prairie Tech. Assn., Am. Technion Soc. (bd. dirs.). Home: 9609 Linden Shawnee Mission KS 66207 Office: Vision Connections 4210 Shawnee Mission Pky # 102B Shawnee Mission KS 66205-2506

MINNELLI, LIZA, singer, actress; b. Los Angeles, Mar. 12, 1946; d. Vincente and Judy (Garland) M.; m. Peter Allen, 1967 (div. 1972); m. Jack Haley, Sept. 15, 1974 (div.); m. Mark Gero, Dec. 4, 1979 (div. 1992). Appeared in Off-Broadway revival of Best Foot Forward, 1963; recorded You Are For Loving, 1963, Tropical Nights, 1977, Liza Minelli at Carnegie Hall, 1987; appeared with mother at London Palladium, 1964; appeared in Flora, the Red Menace, 1965 (Tony award), The Act, 1977 (Tony award), The Rink, 1984; nightclub debut at Shoreham Hotel, Washington, 1965; films include Charlie Bubbles, 1967, The Sterile Cuckoo, 1969, Tell Me That You Love Me, Junie Moon, 1970, Cabaret, 1972 (Oscar award), That's Entertainment, 1974, Lucky Lady, 1975, A Matter of Time, 1976, Silent Movie, 1976, New York, New York, 1977, Arthur, 1981, Rent A Cop, Arthur on the Rocks, 1988, Stepping Out, 1991; albums include: Results, 1989; appeared on TV in own spl. Liza With a Z, 1972 (Recipient Emmy award); other TV appearances include Goldie and Liza Together, 1980, Baryshnikov on Broadway, 1980, The Princess and the Pea, Showtime, 1983, A Time to Live, 1985, Sam Found Out, 1988, Liza Minnelli Live from Radio City Music Hall, PBS (Emmy nomination, Music Program Performance, 1993); internat. tour with Frank Sinatra, Sammy Davis Jr., 1988. Awarded the Brit. equivalent of the Oscar for Best Actress, 1972, Italy's David di Donatello award (twice), the Valentino award. Office: care PMK 1776 Broadway Fl 8 New York NY 10019-2002*

MINNER, RUTH ANN, state senator; b. Milford, Del., Jan. 17, 1935; m. Roger Minner. Student Del. Tech. and Community Coll. Office receptionist Gov. of Del., 1972-74; mem. Del. Ho. of Reps., 1974-82; mem. Del. Senate, 1982-92; lt. gov. State of Del., Dover, 1993—; mem. Dem. Nat. Com., 1988. Home: RD 3 Box 694 Milford DE 19963 Office: Office Lt Gov Tatnall Bldg 3rd Fl Dover DE 19901*

MINNICH, DIANE KAY, state bar executive; b. Iowa City, Feb. 17, 1956; d. Ralph Maynard Minnich and Kathryn Jane (Obye) Tompkins. BA in Behavioral Sci., San Jose State U., 1978. Tutorial program coord./instr. Operation SHARE/La Valley Coll., Van Nuys, Calif., 1979-81; field exec. Silver Sage Girl Scout Coun., Boise, Idaho, 1981-85; continuing legal edn. dir. Idaho State Bar/Idaho Law Found. Inc., Boise, 1985-88, dep. dir., 1988-90, exec. dir., 1990—. Mem. CLE Adminstrs., Chgo., 1985-90; bd. dirs. Silver Sage coun. Girl Scouts, Boise, 1990-93, nominating com. mem., 1990-94, chair nominating com., 1991-92. Named one of Outstanding Young Women in Am., 1991. Mem. Nat. Orgn. Bar Execs. (membership com. 1992), Zonta Club Boise (prs. 1991-92, bd. dirs. 1989-93, chair long range planning com.), Rotary Club Boise (chair mem. com. 1994-96, bd. dirs. 1996—). Office: Idaho State Bar/Idaho Law Found PO Box 895 525 W Jefferson St Boise ID 83702-5931

MINNICK, KATHLEEN T., banker; b. Conshohocken, Pa., Aug. 26, 1953; d. Joseph K. and Anne T. (Bolger) Thomas; divorced; children: Alicia, Matthew. Degree, Am. Inst. Banking, 1983. Teller Am. Bank & Trust Co., Lafayette Hill, Pa., 1972-73; from mktg. rep. to asst. br. mgr. Corestates Bank., Phila., 1973-88; br. mgr. Progress Bank, Plymouth Meeting, Pa., 1988-91; from comml. loan officer to v.p. comml. lending Progress Bank, 1991—; sr. assoc. Robert Morris Assocs., Phila., 1992—. Bd. dirs. Fellowship House Found., 1994—, Greater Conshohocken Econ. Devel. Corp., 1991—. Mem. Vis. Nurse Assn., Montgomery County C. of C. Roman Catholic. Office: Progress Bank Ste 200 Four Sentry Pkwy Blue Bell PA 19422

MINNIE, JANET KAY, nursing administrator, educator; b. Centralia, Ill., Jan. 26, 1951; d. Norman M. and Vivian L. (Piercy) Knight.; m. John W. Minnie, Aug. 5, 1972; children: Tricia L., Joshua W. Diploma, Galesburg Hosp. Sch. Nursing, 1972; postgrad., Carl Sandburg Coll., Galesburg; pediatrics 8 week program, Cook County Hosp., Chgo.; psychiatric study, Galesburg Mental Health Ctr. RN Iowa. From staff nurse to charge nurse intensive care Cottage Hosp., Galesburg, 1972-77, pre-ops. nursing instr., 1977-78; staff nurse New London (Iowa) Care Ctr., 1979-83; cons. New London and Danville (Iowa) Care Ctrs., 1983-86; dir. nursing New London Care Ctr., 1986—; panel mem. Joint Commn. on Accreditation Healthcare Orgns., Des Moines, 1990; nurse cons. HealthCare of Iowa, 1995. Sunday sch. tchr. Presbyn. ch., New London, Iowa, 1986-92; bd. dirs. pub. libr., 1996. Mem. Iowa Nurses of Long Term Care, Iowa Health Care Assn. Home: 103 Hillcrest Dr New London IA 52645 Office: New London Care Ctr S Pine St New London IA 52645

MINNOTTE, LINDA DERR, mental health services professional; b. Moline, Ill., Apr. 11, 1955; d. Howard Lyle and Marilyn Elenor (Lundgren) Derr; m. Richard Tilbrook Minnotte, Dec. 22, 1976; 1 child, Kimberly Jayne. BS in Music Edn., Duquesne U., 1977. Supr. therapeutic activities forensic ctr. Mayview State Hosp., Bridgeville, Pa., 1978—; owner LDM Sports, 1992—; mem. state employee combined appeal United Way steering com. Mayview State Hosp., 1994—, investigator patient abuse investigation com., 1993—. Chairperson Mt. Lebanon (Pa.) H.S. Alumni Band, 1987; dir. adult handbell choir Mt. Lebanon United Meth. Ch., Pitts., 1989—. Mem. Pa. Social Svcs. Union, Mortar Bd. Republican. Home: 115 Abington Dr Pittsburgh PA 15216-1701 Office: Mayview State Hosp 1601 Mayview Rd Bridgeville PA 15017-1581

MINOR, MARIAN THOMAS, elementary and secondary school educational consultant; b. Richmond, Va., Apr. 16, 1933; d. James Madison and Florence Elwood (Edwards) M. BS, U. Va., 1955; MEd, William and Mary Coll., 1968; postgrad., Va. Commonwealth U., 1987-88. Cert. guidance, health and phys. edn. Educator Richmond (Va.) Pub. Schs., 1955-90, ednl. cons., 1990—; educator Sch. Nursing Med. Coll. Va., Richmond, 1958-68; camp dir. Manakin, Va., 1956-68; nat. basketball ofcl. Richmond (Va.) Bd. Ofcls., 1952-77; mem. faculty adv. com. Albert Hill Middle Sch., Richmond, 1965-90, dept. chmn., 1960-90, Tchr. of Yr., 1980; textbook adoption Richmond (Va.) Pub. Sch., 1975, 85, curriculum planner, 1978-79, 82-83, 84-85; PTA coord. Albert Hill Middle Sch., Richmond, 1985-89, chmn. self-study and accreditation team, 1987-88. Mem. Sherwood Park Civic Assn., Richmond, 1960-75; v.p. alumni weekend Mary Washington Alumni Assn., Fredericksburg, Va., 1965, 66, v.p. annual giving, 1967; chmn. basketball ofcl. examiners Richmond Bd. Women Ofcls., 1966-76; bd. dirs., homeowner adv., constrn. crewman Habitat for Humanity, 1994—; mem. Albert Hill PTA (Outstanding Svc. award 1988); mem. exec. com. Northminster Bapt. Ch., 1991-94, deacon, 1989—, premises chair, 1991-94, mem. by-laws revision com., 1986. Mem. AAUW, AAHPERD, Va. Health Phys. Edn. Assn., Va. Ret. Tchrs. Assn., Train Collectors Assn., Nat. Hist. Preservation Soc., Va. Hist. Soc., King and Queen Hist. Soc., Mortar Bd., Alpha Phi Sigma, Kappa Delta Pi. Republican. Home: 1507 Brookland Pky Richmond VA 23227-4707

MINOR, MARY ELLEN, civilian military employee; b. Konawa, Okla., Jan. 11, 1947; d. Tom Loye and Barbara Anna (Wheeler) Bounds; 1 child, Rose Mary Minor Wright. BS in Math., East Ctrl. State U., Ada, Okla., 1968; MS in Math., U. Ark., 1970; postgrad., U. Utah, 1970-72. Ops. rsch. analyst U.S. Army Comm. Command, Ft. Huachuca, Ariz., 1974-78; mathematician U.S. Dept. Treasury, Washington, 1978-79; ops. rsch. analyst U.S. Army Concepts Analysis AG., Bethesda, Md., 1979-80, Office Chief of Staff of Army, Washington, 1980-82; program integration specialist U.S. Army Materiel Command, Alexandria, Va., 1982-88, supervisory ops. rsch. analyst, 1988-93; supervisory ops. rsch. analyst U.S. Army Logistics Integration Agy., Alexandria, 1993—. Parent sponsor Girl Scouts U.S., Annandale, Va., 1981-84. Mem. Am. Def. Preparedness Assn. Home: 20583 Snowshoe Sq Apt 302 Ashburn VA 22011-3964 Office: US Army Logistics Integration Agy 5001 Eisenhower Ave Alexandria VA 22333

MINOW, MARTHA LOUISE, law educator; b. 1954. AB, U. Mich., 1975; EdM, Harvard U., 1976; JD, Yale U., 1979. Bar: Mass. 1981. Law clk. to Judge David L. Bazelon U.S. Ct. Appeals (D.C. cir.), 1979-80; law to Assoc. Justice Thurgood Marshall U.S. Supreme Ct., 1980-81; asst. prof. Harvard U., Cambridge, Mass., 1981-86, prof., 1986—; trustee William T. Grant Found.; bd. dirs. Judge David L. Bazelon Ctr. for Mental Health Law, The Covenant Found. Trustee emeritus Judge Baker Children's Ctr.; bd. dirs. ABF, 1985-94; mem. Harvard Project on Schooling and Children. Sr. fellow Ethics and Professions Harvard U. Mem. Law and Soc. Assn. Office: Harvard Law Sch Cambridge MA 02138

MINTER, JIMMIE RUTH, accountant; b. Greenville, S.C., Sept. 28, 1941; d. James C. and Lois (Williams) Jannino; BS Acctg., U. S.C., 1962; m. Charles H. Minter, Nov. 3, 1972; 1 child, Regina M.; stepchildren: Rhonda, Julie, Gregg; adopted child, Michael Minter. Asst. controller Package Supply & Equipment Co., Greenville, 1964-70, Olympia Knitting Mills, Spartanburg, S.C., 1970-72; controller Diacou Knitting Mills, Spartanburg, 1972-74; adminstr. Atlanta Med. Specialists, P.C., Riverdale, Ga., 1974-79; adminstr., corp. sec. David L. Cooper, M.D. P.C., Riverdale, 1979-89; acct. Ted L. Griffin Enterprises, Jonesboro, Ga., 1988-93; chief tax acct. Clayton County Tax Commn., Jonesboro, 1993—. Program chmn. 4th of July Celebration and Beauty Pageant, City of Riverdale; mem. exec. com. Clayton County Dem. Party, 1987—; Ga. State Dem. treas.; active Clinton Campaign Com.; active local and state election campaign fund raising; bd. dirs. Clayton County Human Rels. Coun. Mem. Am. Bus. Women's Assn. (chpt. Bus. Woman of Yr. 1969), Nat. Assn. Female Execs. Am. Cancer Soc. (silent auction com.), Clayton County Alzheimers Assn. (bd. dirs.). Home: 1244 Branchfield Ct Riverdale GA 30296-2148 Office: PO Box 1119 Riverdale GA 30274-1119

MINTON, KATHY DICKERSON, rehabilitation administrator; b. Peru, Ind., Sept. 22, 1952; d. Paul Eugene and Mary Magdeline (Flamm) Dickerson; m. Roger Owen Minton, Aug. 25, 1973; children: Heather Caryn, Leslie Frances. BS in Nursing, Murray State U., 1974; MBA, Jacksonville State U., 1989. RN Ky., Tex. Staff nurse West Paces Ferry Hosp., Atlanta, 1975-76; nurse mgr. Doctor's Hosp., Tucker, Ga., 1976-78; dir. nursing Body Nursing Ctr., Woodstock, Ga., 1978-80, The Jewish Home, Atlanta, 1980-82; cons. Nat. Healthcare Linen Svc., St. Louis, 1983-86; chmn. of vols. ARC, Ft. McClellan, Ala., 1987-89; nurse mgr. Warm Springs Rehab. Hosp., San Antonio, Tex., 1990-92; dir. nursing Warm Springs Rehab. Hosp., San Antonio, 1992-94, dir. patient care svcs., 1994-95, asst. adminstr. patient care svcs., 1995—; mem. S.W. Tex. Regional Adv. Coun., San Antonio, 1994—. Author: (3 day rev. course) An Overview of Rehab Concepts: Preparation for the CRRN Exam, 1994. 1st v.p. Army Pers. Ctr. Officers' Wives Club, St. Louis, 1985, Ft. McClellan Officers Wives Club, 1986; Ft. McClellan rep. Army Family Action Planning Conf, Washington, 1986; progam chmn. Ga. Assn. Nurses in Long Term Care, Atlanta, 1981-82. Recipient ARC Nurse Pin, 1989. Mem. Assn. Rehab. Nurses (cert., bd. dirs. 1993—), Alamo Area Nurse Execs. (sec.-treas. 1994-95, pres. 1996—). Office: Warm Springs & Bapt Rehab Network 5101 Med Dr San Antonio TX 78229

MINTY, JUDITH M., poet, English language educator; b. Detroit, Aug. 5, 1937; d. Karl Jalmer and Margaret (Hunt) Makinen; m. Edgar Sheldon Minty; children: Lora Ann, John Reed, Ann Sheldon. BS, Ithaca Coll., 1957; MA, Western Mich. U., 1973. Asst. prof., vis. poet-in-residence Ctrl. Mich. U., Mount Pleasant, Mich., 1977-78; assoc. prof., vis. poet-in-residence Syracuse U., N.Y., 1979; prof., poet-in-residence Humboldt State U., Arcata, Calif., 1982-93, prof. emerita English, 1993—; guest lectr. English Grand Valley State U., Allendale, Mich., 1974-77; poet-in-prison pilot project Muskegon Correctional Facility, Mich., 1977; vis. poet-in-residence Interlochen Ctr. for Arts, Mich., 1980, U. Oreg., Eugene, 1983, U. Nebr., Lincoln, 1994; vis. lectr. English U. Calif., Santa Cruz, 1981-82. Author: (books of poetry) Lake Songs and Other Fears, 1974 (U.S. award 1973), Yellow Dog Journal, 1979, reprinted 1992, Letters to My Daughters, 1980, In the Presence of Mothers, 1981, Counting the Losses, 1986, Dancing the Fault, 1991, The Mad Painter Poems, 1996. John Atherton fellowship in poetry Breadloaf Writers Conf., 1974, Yaddo fellowships, 1978, 79, 82; recipient Eunice Tietjens award Poetry mag., 1974, Villa Montalvo award Villa Montalvo Hackley Libr., Muskegon, Mich., 1996, Montalvo award for Excellence in Poetry, 1989; Creative Artists grants Mich. Coun. for Arts, 1981-83, Found. for Women Residency grant Hopscotch House, 1994; Charles H. Hackley Disting. lectureship, Hackley Libr. Mem. PEN (syndicated fiction awards 1985, 86, Calif. fiction award 1987), Poetry Soc. Am.,

Acad. Am. Poets, Associated Writing Programs, Nat. Audubon Soc., Wilderness Soc., Sierra Club, Nature Conservancy. Home: 7113 S Scenic Dr New Era MI 49446

MINTZ, DALE LEIBSON, health foundation executive; b. Bronx, July 28, 1944; d. Jack and Martha (Tobin) Leibson; m. Stephen Allan Mintz, June 19, 1966; children: Eric Michael, Jaclyn Leibson. BA, SUNY, Purchase, 1982; MPA, Bernard M. Baruch Coll., 1991. Cert. health edn. specialist. Corp. art cons. Merryl Wilson Assoc., N.Y.C., 1982-85; asst. to CEO New Am. Libr., N.Y.C., 1985-86; estates coord. Sotheby's, N.Y.C., 1986-87; program dir. Am. Heart Assn., Purchase, 1987-94; field svcs. exec. Nat. Hemophilia Found., N.Y.C., 1994-95; nat. health edn. dir. Hadassah, Women's Zionist Orgn. of Am., N.Y.C., 1995—; chair task force COMMIT, Yonkers, N.Y., 1988-93. Trustee Cmty. Synagogue, Rye, N.Y., 1975-78, Rye Arts Ctr., 1980-89, Rye Hist. Soc., 1994—. Mem. Nat. Assn. Exec. Women, N.Y. State Profl. Health Educators. Office: Hadassah 50 W 58th St New York NY 10019

MINTZ, LENORE CHAICE (LEA MINTZ), personnel company executive; b. N.Y.C., Aug. 6, 1925; d. Abraham and Eva (Kornblith) Chaice; m. Lewis R. Mintz, July 4, 1944; children: Richard Lewis, Alan Lee, Douglas Chaice. Student, U. Mich., 1942-44; BA magna cum laude, U. Bridgeport, 1976. Cert. personnel cons. Office mgr., personnel cons. Golden Door, Inc., Norwalk, Conn., 1970-78; v.p. permanent div. Aubrey Thomas, Inc., Stamford and Norwalk, 1978-84; sr. v.p. Aubrey Thomas Temps., N.Y., N.J., Conn., Pa., 1984-88; area v.p. Mid-Atlantic div. Talent Tree Personnel Svcs., 1988-89; v.p. bus. devel. Human Resources, Inc., Norwalk, Stamford, Statford and North Haven, 1989-90; prin. Lea Mintz & Assocs., Norwalk, 1990—; speaker, panel mem., condr. workshop and seminars in field; justice of peace Fairfield County, Conn., 1954-94; bd. corporators Norwalk Savs. Soc., Animal Care com. U.S. Surgical Corp. Loaned exec. United Way of Norwalk & Wilton, Conn., 1991-92; mem., chmn. Norwalk Bd. Edn., 1966-72; mem. Norwalk Planning and Zoning Commn., 1971-73, Conn. Edn. Coun., 1979-83, Conn. Small Bus. Adv. Coun., 1984-86; mem. regional adv. coun. Norwalk State Tech. Coll., 1988-90; past pres. Norwalk C.C. Found., 1988-90, bd. dirs. 1964-94, life hon. bd. dirs., 1995—; del. numerous Dem. state and county convs.; Clinton del. Dem. Nat. Conv., 1992; mem. adv. coun. displaced homemakers Bridgeport YWCA, 1988-90; v.p. Greater Norwalk Cmty. Coun., 1973-75; life mem. Women's Aux. Jewish Home for Aged in Conn.; cmty. rels. cons. Family & Children's Aid Mid-Fairfield County, Conn., 1992—; active numerous other orgns. Recipient numerous awards including Woman of Yr. award Norwalk Bus. and Profl. Womens Club, 1984, Outstanding Woman of Decade award UN Assn. Conn., 1987, Outstanding Svc. award Conn. Community and Tech. Coll. Bd. Trustees, 1991 (1st honoree). Mem. Women in Mgmt. (pres. 1990, Ann. Recognition award Conn. and Met. N.Y. area 1988), Internat. Assn. Personnel Women, Greater Norwalk C. of C. (bd. dirs. 1980-84, Athena award 1986), Nat. Coun. Jewish Women (life), LWV, Midday Club Stamford, B'nai B'rith (life), Alpha Sigma Lambda. Home and Office: Silvermine 4 May Dr Norwalk CT 06850-1033

MINTZ, PATRICIA POMBOY, secondary education educator; b. N.Y.C., Sept. 1, 1934; d. Emil and Bertha (Armel) Pomboy; m. Edward A. LeVay Jr.; 1 child from previous marriage, Peter Graham Mintz. AB in History with honors, Barnard Coll., 1956; AM in English, Tchrs. Coll., N.Y.C., 1967, EdD, 1980. Cert. English tchr., adminstr. and supr. dist. level. English, history tech. Fieldston Sch., N.Y.C., 1960-67; English chmn. Byram Hills Schs., Armonk, N.Y., 1967-72; supr. dist. English/lang. arts North Shore Schs., Glen Head, N.Y., 1972—; instr. English Columbia U., 1966; dir. Upward Bound English Program, Fieldston Sch., 1967; program chmn. L.I. Writing Conf., 1984-90; program chair N.Y. State English Coun. Conf., 1993. Editor: America, The Melting Pot Anthology, 1969; author: Film Guides for Educational Films, 1972-73. N.Y. Found. for Arts grantee, 1988—, Title III Matching Grant, Writing Program for North Shore Schs., 1977-78. Mem. ASCD, Nat. Coun. Tchrs. English, N.Y. State English Coun., L.I. Lang. Arts Coun., Coun. Adminstrs. and Suprs.

MINTZ, SUSAN ASHINOFF, menswear manufacturing company executive; b. N.Y.C., Dec. 7, 1949; d. Lawrence Lloyd and Thelma B. (Rubens) A.; m. Robert Beier Mintz, June 18, 1983; children: Geoffrey Harrison, Tyler Edward Richard. BA, Finch Coll., 1971; MPA, NYU, 1977. Menswear advt. asst. New Yorker Mag., N.Y.C., 1971-72; assoc. Staub, Warmbold & Assocs., Inc., exec. search co., N.Y.C., 1972-80; exec. v.p. Muhammad Ali Sportswear, Ltd., N.Y.C., 1980-81; pres. Forum Sportswear, Ltd., N.Y.C. and Portsmouth, Va., 1981—; group v.p. Coronet Casuals, Inc., Portsmouth, 1985—, also bd. dirs. Trustee Dean Jr. Coll. Named to Outstanding Young Women Am., U.S. Jaycees, 1980. Mem. Nat. Assn. Men's Sportswear Buyers, Men's Apparel Guild Calif., Beacon Hill Club. Office: 2615 Elmhurst Ln Portsmouth VA 23701-2736

MINUDRI, REGINA URSULA, librarian, consultant; b. San Francisco, May 9, 1937; d. John C. and Molly (Halter) M. BA, San Francisco Coll. for Women, 1958; MLS, U. Calif.-Berkeley, 1959. Reference libr. Menlo Park (Calif.) Pub. Libr., 1959-62; regional libr. Santa Clara County (Calif.) Libr., 1962-68; project coord. Fed. Young Adult Libr. Svcs. Project, Mountain View, Calif., 1968-71; dir. profl. services Alameda County (Calif.) Libr., 1971, asst. county libr., 1972-77; libr. dir. Berkeley Pub. Libr., 1977-94; lectr. U. San Francisco, 1970-72, U. Calif., Berkeley, 1977-81, 91-93; lectr. San Jose State U., 1994—; cons., 1975—; adv. bd. Miles Cutter Ednl., 1992—. Bd. dirs. No. Calif. ACLU, 1994-96, Cmty. Memory, 1989-91, Berkeley Cmty. Fund, 1994—, chair youth com., 1994—, Berkeley Pub. Libr. Found. Bd., 1996—; mem. bd. mgrs. cen. br. Berkeley YMCA, 1988-93. Recipient proclamation Mayor of Berkeley, 1985, 86, 94, Citation of Merit Calif. State Assembly, 1994; named Woman of Yr. Alameda County North chpt. Nat. Women's Polit. Caucus, 1986, Outstanding Alumna U. Calif. Sch. Libr. and Info. Scis., Berkeley, 1987. Mem. ALA (pres. 1986-87, exec. bd. 1980-89, coun. 1979-88, 90-94, Grolier award 1974), Calif. Libr. Assn. (pres. 1981, coun. 1965-69, 79-82), LWV (dir. Berkeley chpt. 1980-81, v.p. comm. svcs. 1995—). Author: Getting It Together, A Young Adult Bibliography, 1970; contbr. articles to publs. including School Libr. Jour., Wilson Libr. Bull. Office: Reality Mgmt 836 The Alameda Berkeley CA 94707-1916

MINZNER, PAMELA B., judge; b. Meridian, Miss., Nov. 19, 1943. BA cum laude, Miami U., 1965; LLB, Harvard U., 1968. Bar: Mass. 1968, N.Mex. 1972. Pvt. practice Mass., 1968-71, Albuquerque, 1971-73; adj. prof. law U. N.Mex., Albuquerque, 1973-77, assoc. prof., 1977-80, prof. law, 1980-83; judge N.Mex. Ct. Appeals, Albuquerque, 1983; now justice N.Mex. Supreme Ct., Albuquerque; mem. faculty Inst. Preparativo Legal U., N.Mex. Sch. Law, 1975, 79; participant Ad Hoc Com. on Women in Judiciary, NEH Summer Seminar for Law Tchrs. Stanford Law Sch., 1982, U. Chgo. Law Sch., 1978. Co-author (Robert T. Lawrence) A Student's Guide to Estates in Land and Future Interests: Text, Examples, Problems & Answers, 1981. Mem. ABA, State Bar N.Mex. (co-editor 1979-83, bd. dirs. 1983—, sect. on women's legal rights and obligations), Gamma Phi Beta. Democrat. Office: PO Box 848 Santa Fe NM 87504-0848*

MIPOS, DEBRA, adult education educator; b. L.A., June 26, 1947; d. Abraham and Ida M. BA, UCLA, 1967; MPA, Golden Gate U., 1986. Eligibility worker Dept. Pub. Social Svcs., L.A., 1970-71; recruitment specialist Action/OEO, San Francisco, 1971-72; tng. specialist Volt Tng., Inc., San Francisco, 1972-74; freelance cons. San Francisco, 1974-77; coord. edn. Kaiser Permanente Med. Ctr., Hayward, Calif., 1977-79; mgr. employee devel. Kaiser Permanente Regional HRD, Oakland, Calif., 1979-88; dir. edn. & tng. Kaiser Permanente Med. Ctr., San Francisco, 1989-91; mgr. physician mgmt. devel. Kaiser Permanente, Oakland, 1991—; cons. in field. Co-author: (workbook) Toward Living in Another Culture, 1979. Mem. Com. Health Rights, San Francisco, 1985—. Mem. Am. Soc. Tng. & Devel. (v.p. 1982), Am. Soc. Health Educators (pres. local chpt. 1981), Orgn. Devel. Network.

MIR, MARILYN, retired educator; b. Upland, Ind., Dec. 9, 1927; d. Robert Heavin Thompson and Lenora Hults; m. Hashem Robert Mir-Afzali, May 12, 1957 (div. 1976); children: Michael Robert Mir-Afzali, Susan Marie Farrell. BS, Ball State U., 1947; postgrad., U. Colo., 1948; MS, Ind. U., 1950; postgrad., U. Wash., 1951, U. Calif., 1952-53, San Francisco State U., 1984-85. Tchr. bus. Ind., 1947-50, Wenatchee (Wash.) High Sch., 1950-52; exec. sec. Fritzi of Calif., San Francisco, 1958-63; engring. sec. Div. of Westinghouse, San Francisco, 1963-68; tchr. bus. and English San Francisco Unified Schs., 1968-85, attendance coord., 1985-87, cons., 1987-90. Vol. libr. Grossmont High Sch. Dist., El Cajon, Calif., 1990—, San Carlos Pub. Libr., San Diego, 1985; ednl. missionary Utah Presbyn. Schs., 1985, N.Mex. Presbyn. Schs., 1987, N.C. Presbyn. Schs., 1989. Mem. AAUW, San Carlos Women's Club (edn. com.). Democrat. Presbyterian. Home: 7912 June Lake Dr San Diego CA 92119-3120

MIRABAL, ANGELA PRINCE, special education educator; b. Tuscaloosa, Ala., Jan. 25, 1967; d. Bennie Andrew and Mary Clara (McCollum) Prince; m. Daniel Mirabal. BS in Specific Learning Disabilities, U. Ala., 1991; MA in Reading, Nova Southeastern U., Ft. Lauderdale, Fla., 1994; EdS in Ednl. Leadership, Nova U., Ft. Lauderdale. Tchr. Coral Springs (Fla.) Mid. Sch., 1991-95; ESE specialist Ft. Lauderdale H.S., 1995—; trainer N.J. Writing Project of Tex., Ft. Lauderdale, 1994—; dept. head exceptional student edn. Coral Springs Mid. Sch., 1994-95. Mem. ASCD, Nat. Reading Assn., Fla. Reading Assn. Democrat. Baptist. Home: 6811 Bayfront Cir Margale FL 33063-7031 Office: Fort Lauderdale HS 1600 NE 4th Ave Fort Lauderdale FL 33305

MIRABELLA, GRACE, magazine publishing executive; b. Maplewood, N.J., June 10, 1929; d. Anthony and Florence (Belfatto) M.; m. William G. Cahan, Nov. 24, 1974. BA, Skidmore Coll., 1950. Mem. exec. tng. program Macy's, N.Y.C., 1950-51; mem. fashion dept. Saks Fifth Ave., N.Y.C., 1951-52; with Vogue mag., N.Y.C., 1952-54, 56-88; assoc. editor Vogue mag., 1965-71, editor-in-chief, 1971-88; founder, publ. dir. Mirabella Mag., 1988—; mem. pub. relations staff Simonetta & Fabiani, Rome, Italy, 1954-56; hon. bd. dirs. Catalyst; lectr. New Sch. Social Rsch.; adv. bd. mem. Columbia Grad. Sch. Journalism, Leeds Castle, London. Mem. Meml. Sloat-Kettering Cancer Ctr. Women's Soc., bd. adv. Harvard Sch. Pub. Health Ctr. for Cancer Prevention. Decorated cavalier Order of Merit Republic of Italy; recipient Outstanding Grad. Achievement award Skidmore Coll., 1972, Coty Fashion Critics award, 1980, Fashion Critics award Parsons Sch. Design, 1985; Woman of Distinction award Birmingham-So. Coll., 1985, Girl Scouts Am. Leadership award, 1987, Excellence in Media award Susan G. Komen Found., 1987, Equal Opportunity award NOW, 1987; officer Order of Merit, Republic of Italy, 1987; Mary Ann Magnin award, 1988; Achievement award Am. Assn. Plastic and Reconstructive Surgery, 1988; Spl. Merit award Coun. Fashion Designers Am., 1989, Life and Breath award N.Y. Lung Assn., 1990, Matrix award Assn. Edn. in Journalism Mass Comm., 1991, AEJMC award, 1992, St. Francis Cabrini Humanitarian award, 1992, Heart of N.Y. award Am. Heart Assn., N.Y.C. Meals-on-Wheels honor, 1994, Nat. Italian-Am. Found. hon., 1994, Barnard award, 1995, Neiman Marcus award, 1995. Mem. Women's Forum N.Y. Office: Mirabella Mag 1633 Broadway New York NY 10019

MIRACLE, BARBARA LYNN, editor; b. St. Petersburg, Fla., Sept. 7, 1954; d. John Joseph and Lila Alberta (Davis) M. BA, U. Fla., 1976, MA, 1980. Rsch. assoc. Congl. Quar. Inc., Washington, 1981-85, asst. rsch. dir., 1985-87, dir. profl. edn. svc., 1987-89; book divsn. mgr. Fla. Trend mag., St. Petersburg, Fla., 1989-91, assoc. editor, 1991-96, small bus. editor, 1996—; lectr. Govt. Exec. Inst., U.S. Office Personnel Mgmt., Washington, 1986-89. Office: Florida Trend 8th Flr 490 1st Ave South Saint Petersburg FL 33731

MIRAGLIO, ANGELA MARIA, dietitian; b. Chgo., Sept. 12, 1944; d. Charles A. and Rose C. (Moles) M.; m. Robert S. Schwartz, Oct. 22, 1983. BS, Mundelein Coll., 1966; MS, U. Chgo., 1975. Registered dietitian. Clin. nutrition dir. West Suburban Kidney Ctr., Oak Park, Ill., 1974-78; clin. nutritionist Pediatric Outpatient Clinics U. Chgo., 1978-83; owner AMM Nutrition Services, Chgo., 1984—; treas. Cons. Nutritionist Dietetic Practice Group, 1989-91; part-time instr. Chgo. City-Wide Coll., 1979-81; lectr. De Paul U. Sch. Nursing, Chgo., 1978-80. Author: Food Composition Tables for Renal Diets, 1978; contbr. articles to profl. jours. Bd. dirs. Dorridge Condominium Assn., Chgo. Mem. Am. Dietetic Assn., Am. Assn. Diabetes Educators, Soc. for Nutrition Edn., Chgo. Dietetic Assn. (sec. 1969-71), Chgo. Nutrition Assn. Roman Catholic. Home and Office: 290 King Ln Des Plaines IL 60016-5976

MIRANDA, MARIA F., school principal; b. Portugal, June 22, 1948; came to U.S., 1952; d. Joseph and Joaquina (Duarte) Afonso; m. Manuel D. Miranda, Dec. 19, 1970; children: Daniel, Mark. BS, U. Conn., 1970; MS, U. Hartford, 1973; postgrad., U. Bridgeport, 1982. Cert. sch. adminstr., Conn. Tchr. pub. schs., Norwalk, Conn., 1970-79; curriculum specialist pub. schs., Bridgeport, Conn., 1979-86, dir. migratory children's program, 1986-89, prin., 1989—; bd. dirs. Ednl. Leadership Inst., Trumbull, Conn., 1994—; mem. State of Conn. Fgn. Lang. Curriculum Adv. Com., Hartford, 1995—. Bd. dirs. Portuguese Found., Hartford, 19946. Mem. NELMS. Office: Multicultural Magnet Sch 700 Palisade Ave Bridgeport CT 06610

MIRANDA-FOSTER, ELENA, educator, journalist; b. Callao, Lima, Peru, Jan. 9, 1958; came to U.S., 1985; d. Esteban Miranda and Pilar Cardenas; m. Robert James Foster, May 19, 1985 (div. July 1994); 1 child, Mitchel Robert. BA, Jaime Bausate U. Sch. of Journalism, 1982, San Martin De Porres U., Lima, 1989. Tchr. art Dalton Pvt. Sch., Lima, Peru, 1979-82; journalist Ministry of Defense, Lima, Peru, 1982-85; protor Boces-Teach Adult Ctr., Nassau County, N.Y., 1988; tchr. presch. Child Care UN Employees, N.Y.C., 1985-88; substitute tchr. N.C., 1989-90; tchr. Spanish, English as 2d lang. Brunswick C.C., Supply, N.C., 1989-91; tchr. Spanish South Brunswick High Sch., Southport, N.C., 1990-91, Union Elem. & Shallotte (N.C.) Mid. Schs., 1991—; mem. adv. bd. Adult Basic Skills in Brunswick C.C., 1994—. Editor: Sara-Sara, 1982, Que Pasa, 1990. Mem. N.C. Advancement of Tchrs., Fgn. Lang. Assn., Hispoanic Culture Assn. of Women (pres. 1994), B County Western For Minority Recruitment (task force com.). Roman Catholic. Home: 208 Evergreen Ln Middleburg FL 32068

MIRELES, LETICIA EDNA, nursing administrator; b. Houston, Dec. 18, 1953; d. Thomas M. and Beatriz (Montalvo) M. Diploma in Vocat. Nursing, Hermann Hosp. Sch. Vocat. Nursing, 1974; BSN, Tex. Woman's U., 1993. Lic. vocat. nurse, RN, Tex. Staff lic. vocat. nurse surg. intermediate care Hermann Hosp., Houston, 1974-75; staff lic. vocat. nurse ICU-CCU Plaza Del Oro Hosp., Houston, 1975-80; lic. vocat. nurse instr. med.-surg. and pharmacology Hosp. Corp. Am. Sch. Vocat. Nursing, Houston, 1980-83; home health nurse Nursing Svcs. Internat., Houston, 1983; staff lic. vocat. nurse dept. dermatology Baylor Coll. Medicine, Houston, 1983-93, nurse, sr. adminstr. asst. divsn. plastic surgery, 1993—. Vol. Houston Proud Orgn. Mem. Am. Soc. Plastic and Reconstructive Nurses, Tex. Nurses Assn., Plastic Surgery Adminstrv. Assn., Dermatology Nurses Assn. (mem. nomination com. 1985), Baylor Coll. Medicine Clin. Practice Adminstrs. Assn. (mem. nomination com. 1993—). Roman Catholic. Office: Baylor Coll Medicine Divsn Plastic Surgery 6560 Fannin St Ste 800 Houston TX 77030-2725

MIRICK, KARLA JEAN, artist; b. Rhinelander, Wis., May 4, 1954; d. Harold Carl and Violet Marie (Engstrom) Peterson; m. Mark J. Mirick, May 19, 1979; children: Patrick, Anika, Mats. BA, Hamline, St. Paul, 1976. Cert. secondary edn., Minn. Grip/asst. Midwestern Films, Mpls., 1977; display asst. Wickes Furniture, Fridley, Minn., 1978; part-time set designer Sta. WCCO TV, Mpls., 1978. 2-person show Ctr. for Visual Arts, Wausau, 1994; 1 person show Gateway Hotel, Land O'Lakes, Wis.; exhibited in group shows Gateway Hotel, Land O'Lakes, Wis., 1977. Bd. dirs. Susan Peterson Prodns., Washington, Cen. Wis. Ballet Found., Wausau, Wis., Performing Arts Found. Affiliate Bd., Wausau; docent Walker Art Ctr., Mpls., 1976, 79. Recipient Regional Rosemaling Show award, 1979. Mem. AAUW, Nat. Mus. Women in Arts. Home: T 6793 N Troy St Wausau WI 54403

MIRIPOL, JERILYN ELISE, poet, writer, writing therapist; b. Chgo., Jan. 22; d. Albert and Janice (Tuchin) M.; m. Richard Palmer Van Duyne, Dec. 30, 1986. BA in English Lit., Northeastern Ill. U., 1974. Writing therapist Northshore Retirement Hotel, Evanston, Ill., 1983; creative writing tchr. Oakton Community Coll., Evanston, 1985—; writing therapist St. Francis Hosp., Evanston, 1989—; artist-writer-in-residence Dawes Sch., Evanston, 1985; artist-in-residence Evanston Twp. High Sch., 1988; writing facilitator for individual students, Chgo., 1987—; tchr. writing therapy to mental health profls. and caregivers U. Wis., Milw., 1989; presenter writing therapy workshop, 1990, Nat. Assn. Poetry-Therapy, Chgo., 1991. Author: Discovering Self-Awareness Through Poetry, 1987, (poetry) The Sounds Were Distilled, 1977; author numerous poems; contbr. articles to profl. jours. Vol. Ridgeview Nursing Home, Evanston, 1982-83; advocate of children of abuse, human and civil rights. Talent scholar in creative writing Northeastern Ill. U., Squaw Valley Community Writers scholar, 1980, Radgale Found. scholar, 1985, Aspen Writer's Workshop Breadloaf Writer's Conf. scholar; Danforth fellow nominee; Dawes Sch. grantee, 1987. Mem. NOW, PEN, UNICEF, ACLU, Nat. Assn. Poetry Therapy, Women's Internat. League for Peace, Humanitas Internat. (human rights com.), Amnesty Internat., Am. Acad. Poets, Ill. Alliance of Arts, 11th Ann. Poetry Therapy Conf. (keynote speaker), Greenpeace, Death Penalty Foes. Home: 1520 Washington Ave Wilmette IL 60091-2417

MIRISOLA, LISA HEINEMANN, air quality engineer; b. Glendale, Calif., Mar. 25, 1963; d. J. Herbert and Betty Jane (Howson) Heinemann; m. Daniel Carl Mirisola, June 27, 1987; 1 child, Ian Cataldo. BSME, UCLA, 1986. Cert. engr.-in-tng., Calif. Air quality engr. South Coast Air Quality Mgmt. Dist., Diamond Bar, Calif., 1988—. Chancellor's scholar UCLA, 1981. Mem. ASME, NSPE, Soc. Women Engrs. Office: South Coast Air Quality Mgmt Dist 21865 Copley Dr Diamond Bar CA 91765-4178

MIROW, SUSAN MARILYN, psychiatry educator; b. Manhattan, N.Y., Feb. 15, 1944. BA in Biology, Temple U., 1964; PhD in Anatomy, N.Y. Med. Coll., 1970; MD, Med. Coll. Pa., 1973. Diplomate Nat. Bd. Med. Examiners, Am. Bd. Psychiatry and Neurology. Intern in medicine and psychiatry Temple U. Hosp., Phila., 1973-74, resident in psychiatry, 1973-75; pvt. practice psychiatry Salt Lake City, 1976—; clin. asst. prof. psychiatry U. Utah Sch. Medicine, Salt Lake City, 1976—; clin. asst. prof. psychiatry Neuropsychiat. Inst. U. Utah; mem. staff Salt Lake Regional Med. Ctr., 1976—, Latter Day Saints Hosp., 1985—; prin. investigator Marine Biol. Lab., Woods Hole, Mass., 1968; research investigator Temple U., Dept. Biology, summer 1971, Hosp. Joint Diseases, N.Y.C., 1969-70; clin. dir. Utah State Hosp., Provo, 1980-82; psychiat. extern Phila. Child Guidance Clin, 1973, neurology clk. Med. Coll. Pa. Dept. Neurology, 1973, cons. psychiatrist Adolescent Residential Treatment Ctr., Salt Lake City, 1976-77; vis. prof. St. George's U., Grenada, 1990—; psychiat. cons. Divsn. Youth Corrections, Salt Lake City, 1992—; lectr. in field. Contbr. articles to profl. jours. NSF fellow 1965-69; grantee John Polachek Rsch. Found., 1969-70; recipient Weisman award Excellence Child Psychiatry, 1973. Fellow Am. Psychiat. Assn.; mem. AAAS, AMA, Utah State Med. Assn. (impaired physician's com. 1983), Salt Lake County Med. Soc., N.Y. Acad. Scis., Soc. Clin. and Exptl. Hypnosis, Internat. Soc. Clin. Hypnosis, Utah Soc. Clin. Hypnosis (sec. 1982-83), Am. Soc. Clin. Hypnosis, The Internat. Soc. for Traumatic Stress Studies. Office: 73 G St Salt Lake City UT 84103-2951

MIRRA, SUZANNE SAMUELS, neuropathologist, researcher; b. N.Y.C., Feb. 16, 1943. BA, Hunter Coll., 1962; MD, SUNY, Bklyn., 1967. Instr. pathology Yale U. Sch. Medicine, New Haven, 1971-73; staff pathologist Atlanta VA Med. Ctr., Decatur, Ga., 1973—; asst. prof. pathology Emory U. Sch. Medicine, Atlanta, 1973-80, assoc. prof. pathology, 1981-93, prof. pathology, 1993—; dir., prin. investor Emory Alzheimer's Disease Ctr., Atlanta, 1991—. Mem. editl. bd. Arch Pathol. Lab. Med., 1988—, Jour. Neuropathology Exptl. Neurology, 1991-95, Brain Pathology, 1995—, Alzheimer's Disease Reviews, 1995—. Recipient Albert E. Levy Sci. Faculty Rsch. award Emory U., 1987, Disting. Alumnus Achievement award SUNY, 1992; named to Hunter Coll. Hall of Fame, 1996. Fellow Coll. Am. Pathologists (Presdl. award 1987,89, Herbert Lansky award 1990, chair neuropathology commn. 1992-95)); mem. Am. Assn. Neuropathologists (v.p. profl. affairs 1992—), Alzheimer's Assn. (bd. dirs. Atlanta chpt. 1987—). Office: VA Med Ctr 113 Emory U 1670 Clairmont Rd Decatur GA 30033-4004

MIRREN, HELEN, actress; b. London, 1946. First appeared with Nat. Youth Theatre; appeared as Cleopatra in Antony and Cleopatra, Old Vic, 1965; joined Royal Shakespeare Co., 1967; appeared as Castiza in The Revenger's Tragedy and Diana in All's Well That Ends Well; other roles include: Cressida in Troilus and Cressida, Royal Shakespeare Co., Stratford, Eng., 1968; Hero in Much Ado About Nothing, Stratford, 1968; Win-the-Fight Littlewit in Bartholomew Fair, Aldwych, 1969; Lady Anne in Richard III, Stratford, Ophelia in Hamlet, Julia in The Two Gentlemen of Verona, Stratford, 1970 (last part also at Aldwych); Tatyana in Enemies, Royal Shakespeare Co., Aldwych, 1971; title role in Miss Julie, Elynae in The Balcony, The Place, 1971; with Peter Brook's Centre Internationale de Recherches Theatrales, Africa and U.S., 1972-73; Lady Macbeth, Royal Shakespeare Co., Stratford, 1974, and Aldwych, 1975; Maggie in Teeth 'n' Smiles, Royal Ct., 1975; Nina in The Seagull and Ella in The Bed Before Yesterday, Lyric for Lyric Theatre Co., 1975, Antony and Cleopatra, The Roaring Girl, Henry VI-Parts 1, 2, 3, 1977-78, Measure for Measure, 1979, The Duchess of Malfi, 1980-81, Faith Healer, 1981, Royal Shakespeare Co., Barbican, 1983, Extremities, 1984, Madame Bovary, 1987, Two Way Mirror, 1988, Sex Please We're Italian, 1991, A Month in the Country, 1994 (Tony nominee - Lead Actress in a Play, 1995); films include: Age of Consent, 1969, Savage Messiah, O Lucky Man!, 1973, Caligula, 1977, The Long Good Friday, Excalibur, 1981, Cal, 1984 (Best Actress award Cannes Film Festival 1984), 2010, 1984, White Knights, 1984, Heavenly Pursuits, 1985, The Mosquito Coast, 1986, Pascali's Island, 1987, When The Whales Came, 1988, Bethune, Making of a Hero, 1988, The Cook, The Thief, His Wife, and Her Lover, 1989, The Comfort of Strangers, 1990, Where Angels Fear to Tread, 1991, The Gift, 1991, The Hawk, 1991, The Prince of Jutland, 1991, The Madness of King George, 1994 (Acad. award nominee for Best Supporting Actress), Prime Suspect: Scent of Darkness (Emmy award 1996); TV appearances include: Behind the Scene, Cousin Bette, Coffin for the Bride, Jackanory, The Changeling, Bellamira, The Philanthropist, Mussolini And Claretta Petacci, The Collection, The Country Wife, Blue Remembered Hills, The Serpent Son, Quiz Kids, Midsummer Night's Dream, After the Party, Cymbeline, Coming Through, Cause Celebre, Miss Julie, The Apple Cart, The Little Minister, As You Like It, Mrs. Reinhardt, Soft Targets, 1982, Heavenly Pursuits, 1985, Red King White Knight, 1988, Prime Suspect, 1991 (Best Actress award BAFTA 1991), Prime Suspect 2, 1992, Prime Suspect 3, 1993 (Emmy award, 1994), Prime Suspect 4, 1994, Chase in Losing Chase, 1995, Some Mothers Son, 1995, A Month in the Country, 1995. Mem. PTO. Office: Ken McReddie Ltd, 91 Regent St, London WIR TTB, England*

MIRSEPASSI-TOLOUI, SHIRLEY SHIRIN, pathologist, educator; b. Tehran, Iran, Apr. 13, 1944; came to U.S., 1972; d. Morteza and Esmatelmolook (Bahrami) Mirsepassi; m. Gerald Javad Toloui, Apr. 23, 1970; children: Kenneth, Sam. MD, Tehran U., 1969. Diplomate Am. Bd. Anatomic and Clin. Pathology and Cytopathology. Asst. prof. N.Y. Med. Coll., Valhalla, 1990—; assoc. pathologist St. Vincent's Hosp., Staten Island, N.Y., 1994—. Fellow Coll. Am. Pathologists, Am. Soc. Clin. Pathologists. Republican. Office: St Vincent's Hosp 355 Bard Ave Staten Island NY 10310

MIRSKY, SONYA WOHL, librarian, curator; b. N.Y.C., Nov. 12, 1925; d. Louis and Anna (Steiger) Wohl; m. Alfred Ezra Mirsky, Aug. 24, 1967 (dec. June 1974). B.S. in Edn., CCNY, 1948; M.S.L.S., Columbia U., 1950. Asst. libr. Rockefeller U., N.Y.C., 1949-60, assoc. libr., 1960-77, univ. libr., 1977-91, univ. libr. emeritus, 1991—; trustee Med. Libr. Ctr. N.Y., 1965-91, v.p., 1980-88; cons. libr. mgmt. Mem. Bibliog. Soc. Am., Bibliog. Soc. Can., Bibliog. Soc. Gt. Britain, Soc. Bibliography of Natural History. Home: Sutton Ter 1161 York Ave Apt 4F New York NY 10021-7945 Office: Rockefeller U Libr 1230 York Ave New York NY 10021-6300

MIRZA, LEONA LOUSIN, educator; b. Chgo., July 1, 1944; d. Max B. and Opal Lousin; m. David B. Mirza; children: Sara Anush, Elizabeth Ann. BA in Math., North Park Coll., Chgo., 1965; MA in Edn., Western Mich. U., Kalamazoo, 1967, EdD in Edn., 1972; cert. in computer studies, North Park Coll., 1983. Tchr. Kalamazoo Pub. Schs., 1965-69; prof. math. edn. North Park Coll., 1969—. Editor The Illinois Mathematics Teacher, 1992—; contbr. articles to profl. jours. Chmn. adv. com. on edn. in Ill., 1975-77. Mem. Nat., Ill. Coun. Tchrs. Math., Ill. Assn. Colls. of Tchr. Edn., Ill. Assn. Tchrs. Edn. in Pvt. Colls. (officer 1974-86). Specialist in elem. curriculum and adminstrn. Home: 795 Lincoln Ave Winnetka IL 60093-1920 Office: 3225 W Foster Ave Chicago IL 60625-4810

MIRZA, NANCY KAYE, writer/consultant; b. Madison Wis., May 26, 1939; d. Woodrow Earl Jacobson and Betty Jane (Kline) Jackson; m. Jerome Mirza, Apr. 14, 1958 (div.); 1 child, Candace Renée. BS, Ill. State U., 1970, MS, 1971. Lic. sch. psychologist, Ill. Model Patrice Vance Agy./Radio City Talent, Chgo., 1944-49; actor Cmty. Theater, Ill., 1947-74; writer New Trier/Ill. Wesleyan U., Bloomington, 1954-59; social activist Unitarian Universalist Assn., Bloomington, 1963-72; sch. psychologist pub. schs. Peoria, Chgo., 1971-74; actor/writer LaMama-Hollywood/I.C.M., L.A., 1974-76; vocat. cons. various locations, Calif., 1976-84; tchr. L.A. Unified Sch. Dist., 1983-88; media advisor/cons./writer Nancy Kaye Mirza, Santa Monica, Calif., 1988—; dir. Playwrites Workshop, L.A., 1974-76. Author: (play) Love on Trial, 1956; cons. (play) Kennedy's Children, 1974 (Tony 1976), Entebe, 1975 (Drama Critics Cir. 1976). Bd. dirs. Unitarian Universalist Assn., Chgo., 1969-72. Recipient Recognition of Outstanding Svc. award Ill. Coun. Exceptional Children, 1973; Ill. State scholar, 1969. Mem. ACA, ACLU, Screen Actors Guild, Actors Equity Assn. (small theatre rep. 1974-75), Am. Contract Bridge League, UCLA Alumni Assn. Unitarian-Universalist.

MISETICH, IONE HOZENDORF, business services company executive, enrolled agent, financial planner, accountant; b. Jackson, Miss., Sept. 19, 1937; d. Glenn Frederick and Ione Belle (Lowry) Hozendorf; m. Francis John Reget, Jan. 17, 1967 (div. 1986); m. Charles Drago Misetich, May 28, 1993; children: Diane Michele, Philip Francis, Michael Trahern. BA cum laude, U. Minn., 1959. CFP; CPA, Calif. Pres., Ea. Sierra Bus. Svcs., Inc., Bishop, Calif., 1980—; sec.-treas. Meyer Cookie Co., Inc. Soprano, Bishop Cmty. Chorus, 1974-78; treas. Calvary Bapt. Ch., Bishop, 1975—, choir dir., 1980—; chmn. Civic Arts Commn., City of Bishop, 1984-87; bd. dirs. Inyo Council for the Arts, 1987-90; pres. Bishop Com. Concert Assn., 1989—. Mem. Nat. Assn. Enrolled Agts., Calif. Soc. Enrolled Agts., Calif. Assn. Ind. Accts., Internat. Assn. Fin. Planners, Inst. CFP, Aircraft Owners and Pilots Assn., DAR, Mensa, Playhouse 395, Bishop Toastmasters Club, Bishop Rotary Club. Republican. Home: 146 North St RR 1 Bishop CA 93514-0728 Office: 130 Short St Bishop CA 93514-0728 Address: PO Box 728 Bishop CA 93515-0728

MISHNE, JUDITH MARKS, social work educator, psychotherapist; b. Cleve., Feb. 21, 1932; d. Moses Isaac and Lillian (Kemelman) Marks; (div.); 1 child, Jonathan. BS, U. Wis., 1953; MSW, Case Western Res. U., 1955; cert., Inst. of Psychoanalysis, Chgo., 1974; DSW, CUNY, 1981. Caseworker Akron (Ohio) Child Guidance Ctr., 1955-56, Cleve. Child Guidance Ctr., 1956-58, Jewish Family Svc., Cleveland Heights, 1959-62; sch. social worker Orange Bd. Edn., Pepper Pike, Ohio, 1962-66; unit supr. Bellefaire of Jewish Children's Bur., Cleve., 1964-66; assoc. prof. sch. of social svcs. adminstrn. U. Chgo., 1966-76; assoc. prof. sch. social work Columbia U., N.Y.C., 1977-79; from assoc. prof. to prof. sch. social work NYU, 1979—; summer faculty mem. sch. social work Smith Coll., Northampton, Mass., 1975-82; cons. Pritzker Children's Hosp., Chgo., 1968-74, Madden Hosp., Chgo., 1973-75, Queens Child Guidance Clinic, Jamaica, N.Y., 1979-80, Roosevelt Hosp., N.Y.C., 1983, Jewish Family Svc., Hackensack, N.Y., 1986-87; vis. lectr. U. Haifa (Israel) Sch. Social Work, 1994. Author: Clinical Work With Children, 1983, Clinical Work With Adolescents, 1986, Evolution and Application of Clinical Theory: Perspectives From Four Psychologies, 1993, The Learning Curve: Elevating Children's Academic and Social Competence, 1996; editor: Psychotherapy and Training in Clinical Social Work, 1980; co-editor: (with others) Ego and Self Psychology: Group Intervention With Children and Adolescents, 1983. Named Disting. Practitioner in Social Work Nat. Academies of Practice, 1983; recipient Spencer Found. award NYU, 1987, Spl. Achievement award PhD Alumni Assn. CUNY, 1996; Vis. scholar Bar Ilan U. Sch. of Social Work, Israel, 1993, 94. Mem. Assn. of Child and Adolescent Therapists, Nat. Fedn. Socs. for Social Work, Coun. on Social Work Edn., Nat. Acad. of Practice in Social Work, Assn. for Psychoanalytic Self Psychology. Democrat. Home: #4E 225 W 88th St New York NY 10024-2303 Office: NYU Sch of Social Work 2 Washington Sq N New York NY 10003-6635

MISHRA, KAREN ELIZABETH, marketing educator, corporate sales trainer; b. Lansing, Mich., July 4, 1963; d. Thomas William and Martha Lynne (Isbell) Repaskey; m. Aneil Kumar Mishra, June 22, 1985. BA, Albion Coll., 1985; MBA, U. Mich., 1988. Coop. edn. Buick Olds Cadillac Group, Lansing, Mich., 1982-85; promotions intern N.Y. Arts program, 1983; coll. grad. in tng. Buick Olds Cadillac, Gen. Motors, Lansing, Mich., 1985-86; coord. summer student program Buick Old Cadillac, Gen. Motors, Lansing, Mich.; promotions coord. Jacobson Stores, Jackson, Mich., 1987; mkt. analyst Johnson Controls, Inc., Manchester, Mich., 1988-89, sales analyst, 1989-90, price adminstrn./promotions mgr., 1990-91, nat. account mgr., 1991-92; prin. AKM Cons. & Rsch., 1992—; pres. U. Mich. Bus. Sch. Student Coun., Ann Arbor, 1987-88; mktg. instr. Pa. State U., 1992—. Composer Born Today, 1980, Let Your Light So Shine, 1981. Vol. William Lucas for Gov. campaign, Lansing, Mich., 1985; mem. Lange Early Music Ensemble, Lansing, 1985; adv. Mortar Bd. Nat. Honor Soc., Ann Arbor, 1986-88, Pa. State U., 1992-96; com. mem. Episc. Ch. Planned Giving, Detroit, 1989; chorister St. Clares Ch. Choir, Ann Arbor, 1988-91; rec. sec. Jr. Women's Club, 1993; mktg. vol. Pub. Radio WPSU, 1993-94; vol. pub. rels. State Coll. Centennial, 1995-96, vol. Bush for Pres. Re-election campaign, 1992; leader Weight Watchers, 1993—; dir. children's choir Grace Luth. Ch., 1993—; mem. Nittany Valley Symphony Guild, 1995—. Mem. Am. Mktg. Assn. (programs v.p.). Republlican. Episcopalian. Home: 965-1 Southgate Dr State College PA 16801 Office: AKM Cons & Rsch PO Box 8057 State College PA 16803

MISIOREK, MARY MADELYN, social worker; b. Mt. Holly, N.J., Sept. 7, 1950; d. Frank and Anna (Dudek) M. BA, Trenton (N.J.) State Coll., 1972; MSW, Rutgers U., 1993. Social worker State of N.J., Pemberton, 1973-79; psychiat./med. social worker Rancocas Hosp., Willingboro, N.J., 1980-95; clin. mgr. The Counseling Program, Marlton, N.J., 1995—. Mem. NASW, LCSW, ACSW, Alpha Beta Mu. Office: The Counseling Program Clinical Dept Marlton NJ 08053

MISKOLCZI, ELISABETA (KLÁRA TAMÁS), artist; b. Tirgu-Mures, Romania, Aug. 20, 1946; came to U.S., 1992; d. József and Sarolta Margit (Plavenszky) Tamás; m. Andrei Blaier, Nov. 29, 1973 (div. June 1989); m. Tiberiu R. Miskolczi, Dec. 16, 1992; 1 stepchild, Christopher Miskolczi. Degree in fine arts, Tirgu-Mures, 1964; MFA, Acad. Fine Art, Cluj, Romania, 1970. Graphic artist packaging design co., Bucharest, Romania, 1970-72; art dir. Meridiane pub. house, Bucharest, 1972-75, Kriterion pub. house, Bucharest, 1975-89; fine artist Fine Artists Union, Bucharest, 1973—; v.p. Symbol Corp., Woodhaven, N.Y., 1993—; dir. Virtual Symbol Gallery/Internet/Netscape, 1995—; dir. weaving studio Dante Divina Commedia, Bucharest, 1989—. One-woman shows at Gallateea, Bucharest, 1974, Simeza, Bucharest, 1979, Theater Gallery, Esslingen, Germany, 1984, Xenia, Athens, Greece, 1984, Pécsi Galeria, Pécs, Hungary, 1991, Nicolae Gallery, Columbus, Ohio, 1992; group exhbns. at Rotterdam, 1977, Oxford, Eng., 1978, Lysaker, 1979, San Francisco, 1982, Stockholm, 1988, Heidelberg, Germany, 1988, Eisenstadt, 1990, Munich, 1990, Belgium, 1991, C&A Gallery, N.Y.C., 1993, La Jolla, Calif., 1995; represented in permanent collections at Albertina Mus., Vienna, Bucharest, Budapest, Warsaw, Poland, Lahti, Toyama. Recipient Purchase prize Cracow, Poland, 1976, prize Szczecin Mus., Cracow, 1980, Grand Prize Gold Hugo, Chgo., 1984, Ctr. George Pompidou, 1986, Audience award Tuzla, 1988. Mem. Fine Artists Union (Young Talents fellow 1973). Roman Catholic. Home and Office: 85-04 Park Lane S Apt 4 Woodhaven NY 11421

MISNER, CHARLOTTE BLANCHE RUCKMAN, community organization administrator; b. Gifford, Idaho, Aug. 30, 1937; d. Richard Steele and Arizona (Hill) Ruckman; m. G. Arthur Misner, Jr., Aug. 29, 1959; children: Michelle, Mary, Jennifer. BS in Psychology, U. Idaho, 1959. Vol. numerous orgns. India, Mexico, The Philippines, 1962-70; sec., v.p., pres., trustee St. Luke's Hosp., Manila, 1970-84; founding mem., 3d v.p., pres. Am. Women's Club of Philippines, 1980-84; exec. adminstr. Friends of Oakland (Calif.) Parks and Recreation, 1986-92, exec. dir., 1992—. Active Lincoln Child Ctr., Oakland, 1984—. Recipient Vol. Svc. award Women's Bd. St. Luke's Hosp., 1977, Mid. Sch. Vol. award Internat. Sch.-Manila, 1980. Me. Alpha Gamma Delta (alumnae treas., pres. East Bay 1985-89, province dir. alumnae 1989—), Cum Laude Soc. (hon.). Home: 481 Ellita Ave Oakland CA 94610-4808 Office: Friends of Oakland Parks & Recreation 1520 Lakeside Dr Oakland CA 94612-4521

MIENER, LORRAINE, laboratory technologist; b. Fitchburg, Mass., June 24, 1948; d. Cedric Winfield and Pearl Erma (Hallisey) M. BA in Biology, Fitchburg State Coll., 1971; MS in Med. Technology, Anna Maria Coll., 1983. Lab. technologist Leominster (Mass.) Hosp., 1971-87; research asst. U. Lowell Rsch. Found. (now U. Mass. Lowell Rsch. Found.), 1987—. Piccolo Townsend (Mass.) Mil. Band, 1964-93; mem. choir United Ch. of Christ, 1961—. Mem. Am. Soc. Clin. Pathologists (assoc., registrant), Am. Soc. for Clin. Lab. Sci., Mass. Soc. for Med. Tech., Am. Assn. Clin. Chemistry.

MISSAKIAN, ILONA VIRGINIA, English educator, bookkeeper; b. Huntington Park, Calif., July 16, 1968; d. Garo Garabed and Brigitte Renata Anne Marie (Kunkel) M. AA with honors, Mt. San Antonio Coll., 1991; BA with honors, Calif. State U., Fullerton, 1993, postgrad., 1993—. Tchg. credential. Instr. Alexandra Ballet Acad., Hacienda Heights, Calif., 1985-92, Dellos Dance and Performing Arts Ctr., Walnut, Calif., 1989-91; apprentice Les Ballets Classiques, Montreal, Can., 1987-88; bookkeeper Garo's German Auto Repair, Walnut, 1986—; instr. Brea (Calif.) Olinda H.S., 1994—. Mem. MLA, Calif. Lit. Project, Calif. State Fullerton Alumni, Alpha Gamma Sigma (sec., news editor 1988-91). Office: Brea Olinda HS 789 N Wildcat Way Brea CA 92621

MISSIMORE, MAUREEN MARGARET, sales professional; b. St. Louis, Apr. 22, 1959; d. Amos Sawyer and Kathleen Blanche (McCotter) M.; m. Terrence R. Fournier, June 22, 1979 (div. 1981). AA in Retailing, St. Louis Community Coll., 1980; BS in Bus., Fontbonne Coll., 1991, MBA, 1995. Sales rep. various retail stores St. Louis, 1975-79; store mgr. Lerner's, St. Louis, 1979-81; sales rep. Eisenhart Brokerage, St. Louis, 1981-83, O'Brien & Assocs., Food Broker, St. Louis, 1983-85, Best Foods-CPC Internat., St. Louis, 1985-87; mktg. asst. Fantasy Coachworks, Ltd., St. Louis, 1990; sales rep. Dillard's, St. Louis, 1991; rep. OPTIONS program Fontbonne Coll., Clayton, Mo., 1992-95; with Burt & Assocs., Dallas, 1996—; cons. Small Bus. Inst., St. Louis, 1988-91. Vol. Humane Soc. Mem. Women's Commerce Assn. (mktg. 1989—), Delta Mu Delta (v.p. 1990—), Kappa Gamma Pi. Democrat. Roman Catholic. Home: 14827 Preston Rd Apt 1202 Dallas TX 75240

MISSIRIOTIS, IRENE, activities director, artist; b. North Charleroi, Pa., Nov. 12, 1938; d. Alexander and Athena (Stirou) M. Diploma in fashion illustration, Art Inst. Pitts., 1960; BS in Psychology-English, writing cert., U. Pitts., 1976. Artist Livingston's, Youngstown, Ohio, 1961-63; layout artist O'Neils, Akron, Ohio, 1963-67; tchr. art Art Inst. Pitts., 1967-73; reporter, typographer, layout artist, illustrator Night Times, Pitts., 1973-76; art coord. Cmty. Human Svcs. Corp., Pitts., 1977-78; recreation leader Pitts. Parks and Recreation Dept., summers 1979-80; program mgr. United Cerebral Palsy Assn., Pitts., 1981; adult day care attendant Hill House Assn., Pitts., 1985-87; therapeutic recreation asst. Angelus Convalescent Ctr., Pitts., 1987-89; activities coord. Canterbury Place, Pitts., 1989-90; activities dir. The Woodwell, Pitts., 1991—; freelance artist, 1956—; designer brochures, booklets, flyers. Vol. Mondale-Ferraro Presdl. Campaign, Pitts., 1984; activist mem. NOW, 1974—. Mem. Pitts. Assn. for Arts in Edn. and Therapy, Assn. for Women in Psychology, Nat. Mus. Women in Arts (charter), Nat. Mus. Am. Indian (charter, cert. of appreciation), Waterford Soc. (charter), World Wildlife Fund, Alpha Sigma Lambda (charter). Democrat. Greek Orthodox. Home: 4733 Centre Ave Apt 1A Pittsburgh PA 15213

MISTELE, PRISCILLA DEBORAH, computer company administrator; b. Detroit, Sept. 18, 1968; d. Otto and Priscilla Maxine (Branham) Collins; m. Bryan Peter Mistele, Aug. 28, 1992. BS in Engring., U. Mich., 1990, MBA with high distinction, 1993. Engring. intern GM, Tarrytown, N.Y., summer 1989; sys. cons. UNISYS Corp., Plymouth, Mich., 1990-92; prin. mktg. specialist AEG Schneider Automation, North Andover, Mass., 1993-95; product mgr. Microsoft Corp., Redmond, Wash., 1995—; owner, co-founder Harvard Software Assoc., Cambridge, Mass., 1994-96. Designer, developer (software) Job-Score, 1995. Mem. NAFE, Alpha Phi Mu. Home: 3504 167th Ave SE Bellevue WA 98008

MITCHELL, ANDREA, journalist; b. N.Y.C., Oct. 30, 1946; d. Sydney and Cecile Mitchell. B.A., U. Pa., 1967. Polit. reporter KYW Newsradio, Phila., 1967-76; polit. corr. Sta. KYW-TV, Phila., 1972-76; corr. Sta. WTOP-TV, Washington, 1977-78; gen. assignment and energy corr. NBC News, Washington, 1978-81; White House corr. NBC News, 1981-88, chief congl. corr., 1989-92, chief White House corr., 1993-94; chief fgn. affairs corr. NBC News, Washington, 1995—, 1994—; instr. Gt. Lakes Colls. Assn., 1974-76; co-anchor Summer Sunday, USA, NBC-TV News, 1984, substitute anchor Meet the Press, 1988—. Overseer, Sch. of Arts and Scis., U. Pa., 1989-95, trustee, 1995—; mem. nat. adv. bd. Girl Scouts U.S. Recipient award for pub. affairs reporting Am. Polit. Sci. Assn., 1969, Pub. Affairs Reporting award AP, 1976, AP Broadcast award, 1977; named Communicator of the Yr., Phila. chpt. Women in Comms., 1976, Woman of the Yr., Phila. chpt. Am. Women in Radio and TV, 1989, Lucretia Mott award Woman's Way, 1991. Mem. White House Corrs. Assn. Office: NBC News 4001 Nebraska Ave NW Washington DC 20016-2733

MITCHELL, BARBARA IRENE, scientific recruiter; b. L.A., May 19, 1942; d. Norman Bailey and Dorothy Elizabeth (Behm) Forster; m. Alexander Rebar Mitchell, Aug. 25, 1963; 1 child, Nicole Anne. BA, Mills Coll., 1963; PhD, Ind. U., 1974; MBA, U. Calif., Berkeley, 1982. Instr. Coll. Mt. St. Vincent, Riverdale, N.Y., 1970-76, J.F. Kennedy U., Orinda, Calif., 1979-80; mgr. indsl. sales Brampton-Mathiesen, San Leandro, Calif., 1982-85; dir. mktg. Shakow & Mitchell Internat., Albany, Calif., 1985-87; recruiter Bridge-Gate Group, San Jose, Calif., 1987-92; prin. Life Sci. Resources, Livermore, Calif., 1992—; invited speaker in field. Kress Found. grantee, 1972-73, NEH grantee, 1976. Mem. AWIS (mentor 1993—), Alumnae Assn. Mills Coll. (bd. govs. 1986-89). Republican. Roman Catholic. Office: Life Sci Resources 5577 Bridgeport Cir Livermore CA 94550-1101

MITCHELL, BETTIE PHAENON, religious organization administrator; b. Colorado Springs, Colo., June 6, 1934; d. Roy William and Laura Lee (Costin) Roberts; m. Gerald Mitchell, May 3, 1952; children: Michelle Smith, Laura Sweitz, Jennie Grenzer, Mohammad Bader. BS in Edn., Lewis & Clark Coll., 1954; postgrad., Portland State U., 1962-72; MA in Religion summa cum laude, Warner Pacific Coll., 1979. Cert. counselor, Oreg. Elem. tchr. Quincy Sch. Dist., Clatskanie, Oreg., 1955-56; substitute tchr. Beaverton (Oreg.) and Washington County Schs., 1956-77; tchr. of the Bible Portland (Oreg.) C.C., 1974-92; counseling and healing ministry, 1977-79; founder, exec. dir. Good Samaritan Ministries, Beaverton, 1979-88, founder, internat. exec. dir., 1988—; tchr. Christian Renewal Ctr. Workshops, 1977-85; speaker, presenter in field; leader tours in the Mid. East; developing counselor edn. programs Pakistan, Ukraine, Jordan, Egypt, Kenya, Uganda, Tanzania, Zambia, Malawi, South Africa, Nigeria, Burundi, Sierra Leone. Author: Who Is My Neighbor? A Parable, 1988, The Power of Conflict and Sacrifice, A Therapy Manual for Christian Marriage, 1988, Good Samaritan Training Handbook, 1989, Be Still and Listen to His Voice, The Story of Prayer and Faith, 1990, A Need for Understanding - International Counselor Training Manual, 1993. Mem. Israel Task Force, Portland, 1974-80; Leader Camp Fire Internat., 1962-73, elem. sch. coord., 1962-68; asst. dir. Washington County Civil Def., 1961-63; precinct committeewoman Rep. Party, 1960; bd. dirs. Beaverton Fish, 1966-74; v.p. NCCJ, Portland, 1983-85; chmn., speaker's bur. Near East Task Force for Israel; chmn. fire bond issue campaign City of Beaverton, mgr. mayoral campaign, 1960; sunday sch. tchr., speaker, organizer Sharing and Caring program Bethel Ch., 1974-79. Mem. ACA, Christian Assn. for Psychol. Studies, Oreg. Counseling Assn. Republican. Home: 6550 SW Imperial Dr Beaverton OR 97008 Office: Good Samaritan Ministries 7929 SW Cirrus Dr # 23 Beaverton OR 97008

MITCHELL, BETTY JEAN, special education educator; b. Harlan, Ky., July 10, 1945; d. Wayne Sidney and Minnie (Harris) Huddleston; m. Don Clark White, Oct. 15, 1965 (div. Jan. 1984); 1 child, Todd Edward White; m. Vernon Ray Mitchell, Dec. 21, 1985. BS in Elem. Edn., Ea. Ky. U., 1976; MEd, Union Coll., Barbourville, Ky., 1978. Cert. tchr. trainable mentally handicapped, cert. elem. prin., cert. supr. of instrn., cert. learning behavior disorder, Ky. 2d grade tchr. Laurel County Bd. Edn.-Sublimity Elem., London, Ky., 1976-78; spl. edn. tchr. Laurel County Bd. Edn.-London Elem. and North Laurel Middle, London, Ky., 1978—; dept. head edn. dept. North Laurel Middle Sch., London, 1992—; com. mem. County Spl. Edn. Planning Com., London, 1994—. Chair Citizens for a Cleaner Laurel County, London, 1992-94; mem. com. Laurel County Vision 2000. Mem. ASCD, Phi Kappa Phi, Delta Kappa Phi, Laurel County C. of C. (edn. com.). Republican. Home: PO Box 833 London KY 40743-0833

MITCHELL, BETTY JO, writer, publisher; b. Coin, Iowa, May 2, 1931; d. Edith Darrah McWilliams; B.A., S.W. Mo. State U., Springfield; M.S.L.S., U. So. Calif. Asst. acquisitions librarian Calif. State U., Northridge, 1967-69, librarian for personnel and fin., 1969-71, acting asso. library dir., 1971-72, asso. dir. univ. libraries, 1972-81; owner Viewpoint Press, Tehachapi, Calif.; cons. Western Interstate Commn. for Higher Edn. USOE Inst. for Tng. in Staff Devel. Problem Solving; participant workshops in field. Bd. dirs. San Fernando Valley council Girl Scouts U.S.A., 1974-77, employed personnel com., 1979-81; bd. dirs. Bear Valley Springs Condominium Owners Assn., 1978, Empyrean Found., 1978-81. Mem. Assn. Women in Computing (bd. dirs. 1987-89), ALA (mem., chmn. various coms.), Nat. Library Assn., Calif. Library Assn., Assn. Calif. State U. Profs. (sec., exec. com., 1971-72), AAUP, Pi Beta Chi, Alpha Mu Gamma. Author: ALMS: A Budget Based Library Management System, 1982, The Secret of Hilhouse: An Adult Book for Teens; co-author: Cost Analysis of Library Functions: A Total System Approach, 1978, How to See the U.S. on $12 a Day; speaker profl. confs.; contbr. writings to profl. publs.; editor Staff Development column in Special Libraries, 1975-76. Home: 29650 Starland Star Route 3 Box 4600-7 Tehachapi CA 93561 Office: PO Box 1090 Tehachapi CA 93581-1090

MITCHELL, BEVERLY ANN BALES, insurance agency owner, women's rights advocate; b. Fremont, Nebr., July 27, 1944; d. Richard Lee Roy Stillwell Bales and Thelma May (Nelson) Lemen (dec.). BA, Midland Luth. Coll., 1967; postgrad., U. Iowa, 1970, 71. Reporter, film columnist, entertainment sect. editor Fremont (Nebr.) Daily Guide and Tribune, 1961-66; tchr. H.S. English Cedar Bluffs (Nebr.) Valley PUb. Schs., 1967-71; dir. quality control, dir. field ops. Frank N. Magid Assocs., Marion, Iowa, 1971-76; employment specialist U.S. Dept. Labor, Cedar Rapids, Iowa, 1976-78; owner, gen. agy. Mitchell Ins., Cedar Rapids, 1978—. Founder, editor: (monthly periodical) Lilith Speaks, 1971-76, 88—; contbr.: Strong Minded Women, 1992. Co-founder, pres. Cedar Rapids (Iowa) Womens Caucus, 1971-76; commr. Cedar Rapids Civil Rights Commn., 1976-80, Cedar Rapics Charter Commn., 1995-96; pres. Linn County (Iowa) Women's Polit. Caucus, 1977-79; mem. Linn County Bd. Condemnation and Compensation, 1994—. Recipient Creighton By-Line award Creighton U., Omaha, 1963, Best Editorial award Nebr. Press Assn., Lincoln, 1963; named Women of the Yr., Cedar Rapids (Iowa) Women's Orgns., 1977. Mem. NRA, NOW (coord. Iowa state divsn. 1973-76, pres. Cedar Rapids chpt. 1994—), Bus. and Profl. Women (bd. dirs. 1994-95), Dodge County Humane Soc. Lutheran. Unitarian. Office: Mitchell Ins 1000 Maplewood Dr NE Cedar Rapids IA 52402-3807

MITCHELL, CAROL ANN, nursing educator; b. Portsmouth, Va., Aug. 31, 1942; d. William Howell and Eleanor Bertha (Wesarg) M.; m. David Alan Friedman, June 17, 1971 (div. 1988). Diploma, NYU, 1963; BS, Columbia U., 1968, MA, 1971, EdM, 1974, EdD, 1980; MS, SUNY, Stony Brook, 1990. Charge nurse Nassau County Med. Ctr., East Meadow, N.Y., 1963-65; staff nurse Meml. Hosp., N.Y.C., 1965-68; head nurse, supr. Community Hosp. at Glen Cove (N.Y.), 1969-71; assoc. prof. dept. nursing Queensborough Community Coll. CUNY, Bayside, 1971-80; assoc. prof. Marion A. Buckley Sch. Nursing Adelphi U., Garden City, N.Y., 1981-88; ednl. cons. Nat. League for Nursing, N.Y.C., 1980-81; prof. sch. nursing SUNY, Stony Brook, 1988-92, chmn. adult nursing, 1988-92; prof. chair Coll. Nursing East Tenn. State U., 1992-95, mem faculty, 1995—; mem. faculty Regents Coll. degrees in nursing program USNY, Albany, 1978-91, cons., 1978—; faculty cons. geriatrics Montefiore Med. Ctr., 1991-93. Editor emeritus: Scholarly Inquiry in Nursing Practice, 1983—; contbr. articles to profl. jours. Robert Wood Johnson clin. nurse scholar postdoctoral fellow U. Rochester (N.Y.), 1983-85. Mem. Am. Nurses Assn., Nat. League for Nursing, Gerontol. Soc. Am., N.Am. Nursing Diagnosis Assn., Soc. for Research in Nursing Edn.

MITCHELL, CAROL ELAINE, publishing executive, writer, educator; b. Columbus, Aug. 11, 1949; d. William Earl and Betty Jane (Tyson) Johnson; m. Larry Lindsay Mitchell, Mar. 3, 1973; 1 child, Mark Lindsay. BS, Ohio State U., 1971. Cert. English tchr. 7-12. Pres. Sparrow House Pub., Columbus, 1990—; instr. adult edn. Columbus Pub. Schs., 1991—; judge Excellence in Writing Columbus Pub. Schs., 1993. Author: Path of Blessings, 1991; editor, writer, prodr.: Columbus pub. schs. adult and juvenile literacy ednl. t.v., 1993. Mem. NAFE, Nat. Edn. Assn., Ohio Edn. Assn. Home: 228 Sherborne Dr Columbus OH 43219 Office: 342 Sherborne Dr Columbus OH 43219

MITCHELL, CAROLYN COCHRAN, college official; b. Atlanta, Dec. 27, 1943; d. Clemern Covell and Agnes Emily (Veal) Cochran; m. W. Alan Mitchell, Aug. 30, 1964; 1 child, Teri Marie. AB magna cum laude, Mercer U., 1965, M in Svc. Mgmt., 1989. Caseworker Ga. Dept. Family & Children Svcs., Macon, 1965-67, Covington, 1967-69; presch. dir. Southwestern Theol. Sem., Ft. Worth, 1969-70; presch. tchr., dir. Noah's Ark Day Care, Bowden, Ga., 1970-72, First Bapt. Ch., Bremen, Ga., 1972-75, Roebuck Park Bapt. Ch., Birmingham, Ala., 1975-79; freelance office mgr. and bookkeeper Macon, 1979-84; asst. to pres. Ga. Wesleyan Coll., Macon, 1984—; exec. dir. Ga. Women of Achievement, 1991-95; dir. Macon Arts Alliance, 1987-91; mem. Cultural Plan Oversight Com., 1989-90. Mem. Get Out the Vote Task Force, Macon, 1981—, Macon Symphony Guild, 1986-91; dep. registrar Bibb County Bd. Elections, Macon, 1981-95. Mem. AAUW (bd. dirs. Ga. chpt., v.p. 1991-93, chair coll.-univ. rels. com. 1993-94, bylaws com. 1996-97, state ednl. found. chair 1996—, v.p., treas., historian, Macon chpt., Named Gift Honoree 1988), NAFE, NOW, Women's Network for Change, Am. Mgmt. Assn., Presdl. Assts. in Higher Edn., Religious Coalition for Reproductive Choice, The Interfaith Alliance, Women's Polit. Orgn. Macon, Sigma Mu. Democrat. Unitarian. Office: Ga Wesleyan Coll 4760 Forsyth Rd Macon GA 31210-4407

MITCHELL, CHERYL ELAINE, marketing executive; b. Oceanside, N.Y., Dec. 27, 1951; d. Harold Bertram and Doris Meredith (Hose) M. BA in History, Polit. Sci., Hartwick Coll., 1973; postgrad., Syracuse U., 1973-75. Campaign staffer Udall for Pres., N.Y., 1975-76; sr. writer Syracuse (N.Y.) Record, 1976-78; assoc. nat. dir. pub. relations Cushman & Wakefield, Inc., N.Y.C., 1978-81; sr. account exec. JP Lohman Orgn., N.Y.C., 1981-84; v.p. SPGA Group, N.Y.C., 1984-86; pres. Mitchell & Assocs., N.Y.C., 1986—; vis. lectr. Pratt Inst.; lectr. in field; press agt. to internat. real estate developers, sports product mgrs., major league sports, archs., catering, gourmet and internat. fast foods, and filmmakers. Contbr. articles to profl. jours; prin. works include strategic mktg. plans numerous corp. and product brochures, advt. and publicity. Dep. press sec. N.Y. Area, Tsongas for Pres. Campaign, 1992. Recipient ANDY award Art Dirs. N.Y., 1983, Champion award of excellence Graphic Arts Exhbn., 1985, Award of Merit Design and Mktg. Comm., 1986, Tech. Difficulty award Assn. Graphic Arts, 1992; co-winner 1990 AIGA Best of Show Bus. to Bus. Category. Mem. NAFE, Alliance of Bldg. Cmty. (bd. dirs.), Urban Solutions (bd. dirs.), N.Y. Bldg. Congress. Democrat. Lutheran. Office: Mitchell & Assocs 19 W 21st St New York NY 10010

MITCHELL, EVELYN, artist; b. Chgo., Dec. 1, 1924; d. Jacob and Anne (Levinberg) M.; m. Yale Solomon, Aug. 17, 1946 (div. Sept. 1977); children: Barry Mitchell Solomon, Paula Harriet Solomon, Roy Blair Solomon. Student, Art Inst. Chgo., 1942, Chgo. Acad. Fine Art, 1943-44. Instr. printmaking Pitts. Ctr. for Arts, 1966-68; instr. Art Inst. Pa., Pitts., 1968-82, Art Inst. Ft. Lauderdale, Fla., 1982-91; workshop presenter Armory Art Ctr., West Palm Beach, Fla., 1993, Art and Culture Ctr., Hollywood, Fla., 1993-96, Mus. Art, Ft. Lauderdale, 1995; art cons. Vocat. Svcs., Pitts. One-woman shows include Pitts. Lab. Theatre Gallery, 1975, Pitts. Ctr. for Arts, Upstairs Gallery, 1969, 78, Country Studio, Hadley, Pa., 1979, Art Inst. Ft. Lauderdale, 1983, 89; exhibited in group shows at Mus. Art, Carnegie Inst., Pitts., 1967, 74, William Penn Meml. Mus., Harrisburg, Pa., 1968, 71, Pitts. Water Color Soc., Three Rivers Arts Festival, Pitts., (Westinghouse Purchase awards 1967, 68); exhibited in group shows at Duquesne U., Duquesne Union Gallery, Pitts., 1970, Pitts. Ctr. for Arts, 1972, Mus. Without Walls, Md., Pa. and W.Va., 1975, Pitts. Print Group Arts and Crafts Ctr., 1976-82, Continuum Art Ctr., Miami Beach, Fla., 1985, Barbara

Gillman Gallery, Miami, Fla., 1986, Mus. Art, Ft. Lauderdale, 1990, Art and Culture Ctr., Hollywood, 1990, 95, 96, Boca Mus., Boca Raton, Fla., 1994, LaDuce Gallery, Ft. Lauderdale, 1995; represented in pub. and corp. collections, including Mount Mercy Coll., Pitts., 1967, Westinghouse Electric Corp., Monroeville, Pa., 1968, Pitts. Bd. Edn., 1969, Pitts. Nat. Bank, 1970, PPG Industries, Pitts., 1979, Art Inst. Pitts., 1981, Miami-Dade Pub. Libr. Sys., 1986, Art Inst. Fla., 1987. Mem. adv. bd. Arts Renaissance Ctr., Pa.; scenery painter Chalk River Drama Group, 1951-52; troop leader Girl Scouts U.S., Pitts., 1961-62; vol. Broward County Libr., Ft. Lauderdale, 1985-88, Salvation Army, Ft. Lauderdale, 1993; chair nat. exhbn. Palm Beach C.C., Lake Worth, Fla., Fine Art Gallery, Broward C.C., Devie, Fla. Recipient Merit award Pitts. Soc. of Artists, Carlow Coll. Gallery, 1970, Award Associated Artists of Pitts., 1967, 68. Mem. 2 + 3 Artists Orgn. (chmn. exhbns. task force), Pa. Crafts Mktg. Coop. (chmn. mus. pub. rels., bd. dirs.), Pitts. Soc. Artists (charter), Associated Artists Pitts. (social chmn.), Pitts. Print Group (charter, edn. chmn., bd. dirs.). Home and Studio: 1201 River Reach Dr # 318 Fort Lauderdale FL 33315

MITCHELL, GLORIA JEAN, elementary school principal, educator; b. Plant City, Fla., Oct. 14, 1945; d. Jessie Mae (Anderson) Smith; m. Thero Mitchell, Sept. 19, 1969; children: Tarra Shariss Patrick, Thero Jr. BS, Bethune-Cookman Coll., 1967; MA, U. Detroit, 1974; postgrad., U. Wash., 1990. Cert. tchr., adminstr. Wash. Tchr. Dade County Schs., Miami, Fla., 1967-71, Agana (Guam) Presch., 1971-72, Detroit Pub. Schs., 1973-76, Prince Williams Schs., Dale City, Va., 1976-81; counselor/tchr. State of Alaska, Ketchikan, 1981-84; tchr. Bellevue (Wash.) Schs., 1985-90, prin., 1992—; bd. dirs. YMCA Bothell, Wash., chair sustaining drive, 1994-95; bd. dirs. Cascadia C.C., Bothell. Recipient Golden Acorn award PTA-Lake Hills Schs., 1986, Golden Apple award KCTS TV, Seattle, 1994-95; named West Field Vol. of Yr., YMCA, Bothell, Wash., 1987, Woman of Yr., Woodinville (Wash.) Region II Prin. of Yr., Bellevue, 1994. Mem. ASCD, Nat. Alliance Black Sch. Educators, Wash. Alliance Black Sch. Educators,. Office: Bellevue Pub Schs 14220 NE 8th St Bellevue WA 98007-4103

MITCHELL, JANET ALDRICH, fund raising executive, reference materials publisher; b. Providence, Jan. 12, 1928; d. Norman Ackley and Janet (Gordon) Aldrich; m. Raymond Warren Mitchell, Jan. 9, 1954 (div. 1967); children—Lydia Aldrich, Polly Burbank. A.B., Smith Coll., 1949; M.Ed., Rutgers U., 1975. Engaged in devel. various non-profit orgns., 1954-72; dir. devel. Wilson Fellowship Found., Princeton, N.J., 1972-74; dir. spl. projects N.J. Dept. Higher Edn., Trenton, 1974-76; pub., editor-in-chief Mitchell Guide, 1976-87, 93—; pres., chmn. Mitchell Guide, 1987—; cons. to numerous non-profit orgns., 1976-86; lectr. Adult Sch., Princeton, 1983-84. Editor: Directory of Woodrow Wilson Fellows, 1968; Guide to Federal Aid to Higher Education, 1975; Higher Education Exchange, 1978; A Community of Scholars, 1980. Exec. officer Princeton Community Democratic Orgn., 1984-86; elected mem. Princeton Twp. Com., 1987-89; mem. NAACP Legal Def. Fund, 1980-86; trustee N.J. Hist. Soc., 1984-86. Episcopalian. Clubs: Smith Coll. (pres. 1968-70), Princeton Dog (bd. dirs. 1962-68). Avocation: breeding and showing standard poodles. Home and Office: 430 Federal City Rd Pennington NJ 08534-4209

MITCHELL, JO KATHRYN, hospital technical supervisor; b. Clarksville, Ark., Dec. 1, 1934; d. Vintris Franklin and Melissa Lucile (Edwards) Clark; m. James M. Mitchell, June 4, 1955 (dec. Feb. 1973); children: James, Karen Ann, Leslie Kay, Vicki Lynn. Student, U. Ark., Fayetteville, 1952-53; student, Coll. Ozarks, 1953-54, U. Ark., 1954-55, Little Rock U., 1958. Technologist clin. chemistry U. Hosp., Little Rock, 1956-57, asst. supr., 1957-59, rsch. technologist, 1960-62, asst. supr. clin. chemistry, 1979-82, supr. clin. chemistry, 1982—; technologist Conway County Hosp., Morrilton, Ark., 1959; office mgr., co-owner Medic Pharmacy, Little Rock, 1962-71; owner The Cheese Shop, Little Rock, 1977-80. Adult advisor Order Rainbow Girls local, Little Rock, 1970-84, state, Ark., 1977-84. Mem. Pharmacy Aux. (pres. 1967-69), Order Eastern Star. Methodist. Home: 6908 Lucerne Dr Little Rock AR 72205-5029

MITCHELL, KAREN E., human resources specialist; b. Wichita Falls, Tex., Nov. 6, 1943; d. Floyd L. and Mildred V. (Smith) Watson; m. Raymon C. Mitchell; children: Karla D. Mitchell Templeton, Jeffrey R. Student, Ind. U.- Purdue U., Indpls., 1992. Mgr. license br. Ind. Bur. Motor Vehicles, Seymour, 1976-89; polit. dir. Ind. Reps., Indpls., 1989-93; client svc. mgr. Norrell Staffing Svc., Seymour, 1995—. Sec. Jackson County Rep. Com., Seymour, 1976-80, vice chair, 1980-93; with platform com. Ind. Rep. State Com., Indpls., 1984, del. to nat. conv., 1986, 9th dist. vice chair, sec., 1989-93; pol. cons. Seymour City Campaign, 1990. Commd. Ky. Col., Gov. Julian Carroll, 1979; named Hon. Sec. of State, Sec. of State Edwin J. Simcox, Ind., 1980, Sagamore of the Wabash, Ind. Gov. Otis Bowen, 1980, Ind. Gov. Robert D. Orr, 1986; recipient Tribute to Women award Rep. Women, 1988. Mem. Seymour C. of C., Seymour Rep. Women's Club (sec. 1978-80). Home: 338 Mutton Creek Dr Seymour IN 47274-4042 Office: Norrell Staffing Svcs 50 Hancock-Ste 7 Seymour IN 47274

MITCHELL, MARY LU, information researcher, civic volunteer; b. Madisonville, Ky., June 8, 1938; d. John Walter and Augusta J. Wright; m. Wade Treutlen Mitchell, Aug. 18, 1966; children: Wade Wright, Catherine W. BA in Polit. Sci., Duke U., 1960. Dir. job placement libr. Harvard U. Bus. Sch., Cambridge, Mass., 1960-62; rschr., writer UN, N.Y.C., 1962-65; dir. pub. info. Econ. Opportunity Atlanta, 1965-69; rschr. N.Y. Times, Atlanta, 1984-91; cons. govtl. and social svc. agys., Atlanta, 1969-84. Mem., former chair, trustee Atlanta Pub. Libr., 1979—; founding mem., former chair Friends of Atlanta Pub. Libr., 1974-79; pres. Ga. Libr. Trustees and Friends, Atlanta, 1981-85; bd. dirs. Friends of Libraries USA, Phila., 1981-85; bd. dirs., vol. other civic and ednl. programs, Atlanta, 1970—. Named Atlanta Woman of Yr. in the Profns., civic and profl. leaders of Atlanta, 1969; recipient Pres.' award Friends of Librs. USA, 1991; mem. Leadership Atlanta, 1974—.

MITCHELL, MOZELLA GORDON, English language educator, minister; b. Starkville, Miss., Aug. 14, 1936; d. John Thomas and Odena Mae (Graham) Gordon; m. Edrick R. Woodson, Mar. 20, 1951 (div. 1974); children: Cynthia LaVern, Marcia Delores Woodson Miller. AB, LeMoyne Coll., 1959; MA in English, U. Mich., 1963; MA in Religious Studies, Colgate-Rochester Divinity Sch., 1973; PhD, Emory U., 1980. Instr. in English and Speech Alcorn A&M Coll., Lorman, Miss., 1960-61; instr. English, chmn. dept. Owen Jr. Coll., Memphis, 1961-65; asst. prof. English and religion Norfolk State Coll., U. Norfolk, Va., 1965-81; assoc. prof. U. South Fla., Tampa, 1981-93, prof., 1993—; pastor Mount Sinai AME Zion Ch., Tampa, 1982-89; presiding elder Tampa dist. AME Zion Ch., 1988—; vis. assoc. prof. Hood Theol. Sem., Salisbury, N.C., 1979-80, St. Louis U., 1992-93; vis. asst. lectr. U. Rochester, N.Y., 1972-73; co-dir. Ghent VISTA Project, Norfolk, 1969-71; cons. Black Women and Ministry Interdenominational Theol. Ctr; lectr. Fla. Humanities Coun., 1994-95. Author: Spiritual Dynamics of Howard Thurman's Theology, 1985, Howard Thurman and the Quest for Freedom, Proc. 2d Ann. Howard Thurman Convocation (Peter Lang), 1992, African American Religious History in Tampa Bay, 1992;, New Africa in America: The Blending of African and American Religious and Social Traditions Among Black People in Meridian, Mississippi and Surrounding Counties (Peter Lang), 1994, also articles, essays in field; editor: Martin Luther King Meml. Series in Religion, Culture and Social Devel.; editorial bd. Cornucipia Reprint Series. Mem. connectional coun. A.M.E. Zion Ch., Charlotte, 1984—, staff writer Sunday sch. lit., 1981—, mem. jud. coun.; mem. Tampa-Hillsborough County Human Rels. Coun., 1987—; pres. Fla. Coun. Chs., Orlando, 1988-90; del. 7th assembly World Coun. Chs., Canberra, Australia, 1991, 17th World Meth. Coun., Rio de Janiero, 1996; founder Women at the Well, Inc. Recipient ecumenical leadership citation Fla. Coun. Chs., 1990, Inaugural lectr. award Geddes Hanson Black Cultural Ctr. Princeton Theol. Sem., 1993; fellow Nat. Doctoral Fund, 1978-80; grantee NEH, 1981, Fla. Endowment for Humanities, 1990—, U. South Fla. Rsch. Coun., 1990—. Mem. Coll. Theology Soc., Am. Acad. Religion, Soc. for the Study of Black Religion (pres. 1992-96), Joint Ctr. for Polit. Studies, Black Women in Ch. and Soc., Alpha Kappa Alpha. Phi Kappa Phi. Democrat. Methodist. Office: U South Fla 301 CPR Religious Studies Dept Tampa FL 33620

MITCHELL, PAMELA ANN, airline pilot; b. Otis AFB, Mass., May 6, 1955; d. Gene Thomas and Rose Margaret (Jones) Mitchell; m. Robert Carroll Stephens, May 26, 1984 (div. Dec. 1992). BFA, Colo. State U., 1975; postgrad., Webster Coll., 1981. Lic. pilot Ill., comml. instr., airline transport pilot, jet rating, Boeing 747 and 727, Boeing 747-400. Flight attendant United Airlines, Chgo., 1976-80; charter pilot Air Aurora, Sugar Grove, Ill., 1978-80; owner, operator Deliverance, Unltd. Ferry Co., Aurora, Ill., 1978-81; flight test pilot Cessna Aircraft Co., Wichita, Kans., 1981-82, nat. spokeswoman, 1982-83; airline pilot Rep. Airlines, Mpls., 1983-84, Northwest Airlines, Mpls., 1985—; pres., ptnr., artist Aerographics Jacksonville, Fla., 1986-90. Mem. Safety Coun. Airline Pilots Assn., 99's Internat. Women Pilots Assn., Mooney Aircraft Pilots Assn., Internat. Soc. Women Airline Pilots (bd. dirs. 1994-96), Nat. Aviation Club, N.W. Airline Ski Team (capt. 1989-94), Kappa Kappa Gamma. Republican. Presbyterian. Home: 12502 Mission Hills Cir Jacksonville FL 32225 Office: Northwest Airlines Minn/St Paul Internat Airport Saint Paul MN 55111

MITCHELL, PATSY MALIER, religious school founder and administrator; b. Greenwood, Miss., Aug. 28, 1948; d. William Lonal and Lillian (Walker) Malier; m. Charles E. Mitchell, Apr. 20, 1970; children: Christopher, Kara, Angela. BS in Edn., Delta State U., 1970, MEd, 1974, Edn. Specialist, 1979; MA in Ch. Ministries, Ch. of God Sch. Theology, 1990; PhD in Psychology and Counseling, La. Bapt. U., 1994; D in Edn. Christian Sch. Adminstrn., Baptist Christian U., 1992. Cert. sch. adminstr. Youth, Christian edn. dir. Ch. of God, Minter City, Miss., 1975—; teen talent dir. Ch. of God, Minter City, 1983—, missions rep., 1975—; dist. Christian edn. dir. Ch. of God, Cleveland, Miss., 1983-85; sch. adminstr. Ch. of God, Cleveland, 1985—; del. Ch. of God Edn. Leadership, Cleveland, Tenn., 1990; del., speaker Christian Schs. Internat., Chattanooga, Tenn., 1991. Contbr. articles to profl. jours. Dir. St. Jude Children's Hosp., Memphis, 1991; vol. 4-H Club, Greenwood, Miss., 1985-91. Named to Outstanding Young Women of Am., 1983; recipient Community Pride award Chevron, 1988, Internat. Woman of Yr. award, 1993. Mem. Christian Sch. Adminstrs., Christian Schs. Internat., Ch. of God Edn. Assn., Delta State Alumni Assn., Ch. of God Sch. of Theology Alumni Assn, Gospel Music Assn. Republican. Home: RR 1 Box 72A Minter City MS 38944-9714

MITCHELL, PAULA KAY, elementary education educator; b. Houston, May 26, 1966; d. Carl Kenneth and Sandra Jean (O'Gilvie) Blacksher; m. John Eugene Mitchell, July 15, 1989. BS in Curriculum and Instrn. cum laude, Tex. A&M U., 1989; M in Lang. Literacy, Tex. Tech U., 1996. Cert. classroom edn. 1st and 4th grade tchr., sci. coord. Babenhausen (German) Elem., Dept. Def. Dept. Schs., 1990-91; 6th grade math and sci. tchr. Spangdahlem (German) Middle Sch., Dept. Def. Dept. Schs., 1991-92; 5th grade lang. arts tchr. St. Mary's Hall, San Antonio, 1992-93; 4th grade lang. arts and 6th grade sci. tchr. All Saints Episcopal Sch., Lubbock, Tex., 1993—; young astronauts co-dir. All Saints Episcopal Sch., Lubbock, 1993—, coord. campus literary mag., 1994—. Campaign vol. San Antonio (Tex.) Rep. Party, 1991-92; reading instr. vol. San Antonio Literacy Coun., 1992. Mem. Nat. Coun. Tchrs. English, Internat. Reading Assn., Caprock Area Writing Project (presenter), Kappa Delta Pi, Phi Kappa Phi. Episcopalian. Office: All Saints Episcopal Sch 3222 103rd St Lubbock TX 79423-5200

MITCHELL, PAULA RAE, nursing educator; b. Independence, Mo., Jan. 10, 1951; d. Millard Henry and E. Lorene (Denton) Gates; m. Ralph William Mitchell, May 24, 1975. BS in Nursing, Graceland Coll., 1973; MS in Nursing, U. Tex., 1976; EdD in Ednl. Adminstrn., N.Mex. State U., 1996. RN, Tex., Mo.; cert. childbirth educator. Commd. capt. U.S. Army, 1972; ob-gyn. nurse practitioner U.S. Army, Seoul, Korea, 1977-78; resigned, 1978; instr. nursing El Paso (Tex.) C.C., 1979-85, dir. nursing, 1985—, acting div. chmn. health occupations, 1985-86, div. chmn., 1986—, curriculum facilitator, 1984-86; ob-gyn. nurse practitioner Planned Parenthood, El Paso, 1981-86, mem. med. com., 1986—; cons. in field. Author: (with Grippando) Nursing Perspectives and Issues, 1989, 93; contbr. articles to profl. jours. Founder, bd. dirs. Health-C.R.E.S.T., El Paso, 1981-85; mem. pub. edn. com. Am. Cancer Soc., El Paso, 1983-84, mem. profl. activities com., 1992-93; mem. El Paso City-County Bd. Health, 1989-91; mem. Govt. Applications Rev. Com., Rio Grande Coun. Govts., 1989-91; mem. collaborative coun. El Paso Magnet H.S. for Health Care Professions, 1992-94. Decorated Army Commendation medal, Meritorious Svc. medal. Mem. Nat. League Nursing (mem. resolutions com. Assocs. Degree coun. 1987-89, accreditation site visitor, AD coun. 1990—, mem. Tex. edn. com. 1991-92, Tex. 3rd v.p. 1992-93), Am. Soc. Psychoprophylaxis Obstetrics, Nurses Assn. Am. Coll. Obstetricians & Gynecologists (cert. in ambulatory women's health care; chpt. coord. 1979-83, nat. program rev. com. 1984-86, corr. 1987-89), Advanced Nurse Practitioner Group El Paso (coord. 1980-83 legis. committee 1984), Am. Phys. Therapist Assn. (commn. on accreditation, site visitor for phys. therapist assistant programs 1991—), Orgn. Assoc. Degree Nursing (Tex. membership chmn. 1985-89, chmn. goals com. 1989—, mem nat. by-laws com., 1990—), Am. Vocat. Assn., Am. Assn. Women Community & Jr. Colls., Tex. Orgn. Nurse Execs., Nat. Coun. Occupational Edn. (mem. articulation task force 1986-89, program standards task force 1991-93), Nat. Coun. Instructional Adminstrs., Tex. Soc. Allied Health Profls., Tex. Nurses Assn., Nat. Soc. Allied Health Profls. (mem. edn. com. 1993—), Sigma Theta Tau, Phi Kappa Phi. Mem. Christian Ch. (Disciples of Christ). Home: 4616 Cupid Dr El Paso TX 79924-1726 Office: El Paso C C PO Box 20500 El Paso TX 79998-0500

MITCHELL, ROSA LOUISE, director; b. Appomattox, Va., Jan. 18, 1966; d. Otis Tucker and Mozell Harvey; m. Parker Mitchell, June 3, 1995. BS in Bus., Bloomfield Coll., 1991; MA in Counseling, Montclair State U., 1995. Youth mentor program coord. Bloomfield (N.J.) Coll., 1993-95, ednl. opportunity fund dir., 1995—; adj. prof., workshop facilitator Bloomfield Coll., 1993—, womens support group coord., 1994-95. Mem. ACA, N.J. Counseling Assn. Office: Bloomfield Coll 23 Austin Pl Bloomfield NJ 07003

MITCHELL, RUTH SHERWOOD, retired nurse; b. Buffalo, Nov. 11, 1929; d. Richard Hamilton and Ruth Amanda (Sykes) Sherwood; m. Ronald Alexander Mitchell Jr., Feb. 29, 1964. BSN, Columbia U., 1960; RN, Presbyn. Hosp. Sch. Nursing, 1952. Grad. head nurse Psycho-Surg. N.Y. State Psychiat Inst., N.Y.C., 1952-53; grad. head nurse supr. oper. rm. Presbyn. Hosp., N.Y.C., 1953-64; instr. Charles H. McCann Vocat. Sch., North Adams, Mass., 1981, staff coord., asst. supr., supr. med.-surg., 1964-93, charge nurse cen. svc., 1964-93; bd. dirs. Ambulance Svc., Adams. Mem. Town Meeting, Adams. Mem. Mass. Nurses Assn. Home: 332 West Rd Adams MA 01220-9736

MITCHELL, VERNICE VIRGINIA, nurse, poet, author; b. Scott, Miss., Mar. 11, 1921; d. Isaiah and Martha Magdalene (Edwards) Smith; m. Willis Mitchell, Aug. 17, 1940; children: Elaine, Kenneth, Liethia, John, Ransom, Paul. Diploma, Princeton Continuation Coll., 1955. Nurse Cook County Sch. Nursing, Chgo., 1951-59, U. Ill. Hosp., Chgo., 1959-67, Grant Hosp., Chgo., 1967-78, Northwestern Meml. Hosp., Chgo., 1979-84; with U. Ill. Hosp. Aetna Nurse's Registry, Chgo., 1984—. Author: The Book Success Through Spiritual Truths, 1987, Details Through Rose-Colored Glasses, 1995, (poems) A Woman, chicago, The 12 Months; also numerous poetry and musical lyrics; poems submitted to Dial-A-Poem, Chgo., 1988-89. Chmn. cookbook project 1988-89. Recipient merit cert. Am. Poetry Assn., 1982, merit cert. World of Poetry, 1983, 85, Golden Poet award 1986, 87, 88, Silver Poet award, 1989, 90; inducted into the Hall of Fame for Sr. Citizens, Chgo., 1991. Mem. 6700 Emerald Ave. Block Club (pres. 1971-92).

MITCHELL-CHAVEZ, BETTIANNE (BA MITCHELL-CHAVEZ), franchise executive; b. Washington, Nov. 27, 1952; d. Noriar and Marylou (Lenk) Pahigian; m. John J. Stabers (div.); 1 child, John Chad; m. Robert Franklin Chavez, Mar. 11, 1991; stepchildren: Andrea, Julia. BS in English cum laude, Suffolk U. Cert. Wilson sales trainer; cert. in Brian Tracy sales and sales mgmt. instrn.; cert. instr. internat. bus., sales mgmt. Sr. account rep. Letter Men Inc., pub., mktg., advt., Burlington, Mass., 1978-82; mgr. Boston sales br. The Boston Herald, 1982-83; telemktg. ter. mgr. Compugraphic Corp. div. AGFA Corp., Wilmington, Mass., 1983-85; pres., mktg. cons. Advance Inc., mktg., recruitment and search co., Marlboro, Mass., 1985-88; dir. sales devel. AlphaGraphics Printshops of Future Inc. affiliate R.R. Donnelly and Sons, Tucson, v.p. tng. and support, 1991-93, v.p. franchise devel., 1993-94; COO, software developer and licensor INVZN, 1994—; adj. bus. prof. Pima C.C.; presenter in field. Mem. ASTD, NAFE, AAUW, Ariz. Franchisor and Licensor Assn. (bd. dirs., program chairperson 1994—, licensor, liaison to Internat. Franchisor Assn. 1993—, pres.-elect, bd. dirs.), The Consortium, Inc. (CEO, founder). Office: AlphaGraphics 3760 N Commerce Dr Tucson AZ 85705-6907 Address: 1338 N Palmsprings Dr Gilbert AZ 85234-8511

MITCHEM, MARY TERESA, publishing executive; b. Atlanta, Aug. 31, 1944; d. John Reese and Sara Letitia (Marable) Mitchem. BA in History, David Lipscomb Coll., 1966. Sch. and library sales mgr. Chilton Book Co., Phila., 1972-79; dir. market devel. Baker & Taylor Co. div. W.R. Grace, N.Y.C., 1979-81; dir. mktg. R.R. Bowker Co. div. Xerox Corp., N.Y.C, 1981-83, dir. mktg. research, 1983-85; mktg. mgr. W.B. Saunders Co. div. Harcourt, Brace & Jovanovich, Phila., 1985-87; mktg. dir. Congl. Quarterly Inc., Washington, 1987-89; dir. mktg. rsch. and devel. Bur. Nat. Affairs, Inc., Washington, 1990-96; account exec. Hughes Rsch. Corp., Rockville, Md., 1996—. Mem. Book Industry Study Group, Inc. (chairperson stats. com. 1984-86), Mktg. Research Assn., Soc. Competitive Intelligence Profls. Home: 4625 Tilden St NW Washington DC 20016-5617 Office: Hughes Rsch Corp 4 Research Pl Ste 140 Rockville MD 20850

MITCHUSSON, LINDA CAMPBELL, dean; b. Shawnee, Okla., Mar. 9, 1946; d. Willard H. and Jewell S. (France) C. BS, East Ctrl. U., 1968; MBA, U. Ark., 1969, PhD, 1975. Cert. mgmt. acct. Instr. acctg., econs. U. Ark., Fayetteville, 1969-72; asst. prof. acctg., fin. U. Tulsa, 1973-77; asst. prof. acctg. Wichita State U., 1977-82, assoc. prof. acctg., 1982-95, dir. sch. accountancy, 1986-89; dean sch. bus., prof. acctg. East Ctrl. U., Ada, Okla., 1996—; bd. dirs. Inst. Mgmt. Accts., exec. com., 1995—, v.p., 1995-96, chair edn. com., 1996—, ethics com., 1994-95, edn. com., 1988-89, 91-94, cmty. svc. com., 1985-88. Contbg. author: Guide to Strategic Planning, 1980, Personal Investing, 1987, Basics of Investing, 1989. Recipient Disting. Educator award Inst. Mgmt. Accts., 1990. Mem. Am. Acctg. Assn. (membership chair 1984-85), Southwestern Bus. Deans' Assn., So. Bus. Adminstrn. Assn., Inst. Mgmt. Accts. (numerous nat., regional & local positions 1978—), Inst. Cert. Mgmt. Accts., Stuart Cameron McLeod Soc., Kiwanis, Beta Alpha Psi (v.p. 1979-84, Faculty Recognition award 1994, Outstanding Educator award 1985), Beta Gamma Sigma, Omicron Delta Epsilon, Delta Mu Delta, Alpha Chi. Office: East Ctrl U Sch Bus Ada OK 74820

MITELMAN, BONNIE COSSMAN, public relations executive, writer, lecturer; b. Flint, Mich., Feb. 15, 1941; d. Maurice B. and Frieda H. (Ragir) Cossman; student U. Mich., 1958-61; BA, Northwestern U., 1969; MA, Manhattanville Coll., 1977; m. Stanley D. Lelewer, Mar. 12, 1961 (div. 1969); children: Joanne, Stephen (dec.); m. Alan N. Mitelman, July 23, 1972; 1 son, Geoffrey. Copywriter trainee Dancer-Fitzgerald-Sample, Inc., Chgo., 1956-60; advt. copywriter Spiegel, Inc., Chgo., 1961-63; freelance advt. and public relations writer, Chgo., N.Y., 1963—; co-founder Mitelman & Assocs., Briarcliff Manor, N.Y., 1972-92; with pub. rels. dept. Anti-Defamation League, N.Y.C., 1992—; adj. lectr. dept. history Mercy Coll., Dobbs Ferry, N.Y., 1979—; contbr. articles to N.Y. Times, Reform Judaism, 1977—. Mem. Am. Hist. Assn., Women in Comm., Authors Guild. Author: Mothers Who Work: Strategies for Coping; mem. editorial bd. Reform Judaism, 1977—. Home: 639 Pleasantville Rd Briarcliff Manor NY 10510-1925

MITGANG, IRIS FELDMAN, lawyer, educator; b. Chgo., Sept. 2, 1937; d. Harry and Leanore (Nelson) Feldman; m. Robert Newton Mitgang, Sept. 9, 1956 (div. Dec. 1974); children: Alix Susan, Steven Ross, Jennifer Lynn. AB, U. Chgo., 1958; MA, U. Rochester, 1967; JD, U. Calif., Davis, 1976. Bar: Calif. 1976, U.S. Dist. Ct. (no. and ea. dists.) Calif.; cert. specialist family law. Ptnr. Dodge, Reyes, Brorby, Randall, Mitgang & Titmus, Walnut Creek, Calif., 1978-90; prin. Law Office Iris F. Mitgang, Walnut Creek, Calif., 1990—; instr. legal writing Sch. Law U. Calif., Davis, 1975-76; adj. prof. family law Sch. Law John F. Kennedy U., Walnut Creek, 1977-87, Sch. Law Golden Gate U., San Francisco, 1987; mem. pro tempore judges panel Contra Costa Superior Ct.; spkr. in field. Mem. editorial bd. Law Rev. U. Calif., Davis Sch. Law, 1976; contbr. various articles to profl. jours. Bd. dirs. Leadership Conf. Civil Rights, Washington, 1979-81, ACLU, Northern Calif.; founding mem. Rape Crisis Ctr. Contra Costa County. Recipient Woman of Yr. award Bus. and Profl. Women, 1979, Women's Leadership award State of Calif., 1980. Mem. State Bar Calif., Nat. Women's Polit. Caucus (nat. chair 1979-81, nat. adv. bd. chair 1981-85, vice chair 1977-79, politic. action chair 1977-79), Am. Acad. Family Mediators, Contra Costa Bar Assn. (co-chair fam. law mediation sect. 1992—), Calif. Women Lawyers, Alameda Contra Costa Trial Lawyers (bd. dirs. 1992-95, chair mentors program), Assn. Family and Conciliation Cts., Assn. Cert. Family Law Specialists, Calif. Dispute Resolution Coun., Soc. Profls. in Dispute Resolution. Democrat. Jewish. Office: Law Offices Iris F Mitgang 1850 Mount Diablo Blvd Ste 605 Walnut Creek CA 94596-4427

MITRANY, DEVORA, marketing consultant, writer; b. Oak Park, Ill., Mar. 20, 1947; d. John Joseph and Frances Elizabeth (Kirke) Lang; m. Douglas Allen Braun, Sept. 16, 1967 (div. Sept. 1976); m. Stanton Mitrany, Feb. 7, 1988 (div. Aug. 1995). BA cum laude, Beloit Coll., 1969; postgrad., Boston U., 1971-72. Elem. and presch. tchr., Oak Park, Ill. and Boston, 1969-72; regional adminstr. TRW Fin. Systems, Wellesley, Mass., 1972-76; mgr. mktg. communications Computer Sharing Svcs., Denver, 1976-82; dir. corp. communications Corp. Mgmt. Systems, Denver, 1982-85; sr. copywriter On-Line Software Internat., Fort Lee, N.J., 1985-86; mgr. corp. communications Health Mgmt. Systems, N.Y.C., 1986-89; dir. pub. rels. Am. Sephardi Fedn., 1989-92; pres. The Mitrell Group, 1992-94; U.S. mktg. dir. The Best of Israel, 1994-95; sr. proposal analyst PCS Health Systems, Inc., 1995—; press release chmn. Nassau Region Hadassah, 1992-94. Warden, vestry mem. Trinity Ch., Wrentham, Mass., 1974-76; mem. vestry St. Philip and St. James Episcopal Ch., Denver, 1983; vol. Hospice of Holy Spirit, Lakewood, Colo., 1980-83; bd. dirs. Talia Hadassah, 1986-94, co-pres., 1990-92; v.p. edn. Long Beach Hadassah, 1992-94; dir. pub. rels. Bus. Roundtable on Nat. Security, Colo., 1983-84. Recipient Nat. Leadership award, Long Beach Hadassah, 1991-92, Nat. Leadership award Talia Hadassah, 1993-94; named Woman of Yr. Talia Hadassah, 1993. Mem. Denver Advt. Fedn. (bd. dirs. 1981-83, Alfie award 1984), Colo. Conf. Communicators (Denver Advt. Fedn. liasion 1981-84), Am. Sephardi Fedn. (edn. com. 1987-89). Jewish. Democrat.

MITTLER, DIANA (DIANA MITTLER-BATTIPAGLIA), music educator and administrator, pianist; b. N.Y.C., Oct. 19, 1941; d. Franz and Regina (Schilling) Mittler; m. Victor Battipaglia, Sept. 5, 1965 (div. 1982). BS, Juilliard Sch., 1962, MS, 1963; DMA, Eastman Sch. Music, 1974. Choral dir. William Cowper Jr. High Sch. and Springfield Gardens Jr. High Sch., Queens, N.Y., 1963-68, coordinator of music Flushing High Sch., Queens, 1968-79; asst. prin. music Bayside High Sch., Queens, 1979-86; assoc. prof. music Lehman Col. CUNY, 1986-87, prof., 1987—, choral dir., 1986—; dir. ednl. projects New World Records, 1987—; ednl. cons. Flushing Coun. on Culture and the Arts; cons. Sta. WNET; assoc. condr. Queens Borough-Wide Chorus, 1964-70; pianist, founder Con Brio Chamber Ensemble, 1978; faculty So. Vt. Music Festival, 1979-83; soloist with N.Y. Philharmonic, 1956; solo and chamber music appearances; examiner N.Y.C. Bd. Edn. Bd. Exams., 1985—. Author: 57 Lessons for the High School Music Class, 1983, Franz Mittler: Austro-American Composer, Musician and Humourous Poet, 1993. Choral dir. and accompanist various charitable, religious, mil., civic holiday functions. N.Y. State Regents scholar, 1958-62; scholarships, Juilliard Sch. and Eastman Sch. Music. Contbr. articles to music publs.; performance Internat. Summer Acad. Mozarteum, Salzburg, Austria, 1995. Mem. Golden Key Soc., Am. Choral Dirs. Assn., Music Edn. Nat. Conf., Sonneck Soc. Democrat. Home: 10857 66th Ave Flushing NY 11375-2247 Office: Lehman Coll Music Dept Bedford Pk Blvd W Bronx NY 10468

MITTS, MARYBETH FRAZIER, real estate company executive, consultant; b. Hartford, Conn., Sept. 4, 1963; d. Robert Lee and Patricia Ann (Casey) Frazier. m. Kevin Garry Mitts, July 14, 1990; children: Margaret, Elizabeth. BA, Mount Holyoke Coll., Mass., 1985; M in Pub. Mgmt., U. Md., 1987. Notary Pub., Calif., 1995—. Rehab. mgmt. specialist U.S. Dept. Housing and Urban Devel., Washington, 1987-90; budget analyst Office of the Comptr., U.S. Dept. Navy, Crystal City, Va., 1990-91; fiscal officer MCAS, U.S. Dept. Navy, Camp Pendleton, Calif., 1991; dep. comptr. MCAS, U.S. Dept. Navy, Tustin, Calif., 1991-92; sr. cons. Comprehensive Housing Svcs., Fountain Valley, Calif., 1992-95; prin. Affordable Housing Profls., San Diego, Calif., 1995—. Bd. dir. Summerset Court Homeowners Assn., San Diego, 1995—. Mem. Mount Holyoke Club San Diego (chmn.

pres. 1994—). Republican. Roman Catholic. Office: Affordable Housing Profls 6953 Schilling Ave San Diego CA 92126

MITZEN, PHYLLIS BASS, social welfare administrator; b. Chgo., Mar. 27, 1942; d. Herbert and Eleanore (Goodman) Bass; m. Michael Allen Mitzen, Dec. 24, 1961; children: Matthew Gary, Jennifer Joy Mitzen Stompor, Joshua Frederick. BA, Northeastern Ill. U., 1976; MA, U. Chgo., 1980; postgrad., Ill. Inst. Tech., 1990-92. Lic. social worker, Ill. Supr. family support Coun. for Jewish Elderly, Chgo., 1980-82, dir. social svcs., 1982-93, dir. home and cmty. based svcs., 1993—; co-chair adv. coun. Cmty. Care Program, Springfield, Ill., 1994-96. Mem. Gov.'s Cmty. Based Long Term Care Task Team, Springfield, 1995-96, Mayor's Commn. on Extreme Weather Conditions, Chgo., 1995; del. White House Conf. on Aging, Washington, 1995; chair Evanston (Ill.) Commn. on Aging, 1976-82. Mem. NASW, Am. Soc. on Aging, Gerontological Assn. of Am., Am. Jewish Com. (v.p. 1992-95, bd. mem. 1995—), Ill. Assn. Cmty. Care Home Care Providers (pres. 1995—). Democrat. Jewish. Office: Council for Jewish Elderly 3003 W Touhy Chicago IL 60645

MIXON, DEBORAH LYNN BURTON, elementary school educator; b. Charleston, S.C., Mar. 26, 1956; d. Harold Boyd and Peggy Wynell (Seagraves) Burton; m. Steven Douglas Schmidt (div. Mar. 1982); 1 child, Julie Ann Schmidt; m. Timothy Lamar Mixon, Oct. 11, 1982; children: Phillip Lamar, Catherine Elizabeth. BS in Edn., U. Ga., 1994. Cert. early childhood educator, Ga. Office coord. Morrison's Cafeteria, Athens, Ga., 1974-76; cashier Winn-Dixie, Athens, 1976-78; data entry clk. Athens Tech. Data Ctr., 1978-79; adminstrv. sec. U. Ga., Athens, 1980-86; sec. to plant mgr. Certain Teed Corp., Athens, 1986-87; s. adminstrv. sec. U. Ga., Athens, 1987-93; tchr. 4th grade Hall County Sch. Sys., Gainesville, Ga., 1994—. Leader Cub Scouts den Boy Scouts Am., 1993-94; troop vol. Girl Scouts U.S., 1992—; vol. leader 4-H Clarke County, Athens, 1992-94. Presdl. scholar U. Ga., 1993-94. Mem. Assn. for Childhood Edn. Internat., Profl. Assn. Ga. Educators, Golden Key, Kappa Delta Epsilon (perfect scholar 1994). Home: 171 Scottwood Dr Athens GA 30607-1338

MIYAMAE, YUKARI, communications consultant, mediator; b. Sapporo, Hokkaido, Japan, June 5, 1950; came to U.S., 1978; Student, Fuji Women's Coll., Sapporo, 1970-74. Adminstr. Am. Soc. for Continuing Edn., Charles Town, W.Va., 1985-88; coord. USAASSIST, Washington, 1988-89; adminstr., rschr. Chubu Electric Power Co., Washington, 1989-92; rschr. Knight-Ridder Info. Design Lab., Boulder, Colo., 1992-95; prin. Open Pacific, Boulder, 1994—. Dir. plays Snow Woman, 1987, Conference of Birds, 1989, Coyote Story, 1990. Bd. dirs. Gaia Found., Denver, 1995—; com. mem. Colo. Sustainable Project, Denver, 1995—, Colo. Environ. Bus. Inst., Denver, 1995—. Mem. Am. Translators Assn., Women in Comm., Colo. Coun. Mediators, Colo. Tech. Transfer Soc., Japan Am. Soc., Boulder C. of C. Home and Office: Open Pacific PO Box 4795 Boulder CO 80306

MIYASHIRO, RUTH E., bank executive; b. 1936. With Boysen Paint Co., Honolulu, 1955-56, Occidental Life Ins. Co., L.A., 1956-58; officer Bank of Hawaii, Inc., Honolulu, 1958-95; v.p., sec. Bancorp Hawaii, Inc., Honolulu, 1971-95. Office: Bancorp Hawaii Inc 130 Merchant St Honolulu HI 96813-4408

MIZELL, JOY REGISTER, critical care nurse; b. Canal Point, Fla., Dec. 3, 1936; d. Noonan A. and Opal A. (Duncan) Register; children: Sandra, Randa, William Michael. Student, Cook County Coll., Gainesville, Tex., 1977, 81; BS in Nursing, Tex. Womans U., Denton, 1978. Nurse Mariners Hosp., Tavernier, Fla., 1980-81; founder, owner, operator The Silk Leaf, Lewisville, Tex., 1981-83; sales exec. Sea Pines Real Estate, Fernandina Beach, Fla., 1984-85; developer's rep. Excel-Edco Investments, Inc., Palataka, Fla.; pub. rels. officer Bank of Burke County, Waynesboro, Ga., 1987-88; nurse critical care unit/ICU Kennestone Hosp., Marietta, Ga., 1988-90; nurse ICU Nassau Gen. Hosp., Fernandina Beach, Fla., 1990—; contract field RN Vis. Nurse Assn., 1991-93; community educator Assoc. Home Health, West Palm Beach, Fla., 1993-95; owner Your Daily Care, West Palm Beach, Fla., 1995—. Mem. Nat. Assn. Geriatric Care Mgrs. (Fla. chpt.), Fla. Assisted Living Assn., Pres. Round Table for Women in Bus., Lewisville C. of C., Ambassador's Club (Lewisville), Fernandina Beach Builders Assn. (co-founder), Sardis (pres. 1986-87), Sardis Bus. Assn. (sec. 1987-88), Waynesboro Bus. Assn. (sec., bd. dirs.), Broadway Home Health Bd., Profl. Resource Network. Office: Your Daily Care 931 Village Blvd Ste 905-300 West Palm Beach FL 33409

MIZES, MARIA GABRIELA, cultural organization administrator, art historian; b. Buenos Aires, July 11, 1961; d. Jimmy M. and Beatriz Adot. BAin Art History magna cum laude, Columbia U., 1992. Asst. registrar Mus. Nacional de Bellas Artes, Buenos Aires, 1982-83, asst. curator, 1983-85, asst. dir., 1985-87, registrar, 1987-90; exhbn. asst. Lat. Am. Artists of the Twentieth Century Mus. Modern Art, N.Y.C., 1991-93; assoc. registrar Am. Fedn. Arts, N.Y.C., 1993-94, registrar, 1994-96; registrar Trust for Mus. Exhbns., Washington, 1996—. Mem. Am. Assn. Muss. (registrars com. 1990), Internat. Coun. Muss., Internat. Documentation Com., Phi Beta Kappa. Roman Catholic. Home: 8747 Kelso Terr Gaithersburg MD 20877 Office: Trust for Mus Exhbns 1424 16th St NW Washington DC 20036

MLAY, MARIAN, government official; b. Pitts., Sept. 11, 1935; d. John and Sonia M.; A.B., U. Pitts., 1957; postgrad. (Univ. fellow) Princeton U., 1969-70; J.D., Am. U., 1977. Mgmt. positions HEW, Washington, 1961-70, dep. dir. Chgo. region, 1971-72, dir. div. consol. funding, 1972-73, dep. dir. office policy devel. and planning USPHS, Washington, 1973-77; dir. program evaluation EPA, Washington, 1978-79, dep. dir. Office of Drinking Water, 1979-84, dir. Office of Ground Water Protection, 1984-91, dir. Oceans and Coastal Protection, 1991-95; sr. rschr. Nat. Acad. Pub. Adminstrn. 1995—. Bd. dirs. D.C. United Fund, 1979-80. Recipient Career Edn. award Nat. Inst. Public Affairs, 1969. Mem. ABA, D.C. Bar (steering com. energy, environment and natural resources sect.). Author articles in field. Home: 3747 1/2 Kanawha St NW Washington DC 20015-1838 Office: Nat Acad Pub Adminstrn 1120 G St NW Ste 850 Washington DC 20005-3801

MLOCEK, SISTER FRANCES ANGELINE, financial executive; b. River Rouge, Mich., Aug. 4, 1934; d. Michael and Suzanna (Bloch) M. BBA, U. Detroit, 1958; MBA, U. Mich., 1971. CPA, Mich. Bookkeeper Allen Park (Mich.) Furniture, 1949-52, Gerson's Jewlery, Detroit, 1952-53; jr. acct. Meyer Dickman, CPA, Algaze, Staub & Bowman, CPAs, Detroit, 1953-58; acct., internal auditor Sisters, Servants of Immaculate Heart of Mary Congregation, Monroe, Mich., 1959-66, asst. gen. treas., 1966-73, gen. treas., 1973-76; internal auditor for parishes Archdiocese of Detroit, 1976-78; asst. to exec. dir. Leadership Conf. of Women, Silver Spring, Md., 1978-83; dir. of fin. Nat. Conf. of Cath. Bishops/U.S. Cath. Conf., Washington, 1989-94; CFO Sisters Servants of the Immaculate Heart of Mary, Monroe, Mich., 1994—; trustee Sisters, Servants of Immaculate Heart of Mary Charitable Trust Fund, Monroe, 1988—. Author: (manual) Leadership Conference of Women Religious/Confernce of Major Superiors of Men, 1981. Treas. Zonta Club of Washington Found., Washington, 1983-88, pres., 1992-93; bd. dirs. Our Lady of Good Counsel High Sch., Wheaton, Md., 1983-89. Mem. AICPA, D.C. Inst. CPAs (mem. not-for-profit com. 1992-94, CFOs com. 1990-94. Democrat. Roman Catholic. Office: Sisters Servants Immaculate Heart Mary 610 W Elm Ave Monroe MI 48162-7909

MOAK-MAZUR, CONNIE JO, investment consultant, marketing professional; b. Ft. Worth, Feb. 5, 1947; d. David Clark and Dorothy Carol (Jackson) Moak; m. Jay Mazur, May 31, 1987. BBA, N. Tex. State U., 1969. Cert. bus. edn. tchr. V.p. Lionel D. Edie & Co., N.Y.C., 1969-77; mgr. Peat, Marwick, Mitchell & Co., N.Y.C., 1977-80; v.p. Shaw Data, N.Y.C., 1980, Fred Alger Mgmt., N.Y.C., 1980-82; ptnr. Glickenhaus & Co., N.Y.C., 1982-93; mng. dir. Wasserstein Perella Capital, 1993-95; group v.p. mktg. client svc. Schroder Wertheim Investment Svcs., N.Y.C., 1993-95; spkr. in field. Contbr. articles to profl. jours. Mem. Fin. Women's Assn., Am. Pension Conf., Internat. Found. Employee Benefit Plans, Assn. Investment Mgmt. Sales Execs. (bd. dirs., pres.). Home: 150 E 69th St Apt 19C New York NY 10021-5704 Office: Schroder Wertheim Investment Svcs 787 7th Ave New York NY 10190

MOATES, BETTY CAROLYN, microbiologist, computer consultant; b. Rector, Ark., Sept. 27, 1937; d. Hubert E. and Edith R. (Robertson) Dawson; m. James J. Moates, Nov. 11, 1972 (dec.). BA, San Jose State U. Lic. clin. lab. scientist, Calif.; cert. med. technologist. Med. technologist O'Connor Hosp., San Jose, Calif., 1960, Vets. Hosp., Palo Alto, Calif., 1961; lab. supr. San Jose Med. Clinic, 1961-67; microbiology supr. Alexian Bros. Hosp., San Jose, 1967-74; microbiologist Good Samaritan Health Sys., San Jose, 1976-96, coord. clin. data sys., 1994-96; sr. microbiologist and microbiology system data coord. Columbia Good Samaritan Health System, Med. Ctr., San Jose, Calif., 1996—. co-author, co-developer: (data users guide) Dogwood Information Management System for County Recorders, 1992, Dogwood Information Management System for the Rebekah Title Insurance Companies, 1992. Pres. Rep. Assembly Calif., 1974-75, Internat. Assn. Rebekah Assemblies, 1988-89. Mem. Calif. Assn. Microbiologists, Calif. Assn. Med. Technologists (sec. 1960-75), Sunnyvale Rebekah Lodge (past presiding officer). Home: 1975 Kobara Ln San Jose CA 95124-1517

MOATES, MARIANNE MERRILL, writer; b. Andalusia, Ala., July 12, 1942; d. Walter O. Merrill and Mary Jim (Hilson) Merrill Pianowski; m. James T. Moates Jr., June 2, 1959; children: Benjamin, Michael, Seth, Mary Elizabeth. BSW, U. Ala., Tuscaloosa, 1975; postgrad., U. Ala., Birmingham, 1976-77. Freelance writing cons. Birmingham, 1976—; assoc. Power of Positive Students, Birmingham, 1986-87; ptnr. Comms. Skills Cons., Birmingham, 1992—; pres. Moates & Assocs., Sylacauga, Ala., 1993—; lectr. in field; cons. arts and humanities projects, Birmingham, 1980—; cons. Ctr. for Adult and Exptl. Learning, Chgo., 1995. Author: A Bridge of Childhood, 1989, Truman Capote: Eine Kindheit in Alabama, 1991, Truman Capote's Southern Years, 1996. Pres. Ala. Writers, Samford U., Birmingham, 1987; chmn. Birmingham-So. Coll. Writing Today, 1994. Grantee Ala. State Coun. on Arts, 1994; Truman Capote scholar, 1987. Mem. AAUW, NOW, Am. Soc. Journalists and Authors. Democrat. Episcopalian. Home and Office: 640 Peckerwood Creek Tr Sylacauga AL 35151

MOAZED, TERESA CLARK, veterinarian, researcher; b. Charlotte, N.C., Mar. 20, 1956; d. Harold Eugene and Frances Willie (Miller) Clark; m. David Charles Moazed, May 20, 1978. DVM, N.C. State U., 1988; MSc, U. Wash., 1992, PhD, 1996. Lic. vet., N.C., Wash. Postdoctoral fellow dept. comparative medicine U. Wash., Seattle, 1988-91; rsch. asst. dept. of pathobiology U. Wash., Seattle, 1992—. Recipient Outstanding Student scholarship U. Wash. Sch. Pub. Health, 1992. Mem. Am. Vet. Med. Assn., Am. Assn. for Lab. Animal Sci., Am. Soc. Lab. Animal Practitioners, Assn. Women Veternarians, Wash. Assn. for Biomed. Rsch., Am. Soc. Microbiology. Home: 1220 NW 77th St Seattle WA 98117

MOBLEY, BARBARA JEAN, state legislator; b. Dec. 1, 1947; m. James L. Savage, Jr. BS, Savannah State Coll.; MSW, U. Ill.; JD, So. Meth. U. Atty.; mem. Ga. Ho. of Reps., 1992—; mem. univ. systems com., sec. spl. judiciary and transp. coms. Democrat. Baptist. Home: PO Box 371442 Decatur GA 30037-1442 Office: Ga Ho of Reps 511-C Legis Office Bldg Atlanta GA 30334

MOCCIA, MARY KATHRYN, social worker; b. Harrisburg, Pa.; d. John Joseph and Winifred Louise Trephan. BEd, U. Hawaii, 1978, MSW with distinction, 1980; postgrad., Fuller Theol. Sem., 1987. Diplomate clin. social work. Intern Koko Head Mental Health Clinic, Honolulu, 1978-79, Dept. Social Services and Housing, Honolulu, 1979-80; vol. worker, group coleader Waikiki Mental Health Ctr., Honolulu, 1979, social worker, 1980; workshop facilitator St. Louis-Chaminade Edn. Ctr. Dept. Insts. and Workshops, Honolulu, 1980-83; founding mem. Anorexia and Bulimia Ctr. Hawaii, Honolulu, 1983, pvt. practice psychotherapy and cons., 1983—; personal counselor Chaminade U. Honolulu, 1980-88; clin. social worker Queen's Med. Ctr., 1988—; practicum instr. U. Hawaii, 1992—; guest lectr. U. Hawaii Sch. Social Work, Honolulu, 1980-81; vol. telephone specialist Suicide and Crisis Ctr. and Info. and Referral Service, Honolulu, 1981-83; group leader obesity program Honolulu Med. Group, 1988—; mem. Hawaii Coun. Self Esteem, 1993; condr. various workshops on anorexia and bulimia. Guest appearances on local tv and radio programs. Mem. Manoa Valley Ch. Mem. NASW, Nat. Assn. Christians in Social Work, Acad. Cert. Social Workers, Registry Clin. Social Workers, Mortar Bd. (pres., nat. del. 1978), Phi Kappa Phi, Pi Lambda Theta, Alpha Tau Delta (pres. 1970). Office: Queens Med Ctr Dept Social Work 1301 Punchbowl St Honolulu HI 96813-2413

MOCEANU, DOMINIQUE, gymnast, Olympic athlete; b. Hollywood, Calif., Sept. 30, 1981. Mem. Nat. Team, 1992-93, 93-94, 94-95, 95-96. Recipient Silver and Bronze medals World Championships, 1995, Gold medal team competition Olympic Games, Atlanta, 1996; placed 1st in balance beam U.S. Classic, Salt Lake City, 1991, 2d in balance beam jr. divsn. U.S. Gymnastics Championships, Columbus, 1992, 2d in all around, 1st team, vault, uneven bars and floor exercise Jr. Pan Am. Games, 1992, 1st in team and balance beam, 3rd in uneven bars Internat. Tournament of Jr. Women's Gymnastics, Charleroi, Belgium, 1993, 1st in all around, vault and team floor exercise, 3rd in uneven bars and balance beam jr. divsn. Coca-Cola Nat. Championships, Nashville, 1994, 2d in team all around, 1st in vault, 3rd in balance beam and floor exercise Am. Classic-Pan Am. Games Trials, Oakland, Calif., 1995, 1st in all around, 2d in floor exercise, 3rd in vault Coca-Cola Nat. Championships, New Orleans, 1995, 1st in all around World Team Trials, Austin, 1995, 1st in uneven bars, 3rd in balance beam Reese's Internat. Gymnastics Cup, Portland, 1995, 1st in all around, team and floor exercise, 3rd in vault and balance beam, 2nd in uneven bars Visa Challenge, Fairfax, Va., 1995, 3rd all around for team, 2d for team balance beam World Championships, Sabae, Japan, 1995; named USOC SportsWoman of Month, Apr. and Sept. 1995. Office: care USA Gymnastics Pan Am Plz 201 S Capitol Ave Ste 300 Indianapolis IN 46225*

MOCHARY, MARY VERONICA, lawyer; b. Budapest, Hungary, Sept. 7, 1942; d. Alexander and Elizabeth (Aranyi) Kasser; m. Stephen E. Mochary, Sept. 25, 1965 (div. 1990); children: Alexandra Veronica, Matthew Neal. BA, Wellesley Coll., 1963; JD, U. Chgo., 1967. Bar: Ark. 1968, N.J. 1970. Ptnr. Fayetteville, Ark., 1968-70, Mochary & Mochary, Montclair, N.J., 1970-85, Cerny & Mochary, Montclair, 1980-84, Lane & Mittendorf, Woodbridge, N.J., 1984-85; legal advisor U.S. Dept. State, Washington, 1985-89, spl. negotiator real estate issues, 1989-92; ptnr. Wine & Assocs., Washington, 1990—; cons. Hughes, Hubbard & Read, Washington; pres. Technopulp, Inc., Montclair, 1982—, Iamco, Inc., Montclair, 1982—; ptnr. Kand M Co., Montclair, 1982—, Atlantic Highlands Real Estate, Montclair, 1982-89. Mayor Twp. of Montclair, 1980-84; mgr. Kasser Art Found., Montclair, 1982—; Rep. candidate U.S. Senate, State of N.J., 1984; co-chmn. re-election campaign Tom Kean for Gov., N.J., 1985; treas. Com. N.J. Rep. Women in 1985; mem. regional adv. bd. Anti-Defamation League of B'nai B'rith, Montclair Library Bd., 1980—, Montclair Twp. Council, 1980—; chmn. Rep. Task Force Women's Polit. Caucus N.J., Overseas Neighbors Internat., 1985; bd. dirs. Am. Hungarian Found., 1970—, Found. Ednl. Alternatives, Urban League, 1985—. Raoul Wallenberg Com. of U.S., 1985—, Nat. Mus. for Women in the Arts, Washington, 1994—; mem. Women's Internat. Forum, 1992—; founder, bd. dirs. WISH;. Recipient Disting. Service award Am. Hungarian Found., 1984. Mem. ABA, N.J. Bar Assn., Ark. Bar Assn., N.J. Conf. Mayors, N.J. Elected Women Ofcls., Suburban Essex Bus. and Profl. Women (named Woman of Yr. 1985), Wellesley Club (pres. N.J. chpt. 1983-84), Women's Internat. Forum, Adirondack League Club, Ocean Reef Club, Angler's Club (Key Largo, Fla.), Rappahannock County Garden Club. Office: 26 Park St Montclair NJ 07042-3443 also: 2700 Virginia Ave NW Washington DC 20037-1908

MOCK, MELINDA SMITH, orthopedic nurse specialist, consultant; b. Austell, Ga., Nov. 15, 1947; d. Robert Jehu and Emily Dorris (Smith) Smith; m. David Thomas Mock, Oct. 20, 1969. AS in Nursing, DeKalb Coll., 1972. RN, Ga.; cert. orthopedic nurse specialist, orthopedic nurse. Nursing technician Ga. Baptist Hosp., Atlanta, 1967, staff nurse, 1979; asst. corr. Harcourt, Brace & World Pub. Co., Atlanta, 1968-69; receptionist-sec. Goodbody & Co., Atlanta, 1969-70; nursing asst. DeKalb Gen. Hosp., Decatur, Ga., 1970-71; staff nurse Doctor's Meml. Hosp., Atlanta, 1972-73; staff nurse Shallowford Cmty. Hosp., Atlanta, 1973, relief charge nurse, 1973, charge nurse, 1973-76, head nurse, 1976-79, orthopedic nurse specialist emergency room, 1979; rehab. specialist Internat. Rehab. Assocs., Inc., Norcross, Ga., 1981, sr. rehab. specialist, 1981, rehab. supr., 1981-82; cons., founder, propr. Healthcare Cost Cons., Alpharetta, Ga., 1982-83; cons., founder, pres. Healthcare Cost Cons., Inc., Alpharetta, 1983—; mem. legis. com. of adv. coun. Ga. Bd. Nursing, Atlanta, 1984-85; mem. adv. coun. Milton H.S. Coop. Bus. Edn., 1986-89; mem. Congressman Patrick Swindall Sr. Citizen Adv. Coun., 1988, Congressman Ben Jones Vets. Affairs Adv. Com., 1989-92, White House Conf. on Small Bus. (appointed by Newt Gingrich 1995), Nat. Fedn. Specialty Nursing Orgns. Task Force on Profl. Liability Ins., 1987-89, Dep. voter registrar Fulton County, Ga., 1983-87; Rep. treas. 23d house dist., mem. Fulton County Rep. Com., 1989—, nominating com., 1991, 92, 93, 95, 96, chmn. polit action com., 1993-95, asst. treas., 1994-95, sec., 1995—; treas. 41st House Dist. Rep. Party, 1993—; 1st vice chairwoman 6th Congl. Dist. Rep. Party, 1993—; mem. State Com. Ga. Rep. Party, 1993—; del. Fulton County Rep. Conv., 1991, 92, 94, 95, 96, del. Ga. 4th Congrl. Dist., 1991, 92, parliamentarian, 1992, credentials com., 1992, Ga. Rep. Conv., 1991, 92, 93, 95, 96, del. Ga. 6th Congrl. Dist. Rep. Party Convention, 1993, 95, 96; alt. del.-at-large Nat. Rep. Conv., 1996; mem. Chattahoochee Rep. Women, 1989—, chmn. campaign com., 1992-94, rec. sec., 1995—; chmn. nominating com. House Dist. 23, 1990; mem. steering com. to re-elect state rep. Tom Campbell, 1990; mem. campaign staff to re-elect state senator Sallie Newbill, 1990, 92, 94; health advisor campaign to elect Matt Towery for lt. gov., 1990, health adv. compaign to elect Bob Barr U.S. Senate, 1991-92; mem. election com. Mark Burkhalter for State Rep.; vol. campaign staff to re-elect Congressman Newt Gingrich, 1992, 94, 96; mem. campaign staff to elect Jim Hunt as state rep., 1996; vol. campaign to elect Tom Price to state senate, 1996. Recipient Nat. Disting. Service Registry award, 1987; named one of Outstanding Young Women Am., 1984. Mem. NAFE, Nat. Assn. Orthopedic Nurses (nat. policies com. 1981-82, chmn. govt. rels. com. 1987-90, nat. treas. 1991-95, nurse Washington intern 1987, legis. contbr. editor news 1989, chmn. legis. workshop, 1989, co-chmn. legis. workshop, 1990, guest editl. Orthopaedic Nursing Jour. 1988, spkr. 1990, 92, 93, 94, Ann. Congress, del. 1982, 91, 92, 93, 94, 96, Pres's. award 1992, Outstanding Contbn. to NAON award 1996, chmn. budget and fin. com. 1991-95, nat. bylaws and policies com. 1995—, bylaws and policies com. Altanta chpt. 1994—, pres.-elect Atlanta chpt. 1996—), Orthopedic Nurses Assn. (nat. bd. dirs. 1977-79, nat. treas. 1979-81, Coun. Splty. Nursing Orgns. Ga. (nominating com. 1976-77), Ga. Med. Auditors Assn., Nat. Nurses in Bus. Assn., Assn. Rehab. Nurses (bd. dirs. Ga. chpt. 1980-81, del. people-to-people program to China 1981), Nat. Fed. Ind. Bus. (guardian 1988—, adv. coun. 1990—, healthcare task force chmn. 1992—, vice-chmn./fed. liaison Ga. adv. coun. 1995—), Am. Bd. Nursing Specialities (chmn. nominating com. 1993-94, 94-95, chmn. com. on specialty bd. rev. 1993-95), Ga. Jaycees (dist. 4C rep. Ga. Jaycee Legis. 1984, 85), Ga. Seatbelt Coalition, Orthopaedic Nurses Cert. Bd. (bd. dirs. 1991-96, pres. 1992-93, task force on advanced practice certification 1991-92), North Fulton C. of C. (vice chmn. health service effectiveness alliance 1984-85, chmn. 1985-86, co-chmn./editor periodical 1985, 3rd Quarter Workhorse award 1985), Alpharetta Jaycees (adminstrv. v.p. 1984-85, internal v.p. 1985-86), Alpharetta Jaycee Women (bd. dirs. 1983). Baptist. Avocations: reading, boating, cmty. svc. activities. Home: 424 Michael Dr Alpharetta GA 30201 Office: Healthcare Cost Cons Inc PO Box 466 St Alpharetta GA 30239

MOCK, MELODY, art historian, educator; b. Alpine, Tex., Dec. 6, 1965; d. Jeremy H. and Ruth E. (Ray) M. BFA, Sul Ross State U., 1991; MA, U. North Tex., 1996. Cert. mus. educator. Editor Sage Lit. Mag., Alpine, 1988-91; rsch. asst. art dept. U. North Tex., Denton, 1994, tchg. fellow art dept., 1994-95, visual resources asst. visual resources collection, 1995-96, gallery asst. Art Gallery, 1995-96; grad. intern Amon Carter Mus., Ft. Worth, 1995-96. Mem. Am. Assn. Mus., Nat. Art Educators Assn., Coll. Art Assn. Home: 12916 Constitution NE Albuquerque NM 87112

MOCKARD, JANET, advertising executive. Sr. v.p. broadcast prodn. dir. W.B. Doner & Co. Office: 400 E Pratt St Baltimore MD 21202*

MODELAND, PHYLLIS JO, author; b. Carthage, Mo., Dec. 22, 1938; d. Howard Levi and Pauline (Crawford) Anderson; m. Dennis L. Rossiter, Mar. 30, 1968 (dec. Apr. 1992); 1 child, Eric Shawn; m. Vernon L. Modeland, May 29, 1996. Head libr. Trs. Regional Libr. Br., Odessa, Mo., 1979-83; editor, gen. mgr. Ozark County Times Newspaper, Gainesville, Mo., 1989; freelance writer, tchr., editor, lectr., photographer. Author: On the Scent of Danger, 1989, Moxie, 1990, A Living History of the Ozarks, 1992; contbr. articles to profl. jours., periodicals, short story anthologies. Mem. Soc. Children's Book Writers, Authors Guild, Western Writers of Am., Women Writing the West, Rocky Mountain Fiction Writers, Heartland Writers Guild, Ozarks Writers League (v.p. 1990, Dan Saults award 1988, 93), Mo. Writers Guild (Best Column. 1989, Best Book 1991, Best Major Work 1992). Home: Box 1299 Flippin AR 72634

MODLEY, VERONICA SUE, insurance representative; b. Beckley, W.Va., Aug. 8, 1962; d. Charles Lowell Helvey and Wanda Marie Adkins; m. Mark Dion Peery, Sept. 1, 1979 (div. Aug. 1982) 1 child, Misty Dawn; m. Robert Wayne Modley, Oct. 23, 1982; children: Ashley Nichole, Robert Wayne II. AS in Secretarial Scis., AS in Med. Sci., Beckley Coll., 1990. Mgr. Hunter Ridge Apts., Mt. Hope, W.Va., 1985-86; receptionist, customer svc. rep. Beckley Ins. Assn., 1986-89; personal lines mgr. Richard M. Lewis Ins., Beckley, 1990-91; ins. agt. Amato Ins., Crab Orchard, W.Va., 1991; customer svc. rep. Acordia Ins. of W.Va., Beckley, 1991—. Mem. Ins. Women of W.Va., Ins. Women of Beckley (sec. 1993-94). Office: Acordia of WVa 328 Neville St Beckley WV 25801

MOE, VIDA DELORES, civic worker; b. Ryder, N.D., Feb. 29, 1928; d. John Nelson and Inga Marie (Lewis) Ahlgran; m. Placido Ferdinand, July 28, 1950 (div.); children: Terrence Paul, Star Marie; m. Edgar Louis Moe, May 24, 1970 (dec. 1983). Student, Minot State U., 1964-66; diploma interior decorating, LaSalle Extension U., 1976. Sec. Raleigh Ins., Tacoma, 1949-50; clk. stenographer Army Transp. Office, San Francisco, 1951-51; clk.-typist Base Supply, Minot AFB, N.D., 1960-61, clk.-stenographer Base Housing, 1961-62, 74, sec. MIADS Direction Ctr., 1962-63, sec. QC Br., 1963-64, sec. dept. acctg. and fin., 1964-65, med. sec. USAF Regional Hosp., 1965-66, sec. Minuteman AFSC, 1966-67, 74-75, sec. 5th Bomb Wing, 1967-70, sec. 1st Missile Wing, 1973-74, sec. dept. mil. personnel, 1975-76, sec. disaster preparedness, 1987-93; sec., salesperson Allen Realty, Minot, 1980-85. Pres. City Art League, 1977-79, 86-87; chmn. Carnegie Restoration and Art Ctr. Project, 1980-87; bd. dirs. Patrons of Libr., Minot, 1978-87, sec., 1979-80, v.p., 1981, pres., 1982-83; v.p. 40/50 Rep. Women Minot, 1982, chair decorations com., 1983; historian Minot Rep. Women, 1984-86. Recipient Superior Performance award 5th Bomb Wing, Minot AFB, 1968, Devotion to Vol. Duty award USAF Regional Hosp., Minot, 1983, 86, Superior Performance Cash award Dept. of Air Force 857 Combat Support Group, 1988-91. Mem. AARP (dir. 1995-96), Nat. Assn. Retired Fed. Employees, N.D. Bus. and Profl. Women's Club (rec. sec. 1978-79, 81-82), Minot Bus. and Profl. Women's Club (pres. 1981-82), Am. Legion Aux. (judge jr. art posters contest 1980-82, pres. 1982-84), Minot Shrine Hosp. Aux. (v.p. 1984, 85, pres. 1986, 87), Beta Sigma Phi (v.p. Laureate Epsilon chpt. 1981-82, pres. 1983-85, Valentine Queen 1985, Girl of Yr. 1985, preceptor Eta chpt., Girl of Yr., 1980, life), MidState Porcelain Artists Guild (v.p. 1983 89, pres. 1984), Order Eastern Star (North Dakota Grand chpt., grand rep. 1979-81, dist. dep. 1982-83, chair credentials com. 1983-84, Grand Martha 1984-85, Grand Electa 1985-86, chmn. registration com. 1986-87, assoc. Grand Conductress 1987-88, Grand Conductress 1989-90, assoc. Grand Matron 1990-91, Worthy Grand Matron 1991-92, Worthy Matron Minot Venus chpt. 1976, 87, 88-89, sec. 1993-94, chaplain 1994-95, assoc. conductress 1995-96, conductress 1996—), Elketts (2nd. v.p. 1988-89, sec. 1993-94), Sons Norway (social dir. 1993-94, chmn. social dirs. 1994), Eagles Aux. (conductor 1993-94, chaplain 1994-95, v.p. 1995-96, pres. 1996—). Lutheran. Avocations: porcelain painting, oil painting, sewing, tennis, embroidery. Home: 705 25th St NW Minot ND 58703-1733

MOE-FISHBACK, BARBARA ANN, counseling administrator; b. Grand Forks, N.D., June 24, 1955; d. Robert Alan and Ruth Ann (Wang) Moe; m. William Martin Fishback; children: Kristen Ann, William Robert. BS in Psychology, U. N.D., 1977, MA in Counseling and Guidance, 1979, BS in Elem. Edn., 1984. Cert. elem. counselor, Ill. Tchr. United Day Nursery, Grand Forks, 1977-78; social worker Cavalier County Social Services, Langdon, N.D., 1979-83; elem. sch. counselor Douglas Sch. System, Ellsworth AFB, S.D., 1984-87, Jacksonville (Ill.) Sch. System, 1987—. Vol. Big Sister Program, Grand Forks, 1978-84; leader Pine to Prairie Girl Scout council, Langdon, N.D., 1980-82; tchrs. asst. Head Start Program, Grand Forks, 1979. Mem. Am. Assn. Counseling and Devel., NEA, Ill. Assn. Counseling and Devel., Ill. Sch. Counselor Assn., AAUW (local br. newsletter editor 1980-81, br. sec. 1981-83), Ill. Edn. Assn., Am. Sch. Counselor Assn., Kappa Alpha Theta (newsletter, magazine article editor 1976-77). Club: Jaycettes (Langdon) (dir. 1982-83). Avocations: cooking, camping, curling, ceramics, creative writing. Home: 291 Sandusky St Jacksonville IL 62650-1844 Office: Jacksonville Sch Dist Jacksonville IL 62650

MOELLER, MARY ELLA, retired home economist, educator, radio commentator; b. Southampton, N.Y., Mar. 11, 1938; d. Harry Eugene and Edith Leone (Reester) Parsons; m. James Myron Moeller, Aug. 5, 1961; 1 child, Mary Beth. BS in Home Econs., U. Nebr., 1960; MLS, SUNY, Stony Brook, 1977. Tchr. home econs. Port Jefferson Schs., N.Y., 1960-70; home econs. program asst. Suffolk County Coop. Extension of Cornell U., Riverhead, N.Y., 1972-82; tchr. home econs. Eastport High Sch., Riverhead, 1982-85, South County Schs., Bellport Middle Sch., N.Y., 1985-93; sch. coord. N.Y. state mentoring program Bellport Middle Sch., 1992-95; host Ask Your Neighbor, Sta. WRIV, Riverhead, 1982-87; trainer Home Econs. Entrepreneurship N.Y. State Edn. Dept., 1986-95; mem. home and career skills regional team N.Y. State Edn. Dept., 1984-86; mem. consumer homemaking adv. bd. Bd. Coop. Edn.; friendly svc. chmn. N.Y. State Ret. Tchrs. L.I. Zone, 1995—. Contbr. monthly articles to consumer publs. Mem. N.Y. State Home Econs. Assn., Am. Home Econs. Assn. (cert. home economist), Suffolk County Home Econs. Assn., DAR (historian 1985), Eastern Star (matron 1970). Home: PO Box 377 Miller Place NY 11764-0377 Office: Bellport Mid Sch Kreamer St Bellport NY 11713

MOELY, BARBARA E., psychology researcher, educator; b. Prairie du Sac, Wis., July 17, 1940; d. John Arthur and Loretta Ruth (Giese) M.; children: John Jacob Moely Wiener, David Andrew Moely Wiener. Student Carroll Coll., 1958-60; BA, U. Wis., 1962, MA, 1964; PhD, U. Minn., 1968. Asst. prof. U. Hawaii, Honolulu, 1967-71; rsch. psychologist UCLA, 1971-72; asst. prof. Tulane U., New Orleans, 1972-75, assoc. prof. psychology, 1975-85, prof., 1985—, dept. chmn., 1992-96. Contbr. articles to profl. jours. Grantee U.S. Office Edn., Handicapped Pers. Preparation, 1977-80, Tulane U., 1973, 75, 77, 78, 83-84, Inst. for Mental Hygiene, City of New Orleans, 1983-84, Nat. Inst. Edn., 1983-84, La. Edn. Quality Support Fund, 1988, 89, 91, 92, 96. Mem. AAUP (v.p. La. conf. 1992-93, sec. 1993—, pres. Tulane 1992-94), APA, Soc. Rsch. in Child Devel., Am. Ednl. Rsch. Assn., Southwestern Soc. for Rsch. in Human Devel. (pres. 1986-88), Phi Beta Kappa (pres. Alpha chapter La. 1981-82, sec. 1995—). Office: Tulane Univ Dept Psychology New Orleans LA 70118

MOFFAT, MARYBETH, automotive company executive; b. Pitts., July 25, 1951; d. Herbert Franklin and Florence Grafe (Knerem) M.; m. Brian Francis Soulier, Nov. 30, 1974 (div.). BA, Carroll Coll., 1973. Indsl. engring. technician Wis. Centrifugal Co., Waukesha, Wis., 1976-77; indsl. engr. Utility Products, Inc., Milw., 1977-79; mgr. indsl. engring. Bear Automotive (div. SPX Corp.), Bangor, Pa., 1980-90; program mgr. Toyota Johnson Controls, Inc. Automotive Systems Group, 1990—. Group home house parent Headwaters Regional Achievement Ctr., Lake Tomahawk, Wis., 1974. Mem. Am. Inst. Indsl. Engrs., MTM Assn. for Standards Rsch., Indsl. Mgmt. Soc., Alpha Gamma Delta (standards chmn. 1971-72). Republican. Methodist. Avocations: skiing, horseback riding, swimming, reading. Office: Johnson Controls Inc Automotive Systems Group One Quality Drive Georgetown KY 40324-2011

MOFFATT, ELIZABETH KATHRYN, journalist, photographer, newspaper editor; b. Harrisburg, Pa., Dec. 6, 1967; d. William Thomas and Kathryn Elizabeth (Gensler) M. BA in English Lit., U. Pitts., Johnstown, 1991. Reporter West Perry Sch. Dist., Elliottsburg, Pa., 1992; stringer Swank-Fowler Publs., Inc., Duncannon, Pa., 1991-92; staff and sports writer, photographer Swank-Fowler Publs., Inc., New Bloomfield, Pa., 1992—; assoc. editor Duncannon Record, Swank-Fowler Publs., Inc., 1994—. Reading tutor Perry County Literacy Coun., Newport, Pa., 1992—, bd. dirs. 1993-95; mem. Laubach Literacy Action, 1993—. Recipient 2d place award for writing, 1994, 95, 1st place for photograph, 1995. Mem. Women in Comm., Ea. U.S. Pipe Band Assn., Amateur Speedskating Union, Lions. Republican. Lutheran. Home: RD 1 Box 350 Lyons Rd Millerstown PA 17062 Office: Duncannon Record 217 N High St Box A Duncannon PA 17020

MOFFATT, JOYCE ANNE, performing arts executive; b. Grand Rapids, Mich., Jan. 3, 1936; d. John Barnard and Ruth Lillian (Pellow) M. BA in Lit., U. Mich., 1957, MA in Theatre, 1960; HHD (hon.), Sch. Psychology, San Francisco, 1991. Stage mgr., lighting designer Off-Broadway plays, costume, lighting and set designer, stage mgr. stock cos., 1954-62; nat. subscription mgr. Theatre Guild/Am. Theatre Soc., N.Y.C., 1965-67; subscription mgr. Theatre, Inc.-Phoenix Theatre, N.Y.C., 1963-67; cons. N.Y.C. Ballet and N.Y.C. Opera, 1967-70; asst. house mgr. N.Y. State Theater, 1970-72; dir. ticket sales City Ctr. of Music and Drama, Inc., N.Y.C., 1970-72; prodn. mgr. San Antonio's Symphony/Opera, 1973-75; gen. mgr. San Antonio Symphony/Opera, 1975-76, 55th St. Dance Theater Found., Inc., N.Y.C., 1976-77, Ballet Theatre Found., Inc./Am. Ballet Theatre, N.Y.C., 1977-81; v.p. prodn. Radio City Music Hall Prodns., Inc., N.Y.C., 1981-83; artist-in-residence CCNY, 1981—; propr. mgmt. cons. firm for performing arts N.Y.C., 1983—; exec. dir. San Francisco Ballet Assn., 1987-93; mng. dir. Houston Ballet Assoc., 1993-95; gen. mgr. Chgo. Music and Dance Theater, Inc., 1995—; cons. Ford Found., N.Y. State Coun. on Arts, Kennedy Ctr. for Performing Arts.; mem. dance panels N.Y. State Coun. on Arts, 1979-81; mem. panels for Support to Prominent Orgns. and Dance, Calif. Arts Coun., 1988-92. Appointee San Francisco Cultural Affairs Task Force, 1991; chmn. bd. Tex. Inst. for Arts in Edn., 1994—; trustee of I.A.T.S.E. Local 16 Pension and Welfare Fund, 1991-94. Mem. Assn. Theatrical Press Agts. and Mgrs., Actors Equity Assn., United Scenic Artists Local 829, San Francisco Visitors and Conv. Bur. (bd. dirs.). Club: Argyle (San Antonio). Office: Chicago Music & Dance Theater Mezz Level 203 No LaSalle Chicago IL 60601

MOFFATT, KATY (KATHERINE LOUELLA MOFFATT), musician, vocalist, songwriter; b. Ft. Worth, Nov. 19, 1950; d. Lester Huger and Sue-Jo (Jarrott) M. Student, Sophie Newcomb Coll., 1968, St. John's Coll., 1969-70. Rec. artist Columbia Records, 1975-79, Permian/MCA Records, 1982-84, Enigma Records, L.A., 1985, Wrestler Records, L.A., 1987-88, Red Moon Records, Switzerland, 1988-93, Philo/Rounder Records, 1989-93, Round Tower Music, U.K., Ireland, Europe, 1993—, Watermelon Records, U.S., 1994—. Folksinger, Ft. Worth, 1967-68; musician, vocalist, songwriter, rec. artist: (films) Billy Jack, 1970, Hard Country, 1981, The Thing Called Love, 1993; prodn. asst. film, Sta. KIII-TV, Corpus Christi, 1970, audio engr., Sta. KRIS-TV, Corpus Christi, 1970; musician, vocalist in blues band, Corpus Christi, 1970; receptionist, bookkeeping asst., copywriter, announcer, Sta. KFWT, Ft. Worth, 1971, musician, vocalist, songwriter, Denver, 1971-72, on tour, 1973, 75—, Denver, 1974, on tour, 1976-79, European tour, 1977, Can. tour, 1984-85, on tour in Europe, U.S., Can. and Asia, 1985—; albums include Katy, 1976, Kissin' In The California Sun, Am. release, 1977, internat. release, 1978, A Town South of Bakersfield, 1985, Walkin' on the Moon, European release, 1988, U.S. release, 1989, Child Bride, 1990, (duet album with brother Hugh) Dance Me Outside, 1992, (Switzerland only) Indoor Fireworks, 1992, The Greatest Show On Earth A.K.A. The Evangeline Hotel, 1994, Hearts Gone Wild, 1994, Tulare Dust, 1995, (duet album with Kate Brislin) Sleepless Nights, 1996; singles include Take it as it Comes, 1981, Under Loved and Over Lonely, 1983; songs include The Magic Ring, 1971; Gerry's Song, 1973, Kansas City Morning, 1974, Take Me Back To Texas, 1975, (Waitin' For) The Real Thing, 1975, Didn't We Have Love, 1976, Kissin' in the California Sun, 1977, Walkin' on the Moon, 1989. Recipient Record World Album award, 1976; named one of 4 Top New Female Vocalists, Cashbox Singles Awards, 1976; nominee for Top New Female Vocalist, Acad. Country Music, 1985. Mem. AFTRA, SAG, NARAS, Am. Fedn. Musicians.

MOFFATT, MINDY ANN, middle school educator, educational training specialist; b. Mpls., Aug. 3, 1951; d. Ralph Theron and La Vone Muriel (Bergstrom) M. Student, UCLA, 1972-73; BA, Calif. State U., Fullerton, 1975, MS in Edn., 1991. Cert. elem. tchr. and adminstr., Calif. Tchr. early childhood edn. program Meadows Elem. Sch., Valencia, Calif., 1977-78; tchr. United Parents Against Forced Busing, Chatsworth, Calif., 1978-80; founding tchr. Gazebo Two Sch. for Young Gifted and Creative Children, Summerville, S.C., 1980-81; tchr. Anaheim Union High Sch. Dist., Anaheim, Calif., 1981-89, mentor, tchr., 1985-88; tchr. Greentree Elem. Sch., Irvine, Calif., 1989-90; with Thurston Mid. Sch., Laguna Beach, Calif., 1990-92; editor Cypress Pub. Group, Laguna Hills, Calif., 1992; tng. specialist Scripps Clinics and Rsch. Found., LaJolla, Calif., 1993-94; tchr. White Hill Mid. Sch., Ross Valley Sch. Dist., San Anselmo, Calif., 1994-95; cons. writing project U. Calif., Irvine, 1982—; textbook cons. McDougal, Littell & Co., Evanston, Ill., 1984-86; facilitator Summer Tech. Tng. Inst., Irvine, 1987. Co-author: Practical Ideas for Teaching Writing as a Process, 1986, 87, Thinking/Writing: Fostering Critical Thinking Through Writing, 1991, Reading, Thinking, and Writing About Culturally Diverse Literature, 1995. Mem. Our Ultimate Recreation (Orange County, Calif., chairperson social com. 1983, chairperson backpacking 1983, v.p. 1993-94). Democrat. Mem. Unity Ch. of Truth.

MOFFETT, KAREN ELIZABETH, physical education educator, guidance counselor; b. Indpls., June 29, 1958; d. Charles Richard and Julie V. (Godo) Tiede; m. Monte Joe Moffett, June 25, 1988. BS, Ind. U., 1981, MS, 1987; MA, Ball State U., 1995. Tchr., coach Delphi (Ind.) Cmty. Schs., 1981-87, Whitko Cmty. Schs., South Whitley, Ind., 1987-95; guidance counselor New Prairie H.S., New Carlisle, Ind., 1995—. Mem. AAHPERD, Ind. Assn. Health, Phys. Edn., Recreation and Dance, Ind. Assn. Track and Cross-Country Coaches, Ind. Coaches of Girl's and Women's Sports, Ind. Counselor's Assn., Phi Delta Kappa. Home: 1556 Admiral Ct Porter IN 46304

MOGGE, HARRIET MORGAN, educational association executive; b. Cleve.; d. Russell VanDyke and Grace (Wells) Morgan; m. Robert Arthur Mogge, Aug. 17, 1948 (div. 1977); 1 child, Linda Jean. BME, Northwestern U., 1959; postgrad., Ill. State U., 1969. Instr. piano, Evanston, Ill., 1954-58; instr. elem. music pub. schs., Evanston, 1959; editorial asst. archivist Summy-Birchard Co., Evanston, 1964-66, asst. to editor-in-chief, 1966-67, cons., 1968-69, ednl. dir., 1969-74, also historian, 1973-74; supr. vocal music jr. high sch., Watseka, Ill., 1967-68; asst. dir. profl. programs Music Educators Nat. Conf., Reston, Va., 1974-84, dir. meetings and convs., 1984-94, mgr. direct mktg. svc., 1981-89; sr. cons. Convention Consulting Svc., 1993—. Mng. editor Am. Suzuki jour., 1972-74, Gen. Music Today, 1987-91; mgr. diplay advt. Model T Times, 1971—; vice chair editorial bd. Exposition Mgmt., 1991-93; Active various community drives. Mem. Music Educators Nat. Conf., Am. Choral Dirs. Assn., In and About Chgo., Music Educators Assn. (bd. dirs.), Suzuki Assn. Ams. (exec. sec. 1972-74), Internat. Assn. Expn. Mgmt. (cert.; mem. edn. com. 1979-88, chmn. edn. com. 1985-87, bd. liaison edn. com. 1987-88, bd. dirs. Washington chpt. 1983-85, nat. bd. dirs. 1986-91, del. to conv. liaison coun. 1989-90, nat. v.p. 1989, nat. pres. 1990, nat. past pres. 1991), Mu Phi Epsilon, Kappa Delta (province pres. 1960-66, 72-76, regional chpts. dir. 1976-78, nat. dir. scholarship 1981-84). Republican. Presbyterian. Clubs: Bus. and Profl. Women's (Watseka) (bd. dirs. 1968-70); Antique Automobile (registrar ann. meeting 1961-86), Model T Ford Internat. (v.p. 1971-72, 76-77, pres. 1981, treas. 1983-87, bd. dirs. 1971-87). Home: 1919A Villaridge Dr Reston VA 20191-4824 Office: PO Box 3362 Reston VA 20195-1362

MOGGIO, BARBARA JEAN, health education specialist; b. Bronx, N.Y., July 7, 1953; d. Thomas Francis and Barbara Margaret (Lang) O'Meara; m. Richard Albert Moggio, July 28, 1984; stepchildren: Samuel A., Jonathan F. ADN, Pace U., 1976; BS, Mercy Coll., Dobbs Ferry, N.Y., 1985; MPH, Yale U., 1987. RN, N.Y.; cert. health edn. specialist. Critical care nurse, nursing care coord. Westchester Med. Ctr., Valhalla, N.Y., 1974-85; adj. asst. prof. Iona Coll., New Rochelle, N.Y., 1988-94; proprietor, CEO Health Wave, Inc., Stamford, Conn., 1990—. Author health curriculum Health Promotion Wave, 1987, 88, 95, 96. Mem. APHA, AAUW, Am. Sch. Health Assn., Assn. Advancement of Health Edn. Home: PO Box 120 446 Long Ridge Rd Pound Ridge NY 10576 Office: Health Wave Inc. 1084 Hope St Stamford CT 06907

MOGUL, LESLIE ANNE, business development and marketing consultant; b. Balt., Mar. 9, 1948; d. Harry and Elaine Mogul; m. William Kasper. AS, Miami Dade Jr. Coll., 1969; BA, Temple U., 1976; MBA, U. Phoenix, 1996. Accredited pub. rels. Account exec. Gray & Rogers, Inc., Phila., 1976-80; pres. Leslie Mogul, Inc., Phila., 1980-84; v.p. McKinney, Inc., Phila., 1984-87; assoc. dir. comm. Scripps Meml. Hosps., San Diego, 1987-93; dir. pub. rels. Scripps Health, San Diego, 1993, dir. customer rels. and mktg., 1994-95; dir. bus. devel. Harborview Med. Ctr. Hosp., San Diego, 1995—. Recipient over 25 awards local and nat. pub. rels. and comm. orgns. Mem. Pub. Rels. Soc. Am. (dir.-at-large 1993-94), Alumni Leadership Calif. Office: Harborview Med Ctr 1855 1st Ave San Diego CA 92101

MOHALLEY, PATRICIA JOANN, library media specialist; b. Lafayette, Ind., Aug. 24, 1951; d. Robert Dean and Alta Mae (Hancock) Clerget; m. Jeremiah J. Mohalley, Mar. 17, 1979; Sarah Frances and Jeremiah J. Jr. BA in Edn., Purdue U., 1973, MS in Edn., 1978. Cert. edn.-libr. media specialist, Ind., Tex. Tchr. grade 5 Crown Point (Ind.) Sch. Corp., 1973-74; tchr. grades 5 and 6 South Newton Sch. Corp., Kentland, Ind., 1974-77; dir. elem. librs. Community Sch. Corp. of Ea. Hancock County, Wilkinson, Ind., 1977-80; libr. media specialist Met. Sch. Dist. of Lawrence Twp., Indpls., 1980-81, Spring Br. Ind. Sch. Dist., Houston, 1981-89, Klein (Tex.) Ind. Sch. Dist., 1989—. Active Cypress Creek Friends Libr., Spring, Tex., 1988—; life mem. Tex. PTA, 1989—. Mem. ALA, Tex. Libr. Assn. Home: 7814 Springberry Ct Spring TX 77379-4084

MOHAMED, DONNA FAHIMAH, counselor; b. Chapel Hill, N.C., Oct. 19, 1959; d. Thomas Lloyd and Helen Eleanor (Helms) Pendergraft; m. Dilip Gandhi, Aug. 19, 1978; 1 child, Sundeep; m. Mustafa Hussein Al-Bar, Apr. 15, 1991; 1 child, Maidah Nasreen. BA in Religious Studies with high honors and distinction, U. N.C., 1994. Rehab. therapist John Umstead Hosp. Continuing Treatment, Butner, N.C., 1985-86; immigration paralegal Law Offices of Douglas Holmes, Durham, N.C., 1986-87; immigration specialist Law Offices of Manlin Chee, Greensboro, N.C., 1987-92; program dir., accredited counselor Immigration & Minority Assistance Network, Durham, 1992—; pro bono project rep. Lawyers Com. for Human Rights, Fredericksburg, Va., 1988-88; minority devel. counselor, Ibad Ar-Rahman Sch., Durham, 1990-91; immigration cons. to bd. dirs. Jamaat Ibad Ar-Rahman, Inc., Durham, 1990-94; dir. cmty. counseling IMAN, Durham, 1991—; speaker N.Am. Coun. for Muslim Women, Chgo., 1994; panelist on cultural awareness, Dept. Edn. and Counseling, U. N.C., Chapel Hill, 1994; organizer, presenter ann. workshops Coll. Bound Program for Youth, Chapel Hill, 1992—. Recipient 1st prize ann. cooking contest Triangle Muslim Women's Group, 1992. Mem. Am. Muslim Coun., Am. Immigration Lawyers Assn. (pro bono affiliation), Muslim Women's Orgn. (pres. Chapel Hill, N.C. chpt. 1991-93), Muslim Student's Assn. (exec. dir. Chapel Hill chpt. 1992-93), Islamic Soc. N.Am., Social Scientists Am., Golden Key Nat. Honor Soc. Democrat.

MOHLE, BRENDA SIMONSON, art appraiser; b. Dallas, May 9, 1959; d. Harold Lee and Lila Faye (Adair) Simonson; m. Robert F. Mohle, Mar. 28, 1981; children: Aaron, Alexandra. BA with high honors, U. Tex., 1980. Sales advisor Newman Gallery, Dallas, 1981-84; gallery mgr. Omni Art, Dallas, 1984-87; owner Signet Art, Carrollton, Tex., 1987—; docent Dallas Mus. Art, 1985—. Mem. Appraisers Assn. Am., Internat. Soc. Appraisers (accredited, treas. North Tex. chpt. 1993-94, sec. North Tex. chpt. 1994-95, v.p. North Tex. chpt. 1995-96, nat. fine art chair). Office: Signet Art 2211 High Point Dr Carrollton TX 75007

MOHLER, GEORGIA ANN, geriatrics nurse practitioner; b. Iowa Falls, Iowa, Mar. 11, 1941; d. George Edward and Norma Dorothy (Wolf) M. Diploma, Meth.-Kahler, Rochester, Minn., 1962; BSN, U. Wash., 1971. RN, Wash.; cert. geriatric nurse practitioner. Relief charge nurse, team leader Swedish Hosp., Seattle, 1963-72; pub. health nurse Vis. Nurse Svc., Seattle, 1971-72; relief charge nurse and medicare coord. Restorative Care Ctr., Seattle, 1972-81; unit coord. Tacoma Luth. Home and Retirement Ctr., Tacoma, 1981-82; nurse practitioner Tacoma Luth. Home, 1983—, dir. home health agy. and nurse practitioner, 1993—. Contbr. to profl. jours. Mem. Pierce County Nurse Practitioner Group, Nat. Conf. Gerontol. Nurse Practitioners. Lutheran. Home: 909 N I St Apt 401 Tacoma WA 98403-2136

MOHLER, MARIE ELAINE, nurse educator; b. Norma, N.D., Mar. 2, 1946; d. Ervin and Katie M. (Nichol) Hansen; children: Zane, Tracy, KyLynn, Todd, Lynnette. Diploma in nursing, Trinity Hosp. Sch. Nursing, Minot, 1967; BSN, Mont. State U., 1969, M in Nursing, 1970; diploma nurse midwifery, SUNY, Bklyn., 1973. RN, N.D.; cert. nurse midwife Am. Coll. Nurse Midwifes. Staff nurse pediatrics Trinity Hosp., Minot, 1967; resident nurse girl's dormitory Mont. State U., Bozeman, 1967-68; staff nurse med.-surg. wards Bozeman (Mont.) Deaconess Hosp., 1969; relief nurse Student Health Ctr. Mont. State U., Bozeman, 1970; camp nurse Camp Pinemore Minoqua, Wis., 1971; part-time staff nurse labor & delivery-maternity-newborn Bannock Meml. Hosp., Pocatello, Idaho, 1972-75; cons. maternal-newborn, pediatric wards Bannock Meml. Hosp., Pocatello, 1972-75; staff nuse maternity-newborn ward John Moses Hosp., Minot, 1977; part time staff nurse maternal-newborn ward St. Joseph's Hosp., Minot, 1978-81; nurse assessor Luth. Social Svc. N.D. and Family Care Network, 1991-93; instr. Ariz. State U., Tempe, 1971-72, No. Ariz. U., Flagstaff, 1972, Idaho State U., Pocatello, 1972-75; asst. prof. Minot (N.D.) State Coll. divsn. Allied Health, 1975-76; instr. medicine U. Miss. Med. Ctr., Jackson, 1976-77; assoc. prof. Minot (N.D.) State U. Coll. Nursing, 1977—; pres. coun. coll. faculties N.D. U. Sys., 1993-94, chair faculty compensation com., 1993-94, 96—, others; mem. budget and salary com., constl. rev. com. Minot State U., 1993-94, others. Author of various videotapes and slide series. Recipient Minot C. of C. Disting. Prof. award, 1986; Burlington No. Found. Faculty Achievement award, 1987; grantee in field. Mem. Assn. Women's Health, Obstetric and Neonatal Nurses (chair legis. chpt.), Alpha Tau Delta. Office: Minot State Univ Coll Nursing 500 University Ave Minot ND 58701

MOHLER, MARY GAIL, magazine editor; b. Milaca, Minn., Dec. 15, 1948; d. Albert and Deane (Vedders) M.; m. Paul Rodes Trautman, June 5, 1976 (div. 1994); children: Elizabeth Deane, David Albert Rodes, Theodore DeForest Lloyd. B.A., U. Calif.-Davis, 1974; M.A. in Lit., SUNY-Stony Brook, 1976. Asst., then editor-reporter Family Circle Mag., N.Y.C., 1979-81; editorial coordinator Ladies' Home Jour., N.Y.C., 1981, assoc. articles editor, 1982, mng. editor, 1982-93, sr. editor, 1994—; editor in chief Ladies' Home Jour. Parent's Digest. Medieval philosophy fellow SUNY-Binghamton, 1978. Mem. MLA, Am. Soc. Mag. Editors, Phi Beta Kappa. Clubs: Medieval; Overseas Press. Office: Ladies Home Jour 125 Park Ave New York NY 10017-5529

MOHNER LANGHAMER, WILMA MARIA, artist; b. Karlsbad, Germany, Apr. 7, 1942; came to U.S. 1979; d. Hugo and Juliane (Satzer) Langhammer; m. Carl Martin Rudolf Mohner, Dec. 9, 1978. RN, City of Munich, 1975. Pres. Orange Hill Studio, Inc., Mission, Tex., 1986—; pub. agreement with Gray Stone Press Pubr., Nashville, 1981-84, HMK Fine Art, N.YC., 1984-85, Unicef, Geneva, Switzerland, 1985; commn. Winter Dreams, Squibb Pharm. Co., world hdqrs., Princeton, N.J. Exhbns. include BMW Gallery, Munich, Reyn Gallery, N.Y.C., Phillips Gallery, Dallas and Palm Beach, Fla.,, Knightsbridge Gallery, Wichita, Kans., McAllen Internat. Mus., Tex., Neiman Marcus, Houston and Dallas, Miniatures '84, Mpls.; comms. incl. BMW, McAllen Internat. Mus, Nat. Christmas Pageant of Peace, White House, 1983, Heye art calendars, 1976—; works in permanent collections in City of Munic, BMW Hdqrs., Smithsonian Instn., Library of Congress, Bibliotheque Nationale, Paris. Invited to paint Easter Egg, White House Easter Egg Roll, Washington, 1984, 85, Honored with letter, Pres.-elect. Ronald Reagan, 1981. Address: RR 1 Box 322 Mission TX 78572-9773

MOHR, BARBARA JEANNE, educator; b. Santa Monica, Calif., Jan. 26, 1953; d. Edgar Kirchner and Beatrice Jeanne (Anderson) M. BA, Calif. State U., Fullerton, 1976; MS, Calif. State U., 1982. Multiple Subject Teaching Credential, 1977, Single Subject Tchr. Credential, 1977. Substitute tchr. Fullerton (Calif.) Sch. Dist., 1977-78, tchr., 1978—, mentor, 1984-96; tchr. calligraphy Laguna Rd. Sch., 1985-92, student coun. advisor, 1988-92, advisor Just Say No Club, 1986-94. Named Tchr. of Yr. Fullerton Sch. Dist., 1989; recipient Hon. Svc. award Laguna Rd. Sch. PTA, 1989; Weingart fellow Nat. Gallery of Art Tchr. Inst., 1996. Mem. NEA, Calif. Tchrs. Assn., Fullerton Elem. Tchrs. Assn., Calif. State U. Alumni Assn., Phi Kappa Phi.

MOHR, ELLEN G., English language educator; b. Mt. Pleasant, Iowa, Dec. 5, 1942; d. F.W. and Martha Margaret (Desenberg) Grube; m. Jan A. Mohr, Aug. 18, 1972; children: Jon, Jennifer. BS in Edn., N.W. Mo. U., 1964, MA in English, 1970. English instr. George Washington Middle Sch., Ridgewood, N.J., 1968-69, Excelsior Springs (Mo.) High Sch., 1970-71, Greenfield Middle Sch., Cin., 1972-73; writing ctr. dir. Johnson County Community Coll., Overland Park, Kans., 1980—; staff devel. intern Johnson County Comm. Coll., Overland Park, Kans., 1994-95, faculty dir. Ctr. for Teaching and Learning, 1995—. Author: Midwest Writing Center Association Proceedings Book, Writing Lab., Newsletter. Recipient Faculty Recognition award Mich. Consortium for C.C.'s, 1991-92, Disting. Status award Johnson County C.C., 1994-96. Mem. Midwest Writing Ctr. Assn. (chair bd. dirs. 1986-91), Nat. Writing Ctr. Assn. (exec. bd. 1989-92, named peer tutor cons.), Kans. Assn. Tchrs. of English, Phi Delta Kappa.

MOHR, VIOLET B., small business owner, farmer; b. Peoria, Ill., Feb. 22, 1901; d. Fred and Mary Jane (Johnson) Zimmerman; m. Leslie F. Shrull (div. May 1, 1925); children: Roswald, Janis; m. Ralph R. Mohr, Febr. 25, 1950. Student, Tri-State Coll., 1930. Owner 5& 10store, Delta, Ohio, 1925-50, Mohr's Shoe Store, Delta, Ohio, 1950-95. Named Citizen of the Year Delta, 1992.

MOHRAZ, JUDY JOLLEY, college president; b. Houston, Oct. 1, 1943; d. John Chesler and Mae (Jackson) Jolley; m. Bijan Mohraz; children: Andrew, Jonathan. BA, Baylor U., 1966, MA, 1968; PhD, U. Ill., 1974. Lectr. history Ill. Wesleyan U., 1972-74; asst. prof. history So. Meth. U., Dallas, 1974-80, coord. women's studies, 1977-81, assoc. prof. history, 1980-94, asst. provost, 1983-88, assoc. provost for student academics, 1988-94; pres. Goucher Coll., Towson, Md., 1994—; cons. Ednl. Testing Svc., Princeton, N.J., 1984-93, Nat. Park Svcs., Seneca Falls, N.Y., 1992-93. Trustee The Lamplighter Sch., 1991-94, St. Mark's Sch. Tex., 1993-94; adv. bd. U. Tex. Southwestern Med. Sch., 1992-94; active Leadership Dallas, 1994. Recipient Disting. Alumni award Baylor U., 1993; named Woman of Merit, Omicron Delta Kappa, 1993. Office: Goucher Coll Office of Pres 1021 Dulaney Valley Rd Baltimore MD 21204

MOHRDICK, EUNICE MARIE, nurse, consultant, health educator; b. Alameda, Calif.; d. Walter William and Eunice Marie (Connors) M. BS in Nursing Edn., U. San Francisco, 1955; MA in Edn. spl interest, San Francisco State Coll., 1967; Pub. Health Cert., U. Calif., San Francisco, 1968; EdD, Western Colo. U., 1977. RN, Calif. Supr. oper. rm. St. John's Hosp., Oxnard, Calif., 1947-50, supr. maternity, delivery and nursery rms., 1950-53; nurse, supr. St. Mary's Hosp., San Francisco, 1943-45, supr., instr., 1955-60, 62-65; asst. dir. nursing, tchr. nursing history St Mary's Coll. of Nursing, San Francisco, 1953-55; tchr. home nursing Mercy High Sch., San Francisco, 1960-61; tchr. Health, Family Life San Francisco Unified Schs., 1968-83; tchr. holistic health Contra Costa Coll., 1981-86; cons. pvt. practice Albany, Calif., 1986—; tchr. El Cerrito (Calif.) Senior Ctr., 1986-88. Author: Elementary Teacher Handbook, How to Teach Sex Education, Grades, 4,5,6, 1977. Mem. Madonna Guild, San Francisco, 1986—, v.p., 1989—; mem. Half Notes' Singing Club to Sick and Spl. Needy, 1970—. Recipient Title I Grant U. Calif. San Francisco, 1968, Workshop Grant for Culture Inter-relationship Study, Singapore, UNESCO, Washington U., St. Louis, 1973. Mem. AAUW, San Francisco State U. Alumna, U. San Francisco Nursing Alumni (charter mem., bd. dirs. 1974-88), Mensa. Republican. Roman Catholic. Home & Office: 555 Pierce St Apt 129 Albany CA 94706-1011

MOHRMAN, KATHRYN, academic administrator. Pres. The Colo. Coll., Colo. Springs. Office: Colorado College Office of the President 14 E Cache La Poudre St Colorado Springs CO 80903-3294

MOJAS, KATHLEEN MARIE, psychologist; b. Santa Monica, Calif., July 1, 1961; d. Peter William and Mary Elizabeth (Simpson) M. BA in Comms., UCLA, 1987; PhD in Clin. Psychology, Calif. Grad. Inst., 1992. Lic. psychologist, Calif., 1994. Intern, tutor, counselor Dr. Gardner Child Psychologist, Brentwood, Calif., 1988-90; psychol. asst. Calif. Grad. Inst.

Counseling Ctr., L.A., 1988-89; psychol. asst. Options Counseling Ctr., Beverly Hills, Calif., 1989-94, seminar leader, spkr., writer, 1989—; rsch. asst. UCLA, 1987, Artists and Educators for Self-Esteem, L.A., 1987-89, Dick Clark Prodns., L.A., 1987; behavior edn. counselor Nutrisys., Northridge, Calif., 1986-87; media psychologist nat. talk, news shows. Contbr. articles to profl. jours., mags. Assoc. mem. APA, Golden Key. Democrat. Office: 449 S Beverly Dr Ste 212 Beverly Hills CA 90212

MOJICA, AURORA, trade association administrator; b. Mayaguez, P.R., Feb. 19, 1939; d. Luis Martinez and Anna Celida Montalvo; m. Aristides Mojica, Jan. 19, 1957 (div. July 1967); children: Ty, Marc Anthony, Raymond Francis, Sharai, Angeles. BS in Mgmt. and Labor Rel., Cornell U., 1979; postgrad., Boston U.; M in Tng. and Edn., 1996. Asst. dir. Attica Commn., N.Y.C., 1974, South Bklyn. Health Ctr., N.Y.C., 1975-79; sec. to the dept., dir. cmty. rels. (1st woman apptd.) Fire Dept. N.Y.C., 1979-81; dir. pub. cmty. rels. WYC Koff Heights Hosp., N.Y.C., 1981-84, Interfaith Adopt-A-Bldg., N.Y.C., 1984-86; dir. women health svcs. Woodhull Med. and Mental Health Ctr., N.Y.C., 1986-87; dir. individual and family grants program Fed. Emergency Mgmt. Agy., P.R., 1987-88; exec. dir. Nat. Image, Inc., Washington, 1988-90; pres. Wall St. chpt. Nat. Image, Inc.; regional tng. dir., safety rep. N.Y. State Dept. Transp., Long Island City, 1990-96; ind. cons., corp. trainer and developer, 1996—; cons. Agy. for Internat. Devel., Mex., Costa Rica and Peru, 1981; trainer Venezuala and P.R., Cornell U. P.R. Studies, N.Y., 1971—; trainer and bd. dirs. Neighborhood Reinvestment, N.Y.C., 1984-86; freelance corp. trainer/developer Marymount Manhattan Coll., Suffolk County Coll., various city, state and fed. govt. groups, nonprofit and profit corps. Bd. dirs. Dialogue on Diversity, Washington; founding mem. 100 Hispanic Women, Inc. Recipient Susan B. Anthony award for Pub. Svc., NOW, N.Y.C., 1981, Pub. Svc. award U.S. Dept. Labor, 1985, Gov. award for excellence, 1994, Women of Achievement award N.Y. State Dept. Transportation, 1994, Advisors Program for Women award Gov. N.Y., 1994; cert. of Recognition Sesame Street CTW, N.Y.C. 1983,; Named Hispanic Woman of the Yr. in Health Hispanic Woman's Network, Bklyn., 1987; Nat. Hispana Leadership Inst. fellow, 1990, 91. Roman Catholic.

MOJO, MELISSA ANNE, corporate communications executive; b. N.Y.C., Nov. 27, 1953; d. Arthur Octavius and Diane Ard (Smith) M.; m. Sean Wester Laakso, Sept. 26, 1992. BFA, Parsons Sch. Design, 1976. Editl. copy person N.Y. Daily News, N.Y.C., 1976-78, asst. mgr. pub. rels., 1978-81; promotions mgr. United Media Enterprises, N.Y.C., 1982; account exec. G.S. Schwartz & Co. Pub. Rels., N.Y.C., 1982-84, v.p. group supr., 1984-88; mgr. editl. svcs. MasterCard Internat., N.Y.C., 1988-89, dir. corporate pub. rels., 1989-92, v.p. corp. comm., 1992—. Recipient Bronze award Fin. World, 1985, 90, Merit and Excellence awards Inside Pub. Rels., 1991, 92, 93, CIPRA award of Excellence, 1995, Clarion award, 1995, Dalton Pen Comm. award, (3) Awards of Merit, 1995; named ABC Gold Quill Finalist, 1995. Mem. Internat. Assn. Bus. Communicators (chpt. newsletter editor 1984-85, co-chair prodl. devel. seminars 1985-86, v.p. spl. programs 1986-87, sec. 1987-88, bd. dirs. 1985-88, awards 1984, 85, 90, 91, Excellence award 1993, Merit award 1994, Excellence award U.S. Dist. One, 1993, 94), Women in Comm. Office: MasterCard Internat 200 Purchase St Purchase NY 10577

MOLAND-BOOTH, KATHRYN JOHNETTA, computer scientist, software engineer; b. Tallahassee, Nov. 5, 1961; d. John and Kathryn Vastavia (Gadson) M.; m. Ronald Lynn Booth, May 7, 1994. BS in Sociology, Fla. A&M U., 1982; MS in Computer Sci., Southern U., 1987; PhD in Info. Systems, Nova U., 1996. Programmer, summer intern IBM, Lexington, 1985; mem. tech. staff Bell Communications Rsch., Piscataway, N.J., 1986; programmer Logos Corp., Mount Arlington, N.J., 1987-88, Telecommunications Inds., Vienna, Va., 1988; systems analyst Advanced Tech., Inc., Reston, Va., 1988; project leader Advanced Tech., Inc., Aiken, S.C., 1989-90; sr. systems analyst, project leader Westinghouse Savannah River Co., Aiken, S.C., 1990-94; devel. mgr. SCT Utility Systems, Inc., Columbia, S.C., 1994—; tech. mem. Occurrence Reporting Spl. Interest Group, Oak Ridge, Tenn., 1991-94. Bd. govs. Am. Biog. Inst. Rsch. Assn. Mem. IEEE (treas. 1991-92, vice chair 1992-93, chair 1993-94, mem. tech. coun. software engring.), NAFE, Nat. Mgmt. Assn., Project Mgmt. Inst., Assn. Computing Machinery. Home: 3315 Camak Dr Augusta GA 30909-9431 Office: SCT Utility Systems Inc 9 Science Ct Columbia SC 29203

MOLDOCH, BERNADINE ELIZABETH, school system administrator; b. Buffalo, Aug. 10; d. Bernard Michael and Helen S. (Kustra) Karpik; m. Michael James Moldoch. BS, D'Youville Coll., Buffalo, N.Y., 1970; MS in Edn., SUNY, Buffalo, 1974, cert. in advance studies, 1987. Tchr. 3d grade St. Mary's of the Lake, Hamburg, N.Y., 1963-64; tchr. 3d and 4th grades St. Theresa, Rochester, N.Y., 1964-69; tchr. 1st thru 6th grades Frontier Ctrl. Sch. Dist., Hamburg, 1969-87; adminstr. Kenmore (N.Y.) Union Free Sch. Dist., 1987—, chairperson gifted/talented rev. bd., 1992-94, dist. lang. arts supr., 1994—. Editor newsletter Phi Delta Kappa Common Ground, 1993—. Mem. policy bd. Kenmore Staff Devel. Ctr., 1988—. Mem. Southtowns Tchrs. Ctr. (chairperson 1984, Svc. award 1987), Phi Delta Kappa (rsch. rep. 1988-89, historian 1993—). Home: 1501 Maple Rd Williamsville NY 14221-3646 Office: Kenmore Union Free Sch Dist 199 Thorncliff Rd Buffalo NY 14223

MOLENDA, SANDRA LORRAINE, aviculturist, small business owner; b. San Jose, Calif., Mar. 22, 1960; d. Edmond Anthony and Joan Marie (Ferrarelli) Foglia; m. Robert Wayne Molenda, June 19, 1983. Cert. avian specialist Pet Industry Joint Adv. Coun.; cert. aviculturist Model Aviculture Program. Owner, mgr. The Parrotlet Ranch, Aptos, Calif.; mem. adv. bd. Bird Clubs Am., Yorktown, Va., 1996—. Contbr. articles to profl. publs. Mem. Am. Fedn. Aviculture (del. 1992—), Internat. Aviculturists Soc. (bd. dirs. 1995—), Internat. Parrotlet Soc. (co-founder, sec. 1992—), Soc. Parrot Breeders and Exhibitors, Avicultural Soc. Am., Exotic Bird Breeders Assn. Democrat.

MOLER, ELIZABETH ANNE, federal agency administrator, lawyer; b. Salt Lake City, Jan. 24, 1949; d. Murray McClure and Eleanor Lorraine (Barry) M.; m. Thomas Blake Williams, Oct. 19, 1979; children: Blake Martin Williams, Eleanor Bliss Williams. BA, Am. U., 1971; postgrad., Johns Hopkins U., 1972; JD, George Wash. U., 1977. Bar: D.C. 1978. Chief legis. asst. Senator Floyd Haskell, Washington, 1973-75; law clk. Sharon, Pierson, Semmes, Crolius & Finley, Washington, 1975-76; profl. staff mem. com. on energy and natural resources U.S. Senate, Washington, 1976-77, counsel, 1977-86, sr. counsel, 1987-88; commr. FERC, Washington, 1988-93, chair, 1993—. Mem. ABA, D.C. Bar Assn. Democrat. Home: 1537 Forest Ln Mc Lean VA 22101-3317 Office: FERC Ste 11A 888 First St NE Ste 11A Washington DC 20426

MOLESWORTH, KELLY JEAN, Spanish educator; b. Syracuse, N.Y., Aug. 13, 1969; d. Joseph Lawrence and Barbara Marie (Britten) M. BS, SUNY, Oswego, 1990; MS, SUNY, Cortland, 1992. Cert. elem. edn. tchr., Spanish tchr. Jr. and sr. high Spanish tchr. N. Syracuse (N.Y.) CS, 1992-93, Lowville (N.Y.) Acad. CS, 1993-95; volleyball coach Lowville Acad., 1993-95. Recipient Paul Douglas Teaching scholarship HESC, 1987-91. Mem. N.Y. State Assn. Fgn. Lang. Tchrs., Kappa Delta Pi. Home: 208 Hoover Dr Syracuse NY 13205-3241

MOLINAR, LUPE RODRIQUEZ, librarian, library director; b. Marathon, Tex., June 6, 1942; d. Luciano and Ignacia (Ramirez) Rodriquez; m. Victor O. Molinar, July 29, 1961; 1 child, Lynn Molinar Boutwell. AA, N.Mex. Jr. Coll., 1989. Cert. libr., Tex. Store clk., waitress Big Bend (Tex.) Nat. Pk., 1960-64; cafeteria worker Sul Ross State U., Alpine, Tex., 1964-65; nurse's aide Twilight Acres, Seminole, Tex., 1969-75; circulating clk. Gaines Co. Libr., Seminole, Tex., 1975-76, processing clk., 1976-91, libr., 1991—. Vol. Voters Registration, Seminole, 1980—; chair St. James Fall Festival, Seminole, 1994; bd. trustees Seminole Ind. Sch. Dist., 1994—. Mem. Tex. Libr. Assn., Guadalupanas Soc. (pres. 1988-89). Democrat. Roman Catholic. Home: 400 NW H Seminole TX 79360 Office: Gaines County Libr 704 Hobbs Hwy Seminole TX 79360-3402

MOLINARI, SUSAN, congresswoman; b. S.I., N.Y., Mar. 27, 1958; d. Guy V. and Marguerite (Wing) M.; m. Bill Paxon, 1994. BA, SUNY, Albany, 1980, MA, 1982. Former intern for State Senator Christopher Mega; former rsch. analyst N.Y. State Senate Fin. Com.; former fin. asst. Nat. Rep. Gov.'s Assn.; ethnic community liaison Rep. Nat. Com., 1983-84; minority leader N.Y.C. Council, 1986-90; mem. 101st-104th Congresses from 14th (now 13th) N.Y. dist., 1990—; vice-chair House Rep. Conf., mem. budget com., chmn. transp. and infrastructure subcom. on railroads. Roman Catholic. Office: US Ho of Reps 2435 Rayburn HOB Washington DC 20515

MOLINARO, VALERIE ANN, lawyer; b. N.Y.C, Oct. 21, 1956; d. Albert Anthony and Rosemary Rita (Zito) M.; m. Howard Robert Birnbach; 1 child, Michelle Annalise Birnbach. BA with honors, SUNY, 1978; JD, Syracuse U., 1980, MPA, 1980. Asst. counsel. New York State Housing Finance Agy., N.Y.C., 1980-82; assoc. counsel, asst. secy. N.Y. State Urban Devel. Corp., N.Y.C., 1982-85; assoc. Mudge Rose Guthrie Alexander & Ferdon, N.Y.C., 1985-87, Bower & Gardner, N.Y.C., 1988, Hawkins, Delafield & Wood, N.Y.C., 1988-91; of counsel McKenzie, McGhee & Harper, N.Y.C., 1991—. Author: Am. Bar Assn. Jour., 1981. Mem. N.Y.C. Commn. on Status of Women, 1995—. Mem. N.Y. State Bar Assn., (tax exempt fin. com.), Assn. Bar City of N.Y., Nat. Assn. Bond Lawyers, N.Y.C. Commn. on the Status of Women (legis. chmn.). Office: McKenzie McGhee et al 888 Seventh Ave Ste 1809 New York NY 10019

MOLINE, SANDRA LOIS, librarian; b. San Antonio, Dec. 13, 1938; d. Udo F. and Olivia Marie (Link) Reininger; m. Jon Nelson Moline, Aug. 13, 1960; children: Kevin, Eric. BA in Chemistry, Austin Coll., 1960; postgrad., Duke U., 1962-64; MA in History of Sci., U. Wis., 1976, MLS, 1977. Tchr. chemistry and physics Durham (N.C.) High Sch., 1960-64; head physics libr. U. Wis., Madison, 1977-88; head reference svcs. Sci. and Engring. Libr. U. Minn., Mpls., 1988-94; libr. Reader's Svcs. Libr., Luth. Coll., Seguin, 1994—. Bd. dirs. Mid-Tex. Symphony, 1995—; trustee Seguin-Guadalupe County Pub. Libr., 1996—. Mem. Spl. Librs. Assn. (physics, astronomy, math, sci.-tech. divsns.), Librs. Assembly (sec., treas. 1980, pres. 1983), Madison Acad. Staff Assn. (steering com. 1980-83, pres. 1982). Home: 605 Fleming Dr Seguin TX 78155-3413

MOLINI, BARBARA SYMONDS, elementary educator; b. San Francisco, Dec. 15, 1941; d. Percival Lionel and Margaret Lena (Karsten) S.; children: Jennifer Nicole, Justin Karsten. BA in Elem. Edn. cum laude, San Francisco State U., 1965; postgrad., Calif. State U., Sonoma, U. Calif., Davis, Pepperdine U. Cert. reading specialist, Calif. Tchr. grade 7 Ctrl. Sch., San Carlos, Calif., 1965-70; tchr. grade 6 Burns Valley Sch., Clearlake, Calif., 1971-72; tchr. grades 7-8 Lower Lake (Calif.) Jr. High Sch., 1972-84, Oak Hill Middle Sch., Clearlake, 1984—; tchr. pilot program San Carlos Elem. Sch. dist., Calif., 1968-70; mentor in art Konocti Unified Sch. Dist., Clearlake, 1990-93, cons. program quality rev., 1994; judge Odyssey of the Mind, Calif., 1992-94; mem. numerous adv. coms. Mem. Calif. Tchrs. Assn., NEA, Calif. League Middle Schs., Calif. Art Educators Assn., Calif. Assn. for Gifted, Nat. Coun. Tchrs. English. Office: Oak Hill Middle Sch PO Box 920 Clearlake CA 95422

MOLLER, JACQUELINE LOUISE, elementary education educator; b. Oneida, N.Y., June 21, 1942; d. Charles and Mary Louise (Dunne) M. BS, SUNY, Oswego, 1964. Cert. tchr., N.Y. Tchr. Oneida Sch. Dist., 1964—. Recipient 1st Pl. award WCNY TV, 1993, Outstanding award, 1995, Case award for innovative teaching with telecomm. N.Y. State Pub. TV, 1992, 94; Mid. State Tchrs. Ctr. grantee, 1992, 94, 95. Mem. Oneida Tchrs. Assn. (former sec. 1966-70), Parent-Tchr-Student Assn. (life, sec.), Delta Kappa Gamma (former pres., treas.). Home: 588 Stoneleigh Rd Oneida NY 13421-1814 Office: Willard Prior Elem Sch East Ave Oneida NY 13421

MOLLES, EMILY D., artist, real estate broker; b. Norwalk, Conn., Mar. 20, 1938; d. Frank and Mary Louise (Perriffo) De Martino; m. Eugene Joseph Molles, Dec. 1, 1956 (div. 1976); children: Deborah Lynn Molles Boy'er, Eugene Scott. Student, Sacred Heart U., 1973, U. Conn., 1975; cert. in real estate law, Fairfield U., 1976; BFA, Ringling Sch. Art and Design, 1995. Cert. Nat. Assn. Realtors. Pres. PRM, Inc., Norwalk, 1976—; realtor June Scott's Assocs., Beverly Hills, Calif., 1980-82, Len Hoff Realty, Marina Del Rey, Calif., 1982-84; founder, owner Country Homes, Milford, Conn., 1984-89, Country Homes of Saugatuck Shores, Westport, Conn., 1989-91. Mem. Sarasota Visual Arts Ctr., Nat. Mus. Women in Arts (assoc.). Home: 2425 Gulf of Mexico Dr 2B Sarasota FL 34228

MOLLICK, LINDA SUGERMAN, artist, educator; b. Bklyn., Dec. 10, 1949; d. Lewis and Celia (Gamburg) Sugerman; m. Sheppard B. Mollick, June 26, 1971; children: Ethan, Jordana, Ariel. BS in Edn. cum laude, Temple U., 1971. Coord. ednl. comm. Hempstead (N.Y.) High Sch., 1971-72; tchr. English N.Y.C. Pub. Schs., 1972-74; instr. acrylic painting LaFarge Inst., Milw., 1992—. One person shows include Fishman Gallery, Milw., 1990, 95, Fire Station Gallery, Milw., 1991, West Bank Cafe, Milw., 1993; exhibited in group show at Milw. Art Mus., 1989; represented in permanent archives Nat. Mus. Women in the Arts, Washington. Bd. dirs. Milw. Jewish Coun., 1980; pres. Maple Dale Indian Hill PTO, Milw., 1990; contbg. artist Art for AIDS, Milw., 1991, 92, 93, 94, 95; campaign coord. Com. to elect Mollick Nicolet, Milw., 1991, 96; bd. dirs. Nat. Coun. Jewish Women, Milw., 1992; active cultural arts divsn. Jewish Cmty. Ctr., Milw., 1994—. Recipient Best Thematic Work award Jury Contemporary Wis. Jewish Art, 1992, First Place award Wis. State Fair, 1992; named Baron Mus. Artist, Congregation Emanuel, Milw., 1993. Mem. Wis. Painters and Sculptors (profl.). Jewish. Home: 225 E Ravine Baye Rd Milwaukee WI 53217

MOLNAU, CAROL, state legislator; b. Sept. 17, 1949; m. Steven F. Molnau; 3 children. Attended, U. Minn. Mem. Minn. Ho. of Reps., 1992—. Active Our Saviors Luth. Ch., 4-H, Chaska City Coun. Mem. Agrl. Com., Econ. Devel., Infrastructure & Regulation Fin.-Transportation Fin. Divsn., Fin. Inst. & Ins.: Internat. Trade & Economic Devel. Republican. Home: 495 Pioneer Trl Chaska MN 55318-1151 Office: 287 State Office Bldg Saint Paul MN 55155

MOLTO, LINDA ANNE LORETTA, artist; b. Toronto, Ont., Can., Dec. 13, 1944; came to the U.S., 1965; d. Delmar Joseph and Marjorie Ellen (Howard) M.; m. Walter Rockwood Ferris II, Oct. 31, 1975 (div. 1985). Co-owner Am. Sch. Broadcasting, St. Petersburg, Fla., 1970-72; with advt. agy. Sumner Comm., St. Petersburg, 1972-74; owner advt. agy. Molto-Pifano, St. Petersburg, 1974-76; pvt. practice artist asst. Orlando, Fla., 1976-80; pvt. practice artist, printmaker Cortez, Fla., 1980—; advisor, art festival com. Anna Maria Island Fine Arts Festivals, Holmes Beach, Fla., 1992-95. Exhbns. include Ann Arbor St. Art Fair, Old Town Art Festival, Chgo., Coconut Grove Art Festival, Upham Gallery, St. Petersburg Beach, Fla. Ctr. Contemporary Art, Tampa, U. South Fla. Libr. Sec. Cortez Village Hist. Soc., 1991-95; bd. mem. Tingley Meml. Libr., Bradenton Beach, Fla., 1993-95, Cortez Cmty. Ctr., 1995. Recipient numerous awards including Best of Show/All Media, Englewood (Fla.) Fine Arts Fest, 1995, award of Excellence, Mainsail Art Festival, St. Petersburg, Fla., 1995, award of Distinction, Riverside Art Festival, Jacksonville, 1995. Mem. Anna Maria Island Art League, Manatee County Cultural Alliance. Home: 4519 124 St W Cortez FL 34215

MONACO, PAMELA MARIE, biology educator; b. Bklyn., May 29, 1961; d. Carmine and Mary Monaco; m. Peter Caparelli, Oct. 12, 1991. BS, St. John's Univ., 1982; MD, Universidad del Noreste, Tamalipis, Mex., 1987. Adj. asst. prof. biology St. John's U., Jamaica, N.Y., 1990-91; asst. prof. biology St. John's U., Jamaica, 1991-93; adj. asst. prof. bilogy Molloy Coll., Rockville Ctr., N.Y., 1992-93; asst. prof. biology Molloy Coll., Rockville Ctr., 1993—. Author: Introduction to Biology, 1991; editor (newsletter) IN VIVO, 1995—. Mem. AAUP, Met. Assn. Coll. & Univ. Biologists (bd. mem.), Assn. Women in Sci., Nat. Mus. Women in Art, Chi Beta Phi. Office: Molloy Coll 1000 Hempstead Ave Rockville Centre NY 11570

MONAGHAN, EILEEN, artist; b. Holyoke, Mass., Nov. 22, 1911; d. Thomas F. and Mary (Doona) Monaghan; m. Frederic Whitaker. Student, Mass. Coll. Art. Represented in collections NAD, Okla. Mus. Art, Hispanic Soc., High Mus. Art, Atlanta, Norfolk museums, U. Mass., Springfield (Mass.) Mus. Fine Art, Reading (Pa.) Art Mus., Charles and Emma Frye Art Mus., Seattle, Kans. State U., Wichita, St. Lawrence U., N.Y., NAD, also in numerous pvt. collections, ann. exhbns., nat. and regional watercolor shows; author: Eileen Monaghan Whitaker Paints San Diego, 1986. Recipient Wong award Calif. Watercolor Soc., Ranger Fund purchase Nat. Acad. Design, Allied Artists Am., DeYoung Mus. show award, Soc. Western Artists award, 1st award Springville (Utah) Mus., William P. and Gertrude Schweitzer prize for excellence in a watercolor NAD, 1996, numerous others. Mem. NAD (academician, Obrig prize, Walter Biggs Meml. award), Am. Watercolor Soc. (Silver medal, Dolphin fellow), Watercolor West Soc. (hon.), San Diego Watercolor Soc. (hon.), Providence Watercolor Club (award), Phila. Watercolor Club. Address: 1579 Alta La Jolla Dr La Jolla CA 92037-7101

MONAHAN, MARIE TERRY, lawyer; b. Milford, Mass., June 26, 1927; d. Francis V. and Marie I. (Casey) Terry; m. John Henry Monahan, Aug. 25, 1951; children: Thomas F., Kathleen J., Patricia M., John Terry, Moira M., Deirdre M. AB, Radcliffe Coll., 1949; JD, New Eng. Sch. Law, 1975. Bar: Mass. 1977, U.S. Dist. Ct. Mass. 1978, U.S. Supreme Ct. 1982. Tchr. French and Spanish Holliston (Mass.) High Sch., 1949-52; pvt. practice Newton, Mass., 1977—. Mem. Mass. Assn. Women Lawyers (pres. 1986). Home and Office: 34 Foster St Newton MA 02160-1511

MONCADA, L. PATRICIA, computer company executive. Sr. corp. counsel, asst. sec. Oracle Corp., Redwood City, Calif. Office: Oracle Corp Box 659507 500 Oracle Pkwy Redwood City CA 94065*

MONCHARSH, JANE KLINE, rehabilitation counselor, vocational specialist, mediator; b. Boston, Jan. 15, 1943; d. Paul Kline and Helen (Chartoff) Kline-Gray; m. Philip C. Moncharsh, Dec. 12, 1965; children: Peretz, Mariasha, Yona, Shira. Student, U. Mass., 1960-62; BA, Boston U., 1965. Cert. rehab. counselor and cons., vocat. expert, case mgr. Rsch. asst. Mass. Mental Health Ctr., Harvard U., Bostn, 1964-65; vocat. evaluator Opportunity Workshop, Mpls., 1965-66, sr. vocat. evaluator, 1966-67, rehab. counselor, 1967-71; vocat. expert Social Security Adminstrn. and R.R. disability hearings, third party and div. litigation HHS, Mpls., 1971—; rehab. counselor and cons., Mpls., 1971—; instr. Minn. Inst. Legal Edn., Mpls., 1991, 92; interviewer Boston U., 1989—. Bd. dirs. Mpls. Fedn., 1989-90; mem. adv. com., bd. dirs. Mpls. Jewish Family and Children Svcs., 1990-94. Mem. AACD, Nat. Assn. Rehab. Providers, Minn. Assn. for Counseling and Devel., Am. Counseling Assn., Assn. for Assessments in Counseling, Nat. Career Devel. Assn., Nat. Disting. Registry (Libr. Cong.), Med. and Vocat. Rehab., Psi Chi. Office: 1433 Utica Ave S Ste 57 Minneapolis MN 55416-3849

MONCRIEF, MARY KATHRYN, rehabilitation counselor; b. Houston, Aug. 10, 1955; d. Malcolm Joseph and Dorothy Earlene (King) LeGrande; m. Theodore James Moncrief, Dec. 19, 1987; children: Barry Lee, Anthony Theodore, Mark, Patricia Ann. BS, Sam Houston State U., 1977; cert., Inst. Child Lit., 1988; postgrad., San Jacinto Coll., 1993. Cert. elem. tchr., Tex.; lic., 1996. Med. records Green Acres Convalescent Home, Huntsville, Tex., 1979-80, 81-82; tchr. Magnolia (Tex.) High Sch., 1980-81; sec. Harris Engring., Huntsville, 1982-83; artist M&M Design, Huntsville, 1983-84; fin. sec. First United Meth. Ch., Huntsville, 1984-87, nursery sch. coord., 1986-87; contractor Tex. Rehabilitation Commn., Huntsville, 1986-87, Pasadena, Tex., 1990-92; counselor Houston Substance Abuse Clinic, Pasadena and Houston, 1992-93, Lake Charles Substance Abuse Clinic, 1992-93; adminstr. Johnson Glass & Mirror, Pasadena, 1993-96; contractor Tex. Rehab. Commn., Pasadena, 1996—. Author poetry, 1985. Ballot counter Voting Polling places, Huntsville, 1977, 78, 79. Recipient Lady Kentiggerma Soc. Creative Anachronism, 1986, Sable Comet, 1986. Mem. NAFE. Republican.

MONDA, MARILYN, quality improvement consultant; b. Paterson, N.J., Aug. 11, 1956; d. Thomas John and Lydia Mary (Dal Santo) M.; m. Lawrence G. Gifford, Jr., Aug. 25, 1984. BA, San Diego State U., 1980; MA, Baylor U., 1984. Math. statistician Navy Personnel Rsch. and Devel. Ctr., San Diego, 1984-86; quality engr. Info. Magnetics, Inc., San Diego, 1986-87; mgmt. cons. Process Mgmt. Inst., Inc., Mpls., 1987-89; staff assoc. Luftig & Assocs., Inc., Detroit, 1989-92; founder Quality Disciplines, San Diego, 1992—; bd. dirs. Deming Users Group, San Diego, 1985-87; lecturer in the field. Contbr. articles to profl. jours. Mem. San Diego Deming Users Group, Am. Soc. Quality Consultants, Am. Statistical Assn., Phi Beta Kappa.

MONDALE, JOAN ADAMS, wife of former vice president of U.S.; b. Eugene, Oreg., Aug. 8, 1930; d. John Maxwell and Eleanor Jane (Hall) Adams; m. Walter F. Mondale, Dec. 27, 1955; children—Theodore, Eleanor Jane, William Hall. BA, Macalester Coll., 1952. Asst. slide librarian Boston Mus. Fine Arts, 1952-53; asst. in edn. Mpls. Inst. of Arts, 1953-57; weekly tour guide Nat. Gallery of Art, Washington, 1965-74; hostess Washington Whirl-A-Round, 1975-76. Author: Politics in Art, 1972. Mem. bd. govs. Women's Nat. Dem. Club; hon. chmn. Fed. Coun. on Arts and Humanities, 1978-80; bd. dirs. Associated Coun. of Arts, 1973-75, Reading Is Fundamental, Am. Craft Coun., N.Y.C., 1981-88, J.F.K. Center Performing Arts, 1981-90, Walker Art Ctr., Mpls., 1987-93, Minn. Orch., Mpls., 1988-93, St. Paul Chamber Orch., 1988-90, Northern Clay Ctr., 1988-93, St. Paul, 1988-93, Nancy Hauser Dance Co., Mpls., 1989-93, Minn. Landmarks, 1991-93; trustee Macalester Coll., 1986—. Presbyterian. Office: Unit 45004 Box 200 APO AP 96337-5004

MONDAY, DELORES FAYE, operating room staff nurse; b. Mt. Ayr, Iowa, July 6, 1961; d. James Andrew and Marilyn (Olney) M. BSN, William Jewell Coll., 1983. RN, Hawaii; cert. BLS, ACLS, operating rm. nurse. Operating rm. staff nurse Med. Ctr. of Independence, Mo., 1983-88; staff nurse oper. room Kuakini Med. Ctr., Honolulu, 1988-93, staff nurse oper. room open heart team, 1988-89; pvt. scrub nurse Dr. Harvey S. Takaki, Honolulu, 1988-92; operating rm. staff nurse evening charge Pali Momi Med. Ctr., Aiea, Hawaii, 1992-94; staff nurse oper. room, nurse 1st asst. Kapiolani Med. Ctr. at Pali Momi, Aiea, Hawaii, 1994—. Named Outstanding Patient Care Svc. Employee for Oper. Room, Kapiolani Med. Ctr. at Pali Momi, 1995. Mem. ANA, RNFA (mem. special assembly), Assn. Operating Rm. Nurses. Home: 99-801 Aumakiki Loop Aiea HI 96701 Office: Kapiolani Med Ctr at Pali Momi 98-1079 Moanalua Rd Aiea HI 96701-4713

MONDY, LINDA M., elementary school counselor, librarian; b. Houston, Mo., Apr. 23, 1958; d. Charles Louis and Hazel Leona (Wallace) Vestal; m. Kerry Layne Mondy, Dec. 22, 1990. BS Edn., Southwest Mo. State U., 1980, MS in Guidance Counseling, 1991. Cert. English tchr., 7-12, libr. K-12, elem. edn. K-8, counseling K-12. Asst. libr. Southwest Mo. State U. Collection Mgmt. Office, Springfield, 1979-80; tchr. lang. arts Phelps County R-3 Sch., Edgar Springs, Mo., 1980-94, guidance counselor, 1994—; coord. Phelps County R-3 Guidance and Counseling Adv. Bd., Edgar Sprngs, 1993-95. Mem. Phelps County Mental Health Coalition, Mo. Sch. Counselors Assn., Nat. Coun. Tchrs. English, Kappa Delta Pi, Sigma Tau Delta. Democrat. Mem. Assembly of God. Home: 15395 Slab Springs Dr Licking MO 65542 Office: Phelps Co R-3 17790 State Rt M Edgar Springs MO 65462

MONEK, DONNA MARIE, pharmacist; b. New Brunswick, N.J., Aug. 9, 1947; d. James Frank and Angeline Eleanor (Marzella) M. BS, Phila. Coll. of Pharmacy, 1970; MBA, Fairleigh Dickinson U., East Rutherford, N.J., 1976. Reg. pharmacist, N.J. Staff pharmacist Freehold (N.J.) Area Hosp., 1971-72, dir. pharmacy, 1972-76; dir. pharmacy Rahway (N.J.) Hosp., 1976—; cons. home health care intravenous therapy, Rahway, N.J., 1985. Rep. committeewoman Middlesex County, 1972-86, 92—; mem. Bd. Health, Metuchen, N.J., 1987—. Mem. Am. Soc. Hosp. Pharmacists, N.J. Soc. Hosp. Pharmacists, N.J. Hosp. Assn. (group purchasing 1980, chairperson profl. stds. 1989-90, vice chairperson state pharmacy com. 1990-91, chairperson 1992), Am. Pharm. Assn., N.J. Pharm. Assn., Metuchen Rep. Club, Cranford Dramatic Club, Kappa Epsilon. Roman Catholic. Office: Rahway Hosp 865 Stone St Rahway NJ 07065-2797

MONETA, DANIELA PATRICIA, librarian, archivist; b. Santa Monica, Calif., Dec. 12, 1941; d. Gerald Dean and Elizabeth Elena (Phy) Pugh; 1 child, Howard Cristiano. BFA, UCLA, 1964, M Libr. and Info. Sci., 1980. Freelance artist L.A., 1964-67; paper restorer Com. to Rescue Italian Art, Florence, 1967-69; freelance book conservator Italy and U.S., 1969-78; head libr. S.W. Mus. Libr., L.A., 1982-89; archivist Subud Archives Internat., Jakarta, Indonesia, 1989-94; cataloger Ariz. newspaper project Ariz. State Libr., Phoenix, 1995-96, head collection devel., 1996—. Author: Charles F.

Lummis, 1985; contbr. articles to profl. publs. Mem. Family History Soc. Ariz., Upper Cumberland Geneal. Soc., Tenn. Geneal. Soc., Cumberland County Hist. Soc., Owen County History and Geneal. Soc.

MONEY, RUTH ROWNTREE, child development specialist, consultant; b. Brownwood, Tex.; m. Lloyd Jean Money; children: Jeffrey, Meredith, Jeannette. BA in Biology, Rice U., 1944; MA in Devel. Psychology, Calif. State U., Long Beach, 1971; BA in Early Childhood Edn., U. D.C., 1979. Rsch. psychologist Early Edn. Project, Capitol Heights, Md., 1971-73; lectr. No. Va. C.C., Anandale, 1973-74; tchr. preschs. Calif. and Va., 1979-81; dir. various preschs., Washington and Va., 1981-85; instr. guided studies Pacific Oaks Coll., Pasadena, Calif., 1986-88; cons. parent/infant programs Resources for Infant Educarers, L.A., 1986—; founder, dir. South Bay Infant Ctr., Redondo Beach, Calif., 1988-92; instr. child devel. Harbor Coll., L.A., 1992-93; bd. dirs. Resources for Infant Educarers, 1986—; pres. bd. dirs. South Bay Infant Ctr., Redondo Beach, 1988-94, treas., 1994—. Producer (ednl. videos) Caring for Infants, 1988—. Mem. League of Women Voters, 1956—, v.p., 1972-76. Mem. Nat. Assn. for Edn. of Young Children, Assn. for Childhood Edn. Internat. Home: 904 21st St Hermosa Beach CA 90254-3105 Office: Resources for Infant Educarers 1550 Murray Cir Los Angeles CA 90026-1644

MONFERRATO, ANGELA MARIA, entrepreneur, investor, writer, designer; b. Wissembourg, Alsace-Loraine, France, July 19, 1948; came to U.S., 1950; d. Albert Carmen and Anna Maria (Vieri) M. Diplomate, Pensionnat Florissant, Lausanne, Switzerland, 1966-67; BS in Consumer Related Studies, Mktg., Pa. State U., 1971, postgrad. in speech and comms., 1971-72. Simultaneous translator fgn. langs. Inst. for Achievement of Human Potential, Phila., 1976-78; art dir. The Artworks, Sumneytown, Pa., 1975-76; asst. productionist Film Space, State College, Pa., 1976; real property mgr. Pla. 15 Condominium, Ft. Lauderdale, Fla., 1979-80; legal asst. Ft. Lauderdale, Fla., 1981-85; owner Rising Sun the Real Estate Corp. South Fla., Ft. Lauderdale, 1986—; pres. Kideos Video Prodns., 1985—; designer Colo. Remodel & Design, 1988-92; owner, designer Monferrato Designs, 1993-95. Office: Monferrato Designs Telluride 200 Front St Placerville CO 81430

MONFILS-CLARK, MAUD ELLEN, analyst; b. Amstelveen, The Netherlands, June 7, 1955; d. Wouter William Frederic and Jeane Albertina (Verbauwen) Monfils; m. Harry Carl Clark, Nov. 26, 1983 (div. 1993). BSBA, Calif. State U., L.A., 1990. Physicians assocs. mgr. L.A. County Health Dept., L.A., 1990-92, fin. mgr., 1992-93, health planning analyst, 1993-95; contract officer Gen. Relief Health Care Program, 1995—; active Comm. Strategy Group, L.A., 1994—, Workforce Devel., L.A., 1994—; mem. staff Stragetic Planning Leadership Team, L.A., 1994—, High Desert Hosp. Strategic Planning Com., L.A., 1994—. Co-recipient Nat. Assn. Counties award, 1994, Pub. Svc. Excellence award, 1994.

MONGAN, AGNES, museum curator, art historian, educator; b. Somerville, Mass., 1905. B.A., Bryn Mawr Coll., 1927; spl. student, Fogg Mus., Harvard U., 1928-29; A.M., Smith Coll., 1929, L.H.D. (hon.), 1941; Litt.D. (hon.), Wheaton Coll., 1954; L.H.D. (hon.), U. Mass., 1970; D.F.A. (hon.), LaSalle Coll., 1973, Colby Coll., 1973, U. Notre Dame, 1980, Boston Coll., 1985. Research asst. Fogg Mus., Harvard U., Cambridge, Mass., 1929-37; keeper of drawings Fogg Mus., Harvard U., 1937-47, curator of drawings, 1974-75, asst. dir., 1951-64, assoc. dir., 1964-68, acting dir., 1968-69, dir., 1969-71, cons., 1972—; Martin A. Ryerson lectr. fine arts Harvard U., 1960-75; vis. dir. Timken Art Gallery, San Diego, 1971-72; Kreeger-Wolf disting. vis. prof. Northwestern U., 1976; Bingham vis. prof. U. Louisville, 1976; Waggoner vis. prof. U. Tex., Austin, 1977, vis. prof. fine arts, 1981; Samuel H. Kress prof.-in-residence Nat. Gallery Art, Washington, 1977-78; vis. prof. fine arts U. Calif.-Santa Barbara, 1979; vis. dir. Met. Mus. and Arts Ctrs., Coral Gables, Fla., 1980; Brazilian Govt. lectr., 1954; Amy Sackler Meml. lectr. Mt. Holyoke Coll., 1966-67; vis. prof. fine arts U. Tex. Austin, 1981; Baldwin lectr. Oberlin Coll., 1966; lectr. throughout U.S., Can., Japan; organized numerous exhbns.; leader, lectr. yearly tours Europe to Friends of the Fogg groups. Former mem. editorial bd. Art Bull.; mem. adv. bd. Arte Veneta, Venice; editor: Heart of Spain (Georgiana Goddard King), 1941; One Hundred Master Drawings, 1949; contbr. to exhbn. and catalogue In Pursuit of Perfection: The Art of J.-A.-D.-Ingres, 1983; contbr. catalogue In Quest of Excellence, 1983; intro. to catalogue The Fine Line, 1985, exhbn. catalogue Ingres and Delacroix, Germany and Belgium, 1986; contbr. Silverpoint Drawings in the Fogg Art Museum, 1987, Some Brief Comments on Left-Handedness for Fogg Old Master Drawings Symposium, 1987; contbr. to books in field. Trustee, mem. corp. Inst. Contemporary Art, Boston, 1940-60; a founder, v.p. Pan-Am. Soc. New Eng., 1940-62; mem. U.S. Nat. Commn. for UNESCO, 1954-57, White House Com. for Edn. in Age of Sci., 1961; trustee Chaplebrook Found.; mem. vis. com. art dept. Wheaton Coll., 1961-68; mem. vis. com. to Art Mus., Smith Coll., to 1970; mem. council for arts MIT; mem. adv. bd. Skowhegan Sch. Painting and Sculpture, 1974—; mem. exec. com. Save Venice, Council for Villa I Tatti; mem. vis. com. dept. textiles Boston Mus. Fine Arts; bd. dirs. Brit. Inst.; mem. exec. com. Somerville Hist. Soc.; vice chmn. Com. for Restoration of Italian Art. Decorated Palms d'Academie (France), cavaliere ufficiale (Italy); recipient Julius Stratton award Friends of Switzerland, 1978, Signet Soc. Medal for Achievement in the Arts Harvard U., 1986, 350th Harvard medal for Extraordinary Service, 1986, Benemerenti medal Vatican, 1987; honored by Women's Caucus for the Arts, 1987; Benjamin Franklin fellow Royal Acad. Art; Inst. Internat. Edn. grantee, 1935; Fulbright scholar, 1950. Fellow Am. Acad. Arts and Scis.; mem. Coll. Art Assn. (bd. dirs. 1949-54), Am. Assn. Art Mus. Dirs. (assoc.), Academie de Montauban, Phi Beta Kappa (hon.). Office: Fogg Museum Harvard U Art Museums Cambridge MA 02138

MONGOLD, CHERYL ANN, elementary education educator; b. Jamestown, Ohio, Dec. 25, 1948; d. H. Andrew and Janet Bernice (Rulon) Cluxton; m. Robert Leslie Mongold, June 20, 1970; 1 child, R. Ashley. BS, Wilmington (Ohio) Coll., 1973; MS, U. Dayton, 1980. Tchr. phys. edn. Greenfield (Ohio) Exemped Village Sch., 1970-74; tchr. K-8 East Clinton Schs., New Vienna, Ohio, 1977—. Clk.-treas. Village of New Vienna, 1991—. Martha Holden Jennings scholar, 1983-84. Mem. Phi Delta Kappa (v.p. membership 1984). Home: 113 W Church St # 119 New Vienna OH 45159-9671 Office: New Vienna Elem Sch 204 S 2nd St New Vienna OH 45159-9306

MONGOLD, SANDRA K., corporate executive; b. Springfield, Ohio, Aug. 14, 1947; d. Robert Harold and Norma Jean (Fennessy) Rine; m. Alan Darrell Mabry, Aug. 18, 1968 (div. 1977); m. Danny Willard Mongold, Nov. 16, 1979; children: Brian Alan Mabry, Krista Marie Mabry. Student, Wright State U., Urbana Coll., So. State Coll., Ohio. Acctg. clk. Irwin Co. (now Am. Tool Cos., Inc.), Wilmington, Ohio, 1968-80, asst. treas., 1980-85, treas., 1985-94, new product com., 1985-93, corporate dir. tng. and devel., 1994—. Mem. adv. bd. So. State Coll.; elected to Wilmington City Coun., 1991—; mem. bus. adv. coun. Wilmington City Schs.; mem. Regional Planning Commn. Mem. NAFE, Nat. Assn. Accts., Am. Mgmt. Assn., Nat. Corp. Cash Mgmt. Assn., Wilmington C. of C. (dir., bd. dirs., treas. 1990, pres. 1991), Wilmington 2001 Com. (bd. dirs. 1992), Clinton County Women's Rep. Club. Republican. Presbyterian. Avocations: golf, bowling. Home: 330 Washington Ave Wilmington OH 45177-1132 Office: Am Tool Cos Inc 92 Grant St Wilmington OH 45177-2324

MONIA, JOAN, management consultant; b. Teaneck, N.J., Mar. 20, 1938; d. James Anthony and Anne Linden (Cairns) McCaffrey; m. Charles Anthony Monia, Dec. 30, 1961; 1 child, Clare Ann Woodman. BA, Ohio Dominican U., 1960. Info. specialist Battelle Meml. Inst., Columbus, Ohio, 1960-62; project leader Douglas Aircraft Corp., Huntington Beach, Calif., 1962-64; programmer analyst McDonnell Aircraft Corp., St. Louis, 1965-66; project mgr. Sanders Assocs., Nashua, N.H., 1968-70; database adminstrn. project leader Mass. Blue Cross, Boston, 1970-74; data strategist Factory Mut. Engring. Corp., Norwood, Mass., 1974-78; mgr. data resource planning Digital Equipment Corp., Maynard, Mass., 1978-84; sr. mem. tech. staff GTE Govt. Systems Corp., Needham, Mass., 1984-91; prin. DMR Group, Inc., Waltham, Mass., 1991—. Recipient Sci. medal Bausch & Lomb, 1956. Home: 175 Anderson Rd Marlborough MA 01752-1474 Office: DMR Group Inc 404 Wyman St Waltham MA 02154-1264

MONK, DEBRA, actress. Stage appearances include (Broadway) Company, Nick & Nora, Prelude to a Kiss, Pump Boys and Dinettes (also co-author), Redwood Curtain (Tony award featured actress in play 1993), Picnic (Tony nomination featured actress 1994), (off-Broadway) Death Defying Acts, 3 Hotels (Helen Hayes award leading actress 1994), Assassins, Man in His Underwear, The Innocent's Crusade, Molieère in Spite of Himself, Oil City Symphony (co-author, Drama Desk award Best Ensemble 1988); TV appearances include NYPD Blue, Women and Wallace, The Becky Bell Story, Law and Order, Redwood Curtain; film appearances include Mrs. Winterbourne, 1996, Substance of Fire, 1996, Prelude to a Kiss, for Love or Money, 1993, Fearless, 1993, Quiz Show, 1993, Jeffery, 1994, The Bridges of Madison County, 1994, Bed of Roses, 1996, Reckless, 1995. Office: Gage Group 315 W 57th St Apt 4H New York NY 10019-3147

MONK, DIANA CHARLA, artist, stable owner; b. Visalia, Calif., Feb. 25, 1927; d. Charles Edward and Viola Genevieve (Shea) Williams; m. James Alfred Monk, Aug. 11, 1951; children: Kiloran, Sydney, Geoffrey, Anne, Eric. Student, U. Pacific, 1946-47, Sacramento Coll., 1947-48, Calif. Coll. Fine Arts, San Francisco, 1948-51, Calif. Coll. Arts & Crafts, Oakland, 1972. Art tchr. Mt. Diablo Sch. Dist., Concord, Calif., 1958-63; pvt. art tchr. Lafayette, Calif., 1963-70; gallery dir. Jason Aver Gallery, San Francisco, 1970-72; owner, mgr. Monk & Lee Assocs., Lafayette, 1973-80; stable owner, mgr. Longacre Tng. Stables, Santa Rosa, Calif., 1989—. One-person shows include John F. Kennedy U., Orinda, Calif., Civic Arts Gallery, Walnut Creek, Calif., Vallery Art Gallery, Walnut Creek, Sea Ranch Gallery, Gualala, Calif., Jason Aver Gallery, San Francisco; exhibited in group shows at Oakland (Calif.) Art Mus., Crocker Nat. Art Gallery, Sacramento, Le Salon des Nations, Paris. Chair bd. dirs. Walnut Creek (Calif.) Civic Arts, 1972-74, advisor to dir., 1968-72; exhibit chmn. Valley Art Gallery, Walnut Creek, 1977-78; juror Women's Art Show, Walnut Creek, 1970, Oakland Calif. Art. Home and Office: Longacre Tng Stables 1702 Willowside Rd Santa Rosa CA 95401-3922

MONK, MEREDITH JANE, artistic director, composer, choreographer, film maker, director; b. N.Y.C., Nov. 20, 1942; d. Theodore G. and Audrey Lois (Zellman) M. BA, Sarah Lawrence Coll., 1964; ArtsD (hon.), Bard Coll., 1988, U. of the Arts, 1989. Artistic dir., founder House Found. for Arts, N.Y.C., 1968—. Prin. works include Vessel, 1971, Quarry, 1976, Turtle Dreams, 1983, Recent Ruins, 1979, The Games, 1983, Book of Days, 1988, Facing North, 1990, Atlas, 1991, Three Heavens and Hells, 1992, Volcano Songs, 1994, American Archeology, 1994. Guggenheim fellow, 1972, 86, Norton Stevens fellow, 1993-94; Recipient Obie award Village Voice, 1972, 76, 85, Creative Arts award Brendeis U., 1974, Deitches Kritiker Preis for best record, 1981, 86, Bessie award N.Y. Dance and Performance awards, 1985, Nat. Music Theatre award, 1986, Dance Mag. award, 1992, John D. and Catherine T. MacArthur award, 1995, 1st Sarah Lawrence Alumna Achievement award, 1995, Samuel Scripps award, 1996. Fellow MacDowell Colony (Sigma Phi Omega award 1987); mem. ASCAP. Office: House Found for Arts 131 Varick St New York NY 10013-1410

MONK, SUSAN MARIE, physician, pediatrician; b. York, Pa., May 7, 1945; d. John Spotz and Mary Elizabeth (Shelly) M.; m. Jaime Pacheco, June 5, 1971; children: Benjamin Joaquin, Maria Cristina. AB, Colby Coll., 1967; MD, Jefferson Med. Coll., 1971. Diplomate Am. Bd. Pediatrics. Pediatrician Children's Med. Ctr., Dayton, Ohio, 1975—; assoc. clin. prof. pediatrics Wright State U., Dayton. Mem. bd. dirs. Children's Med. Ctr., Dayton, 1991-96, chief-of-staff, 1992-94. Mem. Am. Acad. Pediatrics, We. Ohio Pediatric Soc., Pediatric Ambulatory Care Soc. Office: Childrens Health Clinic 536 Valley St Dayton OH 45404-1845

MONKS, LINDA ANN, art educator; b. Montclair, N.J., Aug. 28, 1949; d. Charles and Lillian Bieksha; m. Robert Norman Monks, Apr. 17, 1971; children: Alyson, Shelly, Clayton. BFA, Montclair State Coll., 1972; MAT, Montclair State U., 1996. Subsitute tchr. Byram Bd. of Edn., 1980; driver Frank L. Black, Inc., Andover, N.J., 1985-90; tech. asst. Montclair State Coll., Upper Montclair, N.J., 1993-94; substitute tchr. Hopatcong (N.J.) Bd. Edn., 1995, Lenape Valley Regional H.S., Stanhope, N.J., 1990-95; art instr. Lakeview Learning Ctr., Wayne, N.J., 1995-96, Future Kids, Cresskill, N.J., 1996—; steering com. Crayola Dream-Makers, Upper Montclair, N.J., 1993; treas. Montclair State Art Educators, Upper Montclair, 1993; pub. rels. rep. Children With Attention Deficit Disorders, Newton, N.J., 1988. Pres. Cranberry Lake Fire Dept. Women's Aux., Byram, 1987-94, treas., mem. Recipient Merit scholarship State of N.J., 1967. Mem. Nat. Art Edn. Assn., N.J. Art Edn. Assn., Phi Kappa Phi, Kappa Delta Pi. Home: 22 Laurel Trail Andover NJ 07821-3611

MONROE, BETTY ROSE, costume designer, educator; b. Pensacola, Fla.; m. G. Ervin Monroe (div. 1981); children: David C., Kevin, Lonn, Brittian. BFA, Wayne State U., 1983; MFA, Mich. State U., 1987. Costume designer Boarshead Theater, Lansing, Mich., 1987; asst. prof., costume designer Oakland U., Rochester, Mich., 1989-91, Wichita (Kans.) State U., 1991—. Mem. Am. Coll. Theater Festival, U.S. Inst. Theatre Tech. Office: Wichita State U Sch Performing Arts Wichita KS 67208-1595

MONROE, LEONORA, surgeon; b. Hazleton, Pa., Apr. 11, 1940; d. James and Ruth (Cuozzo) M.; 1 child, Franc. RN, U. Pa., 1960, BA, 1973; MD, Med. Coll. Pa., 1980. Bd. cert. in surgery Am. Bd. Surgery. Head nurse oper. rm. Columbia Presbyn. Hosp., N.Y.C., 1960-62; head nurse med.-surg. U. Pa. Grad. Hosp., Phila., 1963-68, head nurse emergency rm., 1972-75; head nurse labor and delivery Pa. Hosp., Phila., 1968-72; surg. resident Hahnemann U. Hosp., Phila., 1980-83, Polyclinic Med. Ctr., Harrisburg, Pa., 1983-86; attending surgeon Guiffré Med. Ctr., Phila., 1986-88; attending surgeon, instr. surgery Wyckoff Heights Med. Ctr., Bklyn., 1990—; oper. rm. com. Wyckoff Heights Med. Ctr., Bklyn., 1992-96, med. records com., 1994-96, autopsy com., 1996. Mem. Am. Soc. Gen. Surgeons, Soc. Laparoendoscopic Surgeons, Womens Med. Soc. N.Y.C., Am. Coll. Surgeons. Office: Family Health Ctr Ridgewood 68-52 Fresh Pond Rd Ridgewood NY 11385

MONROE, LINDA SUE, newspaper editor; b. Elwood, Ind., Sept. 6, 1954; d. George M. and Helen L. (Palmer) M.; m. Jon R. Talton, Apr. 16, 1988 (div. 1993). BS, Ball State U., 1975; postgrad., Dayton Art Inst., 1988, Poynter Inst., 1990. Reporter, editor Nixon Newspapers, Wabash, Ind., 1975-76; asst. news editor Richmond (Ind.) Palladium-Item, 1976-83; graphics editor Dayton (Ohio) Daily News, 1983-93; asst. mng. editor Courier-News, Bridgewater, N.J., 1993—; prin. Phoenix Designs, High Bridge, N.J., 1994—. Project coord. Lives on the Line Dayton Daily News, 1992. Hist. preservationist Neighborhood Preservation Svcs., Richmond, 1978-80. Recipient Best Newspaper award N.J. Press Assn., 1994-96; Indpls. Press Club scholar, 1974, Ball State U. scholar, 1972-73, Demotte scholar. Mem. Soc. Newspaper Design (bd. dirs. 1996—, editor SND Update 1993-95, Pres. award 1995). Office: Courier-News 1201 Rte 22 W Bridgewater NJ 08807

MONROE, MELROSE, retired banker; b. Flowery Branch, Ga., Apr. 13, 1919; d. Willis Jeptha and Leila Adell Cash; m. Lynn Austin, June 14, 1942. AB in Edn., Ga. State U., 1968. Negotiator Trust Co. Bank, Atlanta, 1962-89, ret., 1989. Mem. Nat. Women's C. of C. (pres. 1987-88), Atlanta Women's C. of C. (dir. 1965-66, pres. Fidelis SS class 1962-63), Am. Legion Aux. (pres. 5th dist. 1986-87, Ga. state chaplain 1989-90, state historian 1991-92, state 2d v.p. 1992-93, 1st v.p. 1993-94, pres. 1994-95), Order of Ea. Star (worthy matron 1951-52). Democrat. Home and Office: 6243 Spout Springs Rd Flowery Branch GA 30542-5032

MONROE, PAULA RUTH, psychologist; b. Worcester, Mass., Dec. 23, 1951; d. Dudley Benson and Gladys Elinor (Norbery) Sherry; m. David Michael Monroe, Feb. 19, 1977; 1 child, Allison. BA, U. North Tex., 1974; MA, U. Tulsa, 1980, PhD, 1990. Lic. psychologist, Okla. Asst. dean Coll. Arts and Scis. U. Tulsa, 1983-85; staff psychologist, mgr. psychol. testing ctr. Children's Med. Ctr., Tulsa, 1990-95; pvt. practice Psychosocial Enhancement Svcs., Inc., Tulsa, 1995—. Contbr. articles to profl. jours. Mem. APA.

MONROY, GLADYS H., lawyer; b. N.Y., Aug. 29, 1937; d. Henry B. and Leonora E. (Low) Chu; m. Jaime L. G. Monroy (div.); m. C. Lawrence Marks, Nov. 29, 1980. BA, Hunter Coll., N.Y., 1957; MS, NYU, 1968, PhD, 1973; JD, U. San Francisco, 1986. Bar: Calif. Lab. technician Sloan-Kettering Inst., N.Y., 1957-60; lab. technician Pub. Health Rsch. Inst., N.Y., 1960-63, rsch. asst., 1963-68; post doctoral fellow Albert Einstein Coll. Medicine, Bronx, N.Y., 1973-77; asst. prof. N.Y. Med. Coll., Valhalla, 1977-79; acquisitions editor Acad. Press, Inc., 1979-81; reseach assoc. U. Calif., San Francisco, 1981-83; atty. Irell & Manella, Menlo Park, Calif., 1986-90, ptnr., 1990-91; ptnr. Morrison & Foerster, Palo Alto, Calif., 1991—. Contbr. articles to profl. jours. Mem. bd. dirs. Project Hogar De Los Ninos, Menlo Park, Calif., 1987, mem. Profl. Women's Network, San Francisco, 1988—; mem. bd. dirs. Child Advocates of Santa Clara and San Mateo Counties, 1995—. Mem. ABA, Am. Intellectual Property Law Assn., Am. Soc. Human Genetics, Am. Chem. Soc., Calif. Bar Assn., San Francisco Intellectual Property Law Assn. (chair patent com. 1992-94), Peninsula Patent Law Assn. (program chair 1993-94, treas. 1994-95), Am. Soc. Microbiology, Phi Alpha Delta. Office: Morrison & Foerster 755 Page Mill Rd Palo Alto CA 94304-1018

MONSEN, ELAINE RANKER, nutritionist, educator, editor; b. Oakland, Calif., June 6, 1935; d. Emery R. and Irene Stewart (Thorley) Ranker; m. Raymond Joseph Monsen, Jr., Jan. 21, 1959; 1 dau., Maren Ranker. B.A., U. Utah, 1956; M.S. (Mead Johnson grad. scholar), U. Calif., Berkeley, 1959, Ph.D. (NSF fellow), 1961; postgrad. NSF sci. faculty fellow, Harvard U., 1968-69. Dietetic intern Mass. Gen. Hosp., Boston, 1956-57; asst. prof. nutrition, lectr. biochemistry Brigham Young U., Provo, Utah, 1960-63; mem. faculty U. Wash., 1963—, prof. nutrition and medicine, 1984—, prof. nutrition, adj. prof. medicine, 1976-84, chmn. div. human nutrition, dietetics and foods, 1977-82, dir. grad. nutritional scis. program, 1994—, mem. Council of Coll. Arts and Scis., 1974-78, mem. U. Wash. Press com., 1981—; chmn. Nutrition Studies Commn., 1969-83; vis. scholar Stanford U., 1971-72; mem. sci. adv. com. food fortification Pan-Am. Health Orgn., São Paulo, Brazil, 1972; tng. grant coordinator NIH, 1976—. Editor Jour. Am. Dietetic Assn., 1983—; mem. editorial bd. Coun. Biology Editors, 1992-96; author research papers on lipid metabolism, iron absorption. Bd. dirs. A Contemporary Theatre, Seattle, 1969-72; trustee, bd. dirs. Seattle Found., 1978-95, vice chmn., 1987-91, chmn., 1991-93; pres. Seattle bd. Santa Fe Chamber Music Festival, 1984-85; mem. Puget Sound Blood Ctr. Bd., 1996—. Grantee Nutrition Found., 1965-68, Agrl. Rsch. Svc., 1969—; recipient Disting. Alumnus award U. Utah, F. Fischer Meml. Nutrition Lectr. award, 1988, L.F. Cooper Meml. Lectr. award, 1991, L. Hatch Meml. Lectr. award, 1992. Mem. Am. Inst. Nutrition, Am. Soc. Clin. Nutrition (sec. 1987-90), Am. Dietetic Assn., Soc. Nutrition Edn., Am. Soc. Parenteral and Enteral Nutrition, Wash. Heart Assn. (nutrition council 1973-76), Phi Beta Kappa, Phi Kappa Phi. Office: U Wash 306 Raitt Hall Box 353410 Seattle WA 98195

MONSIVAIS, DIANE B., surgical nurse, writer; b. White Plains, N.Y., Feb. 9, 1951; d. C. Neilson and Evelyn Thoben (Goerke) Burn; m. Jose J Monsivais, Jun. 26, 1983; children: Daniel, Sharon, Suzanne. BSN, Duke U., 1972; MSN, U. Tex., El. Paso, 1988. Cert. RN. Staff nurse, head nurse adminstrn. U.S. Army Nurse Corps., 1972-81; clin. nurse mgr., pubs. mgr. Hand & Microsurgery Ctr. of El Paso, Tex., 1988—. Contbr. to profl. jours. Mem. Tex. Nurses Assn. (bd. dirs. 1993-94, v.p. 1995-96, pres. dist. I 1996—), Am. Med. Writers Assn. (cert. in writing/editing), Assn. Hand Care Profls. (program chair 1994-95, edn. chair 1995-96, pres.-elect 1996—), Coun. Biology Editors (cert. editor life scis.). Home: 716 Twin Hills Dr El Paso TX 79912-3412 Office: Hand & Microsurgery Ctr El Paso 10525 Vista del Sol #200 El Paso TX 79925

MONSON, DIANNE LYNN, literacy educator; b. Minot, N.D., Nov. 24, 1934; d. Albert Rachie and Iona Cordelia (Kirk) M. BS, U. Minn., 1956, MA, 1962, PhD, 1966. Tchr., Rochester Pub. Schs. (Minn.), 1966-59, U.S. Dept. Def., Schweinfurt, W.Ger., 1959-61, St. Louis Park Schs. (Minn.), 1961-62; instr. U. Minn., Mpls., 1962-66; prof. U. Wash., Seattle, 1966-82; prof. literacy edn. U. Minn., Mpls., 1982—, chmn. Curriculum and Instrn., 1986-89. Co-author: New Horizons in the Language Arts, 1972, Children and Books, 6th edit., 1981; Experiencing Children's Literature, 1984; (monograph) Research in Children's Literature, 1976; Language Arts: Teaching and Learning Effective Use of Language, 1988; Reading Together: Helping Children Get A Good Start With Reading, 1991; assoc. editor Dictionary of Literacy, 1995. Recipient Outstanding Educator award U. Minn. Alumni Assn., 1983, Alumni Faculty award, 1991. Fellow Nat. Conf. Rsch. in English (pres. 1990-91); mem. Nat. Coun. Tchrs. of English (exec. com. 1979-81), Internat. Reading Assn. (dir. 1980-83, Arbuthnot award 1993), ALA, U.S. Bd. Books for Young People (pres. 1988-90). Lutheran. Home: 740 River Dr Saint Paul MN 55116-1069 Office: U Minn 350 Peik Hall Minneapolis MN 55455

MONSON, NANCY PECKEL, writer, editor; b. N.Y.C., Mar. 11, 1959; m. John C. Monson, June 18, 1988. BS magna cum laude, Boston U., 1979. Actress, 1979-86; adminstrv. asst. MIT, Cambridge, 1981; assoc. editor Profl. Postgrad. Svcs., Secaucus, N.J., 1984-87; writer, contbg. editor Cardiology Product News, East Orange, N.J., 1985-86; assoc. editor, reporter The Convention Reporter Group, Secaucus, 1985-88, editor, 1988-90; freelance health writer and editor Pomona, N.Y., 1984—; freelance entertainment writer Pomona, 1988—. Contbr. articles to mags. including Glamour, First for Women, Fitness, Redbook, McCall's, Woman's Day and New Woman, Bottom Line/ Personal. Mem. AFTRA, SAG, Am. Assn. Journalists and Authors, Am. Med. Writers Assn. Office: 1844 South Hill Rd Ludlow VT 05149

MONTAGUE, MARCIA, artist; b. Brookings, S.D., Sept. 21, 1952; d. Clyde Ray and Diane Barbara (Montague) Burnett; m. Benjamin Espinoza, Apr. 17, 1976 (div. Sept. 1978); 1 child, Hilario Montague. Student, U. Wis., 1975, Spokane Falls Coll., 1988, Occidental Coll., U. N.Mex.; BA in Art History, Ea. Wash. U., 1975; AAS in Graphic Design, Spokane Falls C.C., 1988. Artist Times Tribune, Palo Alto, Calif., 1988-93, Food for the Poor, Deerfield Beach, Fla., 1995—, Health Crisis Network, Miami, Fla., 1995-96, ARC, Pompano, Fla., 1996; artist-in-residence Artifactory, Palo Alto, Calif., 1992. Group shows include Albuquerque Juried Art Fair, 1976. Vol. ARC, Pompano, 1996, Horses for Handicapped, Pompano, 1995—. Mem. NOW, Amnesty Internat., Phi Beta Kappa. Democrat. Home: 1893 Discovery Way Pompano FL 33064 Office: Food for the Poor 550 SW 12th Ave #4 Deerfield Beach FL 33442

MONTALVO LOFFREDO, MARY LEE, social welfare administrator; b. Staten Island, N.Y., Mar. 31, 1962; d. Israel and Mary Christina (Rivera) Montalvo; m. Mark D. Loffredo, Sept. 23, 1995. BA, Rutgers U., Newark, 1988; cert. pub. rels., NYU, 1995; cert., Hispanic Women Leadership Inst, Rutgers U., 1995. Pub. rels. asst. Staten Island (N.Y.) U. Hosp., 1986-88, Staten Island Hist. Soc., 1988-90; dir. comty. edn. Staten Island Mental Health Soc., 1990-93; dir. ARC Staten Island chpt., 1994—; co-chairperso HIV Care Network, Staten Island, 1994—; bd. dirs. Interagy. Coun. for the Aging, Staten Island, 1995—. Mem. com. Richmond County Fair, Staten Island, 1988—, founding corr. sec., Latino Civic Assn., Staten Island, 1993—; mem. bd. dirs. Trinity Luth. Sch., Staten Island, 1995—. Recipient Comm. award Nat. Assn. Mental Health Info. Officers, 1991, Raymond C. Fingado award, Staten Island Hist. Soc., 1993, Comty. Hero and Heroine award, N.Y. State Assembly, 1995. Mem. Bus. and Profl. Women's Club (pres. Staten Island 1993-94, Young Careerist 1990), Rotary Club of Staten Island. Office: Am Red Cross 75 Vanderbilt Ave Staten Island NY 10304

MONTANARO, LINDA, secondary education educator; b. Painesville, Ohio, Feb. 15, 1945; d. Lunda and Mary Ann (Tabone) Brafford; children: Melinda, Joseph, Melissa, Jason. BS, Kent State U., 1968; M, Ariz. State U., 1983. Bookkeeper, credit investigator Sears Roebuck, Ashtabula, Ohio, 1963-66; tchr. Geniva (Ohio) H.S., 1967-73, Geneva (Ohio) H.S., Met. TEch. Vocat. Inst., Phoenix, 1979—, Pohenix Union H.S. Named Ariz.'s Secondary Bus. Edn. Tchr. of Yr., 1993, Ariz.'s Vocat. Edn. Tchr. of Yr., 1993, Vocat. Tchr. of Yr., State Coun. on Vocat. Edn., 1994, Vocat. Bus. Dept. of Yr., State Coun. on Vocat. Edn., 1994. Mem. NEA, NAFE, ASCD, NOW, DAV Aux., Nat. Bus. Edn. Assn. (spkr./presenter 1989, 91), Ariz. Bus. Edn. Assn. (state treas. 1989-93, ctrl. rep. 1993-95, pres.-elect 1995-96, pres. 1996-97), Western Bus. Edn. Assn. (Outstanding Bus. Educator 1995), Internat. Soc. Bus. Educators, Ariz. Edn. Assn. (del. Assembly 1991-94), Am. Vocat.

Edn. Assn. (voting del. 1991-92), Ariz. Vocat. Assn. (state v.p. 1991-93, Vocat. Program of Yr. 1993).

MONTAS, CARMEN IRIS, sales promotion manager; b. Bonao, Dominican Republic, Nov. 18, 1964; came to U.S., 1969; d. Segido and Modesta (Abreu) Peña; m. Reinaldo A. Montas. BS in Acctg., St John's U., Jamaica, N.Y., 1985. Staff acct. Ernst & Young, N.Y.C., 1985-89, sr. auditor, 1989; budget analyst Lever Bros. Co., N.Y.C., 1989-91, supr. advt. and promotion acctg., 1991-93, assoc. promotion mgr., 1993-95, promotion mgr., 1995—; mem. Unilever Coupon Com., N.Y.C., 1994-96. Mem. Take Our Daughters to Work Com., N.Y.C., 1996—. Office: Lever Bros Co 390 Park Ave New York NY 10022

MONTBERTRAND, LOIS SHINER, lawyer; b. Lakewood, N.J.; d. Robert Lamont and Anne Shiner; children: Carine Montbertrand, Michelle Montbetrand; m. Alan Paul Poland, Feb. 18, 1996. Grad., Mt. Sinai Hosp. Sch. Nursing, N.Y.C., 1961; diploma Prof. Francais a l'Etranger, U. Aix-Marseilles, France, 1964; BA, Wellesley Coll., 1976; JD, Yale U., 1985. Bar: Conn. 1985, Wis. 1991; RN, N.Y., Pa., Conn., Wis. Assoc. Wiggin & Dana, New Haven, 1985-87, Susman, Duffy & Segaloff, New Haven, 1988-89; atty. Aetna, Hartford, Conn., 1989-90; pvt. practice, Madison, Wis., 1990-91; gen. counsel Office Sec. of State, State of Wis., Madison, 1992-96, UCC counsel dept. fin. instns., 1996—. Active Faircrest Neighborhood Assn. Mem. Wis. Bar Assn. (mediation adv. group, govt. lawyers group), Dane County Bar Assn. (govt. lawyers group steering com.). Office: Dept Fin Instns State Of Wis 30 W Mifflin St Madison WI 53703

MONTEALEGRE, INGRID, computer educator, specialist; b. Santiago, Chile, Mar. 27, 1965; came to U.S., 1969; d. Marcelo and Doris (Dillems) M.; m. John Scott Swierzbin, June 24, 1989. BA in Computer Art, Oberlin Coll., 1987; MS in Computer, N.Y. Inst. Tech., 1991; MA in Edn., NYU, 1996. Cert. tchr. nursery through Kindergarten, grades 1-6, N.Y. state. Cons. Dr. Hector Valdes, Santiago, Chile, 1991-93; computer specialist P.S. 3 Bd. of Edn., N.Y.C., 1993—.

MONTEALEGRE, JANET JOAN, artist, educator; m. Juan C. Montealegre, 1961; children: Mario, Rachel, Michael, Francisco. AA, San Diego C.C., 1979; BA, San Diego State U., 1982, MFA, 1987. Cert. c.c. instr. Instr. Assoc. Students Leisure Connection San Diego State U., 1983; prof. San Diego C.C., 1986; tchr., artist, film coord. Natural History Mus., San Diego, 1981-88; assoc. prof. Mesa C.C., San Diego, 1989-91, Miracosta Coll., Oceanside, Calif., 1990—; assoc. prof., assoc. faculty Nat. Univ., San Diego, 1992—; tchr. asst. edn. cultural complex San Diego C.C., 1986-87; rschr. Cedar of Lebanon Hosp., L.A., 1960-70; sr. staff Martin L. Kin County Hosp., L.A., 1971-74. Patentee in field; exhibits include African Am. Artists 1994 exhibit Kruglak Gallery, 1994, Signature Gallery, 1995. Curator, guild coord. African Am. Mus., San Diego, 1994; conf. coord. Politics of Race in The Cmty., presenter various confs., seminars. Stanford U. fellow, 1994. Mem. Women's Caucus for Art, Nat. Mus. of Women in the Arts. Office: National University 4125 Camino del Rio S San Diego CA 92108

MONTEFERRANTE, JUDITH CATHERINE, cardiologist; b. N.Y., Jan. 27, 1949; d. Stanley and Monica (Vinckus) Sosaris; m. Ronald J. (div. 1983); 1 child, Jason Paul; m. Roger E. Salisbury, Mar. 3, 1990. BS, Adelphi U., Garden City, 1970; MS, SUNY, Buffalo, 1973; MD, Mt. Sinai, N.Y.C., 1978. Attending N.Y. Med. Coll., Valhalla, N.Y., 1983-84; pvt. practice White Plains, N.Y., 1984--; pres. Am. Heart Assn., 1984-86, bd. dirs. Westchester, N.Y., 1987—. Contbr. articles to profl. jours. fellow Am. Colls. of Cardiology, Am. Coll. of Physicians. Fellow Council on Clinical Cardiology of AHA, N.Y. Cardiological Soc.; mem. AMA, FACC, FACP, Soc. of Critical Care Medicine. Office: 222 Westchester Ave # 405 White Plains NY 10604-2906

MONTEIRO, MARILYN DONALDA, university program administrator; b. Washington, Feb. 22, 1941; d. George and Mildred Elaine (Gleaves) Canada; div.; 1 child, Chinyelu A. Ayodele. BA in Polit. Sci., Sociology, U. Mass., 1970; EdM in Learning Environ., Harvard U., 1973, EdD in Ednl. Adminstrn., Planning and Social Policy, 1982. Tchr., tchr. trainer Delta Opportunities Corp., Greenville, Miss., 1970-71; program dir. YMCA-Roxbury Br., Boston, 1973-74; instr. African Am. studies, dir. Affirmative Action Mass. Coll. Art, Boston, 1980-83; adj. asst. prof. Coll. of Edn., dir. Affirmative Action programs U. No. Iowa, Cedar Falls, 1983-87; adj. asst. prof. Coll. of Edn., dir. Affirmative Action No. Ill. U., DeKalb, 1987—; lectr. U. Mass., Boston, 1970, instr., 1974-80; instr. Simmons Coll., 1975-76, Antioch U./Cambridge Inst. of Open Edn., 1980, Mass. Coll. of Art, Boston, 1981-83; workshop leader Ill. Inst. Tech., Chgo., 1994, Nat. Inst. for Employment Equity, Chgo., 1993, Coll. of Lake County, Grayslake, Ill., 1993; cons. Mass. Exptl. Sch. System, 1971-72, Boston Cmty. Sch. Project, 1979-80, Parco Ltd., Cedar Falls, Iowa, 1984, City of Waterloo, 1984, 86, Sterling (Ill.) Pub. Schs., 1992; grants evaluator Mass. Found. for Humanities and Pub. Policy, 1980, Am. Assn. Colls., N.Y.C., 1982-83; presenter in field. Book reviewer; mem. editl. bd. Jour. of African Am. Thought, 1993—, Harvard Ednl. Review, 1976, 77. Bd. dirs Chgo. Metro. YWCA. Recipient Disting. Svc. award City of Cedar Falls, 1987, Ford Found. Nat. fellow, 1975-80, scholarship Harvard U., 1972-73, Disting. Svc. award Sigma Lambda Gamma Internat. Sorority No. Ill. U., 1995. Mem. Nat. Women Studies Assn., Nat. Assn. for Women Educators, Am. Assn. for Affirmative Action, Am. Assn. of Higher Edn., Chgo. Area Women Studies Assn. (chair), Ill. Commn. on Black Concerns in Higher Edn., Harvard Club Chgo., Phi Delta Kappa. Office: No Ill U Affirmative Action Office 302 Lowden Hall De Kalb IL 60115

MONTELEONE, PATRICIA, academic dean. Dean. assoc. v.p. St. Louis u. Sch. Medicine. Office: St Louis U Sch Medicine 1402 S Grand Blvd Saint Louis MO 63104

MONTEVERDE, ROSEMARY, English educator; b. Passaic, N.J., July 9, 1943; d. Thomas E. and Angela M. BA, Douglass Coll., 1965; MEd, Rutgers U., 1969. Tchr. English East Brunswick (N.J.) Bd. Edn., 1965-96; cons. Nat. Bd. for Profl. Teaching Standards, 1996—; cons. in field. Mem. Alpha Delta Kappa (rec. sec. local chpt., pres. local chpt. 1992-94, rec. sec. N.J. state chpt. 1994-96). Home: 38 Bramble Ln Matawan NJ 07747

MONTGOMERY, ANNA FRANCES, elementary school educator; b. Spokane, Wash., Nov. 5, 1945; d. Carl Jacob and Edna Frances (Evans) Kuipers; m. William Lee Montgomery Jr., Oct. 7, 1989. AA, Mid. Ga. Coll., 1965; BS in Elem. Edn., Woman's Coll. of Ga., 1966; MEd, Ga. Coll., 1969, specialist in edn., 1973. Cert. elem. tchr., Ga. Classroom tchr. Muscogee County Sch. Dist., Columbus, Ga., 1966—, reading tchr. Title 1 tutorial program, summer 1975, instr. staff devel. program, 1977-80; social sci. lead tchr. Wesley Heights Elem. Sch., Columbus, 1992—; tennis and athletic instr. Camp Tegawitha, Tobyhanna, Pa., summer 1970; presenter workshop Chattahoochee Valley Coun. for Social Studies, 1977; mem. social studies textbook adoption com. Muscogee County Sch. Dist., 1977-78, 82-83, sick leave com., 1993-95; judge Columbus Regional Social Sci. Fair, 1977, 93-96. Treas. Wesley Heights PTA, 1983-86; vol. Med. Ctr. Aux., Columbus, 1975-79; pres. pastor's Bible study class St. Luke United Meth. Ch., 1993-94, 96, mem. Sarah cir., cir. #11, sec., 1969-71, 78-80, co-chmn., 1976-78; mem. Bessie Howard Ward Handbells Choir; devel. chmn. Ga. state divsn. Centennial/fellowships com. AAUW, 1974-76. Recipient Valley Forge Tchrs. medal Freedoms Found. at Valley Forge, 1975, Outstanding Tchr. of Yr. award Wesley Hts. Elem. Sch., 1975, Muscogee County Sch. Dist., 1979; named Very Important Lady award Girl Scouts Am., Columbus, 1976, Outstanding Young Woman Am., 1982. Mem. AAUW (chmn. centennial fellowship com. Columbus br. 1973-75), Ga. PTA (hon. life), Profl. Assn. Ga. Educators (bldg. rep. Muscogee County chpt. 1983—, sec. 1992-94, treas. 1994—), Nat. Coun. Social Studies (mem. hostess and registration coms. ann. meeting 1975), Ga. Coun. for Social Studies, Ga. Sci. Tchrs. Assn., Valley Area Sci. Tchrs. (corr. sec. 1996-97), Ga. Coll. Alumni Assn., Mid. Ga. Coll. Alumni Assn., Order of Amaranth (charity com. 1991-93, 95, assoc. conductress 1996), Scottish Rite Ladies Aux., Alpha Delta Kappa (Rho chpt., sec. 1975-76, pres.-elect 1976-78, pres. 1978-80), Delta Kappa Gamma (Beta Xi chpt., pres. 1980-82, chmn. pubs. and publicity 1976-78, chmn. profl. affairs 1978-80, nominations com. chair 1981-82, chmn. world fellowship and fund raising 1984-86, chmn. fin. 1990-92, chmn. membership 1994-96), Wesley Heights Elem. Sch. PTA. Home: 5134 Stone Gate Dr Columbus GA 31909-5573

MONTGOMERY, BETTY D., state official, former state legislator. BA, Bowling Green State U.; JD, U. Toledo, 1976. Former criminal clk. Lucas County Common Pleas Ct.; asst. pros. atty. Wood County, Ohio, pros. atty., 1980-88; pros. atty. City of Perrysburg, Ohio; mem. Ohio Senate, 1989-94; atty. gen. State of Ohio, Columbus, 1995—. Mem. Nat. Dist. Atty. Assn., Ohio Bar Assn., Toledo Bar Assn., Wood County Bar Assn. Address: 1164 Dawn Dr Reynoldsburg OH 43068-9999 Office: Attorney Generals Office State Offical Tower 30 E Broad St Columbus OH 43215-3428*

MONTGOMERY, CAROL L., principal; m. Bob Montgomery; children: Carrie, Chris. Student in Elem. Edn., U. North Tex.; BA in Elem. Edn., U. Wichita, 1971; MA in Counseling, Guidance and Psychology, U. No. Colo., 1976; postgrad. in Sch. Adminstrn., Tex. A & M; postgrad., U. S.C.; EdD, U. Louisville, 1993. Tchr. Little Elem. Sch. and Linwood Elem Sch., Wichita, Kans., 1971-73, Pioneer Park Elem. Sch., Cheyenne, Wyo., 1973; substitute tchr. Cheyenne Ind. Sch. Dist., 1974-75; tchr. Cole Elem. Sch., Cheyenne, 1975, Nola Dunn Elem Sch., Burleson, Tex., 1976-78, Cranfills Gap (Tex.) Elem. Sch., 1978-79, Clifton (Tex.) Elem. Sch., 1979; dir. student svcs. Ctrl. Tex. C. C., Killeen, 1979-82; counselor Pelion (S.C.) Elem. Sch., 1982-84, Dutch Fork Elem. Sch., Irmo, S.C., 1984-88; tchr. Middletown Elem. Sch., Louisville, 1987-88; counselor We. Middle Sch., Louisville, 1988-90; prin. Fern Creek Elem. Sch., Louisville, 1990—; bd. dirs. Fern Creek Elem. PTA. Active numerous civic and community orgns. Named to Honorable Order of Ky. Cols.; fellow Scottish Rite Found. Ky., 1990-93. Mem. ASCD (conf. presenter 1993), NAFE, Am. Assn. Counseling and Devel. (Nat. award Human Rights Work 1985-86), Am. Assn. Sch. Adminstrs., Nat. Assn. Elem. Sch. Prins., Nat. Bd. Cert. Profl. Counselors, So. Assn. Accreditation Vis. Teams, Nat. Bd. Cert. Sch. Counselors, Lic. Profl. Counselors Tex., Lic. Profl. Counselors S.C., Ky. Assn. Sch. Adminstrs., Ky. Assn. Elem. Sch. Prins., Ky. Inst. Women in Sch. Adminstrn., Jefferson County Assn. Sch. Adminstrs., Jefferson County Assn. Elem. Sch. Prins., Kappa Delta Pi. Address: 8703 Ferndale Rd Louisville KY 40291

MONTGOMERY, DENISE KAREN, nurse; b. N.Y.C., Dec. 23, 1951; d. Thomas Cornell and Dorothy Marie (Castine) Simons; m. Timothy Bruce Montgomery, July 19, 1974 (div. Feb. 1981); m. Joseph Samuel Montgomery, Aug. 20, 1983. A in Nursing, San Jacinto Coll., 1971. RN, Tex. Charge nurse Aaron's Women's Clinic, Houston, 1977; rsch. asst. dept. ob-gyn. Baylor Coll. Medicine, Houston, 1977-81, nursing supr., 1979-81, program coord. population control program, 1979-81; nurse Dr. Eric J. Haufrect, Houston, 1982-83; office mgr., supr. Dr. J.S. Montgomery III, 1987—, Dr. Samuel Law, Houston, 1983-84. Contbr. articles to med. jours. Recipient Disting. Pub. Svc. award Am. Heart Assn., 1976; recipient several grants. Mem. Nat. Assn. Coll. Ob-Gyn. Democrat. Roman Catholic. Home: 8202 N Tahoe Dr Houston TX 77040-1256

MONTGOMERY, KATHLEEN STANFORD, reading resource educator; b. Calgary, Alb., Can., July 12, 1968; d. Walter William and Myrna Louise Stanford; m. Christopher James Montgomery, June 15, 1989; children: Paige Helen, Hunter David. BEd in Spl. Edn., U. Alberta, 1990; MEd, Seattle U., 1993. Cert. tchr., Wash., Va. Tchr. kindergarten Sammanish Montessori, Redmond, Wash., 1990-92; tchr. early elem. Lake Forest Park Montessori Acad., Seattle, 1992-93, libr. cons., 1994, libr., 1994—, reading and lit. specialist, 1993—; pvt. tutor Seattle, 1992-95, Alexandria, Va., 1996—. Rutherford scholarship Govt. of Alberta, 1986. Mem. Internat. Reading Assn. Home: 7102 Cold Spring Ct Alexandria VA 22306

MONTGOMERY, LINDA STROUPE, county official; b. Havaco, W.Va., Feb. 12, 1943; d. James Allen Stroupe and Opal Marie (Daugherty) Leif; m. James R. Sutliff, Aug. 9, 1960 (div. Feb. 1982); children: Mark S., Debra Lynn, Amy Sutliff Sweckard; m. Paul L. Montgomery, Apr. 23, 1983. Student, S.W. Mo. State U., 1979-93. Sec. Va. Poly. Inst., Blacksburg, 1961-64; office mgr., parlegal William H. Wendt, Springfield, Mo., 1973-84; office adminstr. Greene County Commn., Springfield, 1984-94; recorder of deeds Greene County, 1995—; mem. legis. com. Local Area Govt. Employees Retirement Sys., State of Mo., 1993—. Bd. dirs. Springfield-Greene County Libr. Dist., 1991—, also past pres.; mem. allocations com., sect. chmn. United Way Ozarks, Springfield, 1990—; committeewoman, legis. chmn. Greene County Rep. Ctrl. Com., 1987—. Mem. ALA, Internat. Assn. Clks., Recorders, Election Ofcls. and Treas., Recorder's Assn. Mo., Mo. Libr. Assn., Springfield Area C. of C., Grand Order Pachyderms (past pres.), Phi Kappa Phi. Methodist. Home: 5209 S Shari Ln Rogersville MO 65742 Office: Greene County Govt 940 Boonville Springfield MO 65802

MONTGOMERY, LISA LOUISE, management professional; b. Buffalo, N.Y., Aug. 7, 1966; d. Robert L. and Carolyn H. (Hansen) M. Student, Warnborough Coll., Oxford, Eng., 1987; BA in Math., Wells Coll., 1988; MPA, SUNY, Albany, 1992; advanced health policy cert., U. Md., 1996. Teaching asst. Wells Coll., Aurora, N.Y., 1987-88; statis. analyst Blue Shield of Western N.Y., Buffalo, 1988-90; intern Blue Shield of Northeastern N.Y., Albany, 1990-91; supr. computer lab. Rockefeller Coll., SUNY, Albany, 1991; grad. asst. N.Y. State, Albany, 1991-92; presdl. mgmt. intern Health Care Fin. Adminstrn., Balt., 1992-94, health ins. specialist, 1994—. Mem. NOW, Am. Soc. Pub. Adminstrn. Democrat. Methodist. Office: Health Care Fin Adminstrn 7500 Security Blvd Baltimore MD 21244

MONTGOMERY, MARTHA M., nursing educator; b. Kalkaska, Mich., Feb. 23, 1934; d. Alvah James Montgomery and Genevieve (Ragan) Shaffer. Dipl., Henry Ford Hosp., Detroit, 1955; BSN, Wayne State U., 1962, MSN, 1964. Cert. orthopedic nurse. Staff nurse, head nurse Henry Ford Hosp., Detroit, 1955-59; faculty, staff nurse Evang. Deaconess Hosp., Detroit, 1961-65; staff nurse, rsch. asst. Wayne State U., Detroit, 1963, 75-76; cmty. health nurse Vis. Nurse Assn., Detroit, 1988—; instr. nursing Henry Ford C.C., Dearborn, Mich., 1964—. Instrl. designer and formative evaluator (tv prodn.) Newer Media Approaches to Edn. for Nursing, 1968-71; co-author, editor, cons. in design (brochure) The Curriculum Master Plan, 1981. Grantee Helene Fuld Health Trust, 1990, 93. Mem. ANA, N.Am. Nursing Diagnosis Assn., Am. Fedn. Tchrs., Assn. Ednl. Comm. and Tech., Assn. for Devel. Computer-Based Instrl. Sys., Nat. Assn. Orthopedic Nurses, Sigma Theta Tau (Lambda chpt.). Office: Henry Ford Cmty Coll 5101 Evergreen Rd Dearborn MI 48128-2407

MONTGOMERY, ROBIN VERA, realtor; b. Boise, Idaho, July 21, 1928; d. Bruce Cameron and Grace Evangeline (Matthews) M.; m. Lewis Robert Goldberg, June 10, 1956 (div. June 1978); children: Timothy, Holly, Randall. BA in Journalism, U. Mich., 1957; BArch, U. Oreg., 1972. Architect Robin's Roost, Eugene & Florence, Oreg., 1972-82; realtor Exclusive Realtors, L.A., 1989—. Program chair Hadassah, Eugene, 1968; pres. Elec. Wires Underground, Eugene, 1967. With USN, 1949-53. Mem. Calif. Assn. Realtors, Theta Sigma Phi. Democrat. Home: 1334 S Carmelina Ave Apt 7 Los Angeles CA 90025-1962

MONTGOMERY, ROSE ELLEN GIBSON, secondary education educator, organist; b. Barbourville, Ky.; d. Charles Butler and Mattie Cecilia (Corey) Gibson; m. William Goebel Montgomery; children: Pamela Janeese, Leilani Rose, William Goebel Jr. (dec.). BS, Hawaii Pacific U., 1965; MEd, Bowie (Md.) State U., 1970; postgrad., U. Philippines, 1970-73, U. Md., 1980-82; PhD, Am. Internat. U., 1995. Cert. tchr., Md. Tchr. Pearl Harbor Luth. Elem. Sch., Honolulu, 1965-67, Dept. Def. Schs., Luzon, The Philippines, 1973-92; tchr. Prince George's County Schs., Bowie, 1967-70, 73-92, Laurel, Md., 1992-96; ch. organist Pearl Harbor Meml. Ch., 1963-67, Clark Air Base Chapel, Luzon, 1970-73. Co-author: (handbook) World of Work, 1972; inventor 6-string guitar chord stamp for tchg. guitar. Active Girl Scouts U.S. and Boy Scouts Am., Honolulu; developer Meml. Garden, Bowie, 1973-74. Named Outstanding Organist, Pearl Harbor Christian Ch., 1966; recipient base comdr.'s award Clark Air Base, 1970-73, Outstanding Tchr. of Yr. award City of New Carrollton, Md., 1987, Md. Tchr. of Yr. for Prince George's County, 1993. Mem. NEA (life), Prince George's County Edn. Assn. (del.). Republican. Roman Catholic. Home: 2802 Stonybrook Dr Bowie MD 20715-2157 Office: Dwight David Eisenhower Mid Sch 13725 Briarwood Dr Laurel MD 20708-1301

MONTOOTH, SHEILA CHRISTINE, state agency administrator; b. Pasadena, Calif., Mar. 12, 1952; d. Gerald Frank and Janet Laura (Ebert) M. BS, Calif. State U., L.A., 1974; MPA, Calif. State U., 1985. CPA, Calif. From auditor 1 to tax auditor IV State Bd. Equalization Calif. Bd. Equalization, Pasadena, 1974-81; supr. tax auditor 1 State Bd. of Equalization Calif. Bd. of Equalization, West Los Angeles, 1981-83; bus. taxes adminstr. III State Bd. of Equalization Calif. Bd. Equalization, Lakewood, 1984-87; bus. taxes adminstr. IV State Bd. of Equalization Calif. Bd. Equalization, Downey, 1987-92; bus. taxes adminstr. V State Bd. of Equalization, Hollywood, 1992-93, Arcadia, 1994; bus. taxes adminstr. V State Bd. of Equalization, City of Industry, 1994—. Active Futures for Children. Recipient Bronze award United Way, Los Angeles, 1984, Gold award, 1985. Mem. Nat. Mus. Am. Indian Smithsonian Instn. (charter). Democrat. Roman Catholic. Office: State Bd Equalization 12820 Crossroads Pky S La Puente CA 91746-3411

MONTOYA, VELMA, federal agency administrator; b. L.A., Apr. 9, 1938; d. Jose Gutierrez and Consuelo (Cavazos) Montoya; m. Earl A. Thompson; 1 child, Bret L. Thompson. BA in Diplomacy and World Affairs, Occidental Coll., 1959; MA in Internat. Rels., Fletcher Sch. of Law and Diplomacy, 1960; MS in Econs., Stanford U., 1965; PhD in Econs., U. Calif., L.A., 1977. Asst. prof. Econs. Calif. State U., L.A., 1965-68; vis. assoc. prof. U. So. Calif., 1979; instr. U. Calif., L.A., 1981-82; staff economist The Rand Corp., Santa Monica, Calif., 1973-82; asst. dir. for strategy, White House Office of Policy Devel. Exec. Office of the Pres., 1982-83; expert economist, Office of Regulatory Analysis, Occupational Safety and Health Adminstrn. U.S. Dept. of Labor, 1983-85; dir. of Studies in Pub. Policy and Assoc. Prof. of Political Economy, Sch. of Bus. Mgmt. Chapman U., 1985-87; adj. prof., Sch. of Bus. Mgmt. Pepperdine Univ., 1987-88; pres. Hispanic-Am. Pub. Policy Inst., 1984-90; assoc. prof. of Fin., Sch. of Bus. Adminstrn. Calif. State Polytechnic Univ., Pomona, 1988-90; commr. Occupational Safety and Health Review Commn., 1990—; cons. Urban Inst., 1974, Mexican-Am. Study Project UCLA, 1966, Graduate and Profl. Fellowships to the Office of Post Secondary Education, U.S. Dept. of Edn.; editorial referee Contemporary Policy Issues, Economic Inquiry, Policy Analysis, The Journal of Economic Literature; discussion leader Am. Assembly on Rels. Between the U.S. and Mex.; pres. del. White House Conf. on Aging, 1981; reader of 1988 proposals for the U.S. Dept of Edn. for the Improvement and Reform of Schs. and Teaching; research participant U.S. Dept. of Edn. Delphi Assessment of Drug Policies for Use in Minority Neighborhoods, 1989; mem. hispanic adv. panel Nat. Commn. for Employment Policy, 1981-82; lectr. Brookings Inst. Seminars for U.S. Bus. Leaders; bd. adv. Close-Up Found., 1982-83; discussant Western Economic Assn. Meetings, 1985, 93; bd. adv. Nat. Rehab. Hosp., 1991-94; mem. nat. exec. adv. bd. Harvard Jour. of Hispanic Policy, 1993-95. Bd. regents U. Calif., 1994—; mem. adv. com. U.S. Senate Rep. Conf. Task Force on Hispanic Affairs, 1991—; mem. census adv. com. on Hispanic Population for 1990 Census, US. Dept. of Commerce, 1988-93, bd. advisors Nat. Rehab. Hosp., 1991-94, adv. com. U.S. Senate Rep. Conf. Task Force on Hispanic Affairs, 1991—, nat. exec. adv. bd. Harvard Jour. Hispanic Policy, 1993-95, bd. regents U. Calif., 1994—. Named One of the 100 U.S. Hispanic Influentials Hispanic Bus. Mag., 1982, 90, Woman of the Yr. Mex.-Am. Opportunity Found., 1983, The East L.A. Com. Union, 1979, Marshall scholar, Fulbright scholar; recipient Freedom Found. at Valley Forge Honor Econ. Edn. Excellence Cert., 1986, Univ. fellow Stanford Univ., Internat. Rels. fellow Calif. PTA, John Hay Whitney Opportunity fellow; Calif. State Univ. Found. Faculty Rsch. grantee. Mem. ASTM (com. on rsch. and tech. planning 1985-87), Am. Econ. Assn. (session chair ann. meetings 1995), Nat. Coun. of Hispanic Women, State Bar of Calif., Calif. State Bar Ct. (exec. com. 1987-89, disciplinary bd. 1986-89), Western Econ. Assn., Indsl. Rsch. Inst. for Pacific Nations (adv. bd. 1988-89), Salesian Boys and Girls Club (bd. dirs 1989—), Vets. in Com. Svc. (adv. com. 1989-94), Phi Beta Kappa, Omicron Delta Epsilon, Phi Alpha Theta. Home: 6970 Los Tilos Rd Los Angeles CA 90068

MONTS, ELIZABETH ROSE, insurance company executive; b. LaPorte, Ind., June 13, 1955; d. William David and Marguerite Elizabeth (Burge) Miller; m. James Edwin Monts, May 26, 1978 (div. Aug. 1982); 1 child, Katherine Elizabeth. AA with highest honors, Coll. of Mainland, 1984; BS magna cum laude, U. Houston, Clear Lake, 1989. CPA. Credit adjustment asst. Jaymar-Ruby, Inc., Michigan City, Ind., 1974-79; acctg. clk. Am. Indemnity Co., Galveston, Tex., 1979-80, staff acct., 1980-81, adminstrv. acct., 1981-85, asst. treas., 1985-86, asst. treas., asst. dept. mgr., 1986-87, sec., asst. dept. mgr., 1987-91, asst. v.p., asst. dept. mgr., 1991—. V.I.P. escort Rep. Nat. Conv., Houston, 1992. Mem. AICPA, Fedn. Ins. Women Tex. (regional dir. 1992-94), Tex. Soc. CPA's, Ins. Women Galveston County (pres. 1987-88, 90-91), Beta Gamma Sigma, Phi Kappa Phi, Alpha Chi. Republican. Methodist. Office: Am Indemnity Co PO Box 1259 Galveston TX 77553-1259

MONZINGO, AGNES YVONNE, veterinary technician; b. Mangum, Okla., July 16, 1942; d. Ira Lee and Opal Alice (McAlexander) Mayfield; m. Monty Brent Monzingo, Dec. 19, 1959; children: Tara, Dawn, Michael, Kermit. AS, San Antonio Coll., 1969. Mgr. Tupperware Corp., Wichita Falls, Tex., 1966-69; with La Louisiane, San Antonio, 1974-79; counselor Diet Ctr., Duncanville, Tex., 1984-87; vet. technician DeSoto (Tex.) Animal Hosp., 1985—. Author: (weekly column) Happy Tracks, 1981. Pres. Dallas Stake Primary, 1983-88; commr. Boy Scouts Am., 1988-93. Recipient Wood badge Boy Scouts Am., 1987, Wisdom Trail Dist. award of merit, 1990, Silver Beaver award Boy Scouts Am., 1993. Mem. Tex. Assn. Registered Vet. Technicians (v.p. 1991), Tex. Assn. Animal Technicians (pres. 1988, com. chair 1990-92), Tex. Assn. Registered Technicians (pres. 1992), Am. Boxer Club, Dallas Boxers Club (sec. 1982-92), Metroplex Vet. Hosp. Mgrs. Assn. Mem. LDS Ch.

MOOCHNEK, CECILE, art gallery owner, writer, educator; b. Newark, Apr. 5, 1935; d. Harry Moochnek and Fannie Hoch; m. Tom Ehrlich, June 27, 1964 (div.); children: Michael Jonathan Ehrlich, Kenneth Paul Ehrlich. BA, Bklyn. Coll., 1956, MA, 1958. Tchr. New Utrecht H.S., Bklyn., 1957-67; art dir. Stables Gallery, Taos, N.Mex., 1970-76, Santa Fe, 1976-89; tchr. creative writing Berkeley, Calif., 1989—; art gallery owner Cecile Moochnek Gallery, Berkeley, Calif., 1993—. Contbr. articles to profl. jours. Mem. Mus. Modern Art (San Francisco), Mus. U. Calif., Asian Art Mus. Home and Office: 1809D 4th St Berkeley CA 94710

MOOD, LILLIAN HARRIETT, public health nurse; b. Columbia, S.C., Aug. 12, 1940; d. Francis Palmer and Lula Sue (Rigby) M.; m. Tony Ryan McCreight, Sept. 14, 1963 (div. 1982); children: Wynn Redpath, Susan Liles, Elizabeth Elliott. BSN, U. S.C., 1962, MPH, 1975. RN, S.C. Clin. instr. U. S.C. Coll. Nursing, Columbia, 1962-63; staff and charge nurse Cmty. Hosp. and State TB Hosp., Georgetown and Manning, S.C., 1962-70; supervision/cons. home health svcs. S.C. Dept. Health and Environ. Control, Georgetown and Columbia, 1970-78; project dir. cmty. long term care S.C. Dept. Social Svcs., Columbia, 1978-79; asst. commr. and state dir. pub. health nursing S.C. Dept. Health and Environ. Control, Columbia, 1979-88, dir. assessment and quality assurance, 1988-93, dir. risk comm. and cmty. liaison Environ. Quality Control, 1993—; bd. dirs. Palmetto Sr. Care, Columbia; pres. Assn. State and Territorial Dirs. of Nursing, 1984-86; mem. 10M Com. on Future of Pub. Health. Chair, editor: Nursing, Health and Environment, 1995. Active Friends of Mus., Columbia, Riverbanks Soc., Columbia, S.C. Healthy People Coalition, S.C. Recipient First award of merit Assn. State and Territorial Dirs. of Nursing, 1989; award for excellence S.C. League for Nursing, 1990; Cmty. Leadership fellow W.K. Kellogg Found., 1992-94; fellow Salzburg (Austria) Seminar, 1994. Fellow Am. Acad. Nursing; mem. APHA (governing coun. 1985-86, 89-90), ANA, S.C. Nurses Assn., S.C. Pub. Health Assn. (pres. 1978-79), Nat. League for Nursing (governing bd. 1982, 87-90). Methodist. Home: 628 Shallow Cove Ct Chapin SC 29036 Office: SC Dept Health & Environ Control 2600 Bull St Columbia SC 29201

MOODY, CHERYL ANNE, social services administrator, social worker, educator; b. Winston-Salem, N.C., July 31, 1953; d. Fred Bertram and Mary Edna (Weekley) M. BSW with honors, Va. Commonwealth U., 1975; MSW, U. Mich., 1979. Social worker Family Svcs., Inc., Winston-Salem, 1974-77; sch. social work intern Huron Valley Jr. H.S., Milford, Mich., 1977-78; children's social work intern Downriver Child Guidance Clinic, Allen Park, Mich., 1978-79; children's svcs. specialist Calhoun County Dept. Social

Svcs., Battle Creek, Mich., 1979-81; children's psychiat. social worker Eastern Maine Med. Ctr., Bangor, 1981-82, sr. med. social worker, 1982-85; clin. social worker Ctr. for Family Svcs. in Palm Beach County, Inc., West Palm Beach, Fla., 1988-89, Jupiter, Fla., 1989-91; dir. children's programs Children's Home Soc. of Fla., West Palm Beach, 1985—; asst. prof. social work Fla. Atlantic U., Boca Raton, 1993—. Vol. group leader Lupus Found., Boca Raton, 1994—. Mem. NASW, Acad. Cert. Social Workers. Democrat. Methodist. Home: 6212 62nd Way West Palm Beach FL 33409-7130 Office: Children's Home Soc of Fla 3600 Broadway West Palm Beach FL 33407-4844

MOODY, JANET ANN, special education educator; b. N.Y.C., Dec. 26, 1957; d. John D. and Joan E. (Hartl) M. BS in Speech and Lang. Pathology, Mercy Coll., 1979; MS in Spl. Edn., Manhattan Coll., 1982. Cert. tchr. spl. edn., nursery-6th tchr., N.Y. Spl. edn. tchr. Shield Inst., Bronx, N.Y., 1982-88, master tchr., tchr. trainer, 1988-91, ednl. evaluator, 1989-90, curriculum developer, 1984-85; staff developer Shield Inst., Bronx, 1984, 85, 89-91; spl. edn. educator P.S. 161, Bronx, 1991—; mem. early childhood conv. N.Y.C. Bd. Edn., 1992-94; mem. Compact for Learning adv. bd. P.S. 161, 1994—; presenter in field; mem. Com. for Spl. Edn. Standards, Dist. 75 Citywide, 1995. Contbr. articles to profl. jours. Mem., organizer Bronx divsn. Spl. Olympics, 1986-89. Mem. Alpha Chi, Kappa Delta Pi. Home: 453 E 14th St Apt 9C New York NY 10009 Office: PS 161 628 Tinton Ave Bronx NY 10455-3218

MOODY, LIZABETH ANN, law educator; b. Johnson City, Tenn., July 11, 1934; d. Robert Alexander and Clara Pauline (Fine) M.; m. Alan Paul Buchmann, Sept. 5, 1959. AB, Columbia U., 1956; LLB, Yale U., 1959. Bar: Conn. 1959, Ohio 1960, U.S. Dist. Ct. Conn. 1960, U.S. Supreme Ct. 1977, U.S. Dist. Ct. (no. dist.) Ohio 1961. Assoc. Goldstein & Peck, Bridgeport, Conn., 1959-60, Slough & Slough, Cleve., 1960-61, 63-66, Ginsberg, Guren & Meritt, Cleve., 1962; ptnr. Metzenbaum, Gaines, Finley & Stern, Cleve., 1967-71; assoc. prof. Cleve. State U., 1970-73, prof., 1973-94, interim dean and prof., 1987-88; vis. prof. U. Toledo, Ohio, 1976-77; v.p., dean Coll. Law, prof. Stetson U., 1994—; rev. authority on civil rights HEW, Washington, 1973-79; vis. prof. Nat. Law Ctr. George Washington U., 1981-82, U. Hawaii, Honolulu, 1988. Author: (books) Smith's Review of Corps, 1987, Smith's Review of Estates, 1987; contbr. articles to profl. jours. Pres. Cuyahoga County Econ. and Community Devel., Cleve., 1984-88, Task Force on Violent Crime, Cleve., 1987-88; chmn. audit com. Law Sch. Admission Coun., New Town, Pa., 1988-89, bd. trustees Law Sch. Admission Svc., 1989-94, exec. dir., 1991-93, pres. Law Sch. Admission Svc., 1991-93; commr. Ohio Ethics Commn., Columbus, Ohio, 1988-91, Ohio Pub. Defender Commn.; v.p., trustee Gt. Lakes Theatre Festival, Cleve., 1972-90; dir. Cleve. Growth Assn., 1987-88. Recipient New Frontier award Ams. for Dem. Action, 1977, YWCA Women of Distinction award, 1988, Josephine Irwin award, 1990; Day named in her honor, May 8, 1990, Cleve. Mem. ABA (chair non-profit corp. com. 1987-91, house of dels. 1994—, accreditation com. 1994—), Assn. Am. Law Schs. (exec. com. 1977-81), Ohio State Bar Assn. (coun. of dels. 1981-91, Ohio Bar medal 1992), Cleve. Bar Assn. (pres. 1987-88, meritorious svc. award 1987), Assn. Univ. Profs., Univ. Club, English Speaking Union (trustee 1986-89). Office: Stetson U Coll Law 1401 61st St South Saint Petersburg FL 33707

MOODY, MARILYN DALLAS, librarian; b. Little Rock, Aug. 28; d. Corbin Luther and Marian (Ricks) Dallas; m. W.I. Moody Jr., June 1, 1970 (div. 1987); m. Jeffry Baumann, 1988. Student, Hendrix Coll, Conway, Ark., 1959, U. Ark., 1960, Drexel U., 1964. Librarian Free Library of Phila., 1964-70, cons. librarian, 1971-76, coordinator dist. library ctr. services, 1976-82, chief extension services div., 1982-91; exec. dir. Bucks County Free Lib., Doylestown, Pa., 1991—. Recipient Cert. of Merit, 1981. Mem. ALA (councilor 1983-86), Pub. Libr. Assn. (legis. com. 1989-93), Pa. Libr. Assn. (legis. com. 1988-90, chair legis. com. 1980-82, coord. Legis. Day 1980-82, 87, 92, pres. pub. libr. divsn. 1995—, chair scholarship com.). Office: Bucks County Free Lib 150 S Pine St Doylestown PA 18901-4931

MOODY, PATRICIA ANN, psychiatric nurse, artist; b. Oceana County, Mich., Dec. 16, 1939; d. Herbert Ernest and Dorothy Marie (Allen) Baesch; m. Robert Edward Murray, Sept. 3, 1960 (div. Jan. 1992); children: Deanna Lee Cañas, Adam James Murray, Tara Michelle Murray, Danielle Marie Murray; m. Frank Alan Moody, Sept. 26, 1992. BSN, U. Mich., 1961; MSN, Washington U., St. Louis, 1966; student, Acad. of Art, San Francisco, 1975-78. RN; lic. coast guard, ocean operator. Psychiat. staff nurse U. Mich., Ann Arbor, 1961-62, Langley-Porter Neuro-Psychiat. Inst., San Francisco, 1962-63; instr. nursing Barnes Hosp. Sch. Nursing, St. Louis, 1963; psychiat. nursing instr. Washington U., St. Louis, 1966-68; psychiat. nurse instr. St. Francis Sch. Nursing, San Francisco, 1970-71; psychiat. staff nurse Calif. Pacific Med. Ctr., San Francisco, 1991—; psychiat. staff nurse Charter Heights Behavioral Health Sys., Albuquerque, 1996—; owner, cruise cons. Cruise Holidays Albuquerque, 1995—. Oil and watercolors included in various group exhbns., 1982-93. V.p. Belles-Fundraising Orgn., St. Mary's Hosp., San Francisco, 1974; pres. PTO, Commodore Sloat Sch., 1982. Recipient Honor award Danforth Found., 1954, Freshman award Oreon Scott Found., 1958; merit scholar U. Mich., 1957. Mem. San Francisco Women Artists (Merit award for oil painting 1989), Artist's Equity (bd. dirs. No. Calif. chpt. 1987-89, pres. No. Calif. chpt. 1990), Met. Club. Republican. Lutheran. Home: 219 Spring Creek Ln NE Albuquerque NM 87122 Office: Cruise Holidays Albuquerque 11032 Montgomery Blvd NE Albuquerque NM 87111

MOODY, SUSAN S., bank executive. Exec. v.p. corp. banking NBD Bancorp, Inc., Detroit; exec. v.p. corp & instl. banking First Chgo. NBD Corp. (merger of First Chgo. Corp. and NBD Bancorp, Inc.). Office: First Chgo NBD Corp One First National Plz Chicago IL 60670*

MOON, MONA MCTAGGART, speaker, trainer, consultant, educator; b. Buffalo, N.Y., Oct. 4, 1934; d. William Daniel and Helen Violet (Dubin) McTaggart; m. James McCallum Moon, July 14, 1957; children: Douglas, Melisa, Bruce. BA, UCLA, 1955; MA, San Diego State U., 1985. Lic. tchr., Calif., cert. adminstrn., supervision, Calif. Tchr. high sch. Acalanes High Sch., Lafayette, Calif., 1956-61, San Diego Unified Sch. Dist., 1967-82; pres. Motivation Dynamics, San Diego, 1982—. Contbr. articles to profl. jours. Dir. LWV San Diego, 1967-72. Recipient Outstanding Contbn. award Calif. Assn. Dirs. of Activities; named San Diego County Tchr. of Yr., 1980. Mem. ASCD, ASTD, Nat. Speakers Assn., Phi Beta Kappa. Republican. Presbyterian. Office: 7910 Ivanhoe Ave Ste 29 La Jolla CA 92037-4511

MOON, TAE-HYUN, psychologist; b. Taegu, South Korea, July 1, 1957; came to U.S., 1965; d. Chang Su Moon and Jung Sook (Kim) Faye; m. Gregory Lewis Tietbohl, Aug. 22, 1991; children: Stephanie Kim, Caroline Kim. BA, U. Del., 1979; MS, U. Mass., 1981, PhD, 1984. Lic. psychologist Calif. Clin. supr. Worcester (Mass.) Area CMHC, 1984-85; psychologist pvt. practice, Pleasanton, Calif., 1986—. Recipient Halsey McPhee award U. Del., 1979. Mem. APA, L.A. Psychol. Assn., Alameda County Psychol. Assn. (chair info. & reference 1987-88), Phi Beta Kappa, Psi Chi. Office: 5674 Stoneridge Dr Ste 217 Pleasanton CA 94588

MOON, TESSIE JO, mechanical engineering educator; b. Butler, Pa., Dec. 7, 1961; d. Edward Vincent and Verda Viola Moon; m. Glenn Y. Masada; 1 child, Kendall M. Masada. BS, Grove City Coll., 1983; MS, U. Ill., 1986, PhD, 1989. Jr. engr. AMP Inc., Harrisburg, Pa., 1982; devel. engr. AMP Inc., Winston-Salem, N.C., 1983-84; grad. teaching asst. U. Ill., Urbana-Champaign, 1984-86, grad. rsch. asst., 1986-89; postdoctoral rsch. assoc. Office Naval Rsch.-U. Rsch. Inst. Nat. Ctr. for Composite Materials Rsch., Urbana-Champaign, 1989; asst. prof. U. Tex., Austin, 1989-95, assoc. prof., 1995—; faculty fellow Naval Surface Warfare Ctr. Carderock Divsn., Annapolis, Md., 1991. Editor: Mechanics in Materials Processing and Manufacturing, 1994. Recipient Young Investigator award NSF, 1992-97; initiation grantee Engring. Found., 1992-93, rsch. grantee Office of Naval Rsch., 1992—. Mem. ASME (mem. heat transfer divsn. tech. com. on heat transfer materials processing and mfg. 1991—, vice chmn. applied mechanics divsn. tech. com. on mechanics of materials processing and mfg. 1992—, contbr. articles to jours.), AAUP, AAUW, Am. Acad. Mechanics, Am. Soc. Engring. Edn. (Outstanding New Mechanics award 1992-93), Am. Soc. Materials, The Minerals, Metals and Materials Soc. of AIME, Soc. for the Advancement of Material and Processing Engring. Republican. Office: U Tex Mech Engring Dept ETC 5 160 Austin TX 78712-1063

MOONEY, CATHERINE LEE, real estate broker; b. Newark, Mar. 29, 1953; d. Robert Edward Lee and Catherine Mary (Sorrentino) Gosnell; m. Marvin Granville Coleman, May 20, 1972 (div. 1978); m. Jerome Henri Mooney, May 3, 1986 (div. 1995); 1 child, Stephen Lloyd Coleman. Student, Strayer Coll., 1972. Cert. residential specialist; lic. real estate agt., broker, Utah, Fla. Legal sec., 1976-82; mktg. asst. BSD Med. Corp., Salt Lake City, 1983; dir. investor rels. Kenman Corp., Salt Lake City, 1983-85; realtor, 1986-88; owner, broker Cathy Mooney Real Estate, Salt Lake City, 1988—. Del. Dem. Cen. Com., Salt Lake City, 1989. Mem. Women's Coun. Realtors (edn. chair 1991, Utah state treas. 1994), Residential Sales Coun., Nat. Assn. Realtors, Salt Lake Bd. Realtors (equal opportunity com. 1989, edn. com. 1989, realtor svcs. exec. com. 1992-94, grievance com. 1996—), Utah Assn. Realtors. Roman Catholic. Home and Office: 3066 S Plateau Dr Salt Lake City UT 84109

MOONEY, LORI, county official; b. Atlantic City, Aug. 22, 1929; d. Joseph Aloysius and Alice Marie Inemer; m. Charles H. Calvi (div.); children: Joseph P., Stephen C., Christina L.; m. Thomas Christopher Mooney; children: Thomas C., Timothy C. Service rep. Bell Telephone Co., Atlantic City, 1950-58; sr. evaluator U.S. Census Bur., N.J., 1960-63; coordinator Nat. Small Bus. Com. for Johnson and Humphrey, Washington, 1964; owner, mgr. Lori Mooney & Co., Realtors, Atlantic County, N.J., 1965-77; commr. Atlantic County Bd. Elections, from 1970, also chmn. 5 yrs.; county clk. County of Atlantic, Mays Landing, 1978—; mem. Active Corps Execs., Nat. SBA; chmn. county clk. liaison com. N.J. Supreme Ct., 1984-86. Del. Dem. Nat. Conv., 1972, 76, 84, 88, 96; mem. congl. liaison com. Acad. for State and Local Govts., 1989—; mem. U.S. Senator Bill Bradley's Citizen Adv. Com. Recipient Woman of Achievement award N.J. Fedn. Bus. and Profl. Women, 1985, Role Model award The Sun newspaper, 1989. Mem. Internat. Assn. Clks., Recorders, Election Ofcls. and Treas. (N.J. dir. 1988—), Atlantic County Realtors Assn., Bus. and Profl. Women Atlantic County (scholarship chmn. 1982-85), County Officers Assn. N.J. (bd. dirs. 1978—, pres. 1991-92, 92-93), N.J. Assn. County Clks. (chmn. 1984-86), N.J. Assn. Realtors, Nat. Assn. Realtors, Nat. Assn. Counties, N.J. League Municipalities, Assn. Records Mgrs. and Administrs., Atlantic City Women's C. of C. Home: 100 Carol Rd Linwood NJ 08221-2502 Office: Atlantic County Clks Office Main St Mays Landing NJ 08330-1702

MOONEY, MARILYN, lawyer; b. Pitts., July 29, 1952; d. James Russell and Mary Elizabeth (Cartwright) M. BA summa cum laude, U. Pa., 1973, JD, 1976. Bar: Mass. 1977, D.C. 1985, Pa. 1990, U.S. Dist. Ct. D.C. 1985, U.S. Ct. Appeals (D.C. cir.) 1985, U.S. Supreme Ct. 1986. Atty. E. I. du Pont de Nemours & Co., Wilmington, Del., 1976-84, Washington, 1985; assoc. Fulbright & Jaworski L.L.P., Washington, 1985-90, ptnr., 1990—. Contbr. articles to profl. jours. Active Greater Washington Bd. Trade, D.C. Pub. Affairs Coun., 1992—. Mem. ABA, Fed. Regulation of Securities Com. (subcom. registration statements-1933 Act 1986—), Internat. Bar Assn. Office: Fulbright & Jaworski LLP 807 Pennsylvania Ave NW Washington DC 20004-2604

MOONEY, PATRICIA ANNE, sales professional; b. Bronx, N.Y., June 6, 1948; d. Peter Joseph and Helen (Houlihan) M.; m. Anthony John Grasso, Nov. 21, 1970 (div. 1977); 1 child, A. Benjamin. BA, Coll. New Rochelle, N.Y., 1970, MS, 1975. Tchr. Archdiocese of N.Y., Harrison, 1970-78; salesperson N.Y. Telephone, N.Y.C., 1978-82; instr. AT&T, Aurora, Colo., 1983; sales mgr. AT&T, N.Y.C., 1984, mgr. sales support dept., 1985; mgr. pricing and contract support dept. AT&T, Morristown, N.J., 1986; mgr. new bus. support dept. AT&T, Bridgewater, N.J., 1987; sales br. mgr. AT&T, Englewood, Colo., 1988-92; change mgmt. orgn. AT&T, Bridgewater, N.J., 1993; data networking customer svc. AT&T, Bedminster, N.J., 1994, customer svc. strategy, 1995—; mem. adv. bd. Coll. New Rochelle M. Program in Com.; mem. bd. dirs. Camp Rising Sun Internat. Teenage Leadership Program. Mem. Coll. New Rochelle Alumnae (bd. dirs.). Roman Catholic. Home: 27 Woodruff Rd Morristown NJ 07960-4623

MOOR, ANNE DELL, education director; b. Atlanta, Mar. 29, 1947; d. Kenneth Orman and Lida Louise (Springer) Dupree; m. Philip Ellsworth Moor, June 6, 1970; children: Andrew, Laura. BA, La Grange Coll., 1968. Cert. elem. edn. tchr., Tenn. Tchr. DeKalb County Bd. Edn., Atlanta, 1968-71, Briarcliff Bapt. Presch., Atlanta, 1972-73, Tates Sch., Knoxville, 1973-76; dir. after sch. care Cedar Springs Presbyn., Knoxville, 1993—. Discussion leader Bible Study Fellowship, Knoxville, 1980-93. Mem. Assn. for Childhood Edn. Internat., Tenn. Assn. for Young Children, Knoxville Area Assn. for Young Children. Presbyterian. Office: Cedar Springs Presbyn Ch 9132 Kingston Pike Knoxville TN 37923-5227

MOORE, ALDERINE BERNICE JENNINGS (MRS. JAMES F. MOORE), association and organization administrator; Sacramento, Apr. 17, 1915; d. James Joseph and Elise (Thomas) Jennings; BA, U. Wash., 1941; m. James Francis Moore, Aug. 14, 1945. Sec. to div. Plant supr. Pacific Tel. & Tel. Co., Sacramento, 1937-39; exec. sec. Sacramento Community Chest Fund Raising Dr., 1941; sec. USAAF, Mather Field, Sacramento, 1942; statistician Calif. Western States Life Ins. Co., 1943; treas. Women's Aux. Stranger's Hosp., Rio de Janeiro, Brazil, 1964-65. Vice pres. Douglaston (N.Y.) Women's Club, 1955; mem. Douglaston Garden Club, 1951-55; pres. Nina Opland chpt. Women's Cancer Assn. U. Miami, 1960-61; corr. sec. Coral Gables (Fla.) Garden Club, 1960-62; pres. Miami Alumnae Club of Pi Beta Phi, 1961-62; mem. Putnam Hill chpt. D.A.R., Greenwich Conn., 1967-75, Palm Beach chpt., 1978—; mem. Woman's Club, Greenwich, Conn., 1967-75; mem. Women's Panhellenic Assn., Miami, 1961-62; internat. treas. Ikebana Internat., Tokyo, Japan, 1966-67, parliamentarian Tokyo chpt., 1966-67, N.Y. chpt., 1968-69; mem. Coll. Women Assn. Japan, 1965-66; mem. Tchrs. Assn. Sogetsu Sch. Japanese Flower Arranging, 1966—, Atlantis Golf Club. Served to 1st.lt. WAVES, 1943-45. Mem. Internat. Platform Assn., AAUW, Pi Beta Phi (local v.p. alumnae club 1969-71). Baptist. Club: Steamboat Investment (pres. 1972-73). Home: 316 Fairway Ct Lake Worth FL 33462

MOORE, ALMA C., publishing executive; b. Cin.; d. Henry Paul and Helena Anne (Link) Clausing; m. Roy Moore. Student, Stephens Coll., Parsons Sch. Design, New Sch. Social Rsch., N.Y.C. Women's editor TV Guide mag., N.Y.C., 1962-70; dir. advt., promotion and pub. rels. Yves Saint Laurent Parfums, 1971-72; v.p., promotion and editorial dir. Viva/Omni mags., 1974-80; dir. mktg. communication Redbook mag., 1980-83; editor, pub. Woman Entrepreneur mag., 1983-85; pres. Alma C. Moore & Assocs. Mag. Cons., N.Y.C., 1983—. Mem. ind. jud. screening panel N.Y.C. Civil Ct. Judges Dem. Com., 1985, Women's Campaign Fund; sponsor Children's Aid Soc. Mem. ACLU, NOW, LWV, Nat. Trust Hist. Preservation, Advt. Women N.Y., Women's Econ. Roundtable (N.Y.), Nat. Women's Polit. Caucus, Women's City Club of N.Y. Home and Office: 171 E 62nd St New York NY 10021-7605

MOORE, AMY NORWOOD, lawyer; b. Durham, N.C., Sept. 24, 1953. AB summa cum laude, Mt. Holyoke Coll., 1976; MA, U. Va., 1978, JD, 1983. Bar: D.C. 1984, U.S. Ct. Appeals (D.C. and 6th cirs.) 1985. Law clk. to Frank M. Coffin, U.S. Ct. Appeals (1st cir.), 1983-84; ptnr. Covington & Burling, Washington. Articles editor Va. Law Rev., 1982-83. Mem. Phi Beta Kappa. Office: Covington & Burling PO Box 7566 1201 Pennsylvania Ave NW Washington DC 20044-7566

MOORE, ANDREA S., state legislator; b. Libertyville, Ill., Sept. 2, 1944. Attended, Drake U. m. William Moore; 3 children. Mem. Ill. Ho. of Reps., 1993—; mem. com. on elections and state govt., mem. com. on aging, mem. cities and villages com., mem. environ. and energy com., mem. labor and commerce com. Republican. Home: 361 S Saint Marys Rd Libertyville IL 60048-9407 Office: Ill Ho of Reps State Capitol Springfield IL 62706 also: 2014-H Stratton Bldg Springfield IL 62706 also: 733 N Milwaukee Ave Libertyville IL 60048-1913*

MOORE, ANN S., magazine publisher; b. McLean, VA, 1950; d. Monty and Bea Sommovigo; m. Donovan Moore; 1 son, Brendan. MBA, Harvard U., 1978. With Time, Inc., New York, NY, 1978—; founding publisher Sports Illustrated For Kids, 1989-91; publisher People Weekly, 1991-94, pres., 1994—. Office: People Magazine Rockefeller Ct Time & Life Building New York NY 10020-1393*

MOORE, ANNE FRANCES, museum director; b. Jan. 6, 1946; d. William Clifton and Frances Woods Moore; m. Michael P. Mezzatesta, Mar. 14, 1970 (div. 1987); children: Philip Moore, Alexander Woods, Marya Frances; m. Ernest Watson Hutton Jr., Apr. 20, 1996. BA in Art History, Columbia U., 1969, MA, 1971, MEd in Fine Arts, 1971, MA in Art History, 1982. Tchr. Manassas (Va.) High Sch., 1971-72, Poly. Prep. Country Day Sch., Bklyn., 1972-74; edn. instr. Kimbell Art Mus., Ft. Worth, 1980-83, rsch. assoc., lectr., 1983; assoc. mus. educator, outreach dir. Dallas Mus. Art, 1986-88; curator of edn., lectr. dept. art Oberlin (Ohio) Coll., 1988-90, curator acad. programs, lectr. dept. art, 1991-92; acting dir. The Allen Meml. Art Mus. at Oberlin Coll., 1991-92, dir., 1992—. Bd. trustees Intermus. Conservation Assn. Mem. Assn. Art Mus. Dirs., Assn. Coll. and Univ. Mus. and Galleries, Am. Assn. Mus. (edn. com.), Ohio Mus. Assn., Coll. Art Assn. Office: Allen Memorial Art Museum Oberlin College Oberlin OH 44074

MOORE, BEATRICE, religious organization administrator; b. Somerville, Mass., Oct. 6, 1928; d. George and Christina Turner; m. Wendell Moore, May 9, 1953; children: Karl C., Linda Moore Flewelling, Diane Pearl, Larry. BS in Theology and English, Berkshire Christian Coll., Lenox, Mass., 1950. Pres. The Woman's Home and Foreign Mission Society, Loudon, N.H.; nat. pres. The Woman's Home and Foreign Mission Society, Charlotte, N.C. Sunday sch. tchr., deaconess Loudon Ridge Family Bible Ch.; active Women's Home and Fgn. Mission Soc., Loudon, past pres. N.H. Soc., past pres. ea. region; contee guide Stonecroft Ministries; leader 4-H Club. Office: Woman's Home & Foreign Mission 845 Loudon Ridge Rd Loudon NH 03301-1712

MOORE, BETTY JEAN, retired education educator; b. L.A., Apr. 4, 1927; d. Ralph Gard and Dora Mae (Shinn) Bowman; m. James H. Moore, Nov. 25, 1944 (div. 1968); children: Barbara, Suzanne, Sandra; m. George W. Nichols, Oct. 15, 1983. BA, Pasadena Coll., 1957; MA, U. Nev., 1963; PhD, U. Ill., 1973. Tchr. Calif. pub. schs., 1953-63, sec. tchr., 1963-68; asst. prof. Ea. Ill. U., Charleston, 1968-71; grad. teaching asst. U. Ill., Champaign, 1971-73; asst. prof. to assoc. prof. S.W. Tex. State U., San Marcos, 1973-83, prof. edn., 1983-89, ret., 1989, prof. emeritus, 1995—; sch. evaluator; cons. in field; reading clinic dir. S.W. Tex. State U., 1974-85; cons. Min. Edn., Rep. of Singapore, 1980. Contbr. articles to profl. jours.; author: Teaching Reading, 1984; producer/dir. 5 ednl. videos. Active fund raising various charitable orgns. Mem. Internat. Reading Assn. (chpt. pres. 1964-65), Nat. Council Tchrs. English, AAUP. Presbyterian. Office: Southwest Tex State U C & I Dept San Marcos TX 78666

MOORE, BETTY JO, legal assistant; b. Medicine Lodge, Kans., July 10; d. Joseph Christy and Helen Blanche (Hubbell) Sims; m. Harold Frank Moore, June 19, 1941; children: Terrance C., Harold Anthony, Trisha Jo. Cert., U. West L.A., 1978; student, Wichita (Kans.) U., 1940-41. Cert. legal asst./escrow officer. Sec. UCLA, 1949-59; escrow officer Security Pacific Nat. Bank, L.A., 1959-62, Empire Savs. & Loan Assn., Van Nuys, Calif., 1962-64; escrow supr. San Fernando Valley Bank, Van Nuys, 1964; escrow officer Heritage Bank, Westwood, Calif., 1964-66; escrow coord. Land Sys. Corp., Woodland Hills, Calif., 1966-67; escrow officer/asst. mgr., real estate lending officer Security Pacific Nat. Bank, L.A., 1967-80; real estate paralegal Pub. Storage, Pasadena, 1980-81; asst. mgr. escrow dept. First Beverly Bank, Century City, Calif., 1982-84; escrow trainer/officer Moore's Tng. Temps Inc., Canoga Park, Calif., 1984—; participant People to People Ambassador Program/Women in Mgmt. to USSR, 1989; observer Internat. Fedn. Bus. and Profl. Women's Congress, Washington, 1965, 81, Nassau, Bahamas, 1989, Narobi, Kenya, 1991. Adv. bd. escrow edn. Pierce Coll., Woodland Hills, Calif., 1968-80. Recipient Cert. of Appreciation, Pierce Coll., 1979, Calif. Fedn. Bus. and Profl. Women, 1989, Nat. Women's History Project, 1995. Mem. Nat. Fedn. Bus. and Profl. Women's Clubs, Calif. Fedn. Bus. and Profl. Women (pres. dist. 1987-88, Calif. Found. chmn. 1988-89, internat. concerns chmn. 1996—), Woodlands Hills Bus. and Profl. Women ((pres. 1991-92, 94-95), Tri Valley Dist. Bus. and Profl. Women (legis. chair 1992-93, exec./corr. sec. 1993-94, 94-95), Internat. Fedn. Bus. and Profl. Women, Nat. Women's Polit. Caucus (coord., sec. San Fernando Valley caucus 1986-87, legis. co-chair 1991-92, 92-93), Women's Orgn. Coalition San Fernando Valley (sec. 1992, mem. exec. com. L.A. Women's Equality Day 1995), San Fernando Valley Escrow Assn. (bd. dirs. 1962-64), Woodland Hills C. of C. (assoc.), San Fernando Valley Bd. Realtors, L.A. Women's Legis. Coalition, U. West L.A. Alumni Assn. Democrat. Methodist.

MOORE, BOBBIE FAY, geriatrics nurse practitioner, nurse administrator; b. Woodward, Okla., Jan. 21, 1943; d. Marion Byron and Lelah Catherine (Anderson) Carey; m. Donald Kent Strickland, Apr. 2, 1959 (div. June 1968); children: Donald, Michael; m. Myrl Lynn Moore, Apr. 15, 1988. ADN, N.Mex. State U., Carlsbad, 1983; geriatric nurse practitioner, U. Colo., Denver, 1985. Cert. geriatric nurse practitioner, Am. Nurses Credentialing Ctr., N.Mex. Charge nurse Landsun Homes, Carlsbad, 1971-76; office nurse Dr. C. Munkers, Marquette, Mich., 1976-78; staff and treatment rm. nurse Guadalupe Med. Ctr., Carlsbad, 1978-83; nursing supr., nurse practitioner Landsun Homes, Carlsbad, 1985—, lic. nursing home adminstr., 1990—; mem. nursing adv. bd. N.Mex. State U., 1985—. Tchr. Sunday sch. Meth. Ch., Carlsbad; treas. Continuing Edn. Commn., Carlsbad, 1988—; counselor Boy Scouts Am., Carlsbad, 1989—; youth sponsor 1st United Meth. Ch., Carlsbad, 1990—. Mem. N.Mex. Nurse Practitioner Coun. Home: 103 E Riverside Dr Carlsbad NM 88220-5231

MOORE, CAROLYN LANNIN, video specialist; b. Hammond, Ind., Aug. 14, 1945; d. William Wren and Julia Audrey (Mathews) Lannin; m. F. David Moore, Oct. 21, 1967; children: Jillian Winter Moore Mirise, Douglas Mathew, Owen Glen. BA, Ind. U., 1967; MA, Purdue U., 1991. Stockholders corr. Sears Roebuck and Co., Chgo., 1967-68; caseworker Lake County Dept. of Pub. Welfare, Hammond, Ind., 1968-71; field dir. Campfire Girls Inc., Highland, Ind., 1975-77; project dir. Northwest Ind. Pub. Broadcasting, Highland, 1984-85, interim exec. dir., 1985-87; cons. Telecom. and Grant Writing, Munster, Ind., 1981-85; prin. Carolyn Moore and Assocs.-Laughing Cat Prodns., Munster, Ind., 1987—; instr. Purdue U.-Calumet, Ind., 1989; instr. Valparaiso (Ind.) U., 1990-91; lectr. in field. Prodr. TV series Visclosky Viewpoint, 1985-87; video prodr. A Kid's Eye View of the Symphony, 1987; vol. on-air talent Sta. WYIN Channel 56; co-host This Week in Munster. Mem. Munster Cable TV Commn., 1984—; bd. dirs. N.W. Ind. Literacy Coalition, Inc.; mem. Lake County Master Gardeners; bd. dirs. Ednl. Referral Ctr.. Mem. AAUW, NAFE, Alliance for Cmty. Media, Assn. Ind. Video and Filmmakers Inc., Munster C. of C., Communicators N.W. Ind. (treas. 1996), N.W. Ind. World Trade Coun. (bd. dirs.), Ind. U. Alumni Assn., Sherwood Ladies Golf Leagues, Wicker Park Ladies Golf League (pres.). Democrat. Catholic. Home and Office: Carolyn Moore & Assocs Laughing Cat Prodns 9604 Cypress Ave Munster IN 46321-3418

MOORE, CHERYL MARIE, artist; b. Roanoke, Va., June 30, 1971; d. Timothy Owen and Sharon Lynn (Moore) Beasley; m. Eric Eugene Kalman, June 19, 1992 (div. Sept. 1995); 1 child, Jacob Durham Moore-Copeland. Student, Old Dominion U., Norfolk, Va., 1995. Owner Silver Springs, Virginia Beach, Va., 1992-94, The Conjured Night, Chapel Hill, N.C., 1995—; creator/spkr. workshop "Honoring Your Moontime, 1995, 96. Author articles/poetry to Circle Network News, 1993—; pub./creator Night Queen jour.; singer band Lollygag. Advisor Grass Roots Arts and Crafts, Chapel Hill, 1996—; mem. N.C. Arts Coun., 1996, Of a Like Mind, Madison, Wis. Mem. NOW, Parents and Friends of Lesbians and Gays. Democrat. Dianic Religion. Home: PO Box 154 Saxapahaw NC 27340 Office: The Conjured Night PO Box 16844 Chapel Hill NC 27516

MOORE, COLLEEN FAYE, professional counselor, educator; b. Sault Ste. Marie, Mich., Sept. 16, 1947; d. Fredrick Joseph and Elda Virginia (Nordquist) Smith; m. Donald Melville Moore, June 12, 1965; children: William Melville, Donald Scott, Nancy Louise. Cert. in acctg., Lansing (Mich.) C.C., 1983; assoc. in bus., Kirtland C.C., Roscommon, Mich., 1986; BS in Bus. Edn., Ferris State U., 1990; MA in Counseling, Ctrl. Mich. U., 1994. Lic. profl. counselor. Real estate appraiser Quadrant Northwest Appraisal Svc., Cadillac, Mich., 1984-87; tax preparer H&R Block, Cadillac, 1986-87;

asst. to adminstr. County of Wexford, Cadillac, 1987-89; tchr. Cadillac Cmty. Schs., Cadillac, 1990—; instr. Baker Coll., Cadillac, 1991-93; counselor in pvt. practice Cadillac, 1994—; instr. Northwestern Mich. Coll. Cadillac br., 1996—. Mem. Mich. Counseling Assn., Mich. Sch. Counselor's Assn., Mich. Career Devel. Assn., Am. Counseling Assn., Am. Profl. Soc. on Abuse of Children, Delta Pi Epsilon. Office: Profl Counseling Svcs 2019 Michigan Ave Cadillac MI 49601

MOORE, DARGAN FISHBURNE, poet; b. Walterboro, S.C., Apr. 14, 1940; d. Lucius Gaston and Florence Barnwell (Dargan) Fishburne; m. Austin, Dargan, Walker Gage, Lucius. Student, St. Mary's Jr. Coll., Raleigh, N.C., U. S.C. Probation officer S.C. Juv. Dept., Walterboro; tennis instr. Walterboro; freelance interior decor and social etiquette, Walterboro, 1993-96. Author poetry. Bd. dirs. Network for Youth Svcs., Walterboro, 1985-95; active Casa Little Theatre, Walterboro; bd. dirs. Hampton St. Auditorium Renovation, 1994-96; promoter Jr. League Placement in Orthopedic Sch., Cola, S.C., 1968, sustainer Cola Jr. League. Mem. Colonial Dames. Episcopalian. Home: 508 Hampton St Walterboro SC 29488-4015

MOORE, DEBRA WHITE, music educator; b. Lansdale, Pa., Apr. 19, 1967; d. Eugene Allen and Constance (Painter) White; m. Robert Scott Moore, Aug. 1, 1987. B in Music Edn., U. N.C., 1989; postgrad., Ohio State U., 1992—. Cert. level I Orff; spl. cert. std. Ohio Dept. Edn. Tchr. music Pitt County Schs., Greenville, N.C., 1989-91; substitute tchr. Columbus (Ohio) Pub. Schs., 1991; tchr. music Westerville (Ohio) Schs., 1992—; choir dir. Immanuel Bapt. Ch., Greenville, 1989-91, Scottwood Congl. Ch., Columbus, 1991—; guest tchr. Ohio Dominican Coll., summer 1983. co-researcher: Ohio State Dept. of Edn. Arts for Students With Special Needs, 1994. Music dir. Westerville Peace Sch., 1992. Paul Douglas Teaching fellow U.S. Dept. Edn., 1987-88. Mem. Ohio Educators Assn., Westerville Educators Assn., Music Educators Assn., Ohio Music Educators Assn., N.C. Educators Assn., N.C. Music Educators Assn. Office: Pointview Elem Sch 720 Pointview Dr Westerville OH 43081-3435

MOORE, DEMI (DEMI GUYNES), actress; b. Roswell, N.Mex., Nov. 11, 1962; d. Danny and Virginia Guynes; m. Bruce Willis, Nov. 21, 1987; 3 daughters: Rumer Glenn, Scout LaRue, Tallulah Belle. Studies with Zina Provendie. Actress: (feature films) Choices, 1981, Parasite, 1981, Young Doctors in Love, 1982, Blame it on Rio, 1984, No Small Affair, 1984, St. Elmo's Fire, 1985, About Last Night..., 1986, Wisdom, 1986, One Crazy Summer, 1987, The Seventh Sign, 1988, We're No Angels, 1989, Ghost, 1990, Mortal Thoughts, 1991 (also co-producer), The Butcher's Wife, 1991, Nothing But Trouble, 1991, A Few Good Men, 1992, Indecent Proposal, 1993, Disclosure, 1994, The Scarlet Letter, 1995, Now and Then, 1995 (also prodr.), Undisclosed, 1996, Striptease, 1996, The Juror, 1996; (TV series) General Hospital, 1982-83; (TV movies) If These Walls Could Talk, 1996 (also exec. prodr.); (voice) The Hunchback of Notre Dame, 1996. Office: Creative Artists Agy Inc 9830 Wilshire Blvd Beverly Hills CA 90212-1804*

MOORE, DIANNE J. HALL, insurance claims administrator; b. Wadsworth, Ohio, June 9, 1936; d. Glenn Mackey and Dorothy Laverne (Broomall) Hall; widowed; children: Christine M. Gardner Fiocca, Jon R. Gardner. BA in Speech, Heidelberg Coll., Tiffin, Ohio, 1958. Receptionist Buckeye Union Ins. Co., Akron, Ohio, 1966-67; adjuster Liberty Mut. Ins. Co., Akron, 1967-69; claims liaison Ostrov Agy., Akron, 1969-70; underwriter Clark Agy., Wadsworth, 1971-72; adjuster Celina Group, Wadsworth, 1972-73, Nationwide, Canton, Ohio, 1973-77; asst. claim mgr. Motorist Mut. Ins. Co., Akron, 1977-87; claim rep. Ohio Casualty Ins. Co., San Diego, 1987-88; claims adminstr. Riser Foods, Inc. Risk Mgmt., Bedford Heights, Ohio, 1989—. Mem. Ohio Hist. Soc., Friends of Gettysburg. Mem. Ohio State Claims Assn., Akron Claims Assn. (pres. 1985), Canton Claims Assn. Office: Riser Foods Inc 5300 Richmond Rd Bedford OH 44146-1335

MOORE, EILEEN MARIE, dietitian; b. Buffalo, Feb. 27, 1959; d. Norman J. and Dorothy Phyllis (Kasperek) M. AS in Food Svc. Adminstrn., Erie Community Coll., 1979; BS in Clin. Dietetics, SUNY, Oneonta, 1982. Registered and lic. dietician, Ohio; cert. nutrition support dietitian, Ohio. Clin. dietician Cleve. Metrohealth Systems, 1983-94; clin. dietitian home health svcs. Home Intensive Care Inc., 1991—; cons. home health care quality assurance Care Plus, Inc., Beachwood, Ohio, 1988-89; mem. med. intensive care quality assurance com. Metrohealth Med. Ctr., Cleve., 1987-94, mem. home health care com., 1990-91. Statler Hilton Found. scholar, 1979. Mem. Am. Dietetic Assn., Dietitians in Critical Care, Am. Soc. Parenteral And Enteral Nutrition (cert.). Roman Catholic. Home: 950 Tollis Pky Apt 608 Cleveland OH 44147-1848

MOORE, (MARGARET) ELEANOR MARCHMAN, retired librarian; b. Pinckard, Ala., Nov. 6, 1913; d. Robert Lee and Eleanor Rowena (Paris) Marchman; A.B., Fla. State Coll. for Women, 1936; B.S. in L.S., George Peabody Coll. for Tchrs., 1947, M.A. in Library Sci., 1962; m. James William Moore, Feb. 22, 1934 (div. 1940); 1 son, John Robert. Tchr. Alva (Fla.) High Sch., 1938-40, Wacissa (Fla.) Jr. High Sch., 1940-43; librarian Bartow (Fla.) Sr. High Sch., 1943-45, 48-67, Bartow Pub. Library, 1945-48; cataloger Roux Library, Fla. So. Coll., Lakeland, 1967-70, reference librarian, 1970-75; co-sponsor Polk County Student Library Assn., 1957-59; intern tchr. Fla. State U.; former mem. evaluating team So. Assn. Secondary Schs. and Colls. Recipient Polk County Career Increment award, 1961. Mem. NEA, Beta Phi Mu, Delta Kappa Gamma. Democrat. Baptist. Address: 251 Marilyn Dr Lafayette LA 70503-3968

MOORE, EMMA SIMS, executive secretary; b. Branford, Fla., Oct. 27, 1937; d. Lawton Edward and Annie Ruth (Hewitt) Sims; m. H. Dean Moore, Sr., Sept. 30, 1961; 1 child, H. Dean Jr. Secretarial sci., Jones Coll., 1955; B., Butler U., 1984; MS, Ind. Wesleyan U., 1989; MA, The Fielding Inst., 1995, EdD, 1996. Cert. profl. sec.; cert. adminstrv. mgr. Sec. to svc. mgr. Buick Motor div. GM, Jacksonville, Fla., 1956-72, Charlotte, N.C., 1972-74; sec. to br. mgr. Motors Holding div. GM, Washington, 1974-78, Phila., 1978-82; exec. sec. to dir. product support Allison Gas Turbine div. GM, Indpls., 1982-92; ret., 1992; mem. faculty Ind.- Wesleyan U., 1993-94, Southern Wesleyan Univ. Central, S.C., 1995—. Mem. exec. com. Boy Scouts Am., West Chester, Pa., 1981-82. Mem. AAUW, NAFE (profl. secs. internat. goodwill people to people del. to People's Republic of China, Singapore, Thailand, Indonesia and Hong Kong), Profl. Secs. Internat. (v.p. 1986-87, pres. 1987-89, 500 chpt., Sec. of Yr. 1986 500 chpt., 1989 Ind. divs.), CPS Acad., Inst. Certification. Wesleyan. Home: 107 Catawbah Rd Clemson SC 29631-2826

MOORE, FAY LINDA, software quality engineer; b. Houston, Apr. 7, 1942; d. Charlie Louis and Esther Mable (Banks) Moore; m. Noel Patrick Walker, Jan. 5, 1963 (div. 1967); 1 child, Trina Nicole Moore. Student, Prairie View Agrl. and Mech. Coll., 1960-61, Tex. So. U., 1961, Our Lady Lake U., 1993, Thomas Edison State Coll., 1995-96; capability maturity model assessor tng. Software Engring. Inst., 1995. Cert. ISO 9000 Internal Auditor. Instr. Internat. Bus. Coll., Houston, 1965; keypunch operator IBM Corp., Houston, 1965-67, sr. keypunch operator, 1967-70, programmer technician, 1970-72, asst. programmer, 1972-73, assoc. programmer, 1973-84, sr. assoc. programmer, 1984-87, staff programmer, 1987-94, staff systems analyst, 1994—; sr. software quality engineer Loral Space Info. Systems, Houston, 1994-96; owner, pres. AFT Co., Houston, 1993—; sr. software quality engr. Lockheed Martin Corp., Houston, 1996—; mem. space shuttle flight support team IBM, 1985-92; mem. space sta. team IBM, 1992-93. Recipient Apollo Achievement award NASA, 1969, Quality and Productivity award NASA, 1986, 1992. Mem. NAFE, Soc. Software Quality, Booker T. Washington Alumni Assn., Ms. Found. for Women, Inc. Democrat. Roman Catholic. Avocations: personal computing, board games. Office: Lockheed Martin Corp Mail Stop F6M1A 1322 Space Park Dr Houston TX 77058-3410

MOORE, GISELLE JOSEPHINE, nurse practitioner; b. Nassau, Bahamas; d. John Palmer and Valerie Irene (Merrells) M. BSN, Barry Coll., 1981; MSN, U. Fla., 1990. Advanced registered nurse practitioner, Fla. RN Shands Hosp., Gainesville, Fla., 1982-87; advanced registered nurse practitioner U. Fla./Shands, Gainesville, 1987—; . Fla., Gainesville. Editor: Women's Cancer: A Gynecological Oncology Perspective, 1996—; mem. editl. bd. Cancer Nursing Jour., 1993—. Cons. Am. Cancer Soc., Gainesville, 1993—. Mem. Soc. Gyn. Nurse (chmn. publs.), Oncology Nurse Soc., Am. Holistic Nurses Assn., Fla. Nurses Assn., Sigma Theta Tau. Republican. Ch. of England. Home: 2317 NW 69th Ter Gainesville FL 32606-6393

MOORE, HEATHER PAGE, accountant; b. Birmingham, Ala., Mar. 13, 1969; d. John Coleman Allman and Barbara (Rushing) Prater; m. Stewart Bradford Moore, Aug. 3, 1991. BS, Auburn U., 1989, MBA, 1990; postgrad., U. Ala. Acct. EBSCO Industries, Inc., Birmingham, 1991—. Mem. Inst. Mgmt. Accts. Home: 2410 Park Ln S Mountain Brook AL 35213 Office: EBSCO Industries Inc PO Box 1943 Birmingham AL 35201

MOORE, HELEN ELIZABETH, reporter; b. Rush County, Ind., Dec. 19, 1920; d. John Brackenridge and Mary Amelia (Custer) Johnson; m. John William Sheridan, July 6, 1942 (dec. Jan. 1944); m. Harry Evan Moore, May 15, 1954; 1 child, William Randolph. BS, Ind. U., 1972, MS, 1973. Ofcl. ct. reporter 37th Jud. Cir., Brookville, Ind., 1950-60; freelance reporter Rushvile, Ind., 1960—; conv. reporter various assns. With USMC, 1943. Recipient Sagamore of the Wabash award Gov. Ind., 1984. Mem. Women Marines Assn. (charter, nat. pres. 1966-68), Am. Legion Aux. (various offices 1950— including Eight Forty nat. sec.-treas., pres. Ind. dept. 1966-67, conv. reporter), Bus and Profl. Women (dist. dir., various offices 1967—), Nat. Shorthand Reporters Assn. (registered profl. reporter), Ind. Shorthand Reporters Assn. (state treas., editor Hoosier Reporter, chmn. legal directory), German Geneal. Soc. Am., Ind. German Heritage Soc. (state dir. 1984-92, pres. 1990-92), Ind. U. Alumni Assn. Democrat. Methodist. Home and Office: PO Box 206 Rushville IN 46173-0206

MOORE, HONOR, writer, educator; b. N.Y.C., Oct. 28, 1945; d. Paul and Jenny (McKean) M. BA, Harvard U., 1967. Tchr. Young Writers Inst., Hartford, Conn., 1993—, Women Writing/Women Telling, Kent, Conn., 1994—, Poetry Workshops, Kent, 1994—. Author: Mourning Pictures, 1974 (Creative Artists Pub. Svc. grant 1975), Memoir (collection of poems), 1989, The White Blackbird, a life of the painter Margarett Sargent by her granddaughter, 1996; guest curator Margarett Sargent: A Modern Temperament, 1996. Mem. steering com. Women Writing Women's Lives seminar; vol. N.Y. Ctr. for Humanities, 1991-93, Ctr. for the Humanities, CUNY, 1993-95; bd. dirs. Jenny McKean Moore Fund for Writers, Washington, 1975—, Manhattan Theatre Club, N.Y.C., 1972-76, Music Theatre Group, N.Y.C., 1976-93. Artists grantee Conn. Commn. on Arts, 1992; Nat. Endowment for Arts Creative Writing fellow, 1981; N.Y. Coun. on the Arts grantee, 1976. Mem. Poets and Writers Inc. (bd. dirs. 1974-93), Poetry Soc. Am., PEN Am. Ctr. Home and Office: PO Box 305 Kent CT 06757-0305

MOORE, JACKIE LOU, nurse; b. Blytheville, Ark., Oct. 29, 1955; d. Earl E. and Tommie L. (DeBerry) Brooks; m. Richard D. Moore, May 8, 1982; children: Jamie Lee, Mary Grace. BSN, Miss. Coll., 1977. RN, Miss.; cert. rehab. RN. Staff nurse, clinician Meth. Rehab. Ctr., Jackson, Miss., 1977-83; cons. med. svcs. Crawford Health & Rehab., Jackson, Miss., 1983-88; cons. rehab. nurse Sims & Assocs., Jackson, Miss., 1988-91; med. case mgr. Rehab., Inc., Brandon, Miss., 1991—. Vol. Stewpot Soup Kitchen, Jackson, 1994, Heart Assn. Jackson, 1992. Mem. Nat. Assn. Rehab. Profls. (program chmn. 1986-88, bd. dirs. 1992-94), Miss. Assn. Rehab. Nurses (bd. dirs. 1988-89), Assn. Rehab. Nurses (sec. Miss. chpt. 1992—), Case Mgmt. Assn., Am. Assn. Legal Nurse Cons. Office: Rehab Inc PO Box 4244 Jackson MS 39296-4244

MOORE, JANE ROSS, librarian; b. Phila., Apr. 24, 1929; d. John William and Mary (McClure) Ross; m. Cyril Howard Moore, Jr., June 1, 1956 (div. Mar. 1967). A.B., Smith Coll., 1951; M.S. in L.S., Drexel U., 1952; postgrad., Columbia U.; M.B.A. with distinction, NYU, 1965; Ph.D., Case Western Res. U., 1974. Cataloguer, Yale U. Library, 1952-54; chief tech. processes librarian Lederle Labs., Am. Cyanamid Co., Pearl River, N.Y., 1954-58; chief serials catalog librarian Bklyn. Coll. Library, 1958-65, asst. prof., chief catalog div., 1965-70, asso. prof., chief catalog div., 1971-73, asso. prof. asso. librarian adminstrv. services, 1973-76; prof., chief librarian Mina Rees Libr., Grad. Sch. and Univ. Center, CUNY, 1976-91, prof., chief libr. emerita, 1991—; lectr. Syracuse U. Grad. Sch. Libr. Sci., summer 1967, 69, Queens Coll. Grad. Sch. Libr. and Info. Studies, 1967-69; adj. assoc. prof., 1974-76, adj. prof., 1977-86; HEW Title IIB fellow Case Western Res. U. Sch. Library Sci., 1970-72; trustee N.Y. Met. Reference and Rsch. Libr. Agy., 1984-93, 2d v.p., 1985-88, v.p., 1988-90, treas. 1991-93; mem. chancellor's task force on librs. CUNY, 1979-81. Bd. dirs. Vis. Nurse Assn. of Bklyn., 1984—, mem. exec. com., 1987—; elder, clk. of session, pres. of corp. Presbyn. Ch. Mem. N.Y. Library Assn. (pres. 1979-80, pres. resources and tech. services sect. 1966-67, councilor 1966-67, 75-76, 78-81, sec.-treas. acad. and spl. libraries sect. 1973-75), ALA (membership com. 1967-71, chmn. council regional groups, resources and tech. services div. 1968-69, dir. div. 1968-70, 75-76, chmn. div. cataloging and classification sect. 1975-76), N.Y. Tech. Services Librarians (pres. 1963-64, award 1976), Assn. Coll. and Research Libraries (chmn. univ. libraries sect. 1983-84), N.Y. Library Club (sec. 1964-66, pres. 1980-81, council 1966-70, 73-77, 79-82), OCLC Users Council (SUNY del. 1981-85), AAUP, AAUW, Am. Printing History Assn., Am. Soc. Info. Sci., Archons of Colophon, Library Assn. of Great Brit., Spl. Libraries Assn., The Typophiles, NYU Grad. Sch. Bus. Adminstrn. Alumni Assn. (rec. sec. 1967-69, dir. 1969-70, 75-79), Smith Coll. Club Bklyn. (pres. 1966-67, 67-68, class treas. 1976-81), Smith Coll. Club N.Y., Princeton Club N.Y., Phi Kappa Phi. Home: 35 Schermerhorn St Brooklyn NY 11201-4826 Office: CUNY Mina Rees Libr Grad Sch & U Ctr 33 W 42nd St New York NY 10036-8003

MOORE, JANET MARIE, accountant, state official; b. Butler, Pa., Mar. 13, 1947; d. Jesse Robert and Katherine Mae (Pisor) Moore. A in Specialized Bus., New Castle Bus. Coll., 1972. Cost accountant Package Products Inc., Pitts., 1967-68; audit clk. Liberty Mut. Ins. Co., New Castle, Pa., 1968-71; acct. S.R. Snodgrass & Co., CPAs, New Castle, 1971-74; clerical supr. Pa. vital records Pa. Dept. Health, New Castle, 1974—; pvt. practice acctg., Volant, Pa., 1974—. Mem. NRA (life), Owner Handler Assn., Am. Numismatic Assn., Studebaker Family Nat. Assn. (life), New Castle Kennel Club (sec. 1978, dir. 1977-81, v.p. 1979-81). Democrat. Presbyterian. Home: RR 3 Box 101 Volant PA 16156-8815 Office: PO Box 1528 New Castle PA 16103-1528

MOORE, JANET RUTH, nurse, educator; b. Bridgeport, Conn., Sept. 19, 1949; d. Robert Hartland and Florence (Merritt) Bessom; m. William James Moore, Sept. 5, 1971; children: Jeffrey, Gregory. AA, Green Mountain Coll., 1969; diploma, Mass. Gen. Hosp., 1974; BS in Nursing, Am. Internat. Coll., 1980; MS in Nursing, U. Mass., 1993. RN, Mass.; cert. gerontol. nurse, gerontol. clin. nurse specialist ANCC. Nurse's aide Lynn (Mass.) Hosp., 1967-69, staff nurse, 1972-73; nursing asst. U.S. Army Hosp., Ft. Polk, La., 1971-72; staff nurse Ludlow (Mass.) Hosp., 1980-85; staff edn. instr. Springfield (Mass.) Mcpl. Hosp., 1985-88; dir. staff edn. Jewish Nursing Home, Longmeadow, Mass., 1988-93; instr. Baystate Med. Ctr. Sch. Nursing, Springfield, Mass., 1993—; nurse Camp Wilder, Springfield, 1981-84; clin. instr. Holyoke (Mass.) Community Coll., 1990. Mem. Jr. League of Springfield, 1981-88, Community Health Edn. Council for Children and Adolescents; bd. dirs. Mass. Soc. for Prevention of Cruelty to Children, Springfield, 1985-90, Coun. of Chs., chairperson, Div. on Aging, 1989-90. Mem. ANA, Wilbraham Jr. Women's Club, Sigma Theta Tau, Alpha Chi. Home: 104 Burleigh Rd Wilbraham MA 01095-2620 Office: Baystate Med Ctr Sch of Nursing Springfield MA 01199

MOORE, JEANNE, arts educator and administrator; b. L.A., Aug. 28, 1932; d. George E. and Ellen Kearny (Patrick) M. AA, Pasadena (Calif.) City Coll., 1952; BA with honors, UCLA, 1954; MM, U. So. Calif., 1965, DMA, 1970. Music tchr. Arvin (Calif.) H.S., 1955-60, Santa Maria (Calif.) H.S., 1960-65, Arroyo H.S., El Monte, Calif., 1965-66; asst. prof. edn. U. Victoria, B.C., Can., 1968-70; asst. prof. music edn. Bowling Green (Ohio) State Coll., 1970-71; prof. music West Chester (Pa.) State Coll., 1971-72; lectr. music San Jose (Calif.) State U., 1972-73; asst. prof. music Madison Coll., Harrisonburg, Va., 1974-76; coord. fine arts W.Va. Dept. Edn., Charleston, 1977—; choral dir. Santa Maria Choral Soc., 1963-64, Silver Lake Presbyn. Ch., L.A., 1966-67, Wesley United Meth. Ch., San Jose, 1972-74; contbr./cons. Nat. Study of Sch. Evaluation, Falls Church, Va., 1983-85, 89. Author, editor more than 40 books/monographs; editor, project coord.: (6 books, audio and video) West Virginia Music Test Item Bank, K-4, 1989, (2 books, slides and video) West Virginia Museum Resources for Teaching Art, 1991; co-author: Beyond the Classroom: Informing Others, 1987. Staff mem. Gov.'s Task Force on Arts Edn., W.Va., 1990-94. Nat. Endowment for Arts grantee, 1989-90, 91-92. Mem. Nat. Art Edn. Assn., Nat. Coun. State Suprs. Music (pres. 1984-86), Music Educators Nat. Conf., W.Va. Music Educators Assn. (bd. dirs. 1977—, Presdl. award 1990), W.Va. Art Edn. Assn. (bd. dirs. 1986—, Outstanding Adminstr. award 1991, 92, 93), Phi Delta Kappa, Pi Kappa Lambda, Mu Phi Epsilon. Episcopalian. Home: 102 Brammer Dr Charleston WV 25311-1738 Office: WVa Dept Edn 1900 Kanawha Blvd E Rm B-330 Charleston WV 25305-0002

MOORE, JENNIFER BROWN, lawyer; b. Tuscaloosa, Ala., Jan. 12, 1958. BA, U. N.C., 1983; JD, U. Ga., 1986. Bar: Ga. 1986, U.S. Ct. Appeals (11th cir.) 1986, U.S. Dist. Ct. (no. dist.) Ga. 1986, Ga. Ct. Appeals 1986, U.S. Ct. Appeals (5th cir.) 1986, Ga. Supreme Ct., Ga. Superior Ct. Ptnr. Alston & Bird, Atlanta. Mem. editl. bd. Ga. State Bar Jour., 1991-95; contbr. articles to profl. jours. Mem. Atlanta Bar Assn., State Bar Ga., Phi Beta Kappa, Phi Eta Sigma, Psi Chi, Phi Alpha Delta. Office: Alston & Bird 1 Atlantic Ctr 1201 W Peachtree St Atlanta GA 30309-3424*

MOORE, JOAN L., radiology educator, physician; b. Belmont, Mass., Oct. 26, 1935; d. Frank Joseph and Maria L. Mazzio; children: James Thomas, Edwin Stuart. BA in Chemistry and Theology, Emmanuel Coll., 1957; MA in Genetics and Physiology, Mass. Wellesley Coll., 1961; PhD in Genetics, Bryn Mawr (Pa.) Coll., 1964; MD, Phila. Coll. of Medicine, 1977, MSc in Radiology, 1981. Instr. in biochemistry Gwynedd Mercy Coll., Springhouse, Pa., 1963-65; instr. in genetics Holy Family Coll., Phila., 1965-66; instr. in anatomy Phila. Coll. of Medicine, 1971-77, tchr., 1973-77, asst. prof., 1977-84; prof. W.Va. Sch. of Medicine, 1984—; rotating intern Phila. Coll. of Medicine Hosp., 1977-78, resident in radiology, 1978-81; lt. col. USAR, 1984—; prof. W.Va. Sch. of Medicine, Lewisburg, 1984—. Author: (with Dr. DiVirgilito) Essentials of Neuropathology, 1974. Lector St. Ann's Cath. Ch., Phoenixville, Pa., 1981-84; treas. Hist. Soc. of Frankford, Phila., 1968-75, Sch. Mother's Assn., Devon (Pa.) Prep., 1980-81. Lt. col. U.S. Army Med. Corps, 1992. Mem. AAUP, Am. Acad. Family Physicians, Am. Assn. Women Radiologists, Am. Med. Women's Assn., Am. Osteo. Coll. of Radiology, Am. Soc. Clin. Oncology, Am. Soc. Therapeutic Readiologists, Hist. Soc. of Lewisburg (life), Pa. Osteo. Med. Assn., Pa. Osteo. Gen. Practitioner's Soc., Radiol. Soc. N.Am., Radiation Rsch. Soc., Res. Officers Assn. (life), W.Va. Soc. Osteo. Medicine, Greenbrier River Hike and Bike Trail. Home: RR 1 Box 123 Frankford WV 24938 Office: WVa Sch of Medicine 400 N Lee St Lewisburg WV 24901-1128

MOORE, JOANNE IWEITA, pharmacologist, educator; b. Greenville, Ohio, July 23, 1928; d. Clarence Jacob and Mary Edna (Klepinger) M. A.B., U. Cin., 1950; Ph.D., U. Mich., 1959. Rsch. asst. Christ Hosp. Inst. Med. Rsch., Cin., 1950-55; rsch. asst. U. Mich., Ann Arbor, 1955-57, teaching fellow, 1957-59; postdoctoral fellow in pharmacology Emory U., Atlanta, 1959-61; asst. prof. pharmacology U. Okla. Coll. Medicine, Oklahoma City, 1961-66, assoc. prof., 1966-71, acting chmn., 1969-71, prof., interim chmn., 1971-73, prof., chmn. dept., 1973—, David Ross Boyd prof., chair, 1993; mem. gen. rsch. support rev. com. NIH, 1975-79, mem. biomed. scis. study sect., 1986-90; mem. adv. bd. Fogarty Internat. Ctr., 1992-94. Contbr. articles to profl. jours. USPHS grantee, 1963-69, 72-74, 79-87. Mem. AAAS, Am. Soc. Pharmacology and Exptl. Therapeutics, Assn. Med. Sch. Pharmacology, Am. Heart Assn. (bd. dirs. Okla. affiliate 1973-78, pres. 1979-80, chmn. bd. 1983-85, bd. dirs. Oklahoma City div. 1988-91, pres. 1989-90), Sigma Xi. Office: U Okla Coll Medicine Dept Pharmacology 753 BMSB OUHSC Oklahoma City OK 73190

MOORE, JOY RENÉE, pharmaceutical sales representative; b. St. Charles, Mo., May 31, 1957; d. James Leroy and Velma Lee (Schlote) M. BS in Biology, Lindenwood Coll. for Women, 1979, postgrad. in Health Care Mgmt., 1996—. Svc. rep., ground hostess Airport Terminal Svcs. of St. Louis Internat. Airport, 1976-77; svc. rep., passenger sales Am. Air Lines, Inc., St. Louis, 1977-78; relief passenger svcs. mgr., passenger sales Ea. Air Lines, Inc., St. Louis, 1978-91; med. equip. sales rep. Americair, St. Louis, 1991-92; pharm. sales rep. Schering-Plough/Key Pharms. of Kenilworth N.J., St. Louis, 1992—. Goodwill amb. Silver Liners, St. Louis and Kansas City, 1986-91; patron, exhibitor Charity Horseshows, St. Louis. Biology scholar Lindenwood Coll. for Women, 1975. Republican. Roman Catholic. Home: 4873 Greenburg Dr Saint Charles MO 63304-7555 Office: Schering Plough Corp Key Pharms 2000 Galloping Hill Rd Kenilworth NJ 07033-5030

MOORE, JUDY KAY, media relations specialist; b. Mt. Clemens, Mich., July 20, 1963; d. Elmer Michael and Sharon Ann (Moore) Zurakowski. BA, Albion Coll., 1985. News reporter Green Bay (Wis.) News-Chronicle, 1985-87; chief legislative aide Wis. State Leg., Madison, 1987-90; sr. media relations specialist Univ. Wis. Hosp. Medical Sch., Madison, 1990—. Cons. Am. Heart Assn. Fundraiser, Madison, 1995; co-chair campaign State Rep. Mary Lou Van Dreel, Green Bay, 1988; mem. publicity com. Health Emotions Rsch. Inst. U. Wis., 1996, Med. Flight Critical Care Helicopter 10th Anniv. U. Wis., 1995. Recipient Merit for PR Campaign award Wis. Pub. Rels. Soc. of Am., 1995, Newswriting award Wis. Newspaper Assn., 1986. Mem. Women in Communications (membership com. 1995—), Wis. Communicators Council, Inc., Wis. Healthcare Pub. Rels. and Mktg. Soc. Office: Univ Wis Hosp Medical Sch 610 Walnut St Rm 758 Warf Madison WI 53705

MOORE, KAREN NELSON, judge; b. Washington, Nov. 19, 1948; d. Roger S. and Myrtle (Gill) Nelson; m. Kenneth Cameron Moore, June 22, 1974; children—Roger C., Kenneth N., Kristin K. A.B. magna cum laude, Radcliffe Coll., 1970, J.D. magna cum laude, Harvard U., 1973. Bar: D.C. 1973, Ohio, 1976, U.S. Ct. Appeals (D.C. cir.) 1974, U.S. Supreme Ct. 1980, U.S. Ct. Appeals (6th cir.) 1984. Law clk. Judge Malcolm Wilkey, U.S. Ct. Appeals (D.C. cir.), 1973-74; law clk. Assoc. Justice Harry A. Blackmun, U.S. Supreme Ct., Washington, 1974-75; assoc. Jones, Day, Reavis & Pogue, Cleve., 1975-77; asst. prof. Case Western Res. Law Sch., Cleve., 1977-80, assoc. prof., 1980-82, prof., 1982-95; judge U.S. Ct. Appeals (6th cir.), Cleve., 1995—; vis. prof. Harvard Law Sch., 1990-91. Mem. Harvard Law Rev., 1971-73. Contbr. articles to legal publs. Trustee Lakewood Hosp., Ohio, 1978-85, Radcliffe Coll., Cambridge, 1980-84. Fellow Am. Bar Found.; mem. Cleve. Bar Assn. (trustee 1979-82), ABA (standing com. jud. selection, tenure and compensation 1978-82), Am. Law Inst., Am. Assn. Law Schs. (chmn. civil procedure sect. 1985, academic freedom and tenure com. 1985-89, chmn. 1987-89), Harvard Alumni Assn. (bd. dirs. 1984-87), Phi Beta Kappa. Office: US Ct Appeals 6th Cir 256 US Courthouse 201 Superior Ave Cleveland OH 44114

MOORE, KIMBERLEE CHERYL, middle school educator; b. Denver, Oct. 23, 1967; d. Larry William and Elizabeth (Wood) M. BA in History, Tex. A&M U., 1990. Middle sch. tchr. Rio Vista (Tex.) Ind. Sch. Dist., 1992—. Grantee Ft. Worth Star Telegram, 1993. Mem. NEA, Tex. State Tchrs. Assn. Home: 808 Coury Rd Everman TX 76140-4308

MOORE, LINDA KATHLEEN, personnel agency executive; b. San Antonio, Tex., Feb. 18, 1944; d. Frank Edward and Louise Marie (Powell) Horton; m. Mack B. Taplin, May 25, 1963 (div. Feb. 1967); 1 child, Mack B.; m. William J. Moore, Mar. 8, 1967 (div. Nov. 1973). Student, Tex. A&I Coll., 1962-63. Co-owner S.R.O. Internat., Dallas, 1967-70; mgr. Exec. Girls Pers. & Modeling Svcs., Dallas, 1970-72, Gen. Employment Enterprises, Atlanta, 1972-88; owner, mgr. More Pers. Svcs., Inc., Atlanta, 1988-94, pres., chmn. bd., 1994—; Contbr. short story to Writer's Digest. Mem. NAFE, Nat. Fedn. Bus. and Profl. Women, Am. Soc. Profl. and Exec. Women, Women Bus. Owners, Nat. Assn. Women Cons., Nat. Assn. Personnel Svcs., Ga. Assn. Personnel Svcs., Women's Clubs, Atlanta C. of C. (speaker's bur.), Better Bus. Bur., Cobb County C. of C. Office: More Pers Svcs Inc Ste A-1190 4501 Circle 75 Pkwy Atlanta GA 30339

MOORE, LINDA PERIGO, writer; b. Evansville, Ind., Nov. 25, 1946; d. John Myrl and Loraine Jeannette (Hudson) Perigo; 1 child, Jackson Stuart Moore. BS, Miami U., Oxford, Ohio, 1968; MS, MEd, U. Louisville, 1973. Instr., St. Joseph Infirmary, Louisville, 1969-71; tng. dir. Park-DuValle Neighborhood Health Ctr., Louisville, 1971-74; counselor Charlestown High Sch. (Ind.), 1974-75; tng. dir. Midtown Mental Health Ctr., Indpls., 1977-79; freelance writer, 1980—; cons. Kelly & Assocs., Indpls., 1977-81; instr. Ind. U., Indpls., 1979-81, instr., U. So. Ind., 1986. Bd. dirs. Jr. League Evansville,

1982-84, Mothers Assn. Evansville Day Sch., 1985-87; bd. dir. Evansville Mus. Arts and Sci. Guild, 1982-88, treas. 1994—; pres. Parent, Tchr., Student Assn., Cen. High Sch., 1989-91; sec. U. Evansville Theatre Soc., 1994—. Author: Does This Mean My Kid's a Genius?, 1981; co-author: On People Management, 1984, 2d edit., 1986, Mary Kay; You're Smarter Than You Think, 1985, Japanese and Swedish edits., 1986, Winning the Gold, 1985, Reach for Fitness, 1986, We Live Too Short and Die Too Long, 1991, From Stress to Strength, 1994; Tootie Tittlemousie and the Lights of Christmas, 1988 (Ohio State award 1989); (play) Ektroma, USC dept. theatre, 1996; contbr. articles in mags. and trade jours; tv appearances include: Oprah Winfrey Show, Today, Sonya Live, Larry King.

MOORE, LINDA PICARELLI, insurance executive; b. Bklyn., Jan. 13, 1943; d. Anthony Joseph and Alma Patricia (D'Angio) Picarelli; m. William H. Moore, Nov. 11, 1962 (div. 1974); 1 child, David A.; m. Spiro D. Demetriou, Dec. 9, 1977. Student, Wagner Coll., 1976, Coll. Ins., 1977-80. Licensed ins. broker. Ins. clk. Tchrs. Ins. and Annuity Assn., N.Y.C., 1959-61; claim examiner Aetna Life and Casualty Co., N.Y.C., 1961-63; claim supr. Northeastern Life Ins. Co., N.Y.C., 1963-66; corr. collector Dun and Bradstreet, S.I., N.Y., 1972-73; asst. underwriter Duncanson and Holt, Inc., N.Y.C., 1973-76; underwriting mgr. CNA Ins. Cos., N.Y.C., 1976-85; account mgr. Marsh and McLennan Group Assn., N.Y.C., 1985-87; asst. mgr. Home Ins. Co., N.Y.C., 1987-89; dir. spl. risk underwriting Cigna Ins. Co., Phila., 1989—. Mem. NOW, Amnesty Internat., Am. Spl. Risk Assn. Democrat. Roman Catholic.

MOORE, LOIS JEAN, health science facility administrator; married; 1 child. Grad., Prairie View (Tex.) Sch. Nursing, 1957; BS in Nursing, Tex. Woman's U., 1970; MS in Edn., Tex. So. U., 1974. Nurse Harris County (Tex.) Hosp. Dist., 1957—; pres., chief exec. officer Harris County Hosp.; adminstr. Jefferson Davis Hosp., Houston, 1977-88, exec. v.p., chief ops. officer, 1988—; Mem. adv. bd. Tex. Pub. Hosp. Assn. Contbr. articles to profl. jours. Mem. Mental Health Needs Council Houston and Harris County, Congressman Mickey Leland's Infant Mortality Task Force, Houston Crack-down Com., Gov.'s task force on health care policy, 1991; chairperson Tex. Assn. Pub. and Nonprofit Hosps., 1991, subcom. of Gov.'s task force to identify essential health care svc., 1992; bd. dirs. ARC, 1991—, Greater Houston Hosp. Coun., March of Dimes, United Way. Recipient Pacesetter award North-East C. of C., 1991; named Nurse of Yr. Houston Area League Nursing, 1976-77, Outstanding Black Achiever YMCA Century Club, 1974, Outstanding Women in Medicine YWCA, 1989. Mem. Am. Coll. Hosp. Adminstrs., Tex. Hosp. Assn. (chmn. pub. hosp. com.), Young Hosp. Adminstrs., Nat. Assn. Pub. Hosps. (bd. dirs., mem. exec. com. Tex. assn.), License Vocat. Nurses Assn., sigma Theta Tau. Home: 3837 Wichita St Houston TX 77004-6536 Office: Harris County Hosp Dist PO Box 66769 Houston TX 77266-6769

MOORE, LORETTA WESTBROOK, banker; b. Cameron, Tex., Jan. 2, 1938; d. Merrill Holman and Gladys Evangeline (Strelsky) Westbrook; m. Joe Gregg Moore Jr., Sept. 22, 1956; children: Terri Lynn, Joe Gregg III. Grad. high sch., Hearne, Tex. With Planters & Merchants State Bank, Hearne, Tex., 1956—, v.p., cashier, 1980—, also bd. dirs.; group pres. Nat. Assn. Bank Women (now Fin. Women Internat.), Waco, Tex., 1980-81. Vocat. adv. coun. Hearne Pub. Schs., 1984—. Named Hon. Chpt. Farmer Future Farmers Am., 1984, Notable Women of Tex., 1984. Mem. Bank Adminstrn. Instn. (pres. Brazos Valley chpt. 1983-84), Am. Inst. Banking (bd. dirs. Brazos Valley chpt., charter), Order Eastern Star (past matron). Methodist. Home: RR 1 Box 395 Hearne TX 77859-9617 Office: Planters & Mchts State Bank 122 E 4th St Hearne TX 77859

MOORE, LOU ANNA, elementary educator; b. Richmond, Ind., June 12, 1946; d. Donald William and Clara Anna (Hatler) Meredith; m. Jerold Marvin Moore, Feb. 19, 1966; children: Kelley Renée, Christopher Allen. BS in Elem. Edn., Ind. U., 1981; MEd, Miami U., Oxford, Ohio, 1986, PhD in Curriculum Supervision and Devel., 1996. Elem. edn. cert., gen sci cert., adminstrv. cert., edn. specialist cert. Elem. tchr. Richmond (Ind.) Cmty. Schs., 1983-88, higher order thinking skills computer lab. tchr., 1988-92, program improvement facilitator, consulting tchr., 1992-95, instructional specialist, 1995-96; prin. Baxter Elem. Sch., Richmond, 1996—; rschr. assessment/classroom/sch. practice, Richmond Cmty. Schs., 1992—. Named One of Outstanding Young Women Am. Mem. ASCD, AAUW (past-pres.), Am. Edn. Rsch. Assn., Ind. State Reading Assn. (voting del., honor coun. 1994-95), Ind. Assn. Curriculum Supervision & Devel., Internat. Reading Assn. (honor coun. 1994-95), Richmond Area Reading Coun. (past pres.), Mid-West Edn. Rsch. Assn. Methodist. Home: 30 S 25th St Richmond IN 47374 Office: Baxter Elementary School 315 NW 3d St Richmond IN 47374

MOORE, MARGARET BEAR, American literature educator; b. Zhenjiang, China, Mar. 14, 1925; came to U.S., 1929; d. James Edwin Jr. and Margaret Irvine (White) Bear; m. Rayburn S. Moore, Aug. 30, 1947; children: Margaret Elizabeth Moore Kopcinski, Robert Rayburn. BA, Agnes Scott Coll., 1946; MA, U. Ga., 1973. Book rev. editor East Ark. Record, Helena, Ark., 1948-50; bibliographer Perkins Libr. Duke U., Durham, N.C., 1950-52; instr. in English Hendrix Coll., Conway, Ark., 1955-56, U. Ctrl. Ark., Conway, 1958-59; editor Inst. Cmty. & Area Devel. U. Ga., Athens, 1974-79; tchr. Latin Athens Acad., 1980-81; ind. scholar Athens, 1981—. Author (book revs.) Am. Lit., 1989, 94, Nathaniel Hawthorne Rev., 1992; contbr. articles to profl. jours. Tchr. Presbyn. Ch., Va., Ark., N.C. and Ga., 1945—; deacon, elder First Presbyn. Ch., Athens, 1974—. Mem. MLA, Am. Lit. Assn., Philol. Assn. Carolinas, Soc. for Study So. Lit., South Atlantic MLA, Nathaniel Hawthorne Soc. (exec. com. 1987-90), William Gilmore Simms Soc., Peabody Essex Mus., House of Seven Gables, Va. Hist. Soc., Mortar Bd., Phi Beta Kappa, Phi Kappa Phi. Home: 106 Saint James Dr Athens GA 30606-3926

MOORE, MARGARET HOLLIS, nursing educator; b. Gainesville, Ga., Sept. 22, 1963; d. John Palmour and Paula ann (Howard) M. BSN, Oral Roberts U., 1986. RN, Ga. Staff nurse ICU St. Francis Hosp., Tulsa, 1986-87; emergency dept. staff/relief charge nurse N.E. Ga. Med. Ctr., Gainesville, 1988-91; med./surg. staff devel. instr. Grady Meml. Health Sys., Atlanta, 1993-94; IV nurse edn. specialist Pharmacy Corp. Am., Atlanta, 1994—; BLS instr. Am. Heart Assn., Ga., 1993—. Vol. nurse clinic for underprivileged Oral Roberts U., Kingston, Jamaica, 1987-88; vol. nurse Mercy Ships, West Africa, 1991-93. Mem. Intravenous Nurses Soc. (cert.). Office: Pharmacy Corp Am 1100 Wilson Way Smyrna GA 30082

MOORE, MARIANNA GAY, law librarian, consultant; b. La Grange, Ga., Sept. 12, 1939; d. James Henry and Avanelle (Gay) M. AB in French, English, U. Ga., 1961; MLS, Emory U., 1964; postgrad., U. Ga., 1965-66, U. Ill., 1967-68. Asst. law libr. U. Ga., Athens, 1964-66; asst. libr. Yavapai Coll. Libr., Prescott, Ariz., 1969-72; libr. U. Ill. Law Libr., Urbana, 1966-68; law libr. Leva, Hawes, Symington, Washington, 1972-75; libr. project coord. Wash. Occupational Info. Svc., Olympia, 1976-80, Wash. State Health Facilities Assn., Olympia, 1981-82; mgr. Wash. State Ret. Tchrs. Assn., Olympia, 1982-83, exec. dir., 1984-89; exec. dir. Wash. State Retired Tchrs. Found., Olympia, 1986-89; law libr. Solano County Law Libr., Fairfield, Calif., 1989—; libr. LIBRARY/USA N.Y. World's Fair, N.Y.C., 1965; consulting law libr. Dobbins, Weir, Thompson & Stephenson, Vacaville, Calif., 1989—; law libr. cons. Coconino County Law Libr., Flagstaff, Ariz., 1968-70. Author: Guide to Fin. Aid for Wash. State Students, 1979; tng. package to introduce librs. to Wash. State Info. Svc., 1980. Bd. dirs. Thurston County Sr. Ctr., Olympia, 1976-84, Thurston-Mason Nutrition Program, Olympia, 1977-79, Wash. Soc. Assn. Execs., Edmonds, 1987-89. Mem. Am. Assn. Law Librs., No. Calif. Assn. Law Librs., Calif. Coun. of County Law Librs. Office: Solano County Law Libr Hall of Justice 600 Union Ave Fairfield CA 94533-6324

MOORE, MARY ANN, chiropractor; b. St. Paul, May 29, 1953; d. Lyman Maurice and Louise Elizabeth (Braymen) M.; m. Stephen Michael Batson, June 21, 1981; children: Michael Stephen, Fauna Louise. Degree summa cum laude, Life Chiropractic Coll., Marietta, Ga., 1981. Nurse's aide Highland Park Nursing Home, St. Paul, 1971; phys. therapy asst. U. Minn. Hosp., Mpls., 1973-74; nurse's aide Pleasant Hill Nursing Home, St. Paul, 1975; sales clk. Dayton's Dept. Store, St. Paul, 1976; waitress, gift shop clk. Yellowstone Nat. Park, Wyo., 1976-77; asst. mgr. Shangri-La Health Resort, Bonita Springs, Fla., 1977-78; nurse's aide Marietta Nursing Home, 1979-80; pvt. practice Chesterfield, S.C., 1986—. Contbr. articles to newspapers. Mem. Chesterfield C. of C. Jehovah's Witness. Home: RR 1 Box 245A Ruby SC 29741-9799 Office: Moore Chiropractic Ctr 102 Marshal St Chesterfield SC 29709-1618

MOORE, MARY FRENCH (MUFFY MOORE), potter, community activist; b. N.Y.C., Feb. 25, 1938; d. John and Rhoda (Teagle) Walker French; m. Alan Baird Minier, Oct. 9, 1982; children: Jonathan Corbet, Jennifer Corbet, Michael Corbet. BA cum laude, Colo. U., 1964. Ceramics mfr., Wilson, Wyo., 1969-82, Cheyenne, Wyo., 1982—; commr. County of Teton (Wyo.), 1976-83, chmn. bd. commrs., 1981, 83, mem. dept. pub. assistance and social svc., 1976-82, mem. recreation bd., 1978-81, water quality adv. bd., 1976-82. Bd. dirs. Teton Sci. Sch., 1968-83, vice chmn., 1979-81, chmn., 1982; bd. dirs. Grand Teton Music Festival, 1963-68, Teton Energy Coun., 1978-83, Whitney Gallery of Western Art, Cody, Wyo., 1995—; mem. water quality adv. bd. Wyo. Dept. Environ. Quality, 1979-83; Dem. precinct committeewoman, 1978-81; mem. Wyo. Dem. Cen. Com., 1981-83; vice chmn. Laramie County Dem. Cen. Com., 1983-84, Wyo. Dem. nat. committewoman, 1984-87; chmn. Wyo. Dem. Party, 1987-89; del. Dem. Nat. Conv., 1984, 88, mem. fairness commn. Dem. Nat. Com., 1985, vice-chairwoman western caucus, 1986-89; chmn. platform com. Wyo. Dem. Conv., 1982; mem. Wyo. Dept. Environ. Quality Land Quality Adv. Bd., 1983-86; mem. Gov.'s Steering Com. on Troubled Youth, 1982, dem. nat. com. Compliance Assistance Commn., 1986-87; exec. com. Assn. of State Dem. Chairs, 1989; mem. Wyo. Coun. on the Arts, 1989-95, chmn., 1994-95, Dem. Nat. Com. Jud. Coun., 1989—; legis. aide for Gov. Wyo., 1985, 86; project coord. Gov.'s Com. on Childrens' Svcs., 1985-86; bd. dirs. Wyo. Outdoor Coun., 1984-85; polit. dir., dep. mgr. Schuster for Congress, 1994-95. Recipient Woman of Yr. award Jackson Hole Bus. and Profl. Women, 1981, Dem. of Yr. Nellie Tayloe Ross award, Wyo. Dems., 1990. Mem. Alden Kindred of Am., Jackson Hole Art Assn. (bd. dirs., vice chmn. 1981, chmn. 1982), Assn. State Dem. Chairs, Soc. Mayflower Descendents, Pi Sigma Alpha. Home: 8907 Cowpoke Rd Cheyenne WY 82009-1234

MOORE, MARY JULIA, educator; b. Pitts., Oct. 10, 1949; d. Edward Henry and Julia Ann (Polkabla) Sauer; 1 child, Jason Michael Sauer; m. John Harold Moore, Oct. 27, 1990. BS in Art Edn., Edinboro State Coll., 1971; MS in Spl. Edn., Clarion State Coll., 1980; postgrad. U. Pitts., 1988—. Cert. art tchr., spl. edn. tchr. for mentally retarded. Tchr. Polk (Pa.) State Sch. & Hosp., 1971-72; vol. VISTA, Bath, N.Y., 1972-73; tchr. Polk Ctr., 1973-80, program specialist, 1980-92; residential svc. supr., qualified mental retardation prof. Polk (Pa.) Ctr., 1992—; lectr., speaker, video on local TV on history of Polk Ctr., 1987. Patentee beer bottle shaped cake pan; cakes displayed in TV videos and in various mags.; creator history video Polk Ctr. Active Big Bros./Big Sisters. Mem. Internat. Cake Exhbn. Soc. Democrat. Roman Catholic. Home: RR 3 Box 232-AI Franklin PA 16323-9803

MOORE, MARY KATHRYN, counselor; b. Douglas, Wyo., Jan. 8, 1947; d. John Richard and Hazel May (Slichter) Lewis; children: Kathryn Noelle Moore Huckins, Nicole Marie. BS, Black Hills State U., 1970; MS, S.D. State U., 1993. Lic. profl. counselor; cert. sch. counselor. Tchr. Natrona Sch. Dist., Casper, Wyo., 1968-69, Rapid City (S.D.) Sch. Dist., 1969-70; tchr. Rapid City Christian H.S., 1982-93, counselor, 1992-93; counselor Black Hills Childrens Home Soc., Rockerville, S.D., 1995-96, Meade Sch. Dist., Sturgis, S.D., 1993-96; dir. Home Alone Program, Meade Sch. Dist., 1993-96; dir. Crisis Intervention Team, Sturgis Elem., 1993-96. Mem. ACA, Sch. Counselor's Assn., Phi Delta Kappa. Republican. Home: PO Box 514 Hulett WY 82720

MOORE, MERRY ANN, freelance writer, environmental issues consultant; b. Daytona Beach, Fla., Dec. 25, 1961; d. Albert Mitchell Moore and Elaine (Thomas) Kershaw; m. Robert W. Corrigan, May 1, 1993. BA, Harvard Coll., 1984; License, Universite de Paul Valery, Montpellier, France, 1985. Account rep. McGuire, Barnes, Inc., San Francisco, 1985-87; sr. mktg. specialist PMI Mortgage Ins. Co., San Francisco, 1987-90; prin. Moore Creative, San Francisco, 1990—. Recipient Elizabeth Carey Agassiz Merit award Harvard U., 1981-82, Nat. Special Achievement award Sierra Club, 1994; John Harvard scholar, 1983. Mem. Media Alliance, Fairness and Accuracy in Reporting, Profl. Environ. Marketers Assn., Internat. Assn. Bus. Communicators (Independents' Roundtable), Sierra Club (exec. com. Mateo), Calif. Econ. Recovery and Environ. Restoration Project. Democrat.

MOORE, MICHELE CLAIRE, physician; b. Watertown, N.Y., Sept. 15, 1942; d. Arthur Clair and Jeanne Marilyn (Keib) M.; m. Marcus Christian Hansen, Nov. 27, 1976; children: Martin C., Anneke K. BS, Le Moyne Coll., 1964; MD, Royal Coll. Surgeons Ireland, Dublin, 1974. Sci. tchr. Jamesville-DeWitt Ctrl. Sch., DeWitt, N.Y., 1964-65; rsch. asst. St. Luke's Hosp., N.Y.C., 1965-69; pvt. practice Crown Point, N.Y., 1976-82; town health officer Crown Point, 1977-82; physician Valley Family Physicians, Charlestown, N.H., 1982-84; physician, owner holistic health practice Keene, N.H., 1984—; clinician So. Adirondack Planned Parenthood, Crown Point, 1976-82; clin. instr. SUNY Upstate Med. Sch., Syracuse, 1980-90; adj. assoc. prof. Dartmouth Med. Sch., Hanover, N.H., 1990—; cons. physician PMS/ACT, Bow, N.H., 1991—; speaker in field. Contbr. articles to profl. jours. Steering com. Hospice of Sullivan County, Claremont, N.H., 1983-84; trustee N.E. Coll. Healing Arts and Sci., Bellows Falls, Vt., 1993—. Fellow Am. Acad. Family Physicians; mem. Am. Acad. Environ. Medicine, Am. Med. Women's Assn., New England Soc. Clin. Hypnosis, N.H. Med. Soc., Am. Cancer Soc. (bd. dirs. Essex County, N.Y. chpt. 1976-82). Home: PO Box 27 Alstead NH 03602 Office: 103 Roxbury St Keene NH 03431

MOORE, MYRA LEA, economist educator; b. Atlanta, Feb. 9, 1962; d. Carroll Gene and Joan Patricia (Withers) M.; m. David Rankin Lynn, Apr. 9, 1988. BS in Econs., Radford U., 1984; PhD in Econs., U. Ga., 1994. Instr. U. Ga., Athens, 1993-94; asst. prof. Tex. Christian U., Fort Worth, 1995—. Recipient Outstanding Teaching award U. Ga., 1993. Office: Tex Christian U Dept of Economics Fort Worth TX 76129

MOORE, NANCY FISCHER, elementary school educator; b. Milw., Nov. 26, 1937; d. Herbert Conrad and Erma Emma (Schroeder) Fischer; m. William Stang Moore (dec.). BS, U. Wis., Milw., 1958; MS, U. So. Calif., 1969; cert. in reading edn., U. Ga., 1973, cert. in gerontology edn., 1983, postgrad., 1982-91. Tchr. Grand Rapids (Mich.) Bd. Edn., 1958-61; tchr. U.S. Dept. Def. Overseas Schs., Nfld., Can., 1961-62, Bermuda, 1962-64, Japan, 1964-66; dir. handicapped day camp, tchr. 1st grade/trainable MR U.S. Dept. Def. Overseas Schs., Fed. Republic of Germany, 1966-70, Japan, 1970-71; classrm. tchr. Richmond County Bd. Edn., Augusta, Ga., 1971-95, tchr. remedial reading, 1973-77, 78-79, Title I resource tchr., 1977-78; pres. Cen. Savannah River Area Reading Coun., Augusta, 1977-78; instr. Art in the Elem. Sch. Workshop, Augusta, 1979-80; tchr. conversational English to architecture students, Japan, 1964-66, to co. employees, Japan, 1966; instr. Augusta Coll., 1995—. Active Ft. Gordon Retiree Coun., 1991—; vol. Ombudsman, Augusta, 1982-83, Shelter for Abused Children. Mem. NEA, Ga. Assn. Educators, Richmond County Assn. Educators (pres. 1976-77, membership chairperson 1972-74, bldg. rep.). Home: 2346 New Mcduffie Rd Augusta GA 30906-9026

MOORE, NANCY NEWELL, English language educator; b. Deadwood, S.D., Apr. 11, 1939; d. Harold Richard and Laura Mae (Howe) Newell; m. John Howard Moore, Feb. 23, 1962 (div. Oct. 1980). BA, Lake Forest Coll., 1961; MA, Northwestern U., 1963; PhD, U. Ill., 1968. Instr. of English U. Ill., Champaign-Urbana, 1967-68; asst. prof. of English U. Wis., Stevens Point, 1968-72, assoc. prof., 1972-76, prof., 1976—, asst. to chancellor for women, 1972-74, dept. chmn., 1974-77, chmn. faculty senate, 1981-84. Contbr. articles to profl. jours. Recipient grant for Canadian Studies, Can. Govt., 1986. Mem. AAUW, NOW, Midwest MLA, Assn. for Can. Studies in U.S., Shakespeare Assn. Am., Women in Higher Edn., Phi Eta Sigma. Unitarian. Office: Univ Wisconsin Stevens Point WI 54481

MOORE, NINA-JO, communication educator; b. Balt., Oct. 14, 1951; d. Robert Eastman and Eugenia Josephine (von Janinski) M. BA, U. South Fla., Tampa, 1973; MA, U. Ga., Athens, 1982; PhD, U. Md., College Park, 1987. Tchr. Citrus H.S., Inverness, Fla., 1973-75, 76-77; grad. tchg. asst. U. Ga., Athens, 1975-76; grad. asst., adj. prof. U. Md., College Park, 1977-79; tchr. Oakland Mills H.S., Columbia, 1979-80; youth dir., coord. lay ministry St. Paul's Episcopal Ch., Shreveport, La., 1980-82; coll. prof. La. State U., Shreveport, 1982-84, U. Richmond, Va., 1984-87, Appalachian State U., Boone, N.C., 1987—; camp adminstr. Camp Fernwood, Oxford, Maine, 1975-87, Kamp Kohut, Oxford, Maine, 1993-96. Contbr. articles to profl. jours. Mem. Lions Club, Boone, N.C., 1992—, pres. 1996—. Mem. Carolina Communication Assn. (pres. 1987—), So. States Communication Assn. (com. chair 1972—, pres.), Speech Communication Assn. (com. chair 1972—). Democrat. Episcopalian. Office: Dept Communication Appalachian State U Boone NC 28608

MOORE, NORMA JEAN, real estate associate broker; b. Keota, Iowa, Mar. 23, 1935; d. George E. and Eula Margaret (Martin) Dillon; m. Gordon George Moore, Sep. 1, 1956; children: Steven, Ronald, Cynthia Wojcik. BS, Iowa State U., 1957. Tchr. N. Haven H.S., North Haven, Conn., 1957-60, Hicksville (N.Y.) Jr. High, 1960-61; real estate assoc. Brucker Real Estate, Hatboro, Pa., 1978-82; assoc. broker Prudential Felte Real Estate, Willow Grove, Pa., 1982—. Mem. Ea. Montgomory County Bd. of Realtors, Pa. Assoc. of Realtors, Nat. Assoc. of Realtors. Presbyterian. Home: 163 Greyhorse Rd Willow Grove PA 19090

MOORE, PATRICIA ANN, medical technology investor, consultant; b. Huntington, N.Y., July 16, 1954; d. Joseph Nicholas and Dorothy Patricia (Olszewski) Mamola; m. William Martin Moore, Feb. 15, 1986; children: William Eric, Kyle Martin. BS, U. Santa Clara, 1976. Ops. mgr. Laguna Fed. Savs. & Loan, Orange, Calif., 1977-79; customer svc. rep. Bentley Labs., Irvine, Calif., 1979-80, mgr. custom products, 1980-82, internat. custom product specialist, 1981-82; dist. sales mgr. Am. Bentley Labs., San Francisco, 1982-83, Nellcor, Inc., San Francisco, 1983-84; product mgr. Nellcor, Inc., Hayward, Calif., 1984-85, nat. accounts mgr., 1986-88, internat. distbn. mgr., 1985-88; dir. internat. mktg. and sales NATUS Med., Inc., Foster City, Calif., 1989-92; mng. ptnr. Alpine Ptnrs., Incline Village, 1992—; CEO Responsive Med. Applications, Incline Village, 1996—. Mem. Nat. Account Mktg. Assn., Med. Mktg. Assn., NAFE. Home and Office: Alpine Ptnrs Ste 16L 120 Country Club Dr Incline Village NV 89451

MOORE, PATRICIA KAY, investment relations director; b. Peoria, Ill., Jan. 20, 1947; d. David Harold and Mary Jane (Gregoryk) Jenkins; m. James Christopher Moore, Jan. 11, 1980. BS in Bus. Adminstrn., U. Mo., 1978, MBA, 1981. Planning analyst Emerson Electric Corp., St. Louis, 1972-79; mgr. mktg. adminstrn. Emerson Electric WED, Houston, 1979; dir. mktg. adminstrn. HBE Corp., St. Louis, 1979-82; mgr. market rsch. Emerson Electric ESD, St. Louis, 1982-92; dir., investor rels. ESCO Electronics, St. Louis, 1992—. Mem. U. Mo. Alumni Assn. Home: 712 Sherwood Dr Webster Groves MO 63119-3756 Office: ESCO Electric Corp 8888 Ladue Rd Ste 200 Saint Louis MO 63124

MOORE, PATSY SITES, food services director; b. San Marcos, Tex., Mar. 29, 1939; d. Sam W. and Hilda (Wiede) Sites. BS in Home Econs. Edn., S.W. Tex. State U., 1970. Owner, operator Westoner Kindergarten & Nursery Sch., San Marcos, 1965-68; food svc. dir. San Marcos Consol. Ind. Sch. Dist., 1975—. Mem. steering com. Play Scape/Children's Park, San Marcos, 1992. Mem. Am. Sch. Food Svc. Assn., Tex. Sch. Food Svc. Assn., Ctrl. Tex. Sch. Food Svc. Dirs. Assn. (founder, past pres.), Order Eastern Star. Lutheran. Home: 285 Hilliard Rd San Marcos TX 78666-8905 Office: San Marcos Consol Ind Sch Dist PO Box 1087 San Marcos TX 78667-1087

MOORE, PEGGY SUE, corporation financial executive; b. Wichita, Kans., June 16, 1942; d. George Alvin and Marie Aileene (Hoskinson) M. Student, Wichita State U., 1961-63, Wichita Bus. Coll., 1963-64. Contr. Mears Electric Co., Wichita, 1965-69; exec. v.p., sec., treas., chief fin. officer CPI Corp., Wichita, 1969—, also bd. dirs.; Trustee Fringe Benefits Co., Kansas City, Mo., 1984-85. Active Rep. Nat. Com., Washington, 1985-86, task force, 1986—; treas., bd. dirs. Good Shepherd Luth. Ch., Wichita, 1980-85, mem., 1977—; active Wichita Commn. on Status of Women, 1988. CPI Corp. recipient of Blue Chip Enterprise prize U.S. C. of C., 1996. Mem. NAFE, DAR, Nat. Assn. of Women Bus. Owners, Wichita C. of C., Women's Nat. Bowling Assn. (bd. dirs., pub. com. 1969-76), Internat. Platform Assn., Kans. Purveyors Assn. (bd. dirs. 1988-89), Women's Speakers Bur. Office: CPI Corp 816 E Funston St Wichita KS 67211-4309

MOORE, SALLY FALK, anthropology educator; b. N.Y.C., Jan. 18, 1924; d. Henry Charles and Mildred (Hymanson) Falk; m. Cresap Moore, July 14, 1951; children: Penelope, Nicola. B.A., Barnard Coll., 1943; LL.B., Columbia U., 1945, Ph.D., 1957. Asst. prof. U. So. Calif., Los Angeles, 1963-65, assoc. prof., 1965-70, prof., 1970-77; prof. UCLA, 1977-81; prof. anthropology Harvard U., Cambridge, Mass., 1981—, Victor Thomas prof. anthropology, 1991—, dean Grad. Sch. Arts and Scis., 1985-89. Author: Power and Property in Inca Peru, (Ansley Prize 1957), 1958, Law as Process, 1978, Social Facts and Fabrications, 1986, Moralizing States, 1993, Anthropology and Africa, 1994. Trustee Barnard Coll., Columbia U., 1991-92; master Dunster House, 1984-89. Rsch. grantee Social Sci. Rsch. Coun., 1968-69, NSF, 1972-75, 79-80, Wenner Gren Found., 1983; Guggenheim fellow, 1995-96. Fellow Am. Acad. Arts & Scis., Am. Anthrop. Assn., Royal Anthrop. Inst.; mem. Assn. Polit. and Legal Anthropology (pres. 1983), Am. Ethnological Soc. (pres. 1987-88), Assn. Africanist Anthropologists (pres.-elect 1995). Democrat. Office: Harvard U 348 William James Hall Cambridge MA 02138

MOORE, SALLY JO, behavioral scientist, nurse, educator, minister; b. Chgo., June 13, 1937; d. Clyde Charles and Elizabeth (Lynk) Knudson; m. James Harrington Richards, Sept. 3, 1958; children: Jill Louise, Jeffrey James; m. James Harold Moore, Aug. 5, 1978. AA, RN, Hennipen State Coll., 1974; BA in Bus., Human Svcs., Met. State U., 1979, MA in Religion, 1983; PhD in Behavioral Sci., Nat. Christian U. Mo., 1983. Ordained min. Light of Christ Sem., 1983. Surgical technician No. Meml. Hosp., Golden Valley, Mn., 1973-74; RN U. Minn., 1974-75, Sacred Heart Med. Ctr., Spokane, Wa., 1975-76, St. Mary's Hosp., Mpls., 1976-78; internat. speaker, pres. Braintree, Mpls., 1977-94; pres. Personal Growth Found., Mpls., 1978-85; RN Golden Valley (Minn.) Health Ctr., 1980-86; psychotherapist, 1986-94; nurse U. Colo., 1994-95, Boulder (Colo.) Mental Health Ctr., 1994-96, Luth. Med. Ctr., Colo., 1995; field nurse Total Care, Charlotte, N.C., 1996; specialized youth svcs. nurse Mecklenburg County, N.C., 1996—; apprentice Sioux Medicine Woman, 1989; master practitioner neuro-linguistics, 1991, Level IV transformational kinesiology, 1992; clin. pastoral edn., Denver, 1995; victim advocate Boulder County Sheriff's Dept., 1995. Author: Patterns for Change, 1982, The Pentagonal Brain, 1984, Intuition-How to Develop and Trust It, 1984, Color Sense, 1984, Inner Space, 1986, Wakankana-Keeper of the Sun, 1989, Seasons of the Red Bear, 1991, Onion Peelings, 1992, Love Me and Let Me Go, 1995; founder, dir. Peers Optimal Health Program, 1992-94. Mem. Internat. Assn. Neuro-Linguistics, Amnesty Internat. Office: Colo Law Enforcement Officers Assn 6637 Brynwood Dr Charlotte NC 28226

MOORE, SANDRA KAY, counselor, administrator; b. Sellersville, Pa., June 28, 1943; d. Sheldon Ellsworth and Olive (Moyer) McElroy; m. Thomas Van Moore, June 8, 1963; children: Thomas Shawn, Tara Quinn, Tammy Colleen, Thador Shelby. Student, East Stroudsburg (Pa.) U., 1961-63; BA, Gwynedd-Mercy Coll., 1986; MS, Chestnut Hill Coll., 1990. Cert. in student assistance program. Crisis counselor Archbishop Ryan H.S., Phila., 1989-90; guidance counselor Mt. St. Joseph Acad., Flourtown, Pa., 1990-93; dir. guidance Mt. St. Joseph Acad., Flourtown, 1993—; lectr. Gwynedd-Mercy Coll., Gwynedd, Pa., 1995—; lectr. in field. Author: So You Want to Go to College, 1994. Bd. dirs. Today, Inc., Hilltown, Pa., 1976-80; mem. Hilltown (Pa.) Civic Assn., 1975-85; pres. Bux-Mont Neighbors, Souderton, Pa., 1985, John M. Grasse Home and Sch. Assn., Perkasie, Pa., 1981; chairwoman Christian Edn. Com., Perkasie, 1994. Mem. APA, Ind. Counselors Assn., Nat. Assn. for Coll. Admissions Counselors, Specialists in Schs., Pa. Assn. Secondary Sch. and Coll. Admission Counselors. Democrat. Lutheran. Office: Mount Saint Joseph Academy 120 W Wissahickon Ave Flourtown PA 19031

MOORE, SHERYL STANSIL, medical nurse; b. Birmingham, Ala., May 17, 1963; d. Willie Caesar and Irene (Fisher) Stansil; m. Kyle R. Moore, Aug. 5, 1994; children: Tyler Christina Lowe, Danladi, William. BSN, Dillard U., 1987; MSN in Trauma Nursing, U. Ala. in Birmingham, 1992. Staff nurse Nursefinders, Colorado Springs, Colo., 1994—, Progressive Care Ctr., Terrace Gardens, Colo., 1995—; instr. clin. nursing Beth-El Coll. Nursing,

1995; past instr. clin. nursing Beth-El Coll. Nursing; beauty cons. Mary Kay Cosmetics, 1996—. Named one of Outstanding Young Women of Am., 1988. Mem. ANA, AACN, State Nurses Assn., AMSN. Home: 1985 Mittenwald Dr #102 Colorado Springs CO 80918

MOORE, SHIRLEY THROCKMORTON (MRS. ELMER LEE MOORE), accountant; b. Des Moines, July 4, 1918; d. John Carder and Jessie (Wright) Throckmorton; student Iowa State Tchrs. Coll., summers 1937-38, Madison Coll., 1939-41; M.C.S., Benjamin Franklin U., 1944; CPA, Mc.; m. Elmer Lee Moore, Dec. 19, 1946; children: Fay, Lynn Dallas. Asst. bookkeeper Sibley Hosp., Washington, 1941-42, Alvord & Alvord, 1942-46, bookkeeper, 1946-49, chief accountant, 1950-64, fin. adviser to sr. ptnr., 1957-64; dir. Allen Oil Co., 1958-74; pvt. practice acctg., 1964—. Mem. sch. bd. Takoma Acad., Takoma Park, Md., 1970—; mem. hosp. bd. Washington Adventist Hosp., 1974-85; chmn. worthy student fund Takoma Park Seven Day Adventist Ch., 1987—; trustee Benson Found., 1963—; vol. Am. Women's Voluntary Svc., 1942-45. Recipient Disting. Grad. award Benjamin Franklin U., 1961. Mem. Am., D.C. (pub. rels. com. 1976—) insts. CPAs, Am. Women's Soc. CPAs, Am. Soc. Women Accts. (legislation chmn. 1960-62, nat. dir. 1952-53, nat. treas. 1953-54), Bus. and Profl. Women's Club (treas. D.C. 1967-68), Benjamin Franklin U. Alumni Assn. (Disting. Alumni award 1964, charter, past dir.), D.A.R., Md. Assn. CPAs (charter chmn. membership com. Montgomery Prince George County 1963-64, chmn. student rels. com. 1964-67, pres. 1968-69, mem. fed. tax com. 1971-73). Mem. Seventh Day Adventist Ch. Contbr. articles to profl. jours. Home and Office: 1007 Elm Ave Silver Spring MD 20912-5839

MOORE, SUSAN LYNN, television producer; b. Victoria, Tex., Aug. 17, 1944; d. Carl William and Marjorie Louise (Roberts) Schoepfle; m. Robert Clark, June 6, 1964 (div. 1975); m. Gregory Moore, Apr. 7, 1977 (div. 1987); children: Cynthia, Wendy, Christina. Student, Marietta (Ohio) Coll., 1962-65, U. Ariz., 1965-67, Houston Mus. Fine Arts, 1972-75, U. Houston, 1975-78, Edmonds Community Coll., 1985-88. Art tchr. Mus. Modern Art, Houston, 1973-76; tech. writer applied physics lab. U. Wash., Seattle, 1978-80; founder, owner Moore Prodns., Lake Stevens, Wash., 1980—; exec. dir. Casa de Maria Ctr., Everett, 1991-95; founder, exec. dir. One Life Ctr., Everett, 1994—; reporter, writer Reader's Digest Books, N.Y.C., 1986. Prin. works include Division of Aeronautics, 1991, Evacuation of Elderly and Disabled Passengers from Public Transportation Emergencies, 1990, Cold Expansion of Holes in Metals, for Engineers, 1989, Nisqually Destiny, 1989, Rails to Trails, 1988, Lynnwood, 1988, Edmonds, 1988, Hospice of Snohomish County, 1987, Household Hazardous Waste, 1987, Small Quantity Generators, 1987, Salhus Bridge, 1987, Principles of Eddy Current Testing, 1987, Long Beach Peninsula-Its Future is Now, 1986, others. Founder Snohomish County Visitor Ctr., Everett, Wash., 1984. Mem. N.W. Wash. Tourism Assn. (bd. dirs. 1983-89, chmn. 1986, chair mktg. 1987-89). Home and Office: 1609 Emerald Lake Way Bellingham WA 98226

MOORE, SUSANNA, writer; b. Bryn Mawr, Pa., Dec. 9, 1948; d. Richard Dixon and Anne (Shields) M.; 1 child, Lulu Lenane Sylbert. Author: My Old Sweetheart, 1982 (Am. Book award nomination for best first novel 1983, Sue Kaufman prize for first fiction Am. Acad. Inst. Arts and Letters 1983), The Whiteness of Bones, 1989, Sleeping Beauties, 1993, In the Cut, 1995. Recipient Literary Lion award N.Y. Pub. Libr., 1993. Office: Wylie Aitken & Stone 250 W 57th St New York NY 10107

MOORE, SYLVIA MORRIS, school counselor; b. Bethel, N.C., Aug. 18, 1950. BA, Meredith Coll., 1972; MEd, N.C. State U., 1977. Cert. tchr., N.C.; lic. profl. counselor, N.C.; nat. cert. counselor. Tchr. Wilson (N.C.) Schs., 1972-73, Mid-Way Acad., Raleigh, N.C., 1974-76; counselor South Edgecombe Sch., Pinetops, N.C., 1979-87; industry/edn. coord. North Pitt H.S., Bethel, N.C., 1989-91; counselor West Edgecombe Sch., Rocky Mountain, N.C., 1992-93, Martin Mid. Sch., Tarboro, N.C., 1994—. Mem. ACA, N.C. Counseling Assn., N.C. Assn. Educators. Home: 3984 Buck Moore Rd Macclesfield NC 27852 Office: Martin Mid Sch 400 E Johnston St Tarboro NC 27886

MOORE, TANNA LYNN, business development executive; b. Columbus, Ohio, Oct. 19, 1954; d. Richard Owen and Marianne Ruth (Daries) M.; m. Craig Thomas Swaggert, Aug. 31, 1986; stepchildren: Mitchell, Nickolas. BA in Econs., Kenyon Coll., 1976; MBA, Dartmouth Coll., 1978. With product mgmt. Gen. Mills Inc., 1978-82; account exec., v.p., sr. v.p. U.S. Communications Corp., Mpls., 1982-90; sr. v.p. Keewaydin Group, Inc., Mpls., 1990-91; v.p. planning and bus. devel. Ceridian Corp. (formerly Control Data Corp.), Mpls., 1991-93; v.p., gen. mgr. human resource svcs. and mktg., 1993—; lectr. St. Thomas Coll., St. Paul, prof., 1987; lectr. U. Minn., St. Paul; lectr. promotional mktg., client relationships and career planning to ednl. instns.; bd. dirs. Sta. KTCA-TV, Mpls. Bd. dirs. Illusion Theatre, Mpls., 1979-86, chairperson Crystal Ball, 1987; bd. dirs. Downtown YMCA, Mpls.; commr. Minn. Amateur Sports Commn. Home: 1783 Irving Ave S Minneapolis MN 55403-2820 Office: Ceridian Corp 8100 34th Ave S Bloomington MN 55425-1672

MOORE, TRESI LEA, lawyer; b. Brownwood, Tex., Dec. 3, 1961; d. Dean Moore and Patsy Ruth (Evans) Adams. BA in Fgn. Svc., BA in French, Baylor U., 1984, JD, 1987. Bar: Tex. 1987, U.S. Dist. Ct. (no. dist.) Tex. 1988, U.S. Ct. Appeals (5th cir.) 1989. Atty. Richard Jackson & Assocs., Dallas, 1987-91, Amis & Moore (and predecessor firm), Arlington, Tex., 1992—. Vol. Legal Svcs. of North Tex., Dallas, 1988—, Dallas Com. for Fgn. Visitors, 1989-92; bd. dirs. Plano Internat. Presch. Recipient Pro Bono Svc. award Legal Svcs. of North Tex., 1989, 90, 91. Mem. AAUW (pub. policy dir. Plano, Tex. br. 1992, 93-94, v.p. 1994-95), ABA, State Bar Tex. (mem. mentor program for lawyers com. 1994—, mem. local bar svcs. com. 1994-96), Dallas Bar Assn., Tarrant County Bar Assn., Dallas Women Lawyers Assn. (bd. dirs. 1989-90, v.p. 1992, pres. 1993). Office: Amis Moore & Davis 2301 E Lamar Blvd Ste 250 Arlington TX 76006-7416

MOORE, VIRGINIA BRADLEY, librarian, educator, consultant; b. Laurens, S.C., May 13, 1932; d. Robert Otis Brown and Queen Esther (Smith) Bradley; m. David Lee Moore, Dec. 27, 1957 (div. 1973). B.S., Winston-Salem State U., 1954; M.L.S., U. Md., 1970. Cert. in libr. sci. edn. Tchr. John R. Hawkins High Sch., Warrenton, N.C., 1954-55, Happy Plains High Sch., Taylorsville, N.C., 1955-58, Young and Carver elem. schs., Washington, 1958-65; libr. Davis and Minor elem. schs., Washington, 1965-72, Ballou Sr. High Sch., Kramer Jr. High Sch., Washington, 1972-75, 78-80, Anacostia Sr. High Sch., Washington, 1975-77, 80-95; ret., 1995; dir. ch. libr. workshops Asbury United Meth. Ch., Washington, 1972-74, 76; speaker, presenter Ch. and Synagogue Libr. Assn., 1975, 80, 83; chmn.-competency based curriculum D.C. pub. schs., 1978-93; chair local arrangements launching Nat. Sch. Libr. Media Month, U.S. Capitol, 1985; mem. 1st libr. and info. sci. del. to People's Republic China, 1985, mem. faculty 1st established pub. svc. acad. in nation Anacostia Sr. H.S., 1990-95; presenter Delta Kappa Gamma Soc. Internat. N.E. Regional Conf., Buffalo, 1995, Mid. Atlantic Intellectual Freedom Leadership Devel. Inst., 4H Club, Chevy Chase, Md., 1995; other presentations. Author: (bibliography) The Negro in American History, 1619-1968, 1968, (with Helen E. Williams) Books By African-American Authors and Illustrators for Children and Young Adults, 1991; TV script for vacation reading program, 1971, sound/slide presentation D.C. Church Librs.' Bicentennial Celebration, 1976; video script and tchr.'s guide for Nat. Libr. Week Balloon Launch Day, 1983; bibliography Black Literature/Materials, 1987; contbr. articles to profl. jours. Rec. sec. Washington Pan-Hellenic Coun., 1975; libr. Mt. Carmel Bapt. Ch., Washington, 1984, Sunday Sch. Mother's Day Coord., 1990-94, Jr. Ch. pianist, 1994—, Sunday Sch. adult dept. pianist, 1984—, co-chair African-Am. History Mo. commn., 1996; co-chair nat. libr. involvement com. Martin Luther King, Jr. Fed. Holiday Commn., 1990—, chair, 1996—. Recipient certs. of award D.C. Pub. Libr., 1980, D.C. Pub. Schs., 1983; NDEA scholar Central State Coll., Edmond, Okla., 1969, U. Ky., 1969, honor as outstanding educator Mt. Carmel Bapt. Ch., 1984; scholar Ball State U., 1969; grad. fellow U. Md., 1969. Mem. ALA (councillor-at-large 1983-91), LWV, AARP, Internat. Assn. Sch. Librs., NEA (life), Am. Assn. Sch. Librs. (coms., 1973-83, 1987—), D.C. Assn. Sch. Librs. (pres. 1971-73, citation 1973, newsletter editor, 1971-75, 83), Freedom to Read Found., Soc. Sch. Librs. Internat. (charter), Intellectual Freedom Roundtable (bd. dirs. exec. com. 1989-91), D.C. Libr. Assn., Md. Libr. Assn., Md. Ednl. Media Orgn., Internat. Platform Assn., S.E. Neighbors Club, Am. First Day Cover Soc., Zeta Phi Beta (v.p. chpt. 1972-74), Delta Kappa Gamma Soc. Internat. (v.p. Alpha chpt. 1990-92, pres. 1992-95, N.Y. State mem. chair, 1991-92, rec. sec. 1994-95, v.p. 1995—, liason U.S. Forum 1995—, spkr.). Democrat. Home: 2100 Brooks Dr Apt 721 Forestville MD 20747-1016

MOORE, VIRGINIA LEE SMITH, elementary education educator; b. Middletown, N.Y., May 13, 1943; d. James William and Anna Van Alst (Suydam) Smith; m. Thomas J. Moore, Oct. 16, 1965 (div. Apr. 1980); 1 child, Christian Thomas. AA in Liberal Arts, Orange County C.C., 1963; BA in Sociology magna cum laude, SUNY, Buffalo, 1965; MS in Edn., SUNY, New Paltz, 1980; MS in Edn. of Gifted, Coll. New Rochelle, 1990, cert. elem. edn., staff devel., 1994; cert. sch. adminstrn., 1994. Cert. elem. tchr., N.Y. Spl. edn. tchr. The Devereux Found., Glen Loch, Pa., 1965-66; elem. tchr. Harris Sch., Coatesville, Pa., 1967; elem. tchr. Pine Bush (N.Y.) Cen. Schs., 1967-70, 78—, substitute tchr., 1970-71; nursery sch. tchr. Olivet Meth. Nursery Sch., Coatesville, Pa., 1976-78; presenter ednl. workshops Pine Bus Sch. Dist., Haldane Sch. Dist., Cold Spring, N.Y., Eldred Sch. Dist., Marlboro, N.Y., Middletown (N.Y.) Tchr. Ctr., 1988; coord. Invent Am. Program, Pine Bush Sch. Dist., 1988-92. Pres. Redtown Residents' Assn. , Middletown, 1988—. Recipient Dean's Acad. Excellence award Coll. of New Rochelle, 1991, Orange County Conservation Tchr. of Yr., 1993, N.Y.S. Conservation Tchr. of Yr., 1993; Partnership in Edn. grantee Area Fund Orange County, N.Y., 1991, Energy grantee Orange and Rockland Utilities, 1995. Mem. ASCD, NSTA, N.Y. State United Tchrs., Sci. Tchrs. Assn. N.Y. State (Outstanding Sci. Tchr. award 1992, Excellence in Sci. Tchg. award 1995), N.Y. State Tech. Edn. Assn., Phi Beta Kappa. Baptist. Home: RR 2 Box 358 Middletown NY 10940-9609 Office: Pakanasink Elem Sch PO Box 148 Circleville NY 10919-0148

MOORE, YVONNE LAUGHLIN HOWARD RICHARDSON, retail manager; b. Newark, N.J., July 24, 1943; d. Marion and Ola D. (Johnson) Laughlin; m. Jesse Moore, Sept. 23, 1984 (div. 1996); children: Durand, Anthony, Yvette. Student, Essex County Coll., 1978, 91—. Lic. life ins. producer. Store mgr. Lerner Ltd., N.Y.C., N.J., 1961-87, A & E Stores, Ridgefield, N.J., 1987-88; entrepreneur sponsoring social affairs Oldie But Goodies, N.J., 1990—. Writer of poetry. Mem. NAFE, NAACP, DAV (life aux.).

MOORE-BERRY, NORMA JEAN, secondary school educator; b. Hampton, Ark., Jan. 7, 1949; d. James E. and Alma Lee (McRae) Moore, Sr.; children: Rhemona Moore, Nerissa Moore. BA in English Edn., U. Ark., Pine Bluff, 1971; MA in Reading Edn., So. Ark. U., 1985; postgrad., Henderson State U., 1986, U. Ark., 1989-90. Cert. mid. and secondary English tchr., adult edn., all levels reading. Tchr. English Chidester (Ark.) Sch. Dist., 1971-73; tchr. English, adult edn. instr. Lewisville (Ark.) Sch. Dist., 1973-92, secondary tchr., 1973-93, reading tutor, 1991—; instr. adult edn. Texarkana (Ark.) Pub. Sch. Dist., 1984-91; tchr. English Ctrl. High Sch., 1984-93, Hall Sr. High Sch., Little Rock, 1987-90; chmn. English dept. Lewisville Sch. Dist.; instr. English Ctrl. High Sch., summer 1992; tchr. Ctrl. High Sch. Summer Sch., Little Rock Sch. Dist., summer 1994; English and reading secondary instr., 1994-95. Sponsor sr. class; active sch. charity fund-raising; organizer, sponsor Lewisville Reading Club, Lewisville English Club; mem. bible study group Bethel CME Ch., Stamps, Ark., sponsor, sec. ceo com. Ethnic Club Lewisville High Sch. Named Tchr. Yr., 1984, Lewisville Mid. Sch. Reading/English Tchr., Woman of Yr. ABI, 1993-94. Mem. ASCD, Nat. Coun. Tchrs. English, Ark. Edn. Assn., Ark. Tchr. Retirement Assn., Ark. Reading Coun. Assn. (lit. coun.), Lewisville Edn. Assn. (treas. 1993-94), Phi Delta Kappa. Home: 507 Hope Rd Stamps AR 71860-2017

MOORE DE GOLIER, DANIELLE, political activist; b. Valhalla, N.Y., Dec. 6, 1947; d. Daniel Livingston and Lucy Ann (Collesano) Wilson; m. David Frederick DeGolier, Apr. 8, 1967 (div. 1984); children: Andrea Lynn, Jeffrey David; m. Charles Edward LaGreca, Feb. 14, 1986 (div. May 1993); m. Steven Tracey Moore, July 7, 1996. AA in Liberal Arts Human and Social Scis., Niagara County C.C., 1991. Founder, pres. Citizens Against Pollution Niagara County, 1980-82; founder, facilitator Love Addicts Anonymous Niagra Falls, 1982-88. Author: (children's book) A Lap for Leonard, 1977; columnist The Niagara Gazette, 1975-76, Nat. Women's Polit. Caucus, 1978. Lobbyist state/fed. upgrade adoption laws granting adopted adults access to med. info. via anonymous computer network, 1975; founder, pub. rels. dir. Peoples Animal Lovers Soc., 1975-76; pres. Niagara Area chpt., pub. rels. dir. Animal Birth Control Soc. Western N.Y., 1976; founder, pres. Citizens Against Pollution, Niagara County, 1980-82, Love Addicts Anonymous, Niagara Falls, 1982-89; lobbyist state/fed. stalkers act., Niagara Falls, 1991-93, fed. sponsorship to upgrade domestic violence laws, 1990-94. Statue erected in honor of her Citizens Against Pollution work, Lewiston, N.Y., 1982. Mem. NOW (pres. Niagara County chpt. 1993-94); People Animal Lovers Soc. (founder, pub. rels. dir. 1975-76), Animal Birth Control Soc. Western N.Y. (pres. Niagara County chpt., pub. rels. dir. 1975-77.

MOOREFIELD, CLAUDIA CANDYCE, confectionary marketing professional; b. Fresno, Calif., Nov. 24, 1949; d. Ernest Karl and Alice Vanoosh (Karoglanian) Hosepian; m. Kenneth Gene Moorefield, Dec. 9, 1978; 1 child, Kyle Zachary. BA summa cum laude, Calif. State U., Fresno, 1972, Cert. tchg., 1988. Assoc. editor Autoweek Mag., Reno, Nev., 1972-74; public rels. specialist Toyota Mtr. Sales, USA, Torrance, Calif., 1974-77; acct. exec. Bob Thomas & Assoc., Redondo Beach, Calif., 1977; sales rep. L'Oreal Cosmetics, Fresno, 1979-87; banking svcs. exec. Bank of Fresno, 1989; sales assoc. SRA Sch. Group, Fresno, 1989-95; sales rep. See's Candies, Fresno, 1995—. Author and editor: (book) 50 Years of Our Union, 1970. mayoral appointee Meux Home Adv. Com., Fresno, 1976-78; mem. Friends of the Library, 1992—. Recipient Newswriting award William Randolph Hearst Found., 1969. Mem. Fresno C. of C., Phi Kappa Phi, Kappa Alpha Theta. Home: 2175 Morris Ave Clovis CA 93611 Office: Sees Candies 380 W Shaw Ave Clovis CA 93612

MOOREFIELD, JENNIFER MARY, legislative staff member; b. Danville, Va., Nov. 10, 1950; d. Folger Lester and Mildred (Cox) M. BA in Psychology, Averett Coll., 1972; A in Applied Sci., Danville C.C., 1986; postgrad., Longwood Coll., 1995—. Social worker Henry County Social Svcs., Collinsville, Va., 1972-75, sr. social worker, 1975-80; clk. inventory control Dan River, Inc., Danville, Va., 1981-83; staff asst. U.S. Congressman Dan Daniel, Danville, 1984-88; staff asst. U.S. Congressman L.F. Payne, Danville, 1988-91, casework supr., 1991—; office mgr. U.S. Congressman L.F. Payne, Danville, 1991—. Bd. recording sec. Danville Speech & Hearing Ctr., 1988; Sunday Sch. tchr. Emmanuel Wesleyan Ch., Danville, 1975—; dir. Wesleyan Kids for Missions, Danville, 1993—, Ch. Vacation Bible Sch., Danville, 1993. Mem. Luncheon Pilot Club of Danville, Inc. (recording sec. 1988-89, pres.- elect 1989-90, pres. 1990-91), Va. Dist.- Pilot Internat. (area fundraising leader 1990-91, dist. chaplain 1993-94). Home: 136 Brookview Rd Danville VA 24540-3408 Office: Office of Congressman LF Payne 700 Main St Ste 301 Danville VA 24541-1819

MOORE-RIESBECK, SUSAN, osteopathic physician; b. Joliet, Ill., Jan. 23, 1963; d. Roy W. and Rita M. (Gondek) Moore; m. David E. Riesbeck. BS in Chemistry, Loyola U., Chgo., 1984; DO, Kirksville Coll. Osteo. Med., 1990. Diplomate Am. Bd. Family Practice. Chief resident in family practice Michiana Cmty. Hosp., South Bend, Ind., 1990-92, asst. residency dir., 1993—; med. dir. Transitional Health Svcs. Shamrock Gardens, South Bend, Ind., 1994—, Healthwin Nursing Home, South Bend, Ind., 1995—; Healthwin, South Bend; chair family practice dept. St. Mary Cmty. Hosp., South Bend, Ind., 1994—; med. advisor House Call, Mishawaka, Ind. Ann Wright Hazen scholar, 1987-90, Quad City Osteo. Assn. scholar, 1987; recipient Janet M. Glasgow Meml. Achievement citation AMA, 1990. Mem. Am. Osteo. Assn., Ind. Assn. Osteo Physicians and Surgeons (orgnl. affairs com. 1996—), Am. Coll. Family Practitioners in Osteo. Medicine and Surgery, Phi Sigma Alpha. Office: 2515 E Jefferson Blvd South Bend IN 46615-2635 also: 150 W Angela South Bend IN 46617-1101

MOORES, ANITA JEAN YOUNG, computer consultant; b. Poplar Bluff, Mo., Oct. 11, 1944; d. Joseph Samuel and Irene Anita (Sollars) Young; m. James Stephen Moores, June 5, 1965 (div. Jan. 1979); 1 child, Carolyn Terra. BS in Edn., So. Ill. U., 1972, MS in Edn., 1979. Cons. edn. and bus., sales Forsythe Computers, St. Louis, 1979-81; floor sales mgr., bus. cons., sales Computerland of Southwest Houston-Westheimer, 1981-82; bus. cons., sales Bus. Computer Systems and Software, Houston, 1982-83, MicroTask Computers, 1983-84; adminstrv. asst., tech. support Computerland-Techtron, 1984-85; distributer sales Cyber/Source, Houston, 1985; southwest regional sales mgr. Professions Info. Network, Houston, 1987; adminstrv. asst., computer specialist Human Affairs Internat. Inc., Houston; owner Moores' Consulting, Houston, 1986—. Author: (manuals) Choosing a Business Computer, 1983, Career Management, 1984, Training Manual-Computer, 1989; editor: Hounix Newsletter, 1988-89; artist oil paintings. Cons., trainer Meml. Luth. Ch., Houston, 1980-85; adminstr. Olympic Devel.-Soccer, Houston, 1988-89. So. Ill. U. Grad. fellow, 1975-76; named Outstanding Young Women Athlete, So. Ill. U., 1972.

MOORE-WARNER, NANCY MAE, business educator; b. Pontiac, Mich., Dec. 20, 1942; d. William Lewis and Florence Mae (Love) Robinson; m. Richard Glenn Moore, Sept. 7, 1963 (div. Apr. 1980); children: Richard Glenn, David Lawrence; m. Stephen James Warner, Mar. 9, 1987. BS, Mich. State U., 1963, MA, 1968. Various office positions Mich. State U., East Lansing, 1962-63, 66-67, Ferris State U., Big Rapids, Mich., 1966-67, Pontiac Motors, 1963-65; prof. bus. Mott C.C., Flint, Mich., 1968—. Named Tchr. of Yr. student govt. Mott C.C., 1993. Office: Mott C C 1401 E Court St Flint MI 48503-6208

MOORHATCH, JENNIFER ANNE, secondary education educator; b. Woodbury, N.J., Dec. 6, 1970; d. Harry Honsford and Joanne Catherine (Schlicht) Johnson; m. Stephen Joseph Moorhatch, Dec. 30, 1993. BEd in Music, Taylor U., 1992. Cert. profl. instr., Pa. Music tchr. Melmark Home and Sch., Berwyn, Pa., 1993, The Christian Acad., Media, Pa., 1993—; tchr. piano and voice pvt. practice, Drexel Hill, Pa., 1994—. Pianist, soloist, mem. exultante ringers, sanctuary choir, Aldan (Pa.) Union Ch., 1994—. Republican. Office: The Christian Acad 704 S Old Middletown Rd Media PA 19063

MOORHEAD, ROLANDE ANNETTE REVERDY, artist, educator; b. Périgueux, France, Sept. 24, 1937; d. RémyJean and Andrée Marcelle (Lavollée) Reverdy; liberal arts degree Coll. Technique, Nice, France, 1954; m. Elliott Swift Moorhead, III, Sept. 30, 1960; children: Edward Marc, Roland Elliott, Rémy Bruce. Bi-lingual sec., France, 1957-58, French Embassy, 1959-60, 1968-70; chmn. exhibit com. Lauderdale-By-The-Sea Art Guild, Ft. Lauderdale, Fla., 1972-75, v.p., 1972-74; founder group 5 Women Artists; charter mem. Gold Coast Water Color Soc., Ft. Lauderdale, 1976; mem. exhibit com. Broward Art Guild, Ft. Lauderdale, 1976; treas., dir. Alliance Française, Miami, Fla., 1973-75; one-woman shows include: numerous banks Ft. Lauderdale area, 1971—, Ocean Club Art Gallery, Ft. Lauderdale, 1971-74, Pier 66 Gallery, Ft. Lauderdale, 1973, 75, 76, Ft. Lauderdale City Hall, 1974, 77-78, 81-88, 91-94, St. Basil Orthodox Ch., North Miami Beach, 1977, Galerie Vallombreuse, Biarritz, France, 1977, Galerie du Palais des Fêtes, Périgueux, 1978, 88, Le Club Internationale, Ft. Lauderdale, 1979, Leonard Gallery, Ft. Lauderdale, 1990-92, Tallahassee (Fla.) Capitol Bldg., 1990, Lighthouse Pt. (Fla.) Gallery, 1990, Hollywood (Fla.) Art and Cultural Ctr., 1990, 91, Ft. Lauderdale Arts Inst., 1991, Dover Gallery, Boca Raton, Fla., 1992; exhibited in group shows: Broward Art Guild, Ft. Lauderdale, 1971, 73, 74, Point of Am. Gallery, Ft. Lauderdale, 1971, 73, Internat. Festival, Miami, 1976, Internat. Salon, Biarritz, 1977, Internat. Summer Salon, Paris, 1977, Fine Art Gallery Show and Competition, Long Galleries, Ft. Lauderdale, 1979, Pembroke Pines (Fla.) City Hall, 1982, Hollywood (Fla.) City Library, 1982, also area banks, chs. and libraries, numerous local art festivals; represented in permanent collections: Ft. Lauderdale City Hall, DAV Hdqrs., Washington, Associated Aircraft Co., March of Dimes Bldg. (both Ft. Lauderdale), Oakland Park Lib., Fla., St. Joseph Convent, St. Augustine, Fla., U.S. Air Force Mus., Ohio, Main Line Fleets, Inc., Palm Beach, Fla., Creditre forum, Dusseldorf, W.Ger., St. Front Cathedral, Périgueux, St. Sacerdoce Cathedral, Sarlat, France, also numerous pvt. collections, U.S. and Europe. Recipient Best in Show award Internat. Salon, Biarritz, 1977; named artist in residence Broward County Sch., 1985. Mem. Am. Soc. Portrait Artists, Nat. Assn. Women Artists, Fla. Watercolor Soc., Miami Watercolor Soc., Palm Beach Watercolor Soc., Nat. League Am. Penwomen, Art 24, Périgueux, Internat. Soc. Marine Painters, The Ann White Theatre, Am. Watercolor Soc., Nat. Mus. Women in Arts, Nat. Mus. Am. Indian, Broward Art Guild, Boca Raton Center for Arts, Gold Coast Water Color Soc. (pres. 1984-87), 2+3 The Artist's Orgn., Union des Français de l'Etranger. Office: PO Box 8692 Fort Lauderdale FL 33310-8692

MOORMAN, ROSE DRUNELL, county administrator, systems analyst; b. Miami, Fla., May 13, 1945; d. Willie and Claudia (Fluker) M. BA in Mathematics, Fisk U., 1967; MSE in Computer and Info. Scis., U. Pa., 1976. Computer programmer GE, Valley Forge, Pa., 1967-70; programmer/analyst Price Waterhouse Co., Phila., 1970-72; sr. programmer/analyst Inst. Environ. Medicine U. Pa., Phila., 1972-77; systems analyst Honeywell, Ft. Washington, Pa., 1977-78; dir. tech. svcs. Gill Assocs., Inc., Washington, 1978-83; owner, CEO Computer and Info. Mgmt., Inc., Miami, 1983-88; mgr. tech. support City of Miami, 1988-94, coord. diversity, 1994-95; exec. adminstr. to county commr. Metro-Dade County, 1996—; facilitator Women in Info. Processing, Washington, 1979-83; computer edn. adv. panel Dade County Pub. Schs., 1984-88. Editor: (newsletter) Bits and Bytes, 1979-82; co-editor: (newsletter) Ebenezer Speaks, 1992—. Active Ebenezer United Meth. Ch., Miami, 1954—, treas., chair fin. com., 1992—, Family Christian Assn., 1989-94; troop leader Girl Scouts Am., 1990—; pres. Loran Park Sch. PTA, Miami, 1991-93; treas., bd. dirs. Overtown Comty. Health Clinic, Miami, 1992—, New Miami Group, Inc., 1994—; mem. Dade Heritage Trust, Miami, 1994—; mem. Dade County Hist. Preservation Bd., 1996—. Recipient Leadership award ARC, 1957, 63, Bronze medallion for Community Svc. NCCJ, 1963, Svc. Excellence award Delta Sigma Theta, 1986. Meritorious Svc. award Fisk U., 1992. Mem. NAACP, Nat. Forum Black Pub. Adminstrs. (bd. dirs., 2d v.p. 1993—), Nat. Coun. Negro Women. Republican. Home: 820 NW 172nd Ter Miami FL 33169-5305 Office: Metropolitan Dade County Ste 220 111 NW 1st St Miami FL 33128

MOORMANN, VIKKI PATRICIA, secondary education educator; b. Spokane, Wash., Oct. 1, 1946; d. Victor Charles and Patricia E. (Billberg) Lamb; m. Donald B. Moormann, May 29, 1976. BA, Gonzaga U., 1968; postgrad., U. Idaho, 1995—. Tchr. secondary English Coeur d' Alene (Idaho) Sch. Dist., 1969—; cons. Dept. Edn. Nat. Diffusion Network, Washington, 1983—, Tchr.'s Inc. Author: Save Our Sanity, 1994. Mem. ASCD, NEA, Idaho Edn. Assn., Coeur d' Alene Edn. Assn. (chair various coms. 1976—), Delta Kappa Gamma. Democrat. Office: Coeur d' Alene Sch Dist 271 311 N 10th St Coeur D Alene ID 83814-4280

MOOS, SHEILA MARIE, elementary education educator; b. Pensacola, Fla., July 18, 1970; d. Donal Dwight and Nancy Marie (Davis) M. BS in Edn., Mont. State U., 1992. 3d and 4th grade tchr. St. Mary's Sch., Malta, Mont., 1993—. Mem. Communities Organizing Responsible Events (pres. 1994-95), Delta Gamma. Office: St Marys Sch PO Box 70 Malta MT 59538

MOOS, VERNA VIVIAN, special education educator; b. Jamestown, N.D., July 1, 1951; d. Philip and Violena (Schweitzer) M. BS in Edn., Valley City State U., 1973; MEd, U. So. Miss., 1983, EdS, 1988; AA, Minot State U., 1987; postgrad., East Tex. State U., U. Tex., N.D. State U., U. N.D., Kans. State U., McGill U. Supr. recreation Valley City (N.D.) Recreation Dept., 1969-73; tchr. Harvey (N.D.) Pub. Schs., 1973-75; tchr. spl. edn. Belfield (N.D.) Pub. Schs., 1975-77; edn. therapist N.D. Elks Assn., Dawson, 1976-77; tchr. spl. edn. Dickinson (N.D.) pub. Schs., 1977-87; ednl. technician ABLE, Inc., Dickinson, 1984-87; tchr. spl. edn. Pewitt Ind. Sch. Dist., Omaha and Naples, Tex., 1987—; tchr. adult edn. N.E. Tex. C.C., Mt. Pleasant, 1989—. Local and area dir. Tex. Spl. Olympics, Austin, 1988—; local, regional and state dir. N.D. Spl. Olympics, 1972-87; local coord. Very Spl. Arts Festival; mem. Am. Heart Assn., 1979-87, N.D. Heart Assn., 1979-87; mem. adminstrv. bd. First United Meth. Ch., Naples, Tex., 1994—. Named Dickinson Jaycees Outstanding Young Educator, 1979, Dickinson C. of C. Tchr. of Yr., 1985, Dallas area Coach of Yr., Tex. Spl. Olympics, 1993, Dir. of Yr., N.D. Spl. Olympics, 1985. Mem. NEA, Coun. Exceptional Children, Naples C. of C., Delta Kappa Gamma (scholar), Phi Delta Kappa, Kappa Delta Pi. Home: PO Box 788 Omaha TX 75571-0788 Office: Pewitt CISD PO Box 1106 Omaha TX 75571-1106

MOOSBURNER, NANCY, nutritionist; b. Houston, Tex., Apr. 6, 1943; d. Henry Fenno and Shirley Louise (McCandless) Laughton; m. Stephen Weinert, Nov. 1964 (div. Nov. 1974); children: Catherine, Jeffery; m. Otto Moosburner, Feb. 7, 1976; 1 child, Brian. BS, U. Nevada Reno, 1979, MS, 1982. Edn. specialist Nev. Dept. of Edn., Carson City, 1980-83, state dir., 1983-84; sch. nutrition program supr. Douglas Co. Sch. Dist., Minden, Nev., 1987-93; dir. sch. nutrition St. Helens (Oreg.) Sch. Dist., 1993-94; instr. Truckee Meadows C.C., Reno, Nev., 1982-83, Portland C.C., St. Helens, 1993-94; child nutrition program supr. Auburn (Wash.) Sch. Dist., 1994—; state pres Nev. Sch. Food Svc. Assn., Minden, 1992-93. Contbr. articles to profl. jours. Recipient Excellence in Food Svc. award U.S. Dept. Agri., 1989; named Outstanding Women of Am., 1977. Mem. Am. Dietetic Assn., Am. Sch. Food Svc. Assn. (dir. West region 1991-93, mem. exec. bd.), Soc. for Nutrition Edn., Am. Family and Consumer Svcs. Assn. (formerly Am. Home Econs. Assn.), Oreg. Sch. Food Svc. Assn. (pub. communication 1993-94). Democrat. Home: PO Box 2628 Longview WA 98632-8665

MORACA-SAWICKI, ANNE MARIE, oncology nurse; b. Niagara Falls, N.Y., Sept. 28, 1952; d. Joseph R. and Joan (Forgione) Moraca; m. Richard L. Sawicki, Sept. 15, 1979. BSN, D'Youville Coll., 1974; MS in Nursing, SUNY at Buffalo, 1977. Asst. prof. nursing D'Youville Coll., Buffalo, 1977-81; clin. editor Springhouse (Pa.) Corp., 1981-82; charge nurse Mt. St. Mary's Hosp., Lewiston, N.Y., 1982-84; surg. coord., adminstrv. asst. Dr. Richard L. Sawicki, Niagara Falls, N.Y., 1983—; part-time faculty mem. Niagara County C.C., Sanborn, N.Y.; bd. dirs. adult day care program Health Assn. Niagara County Inc. Contbr.: Nurses Legal Handbook, 1985, Pharmacotherapeutics: A Nursing Process Approach, 1986, 4th edit., 1996; clin. editor, contbr. Nurses Ref. Libr. Series Vols. on Drugs, Definitions, Procedures and Practices; clin. reviewer Manual of Med./Sug. Nursing, 1995, contbr., 1996; clin. reviewer Critical Care Handbook and IV Drug Handbook, 1995; clin. cons. Critical Care Plans, 1987, Taber's Cyclopedic Med. Dictionary, 16th edit., 1989. Recipient Cert. of Appreciation Niagara County C.C., 1988, 91, 92, Cmty. Svc. award Am. Cancer Soc., 1978, Miss Hope award, 1977, Am. Cancer Soc. Nursing Fellowship Grant, 1977; Grad. fellow SUNY, Buffalo, 1976-77. Mem. AAUP, N.Y. State Nurse's Assn., Health Assn. Niagara County (chairperson elect 1995, bd. dirs. adult day care program), Sigma Theta Tau. Home: 4658 Vrooman Dr Lewiston NY 14092-1049

MORAGNE, KATHY ANN STEVENS, educator; b. Cleve., Oct. 16, 1951; d. George Tomlinson and Bernice Caroline (Brand) Stevens; m. James Charles Moragne, June 28, 1975; children: Steven A., John D. MusB, State U. Coll., 1974; postgrad., SUNY, Postdam and Cortland. Tchr. music Ilion (N.Y.) Ctrl. Schs., 1974-93, 94—; acting dir. edn. N.Y. Cmty. Arts Coun., Utica, 1993-94. Contbr. articles to profl. jours. Dir. music Trinity Luth. Ch., Herkimer, N.Y., 1976-81; deacon Trinity Luth. Ch., 1991—. Mem. N.Y. State Sch. Music Tchrs. Assn., Herkimer County Music Educators Assn. (sec. 1985-89), Music Educators Nat. Conf., Delta Kappa Gamma. Office: Ilion Ctrl Schs 77 E North St Ilion NY 13357

MORAHAN-MARTIN, JANET MAY, psychologist, educator; b. N.Y.C., Jan. 13, 1944; d. William Timothy and May Rosalind (Tarangelo) Morahan; m. Curtis Harmon Martin, June 2, 1979; 1 child, Gwendolyn May. AB, Rosemont (Pa.) Coll., 1965; MEd, Tufts U., 1968; PhD, Boston Coll., 1978. Asst. mkt. rsch. analyst Compton Advt. Co., N.Y.C., 1965-67; mkt. rsch. analyst Ogilvy & Mather Advt., N.Y.C., 1967; ednl. rsch. asst. Tufts U., Medford, Mass., 1968-69; counselor Psychol. Inst. Bentley Coll., Waltham, Mass., 1971-72; dir. counseling svcs. Bryant Coll., Smithfield, R.I., 1972-75, psychology instr., 1972-76, asst. prof. psychology, 1976-81, assoc. prof. psychology, 1981-91, prof. psychology, 1991—; bd. dirs. Multi-Svc. Ctr., Newton, Mass., 1980-82. Contbr. articles to profl. jours., chpts. to books; reviewer APA Conv., 1985—, Teaching of Psychology Jour., 1988—, Collegiate Micro-Computer Jour., 1991, 93, Nat. Soc. Sci. Jour., 1991. Bd. dirs. Wellesley (Mass.) Community Children's Ctr., 1986-90, Coun. for Children, Newton, Mass., 1984-86. NIMH fellow, 1967-68; NSF grantee, 1974-76, U.S. Office Edn. grantee, 1980. Mem. Am. Psychol. Assn., Mass. Audubon Soc., Nat. Social Sci. Assn., Mass. Hort. Soc., N.E. Soc. for Behavioral Analysis and Therapy. Home: 17 Fuller Brook Rd Wellesley MA 02181-7108 Office: Bryant Coll 1150 Douglas Pike Smithfield RI 02917-1291

MORALES, CARLOTA ELOISA, principal; b. Havana, Cuba, Oct. 18, 1946; came to U.S., 1961; d. Jose Ramon and Rosa (Paradela) M. AA, Miami Dade Jr. Coll., 1964; BEd in Secondary Edn. Adminstrn., U. Miami, 1966, MEd, 1969, EdD in Adminstrn., 1984. Cert. Math. and langs. tchr., Fla. Tchr. Spanish Acad. of the Assumption, Miami, Fla., 1967-68; tchr. 6th grade Sts. Peter and Paul Sch., Miami, 1968-71, tchr. math., 1971-81, asst. prin., 1981-90; lectr. in Spanish Barry U., Miami Shores, Fla., 1981-82; prin. St. Agatha Sch., Miami, 1990—; judge literary contest Patronato de Cultura Pro-Cuba, Miami, 1973; judge Dade County Youth Fair, Miami, 1985-86; curriculum writer Archdiocese of Miami, 1983—; mem. vis. team Fla. Cath. Conf., Tallahassee, 1982—. Chairperson Sts. Peter and Paul Ann. Festival, Miami, 1971—. Mem. Assn. for Supervision and Curriculum Devel., Phi Delta Kappa. Roman Catholic. Home: 1400 SW 14th Ave Miami FL 33145-1541 Office: St Agatha Sch 1111 SW 107th Ave Miami FL 33174-2506

MORALES, CONCETTA, artist, arts educator; b. Bklyn., June 6, 1960; d. Arthur Thomas and Anna (Zampella) Mo.; m. Thomas Miles Rothwell, Jan. 11, 1992; children: Blaise Morales Rothwell, Cianna Jone Rothwell. BS, Skidmore Coll., 1982; MFA, Sch. of Art Inst. of Chgo., 1986. Instr. Des Moines Art Ctr., 1987-92; asst. prof. Coll. Art and Design, Iowa State U., Ames, 1989-92; rostered artist Artist-in-the-Schs./Cmtys., Iowa Arts Coun., 1987-96. Exhibited in solo shows at Fairfield (Iowa) Art Ctr., 1991, Iowa Wesleyan U., Mt. Pleasant, 1991, Embassy Club, Des Moines, 1994, U. La Crosse, Wis., 1994, Heartland Gallery, Des Moines, 1994, others; exhibited in group shows at Sioux City Art Ctr., 1990, Iowa State U., 1991, Plaza Art Fair, Kansas City, Mo., 1993, Laumeier Contemporary Art and Craft Fair, St. Louis, 1993, Drake U., Des Moines, 1994, Blanden Mus., Ft. Dodge, Iowa, 1995, Brunnier Mus./Iowa State U., Ames, 1995, others; represented in numerous corp. and pvt. collections. Recipient numerous awards including Best of Show Iowa State Fair Cultural Ctr. Exhibit, 1989, Grand Champion award Art-in-the-Park, Des Moines, 1993, Best in Painting, Iowa Exhibited/Heritage Gallery, 1995; executed murals and commns. Home: 6609 New York Cir Des Moines IA 50322-4981 Studio: 304 15th St # 401 Des Moines IA 50309

MORALES, HILDA MARIA, dancer, educator; b. N.Y.C., June 17, 1946; d. Héctor Santiago and Haydeé (Flores) M.; m. Walter Eugene Blake; 1 child, Alana Ruth Blake. Student, Ballet de San Juan Sch., Puerto Rico, 1955-60, Sch. of Am. Ballet, 1960-65. Prin. dancer Pa. Ballet Co., Phila., 1965-73; soloist Am. Ballet Theatre, N.Y.C., 1973-82; artist in residence Colo. Ballet, Denver, 1983-86; ballet instr. Hudson Valley Conservatory, 1995—, Ctrl. Pa. Youth Ballet, 1980—; ballet instr. Vassar Coll., Ind. U. and numerous others. Appeared in Turning Point (film), The Nutcracker (tv), Swan Lake (tv), Sleeping Beauty (tv), Les Grandes Ballets Canadiens, Long Beach Ballet, Indpls. Ballet Theatre, Alburquerque Ballet, Balt. Ballet, Eglevsky Ballet, Dance in America (interview); choreographer Piece d'Occasion (internat. ballet); director Stars of the American Ballet; lecturer Life Behind the Curtain, The Career in Dance: A Preparation, The Ballet Costume: It's History & Construction; appointed ballet mistress by Mikhail Baryshnikov, 1981-82. Ford Found. scholar, Sch. of Am. Ballet, 1960-65. Home: 32 Bayview Terr Newburgh NY 12550

MORALES, SANDRA LEE, educator; b. Sunnyside, N.Y., Oct. 15, 1934; d. John Joseph and Mabel Marnes (O'Brien) Lee; m. Hernan Morales, July 19, 1958; children: Martita Morales Sageser, Anita Morales Frost, Michael, Kathryn, Christina. BA in Chemistry, St. John's U., 1955; MS in Sci. Edn., U. Colo., 1972. Tchr. sci. St. Joseph's High Sch., Bklyn., 1955-56; tchr. algebra, biology All Saints High Sch., Bklyn., 1956; tchr. physics, gen. sci., math. Adelphi Acad., Bklyn., 1956-58; tchr. A.P. chemistry, gen. sci., sr. sci. Antilles H.S., San Juan, P.R., 1958-64, head dept. chemistry, 1962-64; sci. dept. head, tchr. life scis., earth scis. Pauline Meml. Sch., Colorado Springs, Colo., 1981-95; tutor pvt. practice, Colorado Springs, Colo., 1995—. Mem. Pauline Meml. PTO, 1973-95, pres., 1977-79; bd. dirs. Pointe Sublime Water Bd., Colorado Springs, 1980-92; pres. Colorado Springs Intercity Tennis, 1977-79; vol. Humane Soc., Colorado Springs, 1996—, Outdoor Colo., 1996—. Mem. AAUW, Colo. Tennis Assn., Am. Audubon Soc. Republican. Roman Catholic.

MORAN, BARBARA BURNS, librarian, educator; b. Columbus, Miss., July 8, 1944; d. Robert Theron and Joan (Brown) Burns; m. Joseph J. Moran, Sept. 4, 1965; children: Joseph Michael, Brian Matthew. AB, Mount Holyoke Coll., S. Hadley, Mass., 1966; M.Librarianship, Emory U., Atlanta, 1973; PhD, SUNY, Buffalo, 1982. Head libr. The Park Sch. of Buffalo, Snyder, N.Y., 1974-78; prof. Sch. Info. and Libr. Sci. U. N.C., Chapel Hill, 1981—, asst. dean, 1987-90; dean Sch. Info. and Libr. Sci., U. N.C., Chapel Hill, 1990—; participant various seminars; evaluator various edn. progs.; cons. in field. Author: Academic Libraries, 1984; co-author: (with Robert D. Stueart) Library Management, 4th edit., 1993; contbr. articles to profl. jours., chpts. to books; mem. editl. bd. Jour. Acad. Librarianship, 1992-94, Coll. and Rsch. Libraries, 1996—. Coun. Libr. Resources grantee, 1985, Univ. Rsch. Coun. grantee, 1983, 89, others. Mem. ALA, Assn. for Libr. and Info. Sci. Edn., Popular Culture Assn., N.C. Libr. Assn., Beta Phi Mu. Home: 1307 Leclair St Chapel Hill NC 27514-3034 Office: Univ NC Sch Info & Libr Sci Chapel Hill NC 27599-3360

MORAN, JOAN JENSEN, physical education and health educator; b. Chgo., Sept. 25, 1952; d. Axel Fred and Mary J. (Maes) J.; m. Gregory Keith Moran. BS in Edn., Western Ill. U., 1974; MS in Edn., No. Ill. U., 1978. Cert. tchr., Ill. Tchr., coach East Coloma Sch., Rock Falls, Ill., 1974—; part-time recreation specialist Woodhaven Lakes, Sublette, Ill., 1975-79; cons. Ill. State Bd. Edn., Springfield, 1984—; instr. NDEITA, Ill., 1988—; facilitator Project Wild, Ill., 1990—. Instr. ARC, Rock Falls, 1978—, Am. Heart Assn., Rock Falls, 1978—; exec. bd. East Coloma Cmty. Club; fitness del. to Russia and Hungary, 1992; cons. Alcohol Awareness & Occupant Restraint Ill. State Bd. Edn., Substance Abuse Guidance Edn. Com., Rock Falls Drug Free Cmty. Grant com., Whiteside County CPR Coord. com. Recipient Western Ill. U. Alumni Achievement award, 1993, Western Ill. Master Tchr. award, 1993, Svc. award Ill. Assn. Health, Phys. Edn., Recreation and Dance, 1991, 92, Outstanding Young Woman award, 1986, Phys. Educator of Yr. award, 1988; named Mid. Sch. Phys. Edn. Tchr. of Yr. Midwest AAHPERD, 1993, Ill. Assn. Health, Phys. Edn., Recreation and Dance, 1992, Gov.'s Coun. Health and Phys. Edn. award, 1991, Am. Tchr. of Yr. award Walt Disney Co., 1993, Excel award ISBE, 1995. Mem. AAHPERD, NEA, Ill. Assn. Health, Phys. Edn., Recreation and Dance (v.p. teenage youth 1988-90, pres. 1994, past pres., conv. coord. 1995), No. Dist. Ill. Assn. Health, Phys. Edn., Recreation and Dance, Ill. Edn. Assn. (newsletter editor 1984-85, exec. bd. 1985-90, treas. 1985-90), East Coloma Edn. Assn. (pres., pub. rels., v.p. 1993-94, Environ. Edn. Assn. Ill. Democrat. Lutheran. Home: 1903 E 41st St Sterling IL 61081-9449

MORAN, LINDA BARKER, environmental engineer, biology educator; b. New Orleans, Dec. 2, 1957; d. William Barker and Doll Lenderman Watson; m. John Patrick Moran, June 8, 1990; children: Alan Lenderman Robert, Edward O'Day Robert. BS, Tulane U., 1978; MS, McNeese State U., 1991. Chem. engr. PPG Industries, Lake Charles, La., 1977-79; environ. project engr. W.B. Grace/Davison Chem., Lake Charles, 1989; tech. svc. rep. Dearborn Chem., Lake Charles, 1990-91; environ. specialist La. Dept. Environ. Quality, Lake Charles, 1991-92; acting dir. sml. bus. assistance program Md. Dept. Environment, Balt., 1993—; adj. prof. biology Loyola Coll., Balt., 1993-94, Essex C.C., Balt., 1993—. Recipient Award of Appreciation for outreach Korean Drycleaners of Md., 1995, Korean Drycleaners of Greater Washington, 1995. Republican. Episcopalian.

MORAN, PATRICIA GENEVIEVE, corporate executive; b. Evanston, Ill., July 26, 1945; d. James M.; children: Christine Coyle, Thomas Beddia, Donald Beddia. Attended, Marquette U. Pers. mgr. Sesco, 1983-84, dir. corp. transp., assoc. rels. dir., 1984-85, v.p. assoc. rels., 1985-88; group v.p. sales Southeast Toyota, Deerfield Beach, Fla., 1988-89, pres., 1989-94; v.p. H.R. JM Family Enterprises, Inc., Deerfield Beach, pres., 1989-94. Dir. Beacon Coun., Miami, Fla., 1992—, Broward Econ. Devel., Ft. Lauderdale, Fla., 1991—, Youth Automotive Tng. Ctr., Hollywood, Fla., 1985—. Named Top 50 Working Women by Working Woman's Mag. Mem. Ft. Lauderdale C. of C. (dir. 1991—), Tower Club, The Haven (adv. bd. 1994-95). Office: JM Family Enterprises 100 NW 12th Ave Deerfield Beach FL 33442-1702*

MORAN, RACHEL, lawyer, educator; b. Kansas City, Mo., June 27, 1956; d. Thomas Albert and Josephine (Portillo) M. AB, Stanford U., 1978; JD, Yale U., 1981. Bar: Calif. 1984. Assoc Heller, Ehrman, White & McAuliffe, San Francisco, 1982-83; prof. law U. Calif., Berkeley, 1984—; vis. prof. UCLA Sch. Law, 1988, Stanford (Calif.) U. Law Sch., 1989, N.Y.U. Sch. of Law, 1996, U. Miami Sch. Law, 1997; ann. civil rights lectr. Creighton U. Sch. Law, Omaha, 1989; Pirsig lectr. William Mitchell Coll. St. Paul, 1989, others; mem. steering com. Nat. Resource Ctr., Berkeley, 1988-89; chair Chicano/Latino Policy Project, 1993-96. Contbr. numerous articles to profl. jours. Grantee Joseph and Polly Harris Trust Inst. Govtl. Studies, Berkeley, 1987-89, Faculty Devel. U. Calif., Berkeley, 1985-86; recipient Disting. Tchg. award U. Calif. Mem. ABA, AAUP, Calif. Bar Assn., Phi Beta Kappa. Democrat. Unitarian. Office: U Calif Sch Law Boalt Hall Berkeley CA 94720

MORAN, SARAH JUDSON, independent option speculator; b. Newport, R.I., July 1, 1956; d. Richard E. and Norma K. (Judson) Brown; m. John P. Moran Jr., Oct. 3, 1988. BA in Anthropology/Geology, U. Mass., 1981. Sales analyst Silas Brown Inc., Westport, Mass., 1982-85, buyer, 1985—; speculator equity options Westport, 1982—. Mem. Assn. to Overcome Multiple Sclerosis, Phi Beta Kappa. Mem. Soc. of Friends. Home: 1145 Main Rd Westport MA 02790-4412 Office: Angle Assets PO Box 3352 Westport MA 02790-0702

MORAND, KATE MEGAN, speech and language pathologist; b. Evanston, Ill., Mar. 13, 1956; d. Laurence Thomas and Joanne Harriet (Byrnes) M.; m. Donald William Rodd, Oct. 25, 1980 (div. 1985); m. John Regis Penn, July 9, 1988; 1 child, Maureen Nicole. BS, Marquette U., 1978, MS, 1980. Cert. speech and language pathologist, Wis.; lic. supr., dir., coord. of instrn. K-12. Speech and lang. pathologist Cedarburg (Wis.) Pub. Schs., 1980, Milw. Pub. Schs., 1980-87, Slinger (Wis.) Sch. Dist., 1987-92, Pewaukee (Wis.) Pub. Schs., 1992—; speech and lang. pathologist MJ Therapy, Racine, Wis., 1984-85, Luth. Social Svcs., Waukesha, Wis., 1987, Easter Seals Southeastern Wis., Milw., 1987; clin. supr. speech Marquette U., Milw., 1992; diagnostics case mgr. Sch. Dist. Menomonee Falls, Wis., 1992—; fitness instr. YMCA, Menomonee Falls, 1988—; skin care cons. Mary Kay Cosmetics, Dallas, 1988—. Mem. parent bd. Menomonee Falls Swim Club, 1993-96, chair fundraising and pub. rels.; asst. leader, Girls Scouts U.S.A., Waukesha, 1990-93; former parent adv. gifted and talented students Lannon Sch.; religious edn. tchr. Good Shepherd Congregation, Menomonee Falls, 1989-90. Mem. ASCD, Am. Speech-Lang.-Hearing Assn., Wis. Speech-Lang.-Hearing Assn., Phi Delta Kappa. American Catholic. Home and Office: 1385 N Victoria Cir Elm Grove WI 53122

MORANG, DIANE JUDY, writer, television producer, business entrepreneur; b. Chgo., Apr. 28, 1942; d. Anthony Thomas Morang and Laura Ann Andrzejczak. Student, Stevens Finishing Sch., Chgo., 1956, Fox Bus. Coll., 1959-60, UCLA, 1967-69. Mem. staff Drury Ln. Theatre, Chgo., 1961-62; staff AM Show ABC-TV, Hollywood, Calif., 1970-71; chair, mem. judging panel Regional Emmy awards, 1989, judge 2 categories, 1985. Author: How to Get into the Movies, 1978; author, creator: The Rainbow Keyboard, 1991. Bd. dirs., mem. scholarship com. Ariz. Bruins UCLA Alumni Assn. Mem. NATAS (mem. Emmy-award winning team 1971), Ariz. Authors Assn. (bd. dirs.). Roman Catholic.

MORATH, INGE, photographer; b. Graz, Austria, May 27, 1923; d. Edgar Eugen and Mathilde (Wiesler) M.; m. Arthur Miller, Feb. 1962; 1 child, Rebecca Augusta. BA, U. Berlin; DFA (hon.), U. Hartford, 1984. Formerly translator and editor ISB Feature Sect., Salzburg and Vienna, Austria; later editor lit. monthly Der Optmist, Vienna and Austrian editor Heute Mag.; former free-lance writer for mags. and Red White Red Radio Network; with Magnum Photos, Paris and N.Y.C., 1952—; mem. Magnum Photos, 1953—; tchr. photography course Cooper Union, 2 years; lectr. at various univs. including U. Miami, U. Mich. Exhibited photographs one-woman shows Wuehrle Gallery, Vienna, 1956, Leitz Gallery, N.Y.C., 1958, N.Y. Overseas Press Club, 1959, Chgo. Art Inst., 1964, Oliver Woolcott Meml. Library, Litchfield, Conn., 1969, Art Mus., Andover, Mass., 1971, U. Miami, 1972, U. Mich., 1973, Carlton Gallery, N.Y.C., 1976, Neikrug Galleries, N.Y.C., 1976, 79, Grand Rapids (Mich.) Art Mus., 1979, Mus. Modern Art, Vienna, 1980, Kunsthaus, Zurich, Switzerland, 1980, Burden Gallery Aperture Inc., N.Y.C., 1987, Moscow Ctr. Photojournalists, 1988, Sala del Canal, Madrid, 1988, Cathedral, Norwich, Eng., 1989, Am. Cultural Ctr., Brussels, 1989, Kolbe Mus., Berlin, 1991, Mus. Rupertinum, Salzburg, 1991; retrospective Neue Galerie, Linz, Austria, Amerika House, Berlin, 1993, Hradčin, Prague, 1993, Royal Photographic Soc., Bath, Eng., 1994, Mus. Contemporary Art, Madrid, 1995, Book Fair, Frankfurt, 1995, Leica Gallery, N.Y.C., 1996; numerous group shows include Photokina, Cologne, Ger., World's Fair, Montreal, Que., Can.; represented in permanent collections Met. Mus. Art, Boston Mus. Art, Art Inst. Chgo., Bibliothèque Nationale, Paris, Kunsthaus, Zurich, Prague (Czechoslovakia) Art Mus., Rupertinum Mus., Salzburg, Austria; photographer for books Guerreà la Tristesse (Dominique Aubier), 1956, Venice Observed (Mary McCarthy), 1956, (with Yul Brynner) Bring Forth the Children (Yul Brynner), 1960, From Persia to Iran (Edouard Sablier), 1961, Tunisia (Claude Roy, Paul Sebag), 1961, Le Masque (drawings by Saul Steinberg), 1967, In Russia (Arthur Miller), 1969, East West Exercises (Ruth Bluestone Simon), 1973, Boris Pasternak: My Sister Life (O. Carlisle, translator), 1976, In the Country (Arthur Miller), 1977, Chinese Encounters (Arthur Miller), 1979, Salesman in Beijing (Arthur Miller), 1984, Images of Vienna (Barbara Frischmuth, Pavel Kohout, Andre Heller, Arthur Miller), 1981, Inge Morath: Portraits, 1987, In Our Time, 1990, Russian Journal (E. Yevtushenko, A. Voznesensky, O. Andreyev Carlisle), 1991, Inge Morath: Fotografien 1952-92, Inge Morath: Spain in the 50s, 1994, The Danube, 1995; editor, co-photographer books Paris/Magnum, Aperture Inc., biography Grosse Photographen unserer Zeit, 1975; contbr. numerous photographs to European, U.S., S. Am., Japanese mags., and to numerous anthologies including Life series on photography and photographic yearbooks. Recipient Great Austrian State Prize for photography, 1991, various citations for shows. Mem. Am. Soc. Mag. Photographers. Home: Tophet Rd PO Box 232 Roxbury CT 06783 Office: Magnum Photos 151 W 25th St New York NY 10001-7204

MORAWETZ, CATHLEEN SYNGE, mathematician; b. Toronto, May 5, 1923; came to U.S., 1945, naturalized, 1950; d. John Lighton and Elizabeth Eleanor Mabel (Allen) Synge; m. Herbert Morawetz, Oct. 27, 1945; children: Pegeen Morawetz Rubinstein, John Synge, Lida Morawetz Jeck, Nancy. BA, U. Toronto, 1945; SM, MIT, 1946; PhD, NYU, 1951; hon. degree, Eastern Mich. U., 1980, Smith Coll., 1982, Brown U., 1982, Princeton U., 1986, Duke U., 1988, N.J. Inst. Tech., 1988, U. Waterloo, 1993, U. Dublin, 1996. Research assoc. Courant Inst., NYU, 1952-57, asst. prof. math., 1957-60, assoc. prof., 1960-65, prof., 1965—, assoc. dir., 1978-84, dir., 1984-88. Editor Jour. Math. Analysis and Applications, Comms. in PDE; author articles in applications of partial differential equations, especially transonic flow and scattering theory. Trustee Princeton U., 1973-78, Sloan Found., 1980—. Guggenheim fellow, 1967, 79; Office Naval Rsch. grantee, until 1990. Fellow AAAS; mem. NAS, Am. Math. Soc. (term trustee 1975-85, pres. 1995—), Am. Acad. Arts and Scis., Soc. Indsl. and Applied Math. Office: 251 Mercer St New York NY 10012-1110

MORBY, JACQUELINE, venture capitalist; b. Sacramento, June 19, 1937; d. Junior Jennings and Bertha (Backer) Collins; m. Jeffrey L. Morby, June 21, 1959; children: Andrew Jennings, Michelle Lorraine. BA in Psychology, Stanford U., 1959; M in Mgmt., Simmons Grad. Mgmt. Sch., Boston, 1978. Assoc. TA Assocs., Boston, 1978-81, gen. ptnr., 1982-89, mng. dir., 1989—; bd. dirs. Ontrack Computer Sys., Mpls., Axent Tech., Inc., Rockville, Md., Pivotpoint, Inc., Waltham, Mass., R&D Sys., Inc., Colorado Springs, Colo., Ansys, Inc., Houston, Pa., Pacific Mutual Life Ins., Co., Newport Beach, Calif. Trustee Chatham Coll.; mem. Mass. Gov.'s Coun. on Growth and Tech. Mem. Nat. Venture Capital Orgn. Office: TA Assocs 125 High St Boston MA 02110-2704

MOREHOUSE, GEORGIA ANN, microbiologist, researcher; b. Guatamala City, Nov. 1, 1933; d. Bevan Blau and Margaret Julia (Ward) Lewis; m. Lawrence Glen Morehouse, Oct. 6, 1956; children: Timothy Lawrence, Glenn Ellen. BS, Purdue U., 1955. Microbiologist Purdue U., West Lafayette, Ind., 1955-60, Nat. Animal Disease Lab., Ames, Iowa, 1960-63; rsch. specialist dept. of dairy sci. U. Mo., Columbia, 1978-84; videographer, owner Great Moments in Video, Inc., Columbia, 1984-87; adminstr. auxiliary loan fund Mo. Vet. Med. Auxiliary, Columbia, 1987—. Contbr. articles to profl. jours. Chair of nom. com. and fund raising PTA Shepard Blvd. Sch., Columbia, 1968-70, co-chair Columbia Jr. Cotillion, Columbia, 1977-78; bd. dirs. Koinonia House, Columbia, 1978-82, vol. The Wardrope, Columbia, 1972—, coord. latch key program Trinity Presbyn. Ch., Columbia, 1992-94; chair, bd. dirs. Friends of Music, U. Mo., 1996—; pres. Women's Symphony League, Mo. Symphony Soc., Columbia, 1996—; tutor adult reading ctr. Columbia Pub. Schs., 1989—. Home: 916 Danforth Dr Columbia MO 65201

MORELLA, CONSTANCE ALBANESE, congresswoman; b. Somerville, Mass., Feb. 12, 1931; d. Salvatore and Mary Christine (Fallette) Albanese; m. Anthony C. Morella, Aug. 21, 1954; children: Paul, Mark, Laura; guardians of: Christine, Catherine, Louise, Rachel, Paul, Ursula. AA, Boston U., 1950, AB, 1954; MA, Am. U., 1967, D of Pub. Svc. (hon.), 1988; D of Pub. Svc. (hon.), Norwich U. and Dickinson Coll., 1989. Tchr. Montgomery County (Md.) Pub. Schs., 1956-60; instr. Am. U., 1968-70; prof. Montgomery Coll., Rockville, Md., 1970-86; mem. Md. Ho. Dels., Annapolis, 1979-86, 100th-103rd Congresses from 8th Md. dist., 1987—; adv. bd. Am. Univ., Washington; trustee Capitol Coll. Laurel, Md. Trustee Capitol Coll, Laurel, Md., 1977—; chair Sci. Com. Tech. Subcom., Basic Rsch. Subcom., coun. mem. Montgomery County United Way; adv. coun. Montgomery County Hospice Soc.; hon. bd. mem. Nat. Kidney Found; active Human Rights Caucus, co-chair Congressional Women's Caucus, Black Caucus; chair Gov. Reform and Oversight Com. Office: US Ho of Reps 106 Cannon House Office Bu Washington DC 20515 also: 51 Monroe St Rockville MD 20850-2417*

MORELOCK, JASMINE CRAWFORD, artist, art educator; b. Boise, June 30, 1925; d. Graydon Clemson and Doris Cecile (Dinwiddie) Crawford; m. Max Maurice Morelock, Apr. 8, 1950; 1 child, Maurice Max. AA, Stephens Coll., 1945; BA, La. State U., 1949; MA, La. Sch. Tech., 1979; MFA cum laude, Inst. Allende, San Miguel Allende, Guanajuato, Mexico, 1978. Cert. tchr. speech and art, La. Advtsg. writer programming dept. KRMD Radio Sta., Shreveport, La., 1945-48; with Bozell and Jacobs Nat. Advtsg. Agy.; with comml. design Glen Mason Advtsg. Agy.; asst. prof. fine arts La. State U., Baton Rouge, 1948-49; head art dept. Southfield Sch., Shreveport, La., 1972-74; tchr. portrait classes Bossier C. C., Bossier City, La., 1989-91; tchr. art Caddo Parish Sch. Bd., Shreveport, La., 1975-80; represented by Gallery on the Green, Lexington, Mass., Juleaux Gallery of Fine Arts, Kansas City, WLR Design Company, Shreveport, La., Lytle's, Shreveport, La., Riverwalk Gallery, New Orleans; Presenter workshops Barnwell Art Ctr., Shreveport, La., J&M Studio Groups, Shreveport, Women's Dept. Club, Shreveport, Springhill (La.) Art Assn., 1993. One woman exhbns. include La. State U. Shreveport Gallery, 1992, Cambridge Club, Shreveport, 1993, The Glen Gallery, Shreveport, 1995, Shreve Meml. Libr., Shreveport, 1995, numerous others; group exhbns. include Valerie Originals, KJ's Antiques and Silks, Hot Springs, Ark., 1986, Women Artists of La., Baton Rouge, 1987, Boots Pharmaceutical Co., Cambridge Club, Shreveport, La., 1988, 90, 92, Stoner Arts Ctr., Shreveport, 1989, 90, Gallery on the Green, Lexington, Mass., 1989, Simmers Gallery, Shreveport, 1989, La. Artist Group Show, 1990, Barksdale Air Base, 1990, Turner Art Ctr., 1990, Artport, Shreveport, 1990, 92, 93, 94, Riverside Galleries, Shreveport, Southwestern Watercolor Soc., 1992, 94, Nat. Mus. Art, Washington, 1993, Still River Artists, Danbury, Conn., 1993, Okla. 12th Annual Juried Show, 1995, numerous others; represented in pvt. and pub. collections La. State U. Ctr., St. Luke's Hosp., St. Vincent's Acad., U. Club, Seagull Cos., McGoldrick Oil Co., numerous others; featured in (cover) (Goodloe Stuck) The Shreveport Madam, 1986, Boots Pharm. Art Catalogue, 1990, Behold, I Make All Things New, 1991, Artists of La. Catalogue, 1991, (t.v. show) Focus on the Arts, The Shreveport Times, 1995. Recipient Special Selection award Ark. Arts Ctr., Little Rock, 1984, First Purchase Prize Izora and Thilo Steinschulte Meml. award First Meth. Ch. Alexandria (La.), 1984, First Place Ark-La-Tex-Okla Competition First Meth. Ch., Shreveport, 1984. Mem. Nat. Watercolor Soc.,

Nat. Assn. Women Artists, Southwestern Watercolor Soc. (Elizabeth Shanon Meml. award 1991), La. Watercolor Soc. Soc. Exptl. Artists, Hoover Watercolor Soc. (v.p., First Place 1984, H.M. award 1993), Registry of La. Artists, La. Artists, Inc., Southeastern Ctr. for Contemporary Art, Coalition of Women's Art (nat., Dallas). Home and Studio: 427 Monrovia St Shreveport LA 71106

MORENCY, PAULA J., lawyer; b. Oak Park, Ill., Mar. 13, 1955. AB magna cum laude, Princeton U., 1977; JD, U. Va., 1980. Bar: Ill. 1980, U.S. Dist. Ct. (no. dist.) Ill. 1980, U.S. Ct. Appeals (7th cir.) 1981, U.S. Ct. Appeals (5th cir.) 1990. Assoc. Mayer, Brown & Platt, Chgo., 1980-86, ptnr., 1987-94; ptnr. Schiff Hardin & Waite, Chgo., 1994—. Contbr. author: Federal Litigation Guide Vol. 3, 1985. Mem. ABA, Chgo. Coun. of Lawyers (bd. govs. 1989-93). Office: Schiff Hardin & Waite 7200 Sears Tower Chicago IL 60606

MORENO, IGNACIA SOLEDAD, lawyer; b. Cartagena, Colombia, May 8, 1961; came to U.S., 1967; d. Carlos J. and Zenith (Juliao) M. BA in English Lit. and Polit. Sci., NYU, 1986, JD, 1990. Bar: Va. 1990, D.C. 1992, U.S. Dist. Ct. Md. 1992, U.S. Dist. Ct. P.R. 1995, U.S. Supreme Ct. 1995. Intern La Caisse Nacionale de Credit Agricole, Paris, 1982; intern Dept. Internat., Econ. and Social Affairs UN, N.Y.C., 1982; trial preparation asst. N.Y. County Dist. Attys. Office, N.Y.C., 1986-87; law clk. U.S. Senate Com. on Judiciary, Washington, summer 1988; summer assoc. Kaye, Scholer, Fierman, Hayes & Handler, Washington, summer 1989; rsch. asst. NYU Program on Philanthropy and the Law, N.Y.C., 1989-90; law clk. U.S. Attys. Office (so. dist.) N.Y., N.Y.C., 1990; assoc. Hogan & Hartson, LLP, Washington, 1990-94; spl. asst. to asst. atty. gen. environ. and natural resources divsn. U.S. Dept. Justice, Washington, 1994-95, counsel to asst. atty. gen., 1995—; pro bono on behalf of Mexican Am. Legal Def. and Ednl. Fund, 1991, 92, ACLU, 1991, ABA, D.C. Homeless Clinic, 1991, migrant workers, 1991-92, youth (D.C. works), 1993, 94), mentor program Spingarn H.S., D.C., 1990-93, indigent individuals. Vol. numerous N.Y. state and nat. campaigns, 1982-93; mem. exec. com. Mid-Manhattan New Democratic Party, N.Y.C., 1984-85. Recipient Bronze medal for Commendable Svc. EPA, Washington, 1995, Latina Excellence Environ. award Hispanic Mag., 1996; named among 100 Most Influential Hispanics in U.S., Hispanic Bus. Mag., 1995. Mem. ABA (bd. dirs.), Hispanic Bar Assn. D.C. Democrat. Office: US Dept Justice ENRD 10th St & Constitution Ave Washington DC 20530

MORENO, RITA, actress; b. Humacao, P.R., Dec. 11, 1931; m. Leonard I. Gordon, June 18, 1965; 1 child, Fernanda Luisa. Spanish dancer since childhood, night club entertainer; appeared on Broadway in The Sign in Sidney Brustein's Window, 1964-65, Gantry, 1969-70, The Last of the Red Hot Lovers, 1970-71, The National Health, 1974, The Ritz, 1975, Wally's Cafe, 1981, The Odd Couple, 1985; (off Broadway) After Play, 1995; motion picture debut, 1950, and appeared in numerous films including West Side Story, Carnal Knowledge, The King and I, Singing in the Rain, The Four Seasons, I Like it Like That, 1994, Angus, 1995, Wharf Rat, 1995. Recipient Acad. Award for best supporting actress, 1962; Grammy award for best rec., 1973; Antoinette Perry award for best supporting actress Broadway play, 1975; Emmy award, 1977, 78. Address: care Agency for Performing Arts 9000 W Sunset Blvd Los Angeles CA 90069-5801

MORENO, ZERKA TOEMAN, psychodrama educator; b. Amsterdam, The Netherlands, June 13, 1917; d. Joseph and Rosalia (Gutwirth) Toeman; m. Jacob L. Moreno (dec.); 1 child, Jonathan D.; 1 stepchild, Regina. Student, Willesden Tech. Coll., 1937-38, NYU, 1948-49. Cert. trainer, educator, practitioner of psychodrama and group psychotherapy Am. Bd. Examiners. Rsch. asst. Psychodramatic and Sociometric Insts., N.Y.C., 1942-51; pres. Moreno Inst., N.Y.C. and Beacon, N.Y., 1951-82; trainer in psychodrama Studiefrämjandet, Stockholm, 1976-83, Finnish Psychodrama Assn., Lahti, Finland, 1976-83; lectr., trainer, Gt. Britain, Australia, New Zealand, Norway, Sweden, Italy, Germany, Japan, 1976-96, Argentina, Brazil, Greece, The Netherlands, Denmark, Belgium, Spain, Israel, Korea and Taiwan, 1977—; hon. pres. Chinese Zerka Moreno Inst., Nanjing, China. Author: (book of poetry) Love Songs to Life, 1971, 93; co-author: Psychodrama, 1967, 69. Named hon. citizen Comune di Roma, Assessorato Alla Cultura, 1983, Municipalidad de la Ciudad de Buenos Aires, 1984, Federacao Brasiliero de Psicodrama, Sao Paulo, 1996. Fellow Am. Soc. Group Psychotherapy and Psychodrama (pres. 1967-69, hon. v.p. 1988—, sec.-treas. 1955-66, hon. pres.); mem. Internat. Assn. Group Psychotherapy (treas. 1974-76, bd. dirs. 1976-80), Soc. Psicodrama Sao Paulo (hon.), Sociedad Argentina Psicodrama (hon.). Home: 259 Wolcott Ave Beacon NY 12508-3711

MOREY, DIANE P., curriculum specialist, educator; b. Rhinelander, Wis., Sept. 5, 1949; d. Chester L. and Patricia (Naylor) M. AA in Liberal Arts, Nicolet Coll., 1978; Cert. in Dental Hygiene, U. Louisville, 1980, BS in Dental Hygiene, 1981; MS in Curriculum and Supervision, U. Wis., 1992. Registered dental hygienist. Civilian dental hygienist Dept. of Army, Ft. Knox, Ky., 1980-81; clin. dental hygienist Green Bay and Oshkosh, Wis., 1981-88, 89-93; dental hygiene coord. Advance Dental Mgmt., Green Bay, 1988-89; instr., curriculum specialist Pearl River Coll., Hattiesburg, Miss., 1993—; mem., advisor young dental adv. bd. Student Am. Dental Hygienists' Assn., Hattiesburg, 1992—. Recipient Cert. of Appreciation Wis. Dental Hygienists' Assn., 1990. Mem. Am. Dental Hygienists' Assn., Miss. Dental Hygienists' Assn., Kappa Delta Pi, Phi Kappa Phi, Sigma Phi Alpha. Home: 6490 US Hwy 49N # 266 Hattiesburg MS 39401 Office: Pearl River Coll 5448 US Hwy 49 S Hattiesburg MS 39401

MORFORD, LYNN ELLEN, state official; b. Peoria, Ill., June 17, 1953; d. Raymond Scott Jr. and Georgiana (Woodhall) M. BA, Millikin U., 1975; MA, Sangamon State U., Springfield, Ill., 1984. News reporter Stas. WJBC-WBNQ, Bloomington, Ill., 1975-76, Sta. WSOY-AM-FM, Decatur, Ill., 1976-78, Stas. WXCL-WZRO-FM, Peoria, 1978, Sta. KACY-AM-FM, Ventura, Calif., 1978, Sta. WKAN, Kankakee, Ill., 1979-82; freelance news reporter Sta. WMAQ, Chgo., 1982; news dir. Stas. WXCL-WKQA-FM, Peoria, 1983; press sec. Ill. Ho. of Reps. Rep. Press Office, Springfield, 1984-85; chief Press Office, Ill. Dept. Commerce and Community Affairs, Springfield, 1986-95, comms. mgr., 1995—; mem. adv. bd. Ill. AP, 1983; radio news contest judge Okla. AP, 1983; bd. dirs. Ill. News Broadcasters Assn., 1980-84. Chmn. pub. rels., mem. adv. bd. Leadership Ill., 1992—, spring conf. chair, 1994; chmn. pub. rels. Springfield St. Patrick's Day Parade Com., 1991—; chmn. pub. rels. film fund raiser Vachel Lindsay Assn., Springfield, 1989; mem. Springfield Jr. League, 1990-91; mem. Samaritans St. John's Hosp., Springfield, 1995—, Ill. River Econ. Devel. Action Team, 1996—, Orlene Moore Scholarship Com., 1996—, Student of Yr. Selection Com., 1996—; pres., bd. trustees Sherman Pub. Libr. Dist., 1995—. Recipient Best Contbr. award Ill. AP, 1983; Robert Howard scholar Sangamon State U., 1983; named to Hon. Order of Ky. Cols., 1992. Methodist. Home: 2 Willow Hill Dr Sherman IL 62684-9769 Office: Ill Dept Commerce and Community Affairs 620 E Adams St Springfield IL 62701-1615

MORFORD-BURG, JOANN, state senator, investment company executive; b. Miller, S.D., Nov. 26, 1956; d. Darrell Keith Morford and Eleanor May (Fawcett) Morford-Steptoe; m. Quinten Leo Burg, Nov. 12, 1983. BS in Agrl.-Bus., Comml. Econs., S.D. State U., 1979; cert. in personal fin. planning, Am. Coll., 1992. Agrl. loan officer 1st Bank System, Presho, S.D., 1980-82, Wessington Springs, S.D., 1982-86; agrl. loan officer Am. State Bank, Wessington Springs, 1986; registered investment rep. SBM Fin. Svcs. Inc., Wessington Springs, 1986—; mem. S.D. State Senate, Wessington Springs, 1990—, majority whip, 1993-94, minority whip, 1994—; mem. senate appropriations com. 1993—; chair senate ops. and audit com. 1993, 94; mem. ops. and audit com., 1995—; active Nat. Conf. State Legislators' Assembly of Fed. Issues Environ. Com., 1995—. Mem. Midwestern-Can. task force Midwest Conf., 1990-94; mem. transp. com., commerce com., taxation com. S.D. State Senate, Pierre, 1990-92; treas. twp. bd. Wessington Springs, 1990-92; mem. Wessington Springs Sch. Improvement Coun. Mem. Future Farmers Am. (adv. bd. Wessington Springs chpt.), S.D. State U. 4-H Alumni Assn., Nat. Life Underwriters Assn. (Huron chpt.), Order Ea. Star (various offices 1980—). Democrat. Methodist. Home and Office: 38678 SD Highway 34 Wessington Springs SD 57382-5806

MORGA BELLIZZI, CELESTE, editor; b. N.Y.C., Mar. 8, 1921; d. Louis and Emma (Macari) Morga; m. John J. Bellizzi, Sept. 1, 1942; children: John J., Robert F. Student, Columbia U., 1940-41, SUNY, Albany, 1970. Cert. med. lab. technician. Medical lab. technician USMC Hosp., N.Y.C., 1942, Woman's Hosp., N.Y.C., 1942-52; spl. investigator N.Y. State Atty. Gen.'s Office, Albany, 1958-65; editor Internat. Drug Report publ., The Narc Officer publ. Internat. Narcotic Enforcement Officers Assn., Albany, 1965—. Dir. Albany Inst. History and Art, 1988-90, N.Y. State Press Women, Albany, 1987; advisor UN Non-govtl. Orgns. Drug Com., N.Y.C., 1980-90, White House Conf. Drug Free Am., Washington, 1987; mem. com. Bethlehem Drug Prevention Program, Delmar, N.Y., 1987-90, Action Commn. Narc Edn., Delmar, 1984-90; v.p. Women's Rep. Party Albany, 1972. Recipient Pres.'s award INEOA, 1982, Disting. Svc. award Houston Police Dept., 1981. Mem. Nat. Fedn. Press Women, Nat. Press Club, Univ. Club, Albany Country Club, Aberdeen Country Club. Office: Internat Narcotic Enforcement Officers Assn 112 State St Albany NY 12207-2005

MORGAN, ALICE RUTH, retired treasurer; b. Petersburg, Tex., Apr. 1, 1934; d. Cloyd D. and Lula Belle (Jay) Smith; m. Leroy Edward Miner, Aug. 6, 1955 (div. Dec. 1974); children: Steven Dale, Kevin Guy; m. Alfred Curtis Morgan, Apr. 29, 1978. BBA, U. N.Mex., 1956, MBA, 1969. With Sandia Nat. Labs., Albuquerque, 1963-73, mgnr. acctg., 1973-84, asst. treas., 1984-93; ret., 1993. Bd. dirs. Family & Children Svcs., Albuquerque, 1974-88. Mem. Inst. Mgmt. Accts. (ret., bd. dirs. 1990-96). Republican. Episcopal. Home: 9021 Natalie NE Albuquerque NM 87111

MORGAN, ANNETTE N., state legislator; b. Kennett, Mo., Aug. 31, 1938; m. William P. Morgan, 1961; children: John, Katherine. BA, U. Mo., MA. Tchr. adult edn.; mem. Mo. Ho. of Reps. Mem. Adult Edn. Assn. Democrat. Presbyterian. Home: 221 W 48th St #1601 Kansas City MO 64112 Office: Mo Ho of Reps State Capitol Building Jefferson City MO 65101-1556

MORGAN, BARBARA TAYLOR, artist; b. Cedar Rapids, Iowa, July 5, 1946; d. Arthur Dale and Dorothy Jane (Long) Taylor; m. William Steele Morgan, June 12, 1981; 1 child, Austin Kellett Letson, III. BA, U. Ala., 1981; MSEd, Bank St. Coll. Edn. and, Parsons Sch. Design, N.Y.C., 1987; MFA in Painting and Photography, U. Ala., 1992. Cert. tchr. art edn., K-12, Ala., English 7-12. Tchr. art and English The Donoho Sch., Anniston, Ala., 1980-90; instr. dept. art U. Ala., Birmingham, 1992—; mem. exhbns. com. Visual Arts Gallery, Birmingham, 1994—. Solo exhibits include Denise Bibro Fine Arts Gallery, N.Y.C., 1994, Woods Hall Gallery, U. Ala., Tuscaloosa, 1995; group shows include Hammond Hall Gallery, Jacksonville State U., 1993, Ala. Artists Gallery, 1995. Pres. Anniston Coun. for the Arts, Ala., 1981; lectr. Birmingham Mus. of Art, 1995, Birmingham Civil Rights Inst., 1994, Birmingham chpt. AAUW, 1994. Exhbn. grantee Ala. Humanities Found., 1996, Best of Show award Denise Bibro Fine Arts Gallery, 1993. Mem. Jacksonville State U. Fine Art Soc., Ala. Humanities Found., Birmingham Art Assn. (bd. dirs., parliamentarian 1995—), Soc. for Photographic Edn., Birmingham Mus. of Art Photography Guild. Home: 744 Linwood Rd Birmingham AL 35222 Office: U Ala Dept Art and Art History 900 13th St 113 Humanities Birmingham AL 35294-1260

MORGAN, BERNICE MCBORROUGH, accountant; b. Monrovia, Liberia, Apr. 27, 1967; came to U.S., 1993; d. William Jefferson and Bertha Rosamond (Walker) McBorrough; m. Michael Tubman Morgan, June 11, 1960; 1 child, Grace Puate. AA in Liberal Arts and Acctg., Ricks Jr. Coll., 1985; BSBA, U. Liberia, Monrovia, 1989; MS in Profl. Acctg., Strayer Coll., 1995. Computer operator Modern Data Sys., Monrovia, 1988; cost/mgmt. acctg. supr. Keene Industries/Liberian Agrl. Comp., Middlebury, Conn., 1989-93; acct. Parker Whitfield Assocs., Roslyn, Va., 1994-95, Strayer Coll., Alexandria, Va., 1993-95; sr. acct. Telesystems Mktg., Inc., Fairfax, 1995—. Mem. Inst. Mgmt. Accts. Office: Telesystem Mktg Inc Ste 200 13320 Random Hills Rd Fairfax VA 22020

MORGAN, BEVERLY HAMMERSLEY, middle school educator, artist; b. Wichita Falls, Tex.; d. Vernon C. and Melba Marie (Whited) Hammersley; m. Robert Lewis Morgan, Sept. 21, 1957 (div. 1972); children: Janet Claire, Robert David. BA, So. Meth. U.; MA, U. Ala., 1980, AA certification, 1982; postgrad., U. Tex., 1991—. Cert. art tchr., Tex., Ala.; cert. elem. tchr., Ala. Art tchr. Ft. Worth Pub. Schs., 1955-60; English tchr. Lincoln County Schs., Fayetteville, Tenn., 1961-62; 6th grade tchr. Huntsville (Ala.) Pub. Schs., 1960-61, 62-68, art tchr., 1972-92, 93-94. One man shows include U. Ala., 1980, Huntsville Art League, 1981. Mem. Huntsville-Madison County Art Tchrs., Huntsville Mus. Art, Internat. Platform Assn. Republican. Home: 12027 Chicamauga Trl SE Huntsville AL 35803-1544

MORGAN, CAROLYN F., lawyer; b. Gadsden, Ala., Nov. 23, 1945; d. Sephes Jonah and Garnet Sylvia (Watson) M.; m. Galen Kennah, Dec. 16, 1967 (div. Nov. 1979); children: Jason, Jennifer; m. David Cummings, May 6, 1995. BS, Jacksonville State U., 1970; JD, Cumberland Sch. of Law, 1983. Bar: Ala., U.S. Dist. Ct. (no. dist.) Ala., U.S. Ct. Appeals (11th cir.), U.S. Supreme Ct. Social worker II State of Ala., Gadsden, Birmingham, 1969-80; asst. city atty. City of Gadsen, 1983-84; asst. dist. atty. State of Ala., Anniston, 1984-90; corp. counsel BE & K, Inc., Birmingham, 1990-95; asst. gen. counsel BE&K Inc, Birmingham, 1995—. Office: BE&K Inc 2000 Internat Park Dr Birmingham AL 35243

MORGAN, CATHERINE LOUISE, writer; b. Kewanee, Ill., Sept. 21, 1938; d. Norris Goold and Margaret Lucy (Clark) M.; m. Ronald Henry Osowski, Mar. 22, 1970 (dec. Apr. 1972). BA, U. No. Colo., 1960; MA, U. Calif., Berkeley, 1964; MPhil, Columbia U., 1969. Instr. Italian San Francisco State Coll., 1963; instr. French and Italian U. Wyo., Laramie, 1964-67; instr. Italian CUNY-Lehman Coll., Bronx, N.Y., 1969-71, U. Wyo., Laramie, 1971-72; printer Marie Runyon Assocs., N.Y.C., 1972-74; mng. editor Heights and Valley News Newspaper, N.Y.C., 1973-78; editor Tenant Newspaper, N.Y.C., 1977-79; mng. editor Our Town Newspaper, N.Y.C., 1979-81; pvt. practice writing and editing N.Y.C., 1981—; investigative reporter Our Town Newspaper, 1980. Founder, pres. Com. to Impeach Nixon, N.Y.C., 1973; chmn. Columbia Tenants Union, N.Y.C., 1973-75, organizer, 1973-78, Com. to Save Columbia Br. Libr., N.Y.C., 1975, 80; tenant counselor Met. Coun. on Housing, N.Y.C., 1978-80. NDEA Title IV fellowship in Italian, U.S. Govt., Berkeley, 1961-64, Columbia U. fellowship in Italian Columbia U., N.Y.C., 1967-69. Mem. N.Y. Recorder Guild, N.Y. Audubon Soc., Bat Conservation Internat. Democrat.

MORGAN, DONNA JEAN, psychotherapist; b. Edgerton, Wis., Nov. 16, 1955; d. Donald Edward and Pearl Elizabeth (Robinson) Garey. BA, U. Wis., Whitewater, 1983, MS, 1985. Cert. psychotherapist, Wis.; cert. mental health alcohol and drug counselor; nat. cert. alcohol and drug abuse counselor; lic. marriage and family therapist, Wis.; lic. ind. social worker; lic. clin. social worker; nat. cert. counselor; lic. profl. counselor. Pvt. practice Janesville, Wis., 1988-91, New Focus, Waukesha and Mukwonago, Wis., 1996—; clin. supr. Stoughton (Wis.) Hosp., 1985-88; prin. Morgan and Assocs., Janesville, Wis., 1991—. Mem. underaged drinking violation alternative program Rock County, 1986—; co-chmn. task force on child sexual abuse, 1989-91; mem. Rock County Multi-disciplinary Team on Child Abuse, 1990—; mem. spkrs. bur. Rock County C.A.R.E. House, 1990—. Mem. APA, Am. Counseling Assn., Am. Profl. Soc. on the Abuse of Children, Wis. Profl. Soc. on the Abuse of Children (bd. dirs. 1994—), Rock County Mental Health Providers, Am. Assn. Mental Health Counselors, Wis. Assn. Mental Health Counselors, South Ctrl. Wis. Action Coalition, Am. Assn. Marriage and Family Therapy (clin. mem.), Am. Assn. Christian Counselors. Office: 321 E Milwaukee St Janesville WI 53545 also: 2717 N Grandview Blvd Ste 200 Waukesha WI 53188 also: 211 N Rochester St Mukwonago WI 53149

MORGAN, ELIZABETH, plastic and reconstructive surgeon; b. Washington, July 9, 1947; d. William James and Antonia (Bell) M.; children: 1 dau., Ellen. BA magna cum laude, Harvard U., 1967; postgrad. (fellow), Oxford U., Somerville Coll., 1967, 70; MD, Yale U., 1971; law student, Georgetown U., 1986-87; PhD in Psychology, U. Canterbury, Christchurch, New Zealand, 1995. Diplomate Am. Bd. Surgery, Am. Bd. Plastic Surgery. Intern Yale-New Haven Hosp., 1971-72, resident, 1972-73, 76-77; resident Tufts-New Eng. Med. Center, Boston, 1973-76, Harvard-Cambridge (Mass.) Hosp., 1977-78; columnist Cosmopolitan mag., 1973-80; practice medicine specializing in plastic and reconstructive surgery Washington, 1978-86, McLean, Va., 1978-86. Author: The Making of a Woman Surgeon, 1980, Solo Practice, 1982, Custody, A True Story, 1986, The Complete Book of Cosmetic Surgery for Men, Women and Teens, 1988, To Save My Child, 1996. Trustee Kent (Conn.) Sch. Fellow ACS, Am. Soc. Plastic and Reconstructive Surgeons; mem. Internat. Soc. for Study Dissociation., New Zealand Psychol. Soc. Episcopalian.

MORGAN, EVELYN BUCK, nursing educator; b. Phila., Nov. 3, 1931; d. Kenneth Edward and Evelyn Louise (Rhineberg) Buck; m. John Allen McGeary, Aug. 15, 1958 (div. 1964); children—John Andrew, Jacquelyn Ann McGeary Keplinger; m. Kenneth Dean Morgan, June 26, 1965 (dec. 1975). R.N., Muhlenberg Hosp. Sch. Nursing, 1955; B.S. in Nursing summa cum laude, Ohio State U., 1972, M.S., 1973; Ed.D., Nova. U., 1978. R.N., N.J., Ohio, Fla., Calif.; cert. clin. specialist Am. Nurses Assn. Psychiat.-Mental Health Clin. Specialists; advanced R.N. practitioner Fla. Bd. Nursing. Staff nurse Muhlenberg Hosp., Plainfield, N.J., 1955-57; indsl. nurse Western Electric Co., Columbus, Ohio, 1957-59; supr. Mt. Carmel Hosp., Columbus, 1960-65; instr. Grant Hosp. Sch. Nursing, 1965-72; cons. Ohio Dept. Health, 1972-74; prof. nursing Miami (Fla.)-Dade Community Coll., 1974-96, ret., 1996; family therapist Hollywood Pavilion Hosp., 1977-82; pvt. practice family therapy, Ft. Lauderdale, Fla., 1982—. Sustaining mem. Democratic Nat. Com., 1975—. Mem. Am. Nurses Assn., Fla. Council Psychiat.-Mental Health Clin. Specialists, Nat. Guild Hypnotists, Am. Nurses Found., Am. Holistic Nurses Assn., Sigma Theta Tau. Democrat. Roman Catholic.

MORGAN, GRETNA FAYE, retired automotive executive; b. Galveston, Ind., Aug. 24, 1927; d. Fred Monroe and Vera Arnetha (Oakley) Goodier; m. Marvin L. Morgan, Mar. 30, 1946; children: Gary Lynn, Vonna Annette, Marvin Richard, Darla Sue, Janice Arnetha. Diploma in cosmetology, Approved U., Indpls., 1946. Sales distributor Kirby Co., Ft. Wayne, Ind., 1955-62; with Dana Corp., Churubusco, Ind., 1962—; plant mgr. Dana Corp., Athens, Ga., 1978-81, Churubusco, Ind., 1981-90; ret., 1990; bd. dirs. Passages, Inc., Whitley County. Chmn. mayor's com. Employment Handicapped, Athens, Ga., 1980-81; mem. interview bd. selection com. Congressman Dan Coats Mil. Acad., Ft. Wayne, 1985-88, bus. adv. bd. Whitley County Opportunity Ctr., Columbia City, Ind., 1986-90, Chem. Dependency Task Force Whitley County, Ind. Gov.'s Task Force on Drunk Driving, budget com. Whitley County United Way; bd. regents Dana U., Toledo, 1978-82; bd. dirs., pres. Whitley County Jr. Achievement, 1977-78; bd. dirs. Passages, Inc., Columbia City, Ind., 1989—, Whitley County Meml. Hosp. Found., Columbia City, 1989—; mem. Noble County Friends of the Libr., 1990—. Mem. Churubusco C. of C. (pres. 1975-76), Dana Retirees of Fla. Club (pres. 1993—), Calvary Temple Worship Ctr. Home: 1981 Carbonata Dr Alva FL 33920-3647 Office: Dana Corp PO Box 245 Churubusco IN 46723-0245

MORGAN, JACQUI, illustrator, painter, educator; b. N.Y.C., Feb. 22, 1939; d. Henry and Emily (Cook) Morganstern; m. Onnig Kalfayan, Apr. 23, 1967 (div. 1972); m. Tomás Gonda, Jan. 1983 (dec. 1988). B.F.A. with honors, Pratt Inst., Bklyn., 1960; M.A., Hunter Coll., CCNY, 1978. Textile designer M. Lowenstein & Sons, N.Y.C., 1961-62, Fruit of the Loom, N.Y.C., 1962; stylist-design dir. Au Courant, Inc., N.Y.C., 1966—; assoc. prof. Pratt Inst., Bklyn., 1977—; guest lectr. U. Que., Syracuse U., Warsaw TV & Radio, Poland, NYU, Parsons Sch. Design, N.Y.C., Sch. Visual Arts, N.Y.C., Va. Commonwealth U., others; mem. profl. juries; curator Tomás Gonda retrospective exhbn.; condr. workshops. One-person shows include Soc. Illustrators, N.Y.C., 1977, Art Dirs. Club, N.Y.C., 1978, Gallerie Nowe Miasto, Warsaw, 1978, Gallerie Baumeister, Munich, W.Ger., 1978, Hansen-Feuerman Gallery, N.Y.C., 1980; group shows include Mus. Contemporary Crafts, N.Y.C., 1975, Smithsonian Instn., Washington, 1976, Mus. Warsaw, 1976, 78, Mus. Tokyo, 1979, Nat. Watercolor Soc., 1989, Salmagundi Club, 1990, New Eng. Watercolor Soc. Open, 1990, Miss. Watercolor Grand nat., 1990, Illustration West 29, 1990, Adirondack Nat., 1990, Die Verlassenen Schuhe, 1993, N.Y. restaurant Sch., 1994, Lizan-Tops Gallery, 1996; represented in permanent collections: Smithsonian Instn., Mus. Warsaw; author-illustrator: Watercolor for Illustration; produced three of seven instrnl. watercolor videos; series of prints pub., 1995; series of plates publ., 1995; co-curator Tomas Gonda Retrospective, Va. Commonwealth U., Rutgers U., Carnegie Mellon U., others in U.S., Museo Del Arte Modernon, Buenos Aires/to be exhibited and become part of the permanent collection of the Ulmer Mus./HFG Archive; contbr. articles to profl. jours. Recipient more than 150 awards from various orgns. including Soc. Illustrators, Fed. Design Coun., Comm. Arts Mag., Am. Inst. Graphic Arts, N.Y. Art Dirs. Club, Print Design Ann. Mem. Graphic Artists Guild (dir. 1975-79), Soc. Illustrators, Women Artists of the West, Pa. Watercolor Soc. Studio: 692 Greenwich St New York NY 10014-2876

MORGAN, JANE HALE, retired library director; b. Dines, Wyo., May 11, 1926; d. Arthur Hale and Billie (Wood) Hale; m. Joseph Charles Morgan, Aug. 12, 1955; children: Joseph Hale, Jane Frances, Ann Michele. BA, Howard U., 1947; MA, U. Denver, 1954. Mem. staff Detroit Pub. Library, 1954-87, exec. asst. dir., 1973-75, dep. dir., 1975-78, dir., 1978-87; mem. Mich. Libr. Consortium Bd.; exec. bd. Southeastern Mich. Regional Film Libr.; vis. prof. Wayne State U., 1989—. Trustee New Detroit, Inc., Delta Dental Plan of Mich., Delta Dental Plan of Ohio; v.p. United Southwestern Mich.; pres. Univ.-Cultural Center Assn.; bd. dirs. Rehab. Inst., YWCA, Met. Affairs Corp., Literacy Vols. Am., Detroit, Mich. Ctr. for the Book, Interfaith Coun.; bd. dirs., v.p. United Community Svcs. Met. Detroit; chmn. Detroiters for Adult Reading Excellence; chmn. adv. coun. libr. sci. U. Mich., mem. adv. coun. libr. sci. Wayne State U.; dir. Met. Detroit Youth Found.; chmn. Mich. LSCA adv. coun.; mem. UWA Literacy Com., Attys. Grievance Com., Women's Commn., Mich. Civil Svc. Rev. Com.; vice chair Mich. Coun. for Humanities; mem. Commn. for the Greening of Detroit; adv. com. Headstart; mem. Detroit Women's Com., Detroit Women's Forum, Detroit Exec. Svc. Corps. Recipient Anthony Wayne award Wayne State U., 1981, Summit award Greater Detroit C. of C.; named Detroit Howardite of Year, 1983. Mem. ALA, Mich. Library Assn., Women's Nat. Book Assn., Assn. Mcpl. Profl. Women, NAACP, LWV, Women's Economic Club, Alpha Kappa Alpha. Democrat. Episcopalian.

MORGAN, JANET ARLEEN, chemistry educator, consultant; b. Altus AFB, Okla., June 29, 1958; d. Truman Henry and Naomi Evelyn (Kunkle) Palmer; m. James Kenneth Lee, Apr. 25, 1987 (dec. Apr. 19, 1992); m. Craig Allen Morgan, Mar. 26, 1993. AA, Brevard C.C., 1977; BA, U. Ctrl. Fla., 1980, MA, 1984. Cert. secondary chem. tchr., secondary biology tchr.; cert. coach. Chemistry tchr. Trinity Prep. Sch., Winter Park, Fla., 1980-87, Dr. Phillips H.S., Orlando, Fla., 1987—; text reviewer Addison Wesley, 1990; nursing instr. Fla. So. Coll., Lakeland, 1990-93; advanced placement chemistry cons. Seminole C.C., Sanford, Fla., 1993—. Sec. Spring Lake Homeowners Assn., Orlando, 1987-92. Recipient Challenger grant Dept. Edn., 1989. Mem. Nat. Sci. Tchrs. Assn., Am. Chem. Soc. (sec. 1993-94, Outstanding H.S. Tchr. 1993), Fla. Assn. Sci. Tchrs. Presbyterian. Home: 5850 Lokey Dr Orlando FL 32810-3217 Office: Dr Phillips HS 6500 Turkey Lake Rd Orlando FL 32819-4718

MORGAN, JOAN, financial planner; b. Key West, Fla., Dec. 4, 1953; d. Henry Sturgis Morgan and Fanny Gray Little Pratt. BA, Barnard Coll., 1975; MBA, Columbia U., 1977; postgrad., Adelphi U., 1983. Cert. fin. planner. Assoc., syndicate dept. Morgan Stanley & Co., N.Y.C., 1977-80; fin. planner, asst. v.p. Bankers Trust, N.Y.C., 1983-86; prin. Joan Morgan Adminstrv. Svcs., N.Y.C., 1986-93; fin. planner Am. Express Fin. Advisors, Inc., Washington, 1993-95. Bd. dirs. The Madeira Sch., McLean, Va., 1993—; mem. adv. bd. dirs. DearKnows, Ltd., N.Y.C., 1985—. Mem. Inst. Cert. Fin. Planners, Internat. Assn. Fin. Planners, Nat. Assn. Women Bus. Owners, Columbia Bus. Sch. Club of Washington (pres. 1991-92). Republican. Episcopalian. Home: 5044 Millwood Ln NW Washington DC 20016

MORGAN, LORRIE (LORETTA LYNN MORGAN), country singer; b. Nashville, June 27, 1959; d. George Morgan; divorced; m. Keith Whitley (dec. 1989); children: Morgan, Jesse. Rec. artist RCA, 1989—. Albums: Leave the Light On, 1989, Something in Red, 1991, Tell Me I'm Dreaming, 1992, Watch Me, 1992, Trainwreck of Emotion, 1993, Greatest Hits, 1995; (with Sammy Kershaw) War Paint, 1994; #1 Song: I Didn't Know My Own Strength; #1 gold single: Something in Red, 1991; TV movies include:

Proudheart, 1993, ABC Movie of the Week - The Enemy Within, 1995. Office: care Susan Nadler Mgmt 1313 16th Ave S Nashville TN 37212

MORGAN, LUCY W., journalist; b. Memphis, Oct. 11, 1940; d. Thomas Allin and Lucile (Sanders) Keen; m. Alton F. Ware, June 26, 1958 (div. Sept. 1967); children—Mary Kathleen, Andrew Allin; m. Richard Alan Morgan, Aug. 9, 1968; children—Lynn Elwell, Kent Morgan. A.A., Pasco Hernando Community Coll., New Port Richey, Fla., 1975; student, U. South Fla., 1976-80. Reporter Ocala Star Banner, Fla., 1965-68; reporter St. Petersburg Times, Fla., 1967-86, capitol bur. chief, 1986—; assoc. editor and bd. dirs. Times Pub. Co. Recipient Paul Hansel award Fla. Soc. Newspaper Editors, 1981, First in Pub. Service award Fla. Soc. Newspaper Editors, 1982, First Place award in pub. service Fla. Press Club, 1982, Pulitzer award for investigative reporting Columbia U., 1985, First Place award in investigative reporting Sigma Delta Chi, 1985; named to Kappa Tau Alpha Hall of Fame, 1992. Home: 1727 Brookside Blvd Tallahassee FL 32301-6769 Office: St Petersburg Times 336 E College Ave Tallahassee FL 32301-1551

MORGAN, M. JANE, computer systems consultant; b. Washington, July 21, 1945; d. Edmond John and Roberta (Livingstone) Dolphin; 1 child, Sheena Anne. Student U. Md., 1963-66, Montgomery Coll., 1966-70; BA in Applied Behavioral Sci. with honors, Nat.-Louis Univ., 1987, MS in Mgmt., 1991, diploma in info. resource mgmt. Am. U., 1995, postgrad. info. resource mgmt. U.S. Gen. Svcs. Adminstrn., 1995—. With HUD, Washington, 1965-84, computer specialist, 1978-84; pres., chief exec. officer Systems and Mgmt. Assocs., 1983-91; dir. systems engring. Advanced Technology Systems, Inc., Vienna, Va., 1984-86; chief tech. staff Tech. and Mgmt. Services, Inc., 1986-89; sr. cons. Advanced Tech. Systems Inc., Vienna, 1989; sr. computer scientist Integrated Systems div. Computer Scis. Corp., 1989-90; computer systems specialist gen. svcs. adminstrn. U.S. Govt., 1991—; mgmt. cons. Mem. Federally Employed Women, Am. Assn. U. Women. Episcopalian. Club: Order Eastern Star.

MORGAN, MARABEL, author; b. Crestline, Ohio, June 25, 1937; d. Howard and Delsa (Smith) Hawk; m. Charles O. Morgan, Jr., June 25, 1964; children—Laura Lynn, Michelle Rene. Ed., Ohio State U. Pres. Total Woman, Inc., Miami, Fla., 1970—; pub. speaker. Author: The Total Woman, 1973, Total Joy, 1976, The Total Woman Cookbook, 1980, The Electric Woman, 1985. Office: care Total Woman Inc 1300 NW 167th St Miami FL 33169-5738

MORGAN, MARY DAN, social worker; b. Tallulah, La., Nov. 30, 1943; d. Daniel Boone and Mary Louise (McLeod) M.; m. William Jefferson Day (div. Dec. 1995); 1 child, Forrest Jefferson Day. BA, La. Coll., 1965; MS in Libr. Sci., La. State U., 1968; MA in Edn., Murray State U., 1976; MS in Social Work, U. Louisville, 1992. Cert. social worker, Ky., Ind. Libr. Ascension Parish Schs., Donaldsonville, La., 1966-68, Jefferson County Schs., Louisville, 1968-75; tchr. Webster County Schs., Dixon, Ky., 1975-79; tchr. Hardin County Schs., Elizabethtown, Ky., 1979-82, dir. media ctr., 1982-87, tchr. day and residential juvenile facilities, 1987-91, tchr. mid. and sr. high alt. schs., 1991-93; social worker Hospice of Cen. Ky., Elizabethtown, 1993—; pres. Webster County Tchrs. Assn., Dixon, Ky., 1977-78; sec. Ky. Libr. Network Bd., Frankfort, 1986-87. Mem. NEA (life), NASW, AAUW, Filson Club. Office: Hospice of Cen Ky 105 Diecks Dr Elizabethtown KY 42701

MORGAN, MARY LOU, retired education educator, civic worker; b. Chgo., Mar. 5, 1938; d. William Nicholas and Esther Lucille (Galbraith) Wanmer; m. James Edward Morgan, May 30, 1963. BA in Bus. Edn. and Econs., Wichita State U., 1971, MEd in Student Pers. and Guidance, 1974; postgrad., Kans. State U., 1986. Cert. bus. tchr., Kans. Reservationist Braniff, Wichita, Kans., 1961-62; stenographer, fin. analyst, clk.-typist Boeing Co., Wichita, 1962-68, tng., pers. and records positions, 1979-93; pers. cons. Rita Pers. Svc., Wichita, 1974-75; adminstrv. aide, manpower specialist, job developer City of Wichita, 1975-76; account exec., employment counselor Mgmt. Recruiters, 1976-77; pers. mgr., patient cons. Women's Clinic, 1977; vocat. rehab. counselor State of Kans., Parsons, 1977-79; pvt. detective Investigation Svcs., Wichita, 1981-84; instr. career devel. Wichita State U., 1988-90; paralegal asst. Turner & Hensley, Wichita, 1975. Precinct committeewoman Wichita Dem. Com., 1992-94; founder, 1st pres., v.p. program chmn. NOW, Wichita, 1969-93, asst. state coord. polit. action com., Wichita, 1993-95, at-large state bd., Joplin, 1994-95; mem. Jasper County-Newton County Dems., 1993-96; coord. funding Women's Crisis Ctr., Wichita, 1975; docent Carver Mus., Hoover Mus.; bd. dirs. for City of Wichita, Wichita Commn. on Status of Women, 1988-91; bd. commr. Hist. Preservation Commn. Mem. AAUW, Am. Assn. Ret. Persons (legis. coms.), Hillary Clinton Women's Dem. Club.

MORGAN, MARY LOUISE FITZSIMMONS, fund raising executive, lobbyist; b. N.Y.C., July 22, 1946; d. Robert John and Mary Louise (Gordon) Fitzsimmons; m. David William Morgan, Aug. 7, 1971; children: Mallory Siobhan, David William. BA, Marquette U., 1964; MA, Catholic U., Wash., 1966. Asst. prof. Monmouth Coll., West Long Branch, N.J., 1966-69; campaign dir. United Way, N.Y.C., 1969-80; pres. Morgan Communications, N.Y.C., 1980-82; capital campaign dir. YMCA of Greater N.Y., 1982-85; dir. devel. N.Y. Med. Coll., Valhalla, 1985-88; counsel Challenger Ctr., Va., 1988—; v.p. Ctr. Molecular Medicine & Immunology, Newark, 1989—, Garden State Cancer Ctr., Newark, 1990-93; chief devel. and pub. affairs officer Mental Health Assn., White Plains, N.Y., 1993-95; v.p. Missing Kids Internat., Inc., Mc Lean, Va., 1995—; dir. external svcs. St. Vincents Svcs., 1996—; adj. prof. Iona Coll., New Rochelle, N.Y., 1994—; dir. Meth. Ch. Home for Aged, Riverdale, N.Y., Casita Maria Inc., N.Y.C., 1975—; pres., founding dir. Achievement Rewards for Coll. Scientists Inc., N.Y.C., 1978-80. Sec. Darien (Conn.) Dem. Town Com., 1984—, vice chmn. Darien nominating com. 1986—. Recipient 50th Anniversary award Casita Maria Inc., N.Y.C., 1984, Iris award Bus. Communicators of Am., 1991, Nat. Depression Awareness Campaign award NMHA, 1994. Mem. Nat. Soc. Fund Raising Execs., Nat. Soc. Hosp. Adminstrn., Spring Lake (N.J.) Bath and Tennis Club. Democrat. Roman Catholic. Office: 14 Anthony Ln Darien CT 06820

MORGAN, MELANIE KARYN, lawyer; b. Kans. City, Mo., July 29, 1962; married; 2 children. BA in Philosophy, Coll. of William and Mary, 1984, JD, 1987. Bar: Tex. 1987. Assoc. atty. Geary, Stahl & Spencer, Dallas, 1987-89; atty. PepsiCo, Inc.-Frito-Lay, Inc., Dallas, 1989-91, sr. atty., 1991-94, of counsel, 1994—. Mem. ABA, Dallas Bar Assn., Dallas Assn. Young Lawyers, Collin County Bar Assn., Promotion Mktg. Assn. of Am. (legal com.).

MORGAN, PAULETTE ELISE, research associate; b. Fremont, Mich., Oct. 7, 1959; d. Walter and Janet Ann (Strzyz) M.; m. William Francis Howard, Sept. 17, 1988; 1 child, Katherine Eliza Howard. BA in English Lit. and Polit. Sci. summa cum laude, U. Cin., 1983; MA in Polit. Sci., Syracuse U., 1985. Rsch. assoc. N.Y. State Senate Rsch. Svc., Albany, N.Y., 1985-91, prin. analyst, 1991-95; rsch. assoc. N.Y. State Dept. Social Svcs., Albany, 1995—. Mem. Tau Beta Sigma (lifetime).

MORGAN, REBECCA QUINN, business executive; b. Hanover, N.H., Dec. 4, 1938; d. Forrest Arthur and Rachel (Lewis) Quinn; m. James C. Morgan, June 10, 1960; children: J. Jeffrey, Mary Frances. BS, Cornell U., 1960; MBA, Stanford U., 1978. Trustee Palo Alto (Calif.) Bd. Edn., 1973-78; asst. v.p. Bank of Am., Sunnyvale, Calif., 1978-80; county supr. Santa Clara County, San Jose, Calif., 1980-84; state senator State of Calif., Sacramento, 1984-93; pres., CEO Joint Venture: Silicon Valley Network, San Jose, Calif., 1993—; bd. trustees Stanford U., 1993—, bd. dirs. PG&E. Mem. adv. bd. YWCA, Palo Alto, 1983—, Palo Alto Adolescent Svcs., 1975—, Stanford Bus. Sch., 1989—. Named Calif. Legislator of Yr, Sch. Bd. Assn. of Sacramento, 1987, Calif. Probation Parole and Correctional Assn., 1987-88, Calif. Sch. Age Consortium, 1989, Calif. NOW, 1990, Woman of Achievement Santa Clara County, 1983; Am. Leadership fellow, 1993-94. Mem. Calif. Elected Women's Assn. Republican. Office: 99 Almaden Blvd Ste 610 San Jose CA 95113-1605

MORGAN, RENEE MAUREEN, elementary education educator; b. N.Y.C., Jan. 31, 1962; d. Morris Donald Jones and Joan Loretta (Bennett) Murrell; m. Daryl Charles Morgan, Aug. 10, 1991; 1 child, Eric Denzel. BA, Hunter Coll., 1985, MS in Edn., 1993. Cert. early childhood and elem. tchr., Ga., N.Y. 1st grade tchr. PS 160, Bronx, N.Y., 1985-87; art tchr. Abyssinian Bapt. Ch., N.Y.C., 1985-93; kindergarten tchr. College Heights Elem. Sch., Decatur, Ga., 1987-88; 4th grade tchr. PS 103, Bronx, 1988-90, 3d grade tchr., 1990-92; sci. tchr. Grace Ch. Sch., N.Y.C., 1992-93; 4th and 5th grades remedial tchr. Seaborn Lee Elem. Sch., College Park, Ga., 1995; 1st grade tchr. Woodland Elem. Sch., Dunwoody, Ga., 1995—; cons. Ednl. Consulting, Bronx and Norcross, Ga., 1994—. Active Black Women's Health Program, 1995. Mem. Schomburg Soc. for Rsch. in Black Culture. Office: Woodland Elem Sch 1190 Spalding Dr Dunwoody GA 30350

MORGAN, ROBIN EVONNE, poet, author, journalist, activist, editor; b. Lake Worth, Fla., Jan. 29, 1941; 1 child, Blake Ariel. Grad. with honors, The Wetter Sch., 1956; student, pvt. tutors, 1956-59, Columbia U.; DHL (hon.), U. Conn., 1992. Free-lance book editor, 1961-69; editor Grove Press, 1967-70; editor, columnist World column Ms. Mag., N.Y.C., 1974-87, editor in chief, 1989-93, internat. cons. editor, 1993—; vis. chair and guest prof. women's studies New Coll., Sarasota, Fla., 1973; disting. vis. scholar, lectr. Ctr. Critical Analysis of Contemporary Culture, Rutgers U., 1987, U. Denver Grad. Sch. Internat. Affairs, 1996-97; invited spl. cons. UN com. UN Conv. to End All Forms Discrimination Against Women, Sao Paulo and Brasilia, Brazil, 1987; mem. adv. bd. ISIS (internat. network women's internat. cross-cultural exch.); spl. advisor gen. assembly conf. on Gender UN Internat. Sch., 1985-86; free-lance journalist, lectr. cons., editor, 1969—; invited speaker numerous confs., orgns., acad. meetings, U.S. and abroad. Author, compiler, editor: Sisterhood Is Powerful: An Anthology of Writings from the Women's Liberation Movement, 1970, Swedish edit., 1972, Sisterhood Is Global: The International Women's Movement Anthology, 1984, U.K. edit., 1985, Spanish edit., 1994; author: (nonfiction) Going Too Far: The Personal Chronicle of a Feminist, 1978, German edit., 1978, The Anatomy of Freedom: Feminism, Physics and Global Politics, 1982, 2d edit., 1994, fgn. edits. U.K., 1984, Germany, 1985, Argentina, 1986, Brazil, 1992, The Demon Lover: On the Sexuality of Terrorism, 1989, U.K. edit., 1989, Japanese edit., 1992, The Word of a Woman: Feminist Dispatches 1968-91, 1992, 2d edit., 1994, U.K. edit., 1992, Chinese edit., 1996, A Woman's Creed, English, Arabic, French, Russian, Spanish, Portuguese, Chinese and Persian edits., 1995, (fiction) Dry Your Smile: A Novel, 1987, U.K. edit., 1988, The Mer-Child: A New Legend, 1991, German edit., 1995 (poetry) Monster: Poems, 1972, Lady of the Beasts: Poems, 1976, Death Benefits: Poems, 1981, Depth Perception: New Poems and a Masque, 1982, Upstairs in the Garden: Selected and New Poems, 1968-88, 1990, (plays) In Another Country, 1960, The Duel, 1979; co-editor: The Woman: Anthology, 1969; contbr. numerous articles, essays, book revs., poems to various publs.; presenter poetry readings, univs., poetry ctrs., radio, TV, others, 1970—. Mem. 1st women's liberation caucus CORE, 1965, Student Nonviolent Coordinating Com., 1966; organizer 1st feminist demonstration against Miss Am. Pageant, 1968; founder, pres. The Sisterhood Fund, 1970; founder, pres. N.Y. Women's Law Ctr., 1970; founder N.Y. Women's Ctr., 1969; co-founder, bd. dirs. Feminist Women's Health Network, Nat. Battered Women's Refuge Network, Nat. Network Rape Crisis Ctrs.; bd. dirs. Women's Fgn. Policy Coun.; adv. trustee Nat. Women's Inst. for Freedom of Press; founding mem. Nat. Mus. Women in Arts; co-founder Sisterhood is Global Inst. (internat. think-tank), 1984, officer, 1989—, co-organizer, U.S. mem. official visit Coalition of Philippines Women's Movement, 1988; chair N.Y. state com. Hands Across Am. Com. for Justice and Empowerment, 1988; mem. adv. bd. Global Fund for Women. Recipient Front Page award for disting. journalism, Wonder Woman award for internat. peace and understanding, 1982, Feminist of Yr. award Fund for Feminist majority, 1990; writer-in-residence grantee Yaddo, 1980; grantee Nat. Endowment for Arts, 1979-80, Ford Found., 1982, 83, 84. Mem. Feminist Writers' Guild, Media Women, N.Am. Feminist Coalition, Pan Arab Feminist Solidarity Assn. (hon.), Israeli Feminists Against Occupation (hon.). Office: Ms Mag 230 Park Ave New York NY 10169-0005

MORGAN, RUTH PROUSE, academic administrator, educator; b. Berkeley, Calif., Mar. 30, 1934; d. Ervin Joseph and Thelma Ruth (Prcesang) Prouse; m. Vernon Edward Morgan, June 3, 1956; children: Glenn Edward, Renée Ruth. BA summa cum laude, U. Tex., 1956; MA, La. State U., 1961, PhD, 1966. Asst. prof. Am. govt., politics and theory So. Meth. U., Dallas, 1966-70, assoc. prof., 1970-74, prof., 1974-95; prof. emeritus, 1995—; asst. provost So. Meth. U., Dallas, 1978-82, assoc. provost, 1982-86, provost ad interim, 1986-87, provost, 1987-93, provost emerita, 1993—; pres. RPM Assocs., 1993—; v.p. ABATECH, Inc., 1995—; Tex. state polit. analyst ABC, N.Y.C., 1972-84. Author: The President and Civil Rights, 1970; mem. editorial bd. Jour. of Politics, 1975-82, Presdl. Studies Quar., 1980—; contbr. articles to profl. jours. Active Internat. Women's Forum, 1987—; trustee Hockaday Sch., 1988-94; trustee The Kilby Awards Found., 1993-95; bd. dirs. United Way, Met. Dallas, 1993—; mem. adv. com. U.S. Army Command and Gen. Staff. Coll., 1994—; chmn. adv. com. Archives of Women of the Southwest, 1995—. Mem. Am. Polit. Sci. Assn., So. Polit. Sci. Assn. (mem. exec. coun. 1979-84), Southwestern Polit. Sci. Assn. (pres. 1982-83, mem. exec. coun. 1981-84), The Dallas Forum of Internat. Women's Forum (pres. 1996-98), Charter 100 Club (pres. 1991-92), Dallas Summit Club (pres. 1992-93), Phi Beta Kappa, Pi Sigma Alpha, Phi Kappa Phi, Theta Sigma Phi.

MORGAN, SHIRLEY ANN, information systems executive; b. Farmington, Mich., Mar. 13, 1940; d. Clyde Elmer and Callie Mae (Morgan) Card; children: Cindy Jeanne, Dennis Carl, Vicki Anne. BBA, Orlando (Fla.) Coll., 1992. Cert. prodn. and inventory mgmt. With Anchor Coupling Co., Plymouth, Mich., 1959-74; data processing supt. Photon Sources, Livonia, Mich., 1976-80; data processing mgr. S&H Fabricating, Sanford, Fla., 1980-85; MIS mgr. ABB Power Distbn., Sanford, 1985-92, Wheeled Coach, Inc., Winter Park, Fla., 1992-94; dir. info. systems Crane Tech. Group Inc., Daytona Beach, Fla., 1994—. Republican. Office: Crane Tech Group Inc 530 Fentress Blvd Daytona Beach FL 32114-1210

MORGAN, SUSAN MCGUIRE MCGRATH, psychotherapist; b. New London, Jan. 11, 1937; d. Francis Foran and Helen Cuseck (Connolly) McGuire; m. Robert L. McGrath, Sept. 16, 1959 (div. May 1992); children: Robert L., Swithin, Charles Felix, William Ambrose. BA, Smith Coll., 1959, MSW, 1992; MA in Liberal Studies, Dartmouth Coll., 1982; postgrad., C.G. Jung Inst., 1993—. Lic. social worker, Vt. Alcohol educator Dartmouth Med. Ctr., Hanover, N.H., 1972-77; program dir. Pub. Affairs Ctr. Dartmouty Coll., Hanover, 1978-82; cons. Alice Peck Day/Dartmouth Alcohol Program, Hanover, 1982-83; psychotherapist Orange County Mental Health Ctr., Randolph, Vt., 1993—; pvt. practice psychotherapy Norwich, Vt., 1996—; tchr. Inst. for Lifelong Edn. at Dartmouth program Dartmouth Coll., 1993—; spkr. in field. Contbr. to book: Understanding Alcohol, 1979, Loosening the Grip. Pres. Vt. Alcohol Counselors Assn., 1982-84; sec. Norwich Conservation Commn., 1972-82. Mem. NASW, C.G. Jung Soc. of Vt., Assn. for Study of Dreams. Office: PO Box 772 Beaver Meadow Rd Norwich VT 05055

MORGAN, VIRGINIA, magistrate judge; b. 1946. BS, Univ. of Mich., 1968; JD, Univ. of Toledo, 1975. Bar: Mich. 1975, Federal 1975, U.S. Ct. Appeals (6th cir.) 1979. Tchr. Dept. of Interior, Bur. of Indian Affairs, 1968-70, San Diego Unified Schs., 1970-72, Oregon, Ohio, 1972-74; asst. prosecutor Washtenaw County Prosecutor's Office, 1976-79; asst. U.S. atty. Detroit, 1979-85; magistrate judge U.S. Dist. Ct. (Mich. ea. dist.), 6th circuit, Detroit, 1985—. Recipient Spl. Achievement award Dept. of Justice, Disting. Alumni award U. Toledo, 1993. Fellow Mich. State Bar Found.; mem. Nat. Assn. Women Judges, Mich. Bar Assn., Fed. Magistrate Judges Assn. (pres. 1995—), Fed. Bar Assn. (chpt. pres.-elect 1995—). Office: US Courthouse 231 W Lafayette Blvd Detroit MI 48226-2719

MORGAN, WANDA BUSBY, health care executive, educator; b. Cromwell, Okla., Aug. 27, 1930; d. Charles C. and Gladys J. (Beaty) Busby; m. James O. Morgan, Oct. 23, 1954; children: Terri, Kathleen, Martha. BA, Lincoln (Ill.) Christian Coll., 1954; MA, Kans. State U., 1973; postgrad., Cen. State U., Edmond, Okla., 1977-79, U. Okla., 1980-84, Purdue U., 1983. Prof. Manhattan (Kans.) Christian Coll., Manhattan, 1970-74; instr. Seminole (Okla.) Jr. Coll., 1978-80; prof. Bethany (Okla.) Nazarene Coll., 1980-84; instr. Moravian Coll., Bethlehem, Pa., 1984-85, Allentown Coll., Center Valley, Pa., 1985-88; edn. coordinator Sacred Heart HealthCare System, Allentown, Pa., 1985-87; v.p. Sacred Heart Health Care System, Allentown, Pa., 1987-95; instr. Ctrl. Ala. C.C., Alexander City, Ala., 1995-96; dir. investor rels. Guilford Capital Corp., Montgomery, Ala., 1996—; cons. Communication Arts, Ltd., Allentown, 1978-95; advisor Okla. Dept. Edn., Oklahoma City, 1981; tchr., cons. U. Okla. Dept. Edn., Norman, 1980-84, Okla. Writing Project, 1980-84; instr. Lehigh County Cmty. Coll., 1989-91. Author: Bridging the English Gap, 1983; co-author: Grammar, Ltd., 1983. Mem. adv. bd. Lehigh County (Pa.) Human Svcs. Dept., 1986-89, chmn., 1988-89; mem. Lehigh Valley Action Com. United Way, 1992-94, Children's Coalition Lehigh Valley, 1993-94. Fellow U. Okla., 1980. Mem. Am. Soc. Healthcare Mktg. and Pub. Rels., Okla. Coun. Tchrs. English (vice chair coll. sect. 1983-84), Rotary. Democrat. Presbyterian.

MORGART, MICHELE, psychologist, consultant; b. Phila., July 2, 1947; d. Robert Paul and Elizabeth (Byrne) M.; divorced; 1 child, Michael Paul. BA in Psychology and English, U. Akron, Ohio, 1981, MA in Psychology, 1984. Cert. tchr., Ohio; lic. profl. clin. counselor; cert. employee assistance profl. Counselor and edn. specialist Columbia Mercy Med. Ctr., Canton, Ohio, 1984—; dir. concern: Employee Assistance Program Columbia Mercy Med. Ctr., Canton, 1992—; cons. Summit County Adolescent Task Force Svcs. Network, Akron, 1988—; cons. C.A.R.E. Cmty. Drug Edn., Cuy Falls, Ohio, 1984; cons., chmn. City Ethics Adv. Bd., 1994. Vol. Summit County Drug Bd., Akron, 1978-81. Mem. APA (cert.), Employee Asst. Profl. Assn., Psi Chi, Phi Sigma Alpha. Office: Columbia Mercy Med Ctr 1320 Mercy Dr NW Canton OH 44708-2614

MORGEN, LYNN, public relations executive. Grad., CCNY. Former rep. Gruntal & Co., First Manhattan Co.; assoc. ECOM Cons., 1978-79, v.p. investor rels., 1979-82; founding ptnr Morgen-Walke Assocs., 1982—. Office: Morgen-Walke Assocs Inc 380 Lexington Ave Ste 5100 New York NY 10168-0002*

MORGENSTERN, SUSAN, public relations executive. Grad., U. Kans. News editor Nashville (Tenn.) Banner, 1979-85; v.p., dir. publs. Dye, Van Mol & Lawrence, Nashville, 1985-92, sr. v.p., 1992—. Mem. Internat. Assn. Bus. Communicators (dist. bd. dirs.). Office: Dye Van Mol & Lawrence 209 7th Ave N Nashville TN 37219-1802*

MORGENSTERN-LEVINE, LINDA JUNE, manufacturer's representative; b. Bklyn., Aug. 5, 1958; d. Louis and Marilyn (Markovich) Levine; m. Mark Jay Morgenstern, Aug. 28, 1982; children: Kara, Alex, Jamie. BA, SUNY, Binghamton, 1979. Dept. mgr. R.H. Macys, N.Y.C., 1979-80, asst. buyer, 1980-81, group mgr., 1981-82, buyer glassware and lamps, 1982-88; mfr.'s rep. Mikasa, N.Y.C., 1988—; cons. on curtains and homes to home store chain, N.Y.C., 1988-89. Vice pres. fundraising Lindell Elem. Sch. PTA, Long Beach, N.Y., 1994-96, v.p. membership, 1996-98, mem. site based membership com., 1996. Home and Office: 91 Sands Ct Lido Beach NY 11561

MORGENTHAL, BECKY HOLZ, legal association administrator; b. Altadena, Calif., Aug. 5, 1947; d. E. William and Elizabeth (DeLong) Holz; m. Roger Mark Morgenthal, Aug. 12, 1972. AA, Goldey Beacom Coll., 1967; grad., Wilson Coll., 1990. Clk. Hercules, Inc., Wilmington, Del., 1969-71; acct. Beth Products, Lebanon, Pa., 1971-72; adminstrv. asst. Legal Services, Inc., Carlisle, Pa., 1973-76; office mgr. CEMI Corp., Carlisle, 1976-77; acct. Tressler Luth. Services, Camp Hill, Pa., 1978-79, Benatec Assocs., Inc., Camp Hill, 1979-82; fin. analyst Electronic Data Systems, Camp Hill, 1983-87; owner BHM Bus. Svcs., Carlisle, 1982—; exec. dir. Cumberland County Bar Assn., Carlisle; pres. Morgenthal Aviation Corp. Pres. Carlisle Jr. Civic Club, 1979-80; mem. Coun. Cath. Women, Carlisle, 1986—. Mem. AAUW (treas. 1994—, Cen. Pa. chpt. 99's sec. 1994—). Republican.

MORI, HANAE, fashion designer; b. Muikaichi, Shimane, Japan, 1926; m. Ken Mori, May 1947; children: Akira, Kei. BA in Lit., Tokyo Women's Christian Coll., 1947. Pres., founder, designer Hanae Mori Group, N.Y.C., 1951—; uniform designer Japan Airlines, Tokyo, 1967, 70, 73; costume designer Monaco Ballet, 1976, Paris Opera Ballet, 1986, (opera) Madame Butterfly at La Scala, Milan, 1985. Author: Designing for Tomorrow, 1978, A Glass Butterfly, 1984, Hanae Mori 1960-1989, 1989. Adviser Ministry of Cultural Affairs, Tokyo; mem. overseas bd. Boston Symphony Orch.; mem. various cultural coms., Tokyo. Recipient Neiman Marcus award, 1973, Purple Ribbon, Govt. of Japan, 1988, La Croix Chevalier des Arts et Lettres, Govt. of France, 1984, Legion of Honor, 1989. Mem. Chambre Syndicale de Haute Couture Parisienne. Office: Hanae Mori New York Inc 27 E 79th St New York NY 10021-0101

MORIARTY, JUDITH KAY SPRY, state official; b. Fairfield, Mo., Feb. 2, 1942; d. Earl Price and Blanche May (McDavitt) Spry; children: Derek David, Michael Price, Timothy John. Student Central Mo. State U., State Fair C.C.; tng. cert. Elections and County Clks. Assn., Mo., 1985. Motor Vehicle agt. Sedalia Motor Vehicle Registration, Mo., 1977-81; county clk. Pettis County, Sedalia, 1982-93; sec. of state State of Mo., 1993—. Vice regent Daus. Isabella, Sedalia, 1985-86; del. Mo. Dem. Conv., 1980, 84; active Women's Dem. Club Pettis County, Sacred Heart Cath. Ch., Mo. Coun. Econ. Edn., Mo. Hist. Recs. Preservation Bd., Friends of Archives, Local Recs. Bd., State Recs. Commn., Literacy Investment for Tomorrow; bd. dirs. Salvation Army, Sedalia, 1978—, Am. Cancer Soc., Sedalia, 1982—, Sedalia Area Council for Arts, 1980-84. Named Outstanding Young Woman Sedalia, Sedalia Jaycees, 1959. Mem. LWV, Bus. and Profl. Women (legis. chmn. 1984-86), Sedalia Area C. of C. (v.p., bd. dirs. 1982-85), Women's Aglow. Avocations: reading; physical fitness; walking; pen and ink sketching; baking. Office: Office Sec of State PO Box 778 Jefferson City MO 65102-0778*

MORIARTY, MAUREEN C., marketing professional; b. Albany, N.Y., Nov. 4, 1946; d. Richard John and Margaret (Egan) Conners; m. James M. Moriarty, Feb. 1, 1969. BA in History, Coll. St. Rose, 1968; MBA in Mktg., U. Pa., 1976. Sch. tchr. Houston and San Francisco, 1969-74; from asst. product mgr. to group mktg. mgr. Gillette Co., Boston, 1977-86; mktg. dir. men's jean div. Levi Strauss & Co., San Francisco, 1986-92; sr. v.p. mktg. Mattel, Inc., 1992; pres. Global Mktg. Group, Pebble Beach, Calif., 1992—; bd. dirs. Bass Rocks Internat., San Francisco; cons., pub. speaker in field; instr. internat. mktg. Golden Gate U., U. Calif. Extension Program. Author: Goal 4 It, 1988. Bd. dirs. San Francisco Sr. Citizen's Ctr., 1986-89; mktg. adv. bd. United Way, San Francisco, 1990-91, Univ. of Calif. at Berkeley Ext. Prog., San Francisco, 1987-90. Home: PO Box 375 Pebble Beach CA 93953-0375

MORIN, DINA MARIA, customer service professional; b. Hoboken, N.J., Feb. 25, 1968; d. Benjamin and Zora (Lister) Mattessich; m. Lucio Mario Morin, Sept. 5, 1987; 1 child, Ryan Michael. BS in Acctg. magna cum laude, Fairleigh Dickinson U., 1990. Staff auditor The Port Authority of N.Y./N.J., N.Y.C., 1990-93, asst. mgr., 1993—. N.J. State Disting. Scholar, 1986-90, Presdl. scholar Fairleigh Dickinson U., Teaneck, N.J., 1986-90. Mem. NAFE, Inst. Internal Auditors. Office: The Port Authority of NY NJ 4 WTC 4th Floor New York NY 10048

MORISATO, SUSAN CAY, actuary; b. Chgo., Feb. 11, 1955; d. George and Jessie (Fujita) M.; m. Thomas Michael Remec, Mar. 6, 1981. BS, U. Ill., 1975, MS, 1977. Actuarial student Aetna Life & Casualty, Hartford, Conn., 1977-79; actuarial asst. Bankers Life & Casualty, Chgo., 1979-80, asst. actuary, 1980-83, assoc. actuary, 1983-85, health product actuary, 1985-86, v.p., 1986-95; sr. v.p., 1996—; participant individual forum Health Ins. Assn. Am., 1983; spkr. health forum Life Ins. Mgmt. Rsch. Assn., 1992, long-term care conf. Sharing the Burden, 1994. Mem. adv. panel on long term care financing Brookings' Inst. Fellow Soc. Actuaries (conf. spkr. 1988, 94, workshop leader 1990, 93, news editor health sect. news 1988-90); mem. Am. Acad. Actuaries, Health Ins. Assn. Am. (long term care task force 1988—, chair 1993-95, conf. spkr. 1990, 96, tch. adv. com. 1991-93, mem. health care reform strategy com. 1993-95, mem. supplemental ins. com. 1996, mem. legis. policy com. 1996—), Nat. Assn. Ins. Commrs. (ad hoc actuarial working group for long term care nonforfeiture benefits 1992), Chgo. Actuarial Assn. (sec. 1983-85, program com. 1987-89), Phi Beta Kappa, Kappa Delta Pi, Phi Kappa Phi. Office: Bankers Life & Casualty Co 222 Merchandise Mart Plz Chicago IL 60654-1001

MORISSETTE, CAROL LYNNE, healthcare consultant; b. Connellsville, Pa., Apr. 26, 1941; d. Charles Lynn and Iola Grace (Sembower) Sliger; m. George Van Barriger, May 27, 1966 (div. Feb. 1972); m. Richard W. Morissette, Oct. 25, 1991. RN, Montefiore Hosp., 1962; BS, Coll. St. Francis, 1985; MA in Mgmt., Nat. Louis U., 1988. Cert. case mgr. Pub. health nurse Kendall County Health Dept., Yorkville, Ill., 1970-72; team leader Edward Hosp., Naperville, Ill., 1972-73; emergency nurse Cen. Dupage Hosp., Winfield, Ill., 1973-74; staff nurse and head nurse Palos Community Hosp., Palos Heights, Ill., 1974-77, surg. nurse, 1977-82; auditor Med-Charge Analysis, Chgo., 1982-83; mgr. Intracorp CIGNA, Glen Ellyn, Ill., 1983-86, Metlife Healthcare Network, Schaumburg, Ill., 1986; project mgr. Healthcare Intermediaries, Lombard, Ill., 1986-88; dir., provider services Multicare HMO, Chgo., 1988-89; ptnr. Greenberg Assocs., 1989-91; nurse cons. Office Workers' Compensation Programs, U.S. Dept. Labor, Chgo., 1993—; mem. group comparison studies healthcare delivery/costs USSR, 1981, China, 1982, England, 1985, Egypt, 1992. V.p. Indian Oak Condominium Assn., Bolingbrook, Ill., 1972-76; treas. Hickory Heights Condominium Assn., Hickory Hills, Ill., 1978-83, bd. dirs., 1983-95. Mem. NAFE, Women's Health Exec. Network, Am. Coll. Healthcare Execs., Chgo. Health Exec. Forum, Am. Assn. Occupational Health Nurses, Individual Case Mgmt. Assn. (cert. case mgr.). Home: 14136 S Kilpatrick Ave Crestwood IL 60445-2221

MORITZ, JEAN LORIS, educator; b. San Leandro, Calif., July 28, 1934; d. Cyril Sidney and Annabel Alice (Nicholson) Humphrey; m. Arthur Lee Moritz, Oct. 18, 1957; children: Karen Ann Williams, Arthur Lee Moritz Jr., Michele Bird. AA, U. Calif., Berkeley, 1954; BA, Calif. State U., Fresno, 1976. Cert. tchr., Calif.; cert. lang. devel. specialist, Calif. Substitute tchr. Visalia (Calif.) Unified Sch. Dist., 1976-78; tchr. St. Paul's Sch., Visalia, 1978-85, Earlimart (Calif.) Mid. Sch., 1985—. Elder First Presbyn. Ch., Visalia, 1989-93. Mem. AAUW. Office: Earlimart Mid Sch 522 E Sutter Earlimart CA 93219

MORKOVIN, VERA P., physician; b. Syracuse, N.Y., June 9, 1919; d. David Perlmutter and Amelia Barnett Perlmutter-Gorn; m. Dimitry Morkovin, June 9, 1939 (div. 1950); m. Leo A. King, May 4, 1952; children: David, Jesse, Lloyd, Phoebe. BA, Syracuse U., 1939; MD, Rush Med. Coll., 1942. Diplomate Am. Bd. Surgery. Intern gen. surgery Cook County Hosp., Chgo., 1942-43, resident, 1943-46; chief resident surgery Am. Hosp. Chgo., 1946-47; gen. surgery Joslyn Clinic Westlake Hosp. and Gottlieb Meml. Hosp., Melrose Park, Ill., 1947-65; co-founder Med. Emergency Svc. Assocs., Elmhurst, Chgo., Arlington Heights, Ill., 1965; first chair dept. of emergency medicine Ill. Masonic Med. Ctr., Chgo., 1943-83; assoc. prof., chief sect. emergency medicine Coll. Medicine U. Ill., 1975-83; staff emergency physician St. Mary's Hosp., Grand Rapids, Mich., 1983-84; dir. minor emergency clinic Mich. State U., East Lansing, 1984-85; assoc. prof. emergency medicine Mich. State U., 1985—; med. dir. Crossroads Prompt Care Borgess Med. Ctr., Kalamazoo, 1985-95, staff mem. dept. emergency medicine, 1985; family practice Mich., 1996—; co-founder U. Ill. Emergency Medicine Residency; family practice Pennock Hosp., Hastings, Mich., 1996—; med. dir. first project North Side Med. Intesive Care Program, Chgo.; writer, examiner Am. Bd. Emergency Medicine examination; presenter in field. Contbr. articles to profl. jours. Home: 5400 Wilkins Rd Hastings MI 49058-9239

MORLAND, JESSIE PARRISH, retired educator; b. Parrish, Fla., Dec. 3, 1924; d. Jonah and May (Lowry) Parrish; B.A., Fla. Southern Coll., 1947; m. Richard B. Morland, Mar. 17, 1949; 1 child, Laura. Dir. publicity Fla. Southern Coll., 1948-50; editor Dun's Bulletin, Dun and Bradstreet, N.Y.C., 1950-52; feature writer Deland Sun News, Daytona Beach (Fla.) News Jour., 1952-65; tchr. English, journalism Deland (Fla.) Jr. High Sch., 1967-83, tchr. gifted students, 1983-86. Bd. dirs. Deland Mus., 1957-62, Democratic Women's Club, 1952-65; pres. DeLand Cultural Com., 1990-92; sec. exec. bd. DeLand Mus. of Art Guild. Mem. AAUW (dir. 1955-62), Nat. League Am. Pen Women, DeLand Country Club, Alpha Delta Pi. Democrat. Methodist. Home: 524 N Mcdonald Ave Deland FL 32724-3643

MORLEY, DIANE ELIZABETH, artist; b. Las Cruces, N.Mex., Nov. 1951; d. Albert Lewis and Isa Elizabeth (Sherman) Ludy; m. Roy William Morley Jr., July 21, 1979; 1 child, Amanda Elizabeth. BFA, Memphis Coll. Art, 1982. chair bd. dirs. Memphis Ctr. for Contemporary Art, 1990-91; founding mem. Artists Link, Memphis, 1990. Exhibited in group shows including Nelson-Atkins Mus. Art, Kansas City, Mo., 1991, Huntsville (Ala.) Mus. Art, 1992, Nat. Mus. Women in the Arts, Washington, 1993, Kurts Bingham Gallery, 1995; artist presdl. inaugural poster, 1993. Painting fellow Mid-Am. Arts Alliance/NEA, 1990.

MORNEAU, MICHELLE SUSAN, product manager; b. Holyoke, Mass., Feb. 18, 1969; d. Ronald J. and Suzan M. (Bradlinski) M. BS, Syracuse U., 1990; MBA, Boston U., 1995. Catering mgr. Syracuse U., Boston, 1987-90; sr. portfolio acct. Fidelity Investments, Boston, 1990-91, sr. client mgr., 1992-95, product mgr., 1995—. Alumni rep. Syracuse U., 1991—, treas. 93-94; active Jr. League. Home: 12 Ryder Hill Rd Brighton MA 02135

MORNES, AMBER J. BISHOP, computer software trainer; b. Ft. Rucker, Ala., Oct. 20, 1970; d. David Floyd and Holly Brooke (Decker) Bishop; m. David Michael Mornes, May 22, 1993. BA in Psychology, U. Colo., Boulder, 1992. Asst. dir. admissions Rocky Mountain Coll. Art and Design, Denver, 1992-94, placement and alumni svcs. coord., 1995-96; computer software instr. New Horizons Computer Learning Ctr., Aurora, Colo., 1996—. Vol. Colo. Art Educator Assn., 1993—. Mem. APA (student affiliate), Nat. Art Edn. Assn., Colo. Art Edn. Assn. Home: 2500 S York St Apt I1 Denver CO 80210-5245 Office: New Horizons Computer Learning Ctr 2851 S Parker Rd Ste 1300 Aurora CO 80014

MORONEY, LINDA L.S., lawyer, educator; b. Washington, May 27, 1943; d. Robert Emmet and Jessie (Robinson) M.; m. Clarence Renshaw II, Mar. 28, 1967 (div. 1977); children: Robert Milnor, Justin W.R. BA, Randolph-Macon Woman's Coll., 1965; JD cum laude, U. Houston, 1982. Bar: Tex. 1982, U.S. Ct. Appeals (5th cir.) 1982, U.S. Dist. Ct. (so. dist.) Tex. 1982, U.S. Supreme Ct. 1988. Law clk. to assoc. justice 14th Ct. Appeals, Houston, 1982-83; assoc. Pannill and Reynolds, Houston, 1983-85, Gilpin, Pohl & Bennett, Houston, 1985-89, Vinson & Elkins, Houston, 1989-92; adj. prof. law U. Houston, 1989-91, dir. legal rsch. and writing, 1992-96. Fellow Houston Bar Found.; mem. ABA, State Bar Tex., Houston Bar Assn., Assn. of Women Attys., Order of the Barons, Phi Delta Phi. Episcopalian. Home and Office: 3730 Overbrook Ln Houston TX 77027-4036

MORONT, PATRICIA, academic administrator; b. Sagua la Grande, Cuba, Sept. 10, 1956; came to U.S., 1961; d. Antonio and Melba Rosa (Quintero) Moran; children: Kyle Miller, Tyler Miller;. AA, Palm Beach Jr. Coll., 1976; BA in Mass Comms., U. South Fla., 1980. Cert. tchr., Fla. Prodr. and hostess Spanish Pub. Affairs Talk Show (WTOG-TV); pub. svc. dir. WTOG-TV, St. Petersburg, Fla., 1979-82; asst. promtions dir. Busch Gardens, Tampa, Fla., 1983; Spanish/English tchr. Pinellas Sch. Bd., Largo, Fla., 1990-92, Palm Beach Sch. Bd., Boca Raton, Fla., 1990-92; h.s./cmty. rels. dir. New Eng. Inst. Tech. & Fla. Culinary Inst., West Palm Beach, Fla., 1992—; ESOL instr. Adult Vocat. Edn., Lantana, Fla., 1991-92. Mem. tech. prep. mktg. com. P.B. County Sch. Bd. Mem. Women in Comms. Republican. Roman Catholic. Office: Fla Culinary Inst 2400 Metro Centre Blvd West Palm Beach FL 33407

MORPHEW, DOROTHY RICHARDS-BASSETT, artist, real estate broker; b. Cambridge, Mass., Aug. 4, 1918; d. George and Evangeline Booth (Richards) Richards; grad. Boston Art Inst., 1949; children—Jon Eric, Marc Alan, Dana Kimball. Draftsman, United Shoe Machinery Co., 1937-42; blueprinter, advt. artist A.C. Lawrence Leather Co., Peabody, Mass., 1949-51; propr. Studio Shop and Studio Potters, Beverly, Mass., 1951-53; tchr. ceramics and art, Kingston, N.H., 1953—; real estate broker, pres. 1965-81; two-man exhbn. Topsfield (Mass.) Library, 1960; owner, operator Ceramic Shop, West Stewartstown, N.H. Served with USNR, 1942-44. Recipient Profl. award New Eng. Ceramic Show, 1975; also numerous certificates in ceramics. Home: 557 Palomino Trl Englewood FL 34223-3951 Studio: 57 Algonac Rd Cape Neddick ME 03909

MORRILL, JOYCE MARIE, social worker, consultant; b. Rockland, Maine, Dec. 27, 1939; d. Henry Higgins and Julia Ellen (Philbrook) Thompson; BA, U. Hartford, 1964; MSW, Hunter Coll., 1972; m. Edward Morrill, Sept. 7, 1972; 1 son, Gregory Hodgman; step-son Shawn Morrill. Co-host Today in Conn. Program, Sta. WHNB-TV, Hartford, 1964-65; clin. social worker, field instr. Rehab. Inst., N.Y., 1972-78; dir., founder Wellness Svcs., Jamaica Estates, N.Y., 1979-95; pres. Morrill Support, 1996—. Mem. Nat. Assn. Social Workers, Inst. Noetic Scis., N.Am. Menopause Soc. Home and Office: 181-38 Midland Pky Jamaica Estates NY 11432-1400

MORRIN, VIRGINIA WHITE, retired college educator; b. Escondido, Calif., May 16, 1913; d. Harry Parmalee and Ethel Norine (Nutting) Rising; BS, Oreg. State Coll., 1952; MEd, Oreg. State U., 1957; m. Raymond Bennett White, 1933 (dec. 1953); children: Katherine Anne, Marjorie Virginia, William Raymond; m. 2d, Laurence Morrin, 1959 (dec. 1972). Social caseworker Los Angeles County, Los Angeles, 1934-40, 61-64; acctg. clk. War Dept., Ft. MacArthur, Calif., 1940-42; prin. clk. USAAF, Las Vegas, Nev., 1942-44; high sch. tchr., North Bend-Coos Bay, Oreg., 1952-56, Mojave, Calif., 1957-60; instr. electric bus. machines Antelope Valley Coll., Lancaster, Calif., 1961-73; ret., 1974. Treas., Humane Soc. Antelope Valley, Inc., 1968—. Mem. Nat. Aero. Assn., Calif. State Sheriffs' Assn. (charter assoc.), Oreg. State U. Alumni Assn. (life). Address: 3153 Milton Dr Mojave CA 93501-1329

MORRIS, ALICE FAYE, vocal educator; b. Russell, Kans., Dec. 8, 1954; d. Lloyd R. and Marjorie L. (Hoopes) Schneider; m. Derrick Morris, July 24, 1976; children: Zachary, Kyle, Lance, Nathan. AA, Coffeyville C.C., 1974; BS in Music Edn., Kans. State U., 1976; MS in Bldg. and Sch. Adminstrn., Pitts. State U., 1994. Cert. tchr. music, vocal, instrumental and fundamentals. Vocal tchr., bldg. adminstr. Lenapah (Okla.) Sch. Sys., 1977-79, South Coffeyville (Okla.) Sch., 1977-82, Alluwe (Okla.) Sch. Sys., 1983-84, Roosevelt Mid. Sch., Coffeyville, Kans., 1986—. Bd dirs. Am. Cancer Soc., Coffeyville, 1992, youth edn. com., 1983-94; mem. Leadership Coffeyville, 1994-95. Mem. Kans. Music Educators Assn., Beta Sigma Phi (corr. sec. 1989). Republican. Roman Catholic. Home: 505 Centennial St Coffeyville KS 67337-2412 Office: Roosevelt Mid Sch 1000 W 8th St Coffeyville KS 67337-4114

MORRIS, ANN HASELTINE JONES, social welfare administrator; b. Springfield, Mo., Feb. 3, 1941; d. Mansur King and Adelaide (Haseltine) Jones; m. Ronald D. Morris, Nov. 29, 1963 (div. 1990); children: David, Christopher. BA in Edn. and Art, Drury Coll., 1963. Art instr. Ash Grove (Mo.)/Bois D'Arc Pub. Sch. Dist., 1963-64; instr. Drury Coll., Springfield, 1966-67; tchr. Springfield R-12 Sch. Dist., 1974-86; exec. dir. S.W. Ctr. for Ind. Living, Springfield, 1986—; adv. com. Springfield R-12 Spl. Edn., 1993—; tech. cons. and alternative dispute resolution mediator Ams. with Disabilities Act EEOC, Dept. of Justice Network, 1993—. Bd. dirs. Ozark Greenways, 1991-93, Springfield Deaf Relay, 1988-90; adv. task force Allied Health Program Devel. S.W. Bapt Univ., 1988; mem. Drury Coll. Women's Aux., 1984—, conservator of the peace, handicap parking enforcement action team, 1991—; bd. treas. Mo. Parent Act, 1989-91, Diversity Network of the Ozarks, 1990—; svc. coord. Youthnet, 1990—; community adv. bd. Rehab. Svcs., St. John's Regional Health Care Ctr., 1988-91; mem. Springfield Homeless Network, 1989—, others; apptd. to Mo. Gov.'s Coun. on Disability; pres. Statewide Ind. Living Coun. Mem. NOW (sec. 1991), P.E.O., Mo. Assn. of Ctrs. for Ind. Living (v.p. 1990—), Mo. Assn. for Social Welfare (bd. treas. 1989-95), Nat. Assn. of Ind. Living Ctrs. (AIDS task force 1993—), Assn. of Programs for Rural Ind. Living, Nat. Soc. of Fund Raising Execs., Mo. Rehab. Assn., C. of C. (healthcare divsn.), Zeta Tau Alpha. Home: 1748 E Arlington Rd Springfield MO 65804-7742

MORRIS, ANNA ROCHELLE, retail and wholesale executive; b. Lubbock, Tex., Dec. 31, 1957; d. Raphael and JoAnn (Davis) Gillespie; m. Gary Dean Rosselle (div.); m. Randall C. Fraelich (div.); m. Aaron Myles Morris, Nov. 15, 1988. Photographer Miami Seaquarium, Key Biscayne, Fla., 1975-77, Trader Publs., Clearwater, Fla., 1978; salesperson Rex Art Co., Miami, 1979-81, customer svc. rep., 1981-84, asst. purchaser, 1984-87, exec. asst., 1987—. Mem. hospitality com. Miami Film Festival, 1985-86; sec. Freddick Bratcher & Co., South Miami, Fla., 1986—. Democrat. Jewish. Office: Rex Art Co 2263 SW 37th Ave Miami FL 33145-3009

MORRIS, ARLENE MYERS, marketing professional; b. Washington, Pa., Dec. 29, 1951; d. Frank Hayes Myers and Lula Irene (Slusser) Kolcan; m. John L. Sullivan, Feb. 17, 1971 (div. July 1982); m. David Wellons Morris, July 27, 1984. BA, Carlow Coll., 1974; postgrad., Western New England Coll., 1981-82. Sales rep. Syntex Labs., Inc., Palo Alto, Calif., 1974-77; profl. sales rep. McNeil Pharm., Spring House, Pa., 1977-78, mental health rep., 1978-80, asst. product dir., 1981-82, dist. mgr., 1982-85, new product dir., 1985-87, exec. dir. new bus. devel., 1987-89, v.p. bus. devel., 1989-93; v.p. bus. devel. Scios Nova IMC, Mountain View, Calif., 1993—. Mem. Found. of Ind. Colls., Phila., 1989. Mem. Pharm. Advt. Coun., Am. Diabetes Assn., Am. Acad. Sci., Healthcare Bus. Womens Assn., Lic. Execs. Soc. Home: 11701 Winding Way Los Altos CA 94024-6331 Office: Scios Nova 2450 Bayshore Pky Mountain View CA 94043-1107

MORRIS, DOROTHEA LOUISE, nurse midwife; b. Emporia, Kans., Oct. 30, 1944; d. Clarence Earl and Dorothy Ann (Draper) Richardson; m. David B. DeKalb, May 1, 1966 (div. Dec. 1981); children: Michele E. DeKalb, Cheryl L. Lines, David B. DeKalb Jr.; m. James Henry Morris, July 4, 1984. Diploma, Beth-El Sch. Nursing, Colorado Springs, Colo., 1966; BSN, Alaska Meth. U., 1975; MPA, Troy State U., 1988; MSN, U. N.Mex., 1990. RN Colo., N. Mex. Commd. 2d lt. USAF, 1977, advanced through grades to lt. col.; staff nurse Meml. Hosp., Colorado Springs, 1966-67; staff nurse, supr. Albany (Oreg.) Gen. Hosp., 1969; staff nurse, obstetrics Harrisonville (Mo.) Hosp., 1970, USAF Hosp., Anchorage, 1970-75; staff nurse, instr. BOCES, Verona, N.Y., 1976-77; staff nurse, instr. ADN program Mohawk Valley C.C., Utica, N.Y., 1976-77; staff nurse obstetrics Chanute AFB, Rantoul, Ill., 1977-79; nurse-midwife Homestead AFB (Fla.) Hosp., 1980-85, Weisbaden (Germany) Regional Med. Ctr., 1985-88; nurse-midwife, instr. Midwifery Sch., Andrews AFB, Md., 1990—; asst. dir. Air Force Nurse-Midwifery Program, Andrews AFB, 1991—; pres. CNM Svc. Dirs., Inc., 1995-97. Lt. col. USAF, 1977—. Mem. Am. Coll. Nurse Midwives (cert.), Nurses Assn. Obstetrics and Gynecology, NANP in Reproductive Health, Uniformed Nurse Practitioner Assn., Order Ea. Star. Baptist. Home: 4024-2 Ashwood Cir Andrews Air Force Base MD 20762 Office: SGHOM Malcolm Grow 89 MDOS/SGOGM Andrews Air Force Base MD 20762

MORRIS, DOROTHY ELLEN, elementary education educator; b. Twin Falls, Idaho, Aug. 4, 1946; d. Ted Le Roy and Esther (Reid) Baughman; m. Richard Hart Morris, Sept. 17, 1965; children: Shannon Renae, Sheila Kathleen, Nanci Ann. BA in Elem. Edn., Idaho State U., 1970; MEd, Albertson Coll. Idaho, 1990. Tchr. 2d grade Twin Falls (Idaho) Pub. Schs., 1971-73; tchr. 1st grade Filer (Idaho) Sch. Dist., 1974-76, tchr. kindergarten, 1977-79; tchr. kindergarten, 1st grade Buhl (Idaho) Sch. Dist., 1981—; instr. Frame Works, Buhl, 1993—; mem. Eisenhower Grant Group, Twin Falls, 1994; chair artist in edn. com. Buhl Elem. Sch., 1990-93. Leader 4-H Clubs, Buhl, 1978—; pres. Northview Ladies Club, Buhl, 1979. Mem. Buhl Edn. Assn. (treas. 1990-94), Magic Valley Reading Coun. (pres. 1994-95, membership chair 1991-93, vi.p. 1993-94), Delta Kappa Gamma (profl. affairs chair 1992—). Home: 4349 N 1800 E Buhl ID 83316-5318 Office: Popplewell Elem Sch 200 6th Ave N Buhl ID 83316

MORRIS, EDNA K., human resources executive. BS, U. S.C., 1974. Sr. v.p. Hardee's Food Systems, Inc.; v.p. edn. and tng. Flagstar Cos., Inc., 1992-93, sr. v.p. human resources, 1993-95, exec. v.p. human resources, 1995—. Mem. Phi Beta Kappa. Office: The Flagstar Corp 203 E Main St Spartanburg SC 29319

MORRIS, ELIZABETH TREAT, physical therapist; b. Hartford, Conn., Feb. 20, 1936; d. Charles Wells and Marion Louise (Case) Treat; BS in Phys. Therapy, U. Conn., 1960; m. David Breck Morris, July 10, 1961; children: Russell Charles, Jeffrey David. Phys. therapist Crippled Children's Clinic No. Va., Arlington, 1960-62, Shriners Hosp. Crippled Children, Salt Lake City, 1967-69, Holy Cross Hosp., Salt Lake City, 1970-74; pvt. practice phys. therapy, Salt Lake City, 1975—. Mem. nominating com. YWCA, Salt Lake City. Mem. Am. Phys. Therapy Assn., Am. Congress Rehab. Medicine, Am. Alliance for Health Phys. Edn. Recreation & Dance, Nat. Speakers Assn., Utah Speakers Assn., Salt Lake Area C. of C., Friendship Force Utah, U.S. Figure Skating Assn., Toastmasters Internat., Internat. Assn. for the Study Pain, Internat. Platform Assn., World Confederation Phys. Therapy, Medart Internat. Home: 4177 Mathews Way Salt Lake City UT 84124-4021 Office: PO Box 526186 Salt Lake City UT 84152-6186

MORRIS, FLORENCE HENDERSON, auditor; b. Mobile, Ala., Sept. 8, 1964; d. Thomas Gordan Henderson and Joanne Elizabeth (Pfleger) Martin; m. Fred S. Morris, July 28, 1995. BS in Fin., U. Ala., 1986. Payment and receipt rep. SouthTrust Bank of Mobile, 1988-89; internal bank auditor SouthTrust Corp., Birmingham, 1989-90, compliance audit officer, 1990-92; prin. compliance auditor, asst. v.p. SouthTrust Corp. and SouthTrust Bank of Ga., Atlanta, 1992-95; compliance audit supr., v.p. SouthTrust Corp., Birmingham, 1995—. Mem. Inst. Internal Auditors, Bankers Adminstrn. Inst. (cert. bank compliance officer), Am. Bankers Assn., Ala. Fin. Assn., U. Ala. Alumna, Delta Sigma Pi. Office: SouthTrust Corp Audit Dept PO Box 2554 Birmingham AL 35290

MORRIS, GRACE KIRSCHBAUM, psychotherapist, consultant; b. Chgo., Nov. 2, 1933; d. Frederick William and Helen Ann (Cihak) Kirschbaum; m. David Earl Morris, Oct. 18, 1953; children: Michael David, Kathleen Elery Olund. AA, Moraine Valley Community Coll., 1982; BA, Gov.'s State U., 1984, MA, 1988. Newspaper reporter Worth Palos Reporter, Palos Heights, Ill., 1965-75; owner Sch. Psychol. Astrology, Oak Lawn, Ill., 1975—; lectr. various bus., civic groups, 1975—; pvt. practice in counseling Oak Brook, 1992—; owner, pres. Astro Econs., Inc., Oak Brook, 1992—; facilitator self-help workshops, 1977—, fin., bus. workshops, 1979—; co-sponsor World Conf. of Astro-Economics, Chgo., 1987-2007. Author: (textbook) The School of Psychological Astrology, 1987, Working With Businesses, 1990, Company Profiles, 1990, It Looks Like Greek to Me, 1993, How to Choose Stocks That Will Outperform the Market, 1996; editor, publisher 2 newsletters Astro Econs. Stockmarket Newsletter, The Right Time, 1992—. Parliamentarian United Ch. of Christ Conf. Ill., 1975; moderator Chgo. Met. Assn. UCC, 1976; dist. dir. Ill. PTA, 1972-74; pres. Oak Lawn chpt. LWV, 1975. Mem. Am. Assn. Counseling and Devel., Nat. Coun. Geocosmi Rsch. (local edn. chmn. 1982—), Am. Fedn. Astrologers, Fin. Cycles Investment Club (founder 1995). Office: Regency Towers 1415 W 22nd St Tower Fl Oak Brook Mall IL 60521

MORRIS, JANE SHELLEY, art educator; b. July 3, 1946; d. H. F. Sinclair and Anne Leah (Freeman) M. BS in Art Edn., U. N.H., 1968; MEd in Elem. Edn., Plymouth State Coll., 1976. Art tchr. grades 7-9 Needham (Mass.) Pub. Schs., 1968-69; art tchr. grades K-6 Framingham (Mass.) Pub. Schs., 1969-92; ednl. intern Worcester (Mass.) Art Mus., 1988. Mem., advisor Framingham Hist. Soc., 1983-93; campaign worker Dem. Party, Newton, Mass., 1980. Mem. Nat. Art Educators Assn., Inst. Contemporary Art, Mus. Fine Arts Coun.

MORRIS, KATHERINE LANG, counseling psychologist; b. Benson, Minn., Jan. 22, 1947; d. Howard James and Barbara Anne (Bennett) L. BA in Art History, Smith Coll., Northampton, Mass., 1969; MA, Bethel Theol. Sem., St. Paul, 1973; MEd, U. Mo.-Columbia, 1978, Ph.D., 1982. Lic. psychologist, Calif. Tchr., Am. Sch., Barcelona, Spain, 1970-71; campus ministry Univ. Reformed Ch., East Lansing, Mich., 1973-76; counselor Univ. Counseling Ctr., U. Mo., Rolla, 1978-79; coordinator Ctr. for Student Vols. Action, 1979-81; counseling psychologist U. Calif., Davis, 1982-94; pvt. practice counseling psychologist, Sacramento, Calif., 1986-92; dir. counseling dept. health svcs. U. Minn., Duluth, 1994—; cons. in field. Mem. APA. Avocations: skiing, racquetball, writing. Office: U Minn Health Svcs Duluth MN 55811

MORRIS, KIMBERLY SUE, secondary education business educator; b. York, Pa., Apr. 27, 1962; d. Richard Eugene and Betty Lou (Jones) Kiser; m. David Wayne Morris, Oct. 16, 1982; children: Jessica Marie, Katie Lynn. BS, York Coll., 1987, M, 1994. Bus. educator Spring Grove (Pa.) Sch. Dist., 1988-92; bus. educator Red Lion (Pa.) Sch. Dist., 1992—, mentor 9th grade homeroom, 1992-94; yearbook adv. Lion, 1994—; exec. com., 1992-94, discipline com., sec., 1992-94. Mem. Pa. Bus. Edn. Assn., NEA. Home: 13058 Mont Rd Felton PA 17322 Office: Red Lion Area Sch Dist 200 Horace Mann Ave Red Lion PA 17356-2403

MORRIS, LAURA, elementary education educator; b. Santa Monica, Calif., Feb. 26, 1948; d. Maurice and Freida (Shiner) Rosenberg; m. Michael William Morris, Dec. 29, 1968; children: Samantha, Leah M. BA in Elem. Edn., U. Mont., 1970. Cert. elem. tchr., Mont. Elem. tchr. various schs., 1971-75; tchr. 1st grade Our Lady of Sorrows Cath. Sch., Rock Springs, Wyo., 1975-76; piano tchr. Laromor Piano Studio, Rock Springs, 1976-86; instr. Western Wyo. Coll., Rock Springs, 1982-84; tchr. 1st grade Westridge Sch., Rock Springs, 1985-86; tchr., accompanist Baker (Mont.) Pub. Schs., 1986—; mem. gifted and talented adv. com. Baker Elem. Schs., 1994-95. Mem. Am. Legion Aux., Baker, 1993-96. Mem. Music Tchrs. Nat. Assn., Mont. State Music Tchrs. Assn. (v.p. S.E. divsn. 1986—), Internat. Reading Assn., S.W. Wyo. Music Tchrs. Assn. (pres. 1981-83).

MORRIS, LESLIE E., public relations executive; b. Sayre, Pa., Dec. 27, 1965; d. Kenneth Charles and Sandra Kay (Hawley) Edsell; m. Andrew Fay Morris, Oct. 1, 1988. BA in Journalism, Duquesne U., Pitts., 1988; postgrad., Elmira (N.Y.) Coll., 1992—. Editor The Evening Times, Sayre, 1988-89; editor/graphic designer Stewart Howe Alumni Svc., Ithaca, N.Y., 1989-92; dir. comm. Elmira Coll., 1992—. Editor: Campus mag., 1994 (Apex award excellence); author (video script): The Elmira College Experience (Apex award for excellence), 1995; contbr. articles to profl. jours. Mem. pub. support com. ARC, Elmira, 1993—. Mem. Am. Mktg. Assn. (membership com. 1993—), Women in Comm. Home: 104 Hanlon Dr Odessa NY 14869 Office: Elmira College One Park Pl Elmira NY 14901

MORRIS, LINDA A. FINTON, English language educator; b. Lansing, Mich., May 22, 1939; d. Marvin D. and Gertrude (Marcussen) Finton; children: Elizabeth Miller, Katherine. BA, Grinnell Coll., 1961; MA, U. Wash., 1965; PhD, U. Calif., Berkeley, 1978. Prof. U. Calif., Davis, 1978—, dir. women's studies, 1992-96, dir. women's ctr., 1989-92, coord. writing, 1987-89; vis. lectr. Denison U., Granville, Ohio, 1965-69, Grinnell (Iowa) Coll., 1969-72. Author: Women's Humor in the Age of Gentility, 1992; co-author: Dorothea Lange-A Woman of Our Generation, 1994; editor: American Women's Humor: Critical Essays, 1994. Bancroft fellow U. Calif., 1976-77, Pres.'s Humanities Rsch. fellow, 1995-96. Mem. MLA, Am. Studies Assn., Western Lit. Soc. Office: U Calif Dept English Davis CA 95616

MORRIS, LOIS LAWSON, education educator; b. Antoine, Ark., Nov. 27, 1914; d. Oscar Moran and Dona Alice (Ward) Lawson; m. William D. Morris, July 2, 1932 (dec.); 1 child, Lavonne Morris Howell. B.A., Henderson U., 1948; M.S., U. Ark., 1951, M.A., 1966; postgrad. U. Colo., 1954, Am. U., 1958, U. N.C., 1968. History tchr. Delight High Sch., Ark., 1942-47; counselor Huntsville Vocat. Sch., 1947-48; guidance dir. Russellville Pub. Sch. System, Ark., 1948-55; asst. prof. edn. U. Ark., Fayetteville, 1955-82, prof. emeritus, 1982—; ednl. cons. Ark. Pub. Schs., 1965-78. Mem. Commn. on Needs for Women, 1976-78, Hist. Preservation Alliance Ark.; pres. Washington County Hist. Soc., 1983-85; pres. Pope County Hist. Assn.; mem. Ark. Symphony Guild; charter mem. Nat. Mus. in Arts; bd. dirs. Potts Inn Mus. Found. Named Ark. Coll. Tchr. of Year, 1972; recipient Plaque for outstanding svcs. to Washington County Hist. Soc., 1984. Contbr. articles to jours. Mem. LWV, AAUW, Ark. Coun. Social Studies (sec.-treas.), Washington County Hist. Soc. (exec. bd. 1977-80), NEA, Nat. Coun. Social Studies, Ark. Edn. Assn., Ark. Hist. Assn., Pope County Hist. Assn. (pres. 1991-92), The So. Hist. Assn., U. Ark. Alumni Assn., Sierra Club, Nature Conservancy, So. Hist. Assn., Ark. River Valley Arts Assn., Phi Delta Kappa, Kappa Delta Pi, Phi Alpha Theta. Democrat. Episcopalian. Address: 1601 W 3rd St Russellville AR 72801-4725

MORRIS, LYNNE LOUISE, psychotherapist; b. Youngstown, Ohio, Nov. 5, 1946; d. Richard Davies and Elsie Margaret Raymond) B.A., Westminster Coll., Pa., 1969; MSW, NYU, 1971. Cert. clin. social worker. Social worker Community Service Soc., N.Y.C., 1971-74, Altro Health and Rehab. Services, Inc., N.Y.C., 1974-79; field instr. Hunter Coll. Sch. Social Work, NYU Grad Sch. Social Work, 1974-79; clin. coordinator Montefiore Hosp. and Med. Center, Bronx, N.Y., 1979-81; asst. dir. II, social service dept. Montefiore Hosp., Bronx, 1981-83; pvt. practice psychotherapy, N.Y.C., 1976—; sr. staff therapist Counseling and Human Devel. Center, N.Y.C., 1979—. Contbr. articles of profl. jours. including Jour. Geriatric Psychiatry, 1975; abstractor Abstracts for Social Workers, 1975. Fellow N.Y. State Soc. Clin. Social Work Psychotherapists; mem. Nat. Assn. Social Workers (clin. diplomate), Acad. Cert. Social Workers, Am. Assn. Pastoral Counselors (profl. affiliate). Home and Office: 161 W 75th St Apt 2C New York NY 10023-1802

MORRIS, MARGARET E., marketing professional; b. N.Y.C., Nov. 1, 1962; d. John Daniel and Jean Bingham (MacCollom) M.; m. Gary E. Musser Jr., May 1, 1993. BA in English, Georgetown U., 1984. Mem. staff mktg. programs AT&T Nat. Fed. Mktg., Arlington, Va., 1985; mktg. tech. cons. AT&T Nat. Fed. Systems, Washington, 1985-87; tech. cons. computer mktg. Cin. Bell Tel. Co., 1987-89, mktg. tech. cons., 1989-95; sr. acct. exec.-strategic accts., 1995—; tutor (vol.) Ptnrs. in Edn. Editor: (newsletter) District Action Project RAP, 1981-82. Intern Citizen's Complaint Ctr., Washington, 1981-82. Mem. NAFE, Cin. Updowntowners, Soroptimist Internat., Telephone Pioneers Am. Office: Cin Bell Tel Co 201 E 4th St Rm 102-1180 Cincinnati OH 45202-4122

MORRIS, MARGRETTA ELIZABETH, government official; b. Oakland, Calif., Sept. 14, 1950; d. Joseph Francis and Mildred Ruth Madeo; m. Dennis Wayne Morris, July 22, 1972; children: Matthew Benjamin, Roseanna A. BA in Geography, Radford U., 1972. Exec. asst. John Hancock Life Ins., Pittsfield, Mass., 1972-79; paralegal Law Office of Henry F. Zwack, Stephentown, N.Y., 1980-91; exec. dir. Ea. Rensselaer County Waste Mgmt. Authority, Stephentown, 1991—; co-founder MDM Prodns., Stephentown, 1986—. Councilperson Town of Stephentown, 1987-92. Mem. N.Y. State Assn. for Solid Waste Mgmt. (rec. sec. 1992—), N.Y. State Assn. for Reduction, Reuse and Recycling (treas. 1992—), Coalition of N.E. Govs., Gamma Theta Upsilon. Republican. Roman Catholic. Office: Ea Rensselaer County Solid Waste Mgmt Authority 389 Main St Stephentown NY 12168

MORRIS, MARTHA JOSEPHINE, nursing administrator; b. LaPorte, Ind., Jan. 16, 1951; d. John J. and Pearl L. Gorski; m. Richard Dale Morris, Sept. 5, 1970; children: Valerie A., Marlene N. ASN, Purdue U., Westville, Ind., 1977; BSN, Nazareth (Mich.) Coll., 1989. Charge nurse alcoholism/med. surg. unit Borgess Med. Ctr., Kalamazoo, 1977-81, asst. clin. mgr. substance abuse, 1981-88, asst. clin. nurse mgr. nephrology, 1988-90, contingency and patient intensity coord., 1990-93, mgr. patient info. tech., 1993—; mem. test devel. com. for informatics nursing Am. Nurses Credentialing Ctr., Washington, 1994—, mem. bd. on cert. for informatics nursing, 1994—. Mem. ANA, Mich. Nurses Assn. Roman Catholic. Office: Borgess Medical Ctr 1521 Gull Rd Kalamazoo MI 49001-1640

MORRIS, MARY ANN, bookkeeper; b. Great Falls, Mont., Feb. 16, 1946; d. Francis Leonard and Dorothy Irene (Howe) De Lacey; m. Donald Edward Wermuth, June 29, 1968 (div. Jan. 1974); 1 child, Deborah Ann; m. Larry Dallas Morris, Apr. 23, 1977; stepchildren: Serena Jo, Bradley Dwayne, Brian Dale, Bruce Dean. Student, North Idaho Coll., 1985. Sales clk. Dundas Office Supply, Great Falls, 1964-68, Stationer's Office Supply, Tacoma, 1969-70; bookkeeper Miller's Office Supply, Puyallup, Wash., 1971-72, Judge Moving & Storage (Allied), Great Falls, 1973-74; bookkeeper, credit mgr. Meadow Gold Dairy, Great Falls, 1974; pro-rate clk. Builders Transport, Great Falls, 1975-77; bookkeeper C&S Glass, Coeur d'Alene, Idaho, 1978-81, Morris Trucking, Coeur d'Alene, 1977-82; bookkeeper LDM Transport, Hayden Lake, Idaho, 1982—, profl. truck driver (class A vehicle), 1988—. Mem. Women's Retail Credit Mgrs. Assn. Republican. Home and Office: PO Box 2350 Hayden ID 83835-2350

MORRIS, M(ARY) ROSALIND, cytogeneticist, educator; b. Ruthin, Wales, May 8, 1920; came to U.S., 1942, naturalized, 1954; d. Aneurin Edmund and Celia Charles (Evans) M. BS in Horticulture, Ont. Agrl. Coll., Guelph, Can., 1942; PhD in Plant Breeding and Genetics, Cornell U., 1947. Mem. faculty U. Nebr., Lincoln, 1947—, prof. agronomy, 1958-90, prof. emeritus, 1990—. Contbr. chpts. to textbooks, articles to sci. jours. U. Nebr. Johnson Faculty fellow, Calif. Inst. Tech., Pasadena, 1949-50; John Simon Guggenheim Found. fellow, Sweden and Eng., 1956-57. Fellow AAAS, Am. Soc. Agronomy, Crop Sci. Soc. Am.; mem. AAUW, Genetics Soc. Can., Nebr. Acad. Sci., Nebr. Ornithologists' Union (editor The Nebr. Bird Rev. 1992—), Lincoln Camera Club, Sigma Xi, Gamma Sigma Delta, Sigma Delta Epsilon. Office: U Nebr Dept Agronomy Lincoln NE 68583-0915

MORRIS, NAOMI CAROLYN MINNER, medical educator, administrator, researcher, consultant; b. Chgo., June 8, 1931; d. Morris George and Carrie Ruth (Auslender) Minner; m. Charles Elliot Morris, June 28, 1951; children: Jonathan Edward, David Carlton. BA magna cum laude, U. Colo., 1952, MD, 1955; MPH magna cum laude, Harvard U., 1959. Diplomate Am. Bd. Preventive Medicine. Rotating intern L.A. County Gen. Hosp., 1955-56; clin. fellow in pediats. Mass. Gen. Hosp., Boston, 1957; pub. health physician Mass. Dept. Health, Boston, 1957-58; clin. pediatrician Norfolk (Va.) King's Daus. Hosp., 1959-61; from asst. prof. to prof. and chair dept. maternal and child health Sch. Pub. Health, U. N.C., Chapel Hill, 1962-77; prof., dir. cmty. pediats. U. Health Scis., Chgo. Med. Sch., 1977-80; prof. Sch. Pub. Health, U. Ill., Chgo., 1980—, dir. cmty. health scis. divsn., 1980-95; mem. liaison com. with Lake County Med. Soc. 1978-80; resource person Ill. 1980 White Ho. Conf. on Children, 1979-80; mem. nursing divsn. adv. com. Lake County Health Dept., 1980—; participant Enrich-A-Life series Chgo. Dept. Health, 1984-85, Ill. Health and Hazardous Substance Registry Pregnancy Outcome Task Force, 1984-86; mem. profl. adv. bd. Beethoven Project Ctr. Child Devel., 1986—; mem. planning com. for action to reduce infant mortality Chgo. Inst. Medicine, 1986-89; founding mem. Westside Futures Infant Mortality Network, 1986; mem. Ill. vital stats. supplement Ill. Dept. Pub. Health, 1987; investigator and team leader Rev. Mo. Families Maternal and Child Health State Svcs., 1989; mem. children and youth 2000 task force MacArthur Found., 1992—; active Ill. Caucus on Teenage Pregnancies, 1978—, Chgo. Dept. Health Child Health Task Force, 1982-83, HSC Interprofessional Edn. Com., 1983-84, Med. Task Force Project Life, 1983-88, Women's Studies Curriculum Com., 1985-90, Com. Rsch. on Women, 1985-90, Mayor's Adv. Com. on Infant Mortality, 1986—, Gov. Adv. Coun. on Infant Mortality, 1988—, Ctr. for Rsch. on Women Fellowship Com., 1993—; cons. pediat. nursing resources group Ill. Dept. Pub. Health, 1983-84; cons. Cook County Hosp. Study of Preventive Childhood Obesity, 1983-84. Author 8 book chpts; contbr. articles to profl. jours. Fellow APHA (mem. task force on adolescence maternal and child health sect. 1977-85, sec. 1979-80, cons. manpower project 1982-83, mem. publ. bd. 1985-87, mem. coun. pediat. rsch. to Am. Acad. Pediats. 1985-92), Am. Coll. Preventive Medicine, Am. Acad. Pediats. (mem. Ill. chpt. com. on sch. health and com. adolescent health 1993—); mem. Ambulatory Pediat. Assn., Assn. Tchrs. Maternal and Child Health (mem. exec. com. 1981-87, mem. com. on tng. and continuing edn. needs of MCH/CCS dirs. 1982-83, mem. liaison com. to fed. DCMH office 1983-87, pres. 1983-85). Office: U Ill Chgo Sch Pub Health 2035 W Taylor St Chicago IL 60612-7257

MORRIS, PATRICIA ANN, secondary education educator, counselor; b. N.Y.C., May 26, 1957; d. Lawrence and Kitty (Geaneas) M. BA, Rutgers U., 1979; MEd, Ga. State U., 1987. Cert. 7-12 French and Spanish tchr., P-12 counselor, Ga. Tchr. ESOL, Edn. and Tng. Cons., Inc., East Orange, N.J., 1980-81; tchr. French and Spanish, Teaneck (N.J.) Pub. Schs., 1981-82, Fulton County Pub. Schs., Atlanta, 1982—; tennis coach M.D. Collins H.S., College Park, 1986-87, B.E. Banneker H.S., College Park, 1988-90, 94-95. Treas. mem. steering com. archdiocesan conf. Greek Orthodox Young Adult League, Atlanta, 1983—. Mem. ASCD, Am. Assn. Tchrs. French, Am. Assn. Tchrs. of Spanish and Portuguese, Fgn. Lang. Assn. Ga., Greek Orthodox Ladies Philoptochos Soc. Home: 2037 Brian Way Decatur GA 30033 Office: BE Banneker HS 5935 Feldwood Rd College Park GA 30349

MORRIS, PHYLLIS SUTTON, philosophy educator; b. Quincy, Ill., Jan. 25, 1931; d. John Guice and Helen Elizabeth (Provis) Sutton; m. John Martin Morris, Feb. 4, 1950; children: William Robert, Katherine Jill. Student, U. Mich., 1948-51; AB, U. Calif., 1953; MA, Colo. Coll., 1963; PhD, U. Mich., 1969. Instr. humanities Mich. State U., East Lansing, 1968-69; from lectr. to assoc. prof. Kirkland Coll., Clinton, N.Y., 1969-78; assoc. prof. Hamilton Coll., Clinton, 1978-83; adj. assoc. prof. LeMoyne Coll., Syracuse, N.Y., 1983-85; rsch. assoc. in philosophy Oberlin (Ohio) Coll., 1995—; vis. prof. philosophy Oberlin Coll., 1989-91, 93, 94-95, U. Mich., Ann Arbor, 1996. Author: Sartre's Concept of a Person, 1976; revs. editor Sartre Studies Internat. jour., 1995; contbr. articles to profl. jours. Travel grantee Am. Coun. Learned Socs., 1988, Summer Seminar grantee NEH, 1974, 82. Mem. Am. Philos. Assn., Sartre Cir., Sartre Soc. N.Am. (co-founder 1985, exec. com. 1985-91), Soc. for Phenomenology and Existential Philosophy, Soc. for Women in Philosophy. Democrat. Home: 2116 Runnymede Blvd Ann Arbor MI 48103-5034

MORRIS, REBECCA ROBINSON, lawyer; b. McKinney, Tex., July 27, 1945; d. Leland Howell and Grace Laverne (Stinson) Robinson; m. Jesse Eugene Morris, July 18, 1964; children: Jesse III, Susan, John. BBA in Acctg., So. Meth. U., 1974, JD, 1978. Bar: Tex. 1979, U.S. Dist. Ct. (no. dist.) Tex. Acct. Electronic Data Systems Corp., Dallas, 1975; assoc. atty. Dresser Industries, Inc., Dallas, 1978-81, staff atty., 1981-83, corp. atty., 1983-86, asst. sec., 1984-90, sr. atty. corp. adminstrn., 1986-87, corp. counsel, 1987—, sec., 1990—, v.p., 1994—. Trustee Plano (Tex.) Ind. Sch. Dist., 1979-91, 93-94, pres., 1980-85, sec., 1986-91; bd. dirs. Plano Futures Found., Inc., 1992—, pres., 1992-93. Mem. ABA, AICPA, Tex. State Bar, Dallas Bar Assn., Tex. Soc. CPAs, Am. Soc. Corp. Secs. (mem. securities law com. 1988—, proxy system com. 1990-93, exec. steering com. 1993-94, budget com. 1993—, chmn. 1995—, bd. dirs. 1991-94, chmn. mem. com. Dallas chpt. 1986, treas. 1987, v.p. 1988, pres. 1989), Am. Corp. Counsel Assn. (corp. and securities law com. 1991—), SMU Law Rev. Corp. Counsel Symposium (bd. advisors 1996—). Methodist. Home: 1718 14th Pl Plano TX 75074-6404 Office: Dresser Industries Inc 2001 Ross Ave Box 718 Dallas TX 75221-0718

MORRIS, RUSTY LEE, architectural consulting firm executive; b. Glenwood Springs, Colo., Nov. 28, 1940; d. Raymond M. and Raylene Pearl Marie (Hendrick) Morris; m. Robert W. Sosa, Nov. 20, 1995; children: Thomas John, Michael Joseph (dec.), Michelle Renee Bentley. Student, York Christian Coll., 1974-75, U. Nebr., 1975-76, Mesa State Coll., 1992-95; BS in Orgnl. Mgmt. summa cum laude, Colo. Christian U., 1996, postgrad., 1996—. Specialist comm. security Martin-Marietta Corp., Larson AFB, 1962-63; communications security specialist classified def. project Boeing Aerospace Div., Larson AFB, Wash., 1963-64; with F.W. Sickles div. Gen. Instrument Corp., Chicopee, Mass., 1965-68; adminstr. judicial affairs J. Arthur Hickerson, Judge, Springfield, Mass., 1969-71; researcher Mont. United Indian Assn., Helena, 1970-72; adminstrv. asst. Vanderbilt U. Hosp., Nashville, 1980-82; paid bus. supr. Sears Svc. Ctr., Grand Junction, Colo., 1987-89; founder, chief exec. officer Vast Spl. Svcs., Grand Junction, 1988—; courier U.S. Census Bur., Grand Junction, 1990; spl. program coord. Colo. Dept. Parks and Recreation, Ridgway, 1990-91; acad. athletic program founder, coord. Mesa State Coll., 1992-93, math. and sci. rep., student govt., 1992—, athletic coun., 1993—, student health ctr. com., 1993—, faculty search com., 1993; founder, CEO Rolling Spokes Assn.; world cons. on archtl. contracts for structural and/or outdoor recreational facilities. Author: Abuse of Women with Disabilities, 1996. Vol. Easter Seals Soc., 1964-67, vol. instr. Adult Literacy Program, 1984-87; vol. T.V. host Muscular Dystrophy Assn. Am., 1975-94; bd. dirs. Independent Living Ctr., 1985-87, Handicap Awareness Week, 1989, trails com. Colo. State Parks and Outdoor Recreation, 1988—; condr. seminars Ams. With Disabilites Act, 1989—; cons. Bur. Reclamation, 1988—, Bur. Land Mgmt., 1989—; staff trainer Breckenridge Outdoor Recreation Ctr., 1989-90; emergency svcs. officer Colo. Civil Air Patrol, Thunder Mountain Squadron, 1989—; bd. dirs. Handicap Awareness, 1989; dir. com. Colo. State Trails Commn., 1989-90; mem. Dem. Nat. Com., 1991—; dist. com. Grand Junction Sch. Dist., 1992—; mem. Restore the Com., Avalon, 1993—; bd. dirs., presenter No. Colo. chpt. Colo. Orgn. of Victim Assistance; with victim assistance Mesa County Sheriff's Dept., 1993—. Recipient Hometown Hero award, 1993. Mem. AAUW, Internat. Platform Assn., Handicap Scholarship Assn. (bd. dirs. 1994, award 1993), Nat. Orgn. Victim Assistance (presenter 1988—), Nat. Coun. Alcoholism and Drug Abuse (vol. 1987—), Mother's Against Drunk Driver's (bd. dirs. Mesa County chpt., v.p. 1985—), Concerns of Policy Survivors, Club 20 of Western Colo. (mem. com. status), Great Outdoor Colo., Grand Junction C. of C., Grand Junction Symphony, Mus. Western Colo., Mesa State Coll. Geology Club, Toastmasters (Able Toastmaster, winner speech contests 1985-87). Home and Office: Vast Spl Svcs 612 N 15th St Grand Junction CO 81501-4422

MORRIS, SHARON LOUISE STEWART, former day care provider; b. Washington, Feb. 9, 1956; d. George Arthur Jr. and Shirley Ann (Dickinson) S.; m. Brian Stanley Morris, Feb. 9, 1979; children: Jessica Kristin, Krystle Maria. BS, Atlantic Christian Coll., Wilson, N.C., 1978. Cert. tchr. elem. edn. and math., N.C. Cashier Safeway Fin., Wilson, 1980-81, Provident Fin., Wilson, 1981-85; mktg. svc. mgr. Beneficial of N.C. Inc., Wilson, 1985-91; ind. carrier Wilson Daily Times, 1991-94; care provider Crestview Day Sch., Wilson, 1994-95; EMT Wilson Meml. Hosp., Elm City, N.C., 1996—; agt. Cen. Nat. Life Ins., Wilson, 1988-91, Olde Republic, 1990. Notary pub. State of N.C., 1986—. Democrat. Methodist. Home: 1201 Herring Ave NE Wilson NC 27893-3319

MORRIS, SYLVIA MARIE, university official; b. Laurel, Miss., May 6, 1952; d. Earlene Virginia (Cameron) Hopkins Stewart; m. James D. Morris, Jan. 29, 1972; children: Cedric James, Taedra Janae. Student, U. Utah, 1970-71. From adminstrv. sec. to adminstrv. mgr. mech. engring. U. Utah, Salt Lake City, 1972—. Mem. Community Devel. Adv. Bd., Salt Lake City, Utah, 1984—; nom. chmn. and del. to Dem. Mass Meeting, 1988. Recipient Presdl. Staff award, 1994. Mem. NAACP, NAFE, Consortium Utah Women in Higher Edn. Baptist. Home: 9696 Pinebrook Dr South Jordan UT 84095 Office: U Utah 3209 MEB Mech Engr Dept Salt Lake City UT 84112

MORRIS ARCHINAL, GRETCHEN SUZANNE, transportation executive, consultant; b. Detroit, May 8, 1963; d. Richard Frederic and Betty Jean (McNaughton) M.; m. Thomas O. Archinal, Nov. 30, 1991; 1 child, Margaret Kelly. BA, U. Mich., 1985; postgrad., Ctr. for Creative Studies, 1987. Account exec. JL Communications, St. Clair Shores, Mich., 1985-87, sr. account exec., 1987-88; pres. Metro Messenger, Grosse Pointe Woods, Mich., 1988—; owner M Graphics, Grosse Pointe Woods, 1988—; real estate agt. R.G. Edgar & Assocs., Grosse Pointe Farms, 1981-88, cons., 1988—; cons. Mack Ave USA, Grosse Pointe, 1988—. Mem. Hill Assn., Grosse Pointe, 1989—; bd. dirs. Mack Ave USA, 1988-89. Mem. Metro E. C. of C., Grosse Pointe Theatre. Republican. Lutheran. Home: 420 Psc 117 APO AE 09080-9998 Office: Metro Messenger Inc 18720 Mack Ave Ste 230 Grosse Pointe MI 48236-2923

MORRISON, ANN MARIE, systems specialist, electronic data processing specialist; b. Grants Pass, Oreg., Mar. 29, 1944; d. Wilbur Lill and Esther Elaine Groner; m. William Charles Hess, July 25, 1969; children: David William Hess, William Albert Hess. BSEE, BS in Math., Oregon State U., 1968. Engr. Lawrence Livermore Lab., Livermore, Calif., 1968-69; mgr., owner RBR Scales, Inc., Anaheim, Calif., 1969-84; lead engr. Rockwell Internat., Seal Beach, Calif., 1984-86, '87-88; software engr. Hughes Aircraft Co., Fullerton, Calif., 1986-87; sr. engr. Logican Eagle Tech., Inc., Eatontown, N.J., 1988-91; owner Holistic Eclectic Software Svc., Orange, Calif., 1991-93; database adminstr. Jacobs Engring Group, 1993—. Active Calif. Master Chorale, Santa Ana, 1990-92. Mem. IEEE, Am. Soc. Quality Control, Phi Kappa Phi, Eta Kappa Nu, Tau Beta Pi. Lutheran. Office: JEG/WSSRAP 7295 Hwy 94 S Saint Charles MO 63304

MORRISON, CONSTANCE FAITH, state legislator, realtor; b. Washington; d. Graham Edward and Cora E. (Smith) Wilson; m. George H. Morrison, May 14, 1955; 4 children. AA, Normandale C.C., 1980. Photojournalist Dakota County Tribune, 1970-76; pub. affairs writer, pub. info. coord. Ind. Sch. Dist. 191, 1976-80; ind. realtor, 1980—; mem. I-R caucus Minn. Ho. of Reps., 1986-94; sec.-treas. I-R caucus, 1993-94; mem. Minn. Ho. of Reps., 1986-94. Mem. Burnsville City Coun., 1977-82; mayor City of Burnsville, 1982-86, chairwoman chem. health com., 1987-92; bd. dirs. Minn. League Cities, 1983-86, Mpls. Area United Way, 1988—, Minn. Citizens League Bd., 1995—, Dakota County Libr. Bd., 1995—, Dakota County Planning Com., 1995—; chair adminstrv. bd. Grace United Meth. Ch., Burnsville, 1986-90, 95—; co-chairwoman com. to Elect Rep. Women, St. Paul, 1987-91. Mem. Burnsville C. of C., Rotary. Home: 909 W 155th St Burnsville MN 55306-5405

MORRISON, DEBORAH JEAN, lawyer; b. Johnstown, Pa., Feb. 18, 1955; d. Ralph Wesley and Norma Jean (Kinsey) Morrison; m. Ricardo Daniel Kamenetzky, Sept. 6, 1978 (div. Nov. 1991); children: Elena Raquel, Julia Rebecca. BA in Polit. Sci., Chatham Coll., 1977; postgrad., U. Miami, Fla., 1977-78; JD, U. Pitts., 1981. Bar: Pa. 1981, Ill. 1985. Legal asst. Klein Y Mairal, Buenos Aires, Argentina, 1978-79; legal intern Neighborhood Legal Svcs., Aliquippa, Pa., 1980-81; law clk. Pa. Superior Ct., Pitts., 1981-84; atty. John Deere Credit Co., Moline, Ill., 1985-89; sr. atty. Deere & Co., Moline, Ill., 1989—. Mem. ABA, Pa. Bar Assn., Phi Beta Kappa, Order of the Coif. Democrat. Mem. United Methodist. Office: Deere & Co John Deere Rd Moline IL 61265

MORRISON, DIANNE ROSE, educator; b. La Crosse, Wis., Jan. 21, 1947; d. Frank D. Mader and Dorothy C. Eden; m. John T. Morrison, July 12, 1969; children: Matthew M., Ryan P. BS, Winona State U., 1964; MBA, U. Wis., LaCrosse, 1987. cons. Tchr. Aquina H.S., 1969-75, Western Wis. Tech. Coll.; asst. prof. Winona U., St. Mary's Coll.; instr. U. Wis., LaCrosse. Contbr. articles to profl. jours. C. of C. coord. Vol. Income Tax Assistance. Grantee U. Wis. Mem. Inst. Mgmt. Accts. Office: U Wis North Hall 406-F La Crosse WI 54601

MORRISON, ELLEN M., writer, researcher; b. Marysville, Calif., Apr. 17, 1954; d. Louis Arch and Mildred Claire (Hansen) Morrison; m. Kenneth William Lann, Jun. 26, 1976; 1 child, Mallory. BA, UCLA, 1977; MA, U. Chgo., 1982, PhD, 1979-87. Rsch. asst. U. Chgo., 1980-82, rsch. analyst, 1982-84; project dir. Northwestern U., Evanston, Ill., 1984-87; postdoctoral fellow U. Calif., San Francisco, 1988-90; program dir. Inst. for the Future, Menlo Park, Calif., 1990-95; author San Carlos, Calif., 1995—. Co-author: Strategic Choices For America's Hospitals (book of the year 1990), 1990; Contbr. articles to profl. jours. Mem. NOW, Amnesty Internat., Greenpeace. Democrat. Home and Office: 142 Plymouth Ave San Carlos CA 94070-1621

MORRISON, GLADYS MAE, pilot training firm executive; b. Balmorhea, Tex., Jan. 5, 1928; d. Edgar Henry and Alice Vivian (Totter) Walk; m. James Martin Morrison, Nov. 25, 1957 (dec. June 1988). Cert. master aviation instr. Pntr., mgr. Davis Flying Svc., Concord, Calif., 1946-56, Desert Air Oasis, Thermal, Calif., 1957-62; asst. mgr. flight dept. Beechcraft West, Van Nuys, Calif., 1962-64; dir. publs. Fowler Aeronautics, aviation textbook pubs., Burbank, Calif., 1964-65; owner-mgr. Aviation Tng., Prescott, Ariz., 1965—; chief-pilot North-Aire, Inc., Prescott, 1974-86, pres., 1988—, bd. dirs.; instr. FAA approved flight engring. sch. Fowler Aeronautics, Burbank, 1964-65. Author aviation text books; contbr. articles to newspapers and mags. Named Nat. Flight Instr. of Yr. FAA, 1982, FAA Western-Pacific Flight Instr. of Yr., 1982, Ariz. Flight Instr. of Yr. FAA, 1982; recipient Cert. of Recognition, Fedn. Aero Nautique Internat., Paris, 1982. Mem. Aircraft Owner & Pilot Assn. (Master Flight Instr. award 1983), Nat. Assn. Flight Instrs. (Flights Inst. of Yr. 1982), Ninety-Nines, Inc., Silver Wings Fraternity, Alpha Eta Rho (hon.). Republican. Office: North-Aire Inc Prescott Mcpl Airport 6500 Maccurdy Dr Ste 7 Prescott AZ 86301-6135

MORRISON, HARRIET BARBARA, education educator; b. Boston, Feb. 23, 1934; d. Harry and Harriet (Hanrahan) M. BS, Mass. State Coll., Boston, 1956, MEd, 1958; EdD, Boston U., 1967. Elem. tchr. Arlington (Mass.) Pub. Schs., 1956-67, U. Mass., summer 1967; asst. prof. No. Ill. U., De Kalb, 1967-71, assoc. prof. edn., 1971-85, prof. edn., 1985—. Author book The Seven Gifts, 1988; editor Vitae Scholasticae. Mem. ASCD, Am. Ednl. Studies Assn., Philosophy of Edn. Soc., Midwest Philosophy Edn. Soc., Ill. Assn. Supervision and Curriculum Devel., Pi Lambda Theta. Home: 834 S 8th St De Kalb IL 60115-4551 Office: No Ill U Coll Edn De Kalb IL 60115

MORRISON, HELENA GRACE, guidance counselor; b. Neillsville, Wis., Aug. 20, 1957; d. Harold Allen and Nettie Stella (Schafer) Freedlund; m. William James Morrison, Sept. 11, 1981; 1 child, Meghan Marie. BS, U. Wis., Stevens Point, 1980; MEd, Nat. Louis U., Evanston, Ill., 1990; cert., Western Ky. U., 1994, postgrad. Cert. guidance counselor; cert. tchr. Tchr. grades 2 through 3 Pittsville (Wis.) Elem. Sch., 1980-82; tchr. grade 2 Vernon Parish Schs., Leesville, La., 1987-88; tchr. grade 3 Dept. Def. Dependant Schs., Vogelweh, Germany, 1989-92; student svcs. specialist, tchr. gifted edn. LaRue County Schs., Hodgenville, Ky., 1993—, gifted coord., 1995—; leader grade 3 team Vogelweh Elem. Sch., 1990-92; editor Hodgenville Elem. Sch. Yearbook, editor HES News, 1993—. Statistician Kaiserslantern Softball, Vogelweh, 1991; coach girls softball LaRue County Softball, Hodgenville, 1994. Mem. ASCD, Nat. Geog. Soc., Ky. Assn. for Gifted Edn., Ky. Counseling Assn. Home: 3220 Dangerfield Rd Hodgenville KY 42748-9223 Office: Hodgenville Elem Sch 208 College St Hodgenville KY 42748-1404

MORRISON, JENNIFER ANN, lawyer, oil company executive; b. Providence, Feb. 22, 1956; d. John Stephen McKnight and Mary Morrison. BA in Polit. Sci., Oakland U., 1976; JD, U. Okla., 1980. Bar: Okla. 1980, Tex. 1988, U.S. Ct. Appeals (5th, 10th, 11th and D.C. cirs.) 1981, U.S. Supreme Ct 1983, U.S. Ct. Appeals (8th cir.) 1985, U.S. Dist. Ct. (no. dist.) Okla. 1986, U.S. Dist. Ct. (so. dist.) Tex. 1994. Atty. Phillips Petroleum Co., Bartlesville, Okla., 1980-88; counsel BP Exploration Inc., Houston, 1988-90; v.p., gen. counsel, sec. Tex./Con Oil & Gas Co., Houston, 1990-92, Plains Mktg. and Transp., Inc., Houston, 1992-93; pvt. practice Houston, 1993—; apptd. by gov. to Commn. on Oil and Gas Practices, 1990-91; mem. legal subcom. Offshore Operators, 1983-87. Editor U. Okla. Law Rev., 1978-80. Pres., adv. council Retired Sr. Vol. Program, Bartlesville, 1982-88; bd. dirs. Bluestem Girl Scout Council, Bartlesville, 1982-88, SunFest, Inc., Bartlesville, 1984-88. Mem. ABA (royalty task force 1983), Houston Bar Assn. (com. law and the arts 1995—), Okla. Bar Assn., Fed. Energy Bar Assn. (commn. on devel. of fed. lands 1989-90, sec. Houston chpt. 1991-92, pres. Houston chpt. 1992-93, vice chair environ. com. 1992-93), Am. Petroleum Inst. (royalty task force 1983-88), Ind. Petroleum Assn. Am. (natural gas com. 1990-93), Tex. Ind. Petroleum Assn., Natural Gas Supply Assn. (legal subcom. 1988-92), Tex. Mid-Continent Oil and Gas Assn. (legal subcom. 1990-92), Am. Corp. Counsel Assn. (chair Houston chpt. oil and gas com. 1992-93, asst. chair litigation com. 1991-92), Nat. Assn. Women Bus. Owners (sec. Houston chpt. 1995—), Houston Bus. Coun., Pilot Internat. (coord. 1985-88), Phi Alpha Delta. Office: 8705 Katy Freeway Ste 105 Houston TX 77024

MORRISON, MARCY, state legislator; b. Watertown, N.Y., Aug. 9, 1935; m. Howard Morrison; children: Liane, Brenda. BA, Queens Coll., 1957; student, Colo. Coll., U. Colo. Mem. Colo. Ho. of Reps., awd, 1992—; mem. judiciary, health, environ., welfare and instns. coms. Mem. Manitou Springs (Colo.) Sch. Bd., 1973-83, pres., 1980-82, County Park Bd., 1976-83, State Bd. Health, 1985-93, pres., 1988-90, Mountain Scar Commn., 1989, Future Pub. Health, 1989-90, Health Policy Commn., 1990-92; commr. El Paso County, 1985-92, chmn., 1987-89; active Citizens Goals, United Way. Named Outstanding Sch. Bd. Mem., Pikes Peak Tchrs. Assn., 1978, Woman of Spirit, Penrose-St. Francis Hosp. Sys., 1991. Mem. LWV, Health Assn. Pikes Peake Area, Women's Edn. Assn., El Paso Mental Health Assn. Republican. Jewish. Home: 302 Sutherland Pl Manitou Springs CO 80829-2722 Office: Colo Ho of Reps State Capitol Denver CO 80203*

MORRISON, MARGARET LOUISE, artist; b. Atlanta, Oct. 6; d. Watson Russell Sr. and Eva (Darnell) Morrison. BS in Edn., U. Ga., 1970. Cert. tchr., Ga. Tchr. City of Decatur, Ga., 1970-71; supr. KPMG Peat Marwick, Atlanta, 1971—. Exhbns. include Coastal Ctr. for the Arts, St. Simons Island, Ga., Gallery One, St. Simons Island, Coastal Ctr. for the Arts, Jekyll Island, Ga., Decatur (Ga.) Arts Alliance, Acad. Midi, Paris, The Glynn County Art Assn. Royal patron Hutt River Province, Queensland, Australia, 1995; active High Mus. Art, Atlanta, 1989—; bd. govs. Internat. Biog. Ctr.; adv. bd. Am. Biog. Inst. Fellow Acad. Midi (hon.); mem. NAFE, AAUW, Internat. Platform Assn., Nat. Mus. Women in Arts, Allied Artists of Ga., Pen and Ink, U. Ga. Alumni Soc. Office: KPMG Peat Marwick 303 Peachtree St Ste 2000 Atlanta GA 30308

MORRISON, MARTHA KAYE, photolithography engineer; b. San Jose, Calif., Oct. 5, 1955; d. Myrle K. and Arthena R. Morrison; 1 child, Katherine A. AA, West Valley Coll., Saratoga, Calif., 1978. Prodn. worker Signetics Co., Sunnyvale, Calif., 1973-75, equipment engr., 1976-78, 79-80, prodn. supr., 1978-79; expediter Monolithic Memories, Sunnyvale, 1975-76; photolithography engr. KTI Chems., 1980-81; founder, chief engr., CEO Optalign, Inc., Livermore, Forest Ranch, Calif., 1981—; participant West Valley Coll. Tennis Team # 1 Singles and Doubles, 1976-78; regional profl. ranking NCTA Opens Singles/Doubles, 1982-85, 93, 94, 95, rankings 15-20 singles/#2-#8 doubles; instr. tennis Chico Racquet Club, 1994, Butte Creek Country Club, 1995—; participant exhbn. tennis match with Rosie Cosals and Billie Jean King, 1994. Dir. benefit Boys & Girls Club of Chico. Named Champion Chico Open Finalist Woodridge Open, 1994, 1993 #2 NCTA Women's Open Doubles, Doubles #3, 1994, Tracy Open, 1996. Mem. USPTA (cert.), Tennis Profl. Chico Racquet Club, Butte Creek Country Club. Office: PO Box 718 Forest Ranch CA 95942-0718

MORRISON, MICHELLE WILLIAMS, nursing educator, administrator, author; b. Reno, Nev., Feb. 12, 1947; d. Robert James and Dolores Jane (Barnard) Williams; m. Harrison Russell Morrison, Dec. 29, 1974. BSN, U. Nev., Reno, 1973; M Health Svc., U. Calif., Davis, 1977. RN, Oreg. Staff nurse VA Hosp., Reno, 1973-77; family nurse practitioner Tri-County Indian Health Svc., Bishop, Calif., 1977-78; instr. nursing Roque C.C., Grants Pass, Oreg., 1978-82; psychiat. nurse VA Hosp., Roseburg, Oreg., 1982; dir. edn. Josephine Meml. Hosp., Grants Pass, 1983-84; geriatric nurse practitioner Hearthstone Manor, Medford, Oreg., 1984-86; chmn. nursing dept. Roque Community Coll., Grants Pass, Oreg., 1986-89; prin. Health and Ednl. Cons., Grants Pass, 1989—; dir. nursing Highland House Nursing Ctr., Grants Pass, 1990; bd. dirs. Tri-County Indian Health Svc.; cons. for nursing svcs. in long term care facilities. Author: Professional Skills for Leadership; contbr.: Fundamental Nursing: Concepts and Skills. Mem. Josephine County Coalition for AIDS, Grants Pass, 1990. With USN, 1965-69. Mem. NAFE, Nat. League Nursing, Oreg. Ednl. Assn., Oreg. State Bd. Nursing (re-entry nursing com. 1992-93). Office: PO Box 89 Williams OR 97544-0089

MORRISON, PATRICE B., lawyer; b. St. Louis, July 8, 1948; d. Frank J. and Loretta (S.) Burgert; m. William Brian Morrison, Aug. 12, 1969; 1 child, W. Brett. AB, U. Miami, 1971, MA, 1972; JD, Am. U., 1975; LLM in Taxation, Georgetown U., 1978. Bar: Fla. 1975, D.C. 1977, N.Y. 1983. Atty. U.S. Dept. Treas., Washington, 1975-79; atty., ptnr. Nixon Hargrave Devans & Doyle, LLP, Palm Beach County, Fla., 1980-89, Nixon, Hargrave, Devans & Doyle, LLP, Rochester, N.Y., 1989—; bd. dirs. Cloverwood Devel., Inc. Author: (jour.) The Practical Lawyer, 1986, 91. Bd. dirs. Alzheimer's Assn., Rochester, 1990-95, Nat. Women's Hall of Fame, 1990-92; mem. Rochester Women's Network; mem. exec. com. Estate Planning Coun. Rochester, 1992-95. Mem. Am. Immigration Lawyers Assn. Republican. Office: Nixon Hargrave Devans & Doyle LLP PO Box 1051 Clinton Sq Rochester NY 14603

MORRISON, PATRICIA KENNEALY, author; b. N.Y.C., Mar. 4, 1946; d. Joseph Gerard and Genevieve Mary (McDonald) Kennely; m. James Douglas Morrison, June 24, 1970 (dec. July 3, 1971). Student, St. Bonaventure U., 1963-65; BA, Harpur Coll., 1967. Editor Jazz & Pop Mag., N.Y.C., 1968-71; sr. copywriter RCA Records, N.Y.C., 1971-73; copy dir. CBS Records, N.Y.C., 1973-79, New Sch., N.Y.C., 1979-81; author, pres./CEO Lizard Queen Prodns., Inc., N.Y.C., 1984—. Author: (novels) The Copper Crown, 1984, The Throne of Scone, 1986, The Silver Branch, 1988, The Hawk's Gray Feather, 1990, The Oak Above the Kings, 1994, The Hedge of Mist, 1996; (autobiography) Strange Days: My Life With and Without Jim Morrison, 1992; contbr.: Rock She Wrote, 1995; tech. advisor, actress The Doors, 1990-91. Mem. Mensa, Ordo Supremus Militaris Templi Hierosolymitani (dame, preceptor 1995—, knight protector 1995—). Democrat. Office: Lizard Queen Prodns Inc 151 1st Ave Ste 120 New York NY 10003

MORRISON, PORTIA OWEN, lawyer; b. Charlotte, N.C., Apr. 1, 1944; d. Robert Hall Jr. and Josephine Currier (Hutchison) M.; m. Alan Peter Richmond, June 19, 1976; 1 child, Anne Morrison. BA in English, Agnes Scott Coll., 1966; MA, U. Wis., 1967; JD, U. Chgo., 1978. Bar: Ill. 1978. Ptnr. Rudnick & Wolfe, Chgo., 1978—, also chmn. real estate dept., mem. governing policy com.; lectr. in field. Bd. dirs. Girl Scouts of Chgo. Mem. ABA, Am. Coll. Real Estate Lawyers, Chgo. Bar Assn. (real property com., subcom. real property fin., alliance for women), Pension Real Estate Assn., Chgo. Fin. Exch., Chgo. Real Estate Women. Office: Rudnick & Wolfe 203 N La Salle St Ste 1800 Chicago IL 60601-1210

MORRISON, SHELLEY, actress; b. N.Y.C., Oct. 26, 1936; d. Maurice Nissim and Hortense (Alcouloumre) Mitrani; m. Walter R. Dominguez, Aug. 11, 1973. Student, L.A. City Coll., 1954-56. Actress: (films) Interns, 1962, The Greatest Story Ever Told, 1964, Castle of Evil, 1965, Divorce, American Style, 1965, How to Save a Marriage, 1966, Funny Girl, 1967, Three Guns for Texas, 1969, Man & Boy, 1971, Blume in Love, 1972, McKenna's Gold, 1967, Breezy, 1973, People Toys, 1973, Rabbit Test, 1975, Max Dugan Returns, 1982, Troop Beverly Hills, 1988, Fools Rush In, 1996, (TV movies) Three's a Crowd, 1969, Once an Eagle, 1974, The Night That Panicked America, 1975, Kids Don't Tell, 1984, Cries From the Heart, 1994, (TV series) Laredo, 1965-67, The Flying Nun, 1966-70, First and Ten, 1987, I'm Home, 1990, The Fanelli Boys, 1990, Love, Lies and Murder, 1990, Playhouse 90, Dr. Kildare, The Fugitive, Gunsmoke, Marcus Welby, and many others, 1960-70, Man of the People, Sisters, 1991, 92, Murder She Wrote, 1992, Johnny Bago, 1993, Columbo, 1993, L.A. Law, 1994, Live Shot, 1995, Courthouse, numerous others, (stage prodns.) Pal Joey, 1956, Bus Stop, 1956, Only in America, 1960, Orpheus Descending, 1960, Spring's Awakening, 1962, over 65 other prodns., 1956-1970; prodr., writer live shots, 1975—. Condr. seminars (with husband Walter Dominquez) about Native Americans to keep traditions and ceremonies flourishing. Honored (with husband Walter Dominquez) for work with homeless City of L.A., 1985, for work during L.A. riots, 1992. Mem. SAG, AFTRA, Actors Equity Assn. Democrat.

MORRISON, SHIRLEY ANNE LYNN, purchasing agent; b. Bainbridge, Ga., Jan. 20, 1951; d. Ellis Carroll and Mary Christine (Kelley) L.; m. Garry Brooks, June 12, 1969 (div. May 1978); m. Joseph James Morrison, May 6, 1979; children: Tonya Lee, William Cody Joseph, James Derek. Student, Bainbridge Coll., 1985. Sec., bookkeeper Adams Lumber Co., Bainbridge, 1973-77; sec. to purchasing agt. City of Bainbridge, 1977-80, purchasing dir., 1980—. Mem. Nat. Inst. Govt. Purchasing, Govt. Purchasing Assn. Ga. Baptist. Office: City of Bainbridge 240 N Donalson St PO Box 158 Bainbridge GA 31718

MORRISON, SHIRLEY MARIE, nursing educator; b. Stuttgart, Ark., June 13, 1927; d. Jack Vade Wimberly and Mabel Claire (Dennison) George; m. Dana Jennings Morrison, Mar. 12, 1951 (dec. Dec. 1995); children: Stephen Leslie, Dana Randall, William Lee, Martha Ann Morrison Carson. Diploma, Bapt. Hosp. Sch. Nursing, Nashville, 1949; BSN, Calif. U., Fullerton, 1977; MSN, Calif. U., L.A., 1980; EdD, Nova Southeastern U., 1987. RN, Tex., Calif.; cert. pub. health nurse, Calif.; cert. secondary tchr., Calif. Staff nurse perinatal svcs. Martin Luther Hosp., Anaheim, Calif., 1960-77, relief 11-7 house supr., 1960-77; dir. vocat. nursing program Inst. Med. Studies, 1978-81; mem. faculty BSN program Abilene (Tex.) Intercollegiate Sch. Nursing, 1981-92, dir. ADN program, 1992—; mem. profl. adv. bd. Nurse Care, Inc., Abilene, 1988—. Mem. adv. bd. parent edn. program Abilene Ind. Sch. Dist., 1985—; active Mar. Dimes, Abilene, 1990—, Ednl. Coalition for Bob Hunter, Abilene, 1994; bd. dirs. Hospice Big Country, Abilene, 1987—. Grantee NIH, 1992. Mem. Nat. Orgn. Assn. Degree Nurses (mem. program com. 10th anniversary nat. conv.), Tex. Orgn. Assoc. Degree Nurses, So. Nursing Rsch. Soc. (rsch. presenter), Health Edn. Resource Network Abilene (founding mem., pres. elect, pres. 1995-96). Democrat. Methodist. Home: PO Box 2583 Abilene TX 79604 Office: Abilene Intercollegiate Sch Nursing 2149 Hickory St Abilene TX 79601-2339

MORRISON, SUSAN JOAN, microbiology educator; b. Boston, June 5, 1947; d. Sumner M. and Mary L. Morrison. BS, Colo. State U., Ft. Collins, 1969, MS, 1971; PhD, Fla. State U., Tallahassee, 1980. Grad. teaching and rsch. asst. Colo. State U., 1969-71; asst. scientist The Hormel Inst., U. Minn., Austin, 1971-73; grad. rsch. asst., NIEHS trainee Fla. State U., 1973-79; asst. prof. biology Coll. of Charleston, S.C., 1979—, allied health coord., acad. advisor, 1980—; coord. minor in environ. studies program Coll. of Charleston, 1993—; adj. asst. prof. Med. U. S.C., Charleston, 1994—. Contbr. articles to profl. jours. Recipient Disting. Svc. award Coll. of Charleston, 1991. Mem. Am. Soc. for Microbiology (councilor 1986-89, newsletter editor S.C. br. 1982-91, pres. S.C. br. 1991-93), Nat. Assn. Advisors for the Health Professions (so. bd. dirs. 1985-88, 91-92, 93—), S.C. Acad. Sci., Sigma Xi, Phi Kappa Phi (sec.-treas. chpt.), Omicron Delta Kappa. Office: Coll of Charleston Dept Biology 66 George St Charleston SC 29424-0001

MORRISON, TONI (CHLOE ANTHONY MORRISON), novelist; b. Lorain, Ohio, Feb. 18, 1931; d. George and Ella Ramah (Willis) Wofford; m. Harold Morrison, 1958 (div. 1964); children: Harold Ford, Slade Kevin. B.A., Howard U., 1953; M.A., Cornell U., 1955. Tchr. English and humanities Tex. So. U., 1955-57, Howard U., 1957-64; editor Random House, N.Y.C., 1965—; assoc. prof. English SUNY, Purchase, NY, 1971-72; Schweitzer Prof. of the Humanities SUNY, Albany, NY, 1984-89; Robert F. Goheen Prof. of the Humanities Princeton Univ., Princeton, NJ, 1989—; Visiting prof., Yale Univ., 1976-77, Bard Coll., 1986-88. Author: The Bluest Eye, 1969, Sula, 1973 (National Book award nomination 1975, Ohioana Book award 1975), Song of Solomon, 1977 (National Book Critics Circle award 1977, American Acad. and Inst. of Arts and Letters award 1977), Tar Baby, 1981, (play) Dreaming Emmett, 1986, Beloved, 1987 (Pulitzer Prize for fiction 1988, Robert F. Kennedy Book award 1988, Melcher Book award Unitarian Universalist Assn. 1988, National Book award nomination 1987, National Book Critics Circle award nomination 1987), Jazz, 1992, Playing in the Dark: Whiteness and the Literary Imagination, 1992, Nobel Prize Speech, 1994; editor: The Black Book, 1974, Race-ing Justice, En-Gendering Power: Essays on Anita Hill, Clarence Thomas, and the Construction of Social Reality, 1992; lyricist: Honey and Rue, 1992. Recipient New York State Governor's Art award, 1986; Washington College Literary award, 1987; Elizabeth Cady Stanton award National Organization for Women; Nobel prize in Literature Nobel Foundation, 1993. Mem. Author's Guild (council). Office: Princeton U Dept Creative Writing 185 Nassau St Princeton NJ 08544-2003 also: care Suzanne Gluck Internat Creative Mgmt 40 W 57th St New York NY 10019-4001*

MORRISSEY, CLAUDIA SUSAN, internist, public health specialist; b. Alliance, Nebr., Apr. 8, 1947; d. Thomas James and Geraldine Esther (Ekhoff) Peterson; m. Joseph Lawrence Morrissey (div.); m. Kevin Charles Conlon; children: Erin C., Bridget E., Liam T. BA in History, U. No. Iowa, 1970; premed. student, Drake U., Des Moines, 1977-78; MD, Chgo. Med. Sch., 1982; MPH, Johns Hopkins Sch. Pub. Health, 1992. Diplomate Am. Bd. Internal Medicine. Resident in internal medicine U. Iowa Hosps. and Clins., 1985; assoc. planner N.Mex. State Planning Office, Santa Fe, 1972-73; staff internist Nat. Health Svcs. Corps., Erie Family Health Ctr., Chgo., 1985-87; instr. clin. cmty. health Northwestern U., Chgo., 1985-87; practicing internist various locations, 1987-95; health and child survival fellow, repro. health advisor U.S. Agy. Internat. Devel., Washington, 1995—; bd. dirs. Orgn. Student Reps., Am. Assn. Med. Colls., 1979-80; spkr. on women's health and devel., and on health care reform, 1970—. VISTA vol., Reno, Nev., 1970-72; exec. dir. ACLU, Iowa, 1974-76. Recipient Woman of Distinction award Soroptimists Internat., 1994. Mem. APHA, Am. Med. Women's Assn. (rep. to UN 4th World Conf. on Women 1995, rep. to UN Internat. Conf. on Population and Devel. 1994), Nat. Coun. Internat. Health, NOW, Amnesty Internat., Oxfam Am., Greenpeace, Delta Omega. Office: Johns Hopkins U Health & Child Surv Program Ste 2B 103 E Mt Royal Ave Baltimore MD 21202

MORRISSEY-CABAJ, EILEEN, finance director, consultant; b. Bayshore, N.Y., Jan. 7, 1957; d. John D. and Dorothy T. (Considine) Morrissey; m. Chris R. Cabaj, May 26, 1991. BS in Acctg., SUNY, Binghamton, 1979; M in Info. Sys., NYU, 1987. CPA, N.Y., Colo. Acct. Field, Tiger, Krell & Werber, N.Y.C., 1979-81; sr. mgr. KPMG Peat Marwick, N.Y.C., 1981-91, Price Waterhouse, Santa Ana, Calif., 1991-94; dir. advanced cost mgmt. AlliedSignal, Torrance, Calif., 1994—; spkr. in field. Co-author Implementing Activity Based Management Moving from Analysis to Action, 1990 (mgmt. acctg.'s literary award 1991); contbr. articles to profl. jours. Mem. AICPAs (mem. mgmt. acctg. exec. bd. industry rep., strategic performance measures task force industry rep., benchmarking task force rep.), Inst. Mgmt. Accts. NJ. Home: 17291 Lee Cir Huntington Beach CA 92647

MORROW, CHERYLLE ANN, accountant, bankruptcy, consultant; b. Sydney, Australia, July 3, 1950; came to U.S., 1973; d. Norman H. and Esther A. E. (Jarrett) Wilson. Student, U. Hawaii, 1975; diploma Granville Tech. Coll., Sydney, 1967. Acct., asst. treas. Bus. Investment, Ltd., Honolulu, 1975-77; owner Lanikai Musical Instruments, Honolulu, 1980-86, Cherylle A. Morrow Profl. Svcs., Honolulu, 1981—; fin. managerial cons. E.A. Buck Co., Inc., Honolulu, 1981-84; contr., asst. trustee THC Fin. Corp., Honolulu, 1977-84, bankruptcy trustee, 1984-92; v.p., sec., treas. Innervation, Inc., 1989—; panel mem. Chpt. 7 Trustees dist. Hawaii U.S. Depart. Justice, 1988-91; co-chair Small Bus. Hawaii Legislative Action Com., 1990-92. Mem. Small Bus. Hawaii PAC, Lanikai Community Assn., Arts Coun. Hawaii; vol., mem. Therapeutic Horsemanship for Handicapped, program chair, 1990-92, vice chair, 1990-95, chair, 1995—; vol., mem. Small Bus. Adminstrn. Women in Bus. Com. 1987—; vol. tax preparer IRS VITA, 1990—. Recipient City and County of Honolulu award, State of Hawaii award, 1996, Women in Bus. Advocate award U.S. Small Bus. Adminstrn., 1996, Small Bus. Booster award Small Bus. Hawaii, 1996. Mem. AARP (vol. tax preparer TCE 1991—), NAFE, Australian-Am. C. of C. (bd. dir. 1985-92, corp. sec. 1986-92, v.p. 1988-92), Pacific Islands Assn. Women (corp. sec./treas. 1988-90), Pacific Islands Assn. (asst. treas. 1988—). Avocations: reading, music, dancing, sailing, gardening. Office: Innervation, Inc 145 Hekili St Ste 300 Kailua HI 96734-2804

MORROW, DEBRA D., accountant; b. Louisville, Dec. 9, 1962; d. Ernest D. and Beatrice M. (Wallace) Watkins; m. Thomas E. Morrow, June 12, 1982; children: Michael T., Robert E. BS in Accountancy, No. Ky. U., 1996. Bookkeeper New Haven Moving Equipment, Louisville, 1984-96; acct., office mgr. Mackey McNeill Mohr, PSC, Ft. Mitchell, Ky., 1996—. Active YMCA. Recipient Bus. Merit award Nat. Collegiate Bd., 1995,; All Am. scholar Nat. Scholarship Found., 1995; scholar Becker Rev. Course, 1996. Mem. Inst. Managerial Accts., Nu Kappa Alpha (bd. mem.). Republican. Home: 21 Crystal Lake Dr Taylor Mill KY 41017 Office: Mackey McNeill Mohr PSC Ste 130 211 Grandview Dr Fort Mitchell KY 41017

MORROW, ELIZABETH HOSTETTER, business owner, sculptress, museum association administrator, educator; b. Sibley, Mo., Feb. 28, 1947; d. Elman A. and Lorine (Hostetter) Morrow; married, 1970 (div. 1979); children: Jan Pawel, Lorentz Arthur. Student, William Jewell Coll., 1958-59, Colo. Coll., 1959-60, U. Okla., 1960-62; BFA, U. Kans., 1964, MFA, 1967; postgrad., U. Minn., 1965, U. Kans., 1968. Pres. E. Morrow Co., Kansas City, Mo., 1966-67; head dept. art U. Hawaii, Honolulu, 1968-69, Tarkio (Mo.) Coll., 1970-74; exec. dir. Pensacola (Fla.) Mus. Art, 1974-76; pres., owner Blair-Murrah Exhbns., Sibley, Mo., 1980—; pres. bd. trustees, chief exec. officer Blair-Murrah, Inc., 1991—; sec.-treas. Coun. for Cultural Resources, 1995—. Del. White House Conf. on Small Bus., 1986. Lew Wentz scholar U. Okla., 1960-62. Mem. AAUW, Internat. Coun. of Mus., Internat. Coun. Exhbn. Exch., Internat. Soc. Appraisers, Am. Assn. Mus., Nat. Orgn. of Women Bus. Owners, Nat. Assn. Mus. Exhibitions, Ft. Osage Hist. Soc., Friends Art, Internat. Com. Fine Arts, Internat. Com. Conservation, Internat. Sculpture Ctr., DAR, Delta Phi Delta. Republican. Home: Vintage Hill Orch Sibley MO 64088 Office: Blair-Murrah Vintage Hill Orch Sibley MO 64088 also: 7 rue Muzy, PO Box Nr 554, 1211 Geneva 6 Switzerland

MORROW, JENNIFER LEIGH See LEIGH, JENNIFER JASON

MORROW, SHARON L., English educator; b. Mobile, Ala., Mar. 5, 1943; d. Sherwin William Agee and Mildred Johnson (Jones) Dillard; divorced; children: Lori Lynn Morrow Kelley, Leigh Diane. BS, North Tex. State U., 1965; MEd, Tex. Tech. U., 1981. Tchr. Lubbock (Tex.) Ind. Sch. Dist., 1965-81, Hurst-Euless-Bedford (Tex.) Ind. Sch. Dist., 1981—; newsletter editor Ednl. Svc. Ctr. Region II, Ft. Worth, 1991-95; publ. editor IBM, Las Colinas, Tex., 1984-85. Recipient thanks to tchrs. award Apple Computer, 1990. Mem. NEA, Nat. Coun. Tchrs. English, Tex. Coun. Tchrs. English. Democrat. Methodist. Home: 1610 Creek Bank Ln Arlington TX 76014 Office: Hurst-Euless-Bedford ISD Harwood Jr High 300 Martin Dr Bedford TX 76021

MORROW, SUSAN BRIND, writer; b. Geneva, N.Y., Apr. 30, 1958; d. David Hutchison and Shirley Jean (Hodgins) Bring; m. Lance Morrow, Oct. 19, 1988. BA, Barnard Coll., 1978; MA, Columbia U., 1983. Fellw Inst. Current World Affairs, Hanover, N.H., 1988-90. Author article for Ency. of Mil. History. Fellow Explorers Club; mem. Soc. Women Geographers, Inst. Human Origins. Home and Office: RR 1 Box 214 Dover Plains NY 12522

MORROW, SUSAN DAGMAR, psychic, educator, writer, consultant; b. Harrisburg, Pa., July 10, 1932; d. William Lime and Margaret Louise (Deckard) Brubaker; m. Henry Taylor Morrow, June 9, 1952 (div. Mar. 1984); children: Quenby Anne, Christopher Brian. Student Carnegie Inst. Tech., 1950-52, U. Ariz., 1952-54, U. Calif., Berkeley Ext., 1960-72, Foothill Coll., 1980-81. Self-employed psychic, psychic tchr., Palo Alto, Calif., 1976-80, Mountain View, Calif., 1980—; medium, psychic, tchr. Seekers Quest Profl. Ctr., San Jose, Calif., 1983—; tchr. Sunnyvale Community Ctr., 1977-87; tchr. San Andreas Health Coun., Palo Alto, 1981-83; lectr. U. Calif., Berkeley, 1978, Foothill Coll., Los Altos, Calif., 1980; lectr. in field; medium, cons. in cases of mental disorientation to psychologists, Palo Alto and Mountain View, 1978—, to detectives and police in cases of missing persons, animals or property, 1983—, pvt. tutor, medium, cons. past lives, archeological information, 1990—. Contbr. articles on psychic awareness to various publs. Mem. Assn. Psychic Practitioners (co-founder, v.p. 1982-83, editor and writer newsletter 1982-83), Mountain View C. of C., Mind Being Found., Assn. Rsch. and Enlightenment, Inst. Noetic Sci., Friends of the Animals. Democrat. Methodist. Avocations: physical mediumship, painting, swimming, sailing.

MORROW, SUSAN H., interior designer; b. Bklyn., Aug. 27, 1943; d. Murray and Roslyn (Benjamin-Polsky) Chalkin; m. Robert Morrow (div.); children: Christopher, Andrew. BFA, Syracuse U., 1964; MA, NYU, 1965; cert. Post Coll. With Bagatelle Assocs., Roslyn, N.Y., 1972-74, The Wallpaper Place, Roslyn, 1974-75, Trio Designs, Huntington, N.Y., 1975-80, SHS Designs, Inc., North Hills, N.Y., 1980—; designer Designs For ..., Manhasset, N.Y., 1981—, ptnr., 1982—; pres. Wallpapers and ..., 1985—; designer Cinderella Project, Bklyn. Union Gas Urban Renewal, 1979, Human Resources, Ind. Living Project, 1982—; designer Designs For..., Roslyn, N.Y.; designer and converter Class Reunion, 1987. Designer Showcase Mansions; contbr. articles to mags. Co-chairperson budget adv. com. Roslyn Schs.; v.p. Norgate Civic Assn., Roslyn. Named Woman of Yr., Hadassah, 1974. Mem. Am. Soc. Interior Designers, 110 Assn. Profl. Women, Assn. Environ. Designers, Mensa, Internat. Platform Assn., LWV (v.p.). Home: PO Box H Sea Cliff NY 11579-0707 Office: Designs For... 24 Skillman St Roslyn NY 11576-1183

MORSE, CONNI GOODWILL, university communications educator; b. Zanesville, Ohio, May 11, 1959; d. Robert Eugene and Patricia Lou (Jones) Goodwill; m. Perry Morse, Dec. 26, 1981; 1 child, Quinn. BA in Political Sci., Am. Univ., 1981, MS in Mktg., 1987. Lectr. Am. Univ., Washington, 1988-90, Hood Coll., Frederick, Md., 1991-93, Coll. of Notre Dame, Balt., 1994-95, U. Richmond, Va., 1996—; instr. Women's Resource Ctr. U. Richmond, 1996. Mem. Am. Assn. Univ. Women (Frederick County br., pres. 1993-94), Omicron Delta Kappa. Democrat. Methodist. Home: 11324 Stonecrop Pl Richmond VA 23236

MORSE, JULIE H., banker; b. Douglas, Ga., Jan. 14, 1950; d. Frank R. and Dean (Bulkins) Hutchinson; m. Paul Caudill, Feb. 13, 1970 (div. Apr. 1973); m. Jesse R. Morse, Sept. 3, 1976; 1 child, Sheridan Rae. Degree in edn., U. Fla. Banker Family Savs. Bank., Seattle, 1983-86, Great Western Savs. Bank., Seattle, 1986-88, Security Pacific Bank, Seattle, 1989-93, U.S. Bankcorp, Seattle, 1993—. Pres. Bitter Lake Adv. Coun., Seattle, 1992—; v.p. Crown Hill C. of C., Assoc. Recration Coun., Seattle, 1995—, Luther Child Ctr. Found., Everett, Wash., 1994—. Mem. Assn. Women in Computing (pres. Puget Sound chpt. 1990-96, nat. bd. dirs. chpts. v.p. 1994—). Home: 15122 46th Pl W Lynnwood WA 98037

MORSE, KAREN WILLIAMS, academic administrator; b. Monroe, Mich., May 8, 1940; m. Joseph G. Morse; children: Robert G., Geoffrey E. BS, Denison U., 1962; MS, U. Mich., 1964, PhD, 1967; DSc (hon.), Denison U., 1990. Rsch. chemist Ballistic Rsch. Lab., Aberdeen Proving Ground, Md., 1966-68; lectr. chemistry dept. Utah State U., Logan, 1968-69, from asst. to assoc. prof. chemistry, 1969-83, prof. chemistry dept., 1983-93, dept. head Coll. Sci., 1981-88, dean Coll. Sci., 1988-89, univ. provost, 1989-93; pres. Western Wash. U., Bellingham, 1993—; mem., chair Grad. Record Exam in chemistry com., Princeton, N.J., 1980-89, Gov.'s Sci. Coun., Salt Lake City, 1986-93, Gov.'s Coun. on Fusion, 1989-91, ACS Com. on Profl. Tng., 1984-92; cons. 1993; nat. ChemLinks adv. com. NSF, 1995; bd. advisor's orgn. com. 2008 summer Olympic Games, Seattle, 1995; faculty Am. Assn. State Colls. and Univs. Pres.'s Acad., Aug. 1995; chair Coun. of Pres., 1995—. Contbr. articles to profl. jours.; patentee in field. Mem. Cache County Sch. Dist. Found., Cache Valley, Logan, 1988-93; swim coach, soccer coach; trustee First United Presbyn. Ch., Logan, 1979-81, 82-85; adv. bd. Sci. Discovery Ctr., Logan, 1993; mem. bd. dirs. United Way, Whatcom County, 1993—; exec. com. Fourth Corners Econ. Devel. Bd., 1993—; mem. policies and procedures com. AASCU, 1993—. Recipient Disting. Alumni in Residence award U. Mich., 1989. Fellow AAAS; mem. Am. Chem. Soc. (Utah award Salt Lake City and Cen. dists. 1988), Bus. and Profl. Women Club (pres. 1984-85), Philanthropic Edn. Orgn., Phi Beta Kappa, Sigma Xi, Phi Beta Kappa Assocs., Phi Kappa Phi, Beta Gamma Sigma. Office: Western Washington Univ Office of Pres Bellingham WA 98225-5996

MORSE, SUSAN EDWINA, film editor; b. Bklyn., Mar. 4, 1952; d. Rogers Watrous and Marian Edwina (Davis) M.; m. Jack Carter Richardson, July 11, 1987; 1 child, Dwight Rogers Richardson. BA, Yale U., 1974; grad., NYU, 1976. Film editor Rollins & Joffe Prodns., N.Y.C., 1976-93, Sweetheart Prodns., N.Y.C., 1994—. Editor (films) Manhattan, 1979 (Brit. Acad. Award Nomination), Stardust Memories, 1980, Arthur, 1981, A Midsummer Night's Sex Comedy, 1982, Zelig, 1983 (Brit. Acad. Award Nomination), Broadway Danny Rose, 1984, The Purple Rose of Cairo, 1984, Hannah and Her Sisters, 1985 (Brit. Acad. Award Nomination, Oscar Nomination), Radio Days, 1986 (Brit. Acad. Award Nomination), September, 1987, Another Woman, 1988, New York Stories (Oedipus Wrecks), 1989, Crimes and Midsemeanors, 1989 (Brit. Acad. Award Nomination), Alice, 1990, Shadows and Fog, 1991, Husbands and Wives, 1992, Manhattan Murder Mystery, 1993, Bullets Over Broadway, 1994, Mighty Aphrodite, 1995, Everyone Says I Love You, 1996, (TV films) The Greatest Man in the World, 1978, Don't Drink the Water, 1994; co-editor (with Dennis Virkler) Miracles, 1985; assoc. editor (with David Holden) The Warriors, 1978, (with Thelma Schoonmaker) Raging Bull, 1979. Coach youth baseball team; referee youth soccer team. Mem. Acad. Motion Picture Arts and Scis., Am. Cinema Editors.

MORSELLI, MARIAFRANCA C., botany educator, consultant; b. Milan, Aug. 17, 1922; U.S. citizen, 1961; d. Lorenzo Carpaneda and Attilia Baranzini; m. Mario Morselli, June 8, 1949; children: Olga, Giovanna, Francesca. BA in Humanities-Sci., Lyceum Parini, Milan, 1941; PhD in Natural Sci.-Botany, Milan U., 1946. Prof. natural sci. Lyceum Virgilio, Milan, 1945-47; asst. prof. Quincy (Ill.) Coll., 1947-49; rsch. assoc. N.Y. Botanical Garden, Bronx, 1960-61; rsch. asst. botany dept. U. Vt., 1964-70; instr. Italian lang. romance lang. dept. UVM, 1969-70, sr. technologist, 1970-72, rsch. assoc., 1972-78, rsch. assoc. prof., 1978-85; dir. Maple Rsch. Lab. Harvard Biol. Lab., 1978-88; rsch. prof. UVM, 1985-88, rsch. prof. emerita botany dept., 1988—; mem. adj. faculty in vitro cell biology program SUNY, Plattsburgh, 1982-85; cons. Maple Sci. and Women in Sci., 1988—; spkr. in field. Contbr. articles to profl. jours.; editor: Sugar Maple Rsch. News, 1979-88; reviewer: Can. Jour. Botany, Can. Jour. Forest Rsch., Jour. Assn. Ofcl. Analytical Chemists, USDA Forest Svc., Forestry Chronicle, Plant Sci. Bulletin, others. Recipient fellow Ctr. for Rsch. on Vt., 1980, WYCA Susan B. Anthony award to outstanding women, 1996; inductee Am. Maple Mus.

Hall of Fame, 1991. Fellow Vt. Acad. Arts and Scis.; mem. NOW, LWV, YWCA, AAAS, AAUP, AAUW (officer Burlington br., state and assn. name grant awards 1980, 84, 85, 86, 89, 96), Am. Soc. Plant Physiologists, Am. Inst. Biol. Sci., Botany Soc. Am., Nat. Women's Polit. Caucus, Older Women League, N.Am. Maple Syrup Coun. (life, award for outstanding svc. in rsch. for the maple industry 1983), Can. Soc. Plant Physiologists, Assn. Offcl. Analytical Chemists, Tissue Culture Assn., Bus. Profl. Women (One of Vt. Most Exciting Women 1985), Internat. Plant Tissue Culture Assn., Internat. Soc. Arboriculture (mem. NE chpt.), Internat. Maple Syrup Inst. (rsch. svc. award 1988), Italian Bot. Soc., Torrey Botany Club, Assn. Women in Sci., The Nature Conservancy, Vt. Natural Resources Coun., Vt. Maple Industry Coun. (maple person of 1987 award 1988), Vt. Maple Sugar Makers Assn. (maple syrup prodr. of 1987 award 1988), Vt. Coun. World Affairs, Vt. Assn. Retarded Citizens, Chittenden County Sugar Makers Assn., Women of UVM, Klifa Club, Sigma Delta Epsilon.

MORTENSEN, NANCY LEE, artist; b. Balt., Aug. 17, 1945; d. Martin Byron and Iduma (Chitwood) M. BS, East Stroudsburg Univ., 1967. Cert. tchr. freelance writer, artist. Author, reader: (book on tape) Tales from the Grave, 1994; reader: (book on tape) Serendipity, 1994. Recipient Spl. Svcs. award Small Press Writers and Artists Orgn. Mem. Genre Writers Am. (reviewer), Sci. Fiction and Fantasy Workshop, Kappa Delta Pi. Home and Office: 408 Dalewood Rd Dalton GA 30720

MORTENSEN-SAY, MARLYS (MRS. JOHN THEODORE SAY), school system administrator; b. Yankton, S.D., Mar. 11, 1924; d. Melvin A. and Edith L. (Fargo) Mortensen; BA, U. Colo., 1949, MEd, 1953; adminstrv. specialist U. Nebr., 1973; m. John Theodore Say, June 21, 1951; children: Mary Louise, James Kenneth, John Melvin, Margaret Ann. Tchr. Huron (S.D.) Jr. High Sch., 1944-48, Lamar (Colo.) Jr. High Sch., 1950-52, Norfolk Pub. Sch., 1962-63; sch. supt. Madison County, Madison, Nebr., 1963—. Mem. NEA (life), AAUW, Am. Assn. Sch. Adminstrs., Dept. Rural Edn., Nebr. Assn. County Supts., N.E. Nebr. County Supts. Assn., Assn. Sch. Bus. Ofcls., Nat. Orgn. Legal Problems in Edn., Assn. Supervision and Curriculum Devel., Nebr. Edn. Assn., Nebr. Sch. Adminstrs. Assn. Republican. Methodist. Home: 4805 S 13th St Norfolk NE 68701-6627

MORTHAM, SANDRA BARRINGER, state official; b. Erie, Pa., Jan. 4, 1951; d. Norman Lyell and Ruth (Harer) Barringer; m. Allen Mortham, Aug. 21, 1950; children: Allen Jr., Jeffrey. AS, St. Petersburg Jr. Coll., 1971; BA, Eckerd Coll. Cons. Capital Formation Counselors, Inc., Bellair Bluffs, Fla., 1972—; commr. City of Largo, Fla., 1982-86, vice mayor, 1985-86; mem. Fla. Ho. of Reps., 1986-94, Rep. leader pro tempore, 1990-92, minority leader, 1992-94; Sec. of State State of Fla., 1995—. Bd. dirs. Performing Arts Ctr. & Theatre, Clearwater, Fla.; exec. com. Pinellas County Rep. Com., Rep. Nat. Com. Named Citizen of Yr., 1990; recipient Tax Watch Competitive Govt. award, 1994, Bus. and Profl. Women "Break the Glass Ceiling" award, 1995, Fla. League of Cities Quality Floridian award, 1995, also numerous outstanding legislator awards, achievement among women awards from civic and profl. orgns. Mem. Am. Legis. Exch. Coun., Nat. Rep. Legislators Assn., Largo C. of C. (bd. dirs. 1987—, pres.), Largo Jr. Woman's Club (pres., Woman of Yr. award 1979), Suncoast Community Woman's Club (pres., Outstanding Svc. award 1981, Woman of Yr. award 1986), Suncoast Tiger Bay, Greater Largo Rep., Belleair Rep. Woman's, Clearwater Rep. Woman's. Presbyterian. Home: 6675 Weeping Willow Dr Tallahassee FL 32311 Office: Secretary of State The Capitol, PL-02 Tallahassee FL 32399-0250

MORTIMER, PAMELA S., printing company executive; b. Oil City, Pa., May 17, 1966; d. Paul D. and Joan L. (Orszulak) M. Cert. graphic artist, Jeff Tech., 1984. Gen. mgr. Pat's Printing, DuBois, Pa., 1989—; pub., editor-in-chief Poetic Justice, Penfield, Pa., 1990-95; owner, pub. Premier Pub., DuBois, Pa., 1991-94; cons., pres. DuBois Area Coun. Arts, 1992—; lit. judge Nat. PTA, 1994-96. Author: Emma, 1992, Blue Jazz Moon, 1996; contbr. poetry to jours. Campaign fundraiser YMCA, DuBois, 1995, vice chair, sr. vol. Hope for Victims Violence, DuBois, 1989-94. Named Poet of Yr World of Poetry, 1990 92; recipient Blue Ribbon award So. Poetry Assn., 1989, Merit award, 1990. Mem. NOW, Writers Revue (founder), Amnest Internat., Great Lakes Nordic Soc. Home: PO Box 46 Penfield PA 15849 Office: Pats Printing 309 W Long Ave Du Bois PA 15801

MORTON, CAROLINE JULIA, marketing executive; b. N.Y.C.; BS in Edn., U. Pa.; MBA, N.Y. U.; grad. cert. in profl. writing and effective communication, CCNY. Vice pres. mktg. mgmt. V-TEC Corp., Hopewell, Va.; pres. CMR Co., Hopewell; past cons. Advt. Women of N.Y. Mem. AAWU, Am. Mktg. Assn. (past dir.), Advt. Women of N.Y., Fedn. Profl. Bus. Women, Am. Mgmt. Assn., Women in Communications. Contbr. articles to profl. jours.

MORTON, CLAUDETTE, higher education administrator, education educator; b. Billings, Mont., Jan. 21, 1940; d. Hugh Wesley and Timey Delacy (Hopper) M.; m. Larry Roy Johnson, July 5, 1959 (div. 1987); 1 child, Eric Roy Johnson; m. George Miller, Sept. 3, 1987. BA in Drama, U. Mont., 1963, MA in Drama, 1964, EdD in Edn., 1990. Cert. tchr., adminstrv., Mont. Tchr. English, supr. Moorhead (Minn.) State U., 1964-65; sub. tchr. Missoula and Glassgow (Mont.) Sch. Dists., 1965-70; English tchr., dir. speech, drama Glasgow H.S., 1970-78; English specialist, liaison to county supr. Office of Public Instrn., Helena, Mont., 1978-86; exec. sec. and state agy. dir. Bd. of Pub. Edn., Helena, 1986-90; dir. Mont. rural edn. ctr. and western Mont. coll. assoc. prof. edn. U. Mont., Dillon, 1990-96; exec. dir. Mont. Small Schs. Alliance, Helena, 1996—; mem. rural edn. adv. com. Northwest Reginal Edn. Lab., Portland, 1991—, adv. bd. Ctr. for Study of Small and Rural Schs. U. Okla., 1993—. Editor: Visions: Healthy Living for the 21 Century, 1992; contbr. articles to profl. jours. Mem. Ch. Pub. Policy Mont. Arts Coun., 1978-86, chair Mont. Cult. Advocacy, 1982-86; state. pres. AAUW, Mont., 1988-90, theatre content ch. arts assessment planning com. Coun. of Chief State Sch. Officers. Mem. Nat. Assessment Ednl. Progress (arts assessment, oversight com.), Nat. Rural Edn. Assn. (Howard A. Dawson award for svc. 1995), Nat. Coun. of Tchrs. of English, Am. Assn. Colls. of Tchr. Educators, Am. Edn. Rsch. Assn., Mont. Alliance for Arts Edn., Delta Kappa Gamma, Phi Delta Kappa. Democrat. Congregationalist. Office: Mont Small Schs Alliance 15 Montana Ave Helena MT 59601

MORTON, HENRIETTA OLIVE, academic administrator; b. Elbert, Colo., May 22, 1937; d. Henry Oliver and Mary Irene (Wasson) Pearson; m. Wayne Wilbur Morton, Dec. 29, 1956 (div. Aug. 1987); children: Lonnie Wayne, Vicki Rae. BA in Adult Edn. Adminstrn., Loretta Heights Coll., 1984; MA in Edn., Regis U., 1995. Supr. of cmty. edn. and adminstrn. Colo. Northwestern C.C., Steamboat Springs, 1975-80; dir. of cmty. edn. Colo. Mountain Coll., Steamboat Springs, 1980—; mchts. coun. mem. Steamboat Chamber Resort Assn., 1985—, econ. devel. coun. mem. V.p., treas. Routt County Sch. Dist. RE-1, 1967-75; vice-chair Rep. Party, 1988-94, chair, 1995—. Mem. Colo. Assn. Sch. Bds. (honor roll 1975), Mountain Plains Adult Edn. Assn., Nat. Coun. Cmty. Svcs. and Continuing Edn. Republican. Office: Colo Mountain Coll 1370 Bob Adams Dr Steamboat Springs CO 80487-5029

MORTON, JOANNE MCKEAN, computer educator, consultant; b. New London, Conn., Dec. 3, 1953; d. Newton Hubbard and Lucille (Paganetti) McK.; m. Michael McNally Morton, Sept. 16, 1978. BA, Conn. Coll., 1976; MBA, Rensselaer Poly. Inst., 1985. Dept. mgr. Great Atlantic & Pacific Tea Co., Inc., Springfield, Mass., 1976-84; research asst. Hartford Grad. Ctr., Conn., 1985, adj. lectr. Sch. Mgmt., 1986—; lectr. courses in mktg. and computer applications; founder, pres. Morton & Assocs. Income Tax Svcs., 1986—; enrolled agent Dept. Treasury, 1990. Fellow Nat. Tax Practice Inst., Nat. Assn. Enrolled Agts., Conn. Soc. of Enrolled Agts. Home and Office: Morton & Assocs 19 Twin Lakes Dr Waterford CT 06385-4141

MORTON, LAUREL ANNE, elementary education educator; b. Cin., July 27, 1954; d. James William and Rosemary (Danner) M. BA in Social Sci., Calif. State U.-Stanislaus, Turlock, 1978; teaching credential, Calif. State Polytech U., Pomona, 1986; MA in Edn., Calif. State Poly. U., Pomona, 1992. Cert. tchr., Calif., Colo. Sr. loan clk. Shearson Am. Express Mortgage Corp., Newport Beach, Calif., 1978-82; adminstrv. asst. Investco Corp., Santa Barbara, Calif., 1982-83; supr. loan servicing dept. County Savs. Bank, Santa Barbara, 1983-84; comm. asst. Fuller Theol. Sem., Pasadena, Calif., 1984-85; elem. tchr. Howard Sch., Ontario, Calif., 1986-91; tchr. Bon View Elem. Sch., Ontario, 1992—, 4th grade team leader, 1993-94, track leader, 1995-96. Mem. Nat. Honor Soc., Phi Kappa Phi, Zeta Tau Alpha. Home: 1919 Stonehouse Rd Sierra Madre CA 91024-1409 Office: Bon View Elem Sch 2121 S Bon View Ontario CA 91761-4408

MORTON, LINDA, mayor; b. Dec. 7, 1944; married; 2 children. BA with honors, U. Nebr., 1966. Lic. real estate broker. Tchr. Sunnyvale (Calif.) Elem. Sch., 1967-69, Jefferson County (Colo.) Sch. Dist., 1966-67, 69-70; real estate agt. Crown Realty, Lakewood, Colo., 1979-82, Van Schaack & Co., Lakewood, 1982-83, Re-Max Profls., Lakewood, 1983-91. Mem. city coun. City of Lakewood, 1981-91, mayor, 1991—; chair Denver Metro Mayors Caucus; appts. by Gov. to Blue Ribbon Panel on State Transp. Needs, 1995; represented Lakewood on Bd. Denver Regional Coun. of Govts., from 1981, chair, 1986-87; chair Jefferson City C. of C., 1989-90; apptd. by Gov. Colo. to Met. Air Quality Coun., 1985; bd. dirs. Nat. Assn. Regional Coun. Govts., 1986-90, CML, 1993—. Office: City of Lakewood 445 S Allison Pky Lakewood CO 80226-3106

MORTON, MALVIN, social welfare administrator, consultant; b. Temeha, Tex., June 24, 1906; d. Charles Newton and Bessie Howell (Warner) M. MA in Social Svcs., U. Pitts., 1945. Caseworker Fed. Emergency Relief Adminstrn., Ft. Worth, 1933-35; program dir. YWCA, Greensboro, N.C., 1935-40; dir. teenage girls program YWCA, Indpls., 1940-43; social work cons. Community Chest Welfare Fedn., Pitts., 1945-47; pub. rels. dir. United Charities, Chgo., 1947-52; exec. dir. Chgo. Fedn. of Settlements & Neighborhood Ctrs., Chgo., 1952-61; publs. dir. Am. Pub. Welfare Assn., Chgo., 1961-71; dir. communications Florence Crittendon Assn. of Am., Chgo., 1971-74, ret., 1974; founder, bd. dirs. Contact Chgo.; attendance internat. social welfare confs., Munich, Athens, Washington, Copenhagen, Helsinki. Editor Pub. Welfare, 1952-61. Patron Olive Branch Mission, Chgo., 1963—; founder, adviser Citizenship Coun. Greater Chgo., 1956—; exec. dir. Chgo. Mayor's Civic Com. for Jane Addams Centennial, 1960; bd. dirs. Friends of Lit., 1978—, pres. 1990-92. Recipient honors Am. Assn. S.W. with Groups, 1993, U. Pitts. Sch. Social Work, 1993, Tex. Wesleyan U., 1993. Mem. NASW (life), Am. Med. Writers Assn. (life, Chgo. chpt.), Lyric Opera Chgo., Goodman Theater Chgo., Art Inst. Chgo. Democrat. Methodist. Home: Bethany Home 4950 N Ashland Ave # 478 Chicago IL 60640-3417

MORTON, MARILYN MILLER, genealogy and history educator, lecturer, researcher, travel executive, director; b. Water Valley, Miss., Dec. 2, 1929; d. Julius Brunner and Irma Faye (Magee) Miller; m. Perry Wilkes Morton Jr., July 2, 1958; children: Dent Miller Morton, Nancy Marilyn Morton Driggers, E. Perian Morton Ethridge. BA in English, Miss. U. for Women, 1952; MS in History, Miss. State U., 1955. Cert. secondary tchr. Tchr. English, speech and history Starkville (Miss.) H.S., 1952-58; part-time instr. Miss. State U., 1953-55; mem. spl. collection staff Samford U. Libr., Birmingham, Ala., 1984-92; lectr. genealogy and history, instr. Inst. Genealogy & Hist. Rsch., Samford U., Birmingham, 1985-93, assoc. dir., 1985-88, exec. dir., 1988-93; founding dir. SU British and Irish Inst. Genealogy & Hist. Rsch. Samford U., Birmingham and British Isles, 1986-93; owner, dir. Marilyn Miller Morton Brit-Ire-U.S. Genealogy, Birmingham, also British Isles, 1994—; instr. genealogy classes Samford U. Metro Coll., 1989-94; lectr. nat. conf. Fedn. of Geneal. Socs. Contbr. articles and book revs. to profl. jours. Active Birmingham chpt. Salvation Army Aux., 1982—. Inducted into Miss. U. for Women Hall of Fame, 1952. Fellow Irish Geneal. Rsch. Soc. London; mem. Internat. Soc. Brit. Genealogy and Family History, Nat. Geneal. Soc. (mem. nat. program com. 1988—, lectr. nat. mtgs.), Assn. Profl. Genealogists, Soc. Genealogists London, Antiquarian Soc. Birmingham (sec., 2d v.p. 1982-84), DAR (regent Cheaha chpt. 1977-78), Daus. Am. Colonists (regent Edward Waters chpt. 1978-79), Nat. League of Am. Penwomen, Phi Kappa Phi (charter mem. Samford U. chpt. 1972). Home and Office: 3508 Clayton Pl Birmingham AL 35216-3810

MOSCHETTI, SYBIL IDA, artist; b. Austin, Colo., Feb. 19, 1915; d. William Thomas and Lavene Ella (Woolley) Grow; m. Ubaldo Antonio Moschetti, Aug. 15, 1942 (dec. May 1994); children: Elizabeth, Gary, Gentina. BA, U. Colo., 1936. Author: Exploring Painting, 1988, Transparent Watercolor, 1993, Best of Watercolor, 1995. Recipient Top award in watercolor Adirondacks Nat. Exhbn., Old Forge, N.Y., 1984, Top award in watercolor San Diego Watercolor Soc., 1987. Mem. Am. Watercolor Soc. (Bloomingdale award in watercolor 1981, Stroud award in watercolor 1991), Nat. Watercolor Soc., Mont. Watercolor Soc. (Silver medal in watercolor 1987), Rocky Mountain Nat. Watercolor Soc., Watercolor West (2d place in watercolor 1986), Soc. Layerists in Multi-Media. Republican. Roman Catholic. Home: 1024 Eleventh St Boulder CO 80302-7207

MOSELEY, KAREN FRANCES F., school system administrator, educator; b. Oneonta, N.Y., Sept. 18, 1944; d. Albert Francis and Dorothy (Brown) Flanigan; m. David Michael McLaud, Sept. 8, 1962 (div. Dec. 1966); m. Harry R. Lasalle, Dec. 24, 1976 (dec. Feb. 1990); 1 child, Christopher Michael; m. Kel Moseley, Jan. 22, 1994. BA, SUNY, Oneonta, 1969, MS, 1970. Cert. secondary edn. tchr., Fla., Mass., N.Y. Tchr. Hanover (Mass.) Pub. Schs., 1970-80; lobbyist Mass. Fed. Nursing Homes, Boston, 1980-84; tchr., dept. chair Palm Beach County Schs., Jupiter, Fla., 1985-95; chair of accredidation Jupiter H.S., 1990-91; Fulbright tchr., Denmark, 1994-95. Author: How to Teach About King, 1978, 10 Year Study, 1991. Del. Dem. Conv., Mass., 1976-84; campaign mgr. Kennedy for Senate, N.Y., 1966, Tsongas for Senate, Boston, 1978; dir. Plymouth County Dems., Marshfield, Mass., 1978-84; Sch. Accountability Com., 1991-95; polit. cons. Paul Tsongas U.S. Senate, Boston, 1978-84, Michael Dukakis for Gov., Boston, 1978-84. Mem. AAUW, NEA, Nat. Honor Soc. Polit. Scientists, Classroom Tchrs. Assn., Mass. Coun. Social Studies (bd. dirs. Boston chpt. 1970-80), Mass. Tchrs. Assn. (chair human rels. com. Boston chpt. 1976-80), Plymouth County Social Studies (bd. dirs. 1970-80), Mass. Hosp. Assn. (bd. dirs. Boston chpt. 1980-84), Nat. Coun. for Social Studies, Fulbright Alumni Assn. Roman Catholic. Home: 369 River Edge Rd Jupiter FL 33477-9350

MOSELEY, PAMELA DENISE, nurse, educator; b. L.A., Oct. 4, 1961; d. Harold and Patsy Ruth (Givens) M. BSN, San Jose State U., 1985; MNursing, UCLA, 1989, cert. lactation educator, 1992; postgrad., Pepperdine U., 1996—. RN, Calif.; cert. childbirth educator Am. Soc. Psychoprop ylaxis in Obstetrics. Clin. nurse, charge nurse Kaiser Found. Hosp., L.A., 1986-89; clin. nurse specialist Kaiser Permanente, L.A., 1989-93; nurse educator, clin. nurse specialist Kaiser Permanente, Bellflower, Calif., 1993—; childbirth educator Crittenton Ctr. for Young Women and Infants, L.A., 1990—; cons. ednl. program Beverly Hosp., Montebello, Calif., 1993—; instr. nursing U. Phoenix, L.A., 1993—. Vol. AIDS Project, L.A., 1993—; panel judge Nancy Susan Reynolds media awards Ctr. for Youth Advocacy, L.A., 1991-94; team mem. teen pregnancy task force Gt. Beginnings for Black Babies, L.A., 1990—; mem. perinatal adv. coun. L.A. Cmtys., 1993-96. Mem. Toastmasters (v.p. pub. rels. 1992-93), Sigma Theta Tau, Chi Eta Phi (pres. pledge club 1992—). Democrat. Home: 9781 Via Zibello Burbank CA 91504 Office: Kaiser Permanente 12200 Bellflower Blvd Downey CA 90242

MOSELEY, THERESA, guidance counselor, actress; b. Ft. Bragg, N.C., Feb. 27, 1958; d. Clarence B. and Hazel Mae (Stinney) M. BA, Ga. State U., 1988; MEd, Bowie State U., 1994; postgrad., Am. U. Receptionist Brannell Coll., Atlanta, Ga., 1981-84; red coat Continental Airlines, Newark, N.J., 1988-93; counselor U. Md., College Park, 1994; counselor, tchr. Prince Georges County Sch., Upper Marlboro, 1995—; mem. Assn. for Multi-cult. counseling and devel., 1993—, Md. Assn. for Counseling and Devel., 1993—, v.p. Montgomery County Parent Policy Coun., Rockville, Md., 1994-95. vol. Dem. Convention, Atlanta, 1988. With U.S. Army, 1976-80. Recipient Career Day Appreciation award John Burrough Elem., Washington, 1995, others. Mem. ACA, Am. Sch. Counseling Assn., Nat. Assn. for the Edn. of Young Children, Md. Assn. for Counseling and Devel., Prince Georges County Edn. Assn., AFTRA, SAG, Chi Sigma Iota. Democrat. Protestant. Home: 1131 University Blvd W Silver Spring MD 20902

MOSELEY-BRAUN, CAROL, senator; b. Chgo., Aug. 16, 1947; d. Joseph J. and Edna A. (Davie) Moseley; m. Michael Braun, 1973 (div. 1986); 1 child, Matthew. BA, U. Ill., Chgo., 1969; JD, U. Chgo., 1972. Asst. U.S. atty. U.S. Dist. Ct. (no. dist.) Ill., 1973-77; mem. Ill. Ho. of Reps., 1979-88; recorder of deeds Cook County, Ill., 1988-92; U.S. senator from Ill. Washington, 1993—; mem. fin. com., subcom. on social security and family policy, subcom. on medicare, long-term care and health ins., mem. com. on banking, housing and urban affairs, subcom. on HUD oversight and structure, subcom. on internat. fin. and monetary policy, subcom. on fin. instns. and regulatory relief. Office: US Senate 320 Hart Senate Bldg Washington DC 20510

MOSER, MARCIA J., accountant; b. Pitts., Jan. 28, 1966; d. Richard V. and Dorothy K. (Wisniewski) Wolf; m. Warren D. Moser, Dec. 14, 1991. BS in Bus. Acctg., U. Pitts., 1991. Acctg. clk. Rite-Way Tool Co., Inc., Pitts., 1985-92; accounts receivable clk. Vista Metals, Inc., McKeesport, Pa., 1992-95; cash processor Harbison-Walker Refractories Co., Pitts., 1995—. Mem. Nat. Assn. Credit Mgmt. Office: Harbison-Walker Refractories Co 600 Grant St Rect Pittsburgh PA 15219

MOSER, SUZAN ANNE, nurse, researcher, analyst; b. St. Louis, June 21, 1959; d. Mark David Sr. and Betty Jane (Ziercher) Kaskus; m. Charles Edward Moser, May 22, 1981; 1 child, Alexander Charles. Diploma in nursing, Barnes Hosp. Sch. of Nursing, 1980; BSN, SUNY, Albany, 1986; MBA, U. Minn., 1991. RN, Calif. Staff nurse pediatric cardiology unit St. Louis Children's Hosp., 1980-81; staff nurse cardiology dept. U. Mo., Columbia, 1981-83; clin. rsch. rep. Intec Systems, Inc., Pitts., 1983-85; clin. rsch. assoc. Cardiac Pacemakers, Inc., St. Paul, 1985-86, clin. programs specialist, 1986-87, mgr. clin. programs, 1988-89, clin. project mgr., 1989-90, market analyst, 1990-92, bus. analyst, 1992; dir. clin. affairs/ventricular tachycardia ablation programs Medtronic CardioRhythm, San Jose, Calif., 1992—; mem. coun. on cardiovascular nursing Am. Heart Assn., Dallas, 1988—. Author: Automatic Implantable Cardioverter Defibrillator System Evaluation, 1988; editor: (chpt. in book) Cardiac Crisis, 1984, Implantable Cardioverter-Defibrillators, 1993; contbr. articles to profl. jours. Brazil outreach nurse Redeemer Luth. Ch., Fridley, Minn., 1990. Mem. Am. Acad. Med. Adminstrs., N.Am. Pacing and Electrophysiology, Am. Heart Assn., Cardiovasc. Nursing Coun. Home: 2998 Heidi Dr San Jose CA 95132-2719 Office: Medtronic CardioRhythm 130 Rio Robles San Jose CA 95134-1813

MOSES, GLORIA JEAN, artist; b. St. Louis, Apr. 10, 1940; d. Harry and Pearl (Greenberg) Wittelstein; children: Joel Michael, Glenna Marie, Sharon Madeline. Student, Santa Monica City Coll., L.A., 1957-61, Washington U., St. Louis, 1957-61. Artist Saddle and Bridle Mag., St. Louis, 1957-61; self employed, 1961—. Exhibited works at County Mus. L.A., Long Beach Mus., 1961—, Orlando Gallery, L.A., 1987, 94, 96, Ariana Gallery, Detroit, 1994—, Valley Miller Gallery, Palm Springs, 1994—. Mem. Nat. Watercolor Soc. (signature, bd. dirs. 1982), Watercolor USA (Patron award 1980), Nat. Print Soc., Ceramic Soc. Democrat. Jewish. Office: Moses and Assocs 493 S Robertson Blvd Beverly Hills CA 90211

MOSES, PATRICIA ANN, nurse; b. Syracuse, N.Y., Jan. 24, 1960; d. Naif Elias and Mary (Mobarak) M. Grad. in nursing, Crouse Irving Meml. Hosp., Syracuse, 1982; BSN, SUNY, Utica, 1989. RN, N.Y.; cert. in med.-surg. nursing ANCC, 1991. Permanent shift charge nurse Crouse Irving Meml. Hosp., 1981-88, staff nurse, 1982—, staff nurse orientor, 1983-88, mem. speakers. bur., 1989—. Mem. Greater Baldwinsville (N.Y.) Vol. Ambulance Corps, 1978—, basic EMT, 1979-90, advanced EMT, 1991—, coord. OSHA trainer program, 1992—, mem. nominating com., 1985—, life mem., 1993—; guest speaker-instr. for emergency medicine pre-hosp. classes Onondaga C.C., 1994, 95; vol. camp nurse, 1993—. Named Vol. of the Yr. Baldwinsville Vol. Ambulance Corps, 1996. Office: Crouse Irving Meml Hosp 736 Irving Ave Syracuse NY 13210

MOSES, YOLANDA T., academic administrator; b. Los Angeles, CA; m. James F. Bawek; 2 daughters: Shana and Antonia. BS Sociology, Calif. State Coll., San Bernardino, 1968; M.A., Ph.D Anthropology, UC Riverside, 1976. Dean Coll. of Arts, prof. of soc. sci. Calif. State Polytechnic U., 1982-88; v.p. academic affairs, prof. of anthropology Calif. State U., Dominguez Hills, 1988-93; pres. City Coll. of N.Y./CUNY, 1993—. chair United Negro Coll. Fund Advisory Bd for Service Learning, mem. Women's Forum, Inc., Amer. Anthropological Assn (pres. 1995). Office: City Coll of NY/CUNY Office of the Pres Convent Ave at 138th St New York NY 10031

MOSHER, SALLY EKENBERG, lawyer; b. N.Y.C., July 26, 1934; d. Leslie Joseph and Frances Josephine (McArdle) Ekenberg; m. James Kimberly Mosher, Aug. 13, 1960 (dec. Aug. 1982). MusB, Manhattanville Coll., 1956; postgrad., Hofstra U., 1958-60, U. So. Calif., 1971-73; JD, U. So. Calif., 1981. Bar: Calif., 1982. Musician, pianist, tchr., 1957-74; music critic Pasadena Star-News, 1967-72; mgr. Contrasts Concerts, Pasadena Art Mus., 1971-72; rep. Occidental Life Ins. Co., Pasadena, 1975-78; v.p. James K. Mosher Co., Pasadena, 1961-82, pres., 1982—; pres. Oakhill Enterprises, Pasadena, 1984—; assoc. White-Howell, Inc., Pasadena, 1984—; real estate broker, 1984—; harpsichordist, lectr., 1994—. Contbr. articles to various publs. Bd. dirs. Jr. League Pasadena, 1966-67, Encounters Concerts, Pasadena, 1966-72, U. So. Calif. Friends of Music, L.A., 1973-76, Calif. Music Theatre, 1988-90, Pasadena Hist. Soc., 1989-91, I Cantori, 1989-91; bd. dirs. Pasadena Arts Coun., 1986-92, pres., 1989-92, chair adv. bd., 1992-93; v.p., bd. dirs. Pasadena Chamber Orch., 1986-88, pres., 1987-88; mem. Calif. 200 Coun. for Bicentennial of U.S. Constn., 1987-90; mem. Endowment Adv. Commn., Pasadena, 1988-90; bd. dirs. Foothill Area Cmty. Svcs., 1990-95, treas., 1991, vice chair, 1992-94, chair, 1994-95. Manhattanville Coll. hon. scholar, 1952-56. Mem. ABA, Calif. Bar Assn., Assocs. of Calif. Inst. Tech., Athenaeum, Kappa Gamma Pi, Mu Phi Epsilon, Phi Alpha Delta. Republican. Home: 1260 Rancheros Rd Pasadena CA 91103-2759 Office: 711 E Walnut St Ste 407 Pasadena CA 91101-4403

MOSHER, SUE A., computer consultant; b. Havre, Mont., Aug. 21, 1953; d. Richard B. and Malinda Grace (Simpson) Billingsley; m. Robert Allen Mosher, June 21, 1986; 1 child, Ann Maura. BA in Sociology, Coll. of William & Mary, Williamsburg, Va., 1974. Asst. music dir. Sta. WOWI-FM, Norfolk, Va., 1974-75; news dir. Sta. WNOR-AM/FM, Norfolk, Va., 1976-77; reporter, editor, writer Sta. WSOC-AM/FM, Charlotte, N.C., 1977-79; editor, writer AP Broadcast Svcs., N.Y.C., 1979-82, asst. broadcast editor, 1982-83; gen. broadcast editor AP Broadcast Svcs., N.Y.C. and Washington, 1983-85; asst. dir. adminstrn. AP Broadcast Svcs., Washington, 1985-87, asst. dir. tech. devel., 1989-94; prin. Slipstick Sys., Moscow, 1994—. Author: AP NewsDesk User's Manual, 1991, Microsoft Exchange User's Handbook, 1996; contbg. editor: Inside Windows: Networking Edition, 1994; contbr.: Spl. Edition Using Windows NT Workstation 3.51, 1996, Spl. Edition Using Windows NT Workstation 4.0, 1996. Microsoft Office Expert Solutions, 1996. Trustee, Universalist Nat. Meml. Ch., Washington, 1990-91. Mem. Radio-TV News Dirs. (data transmission guidelines com. 1986-96). Home and Office: care US Embassy Moscow PSC 77 APO AE 09721

MOSHIER, MARY BALUK, patent lawyer; b. Pitts., Aug. 20, 1905; d. Andrew and Johanna (Hlebasko) Baluk; m. Ross Warren Moshier; children: Thomas, Stephen. BA, U. Ark., 1929; postgrad., U. Chgo., 1945-46; JD, No. Ky. U., 1962. Bar: U.S. Patent Office 1944, Ohio 1962. Tchr. Gary (Ind.) Pub. Schs., 1930-35; tech. libr. Monsanto Co., Dayton, Ohio, 1936-41, patent chemist, 1942-45, agt., atty., 1949-66; patent adviser U.S. Office of Naval Rsch., San Francisco, 1948-49; patents cons., pvt. practice, 1969—. Co-author: Anydrous Aluminum Chloride in Organic Chemistry, 1941. Mem. AAAS, AAUW, NOW, Lawyers Club of Sun City, Nat. Assn. Ret. Fed. Employees, U.S. Chess Fedn., Phi Alpha Delta Legal Frat. Internat. Democrat. Episcopalian. Home and Office: 17300 N 88th Ave Apt 238 Peoria AZ 85382-3505

MOSK, SUSAN HINES, lawyer; b. Pitts., Dec. 14, 1946; d. William James and Catherine Elizabeth (Cook) Hines; m. Stanley Mosk, Aug. 27, 1982 (div. Jan. 1995). B in Music Edn., Fla. State U., 1968, M in Music Edn., 1970; JD, U. Calif., San Francisco, 1990. Bar: Calif. 1990, U.S. Dist. Ct. (no. dist.) Calif. 1990, U.S. Ct. Appeals (9th cir.) 1990. Assoc. Payne, Thompson & Walker, San Francisco, 1990-94; of counsel Knecht, Haley, Lawrence & Smith, San Francisco, 1994-95; prin. Law Offices of Susan H. Mosk, San Francisco, 1995—; commr. Jud. Nominees Evaluation Commn., 1992-96. Author/editor: Rainmaking Guide to Corporate Counsel, 1993. Mem. steering com. Women's Leadership Coun. for U.S. Senator Diane Feinstein, 1992—; chair No. Calif. Women's Cabinet for Kathleen Brown

Gubernatorial Campaign, San Francisco, 1994; co-chair fin. Willie L. Brown Mayoral Campaign, 1995. Mem. State Bar of Calif., Calif. Women Lawyers (bd. govs. 1992-94, 1st v.p. 1993-94), Queen's Bench. Democrat. Office: Law Offices of Susan H Mosk 185 Post Ste 300 San Francisco CA 94108

MOSKAL, JANINA, high technology manufacturing executive; b. Czerna, Poland, June 6, 1944; came to U.S., 1963; d. Stanislaw and Agata (Kleczek) Kot; m. Tadeusz J. Moskal, Dec. 29, 1960 (div. 1981); children: Robert R., Thomas L. Student, L.I. U., 1976-78; AAS, Nassau Community Coll., 1980. Machine operator Photocircuits Corp., Glen Cove, N.Y., 1966-70, programmer, 1970-72, supr., 1972-81, engr. process support, 1981-83, systems mgr. laser graphics, 1984-86; gen. mgr., ptnr. NC Design Corp., Williston Park, N.Y., 1983-84; systems mgr. Parlex Corp., Methuen, Mass., 1984-87; mfg. specialist Rothtec Engraving Corp., New Bedford, Mass., 1987—; owner, prin. JM Cons., Glen Cove, 1987—; organizer, instr. tech. courses and seminars, 1980-81, 1986-87. Officer Polish Nat. Home, Glen Cove, 1975-79, Polonia, Glen Cove, 1978. Republican. Roman Catholic. Office: JM Cons Co 109 Shore Rd Glen Cove NY 11542-3428

MOSKOWITZ, FRAN LEIGHT, educator; b. Bklyn., Jan. 12, 1952; d. Oscar and Louise (Vidro) Leight; m. William Alan Moskowitz, May 29, 1972 (div. 1995); children: Danielle, Magan, Lindsey. BA, Monmouth Coll.; postgrad., Fordham U. Cert. advanced hypnologist, holistic health counselor, Gestalt techniques. Creator, tchr., program dir. YWHA, Morganville, N.J., 1976-84; artistic creator, mfr., distbr. From Me to You Greeting Cards, N.J., 1984-86; writer, prodr., dir. Look At Me, Marlboro, N.J., 1986-87; creative writing tchr. Brookdale C.C., Lincroft, N.J., 1986—; creator, host Bridging Gaps Pub. Radio Brookdale C.C., Lincroft, N.J., 1986—; facilitator communications workshops, N.J., 1986—; communications cons. Step Family Assn., Red Bank, N.J., 1988; facilitator ednl. workshops Brick (N.J.) Hosp., 1995—; mem. adv. bd. Women Against Violent Encounters, N.J., 1996. Counselor Howell (N.J.) Youth and Family Svcs., 1987-88; recreational vol. Renaissance House, Morganville, 1988-89. Mem. AAUW, Am. Counseling Assn., NASW, Internat. Assn. Counselors and Therapists, New Approaches to Wellness, NOW. Home: 52 Girard St Marlboro NJ 07746

MOSKOWITZ, RANDI ZUCKER, nurse; b. N.Y.C., Oct. 19, 1948; d. Seymour and Gertrude (Levy) Zucker; R.N., Jewish Hosp. & Med. Center Sch. Nursing, 1969; BA, Marymount Manhattan Coll., 1975; MS, Hunter Coll., 1979; MBA, Columbia U., 1990; m. Marc N. Moskowitz, July 11, 1976. Gen. staff nurse neurosurgery unit, N.Y. Hosp., N.Y.C., 1969-71, sr. staff nurse Recovery Room, 1971-76, nurse coordinator utilization rev., 1976-79; health educator Office of Cancer Communications, Meml. Sloan-Kettering Cancer Center, 1979-81; adminstrv. nurse oncologist Bklyn. Community Hosp. Oncology Program, Meth. Hosp., 1981-83, grants coordinator radiotherapy dept., 1983-86; adminstr. Ambulatory Oncology Ctr., Columbia-Presbyn. Med. Ctr., N.Y.C., 1986-89; adminstr. Surg. Day Hosp., Meml. Sloan-Kettering Cancer Ctr., 1990—; Masters prof. oncology Columbia U. Sch. Nursing. Co-editor Oncology Nursing: Advances, Treatments and Trends into the Twenty-first Century; contbr. articles to profl. jours. Mem. Soc. Ambulatory Care Profl., Oncology Nursing Soc. (sec. N.Y.C. chpt. 1983-87, pres. 1988-89). Home: 446 E 86th St Apt 5-F New York NY 10028-6466 Office: Meml Sloan-Kettering Cancer Ctr 1275 York Ave New York NY 10021-6007

MOSLEY, JULIE LYNN, secondary school educator; b. Lebanon, Mo., Oct. 10, 1969; d. John Crawford and Janie Lou (Varble) Cook; m. Clay Robert Mosley, Aug. 17, 1971. BA in English and Edn., Culver-Stockton Coll., 1992; mid. sch. certification, S.W. Mo. State U., 1995. Cert. tchr. 7-12, Mo. Tchr. English, chair dept. Laclede County R.I. Sch., Conway, Mo., 1993—. Recipient 1st place short story category Quincy (Ill.) Writer's Guild, 1992. Mem. Nat. Coun. Tchrs. of English. Home: RR 1 Box 30 Phillipsburg MO 65722 Office: Laclede County RI Sch Rt 2 Box 82 B Conway MO 65632

MOSLEY, SHARON ELAINE, elementary education educator; b. Dover, Del., Aug. 10, 1968; d. Coleman Watson and Elaine Virginia (Burton) M. BS in Music Edn., Shenandoah Conservatory Music, Winchester, Va., 1989; MA in Music Edn., NYU, 1991. Lic. K-12 music tchr., N.Y. Tchr. music Longwood Jr. H.S., Middle Island, N.Y., 1990-91; tchr. elem. music East Meadow (N.Y.) Union Free Sch. Dist., 1991—, dir. cultural arts program, 1994—; mus. dir. McVey Drama Club, East Meadow, 1992—. Bassoonist Cmty. Orch. Mem. NAFE, Mus. Educators Nat. Conf., Nassau Music Educators Assn. Democrat. Methodist. Home: 150 S Ocean Ave Freeport NY 11520

MOSS, BARBARA ELLEN, executive recruiter; b. St. Louis, Nov. 16, 1947; d. Charles Monville and Virginia Belle (Poston) Schwarz; m. Merrill L. Moss, Oct. 3, 1974; children: Michelle and Jennifer. Student, Southeast Mo. State U., 1965-68, U. Mo., St. Louis, 1968-69. Exec. sec. to pres. Laura McCarthy Realtors, St. Louis, 1974-75; title abstractor Record Data Mo., St. Louis, 1976-79; dir. planning First City Equities, Seattle, 1980-88; dir. mktg. Berkeley Engrng. & Constrn., Seattle, 1988-89; owner Moss & Co., Bainbridge Island, Wash., 1989—. Mem. Valley Area Transp. Alliance, Seattle, 1988; violinist Bainbridge Island Orch. Mem. Nat. Assn. Indsl. & Office Properties (Golden Gavel 1996), Nat. Assn. Corp. Real Estate Execs., Comml. Real Estate Women, Master Builders Assn., Bldg. Owners and Mgrs. Assn. Home and Office: Moss & Company 12145 Arrow Point Loop Bainbridge Island WA 98110

MOSS, CHRISTINE JOANN, fundraiser; b. Modesto, Calif., Jan. 30, 1956; d. R.C. and Elsie Jean (Whitehead/Hass) Smallwood; m. Mitchell Curtis Berry, Jan. 7, 1978 (div. May 1988); children: Vanessa, Graham, Shannon; m. Edward Richard Moss, June 18, 1994; stepchildren: Matthew, Lindsey, Megan. Student, Calif. State U., San Bernardino, 1990. Instr. Profl. Golfers Career Coll., Murietta, Calif., 1992-94; vocat. evaluation assoc. Testing, Evaluation and Mgmt., Temecula, Calif., 1992-94; admissions rep., instr. Yorktowne Bus. inst., York, Pa., 1994-95; devel. officer Hanover (Pa.) Hosp., 1995—. Vol. allocations and spl. gifts com. United Way of York County, Hanover, 1996; vol. maj. gifts com. YMCA, Hanover, 1996. Mem. Assn. for Hosp. Philanthropy, Hanover C. of C. Republican.

MOSS, CYNTHIA, wildlife researcher; b. Ossining, N.Y., July 24, 1940; d. Julian B. and Lillian (Drion) M. BA, Smith Coll., 1962. Reporter, researcher Newsweek, N.Y.C., 1964-68; rsch. asst. elephant behavior and ecology Lake Manyara, Tanzania, 1968; asst. to vet. researchers Nairobi, Kenya, 1969; rsch. asst. Athi Plains, Kenya, 1970, Tsavo Nat. Park, Kenya, 1970; freelance journalist, 1970-71; editor Wildlife News, Washington, 1971—; co-dir. rsch. project Amboseli (Kenya) Elephant Rsch. Project, 1972—; sr. assoc. African Wildlife Found.; rsch. fellow Animal Rsch. and Consercation Ctr., N.Y. Zool. Soc. Author: Portraits in the Wild: Behavior Studies of East African Mammals, 1975, Thirteen Years in the Life of an Elephant Family, 1988; editor: Relationships and Social Structure of Some Non-human Primates, 1984. African Wildlife Leadership Found. grantee, 1975. Mem. East African Natural History Soc. Office: African Wildlife Found, PO Box 48177, Nairobi Kenya*

MOSS, ELIZABETH LUCILLE (BETTY MOSS), transportation company executive; b. Ironton, Mo., Feb. 13, 1939; d. James Leon and Dorothy Lucille (Russell) Rollen; m. Elliott Theodore Moss, Nov. 10, 1963 (div. Jan. 1984); children: Robert Belmont, Wendy Rollen. BA in Econs. and Bus. Adminstrn., Drury Coll., 1960. Registrar, transp. mgr. Cheley Colo. Camps, Inc., Denver and Estes Park, 1960-61; office mgr. Washington Nat. Ins. Co., Denver, 1960-61; sec. White House Decorating, Denver, 1961-62; with Ringsby Truck Lines, Denver, Oakland, Calif., and L.A., 1962-67, System 99 Freight Lines, L.A., 1967-69; terminal mgr. System 99 Freight Lines, Stockton, Calif., 1981-84; with Yellow Freight System, L.A., 1969-74, Hayward, Calif., 1974-77; ops. mgr. Yellow Freight System, Urbana, Ill., 1977-80; sales rep. Calif. Motor Express, San Jose, 1981; regional sales mgr. Schneider Nat. Carriers, Inc., No. Calif., 1984-86; account exec. TNT-Can., Nev. and Cen. Calif., 1986-88; mgr. Interstate-Intermodal Divs. HVH Transp., Denver, 1988-89; regional sales mgr. MNX, Inc., Northern Calif., 1989-91; dir. sales Mountain Valley Express, Manteca, Calif., 1992—; chmn. op. coun. for San Joaquin and Stanislaus Counties Calif. Trucking Assn., 1983-84; planning adv. com. Truck Accident Reduction Projects, San Joaquin County, 1987-88. Mem. Econ. Devel. Coun. Stockton C. of C., 1985-86; active Edison High Sch. Boosters, 1982-88. Mem. Nat. Def. Transp. Assn. (bd. dirs. 1986-87), Stockton Traffic Club (bd. dirs. 1982-84, Trucker of Yr.), Ctrl. Valley Traffic Club, Oakland Traffic Club, Delta Nu Alpha (bd. dirs. Region 1 1982-84, v.p. chpt. 103 1984-85, pres. 1985-86, chmn. bd. 1985-87, regional sec. 1987-88, Outstanding Achievement award 1986, 88). Methodist. Home: 455 E Ocean Blvd Apt 602 Long Beach CA 90802-4940

MOSS, MYRA ELLEN (MYRA MOSS ROLLE), philosophy educator; b. L.A., Mar. 22, 1937; m. Andrew Frank Rolle, Nov. 5, 1983. BA, Pomona Coll., 1958; PhD, The Johns Hopkins U., 1965. Asst. prof. Santa Clara (Calif.) U., 1968-74; prof. Claremont McKenna Coll., 1975—, chmn. Dept. of Philosophy, 1992-95; assoc. dir. Gould Ctr. for Humanities, Claremont, Calif., 1993-94; adv. coun. Milton S. Eisenhower Libr./Johns Hopkins U., 1994-96. Author: Benedetto Croce Reconsidered, 1987; translator Benedetto Croce's Essays on Literature & Literary Criticism, 1990; assoc. editor Special Issues; Symposia Journal of Value Inquiry, 1991, 92, 93 (Honorable Mention, Phoenix award). Dir. Flintridge (Calif.) Riding Club, 1991. Mem. Am. Philos. Assn., Am. and Internat. Soc. for Value Inquiry, Soc. for Aesthetics, Phi Beta Kappa (hon.). Office: Claremont McKenna Coll 890 Columbia Ave Claremont CA 91711-3901

MOSS, SIDNEY LOUISE GILL, county official; b. Tampa, Fla., June 29, 1943; d. Fred Bertram and Marth Louise (Braswell) Gill; m. Lewis C. Moss; 1 child, leLainya. BA in Elem. Edn., U. South Fla., 1964. Tchr. elem. Hillsborough, Palm Beach, Alachua Counties, Fla., 1964-69; job placement counselor, sr. cmty. worker Hosp. Welfare Bd. Welfare Cmty. Action Agy., Hillsborough County, Fla., 1969-75; field supr. Cmty. Act. Agy., Hillsborough County, 1977-80; mgr. Ruskin Cmty. Svc. Ctr. Social Svcs. Dept., Hillsborough County, 1980-82; asst. project dir. svcs. dept. Homemaker Svcs. Aging, Hillsborough County, 1982-84; resource program developer Health and Social Svcs. Dept., Hillsborough County, 1984-86, dir. social svcs. divsn., 1986—. Commr. Commn. for Transp. Disadvantaged, Fla., 1992-95. Mem. Fla. Assn. for Coordinated Transp. Sys. (v.p. 1992), Keystone Civic Assn. Democrat. Methodist. Home: 12834 Olive Jones Rd Tampa FL 33625 Office: Hillsborough County Govt Dept Social Svcs 601 E Kennedy 24th Fl Tampa FL 33602

MOSS, SUSAN, nurse, retail store owner; b. Youngstown, Ohio, Aug. 17, 1940; d. Jarlath G. and Sara G. (Curley) Carney; divorced; children: John P., Jerri Ann Moss Williams. Lic. nurse, Choffin Sch., 1973; AS in Am. Bus. Mgmt., Youngstown State U., 1992. Surg. scrub nurse St. Elizabeth Hosp., Youngstown, 1972-78; office mgr. Moss Equipment Co., North Jackson, Ohio, 1978-83; pvt. duty nurse Salem, Ohio, 1979—; night nurse supr. Gateways for Better Living, Youngstown, 1982-84; owner Laura's Bride and Formal Wear, Salem, 1987—; CEO Strawberry Sunshine Svcs. Co., Salem, 1994—; cons. Edith R. Nolf, Inc., Salem. Author: (novelette) Turlaleen. Water therapy aide Easter Seal Soc., Youngstown, 1970-75, bd. trustees, 1973-75; mem. Hear, Now, Denver, 1989. Mem. LPN Assn. Ohio, Bus. and Profl. Women, Youngstown State U. Alumni Club, Short Hills Lit. Soc., Beta Sigma Phi (v.p., Silver Circle award 1986, Order of the Rose 1987). Democrat. Roman Catholic. Office: Lauras Bride & Formal Wear 1271 E Pidgeon Rd Salem OH 44460-4364

MOSS, SUSAN HECHT, artist, writer; b. Chgo., May 6, 1944; d. Benjamin Franklin and Amy (Hecht) M.; m. Glen Galloway, Jan. 15, 1964 (div. Sept. 1974). BA in Art/Psychology with honors, U. Nev., 1966; MFA, Otis Art Inst., 1970. Author: Keep Your Breasts! Preventing Breast Cancer the Natural Way, 1994; contbr. poetry to profl. publs.; exhibited in permanent collections at L.A. County Mus. of Art, Skirball Mus., L.A., Laguna Mus. of Art.; exhibited David Findlay Gallery, N.Y., Albright-Knox Mus., Forum Gallery, N.Y. Mem. Cancer Ctrl. Soc. (spkr. 1996), Nat. Breast Cancer Coalition. Democrat. Jewish. Studio: 4767 York Blvd Los Angeles CA 90042 Home: 1979 Montiflora Ave Los Angeles CA 90041

MOSSBERG, BARBARA CLARKE, educational writer and speaker; b. Hollywood, Calif., Aug. 9, 1948; d. Gerard Theodore and Antonina Rose (Rumore) Clarke; m. Christer Lennart Mossberg, June 21, 1974; children: Nicolino Clarke Mossberg, Sophia Antonina Clarke Mossberg. BA, UCLA, 1970; MA, Ind. U., 1972, PhD, 1976. From asst. to assoc. prof. U. Oreg., Eugene, 1976-88, assoc. and acting dean Grad. Sch., 1984-85, dir. Am. studies, 1984-86; exec. dir. VIA Internat., Washington, 1988-93; assoc. provost and dir. external rels. Hobart and William Smith Colls., Geneva, N.Y., 1993-94; sr. fellow Am. Coun. Edn., Washington, 1993—; prof., bicentennial chair U. Helsinki, Finland, 1982-83, sr. Fulbright Disting. lectr., 1990-91; Mellon fellow, moderator, resource fellow Aspen Inst., 1984, 88, 89; U.S. scholar in residence U.S. Info. Agy., Washington, 1986-88; dir. Am. studies summer inst. Swedish Ministry of Edn. and Culture, Uppsala U., 1986, 87, 88; dir. M. R. Smith coun. scholars Am. Coun. on Edn., Washington, 1994; cons. in field. Author: Emily Dickinson, 1983 (Choice award 1983); contbr. articles to profl. jours. U.S. rep. The Lahti (Finland) Internat. Writer's Reunion, 1983, Can. Couchiching Conf., 1994; spkr. Oreg. Commn. for the Humanities, Oreg., 1983-86; adv. bd. mem., moderator The Next Stage, Washington, 1993. Rsch. grantee U. Oreg., 1979, Nat. Endowment for the Humanities, Sweden, 1980, Am. Coun. Learned Socs., U. Manchester, 1985; Disting. Inst. scholar Mt. Vernon Inst., Washington, 1994, others. Mem. Emily Dickinson Soc. (founding mem., bd. mem., v.p. and program chair 1988-90), Soc. for Values in Higher Edn., Soc. Women Geographers, Women's Fgn. Policy Group, The Writer's Ctr. Office: Am Coun on Edn One Dupont Circle NW Washington DC 20036

MOSSEL, PATRICIA FLEISCHER, opera executive; b. N.Y.C., Nov. 19, 1933; d. Burnet Thomas and Martha Camille (Leigh) Kraut; m. Allan A Fleischer, Dec. 30,. 1956 (div. 1987); children: Hillary Lee, Jason Allan; m. John W. Mossel, Sept. 4, 1993. BA, U. Rochester, 1955; MA, Yale U., 1956. Cert. fund raising exec. Tchr. Colby Coll., New London, N.H., 1956-57; editor Far Eastern Pub.-Yale U., New Haven, 1957-60; dir. devel. San Francisco Opera, 1979-84; dir. devel., mktg. and pub. relations The Wash. Opera, 1984-95, exec. dir., 1995—; mem. bd. San Francisco Symphony and Opera; bd. chmn., exec. dir. Mt. Diablo Rehabilitation Ctr.; co-founder Medi-Physics, Inc.; cons. D.C. Humanities Council, 1989—. Editor: Western Lit. on China, 1959. Mem. adv. council Fund Raising Sch., Indpls.; v.p. Nat. Soc. Fund Raising Exec. Found. bd. dirs., Washington, 1985-87. Mem. Nat. Soc. Fund Raising Execs. (named Fund Raising Exec. of Yr. 1986), Assocs. of Yale Alumni (del. 1988-91), Yale Club, Phi Beta Kappa. Republican. Presbyterian. Office: Washington Opera/Eisenhower Theater 2209 Kennedy Ctr Washington DC 20566-0012*

MOSSMAN, HELEN MARIE, journalist, columnist; b. Isabela, N.O., The Philippines, Aug. 2, 1933; came to U.S., 1945; d. Jorge Arzaga and Iva (Harrison) Madamba; m. Dean Seeman, Aug. 21, 1954 (div. June, 1974); children: Jayne, Kevin, Saralee, Daniel; m. Romain S. Mossman, Apr. 3, 1977. BA, Okla. State U., 1954; postgrad., Calif. State U., Chico, 1973-75. Copywriter WKY Radio, Okla. City, 1954-55, WKY-TV, Okla. City, 1954-56; affirmative action coord. Butte County, Oroville, Calif., 1974-76; exec. v.p. Woodward (Okla.) C. of C., 1976-79; owner-mgr. Visa Personnel, Inc., Woodward, 1979-84; reporter Woodward News, 1984-87, mng. editor, 1987-92, cmty. editor, 1992—, columnist, 1987—; bd. dirs. Freedom of Info. Okla., 1991—; William Randolph Hearst vis. profl. U. Tex., 1993. Field worker Okla. ERA, 1980-82. Recipient Assoc. Press awards, 1984—, Okla. Press awards, 1984—, Marshall Gregory award Okla. Edn. Assn., 1984. Mem. AAUW (pres. Woodward 1976, 86), Rotary Internat. (Group Study Exchange, Japan 1996). Episcopalian. Home: 1846 20th Woodward OK 73801 Office: Woodward News 904 Oklahoma Woodward OK 73801

MOSSO, CLAUDIA GRUENWALD, journalist, translator; b. Frankfurt, West Germany, Sept. 26, 1952; came to U.S., 1955; d. Geza and Marianne (Pabst) Gruenwald; m. Craig W. Mosso, May 28, 1976 (div. 1984); 1 child, Brent. BA in Journalism, Pa. State U., State Coll., 1974. Dir. pub. rels. United Way of Erie County, Pa., 1975-76; pres. Translation & Interpreter Svc., North East, Pa., 1976—; reporter North East Breeze, 1986-92; editor Millcreek (Pa.) Sun, 1992—; cons. fgn. langs. and customs usage. Translator, abstracter numerous articles, 1976—. Mem. AAUW (fin. sec. 1982-84), Am. Translators Assn., Assn. Profl. Translators, N.E. Ohio Translators Assn., Soc. Profl. Journalists. Office: 10134 Ashton Rd North East PA 16428-5843

MOSTER, MARY CLARE, public relations executive; b. Morristown, N.J., Apr. 7, 1950; d. Clarence R. and Ruth M. (Duffy) M.; m. Louis C. Williams, Jr., Oct. 4, 1987. BA in English with honors, Douglass Coll., 1972; MA in English Lit., Univ. Chgo., 1973. Accredited pub. rels. specialist. Editor No. Trust Bank, Chgo., 1973-75, advt. supr., 1975-77, communications officer, 1977-78; account exec. Hill & Knowlton, Inc., Chgo., 1978-80, v.p., 1980-83, sr. v.p., 1983-87, sr. v.p., mng. dir., 1987-88; staff v.p. comms. Navistar Internat. Corp., Chgo., 1988-93; v.p. corp. comms. Comdisco, Inc., Rosemont, Ill., 1993—; mem. bd. dirs. The Pegasus Players, 1993—. Author poetry, poetry translation. Bd. govs. Met. Planning Coun., Chgo., 1988-94; fellow Leadership Greater Chgo., 1989-90; bd. dirs. New City YMCA, Chgo., 1986-92; corp. devel. bd. Steppenwolf Theatre Co., Chgo., 1988-90; mem. The Chgo. Network, 1994—, bd. dirs., 1996—. Mem. Nat. Investor Rels. Inst. (bd. dirs. 1988-89, 90-93), Arthur W. Page Soc., Pub. Rels. Soc. Am., Internat. Women's Forum, Equipment Leasing Assn. Am. (mem. pub. rels. adv. com.). Office: Comdisco Inc 6111 N River Rd Rosemont IL 60018-5158

MOSZKOWSKI, LENA IGGERS, secondary school educator; b. Hamburg, Mar. 8, 1930; d. Alfred G. and Lizzie (Minden) M.; m. Steven Alexander, Aug. 29, 1952 (div. Oct. 1977); children: Benjamin Charles, Richard David (dec.), Ronald Bertram. BS, U. Richmond, 1948; MS, U. Chgo., 1953; postgrad., UCLA, 1958. Tchr. Lab. asst. U. Chgo. Ben May Cancer Research Lab., Chgo., 1951-53; biology, sci. tchr. Bishop Conaty High Sch., Los Angeles, 1967-68; chemistry, sci. tchr. St. Paul High Sch., Santa Fe Springs, Calif., 1968-69; chemistry, human ecology tchr. Marlborough Sch., Los Angeles, 1969-71; tchr. biology and sci. ecology L.A. Unified Sch. Dist., 1971—. Author: Termite Taxonomy Cryptotermes Haviland and C. Krybi, Madagascar, 1955, Ecology and Man, 1971, Parallels in Human and Biological Ecology, 1977, American Public Education, An Inside Journey, 1991-92. Founder, adminstr., com. mem. UCLA Student (and Practical Assistance Cooperative Furniture), Los Angeles, 1963-67; active participant UCLA Earth Day Program, Los Angeles, 1970. Recipient Va. Sci. Talent Search Winner Va. Acad. of Sci., 1946; Push Vol. Tchr. award John C. Fremont High Sch., Los Angeles, 1978. Mem. Calif. Tchrs. Assn., United Tchrs. L.A., Sierra Club. Democrat. Jewish. Home: 3301 Shelburne Rd Baltimore MD 21208-5626

MOTLEY, CONSTANCE BAKER (MRS. JOEL WILSON MOTLEY), federal judge, former city official; b. New Haven, Sept. 14, 1921; d. Willoughby Alva and Rachel (Huggins) Baker; m. Joel Wilson Motley, Aug. 18, 1946; 1 son, Joel Wilson, III. AB, NYU, 1943; LLB, Columbia U., 1946. Bar: N.Y. bar 1948. Mem. Legal Def. and Ednl. Fund, NAACP, 1945-65; mem. N.Y. State Senate, 1964-65; pres. Manhattan Borough, 1965-66; U.S. dist. judge So. Dist. N.Y., 1966-82, chief judge, 1982-86, sr. judge, 1986—. Mem. N.Y. State Adv. Council Employment and Unemployment Ins., 1958-64. Mem. Assn. Bar City N.Y. Office: US Dist Ct US Courthouse 500 Pearl St New York NY 10007-1501

MOTT, EVELYN LOUISE, librarian; b. Flint, Mich., Nov. 10, 1933; d. Cyril August and Elizabeth J. (Smith) Schmidt; m. Frederick E. Sanocki, Oct. 13, 1956 (div. 1974); children: Tom, Julie, Elizabeth, Marie; m. Robert A. Mott, July 3, 1975 (dec. 1996). BS summa cum laude, Nazareth Coll., 1955; MLS, U. Mich., 1974. Cert. med. asst.; cert. med. technologist Am. Soc. Clin. Pathology; tchrs. cert., Mich., Fla. Med. technologist St. Joseph Hosp., Flint, 1955-58; tchr. Flint Pub. Schs., 1968-72; dist. libr. Genesee (Mich.) Schs., 1974-80; med. asst. inst. Pontiac Bus. Inst., Oxford, Mich., 1982-84; libr. Palm Beach County Libr. Sys., West Palm Beach, Fla., 1985—; legis. liaison Flint Fedn. Tchrs., 1968-72; presenter med. reference workshops Palm Beach County Libr., West Palm Beach. Reviewer Libr. Jour., 1988-91, Profl. Med. Asst., 1982. Chairperson Christian Family Movement, Lansing, Mich., 1961-63, McCarthy for Pres., Genesee County, 1966-68; alternate del. Dem. Nat. Conv., Chgo., 1968. Bishop Alburs scholar, 1951-55. Mem. AAUW, ALA (Charles Scribner's Sons award 1977), NOW, Kappa Gamma Pi. Office: Okeechobee Blvd Br Libr 5689 Okeechobee Blvd West Palm Beach FL 33417

MOTT, MARY ELIZABETH, educational administrator; b. West Hartford, Conn., July 10, 1931; d. Marshall Amos and Mary Salome (Herman) M. B.A., Conn. Coll. Women, 1953; M.A., Western Res. U., 1963. Cert. tchr., Ohio; cert. computer tchr., Ohio. Mgr. sales promotion Cleve. Electric Illuminating Co., 1953-60; tchr. Newbury Bd. Edn., Ohio, 1960-67, West Geauga Bd. Edn., Chesterland, Ohio, 1967—; chmn. state certification com. in computers ECCO, Mayfield, Ohio, 1983—, exec. bd., 1980—. Asst. dir. West Geauga Day Camp, Chesterland, 1968. Mem. Ednl. Computer Consortium Ohio, West Geauga Edn. Assn. (mem. exec. bd. 1975—), Delta Kappa Gamma. Republican. Clubs: MAC Users Group, Nat. Assn. Playing Card Collectors. Avocations: golf, travel, reading, gardening, computers. Office: Westwood Sch 13738 Caves Rd Chesterland OH 44026-3415

MOTT, PEGGY LAVERNE, sociologist, educator; b. Stephenville, Tex., Mar. 23, 1930; d. Artemis Victor Dorris and Tempie Pearl (Price) Hickman; m. J.D. Mott, Sept. 11, 1947 (dec. Apr. 1988); children: Kelly A. Wilcoxson, Kimberly S. Minesinger. BA, Southwest Tex. State U., 1980, MA, 1982. Cert. instr. ceramic arts Nat. Ceramic Art Inst., 1972. Instr. ceramics Arts & Crafts Ctr. Lackland AFB, San Antonio, 1969-72, dir. sales Arts & Crafts Ctr., 1972-77; asst. instr. S.W. Tex. State U., San Marcos, 1980-82; instr. sociology Palo Alto Coll., San Antonio, 1991—. Author: Screaming Silences, 1994, (poem) Concho River Rev., 1993, Inkwell Echos, 1989-95, Lucidity, The T.O.P. Hwupp, 1994-95, Hwap, Patchwork Poems, 1995. Vol. coord. Fisher Houses, Inc., Lackland AFB, 1992—. Named Vol. of Month, USAF, 1976, 77, 78, Vol. of Quarter, 1976, 77, 78, 84, Vol. of Yr., 1980. Mem. Internat. Soc. Poets, Clipper Ship Poets, San Antonio Poets Assn. (v.p. 1991-92, pres. 1992-93, Poet Laureate 1994-95), San Antonio Ethnic Arts. Home: 1307 Canyon Ridge Dr San Antonio TX 78227-1727

MOTTLEY, MELINDA, secondary education educator; b. Richmond, Va., Mar. 11, 1948; d. Samuel Morton and Zoa (Robinson) M. BS, Longwood Coll., 1970; MA in Art Edn., Va. Commonwealth U., 1982; postgrad., Parsons Sch. Design, 1984. Tchr. art and jewelry Thomas Jefferson H.S., Richmond, 1972-83; art resource tchr. Arts and Humanities Ctr., Richmond, 1983-87; tchr. art and jewelry John Marshall H.S., Richmond, 1988—; adj. instr. Va. Commonwealth U., Richmond, 1985-89; art cons. Richmond Pub. Schs., 1970-71; mem. tchrs. adv. bd. Va. Mus. Fine Arts, Richmond, 1993-97. Exhibited jewelry in group shows at Hand Workshop, Richmond, 1985, 86, 87, Va. Craftsmen, 1989, Va. Mus. Fine Art, 1990, 91, 92, Arts on the Square Gallery, Richmond, 1993, 94, Women's Caucus, Logan Fine Arts Gallery, Midlothian, Va., 1996, Nations Bank Richmond, 1990, others. Bd. dirs. Comty. Sch. for Arts, 1994-97. Grantee Va. Commn. for Arts, 1987, 96, Ptnrs. in the Arts Richmond Arts Coun., 1995, Tchr. Incentive grantee Richmond Pub. Schs., 1996. Mem. Va. Art Edn. Assn. (sec., pres. Ctrl. region 1990-95, state sec. 1993-95, Secondary Tchr. of Yr. award 1990, John Marshall H.S. Tchr. of the Yr. award 1994), Richmond Craftsmans Guild (v.p. 1988-90), Women's Caucus for Art, Va. Alliance for Arts, Soc. N. Am. Goldsmiths. Presbyterian. Office: John Marshall HS 4225 Old Brook Rd Richmond VA 23227-3802

MOTZ, DIANA GRIBBON, federal judge; b. Washington, July 15, 1943; d. Daniel McNamara and Jane (Retzler) Gribbon; m. John Frederick Motz, Sept. 20, 1968; children: Catherine Jane, Daniel Gribbon. BA, Vassar Coll., 1965; LLB, U. Va., 1968. Bar: U.S. Dist. Ct. Md. 1969, U.S. Ct. Appeals (4th cir.) 1969, U.S. Supreme Ct. 1980. Assoc. Piper & Marbury, Balt., 1968-71; asst. atty. gen. State of Md., Balt., 1972-81, chief of litigation, 1981-86; ptnr. Frank, Bernstein, Conaway & Goldman, Balt., 1986-91; judge Md. Ct. of Special Appeals, Md., 1991-94, U.S. Ct. Appeals (4th Cir.), 1994—. Mem. ABA, Md. Bar Assn., Balt. City Bar Assn. (exec. com. 1988), Am. Law Inst., Am. Bar Found., Md. Bar Found., Lawyers Round Table, Fed. Cts. Study Com., Wranglers Law Club. Roman Catholic. Office: 101 W Lombard St Ste 920 Baltimore MD 21201-2626

MOUDON, ANNE VERNEZ, urban design educator; b. Yverdon, Vaud, Switzerland, Dec. 24, 1945; came to U.S., 1966; d. Ernest Edouard and Mauricette Lina (Duc) M.; m. Dimitrios Constantine Seferis, Dec. 30, 1982; children: Louisa Moudon, Constantine Thomas. BArch with honors, U. Calif., Berkeley, 1969; DSc, Ecole Poly. Fed., Lausanne, Switzerland, 1987. Fed. Register of Swiss Architects. Rsch. assoc. Bldg. Systems Devel., Inc.,

San Francisco, 1969-70; sr. project planner J. C. Warnecke and Assocs., N.Y.C., 1973-74; archtl. cons. McCue, Boone & Tomsick, San Francisco, 1974-76; asst. to assoc. prof. architecture MIT, Cambridge, Mass., 1975-81, Ford internat. career chair, 1977-79; sec. Assn. Collegiate Schs. Arch., 1978-80; assoc. prof. urban design U. Wash., Seattle, 1981-87, prof. architecture, landscape architecture, urban design and planning, 1987—, dir. urban design program, 1987-93, assoc. dean acad. affairs Coll. Arch. & Urban Planning, 1992-95; dir. Cascadia Cmty. and Environ. Inst., Seattle, 1993—; lectr. in architecture U. Calif., Berkeley, 1973-75; sr. rschr. Kungl Tekniska Hogskolan, Sch. of Architecture, Stockholm, 1989. Author: Built for Change, 1986; editor: Public Streets for Public Use, 1987, 91, (monograph) Master-Planned Communities, 1990; contbr. articles to profl. jours. Recipient seven rsch. grants Nat. Endowment for the Arts, Washington, 1976-89, individual fellowship, 1986-87, Applied Rsch. award Progressive Architecture, 1983, two rsch. grants Wash. State Dept. Transp., Seattle, 1991-92. Fellow Inst. for Urban Design; mem. Internat. Assn. for the Study of People in Their Phys. Surroundings, Orgn. Women Architects, Tau Sigma Delta. Home: 3310 E Laurelhurst Dr NE Seattle WA 98105-5336 Office: U Wash Urban Design JO-40 Gould Hall Seattle WA 98195

MOUL, MAXINE BURNETT, state official; b. Oakland, Nebr., Jan. 26, 1947; d. Einer and Eva (Jacobson) Burnett; m. Francis Moul, Apr. 20, 1972; 1 child, Jeff. BS in Journalism, U. Nebr., 1969; DHL (hon.), Peru State Coll., 1993. Sunday feature writer, photographer Sioux City Iowa Jour., 1969-71; reporter, photographer, editor Maverick Media, Inc., Syracuse, Nebr., 1971-73, editor, pub., 1974-83, pres., 1983-90; grant writer, asst. coord. Nebr. Regional Med. Program, Lincoln, 1973-74; lt. gov. State of Nebr., Lincoln, 1991-93; dir. Dept. Econ. Devel., Lincoln, 1993—. Mem. Dem. Nat. Com., Washington, 1988-92, Nebr. Dem. State Ctrl. Com., Lincoln, 1974-88; del. Dem. Nat. Conf., 1972, 88, 92; mem. exec. com. Nebr. Dem. Party, Lincoln, 1988-93. Recipient Margaret Sanger award Planned Parenthood, Lincoln, 1991, Champion of Small Bus. award Nebr. Bus. Devel. Ctr., Omaha, 1991, Toll fellowship Coun. State Govts., Lexington, Ky., 1992. Mem. Bus. and Profl. Womem, Nebr. Mgmt. Assn. (Silver Knight award 1992), Nat. Conf. Lt. Govs. (bd. dirs. 1991-93), Nebr. Press Women, Women Execs. in State Govt., Cmty. Devel. Soc., U. Nebr.-Lincoln Journalism Alumni. Democrat. Office: State of Nebr PO Box 94666 Lincoln NE 68509-4666

MOULTON, GRACE CHARBONNET, physics educator; b. New Orleans, Nov. 1, 1923; d. Wilfred J. and Louise A. (Hellmers) Charbonnet; m. William Gates Moulton, June 1, 1947; children: Paul Charbonnet Moulton, Nancy Gates Moulton. BA, Tulane U., 1944; MS, U. Ill., 1948; PhD, U. Ala., 1962. Asst. prof. physics U. Ala., Tuscaloosa, 1962-65; asst. prof. physics Fla. State U., Tallahassee, 1965-74, assoc. prof. physics, 1974-80, prof. physics, 1980—; cons. State Bd. Regents, Fla., 1984-85, Fla. Univ. System, 1989-90. Referee jour. articles Jour. Chem. Physics, Radiation Rsch.; contbr. many sci. rsch. articles to profl. jours. Four Yr. Undergrad. scholar Tulane U., scholar U. Ill.; rsch. grantee NIH. Mem. Am. Phys. Soc., (mem. coun. southeastern sect. 1988—). Office: Fla State U Dept Physics Tallahassee FL 32304

MOULTON, KATHERINE KLAUBER, hotel executive; b. Buffalo, Nov. 28, 1956; d. Murray Joseph and Joanna (Brown) Klauber; m. Michael Arthur Moulton, July, 10, 1982. BS, Cornell U., 1978. Hotel and restaurant designer Cini-Grissom Assoc., Potomac, Md., 1978-82; pres., gen. mgr. Colony Beach & Tennis Resort, Longboat Key, Fla., 1982—; owner Le Tennique, Longboat Key, 1982—; exec. v.p., cons., designer Total Environments, Longboat Key, 1982—. Contbr. articles to restaurant and hotel design mags. Mem. Coquille, Sarasota, Fla., 1982; organizer, fund raiser St. Jude's Children's Rsch. Hosp., 1982; mem. found. bd. Girls Inc.; mem. resources com. John and Mabel Ringling Mus.; mem. Sarasota County Tourist Devel. Coun. Recipient Region IV Advocacy award Girls Inc., 1993. Mem. Am. Hotel Motel Assn., Fla. Hotel Motel Assn., Cornell Soc. Hotelmen, Sarasota C. of C. (bd. dirs.), Southern Innkeepers Assn. (bd. dirs.). Office: Colony Beach & Tennis Resort 1620 Gulf Of Mexico Dr Longboat Key FL 34228-3403

MOUNT, MARSHA LOUISE, management consultant; b. Newark, May 26, 1962; d. Huston Ellis and Katherine Ellery (Lyman) M. BA, Columbia U., 1984, MBA, 1990. Rsch. asst. Gen. Bd. Global Ministries, N.Y.C., 1984-85; analyst Bristol-Myers, N.Y.C., 1986-88; assoc. staff analyst N.Y.C. Dept. Transp., 1990-94, dep. dir. analytical svcs., 1992-94; sr. mgmt. cons. George S. May Internat. Co., San Jose, Calif., 1994—. Mem. Nat. Mus. Women in Arts, Washington. Recipient Cert. of Merit Nat. Merit Scholarship Corp., 1980, Cert. of Distingction Barnard Coll., N.Y.C., 1984, Lead auditor Quality Assessment, 1995, Staff Exec. of Yr., 1995. Mem. Nat. Mus. Women in Arts, Washington, Amnesty Internat.

MOUNTZ, LOUISE CARSON SMITH, retired librarian; b. Fond Du Lac, Wis., Oct. 20, 1911; d. Roy Carson and Charlotte Louise (Scheurs) Smith; m. George Edward Mountz, May 4, 1935 (dec. Oct. 3 1951); children: Peter Carson, Pamela Teeters Mountz McDonald. Student, Western Coll. for Women, 1929-31; AB, The Ohio State U., 1933; MA, Ball State U., 1960; postgrad., Manchester Coll., 1954, Ind. U., 1960-61. Cert. tchr., Ind. Tchr. Monroeville (Ind.) High Sch., 1953-54, Riverdale High Sch., St. Joe, Ind., 1954-55; libr. High Sch., Avilla, Ind., 1955-58; head libr. Penn High Sch., Mishawaka, Ind., 1958-67, Northwood Jr. High Sch., Ft. Wayne, Ind., 1967-69, McIntosh Jr. High Sch., Auburn, Ind., 1969-74; dir. Media Ctr. DeKalb Jr. High Sch., Auburn, Ind., 1974-78; ret., 1978; cons. media ctr. planning Penn-Harris-Madison Sch. Corp., Mishawaka, 1966-67. Author: Biographies for Junior High Schools and Correlated Audio-Visual Materials, 1970; contbr. articles to profl. jours. Bd. dirs. DeKalb County chpt. ARC, 1938-42, 51-53, DeKalb County Heart Assn., 1946-52, DeKalb County Cmty. Concert Assn., 1946-58, Am. Field Svc. Mishawaka chpt., 1960-67; active Ft. Wayne Philharmonic Orch. Assn., Ft. Wayne Art Mus., Ft. Wayne Hist. Soc., DeKalb County Hist. Soc., Garrett Hist. Soc., DeKalb County Genealogy Soc., Preservation of DeKalb County Heritage Assn., DeKalb Meml. Hosp. Women's Guild, also life mem. Mem. AAUW, ALA, NEA, World Confedn. Orgns. Teaching Professions, Nat. Coun. Tchrs. English, Ind. Sch. Librarians Assn. (dir. 1963-67), Internat. Assn. Sch. Librarianship, Ind. Assn. Ednl. Communication and Tech., Assn. Ind. Media Educators, Nat. Ret. Tchrs. Assns., Nat. Trust Hist. Preservation, Hist. Landmarks Found. Ind., Delta Kappa Gamma (charter mem., Beta Beta chpt.), Kappa Kappa Kappa (pr. officer 1941-45, pres. Alpha Chi chpt. 1938-40, Garrett Assoc. chpt. 1971-73), Delta Delta Delta (house pres.). Methodist. Lodge: Order Ea. Star. Clubs: Greenhurst Country, Ft. Wayne Women's, Athena Lit. (hon. mem.), Ladies Lit. of Auburn. Home: 19 Castle Ct Auburn IN 46706-1439

MOURNING, ELIZABETH ANNE, financial advisor, accountant; b. Boulder, Colo., May 7, 1964; d. Donald Boyce and Sondra Lillian (Wells) M. BS in Acctg., U. Wyo., 1989; MS in Acct., U. Colo., Denver, 1993, MBA, 1993. CPA. Acct., tax preparer Nature's Lawn, Englewood, Colo., 1991-92; audit mgr. U.S. West, Englewood, Colo., 1993-96; fin. advisor U.S. West, Denver, 1996—; ski instr., Winter Park, Colo., 1989-92. Ski tchr. Nat. Sports Ctr. Disabled, Winter Park, 1992—; tchr. Jr. Achievement, Denver, 1993-94; organizer Spl. Olympics, Denver, 1993—. Mem. Am. Inst. CPAs, Colo. Soc. CPAs, Inst. Mgmt. Accts. Episcopalian. Office: US West 1999 Broadway Denver CO 80202

MOUSSEAU, DORIS NAOMI BARTON, retired elementary school principal; b. Alpena, Mich., May 6, 1934; d. Merritt Benjamin and Naomi Dora Josephine (Pieper) Barton; m. Bernard Joseph Mousseau, July 31, 1954. AA, Alpena Community Coll., 1954; BS, Wayne State U., 1959; MA, U. Mich., 1961, postgrad., 1972-75. Profl. cert. ednl. adminstr., tchr. Elem. tchr. Clarkston (Mich.) Community Schs., 1954-66; elem. sch. prin. Andersonville Sch., Clarkston, 1966-79, Bailey Lake Sch., Clarkston, 1979-94; ret., 1994; Oakland County rep. Mich. Elem. and Mid. Schs. Prins. Assn. Retirees Task Force, 1996. Cons., rsch. com. Youth Assistance Oakland County Ct. Svcs., 1968-88; leader Clarkston PTA, 1967-94; chair Clarkston Sch. Dist. campaign, United Way, 1985, 86; mem. allocations com. Oakland County United Way, 1987-88. Recipient Outstanding Svc. award Davisburg Jaycees, Springfield Twp., 1977, Vol. Recognition award Oakland County (Mich.) Cts., 1984. Fellow ASCD, MACUL (State Assn. Ednl. Computer Users); mem. NEA (del. 1964), Mich. Elem. and Middle Sch. Prins. Assn. (treas., regional del. 1982—, pres.-elect Region 7 1988-89, program planner, pres. 1989-90, sr. advisor 1990-91, Honor award Region # 7 1991), Mich. Edn. Assn. (pres. 1960-66, del. 1966), Clarkston Edn. Assn. (author, editor 1st directory 1963), Women's Bowling Assn., Elks, Spring Meadows Gold Club, Phi Delta Kappa, Delta Kappa Gamma (pres. 1972-74, past state and nat. chmn., Woman of Distinction 1982). Republican. Home: 6825 Rattalee Lake Rd Clarkston MI 48348-1955

MOVIUS, ALISON WHITNEY BURTON (ALISON WHITNEY), writer, educator, publisher, speaker, poet, songwriter; b. Billings, Mont., Apr. 4, 1945; d. William Robert and Alice Whitney (Burton) Movius; divorced; children: David Lindley, Elisabeth Whitney. BA in Humanities, U. Calif., Berkeley, 1967. Staff mem. Campus Crusade for Christ, various locations, 1967-78; dir. The Happy Place Nursery Sch., Ann Arbor, Mich., 1978-80; curriculum writer, children's songwriter, seminar spkr., 1976-85; founder, owner pub. co. Whitney Works!, La Jolla, Calif., 1992-96; writer, founder, pres. Abuse Survivor's Friendship Network, La Jolla, 1992-96. Author: (workbook, lectures) The Challenge of Being a Woman, 1976, Poems that Tell a Story, 1996, Poems for Battered Women, 1996, When There's Abuse..., 1996, When Hard Things Happen, 1996, Happy Little Scripture Songs, vol. I (for young children), 1996, On Love and Loving, vol. I, 1996; songwriter 1, 500 children's songs. Named to Outstanding Young Women of Am., 1978. Office: Whitney Works! PO Box 13191 La Jolla CA 92039-3191

MOWATT, E. ANN, women's voluntary leader. BA in History, Dalhousie U., Halifax, Nova Scotia, 1982; BL, 1985. Barrister, solicitor Patterson Palmer Hunt Murphy, 1986—; ptnr. Palmer, O'Connell, Leger, Roderick, Glennie, 1991. Bd. dirs. YMCA-YWCA of Saint John N.B., Can., 1987-93, also mem. exec., fin., social action, and camp coms., pres., 1991; bd. dirs. YWCA of Can., 1989—, also chair constn. task force, mem.-at-large, treas., v.p., now pres., 1995—; bd. dirs. Coalition of Nat. Vol. Orgns., 1994—; pres. Saint John chpt. Multiple Sclerosis Soc. Can., 1987-88, bd. dirs. Atlantic divsn., 1988—, mem. nat. bd. dirs., 1992-95, pres. Atlantic divsn., 1993—. Mem. Can. Bar Assn. (mem. N.B. coun. 1986-89), Law Soc. N.B. (mem. legal aid com. 1989-92). Home: 1054 Mollins Dr Apt 3, Saint John, NB Canada E2M 4L8 Office: 80 Gerard St E, Toronto, ON Canada 1G6 also: PO Box 1425, Saint John, NB Canada E2L 4H8

MOWER, MELISSA BEE, magazine editor, writer; b. South Weymouth, Mass., July 16, 1959; d. Robert Ellis and Virginia Keith. BA, Calif. State U., Chico, 1982. Reporter Lassen Advocate, Susanville, Calif., 1982-84; reporter Oakdale (Calif.) Leader, 1984; reporter/editor MPG Newspapers, Plymouth, Mass., 1986-89; southwestern editor Message Mag., Davis, Calif., 1990—; sr. editor Message Mag., Santa Rosa, Calif., 1990-94; media rels. coord. Sohnen-Moe Assocs., Tucson, 1994—. Democrat. Office: 1223 College Ave Ste 2 Santa Rosa CA 95401

MOY, AUDREY, retail buyer; b. Bronx, N.Y., May 6, 1942; d. Ferdinand Walter Melkert and Stella (Factorow) Schroff; m. Edward Moy, Aug. 16, 1974. BA in Biology, Hunter Coll., 1964, MA in Biology, 1966. Asst. buyer Bonwit Teller, N.Y.C., 1961-68; dept. mgr. Franklin Simon, N.Y.C., 1968; asst. buyer Saks Fifth Ave., N.Y.C., 1968-73; buyer Martins, Bklyn., 1973, Belk Store Svcs., N.Y.C., 1974—. Mem. NAFE. Avocations: cooking, fishing, gardening.

MOYA, OLGA LYDIA, law educator; b. Weslaco, Tex., Dec. 27, 1959; d. Leonel V. and Genoveva (Tamez) M.; m. James Troutman Byrd, Aug. 24, 1985; children: Leanessa Geneva Byrd, Taylor Moya Byrd. BA, U. Tex., 1981, JD, 1984. Bar: Tex. 1984. Legis. atty. Tex. Ho. of Reps., Austin, 1985; atty. Tex. Dept. Agr., Austin, 1985-90; asst. regional counsel U.S. EPA, Dallas, 1990-91; asst. prof. law South Tex. Coll. of Law, Houston, 1992-95, assoc. prof. law, 1995—. Co-author: (with Andrew L. Fono) User's Guide to the Federal Environmental Laws, 1996. Bd. dirs. Hermann Children's Hosp., Houston, 1993—; mem. Leadership Tex., Austin, 1991—; bd. dirs. Tex. Clean Water Coun., Austin, 1992; U.S. del. to UN Conf. on the Environ. for Latin Am. and the Caribbean, San Juan, P.R., 1995. Recipient Vol. of Yr. award George H. Hermann Soc., 1995, Hispanic Law Prof. of Yr. Hispanic Nat. Bar Assn., 1995. Mem. ABA (environ. law sect.), Hispanic Bar Assn. (bd. dirs. 1992—, Excellence award 1995, 96), Mex.-Am. Bar Assn. Office: South Tex Coll of Law 1303 San Jacinto St Houston TX 77002

MOYA, SARA DREIER, municipal government official; b. N.Y.C., June 9, 1945; d. Stuart Samuel and Hortense (Brill) Dreier; m. P. Robert Moya, May 30, 1966; children: J. Brill, Joshua D. BA, Wheaton Coll., Norton, Mass., 1967; postgrad., Mills Coll., Oakland, Calif., 1967-68; MPA, Ariz. State U., 1995, postgrad., 1995—. Mem. Paradise Valley (Ariz.) Town Coun., 1986—, vice mayor, 1990-92; chmn. Gov.'s Homeless Trust Fund Oversight Com., 1991—; pres. Ctr. for Acad. Precosity, Ariz. State U., Tempe, 1987—; bd. dirs. Ariz. Assn. Gifted and Talented; participant 3d session Leadership Am., 1990. Mem. Citizens Adv. Bd. Paradise Valley Police Dept., 1984-86, Valley Citizens League Task Force on Edn.; chair Maricopa Assn. Govts. Task Force on Homeless, 1989-92, 95—; mem. FEMA bd. Maricopa County and Ariz., 1989—; bd. dirs. Valley Youth Theater, 1990-93, Maricopa County Homeless Accomodation Sch., 1991—. Mem. ASPA, Ariz. Women in Mcpl. Govt. (sec. 1988-89, bd. dirs. 1986—, pres. 1989-90), Maricopa Assn. Govts. (regional coun. 1988—, vice-chmn. mag. regional devel. policy com. 1989-91, chair 1992—, mag. joint econ. devel./human resources subcom., mag. youth policy com. 1994—), Maricopa Assn. Govts. (air quality policy com. 1994—), Ariz. Acad., Ariz. Planning Assn. (bd. dirs., citizen planner, 1996—), Paradise Valley Country Club, Phi Kappa Phi, Pi Alpha Alpha. Republican. Home: 5119 E Desert Park Ln Paradise Valley AZ 85253-3055 Office: Town Paradise Valley 6401 E Lincoln Dr Paradise Valley AZ 85253-4328

MOYER, CHERYL LYNN, non-profit administrator; b. St. Petersburg, Fla., Apr. 4, 1953; d. Joseph Paul Safko and Doris Marie (Wolf) Sniegocki; m. John Arthur Weber (div. 1982); m. Ross Allen Moyer, June 21, 1983; children: Deborah, Martin, Brian, Spencer. BS, Lock Haven U., 1986; MPA, Pa. State U., 1987. Office mgr. Piper Aircraft Corp., Lock Haven, Pa., 1974-76; radio rep. Sta. WTGC Radio, Lewisburg, Pa., 1976-77; sales rep. Sears, Lycoming Mall, Pa., 1977-83; ptnr., dir. The Trading Post, Williamsport, Pa., 1983-85; mgr., founder Lock Haven U. Day Care, 1985-86; field mgr. Pa. Pub. Interest Coalition, State Coll., Pa., 1987-88; exec. dir. Pa. Assn. Families, Harrisburg, Pa., 1988-91; unit dir.-residential Resources for Human Devel., Phila., 1989-93; mgr. ob-gyn. clinic Meth. Hosp., Phila., 1993-94, bus. analyst, 1994; owner Family Fin. Svcs., 1994-95; chair bd. dirs., fin. dir. Matchmaker Internat. Midlantic; Nat. reg. lobbyist. Grantee Family Planning Svcs., 1994. Mem. Nat. Assn. Dual Diagnosis, Pa. State Alumni Assn., Interfaith Assn., Mensa. Home: 79 Tallowood Dr Medford NJ 08055

MOYER, LOUISE EILEEN, lawyer; b. Reading, Pa., Feb. 22, 1967; d. Carson E. and Lillian R. (Dornmoyer) S.; m. Brian Keith Moyer, Sept. 30, 1995. BS magna cum laude, Drexel U., 1989; JD summa cum laude, Villanova U., 1992. Bar: Pa. 1992, U.S. Ct. Appeals (3rd cir.) 1994. Jud. law clk. U.S. Ct. Appeals for the Third Cir., Phila., 1992-94; assoc. Dechert Price & Rhoads, Phila., 1994—. Mem. ABA, Pa. Bar Assn., Order of the Coif. Home: 25 College Ave Trappe PA 19426 Office: Dechert Price & Rhoads 4000 Bell Atlantic Tower 1717 Arch St Philadelphia PA 19103

MOYER, MARY LOUISE, internist; b. Phila., Dec. 14, 1961; d. John Henry and Mary Elizabeth (Hughes) M. Student, U. Pitts., 1980-82; BA summa cum laude, Temple U., 1985, MD, 1989. Diplomate Am. Bd. Internal Medicine. Intern Hahnemann Univ. Hosp., Phila., 1989-90, resident, 1990-92; staff physician critical care St. Anthony Hosp., Denver, 1992-94; primary care physician Luth. Hosp., Wheat Ridge, Colo., 1994-96, St. Anthony Hosp., Denver, 1996—. Presdl. scholar Temple U., 1985. Mem. ACP. Republican. Office: North Denver Med Clinic 4301 Lowell Blvd Denver CO 80211

MOYERS, JUDITH DAVIDSON, television producer; b. Dallas, May 12, 1935; d. Henry Joseph and Eula E. (Dendy) Davidson; m. Bill D. Moyers; children: William Cope, Suzanne, John. BS, U. Tex., 1956; LittD (hon.), L.I. U., 1989, SUNY, 1990. Pres., exec. prodr. Pub. Affairs T.V., N.Y.C., 1987—; Bd. dirs. Paine Webber Mut. Funds, Ogden Corp. Exec. prodr. numerous T.V. documentaries (Emmy 1980, 93); contbr. articles to profl. jours., newspapers, mags. Trustee SUNY, 1976-90; commr. U.S. Commn. UNESCO, Washington, 1977-80, White House commn. Internat. Yr. of Child, Washington, 1978-80; mem. jud. selection com. State N.Y., 1992-93; dir. Pub. Agenda Found. Mem. Century Club. Mem. Congregational Ch. Office: Pub Affairs TV Inc 356 W 58th St New York NY 10019-1804

MOYZIS, VIRGINIA FRANCES, elementary school educator; b. Chgo., May 21, 1921; d. Frank John and Emily (Sulan) Spurney; m. Raymond Moyzis, Dec. 2, 1945; children: Kathleen Dalton, Jeanne Curry, Michael. AA, Bogan Jr. Coll., Chgo., 1967; BA in Edn., Chgo. State U., 1969. Jr. high tchr. St. Rene Sch. Chgo. Archiocese, 1969-75; jr. high tchr. St. Bruno Sch., Chgo., 1976-95; substitute tchr. Chgo. Archdiocese Schs., 1995—. Pres. PTA, Chgo. Mem. Retired Tchrs. Orgn.

MOZLEY, DORIS NEILL, financial planner; b. Huntsville, Ala., Aug. 24, 1927; d. James M. and Rena (Simpson) Neill; m. Paul D. Mozley, June 15, 1952 (div. Mar. 1983); children: Susan Harris, Sally Dalzell, Paul D. Jr. BS in Edn., U. Ala., 1952; MA in History, Old Dominion U., 1975; postgrad., Coll. William and Mary, 1976. Tchr. Ala. Pub. Sch. System, Birmingham, 1952-55; stockbroker Dean Witter Reynold, 1983-90, Anderson & Studich, 1990-92; fin. planner Investors Securities, Suffolk, Va., 1992—. Contbr. articles to profl. publs. Lobbyist Com. for Equality and Justice for Mil. Wives, Norfolk, Va., 1985—. Office: Investors Security Co Inc 110 Bank St PO Box 546 Suffolk VA 23434

MUCHMORE, CAROLIN MARIE, real estate corporation officer; b. Aug. 18, 1944; d. Alfred G. and Mary K. (Lang) Columbo; m. Robert W. Muchmore, Mar. 17, 1962; children: Kim A. Wimmer, Dana A., Robert Jr. Cert. real estate broker. Mgr. guest rels. Great Adventure, Jackson, N.J., 1974-79; sales rep. Mut. of Omaha, Ins., Freehold, N.J., 1980-81; sales assoc. Sterling Thompson Realtors, Howell, N.J., 1979-82, Weichert Realtors, Manalapan, N.J., 1982-84; br. mgr. Weichert Realtors, Howell, 1984—; hosting dir. Sister Cities, Howell, 1988—; instr. Cuyohoga Anti-Discrimination, Aberdeen, N.J., 1989, Weichert-Orientation Sch., Aberdeen, 1984-93; v.p. Broker Mgr. Realty Execs. 100, Howell, 1993—. Com. Muscular Dystrophy, Ocean Twp., 1979-85, Spl. Olympics, Monmouth County, 1983-86; chmn. Toys for Tots, Monmouth and Ocean County, 1988-89. Recipient N.J. State Million Dollar Club, N.J. Assn. Realtors, 1981-93, N.J. State Pres. Club, 1985-86. Mem. Grad. Realtors Inst., Womens Coun. Realtors (pub. rels. officer), Howell C. of C., Jackson C. of C., BPOE (hon. mem.), Real Estate Brokerage Coun., Nat. Assn. Real Estate Owned Brokers, N.J. Assn. Realtors, Monmouth County Bd. Realtors (dir. 1992—). Home: 2 Cuomo Ct Englishtown NJ 07726-8500

MUDD, ANNE CHESTNEY, small business owner, mathematics educator, real estate agent; b. Macon, Ga., June 30, 1944; d. Bard Sherman Chestney and Betty (Bartow) Houston; children: Charles Lee Jr., Richard Chestney, Robert Jason. BA, U. Louisville, 1966, MA, 1976; postgrad., John Marshall Law Sch., 1995—. Math statistician U.S. Bur. Census, Jeffersonville, Ind., 1966-70; instr. math. U. Louisville, 1975-77, Coll. DuPage, Glen Ellyn, Ill., 1978-85, 92; tchr. math and substitute tchr. Lyons Twp. High Sch., La Grange, Ill., 1986-91; realtor First United Realtors, Western Springs, Ill., 1989-92; owner, mgr. retail bus., 1992—; math tutor Louisville 1969-77, Western Springs, Ill. 1977—. editor: Mathematics Textbook, 1991-92. Mem. steering com. Village Western Springs, 1986-87; bd. dirs. Children's Theater Western Springs, 1987-91; mem. Lyons Twp. H.S. Com. Student Discipline. Mem. NAFE, LWV (pres. 1983-85, bd. dirs.), Western Springs Hist. Soc. Home: 3958 Hampton Ave Western Springs IL 60558-1011

MUDGE, LOIS CORDELLA, primary grades educator; b. Bridgewater, S.D., Aug. 11, 1936; d. Paul G. and Margaret (Wurz) Walter; m. Lyle K. Mudge, Dec. 22, 1957; children: Kenneth (dec.), Thomas. BA, Ctrl. Wash. U., 1977; MEd, Heritage U., 1995. Country sch. tchr. Hitchcock, S.D., 1955-56; 4th grade tchr. Rapid City (S.D.) Sch. Dist., 1956-58; 1st grade tchr. Kiona Benton Sch. Dist., Benton City, Wash., 1963-64; 2d, 3d, k tchr. Richland (Wash.) Sch. Dist., 1977—. Recipient Learner Profile award, Richland Edn. Found., 1994. Mem. ASCD. Baptist. Office: Richland Sch Dist 1525 Hunt Ave Richland WA 99352

MUDGETT, ELIZABETH ERSKINE, patient educational coordinator, nurse; b. Boston, May 3, 1961; d. Alan Laurie and Janice (Farrell) Erskine; m. Mark Kenneth Mudgett, June 21, 1986; children: Lauren Elizabeth, Matthew Erskine. BSN, Skidmore Coll., 1983. RN, Mich., Mass.; BCLS, Am. Heart Assn. Student nurse internship NYU Hosp., N.Y.C., 1982; nursing asst. Mass. Gen. Hosp., Boston, 1982; grad. nurse Suburban Manor Nursing Home, Acton, Mass., 1983; grad. nurse U. Mass. Med. Ctr., Worcester, 1983-84, resource/primary care nurse in neurology, 1984-86; neuro ICU charge nurse U. Mich. Med. Ctr., Ann Arbor, 1986-88, clin. rsch. coord. nuclear medicine, 1988-91, clin. care coord., 1991—. Author, producer, dir. video Home Parenteral Therapy, 1992; contbr. articles to profl. jours. Mem. Home Care Coordination, Ann Arbor, 1991—, Patient Care Adv. Com., Ann Arbor, 1991—. Mem. ANA, Mich. Nurses Assn., Intravenous Nurses Soc. Home: 5135 Kierston Dr Brighton MI 48116-9050 Office: U Mich Med Ctr 1500 E Medical Center Dr Ann Arbor MI 48109-0802

MUEHLNER, SUANNE WILSON, library director; b. Rochester, Minn., June 29, 1943; d. George T. and Rhoda (Westin) Wilson. Student Smith Coll., 1961-63; A.B., U. Calif.-Berkeley, 1965; M.L.S., Simmons Coll., 1968; M.B.A., Northeastern U., Boston, 1979. Librarian, Technische Univ. Berlin, Germany, 1970-71; earth and planetary scis. librarian MIT Libraries, Cambridge, 1968-70, 1971-73; personnel librarian, 1973-74, asst. dir. personnel services, 1974-76, asst. dir. pub. services, 1976-81; dir. libraries Colby Coll., Waterville, Maine, 1981—. Mem. ALA, New Eng. Assn. Coll. and Research Librarians (sec.-treas. 1983-85, pres. 1986-87), Maine Libr. Assn. (chmn. intellectual freedom com. 1984-88, OCLC Users Coun., 1988-95), Nelinet (bd. dirs. 1985-91, chair 1989-91). Office: Colby Coll Miller Libr Waterville ME 04901

MUEHRCKE, JULIANA OBRIGHT (JILL MUEHRCKE), publisher, editor; b. Aurora, Ill., Sept. 3, 1945; d. Russell B. and Constance (Rennels) Obright; m. John Evans, Sept. 24, 1965 (div. 1968); 1 child, Andrea Marit; m. Phillip C. Muehrcke, July 22, 1969. Student, U. Colo., 1963-67; BA, U. Wash., 1971. Author textbooks Prentice Hall Textbooks, Englewood Cliffs, N.J., 1967-80, Macmillan Co., N.Y.C., 1973-74, Denoyer-Geppert, Chgo., 1980-82, Harcourt Brace, N.Y.C., 1981-82, Scott Foresman, Glenview, Ill., 1982-83; owner JP Publs., Madison, Wis., 1978—; mng. editor Sunshine Newspaper, Madison, 1981-83, Nonprofit World Jour., Madison, 1983—. Mem. Friends of the Madison Pub. Libr., 1987—, Madison Literacy Coun., 1988—. Mem. Women in Communications Inc. (v.p., membership chair 1987—), Am. Assn. Suicidology (bd. sec. Wis. chpt. 1988—), Alliance for the Mentally Ill, Dane County Mental Health, Univ. League (events chair 1972—). Office: Soc for Nonprofit Orgns 6314 Odana Rd Ste 1 Madison WI 53719-1129

MUELLER, ANNE, legislator; b. Atlanta, Oct. 5, 1929; d. Howard Raymond O'Quin and Bessie Kate (Bell) Brace; m. Hans Kurt Mueller, June 23, 1953; children: Yvonne Marie Key, Heidi Spivey, Mark Jennings. BS in Zoology, U. Ga., 1951. Registered med. technologist. Med. technologist Grady Hosp., Atlanta, 1953—, St. Joseph Hosp., Atlanta, 1957, Meml. Hosp., Waycross, Ga., 1958-59; legislator Ga. Ho. of Reps., 1983—. Mem. Savannah (Ga.) area Rep. Women, sec., 1980-81, v.p., 1981-82, Ga. Fedn. of Rep. Women, Savannah, dist. dir., 1986—. Republican. Baptist. Home: 13013 Hermitage Rd Savannah GA 31419-2850 Office: GA House of Reps State Capitol Atlanta GA 30334-9003

MUELLER, BARBARA STEWART (BOBBIE MUELLER), youth drug use prevention specialist, volunteer; b. Weslaco, Tex., Oct. 5, 1934; d. Roy Wesley Stewart and Marjorie Eleanor (Crossley) Willis; m. Charles Paul Mueller, Sept. 5, 1957 (div. 1985); children: Kathryn Anne, John Stewart. BA, U. Tex., 1957. cons. Parent Music Resource Ctr., Washington, 1986; edn. prevention chmn. U.S. Attys. Office, San Antonio, 1989-90; prevention chmn. Mayor's Alcohol and Drug Task Force, San Antonio,

1986-88. Author: (childrens TV): Henry Blue Shoe KONO-TV San Antonio, 1957; contbr. articles to profl. publs. Sec. Alamo Heights (Tex.) Recreation Coun., 1977-78; pres. San Antonio Petroleum Aux., 1978-79; founder, pres. Community Families in Action, 1980-89; trustee Youth Alternatives, Inc., 1983-85; mem. allocation panel United Way, 1988-90; mem. alcohol and drug adv. com. N.E. Ind. Sch. Dist., 1986-91; mem. drug free schs. com. S.W. Ind. Sch. Dist., 1991-92; regional coord. Texans War on Drugs, 1988-92; vol. U.S. Dept. Justice, San Antonio, 1984-88; mem. proclamation com. Stop Tex. Epidemic, 1982; active Trinity Bapt. Ch. Recipient Yr. award Drug Awareness Ctr., San Antonio, 1984, Bexar Co. Med. Soc. Aux., San Antonio, 1984, Gov.'s Cert., Texans War on Drugs, Austin, 1982, Commendation U.S. Pres. Child Safety Partnership, Washington, 1986. Mem. Women in Communications, Inc. (hon.) (Pub. Awareness award 1984), Zeta Tau Alpha (sec., v.p., pres. San Antonio chpt. 1969-77, Nat. Merit award 1980).

MUELLER, BETTY JEANNE, social work educator; b. Wichita, Kans., July 7, 1925; d. Bert C. and Clara A. (Pelton) Judkins; children—Michael J., Madelynn J. MSSW, U. Wis., Madison, 1964, PhD, 1969. Asst. prof. U. Wis., Madison, 1969-72; vis. asso. prof. Bryn Mawr (Pa.) Coll., 1971-72; asso. prof., dir. social work Cornell U., Ithaca, N.Y., 1972-78, 92-94, prof. human services studies, 1978—; nat. cons. Head Start, Follow Through, Appalachian Regional Commn., N.Y. State Office Planning Services, N.Y. State Dept. Social Services, N.Y. State Div. Mental Hygiene, Nat. Congress PTA, ILO. Author: (with H. Morgan) Social Services in Early Education, 1974, (with R. Reinoehl) Computers in Human Service Education, 1989, Determinants of Human Behavior, 1995; contbr. articles to profl. jours. Grantee HEW, 1974-76, 79-80, State of N.Y., 1975—, Israeli Jewish Agy., 1985-87, Israeli Nat. Council for Research, 1986-87; Fulbright Research award, 1990. Mem. Leadership Am., Chi Omega. Democrat. Unitarian. Home: 412 Highland Rd Ithaca NY 14850 Office: Cornell U Human Services Studies N139MVR Hall Ithaca NY 14853

MUELLER, DONNA MARIE WITT, reading specialist, gifted coordinator; b. Youngstown, Ohio, May 5, 1949; d. Francis John Jr. and Mary Louise (Murray) Witt; m. Zane Gerald Mueller, Oct. 28, 1972; children: Teresa J., Christina M., Jessica L. BS in Edn., St. John Coll., 1972, Reading Specialist Cert., 1975; MEd in Gifted Edn., Kent State U., 1993. Grade 8 reading and math tchr. Marycrest Sch., Independence, Ohio, 1972-74; reading specialist Moody Jr. High Sch., Bedford, Ohio, 1974-76, St. Ambrose Sch., Brunswick, Ohio, 1978-81, The Learning Connection, Brunswick, 1981-87; reading specialist, gifted coord. St. Albert the Great Sch., North Royalton, Ohio, 1987—; dir. Camp Invention, Akron, Ohio, 1993—; judge Odyssey of the Mind, Cuyahoga County, Ohio, 1994—; career day coord. St. Albert the Great Sch., 1992—, young author's conf. coord., 1994—. Lay minister St. John Neuman Ch., Strongsville, Ohio, 1987—; fgn. exch. student host mother Padua Franciscan High, Parma, Ohio, 1994, 96. Mem. Nat. Cath. Edn. Assn., Internat. Reading Assn., Ohio Assn. for Gifted children. Home: 11702 Park Pt Strongsville OH 44136-4520

MUELLER, GAIL DELORIES, forensic chemist, toxicologist; b. Chgo., Sept. 30, 1957; d. Roger George and Delories B. (Reppert) Johnson; m. Joseph E. Mueller, Jan. 26, 1991. BS in Chemistry, No. Ill. U., 1980. Quality control chemist Standard Pharmacal Corp., Elgin, Ill., 1980; forensic chemist Ill. Racing Bd. Lab., Elgin, 1980-82, Analytical Techs., Inc., Tempe, Ariz., 1982-84; analytical chemist Nichols Inst., San Juan Capistrano, Calif., 1985-87; forensic chemist, toxicologist, GC/MS group leader Damon Reference Labs., Rancho Cucamonga, Calif., 1987-94; forensic chemist, toxicologist Associated Pathologists Labs., Las Vegas, Nev., 1994-95; rsch. chemist Ansys, Inc., Irvine, Calif., 1995—. Fellow Am. Inst. Chemists; mem. Am. Chem. Soc., Calif. Assn. Toxicologists. Home: 7834 Settlers Ridge Las Vegas NV 89128 Office: Ansys Inc 2 Goodyear Irvine CA 92718

MUELLER, JEAN MARGARET, nursing consultant; b. Huntington, N.Y., June 3, 1951. Diploma in Nursing, Pilgrim State Hosp., 1973; BSN, SUNY, Stony Brook, 1979; M in Profl. Studies, New Sch. for Social Rsch., 1986. RN, N.Y. Nurses aide Huntington Hosp., N.Y., 1971, LPN, 1972, RN, charge ICU/CCU, MICU/SICU, telemetry, 1973-77; charge nurse, MICU North Shore U. Hosp, Manhasset, N.Y., 1977-78; private duty cases, Holter monitor scanning, 1978-84; dir. nursing svcs., assoc. dir. nursing svcs. Nesconset (N.Y.) Nursing Ctr., 1984-86; nursing edn. instr. St. Charles Hosp., Port Jefferson, N.Y.; labor and delivery nurse SUNY, Stony Brook; teaching and rsch. nurse II Diabetes Ctr., SUNY, Stony Brook; tchg. hosp. insvc. educator I SUNY, Stony Brook, 1990-94; hosp. nursing svcs. cons. Office Health Sys. Mgmt., N.Y. State Dept. Health, Hauppauge, N.Y., 1994—; mem. adj. faculty Sch. of Nursing SUNY, Stony Brook, 1992—, St. Joseph's Coll., 1994; rsch. com. dept. family medicine with E. Stark, E.A.P.; hosp. nursing svcs. cons. office health sys. mgmt. N.Y. State Dept. Health, 1994—; lectr. Med., Emotional and Psychol. Indicators of Family Violence. Contbr. articles to profl. jours. Active Mothers Against Drunk Driving; mem. Suffolk County Family Violence Task Force. Recipient President's award for leadership tng. programs SUNY, 1993, for spl. needs of elderly tng. programs and humanistic approach to health care tng. programs, 1994. Mem. Nat. Nurses Assn., Sigma Theta Tau. Home: 234 Hallock Rd Stony Brook NY 11790-3026

MUELLER, LINDA KING, writer; b. Indpls., June 17, 1952; d. William Z. and Sherry LaVonne (McDowell) King; m. William Paul Mueller, Sept. 6, 1975; 1 child, Melinda Kay. BA in Journalism, Purdue U., 1974. Pub. info. officer Ind. Dept. Pub. Instrn., Indpls., 1974-75; mng. editor Portage (Ind.) Press, 1976-80; coord. pub. rels. Portage Twp. Schs., 1977-83; reporter, feature writer Gary (Ind.) Post-Tribune, 1981-83; editor Our Town Mag., Pitts., 1984-85; dir. pub. rels. Pitts. Children's Mus., 1986-90; coord. cmty. rels. Hampton Tow. Sch. Dist., Allison Park, Pa., 1990—; assoc. editor Hampton & McCandles Mag., Allison Park, Pa., 1994—; free-lance writer, pub. rels. cons. PR on A Showstring, Pitts., 1989—; presenter in field. Humor columnist Portage (Ind.) Press, 1976-80, 93—. Rep. Shaler Area Dist. Parent Coun., Glenshaw, Pa., 1990—, Pitts. Mus. Coun., 1986-90; pres. Shaler Area High Sch. Parents Assn., Pitts., 1994—, Shaler Area Mid. Sch. Parent Assn., Glenshaw, 1993-94; dir. pub. rels. Act One Theatre Sch., Glenshaw, 1988-95. Mem. Nat. Sch. Pub. Rels. Assn., Pa. Sch. Pub. Rels. Assn., North Pitts. Bus. and Profl. Women (pres. 1986-87), Women in Communications (Matrix award 1986, 72), Home Bus. Assn., Edn. Press. Assn. Home and Office: 124 Loire Valley Dr Pittsburgh PA 15209

MUELLER, LOIS M., psychologist; b. Milw., Nov. 30, 1943; d. Herman Gregor and Ora Emma (Dettmann) M.; BS, U. Wis.-Milw., 1965; MA, U. Tex., 1966, PhD, 1969. Cert. family mediator. Postdoctoral intern VA Hosp., Wood, Wis., 1969-71; counselor, asst. prof. So. Ill. U. Counseling Center and dept. psychology, Carbondale, 1971-72, coordinator personal counseling, asst. prof., 1972-74, counselor, asst. prof., 1974-76; individual practice clin. psychology, Carbondale, 1972-76, Clearwater, Fla., 1977-90, Port Richey, Fla., 1990—; family mediator, 1995—; mem. profl. adv. com. Mental Health Assn. Pinellas County, 1978, Alt. Human Services, 1979-80; cons. Face Learning Center, Hotline Crisis Phone Service, 1977-87; advice columnist Clearwater Sun newspaper, 1983-90; pub. speaker local TV and radio stas., 1978, 79; talk show host WPLP Radio Sta., Clearwater, 1980-83, WTKN Radio Sta., Tampa Bay, 1988-89, WPSO Radio Sta., New Port Richey, 1991. Campaign worker for Sen. George McGovern presdl. race, 1972. Lic. psychologist, Ill., Fla. Mem. Am., Fla., Ill., Pinellas (founder, pres. 1978) psychol. assns., Am. Soc. Clin. Hypnosis, Fla. Soc. Clin. Hypnosis, West Pasco C. of C., Calusa Bus. & Profl. Women. Contbr. articles to profl. jours. Office: 9501 US Highway 19 Ste 212 Port Richey FL 34668-4641

MUELLER, MARILYN JEAN, insurance company executive; b. Shawano, Wis., Mar. 19, 1946; d. Raymond Walter and Kathryn Ruth (Arveson) M. BA in English, U. Wis., Oshkosh, 1968, BA in Spanish, 1968. CLU; chartered fin. cons. Group rep. Wash. Nat. Ins. Co., Columbus, Ohio, 1968-73, asst. mgr., 1973-79; asst. mgr. Wash. Nat. Ins. Co., Phila., 1979-82, group mgr., 1982—; with Field Mgmt. Coun., Evanston, Ill., 1982-83, sec., 1988, Therapy Dogs, Inc. Tutor Literacy Vols. of Am., Voorhees, N.J., 1986—. Mem. CLU/Chartered Fin. Cons. South Jersey (bd. dirs. 1992-94), N.J. Prins. and Supervision Assn./Corp. Allied Ptnrs. (chairperson). Republican. Lutheran. Office: Wash Nat Ins Co Commerce Ctr 1810 Chapel Ave W Ste 260 Cherry Hill NJ 08002-4608

MUELLER, MONICA LYNN, special education educator; b. Melbourne, Fla., July 23, 1969; d. Lester Walter and Marilyn Price M. BA, San Diego State U., 1991; MA, Nat. Univ., 1993. Cert. tchr., Calif. Tchr. K-12 San Diego (Calif.) Community Schs., 1992-96; prof. U. San Diego, 1996; active Challenger Program Wis. Hart, 1996-97. Author: (guide) Oak Creek Curriculum Guide, 1994, 95, Challenger Curriculum Guide, 1996. Decorating chair Share Bear Gift Drive, San Diego, 1993, 94, 96, procurement chair, 1993; Calif. del. Libertarian Party, Salt Lake City, 1993. Office: La Mesa Jr High Challenger Program 26623 May Way Santa Clara CA 91351

MUELLER, NANCY SCHNEIDER, retired biology educator; b. Wooster, Ohio, Mar. 8, 1933; d. Gilbert Daniel and Winifred (Porter) Schneider; m. Helmut Charles Mueller, Jan. 27, 1959; 1 child, Karl Gilbert. AB in Biology, Coll. of Wooster, 1955; MS in Zoology, U. Wis., 1957, PhD in Zoology, 1962. Instr. zoology U. Wis., Madison, 1966; asst. prof. poultry sci. and zoology N.C. State U., Raleigh, 1968-71; vis. prof. biology N.C. Ctrl. U., Durham, 1971-73, assoc. prof., 1973-79, prof., 1979-93; ret., 1993; vis. scientist U. Vienna, Austria, 1975. Contbr. articles, abstracts to profl. publs. Mem. Am. Soc. Zoologists, Am. Ornithologists Union, Cooper Ornithol. Soc., Wilson Ornithol. Soc., Wis. Acad. Sci., Arts and Letters, N.C. Acad. Sci., LWV (bd. dirs. 1988—, natural resources com. 1988—), Sigma Xi. Home: 409 Moonridge Rd Chapel Hill NC 27516-9385

MUELLER, PEGGY JEAN, dance educator, choreographer, rancher; b. Austin, Tex., June 14, 1952; d. Rudolph George Jr. and Margaret Jean (Locke) M.; m. John Yerby Tarlton, June 24, 1972 (div. June 1983). BS in Home Econs., Child Devel., U. Tex., Austin, 1974. Dance tchr. Shirley McPhail Sch. Dance, Austin, 1972-75; dance tchr. Jean Tarlton Sch. Dance, Alpine, Tex., 1975-77, College Station, Tex., 1977-80; dance tchr. Sul Ross State U., Alpine, 1975-77, Tex. A&M U., College Station, 1977-80, A&M Consol. Community Edn., Coll. Station, 1977-78, Jean Mueller Sch. Dance, Austin, 1980—, U. Tex., Austin, 1980—; dancer, contest judge Gt. Tex. Dance-Off, Austin, 1985-86; mem. equestrian com. Austin-Travis County Livestock Show and Rodeo, 1980-92, chmn. trail ride, 1986—; trail boss, pres. Austin Founders Trail Ride, 1986—; trail boss Bandera Longhorn Cattle Drive and Trail Ride, 1990, 91; choreographer, head cheerleader Austin Texans Pro Football Team, 1981; dance tchr. Austin Ballroom Dancers, 1988; dancer, agt. George Strait/Bud Light Comml. Auditions, 1990; head contest judge Am.'s Ultimate Dance Contest, Austin, 1994; contest judge Two-Stepping Across Am., Austin, 1994; speaker in field. Dancer Oklahoma, Austin, 1969, Kiss Me Kate, Austin, 1970; choreographer, lead role Cabaret, Alpine, 1976. Active Women's Symphony League Austin, 1972—, Settlement Club, Austin, 1987—; recreation chmn. St. Martin's Evang. Luth. Ch., Austin, 1972—; hon. trail boss St. Jude Children's Rsch. Hosp. Trail Ride, Austin and Kyle, Tex., 1991. Recipient Outstanding Trail Rider of Yr. award Wild Horse Trail Ride, Okla., 1984; named Tex. First Lady Trail Boss, Gov. Mark White, Mayor Frank Cooksey, Austin City Coun., 1986, Judge Bill Aleshire, Travis County Commrs., 1989, Outstanding Intramural Sports Team Mgr.-Player, Tex. A&M U., 1978-79. Mem. Tex Assn. Tchrs. of Dancing, Inc., U.S. Twirling and Gymnastics Assn., Univ. Tex. Ex-Students Assn., Tex. Execs. in Home Econs., Am. Vet. Med. Assn. Aux. (v.p. 1978-79, pres. 1979-80), Am. Horse Shows Assn., Internat. Arabian Horse Assn., Austin Women's Tennis Assn. (v.p. 1985-86, pres. 1986-90, spl. events chmn. 1990-92, advisor 1990—, winner 2d ann. Harriet Crosson Outstanding Player & Community Svc. award), Women's Team Tennis of Austin Assn. (pres.-elect 1992-93, pres. 1993-94), Capital Area Tennis Assn. (membership com. 1991, 92), Houston Salt Grass Trail Ride Assn., San Antonio Alamo Trail Ride Assn., Ft. Worth Chisholm Trail Ride Assn., U. Tex. Longhorn Alumni Band, Austin C. of C., Am. Bus. Women's Assn., Austin Alumnae Panhellenic Assn. (1st v.p. 1989-90, rush forum chmn. 1990, pres. 1990-91, parliamentarian 1991-92), Omicron Nu (v.p. 1973-74), Jr. Austin Woman's Club (historian 1990-91), Austin Country Club (team tennis captain 1994—), Zeta Tau Alpha (Austin Alumnae Chpt., alumnae photographer, social advisor 1982-87, treas. 1987-89, publicity chmn. 1989, Easter Seals fundraiser, Honor Cup winner 1990, pres. 1991-92, internat. convention official del. 1988, 92, nominating chmn. 1992-93, mem. yearbook com. 1992-94, 2d v.p. 1993-94). Republican. Clubs: Cen. Tex. Arabian Horse, Capitol Area Quarter Horse Assn., Jr. Austin Woman's, Austin Country. Home and Office: PO Box 14762 Austin TX 78761-4762

MUELLER-FITCH, HEATHER MAY, priest; b. Radford, Va., Apr. 28, 1942; d. Robert Rohn and Esther Helen (Schmidt) Selfridge; m. John Scott Mueller, Aug. 17, 1962 (div. May 1973); children: Anne Elizabeth, Heidi Michelle; m. Richard Keelor Fitch, Apr. 25, 1992. BS, Mich. State U., 1967; MDiv, Ch. Div. Sch. of the Pacific, Berkeley, 1978. Seminarian intern All Saints Episcopal Ch., Kapaa, Hawaii, 1976-77; chaplain Seabury Hall, Makawao, Hawaii, 1978-81; assoc. priest Holy Innocent's Episcopal Ch., Lahaina, Hawaii, 1981; rector St. John's Episcopal Ch., Kula, Hawaii, 1981—; bd. mem. Episcopal Women's Caucus, N.Y.C., 1983-85. Founder Kula Cmty. Assn., 1985, Malama Makua Keiki, Wailuku, Hawaii, 1991; cofounder Hawaii Clergy Assn., Honolulu, 1993. Mem. Nat. Network Episcopal Clergy Assn. (bd. dirs. 1990-95), Hawaii Com. Chs. (pres. 1992-96), Interfaith Clergy Assn. (pres., founder 1993-95), Rotary (Paul Harris fellow 1994). Democrat. Episcopalian. Home: RR 2 Box 212 Kula HI 96790

MUFFOLETTO, MARY LU, retired school program director, consultant, editor; b. Chgo., May 25, 1932; d. Anthony Joseph and Lucile (Di Giacomo) M. B in Philosophy, DePaul U., 1959; ME, U. Ill., 1967. Tchr. elem. edn. Community Cons., Palatine, Ill., 1959-65; tchr. gifted children Sch. Dist. 15, Palatine, 1965-67, curriculum supr., 1967-75; dir. gifted edn. program Sch. Dist. 15, Palatine, Ill., 1972-95; coord. state and fed. programs Sch. Dist. 15, Palatine, 1975-95; asst. prin. Sch. Dist. 15, Palatine, Ill., 1975-95, retired, 1995; assoc. prof. Nat. Coll. Edn., Evanston, Ill., 1979-95; editor Tchg. Ink, Inc., 1995—; chairperson State Bd. of Edn. Adv. Com. on Gifted Edn., Springfield, Ill., 1977-85; pres. No. Ill. Planning Commn. for Gifted, 1978-80. Editor: (tchr. activity books) Teaching Inc., 1995—. Mem. Nat. Coun. for Social Studies, Assn. for Curriculum and Supervision, Coun. for Exceptional Children, U. Ill. Alumni Assn. (pres. Champaign chpt. 1982-85, Loyalty award), Kiwanis, Phi Delta Kappa (sec. 1985-87). Home: 21302 W Brandon Rd Kildeer IL 60047-8618

MUFTIC, FELICIA ANNE BOILLOT, consumer relations professional; b. Muskogee, Okla., Feb. 27, 1938; d. Lowell Francois and Geneva Margaret (Halstead) Boillot; m. Michael Muftic, Sept. 6, 1961; children: Tanya Muftic-Streicher, Theodore B., Mariana C. BA, Northwestern U., 1960. Exec. dir. Metro Dist. Atty.'s Consumer Office, Denver, 1973-79; talk show host KNUS, Denver, 1981-83; clk., recorder City and County of Denver, Colo., 1984-91; spl. projects dir. Consumer Credit Counseling, Denver, 1991-95; cons. consumer affairs pvt. practice, Denver, 1995—; pres. Muftic and Assocs., Denver, 1980-83; commr. Uniform Consumer Credit Code, Colo., 1991—. Author: Colorado Consumer Handbook, 1982. Candidate for mayor, Denver, 1979. Named Media person of Yr., NASW, Colo., 1982; recipient Outstanding Contbrn. in Consumer Affairs award Denver (Colo.) Fed. Exec. Bd., 1982. Mem. Am. Arbitration Assn. (chmn. regional dispute settlement bd. 1993-96), Inst. Internat. Edn. (bd. mem. 1980—), Rotary Internat. Democrat. Home and office: 3671 S Pontiac Way Denver CO 80237-1326

MUHAMMAD, KHALEEDAH, entrepreneur, sales and marketing consultant, community activist; b. Berkeley, Calif., Nov. 2, 1943; d. Samuel Taylor Odom and Robbie Lee (Taylor) Gordon; m. O.B. Britt, Jan. 2, 1963 (div. 1972); children: Raymie, Jamal; m. Ansar El Muhammad, June 12, 1974; children: Tamishi, Ansar El II. BA, Los Angeles State Coll., 1965; postgrad., Calif. State, Hayward, 1971-72. Caseworker Pacoima (Calif.) Child Guidance Clinic, 1965-68; probation officer Los Angeles Probation Dept., 1968-72; ednl. opportunity program counselor U. Calif., Berkeley, 1974-79; community cons. YWCA, Richmond, Calif., 1979-81; owner, sales mgr. Touch of Class Boutique, Richmond, 1981-84; owner, mktg. cons. Nature's Co., Richmond, 1982-84; owner Unique Home Services, Richmond, 1984—; part-owner, mktg. cons. Cora's Kitchen, Oakland, Calif., 1987—, Halal Mktg. Services, Oakland, 1987—; sales, mktg. cons. The Fox Factory, Richmond, 1985-87. Author: (pamphlet) It's Not Easy Being a Parent, 1979. Vice chairperson Unity Orgn., Richmond, 1979-83; founder People United For Coops., Richmond, 1983; bd. dirs. Richmond chpt. Reading Is Fundamental, 1979-83, Minority Arts Network, Contra Costa, Calif., 1987; ct. apptd. spl. rep. Adv. for Wards of the Ct., 1990-91; co-founder Loving Care Inc.; exec. dir. Ansari House Residential Treatment Facility for Teenage Girls. Mem. Nat. Assn. Female Execs. Democrat. Islam.

MUHLERT, JAN KEENE, art museum director; b. Oak Park, Ill., Oct. 4, 1942; d. William Henry and Isabel Janette (Cole) Keene; m. Christopher Layton Muhlert, Jan. 1, 1966; 1 son, Michael Keene. B.A. in Art and French, Albion (Mich.) Coll., 1964; M.A. in Art History, Oberlin (Ohio) Coll., 1967; student, Neuchatel (Switzerland) U., Inst. European Studies, Paris, Inst. de Phonetique, Acad. Grande Chaumiere. Asst. curator Allen Meml. Art Mus., Oberlin, 1967-68; asst. curator 20th Century painting and sculpture Nat. Collection Fine Arts, Smithsonian Instn., Washington, 1968-73; assoc. curator Nat. Collection Fine Arts, Smithsonian Instn., 1974-75; dir. U. Iowa Mus. Art, 1975-79, Amon Carter Mus., Ft. Worth, 1980-95, Palmer Museum of Art, University Park, PA, 1996-. Author museum brochures, catalogues. Mem. Nat. Mus. Act Adv. Council, 1980-83, vis. com. Allen Meml. Art Mus. of Oberlin (Ohio) Coll., 1987—. Grantee Nat. Endowment Arts-Donner Found., 1979; recipient Friend of Art Edn. award Tex. Art Edn. Assn., 1994. Mem. Assn. Art Mus. Dirs. (trustee 1981-82, 84-86, 92-93, chmn. govt. and art com. 1982-84, chmn. profl. practices com. 1990-92), Western Assn. Art Mus. (regional rep. 1978-79), Am. Assn. Mus. (commn. for new century 1981-84, gen. co-chair 1993 ann. meeting), Am. Arts Alliance (dir. 1980-86, vice-chmn. 1982-84). Office: Palmer Museum of Art Penn State University Park State College PA 16802-2507*

MUICO-MERCURIO, LUISA, critical care nurse; b. Caloocan, Manila, Philippines, Nov. 17, 1955; d. Amado B. and Eustaquia (Buenavista) Muico; m. Wilfred Tongson Mercurio, Dec. 28, 1974; children: Elyjah Matthew, Kristoffer Ross, Mercurio. ADN, Harbor City Coll., 1978; BSN, Calif. State U., 1990, postgrad., 1992—. Cert. ACLS instr., BLS instr; CCRN; cert. pub. health nurse. Staff nurse ICU Long Beach (Calif.) Meml. Med. Ctr., 1978-80; staff nurse CVT/ICU Cedar Sinai Med. Ctr., L.A., 1980-84; staff nurse ICU, critical care unit, emergency rm., cath. lab. Long Beach Community Hosp., 1982-86; ICU, CCU coord. Pioneer Hosp., Artesia, Calif., 1986-87; staff nurse CSU Kaiser-Permanente, L.A., 1988-90, pub. health nurse, 1990, asst. dept. adminstr., 1990-92; asst. dept. adminstr. Kaiser-Permanente, Sunset and Bellflower, Calif.; cardiovascular/thoracic surgery nurse coord. Kay Med. Group/Hosp. Good Samaritan, L.A., 1992—; adminstrv. supr. Barlow Respiratory Hosp., L.A., 1993; staff nurse critical care unit UCLA, 1994—; nursing faculty Pacific Coast Coll., 1994—, ICU-Kaweah Delta Dist. Hosp., Visalia, Calif., 1996—; adminstr., cons. Welco Guest Homes, Porterville, Calif., 1996—. Named to Dean's list Harbor City Coll., 1976-78, Dean's list Calif. State U., 1988-90. Mem. AACN (cert.), Nat. Golden Key Honor Soc., Nursing Honor Soc., Sigma Theta Tau (Nu Mu chpt.). Republican.

MUIR, HELEN, journalist, author; b. Yonkers, N.Y., Feb. 9, 1911; d. Emmet A. and Helen T. (Flaherty) Lennehan; student public schs.; m. William Whalley Muir, Jan. 23, 1936; children: Mary Muir Burrell, William Torbert. With Yonkers Herald Statesman, 1929-30, 31-33, N.Y. Evening Post, 1930-31, N.Y. Evening Jour., 1933-34, Carl Byoir & Assos., N.Y.C., and Miami, Fla., 1934-35; syndicated columnist Universal Svc., Miami, 1935-38; columnist Miami Herald, 1941-42; children's book editor, 1949-56; women's editor Miami Daily News, 1943-44; freelance mag. writer, numerous nat. mags., 1944—; drama critic Miami News, 1960-65. Trustee Coconut Grove Libr. Assn., Friends U. Miami Libr., Friends Miami-Dade Pub. Libr.; vis. com. U. Miami Librs.; bd. dirs. Miami-Dade County Pub. Libr. System; past chmn., mem. State Libr. Adv. Coun., 1979-91, past chmn. Recipient award Delta Kappa Gamma, 1960; Fla. Libr. Assn. Trustees and Friends award, 1973, Coun. Fla. Librs. award, 1990; trustee citation ALA, 1984, Spirit of Excellence award, 1988; named to Fla. Women's Hall of Fame, 1984, Miami Centennial '96 Women's Hall of Fame. Mem. Women in Communications (Cmty. Headliner award 1973), Soc. Women Geographers (Meritorious Svc. award 1996), Author's Guild. Clubs: Florida Women's Press (award 1963); Cosmopolitan (N.Y.C.); Biscayne Bay Yacht. Author: Miami, U.S.A., 1953, 3d rev. edit., 1990, Biltmore: Beacon for Miami, 1987, 2d rev. edit., 1993, Frost In Florida: A Memoir, 1995. Home: 3855 Stewart Ave Miami FL 33133-6734

MUIR, ROBIN DENISE, secondary education educator; b. Red Bank, N.J., Dec. 28, 1966; d. Allan Koen and Alice Merrill M. BS Edn., Tex. Tech. U., 1989. Cert. tchr. social studies, gifted/talented edn. Sales mgr. Pretty Balloons Unltd., Houston, 1980-89; tech. ctr. Helpdesk Asst., Lubbock, Tex., 1985-87; student mgr. U. C. Food Svc., Lubbock, 1987-89; office mgr. Alliance Gift Cons., Houston, 1990; tchr. econs. Klien Ind. Sch. Dist., Houston, 1990; tchr. Am. history Cypress Fairbanks Ind. Sch. Dist., Houston, 1990-92, tchr. world history, 1992-93, tchr. govt. and econs., 1993—, tchr. world area studies, 1994-95, tchr. world geography, 1995—; v.p. Cy-Fair Coun. for Social Studies, Houston, 1994-95, sec., 1993-94, state bd. reps., 1995—; chmn. Cy-Creek History Fair, 1993-95. Editor: (newsletter) UC Programs, 1987-88; author/editor: Endymion mag., 1983-85. Sponsor Model UN, Houston Area, 1994-95, SPARKS, Cy-Fair Area, 1992-94. Fellowship Hatton Sumners Inst., Houston, 1994; participant Roger Taylor Seminar, Alief, Tex., 1994. Mem. UN Assn. (sponsor), Tex. Coun. for the Social Studies (com. mem. 1991-94), Nat. Coun. for the Social Studies, Nat. Trust, World History Assn., Orgn. of Am. Historians. Office: Cypress Creek High Sch 9815 Grant Rd Houston TX 77070-4501

MUIR, RUTH BROOKS, counselor, substance abuse service coordinator; b. Washington, Nov. 27, 1924; d. Charles and Adelaide Chenery (Masters) B.; m. Robert Mathew Muir, Nov. 26, 1947 (dec. Feb. 20, 1996); children: Robert Brooks, Martha Louise, Heather Sue. BA in Art, Rollins Coll., Winter Park, Fla., 1947; MA in Rehab. Counseling, U. Iowa, 1979. Cert. substance abuse counselor, Iowa. Program advisor Iowa Meml. Union, Iowa City, 1959-66; counselor, coord. Mid Eastern Coun. on Chem. Abuse, Iowa City, 1976-81; patient rep. Univ. Hosp., Iowa City, 1982-85; rsch. project interviewer dept. psychiatry, U. Iowa Coll. Medicine, 1985-88. Art exhibited at Iowa City Sr. Ctr., 1987, 92, Iowa City Art Ctr., 1989, U. Iowa Hosp., 1991, Great Midwestern Ice Cream Co., 1991, Summit St. Gallery, 1995; creator, coord. therapeutic series Taking Control, Iowa City Sr. Ctr., 1986-87. Vol. coord. art exhibits Sr. Ctr., Iowa City, 1992-94; treas. bd. dirs. Crisis Ctr., Iowa City, 1975-77; sec. coun. elders Sr. Citizens Ctr., Iowa City, 1976-78; pres. Unitarian-Universalist Iowa City Women's Fedn., 1985; friend of U. of Iowa Mus. Art; mem. Johnson County Arts Coun., Opera Supers, Iowa City Unitarian U.N. Envoy; fgn. rels. coun., bd. dirs. annual changing family conf. U. Iowa, 1986-92; non-govtl. rep. Earth Summit Global Forum, 1992. Mem. AAUW (state cultural rep. 1990-92, painting presented to young leader 1996), Iowa City Unitarian Soc. (mem. adult program com. 1993-94, mem. unitarian care com. 1993-96), Pi Beta Phi (pres. alumnae club 1995—), U. Iowa Print and Drawing Study Club. Home and Office: 6 Glendale Ct Iowa City IA 52245-4430

MUJAHED, MARY ELIZABETH, small business owner; b. Cheyenne, Wyo., Mar. 16, 1929; d. Frank Ralph and Elsie Fern (Patterson) Yager; m. Saleh Ramadan Mujahed, July 24, 1952; children: Susan Elizabeth, David Saleh. BA in Liberal Arts, Scripps Coll., 1951. Libr. asst. Contra Costa (Calif.) County Libr. System, 1965-69; pub. Willoughby Pub. Co., Walnut Creek, Calif., 1995—; owner Orion Pub. Co., Walnut Creek, Calif., 1982-83. Editor: How To Stop Smoking, 1982. Mem. Nat. Congl. Rep. Com., Washington, 1977-90; sustaining mem. Nat. Rep. Com., 1977-90, Nat. Rep. Senatorial Com., 1977-92, Rep. Presdl. Task Force, 1982-96. Recipient Medal of Merit, Rep. Presdl. Task Force, 1982; Disting. benefactor Afghan Mercy Fund. Mem. Am. Assn. Polit. and Social Sci., Nat. Acad. Polit. Sci.

MUKHERJEE, BHARATI (MRS. CLARK BLAISE), author, English educator; b. Calcutta, India, July 27, 1940; d. Sudhir Lal and Bina (Banerjee) M.; m. Clark L. Blaise, Sept. 19, 1963; children: Bart Anand, Bernard Sudhir. BA, U. Calcutta, 1959; MA, U. Baroda, India, 1961; MFA, U. Iowa, 1963, PhD, 1969. Instr. in English Marquette U., Milw., 1964-65; instr. U. Wis., Madison, 1965; lectr. McGill U., Montreal, Que., Can., 1966-69; asst. prof. English McGill U., Montreal, Can., 1969-73, assoc. prof., 1973-78, prof., 1978-79; prof. Skidmore Coll., Saratoga Springs, N.Y., 1979-84; assoc. prof. Montclair (N.J.) State College, 1984-87; prof. CUNY, 1987-89, U. Calif., Berkeley; vis. prof. of writing U. Iowa, Iowa City, 1979, 82; vis. prof. Emory U., Atlanta, 1983. Author: The Tiger's Daughter, 1972, Wife, 1975, (with Clark Blaise) Days and Nights in Calcutta, 1977, Darkness, 1985, The Middleman and Other Stories, 1988 (Nat. Book Critics Circle award 1989), The Sorrow and the Terror, 1988, Jasmine, 1989, The Holder of the World, 1993; contbr. short stories, essays and book revs. to several jours. Grantee McGill U., 1968, 70, Can. Arts Coun., 1973-74, 77, Shastri Indo-Can. Inst., 1976-77, Guggenheim Found., 1978-79, Can. Govt., 1982; recipient 1st prize Periodical Distbn. Assn., 1980, NEA award, 1986. Mem. PEN. Hindu. Office: U Calif Dept English 322 Wheeler Hall Berkeley CA 94720-4714

MULAC, PAMELA ANN, priest, pastoral counselor; b. Salem, Ohio, Dec. 6, 1944; d. Elmer John and Dorothy Adelaide (McGee) M.; m. George Robert Larsen, Aug. 8, 1987. Student, Bryn Mawr Coll., 1962-64; AB, U. Chgo., 1966; MDiv, Seabury-Western Theol. Sem., 1974; PhD, Garrett Evang. Theol. Sem., Northwestern U., 1988. Ordained to ministry Episcopal Ch. as priest, 1978. Asst. deacon, priest St. Luke's Ch., Evanston, Ill., 1974-84; asst. priest St. Mark's Ch., Upland, Calif., 1984-88, St. Ambrose Ch., Claremont, Calif., 1988-90; assoc. priest for pastoral care All Saints Ch., Pasadena, Calif., 1991-93; asst. interim pastor St. George's, La Canada, Calif., 1994-95; chaplain Foothill Presbyn. Hosp., Glendon, Calif., 1994-95; interim pastor St. Timothy's Ch., Apple Valley, Calif., 1995-96; pastoral counselor Swedish Covenant Hosp., Chgo., 1975-84; adj. lectr. Seabury-Western Theol. Sem., Evanston, 1981-82, trustee, 1981-84; pastoral counselor Walnut (Calif.) Valley Counseling Ctr., 1984-89; adj. lectr. marriage and family therapy program Azusa Pacific U., 1988-89, adj. lectr. operation impact, 1991-92; adj. prof. Sch. of Theology at Claremont, 1994-95; adj. prof. Episc. Theology Sch., Claremont, 1994-96. Bd. dirs. Cathedral Shelter Chgo., 1980-84; co-chairperson Leader's Sch. Cursillo, Chgo., 1981-83; mem. Commn. on Alcoholism, Diocese of L.A., 1985-87. Episcopal Ch. Found. fellow, 1978-81. Mem. Am. Assn. Pastoral Counselors (sec. Pacific region 1984-85, treas. 1984-91, fin. chair 1988-91), Assn. Clin. Pastoral Edn. Home and Office: 2964 Gambrel Gate La Verne CA 91750-2372

MULAY, SHAWNA RAE, public relations director; b. Denver, Nov. 28, 1968; d. Carl Raymond Joseph and Marilyn Dawn (Resseguie) M. BA, Cornell Coll., 1991. Dir. pub. rels. Grubb-Ellis Co., Denver, 1991—; mem. adv. bd. Alameda H.S., Lakewood, Colo., 1993—; local, state judge Colo. Distributive Edn. Clubs Am., Denver, 1992—. Author, editor: Denver Commercial Real Estate, 1993, 94, 95 (Nat. Class "A" award for excellence in comms. 1995). Mem. Nat. Assn. Indsl. and Office Pks. (event dir. 1994—, hon. co-chair 1994, 95, dir. property tour 1994—). Office: Grubb & Ellis Co Ste 2000 1 Tabor Ctr Denver CO 80202

MULCAHY, LUCILLE BURNETT, freelance writer; b. Albuquerque, Nov. 10, 1918; d. Harry Leland and Grace Ruth (Lomax) Burnett; m. Clemons David Mulcahy Jr., Sept. 1, 1939 (div. May 1957); children: Burnette Anne, DeeAnn Eileen. Student, N.Mex. State U., 1947, U. Albuquerque, 1975. Freelance writer, 1953—; procurement officer Albuquerque Pub. Libr., 1963-76; storyteller various schs. Author: (childrens books) Dark Arrow, 1953, 95, Pita, 1954, Magic Fingers, 1958 (Jr. Lit. Guild award), Blue Marshmallow Mountains, 1959, Natoto, 1960, Fire on Big Lonesome, 1967, (under pseudonym) Dale Evans and Danger in Crooked Canyon, 1958. Recipient Zia award N.Mex. Press Women, 1967. Home: 505 Doe Ln SE Albuquerque NM 87123

MULDAUR, DIANA CHARLTON, actress; b. N.Y.C., Aug. 19, 1938; d. Charles Edward Arrowsmith and Alice Patricia (Jones) M.; m. James Mitchell Vickery, July 26, 1969 (dec. 1979); m. Robert J. Dozier, Oct. 11, 1981. B.A., Sweet Briar Coll., 1960. Actress appearing in: Off-Broadway theatrical prodns., summer stock, Broadway plays including A Very Rich Woman, 1963-68; guest appearances on TV in maj. dramatic shows; appeared on: TV series Survivors, 1970-71, McCloud, 1971-73, Tony Randall Show, 1976, Black Beauty, 1978; star: TV series Born Free, 1974, Hizzoner, 1979, Fitz & Bones, 1980, Star Trek: The Next Generation, 1988-89; NBC miniseries and TV series A Year in the Life, 1986; TV movie Murder in Three Acts, The Return of Sam McCloud, 1989; TV series L.A. Law, 1989-91; motion picture credits include McQ, The Lawyer, The Other, One More Train to Rob, Matt, etc. Bd. dirs. Los Angeles chpt. Asthma and Allergy Found. Am.; bd. advisors Nat. Ctr. Film and Video Preservation, John F. Kennedy Ctr. Performing Arts, 1986. Recipient 13th Ann. Commendation award Am. Women in Radio and TV, 1988, Disting. Alumnae award Sweet Briar Coll., 1988. Mem. Acad. Motion Picture Arts and Scis., Screen Actors Guild (dir. 1978), Acad. TV Arts and Scis. (exec. bd., dir., pres. 1983-85), Conservation Soc. Martha's Vineyard Island. Office: The Artists Group Ltd 1930 Century Park W Ste 403 Los Angeles CA 90067-6803

MULDER, ANN ELIZABETH, health careers educator, secondary education educator, nurse; b. Washington, Iowa, Feb. 20, 1961; d. Thomas John and Aileen Delores (Peterson) Sandell; m. Tom Alan Mulder, July 3, 1983; children: Jacob, Stephen. AS in Nursing, Iowa Cen. C.C., 1982; BS in Tech. Edn., Tex. A&M U., 1990; MS in counseling, U. Houston, Clear Lake, 1995. RN St. Luke's Hosp., Cedar Rapids, Iowa, 1982-83; RN Humana Hosp. of Clear Lake, Webster, Tex., 1984-85, asst. head nurse, 1986; coord. health occupations Pearland (Tex.) H.S., 1986-89, Clear Lake H.S., Houston, 1989—; mentoring cons. Tex. Edn. Agy., Austin, 1989-93. Instr. CPR, Am. Heart Assn., Houston, 1988—; RN crisis vol. ARC, Clear Lake, 1992-93. Mem. Tex. Health Occupations Assn. (pres. Area VI, 1992-93, sec. to coord. bd. 1993, gov. coun. 1994—). Democrat. Lutheran. Office: Clear Lake HS 2929 Bay Area Blvd Houston TX 77058-1005

MULDER, ARLENE JOANN, mayor; b. Tulare, Calif., Oct. 13, 1944; d. Joseph R. and Anna W. (Lorenzo) Borges; m. Albert John Mulder, June 18, 1966; children: Michelle, Alison, Michael. BS, San Francisco State U., 1966, postgrad., 1967. Cert. secondary tchr., Calif., Ill. Tchr. pub. schs., Anaheim, Calif., 1967-69; tchr. Niles Twp. Dist. 219, Skokie, Ill., 1972-78, coach, 1973-78; mem. Arlington Heights (Ill.) Park Dist. Commn., 1979-91; village trustee Village of Arlington Heights, 1991-93, mayor, 1993—; coach Sch. Dist. 25, Arlington Heights, 1990-92. Mem. Arlington Heights Centennial Commn., 1984-89. Office: Village Arlington Heights 33 S Arlington Heights Rd Arlington Heights IL 60005

MULDER, PATRICIA MARIE, education educator; b. South Bend, Ind., Dec. 28, 1944; d. Ervin James and Carmen Virginia (Sheeley) Anderson; m. James R. Mulder, Dec. 27, 1964; children: Todd Alan, Scott Robert. BA, Western Mich. U., 1967. Freelance writer, photographer Berrien Springs, Mich., 1980—; tchr. Eau Claire (Mich.) Pub. Schs., 1969-70; staff writer, sales rep. Jour. Era, Berrien Springs, 1979-81; sales rep. Berrien County Record, Buchana, Mich., 1981-82; account exec. WHFB Radio Palladium Pub. Co., St. Joseph, Mich., 1982-86; substitute tchr. Berrien County Intermediate Dist., 1986-89; instr. Southwestern Mich. Coll., Dowagiac, 1989—. Editor The Positive Image newsletter, 1980—, The F Stop, 1982-90; author: Poetry Anthologies, 1989—; staff writer Decision Point, 1988-89; newsletter editor Fernwood Nature Photographers, 1980—. Ofcl. photographer Ind. and Internat. Spl. Olympics, Notre Dame, 1986. Named Emerging Artist Ind. Coun. for the Arts, 1989, Honor award Southwestern Coun. of Camera Clubs, 1988, Photographer of the Yr. Berrien County Photographic Artists, 1987, 90. Mem. AAUW, Nat. Authors Registry, Meth. Profl. Women (sec. 1990—), Berrien County Artists (v.p. 1986), Berrien County Photographic Artists (v.p. 1984), Southwestern Mich. Coun. Camera Clubs, Berrien Springs Camrea Club (v.p. 1980—). Methodist. Home: 10252 Castner Dr Berrien Springs MI 49103-9602 Office: Southwestern Mich Coll 58900 Cherry Grove Rd # 316L Dowagiac MI 49047-9726

MULDOON, PATRICIA, special education administrator; b. Urbana, Ill., Mar. 17, 1940; d. Maurice Elwood and Marie Ann (Craig) Turner; m. Patrick John Muldoon, Aug. 4, 1962; children: Shaena, Patrick, Meghan, Bronwyn, Sean. BA, Mich. State U., 1962; MS, Radford Coll., 1976. Spl. edn. tchr. Giles County Pub. Schs., Pearisburg, Va., 1971-80, spl. edn. supr., 1980-88, dir. spl. programs, 1989—; adv. coun. NRV Head Start, Christiansburg, Va., 1993-96. Bd. dirs. New River Valley Hospice, Christiansburg, 1994-97, New River Valley Mental health Assn., Christiansburg, 1995-96. Named Outstanding Tchr. of the Yr. Giles County Assn. for Retarded Citizens, Pearisburg, 1976, Grace Maynard award Va. Coun. for Exceptional Children, 1982, 95. Mem. Coun. for Exception Children (sect., chpt. pres. 1990-95), Learning Disabilities Assn. of Am., Coun. for Learning Disabilities, Delta Kappa Gamma (sec. 1979-95), Phi Delta Kappa. Home: Rte 1 Box 149 Pembroke VA 24136 Office: Giles County Pub Schs Rte 1 Box 52 Pearisburg VA 24134

MULDROW, TRESSIE WRIGHT, psychologist; b. Marietta, Ga., Feb. 1, 1941; d. Festus Blanton and Louise Williams Wright Summers; BA, Bennett Coll., 1962; MS, Howard U., 1965, PhD, 1976; 1 child, DeJuan Denise. Research asst. W.C. Allen Corp., Washington, 1966-68; personnel research psychologist Dept. Navy, Washington, 1968-73, Office Personnel Mgmt., CSC, 1973-79; chief, adv. council on alternative selection procedures Office Personnel Mgmt., Washington, 1979-86, chief consultative services, 1986-91, chief multidimentional assessment br., 1992-94; spl. advisor Office of Diversity, 1994-95; leader Bus. Re-engring. Task Force, 1995—, acting divsn. dir. Assessment Svcs. Divsn. lectr. Howard U., 1979. Mem. Washington Inter-Alumni council United Negro Coll. Fund, 1970—, pres., 1988-92; trustee Bennett Coll., vice chmn., 1985-90; v.p. Family Life Ctr. Br., Boys and Girls Clubs of Washington, 1984-90. Named Alumnae of Yr., United Negro Coll. Fund, 1971, Outstanding Alumnae, Morehouse Coll., 1978, Outstanding Alumnae, Bennett Coll., 1993, Outstanding Woman, Am. Bus. Women Assn., 1994; recipient UNCF Individual Achievement award, 1985, Exemplary Performance award UNCF, 1996. Mem. Bennett Coll. Alumnae Assn. (nat. pres. 1978-85, 93—, Alumnae of Yr. award 1987), Am. Psychol. Assn., Delta Sigma Theta. Presbyterian. Contbr. articles to profl. publs. Office: 1900 E St NW Washington DC 20415-0001

MULKEY, SHARON RENEE, gerontology nurse; b. Miles City, Mont., Apr. 14, 1954; d. Otto and Elvera Marie (Haglof) Neuhardt; m. Monty W. Mulkey, Oct. 9, 1976; children: Levi, Candice, Shane. BS in Nursing, Mont. State U., 1976. RN, Calif. Staff nurse, charge nurse VA Hosp., Miles City, Mont., 1976-77; staff nurse obstetrics labor and delivery Munster (Ind.) Cmty. Hosp., 1982-83; nurse mgr. Thousand Oaks Health Care, 1986-88; unit mgr. rehab. Semi Valley (Calif.) Adventist Hosp., 1988-89, DON TCU, 1989-91; DON Pleasant Valley Hosp. Extended Care Vacility and Neuro Ctr., 1991-93; dir. nurses Victoria Care Ctr., Ventura, Calif., 1993—; clin. supr. Procare Home Health, Oxnard, Calif., 1996—. Mem. ANA, Nat. Gerontol. Nursing Assn., Internat. Platform Assn., Alpha Tau Delta (pres. 1973-75), Phi Kappa Phi. Home: 3461 Pembridge St Thousand Oaks CA 91360-4565

MULL, JOCELYN BETHE, school administrator; b. Nassau, N.Y., Oct. 21, 1968; divorced; 1 child, Eron Michael. BA, SUNY, Buffalo, 1981, MA, 1989. Dir. edn. Ctr. for Positive Thought, Mus. African Am. Arts and Antiquities, Buffalo, 1978-83; tchr. English, Buffalo Bd. Edn., 1980—, cons. tchr. inclusion project, 1991-93, fed. magnet curriculum specialist Futures Acad., 1993—; case mgr. spl. edn., gifted and comprehensive programs Crenshaw H.S., L.A.; case mgr. spl. edn. and GATE coord. Crenshaw H.S. Author: (poetry) Goti, Paja, Mguu-The Knee, A Thigh and The Leg, 1980, Strength in the Water, 1995. Rec. coord., publicist Lighthouse Interdenominational Choir, 1988-94; project coord. Performing Artists Collective, Western N.Y. United Against Drugs, Buffalo, 1993—; mem. Mayor's Arts and Adv. Coun. Against Drugs and Violence, 1995. Recipient Educator of Excellence award PUSH Excel, Operation PUSH, 1981, N.Y. State English Coun., 1994, Creative Arts award, 1980, citation Martin Luther King Jr. Arts and Scis. award, 1986—, Outstanding Commemorative Youth award for performing arts and cmty. svc., 1980. Mem. ASCD, NEA (spl. edn. com.), Buffalo Tchrs. Fedn. (multicultural com.), AAUW, Phi Delta Kappa. Office: Crenshaw High School 5010 11th Ave Los Angeles CA 90043

MULLAGHY, ANN MARGARET, fiscal policy analyst; b. Evanston, Ill., Jan. 16, 1969; d. Patrick Brendan and Nancy Theresa (Gibbons) M. BA in Econs., Ea. Ill. U., 1991; postgrad., DePaul U., 1992—. Budget analyst City of Chgo. Office of Budget and Mgmt., 1992-93, fiscal policy analyst, 1994, chief revenue analyst, 1995, asst. budget dir., 1996—. Mem. 40th Ward Dem. Orgn. Mem. Govt. Fin. Officers Assn. Democrat. Roman Catholic.

MULLANEY, JOANN BARNES, nursing educator; b. Newport, R.I., Dec. 7, 1943; d. Elliott Calvert and Betty (Dawson) Barnes; m. Charles Patrick Mullaney, June 3, 1967 (div. 1973); 1 child, Mark Andrew. Diploma in Nursing, Newport Hosp. Sch. Nursing, 1965; BSN, Salve Regina Coll., Newport, 1976; BSN/MS in Psychiat. Mental Health Nursing, Boston Coll., 1977; PhD in Edn., U. Conn., 1983. RN, R.I.; clin. specialist, ANCC. Instr. Salve Regina U., Newport, 1979-83, asst. prof., 1983-85, sr. level coord., 1983-94, assoc. prof. nursing, 1985-95, prof., 1995—; psychiat. clin. specialist in pvt. practice The Center, Middletown, R.I., 1990—, utilization reviewer, Providence, 1990-92, ednl. cons., 1990—. Contbr. to book: Psychiatric Care Planning, 1989 (ASN Book of Yr. 1988). Mem. Atty.-Gen.'s Task Force on Domestic Violence, Providence, 1994; mem. Health Care Reform Coalition, Providence, 1993—, Nat./R.I. Action Not Gridlock Coun., 1993—; mem. R.I. House and Senate Women's Health Issues Commn., 1995. Recipient Air Force Nurse Educator award, 1988; grantee HEW, 1976, NIMH, 1977, 91-94, Lilly Co., 1994; M.A.C.N. scholar, 1995. Mem. ANA, AAUW, AAUP, NEON, ENRS, SERPA, RISNA (pres.-elect 1992-93, pres. 1993-95, pres. ex-officio 1995—), Mass. Assn. Coll. Nursing Rsch., Sigma Theta Tau (Delta Upsilon chpt.), Phi Lambda Theta. Home: 242 Gibbs Ave Newport RI 02840-2829

MULLARKEY, MARY J., state supreme court justice; b. New London, Wis., Sept. 28, 1943; d. John Clifford and Isabelle A. (Steffes) M.; m. Thomas E. Korson, July 24, 1971; 1 child, Andrew Steffes Korson. BA, St. Norbert Coll., 1965; LLB, Harvard U., 1968; LLD (hon.), St. Norbert Coll., 1989. Bar: Wis. 1968, Colo. 1974. Atty.-advisor U.S. Dept. Interior, Washington, 1968-73; asst. regional atty. EEOC, Denver, 1973-75; 1st atty. gen. Colo. Dept. Law, Denver, 1975-79, solicitor gen., 1979-82; legal advisor to Gov. Lamm State of Colo., Denver, 1982-85; ptnr. Mullarkey & Seymour, Denver, 1985-87; justice Colo. Supreme Ct., Denver, 1987—. Recipient Alumni award St. Norbert Coll., De Pere, Wis., 1980, Alma Mater award, 1993. Fellow ABA Found., Colo. Bar Found.; mem. ABA, Colo. Bar Assn., Colo. Women's Bar Assn. (recognition award 1986), Denver Bar Assn., Thompson G. Marsh Inn of Ct. (pres. 1993-94). Office: Supreme Ct Colo 2 E 14th Ave Denver CO 80203-2115

MULLEEDY, JOYCE ELAINE, nursing service administrator, educator; b. Paterson, N.J., Aug. 30, 1948; d. Edward and Jane (Van De Weert) Schuurman; m. Philip Anthony Mulleedy, May 14, 1982. BS, Paterson State Coll., 1970. RN, cert. emergency nurse, emergency med. technician, paramedic. Pub. health nurse Vis. Nurse Assn. of No. Bergen County, Ramsey, N.J., 1970-72; health dir. Camp Fowler Assn., Speculator, N.Y., 1973-76; exec. dir. Am. Cancer Soc., Speculator, 1976-77; pub. health nurse Hamilton County Nursing Service, Lake Pleasant, N.Y., 1977-80, supervising pub. health nurse, 1980-82, dir. patient svcs., 1982-86; quality improvement coord. Susquehanna-Adirondack Regional Emergency Med. Svcs. Program, 1986-96; dir. ednl. svcs. Adirondack Appalachian Regional Emergency Med. Svcs. program, 1996—. mem. profl. adv. com. Hamilton County Nursing Svc., Indian Lake, N.Y., 1992—. Author instructional booklet: Assessing Your Patients, 1983, (pamphlet) A Note to Parents, 1985, Advanced Assessment and Treatment of Life Threatening Pediatric Emergencies, 1995, Orientation to EMS for Emergency Dept. Physicians and Nurses, 1996. Bd. dirs. Am. Cancer Soc.-Hamilton County Unit, Speculator, 1972-76, Speculator Vol. Ambulance Corps, Inc., 1974—, ARC-Hamilton County chpt., Lake Pleasant, N.Y., 1981-88; mem. administrv. bd. dirs. Grace United Meth. Ch., Speculator, 1982—, Rainbow Christian Children's Ctr., 1992—. Martha Hazen Scholar Am. Legion, 1966; recipient Svcs. award Am. Legion, 1977. Mem. N.Y. State Assn. County Health Ofcls., Adirondack-Appalachian Regional Emergency Med. Svcs. Coun. (chmn. 1982-87, chmn. tng. com. 1982—), Emergency Nurses Assn., Hamilton County Emergency Med. Svcs. Coun. (sec.-treas. 1974-90, instr. 1974—). Republican. Home: PO Box 203 Speculator NY 12164-0203 Office: Adirondack-Appalachian Regional Emergency Med Svcs Prog PO Box 212 Speculator NY 12164-0212

MULLEN, EILEEN ANNE, staff training and development executive; b. Phila., Feb. 14, 1943; d. Joseph Gregory and Helen Rita (Kane) M. BS in English, St. Joseph U., 1967; MA in English, Villanova U., 1978. Cert. tchr., Pa. Tchr., St. Anastasia Sch., Newtown Square, 1960-67, West Cath. Girls High Sch., 1967-74; mgr. staff tng. and devel. ASTM, Phila., 1974—; instr. lit., speech and communications Widener U. Weekend Coll., Chester, Pa. and Wilmington, Del. Author: Speech Command, 1995; contbg. author articles on communications tng. programs; contbr. articles to profl. publs. Mem. ASTD (pres. Phila./Delaware Valley chpt. 1980-81, award for outstanding leadership as pres. 1981), Am. Soc. Assn. Execs. (Delaware Valley chpt.). Democrat. Roman Catholic. Office: ASTM 100 Barr Harbor Dr West Conshohocken PA 19428

MULLEN, M. DENISE, art educator, higher education administrator, photographer, artist; b. Lawton, Okla., July 25; d. T.L. and Leila Virginia (Wyatt) M. BA, Sweet Briar Coll., 1970; MFA, Pratt Inst., 1973. Asst. prof. art Sweet Briar (Va.) Coll., 1974-75; instr. art County Coll. of Morris, Dover, N.J., 1977-78, adj. instr. art, 1977, 78; adj. instr. art Jersey City State Coll., 1977-86, asst. prof. art, coord. photography, 1986-93, chair dept. art, assoc. prof., 1994—; vis. evaluator Nat. Assn. Schs. Art and Design, Reston, Va., 1994—; mem. exec. bd., art dir. Printmaking Coun. N.J., Sommerville, 1986-89, mem. adv. bd., 1985, 90. Solo exhbns. include Jersey City Mus., 1996, Mednick Gallery, U. of the Arts, Phila., 1996; exhibited works in group shows at ARTspace Gallery, Richmond, Va., 1994, Ctr. for Book Arts, N.Y.C., 1994, Galerie Mesa, 1995. Trustee N.J. Ctr. for the Visual Arts, Summit, 1996. Recipient various merit and purchase awards. Mem. Nat. coun. Arts Adminstrs., Ctr. for Book Arts, Dieu Donne Paper Mill, Coll. Art Assn., Soc. Am. Graphic Artists, Guild of Bookworkers. Office: Jersey City State Coll Art Dept 2039 Kennedy Blvd Jersey City NJ 07305

MULLEN, REGINA MARIE, lawyer; b. Cambridge, Mass., Apr. 22, 1948; d. Robert G. and Elizabeth R. (McHugh) M. BA, Newton Coll. Sacred Heart, 1970; JD, U. Va., 1973. Bar: Pa., Del., U.S. Dist. Ct. Del., U.S. Ct. Appeals (3d cir.), U.S. Supreme Ct. Dep. atty. gen. State Del. Dept. Justice, Wilmington, 1973-79, state solicitor, 1979-83, chief fin. unit, 1983-88; v.p., counsel MBNA Am. Bank, N.A., Newark, Del., 1988-91, 1st v.p., sr. v.p., counsel, 1991—; Mem. bd. Bar Examiners, State Del., 1979-89; bd. dirs. Del. Cmty. Investment Corp., Wilmington, 1994-96, Wilmington Music Festival, 1992—; mem. bd. profl. responsibility State of Del., 1996—. Bd. dirs. Wilmington Music Festival, 1992—; mem. fin. com. Chesapeake Bay Girl Scout coun. Wilmington, 1985-94, bd. dirs., 1988-94, v.p., 1990-94, mem. fund devel. com., 1994—, chair personnel com., 1996—; bd. dirs. Comty. Legal Aid Soc., 1994—, treas., 1995—. Mem. ABA, Del. State Bar Assn. (chair adminstrv. law sect. 1983-85). Democrat. Roman Catholic. Office: 400 Christiana Rd Newark DE 19713-4217

MULLENIX, KATHY ANN, relocation company executive; b. Goodland, Ind., Mar. 8, 1955; d. Boyd Dale and Edith Marie Hoaks; 1 child, Joseph F. Hamburg IV. Diploma, South Newton Jr./Sr. H.S., Goodland, Ind., 1973. Asst. to pres. Planes Moving, Cin., 1981-88; sales mgr. Tru-Pak Moving, Greenville, S.C., 1988-89; account exec. Armstrong Relocation, Atlanta, 1989—. Den leader Cub Scouts, Blue Ash, Ohio, 1982-86; coach's asst. Soccer Assn., Mason, Ohio, 1985-88; treas. PTA Mason Mid. Sch., 1988; tutor Gwinnette Co. Adult Literacy, Lawrenceville, Ga., 1994. Mem. NAFE. Office: Armstrong Relocation 6950 Business Ct Atlanta GA 30340-1429

MULLER, ALEXANDRA LIDA, real estate management director; b. N.Y.C., June 9, 1949; d. John William and Elisa (Bianco) M. BA in Math., Western N.E. Coll., 1971; Cert. in Real Estate, NYU, 1982, Cert. as Real Estate Broker, 1991. Lic. notary pub. Ptnr. Raffles, Florence, Italy, 1972-74; bookkeeper Emmeti, Florence, Italy, 1974-76; tchr. English and Italian Berlitz Sch. Langs., Florence, Italy, 1976-77; tchr., interpreter, translator Italy, 1977-84; office mgr. UNICEF, Milan, Italy, 1982-83; dir. Barhite & Holzinger, N.Y.C., 1985-89; dir., office mgr. The Robert-Thomas Co., N.Y.C., 1990-92; assoc. broker The Thomas Campenni Co., N.Y.C., 1992—; ind. real estate broker. Pres. Gallery House Condominium. Office: The Thomas F Campenni Co 21 W 46th St New York NY 10036-4119

MULLER, FREDERICA DANIELA, psychology educator; d. Leopold and Elena; m. Dr. L. Muller; children: Daniela, Adrian. Grad., Med. Inst. Radiology, Romania, 1962, PsyD in Clin. Psychology, 1965, M in Internat. Law and Bus., 1966; specialization courses in Psychodrama, Moreno Inst., Vienna, 1969; grad., Inst. Rsch. in Aging, Rome, 1970, Miami Inst. Psychology, 1987. Diplomate Am. Bd. Forensic Medicine, Am. Bd. Forensic Examiners; lic. psychologist, Pa.; lic. psychotherapist, Fla.; cert. family mediator, Fla. Supreme Ct. continuing edn. units provider psych. Prof. Sch. Continuing Edn. Barry U., North Miami, Fla.; instr. advanced courses in psychology, psychodrama, med. ethics, social manners; guest speaker Colloque Internat., Bucharest, Romania, 1989-93; guest lectr. U. Arboga, Sweden 1968-72; founder Internat. Studies for Biopsychosocial Issues, 1991; cons. dept. of marriage, family and child devel. systemic studies, Nova U., 1992; founder Euro Am. Exch. Co., 1980; with Santé Internat., Switzerland, 1982-85; dir. Ctr. Biopsychosocial Medicine, 1995. Conducted rsch. on stress and aging with Dr. Anna Aslan, world renowned author; developed 45 minute stress reduction program for use in the work place. Author: The Management of Occupational Stress and Its Linkage to Social Pressures; contbr. articles to profl. jours. Mem. APA, Medicins du Monde (hon.), Am. Soc. Group Psychotherapy and Psychodrama, Soc. Psychol., Studies Social of Issues, World Fedn. for Mental Health.

MULLER, MARGIE HELLMAN, financial services consultant; b. L.A., Nov. 30, 1927; d. S. Jack and Marjorie (Ullman) Hellman; m. Steven Muller, June 19, 1951; children: Julie, Elizabeth. BA, UCLA, 1949. Sales promotion asst. Joyce (Calif.) Ltd., London, 1950-51; copywriter Hamrick Advt., Ithaca, N.Y., 1951-54; sr. assoc. Conant and Co., N.Y.C., 1954-57; mgr. advt. and pub. relations Theodore Presser Co., Bryn Mawr, Pa., 1957-58; acct. exec. Laux Advt., Ithaca, 1959-60; asst. v.p. mktg. Tompkins County Trust Co., Ithaca, 1960-71; v.p. Md. Nat. Bank, Balt., 1971-77; sr. v.p. Union Trust Bancorp., Balt., 1977-83; state bank commr. Balt., 1983-96. Contbr. articles to profl. jours. Bd. dirs. The Leadership Balt., 1985-87; pres. Balt. Promotion Coun., 1974-75, Health and Welfare Coun., Ctrl. Md., 1982-85; mem. adv. commn. Md. Dept. Econ. and Cmty. Devel., 1975-83; mem. adv. coun. Credit Rsch. Ctr., Krannert Grad. Sch. Mgmt., Purdue U., vice chmn., 1993-94, chmn., 1994-95. Mem. Bank Mktg. Assn. (bd. dirs. 1974-78, exec. com. 1977-78, nat. conv. chmn. 1977), Nat. Assn. State Credit Union Suprs. (bd. dirs. 1984-88), Conf. State Bank Suprs. (bd. dirs. 1988-94, vice chmn. 1990-91, chmn. 1991-93), Fed. Fin. Instns. Exam. Coun. (state liaison com. 1991-94, chmn. 1993-94).

MÜLLER, REBECCA C., financial planner; b. Springfield, Ohio, July 21, 1956; d. James and Carol (Kuck) Moss; m. Larry G. Müller, Dec. 19, 1981; children: Eric Lloyd and Michael Kuck. Student, Purdue U., Fort Wayne, Ind., 1974-75; BA in Math. cum laude, Graceland Coll., 1978, BA in Recreation and Outdoor Edn., 1978. Cert. fin. planner, Colo. Math tchr. Nickerson (Kans.) High Sch., 1978-83, asst. coach boy's tennis, 1978-81, head coach women's volleyball, 1978-81; pres. Money Concepts Fin. Planning Ctr., Indpls., 1983—; city playgrounds dir. Hutchinson (Kans.) Recreation Commn., 1979-83; pres. regional hdqs. MC-TIP, Inc. dba Money Concept, Indpls., 1985—. Treas. Lawrence Town Kindergarten PTO, Indpls., 1990-91 92-93; vice chmn. Castleton United Meth. Endowment Fund Com., Indpls., 1993—. Mem. Internat. Assn. Fin. Planners. Office: Money Concepts 7155 Shadeland Sta Ste 120 Indianapolis IN 46256

MULLETTE, JULIENNE PATRICIA, television personality and producer, astrologer, author, health center administrator; b. Sydney, Australia, Nov. 19, 1940; came to U.S., 1953; d. Ronald Stanley Lewis and Sheila Rosalind Blunden (Phillips) M.; m. Fred Gillette Sturm, Nov. 24, 1964 (div. Dec. 1969); m. Kenneth Walter Gillman, Dec. 28, 1971; children: Noah Khristoff Mullette-Gillman, O'Dhaniel Alexander Mullette-Gillman. BA, Western Coll. for Women, Oxford, Ohio, 1961; postgrad., Harvard U., 1964, U. Sao Paulo, Brazil, 1965, Inst. de Filosofia, Sao Paulo, 1965, Miami U., Oxford, 1967-69. Tchr. English, High Mowing Sch., Wilton, N.H., 1962-64, Stoneleigh-Prospect Hill Sch., Greenfield, Mass., 1964; seminar dir. Western Coll., Oxford, Ohio, 1967-69; pres. Family Tree, The Home Univ., Montclair, N.J., 1978-80; dir. Pleroma Holistic Health Ctr., Montclair, 1980—; dir. Astrological Rsch. Ctr., Sydney, Australia, 1983; hostess (radio talk show) You and the Cosmos Sta. WFMU, East Orange, N.J., 1985, Sta. WJFF, Jeffersonville, N.Y., 1992—, The Juliette Mullette Show, Connections TV, Newark, 1985—, The Juliette Mullette Show Sta. WFDU, Fairleigh Dickinson U., N.J., 1986—, (TV program) You and the Cosmos, Woodstock, N.Y., 1992—; founder Spiritual Devel. Rsch. Group 191986—; pvt. astrology counselor, 1962—; lectr., speaker worldwide, 1968—; guest on radio and TV shows, U.S. and Can., 1962—; host syndicated radio talk show The Juliette Mullette Show, N.Y., N.J., 1987—; host The Juliette Mullette Show You and The Cosmos, WJFF Radio, 1992—, WKNY Radio, 1994—;

in charge of programming WPAC Woodstock, 1993—. owner, pres. Moonlight Pond, Woodbourne, N.Y., 1988—; founder The Spiritual Devel. Ctr., 1986—, Pleroma Found. for Astrological Rsch. and Studies, 1990; breeder, trainer llamas, alpacas and other exotic animals; apptd. Woodstock Pub. Access Com., 1993—. Author: The Moon-Understanding the Subconscious, 1973; also articles, 1968—; founding editor KÓSMOS mag., 1968-78, The Jour. of Astrological Studies, 1970; contbg. columnist I Love Cats, 1988—, Aspects mag., Mountain Astrologer. Founder local chpt. La Leche League, Montclair, 1974. Mem. AAUW (chair cultural affairs Montclair chpt.), Spiritual Devel. Group (founder 1987), Internat. Soc. Astrological Research (founding pres. 1968-78), Cosmos Hyperspace Astrological Origins and Supergravity Studies (founder 1994—), Am. Fedn. Astrologers (cert.), Société Belge d'Astrologie, Am. Assn. Humanistic Psychology, AAUW (dir. cultural affairs 1987—), NAFE, Internat. Llamas Assn. Avocations: competitive tennis, local theatre, singing. Home: 89 Clinton Ave Montclair NJ 07042

MULLICAN, JUDITH GUIN, educational writer; b. Russellville, Ala., Apr. 19, 1952; d. J. Foy and Dorace Jean (Caldwell) Guin; m. Jim D. Mullican, May 27, 1972; children: Catherine Elizabeth, Lyle David. BA in Tchg., Sam Houston State U., 1974; BS in Edn., Western Carolina U., 1988, MA in Edn., 1989. Speech pathologist Brenham (Tex.) State Sch., 1974-75; speech and lang. pathologist Lyons (Ga.) Elem. Sch., 1975-76; tchr. kindergarten Gingerbread Sch., Gautier, Miss., 1981-85, Haywood County Schs., Waynesville, N.C., 1989-90; tchr. spl. edn. Cherokee (N.C.) Reservation Schs., 1990-91; tchr. Head Start, Waynesville, N.C., 1991-93; writer HighReach Learning, Arden, N.C., 1993—. Vol. Girl Scouts U.S.A., Miss., N.C., 1982-89; coord. United Way, Buncombe County, N.C., 1993. Chancellor's fellow Western Carolina U., 1988-89. Mem. Ch. of Christ. Office: HighReach Learning 36 Old Shoals Rd Arden NC 28704-8438

MULLIGAN, DEANNA MARIE, management consultant; b. West Point, Nebr., July 24, 1963; d. Paul Arthur and Judith Maureen (Bottger) Predoehl; m. Stephen Edward Mulligan, Dec. 26, 1985. BS in Bus., U. Nebr., 1985; MBA, Stanford U., 1989. Cons. Woodmen Accident and Life, Hayward, Calif., 1985-87; intern Hewlett-Packard, 1988; dir., corp. planning N.Y. Life, N.Y.C., 1989-90, asst. v.p., 1990-92; assoc. McKinsey & Co., Inc., N.Y.C., 1992—. Vol. Friendly Visitor Program, Napa, Calif., 1987; mem. planning forum, N.Y.C. Nat. Merit scholar, 1981. Office: McKinsey and Co 55 E 52nd St New York NY 10055-0002

MULLIGAN, ELINOR PATTERSON, lawyer; b. Bay City, Mich., Apr. 20, 1929; d. Frank Clark and Agnes (Murphy) P.; m. John C. O'Connor, Oct. 28, 1950; children: Christine Fulena, Valerie Clark, Amy O'Connor, Christopher Criffan O'Connor; m. William G. Mulligan, Dec. 6, 1975. BA, U. Mich. 1950; JD, Seton Hall U., 1970. Bar: N.J., 1970. Assoc. Springfield and Newark, 1970-72; pvt. practice, Hackettstown, N.J., 1972; ptnr. Mulligan & Jacobson, N.Y.C., 1973-91, Mulligan & Mulligan, Hackettstown, 1976—; atty. Hackettstown Planning Bd., 1973-86, Blairstown Bd. Adjustment, 1973-95; sec. Warren County Ethics Com., 1976-78, sec. Dist. X and XIII Fee Arbitration Com., 1979-87, mem. and chair., 1987-91, mem. dist. ethics com. XIII, 1992—; mem. spl. com. on atty. disciplinary structure N.J. Supreme Ct., 1981—. lectr. Nat. Assn. Women Judges, 1979. Contbr. articles to profl. jours. Named Vol. of Yr. Attys. Vols. in Parole Program, 1978. Fellow Am. Acad. Matrimonial Lawyers (pres. N.J. chpt. 1995—); mem. ABA, Warren County Bar Assn. (pres. 1987-88), N.J. State Bar Assn., N.J. Women Lawyers Assn. (v.p. 1985—), Am. Mensa Soc., Kappa Alpha Theta, Union League Club (N.Y.C.), Baltusrol Golf Club (Springfield, N.J.), Panther Valley Golf and Country Club (Allamuchy, N.J.). Republican. Home: 12 Goldfinch Way Hackettstown NJ 07840-3007 Office: 480 Hwy 517 PO Box 211 Hackettstown NJ 07840-0211

MULLIGAN, ROSEMARY ELIZABETH, paralegal; b. Chgo., July 8, 1941; d. Stephen Edward and Rose Anne (Sannasardo) Granzyk; children: Daniel R. Bonaguidi, Matthew S. Bonaguidi. AAS, Harper Coll., Palatine, Ill., 1982; student, Ill. State U., 1959-60. Paralegal Miller, Forest & Downing Ltd., Glenview, Ill., 1982-91; ind. contractor mcpl. law, 1991—; paralegal seminar educator Harper Coll. Pro-choice activist and mem. Ill. Ho. of Reps., 1993—, chmn. human svcs. appropriations com.; gov.'s workgroup on early childhood. Recipient Disting. Alumnus award Ill. C.C. Trustee Assn., 1993, Legislator of Yr. award Ill. Assn. Cmty. Mental Health Agys., 1996, Heart Start award Nat. Ctr. Clin. Infant Programs; Flemming fellow Ctr. for Policy Alts., 1995. Mem. LWV, Nat. Women's Polit. Caucus, Ill. Fedn. Bus. and Profl. Women, Ill. Women in Govt., Chgo. Women in Govt. Rels., Ill. Fedn. Bus. and Profl. Women (nat. legis. platform rep. 1991-92, chair Outstanding Working Women of Ill. 1991-92, state membership chair 1989-90, state legis. co-chair, nat. platform rep. 1988-89, state legis. chair, nat. platform rep. 1987-88). Roman Catholic. Home: 856 E Grant Dr Des Plaines IL 60016-6260 Office: Ill Ho of Reps State Capitol Springfield IL 62706 also: 932 Lee St Ste 204 Des Plaines IL 60016

MULLIN, MARIAN VERONICA, accounting educator; b. Pitts., Aug. 11, 1941; d. Peter and Marie Ann (Grosdeck) Gramba; m. Richard Patrick Mullin, Jr., Nov. 24, 1966; children: Matthew, Marcus, Richard III. BS in BA, Duquesne U., 1963, MA in Econs., 1968; BA in Acctg., St. Bernard Coll., Cullman, Ala., 1974; MS in Taxation, Robert Morris Coll., 1985; M.Profl. Accountancy, W.Va. U., 1993. CPA, W.Va.; CMA. Instr. St. Bernard Coll., Cullman, 1967-69, Robert Morris Coll., Pitts., 1969-72; assoc. prof. acctg. West Liberty (W.Va.) State Coll., 1974—. Lector St. Michael Ch. Recipient Outstanding Tchr. award Delta Sigma Pi, 1987. Mem. AICPA, Inst. Mgmt. Accts., Soroptimists Internat., Beta Gamma Sigma. Roman Catholic. Home: 37 Maple Ave Wheeling WV 26003 Office: West Liberty State Coll West Liberty WV 26074

MULLIN, MARSHA ANN, curator; b. Rushville, Ind., June 30, 1951; d. Dixie and Norna Joan (Ruby) M. BA, Ind. U., 1973; MA, Tex. Tech U., 1976, U. Notre Dame, 1986. Curator Discovery Hall Mus., South Bend, Ind., 1976-86, The Hermitage, Hermitage, Tenn., 1986—. Mem. Am. Assn. Mus., Am. Assn. State and Local History. Democrat. Mem. Disciples of Christ. Office: The Hermitage 4580 Rachels Ln Hermitage TN 37076

MULLIN, MARY ANN, career counselor; b. Passaic, N.J., Feb. 9, 1943; d. M. Joseph and Rose M. (Rienzi) DeVita; m. John G. Mullin Jr.; children: Kathleen, John, Robert. BA in Comms., William Paterson Coll., 1991, MA in Urban Studies, 1994; postgrad., Jersey City State U., 1995—. Office mgr. Joseph DeVita, Inc., Paterson, N.J., 1978-94; grad. rsch. asst. William Paterson Coll., Wayne, N.J., 1992-94; ednl. broker/counselor Bergen County Tech. Inst., Hackensack, N.J., 1994-95; grad. admissions counselor Sch. Arch. N.J. Inst. Tech., Newark, 1995—. Pres., bd. dirs. Lenni Lenape Girl Scout Coun., Bulter, N.J., 1989-96; pastoral care/eucharistic min. St. Anthony's Ch., Hawthorne, N.J., 1978—; eucharistic min. Wayne (N.J.) Gen. Hosp., 1978—. Recipient Thanks badge Girl Scouts Am., 1996, Honor pin Lenni Lenape Girl Scout Coun., 1991, Outstanding Vol. Svc. award Paterson Task Force, 1994; named Vol. of Week, The Record, 1993. Mem. Pi Lambda Theta (dir. rsch. projects Beta Chi chpt. 1994-96, Outstanding Svc. award 1995, regional chair N.E. conf. Beta Chi chpt. 1996). Democrat. Roman Catholic. Home: 519 Goffle Hill Rd Hawthorne NJ 07506 Office: N J Inst Tech Sch Arch Martin L King Blvd Newark NJ 07102

MULLINEAUX, JEWEL E., retired educator; b. N.Y.C.; d. Aubrey Vibbert and Bertye (Winterling) Brooks; m. Donald Hammond Mullineaux, Sept. 15, 1948. BA in Spanish with honors, Goucher Coll., 1938; postgrad., Temple U., 1938, U. Pa., 1940; MA, U. Md., 1954. Counselor, tchr., interviewer City of Balt., 1938-42; supr., counselor War Man Power Commn., Balt., 1942-48; chief exams. and recruitment Civil Svc. Commn. Balt., 1948-67; assoc. prof. career selection, career counselor Community Coll. Balt., 1967-74; cons. police patrolmen selection, various U.S. cities. Editor Macca Media jour., 1970-73; contbr. articles to profl. jours.; co-author: (novel) Shadow and Shield, 1981; author short stories and poetry. Sec.-treas. Am. Soc. Pub. Adminstrs., Balt., 1950-52; mem. Mid.-Atlantic Assn. Jr. Colls., 1967-74, Mid-Atlantic Career Counseling Assn., 1967-74, Senator John Marshall Butler's Com. Disting. Women Leaders, 1954; pres. city coun. Beta Sigma Phi, Balt., 1947; all offices local chpt. Beta Sigma Phi, Balt., 1938-50; mentor teenagers Nu Phi Mu, Balt., 1948-50; mem. Halifax Humane Soc., Daytona Beach, Fla., 1980—, Nat. Wildlife Fedn., 1985—. Recipient Cert. Appreciation personnel dept. City of Phila., 1966, Cert. of Award, Ga. State Writing Competition, 1989, Goldkey, Phi Kappa Phi, 1954. Mem. AAUW (mentor creative writers' group, Book award), Halifax River Yacht Club. Christian Scientist. Home: The Landmark 404 S Beach St Apt 202 Daytona Beach FL 32114-5010

MULLINS, BARBARA, advertising executive. Sr. v.p., dir. TV prodn. N.Am. BBDO, N.Y.C. Office: BBDO NY 1285 Avenue Of The Americas New York NY 10019-6028*

MULLINS, BARBARA ANN BURDO, professional development center coordinator; b. Mineola, N.Y., Jan. 6, 1963; d. Joseph and Alice (Digsby) Burdo; m. Jeffery L. Mullins, July 28, 1991. BS, Liberty Bapt. Coll., 1984; MEd, Liberty U., 1988; EdD, U. Va., 1992. Cert. elem. tchr., Va. Elem. tchr. Lynchburg (Va.) Christian Acad., 1984-90; adj. prof. Syracuse (N.Y.) U., 1992; profl. devel. ctr. coord. U. Md., College Park, 1992—; cons. Classroom Orgn. and Mgmt. Program Vanderbilt U., Tenn., 1993—; mem. adv. bd. Office Lab. Experiences, U. Md., College Park, 1994-95. Gov.'s fellow U. Va., 1990-92. Mem. ASCD, Am. Edn. Assn., Internat. Reading Assn., Christian Educator's Assn. Office: U Md Benjamin Bldg College Park MD 20742

MULLINS, BETTY JOHNSON, realtor; b. Killen, Ala., Dec. 29, 1925; d. James E. and Vernie (Muse) Johnson; m. Charles Harvey Mullins, Nov. 18, 1944; children: Charles Harvey Jr., Susan. BS, U. North Ala., 1945. Tchr. Biloxi (Miss.) City Schs., 1945-46, Elizabeth City County Schs., Buckroe Beach, Va., 1946-47, Sheffield (Ala.) City Schs., 1949-58; with family automobile bus., 1958-86; real estate assoc. Neese Real Estate, Inc., Florence, Ala., 1986—. Pres. Project Courtview, Florence, 1980, Heritage Found., Florence, 1994—, Concert Guild, Florence, 1994; mem. Tenn. Valley Art Guild, Tuscumbia, Tenn. Valley Art Ctr., Tuscumbia, Friends of Kennedy Douglas Art Ctr., Florence; v.p. Salvation Army Aux., 1991-92; mem., past pres. United Meth. Women, First Meth. Ch., Florence, mem. adminstrv. bds.; bd. dirs. Friends of Libr., Florence, 1993—, Downtown Florence Unltd., Florence Main St., Bd. Rape Response; mem., past pres. Lauderdale-Colbert-Franklin Foster Grandparent Adv. Bd., Russellville, Ala., Ret. Sr. Vol. Program Adv. Bd.; pres. cabinet U. North Ala., mem. found. bd., 1994, 95, 96; trustee United Way, Shoals, 1992—; family built and maintains garden at First Meth. Ch., Florence in memory of Charles Mullins, Jr. Recipient Shoals Area Citizen of Yr., 1984, Shoals Area Top Prodr. Muscle Shoals Area Bd. Realtors, 1991, 92, 93, 94, Cmty. Svc. award U. North Ala., 1994; named Woman of Yr. Bus. and Profl. Women, 1980. Mem. LWV, Shoals-AAUW (pres. 1990-91), Nat. Bd. Realtors, U. North Ala. Alumni Assn. (past pres., bd. dirs., Alumni of Yr. award 1985, Cmty. Svc. award 1994, Found. Bd. 1994, 95, 96), Internat. Fertilizer Devel. Ctr. Century Club (past pres. Muscle Shoals, Ala. chpt.), Shoals C. of C. (past bd. dirs.), Tenn. Valley Hist. Assn., U. North Ala. Sportsman Club, Muscle Shoals Bd. Realtors, Ala. Bd. Realtors. Republican. Methodist. Home and Office: PO Box 70 Florence AL 35631-0070

MULLINS, OBERA, microbiologist; b. Egypt, Miss., Feb. 15, 1927; d. Willie Ree and Maggie Sue (Orr) Gunn; BS, Chgo. State U., 1974; MS in Health Sci. Edn., Governors State U., 1981; m. Charles Leroy Mullins, Nov. 2, 1952; children: Mary Artavia, Arthur Curtis, Charles Leroy, Charlester Teresa, William Hellman. Med. technician, microbiologist Chgo. Health Dept., Chgo., 1976—, now pers. asst. III. Mem. AAUW, Am. Soc. Clin. Pathologists (cert. med. lab. technician), Ill. Soc. Lab. Technicians. Roman Catholic. Home: 9325 S Marquette Ave Chicago IL 60617-4131 Office: Westtown Neighborhood Health Ctr 2418 W Division St Chicago IL 60622-2940

MULLINS, RUTH GLADYS, nurse; b. Westville, N.S., Can., Aug. 25, 1943; d. William G. and Gladys H.; came to U.S., 1949, naturalized, 1955; student Tex. Womans U., 1961-64; BS in Nursing, Calif. State U.-Long Beach, 1966; MNursing, UCLA, 1973; m. Leonard E. Mullins, Aug. 27, 1963; children: Deborah R., Catherine M., Leonard III. Pub. health nurse, L.A. County Health Dept., 1967-68; nurse Meml. Hosp. Med. Center, Long Beach, 1968-72; dir. pediatric nurse practitioner program Calif. State U., Long Beach, 1973—, asst. prof., 1975-80, assoc. prof., 1980-85, prof., 1985—; health svc. credential coord. Sch. Nursing Calif. State U., Long Beach, Calif., chmn., 1979-81, coord. grad. programs, 1985-92; mem. Calif. Maternal, Child and Adolescent Health Bd., 1977-84; vice chair Long Beach/Orange County Health Consortium, 1984-85, chair 1985-86. Tng. grantee HHS, Divsn. Nursing Calif. Dept. Health; cert. pediatric nurse practitioner. Fellow Nat. Assn. Pediatric Nurse Assocs. and Practitioners (exec. bd., pres. 1990-91), Nat. Fedn. Nursing Specialty Orgns. (sec. 1991-93); mem. Am. Pub. Health Assn., Nat. Alliance Nurse Practitioners (governing body 1990-92), Assn. Faculties Pediatric Nurse Practitioner Programs, L.A. and Orange County Assn. Pediatric Nurse Practitioners and Assocs., Am. Assn. U. Faculty, Ambulatory Pediatric Assn. Democrat. Methodist. Author: (with B. Nelms) Growth and Development: A Primary Health Care Approach; contbg. author: Quick Reference to Pediatric Nursing, 1984; asst. editor Jour. Pediatric Health Care. Home: 6382 Heil Ave Huntington Beach CA 92647-4232 Office: Calif State U Dept Nursing 1250 N Bellflower Blvd Long Beach CA 90840-0006

MULLIS, MADELINE GAIL HERMAN, music educator, choir director; b. Lenoir, N.C., Oct. 26, 1936; d. William Richard and Madeline Edythe (Harris) Herman; m. Thad McCoy Mullis Jr., Dec. 18, 1960 (div. Oct. 1978); children: Thad McCoy III, Myra Lynn, Martin Harper. MusB, U. N.C., Greensboro, 1958; MA, Appalachian State U., 1963; level I Orff cert., Memphis State U. Cert. elem., secondary instrumental and choir music tchr. N.C. Jr. choir dir. St. Stephens Luth. Ch., Lenoir, 1969-80, sr. choir dir., 1960—, handbell choir dir., 1970—, deacon, 1980-82, 84-86;, 88-90; Sunday sch. tchr. St. Stephens Luth. Ch., Lenoir, 1983-86; tchr. classroom music, chorus, band Caldwell County Schs., Lenoir, 1958-65, 77—, chair St. Stephens Worship and Music, Lenoir, 1988-93; del. N.C. Synod Conv., Hickory, N.C., 1990; pres. Agape Women's Circle, Lenoir, 1991-92. Chairperson Sesquicentennial Children's Chorus, Caldwell County, 1991; coord. 1st Caldwell County Children's Choral Festival, 1993. Recipient 24 Superior Ratings at Jr. H.S. Choral Festivals. Mem. NEA, N.C. Ctr. for Advancement of Tchg. (hon.), Assn. Luth. Musicians, N.C. Assn. Educators, Music Educators Nat. Conf., N.C. Music Educators Assn., Am. Orff-Schulwerk Assn., Cmty. Music Club (pres. 1993-95), Caldwell County Hist. Soc., Alpha Delta Kappa (hon.). Republican. Home: 119 Ellison Pl NE Lenoir NC 28645-3716 Office: 1406 Harper Ave NW Lenoir NC 28645-5059 also: Happy Valley Sch PO Box 130 Patterson NC 28661

MULROY, KATHLEEN COLSON, library director; b. Pitts., May 2, 1951; d. Frank J. and Esther A. (Roche) Colson; m. William T. Mulroy Jr., Apr. 31, 1977. BA in History and Polit. Sci., U. Ky., 1973; MSLS, 1974. Cert. profl. libr., Pa., N.J. Libr. Pub. Libr. of Youngstown (Ohio) and Mahoning County, 1974-78; cons. Nola Regional Libr. Sys., Youngstown, 1978-82, Newcastle (Pa.) Pub. Libr. and Dist. Ctr., 1982-83, Delaware County Libr. Sys., Media, Pa., 1984-87; network cons. N.J. State Libr., Trenton, 1987-91; dir. libr. svcs. Holy Family Coll., Phila., 1991—; bd. trustees Palinet, Inc., Phila., 1992—; grant reviewer N.J. State Libr., Trenton, 1992—; exec. bd. Tri State Coll. Libr. Coop., Rosemont, Pa., 1992-94, 95—; presenter in field. Co-author: Automating Your Library, 1994; compiler Native Americans: Recommended Books for Children and Young Adults, 1983. Mem. ALA, Cath. Libr. Assn., Pa. Libr. Assn. (chpt. bd. mem. 1994—, past state bd. mem., past pub. rels. com. chair), Internat. Reading Assn. Republican. Home: 424 Tennis Ave Ambler PA 19002-3518 Office: Holy Family Coll Libr Grant & Frankford Aves Philadelphia PA 19114

MULTHAUP, MERREL KEYES, artist; b. Cedar Rapids, Iowa, Sept. 27, 1922; d. Stephen Dows and Edna Gertrude (Gard) Keyes; m. Robert Hansen Multhaup, Apr. 7, 1944; children: Eric Stephen, Robert Bruce. Student fine art, State U. of Iowa, 1942-43; student color theory, Rice U., 1971. Mem. teaching faculty Summit (N.J.) Art Assn., 1956-60; art instr. studio classes Springfield, N.J., 1954-55, Bloomfield (N.J.) Art Group, 1955-56, Westport, Conn., 1962-63; mem. teaching faculty Hunterdon Art Ctr., Clinton, N.J., 1985-92. One woman exhbns. include Coriell Gallery, 1995; exhibited in group shows at Nat. Assn. Women Artists, N.Y.C., 1957-93 (awards in figure painting), Hartford (Conn.) Athanaeum Mus., 1961 (1st prize), Highgate Gallery, N.Y.C., Waverly Gallery, N.Y.C., Leicester Gallery, London, Silvermine Gallery, Conn., Pendut Gallery, Tex., Benedict Gallery, Sidney Rothman Gallery, N.J., Stamford (Conn.) Mus., Bridgeport (Conn.) Mus., Montclair (N.J.) Mus., Newark Mus., Coriell Gallery, Albuquerque; included in traveling exhibit Nat. Assn. Women Artists, 1996-98. Bd. dirs., exhbn. chmn. Summit Art Assn., 1950-60, Silvermine Guild of Art, New Canaan, Conn., 1960-64; bd. dirs. Artist's Equity of N.J., 1977-84, chmn. state-wide event, 1983, 86; artist's adv. coun. Hunterdon Art Ctr., Clinton, 1988-92. Recipient awards in juried exhbns. in Iowa, Pa., N.J., Conn., N.Y.C. Mem. Nat. Mus. for Women in Arts (charter mem.), Nat. Assn. Women Artists Inc. (awards for figure painting 1957, 80, 89), Albuquerque United Artists. Home and Studio: 1321 Stagecoach Rd SE Albuquerque NM 87123-4320

MULVANEY, MARY FREDERICA, systems analyst; b. N.Y., Nov. 27, 1945; d. Michael Joseph and Mary Catherine (Clapper) M. BA, Marymount Coll., 1967; MA, U. Va., 1968. Cert. data processor Inst. Certification of Computer Profls., Ill. Computer systems analyst Dept. of Def., Ft. Meade, Md., 1968-74; sr. programmer analyst Planning Rsch. Corp., McLean, Va., 1974-83; mem. tech. staff Fed. Systems Group TRW Inc., Fairfax, Va., 1983-90; sr. mem. tech. staff GTE Govt. Systems Corp., Rockville, Md., 1990-94; engr., sci. TRW, Inc., Fairfax, Va., 1994—. Mem. IEEE, Data Processing Mgmt. Assn., Computer Measurement Group, Cath. Assn. of Scientists and Engrs. Roman Catholic. Office: TRW Sys Integration Group One Federal Systems Park Dr Fairfax VA 22033

MULVANEY, SUSAN S., adult education educator, researcher; b. Langdale, Ala., Nov. 4, 1954; d. Charles L. Spraggins and Nancy J. (Stewart) Mulheirn; 1 child, Kaela S. BA, Radford (Va.) Coll., 1977; MA, U. So. Calif., L.A., 1984; PhD, UCLA, 1995. Asst. prof. West Coast U., L.A., 1981-84; asst. lectr. U. So. Calif., L.A., 1982-84; dir. English dept. West Coast U., L.A., 1984-94, dir. gen. studies, 1994-96, dean student affairs, 1996—. Co-author: (book) Computer Notions, 1985. Campaigner Dem. Party, L.A., 1992; pres. PTA Franklin Ave. Elem., L.A., 1995—. Mem. AAUW, Am. Sociological Assn., Am. Ednl. Rsch. Assn., Phi Kappa Phi. Democrat. Office: West Coast U 440 Shatto Pl Los Angeles CA 90020

MULVEY, HELEN FRANCES, emeritus history educator; b. Providence, Feb. 22, 1913; d. William James and Anna (Nelson) M. A.B., Pembroke Coll., 1933; A.M., Columbia U., 1934; A.M., Radcliffe Coll., 1942; Ph.D., Harvard U., 1949. Instr. history Russell Sage Coll., Troy, N.Y., 1944-46; asst. prof. to prof. history, Conn. Coll., New London, 1946-83, prof. emeritus, 1983—, Brigida Pacchiana Ardenghi chair, 1975-78; vis. prof. Brit. history, U. Wis., Madison, 1971-72; vis. lectr. Yale U., 1974-83; lectr. Irish history, Pfizer Adult Edn., Groton, Conn., 1983-84; vis. scholar Phi Beta Kappa, Washington, 1982-83. Author articles, essays Irish and Brit. history; co-editor bibliog. vol. in A New History of Ireland, 9 vols. Anne Crosby Emery fellow, Brown U., 1933. Mem. Am. Hist. Assn., Am. Conf. for Irish Studies, North Am. Conf. on Brit. Studies, AAUP (chpt. pres. 1962-64), Phi Beta Kappa. Clubs: Harvard. Office: Conn Coll PO Box 5508 New London CT 06320

MULVEY, MARY C., retired adult education director, gerontologist, senior citizen association administrator; b. Bangor, Maine, Aug. 17, 1909; d. Michael J. and Ann Loretta (Higgins) Crowley; m. Gordon F. Mulvey, Jan. 25, 1940. BA, U. Maine, 1930; MA, Brown U., 1953; EdD, Harvard U., 1961; LHD (hon.), U. Maine, 1991. Dir. adminstrn. on aging State of R.I., SS, R.I., 1960-63; co-founder Nat. Coun. Sr. Citizens, 1961; pres. Nat. Sr. Citizens Edn. and Rsch. Ctr., Washington, 1963—; 1st v.p. Nat. Coun. Sr. Citizens, 1976—; guidance counselor Providence Sch. Dept., 1963-65; dir. adult edn. City of Providence Sch. Dept., 1965-79; reg. prog. rep. Title V, Older Ams. Act, Nat. Coun. Sr. Citizens, Washington, 1980-94; major role in enactment of Medicare and Older Americans Act, 1950-65; del., adv. com. White House Conf. on Aging, 1961, 71, 81, 95; cons. Fed. Housing for the Aging, Washington, 1963-65, mem. tech. rev. com. Older Ams. Act Title IV, 1966-70; instr. preparing retirement, developer women's program U. R.I., 1963-80; appt. by Pres. Carter to Fed. Coun. Aging, 1979, by Pres. Clinton, 1995; pres. R.I. State Coun. Sr. Citizens, 1982—; charter mem. adv. bd. Coll. Arts, Humanities, U. Maine, 1992—; mem. various coms. state and nat. level. Publs. and contbr. articles to profl. jours. Recipient Soroptomists fellow award in rsch. in gerontology Harvard U., 1955, 57, 59, Cert. of award as Project Dir. of Sr. AIDES Employment Program, 1968-79, Medicare award R.I. State Coun. Sr. Citizens and Nat. Coun. Sr. Citizens, 1985, Disting. Achievement award U. Maine, 1980, Disting. Achievement award Berwick Acad., 1981, Justice for All award R.I. Bar Assn., 1981, Woman of Yr. award Nat. Sr. Pageant, 1982, R.I. Women 1st R.I. Sec. of State, 1991, citation Syracuse U., 1991, R.I. Dept. Elderly Affairs, 1993, 25th Anniversary Title V Sr. Employment award Nat. Coun. Sr. Citizens, 1993, Lifetime Achievement award Nat. Coun. Sr. Citizens, 1994, Co-Founder and Continuing Bd. Mem. award Nat. Coun. Sr. Citizens, 1995, Svcs. for St. Citizens award, 1995; inducted into R.I. Heritage Hall of Fame, 1993. Fellow Gerontol. Soc. Am.; mem. ACA, AAUW, Am. Assn. Adult and Continuing Edn., Harvard U. Alumni Assn. (Alumni award R.I. chpt. 1986), U. Maine Alumni Assn., Brown U. Alumni Assn., Pi Lambda Theta, Delta Delta Delta. Home: 95 Plymouth Rd East Providence RI 02914-1943

MUNAT, FLORENCE HOWE, writer, librarian; b. Evanston, Ill., Mar. 28, 1947; d. Edward Cole and Carol Whiting (Bourne) Howe; m. Charles Elliot Munat, Nov. 13, 1969; children: Charles F., Isabel A., Benedict J., Edward C. BA, Lawrence U., 1969; MLS, So. Conn. State Coll., 1981; Certificate short stories and articles, Inst. Children's Literature, 1993, Certificate novels, 1996. Tchr. English Middletown (Conn.) H.S., 1969-70; asst. promotion dept. Wesleyan U. Press., Middletown, Conn., 1970-71; reference librarian Russell Pub. Libr., Middletown, Conn., 1971-89; writer children's materials Bainbridge Is., Wash., 1989—. Author: FACT-ination, 1976, Incredible Sports Facts, 1981; contbr. articles, short stories to literary mags.; book reviewer Voice of Youth Advocates, Metuchen, N.J., 1990—; vol. host radio show Wash. Talking Book and Braille Libr., Seattle, 1990—. Host parent Am. Field Svc., N.Y., 1973-74, 80-81, 83-84, 86-87; pres. student liaison, head publicity Am. Field Svc. Internat./Intercultural, Middletown, Conn ., 1975-89; pres., head publicity Hark Wright Scholarship Com., Middletown, 1974-89. Mem. Soc. Children's Book Writers and Illustrators, Pacific N.W. Writers' Conf., Soc. Children's Book Writers and Illustrators (Wash. chpt.). Home: 11702 NE Sunset Loop Bainbridge Island WA 98110

MUNCEY, BARBARA DEANE, university official, consultant; b. Welch, W.Va., July 12, 1952; d. Juan Irvin and June Henryetta (Dowse) M. AB, Marshall U., Huntington, W.Va., 1974; postgrad., U. Ill., 1980; postgrad, U. Mich, 1984-85; postgrad., U. Oklahoma, 1987; MA, Western Mich. U., 1994. Asst. dir. Heartside Neighborhood Assn., Grand Rapids, Mich., 1979-80, Muncey Devel. Corp., Grand Rapids, Mich., 1979-80; coord. Northeast Mich. Econ. Devel. Assn., Gayland, Mich., 1980-81; dir. of econ. devel. Grand Rapids Internat Tribal Coun., Mich., 1984-86; dir. Sterling Indsl. Devel. Com., Ill., 1986-89; pres. Muncey Cons. Svcs., 1989-90; grad. asst. coord. Office Field Experiences, Western Mich. U., Kalamazoo, 1990-93; mem. grad. studies coun., grad. curriculum com. Western Mich. U., 1992-93, mem. com. to adviser pres. on acad. affairs, 1993; v.p. Sauk Valley Area Econ. Devel. Assn., 1989-90; mem. Whiteside County Regional Planning Commn., 1987-90. Mem. Rep. Women's Club. Mem. NAFE, Am. Econ. Devel. Coun., Ill. Devel. Coun., Mich. Indsl. Devel. Coun., Mid-Am. Econ. Devel. Coun., Phi Kappa Phi. Baptist. Office: Western Mich U The Grad Coll Grad Student Adv Com Kalamazoo MI 49008-5121

MUNCY, MARTHA ELIZABETH, retired newspaper publisher; b. Dodge City, Kans., Nov. 5, 1919; d. Jess C. and Juliet Mildred (Pettijohn) Denious.; m. Howard E. Muncy, June 5, 1943 (div. 1969); children: Martha Juliet, Suzanne M. Kerr, Howard E. Jr. Student, Lindenwood Coll. for Women, 1937-38; BA, U. Kans., 1941. Advt. mgr. Dodge City Broadcasting Co., 1942-43, copywriter, 1944-46, pres., 1973-88; saleswoman Boot Hill Mus., Inc., Dodge City, 1963; pub., pres. Dodge City Daily Globe, 1973-88. Mem. Kans. Cavalry, Topeka, 1976—; bd. dirs. Arrowhead West, Inc., Dodge City, 1976-90, Dodge City Roundup, Inc., 1976-89, Dodge City Crimestoppers, 1985—; bd. dirs., sec. Ford County Hist. R.R. Preservation and Found., Dodge City, 1984-90; trustee William Allen White Found., Lawrence, Kans., 1984—. Recipient Outstanding Service award Dodge City Lions, 1981; named Kans. Outstanding Rehab. vol. Kans. Rehab. Assn., 1985. Mem. AAUW, Kans. Press Women (Woman of Achievement award 1984), S.W. Kans. PressWomen, Dodge City Media Pros, Dodge City

Women's C. of C. (Athena award 1989), Dodge City C. of C., The Philomaths, DAR, PEO, Salvation Army Aux., Sigma Delta Chi, Kappa Alpha Theta. Republican. Presbyterian. Home: 511 Annette St Dodge City KS 67801-2811

MUND, GERALDINE, bankruptcy judge; b. L.A., July 7, 1943; d. Charles J. and Pearl (London) M. BA, Brandeis U., 1965; MS, Smith Coll., 1967; JD, Loyola U., 1977. Bar: Calif. 1977. Bankruptcy judge U.S. Cen. Dist. Calif., 1984—. Past pres. Temple Israel, Hollywood, Calif. Mem. ABA, L.A. County Bar Assn. Office: Roybal Bldg 255 E Temple St Los Angeles CA 90012-3334

MUNDELL, SUSAN BELLE, special education educator; b. Denver, July 15, 1950; d. Robert James and Hazel F. (Foster) Hermes; m. James Lee Mundell; children: Jeffrey, Jenna. BS, Colo. State U., 1973; MA, U. No. Colo., 1979; cert. endorsement Ednly. Handicapped, U. Colo., Denver, 1984. Lic. tchr. Colo; K-12 spl. edn., 7-12 occupl. home econs. Tchr. Jefferson County Pub. Schs., Arvada, Colo., 1979—. Co-author: (book) Practical Portfolios: Reading, Writing, Math. and Life Skills, 1994. Flutist Cmty. Concert Band, Arvada, 1990—. Mem. Colo. Coun. Internat. Reading Assn. (Star Grant award 1994), Coun. Learning Disabilities (1 of 8 Nat. Tchrs. of Yr. 1993, Colo. Tchr. of Yr. 1993). Office: Thomson Elem Sch 7750 Harlan Arvada CO 80003

MUNDER, BARBARA A., publishing executive. BA in Polit. Sci., Elmira Coll.; MBA, NYU. V.p., contbg. editor Instnl. Investor Mag.; from dir. conf. and exposition ctr. to dir. Bus. Week McGraw-Hill Cos., Inc., N.Y.C., 1976-86, v.p. planning and devel. mgmt. group, 1986-95, sr. v.p. corp. affairs, 1995—. Co-author: Joe Louis: 50 Years, An American Hero, 1988. Mem. Information Industry Assn. (chair 1996). Office: McGraw-Hill Inc 1221 Avenue of the Americas New York NY 10020-1001

MUNDORFF SHRESTHA, SHEILA ANN, cariologist; b. Rochester, N.Y., Dec. 14, 1945; d. Karl Mundorff and Elizabeth Mary (Braun) Ross; m. Buddhi Man Shrestha, June 18, 1988. BS in Biology, Nazareth Coll., Rochester, 1967; MS in Microbiology, U. Rochester, 1984. Lab. technician Eastman Dental Ctr., Rochester, 1967-69, rsch. asst., 1969-71, rsch. assoc., 1971-92, small animal expt. coord., 1984-92, sect. head animal/microbiol. rsch., 1987—, chmn. Instl. Animal Care and Use Com., 1990—, vivarium dir., 1990—, med. emergency program dir., 1991-92, asst. prof., 1992—; mem. animal resource group ADA Health Found., Chgo., 1981-83; cons. working group Sci. Consensus Conf.-Assessment Cariogenic Potential of Foods, San Antonio, 1985; participant, reactor, co-chair animal caries models working groups Conf. on Clin. Aspects of Demineralization of Teeth, Rochester, N.Y., 1994. Patentee in field. CPR instr. ARC, Rochester, 1978-94, cert. 1st responder, N.Y.S., 1992-95. NIH, Nat. Inst. Dental Rsch. grantee, 1986, 87, 88. Mem. Am. Assn. Dental Rsch. (sec.-treas. Rochester sect. 1977-92). Roman Catholic. Office: Eastman Dental Ctr 625 Elmwood Ave Rochester NY 14620-2913

MUNDY, DORIS JEAN, city clerk; b. Philippi, W.Va.; d. Franciscus Joe and Bonnie Ruth (Jones) Shockey; m. Freddie Eugene Mundy, Mar. 4, 1955; children: Joseph, Jeanne, Ronnie, Robbie. BA, Fairmont State Coll., 1980. Cert. mcpl. clk. IIMC. Sec., resource dir. Barbour County Bd. of Edn., Philippi, 1955-74; clk., conservation technician USDA Soil Conservation Svc., Philippi, 1974-82, USDA Farmers Home Adminstrn., Philippi; city clk. City of Philippi, 1990—. Mem. Internat. Inst. Mcpl. Clks. (cert., W.Va. membership chmn. 1994-95), W.Va. Assn. Mcpl. Clks. and Recorders (dir. 1993, pres. 1994), Soil Conservation Soc. Am. Methodist. Office: PO Box 460 108 N Main St Philippi WV 26416

MUNDY, PHYLLIS, state legislator; b. Evansville, Ind., Jan. 31, 1948. BS, Bloomsburg State Coll., 1970. Mem. Pa. Ho. of Reps. Home: 157 N Gates Ave Kingston PA 18704-5516 Office: Pa Ho of Reps State Capitol Harrisburg PA 17120 also: Park Bldg Ste 109 400 3rd Ave Kingston PA 18704-5816

MUNEIO, PATRICIA ANNE, public health nurse; b. Detroit, Oct. 7, 1949; d. Charles Eli and Mary Jane (Voletti) M. BSN, Wayne State U., 1973; MS, Calif. Coll. for Health Scis., San Diego, 1994. RN, Mich. Staff nurse to head nurse Detroit Osteo. Hosp., Highland Park, Mich., 1974-75; nurse emergency rm. Grace Hosp., Detroit, 1975-77; pub. health nurse, team leader Detroit VNA, Detroit, 1977-83; staff nurse, head nurse Comprehensive Health Svcs. of Detroit, 1983-85; pvt. duty nurse AbCare, Inc., Detroit, 1985; pub. health nurse, supr. Cmty. Home Care, Sterling Heights, Mich., 1985-88; home care supr. Med. Personnel Pool, Southfield, Mich., 1988-89; pub. health nurse III Macomb County Health Dept., Mt. Clemens, Mich., 1989-96; health care surveyor spl. svcs. sect. Mich. Dept. Consumer and Industry Svc., Lansing, 1996—. Mem. ANA, Mich. Nurses Assn. (rep. 1992, Bue Water Dist. v.p. 1990-92, pres. 1992-96), Macomb County Health Dept. Staff Coun. (pres. 1990-94). Democrat. Roman Catholic. Home: 8669 Crestview Dr Sterling Heights MI 48312-6028 Office: Mich Dept Consumer and Industry Svc Spl Svcs Section 1808 W Saginaw Lansing MI 48915

MUNGER, SHARON, market research firm executive; M. Robert Munger; 3 children: Shawn, Shane, Blair. Grad. Vanderbilt U. Sec., data processor, acct. exec. M/A/R/C, Inc., Irving, Tex., from 1973; now pres., chief operating officer Irving, Tex. Office: M-A-R-C Inc 7850 N Belt Line Rd Irving TX 75063-6064*

MUNNELL, ALICIA HAYDOCK, economist; b. N.Y.C., Dec. 6, 1942; d. Walter Howe Haydock and Alicia (Wildman) Haydock Roux; m. Thomas Clark Munnell (div.); children: Thomas Clark Jr., Hamilton Haydock; m. Henry Scanlon Healy, Feb. 2, 1980. BA in Econs., Wellesley, 1964; MA in Econs., Boston U., 1966; PhD in Econs., Harvard U., 1973. Staff asst. bus. rsch. div. New Eng. Tel. Co., Boston, 1964-65; teaching fellow econs. dept. Boston U., 1965-66; rsch. asst. for dir. econ. studies program Brookings Instn., Washington, 1966-68; teaching fellow Harvard U., Cambridge, Mass., 1971-73; asst. prof. econs. Wellesley Coll., Mass., 1974; economist Fed. Res. Bank Boston, 1973-76, asst. v.p., economist, 1976-78, v.p., economist, 1979-84, sr. v.p., dir. rsch., 1984-93; asst. sec. for econ. policy Dept. Treasury, Washington, 1993-95; mem. Coun. of Econ. Advisors, 1995—; mem. Gov.'s Task Force on Unemployment Compensation, Mass., 1975; mem. spl. funding adv. com. for Mass. pensions, 1976; mem. Mass. Retirement Law Commn., 1976-82; staff dir. joint com. on pub. pensions Nat. Planning Assn., 1978; mem. adv. com. for urban inst. HUD grant on state-local pensions, 1978-81; mem. pension rsch. council Wharton Sch. Fin. and Commerce, U. Pa., 1979—; mem. adv. group Nat. Commn. for Employment Policy, 1980-81; mem. adv. bd. Nat. Aging Policy Ctr. in Income Maintenance, Brandeis U., 1980-84; participant pvt. sector retirement security and U.S. tax policy roundtable discussions Govt. Rsch. Corp., 1984; mem. supervisory panel Forum Inst. of Villers Found., 1984; mem. Medicare working group, div. of health policy rsch. and edn. Harvard U., 1984-87; mem. Commn. on Coll. Retirement, 1984-86; mem. com. to plan major study of nat. long term care policies Inst. Medicine, Nat. Acad. Scis., 1984-87; mem. steering com. Am. Assn. Ret. Persons, 1987—; mem. adv. council Am. Enterprise Inst., 1987—; com. mem. Inst. Medicine, Nat. Acad. Scis. Human Rights Com., 1987—; co-founder, pres. Nat. Acad. Social Ins., 1986—; bd. dirs. Pension Rights Ctr.; mem. program rev. com. Brigham and Women's Hosp., 1988—; mem. Commn. to Rev. Mass. Anti-Takeover Laws, 1988-89, econs. vis. com. MIT, 1989—. Author: The Impact of Social Security on Personal Saving, 1974, Future of Social Security, 1977 (various awards), Pensions for Public Employees, 1979, The Economics of Private Pensions, 1982; co-author: Options for Fiscal Structure Reform in Massachusetts, 1975; editor: Lessons from the Income Maintenance Experiments, 1987, Is There a Shortfall in Public Capital Investment?, 1991, (conf. proc.) Retirement and Public Policy, 1991, Pensions and the Economy: Sources, Uses, and Limitations of Data, 1992, co-editor: Pensions and the Economy: Sources, Uses, and Limitations of Data; contbr. articles to profl. jours., chpts. to books. Mem. Inst. Medicine of NAS, Nat. Acad. Pub. Adminstrn. Office: Council of Econ Advisers Old EOB Exec Office of the Pres Washington DC 20502

MUNOZ, HEATHER TAMARA, non-profit administrator; b. New Haven, Conn.; d. James John and Cynthia Ann (Sias) Close; m. Glenn Joseph Munoz. BA, Columbia Coll., 1991. Asst. dir. Met. Rsch., N.Y.C., 1991-93; mem., program officer Riverside Park Fund, N.Y.C., 1993—; project coord. Dial Svc. Internat., N.Y.C., 1991-92. Rsch., designer Columbia and the City, 1993. Mem. Nat. Archery Assoc.

MUÑOZ, MARGARET ELLEN, reading specialist; b. Jacksonville, Ill., Jan. 30, 1947; d. George William and Lois Lottie (Ankrom) Greene; m. Juan James Muñoz, Mar. 31, 1972; children: Aaron Joseph, Lauri Elizabeth. BA, Culver-Stockton Coll., 1969; MA, Western Ill. U., 1971. Cert. tchr. reading K-12 and English 7-12, Mo. Tchr. lang. arts 10-12 Quincy (Ill.) Sr. H.S., 1970-72; tchr. lang. arts 7-12 Sch. Dist. R-S, New Raymer, Colo., 1972-73; tchr. lang. arts 9-12 Kansas City (Mo.) Sch. Dist., 1973-78; tchr. lang. arts 10-12 Ft. Osage Sch. Dist., Independence, Mo., 1978-80; Tchr. Title I Reading 7-8 Independence Pub. Schs., 1980-81, 89—, tchr. ESL and Am. Indian K-12, 1985-89; chairperson Profl. Devel.-Palmer, Independence, 1993—; sponsor Sharing Stories With Children, Independence, 1993—; presenter reading strategies Ottawa U., Overland Park, Kans., 1994, Chpt. I State Conf., 1994, Ann. Assessment & Authentic Performance Conf., Olathe, Kans., 1996; mem. Dist. Profl. Devel., Independence, 1994—; mem. adv. bd. Kansas City Regional Profl. Devel. Ctr., 1995-96. Active Blue Ridge Blvd. United Meth. Ch., Kansas City, 1982—; officer Mothers' Coun., Boy Scouts Am., Kansas City, 1993—. Mem. ASCD, Mo. Nat. Edn. Assn., Independence/Ft. Osage Internat. Reading Assn. (com. chair 1984—), PTA (life). Office: Palmer Jr HS 218 N Pleasant St Independence MO 64050-2655

MUÑOZ DONES CARRASCAL, ELOISA, hospital administrator, pediatrician, consultant, educator; b. San Lorenzo, P.R., Oct. 25, 1922; d. Pedro and Maria (Dones) Muñoz; m. José D. Carrascal, Dec. 7, 1962; children: Lilia, Maria. BA in Edn. cum laude, BS in Chemistry cum laude, U. P.R., Rio Piedras, 1943; MD, Tulane U., 1948. Diplomate Am. Bd. Pediatrics. Intern Arecibo Charity Dist. Hosp., 1948-49; resident in pediatrics San Juan (P.R.) City Hosp., 1949-51, chief newborn svc., attending pediatrician, 1951—, dir. neonatal-perinatal medicine, 1965—, dir. fellowship tng. program, 1972—; from instr. to assoc. prof. clin. pediatrics sch. medicine U. P.R., 1951-89, prof., 1989—; courtesy pediatrician neonatologist Tchrs. Hosp., Hato Rey, P.R., 1951-76, Ashford Presbyn. Drs. Hosp., Santurce, P.R., 1951-76, San Jorge H. H. Pavia Fernandez, Santurce, 1951-76; cons. pediatrician neonatologist Tchrs. H. Auxilio Mutuo H., Hato Rey, 1976—, Drs. H. San Jorge H. Ashford, San Juan, 1976—; mem. exec. com. San Juan City Hosp., 1976—, pres. med. faculty, 1976-77, 87-89, mem. instl. rev. bd., mem. ednl. rev. bd., mem. various coms.; lectr. in field. Contbr. articles to profl. jours. U.S. del. Care Orgn. Latin Am., 1962-63. Recipient Bronze medal Brazilian Acad. Human Scis., 1975, Hon. Cert. Internat. Yr. Women, City Mayor Lodo Carlos Romero Barceló, 1975, Hon. Cert. Disting. Svc. to Cmty., Julio Sellés Solá Elem. Sch., 1976, Pioneer Pediatrician award P.R. Pediat. Sect. Convention, 1993, Pioneer in Neonatology award P.R. Pediat. Sect. Convention, 1995, Pioneer Pidiat. Critical Care award Pediat. Critical Care Assn., 1996; grantee NIH, 1962. Fellow Am. Acad. Pediatrics (neonatal perinatal sect., mem. com. fetus and newborn P.R. chpt. 1956—, sec.-treas. 1962-64, mem. com. history perinatal sect. 1992—, Plaque in Recognition Disting. Pediatrician and Tchr. 1985), Pan Am. Pediatrics; mem. Am. Med. Women Assn., P.R. Med. Assn. (pediat. sect., mem. chamber of dels. 1962-63, Bronze plaque 1967, 91, Gold Pin 1980), P.R. Med. Women Assn. (sec.-treas. 1957-60, pres. 1960-64), Pan Am. Med. Women Assn. (pres. P.R. chpt. 1960-64, P.R. del. VIII Congress Manizales Colombia 1962), Pan Am. Med. Women Alliance (vis. lectr. 1962), Tulane Med. Alumni, London Royal Soc. Health, Colegio de Químicos, Soc. Dominicana de Pediatría (hon., vis. lectr. 1971), Dominican Rep. Soc. (hon.). Home: Duke C 12 Esq Tulane Santa Ana Rio Piedras San Juan PR 00927 Office: Las Americas Profl Ctr Domenech 400 Ste 309 Hato Rey San Juan PR 00918

MUÑOZ-SOLÁ, HAYDEÉ SOCORRO, library administrator; b. Caguas, P.R., Dec. 27, 1943; d. Gilberto Muñoz and Carmen Haydeé (Solá) de Muñoz; m. Juan M. Masini-Soler, Jan. 8, 1966 (div. 1979); children: Juan Martín Masini-Muñoz, Haydeé Milagros Masini-Muñoz. BA in Psychology, U. P.R., Río Piedras, 1965, MLS, 1970; D in Libr. Sci., Columbia U., 1985. Asst. libr. U. P.R., Río Piedras, 1964-67; dir. libr. Interam. U., Aguadilla, P.R., 1974-75; head svcs. to pub. U. P.R., Aguadilla, 1975-76; cataloguer Cath. U., Ponce, P.R., 1976-79; catalogue U. P.R., Río Piedras, 1982-84, head libr. and info. sci. libr., 1984-85, prof. grad. libr. sch., 1986, dir. libr. sys., 1986-93; coord. external resources libr. sys. U. P.R.; dir. P.R. Newspaper Project, Río Piedras, 1986-90; mem. Adv. Com. on Pub. Librs., San Juan, 1987-93; proposal reviewer NEH, 1990—; chmn. Puerto Rican Del. to Nat. White House Conf. on Libr. and Info. Svcs., 1991. Author: La Información y la Documentación Educativa/Informe Sobre la Situación Actual en Puerto Rico, 1991, Memorias: Sequnda Pre-Conferencia de Casa Blanca Sobre Bibliotecas y Servicios de Información en Puerto Rico, 1991; contbr. articles to profl. jours. Mem. Ponce Sport Club, 1976-83, ARC, Ponce, 1978. Recipient plaque White House Pre-Conf. on Libr. and Info. Scis., 1990; French Alps Study Tour scholar Assn. Caribbean Univ. Rsch. and Instl. Librs., 1989, Germany Study Tour scholar Fgn. Rels. Office, Germany, 1991. Mem. ALA, Am. Mgmt. Assn., Grad. Sch. Libr. and Info. Sci. Alumni Assn. (pres. 1988-90), Seminar for Acquisitions L.Am. Libr. Materials, Iberoamerican Nat. Librs. Assn. (pres. 1992-93), Puerto Rican Librs. Soc. (coord. So. area 1974, Lauro award 1989), Assn. Caribbean U. Rsch. and Instnl. Librs. (Parchment award 1988), Asoc. para las Comunicaciones y Tecnología Educativa, Mid. States Assn. Colls. and Schs. (collaborator), Am. Women Assn., Phi Delta Kappa (chair P.R. com. 1988-90, Kappan of Yr. 1990), Eta Gamma Delta. Roman Catholic. Office: U of PR Library System PO Box 23302 University Sta San Juan PR 00931-3302

MUNRO, ALICE, author; b. Wingham, Ont., Can., July 10, 1931; d. Robert Eric and Anne Clarke (Chamney) Laidlaw; m. James Armstrong Munro, 1951 (div. 1976); children: Sheila, Jenny, Andrea; m. Gerald Fremlin, 1976. BA, U. Western Ont., 1952, DLitt (hon.), 1976. Author: (short stories) Dance of the Happy Shades, 1968 (Gov.-Gen.'s Lit. award 1969), A Place for Everything, 1970, Lives of Girls and Women, 1971 (Can. Booksellers award, 1972), (short stories) Something I've Been Meaning To Tell You, 1974, Who Do You Think You Are?, 1979 (pub. in U.S. as Beggar Maid: Stories of Flo and Rose, 1984, Gov.-Gen.'s Lit. award 1978), The Moons of Jupiter, 1982, The Progress of Love, 1986 (Gov. Gens. Lit. award 1987), Friend of My Youth, 1990, (short stories) Open Secrets, 1994, A Wilderness Station, 1994, Selected Stories, 1996; TV scripts: A Trip to the Coast, 1973, Thanks For The Ride, 1973, How I Met My Husband, 1974, 1847: The Irish, 1978. Recipient Can.-Australia Lit. Prize 1994, Marian Engel award, 1986. Home: PO Box 1133, Clinton, ON Canada N0M 1L0 Office: care Alfred A Knopf Inc 201 E 50th St New York NY 10022-7703*

MUNRO, BARBARA HAZARD, nursing educator, college dean, researcher; b. Wakefield, R.I., Nov. 28, 1938; d. Robert J. and Honore (Egan) Hazard; m. Bruce Munro, June 1, 1961; children: Karen Aimee, Craig Michael, Stephanie Anne. BS, MS, U. R.I., Kingston; PhD, U. Conn. RN, Conn. Asst. prof. U. of R.I. Coll. of Nursing, Kingston; assoc. prof., chmn. program in nursing rsch. Yale U., New Haven, Conn.; assoc. prof., asst. dir. Ctr. for Nursing Rsch. U. Pa., Phila.; dean, prof. Boston Coll. Sch. Nursing, 1990—; presenter and workshop leader various nursing confs. and seminars in U.S. Contbr. articles and rsch. to profl. pubs. Trustee St. Elizabeth's Med. Ctr. Boston, 1994—. Recipient Nat. Rsch. Svc. award. Fellow Am. Acad. Nursing; mem. ANA, Nat. League for Nursing, Sigma Theta Tau, Pi Lambda Theta, Phi Kappa Phi.

MUNRO, CRISTINA STIRLING, artistic director; b. London, May 22, 1940; came to U.S., 1977; m. Richard Munro (div. 1986); children: Alexandra, Nicholas. Attended various artistic schs., London. Mem. ballet corps Sadlers Wells Opera Ballet, London, 1960-62, Het Nederlands Ballet, The Hague, Holland, 1962-63; soloist London Festival Ballet, 1963-72; prin. soloist Eliot Feld Ballet, N.Y.C., 1972-75; prin. dancer, artistic dir. Old Dominion U., Norfolk, Va., 1975; artistic dir. Louisville Ballet Co., 1975-79; ballet mistress Houston Ballet, 1979-85; dir. Munro Ballet Studies, Corpus Christi, Tex., 1985—; artistic dir. Corpus Christi Ballet, 1985—; guest artist and choreographer numerous cos. in U.S. Recipient Giovanni Martini award Louisville, 1978. Mem. Imperial Soc. Tchrs. of Dance, Royal Acad. Dancing, Brit. Actors Equity Assn., Am. Guild Mus. Artists. Office: Munro Ballet Studios Corpus Christi Ballet 5610 Everhart Rd Corpus Christi TX 78411-4905

MUNRO, ELEANOR, writer, lecturer; b. Bklyn., Mar. 28, 1928; d. Thomas and Lucile (Nadler) Munro; m. Alfred Frankfurter (dec. 1965); children: David, Alexander (dec.); m. E.J. Kahn, Jr. (dec.). BA, Smith Coll., 1949; MA, Columbia U., 1968. Staff writer, editor Art News Mag., N.Y.C., 1952-59; freelance writer, art critic, lectr. N.Y.C., 1960—; vis. fellow Woodrow Wilson Nat. Fellowship Fedn., Princeton, N.J., 1990—; cons., juror Bush Fdn., St. Paul, 1994; resident fellow Bellagio Study Ctr., Lake Como, Italy, 1991, Yaddo, Saratoga Springs, N.Y., 1984. Author: Encyclopedia of Art, 1961, Through the Vermilion Gates, 1971, Originals: American Women Artists, 1979 (a N.Y. Times Notable Book of Yr.), Memoir of a Modernist's Daughter, 1988, On Glory Roads: A Pilgrim's Book about Pilgrimage (a N.Y. Times Notable Book of Yr.); author articles, criticism, fiction and poetry. Bd. dirs. Truro (Mass.) Ctr. for Arts, 1979—, The Living Theater, N.Y.C., 1989—, Nat. Alliance Rsch. into Schizophrenia and Depression, N.Y.C., 1995—. Recipient Cleve. Arts prize, 1988, medal of honor Smith Coll., 1990. Mem. PEN Am., Am. Internat. Assn. Art Critics, Authors Guild. Home: 176 E 71st St #3B New York NY 10021

MUNRO, HEDI See MESNEY, DOROTHY TAYLOR

MUNRO, JANET ANDREA, artist; b. Woburn, Mass., Dec. 8, 1949; d. John Lehne, Jr. and Celina (Herbert) Baehr; m. Charles Eldon Munro, II, May 16, 1968; children Jacquelyn, David, Chad. Represented by Jay Johnson Gallery, N.Y.C., 1979-89, Frank Miele Gallery, N.Y.C., 1990—, Sternberg Galleries, Chgo., 1990—, Gallery 53 Artworks, Cooperstown, N.Y., 1990—, Toad Hall Gallery, N.Y.C., 1990—. Exhbns. include: Bloomingdales Dept. Store, N.Y.C., The MacArthur Found., West Palm Beach, Fla., 1987, Squibb Gallery, Princeton, N.J., 1983, Marshall Fields Dept. Store, Chgo., 1983, Jay Johnsons America's Folk Heritage Gallery, N.Y.C., 1982-84, Galerie Pro Arte Kasper, Morges, Switzerland, 1983-84, Occidental Oil Corp., San Francisco, 1980, Nassau County Mus. Fine Arts, Roslyn, N.Y., Silver Guild Ctr. Arts, New Canaan, Conn., John Judkyn Meml. Am. Mus. in Britain, Bath, Eng., Central Sch. Art and Design, London, Haworth Gallery, London, numerous others; featured in numerous publs.; represented in permanent collections: The White House, Smithsonian Inst., The Wallace House Mus., Somerset County, N.J., Fenimore House, N.Y. State Hist. Assn., Cooperstown, N.Y.; represented in numerous pub. and pvt. collections; featured in numerous newspapers and mags. Recipient Diploma award Internat. Naive Art Exhibit, Morges, Switzerland, 1983, 84. Active Cooperstown PTA, N.Y., 1985. Home: PO Box 303 Portlandville NY 13834-0303 also: 212 Coolidge Dr Sarasota FL 34236-2021

MUNSEN, JOY DIANE, secondary education educator; b. Syracuse, Kans., Dec. 29, 1947; d. Delmar Jay and Norva Elinor (Martin) Pelton; m. Paul Thomas Munsen Jr., Dec. 28, 1968; children: Mark Garrison, Matthew Jay. BS in Edn., Ctrl. Mo. State U., Warrensburg, 1970; MA in Secondary Edn., U. Mo., Kansas City, 1987. Cert. in social studies, English, core curriculum 7-12, Mo. Tchr. R-7 Sch. Dist., Lee's Summit, Mo., 1971-73, 81—; social studies lead tchr., technology chair Campbell Jr. High Sch., Lee's Summit, 1991—; presenter in field. Team mother Lee's summit Baseball/Soccer Assn.; supporter Safety Town, Lee's Summit, 1979. Recipient Excellence in Teaching award Lee's Summit C. of C., 1988, other awards. Mem. Nat. Coun. Social Studies, Parent-Tchr. Student Assn., Nat. Assn. for Gifted Children, Mo. Coun. for Gifted Children, Mortar Board, Delta Kappa Gamma (1st v.p. 1982), Sigma Kappa. Office: Bernard C Campbell Jr HS 1201 NE Colbern Rd Lees Summit MO 64086-5816

MUNSON, CHRISTINE B., bank executive; b. Jackson, Miss., Sept. 3, 1953; d. John Lyman and Frances (Gholson) Blakeslee; m. Glenn Walter Munson, July 10, 1976; children: Patrick, Courtney, Kelly. BA in Econ. magna cum laude, U. Memphis, 1979, postgrad. in Bus. Adminstr.-Finance. Sr. credit analyst Union Planters Nat. Bank, Memphis, 1979-80, comml. lending officer, 1980-81; v.p., sr. comml. lender First Tenn. Bank, Memphis, 1981-88, sr. v.p., mgr. Met. divsn., 1988-94, exec. v.p., mgr. Met. banking and real estate divsn., 1994—; bd. dirs. Ctr. City Devel. Corp., Memphis, 1994—. Bd. chmn. Shelby Residential and Vocat. Svcs., Memphis; treas., bd. dirs. Leadership Memphis Inc.; com. chair, bd. dirs. Memphis Depot Redevel. Bd.; treas., bd. dirs. Grace St. Luke's Sch., Memphis. Name of one Outstanding Young Women in Am., 1983. Mem. Memphis Rotary. Office: First Tenn Bank 165 Madison Memphis TN 38101

MUNSON, HELEN CRANE (KIT MUNSON), marriage and family therapist, mediator, consultant; b. Batavia, N.Y., Aug. 6, 1936; d. Thomas Patrick and Helen E. (Elliott) Crane; m. Hugh W. Munson; children: R. Michael, Dorie, Pat, Denise, Catherine, Joe, Maggie, Alex. BS in Psychology summa cum laude, Ind. Tech., 1977; MS in Marriage and Family Therapy, Va. Tech., 1984. Lic. profl. counselor, Va. Caseworker, head adoptions, interim exec. dir. Cath. Charities Southwestern Va., 1987-94; cons. New River Valley, Va., 1994—. Foster care worker Cath. Children's Svcs., Seattle, 1968-72, Rape Crisis, Ft. Wayne, Ind., 1972-77; bd. dirs. Shelter Home, New River Valley, Va., 1978—. Mem. Am. Mental Health Counselors Assn., Va. Mediation Network, Va. Counselors Assn., Acad. Family Mediators, Va. Tech. Faculty Women's Club, Blacksburg Intermediate Women's Club (sec. 1995—), Chi Sigma Iota. Office: 2749 Market St Christiansburg VA 24073

MUNSON, LUCILLE MARGUERITE (MRS. ARTHUR E. MUNSON), real estate broker; b. Norwood, Ohio, Mar. 26, 1914; d. Frank and Fairy (Wicks) Wirick; R.N., Lafayette (Ind.) Home Hosp., 1937; A.B., San Diego State U., 1963, student Purdue U., Kans. Wesleyan U.; m. Arthur E. Munson, Dec. 24, 1937; children—Barbara Munson Papke, Judith Munson Andrews, Edmund Arthur. Staff and pvt. nurse Lafayette Home Hosp., 1937-41; indsl. nurse Lakey Foundry & Machine Co., Muskegon, Mich., 1950-51, Continental Motors Corp., Muskegon, 1951-52; nurse Girl Scout Camp, Grand Haven, Mich., 1948-49; owner Munson Realty, San Diego, 1964—. Mem. San Diego County Grand Jury, 1975-76, 80-81, Calif. Grand Jurors Assn. (charter). Office: 2999 Mission Blvd Ste 102 San Diego CA 92109-8070

MUNSON, NANCY KAY, lawyer; b. Huntington, N.Y., June 22, 1936; d. Howard H. and Edna M. (Keenan) Munson. Student, Hofstra U., 1959-62; JD, Bklyn. Law Sch., 1965. Bar: N.Y. 1966, U.S. Supreme Ct. 1970, U.S. Ct. Appeals (2d cir.) 1971, U.S. Dist. Ct. (ea. and so. dists.) N.Y. 1968. Law clk. to E. Merritt Weidner Huntington, 1959-66, sole practice, 1966—; mem. legal adv. bd. Chgo. Title Ins. Co., Riverhead, N.Y., 1981—; bd. dirs., legal officer Thomas Munson Found. Trustee Huntington Fire Dept. Death Benefit Fund; pres., trustee, chmn. bd. Bklyn. Home Aged Men Found.; bd. dirs. Elderly Day Svcs. on the Sound. Mem. ABA, N.Y. State Bar Assn., Suffolk County Bar Assn., Bklyn. Bar Assn., NRA, DAR, Soroptimists (past pres.). Republican. Christian Scientist. Office: 197 New York Ave Huntington NY 11743-2711

MUNZ, ANN CAROL, sales executive; b. Cin., Feb. 11, 1956; d. Wayne Dudley and Helen Laurel (Kisker) Martin; m. Roger Garland Munz, Mar. 17, 1984. BS in Edn., Miami U., 1978, MA in Edn., 1979. Dir. sports medicine, sports schs. Miami U., Oxford, Ohio, 1978-80; phys. therapy asst. McCullough-Hyde Meml. Hosp., Oxford, 1979-83; sales rep. Wil-Med, Inc., Cin., 1982-84, Mediwell, Inc., Ft. Worth, 1984; mfr.'s rep. Dynasplint Sys., Inc., Balt., 1985-86, regional sales mgr., 1986-92; regional sales mgr. Autogenesis, Inc., Anchorage, 1992—; health svcs. coord. Lifeline Screening, Inc., Largo, Fla., 1994—, regional mgr., 1995—. Asst. to editor NATA Jour., 1979-80; grad. asst. Miami U., 1979. Chmn. membership records Diabetes Found. Inc., Naples, Fla. Mem. NAFE. Home and Office: 10436 Winterview Dr Naples FL 33942-1522

MUNZER, CYNTHIA BROWN, mezzo-soprano; b. Clarksburg, W.Va., Sept. 30, 1948; d. Ralph Emerson and Doris Marguerite (Dixon) Brown; 1 dau., Christina Marie. Student, U. Kans., 1965-69. Adj. prof. voice U. So. Calif., 1994—. Debut, Oxford (Eng.) Opera, 1969, Met. Opera debut, N.Y.C., 1973; performed 1973-96 with: Met. Opera, Phila. Opera, Wolftrap Festival, Washington Opera, Goldovsky Opera, Washington Civic Opera, St. Petersburg Opera, Dallas Opera, Metropolin. Opera-Japan, Boston Concert Opera, Dayton Opera, Chgo. Opera Theatre, Mich. Opera, Kansas City Opera, New Orleans Opera, Houston Grand Opera, Ft. Worth Opera, Florentine Opera-Milw., Minn. Opera, Central City Opera, Aspen Festival, Opera Colo., Boston Festival Orch., Ontario Opera, Salt Lake City Opera,

Nev. Opera, Cleve. Opera, Opera Pacific, Des Moines Opera, Ky. Opera, Mobile Opera, Internat. Artist Series in Kuala Lumpur, Penang, Jakarta; Hong Kong Philharmonic, Shanghai Symphony, Singapore Symphony, Philippine Philharmonic, N.Y.C. Ballet, Am. Symphony, Nat. Symphony, Charleston Symphony, Phila. Orch., New Haven Symphony, Houston Symphony, Ft. Wayne Symphony, El Paso Symphony, San Antonio Symphony, Amarillo Symphony, Wichita Symphony, Milw. Symphony, Minn. Orch., Denver Symphony, Phoenix Symphony, Oreg. Bach. Festival, San Francisco Symphony, L.A. Philharm., Louisville Symphony, Rochester Philharmonic, Binghamton Symphony, Rhode Island Symphony, Carmel Bach Festival, Anchorage Symphony, L'Opera de Montreal, Colo. Opera Festival, New York Mozart Bicentennial Festival, Brattleboro Festival, Knoxville Opera, Gold Coast Opera, Hawaii Opera, Augusta Opera, Berkshire Opera, Madison Opera, Chattanooga Symphony. Recipient Frederick K. Weyerhaeuser award, Gramma Fisher Found. award, Goeran Gentele award, Sullivan Found. award, Geraldine Farrar award. Office: PO Box 77332 Los Angeles CA 90007-0332

MURAWSKI, MARIANNE M., academic administrator; b. Abington, Pa., Mar. 4, 1962; d. Edmund J. and Mary M. (Matonick) M. BA, Rutgers U., 1984; MMus, Temple U., 1992; postgrad., U. Md., 1992—. Acad. advisor Rutgers U., Camden, N.J., 1985-90, music student tchr. supr., 1986-90, vis. lectr. in music, 1991—; coord. acad. advisement Gloucester County Coll., Sewell, N.J., 1990-94, adj. instr. music, 1991-94; divsnl. adminstr. gen. studies Richard Stockton Coll. N.J., Pomona, 1995—, adj. lectr. music, 1994—; tchg. asst. music U. Md., College Park, 1994-95; adj. lectr music Brookdale C.C., Lincroft, N.J., 1994—. Mem. NAFE, Am. Musicological Soc., Coll. Mus. Soc. Office: Richard Stockton Coll NJ Gen Studies Pomona NJ 08240

MURAWSKI, SUSAN, family nurse practitioner; b. Erie, Pa., Dec. 16, 1953; d. Bernard and Lucille (Gorny) Murawski; m. Timothy clarence Lyons, Aug. 13, 1994. B.Elem. Edn., Pa. State U., 1975; BSN, Edinboro U. of Pa., 1991; MSN, U. Pitts., 1994. Cert. nurse practitioner. Tchr. Harborcreek Sch. for Boys, Erie, 1979-80; staff nurse St. Vincent Health Ctr., Erie, 1983-92; family nurse practitioner Cmty. Health Net, Erie, 1994—. Editor/founder Pa. NP Issues newsletter, 1996. Bd. dirs., edn. chairperson Whole Foods Coop. Assn., Erie, 1984-85, then v.p./pres., newsletter editor, 1984-86, 89—. Mem. AAUW, Am. Acad. Nurse Practitioners, Am. Coll. Nurse Practitioners, Pa. Nurse Practitioners Coalition (rec. sec. 1995—), N.W. Pa. Nurse Practitioners Assn. (sec. 1994—, conf. chairperson 1995-96). Office: Community Health Net 1720 Holland St Erie PA 16503

MURDOCK, MICHELLE MARIE, marketing executive; b. Columbus, Ohio, Nov. 18, 1959; d. Louis Joseph and Barbara Jean (Stites) M. BA in Econs., U. Conn., Stamford, 1982. Membership rep. CUC Internat., Inc., Stamford, 1984-85, membership coord., 1985-86, asst. mgr. account mgmt., 1986-87, asst. mgr. mktg. svcs., 1987, mgr. mktg. svcs., 1987-89, dir. mktg. ops., 1989-90, dir. mktg. systems support, 1990-92; v.p. ops. CRRC, Westport, Conn., 1993; v.p. mktg./sales Sayers Pub. Group, Arvada, Colo., 1994-96; mgr. Stroke Ctr. Network Nat. Stroke Assn., Englewood, Colo., 1996—; cons. on young careerists Bus. and Profl. Women's Club, Inc., Stamford, 1990. Recipient cert. of appreciation Bus. and Profl. Women's Club, Inc., 1990. Mem. NAFE. Office: Nat Stroke Assn 8480 E Orchard Rd Ste 1000 Englewood CO 80111-5015

MURDOCK, PAMELA ERVILLA, advertising travel company executive, b. Los Angeles, Dec. 3, 1940; d. John James and Chloe Conger (Keefe) M.; children: Cheryl, Kim. BA, U. Colo., 1962. Pres., Dolphin Travel, Denver, 1972-87; owner, pres. Mile Hi Tours, Denver, 1973—, MH Internat., 1987—, Mile-Hi Advt. Agy., 1986— . Bd. dirs. Rocky Mountain chpt. Juvenile Diabetes Found. Internat. Named Wholesaler of Yr., Las Vegas Conv. and Visitors Authority, 1984. Mem. NAFE, Am. Soc. Travel Agts., Colo. Assn. Commerce and Industry, Nat. Fedn. Independent Businessmen. Republican. Home: 5565 E Vassar Ave Denver CO 80222-6239 Office: Mile Hi Tours Inc 2160 S Clermont Denver CO 80222-5000

MURILLO, JUDITH A., property manager; b. Elmhurst-Queens, N.Y., Aug. 12, 1970; d. Alejandro and Gladys E. (Mejia) M.; m. Louie A. Tomalå, Feb. 25, 1962; 1 child, Jessica A. Tomalå. Grad. h.s., N.Y.C., 1989. Cert. occupancy specialist; cert. assisted housing mgr. Adminstrv. asst. Phipps Houses, Inc., Henry Phipps Plaza West, N.Y.C., 1990-91, recert. specialist, 1991-93; recert. specialist P & L Mgmt., N.Y.C., 1994-95, property mgr., 1995—. Democrat. Roman Catholic. Home: 34-43 Crescent St Apt 2G Long Island City NY 11101

MURILLO, VELDA JEAN, social worker, counselor; b. Miller, S.D., Dec. 8, 1943; d. Royal Gerald and Marion Elizabeth (Porter) Matson; m. Daniel John Murillo, June 25, 1967 (div. Dec. 1987); 1 child, Damon Michael. BS, S.D. State U., 1965; MA, Calif. State U., Bakersfield, 1980. Cert. marriage, family and child counselor. Social worker adult svcs. Kern County Dept. Welfare, Bakersfield, 1965-78, social worker child protective svcs., 1978-84; asst. coord. sexual abuse program Kern County Dist. Atty., Bakersfield, 1985-91, coord. sexual abuse program, 1991—; Mem. Calif. Sexual Assault Investigators, 1982-84, Kern Child Abuse Prevention Coun., Bakersfield, 1982-84; co-developer, presenter Children's Self Help Project, Bakersfield, 1982-87; cons. mem. Sexual Assault Adv. Com., Bakersfield, 1991—. Democrat. Office: Kern County Dist Atty 1215 Truxtun Ave Bakersfield CA 93301

MURPHEY, MARGARET JANICE, marriage and family therapist; b. Taft, Calif., July 24, 1939; d. Glen Roosevelt Wurster and Lucile Mildred (Holt) Lopez; m. Russell Warren Murphey, June 20, 1959; children: Lucinda Kalbfleisch, Rochelle Murphey, Janice Sorenson. BA in Social Sci., Calif. State U., Chico, 1986, MA in Psychology, 1989; postgrad., La Salle U. Sec. Folson State Prison, Calif., 1963-66; tchr. Desert Sands Unified Schs., Indio, Calif., 1969-72; claims determiner Employment Development Dept., Redding, Calif., 1976-78; sec. Shasta County Pers., Redding, 1978-79; welfare worker Shasta County Welfare Office, Redding, 1979-85; therapy intern Counseling Ctr. Calif. State U., Chico, 1989-90; therapist Family Svc. Assn., Chico, 1987-90, Butte County Drug and Alcohol Abuse Ctr., Chico, 1989-90; mental halth counselor Cibecue (Ariz.) Indian Health Clinic, 1990—; mem. Kinisba Child Abuse Com., 1994—. Vol. Pacheco Sch., Redding, 1972-76; Sunday sch. tchr., dir. vacation Bible sch. Nazarene Ch., Sacramento, Indio and Redding, 1958-85. Recipient Sch. Bell award Pacheco Sch. Mem. APA, ACA, Am. Assn. Christian Counselors, Am. Assn. Multi-Cultural Counselors, Psi Chi. Home: PO Box 1114 Show Low AZ 85901-1114 Office: Cibecue Health Ctr Apache Behavioral Health PO Box 1089 Whiteriver AZ 85941-1089

MURPHEY, SHEILA ANN, infectious diseases physician, educator, researcher; b. Phila., July 10, 1943; d. William Joseph and Sara Esther (Mallon) M. AB, Chestnut Hill Coll., 1965; MD, Women's Med. Coll. of Pa., 1969. Diplomate Am. Bd. Internal Medicine, Am. Bd. Infectious Diseases. Intern in internal medicine Mt. Sinai Hosp. of N.Y., 1969-70, resident in internal medicine, 1970-72, instr. internal medicine, 1971-72; fellow infectious diseases U. Pa. Sch. Medicine, Phila., 1972-74, instr. dept. medicine, 1974-75, asst. prof. dept. medicine, 1975-77; chief infectious diseases sect. Phila. Gen. Hosp., 1974-77; attending physician Hosp. U. Pa., Phila. Gen. Hosp., 1974-77; dir. divsn. infectious diseases, asst. prof. medicine Jefferson Med. Coll., Phila., 1977-80, clin. assoc. prof. medicine, 1980—; dir. divsn. infectious diseases Thomas Jefferson U., Phila., 1977-88; infection control officer, attending physician Thomas Jefferson U. Hosp., Phila., 1977—. Contbr. articles to profl. jours. Fellow Coll. Physicians Phila.; mem. Am. Soc. Microbiology, Am. Coll. Physicians, Am. Fedn. Clin. Rsch., Soc. Healthcare Epidemiology of Am., Infectious Diseases Soc. Am., Alpha Omega Alpha. Democrat. Roman Catholic. Office: Jefferson Med Coll 1015 Chestnut St Ste 1020 Philadelphia PA 19107-4316

MURPHY, ANN MARIE, special education educator; b. Phila., Aug. 29, 1953; d. Daniel Joseph and Mary Ann Murphy. BA, Glassboro State Coll., 1975, MA, 1989. Cert. learning disabilities tchr. cons. Tchr. severly retarded Am. Inst. for Mental Studies, Vineland, N.J., 1975-79; tchr. emotionally disturbed and perceptually impaired Woodbury (N.J.) Sch. Dist., 1979-94, resource ctr. tchr./learning disabilities tchr. cons., 1994—; asst. basketball coach Woodbury (N.J.) H.S., 1979-89, Glassboro State/Rowan Coll., 1989-94. Named to Glassboro State/Rowan Hall of Fame, Rowan Coll. N.J., Glassboro, 1989, South Jersey Basketball Hall of Fame, 1992, Gloucester County Sports Hall of Fame, 1996. Mem. Coun. for Exceptional Children, N.J. Edn. Assn. (bldg. rep. 1979-85), Women's Basketball Coaches Assn., Assn. Learning Cons., Delta Kappa Gamma. Office: Woodbury Pub Schs Walnut St Sch Woodbury NJ 08096

MURPHY, ANN PLESHETTE, magazine editor-in-chief. Editor-in-chief Parents mag., N.Y.C. Office: Parents Magazine 685 3rd Ave New York NY 10017-4024*

MURPHY, BARBARA ANN, public relations manager; b. Panama City, Fla., Feb. 2, 1955; d. Francis James and Marian Ann (Jones) M. B of Communications, U. Puget Sound, 1977. Dir. spl. events Restaurant Assn. of Wash., Seattle, 1979-82; pub. rels. officer Wash. Ho. of Reps., Olympia, 1983-86; pub. rels. mgr. Boeing Aerosapce Co., Kent, Wash., 1986-89, Boeing Computer Svcs., Bellevue, Wash., 1989-90; communications mgr. 777 Divsn. Boeing Comml. Airplane Group, Everett, Wash., 1990-95; pub. rels. mgr. Boeing Comml. Airplane Group, Seattle, 1995—; mem. Boeing Mgmt. Assn., 1986—. Mem. Pub. Rels. Soc. Am. Office: Boeing Comml Airplane Group PO Box 3707 M/S 65-47 Seattle WA 98124-2207

MURPHY, BARBARA ANN, protective services official; b. Union City, N.J., Oct. 4, 1922; d. Thomas Henry and Charlotte Ruth (Ticer) Murphy. BS, Jersey City State Coll., 1944; MA, Columbia U., 1949. Ret. educator; chair child placement rev. bd., Hudson County Superior Court of N.J., Chancery Divsn. Family, 1992—. Pres. bd. trustees Weehawken (N.J.) Libr., 1994—. Recipient Gov.'s Tchr. Recognition Program award, Princeton, N.J., 1989; named to Weehawken H.S. Hall of Fame, Weehawken Bd. Edn., 1992. Mem. AAUW (pres. 1988-91), N.J. Schoolwomen's Club (v.p. 1980), Weehawken Hist. Soc. (life mem.), Weehawken Adult Club (charter), Palisade Gen. Hosp. Vols. Home: 107 Hauxhurst Ave Weehawken NJ 07087

MURPHY, BETTY JANE SOUTHARD (MRS. CORNELIUS F. MURPHY), lawyer; b. East Orange, N.J.; d. Floyd Theodore and Thelma (Casto) Southard; m. Cornelius F. Murphy, May 1, 1965; children: Ann Southard, Cornelius Francis Jr. AB, Ohio State U.; student, Alliance Française and U. Sorbonne, Paris; JD, Am. U.; LLD (hon.), Eastern Mich. U., 1975, Capital U., 1976, U. Puget Sound, 1986; LHD, Tusculum coll., 1987. Bar: D.C. 1958. Corr., free lance journalist Europe and Asia, UPI, Washington; pub. relations counsellor Capital Properties, Inc. of Columbus (Ohio), Washington; practiced in Washington, 1959-74; mem. firm McInnis, Wilson, Munson & Woods (and predecessor firm); dep. asst. sec., adminstr. Wage and Hour Divsn. Wage and Hour div. Dept. Labor, 1974-75; chmn. and mem. NLRB, 1975-79; ptnr. firm Baker & Hostetler, 1980—; adj. prof. law Am. U., 1972-80; mem. adv. com. on rights and responsibilities of women to Sec. HEW; mem. panel conciliators Internat. Ctr. Settlement Investment Disputes, 1974-85; mem. Adminstrv. Conf. U.S., 1976-80, Pub. Svc. Adv. Bd., 1976-79; mem. human resouces com. Nat. Ctr. for Productivity and Quality of Working Life, 1976-80; mem. Presdl. Commn. on Exec. Exch., 1981-85. Trustee Mary Baldwin Coll., 1977-85, Am. U., 1980—, George Mason U. Found., Inc., 1990—, George Mason U. Edn. Found., 1993—; nat. bd. dirs. Med. Coll. Pa., bd. corporators, 1976-85; bd. dirs. Ctr. for Women in Medicine, 1980-86; bd. govs. St. Agnes Sch., 1981-87; mem. exec. com. Commn. on Bicentennial of U.S. Constn., chmn. internat. adv. com., 1985-92; vice chmn. James Madison Meml. Fellowship Found., 1989-96; bd. dirs. Meridian Internat. Ctr., 1992-96, Friends of Congl. Law Libr., 1992—, Friends of Dept. of Labor; bd. dirs. Union Internationale des Advocats, 1996—. Recipient Ohio Gov.'s award, 1980, fellow award, 1981, Outstanding Pub. Service award U.S. Info. Service, 1987; named Disting. Fellow John Sherman Myers Soc., 1986. Mem. ABA (adminstrv. law sect., chmn. labor law com. 1980-83, chmn. internat. and comparative law adminstrv. law sect. 1983-88, chmn. customs, tariff and trade com. 1988-90, employment law sect. 1990, chmn. internat. com. dispute resolution sect. 1995—), FBA, Inter-Am. Bar Assn. (editor newsletter, Silver medal 1967, co-chmn. labor law com. 1975-83), Bar Assn. D.C., World Peace Through Law Ctr., Am. Arbitration Assn. (bd. dirs. 1985—, mem. editl. bd. 1992, mem. exec. com. 1995—, mem. internat. arbitration com. 1995—), Rep. Nat. Lawyers Assn. (nat. v.p. 1990-95, nat. vice chmn. 1996—), Supreme Ct. Hist. Soc., Am. U. Alumni Assn. (bd. dirs.), Mortar Bd., Kappa Beta Pi. Republican. Office: Baker & Hostetler 1050 Connecticut Ave NW Washington DC 20036-5303

MURPHY, CARA ANN, journalist; b. Rochester, N.Y., July 16, 1965; d. Edward Joseph and Jacqueline Ann (Smith) M. BA, U. Mich., 1988; MA, U. So. Calif., 1991. From reporter to mng. editor The Beach Reporter, Manhattan Beach, Calif., 1991—. Office: The Beach Reporter 500 S Sepulveda Blvd #215 Manhattan Beach CA 90266

MURPHY, CARYLE MARIE, foreign correspondent; b. Hartford, Conn., Nov. 16, 1946; d. Thomas Joseph and Muriel Kathryn (McCarthy) M. BA cum laude, Trinity Coll., 1968; M in Internat. Pub. Policy, Johns Hopkins U., 1987. Tchr. English, history St. Cecilia Tchr. Tng. Coll., Nyeri, Kenya, 1968-71; reporter Brockton (Mass.) Enterprise, 1972-73; freelance corr. Washington Post, Newsweek, Sunday Times of London, et al, Luanda, Angola, 1974-76; reporter Fairfax County Washington Post, 1976-77, fgn. corr. in South Africa, 1977-82, reporter immigration issues, 1982-85, bur. chief Alexandria, Va., 1985-89; fgn. corr. Mid. East Washington Post, Cairo, 1989-94. Vol. ARC, Washington, 1984, Whitman-Walker Found., Washington, 1988-89. Recipient Courage in Journalism award Internat. Women's Media Found., 1990, George Polk award L.I. U., 1991, Edward Weintal Journalism award Sch. Fgn. Svc., Georgetown U., 1991, Pulitzer Prize for internat. reporting, 1991; Edward R. Murrow fellow Coun. on Fgn. Rels., N.Y., 1994-95. Roman Catholic. Office: Washington Post Fgn Desk 1150 15th St NW Washington DC 20071-0001*

MURPHY, DEBORAH ANN, marketing professional, artist; b. N.Y.C., May 24, 1960; d. Thomas and Carol Ann (O'Fee) C.; m. Sean Joseph Murphy, Apr. 14, 1979; (div. Apr., 1984); 1 child, William. AA with hons., St. Louis C.C. at Meramac, 1987; BFA, Washington U., 1989. Mktg. mgr. JetCorp Aircraft Sales, Inc., St. Louis, 1992-94; mktg. dir. JetBrokers, Inc., Chesterfield, Mo., 1994—. Artist One-person show Mixed Media Prints, 1995. Mem. Art St. Louis (program com. mem.), St. Louis Women's Caucus for Art (pres. 1995-96), Washington U. Alumni Parents Admissions Program. Office: JetBrokers Inc 583 Bell Ave Hangar D Chesterfield MO 63017

MURPHY, DEBORAH JUNE, lawyer; b. Clinton, Tenn., Dec. 19, 1955; d. Robert Carlton and Mary Ruth (Melton) M.; m. Charles L. Beach, Dec. 9, 1987. BS, U. Tenn., 1977; postgrad. Vanderbilt U., 1983; JD, Nashville YMCA Law Sch., 1987. Bar: Tenn. 1987. Tax auditor State of Tenn., Knoxville, 1977-82, Nashville, 1983-85, legal advisor, 1985-86; with office legal services Tenn. Gen. Assembly, Nashville, 1986-87; atty. U.S. Dept. Treasury, 1987—; Mem. ABA, ATLA, Tenn. Trial Lawyers Assn., Anderson County Bar Assn., Lawyers Assn. for Women. Democrat. Methodist. Avocation: travel. Home: PO Box 510 Clinton TN 37717 Office: 710 Locust St Fl 4 Knoxville TN 37902-2540

MURPHY, DEBORAH MARGARET, mental health services professional, social worker; b. Monroe, La., Mar. 10, 1967; d. Ronald Gene and Billie Margaret Farmer; m. Larry Stevens Murphy, Dec. 20, 1992; 1 child, Taylor Woodson. BA, Northeast La. State U., 1989. Admission clk. E.A. Conway Meml. Hosp., Monroe, La., 1986-87, 1988-90; soc. svcs. dir. Teh Oaks Nursing Home, Monroe, La., 1990-93; psychiatric technician St. Francis Hosp., Monroe, La., 1993-94; program dir. Ashley Meml. Hosp., Crossett, Ark., 1994—; adv. bd. social workers U. Ark., Montcello, 1995—. Mem. ethics com. Ashley Meml. Hosp., Crossett, Ark., 1993. Democrat. Baptist. Home: 235 Morgan Hare Rd Monroe LA 71203-8442

MURPHY, DEIRDRE MOIRA, legal secretary, writer; b. Chgo., Aug. 8, 1961; d. Martin R. Sr. and Margaret Louise Murphy; m. James Arthur Rittenhouse, May 28, 1983 (div. Feb. 1992); 1 child, Aislinn Brighid Murphy. BA in Anthropology with honors, U. Notre Dame, 1983. Ops. mgr. AOS Pub. Svcs., Chgo., 1983-86; sr. prodn. asst. AMA Publs. Dept., Chgo., 1986-89; sec. to pres. Martin R. Murphy and Assocs., Chgo., 1989-92; exec. sec. Luth. Social Svcs., Milw., 1992-95; legal sec. Lowe Law Offices, S.C., Milw., 1995—; Spkr. in field. Contbr. articles to publs.; performer, musician. Mem. Sci. Fiction and Fantasy Writers Am. (assoc.), Milw. Area Writer's Guild, Sci. Fiction and Fantasy Workshop, Soc. for Creative Anachronism, Lambda Alpha. Home: 2663 N Pierce St Milwaukee WI 53212-2954

MURPHY, DIANA E., federal judge; b. Faribault, Minn., Jan. 4, 1934; d. Albert W. and Adleyne (Heiker) Kuske; m. Joseph Murphy, July 24, 1958; children: Michael, John E. BA magna cum laude, U. Minn., 1954, JD magna cum laude, 1974; postgrad., Johannes Gutenberg U., Mainz, Germany, 1954-55, U. Minn., 1955-58. Bar: Minn. 1974, U.S. Supreme Ct. 1980. Assoc. Lindquist & Vennum, 1974-76; mcpl. judge Hennepin County, 1976-78, Minn. State dist. judge, 1978-80; judge U.S. Dist. Ct. for Minn., Mpls., 1980-94, chief judge, 1992-94; judge U.S. Ct. of Appeals (8th cir.), Minneapolis, 1994—. Bd. editors: Minn. Law Rev., Georgetown U. Jour. on Cts., Health Scis. and the Law, 1989-92. Bd. dirs. Spring Hill conf. Ctr., 1978-84, Mpls. United Way, 1985—, treas., 1990-94, vice chair, 1996—; bd. dirs. Bush Found., 1982—, chmn. bd. dirs., 1986-91; bd. dirs. Amicus, 1976-80, also organizer, 1st chmn. adv. coun.; mem. Mpls. Charter Commn., 1973-76, chmn., 1974-76; bd. dirs. Ops. De Novo, 1971-76, chmn. bd. dirs., 1974-75; mem. Minn. Constl. Study Commn., chmn. bill of rights com., 1971-73; regent St. Johns U., 1978-87, 88—, vice chmn. bd., 1985-87, chmn. bd. 1995—; mem. Minn. Bicentennial Commn., 1987-88; trustee Twin Cities Pub. TV, 1985-94, chmn. bd., 1990-92; trustee U. Minn. Found., 1990—, treas., 1992—; bd. dirs. Sci. Mus. Minn., 1988-94, vice chmn., 1991-94; trustee U. St. Thomas, 1991—; dir. Nat. Assn. Pub. Interest Law Fellowships for Equal Justice, 1992-95. Fulbright scholar; recipient Amicus Founders' award, 1980, Outstanding Achievement award U. Minn., 1983, Outstanding Achievement award YWCA, 1981, Disting. Citizen award Alpha Gamma Delta, 1985. Fellow Am. Bar Found.; mem. ABA (mem. ethics and profl. responsibility judges adv. com. 1981-88, standing com. on jud. selection, tenure and compensation 1991-94, mem. standing com. on fed. jud. improvements, 1994—, Appelate Judges conf. exec. com. 1996—), Minn. Bar Assn. (bd. govs. 1977-81), Hennepin County Bar Assn. (gov. coun. 1976-81), Am. Law Inst., Am. Judicature Soc. (bd. dirs. 1982-93, v.p. 1985-88, treas. 1988-89, chmn. bd. 1989-91), Nat. Assn. Women Judges, Minn. Women Lawyers (Myra Bradwell award 1996), U. Minn. Alumni Assn. (bd. dirs. 1975-83, nat. pres. 1981-82), Fed. Judges Assn. (bd. dirs. 1982—, v,p. 1984-89, pres. 1989-91), Hist. Soc. for 8th Cir. (bd. dirs. 1988-91), Fed. Jud. Ctr. (bd. dirs. 1990-94, 8th cir. jud. coun. 1992-94, mem. U.S. jud. conf. com. on ct. adminstrn. and case mgmt. 1994—), Order of Coif, Phi Beta Kappa. Office: US Dist Ct 684 US Courthouse 110 S 4th St Minneapolis MN 55401

MURPHY, DIANE GENSHEIMER, real estate broker, educator; b. Erie, Pa., Nov. 12, 1948; d. Herbert F. and Jeanne Lenore (Menz) Gensheimer; m. James J. Murphy, June 6, 1982; 1 child, Jeanne Marie. BA magna cum laude, Gannon U., 1970; MA, U. Md., 1971, PhD, 1978. Lic. real estate broker, Va. V.p. J.D. Internat., Inc., Alexandria, Va., 1980—; pres. DGM Properties, Inc., Alexandria, 1992—; adult edn. instr. Arlington, Alexandria and Fairfax Counties, Va., 1993-96. Contbr. articles to profl. jours. Active Alexandria (Va.) Seaport Found., 1992—. Grad. fellow U. Md., College Park, 1971-72. Mem. Kiwanis Internat. (Alexandria Va. chpt. bd. dirs. 1995-96), No. Va. Assn. Realtors, No. Va. Bd. Realtors. Episcopalian. Office: DGM Properties Inc 104 S Columbus St Alexandria VA 22314

MURPHY, DONNA JEANNE, actress; b. Corona, N.Y., Mar. 7, 1959. Student, NYU Sch. of the Arts. Stage appearances include: (regional theater) Miss Julie, Pal Joey, (off-Broadway) Song of Singapore, Hey Love: The Songs of Mary Rodgers, Privates on Parade, Showing Off, Birds of Paradise, Little Shop of Horrors, A...My Name Is Alice,, Twelve Dreams, Hello Again, 1995, (Broadway) The King and I, 1996 (Best Leading Actress Tony award 1996), Passion (Leading Actress in Mus. Tony award 1994), The Mystery of Edwin Drood, They're Playing Our Song, The Human Comedy; appeared in film Jade, 1995; TV appearances include Law & Order, All My Children, Another World, Murder One, 1995-96, HBO Lifestories, 1996. Office: Silver Massetti & Assocs 145 W 45th St Fl 1204 New York NY 10036-4008

MURPHY, EDRIE LEE, hospital laboratory administrator; b. Redwood Falls, Minn., Dec. 4, 1953; d. Melvin Arthur and Betty Lou (Wenholz) Timm; m. David Joseph Murphy, July 28, 1984; children: Michael David, Scott Christopher. BS in Med. Tech. summa cum laude, Mankato State U., 1976; MBA, U. St. Thomas, 1984. Registered med. technologist. Med. technologist Children's Health Care, St. Paul, 1976-81, chemistry supr., 1981-85, lab. mgr., 1985-95, dir. lab. systems, Mpls., St. Paul's Campus, 1995—. Contbr. articles to profl. jours. Charles H. Cooper scholar, 1975. Mem. Am. Soc. Clin. Lab. Scis., Minn. Soc. Clin. Lab. Scis., Am. Assn. Clin. Chemists, Clin. Lab. Mgmt. Assn. (sec./treas. Minn. chpt. 1994-96, bd. dirs. 1996—), Phi Kappa Phi. Club: Elan Vital Ski (v.p. membership 1981-82) (Mpls.). Avocations: photography, sailing, skiing, tennis, travel. Office: Childrens Health Care 345 Smith Ave N Saint Paul MN 55102-2369

MURPHY, ELVA GLENN, executive assistant; b. Chickasha, Okla., Aug. 21, 1934; d. Elsie Lee (Murphy) Sommer; m. Calvin E. Morgan, Mar. 11, 1972 (dec. Dec. 1976); m. C. Gordon Murphy, Oct. 17, 1981. Student, UCLA, 1954-55, Columbia U., 1973. Various secretarial positions Calif., 1956-67; fgn. svc. sec. U.S. Dept. State, Paris, 1967-69; exec. asst. to Cyrus R. Vance Simpson Thacher & Bartlett, N.Y.C., 1969-77, 80—, U.S. Dept. State, Washington, 1977-80. Mem. Seraphic Soc. (pres. 1990-92). Democrat. Home: 60 Sutton Pl S # 9HN New York NY 10022-4168 Office: Simpson Thacher & Bartlett 425 Lexington Ave New York NY 10017-3954

MURPHY, ERIN ELIZABETH, editor; b. Balt., Oct. 9, 1965; d. John Joseph and Doris Alice (Metzbower) M. BA in English, U. Miami, Coral Gables, Fla., 1987, BS in Computer Sci., 1987. Assoc. editor IEEE Spectrum Mag., N.Y.C., 1987-90; sr. editor, on-line editor Omni mag., Greensboro, N.C., 1990—. Mem. Phi Beta Kappa. Office: Omni Mag 324 W Wendover Ave Ste 200 Greensboro NC 27408-8437

MURPHY, EVELYN FRANCES, healthcare administrator, former lieutenant governor; b. Panama Canal Zone, Panama Canal Zone, May 14, 1940; d. Clement Bernard and Dorothy Eloise (Jackson) M. AB, Duke U., 1961, PhD, 1965; MA, Columbia U., 1963; hon. degrees, Regis Coll., 1978, Curry Coll., Northeastern U., Simmons Coll., Wheaton Coll., Anna Maria Coll., Bridgewater State Coll., Salem State Coll., Emmanuel Coll.; hon. degree, Suffolk U. Pres. Ancon Assocs., Boston, 1971-72; ptnr. Llewelyn-Davies, Weeks, Forrester-Walker & Bor, London, 1973-74; sec. environ. affairs Commonwealth of Mass., Boston, 1975-79, sec. econ. affairs, 1983-86, lt. gov., 1987-91; mng. dir. Brown Rudnick Freed and Gesmer, Boston, 1991-93; exec. v.p. Blue Cross/Blue Shield of Mass., Boston, 1994—; also bd. dirs. Blue Cross Blue Shield Mass., Boston; vis. pub. policy scholar Radcliffe Coll., 1991; vice chmn./chmn. Nat. Adv. Com. on Oceans and Atmosphere (Presdl. apptd.), 1979-80; bd. dirs. Fleet Bank of Mass., Fleet Bank of Conn., Fleet Bank R.I. Recipient Disting. Svc. award Nat. Sierra Club, 1978, Nat. Govs. Assn. 1978, Outstanding Citizen award Mass. Audubon Soc., 1978; Harvard U. fellow, 1979-80. Mem. Women Execs. in State Govt. (chair 1987). Democrat. Office: Blue Cross Blue Shield Mass 100 Summer St Boston MA 02110-2104

MURPHY, FRANCES LOUISE, II, newspaper publisher; b. Balt.; d. Carl James and L. Vashti (Turley) M.; m. James E. Wood (div.); children: Frances Murphy Wood Draper, James E. Jr., Susan Wood Barnes. BA, U. Wis., 1944; BS, Coppin State Coll., Balt., 1958; MEd, Johns Hopkins U., 1963. City editor Balt. Afro-Am., 1956-57; dir. News Bur., Morgan State Coll., Balt., 1964-71; chmn. bd. dirs. Afro-Am. Newspapers, Balt., 1971-74; assoc. prof. journalism State Univ. Coll., Buffalo, 1975-85, Howard U., Washington, 1985-91; editor Washington Afro-Am., 1951-56, pub., 1987—; bd. dirs. Afro-Am. Newspapers, Balt., 1985-87; mem. adv. bd. Partnership Inst., Washington, 1985-91; treas. African Am. Civil War Meml. Freedom Found., African Am. Leadership Summit. Trustee State Colls. Md., 1971-76, U. D.C., 1994—; bd. dirs. Delta Rsch. and Ednl. Found., 1993-95; nat. bd. dirs. NACCP, 1971-76. Named One of 100 Most Influential Black Ams., Ebony mag., 1973, 74, Disting. Marylander, Gov. State of Md., 1975; recipient Ida

B. Wells award Congl. Black Caucus, 1989, Public Svc. award African Methodist Episcopal Ch., 1991, Invaluable Svc. award Martin L. King Jr. Found., 1992, Black Women of Courage award Nat. Fedn. Black Women Bus. Owners, 1993, Black Awareness Ach. award Holy Redeemer Catholic Ch., 1993, Bus. of the Yr. award Bus. and Profl. Women's League, 1993, Oustanding Svc. award Capital Press Club, 1993, Black Conscious Commitment trophy Unity Nation, 1993, Dedicated Cmty. Svc. award Ward I Cmty. and D.C. Pub. Schs., 1994, Women of Strength award Nat. Black Media Coalition, 1994, 95, Outstanding Woman of Yr. award Alpha Gamma chpt. Iota Phi Lambda, 1994, Art Carter Excellence award Capital Press Club, 1994, Excellence in Comm. award Washington Inter-Alumni Coun. United Negro Coll. Fund, 1994, 95, Disting. Cmty. Svc. award The Questers, Inc., 1995, Outstanding Journalist award Masons, 1995, Outstanding Achievement award Beta Zeta chpt. Zeta Phi Beta, 1996, award in recognition of outstanding contbns. made to youth The Soc., 1996, Disting. Black Women award BISA, 1996. Mem. Nat. Newspaper Pubs. Assn. (editl. com. 1987—, Merit award 1987, 89-93), Soc. Profl. Journalists (Disting. Svc. in local journalism award Washington chpt. 1994), Links, Capital Press Club (exec. bd. 1987—, Outstanding Svc. award 1993, Art Carter award of excellence 1994), Delta Sigma Theta (Frances L. Murphy II Comm. award Fed. City Alumnae chpt. 1993, Fortitude Image award Prince George's County chpt. 1994), Kiwanis Club (first woman hon., 1995). Democrat. Episcopalian. Home: 5709 1st St NW Washington DC 20011-2319 Office: Washington Afro-Am 1612 14th St NW Washington DC 20009-4307

MURPHY, GLORIA WALTER, novelist, screenwriter; b. Hartford, Conn., Feb. 22, 1940; d. Frank and Elizabeth (Lemkin) Walter; m. Joseph S. Murphy; children: William Gitelman, Laurie Gitelman, Daniel Gitelman, Julie Gitelman, Caitlin Fleck. Student, No. Essex Community Coll., Haverhill, Mass., 1979-81, Boston U., 1981-82. Columnist Pandora's Box The Peabody (Mass.) Times, 1975; columnist Murphy's Law The Methuen (Mass.) News, 1979. Author: Nightshade, 1986, Bloodties, 1987, Nightmare, 1987, The Playroom, 1987, Cry of the Mouse, 1991, Down Will Come Baby, 1991, A Whisper in the Attic, 1992, A Shadow on the Stair, 1993, Simon Says, 1994, A Stranger in the House, 1995, Summer of Fear, 1996. Mem. Mystery Writers Am., Authors Guild. Address: PO Box 670 Ringwood NJ 07456-0670

MURPHY, GRETA WERWATH, retired college official; b. Milw., Aug. 24, 1910; d. Oscar and Johanna (Seelhorst) Werwath; m. John Heery Murphy, Sept. 18, 1941. Ed. Ohio State U., 1943-45; PhD in Comms. (hon.) Milw. Sch. Engring., 1993 . With Milw. Sch. Engring., 1928—, head admissions dept., 1931-42, dir. pub. rels. 1945-66, v.p. pub. rels. and devel., 1966-77, v.p., cons., 1978—, regent emeritus, 1985—. Mem. Milw. County Planning Commn., 1966—, vice chmn., 1974-75, chmn., 1976-77. Fellow Pub. Rels. Soc. Am. (founder, past pres. Wis. chpt.); mem. Am. Coll. Pub. Rels. Assn. (past dir., sec., trustee), Women's Advt. Club (pres.). Club: Womans of Wis. Home: 1032 Malaga Ave Miami FL 33134-6319 also: 5562 Cedar Beach S Belgium WI 53004-9646

MURPHY, JOANNE BECKER, writer; b. Detroit; d. Louis Norman and Gertrude Margaret (Kornmeier) Becker; m. Joseph A. Murphy, Jr., June 24, 1961; children: Michael Ellis, Joseph A. III. BA in Journalism, Mich. State U., 1958; MA in Humanities, Wayne State U., 1975. With pub. rels. dept. WBZ TV, Boston, 1958-60, The Jam Handy Orgn., Detroit, 1960-62, Detroit Symphony Orch., 1969-70; freelance writer, editor Detroit, 1980-90, Washington, 1990—. Contbg. writer: Affecting Change, 1986, Glass: State of the Art, 1989; editor: As Parents We Will, 1985 (1st Pl. award Pub. Svc. Nat. Found. for Alcoholism Comm.); writer, editor publs. for arts and human svcs. orgns.; contbr. articles to mage., newspapers. Mem. program bd. Grosse Pointe (Mich.) War Meml., 1987-90; bd. dirs. Detroit Artists Market, 1982-90, Mich. Metro coun. Girl Scouts U.S.A., 1971-78, Family Svcs. Detroit and Wayne County, 1970-76, All Hallows Guild, Washington Nat. Cathedral, 1993—; bd. canvassers Grosse Pointe Sch. Sys., 1986-90. Named one of 50 Outstanding Women Mich. State U., 1958. Mem. Women in Comms. Inc. (v.p. pub. rels. D.C. chpt. 1992-93), Washington Ind. Writers, Am. News Women's Club (Washington, bd. dirs. 1996), Kappa Alpha Theta. Home and Office: 2717 O St NW Washington DC 20007-3128

MURPHY, JOANNE M., computer company executive; b. Holyoke, Mass., Dec. 31, 1957; d. LeRoy Paul and Rose Marie (Danehey) Miller; m. Dennis Francis Murphy III, June 2, 1979; 1 child, Dennis Francis IV. AS in Bus. Studies, Holyoke Community Coll., 1979; BS in Mktg., U. Mass., 1980; postgrad., U. Hartford. Account rep. Xerox Corp., Hartford, Conn., 1980-82; sr. account exec. Exxon Office Systems, Stamford, Conn., 1983-85; area sales cons. ShareTech, Hartford, 1985-86; sr. mktg. rep. Honeywell Info. Systems, Glastonbury, Conn., 1986-87; nat. account exec. Computer Horizons, Inc., 1987-93, dir. bus devel., 1994-95; solutions mgr. IBM Corp., 1995—; engagement mgr. Horizons Cons., Inc. divsn. Computer Horizons Corp., Mountain Lakes, N.J. Editor shared tenant newsletter, 1985. Mem. Nat. Orgn. Female Execs., Data Processing Mgmt. Assn., Orgn. for Profls. in Telecommunication. Republican. Roman Catholic. Avocations: skiing, tennis, golf, personal computers. Home: 195 Firetown Rd Simsbury CT 06070 Office: Computer Horizons Corp 49 Old Bloomfield Ave Mountain Lakes NJ 07046

MURPHY, JUDITH CHISHOLM, trust company executive; b. Chippewa Falls, Wis., Jan. 26, 1942; d. John David and Bernice A. (Hartman) Chisholm. BA, Manhattanville Coll., 1964; postgrad., New Sch. for Social Research, 1965-68, Nat. Grad. Trust Sch., 1975. Asst. portfolio mgr. Chase Manhattan Bank, N.A., N.Y.C., 1964-68; trust investment officer Marshall & Ilsley Bank, Milw., 1968-72; asst. v.p. Marshall & Ilsley Bank, 1972-74, v.p., 1974-75; v.p., treas. Marshall & Ilsley Invesmtent Mgmt. Corp., Milw., 1975-94; v.p. Marshall & Ilsley Trust Co., Phoenix, 1982—, Marshall & Ilsley Trust Co. Fla., Naples, 1985—; v.p., dir. instnl. sales Marshall & Ilsley Trust Co., Milw., 1994—; coun. mem. Am. Bankers Assn., Washington, 1984-86; govt. relations com. Wis. Bankers Assn., Madison, 1982-88. Contbr. articles to Trusts & Estates Mag., 1980, ABA Banking Jour., 1981, Maricopa Lawyer, 1983. Chmn. Milw. City Plan Commn., 1986—; commr. Milw. County Commn. on Handicapped, 1988-90; bd. dirs. Cardinal Stritch Coll., Milw., 1980-89, Children's Hosp. Wis., Milw., 1989—. Recipient Outstanding Achievement award YWCA Greater Milw., 1985, Sacajawea award Profl. Dimensions, Milw., 1988, Pro Urbe award Mt. Mary Coll., 1988, Vol. award Milw. Found., 1992; named Disting. Woman in Banking, Comml. West Mag., 1988. Mem. Milw. Analysts Soc. (sec. 1974-77, bd. dirs. 1977-80), Fin. Women Internat. (bd. dirs., v.p. 1976-80), Am. Inst. Banking (instr. 1975-78), TEMPO (charter), Profl. Dimensions (hon.), University Club, Woman's Club Wis., Rotary. Democrat. Roman Catholic. Home: 1139 N Edison St Milwaukee WI 53202-3147 Office: Marshall & Ilsley Trust Co 1000 N Water St Milwaukee WI 53202-3197

MURPHY, KATHLEEN ANNE FOLEY, advertising agency executive; b. Fresh Meadows, N.Y., Oct. 15, 1952; d. Thomas J. and Audrey L. (Finn) F.; m. Timothy Sean Murphy, Sept. 26, 1992. BA, Marymount Coll., 1974; postgrad., Smith Coll., 1985. V.p. acct. supr., sr. v.p. mgmt. supr., sr. v.p. group dir. Ogilvy & Mather Inc., N.Y.C., 1974-90; sr. v.p., worldwide account dir. Young & Rubicam, San Francisco, 1990-92, sr. v.p., dir. account svcs., 1992-95, exec. v.p., dir. acct. svcs., 1995—. Mem. San Francisco Advt. Club, Advt. Edn. Fedn. Roman Catholic. Home: One Brookside Ave Berkeley CA 94705 Office: Young & Rubicam 100 1st St San Francisco CA 94105-2634

MURPHY, KATHLEEN MARY, former law firm executive; b. Bklyn., Dec. 16, 1945; d. Raymond Joseph and Catherine Elizabeth (Kearney) M. BA in Edn., [illegible] Coll., 1971; MS in Edn., Bklyn. Coll., 1975. Cert. elem. sch. tchr., N.Y. Elem. sch. tchr. various parochial schs. L.I., Bklyn., Queens, N.Y., 1969-80; from asst. prin. to prin. parochial sch. Queens, 1980-82; supr.-trainer Davis, Polk, Wardwell law firm, N.Y.C., 1982-88; mgr. Schulte Roth & Zabel, N.Y.C., 1988-95; Reiki practitioner, 1995—; trainer program for new employees, 1984; speaker edn. topics, Bklyn., Queens, 1979-81. Mem. NAFE. Democrat. Roman Catholic.

MURPHY, KATHRYN MARGUERITE, archivist; b. Brockton, Mass.; d. Thomas Francis and Helena (Fortier) M. AB in History, George Washington U., 1935, MA, 1939; MLS, Cath. U., 1950; postgrad. Am. U., 1961. With Nat. Archives and Records Svc., Washington, 1940-89, ret., supervisory archivist Ctrl. Rsch. br., 1958-62, archivist, 1962—, mem. fed. women's com. Nat. Archives, 1974, rep. to fed. women's com. GSA, 1975; docent, 1989—; lectr. colls., socs. in U.S., 1950—; lectr. Am. ethnic history, 1978-79; free lance author and lectr. in field. Founder, pres. Nat. Archives lodge Am. Fedn. Govt. Employees, 1965—, del. conv., 1976, 78, 80, recipient award for outstanding achievement in archives, 1980. Recipient commendation Okla. Civil War Centennial Commn., 1965; named hon. citizen Oklahoma City, Mayor, 1963. Mem. ALA, Soc. Am. Archivists (joint com. hosp. librs. 1965-70), Nat. League Am. Pen Women (corr. sec. Washington 1975-78, pres. chpt. 1978-80), Bus. and Profl. Womens' Club Washington, Phi Alpha Theta (hon.). Contbr. articles on Am. ethnic history to profl. publs. Home: 1500 Massachusetts Ave NW Washington DC 20005-1821

MURPHY, LINDA S., city official; b. Lynchburg, Va., June 7, 1948; d. Carter P. and Dorothy L. (Clark) Tucker; m. Daniel K. Murphy, Mar. 25, 1972; 1 child, Krystal. Student, Longwood Coll., 1966-68. Exec. sec. First Nat. Bank of Anchorage, Seward, Alaska, 1976-80; clk. of ct., asst. magistrate Alaska Ct. System, Seward, 1980-81; city clk., pers. officer City of Seward, 1981—. Sec., Seward Concert Assn., 1982; chmn. Seward Sch. Adv. Bd., 1983; v.p. bd. dirs. Seward Life Action Coun., 1983-84, pres. bd. dirs., 1984-86; chmn. Seward-Obihiro Sister City Com., 1984; lt. gov. Transition Team, 1995; chmn. local United Way, 1995. Named Alaska Mcpl. Official of Yr., 1992. Mem. Internat. Inst. Mcpl. Clks. (bd. dirs. 1992-95, 2d v.p. 1995-96, 1st v.p. 1996—), Alaska Assn. Mcpl. Clerks (sec. 1984-85, v.p. 1985-86, pres. 1986-87), Alaska Women in Govt. (v.p. 1985-87), Bus. and Profl. Women's Club (v.p. 1988-89, pres. 1989-90), Rotary (bd. dirs. 1989-96, treas. 1991-93, v.p. 1993-94, pres. 1994-95). Democrat. Home: Nhn Salmon Rd Seward AK 99664 Office: Seward City Hall PO Box 167 Seward AK 99664-0167

MURPHY, LISA MARIE, account executive; b. Washington, Oct. 31, 1961; d. Stuart Ronald and Joan Marie (Kelly) Sklamm; m. John Edward Murphy, Feb. 12, 1989; 1 child, Nicholas Patrick. BS in Journalism and Speech Comm., Towson State U., 1983; MA in Speech Comm., U. Maine, 1985. Lic. to sell group health/life ins. Maine. Sales rep. Well Care New Eng., Bangor, Maine, 1986-87; dir. edn. Career Com. Sch. Bus., Virginia Beach, Va., 1987-88; area rep. Readicare Occupl. Med. Clinics, San Francisco, 1988-89; sales rep. Med. Evaluation Specialists, Walnut Creek, Calif., 1989-91; regional sales rep. Disability Evaluation Group, Oakland, Calif., 1991-93; account exec. Corvel Corp., Concord, Calif., 1993—. Copy editor feature sect. The Towsonian, 1982, copy editor culinary sect. The Balt. Sun, 1982. Mem. Indsl. Claims Assn. San Francisco (editor No. Calif. Resource Directory 1990, 95, 96, dir. edn. 1991, exec. com. 1991-96), San Francisco Indsl. Claims Assn. (cons.), No. Calif. Coun. Self-Insureds (cons.), North Bay Workers Compensation Assn. (cons.), Diablo Valley Indsl. Claims Assn. Democrat. Roman Catholic. Home: 161 Sunnyglen Dr Vallejo CA 94591 Office: Corvel Corp Ste 700 1800 Sutter St Concord CA 94520

MURPHY, MARGARET HACKETT, federal bankruptcy judge; b. Salisbury, N.C., 1948. BA, Queens Coll., Charlotte, N.C., 1970; JD, U. N.C., Chapel Hill, 1973. Bar: Ga. 1973, U.S. Bankruptcy Ct. Assoc. Smith, Cohen, Ringel, Kohler and Martin, Atlanta, 1973-79; ptnr. Smith, Gambrell & Russell (formerly Smith, Cohen, Ringel, Kohler and Martin), Atlanta, 1980-87; U.S. bankruptcy judge U.S. Dist. Ct. (no. dist.) Ga., Atlanta, 1987—. Office: 1290 US Courthouse 75 Spring St SW Atlanta GA 30303-3367

MURPHY, MARGARET MCMAHON, television producer; b. N.Y.C., May 22, 1943; d. Gerard Augustine and Margaret (Nolan) McMahon; m. Eugene John Murphy, Feb. 23, 1965 (div Jan 1979); 1 child, Jane Owen. BS, Fordham U., 1964; postgrad., CUNY Neighborhood Playhouse, 1965-66. Film editor, prodr. Sesame Street Children's TV Workshop, N.Y.C., 1968-72; film editor ABC Sports, N.Y.C., 1975-76, prodr., writer, 1996; prodr. McCann-Erickson, N.Y.C., 1976-79; film editor 60 Minutes, CBS News, N.Y.C., 1979-82; prodr. film editor Smithsonian World Sta. WETA, Washington, 1982-85; prodr. Our World, ABC News, N.Y.C., 1986-87, prodr. Nightline,, 1989-92, prodr. GMA Sunday, 1995; ptnr. Belzberg/Murphy Prodns., N.Y.C., 1987-89; prodr. Dateline-NBC, NBC News, N.Y.C., 1992-94; writer Turner Sports, Atlanta, 1995. Prodr., editor feature documentary They Are Their Own Gifts, 1979 (award N.Y. Film Fest 1979); prodr., dir. interactive videodisc Fun & Games, 1982 (nom. Grammy Award, 1982). Prodr. Prin. for A Day, N.Y.C., 1995. Recipient Spl. Jury award Bklyn. Arts and Cultural Assn., 1972, Nat. Emmy award NATAS, 1976, 84, 90, also Berlin, Edinburgh and Houston Film Festival awards. Democrat. Roman Catholic.

MURPHY, MARY C., state legislator. BA, Coll. St. Scholastica; postgrad. U. Minn., Macalester Coll., U. Wis.-Superior, Am. U., Indiana U. H.s. tchr.; mem. Minn. Ho. of Reps., 1976—, mem. com. chair judiciary fin. com., tourism consumer affairs, labor-mgmt. relations coms.; active del. Duluth Central Labor Body AFL-CIO; mem., lector St. Raphael's Parish; dir. State Democratic Farmer-Labor Party, 1972-74, chmn. 8th Dist. credentials com., 1974—, chmn. St. Louis County Legis. Delegation, 1985-86. Mem. Duluth Fedn. Tchrs. (1st v.p. 1976-77, various coms.), Minn. Fedn. Tchrs. (legis. com. 1972-75), Am. Fedn. Tchrs. (del. nat. convs.), Minn. Hist. Soc., Alpha Delta Kappa. Office: State Office Bldg Saint Paul MN 55155-1201

MURPHY, MARY KATHLEEN, nursing educator; b. Elkins, W.Va., Jan. 27, 1953; d. Wyatt W. and Emma Loretta (Bohan) M.; children: Bridget Allyn, Kelley M. Poling. Diploma, Upshur County Sch. Nursing, Buckhannon, W.Va., 1982; ADN, Davis and Elkins Coll., 1984, BSN magna cum laude, 1986; MSN, W.Va. U. Cert. correctional health profl., substitute vocat. tchr. practical nursing, W.Va. Nurse, asst head nurse in ob-gyn. Meml. Gen. Hosp., Elkins, W.Va.; staff nurse, resource pool in ob-gyn. W.Va. U., Morgantown; DON Correctional Med. Systems, Huttonsville, W.Va.; instr. in nursing Davis and Elkins Coll.; nurse mgr. Elkins Mountain Sch. Randolph County Bd. Edn. Reviewer nursing texts Lippincott-Raven Pub. Mem. ANA, W.Va. Nursing Assn. (reviewer approval unit com. edn.), Inst. Noetic Scis., So. States Correctional Assn., Alpha Chi, Sigma Theta Tau.

MURPHY, MARY KATHLEEN CONNORS, college administrator, writer; b. Pueblo, Colo.; d. Joseph Charles and Eileen E. (McDermott) Connors; m. Michael C. Murphy, June 6, 1959; children: Holly Ann, Emily Louise, Patricia Marie. AB, Loretto Heights Coll., 1960; MEd, Emory U., 1968; PhD, Ga. State U., 1980. Tchr. English pub. schs., Moultrie, Ga., 1959, Sacramento, 1960, Marietta, Ga., 1960-65, DeKalb County, Ga., 1966; tech. writer Ga. Dept. Edn., 1966-69; editorial asst. So. Regional Edn. Bd., Atlanta, 1969-71; dir. alumni affairs The Lovett Sch., Atlanta, 1972-75, dir. publs. and info. svc., 1975-77; coord. summer series in aging Ga. State U., 1979; dir. devel. found. rels. Ga. Inst. Tech., 1980-87, dir. devel., 1987-89; asst. dir. devel. for spl. gifts U Ga., 1989-91; assoc. v.p. for devel. Oglethorpe U., 1991—; state coord. for Ga., Am. Coun. on Edn. nat. identification program for women in higher edn. administrn., 1983-85; presenter profl. confs.; freelance edn. writer, 1968—; co-author: Fitting in as a New Service Wife, 1966; contbr. and contbg. editor numerous articles on teaching, secondary edn., higher edn., and fund raising to profl. publs.; columnist Daily Jour., Marietta, 1963-67, The Atlanta Constn., 1963-68; editor: Cultivating Found. Support for Edn., 1989, Building Bridges: Fund Raising for Deans, Faculty, and Development Officers, 1992. Bd. advisors Bridge Family Counseling Ctr., 1981-86, Northside Sch. Arts, 1981-83; bd. dirs. Atlanta Women's Network, 1982-84, v.p., 1983-84; prin., bd. dirs. Sch. Religion, Cathedral of Christ the King, 1979-84; mem. devel. com. Archdiocese of Atlanta, 1991-94; publicity chmn. Phoenix Soc. Atlanta, 1981-91, adv. bd., 1988-91; mem. allocations com., exec. com. United Way Met. Atlanta, 1983; bd. counseling Fulton Svc. Ctr., Met. Atlanta chpt. ARC, 1982-83; mem. Leadership Atlanta, class of 1983-84; group facilitator, 1984-85, co-chmn. edn. program, 1987; co-chair bldg. fund com. Mary Our Queen Ch., 1996—. NDEA fellow, 1965-66; Adminstrn. of Aging fellow, 1977-79; recipient Image Maker award Atlanta Profl. Women's Directory, Inc. 1984. Mem. Coun. for Advancement and Support of Edn. (publs. com., alumni adv. com., 1974-76, dist. III bd., 1981-95, chmn. corp. and found. support conf., N.Y.C., 1985, maj. rsch. conf., Atlanta, 1986, matching gift conf., Tampa, 1989, dist. III conf. chmn. 1986, chair elect 1989-91, chair dist. III bd., 1991-93, past chair and nonminations com. chair, 1993-95, membership svcs. com. 1989-93, Washington bd. dirs. 1992-96, exec. com., trusteeship com., dist. svcs. and governance com., Alice Beeman Writing award, 1994), Ga. Coun. on Planned Giving (bd. dir., chair edn. com. planned giving com., 1995—), Nat. Assn. Ind. Schs. (publs. com. 1974-76), Edn. Writers Assn., Nat. Soc. Fund Raising Execs. (v.p. Ga. chpt. 1985, pres. 1986-87, mem.-at-large nat. bd. 1985-89, chmn. pub. rels. com. 1985-87, asst. treas., chair audit com., mem. exec. com. 1988-90), Kiwanis (co-chair membership com. Atlanta club 1990-91, chair program com. 1991-96, dir. 1993-94, asst. sec. 1994-95, v.p. 1995-96, pres. elect. 1996—), Phi Delta Kappa, Kappa Delta Pi (pres. 1980-81).

MURPHY, MARY KATHRYN, industrial hygienist; b. Kansas City, Mo., Apr. 16, 1941; d. Arthur Charles and Mary Agnes (Fitzgerald) Wahlstedt; m. Thomas E. Murphy Jr., Aug. 26, 1963; children: Thomas E. III, David W. BA, Avila Coll., Kansas City, 1962; MS, Cen. Mo. State U., 1975. Cert. in comprehensive practice of indsl. hygiene. Indsl. hygienist Kansas City area office Occupational Safety and Health Adminstrn., 1975-78, regional indsl. hygienist, 1979-86; dir. indsl. hygiene Chart Svcs., Shawnee, Kans., 1986-87; dir. indsl. hygiene and hazardous substance control Hall-Kimbrell Environ. Mgmt. and Pollution Control, Lawrence, Kans., 1987-88, mgr. dept. indsl. hygiene div. environ. mgmt. and program control, 1988-89; dir. indsl. hygiene Hazardous Waste divsn. Burns & McDonnell, Engrs., Architects, Kansas City, Mo., 1989-93; mgr. health & safety dept. Burns & McDonnell Waste Cons., Inc., Overland Park, Kansas, 1990-93, dir. indsl. hygiene U.S. Army Corps Engrs., Kansas City, 1993; regional program mgr. environ. & safety ctrl. region FAA, Kansas City, 1993—; asst. dir. safety office U. Kans. Med. Ctr., 1978-79; adj. prof. continuing edn. divsn. U. Kans.; adj. lectr. Ctrl. Mo. State U. Summer talent fellow Kaw Valley Heart Assn., 1961. Mem. AAAS, Am. Indsl. Hygiene Assn. (sec.-treas. Mid-Am. sect. 1978-79, bd. dirs. 1981, mem. auditcom.), Am. Chem. Soc., Am. Conf. Govt. Indsl. Hygienists (mem. chem. agts. threshold limit value com.), Am. Acad. Indsl. Hygiene, Air and Waste Mgmt. Assn., Environ. Audit Roundtable, N.Y. Acad. Scis., Internat. Soc. Environ. Toxicology and Cancer, Am. Coll. Toxicology, Am. Conf. on Chem. Labeling. Home: 10616 W 123rd St Shawnee Mission KS 66213-1952 Office: FAA-ACE 473 601E 12th St Kansas City MO 64106

MURPHY, MICHELE SUSAN, non-profit agency executive; b. Cleve., Aug. 11, 1949; d. Edward Jerry and Violet Agnes (Lozick) M. BS in Journalism, Ohio U., 1971; M Non-Profit Orgns., Case Western Res. U., 1993. Press rep. Cuyahoga Community Coll. West, Parma, Ohio, 1971-75; pub. info. specialist Cuyahoga Community Coll., Cleve., 1975-76, news bur. mgr., 1976-77, asst. dir. info. svcs., 1977-78, cons., 1979; coord. U.S. Senate Campaign, Cleve., 1981-82; communications liaison Cuyahoga County Bd. Elections, Cleve., 1982-94; exec. dir. Crime Stoppers of Cuyahoga County, Inc., Cleve., 1994; founder, exec. dir. Conflict Resolution Ctr. of the West Shore, Inc.; cons. in mktg. The City Club, Cleve., 1991. Mem. Leadership Cleve., Greater Cleve. Growth Assn., 1986; editor Rep. News, Cuyahoga County Rep. Orgn., 1983-84. Recipient Appreciation award Greater Cleve. Crime Prevention Com., 1992, Ohio State Chiefs of Police Assn., 1990, Vol. Achievement award CIVAC, Cleve., 1987, Cert. of Appreciation Community Rels. Bd., City of Cleve., 1987, Sports Promotion award Nat. Jr. Coll. Athletic Assn., 1973, 74, 75. Mem. Ohio Mediation Assn., Acad. Family Mediators, Cuyahoga County Police Chiefs Assn. (hon., named Citizen of Yr. 1995). Office: CRC West Shore Inc 24700 Center Ridge #6 Westlake OH 44145

MURPHY, MILLENE FREEMAN, educator, nurse, business executive; b. Idaho Falls, Idaho, Feb. 3, 1941; d. Eson Milton and Maurine (Dustin) Freeman; m. Stanley Dee Murphy, Aug. 24, 1962; children: Madison Dee, D'Lene, Eric Daniel, Aaron Milton, William Stanley, Sarah Anne, Nona Reen. BSN, Brigham Young U., 1963; MS in Psychiatric Nursing, U. Utah, 1970; PhD in Neuropsychology, Brigham Young U., 1982. Advanced practice RN. Nurses aid LDS Hosp., Idaho Falls, Idaho, 1959-63; pub. health nurse Salt Lake City Health Dept., 1963-64; staff nurse LDS Hosp., Salt Lake City, 1964-68; instr. nursing Brigham Young U., Provo, 1965-67, asst. prof., 1970-83; assoc. prof., dir. nursing SEMO U., Cape Girardeau, Mo., 1983-85; assoc. prof. Brigham Young U., 1985-96; founder, exec. dir. Wellness Consultation and Edn., Richfield, Utah, 1992—; pres. Psychiat. Rehab. Nurses, Nine Mile Falls, Wash.; co-founder Three R's Program for psychiatric rehab. Author: (with others) How to Enter the World of Psychosis, 1994, Recovering from Psychosis; A Wellness Approach, 1996, My Symptom Management Workbook: A Wellness Expedition, 1996. Coach Payson Youth Soccer Program, 1990-93. Mem. ANA, Am. Psychiatric Nurses Assn., Soc. Edn. and Rsch. Psychiatric Nursing, Utah Psycho-Social Nursing Orgn. (pres., chair 1988-92), Utah Coun. Psychiatric Nurses, Phi Kappa Phi, Sigma Theta Tau, Sigma Xi. Mem. LDS Ch. Home: PO Box 502 Richfield UT 84701

MURPHY, PATRICIA A., lawyer; b. Astoria, N.Y., July 7. BA, Fordham U., 1978, JD, 1981. Bar: N.Y. 1982. Ptnr. Brown & Wood, N.Y.C. Office: Brown & Wood One World Trade Ctr New York NY 10048-0557*

MURPHY, PATRICIA ANN, writer, legal consultant; b. Shelton, Wash., June 22, 1940; d. Cyril Daniel and Donna Denio (Driskel) M.; 1 child, Jamie Shoemaker. BA, U. Minn., 1963; MS, St. Cloud State U., 1974; PhD, The Union Inst., Cin., 1991. Diplomate Am. Bd. Vocat. Experts; cert. rehab. counselor Commn. on Rehab. Counselor Certification. Asst. dir. U. Calif. Women's Ctr., Santa Barbara, 1975-78; vocat. rehab. counselor pvt. practice, Santa Monica, Lake Tahoe, Calif., 1978-92; legal cons. pvt. practice, Santa Fe, N. Mex., 1993—. Author: (books) Searching for Spring, 1987, We Walk the Back of the Tiger, 1988, Making the Connections: Women, Work and Abuse, 1993, A Career and Life Planning Guide for Women Survivors, 1996. Bd. dirs. Family Violence Project, Santa Barbara, Calif., 1976-78; chmn. bd. dirs. Making the Connections Intercultural Network, Chgo., 1990—; adv. bd. Standing Against Global Exploitation, San Francisco, 1995—. Named Women's Health Policy fellow John D. and Catherine MacArthur Found., Chgo., Ill. Mem. NOW, Nat. Assn. Rehab. Profls. in Pvt. Sector (Most Innovative Rehab. Counselor 1991), Nat. Rehab. Assn., Nat. Women's Studies Assn. Democrat. Home and Office: 86 Monte Alto Rd Santa Fe NM 87505

MURPHY, PATRICIA ENGLE, art therapist; b. Balt., July 7, 1944; d. Robert Engle and Robin (Hening) Stewart; m. Neil Edward Franklin, June 11, 1988. BA, U. Ala., 1967; MLA, Johns Hopkins U., 1972; MA, Goucher Coll., 1983; PhD, U. Idaho, 1992. Resource devel. officer State of Md., Balt., 1973-79, gov.'s rep., 1979-81; internat. cons. various univs. South Africa and Malawi, 1988—; art therapist Sheppard Pratt Hosp., Balt., 1983-84, U. Idaho, Moscow, 1989-91; pvt. practice Moscow, 1992—. Mem. Am. Assn. Art Therapy (registered art therapist, mem. editl. bd. 1995—). Home: 1207 Nearing Rd Moscow ID 83843

MURPHY, PEREGINE LEIGH, priest, clinical researcher; b. Fowler, Calif., Sept. 29, 1954; d. Elbert Thurman Pitcock Jr. and Patricia (Dolan) Olsen. BA in Human Devel., Calif. State U., Hayward, 1979, MS in Clin. Counseling, 1980; MBA, Coll. Notre Dame, Belmont, Calif., 1982; MDiv, Gen. Theol. Sem., 1990. Ordained priest, Episc. Ch., 1991. Parent educator, tchr. Children's Ctr. of Stanford (Calif.) Community, Stanford U., 1980-83; human resource cons. Continental Corp., N.Y.C., 1983-85; v.p. adminstrn. Continental Internat. Life, Continental Corp., N.Y.C., 1985-86; residency pastoral care Columbia Presbyn. Med. Ctr., N.Y.C., 1988-89; sr. staff assoc. neuromuscular rsch. N.Y. Neurol. Inst. Columbia Presbyn. Med. Ctr., N.Y.C., 1990—; asst. min. Cathedral Ch. of St. John the Divine, N.Y.C., 1991-95, Ch. of the Incarnation, 1995—; resource cons. in amyotrophic lateral sclerosis N.Y. Neurol. Inst., N.Y.C., 1990—. Contbr. med. articles to profl. jours. Mem. commn. on ministry Episcopal Diocese, 1995—. Mem. Am. Psychol. Assn. (assoc.), Am. Acad. Neurology (affiliate), Nat. Hospice Orgn. Office: NY Neurol Inst 710 W 168th St New York NY 10032-2603

MURPHY, ROBIN ROBERSON, computer science educator; b. Mobile, Ala., Aug. 25, 1957; d. Fred Blakely and Ada Lee (Wills) Roberson; m. Kevin Eddy Murphy, Aug., 27, 1982; children: Kathleen Freebern, Allan Roberson. B in Mech. Engring., Ga. Inst. Tech., 1980, MS in Computer Sci., 1989, PhD in Computer Sci., 1992. Project engr. Dow Chem. USA, Plaquemine, La., 1980-84; software project engr. Turbitrol Co., Atlanta, 1984-86; asst. prof. dept. math. and comp. sci. Colo. Sch. Mines, Golden,

1992—, assoc. dir. Ctr. Robotics and Intelligent Systems, 1994-95; mem. NSF vis. com. on computer sci. curriculum U. Va., Charlottesville, 1992-95. Author: (with others) The Handbook of Brain Theory and Neural Networks, 1995; contbr. articles to profl. jours. Rsch. grantee NSF, 1994—, Advanced Rsch. Projects Agy., 1994—, NASA, 1994—. Mem. AAAI, IEEE, AIAA, Assn. Computing Machinery. Office: Colo Sch Mines Dept Math and Computer Sci Golden CO 80401-1887

MURPHY, SHARON MARGARET, university official, educator; b. Milw., Aug. 2, 1940; d. Adolph Leonard and Margaret Ann (Hirtz) Feyen; m. James Emmett Murphy, June 28, 1969 (dec. May 1983); children: Shannon Lynn, Erin Ann. BA, Marquette U., 1965; MA, U. Iowa, 1970, PhD, 1973. Cert. K-14 tchr., Iowa. Tchr. elem. and secondary schs., Wis., 1959-69; dir. publs. Kirkwood C.C., Cedar Rapids, Iowa, 1969-71; instr. journalism U. Iowa, Iowa City, 1971-73; asst. prof. U. Wis., Milw., 1973-79; assoc. prof. So. Ill. U., Carbondale, 1979-84; dean/prof. Marquette U., Milw., 1984-94; provost, v.p. acad. affairs, prof. Bradley U., Peoria, Ill., 1994—; pub. rels. dir., editor Worldwide mag., Milw., 1965-68; reporter Milw. Sentinel, 1967; Fulbright sr. lectr. U. Nigeria, Nsukka, 1977-78. Author: Other Voices: Black, Chicano & American Indian Press, 1971; (with Wigal) Screen Experience: An Approach to Film, 1968, (with Murphy) Let My People Know: American Indian Journalism, 1981, (with Schilpp) Great Women of the Press, 1983; editor: (book, with others) International Perspectives on News, 1982. Bd. dirs. Dow Jones Newspaper Fund, N.Y., 1986-95, Peoria Symphony; v.p. women's fund Peoria Cmty. Found.; mem. Peoria Riverfront Commn. Recipient Medal of Merit, Journalism Edn. Assn., 1976, Amoco Award for Teaching Excellence, 1977, Outstanding Achievement award Greater Milw. YWCA, 1989; named Knight of Golden Quill, Milw. Press Club, 1977; Nat. headliner Women in Communication, Inc., 1985. Mem. Assn. Edn. in Journalism and Mass Comm. (pres. 1986-87), Internat. Comm. Assn., Tempo, Newspaper Assn. Am. Found. (trustee 1993-96), Peoria C. of C. (bd. dirs.), Soc. Profl. Journalists, Nat. Press Club. Democrat. Roman Catholic. Office: Bradley U Office of Provost Peoria IL 61625

MURPHY, SHIRLEY HUNTER, reading specialist; b. Atlanta, June 29, 1947; d. John Henry and Ruby Lee (Wilson) Hunter; m. Robert Leslie Murphy, July 10, 1979 (May 1979); children: Lisa Denise, Ricardo Leslie. BS in Elem. Edn., Morris Brown Coll., 1969; M in Reading, Atlanta U., 1978; Cert. in Adminstrn., West Ga. Coll., 1991; Edn. Specialist in Adminstrn., Jacksonville State U., 1994; postgrad., U. Sarasota, 1995—. Cert. tchr., Ga. Tchr. Social Circle (Ga.) City Schs., 1969-70; tchr. DeKalb County Sch. Sys., Decatur, Ga., 1970-80, reading specialist, 1980—. Fin. sec. Am. Bus. Women's Assn., Atlanta, 1989-94. Mem. NAACP, Internat. Reading Assn., Profl. Assn. Ga. Educators, DeKalb Assn. Educators. Baptist. Home: 3441 Columbia Ct Decatur GA 30032

MURPHY, S(USAN) (JANE MURPHY), small business owner; b. Williamsport, Pa., Dec. 26, 1950; d. Jack W. and Edythe J. (Grier) M.; m. Michael J. Sanchez, Dec. 30, 1979. BBA, Pa. State U., 1978. Gen. mgr. Murphy Swift Homes, Hummelstown, Pa., 1970-75; owner, operator Murphy's Home Ctr., Hummelstown, 1975-79, 85-91; mgr. Builder's Emporium, San Diego, 1979-80; entrepreneur Castle in the Sand, San Diego, 1980-83; adminstr. Sohio Constrn., Prudhoe Bay, Alaska, 1983-85; fin. systems analyst Blue Shield, San Francisco, 1991-93; entrepreneur Pacific Bay Svcs., San Francisco, 1993—; owner, operator Murphy's Home Ctr., Hummelstown, Pa., 1994—; cons. in field; dealer Servistar Home Ctrs. Photographs displayed at San Diego Art Inst. Vol. Hershey (Pa.) Free Ch. Donald MacIntyre scholar, 1979, Class of 1920 scholar, 1979, Congressman Kunkel scholar, 1979. Mem. Pa. Hardware Assn., Hummelstown C. of C., Better Bus. Bur. Evangelical Christian. Office: Murphy's Home Ctr Hummelstown PA 17036

MURPHY, SUSAN LYNN JAYCOX, construction executive; b. Bay Shore, N.Y., Aug. 26, 1961. BS, U. Ala., 1984; MBA, Dowling Coll., 1987. Pres. Constrn. Materials Testing, Inc., Bethpage, N.Y., 1987. Mem. ASTM, Am. Soc. Quality Control, Am. Concrete Inst., Delta Mu Delta. Mem. Christian Ch. Office: Constrn Materials Testing Inc PO Box 355 Bethpage NY 11714-0355

MURPHY, SUZANNE GAIL, writer, psychotherapist, clinical social worker; b. N.Y.C., Mar. 13, 1942; d. Benjamin H. and Blanche (Dickes) Rubin; m. Paul Felzen, June 25, 1966 (div. July 1972); m. John Anthony Murphy, May 25, 1986. BS, Boston U., 1963; MA, NYU, 1966; MSW, Yeshiva U., 1985. Lic. ind. social worker, Ariz.; cert. social worker, N.Y. Freelance mag. writer, 1975—; psychotherapist for adult women molested as children Las Familias, Tucson, 1989—. Author: (fiction) Denise, by Herself, 1983. Mem. NASW, Soc. for Southwestern Authors. Democrat. Home: 3 Harrington St New Paltz NY 12561

MURPHY-BARSTOW, HOLLY ANN, financial consultant; b. St. Joseph, Mo., Jan. 16, 1960; d. Roy Edward and Kathryn Louise (Bachle) Murphy; m. Bruce William Barstow, Oct. 1, 1983; children: Brett Murphy, Taylor Lin. Student, U. Mo., 1978-79; BS, N.W. Mo. State U., 1981. Acct. exec. S.C. Johnson, Omaha, Nebr., 1982-83; dir. mktg. YMCA, Omaha, Nebr., 1983-85; fin. cons. Merrill Lynch, Omaha, Nebr., 1985-89, Smith Barney, Omaha, Nebr., 1989—; instr. fin. seminar Creighton U., Omaha, 1993—, Dana Coll., Blair, Nebr., 1993—; fin. corres. KMTV-3, KETV-7, WOWT-6, Omaha, 1993—. Pres. Am. Lung Assn. Nebr., Omaha, 1992-96; vice chair bd. trustees First Presbyn. Ch., Omaha, 1989-93; membership chair bd. mgrs. West YMCA, Omaha, 1991—; mem Columbian Sch. PTA; campaign chair Toys for Tots, 1994—; founding mem. Omaha Women's Fund. Named one of Ten Outstanding Young Omahans, Omaha Jaycees, 1994. Mem. Omaha Panhellenic Assn., Leadership Omaha (grad.), River City Roundup (trail boss 1989), Sigma Sigma Sigma. Office: Smith Barney 9394 W Dodge Rd # 250 Omaha NE 68114-3319

MURPHY-SPENCER, AMY EVELYN, university services coordinator; b. Liberty, Ky., Sept. 16, 1966; d. John Wallace Jr. and Evelyn Joyce (Bastin) Murphy; m. Mark Christopher Spencer, June 5, 1993. BA in Psychology and Sociology, U. Ky., 1988, MS in Counseling Psychology, 1991, EdS in Counseling Psychology, 1992. Mental health assoc. Fayette County Comprehensive Care, Lexington, Ky., 1989-90; program dir. childrens home Scott County Comprehensive Care, Georgetown, Ky., 1991; rsch. asst. dept. surgery U. Ky., Lexington, 1991-92; curriculum evaluation specialist U. Ky. Coll. Medicine, Lexington, 1992-94, coord. testing and assessment, 1994—; cons. to faculty U. Ky. Coll. Medicine, Lexington, 1994—. Mem. ACA, Assn. Am. Med. Coll., Generalists in Med. Edn., Am. Ednl. Rsch. Assn., Phi Beta Kappa (hon.), Sigma Xi (hon.). Republican. Southern Baptist. Office: Univ Ky Coll Medicine 800 Rose St MN 104 Lexington KY 40536-0084

MURRAY, ABBY DARLINGTON BOYD, psychiatric clinical specialist, educator; b. Johnstown, Pa., Mar. 1, 1928; d. Frank Reynolds and Marion (Gasson) Allen; m. Joseph Christopher Murray, Sept. 16, 1950; children: Anne, Joseph Jr., Mary, John, James. BSN, Georgetown U., 1950; MS Edn. in Guidance and Counseling, L.I. Univ., Brookville, N.Y., 1976; MEd Psychiat. Clin. Specialist, Columbia U., 1977; postgrad., Ctr. for Family Learning, New Rochelle, N.Y., 1981-82. Sch. nurse Huntington (N.Y.) Pub. Schs.; with VA Med. Ctr., Northport, Va., 1973-76; prof. U. Md., Balt., 1978-79, L.I. Univ., Brookville, 1979-81; psychiat. clin. specialist VA Med. Ctr., Brooklyn, Va., 1984-87, East Orange, N.J., 1987-89; nurse educator Ft. Monmouth, N.J., 1989—; family therapist Family & Cmty. Counseling Agy., Red Bank, N.J., 1989—; program planner, Ft. Monmouth. Republican. Roman Catholic. Home: 91 Tanyard Ln Huntington NY 11743 also: 116 Manor Dr Red Bank NJ 07701

MURRAY, ANNE, country singer; b. Springhill, N.S., Can., June 20, 1945; d. Carson and Marion (Burke) M.; m. William M. Langstroth, June 20, 1975; children: William Stewart, Dawn Joanne. B.Phys. Edn., U. N.B., 1966, D.Litt. (hon.), 1978; D.Litt. (hon.), St. Mary's U., 1982. Rec. artist for, Arc Records, Can., 1968, Capitol Records, 1969—; appeared on series of TV spls., CBC, 1970-81, 88-93; star CBS spls., 1981-85; toured N. Am., Japan, England, Germany, Holland, Ireland, Sweden, Australia and New Zealand, 1977-82; released 31 albums including: A Little Good News, 1984, As I Am, 1988, Greatest Hits, vols. I, 1981, vol. II, 1989, Harmony, 1987, You Will, 1990, Yes I Do, 1991, Croonin', 1993, others. Hon. chmn. Can. Save the Children Fund, 1978-80. Recipient Juno awards as Can.'s top female vocalist, 1970-81; Can.'s Top Country Female Vocalist, 1970-86; Grammy award as top female vocalist-country, 1974; Grammy award as top female vocalist-pop, 1978; Grammy award as top female vocalist-country, 1980, 83; Country Music Assn. awards, 1983-84; named Female Rec. Artist of Decade, Can. Rec. Industry Assn., 1980, Top Female Vocalist 1970-86; star inserted in Hollywood Walkway of Stars, 1980; Country Music Hall of Fame Nashville; decorated companion Order of Can.; inducted Juno Hall of Fame, 1993. Mem. AFTRA, Assn. Canadian TV and Radio Artists, Am. Fedn. Musicians. Office: Balmur Ltd, 4950 Yonge St Madison Ctr 2400, Toronto, ON Canada M2N 6K1*

MURRAY, ANNE FIRTH, corporate executive; b. Wanganui, New Zealand, June 23, 1935; d. Roberts Mathew and Eleanor Mary (Doyle) Firth; m. Douglas P. Murray (div. 1978); 1 child, Gwyn. BA, U. Calif., Berkeley, 1955; MPA, NYU, 1977. Editor Stanford (Calif.) U. Press, 1960s; writer/editor UN, N.Y.C., 1971-77; cons. N.Y.C., 1977-78; program dir. Hewlett Found., Calif., 1978-87; cons. prof. Stanford U., Calif., 1994—; pres. The Global Fund for Women, Menlo Park, Calif., 1987—; trustee Ind. Sector, Washington, IPAS, N.C. Editor/co-author: Ending Violence Against Women, 992, Neighborhood Government in New York City, 1974; author: (booklet) A Woman's Fundraising Handbook, 1995. Recipient Carl Schultz award Am. Pub. Health Assn., 1987, Women of Excellence award N.C. Woman's Mag., 1992; honoree World Assn. of UN Interns and Fellows, 1995.

MURRAY, BARBARA P., financial company executive; b. Boston, Dec. 30, 1948; d. William J., Jr. and Claire P. (Porter) P.; m. Richard B. Murray, July 29, 1977; children: Joshua P. Messina, Jesse P. Murray. Student, Bentley Coll., 1977—, Northeastern U. Exec. sec. Eaton & Howard, Boston, 1966-72, Coopers & Lybrand, Boston, 1972-77; adminstrv. asst. Greylock, Boston, 1977-80, chief adminstrv. officer, 1980—. Office: Greylock One Federal St Boston MA 02110-2065

MURRAY, BERTHA FLOWERS, college administrator; b. Tallapoosa County, Ala., July 20, 1939; d. Daniel and Mae Frances (Fuller) Flowers; children: Carmen Louise, Bernard. BS, Ala. A&M U., 1960; MEd, U. Fla., 1973; MS, Fla. State U., 1976, PhD, 1991. Cert. devel. edn. specialist. Isntr. English, math. Morgan County Tng. Sch., Hartselle, Ala., 1960-61; instr. social studies Hannah Mallory Jr. H.S., Goodwater, Ala., 1961-64; instr. English, math. Speight H.S., Ft. Gaines, Ga., 1964-66, 67-69, Buchholz H.S., Gainesville, Fla., 1970-71; lang. arts instr. P.K. Yonge Lab Sch., Gainesville, Fla., 1971-73, 74-75; instr. English, civics Fla. A&M H.S., Tallahassee, 1973-74; instr. English Mineral Springs H.S., Ellerbe, N.C., 1966-67; instr., adminstr. Tallahassee C.C., 1976—; reader/evaluator for coll. level acad. skills test State of Fla., Tallahassee, 1986-94. Pres. Nat. Hook-up of Black Women, Tallahassee, 1988-90, sec., 1995—; Sunday sch. tchr. Bethel Missionary Bapt. Ch., Tallahassee, 1973—. Recipient Cert., Bethel Christian Acad., 1992, Kellogg Leadership scholar Ctr. for Devel. Edn., 1985. Mem. NAACP (Black Achiever award 1995), Nat. Assn. for Devel. Edn. (pres. 1992-93), Fla. Devel. Edn. Assn. (pres. 1987-88), Alpha Kappa Alpha (chair-nominating 1994-96). Office: Tallahassee CC 444 Appleyard Dr Tallahassee FL 32304

MURRAY, CHERRY ANN, physicist, researcher; b. Ft. Riley, Kans., Feb. 6, 1952; d. John Lewis and Cherry Mary (Roberts) M.; m. Dirk Joachim Muehlner, Feb. 18, 1977; children: James Joachim, Sara Hester. BS in Physics, MIT, 1973, PhD in Physics, 1978. Rsch. asst. physics dept. MIT, Cambridge, 1969-78; rsch. assoc. Bell Labs., Murray Hill, N.J., 1976-77; mem. tech. staff AT&T Bell Labs., Murray Hill, 1978-85, disting. mem. tech. staff, 1985-87, dept. head low-temperature and solid-state physics rsch., 1987-90, dept. head condensed matter physics rsch., 1990-93, dept. head semicond. physics rsch., 1993—; co-chair Gordon Rsch., Wolfeboro, N.H., 1982, chair, 1984. Contbr. numerous articles to profl. jours. and chpts. to books. NSF fellow, 1969; IBM fellow MIT, 1974-76. Fellow Am. Phys. Soc. (Maria Goeppart-Mayer award 1989), Sigma Xi. Office: Bell Labs Lucent Techs 700 Mountain Ave Rm ID-334 New Providence NJ 07974

MURRAY, COLETTE MORGAN, healthcare executive, fundraising consultant; b. San Francisco, July 28, 1935; d. Thomas Ralph and Althea L. (Bail) Morgan; m. J. Roger Samuelsen, Sept. 14, 1959 (div. 1969); 1 child, Thea S. Kano; m. Richard Arlan Murray, Nov. 4, 1983. AB, U. Calif., Berkeley, 1959; JD, U. San Francisco, 1964; cert. in mgmt., U. Calif., Davis, 1975, U. Tex., 1989. Cert. fund raising exec. Pvt. practice law Walnut Creek, Calif., 1965-73; exec. dir. Calif. Alumni Assn., Berkeley, 1973-78; asst. chancellor univ. rels. U. Calif., Santa Cruz, 1978-85; v.p. for devel. and alumni U. Louisville, Ky., 1985-88; v.p. for devel. and univ. rels. Tex. Tech. U., Lubboch, 1988-90; corp. v.p. for philanthropy and community devel. Henry Ford Health System, Detroit, 1990-95; CEO Sharp Healthcare Found., San Diego, 1995—; cons. Coun. for the Advancement and Support of Edn., Washington, 1980—, NSFRE, Washington, 1992—; bd. dirs. Leadership Detroit, 1992-95, pres. Leadership Am. Assn., Washington, 1993-94. Bd. dirs. CATCH, Detroit, 1990-95. Recipient Dorothy Shaw award Alpha Delta Pi, 1958; named Citizen of Yr., Santa Cruz C. of C., 1981. Mem. NSFRE (pres. 1994), Coun. for Advancement and Support of Edn. (chair bd. 1981-82, Hesburgh award 1984), Univ. Club, San Diego Country Club. Office: Sharp Healthcare Found Ste 302 8525 Gibbs Dr San Diego CA 92123

MURRAY, CONNIE WIBLE, state legislator; b. Tulsa, Oct. 13, 1943; d. Carl Prince Lattimore and Jimmie Bell Henry; m. Jarrett Holland Murray, May 4, 1995. Cert. of oral hygiene, Temple U., 1965; BA, Loyola Coll., 1975; JD, U. Md., 1980. Registered dental hygienist Bethlehem, Pa., 1965-66, Joppa, Md., 1966-77; law clk. Hon. Albert P. Close, Belair, Md., 1980-81; atty., 1981-85, realtor, 1985-90; mem. Mo. Ho. of Reps., Jefferson City, 1990—; house mgr. Articles ot Impeachment of Judith Moriarty, Mo. Sec. of State, 1994; mem. budget com. Mo. Ho. of Reps., also mem. appropriations social svcs. and corrections com., judiciary and ethics com., civil and criminal law and accounts, opers. and fin. com., interim com. for fed. funds and block grants, commn. on intergovtl. affairs, commn. on mgmt. and productivity, legis. oversight com. for ct. automation, ho. automation com. Bd. dirs. North Springfield Betterment Assn., 1989; vocat. adv. bd., dir. house intern programs Nat. Conf. State Legislators. Named Outstanding Freshman Legis. on Health Care Issues, Mo. Rep. Caucus, 1992; recipient Jud. Conf. Legis. award Mo. Jud. Conf., 1994, Outstanding Woman Legis. award Assn. Probate and Assoc. Cir. Judges, 1995. Mem. LWV (bd. dirs. Springfield 1989, treas.), Nat. Order Women Legis., Nat. Conf. State Legis., Nat. Women's Polit. Caucus, Women Legis. Mo., Mo. Bar Assn. (Adminstr. for Justice award), Am. Legis. Exch. Counsel, Ctr. for Am. Women in Politics, Greene County Bar Assn., Forum-A Women's Natwork, Women in Govt. Home: 2118 S Catalina Ave Springfield MO 65804-2829 Office: Mo Gen Assembly State Capitol Office Bldg Jefferson City MO 65101-6806

MURRAY, DAVINA ANN, financial analyst; b. Sabetha, Kans., Nov. 12, 1951; d. Jim R. and Shirley A. (Ellington) Murphy; m. Brian C. Murray, July 2, 1981; 1 child, Bria Lynne. AS in Bus., Point Park Coll., 1992, BS in Acctg., 1992; postgrad., Robert Morris Coll., 1996—. With Integra Fin. Corp., Pitts., 1978-96, past acctg. clk., 1978-79, adminstrv. asst., 1980-86, fin. analyst, 1986-96; sr. acctg. officer fixed assets Pitts. Nat. Corp, 1996—. Mem. com. Pitts. City Sch. Redistricting, 1993. Mem. Inst. Mgmt. Accts., Alpha Sigma Lambda. Office: Pitts Nat Corp 2 PNC Plz Pittsburgh PA 15265

MURRAY, DIANE ELIZABETH, librarian; b. Detroit, Oct. 15, 1942; d. Gordon Lisle and Dorothy Anne (Steketee) LaBoueff; m. Donald Edgar Murray, Apr. 22, 1968. AB, Hope Coll., 1964; MLS, Western Mich. U., 1968; MM, Aquinas Coll., 1982; postgrad., Mich. State U., East Lansing, 1964-66. Catalog libr., asst. head acquisitions sect. Mich. State U. Librs., East Lansing, 1968-77; libr. tech. and automated svcs. Hope Coll., Holland, Mich., 1977-88; dir. librs. DePauw U., Greencastle, Ind., 1988-91; acquisitions libr. Grand Valley State U., Allendale, Mich., 1991—; sec., vice chair, chairperson bd. trustees Mich. Libr. Consortium, Lansing, 1981-85. Vice pres. Humane Soc. of Putnam County, Greencastle, 1990-91. Mem. ALA. Methodist. Office: Grand Valley State U Zumberge Libr Allendale MI 49401

MURRAY, ELEANOR F., educator, freelance writer; b. Omaha, Nov. 30, 1916; d. Fred Blatchford and Calista June (Reynolds) Greusel; m. Jack Earl Buckley, June 15, 1970 (dec. Nov. 1977); m. Hubert Larkin Murray; children: Thomas M. B. Hicks, Mary E. Sharp, Barbara R. Wilke. BS in Edn., U. Nebr., 1939. Cert. tchr. of English. Newswriter Etowah Observer, Alabama City, Ala., 1939-40; feature writer Stars 'n Stripes, Tokyo, 1947-51; columnist Japan Times, Tokyo, 1949-51; in pub. relations Am. Internat. Underwriters, Tokyo, 1948-51; writer news and features Paterson (N.J.) Evening News, 1952-54; tchr. Riverdale (N.J.) Sch., 1954-55, Panama Canal Zone Schs., 1955-60, Skokie (Ill.) Schs., 1961-66; freelance writer Sebring, Fla., 1980—. Author: (non-fiction) Bend Like the Bamboo, 1982, Growing Up In Aunt Molly's Omaha, 1990; (poetry) Cherokee County Summer, 1981, God's Green Valley, 1983; author articles. Democrat. Presbyterian. Home: 1418 NE Lakeview Dr Sebring FL 33870-2700

MURRAY, FLORENCE KERINS, state supreme court justice; b. Newport, R.I., Oct. 21, 1916; d. John X. and Florence (MacDonald) Kerins; m. Paul F. Murray, Oct. 21, 1943 (dec. June 2, 1995); 1 child, Paul F. AB, Syracuse U., 1938; LLB, Boston U., 1942; EdD, R.I. Coll. Edn., 1956; grad., Nat. Coll. State Trial Judges, 1966; LLD (hon.), Bryant Coll., 1956, U. R.I., 1963, Mt. St. Joseph Coll., 1972, Providence Coll., 1974, Roger Williams Coll., 1976, Salve Regina Coll., 1977, Johnson and Wales Coll., 1977, Suffolk U., 1981, So. New Eng. Law Sch., 1995. Bar: Mass. 1942, R.I. 1947, U.S. Dist. Ct. 1948, U.S. Tax Ct. 1948, U.S. Supreme Ct. 1948. Sole practice Newport, 1947-52; mem. firm Murray & Murray, Newport, 1952-56; assoc. judge R.I. Superior Ct., 1956-78; presiding justice Superior Ct. R.I., 1978-79; assoc. justice R.I. Supreme Ct., 1979—; staff, faculty adv. Nat. Jud. Coll., Reno, Nev., 1971-72, dir., 1975-77, chmn., 1979-87, chair emeritus, 1990—; mem. com. Legal Edn. and Practice and Economy of New Eng., 1975—; former instr. Prudence Island Sch.; legal adv. R.I. Girl Scouts; sec. Commn. Jud. Tenure and Discipline, 1975-79; apptd. by Pres. Clinton to bd. dirs. State Justice Inst., 1994—; participant, leader various legal seminars. Mem. R.I. Senate, 1948-56; chmn. spl. legis. com.; mem. Newport Sch. Com., 1948-57, chmn., 1951-57; mem. Gov.'s Jud. Coun., 1950-60, White House Conf. Youth and Children, 1950, Ann. Essay Commn., 1952, Nat. Def. Adv. Com. on Women in Service, 1952-58, Gov.'s Adv. Com. Mental Health, 1954, R.I. Alcoholic Adv. Com., 1955-58, R.I. Com. Youth and Children, Gov.'s Adv. Com. on Revision Election Laws, Gov.'s Adv. Com. Social Welfare, Army Adv. Com. for 1st Army Area; mem. civil and polit. rights com. Pres.'s Commn. on Status of Women, 1960-63; mem. R.I. Com. Humanities, 1972—, chmn., 1972-77; mem. Family Ct. Study Com., R.I. com. Nat. Endowment Humanities; bd. dirs. Newport YMCA; sec. Bd. Physicians Service; bd. visitors Law Sch., Boston U.; bd. dirs. NCCJ; mem. edn. policy and devel. com. Roger Williams Jr. Coll.; trustee Syracuse U.; pres. Newport Girls Club, 1974-75, R.I. Supreme Ct. Hist. Soc., 1988—; chair Supreme Ct. Mandatory Continuing Legal Edn. Com., 1993—. Served to lt. col. WAC, World War II. Decorated Legion of Merit; recipient Arents Alumni award Syracuse U., 1956, Carroll award R.I. Inst. Instn., 1956, Brotherhood award NCCJ, 1983, Herbert Harley award Am. Judicature Soc., 1988, Melvin Eggers Sr. Alumni award Syracuse U., 1992, Merit award R.I. Bar Assn., 1994; named Judge of Yr. Nat. Assn. Women Judges, 1984, Outstanding Woman, Bus. and Profl. Women, 1972, Citizen of Yr. R.I. Trial Lawyers Assn.; Newport courthouse renamed in her honor, 1990. Mem. ABA (chmn. credentials com. nat. conf. state trial judges 1971-73, chair judges adv. com. on standing com. on ethics and profl. responsibility 1991—, joint com. on jud. discipline of standing com. on profl. discipline 1991-94), AAUW (chmn. state edn. com. 1954-56), Am. Arbitration Assn., Nat. Trial Judges Conf. (state chmn. membershiup com., sec. exec. com.), New Eng. Trial Judges Conf. (com. chmn. 1967), Boston U. Alumni Coun., Am. Legion (judge adv. post 7, mem. nat. exec. com.), Bus. and Profl. Women's Club (past state v.p., past pres. Newport chpt., past pres. Nat. legis. com.), Auota Club (past gov. internat., past pres. Newport chpt.), Alpha Omega, Kappa Beta Pi. Office: RI Supreme Ct 250 Benefit St Providence RI 02903-2719

MURRAY, JEANNE See STAPLETON, JEAN

MURRAY, JEANNE EVELYN, insurance executive; b. Phoenix, Dec. 20, 1932; d. Thomas Lott and Bernice O. (Lockhart) Pettus; m. Richard C. Murray, May 2, 1952; children: Donn R., Susan Murray Hopkins. Student, Lamson Bus. Coll., Phoenix, 1950-52, Phoenix Jr. Coll., 1953-54, Scottsdale Community Coll., Ri, Phoenix, 1954. Sec. E. R. Livermore Adjustment Co., Phoenix, 1952-54, Allstate Ins. Co., Phoenix, 1954-56, State Farm Ins., Phoenix, 1956-60; claim adjuster, investigator, pvt. investigator Panarello Adjustment Co., Scottsdale, 1966-88; ins. exec. Farmers Ins. Group, Scottsdale, 1991-93; claim examiner Insurtx, Scottsdale, 1993—. Fundraiser Am. Cancer Soc., Phoenix, 1975-90, Am. Heart Assn., 1975—; vol. in reading program Scottsdale Pub. Schs. Mem. Ariz. Ins. Claims Assn., Ariz. Pvt. Investigation Assn., U.S. Tennis Assn., Amateur Athletic Assn., Scottsdale Racquet Club. Republican. Methodist. Home: 11178 N 109th St Scottsdale AZ 85259 Office: Insurtx Scottsdale AZ 85257-3777

MURRAY, JULIA KAORU (MRS. JOSEPH E. MURRAY), occupational therapist; b. Wahiawa, Oahu, Hawaii, 1934; d. Gijun and Edna Tsuruko (Taba) Funakoshi; m. Joseph Edward Murray, 1961; children: Michael, Susan, Leslie. BA, U. Hawaii, 1956; cert. occupational therapy U. Puget Sound, 1958. Therapist, Inst. Logopedics, Wichita, Kans., 1958; sr. therapist Hawaii State Hosp., Kaneohe, 1959; part-time therapist Centre County Ctr. for Crippled Children and Adults, State College, Pa., 1963; vice chmn. adv. bd. Hosp. Improvement Program, East Oreg. State Hosp., Pendleton, 1974; v.p. Ind. Living, Inc., 1976-79; job search instr.; mem. adv. com. Oreg. Ednl. Coordinating Commn., 1979-82; mem. Oreg. Bd. Engring. Examiners, 1979-87; supr., occupational therapist Fairview Tng. Ctr., Salem, Oreg., 1984-94; occupational therapist U.S. Naval Hosp., Okinawa, Japan, 1994—. Rep. from Umatilla County Commrs. to Blue Mountain Econ. Devel. Council, 1976-78; mem. Ashland Park and Recreation Bd., 1972-73; vice chmn. adv. bd. LINC, 1978; mem. exec. bd. Liberty-Boone Neighborhood Assn., 1979-83. Mem. Am. Occupational Therapy Assn., Oreg. Occupational Therapy Assn., Hawaii Occupational Therapy Assn. (sec. 1960) Occupational Therapy Assn., LWV (bd. dirs. Pendleton 1974, 77-78, pres. 1975-77; bd. dirs. Oreg. 1979-81, Ashland, Wis., 1967-71, Wis. v.p. 1970). Office: Medically Related Svcs US Naval Hosp Okinawa Japan Psc 482 FPO AP 96362-1600

MURRAY, KATHLEEN ANNE, sales representative; b. Neenah, Wis., Aug. 7, 1958; d. Edward Joseph and Mary Margaret (Schaller) M. BBA, U. Wis., 1985. Payroll acct. Fel-Pro, Inc., Skokie, Ill., 1985-93, sales rep., 1993—. Roman Catholic. Home: 716 10th St Baraboo WI 53913 Office: Fel-Pro Inc 7450 N McCormick Blvd Skokie IL 60076

MURRAY, LYNDA BERAN, counselor; b. Richmond, Va., Feb. 29, 1944; d. Lynn Carlyle and Clelia (Crawford) Beran; m. Frank Stephen Murray, Feb. 3, 1968 (dec. 1990); children: Stephanie, Frank Stephen Jr., Rebecca, Jeremy, Anthony, Nicholas. BA, U. Richmond, 1965; MA, U. Ky., 1968; MEd, Lynchburg Coll., 1988; CAGS, Va. Poly. Inst. and State U., 1993, PhD, 1995. Cert. elem. and secondary counselor, Va. Instr. psychology Randolph-Macon Woman's Coll., Lynchburg, Va., 1970-72; contractural sch. psychologist Lynchburg City Schs., 1975-91, elem. sch. counselor, 1989-91; supr. counselor edn. dept. Va. Poly. Inst. and State U., Blacksburg, 1991-93; emergency svcs. clinician New Rivery Valley Community Svcs. Bd., 1993-94; elem. sch. counselor Montgomery County Pub. Schs., Elliston, Va., 1994—; emergency mental health cons. Lynchburg Gen. Hosp., 1986-90. Mem. ACA, Va. Counselors Assn., New River Valley Counselors Assn. (pres. 1996—), Chi Sigma Iota (sec. 1990-91, pres. 1992-93). Home: 310 Cherokee Dr Blacksburg VA 24060-1822 Office: Elliston-Lafayette Elem Sch Dept Counselor Edn 9812 Roanoke Rd Elliston VA 24087-2314

MURRAY, MARCIA, principal; b. Buffalo, Nov. 1, 1950; d. Jacob and Ethel (Tasman) Freedman; m. Alfredo De Avila, Feb. 20, 1970 (div. Mar. 13, 1985); children: Lisa, Esteban, Joaquin; m. Arthur W.S. Murray III, Oct. 16, 1993. BA, Pan Am. U., 1974; MA, Wash. State U., 1977; PhD, Tex. A&M U., 1991. Cert. elem. tchr., Tex., bilingual tchr., Tex., middle mgmt. Elem. tchr. Hidalgo (Tex.) Ind. Sch. Dist., 1978-80; adminstr. Alamo Pub. Libr. City of Alamo, Tex., 1980-84; elem. tchr. Pharr-San Juan-Alamo Ind. Sch. Dist., 1980-84; dir. edn. talent search Pan Am. U., Edinburg, Tex., 1985-89; adult ESL instr. Hidalgo-Starr Adult Edn. Coop., McAllen, Tex., 1988-89; parent educator Bryan (Tex.) Ind. Sch. Dist., 1989-91; adj. faculty Blinn Coll., Bryan, 1993—; adult cmty. edn. coord. Bryan Ind. Sch. Dist.,

1991-93, bilingual/ESL supr., 1993—, prin. Anson Jones Elem., Bryan Acad. Visual and Performing Arts, 1995—; adv. mem. Nat. Ctr. Adult Literacy, Phila., 1991-93; cons. Travel and More, College Station, 1994—. Contbr. articles to profl. jours. Dir., v.p. comms. Literacy Vols. of Am., Bryan, 1993—; 2nd v.p. Hillel at Tex. A&M U., College Station, Tex., 1994—. Mem. Tex. Assn. Bilingual Edn., Tex. Assn. Tchrs. Englishto Speakers of Other Langs., Tex. Assn. Literacy and Adult Edn. (co-chair profl. devel. 1991-93). Office: Anson Jones Elem Bryan Acad Visual & Performing Arts 1400 Pecan St Bryan TX 77803

MURRAY, MARY, early childhood and elementary educator; b. Beverly, Mass.; d. Edward James and Anne (Dowd) M. AS in Nursing, Endicott Coll.; AB, Boston Coll., 1985; MSEd in Early Childhood & Elem. Edn., Wheelock Coll., 1993. Cert. tchr., Mass. Tchr. Glen Urquhart Sch., Beverly Farms, Mass., 1982-87, kindergarten asst., 1982-83; kindergarten tchr., 1983-85, first grade tchr., 1985-87; dir. extended day program Glen Urquhart Sch., Beverly Farms, Mass., 1982-85, coord. summer camp program, 1984-86; lower sch. assoc. Shady Hill Sch., Cambridge, Mass., 1987-88; rsch. asst. Wheelock Coll., Boston, 1987-91; tchr. kindergarten, curriculum coord. Prospect Hill Parents' and Childrens' Ctr., Waltham, Mass., 1988-91; substitute tchr. Marblehead (Mass.) Mid. Sch., 1993—; ednl. cons. Beverly Farms, Mass., 1992—; substitute tchr. Shore Country Day Sch., Beverly, Mass., 1992—; mentor, tchr., faculty summer compass program Lesley Coll. Grad. Sch. of Edn., Cambridge, Mass., 1994—; founder, dir. Summer Enrichment at Lanesville, Mass., 1987-89; certification cons., adv. bd. Power Industries, Wellesley Hills, Mass., 1989—; cons. Activities Club, Inc., Waltham, 1989-91; mem. Early Childhood Adv. Coun., Medford, Mass., 1990-93; lifeguard supr. West Beach Corp., 1980-86; mem. cert. team Nat. Assn. Educators Young Children, 1989-91, Ind. Sch. Assn. Mass., 1983-88; presenter workshops. Author curriculum materials, activity kits for children. Tchr. religious edn. program St. Margaret Parish, Beverly Farms, 1970—, dir., coord., 1989—; synod group leader Archdiocese of Boston, 1987; water safety instr. ARC; coach Christian Youth Orgn. Girls Basketball, St. Joseph Parish, Medford, Mass., 1991-93; active Mass. Spl. Olympics; mem. Youth Activities Coord., Farms/Prides Cmty. Orgn., Feed the Hungry Project, Beverly, Mass., Good Friday Walk Orgnl. Com.; adv. bd. Wenham (Mass.) Mus.; friends-of-com. Fitz Meml. Libr. Endicott Coll., Beverly, Mass. Wheelock Coll. grad. grantee, 1993. Mem. ASCD, Nat. Assn. Edn. Young Childen, Assn. Childhood Edn. Internat., Young Alumni Club Boston Coll. (program coord./spl. events 1988-90), Ste. Chretienne Acad. Alumnae Assn., Wheelock Coll. Alumni Assn. Democrat. Roman Catholic. Home: 650 Hale St Beverly Farms Beverly MA 01915-2117

MURRAY, PAMELA ALISON, business executive; b. Phila., Sept. 22, 1955; d. Everett Hickman Jr. and Laura Frances (Lautenbach) M. BA in Math. cum laude, Gettysburg (Pa.) Coll., 1977; MBA in Mktg., Temple U., 1986; postgrad., U. Del., 1978-80. Asst./assoc. systems programmer Burroughs Corp., Paoli, Pa., 1977-79, cost acctg. analyst, gen. acctg. analyst, 1979-80, sr. tech. analyst, 1980-82, mgr. data ctr. tech. support, 1982-83; mgr. software product assurance Unisys Corp./Burroughs Corp., Paoli, Pa., 1983-86; mgr. product assurance Unisys Corp., Devon, Pa., 1986-88; sr. staff engr. Unisys Corp., Blue Bell, Pa., 1988-90, system quality mgr., 1990-91; mgr. quality assurance Unisys Corp., Paoli and Blue Bell, 1991-92; mgr. requirements assurance Unisys Corp., Paoli, 1992-93; mgr. Bus. Excellence Unisys. Corp., Paoli, 1993-94; mgr. client satisfaction Unisys Corp., Paoli, 1995—; instr. after-hours tng. Burroughs Corp./Unisys, 1983-86; examiner Chmn.'s Total Quality award, 1992. Mem. Pa. Quality Leadership Bd. Examiners, 1994, Malcolm Baldrige Nat. Quality Award Bd. Examiners, 1995, 96; fundraiser Am. Heart Assn., 1987-94, 96, Am. Cancer Soc., 1989, March of Dimes, 1987, 89. Recipient Young Alumni Achievement award Gettysburg Coll., 1989, Phila. Alumni Club Silver Plate, 1988, Svc. award, 1989. Mem. Am. Soc. Quality Control, Phila. Area Coun. for Excellence, Gettysburg Coll. Alumni Assn. (chmn. alumni reunion com. 1992-93, treas. 1991-93, chmn. alumni ctr. task force 1990-93, career rep. 1988—), Phila. Alumni Club (pres. 1986-90, v.p. 1984-86), Jr. League Phila. (treas.-elect 1995-96, treas. 1996-97, chmn. cookbook sales com. 1990-92, 92-93, chmn. cookbook com. 1992 93), Temple U. Alumni Assn. Republican. Mem. Christian Ch. Home: 404 Danor Ct Wayne PA 19087-1232

MURRAY, PATRICIA ANN, child development specialist; b. Joliet, Ill.; d. William Roberts and Elsie M. (Fischer) M.; m. David Johnson Hyslop (div.); children: Alex Hyslop, Kris Hyslop; m. Gerald Dale Preator (div.); Robin Preator. BS in Music, Ithaca Coll., 1965; MEd in Counseling, Lewis and Clark Coll., 1972. Cert. counselor. Music tchr. N.Y., Minn. and Oreg. sch. dists., 1965-80; exec. dir. Chamber Music NW, Portland, Oreg., 1973; family counselor Harry's Mother Counseling Ctr., 1978; child devel. specialist, counselor Portland, 1981-95, therapist, pvt. practice, 1994—; mentoring counselor, Portland, 1995; Hakomi Therapy Tng., Portland, 1993—; students-at-risk tng., Portland, 1995—. Mem. 1st Unitarian Ch., Portland, 1988—. Mem. Oreg. Counseling Assn. (sec. 1988-89), Nat. Coun. Counselors. Democrat.

MURRAY, PATTY, senator; b. Seattle, Wash., Oct. 11, 1950; d. David L. and Beverly A. (McLaughlin) Johns; m. Robert R. Murray, June 2, 1972; children: Randy P., Sara A. BA, Wash. State U., 1972. Sec. various cos., Seattle, 1972-76; citizen lobbyist various ednl. groups, Seattle, 1983-88; legis. lobbyist Orgn. for Parent Edn., Seattle, 1977-84; instr. Shoreline Community Coll., Seattle, 1984—; mem. Wash. State Senate, Seattle, 1989-92, U.S. Senate, Washington, 1993—; ranking minority mem. Appropriations Legis Br.; vice chmn. Senate Dem. Policy Com.; mem. Com. on Banking, Housing and Urban Affairs, Budget Com., Senate Dem. Tech. and Comms. Com., Com. on Vets. Affairs, Select Com. on Ethics. Mem. bd. Shoreline Sch., Seattle, 1985-89; mem. steering com. Demonstration for Edn., Seattle, 1987; founder, chmn. Orgn. for Parent Edn., Wash., 1981-85; 1st Congl. rep. Wash. Women United, 1983-85. Recipient Recognition of Svc. to Children award Shoreline PTA Coun., 1986, Golden Acorn Svc. award, 1989; Outstanding Svc. award Wash. Women United, 1986, Outstanding Svc. to Pub. Edn. award Citizens Ednl. Ctr. NW, Seattle, 1987. Democrat. Office: US Senate 111 Russell Senate Office Bldg Washington DC 20510-4704

MURRAY, PHYLLIS CYNTHIA, educator; b. Farmville, Va., Nov. 3, 1938; d. Claude and Frazure Young; m. Robert William Murray, Dec. 14, 1963; 1 child, Sidney Adolphus. BA, Hunter Coll., 1960; MS, U. Pa., 1961; diploma, Cornell U., 1980; cert., Vassar Coll., 1991. Tchr. D.C. Bd. of Edn., Washington, 1961-63, N.Y. Bd. Edn., 1963—; TV producer TCI, Mamaroneck, N.Y., 1990—; radio host Sta. WVOX Radio, New Rochell, N.Y., 1994—; founder One Love Tennis, White Plains, 1994—. Author: Huggy Bean Visits Ethiopia, 1985; co-author: Enslaved Africans of the North, Encounters in Living History: Activity based lessons on the Enslaved Africans of the North, 1996; contbr. articles to profl. jours. Mem. Town and Village Civic Club, Scarsdale, N.Y., 1994—; mem. UFT-Unity com., N.Y.C., 1994—. Recipient Edn. award Nat. Coun. Negro Women, 1990; Impact II grantee, 1990, 94, 95. Mem. NAACP, United Fedn. of Tchr. (del. unity 1963), Alpha Kappa Alpha (Silver Star 1991). Home: 1181 Post Rd Scarsdale NY 10589-2023 Office: Bd of Edn PS75X 984 Faile St Bronx NY 10459

MURRAY, SANDRA ANN, biology research scientist, educator; b. Chgo., Oct. 7, 1947; d. Charles William and Muggie (Wise) M. BS, U. Ill., 1970; MS, Tex. So. U., 1973; PhD, U. Iowa, 1980. Instr. biology Tex. So. U., Houston, 1972-73; NIH rsch. fellow U. Calif., Riverside, 1980-82; asst. prof. anatomy U. Pitts., 1982-89, assoc. prof. cell biology and physiology, 1989—; assoc. prof. Health Officers Inst. Office Def., Addis Ababa, Ethiopia, 1996—; vis. scientist Scripps Rsch. Inst., La Jolla, Calif., 1991-92, INSERM-INRA Hosp. Debrousse, Lyon, France, 1995; cons. NIH, NSF; vis. sci. cons. Fedn. Am. Soc. Exptl. Biology; invited internat. rsch. lectr. at sci. confs. Contbr. articles to Jour. Cell Biology, Anat. Records, Endocrinology, Am. Jour. Anatomy, Molecular and Cellular Endocrinology, Cancer Rsch. Bd. dirs. NAACP, Riverside, 1980-81. Ford Found. fellow, 1978; Rsch. grantee NSF, 1984—, Beta Kappa Chi, Tri Beta Biol. Soc.; recipient Outstanding Achievment award in Sci., Omega Psi Chi; recipient Faculty award Student Nat. Med. Assn. Mem. Am. Soc. Cell Biology (mem. minority affairs com. 1980—, rsch. award to marine biol. lab. 1986, 87, 88, 89, rsch. presentation travel award 1984), Am. Soc. Biol. Chemists (rsch. presentation travel award 1985), Am. Assn. Anatomists, Tissue Culture Assn. (chairperson internat. sci. com. 1982), Endocrine Soc. (student affairs com.). Home: 5417 Coral St Pittsburgh PA 15206-3413 Office: Univ Pitts Scaife Hall 864A Pittsburgh PA 15261

MURRAY, STANEE PETTIT, photographer; b. Lakewood, N.J., Mar. 14, 1958; d. Stanley Ray and Eleanor Doris (Clayton) Pettit; m. Robert Paul Murray, Oct. 16, 1982. BS in Biology, Georgian Ct. Coll., 1980; MS in Computer Sci., Stevens Inst. Tech., 1986; diploma, NY Inst. Photography, 1990. Nat. cert. profl. photographer. Sr. tech. assoc. AT&T Bell Labs., W. Long Branch, N.J., 1980-85; owner Stanee Rae Studio, Lincroft, N.J., 1990—. Contbr. articles to profl. jours. Vol. Georgian Ct. Coll., Lakewood, N.J., 1990—. Mem. Wedding Photographer Internat. (2 honorable mention ribbons 1992, honorable mention ribbon 1994, 3d pl. award 1994), Profl. Photographers Am., Profl. Photographers N.J. (Blue Ribbon and Judge's Choice award 1995, webmaster). Home and Office: 42 Shelbern Dr Lincroft NJ 07738-1325

MURRAY, SUZANNE MARIE, accountant; b. Frankfurt, Germany, Aug. 12, 1970; (parents Am. citizens); d. Peter A. and Suzanne Marie (Falzo) M. BBA in Acctg., Siena Coll., 1992. CPA, N.Y. Assoc. acct. Bollam Sheedy Torani & Co., LLP, Albany, N.Y., 1992-95, Margolis & Co., PC, Bala Cynwyd, Pa., 1995-96; sr. auditor Wallace Sanders & Co., Dallas, 1996—. Asst. vol. Arsenal City Run, Watervliet, N.Y., 1992-93. Mem. Inst. Mgmt. Accts. (dir. student activities Albany chpt. 1994-95, mem. pub. rels. com. Phila. chpt. 1995—). Home: 17200 Westgrove Dr Apt 1524 Dallas TX 75248 Office: Wallace Sanders & Co 8131 LBJ Freeway Ste 875 Dallas TX 75251

MURRAY-MIHALICH, CONSTANCE YVONNE, gerontology and geropsychiatric nurse, administrator; b. Pitts., Feb. 28, 1953; d. Harry Lawrence Murray and Yvonne Louise (Ploesch) Murray Lelko; m. Thomas Frederick Mihalich, Dec. 6, 1980; children: Stephen Paul, Neil Thomas. AA cum laude, Cuyahoga C.C., Parma, Ohio, 1990, AS cum laude, 1993; Diploma in Nursing, MetroHealth Med. Ctr., Cleve., 1993. RN, Ohio, Fla. Mgmt./pers. cons. Denver, 1973-79; dir. sr. programs Indian Hills Sr. Cmty., Euclid, Ohio, 1979-82; exec. recruiter Cleve., 1984-89; psychiat. staff nurse Western Res. Psychiat. Hosp., Cleve., 1993-94; staff devel. coord. Beneva Nursing Pavilion, Sarasota, Fla., 1994; DON Middlebury Manor, Akron, Ohio, 1994-96, Candlewood Park Health Care Ctr., East Cleveland, Ohio, 1996—; ind. cons./owner CoVon Diversified Healthcare Assocs., 1995—; tchr. adult edn., Denver, 1975-77; seminar developer/facilitator, Cleve., 1984-89. Advocate Rape and Domestic Violence Crisis Intervention Cmty. Mental Health, Denver, 1977-79. Mem. Nat. Assn. Dirs. Nursing Adminstrn., Nat. Nursing Staff Devel. Orgn., Nat. Gerontol. Nursing Assn., Nat. League for Nursing, Ohio League for Nursing, Am. Psychiat. Nurses Assn., Nat. Fedn. Bus. and Profl. Women's Clubs (Young Career Woman award 1976, Outstanding Bus. Woman award 1978). Home: 3311 E Wallings Rd Broadview Heights OH 44147

MURRELL, SUSAN DEBRECHT, librarian; b. St. Louis, Aug. 10, 1951; d. Edward August and Edith (Keeney) DeB.; m. Harry Thornton Murrell, Oct. 18, 1974; children: Brian, Katherine. B, U. Ky., 1973; MLS, U. Mo., 1976. Children's libr. Louisville Free Pub. Libr., 1974-76, talking book libr. head, 1976-83; lower/mid. sch. libr. Ky. Country Day Sch., Louisville, 1983-84; children's libr. Emmet O'Neal Libr., Mountain Brook, Ala., 1984-86, asst. dir., 1986-89, dir., 1989—. Bd. dirs. Mountain Brook Libr. Found., 1993—; active Jefferson County Pub. Libr., mem. publicity com., 1989-92; mem. allocations com. United Way. Mem. ALA (pub. librs. chairperson 1995-96), Ala. Libr. Assn. (mem. publicity com. 1992-93, pub. libr. chair 1995-96), Rotary Internat. Roman Catholic. Office: Emmet O'Neal Libr 50 Oak St Birmingham AL 35213-4219

MUSE, ALEXANDRA VICKREY, art consultant; b. Pitts., Apr. 11, 1967; d. Albert Charles and Nancy Burns (Trainer) M. BA in History magna cum laude, Georgetown U., 1989; MA in Arts Adminstrn., NYU, 1995. Asst. art dealer Ikkan Art Internat., N.Y.C., 1989-92; owner, prin. Vickrey Fine Art, Pitts., 1992-93; asst. curator, exhbn. coord. David Hupert Assoc., N.Y.C., 1994-95; asst. dir. Inst. for Asian Studies, N.Y.C., 1995-96; cons., exhbn. coord. Pamela Auchincloss Gallery, N.Y.C., 1995—. Bd. dirs. Checkerboard Film Found., N.Y.C., 1992—. Mem. Am. Assn. Mus., Coll. Art Assn., Phi Beta Kappa. Home: 322 W 87th St New York NY 10024

MUSE, BELINDA LEIGH, systems analyst; b. Evanston, Ill., July 23, 1962; d. Richard Joseph and Denise Jeannine (Lanphear) Gans; m. Jonathan Matthew Muse, Dec. 28, 1991 (div. Dec. 1994). BS, U. Ill., 1984; MS, DePaul U., 1993. Chem. engr. Jim Walter Rsch. Corp., St. Petersburg, Fla., 1985-90; systems analyst DePaul U., Chgo., 1990-92; bus. analyst Hewitt Assn., Lincolnshire, Ill., 1992-93; programmer analyst Caremark, Lincolnshire, 1993-94; product specialist Andersen Consulting, Northbrook, Ill., 1994—. Nat. Merit scholar, 1980. Home: 816 W Waveland # 18 Chicago IL 60613 Office: 69 W Washington Chicago IL 60602

MUSEKAMP, LINDA NOE, television producer, volunteer; b. Campbellsville, Ky., July 31, 1951; d. Charles Simpson and Audrey Ethel (Akin) Noe; m. George Justin Musekamp, Sept. 8, 1979 (dec.); children: George Brookshire, Charles Oliver Justin. Cert. exec. sec., Patricia Stevens Coll., Tampa, Fla., 1970. Cert. property mgr. Exec. sec. Sta. WLWT-TV, Cin., 1975-77, talent coord., 1977-80; prodr. Musekamp Prodns., Cin., 1980-83, cons., 1983-85; chmn., vol. Am. Cancer Soc., Cin., 1992—, bd. dirs., 1993—; pres., vol. PTO, Cin., 1992—; publicity chmn. Kindervelt, Cin., 1993—; real estate agt., 1994-96. Prodr.: (TV show) Real Cincinnati, 1996—. Republican. Baptist.

MUSETH, JERENE MARION, fisheries technologist; b. Seattle, July 6, 1943; d. Orville LaVern Decker and Jean Kathryn Veeder; m. Henry Amos Museth, Nov. 24, 1967 (div. Feb. 1984); 1 child, Melissa Jean. Student, U. Alaska. EMT; cert. indsl. first aid and CPR instr. Contact rep. VA, Juneau, Alaska, 1967-72; mgmt. technician VA, Junea, Alaska, 1972-73; comml. fisherman Elfin Cove, Alaska, 1973-87; gen. mgr. Elfin Wet Goods/Gen. Supplies, Elfin Cove, 1975-80; constrn. foreman Elfin Cove Boardwalk, 1976-79; adminstrv. asst. Alaska Trollers Assn., Juneau, 1983-86; natural resource technician II Alaska Dept. Fish & Game, Juneau, 1989—; mem. southeast adv. panel Citizen Commn. Fed. Areas, Fairbanks, Alaska, 1981-83; mem. Elfin Cove Fish & Game Adv. Com., 1982-84; bd. mem. Elfin Cove, Incorp., 1982-87, Alaska Bd. of Fisheries, 1984-87. Chmn. Election Bd., Elfin Cove, 1975-84; vice chair Juneau Troll PAC, 1981-83; vol. Alaska Women's Conf., Juneau, 1995-96; mem. Capital City Women's Polit. Caucus, Juneau, 1995—. Mem. LWV, NOW (northwest region), Women in Fisheries Network, Alaska State Employees Assn. (steward, mem. women's com.), Healing Touch Network. Democrat. Home: PO Box 20754 Juneau AK 99802 Office: Alaska Dept Fish and Game PO Box 25526 Juneau AK 99802

MUSGRAVE, THEA, composer, conductor; b. Edinburgh, Scotland, May 27, 1928; m. Peter Mark, 1971. Ed., Edinburgh U., Paris Conservatory; Mus.D. (hon.). Composer: (opera) The Abbot of Drimock, 1955, The Decision, 1964-65, The Voice of Ariadne, 1972-73, Mary, Queen of Scots, 1975-77, (first performed Scottish Opera) A Christmas Carol, 1978-79 (first performed Va. Opera Assn., 1979), An Occurrence at Owl Creek Bridge, 1981, Harriet, The Woman Called Moses, 1981-84 (first performed Va. Opera 1985), Simon Bolivar, (ballet) Beauty and the Beast, 1969, (symphony and orchestral music) Obliques, 1958, Nocturnes and Arias, 1966, Concerto for Orch., 1967, Clarinet Concerto, 1968, Night Music, 1969, Scottish Dance Suite, 1969, Memento Vitae, 1969-70, Orfeo II, 1975, Soliloquy II and III, 1980, From One to Another, 1980, Peripeteia, 1981, The Seasons, 1988, (marimba concerto) Journey through a Japanese Landscape, (bass-clarinet concerto) Autumn Sonata, (oboe concerto) Helios, (chamber and instrumental music) String Quartet, 1958, Trio for flute, oboe and piano, 1960, Monologue, 1960, Serenade, 1961, Chamber concerto No. 1, 1962, Chamber Concerto No. 2, 1966, Chamber Concerto No. 3, 1966, Music for horn and piano, 1967, Impromptu No. 1, 1967, Soliloquy I, 1969, Elegy, 1970, Impromptu No. 2, 1970, Space Play, 1974, Orfeo I, 1975, Fanfare, 1982, Pierrot, 1985, Narcissus, 1987, Niobe, 1987, (vocal and choral music) Two Songs, 1951, Four Madrigals, 1953, Six Songs: Two Early English Poems, 1953, A Suite O'Bairnsangs, 1953, Cantata for a Summer's Day, 1954, Song of the Burn, 1954, Five Love Songs, 1955, Four Portraits, 1956, A Song for Christmas, 1958, Triptych, 1959, Sir Patrick Spens, 1961, Make Ye Merry for Him That Is to Come, 1962, Two Christmas Carols in Traditional Style, 1963, John Cook, 1963, Five Ages of Man, 1963-64, Memento Creatoris, 1967, Primavera, 1971, Rorate Coeli, 1973, Monologues of Mary, Queen of Scots, 1977-86, O Caro M'e Il Sonno, 1978, The Last Twilight, 1980, Black Tambourine, 1985, For the Time Being, 1986, Echoes Through Time, 1988, Wild Winter for Viols & Voices, 1993, On the Underground Sets 1, 2 & 3, 1994, 95, (Robert Burns' poems for soprano & orch.) Songs for a Winter's Evening, 1995. Office: VA Opera Assn PO Box 2580 Norfolk VA 23501-2580

MUSHINSKY, MARY M., state legislator; b. New Haven; m. Martin J. Waters; children: Martin Waters, Edward Waters. Grad., So. Conn. State U.; student, Fla. Atlantic U., Wesleyan U. Mem. Conn. Ho. of Reps., 1981—, mem. environ., fin., revenue and bonding com., chmn., select com. on children. Democrat. Home: 188 S Cherry St Wallingford CT 06492-4016 Office: State House of Reps House of Reps Hartford CT 06106

MUSSELMAN, TRUDI TAYLOR, management executive; b. N.Y.C., June 14, 1947; m. Ronald L. Musselman, Dec. 28, 1983. BS, U. Hartford, 1969. U.S. sales mgr. Courtaulds Fabrics, N.Y.C., 1973-79; div. mgr. Avon Products, Kansas City, Mo., 1980-83, Newark, Del., 1987-91; br. mgr. Adia Pers. Svcs., St. Louis and Lancaster, Pa., 1984-86; pres. Mgmt. Dynamics, Lancaster, 1991—; cons. U.S. and Can., 1991. Author: (manuals) Dynamic Presentations, 1992, Seven Steps to Practically Perfect Presentations, 1993, Service With Style, 1993. Pole watcher Dem. Com., Lancaster, 1992. Mem. ASTD.

MUSTARD, CINDY SINGLETON, social worker, administrator; b. St. Louis, Oct. 29, 1943; d. George Conley and Elizabeth Ann (Nye) Miller; m. Marvin Eugene Mustard, Aug. 9, 1969; 1 child, Katherine Conley. Ba, U. Mo., 1965. Caseworker II Jackson Co. Divsn. Divsn. Family Svcs., Kansas City, Mo., 1965-68; program & tng. dir. Camp Fire Inc., Kansas City, 1969-88; field rep. Am. Cancer Soc., Columbia, Mo., 1988-91; exec. dir. Voluntary Action Ctr., Columbia, 1991—; Bd. dirs. Rusk Rehab. Ctr., Columbia, 1993—. Editor Directory Cmty. Svcs. Boone County. Elder, mission com. mem. 1st Presbyn. Ch., Columbia, 1989-93; sec. bd. dirs. Mo. Vols., 1994—; chair United Way Exec. Dirs. Coun., 1993; co-chair City Bd. Election Proposition I, Columbia, 1994; chair Commn. Cultural Affairs, Columbia, 1994-95, commn. mem., 1994—. Mem. Boone County Related Agys. (v.p. 1993-94), Caring Cmtys. Partnership (co-chair dental trask force), Interfaith Coun., Downtown Rotary (bd. dirs. 1992—), Columbia C. of C. (bd. dirs. 1991-94). Democrat. Home: 600 S Greenwood Columbia MO 65203 Office: Voluntary Action Ctr 800 N Providence Columbia MO 65203

MUSTARD, MARY CAROLYN, financial executive; b. North Bend, Nebr., Sept. 21, 1948; d. Joseph Louis and Rosalie Margaret (Emanuel) Smaus; m. Ronald L. Mustard, Apr. 19, 1969 (div. 1988); children: Joel Jonathan, Dana Marie. Student, Creighton U., 1966-67, C.E. Sch. Commerce, 1967-68, Coll. of St. Mary, 1983-84, Met. C.C., Omaha, 1988-90, Bellevue U., 1991-92. With Platte County Dept. Pub. Welfare, Columbus, Nebr., 1968-69; sec. to plant mgr. B.L. Montague Steel Co., Sumter, S.C., 1969-70; property disposal technician Property Disposal Office, Shaw AFB, S.C., 1970-71; libr. technician Hdqs. Strategic Air Command Librarian, Offutt AFB, Nebr., 1971-76; sec.-steno Hdqs. Strategic Air Command Communications/Frequency Mgmt., Offutt AFB, Nebr., 1976-79; security specialist/program analyst Hdqs. Strategic Air Command Security Police, Offutt AFB, Nebr., 1979-88; budget analyst Hdqs. Strategic Air Command Fin. Mgmt., Offutt AFB, 1988-92; funds control analyst Hdqs. Air Mobility Command, Scott AFB, Ill., 1992-93, chief hdqs. and comm. account, 1993-94, chief hdqs. relocation, transition assistance/comm. programs, 1994-95; chief base realignment and closure program Air Mobility Command, Scott AFB, Ill., 1995-96; systems adminstr. Def. Fin. and Acctg. Svc., Kansas City, Mo., 1996—. Mem. Am. Soc. Mil. Comptrollers (SAC Budget Analyst of Yr. 1990). Democrat. Roman Catholic. Office: DFAS-KC/ALS 1500 E 95th St Kansas City MO 64197-0001

MUSTO, DOREEN, interior designer; b. Rochester, N.Y., Oct. 18; d. Nunzio Edward and Ann (Iaculli) Musto; m. Douglas L. Wink; 1 stepdaughter, Melissa Lynn; 1 child, Douglas III. AAS in Psychology cum laude, Monroe C.C., 1973; BSW cum laude, SUNY, Brockport, 1975. Social worker, dir. mental health Cobbs Hill Nursing Home, Rochester, N.Y., 1975-78; social worker Rochester, N.Y., 1980-89; interior designer for retail stores Washington, 1989-91; CEO Three-D-Wink Inc., Washington, 1991—. Mem. Peerless Rockville (Md.) Hist. Soc.; judge, mem. 4-H Orgn., 1985—; vol. to staff White House, Washington, 1994—; head art dept. Young Reps. Club, Rochester, 1964-69; organizer, pres. Rockshire New Comers Club, Rockville, Md.; active nat., local politics; chmn. Rockshire Arch. Com. Mem. NOW, Nat. Trust for Hist. Preservation, White House Hist. Soc., Decorative Arts Trust (cons.), Nat. Mus. of Women in the Arts (charter), Tex. State Soc. (inaugural ball com. 1985-94), Nat. Am. Italian Found., Smithsonian Instn., Md. Design, Space Planning and Props Soc. (founder, dir.).

MUSTY, ROSE MARIE, exchangor/investment counselor, educator; b. Woodsville, N.H., Feb. 22, 1950; d. Robert Gorham and Alberta Pearl (Mitchell) M. BS in Small Bus. Mgmt. summa cum laude, N.H. Coll., 1995, MS in Bus. Edn. summa cum laude, 1996. Lic. real estate broker. Mgr. gen. ledger and acctg. Concord (N.H.) Savs. Bank, 1975-80; banker officer, internal auditor Dartmouth Savs. Bank, Hanover, N.H., 1981-83; pvt. practice exchangor/investment counselor Hanover, 1983—; pres. Northeast Real Estate Exch., Northampton, Mass., 1991-92; program chmn. Cert. Comml. Investment Mem., Andover, Mass., 1992-93; pub. rels. com. Manchester (N.H.) Arts and Entertainment Zone, 1992-93; edn. and conv. com. mem. N.H. Assn., Realtors, Concord, 1992-93; mktg. com. mem. N.H. Comml. Investment Divsn., Concord, 1993-94; judge N.H. DECA 39th Annual Conf., Manchester, 1996; adj. prof. various colls., 1996—. Scholar Nat. Assn. Bank Women, 1981. Mem. Nat. Bus. Edn. Assn., N.H. Bus. Edn. Assn., Delta Mu Delta (Gamma Nu chpt. v.p. 1996—, 1st Annual Recognition award 1995, del. triennial nat. conv. 1995), Delta Pi Epsilon (Delta Theta chpt., charter mem.). Home: 1112 Black Brook Rd Dunbarton NH 03045 Home (summer): Lake Armington PO Box 143 Piermont NH 03779

MUTAFOVA-YAMBOLIEVA, VIOLETA NIKOLOVA, pharmacologist; b. Svishtov, Bulgaria, Apr. 18, 1954; d. Nikola Anastassov Mutafov and Bogdanka Ivanova (Boteva) Mutafova; m. Ilia Angelov Yamboliev, Mar. 24, 1984; children: Irena, Kalina. MD, Med. Acad., Sofia, Bulgaria, 1978, splty. Pharmacology, 1985, PhD, 1987. Physician Dept. Internal Medicine Dist. Hosp., Svishtov, Bulgaria, 1979-82; rsch. asst. prof. pharmacology Med. Acad., Sofia, 1982-87, Bulgarian Acad. Scis., Sofia, 1987-93; Fogarty Internat. fellow Sch. Medicine Univ. Nev. Reno, 1993-95. Co-author: Trends in Pharmacology and Pharmacotherapy; contbr. articles to profl. jours. Mem. AAAS, Bulgarian Pharmacol. Soc. (exec. com., Best Young Pharmacologist award 1988), Soc. Bulgarian Physicians, N.Y. Acad. Scis.

MUZYKA, JENNIFER LOUISE, chemist, educator; b. Fredericksburg, Va., Nov. 9, 1963; d. Kie Muzyka and Jo Anne (Martin) Cepeda; m. Mark Stephan Meier, June 4, 1994. BS in Chemistry, U. Dallas, 1985; PhD in Organic Chemistry, U. Tex., 1990. Asst. prof. Roanoke Coll., Salem, Va., 1990-94, Centre Coll., Danville, Ky., 1994—; Petroleum Rsch. Fund summer faculty fellow U. Ky., 1992. Contbr. articles to profl. jours. Rsch. grantee Ky. NSF EPSCOR, 1995, rsch. grantee Petroleum Rsch. Fund, 1992; Engrs. Club Dallas scholar, 1981-82. Mem. AAUP, Am. Chem. Soc. (chair-elect Lexington sect. 1995-96, chair 1996—, sec. Va. Blue Ridge sect. 1993-94), Ky. Acad. Sci. (Marcia Athey Rsch. grantee 1995), Coun. Undergrad. Rsch., Sigma Xi, Iota Sigma Pi (sec. Argentum chpt. 1993-94). Office: Centre Coll Chemistry Dept 600 W Walnut St Danville KY 40422

MUZYKA-MCGUIRE, AMY, marketing professional, nutrition consultant; b. Chgo., Sept. 24, 1953; d. Basil Bohdan and Amelia (Rand) Muzyka; m. Patrick J. McGuire, June 3, 1977; children: Jonathan, Elizabeth. BS, Iowa State U., 1975, postgrad., 1978—; registered dietitian, St. Louis U., 1980. Cert. dietitian. Home economist Nat. Livestock and Meat Bd., Chgo., 1975-77; dietary cons. various hosps. and nursing homes, Iowa, 1978-79; supr. foodsvc. Am. Egg Bd., Park Ridge, Ill., 1980-83; assoc. dir., mgr. foodsvc. Cole & Weber Advt., Seattle, 1984-85; prin., owner Food and Nutrition Comms., Federal Way, Wash., 1986—. Co-author: Turkey Foodservice Manual, 1987; editor: (newsletter) Home Economists in Business, 1975-77, Dietitians in Business and Industry, 1982-85; Food Net on Internet, 1995—;

contbr. articles to profl. jours. Active Federal Way Women's Network, 1986-87. Named Outstanding Dietitian of Yr. North Suburban Dietetic Assn., 1983. Mem. Am. Dietetic Assn., Internat. Foodsvc. Editorial Coun., Consulting Nutritionists, Vegetarian Nutrition, Home Economists in Bus. Home: 5340 SW 315th St Federal Way WA 98023-2034

MYATT, SUE HENSHAW, nursing home administrator; b. Little Rock, Aug. 16, 1956; d. Bobby Eugene and Janett Lanell (Ahart) Henshaw; m. Tommy Wayne Myatt; children: James Andrew, Thomas Ryan. BS in Psychology, Old Dominion U., 1978, MS in Ednl. Counseling, 1982. Cert. activity cons. Nat. Cert. Coun. of Activity Profls., gerontol. activity therapy cons., Va. Dir. activity Manning Convalescent, Portsmouth, Va., 1983-84, Camelot Hall, Norfolk, Va., 1984-86; coord. activities Beverly Manor, Portsmouth, 1986-87, Gerogian Manor Assisted Living Facility, 1989-90; dir. activities Huntington Convalescent Ctr., Newsport News, Va., 1990-91; nursing home adminstr.-in-tng. Bayview Healthcare Ctr., Newport News, 1991-92; adminstr. Evangeline of Gates, Gatesville, N.C., 1992-95, Mary Washington Health Ctr., Colonial Beach, Va., 1993-95, Brian Ctr. Health & Rehab., Lawrenceville, Va., 1995—; instr. Tidewater Community Coll., 1990. Mem. Nat. Assn. Activity Profl. (cert. legis. com.), Va. Assn. Activity Profl. (v.p. 1986-87, creator logo), Hampton Roads Activity Profls. Assn. (sec. 1985-86, pres. 1986-87, v.p. 1987-88). Home: 518 Tanglewood Dr Bracey VA 23919

MYCKO, LINDA JEAN, elementary education educator; b. DuBois, Pa., Dec. 3, 1951; d. Eugene D. and Shirley A. (Simpson) Delp; m. Henry J. Mycko, Sept. 7, 1974; children: Henry J. Jr., Kimberly, Jonathan. BS in Elem. Kindergarten Edn., Pa. State U., 1973; MEd in Adminstrn., George Mason U., 1995. Cert. profl. cert. endorsements in Elem. Kindergarten edn., gifted and talented edn., adminstrn., Va. Tchr. Apple Tree Presch., Manassas, Va., 1985-86; substitute tchr. Manassas Pub. Schs., 1986-87, whole lang. trainer, 1992-94; tchr. Weems Elem. Sch., Manassas, 1987—; presenter No. Va. Gifted and Talented Conf., Stafford, 1990—, presenter Intro to Tech. insvcs., 1995; mem. tech. com. City of Manassas, 1994-95. Grantee Dept. Inst. Svcs., 1993. Mem. ASCD. Home: 9508 Natchez Trail Ct Manassas VA 22110-6601 Office: Weems Elem Sch 8750 Weems Rd Manassas VA 22110-4941

MYERBERG, MARCIA, investment banker; b. Boston, Mar. 25, 1945; d. George and Evelyn (Lewis) Katz; m. Jonathan Gene Myerberg, June 4, 1967 (div. Mar. 1994); 1 child, Gillian Michelle. BS, U. Wis., 1966. Corp. trust adminstr. Chase Manhattan Bank, N.Y.C., 1966-67; asst. cashier Glore Forgan, Wm. R. Staats, Phoenix, 1967-68; bond portfolio analyst Trust Co. of Ga., Atlanta, 1969-72; asst. v.p. 1st Union Nat. Bank, Charlotte, N.C., 1973-78; dir. cash mgmt. Carolina Power & Light Co., Raleigh, N.C., 1978-79; sr. v.p., treas. Fed Home Loan Mortgage Corp., Washington, 1979-85; dir. Salomon Bros. Inc., N.Y.C., 1985-89; sr. mng. dir. Bear, Stearns & Co. Inc., N.Y.C., 1989-93; mng. dir. Bear, Stearns Home Loans, London, 1989-93; chief exec. Myerberg & Co., L.P., N.Y.C., 1994—. Home: 201 E 87th St Apt 16R New York NY 10128-1101 Office: 780 3rd Ave New York NY 10017-2024

MYERS, ANN MARGARET, state agency supervisor; b. Meshoppen, Pa., Mar. 9, 1953; d. Jack William and Sara Elizabeth (Walsh) Morgan; m. Randy Cloyd Myers, Oct. 13, 1984 (div. Nov. 25, 1991). AS in Liberal Arts, Keystone Jr. Coll., LaPlume, Pa., 1993; BA cum laude in Sociology, Psychology, Wilkes U., Wilkes Barre, Pa., 1996. Asst. retail mgr. Rite Aid Corp., Tunkhannock, Pa., 1971-78; prodn. technician Procter & Gamble Corp., Mehoopany, Pa., 1978-85; restaurant mgr. Shaffer's Pink Apple, Tunkhannock, 1991-92; secretarial supr. Pa. Dept. Agr., Tunkhannock, 1992—; N.E. Pa. Tri-County rural devel. com. sec., Tunkhannock, 1992—. Mem. Wyoming County Dem. Women's Soc., 1995—, Wyoming County Emergency Mgmt., 1992-95. Mem. Am. Fedn. State, County, Mcpl. Employees Coun. 87 (sec. local 2370, congl. liaison 1995—), Wyoming County Hillary Rodham Clinton Fan Club (coord. 1995—). Roman Catholic.

MYERS, CHARLOTTE WILL, biology educator; b. Harbor Beach, Mich., Jan. 5, 1930; d. Louis John and Ruth (Sageman) Wills; m. John Jay Myers, Dec. 27, 1958; children: Sandra, Andrew, Susan Ruth. BA in Biology, U. Mich., 1951, MS in Edn., 1952. Tchr. biology Birmingham (Mich.) Pub. Schs., 1952-59; tchr. art pvt. practice, Birmingham, 1962-78, Santa Fe, 1979-96; instr. Oakland U. , Pontiac, Mich., 1975-77; demonstrator, coord. Internat. Porcelain Art Teaching, Birmingham and Santa Fe, 1972-96. V.p. PTA, Birmingham, 1957; founder Future Tchrs., Birmingham, 1956; area chmn. Muscular Dystrophy, Birmingham, 1963-64; leader Girl Scouts Am., Birmingham, 1969-71. Mem. N.Mex. State Fedn. Porcelain Artists (sec. 1986-94), Mich. China Painting Tchrs. Orgn. (pres. 1973-77), Rocky Mountain Outdoor Writers & Photographers (bd. dirs. 1995—), Internat. Porcelain Arts Tchrs., Artists Equity (treas. 1981-83), Porcelain Arts Club (pres. 1979-81, treas. 1987-89). Democrat. Presbyterian. Home and office: Rte 3 Box 109JM Santa Fe NM 87505

MYERS, DIANNE LOUISE, gerontology nurse; b. Hanover, Pa., Dec. 24, 1959; d. Clyde R. and Marian L. M. BSN, Pa. State U., University Park, 1980, MSN, 1985. RN, Pa.; cert. gerontol. clin. nurse specialist ANCC. Resident care supr. York (Pa.) Luth. Retirement Village, 1982-84; med. supr. Devon (Pa.) Manor, 1985-86; adminstrv. supr. Bryn Mawr Rehab. Hosp., Malvern, Pa., 1986-88; clin. instr. Chambersburg (Pa.) Hosp., 1988-90, gerontology clin. nurse specialist, 1990—. Trustee Advancing Geriatric Edn. Inst. Recipient award for advanced clin. practice Pa. Nightengale Awards Found., 1993. Mem. Gerontol. Nursing Assn. (treas.), Sigma Theta Tau.

MYERS, ELIZABETH ROUSE, management consultant; b. Grand Island, Nebr., July 14, 1923; d. William Wayne Rouse and Lulu Zella Trout; m. Richard Roland Myers, June 25, 1943; children: Diane Marie Berndt, Richard Wayne. Student, Kearny State Tchrs. Coll., Nebr., 1942-43. Draftsman Borg-Warner Corp., Kalamazooo, 1944; acct. CFI Steel Corp., Pueblo, Colo., 1950-52; sec., treas. Standard Paint, Yakima, Wash., 1954-86; pres. Pied Piper Childrens Books, Yakima, Wash., 1985-96; federal oil leases, 1980—; docent Yakima Valley Mus. & Gilbert House, Wash. 1984—. Editor: H.S. Paper. Tchr., supt. First Presbyn. Ch., Yakima, Wash., 1958-70; mem. bd. Parent Tchrs.; bd. dirs., teen chmn. YWCA; pres. Gilbert House. Mem. Yakima Valley Mus. (awarded Doll 1985, Show 1986, vol. of yr. 1994). Republican. Presbyterian. Home: 106 N 25th Ave Yakima WA 98902-2807

MYERS, JOAN, photographer; b. Des Moines, Iowa, June 11, 1944; d. Henry B. Wallace and Florence (Kling) Smith; divorced; children: Raymond Louis Buetens, Julian Aaron Buetens. BA, Stanford U., 1966, MA, 1967. Photographer: Along the Santa Fe Trail, 1986; author, photographer: Santiago: Saint of Two Worlds, 1992, Whispered Silences, 1996; one-woman shows at Robert Schoelkopf Gallery, N.Y., 1976, Thackrey and Robertson, San Francisco, 1977, Photopia, Phila., 1978, Susan Spiritus Gallery, Newport Beach, Calif., 1978, 80, 84, Stanford (Calif.) U. Mus., 1978, Port Washington (N.Y.) Pub. Libr., 1979, Mancini Gallery, Phila., 1981, Galerie Perspectives, Paris, 1981, Linda Durham Gallery, Santa Fe, 1981, 84, 86, 89, 91, 93, Calif. State U., Long Beach, 1981, Sheldon Art Gallery, U. Nebr., Lincoln, 1982, Etherton Gallery, Tucson, 1982, U. Art Mus. U. N.Mex., Albuquerque, 1983, Palm Springs Desert Mus.,1 984, Dallas Pub. Libr., 1985, Marcuse Pfeifer Gallery, N.Y., 1986, Smithsonian Instn. Traveling Exhbn., 1986-89, Griffin Art Gallery, Nacogdoches, Tex., 1987, Nora Eccles Harrison Mus. Art, Logan, Utah, 1987, Ctr. for Creative Photography, Tucson, 1987, Ark. Art Ctr., Little Rock, 1988, Audubon Naturalist Ctr., Chevy Chase, Md., 1991, Kathleen Ewing Gallery, Washington, 1991, Albuquerque Mus., 1992, Rice U. Media Ctr., Houston, 1992, Corpus Christi (Tex.) U., 1993, Salt Lake City Art Mus., 1994, Vision Gallery, San Francisco, 1994; two-persons shows at Galerie Montesquieu, Agen, France, 1981, Galerie Arpa, Bordeaux, France, 1981, Port Washington Pub. Libr., 1984; represented in numerous permanent and pub. collections, including Mus. Fine Art, Houston, Santa Barbara Mus. Art, Nat. Gallery Art, Smithsonian Instn., Mus. Modern Art, High Mus. Art, Atlanta, others. Mem. N.Mex. Coun. on Photography, 1986—. Grantee NEA, 1982, 90, Ariz. Commn. on Arts, 1990. Home: PO Box 237 Tesuque NM 87574

MYERS, JUDY CASHMAN, accountant; b. Manchester, Md., Feb. 8, 1948; d. Guy Edward and Nadine Rebecca (Feeser) Wine; m. John Edward Cashman, Dec. 31, 1973 (div. 1990); 1 child, Michael Edward Cashman. BS, U. Balt., 1984. CPA, Md. Office mgr., acct. Hertzbach & Co., CPAs, Owings Mills, Md., 1979-84, Elion Concrete, Inc., Balt., 1985-94, O'Meara Constrn. Co., Inc., Finksburg, Md., 1995—; pvt. practice acctg. and tax preparation, Finksburg, 1992—; tchr. adult edn. Balt./Carroll County Schs., Westminster, Md., 1993-95; treas. St. Benjamin's Luth. Ch., 1992, 93, 95, 96. Mem. Carroll County Arts Coun., Westminster, 1994—; mem., contbr. Westminster Writers' Group, 1992—. Mem. Md. Soc. Accts., Inst. Cert. Mgmt. Accts., Aid Assn. Luths. (5 Yr. Officer 1995, treas. 1990-96). Republican. Home: 2664 Sandymount Rd Finksburg MD 21048 Office: O'Meara Constrn Co Inc 3150 Baltimore Blvd Finksburg MD 21048

MYERS, KATHERINE DONNA, writer, publisher; b. L.A., Nov. 10, 1925; d. John Allen Myers and Eulah Caldwell (Myers) Harris; m. Thomas Miller, Feb. 2, 1944 (div. 1963); children: Kathleen JoAnn Content, David Thomas. Teaching credential in bus. edn., U. So. Calif., L.A., 1975; postgrad., Loyola U., Paris, 1980. Cert. pub. adminstr. Dep. field assessor L.A. County Tax Assessor, L.A., 1944-60; sec. L.A. Unified Sch. Dist., 1960-70; br. sec. bank Crocker Nat. Bank, L.A., 1970-78; instr. legal sec. Southland Coll., L.A., 1975-78; exec. sec. ABC, L.A., 1978-89; v.p. spl. projects Glendale (Calif.) TV Studios, 1990-92; writer, publisher Eagles Wings Publishing Co., L.A., 1992—; owner, pres. Success Secretarial Seminar, L.A., 1980-84; pub., author Eagle's Wings Pub. Co., L.A., 1992—; wedding cons., counselor Crenshaw United Meth. Ch., L.A., 1993—. Author, pub.: Wedding Bells, A New Peal, 1994; (instrnl. book) Productivity Guide, Bilingual Special Education, 1980; (biography) The Eagle Flies on Friday, 1988, (hist. newsletter) Eagle Reader's Newsletter, 1993; author: (tech. booklet) Ronnie Knows about Sickle Cell, 1973 (Founder's award 1973). Troop leader, adminstr. Girl Scouts Am., L.A., 1956; chmn. sickle cell com. MLK Hosp. Guild, L.A., 1974; den mother Boy Scouts Am., 1960; lifetime mem. PTA, L.A., 1960. Recipient THANKS badge Girl Scouts Am., 1959, Founder's award MLK Jr. Hosp. Guild, 1974. Mem. Photo Friends Ctrl. Libr., Wilshire C. of C. (bd. dirs. 1980). Democrat. United Methodist. Home: 4215 W Slauson Ave Apt 122 Los Angeles CA 90043-2831 Office: Eagles Wings Publishing Co PO Box 361263 5350 Wilshire Blvd Los Angeles CA 90036

MYERS, LIBBY ANN, retired nurse; b. Hutchinson, Kans., July 22, 1936; d. Edwin Eugene and Verna Maxine (Craig) Schroëder; m. William Wayne Osborne, Apr. 1950 (div. 1960); m. William Andrew Myers III, June 21, 1962; children: Linda Kay, Lloyd Lee, Diana Gaye, Joe Lyle, Delbert Matthew. MSN, Okla. Bapt. U., 1958. RN, Okla. Nurse Bapt. Meml. Hosp., Oklahoma City, 1967-70, Doctors Gen. Hosp., Oklahoma City, 1970-73, Mercy Hosp., Oklahoma City, 1973-79; nurse, team leader PICU Hutchinson (Kans.) Hosp., 1979-87; pvt. practice pvt. duty nurse Oklahoma City, 1987-93; ret., 1993; owner, operator Day Care Facility, Oklahoma City, 1977-79. Precinct poll inspector Precinct 238 Oklahoma City Election Bd., 1988-96, precinct com. chair Precinct 238 Oklahoma City Rep., 1992-96; exec. com. Oklahoma County Rep. Hdqrs., Oklahoma City, 1994-96; pres., former block capt. Epworth Neighborhood Assn., Oklahoma City, 1991-96; counselor Homicide Survivors Support Group, Oklahoma City, 1991-96, lobbist for victims bills, 1992-96; Sunday sch. tchr., Bible sch. tchr. Crestwood Bapt. Ch., Oklahoma City. Mem. Tri-City Rep. Women, Bapt. Women.

MYERS, LINDA SHAFER, secondary education educator; b. Lebanon, Tenn., Apr. 12, 1943; d. Odie and Nellie Irene Shafer; m. C. Bruce Myers (div.); children: James B., Joseph C. BA, Berea Coll., 1965; MA, Austin Peay State U., 1972, postgrad., 1993. Cert. tchr., Tenn. English tchr. Montgomery County Schs., Clarksville, Tenn., 1985—. Mem. Nat. Tenn. Edn. Assn., Nat. Tenn. Coun. of Tchrs. of English, Delta Kappa Gamma Soc. Internat. Office: Clarksville H S 151 Richview Rd Clarksville TN 37043

MYERS, LINDA SUSAN, asset manager, professional mountain bike racer; b. Santa Barbara, Calif., Mar. 2, 1954; d. Bryant and Patricia Lee (Morrison) M.; m. Kenneth Russel Browning (div. 1993); children: Steven Mark, Katherine Patricia. BS in Math., U. Redlands, 1975. Cert. secondary edn. tchr. Tchr. Montclair (Calif.) H.S., 1975-78; property mgr. Simco, Inc., Pasadena and Big Bear Lake, Calif., 1980-92; asset mgr. Big Bear Lake, 1992—. Mem. World Downhill Mountain Bike Team, 1991, 92, 94, 95, World Cross Country Team, 1992. Recipeint Gold medal Nat. Downhill Race, 1990, 91, Bronze medal Nat. Cross Country Race, 1990, 91, World Downhill Race, 1990.

MYERS, LINDA SUSAN, management consultant; b. N.Y.C., June 5, 1955. BA, Goucher Coll., 1976; MA, Columbia U., 1977; EdD, Harvard U., 1994. Mgr. Squibb Corp., Princeton, N.J., 1983-86, Savin Corp., N.Y.C., 1986-88; mgmt. cons. Synapse, Phila., 1989-94; account exec. Forum Corp., Phila., 1994-95; mgmt. cons. Price Waterhouse, Phila., 1995—. Mem. Phila. Orgnl. Devel. Network. Office: Price Waterhouse 30 S 17th St Philadelphia PA 19103

MYERS, MARY KATHLEEN, publishing executive; b. Cedar Rapids, Iowa, Aug. 19, 1945; d. Joseph Bernard and Marjorie Helen (Huntsman) Weaver; m. David F. Myers, Dec. 30, 1967; children: Mindy, James. BA in English and Psychology, U. Iowa, 1967. Tchr. Lincoln H.S., Des Moines, 1967-80; editor Perfection Learning Corp., Des Moines, 1980-87, v.p., editor-in-chief, 1987-93; pres., founding ptnr. orgn. to promote Edward de Bono Advanced Practical Thinking Tng., Des Moines, 1992—. Editor: Retold Classics, 1988-91, (ednl. program) Six Thinking Hats, 1991, Lateral Thinking, 1993; originator numerous other ednl. products and programs. Mem. Gov.'s Commn. to Enhance Ednl. Leadership Iowa, Dept. of Edn., 1991-93. Mem. ASTD, Am. Soc. Quality Control, Assn. for Quality and Participation. Home: 4315 Urbandale Ave Des Moines IA 50310-3460 Office: APTT 10520 New York Ave Des Moines IA 50322-3775

MYERS, MICHELE TOLELA, university president; b. Rabat, Morocco, Sept. 25, 1941; came to U.S., 1964; d. Albert and Lilie (Abecassis) Tolela; m. Pierre Vajda, Sept. 12, 1962 (div. Jan. 1965); m. Gail E. Myers, Dec. 20, 1968; children: Erika, David. Diploma, Inst. Polit. Studies, U. Paris, 1962; MA, U. Denver, 1966, PhD, 1967; MA, Trinity U., 1977; LHD, Wittenberg U., 1994. Asst. prof. speech Manchester Coll., North Manchester, Ind., 1967-68; asst. prof. speech and sociology Monticello Coll., Godfrey, Ill., 1968-71; asst. prof. communication Trinity U., San Antonio, 1975-80, assoc. prof., 1980-86, asst. v.p. for acad. affairs, 1982-85, assoc. v.p., 1985-86; assoc. prof. sociology, dean Undergrad. Coll. Bryn Mawr (Pa.) Coll., 1986-89; pres. Denison U., Granville, Ohio, 1989—; comm. analyst Psychology and Commn., San Antonio, 1974-83; bd. dirs. Am. Coun. on Edn., chair elect. Nat. Assn. Ind. Colls. and Univs., Sherman Fairchild Found.; mem. Fed. Res. Bank of Cleve., 1995—; pres.'s commn. Na. Collegiate Athletic Assn., 1993—. Author: (with Gail Myers) The Dynamics of Human Communication, 1973, 6th and internat. edits., 1992, transl. into French, 1984, Communicating When We Speak, 1975, 2d edit., 1978, Communication for the Urban Professional, 1977, Managing by Communication: An Organizational Approach, 1982, transl. into Spanish, 1983, internat. edit., 1982. Trustee Phila. Child Guidance Clinic, 1988-89; trustee assoc. The Bryn Mawr Sch., Balt., 1987-89; v.p., bd. dirs. San Antonio Cmty. Guidance Ctr., 1979-83. Am. Coun. Edn. fellow in acad. adminstrn., 1981-82, Bank One Columbus, 1990-94. Mem. Am. Coun. Edn. (commn. on women in higher edn. 1990-92, bd. dirs. 1993—, chmn.-elect 1996—). Home: 204 Broadway W Granville OH 43023-1120 Office: Denison U Office of the President Granville OH 43023

MYERS, MONTZ ELAINE, medical and surgical nurse; b. Poplar Bluff, Mo., Nov. 28, 1948; d. Harvey Donald and Patricia Ruth (Ware) Adams; m. Lawrence Leroy Myers, Aug. 13, 1968; children: Michael, Michelle, Melissa. Diploma, Burge Sch. Nursing, Springfield, Mo., 1982; BSN, S.W. Mo. State U., 1986. RN, Mo.; cert. med.-surg. nurse ANCC. Med.-surg. staff nurse Cox Med. Ctr. South, Springfield, Mo., 1982-89, asst. nurse mgr. same day surgery, 1989—. Mem. Nat. League of Nursing. Home: 3839 N Stewart Ave Springfield MO 65803-4838 Office: Cox Med Ctr South 3801 S National Ave Springfield MO 65807-5210

MYERS, PATRICIA ELLEN, English language educator; b. South Bend, Ind., Mar. 28, 1959; d. James Edward Myers and Barbara Louise; ptnr. Celeste Marie Cauley (div. June 1987); 1 child, Kelsey Louise Myers-Cauley; ptnr. Linda Gay Painter. BA in Women's Studies, U. Mich., 1981, MA in Am. Culture, 1987, postgrad., 1985-92. Adminstrv. asst. U. Mich., Ann Arbor, 1985-89, rsch. asst., 1986, cons., 1988-92, advisor, 1991-92, instr., 1986-96; assoc. adj. faculty mem. Ind. U. and Ivy Tech. State Coll., South Bend, 1993-96. Editor: A Certain Terror: Heterosexism, 1993; editl. bd. Green Politics, 1995-96, Green Notes, 1996; contbr. articles to profl. jours. Co-chair LBGQ Caucus Green Party USA, South Bend, 1995-96; mem. TLC St. Joe Valley NOW, South Bend, 1992-96; mem. Pride Action com., South Bend, 1992-96. Mem. Nat. Coun. Tchrs. Eng., Nat. Gay/Lesbian Task Force, Nat. Adj. Faculty Guild, Ind. Coun. Tchrs. Eng. Office: Michiana Homophobia Edn Project 515 S St Joseph St South Bend IN 46601

MYERS, PATRICIA L., business executive; b. Denison, Tex., Mar. 15, 1941; d. Albert Lewis and Ava Alberta (Stogsdill) Cravens; m. Jimmy Dale Myers, May 6, 1960; children: Jimmy Keith, Jeffrey Alden, Gregory Bryan. AA, San Jacinto Coll., Pasadena, Tex., 1986. Substitute tchr. Pasadena (Tex.) Ind. Schs., 1970-75; claims processor Prudential Ins., Houston, 1976-79, training instr. claims, 1979-81, asst. supr. claims, 1981-83; fund adminstr. Sheet Metal # 54 Trust Funds, Houston, 1983-87; adminstrv. mgr. Zenith Adminstrs., Houston, 1987—; bd. dirs. Friends of a Pepper, Inc. Editor: (quarterly newsletter) The Peeper Press, 1995. Pres. JD Parks Elem. PTA, Pasadena, Tex.; pres., v.p. Pasadena Internat. Little League; tng. instr. Ladies Aux. Sam Houston Area Coun., Houston; den leader coach Sam Houston Area Coun. Boy Scouts of Am., Houston; mem. Harrison Sub-Divsn. Property Owners, 1982-84, Treasure Island-Magnolia Point Civic Assn., 1995-96. Office: Zenith Adminstrs 4600 Gulf Freeway # 300 Houston TX 77023

MYERS, PATRICIA LOUISE, utilities administrator; b. Lafayette, Ind., July 18, 1942; d. Lloyd P. and Frances Lucille Sollars; m. Donald Eugene Myers; children: Dirk Eugene, Carey Dean. BS, Purdue U., 1964; MSW, Ind. U., Indpls., 1967. Exec. dir. After Sch. House, Miami, Fla., 1975-76, Alaska Crippled Children and Adults, Fairbanks, 1979-81; city mgr. City of Galena, Alaska, 1981-87; owner Welcome to Fairbanks, Alaska, 1987-95; day care assistance adminstr. Fairbanks North Star Borough, 1988-90; subscriber svcs. mgr. Fairbanks Mcpl. Utilities Sys., 1990—; social worker Marion County Mental Health Assn., Indpls., 1965-67; psychiat. social worker Dayton (Ohio) Mcpl. Ct., 1967-69; owner vending co., Fairbanks, 1976-79. Co-chair com. Mayor's Task Force on Econ. Devel., Fairbanks, 1988-89; mem. Mayor's Task Force on Families and Children, Fairbanks, 1988-89; mem. legis. com. Alaska Mcpl. League, 1983-87. Baha'i. Office: Fairbanks Mcpl Utilities 645 5th Ave Fairbanks AK 99701

MYERS, SHARON DIANE, auditor; b. Lawrence, Kans., Sept. 18, 1955; d. Richard Paul and Helen Carol (Overbey) M. AA, Mt. San Antonio Coll., Walnut, Calif., 1981; BSBA, Calif. State U., Pomona, 1983, MBA, 1986. Cert. fraud examiner; cert. govt. fin. mgr. Revenue agt. IRS, Glendale, Calif., 1984-85; auditor Def. Contract Audit Agy., L.A., 1985-92; auditor Office Inspector Gen. FDIC, Newport Beach, Calif., 1992—; instr. Azusa (Calif.) Pacific U., 1987, 88, West Coast U., San Diego, 1992. Musician, Sunday sch. supt. Covina (Calif.) Bapt. Temple, 1975-95, Liberty Bapt. Ch., Irvine, Calif., 1995—. Mem. Assn. Govt. Accts. Republican. Home: 4885 NW Gustafson Rd Silverdale WA 98383

MYERS, SHIRLEY DIANA, art book editor; b. N.Y.C., Jan. 6, 1916; d. Samuel Archibald and Regina (Edelstein) Levene; m. Bernard Samuel Myers, Aug. 11, 1938 (dec. Feb. 1993); children: Peter Lewis, Lucie Ellen. BA, NYU, 1936, MA, 1938. Editorial asst. Am. Dancer mag., N.Y.C., 1936-38; asst. to dir. Nat. Art Soc., N.Y.C., 1938-42; freelance, art book editor N.Y.C. and Austin, Tex., 1947—. Editor: Modern Art in the Making, 1950, 59, Mexican Painting in Our Time, 1956, The German Expressionists, 1957, 63, Understanding the Arts, 1958, 63, Bruegel, 1976, Manet, 1977, (with B.S. Myers) Dictionary of 20th Century Art, 1974; asst. editor Ency. of Painting, 1955, 70, 79; asst. editor, contbr. McGraw-Hill Dictionary of Art, 5 vols., 1960-69; contbg. editor: Art and Civilization, 1956, 67; coord., picture editor Ency. World Art: Supplement, Vol. XVI, 1982, 83. Vol. archives New Sch. for Social Rsch. Libr., 1993-95. Mem. NOW, Older Women's League (rec. sec. Greater N.Y. chpt. 1993-95, v.p. 1995-97), Quest (coord. archaeology 1995-97, the city in history 1996-97).

MYERS, SUE BARTLEY, artist; b. Norfolk, Va., Aug. 22, 1930; d. Louis and Rena M. Bartley; m. Bertram J. Myers, Nov. 24, 1949; children: Beth R., Mark F., Alyson S. Student, Stephens Coll., Va. Wesleyan. V.p. Jamson Realty Inc., Myers Realty Inc.; ltd. ptnr. Downtown Plaza Shopping Ctr., Warwick Village Shopping Ctr., Suburban Park Assocs. Solo shows at Village Gallery, Newport News, 1988, Artist at Work Gallery, Virginia Beach, Va., 1991, Va. Wesleyan U., Virginia Beach, 1991, 92, Will Richardson Gallery, Norfolk, Va., 1993, 94, Ctrl. Fidelity Bank, Norfolk, Va., 1995. Pres. adv. coun. Va. Wesleyan U., 1992-94; mayor's del. Sister Cities, Norwich, Eng., 1984, Kidikushu, Japan, 1982, Edinburgh, Scotland, 1991, Toulon, France, 1992; mem. entertainment com. Azalea Festival Norfolk, 1984; founder art scholarship Va. Wesleyan; bd. dirs. corp. campaign Va. Zool. Soc., 1996. Mem. Tidewater Artists Assn., Art Odyssey. Jewish. Home: 7338 Barberry Ln Norfolk VA 23505-3001

MYERS, VIRGINIA LOU, education educator; b. Indpls., July 18, 1940; d. John Rentschler and Bonnie Mae (Powell) Jones; m. James W. Rose Jr., Aug. 2, 1966 (div. Nov. 1986); m. Byron P. Myers, Sept. 11, 1987. BS in Edn., U. Indpls., 1966; MS in Edn., Butler U., 1971; PhD in Edn. Psychology, U. South Fla., 1991. Cert. elem. tchr., reading specialist and prin., Ind. Tchr. Indpls. Pub. Schs., 1966-72; pvt. tutor Self, Indpls., 1972-74; tchr.'s tchr. Urban/Rural Sch. Devel. Project, Indpls, 1974-77; reading techr. Mid. sch. dist. Pike Twp., Indpls., 1977-80; curriculum specialist Mid. sch. Dist. Washington Twp., Indpls., 1980-82; tchr. chpt. I Noblesville (Ind.) Pub. Schs., 1982-83; instr. social scis. Manatee C.C., Venice, Fla., 1983-87; asst. prof. edn. Mo. So. State Coll., Joplin, 1990-91, East Carolina U., Greenville, N.C., 1992-96; assoc. prof. edn. Barton Coll., Wilson, N.C., 1996—; cons. Bertie County Schs. (Windsor) N.C., 1994—. Treas. Smart Start Initiative, Greenville, 1993—; chair Birth Through Kindergarten Higher Edn. Consortium, 1994-96. Mem. ASCD, Interat. Reading Assn., Nat. Coun. Tchrs. English, Nat. Assn. for Edn. Young Children, Orton Dyslexia Soc. Presbyterian. Home: 114 Asbury Rd Greenville NC 27858 Office: Barton Coll Dept Edn Wilson NC 27893

MYERS MAURIN, SYLVIA, estate planning specialist; b. Uniontown, Pa., Oct. 28, 1948; d. Charles Albert and Jean Rose (Durant) Schiffbauer; 1 child, Kevin Charles. BS in Comunications, California U. of Pa., 1974, MEd in Reading, 1982, MA in English, 1977; law student, Duquesne U., Pitts., 1980-84. Sec. tchr. of English and communication Albert Gallatin Area Sch. Dist., Point Marion, Pa., 1974-76; dir. devel., pub. and alumni affairs California Univ. of Pa., 1976-85; fin. and estate planning cons. Pitts., 1985—; gift planning specialist Sewickley Valley Hosp., Pa., 1987—, The Pvt. Bank of PNC Bank NA, 1991—; bd. dirs. Nat. Com. on Planned Giving, 1997—. Co-author book series, workbook: Smart Marketing for Non-Profits, 1986, 87; contbr. articles to profl. jours. Officer The Pitts. Planned Giving Coun., 1986—, program chmn. 1990—; mem. Estate Planning Coun. of Pitts., 1986—. Consortium for Internat. Edn. scholar, 1977; named Outstanding Female Exec. Leader, Westmoreland County Community Coll., 1989. Mem. Assn. for Healthcare Philanthropy, Nat. Com. on Planning Giving (liaison for Pitts.), Nat. Assn. Women Bus. Owners (bd. dirs. 1987-89). Home: 7416 Lighthouse Point Pittsburgh PA 15221 Office: The Pvt Bank PNC Bank NA 1 Oliver Plz Fl 27 Pittsburgh PA 15265

MYERS PASQUINO, MARY ELLEN, social worker; b. Rochester, N.Y., Aug. 1, 1963; d. James Cronley and Ellen Therése (O'Brien) Myers; m. Alan Thomas Pasquino, Oct. 19, 1985. BS, Cornell U., 1985; MSW, Va. Commonwealth U., 1991. Cert. family therapist, Va. Coord./teen parent support program New River Cmty. Action, Christianburg, Va., 1989-91; probation counselor 27th Dist. Ct. Svc., Christianburg, 1991-94; dir. Youth Svc. Bur., Waterford, Conn., 1994—. Vice chair, bd. dirs. New River Cmty. Action, Christianburg, 1991-94; bd. dirs. Habitant for Humanity, New River Valley, 1992-94; chair, bd. dirs. Multidisciplinary Team on Child Abuse and Neglect , New River, 1989-94; chair Justice and Peace com., St. Jude's, Radford, Va., 1993-94. Mem. NASW (Social Worker of Yr. 1994), Chil Plan Com. Roman Catholic. Home: 496 Montauk Ave New London CT 06370

MYHRE, KATHLEEN RANDI, nurse; b. Everett, Wash., Apr. 18, 1952; d. Richard Alvin and Beverley Jeanette (Nesbit) M. LPN, Bellingham (Wash.) Tech. Sch., 1970; ADN, Lane C.C., Eugene, Oreg., 1988. RN, Oreg. LPN night charge nurse Island's Convalescent Ctr., Friday Harbor, Wash., 1970-75; LPN float Sacred Heart Gen. Hosp., Eugene, Oreg., 1975-87; charge nurse urgent care unit Eugene Clinic, 1987—. Democrat. Home: 80687 Lost Creek Rd Dexter OR 97431-9742

MYLROIE, WILLA WILCOX, transportation engineer, regional planner; b. Seattle, May 30, 1917; d. Elgin Roscoe and Ruth B. (Begg) Wilcox; m. John Ellis Mylroie (dec. 1947); children: Steven Wilcox Mylroie, Jo Mylroie Sohneronne; m. Donald Gile Fassett, Dec. 30, 1966. BS in Civil Engring., U. Wash., 1940, MS in Regional Planning, 1953. Lic. profl. civil engr. Civil engr. U.S. Engring. Dept. C.E., Seattle, 1941-46; affiliate prof. civil engring. U. Wash., Seattle, 1948-51, research asst. prof. civil engring., 1951-56; assoc. prof. civil engring. Purdue U., Lafayette, Ind., 1956-58; research engr. and planner Wash. State Dept. Hwys., Olympia, 1958-69, head research and spl. assignment div., 1969-81; cons. civil engring. and regional planning Olympia, 1981—; cons. King County Design Commn., Seattle, 1981-89; advisor Coll. Engring. U. Wash., 1978-86, affiliate prof. civil engring., 1981-84; advisor Wash. State U. Coll. Engring., Pullman, 1977-85. Active Girls Scouts U.S. coun., Boy Scouts Am., Olympia, Renton, 1950-60; pres. high sch. PTA, Olympia; commr. Thurston County Planning Commn., Olympia; U.S. Coast Guard Auxilliary, 1982-89, U.S. Power Squadron, 1967—; citizen amb. People to People Trip, Moscow, St. Petersburg, Russia and Muensk, Bolarus. Recipient Profl. Recognition award Women's Transp., Spokane, Spl. Svc. award Transp. Rsch. Bd. Coun., Washington, U. Wash. Coll. Engring. Alumni Achievement award, 1993. Fellow ASCE (ad hoc vis. com. engring. coun. for profl. devel., Edmund Friedman Profl. Recognition award 1978), Inst. Transp. Engrs. (hon. mem., internat. bd. dirs., Tech. Coun. award 1982); mem. Planning Assn. Wash. (bd. dirs.), Sigma Xi. Home and Office: 7501 Boston Harbor Rd NE Olympia WA 98506-9720

MYRDAL, ROSEMARIE CARYLE, state official, former state legislator; b. Minot, N.D., May 20, 1929; d. Harry Dirk and Olga Jean (Dragge) Lohse; m. B. John Myrdal, June 21, 1952; children: Jan, Mark, Harold, Paul, Amy. BS, N.D. State U., 1951. Registered profl. first grade tchr., N.D. Tchr. N.D., 1951-71; bus. mgr. Edinburg Sch. Dist., 1974-81; mem. N.D. Ho. of Reps., Bismarck, 1984-92, mem. appropriations com., 1991-92; lt. gov., State of N.D., Bismarck, 1992—; sch. evaluator Walsh County Sch. Bds. Assn., Grafton, N.D., 1983-84; evaluator, work presenter N.D. Sch. Bds. Assn., Bismarck, 1983-84; mem. sch. bd. Edinburg Sch. Dist., 1981-90; adv. com. Red River Trade Corridor, Inc., 1989—. Co-editor: Heritage '76, 1976, Heritage '89, 1989. Precinct committeewoman Gardar Twp. Rep. Com., 1980-86; leader Hummingbirds 4-H Club, Edinburg, 1980-83; bd. dirs. Camp Sioux Diabetic Children, Grand Forks, N.D., 1980-90, N.D. affiliate Am. Diabetes Assn., Families First-Child Welfare Reform Initiative, Region IV, 1989-92; dir. N.D. Diabetes Assn., 1989-91; chmn. N.D. Ednl. TelecommunicationsCoun., 1989-90; vice chmn. N.D. Legis. Interim Jobs Devel. Commn., 1989-90. Mem. AAUW (pres. 1982-84 Pembina County area), Pembina County Hist. Soc. (historian 1976-84), Northeastern N.D. Heritage Assn. (pres. 1986-92), Red River Valley Heritage Soc. (bd. dirs. 1985-92). Lutheran. Club: Agassiz Garden (Park River) (pres. 1968-69). Home: 121 E Arikara Ave Apt 302 Bismarck ND 58501-2638 Office: 600 E Boulevard Ave Bismarck ND 58505

MYRICK, HELEN ESTELLE, civic worker; b. Vancouver, B.C., Can., Feb. 4, 1952; came to U.S., 1964; d. Guy Vernon and Vera Loretto (Tacey) M. BA in Cmty. Svcs., Seattle U., 1973; MPA, Pacific Luth. U., 1984. Counselor Renton (Wash.) Area Youth Svcs., 1973-79; probation officer Kitsap County, Bremerton, Wash., 1979-82; social worker III, Wash. State Dept. Social and Health Svcs., Tacoma, 1982-85; mgr. human resources Tacoma-Pierce County Health Dept., 1985-93; legis. aide Wash. State Ho. of Reps., Olympia, 1993-94; polit. cons. Save Our Sealife Initiative Campaign, Tacoma, 1994-95; cons., project mgr. Greater Pierce County Cmty. Network, Tacoma, 1995—; employment counselor King County Work Tng. Program, Seattle, summer 1995. Mem. adv. bd. Pierce County Cmty. Action Agy., 1987-95, Tacoma Hate Crimes Task Force, 1991-93; adult advisor Students Against Violence Everywhere, Federal Way, Wash., 1994-95; candidate Wash. State Ho. of Reps., 1990, 94; bd. dirs. Wash. State Women's Polit. Caucus, Seattle, 1993-95, endorsement chmn., 1995-97; rep. legis. action com. 30th Dist. Dems., Federal Way, 1992-94; bd. dirs. Port of Tacoma Citizen's Work Group, 1995—; bd. dirs. Federal Way Youth and Family Svcs., 1990—, also past pres.; mem. tech. adv. bd. Family Policy Coun., 1995—. Recipient Disting. Svc. award N.W. Dispatch newspaper, 1991; leadership fellow Tacoma-Pierce County C. of C., 1988-89. Mem. NOW, Coalition To Stop Gun Violence, Toastmasters (Most Enthusiastic Speaker award Tacoma 1990), City Club Tacoma (bd. dirs. 1991—). Home and Office: Apt 151 4901 Fairwood Blvd NE Tacoma WA 98422

MYRICK, SHARON TONI, contact representative; b. Phila., Apr. 7, 1952; d. Charles William and Clara (Benjamin) Yates; m. Lawrence Winston Myrick, Dec. 26, 1972 (dec. Dec. 1994); children: Jerel Yates, Lawrence Jr., Helen, Yvonne, Rachael. Grad. h.s., Phila. Lic. ins. agt., Pa. Cashier Woolworth's, Phila., 1985-86, sect. merchandiser, 1986-88; asst. mgr. Domino's Pizza, Phila., 1988; mgr. Murry's, Phila., 1988-89; ins. agt. Prim Am., Phila., 1989-91; contact rep. IRS, Phila., 1991—; sole proprietor Sharon's, Phila., 1996; instr. IRSn. Phila., 1994—. Contbr. poetry to anthologies. Recipient Sales Exec. award Masons, 1991, award Greater Mt. Sinai Bapt. Ch., 1995. Mem. Internat. Soc. Poets (Cert. Merit 1994), Internat. Soc. Authors and Artists. Democrat. Roman Catholic. Office: IRS 600 Arch St Philadelphia PA 19106

MYRICK, SUE, congresswoman, former mayor; b. Tiffin, Ohio, Aug. 1, 1941; d. William Henry and Margaret Ellen (Roby) Wilkins; m. Jim Forest (div.); children: Greg, Dan; m. Wilbur Edward Myrick Jr., Sept. 11, 1977. Student, Heidelberg Coll., 1959-60, HHD (hon.). Exec. sec. to mayor and city mgr. City of Alliance, Ohio, 1962-63; dir. br. office Stark County Ct. of Juvenile and Domestic Rels., Alliance, 1963-65; pres. Myrick Agy., Charlotte, N.C., 1971-95; mayor of Charlotte, 1987-91; mem. 104th Congress from 9th N.C. District, Washington, D.C., 1995—; candidate for U.S. Senate from N.C., 1992; active Heart Fund, Multiple Sclerosis, March of Dimes, Arts and Scis. Coun. Fund Dr.; past mem. adv. bd. Uptown Shelter, Uptown Homeless Task Force, bd. dirs. N.C. Inst. Politics; v.p. Sister Cities Internat.; mem. Pres. Bush's Affordable Housing Commn.; founder, coord. Charlotte vol. tornado relief effort; former bd. dirs. Learning How; former mem. adv. bd. U.S. Conf. Mayors; mem.-at-large Charlotte City Coun., 1983-85, Strengthening Am. Commn.; lay leader, Sunday sch. tchr. 1st United Meth. Ch.; treas. Mecklenburg Ministries; former trustee U.S. Conf. of Mayors. Recipient Woman of Yr. award Harrisonburg, Va., 1968; named one of Outstanding Young Women of Am., 1968. Mem. Women's Polit. Caucus, Beta Sigma Phi. Republican. Home: 310 W 8th St Charlotte NC 28202-1704 Office: US House Reps 509 Cannon House Office Bldg Washington DC 20515-3309 also: Myrick Enterprises 505 N Poplar St Charlotte NC 28202-1729

NABHOLZ, MARY VAUGHAN, rehabilitation nurse; b. Memphis, July 4, 1938; d. George E. Jr. and Anna Marie (Hannifin) Vaughan; m. William James Nabholz, Jr., May 30, 1959; children: Kathleen Marie, William James III, Michael Vaughan. Diploma, St. Joseph Hosp., Memphis, 1959; BA, Webster U., 1978. Cert. CIRS, CCM. Staff nurse St. Joseph Hosp., St. Charles, Mo., 1965-77; supr. Always Care Nursing Svc., St. Louis, 1977-78; home care nurse Jewish Hosp., St. Louis, 1979-81; regional med. mgr. Md. Casualty Co., St. Louis, 1981-88; case mgr. Am. Health Network, St. Louis, 1988-91; regional mgr., 1990; cons., owner Nabholz & Assocs., Bridgeton, Mo., 1991—. Bd. dirs. Ctr. Head Injury Svcs. Mem. Nat. Head Injury Assn., Nat. Spinal Cord Assn., Assn. Rehab. Nurses, Nat. Rehab. Assn.

NABORS, PEGGY LEE, educator; b. Houston, Mar. 17, 1946; d. Carroll Wesley and Aileen (Duncan) Tabb; m. Michael Nabors, May 28, 1966 (div. Aug. 1983); children: Michael Drew, Melanie Carroll. BS in Edn., U. Ctrl. Ark., 1971. Owner Safari Campground, Harrison, Ark., 1970-75; tchr. Harrison Sch. Dist., 1970-82, Pulaski City Sch. Dist., Little Rock, 1982-83. Mem. state com. Dem. Party Ark., Little Rock, 1992—; mem. adminstrv. bd. Highland Valley United Meth. Ch., Little Rock, 1995—; bd. trustees Boone County Spl. Svcs., Harrison, 1974-82. Named Outstanding Young Educator Harrison Jaycees, 1975. Mem. NEA, Nat. Staff Orgn., Ark. Edn. Assn. (pres. 1983-85, uniserv dir. 1989—), Ark. Staff Orgn.

NACHMAN, LEAH BADRIAN, elementary education educator; b. N.Y.C., July 31, 1950; d. Henry and Nelle (Budzanover) Badrian; m. Steven Howard Nachman, Apr. 3, 1971; children: Paul David, Rachel Freida. BA, Bklyn. Coll., 1971, MS, 1974; EdD, Nova U., 1988. Cert. elem. tchr., Fla. Tchr. lang. arts Sch. Dist. 307, Bklyn., 1971-72; tchr. Pub. Sch. 187, Bklyn., 1972-73, Pub. Sch. 132, Bklyn., 1973-74, Broadview Elem., Pompano Beach, Fla., 1974-77, Tamarac (Fla.) Elem. Sch., 1979-80; tchr. Nob Hill Elem. Sch., Sunrise, Fla., 1980—, faculty rep., 1984—; tchr. reading St. Vincent's Hall, Bklyn., 1973-74; tchr. adult edn. Dillard H.S., Ft. Lauderdale, Fla., 1974-77; instr. Nova U., Ft. Lauderdale, 1989—; insvc. facilitator cadre Broward Schs., 1990—, clin. educator tng. cadre, 1994—, sch. improvement team chair, 1992—; mem. Nob Hill Literacy Team, 1996—. Author: Kindergarten Handbook, 1990; contbr. articles to profl. jours. Religious sch. chair Temple Emanu-el Ch., Ft. Lauderdale, 1986-91; vol. Girls Scouts U.S., Sunrise, Fla., 1989—. Grantee Broward Edn. Found, 1990, 94, 95, Broward County Schs., 1991, 93, 95, Citibank Success Fund, 1991, 95; finalist Tchr. of Yr. Broward County Fla., 1996. Mem. Internat. Reading Assn., Fla. Reading Assn., Broward County Reading Coun., Phi Delta Kappa. Democrat. Jewish. Home: 9660 NW 24th Ct Sunrise FL 33322-3252 Office: Nob Hill Elem 2100 NW 104th Ave Sunrise FL 33322-3515

NACHTIGAL, PATRICIA, equipment manufacturing company executive, general counsel; b. 1946. BA, Montclair State U.; JD, Rutgers U.; LLM, NYU. Tax atty. Ingersoll-Rand Co., Woodcliff Lake, N.J., 1979-83, dir. taxes and legal, 1983-88, sec., mng. atty., 1988-91, v.p., gen. counsel, 1991—. Office: Ingersoll-Rand Co 200 Chestnut Ridge Rd Westwood NJ 07675*

NACOL, MAE, lawyer; b. Beaumont, Tex., June 15, 1944; d. William Samuel and Ethel (Bowman) N.; children: Shawn Alexander Nacol, Catherine Regina Nacol. BA, Rice U., 1965; postgrad., S. Tex. Coll. Law, 1966-68. Bar: Tex. 1969, U.S. Dist. Ct. (so. dist.) Tex. 1969. Diamond buyer/appraiser Nacol's Jewelry, Houston, 1961—; pvt. practice law, Houston, 1969—. Author, editor ednl. materials on multiple sclerosis, 1981-85. Nat. dir. A.R.M.S. of Am. Ltd., Houston, 1984-85. Recipient Mayor's Recognition award City of Houston, 1972; Ford Found. fellow So. Tex. Coll. Law, Houston, 1964. Mem. Houston Bar Assn. (chmn. candidate com. 1970, chmn. membership com. 1971, chmn. lawyers referral com. 1972), Assn. Trial Lawyers Am., Tex. Trial Lawyers Assn., Am. Judicature Soc. (sustaining), Houston Fin. Coun. Women, Houston Trial Lawyers Assn. Presbyterian. Office: 600 Jefferson St Ste 850 Houston TX 77002-7326

NADA, JUANITA ANN, sociologist educator. BS in English, Bowling Green State U., 1965, MA in Sociology, 1967; PhD in Sociology, U. Minn., 1971. Cert. instr. Calif. C.C. Instr. sociology Normandale C.C., Bloomington, Minn., 1970-76, Palomar Coll., San Marcos, Calif., 1977-84, Golden Gate U., San Francisco, 1985-86; assoc. prof. sociology SUNY, Alfred, 1987-88; asst. prof. sociology St. Leo (Fla.) Coll., 1988-92, San Antonio Coll., 1992—. Grantee NEH, 1974. Mem. Am. Sociol. Assn., Tex. C.C. Tchrs. Assn., Alpha Kappa Delta, Sigma Tau Delta, Kappa Delta Pi.

NADELMAN, CYNTHIA J., writer, editor; b. Naples, Italy, Aug. 2, 1953; (parents Am. citizens); d. E. Jan and Joyce V. (Cavanah) N. AB, Bryn Mawr Coll., 1975. Editl. asst. ARTnews mag., N.Y.C., 1978-80, asst. editor, 1980-81, assoc. editor, 1981-83, sr. editor, 1983-84, freelance writer, editor, 1984—. Assoc. editor Drawing mag., 1984-86, contbg. editor ARTnews mag., 1984—; oral-history interviewer Archives of Am. Art, 1987-91; contbr. articles, reviews, poems to mags. and jours. Fellow Ingram Merrill Found., 1990, N.Y. Found. for the Arts, 1993. Mem. Internat. Art Critics Assn., Authors Guild. Home and Office: 205 W 91st St 5B New York NY 10024

NADELSON, CAROL COOPERMAN, psychiatrist, educator; b. Bklyn., Oct. 13, 1936; m. Theodore Nadelson, July 16, 1965; children: Robert, Jennifer. B.A. magna cum laude, Bklyn. Coll., 1957; M.D. with honors, U. Rochester, N.Y., 1961. Dir. med. student edn. Beth Israel Hosp., Boston, 1974-79, psychiatrist, 1977; assoc. prof. psychiatry Harvard U. Med. Sch., Boston, 1976-79; research scholar Radcliffe Coll., Cambridge, Mass., 1979-80; prof. psychiatry Tufts Med. Sch., Boston, 1979-95; vice chmn., dir. tng. and edn. dept. psychiatry Tufts-New Eng. Med. Ctr., Boston, 1979-93; clin. prof. psychiatry Harvard Med. Sch., Boston, 1995—. Editor: The Woman Patient, Vols. 1, 2 and 3, 1978, 82; Treatment Interventions in Human Sexuality, 1983; Marriage and Divorce: A Contemporary Perspective, 1984, Women Physicians in Leadership Roles, 1986, Training Psychiatrists for the '90s, 1987, Treating Chronically Mentally Ill Women, 1988, Family Violence, 1988, Women and Men: New Perspectives on Gender Differences, 1990, International Review of Psychiatry Vols. 1 & 2, 1993, 96, Major Psychiatric Disorders, 1982, The CHallenge of Change: Perspectives on Family, Work and Education, 1983; editor-in-chief Am. Psychiatric Press, Inc., 1986—, pres., CEO, 1995—; contbr. over 200 articles to profl. jours. Trustee Menninger Found., 1988—. Recipient Gold Medal award Mt. Airy Psychiat. Ctr., 1981, award Case Western Res. U., 1983, Elizabeth Blackwell award Am. Med. Women's Assn., 1985; Picker Found. grantee, 1982-83. Fellow Ctr. for Advanced Study in the Behavioral Scis., Am. Psychiat. Assn. (pres. 1985-86, Seymour D. Vestermark award 1992, Disting. Svc. award 1995); mem. Am. Coll. Psychiatrists (bd. regents 1991-94, Disting. Svc. award 1989), AMA (impaired physicians com. 1984, Sidney Cohen award 1988), Group for Advancement of Psychiatry (bd. dirs. 1984). Office: 30 Amory St Brookline MA 02146-3909

NADLER-HURVICH, HEDDA CAROL, public relations executive; b. Bronx, N.Y., June 15, 1944; d. Julius Louis and Julia (Nemzer) Cohen; m. David George Nadler, Oct. 3, 1965 (div. 1979); 1 child, Laura Lee Nadler; m. Burton Earl Hurvich, Dec. 8, 1984. BBA, Baruch Coll., 1965. V.p., sec. Irving L. Straus Assocs., Inc., N.Y.C., 1965-80; exec. v.p. Mount & Nadler Inc., N.Y.C., 1980—. Office: Mount & Nadler 425 Madison Ave New York NY 10017-1110

NADZICK, JUDITH ANN, accountant; b. Paterson, N.J., Mar. 6, 1948; d. John and Ethel (McDonald) N. BBA in Acctg., U. Miami (Fla.), 1971. CPA, N.J. Staff acct., mgr. Ernst & Whinney, C.P.A.s, N.Y.C., 1971-78; asst. treas. Gulf & Western Industries, Inc., N.Y.C., 1979-83, asst. v.p., 1980-82, v.p., 1982-83; v.p., corp. contr. United Mchts. and Mfrs. Inc., N.Y.C., 1983-85, sr. v.p., 1985-86, exec. v.p., CFO, 1986—, also bd. dirs. 1987—. Mem. AICPAs, Nat. Assn. Accts., N.Y. State Soc. CPAs, U. Miami Alumni Assn., Delta Delta Delta. Roman Catholic. Home: 280 Lincoln Ave Elmwood Park NJ 07407

NAESER, NANCY DEARIEN, geologist, researcher; b. Morgantown, W.Va., Apr. 15, 1944; d. William Harold and Katherine Elizabeth (Dearien) Cozad; m. Charles Wilbur Naeser, Feb. 6, 1982. BS, U. Ariz., 1966; PhD, Victoria U., Wellington, New Zealand, 1973. Geol. field asst. U.S. Geol. Survey, Flagstaff, Ariz., 1966; sci. editor, New Zealand Jour. Geology and Geophysics, New Zealand Dept Sci. and Indsl. Research, Wellington, 1974-76; postdoctoral rsch. assoc., U. Toronto, Ont., Can., 1976-79; postdoctoral rsch. assoc. U.S. Geol. Survey, Denver, 1979-81, geologist, 1981—; adj. prof. Dartmouth Coll., Hanover, N.H., 1985—, U. Wyo., Laramie, 1984—. Editor: Thermal History of Sedimentary Basins - Methods and Case Histories, 1989; contbr. articles on fission-track dating to profl. jours., 1977—. Docent Denver Zoo. Fulbright fellow New Zealand, 1967-68. Fellow Geol. Soc. Am.; mem. Am. Assn. Petroleum Geologists, Geol. Soc. New Zealand, Mortar Bd., Phi Kappa Phi. Methodist. Office: US Geol Survey Mail Stop 926 A 12201 Sunrise Valley Dr Herndon VA 20192

NAGEL, MARIA MARGHERITA LOUISA VISSAT, healthcare administrator; b. Greensburg, Pa., Mar. 18, 1942; d. Peter Louisa and Rose Delores (Episcopo) Vissat; m. Donald Lewis Nagel, Aug. 24, 1963; 1 child, Keith Barrett. BA in Chemistry, Knox Coll., Galesburg, Ill., 1963; MS, U. Nebr., 1986; PhD, 1991. Cert. nuclear medicine technologist. Tchr. Chemistry and Swimming Omaha Bd. Edn., 1970-72; asst. instr. U. Nebr. Med. Ctr., 1977-79; instr., 1979-87; program dir. Nuclear Medicine Tech. Sch. Allied Health Professions, 1977-92; asst. prof., 1987-92; chairperson Dept. Allied Health Nebr. Meth. Coll. Nursing and Allied Health, Omaha, 1992-94, chairperson depts. allied health and gen. edn., 1994-96, assoc. prof., 1992—, dir. grants and new program devel., 1996—; cons. Abelson, Taylor, Fitzsimmons, Inc., Chgo., 1987-88; external examiner Kuwait U., 1989, 90, 95, 96. Author: Nuclear Medicine Technology and Techniques 1st and 2nd edit., 1981, 89; reference editor: Journal of Nuclear Medicine Technology, 1989-93. Mem. Rotary Omaha West, 1993—, Bellevue Postal Adv. Bd., 1994; dir. Am. Cancer Soc., Omaha, 1994-96. Named Outstanding Tchr. of Yr. U. Nebr. Med. Ctr., Omaha, 1983-84. Mem. Soc. of Nuclear Medicine (pres. tech. section 1984-85, chmn. joint rev. com. on edn. in nuclear medicine 1992-94, mem. edn. and rsch. found.). Office: Nebraska Methodist College of Nursing & Allied Health 8501 W Dodge Rd Omaha NE 68114-3426

NAGGAR, CAROLE, artist; b. Cairo, June 16, 1951; came to the U.S., 1987; d. André Victor and Denise (Harari) N.; m. Frederick Kalman Ritchin, May 29, 1988; children: Ariel Solomon, Ezra Samuel. BA in Linguistics, Paris XII U.-Vincennes, 1971; BA in History of Art, Paris X U.-Hanterre, 1971; MA in Anthropology, Paris-Jussien U., 1973. Dir. summer edn. program Internat. Ctr. of Photography, N.Y.C.; adj. tchr. history of photography NYU; adj. tchr. contemporary criticism Sch. Visual Arts. One-woman shows Shelter for Contemporary Art, Suzanne Dellal Ctr., Tel-Aviv, 1991, Riverdale YM-YWHA, 1992, 94, Paris-N.Y.-Kent (Conn.) Gallery, 1993, Pulse Art Gallery, N.Y.C., 1995, Rockland Ctr. for Holocaust Studies, Spring Valley, N.Y., 1995, Adine Fine Arts, N.Y.C., 1996, others; works exhibited in group shows at Museo de Arte Carrillo Gil, Mexico, 1991, Ctr. for Book Arts, N.Y.C., 1991, Woodstock (N.Y.) Guild Kleinert Art Ctr., 1991, State Libr., Salem, Oreg., 1991, 494 Gallery, N.y.C., 1991, N.J. Ctr. for Visual Arts, Summit, 1991, Iztvan Karaly Mus., Budapest, 1992, NYU-Tisch Sch. of the Arts, 1993, 94, 95, Galerie Caroline Corre, Paris, 1993-94, others; represented in permanent collections The Franklin Furnace, N.Y., Ctr. for Book Arts, N.Y., Mus. Modern Art, Book Artists' Books Archive, N.Y., Agence Sygma, N.Y., Denise Cadé Gallery, N.Y., El Archivero, Mexico, Mus. Fine Arts, Budapest, others; contbr.: Mexico Through Foreign Eyes 1890-1990, 1992, Light Readings: Women on Photography, 1996; contbr. articles to profl. jours. Grantee Nat. Ctr. of Lit., Paris, 1981, 87, Rubin Found. Mem. Internat. Assn. Art Critics. Office: Internat Ctr Photography 1130 5th Ave New York NY 10028

NAGLE, DONNA PAAR, secondary and middle school art educator; b. Bethlehem, Pa., Feb. 10, 1967; d. James Frank and Martha Rae (Lockey) Paar; m. Paul George Nagle, Mar. 14, 1992. BS, Pa. State U., 1988; MEd, Kutztown U., 1991. Cert. tchr., Pa. Art tchr. Pa. State U., University Park, 1987, mus. docent trainer, 1987; art tchr. Lower Dauphin Sch. Dist., Hummelstown, Pa., 1988—; jewelry tchr. Harrisburg (Pa.) Art Assn., 1991-94; jewelry designer Knogist Designs, Camp Hill, Pa., 1992—; mem. arts adv. colloquium Pa. Dept. Edn., Harrisburg, 1989; appt. to Nat. Assessment Gov. Bd. Exercise Devel. Project, 1993; elected to Univ. Scholars Mortar Bd. Program, 1987-88. Vis. artist grantee Pa. Coun. for the Arts, 1989. Mem. NEA, Nat. Art Edn. Assn., Pa. Art Edn. Assn. (regional dir. 1989-93, elem. divsn. dir. 1993-94, conf. co-chairperson 1993, outstanding regional rep. award 1992), Harrisburg Art Assn, Alpha Omicron Pi (state dir. 1986-87, edn. chair 1987-88). Home: 54 S 18th St Camp Hill PA 17011-4810 Office: Lower Dauphin Mid Sch 251 Quarry Rd Hummelstown PA 17036-1723

NAGLE, JEAN SUSAN, sociologist, psychologist; b. Detroit; d. Peter and Hedy (Grusczynski) Karabacz; BS in Sociology, Wayne State U., 1952; postgrad. U. Chgo., 1953-55; MA, N.Mex. Highlands U., 1960, MS, 1967; PhD, Union Grad. Sch., 1977; postgrad. Bryn Mawr Inst. Women in Higher Edn. Adminstrn., 1981; m. Robert D. Nagle, Nov. 20, 1956; children—Carl A., Sonya L., Paula E. Diagnostic technician Vocat. Counseling Inst., Detroit, 1952; research technician United Auto Workers-CIO, Detroit, 1958; clin. psychology intern N.Mex. State Hosp., Las Vegas, 1962-63; clin. psychology trainee VA Hosp., Omaha and Lincoln, Nebr., 1963-64; instr. sociology N.W. Mo. State U., Maryville, 1965-70, prof. sociology and psychology, 1971-92. Bd. dirs. Inst. Discourse. N.W. Mo. State U. grantee, 1981, 82. Mem. Am. Psychol. Assn., Am. Sociol. Assn., Am. Psychol. Soc., Midwest Sociol. Soc., Psychology/Sociology Club, Mo. Psychol. Assn., World Federalists, Psi Chi, Pi Gamma Mu. Home: 2327 E Geneva Dr Tempe AZ 85282

NAGLE, SUZANNE KURTZ, human services coordinator; b. Washington, Nov. 8, 1965; d. Thomas Richardson and Marcia Mae (Burch) K.; m. Steven Mark Nagle, Oct. 12, 1991. BA, U. Richmond, 1987; MS, Va. Tech, 1994. Health promotions coord. Montgomery Regional Hosp., Blacksburg, Va., 1991-94, coord. vol. svcs., srs. advisor, 1994—; aerobics instr. Fitness Connection, Blacksburg, 1990—. Mem. safety com. Town of Blacksburg, 1995. Named New River Valley Woman of Distinction, Girl Scouts Am., 1995. Mem. Am. Heart Assn. (sec. 1993-94), Am. Cancer Soc. (pres. 1995—). Office: Montgomery Regional Hosp 3700 S Main St Blacksburg VA 24060

NAGLEE, ELFRIEDE KURZ, retired medical nurse; b. Phila., Mar. 13, 1932; d. Emil and Frida (Keppler) Kurz; m. David I. Naglee, Sept. 6, 1952; children: Joy, Miriam, Deborah, Joanna, David. Grad., Phila. Gen. Hosp., 1952. RN, Ga. Dir. nursing City County Hosp., LaGrange, Ga.; house supr. West Ga. Med. Ctr., LaGrange; staff nurse med. fl. West Ga. Med. Ctr., LaGange; ret., 1995. Mem. Ga. Nursing Assn. Home: 804 Piney Woods Dr La Grange GA 30240-2020

NAGORKA, STEFANIE, artist; b. Munich, Mar. 26, 1954; d. Henry Jozef and Diane Helen (Suchoff) N; m. Yuheng Shang; children: Adam, Michelle. BFA, Pratt Inst., 1974, MFA, 1979. Dir. Mapping No Boundries, Newark, N.Y.C., 1996—. Exhibits include The Drawing Ctr., N.Y.C., 1991, Information Gallery, N.Y.C., 1993-94, N.J. State Mus., Trenton, 1994, Sculpture Ctr. Gallery, N.Y.C., 1995. Mem. Mus. Modern Art. Recipient Excellence award David Adler Cultural Ctr., 1992; grantee Artists Space. Home: 317 Grove St Montclair NJ 07042

NAGTALON-MILLER, HELEN ROSETE, humanities educator; b. Honolulu, June 27, 1928; d. Dionicio Reyes and Fausta Dumbrigue (Rosete) N.; m. Robert Lee Ruley Miller, June 15, 1952. BEd, U. Hawaii, 1951; Diplôme, The Sorbonne, Paris, 1962; MA, U. Hawaii, 1967; PhD, Ohio State U., 1972. Cert. secondary education educator. Tchr. humanities Hawaii State Dept. Edn., Honolulu, 1951-63; supr. student tchrs. French lab. sch. Coll. of Edn. U. Hawaii, Honolulu, 1963-66, instr. French, coord. French courses Coll. Arts and Scis., 1966-69; teaching asst. Coll. Edn. Ohio State U., Columbus, 1970-72; instr. French lab. sch. Coll. Edn. U. Hawaii, Honolulu, 1974-76; adminstr. bilingual-bicultural edn. project Hawaii State Dept. Edn., Honolulu, 1976-77; coord. disadvantaged minority recruitment program Sch. Social Work, U. Hawaii, Honolulu, 1977-84; coord. tutor tng. program U. Hawaii, Honolulu, 1984-86; program dir. Multicultural Multifunctional Resource Ctr., Honolulu, 1986-87; vis. prof. Sch. Pub. Health, ret. U. Hawaii, Honolulu, 1987-92, 92—; bd. dirs. Hawaii Assn. Lang. Tchrs., Honolulu, 1963-66, Hawaii Com. for the Humanities, 1977-83; mem. statewide adv. coun. State Mental Health Adv. Com., Honolulu, 1977-82; task force mem. Underrepresentation of Filipinos in Higher Edn., Honolulu, 1984-86. Author: (with others) Notable Women in Hawaii, 1984; contbr. articles to profl. jours. Chairperson edn. and counseling subcom. First Gov.'s Commn. on Status of Women, Honolulu, 1964; vice chairperson Honolulu County Com. on the Status of Women, 1975-76, Hawaii State Dr. Martin Luther King Jr. Commn., Honolulu, 1982-85; pres. Filipino Hist. Soc. of Hawaii, 1980—; mem. Hawaii State Adv. Com. to U.S. Commn. on Civil Rights, 1981—, chairperson, 1982-85; bd. dirs. Japanese Am. Citizens League Honolulu chpt., 1990—, mem. Hawaiian Sovereignty com., 1994—. Women of Distinction, Honolulu County Com. on Status of Women, 1982; recipient Nat. Edn. Assn. award for Leadership in Asian and Pacific Island Affairs, NEA, 1985, Alan F. Saunders award ACLU in Hawaii, 1986, Disting. Alumni award U. Hawaii Alumni Affairs Office, 1994. Mem. Filipino Am. Nat. Hist. Soc., Filipino Coalition for Solidarity, Gabriela Network (Hawaii chpt.), Filipino Cmty. Ctr., NOW, Alliance Française of Hawaii. Democrat. Home and Office: 3201 Beaumont Woods Pl Honolulu HI 96822-1423

NAGY, CHRISTA FIEDLER, biochemist; b. Marienbad, Czech Republic, July 8, 1943; d. Herbert A. Fiedler and Anna C. (Gluth) Rathmann; m. Bela Imre Nagy, Aug. 22, 1969; 1 child, Byron. BS in Biology, Fairleigh Dickinson U., 1967, MS in Biochemistry, 1974; PhD in Biochemistry, Rutgers U., 1981. Assoc. scientist Hoffmann-La Roche Inc., Nutley, N.J., 1975-80, sr. scientist, 1981-88, assoc. rsch. investigator, 1988-95; contract med. writer

Nutley, 1996—. Mem. AAAS, N.Y. Acad. Scis., Am. Soc. Biol. Chemists, Am. Med. Writers Assn. Roman Catholic. Office: Hoffmann LaRoche Inc 340 Kingsland St Nutley NJ 07110-1150

NAGY, CHRISTINE LEE, rehabilitation, home care and geriatrics nurse, nursing educator; b. N.Y.C., July 11, 1961; d. Augustus Richard Monturo and Martha Kay Childress Ferris; m. William John Nagy, Aug. 19, 1989; 1 child, Alexander Christopher; 1 stepchild, Angeline Nicole. BA in Communications, BSN, Cleve. State U., 1990. Cert. in gerontology, rehab. and nursing adminstrn. Staff/charge nurse Metrohealth Med. Ctr., Cleve., 1988-90; charge nurse Jackson Meml. Hosp., Miami, Fla., 1990-92; unit mgr. geriatric rehab. and long term care Saginaw (Mich.) Community Hosp., 1992; charge nurse, nursing home care and rehab. unit Saginaw VA Hosp., 1992-93; unit mgr. geriatric rehab. unit Mt. Sinai Med. Ctr., Miami Beach, Fla., 1993-94; home care rehab. coord. Marymount Hosp., Garfield Heights, Ohio, 1994—; mem. policy, procedure, nurses wk., long term care coms. and behavior modification team Saginaw Community Hosp., 1992—. BLS instr. ARC/Am. Heart Assn., Cleve., Miami, 1990, 91, continuing edn./insvc. educator, 1990—; active Broward County Schs. PTA, 1993, 94, Garfield Heights Schs. PTA, 1994, Black River Schs. PTA; cub scout den leader, coach Seminole Dist. and Greater Cleve. Dist. Boy Scouts Am.; vol. Lakewood Meals on Wheels, Ohio, 1987-90, Garfield Heights Meals on Wheels; mem. St. Stephen's Ch. Ladies Guild, West Salem, Ohio; coaching asst. youth/boys divsn. Ashland Soccer Assn. Mem. ANA, Nat. League for Nursing, Assn. Rehab. Nurses, Mich. Nurses Assn., Fla. Nurses Assn., Ohio Nurses Assn., Nat. Spinal Cord Nurses. Republican. Roman Catholic.

NAGY, IVONNE LUGO, lawyer; b. Santurce, P.R., Sept. 4, 1949; d. Jose Angel Lugo and Maria Teresa Sandin; m. Joseph Robert Nagy, Sept. 11, 1970 (div. Sept. 1984); children: Steven, Eric, Jennifer. Diploma, U. P.R., 1969; BA, Fordham U., 1980; JD, Yale U., 1983. Bar: N.Y. 1984. Assoc. Chadbourne & Parke, N.Y.C., 1983-87; spl. counsel Am. Stock Exch., N.Y.C., 1987—; Mentor N.Y.C. Partnership, 1992-94. Mem. N.Y. County Lawyers Assn., P.R. Bar Assn., Hispanic Nat. Bar Assn. Democrat. Roman Catholic. Home: 556 17th St Apt 1 Brooklyn NY 11215 Office: Am Stock Exch Inc 86 Trinity Pl New York NY 10006

NAGYS, ELIZABETH ANN, environmental issues educator; b. St. Louis; d. Dallas and Miriam (Miller) Nichols; m. Sigi Nagys, Feb. 7, 1970; children: Eric M., Jennifer R., Alex E. BS., So. Ill. U. Extension, Edwardsville, 1970. Cert. tchr., Mo., Ill. Announcer Sta. KMTY, Clovis, N.Mex., 1970-71; substitue tchr. Ritneour Sch. Dist., Overland, Mo., 1977-78; instr. biology, environ. issues Southwestern Mich. Coll., Dowagiac, Mich., 1988-92; exec. v.p. Profl. Sound Designers, Goshen, Ind., 1994—; customer svc. coord. Meijer, Inc., 1995—; reviewer textbooks Harcourt, Brace & Co., 1993. Bd. dirs. United Meth. Ch., Marvin Park, 1979-84; coord. United Meth. Women, 1980-87; mem. Hazardous Waste Com. for Elkhart County, Ind., 1991-94; charter mem. Holocaust Meml. Mus.; assoc. mem. Art Inst. Chgo.; active Nat. Arbor Day Found. Mem. AAUW (v.p. Goshen 1994-95), Nat. Audubon Soc., Sierra Club, Welcome Wagon Club.

NAGY-ZEKMI, SILVIA MARGIT, foreign languages educator; b. Budapest, Hungary, May 15, 1953; came to U.S., 1980; d. János and Maria (Vajda) Nagy; m. Nadir Zekmi, May 29, 1995. MA in L.Am. Lit., MA in Hungarian Lit., Eötvös Loránd U., Budapest, 1980, PhD in Hispanic Lit. cum laude, 1981. Asst. prof. U. Richmond, Va., 1984-87, Loyola U., New Orleans, 1987-90; asst. prof. dept. modern langs. Cath. U. Am., Washington, 1990—; cons. U. Tex. Press, Austin, 1993. Author: Historia de la Canción Folklórica de los Andes, 1989, Paralelismos Transtlánticos, 1996; m. editl. bd. Scripta Humanistica, 1991—. Rsch. grantee U. Richmond, Chile, 1986, Loyola U., Chile, 1988, Cath. U. Am., Ecuador, 1991. Mem. MLA, L.Am. Studies Assn., Hungarian Am. Educators Assn., L.Am. Indian Lits. Assn., Coun. Francophone Studies, Internat. Assn. Semiotics. Office: Cath U Am Dept Modern Langs Michigan Ave NE Washington DC 20064

NAHEMOW, IRIS STEIN, non-profit administrator, consultant, educator, writer; b. Pitts., June 23, 1938; d. Morris and Rhea (Pearlman) Stein; m. Michael Altman, July 19, 1959 (div. Nov. 1968); m. Martin D. Nahemow, June 1, 1969; children: Deborah Baron, Lisa Young. BS in Edn., U. Pitts., 1960; MS in Edn., U. Pa., 1963; PhD, U. Pitts., 1971. Tchr. Phila. Sch. Dist., 1960-63; dir. cmty. svcs. Alleghany East Mental Health/Mental Retardation, Pitts., 1971-84; exec. dir. Big Bros./Big Sisters, Pitts., 1984-88; regional dir. Jewish Nat. Fund, Pitts., 1989—; prin. Nahemow Assoc., Pitts., 1996—; adj. prof. U. Pitts., 1993—; lectr., workshop instr. U. W.Va., Morgantown, 1991—. Bd. dirs. Riverview Childrens Ctr., Verona, Pa., 1986—. Mem. Nat. Soc. Fund Raising Execs. (cert.). Home: 1238 Bellerock St Pittsburgh PA 15217 Office: Nahemow Assoc 1238 Bellerock St Pittsburgh PA 15217

NAHIGIAN, ALMA LOUISE, technical documentation administrator; b. Peabody, Mass., Sept. 17, 1936; d. Walter Daniel and Alma Edith (Knowles) Higgins; m. Franklin Roosevelt Nahigian, April 30, 1961; daus.: Ellen Elise, Dana Leigh, Catherine Elizabeth. AA, Boston U., 1956, BS, 1958, MS in Journalism, 1963. Editor nat. and spl. projects Boston U. News Bur., 1959-61, 63-64; writer, editor Nutrition Found., N.Y.C., 1961-63; writer, editor, cons. Cambridge (Mass.) Communicators, Tech. Edn. Research Ctr., Harvard U., Cambridge, Smart Software, Inc., Belmont, Mass., 1970-82; tech. editor Digital Equipment Corp., Bedford, Mass., 1979-84; prin. tech. writer, editor Wang Labs, Inc., Lowell, Mass., 1984—, documentation sect. mgr. editorial, 1984-93; sr. adv. tech. editor Dun & Bradstreet Software, Westborough, Mass., 1993-95; prin. tech. editor Info. Resources, Inc., Waltham, Mass., 1995—; instr. Harvard U., Cambridge, 1987-88, Radcliffe Coll., Cambridge, 1979; mem. adj. faculty Northeastern U., Boston, 1989—, guest lectr., 1979, 88. Contbr. numerous articles to profl. pubs. Active LWV, Arlington, Mass., 1963-73. Fellow Soc. Tech. Communication (assoc., bd. dirs., Boston chpt. pres. 1992-93, co-mgr. soc.-level com. 1993-95, mem. 1995—, judge internat. level competitions 1993—, Tech. Pubs. Competition Excellence award 1989, 93, 95, Art Competitions Excellence award 1992, co-presenter). Democrat. Roman Catholic. Home: 30 Venner Rd Arlington MA 02174-8028 Office: Info Resources Inc 200 5th Ave Waltham MA 02154

NAIL, RUBY JEANNE, social worker; b. Longview, Wash., Feb. 20, 1949; d. William Alfred Secor and Vella Dale Wise; m. Gary Dean Nail, Aug. 21, 1979; 1 child, Anna Marie. Grad. high sch., Kelso, Wash. With child protection divsn. Dept. Social Svcs., Honolulu, 1985, with mental health divsn., 1988; subs. tchr. Dept. Edn., Honolulu, 1992; with case mgmt. divsn. CPS, Honolulu, 1988. Author: Beyond The Wall, 1996. Mem. Soc. 173rd Airborne, Reading Oasis Writers Guild (charter). Roman Catholic. Home: 802 Harris St Kelso WA 98626

NAJJAR, TAMARA LITCHFIELD, mail order business owner; b. Elgin, Ill., June 2, 1958; d. Kelmar Thomas and Betty Joan (Light) Litchfield; m. Idris M. Najjar, Jan. 5, 1986; children: Zakariya, Suraya, Ali. AS in Fire Protection, AS in Safety, We. Ky. U., Bowling Green, 1983. Lic. cosmetologist. Asst. supr. Opryland USA Inc., Nashville, 1983-86; asst. mgr. Hitachi Am., Nashville, 1986-91; owner, mgr. TJ Designs, Riverside, Calif., 1993—. Author, pub.: Beauty Shop in A Book, 1993. Fundraising chair Islamic Acad., Riverside, 1993-94, yearbook organizer, 1993. Mem. Mosque of Riverside. Democrat. Muslim. Home and Office: 273 Newell Dr Riverside CA 92507-3106

NAKAGAWA, JEAN HARUE, diversified corporation executive; b. Honolulu, Sept. 21, 1943; d. Herbert Haruo and Dorothy Mitsue (Nishimura) Yorita; m. Melvin Katsumi Nakagawa, July 16, 1966; 1 child, Lisa. BBA, U. Hawaii, 1965, MBA, 1968. Rsch. asst. First Hawaiian Bank, Honolulu, 1965-68; dir. planning AMFAC, Inc., Honolulu, 1968-73; v.p. Island Fed. Savings and Loan, Honolulu, 1973-75; dir. rsch. and planning Servco Pacific Inc., Honolulu, 1975—, asst. v.p., 1975-77, v.p., 1977-79, group v.p., 1979-84, sr. v.p., 1984-88, exec. v.p., 1988—; bd. dirs. Servco Pacific Inc., Servco Fin. Corp. Trustee Honolulu Theater for Youth, 1982-89, Hawaii Pub. Employees Health Fund, 1985-89; mem. devel. com. Hawaii Baptist Acad.; bd. dirs. ARC; mem. Pacific Asian Affairs Coun., Hawaii Econ. Edn. Coun., Hawaii Fgn. Rels. Coun. Mem. Hawaii Soc. Corp. Planners (v.p., pres.), Hawaii Econ. Assn. (pres., v.p.), Planning Execs. Inst. (pres.), Orgn. Women Leaders (v.p.). Club: Plaza.

NAKAJIMA, YASUKO, medical educator; b. Osaka, Japan, Jan. 8, 1932; came to U.S., 1962, 69; d. Isao and Taeko Nakagawa; m. Shigehiro Nakajima; children: Hikeko H., Gene A. MD, U. Tokyo, 1955, PhD, 1962. Intern U. Tokyo Sch. Medicine, 1955-56, resident, 1956-57, instr., 1962-67; assoc. prof. Purdue U., West Lafayette, Ind., 1969-76, prof., 1976-88; prof. anatomy and cell biology U. Ill. Coll. Medicine, Chgo., 1988—; vis. rsch. fellow Coll. Physicians and Surgeons, Columbia U., N.Y.C., 1962-64; asst. rsch. anatomist UCLA Sch. Medicine, 1964-65; vis. rsch. fellow Cambridge U., 1967-69. Contbr. articles to sci. jours. Fulbright travel grantee, 1962-65. Mem. AAAS, Am. Physiol. Soc., Soc. Neurosci., Am. Soc. Cell Biology, Am. Assn. Anatomists, Biophys. Soc., Marine Biol. Lab. Corp. Office: U Ill Coll Medicine at Chgo Dept Anatomy-Cell Biology m/c 512 808 S Wood St Chicago IL 60612-7300

NAKATA, CHERYL LYNNE, physical education educator; b. Chgo., Jan. 28, 1958; d. Hitoshi and Chiyeko Sakurai; m. Gary Yoshio Nakata, July 19, 1980; children: Jennifer Jun, Kaycie Kiku. BS in Phys. Edn., Calif. State U., Long Beach, 1980. Cert. tchr. phys. edn. Phys. edn. tchr., coach L.A. Unified Sch. Dist., Gardena (Calif.) H.S., 1981—; basketball and softball dept. chair Gardena H.S., 1993—, all-city selection com., 1994. Recipient Asian Pacific Island Day of the Tchr. Recognition award Assn. Pacific Island Educators, Inc., 1993. Mem. AAHPERD, NEA, Calif. Tchrs. Assn., Calif. Assn. Phys. Edn., Recreation, and Dance, Coaches of L.A. Women's Sports. Office: Gardena HS 1301 W 182nd St Gardena CA 90248-3322

NAKAYAMA, PAULA AIKO, justice; b. Honolulu, Oct. 19, 1953; m. Charles W. Totto; children: Elizabeth Murakami, Alexander Totto. BS, U. Calif., Davis, 1975; JD, U. Calif., 1979. Bar: Hawaii 1979. Dep. pros. atty. City and County of Honolulu, 1979-82; ptnr. Shim, Tam & Kirimitsu, Honolulu, 1982-92; judge 1st Cir. Ct. State of Hawaii, Oahu, 1992-93; justice State of Hawaii Supreme Ct., Honolulu, 1993—. Mem. Am. Judicature Soc., Hawaii Bar Assn., Sons and Daughters of 442. Office: Ali'iolani Hale 417 S King St Honolulu HI 96813-2902 Address: PO Box 2560 Honolulu HI 96804-2560

NAKER, MARY LESLIE, export transportation company executive; b. Elgin, Ill., July 6, 1954; d. Robert George and Marilyn Jane (Swain). BS in Edn., No. Ill. U., 1976, MS in Edn., 1978, postgrad., 1980; postgrad., Coll. Fin. Planning, 1990. Cert. tchr., Ill., fin. paraplanner. Retail sales clk. Fin'n Feather Farm, Dundee, Ill., 1972-75; self-employed tchr. South Elgin, Ill., 1974-78; teaching asst. Sch. Dist #13, Bloomingdale, Ill., 1976-78, substitute tchr.; office mgr. Tempo 21, Carol Stream, Ill., 1978-82, LaGrange, Ill., 1982-85; sales coord. K&R Delivery, Hinsdale, Ill., 1986-89; fin. planner coord. Elite Adv. Svcs., Inc., Schaumburg, Ill., 1989-90; adminstrv. coord. Export Transports, Inc., Elk Grove Village, Ill., 1990—. Leader Girl Scouts U.S.A., 1972-77, camp counselor, 1972-79. Recipient Music Scholarship PTA, U. Wis., 1967, PTA, U. Iowa, 1968-69. Mem. Nat. Geographic Soc., Smithsonian Assn. Lutheran. Home: 2020 Clearwater Way Elgin IL 60123-2588 Office: Export Transports Inc 611 Eagle Dr Bensenville IL 60106

NALEWAKO, MARY ANNE, corporate secretary; b. Johnstown, Pa., Aug. 15, 1934; d. Charles and Margaret (Timothy) Rooney; m. Michael S. Nalewako, Apr. 8, 1961; 1 child, Michael. BSBA, Coll. St. Elizabeth, Convent Station, N.J., 1987. Adminstrv. asst. to chmn. Gen. Pub. Utilities, Parsippany, N.J., 1975-88, corp. sec., 1988—. Recipient Twin award Central (N.J.) YWCA, 1989, award Exec. Women of N.J., 1992. Mem. Am. Soc. Corp. Secs., Seraphic Soc., Spring Brook Country Club. Office: Gen Pub Utilities Corp 100 Interpace Pky Parsippany NJ 07054-1149

NALL, LUCIA LYNN, controller; b. Jackson, Miss., Nov. 22, 1954; d. Aldert S. and Jean (Eaves) Nall. BA in History, Belhaven Coll., 1975, BS in Acctg., 1981; MBA, Miss. Coll., 1994. Acct. Miss. State Bd. Health, Jackson, 1979-85; asst. contr. Miller-Wills Aviation, Jackson, 1985-87; contr. Alston, Rutherford, Tardy & Van Slyke, Jackson, 1987-96; owner Freight Brokers, Brandon, Miss., 1996—. Mem. NAFE, Inst. Mgmt. Accts. Home: 930 N Livingston Rd Jackson MS 39213-9207 Office: Freight Brokers 108 Office Park Dr Brandon MS 39043

NALLEY, ELIZABETH ANN, chemistry educator; b. Catron, Mo., July 8, 1942; d. Arthur E. and Thelma L. (King) Frazier; m. Robert L. Mullican, Jan. 2, 1986; 1 child, George L. BS, Northeastern Okla. State U., 1965; MS, Okla. State U., 1969; PhD, Tex. Woman's U., 1975. High sch. tchr. Muskogee (Okla.) Ctrl. High Sch., 1964-65; instr. Cameron U., Lawton, Okla., 1969-72; asst. prof. Cameron U., Lawton, 1972-75, assoc. prof., 1975-78, prof., 1978—. Contbr. articles to profl. jours. Recipient Disting. Svc. award Cameron U., 1995. mem. AAAS, Assn. for Advancement of Computers in Edn., Am. Chem. Soc. (councilor 1980—, sec. div. profl. rels. 1987—, sec. divsn. profl. rel. 1987-96, chair-elect divsn. profl. rels. 1996, Okla. Chemist award 1992, divsn. profl. rels. Henry Hill award, 1996), Am. Inst. Chemists (nat. bd. dirs.), Phi Kappa Phi (regent 1981-89, nat. v.p. 1989-92, nat. pres.-elect 1992-95, nat. pres. 1995—, Disting. Faculty award 1978), Sigma Xi, Sigma Pi Sigma, Iota Sigma Pi. Home: RR 3 Box 176-1 Chickasha OK 73018-9544 Office: Cameron U Dept of Chemistry 2800 W Gore Blvd Lawton OK 73505-6320

NALLS, ANNE LINDSAY, gifted and talented education educator; b. Macon, Ga., Oct. 20, 1936; d. Tom Wilson and Elizabeth Furman (Jones) N.; m. Henry Chovine Croom, Aug. 25, 1956 (div.); children: Meagan, Lindsay; m. Stephen Hill McCleary, June 18, 1989. AB, Wesleyan Coll., 1960; M in Counseling, Ariz. State U., 1979; EdD, U. Ga., 1986. English tchr. Willingham Boys' H.S., Macon, Ga., 1960-61; English and Modern Dance tchr. Wesleyan Coll., Macon, 1961-62; dir. religious edn. Unitarian-Universalist Ch., Phoenix, 1976; tchr. Banks County H.S., Homer, Ga., 1979-80; lead tchr. Elbert County Gifted Program, 1980-83; dir., tchr. Athens Middle Sch. for Arts and Scis., 1987-88; spl. edn. coord. N.E. Ga. Regional Ednl. Svc. Agy., 1988-89; coord. program for the gifted and talented Bowling Green (Ohio) City Schs., 1990-95; coord. Sandusky Co. Edn. Svc. Ctr., 1996—; co-chair Ohio Assn. for Gifted Children State Conv., 1993; chair Ohio Future Problem Solving Bowl; adj. asst. prof. Bowling Green State Univ.; part-time assoc. prof. U. Ga., Athens. Bd. dirs. LWV, Bowling Green, 1992-3; vol. Habitat for Humanity, St. Paul's Homeless Shelter; bd. dirs. Unitarian-Universalist Ch., 1994, pres. 1993-94; area rep. Youth for Understanding, Athens, 1980-89, host parent for five exch. students, 1980-89, Ch. sch. tchr., Athens; bd. trustees Phoenix Elem. Sch. Dist. #1, pres. 1978-79, campfire leader, Phoenix; vol. probation officer Maricopa Youth Dept., Phoenix; pres., treas. Kenilworth Sch. PTO; vol. tutor Phoenix Elem. Sch. Torrance scholar Torrance Ctr. for Creative Studies, 1990. Mem. AAUW, Nat. Assn. for Gifted Children, Ohio Assn. of Gifted Children, N.W. Ohio Assn. of Coordinators of Gifted, Amnesty Internat., Greenpeace, Phi Delta Kappa, Delta Kappa Gamma. Office: Sandusky Co Edn Svc Ctr 602 W State St Fremont OH 44320

NALLS, GAYIL LYNN, artist; b. Washington, July 17, 1953; d. Hampton Roberts and Doris Winifred (Fields) N.; m. Winfred Overholser III, Feb. 17, 1979 (dec. Oct. 1983); m. John William Steele, Aug. 15, 1992; 1 child, Morgan Nalls. Student, Va. Commonwealth U., 1971-72, Parsons Sch. Design, 1972-74, Am. U., Washington, 1974, Corcoran Sch. Art, 1975-76. Tchr. Parsons Sch. Design, N.Y.C., 1986—; ptnr. Election Satellite Network, Tribeca Film Ctr., N.Y.C., 1991-94; co-founder Digital Network TV, N.Y.C., 1993—. One-person shows include Susan Caldwell Gallery, N.Y.C., 1983, U. Richmond, Va., 1988, Baumgartner Galleries, Washington, 1990, Phillipe Staib Gallery, N.Y.C., 1992, Downtown Cmty. TV Ctr., N.Y.C., 1992; exhibited in group shows at Indpls. Mus. Art, 1984, Corcoran Gallery Art, Washington, 1988, U.S. Mission, Berlin, West Germany, 1988, Bruce Mus., Greenwich, Conn., 1988, Southeastern Ctr. Contemporary Art, Winston-Salem, 1989, Monastery of Santa Clara, Seville, Spain, 1992, Pretoria Art Mus., South Africa, 1994, Hand Workshop, Richmond, 1995, NGO Forum on Women '95 Film Festival, Huairou, China, 1995, (Internet exhibition) Inst. Studies in the Arts Ariz. State U., 1995, Internat. Ctr. N.Y., 1996; represented in permanent collections at Met. Mus.Art, Nat. Mus. Am. Art, Corocoran Gallery; author: The Laments, 1990, (screenplay) X-tips, 1994; author, producer: Permutatude, 1988-94, Gal Gaia/Mother Right, 1990; producer, dir. The Laments, 1994; dir., prodr. (documentary) A Common Destiny: Thomas Banyacya, The Hopi Prophecy, Jewell Praying Wolfe James, (Talking Head documentary) Walking in Both Worlds, 1989, Tom Doston Speaking for Traditional Chief William Commanda: Message from the Elders of the Seven Fires Prophecy, 1995; choreographer (video) Wheels Over Indian Trails, 1993. Conceiver, designer, constructor Commn. Fine Arts and Landmark, Winfred Overholser III Meml. Sculpture Garden, Georgetown U. Hosp., Washington, 1983-85; conceier The Lab Sch. Portfolio for Lab. Sch. Washington, 1986; bd. dirs., curator 10thAnniversary Exhbn. Washington Project for the Arts, 1985-88. Recipient award EarthPeace Internat. Film Festival, Burlington, Vt., 1991, award of merit 20th Biennial Exhbn., U. Del., Newark, 1982, Purchase award Richard B. Russell Bldg. and U.S. Ct. House, Atlanta, 1982, Bay Bank Valley Trust Co. award 66th Nat. Exhbn. George Walter Vincent Smith Art Mus., Springfield, Mass., 1985; D.C. Commn. Arts. and Humanities fellow, Washington, 1987.

NAMIAS, JUNE, history educator, writer; b. Boston, May 17, 1941; d. Foster and Helen (Needle) N.; m. Peter Edmund Slavin, June 1965 (div. Oct. 1970); 1 child, Robert Victor Slavin. BA with honors, U. Mich., 1962; MA in Tchg., Harvard U., 1963; PhD in History, Brandeis U., 1989. H.s. tchr. history Newton (Mass.) Pub. Schs., 1965-87; vis. asst prof. history MIT, Cambridge, Mass., 1987-91, Wheaton Coll., Norton, Mass., 1991-92; assoc. prof. history U. Alaska, 1992—. Author: First Generation: In the Words of Twentieth-Century American Immigrants, 1978, 92, White Captives: Gender and Ethnicity on the American Frontier, 1607-1862, 1993; editor: A Narrative of the Life of Mrs. Mary Jemison, 1992; contbr. poetry to various jours. Mem. Orgn. Am. Historians, Am. Hist. Assn., Soc. Ethnohistory, Soc. Early Am. History. Jewish. Office: U Alaska Dept History 3211 Providence Dr Anchorage AK 99508

NAMKUNG, XHANA MARIE, advertising executive; b. San Diego, Jan. 15, 1964; d. Paul S. Namkung and Leota Carolyn (Hamilton) Kotler. AA magna cum laude, L.A. Valley Coll., Van Nuys, Calif., 1984; BA with distinction, U. Hawaii, 1988. Office mgr. Kingsound Studios, North Hollywood, Calif., 1984-85; adminstrv. office mgr. Western Equipment Dist. Co., Van Nuys, Calif., 1984-90; legal sec. Northridge, Calif., 1989-92; lead student svc. rep. Learning Tree U., Chatsworth, Calif., 1991-93; exec. asst. fin. EMI Music Distbn., Woodland Hills, Calif., 1992-94, rsch. corr. nat. advt., 1994-95, sr. coord. nat. advt., 1995—. Vol. Musicares, L.A., 1995—. Mem. Women in Comm., Inc. Office: EMI Music Distbn 21700 Oxnard St Ste 700 Woodland Hills CA 91367

NANAGAS, MARIA TERESITA CRUZ, pediatrician, educator; b. Manila, Jan. 21, 1946; came to U.S., 1971; d. Ambrosio and Maria (Pasamonte) Cruz; m. Victor N. Nanagas, Jr.; children: Victor III, Valerie, Vivian. BS, U. of the Philippines, 1965, MD, 1970. Diplomate Am. Bd. Pediat. Intern, resident St. Elizabeth's Hosp., Boston, 1971-74; fellow in ambulatory pediat. North Shore Children's Hosp., Salem, Mass., 1974-75; active staff medicine Children's Med. Ctr., Dayton, Ohio, 1976—, head divsn. gen. pediat., 1988-90, 95—, co-interim head ambulatory pediat., 1989-90, med. dir. ambulatory pediat., dir. ambulatory svcs., 1990—; clin. asst. prof. pediat. Wright State U., Dayton, 1977-83, clin. assoc. prof. pediat., 1983—, head divsn. gen. pediat., 1993—, selective dir., 1989—; dir., preceptor Wright State U. resident's family clinic Children's Med. Ctr., 1989—, attending physician family practice programs, 1978—. Active Miami Valley Lead Poisoning Prevention Coalition, 19926. Fellow Am. Acad. Pediat.; mem. Western Ohio Pediat. Soc. Office: Children's Med Ctr Health Clinic 1 Childrens Plz Dayton OH 45404-1898

NANAVATI, GRACE LUTTRELL, dancer, choreographer, instructor; b. Springfield, Ill., Oct. 2, 1951; d. Curtis Loren and Mary Grace (Leaverton) Luttrell; m. P.J. Nanavati, May 11, 1985; 1 child, William P. BA, Butler U., 1973; MA, Sangamon State U., 1978. Owner, dir. Dance Arts Studio, Springfield, 1973—; artistic dir. Springfield (Ill.) Ballet Co., 1975—; compulsory arts programming com. Sch. Dist. 186, Springfield, 1990—; dance panel Ill. Arts Coun., 1990-92, 94-96. Vol. Meml. Med. Ctr., Springfield, 1980-88. Named Women of Yr., YMCA, Springfield, 1982; recipient Mayor award for Arts, City of Springfield, 1985, Best of Springfield award Ill. Times, Springfield, 1990. Home: 1501 Williams Blvd Springfield IL 62704-2346 Office: Dance Arts Studio Inc 2820 Macarthur Blvd Springfield IL 62704-5017

NANCE, BETTY LOVE, librarian; b. Nashville, Oct. 29, 1923; d. Granville Scott and Clara (Mills) Nance. BA in English magna cum laude, Trinity U., 1957; AM in Library Sci., U. Mich., 1958. Head dept. acquisitions Stephen F. Austin U. Library, Nacogdoches, Tex., 1958-59; librarian 1st Nat. Bank, Fort Worth, 1959-61; head catalog dept. Trinity U., San Antonio, 1961-63; head tech. processes U. Tex. Law Library, Austin, 1963-66; head catalog dept. Tex. A&M U. Library, College Station, 1966-69; chief bibliographic services Washington U. Library, St. Louis, 1970; head dept. acquisitions Va. Commonwealth U. Library, Richmond, 1971-73; head tech. processes Howard Payne U. Library, Brownwood, Tex., 1974-79; library dir. Edinburg (Tex.) Pub. Library, 1980-91; pres. Edinburg Com. for Salvation Army. Mem. ALA, Pub. Library Assn., Tex. Library Assn., Hidalgo County Library Assn. (v.p. 1980-81, pres. 1981-82), Pan Am. Round Table of Edinburg (corr. sec. 1986-88, assoc. dir. 1989-90), Edinburg Bus. and Profl. Womens Club (founding bd. dirs., pres. 1986-87, bd. dirs. 1987-88), Alpha Lambda Delta, Alpha Chi. Methodist. Club: Zonta Club of San Antonio (bd. dirs. 1996—). Home: 5359 Fredericksburg Rd Apt 806 San Antonio TX 78229-3549

NANCE, MARTHA MCGHEE, rehabilitation nurse; b. Huntington, W.Va., Jan. 24, 1944; d. Orme Winford and Sadie Mae (Dudley) McGhee; m. John Edgar Nance, Mar. 17, 1990; children: Laura Beckner, Suzie Brickey. RN, St. Mary's Sch. Nursing, Huntington, W.Va., 1980; student, Marshall U., Huntington, W.Va., 1978-88. Cert. rehab. nurse, cert. case mgr. Surg. head nurse Huntington Hosp. Inc., nursing supr.; quality assurance dir. Am. Hosp. for Rehab., Huntington, 1988-89, DON, 1989-90; rehab. charge nurse Am. Putnam Nursing and Rehab. Ctr., Hurricane, W.Va., 1990—; mgr. health svcs. Mountain State Blue Cross/Blue Shield, Charleston, W.Va., 1995—, mgr. precert., case mgmt. and med. rev., 1995—. Mem. Assn. for Practitioners in Infection Control. Home: RR 4 Box 100 Hurricane WV 25526-9351

NANCE, MARY JOE, secondary education educator; b. Carthage, Tex., Aug. 7, 1921; d. F. F. and Mary Elizabeth (Knight) Born; m. Earl C. Nance, July 12, 1946; 1 child, David Earl. BBA, North Tex. State U., 1953; postgrad., Northwestern State U. La., 1974; ME, Antioch U., 1978. Tchr., Port Isabel (Tex.) Ind. Sch. Dist., 1953-79; tchr. English, Tex., 1965, Splendora (Tex.) High Sch., 1979-80, McLeod, Tex., 1980-81, Bremond, Tex., 1981-84. Vol. tchr. for Indian students, 1964-65, 79. Served with WAAC, 1942-43, WAC 1945. Recipient Image Maker award Carthage C. of C., 1984; cert. bus. educator. Mem. ASCD, NEA, Nat. Bus. Edn. Assn., Tex. Tchrs. Assn., Tex. Bus. Tchrs. Assn. (cert. of appreciation 1978), Nat. Women's Army Corps Vets. Assn., Air Force Assn. (life), Gwinnett Hist. Soc., Hist. Soc. Panola County, Panola County Hist. & Geneal. Assn., Coun. for Basic Edn., Nat. Hist. Soc., Tex. Coun. English Tchrs. Baptist.

NANK, LOIS RAE, financial executive; b. Racine, Wis., Jan. 6; d. Walter William August and Lanora Elizabeth (Freymuth) N. BS in Econs., U. Wis., 1962; postgrad. in profl. mgmt., Fla. Inst. Tech., 1977. Contract specialist U.S. Naval Ordnance Sta., Forest Park, Ill., 1963-66, U.S. Army Munitions Command, Joliet, Ill., 1966-72; plans/program specialist U.S. Army Munitions Command, Joliet, 1972-73, U.S. Army Armament Command, Rock Island, Ill., 1973-77; chief budget office U.S. Army Auto Log Mgmt. System Act, St. Louis, 1977-81; sr. budget analyst U.S. Army Materiel Command, Alexandria, Va., 1981-87; sr. fin. mgr. Def. Mapping Agy., Reston, Va., 1987-93; cons. Springfield, Va., 1993-96, Leesburg, Fla., 1996—. Coun. mem. chairperson bldg. com. Bread of Life Luth. Ch., Springfield, Va., 1986-90, Christ Luth. Ch., Fairfax, Va., 1990—; bd. dirs. Cedar Wood Homeowners' Assn., Bettendorf, Iowa, 1975-77, Oak Homeowners' Assn., Chesterfield, Mo., 1980-81. Mem. NAFE, Am. Soc. Mil. Comptrollers, Va. Assn. Female Execs., Order of Ea. Star.

NANKERVIS, MEDORA B., artist; b. L.A., Oct. 5, 1925; d. Granville Harrison and Sylvia (Tolman) Pierson; m. William Melvin Nankervis, May 9, 1957 (dec. 1995); children: Craig Melvin, Sylvia Kay, Michael Scott. Grad. high sch., Ashland, Oreg. Bookkeeper Pierson Prodn., Lynwood, South Gate, Calif., 1940-50's, Map Brass Products, Lynwood, South Gate, 1940-50's; co-operator Pierson Brass Foundry, South Gate, 1950's, Sunset Beach

Airport, Huntington Beach, Calif., 1955-57; bookkeeper Wm. Nankervis Bldg. Contractors, Garden Grove, Calif., 1958-67; operator, owner Sunnyside Guest Ranch, Rogue River, Oreg., 1968-76, May Hill Tree and Art Farm, Rogue River, 1987—; workshop instr., so. Oreg., 1970's-80's. Founder Woodville Fine Arts Assn. and Gallery, Rogue River, 1968-88; mem. founding bd. Grants Pass (Oreg.) Mus. Art, 1979—; founder Women Artists Cascades, Oreg., 1982—, Hillary Rodham Clinton Fan Club, 1995—, Great We Artists Retreats. Mem. Inst. Noetic Scis., Watercolor Soc. Oreg. Democrat. Quaker. Home: 13525 E Evans Creek Rd Rogue River OR 97537

NANNA, ELIZABETH ANN WILL, librarian, educator; b. Rahway, N.J., Nov. 21, 1932; d. Rudolph Julius and Dorothy Ada (Haulenbeck) Will; m. Antonio Carmine Nanna, June 15, 1963. Cert. in bus. with honors, Stuart Sch. Bus. Adminstrn., 1963; AA, Ocean County Coll., 1980; BA with honors, Georgian Ct. Coll., 1984, MA, 1984, postgrad., 1984-85; postgrad., Jersey City State Coll., 1988, Montclair State Coll., 1988-89. Cert. art, early childhood and spl. edn., media specialist, supr., N.J. Entrepreneur Ye Olde Cedar Inn, Toms River, N.J., 1963-78; tchr. art and history Monsignor Donovan High Sch., Toms River, 1980-82; tchr. art Whiting (N.J.) Elem. Sch./Manchester Twp. Sch. Dist., 1983-84, Ridgeway Elem. Sch./ Manchester Twp. Sch. Dist., Manchester, 1985-87; gifted and talented program tchr., coord., 1984-86; tchr. spl. edn. New Egypt (N.J.) Elem. Sch./ Plumsted Twp. Sch. Dist., 1988, libr. media specialist, 1988—. Author: Fostering Cognitive Growth Through Creativity, 1984; contbr. articles to profl. jours. Mem. Mounmouth Park Ball Com., Monmouth County, N.J., 1974—; dir. teen charm sch. Rutgers U. Extension Svc., Ocean County, N.J., 1965; chmn. Ocean County Fair Queen, 1967-84, Ocean County Heart of Hearts Charity Ball, 1976. Recipient Leadership and Svcs. award Ocean County Fair, Ocean County Heart Fund Assn., 1977. Mem. N.J. Reading Assn. (state coun.), N.J. Libr. Assn., N.J. Edn. Assn., Ednl. Media Assn. N.J., Ocean County Artists Guild, Edn. Media Assn. N.J., Georgian Ct. Coll. Alumni Assn. Republican. Roman Catholic. Home: 15 Mitchell Dr Toms River NJ 08755-5179 Office: Plumsted Twp Sch Dist 44 N Main St New Egypt NJ 08533-1316

NANNEY, CAROL RIDLEY, elementary school educator; b. Huntingdon, Tenn., Dec. 11, 1970; d. Larry Ray and Patricia Ann (Abernathy) Ridley; m. Timothy Douglas Nanney, June 12, 1995. BA, Bethel Coll., 1993. Cert. elem. tchr., Tenn. Announcer WHDM Radio, McKenzie, Tenn., 1985-92; tchr. 2d grade McKenzie Elem. Sch., 1993—; coach Odyssey of the Mind Team, McKenzie, 1993—. Elder First Cumberland Presbyn. Ch., McKenzie, 1994—. Mem. Tenn. Edn. Assn., McKenzie Edn. Assn.

NANNEY, SONDRA TUCKER, dance school executive, small business owner; b. Knoxville, Tenn., Dec. 11, 1937; d. Willard Woodrow and Mary Lou (Pollard) Tucker; m. Red Celestine Nanney, March 11, 1960; children: Stacy Leigh Nanney Courtney, Kristin Kaye. Grad. high sch., Knoxville, 1955. Bookkeeper Miles Siegel, CPA, Knoxville, 1955-56; sales sec. Sta. WBIR-TV, Knoxville, 1956-64, Knoxville News Sentinel, 1965-67; owner Concord Farragut Sch., Knoxville, 1974-79, Knoxville Sch. Dance, 1979-95, Images Dancewear, Knoxville, 1989-95; pres. Knoxville Met. Dance, 1982-95. Mem. Knoxville Symphony League (officer 1982-95, pres. 1989-90, chmn. showcase 1993, nominating com. 1992), Knoxville Met. Dance Theatre (pres. 1995). Republican.

NAPIER, MARTI A., accountant; b. Boise, Idaho, July 11, 1956; d. Charles Roy and Treva Zella (Harris) Malmstrom; m. Eric C. Johns, Jan. 16, 1976 (div. Aug. 1979); m. Brian A. Napier, May 29, 1981. BSBA, Chapman U., 1989; MBT in Acctg., U. So. Calif., 1993. CPA, Calif. Staff acct. Boyce Garvin, P.A., Santa Ana, Calif., 1985-86, Boyle & Daugherty, Orange, Calif., 1986-88; supr. tax dept. Grant Thornton, Irvine, Calif., 1988-93; acct. Sparks & Nelson CPAs, Santa Ana, 1993; ptnr. Marti A. Napier CPA MBT, Yorba Linda, Calif., 1993—. Exec. com., treas. Mary Magdalene Project, Inc., South Gate, Calif., 1994—; exec. com. Olive Crest Christian Outreach Coun., Santa Ana, 1995; bd. deacons Yorba Linda Presbyn. Ch., 1993—. Mem. AICPA, Calif. Soc. CPA, Yorba Linda C. of C. (amb., com. mem. 1994—). Republican. Presbyterian. Home: 16945 Mariah Ct Yorba Linda CA 92686-1537

NAPLES, SUSAN LORRAINE, property management company executive; b. Claremont, N.H., May 15, 1949; d. Robert William Gerrie and Margaret Lorraine (Leavitt) Baney; 1 child, Clinton Eric. Student pub. schs. Santa Ana, Calif. Cert. cmty. assn. mgr., profl. cmty. assn. mgr. Project dir., personnel dir. Cmty. Devel. Council Santa Ana, 1974-76; founding exec. dir. Women's Transitional Living Ctr., Orange, Calif., 1976-78; sr. account exec. Profl. Cmty. Mgmt., El Toro, Calif., 1978-81; CEO Cardinal Property Mgmt., Inc., Anaheim, 1981—. Co-author: How to Start a Shelter for Battered Women, 1977. Participant White House Conf. on Domestic Violence, 1977; founder, dir. Calif. Assn. Cmty. Mgrs., 1992—, AIDS Walk Orange County, 1991-92; del. Dem. Nat. Conv., 1992, 96; mem. Dem. Found. Orange County, 1992—, vice-chair, 1994-96, treas., 1996—; mem. Orange County Dem. Ctrl. Com., 1991—, Calif. Dem. Ctrl. Com., 1992—, mem. exec. bd., 1993-94. Mem. NOW (co-chair Orange County chpt. 1976, co-coordinator domestic violence task force Calif. chpt. 1977), NAFE, Nat. Women's Polit. Caucus, Assn. Traditional Hooking Artists. Office: Cardinal Property Mgmt Inc 1290 N Hancock St Ste 103 Anaheim CA 92807

NAPOLITANO, GRACE F., state legislator; b. Brownsville, Tex., Dec. 4, 1936; d. Miguel and Maria Alicia Ledezma Flores; m. Frank Napolitano, 1982; 1 child, Yolando M., Fred Musquiz Jr., Edward M., Michael M., Cynthia M. Student, Cerritos Coll., L.A. Trade Tech, Tec Southwest Coll. Mem. Calif. Assembly, 1993—. Councilwoman City of Norwalk, Calif., 1986-92, mayor, 1989-90; active Cmty. Family Guidance. Mem. Cerritos Coll. Found., Lions Club. Democrat. Roman Catholic. Home: 12946 Belcher St Norwalk CA 90650-3328 Office: Calif Assembly State Capitol Sacramento CA 95814-4906 also: PO Box 942849 Sacramento CA 94249-0001*

NAPOLITANO, JANET ANN, prosecutor; b. N.Y.C., Nov. 29, 1957; d. Leonard Michael and Jane Marie (Winer) N. BS, U. Santa Clara, Calif., 1979; JD, U. Va., 1983. Bar: Ariz. 1984, U.S. Dist. Ct. Ariz. 1984, Ct. Appeals (9th cir.) 1984, U.S. Ct. Appeals (10th cir.) 1988. Law clk. to hon. Mary Schroeder U.S Ct. Appeals (9th Cir.), 1983-84; ptnr. Lewis & Roca, Phoenix, 1984-93; U.S. atty. Dist. Ariz., Phoenix, 1993—; mem. Atty. Gen.'s Adv. Com., 1993-95, chair, 1995-96. Vice-chair Ariz. Dem. Party, 1991-92; mem. Dem. Nat. Com., 1991-92; State Bd. Tech. Registration, 1989-92; Phoenix Design Standards Rev. Com., 1989-91; bd. dirs. Ariz. Cmty. Legal Svcs. Corp., 1987-92; bd. regents Santa Clara U., 1992—. Truman Scholarship Found. scholar, 1977. Mem. ABA, Am. Law Inst., Ariz. Bar Assn., Maricopa County Bar Assn., Am. Judicature Soc., Ariz. State Bar (chmn. civil practice and procedure com. 1991-92), Phi Beta Kappa, Alpha Sigma Nu. Office: US Attys Office 4000 US Courthouse 230 N 1st Ave Phoenix AZ 85025-0085

NAPPHOLZ, CAROL JANE, academic advisor, educator; b. Canterbury, Kent, Eng., Apr. 11, 1948; came to the U.S., 1983; d. Ronald Stanley and Margaret (Sim) Elphick; m. Tibor Anton Nappholz, Mar. 15, 1975; children: Kim, Tammy. BA, Macquarie U., Sydney, Australia, 1983; MA, U. Denver, 1986, PhD, 1992. Asst. UN Curriculum Devel. Orgn., Fiji, 1970; exec. asst. to dir. of Southwest Pacific Region Sabena Belgian Airlines, Sydney, Australia, 1971-77; instr. U. Denver, 1984-89, asst. to chair English dept., 1988-94, acad. advisor, faculty Univ. Coll., 1994—. Author: Unsung Women: The Anonymous Female Voice in Troubador Poetry, 1994; contbr. articles to English Lang. Notes, Tenso; presenter papers Medieval Acad. Am., Rocky Mountain Medieval and Renaissance Assn. Pres. Colo. Youth Symphony Orchs., Denver, 1994—. Recipient 1st place prize Colo. State Open Women's Squash Championships, 1984. Mem. MLA, Nat. Coun. Tchrs. English, Inst. Linguists (London) (assoc.).

NAQUIN, PATRICIA ELIZABETH, employee assistance consultant; b. Houston, Jan. 28, 1943; d. Louie Dee and Etha Beatrice (English) Price; m. Hollis James Naquin, Mar. 23, 1961; children: Price Naquin, Holli Campbell. BS, U. Houston, 1969, MS, 1982; PhD, Tex. Woman's U., 1988. Lic. profl. counselor; lic. chem. dependency counselor; nat. cert. counselor; cert. chem. dependency specialist; cert. employee assistance profl. Purchasing agt. Internat. Affairs U. Houston, 1966-68; elem. sch. tchr. Pasadena (Tex.) Ind. Sch. Dist., 1969-82; spl. edn. counselor Alvin (Tex.) Ind. Sch. Dist., 1982-85, drug-free schs. coord., 1988-92; marriage and family therapist Lifespan Counseling, Pasadena, 1985-92; employee assistance cons. DuPont, LaPorte, Tex., 1992—; adv. com. mem. Sam Houston U., Huntsville, Tex., 1983; trainer and instr. Bay Area Coun. on Drugs and Alcohol, Houston, 1988-92; cons. Alvin Ind. Sch. Dist., 1989-92, DuPont Valuing People Core Team, 1993—; supr. State Bd. of Profl. Counselors, Houston, 1988—. Co-author: Life is for Everyone Manual, 1990. Com. co-chair Alvin S.A.P. Task Force, 1988-92; com. mem. Tri-Dist. Task Force, Alvin, 1990-91; com. chmn. Alvin Bus./Edn. Partnership, 1992; bd. dirs. Brazoria (Tex.) County Coun. Drugs and Alcohol, 1991. Mem. Am. Assn. Marriage and Family Therapists, Tex. Assn. Counselors of Alcohol and Drug Abuse, Am. Counseling Assn., Employee Assistance Program Assn., Nat. Disting. Svc. Registry/Libr. of Congress, Phi Delta Kappa. Republican. Methodist.

NARAD, JOAN STERN, psychiatrist; b. N.Y.C., June 21, 1943; d. Victor and Grete (Metzger) S.; m. Richard M. Narad; children: Christine, Laurie, Michael. BA, NYU, 1964; MD, Woman's Med. Coll., Pa., 1968. Diplomate Am. Bd. Psychiatry, Am. Bd Child Psychiatry. Intern pediatrics Stanford (Calif.) U. Hosp., 1968-69; resident adult psychiat. Med. Coll., Phila., 1969-71, chief resident in child psychiatry, 1971-73; grad. in psychoanalysis and child psychoanalysis Phila. Psychoanalytic Inst., 1978; practice medicine specializing in child and adolescent psychiatry Westport, Conn., 1979—; chief Adolescent and Young Adult Svc., Silver Hill Found., New Canaan, Conn., 1980-84, 89-93, sr. adolescent cons., 1993-94; unit chief Riverview Hosp. for Children and Youth, Middletown, Conn., 1994—; cons. Cath. Home Girls, Phila., 1971-78, Germantown Friends Sch., 1973-79; asst. prof. Child Psychiat. Med. Coll. Pa., 1975-79; asst. clin. prof. Yale Child Study Ctr., 1979-92, assoc. clin. prof., 1992—. Fellow NIMH, 1968. Fellow Am. Acad. Child and Adolescent Psychiat.; mem. Am. Psychiat. Assn., AMA, Alumnae Assn. Med. Coll. Pa., Am. Psychoanalytic Assn., Western New Eng. Psychoanalytic Soc., Conn. Coun. Child Psychiatry. Home and Office: 3 Colony Rd Westport CT 06880-3703

NARANJO, CAROLYN R., lawyer; b. Far Rockaway, N.Y., Nov. 28, 1954; d. Anthony J. and Mary (Lautazi) Spina; m. James Naranjo, Apr. 28, 1989. BA summa cum laude in Spl. & Elem. Edn., Bklyn. Coll., CUNY, 1976; JD, Temple U., 1981; student, Fordham U., 1980-81. Asst. counsel to head regional counsel First Am. Title Insurance, N.Y.C., 1981-82; legal counsel Creative Abstract Corp., N.Y.C., 1982-84; assoc. firm Friedman & Kornheiser, N.Y.C., 1982-84; assoc. Quinn, Cohen, Shields & Bock, N.Y.C., 1984-86; mng. ptnr. Collier, Cohen, Crystal & Bock, N.Y.C., 1986-94; pvt. practice Garden City, N.Y., 1994—. Mem. ABA, Columbian Lawyers Assn. of Nassau County, Nassau Bar Assn., N.Y. State Bar Assn. Office: 226 7th St Ste 200 Garden City NY 11530

NARASIMHAN, PADMA MANDYAM, physician; b. Bangalore, India, Mar. 19, 1947; came to U.S., 1976; d. Alasingracher Mandyam and Alamela Mandyam Narasimhan; m. Mandyam N. Venkatesh, Mar. 28, 1981 (div.) 1 child, Ravi. Student, Delhi U., New Delhi, 1964, MBBS, 1969; MD, Maulana Azad Med. Coll., New Delhi, 1970. Diplomate Am. Bd. Internal Medicine. Intern in internal medicine Flushing Hosp., N.Y.C., 1976-77; resident in internal medicine Luth. Med. Ctr., N.Y.C., 1977-79; fellow hematology, oncology Beth-Israel Med. Ctr., N.Y.C., 1979-81; asst. prof. King Drew Med. Ctr., L.A., 1983-87, Harbor UCLA, Torrance, 1987—. Mem. editorial bd. Jour. Internal Medicine, 1986—. Mem. ACP, Am. Soc. Clin. Oncology, So. Calif. Acad. Clin. Oncology. Hindu. Home: 6604 Madeline Cove Dr Palos Verdes Peninsula CA 90275-4608 Office: Harbor UCLA 100 W Carson St Torrance CA 90509

NARAYAN, BEVERLY ELAINE, lawyer; b. Berkeley, Calif., June 19, 1961; d. Jagjiwan and Alexandra (Mataras) N.; m. James Dean Schmidt, Jan. 7, 1989; children: Sasha Karan, Kaiya Maria. Student, San Francisco State U., 1979-80; BA, U. Calif., Berkeley, 1983; JD, U. Calif., San Francisco, 1987. Bar: Calif. 1987, U.S. Dist. Ct. (no. dist.) Calif. 1987, U.S. Dist. Ct. (ctrl. dist.) 1988. Atty. Daniels Barratta & Fine, L.A., 1988-89, Kornblum Ferry & Frye, L.A., 1990-91, Clapp Moroney Bellagamba Davis & Vucinich, Menlo Park, Calif., 1991-93, pvt. practice, Burlingame, Calif., 1993—; arbitrator Nat. Assn. Securities Dealers, San Francisco, 1987—, Pacific Stock Exch., San Francisco, 1994—; mediator Peninsula Conflict Resolution Ctr., San Mateo, Calif., 1995—; judge pro tem San Mateo Superior Ct., Redwood City, Calif., 1994—. Candidate Sch. Bd. San Mateo (Calif.) Unified Sch. Dist., 1993. Recipient U. Calif. Hastings Coll. Law Achievement award, 1986. Mem. ABA, San Mateo County Bar Assn. (co-chair women lawyers 1995, bd. dirs. 1994-96), Nat. Women's Polit. Caucus (bd. dirs., diversity chair 1993—), San Mateo County Barristers Club (bd. dirs. 1993—, child watch chair 1995—). Office: 1508 Howard Ave Burlingame CA 94010

NARBONI, BETHANY ALLEN, auditor, educator; b. Columbia, S.C., July 23, 1961; d. Earl Julian and Janis Bethany (James) Allen; m. Edmond Marcel Maurice Narboni. BS in Acctg., U. S.C., 1985. CPA, S.C.; cert. info. sys. auditor; cert. internal auditor. Sr. auditor internal audit dept. U. S.C., Columbia, 1986-89; auditor S.C. Legis. Audit Coun., Columbia, 1989-94, SCANA Corp., Columbia, 1994—; instr. Midlands Tech. Coll., Columbia, 1995—. Mem. Hist. Elmwood Park Neighborhood Assn. (pres. 1993, chair publicity com. 1991-92, chair home tour com. 1993). Recipient Methodology award Nat. Legis. Program Evaluation Soc., 1991, Concurrent Resolution of Commendation S.C. Gen. Assembly, 1992. Mem. AICPA, Inst. Internal Auditors, S.C. Assn. CPAs, Info. Sys. Audit and Control Assn. Republican. Episcopalian. Office: SCANA Corp Audit Svcs Dept 1426 Main St Columbia SC 29201

NARDI, GRACIELA HORNE, cosmetics team manager, artist; b. Buenos Aires, Sept. 29, 1946; came to U.S., 1984; d. Carlos Alberto Horne and Nelida (Ferrari) Barbarossa; m. Norberto Nardi, Jan. 11, 1976; 1 child, Matias; stepchildren: Moira, Pablo, Nicolas. Student, Buenos Aires Sch. Law, Vinci Art Sch., Boca, Argentina; AA, Citrus Coll., Asuza, Calif. Conv. bidding supr. Hosp. Jose San Martin, Buenos Aires, 1966-72; gen. dir. Bestline Co., Buenos Aires, 1973-80; owner Corondo Travel Agy., Argentina, 1980-84, Cafe Dell'Arte, New Orleans, 1985-89; asst. mgr. Griswold's Hotel, Claremont, Calif., 1985-89; team mgr. Mary Kay Cosmetics, Claremont, Calif., 1989—; art cons. Claremont Art Assn., 1992—. Exhbns. include Pomona Valley (Calif.) Art Assn., 1992 (2d prize), 93, 94, 95, Upland (Calif.) Art Assn., 1993 (2d prize), 94, 95, Cafe Buenos Aires, 1995. Mem. Pomona Valley Art Assn., Upland Art Assn., Claremont Art Assn. Roman Catholic. Home: 411 Lee Ave Claremont CA 91711

NARDI, THEODORA P., former state legislator; b. Warwick, R.I., Aug. 28, 1922; widow; 4 children. Attended, Manhattanville Coll. Mem. N.H. Ho. of Reps., 1973-83, mem. appropriations com., 1989-94, ret., 1994. Chmn. Hills County Dem. Com., 1977-78; pres. N.H. Owl, 1979-80; chmn. Manchester (N.H.) Legis. Del., 1979-82; bd. dirs. N.H. Soup Kitchen, 1985-90, New Horizons Soup Kitchen, 1989-93; active N.H. Cath. Charities, 1986—, Manchester Housing Coun., 1986-92. Democrat. Roman Catholic. Home: 776 Chestnut St Manchester NH 03104-3012

NARDI RIDDLE, CLARINE, association administrator, judge; b. Clinton, Ind., Apr. 23, 1949; d. Frank Jr. and Alice (Mattioda) Nardi; m. Mark Alan Riddle, Aug. 15, 1971; children: Carl Nardi, Julia Nardi. AB, Ind. U., 1971, JD, 1974; LHD (hon.), St. Joseph Coll., 1991. Bar: Ind. 1974, Conn. 1979, U.S. Dist. Ct. Ind. 1974, Fed. Dist. Ct. Conn. 1980, U.S. Ct. Appeals (2d cir.) 1986, U.S. Ct. Appeals (D.C. cir.) 1994, U.S. Supreme Ct. 1980. Staff atty. Ind. Legis. Svc. Agy., Indpls., 1974-78, legal counsel, 1978-79; dep. corp. counsel City of New Haven, 1980-83; counsel to atty. gen. State of Conn., Hartford, 1983-86, dep. atty. gen., 1986-89, acting atty. gen., 1989, atty. gen., 1989-91; judge Superior Ct. State of Conn., 1991-93; sr. v.p. for govtl. affairs, gen. counsel Nat. Multi-Housing Coun., Nat. Apartment Assn., 1995—; asst. counsel state majority Conn. Gen. Assembly, Hartford, 1979, legal rsch. asst. to prof. Yale U., New Haven, 1979; legal counsel com. on law revision Indpls. State Bar Assn., 1979; mem. Chief Justice's Task Force on Gender Bias, Hartford, 1988-90; mem. ethics and values com. Ind. Sector, Washington, 1988-90. Bd. visitors Ind. U., Bloomington, 1974-92; mem. Gov.'s Missing Children Com., Hartford, Conn. Child Support Guidelines Com., Gov.'s Task Force on Justice for Abused Children, Hartford, 1988-90. Named Conn. History Maker Women's Bur. & Permanent Commn. on Status of Women, U.S. Dept. Labor, 1989; recipient Citizen award Nat. Task Force on Children's Constl. Rights. Mem. ABA, Conn. Bar Assn. (chair com. on gender bias, Citation of Merit women and law sect. 1989), Nat. assn. Attys. Gen. (chair charitable trusts and solicitation 1988-90), New Haven Neighborhood Music Sch. (bd. dirs.), Am. Arbitration Assn. (arbitration panel 1994). Democrat. Presbyterian.

NARTONIS, CYNTHIA, artist; b. Roseburg, Oreg., Nov. 4, 1943; d. Charles Sheets and Olive Ruth (Gilmore) Collins; m. David Kallman Nartonis; children: Katherine Ann, Constance. BA, Williamette U., Salem, Oreg., 1965. Adjunct lectr. Mus. Fine Arts, Boston, 1966-70; dir. Slide Libr., 1969-70; curator Mus. Principia Coll., Elsah, Ill., 1974-78; lectr. Fine Arts and Art History Principia Coll., 1974-78, 76-88; artist, 1988—; juror Elder Gallery Nebr. Wesleyan U., Lincoln, 1990. bd. dirs. The Art Connection, Inc., Boston, 1995—. Named Guest Artist Tamarind Inst., Albuquerque, 1993; recipient Juror's Merit award Laguna Gloria Art Mus., Austin, Tex., 1990; grantee The E.D. Found., Ridgefield, N.J., 1988. Mem. Boston Print Club, Mary Ryan Gallery N.Y., Elliot Smith Gallery St. Louis, Elizabeth Leach Gallery Portland, Fletcher Priest Gallery, Alexa Lee Gallery. Home: 68 Waltham St Boston MA 02118

NARVÁEZ, JOLENE DENISE, choir director, music educator; b. Richmond, Ind., Oct. 7, 1959; d. John Raleigh Webster and Lois Elvina (Cramer) Lewis; m. John Samuel Maples, June 25, 1977 (div. 1988); children: Emily Jo, John Lester; m. Tony Felix Narváez, Feb. 23, 1990; 1 child, Bethany Joy. Diploma Ch. Music, Clear Creek Bapt. Coll., 1985, BRE, 1985; MM in Music, Southwestern Bapt. Theol. Seminary, 1988. Cert. tchr., Tex. Minister of music Ctrl. Bapt. Ch., Richmond, Ind., 1983-85; dir. choral music edn. Coppell (Tex.) Middle Sch., 1989-92; minister of music Wesley Evangelical Methodist Ch., Hurst, Tex., 1990-92, Rejoice Luth. Ch., Coppell, Tex., 1993—; dir. choral music edn. Coppell (Tex.) H.S., 1991—. Mem. Am. Choral Dirs. Assn., Tex. Music Educators Assn., Tex. Choral Dirs. Assn. Baptist. Office: Coppell H S 185 W Pkwy Blvd Coppell TX 75019

NASCA, ANGELA MARIE, clinical specialist of psychology; b. Bklyn., June 27, 1971; d. Richard Lawrence and Connie Marie (Sabia) N. BA, U. Del., 1993; MA in Edn., Seton Hall U., 1995, postgrad., 1995—. Office asst. Display Factory Inc., Spotswood, N.J., summers 1989—; group leader YMCA, Newark, Del., 1992-93; support counselor Cmty. Access Unltd., Elizabeth, N.J., 1993-95; clin. specialist Beth Israel Med. Ctr., Newark, N.J., 1995—; rschr. Human Emotions Lab., Newark, Del., 1992-93, Nonverbal Behavior, Newark, 1993. Vol. Parents' Anonymous, Newark, Del., 1992-93; sr. rep. Psi Chi Psychology Honors Fraternity, Newark, 1993. Mem. APA (affiliate), ACA (affiliate), Kappa Delta Pi. Republican. Roman Catholic. Office: Beth Israel Med Ctr 201 Lyons Ave Newark NJ 07112

NASH, ALANNA KAY, critic, writer; b. Louisville, Aug. 16, 1950; d. Allan and Emily Kay (Derrick) N. BA, Stephens Coll., 1972; MS, Columbia U., 1974. Music critic Louisville Courier Jour., 1977; writer, producer Sta. WHAS, Louisville, 1980; pres. Alandale Prodns., Louisville, 1981—; freelance writer specializing in the arts Stereo Rev., Esquire, N.Y. Times, Entertainment Weekly, TV Guide, Ms., Glamour, Working Woman, Saturday Evening Post, Video Rev., 1964—. Author: Dolly, 1978, rev. edit. Dolly Parton: The Early Years, 1994, Behind Closed Doors: Talking with the Legends of Country Music, 1988, Golden Girl: The Story of Jessica Savitch, 1988, 96, Elvis Aaron Presley: Revelations from the Memphis Mafia, 1995; (ghostwriter) Elvis: From Memphis to Hollywood, 1992; co-producer: (TV documentary) The Deaners: Cause without a Rebel; writer, producer: network and syndicated specials; contbr. to books. Recipient Nat. Prodn. awards Alpha Epsilon Rho, 1971. Mem. Soc. Profl. Journalists (bd. dirs. Louisville chpt. 1987—, v.p. 1992-93, pres. 1993-94, Nat. Mem. of Yr. award 1994, Howard Dubin award 1994), Authors Guild, Am. Soc. Journalists and Authors, Country Music Assn. Republican. Methodist. Home and Office: 649 Breckenridge Ln Louisville KY 40207

NASH, ANNE-MARIE, publisher; b. Portland, Oreg., Nov. 29, 1970; d. James Thomas Jr. and Barbara Ann (Thoming) Bradshaw; m. Michael Keirn Nash, July 16, 1995. BA in Mass Comms., Linfield Coll. Reporter, editor The Linfield Rev., McMinnville, Oreg., 1991-93; reporter The McMinnville News Register, 1991-93; intern Sta. KATU Channel 2, Portland, 1993; project mgr. Oak Tree Publs., Beaverton, Oreg., 1993-96. Editor: (online catalogs) The Intel Client/Server Solutions Catalog, 1994—, The Intel Internet Resource Directory, 1995—, (online directory) Intel: What's Cool on and Off the 'Net, 1996. Democrat. Office: Oak Tree Publs Ste 251 3800 SW Cedar Hills Blvd Beaverton OR 97005

NASH, DONNA LOUISE, secondary school educator; b. Jacksonville, Tex., Mar. 24, 1940; d. H. Don and Louise (Jared) Jenkins; m. M. Brooks Nash, June 1, 1963; children: Brooklynn, Mike. BA in Edn., U. Ark., 1962; MS in Edn., U. Ctrl. Ark., 1971. Cert. tchr., Ark. 1st grade tchr. Cloverdale Elem. Sch., Little Rock, 1962-69; kindergarten tchr. Pulaski Heights Bapt. Sch., Little Rock, 1973-76; reading tchr. Cabot (Ark.) Jr. H.S., 1977-80, geography tchr., 1981—, geography bee coord., mock election coord., 1988—, geography awareness coord., 1992—. Mem. Nat. Coun. for the Social Studies, Ark. Humanities Assn. Republican. Methodist. Office: Cabot Jr HS 38 Panther Trl Cabot AR 72023-9436

NASH, JUDITH KLUCK, mathematics educator; b. Manchester, Conn., Dec. 26, 1946; d. Erwin John and Eleanor May (Starke) Kluck; m. Stephen T. Nash, Apr. 7, 1990. BS, So. Conn. State U., 1969; MS, 1976. Math. tchr. Cheshire (Conn.) Pub. Schs., 1969-93, Tunxis Cmty.-Tech. Coll., Farmington, Conn., 1994—. Home: 72 Tunxis Path Plantsville CT 06479-1348 Office: Tunxis Cmty-Tech Coll 271 Scott Swamp Rd Farmington CT 06032

NASH, JUNE CAPRICE, anthropology educator; b. Salem, Mass., May 30, 1927; d. Joseph and M. Josephine Bousley; children: Eric, Laura; m. Herbert Menzel, July 1, 1972. BA, CUNY, 1948; MA, U. Chgo., 1953, PhD, 1960. Asst. prof. Chgo. Tchrs. Coll., Chgo., Ill., 1960-63, Yale U. New Haven, Conn., 1963-68; assoc. prof. NYU, 1968-72; prof. CUNY, 1972—; disting. vis. prof. Am. U., Cairo, 1978, U. Colo., Boulder, 1988—; vis. prof. SUNY, Albany, 1988-89; disting. prof. CUNY, N.Y.C., 1990. Author: In the Eyes of the Ancestor, 1970, We Eat the Mines and the Mines Eat Us: Dependency and Exploitation in Bolivian Mining Communities, 1979, From Tank Town to High Tech: The Clash of Community and Industrial Cycles, 1989; editor: Crafts in the World Market: The Impact of Global Exchange on Middle American Artisans, 1993, La explosión de comunidades en chiapas, México, 1995; co-editor: (with Helen I. Safa) Sex and Class in Latin America, 1976, Women and Change in Latin America, 1986, (with Juan Carradi and Hobard Spaldine) Ideology and Change in Latin America, 1976, (with Jorge Dandler and Nicholas Hopkins) Popular Participation in Change: Cooperatives, Collectives and Self-Management, 1976. Mem. Soc. for the Anthropology of Work (pres. 1988—), Assn. Polit. and Legal Activities (pres. 1983), Am. Anthropology Assn. (Disting. Svc. award 1995), Am. Ethnographic Soc., Assn. for Feminist Anthropology (pres. 1990-93). Home: 2166 Broadway 18D New York NY 10024 Office: CUNY 137th Convent New York NY 10031

NASH, MARLENE DIANNE, accountant, consultant; b. Bridgeport, Conn., June 19, 1952; d. Weston Montgomery and Mary Agnes (Grant) Nash; 1 child, Trevis Jonathan; m. James Alfred Robinson, Jr., Sept. 4, 1970 (div. Nov. 1977); children: Trela Jamene Robinson, Michele Charise Fernandez. AAS in Acctg., Thomas Nelson C.C., Hampton, Va., 1993. Payroll clk., cost acct. Action for Bridgeport Cmty. Devel., 1978-83; acct. Hall Neighborhood House, Bridgeport, 1984-86; accounts payable clk. Greater Bridgeport Transit, 1986-89; accounts receivable clk. Selectemps, Hampton, Va., 1993; accounts payable clk. Olsten, Newport News, Va., 1994; adminstrv. asst. Prodn. Support Svcs., Newport News, 1995; account clk. Commr. of the Revenue, Newport News, 1994—. Mem. Inst. Mgmt. Accts. Democrat. Episcopalian. Office: Commr of the Revenue 2400 Washington Ave Newport News VA 23607

NASH, MARY HARRIET, artist; lecturer; b. Washington, May 8, 1951; d. Richard Harvey and Janet Rose (Nivinski) N. BA, George Washington U.,

1973; MFA, Washington State U., 1976. Guest lectr. Mus. Art, Wash. State U., Pullman., 1976, 2d St. Gallery, Charlottesville, Va., 1980, U. Ala., Tuscaloosa, 1981, SEWSA Conf., Charlottesville, 1983; artist-in-residence Va. Mus. Fine Arts, Richmond, 1984—; guest juror Twinbrook Art Show, Fairfax, Va., 1978; tchg. asst. Wash. State U., 1975-76 vis. artist, lectr. Johnson (Vt.) State Coll., 1995; guest lectr. Julian Scott Meml. Gallery Johnson State Coll., Vt., 1995. Author art show catalogue: Personal Paintings, 1978, artist's book: Skulls Are Forever, 1986; contbr. articles to profl. jours. Recipient Cert. Outstanding Achievement, Women in Design Internat., 1983; MacDowell Colony fellow, 1977; recipient 3 gubernatorial citations Gev. George Allen, Richmond, 1995-96; nominee Cultural Olympiad, Atlanta, 1995. Mem. Southeastern Ctr. for Contemporary Art (hon. mention 1979), Phi Kappa Phi.

NASH, MILDRED JEAN, English educator, poet; b. Sharon, Pa., Aug. 3, 1938; d. Merrill G. and Mary (Dallas) Leonard; m. James A. Nash, Aug. 14, 1960; children: Noreen Elizabeth, Rebecca Anne. AB, Grove City (Pa.) Coll., 1960; EdM, Harvard U., 1977. Tchr. English Rockport (Mass.) H.S., 1960-61, Burlington (Mass.) H.S., 1979-84; dir. BEAM (Burlington's Extended Acad. Model) Marshall Simonds Mid. Sch., 1984—. Author: (poetry) Beyond Their Dreams, 1989; contbr. numerous poems to mags., jours. and anthologies. Rep. Town Meeting, Burlington, 1975—. Recipient awards World Order of Narrative Poets, 1994. Mem. Poetry Soc. Am. (Emily Dickinson award 1979), New Eng. Poetry Club (sec. 1978-89, Power Dalton Meml. award 1980, Leighton Rollins Meml. award 1980). Home: 39 Sunset Dr Burlington MA 01803 Office: Marshall Simonds Mid Sch Winn St Burlington MA 01803

NASH, RENEA DENISE, public information officer; b. Morehead, Miss., Dec. 14, 1963; d. James O. and Eunice P. N. BAA, Ctrl. Mich. Univ., 1986; MMC, Ariz. State Univ., 1993. Bus. reporter Register, Sandusky, Ohio, 1987-88; news publ. specialist U-Haul Internat., Phoenix, 1988-89; pub. info. specialist Ariz. State Univ., Tempe, 1989-90; substitute tchr. Phoenix Elem. Sch. Dist., 1991-93; mgr. comm. Ariz. Spl. Olympics, Phoenix, 1993-94; pub. info. officer City of Phoenix, 1994—; adj. prof. Ariz. State Univ., 1994—; court appointed spl. advocate Ariz. Supreme Ct. Freelance writer; author: Coping with Interracial Dating, 1993 (1994 Books for the Teen Age citation N.Y. Pub. Libr.), Coping as a Biracial Child, 1994, Everything You Need to Know as a Multiethnic Child, 1994. Mem. Internat. Assn. Bus. Comm. (Phoenix chpt.). *

NASH, SHEENA ANN HARGIS, flight nurse; b. Taipei, Taiwan, China, July 11, 1966; came to U.S., 1968; d. Joseph Scott and Julia Ann (Barnes) Hill; m. Earnest Harold Hargis, Jr., July 20, 1985 (div. Mar. 1990); 1 child, Sheena Marie; m. Shannon T. Nash, May 10, 1996. BSN, Tenn. Tech. U., 1990. Cert. emergency med. technician, Tenn. Emergency med. technician Putnam County Ambulance Svc., Cookeville, Tenn., 1985—; staff nurse transplant unit St. Thomas Hosp., Nashville, 1990-92; staff nurse, supr., educator critical care Cookeville Gen. Hosp., 1992—; flight nurse Erlanger Med. Ctr.-Life Force Air Med., Chattanooga, 1995—; preceptor for nursing student Tenn. Tech. U., Cookeville, 1992—; BLS instr., ACLS instr., pediat. advanced life support instr., prehosp. trauma life support instr., 1990—. Mem. PTO Parkview, Cookeville, 1992-96; mem. Cookeville Women's Bowling Assn., team capt., 1992-94, pres., 1994-95; mem. Putnam County Vol. Fire Fighter; asst. coach Boxter T-Ball Assn., 1992-94. Mem. AACN (CCRN), ANA, Emergency Nurses Assn., Nat. Flight Nurses Assn., Tenn. Nurses Assn. (bd. dirs. 1990-92, sec. 1994—), Nat. Wildlife Assn. Home: 4049 Ditty Rd Cookeville TN 38506

NASH, SYLVIA DOTSETH, religious organization executive, consultant; b. Montevedio, Minn., Apr. 25, 1945; d. Owen Donald and Selma A. (Tollefson) Dotseth; divorced; 1 child, Elizabeth Louise; m. Thomas L. Nash, Dec. 20, 1986. Grad., Calif. Luth. Bible Sch., 1965; doctorate (hon.), Pilgrims Theol. Seminary, 1994. Office mgr. First Congl. Ch., Pasadena, Calif., 1968-75; adminstrv. asst. Pasadena Presbyn. Ch., 1975-78; dir. adminstrv. svcs. Fuller Theol. Sem., Pasadena, 1978-81; CEO Christian Mgmt. Assn., Diamond Bar, Calif., 1981-94; pres. Christian Healthcare Network, La Mirada, Calif., 1994-95; sr. cons. Lillestrand and Assocs., La Mirada, Calif., 1996—; cons. various orgns., 1985—. Author: Inspirational Management, 1992 (Your Church Mag. award 1992); editor: The Clarion, 1975-78, The Christian Mgmt. Report, 1981-94; mem. editl./adv. bd. Your Church Mag.; mem. edtl. bd. Jour. Ministry Mktg. and Mtmg.; contbr. articles to profl. jours. Bd. dirs. Evang. Coun. for Fin. Accountability, Campus Crusade for Christ Internat. Sch. Theology, Nat. Network of Youth Ministries, The Mustard Seed, Inc., Nat. Assn. of Ch. Bus. Adminstrn., Found. for His Ministry, Lamb's Players, Gospel Lit. Internat., Rosemead, Calif. Mem. NAFE, Nat. Assn. Ch. Adminstrs. (sec. 1979-81), Am. Soc. Assn. Execs. Office: Lillestrand and Assocs PO Box 1361 La Mirada CA 90637-1361

NASON, DOLORES IRENE, computer company executive, counselor, eucharistic minister; b. Seattle, Jan. 24, 1934; d. William Joseph Lockinger and Ruby Irene (Church) Gilstrap; m. George Malcolm Nason Jr., Oct. 7, 1951; children: George Malcolm III, Scott James, Lance William, Natalie Joan. Student, Long Beach (Calif.) City Coll., 1956-59; cert. in Religious Edn. for elem tchrs., Immaculate Heart Coll., 1961, cert. teaching, 1962, cert. secondary teaching, 1967; attended, Salesian Sem., 1983-85. Buyer J. C. Penney Co., Barstow, Calif., 1957; prin. St. Cyprian Confraternity of Christian Doctrine Elem. Sch., Long Beach, 1964-67; prin. summer sch. St. Cyprian Confraternity of Christian Doctrine Elem. Sch., Long Beach, 1965-67; pres. St. Cyprian Confraternity Orgn., Long Beach, 1967-69; dist. co-chmn. L.A. Diocese, 1968-70; v.p. Nason & Assocs., Inc., Long Beach, 1978—; pres. L.A. County Commn. on Obscenity & Pornography, 1984—; eucharistic minister St. Cyprian Ch., Long Beach, 1985—; bd. dirs. L.A. County Children's Svcs., 1988—; part-time social svcs. counselor Disabled Resources Ctr., Inc., Long Beach, 1992—; vol. Meml. Children's Hosp., Long Beach, 1977—; mem. scholarship com. Long Beach City Coll., 1984-90, Calif. State U., Long Beach, 1984-90. Mem. adv. bd. Pro-Wilson 90 Gov., Calif., 1990; mem. devel. bd. St. Joseph High Sch., 1987—; pres. St. Cyprian's Parish Coun., 1962—; mem. Long Beach Civic Light Opera, 1973—, Assistance League of Long Beach, 1976—. Mem. L.A. Fitness Club, U. of the Pacific Club, K.C. (Family of the Month 1988). Republican. Roman Catholic.

NASSAR-MCMILLAN, SYLVIA C., educator; b. Detroit, Aug. 29, 1963; d. Albert S. Nassar and Erika L. Strunk; m. Ian Johnson McMillan, July 17, 1994. BA, Oakland U., 1984; MA, Ea. Mich. U., 1986; PhD, U. N.C., Greensboro, 1994. Grad. asst. Ea. Mich. U., Ypsilanti, 1985-86; bi-lingual officer mgr. Motion Mfg., Detroit, 1986-87; counselor UAW/GM Human Resource Ctr., Pontiac, Mich., 1987-88; program coord. women's ctr. We. Mich. U., Kalamazoo, 1988-89, coord. career planning, 1989-90; career counselor, intern Loyola U., Chgo., 1990; counselor, site supr. Charlevoix Publ Schs., Beaver Island, Mich., 1991; asst. prof., counseling coord. Austin Peay State U., Clarksville, Tenn., 1994-96; asst. prof. counselor edn. U. N.C., Charlotte, 1996—; mem. sexism com. Austin Peay State U., 1995-96, mem. critical incident stress mgmt., 1994-96, mem. univ. hearing bd., 1994-96. Workcamp leader Vols. for Peace, Baxter State Park, Mich., 1990, Girl Scouts Am., Kalamazoo, 1990; group counselor/cmty. edn./vol. tng. HAVEN-Domestic Violence Shelter, Oakland County Mich., 1986-88. Doctoral fellow Residence Life U. N.C., Greensboro, 1991-94; recipient Profl. Devel. award Mich. Coll. Personnel Assn., 1989-90. Mem. Am. Counseling Assn. (editl. bd. Jour. of Counseling and Devel. 1996—, professionalism com. 1995—), Am. Psychol. Assn., So. Assn. counselor Edn. & Supervision, Assn. Counselor Edn. & Supervision, Chi Sigma Iota. Office: Dept Counselor Edn Spl Edn & Child Devel U NC Charlotte NC 28223

NASSAU, CAROL DEAN, educator; b. Omaha, Nebr., Jan. 16, 1953; d. Robert Paulus and Dorothy Ann (Peterson) Dean; 1 child, William Dean Nassau. BA in Translation, U. Nebr., 1976; MA in Comparative Lit., Binghamton (N.Y.) U., 1983, MAT in Fgn. Lgn., 1987. Cert. tchr., N.Y. Translator Mutual of Omaha Ins. Co., Omaha, 1976-78; tchr. Unatego Ctrl. Schs., Wells Bridge, N.Y., 1987-88, Oneonta (N.Y.) City Schs., 1988—. Contbr. articles to profl. jours.; actress (TV series) Susquehanna Stories, 1990. Couper fellowship Bringhamton U., 1994. Mem. Am. Ednl. Rsch. Assn., N.Y. State Assn. for Fgn. Lang. Tchrs. (presenter confs. 1987, 95, Outstanding Svc. award 1988). Democrat. Home: 2 Washburn St Oneonta NY 13820

NASSER, GISELLE L., marketing professional; b. Bogotá, Colombia, July 29, 1970; d. Salim and Olga Lucia (Posada) N. Student, U. Houston, 1991; Degree in Advt., U. Bogotá, Colombia, 1994. Gen. mgr. S.N. Indsl., Bogotá, Colombia, 1991; comml. dir. Jamaica Tourist Bd., Bogotá, Colombia, 1991-94; producer Monumental Sculptures & Scripts Fernando Botero, Ft. Lauderdale, Fla., 1995, Gold Italia-Miami, Miami, Fla., 1995; mktg. dir. S.N. Indsl., Miami, Fla., 1994-95; creator and producer Advt. Campaign for S.N. Indsl., Bogotá, 1993; producer Fernando Botero Monumental Sculptures & Drawings, Ft. Lauderdale, 1994; assoc. producer Gold Italia Miami '95, Miami, 1995. Vol. Miami Project to Cure Paralysis, 1994-95, Star Art Found., Miami, 1994. Home: 15401 SW 88 Ave Miami FL 33157

NASSOURA, NANCY KATHRYN, special education educator; b. N.Y.C., Oct. 16, 1968; d. Robert Emmett and Winifred Kathryn (Flynn) Bozzomo; m. Khaled Nassoura, July 8, 1995. BA, Coll. St. Elizabeth, 1991; MA in Spl. Edn., Kean Coll. N.J., 1994. Tchr. handicapped, elem. edn., secondary English. Permanent substitute Clifton (N.J.) Pub. Schs., 1992; resource ctr. tchr. Bedwell Elem. Sch., Bernardsville, N.J., 1992-94, Hilltop Elem. Sch., Mendham, N.J., 1994—; head tchr. summer program, YMCA, Livingston, N.J., 1991—, morning program, Basking Ridge, N.J., 1992-94. Mem. Coun. Exceptional Children, Coun. for Children with Behavorial Disorders, Coun. for Children with Learning Disabilities, Orton Dyslexia Soc., N.J. Edn. Assn., N.J. Coun. for Social Studies, Kappa Delta Pi. Office: Hilltop Elem Sch 12 Hilltop Rd Mendham NJ 07945-1215

NASTASI, KATHLEEN PATRICIA, systems analyst; b. Rochester, N.Y., July 13, 1960; d. Donald P. and Nancy K. (Kleinhans) N. BA in Math., Nazareth Coll., Rochester, N.Y., 1982, BA, 1982; postgrad., St. John Fisher Coll., Rochester, N.Y., 1994—. Cert. notary pub., N.Y. Title exam, bookkeeper Pub. Abstract Corp., Rochester, 1982-83; v.p., office mgr. Colon Abstract Corp., Rochester, 1983-86; systems adminstr. First Fed. S & L, Rochester, 1986-95; analyst, cons. Ciber, Inc., Rochester, 1995—; facilitator devel. team meetings Xerox Corp., Rochester, 1995—. Musician in field. Recipient Achievement in Maths. award Bishop Kearney, 1978; faculty scholar Nazareth Coll., Kodak Co. scholar, 1978-82. Mem. NAFE, Nat. Honor Soc. Home: 153 Lake Rd Webster NY 14580 Office: Ciber Inc 345 Woodcliff Dr Fairport NY 14450

NATAL, DOTTIE LOUISE, educational software publisher, educational technology researcher; b. Toledo, Dec. 8, 1955; d. John Robert and Jeanette Alice (Bauer) Ermlich; m. David Natal; children: Jovena, Alisa. BA in Math., U. Calif., Santa Barbara, 1980, MA in Ednl. Psychology, 1990, PhD in Ednl. Psychology, 1995. Cert. tchr., Calif. Math. tchr. Santa Barbara Pub. Schs., 1980-83; programmer, nuclear physicist Mission Rsch. Corp., Santa Barbara, 1983-88; ednl. software pub. Imagen Multimedia, Lompoc, Calif., 1990—. Developer (software) Coop. Group Tools, 1994. Treas. Lompoc Dem. Club, 1990—. Mem. Am. Ednl. Rsch. Assn., Multimedia Developers Group, Computer Using Educators. Office: Imagen Multimedia Corp 2351 Sweeney Rd Lompoc CA 93436-9650

NATALE, ROSE ANNE, elementary education educator; b. Chester, Pa., Dec. 15, 1955; d. Lawrence Joseph and Margaret (Farr) N. BA in Polit. Sci., U. Del., 1977; MS in Edn., St. Joseph's U., Phila., 1993. Cert. secondary social studies, elem. edn., elem. prin., supr. curriculum and instrn. Clk. F.B.I., Phila., 1977-81; fraud investigator Phila. (Pa.) Nat. Bank, 1981-83; tchr. S.E. Delco Sch. Dist., Folcroft, Pa., 1988—. Vol. Spl. Olympics Delaware County, Pa., 1994. Mem. ASCD, Nat. Coun. Tchrs. Math. Office: Ashland Middle Sch Ashland & Bartram Aves Glenolden PA 19036

NATALIA, RUSAK, lawyer; b. New Brunswick, N.J., May 24, 1961; d. Vasil and Halina (Rodzko) R.; m. Christopher Joseph Gernat, Oct. 20, 1990; children: Roman, Natasia, Kiprian. BA in English Lit. and Anthropology, Rutgers U., 1983; JD, Hofstra U., 1986. Bar: N.J. 1987, N.Y. 1987. Assoc. Jacobs, Katz & Lurie, P.C., Bklyn., 1987, Voorhees, Bennett & Wherry, Pennington, N.J., 1987-89; ind. cons. Somerset, N.J., 1989-90; assoc. Bloom Borenstein, P.C., Springfield, N.J., 1990-92; ind. cons. Bridgewater, N.J., 1992—. Assoc. producer: (TV program) The Law Journal, 1993-94; asst. editor: Belarussian Rev., 1993—; contbr. to profl. publs. Speaker for Christian Dem. Women's Orgn., 1st World Conf. of Belarussian, Miensk, 1992; bd. dirs. Belarusan-Am. Cultural and Ednl. Soc., 1994—; vol. Legal Clin. Women's Resource Ctr., Bridgewater, 1993—; vol. Rape Crisis Ctr., Somerville, N.J., 1995—. Mem. N.J. Bar Assn. Home: 1268 Crim Rd Bridgewater NJ 08807

NATALICIO, DIANA SIEDHOFF, academic administrator; b. St. Louis, Aug. 25, 1939; d. William and Eleanor J. (Biermann) Siedhoff. BS in Spanish summa cum laude, St. Louis U., 1961; MA in Portuguese lang., U. Tex., 1964, PhD in Linguistics, 1969. Chmn. dept. modern langs. U. Tex., El Paso, 1973-77, assoc. dean liberal arts, 1977-79; acting dean liberal arts, 1979-80; dean Coll. Liberal Arts U. Tex., El Paso, 1980-84, v.p. acad. affairs, 1984-88, pres., 1988—; bd. dirs. El Paso br. Fed. Res. Bd. Dallas, chmn., 1989; mem. Presdl. Adv. Commn. on Ednl. Excellence for Hispanic Ams., 1991; bd. dirs. Sandia Corp., Enserch Corp.; bd. dirs. Nat. Action Coun. for Minorities in Engring., 1993-96; mem. Nat. Sci. Bd. 1994-2000; mem. NASA Adv. Coun., 1994-96; bd. mem. Fund for Improvement of Post-Secondary Edn., 1993-97; bd. dirs. Fogarty Internat. Ctr. of NIH, 1993-96; bd. chair Am. Assn. Higher Edn., 1995-96; bd. dirs. U.S.-Mexico Commn. for Ednl. and Cultural Exch., 1994-96. Co-author: Sounds of Children, 1977; contbr. articles to profl. jours. Bd. dirs. United Way El Paso, 1990-93, chmn. needs survey com., 1990-91, chmn. edn. divsn., 1989; chmn. Quality Edn. for Minorities Network in Math. Sci. and Engring., 1991-92; chairperson Leadership El Paso, Class 12, 1989-90, mem. adv. coun., 1987-90, participant, 1980-81; mem. Historically Black Colls. and Univs./Minority Instns. Consortium on Environ. Tech. chairperson, 1991-93. Recipient Torch of Liberty award Anti-Defamation League B'nai B'rith, 1991, Conquistador award City of El Paso, 1990, Humanitarian award Nat. Coun. Christians and Jews, El Paso chpt., 1990; mem. El Paso Women's Hall of Fame, 1990. Mem. Philos. Soc. Tex. Home: 711 Cincinnati Ave El Paso TX 79902-2616 Office: U Tex at El Paso Office of the President El Paso TX 79968-0500

NATHAN, DEBBIE, writer; b. Houston, Aug. 27, 1950; d. Charles Carb and Sylvia Ruth (Laufe) N.; m. Morten Naess, Dec. 28, 1982; children: Sophia, William. BA in Social Scis., Temple U., 1972; MA in Linguistics, U. Tex., El Paso, 1978. Writer Chgo., 1980-84, El Paso, 1984—; staff reporter El Paso Times, 1985-86. Co-author: Satan's Silence, 1995; author: Women and Other Aliens, 1991; contbr.: The Satanism Scare, 1991; contbr. articles to mags. Founder, coord. League for Immigration/Border Rights Edn., El Paso, 1986-89; active Border Rights Coalition, El Paso, 1989—; bd. dirs. Planned Parenthood, El Paso, 1988-90; mem. immigration com. ACLU, El Paso, 1988—. Recipient J.L. Mencken award Free Press Assn., 1988, Hugh Hefner 1st Amendment award Playboy Found., 1991, S.W. Book award El Paso Pub. Libr. Assn., 1992. Mem. Nat. Writers Union (at-large del. 1995—), PEN-West. Office: 109 N Oregon # 412 El Paso TX 79901

NATHAN, HELEN SIGUR, group travel coordinator; b. New Orleans, Oct. 17, 1962; d. Arthur Alexander Jr. and Jacquelyn Elaine (Vedrenne) Sigur; m. Mitchell Alan Nathan, May 28, 1990. BS, La. State U., 1984; BS magna cum laude, Towson State U., 1994. Coord. media, pub. rels. Nat. Sports Festival VI (now U.S. Olympic Festival), Baton Rouge, La., 1984-85; acct. exec. S.R. Publs./Baton Rouge Mag., 1985-86; advt. sales assoc. L.M. Berry (yellow pages), Metairie, La., 1986-87; group travel cons., tour dir. Alexander Travel, Metairie, La., 1987-88; group travel coord. AESU Travel, Inc., Balt., 1988—; tchr. music George Fox Mid. Sch., Pasadena, Md., 1994; musical dir. Jewish Cmty. Ctr., Balt., 1993, 96; dir., soprano AESU Christmas Chorus, Balt., 1995—; soprano, charter mem. O Christmas Trio, Balt., 1991—. Author, dir., producer (one-act musical) Swamp Trek, 1984. Cantor St. Charles Borromeo Ch., Balt., 1989—. Towson State U. scholar, 1991-94. Mem. Md. Music Educators Assn., Music Educators Nat. Conf., Delta Zeta (historian, chaplain, activities chmn. 1980—), Kappa Delta Pi (historian 1993-94). Republican. Roman Catholic.

NATHANS, SARI RODA, computer consultant; b. Paterson, N.J., May 19, 1961; d. Jerome and Rita (Kitzis) N. BSBA in Computer Info. Sys., Ohio State U., 1983; MS in Computer Info. SCI., Nova S.E. U., 1996. Analyst Mellon Bank, N.A., Pitts., 1983-84, Coca-Cola Co., Atlanta, 1984-87; sr. sys. engr. Contel Corp., Atlanta, 1987-91; adv. sys. engr. GTEDS, Tampa, Fla., 1991-95, prin. cons. Informix Software, Tampa, 1995—. Office: Informix Software Inc 8675 Hidden River Pkwy #100 Tampa FL 33637

NATHANSON, LINDA SUE, publisher, author, technical writer; b. Washington, Aug. 11, 1946; d. Nat and Edith (Weinstein) N.; m. James F. Barrett. BS, U. Md., 1969; MA, UCLA, 1970, PhD, 1975. Tng. dir. Rockland Research Inst., Orangeburg, N.Y., 1975-77; asst. prof. psychology SUNY, 1978-79; pres. Cabri Prodns., Inc., Ft. Lee, N.J., 1979-81; research supr. Darcy, McManus & Masius, St. Louis, 1981-83; mgr. software tng., documentation On-Line Software Internat., Ft. Lee, 1983-85; pvt. practice cons. Ft. Lee, 1985-87; founder, exec. dir. The Edin. Group, Inc., Gillette, N.J., 1987—; founder, pres. Edin Books, Inc., Gillette, N.J., 1994—. Author: (with others) Psychological Testing: An Introduction to Tests and Measurements, 1988; pub. A Funny Thing Happened at the Interview (G.F. Farrell), 1996, Angel Talk, 1996. Recipient Research Service award 1978; Albert Einstein Coll. Medicine Research fellow, 1978-79. Jewish. Home and Office: 102 Sunrise Dr Gillette NJ 07933-1944

NATORI, JOSIE CRUZ, apparel executive; b. Manila, May 9, 1947; came to U.S., 1964; d. Felipe F. and Angelita A. (Almeda) Cruz; m. Kenneth R. Natori, May 20, 1972; 1 child, Kenneth E.F. BA in Econs., Manhattanville Coll., 1968. V.p. Merrill-Lynch Co., N.Y.C., 1971-77; pres. The Natori Co., N.Y.C., 1977—; bd. dirs. Dreyfus Third Century Fund, The Alltel Corp., Calyx and Corolla. Bd. dirs. Philippine Am. Found., Jr. Achievement, Inc., 1992, Ednl. Found. for Fashion Industries; trustee Manhattanville Coll. Recipient Human Relations award Am. Jewish Com., N.Y.C., 1986, Harriet Alger award Working Woman, N.Y., 1987, Castle award Manhattanville Coll., Purchase, 1988, Galleon award Pres. Philippines, N.Y.C. Asian-Am. award, Friendship award Philippine-Am. Found., Hall of Fame award Mega Mags., Salute to Am. Fashion Designers award Dept. of Commerce. Mem. CFDA, Young Pres.'s Orgn., Fashion Group, Com. of 200. Home: 45 E 62nd St New York NY 10021-8025 Office: Natori Co 40 E 34th St Fl 18 New York NY 10016-4501*

NATOW, ANNETTE BAUM, nutritionist, author, consultant; b. N.Y.C., Jan. 30, 1933; d. Edward and Gertrude (Jackerson) Baum; m. Harry Natow, Nov. 30, 1955; children: Allen, Laura, Steven. BS, CUNY Bklyn. Coll., 1955; MS, SUNY Coll. Plattsburg, 1960; PhD, Tex. Women's U., 1963. Registered dietitian, N.Y. Asst. prof. SUNY Coll. Plattsburg, 1967-69, CUNY Coll. Lehman, N.Y.C., 1969-70; assoc. prof., chmn. dept. SUNY Downstate Med. Ctr., Bklyn., 1970-76; prof., dir. nutrition programs Adelphi U., Garden City, N.Y., 1976-90, prof. emerita, 1991—; intern Montreal Diet Dispensary, March of Dimes, 1980; pres., writer, cons. NRH Nutrition Cons., Inc., Valley Stream, N.Y., 1980—. Author: No-Nonsense Nutrition, 1978, Geriatric Nutrition, 1980, Nutrition for the Prime of Your Life, 1983, No-Nonsense Nutrition for Kids, 1985, Megadoses: Vitamins as Drugs, 1985, Nutritional Care of the Older Adult, 1986, Pocket Encyclopedia of Nutrition, 1986, The Cholesterol Counter, 1989, 1988, 2d edit., 1989, The Fat Counter, 1989, The Fat Attack Plan, 1990, The Diabetes Carbohydrate and Calorie Counter, 1991, The Pregnancy Counter, 1992, The Iron Counter, 1993, The Sodium Counter, 1993, The Antioxidant Vitamin Counter, 1994, The Fast Food Counter, 1994, The Supermarket Nutrition Counter, 1995; editor Jour. Nutrition for Elderly, 1983—; mem. editorial bd. Environ. Nutrition Newsletter, 1985—; mem. editorial adv. bd. Prevention, 1984-86; contbr. numerous articles to profl. jours. United Hosp. Fund grantee, 1978. Mem. Am. Dietetic Assn., N.Y. State Dietetic Assn., N.Y. State Nutrition Coun. (sec. 1973-74). Home: 100 Rosedale Rd Valley Stream NY 11581-2802 Office: NRH Nutrition Cons Inc 100 Rosedale Rd Valley Stream NY 11581-2802

NATZKE, PAULETTE ANN, manufacturing executive; b. Wausau, Wis., Oct. 23, 1943; d. Milton L. and Geraldine J. (Henrichs) Marth; m. Kenneth A. Natzke, June 29, 1963; children: Jerome E., Julie J. Cert. ceramic tchr. Sec. Marth Wood Shavings Supply, Marathon, Wis., 1973-85; pres. Marth Wood Shavings Supply, Marathon, 1985—; v.p. Marth Transp. Inc., Marathon, 1984—; bd. dirs. Marth Found., Marathon, 1982—; owner Privacy Point on Lake Nokomis, Tomahawk, Wis., 1992—. Republican. Lutheran. Home: 6752 State Highway 107 Marathon WI 54448-9444 Office: Marth Wood Shavings Supply Inc Marathon WI 54448-9802

NAUEN, ELINOR JUDITH, writer, editor, poet; b. Sioux Falls, S.D., Feb. 18, 1952; d. Hans and Joyce (Phillips) N.; m. John J. Stanton, Dec. 23, 1991; stepchildren: Sean, Sam, Tara. Student, Mich. State U., 1970-73, CCNY, 1977-79. Editor Bauer Pub., Englewood, N.J., 1985-90; sr. editor First Mag., Englewood Cliffs, N.J., 1991-93; freelance editor, freelance writer N.Y.C., 1993—; coord. theater series Poetry Project, N.Y.C., 1985-88, dir., 1995—; cons. Newsweek Internat., N.Y.C., 1994—. Author: American Guys, 1996; author of numerous poems; editor: Diamonds are a Girl's Best Friend: Women Writers on Baseball, 1994, Ladies, Start Your Engines: Women Writers on Cars and the Road, 1996. Tutor Rhinelander Children's Aid Soc., N.Y.C., 1983-88; dir. Tzvi Aryeh AIDS Found., N.Y.C., 1994—. Mem. Nat. Writers Union. Office: 27 1st Ave # 9 New York NY 10003

NAUGHTON, FRANCINE RACINE, secondary education educator; b. Yonkers, N.Y., Nov. 12, 1943; d. William D. and Helen (Gernicara) Racine; m. John P. Naughton, Oct. 1, 1966; children: Jeanane Naughton Carr, John, Thomas, Katherine, Annie. BA, CUNY, 1966; MS in Edn. with honors, Iona Coll., 1990. Cert. secondaray social studies tchr., N.Y. Tchr. sociala studies Our Lady of Fatima Sch., Scarsdle, N.Y., 1984—. Mem. adv. bd. Scarsdale Summer Music Theater, 1985-95, v.p., 1995—. Home: 9 Roosevelt Pl Scarsdale NY 10583 Office: Our Lady of Fatima Sch 963 Scarsdale Rd Scarsdale NY 10583

NAUGHTON, MARIE ANN, corporate executive; b. Boston, Feb. 19, 1954; d. Robert J. and Beatrice T. (McDonald) N. BS in Speech magna cum laude, Emerson Coll., 1976; MA, Ind. U., 1977; Cert. spl. studies bus. and adminstrn. Harvard U., 1989. Speech-lang. pathologist Dedham (Mass.) pub. schs., 1977-79, Mass. Gen. Hosp., Boston, 1979-81; speech pathologist Mt. Auburn Hosp., Cambridge, Mass., 1982-84; v.p. Curtis-Newton Corp., 1984—. Author: A Coarticulation Manual for the Remediation of /S/, 1979. Elected Dedham Sch. Com., 1993-96. Fellow Soc. for Ear, Nose and Throat Advances in Children; mem. LWV (sec.), Am. Speech, Lang. and Hearing Assn. (cert. clin. competence), Northeastern Retail Lumber Assn., Mass. Retail Lumber Assn. (bd. dirs. 1996—), Zeta Phi Eta. Home: 77 Circuit Rd Dedham MA 02026-3605 Office: 41 River St Dedham MA 02026-2935

NAUGLE, JOAN CAROL, elementary education educator; b. St. Louis, Mar. 30, 1951; d. Richard Edward and June (Hollis) Savage; m. Karl E. Naugle, July 14, 1979; children: Karl Edward, Kathryn Elizabeth, Karen Ellen. BA in Edn., S.W. Mo. State U., 1973; MEd, John Carroll U., 1976. Data processor Sunnen Products Co., St. Louis, 1970-72; receptionist, sec. Crawford House Hotel, Crawford Notch, N.H., 1973; 6th grade tchr. Mayfield Middle Sch., Mayfield Heights, Ohio, 1973-81, Newington Elem. Sch., Summerville, S.C., 1982-83; 3d grade tchr. Knightsville Elem. Sch., Summerville, 1983-87; with profl. devel. dept. Dorchester Sch. Dist. 2, Summerville, 1987—. Dir. swim team Quail Arbor Civic Club, Summerville, 1994; active dist. pub. rels. United Meth. Women, 1991—; pres. Summerville Elem. PTO, 1989-91, manpower chmn., 1991—; legis. chair Rollings Elem. PTA, 1993-95, v.p., 1990-91. Named Outstanding Wellness Coord. Carolina Healthstyles, 1994. Mem. Phi Delta Kappa, Alpha Delta Kappa (mems. chair 1986—). Republican. Home: 107 Spring St Summerville SC 29485-4825 Office: Dorchester Sch Dist 2 805 S Main St Summerville SC 29483-5913

NAUMAN, MARY JEAN RITA, elementary school educator; b. Peoria, Ill., Aug. 9, 1941; d. Valentine Laurence and Margaret Cecilia (Stenger) N. BA, Mount Mary Coll., Milw., 1969; MS, No. Ill. U., 1975; Reading Recovery Cert., Ill. State U., Normal, 1992. Cert. tchr. K-8, lang. arts, reading, vocal music, social studies. Tchr. grades 6-8 St. James Sch., Belvidere, Ill., 1963-67; tchr. grades 2-8 Diocese of Peoria, 1967-74; tchr. grades 1-2 Springlake Dist. 606, Manito, Ill., 1974-75; tchr. Title I Dist. #108, Pekin, Ill., 1975-77; tchr. grade 1 Dist. # 108, Pekin, Ill., 1977-91, tchr. Chpt. I/reading recover, 1991—; instr. night classes Ill. Ctrl. Coll., East Peoria, 1972-73; bd. cons. Ill. State Bd. Edn., Springfield, 1988-90, Ill. Reading Coun., Bloomington, 1978-82; diagnostic cons. Dist. #108, 1976-77. Publicity chair, bd. dirs. Cmty. Concert Assn., Pekin, 1985—. Recipient

Master Tchr. award State of Ill., Tazewell County, 1984; grantee Alpha Delta Kappa, North Ctrl. area, Des Moines, 1993, Pres.'s Coun., Peoria, 1994. Mem. NEA, Ill. Edn. Assn., Edn. Assn. Pekin, Internat. Reading Assn., Ill. Reading Coun., Ill. Valley Reading Coun. (corres. sec., pres.), Alpha Delta Kappa (exec. bd., corres. sec. 1982—, rec. sec., pres. 1988-90). Democrat. Roman Catholic. Office: Willow Elementary School 1110 Veerman St Pekin IL 61554-2442

NAUTS, HELEN COLEY, health science association administrator; b. Sharon, Conn., Sept. 2, 1907; d. William Bradley and Alice (Lancaster) Coley; m. william Boone Nauts, Sept. 22, 1928; children: Nancy Coley, Phyllis Lancaster. Student sch. landscape architecture, Columbia U., 1927-28; DSc (hon.), Hartwick Coll., 1986. Pvt. practice landscape architecture N.Y. and Conn.; founder, exec. dir. Cancer Research Inst., N.Y.C., 1953-82, dir. Sci. Med. Communications, 1982-95; exec. dir. Brearley Alumnae Assn., N.Y.C., 1940-48, mng. editor Brearley Bull., 1946-48; trustee Cancer Rsch. Inst., 1953-66; lectr. cancer confs. France, Germany, Eng., Japan, China, U.S., Sweden, Denmark. Author, editor sci. papers in cancer rsch., monographs on cancer immunology. Recipient William B. Coley Meml. award, 1985, Commandeur de l'Ordre Nat. de Merite Pres. Valery Giscard d'Estaing, 1981, Francis Riker Davis Alumnae award Brearley Sch., 1980. Democrat. Presbyterian. Club: Cosmopolitan (N.Y.C.). Home and Office: Cancer Research Inst 1225 Park Ave New York NY 10128-1758

NAVA, CYNTHIA D., state legislator. BS, Western Ill. U.; MA, Ea. Ill. U. Dep. supt. Gadsden Schools; mem. N.Mex. Senate; mem. rules com., fin. com. Home: 3002 Broadmoor Dr Las Cruces NM 88001-7501 Office: N Mex Senate State Capitol Santa Fe NM 87503*

NAVARRA, LISA M. TERRUSO, gifted/talented education educator; b. Freeport, N.Y., June 23, 1964; m. Christopher Navarra, May 18, 1991. BS, Adelphi U., 1987; MEd, St. John's U., 1993. Cert. gifted/talented educator, N.Y. 6th grade tchr. Our Lady of Grace, Bklyn., 1987-89; lang. arts tchr., grades 5-8 St. Bernard's Acad., Bklyn., 1990—; moderator of newspaper, 1990-93, yearbook, 1993-94; chairperson lang. arts dept. St. Bernard's Acad., 1990-94. Recipient Adelphi U. Leadership award, 1986. Mem. ASCD.

NAVARRA, TOVA, nurse; b. Newark, July 10, 1948; d. Joe and Rose Leslie Treihart; m. John G. Navarra Jr., Aug. 26, 1967; children: Yolanda, John G. III. BA magna cum laude, Seton Hall Univ., 1974; AAS with honors, Brookdate C.C., Lincroft, N.J., 1984; student, Fairleigh Dickinson U. Elem. sch. tchr. Jersey City, 1967-69; corr. Village Times, Long Island, N.Y., 1974-75; tchr. music, humanities, German, art, art history Seton Hall Pres. Sch., South Orange, N.J., 1975-78; entertainment, feature writer, press corr. Asbury Park Press, Neptune, N.J., 1978-85; feature writer, art critic, family writer Asbury Park Press, Neptune, 1985-92; feature writer, art columnist Two River Times, Red Bank, N.J., 1993-94; psychiatric charge nurse, 1985; supr. grant rsch. Vis. Nurse Assn. Ctrl. Jersey, Red Bank, N.J., 1993-94; lectr. at writing confs. Author: The New Jersey Shore: A Vanishing Splendor, 1985, Jim Gary: His Life and Art, 1987, Your Body: Highlights of Human Anatomy, 1990, Playing It Smart: What to Do When You're on Your Own, 1989, also, pub. On My Own: Helping Kids Help Themselves, 1994, Themselves, 1994, A Practical Guide for Health Professionals, An Insider's Guide to Home Health Care: An Interdisciplinary Approach, 1995, Wisdom for Caregivers, 1995, (staged readings) Through the Kunai Grass with Dad, 1988, Don't Cry, Pandora, 1989; co-author: (with Myron A. Lipkowitz and John G. Navarra) Therapeutic Communication: A Guide to Effective Interpersonal Skills for Health Care Professionals, 1990, Encyclopedia of Vitamins, Minerals, and Supplements, 1995, (with Lipkowitz), Allergies A-Z, 1994; (with Margaret Lundrigan) Interdisciplinary Approach, 1996, Images of America: Howell and Farmingdale 1996; illustrator Drugs and Man, 1973; editor in chief Shore Affinity, 1979-81; contbg. editor Am. Jour. Nursing, 1990-94; staff writer, illustrator, photographer N.J. Music and Arts, 1978-81; editor Associated Univ. Presses, 1981-82; copywriter, photographer Jersey Shore Med. Ctr., 1985; feature writer, columnist Copley News Svc., 1988-93; health trend columnist Personal Fitness, 1989-90; photography exhbns. in N.Y., N.J., Pa., guest various radio and TV programs; contbr. photographs to books, articles and photogs. to mags., newspapers; solo exhibits include Atlantic City Art Ctr., 1982, O.K. Harris Works of Art, N.Y.C., 1990, Gallery Axiom, Phila., 1991, Moumouth U., 1991, M. Thomson Kravetz Gallery, Bay Head, N.J.; group shows at Moravian Coll., Bethlehem, Pa., 1992, Art Forms, Red Bank, 1991. Mem. Gov.'s Coun. on Alcoholism and Drug Abuse Prevention, co-chair Later Childhood subcom., 1992. Mem. N.J. Playwrights Workshop (charter), N.J. State Nurses Assn. Office: Sanford J Greenburger Assocs care Faith H. Hamlin 55 Fifth Ave New York NY 10003*

NAVARRO, JANYTE JANINE, environmental educator; b. LaJara, Colo., Apr. 14, 1935; d. John Charles Blissard and Mary Margaret (Mathias) Tedesco; m. Daniel David Myers (div. 1968); children: Kelli, Keith, Kim; m. Rafael Fowler Navarro (div. Sept. 1994); children: Eric, Marshall, Laura Lynne, Mitchell. Student, Colo. U., 1954-55, U. N.Mex. Owner Poodle Breeding Bus., Albuquerque, 1964-67, Jan-Knits, Albuquerque, 1973-74, Sharing Is Caring, Albuquerque, 1980—; mng. ptnr. Land-Ho Enterprises, 1988—; regional dir. EXCEL Telecoms., 1996; bd. dirs. Fieseta de Shaklee, Albuquerque. Producer: (video) The Sponsoring Process, 1981; articles, newsletters in field. Bd. dirs. Sandia Ch. Religious Sci. Mem. Rio Grande Sales Leaders Assn. (pres. 1984, 86). Home and Office: 1505 Gretta St NE Albuquerque NM 87112-4319

NAVEH, MARCIA SPIEGEL, physician; b. Miami, Fla., Feb. 11, 1949; d. Bernhard and Constance (Stern) Spiegel; m. Aaron Naveh, June 6, 1971; children: Dahlia, Elan. BS, Tulane U., 1971, MS, 1972; MD, Albert Einstein Coll. Medicine, 1977. Diplomate Nat. Bd. Med. Examiners, Am. Bd. Internal Medicine. Attending physician Presbyn. Hosp., N.Y.C., 1980-84, St. Lukes-Roosevelt Hosp. Ctr., N.Y.C., 1984—; physician N.Y. Med. Group, N.Y.C., 1984—, bd. dirs., 1995—; physician mem. Assocs. in Internal Medicine, Columbia U., N.Y.C., 1980-84; asst. prof. clin. medicine, Columbia U., 1980—; bd. dirs. Group Coun. Mut. Ins. Co., N.Y.C., N.Y. Med. Group. Mem. ACP, Am. Med. Womens Assn.

NAVEJA-ELLIS, FRANCESCA ANGELA, mental health counselor and clinic administrator; b. N.Y.C., June 23, 1939; d. Antonio and Jeannette Marie (Thomas) Naveja; m. David H. Ellis, Oct. 21, 1957; children: Theresa Fae Ann Zendejas, David Cary Ellis. AA with Honors, Allan Hancock Coll., 1985; BS, Columbia Pacific U., 1988; MA, U. San Francisco, 1989. Adminstr. Community Ministry Ctr., Chino, Calif., 1977-79; bus. mgr. Humanistic Mental Health, Santa Maria, Calif., 1984-85; med. sec. A. Edward Hoctor, MD., Santa Maria, 1985; bus. mgr. Affiliated Psychotherapist, Santa Maria, 1985-87; founder, exec. dir., psychotherapist, C.E.O. AP Inst., Inc. Community Counseling Ctr., Santa Maria, 1988—; program dir. Safe Interventions, Santa Maria, Case Mgmt. and Consulting Assocs., Santa Maria; mem. adj. faculty Columbia Pacific U., Sierra U.; founder, dir. Trias Inst., Santa Maria, 1984—, AP Inst., Santa Maria, 1986-87, AP Inst. Valley Counseling Ctr., 1986-95; bd. dirs. Friends of Ruth Women's Shelter, Santa Maria, 1985; cons. St. Joseph's High Sch., 1990, Ctrl. Coast Cons. Assocs., 1991—. Editor, author quar. newsletter Pride, 1990—. Vol. Dem. Women's Caucus 1986; mem. Women's Network, Santa Maria, 1986-89; mental health adv. coun. Santa Barbara County, 1990, with Domestic violence Edn./Elimination Svcs., 1992-95. Mem. Am. Mental Health Counseling Assn., Assn. Christian Therapists (regional coord., 1988-90), Calif. Assn. Marriage Family Therapists, Cen. Coast Jung Soc., Western Assn. Spiritual Dirs., Cen. Coast Hypnosis Soc. Mem. Am. Assn. Prof. Hypnotherapists. Office: Lovelock Mental Health PO Box 1046 Lovelock NV 89419

NAVRATILOVA, MARTINA, former professional tennis player; b. Prague, Czechoslovakia, Oct. 18, 1956; came to U.S., 1975, naturalized, 1981; d. Miroslav Navratil and Jana Navratilova. Student, schs. in Czechoslovakia; Hon. doctorate, George Washington U., 1996. Profl. tennis player, 1975-94; tennis commentator/broadcaster HBO Sports, 1995. Author: (with George Vecsey) Martina, 1985, (with Liz Nickels) The Total Zone, 1995, (with Liz Nickels) The Breaking Point, 1996. Vol. Rainbow Found. Winner Czechoslovak Nat. singles, 1972-74, U.S. Open singles, 1983, 84, 86, 87, U.S. Open doubles, 1977, 78, 80, 83, 84, 87, 90, U.S. Open mixed doubles, 1987, Va. Slims Tournament, 1978, 83, 84, 85, 86, Va. Slims doubles, 1991, Wimbledon singles, 1978, 79, 82, 83, 84, 85, 86, 87, 90, Wimbledon women's doubles, 1976, 79, 81, 82, 83, 84, 86, Wimbledon mixed doubles, 1985, 94, 95, French Open singles, 1982, 84, Australian Open singles, 1981, 83, 85, Australian Doubles (with Nagelsen) 1980, (with Shriver), 1982, 84, 85, 87, 88, 89, Grand Slam of Women's Tennis, 1984, Roland Garros (with Shriver), 1985, 87, 89, Italian Open doubles (with Sabatini), 1987, (with Shriver) COREL WTA Tour doubles team of yr., 1981-89, triple Crown at U.S. Open, 1987; recipient Women's Sports Found. Flo Hyman award, 1987; named Female Athlete of the Decade (1980s) The Nat. Sports Review, UPI, and AP, WTA Player of Yr., 1978-79, 82-86, Women's Sports Found. Sportswoman of Yr., 1982-84, Hon. Citizen of Dallas, AP Female Athlete of Yr., 1983, Chgo. Hall of Fame, 1994; Martina Navratilova Day proclaimed in Chgo., 1992. Mem. Women's Tennis Assn. (dir., exec. com., pres.). Address: IMG 1 Erieview Plz Cleveland OH 44114-1715

NAWROCKI, MARYANN G., elementary school educator; b. Chgo., July 9, 1969; d. Frank J. and Harriet C. Nawrocki. BA, U. Chgo., 1991; MEd, U. Ill., Chgo., 1993. Cert. elem. tchr., Ill. 5th grade tchr. Blessed Kateri Tekawithe Acad., Thoreau, N.Mex., 1993-94; 2d grade tchr. St. Thomas the Apostle Grade Sch., Chgo., 1994—. Mem. Nat. Coun. Tchrs. of Math., Internat. Reading Assn., Nat. Sci. Tchrs. Assn. Office: St Thomas the Apostle Sch 5467 S Woodlawn Ave Chicago IL 60615

NAYER, JO ANN ELIZABETH, executive, multimedia producer; b. Rome, N.Y., May 28, 1954; d. Veto Philip and Josephine Spohn; children: Tracy, Matthew. BA, SUNY, Binghamton, 1976; MLS, U. Md., 1978. Media libr. Langston Hughes Libr., Corona, N.Y., 1978-80; prodn. mgr. Showtime Networks, N.Y.C., 1980-87; dir. post prodn. Lifetime TV, N.Y.C., 1987-94; owner, multimedia producer Tama Interactive Design, Inc., Bklyn., 1995—. Office: Tama Interactive Design 230 11th St Brooklyn NY 11215

NAYLOR, PHYLLIS REYNOLDS, author; b. Anderson, Ind., Jan. 4, 1933; d. Eugene Spencer and Lura Mae (Schield) Reynolds; m. Thomas A. Tedesco, Jr., Sept. 9, 1951 (div. 1960); m. Rex V. Naylor, May 26, 1960; children: Jeffrey, Michael. Diploma, Joliet Jr. Coll., 1953; BA, Am. U., 1963. Author: 90 books including Crazy Love: An Autobiographical Account of Marriage and Madness, 1977, Revelations, 1979, A String og Chances, 1982 (ALA notable book), The Gaony of Alice, 1985 (ALA notable book), The Keeper, 1986 (ALA notable book), Unexpected Pleasures, 1986, Send No Blessings, 1990 (YASD best book for young adults), Shiloh, 1991 (ALA notable book, John Newbery medal 1992). Recipient Golden Kite award Soc. Children's Book Writers Am., 1985, Child Study award Bank St. Coll., 1983, Edgar Allan Poe award Mystery Writers Am., 1985, Internat. book award Soc. Sch. Librs., 1988, Christopher award, 1989, Newbery award ALA, 1992, Nat. Endowment of Arts Creative Writing fellow, 1987. Mem. Children's Book Guild of Washington (pres. 1974-75, 83-84), Soc. Children's Book Writers, Authors Guild, PEN, Council for a Livable World, SANE, Physicians for Social Responsibility, Amnesty International. Unitarian. Home and Office: 9910 Holmhurst Rd Bethesda MD 20817-1618

NAYOR, NANCY, film company executive. Sr. v.p. feature casting Universal Pictures, Universal City, Calif. Office: MCA-Universal 100 Universal City Plz Bldg 463 Universal City CA 91608-1014*

N'COGNITA, VERNITA See NEMEC, VERNITA ELLEN MCCLISH

NEACSU, MARIA, artist; b. Manoleasa, Romania, Aug. 15, 1948; d. Ioan and Valeria (Busuioc) Grosu; m. Marius C. Neacsu, Aug. 15, 1970; 1 child, George Mircea. BSBA, Acad. Econ. Study, Bucharest, 1973; BS in Art, U. Calif., Berkeley, 1993; MFA, U. Calif., 1995. Econ. Iprochim, Bucharest, 1973-81; sr. acct. Bechtel, Inc., San Francisco, 1981-83; acctg. mgr. West Mgmt. Co., Oakland, Calif., 1983-86; sr. acct. Kaiser Engring. Inc., Oakland, 1986-89; artist Walnut Creek, Calif., 1989—. Jack K. and Gertrude Murphy fine arts fellow San Francisco Found., 1994. Republican. Home: 505 Pimlico Ct Walnut Creek CA 94596-3677

NEAGOY, MARY, broadcast executive. V.p. comm. VH1, N.Y.C. Office: NBC 30 Rockefeller Plz New York NY 10112*

NEAL, BONNIE JEAN, real estate professional; b. Kansas City, Mo., Apr. 24, 1930; d. David Ira and Juanita Mae (Duncan) Johnson; m. Howard Stranton Neal, July 24, 1948 (div. Oct. 1972); children: Randall Stranton, William Scott, Douglas Kelly. Student, U. Omaha, 1980-86, Londay Sch. Real Estate, Omaha, 1987. Data processing supr. Enron Corp., Omaha, 1980-85, adminstrv. support analyst, 1985-86; real estate sales agt. Allen, Young Assocs., Omaha, 1987, Home Real Estate (merger Allen Young Assocs. and Wurdeman & Maenner), Omaha, 1988; with Coldwell Banker Action Real Estate, 1988-91, Coldwell Banker BJ Brown, La Vista, Nebr., 1991-92. Active PTA, Council Bluffs, Iowa, 1957-59; vol. March of Dimes, Council Bluffs, 1963; mem. Realtors Polit. Action Com.; mem. pub. rels. com. Bd. Realtors, 1994-96, mem. forms com., 1995-96. Fellow Omaha Bd. Realtors, Women's Bowling Assn., Order Ea. Star (25-Yr. award 1980); mem. Women's Coun. Realtors. Democrat. Baptist. Home and Office: Home Real Estate 14250 W Maple Rd Omaha NE 68164-2436

NEAL, DARWINA LEE, government official; b. Mansfield, Pa., Mar. 31, 1942; d. Darwin Leonard and Ina Belle (Cooke) N. BS, Pa. State U., 1965; postgrad., Cath. U, 1968-70. Registered landscape architect. Landscape architect nat. capital region Nat. Pk. Svc., 1965-69, office of White House liaison, 1969-71, office of profl. services, 1971-74, div. design svcs., 1974-89, chief design svcs., 1989-95; landscape architect office of stewartship & partnership Nat. Pk. Svc., Washington, 1996—; judge numerous award juries. Contbr. articles to profl. jours.; co-author sects. of profl. bull., mag.; author introduction to book Women, Design and the Cambridge School; columnist: Land monthly, 1975-79. Mem. Women's Coun. on Energy in Environment. Recipient Merit award Landscape Contractors Met. Washington; recipient hon. mention Les Floralies Internationales de Montreal, 1980 Alumni Achievement award Pa. State U. Arts and Architecture Alumni Soc., 1981. Fellow Am. Soc. Landscape Architects (v.p. 1979-81, pres. elect 1982-83, pres. 1983-84, trustee 1976-77, nat. treas. 1977-79, legis. coordinator 1975-79, sec. Coun. Fellows 1988-90, (del. to Internat. Fedn. Landscape Architects, del. 1989—, ex-officio rep. to U.S./internat. com. on monuments and sites, liaison to historically black coll. and univ. program Dept. Interior, recipient Pres.' medal 1987); mem. Landscape Archtl. Accreditation Bd. (roster vis. evaluators), Nat. Recreation and Parks Assn., Nat. Soc. Park Resources (bd. dirs. 1978-80), Nat. Trust Hist. Preservation, Pa. State U. Alumni Assn. (Washington met. chpt. trustee 1972-74), Am. Arbitration Assn. (nat. panel arbitrators), Com. 100 for the Fed. City, Preservation Action, Nat. Assn. Olmsted Parks, Beekman Pl. Condominium Assn. (bd. dirs. 1985-91, archtl. control com.), Nat. Parks and Conservation Assn., Alliance for Historic Preservation, World Watch, Worldwide. Office: Nat Park Svc/Nat Capital Area Off Stewardship & Ptnrships 1100 Ohio Dr SW Washington DC 20242

NEAL, IRENE COLLINS, artist, educator; b. Greensburg, Pa., May 14, 1936; d. Oliver Shupe and Betsey Cowap (Mann) Collins; m. Paul Whitaker Neal, Nov. 24, 1960; children: Paul Collins Gordon, Betsey Whitaker. BA, Wilson Coll., 1958; student, Sch. Visual Arts, Rio de Janeiro, 1976-77, Memphis State U., 1979-80, U. Bridgeport, 1982-83; participant, Triangle Art Workshop, Pine Planes, N.Y., 1985. guest spkr. Coll. Santa Fe, Albuquerque, N.Mex., 1994. Solo exhbns. include Allied Chem. Corp., Morristown, N.J., 1975, Planetarium of Rio de Janeiro, 1977, The Pat Ackerman Gallery, Mphs., 1980, Westmoreland Mus. Art, Greensburg, 1986, Wilson Coll., 1993; group exhbns. include Jersey City Mus., 1975, N.J. State Mus., 1975, Somerset (N.J.) Tri-State Mus., 1975, Nat. Arts Club, N.Y.C., 1975, Garden State Watercolor Soc., 1975, Salao de Marinhas, Rio de Janeiro, 1977, Stamford (Conn.) Mus., 1984, 85, 89, Branchville Soho Gallery, Ridgefield, Conn., 1984, Silvermine Guild, New Canaan, Conn., 1984, Stamford Libr., 1985, Shippee Gallery, N.Y.C., 1986, 110 Greene St., N.Y.C., 1986, Wilton (Conn.) Libr., 1986, Aldrich Mus. Contemporary Art, Ridgefield, 1987, Ariel Gallery, N.Y.C., 1988, 89, Visual Arts Festival, Edmonton, Can., 1989, Mus. Art., Ft. Lauderdale, Fla., 1991-92, Salander-o'Reilly Galleries, Inc., N.Y., 1994, Vanderleelie Gallery, Edmonton, Can., 1996, Galerie Piltzer, Paris, France, 1996, Fine Art 2000, Stamford, Conn., 1996; represented in collections Planetarium Rio de Janeiro, Internat. Paper, N.Y.C., Westmoreland Mus. Art, Greensburg, Pepperdine U., Malibu, Calif., Newport Harbor Art Mus., Newport Beach, Calif., Hoover Instn. Stanford (Calif.) U., St. Matthew's Episcopal Ch., Wilton, Conn., Columbia U., N.Y.C., Ctr. Arts, Vero Beach, Fla., Mus. Art., Ft. Lauderdale, Alamo Rent A Car, Ft. Lauderdale, Denver Ctr. Performing Arts, Louis P. Cabot, Boston. Republican. Episcopalian. Home and Studio: 700 River Rd Cos Cob CT 06807

NEAL, JOYCE OLIVIA, utility company executive; b. Jamaica, N.Y., Aug. 11, 1943; d. Nathaniel Grant and Ernestine (Wilson) Thomas; m. Robert Lee Neal Jr., Dec. 16, 1959 (div. Dec. 1972); children: Cheryl Ann, Robin Crystal, Sylvia Lenore. AAS, SUNY, Farmingdale, 1979; BBA, Hofstra U., 1983. Keypunch operator E.B.S. Data Processing, Amityville, N.Y., 1968-71, asst. supr., 1971-72; keypunch operator Long Island Lighting Co., Hicksville, N.Y., 1972-78, asst. systems designer, 1978-79, assoc. systems designer, 1979-81, systems designer, 1981-84, systems analyst, 1984-85, project leader, 1985-89, sect. supr., 1989-95, project mgr., 1995—. Tutor Literacy Vols. Am., Nassau County, N.Y., 1988-90; vol. United Negro Coll. Fund, Nassau County, 1985—; bd. dirs. Suffolk County Housing Authority, Hauppauge, N.Y., 1985. Walter A. Lynch scholar SUNY, Farmingdale, 1979; recipient Cert. Appreciation, U.S. Assn. Evening Students, 1978-82, nat. sec. 1982. Mem. NAFE, NAACP, Coll. Scholarship Svc. (Cert. Appreciation, Talent Roster 1979), Black Women's Alliance Inc. (co-founder, pres. 1979-81, 84-85, 90-92, treas. 1986-89, sec. 1994—, Appreciation award 1989), Take Off Pounds Sensibly (founder Amityville chpt., leader 1974-78, 81-84, 86-87), Phi Theta Kappa, Alpha Beta Gamma, Alpha Sigma Lambda. Baptist. Office: Long Island Lighting Co 175 E Old Country Rd Hicksville NY 11801-4257

NEAL, LEORA LOUISE HASKETT, social services administrator; b. N.Y.C., Feb. 23, 1943; d. Melvin Elias and Miriam Emily (Johnson) Haskett; m. Robert A. Neal, Apr. 23, 1966; children: Marla Patrice, Johnathan Robert. BA in Psychology and Sociology, City Coll. N.Y., 1965; MS in Social Work, Columbia U., 1970, cert. adoption specialist, 1977; IBM cert. community exec. tng. program, N.Y., 1982. Cert. social worker N.Y. state. Caseworker N.Y.C. Dept. Social Service, 1965-67, Windham Child Care, N.Y.C., 1967-73; exec. dir. Assn. Black Social Workers Child Adoption Counseling and Referral Service, N.Y.C., 1975—; cons. adoption, adoption tng. N.Y. State Dept. Social Svc., Columbia U. Sch. Social Work, N.Y.C. Human Resources Adminstrn., U. La., New Orleans; founder Haskett-Neal Publs., Bronx, N.Y., 1993. Co-author: Transracial Adoptive Parenting: A Black/White Community Issue, 1993; contbr. articles in field to profl. jours. Child Welfare League Am. fellow, 1976; recipient cert. No Time to Lose cert. N.Y. State Dept. Social Svcs., 1989. Mem. NAFE, Columbia U. Alumni Assn., CCNY Alumni Assn., Missionary Com. Revival Team (outreach chairperson 1982-88). Democrat. Office: Assn Black Social Workers 1969 Madison Ave New York NY 10035-1549

NEAL, LOUISE KATHLEEN, life insurance company executive, accountant; b. Seattle, Nov. 25, 1951; d. Paul Bradford and Ruth Catherine (Park) Johnson; m. William Steven Neal, Oct. 25, 1974. B.A. in Bus. Adminstrn. and Acctg., U. Wash., 1974. Sr. acct. Touche Ross & Co., Seattle, 1974-77; internal auditor No. Life Ins. Co., Seattle, 1977-83; auditor Northwestern Nat. Life Ins. Co., Mpls., 1983-84, 2d v.p., auditor, 1984-88; sr. v.p., gen. auditor Transam. Occidental Life Ins. Co., L.A., 1988-89, sr. v.p., 1990-92, sr. v.p., chief adminstrv. officer, 1992-95; pres. USA Admin Svcs. Inc. sub. Transam. Occidental Life Ins. Co., Overland Park, Kans., 1995—. Fellow Life Mgmt. Inst.; mem. AICPA. Office: USA Admin Svcs Inc PO Box 2948 Overland Park KS 66201-1348

NEAL, MARGARET SHERRILL, writer; b. Memphis, Apr. 13, 1950; d. Wilburn Franklin and Merle Aileen (Willis) N. BA, Memphis State U., 1972, postgrad., 1973; MS, Columbia Pacific U., 1984. Air traffic controller FAA, Memphis, 1974-76, New Bern, N.C., 1976-81, Vero Beach, Fla., 1981-83; detection systems specialist U.S. Customs Service, Miami, 1983-87, intelligence rsch. specialist, 1987-89; ret., 1989. Mem. NOW, Smithsonian Instn., Mensa, Nat. Trust Hist. Preservation, Greenpeace, Clan Macneil Soc., Nature Conservancy, Save the Manatee Club. Republican. Presbyterian.

NEAL, MO (P. MAUREEN NEAL), sculptor; b. Houston, Oct. 26, 1950, d. Gordon Taft and Mary Louise (O'Connor) N.; m. Thomas Alan Buttars, Jan. 2, 1984. BA cum laude, Wash. State U., 1988; MFA, Va. Commonwealth U., 1991. Asst. prof. dept. art & art history U. Nebr., Lincoln, 1994—; adj. faculty dept. fine arts U. S.D., Vermillion, 1991-92. Grantee S.D. Arts Coun., 1992, 94, Nat. Endowment for Arts, 1994. Mem. South East Coll. Art Assn., Mid Am. Coll. Art Assn., Phi Beta Kappa. Democrat. Office: U Nebr Dept ARt & Art History Rm 207 Woods Hall Lincoln NE 68588-0114

NEAL, SUSAN KAY, accountant; b. Inglewood, Calif., Nov. 4, 1958; d. James Hampton and Betty Kay (Frydenlund) Neally; m. Lawrence Patrick Neal, June 4, 1990; children: Kate Alexa, Megan Elizabeth. BS in Acctg., Loyola Marymount U., 1980; MS in Tax, Golden Gate U., 1994. CPA, Calif., Tex. V.p. Gumbiner, Savett, Finkel, FIngleson & Rose, Inc., Santa Monica, Calif., 1980-94; pvt. practice Round Rock, Tex., 1994—. Co-editor: Propsed Audit and Accounting Guide: Audits of Future Commission Merchants and Commodity Pool, 1986. Counselor Tax Counseling for Elderly, Round Rock, 1996. Mem. AICPA, Calif. Soc. CPAs, Tex. Soc. CPAs, Better Bus. Bur., Round Rock C. of C. Republican. Lutheran. Home and Office: 16910 Judy Scholl Way Round Rock TX 78681

NEAL, TERESA SCHREIBEIS, secondary education educator; b. Wheatland, Wyo., Mar. 19, 1956; d. Gene L. and Bonnie Marie (Reed) Schreibeis; m. Michael R. Neal, Apr. 7, 1990; 1 child, Rianna Michelle. BA in Am. Studies and English Edn., U. Wyo., 1978; MA in History, U. So. Calif., 1989, PhD, 1994. Cert. secondary edn. tchr., Wyo., Colo. Tchr. lang. arts and social studies, asst. coach Carbon County Sch. Dist. 1, Rawlins, Wyo., 1978-86; asst. lectr. freshmen writing program U. So. Calif., L.A., 1986-90; prof. history Palomar (Calif.) Community Coll., San Diego, 1991; software support specialist Dynamic Data Systems, Westminster, Colo., 1992-93; tchr. humanities/gifted and talented classes Arvada (Colo.) West High Sch., 1993—; participant critical thinking and humanities secondary edn. project NEH, Wyo., 1985-86. Mem., chair Reading Is Fundamental Program, Rawlins, 1983-85. Mem. AAUW, Western Assn. Women Historians, G. Autrey Mus. Western Art, Phi Beta Kappa. Office: 11325 Allendale Dr Arvada CO 80004-4477

NEALE, DIANE YUNCK, artist; b. Olney, Ill., Dec. 1, 1944; d. George Feick and Dorothy (Phillips) Yunck; m. Latimer Ford Neale, June 14, 1967; children: Georgia Ford, Jules Arthur. BA in Art, French, Coll. Wooster, 1966; postgrad., Pratt Inst., 1967. Presch. and elem. art tchr. So. Calif. Sch. Dists., 1966-78. One-woman shows include Helen Drue Gallery, 1989, Arabesque-Stearns & Black Gallery, 1990, Valentine Owens Gallery, 1992; group exhibitions include Brushworks Gallery, San Diego, 1994-95, Gallery Viva, Kawasaki City, Japan, 1994, C.G Rein Gallery, Scottsdale, Ariz., 1993-94, Gallery Milieu, 1992. Bd. trustees Malibu (Calif.) United Meth., 1990, Sunday sch. tchr., choir mem., 1983-90. Methodist. Office: Diane Neale Studio 3525 Decker Rd Malibu CA 90265

NEALE, GAIL LOVEJOY, educational administrator; b. Detroit, Feb. 8, 1935; d. Elijah Parish and Jane Appleton (Howell) Lovejoy; m. Richard Potter (div.); m. Anthony Astrachan (div.); children: Owen Lovejoy, Joshua Howell; m. Robert Edward Neale, June 23, 1984. Student, Vassar Coll., 1952-54. Rsch. aide, dir. devel., corp. sec., v.p. Hudson Inst., Inc., Croton on Hudson, N.Y., 1962-76; v.p. Aspen Inst., N.Y.C., 1976-78; dir. external affairs Middlebury (Vt.) Coll., 1978-80; pres. Hudston Inst., Croton on Hudson, 1980-82; corp. sec. Commonwealth Fund, N.Y.C., 1983-86; project adminstr. Mt. Holyoke Coll., South Hadley, Mass., 1986-88; dir. devel. Hampshire Coll., Amherst, Mass., 1988-91; exec. v.p., COO Salzburg Seminar, Middlebury, Vt., 1991—; bd. dirs. JL Found., L.A., Capital Income Builder, L.A., Capital World Growth and Income Fund, L.A., AmcapFund, L.A., Fundamental Investors, L.A., Vera Inst. for Justice, N.Y.C. Bd. dirs. Conern for Dying, N.Y.C., 1986-90. Mem. Origami Soc. Am., Cosmopolitan Club. Democrat. Episcopalian. Home: 154 Prospect Pky Burlington VT 05401 Office: Salzburg Seminar PO 886 Marbleworks Middlebury VT 05753

NEAL-PARKER, SHIRLEY ANITA, obstetrician and gynecologist; b. Washington, Aug. 28, 1949; d. Leon Walker and Pearl Anita (Shelton) Neal; m. Andre Cowan Dasent, June 21, 1971 (div. Feb. 1978); 1 child, Erika Michelle Dasent; m. James Carl Parker, Feb. 11, 1979; 1 child, Amirah Nabeehah. BS in Biology, Am. U., 1971; MD, Hahnemann U., 1979. Med. lic. Md., W.Va., Calif., Wash. Intern Howard U. Hosp., 1979-80, resident, 1980-84; physician Nat. Health Svc. Corp., Charleston, W. Va., 1984-86; clin. instr. W. Va. U., Charleston, 1985-86; pvt. practice ob./gyn. Sacramento, 1986-95; pvt. practice Chehalis, Wash., 1995—. Mem. bd. Ruth Rosenberg Dance Ensemble, Sacramento, 1992-95, Chehalis Ballet Ctr., 1995, Human Response Network, Chehalis, 1995. Mem. Nat. Med. Assn., Am. Md. Women's Assn. (comty. svc. award Mother Hale br. 1994), No. Calif. Ob-Gyn. Soc., Nat. Assn. Gynecol. Laparoscopists, Nat. Assn. Reproductive Profls., Calif. Med. Assn., Wash. State Med. Assn., Lewis County Med. Soc., Soroptomist Internat. Home: 221 Vista Rd Chehalis WA 98532 Office: Shirley A Neal-Parker MD 171 S Market Blvd Chehalis WA 98532

NEAL-VITTIGLIO, CYNTHIA KAREN, clinical psychologist; b. Detroit, Dec. 30, 1952; d. Gaston O. and Evelyn Jewel (Dunn) N.; m. Thomas Anthony Vittiglio, July 10, 1988; 1 child, Anthony. BA, Wayne State U., 1975, MA, 1977, PhD, 1983. Licensed psychologist. Clin. researcher Sinai Hosp., Detroit, 1977-78; clin. asst. Dept. Neuropsychology Lafayette Clinic, 1974-75; faculty mem. Inst. for Sex Rsch., Bloomington, Ind., 1975, 80; sch. psychologist Lakeshore Pub. Schs., St. Clair Shores, Mich., 1979-80; staff psychologist Evergreen Counseling Ctr., St. Clair Shores, 1979—; consulting psychologist St. John Hosp., Detroit, 1983—. Mem. Jr. Coun., Founders Soc., Detroit, 1985—, Cranbrook Women's Soc., Bloomfield Hills, Mich., 1987—, Am. Ballet Soc., N.Y.C., 1980—. Recipient Grad. Fellowship Wayne State U., 1988. Mem. APA, DAR (Louise St. Clair chpt.). Republican. Office: Evergreen Counseling Svcs 19900 Ten Mile Saint Clair Shores MI 48009

NEARY, PAMELA, state legislator; b. Mar. 16, 1955; m. Court Storey; 4 children. BS in Biology and Polit. Sci., Ft. Lewis St. Coll.; MA in Pub. Affairs, Humphrey Inst. Mem. Minn. Ho. of Reps., 1992—; mem. health and human svcs. com., mem. regulated industries and energy com., mem. transp. and transit com. Active Citizens League. Mem. Minn. Women's Polit. Caucus, Minn. Women's Consortium. Democrat. Home: 1033 Indian Trl S Afton MN 55001-9705 Office: Minn Ho of Reps State Capital Building Saint Paul MN 55155-1606*

NEARY, PATRICIA ELINOR, ballet director; b. Miami, Fla.; d. James Elliott and Elinor (Mitsitz) N. Corps de ballet Nat. Ballet of Can., Toronto, Ont., 1957-60; prin. dancer N.Y.C. Ballet, 1960-68; ballerina Geneva Ballet (Switzerland), 1968-70, ballet dir., 1973-78; guest artist Stuttgart Ballet, Germany, 1968-70; asst. ballet dir., ballerina West Berlin Ballet, 1970-73; ballet dir. Zurich Ballet (Switzerland), 1978-86, La Scala di Milano ballet co., Italy, 1986-88; tchr., Balanchine ballets, Balanchine Trust, 1987—.

NEASE, JUDITH ALLGOOD, marriage and family therapist; b. Arlington, Mass., Nov. 15, 1930; d. Dwight Maurice Allgood and Sophie (Wolf) Allgood Morris; student Rockford Coll., 1949-50; BA, NYU, 1953, MA, 1954; MS, Columbia U. Sch. Social Work, 1956; m. Theron Stanford Nease, Sept. 1, 1962; children: Susan Elizabeth, Alison Allgood. Social worker, psychiatric social worker Bellevue Psychiat. Hosp., N.Y.C., 1956-59; psychiat. social worker St. Luke's Hosp., N.Y.C., 1959-62; asst. psychiat. social work supr. N.J. Neuropsychiat. Inst., Princeton, 1962-64; group co-leader Ctr. for Advancement of Personal and Social Growth, Atlanta, 1973-76, asst. dir., social work supr., group co-leader Druid Hills Counseling Ctr., Columbia Theol. Sem., 1973-82; marriage and family therapist Cath. Social Svcs., Atlanta, 1978-87; chief Cmty. Mental Health Svc., Ft. McPherson, Atlanta, Ga., 1987-92; master's level clinician Ctr. for Psychiatry, Smyrna, Ga., 1990-92; pvt. practice marriage and family therapy. Mem. NASW, Acad. Cert. Social Workers, Am. Assn. Marriage and Family Therapy, Am. Group Psychotherapy Assn. Republican. Episcopalian. Home and Office: 1557 Bennett Road Grayson GA 30221

NEBLETT, CAROL, soprano; b. Modesto, Calif., Feb. 1, 1946; m. Philip R. Akre; 3 children. Studies with, William Vennard, Roger Wagner, Esther Andreas, Ernest St. John Metz, Lotte Lehmann, Pierre Bernac, Rosa Ponselle, George London, Jascha Heifetz. Soloist with Roger Wagner Chorale; performed in U.S. and abroad with various symphonies; debut with Carnegie Hall, 1966, N.Y.C. Opera, 1969, Met. Opera, 1979; sung with maj. opera cos. including Met. Opera, N.Y.C., Lyric Opera Chgo., Balt. Opera, Pitts. Opera, Houston Grand Opera, San Francisco Opera, Boston Opera Co., Milw. Florentine Opera, Washington Opera Soc., Covent Garden, Cologne Opera, Vienna (Austria) Staatsoper, Paris Opera, Teatro Regio, Turin, Italy, Teatro San Carlo, Naples, Italy, Teatro Massimo, Palermo, Italy, Gran Teatro del Liceo, Barcelona, Spain, Kirov Opera Theatre, Leningrad, USSR, Dubrovnik (Yugoslavia) Summer Festival, Salzberg Festival, others; rec. artist RCA, DGG, EMI; appearances with symphony orchs., also solo recitals, (film) La Clemenza di Tito; filmed and recorded live performance with Placido Domingo, La Fancivila del West; numerous TV appearances. Office: DA CAPO PO Box 180-369 Coronado CA 92118*

NEBORSKY, STEPHANIE JOY, reading and language arts consultant, educator; b. Putnam, Conn., June 14, 1950; d. Stephen Frank and Dorothy Elizabeth (Angelott) N. AS, Manchester (Conn.) C.C., 1968-70; BS in Intermediate Edn., Eastern Conn. State U., 1972, MS in Lang. Arts, 1978; cert. supervision and adminstrn., Sacred Heart U., 1991. Cert. reading and lang. arts cons., supervision and adminstrn., Conn. Tchr. English and reading Dr. Helen Baldwin Sch., Canterbury, Conn., 1972-86, 94-95, tchr. 5th-8th grades, 1986-89, 95—, 5th grade tchr., writing coach, 1989-90, lang. arts coord., 1990-94; adult edn. instr. Putnam (Conn.)-Thompson Cmty. Coun., 1975-76; tchr. Summer Youth Employment Tng. Program East Conn./Brandeis U., Hampton, 1993; adj. instr. Sacred Heart U., Lisbon, Conn., 1993—; presenter numerous edn. confs.; scorer and resolution reader Conn. State Dept. Edn., 1980-90. Contbr. articles to profl. jours. Named Dist. Tchr. of Yr., Canterbury Pub. Schs., 1989, Finalist Conn. Tchr. of Yr., 1989. Mem. ASCD, Ea. Conn. Reading Assn. (pres. 1995-96), Canterbury Edn. Assn. (governing bd. sec. 1995—), Internat. Reading Assn., New Eng. Reading Assn., Nat. Coun. Tchrs. English, Whole Lang. Umbrella, Conn. TAWL, Delta Kappa Gamma (rec. sec. 1994-96). Home: 314 Hampton CT 06247-1416 Office: Dr Helen Baldwin Mid Sch PO Box 100 45 Westminister Rd Canterbury CT 06331

NECCO, E(DNA) JOANNE, school psychologist; b. Klamath Falls, Oreg., June 23, 1941; d. Joseph Rogers and Lillian Laura (Owings) Painter; m. Jon F. Puryear, Aug. 25, 1963 (div. Oct. 1987); children: Laura L., Douglas F.; m. A. David Necco, July 1, 1989. BS, Cen. State U., 1978, MEd, 1985; PhD in Applied Behavioral Studies, Okla. State U., 1993. Med.-surg. asst. Oklahoma City Clinic, 1961-68; spl. edn. tchr. Oklahoma City Pub. Schs., 1978-79, Edmond (Okla.) Pub. Schs., 1979-83; co-founder, owner Learning Devel. Clinic, Edmond, 1983-93; asst. prof. profl. tchr. edn. U. Ctrl. Okla., Edmond, 1993—; adj. instr. Ctrl. State U., Edmond, 1989-93, Oklahoma City U., 1991-93; mem. rsch. group Okla. State U., Stillwater, 1991-93; presenter in field. Contbr. articles to profl. jours. Com. mem. Boy Scouts of Am., SCUBA Post 604, Oklahoma City, 1981-86; mem. Edmond Task Force for Youth, 1983-87, Edmond C. of C., 1984-87; presenter internat. conf. Okla. Ctr. for Neurosci., 1996; evaluator for Even Start Literacy Program, 1994—, presenter internat. conf., Singapore, 1996. Mem. Assn. Supervision and Curriculum Devel., Nat. Assn. for Sch. Psychologists, Am. Bus Women's Assn., Coun. for Exceptional Children, Learning Disabilities Assn., Am. Assn. for Gifted Underachieving Students, Okla. Learning Disabilities Assn., Okla. Assn. for Counseling and Devel., Golden Key Nat. Honor Soc., Internat. Soc. for Scientific Study of Subjectivity, Am. Coun. on Rural Spl. Edn., Ctrl State U. (Okla., life), Phi Delta Kappa. Republican. Home: 17509 Woodsorrel Rd Edmond OK 73003-6951 Office: U Ctrl Okla Coll Edn 100 N University Dr Edmond OK 73034

NEDDERMAN, NORMA FAYE SANDBERG, government official; b. Kansas City, Mo., Oct. 15, 1954; d. Max B. and Lillian Beatrice (Walters) Holt; m. Steven Dale Sandberg, Nov. 20, 1976 (div. Feb. 1984); 1 child, Gregory Louis; m. Jeff Paul Nedderman, July 27, 1990; children: Wade Howard, Laura Anne. BS in Environ. Health, U. Kans., 1975, MS in Environ. Sci., 1977. Environ. engr. Kans. Dept. Health and Environ., Topeka, 1976-79, EPA, Kansas City, Kans., 1979-87; chief safety and environ. mgmt. br. Gen. Svcs. Adminstrn., Ft. Worth, 1987-91; mgr. Ark.-La. Airport Devel. Office, FAA, Ft. Worth, 1991—; exec. bd. Dallas/Ft. Worth Fed. Safety Coun., Arlington, 1989-90; lectr. in field. Arbitrator Better Bus. Bureau, Kansas City, Mo., 1985-87; active PTA, Arlington, 1987—. NASA fellow, 1976; named one of Outstanding Young Women of Am., 1978. Mem. LWV, Exec. Women in Govt. (v.p. 1991, pres. 1993-94), Air and Waste Mgmt. Assn., Fed. Women's Program Com. (program chmn. 1990—), Fed. Bus. Assn. (v.p. 1992, chmn. scholarship com. 1992-96), Nat. Fire Protection Assn., Toastmasters (pres. 1990, Competetent Toastmaster award 1988, Able Toastmaster award 1992). Methodist. Office: FAA Fort Worth TX 76193

NEDERVELD, RUTH ELIZABETH, retired real estate executive; b. Hudsonville, Mich., Oct. 29, 1933; d. Ralph and Hattie (Ploeg) Schut; m. Terrill Lee Nederveld, June 6, 1952; children: Courtland Lee, Valerie Lynn Nederveld Heisey, Darwin Frederic. Degree in Real Estate, U. Mich., 1979; student, Pa. State U., Centre Hall, 1973, Aquinas Coll., Grand Rapids, Mich., 1974; degree, Grad. Realtors Inst., 1979. Cert. residential specialist; registered securities agt. With sales dept. Field Enterprises, Lancaster, Pa., 1962-72; sales assoc. E. James Hogan, Lancaster, 1972-74, C-21 Packard, Grand Rapids, Mich., 1974-80; assoc. broker comml. divsn. Markland Devel., Inc., Grand Rapids, 1980-86, Am. Acquest Realty, Inc., Grand Rapids, 1986-89; broker, owner R.E. Nederveld Realtors, Ada, Mich., 1989-94; ret., 1994. Pres. Civic Nucomers of Grand Rapids, 1978; trustee, elder Forest Hills Presbyn. Ch., Cascade, Mich., 1983-86. Mem. Nat. Assn. Realtors (mem. comml. dept. 1973—), Mich. Assn. Realtors, Grand Rapids Real Estate Bd., Woman's Council Realtors (corr. sec. 1986-87), Nat. Assn. Female Execs., Assn. Sales and Mktg. Execs. (exec. dir. internat. chpt. 1977-84, pres. Grand Rapids chpt. 1986-87). Republican. Lodge: Order of Eastern Star.

NEDZA, SANDRA LOUISE, manufacturing executive; b. Chgo., Aug. 20, 1951; d. Thomas and Ina Louise (Wilson) Ingle; m. James Owen Earnest, May 5, 1973 (div. Nov. 1984); m. Ronald Edward Nedza, Nov. 22, 1986; 1 child, Thomas Edward. Student acctg., Met. Sch. Bus., Chgo., 1970. Accounting clk. Gane Bros. & Lane, Inc., Chgo., 1967-72; advanced from expeditor to buyer Hammond Organ Co., Chgo., 1972-84; purchasing/prodn. control supr. IRP-Profl. Sound Products, Elk Grove Village, Ill, 1984-94, Bensenville, Ill., 1994—. Mem. Jobs Daughters, 1967—. Mem. Lion, Alpha Iota (scholarship key 1970). Lutheran. Clubs: Juke Box Sno-Riders (sec. 1986-87) (Fox Lake, Ill.), Lakeview Sno-Riders. Lodge: Lioness (v.p. 1985-88, pres. 1988-89) (Chgo.). Home: 1418 S Robert Dr Mount Prospect IL 60056-4542 Office: IRP-Profl Sound Products 1111 Tower Ln Bensenville IL 60106-1027

NEECE, OLIVIA HELENE ERNST, real estate company executive, consultant; b. L.A., Jan. 3, 1948; d. Robert and Beatrice Pearl Ernst; m. Huntley Lee Bluestein, 1967 (div. 1974); children: Melissa Dawn, Brendon Wade; m. Anthony Ray Neece, Mar. 20, 1976. Cert. interior design, UCLA, 1972-75; BSBA, U. So. Calif., 1990; MBA, UCLA, 1993. Cert. interior designer Calif. Coun. for Interior Design; lic. gen. contractor, real estate broker, Calif. Staff designer Frances Lux Designs, L.A., 1974; project designer Yates Silverman Inc., L.A., 1974-77; owner Olivia Neece Planning & Design, Tarzana, Calif., 1977-86; v.p. project devel. Design Services/Aircoa, Englewood, Colo., 1986-87; v.p. project adminstrn. Hirsch-Bedner Assoc., Santa Monica, Calif., 1987-88; treas.-sec. EON Corp., L.A., 1980—; owner Olivia Neece Planning & Design, Tarzana, 1988-93; dir. ops. The Ernst Group, L.A., 1980—; ptnr. Neece Assocs., L.A., 1993—; prof. Calif. State U., Northridge, part-time, 1994—; speaker in field; instr. ext. program UCLA, 1981-83. Co-author: A Step by Step Approach to Hotel Development, 1988; conbtr. articles to profl. jours. Bd. dirs., chmn. advt. L.A. Music Ctr. Opera League; co-chair L.A. Master Chorale Gala; mem. L.A. Music Ctr. Club 100, Gold Guild of Ctr. Theatre Group/Ahmanson of L.A. Music Ctr., Friends of the Hollywood Bowl; charter mem. Los Angeles County Mus. Art; vol. restoration of San Diego R.R. Mus., 1985-92. Recipient Holiday Inn Devel. award, Foster City, Calif., 1986, Warwick, R.I., 1988, 1st and 2d place awards Lodging Hospitality Designers Circle, 1987, Gold Key award Russell St. Inn, 1986. Mem. Am. Soc. Interior Designers (1st pl. portfolio competition 1974), Inst. Bus. Designers (profl., v.p., bd. dirs.), Nat. Restaurant Assn., Urban Land Inst., Am. Hotel and Motel Assn., Decorative Arts Coun., Nat. Coun. Interior Design Qualifications. Office: Neece Assoc 18200 Rosita St Tarzana CA 91356-4622 also: The Ernst Group 12401 Helena St Los Angeles CA 90049-3907

NEEDHAM, JUDY LEN, artist, art educator; b. Big Spring, Tex., Dec. 1, 1941; d. Carl Granvil and Mary Louise (Grilliette) Hill; m. Andrew James Needham III, Jan. 1, 1960; children: Andy, Jack, Johnny, Joshua. Grad. high sch., Tuscola, Tex. workshop dir., coord. Fine Arts League Coleman (Tex.) County, 1990-96, art exhbn. dir. 1992-96, pres., 1992, 93. Exhibited in group shows Citizens Nat. Bank, Brownwood, Tex., 1992, 1st Coleman (Tex.) Nat. Bank, 1992-95, Coleman County State Bank, 1992-96, Security State Bank, Abilene, Tex., 1995, John Selmon Gallery, Stamford, Tex., 1995, Gage Hotel Emporium, Marathon, Tex., 1994-95, West Tex. Art Gallery, San Angelo, 1994-95, Kendall Art Gallery, San Angelo, 1995, Breckenridge (Tex.) Fine Arts Gallery, 199.4. troop leader Heart of Tex. coun. Girl Scouts Am., Brownwood, 1965-70; den mother, asst. camp dir. Chisholm Tr. coun. Boy Scouts Am., Abilene, 1972-79; pres. Band Boosters Coleman H.S., 1990, 91, 92. Recipient Dist. Award of Merit Boy Scouts Am. Chisholm Trail Coun., 1979, Best of Show Cross Plains (Tex.) Paint and Palett, 1993, Best of Show Coleman County Fine Arts League, 1994, Best of Show Comanche County Art Assn., 1995. Home: 427 Sunrise Ln Coleman TX 76834

NEEDHAM, LILLIE DULCENIA, secondary education educator, business educator; b. Chgo., June 12, 1949; d. Clarence R. Sr. and Deborah Lee (Morris) Needham; 1 child, Aston R. Needham-Watkins. BS in Edn., Chgo. State Coll., 1970, MS in Edn., 1974. Tchr. Chgo. Pub. Schs., 1970—, office occupations coord., 1976-77, 78-90, 91—, S.W.A.T. shop founder, coord. info. processing, 1992—, bus./computer dept. chair. Mem. NAFE, ASCD, Chgo. Bus. Edn. Assn. (sec. 1994-95, v.p. 1995—), Nat. Bus. Edn. Assn. Internat. Soc. Bus. Educators, Chgo. Computer Soc., Bus. Profls. Am., Am. Entrepreneur Assn.

NEEDLER, PRISCILLA A., real estate agent, relocation administrator; b. Hartford City, Ind., July 3, 1940; d. Paul R. Cheeseman and Ursula W. (DeHaven) Dobbs; m. Marvin A. Needler, Apr. 29, 1960; children: Veronica Kay, Elizabeth Ann. Student, Ball State U., 1958-60, Ind. Bus. Coll., 1960-62; Lic. realtor, Barrett Real Estate Licensing, 1989. Receptionist Purdue U., West Lafayette, Ind., 1962-64; asst. dir. Metro Area Citizens Orgn., Indpls., 1977-80; mktg. specialist Ventura Homes, Inc., Indpls., 1980-83; gen. contr. Indpls., 1984-89; realtor Century 21 Gold Key, Indpls., 1989—, dir. relocation, 1993—; mem. com. Greviance II, Indpls., 1995—; mem. governing bd. Women's Coun. Realtors, Indpls., 1993—. Mem. governing bd. PTO, Indpls., 1971-81; pres. N.E. Neighborhood Orgn., Indpls., 1976-78, block capt., 1979-84; block capt. Avalon Hills Civic Assn., Indpls., 1991-94. Recipient Award of Honor, Arlington H.S., 1979, Outstanding Neighbor award N.E. Neighborhood Orgn., 1979. Mem. Builders Assn. Indpls., Met. Indpls. Bd. Realtors. Home: 6649 E 65th St Indianapolis IN 46220

NEEL, EULA BARNEYCASTLE, state purchasing agent; b. Votaw, Tex., Feb. 24, 1928; d. Elzie and Susan Viola (Bass) Barneycastle; m. Walter Lee Neel, Dec. 18, 1953 (dec.). Student, Durham's Bus. Coll., 1945-46. Lic. Real Estate Agent, Utah. Sec. E.I. Du Pont Co., La Porte, Tex., 1947-49, asst. to plant buyer, 1949-70, sr. buyer, 1970-76, regional buyer, 1976-78; vol. missionary LDS Ch., Nitro, W.Va., 1979-80; civic/religious activist Salt Lake City, 1980-84; dept. corrections purchasing technician State of Utah, Draper, 1984-87; purchasing agt. State of Utah, Salt Lake City, 1987—; com. chair UCI Furniture Mfg.-State, Salt Lake City, 1988—; mgr. Pharm. Com.-State, Salt Lake City, 1988—. Author: (contract) Rotenone-Treatment of Water Reservoirs, 1991 (Hero Award); composer: (pub.) Development and Self-Esteem, 1975 (hon. mention). Pres. LDS Young Women, Houston, 1962-78; advancement chair Boy Scout of Am., Sandy, Utah, 1985-86. Mem. Nat. Assn. Purchasing Mgmt. Republican. Mem. LDS Ch.

NEELY, BECKIE DENISE, social services administrator; b. Lynnwood, Calif., Feb. 25, 1954; d. James Richard and Betty Mae (Tucker) Black; m. Robert Vernon Neely, Jan. 24, 1976; children: Christi Lynn, John Robert. AA in Child Devel., Adminstrn., Grossmont Coll., 1982; BA in Behavioral Sci., Nat. U., 1994, MS, 1995. Lead tchr., asst. dir. Navajo Child Devel. Ctr., El Cajon, Calif., 1984-86; lead tchr. Little Acorn Presch., El Cajon, Calif., 1986-89; site supr., dir. Davis-Grossmont YMCA, La Mesa, Calif., 1989—; cons. YMCA, La Mesa, 1989—. Youth choir dir. Christian Ch. of Lemon Grove, Calif., 1986-88, jr. high Sunday sch. tchr., 1987-89; band bd. dirs. Lemon Grove Mid. Sch., 1987-90, Helix H.S., La Mesa, 1991-93. Recipient Caring Power award YMCA, San Diego, 1990, Inspiring Leader award, 1994. Mem. Nat. Assn. for Edn. Young Children, Nat. U. Alumni Assn. Home: 7648 Church St Lemon Grove CA 91945

NEELY, SALLY SCHULTZ, lawyer; b. L.A. BA Stanford U., 1970, JD, 1971. Bar: Ariz. 1972, Calif. 1977. Law clk. to judge U.S. Ct. Appeals (9th cir.), Phoenix, 1971-72; assoc. Lewis and Roca, Phoenix, 1972-75; asst. prof. Harvard U. Law Sch., Cambridge, Mass., 1975-77; assoc. Shutan & Trost, P.C., Los Angeles, 1977-79, ptnr., 1979-80, Sidley & Austin, L.A., 1980—; faculty Am. Law Inst.-ABA Chpt. 11 Bus. Reorgns., 1989-95, Bankruptcy Law Inst. and Bankruptcy Litigation Inst., 1987-92, Nat. Conf. Bankruptcy Judges, 1988, 90, 95, Fed. Jud. Ctr., 1989, 90, 94-95, Workshop Bankruptcy and Bus. Reorganization NYU, 1992—; rep. 9th cir. jud. conf., 1989-91; mem. Nat. Bankruptcy Conf., 1993—. Chair Stanford Law Sch. Reunion Giving, 1986; bd. visitors Stanford Law Sch., 1990-92. Fellow Am. Coll. Bankruptcy; mem. ABA, Calif. State Bar Assn. (debtor-creditor rels. and bankruptcy subcom. bus. law sect. 1985-87). Office: Sidley & Austin 555 W 5th St Ste 4000 Los Angeles CA 90013-3000

NEELY, STEPHANIE ANN, mathematics educator; b. Jonesboro, Ark., Sept. 24, 1953; d. James Vondal and Bobbie Jean (Hutchison) Broadway; m. Marion Keith Neely, June 29, 1979; 1 child, Joshua James. BSE in Math., Ark. State U., 1975, MSE in Curriculum and Instrn., 1991. Jr. high math. educator Marked Tree Middle Sch., Ark., 1975-79; 8th grade math. tchr. Westside H.S., Jonesboro, Ark., 1979—; sponsor Westside H.S. Student Coun., Jonesboro, Ark., 1991—; chairperson NCA/COE High Expectation Com., Westside H.S., 1992—. Mem. Nat. Coun. Tchrs. Math. Baptist. Home: 210 Woody Ln Jonesboro AR 72401 Office: Westside HS 1630 Hwy 91 W Jonesboro AR 72404

NEFF, DIANE IRENE, naval officer; b. Cedar Rapids, Iowa, Apr. 26, 1954; d. Robert Mariner and Adeline Emma (Zach) N. BA in Psychology and Home Econs., U. Iowa, 1976; MA in Sociology, U. Mo., 1978; MEd in Ednl. Leadership, U. West Fla., 1990. Contract compliance officer, dir. EEO, City of Cedar Rapids, 1979-81; commd. ensign USN, 1981, advanced through grades to lt. comdr.; asst. legal officer Naval Comm. Area Master Sta., Guam, 1982-83; comm. security plans and requirements officer Comdr.-in-Chief US Naval Forces in Europe, London, 1983-85; dir. standards and evaluation dept. Recruit Tng. Command, Orlando, Fla., 1985-89; rsch. and analysis officer Naval Res. Officers Tng. Corps Office Chief Naval Edn. and Tng., Pensacola, Fla., 1989-91; tech. tng. officer Recruit Tng. Command, Great Lakes, Ill., 1991-92, mil. tng. officer, 1992-93, dir. apprentice tng., 1993-95; coord. ednl. and tng. programs U. Ctrl. Fla., Orlando, 1995—. Founding mem. Unity of Gulf Breeze, Fla., 1990; performer various benefits for chs., mus., others, Orlando, 1988, 91, 95, 96. Fellow Adminstrn. on Aging, 1977. Unitarian.

NEFF, GLENDA KAY, tax specialist; b. Libby, Mont., Nov. 19, 1957; d. John J. and Rosalie M. (Sisich) Drynan; m. Danny L. Neff, June 14, 1980; children: Christopher J., Erica R. AA in Bus. Adminstrn., Flathead C.C., Kalispell, Mont., 1978; BSBA in Acctg., U. Mont., 1980. Enrolled agt. IRS; cert. Health Ins. Assn. Staff acct. Kindrid Holland & Booker CPAs, Helena, Mont., 1980-82; revenue agt., tax examiner State of Mont., Helena, 1982-91; corp. tax mgr., corp. fin./tax mgr., mgr. mem. acctg. Blue Cross Blue Shield of Mont., Helena, 1991—; leader Blue Cross Blue Shield Sch./Bus. Partnership, 1993-96, leader nat. and regional tax adv. groups, 1994-96, alternate emergency disaster relief coord., 1996. Mem. Inst. Mgmt. Accts. (cert.), Nat. Soc. Tax Profls., Nat. Assn. Enrolled Agts. Office: Blue Cross Blue Shield Mont 404 Fuller Helena MT 59601

NEFF-ENCINAS, JULIE GAY, bilingual education specialist, consultant; b. Chgo., June 21, 1957; d. Wesley Miles and Betty Ann (Pitts) Neff; m. Ernesto Valenzuela Encinas, July 5, 1980; children: Ariella, Gerard, Martin. BA, Hanover Coll., 1978; MEd, U. Ariz., 1979. Cert. secondary tchr. with bilingual edn. endorsement. 7th and 8th grade tchr. Cath. Diocese of Tucson, 1979-80; bilingual edn. tchr. Tucson Unified Sch. Dist., 1980-89, bilingual edn. curriculum specialist, 1989—; adj. faculty No. Ariz. U., Flagstaff, 1993—; cons. S.W. Regional Lab., Los Alamitos, Calif., 1993—. Co-author Tucson Unified Sch. Dist. Compliance Procedures Manual for Bilingual Edn., 1993, Tucson Unified Sch. Dist. Comprehensive Plan for Bilingual Edn., 1993. Title VII Short Term Tng. grantee U.S. Dept. Edn., 1991-94, Title VII Systemwide Improvement grantee U.S. Dept. Edn., 1995—. Mem. Nat. Assn. for Bilingual Edn., Ariz. Assn. for Bilingual Edn., Tucson Assn. for Bilingual Edn., Nat. Audubon Soc. Home: 4040 S Silver Bridle Ln Tucson AZ 85735 Office: Tucson Unified Sch Dist 1010 E 10th St Tucson AZ 85719

NEGA, NANCY KAWECKI, middle school science educator; b. Chgo., Mar. 16, 1946; d. John Sebastian and Irene M. (Wantuch) Kawecki; m. Lance J. Nega, Feb. 24, 1968; children: Sandi Kawecka Nenga, Todd J. BA in Biology, Ill. Coll., 1968; MS Tchg. in Elem. Math., U. Ill., Chgo., 1991. Rschr. Morton-Norwich, Inc., Woodstock, Ill., 1968-72; tchr. Elmhurst (Ill.) Unit Dist. 205, 1986—; trainer Globe Program, Washington, 1995—; Internet trainer Argonne (Ill.) Nat. Lab., 1996—. Recipient Presdl. award of excellence in sci. and math. tchg. NSF, 1995. Mem. Nat. Sci. Tchrs. Assn., Ill. Sci. Tchrs. Assn. (award of excellence 1994), Nat. Mid Level Sci. Tchrs. Assn. Office: Churchville Jr HS 155 Victory Pkwy Elmhurst IL 60126

NEGRO, JANE ANN, elementary education educator; b. Bay City, Mich., Oct. 3, 1953; d. Francis William and M. Noreen (Cole) Fredenburg; m. Charles John Negro, Feb. 21, 1981; children: Anne, John, Mark, Margaret. BS, Ctrl. Mich. U., 1975, MA, 1986, student, 1991. Tchr. 2d and 3d grades Oscoda Area Schs., Glennie, Mich., 1978-79, kindergarten tchr., 1979-81; jr. primary tchr. Oscoda Area Schs., Oscoda, Mich., 1981-82, tchr. 1st grade, 1982-83, kindergarten tchr., 1983-88, reading specialist, 1989-93, Chpt. One coord., Title I coord., 1993—, Title I coord., multiage tchr., 1995-96; chair Early Childhood Com., Oscoda, 1993—. Active Miss Iosco Scholarship Pageant, 1988; judge Miss Mich. Scholarship Pageant, 1994. Mem. Nat. Coun. Tchrs. English, Nat. Coun. Tchrs. Maths., Internat. Reading Assn., Mich. Edn. Assn., Sunrise Asns. Edn. of Young Children (v.p. pres.-elect 1993-95), Mich. Assn. Edn. of Young Children, Mich. Reading Assn., Iosco Reading Coun. (past pres., Educator of Yr. 1992), Delta Kappa Gamma (Woman of Distinction 1992). Office: Oscoda Area Schs 110 Pearl St Oscoda MI 48750

NEGUS, LUCY NEWTON BOSWELL, foundation executive; b. Charlottesville, Va., Apr. 27, 1937; d. William Ward and Lucy Tyler (Newton) Boswell; m. Sidney Stevens Negus, Jr., Dec. 23, 1957 (div. Nov. 1971); children: Sidney Stevens III, Lucy Tyler Negus Snidow, Tayloe Newton. Student, Randolph-Macon Woman's Coll., 1955-57; BS in Mass. Comm., Va. Commonwealth U., 1985. Adminstrv. asst. St. Paul's Episcopal Ch., Richmond, Va., 1972-77; coord. comm. Westminster-Canterbury Corp., Richmond, 1977-78; corp. sec. Westminster-Canterbury Found., Richmond, 1980—; dir. cmty. rels. and devel. Westminster-Canterbury Mgmt. Corp., Richmond, 1978-95, dir. devel., 1995—. Writer/editor Coming of Age insert Va. Churchman, 1978-79, The Lamp, 1978-95; contbr. articles, poetry to profl. jours.; writer/rschr. books by other authors including: Christpower, 1974. Mem. Leadership Metro Richmond Class, 1966, Citizens Coalition for Greater Richmond, 1966; exec. bd. Collegiate Schs. Alumni Assn., Richmond, 1980-83, 91-94; bd. assocs. St. Paul's Coll., Lawrenceville, Va., 1985-88. Mem. Va. Assn. Fundraising Execs. (founding mem., pres. 1983-84, Devel. Recognition award 1993), Va. Planned Giving Study Group (bd. dirs. 1992-95), Estate Planning Coun. of Richmond, The Woman's Club The Laurels Honor Soc., Phi Kappa Phi, Kappa Tau Alpha. Republican. Episcopalian. Home: 5404 Queensbury Rd Richmond VA 23226-2120 Office: Westminster-Canterbury Mgmt 1600 Westbrook Ave Richmond VA 23227

NEIDHARDT, ERIKA JOHANNA, art educator; b. Denver, Pa., Dec. 21, 1930; d. Paul Alfred and Johanne Helene (Döhler) N. BS in Art Edn., Kutztown (Pa.) U., 1952; MS of Arts in Art, San Diego U., 1963; postgrad., various univs. Cert. tchr., Pa. Tchr. art Caernarvon Sch. Dist., Morgantown, Pa., 1952-53, Cocalico Union Sch. Dist., Denver, Pa., 1953-63; tchr. art Marple Newtown Sch. Dist., Newtown Square, Pa., 1963-93, tchr. art adult evening classes, 1985-92, mem. profl. devel. com., task force excellence, adv. coun., mentor new tchr. program. Mem. Chapel of Four Chaplains, Phila. Mus. of Art. Mem. NEA, Pa. State Edn. Assn., Nat. Art Edn. Assn., Pa. State Art Edn. Assn., Marple Newtown Edn. Assn. (adv. coun. 1990-93, Tchr. of Yr. 1987-88), Howard Pyle Studio Group. Home: 3001 Hillingham Cir Chadds Ford PA 19317-9255

NEIKIRK, MARY MARGARET, mathematics educator, curriculum consultant; b. San Angelo, Tex., Nov. 30, 1946; d. Charles Edward and Dorotha Esther (Meier) N. BS, U. Tex., 1968; MS, U. N.C., Greensboro, 1974; EdD, U. Ga., 1985. Cert. math., phys. edn. tchr. Phys. edn. tchr., coach Devine (Tex.) Jr. H.S., 1968-70; tchg. asst. U. N.C., Greensboro, 1970-72; asst. prof. Smith Coll., Northampton, Mass., 1974-76; rsch. asst. U. Ga., Athens, 1976-78, 80-81; asst. prof., curriculum specialist Ea. Ky. U., Richmond, 1978-79; registrar, adj. faculty Southwestern Coll., Santa Fe, 1985-87; vol. svcs. specialist Santa Fe C.C., 1987-89; math. instr. Coll. of Santa Fe, 1989—; bd. dirs., v.p. Lit. Vols. Santa Fe, 1985-88; mem. program com. 1987 Internat. Conf., Assn. for Exptl. Edn., Santa Fe, 1987. Author/co-author: Physical Educators for Educational Equity, 1979; co-author: (essay) Rivers Running Free, 1987; contbr. articles to profl. jours. Mem. Women's Caucus, Richmond, Ky., 1978-79; AIDS activist N.Mex. AIDS Svcs., 1991—. Mem. Nat. Coun. Tchrs. Math, Life Edn. Network of S.W., Cluster Permaculture Cohousing Project, Hand in Hand, Orton Dyslexia Soc. Green Party. Office: Coll Santa Fe 1600 Saint Michaels Dr Santa Fe NM 87505-7615

NEILAND, BONITA JUNE, botanist, educator; b. Eugene, Oreg., June 5, 1928; d. Herbert Eugene and Ann Lavina (Thompson) Miller; m. Kenneth Alfred Neiland, Dec. 23, 1955. BS in Biology, U. Oreg., 1949; MA in Botany, Oreg. State Coll., 1951; diploma in rural sci., U. Coll. Wales, 1952; PhD of Botany, U. Wis., 1954. Instr. biology U. Oreg., Eugene, 1954-55; asst. prof. biology State Sys. Higher Edn. Gen. Ext. Divsn., Eugene, 1955-60; from asst. prof. to prof. Botany and Land Resources U. Alaska, Fairbanks, 1961-87; ret., 1987; cons. plant ecology. Contbr. articles to profl. jours. Bd. dirs. Deschutes Soil and Water Conservation Dist., Bend, Oreg. Fulbright fellow, 1951-52; grantee NSF, 1955—, John Muir Inst., 1955. Mem. AAAS (fellow 1975), Brit. Ecol. Soc., Soil and Water Conservation Soc., Sigma Xi, Phi Beta Kappa, Phi Kappa Phi. Home: 69715 Holmes Rd Sisters OR 97759

NEILL, DEBRA ANNE, nurse, home health marketing consultant; b. Phila., July 7, 1958; d. John Glenn Wise, Ruth Ann (Biel) Lamb; m. James Patrick Neill, May 7, 1988; 1 child, Lorielle Kristine. BS in Nutrition, U. Md., 1981; BSN, U. Md., Balt., 1983. RN, Fla. Staff nurse, team leader Manatee Meml. Hosp., Bradenton, Fla., 1983-84; charge nurse Manatee Meml. Hosp., Bradenton, 1984-85; staff nurse, team leader Venice (Fla.) Hosp., 1985-86, relief charge nurse, 1986-89; team coord. Home Health Svc. of Sarasota, Fla., 1989-90, mktg. coord., 1990-92, patient care supr., 1992-95, regional dir. mktg., 1995-96; mktg. cons. Home Health Svc. of Arcadia, Fla., 1996—, Home Health Svcs. of Sarasota North, Ctrl. and South Offices, 1996—. Mem. Fla. Health Care Social Workers Assn., Sarasota County Aging Network, Am. Morgan Horse Assn., Alzheimer's Assn. Republican. Baptist. Home: 7864 Saddle Creek Trail Sarasota FL 34241 Office: Home Health Svc of Sarasota 4020 Beneva Rd Sarasota FL 34233

NEIMAN, NORMA, insurance agent, retired; b. Louisville, Mar. 12, 1923; d. Sam and Sarah (Bordofsky) Berlin; m. Jacob B. Neiman, July 26, 1942 (dec. Mar. 24, 1993); children: Bennett A., Anna L. Bever, James C. Student, U. Louisville, 1941-43; student creative writing program, U. Cin., 1975. Asst., gen. support Diversified Coverage Brokerage Agy., 1956-87, gen. agt. various ins. cos., 1987-96; gen. agt. Sovereign Life, First Colony Life Inst., Jackson Life Ins. Contbr. poetry to anthologies. Tutor Matthew Duvall Elem. Sch., Cin., 1990-92, Jane Hoop Elem. Sch., Cin., 1993; charter mem. Citizens Against Govt. Waste, 1990. Named Citizen of the Yr., Hutt river Principality, 1996. Mem. NAFE, Pan Am. Soc. Cin. (co-founder), Internat. Platform Assn., Internat. Soc. Poets.

NEIMAN, SUSAN, philosophy educator; b. Atlanta, Mar. 27, 1955; children: Benjamin Wagner, Shirah Wagner, Leila Wagner. AB, Harvard U., 1977, AM, 1980, PhD, 1986. Assoc. prof. Yale U., New Haven, 1989-96, Tel Aviv U., 1996—. Author: Slow Fire, 1992 (PEN award 1993), The Unity of Reason, 1994. Sheldon fellow, 1982, Fulbright fellow, 1983, Henrich Heine fellow, 1984. Mem. Phi Beta Kappa. Office: Dept Philosophy, Tel Aviv U, 69978 Tel Aviv Israel

NEIMARK, VASSA, interior architect; b. Miami, Fla., Dec. 9, 1954; d. William Rolla and Bettijean (Davison) Meyer; m. Philip John Neimark, Oct. 29, 1982; children: Dashiel Charles, Darq-Amber. Student, Art Inst. Ft. Lauderdale, 1974, Art Inst. Chgo., 1980. Owner, prin. Vassa Inc., Chgo., 1979—. Contbr. articles to local mag. Bd. dirs. M.R.I.C. Michael Med. Found., Chgo., Expressways Mus., Chgo., Orchard Village Home for Retarded Adults, Park Ridge Youth Campus, Des Plaines, Ill. Recipient Star on Horizon award Chgo. Mdse. Mart-Chgo. Design Sources, 1985, Spl. Recognition in Design award, 1987. Mem. Internat. Soc. Interior Designers (bd. dirs. 1985-86), Women in Design Industry, IFA Found. N. Am. (v.p.), Internat. Inst. for Bau-Biologie and Ecology, Inc., Carlton Club, Club International.

NEISWANDER, LINDA CAROL, realtor, interior decorator; b. Lansing, Mich., Jan. 1, 1951; d. Gordon Field and Phyllis Blanche (Bedell) Priest; m. Paul Clair Neiswander, Aug. 19, 1972; children: Kristin Anne, Ashley Marie. Student, Ea. Mich. U., 1969-71; grad., Realtors Inst., 1996. Lic. notary pub., S.C. Owner Designs by Linda C. Neiswander, Midland, Mich., 1978-84; tchr. Sawtooth Ctr. for Visual Design, Winston-Salem, N.C., 1986-88; realtor, ptnr. Eulalie Salley & Co., 1988—; cons. Mary Kay Cosmetics, Aiken, 1994—; designer Dogwood Flories, Aiken, 1995—. Mem. Gathering Choir, St. Mary's Cath. Ch., Aiken, 1989—, food coupon coord., 1990-96; v.p., mem. adv. bd. Nuture Home-Cmty. United for Tomorrow's Future, Aiken, 1992—. Recipient cert. of professsionalism S.C. Assn. Realtors, 1993, 94, cert. of scholastic achievement Nat. Assn. Realtors, 1994. Mem. Aiken Bd. Realtors (chmn. cmty. svc. 1991-93, co-chmn. casino night Habitat for Humanity 1991-94, co-chmn. hospitality, 1992-94, sec. 1994-95, President's Club 1992-94), Lions. Republican. Home: 1017 Water Oak Dr Aiken SC 29803 Office: Eulalie Salley & Co 108 Laurens St NW Aiken SC 29801

NEJIB, PERRI UMID-RASHID, electrical engineer; b. Pitts., Nov. 30, 1964; d. Umid Rashid Nejib and Mary Margaret (Grubb) Swaback. BSEE, Wilkes U., 1986; MSEE, Johns Hopkins U., 1989. Electronics engr. Harry Diamond Labs, Adelphi, Md., 1986-90; project officer Army Rsch. Lab., Adelphi, 1990-95, project leader, 1995—; mem. women's advisory coun. Harry Diamond Labs., Adelphi, 1989-93; tech. recruiter HDL/ARL, Adelphi, 1990—; cons. Macintosh Systems, Adelphi, 1989—; mediator Mid-Level Employee Com., Adelphia, 1991—. Contbr. articles to profl. jours. Asst. coach Howard County Youth Soccer, Columbia, Md., 1994—; registrar Md. Soccer Assn., Balt., 1993—, team mem. Strike-Hers Soccer Club, capt. 1988—; mem. Chesapeake Bay Lightning Women's Hockey Club; asst. sci. instr. Prince George's Schs., Md., 1986-90; mem. N.E. Pa. Assn. of Arab Ams., Wilkes-Barre, Pa., 1982—. Mem. Mac Sci. Tech., Md. State Soccer Assn. (women's program coord., del. 1993-95). Republican. Moslem. Home: # 805 11430 Little Patuxent Pkwy Columbia MD 21044 Office: US Army Rsch Lab AMSRL-LT 2800 Powder Mill Rd Adelphi MD 20783

NELIPOVICH, SANDRA GRASSI, artist; b. Oak Park, Ill., Nov. 22, 1939; d. Alessandro and Lena Mary (Ascareggi) Grassi; m. John Nelipovich Jr., Aug. 19, 1973. BFA in Art Edn., U. Ill., 1961; postgrad., Northwestern U., 1963, Gonzaga U., Florence, Italy, 1966, Art Inst. Chgo., 1968; diploma, Accademia Universale Alessandro Magno, Prato, Italy, 1983. Tchr. art Edgewood Jr. High Sch., Highland Park, Ill., 1961-62, Emerson Sch. Jr. High Sch., Oak Park, 1962-77; batik artist Calif., 1977—; illustrator Jolly Robin Publ. Co., Anaheim, Calif., 1988—; supr. student tchrs., Oak Park, 1970-75; adult edn. tchr. ESL, ceramics, Medinah, Ill., 1974; mem. curriculum action group on human dignity, EEO workshop demonstration, Oak Park, 1975-76; guest lectr. Muckenthaler Ctr., Fullerton, Calif., 1980, 92, Nigüel Art Group, Dana Point, Calif., 1989, Carlsbad A.A., 1990, ARt League, Oceanside Art Group, 1992; 2d v.p. Anaheim Hills Women's Club, 1990-91, rec. sec. 1991-92; fabric designer for fashion designer Barbara Jax, 1987. One-Woman shows include Lawry's Calif. Ctr., L.A., 1981-83, Whittier (Calif.) Mus., 1985-86, Anaheim Cultural Ctr., 1986-88, Ill. Inst. Tech., Chgo., 1989, Muckenthaler Cultural Ctr., Fullerton, 1990; also gallery exhibits in Oak Brook, 1982, La Habra, Calif., 1983; represented in permanent collections McDonald's Corp., Oak Brook, Glenkirk Sch., Deerfield, Ill., Emerson Sch., Oak Park, galleries in Laguna Beach, Calif., Maui, Hawaii, Mich., N.J.; poster designer Saratoga Fine Arts. Active Assistance League, Anaheim, Calif., 1992—, 2d v.p. ways and means com., 1995-96. Recipient numerous awards, purchase prizes, 1979—; featured in Calif. Art Rev., Artists of So. Calif., Vol. II, Nat. Artists' Network, 1992. Mem. AAUW (hospitality chmn. 1984-85), Soc. Children's Book Writers and Illustrators, Assistance League Anaheim, Oak Park Art League, Orange Art Assn. (jury chairperson 1980), Anaheim Art Assn., Muckenthaler Ctr. Circle, Anaheim Hills Women's Club. Roman Catholic. Home and Office: 5922 E Calle Cedro Anaheim CA 92807-3207

NELLERMOE, LESLIE C., lawyer; b. Oakland, Calif., Jan. 26, 1954; d. Carrol Wandell and Nora Ann (Conway) N.; m. Darrell Ray McKissic, Aug. 9, 1986; 1 child, Devin Anne. BS cum laude, Wash. State U., 1975; JD cum laude, Willamette U., 1978. Bar: Wash. 1978, U.S. Dist. Ct. (ea. dist.) Wash. 1979, U.S. Dist. Ct. (we. dist.) Wash. 1983. Staff atty. Wash. Ct. Appeals, Spokane, 1978-79; asst. atty. gen. Wash. Atty. Gen. Office, Spokane, 1979-83, Olympia, 1983-85; assoc. Syrdal, Danelo, Klein, Myre & Woods, Seattle, 1985-88; ptnr. Heller Ehrman White & McAuliffe, Seattle, 1989—. Bd. dirs. Campfire Boys & Girls, Seattle, 1991—. Mem. ABA, Wash. State Bar Assn., King County Bar Assn. Wash. Environment Industry Assn. (bd. dirs.). Office: Heller Ehrman White & McAuliffe 701 5th Ave 6100 Columbia Ctr Seattle WA 98104

NELLETT, GAILE L., mental health nurse; b. Ottawa, Ill., Nov. 5, 1941; d. Edwin Edward and Mabel Delia (Higgins) Hausaman; children: Anne Marie, James, Sarah, Susan, Julie; m. Henry H. Nellett, Aug. 8, 1988. BSN, Governors State U., University Park, Ill., 1993; MS in Nursing Adminstrn., Loyola U., Chgo., 1995, postgrad., 1996—. RN, Ill. Staff nurse med.-surg. and psychiat. units Cmty. Hosp. Ottawa, 1974-75, asst. head nurse, 1975-77, head nurse psychiat. unit, 1977-79, head nurse psychiat. and chem. dependency units, 1979-84, nursing mgr. psychiat. and chem. dependency units, 1984-92, program mgr. psychiat. and chem. dependency units, 1987-92, part-time home health nurse, 1992-94; rsch. asst. Loyola U., 1993-96. Bd. dirs. Ottawa area United Way, 1976-92, v.p., 1985, sec., 1984, 86. Nursing Adminstrn. fellow Edward Hines Jr. VA, Hines, Ill., 1994, tuition fellow Loyola U., 1993-96. Mem. ANA, Nat. Nurses Soc. on Addictions, Ill. Nurses Assn. (bd. dirs. dist. 4 1974-80), Peer Assistance Network for Nurses (regional support person dist. 2 1988-96), Am. Psychiat. Nurses Assn., Sigma Theta Tau. Roman Catholic. Home: PO Box 730 108 S Wabena Ave Minooka IL 60447

NELLIGAN, ANNETTE FRANCES, caseworker supervisor; b. Bangor, Maine, Sept. 20, 1954; d. Paul James and Laura Jenny (Sumner) N.; m. Peter Jamie Smith, June 22, 1985; children: Angelica Grace Nelligan-Smith, Acatia Faith Nelligan-Smith. AA, U. Maine, Bangor, 1974; BS, U. Maine, 1977, MEd, 1978, EdD, 1995. Lic. clin. profl. counselor; lic. marriage and family counselor; lic. social worker; cert. secondary sch. tchr., Maine. Tchr. Bangor H.S., 1978, Etna (Maine)-Dixmont Sch., 1979-80; residential advisor Penobscot Job Corps, Bangor, 1980-84; group life worker St. Andre's Home, Bangor, 1984; caseworker, supr. Maine Dept. Human Svcs., Bangor, 1984—; mem. Homeless Edn. Adv. Bd., Bangor, 1992-95. Mem. ACA, Assn. for Specialists in Group Work. Roman Catholic. Home: 385 Hancock St Bangor ME 04401 Office: Maine Dept Human Svcs 396 Griffen Rd Bangor ME 04401

NELLIGAN, KATE (PATRICIA COLLEEN NELLIGAN), actress; b. London, Ont., Can., Mar. 16, 1951; d. Patrick Joseph and Alice (Dier) N. Attended, York U., Toronto, Ctrl. Sch. Speech and Drama, London. Appeared in plays in Bristol, London, and New York: Barefoot in the Park, 1972, Misalliance, A Streetcar Named Desire, The Playboy of the Western World, London Assurance, Lulu, Private Lives, Knuckle, 1974, Heartbreak House, 1975, Plenty, 1975, As You Like It, A Moon for the Misbegotten, 1984, Virginia, 1985, Serious Money, 1988, Spoils of War, 1988, BAd Habits; films include: The Count of Monte Cristo, 1979, The Romantic Englishwoman, 1979, Dracula, 1979, Mr. Patman, 1980, Eye of the Needle, 1980, Agent, 1980, Without a Trace, 1983, Eleni, 1985, White Room, 1990, Bethune: The Making of a Hero, 1990, Frankie and Johnnie, 1991, The Prince of Tides, 1991, Shadows and Fog, 1992, Fatal Instinct, 1993, Wolf, 1994, Into the Deep, 1994, How to Make an American Quilt, 1995, Margaret's Museum, 1995, Up Close and Personal, 1996; TV appearances include: The Arcata Promise, 1974, The Onedin Line, The Lady of the Camellias, Licking Hitler, Measure for Measure, Therese Raquin, 1980, Forgive Our Foolish Ways, 1980, Kojak: The Price of Justice, 1987, Control, 1987, Love and Hate: A Marriage Made in Hell, 1990, Terror Strickes the Class Reunion, 1992, The Diamond Fleece, 1992, Liar Liar, 1993, Shattered Trust: The Shari Karney Story, 1993, Spoils of War, 1994, Million Dollar Babies, 1994, A Mother's Prayer, 1995, Captive Heart: The James Mink Story, 1996. Recipient Best Actress award Evening Standard, 1978. Office: Internat Creative Mgmt c/o Joe Funicello 8942 Wilshire Blvd Beverly Hills CA 90211*

NELLIS, BARBARA BROOKS, trust company executive; b. Akron, Ohio, Mar. 16, 1935; d. Frank and Alice (Woodhall) Brooks; m. William J. Waltenbaugh, Oct. 31, 1953 (div. 1965); children: Bonnie, Becky, Brooks; m. Robert E. Nellis, June 25, 1971; children: Cheryl, Jack Lori, Kathryn, Robert. Student, Kent State U., 1964, Akron U., 1965, Purdue U., 1977, Malone Coll., 1978-88; DSc (hon.), U. Akron, 1989. Sec. Goodyear Tire and Rubber Co., Akron, 1952-62; exec. sec. Morgan Adhesives Co., Stow, Ohio, 1969-71; mgmt. cons. Brouse McDowell Hunsicker and Assocs. Law Firm, Akron, 1971-88; real estate agt. Kallstrom Realty, Akron, 1978; pres. TMI and D Co. Inc., Akron, 1978-88, T.M. Investment and Devel., Akron, 1978-88; real estate agt. Marting Realty, Akron, 1982, 1987; sales mgr. Coldwell Banker. Recipient Presdl. citation, 1988. Fellow Akron Area Com., Nat. Assn. Realtors, Ohio Assn. Realtors. Democrat. Home: 664 Pebble Beach Dr Akron OH 44333-2849 Office: Omar Corp PO Box 311 Bath OH 44210

NELSEN, EVELYN RIGSBEE SEATON, retired educator; b. Jonesboro, Ark., Nov. 9, 1930; d. Glen Brown and Ruby Beatrice (Minton) Rigsbee; m. Frank W. Seaton, Apr. 19, 1952 (div. Aug. 1980); children: Susanna, Frank, Caroline, Rebecca, Elizabeth; m. David Allen Nelsen, July 25, 1981. BS in Edn., Ark. State U., 1968, MS in Edn., 1976; postgrad., U. Miss., 1968, U. Ark., Little Rock, 1989-90, U. Ctrl. Ark., 1990-92. Cert. English, French and gifted edn. tchr., adminstrn., secondary prin., Ark. Saleswoman Fan-Craft, Inc., Plainville, Conn., 1955-61; pers. dir. St. Bernard's Hosp., Jonesboro, 1961-68; tchr. Jonesboro Pub. Schs., 1968-81, Hazen (Ark.) Schs., 1985-92; remodeler, Little Rock, 1981-85, Hazen and Jonesboro, 1992—; tchr. Gov.'s Sch. for Gifted, summer 1983; former mem. English Planning Commn., State of Ark, former mem. Gifted Edn. Commn. Author: (novel) Tori; contbr. numerous articles to trade jours., essays to newspaper. Vol. various Dem. polit. campaigns, Ark., 1968—, Clinton Presdl. Campaign, Little Rock, 1992, Dem. Nat. Com. Grantee U. Miss., summer 1968. Mem. Am. Assn. Ret. Persons, Ark. Assn. Ret. Tchrs., Royal Trust, Nat. Trust, Phi Delta Kappa, Delta Kappa Gamma, Lambda Iota Tau. Home: Nelsen Grove Box 811 Hazen AR 72064 also: 301 S McClure Jonesboro AR 72401

NELSON, AÏDA Z., artist; b. Nov. 5, 1939; d. Jacob S. and Rachel R. (Lutzio) Iscovit; widowed; children: Joshua, Deborah. Student, Art Students League, 1954-58; MFA, U. Buenos Aires, 1962. art tchr. NYU, Sch. Visual Arts, N.Y., Coll. New Rochelle, N.Y., N.Y. Inst. Tech., William Patterson Coll., N.J., Fashion Inst. Tech., N.Y. One-woman shows at Galeria Zilzer, Buenos Aires, 1987, Galerie Neufville, Paris, 1988, Galerie Claude Levin, Paris, 1989, Galerie Le Gron, San Miguel de Allende, Mex., 1990, Mus. San Miguel de Allende, 1996; group exhbns. include Ctr. Culturel Americain, Paris, 1964, Galerie Sorbonne, Paris, 1964, Mus. Art Moderne, Salon de Jeune Peinture, Paris, 1965 (award), Galerie Claude Levin, Paris, 1966, Mus. D'Art Moderne, Salon Interministeriel, Paris, 1967, Galerie Neufville, 1970, Cimaise de Paris, 1972 (award), Orgn. Ind. Artists, N.Y.C., 1991, The Emerging Collector, N.Y.C., 1993, Ctr. for Arts and Culture, L.A., 1993, Gallery 33, N.Y.C., 1994, Galleria Juan Leny, San Miguel de Allende, 1994, Sta. Gallery, Katonah, N.Y., 1994, Tribeca Gallery, N.Y.C., 1994, Prince St. Gallery, N.Y.C., 1994, MBM Gallery, N.Y.C., 1995, Gallery 33, n.Y.C., 1995, PDQ Gallery, N.Y.C., 1995; represented in numerous pvt. collections. Mem. Women's Caucus for Arts, Orgn. Ind. Artists, Art Inst. N.Y.C. Home: 444 Central Park West New York NY 10025-4378

NELSON, ALICE CARLSTEDT, retired nurse educator; b. Strandquist, Minn., May 25, 1921; d. Peter Gustaf and Florence Olivia (Berg) Carlstedt; m. Armour Halstead Nelson June 5, 1954 (dec. Dec. 1993). RN, Bethesda Hospital, St. Paul, 1944; BS, Augustana Coll., Rock Island, Ill., 1948; MA, U. Chgo., 1954. RN, Minn., Ill., N.D., Iowa, Calif.; cert. lactation educator, cert. lifetime cmty. coll. tchr. Asst. night supr. Bethesda Hosp., St. Paul, 1944-45; with Army Nurse Corps, 1945-46; jr. grade nurse Wadsworth VA Hosp., L.A., 1947-48, intermediate grade nurse, 1967-68; head nurse Crippled Children's Sch., Jamestown, N.D., 1948-50, Sch. for Handicapped Children U. Iowa, Iowa City, 1950-51; clin. instr. Chgo. Lying-In Hosp., 1951-54, St. Luke's Hosp., Fargo, N.D., 1954-60; tchr., supr. lab. pre-sch. N.D. State U., Fargo, 1962-64; coll. health svc. Calif. Luth. U., Thousand Oaks, 1968-74, faculty dept. nursing, 1982-85; private duty nurse Thousand Oaks, 1976-81; retired, 1990; obstetric nurse Moline (Ill.) Luth. Hosp., Miller Hosp., St. Paul, 1947-48; state sec. League for Nursing, N.D., 1956-64; team mem. preparation Nat. Achievement Test in Nursing of Children, N.Y., 1959. Contbr. articles to profl. and popular publs. Various offices including Ch. Coun. Holy Trinity Luth. Ch., Thousand Oaks, 1964-90; founding bd. dirs. Honey Tree Pre-Sch., Thousand Oaks, 1972; mem. task force on aging S.W. Pacific Luth. Synod Office, L.A., 1979; parent-aide, hotline, etc. Child Abuse & Neglect, Ventura County, Calif., 1979-82; bd. dirs. La Serena Retirement Ctr., Thousand Oaks, 1985-88; mem. ch. choir Salemsborg Luth. Ch., Smolan, Kans., 1990—, mem. ch. coun., 1996—. Recipient award Am. Jour. Nursing, 1969, Calif. Nurse, 1987, Outstanding Vol. award Ventura County Child Abuse & Neglect, 1982. Mem. Am. Assn. Univ. Women, Bethany Bibliophiles Book Club, Writer's Cramp Group. Democrat.

NELSON, ALICE ELIZABETH HILL, museum docent; b. Oakland, Calif., Jan. 19, 1921; d. George Clayton Hill and Netha Alice (Hall) Hill-Kinkead; m. James Walter Nelson, Jr., June 13, 1942; children: James W. III, Georgeanne Cusic, Susan Brewster, Karen McCormick, Marjorie Moon. BA, U. Calif., Berkeley, 1942; BFA, Cardinal Stritch Coll., 1968. Pres. Literary League, Meadville, Pa., 1972-74; docent Milw. Art Mus., 1978-96, hon. docent, 1996, lectr. Art History, 1984-96; docent Villa Terrace 18th C Decorative Arts Museum, Milw., 1990—; artist in residence Herb Soc. Am., Milw., 1975-85. One woman show, paintings, sculptures Studio San Damiano, Milw., 1968; two women show, paintings, sculptures Meadville, Pa., 1973. Bd. dirs. Milw. Symphony Women's League, 1960-69; docent (hon.) Milw. Art Mus., 1996. Named Docent of Year Milw. Art Mus., 1984. Mem. League of Milw. Artists, AAUW (bd. dirs., sec. Wis. chpt. 1963-66), Women's Club of Wis. (Art Com. 1987-89, docent 1991-92), Alpha Omicron Pi, Prytanean (pres. 1941-42). Republican. Episcopalian. Home: 3366 N Lake Dr Milwaukee WI 53211-2909 Studio: N67w32426 Wildwood Point Rd Hartland WI 53029-9712

NELSON, ANITA JOSETTE, educator; b. San Francisco, June 10, 1938; d. George Emanuel and Yvonne Louise (Borel) N. BA, San Francisco State Coll., 1960; MA, U. Denver, 1969. Dir. Community Ctr., Nurenberg, W.Ger., 1961-63; dir. program spl. services Cmty. Ctr., Tokyo, 1964-66; resident counselor U. Denver, 1967-69; dir. student activities Maricopa (Ariz.) Tech. Coll., 1969-72, coach women's varsity tennis, coordinator campus activities, 1972-75; counselor, fgn. student advisor Scottsdale (Ariz.) C.C., 1975-94, divsn. chair counseling, 1989-91. Named Phoenix Mgmt. Council Rehabilitator of Year, 1977. Republican. Address: 351 Molino Ave Mill Valley CA 94941

NELSON, ANNA MASTERTON, writer; b. West Covina, Calif., July 16, 1969; d. Richard Frederick and Mary Winifred (Denk) N. BA in Psychology, U. So. Calif., L.A., 1994. With Fox Broadcasting Corp. Page; writer's asst., sr. v.p. devel. Dick Clark Prodns., Inc., exec. asst.; spl. effects prodn. asst. Set Shop, Arroyo Studios; asst. script supr. Mike Young Prodns./Baytide Filmworks; asst. dir. admissions Calif. Internat. U.; asst. to dir. Gettysburg; adminstrv. asst. Acuity Entertainment; rsch. session supr. Columbia Broadcasting Sys.; radio promotions asst. Rocky & Laurie Show WPOC FM, Balt.; lectr. dept. anthropology U. So. Calif., L.A., 1994—, cons., dept. psychology, 1995-96. Editor (newsletters) Trojan Cailleach, 1995, 96, The Smoking Gun, 1996. Active Malibu (Calif.) Rep. Womens Club, 1993—, Project AIDS, L.A., 1993-95; counselor DiverSCity, L.A., 1993-96. Mem. Am. Sociol. Soc., St. Andrew's Soc., Clan Gunn Soc. So. Calif. (editor 1995—), Ancient Religions Soc. (pres., editor 1994—). Office: 2265 Westwood Blvd #153 Los Angeles CA 90064

NELSON, BARBARA ANNE, lawyer; b. Mineola, N.Y., Jan. 16, 1951; d. Richard William and Dorothee Helen (Thorne) N. BA, Inter Am. U. P.R., 1972; JD, New Eng. Sch. Law, 1975. Legal editor Prentice Hall Pub. Co., Englewood Cliffs, N.J., 1976-77; assoc. Antonio C. Martinez Law Firm, N.Y.C., 1977-79, Pollack & Kramer, N.Y.C., 1979-83; pvt. practice N.Y.C., 1983-95; immigration judge U.S. Immigration, N.Y.C., 1995—. Author, speaker tng. film. Mem. ACLU, Am. Immigration Lawyers Assn., Legal Aid Soc. N.Y., Amnesty Internat., Asia Soc. Home: 324 W 14th St Apt 5A New York NY 10014-5003 Office: 26 Federal Plz New York NY 10278

NELSON, BARBARA JONES, food service and theatre professional; b. Augusta, Ga., Feb. 3, 1954; d. Robert F. and Margaret H. (Hill) Jones; divorced; children: Candice, Russell. Diploma, Dallas Fashion Mdse. Coll. Pres. Bo-Mar, Inc., Gallup, N.Mex., Cinebar, Inc. Mem. McKinley County Rep. Party, Gallup, 1991—; sec. Gallup Downtown Devel. Group.; sec. McKinley County Crimestoppers Bd. Named Employer of Yr. by Connections/Nat. Assn. Retarded Citizens, Durango, Colo., 1991, N.Mex. Mainstreet Vol. of Yr., 1995, Woman of Yr., AAUW, 1995. Mem. NAFE, Soroptimist, Am. Mgmt. Assn., Nat. Restaurant Assn., Nat. Fedn. Ind. Bus., Gallup-McKinley C. of C. (sec.). Episcopalian. Office: Bo-Mar Inc 914 E 66 Ave Gallup NM 87301

NELSON, BARBARA KAY, insurance agent, financial services consultant; b. Dayton, Ohio, May 20, 1947; d. Orville James and Catherine Ann (Pentenburg) Weber; m. Theodore Joseph Nelson II, Nov. 8, 1969 (div. Nov. 1990); children: Theodore Joseph III, Jason Michael. BA, U. Dayton, 1969; MA, Webster U., 1985. CLU. TV co-host Sta. WHIO-TV, Dayton, 1969; dept. mgr. Elder-Beerman, Dayton, 1969-70; customer service rep. Ohio Bell Telephone, Dayton, 1970; adminstrv. coordinator AmeriSource, San Antonio, 1984-86; agt. N.Y. Life Ins., 1986-89; sales mgr. John Hancock Fin. Svcs., 1989-93; dir. tng. San Antonio regional mktg. office Lincoln Nat., 1993-96, long term care specialist, 1995-96, USAA, 1996—; chair bd. San Antonio Women's C. of C. Tex., 1988-91; sec. bd. dirs. Network Power Tex., 1987-90. Mem. exec. bd. Oak Grove Elementary Sch. PTA, San Antonio, 1981-83; mem. San Antonio Assn. Life Underwriters, San Antonio C. of C., local govt. com., 1991—; mem. religious edn. com. St. Mark's Ch., San Antonio, 1983-84; mem. North San Antonio Chamber/Pub. Art, 1984-85. Mem. NAFE, Women Life Underwriters Confederation (pres. 1992—). Club: FLW Officers Wives (pres. 1980-81). Avocations: art; jogging; bicycling; racquetball; reading.

NELSON, BETH CARLSON, educator, consultant; b. Crofton, Nebr., Dec. 31, 1926; d. Harold and Alta Iona (Jones) Carlson; m. Sidney Hascue Nelson, Apr. 8, 1946; children: Judith Nelson DeBordones, Jeanie Anderson, Betty Whitley. BS, Radford (Va.) U., 1958; MS, Va. Poly. Inst. and State U., 1964; EdD, U. Va., 1972. Cert. tchr., adminstr., supr., supt., Va. Classrm. tchr. Radford City Schs., 1958-66; supr. reading Pulaski County Schs., Pulaski, Va., 1966-69; supr. elem. edn. Pulaski County Schs., Va., 1969-74; pres. Va. Edn. Assn., Richmond, 1975-76; prof. edn. Radford U., 1974-91; ednl. cons., 1991—; pres. U. Va. Edn. Found., Charlottesville; instr., cons. Am. Schs., Sao Paulo, Brazil, 1977-79; dir. Region 1, Beginning Tchrs. Assn. Program, Va. State Dept. Edn., 1985-91. Vice chmn. sch. bd. Pulaski County, 1996—; bd. dirs. Fine Arts Ctr. for NRV, Pulaski, 1978—;

vice chair Pulaski County Dem. Com., 1994—. Recipient Outstanding Svc. award Radford U., 1985. Mem. NEA (bd. dirs. 1977-83, Outstanding Woman Educator award 1976), Va. Congress PTA (hon.), Delta Kappa Gamma (chpt. pres.). Methodist. Home: 6800 Viscoe Rd Radford VA 24141

NELSON, CANDACE ANN, network associate, former educator; b. Grand Rapids, Mich., July 20, 1954; d. Willis John and Valerie (Boisseau) N.; m. Peter William Siebert, Sept. 10, 1988; children: Lucas, Elias. BA, Smith Coll., 1976; MS, U. Wis., 1984. Tchr. Minnetonka (Minn.) H.S., 1977-79; ednl. dir. Bridge for Runaway Youth, Mpls., 1979-80; tchr. Colegio Franklin D. Roosevelt, Lima, Peru, 1980-81; program asst. Cath. Relief Svcs., Lima, 1981-82; sr. program officer World Edn., Boston, 1984-91; cons. UN, Aspen Inst., others, Boston, 1991-94; sr. associate SEEP Network, Boston, 1994—; advisor for African program McKnight Found., Mpls., 1993—. Author: Village Banking: The State of the Practice, 1996; writer/editor: (newsletter) Nexus, 1991-96. Mem. Internat. Coalition for Women and Credit (facilitator, founder), Assn. for Women and Devel., Assn. for Enterprise Opportunity. Home: 70 Robbins Rd Arlington MA 02174

NELSON, CARLON JUSTINE, engineering and operations executive; b. Siloam Springs, Ark., May 26, 1960; d. Robert F. and Jean (Caroom) Toenges. BS in Indsl. Engring., U. Ark., 1982; MBA, Houston Bapt. U., 1988. Registered profl. engr., Tex. Supr. codes and regulatory compliance Tex. Ea., Houston, 1982-85, supr. ops. spl. projects, 1985-87, mgr. project devel., 1987-90; dir. spl. projects, tech. asst. to pres. Enron, Houston, 1990-91, dir. throughput engring., 1991-92, project dir., 1992-95; v.p. engring. So. Union Gas Co., Austin, Tex., 1995-96; v.p. ops. Mo. Gas Energy, Kansas City, Mo., 1996—. Mem. NSPE, Tex. Soc. Profl. Engrs. Home: 5601 NE Northgate Crossing Lees Summit MO 64064 Office: Mo Gas Energy 3420 Broadway Kansas City MO 64111

NELSON, CHARLENE DESS, elementary education educator; b. Akron, Ohio, June 11, 1963; d. Roy Jefferson and Judith Charlene (Bittinger) N.; m. Robert Scott Forbes, May 20, 1989. BA in Elem. Edn., U. Akron, 1987, MA in Edn. Founds., 1989. Cert. elem. and music tchr., Ohio. Media specialist U. Akron, 1989; tchr. elem. music and band Akron Pub. Schs., 1991-92, tchr. music, 1992-93, 6th grade tchr., 1993—; audio-visual coord. Crosby Elem. Sch., Akron, 1994-95; video news dir. Crosby Elem./Akron Pub. Sch., 1994-95; newspaper editor Akron Pub. Schs., 1993-95. Dir. bell choir Firestone Park United Meth. Ch., Akron, 1993-95. Mem. ASCD, Nat. Coun. Tchrs. Math., Ohio Ednl. Libr. and Media Assn. (internship 1986), Phi Delta Kappa (v.p. membership).

NELSON, CHARLOTTE BOWERS, public administrator; b. Bristol, Va., June 28, 1931; d. Thaddeus Ray and Ruth Nelson (Moore) Bowers; m. Gustav Carl Nelson, June 1, 1957; children: Ruth Elizabeth, David Carl, Thomas Gustav. BA summa cum laude, Duke U., 1954; MA, Columbia U., 1961; MPA, Drake U., 1983. Instr. Beaver Coll., 1957-58, Drake U., Des Moines, 1975-82; office mgr. LWV of Iowa, Des Moines, 1975-82; exec. asst. Iowa Dept. Human Svcs., Des Moines, 1983-85; exec. dir. Iowa Commn. on Status of Women, Des Moines, 1985—. Bd. dirs., pres. LWV, Beloit, Wis., 1960-74; bd. dirs. LWV, Des Moines, 1974-82, Westminster House, Des Moines, 1988—, pres. 1996. Named Visionary Woman, Young Women's Resource Ctr., 1994. Mem. Am. Soc. Pub. Adminstrn. (pres. exec. coun. 1984-86, past pres., Mem. of Yr. 1993), Phi Beta Kappa. Home: 1141 Cummins Cir Des Moines IA 50319-0090 Office: Human Rights Dept Lucas State Office Bldg 321 E 12th St Des Moines IA 50309-5636

NELSON, CHARLOTTE COLEEN, special education educator; b. Belleville, Kans., Nov. 21, 1942; d. Clarence George and Sybil Evelyn (Davidson) Rahe; m. Phillip Allen Truby, May 30, 1965 (div. 1976); children; Gregory Brent, Michelle Diane Truby Swenson; m. Maynard Eugene Nelson, Oct. 7, 1978. BS, Kans. State U., 1964; MA, U. Mo., Kansas City, 1970; MS, Kans. State U., 1981, EdD, 1994. Elem. tchr. Republic (Kans.) Elem. Sch., 1964-65, Unified Sch. Dist. # 110, Overland Park, Kans., 1966-67; chpt. 1 reading tchr. CSD # 1, Hickman Mills, Mo., 1970-73; elem. tchr. Unified Sch. Dist. # 271, Beloit, Kans., 1973-79; gifted edn. cons. Unified Sch. Dist. # 305, Salina, Kans., 1979-91, coord. for assistive tech. and gifted edn., 1991—. Mem. ASCD, NAFE, Coun. for Exceptional Children, Nat. Assn. for Gifted Children, Delta Kappa Gamma (pres. chpt. 1988-90). Home: 160 S Estates Dr Salina KS 67401-3562 Office: Ctrl Kans Cooperative Edn 3023 Canterbury Dr Salina KS 67401-8038

NELSON, CHRISTINE SMITH, municipal employee; b. Cleve., Mar. 27, 1970; d. Joseph Ford and Livia Leonilda (DeSanto) Smith; m. Steven James Nelson, May 29, 1993. BA, Hiram Coll., 1992; MPA, Cleve. State U., 1996. Econ. devel. dir. City of Beford, Ohio, 1993—. Troop leader Girl Scouts U.S., Lakewood, Ohio, 1994—. Mem. Internat. City Mgrs. Assn., Am. Econ. Devel. Assn., Bedford C. of C. (bd. dirs. 1993—, treas. 1996), Rotary Internat. Democrat. Roman Catholic. Office: City of Bedford 65 Columbus Rd Bedford OH 44146

NELSON, CLARA SINGLETON, aerospace company executive; b. Union Ridge, Tenn., Apr. 10, 1935; d. Ernest Caldwell and Willie Emma (Hord) Singleton; m. Joe Edward Nelson, July 26, 1953; children: Drexel Edward, Dorissia Lynett. Student Tenn. State U., 1961-62, Middle Tenn. State U., 1984; AS, Motlow Coll., 1978; BS in Edn. with highest honors U. Tenn., Knoxville, 1991. Cert. personnel specialist. Sec., adminstrv. asst. Bedford County Sch., Shelbyville, Tenn., 1957-64; sec., personnel asst. Aro, Inc., Arnold Air Force Sta., Tenn., 1964-71; mem. pub. relations staff, job interviewer Employment Security, Shelbyville, 1971-81; mgr. employment EE Calspan Corp., Arnold Air Force Sta., 1981-94; with Micro Craft Tech, 1994-95; employment & recruiting mgr. Sverdrup Tech., 1995—; mem. adv. bd. Tenn. Area Vocat. Sch., Shelbyville, 1979—, Bedford Moore Vocat. Ctr., Shelbyville, 1979—; cons., dir. Career Devel. Workshops, Shelbyville. Chmn. adv. commn. Equal Employment Opportunity, 1983—, chmn. employer com. Tullahoma Job Service, Tenn., 1985—; former mem. Patrons Council Argie Cooper Libr., Shelbyville; Bus. Adv. Group Motlow State Coll., Tullahoma; trustee Motlow Coll. Found.; mem. Shelbyville Regional Planning Commn. Recipient cert. of appreciation ARC, 1985. Mem. Am. Mgmt. Assn., Highland Rim Human Resource Mgmt. Assn. (treas. 1983-84, 87, sec. 1988, 94, chair program com. 1989, 1994—), Nat. Assn. Female Execs. (network dir. 1985, charter), Nat. Mgmt. Assn., Nat. Assn. Bus. and Profl. Women's Clubs, Inc. (chair membership 1991-93), Am. Assn. Affirmative Action, Tenn. State U. Cluster (chmn. com. 1984—), Better Homes and Gardens Shelbyville Club. Methodist. Avocations: reading, gardening. Home: 118 Scotland Hts Shelbyville TN 37160-2912 Office: Sverdrup Tech 877 Ave E Arnold AFB TN 37389-5051

NELSON, CYNTHIA KAYE, training professional; b. Kearney, Nebr., May 8, 1949; d. LeRoy J. and W. Eileen (Schmidt) Wacker; m. James C. Nelson (div. 1987); children: Alexis Ann, Whitney Eileen. BA, U. No. Iowa, 1971; postgrad., No. Ill. U., 1973. Cert. tchr., Ill., Mo. Tchr. Dixon (Ill.) Pub. Schs., 1972-74, Maplewood (Mo.)-Richmond Heights Sch. Dist., 1974-75; counselor Mo. Bus. Men's Clearing House, St. Louis, 1975-76; dir. edn. Deltex Co., Naperville, Ill., 1982-84; trainer Electronic Data Systems Co., LaGrange, Ill., 1985-86; learning technologist Bellcore Tng. and Edn. Ctr., Lisle, Ill., 1988-90; sr. tech. tng. engr. Fujitsu Network Comm., Raleigh, N.C., 1990—. Mem. ASTD, AAUW, Internat. Soc. of Performance and Improvement, Alpha Chi Omega, Beta Sigma Phi. Republican. Lutheran. Office: Fujitsu Network Comm 7404 Rainwater Rd Raleigh NC 27615

NELSON, DAWN MARIE, middle school science and math educator; b. Norristown, Pa., Mar. 29, 1960; m. Peirce Watson Nelson, Aug. 12, 1978; children: Adam Christopher, Joshua Peirce. Student, Montgomery County C.C., Blubell, Pa., 1977-78, Temple U., 1979-80, Ursinus Coll.; BS in Edn. summa cum laude, Cabrini Coll., Radnor, Pa., 1992, postgrad., 1996—; postgrad., St. Joseph's U., 1995. Cert. elem. tchr., Pa.; cert. ASCI. Tchr. Penn Christian Acad., Norristown, 1992—; asst. curriculum and program developer; accreditation steering com.; supr. Math. Olympics, co-chmn.; mentor, student tchr. supr. Vol. pub. and pvt. schs., ch. orgns. Mem. ASCD, ACSI, Alpha Sigma Lambda. Office: Penn Christian Acad 50 W Germantown Pike Norristown PA 19401-1565

NELSON, DEBBIE LOUISE, tooling designer; b. Rolla, MO, Sept. 15, 1954; d. Martin Alfred Fleischmann and Esther Magretha (Tiede) Harris; m. Roy Allen Nelson, March 24, 1972 (div. Oct. 1991), 1 child, Melissa Beth. A in Tech., Linn (Mo.) Tech. Coll., 1991. In product design, quality control and tooling design Holland/Binkley Co., Warrenton, Mo., 1991—. Democrat. Methodist. Home: Rt 3 Box 101 Owensville MO 65066 Office: Binkley Co PO Box 370 Warrenton MO 63383-0370

NELSON, DEBRA JEAN, journalist, public relations executive, consultant; b. Birmingham, Ala., Nov. 12, 1957; d. James Eric Nelson. BA, U. Ala., Tuscaloosa, 1980. Dir. pub. afffairs Sta. WSGN Radio, Birmingham, 1980-84, news anchor, reporter, 1982-84; dir. community affairs Sta. WBRC-TV, Birmingham, 1984-88, producer, anchor, 1986-88; instr. spl. studies U. Ala., Birmingham, 1988—; dir. media rels. U. Ala. System, Tuscaloosa, 1991-94; adminstr. external affairs Mercedes-Benz U.S. Internat., Inc., Tuscaloosa, 1994—. Pub. affairs prodr./host Sta. WUAL-FM/WQPR, Tuscaloosa, 1991—. Pres.-elect Found. Women's Health in Ala., Inc., 1993—; mem. U.S. libr. lieracy rev. panel Dept. Edn., Washigngton, 1987-92; mem. Leadership Birmingham, 1991-92; bd. dirs., mem. exec. com. Ala. affiliate Am. Heart Assn., 1986-91; mem. U.S. Mil. Rev. Panel for 6th Congl. Dist., 1987; mem. gen. campaign com. Ala. campaign United Negro Coll. Fund, 1992. Recipient award of distinction Internat. Assn. Bus. Communicators, 1985, Disting. Leadership award United Negro Coll. Fund, 1985, 87, 88, Outstanding Achievement award Delta Sigma Theta, 1986, Outstanding Vol. Svc. award ARC, Birmingham, 1987, Woman of Distinction award Iota Phi Lambda, 1987, Human Rights award So. Christian Leadership Conf. Mem. Assn. Black Women in Higher Edn. (bd. dirs. 1993—, chair com. on pub. rels.), Am.-Japan Soc., Coun. for Advancement and Support of Edn. Home: 1129 Amberley Woods Dr Helena AL 35080 Office: Mercedes-Benz US Int Inc PO Box 100 Tuscaloosa AL 35403

NELSON, DIANA, former state legislator, educational association executive; b. Berlin, Wis., Oct. 15, 1941; d. Llewellyn James and Virginia Laurel (Shaver) Walker; B.S., U. Wis., 1963; children: Stephanie, Brian. Mem. Ill. Ho. of Reps., 1981-85; exec. dir. Mental Health Assn. Ill., 1986-88; v.p. pub. affairs Harris Bank, Chgo., 1988-92; pres. Leadership for Quality Edn., 1992-94; dir. pub. affairs Union League Club Chgo., 1994—. Congl. candidate Ill. 13th Dist., 1984; candidate Cook County Clk., 1986; Dole del., primary election, 1988. Republican. Congregationalist. Office: Union League Club 65 W Jackson Blvd Chicago IL 60604

NELSON, DOREEN KAE, mental health counselor, reserve military officer; b. Duluth, Minn., Oct. 18, 1957; d. Norman G. Nelson and Carola Gerene (Sunneli) Cooper. B Applied Scis., U. Minn., 1983; MS in Human Resources Mgmt. Devel., Chapman U., 1988; MAEd in Mental Health Counseling, Western Ky. U., 1995. Commd. 2nd lt. U.S. Army, 1983, advanced through grades to maj., 1994; pers. officer 62nd Med. Group U.S. Army, Ft. Lewis, Wash., 1987-88; med. pers. officer Acad. Health Scis. U.S. Army, Ft. Sam Houston, Tex., 1989, chief adminstrv. svcs. div. Med. Dept. Ctr. and Sch., 1989-92; med. advisor Readiness Group Knox, Ft. Knox, Ky., 1992-94; counselor intern Ireland Army Hosp., Ft. Knox, 1995; mental health counselor IV Meridian Behavioral HealthCare, Inc., Gainesville, Fla., 1995—. Lutheran. Home: PO Box 807 Newberry FL 32669-0807

NELSON, DOROTHY WRIGHT (MRS. JAMES F. NELSON), federal judge; b. San Pedro, Calif., Sept. 30, 1928; d. Harry Earl and Lorna Amy Wright; m. James Frank Nelson, Dec. 27, 1950; children: Franklin Wright, Lorna Jean. B.A., UCLA, 1950, J.D., 1953; LL.M., U. So. Calif., 1956; LLD honoris causa, Western State U., 1980, U. So. Calif., 1983, Georgetown U., 1988, Whittier U., 1989, U. Santa Clara, 1990; LLD (honoris causa), Whittier U., 1989. Bar: Calif. 1954. Research assoc. fellow U. So. Calif., 1953-56; instr., 1957, asst. prof., 1958-61, assoc. prof., 1961-67, prof., 1967, assoc. dean., 1965-67, dean., 1967-80; judge U.S. Ct. Appeals (9th cir.), 1979—; cons. Project STAR, Law Enforcement Assistance Adminstrn.; mem. select com. on internal procedures of Calif. Supreme Ct., 1987—; co-chair Sino-Am. Seminar on Mediation and Arbitration, Beijing, 1992; dir. Dialogue on Transition to a Global Soc., Weinacht, Switzerland, 1992. Author: Judicial Adminstration and The Administration of Justice, 1973, (with Christopher Goelz and Meredith Watts) Federal Ninth Circuit Civil Appellate Practice, 1995; Contbr. articles to profl. jours. Co-chmn. Confronting Myths in Edn. for Pres. Nixon's White House Conf. on Children, Pres. Carter's Commn. for Pension Policy, 1974-80, Pres. Reagon's Madison Trust; bd. visitors U.S. Air Force Acad., 1978; bd. dirs. Council on Legal Edn. for Profl. Responsibility, 1971-80, Constnl. Right Found., Am. Nat. Inst. for Social Advancement; adv. bd. Nat. Center for State Cts., 1971-73; chmn. bd. Western Justice Ctr., 1986—; mem. adv. com. Nat. Jud. Edn. Program to promote equality for woman and men in cts. Named Law Alumnus of Yr. UCLA, 1967; recipient Profl. Achievement award, 1969; named Times Woman of Yr., 1968; recipient U. Judaism Humanitarian award, 1973; AWARE Internat. award, 1970; Ernestine Stalhut Outstanding Woman Lawyer award, 1972; Pub. Svc. award Coro Found., 1978, Pax Orbis ex Jure medallion World Peace thru Law Ctr., 1975, Hollzer Human Rights award Jewish Fedn. Coun., L.A., 1988, Medal of Honor UCLA, 1993; Lustman fellow Yale U. 1977. Fellow Am. Bar Found., Davenport Coll., Yale U.; mem. Bar Calif. (bd. dirs. continuing edn. bar commn. 1967-74), Am. Judicature Soc. (dir., Justice award 1985), Assn. Am. Law Schs. (chmn. com. edn. in jud. adminstrn.), Am. Bar Assn. (sect. on jud. adminstrn., chmn. com. on edn. in jud. adminstrn. 1973-89), Phi Beta Kappa, Order of Coif (nat. v.p. 1974-76), Jud. Conf. U.S. (com. to consider standards for admission to practice in fed. cts. 1976-79). Office: US Ct Appeals Cir 125 S Grand Ave Ste 303 Pasadena CA 91105-1652

NELSON, EDITH ELLEN, dietitian; b. Vicksburg, Mich., Sept. 26, 1940; d. Edward Kenneth and Anna (McManus) Rolffs; m. Douglas Keith Nelson; children: Daniel Lee, Jennifer Lynn. BS, Mich. State U., 1962; MEd in Applied Nutrition, U. Cin., 1979. Lic. dietitian, Fla. Clin. dietitian Macon (Ga.) Gen. Hosp., Blodgett Meml. Hosp., Grand Rapids, Mich.; grad. teaching asst. U. Cin., 1978-79; dir. nutrition svcs. Dialysis Clinic, Inc., Cin., 1979-88; cons. dietitian Panama City Devel. Ctr., Ft. Walton Beach Devel. Ctr., Fla., 1988-94, N.W. Fla. Community Hosp., Chipley, Fla., 1993-94, Beverly Enterprises, Panama City Beach, 1994—; renal dietitian Dialysis Svcs. Fla., Ft. Walton Beach, 1989-92. Mich. Edn. Assn. scholar, 1958; Nat. Kidney Found. grantee, 1986. Mem. Am. Dietetic Assn., Fla. Dietetic Assn., Panhandle Dist. Dietetic Assn., Nat. Kidney Found. (coun. on renal nutrition, Fla. coun. on renal nutrition), Omicron Nu. Home: 150 Grand Lagoon Shores Dr Panama City FL 32408

NELSON, ELAINE EDWARDS, lawyer; b. Waco, Tex., Sept. 16, 1947; d. Bedford Duncan and Joyce (Harlan) Edwards; m. David A. Nelson, Apr. 12, 1969; children: Carol Christine, Harlan Claire. BA, Baylor U., 1969, JD, 1978. Bar: Tex. 1978. Gen. counsel Austin Industries, Inc., Dallas, 1978—. Office: Austin Industries Inc 3535 Travis St Ste 300 Dallas TX 75204-1466

NELSON, ESTHER, dance educator; b. N.Y.C., Sept. 9, 1928; d. Rubin and Freda (Seligman) N.; m. Leon Sokolsky, Nov. 18, 1949 (dec. May 1992); children; Mara, Risa. BA in psychology, Bklyn. Coll., 1949; MA in dance edn., N.Y. Univ., 1950. Dance educator Fieldston Arts Ctr., Riverdale, N.Y., 1949-64, Scarsdale (N.Y.) Dance Inc., 1953-68, Knollwood Sch., Elmsford, N.Y., 1953-70, Mid-Westchester YM&WHA, Scarsdale, 1968-78; tchr. trainer workshops Title XX Grant, Millersville, Pa., 1979-81; dance and music educator Horace Mann Preschool, N.Y.C., 1992—; adj. prof. music and dance Bklyn. Coll., 1982-85, workshop and speaker Libr. Conf., 1981—. Author: Everybody Sing and Dance!, 1989, The World's Best Funny Songs, 1988, The Fun-to-Sing Songbook, 1986, The Great Rounds Songbook, 1985, The Funny Songbook, 1984, The Silly Songbook, 1981, Holiday Singing & Dancing Games, 1980, Singing and Dancing Games for the Very Young, 1977, Musical Games for Children of All Ages, 1976, Movement Games for Children, 1975, Dancing Games for Children of All Ages, 1973; produced numerous cassette tapes. Mem. Am. Dance Guild, Dalcroze Soc. Democrat. Jewish. Home: 3605 Sedgwick Ave # A32 Bronx NY 10463 Office: Dimension 5 Box 403 Kingsbridge Station Bronx NY 10463

NELSON, ETHELYN BARNETT, civic worker; b. Bessemer, Ala., Jan. 16, 1925; d. Laurence McBride and Ethel Victoria Fortesque (King) Barnett; student Huntingdon Coll., 1943, U. Ala., 1948, George Washington U., 1948-49, 74; m. Stuart David Nelson, May 6, 1949; children—Terryl Lynn, Cynthia Dianne, Jacqueline Margo. Sec., U.S. Air Force, Montgomery, Ala. and Panama Canal Zone, 1944-49; sec. to dep. undersec. U.S. Dept. State, Washington, 1951-53, U.S. Ho. of Reps. and U.S. Senate, 1959-60; adminstrv. asst. editorial div. Nat. Geog. Soc., Washington, 1962-65; rec. sec. Dist. IV, Nat. Capital Area Fedn. Garden Clubs, Inc., Washington, 1981-83. Mem. Women's Com. Nat. Symphony Orch., The English-Speaking Union, Vols. for Washington Ballet, Washington Opera Guild. Mem. Salvation Army Aux., Suburban Hosp. Assn. Republican. Clubs: Landon Woods Garden (pres. 1978-80), Congressional Country; Capital Speakers (Washington). Patentee. Home: 6410 Maiden Ln Bethesda MD 20817-5612

NELSON, FRANCES PATRICIA, food service executive; b. Denver, Jan. 15, 1948; d. Wilbur Jordan and Margaret Emma Anna (Kruger) Cannon; m. Kenneth Roy Nelson, Sept. 2, 1972; children: Krista, Erin, Michael. BS, Colo. State U., 1970; MA, U. No. Colo., 1981. Asst. dir. child nutrition Colo. Dept. Edn., Denver, 1971-77; dir. nutrition svc. Denver Head Start, 1981-83; dir. food svc. Englewood (Colo.) Pub. Schs., 1988-91, Jefferson County Schs., Golden, Colo., 1991—; cons. Wildwood Child Care, Englewood, 1984-88, Mile High Child Care Assn., Denver, 1981-83, Colo. Dept. Edn., Denver, 1976, Denver Pub. Schs., 1979. Contbr. articles to profl. jours. Leader Girl Scouts Am., Denver, 1982-88, Boy Scouts Am., 1991; team adminstr. Aurora (Colo.) Soccer Club, 1981-88. Mem. Am. Dietetic Assn., Am. Sch. Food Svc. Assn., Colo. Sch. Food Svc. Assn. (pres.-elect 1991-92, pres. 1992-93). Home: 6227 S Netherland Cir Aurora CO 80016-1323 Office: Jefferson County Pub Schs 1829 Denver West Dr # 27 Golden CO 80401-3146

NELSON, FREDA NELL HEIN, librarian; b. Trenton, Mo., Dec. 16, 1929; d. Fred Albert and Mable Carman (Doan) Hein; m. Robert John Nelson, Nov. 1, 1957 (div. Apr. 1984); children: Thor, Hope. Nursing diploma, Trinity Luth. Hosp., Kansas City, Mo., 1950; B. Philosophy, Northwestern U., 1961; MS in Info. and Libr. Sci., U. Ill., 1986. RN. Operating rm. nurse Trinity Luth. Hosp., Kansas City, Mo., 1950-52, Johns Hopkins Hosp., Balt., 1952, Wesley Meml. Hosp., Chgo., 1952-58, Tacoma Gen. Hosp., 1958-59, Chgo. Wesley Hosp., 1959-61; libr. asst. Maple Woods Campus Met. Community Colls., Kansas City, 1987-89, libr., libr. mgr. Blue Springs Campus, 1989—; co-founder Coll. for Kids, Knox Coll., Galesburg, Ill., 1982. Nurses scholar Edgar Bergen Found., 1947; recipient Award of Merit, Chgo. Bd. Health, 1952. Home: 7000 N Elm St Pleasant Valley MO 64068 Office: Blue Springs Campus Libr 1501 W Jefferson St Blue Springs MO 64015-7242

NELSON, HEDWIG POTOK, financial executive; b. Detroit, Oct. 6, 1954; m. Richard Alan Nelson. BA with honors, U. Mich., 1976; MBA, Am. U., 1980. Fin. asst. antitrust div. U.S. Dept. Justice, Washington, 1979-80; fin. analyst corp. treasury Martin Marietta Corp., Bethesda, Md., 1980-81, fin. adminstr. aggregates div., 1981-83, sr. fin. adminstr. bus. devel. data systems div., 1983, mgr. fin. planning and analysis, 1983-85; mgr. mergers and acquistions M/A-COM Devel. Corp., Rockville, Md., 1985-88; sr. analyst group fin. Marriott Corp., Bethesda, 1988-89, mgr. bus. planning, hotel div., 1989-90; mgr. planning and analysis, geon vinyl div. BF Goodrich, Cleve., 1990-91, bus. contr. molding, geon vinyl div., 1991-93; bus. mgr. extrusions The GEON Co., Cleve., 1993-96; dir. planning and anlysis Elsag Bailey, Inc., Wickliffe, Ohio, 1996—. Mem. NAFE (treas. Montgomery County chpt. 1987-88). Home: 325 Middlebush Cir Akron OH 44321-2778 Office: Elsag Bailey Inc 29801 Euclid Ave Wickliffe OH 44092

NELSON, HELAINE QUEEN, lawyer; b. Hamtramck, Mich., Mar. 15, 1945; d. Willard Myron and Helen Victoria (Nebraska) Bowers; m. William Michael Nelson, Apr. 19, 1970; 1 child, Lindsey Paige. BS, Western Mich. U., 1969, MS, 1971; JD, U. Detroit, 1977. Bar: Ohio 1977, U.S. Dist. Ct. (no. and so. dists.) Ohio 1978, Ill. 1985, Mich. 1996. Corp. counsel Beverage Mgmt., Inc., Columbus, Ohio, 1977-79, assoc. gen. counsel, 1979-80, gen. counsel, 1980-84; sr. atty. Abbott Labs., Abbott Park, Ill., 1984-87; sr. counsel Abbott Labs., Abbott Park, 1995—; divsn. counsel Abbott Labs., Columbus, 1987-95; sr. counsel Abbott Labs., Abbott Park, Ill., 1995—; pvt. practice Mich., 1996—. Mem. Ohio Bar Assn., Am. Corp. Counsel Assn. Unitarian. Office: 16940 Riley St Holland MI 49424-6018

NELSON, HOPE LINDA, pilot; b. Plainfield, N.J., Nov. 25, 1964; d. Ralston J. and Eileen M. (Creed) N. BS in Aviation Mgmt., Fla. Inst. Tech., 1986. Capt. Am. Eagle, Raleigh, N.C., 1990-95, Nashville, 1995-96; fist officer Northwest Airlines, Mpls., 1996—. Mem. Airlines Pilots Assn., Aircraft Owners Pilots Assn. Home: 2 70th St Harvey Cedars NJ 08008

NELSON, JANE D., opera company executive. Artistic dir. Dayton Opera Assn., Dayton, Ohio. Office: Dayton Opera Assn Memorial Hall 125 E 1st St Dayton OH 45402-1214*

NELSON, JANE GRAY, small business owner, educator; b. Hamilton, Ohio, Oct. 5, 1951; d. Robert Allen and Edna Mae (Allen) Gray; m. James Michael Nelson, Sept. 27, 1978; children: Brian, Elizabeth, Christina, Michelle, Jennifer. Student, U. Tex., Arlington, 1969-70; BS in Edn. and Linguistics, N. Tex. State U., 1972, postgrad., 1973-75; postgrad., So. Meth. U., 1973-75. Cert. tchr. Tchr. Arlington (Tex.) Ind. Sch. Dist., 1973-78; instr. community edn. Lewisville (Tex.) Ind. Sch. Dist., 1980—; owner, pres. Connections, Lewisville, 1987-92; owner Mayday Mfg., 1992—; chmn. Lewisville Community Edn. Adv. Coun., 1986-89; mem. steering com. Tex. Coummunity Edn. Counel of Couns., 1986; pres. Tex. Community Edn. Adv. Coun. Assn., 1986-88; bd. dirs., founder INFOHELP, Lewisville; mem. Tex. Bd. Edn., 1988-90; mem. adv. com. Tex. Ctr. for Ednl. Rsch.; mem. Nat. Com. for Tech. Edn. Excellence. Author: Drill Team, 1985; mem. editorial adv. bd. Tex. Researcher. Chmn. cultural arts Lewisville Ind. Sch. Dist. Community Edn. Adv. Council, 1984-89, ticket sales fundraiser, 1984-85, nominating com., 1986, sci. fair, 1985, ednl. com. Congressman Armey's Drug Abuse Task Force, Denton County, Tex., 1986-89, communications Lewisville Bond Election Steering Com., 1986, talent com. Red Stockings Follies Prodn., Lewisville, 1985, student com. Tex. State Bd. Edn., 1988-90; adv. com. Tex. Ctr. Ednl. Rsch.; nat. com. Tech. Edn. Excellence; editorial adv. bd. Tex. Researcher; founder, charter mem. Community Against Substance Abuse, Lewisville, 1987-89; mem. Lewiston Ind. Sch. Dist. Drug and Alcohol Abuse Task Force, 1986-89, Community Action League Lewisville, 1979—, v.p., 1980-81; active Lewisville Ind. Sch. Dist. Council PTA's, Highland Village Elem. PTA, (PTA Tex. Life Membership award 1987), Am. Cancer Soc.; bd. dirs. Dist.-Wide Drill Team and Baton Twirling Corps, 1980-86, edn. work com. 1st United Meth. Ch., Parent Support, Friends of Hospice, Denton, Tex., 1986—; Republican candidate from dist. 11 Tex. State Bd. Edn., 1988; mem. Tex. Cancer Coun., 1995—, Tex. Conservative Coalition Bd., 1993—. Named to Tex. Honor Roll, Young Conservatives of Tex., 1993, 95, Top Ten Legislator, Free Market Found., 1993, 95. Mem. Nat. Community Edn. Assn. (Citizen Leadership award 1986), Tex. Community Edn. Assn. (Citizen Leadership award 1987), Tex. Community Edn. Adv. Coun. Assn. (pres. 1986-88), Tex. Tchrs. Assn. (chmn. textbook adoption com. 1975-76), North Tex. State U. Alumnae Assn., Delta Zeta (founder Lewisville-Lake Cities chpt., bd. dirs. Province XVII 1975-81). Republican. Office: 3700 Forums Dr Flower Mound TX 75028

NELSON, KAREN ELIZABETH, lawyer; b. Gouverneur, N.Y., Apr. 1, 1966; d. David Sprague and Constance Ann (Moore) N. BA, U. Vt., 1988; JD, Suffolk U., 1993. Bar: Mass. 1993, Conn. 1994. Litigation paralegal Bingham, Dana & Gould, Boston, 1989-92, assoc., 1993—; pro se law clk., intern U.S. Dist. Ct. Mass., Boston, 1992-93. Mem. ABA, Mass. Bar Assn., Mass. Women's Bar Assn., Boston Bar Assn. Democrat. Unitarian Universalist. Office: Bingham, Dana & Gould 150 Federal St Boston MA 02110

NELSON, KARIN BECKER, child neurologist; b. Chgo., Aug. 14, 1933; d. George and Sylvia (Demansly) Becker; m. Phillip G. Nelson, Mar. 20, 1955; children: Sarah Nelson Hammack, Rebecca Nelson Miller, Jenny Nelson Walker, Peter. MD, U. Chgo., 1957; Student, U. Minn., 1950-53. Cert. child neurology Am. Bd. Psychiatry and Neurology. Intern rotating Phila. Gen. Hosp., 1957-58; asst. resident neurology U. Md. Sch. Medicine, Balt., 1958-59; resident neurology George Washington U. Sch. Medicine, Washington, 1959-62; cons. in med. neurology St. Elizabeth's Hosp., Washington, 1960-62; registrar to outpatients Nat. Hosp., Queen Sq., London, 1963; med. officer perinatal rsch. br. Nat. Inst. of Neurol. Disorders and Blindness, NIH, 1964-67; asst. prof. neurology George Washington U., Washington,

1970-72; assoc. neurologist Children's Hosp. of D.C., Washington, 1967-71; instr. neurology George Washington U., Washington, 1967-70; attending neurologist Children's Hosp., Washington, 1971-73, 78—; assoc. clin. prof. neurology George Washington U., Washington, 1972—; mem. orphan products devel. initial rev. group FDA, 1983-86, Boston Collaborative Drug Surveillance Group, 1985-86, vaccine Am. Acad. Pediatrics, 1985, 87, Dept. Health, State of Calif. Birth Monitoring Group, 1986—, Ctr. for Disease Control Birth Defects Monitoring Com., 1987; med. officer Nat. Inst. Neurol. Disorders and Blindness, NIH, Bethesda, 1972—; med. staff Children Hosp., Washington, 1962—; mem. adv. bd. Internat. Sch. Neuroscis., Venice, Italy, Little Found./World Fedn. Neurology, 1992—, rev. bd. Nat. Inst. Aging; mem. epidemiology steering com. NIH, 1993—. Editor: Workshop on the Neurobiological Basis of Autism, 1979, (with J.H. Ellenberg) Febrile Seizures, 1981; editorial bd. Pediatric Neurology, 1984-90, Brain and Development, 1984—, Neurology, 1985-88, Paediatric and Perinatal Epidemiology, 1987—, Developmental Medicine and Child Neurology, 1988; field editor Epilepsy Advances; contbr. papers to profl. jours. Recipient Spl. Recognition award USPHS, 1977, Spl. Achievement award 1981, United Cerebral Palsy Weinstein-Goldenson Rsch. award 1990, Dirs. award NIH, 1992. Fellow Am. Acad. Neurology (exec. bd. 1989-91, councillor); mem. Soc. Perinatal Obstetricians (hon.), Child Neurology Soc. (program chmn. 1973, liaison nat. Inst. of Neurol. and Communicative Disorders and Blindness 1975-80, ethics com. 1985-87, by-laws com. 1990—, ad hoc com. for consensus statement of DPT immunications and the cen. nervous system 1990, long range planning com. 1991—, Hower award 1991), Am. Acad. for Cerebral Palsy and Devel. Medicine (program chmn. 1985), Am. Epilepsy Soc. (Disting. Basic Neuroscientist Epilepsy Rsch. award 1992), Am. Neurol. Assn. (membership com. 1994—), Internat. Child Neurology Assn. (sci. selection com. 1993-94), Can. Assn. Child Neurology (hon.), Soc. Perinatal Obstetricians (hon.), Baltic Child Neurology Soc., Dana Alliance Brain Initiatives, Alpha Omega Alpha. Democrat. Jewish. Office: NIH 7550 Wisconsin Ave Rm 700 Bethesda MD 20892-9130

NELSON, KAY ELLEN, speech and language pathologist; b. Milw., Apr. 14, 1947; d. John A. and Margaret B. (Janke) Strobel; m. Kuglitsch Dale, Mar. 2, 1974 (div. Dec. 1981); 1 child, Ashley Lara. BA with distinction, U. Wis., Madison, 1969; MA, U. Wis., Milw., 1972. Speech and lang. pathologist Sch. Dist. 146, Dolton, Ill., 1970-71, Waukesha County Handicapped Children's Edn. Bd., Waukesha, Wis., 1972-77, 79-80, Kettle Moraine Area Schs., Wales, Wis., 1980-94; dir. speech/lang. pathology MJ Care, Inc., Fond du Lac, Wis., 1994-96; speech-lang. pathologist, clin. specialist NovaCare, Inc., New Berlin, Wis., 1996—; pvt. practice Dousman, Wis., summers 1991-93. Fellow Herb Kohl Found., 1993. Mem. Am. Speech, Lang. and Hearing Assn. (cert. of clin. competence, ACE awards 1990, 91, 92, 94, 95), Wis. Speech., Lang. and Hearing Assn. (sch. rep. dist VII 1991—, chmn. sch. svcs. com. 1992-94, v.p. sch. svcs. 1994-95, rep.-at-large 1995-96), Internat. Soc. for Augumentive and Alternative Comm., U.S. Soc. for Augumentive and Alternative Comm., Wis. Soc. for Augumentive and Alternative Comm. (sec. 1990-92, membership chmn. 1990-93, v.p. profl. affairs 1993). Unitarian. Office: NovaCare Inc 13700 W National Ave New Berlin WI 53151

NELSON, LAURA, secondary education educator; b. New Haven, Conn., Jan. 6, 1954; d. Louis Elias and Louise Janet (Biondella) Birbarie; m. Stephen Barry Nelson, June 19, 1976; 1 child, Erik Stephen. BA in Biology, Wheaton Coll., Norton, Mass., 1976; MS in Edn., Old Dominion U., 1991. Cert. seondary tchr. and adminstr., Va. Tchr. Norfolk (Va.) City Schs., 1976—. Den leader Boy Scouts Am., Norfolk, 1986-88. Recipient Tchr. of Yr. award Tidewater Sci. Congress, 1993, Gov.'s Sch. Outstanding Educator award Va. Dept. Edn., 1994, Sch. Bell award Va. Dept. Edn., 1993, 95; grantee Dept. of Justice, 1992, grantee Tech. Prep., 1994, 95, grantee Eisenhouwer Math./Sci., 1994, 95. Mem. NEA, ASCD, Nat. Assn. Secondary Prins., Nat. Sci. Tchrs. Assn., Va. Assn. Sci. Tchrs., Tidewater Assn. Chemistry Tchrs. Home: 409 Charlotte Dr Portsmouth VA 23701-1021 Office: Norview HS 1070 Middleton Pl Norfolk VA 23513

NELSON, LEANN LINDBECK, small business owner; b. McCook, Nebr., Jan. 27, 1937; d. Clifford Roy Lindbeck and Elizabeth J. (Downs) Rollstin; m. Lawrence L. Nelson, June 21, 1958; children: Glen Lindbeck, Todd Alan. BS in Dietetics, U. Tex., 1960. Dietitian Parkview Bapt. Hosp., Yuma, Ariz., 1960-61; instr. foods and nutrition Jefferson County Schs., Lakewood, Colo., 1969-71; dir. education and consumer programs, cons. nutrition Dairy Coun., Inc., Denver, 1971-74; coord. low-income foods and nutrition programs Emily Griffith Opportunity Sch., Denver, 1974-76; dir., asst. dir. edn./info. and product publicity Am. Sheep Prodrs. Coun., Denver, 1976-83; pres. Natural Accents, Denver, 1983-90; cons. fixed income counseling program City of Denver, Denver County, 1975-76, comm. cons., 1989—; pres., owner LeAnn Nelson Presents, 1988—; co-chairperson Home Econs. Nat. Task Force on Profl. Unity and Identity, 1992-93; prof. home econs., mem. adv. com. Coll. Applied Human Scis., Colo. State U., 1994-96. Author: Accessories... What a Finish!, 1988. Chmn. home econs. adv. com. U. No. Colo., 1980-82; v.p. Clock Tower Mchts. Assn., Denver, 1983-85; chmn., buyer Denver Symphony Guild Gift Shop, 1984-87; mem. adv. bd. State Bd. Cmty. Colls. Occupational Edn., Home Econ. Tech. Adv. Com., 1986-95, Coll. Applied Human Scis. Colo. State U., Ft. Collins, 1986-87; mem. consumer & family studies adv. com. Emily griffith Opportunity Sch., 1993—. Named Colo. Home Economist of Yr. Colo. Home Econs. Assn., 1979, Colo. Bus. Home Economist of Yr. Colo. Home Econs. Assn., 1980; recipient Leadership award Colo. Home Econs. Assn. Mem. Nat. Assn. Women Bus. Owners, Home Economists in Bus. (nat. chmn.-elect 1981-82, nat. chmn. 1982-83, Nat. Bus. Home Economist of Yr. 1986), Colo. Assn. of Profl. Saleswomen, Profl. Aux. Assistance League of Denver, Denver Fashion Group (regional dir. 1984-86), Am. Women in Radio & TV (treas. Denver chpt. 1978-79). Clubs: Penrose, Executive. Home and Office: 1250 Humboldt St Apt 1001 Denver CO 80218-2416

NELSON, LINDA SHEARER, child development and family relations educator; b. New Kensington, Pa., Dec. 8, 1944; d. Walter M. and Jean M. (Black) Shearer; m. Alan Edward Nelson, Dec. 29, 1973; children: Amelia (Amy), Emily. BS in Home Econs. Edn., Pa. State U., 1966; MS in Child Devel. and Family Rels., Cornell U., 1968; PhD in Higher Edn. and Child Devel., U. Pitts., 1982. Head tchr.-lab. nursery sch. Dept. of Psychology, Vassar Coll., Poughkeepsie, N.Y., 1968-69; instr. child devel. dept. home econs. edn. Indiana U. Pa., 1969-72, asst. prof., 1972-77, assoc. prof., 1977-84, prof. child devel. and family rels., 1984—, dept. chair, 1991-93, prof. child devel. and family rels., 1993—, mem. values task force, strategic planning com., 1995-96; mem. refocusing II com. Indiana U. Pa., 1994-95, strategic planning com. mem. values task force, 1995-96; ind. cons., trainer Head Start Programs, Pa., 1970—, Child Care Programs and Agys., Pa., 1970—; child devel. assoc. rep. Coun. for Early Childhood Profl. Recognition, Washington, 1989-91; field rep. Keyston U. Rsch. Corp., Erie, 1990-91; keynote/guest spkr. child devel./child care and home econs. confs., Pa. and nat., 1985—. Mem. adv. bd. Early Childhood Edn., Annual Edits., 1985—; mem. adv. bd. Interface: Home Economics and Technology Newsletter, 1993-96; contbr. articles to profl. jours. Bd. dirs. Indiana County Child Care Program, 1970-92; guest spkr. Delta Kappa Gamma, Indiana, 1990, Bus. and Profl. Women, Indiana, 1991, IUP's The Marriage Project, 1996. Grantee in field, 1985—. Mem. AAUW (guest spkr. 1996), Nat. Assn. for Edn. Young Children, Pitts. Assn. for Edn. Young Children (conf. co-chair 1983-85, in-svc. tng. spkr. 1995), Assn. Pa. State Coll. and Univ. Faculties, Kappa Omicron Nu. Democrat. Presbyterian. Office: Indiana U of Pa Human Devel and Environ Studies Dept 207 Ackerman Hall Indiana PA 15705

NELSON, MARCELLA SIMONETTA, artist; b. Rochester, N.Y., Mar. 13, 1955; d. John Charles and Bruna (Marchi) N. BA in Liberal Arts, Sarah Lawrence Coll., 1977; MA in Painting, NYU, 1979. Tchr. art St. Ann's Sch., Brooklyn Heights, N.Y., 1979-82; apprentice, part-time asst. John Kacere, N.Y.C., 1979-82. One-woman show 80 Washington square East Gallery, NYU, 1979; 2-person show Joy Berman Gallery, Phila., 1991; exhibited in group shows NYU, 1979, 80, Kamikaze, nightclub, N.Y.C., 1984, RVS Gallery, Southampton, N.Y., 1988, SUNY, L.I., 1988, Keith Green Gallery, N.Y.C., 1988, Jo Berman Gallery, Phila., 1989, Gallery Madison 90, N.Y.C., 1990, 92, Max Fish, N.Y.C., 1991, Hampton Square Gallery, Westhampton, N.Y., 1993. Recipient hon. mention NYU Ann. Small Works Competition, 1980. Home and Studio: 209 Elizabeth St 3d Fl New York NY 10012

NELSON, MARGUERITE HANSEN, special education educator; b. S.I., N.Y., June 23, 1947; d. Arthur Clayton and Marguerite Mary (Hansen) Nelson. AB magna cum laude, Boston Coll., 1969; MS in Edn., SUNY, Plattsburgh, 1973; post master's cert. in gerontology, Yeshiva U., 1982; PhD, Fordham U., N.Y.C., 1995. Cert. elem. and spl. edn. tchr., N.Y. Pre-primary tchr. Pub. Sch. 22R S.I., N.Y.C. Bd. Edn., 1969-70; primary tchr. Oak Street Sch., Plattsburgh, N.Y., 1971-73, Laurel Plains Sch., Clarkstown Cen. Schs., New City, N.Y., 1973-78, Resource Rm. Lakewood Sch., Congers, N.Y., 1978—; mem. adj. faculty St. Thomas Aquinas Coll., Sparkill, N.Y., 1985-89, 95—, Fordham U., Lincoln Ctr., N.Y.C., 1990; presenter in field internat. and nat. confs., seminars. Author: Teacher Stories, 1993, Research on Teacher Thinking, 1993; contbr. articles to profl. jours. and textbooks. Recipient Impact II Tchr. Recognition award, 1984; grantee Chpt. II, 1983-84, Clarkstown Ctrl. Schs., 1986-91, Office of Spl. Edn., 1992, 95. Mem. AAUW, Am. Ednl. Rsch. Assn., Assn. for Children with Learning Disabilities, N.Y. State Congress of Parents and Tchrs. (hon. life), Assn. for Retarded Citizens. Home: PO Box 395 Valley Cottage NY 10989 Office: Lakewood Elem Sch 77 Lakeland Ave Congers NY 10920-1733

NELSON, MARJORIE LOIS RAMEY, retired medical technician; b. Salmon, Idaho, Feb. 4, 1914; d. Louis Francis and Clara Frances (Blume) Ramey; m. Carl Frederick Nelson, Oct. 11, 1937; children: Fred Louis, Lorenzo John, Frances Anne Nelson Jeffery. Student, Tucson C.C., 1974. Accredited med. record technician. Stenographer, transcriptionist State Hosp. South Idaho State Employees, Blackfoot, Idaho, 1932-35; bookkeeper, stenographer State Ins. Fund Idaho State Employees, Boise, Idaho, 1935-37; stenographer, asst. bookkeeper State Hosp. South Idaho State Employees, Blackfoot, Idaho, 1962-65; med. stenographer-recorder Pinal County Hosps., Casa Grande and Florence, Ariz., 1965-67; med. transcriber U.S. Civil Svc., Papago, Ariz., 1967-70; med. transcriber, coder Indian Health Svc., Papago, 1970-77, R&D profl., 1970-77; med. records technician Computerized Analytical Co., Indian Health, Tucson, 1977-79; description pers. med. records person U.S. Health and Welfare Indian Health Svc., San Xavier, Tucson Papago Reservation, 1976. Author: Footprints on Mountain Trails, 1993. Sec., dep. state organizer Idaho State and Local Granges, Salmon, 1928-32; pres. Ladies' Aid Bethel Luth. Ch., Firth, Idaho, 1934—; mem. Ch. Women United, Land of Yankee Fork Hist. Assn. Mem. Order Ea. Star (pres. and sec. 1937, past matron, Grand Martha, grand rep. 1940). Lutheran.

NELSON, MARTHA JANE, magazine editor; b. Pierre, S.D., Aug. 13, 1952; d. Bernard Anton and Pauline Isabel (Noren) N. BA, Barnard Coll., 1976. Mng. editor Signs: Jour. of Women in Culture, N.Y.C., 1976-80; editor Ms. Mag., N.Y.C., 1980-85; editor-in-chief Women's Sports and Fitness Mag., Palo Alto, Calif., 1985-87; exec. editor Savvy, N.Y.C., 1988-89, editor-in-chief, 1989-91; asst. mng. editor People, 1993; editor In Style Mag., N.Y.C., 1993-96. Editor: Women in the American City, 1980; cons. editor Who Weekly, Sydney, 1992; contbr. articles to profl. publs. Bd. dirs. Painting Space 122, N.Y.C., 1982-85, Urban Athletic Assn. Mem. Am. Soc. Mag. Editors, Women in Film.

NELSON, MARY CARROLL, artist, author; b. Bryan, Tex., Apr. 24, 1929; d. James Vincent and Mary Elizabeth (Langton) Carroll; m. Edwin Blakely Nelson, June 27, 1950; children: Patricia Ann, Edwin Blakely. BA in Fine Arts, Barnard Coll., 1950; MA, U. N.Mex., 1963. Juror Am. Artist Golden Anniversary Nat. Art Competition, 1987, Don Ruffin Meml. Art Exhbn., Ariz., 1989, 96, N.Mex. Arts and Crafts Fair, 1989; guest instr. continuing edn. U. N.Mex., 1991; conf., organizer Affirming Wholeness, The Art and Healing Experience, San Antonio, 1992, Artists of the Spirit Symposium, 1994. Group shows include N.Mex. Mus. Fine Arts Biennial, 1987, N.Mex. Lightworks, 1990, Level to Level, Ohio Layering, 1987, Artist as Shaman, Ohio, 1990, The Healing Experience, Mass., 1991, A Gathering of Voices, Calif., 1991, Art is for Healing, The Universal Link, San Antonio, Tex., 1992, Biennial, Fuller Lodge Art Ctr. Los Alamos, N.Mex., 1993, Layering, Albuquerque, 1993, Crossings, Bradford, Mass., 1994, The Layered Perspective, Fayetteville, Ark., 1994, Tree of Life, San Miguel de Allende, Mex., 1996; represented in pvt. collections in: U.S., Fed. Republic of Germany, Eng. and Australia; author: American Indian Biography Series, 1971-76, (with Robert E. Wood) Watercolor Workshop, 1974, (with Ramon Kelley) Ramon Kelley Paints Portraits and Figures, 1977, The Legendary Artists of Taos, 1980, (catalog) American Art in Peking, 1981, Masters of Western Art, 1982, Connecting, The Art of Beth Ames Swartz, 1984, Artists of the Spirit, 1994, Doris Steider, A Vision of Silence, 1996, (catalog) Layering, An Art of Time and Space, 1985, (catalog) Layering/Connecting, 1987; contbg. editor Am. Artist, 1976-91, Southwest Art, 1987-91; editor (video) Layering, 1990; arts correspondent Albuquerque Jour., 1991-93. Mem. Albuquerque Arts Bd., 1984-88. Mem. Soc. Layerists in Multi-Media (founder 1982). Home: 1408 Georgia St NE Albuquerque NM 87110-6861

NELSON, MARY ELLEN GENEVIEVE, adult education educator; b. Milw., Sept. 13, 1948; d. William Paul and Evelyn Marie (Saduske) Naber; m. Kenneth Arthur Nelson, July 22, 1972; children: William Norris, Victoria Marie. BS in Edn., Mt. Mary Coll., 1970; MEd, Carroll Coll., 1994. Cert. tchr., Wis. Clk. Oldline Life Ins., Milw., 1967-70; math. tchr. Menomonee Falls (Wis.) East H.S., 1970-76; math. and adult basic edn. tchr. Waukesha County Tech. Coll., Pewaukee, Wis., 1978-82; math. tchr., goal instr. Waukesha County Tech. Coll., 1982-88; lead adult basic edn. tchr. and goal instr. Waukesha campus Waukesha County Tech. Coll., Menomonee Falls, 1988—. Dir. presch. program St. Agnes Cath. Ch., Butler, Wis., 1979-82, presch. tchr., 1977-79; den mother cub scout Pack 72, Boy Scouts Am., Butler, 1983-84, candy fundraiser chmn., 1985, 86; mem. Leadership Menomonee Falls, 1995-96. Mem. Nat. Coun. Tchrs. Math., Wis. Math. Coun., Wis. Adult and Continuing Edn. Assn., Menomonee Falls C. of C. (Waukesha County Tech. Coll. rep. 1993—, edn. com. 1986—), Rotary (partnership). Roman Catholic. Home: W152 N8645 Margaret Rd Menomonee Falls WI 53051-6716 Office: Menomonee Falls Campus Cmty Ctr Menomonee Falls WI 53051

NELSON, NANCY ELEANOR, pediatrician, educator; b. El Paso, Apr. 4, 1933; d. Harry Hamilton and Helen Maude (Murphy) N. BA magna cum laude, U. Colo., 1955, MD, 1959. Intern, Case Western Res. U. Hosp., 1959-60, resident, 1960-63; pvt. practice medicine specializing in pediats., Denver, 1963-70; clin. prof. U. Colo. Sch. Medicine, Denver, 1988—, asst. dean Sch. Medicine, 1982-88, assoc. dean, 1988—. Mem. Am. Acad. Pediats., AMA (sect. med. schs. governing coun. 1994—), Denver Med. Soc. (pres. 1983-84), Colo. Med. Soc. (bd. dirs. 1985-88, judicial coun. 1992—). Home: 1265 Elizabeth St Denver CO 80206-3241 Office: 4200 E 9th Ave Denver CO 80262

NELSON, NANCY FAYE, mathematician, educator; b. Nashville, May 21, 1965; d. Walter Davis Jr. and Helen (Feinmel) N. BS in Math., Coll. William and Mary, 1987. Cert. secondary tchr., Va. Tchr. substitute Henrico County Schs., Richmond, Va., 1987-88, Richmond Pub. Schs., 1987-88; tchr. math. Charles City (Va.) County Schs., 1988-89, Richmond Pub. Schs., 1989—; tchr. Hebrew Congregation Beth Ahabah, Richmond, 1992—. Vol. Daily Planet, Richmond, 1991—, CARITAS, Richmond, 1989—. Grantee Benjamin Banneker Orgn., 1993-94. Mem. NEA, Nat. Coun. Tchrs. Math., Va. Edn. Assn., Va. Coun. Tchrs. Math., Richmond Edn. Assn., Greater Richmond Coun. Tchrs. Math. (bd. dirs. 1992-93), Benjamin Banneker Orgn.. Democrat. Office: George Wythe HS 4314 Crutchfield St Richmond VA 23225-4767

NELSON, NETTE ADALINE, finance company executive; b. Hood River, Oreg., June 23, 1939; d. Burt Cheney and Ethel Gertrude (Taylor) Nelson; m. Charles Luther Blaylock, July 1961 (div. 1968); children: Charles Wayne, Dennis Ray, Meri Jo. Student, Oreg. State U., 1957-59; BA, U. Nebr., 1983; MPA, Harvard U., 1984. With Lockheed, Sunnyvale, Calif., 1959-62; asst. to mgr. Fairchild Semiconductor, Mountain View, Calif., 1962-68; asst. to state planner Office of Gov., Salem, Oreg., 1968-69; assoc. planner Daniel, Mann, Johnson & Mendenhall, Portland, 1969-74; exec. asst. to dir. Dept. Land Conservation & Devel., Portland/Salem, Oreg., 1974-75; dir. statewide progs. Exec. Dept., State of Oreg., Salem, 1975-80; dir./cons. Nebr. Telecom & Info. Ctr., Lincoln, 1984-87; v.p. Nebr. R&D Authority, Lincoln, 1987-89, pres., 1989-90; pres. The Nelson Group, Lincoln, 1991—; lobbyist various orgns. Contbr. articles to profl. jours. V.p., bd. dirs. Heartland Ctr. for Leadership Devel., Lincoln, 1988—; bd. dirs. Network Nebr., 1991—, Nebr. Venture Group, 1990, Prairie Fire, 1987-90, Lincoln YWCA, 1995—; advisor to Legis. New Horizons for Nebr. project, Lincoln, 1987-90; chmn. Nebr. Edn. Tech. Consortium, Lincoln, 1984—; mem. New Seeds for Nebr. project, Lincoln, 1988-90. Recipient Tribute to Women, Lincoln YWCA, 1994. Mem. Cmty. Devel. Soc., Internat. Women's Inst. Theology, Torch Club. Office: 411 S 44th St Lincoln NE 68510-1862

NELSON, NEVIN MARY, interior designer; b. Cleve., Nov. 5, 1941; d. Arthur George Reinker and Barbara Phyllis (Gunn) Parks; m. Wayne Nelson (div. 1969); children: Doug, Brian. BA in Interior Design, U. Colo., 1964. Prin. Nevin Nelson Design, Boulder, Colo., 1966-70, Vail, Colo., 1970—; program chmn. Questers Antique Study Group, Boulder, 1969. Coord. Bob Kirscht for Gov. campaign, Eagle County, Colo., 1986; state del. Rep. Nat. Conv., 1986-88; county coord. George Bush for U.S. Pres. campaign, 1988, 92; chmn. Eagle County Reps., 1989-93; v.p. bd. dirs. Park Lane Condo Assn., Denver, 1995-96. Mem. Am. Soc. Interior Designers. Episcopalian. Home: PO Box 1212 Vail CO 81658-1212 Office: 2498 Arosa Dr Vail CO 81657-4276

NELSON, NORMA RANDY DEKADT, psychotherapist, consultant; b. Irvington, N.J., Nov. 10, 1930; d. Ralph Joseph and Irma Marie (Richardson) Miele; m. Pieter Pim deKadt, Sept. 15, 1956 (div. 1984); children: Sharon, David, John; m. Ronald Prescott Nelson, July 27, 1985. BS, Northwestern U., Evanston, Ill., 1953; MS, Bridgeport U., 1974; cert. therapist, Found. Religion & Mental Heath, 1980; M in Neuro Linguistics, U. Calif., Santa Cruz, 1996. Pers. trainer B. Altman & Co., N.Y.C., 1953-54, asst. to merchandise mgr., 1954-55; dir. promotion Operation Home Improvement U.S. C of C and Time Inc., N.Y.C., 1955-57; counselor Stamford Counseling Ctr., Conn., 1975-80; trainer cons. N.Y.C., 1980-95; psychotherapist, cons. Stamford (Conn.) Counseling Ctr., 1976-82; pvt. practice Old Greenwich, Conn., 1980—; condr. positive parenting programs; keynote spkr. on raising self-esteem, development of motiviation, personal and spirit in the work place; seminar leader personality profile styles and teamwork, work and family life, motivation nd mental attitude, Open to Spirit seminars; founder, pres. Positive Parenting Program, Ctr. Well-Being, 1995; founder Family Re-entry Fathers Helping Fathers Program, 1995. Author: Magic of Attitude, 1995; contbr. articles to profl. jours. Pres. Old Greenwich (Conn.) Riverside Community Ctr., 1960; bd. dirs. YWCA, Greenwich, 1968-76, Parents Together, Greenwich, 1980-86; chmn. Women Together, Christ Ch., Greenwich, 1989-90; speaker PTAs, Greenwich, 1980-95; vol. Jr. League, 1956-75. Recipient Environ. Beautification award Old Greenwich, Conn., 1975. Mem. Assn. Carlton Learning Systems, Capr. Assn. Bus. Orgn. Colls., Transactional Analysis Assn., Trains Values Realization Inst., Kripalu Cons. Collaborative. Episcopalian. Home and Office: 8 Middle Way Old Greenwich CT 06870-2405

NELSON, ROBERTA JEAN, artist, art educator; b. Harrisburg, Pa., Aug. 16, 1942; d. C. Robert and Dorothy Helen (Spangler) Budd; m. Eric V. Nelson, July 2, 1966. BS in Art Edn., Pa. State U., 1964; postgrad., Elmira Coll., 1975, SUNY, Oswego, 1974. Cert. tchr., N.Y. Elem. and jr. H.S. art tchr. Bainbridge (N.Y.) Ctrl. Sch., 1965; jr. H.s. art tchr. West Jr. H.S., Binghamton, N.Y., 1966-67; elem. art tchr. Chenango Valley Ctrl. Sch., Binghamton, 1967-71, Mexico (N.Y.) Ctrl. Schs., 1971-74; jr.-sr. H.S. art tchr. Romulus (N.Y.) Ctrl. Sch., 1974—; mem. Am. Craft Coun., N.Y.C., 1995-96, Meml. Art Gallery, Rochester, N.Y., 1992—, Seneca County Arts Coun., Seneca Falls, N.Y., 1996. Mem. Am. Fedn. Tchrs., Nat. Mus. Women in Arts (charter), N.Y. State Art Tchrs. Assn., N.Y. State United Tchrs., Delta Kappa Gamma (2d v.p., various chairperson posts). Home: 3261 Canoga St Seneca Falls NY 13148 Office: Romulus Ctrl Sch 4505 Main St Romulus NY 13148

NELSON, RUTH NAOMI, marketing professional; b. Beaumont, Calif., Oct. 11, 1948; d. Ashel LeRoy and Hazel J. (Cain) N. BA in Phys. Edn. and Psychology, U. No. Colo., 1970; MS in Phys. Edn., George Williams Coll., 1973; postgrad., Concordia Coll., Montreal, Can., 1978. Head women's volleyball coach, head men's tennis coach, instr. phys. edn. George Williams Coll., Downers Grove, Ill., 1970-72; mem. U.S. Nat. Volleyball Team, 1972, 75; head women's tennis coach U. Houston, 1974-76, head women's volleyball coach, instr. phys. edn., supr. student tchrs., advisor men's volleyball club team, 1974-81; pres., dir. jr. devel. program, camps, clinics, and coaches devel. program Houston Stars Volleyball Club, 1977-81; head women's volleyball coach, advisor to men's volleyball club team, instr. phys. edn., supv. student tchrs. La. State U., Baton Rouge, 1981-85; volleyball dir. Spl. Olympics Internat., Washington, 1985-91, sport mktg. mgr., 1991-92, 94—, sports mktg. dir., 1992-93, corp. mktg. dir., 1993-94; dir. nonprofit and sports mktg. Intellicall, Inc., 1995—; head volleyball coach Dallas Belles women's profl. team Major League Volleyball, Dallas, 1987; head women's vollyball coach, instr. phys. edn., advisor to men's volleyball club team U. Iowa, 1989-91; dir. nonprofit & sports mktg. Intellicall, Inc., Dallas, 1995-96; dir. nonprofit and sports mktg. Global Affinity Group, Dallas, 1996—; coach top 3 Olympic players Flo Hyman, Rita Crockett, Rose Magers, 1974-81; asst. coach U.S. Women's Nat. Volleyball Team, 1977; mem. adv. bd. Volleyball Enterprises, 1978; head coach U.S. World Univ. Games Team, 1979, South and Midwest Sports Festival Teams, 1979, Houston Stars Volleyball AAU Jr. Olympic Team, 1979, U.S. Jr. Nat. Volleyball Team, 1984; volleyball dir. La. Spl. Olympics, 1982, 83, 84, 85, volleyball advisor, 1986, 87, 88; pres. sales, mktg., cons. on weight tng., dir. for players' and coaches' clinics Baton Rouge Volleyball Club, 1981—; pres. not-for-profit La. Volleyball Club, 1986—; tech. expert U.S. Women's Nat. Team, 1983; volleyball rules chairperson Spl. Olympics Internat., 1984-91, volleyball dir., 1985-91, dir. model chpt. programs, 1989, volleyball advisor, 1991-94; cons. sales and mktg. for splty. advt. and promotional programs Acadian Advt., 1985-89, cons. mktg., promotion and sales, 1989—; cons. advanced jump tng. and rehab. Plyometric Inc., 1989-90; instr. volleyball for coaches cert. U.S. Volleyball Assn., 1990-91; volleyball color analyst Iowa Pub. TV, Des Moines, 1985, 86, 87, 88; dir. placement U.S. men's and women's profl. volleyball players in Europe Internat. Players Promotion, Mulhouse, France, 1989; cons. disability players in France and Switzerland Inst. Internat. Sports, Kingston, R.I.; head coach jrs. Springfield Jr. Volleyball Club, 1989; mem. adv. bd. Women's Sports Found., 1992-95; dir. Hawkeye Challenge Jr. Volleyball Clinic, U. Iowa, 1990, U. Iowa Overnight Camp, 1991; bd. dirs. Wallyball, Inc., 1992—; numerous others; presenter in field; cons. in field. Contbr. articles to profl. publs. Sponsor West Germany vs. Houston Stars, 1978; co-sponsor Volleyball Enterprises-Japan vs. U.S. Women's Olympic Team, 1979, USA vs. Japan Olympic Team, 1982, Aspri Sports-USA vs. Korean Olympic Team, 1983, Audubon Ford-USA vs. Japan Olympic Team, 1984, United Cos., Piccadilly and Episcopal H.S., Pelican State Games, 1985-86; cons. Iowa Spl. Olympics Tng. Sch., 1989-91. Recipient Tachikara Victory Club award for 500 wins, 1985, U.S.A. Volleyball Meritorious Svc. award Spl. Olympics Internat. Volleyball, 1994; named one of Outstanding Young Women of Am., 1980, 84; named Outstanding Prof., U. Houston, 1981. Mem. AAHPERD, AAUP, USTA, Nat. Assn. Phys. Edn. Coll. Women, Assn. Intercollegiate Athletics for Women (nat. volleyball chair 1979-80), U.S. Volleyball Assn. Delta Region (jr. volleyball devel. dir. 1986), Collegiate Volleyball Coaches Assn. (nat. seedling com. 1981-84), Am. Volleyball Coaches Assn. (profl. mem.), Am. Mktg. Assn. (profl. mem.), So. Assn. Phys. Edn. Coll. Women, Women's Sports Found. (mem. adv. bd. 1991—), La. Volleyball Coaches Assn. (co-founder, bd. dirs. 1983-87), Tex. Assn. Intercollegiate Athletics for Women (mem. sending com., Tex. state volleyball sports dir. 1979-80), S.W. Assn. Intercollegiate Athletics for Women (mem. regional sending com., mem. region 4 volleyball rep. 1978-80), Assn. Intercollegiate Athletics for Women (nat. volleyball chairperson 1979-80), Tex. Assn. for Health, Phys. Edn. and Recreation, La. Volleyball Club (pres. 1985—), Baton Rouge Volleyball Club, 1981—. Home: PO Box 829 Merrifield VA 22116-2829

NELSON, SARAH MILLEDGE, archaeology educator; b. Miami, Fla., Nov. 29, 1931; d. Stanley and Sarah Woodman (Franklin) M.; m. Harold Stanley Nelson, July 25, 1953; children: Erik Harold, Mark Milledge, Stanley Franklin. BA, Wellesley Coll., 1953; MA, U. Mich., 1969, PhD, 1973. Instr. archaeology U. Md. extension, Seoul, Republic Korea, 1970-71; asst. prof. U. Denver, 1974-79, assoc. prof., 1979-85, prof. archaeology, 1985—, chair dept. anthropology, 1985-95, dir. women's studies program, 1985-87, John Evans prof., 1996; vis. asst. prof. U. Colo., Boulder, 1974; resident Rockefeller Ctr. in Bellagio, Italy, 1996. Co-editor: Powers of Observation, 1990, Equity Issues for Women in Archaeology, 1994; author: Archaeology of Korea, 1993; editor: The Archaeology of Northeast China, 1995. Active

Earthwatch, 1989. Recipient scholarly comm. award from China, NAS, 1988, Outstanding Scholar award U. Denver, 1989; grantee S.W. Inst. Rsch. on Women, 1981, Acad. Korean Studies, Seoul, 1983, Internat. Cultural Soc. Korea, 1986, Colo. Hist. Fund, 1995-97, Rockefeller Found. Residency, Bellagio, Italy. Fellow Am. Anthrop. Assn.; mem. Soc. Am. Archaeology, Assn. Asian Studies, Royal Asiatic Soc., Sigma Xi (sec.-treas. 1978-79), Phi Beta Kappa. Democrat. Home: 5878 S Dry Creek Ct Littleton CO 80121-1709 Office: U Denver Dept Anthropology Denver CO 80208

NELSON, SONJA DIANN, research psychologist; b. St. Louis, Sept. 18, 1968; d. Carroll Dean and Norma Lenore (Kincannon) N. BA, Harding U., 1990; MS, Tulane U., 1994. Intern, rsch. asst. Cen. Ark. Screening and Assistance Ctr., Little Rock, 1989-90; tchg. asst. dept. psychology Tulane U., New Orleans, 1990-94; rsch. specialist Inst. on Disability and Human Devel., Chgo., 1994-95, Program for Mental Health Svcs. Rsch. on Women and Gender, Chgo., 1995—; substitute tchr. Ft. Zumwalt Sch. Dist., St. Peters, Mo., 1993. Mem. Women's Action Coalition, Chgo., 1994; vol. Debra's Place, Chgo., 1996. Full tuition scholar/tchg. assistantship Tulane U., 1990-94. Mem. AAUW, NOW. Office: Program Mtl Hlth Svcs Rsch MC 912 1601 W Taylor Chicago IL 60612

NELSON, SUE A., legislative staff member. BA, U. Mich., 1974; MPA, U. Tex., 1980. Rsch. asst. Multi-Ethnic Curriculum Revision Project, Ann Arbor, Mich., 1975; program mgr. Capital Area Planning Coun., Austin, Tex., 1977-78; presdl. mgmt. intern Treasury Dept., 1980-82; budget analyst Office Mgmt. and Budget, 1982-85; dir. budget rev. Senate Budget Com., 1985—; assoc. dir. Nat. Econ. Commn., 1988-89. Office: Com Budget 630 Senate Dirksen Office Bldg Washington DC 20510

NELSON, THERESA, writer; b. Beaumont, Tex., Aug. 15, 1948; d. David Rogers Jr. and Alice Carroll (Hunter) N.; m. Kevin Cooney, Sept. 26, 1968; children: Michael Christopher, Brian David, Errol Andrew. BA magna cum laude, U. St. Thomas, 1972. Actor, tchr. creative dramatics Theatre Under The Stars, Houston, 1971-80; dir. glee club St. Mary's Sch., Katonah, N.Y., 1983-90; spkr. in schs., librs., lit. groups, 1983—. Author: The Twenty-Five Cent Miracle, 1986 (Best Book of Yr. citation Sch. Libr. Jour., 1986, Washington Irving Children's Choice award, 1988), Devil Storm, 1987 (Notable Children's Trade Book in the field of social studies citation Nat. Coun. Social Scis. Children's Book Coun. 1987), And One For All, 1989 (Notable Children's Book citation, Best Book for Young Adults citation ALA, Best Book of Yr. citation Sch. Libr. Jour., Editor's Choice citation Booklist, Fanfare citation Horn Book, Pick of the Lists citation Am. Bookseller, Books for Children citation Libr. Congress/Children's Lit. Ctr., others), The Beggar's Ride, 1992 (Notable Children's Book citation, Best Book for Young Adults ALA, Best Book of Yr. citation Sch. Libr. Jour., Fanfare citation Horn Book, others), (short story) Andrew, Honestly, 1993, (novel) Earthshine, 1994 (Child Study award Bank St. Coll., 1995, Boston Globe/Horn Book honor, Notable Children's Book citation, Best Book for Young Adults ALA, Best Book of Yr. citation Sch. Libr. Jour., others). Mem. Authors Guild, Authors League of Am., Soc. Children's Book Writers and Illustrators, Golden Triangle Writers Guild, So. Calif. Coun. Lit. for Children and Young People. Democrat. Roman Catholic. •

NELSON, VALARIE DAPHINE, physical education educator; b. Little Rock, Oct. 16, 1963; d. Johnnie Lee Freeman and Mary Lee Franklin Freeman Harris. Diploma, Adult Edn. Ctr., 1992; BS in Therapeutic Recreation summa cum laude, U. Ark., Pine Bluff, 1996. CNA; cert. therapeutic recreation specialist. Nursing asst. Pine Bluff Nursing Home, 1982-85, activity asst. dir., 1985-87; floor supr. Wyatt's Cafeteria, Pine Bluff, 1987-90; cert. nursing asst. Jefferson Regional Med. Ctr., Pine Bluff, 1988-91; aerobics instr. U. Ark., Pine Bluff, 1992-95, Shaping Up With Valarie Aerobics Studio, Pine Bluff, 1992-96; intern Little Rock VA Med. Ctr., 1996; with City of Little Rock; aerobics instr. Dunbar Cmty. Ctr., Pine Bluff; aerobic fitness specialist Merrill Cmty. Ctr., Pine Bluff. Host (TV show) Shaping Up with Valarie. Vol. United Way, Pine Bluff, 1986—, Women's Shelter, Pine Bluff, 1991, Corner Stone Project, Pine Bluff, 1991-92, Pine Bluff Nursing Home, 1980-88, RIF Reading is Fun, Pine Bluff, 1987, Neighbor to Neighbor, Pine Bluff, 1992-93, Jump Rope for Heart, Pine Bluff, 1993, Gt. Am. Cancer Lockup, Pine Bluff, 1992-93, Drug Free Am. Campaign, Pine Bluff, 1990-93, North Little Rock VA; motivational spkr. youth groups; pres. Off-Campus Club, Pine Bluff, 1989-90; mem. Interested Voter Registration, Pine Bluff, 1989—; active College Heights Ch. of Christ. Named Queen Off-Campus Club, 1989-90, October Calender Pageant, 1995; recipient 1st Good News award, 1993; named to All Am. Acad. Team, 1995. Mem. AAHPERD, NAACP, Am. Therapeutic Recreation Assn., Am. Therapeutic Assn., Ark. Therapeutic Recreation Assn., La. Torrence Inst. (exec. leader 1993—), HPER Club (v.p. 1993—). Mem. Ch. of Christ. Home: 1202 E 7th Ave Pine Bluff AR 71601-5103

NELSON, VIRGINIA SIMSON, pediatrician, physiatrist, educator; b. L.A.; d. Jerome and Virginia (Kuppler) Simson; children: Eric, Paul. AB, Stanford U., 1963, MD, 1970; MPH, U. Mich., 1974. Diplomate Am. Bd. Pediatrics, Am. Bd. Phys. Medicine and Rehab. Pediatrician Inst. Study Mental Retardation and Related Disabilities, U. Mich., Ann Arbor, 1973-80; mem. faculty phys. medicine and rehab. dept. U. Mich. Med. Ctr., Ann Arbor, 1980-83, resident PM&R, 1983-85, chief pediatric PM&R, 1985—. Contbr. articles to profl. jours. Office: Univ Mich Med Ctr F7822 Mott Hospital Ann Arbor MI 48109-0230

NELSON-MAYSON, LINDA RUTH, art museum curator; b. Vincennes, Ind., Jan. 9, 1954; d. Robert Arthur and Darleen Marie (Andrews) N.; m. William A. Mayson, June 12, 1982; 1 child, Eric Nelson. BFA, Miami U., Oxford, Ohio, 1976; MFA, Ohio State U., 1981. Co-dir. Artreach Gallery, Columbus, Ohio, 1980-82; art instr., gallery asst. Ohio U., Chillicothe, 1982-83; asst. curator Ross County Mus., Chillicothe, 1982-83; art dir. Aaron Copland Music & Arts Program, White Plains, N.Y., 1982-85; artist-in-edn. Nebr. Arts Council, Omaha, 1983-85; curator Art Mus. South Tex., Corpus Christi, 1985-89; curator collections Columbia (S.C.) Mus. Art, 1989-92, dep. dir. curatorial svcs., 1992-94; supr. curatorial projects Minn. Mus. Am. Art, St. Paul, 1994—; juror art exhibits Corpus Christi Arts Found., 1986-88, Hardin Simmons U., 1987, Anderson Coll., 1989, Hilton Head Art League, 1994; mem. pub. art selection panel S.C. Arts Coun., 1990; mem. steering com. South Tex. Regional Arts Conf., 1986-88; adj. lectr. art history U. S.C., 1989-94; chmn. curators com. S.E. Mus. Conf., 1991-93, chmn. local program com., 1992, mem. program com., 1992-93. Grantee NEA, S.C. Arts Coun., Tex. Coun. on Arts, Kress Found., Inst. Mus. Svcs. Mem. am. Assn. Mus. (co-chmn. exhibits competition 1991-93, chmn. curator's com. 1993-95, chmn. of SPC com. 1994-95, nominating com. 1994-95), Minn. Assn. Mus., Midwest Mus. Assn., Coll. Art Assn. Democrat. Office: Minn Mus Am Art Landmark Ctr 75 W 5th St Saint Paul MN 55102

NELSON-PEÑA, KRISTINE, college program director; b. Seattle, Nov. 2, 1951; d. Richard Christian and Mildred Marie (Cunningham) Nelson; m. Miguel Angel Peña, Nov. 29, 1994. AA, East L.A. Coll., 1972; BA, Calif. State U., L.A., 1977, MS, 1981. Dorm counselor Ramona Convent, Alhambra, Calif., 1976-77; counselor Glendale (Calif.) Coll., 1977-90; matriculation coord. Cypress (Calif.) Coll., 1990—. Author Cypress Coll. Student Handbook, 1991—, campus newsletter Matriculation Matters, 1991—, Latino newsletter Latino Advocate, 1990-92. Bd. dirs. Glendale YWCA, 1978-80; mem. Glendale Human Rels. Coun., 1987-89. Mem. NOW. Democrat. Roman Catholic. Office: Cypress College 9200 Valley View Stq Cypress CA 90630

NELSON-SMALL, KATHY ANN, foundation administrator; b. Williamsport, Pa., Sept. 21, 1954; d. Dan LeRoy and Shirley Joann (Klein) Hoover; m. Robert Joseph Small, Feb. 14, 1996. BS in German Edn., Ind. U. of Pa., 1976; postgrad., Pa. State U., 1978-83. Tchr. German Hollidaysburg (Pa.) Area Sch. Dist., 1977-85; adminstr. Carlisle (Pa.) Project, 1985; dir. fin. devel. and pub. rels. Am. Lung Assn., York, Pa., 1986; chief profl. officer Adams County United Way, Gettysburg, Pa., 1987—. Press sec. Nancy Kulp's campaign for 9th Congl. Dist., Pa., 1984; mem. Downtown Gettysburg, 1987—, 125th Battle of Gettysburg Anniversary Commn., 1988; treas. Adams County Coun. Cmty. Svcs., 1987—, Pa. State Club of Adams County, 1989-91; mem. adv. bd. Adams County Job Ctr., 1989—, Minority Youth Ednl. Inst., 1988-91, Intercultural Resource Ctr., Gettysburg Coll., 1989-91; mem. Adams Area Postal Customer Coun., 1987-89; dir. Adams Cmty. TV, 1988-89; mem. profl. adv. coun., chairperson small cities task force United Way Pa., 1990—, mem. network com., 19992-94; mem. planning com. United Way Leaders' Conf., 1995; mem. pub. rels. com. Main St. Gettysburg, 1996—; participant United Way Leaders Conf. Fulbright/Goethe Haus scholar, Stuttgart, Germany, 1982. Mem. NAFE, Bus. and Profl. Women, Ctrl. Pa. Assn. Women Execs. (charter), Kiwanis (pres. Hist. Gettysburg chpt. 1991-92, chmn. dist. conv. Pa. chpt. 1992, dist. maj. emphasis program chairperson 1992-93), Pa. Stat Alumni Assn. (life), Alpha Omicron Pi (endowment chairperson 1993—). Democrat. Lutheran. Home: 2566 Old Route 30 Orrtanna PA 17353-9759 Office: Adams County United Way PO Box 3545 Gettysburg PA 17325-0545

NELSON-WALKER, ROBERTA, management software company executive; b. N.Y.C., Sept. 1, 1936; d. Richard E. and Esther (McBride) Martin; m. Robert L. Nelson, July 20, 1957 (div.); children: Carol, Craig, Robert H.; m. Dan Walker, Nov. 1978 (div.). BA, DePaul U., 1976, MS in Mgmt. with distinction, 1977. Dir. devel. Ray Graham Assocs., Elmhurst, Ill., 1970-76; dir. human resources Nat. Easter Seal Soc., Chgo., 1979-81; v.p. Butler Walker Inc., Oak Brook, Ill., 1981-85; pres. CNR, Inc., Oak Brook, Ill., 1985-91; spl. agt. Prudential Ins., Oak Brook, Ill., 1991-95; mng. dir. Visimark L.L.C., Oak Brook, Ill., 1995—. Author: Creating Acceptance for Handicapped People, 1975, Creating, Planning, and Financial Housing for Handicapped People, 1979. Founder, organizer Found. for Handicapped, 1970-76,; pres. DuPage County Pub. Health Coun., 1974; bd. dirs. DuPage County Mental Health Assocs., 1970, Forest Found. DuPage County, 1976-86, Shakespeare Globe, London and Chgo., 1982—; mem. DuPage County Bd. Health, 1975, Ill. Gov.'s Com. for Handicapped, 1976, women's coun. Chgo. Heart Assn., 1979—. Recipient Meritorious Svc. award, Chgo. Heart Assn., 1968, 70, Fond du Coer award AHA, 1968, Cursade of Mercy Achievement awards, 1974-76, State of Ill. procalmation by Gov. James Thompson, Ill. Epilepsy Assn., 1978. Office: Visimark LLC 2100 Clearwater Dr Oak Brook IL 60521

NEMAN, BETH S., English educator; b. Detroit, Dec. 2, 1931; d. Louis I. Smilansky and Harriet (Feldman) Smilansky Plaut; m. Albert H. Neman, July 12, 1953; children: David G., Daniel L. AB, U. Mich., 1953; MA, U. Cin., 1963; PhD, Miami U., 1976. Cert. elem. and secondary tchr., Ohio, Mich. Tchr. Cleve. Pub. Schs., 1953-55, Princeton Pub. Schs., Sharonville, Ohio, 1955-57; co-head, tchr. English dept. Madeira (Ohio) High Sch., 1963-70; teaching assoc. Miami U., Oxford, Ohio, 1971-76, asst. prof., 1976-80; asst. prof. English Wilmington (Ohio) Coll., 1980-86, assoc. prof., 1986-93, prof. English, 1993—; cons. in field. Author: Teaching Students to Write, 1980, 96, Writing Effectively, 1983, 90, Writing Effectively in Business, 1992; contbr. articles to encys., scholarly jours. Rsch. fellow Miami U., 1974-75; Ohio Bd. Regents grantee, 1990-91, 92-93. Mem. Nat. Coun. Tchrs. English, Coll. Composition and Communication Conf., Am. Soc. Eighteenth Century Studies, Phi Beta Kappa. Jewish. Home: 1101 Lois Dr Cincinnati OH 45237-5121 Office: English Dept Wilmington Coll Wilmington OH 45177

NEMEC, VERNITA ELLEN MCCLISH (VERNITA N'COGNITA), mixed-media artist, educator, arts administrator, curator; b. Painesville, Ohio, Nov. 30, 1942; d. Vernon William and Ellen (Ludway) McClish; m. David Joseph Nemec, Apr. 18, 1964 (div. 1970). B.F.A. cum laude, Ohio U., 1964; postgrad. Cleve. Inst. Art, 1964-65; M.A., NYU, 1966; postgrad. Bklyn. Mus. Sch. Art, 1967-68, Fashion Inst. Tech., 1969-70, Sch. Visual Arts, 1970-71, Naropa Inst., 1978-79. Art specialist pub. schs., N.Y.C., 1967-68; prof. fine arts Rockland Community Coll., Suffern, N.Y., 1970-71, CUNY, 1973-79, Sch. Visual Arts, N.Y.C., 1977-78, Hunter Coll.; ednl. cons. Middlesex Arts and Edn. Coun., Highland Park, N.J., 1988—; curator Mus. Project for Living Artists, N.Y.C., 1970; co-dir. Whitney Counterweight, N.Y.C., 1977, 81, 83; asst. dir. Susan Caldwell Gallery, 1982; design asst. John Haines Design, N.Y.C., 1983; bd. dirs. Found. New Ideas, 1985; vis. artist Lake Erie Coll., Painesville, 1975, Jersey City State Coll., 1976, U. Calif.-Santa Barbara, 1983; artist-in-residence Millay Colony for Arts, Austerlitz, N.Y., 1981; exec. dir., pres. Artists Talk on Art, 1989—; v.p. Heresies Collective, 1992-96; curator Art from Detritus: Recycling with Imagination, 1994-96. Solo exhbns. include: Soho 20 Gallery, N.Y.C., 1975, 77, Jersey City State Coll., 1976, Jersey City Mus., 1977, Fiatal Muveszek Klubia, Budapest, Hungary, 1980, 10 on 8 Gallery, N.Y.C., 1984, Los Angeles Women's Bldg., 1985, Amsterdam's Grand, N.Y.C., 1990, 91, 92, Artpol, Budapest, 1993, NIH, Bethesda, Md., 1995; group exhibits include: Landmark Gallery, N.Y.C., 1976, Bronx Mus. Art, 1976, David & Long Gallery, N.Y.C., 1977, Willoughby Fine Arts Ctr., Ohio, 1974, Joseloff Gallery, Hartford, Conn., 1980, Franklin Furnace, N.Y.C., 1991, Baruch Coll., N.Y.C., 1992, Ea. Mont. Coll., Billings, 1992; exhibits in Europe; pvt. and pub. collections include Mus. Modern Art, N.Y. Savaria Mus., Szombathely, Hungary, Franklin Furnace, Grupa Junij Belgrade, Asian Art Ctr, N.Y.C., Queensboro Coll. Author: Unmaled, 1978, The Hole Burned Book, 1991; playwright: Private Places, 1985, The Last Confession, 1982, The Autumn of Her Descent, 1984, Micro-Soft Woman, Giovanni's Box, 1990; founder, artistic dir. The Floating Performance, 1985—. NDEA fellow, 1965-66, Cultural Council Found. fellow, 1978, 79, 84; Jerome Found. grantee, 1988. Mem. Nat. Abortion Rights Action League, NOW, Women's Caucus for Art, Lower Manhattan Loft Tenants Assn., Orgn. Ind. Artists. Address: 361 Canal St New York NY 10013-2216

NEMIROFF, MAXINE CELIA, art educator, gallery owner, consultant; b. Chgo., Feb. 11, 1935; d. Oscar Bernard and Martha (Mann) Kessler; m. Paul Rubenstein, June 26, 1955 (div. 1974); children: Daniel, Peter, Anthony; m. Allan Nemiroff, Dec. 24, 1979. BA, U. So. Calif., 1955; MA, UCLA, 1974. Sr. instr. UCLA, 1974-92; dir., curator art gallery Doolittle Theater, Los Angeles, 1985-86; owner Nemiroff Deutsch Fine Art, Santa Monica, Calif.; leader of worldwide art tours; cons. L'Ermitage Hotel Group, Beverly Hills, Calif., 1982—, Broadway Dept. Stores, So. Calif., 1979—, Security Pacific Bank, Calif., 1978—, Am. Airlines, Calif. Pizza Kitchen Restaurants; art chmn. UCLA Thieves Market, Century City, 1960—, L.A. Music Ctr. Mercado, 1982—; lectr. in field. Apptd. bd. dirs. Dublin (Calif.) Fine Arts Found., 1989; mem. Calif. Govs. Adv. Coun. for Women, 1992. Named Woman of Yr. UCLA Panhellenic Council, 1982, Instr. of Yr. UCLA Dept. Arts, 1984. Mem. L.A. County Mus. Art Coun., UCLA Art Coun., UCLA Art Coun. Docents, Alpha Epsilon Phi (alumnus of yr. 1983). Democrat. Jewish.

NENSTIEL, SUSAN KISTHART, insurance professional office administrator; b. Hazleton, Pa., Aug. 21, 1951; d. Frank W. and Mary A. (Price) Kisthart; m. David W. Nenstiel, June 4, 1977. BS, Pa. State U., 1973; MBA, Wilkes (Pa.) Coll., 1982. Control mgr. Barrett, Haentjens & Co., Hazleton, 1973-79, export mgr., 1979-86; exec. dir. Leadership Hazleton, 1986-87; devel. officer Planned Parenthood of NE Pa., Wilkes-Barre, 1986-87; ins. broker, office mgr. Nenstiel & Nenstiel, West Hazleton, Pa., 1988—. Spl. events coord. Hospice Saint John, 1996—; pres. YWCA, Hazleton, 1983-85, Women's Coalition of Greater Hazelton, 1987-91; sec. Govt. Study Commn., Hazleton, 1986; trustee Hazleton Area Pub. Libr., sec., 1987-89, v.p., 1990-91, pres., 1991-93; chmn. Luzerne County Commn. for Women, 1988-91; mem., chmn. Hazleton City Zoning Bd., 1988-92; treas. Pa. Women's Campaign Fund, 1987-91, pres., 1991-92; mem. Leadership Hazleton Adv. Coun., 1988-92; mem. Pa. Pub. Libr. Project, 1992-94; bd. dirs. Hazleton Health Care Found., 1992—, chairperson, 1994—, Cmty. Banks, Inc., 1996—; mem. Greater Hazelton Health Alliance Bd., 1995—, Luzerne County Regional Bd. Cmty. Banks, N.A., 1993—. Named one of Outstanding Women Penns Woods Coun. Girl Scouts USA, 1977, Outstanding Young Women in Am., 1985, Woman of Yr. Soroptimist Internat., 1984, Greater Hazleton Jaycee Disting. Svc. award, 1990; recipient Luzerne County Pathfinder's award, 1990, Hon. P.E.A.R.L. award YWCA, 1996; named to Pa. Honor Roll of Women, 1996. Mem. AAUW (br. pres. 1977-79, state sec. 1981-83, state treas. 1983-85, state pres. 1992-96, Br. Outstanding Woman of Yr. 1980, assn. program com. 1995—, assn. women's issue com. 1989-91, chairperson assn. conf. state pres. 1994, mem. state bd. 1989—), NAFE, Nat. Assn. Ins. Women, Greater Hazleton C. of C. (bd. dirs. 1995—). Republican. Home: 21 Poolside Dr Hazleton PA 18201-9409

NERENBERG, ARLENE IRIS, lawyer, social worker; b. Phila., Nov. 4, 1951; d. Ralph and Ruth (Kellman) Steinman; m. Sheldon Glen Nerenberg, Dec. 24, 1985; 1 child, Bonnie Renee. AA, C.C. of Phila., 1988; BA, Temple U., 1992, JD, 1996. Bar: Pa., N.J. Supr. social workers Commonwealth of Pa., Phila., 1990—; assoc. Law Offices of Sheldon G. Nerenberg, Phila., 1993—; mem. Family and Landlord/Tenant Ct., 1994—. Editor newspaper Trumpet, 1994-96. Tchr., mem. adv. bd. Mayor's Commn. on Literacy, Phila., 1990—; chief shop stewar, Phila. chpt. bd. Pa. Social Svc. Union, 1993—; vol. re-election bd. Dem. Party, Phila., Harrisburg, Pa. and Washington, 1993—; mem. steering com. Frankford/Torresdale Hosp., Phila., 1995—; active Spl. Olympics, 1994—; mem. Holocaust Mus. of Washington, 1994—; diplomate World Jewish Congress, Washington, 1995—. Mem. ABA (contbr. to mag. Phila. Lawyer 1995, mem. family law, criminal law, and employment law sects.), ATLA (mem. constitutional law, family law, and criminal law sects.), U.S. Holocaust Mus. (assoc., charter), Pa. Bar Assn., Phila. Bar Assn., Phila. Paralegal Assn., Pa. Trial Lawyers Am., Women in the Arts, MADD, Phi Theta Kappa. Home: 10117 Wilbur St Philadelphia PA 19116 Office: Law Office of S G Nerenberg 9925 Bustleton Ave # 51174 Philadelphia PA 19115

NESBARY, CONNIE ROSE, clinical therapist, consultant; b. Fremont, Mich., Dec. 26, 1954; m. Dale Kevin Nesbary, Aug. 17, 1979; children: Nicole Cora, Matthew Dale. BA, Mich. State U., 1977; MA, Lesley Coll., 1992. Lic. profl. counselor, Mich.; limited lic. psychologist, Mich. Personnel mgmt. analyst Mich. Dept. of Mental Health, Lansing, 1979-82; self employed, 1983-92; MA psychol. Dorchester Counseling Ctr., Boston, 1992-93, Beaverbrook Guidance Ctr., Waltham, Mass., 1993-94, Devel. Ctrs., Inc., Detroit, 1994—; dir. Rose Counseling, Southfield, Mich., 1996—. Bd. dirs. Women's Ctr., Cambridge, Mass., 1992-93, Southfield Swim Club, Southfield, 1995-96. Mem. Northamerican Assn. of Masters in Psychol., Mich. Assoc. of Profl. Psychol. (bd. dirs., treas. 1995-96), Mass. Mental Health Counselors Assoc. (bd. dirs., treas. 1992-94), Internat. Women's Writers Guild. Office: Rose Counseling PC PO Box 2618 Southfield MI 48037

NESBIT, WENDY MICHELLE, secondary school educator; b. St. Louis, Mar. 10, 1972; d. Donny Lee and Karen Ann (O'Shea) N.; m. Bryan Mickley, June 24, 1995. BS, So. Ill. U., 1993. Cert. math. tchr. 7-12, Mo. 7th and 8th grades math. tchr. St. Gabriel the Archangel Sch., St. Louis, 1993-94; math. tchr. Festus (Mo.) H.S., 1994—; summer sch. tchr. Bishop DuBourg H.S., St. Louis, 1993-94; cheerleading coach Festus H.S., 1994—. Mem. NEA, Ill. Coun. Tchrs. Math. (speaker at conf. 1993), Mo. Coun. Tchrs. Math., Nat. Coun. Tchrs. Math., Math Assn. Am., Mo. Cheerleading Coaches Assn. Office: Festus HS 1515 Mid Meadow Ln Festus MO 63028

NESBITT, DEETTE DUPREE, small business owner, investor; b. Houston, May 5, 1941; d. Raymond Benjamin DuPree and Alice Lula (Cade) Foster; children: Alice L., Charles S. Massey Nesbitt; m. Ernest V. Nesbitt, Aug. 20, 1971. Student, Sam Houston State U., 1960-61, U. Houston, 1961-62, 81-83. Lic. real estate, Tex. Co-owner K & N Perforators, Inc., Houston; vol. adminstrv. asst. numerous orgns., Houston. Contbr. articles to various publs. Former bd. trustees Pace Soc. Am., Inc., Ladies Oriental Shrine N.Am., Inc.; bd. dirs. Evergreen Friends, Inc., 1991—; dir., sec. competitive swim team Dad's Club YMCA, Houston, 1981-83; vol. adminstrv. asst. numerous orgns., Houston. Recipient Varina Howell Davis medal Mil. Order Stars and Bars, 1992, Silver Good Citizenship medal SAR, 1992, Honor award Tex. Sons of Confederate Veterans, 1992; featured on Eyes of Texas, NBC, 1992. Mem. Nat. Soc. DAR, Huguenot Soc., S.C. Soc. Descendants of the Colonial Clergy, Nat. Soc. Magna Charta Dames, Plantagenet Soc., Col. Order of the Crown, The Sovereign Colonial Soc. Am. Royal Descent, Nat. Jamestown Soc. (mem. coun. 1993-95, auditor gen. 1995—), First Tex. Co. Jamestowne Soc. (lt. gov., gov. 1985-93, hon. gov. life), Soc. First Families of Ga. 1733-1797 (v.p. gen. Tex. State Soc. 1987—), Soc. First Families of S.C. 1670-1700 (life), Order of First Families of Va. 1607-1624/5 (life), Order of First Families of Miss. 1699-1817 (life), Daus. Rep. Tex. (Tex. Star chpt., Appreciation award 1996), Colonial Dames Am. (pres. chpt. VIII 1995—), United Daus. Confederacy (Jefferson Davis chpt., Confederate Ball com. 1985-95, co-chmn. ball 1988, advisor to chmn. 1989, 90, Jefferson Davis Hist. award, Winnie Davis medal, Spl. Recognition award, honorary chmn. Houston's Confederate Ball 1995), Sons and Daus. of Pilgrims (mem. nat. com. 1993-97), Freedoms Found. Valley Forge (George Washington Honor medal 1994), Harris County Hist. Commn., Petroleum Club Houston, Galveston Yacht Club. Republican. Episcopalian. Home: 15411 Old Stone Trl Houston TX 77079-4206

NESBITT, JUANITA, occupational health nurse, medical and surgical nurse; b. Conecuh County, Ala., Dec. 27, 1950; d. Moses Jr. and Willie Belle (Turner) Nolan; m. William E. Nesbitt, Aug. 24, 1974; children: Cedric, Titus, Matthew. AAS in Nursing, Parkland Coll., Champaign, Ill., 1972; BSN, St. Xavier Coll., Chgo., 1975. RN, Ill.; cert. coll. health nurse. Staff nurse U. Chgo. Hosps. and Clinics, 1975-76, Mercy Hosp. (now Covenant Med. Ctr.ú, Urbana, Ill., 1977-78; staff nurse preventive medicine clinic-ambulatory clinic McKinley Health Ctr., U. Ill., Urbana, 1978—; staff nurse Alpha Christian Nurse Registry, Champaign, 1984-86; patient adv. nurse Carle Clinic, Urbana, 1993—. Blood drive vol. ARC, 1975, instr. CPR, 1987; bd. dirs. Self Help, Inc., Champaign County, 1988. 1st lt. USAR, 1983-92. Mem. Sickle Cell Soc. Champaign County (organizer), Sigma Theta Tau. Home: 1803 Broadmoor Dr Champaign IL 61821-5853

NESBITT, LENORE CARRERO, federal judge; m. Joseph Nesbitt; 2 children: Sarah, Thomas. A.A., Stephens Coll., 1952; BS, Northwestern U., 1954; student U. Fla. Law Sch., 1954-55; LLB, U. Miami, 1957. Rsch. asst. Dist. Ct. Appeal, 1957-59, Dade County Cir. Ct., 1963-65; pvt. practice Nesbitt & Nesbitt, 1960-63; spl. asst. attorney gen., 1961-63; with Law Offices of John Robert Terry, 1969-73; counsel, Fla. State Bd. Med. Examiners, 1970-71; with Petersen, McGowan & Feder, 1973-75; judge Fla. Cir. Ct., 1975-82, U.S. Dist. Ct. (so. dist.) Fla., Miami, 1983—. Bd. trustees U. Miami; bd. dirs. Miami Children's Hosp. Mem. FBA, Fla. Bar Assn., U.S. Jud. Conf. Com. on Criminal Law and Probation Adminstrn. Office: US Dist Ct 301 N Miami Ave Miami FL 33128-7702•

NESBITT, VERONICA A., management executive; b. Henderson, Tenn., June 10, 1959; d. Hiawatha Daniel and Laura Mae (Green) Thompson; m. Darryl L. Nesbitt, Nov. 12, 1992; children: Shemenya A. Davis, Maleka L. Cert. stenographer, Miller-Hawkins B. Coll., 1979; Cert. data transcriber, IRS, Memphis, Tenn., 1981; Cert. computer operator, U.S. Army, Newport News, Va., 1985, Cert. computer programmer, 1987; postgrad., Columbia Coll., 1990. Stenographer Memphis & Shelby County Health Dept., Memphis, 1979-80; cash clk./data transcriber IRS, Memphis, 1980-82; data transcriber U.S. Army, Fort Sheridan, Ill., 1982-83; work order clk. U.S. Army, Fort Sheridan, 1984-85, quality control clk., 1985-89; mgmt. asst. HQ USAREC, Fort Sheridan, Ill., 1989-92; data transcriber Selective Svc., North Chicago, Ill., 1983-84; telemarketer Allstate Ins. Co., Northbrook, Ill., 1986-88; unit supr. Allstate Ins. Co., Glenview, Ill., 1988-92; employee coun., 1994; total quality facilitator Allstate Ins. Co., Glenview, Ill., 1992; mgmt. asst. Hdqs. US Army Recruiting Command, Ft. Knox, Ky., 1992-94, 233d Base Support Bn., Darmstadt, Germany, 1994—; chmn. task force Allstate, Glenview, 1990. Mem. Am. Heart Disease Found., 1991-92, Easter Seal Soc., 1991-92, March of Dimes, 1991—, Nat. Heart Rsch., 1991-95; mem. Nat. Cancer Rsch., 1991-95, fed. women's program mgr., 1995—; treas. Second Glance Thrift Store, 1996—; welfare com., continuing edn. grants Darmstadt Women's Club, 1995-96, chmn. Second Glance Thrift Store; counselor Equal Employment Opportunity, 1995—; mem. Equal Opportunity Adv. Action Team, 1995—. Mem. NAFE, Am. Cancer Soc., Am. Heart Disease Prevention Found., Jack Anderson Internat. Platform Assn. Baptist. Office: CMR 431 233d Base Support Battalion APO AE 09175 also: HHC 440th Signal BN CMR 431 Box 2557 APO AE 09175

NESBITT-GUERRERO, TAMARA JOY, adult education educator; b. Cobleskill, N.Y., Sept. 13, 1968; d. Thomas Francis and Sharon Ann (Jenkins) Nesbitt; m. Ramon Guerrero, Dec. 10, 1994. AAS, Genesee C.C., Batavia, Coll., 1988; BS summa cum laude, The Coll. of St. Rose, 1992, MS, 1994. Cert. spl. edn. and elem. tchr., N.Y. Residential counsel Schoharie (N.Y.) ARC, 1988-89, asst. mgr., 1989-90; residential counselor Rehab. Support Svcs., Albany, N.Y., 1990-93; tchr. adult edn. Albany Bd. Coop. Ednl. Svcs., N.Y., 1992—; advocate Schoharie County ARC, Schoharie, 1990—. N.Y. State Challenger scholar, 1991. Mem. Coun. Exceptional Children, Delta Kappa Pi. Lutheran. Home: 41 Hurlbut St Albany NY 12209-2110 Office: Albany Bd Coop Ednl Svcs 1015 Watervliet Shaker Rd Albany NY 12205

NESIN, BARBARA, artist, art educator; b. N.Y.C., Jan. 5, 1951; d. Lazare and Simone (Esteve) N. BFA, Pratt Inst., 1974; MBA, L.I. U., Bklyn., 1984; MFA, Ind. State U., 1996. Cert. tchr. visual art K-12, Maine; cert. tchr. visual art, mktg. and econs., Wash. Instr. art N.H. Coll., Brunswick, Maine, 1988-90; art specialist K-3 MSAD 75, Topsham, Maine, 1988-90; art specialist K-8 Augusta (Maine) Sch. System, 1990-91; youth program coord. Stanwood (Wash.)-Camano Family Ctr., 1992-93; instr. art Whidbey Island Naval Air Sta., Oak Harbor, 1993, Skagit Valley Coll., Oak Harbor, 1991-93; grad. teaching asst. Ind. State U., Terre Haute, 1993-96; visual arts faculty Front Range Cmty. Coll., Fort Collins, Colo., 1996—; pub. rels. coord. Tedford-Oasis Programs, Brunswick, Maine, 1988-90; panel presenter Founds. Art Theory and Edn. Conf., St. Louis, 1995; mem. gallery com. Ctr. for Arts at the Chocolate Ch., Bath, Maine, 1989-91; intern cross-cultural visual literacy program Bronx (N.Y.) Mus. of Arts, 1995; panel presenter Ctr. Caribbean Studies, Havana, 1995. Exhibited in shows at Ind. State U., 1994-96, Arts Illiana, 1995, Miss. State U., 1995, Ind. U. Gallery, Bloomington, 1994-95, Indpls. Mus. of Art Rental Gallery, 1995, Art Place, Chgo., 1996, St. John's U., Jamaica, N.Y., 1996, SFA Gallery, Nacogdoches, Tex., 1996, Jardin Culturel, Cambria Heights, N.Y., 1996, St.-Mary-of-the-Woods Coll. Art Gallery, 1996, Ashwell Gallery, Beverly, Mass., 1996, others; represented in permanent collection at U. Ill., Ind. State U. Recipient Cmty. Svc. (VISTA) award State of Maine, 1988, Peoples Choice award Nat. Womens Music Festival, 1994; grad. rsch. grantee, 1995-96. Mem. Coll. Art Assn. (cultural diversity com.), Haitian Studies Assn., Founds. in Art Theory and Edn. Office: Front Range Cmty Coll Dept Arts & Humanities 1400 Remington St Rm 229 Fort Collins CO 80525

NESMITH, AUDREY MARIE, military housing manager (retired), writer; b. Washington, Apr. 6, 1937; d. John Wallace and Elsie Mae (Welsh) Cullins; m. Adolfo Mier Delhierro, May 11, 1960; (dec. Mar., 1978), children: Alicia Marie Delhierro Carver, Julia Mae Delhierro Crawford; m. Benjamin Rea Nesmith, Jan. 9, 1985. Student, U. Md., 1982-86. Chief bachelor officers qtrs. U.S. Army White Sands Missile Range, WSMR, N. Mex., 1978-80; chief housing referral office U.S. Army, Ft. Sam Houston, Tex., 1980-82; chief housing divsn. U.S. Army-U.S. Army Mil. Command, Garmisch, Fed. Republic Germany, 1982-85; dep. dir. housing divsn. U.S. Navy Washington Naval Dist., 1985-89; Equal Employment Opportunity officer, Garmisch, Fed. Republic Germany, 1984-85; v.p. Profl. Housing Mgmt. Assn., Garmisch, 1983-84. Author: (book) Loved into Life, 1985. Treas. First Ch. Christian and Missionary Alliance, 1994-96. Republican. Home: 1533 Merion Way #26-E Seal Beach CA 90740

NESMITH, FRANCES JANE, education consultant; b. Tulsa, Nov. 6, 1926; d. George W. and Frances Pearl (Hendrix) N. BA, U. Houston, 1947; MA in Polit. Sci., Columbia U., 1951; postgrad., U. Tex., 1957, 58, 61-64; EdD, Columbia U., 1968. Cert. ednl. adminstr. Tchr. Houston Ind. Sch. Dist., 1947-58; lectr. U. Houston, 1956-58; tchr. Austin (Tex.) Ind. Sch. Dist., 1958-69; instr. Columbia U., N.Y.C., 1964-66, Austin Community Coll., 1973-74; coord. secondary social studies Austin Ind. Sch. Dist., 1969-86; adj. assoc. prof. Coll. Edn. U. Tex., Austin, 1986—; edn. cons. Austin, 1986—; cons. Addison-Wesley Pub. Co., Menlo Park, Calif., 1987—, State Bar Tex., Austin, 1989—, Learned & Tested, Inc., Orlando, Fla., 1986. Author: Texas Teacher Appraisal Systems-Economics, 1987, World History, 1988, Economics, U.S. History and Government—A Law-Related Education Resource Guide, 1992; co-auuthor: The Story of Texas, 1963; guest editor Southwestern Jour. Social Edn., 1981. Pub. mem. Citizens and Law Focused Edn. Com. State Bar Tex., Austin, 1983-86; mem. adv. coun. Lifetime Learning Inst., Austin, 1989—. Heft scholar Columbia U., N.Y.C., 1966; recipient Leon Jaworski award Tex. Young Lawyers, State Bar Tex., Austin, 1986, George Washington medal Freedoms Found., Valley Forge, Pa., 1986. Mem. Nat. Coun. Social Studies, Tex. Coun. Social Studies, Austin Coun. Social Studies (exec. sec. 1969-86), Tex. Tchrs. Assn. (life), Tex. Hist. Assn., Delta Kappa Gamma (internat. fellow 1965), Phi Delta Kappa. Democrat. Methodist. Home and Office: 2605 Salado St Austin TX 78705-3911

NESMITH, LYNN SHIELDS, language arts educator; b. Jacksonville, Fla., June 18, 1942; d. William Charlton and Erma Jean (Shields) N. BA, Jacksonville U., 1964; MEd, U. N. Fla., 1975. cert. tchr., Fla. Tchr. Duval County Sch. Sys., Jacksonville, 1965—; counselor Shenck Job Corps Ctr., Pisgah Forest, N.C., 1996—. Mem. Am. Mus. Women Arts, Am. Fedn. Tchrs., Fla. Edn. Assn., Duval Tchrs. United (bldg. rep., exec. coun. 1968-88). Democrat. Methodist. Office: Southside Middle Sch 2948 Knights Lane E Jacksonville FL 32216

NESTOR CASTELLANO, BRENDA DIANA, real estate executive; b. Palm Beach, Fla., Nov. 10, 1955; d. John Joseph and Marion O'Connor Nestor; m. Robert Castellano. Student, U. Miami, Fla., 1978. Lic. real estate broker, Fla. Salesman Oscar E Dooley, Inc., Miami, Fla., 1978-80; prin. Brenda Nestor Assocs, Inc., Miami Beach, Fla., 1980—; exec. v.p., bd. dirs. D.W.G. Corp., N.V.F. Corp., Salem Corp., Southeastern Pub. Svc., Graniteville Corp., Essex Ins., Chesapeake Ins.; exec. v.p., dir. Security Mgmt. Named Ms. Charity, City of Miami, 1985. Mem. Miami Beach Bd. Realtors (bd. dirs. 1984—), Real Estate Securities and Exch. Com., Le Club (N.Y.C.), La Gorce Country Club, Fisher Island Club. Roman Catholic. Home and Office: 6917 Collins Ave Miami FL 33141-3263

NETTER, MIRIAM MACCOBY, lawyer; b. Mt. Vernon, N.Y., Nov. 30, 1935; d. Max and Dora Maccoby; m. Howard R. Netter, June 24, 1956; children: Mark, Beth Ann. BA, Brown U., 1956; JD cum laude, Union U., Albany, N.Y., 1972. Bar: N.Y. 1973, U.S. Dist. Ct. (no. dist.) N.Y. 1973, U.S. Ct. Appeals (2d cir.) 1990, U.S. Supreme Ct. 1984. Unemployment ins. claims examiner Dept. Labor State of N.Y., Rochester, 1956-59; tchr. Rush-Henrietta Sch., Rochester, 1959-60; assoc. Harvey M. Lifset, Esquire, Albany, 1973; assoc. Pattison, Herzog, Sampson & Nichols, 1974-79; ptnr. Pattison, Sampson, Ginsberg & Griffin, P.C., Troy, N.Y., 1974-92; pvt. practice, 1992—; mem. Com. on Character and Fitness 3d Jud. Dept. N.Y. State Supreme Ct., Albany, 1981—. Lead articles editor Albany Law Rev., 1971-72. Mem. exec. com. Legal Aid Soc. Northeastern N.Y., Albany, 1977-86, 1st v.p., 1982-84, pres. 1984-86; legal advisor, dir. Kidney Found. N.E. N.Y., Albany, 1983—. Mem. ABA, N.Y. State Bar Assn. (chair membership com. 1986-89, Ho.of Dels. 1988-92, 93—, nominating com. 1992—, com. judicial selection 1988—, women in law 1992—), Women's Bar Assn. N.Y. (capital dist. charter), Albany County Bar Assn., Rensselaer County Bar Assn. (v.p. 1990—, pres. 1993—), Phi Kappa Phi. Home: 28 Devon Rd Delmar NY 12054-3534 Office: care MapInfo 1 Global Vw Troy NY 12180-8371

NETTER, VIRGINIA THOMPSON, produce company owner; b. Hardyville, Ky., Nov. 2, 1931; d. Duluth Sydnor and Vera (Asbury) Thompson; m. S. Mitchell Netter, Oct. 4, 1947; children: Ronald Lee, Candace Netter Harrison. BA, U. Louisville, 1982; MA in Counseling/Clin. Psychology, Spalding U., 1989. Owner, Netter Produce Co., Louisville, 1954—, Big Four Farms, Belmont, Ky., 1959—. Named to Hon. Order Ky. Cols., 1982. Mem. AAUW, Woodcock Soc., Psi Chi, Phi Kappa Phi. Avocations: ballroom dancing, riding, golf, travel. Home: 1029 Alta Vista Rd Louisville KY 40205-1727 Office: Netter Produce Co 331-335 Produce Plz Louisville KY 40202

NETTLES, BEATRICE, artist, photography educator; b. Gainesville, Fla., Oct. 17, 1946; d. Victor Fleetwood and Grace Beatrice (Noble) N.; m. Lionel Suntop; children: Rachel Starr, Gavin Lazar. BFA, U. Fla., 1968; MFA, U. Ill., 1970. Instr. Nazareth Coll., Rochester, N.Y., 1970-71; asst. prof. Rochester (N.Y.) Inst. Tech., 1971-72, assoc. prof., 1976-84; asst. prof. Tyler Sch. Art, Temple U., Phila., 1972-74; prof., chair photography U. Ill., Champaign/Urbana, 1984—. Author, photographer: Life's Lessons: A Mother's Journal, 1990, Complexities: Photographs and Text by Bea Nettles, 1991, Turning 50, 1995, Breaking the Rules: A Photo Media Cookbook, 3d edit., 1995. Fellow Nat. Endowment for the Arts, 1979, 86; univ. scholar U. Ill., Champaign/Urbana. Home: Box 725 Urbana IL 61803 Office: Univ Ill Art and Design 408 E Peabody Dr Champaign IL 61820

NETTLES, TONI OLESCO, non-commissioned officer; b. Ensley, Ala., Sept. 14, 1961; d. Willie Edward and Rosie Lee (Cooke) Pace; m. Jonathan Paul Nettles, Dec. 25, 1980 (div. Dec. 1991); 1 child, Ashley. AS in Applied Sci., Cmty. Coll. of the Air Force, 1988; AA, U. Md., 1990, BS, 1996. Computer operator 2162CS USAF, Buckley, Colo., 1979-84; COMSEC acct. USAF, Lowry AFB, Colo., 1984-85; facility chief 3d Combat Comm. Group USAF, Tinker AFB, Okla., 1985-88; non-commd. officer in charge 603rd Aerial Port Squadron USAF, Kadena, Japan, 1988-92; non-commd. officer in charge 305th CS USAF, Grissom AFB, Ind., 1992-94; supt. ops. 55th Computer Sys. Squadron USAF, Offutt AFB, Nebr., 1994—, master sgt. 55th computer sys. squadron, 1995-96; base Comsec mgr. 55 Comm. Squadron, 1996—; instr. total quality mgmt., 1992-94. Leader troop Girl Scouts Am., West Pacific, 1990; mem. PTA, Omaha, 1994—; vol. Nebr. Spl. Olympics, Omaha, 1995, United Way/CHAD, Omaha, 1994-95. Recipient Letter of appreciation MADD Nat. Pres., 1995, 96, Letter of Appreciation regional commr. Girl Scouts U.S., West Pacific, 1990. Mem. Vis. Nurse Assn. (vol. 1994-95), Black Heritage Com. (citation, letter of appreciation, 1989). Home: 2802 Lynnwood Dr Omaha NE 68123 Office: Base COMSEC Mgr 55 Communications Sq #206 201 Lincoln Hwy Omaha NE 68113-2040

NETTROUR, LILA GROFF, biology educator; b. San Francisco; d. Arthur and Mary Ellen (Anderson) Groff; m. Lewis F. Nettrour, Oct. 22, 1966; children: John, Barbara. BA, St. Olaf Coll., 1964; MEd, U. Pitts., 1966. Microbiologist Mayo Clinic, Rochester, Minn., 1964-65; sci. tchr. Dover Eyota (Minn.) High Sch., 1966-67; part-time instr. Community Coll. Allegheny County, Pitts., 1980-90, assoc. prof. biol. scis., 1991—. Dir. YMCA North Hills, Pitts., 1974-80, chmn. 1980; bd. dirs. St. John's Luth. Ch. Living Gifts and Meml. Fund, Pitts. Mem. AAUW, North Hills Environ. Coun. Office: Community Coll Allegheny Co 8701 Perry Hwy Pittsburgh PA 15237-5353

NETZ, DEBORAH RUDDER, psychologist; b. Freeport, Tex., July 4, 1953; d. Leroy Brooks and Lois Carol (Mann) Rudder; m. Charles E. Netz, Dec. 30, 1977 (div. 1990); children: Elizabeth Anne, Andrew Charles. BFA, U. North Tex., 1975; MS, Angelo State U., 1992. Employment spl. Concho Resource Ctr., San Angelo, Tex., 1991-93; assoc. psychologist Denton (Tex.) State Sch., 1993-96; Children's counselor Ann's Haven Hospice Bereavement Group, Denton, 1993-96; counselor Hospice of San Angelo (Tex.) Children's Bereavement Group, 1991-93. Mem. Pi Gamma Mu. Democratic. Methodist. Office: Denton State Sch State Sch Rd Denton TX 76201

NETZER, LANORE A(GNES), retired educational administration educator; b. Laona, Wis., Aug. 27, 1916; d. Henry N. and Julia M. (Niquette) Netzer; m. Glen G. Eye, 1979. Diploma, Oconto County Normal Sch., 1935; BS, State Tchrs. Coll., Oshkosh, Wis., 1943; MS, U. Wis., 1948, PhD, 1951. Tchr. Goldhorn Rural Sch., Pound, Wis., 1935-36; tchr. Goldfield Sch., Pound, 1936-37, tchr., acting prin., 1937-39; tchr., prin. Spruce (Wis.) Grade Sch., 1939-41; tchr. pub. schs. Neenah, Wis., 1943-46; demonstration and critic tchr. Campus Sch. State Tchrs. Coll., Oshkosh, 1946-48; supr. student tchrs.' coll. instrn. State Tchrs. Coll., Milw., 1950-55; teaching asst. U. Wis., Madison, 1948-50; assoc. prof. edn. U. Wis., Milw., 1955-63; prof. ednl. adminstrn. U. Wis., Madison, 1963-77, emeritus prof., 1977—; rsch. assoc. U.S. Office Edn., 1963-66; supr. student tchrs. coll. instrn. State Tchrs. Coll., Milw., 1950-55; mem. curriculum adminstrn. com. Wis. Coop. Curriculum Planning Program, 1945-52; mem. Wis. Joint Com. on Edn., 1957-59, E.B. Fred Fellowship Com., U. Wis., 1966—; ednl. cons. Educators Progress Svc., 1970—. Author: The Use of Industry Aids in Schools, 1952, (with Glen G. Eye) Supervision of Instruction: A Phase of Administration, 1965, 2d. edit., 1971, (with others) Interdisciplinary Foundations of Supervision, 1969, (with G. Eye) School Administrators and Instruction, 1969, (with others) Education Administration and Change, 1970, (with others) Supervision of Instruction, 1971, Strategies for Instructional Management, 1977; contbr. articles to profl. jours. Rsch. grantee Hill & Knowlton, Inc., N.Y.C., 1949; grantee Wis. Mfrs. Assn., 1954; recipient award of Distinction Nat. Coun. of Adminstrv. Women in Edn., 1975. Mem. AAUP, Wis. Edn. Assn. (life), So. Wis. Edn. Assn., Nat. Assn. Supervision and Curriculum Devel., Wis. Assn. Supervision and Curriculum Devel., Southwestern Assn. Supervision and Curriculum Devel., Wis. Elem. Sch. Prins. Assn., Am. Assn. Sch. Adminstrs., Wis. Assn. Sch. Dist. Adminstrs., Am. Edn. Rsch. Assn., Wis. Edn. Rsch. Assn., Univ. Coun. Ednl. Adminstrn., U. Wis. Alumni Assn. (life), U. Wis. Meml. Union (life), Phi Beta Sigma, Kappa Delta Pi, Pi Lambda Theta, Phi Delta Kappa. Home: 110 S Henry St Apt 1506 Madison WI 53703-3168 Office: U Wis Dept Ednl Adminstrn 1025 W Johnson St Madison WI 53706-1706

NEUFELD, ELIZABETH FONDAL, biochemist, educator; b. Paris, Sept. 27, 1928; U.S. citizen; m. 1951. PhD., U. Calif., Berkeley, 1956; D.H.C. (hon.), U. Rene Descartes, Paris, 1978; D.Sc. (hon.), Russell Sage Coll., Troy, N.Y., 1981, Hahnemann U. Sch. Medicine, 1984. Asst. research biochemist U. Calif., Berkeley, 1957-63; with Nat. Inst. Arthritis, Metabolism and Digestive Diseases, Bethesda, Md., 1963-84, research biochemist, 1963-73, chief sect. human biochem. genetics, 1973-79, chief genetics and biochem. br., 1979-84; prof., chmn. dept. biol. chemistry UCLA Sch. Medicine, 1984—. Passano Found. sr. laureate, 1982; named Calif. Scientist of Yr., 1990; recipient Dickson prize U. Pitts., 1974, Hillenbrand award, 1975, Gairdner Found. award, 1981, Albert Lasker Clin. Med. Rsch. award, 1982, William Allan award, 1982, Elliott Cresson medal, 1984, Wolf Found. prize, 1988, Christopher Columbus Discovery award for biomed. rsch., 1992, Nat. Medal of Sci., 1994. Fellow AAAS; mem. NAS, Inst. Medicine of NAS, Am. Acad. Arts and Scis., Am. Soc. Human Genetics, Am. Chem. Soc., Am. Soc. Biochemistry and Molecular Biology (pres. 1992-93), Am. Soc. Cell Biology, Am. Soc. Clin. Investigation. Office: UCLA Sch Medicine Dept Biol Chemistry Los Angeles CA 90024-1737

NEUGARTEN, BERNICE LEVIN, social scientist; b. Norfolk, Nebr., Feb. 11, 1916; d. David L. and Sadie (Segall) Levin; m. Fritz Neugarten, July 1, 1940; children: Dail Ann, Jerrold. B.A., U. Chgo., 1936, Ph.D., 1943; D.Sc. (hon.), U. So. Calif., 1980; PhD (hon.), Cath. U., Nijmegen, 1988. Rsch. assoc. Com. on Human Devel., U. Chgo., 1948-50; asst. prof. U. Chgo., 1951-60, assoc. prof., 1960-64, prof., 1964-80, chmn., 1969-73, prof. social svc. adminstrn., 1978-80, mem. com. on policy studies, 1979-80, Rothschild disting. scholar, prof. emeritus, 1988—; prof. emerita Northwestern U., 1980-88; mem. council U. Chgo. Senate, 1968-71, 72-75, 78-80, chmn. council com. on univ. women, 1969-70; nat. adv. council Nat. Inst. on Aging, 1975-76, 78-81, Fed. Council on Aging, 1978-81; dep. chmn. White House Conf. on Aging, 1980-81. Author: (with R.J. Havighurst) American Indian and White Children: A Social-Psychological Investigation, 1955, reprint, 1969, (with R.J. Havighurst) Society and Education, 1957, rev., 1962, 67, 75, (with Assocs.) Personality in Middle and Late Life, 1964, reprint, 1980, (with J.M.A. Munnichs et al) Adjustment to Retirement, 1969, (with R.P. Coleman) Social Status in the City, 1971, Middle Age and Aging, 1968; co-editor: (with H. Eglit) Age Discrimination, 1981, Age or Need? Public Policies for Older People, 1982; assoc. editor Jour. Gerontology, 1958-61, Human Devel., 1962-68; adv. or cons. editor other profl. jours., 1959—; author monographs, research papers and reports. mem. various adv. bodies. Recipient Am. Psychol. Found. Disting. Tchg. award, 1975, Disting. Psychologist award Ill. Psychol. Assn., 1979, Sandoz Internat. Prize for Gerontol. Rsch., 1987, Ollie Randall award Nat. Coun. on Aging, 1993, Gold Medal award for lifetime contbn. as a psychologist in the public interest Am. Psychol. Found., 1994. Fellow AAAS, Am. Psychol. Assn. (coun. rep. 1967-69, 73-76, Disting. Sci. Contbn. award 1980, honoree Women's Heritage Exhibit 1992, Gold Medal award 1994), Am. Sociol. Assn., Gerontol. Soc. Am. (pres. 1968-69, Kleemeier award 1971, Brookdale award 1982, Disting. Mentor award 1988), Am. Acad. Arts and Scis., Internat. Assn. Gerontology (governing coun. 1975-78, chmn. N.Am. exec. com. 1983-85, disting. creative contrbn. to gerontology award); mem. Inst. Medicine of NAS. Home: # 1202 1551 Larimer St Denver CO 80202

NEUGEBAUER, MARCIA, physicist, administrator; b. N.Y.C., Sept. 27, 1932; d. Howard Graeme MacDonald and Frances (Townsend) Marshall; m. Gerry Neugebauer, Aug. 25, 1956; children: Carol, Lee. B.S., Cornell U., 1954; M.S., U. Ill., 1956. Grad. asst. U. Ill., Urbana, 1954-56; vis. fellow Clare Hall Coll., Cambridge, Eng., 1975; sr. research scientist Jet Propulsion Lab. Calif. Inst. Tech., Pasadena, 1956—; vis. prof. planetary sci. Calif. Inst. Tech., Pasadena, 1986-87; mem. com. NASA, Washington, 1960—, NAS, Washington, 1981—; Regents lectr. UCLA, 1990-91. Contbr. numerous articles on physics to profl. jours. Named Calif. Woman Scientist of Yr. Calif. Mus. Sci. and Industry, 1967; recipient Exceptional Sci. Achievement medal NASA, 1970, Outstanding Leadership medal NASA, 1993. Fellow Am. Geophys. Union (sec., pres. solar planetary relationships sect. 1979-84, editor-in-chief Rev. Geophysics 1988-92, pres.-elect 1992-94, pres. 1994-96)mem. governing bd. Amer. Inst. Physics, 1995—. Democrat. Home: 1720 Braeburn Rd Altadena CA 91001-2708 Office: Calif Inst Tech Jet Propulsion Lab/MS 169-506 4800 Oak Grove Dr Pasadena CA 91109-8001

NEULS-BATES, CAROL, business executive, musicologist; b. Bklyn., Dec. 1, 1939; d. Frederick Carl and Edith Tindall Neuls; B.A. cum laude, Wellesley Coll., 1961; Ph.D., Yale U., 1970; postgrad. N.Y.U. Sch. Bus. Adminstrn., 1979; m. William Boulton Bates, Jr., Sept. 1, 1962; 1 dau., Julia Barstow. Mng. editor RILM: Abstracts of Music Lit., Grad. Center City U. N.Y., 1972-75, project dir., co-prin. investigator Women in Am. Music, 1976-79; adj. asst. prof. music Hunter Coll., City U. N.Y., 1973-75; asst. to curator Lincoln Center Library Performing Arts, 1975-76; asst. editor Coll. Music Symposium, 1975-78; asst. prof. music Bklyn. Coll. City U. N.Y., 1978-82; account supr. John O'Donnell Co., N.Y.C., 1982-85, v.p., 1986—. Yale U. fellow, 1962-67; Radcliffe Inst. grantee, 1968-70; research grantee Nat. Endowment Humanities, 1976-79, Ford Found., 1977-79, Nat. Fedn. Music Clubs, 1978. Mem. Coll. Music Soc. (council 1975-78), Am. Musicol. Soc., Sonneck Soc., Inst. Research in History, Nat. Women's Studies Assn., Nat. Soc. Fund Raising Execs., Women in Fin. Devel., NOW. Author: Women in Music: An Anthology of Source Readings from the Middle Ages to the Present, 1982, rev. edit., 1995; Women in American Music: A Bibliography of Music and Literature, 1979; contbr. articles to music and women's studies jours., 46 articles to New Grove's Dictionary of Music and Musicians series.

NEUMAN, JOHANNA C., journalist, author; b. L.A., May 7, 1949; d. Seymour I. and Evelyn Abigail (Zamichow) N.; m. Ronald H. Nessen, Feb. 14, 1988. BA, U. Calif., 1970, MA in journalism, 1973. City hall corr. L.A. Daily Jour., 1973-75, capitol corr., 1975-76; capitol bur. chief Clarion-Ledger, Jackson, Miss., 1976-79, Washington corr., 1979-81; congl. corr. Gannett Nes Srvs., Arlington, Va., 1982-84; white house corr. USA Today, Arlington, Va., 1984-90, sr. diplomatic corr., 1990-93, fgn. editor, 1994—; rsch. fellow Atlantic Coun., Washington, 1989-91, adj. lectr. George Washington U., Washington, 1995—. Author: Lights, Camera, War: Is Media Technology Driving International Politics, 1996; co-author: Knight and Day, 1995, Press Corpse, 1996; contbr. articles to profl. jours. Recipient Nieman fellow. Haryard U., 1981-82, Freedom Forum fellow. Columbia U., 1993-94. Mem. White House Corr. Assn. (pre. 1989-90). Office: USA Today 1000 Wilson Blvd Arlington VA 22229

NEUMAN, LINDA KINNEY, state supreme court justice; b. Chgo., June 18, 1948; d. Harold S. and Mary E. Kinney; m. Henry G. Neuman; children: Emily, Lindsey. BA, U. Colo., 1970, JD, 1973. Lawyer Betty, Neuman, McMahon, Hellstrom & Bittner, 1973-79; v.p., trust officer Bettendorf Bank & Trust Co., 1979-80; dist. ct. judge, 1982-86; supreme ct. justice State of Iowa, 1986—; mem. adj. faculty U. Iowa Grad. Sch. of Social Work, 1981; part-time jud. magistrate Scott County, 1980-82; mem. Supreme Ct. continuing legal edn. commn.; chair Iowa Supreme Ct. commn. planning 21st Century; mem. bd. counselors Drake Law Sch., time on appeal adv. com. Nat. Ctr. State Cts. Dir. Nat. Assn. Women Judges. Recipient Regents scholarship. Fellow ABA (chair appellate judges conf., mem. appellate standards com., JAD exec. coun.); mem. Am. Judicature Soc., Iowa Bar Assn., Iowa Judges Assn., Scott County Bar Assn. Office: Iowa Supreme Ct State Capitol Des Moines IA 50319

NEUMAN, NANCY ADAMS MOSSHAMMER, civic leader; b. Greenwich, Conn., July 24, 1936; d. Alden Smith and Margaret (Mevis) Mosshammer; BA, Pomona Coll., 1957, LLD, 1983; MA, U. Calif. at Berkeley, 1961; LHD, Westminster Coll., 1987; m. Mark Donald Neuman, Dec. 23, 1958; children: Deborah Neuman Metzler, Jennifer Fuller, Jeffrey Abbott. William A. Johnson Disting. lectr. Am. govt. Pomona Coll., 1990; disting. vis. prof. Washington and Jefferson Coll., 1991, 94, Bucknell U., 1992. Pres., Lewisburg (Pa.) area League Women Voters, 1967-70; bd. dirs. LWV Pa., 1970-77, pres., 1975-77; bd. dirs. LWV U.S., 1977-90, 2d v.p., 1978-80, 1st v.p., 1982-84, pres., 1986-90; bd. dirs. Pathmakers, Inc., 1993—, pres. 1993-95; mem. Pa. Gov.'s Commn. on Mortgage and Interest Rates, 1973, Pa. Commonwealth Child Devel. Com., 1974-75, Nat. Commn. on Pub. Svc., 1987-90; bd. dirs. Housing Assistance Council, Inc., Washington, 1974—, pres., 1978-80; bd. dirs. Nat. Council on Agrl. Life and Labor, 1974-79, Nat. Rural Housing Coalition, 1975-95, Pa. Housing Fin. Agy., 1975-80, Jud. Inquiry and Rev. Bd. Pa., 1989-93, Disciplinary Bd. Supreme Ct. Pa., 1980-85; mem. Pa. Gov.'s Task Force on Voter Registration, 1975-76, Nat. Task Force for Implementation Equal Rights Amendment, 1975-77; mem. adv. com. Pa. Gov.'s Interdepartmental Council on Seasonal Farmworkers, 1975-77; mem. Appellate Ct. Nominating Commn. Pa., 1976-79; mem. Fed. Jud. Nominating Commn. Pa., 1977-85, chmn., 1978-81, 82-83; mem. Pa. Gov.'s Study Commn. on Pub. Employee Relations, 1976-78; del. Internat. Women's Yr. Conf., 1977; bd. dirs. ERAmerica, Inc., 1st v.p., 1977-79, Nat. Low Income Housing Coalition, 1979-82; Rural Am., 1979-81, Fed. Home Loan Bank Pitts., 1979-82; mem. Nat. Adv. Com. for Women, 1978-79; mem. nat. adv. com. Pa. Neighborhood Preservation Support System, 1976-77; bd. dirs. Pa. Women's Campaign Fund, 1984-86, 92—, pres., 1992-96, Rural Coalition, Washington, 1984-90, Com. on the Constitutional System, 1988-90, Am. Judicature Soc., 1989-93; exec. com. Leadership Conf. Civil Rights, 1986-90; bd. dirs. Pennsylvanians for Modern Cts., 1986— trustee Citizen's Rsch. Found., 1989 ; mem. mid. dist. Pa. adv. com. judicial and U.S. atty nominations, 1993-94. Editor: A Voice of Our Own: Leading American Women Celebrate the Right to Vote, 1996. Virginia Travis lectureship Bucknell U., 1982. Recipient Disting. Alumna award MacDuffie Sch. for Girls, 1979, Liberty Bell award Pa. Bar Assn., 1983, Barrows Alumni award Pomona Coll., 1987, Thomas P. O'Neill Jr. award for exemplary pub. svc., 1989; named Disting. Daughter of Pa., 1987 Woodrow Wilson vis. fellow, 1993—. Mem. ABA (com. election law and voter participation, 1986-90, accreditation com. 1990-96). Home: 132 Verna Rd Lewisburg PA 17837-8747

NEUMAN, SUSAN CATHERINE, public relations and marketing consultant; b. Detroit, Jan. 29, 1942; d. Paul Edmund and Elsie (Goetz) N.; AB, U. Miami (Fla.), 1964; MBA, Barry U., Miami Shores, Fla., 1985. APR (PRSA), 1973. Journalist, writer The Miami Herald (Fla.), 1962-65; editor Miamian Mag., 1965-69; pres. Susan Neuman Inc., Miami, 1969—. Mem. Fla. Gov.'s Pub. Relations Adv. Council, 1978-86. Mem. Pub. Relations Soc. Am. (accredited, past officer, bd. dirs. Miami chpt.), Ins. Exchange of Ams. (founding mem.), Econ. Soc. South Fla. (past officer, bd. dirs.), Miami C. of C., Counselor's Acad. Democrat. Roman Catholic. Clubs: Miami City (founder), Miami Internat. Press (charter, founder, pres. 1985-86) (Miami), Com. of One Hundred. Home: 13540 NE Miami Ct Miami FL 33161-2739 Office: Susan Neuman Inc Pla Venetia 25th Fl 555 NE 15th St Apt 25K Miami FL 33132-1405

NEUMAYR, SHARON, land developer, author; b. Parkston, S.D., July 27, 1942; d. Herbert and Edna K. (Schumacher) N. BS in Edn., No. State U., Aberdeen, S.D., 1964; MA, Western State Coll., Gunnison, Colo., 1970. Cert. profl. tchr. Colo. Tchr. English Marshall (Minn.) High Sch., 1964-67, Risley Jr. High, Pueblo, Colo., 1967-73, Ctrl. High Sch., Pueblo, 1973-95; tchr. composition/lit. Pueblo C.C., 1991-95; tchr. composition U. So. Colo., Pueblo, 1994; land developer Pueblo County, 1996—. Author: (workbooks) American Literature Activities, 1992, World Literature Activities, 1994. Bd. dirs. Pueblo Ballet, 1987-89, Pueblo Symphony, 1989-93, Animal Welfare, Pueblo, 1993-95. Mem. NEA, Nat. Coun. Tchrs. of English. Democrat. Home: PO Box 1653 Pueblo CO 81002

NEUNZIG, CAROLYN MILLER, elementary, middle and high school educator; b. L.I., May 5, 1930; kd. Stanley and Grace (Walsh) Miller; m. Herbert Neunzig, May 28, 1955; children: Kurt Miller, Keith Weidler. BA, Beaver Coll., Glen Side, Pa., 1953; MSSc, Syracuse U., 1989; postgrad., Adelphi U.; Cert., N.C. State U., Raleigh. Cert. in elem. edn., reading, history and English, N.C. Reading tchr. grades K-6 St. Timothy's Sch., Raleigh, N.C., 1971-83, 5th grade tchr., 1983-88, 5th grade lead tchr., 1986-88; tchr. English and geography 7th grade St. Timothy's Mid. Sch., Raleigh, 1991—; tchr Am. govt. 12th grade St. Timothy's Mid. Sch./Hale High Sch., Raleigh, 1991-93; instr. continuing edn. program history Meredith Coll., Raleigh, 1990-91, spl. high sch. registration commr., 1991-93, instr. continuing edn. program in history, 1995-96. Mem. Am. Acad. Polit. and Social Sci., Acad. Polit. Sci., Nat. Coun. for Social Studies, Nat. Coun. Tchrs. English.

NEUSTADT, BARBARA MAE, artist, illustrator, etcher; b. Davenport, Iowa, June 21, 1922; d. David and Cora (Wollensky) N.; children: Diane Elizabeth Walbridge Wheeler, Laurie Barbara Meyer Hall. B.A., Smith Coll., 1944; postgrad., U. Chgo., 1945-46; Art Student's League scholar, Ohio U. Sch. Fine Arts, 1952. Art dir., designer Shepherd Cards, Inc., N.Y.C., 1956-63; dir., instr. Studio Graphics Workshop, Woodstock, N.Y., 1970—; lectr. on printmaking; participant artist in schs. program N.Y. State Schs., 1972-74; Bd. dirs., editor bull. LWV of Woodstock, 1969-70. Illustrator: The First Christmas, 1960, A Dream of Love (by Joseph Langland), 1986 (exhibited in Sarasota, Fla., 1986, Ga. So. Coll., Statesboro, 1987), Nat. Mus. Women in the Arts, Washington, 1993-94; commd. etching edits to Collectors Am. Art, N.Y.C., 1956, 58, 61, Internat. Graphic Arts Soc., N.Y.C., 1960, N.Y. Hilton Art Collection, N.Y.C., 1961; one-man shows include Ruth White Gallery, N.Y.C., 1958, Phila. Art Alliance, 1959, Portland (Maine) Mus. Art, 1965, L.I. U., Bklyn., 1973, Smith Coll., Northampton, Mass., 1974, Manatee Art League, Bradenton, Fla., 1980, 91, Sarasota, Fla., 1985, 86, Unity Gallery, Sarasota, 1994; group shows include Mus. Modern Art, N.Y.C., 1958-59, Yale U. Art Gallery, New Haven, 1960, Soc. Am. Graphic Artists nat. and internat. exhbns., 1954, 55, 57, 59, 60, 61, 73, 75, 76, 78, L'Antipoete Galerie Librairie, Paris, 1961, Quito, Ecuador, S.Am., 1987, Fla. Printmakers, 1987, 88, So. Printmakers, U. of S. Ala., 1988, Springfest '89, Bradenton, Fla., 1989, Invitational Manatee Art League, Bradenton, 1992, 93, 94, Soc. Exptl. Artists, Longboat Key, juried 1992, juried Shreveport, La., 1993, Nat. Mus. Women Arts, Washington, 1993-94, Longboat Key Art Ctr., 1994; represented in permanent collections including Met. Mus. Art, N.Y.C., Library of Congress, Nat. Gallery Art, Washington, Phila. Mus. Art, USIA, Bonn, Germany, N.Y. Public Library N.Y.C., Rare Book Rm., William A. Neilson Libr., Smith Coll., Henderson Libr., Ga. So. Coll. Found., Statesboro, Ga., McFarlin Libr., Spl. Collections, U. of Tulsa, 1990, Ward Meml. Collection, Gilkey Ctr. for Graphic Arts, Portland (Oreg.) Art Mus., 1992, Nat. Mus. Women Arts. Recipient prize Boston Printmakers, 1957, Joseph Pennell Meml. medal Phila. Watercolor Club, 1972; Yasuo Kuniyoshi Meml. award, 1978; Am. the Beautiful Fund of N.Y. of Natural Area Council grantee, 1973. Mem. Soc. Am. Graphic Artists (prize 1954, 78), Phila. Water Color Club (prize 1972), Fla. Printmakers, The So. Graphics Coun., Art Uptown Inc. Gallery (Sarasota, Fla.), Gallery Two (Rockville, Md.). Studio: Pleiades Press/ Studio Graphics 3014 Ave C Holmes Beach FL 34217

NEUWIRTH, BEBE, dancer, actress; b. Newark, Dec. 31; d. Lee Paul and Sydney Anne Neuwirth. Student, Juilliard Sch., 1976-77. Appeared on Broadway and internationally as Sheila in A Chorus Line, 1978-81; other stage appearances include West Side Story, 1981, (on Broadway) Little Me, 1982, Upstairs at O'Neal's, 1982-83, The Road to Hollywood, 1984, Just So, 1985, (on Broadway) Sweet Charity, 1985-87 (Tony award for Best Supporting Actress in a Musical 1985-86), Waiting in the Wings: The Night the Understudies Take the Stage, 1986, Showing Off, 1989, Chicago, 1992 (L.A. Drama Critics Circle award), Kiss of the Spider Woman (London), 1993, (on Broadway) Damn Yankees, 1994, Pal Joey, 1995; prin. dancer on Broadway Dancin', 1982; leading dance role Kicks, 1984; TV series Cheers, 1984-93 (Emmy award for Best Supporting Actress in a Comedy Series 1990, 91); TV guest appearances Frasier, 1994, Aladdin, 1994; TV movies Without Her Consent, 1990, Unspeakable Acts, 1990, Wild Palms, 1993; films Say Anything, 1989, Green Card, 1990, Bugsy, 1991, Painted Heart, 1992, Malice, 1993, Jumanji, 1994, Pinocchio, 1995. Vol. performances for March of Dimes Telethon, 1986, Cystic Fibrosis Benefit Children's Ball, 1986, Ensemble Studio Theater Benefit, 1986, Circle Repertory Co. Benefit, 1986, all in N.Y.C. Democrat. Office: Internat Creative Mgmt 8942 Wilshire Blvd Beverly Hills CA 90211-1934 Office: Internat Creative Mgmt 40 W 57th St New York NY 10019-4001

NEVANS-PALMER, LAUREL SUZANNE, rehabilitation counselor; b. N.Y.C., Aug. 1, 1964; d. Roy N. and Virginia (Place) Nevans; m. Russell Baird Palmer III, Oct. 12, 1991. BA in English, Secondary Edn. cum laude, U. Richmond, 1986, postgrad., 1989-92; MA in Edn. and Human Devel., George Washington U., 1991, cert. in job devel. and placement, 1992. Group leader S.E. Consortium for Spl. Svcs., Larchmont, N.Y., 1980-85; vocat. instr. Assn. for Retarded Citizens Montgomery County, Rockville, Md., 1986-89; edn. specialist George Washington U. Out of Sch. Work Experience Program, Washington, 1989-90; rsch. asst. George Washington U. Dept. Tchr. Prep. & Spl. Edn., Washington, 1989-91; employability skills tchr., rsch. intern Nat. Rehab. Hosp. Rehab. Engring. Dept., Washington, 1991; vocat./ind. living skills specialist The Independence Ctr., Rockville, Md., 1991-93; leadership team mgr. Career Choice project The Endependence Ctr. of No. Va., Arlington, 1993-94; program dir. United Cerebral Palsy of D.C. and No. Va., Washington, 1994—; teaching asst. Rehab. Counseling Program, George Washington U., 1991. Recipient traineeship GWU Counseling Dept., 1990, 91. Mem. Nat. Rehab. Assn., Nat. Rehab. Counselors Assn., D.C. Met. Area Assn. Person's in Supported Employment (editor newsletter 1995—), Nat. Career Devel. Assn., Nat. Employment Counseling Assn., Nat. Assn. Ind. Living, Am. Assn. Counseling and Devel., Am. Rehab. Counseling Assn. Democrat. Home: 611 Woodside Pky Silver Spring MD 20910 Office: United Cerebral Palsy 3135 8th St NE Washington DC 20017

NEVES, JOYCE, elementary school educator; b. Central Falls, R.I., Sept. 17, 1948; d. Joaquim Almeida and Maria Rosa (Pires) N. BA, R.I. Coll., 1969, MEd, 1972. Tchr. grade 4 Town of Cumberland (R.I.) Sch. Dept., 1969-72, Chpt. I reading tchr., 1972-79, reading specialist, 1979—. Mem. Internat. Reading Assn. (R.I. coun., No. R.I. coun. treas., membership chair), New Eng. Reading Assn., Alpha Delta Kappa (chpt. treas., state treas.). Home: 135 Clark St Cumberland RI 02864

NEVES-ELBAUM, STELLA BOUDRIAS, temporary services executive; b. Boston, Mar. 3, 1949; d. Albert Joseph and Stella Ann (Shimkus) Boudrias; m. Alfred F. Neves, June 14, 1969 (div. 1978); children: Alexandria Lee, Jennifer Lynn; m. Marvin B. Elbaum, July 23, 1994. BA, U. Hartford, 1970. Pres. Home Nursing Svc., Hartford, 1973-80; pres. Koenig's Art Supply, Old Saybrook, Conn., 1980-83; pres. The Freelance Exchange, Inc., Farmington, Conn., 1983—. Chmn. bd. dirs. ARC, Hartford, 1984-85. Mem. Conn. Women's Coun. (bd. dirs.), Les Chefs Femmes, Inc. (bd. dirs.). Democrat. Avocations: Skiing, gourmet cooking, gardening, golf. Office: Freelance Exchange Inc PO Box 1165 Glastonbury CT 06033

NEVIASER, MYRA, program evaluation specialist; b. Washington, Aug. 26, 1947; d. Edward and Sylvia Singer; m. Alvin Mayer Neviaser, Aug. 20, 1972; children: Robin, Leslie. BS in Elem. Edn., U. Mich., 1969; MA in Edn., U. Md., 1973. Tchr. Montgomery County Pub. Schs., Rockville, Md., 1969-78, reading specialist, 1978-85, tchr. specialist chpt. 1, 1985-92, title I program evaluation specialist, 1992—. Mem. NEA, Internat. Reading Assn., Alpha Delta Kappa. Office: Montgomery County Pub Schs 850 Hungerford Dr Rockville MD 20850

NEVILLE, ELISABETH, computer applications specialist; b. Winchester, Mass., Dec. 5, 1967; d. Joseph and Elinor (Lindsey) N. BA in Graphic Design, Northeastern U., 1993. Adminstr. art room Mercer Photography, Danvers, Mass., 1985-92; photograph restorer Take Two, Arlington, Mass., 1991-94; prodn. artist Ligature Inc., Boston, 1993-94; computer applications specialist Scitex Am. Corp., Bedford, Mass., 1994—. Active Big Sister Assn., 1993-94. Mem. NAFE, Northeastern U. Alumni Assn., Shore Country Day Sch. Alumni Assn., Lawrence Acad. Alumni Assn. Mem. United Ch. of Christ. Home: 6 Stafford Rd Danvers MA 01923

NEVILLE, EMILY CHENEY, author; b. Manchester, Conn., Dec. 28, 1919; d. Howell and Anne (Bunce) Cheney; m. Glenn Neville; children—Emily Tam, Glenn H.H., Dessie, Marcy, Alec. A.B., Bryn Mawr Coll., 1940; J.D., Albany Law Sch., 1976. Bar: N.Y. bar 1977. Feature writer N.Y. Mirror, 1941-42. Author books including: Seventeen Street Gang, 1966, Traveler from a Small Kingdom, 1968, Fogarty, 1969, Garden of Broken Glass, 1975, The Bridge, 1988, The China Year, 1991. Recipient Newbery award for It's Like This Cat 1964, Jane Addams award for Berries Goodman 1966. Address: 333 Market St Keene Valley NY 12943

NEVILLE, MARGARET COBB, physiologist, educator; b. Greenville, S.C., Nov. 4, 1934; d. Henry Van Zandt and Florence Ruth (Crozier) Cobb; m. Hans E. Neville, Dec. 27, 1957; children: Michel Paul, Brian Douglas. BA, Pomona Coll., 1956; PhD, U. Pa., 1962. Asst. prof. physiology U. Colo. Med. Sch., Denver, 1968-75, assoc. prof., 1975-82, prof., 1982—, dir. med. scientist tng. program, 1985-94. Editor: Lactation: Physiology, Nutrition, Breast Feeding, 1983 (Am. Pubs. award 1984), Human Lactation I, 1985, The Mammary Gland, 1987, Jour. Mammary Gland Biology and Neoplasia, 1995—; contbr. numerous articles to profl. jours. Recipient Rsch. Career Devel. award NIH, 1975, NIH merit award, 1993. Mem. AAAS, Am. Physiol. Soc., Am. Soc. Cell Biology, Internat. Soc. Rsch. in Human Milk and Lactation, Phi Beta Kappa. Office: U Colo Dept Physiology PO Box 240C Denver CO 80262

NEVILLE, MONICA MARY, state assembly program executive; b. Phila., Jan. 4, 1949; d. Edward Joseph and Mary Monica (Auletta) N.; m. William H. Pickens III, May, 1993; children: Jennifer Kathryn Gamber, John Blair Gamber, Jr. Student, Rutgers U., 1967-69; AB, U. Calif., Berkeley, 1977. Intern Gov.s' Office, Sacramento, Calif., 1976-77; press asst. Gov. Edmund G. Brown, Jr., Sacramento, 1977-80; pub. info. officer Protection and Adv., Inc., Sacramento, 1980-81; asst. press sec. Calif. Assembly Speaker Willie L. Brown, Jr., Sacramento, 1981-84; press sec. Speaker Willie L. Brown, Jr., Sacramento, 1984-86, spl. asst., 1986-88; prin. cons. Assembly Floor Analysis Unit, Sacramento, 1988-91; dir. Calif. Assembly Fellows Program, Sacramento, 1991—; coord. Calif. Assembly Intern Program, Sacramento, 1991—. Editor: Jesse Marvin Unruh Assembly Fellowship Jour., 1991—. Mem. Calif. Studies Assn., Sacramento, Sacramento (Calif.) Symphony Assn. Mem. Sacramento Press Club, U. Calif. Berkeley Alumni Assn. (life mem.). Home: 1914 Selby Ave # 402 Los Angeles CA 90025 Office: Assembly Fellow Program Legis Office Bldg 1020 N St Ste 402 Sacramento CA 95814-5624

NEVILLE, PHOEBE, choreographer, dancer, educator; b. Swarthmore, Pa., Sept. 28, 1941; d. Kennith R. and Marion (Eberbach) Balsley. Student, Wilson Coll., 1959-61. Cert. practitioner body-mind centering; registered movement therapist. Instr. Bennington (Vt.) Coll., 1981-84, 87-88; vis. lectr. UCLA, 1984-86. Dancer, choreographer Judson Meml. Ch., N.Y.C., 1966-70, Dance Uptown Series, N.Y.C., 1969, Cubiculo Theatre, N.Y.C., 1972-75, Delacorte Dance Festival, N.Y.C., 1976, Dance Umbrella Series, N.Y.C., 1977, Riverside Dance Festival, N.Y.C., 1976, 78, N.Y. Seasons, 1979—; dancer, artistic dir. Phoebe Neville Dance Co., N.Y.C., 1975—, Jacob's Pillow Splash! Festival, 1988, Dance Theater Workshop Winter Events, 1988. Recipient Creative Artist Public Svc. award, 1975; Nat. Endowment for Arts fellow, 1975, 79, 80, 85-87, 92-94, Choreographic fellow N.Y. Found. for Arts, 1989. Mem. Laban Inst. Movement Studies, Dance Theater Workshop, Body-Mind Centering Assn. (cert. practitioner and tchr.), Internat. Movement Therapy Assn. (registered), Internat. Assn. Healthcare Practitioners. Buddhist. Club: Recluse.

NEVIN, JEAN SHAW, artwear and jewelry designer; b. Bklyn., Dec. 21, 1934; d. Marshall Robert and Dorothy Frances (Brown) Shaw; m. Robert Stephen Nevin, Dec. 9, 1955. BA in English, SUNY, Albany, 1956. Textbook and freelance editor, 1959-74; printmaker, papermaker Jean Nevin Graphics, Indpls., 1969-84; owner, mgr., knitwear designer Chameleon, Indpls., 1985-88; pres., knitwear designer Knitting Machine Shop, Inc., Indpls., 1988-91; owner Knitwearables, Albuquerque, 1991—; instr. print and paper making Indpls. Art League, 1974-83, exhibits coord., 1969, 73, edn. coord., 1979-80, editor Artifacts, 1968-69, 72-73; editor, pub. Swatchnotes, 1987-91. Exhibited to nat. group shows and galleries prints and handmade paper, 1970-84, garments and jewelry, 1992—; designer wearable art. Mem. Facets Artwear Designers. Home and Office: 9641 Mendoza Ave NE Albuquerque NM 87109-6614

NEVINS, LYN (CAROLYN A. NEVINS), educational supervisor, trainer, consultant; b. Chelsea, Mass., June 9, 1948; d. Samuel Joseph and Stella Theresa (Maronski) N.; m. John Edward Herbert, Jr., May 1, 1979; children: Chrissy, Johnny. BA in Sociology/Edn., U. Mass., 1970; MA in Women's Studies, George Washington U., 1975. Cert. tchr., trainer. Tchr. social studies Greenwich (Conn.) Pub. Schs., 1970-74; rschr. career/vocat. edn. Conn. State Dept. Edn., Hartford, 1975-76; rschr., career/vocat. edn. Area Coop. Edn. Svcs., Hamden, Conn., 1976-77; program mgr., trainer career edn. and gender equity Coop. Ednl. Svcs., Norwalk, Conn., 1977-83; trainer, mgr., devel., Beginning Educator Support and Tng. program Coop. Ednl. Svcs., Fairfield, Conn., 1987—; state coord. career edn. Conn. State Dept. Edn., Hartford, 1982-83; supr. Sacred Heart U., Fairfield, 1992—; mem. bias com. Conn. State Dept. Edn., Hartford, 1981—; mem. vision com. Middlesex Mid. Sch., Darien, Conn., 1993-95; mem. ednl. quality and diversity com. Town of Darien, 1993-95; cons., trainer career devel./pre-retirement planning Cohen and Assocs., Fairfield, 1981—, Farren Assocs., Annandale, Va., 1992—, Tracey Robert Assocs., Fairfield, 1994—; freelance cons., trainer, Darien, 1983-87; presenter Nat. Conf. GE, 1980, Career Edn., 1983, Am. Edn. Rsch. Assn., 1991; lectr. in field. Coach Spl. Olympics, 1993—, Darien (Conn.) Girls' Softball League, 1992—. Mem. NOW (founder, state coord. edn. 1972-74), ASCD. Home: 4 Hollister Ln Darien CT 06820-5404 Office: Coop Ednl Svcs 25 Oakview Dr Trumbull CT 06611

NEVINS, SHEILA, television programmer and producer; b. N.Y.C.; d. Benjamin and Stella N.; B.A., Barnard Coll., 1960; M.F.A. (Three Arts fellow), Yale U., 1963; m. Sidney Koch; 1 son, David Andrew. TV producer Great Am. Dream Machine, NET, 1970-72, The Reasoner Report, ABC, 1973, Feeling Good, Children's TV Workshop, 1975-76, Who's Who, CBS, 1977-78; v.p. documentary and family programming HBO, N.Y.C., 1978-82, dir. documentary programming Home Box Office, N.Y.C., 1986-95, sr. v.p. documentary and family programming, 1995—. Bd. dirs. Women's Action Alliance. Recipient Peabody award, 1986, 92, Acad. Award Documentary, 1993, Emmy award, 1994, 1995; named Woman of Achievement YWCA, 1991. Mem. Writers Guild Am., Women in Film.

NEW, ANNE LATROBE, public relations, fund raising executive; b. Evanston, Ill., May 10, 1910; d. Charles Edward and Agnes (Bateman) N.; m. John C. Timmerman, Sept. 30, 1933; 1 child, Jan LaTrobe. AB, U. S.C., 1930; postgrad., Hunter Coll., 1930-31, NYU, 1932-33. APR (Accredited Pub. Relatons Practitioner). Editorial asst. Pictorial Review Mag., N.Y.C., 1930-32; copy asst. J. Walter Thompson Co., N.Y.C., 1932-33; sub editor Cosmopolitan Mag., N.Y.C., 1933-37; with Girl Scouts of the U.S., N.Y.C., 1937-57, chief pub. rels. officer, 1945-57; dir. pub. info. edn. Nat. Recreation and Park Assn., 1957-66; special asst. gen. dir. Internat. Social Svc. Am. Branch, N.Y.C., 1966-68; dir. devel. Nat. Accreditation Coun. for Agys. Serving Blind and Visual Handicapped, N.Y.C., 1969-78; pres. Timmerman & New Inc., Mamaroneck, N.Y., 1980—; cons. dept. pub. adminstrn. Baruch Coll., CUNY, 1987-94, Sch. Pub. Affairs, 1994—. Author: Service For Givers, The Story of the National Information Bureau, 1983, Raise More Money for Your Nonprofit Organization, 1991; contbr. articles to profl. jours. Mem. Westchester Dem. Com. Westchester County, 1963-67, 89—; bd. dirs. Mamaroneck (N.Y.) United Fund, 1963-64; chmn. nominating com. LWV, Mamaroneck, 1988, chmn. by-law com., 1989; warden emerita, vestry mem. St. Thomas' Episc. Ch., Mamaroneck. Recipient Marzella Garland award for outstanding achievement in promotion of improved housing conditions in Mamaroneck Village, 1995. Mem. Pub. Rels. Soc. Am. (bd. dirs. N.Y. chpt. 1958-72), Women Execs. Pub. Rels. (sec. 1962-63), Nat. Soc. Fund Raising Execs. (bd. dirs. greater N.Y. chpt. 1978-84), Phi Beta Kappa (Scarsdale/Westchester Phi Beta Kappa Assn.). Democrat. Office: Timmerman & New Inc 235 S Barry Ave Mamaroneck NY 10543-4104

NEW, MARGARET ANN, education educator, consultant; b. Stevens Point, Wis., Jan. 26, 1940; d. Robert Byron and Millicent (Coombs) Freed; m. William New Jr., Oct. 1, 1966 (div. 1982); 1 child, Catherine Ann. BS, U. Wis., 1962; MA, Stanford U., 1966; EdD, UCLA, 1972. Asst. dean housing UCLA, 1969-72; dean students Marlborough Sch., L.A., 1972-73; head counselor Half Moon Boy (Calif.) H.S., 1973-75; real estate profl. Cornish & Carey, Pardoe, Calif., D.C., Va., 1975-85; dir. devel. Foxcroft Sch., Middleburg, Va., 1985-87, Youth Svc. Am., Washington, 1987-89; cons. Middleburg Group, 1989-93; mktg., devel. mgr. Am. Soc. Naval Engrs., 1993-95; career cons. Middleburg (Va.) Group, 1987—; bd. dirs. Stanford (Calif.) U. Eastern Coun. Vice chair Middleburg Planning Commn., 1994—, Action on Smoking & Health, Washington, 1993—; mem. gov.'s club Alexander for Pres., Nashville, 1995—; pres. Meadowbrook Homeowners Assn., Middleburg, 1995—. Mem. Am. Counseling Assn., Met. Area Career/Life Planners Network, Internat. Assn. Career Mgmt. Profls., Colonial Dames Am., Met. Club. Republican. Episcopalian. Office: Middleburg Group PO Box 933 Middleburg VA 20118

NEW, PAMELA ZYMAN, neurologist; b. Chgo., Jan. 24, 1953; d. HIllard Anthony and Virginia Lillian (Drechsler) Zyman; m. Joseph Keith New, Sept. 12, 1982; children: Matthew, Anneliese, Theresa. BS in Medicine, Northwestern U., 1973, MD, 1976. Resident in internal medicine Baylor Affiliated Hosps., Houston, 1977-80, resident in neurology, 1983-85; mem. staff dept. medicine VA Hosp., Houston, 1980-81; resident in gen. surgery N.Y. Hosp., Cornell Med. Ctr., N.Y.C., 1981, resident in neurosurgery, 1981-83; fellow neuro-oncology M.D. Anderson Hosp. and Tumor Inst., Houston, 1985-87; asst. prof. divsn. neurology dept. medicine U. Tex. Health Sci. Ctr., San Antonio, 1987—; staff physician Audie L. Murphy Meml. VA Hosp., San Antonio, 1987—; lectr., researcher in field. Contbr. articles to profl. publs., chpts. to books. Mem. ACP, S.W. Oncology Group, Assn. VA Investigators and Rsch. Adminstrs., Am. Acad. Neurology, Am. Parkinson's Disease Assn. (co-dir. Parkinson's Disease Info. Referral Ctr.), Movement Disorders Soc., Soc. of Neuro-Oncology. Roman Catholic. Office: U Tex Health Sci Ctr 7703 Floyd Curl Dr San Antonio TX 78284-6200

NEW, ROSETTA HOLBROCK, home economics educator, nutrition consultant; b. Hamilton, Ohio, Aug. 26, 1921; d. Edward F. and Mabel (Kohler) Holbrock; m. John Lorton New, Sept. 3, 1943; 1 child, John Lorton Jr. BS, Miami U., Oxford, Ohio, 1943; MA, U. No. Colo., 1971; PhD, The Ohio State U., 1974; student Kantcentrum, Brugge, Belgium, 1992, Lesage Sch. Embroidery, Paris, 1995. Cert. tchr., Colo. Tchr. English and sci. Monahans (Tex.) H.S., 1943-45; emergency war food asst. U.S. Dept. Agr., College Station, Tex., 1945-46; dept. chmn. home econs., adult edn. Hamilton (Ohio) Pub. Schs., 1946-47; tchr., dept. chmn. home econs. East H.S., Denver, 1948-59, Thomas Jefferson H.S., Denver, 1959-83; mem. exec. bd. Denver Pub. Schs.; also lectr.; exec. dir. Ctr. Nutrition Info. U.S. Office of Edn. grantee Ohio State U., 1971-73. Mem. Cin. Art Mus., Nat. Trust for Historic Preservation. Mem. Am. Home Econs. Assn., Am. Vocat. Assn., Embroiders Guild Am., Hamilton Hist. Soc., Internat. Old Lacers, Ohio State U. Assn., Ohio State Home Econs. Alumni Assn., Fairfield (Ohio) Hist. Soc., Republican Club of Denver, Internat. Platform Assn., Phi Upsilon Omicron. Presbyterian. Lodges: Masons, Daughters of the Nile, Order of Eastern Star, Order White Shrine of Jerusalem. Home and Office: 615 Crescent Rd Hamilton OH 45013-3432

NEWBERG, DOROTHY BECK (MRS. WILLIAM C. NEWBERG), portrait artist; b. Detroit, May 30, 1919; d. Charles William and Mary (Labedz) Beck; student Detroit Conservatory Music, 1938; m. William C. Newberg, Nov. 3, 1939; children: Judith Bookwalter Bracken, Robert Charles, James William, William Charles. Trustee Detroit Adventure, 1967-71, originator A Drop in Bucket Program for artistically talented inner-city children. Cmty. outreach coord. Reno Police Dept.; bd. dirs. Bloomfield Art Assn., 1960-62, trustee 1965-67; bd. dirs. Your Heritage House, 1972-75, Franklin Wright Settlement, 1972-75, Meadowbrook Art Gallery, Oakland U., 1973-75; bd. dirs. Sierra Nevada Mus. Art, 1978-80; bd. dirs. Nat. Conf. Christians and Jews, Gang Alternatives Partnership. Recipient Heart of Gold award, 1969; Mich. vol. leadership award, 1969, Outstanding Vol. award City of Reno, 1989-90. Mem. Nevada Mus. Art, No. Nev. Black Cultural Awareness Soc. (bd. dirs.), Hispanic 500 C. of C. No. Nev. Roman Catholic. Home: 2000 Dant Blvd Reno NV 89509-5193

NEWBERY, ILSE SOFIE MAGDALENE, German language educator; b. Darmstadt, Germany, Nov. 15, 1928; came to U.S., 1965; d. Otto and Charlotte (Brill) Brusius; m. A.C.R. Newbery, Dec. 28, 1954; children: Martin Roger, Frances Janet. Diplom akad. gepr. Übersetzer, U. Mainz, Germany, 1949; Staatsexamen Höh. Lehrfach, U. Frankfurt, Germany, 1954; PhD, U. B.C., Vancouver, Can., 1964. Part-time lectr. Queen's U., Belfast, Ireland, 1955-56; grad. asst. U. B.C., 1958-62; lectr. U. Calgary, Can., 1964-65; asst. prof. Georgetown (Ky.) Coll., 1965-67, assoc. prof., 1968-83, prof. German, 1983-94, chair langs. dept., 1989-94, prof. emeritus, 1994—; examiner Goethe Inst., 1983-87; oral proficiency tester ACTFL, 1985-87; rsch. in German exile lit. Author software in field, 1989—. Founding mem. internat. folk ensemble Singing Hons, Lexington, 1977—. Recipient KCTFL Project award, Ky. Coun., 1994, Rollie Graves Tech. Excellence award, 1993. Mem. Am. Assn. Tchrs. German (v.p. Ky. chpt. 1979-81, pres. 1981-83), Am. Coun. Tchrs. Fgn. Langs., Ky. Coun. Tchrs. Fgn. Langs. (bd. dirs. 1979-83).

NEWBILL, STACIE MICHELE, dental hygienist; b. Augsburg, Germany, Mar. 14, 1967; d. Jon R. Newbill and Mary A. Spencer. AAS in Dental Hygiene, Charles Stewart Mott C.C., Flint, Mich., 1990. Registered dental hygienist, Mich., Calif. Dental hygienist USN Dental Clinic, San Diego, 1991-92, Office of D. Douglas Cassat D.D.S., San Diego, 1992—. Vol. Mich. Acad. of Dentistry for the Handicapped, 1990. Mem. San Diego County Dental Hygienists Soc. (chair cmty. dental health/pub. rels., pres. 1995—), Am. Dental Hygienists Assn. Home: 5750 Friars Rd # 304 San Diego CA 92110 Office: Dr Steven Olmos DDS 7811 La Mesa Blvd Ste # C La Mesa CA 91941

NEWBORN, KAREN B., lawyer; b. Cleve., Oct. 30, 1944. BA, Goucher Coll., 1966; JD summa cum laude, Cleve. State U., 1976. Bar: Ohio 1976, U.S. Dist. Ct. (no. dist.) Ohio 1976, U.S. Ct. Appeals (6th cir.) 1978, U.S. Dist. Ct. (ea. dist.) Mich. 1984, U.S. Supreme Ct. 1988. Ptnr. Baker & Hostetler, Cleve.; asst. law dir. City Cleve., 1976-79; adj. instr. teaching trial advocacy, 1987. Mem. ABA, Ohio State Bar Assn., Cleve. Bar Assn. (bd. trustees 1989-92, chair commn. women in the law 1987-90), Inn of Ct. Office: Baker & Hostetler 3200 Nat City Ctr 1900 E 9th St Cleveland OH 44114-3401*

NEWBURG, ANNE COLBY, writer; b. Paris, Dec. 24, 1957; d. Andre W.G. and Ellen French (Vanderbilt) N.; m. Jeffrey Andrew Wasserman, Jan. 2, 1990; 1 child, Jane Olga. BA, Trent U., Peterborough, Ont., 1977; MA in Philosophy, McGill U., Montreal, Que., 1987. Contbr. short stories to The Antioch Rev., Other Voices, American Short Fiction, Turnstile. Teaching fellow McGill U., 1985-87; McDowell Colony fellow, Peterborough, 1992. Democrat.

NEWBURG, CHARLENE O., career counselor; b. Sioux Falls, S.D., Sept. 18, 1927; d. Abraham I. and Sarah (Agrant) Obstfeld; m. Mortimer Newburg, Apr. 16, 1950; children: Janet N. Smalley, Patricia N. Stiffman. BA, Bard Coll., 1949; student, Columbia U., 1949-51; MA, NYU, 1966. Cert. counselor; nat. cert. career counselor; N.Y. state cert. guidance counselor. Counselor, coord. Manpower Devel. and Tng., White Plains, N.Y., 1966-70; career advisor White Plains Adult Edn., N.Y.C., 1971-72; psychology instr. Westchester Community Coll., Valhalla, N.Y., 1971-72, interviewer, 1986-87; guidance counselor Fox Lane Middle Sch., Bedford, N.Y., 1972-75; project dir. Catlayst, N.Y.C., 1976-78; program specialist Westchester County Office for Women, White Plains, 1987-92; pres. Career Transitions Svcs., New Rochelle, N.Y., 1992—; cons., trainer Nat. Ctr. for Vocat. Edn., Columbus, Ohio, 1980. Trustee Bard Coll., 1962-65, trustee assoc., 1962—; dir./v.p. Pelham Art Ctr., N.Y., 1980-87. Named John Bard scholar Bard Coll., 1948; recipient Wm. Lockwood prize, 1949. Mem. AACD, Nat. Career Devel. Assn., League Women Voters, Westchester Assn. Continuing Edn., Sr. Community Svc. Employment Com., Office for Aging. Office: Career Transitions Svcs 38 James Dr New Rochelle NY 10804

NEWBURGE, IDELLE BLOCK, psychotherapist; b. Bklyn.; m. Lawrence G. Newburge; children: Geri, Scott. AB magna cum laude, U. Miami, 1972, MEd, 1973. Lic. mental health counselor; nat. cert. counselor. Acting supr., lead counselor Office Vocat. Rehab., Miami, 1973-79, supr. mental health unit, 1985-87; vocat., edn. specialist Spectrum Programs, Inc., Miami, 1979-81, outpatient supr., 1981-85; psychotherapist Alan Jaffe, PhD and Assoc., Lauderhill, Fla., 1985-88, A.C.S. Pvt. Counseling, Plantation, Fla., 1988-91, KPK Counseling Svcs., Plantation, 1992—; community adv. bd. Fellowship House, Miami, 1985-87; chmn., com. mem. Parent Resource Ctr., Miami, 1979-82. Active Nat. Mus. for Women in the Arts (charter), Washington, 1991—, U.S. Holocaust Meml. Mus. (charter), Washington, 1991—, Greenpeace, Humane Soc., Nat. Wildlife Fedn., NOW, N.Am. Vegetarian Soc. Fellow Am. Bd. Cert. Managed Care Providers (cert. rehab. counselor, master addiction counselor, cert. criminal justice specialist); mem. NASW, ACA, Am. Mental Health Counselors Assn., Fla. Alcohol and Drug Abuse

Assn., Fla. Mental Health Counselors Assn., , Mental Health Assn. Broward County (Listen to Children Programs cons. 1988—), Mental Health Assn. Broward County (profl. mem., bd. dirs., chair), Fla. Soc. Clin. Hypnosis, Lauderhill C. of C. (charter), Plantation C. of C., Women's Forum (charter). Office: KPK Counseling Services 8030 Peters Rd # D106 Plantation FL 33324-4038

NEWCOMB, PATRICIA ANN, commercial banker, consultant; b. Wilmington, Ohio, Jan. 15, 1952; d. Robert Peter and Julia Gaynell (Butt) N. BA, Rockford (Ill.) Coll., 1974; MA, Ohio State U., Columbus, 1979; MBA, Georgetown U., Washington D.C., 1986. Tchr. math U.S. Peace Corps., The Gambia, West Africa, Lima City (Ohio) Schs.; credit analyst Nat. Bank of Detroit, 1986-88; loan officer Nat. Bank of Detroit-Mich., 1988-91; 2d v.p., comml. loan officer NBD Bank, Dayton, Ohio, 1991-96; asst. v.p., mgr. small bus. group Fifth Third Bank, Dayton, 1996—; adv. bd. mem. Downtown YMCA Branch, Dayton; mem. coord. com. Montgomery Free Tree Program, Dayton. Mem. Nat. Peace Corps Assn., Cityfolk (dir. 1996—), Robert Morris Assocs., Citywide Devel. Microenterprise Program (mem. adv. bd. 1994-95, named Vol. of the Yr. 1995). Home: 230 Snowhill Ave Kettering OH 45429 Office: The Fifth Third Bank 1 S Main St Dayton OH 45402

NEWELL, BARBARA WARNE, economist, educator; b. Pitts., Aug. 19, 1929; d. Colston E. and Frances (Corbett) Warne; m. George V. Thompson, June 15, 1954 (dec. 1954); m. George S. Newell, June 9, 1956 (dec. 1964); 1 dau., Elizabeth Penfield. BA, Vassar Coll., 1951; MA, U. Wis., 1953, PhD, 1958, D. Pub. Svc.; LHD, Trinity Coll., 1973, Lesley Coll., 1978; LLD, Central Mich. U., 1973, Williams Coll., 1974, Rollins Coll., 1981, Butler U., 1983, Monmouth Coll., 1986; DLitt, Northeastern U., 1974, Mt. Vernon Coll., 1975, Lesley Coll., 1978, Denison U., 1978, Eckerd Coll., 1982, Gettysburg Coll., 1982, Dennison U., 1978; D.Adminstrn., Purdue U., 1976; DSc, Fla. Inst. Tech., 1981; LHD, Eckerd Coll., 1982; LLD, Butler U., 1983; D Pub. Service, Alaska Pacific U., 1986; DsPS, U. Md., 1987. Asst. to chancellor U. Wis., 1965-67; research, teaching asst., assoc. U. Ill., 1954-59; asst. prof., then assoc. prof. econs. Purdue U., 1959-65; asst. to pres., assoc. prof. econs. U. Mich., Ann Arbor, 1967-71, acting v.p. student affairs, 1968-70; prof. econs., assoc. provost grad. study and research U. Pitts., 1971; pres. Wellesley (Mass.) Coll., 1972-79; U.S. rep. with rank ambassador to UNESCO, Paris, 1979-81; chancellor State U. System Fla., Tallahassee, 1981-85; Regents prof. Fla. State U., 1985—; vis. scholar Harvard U., 1985-86, vis. lectr., 1986-87. Author: Chicago and the Labor Movement, 1961, (with Lawrence Senesh) The Pulse of the Nation, 1961, Our Labour Force, 1962; editorial bd.: (with Lawrence Senesh) Labor History, 1975—; mem. editorial bd. Jour. for Higher Edn. Mgmt., 1984—; contbr. articles and revs. to profl. jours. and mags. Trustee Carnegie Endowment for Internat. Peace, 1973—; bd. dirs. Americans for the Universality of UNESCO, 1984—; mem. Fla. State Job Tng. com., 1991—, mem. Fla. Edn. and Employment Coun. for Women and Girls, 1992—. Wells fellow, 1981. Office: Florida State U Dept of Econ Tallahassee FL 32306-2045

NEWELL, CHARLDEAN, public administration educator; b. Ft. Worth, Oct. 14, 1939; d. Charles Thurlow and Mildren Dean (Looney) N. BA, U. North Tex., 1960, MA, 1962; PhD, U. Tex., 1968; cert., Harvard U., 1988. Instr. U. North Tex., Denton, 1965-68, asst. prof., 1968-72; assoc. prof., dir. Fedn. North Tex. Area Univs., Denton, Dallas, 1972-74; assoc. prof., assoc. v.p. acad. affairs U. North Tex., Denton, 1974-76, assoc. prof., chair dept. polit. sci., 1976-80, prof. polit. sci., 1980-92, assoc. v.p., spl. asst. to chancellor, 1982-92, regents prof. pub. adminstrn., 1992—; cons. Miss. Bd. Trustees State Instns. Higher Learning, Jackson, 1983-84, Ednl. Testing Svc., Princeton, N.J., 1980, 82, 85, Spear, Down & Judin, Dallas, 1994-95, North Tex. Inst. Edn. in Visual Arts, Denton, 1993-94; bd. dirs. Mcpl. Clks. Ednl. Found., San Dimas, Calif.; bd. regents Internat. City/County Mgmt. Assn., Washington. Author: (with others) City Executives: Leadership Roles, Work Characteristics and Time Management, 1989, The Effective Local Government Manager, 1993, Essentials of Texas Politics, 1995, Texas Politics, 1996; contbr. articles to profl. jours. Chmn. Denton Charter Rev. Com., 1978-79; mem. Denton CSC, 1989—, chmn., 1992—; mem. adv. com. Ann's Haven Hospice, Denton, 1981-85; mem. exec. coun. Episcopal Diocese Dallas, 1985-88; mem. Denton Blue Ribbon Capital Improvements Com., 1995-96. Recipient Elmer Staats Career Pub. Svc. award Nat. Assn. Sch. Pub. Affairs Adminstrn., 1993. Mem. ASPA (sect. chmn. 1982-83, mem. editl. bd. 1985-88), Internat. Pers. Mgmt. Assn. (regional program com. 1982-83), Am. Polit. Sci. Assn., Southwestern Polit. Sci. Assn. (sec., treas. 1975-79), Denton C. of C., Denton Tennis Assn., Pi Sigma Alpha (exec. coun. 1988-92), Pi Alpha Alpha (exec. coun. 1995—). Democrat. Home: 709 Mimosa Dr Denton TX 76201-8814 Office: U North Tex PO Box 5367 Denton TX 76203-0367

NEWELL, JANE ANN, elementary educator; b. Joplin, Mo., May 23, 1938; d. Earnest and Ruth Madge (Turner) Kirkpatrick; m. Max G. Newell, Nov. 7, 1957; children: Terry, Tamera, Shari, David. BA in Edn., Wichita State U., 1975; MS in Edn., Pittsburg (Kans.) State U., 1981. Cert. elem. tchr., Kans., Mo. Elem. sch. tchr. Galena (Kans.) Unified Sch. Dist. 499, 1976—; piano and organ tchr. Organist Meth. Ch. Mem. NEA, Kans. Edn. Assn. Democrat.

NEWFIELD, JOANNE HELENE, accountant; b. Bronx, N.Y., May 5, 1957; d. Howard B. and Bea Newfield; 1 child, Syrena A. Mattioli. BBA, U. Pa., 1985. Program mgr. Pa. Psychol. Svcs., Phila., 1981-90; staff acct. Holmes & Holmes, Flourtown, Pa., 1985; acct. asst. Kuljian Corp., Phila., 1985-87; acctg. mgr. Rulyn, Inc., Cherry Hill, N.J., 1990-91; payroll mgr. Stout Environ., Thorofare, N.J., 1991-92; cons. Manadu, Inc., Ft. Lauderdale, Fla., 1993-95; mgr. acctg. dept. Videoland, Inc., West Lafayette, Ind., 1995-96; dir. fin. RMC, West Lafayette, 1995—. Treas. YMCA Newcomers, 1995-96. Mem. NAFE, Am. Soc. Women Accts., Inst. Mgmt. Accts. Home and Work: 52 Mara Ct Cherry Hill NJ 08002

NEWLAND, JANE LOU, nursing educator; b. Toledo, July 18, 1931; d. Clarence Charles Meinen and Bernice Isabell (Floyd) Scott; m. Byron Merle Newland, Aug. 4, 1962; children: Jeffrey Bruce, Brian James. Diploma in nursing, Lima (Ohio) Meml. Hosp., 1952; BSN, Ohio State U., 1959; M Vocat. Edn., U. South Fla., 1983, EdS in Vocat. Edn., 1989. RN, Ohio, Fla.; cert. tchr., Fla. Stewardess nurse Balt. & Ohio R.R., Cin., 1953-56; dir. nursing Lima State Hosp., 1960-67, dir. nursing edn., 1967-72; renal nurse children's svc. Health and Rehabilitative Svcs. Fla., Ft. Myers, 1975-78; practical nursing instr. Lee High-Tech. Ctr. Ctrl., Ft. Myers, 1979—; mem. adv. bd. Practical Nurse Assn., Lima, 1966-71. Mem., sec. St. James City Civic Assn., 1973-76; den leader Boy Scouts Am., St. James City, 1970-76; treas. PTA Pine Island Elem. Sch., Pine Island Center, Fla., 1973-75. Recipient Assoc. Master Tchr. award Fla. State Bd. Edn., 1986. Mem. Assn. Practical Nurse Educators Fla., Nat. Assn. health Occupations Tchrs., Lee County Vocat. Assn. (Outstanding Health Occupation Tchr. award 1985, Outstanding Vocat. Edn. Tchr. award 1990), Fla. Vocat. Assn., Health Occupation Educators Assn. Fla., Ladies Aux. VFW, Ladies Oriental Shrine, Order Ea. Star, Niobians of Cape Coral (Fla.), Kappa Delta (v.p. 1983-85, pres. 1993—), Phi Kappa Phi. Lutheran. Home: 2261 Carambola Ln Saint James City FL 33956 Office: Lee County High Tech Ctr 3800 Michigan Ave Fort Myers FL 33916-2202

NEWLAND, LINDA CLAIRE (MICKI NEWLAND), secondary education educator; b. St. Louis, Nov. 23, 1948; d. Paul George and Clara Louise (Busboom) Kiehl; m. David Alan Newland, Dec. 26, 1970; children: Stephanie, Joshua, Christina, Paul, Rachel. AA in Liberal Arts, St. John's Coll., Winfield, Kans., 1968; BS in Secondary Edn., Concordia Coll., Seward, Nebr., 1970; postgrad., Calif. State U., Dominguez Hills. Cert. in secondary edn. English and math., Calif., Ark. Tchr. Luth. H.S., L.A., 1970-71; statis. analyst Grey Advt., L.A., 1971-78; math./computer tchr. Phillips County C.C., Helena, Ark., 1982-85; tchr. math. Stuttgart (Ark.) H.S., 1981-86; tchr., chair dept. math. Hoover H.S., Glendale, Calif., 1987—, mentor tchr., 1996—; freelance mktg. rschr., L.A., 1986; tutor Glendale Unified Sch. Dist., 1991—. Patroness of preludes Glendale Symphony Orch., 1993, 94; adult literacy tutor Glendale Pub. Libr., 1992, 93; treas. Purple Cir. of Hoover H.S., 1993—; mem. planning team Glendale 2000/Hoover 2000, 1992, 94. Named Outstanding Mem., Verdugo Gymnastics Club, Glendale, 1989, Hoover Hero, 1994, 96. Mem. Nat. Coun. Tchrs. Math., Calif. Tchrs. Math., Foothill Math. Coun., Women's Orgn. of Glendale Symphony Orch. Lutheran. Home: 27547 Open Crest Dr Saugus CA 91350-1624 Office: Hoover HS 651 Glenwood Rd Glendale CA 91202-1552

NEWLAND, RUTH LAURA, small business owner; b. Ellensburg, Wash., June 4, 1949; d. George J. and Ruth Marjorie (Porter) N. BA, Cen. Wash. State Coll., 1970, MEd, 1972; EdS, Vanderbilt U., 1973; PhD, Columbia Pacific U., 1981. Tchr. Union Gap (Wash.) Sch., 1970-71; ptnr. Newland Ranch Gravel Co., Yakima, Wash., 1970—, Arnold Artificial Limb, Yakima, 1981-86; owner, pres. Arnold Artificial Limb, Yakima and Richland, Wash., 1986—; ptnr. Newland Ranch, Yakima, 1969—. Contbg. mem. Nat. Dem. Com., Irish Nat. Caucus Found.; mem. Pub. Citizen, We The People, Nat. Humane Edn. Soc.; charter mem. Nat. Mus. Am. Indian. George Washington scholar Masons, Yakima, 1967. Mem. NAFE, NOW, Am. Orthotic and Prosthetic Assn., Internat. Platform Assn., Nat. Antivisection Soc. (life), Vanderbilt U. Alumni Assn., Peabody Coll. Alumni Assn., Columbia Pacific U. Alumni Assn., World Wildlife Fund, Nat. Audubon Soc., Greenpeace, Mus. Fine Arts, Humane Soc. U.S., Wilderness Soc., Nature Conservancy, People for Ethical Treatment of Animals, Amnesty Internat., The Windstar Found., Rodale Inst., Sierra Club (life), Emily's List. Independent. Home: 2004 Riverside Rd Yakima WA 98901-9564 Office: Arnold Artificial Limb 9 S 12th Ave Yakima WA 98902-3106

NEWLANDS, SHEILA ANN, consumer products company executive, controller; b. Worcester, Mass., Mar. 8, 1953; d. Joseph and Doris Edna (Bachand) N.; m. Domenic V. Testa Jr., Oct. 2, 1976 (div. 1983). BA summa cum laude, Worcester State Coll., 1975; cert. interior design, Bunkerhill Community Coll., 1976; MS, Simmons Coll., 1976; MBA, Suffolk U., 1983. Cert. real estate broker, Mass.; CPA, Wash. Dir. health scis. library Lynn Hosp., Mass., 1976-78, Mt. Auburn Hosp., Cambridge, 1978-81; assoc. fin. analyst Data Gen., Westboro, Mass., 1981-82, fin. analyst, 1982-84, sr. fin. analyst, 1984; fin. analyst Stimson Lane Wine and Spirits, Woodinville, Wash., 1985-86, dir. fin., 1986-91, v.p., contr., 1991—; guest lectr. Simmons Coll. Sch. Library Sci., Boston, 1980-81. Mem. Burlington (Mass.) Conservation Commn., 1978-84. Mem. Fin. Mgmt. Honor Soc., Phi Alpha Theta. Home: PO Box 514 Issaquah WA 98027-0514 Office: Stimson Lane Wine & Spirits One Stimson Ln Woodinville WA 98072

NEWMAN, BARBARA POLLOCK, journalist, television writer, producer; b. N.Y.C., June 15, 1939; d. Irving G. and Jeanne (Ginsberg) Pollock; div.; 1 child, Penelope. BA, Mount Holyoke Coll., 1960; MA, Columbia U., 1962. Legis. asst. Rep. James Scheuer, Washington, 1964-65, Mayor John Lindsay, N.Y.C., 1965-67; mem. President's Nat. Adv. Commn. on Civil Disorders, Washington, 1967-79; reporter, interviewer Nat. Pub. Radio, N.Y.C., 1971-78; investigative reporter, producer "20/20" ABC News, Washington, 1978-81; exec. producer Jack Anderson Confidential, Washington, 1982-83; pres. Praetorian Prodns., Inc., Washington, 1984—; moderator Nat. Town Meetings, Pub. TV, 1975-78; Hostess McNeill Lehrer Report, Aug. 1977; mem. adv. bd. Washington Journalism Review, 1977-80. Author: The Covenant: Love and Death in Beirut, 1989; contbr. news and editl. articles to newspapers and popular jours.; sr. prodr. Now It Can Be Told, 1991; prodr. documentaries for investigative reports Arts and Entertainment Network; prodr. Channel 4 and Ctrl. TV, London. Recipient Peabody award thorugh Nat. Pub. Radio, 1972, Ohio State award, 1973, 74, 76, Silver Gavel award, ABA, 1974, Cadmus award, Am. Lebanese League, 1981; Emmy nominee, 1981 for investigative reporting. Home: 5336 29th St NW Washington DC 20015-1332

NEWMAN, BETTY LOUISE, accountant; b. Llano, Tex., Dec. 1, 1946; d. Travis Alger and Edith Lucile (Tate) N.; m. Vernon George Mangold (div. July 1981); 1 child, Ian Keith. Student, San Antonio Jr. Coll., 1965-66; BBA, U. Tex., San Antonio, 1985. Data claims analyst Blue Cross/Blue Shield, San Antonio, 1980-82; regional sec., acct. BioMed. Applications, San Antonio, 1982-83; with acctg. dept. Comprehensive Bus. Svcs., Boerne, Tex., 1983-84; acct. Cadwallader Ins. Agy., San Antonio, 1986, Data Processing Support, Inc., San Antonio, 1986-87, Archive Retrieval Sys., Inc., San Antonio, 1986-87; pvt. practice acctg. San Antonio, 1987—; acct. atty., 1989-92; acct. Night in Old San Antonio, 1996. Vol. Boy Scouts Am., San Antonio, 1978-89, unit commr., 1989; bd. dirs. San Antonio Met. Ministries, 1987-90. Scholar Women in Bus., 1983. Mem. NAFE, Nat. Assn. Accts. (assoc. bd. dirs. 1988-90), Inst. Mgmt. Accts., Leon Springs Bus. Assn., Am. Luth. Women. Home and Office: 25403 Brewer Dr San Antonio TX 78257-1139

NEWMAN, CAROL L., lawyer; b. Yonkers, N.Y., Aug. 7, 1949; d. Richard J. and Pauline Frances (Stoll) N. AB/MA summa cum laude, Brown U., 1971; postgrad. Harvard U. Law Sch., 1972-73; JD cum laude, George Washington U., 1977. Bar: D.C., 1977, Calif., 1979. With antitrust div. U.S. Dept. Justice, Washington and L.A., 1977-80; assoc. Alschuler, Grossman & Pines, L.A., 1980-82, Costello & Walcher, L.A., 1982-85, Rosen, Wachtell & Gilbert, 1985-88, ptnr., 1988-90; ptnr. Keck, Mahin & Cate, 1990-94; pvt. practice, L.A., 1994—; adj. prof. Sch. Bus., Golden Gate U., spring 1982. Candidate for State Atty. Gen., 1986; L.A. city commr. L.A. Bd. Transp. Commrs., 1993—, v.p., 1995—. Mem. ABA, State Bar Calif., L.A. County Bar Assn., L.A. Lawyers for Human Rights (co. pres. 1991-92), Log Cabin (bd. dirs. 1992—, pres. 1996—), Calif. Women Lawyers (bd. dirs., bd. govs. 1991-94), Women's Progress Alliance (bd. dirs. 1996—), Order of Coif, Phi Beta Kappa.

NEWMAN, DEANNE LEE KREIS, psychotherapist; b. Cleve., June 17, 1938; d. Milton Fred and Mildred Marie Elizabeth (Monson) Kreis; m. Philip Hersh Newman, Aug. 14, 1965 (div. Apr. 1985); children: Rachael, Adam. BA, Mills Coll., 1956; postgrad., Boston U., 1966-67; MSW, U. So. Calif., L.A., 1969. Lic. ind. social worker, N.Mex. Children's worker L.A. County Dept. Adoptions, Long Beach, Calif., 1965-66; natural parent worker L.A. County Dept. Adoptions, Long Beach, 1967-68; psychiat. social worker Footlighter Child Guidance Clinic, Hollywood, Calif., 1969-70; psychotherapist Los Alamos (N.Mex.) Family Coun., 1972-77; pvt. practice psychotherapist Santa Fe and Los Alamos, N.Mex., 1977—; chair program com. C.G. Jung Inst. Santa Fe, 1984-86, 92-95, clin. supr., instr., 1993—, exec. bd. mem., 1993-94. Mem. NASW, Inter-Regional Soc. Jungian Analysts (diplomate analytical psychology), Internat. Assn. Analytical Psychology, Eye Movement Desensitization and Reprocessing Internat. Assn. Home: 1626 Paseo de Peralta Santa Fe NM 87501 Office: 2610 Trinity Dr Los Alamos NM 87544

NEWMAN, JANE, advertising agency executive; b. Woking, Surrey, Eng., Oct. 22, 1947; came to U.S., 1978; d. Ronald William and Victoria (Brady) N.; 1 child. BA, Sussex U., Eng., 1969; MA, Lancaster U., Eng., 1970. Account planner Boase Massimi & Pollitt, London, 1970-78; account mgr. Needham Harper & Steers, Chgo., 1978-79, Ammirati & Puris, N.Y.C., 1979-81; vice chmn. Chiat/Day Advt., N.Y.C., 1981-93; ptnr. Merkley Newman Harty Advt. Agy., N.Y.C., 1993—. Office: Merkley Newman Harty 12th Fl 200 Varick St New York NY 10014-4810

NEWMAN, JANICE MARIE, business owner, lawyer; b. N.Y.C., Aug. 11, 1951; d. Robert and Clara (White) Swindler; m. Roger Kevin Newman, Jan. 20, 1972 (div. 1980); 1 child, Germaine M. Swindler-Newman (dec.). BA, Smith Coll., 1973; JD, Rutgers U., 1980. Bar: N.J. 1983, U.S. Supreme Ct. 1987. Adminstrv. asst. Corp. Ann. Reports, N.Y.C., 1972-73; pub. rels. asst. Lippincott & Margulies, N.Y.C., 1973; journalist Essex Forum Newspaper, East Orange, N.J., 1973; pub. info. officer City of Newark, 1974-82; producer, host Newark and Reality TV show, Newark, 1974-85; asst. communications dir. Mayor's Office, Newark, 1982-86; legis. liaison, publ. info. officer N.J. Div. on Women, Trenton, 1988-90, acting dir., 1990, women svcs. coord., 1990-91; environ. issues specialist N.J. Dept. Environ. Protection and Energy, Trenton, 1991-92; comm. specialist Dept. Environ. Protection, Lawrenceville, N.J., 1992-95; pvt. practice South Orange, N.J., 1994—; mem. working group N.J. Supreme Ct. Domestic Violence, 1994-96; pres. JM Newman & Assocs.; chair Interest on Lawyers Trust Accounts, 1995-96, mem., 1986—. Mem. editorial bd. N.J. Lawyer mag., 1987—, The Voice, Episcopal Diocese of Newark, 1992-95; design editor: The Voice, 1993-94; contbr. articles to mags. Bd. dirs. Instrns. Exposures Experiences, 1983-87, Greater Newark Conservancy; 2d v.p. Women's Polit. Caucus, N.J., 1991-92, 1st v.p., 1992-93; appt. to N.J. Supreme Ct. Com. on Women in the Cts., 1990—, Com. on Character, 1992—, N.J. Women Vets. Adv. Com., 1993-94; lay reader, eucharistic lay min., parliamentarian, 1992-94, Episc. Diocese of Newark; sr. warden, House of Prayer Espisc. Ch., Newark, 1992. Recipient Pub. Svc. award N.J. Voice Newspaper, 1977, Achievement award Minority Contractors and Craftsmen Trade Assn., 1982, award Nat. Council Negro Bus. and Profl. Women Legal Achievement, 1987, award N.J. Unit Nat. Assn. Negro Bus. and Profl. Women's Clubs, 1987; named to Outstanding Young Women Am. U.S. Jaycees, 1984. Mem. Nat. Assn. Media Women (rec. sec. 1985-87, Media Woman of Yr. award 1985, pres. N.J. cpt. 1986-88), N.J. State Bar Assn. (Young Lawyers Div. Community Svc. award 1989, mem. pub. rels. com. 1987—, 2d vice-chair women's rights sect., 1990-92, 1st vice chair women's rights sect., 1992-93, chair, 1993-95, bd. trustees minorities in the profession sect.), N.J. State Bar Found. (trustee 1994—), N.J. Women Lawyers Assn. (pres. 1986-88, bd. trustees pub. rels. com., entertainment & arts com., Essex County Bar Assn., Nat. Coun. Negro Women, Garden State Bar Assn., Essex County Women Lawyers (trustee 1991-94). Democrat. Episcopalian. Home: 4 Church St South Orange NJ 07079 also: 4 Sloan St South Orange NJ 07079-1714

NEWMAN, JEANNE JOHNSON, sociolinguistic educator, researcher; b. Twin Falls, Idaho, Dec. 8, 1939; d. Glen Everett Johnson and Alta Ruth (Egbert) Kizer; children: Ronald, Javier. BA, Calif. State U., 1986, MA, 1988; PhD, U. Pa., 1993. ESL tchr., coord. edn. dept. Tulare County Community Action Agy., Visalia, Calif., 1967-69; dir. community devel., dir. planning and evaluation Kings County Community Action Orgn., Hanford, Calif., 1970-75; program planner Community Action Program Tulare County, Visalia, Calif., 1975-79; edn. rev. instr., program specialist, tchr. PROTEUS Adult Tng., Inc., Visalia, Calif., 1979-84; student asst., tutor Calif. State U., Fresno, 1985-86, rsch. asst., 1986-87; rsch. asst. U. Pa., Phila., 1988-89; tchr., workshop facilitator Svc., Commitment, Success Bus. and Tech. Sch., Phila., 1990-93; rsch. assoc. Vocational Rsch. Inst., divsn. Jewish Employment & Vocational Svcs., Phila., 1993-95; acad. dir. Stage Lang. Acad., Seoul, Korea, 1995—; presenter rsch. papers Second Lang. Rsch. Forum, Eugene, Oreg., L.A., 1989, 90, Boston U. Lang. Devel., 1989, 90, TESOL Internat., N.Y.C., 1991, Balt., 1994, Long Beach, Calif., 1995, Pa. chpt. PENN-TESOL East, 1994; cons. SCS Bus. and Tech. Sch., Phila., 1990-93; mem. staff Literacy Rsch. Ctr., newsletter editor, 1990; contbg. mem. Working Papers in Ednl. Linguistics, editor, 1989-91. Author rsch. papers. Visitor Presbyn. Home Elderly, Phila., 1988-91; mem., organizer Tri-County Sr. Citizens, Commn. on Aging, Fresno, Kings and Tulare County, 1980-85. Calif. State U. Alumni Assn. scholar, 1987-88, U. Pa. Grad. Sch. Edn. scholar, 1988-93. Mem. TESOL Internat. (vol. Pa. chpt. 1989-94), Am. Assn. Ret. Educators, Am. Assn. Applied Linguistics, AAUW, NAFE, Internat. Platform Assn., Modern Lang. Assn. Home and Office: 831-3 Yeoksam-Dong, Gangnam-Ku, Seoul Korea 135-080

NEWMAN, JOAN FINEGAN, guidance counselor; b. Phila., Feb. 22, 1933; d. James Leo and Madelyn (Daley) Finegan; m. Albert J. Newman, Nov. 20, 1954; children: James, Michael, Kathleen. BS in Elem. Edn., West Chester U., 1954, MEd, 1976; supervisory cert., Villanova U., 1985. Elem. tchr. Phila. Sch. Dist., 1954-57; elem. tchr. Upper Darby (Pa.) Sch. Dist., 1968-76, sch. social worker, 1976-82, sch. guidance counselor, 1982—, student assistance team leacer, supr. counselors, 1984—. Recipient drug and alcohol prevention award State of Pa., 1995, Pa. Counselor of the Year Pa. Sch. Counselor Assn., 1995-96. Mem. ACA (lic.), Am. Group Counseling Assn., Nat. Cert. Counselor Assn., Nat. Edn. Assn., Pa. State Edn. Assn., Pa. Edn. Assn., Upper Darby Edn. Assn. Republican. Roman Catholic. Home: 3701 Taylor Ave Drexel Hill PA 19026 Office: Drexel Hill Mid Sch 3001 State Rd Drexel Hill PA 19026

NEWMAN, JOAN MESKIEL, lawyer; b. Youngstown, Ohio, Dec. 12, 1947; d. John F. and Rosemary (Scarmuzzi) Meskiel; m. Charles Andrew Newman, Aug. 8, 1971; children: Anne R., Elyse S. BA in Polit. Sci., Case-Western Reserve U., 1969; JD, Washington U., St. Louis, 1972, LLM in Taxation, 1973. Bar: Mo. 1972. Assoc. Lewis & Rice, St. Louis, 1973-80, ptnr., 1981-90; ptnr. Thompson Coburn, St. Louis, 1990—; adj. prof. law Washington U. Sch. Law, St. Louis, 1975-92; past pres., mem. Midwest Pension Conf., St. Louis chpt., lectr. in field. chmn. bd. dirs. Great St. Louis coun. Girl Scouts U.S., 1988-92, officer, 1978-92; mem. bd. dirs. and exec. com. Girl Scouts U.S., 1993—; chmn. bd. dirs. Met. Employment and Rehab. Svcs., 1994—; bd. dirs. Jewish Fedn. St. Louis, 1991—, Jewish Ctr. Aged, 1990-92; chmn. bd. dirs. Women of Achievement, 1993-96; mem. cmty. wide youth svcs. panel United Way Greater St. Louis, 1992-96, fin. futures task force Kiwanis Camp Wyman, 1992-93; mem. nat. coun. Washington U. Sch. Law, 1988-91; chmn. staff blue ribbon fin. com. Sch. Dist. Clayton, 1986-87; vol. Women's Self Help Ctr. Named Woman of Achievement St. Louis, 1991. Mem. Mo. Bar Assn. (staff pension and benefits com. 1991—), Bar Met. St. Louis (past chmn. taxation sect.), St. Louis Forum, Order of Coif (hon.). Office: Thompson Coburn 1 Mercantile Ctr Ste 3300 Saint Louis MO 63101-1643

NEWMAN, JODY, association executive. Exe dir National Women's Political Caucus, Washington DC. Office: National Womens Political Caucus 1275 K St NW Ste 750 Washington DC 20005-4006*

NEWMAN, MARGARET ANN, nursing educator; b. Memphis, Oct. 10, 1933; d. Ivo Mathias and Mamie Love (Donald) N.; BSHE, Baylor U., 1954; BSN, U. Tenn., Memphis, 1962; MS, U. Calif., San Francisco, 1964; PhD, NYU, 1971. Dir. nursing, asst. prof. nursing Clin. Research Center, U. Tenn., 1964-67; asst. prof. N.Y.U., 1971-75, assoc. prof., 1975-77; prof. in charge grad. program and research dept. nursing Pa. State U., 1977-80, prof. nursing, 1977-84; prof. nursing U. Minn., 1984-96, prof. emeritus 1996—; disting. resident Westminster Coll., Salt Lake City Utah, 1991. Travelling fellow New Zealand Nursing Ednl. & Rsch. Fund, 1985; Am. Jour. Nursing scholar, 1979-80; recipient Outstanding Alumnus award U. Tenn. Coll. Nursing, 1975, Disting. Alumnus award NYU Div. Nursing, 1984; Disting. Scholar in Nursing award NYU Div. Nursing, 1992, Sigma Theta Tau Founders Rsch. award, 1993, Nursing Scholar award St. Xavier U., 1994, E. Louise grant award for nursing excellence U. Minn., 1996, Margaret Newman scholar award Zeta chpt. Sigma Theta Tau, 1996—. Fellow Am. Acad. Nursing. Author: Theory Development in Nursing, 1979, Health as Expanding Consciousness, 1986, 2nd edit., 1994, A Developing Discipline, 1995; editor: (with others) Source Book of Nursing Research, 1973, 2d edit., 1977. Research on patterns of person-environment interaction as indices of health as expanding consciousness; also models of profl. practice. Home: 289 5th St E Saint Paul MN 55101-1995

NEWMAN, MARJORIE YOSPIN, psychiatrist; b. Bklyn., July 8, 1945; d. Toby and Audrey (Kreinik) Yospin; children: Eric, David. Student, Smith Coll., 1963-64; AB, Barnard Coll., 1967; MD, Med. Coll. Pa., 1971. Diplomate Am. Bd. Psychiatry and Neurology. Psychiatry intern, resident Albert Einstein Coll. Medicine, N.Y.C., 1971-75; asst. prof. psychiatry U. Tex. Health Sci. Ctr., San Antonio, 1975-77; asst. prof. psychiatry Sch. Medicine UCLA, 1977-79, 1977-79, asst. clin. prof. Sch. Medicine, 1979—; dir. residency tng. in psychiatry Med. Ctr. Harbor-UCLA Med. Ctr., 1977-79; pvt. practice Pasadena, Calif., 1983—. Grantee NSF, 1969; Am. Field Svc. Internat. scholar, 1963. Mem. Am. Psychiat. Assn., So. Calif. Psychiat. Soc., Smith Coll. Alumna Assn., Barnard Coll. Alumna Assn., Columbia U. Alumna Assn., Ivy League Assn. So. Calif. Office: Cotton Med Ctr South 50 Alessandro Pl Ste 340 Pasadena CA 91105-3149

NEWMAN, MARY ALICE, county official; b. Newark, Mar. 8, 1946; d. Stanley L. and Estelle C. (Forrest) Senk; m. Jack David Newman, Oct. 7, 1967; children: Jonathan Christopher, Alison Marie. AA, Newark State Coll., Union, N.J., 1967. Editor R.L. Polk, Portland, Oreg., 1969-71; clk. U.S. Forest Svc., Portland, 1971-74; sec. Def. Contract Adminstrn., Portland, 1974-76; vets. svcs. clk. VA, Portland, 1976-82; intake officer Clackamas County Community Corrections, Oregon City, Oreg., 1982-84; vets. svc. officer Clackamas County Vets. Svcs., Oregon City, 1984—. Co-author: The Horsekeeper, 1985; editor Union Label newsletter, 1980-82, VA Employee newsletter, 1980-82; co-editor: Oreg. 4-H Horse Contest Guide, Learning to Jump Annual. Mem. Clackamas County Horse Adv., 1989—; judge Oreg. 4-H Horse Program, 1990—; chmn. dressage program Clackamas County 4-H Horse Program, 1989-94; chmn. Oreg. State 4-H Dressage Program, 1991—; dist. commr. Lake Oswego Pony Club, Oregon City, 1989-94; treas. Oreg. region U.S. Pony Clubs, Oregon City, 1988-92; leader 4-H Club, 1985—, Oreg. 4-H Horse Devel. Bd., 1993—. Recipient Minuteman Flag and Star award U.S. treas. Dept., 1980, Svc. award West Linn VFW

Post, 1987,. 4-H Leader of Yr. award Clackamas County 4-H Ext., 1990, 92; named County Vets. Svc. Officer of Yr. Oreg. Dept. Vets. Affairs, 1993. Mem. Nat. Assn. County Vets. Svc. Officers (legis. com. 1994—, mem. exec. bd. 1995—), Oreg. County Vets. Svc. Officers (exec. bd. 1988-90, v.p. 1990-91, pres. 1991-94, exec. bd. 1994—), Nat. Assn. Atomic Vets., Western Paraders Assn. (3d v.p. 1988-92, 2d v.p. 1993-95). Home: 20500 S Ridge Rd Oregon City OR 97045-9645 Office: Clackamas County Vets Svcs 719 Main St Oregon City OR 97045-1814

NEWMAN, MARY THOMAS, communications educator, management consultant; b. Howell, Mo., Oct. 15, 1933; d. Austin Hill and Doris (McQueen) Thomas; m. Grover Travis Newman, Aug. 22, 1952 (div. 1967); 1 child, Leah Newman Lane; m. Rodney Charles Westlund, July 18, 1981. BS, S.F. Austin State U., 1965; MA, U. Houston, 1956; PhD, Pa. State U., 1980. Cert. permanent tchr., Tex. Instr. communications South Tex. Coll., Houston, 1965-70; assoc. prof. communications Burlington County Coll., Pemberton, N.J., 1970-72; teaching asst. in communications Pa. State U., University Park, 1972-73; asst. prof. Ogontz Campus Pa. State U., Abington, 1973-80; lectr. mgmt. and communications U. Md., Europe and Asia, 1980-83; mem. vis. faculty dept. communications U. Tenn., Knoxville, 1984-85; asst. prof. human factors U. So. Calif., L.A., 1985-88; assoc. prof. human factors, dir. profl. devel. U. Denver Coll. Systems Sci., 1988-92; assoc. prof. USC, Berlin, Germany, 1992-93; assoc. prof., assoc. dir. Whitworth Coll., Spokane, Wash., 1993-95; assoc. prof. comms. Houston Baptist U., 1995—; pres. Human Resource Communications Group, Easton, Md., 1984—; lectr. Bus. Rsch. Inst., Toyo U., Tokyo, 1983, Saitama Med. U., Japan, 1983; scholar in residence U.S. Marine Corps., Quantico, Va., 1990-92; mem. final phase faculty USC MSSM Troop Draw Down, Berlin, Germany, 1992-93; team mem. Spokane Inter-Collegiate Rsch. & Tech. Inst., 1993-95; dir. Women's Leadership Conf., Moses Lake, Wash., 1993; mem. world svcs. com. YWCA, Spokane; Lilly fellow 1996. Author: Introduction to Basic Speech Communication, 1969; contbr. articles to profl. jours. Program developer U.S. Army Hdqrs. Sch. Age Latch Key Program, Alexandria, Va., 1987; mem. Govt. of Guam Women's Issues Task Force, 1985. Lilly fellow in humanities and arts, summer 1996. Mem. Human Factors Soc., Speech Communication Assn. (legis. com. 1970-73, editl. bd. jour. 1970-76), Ea. Communication Assn. (editl. bd. jours. 1975-80), Univ. Film Assn. (publicity dir. 1978-80), Indsl. Comm. Coun., Chesapeake Women's Network, Easton Bus. and Profl. Women, Alpha Chi, Alpha Psi Omega, Pi Kappa Delta, Delta Kappa Gamma. Office: Houston Baptist U Dept Comms 7502 Fondren Houston TX 77074

NEWMAN, MURIEL KALLIS STEINBERG, art collector; b. Chgo., Feb. 25, 1914; d. Maurice and Ida (Nudelman) Kallis; m. Albert H. Newman, May 14, 1955; 1 son by previous marriage, Glenn D. Steinberg. Student, Art Inst. Chgo., 1932-36, Ill. Inst. Tech., 1947-50, U. Chgo., 1958-65. hon. life trustee, benefactor Met. Mus. Art, N.Y.C., mem. vis. com. dept. 20th Century Art, mem. acquisitions com., 1981—, mem. decorative arts com., 1989; also Costume Inst. Dir., 20th Century Painting and Sculpture Com., Art Inst. Chgo., 1955-80, governing mem. inst., 1955—, major benefactor, 1979—; pioneer collector Am. abstract expressionist art, 1949—, major show of collection, Met. Mus. Art, N.Y.C., 1981, also show of personal collection of costumes and jewelry, 1981. Bd. govs. Landmarks Preservation Council, Chgo., 1966-78; mem. woman's bd. U. Chgo., 1960-81, Art Inst. Chgo., 1953—; trustee Mus. Contemporary Art, 1970—, benefactor, 1970—; trustee Chgo. Sch. of architecture Found., 1971—, Archives Am. Art, 1976—; mem. bd. Bright New City Urban Affairs Lecture Series, 1966—. Recipient Scroll Recognition of Public Service U.S. Dept. State, 1958. Mem. Antiquarian Soc. of Art Inst. Chgo., Chgo. Hist. Soc. (mem. guild 1958—). Clubs: Arts (Chgo.), Casino (Chgo.).

NEWMAN, NANCY MARILYN, ophthalmologist, educator, consultant, inventor, entrepreneur; b. San Francisco, Mar. 16, 1941. BA in Psychology magna cum laude, Stanford U., 1962, MD, 1967. Diplomate Am. Bd. Ophthalmology. NIH trainee neurophysiology Inst. Visual Scis., San Francisco, 1964-65; clin. clk. Nat. Hosp. for Nervous and Mental Disease, London, 1966-67; intern Mount Auburn Hosp., Cambridge, Mass., 1967-68; NIH trainee neuro-ophthalmology, from jr. asst. resident to sr. asst. resident to assoc. resident dept. ophthalmology sch. medicine Washington U., St. Louis, 1968-71; NIH spl. fellow in neuro-ophthalmology depts. ophthalmology and neurol. surgery sch. medicine U. Calif., San Francisco, 1971-72, clin. asst. prof. ophthalmology sch. medicine, 1972; asst. prof., chief divsn. neuro-ophthalmology Pacific Med. Ctr., San Francisco, 1972-73, assoc. prof., chief, 1973-88; physician, cons. dept. neurology sch. medicine U. Calif., VA Med. Ctr., Martinez, Calif., 1978—; prof. dept. spl. edn. Calif. State U., San Francisco, 1974-79; vis. prof. Centre Nat. D'Ophtalmologie des Quinze-Vingts, Paris, 1980; clin. assoc. prof. sch. optometry U. Calif., Berkeley, 1990—; bd. dirs., adv. bd. Frank B. Walsh Soc., 1974-91, Rose Resnick Ctr. for the Blind and Handicapped, 1988-92, Fifer St. Fitness, Larkspur, 1990-92; Internat. Soc. for Orbital Disorders, 1983—, North Calif. Soc. Prevention of Blindness, 1978-88, North African Ctr. for Sight, Tunis, Tunisia, 1988—; pres., CEO Minerva Medica; cons. in field. Author: Eye Movement Disorders; Neuro-ophthalmology: A Practical Text, 1992; mem. editoral bd. Jour. of Clin. Neuro-ophthalmology, Am. Jour. Opthalmology, 1980-92, Soc. Francaise d'Ophtalmogie, Ophthalmology Practice, 1993—; contbr. numerous articles to profl. jours. Recipient NSPI award Self Instrnl. Materials Ophthalmology, Merit award Internat. Eye Found., fellow 1971; Smith-Kettlewell Inst. Vis. Scis. fellow, 1971-72. Mem. AMA (leader Calif. del. continuing med. edn. 1982, 83), San Francisco Med. Soc., Calif. Med. Assn. (sub com. med. policy coms. 1984—, chair com. on accreditation continuing med. edn. 1981-88, chair quality care rev. commn. 1984), Assn. for Rsch. in Vision and Ophthalmology, Pan Am. Assn. of Ophthalmology, Soc. of Heed Fellows, Pacific Coast Oto-Ophthalmology Soc., Lane Medical Soc. (v.p. 1975-76), Internat. Soc. of Neuro-Ophthalmology (founder), Cordes Soc., Am. Soc. Ophthalmic Ultrasound (charter), Orbital Soc. (founder), West Bay Health Systems Agy., Oxford Opthalmology Soc., Pacific Physician Assocs., Soc. Francaise D'Ophtalmologie (mem. editorial bd. jour.). Home: 819 Spring Dr Mill Valley CA 94941-3924

NEWMAN, PAMELA JEAN, home school provider; b. Phila., Feb. 19, 1951; d. James Henry and Marion Reta (McGee) N.; (div.); 1 child, Pamela Jean Newman. Student, U. Pa., 1968. Home sch. supr. Phila., 1983-95, home sch. provider, 1992—; adult literacy tutor, Phila. Ctr. for Literacy, 1986. Vol., site dir. Girl Scouts of Greater Phila., 1989—, troop leader, 1986—; bd. dirs. Oak Tree Health Plan, Phila., 1994—. Recipient award of appreciation Young Great Soc., 1968.

NEWMAN, PATRICIA ANNE, nurse anesthesia educator; b. New Orleans, Aug. 25, 1941; d. Merwyn James and Yvonne Louise (Cannon) Woodson; m. Robert Charles Newman Sr., Dec. 9, 1967 (div. Dec. 1975); 1 child, Robert Charles Jr. Diploma in nursing, Mercy Hosp., New Orleans, 1961; cert. in nurse anesthesia, Charity Hosp., New Orleans, 1963; BA in Health Care, Edn., Ottawa U., 1978; MS in Nurse Anesthesiology, Xavier U., 1992. Cert. RN anesthetist. Staff nurse anesthetist Hotel Dieu Hosp., New Orleans, 1963-70, Oschsner Found. Hosp., New Orleans, 1970-71, Houston Anesthesia Assocs., 1976-81, East Jefferson Hosp., Metairie, La., 1971-76; staff nurse anesthetist, chief nurse anesthetist Stamford (Conn.) Anesthesia Assocs., 1981-91; instr. clin. anesthesia Charity Hosp./Xavier U. Sch. Nurse Anesthesiology, New Orleans, 1991—; adj. instr. in grad. sch. Xavier U., New Orleans, 1992—. Mem. Coun. for Pub. Interest in Anesthesia (chair 1991-92), Am. Assn. Nurse Anesthetists (mgmt. com. 1991-92, nominating com. 1988-89, minutes com. 1985-86, 92-93, pub. rels. com. 1995-96), La. Assn. Nurse Anesthetists (pub. rels. com. 1992, bd. dirs. 1994-95, chmn. govt. rels. com. 1994-95, 95-96, v.p. 1995-96, acting pres. 1995-96, editor LANASCOPE 1995-96), Conn. Assn. Nurse Anesthetists (pres., v.p., various chairs coms.). Roman Catholic. Home: 4007 Saint Elizabeth Dr Kenner LA 70065-1642 Office: Xavier U Charity Hosp Sch Nurse Anesthesiology 1532 Tulane Ave New Orleans LA 70112-2802

NEWMAN, PAULINE, federal judge; b. N.Y.C., N.Y., June 20, 1927; d. Maxwell Henry and Rosella N. B.A., Vassar Coll., 1947; M.A., Columbia U., 1948; Ph.D., Yale U., 1952; LL.B., NYU, 1958. Bar: N.Y. 1958, U.S. Supreme Ct. 1972, U.S. Ct. Customs and Patent Appeals 1978, Pa. 1979, U.S. Ct. Appeals (3d cir.) 1981, U.S. Ct. Appeals (fed. cir.) 1982. Research chemist Am. Cyanamid Co., Bound Brook, N.J., 1951-54; mem. patent staff FMC Corp., N.Y.C., 1954-75; mem. patent staff FMC Corp., Phila., 1975-84, dir. dept. patent and licensing, 1969-84; judge U.S. Ct. Appeals (fed. cir.), Washington, 1984—; bd. dir. Research Corp., 1982-84; program specialist Dept. Natural Scis. UNESCO, Paris, 1961-62; mem. State Dept. Adv. Com. on Internat. Indsl. Property, 1974-84; lectr. in field. Contbr. articles to profl. jours. Bd. dirs. Med. Coll. Pa., 1975-84, Midgard Found., 1973-84; trustee Phila. Coll. Pharmacy and Sci., 1983-84. Mem. ABA (council sect. patent trademark and copyright 1983-84), Am. Patent Law Assn. (bd. dirs. 1981-84), U.S. Trademark Assn. (bd. dirs. 1975-79, v.p. 1978-79), Am. Chem. Soc. (bd. dirs. 1972-81), Am. Inst. Chemists (bd. dirs. 1960-66, 70-76), Pacific Indsl. Property Assn. (pres. 1979-80). Clubs: Vassar, Yale. Office: US Ct Appeals Nat Cts Bldg 717 Madison Pl NW Washington DC 20439-0001*

NEWMAN, RACHEL, magazine editor; b. Malden, Mass., May 1, 1938; d. Maurice and Edythe Brenda (Tichell) N.; m. Herbert Bleiweiss, Apr. 6, 1973 (div. Apr. 1989). BA, Pa. State U., 1960; cert., N.Y. Sch. Interior Design, 1963. Accessories editor Women's Wear Daily, N.Y.C., 1964-65; designer, publicist Grandoe Glove Corp., N.Y.C., 1965-67; assoc. editor McCall's Sportswear and Dress Merchandiser mag., N.Y.C., 1967; mng. editor McCall's You-Do-It Home Decorating, 1968-70, Ladies Home Jour. Needle and Craft mag., N.Y.C., 1970-72; editor-in-chief Am. Home Crafts mag., N.Y.C., 1972-77; fashion dir. Good Housekeeping mag., N.Y.C., 1977-78, home bldg. and decorating dir., 1978-82; editor-in-chief Country Living mag., N.Y.C., 1978—; founding editor Country Cooking mag., 1985—, Dream Homes mag., 1989—, Country Kitchens mag., 1990—, Country Living Gardener Mag., 1993—, Healthy Living mag., 1996—. Pa. State U. Alumni fellow, 1986; recipient Cir. of Excellence award IFDA, 1992, YMCA Hall of Fame, 1992; named Disting. Alumni Pa. State U., 1988. Mem. N.Y. Fashion Group, Nat. Home Fashions League, Am. Soc. Interior Designers, Am. Soc. Mag. Editors. Office: Country Living 224 W 57th St New York NY 10019-3212

NEWMAN, RUTH TANTLINGER, artist; b. Hooker, Okla., May 28, 1910; d. Walter Warren and Jean Louise (Hayward) Tantlinger; m. John Vincent Newman; children: Peter Vincent, Michael John. Student, Pomona Coll; BFA, UCLA, 1932; postgrad., Instituto Allende, U. Guanajuato, Mex. Art tchr. Santa Ana (Calif.) Schs., 1933-34, Santa Ana Adult Edn., 1934-40; watercolor tchr. Ventura (Calif.) Recreation Ctr., 1941-50; pvt. tchr. watercolor Calif., 1950-85. One-woman shows include Ventura County Mus. History and Art, 1993, Santa Barbara Art Assn., Ojai Art Ctr., Ventura Art Club, Oxnard (Calif.) Art Club, Art Club of Westlake Village, Thousand Oaks (Calif.) Art Club, others; commd. to paint 12 Calif. Missions, 1958, watercolors at San Juan Bautista Retreat House, Calif., oils at Ch. of San Bernardino, Mallorca, Spain; book featuring reproductions of selected works, Ruth Newman: A Lifetime of Art, introduced at her solo show in Ventura Mus., 1993. Mem. Westlake Village Art Guild, Thousand Oaks Art Club, Buena Ventura Art Club (charter). Home: 32120 Oakshore Dr Westlake Village CA 91361

NEWMAN, SANDRA SCHULTZ, judge. Grad., Drexel U., Temple U., Villanova U.; hon. doctorate, Gannon U., 1996, Widener U., 1996. Asst. dist. atty. Montgomery County, Pa.; pvt. practice; judge Commonwealth Ct. of Pa., 1993-95; justice Supreme Ct. of Pa., 1995—; chairperson bd. consultors Villanova U. Law Sch.; mem. adv. bd. U. Pa. Biddle Law Libr., Drexel U. Coll. Bus. and Adminstrn.; lectr. in field. Author: Alimony, Child Support and Counsel Fees, 1988; contbr. articles to profl. jours. Recipient Phila. award for Super Achiever Pediatric Juvenile Colitis Found. Jefferson Med. Coll. and Hosp., 1979, award for Dedicated Leadership and Outstanding Contbns. to the Cmty. and Law Employment Police Chiefs Assn. of Southeastern Pa., Drexel 100 award, 1993, Medallion of Achievement award Villanova U., 1993, Susan B. Anthony award Women's Bar Assn. Western Pa., 1996, award Justinian Soc., 1996, award Tau Epsilon Law Soc., 1996; honored by Women of Greater Phila., 1996; named Disting. Daughter of Pa. Office: Supreme Ct Pa 100 Four Falls Corporate Ctr Ste 400 West Conshohocken PA 19428*

NEWMAN, SHARON LYNN, elementary education educator; b. Lewisburg, Tenn., Jan. 9, 1946; d. Hermit Taft and Martha Elizabeth (Pardue) Simmons; m. George Wynne Newman Sr., June 11, 1967; 1 child, George Wynne Jr. BS in Edn., Athens State Coll., 1979. Substitute tchr. Giles County Bd. Edn., Pulaski, Tenn., 1979-81; chpt. 1 reading tchr. Giles County Bd. Edn., Pulaski, 1981-91, chpt. 1 math. tchr., 1991—; chpt. 1 coord. Elkton (Tenn.) Elem. Sch., 1989—, mem. steering com., 1989—, chair math. dept., 1993-95, chpt. title I com., 1995—, mem. disaster preparedness team. Ch. libr. Elkton (Tenn.) Bapt. Ch., 1992—; vol. Giles County Hist. Soc. Libr. and Mus., 1995—. Mem. NEA, Nat. Coun. Tchrs. Math., Giles County Edn. Assn. (rsch. chairperson 1993-95). Home: 1758 Old Stage Rd Ardmore TN 38449 Office: Elkton Elem Sch Elkton TN 38455

NEWMAN, SUZANNE DINKES, advertising agency executive; b. Bklyn., Apr. 28, 1949; d. Philip and Natalie (Hollander) Dinkes; m. Ralph Michael Newman, Mar. 9, 1975. Student, Cooper Union, 1967-71, Sch. Visual Arts, N.Y.C., 1971-72. Asst. art dir. Lincoln Ctr. Programs, N.Y.C., 1973-74; art dir. BimBamBoom Mag., Yonkers, N.Y., 1974, Fairfax Advt., N.Y.C., 1974-75; dir. ops. TBE Advt., Yonkers, 1975-87, CEO, 1987-94; art dir. Time Barrier Express, Yonkers, 1975-80; CEO R.S. Newman & Assocs., Yonkers, 1994—; concert coord. Classic Harmony Prodns., N.Y.C., 1975; spl. event planner The Left Bank, Mount Vernon, N.Y., 1980-81; spl. event cons. Glen Island Casino, New Rochelle, N.Y., 1984-85; event coord., Top Brass, Yonkers, 1986-87; art dir., cons. various music publs., 1974-80. Mem. Yonkers Citizen's Adv. Group, Yonkers Mayorial Transition Com., 1991-92, Alliance Devel. Com., Yonkers Sch. and Bus. Alliance, 1991—, program com., 1991—; mem. Yonkers Coun. Pres.'s Citizens Adv. group, 1992—, Yonkers Dem. Com., dist. leader, 1991-93; jour. chair gala com. Hudson River Mus., 1992; mem. Yonkers Local Bus. Adv. Coun., 1992-94; mem. Yonkers Pvt. Industry Coun., 1992-94, sec. 1993-94; promotion chair Yonkers Hudson Riverfest, 1992-93; bus. adv. com. Yonkers Econ. Devel. Zone, 1993-94; active Yonkers Waterfront Task Force, 1993-94; bd. dirs. Youth Theater Interaction, 1994—; bd. dirs. Westchester divsn. Jewish Guild for Blind, 1994—, gala chair, 1994; events coord. Mayor's Inaugural Ball, 1996. Editor: Rockin' in the Fourth Estate, 1979-80. Art dir.: White and Still All Right!, 1977, Sun Records, 1980, The Buddy Holly Story, 1979. Recipient Disting. Leadership and Svc. award Westchester County C. of C., 1985, Westchester award, Westchester Small Bus. Coun., 1989. Mem. Westchester Small Bus. Coun. (comms. chmn. 1984-85, Westchester winner 1989), Westchester Assn. Women Bus. Owners, Am. Women Entrepreneurs, Yonkers C. of C. (bd. dirs. 1996—), Coun. for Arts Westchester. Democrat. Jewish. Avocations: reading; antiques; gardening. Office: RS Newman & Assocs 72 Highview Ter Yonkers NY 10705-2732

NEWMAN, WENDY SUE, photographer; b. Detroit, Jan. 7, 1956; d. Raphael John and Frances Eugene (Wilson) Cheatham; m. Stephen Alan Newman, Oct. 17, 1986; children: Rachel, William Stephen. AA in Fine Arts Fashion, Internat. Fine Arts Sch., Miami, 1975; AA in Fashion Design, Miami-Dade C.C., 1977. Owner, founder Modeling Connection, Ft. Myers, Gainesville; owner, founder Modeling Connection, Naples, Fla., 1978-87, cons., 1984-89; cons. Modeling Connection, Gainesville, 1985-89; owner, mgr. Newman Photography, Ft. Myers, 1988—. Active Abuse Counseling Treatment, Ft. Myers, Gabrielle House, Ft. Myers. Named Boss of Yr., Working Women's Assn. Lee County, 1982, Sch. Dir. of Yr., Face Finders Internat., 1985; recipient grand prize for black and white photograph Best of Fla. Mem. Lee County Photographers Assn. (pres. 1994-95). Lutheran. Home: 15660 Lightblue Cir Fort Myers FL 33908

NEWNAM, PHYLLIS SUE See SAND, PHYLLIS SUE NEWNAM

NEWPORT, L. JOAN, clinical social worker, psychotherapist; b. Ponca City, Okla., July 5, 1932; d. Crawford Earl and Lillian Pearl (Peden) Irvine; m. Don E. Newport, July 9, 1954 (div. July 1971); children: Alan Keith, Lili Kim. BA cum laude, Wichita State U., 1955; MSW, U. Okla., 1977. Bd. cert. diplomate in clin. social work Acad. Cert. Social Workers; lic. social worker, Okla. Dir. children's work Wesley United Meth. Ch., Oklahoma City, 1969-71; social worker Dept. Human Svcs., Newkirk, Okla., 1972-77; in-sch. suspension counselor Kay County Youth Svcs., Ponca City, Okla., 1977; med. social worker St. Joseph Med. Ctr., Ponca City, 1977-78, dir. social work, 1978-83; pvt. practice Ponca City, 1979—; med. social worker Healthcare Svcs., Ponca City, 1983-84; cons. Blackwell, Perry, Pawhuska, O'Keene Hosps., 1978-85; cons. social work Bass Meml. Hosp., Enid, Okla., 1985; sponsor, organizer Kay County Parents Anonymous, Ponca City, 1976-83; vice chair Okla. State Bd. Lic. Social Workers, Oklahoma City, 1988-90; presentor, lectr. in field; supr. students Okla. U. Sch. Social Work. Mem. Okla. Women's Network, 1989—; mem. adv. bd. Displaced Homemakers, Ponca City, 1985-89; mem. adv. bd. Kay County Home Health, 1979-83, chair, 1979-81. Named Hon. State Life Mem. Burbank PTA, Oklahoma City, 1971; scholar Wichita (Kans.) Press and Radio Women, 1953, Conoco, Inc., Houston, 1951-54. Mem. NASW (Okla. del. Del. Assembly Washington 1987, chmn. vendorship com. 1985-87, pres. Okla. chpt. 1988-90, Social Worker of Yr. 1987), Child Abuse Prevention Task Force (pres. dist. 17 1986-88, mem. grant evaluation com. 1986-96), Zeta Phi Eta. Democrat. Methodist. Home: 109 N Walnut Ave Newkirk OK 74647-2036 Office: 619 E Brookfield Ave Ponca City OK 74601-2804

NEWS, KATHRYN ANNE, editor, educator, writer; b. McPherson County, Kans., Mar. 16, 1934; d. Henry J. and Mary J. (Kauffman) Goering; m. Albert D. Klassen Jr. (div. June 1976); children: Teresa C., Jean A., Eric P., Rachel S.; m. Francis W. News, Mar. 4, 1982. Student, Bethel Coll., 1952-54, Washburn U., 1964-67; BA, Roosevelt U., 1968; MA, Ind. U., 1971. Assoc. editor Holiday mag. Curtis Pub. Co., Indpls., 1973-74, mng. editor, 1974-77; travel page cons. Sat. Evening Post, 1976-77, Country Gentleman, 1976-77; editor Going Places mag. Chilton Publs., Radnor, Pa., 1977-79; mng. editor Réalités mag., 1979-81, Spring mag. Rodale Press, 1981-82; assoc. prof. communications Temple U., Phila., 1982—. Author: Great Escapes: An Executive's Guide to Fine Resorts, 1980. Recipient cert. of merit Atlantic Monthy, 1958; 1st Place Fellowship award Ind. U. Writers Conf., 1970, Golden Basset award, 1973, Chilton Editorial award, 1978. Office: Temple U Dept Journalism Philadelphia PA 19122

NEWSOM, CAROLYN CARDALL, management consultant; b. South Weymouth, Mass., Feb. 27, 1941; d. Alfred James and Bertha Virginia (Roy) Cardall; m. John Harlan Newsom, Feb. 4, 1967; children: John Cardall, James Harlan. AB, Brown U., 1962; MBA, Wharton Sch., 1978; PhD, U. Pa., 1985. Systems engr. IBM, Seattle, 1964-70, Newsom S.E. Services, Seattle, 1970-76; instr. U. Pa. Wharton Sch., Phila., 1978-81; v.p., prin. sr. cons. PA Cons. Group, Princeton, N.J., 1981-88; pres. Newsom Assocs., Yardley, Pa., 1988; ptnr. Bus. Strategy Implementation, Princeton, N.J., 1989-90; pres. Strategy Implementation Solutions, Yardley, Pa., 1990—; examiner N.J. Quality Achievement Award, 1993-94, sr. examiner, 1995-96. Trustee St. Mary Hosp., Langhorne, Pa., 1986-94; bd. dirs. Chandler Hall. Mem. AAUW, Acad. Mgmt., Am. Mgmt. Assn., Am. Soc. for Quality Control, Am. Bus. Women's Assn., Brown Alumni Assn. (pres.-elect 1993-95, pres. 1995-97), Quality N.J. Office: Strategy Implementation Solutions 1588 Woodside Rd Yardley PA 19067-2611

NEWSOM, DOUGLAS ANN JOHNSON, author, journalism educator; b. Dallas, Jan. 16, 1934; d. J. Douglas and R. Grace (Dickson) Johnson; m. L. Mack Newsom, Jr., Oct. 27, 1956 (dec.); children: Michael Douglas, Kevin Jackson, Nancy Elizabeth, William Macklemore; m. Bob J. Carrell, 1993. BJ cum laude, U. Tex., 1954, BFA summa cum laude, 1955, M in Journalism 1956, PhD, 1978. Gen. publicity State Fair Tex., 1955; advt. and promotion Newsom's Women's Wear, 1956-57; publicist Auto Market Show, 1961; lab. instr. radio-tv news-writing course U. Tex., 1961-62; local publicist Tex. Boys Choir, 1964-69, nat. publicist, 1967-69; pub. rels. dir. Gt. S.W. Boat Show Dallas, 1966-72, Family Fun Show, 1970-71, Horace Ainsworth Co., Dallas, 1966-76; pres. Profl. Devel. Cons., Inc., 1976-89; faculty Tex. Christian U., Ft. Worth, 1969—, prof. dept. journalism, chmn. dept., 1979-86, adviser yearbook and mag., 1969-79; dir. ONEOK Inc., diversified energy co., 1980—; Fulbright lectr. in India, 1988. Author: (with Alan Scott) This is PR, 1976, 3d edit., 1984, (with Alan Scott and Judy Van Slyke Turk) 4th edit., 1989, 6th edit., 1995, (with Judy Van Slyke Turk and Dean Kruckeberg), 1996, (with Bob Carrell) Writing for Public Relations Practice, 4th edit., 1994, (with Jim Wollert) Media Writing, 1984, 2d edit., 1988; editor (with Carrell) Silent Voices, 1995; mem. editorial bd. Pub. Rels. Rev., 1978—. Sec.-treas. Pub. Rels. Found. Tex., 1979-80, also trustee; pub. rels. chmn. local Am. Heart Assn., 1973-76, state pub. rels. com. 1974-82, chmn., 1980-82; trustee Inst. for Pub. Rels. Rsch. and Edn., 1985-89; mem. Gas Rsch. Adv. Coun., 1981—. Fellow Pub. Rels. Soc. Am. (chmn. Coll. Fellows 1992, nat. edn. com. 1975, chmn. 1978, nat. faculty adviser, chmn. edn. sect.); mem. Assn. Edn. in Journalism and Mass Communication (pres. pub. rels. div. 1974-75, nat. pres. 1984-85), Women in Communications (nat. conv. treas. 1967, nat. pub. rels. chmn. 1969-71), Tex. Pub. Rels. Assn. (dir. 1976-84, v.p. 1980-82, pres. 1982-83), Mortar Bd. Alumnae (adviser Tex. Christian U. 1974-75), Phi Kappa Phi, Kappa Tau Alpha, Phi Beta Delta. Episcopalian. Home: 4237 Shannon Dr Fort Worth TX 76116-8043 Office: Tex Christian U Dept Journalism PO Box 298060 Fort Worth TX 76129

NEWSOME, SANDRA SINGLETON, elementary education educator, assistant principal; b. Bayboro, N.C., Apr. 4, 1948; d. John Wilson Singleton and Cora Lee (Beasley) Hatchel; m. Edward Newsome Jr., Feb. 14, 1971. BS, Elizabeth City State U., 1970; MS, Bowie State U., 1979; EdD, Pensacola Christian Coll., 1992. Cert. tchr., Washington. Tchr. D.C. Pub. Schs., Washington, 1970-80, reading tchr., 1980-82, reading specialist, 1982—; asst. prin. Calvary Temple Christian Sch., Sterling, Va., 1985-86; prof. Bowie State U., 1994—; adminstrv. intern Roper Mid. Sch. of Math. Sci. and Tech., Washington, 1993-95; cons. Bowie State Spl. Interest Coun., 1991-92, D.C.-Dakar Friendship Coun., 1991-92; mem. adv. bd. Walk In Faith mag., Washington, 1991-92; dir. Acad. Tutorial Program, Temple Hills, Md., 1990-91. Contbr. to profl. publs. Mentor Teen Parenting, Inc., Hyattville, Md., 1989, Valuettes, Washington, 1990-92; dir. Adult Literacy Coun., Temple Hills, 1990; asst. dir. Jr. Toastmasters, Brightwood, 1993; program developer, dir. Visions: A Tour into Values, Washington, 1993; pres. Hellen Lee Dr. Civic Assn., Clinton, 1994-95; dir. Christian Edn., Alexandria (Va.) Christian Ctr., 1994—. Recipient Save Our Youth Am. award Soya, Inc., Washington, 1989, Literacy award Bowie State U., 1991; Teacher-to-Teacher grantee, 1990-92; fellow Cafritz Found., 1991. Mem. ASCD, AFT, AAUW, LEAD Program, Nat. Black Child Devel. Inst., Bowie State Spl. Interest Orgn., Alexandria Christian Ctr., Hellen Lee Dr. Civic Assn. (pres. 1994-95). Home: 2319 Parkside Dr Mitchellville MD 20721 Office: Roper Mid Sch Math Sci Tech 4800 Meade St NE Washington DC 20019

NEWTON, ESTHER, anthropologist, educator; b. N.Y.C., Nov. 28, 1940; d. Saul B. and Virginia N. BA, U. Mich., 1962; MA, U. Chgo., 1964, PhD, 1968. Asst. prof. CUNY, Queens, 1968-71; from asst. prof. to assoc. prof. anthropology SUNY, Purchase, 1971-92, prof. anthropology, 1992—; coord. women's studies program SUNY, Purchase, 1984-86; vis. prof. Yale Univ., 1970, Univ. Amsterdam, 1993; affiliated scholar CUNY, 1992-93; scholar in residence U. Calif., Santa Cruz, 1993; curator exhbn. Gay and Lesbian Cmty. Svcs. Ctr., 1993. Author: Mother Camp: Female Impersonators in America, 1972, reprinted with new introduction, 1979, Cherry Grove, Fire Island: Sixty years in America's First Gay and Lesbian Town, 1993; co-author: (with Shirley Walton) Womanfriends, 1976; contbr. to anthologies including The Lesbian Issue: Essays from Sign, 1985, Hidden from History: Reclaiming the Gay and Lesbian Past, 1989, International Gay Studies: The Amsterdam Conference, 1994, History of Homosexuality in Europe and America, 1994, Writing Lesbian and Gay Culture, 1995; mem. editl. bd. The Cutting Edge: Lesbian Life and Literature Series, Between men, Between Women: Lesbian and Gay Studies Series, GLQ: Jour. of Queer Studies, Jour. of Homosexuality, Jour. Sexuality in History; contbr. to books including Amazon Expedition, 1973, Anthropology and American Life, 1974, Symbolic Anthropology: A Reader in the Study of Symbols and Meaning, 1977, Strategies des femmes, 1984, Pleasure and Danger: Exploring Female Sexuality, 1984, Homosexuality, Which Homosexuality? Vol. 2, 1987, The Lesbian and Gay Studies Reader, 1993; contbr. articles to mags. and jours. La Verne Noyes scholar U. Chgo., 1962-63; training grantee NIH, 1963-65, faculty support grantee SUNY, Purchase, 1987, 92; pre-doctoral fellow NIMH, 1965-67; recipient experienced faculty travel award SUNY, 1987, 91. Mem. Am. Anthrop. Assn. (cochair commn. lesbian and gay issues, 1994-96). Office: Divsn Social Sci SUNY Purchase NY 10577*

NEWTON, LEILANI L., bank executive. BA, U. Wis.; MA, U. Mich. Credit mgr. for Austria and Ea. Europe Dow Chemical, Vienna, 1971-73; computer programmer Export-Import Bank of the U.S., 1973-77, asst. to the treas.-contr., 1977-90; mgr., v.p. Credit Adminstrn., 1990—. Mem. Women in Internat. Trade, Profl. Banker's Assn. Office: Export Import Bank of the US 811 Vermont Ave NW Washington DC 20571-0001

NEWTON, LISA HAENLEIN, philosophy educator; b. Orange, N.J., Sept. 17, 1939; d. Wallen Joseph and Carol Bigelow (Cypiot) Haenlein; m. Victor Joseph Newton, June 3, 1972; children: Tracey, Kit, Cynthia Perkins, Daniel Perkins, Laura Perkins. Student, Swarthmore Coll., 1957-59; BS in Philosophy with honors, Columbia U., 1962, PhD, 1967. Asst. prof. philosophy Hofstra U., Hempstead, N.Y., 1967-69; asst. prof. philosophy Fairfield U., Conn., 1969-73, assoc. prof., 1973-78, prof., 1978—, dir. program in applied ethics, 1983—, dir. program in environ. studies, 1986—; lectr. in medicine Yale U., 1984—; lectr., cons. in field. Author: Ethics in America; co-author: Watersheds, 1994, Wake-Up Calls, 1996; co-editor: Taking Sides: Controversial Issues Business Ethics, 4th edit., 1996; contbr.a rticles to profl. jours. Mem. exec. bd. Conn. Humanities Council, 1979-83. Mem. Am. Soc. Value Inquiry (past pres.), Am. Philos. Assn., Am. Soc. Polit. and Legal Philosophy, Acad. Mgmt., Am. Soc. Law and Medicine, Soc. Bus. Ethics (past pres.), Phi Beta Kappa. Home: 4042 Congress St Fairfield CT 06430-2041 Office: Fairfield U Dept Philosophy Fairfield CT 06430-7524

NEWTON, RHONWEN LEONARD, writer, microcomputer consultant; b. Lexington, N.C., Nov. 13, 1940; d. Jacob Calvin and Mary Louise (Moffitt) Leonard; children: Blair Armistead, Newton Jones, Allison Page, William Brockenbrough III. AB, Duke U., 1962; MS in Edn., Old Dominion U., 1968. French tchr. Hampton (Va.) Pub. Schs., 1962-65, Va. Beach (Va.) Pub. Schs., 1965-66; instr. foreign lang. various colls. and univs., 1967-75; foreign lang. cons. Portsmouth (Va.) Pub. Schs., 1973-75; dir. The Computer Inst., Inc., Columbia, S.C., 1983; pres., founder The Computer Experience, Inc., Columbia, 1983-88, RN Enterprises, Columbia, 1991—. Author: WordPerfect, 1988, All About Computers, 1989, Microsoft Excel for the Mac, 1989, Introduction to the Mac, 1989, Introduction to DOS, 1989, Introduction to Lotus 1-2-3, 1989, Advanced Lotus 1-2-3, 1989, Introduction to WordPerfect, 1989, Advanced WordPerfect, 1989, Introduction to Display/Write 4, 1989, WordPerfect for the Mac, 1989, Introduction to Microsoft Works for the Mac, 1990, Accountant, Inc for the Mac, 1992, Introduction to Filemaker Pro, 1992, Quicken for the MAC, 1993, Quicken for Windows, 1993, WordPerfect for Windows, 1993, Advanced WordPerfect for Windows, 1993, Lotus 1-2-3 for Windows, 1993, Introduction to Quick Books, 1994, Quick Book for Windows, 1994, Introduction to Word for Windows, 1995. Mem. Columbia Planning Commn., 1980-87; bd. dirs. United Way Midlands, Columbia, 1983-86; bd. dirs. Assn. Jr. Leagues, N.Y.C., 1980-82; trustee Heathwood Hall Episcopal Sch., Columbia, 1979-85. Republican. Episcopalian. Home and Office: 1635 Kathwood Dr Columbia SC 29206-4509

NEWTON, VIRGINIA, archivist, historian, librarian; b. Walters, Okla., Oct. 5, 1938; d. John Walter and Reba Catherine (Mawdsley) N.; m. Gary J. Mounce, Dec. 27, 1963 (div. 1982). Student, Inst. Tecnológico y de Estudios Superiores de Monterrey, Nuevo Leon, Mex., 1957; AA in Bus. Adminstrn., Stephens Coll., 1958; BA in History, Okla. State U., 1960; M of Librarianship, U. Wash., 1963; cert. in libr. sci., U. Tex., 1968, MA in History Archives and Libr. Sci., 1975, PhD in History, Archives and Libr. Sci., 1983. Libr. Inst. Pub. Affairs U. Tex., Austin, 1963-65, libr. Art Libr., 1965-67; coord. Sr. Community Svcs. Program Econ. Opportunities Devel. Corp., San Antonio, 1968-69; archivist, spl. collections libr. Trinity U., San Antonio, 1969-73; spl. collections and reference libr. Pan Am. U., Edinburg, Tex., 1974-77; archivist, records analyst Alaska State Archives and Records Svc., 1983-84, dep. state archivist, 1984-87; state archivist Alaska State Archives & Records Mgmt. Svcs., 1988-93; dir. Columbus Meml. Libr. OAS, Washington, 1993—; archives cons. Ford Found. for Brazilian Archivists Assn., 1976, Soc. for Ibero-Latin Thought, 1980, Project for a Notarial Archives Computerized Guide, 1980; reviewer grant proposal NEH, 1978—; chair Alaska State Hist. Records Adv. Bd., 1988-93, coords. steering com., 1991-93. Author: An Archivists' Guide to the Catholic Church in Mexico, 1979; contbr. articles to profl. publs. founder jail libr. Bexar County Jail, San Antonio; hon. dep. sheriff Bexar County, 1972-75; mem. Dem. party; chair Dems. Abroad in Mex., 1979-81; mem. Dems. Abroad Del. The Dem. Nat. Conv., N.Y., 1980; vice- chair Bill Egan Forum Greater Juneau Dem. Precinct, 1986-88. Recipient Commendation award Gov. of Alaska William Sheffield, 1985, Masonic Scholarship for internat. rels. George Washington U., 1960-61; univ. fellow U. Tex.-Austin, 1982-83, post masters fellow U.S. Dept. Edn.-U. Tex., Austin, 1967-68; scholar Orgn. Am. States, 1980, 81, Fulbright-Hays scholar, 1979, 80, scholar Nat. Def. Fgn. Lang.-U. Tex., Austin, 1978-79, scholar Calif. State Libr., 1962-63. Mem. AAUW (bd. dirs. 1983-86, scholar 1983), Nat. Assn. Govt. Archives and Records Adminstrs. (bd. dirs. 1989-93, chair membership com. 1989-93), Alaska Hist. Soc. (bd. treas. 1988-94), Alaska Libr. Assn., Acad. Cert. Archivists (cert. 1989), Rotary, Phi Kappa Phi. Democrat. Unitarian. Home: 2801 Park Center Dr # A909 Alexandria VA 22302-1431 Office: Columbus Meml Libr OAS 19th & Constitution Ave NW Washington DC 20006-4499

NEZU, CHRISTINE MAGUTH, clinical psychologist, educator; b. Passaic, N.J., June 18, 1952; d. Frank Joseph and Alice Anna (Hingstmann) Maguth; m. Arthur Maguth Nezu, June 12, 1983; children: Frank, Alice, Linda. BA, Fairleigh Dickingson U., Rutherford, N.J., 1977; MA, Fairleigh Dickingson U., Teaneck, N.J., 1981, PhD, 1987. Lic. psychologist, N.Y., N.J., Pa. Psychology intern Beth Israel Med. Ctr., N.Y.C., 1985-86; coord. rsch. and clin. supervision Project NSTM, Fairleigh Dickinson U., Teaneck, 1986-87; clin. asst. prof. and supervising psychologist Beth Israel Med. Ctr., Mt. Sinai Sch. Medicine, N.Y.C., 1987-89; asst. prof. Med. Coll. of Pa. and Hahnemann U., Phila., 1989-93, assoc. prof., 1993—, dir. intern tng., 1989-94, assoc. dean for rsch. Sch. of Health Scis. and Humanities, 1995—. Co-author: Problem Solving Therapy, 1989; co-editor Clinical Decision-Making, 1989, Psychotherapy of Persons with Mental Retardation: Clinical Guidelines for Assessment and Treatment, 1992; contbr. articles to profl. jours. Mem. Phila. Mus. of Art, Mus. of the U. of Pa.; vol. Winter Shelter Program for the Homeless, Phila., 1991—. Recipient Bd. Trustees fellowship award Fairleigh Dickinson U., 1985, rsch. fellowships, 1983-86. Fellow Pa. Psychol. Assn.; mem. Am. Psychol. Assn., Am. Assn. on Mental Retardation, Assn. for the Advancement of Behavior Therapy (chair com. on acad. tng. 1990-93, coord. acad. and profl. issues 1993—). Lutheran. Home: 2426 Fitlers Walk Philadelphia PA 19103-5562 Office: Hahnemann U Broad And Pine St Philadelphia PA 19102-5087

NG, HELEN M., financier, civil engineer; b. Santa Ana, Calif., July 27, 1965; d. Steve K. and Evelyna H. (Hung) N. AB in Internat. Rels., BS in Civil Engring., Stanford (Calif.) U., 1988; MBA Sloan Sch. Mgmt., MIT, Cambridge, 1995. Reg. profl. engr. Civil engr. Morrison-Knudsen Engrs., San Francisco, 1989-91, Deleuw-Cather & Co., San Francisco, 1991-92; trans. industry analyst Fed. Railroad Adminstrn., U.S. Dept. Transp., Washington, D.C., 1995-96; assoc. structured finance BZW/Barclays Bank PLC, N.Y., 1996—; lectr. in field. Author: (nat. policy draft for high-speed ground transp.) Fed. Railroad Adminstrn., Dept. Transp., Washington D.C., 1995-96. Named Amb. of Goodwill Rotary Internat., 1992-93, amb. scholar Rimsky-Korsakoff Conservatory of Music Rotary Internat. Mem. NAFE, Women's Transp. Sem. Office: BZW/Barclays Bank PLC 222 Broadway New York NY 10038

NGUYEN, ANN CAC KHUE, pharmaceutical and medicinal chemist; b. Sontay, Vietnam; came to U.S., 1975; naturalized citizen; d. Nguyen Van Soan and Luu Thi Hieu. BS, U. Saigon, 1973; MS, San Francisco State U., 1978; PhD, U. Calif., San Francisco, 1983. Teaching and research asst. U. Calif., San Francisco, 1978-83, postdoctoral fellow, 1983-86; research scientist U. Calif., 1987—. Contbr. articles to profl. jours. Recipient Nat. Research Service award, NIH, 1981-83; Regents fellow U. Calif., San Francisco, 1978-81. Mem. AAAS, Am. Chem. Soc., N.Y. Acad. Scis., Bay Area Enzyme Mechanism Group, Am. Assn. Pharm. Scientists. Roman Catholic. Home: 1488 Portola Dr San Francisco CA 94127-1409 Office: U Calif Box 0989 San Francisco CA 94143

NIAGRO, MARGARET FREE, veterinarian; b. Columbia, S.C., Jan. 19, 1959; d. Samuel Frederick and Margaret Elizabeth (Fogle) F. BS, U.S.C., 1982, MS, 1985; DVM, U. Ga., 1989. Sml. animal intern U. Ga. Vet. Hosp., Athens, 1989-90; assoc. vet. Hidden Hills Animal Hosp., Stone Mountain, Ga., 1990-91, Lilburn (Ga.) Animal Hosp., 1991-96; freelance veterinarian, 1996—; co-owner D.B.F. Interactive. Mem. Am. Vet. Med. Assn., Am. Animal Hosp. Assn., Gwinnett Vet. Med. Assn., Greater Atlanta Vet. Assn., Ga. Vet. Med. Assn.

NIBLACK, NANCY LEE PARHAM, insurance agent, financial consultant; b. Martin, Tenn., Jan. 24, 1941; d. Thomas Anderson Jr. and Helen Rose (Hilliard) Parham; m. John Cumming Watkins Jr., Sept. 26, 1964 (div. Oct. 1971); 1 child, Scott Christopher Watkins Niblack; m. James Frederick Niblack, June 7, 1981 (div. Oct. 1990). AA, St. Johns River Jr. Coll., 1961; BA, U. Fla., 1963; MSW, U. Ala., 1969. CLU, ChFC. Psychiat. social worker Bryce Hosp., Tuscaloosa, Ala., 1965-69; asst. prof. Inst. Contemporary Corrections & Behavioral Sci. Sam Houston State Univ., Huntsville, Ala., 1969-70; clin. social worker Comprehensive Care Ctr., Lexington, Ky., 1971-79, Mental Health Svcs., Inc., Gainesville, Fla., 1979-80; spl. agt. Prudential Preferred Fin. Svcs., Gainesville, 1980-96; life specialist Allstate Life, Gainesville, 1996—; part time lectr. Univ. Ky., Lexington, 1971-79. Elder, treas. Grace Presbyn. Ch., 1987-90; pres., meet coord. Buchholz High Sch. Swim Team. Fellow Life Underwriting Tng. Coun.; mem. NASW, Acad. Cert. Social Workers, Am. Soc. CLUs and ChFCs, Gainesville Assn. Life Underwriters (pres. 1988-89, Key Man award 1988, Agt. of Yr. award 1992), Estate Planning Coun. Gainesville, Gainesville Area Investment Network (pres. 1989), Gainesville Sports Organizing Com., Hon. Order Ky. Cols. (treas. Gator chpt. 1988-94), Kiwanis, Alpha Omicron Pi (corp. treas. 1986-95). Democrat. Office: Allstate PO Box 14404 Gainesville FL 32604-2404

NICCOLINI, DIANORA, photographer, artist; b. Florence, Italy, Oct. 3, 1936; came to U.S., 1946, naturalized, 1960; d. George and Elaine (Augsbury) N. Student Hunter Coll., 1955-62, Art Students League, 1960, Germain Sch. Photography, 1962. B.A magna cum laude, Marymount Manhattan Coll., 1995. Med. photographer Manhattan Eye, Ear and Throat Hosp., 1963-65; organizer med. photography dept., 1st chief med. photographer Lenox Hill Hosp., 1965-67; organizer, head dept. med. and audio visual edn. St. Clare's Hosp., N.Y.C., 1967-76; mem. Third Eye Gallery, N.Y.C., 1974-76; owner Dianora Niccolini Creations, 1976—; instr. photography Camera Club N.Y., 1978-79, Germain Sch. Photography, 1978-79, N.Y. Inst. Photography, 1981-83; one woman shows 209 Photo Gallery, Top of the Stairs Gallery, Third Eye Gallery, 1974, 75, 77, West Broadway Gallery, N.Y.C., 1981, Camera Club N.Y., 1982, Photographics Unltd. Gallery, N.Y.C., 1981, Overseas Press Club, N.Y.C., 1983, Impulse Gallery, Provincetown, Mass., 1992; exhibited in group show at Jacob Javits Fed. Bldg., N.Y.C., 1992, Neikrug Gallery, N.Y.C., 1993, Ward-Nasse Gallery, Internat. Salon, N.Y.C., 1996; project dir., Ward-Nasse Gallery, N.Y.C., 1996, Curio-Spector Gallery, N.Y.C., 1996, Photography over 65, N.Y.C., 1978; pub. portfolios; author: Women of Vision, 1982, Men in Focus, 1983; editor: P.W.P. Times, 1981-82; contbr. to photog. books, 1979, 80; designer greeting cards Flashcards, Inc., 1988-90; contbg. editor Functional Photography, 1979-80, N.Y. Photo Dist. News, 1980; listed in numerous anthologies. Mem. Women Photographers N.Y. (founder 1974), Biol. Photog. Assn., Internat. Ctr. Photography, Am. Soc. Mag. Photographers, Am. Soc. Picture Profls., Profl. Women Photographers (coord. 1980-84), Unity Ctr. Practical Christianity. 1982, Interfaith, 1995. Home: 356 E 78th St New York NY 10021-2239

NICHOLAS, MARY, sculptor; b. N.Y.C., May 4, 1922; d. George and Katherine (Stellakis) N.; m. Julius Kramer, Oct. 14, 1946. Cert. in fine arts, Cooper Union Art Sch., N.Y.C., 1946. Display artist N.Y.C., 1940-60, colorist, 1960-63, staff frame shop, 1964-85. Author of poetry. Mem. Sculptors Guild N.Y., Provincetown Assn. Home: 306 Grand ave Englewood NJ 07631

NICHOLAS, NICKIE LEE, industrial hygienist; b. Lake Charles, La., Jan. 19, 1938; d. Clyde Lee and Jessie Mae (Lyons) N.; B.S., U. Houston, 1960, M.S., 1966. Tchr. sci. Pasadena (Tex.) Ind. Sch. Dist., 1960-61; chemist FDA, Dallas, 1961-62, VA Hosp., Houston, 1962-66, chief biochemist Baylor U. Coll. Medicine, 1966-68; chemist NASA, Johnson Spacecraft Center, 1968-73; analytical chemist TVA, Muscle Shoals, Ala., 1973-75; indsl. hygienist, compliance officer OSHA, Dept. Labor, Houston, 1975-79, area dir., Tulsa, 1979-82, mgr., Austin, 1982—; mem. faculty VA Sch. Med. Tech., Houston, 1963-66. Recipient award for outstanding achievement German embassy, 1958, Suggestion award VA, 1963, Group Achievement award Skylab Med. Team, NASA, 1974, Personal Achievement award Dept. Labor Fed. Women's Program, 1984, Career Achievement award Federally Employed Women, Inc., 1988, Meritorious Performance award DOL-OSHA, 1990, Disting. Career Svc. award Dept. Labor, 1991, Sec.'s Exceptional Achievement award Dept. Labor, 1991, Cert. Appreciation, OSHA, 1991, Asst. Sec.'s Leadership award DOL-OSHA, 1992. Mem. Am. Chem. Soc. (dir. analytical group Southeastern Tex. and Brazosport sects. 1971, chmn. elect 1973), Am. Assn. Clin. Chemists, Am. Conf. Govtl. Indsl. Hygenists, Am. Ind. Hygiene Assn., Am. Soc. Safety Engrs., Am. Harp Soc., Fed. Exec. Assn. (pres. 1984-85), Kappa Epsilon. Home: 1002 Sundance Ridge Rd Dripping Springs TX 78620-9501 Office: 903 San Jacinto Blvd Ste 319 Austin TX 78701-2450

NICHOLAS, ROCHELLE GLORIA, sculptor; b. N.Y.C., Sept. 3, 1933; d. Philip William and Esther (Sugerman) Karp; m. George Peter Nicholas, May 18, 1933; 1 child, Andrea Catherine. BFA, Hunter Coll., N.Y.C., 1957; postgrad., Columbia U., 1957-58. Prin. works include sculpture Provincetown (Mass.) Mus., Nat. Trust for Hist. Preservation at Chesterwood, Stockbridge, Mass., Penson Gallery, N.Y.C., O'Hara Gallery, N.Y.C., Lydon Fine Art, Chgo. Mem. Internat. Sculpture Ctr., N.Y. Artists Equity.

NICHOLS, AVIS B., state legislator; b. Waterbury, Vt.; married; 3 children. Student, Burdett Bus. Coll., U. N.H. Mem. N.H. Ho. of Reps.; mem. ways and means com.; former tchr. Burdett Bus. Coll.; former pvt. sec. Mem. Merrimack County Rep. com. and exec. com., Rep. state com., state boiler adv. coun., Kearsarge Regional Sch. Bd., 1976-89, Warner budget com., 1977-83; co-chair Warner br. ARC, 1972-82, dir. swimming program; former marshal and fin. chair Rebekah Assembly N.H.; mem. Girl Scouts U.S. Mem. Welcome Rebekah Lodge (former noble grand). Home: PO Box 306 Main St Warner NH 03278 Office: NH Ho of Reps State House Concord NH 03301*

NICHOLS, CAROL D., real estate professional, association executive. BA, U. Pitts., 1964; cert. in advanced mgmt., U. Chgo. From mgmt. trainee to buyer May Dept. Stores Co., Pitts., 1964-70; various mgmt. positions, then mng. dir. mortgage and real estate div. Tchrs. Ins. and Annuity Assn. Am., N.Y.C., 1970—; instr. real estate div. continuing edn. Marymount Manhattan Coll., N.Y.C., 1975-76, Woman's Sch. Adult Edn. Ctr., N.Y.C., 1976-77; v.p. instn. owners div. Real Estate Bd. N.Y., past chmn. fin. com., mem. seminar and gen. meetings coms. Trustee, mem. investment com. Nat. Jewish Ctr. for Immunology and Respiratory Medicine. Recipient Nat. Humanitarian award Nat. Jewish Ctr. for Immunology and Respiratory Medicine, Nat. Brotherhood award NCCJ. Mem. Assn. Real Estate Women (past pres.), Urban Land Inst. (trustee, chmn. urban devel. and mixed use coun., coun. coord. and inner city). Home: 165 Winfield St East Norwalk CT 06855-1622 Office: Teachers Ins & Annuity Assn 730 3rd Ave New York NY 10017-3206

NICHOLS, IRIS JEAN, illustrator; b. Yakima, Wash., Aug. 2, 1938; d. Charles Frederick and Velma Irene (Hacker) Beisner; (div. June 1963); children: Reid William, Amy Jo; m. David Gary Nichols, Sept. 21, 1966. BFA in Art, U. Wash., 1978. Freelance illustrator, graphic designer Seattle, 1966—; med. illustrator, head dept. illustration Swedish Hosp. Med. Ctr., Seattle, 1981-86; owner, med. and scientific illustrator Art for Medicine, Seattle, 1986—; part-time med. illustrator U. Wash., Seattle, 1966-67; part-time med. illustrator, graphic coord. dept. art The Mason Clinic, 1968-78; instr. advanced illustration Cornish Coll. Arts, Seattle, 1988—. Illustrator various books including Bryophytes of Pacific Northwest, 1966, Microbiology, 1973, 78, 82, 94, Introduction to Human Physiology, 1980, Understanding Human Anatomy and Physiology, 1983, Human Anatomy, 1984 Regional Anesthesia, 1990, and children's books on various subjects; exhibited in group shows at Seattle Pacific Sci. Ctr., summer 1979, 82, Am. Coll. Surgeons (1st prize 1974), N.W. Urology Conf. (1st prize 1974, 76, 2d prize 1975). Pres. ArtsWest (formerly West Seattle Arts Coun.), 1983; active Seattle Art Mus. Named to West Seattle H.S. Alumni Hall of Fame, 1986, Matrix Table, 1986-96. Mem. Assn. Med. Illustrators (Murial McLatchie Fine Arts award 1981), Nat. Mus. Women in the Arts (Wash. state com., bd. dirs. 1987-95, pres. 1993-94), Women Painters of Wash. (pres. 1987-89), U. Wash. Alumni Assn., Lambda Rho (pres. 1995-96).

NICHOLS, JOAN WILSON, business educator; b. Kansas City, Mo., Mar. 18, 1933; d. William Henry Wilson and Viola Marie Stiles; m. Gilbert William Nichols, Jan. 29, 1952; children: Michael, Stephen, Christopher. BBA, U. Mo., Kansas City, 1961; MA, Webster U., 1991. Cert. fin. mgr. Adminstrv. asst. Emerson Electric, Mt. Pleasant, Iowa, 1966-72; bus. office mgr. Hadley Regional Med. Ctr., Hays, Kans., 1972-74; v.p. Merrill Lynch, Wichita, Kans., 1974-88; instr., dir. Ctr. Mgmt. Devel. Svcs., Ctr. Ins. Edn. Emporia (Kans.) State U., 1988—; cons., spkr., book reviewer in field. Editor: Kansas Insurance Fact Book, 1992, 2nd edit., 1994. Treas. SOS, Emporia, 1993—. Mem. Nat. Bus. Edn. Assn., Nat. Acad. Advisors Assn., Emporia C. of C., Sigma Beta Delta, Delta Phi Epsilon (advisor 1992—). Home: 1925 W 24 # 103 Emporia KS 66801 Office: Emporia State U Campus Box 4058 Emporia KS 66801

NICHOLS, JOANN EDITH HESELTON, retired legal secretary; b. Tinmouth, Vt., Dec. 1, 1930; d. Ward McKinley and Gladys (Gilman) Heselton; m. Alaric George Nichols, Oct. 6, 1973 (dec. May 1991). Office worker Holstein-Friesian Assn., Brattleboro, Vt., 1948-53; bookkeeper Brattleboro Trust Co., 1953-60; sec. Gates Ins. Agy., Brattleboro, 1960-71; from admissions sec. to sec. to pres. Marlboro (Vt.) Coll., 1971-84; legal sec. various law offices, Brattleboro, 1984-87; sec., paralegal John A. Rocray, Brattleboro, 1987-95. Author: Descendants Giles Roberts, Scarborough, Maine, 1994, Index Known Cemetery Listings in Vermont, 1995. Historian Centre Congl. Ch., Brattleboro, 1990—; treas. Blind Artisans of Vt., 1991—. Mem. Nat. Geneal. Soc., Geneal. Soc. Vt. (sec. 1971-75, pres. 1975-93), N.H. Soc. Genealogists, NE Hist. Geneal. Soc. Home: 46 Chestnut St Brattleboro VT 05301-3152

NICHOLS, KYRA, ballerina; b. Berkeley, Calif., July 2, 1958. Studied with Alan Howard, Pacific Ballet, Sch. Am. Ballet, N.Y.C. With N.Y.C. Ballet, 1974—, prin. dancer, 1979—. Created roles in Tricolore, 1978, A Sketch Book, 1978, Jerome Robbins' Four Seasons, 1979, John Taras' Concerto for Piano and Wind Instruments, Stravinsky Centennial Celebration, 1982, Jacques d'Amboise's Celebration, 1983; performed in N.Y.C. Ballet's Balanchine Celebration, 1993. Ford Found. scholar; recipient Dance Mag. award, 1988. Office: Peter S Diggins Assocs 133 W 71st St New York NY 10023-3834 also: NYC Ballet Inc NY State Theater Lincoln Ctr Pla New York NY 10023

NICHOLS, LEE ANN, library media specialist; b. Denver, Apr. 27, 1946; d. Bernard Anthony and Margaret Mary (Pughes) Wilhelm; m. Robert Joseph Nichols, July 12, 1975; children: Rachel, Steven, Sarah. BS in Edn., St. Mary of the Plains, Dodge City, Kans., 1968; MA in Edn., Colo. U., 1978. Cert. type B profl. tchr., Colo. Tchr. So. Tama Sch. Dist. Montour, Iowa, 1968-70, Strasburg (Colo.) Sch. Dist., 1970-73; svc. rep. Montain Bell, Denver, 1973-75; libr., tchr. Simla (Colo) Sch. Dist., 1976-78; dir. Simla Br. Libr., 1978-81; dir. Christian edn. St. Anthony's Ch/, Sterling, Colo., 1983-84; libr. cons. Rel Valley Sch., Iliff, Colo., 1984—, Plateau Sch. Dist., Peetz, Colo., 1986—; mem. Colo. Coun. for Libr. Devel., Denver, 1986-92, chmn. 1991; instr. Northeastern Jr. Coll., Sterling; del. Gov.'s Conf. on Libr. and Info. Scis., 1990. Contbr. articles to profl. jours. Active Sterling Arts Coun., sec., 1982-85, v.p., 1985, pres., 1986-87; chair Northeastern Jr. Coll. Found., Sterling, 1983-87, mem. 1981-91; mem. community adv. coun. Northeastern Jr. Coll., 1991-93, chair, 1993; bd. dirs. Wagon Wheel chpt. Girl Scouts Am., 1975-78. Mem. ALA, Am. Assn. Sch. Librs., Assn. Libr. Svcs. to Children, Colo. Ednl. Media Assn., Colo. Libr. Coun., Internat. Reading Assn. (Colo. Coun.). Home: 12288 County Road 370 Sterling CO 80751-8421 Office: Caliche Jr High Sch RR 1 Iliff CO 80736-9801

NICHOLS, MARGARET IRBY, librarian, educator; b. Maud, Tex., July 9, 1924; d. James Rainwater and Winnie (Pride) Irby; m. Irby Coghill Nichols Jr., Apr. 18, 1953 (div. Jan. 1992); children: Nina Nichols Austin, Irby C. Nichols III. BA, U. North Tex., 1945; MLS, U. Tex., 1957. Libr. Mercedes (Tex.) H.S., 1945-46; cataloger Bethany (W.Va.) Coll., 1946; chief reference libr. Tex. Tech U., Lubbock, 1946-48; ref. libr. El Paso Pl., 1949-51; chief reference libr. N.Mex. Mil. Inst., Roswell, 1951-53; sch. libr. South Jr. H.S., Roswell, 1954-55; acad. dean Selwyn Sch., Denton, Tex., 1965-67; prof. Sch. Libr. and Info. Scis. U. North Tex., Denton, 1968-91, assoc. dean Sch. Libr. and Info. Scis., 1989-91; cons. in field, 1991—. Author: Core Reference Collections, 1986, 2d edit., 1993, Guide to Reference Sources, 4th edit., 1992, Reference Sources for Small and Medium Libraries, 1988, 2d edit., 1994, Texas Information Sources, 1996; contbr. articles to profl. jours. Mem. ALA (mem. coun. 1988-92), Tex. Libr. Assn. (exec. bd. 1983-86, 88-92, pres. 1984-85, Disting. Svc. award 1990, Lois Bebout Outstanding Svc. award Reference Round Table 1995). Home: 2514 Royal Ln Denton TX 76201

NICHOLS, MICHELLE LYNNETTE, medical educator, physician; b. Pascagoula, Miss., June 16, 1962; d. Jerome and Mable (Berry) N. BS, U. So. Miss., Hattiesburg, 1984; MS, 1987; MD, U. Miss. Sch. Med., Jackson, 1990. Resident family medicine U. Miss., 1990-93; emergency room physician Miss. VA Med. Ctr., Jackson, 1991-93; clinic physician Jackson-Hinds Comprehensive Health Ctr., Miss., 1992-93; clin. assoc. Duke U. Med. Ctr., Durham, N.C., 1993-94; attending physician, fellow Duke U. Dept. Family Medicine, Durham, N.C., 1993-94; asst. prof. Morehouse Sch. Medicine, Atlanta, 1994-95; attending physician Morehouse dept. Family Medicine, Atlanta, 1994—, assoc. residency dir., 1995—; obstetrical coord. Morehouse Family Practice Ctr., Atlanta, 1994-95; chair OB Quality Improvement Morehouse Family Practice Ctr., 1994—. Clinic physician Homeless Shelter Cmty. Stewpot for the Homeless, Jackson, Miss., 1991-93. Named Resident rep. Am. Acad. Family Physicians, 1991-93, Assoc. Chief Resident U. Miss. Dept. Family Medicine, Jackson, Miss., 1992-93, Hall of Fame U. So. Miss., Hattiesburg, 1984. Mem. AMA, Am. Acad. Family Physicians, Soc. Tchrs. Family Medicine (New Faculty Orientation award 1995), Ga. Acad. Family Physicians, Nat. Med. Assn., Alpha Kappa Alpha. Office: Morehouse Sch Medicine FM 505 Fairburn Rd SW Atlanta GA 30331

NICHOLS, NANCY STEPHENSON, executive search company executive; b. Wilmington, Del., Dec. 9, 1944; d. Thomas Wilson and Elizabeth (Forster) Stephenson; m. David Finlay Pyle, Oct. 4, 1969 (div. Oct. 1992); children: Courtney T., Lindsey S.; m. Rodney Wayson Nichols, Mar. 13, 1993; 1 stepchild, Christopher M. BA, Smith Coll., 1966; MA, Harvard U., 1977, PhD, 1980. Dir. Mason fellows program Harvard Inst. for Internat. Devel., Cambridge, Mass., 1980-87, assoc. dir. for external affairs, 1987-91; assoc. dir. MPA program Kennedy Sch. Govt., Harvard U., Cambridge, 1980-87, spl. asst. to pres. for internat. affairs, 1987-91, v.p. for planning and devel. Am. U. Beirut, N.Y.C., 1992-93; exec. dir. Norman Broadbent Internat., N.Y.C., 1993-96; ptnr. Heidrick & Struggles, Inc., N.Y.C., 1996—. Editor: (monograph) Converting International Debt to Education, 1991; contbr. articles to profl. jours. Bd. dirs. Amigos de las Ams., Houston, 1990—, Inst. for Social and Econ. Programs in Mid. East, Harvard U. John F. Kennedy Sch. Govt., 1993-96, The North Am. Com. for L'Envol, France, 1995—; mem. Vietnam Fulbright Com., N.Y.C., 1993—, Art Table, 1996—. Fulbright fellow, Turkey, 1978-79, fellow Am. Rsch. Inst. in Turkey, 1978-79. Mem. Coun. on Fgn. Rels., Harvard Club N.Y.C. Episcopalian. Home: 418 E 59th St Apt 14B New York NY 10022 Office: Heidrick & Struggles Inc 245 Park Ave New York NY 10167-0152

NICHOLS, SALLY JO, geriatrics nurse; b. Coldwater, Mich., Jan. 28, 1965; d. Leo Arnold and Charlotte (Ferguson) N. LPN, Pasco-Hernando C.C., 1985, AA, 1986, ASN, 1992; student, U. South Fla., 1990-91, 94—. RN, LPN, Fla. LPN All Cmty. Walk-In Clinic, Spring Hill, Fla., 1986; office mgr. Internat. Clerical Labs., Crystal River, Fla., 1986; LPN, charge nurse Eastbrooke Health Care Ctr., Brooksville, Fla., 1987-91; pvt. duty LPN Nursefinders, Inverness, Fla., 1991; med.-surg. LPN Oak Hill Hosp., Spring Hill, 1991; LPN charge nurse, then RN supr. Avante at Inverness, 1991—, resident assessment coord., care plan asst. coord., 1993-95, care plan coord., 1995-96, utilization rev./Medicare rev. coord., 1995-96, nurse mgr., 1996—. Relief ch. pianist Grace Tabernacle Ind. Bapt. Ch., Brooksville,

1983-91. Mem. ANA, Fla. Nurses Assn., Golden Key Honor Soc. Democrat. Home: 1225 W Highland Blvd Inverness FL 34452 Office: Avante of Inverness 304 N Citrus Ave Inverness FL 34452-4157

NICHOLS, VANESSA TERRY, elementary educator; b. Cleve., June 17, 1955; d. George Andrew and Nora Jane (Cotton) Terry; m. Leonard Allan Nichols, Aug. 2, 1981 (div. Apr. 1995); children: Vanita Lynn, Terry Allen. BS, Ctrl. State U., 1977; MA, Ohio State U., 1991. Cert. tchr., Ohio. Tchr. Our Lady of Lourdes, Atlanta, 1983-85; teller Bank One, Ashland, Ohio, 1985-87; pvt. practice home day care Akron, Ohio, 1987-88; tchr. Akron Pub. Schs., 1988-92, Shaker Hts. (Ohio) Schs., 1992—. Ohio State Minority fellow, 1986. Mem. Delta Sigma Theta. Baptist. Home: 1039 Argonne Rd South Euclid OH 44121

NICHOLS, VICKI ANNE, financial consultant, librarian; b. Denver, June 10, 1949; d. Glenn Warner and Loretta Irene (Chalender) Adams; B.A., Colo. Coll., 1972; postgrad. U. Denver, 1976-77; m. Robert H. Nichols, Oct. 28, 1972 (div.); children—Christopher Travis, Lindsay Meredith. Treas., controller, dir. Polaris Resources, Inc., Denver, 1972-86; controller InterCap Devel. Corp, 1986-87; treas., controller, dir. Transnat. Cons., Ltd., 1986-91; mgr. collection svcs. Jefferson County (Colo.) Pub. Library, 1986—; dir., owner Nichols Bus. Services. Home: 4305 Brentwood St Wheat Ridge CO 80033-4412 Office: 10500 W 38th Ave Wheat Ridge CO 80033

NICHOLS, VIRGINIA VIOLET, insurance agent, accountant; b. Monroe County, Mo., Oct. 26, 1928; d. Elmer W. and Frances L. (McKinney) N.; student Belleville (Ill.) Jr. Coll., 1959-60, Rockhurst Coll., 1964-65, Avila Coll., Kansas City, Mo., 1981-84. Sec., Panhandle Eastern Pipeline Co., Kansas City, Mo., 1964-65, St. Louis County Dept. Revenue, 1965-69, Forest Park Community Coll., 1969-71, Nooney Co., St. Louis, 1971-77, J. A. Baer Enterprises, St. Louis, 1979; acct. Panhandle Eastern Pipe Line Co., Kansas City, Mo., 1979-85. Vol., ARC, 1965—. Mem. Profl. Secs. Internat. (Sec. of Year 1969, sec. Mo. div. 1975-76), Jr. Women's C. of C. (Girl of Year 1975, pres. 1974-75), Soroptimist's Internat. (treas. Kansas City chpt. 1990-91). Republican. Mem. United Ch. of Christ. Home: PO Box 5832 Kansas City MO 64171-0832

NICHOLSON, BARBARA LYNN, communications educator; b. Weston, W.Va., Oct. 3, 1951; d. Thomas Edward and Audra Gladys (Riffle) Ochletree; m. Gregory Charles Nicholson, Jan. 23, 1971; children: Amanda J., Matthew E. BA, Glenville State Coll., 1973; MA, W.Va. Univ., 1978; PhD, Ohio Univ., 1987. Tchr. Gilmer County H.S., Glenville, W.Va., 1973-79; asst. prof. Glenville State Coll., 1979-88; comm. dir. W.VA. Gov.'s Office, Charleston, 1988-91; asst. dir. Satellite Network of W.Va., Institute, 1991-94; assoc. prof. W.VA. Grad. Coll., So. Charleston, 1995—; comm. cons. Univ. Do Espirito Santo, Vittoria, Brazil, 1994; mem. evaluation team H.S. that work So. Region Edn. Bd., 1995—. Author: (chpt.) Meeting The Challenge of Cultural Diversity in Teacher Preparation, 1993; contbr. articles to profl. jours. Exec. bd. W.Va. Civil Liberties Union, Charleston, 1995—; mem. W.Va. Arts Advocacy Orgn., Charleston, 1995—. Fulbright fellow Coun. Internat. Exchange of Scholars, Sweden, 1995, exchange faculty, Russia, 1996; named Alumna of Yr., Glenville State Coll., 1996. Mem. Assn. Grad. Liberal Studies, Humanities and Tech. Assn., Assn. Ednl. Comm. and Tech., W.Va. Ednl. Media Assn. Democrat. Home: 14 Seneca Hills Dr Elkview WV 25071 Office: WV Grad Coll 100 Angus E Peyton Dr South Charleston WV 25303

NICHOLSON, ELLEN ELLIS, clinical social worker; b. Boston, Apr. 1, 1940; d. George Letham and Mary Stirling (Money) McIver; divorced; 1 child, Matthew Norman Ellis. Dental Hygienist, Forsyth Coll., 1959; BS, Northeastern U., 1973, MEd in Counseling, 1974; MSW, Boston U., 1984. Registered dental hygienist, Mass. Dental hygienist, 1959-66; clin. coord., pvt. dental practice Forsyth Dental Ctr., Boston, 1966-70; dir. vol. counseling Solomon Mental Health Ctr., Lowell, Mass., 1974-75; social worker East Boston Social Ctrs., Inc., 1976-77, dir. youth family counseling, 1977-79; supr. family svc. Boston Housing Authority, 1979-81; social worker Mass. Soc. Prevention Cruelty to Children, Hyannis, 1984-86, supr., 1986-93, clinic dir., 1993-95; dir. profl. svcs. Child and Family Svc. of Cape Cod, Hyannis, 1995—; dir. Abuse Prevention Svcs. Child and Family Svc. of Cape Cod, 1995—; psychotherapist Riverview Sch., Sandwich, Mass., 1989-93. Advisor youth group Christ Episcopal Ch., Needham, Mass., 1960-64, St. Paul's Ch., Newburyport, Mass., 1964-65; vol. counselor Solomon Mental Health Ctr., Lowell, 1972-74; chair Barnstable County Children's Task Force; chair adv. com. Carnstable County Sexual Abuse Intervention Network; mem. Barnstable County Juvenile Firesetters Task Force. Mem. ANASW, Am. Profl. Soc. on Abuse of Children, Assn. for Treatment of Sexual Abusers, Sigma Phi Alpha, Sigma Epsilon Rho, Kappa Delta Pi. Office: Child & Family Svc of Cape Cod 1019 Rte 132 Hyannis MA 02601

NICHOLSON, JENNIFER DENISE, workers' compensation claims manager; b. Redlands, Calif., Apr. 30, 1968; d. Jimmie Douglas Crow and Kathleen Ann (Gasponi) Hartman; m. Steven Edgar Nicholson, Dec. 17, 1994. BS in Math., Azusa Pacific U., 1990. Cert. workers' compensation claims profl. Ins. Ednl. Assn., Calif., Wash.; cert. claims, Oreg. Workers' compensation adminstr. GAB Bus. Svcs., San Bernardino, Calif., 1990-92; workers' compensation adjuster Alexsis Risk Mgmt., West Covina, Calif., 1992; workers' compensation sr. adjuster Utica Mut. Ins. Co., Glendora, Calif., 1992-94; workers' compensation claims supr. May Dept. Stores Co., Redondo Beach, Calif., 1994-95, workers' compensation claims mgr., 1995—. Mem. NAFE. Office: May Dept Stores Co We Reg Claims Office Ste 1 1801 Hawthorne Blvd Redondo Beach CA 90278

NICHOLSON, LISA GHOST, banker; b. Grove City, Pa., Jan. 27, 1958; d. William Allen and Sandra (Boyce) Ghost; m. James Elvis Nicholson, Jr., Apr. 15, 1979; children: Amy-Beth, Jacob. BS in BA, Kennedy-Western U., Boise, Idaho, 1994, MS in Mgmt. Info. Systems, 1996. Teller/asst. to treas. First Fed. Savs. and Loan, Front Royal, Va., 1980-81; substitute tchr./tchr.'s aide Warren County schs., Front Royal, 1977-79, 84-85; contract mgmt. asst. Def. Contracts Adminstrn., Vint Hill Farms Station, Va., 1985-86; procurement clk. U.S. Army C.E., Winchester, Va., 1986; contract specialist Shenandoah Studios of Stained Glass, Front Royal, 1986-87; v.p. ops. Va. Savs. Bank FSB, Front Royal, 1987—. Pres., founder Dynamic Youth Program, Inc., Front Royal, 1995—; chair Elem. Sch. Site Based Mgmt., Front Royal, 1994-95; pres. PTA, Front Royal, 1993-94; coord./founder Sch./Bus. Partnership, Front Royal, 1992-95. Bridgewater Coll. Pres.'s scholar, 1976. Mem. Va. Bankers Assn., Home Edn. Assn. of Va. Home: 819 E 6th St Front Royal VA 22630 Office: Virginia Savings Bank 600 N Commerce Front Royal VA 22630-3418

NICHOLSON, MYREEN MOORE, artist, researcher; b. Norfolk, Va., June 2, 1940; d. William Chester and Illeen (Fox) Moore; m. Roland Quarles Nicholson, Jan. 9, 1964 (dec. 1986); children: Andrea Joy, Ross (dec. 1965); m. Harold Wellington McKinney II, Jan. 18, 1981; 1 child, Cara Isadora. AA, William and Mary Coll., 1960; BA Old Dominion U., 1962; MLS, U. N.C., 1971; postgrad. Old Dominion U. 1962-64, 64-67, 75-85, 86-92, 94-96, The Citadel, 1968-69, Hastie Sch. Art, 1968, Chrysler Mus. Art Sch., 1964. English tchr., Chesapeake, Va., 1962-63; dept. head, Portsmouth (Va.) Bus. Coll., 1963-64; tech. writer City Planning/Art Commn., Norfolk, 1964-65; art tchr. Norfolk pub. schs., 1965-67; prof. lit., art Palmer Jr. Coll., Charleston, S.C., 1968; tchr. Penn Sch. John's Island, S.C., 1968; librarian Charleston Schs., 1968-69; asst. to asst. dir. City Library Norfolk, 1970-72, art and audio-visual librarian, 1972-75, rsch. librarian, 1975-83, librarian dept. fiction, 1983-90; dir. W. Ghent Arts Alliance, Norfolk, 1978—. Poet-in-schs., Virginia Beach, Va., 1987. Book reviewer Art Book Revs., Library Jour., 1973-76; editor, illustrator Acquisitions Bibliographies, 1970—, West Ghent newsletter, 1995—; juried exhibits various cities including Grand Hyatt, Mayflower, Washington, by Joan Mondale, Nohra Haime, curator of Freer Gallery, by sr. curator Nat. Mus. Am. Art, curator Phillips Collection, asst. curator, White House; group shows include Yorktown Small Works Show, 1996, Hampton Arts Commn. and Tidewater Artists Assn. Portfolio Show, 1996, Suffolk Artists and Writers Invitational Exhibit, 1996, Virginia Beach Resort and Conf. Ctr. Print Show, 1996, Peninsula Ann. Juried Art Exhibit, 1996, Hampton Bay Days Juried Art Exhibit, 1996; contbr. art and poetry to various publs. and anthologies. Mem. Virginia Beach Arts Ctr., 1978-93, Hampton Art League, 1990—, Suffolk Art League, 1990—; bd. dirs. W. Ghent Art/Lit. Festival, 1979; poetry reader Poetry Soc. Va., Va. Ctr. for Creative Arts, Sweetbriar, 1989, Walden Books, 1991, Christopher Newport U., 1994-95, Caberet Voltaire, 1994, J.M. Prince Books and Coffeehouse, 1995—, Statues St. Mark's Cath. Ch., 1991-92; graphics of hundreds of celebrities from life; curator Va. Winter Show Life Saving Mus., 1991-92; judge Bornstein art scholarship Chrysler Mus., 1992; mem. staff Mid-Atlantic Antiques Mag., 1993—. Recipient awards various art and poetry contests; Coll. William and Mary art scholar, 1958, Tricentenial award for Contbns. to the Arts in Va., 1993; recipient Cert. for Vol. Contbns. to Va. by Gov., 1994. Nat. Endowment Arts grantwriter, 1975; bd. dirs. Tidewater Literacy Coun., 1971-72; bd. dirs. West Ghent League. Mem. ALA (poster sessions rev. com. 1985-96, pub. relations judge, subcom. comm. 1988-90), Pub. Libr. Assn. (com. bylaws and orgns. 1988-90), Va. Libr. Assn. (pub. relations com. 1984-86, grievance and pay equity com. 1986-88, co-winner Paraprofl. Logo award for Norfolk Pub. Libr., 1985, chair elect, 1991-92, chair Pub. Documents Forum, 1992-93, sec. 1994), Southeastern Libr. Assn. (Rothrock award com. 1986-88, com. on coms. 1991-92), Poetry Soc. Va. (ea. pres. 1986-89, nominating com. 1989-90, state corr. sec., editor newsletter 1990-93, dir. publicity 1993-95, 70th Anniversary plaque for Wren Bldg.), Art Librs. Soc. N.Am., Tidewater Artists Assn. (bd. dirs. 1989—, chair grantwriting com. 1990—, pres. 1991-92), Southeastern Coll. Art Assn., Acad. Am. Poets, Irene Leache Soc., Internat. Platform Assn. (artists assn.), Old Dominion U. Alumni Assn. (artistic dir. Silver Reunion), Southeastern Soc. Archtl. Historians, Ikara (pres. 1989—), D'Art Ctr. (Dockside art rev., bd. dirs. 1991—), Ex Libris Soc. (charter), Va. Writers Club (editor West Ghent newsletter). Home and Office: 1404 Gates Ave Norfolk VA 23507-1131

NICKEL, JANET MARLENE MILTON, geriatrics nurse; b. Manitowoc, Wis., June 9, 1940; d. Ashley and Pearl (Kerr) Milton; m. Curtis A. Nickel, July 29, 1961; children: Cassie, Debra, Susan. Diploma, Milw. Inst., 1961; ADN, N.D. State U., 1988. Nurse Milw. VA, Wood, Wis., 1961-62; supervising nurse Park Lawn Convalescent Hosp., Manitowoc, 1964-65; newsletter editor Fargo (N.D.) Model Cities Program, 1970-73; supervising night nurse Rosewood on Broadway, Luth. Hosps. and Homes, Fargo, 1973-92; assoc. dir. nursing Elim Nursing Home, Fargo, 1992-94, night nurse, 1994—. Mem. Phi Eta Sigma. Home: 225 19th Ave N Fargo ND 58102-2352 Office: 3534 S University Dr Fargo ND 58104-6228

NICKEL, ROSALIE JEAN, reading specialist; b. Hooker, Okla., Oct. 10, 1939; d. Edwin Charles and Esther Elizabeth (Wiens) Ollenburger; m. Ted W. Nickel, June 3, 1960; 1 child, Sandra Jean. BA, Tabor Coll., 1961; MA, Calif. State U., Fresno, 1970. Cert. tchr., Calif. Elem. tchr. Visalia (Calif.) Pub. Schs., 1961-62; overseas tchr. Kodaikanal Internat. Sch., Madras State, India, 1963-65; tchr. Mendota (Calif.) Jr. High Sch., 1966; elem. tchr. Fresno Pub. Schs., 1966-68, Inglewood (Calif.) Pub. Schs., 1968-73; spl. reading tchr. Tulsa Pub. Schs., 1974-81; salesperson, mgr. Compaq, Marion, Kans., 1981-85; gifted student tchr. Wichita (Kans.) Pub. Schs., 1986; reading specialist and resource tchr., 1987—, sch. technology coord., 1989—, dist. K-3 literacy task force, 1995—, dist. lang. arts adoption com. 1995——; evaluator State Textbook Com., Tulsa, 1976, 78; mem. quality rev. team Birney Elem. Sch., Fresno. Newsletter editor Marion County Arts Council, 1981-82. Co-dir. Am. Field Svc., Tulsa, 1980-81; v.p. Women's Federated Clubs Am., Marion, 1985-86; pres. Butler Mennonite Brethern Women's Fellowship, 1989-91. Mem. Internat. Reading Assn., Tulsa Reading Assn., Fresno Area Reading Council. Home: 2821 W Compton Ct Fresno CA 93711-1181 Office: Fresno Unified Schs Tulare And M St Fresno CA 93701

NICKELSON, KIM RENÉ, internist; b. Chgo., Feb. 13, 1956; d. Robert William and Carolynn Lucille (Marts) N.; m. Louis Peter Sguros; children: Brian Louis, Justin Robert Peter. BS in Chemistry, U. Ill., 1978; MD, Loyola U., Maywood, Ill., 1981. Diplomate Am. Bd. Internal Medicine. Intern and resident in internal medicine Luth. Gen. Hosp., Park Ridge, Ill., 1981-84; pvt. practice Oakbrook, Ill., 1984-87, Plantation, Fla., 1987—; adj. attending staff Rush-Presbyn. St. Luke's Med. Ctr., Chgo., 1984-87; assoc. attending staff Hinsdale (Ill.) Hosp., 1984-87, Westside Regional Med. Ctr., Plantation, Plantation Gen. Hosp., Fla. Med. Ctr. South, Plantation. Musician Elk Grove (Ill.) Community Band, 1978-87, Hollywood (Fla.) Symphony Orch., 1987—, Sunrise (Fla.) Pops Symphony, 1987—, Deerfield (Fla.) Community Band, 1987—. Mem. ACP, Internat. Horn Soc. Office: Internal Medicine Assocs 499 NW 70th Ave Ste 200 Plantation FL 33317-7573

NICKENS, CATHERINE ARLENE, nurse supervisor; b. Litchfield, Ill., Oct. 30, 1932; d. Harley Lloyd Moore and Ida Mae Reynolds; m. Carl Roland Nickens, Sept. 4, 1954 (div. Apr. 1975); children: Linda Dianne, Carl Roland Jr., Karen Patricia, Eric Moore. Nursing diploma, St. Joseph's Hosp., 1954. RN, Calif. Staff nurse St. Joseph's Hosp., Alton, Ill., 1954-55; staff nurse St. Mary's Hosp., Streator, Ill., 1962-68, supr., acting dir., 1968-70; nursing supr. Illini Hosp., Silvis, Ill., 1970-74; office nurse pediatrician's office Silvis, 1974-75; staff nurse telemetry/drug abuse North Miami Gen. Hosp., Miami, Fla., 1975-80; staff nurse, relief supr. Petaluma (Calif.) Valley Hosp., 1981—; participant women's health study Brigham and Women's Hosp., Boston, 1994-96. Author: (hist. fiction) The Thoroughly Compromised Bride, 1991 (award 1992), The Highwayman, 1993 (award 1994). Mem. ACLU, N.Y.C., 1995, Parents, Families and Friends of Lesbians and Gays, Washington, 1994-96, Nat. Mus. of Am. Indian/Smithsonian Instn., Washington, 1996; friend of the quilt NAMES Project Meml. Quilt, San Francisco, 1992-96; mem. friendship cir. Am. Found. for AIDS Rsch., Washington, 1994-96. Mem. Calif. Nurses Assn., Romance Writers of Am. (mentor to unpublished writers 1995-96). Home: 105 Olive St Santa Rosa CA 95401-6241

NICOL, MARJORIE CARMICHAEL, research psychologist; b. Orange, N.J., Jan. 6, 1929; d. Norman Carmichael and Ethel Sarah (Siviter) N. BA, Upsala Coll., MS, 1978; MPh, PhD, CUNY, 1988. Mgr. advt. prodn. RCA, Harrison, N.J., 1950-58; advt. mgr., writer NPS Advt., East Orange, N.J., 1960-67; pres. measurement and eval., chief exec. officer, psychol. evaluator Nicol Evaluation System, Millburn, N.J., 1967—; CEO Rafiki, Essex County, N.J., 1965—. Author: Nicol Index, Nicol Evaluation System, 1991. Officer Montclair Rehab. Orgn., 1981—; founder, patron Met. Opera at Lincoln Ctr. Republican. Presbyterian. Home: 85 Linden St Millburn NJ 07041-2160 Office: PO Box 111 Millburn NJ 07041-0111

NICOLA, PAULA WATERS, field underwriter, safety professional; b. Pensacola, Fla., Apr. 14, 1970; d. Ronald Douglas and Chris (Marsailis) Waters; m. Steven Doyle Nicola, June 29, 1991. BS in Chemistry, U. So. Ala., 1992. Safety and health specialist State of Fla. Divsn. of Safety, Jacksonville, 1992-93; regional mgr., risk mgmt. and field underwriter U.S. Employer Consumer Self-Insured Fund, Pensacola, Fla., 1993—. Mem. Big Bros./Big Sisters, Pensacola, 1994. Presdl. scholar U. So. Ala., 1988-92, grad. scholar U. West Fla., 1994. Mem. Am. Soc. Safety Engrs. Republican. Baptist. Home and Office: 2110 Saint Andrews Dr Cantonment FL 32533-6844

NICOLAÏ, JUDITHE, international business trade executive; b. Lawrence, Mass., Dec. 15, 1945; d. Victor and Evelyn (Otash) Abisalih. Student in photography, L.A. City Coll., 1967, UCLA, 1971; AA in Fgn. Langs., Coll. of Marin, 1983; hon. degree, Culinary Inst., San Francisco, 1981. Photographer Scott Paper Co., N.Y.C., 1975; owner, operator restaurant The Raincheck Room, West Hollywood, Calif., 1976; prin., pres., chief exec. officer, photographer fashion Photographie sub. Nicolaï Internat. Svcs., Nice, France, 1977—; prin., pres., chief exec. officer, instr. catering and cooking Back to Basics sub. Nicolaï Internat. Svcs., San Francisco, 1980—; chief photographer exhibit and trade show, chief of staff food div. Agri-Bus. U.S.A., Moscow and Washington, 1983; head transp. U.S. Summer Olympics, L.A., 1984, interpreter for Spanish, French, Portuguese, and Italian, 1985; prin., pres., chief exec. officer, interpreter Intertrans subs. (Nicolaï Internat. Svcs.), San Francisco, 1985—; founder, pres. Nicolaï Internat. Svcs., San Francisco, 1985—; pres., CEO Cyprus Personal Care Products, 1994—. Contbr. column on food and nutrition to jour., 1983-84. Mem. Alpha Gamma Sigma. Office: Nicolai Internat Svcs 1686 Union St Ste 203 San Francisco CA 94123-4509 Mailing Address: 2269 Chestnut St Ste 237 San Francisco CA 94123-2607

NICOLAYSEN, LUCILE MARTINEZ, Spanish educator; b. N.Y.C.; d. Bernabe Lago Martínez and Pura (Bellón) Gonçalves; m. John E. Nicolaysen, May 29, 1968; children: Pamela, Cristina. BA in Spanish, Philosophy, Hunter Coll., 1966; MA in Spanish Lit., Montclair State Coll., 1979; MA in Adminstrn. and Edn. Leadership, William Paterson Coll., 1994. Tchr. Spanish Bd. of Edn., N.Y.C., 1966-69; tchr. ESL Bergenfield (N.J.) Bd. of Edn. Adult Sch., 1978-84; tchr. Spanish No. Valley Regional H.S. Dist., Old Tappan, N.J., 1986—; vis. com. Mid. States, Union Hill, 1993; chairperson com. Mid. States at Nurits, Old Tappan, 1993; reader A.P. exams ETS Spanish AP, San Antonio, 1994, Clemson, S.C., 1995. Leader, chairperson Girl Scouts Am., Bergen County. Recipient Tchr. Recognition award Gov. N.J., 1990. Mem. Pi Lambd Theta. Office: No Valley Regional HS Central Ave Old Tappan NJ 07675

NICOLETTI, BETSY A., health facility administrator; b. Erie, Pa., Sept. 19, 1953; d. Anthony Woodrow and Tressa (Brown) N.; m. Christopher S. Allen (div. Feb. 1991); children: David N., Daniel P., Julia E. BS, U. Pitts., 1975, MSW, 1977; MS, Antioch U., 1994. Part time social worker Shadyside Hosp., Pitts., 1975-77; social worker Med. Ctr. Hosp. Vt., Burlington, 1977-79, Family Svcs. of Rochester (N.Y.), 1979-81; office mgr. Christopher Allen, MD, Chester, Vt., 1982-87; COO Network Mgmt. Svcs., Springfield, Vt., 1988—; trustee, treas., 1st v.p., pres. Healthcare and Rehab. Svcs. Southeastern Vt., Bellows Falls, 1991—. Active fundraising com. Whiting Libr., Chester, 1983-86; mem. com. New Am. Schs. Grant Pub. Schs. in Springfield, 1993-94; trustee-treas. Vt. Ctr. for The Book, Chester, 1994-95. Mem. Vt. Blue Cross/Blue Shield Bus. Adv. Group, New England Healthcare Assembly (physician practice mgmt. adv. bd.), Med. Group Mgmt. Assn. Democrat. Home: 115 Parker Hill Rd Springfield VT 05156 Office: Network Mgmt Svcs 252 River St Springfield VT 05156

NICOLINI, GAIL F., mathematics educator secondary school; b. Evergreen Park, Ill., Aug. 25, 1953; d. Rocco and Frances H. (Spiller) Marich; m. Christopher Nicolini, June 7, 1977; children: Stephanie, Dominic, Gina. BA, Coll. St. Francis, Joliet, Ill., 1975; MA in Spl. Edn., Chgo. State U., 1982. Tchr. Andrean H.S., Merrillville, Ind. Vice precinct capt., Merrillville, Ind., 1992-94. Mem. Nat. Coun. Tchrs. Math., Nat. Cath. Edn. Assn., N.W. Ind. Tchrs. of Math., Aquatic Club Merrillville (treas. 1994-95). Roman Catholic. Home: 5617 Massachusetts Merrillville IN 46410 Office: Andrean HS 5959 Broadway Merrillville IN 46410

NICOLL, JUDITH A., retired guidance counselor; b. Port Washington, N.Y., Mar. 28, 1938; d. William J. and Gertrude C. (Crampton) N. BS, Boston U., 1960; MA, Columbia U., 1963, profl. diploma, 1965. Cert. guidance counselor, N.Y. Dance, phys. edn. tchr. Lexington (Mass.) Pub. Schs., 1960-62; jr. h.s. guidance counselor South Huntington (N.Y.) Pub. Schs., 1965-66; h.s. guidance counselor Bellmore (N.Y.)-Merrick Ctrl. H.S. Dist., 1966-94; ret. Bellmore (N.Y.)-Murrick Ctrl. H.S. Dist., 1994. Recipient Nassau County Exec. award, 1989, 94, Svc. award N.Y. State United Tchrs. Assn., 1994; named Outstanding Innovator, Bellmore-Merrick Cultural Arts Coun., 1984, 94. Mem. AAUW, L.I. Pers. and Guidance Assn. (sec. 1970-75), Cow Neck Hist. Roman Catholic. Home: 15 Highland Ave Port Washington NY 11050

NIDA, KATHRYN BETH, artist; b. Anchorage, Mar. 9, 1967; d. Robert Hale and Jeannine Danette (Jensen) Nida; m. Duncan Robert Hughes, July 8, 1989. BA in Studio Art, Comparative Lit., U. Calif., Irvine, 1989. Artist/printmaker San Diego, 1989—; tech. editor Converse Cons., San Diego, 1990-93, Brian F. Smith & Assocs., San Diego, 1993-94, Harcourt Brace & Co., San Diego, 1994-96; freelance editor San Diego, 1996—; exhbn. dir. Art Gallery-Artwalk, San Diego, 1991—. Artist serigraphs: 4 x 4 Plywood, 1991, I Stand Relieved, 1992, Tin Can, 1992, Nervous Breakdown, 1994, Seismically Unstable, 1995; one woman show at U. Calif.-Irvine Women's Ctr., 1990. Mem. Am. Needlepoint Guild, Embroidery Guild of Am., L.A. Printmaking Soc., San Diego Art Inst.

NIEDERMEIER, MARY B., retired nutrition educator; b. Webster Groves, Mo., Oct. 20, 1914; d. Albertus and Daisey May (Christman) Wickersham; m. Walter H. Niedermeier, Sept. 9, 1939; children: Gail Santarelli, Bart Niedermeier. BS, Mich. State U., 1937; MA, Columbia U., 1957, profl. diploma, 1959. Cert. in dietetics, Miami Valley Hosp., Dayton, Ohio, 1938. Dist. nutritionist N.J. State Dept. of Health, Newark; instr. nutrition edn. Sch. of Dentistry Fairleigh Dickinson U., Teaneck, N.J.; instr. nutrition edn. Sch. of Nursing St. Louis U. Pres. PTA, Oradell (N.J.) Pub. Sch., 1954-57; bd. dirs. Rancho Bernardo (Calif.) Oaks North Community Ctr., 1974-76; bd. deacons Rancho Bernardo Presbyn. Ch., 1975-77; treas. PEO-TV chpt., Rancho Bernardo, 1990. Grace McCloud fellow 1957-59 Columbia U. Mem. AAUW, AAUP, Am. Dietetic Assn., Calif. Dietetic Assn., N.J. Dietetic Assn., Alpha Omicron Pi. Republican. Home: 17411 Plaza De La Rosa San Diego CA 92128-2223

NIEDERMEYER, EMILY L., fundraiser; b. Portland, Oreg., Oct. 14, 1968; d. Thomas Joseph and Barbara Louise (Whitehead) N. BA, Whitman Coll., 1990. Alumni officer Whitman Coll., Walla Walla, Wash., 1990-92; asst. dir., spl. asst. to v.p. Reed Coll., Portland, Oreg., 1992-96; dir. ann. giving Pacific U., Forest Grove, Oreg., 1996—. Democrat. Office: Pacific U 2043 College Way Forest Grove OR 97221

NIEKAMP, CHRISTINE MARIE, labor and delivery nurse, educator; b. Freeport, Tex., Jan. 19, 1962; d. Leray Joseph and Helen Agnes (Janca) N. BSN, Incarnate Word Coll., 1984. RN, Tex.; RNC, NCC. Staff nurse, labor and delivery clin. nurse III S.W. Tex. Meth. Hosp., San Antonio, 1984—, neonatal resuscitation instr., 1989—, rotating evening charge nurse, 1988—, chairperson. edn. coun. labor and delivery, 1991-92, mem. edn. coun. labor and delivery, 1991—, mem. quality improvement coun. labor and delivery, 1994. Mem. Assn. Women's Health, Obstetric, and Neonatal Nurses. Roman Catholic. Home: 13121 NW Military Hwy # 623 San Antonio TX 78231 Office: SW Tex Meth Hosp 7700 Floyd Curl Dr San Antonio TX 78229

NIELSEN, GEORGIA PANTER, flight attendant; b. Smith Center, Kans., May 10, 1937; d. Herbert Grover and Mildred P.; m. Dan Erik Nielsen, Jan. 16, 1971. MA, San Jose (Calif.) State U., 1979. Flight attendant San Francisco, 1960—; editor, pub. Air Reporter, San Francisco, San Jose, Calif, 1991—, Oakland, Calif., 1991—; exec. bd. San Mateo Ctrl. Labor Coun. AFL-CIO, 1984-95. Author: From Sky Girl to Flight Attendant Women and the Making of a Union, 1982. Named Spkr. of Yr. People Speaking, 1988; recipient Unity award Honoree San Mateo Ctrl. Labor Coun., 1992. Mem. Assn. of Flight Attendants (union officer 1978-85, nat. historian 1980—, local pres. 1982-85). Office: Air Reporter PO Box 32233 San Jose CA 95152-2233

NIELSEN, JENNIFER LEE, molecular ecologist, researcher; b. Balt., Mar. 21, 1946; d. Leo Jay and Mary Marriott (Mules) N.; divorced; children: Nadja Ochs, Allisha Ochs. MFA, Ecole des Beaux Arts, Paris, 1968; BS, Evergreen State Coll., 1987; MS, U. Calif., Berkeley, 1990, PhD, 1994. Artist Seattle, 1969-78; fish biologist Weyerhaeuser Co., Tacoma, Wash., 1978-89; resource cons. Berkeley, 1989-90; rsch. biologist USDA-Forest Svc., Albany, Calif., 1990—; vis. scientist Stanford U., Pacific Grove, Calif., 1994—; rsch. assoc. U. Calif., Santa Barbara, 1994—; rsch. assoc. U. Calif. Marine Sci. Inst., Santa Barbara, 1994—. Editor: Evolution and the Aquatic Ecosystem, 1995; contbr. articles to profl. jours.; paintings exhibited at Metro. Mus. Modern Art, 1966; represented in numerous pvt. collections, U.S. and Europe. Mem. Am. Fisheries Soc. (pres. chpt. 1993-94), Molecular Marine Biology and Biotech. (regional editor 1995), Animal Behaviour Soc. (policy com. 1993-94). Home: 84 Corona Rd Carmel Highlands CA 93923 Office: Hopkins Marine Sta Oceanview Blvd Pacific Grove CA 93950

NIELSEN, JOYCE, former state legislator; b. Askov, Minn., Nov. 20, 1933; d. Clarey Burnhardt and Dorothy Elaine (Saastad) Jensen; m. Eric Hans Nielsen, June 11, 1955; 1 child, Cindy. Grad., Cloquet (Minn.) H.S. Fin. cons. Nielsen Fin. Cons., Inc., Cedar Rapids, Iowa, 1984-88; mem. Iowa Ho. of Reps., Des Moines, 1989-93; facilitator Parenting Edn. Programs 1993—. Bd. dirs., Vice President, former treas. Peoples Ch., Cedar Rapids, 1994—; bd. dirs., sec. UN Assn., Cedar Rapids, 1988; bd. dirs., mem. exec. com. United Way, Cedar Rapids; founding mem., v.p. Dem. Activist Women's Network, 1995—. Named Woman of Yr., Coalition of Women's Groups; recipient Outstanding Svc. award YWCA, Community Action Agy. Mem.

LWV (bd. dirs., v.p. 1995—). Democrat. Mem. Unitarian Ch. Home: 2702 Q Ave NW Cedar Rapids IA 52405-1439

NIELSEN, NANCY, publishing executive; b. Jeffersonville, Ind., 1950. BA, Univ. Calif., Berkeley, 1975. Asst. city editor, weekend mag. editor Dallas Times Herald, 1975-77; cons. McKinsey & Co. Inc.; dir. office of comm. Capital Cities/ABC Inc., N.Y.C., 1984-86; deputy dir. corp. rels. The N.Y. Times Co., N.Y.C., 1986-88, dir. corp. rels./Pa., 1987-93, v.p. corp. comm., 1992—; bd. dir. Inst. of Journalism Edn. Recipient Alumni Assn. award for outstanding performance in journalism Univ. Calif. Berkeley. Office: The New York Times Co 229 W 43rd St New York NY 10036-3913*

NIELSON, NORMA LEE, business educator; b. Augusta, Ga., Dec. 26, 1953; d. Norman Lyle and Betty Lou (Buckner) Parrott; m. Mark G. Nielson, Nov. 20, 1985 (div. 1988); 1 child, Eric Gordon. BS, Northwest Mo. State U., 1974; MA, U. Pa., 1976, PhD, 1979. CLU. Asst. prof. Iowa State U., Ames, 1977-79, U. So. Calif., L.A., 1979-84; cons. profl. Mercer-Meidinger, L.A., 1984-85; assoc. prof. Oreg. State U., Corvallis, 1985-90; prof. Oreg. State U., 1990—; bd. examiners Internat. Bd. Stds. and Practice for CFP, 1991-94. Developer software; contbg. author: Handbook for Corporate Directors, 1985; contbr. articles to profl. publs. Vol. Linn-Benton Food Share, Corvallis; bd. dirs. Corvallis Cmty. Dare Care, Inc., 1988-91; candidate for Oreg. Ho. of Reps., 1994. Andrus Found. rsch. grantee, 1989-91. Mem. Am. Risk and Ins. Assn. (bd. dirs. 1990—, officer 1993—), Western Risk and Ins. Assn. (officer 1981-84), Risk and Ins. Mgmt. Soc. Office: Oreg State U Coll Bus #200 Bexell Hall Corvallis OR 97331-2603

NIEMAN, VALERIE GAIL, editor; b. Jamestown, N.Y., July 6, 1955; d. Warner Ernest and Eleanor A. (Aiken) N. Student, Jamestown C.C., 1975-76; BS in Journalism, W.Va. U., 1978. Staff writer W.Va. U News Svc., Morgantown, W.Va., 1978; reporter Dominion Post, Morgantown, 1978; reporter Times West Virginian, Fairmont, W.Va., 1979-92, city editor, 1992-95, exec. editor, 1995—; tchr. basic newswriting W.Va. U., Morgantown, 1990, tchr. sci. fiction writing, 1995; lectr., vis. writer tri-state area, 1988—; founding co-editor Kestrel lit. jour., Fairmont, 1992—; co-founder, co-dir. Kestrel Writers Conf., Fairmont, 1993—. Author: (novel) Neena Gathering, 1988, (poetry chpts.) How We Live, 1996, Slipping Out of Old Eve, 1988. W.Va. cir. writer W.Va. Humanities Commn., 1994; mem. Leadership Marion, Fairmont, 1995-96. Recipient award in letters Fairmont Arts and Humanities, 1988, 94; Fellow in poetry NEA, 1991, fellow in fiction Ky. Found. for Women, 1991, fellow in fiction, W.Va. Commn. on Arts, 1992. Mem. Sci. Fiction and Fantasy Writers Am., W.Va. Writers Inc. Democrat. Lutheran. Office: Times West Virginian 300 Quincy St Fairmont WV 26555

NIEMANN, LINDA GRANT, railroad conductor; b. Pasadena, Calif., Sept. 22, 1946; d. Carl George and Mary Grant (Parkhurst) N. BA, U. Calif., Santa Cruz, 1968; PhD, U. Calif., Berkeley, 1975. Brakeman, condr. So. Pacific, 1979—. Author: Boomer: Railroad Memoirs, 1990. Mem. PEN, Nat. Writers Woman. Address: PO Box 7409 Santa Cruz CA 95061-7409

NIEMELA, PEGGY ANN, elementary education educator; b. Hancock, Mich., Apr. 22, 1954; d. Chester A. and Marjorie S. (White) Gibbs; m. James O. Niemela, Sept. 25, 1976; children: Corey J., Mark G. BS, No. Mich. U., 1971-75. cert. elem. and English tchr., Mich. 5th and 6th grade tchr. Adam Twp. Schs., South Range, Mich., 1975-78, elem. counselor, 1976-77; elem. tchr. Lake Linden (Mich.) Hubbell Schs., 1982-89; dir. teaching, learning ctr. Suomi Coll., Hancock, 1989-90; 6th grade tchr. Lake Linden Hubbell Schs., 1991—; chairperson Sch. Improvement Com., Lake Linden, 1993—. Mem. Mich. Reading Assn. Methodist. Home: 90 1st St Laurium MI 49913-2011 Office: Lake Linden Hubbell Schs 601 Calumet St Lake Linden MI 49945-1002

NIEMI, JANICE, lawyer, former state legislator; b. Flint, Mich., Sept. 18, 1928; d. Richard Jesse and Norma (Bell) Bailey; m. Preston Niemi, Feb. 4, 1953 (divorced 1987); children—Ries, Patricia. BA, U. Wash., 1950, LL.B., 1967; postgrad. U. Mich., 1950-52; cert. Hague Acad. Internat. Law, Netherlands, 1954. Bar: Wash. 1968. Assoc. firm Powell, Livengood, Dunlap & Silverdale, Kirkland, Wash., 1968; staff atty. Legal Service Ctr., Seattle, 1968-70; judge Seattle Dist. Ct., 1971-72, King County Superior Ct., Seattle, 1973-78; acting gen. counsel, dep. gen. counsel SBA, Washington, 1979-81; mem. Wash. State Ho. of Reps., Olympia, 1983-87, chmn. com. on state govt., 1984; mem. Wash. State Senate, 1987-95; sole practice, Seattle, 1981-94; superior ct. judge King County, 1995—; mem. White House Fellows Regional Selection Panel, Seattle, 1974-77, chmn., 1976, 77; incorporator Sound Savs. & Loan, Seattle, 1975. Bd. dirs. Allied Arts, Seattle, 1971—, Ctr. Contemporary Art, Seattle, 1981-83, Women's Network, Seattle, 1981-84, Pub. Defender Assn., Seattle, 1982-84; bd. visitors dept. psychology U. Wash., Seattle, 1983-87, bd. visitors dept sociology, 1988— . Named Woman of Yr. in Law, Past Pres.'s Assn., Seattle, 1971; Woman of Yr., Matrix Table, Seattle, 1973, Capitol Hill Bus. and Profl. Women, 1975. Mem. Wash. State Bar Assn., Wash. Women Lawyers, Allied Arts of Seattle Bd. Democrat. Home: PO Box 20516 Seattle WA 98102-1516

NIENHIUS-HORNER, CAROLYN JOANNE, educator, counselor, consultant; b. Akron, Ohio, Oct. 26, 1948; d. James Patrick and Pauline Elizabeth (Beretics) Kintz; m. Ronald Jay Nienhius, Aug. 23, 1970 (div. Dec. 1979); children: Nathan Jeremy, Seth Michael; m. Karl Ford Horner, Jr., Nov. 3, 1983. BS, Ohio State U., 1972; M in Tech. Edn. Guidance, U. Akron, 1988, M in Counseling, 1990. Lic. social worker, Ohio; cert. employee assistance profl.; trained in divorce mediation. Employee devel. trainer Sum County Dept. Human Svcs., Akron, 1984-90; employee assistance counselor Tri-County Employee Assistance Progam, Akron, 1989-90; intrvention program coord. Community Drug Bd., Akron, 1990-91; counselor, consultant, trainer Hop To It (pvt. practice), Hartville, Ohio, 1991—; instr., trainer, practicum supr., program developer, writer Stark Tech. Coll., Canton, Ohio, 1990—; cons. Child Support Enforcement Agy. Akron, 1989—; in-svc. trainer Wadsworth (Ohio) City Schs.; presenter Ohio Welfare Conf., Toledo, 1989, Ohio Counselors Conf., Columbus, 1990; curriculum writer Case Western Res. U. Mandel Sch. Applied Social Scis. Vol. ARC, Akron, 1967-88, Risk Reduction Health Promotion Task Force, Akron, 1984-89, Side Stream Smoke Task Force, 1984-89; coord. Tri County Disabled Citizens Activities, Akron, 1988-89; recorder Stark Tech. Coll. Adv. Bd., 1990—; mem. citizen ambassador program mgmt. Tng. and Incentive Delegation to Russia and Ukraine, 1992. Mem. AACD, ASTD, Ohio Coun. for Self Esteem, Internat. Assn. for Addictions and Offenders Counselors, Toastmasters Internat., Chi Sigma Iota (program chmn. Alpha Upsilon chpt. 1989-90, Pres. award, Akron, 1990). Home and Office: Hop To It Counseling Svcs 7052 Pinedale St NE Hartville OH 44632-9392

NIES, HELEN WILSON, federal judge; b. Birmingham, Ala., Aug. 7, 1925; d. George Earl and Lida Blanche (Erckert) Wilson; m. John Dirk Nies ; children: Dirk, Nancy, Eric. BA, U. Mich., 1946, JD, 1948. Bar: Mich. 1948, D.C. 1961, U.S. Supreme Ct. 1962. Atty. Dept. Justice, Washington, 1948-51, Office Price Stblzn., Washington, 1951-52; assoc. Pattishall, McAuliffe and Hofstetter, Washington, 1960-66, resident ptnr., 1966-77; ptnr. Howrey & Simon, Washington, 1978-80; judge U.S. Ct. Customs and Patent Appeals, 1980-82; cir. judge U.S. Ct. Appeals Fed. Cir., 1982—; chief judge U.S. Ct. Appeals (fed. cir.), 1990-94, sr. status, 1995—; mem. jud. conf. U.S. Com. on Bicentennial of Constn., 1986-92; mem. pub. adv. com. trademark affairs Dept. Commerce, 1976-80; mem. adv. bd. BNA's Patent Trademark and Copyright Jour., 1976-78; mem. bd. visitors U. Mich. Law Sch., 1975-78; adv. for restatement of law and unfair competition Am. Law Inst., 1986—; speaker World Intellectual Property Orgn., Forum of Judges, Calcutta, 1987, European Judges Conf., Hague, 1991, Kyoto (Japan) Comparative Law Ctr., 1992, others. Recipient Athena Outstanding Alumna award U. Mich., 1987, Jefferson medal N.J. Patent Law Assn., 1991, Judicial Honoree award Bar Assn. D.C., 1992, D. of Laws, Honoris Causa, John Marshall Law Sch., Chgo., 1993. Mem. ABA (chmn. com. 203, 1972-74, com. 504, 1975-76), Bar Assn. D.C. (chmn. patent trademark copyright sect. 1975-76, dir. 1976-78), U.S. Trademark Assn. (chmn. lawyers adv. com. 1974-76, bd. dirs. 1976-78), Am. Patent Law Assn., Fed. Bar Assn., Nat. Assn. Women Lawyers, Women's Bar D.C. (Woman Lawyer of Yr. 1980), Order of Coif, Phi Beta Kappa, Phi Kappa Phi. Office: US Ct Appeals Fed Cir 717 Madison Pl NW Washington DC 20439-0001*

NIES, KEVIN ALLISON, physics educator; b. N.Y.C., Apr. 23, 1949; d. Russell Albert and Signe Marie (Rasmussen) N. BS in Physics, U. Calif., Santa Barbara, 1972; postgrad., UCLA, 1979, Pasadena City Coll., 1980-81, Calif. State U., Northridge, 1985-90. Tchg. credential, Calif.; lic. FCC radio telephone 2d class. Rsch. assoc. level 2 UCLA Brain Inst., L.A., summer 1973; TV technician, engr. NBC, N.Y.C., 1978; founder, dir. Calif. Video Inst., L.A., 1980—; tchr. secondary edn. L.A. Unified Sch. Dist., 1985—; judge sci. fair San Fernando H.S., Slymar, Calif., 1994; instr. video prodn. Calif. Video Inst., L.A., 1982-85; mem. Assn. Women in Sci., L.A., 1978-83, 94, NSTA, 1985-88, Nat. Orgn. Broadcasting Engrs. and Technicians, 1978-80. Author, dir.: (video series) Women Physicists and Their Research, 1981, (video programs) Voyager: The Inside Story, 1982, Scientists in Space, 1983, Working Under Volcanos, 1984, Rendezvous with a Comet, 1985; author, illustrator: (book) From Sorceress to Scientist, 1990. Mem. Mus. of Tolerance, L.A., 1995-96. Mem. NOW, United Tchrs. L.A., Calif. Sci. Tchrs. Assn., Am. Film Inst., Nat. Alliance of Breast Cancer Orgns., UCLA Alumni Assn. Democrat. Office: The Calif Video Inst PO Box 572019 Tarzana CA 91357

NIEUWENDORP, JUDY LYNELL, special education educator; b. Sioux Center, Iowa, Jan. 3, 1955; d. Leonard Henry and Jenelda Faith (Van't Hul) N. BA in Religious Edn., Reformed Bible Coll., 1977; BA in Secondary Edn. and Social Scis., Northwestern Coll., 1980; degree edn. of emotional disabilities, Mankato State U., 1984; MEd, Marian Coll., 1989. Tutor, counselor The Other Way, Grand Rapids, Mich., 1976-77; sr. counselor Handicap Village, Sheldon, Iowa, 1978-79; florist Sheldon Greenhouse, 1979-80; K-6 summer sch. tchr. Worthington (Minn.) Sch. Dist., 1982-83; tchr. of emotional/behavioral disabilities class Worthington Sr. H.S., 1981-85, White Bear Lake (Minn.), 1985-89, Northland Pines H.S., Eagle River, Wis., 1989—; negotiator Coop. Edn. Svcs. Agy., Tomahawk, Wis., 1994—; instr. workshop Advanced Learning, Cedar Falls, Iowa, 1991-92; regional rep. for coun. of spl. program devel. Den. Coop. Svc. Unit, 1983-85; basketball/volleyball coach Worthington, White Bear Lake and Three Lakes, Wis., 1981-89. Mem. scholarship com. Profl. Bus. Women Am., Worthington, 1984-85; asst. devel. mem.Hosp. Mental Health Unit, Worthington, 1983-84; founder parent support group for parents of spl. edn. students Worthington Sch. Dist., 1983-84. Mem. Nat. Edn. Coun., Wis. Edn. Assn., Coun. for Exceptional Children, Minn. Educators for Emotionally Disabled, AKF Martial Arts. Home: 5148 Hwy G Eagle River WI 54521

NIEVES, CARMEN, emergency services coordinator; b. Biddeford, Maine, Aug. 26, 1950; d. Roland E. and Yvette T. (Lessard) Therrien; m. Jose E. Nieves, June 27, 1987. Cert. mgmt., Riverside City Coll., 1996. Cert. emergency mgr. Police svcs. rep. Riverside (Calif.) Police, 1986-91, emer. svc. coord., 1991—. Adv. com. local gov., 1990—. Mem. Western Riverside Emer. Council (chair. 1993—), Emergency Mgrs. Assn. (chair 1993-95), Calif. Emergency Svcs. Assn., Earthquake Survival Program. Office: Riverside Police 4102 Orange St Riverside CA 92501

NIEWIAROSKI, TRUDI OSMERS (GERTRUDE NIEWIAROSKI), social studies educator; b. Jersey City, Apr. 30, 1935; d. Albert John and Margaret (Niemeyer) Osmers; m. Donald H. Niewiaroski, June 8, 1957; children: Donald H., Donna, Margaret Anne, Nancy Noel. AB in History and German, Upsala Coll., East Orange, N.J., 1957; MEd, Montgomery County Pub. Schs., Rockville, Md., 1992. Cert. tchr., Md. Tchr. geography Colego Americano, Quito, Ecuador, 1964-66; bd. dirs. Cotopaxi Acad., Quito, 1964-65; tchr. speed reading Escuela Lincoln, Buenos Aires, Argentina, 1966-67; substitute thcr. Montgomery County Pub. Schs., Rockville, 1978-83, tchr. social studies, 1984—; del. Eisenhower People to People Educators' Del. Vietnam, 1993. Author curricula; contbr. chpts. to books, articles to profl. jours.; lectr. at workshops. Bd. dirs. Cotopaxi Acad., Quito, 1964-65; pres. Citizens Assn., Potomac, Md., 1977-81; leader Girl Scouts U.S., 1975-76; adv. coun. Milken Found. Recipient Md. Tchr. of Yr. award State of Md. Edn. Dept., 1993, finalist nat. Tchr. of Yr., 1993, Disting. Alumni award Upsala Coll., 1993, Nat. Educator award Milken Found., 1994; Fulbright fellow, India, 1985, China, 1990, Japan Keizai Koho Ctr. fellow, 1992; UMBC-U. Mex. Art and Culture scholar, 1995. Mem. AAUW, ASCD, Nat. Coun. Social Studies, Md. Coun. for Social Studies, Asia Soc., Smithsonian Instn., Montgomery County Hist. Soc., Spl. Interest Groups-China, Japan and Korea, Md. Bus. Roundtable for Edn., Nat. Social Studies Suprs. Assn., Kappa Delta Pi. Office: R Montgomery High Sch Rockville MD 20852

NIFFENEGGER, CAROL JANE, artist; b. South Haven, Mich.; d. Henry Paul and Esther Theresa (Warskow) N. BA with Distinction, U. Mich., 1971; postgrad. studies, Hunter Coll., 1974; cert. of design, N.Y. Sch. of Interior Design, 1986. Congressional intern Rep. Edward Hutchinson, Washington, 1970; libr. Medtronic France, Paris, 1971-73; asst. to editor-in-chief U.P. Internat., N.Y.C., 1975-77; asst. producer CBS-TV News/Entertainemnt, N.Y.C., 1978-81; conf. dir. continuing edn. dept. L.I. U., 1982; TV prodr. March of Dimes Telethon, White Plains, N.Y., 1983-86; artist, N.Y.C., 1987—. Artist, one woman shows in N.Y.C., 1991, 93, 95, 96, in Conn., 1990; numerous juried and group exhbns. including 7th and 8th Ann. Mich. Statewide Art Competitions. Trustee Am. Philharm. Orch., N.Y.C., 1980-81. Recipient Emmy for undercover rsch. N.Y. chpt. Nat. Acad. TV Arts and Scis., 1980, Best-in-Show award Art Students League, N.Y.C., 1991, Purchase award Holland (Mich.) Area Arts Ctr., 1995. Mem. Club of Budapest (spk. 1st world mem.'s meetiing 1996). Office: Denise Bibro Fine Art Gallery 584 Broadway New York NY 10012

NIGHTINGALE, ELENA OTTOLENGHI, geneticist, physician, administrator; b. Livorno, Italy, Nov. 1, 1932; came to U.S., 1939; d. Mario Lazzaro and Elisa Vittoria (Levi) Ottolenghi; m. Stuart L. Nightingale, July 1, 1965; children—Elizabeth, Marisa. A.B. summa cum laude, Barnard Coll., 1954; Ph.D., Rockefeller U., 1961; M.D., NYU, 1964. Asst. prof. Cornell U. Med. Coll., N.Y.C., 1965-70, Johns Hopkins U., Balt., 1970-73; fellow in clin. genetics and pediatrics Georgetown U. Hosp., Washington, 1973-74; sr. staff officer NAS, Washington, 1975-79, sr. program officer Inst. Medicine, 1979-82, sr. scholar in residence, 1982-83; spl. advisor to pres. Carnegie Corp. N.Y., N.Y.C., 1983-94, sr. program officer, 1989-94; scholar-in-residence Nat. Acad. Scis., Washington, 1995—; vis. assoc. prof. Harvard U. Med. Sch., Boston, 1980-84, vis. lectr., 1984-95; adj. prof. pediatrics Georgetown U. Med. Ctr., 1984—, George Washington U. Med. Ctr., 1994—; mem. recombinant DNA adv. com. NIH, Bethesda, Md., 1979-83. Editor: The Breaking of Bodies and Minds: Torture, Psychiatric Abuse and the Health Professions, 1985, Prenatal Screening, Policies and Values: The Example of Neural Tube Defects, 1987; co-author: Before Birth: Prenatal Screening for Genetic Disease, 1990, Promoting the Health of Adolescents: New Directions for the 21st Century, 1993; contbr. numerous sci. articles to profl. publs. Bd. dirs. Ctr. for Youth Svcs., Washington, 1980-84, Sci. Svc. Inc., Washington, 1985-96, Amnesty Internat., U.S.A., 1989-91. Sloan Found. fellow, 1974-75. Fellow AAAS (chmn. com. on sci. freedom and responsibility 1985-88), N.Y. Acad. Scis., Royal Soc. Medicine; mem. Harvey Soc., Am. Soc. Microbiology, Am. Soc. Human Genetics (social issues com. 1982-85), Genetics Soc. Am., Inst. Medicine of NAS (chmn. com. on health and human rights 1987-90), Phi Beta Kappa, Sigma Xi. Office: Nat Acad Scis 2101 Constitution Ave NW Washington DC 20418-0007

NIHILL, KAREN BAILEY, nursing home executive, nurse clinician; b. Erie, Pa., Mar. 15, 1947; d. William C. and Eleanor (Danielson) Bailey; 1 son, Liam H. R.N., Hamot Med. Center, Erie, 1968; postgrad. SUNY, Gannon U., U. S.C., U. Pa., 1974—. RN, Pa. Critical care nurse Hamot Med. Center, 1968-71, VA Hosp., Phila., 1974-77; dir. nursing Chapel Manor and Nursing Home, Phila., 1977—, also Phila. Protestant Home and Elmira Jeffries Nursing Home; critical care nurse coord., supr. Millcreek Community Hosp., Erie, Pa., 1991—. Active Lutheran Ch. Women's Orgn. Served to lt. Nurse Corps, U.S. Navy, 1971-73. VA grantee, 1974. Mem. ACLS, Am. Assn. Critical Care Nurses, Pa. Nurses Assn. Republican. Home: 5316 Bryant St Erie PA 16509-2404

NIKETIĆ, STEPHANIE NEALE, business executive, consultant; b. Salt Lake City, Nov. 13, 1957; d. Robert Hersel and Luise (Putcamp) Johnson; m. Novak Milorada Niketić; children: Maximilian Novak, Dara Luise. Mktg. adminstr. Western hemisphere R.P.I. Van Leer B.V., Greenwich, Conn., 1977-81; mktg. comm. mgr. Van Leer USA Inc., Woburn, Mass., 1981-83; cons. Yankee Group Rsch., Inc., Boston, 1983-84; Japan br. mgr. Yankee Group Rsch., Inc., Tokyo, 1984-86; v.p. internat. ops. Yankee Group Rsch., Inc., Boston, 1986-89, COO, gen. mgr., 1989-91; pres., founder, owner Sutra, Inc., Newburyport, Mass., 1992—. Home: 93 High St Newburyport MA 01950 Office: Sutra Inc 102 State St Newburyport MA 01950

NILES, BARBARA ELLIOTT, psyanalyst; b. Boston, Jan. 31, 1939; d. Byron Kauffman and Helen Alice (Heissler) Elliott; m. John Denison, June 25, 1960 (div. 1981); children: Catherine, Andrew. AA, Briarcliff Coll., 1958; BA, SUNY, 1984; MSW, Hunter Coll., 1986. Cert. social worker; cert. in psychotherapy and psychoanalysis Inst. Contemporary Psychotherapy and Psychoanalysis, 1990. Exec. com. Legal Aid Soc. Women's Aux., N.Y.C., 1965-67; sec. Water Quality Task Force Scientists' Com. for Pub. Info., N.Y.C., 1973-74; founding dir., sec. Consumer Action Now Inc., N.Y.C., 1970-77; dir. devel. Consumer Action Now's Council Environ., N.Y.C., 1976-77; dir. 170 Tenants Corp., N.Y.C., 1979-81; mem. pub. interest com. Cosmopolitan Club, N.Y.C., 1979-82; dir. INFORM Inc., N.Y.C., 1978-84; pvt. practice psychotherapy and psychoanalysis N.Y.C., 1986—; mem. faculty metro ctr. Empire State Coll., N.Y.C., 1987—. Editor: biography: Off the Beaten Track, 1984. Mem. Nat. Assn. Social Workers. Clubs: Cosmopolitan (N.Y.C.), The Vincent (Boston). Office: 230 Central Park W New York NY 10024-6029

NILSEN, DIANNE, psychologist, researcher; b. Waukegan, Ill., Oct. 10, 1960; d. Gilbert R. and Lorraine L. (Kozlecar) Nilsen; m. Gordon J. Curphy, Mar. 31, 1989; 1 child, Ian Patrick. BS, U. Wis., Parkside, 1982; PhD, U. Minn., 1995. Rsch. analyst State of Minn., St. Paul, 1982-87; rsch. asst. Pers. Decisions Rsch. Inst., Mpls., 1987-89; rsch. assoc. Ctr. for Creative Leadership, Colorado Springs, Colo., 1989—. Co-author: Manual for Campbell Interest and Skill Survey, 1992. U. Minn. Grad. fellow, 1986, 87, 88. Mem. APA, Soc. for Indsl./Orgnl. Psychology, Colo. Wyo. Assn. Indsl./Orgnl. Psychologists. Home: 15485 Pleasant View Dr Colorado Springs CO 80921 Office: Ctr for Creative Leadership 850 Leader Way Colorado Springs CO 80921

NILSSON, NANCY MITCHELL, playwright; b. Milw., Mar. 16, 1928; d. Roy David and Marie Lucille (Toney) Mitchell; m. John Dexter Nilsson, Oct. 29, 1955; 1 child, David Samuel. BA, Huntingdon Coll., Montgomery, Ala., 1949; MA, Vanderbilt U., 1955. Primary tchr. Madison County Sch. Sys., Huntsville, Ala., 1950-58; h.s. tchr. Madison County Sch. Sys., Huntsville, 1964-66; feature writer Huntsville News, 1964; pub. rels. officer Cmty. Chest (United Way), Huntsville, 1964-65; sr. publs. engr. Vitro Corp., Silver Spring, Md., 1980-90. Playwright: Reunion, 1973, All God's Chillun Got Shoes, 1978, Alvin Was a Mean Old Boy, 1984, Very Truly Yours, Mary Lincoln, 1986, This Lemon is Soft, 1988, Clara Barton, 1991, Faulty Genes, 1993, All I Could See, 1995, Great Scott, 1996, others. Founder Huntsville Little Theatre, 1949, bd. dirs., pres., 1949-66, dir., 1949-66; pres. Ala. Theatre Conf., 1965; bd. dirs., dir., pres. Rockville (Md.) Little Theatre, 1967-85; chmn. City of Rockville Humanities Commn., 1980-81. Recipient numerous awards and commns. for plays. Mem. Playwrights Forum 2 of Washington, Chi Delta Phi. Republican. Roman Catholic. Home: 309 Twinbrook Pkwy Rockville MD 20851

NILSSON, SHIRLEY, religious organization administrator, educator. BA in Edn., Bethany Coll., Lindsborg, Kans. Tchr. St. Luke Luth. Weekdale Sch.; 2d v.p. Ch. Women United, Inc., N.Y.C., 1993—. Former Utah res. Ch. Women United, co-facilitator state unit, S.W. regional coord.; mem. nat. jubilee com.; mem. congl. unit Luth. Ch. Women; bd. dirs., sec. Rocky Mountain Synod, Evang. Luth. Ch. in Am.; active Women of Evang. Luth. Ch. in Am.; unit and bd. positions LWV. Office: Ch Women United Inc 475 Riverside Dr Rm 812 New York NY 10115-0050

NINTEMANN, TERRI, legislative staff member; b. Rochester, Minn., Mar. 13, 1963; d. John F. and Janice A. (Blair) Nintemann; m. Vincent J. Kiernan, Aug. 27, 1994. BS, U. Minn., 1985. Legis. asst. Farm Credit Svcs., St. Paul, Minn., 1986; intern, receptionist U.S. Senator Rudy Boschwitz, Washington, 1985, legis. corr., 1986-87, legis. asst., 1987-91; legis. dir. U.S. Rep. Dave Camp, Washington, 1991-92; profl. staff mem. Senate Agrl. Com., U.S. Senate, Washington, 1992—. Mem. U. Minn. Alumni, FFA Alumni (life mem.). Republican. Roman Catholic. Office: Senate Agrl Com 328 A Russell Senate Office Bldg Washington DC 20510

NIPERT, DONNA ANN See BARRETT, JESSICA

NISBETT, DOROTHEA JO, nursing educator; b. Lodi, Tex., May 16, 1940; d. Cecil Robey and Lola Ruby (Pippin) Lovett; m. Leonce Paul Lanoux Jr., June 10, 1966 (div. July 1984); 1 child, Cecil Lance Lanoux; m. James Harris Nisbett, May 12, 1990. Diploma in nursing, Tex. Ea. Sch. Nursing, 1963; BSN, Tex. Christian U., 1965; MS, Tex. Woman's U., 1977. RN, Tex. Asst. charge nurse med./surg. unit Med. Ctr. Hosp., Tyler, Tex., 1963-64, asst. dir. nursing, 1967; instr. nursing Tex. Ea. Sch. Nursing, Tyler, 1965-66; head nurse med./surg. unit Providence Hosp., Waco, Tex., 1966-67; dir. nursing Laird Meml. Hosp., Kilgore, Tex., 1967-69; instr. nursing Kilgore Coll., 1969-73, McLennan C.C., Waco, 1973—. Charter sec. Am. Heart Assn., Kilgore, 1968-69; bd. dirs. Heart of Tex. Soccer Assn., Waco, 1982-85. Mem. Nat. Orgn. Assoc. Degree Nursing, Tex. Jr. Coll. Tchr. Assn., Assn. Profl. and Staff Devel., Beta Sigma Phi (Outstanding Young Woman of Yr. 1981, Sweetheart 1970, 82, 91, Woman of Yr. 1990, Order of the Rose 1980, Silver Cir. award 1990). Methodist. Office: McLennan CC 1400 College Dr Waco TX 76708-1402

NISHIO, LINDA E., artist; b. L.A., June 18, 1952; d. Isamu and Ruby (Hifumi) N.; m. Mark S. Clair, Nov. 22, 1974 (wid. July 1982). Student, UCLA, 1970-73; BFA, U. Kans., 1975; MFA, Rutgers U., 1977. Graphic designer Women's Graphic Ctr., L.A., 1981-86; graphic designer Nishio Design, Pasadena, Calif., 1986—; vis. artist Otis Art Inst., L.A., 1993-94, San Francisco Art Inst., 1994-96, UCLA, 1993-94, others; mem. performance com. L.A. Contemporary Exhbns., 1986-90, others. One-woman shows include: Santa Monica Mus. of Art, 1993, Times Square Messages to the Pub., N.Y., 1989, Embassy Theater, L.A., 1985, U. Kans., Lawrence, 1985, Mus. Contemporary Art, L.A., 1983, U. So. Calif., L.A., 1983, Ohio State U. Gallery of Fine Arts, Columbus, 1983, Woman's Bldg., L.A., 1983, Printer Matter, N.Y., 1982, Mason Gross Sch. of Art, Rutgers U., 1982, Otis Gallery, L.A., 1996, others; group shows include Japanese Am. Mus., L.A., 1995, Gallery IV, L.A., 1994, L.A. Mcpl. Gallery, Barnsdall Park, L.A., 1993, Fed. Reserve Bank, L.A., 1992, The Armory Ctr. for the Arts, Pasadena, 1991, Montgomery Gallery, 1989, Rutgers Art Ctr., New Brunswick, N.J., 1988, others; media works include Meta-tation Sportswear, 1993-94, Meta-tation Gym Workout Tape, 1993-94, meta-tation Labels, 1993-94, posters, postcards, others. Bd. dirs. Woman's Bldg., L.A., 1981-83, L.A. Contemporary Exhbns., L.A., 1988-94; co-chmn. bd. L.A. Contemporary Exhbns., 1990-91. Recipient artist fellowship Nat. Endowment for the Arts, 1987, Brody Arts, L.A., 1986, Art Matters Inc., 1996; Pasadena Arts Commn. grantee, 1990.

NISHITANI, MARTHA, dancer; b. Seattle, Feb. 27, 1920; d. Denjiro and Jin (Aoto) N. B.A. in Comparative Arts, U. Wash., 1958; studied with, Eleanor King, Mary Ann Wells, Perry Mansfield, Cornish Sch., Conn. Coll. Sch. Dance, Long Beach State U. Founder, dir. Martha Nishitani Modern Dance Sch. and Co., Seattle, 1950—; dance dir. Helen Bush Sch. and Central YWCA, 1951-54; choreographer U. Wash. Opera Theater, 1955-65, Intiman Theater, 1972—; dance instr. Elementary and Secondary Edn. Act Program, 1966; dance specialist spl. edn. program Shoreline Pub. Schs., 1970-72; condr. workshops and concerts King County Youth Correctional Instns., 1972-73; Dance adv. counsel Wash. Cultural Enrichment Program; dance adv. bd. Seattle Parks and Recreation. Dancer Eleanor King Co., Seattle, 1946-50, dance films, 1946-51, Channel 9, Ednl. TV, 1967-68; lectr. demonstrator numerous colls., festivals, convs., childrens theater.; author articles on dance; one of the subjects: A Celebration of 100 Years of Dance in Washington, 1989. Trustee Allied Arts Seattle, 1967. Recipient Theta Sigma Phi Matrix Table award, 1968, Asian Am. Living Treasure award Northwest Asian Am. Theater, 1984; listed Dance Archives, N.Y.C. Libr., 1991, N.Y.C. Lincoln Ctr. Dance Archives, 1991, U. Wash. Libr. Archives, 1993, exhibit of Japanese Am. Women of Achievement, Burke Mus., 1994, 42d Anniversary of Martha Nishitani Modern Dance Sch. Mem. Am. Dance Guild (exec. com. 1961-63), Com. Research in Dance, Seattle Art Mus., Internat.

Dance Alliance (adv. council 1984), Smithsonian Assos., Progressive Animal Welfare Soc. Address: 4205 University Way NE PO Box 45264 Seattle WA 98145-0264

NISIVOCCIA, BARBARA, human resource manager; b. Belleville, N.J., Oct. 5, 1965; d. Rocco Michael and Nicolena Delores (Macera) N.; m. Richard Harry Monastersky, May 2, 1993 (div. Mar. 1995). BS in Orgnl. Mgmt. magna cum laude, Nyack Coll., 1991. Tech. recruiter Carter McKenzie, Inc., West Orange, N.J., 1985-89; human resources coord. Booz Allen and Hamilton, Florham Park, N.J., 1990; human resource mgr. Datascape Corp., Montvale, N.J., 1990-92, Schering Plough Pharms., Kenilworth, N.J., 1992-94, Chubb and Son, Inc., Warren, N.J., 1994—. Mem. Corp. Recruiters Exch. Assn. (pres. 1994), Experienced Hire Diversity Task Force (mem. adv. cons. 1995—, Recognition award 1995). Republican. Roman Catholic. Office: Chubb and Son Inc 15 Mountain View Rd Warren NJ 07059

NISLY, LORETTA LYNN, medical and surgical nurse, geriatrics nurse; b. Cheverly, Md., Jan. 26, 1967; d. Mart and Mary (Miller) Overholt; m. Timothy Daniel Nisly, July 18, 1987. AD, Germanna Community Coll., Locust Grove, Va., 1994; LPN, Piedmont Tech. Edn. Ctr., Culpeper, Va., 1989. LPN, RN, Va. Med.-surg. nurse Culpeper Meml. Hosp., 1989-90, 95—; charge nurse Mt. View Nursing Home, Aroda, Va., 1990-92, Orange County Nursing Home, Orange, Va., 1992-94. Recipient Florence Nightengale award Germanna Cmty. Coll., 1995. Mem. Brethren. Home: HC 5 Box 128 Aroda VA 22709-9540

NIST, LINDA LOUISE, secondary school mathematics educator; b. Jersey City, Oct. 6, 1941; d. Charles John and Grace Alice (O'Neill) N. BA in Math., Coll. of St. Elizabeth, 1965; MA in Humanities, Manhattanville Coll., 1970. Cert. tchr. secondary level math., N.J. Tchr. grade 6 Our Lady of All Souls Sch., East Orange, N.J., 1963-65; math. tchr. DePaul H.S., Wayne, N.J., 1965-69, Lakewood (N.J.) H.S., 1977-80, Jonathan Dayton H.S., Springfield, N.J., 1981-82; group underwriter, life, med. U.S. Life Ins. Co., Neptune, N.J., 1987-90; math. tchr. Sci. H.S., Newark, 1990-92, Weequahic H.S., Newark, 1992—; tchr. Scripture House of Prayer Experience, Convent Sta., N.J., 1970-75; dir. Sch. of the Bible, 1973 (summer); tchr. ESL Cath. Cmty. Svcs., Elizabeth, N.J., 1989-90, Linden (N.J.) Bd. Edn., 1990-92. NEH fellow, Dodge NEH fellow San Diego State U., 1994. Mem. Nat. Coun. Tchrs. of Math., N.J. Math. Coalition. Roman Catholic. Home: 134 North St Bayonne NJ 07002-1217 Office: Weequahic HS 279 Chancellor Ave Newark NJ 07112-1201

NITZ, KATHLEEN R., music educator, vocalist; b. St. Louis, Mo., Sept. 2, 1946; d. Johh F. and Ella A. (Gergs) R.; m. Frederic W. Nitz, June 8, 1968 (div. Mar. 1993); children: Frederic Theodore, Anna Louise. BA in Speech and Drama, Valparaiso U., 1976; MA in Music, San Jose State U., 1980. Pvt. vocal instr. Boulder Creek, Calif., 1978-93, Santa Cruz, Calif., 1993—; instr. West Valley Coll., Saratoga, Calif., 1988-92, San Jose (Calif.) State U., 1995—; bd. dirs. Santa Cruz (Calif.) Chamber Players, 1993—. Singer: Opera Outreach and main stage prodns. Opera San Jose, Calif., 1989-92, Opera a la Carte San Francisco Opera Guild, 1989-92, Composers Performing Ensemble NACUSA, Palo Alto, Calif., 1993—; soloist with numerous other opera cos., oratorio socs. and other chamber music series. Mem. Nat. Assn. Tchrs. of Singing, Music Tchrs. Assn. Calif. Office: San Jose State Univ Sch Music and Dance One Washington Sq San Jose CA 95192

NIX, BARBARA LOIS, real estate broker; b. Yakima, Wash., Sept. 25, 1929; d. Martin Clayton and Norma (Gunter) Westfield; A.A., Sierra Coll., 1978; m. B.H. Nix, July 12, 1968; children—William Martin Dahl, Theresa Irene Dahl; step-children—Dennis Leon, Denise Lynn. Bookkeeper, office mgr. Lakeport (Calif.) Tire Service, 1966-69, Dr. K.J. Absher, Grass Valley, Calif., 1972-75; real estate sales and office mgr. Rough and Ready Land Co., Penn Valley, Calif., 1976-77, co-owner, v.p., sec., 1978—, also of Wildwood West Real Estate, Gateway Real Estate. Youth and welfare chmn. Yakima Federated Jr. Women's Club, 1957; den mother Cub Scouts, 1959-60; leader Girl Scouts, 1961-62; mem. Friends of Hospice; mem. Sierra, Nev. Meml. Hosp. Found.; adv. bd. dirs., v.p. Roots and Wings Ednl. Found. Recipient Pres.'s award Sierra Coll., 1973; others. Mem. Lake Wildwood Women's Club, Penn Valley (founder, pres. 1978), Sierra Nevada Meml. Hosp. Aux. Democrat. Roman Catholic. Clubs: Job's Daus. (life). Home: 19365 Wildflower Dr Penn Valley CA 95946-9720 Office: PO Box 191 Rough and Ready CA 95975

NIX, DENISE ELAINE, accountant; b. Atlanta, Feb. 29, 1960; d. Ben A. and Hazel G. (Ingram) Ward; m. James C. Nix, Feb. 14, 1981; children: Jessica E., J. Levi. BS in Bus. Adminstrn. and Acctg. cum laude, Brenau U., 1993. Bookkeeper Lanier Pk. Hosp., Gainesville, Ga., 1981-84; asst. controller, consolidation acct. Protein Foods, Gainesville, 1984-93; asst. controller Turbo Transport, Gainesville, 1993—. Mem. Inst. Mgmt. Accts. Baptist.

NIXON, ANNA JENKINS, newspaper editor; b. Roswell, N.Mex., July 16, 1945; d. Paul William and Elizabeth (Blount) Jenkins; 1 child, Rex Lynn. Student, Ea. N.Mex. U., 1964-66, La. State U., 1980, S.W. Miss. Jr. Coll., 1984. Telephone mfr. AT&T, Shreveport, La., 1972-84; reporter Caddo Citizen News, Vivian, La., 1984-85; reporter, lifestyles editor Columbian-Progress, Columbia, Miss., 1985-88; mng. editor St. Francisville (La.) Dem., 1988-89; lifestyles editor Hobbs (N.Mex.) Daily News, 1989-92, Portales (N.Mex.) News-Tribune, 1992—. Editor, pub. mag. New Beginnings, 1995—. Bd. dirs., sec. Salvation Army, 1989-92. Mem. Roosevelt county Hist. Soc. (pub. rels., publicity chmn. 1994), Kiwanis (charter mem., sec. 1986-89), Beta Sigma Phi (city coun. rep. 1992—). Baptist. Home: PO Box 364 Portales NM 88130 Office: Portales News-Tribune 101 E 1st Portales NM 88130

NIXON, JUANA LYNN WHITLEY, advertising executive; b. LaGrange, Ga., Aug. 11, 1964; d. John Hamilton and Lena Pearl (Knight) W. BA in Math. and Bus. magna cum laude, LaGrange Coll., 1986. Gen. mgr. Unique Advt. Specialties, LaGrange, 1985—. Neighborhood capt. Am. Cancer Soc.; mem. La Fayette Singers, 1st Bapt. Ch. Choir, 3 yr.-old choir dir., 4 yr.-old Sun. sch. tchr., co-dir.; mem. Rep. Presdl. Task Force; mem. adult choir First Bapt. Ch. Ty Cobb scholar, 1985, 86. Mem. NASE, NAFE, Omicron Delta Kappa, Alpha Omicron Pi (chair philanthropy com.). Home: 811 Wisteria Way La Grange GA 30240-1639 Office: Unique Advt Specialties 818 N Greenwood St La Grange GA 30240-1705

NIXON, MARNI, singer; b. Altadena, Calif., Feb. 22, 1930; d. Charles and Margaret (Wittke) McEathron; m. Ernest Gold, May 22, 1950 (div. 1969); children: Andrew Maurice, Martha Alice, Melani Christine; m. Lajos Frederick Fenster, July 23, 1971 (div. July 1975); m. Albert David Block, Apr. 11, 1983. Student opera workshop, Los Angeles City Coll., UCLA, U. So. Calif., Tanglewood, Mass. Dir. vocal faculty Calif. Inst. Arts, Valencia, 1970-72; pvt. tchr., vocal coacn, condr. master classes, 1970—, pvt. voice tchr., coach, condr. master classes, 1970—; head apprentice div. Santa Barbara Music Acad. of West, 1980; formerly dir. opera workshop Cornish Inst. Arts, Seattle.; tchr. in field; judge Met. Opera Internat. Am. Music Awards, Nat. Inst. Music Theatre, 1984, 85-86, 87; panelist New Music, Nat. Assn. Tchrs. Singing, pres. (N.Y. chpt.), 1994—; dialect dir., opera recs. Child actress Pasadena (Calif.) Playhouse, 1940-45, soloist Roger Wagner chorale, 1947-53, appeared with New Eng. Opera Co., Los Angeles Opera Co., also Ford Found. TV Opera, 1948-63, San Francisco Spring Opera, 1966, Seattle Opera, 1971, 72, 73; classical recitals and appearances with symphony orchs. throughout U.S., Can., also Eng., Israel, Ireland; appeared on Broadway as Eliza Doolittle in My Fair Lady, 1964; in motion picture as Sister Sophia in Sound of Music, 1964; also in numerous TV shows and night clubs; star children's ednl. TV show Boomerang, ABC-TV, from 1975; off-Broadway show Taking My Turn, from 1983, Opal, from 1995; appeared in (stage plays) Romeo & Juliet, N.Y.C.; taped for Great Performances PBS-TV Role of Edna, 1994; voice dubbed in for musical motion pictures My Fair Lady, The King and I, An Affair to Remember, West Side Story, and others; rec. artist for Columbia, Mus. Heritage Records, Capital, RCA Victor, Ednl.Records, Reference Recs., Varese-Sarabande, Nonesuch; played violin at age 4; studied in youth orch., 10 yrs; studied voice at age 10. Recipient 4 Emmy awards for best actress, 2 Action for Childrens TV awards, 1977; nominee Drama Desk award; recipient Chgo. Film Festival award, 1977, Gold Record for Songs from Mary Poppins, 2 time Grammy award nominee Nat. Acad. Rec. Arts and Scis. (1st rec. Cabaret Songs and Early Songs by Arnold Schoenberg, RCA, 1977 and 1st rec. Emily Dickinson Songs by Aaron Copland, Reference Recs., 1988. Mem. Nat. Assn. Tchrs. Singing (pres. N.Y. chpt. 1994—).

NIXON, SHIRNETTE MARILYN, pharmaceutical company administrator; b. N.Y.C., Apr. 14, 1947; d. Clifford Bernard and Edna Lucille (Anglin) N. BA in English, Bklyn. Coll., 1969. Pers. asst. Mut. N.Y., N.Y.C., 1969-73; editorial asst. Franklin Watts Inc., N.Y.C., 1973-76; adminstrv. sec. for pers. Pfizer, Inc., N.Y.C., 1976-82, adminstrv. sec. for tax, 1982—, instr. to execs. secs., 1988, 89; instr. to execs. secs. Mabel Dean Bacon H.S., 1990; mem. sec. tng. coun., 1996-97. Mem. YWCA Helpline; spkr. Pfizer Town Meeting, 1996. Recipient Spl. Recognition Letter Mayor David Dinkins. Mem. AAUW, Internat. Tng. in Communication, Bklyn. Coll. Alumni Assn. Office: Pfizer Inc 235 E 42nd St New York NY 10017-5703

NIZNIK, CAROL ANN, electrical engineer, educator, consultant; b. Saratoga Springs, N.Y., Nov. 10, 1942; d. John Arthur Niznik and Rosalia Sopko; m. Donald H. Walter, Jan. 11, 1964. AAS in Engring. Sci., Alfred (N.Y.) State Coll., 1962; BSEE, U. Rochester, N.Y., 1969, MSEE, 1972; PhD in Elec. Engring., SUNY, Buffalo, 1978. Technician Taylor Instrument Corp., Rochester, 1962-64; sr. technician IBM Corp., Poughkeepsie, N.Y., 1964-68; rsch. scientist Eastman Kodak Corp., Rochester, 1969-70; sr. engr. Xerox Corp., Webster, N.Y., 1971-74; rsch. ast. prof. SUNY, buffalo, 1979-80; assoc. prof. elec. engring. U. Pitts., 1980-83; pres., cons. NW Systems, Victor, N.Y., 1975—; adj. prof. math. Rochester Inst. Tech., 1993-94; vis. assoc. prof. Ctr. for Brain Rsch., Sch. Medicine, U. Rochester, 1983-84. Contbr. some 65 articles to profl. jours.; patentee in field. Recipient fellowships, grants and U.S. govt. contracts. Mem. IEEE (sr.), Sigma Xi, Eta Kappa Nu, Tau Beta Pi. Roman Catholic.

NIZZE, JUDITH ANNE, physician assistant; b. L.A., Nov. 1, 1942; d. Robert George and Charlotte Ann (Wise) Swan; m. Norbert Adolph Otto Paul Nizze, Dec. 31, 1966. BA, UCLA, 1966, postgrad., 1966-76; grad. physician asst. tng. program, Charles R. Drew Sch. Postgrad., L.A., 1979; BS, Calif. State U., Dominguez, 1980. Cert. physician asst., Calif. Staff rsch. assoc. I-II Wadsworth Vet. Hosp., L.A., 1965-71; staff rsch. assoc. III-IV John Wayne Clinic Jonsson Comprehensive Cancer Ctr., UCLA, 1971-78; clin. asst. Robert S. Ozeran, Gardena, Calif., 1978; physician asst. family practice Fred Chasan, Torrance, Calif., 1980-82; sr. physician asst. Donald L. Morton prof., chief surg. oncology Jonsson Comprehensive Cancer Ctr., UCLA, 1983-91; administrv. dir. clin. rsch. John Wayne Cancer Inst., Santa Monica, Calif., 1991—. Contbr. articles to profl. jours. Fellow Am. Acad. Physician Assts., Am. Assn. Surgeons Assts., Calif. Acad. Physician Assts.; mem. Assn. Physician Assts. in Oncology, Am. Sailing Assn. Republican. Presbyterian. Home: 13243 Fiji Way Unit J Marina Dl Rey CA 90292-7079 Office: John Wayne Cancer Inst St John's Hosp & Health Ctr 1328 22d St 2 West Santa Monica CA 90404-2032

NNAEMEKA, OBIOMA GRACE, French language and women's studies educator, consultant, researcher; b. Agulu, Anambra, Nigeria; came to U.S., 1974; d. Christopher Egbunike and Jessie Ifemelue (Ogbuefi) Obidiegwu; m. Tony Ikedigbo Nnaemeka, Sept. 25, 1973; children: Ike, Uchenna. BA with honors, U. Nigeria, Nsukka, 1972; MA, U. Minn., 1977, PhD with distinction, 1989. Rsch. fellow U. Nigeria, 1972-74, lectr., 1982-87; asst. prof. Concordia Coll., Minn., 1988-89, Coll. Wooster, Ohio, 1989-91; assoc. prof. Ind. U., Indpls., 1991—; cons. Govt. Senegal, Dakar, 1990-92; commentator Internat. Svc. Radio Netherlands, Hilversum, 1990—; Edith Kreeger Wolf Disting. prof. Northwestern U., 1992. Author: Agrippa d'Aubigne: The Poetics of Power and Change; editor: The Politics of Mothering, 1996, Sisterhood, Feminisms, & Power, 1996; contbr. articles to profl. jours. Founder Assn. African Women's Scholars, 1995; convener, organizer First Internat. Conf. Women in Africa & African Diaspora, 1992. Named Achiever of Yr. Leadership Nigeria Network, 1994; grantee from McArthur Found, Rockefeller Found., Swedish Internat. Devel. Agy., Swedish Agy. for Rsch. Cooperation with Developing Countries, 1991-92. Mem. Am. Assn. Tchrs. French, Ind. Fgn. Lang. Tchrs. Assn., Modern Langs. Assn., African Studies Assn., African Lit. Assn. Office: Ind U French Dept 425 University Blvd Indianapolis IN 46202

NOAH, JULIA JEANINE, retired librarian; b. Craig, Mo., July 14, 1932; d. Hiram Curtis and Eloise Julia (Puckett) True; m. Raymond Laverne Noah, Sept. 5, 1954; children: David Scott, Danny Ray, Deborah Jill, Douglas True. BS, U. Ill., 1953; MA in Library Sci., U. South Fla., 1983. Asst. rsch. librarian Parke, Davis & Co., Detroit, 1953-55; cataloging librarian U. Mo., Columbia, 1955-57; sch. librarian High Point Elem. Sch., Clearwater, Fla., 1968; library aide Clearwater High Sch., 1973-78; reference asst. Dunedin (Fla.) Pub. Library, 1978-84, dir. info. svcs., 1984-88, library dir., 1988-94; ret. Mem. ALA, DAR, Fla. Libr. Assn., Questers, Phi Kappa Phi, Beta Phi Mu. Republican. Presbyterian.

NOAKES, BETTY L., retired elementary school educator; b. Oklahoma City, Okla., Aug. 28, 1938; d. Webster L. and Willie Ruth (Johnson) Hawkins; m. Richard E. Noakes, Apr. 22, 1962 (dec.); 1 child, Michele Monique. Student, Oklahoma City U., MEd, 1971; BS, Cen. State U., 1962; postgrad., Cen. State U., Okla. State U. Elem. tchr. Merced (Calif.) Pub. Schs., 1966-67, Oklahoma City Schs., 1971-73, Mid-Del Schs., Midwest City, Okla., 1973-95; founder, owner Noakes-I Care Day Care, 1995—. 2d v.p. PTA, Pleasant Hill, 1991, cert. recognition, 1992-93; active Nat. PTA, 1991-92; charter mem. Nat. Mus. of Am. Indian-Smithsonian Instn. Recipient Cert. Appreciation YMCA, 1992-92, Disting. Svc. award Mid-Del PTA, 1992. Mem. NEA, AAUW, NAACP, Nat. Therapeutic Recreation Assn., Okla. Edn. Assn., Smithsonian Instn., Oklahoma City U. Alumni Assn., United Meth. Women Assn., Cen. State U. Alumni Assn., Okla. Ea. Star (Lilly of the Valley chpt. 7), Phi Delta Kappa (sgt.-at-arms), Zeta Phi Beta. Home: 5956 N Coltrane Rd Oklahoma City OK 73121-3409

NOBERT, FRANCES, music educator; b. Winston-Salem, N.C., Dec. 12, 1936; d. Henry Carrington and Frances Mozelle (Harrison) Cuningham; m. Jon Marshall Nobert (div. Jan. 1980). BM in Music Edn., Salem Coll., 1959; Fulbright Cert. in Organ, Conservatory of Music, Frankfurt am Main, Germany, 1961; MM in Organ, Syracuse U., 1963; DMA in Choral Music, U. So. Calif., 1980. Organist, choir dir. United Ch., Fayetteville, N.Y., 1961-67; choral an gen. music tchr. Fayetteville Manlius Sch. Dist., 1963-67; vocal music tchr. U.S. Grant H.S., Van Nuys, Calif., 1967-80; organist United Ch. of Christ Congregational, Claremont, Calif., 1981-83; organist, choir dir. St. Matthias Episcopal Ch., Whittier, Calif., 1983-94; prof. music, coll. organist Whittier Coll., 1982—, coord. women's studies' activities, 1995—; choral singer L.A. Master Chorale, 1972-86; vis. instr. of key bd. theory, L.A. Valley Coll., Van Nuys, Calif., 1980-81, spring 1982; bd. dirs., program chair, sub-dean, dean Pasadena chpt. Am. Guild of Organists, Pasadena, Calif., 1991-95; resident dir. for Denmark's Internat. Study Program, Whittier Coll., 1994. Faculty Rsch. grant Whittier Coll., 1984, Devel. grant, 1986, 88, 90, 91, 93. 96, Irvine grant, 1995. Mem. NOW, Am. Guild Organists, Organ Hist. Soc., Rio Hondo Symphony Guild, Whittier Cultural Arts Found., Mader Corp., Feminist Majority. Episcopalian. Office: Whittier Coll Mus Dept 13406 Philadelphia St Whittier CA 90608

NOBLE, MARION ELLEN, retired home economist; b. Blanchardville, Wis., Feb. 18, 1914; d. Dwight Eldridge and Doris Edna (Parkinson) Baker; m. B. Frank Smyth (dec. 1979); children: William, Ann Smyth Marris, Robert, Larry, Margaret Smyth Decker; m. George C. Noble, 1981. BS, U. Wis., Madison, 1936. V.p. Smyth Bus Systems, Canton, Ohio, 1950; womens editor Radio Station WFAH, Alliance, Ohio, 1952-58; home economist extension svc. Stark County, Ohio State U., Canton, 1961-70. Contbr. articles to profl. jours. Named Woman of the Year Urban League, Canton, 1964. Mem. AAUW, Nat. Assn. Extension Home Economists, Pacific Pioneer Broadcasters, Home Econs. Club, Thimble Collectors Internat., Ladies Oriental Shrine of North Am., Phi Upsilon Omicron, Epsilon Sigma Phi. Republican. Methodist. Home: 3240 San Amadeo # A Laguna Hills CA 92653-3037

NOBLE, MARY CATHERINE, English and journalism educator; b. Artesia, N. Mex., May 15, 1939; d. Lester Coleman and Laura Bernice (Durbin) George; m. Charles Noble, Jun. 6, 1962 (div. 1990); children: Larry, Becky, Patti, Greg. BA, N. Mex. Highlands U., 1962. Cert. h.s. tchr., Idaho, N. Mex. Tchr. Highland H.S., Albuquerque, N. Mex., 1963-65, Idaho Falls H.S., 1976—; sec. Idaho Journalism Educators Assn., 1980-84. Brownie Troop Leader Girl Scouts, Idaho Falls, 1972-74. Mem. IJAA/NJEA, Idaho Tchrs. of English, Idaho Vocat. Tchrs. Home: 1135 Austin Ave Idaho Falls ID 83404

NOBLE, PATRICIA ANN, director child care and youth center; b. Fitchburg, Mass., Oct. 9, 1944; d. John William and Mary Catherine (Sweeney) Morrissey; m. Ronald Coleman, Oct. 15, 1967 (div. Dec. 1969); 1 child, Michael; m. Philip Steele Noble, July 9, 1970; children: Jason, Brian. BA, State Coll. Fitchburg, 1967. Substitute tchr. Provincetown (Mass.) Sch. Dist., 1966-67; child care dir. DLM, Denver, 1976-79; referral counselor Child Care Coun. of Suffolk, Southampton, N.Y., 1991; exec. dir. Bridgehampton (N.Y.) Child Care and Recreation Ctr., 1992—. Author: (poetry book) Kitchen Privileges, 1993. Bd. dirs. Bridgehampton Union Free Sch. Dist., 1989-96. Fellow East End Writers. Democrat. Office: Bridgehampton Child Care & Recreation Ctr Inc PO Box 1197 Bridgehampton NY 11932

NOBLE, SUNNY A., business owner; b. Moorhead, Minn., May 22, 1940; m. Eric Scott Noble, Apr. 11, 1980. MBA, U. Calif., Berkeley, 1960; qualified parapsychologist, U. Minn., 1979. Mgr. Spear & Hill Attys., N.Y.C., 1969-70; mgr. exec. property mgmt. May Co. Dept. Stores, La Jolla, Calif., 1981-82; owner, pres. The Computer Tutor, L.A., 1984—. Author: (newspaper column) That Computes, 1984-88, The Storyteller, 1987-91; humor columnist The Westside Examiner, 1996—. Mem. Internat. Platform Assn., Toastmasters Internat. (ednl. v.p. 1988), Mensa, Beta Sigma Phi. Home and Office: 4152 W Avenue L2 Quartz Hill CA 93536-4216

NOBLE, SUSAN ELVIRA, nurse; b. San Francisco, July 27, 1962; d. Brice Esker Noble and Teresita (Cui) Calixto. BSN, Humboldt State U., 1993. RN, Calif. Night supr., relief cmty. psychiat. ctrs. CPC Belmont (Calif.) Hills Hosp., 1993-95; clin. coord. psychiatry/Asian Focus Unit San Francisco Gen. Hosp., 1995—. Mem. Soc. Advancement of Modeling and Role-Modeling. Republican. Roman Catholic. Office: San Francisco Gen Hosp Unit 7C 1001 Potrero Ave San Francisco CA 94110

NOBLITT, DONNA RONE, secondary education educator; b. Greenwood, Miss., Feb. 6, 1950; d. Luther R. and Christine M. (Ivey) Rone; m. Larry Douglas Noblitt, Feb. 3, 1973; children: Michelle E., Alan L. BS in Math., La. Tech U., 1971; MS in Math., Lamar U., 1991. Tchr. math. Glenmora (La.) H.S., 1971-73, Lincoln Jr. H.S., Beaumont, Tex., 1973-74, Huntington (Tex.) H.S., 1974-76, Port Neches (Tex.)-Groves H.S., 1976-86, West Brook H.S., Beaumont, 1986—; coach Channel 6 Challenge, Beaumont, 1991—, Texaco Challenge, Port Arthur, Tex., 1991—, Acad. Decathlon, Beaumont, 1991—; mentor for student tchrs. Lamar U., Beaumont. Named Tchr. of Month, West Brook H.S., 1994. Mem. Nat. Coun. Tchrs. Math., Tex. Classroom Tchrs. Orgn., A&M Mothers Club. Methodist. Home: 116 Sparrow Way Beaumont TX 77707-2024 Office: West Brook HS 8750 Phelan Blvd Beaumont TX 77706-5133

NOBLITT, NANCY ANNE, aerospace engineer; b. Roanoke, Va., Aug. 14, 1959; d. Jerry Spencer and Mary Louise (Jerrell) N. BA, Mills Coll., Oakland, Calif., 1982; M.S. in Indsl. Engring., Northeastern U., 1990. Data red specialist, Universal Energy Systems, Beaver Creek, Ohio, 1981; aerospace engr. turbine engine div. components br. turbine group aero-propulsion lab. Wright-Patterson AFB, Ohio, 1982-84, engine assessment br. spl. engines group, 1984-87; lead analyst cycle methods computer aided engr. Gen. Electric Co., Lynn Mass., 1987-90, Lynn PACES project coord., 1990-91; software systems analyst Sci. Applications Internat. Corp., with artificial intelligence Sci. Applications Internat. Corp., Mc Lean, Va., 1991-92, software engring. mgr., intelligence applications integration, Sci. Applications Internat. Corp., Hampton, Va., 1992-93, mgr. test engring. and systems support, 1993-94, mgr. configuration mgmt., 1994, mgmt. asst. to TBMCS program mgr., 1994-95; sr. simulation engr. Chem Demil, 1995—. Math and sci. tutor Centerville Sch. Bd., Ohio, 1982-86, math. and physics tutor Marblehead Sch. Bd., Mass., 1988-90; tutor math, chemistry & physics Poquoson Sch. Bd., Va., 1994—; rep. alumnae admissions Mills Coll., Boston area, 1987-91; mem. bd. trustees/bd. govs. Mills Coll., 1995—; mem. Citizens for Hilton Area Revitalization, 1994—. Recipient Notable Achievement award U.S. Air Force, 1984; recipient Special award Fed. Lab. Consortium, 1987. Mem. Soc. Mfg. Engrs. Avocation: book collecting. Home: 58 Hopkins St Newport News VA 23601-4034 Office: Sci Applications Internat Corp Hampton VA 23666

NOBOA-STANTON, PATRICIA LYNN, corporate executive; b. Cin., Sept. 6, 1947; d. William Emile and Marie Virginia (Ballbach) Hakes; m. Donald R. Stanton, Nov. 10, 1987; children from previous marriage: Aric Israel, Rene Carlos. Diploma Presbyn.-St. Luke's Sch. Nursing, Chgo., 1967, Nat. Inst. Real Estate, 1989, No. Va. Community Coll., 190. Supr. patient care Alexandria Hosp., Va., 1976-78; pres. Renaissance Reprographics, Inc., Reston, Va., 1985-89; pres. Va. Leasing & Copying Inc., Reston, 1978-89; realtor Wellborn Comml., 1989-91; dir. ops., publ. and health cons. Atlantic Resources Corp., 1991-93, dir. ops. and adminstrn., 1991-93; exec. v.p. Mark Moseley's Travel, 1993-95; CEO Transitions 2000, 1995—. Pres. Reston Bd. Commerce, 1985, founding bd. dirs. 1982-85, v.p. 1984, sec. 1983; v.p. Planned Community Archives, Inc., 1985-88; mem. regional com. United Way, 1985-87; Dulles Area Regional Council steering com., 1985-88; pres. Myterra Home-owners Assn., 1990—; bd. dirs. N. Va. Local Devel. Corp., 1987—; bd. dirs. Fairfax Symphony, Reston Bd. Commerce, 1989. Named Reston Citizen of Yr., 1985; named Small Bus. Person of Yr. Fairfax County Commn. for Women, 1985-87. Mem. Northern Va. Assn. Realtors, Nat. Assn. Realtors, Va. Assn. Realtors, Nat. Assn. Quick Printers (bd. dirs. Capital chpt. 1984—, vice chair 1987—), Internat. Platform Assn., Fairfax County C. of C. (bd. dirs. 1985-86, 87—), Herndon C. of C., Washington-Dulles Task Force. Episcopalian. Lodge: Rotary. Avocations: computers, music, flying. Office: Transitions 2000 12401 Myterra Way Herndon VA 22071

NOCHMAN, LOIS WOOD KIVI (MRS. MARVIN NOCHMAN), educator; b. Detroit, Nov. 5, 1924; d. Peter K. and Annetta Lois (Wood) Kivi; AB, U. Mich., 1946, AM, 1949; m. Harold I. Pitchford, Sept. 6, 1944 (div. May 1949); children: Jean Wood Pitchford Horiszny, Joyce Lynn Pitchford Undiano; m. Marvin A. Nochman, Aug. 15, 1953; 1 child, Joseph Asa. Tchr. adult edn., Honolulu, 1947, Ypsilanti (Mich.) H.S., 1951-52; spl. instr. English, Wayne State U., Detroit, 1953, 54; tchr. Highland Park (Mich.) Coll., 1950-51, instr. English, 1954-83. Mem. exec. bd. Highland Park Fedn. Tchrs., 1963-66, 71-72, mem. 1st bargaining team, 1965-66, 73, del. to Nat. Conv., 1964, 71-74, rep. higher edn. to Mich. Fedn. Tchrs. Exec. Com., 1972-76; mem. faculty adv. com. Gov.'s Commn. on Higher Edn., 1973—. Tchr. Baha'i schs., Davison, Mich., 1954-55, 58-59, 63-66, Beaulac, Que., Can., 1960, Greenacre, Maine, 1965; sec. local spiritual assembly Baha'is, Ann Arbor, 1953, sec., Detroit, 1954, chmn., 1955; mem. nat. com. Baha'is U.S., 1955-68; sec. Davison Bahai Sch. Com. and Council, 1956, 58, 63-68; Baha'i lectr. Subject of local TV show Senior Focus, 1992. Mem. NOW, Modern Lang. Assn., Nat. Coun. Tchrs. English, Mich. Coll. English Assn., Am. Fedn. Tchrs., Nat. Soc. Lit. and Arts, Women's Equity and Action League (sec. Mich. chpt. 1975-79), Alpha Lambda Delta, Alpha Gamma Delta. Contbr. poems to mags. Recipient Women's Movement plaque Women Lawyers Assn. Mich., 1975, Lawrence award Mich. Masters Swimming, 1991, 9 World Master Records In Age Group and short course meters, 1994 Long Course Meters, 1995, 23 Nat. Masters Records, 1994-96, 6 Nat. YMCA records, 1995, 2 U.S. Nat. Sr. Sports Classic Records, 1995, 2 World Sr. Games Records, 1993, All-Am. award, 1990-96, 2 U.S. Nat. Sr. Sports Classic Records, U.S. MS Long Distance All Star, 1995, U.S. MS Finals All Star, 1995; named one of 10 Best of 1995 Swim Mag. Avocation: U.S. Swimming Master Champion.

NODDINGS, NEL, education educator, writer; b. Irvington, N.J., Jan. 19, 1929; d. Edward A. Rieth and Nellie A. (Connors) Walter; m. James A. Noddings, Aug. 20, 1949; children: Chris, Howard, Laurie, James, Nancy, William, Sharon, Edward, Vicky, Timothy. BA in Math., Montclair State

Coll., 1949; MA in Math., Rutgers U., 1964; PhD in Edn., Stanford U., 1973; PhD (hon.), Columbia Coll., S.C., 1995. Cert. tchr., Calif., N.J. Tchr. Woodbury (N.J.) Publ Schs., 1949-52; tchr. math. dept. Matawan (N.J.) High Sch., 1958-62, chair, asst. prin., 1964-69; curriculum supr. Montgomery Twp. Pub. Schs., Skillman, N.J., 1970-72; dir. precollegiate edn. U. Chgo., 1975-76; asst. prof. Pa. State U., State College, 1973; from asst. prof. to assoc. prof. Stanford (Calif.) U., 1977-86, prof., 1986—, assoc. dean, 1990-92, acting dean, 1992-94, Lee L. Jacks prof. child edn., 1992—; bd. dirs. Ctr. for Human Caring Sch. Nursing, Denver, 1986-92; cons. NIE, NSF and various other sch. dists. Author: Caring: A Feminine Approach to Ethics and Moral Education, 1984, Women and Evil, 1989, (with W. Paul Shore) Awakening the Inner Eye: Intuition in Education, 1984, (with Carol Witherell) Stories Lives Tell, 1991, The Challenge to Care in Schools, 1992, Educating for Intelligent Belief or Unbelief, 1993, (with Suzanne Gordon and Patricia Benner) Philosophy of Education, 1995, Caretaking, 1996. Mem. disting. women's adv. bd. Coll. St. Catherine. NSF fellow Rutgers U., 1962-64; recipient Anne Roe award for Contbns. to Profl. devel. of Women, Harvard Grad. Sch. Edn., 1993, medal for disting. svc. Tchrs. Coll. Columbia, 1994. Fellow Philosophy of Edn. Soc. (pres. 1991-92); mem. Am. Ednl. Rsch. Assn., Am. Philos. Assn., John Dewey Soc. (pres. 1994-96), Phi Beta Kappa (vis. scholar), Kappa Delta Pi. Office: Stanford U Sch of Edn Stanford CA 94305

NODDINGS, SARAH ELLEN, lawyer; b. Matawan, N.J.; d. William Clayton and Sarah Stephenson (Cox) Noddings; children: Christopher, Aaron. BA in Math., Rutgers U., New Brunswick, N.J., 1965, MSW, 1968; JD cum laude, Seton Hall U., Newark, 1975; postgrad., UCLA, 1979. Bar: Calif. 1976, Nev. 1976, N.J. 1975, U.S. Dist. Ct. (ctrl. dist.) Calif. 1976, U.S. Dist. Ct. N.J. 1975. Social worker Carteret (N.J.) Bd. Edn., 1970-75; law clk. Hon. Howard W. Babcock, 8th Jud. Dist. Ct., Las Vegas, Nev., 1975-76; assoc. O'Melveny & Myers, L.A., 1976-78; atty. Internat. Creative Mgmt., Beverly Hills, Calif., 1978-81, Russell & Glickman, Century City, Calif., 1981-83; atty. Lorimar Prodns., Culver City and Burbank, Calif., 1983-87, v.p., 1987-93; atty. Warner Bros. TV, Burbank, Calif., 1993—, v.p., 1993—. Dir. county youth program, rsch. analyst Sonoma County People for Econ. Opportunity, Santa Rosa, Calif., 1968-69; VISTA vol. Kings County Cmty. Action Orgn., Hanford, Calif., 1965-66; officer, PTA bd. Casimir Mid. Sch. and Arlington Elem. Sch. Mem. Acad. TV Arts and Scis. (nat. awards com. 1994—), L.A. Copyright Soc. (trustee 1990-91), Women in Film, L.A. County Bar Assn. (intellectual property sect.), Women Entertainment Lawyers. Office: Warner Bros TV 300 Television Plz Burbank CA 91505-1372

NOE, ELNORA (ELLIE NOE), retired chemical company executive; b. Evansville, Ind., Aug. 23, 1928; d. Thomas Noe and Evelyn (West) Dieter. Student Ind. U.-Purdue U., Indpls. Sec., Pitman Moore Co., Indpls., 1946; with Dow Chem. Co., Indpls., 1960-90, pub. rels. asst. then mgr. employee comm., 1970-87, mgr. cmty. rels., 1987-90, DowBrands Inc., 1986-90; vice chmn. corp. affairs discussion group, 1988-89, chmn., 1989-90; mem. steering com. Learn About Bus. Recipient 2d pl. award as Business-woman of Yr., Indpls. Bus. and Profl. Women's Assn., 1980, Indpls. Profl. Woman of Yr. award Zonta, Altrusa, Soroptomist & Pilot Svc. Clubs, 1985, DowBrands Great Things Cmty. Svc. award, 1991. Mem. Am. Bus. Women Assn. (Woman of Yr. award 1965, past pres.), Ind. Assn. Bus. Communicators (hon., Communicator of Yr. 1977), Women in Comm. (Louise Eleanor Kleinhenz award 1984), Zonta (dist. pub. rels. chmn. 1978-80, area dir. 1980-82, pres. Indpls. 1977-79, bd. dirs. 1993-95), Dow Indpls. Retiree Club (pres. 1995—).

NOE, HEATHER A.B., mathematician, educator, language educator; b. Hannibal, Mo., Feb. 6, 1969; d. Charles L. and Sandra J. (Larimore) Bartison; m. Kendall R. Noe, Aug. 10, 1991. BS in Edn., U. Mo., 1991. Cert. tchr. Tchr. math., Spanish Cooper County C-4 Sch., Pilot Grove, Mo., 1991—. Mem. Nat. Coun. Tchrs. Math., Fgn. Lang. Assn. Mo. Home: 212 Spring Valley Rd Columbia MO 65203

NOEL, MACHELLE LYN, catalog marketer; b. Altoona, Pa., Nov. 30, 1967; d. Herbert E. and Linda L. (Noffsker) Grace; m. David T. Noel. BS, Lock Haven (Pa.) U., 1990. Staff acct. JLG Industries, McConnellsburg, Pa., 1990-92; mfg. acct. New Pig Corp., Tipton, Pa., 1992-96; catalog mktg. Internat. Divsn., New Pig Corp., Tipton, 1996—. Bd. dirs. Blair County Red Cross, 1995—, coord. fin. devel. team, 1994—; cmty. rels. coord. Am. Red Cross, 1994—; mem. Alliance Bikers Aimed Toward Edn., 1995—. Named to Outstanding Young Women of Am., 1988. Mem. Inst. Mgmt. Accts. Democrat. Methodist. Office: New Pig Corp 3 Pork Ave Tipton PA 16684

NOEL, TALLULAH ANN, healthcare industry executive; b. Detroit, Oct. 21, 1945; d. Harry Carababas and Ruby Dimple (Gentry) Caruso; m. Vernon E. Noel (div. 1965); children: Cynthia L. Robbins, Kimberly J. Wise. AA in Nursing, Morton Coll., Cicero, Ill., 1976; BS, Coll. St. Francis, Joliet, Ill., 1983; MS in Mgmt., Nat.-Louis U., Evanston, Ill., 1990. RN. Staff nurse Mt. Sinai Hosp., Chgo., 1976-78, head nurse, 1978-79, critical care nurse, 1979-80, oncology clinician, 1980-82; head nurse McNeal Hosp., Berwyn, Ill., 1982-84; dir. nursing Nursefinders of Elmwood Park (Ill.), 1984-86; dir. profl. svcs. Nursefinders of Chgo., Elmwood Park, 1986-87, v.p. profl. svcs., 1987-88, v.p. ops., chief oper. officer, 1988-90; area v.p. Nursefinders, Inc., Hillside, Ill., 1990-91; v.p. Amserv Healthcare, Inc., Riverside, Ill., 1992-94; pres., owner Staffing Team Internat., Inc., Oak Brook, Ill., 1994—. Bd. dirs. Morton Coll. Found., 1987-88, Chgo. Heart Assn., 1985—, Grant Works Children's Ctr., Cicero, 1982-85. Mem. Women's Health Exec. Network, Nat. League Nursing, Oncology Nursing Soc., Am. Fedn. Home Health Agys., Assn. Critical Care Nurses, others. Democrat. Roman Catholic. Office: Staffing Team Internat Inc 1100 Jorie Blvd Ste 234 Oak Brook IL 60521-2244

NOEL, TERRI WEISNER, electronics company executive; b. Durham, N.C., Apr. 2, 1949; d. Charles Joseph and Jewell Lorraine (Parrott) Weisner; children: Kristin Nelda Jensen Gustafson, Etta Bonnin Jensen; m. Franc Edward Noel, Mar. 3, 1984. BS in Computer Sci., N.C. State U., 1972; M in Project Mgmt., George Washington U., 1996. Assoc. programmer Western Electric Co., Greensboro, N.C., 1971-72; staff programmer Rsch. Triangle Inst., Research Triangle Park, N.C., 1972-73; program mgr. IBM Corp., Research Triangle Park, 1973-96, mgr. triangle area edn., 1996—; cons. Rsch. Triangle Inst., 1980-81. Author IBM Tech. Disclosure Bull., 1984 (award). Bd. dirs. Durham (N.C.) Pub. Edn. Network, 1985-86; chair Consortium for Human Devel. and Sch. Improvement, Durham, 1996; mem. N.C. Bus. Com. for Edn., Raleigh, 1996. Mem. Soc. Women Engrs. (sr., chpt. v.p. 1981-90), Project Mgmt. Inst. Home: 4021 Swarthmore Rd Durham NC 27707 Office: IBM Corp LRVA/B632 PO Box 12195 Research Triangle Park NC 27709

NOETH, CAROLYN FRANCES, speech and language pathologist; b. Cleve., July 21, 1924; d. Sam Falco and Barbara Serafina (Loparo) Armaro; m. Lawrence Andrew Noeth Sr., June 29, 1946; children: Lawrence Andrew Jr. (dec.), Barbara Marie. AB magna cum laude, Case Western Res. U., 1963; MEd, U. Ill., 1972; postgrad., Nat. Coll. Edn., 1975—. Lic. speech and lang. pathologist, Ill. Speech therapist Chgo. Pub. Schs., 1965; speech, lang. and hearing clinician J. Sterling Morton High Schs., Cicero and Berwyn, Ill., 1965-82, tchr. learning disabilities/behavior disorders, 1982, dist. ednl. diagnostician, 1982-84; Title I Project tchr., summers 1966-67, lang. disabilities cons., summers 1968-69, in-service tng. cons., summer 1970, dir. Title I Project, summers 1973-74, learning disabilities tchr. W. Campus of Morton, 1971-75, chmn. Educable-Mentally Handicapped-Opportunities Tchrs. Com., 1967-68, spl. edn. area and in-sch. tchrs. workshops, 1967—. Precinct elections judge, 1953-55; block capt. Mothers March of Dimes and Heart Fund, 1949-60; St. Agatha's rep. Nat. Catholic Women's League, 1952-53; collector various charities, 1967, 93-94; mem. exec. bd. Morton Scholarship League, 1981-84, corr. sec., 1981-83; vol. Am. Cancer Soc., 1985—; vol. judge Ill. Acad. Decathlon, 1988—. First recipient Virda L. Stewart award for Speech, Western Res. U., 1963, recipient Outstanding Sr. award, 1963. Mem. Am. (life, cert.), Ill. Speech, Language, and Hearing Assns. (life mem.), Council Exceptional Children (divsn. for learning disabilities, pioneers divsn., chpt. spl. projects chmn., exec. bd. 1976-81, chpt. pres. 1979-80), Council for Learning Disabilities, Profls. in Learning Disabilities, Internat. Platform Assn., Kappa Delta Pi, Delta Kappa Gamma (chmn., co-chmn. chpt. music com. 1979—, mem. state program com. 1981-83, chpt. music rep. to state 1982—, chmn. chpt. promotion com. 1993-94, 96—). Roman Catholic. Clubs: St. Norbert's Women's (Northbrook, Ill.), Case-Western Res. U., U. Ill. Alumni Assns., Lions (vol. Northbrook, 1966—). Chmn. in compiling and publishing Student Handbook, Cleve. Coll., 1962; contbr. lyric parodies and musical programs J. Sterling Morton High Sch. West Retirement Teas, 1972-83. Home and Office: 1849 Walnut Cir Northbrook IL 60062-1245

NOETZELMAN, JULIE ANNE, human services administrator; b. Hastings, Nebr., May 6, 1952; d. Nelson Lorrell and Margie Louise (Johanson) Brown; m. Alfred Earl Noetzelman; children: Nicole, Krystal, Charissa. Student, Mesa Coll., 1970-71. Expediter Occidental Oil Shale, Inc., Grand Junction, Colo., 1974-76; co-mgr. Winners Barn, Spiro, Okla., 1979-80; computer operator Coop. Computing, Inc., Ft. Smith, Ark., 1980; exec. sec. Grace Cmty. Ch., Fruita, Colo., 1983-84; hostess San Miguel Ranch, Nucla, Colo., 1985-86; prevention specialist Cmtys. for a Drug-Free Colo., Nucla, 1988-95; juvenile diversion specialist West End Juvenile Diversion, Nucla, 1992-96; exec. dir. West End Family Link Ctr., Nucla, 1993—. Foster parent Montrose County Dept. Social Svcs., Nucla, 1988—; adult trainer, troop leader Chipeta Coun. Girl Scouts U.S., Nucla, 1986-92; pres. adv. bd. Fruita Day Care Ctr., 1982-83. Mem. NAFE, Nat. Coun. Alcohol-Drug Abuse. Home: PO Box 398 Nucla CO 81424 Office: West End Family Link Ctr PO Box 602 Nucla CO 81424

NOFFSINGER, NANCY LEIGH, special education educator; b. Princeton, Ky., Oct. 20, 1948; d. Charlie H. and Margaree (Oates) N. BS, Murray (Ky.) State U., 1980, masters equivalent, 5th yr. program, 1987. LPN, 1974. Sch. nurse, then spl. edn. tchr. Dawson Springs (Ky.) Bd. Edn., 1980-83; spl. edn. substitute tchr. various counties, Ky., 1983-85; spl. edn. tchr. Critten County Bd. Edn., Marion, Ky., 1985—; mem. site-base decision-making com. Crittenden County Elem. Sch., 1993-96. Mem. NOW, ACLU, Ky. Edn. Assn. (1st dist. pres., mem. human and civil rights diversity com. 1994—), Crittenden County Edn. Assn. (pres. 1992-95, chair KePAC legis. chair 1995—), Caldwell County Dem. Women's Club (chair program com. 1996—), Greenpeace, Amnesty Internat., So. Poverty Law Ctr., Handgun Control Inc., Humane Soc. U.S. Democrat. Baptist. Home: 418 S Seminary St Princeton KY 42445

NOGUERE, SUZANNE, publishing manager, poet; b. Bklyn., Dec. 1, 1947; d. Eugene R. and Virginia Helene (Braun) N.; m. Henry Grinberg, June 5, 1983. BA in Philosophy magna cum laude with honors, Columbia U., 1969. Classified ad. mgr. Printing News/East, Melville, N.Y., 1973—. Author: (children's books) Little Koala, 1979, Little Raccoon, 1981, (poetry collection) Whirling Round the Sun, 1996. Recipient Discovery award The 92d St. Y Unterberg Poetry Ctr. and The Nation mag., 1996. Mem. Acad. Am. Poets, Poetry Soc. Am. (Gertrude B. Claytor Meml. award 1989), Poets House. Home: Apt 12B 27 W 96th St New York NY 10025 Office: Printing News/East 445 Broad Hollow Rd Melville NY 11747

NOKES, MARY TRIPLETT, former university president, counselor, artist; b. Weatherford, Okla., Sept. 6, 1920; d. Ernest Carlton and Eva Hannah (Claridge) Triplett; m. George Willis Malcom Nokes, July 11, 1937; 1 child, William Careton. BA, Cen. State U., 1943; Masters Degree, U. Okla., 1949, Doctors Degree, 1969. Tchr., sec. Okla. Edn. Assn., Oklahoma City, 1943-83; advisor Nat. Honor Soc., Oklahoma City, 1955-83; 1st v.p. Internat. Porcelain Artist, 1966-68, pres., 1968-70, sec. bd., 1979-92; pres. Okla. State U., 1975-91; ret., 1991; legis. rep. for Okla. Edn. Assn., 1979-92; presenter seminars on china painting, 1991—. Sponsor Student Coun., 1955-83; pres. Okla. State China Painting Tchr., 1986-87; dir. Vacation Bible Sch., 1984-95, 96—; pres. Soccer Club, 1995-96, Sooner Art Club, 1996—. Named Vol. Woman of Yr. Salvation Army, Okla., 1992-93, Woman of Yr. Salvation Army, 1995-96, Personality of South, 1994-95, Cmty. Leader for Noteworthy Ams., 1994-95, Cmty. Leader Oklahoma City, 1994-95; recipient proclamation Mayor Oklahoma City, 1994-95, 95-96, named Amb. of Good Will by Governor of Okla. Mem. Internat. Porcelain Art Tchrs. (past v.p., past pres., regional chmn., sec. to internat. bd. dirs.), Intercontinental Biographical Assn., C. of C. (sec.), Les Lefeyetts Home Club (pres. 1941-43), Garden Club (pres.), Sooner Art Club (pres. 1991-97), Kermac Art Club, Alpha Phi Sigma, Kappa Delta Phi, Kappa Kappa Iota. Baptist. Home: 4125 NW 57th St Oklahoma City OK 73112-1505

NOLAN, FABIAN ELIZABETH, principal; b. Pitts., Feb. 18, 1952; d. Clarence and Kathryn Lee (Johnson) N.; divorced, Sept. 1987; children: Tamara Wain, Terence Morris, Burlie Morris IV. BS, U. Pitts., 1980, MEd, 1982. Tchr. Allegheny Intermediate Unit, Pitts., 1986-90; prin. Mars (Pa.) Area Sch. Dist., 1990-91, North Allegheny Schs., Pitts., 1991-95; instr. Slipper Rock (Pa.) U., 1995—; cons. The Nolan Group, Cin., 1994—, R.A.L. Cons., Pitts., 1995. Mem. ASCD, Nat. Assn. Multicultural Edn., Coun. Exceptional Children, Alliance of Black Sch. Educators. Baptist.

NOLAN, JEAN, federal agency official; b. Collingdale, Pa., Oct. 25, 1959; d. John Thomas and Elizabeth (Gillan) N. BA, Temple U., 1981. Reporter Inside Radio, Cherry Hill, N.J., 1978-82; staff reporter Phila. Bus. Jour., 1982-84, Washington Bus. Jour., Tysons Corner, Va., 1984-85, Housing & Devel. Reporter, Washington, 1985-89; dir. publs. Enterprise Found., Columbia, Md., 1989-91, dir. comms., 1991-93; asst. sec. pub. affairs U.S. Dept. HUD, Washington, 1993—. Mem. Comms. Affinity Group Coun. Found. Democrat. Office: US Dept HUD 451 7th St SW Rm 10032 Washington DC 20410-0001

NOLAN, LOUISE MARY, school system administrator, author; b. Boston, Sept. 28, 1947; d. John Joseph and Helen (Spiers) N. BA, Regis Coll., 1969; MEd, Boston U., 1971 postgrad., 1981-82; postgrad Fitchburg State Coll., 1972-74, Salem State Coll., 1977-79; PhD, Boston Coll., 1986, MIT, 1992. Counselor Camp Thoreau, Inc., Concord, Mass., 1964-68; tchr., chmn. sci. dept. John F. Kennedy Meml. Jr. H.S., Woburn, Mass., 1969-86; asst. supt. schs. for curriculum and instrn. Woburn Pub. Schs., 1986—; instr. Boston Coll., 1992—; adj. assoc. prof. sch. edn. 1992—; initiator Woburn-Sci. Specialist Program Middlesex Acad. League, Woburn Expects Excellence in Edn. Reform Act, Let's Take Sci. Home Program, Youth Engaged in Svc.; co-owner Ruth and Louise Silkscreening, Lexington, Mass., Fancypants, Carlisle, Mass.; bd. dirs. ecology program Curry Coll., Milton, Mass., 1977, Mass. Mid. Sch. Sci. Olympics, North Shore Math and Sci. Collaborative, Newspaper in Edn. Boston Globe; mem. MIT High/Middle Sch. Math Sci. Tchr. Program; mem. new standards project Mass. Ednl. Assessment Program Com., Mass. State Sci. & Math. Frameworks Assessment com. Author: Y.E.S.-A Comprehensive Guide to Students Education Youth in Environmental Sciences, 1982; Bioluminscence-An Experimental Guide; Marine Plankton, 1983; Health Physical Science, 1983, 87, Physical Science: A Problem Solving Approach, 1991, Using Literature to Teach Science; Improving Students' Writing, 1995, Opened Assessment, 1995, Elementary School Writing Guide, 1995, Middle School Writing Guide, 1996, High School Writing Guide, 1996. Active New Eng. League Mid. Schs., Nat. League Mid. Schs. Past vice chmn. Mass. Sci. Fair Com.; bd. dirs. North Shore Sci. and Math. Collaborative, Newspaper in Edn. program The Boston Globe. Sci. & engring. fellow MIT Inst. for Mid. and High Sch., 1992; NSF grantee, 1972-73, 77-79, 81-82; chemistry fellow Boston U., 1983-84, edn. fellow MIT, 1992; For a Cleaner Environ. grantee, 1984-86. Mem. NEA, AAAS, Nat. Coun. Social Studies, Nat. Coun. Teaching English, Nat. Coun. Tchrs. Math., Mass. Assn. Sci. Suprs., Mass. Tchrs. Assn., Nat. Assn. Sci. Tchrs., Mass. Assn. Sci. Tchrs., Nat. Assn. Biology Tchrs., Nat. Assn. Rsch. in Sci. Teaching, Middlesex County Tchrs. Assn., Biology Roundtable, Woburn Tchrs. Assn., Mass. Supts. Assn., Beta Beta Beta, Pi Lambda Theta, Mus. Fine Arts Club, Concord Art Assn. Club, Mus. of Sci. Club. Democrat. Roman Catholic. Home: 9 Stevens Rd Lexington MA 02173-4126 Office: Adminstrn Offices 33 Locust St Woburn MA 01801-4033

NOLAN, SUSAN ELIZABETH, journalist; b. Seattle, Oct. 13, 1948; d. Donald Phillip Schmidt and Jean (Waller) McGarry; m. John Joseph Nolan, Nov. 22, 1968; children: Kathrine, Carolynne. Grad., H.B. Plant H.S., Tampa, Fla., 1966. Journalist, columnist Seneca (S.C.) Jour. and Tribune, 1986-88. Contbr. poems to profl. publs. Recipient Feature News Articles of Yr. award S.C. Alliance for Mentally Ill, 1987. Roman Catholic.

NOLAND, ANNGINETTE ROBERTS, retired sales executive; b. Stillwater, Okla., Sept. 30, 1930; d. Cecil Andrew and Gladys Leah (Woods) Roberts; m. Thomas Vaughan Noland, June 11, 1949; children: Nanette Noland Crocker, Thomas Vaughan Noland, Bruce Andrew Noland. Student, Okla. State U., 1948-49; cert. in planning, U. Wis. Chpt. advisor Kappa Delta Sorority, Stillwater, 1953-54, Baton Rouge, 1956-59; province pres. Kappa Delta Sorority, Miss., 1970-77; chpt. dir. II Kappa Delta Sorority, 1977-84, nat. dir. scholarship program, 1984-87, past mem. evaluation com., chmn. conv. scholarship banquet com., 1985, chmn. fellowships evaluation com., 1984-87; accounts receivables clk. Sta. WLOX-TV, Biloxi, Miss., 1973-76, sales asst., 1976-82, nat. sales asst. and polit. sales, 1982-84, nat. sales supr., 1984-95. Recipient award Order of the Emerald Kappa Delta Sorority, 1988. Mem. NAFE, DAR (treas. Biloxi chpt. 1983-89, corr. sec. 1989—), S.C. Geneal. Soc., Okla. Geneal. Soc., Colonial Dames XVII Century (corr. sec. local chpt. 1985-87, pres. 1987-89, 2d v.p. 1989-90, corr. sec. 1991—, state chair Colonial Heritage Week 1989-91, state chmn. yearbooks 1991-93, state organizing sec. 1993-95, corr. sec. 1993—, state insignia chair 1995—), Dau. Am. Colonists (charter mem. local chpt., 1st v.p. 1993—, state chair coll. Ozarks com. 1995—), UDC (1st v.p. local chpt. 1990-94, dist. dir., state conv. chair 1992, state fin. com. chair 1993-94, chpt. pres. 1994-96, state recorder crosses mil. svc. 1994—), Sons and Daus. Pilgrims (state recording sec. 1995—), U.S. Daus. of 1812, Magna Charta Dames, Biloxi Yacht Club (aux. corr. sec. 1986-88, sec. 1989-90). Republican. Episcopalian. Home: 2441 Old Bay Rd Biloxi MS 39531-2113

NOLAND, CHRISTINE A., magistrate judge. BA, La. State Univ., JD. Law clk. to Hon. John V. Parker U.S. Dist. Ct. (La. mid. dist.), 5th circuit; magistrate judge U.S. Dist. Ct. (La. mid. dist.), 5th circuit, Baton Rouge, 1987—. Mem. ABA, La. State Bar, La. trial Lawyers Assn., Baton Rouge Bar Assn., Dean Henry George McMahon Inn of Ct. (counselor). Office: Russell B Long Fed Bldg & Courthouse 777 Florida St Rm 265 Baton Rouge LA 70801-1717

NOLAND, MARIAM CHARL, foundation executive; b. Parkersburg, W.Va., Mar. 29, 1947; d. Lloyd Henry and Ethel May (Beare) N.; m. James Arthur Kelly, June 13, 1981. BS, Case Western Res. U., 1969; M in Edn., Harvard U., 1975. Asst. dir. admissions, fin. aid Baldwin-Wallace Coll., Berea, Ohio, 1969-72; asst. dir. admissions Davidson (N.C.) Coll., 1972-74; case writer Inst. Edn. Mgmt., Cambridge, Mass., 1975; sec., treas., program officer The Cleve. Found., 1975-81; v.p. The St. Paul Found., 1981-85; pres. Community Found. for S.E. Mich., 1985—; chair bd. trustees Coun. of Mich. Founds., Grand Haven, Mich., 1988—. Trustee Coun. on Founds., 1994—, Henry Ford Health System, 1994—, Alma Coll., 1994—. Mem. Detroit Com. Fgn. Rels. Office: Community Found Southeastern Mich 333 W Fort St Bsmt 2010 Detroit MI 48226-3134

NOLES, TAMMY GAYE, writer; b. Fairfield, Calif., Oct. 11, 1965; d. Ellen LaVon (Aldridge) N. AS, Northlake Coll., Irving, Tex., 1986; BA, U. North Tex., Denton, 1989. Intern Las Colinas Weekly, Irving, 1988; free-lance reporter Irving Community TV Network, 1987—; staff writer, news editor, editor Las Colinas People, 1989-92; writer, editor H.D. Vest Fin. Svcs., 1993—. Mem. NAFE, Press Club of Dallas, Alpha Epsilon Rho. Baptist.

NOLLEN, MARGARET ROACH, financial administrator; b. St. Louis, May 3, 1963; d. Jerry Burns and Mary Judith (Moreau) Roach; m. Frederick Walter Nollen II, Jan. 16, 1988; children: Jacob Burns, Patrick James. BBA in Fin., U. Tex., 1984; MBA, S.W. Tex. State U., 1990. Mktg. officer First City-Clear Lake, Houston, 1984-85; corp. svcs. officer, mgr. point of sales svcs. First City-Austin, Tex., 1985-87; investment officer NCNB Tex. Nat. Bank, Austin, 1987-89; fin. analyst U. Tex. System, Austin, 1989-91; dir. adminstrn. for external affairs Rice U., Houston, 1991-92; sr. fin. analyst for corp. fin., risk mgmt. and pensions Transco Energy Co., Houston, 1992-95; dir. fin. and adminstrn. Houston Symphony Soc., 1995—. Patentee in field of comml. monetary payment. Mem. NAFE, U. Tex. Exes, S.W. Tex. State U. Alumni Assn. Home: 10510 Great Plains Ln Houston TX 77064-7100 Office: The Houston Symphony Society 615 Louisiana St Houston TX 77002

NOON, ETHELYN SUE, secondary school educator; b. St. Paul, June 19, 1940; d. Mack and Minnie (Sorkin) Liebo; m. Walter Charles Noon, Jr., Aug. 26, 1962; children: Walter, Michael, Kimberly. BA in English and philosophy, U. Ariz., 1961; MA in Ednl. Adminstrn., Calif. State U., San Bernardino, 1989. Cert. tchr. English. Teller Humboldt Nat. Bank, Eureka, Calif., 1973-74; editor/writer Coast Credit Union, Eureka, 1974-75; tchr. Garden Sch., Riverside, Calif., 1976-82; tchr. English and history St. Catherine's Sch., Riverside, 1982-84; tchr. English Chaffey Joint Union H.S. Dist., Ontario, Calif., 1984—; on-site gifted and talented edn. coord. Montclair H.S., 1987-91. Contbr. articles to profl. jours., poetry to pubs. Tchr. art YWCA, Riverside, 1979-81; spkr. women's history Girls' Found., Riverside, 1993-95; recording sec., v.p. elect LWV, 1969-80. U. Ariz. scholar, 1960-61. Mem. AAUW (recording sec. 1994-95), Phi Kappa Phi. Democrat. Jewish. Home: 562 Campus View Dr Riverside CA 92507

NOONAN, JACQUELINE ANNE, pediatrics educator; b. Burlington, Vt., Oct. 28, 1928. BA, Albertus Magnus Coll., 1950; MD, U. Vt., 1954, DSc (hon.), 1980. Diplomate Am. Bd. Pediatrics, Am. Bd. Pediatric Cardiology. Intern N.C. Meml. Hosp., Chapel Hill, 1954-55; resident in pediatrics Children's Hosp., Cin., 1955-57; rsch. fellow Children's Med. Ctr., Boston, 1957-59; asst. prof. pediatrics State U. Iowa Sch. Medicine, 1959-61; asst. prof. pediatrics cardiology U. Ky. Coll. Medicine, Lexington, 1961-64, assoc. prof., 1964-69, prof., 1969—, chmn. dept. pediatrics, 1974-92; mem. embryology and human devel. study sect. NIH, 1973-78; mem. U.S.-USSR Symposium on Congenital Heart Disease, 1975; mem. sub. bd. pediatric cardiology Am. Bd. Pediatrics, 1977-82; examiner, mem. test. com. Nat. Bd. Med. Examiners, 1984-90, exec. com., 1991-95; participant various confs. in field; vis. prof. Vanderbilt U., Nashville, 1987; spkr. in field. Contbr. articles, revs. to med. publs.; mem. editl. bd. Am. Jour. Diseases Children, 1970-80, Am. Jour. Med. Edn., 1975-78, Pediatric Cardiology, 1978-90, Am. Heart Jour., 1994—, Clin. Pediatrics, 1990—. Mem. AMA, Am. Acad. Pediatrics (cardiology sect. chmn. 1972-74), Am. Coll. Cardiology (gov. Ky. chpt. 1989-92), Am. Fedn. Clin. Rsch., Assn. Med. Sch. Pediatric (dept. chmn. exec. com. 1978-81), Fayette County Med. Soc., Irish-Am. Pediatric Soc., Am. Pediatric Soc., Ky. State Med. Assn., NIH Alumni Assn., Soc. Pediatric Rsch., So. Soc. Pediatric Rsch. (pres. 1972). Office: U Ky Med Ctr Pediatrics Ky Clinic Lexington KY 40536-0284

NOONAN, MELINDA DUNHAM, women's health nurse, educator; b. Peoria, Ill., Feb. 19, 1954; d. Emmett Maxwell Dunham and Dixie Maurine (DeCounter) Widner; m. Robert Joseph Noonan; children: Alissa, Meris. Diploma, Ravenswood Hosp. Sch. Nursing, 1977; BSN cum laude, U. Ill., Chgo., 1989; MS, North Park Coll., 1995. Med. asst. James J. Hines, M.D., S.C., Chgo., 1973-76; staff nurse Northwestern Meml. Hosp., Chgo., 1978-79, asst. head nurse, 1979-80, staff nurse, 1980-86, perinatal and women's health educator, 1983—, coord. Health Learning Ctr., 1989-92; coord. Women's Ctr., Prentice Women's Hosp., Chgo., 1992-94; dir. women's programs Columbus Hosp., Chgo., 1994-96; dir. women's and family svcs. Swedish Convenant Hosp., Chgo., 1996—; founder, bd. dirs. Mothers Organized for Mut. Support, Chgo., 1981-89; creator, coord. Beyond The Birth Experience Program, Chgo., 1983-91. Contbg. author: Drugs, Alcohol, Pregnancy and Parenting, 1988, Clinical Issues of Perinatal and Women's Health Nursing, 1991, Jour. Obstetrical, Gynecological and Neonatal Nursing, 1996. Bd. dirs. Mothers Organized for mut. Support, 1981-88; troop leader Girl Scouts U.S., Chgo., 1991-93. Mem. Assn. Women's Health, Obstetrics and Neonatal Nurses (consumer edn. com. 1992-93, edn. com. 1994-95), Nat. Assn. Women's Health Profls., Am. Orgn. Nurse Execs., Rebekah (vice grand 1981-82, noble grand 1982-83), Sigma Theta Tau. Democrat. Roman Catholic. Home: 3414 W Glenlake Ave Chicago IL 60659-3420 Office: Swedish Covenant Hosp 5145 N California Ave Chicago IL 60625

NOONAN, NORINE ELIZABETH, academic administrator, researcher; b. Phila., Oct. 5, 1948; d. Alaric Edwin and Norine (Radford) Freeman. BA, summa cum laude, U. Vt., 1970; MA, Princeton U., 1972, PhD, 1976. Asst. prof. Coll. Vet. Medicine, U. Fla., Gainesville, 1976-81, assoc. prof., 1981; research assoc. prof. Georgetown U., Washington, 1981-82; Am. Chem. Soc. sci. fellow U.S. Senate Commerce Com., Washington, 1982-83; program and budget analyst Office Mgmt. and Budget, Washington, 1983-87, acting br. chief sci. and space programs, 1987-88, br. chief, 1988-92; v.p. rsch. Fla. Inst.

Tech., Melbourne, 1992—, dean grad. sch., 1993—; bd. advisors U.S. Found. for the Internat. Space U., 1989-90; disting lectr. MITRE Corp. Inst., 1991; vis. faculty Exec. Seminar Ctrs., Office Personnel Mgmt.; cons. Am. Chem. Soc. com. chem. and pub. affairs; mem. NASA space sci. adv. com.; mem. com. Antarctic policy & sci. NRC; mem. future of space sci. DOE environ. mgmt. sci. program NRC; councilor Oak Ridge Assn. Univs.; trustee Southeast Univs. Rsch. Assn., also chair finance com. Contbr. articles to sci. jours. Vol. Balt. City Fair, 1982-91. Bd. dirs. Brevard Symphony Orchestra, 1993-96, Wolf Trap Farm Pk. Assocs., Wolf Trap Farm Pk. for the Performing Arts, 1988-92, exec. com. 1990-92, exec. vice chmn., 1991-92, treas., 1992; mem. adv. coun. Brookings Instn. Ctr. for Pub. Policy Edn., 1989-93; treas. White House Athletic Ctr., 1990-92, Potomac Basset Hound Club, Space Coast Tiger Bay Club, bd. dirs 1996—. Recipient Spl. Performance award Office Mgmt. and Budget, 1987, 88; grantee Fla. div. Am. Cancer Soc., 1977, NIH, 1979, NSF, 1979. Fellow AAAS (mem. at large sect. gen. interest in sci. and tech. 1994—, mem. sci., engring. and pub. policy com.); mem. Am. Soc. Cell Biology, Sigma Xi, Phi Beta Kappa (pres. Fla. chpt. 1980-81). Mem. United Ch. of Christ. Avocations: running, purebred dogs, fishing, cooking, aerobics. Home: 2480 Grassmere Dr Melbourne FL 32904-9715 Office: Fla Inst Tech 150 W University Blvd Melbourne FL 32901-6982

NOONAN, SUSAN ABERT, public relations counselor; b. Lancaster, Pa., May 10, 1960; d. James Goodear and Carole (Althouse) Abert; m. David Lindsay Noonan, July 28, 1986; children: Caroline du Pont, Elizabeth Augusta. BA, Mt. Holyoke Col., 1982. Account exec. Merill Lynch, N.Y.C., 1982-83; sr. v.p. Cameron Assocs., N.Y.C., 1983-88; pres., founder Noonan/Russo Comm., N.Y.C., 1988—. Mem. Nat. Investor Rels. Inst. Office: Noonan/Russo Comm Inc 220 5th Ave New York NY 10001-7708

NORBECK, JANE S., nursing educator; b. Redfield, S.D., Feb. 20, 1942; d. Sterling M. and Helen L. (Williamson) N.; m. Paul J. Gorman, June 28, 1970; 1 child Sara J. Gorman. BA in Psychology, U. Minn., 1965, BSN, 1965; MS, U. Calif., San Francisco, 1971, DNSc, 1975. Psychiat. nurse Colo. Psychiat. Hosp., Denver, 1965-66, Langley Porter Hosp., San Francisco, 1966-67; pub. health nurse San Francisco Health Dept., 1968-69; prof. U. Calif. (San Francisco) Sch. of Nursing, 1975—, dept. chair, 1984-89, dean, 1989—; chair study sect. Nat. Inst. of Nursing Rsch., 1990-93, mem. editl. bd. Archives of Psychiat. Nursing, 1985-95, Rsch. in Nursing and Health, 1987—. Co-editor: Annual Review of Nursing Research, 1996-97; contbr. articles to profl. jours. Mem. ANA, Am. Acad. Nursing, Am. Orgn. Nursing Exec., Am. Assn. Coll. Nursing, Inst. of Medicine, Sigma Theta Tau. Office: U Calif Sch Nursing 501 Parnassus Ave San Francisco CA 94143

NORCEL, JACQUELINE JOYCE CASALE, educational administrator; b. Bklyn., Nov. 19, 1940; d. Frederick and Josephine Jeanette (Bestafka) Casale; m. Edward John Norcel, Feb. 24, 1962. BS, Fordham U., 1961; MS, Bklyn. Coll., 1966; 6th yr. cert. So. Conn. State U., 1980; postgrad. Bridgeport U. Elem. tchr., pub. schs., N.Y.C., 1961-80; prin. Coventry Schs., Conn., 1980-84, Trumbull Schs., Conn., 1984—; guest lectr. So. Conn. State U., 1980—; cons. Monson Schs., Mass., 1984; mem. Conn. State Prin. Acad. Adv. Bd., 1986-88; mem. adj. faculty Sacred Heart U., Fairfield, Conn., 1985—, So. Conn. State U., summer 1991. Editor: Best of the Decade, 1980; mem. editorial adv. bd. Principal Matters; contbr. articles to profl. jours. Chmn. bldg. com. Trumbull Bd. Edn., 1978-80; chmn. Sch. Benefit Com., Trumbull, 1985-86; catechist Bridgeport Diocese, Roman Cath. Ch., Conn., 1975-85, youth minister, 1979-84, coord., evaluator leadership tng. workshops for teens and adults, 1979-84; mem. St. Stephen's Parish Coun., 1993—. Recipient Town of Trumbull Service award, 1982, Nat. Disting. Prin. award, 1988, Joseph Formica Disting. Svc. award EMSPAC, 1994. Mem. ASCD, N.E. Regional Elem. Prins. Assn. (rep. 1984-86, sec. 1986-87), Elem. Mid. Sch. Prins. Assn. (pres. 1985-86, Citizen of Year award, 1991, Pres.'s award 1981-85, state elected rep. 1989-90, fed. rels. coord. 1990-94, dist. dir. 1995-96),Adminstrn. and Supervision Assn. (sec. 1980-81, pres. 1981-82, exec. bd. 1982-93), Hartford Area Prins. and Suprs. Assn. (local pres. 1981-82), Nat. Assn. Elem. Sch. Prins. (zone I dir. 1987-90, del. to gen. assemblies 1984-90, bd. dirs. 1987-90), Conn. Assn. Supervision and Curriculum Devel., Trumbull Adminstrs. Assn. (pres.-elect 1989-91, pres. 1991-93), Eastern Conn. Council of Internat. Reading Assn., New Eng. Coalition Ednl. Leaders, Associated Tchrs. of Math. in Conn., Phi Delta Kappa (Disting. Fellow award 1992, v.p. rsch. and projects 1993-95), Pi Lambda Theta (Beta Sigma chpt.), Delta Kappa Gamma. Republican. Home: 5240 Madison Ave Trumbull CT 06611-1016 Office: Tashua Sch 401 Stonehouse Rd Trumbull CT 06611-1651

NORD, GAIL DIETERICH, mathematician, educator; b. Garfield Heights, Ohio, Dec. 9, 1960; d. Benedict Charles Dieterich and Elizabeth Ann (Easterly) Brown; m. John Faris Nord, Sept. 7, 1984; 1 child, Katie Marie. BS in Secondary Edn., U. Cin., 1983, BA in Math., 1983; MA in Math., Ohio State U., 1985. Asst. prof. math. Gonzaga U., Spokane, Wash., 1987—. Bd. dirs. Expanding Your Horizons, Spokane; vol. The Children's Ark, Spokane, 1995—. Mem. AAUW, Math. Assn. Am., Nat. Coun. Tchrs. Math., Wash. State Math. Coun., Kappa Delta Pi. Office: Gonzaga Univ Dept Math AD Box 41 Spokane WA 99258-0001

NORDGREN, LYNN LIZBETH, elementary education educator, educational administrator; b. Mankato, Minn., Jan. 29, 1951; d. Lee Adolph and Donna Lou (Charles) N.; 1 foster child, Nathan. BS in Tchg., Mankato State U., 1975, postgrad. im Eperiential Edn., 1993—. Cert. tchr. 1-6, spl. edn. k-12, experiential edn., k-12, Minn. Tchr. EMH (intermediate) Spl. Edn. Lincoln Sch., Mpls, 1975-77, 4th grade Lincoln Sch., Mpls, 1977-79, EMH (primary) Spl. Edn. Standish Sch, Mpls, 1979-80, Omega Math. Lab. Holland Sch., Mpls, 1983-84, gifted and talented Olson Elem. Sch., Mpls, 1983-88, 3d and 4th grades Pub. Sch. Acad., Mpls, 1988-91; profl. devel. facilitator Mpls. Pub. Schs., Mpls, 1991—; mem., tchr. rep. dist. leadership team Mpls. Schs., 1990—, Project Racism, 1994—; creator, producer, owner The Learning Bridge (ednl. products), 1994—; field test coord. Nat. Bd. Profl. Tchg. Stds. Pres. People Acting for Indigenous Rights, Mpls., 1990—; network leader Am. Fedn. Tchrs., 1991-93; vol. mem. adv. com. Native Am. Rainbow Network, 1994; sec. Hawthorne Area Cmty. Coun., 1995—. Recipient Tchr. Venture Fund awards Econ. Project, 1985-86, World Hunger Project, 1986-87, Mpls.; grantee: Minn. Environ. Svcs. Found., 1991-96, Nat. Bd. for Profl. Teaching Standards, 1992-94, 94. Mem. Minn. Fedn. Tchrs., Mpls. Fedn. Tchrs. (steward 1991—), Minn. Assn. Supervision and Curriculum Devel., Minn. Staff Devel. Coun., Nat. Staff Devel. Coun. Democrat. Home: 2810 N 4th St Minneapolis MN 55411-1512 Office: 925 Delaware S E Minneapolis MN 55414

NORDHAGEN, HALLIE HUERTH, nursing home administrator; b. Sarona, Wis., Apr. 2, 1914; d. Mathias James and Ethel Elizabeth (Fann) Huerth; B.Ed., U. Wis., Superior, 1938, M.A., 1949; m. Carl E. Nordhagen, May 24, 1947; children: Bruce Carl, Brian Keith. Prin., tchr. Wis. Public Schs., 1932-46; supervising tchr. Wis. Community Coll., 1946-48; psychiat. adminstr. Trempealeau County Health Care Center, psychiat. nursing home, Whitehall, Wis., 1959—; mem. Wis. Nursing Home Adminstrs. Examining Bd.; fellow Menninger Clinic, Topeka, 1979-81; cons. to the bishop Evangelical Lutheran Ch., Wis. Chairperson BRAD Assn./Acohol & Drug Abuse, mem. Trampealeau County Alliance Drug Free Youth; mem. com. cons. to bishop Evangelical Luth. Ch. Am., 1995. Recipient Disting. Service award in edn. and hosp. adminstrn., London, 1967, award for services to human services programs Wis. Assn. Human Services, 1972, award for outstanding services to exceptional children Assn. Retarded Children, 1978, award for accomplishments in human resources Trempealeau County Conservation Service, 1981; Wis. State Senate citation, 1983; citatioin Wis. Gov., 1984. Mem. Wis. Assn. County Homes, Wis. Edn. Assn., Wis. Assn. Human Services Programs, Internat. Platform Assn., Am. Lutheran Ch. Women. Clubs: Whitehall Country, Women's. Author: Wisconsin Indians, 1966. Home: 35681 Claire St Whitehall WI 54773-8430

NORDIN, PHYLLIS ECK, sculptor, painter; b. Chgo. Student Beloit Coll., Wayne State U.; B.S., U. Toledo, 1963, BA cum laude, 1972, MLS, 1992; BA, Sch. Design Toledo Mus. Art, 1972. Instr. Lourdes Coll. Sylvania, Ohio, 1986-89, U. Toledo, 1986-89. Prin. works include large bronze sculptures Lucas County Main Library, Toledo, Christ figure St. Joan of Arc Ch., Maumee, Ohio, Ronald McDonald House, Toledo, First English Evangel. Luth. Ch., Grosse Pointe Woods, Mich., Christ Presbyn. Ch., Covenant Presbyn. Ch., Toledo, Toledo Hosp., Reynolds Br. Libr., Toledo, Port Clinton and Defiance (Ohio) Librs. , stone wall mural Epworth United Methodist Ch., Toledo, Beloit Coll., Wis., bronze fountain U. Toledo, bronze life-size children Treasure Coast Mall, Stuart, Fla., Kingston, Tenn. Pub. Libr., welded steel sculpture Town Ctr. Mall, Port Charlotte, Fla., Carey (Ohio) Bank, Toledo Bank, Bi-Centennial Park, Toledo, wood wall carvings 1st Meth. Ch., LaGrange, Ill., ferro-cement abstract Flower Hosp., Sylvania, Ohio, Rossford (Ohio) Meth. Ch.; numerous others; exhibited Allied Artists Am., Salmagundi Club, Audubon artists, N.Am. Sculpture exhibit; numerous others. Represented by Collectors Corner Toledo Mus. Art, 1970—. Recipient Alpha award Foothills Art Ctr., 1983, 1st prize Ann. Nat. Art Exhbn., 1978, numerous others; named to Lyons Twp. H.S. Hall of Fame, 1996. Mem. Nat. Assn. Women Artists, Nat. Sculpture Soc., Ohio Designer Craftsmen, Ohio Liturgical Art Guild, Catharine Lorillard Wolfe Art Club, Athena Art Soc., Northwestern Ohio Watercolor Soc., Toledo (Ohio) Artists' Club, Phi Kappa Phi (hon.). Home and Studio: 4035 Tantara Dr Toledo OH 43623-3311

NORDLING, JOANNE, parenting educator, writer, consultant; b. Windom, Minn., Nov. 2, 1934; d. Verle Desmond and Dora Marie (Funston) Swenston; m. George D. Nordling, Aug. 17, 1952; children: Dirk, Eric, Chris, Craig. BS in Social Studies, Portland State U., 1966, MS in Edn., 1971; MEd in Counseling, Lewis & Clark Coll., 1976. Cert. tchr., sch. counselor. Media specialist Newberg (Oreg.) Schs., 1971-73, child and family counselor, 1976-78; tchr. and counselor Fanno Creek Children's Ctr., Portland, Oreg., 1974; child and family counselor West Linn (Oreg.) Schs., 1978-87; cofounder Parent Support Ctr., Portland, Oreg., 1988—, sec., 1990-93, pres., 1993—. Author: Dear Faculty, 1976, Taking Charge: A Parent and Teacher Guide to Loving Discipline, 1992, rev. edit., 1996; contbr. chpt. to book. Mem. ACLU, West Hills Unitarian/Universalist Fellowship, Audubon Soc., Planned Parenthood. Recipient Outstanding Svc. award Washington County Cmty. Action, 1989. Democrat. Office: Parent Support Ctr Inc P O Box 80753 Portland OR 97280

NORDMEYER, MARY BETSY, vocational educator; b. New Haven, May 19, 1939; d. George and Barbara Stedman (Thompson) N. ABPhil, Wheaton Coll., Norton, Mass., 1960; MA, San Jose State U., 1968; AS in Computer Sci., West Valley Coll., 1985. Cert. tchr. spl. edn., Calif.; cert. secondary tchr., Calif. Instr. English Santa Clara (Calif.) Unified Sch. Dist., 1965-77, vocat. specialist, 1977—, dir. project work ability, 1984—, also mem. community adv. com.; facilitator Project Work-Ability, Region 5, 1985-86, sec., 1988-90. Author poetry, 1960, Career and Vocat. Edn. for Students With Spl. Needs, 1986; author/designer Career English, 1974, Career Information, 1975. Recipient Outstanding Secondary Educator award, 1975, Award of Excellence, Nat. Assn. Vocat. Edn., 1984; named Tchr. of Yr. in Spl. Edn., Santa Clara Unified Sch. Dist., 1984-85. Mem. Calif. Assn. Work Experience Educators, Sierra Club, Epsilon Eta Sigma. Democrat. Home: 14920 Sobey Rd Saratoga CA 95070-6236 Office: Santa Clara Unified Sch Dist 1889 Lawrence Rd Santa Clara CA 95051-2108

NORDQUIST, SANDRALEE RAHN, lay worker; b. Chgo., Dec. 5, 1940; d. Herbert Henry and Elinor Gertrude (Duben) Rahn; m. George Leczewski, Oct. 13, 1962 (div. Dec. 1968); 1 child, Peter George (dec.); m. David Arthur Nordquist, July 19, 1969; children: Kerilinn D., Sharianne R. AA, Harper Coll., 1982; BS in English, Elmhurst (Ill.) Coll., 1985, BS in Theology, 1988; postgrad., Northestern Ill. U., Chgo., Drake U. Cert. tchr. English, history, learning disordered, behaviorally disordered, Ill. Tchr. English, gen. music and spl. edn. Foreman H.S., Chgo., 1990—; tchr. English summer sch. Luther H.S., Chgo., 1990, 92-94; feature writer Daily Herald, Paddock Publs., 1991—; tchr. sci. summer sch. Weber H.S., 1995, Chgo., 1995. Columnist (newspaper) Pulitzer Pubs. Notebook, 1986-90. Leader Girl Scouts U.S., Chgo. and Elk Grove, 1968-70, 77-81; v.p. Dist. 59 Orch. Assn., Elk Grove Village, Ill., 1985-87; pres. Sch. Dist. 59 Project 444, Elk Grove Village, 1981; confirmation tchr. Evang. Luth. Ch. of the Holy Spirit, Elk Grove, Ill., 1990-91, guild pres., adv. trinity preaching, 1990-91, leader adult Bible study, 1991-93; lector, greeter, actress Trinity Luth. Ch., Roselle, Ill., 1992—, also Drama Guild. Mem. Nat. Coun. Tchrs. of English, Ill. Assn. Tchrs. of English, Sigma Tau Delta. Home: 639 Sycamore Dr Elk Grove Village IL 60007-4624 Office: Foreman High Sch 3235 N Leclaire Ave Chicago IL 60641-4238

NORDYKE, ELEANOR COLE, population researcher, public health nurse; b. Los Angeles, June 15, 1927; d. Ralph G. and Louise Noble (Carter) Cole; m. Robert Allan Nordyke, June 18, 1950; children: Mary Ellen Nordyke-Grace, Carolyn Nordyke-Cozzette, Thomas A., Susan E., Gretchen Nordyke Worthington. BS, Stanford U., 1950; P.H.N. accreditation, U. Calif.-Berkeley, 1952; MPH, U. Hawaii, 1969. RN. Pub. health nurse San Francisco Dept. Health, 1950-52; nurse-tchr. Punahou Sch., Honolulu, 1966-67; clinic coordinator East-West Population Inst., East-West Ctr., Honolulu, 1969-75, population rschr., 1975-82, rsch. fellow, 1982-92; cons. Hawaii Commn. on Population, Honolulu, 1970-83; mem. Hawaii Policy Action Group for Family Planning, Honolulu, 1971-89, chmn., 1976-77. Author: The Peopling of Hawaii, 1977, 2d rev. edit., 1989, A Profile of Hawaii's Elderly Population, 1984, (with Robert Gardner) The Demographic Situation in Hawaii, 1974, mem. editorial bd. Hawaiian Jour. History, 1980—; contbr. articles to profl. jours. Bd. dirs. YMCA, Honolulu, 1970—, vice-chmn. 1978-79, chmn. YMCA Camp Erdman, 1989-92; bd. dirs. Hawaii Planned Parenthood, 1974-78, Friends of Libr. of Hawaii, 1985-87; trustee Hawaiian Hist. Soc., 1978-82, Arcadia Retirement Residence, Honolulu, 1978-87; bd. dirs. Hawaii Pacific U., 1988—, mem. liberal arts coun. Mem. Population Assn. Am., Population Reference Bur., Hawaii Pub. Health Assn., Am. Statis. Assn., Hawaii Econ. Assn., Hawaiian Hist. Soc., Friends of East-West Ctr., Friends of Univ. Hawaii Sch. Medicine, Stanford Nurses Alumni Assn., Stanford Alumni Assn. (bd. dirs. Hawaii chpt.), Friends of Iolani Palace, Gen. Fed. Women's History Club, Book Reading Club, Outrigger Canoe Club, Morning Music Club, Phi Beta Kappa. Democrat. Congregationalist. Home: 2013 Kakela Dr Honolulu HI 96822-2158

NOREK, FRANCES THERESE, lawyer; b. Chgo., Mar. 9, 1947; d. Michael S. and Viola C. (Harbecke) N.; m. John E. Flavin, Aug. 31, 1968 (div.); 1 child, John Michael. B.A., Loyola U., Chgo., 1969, J.D., 1973. Bar: Ill. 1973, U.S. Dist. Ct. (no. dist.) Ill. 1973, U.S. Ct. Appeals (7th cir.) 1974. Assoc. Alter, Weiss, Whitesel & Laff, Chgo., 1973-74; asst. states atty. Cook County, Chgo., 1974-86; assoc. Clausen, Miller, Gorman, Caffrey & Witous P.C., 1986—; mem. trial practice faculty Loyola U. Sch. Law, Chgo., 1980—; judge, evaluator mock trial competitions, Chgo., 1978—; lectr. in field. Recipient Emil Gumpert award Am. Coll. Trial Lawyers, 1982. Mem. Chgo. Bar Assn. (instr. fed. trial bar adv. program young lawyer's sect. 1983-84). Office: Clausen Miller Gorman Caffrey & Witous PC 10 S La Salle St Chicago IL 60603-1002

NORELL, JUDITH REGINA, musician, political administrator; b. N.Y.C.; d. Sandor and Sylvia (Duchin) Hirsch; m. Ian Strasfogel, Feb. 15, 1973; children: Daniella, Gabirelle. MM, Juilliard Sch., 1971. Artistic dir. Bach Gesselschaft N.Y., N.Y.C., 1984-86, Opera Antica, Palm Beach, Fla., 1987-93; exec. dir. Women's Campaign Sch. Yale U., New Haven, 1996—. Ford Found. fellow, 1970; recipient medal Mayor of City of N.Y., 1995. Mem. LWV, NWPC (legis. dir. N.Y. state chpt. 1995—). Office: Yale U Women's Campaign Sch PO Box 686 Westport CT 06881

NOREN-IACOVINO, MARY-JO PATRICIA, insurance company executive; b. N.Y.C., Feb. 20, 1951; d. James Pierce and Grace Virginia (Keating) Keelty; m. Louis T. Iacovino, Sept. 23, 1989. Student, CUNY, 1971-72. Asst. v.p. Huntoon, Paige & Co., Inc., N.Y.C., 1972-79; v.p. Merrill Lynch Capital Mkts., N.Y.C., 1979-85, Security Pacific Merchant Bank, N.Y.C., 1985-89, Oxford Resources Corp., Woodbury, N.Y., 1989-90; securities products coord. Equitable Life, N.Y.C., 1990-94. Mem. Oratorio Soc. N.Y. (bd. dirs., mktg. dir. 1993), Women's Life Underwriters Coun., Nat. Assn. Life Underwriters. Home: 17 Park Ave # 9A New York NY 10016-4306 Office: The Equitable Fl 32 1221 Ave of the Americas New York NY 10020-1088

NORKIN, CYNTHIA CLAIR, physical therapist; b. Boston, May 6, 1932; d. Miles Nelson and Carolyn (Green) Clair; m. Stanislav A. Norkin, Feb. 19, 1955 (dec. 1970); 1 child, Alexandra. BS in Edn., Tufts U., 1954; cert. phys. therapy Bouve Boston Coll., 1954; MS, Boston U., 1973, EdD, 1984. Instr. Bouve-Boston Coll., 1954-55; staff phys. therapist New Eng. Med. Center, Boston, 1954-55; staff phys. therapist Abington Meml. Hosp., Abington, Pa., 1965-70, Eastern Montgomery County Vis. Nurse Assn., 1970-72; asst. prof. phys. therapy Sargent Coll., Boston U., 1973-84; assoc. prof. phys. therapy, dir., founder Sch. Phys. Therapy, Ohio U., Athens, 1984-95; cons. Boston Center Ind. Living, Cambridge Vis. Nurse Assn., Mass. Medicaid Cost Effectiveness Project, 1978; sec. Health Planning Council Greater Boston, 1976-78; book, manuscript reviewer F.A. Davis Co., 1986—; mem. arthritis adv. com. Ohio Dept. Health. Trustee Brimmer and May Sch., 1980. Mem. AAAS, Am. Phys. Therapy Assn. (on site evaluator commn. on accreditation 1986—), Mass. Phys. Therapy Assn. (chmn. Mass. quality assurance com. 1980-83), Am. Public Health Assn., Mass. Assn. Mental Health, Athens County Vi. Nurse Assn. (sec. adv. coun. 1984-95). Episcopalian. Author: (with P. Levangie) Joint Structure and Function: A Comprehensive Analysis, 1983, 2d edit., 1992; (with D.J. White) Joint Measurement: A Guide to Goniometry, 1985, 2d edit., 1995.

NORLEN, PAMELA SUSAN, secondary education educator; b. Omaha, Mar. 8, 1949; d. Raymond Carl and Mildred Adeline (Van Zago) Peterson; m. David Frank Norlen, Feb. 7, 1970; children: Matthew, Scott, Julie. BS, U. Nebr., 1970; postgrad., U. Nebr., Omaha, Wayne State U., Kearney State U. Tchr. jr. h.s. Westside Pub. Schs., Omaha, 1970-71; tchr. social studies Westside H.S., Omaha, 1981-82; tchr. social studies Millard Pub. Schs., Omaha, 1982—, curriculum specialist for social studies, 1993-96, dept. head, 1996—; mem. effective schs. com. Millard South H.S., Omaha, 1989-91, chair action team for site-based mgmt. Mem. ASCD, NEA, Nat. Coun. for Social Studies, Nebr. Edn. Assn., Nebr. State Social Studies Coun., Millard Edn. Assn. Office: Millard Pub Schs 14705 Q St Omaha NE 68137

NORLIST See LUST, ELENORE

NORMAN, ALLINE L., health facility administrator; b. Homerville, Ga., Dec. 20, 1938; d. John F. and Alline D. N. BS, Ga. Coll., 1960; cert. Sch. for Med. Records, U.S. Pub. Health Svc., 1961. U.S. pub. svc. offcr. U. Cin., 1961-65; asst. chief and chief med. records U.S. Pub. Health Svc. Hosps., New Orleans, Chgo., Norfolk, 1965-70; chief med. info. section, Med. Adminstrn. Svc. VA Med. Ctr., N.Y., 1970-72, Miami, 1972-75; asst. chief Med. Adminstrn. Svc. VA Med. Ctr., East Orange, N.J., 1975-80, Miami, 1980-83; chief Med. Adminstrn. Svc. VA Med. Ctr., Augusta, Ga., 1983-85; chief field ops. divsn., Med. Adminstrn. Svc. VA Med. Ctr., Atlanta, 1988-89; from dep. dir. to dir. Med. Adminstrn. Svc. VHA, 1990-93, dir. Adminstrn. Svc. Office, 1993-94; dir. VA Med. Ctr., Lake City, Fla., 1994—; chmn. combined fed. campaign Vets. Health Adminstrn., 1991, co-chmn. chief med. dir.'s adv. com. on diversity, 1992-96, mem. task force subcom. on recommendations of commn. on future structure of vets. health car, 1992; mem. White House Nat. Health Care Task Force on Integration Govt. Sys., 1993, Sec.'s Adv. Group on Sexual Harassment, 1993-96, Interagy. Inst., 1993-94. Bd. dirs. Suwanee United Way, 1994-95, Lake City C.C. Found., 1995-96, Am. Cancer Soc., Lake City, 1995-96. Recipient Fed. Leadership award, 1992, cert. achievement Fed. Women's Interagency Bd., 1993, Sec. Meritorious Svc. award, 1994, Under Sec. Health Honor award, 1994. Mem. VA Sr. Execs. Assn. (bd. dirs. 1994). Methodist. Office: VA Med Ctr Lake City FL 32025

NORMAN, E. GLADYS, business computer educator, consultant; b. Oklahoma City, June 13, 1933; d. Joseph Eldon and Mildred Lou (Truitt) Biggs; m. Joseph R.R. Radeck, Mar. 1, 1953 (div. Aug. 1962); children: Jody Matti, Ray Norman, Warren Norman (dec. May 1993), Dana Norman; m. Leslie P. Norman, Aug. 26, 1963 (dec. Feb. 1994); 1 child, Elayne Pearce. Student, Fresno (Calif.) State Coll., 1951-52, UCLA, 1956-59, Linfield Coll., 1986-95. Math. aid U.S. Naval Weapons Ctr., China Lake, Calif., 1952-56, computing systems specialist, 1957-68; systems programmer Oreg. Motor Vehicles Dept., Salem, 1968-69; instr. in data processing, dir. Computer Programming Ctr., Salem, 1969-72; instr. in data processing Merritt-Davis Bus. Coll., Salem, 1972-73; sr. programmer, analyst Teledyne Wah Chang, Albany, Oreg., 1973-79; sr. systems analyst Oreg. Dept. Vets. Affairs, Albany, 1979-80; instr. in bus. computers Linn-Benton Community Coll., Albany, 1980-95; ret., 1995; computer cons. for LBCC Ret. Sr. Vol. Program, 1995—; presenter computer software seminars State of Oreg., 1991-93, Oreg. Credit Assoc. Conf., 1991, Oreg. Regional Users Group Conf., 1992; computer tchr. Linn-Benton C.C., 1996; computer cons. Oremet Titanium, 1996; computer cons. in field. Mem. Data Processing Mgmt. Assn. (bd. dirs. 1977-84, 89-95, region sect. 1995—, assoc. v.p. 1988, Diamond Individual Performance award 1985). Democrat.

NORMAN, MARDI, computer company executive; b. Oceanside, Calif., June 6, 1968; d. L. Bruce and Marjorie N. Attended, London U., 1989; BS in Bus., Calif. State Polytechnic U., 1992; postgrad., UCLA, 1996—. Front desk mgr. Santa Anita Inn, 1987-89, 89-90; asst. to divsn. mgr. Glen Ellen Winery, 1990-92; promotional mgr. Charles Revson, Inc., 1992-93; v.p., co-owner Dynamic Systems, Inc., 1993—; career advisor Chi Omega, Pomona, Calif., 1995. Recipient Cmty. Svc. award Human Corps., 1991-92. Mem. Inst. Mgmt. Accts. Republican. Roman Catholic. Home: 437 28th Pl Manhattan Beach CA 90266 Office: Dynamic Systems Inc 120 W Bellevue Dr Pasadena CA 91105

NORMAN, MARIANNE DARR, middle school educator; b. Ft. Wayne, Ind., Sept. 1, 1942; d. Eugene Stanton Sr. and Marilyn Alice (Meier) Darr; m. Harold F. Norman, Oct. 26, 1961 (div. Dec. 1989); children: Andrea, John. BS, Manchester Coll., 1965; MS, St. Francis Coll., 1970. Cert. tchr., Ind. 6th grade tchr. Ligonier (Ind.) Elem. Sch., 1964-65; 8th grade English tchr. Marshall Mem. Sch., Columbia City, Ind., 1965-66; 9th grade English tchr. Columbia City Joint H.S., 1966-67, 10th Grade English tchr., 1977-78; freshman composition tchr. Purdue U., Ft. Wayne, Ind., 1978-80; owner The Shirt Cellar, Churubusco, Ind., 1978-87; mid. sch. lang. arts tchr. Washington Ctr. Sch., Columbia City, 1987-92, Thorncreek Ctr. Sch., Columbia City, 1992—; tchr.-cons. Ind. Writing Project, 1991—, also pres. adv. bd., dir. 1995—; mem. steering com. Portfolio Implementation program Columbia City Schs., 1990—; failitator Ind. Dept. Edn., 1994—. Mem. ASCD, NEA, ALAN, Ind. State Tchrs. Assn., Ind. Mid. Level Assn., Nat. Coun. Tchrs. English, Ind. Coun. tchrs. English (Hoosier Tchr. of English 1991, editor newsletter 1993-95). Methodist. Home: 5150 Lakewood Dr Columbia City IN 46725

NORMAN, MARSHA, playwright; b. Louisville, Sept. 21, 1947; d. Billie Lee and Bertha Mae (Conley) Williams; m. Michael Norman (div. 1974); m. Dann C. Byck Jr., 1978 (div.); m. Timothy Dykman; 2 children: Angus, Katherine. B.A., Agnes Scott Coll., 1969; M.A.T., U. Louisville, 1971. Author: (plays) Getting Out, 1977 (John Gassner New Playwrights medallion, Outer Critics Circle award 1979, George Oppenheimer-Newsday award 1979), Third and Oak, 1978, Circus Valentine, 1979, The Holdup, 1980, 'Night, Mother, 1982 (Susan Smith Blackburn prize 1982, Tony award nomination for best play 1983, Pulitzer prize for Drama 1983, Elizabeth Hull-Kate Warriner award Dramatists Guild 1983), Traveler in the Dark, 1984, Sarah and Abraham, 1987, D. Boone, 1992; (book of musical, lyrics) The Secret Garden, 1991 (Tony award for best book of musical 1991, Tony award nominee for best original score 1991, Drama Desk award for best book of musical 1991; Loving Daniel Boone (play) 1992, Trudy Blue (play), 1995, The Red Shoes (book and lyrics), 1992; (screenplay) 'Night, Mother, 1986; (teleplays) It's the Willingness, 1978, In Trouble at Fifteen, 1980, The Laundromat, 1985, Third and Oak: The Pool Hall, 1989, Face of a Stranger, 1991; (novel) The Fortune Teller, 1987; (collection) Four Plays by Marsha Norman, 1988. NEA grantee, 1978-79, Rockefeller playwright-in-residence grantee, 1979-80, Am. Acad. and Inst. for Arts and Letters grantee; recipient Lit. Lion award N.Y. Pub. Libr., 1986. Office: Jack Tantleff 375 Greenwich St Ste 700 New York NY 10013-2338

NORMAN, MARY MARSHALL, counselor, therapist; b. Auburn, N.Y., Jan. 10, 1937; d. Anthony John and Zita Norman. BS cum laude, LeMoyne Coll., 1958; MA, Marquette, U., 1960; EdD, Pa. State U., 1971. Cert. Alcoholism Counselor. Tchr., St. Cecilia's Elem. Sch., Theinsville, Wis., 1959-60; vocat. counselor Marquette U., Milw., 1959-60; dir. testing and counseling U. Rochester (N.Y.), 1960-62; dir. testing and counseling, dean women, asso. dean coll., asst. dean students, dir. student activities, asst. prof. psychology Corning (N.Y.) C.C., 1962-68; rsch. asst. Center for Study Higher Edn., Pa. State U., University Park, 1969-71; dean faculty South

Campus, C.C. Allegheny County, West Mifflin, Pa., 1971-72, campus pres., coll. v.p., 1972-82; pres. Orange County C.C., 1982-90; sr. counselor The Horton Family Program, 1990—. cons. Boricua Coll., N.Y.C., 1976-77; reader NSF, 1977-78; mem. govtl. commn. com. Am. Assn. Cmty. and Jr. Colls., 1976-79, bd. dirs., 1982—; mem. and chmn. various middle state accreditation teams. Bd. dirs. Orange County United Way; bd. dirs. Orange County Alcoholism and Drug Abuse Coun., 1993—. Mem. Am. Assn. Higher Edn., Nat. Assn. Women Deans Counselors, Am. Assn. Women in Community and Jr. Colls. (charter, Woman of Yr. 1981), Pa. Assn. Two-Yr. Colls., Pa. Assn. Acad. Deans, Pitts. Council Women Execs. (charter), Am. Council on Edn. (Pa. rep. identification women for adminstrn. 1978—), Pa. Council on Higher Edn., Orange County C. of C., Gamma Pi Epsilon. Contbr. articles to profl. jours. Home: 8 Crabapple Ln Middletown NY 10940-1006 Office: 406 E Main St Middletown NY 10940

NORMAN, SHERI HANNA, artist, educator, cartographer; b. Chgo., Dec. 15, 1940; d. L.J. and Margaret Maxine (Kuyper Fleischer) Hanna; m. Donald Lloyd Norman, Febr. 28, 1963 (div. 1996); 1 child, Ronald Wayne Norman. BA, U. Wyo., Laramie, 1963; attended, Dayton (Ohio) Art Inst., 1975; MFA, San Francisco Art Inst., 1993. Substitute tchr. Arlington, Va. and Yellow Springs, Ohio Pub. Sch. Dists., 1965-71; tech. illustrator, draftsperson U. Tex. Austin, Geotek, Inc., Denver, 1976-85; cartographer British Petroleum, San Francisco, 1985-87; draftsperson Earth Scis. Assocs., Palo Alto, Calif., 1988-92; intern, printmaking asst. Crown Point Press, San Francisco, 1991-92; freelance cartographer San Francisco, 1993—; educator pub. printmaking & papermaking workshops, San Francisco, 1995—; pub. printmaking demonstrations San Francisco Women Artists Gallery, 1995, 96; leader pub. nature/women's ceremony-ritual, San Francisco, 1991-93; artist in residence Villa Montalvo Ctr. for the Arts, Saratoga, Calif., 1996. Author, illustrator: (book) Envisioning An Unbroken Arc, 1992, Vol. 11, 1992. Contbg. artist Florence Crittenton Svcs., San Francisco, 1995, San Francisco Women Artists Gallery, 1995—. Mem. Calif. Soc. Printmakers (mem. exhbn. com. 1995), No. Calif. Women's Caucus For Art, Graphic Arts Workshop. Home and Studio: 681-B San Bruno Ave San Francisco CA 94107

NORMENT, LISA, writer, educator; b. Everett, Wash., Aug. 9, 1966; d. William L. and Eleanor (Graham) N.; m. Michail Alan Reid, May 27, 1995. BA in English, Syracuse U., 1989. Editl. asst. Avon Books, N.Y.C., 1990-93; tchr. St. Francis of Assisi Sch., Bklyn., 1993-94, St. Aloysius Sch., N.Y.C., 1995—. Author: Once Upon a Time in Junior High, 1994 (One of Best Teenage Books of 1996, N.Y. Pub. Libr. Young Author Librs. 1996). Mem. Soc. Children's Book Writers. Home: 1376 Midland Ave # 707 Bronxville NY 10708

NORMORE, LORRAINE FRANCES, information systems researcher; b. Regine, Sask., Can., Aug. 13, 1946; came to U.S., 1975; d. John Charles and Jean Dorothy (Werstiuk) Dombrowski; m. Calvin G. Normore, May 18, 1969 (div. May 1983); 1 child, Christina. BA in Psychology with honors, McGill U., Montreal, 1967; MLS, U. Toronto, 1975; PhD in Experimental Psychology, Ohio State U., 1986. Rschr. Chem. Abstracts Svc., Columbus, Ohio, 1983—. Troop leader Girl Scouts Am., Columbus, Ohio, 1988-96. Mem. Human Factors and Ergonomics Soc. (TG sec., treas. 1990—, pres. ctrl. Ohio chpt. 1986—, newsletter editor 1991—), Assn. for Computing Machinery Spl. Interest Group on Computer-Human Interaction.

NORRIS, ANDREA SPAULDING, art museum director; b. Apr. 2, 1945; d. Edwin Baker and Mary Gretchen (Brendle) Spaulding. BA, Wellesley Coll., 1967; MA, NYU, 1969, PhD, 1977. Intern dept. western European arts Met. Mus. Art, N.Y.C., 1970, 72; rsch. and editorial asst. Inst. Fine Arts NYU, 1971, lectr. Washington Sq. Coll., 1976-77; lectr. Queens Coll. CUNY, 1973-74; asst. to dir. Art Gallery Yale U., New Haven, 1977-80, lectr. art history, 1979-80; chief curator Archer M. Huntington Art Gallery, Austin, Tex., 1980-88; lectr. art history Dept. Art U. Tex., Austin, 1984-88; dir. Spencer Mus. Art U. Kans., Lawrence, 1988—. Co-author: (catalogue) Medals and Plaquettes from the Molinari Collection at Bowdoin College, 1976; author: (exhbn. catalogues) Jackson Pollock: New-Found Works, 1978; exhbn. The Sforza Court: Milan in the Renaissance 1450-1535, 1988-89. Mem. Renaissance Soc. Am., Coll. Art Assn., Assn. Art Mus. Dirs., Phi Beta Kappa. Office: Spencer Mus Art U Kans Lawrence KS 66045

NORRIS, CAROL BROOKS, librarian, educator; b. Porterdale, Ga., Dec. 22, 1943; d. James P. and Georgia E. (Queen) Brooks; m. Frederick W. Norris, Aug. 30, 1963; children: Lisa C., Mark F. Student, Milligan Coll., Tenn., 1961-63; BA, Phillips U., Enid, Okla., 1965; MLS, U. Md., 1982; postgrad., East Tenn. State U., 1978-80, 91, U. Tenn., 1988, 90. Caseworker Dept. Child Welfare, Enid, 1966-67; homebound tchr. New Haven (Conn.) Pub. Schs., 1967-70; English tchr. Putnam (Okla.) High Sch., 1965-66, U.S. Army, Boeblingen, Germany, 1975-77, Cen. Tex. State Coll., 1977; tchr. adult basic edn. Johnson City (Tenn.) Schs., 1977-79; systems analyst East Tenn. State U., Johnson City, 1980-82, libr., assoc. prof., 1982—, mem. univ. coun., 1989-91, mem. tchr. edn. adv. coun., 1989-92, mem. faculty senate, 1985-88, sec. senate, 1986-87, mem. women's steering com., writing com., rsch. devel. com., 1993—. Author: Library Hi Tech Bibliography, 1987, 90, Read More About It, 1989, (with others) Notable Women in the Life Sciences, 1996; editorial advisor Nat. Forum jour., 1981-86; contbr. articles to profl. jours. Mem. ALA, Southeastern Libr. Assn., Tenn. Libr. Assn., East Tenn. Online Users Group (pres. 1984-85, v.p. 1983-84, sec. 1982-83), Boone Tree Libr. Assn. (v.p. 1986-88), Delta Kappa Gamma, Phi Kappa Phi, Kappa Delta Pi. Democrat. Mem. Christian Ch. Office: East Tenn State Univ 70665 Johnson City TN 37614

NORRIS, DEBORAH OLIN, psychology educator, neurotoxicologist; b. Bethesda, Md., Mar. 24, 1957; d. Charles Hilden and Jacqueline (Smith) Olin; m. Jon William Norris, Sept. 25, 1982; children: Jessie Lind, Jacqueline Lauren, Jon Hilden. BA, Colo. Coll., 1979; MA, Am. U., 1984, PhD, 1988. Asst. prof. psychology Am. U., Washington, 1985—; psychopharmacologist VA Med. Ctr, Washington, 1991-94; neurotoxicologist EPA, Washington, 1994—.

NORRIS, ELIZABETH DOWNE, archivist; b. White Plains, N.Y., Apr. 25, 1914; d. Albro Farwell and Alice Elizabeth (Morse) Downe; B.A., Smith Coll., 1936; M.Div., Yale U., 1939; M.L.S., Columbia U., 1955; 1 son, Donald E. Norris. Asst. residence dir. New Haven YWCA, 1940-42; religious edn. librarian Union Theol. Sem., N.Y.C., 1953-57; librarian NCCJ, N.Y.C., 1957-63; head librarian Nat. Bd. YWCA of the U.S.A., N.Y.C., 1963—, dir. Nat. Bd. Archives Project, 1976—, YWCA historian, 1980—, project dir. traveling exhbn. Women First for 135 Years, 1993—. Recipient Henry Foote Lewis prize in religion, 1934. Mem. Spl. Libraries Assn., Soc. Am. Archivists. Mem. United Ch. Christ. Editor: Feminine Figures: Selected Facts about American Women and Girls, 1968-72; Subject Headings on Women, 1973; Recent Trends in Professionalism, 1973; The YWCA Advances Women's Rights, 1855-1989, 1989; Diary of a Volunteer, 1983; Women and Children First; a Century of YWCA Services to Children, 1984, The YWCA Secretary Searches for Professionalism 1889-1955, 1989; contbg. librarian Mental Health Book Rev. Index, 1961-72; editor, mem. adv. com. Books for Brotherhood, ann. 1957-76; co-editor Reunion: Newsletter for Retired Staff, 1994—; author: (series) Unscholarly Sketches, 1995-96; contbr. articles to jours. Home: 505 Laguardia Pl New York NY 10012-2001 Office: 726 Broadway New York NY 10003

NORRIS, GENIE M., senior government official; b. N.Y.C., July 15, 1951; d. Eugene and Peggy (Carter) Martell; m. Larry Specht, Apr. 22, 1982; children: Amanda Michele, Joshua Albert, Rachel Elizabeth. Adminstr. Senator Patrick Moynihan, N.Y.C., 1976; exec. asst. U.S. Senate, Washington, 1982-86; dep. field dir. Carter/Mondale Presdl. Campaign, Washington, 1979; dep. dir. Dem. Nat. Com., Washington, 1980-81; dir., sr. assoc. Francis Assocs., Ltd., Washington, Germany, 1981-82; exec. asst. Senator Patrick Moynihan, Washington, 1982-86; guest lectr. USIA, Washington, 1987-90; mgr. Amb. Residence, Bonn, Germany, 1987-90; sr. assoc. FMR Group, Washington, 1990; dep. exec. dir. Dem. Congl. Campaign Com., Washington, 1990-91, exec. dir., 1991-94; dep. asst. sec. for ops. Dept. of State, Washington, 1995—; com. rep. Dem. Nat. Com. South Africa, 1980, Dem. Congl. Campaign Com., Republic of China, 1992; Peace Corp. transition team leader Pres. Transition Team, Washington, 1992-93; South Africa elections obs. UN, 1994. With U.S. Army, 1975-78. Democrat. Roman Catholic. Home: 1630 Davidson Rd Mc Lean VA 22101-4306

NORRIS, JOAN CLAFETTE HAGOOD, elementary school educator; b. Pelzer, S.C., June 26, 1951; d. William Emerson and Sarah (Thompson) Hagood; divorced; 1 child, Javiere Sajorah. BA in History and Secondary Edn., Spelman Coll., 1973; MA in Teaching in Edn., Northwestern U., 1974; MA in Adminstrn. and Supervision, Furman U., 1984. Cert. elem. edn. tchr., elem. prin., social studies tchr., elem. supr., S.C.; notary pub., S.C. Clk. typist Fiber Industry, Greenville, S.C., 1970, Spelman Coll. Alumni Office, Atlanta, 1970-73; tchr. Chgo. Bd. Edn., 1973-74, Greenville County Pub. Schs., Greenville, S.C., 1974—, Hollis Acad., Greenville, S.C.; chair black history com. Armstrong Elem. Sch., Greenville, 1991, Am. edn. com., 1992; sch. acad. and student affairs com. St. Josephs H.S., 1995; steering com. N.W. area Greenville County Sch. Dist., 1994-95, chair elem. steering com., 1996, participant Curriculum Leadership I, 1996. Contbr. articles to profl. jour. Sec. Webette's Temple # 1312, Greenville, 1985, parliamentarian, 1986; active NAACP, Greenville, 1989-92. Alliance of Quality Edn. grantee, 1989-90; selected to Potential Adminstrs. Acad., Furman U., 1991; named Tchr. of the Yr., Armstrong Elem. Sch., 1981-82, 90-91. Mem. NEA, AAUW (Greenville br. exec. bd. cmty. rep. 1993-94, v.p. programs 1994-96, pres.-elect. 1996—, nominating com., gift honoree), S.C. Alliance Black Educators, Spelman Alumni Assn., Northwestern Alumni Assn., Phi Kappa Delta (sec. chpt. 1993-94), Phi Delta Kappa (chpt. alt. del. 1992-93, v.p. membership 1996—). Democrat. Baptist. Home: 219 Barrett Dr Mauldin SC 29662-2030 Office: Hollis Acad 14 Eight St Judson Greenville SC 29611

NORRIS, KAREN W., grants specialist; b. Washington, Mar. 5, 1950; d. Jerome J. and Lillian (Pittle) N.; children: Elysa, Mindy. BA, George Washington U., 1972; MBA, Hood Coll., 1994. Tchr. journalism, TV and English Montgomery County Pub. Schs., Rockville, Md., 1972-80; broadcast engr. CBS TV-WDVM-TV, Washington, 1980-83; pvt. practice comm. cons. Washington, 1983-88; mem. grants-dept. mgmt. staff Montgomery County Pub. Schs., Rockville, 1988-94; grants specialist Prince George's County Pub. Schs., Upper Marlboro, Md., 1994—; mem. cultural arts adv. com. Montgomery County Govt., Rockville, 1975; mem. performing arts adv. com. Prince George's County Pub. Schs., Upper Marlboro, 1994—. Bd. dirs. Journalism Edn. Assn., Balt., 1972-75. Recipient Excellence in H.S. Journalism award Montgomery County C. of C., Rockville, 1978; named Md. Journalism Tchr. of Yr., Md. Journalism Edn. Assn., Rockville, 1972; Coll. scholar NEA, Washington, 1968. Mem. Assn. Supervisory and Adminstrv. Pers. Office: Prince Georges County Pub Schs Grants Devel 14201 School Ln Upper Marlboro MD 20772

NORRIS, KATHARINE EILEEN, communications professional, educator; b. Norwalk, Calif., Feb. 2, 1960; d. Curtis Bird and Eileen Patricia N. BA, Salem State Coll., 1982; MA, Brown U., 1987. Feature writer The Enterprise newspaper, Brockton, Mass., 1984, 87-88; editor Assoc. Newspapers, Stoughton, Mass., 1987-88, The Mansfield (Mass.) News, 1988-89; coll. instr. Bristol C.C., Fall River, Mass., 1989—, Mt. Ida Coll., Newton Centre, Mass., 1990-95, Bridgewater (Mass.) State Coll., 1991—; radio talk host WPEP, Taunton, Mass., 1991—; dir. pub. rels. Zeiterion Theatre, New Bedford, Mass., 1995—. Asst. editor: The Guide for Students and Parents to 101 of the Best Values in America's Colleges and Universities, 1993. Mem. NEA, Modern Lang. Assn., Nathaniel Hawthorne Soc. Home: 123 Crane Ave S # 2 Taunton MA 02780-1202

NORRIS, KATHERINE CECELIA, mechanical engineer; b. Syracuse, N.Y., Nov. 7, 1943; d. James Dalton and Bertha Genevieve (Bourque) N.; children: Mary Rose Courtney. BSME, Duke U., 1966; MSME, Mass. Inst. Tech., 1967. Registered profl. engr. Vt., N.Y. Jr. engr. through staff engr. IBM Corp., Hopewell Junction, N.Y., 1967-76; staff engr. IBM Corp., Essex Junction, Vt., 1976-78, project engr., 1978-80, devel. engr., 1980-88, adv. engr., 1988—; project mgr., Sematech, Austin, Tex., 1992-93. Contbr. articles to profl. jours. Awards chair Vt. Engr. Week Com., 1994, 95; vol. Milton Family Com. Ctr., Milton, Vt., 1992; production staff vol. Cmty. Newspaper, Milton, 1990-94; canvasser United Way, 1985-91. Recipient fellowship Nat. Sci. Found., 1966-67. Mem. ASME, NSPE, Soc. Women Engrs. (sr. life; bd. dirs. 1990-92, chair sch. com. 1993-96), Phi Beta Kappa, Tau Beta Pi. Home: 406 Route 7 North Milton VT 05468 Office: IBM Corp Microelectronics Div 1000 River St Essex Junction VT 05452

NORRIS, LOIS ANN, elementary school educator; b. Detroit, May 13, 1937; d. Joseph Peter and Marguerite Iola (Gourley) Giroux; m. Max Norris, Feb. 9, 1962 (div. 1981); children: John Henry, Jeanne Marie, Joseph Peter. BS in Social Sci., Ea. Mich. U., 1960, MA, 1960; cert. adminstr., Calif. State U., Bakersfield, 1983. Kindergarten tchr. Norwalk-LaMirada Unified Sch. Dist., 1960-62; tchr. various grades Rialto Unified Sch. Dist., 1962-66; kindergarten tchr. Inyokern (Calif.) Sch., 1969-82; 1st grade tchr. Vieweg Basic Sch, 1982-92, kindergarten tchr., 1992-96; retired, 1996; head tchr. Sierra Sands Elem. Summer Sch.; adminstrv. intern Sierra Sands Adult Sch., master tchr., head tchr., counselor. Ofcl. scorekeeper, team mother, snack bar coord. China Lake Little League; team mother, statistician Indian Wells Valley Youth Football; bd. mem. PTA; pres. Sch. Site Coun.; treas. Inyokern Parents Club; run coord. City of Hope; timekeeper, coord. Jr. Olympics; mem. planning com. Sunshine Festival; active Burros Booster Club. Recipient Hon. Svc. award PTA, 1994. Mem. Desert Area Tchrs. Assn., Assn. Calif. Sch. Adminstrs., Inyokern C. of C. (sec.), Am. Motorcycle Assn., NRA, Bakersfield Coll. Diamond Club. Republican. LDS Ch. Home: PO Box 163 201 N Brown Rd Inyokern CA 93527 Office: Sierra Sands Unified Sch 113 W Felspar Ave Ridgecrest CA 93555-3520

NORRIS, PAMELA, school psychologist; b. Springfield, Mass., May 11, 1946; d. William Henry Jr. and Loretta Agnes (Houck) N. BA in English, Keuka Coll., 1968; MA in Philosophy, U. Mass., 1969; MEd in Guidance and Counseling, Westfield (Mass.) State Coll., 1973; MA in Clin. Psychology with distinction, Am. Internat. Coll., 1991. Nat. cert. sch. psychologist; cert. sch. psychologist, Mass., Conn.; lic. ednl. psychologist, Mass.; lic. real estate broker, Mass.; cert. guidance counselor, Mass.; cert. English tchr., Mass., Conn. English tchr. Agawa Pub. Schs., Feeding Hills, Mass., 1970-87, sch. psychologist, 1987—. Telephone operator Springfield (Mass.) Hotline, 1970-72; telephone operator, counselor Falmouth (Mass.) Emergency and Referral Svc., 1971, SPAN Ctr., Feeding Hills, Mass, 1972-73, CHEC-Line, West Springfield, Mass., 1974-75; occupational therapist Monson (Mass.) State Hosp., 1976-77. Mem. APA (assoc.), Nat. Assn. of Sch. Psychologists, New Eng. Psychol. Assn., Mass. Sch. Psychology Assn., Western Mass. Sch. Psychology Assn., Sigma Tau Delta, Pi Delta Epsilon. Office: Agawa Pub Schs 1305 Springfield St Feeding Hills MA 01030-2180

NORRIS, REBECCA, design firm executive; b. Balt., Sept. 29, 1955; d. Ray Norman and Peggy Jean (Weeks) N. BA, Bob Jones U., 1977. Designer World Wide Advt.-J. Walter Thompson, Balt., 1978; designer, art dir. M.J. Seidel, Balt., 1979-81; designer Johns Hopkins U., Balt., 1981-86; art dir. Norris, Reynolds & Denham, Balt., 1986—. Vol. Transplant Resource Ctr., Balt., 1990-91, Johns Hopkins Women's Bd., Balt., 1992. Recipient design awards Print mag., 1983, N.Y. Soc. Scribes, 1984, Univ. and Coll. Designers Assn., 1985, Graphis, 1992, others. Mem. Printing Industries Md., Md. Hist. Soc., The Daguerreian Soc., Nat. Trust for Historic Preservation. Office: Norris Reynolds & Denham 112 N Beechwood Ave Baltimore MD 21228-4927

NORRIS, SUSAN ELIZABETH, social worker; b. Lubbock, Tex., Oct. 8, 1952; d. William Oxford and Katherine Burton (Sydnor) N. BA, U. Tex., Arlington, 1974; MSW, U. Conn., 1987. Child protective svcs. social worker Tex. Dept. Human resources, Ft. Worth, 1978-82; temp. word processor various cos., 1983-85; rsch. cons. Hartford, Conn., 1986-89; dir. child care svcs. United Way Conn., Hartford, 1987-92, dir. program svcs., 1992-93; faculty/assoc. dir. child and family studies, pediatrics U. Conn. Health Ctr., Farmington, 1993-94; dir. Americorps CARE, Nat. Assn. of Childcare Resource & Referral Agy's., 1994-96; program mgr. Work/Family Directions, Boston, 1996—. Bd. dirs., sec. Hartford Interval House, 1989-93; pres. bd. dirs. Hartford Area Child Collaborative, 1992-94. Democrat. Office: Work/Family Directions 930 Commonwealth Ave Boston MA 02215-1212

NORSKOG, EUGENIA FOLK, elementary education educator; b. Staunton, Va., Mar. 23, 1937; d. Ernest and Edna Virginia (Jordan) Folk; m. Russell Carl Norskog, Nov. 25, 1967; children: Cynthia, Carl, Roberta, Eric. BA, King Coll., 1958; MEd, George Mason U., 1977. Cert. tchr., Va. Tchr. elem. Bristol (Va.) Pub. Schs., 1958-61, 62-65, Staunton (Va.) Pub. Schs., 1961-62, Fairfax (Va.) County Pub. Schs., 1965-68; with Project 100,000, USAFI, 1966-68; project 100,000 USAF, Fort Ord, Calif., 1969; tchr. elem. Monterey (Calif.) Peninsula Sch. Div., 1970-71, Prince William County Schs., Manassas, Va., 1972—; Va. rehab. sch. Prince William County, Richmond, Va., 1979-82. V.p. Fauquier Gymnastics, Warrenton, Va., 1982-83, pres., 1983-85; coach, bd. dirs., referee Warrenton Soccer Assn., 1980-88; soccer referee Piedmont Referee Assn., Manassas, 1990-95. Mem. NEA, Va. Edn. Assn. Prince William Edn. Assn. (bd. dirs. 1974-77). Home: 7160 Airlie Rd RR 8 Box 398 Warrenton VA 22186-9448

NORSTRAND, IRIS FLETCHER, psychiatrist, neurologist, educator; b. Bklyn., Nov. 21, 1915; d. Matthew Emerson and Violet Marie (Anderson) Fletcher; m. Severin Anton Norstrand, May 20, 1941; children: Virginia Helene Norstrand Villano, Thomas Fletcher, Lucille Joyce. BA, Bklyn. Coll., 1937, MA, 1965, PhD, 1972; MD, L.I. Coll. Medicine, 1941. Diplomate Am. Bd. Psychiatry and Neurology with supplementary cert. in geriatric psychiatry. Med. intern Montefiore Hosp., Bronx, N.Y., 1941-42; asst. resident in neurology N.Y. Neurol. Inst.-Columbia-Presbyn. Med. Ctr., N.Y.C., 1944-45; pvt. practice Bklyn., 1947-52; resident in psychiatry Bklyn. VA Med. Ctr., 1952-54, resident in neurology, 1954-55, staff neurologist, 1955-81, asst. chief neurol. svc., 1981-91, staff psychiatrist, 1991-95; neurol. cons. Indsl. Home for Blind, Bklyn., 1948-51; clin. prof. neurology SUNY Health Sci. Ctr., Bklyn., 1981—; attending neurologist Kings County Hosp., Bklyn., State U. Hosp., Bklyn. Contbr. articles to med. jours. Recipient spl. plaque Mil. Order Purple Heart, 1986, Spl. Achievement award PhD Alumni Assn. of CUNY, 1993, Lifetime Achievement award Bklyn. Coll., 1995, and others. Fellow Am. Psychiat. Assn., Am. Acad. Neurology, Internat. Soc. Neurochemistry, Am. Assn. U. Profs. Neurology, Am. Med. EEG Soc. (pres. 1987-88), Nat. Assn. VA Physicians (pres. 1989-91, James O'Connor award 1987), N.Y. Acad. Scis., Sigma Xi. Democrat. Presbyterian. Home: 7624 10th Ave Brooklyn NY 11228

NORSWORTHY, ELIZABETH KRASSOVSKY, lawyer; b. N.Y.C., Feb. 26, 1943; d. Leonid Alexander and Wilma (Hudgens) Krassovsky; m. John Randolph Norsworthy, June 24, 1961 (div. 1962), m. Nov. 26, 1977 (div. 1984); 1 child, Alexander. AB magna cum laude, Hunter Coll., CUNY, 1965; MA, U. N.C., 1966; JD, Stanford U., 1977. Bar: D.C. 1978, Mass. 1992, U.S. Ct. Appeals (D.C. cir.) 1979. Atty. applications, disclosure rev. and investment adviser regulation, divsn. investment mgmt. SEC, Washington, 1978-79, 80-82, atty. operating brs. and disclosure policy divsn. corp. fin., 1979-80, chief, spl. counsel office of regulatory policy divsn. investment mgmt., 1983-86; assoc. Kirkpatrick & Lockhart, Washington, 1986-90; ptnr. Sullivan & Worcester, Boston, 1990-92; pvt. practice Norfolk, Mass., 1992-95, Concord, Vt., 1996—; pub. arbitrator, chairperson NASD; arbitrator Am. Arbitration Assn.; adj. faculty Roger Williams Sch. Law U. R.I., 1996—. Trustee St. Andrew's Endowment Com., Arlington, Va., 1989—, Boston Region SEC Alumni Assn., 1992—; clk. of the vestry St. Paul's, Millis, Mass., 1993-95; mem.-at-large exec. Millis Cmty. Chorale, 1994-95. Mem. ABA (securities com. 1986—, investment adviser investment co. subcom. 1990—), N.Y. '40 Acts. Com., Union Club of Boston, Trustees of the Reservations, Phi Beta Kappa, Phi Alpha Theta. Democrat. Episcopalian. Office: Winterbrook Farm Box 91 Woodland Rd Concord VT 05824

NORTH, ANITA, secondary education educator; b. Chgo., Apr. 21, 1963; d. William Denson and Carol (Linden) N. BA, Ind. U., 1985; MS in Edn., Northwestern U., 1987. Cert. tchr., Ill. High sch. social studies and English tchr. Lake Park High Sch., Roselle, Ill., 1987-89; high sch. social studies tchr. West Leyden High Sch., Northlake, Ill., 1989—; exch. program coord. West Leyden High Sch., 1989—, head coach boys' tennis team, 1989—, asst. coach girls' tennis team, 1994—, asst. speech coach, 1992-93. Humanities fellow Nat. Coun. Humanities, 1995; recipient Fern Fine Tchg. award West Leyden H.S., 1992. Mem. AAUW, Nat. Coun. for Social Studies, Ill. Coun. for Social Studies, Orgn. Am. Historians, Ill. Tennis Coaches Assn., Phi Delta Kappa. Christian.

NORTH, CAROL SUE, psychiatrist, educator; b. Keokuk, Iowa, May 6, 1954; d. Ray Stemen and Doris Ethelyn (Wood) N. BS in Gen. Sci., U. Iowa, 1976; MD, Wash. U., St. Louis, 1983, M in Psychiatric Epidemiology, 1993. Resident in psychiatry Barnes Hosp., Washington U. Med. Sch., St. Louis, 1983-87; rsch. fellow dept psychiatry Washington U., St. Louis, 1987-90, instr. dept. psychiatry, 1987-89, asst. prof. dept. psychiatry, 1989—; staff psychiatrist Grace Hill Neighborhood Health Ctr., St. Louis, 1987—, Midwest Psychiatry, 1993-95, Adapt of Am., 1995—. Author: Welcome, Silence, 1987, Multiple Personalities, Multiple Disorders: Psychiatric Classification and Media Influence, 1993; contbr. articles to profl. jours. Bd. Dirs. St. Louis Met. Alliance for the Mentally Ill, 1992—; trustee Rosati Stblzn. Ctr. for Homeless and Mentally Ill, 1992-94. Nat. Inst. Alcoholism and Alcohol Abuse grantee, 1988-93, Nat. Hazards Rsch. Applications Info. Ctr. grantee, 1987-88, NIMH grantee, 1991-95. Mem. Am. Psychiat. Assn., Life History Rsch. Soc., Ea. Mo. Psychiat. Soc. (exec. coun. and pres. 1996—), Am. Psychopathol. Assn., Am. Acad. Clin. Psychiatrists, Nat. Alliance for Mentally Ill, Am. Assn. Cmty. Psychiatrists, St. Louis Track Club. Presbyterian. Office: Washington U Sch Medicine Dept Psychiatry 4940 Childrens Pl Saint Louis MO 63110-1002

NORTH, DORIS GRIFFIN, physician, educator; b. Washington, Nov. 30, 1916; d. Edward Lawrence and Ruth Gladys (Spray) Griffin; m. Victor North, Nov. 2, 1940 (dec. 1984); children: James, Daniel, Frederick. BA, U. Kans., 1938, MT, 1939; MD, Kans. U., 1947. Med. tech. Ralph G. Ball, M.D., Manhattan, Kans., 1939-40, St. Francis Hosp., Pitts., 1940-41, John Minor, M.D., Washington, 1941-43; intern Wesly Hosp., Wichita, Kans., 1947-48; resident in pediat. and internal medicine Sedgwick Hosp., Wichita, 1948-49; pvt. practice family physician Wichita, Kans., 1951-96; clin. asst. prof. medicine Kans. State U. Sch. Medicine, Wichita, 1974-96. Mem. AMA, Am. Acad. Family Practice, Kans. Med. Soc., Med. Soc. Sedgwick County, Phi Beta Kappa, Alpha Omega Alpha. Home: 1000 S Woodlawn St Apt 408 Wichita KS 67218-3641 Office: 1148 S Hillside St Wichita KS 67211-4005

NORTH, KATHLEEN JOYCE, economist, state official; b. Omaha, July 31, 1965; d. John Edward and Joyce Marie (Zimmerman) N. BA in Econs., U. Tex., 1987; MS in Econs., Tex. A&M U., 1992. Utility specialist Office Atty. Gen. Tex., Austin, 1990-91; rate analyst Pub. Utility Commn. Tex., Austin, 1988-90, econ. analyst, 1992-94, regulatory specialist Consumer Affairs Office, 1994-95, mgr. Consumer Affairs Office, 1995—. Office: Pub Utility Commn Tex 7800 Shoal Creek Blvd Austin TX 78757

NORTH, KATHRYN E. KEESEY (MRS. EUGENE C. NORTH), retired educator; b. Columbia, Pa., Jan. 25, 1916; d. Isaac and Elizabeth (French) Keesey; B.S., Ithaca Coll., 1938; M.A., N.Y. U., 1950; m. Eugene C. North, Aug. 18, 1938. Dir. music Cairo (N.Y.) Central Sch. Dist., 1938; music edn. cons. Argyle (N.Y.) Central Sch. Dist., 1939; dir. gen. music curriculum Hartford (N.Y.) Central Sch. Dist., 1939; mem. staff Del. Dept. Pub. Instrn., Dover, 1943; dir. music edn. Herricks (N.Y.) Pub. Schs., 1944-71; ret., 1971. Vis. lectr. Ithaca Coll., summers 1959, 60, 62-65, Fairleigh-Dickinson U., Rutherford, N.J., summer 1966, Albertus Magnus Coll., New Haven, summer 1968; instr. Adelphi Coll., 1954-55, Sch.. Edn., N.Y.U., 1964-65. Mem. Music Educators Nat. Conf., N.E.A., N.Y. State Sch. Music Assn., N.Y. State Tchrs. Assn., Nassau Music Educators Assn. (exec. bd. 1947-58), N.Y. State Council Adminstrs. Music Edn. (chpt. v.p. 1967-68), Herricks Tchrs. Assn. (pres. 1948), Sigma Alpha Iota. Mem. Order Eastern Star. Home: 1645 Calle Camille La Jolla CA 92037-7107

NORTHCUTT, BONNIE, sports organization administrator; b. Leakey, Tex., Dec. 2, 1942; d. Jesse Lent and Ada (Bonner) Wells; m. Norvell Waukeen Northcutt, Aug. 25, 1962; children: Elizabeth Leigh, Linda Nicole. BS, U. Tex., 1976; postgrad., S.W. Tex. U., 1977-78. Supr. record room Univ. Hosp. Tex. A&M U., College Station, 1963-67; mgr. Twin Canyon Translator Sys., Campwood, Tex., 1970; adminstrv. clk. Univ. Interscholastic League, Austin, Tex., 1976-78, asst. to athletic dir., 1978-79, asst. athletic dir., 1979-83, asst. to dir., 1983-94, dir. policy, 1995—; mem.

Olympic Game Preparation Com., 1976-80; chmn. rules com. Nat. Fedn. Volleyball, 1981-88; bd. dirs. U.S. Volleyball Assn., 1988-96; founding mem. Nat. Fed. Trust Bd., 1993—. Commr. Western Hills Basketball League, Westlake, Tex., 1981-82; chmn. founding com. chem. awareness program Shepherd of Hills Luth. Ch., Austin, 1985—. Recipient Outstanding Svc. award Nat. Fedn. Volleyball, 1983, Disting. Svc. award S.W. Ofcls. Assn., 1983, Meritorious Svc. award U.S. Volleyball Assn., 1993. Mem. LWV, Smithsonian Assocs., Westlake Ind. Sch. Dist. Booster Club (life). Democrat. Office: Univ Interscholastic League 3001 Lake Austin Blvd Austin TX 78703

NORTHCUTT, KATHRYN ANN, elementary school and gifted-talented educator, reading recovery educator; b. Ft. Worth, Nov. 11, 1953; d. Lawrence William and Eva Jo (McCormick) Lloyd; m. Frank E. Northcutt, Aug. 28, 1980; 1 child, Matthew Adam. Student, North Tex. State U., 1972-75; BS in Edn., U. Tex., Tyler, 1980, MEd, 1986. Cert. elem. educator, music educator, supr. K-8; cert. curriculum and instrn. supr. Tchr. grade 1 Longview (Tex.) Ind. Sch. Dist., Longview, 1980-87, tchr. gifted and talented reading, 1990-92, tchr. 3d grade, 1992-93, tchr. 4th grade, 1993-95, reading recovery tchr., 1995—; tchr. 1st grade Pine Tree Ind. Sch. Dist., 1987-90. Mem. Gregg County Hist. Soc., Longview Opera Guild (pres.). Mem. ASCD, Nat. Coun. Tchrs. Math., Assn. Tex. Profl. Educators, Reading Recovery Coun. N.Am., Jr. League of Longview (sustaining), Phi Beta Kappa, Sigma Alpha Iota. Home: 5 Latonia Ct Longview TX 75605-1537 Office: Longview Ind Sch Dist PO Box 3268 Longview TX 75606

NORTHCUTT, MARIE ROSE, educator; b. White Plains, N.Y., Feb. 2, 1950; d. Carlo and Marcelline Marie Rose (Benoit) DeMarco; m. Kenneth Walter Northcutt, Mar. 17, 1984; children: James Lee, Thomas Joseph. BA, Lynchburg Coll., 1972; MA, Columbia U., 1977. Cert. elem. and secondary tchr., N.Y. Tchr. Petersburg (Va.) Pub. Schs., 1972-74; asst. relocation mgr. Ticor Co., White Plains, 1974-75; 3d grade tchr. Resurrection Sch., Rye, N.Y., 1975-76; 6th grade tchr. Harrison (N.Y.) Cen. Sch. Dist., 1976-78, learning disabilities specialist, 1981—; tchr. of emotionally handicapped N.Y.C. Schs., 1978-80; learning evaluator Empire State Coll., White Plains, 1981-82; ind. evaluation cons., White Plains, 1981—; chair Mid. States Subcom. Active Harrison High Sch. PTA. Mem. Assn. for Children with Learning Disabilities, Westchester County Assn. for Children with Learning Disabilities, Spl. Edn. Parents Tchrs. Assn., Orton Soc., Phi Delta Kappa. Roman Catholic. Home: 81 Griffin Pl White Plains NY 10603-3609 Office: Harrison Cen Sch Dist Union Ave Harrison NY 10528-2108

NORTHROP, MARY RUTH, mental retardation nurse; b. Washington, June 5, 1919; d. William Arthur and Emma Aurelia (Kaech) N. Diploma in nursing, Georgetown U., 1951, BS in Nursing cum laude, 1952; MS, U. Md., 1958; MA in Anthropology, U. Va., 1970. RN, Va. Asst. dir. nursing U. Md. Hosp., Balt., 1958-60; dir. nursing Georgetown U. Hosp., Washington, 1961; nursing rep. ARC, Pa., 1962; regional dir. nursing ARC, New Eng. and N.Y., 1963-68; pediatric nursing cons. Va. Dept. Health, Richmond, 1971-84; clin. nursing specialist Va. Dept. Mental Health and Mental Retardation, Petersburg, Va., 1988—; adj. asst./assoc. prof. U. Md. Sch. Nursing, Balt., 1958-60. Nursing fellow rsch. HEW, U. Md., Bethesda, 1957-68, nursing fellow anthropology U. Va., 1968-70; recipient Recognition Georgetown U. Alumni Assn., Richmond, 1987. Mem. ANA, Va. Nursing Assn., DAR (chpt. regent 1983-86, dist. treas. 1992-95), Mensa, Sigma Theta Tau. Republican. Roman Catholic. Home: 300 W Franklin St # 401E Richmond VA 23220-4904 Office: Southside Va Tng Ctr PO Box 4110 Petersburg VA 23803-0110

NORTHWAY, WANDA I., realty company executive; b. Columbia, Mo., July 11, 1942; d. Herman W. and Goldie M. (Wood) Proctor; m. Donald H. Northway, June 12, 1965; 1 child, Michelle D. Student U. Mo., 1966. Lic. real estate agt., Mo.; grad. Realtors Inst. Realtor, assoc. Gentry Real Estate Co., Columbia, 1969-80; realtor Griffin Real Estate Co., 1980-81; pres., realtor, ptnr. House of Brokers Realty, Inc., Columbia, 1981—; pres., organizer Realtor-Assoc. Sales Club, Columbia, 1975; pres. Columbia Bd. Realtors, 1982. Contbr. articles to realty mags. Sunday sch. tchr., girls' aux. leader Baptist Ch.; vol. ARS, local hosp; campaign worker for Columbia legislators; mem. allocation com. United Way; active vol. Am. Cancer Soc. and Heart Assn. Named Realtor Assoc. of Yr., Columbia Bd. Realtors, 1974, Realtor of Yr., 1980. Mem. Mo. Assn. Realtors (state dir. 1974-77, Realtor Assoc. of Yr. award 1977), Realtors Nat. Mktg. Inst. (cert. residential specialist 1978), Nat. Assn. Realtors, (nat. dir. 1977), Epsilon Sigma Alpha (state corr. sec., local pres.). Republican. Baptist. Clubs: Million Dollar (life); Federation of Women's (pres. Mo. 1980). Office: House of Brokers Realty Inc 1515 Chapel Hill Rd Columbia MO 65203-5457

NORTON, ANDRE ALICE, author; b. Cleve., Sept. 17, 1912; d. Adalbert and Bertha Stemm N. Librarian Cleve. Public Library, until 1951. Author: 125 books including The Sword is Drawn (Dutch Gov. award 1946) 1944, Sword in Sheath (Ohioana Juevenile award Honor Book 1950) 1949, Starhunter (Hugo award nomination World Sci. Fiction Convention 1962) 1961, Witch World (Hugo award nomination World Sci Fiction Convention 1964) 1963, Night of Masks (Boy's Club of Am. Certificate of Merit 1965) 1964; series include Swords Trilogy, Star Ka'at Sci. Fiction Series, Witch World Fantasy Series. Recipient Invisible Little Man award Westercon XVI, 1963, Phoenix award 1976, Gandalf Master Fantasy award World Sci. Fiction Convention, 1977, Andre Norton award Women Writers of Sci. Fiction, 1978, Balrog Fantasy award 1979, Ohioana award, 1980, Fritz Leiber award, 1983, E.E. Smith award, 1983, Nebula Grand Master award Sci. Fiction Writers of Am., 1984, Jules Verne award, 1984, Second Stage Lensman award, 1987; named to Ohio Hall of Fame, 1981. Mem. Sci. Fiction Writers Am.

NORTON, ELEANOR HOLMES, congresswoman, lawyer, educator; b. Washington, June 13, 1937; d. Coleman and Vela (Lynch) Holmes; m. Edward W. Norton (div.); children: Katherine Felicia, John Holmes. BA, Antioch Coll., 1960; MA in Am. Studies, Yale U., 1963, LLB, 1964. Bar: Pa., 1965, U.S. Supreme Ct., 1968. Law clk. to Judge A. Leon Higgonbotham Fed. Dist. Ct., 1964-65; asst. legal dir. ACLU, 1965-70; exec. asst. to mayor City of N.Y., 1971-74; chmn. N.Y.C. Commn. on Human Rights, 1970-77, EEOC, Washington, 1977-81; sr. fellow Urban Inst., Washington, 1981-82; prof. law Georgetown U., Washington, 1982—; mem. 100th-104th Congresses from D.C. dist., 1990—; lead Dem. mem. D.C. subcom., water resources and environ. subcom., pub. bldgs. and econ. devel. subcom. Office: 1424 Longworth HOB Washington DC 20515 also: Georgetown U Law Ctr 600 New Jersey Ave NW Washington DC 20001-2075

NORTON, ELIZABETH WYCHGEL, lawyer; b. Cleve., Mar. 25, 1933; d. James Nicolas and Ruth Elizabeth (Cannell) Wychgel; m. Henry Wacks Norton Jr., July 16, 1954 (div. 1971); children: James, Henry, Peter, Fred; m. James Cory Ferguson, Dec. 14, 1985 (div. Apr. 1988). BA in Math., Wellesley Coll., 1954; JD cum laude, U. Minn., 1974. Bar: Minn. 1974. Summer intern Minn. Atty. Gen.'s Office, St. Paul, 1972; with U.S. Dept. Treasury, St. Paul, 1973; assoc. Gray, Plant, Mooty, Mooty & Bennett, P.A., Mpls., 1974-79, prin., 1980-94, of counsel, 1995-96; mem. Minn. Lawyers Bd. Profl. Responsibility, 1984-89; mem. U. Minn. Law Sch. Bd. Visitors, 1987-92. trustee YWCA, Mpls., 1979-84, 89-91, co-chmn. deferred giving com., 1980-81, chmn. by-laws com., bd. dirs., 1976-77, lectr.; treas. Minn. Women's Campaign Fund, 1985, guarantor, 1982-83; budget and fin. com. bd. dirs., 1984-87; trustee Ripley Meml. Found., 1980-84; treas. Jones-Harrison Home, 1967, bd. dirs., 1962-69, 2d v.p., chmn. fin., 1968-69; mem. Sen. David Durenberger's Women's Network, 1983-88. Durant scholar. Fellow Am. Bar Found.; mem. ABA (mediation task force family law sect. 1983-84), Minn. Bar Assn. (human rights com. family law sect., task force uniform marital property act 1984-85), Minn. Bar Found. (dir. 1991-94), Hennepin County Bar Assn. (pres. 1987-88, chmn. task force on pub. edn. 1984, chmn., mem. exec. com. family law sect. 1979-94), Minn. Inst. Legal Edn., Minn. Women's Lawyers (exec. com.), U. Minn. Law Sch. Alumni Assn. (dir. 1975-81, exec. com. 1981-83), Wellesley Club, Phi Beta Kappa. Home: 4980 Dockside Dr Apt 204 Fort Myers FL 33919-4657 Office: Gray Plant Mooty Mooty & Bennett 33 S 6th St Ste 3400 Minneapolis MN 55402-3705

NORTON, GALE A., state attorney general; b. Wichita, Mar. 11, 1954; d. Dale Bentsen and Anna Jacqueline (Lansdowne) N.; m. John Goethe Hughes, Mar. 26, 1990. BA, U. Denver, 1975, JD, 1978. Bar: Colo. 1978, U.S. Supreme Ct. 1981. Jud. clk. Colo. Ct. of Appeals, Denver, 1978-79; sr. atty. Mountain States Legal Found., Denver, 1979-83; nat. fellow Hoover Instn. Stanford (Calif.) U., 1983-84; asst. to dep. sec. U.S. Dept. of Agr., Washington, 1984-85; assoc. solicitor U.S. Dept. of Interior, Washington, 1985-87; pvt. practice law Denver, 1987-90; atty. gen. State of Colo., Denver, 1991—; Murdock fellow Polit. Economy Rsch. Ctr., Bozeman, Mont., 1984; sr. fellow Ind. Inst., Golden, Colo., 1988-90; policy analyst Pres. Coun. on Environ. Quality, Washington, 1985-88; lectr. U. Denver Law Sch., 1989; transp. law program dir. U. Denver, 1978-79. Contbr. chpts. to books, articles to profl. jours. Participant Rep. Leadership Program, Colo., 1988, Colo. Leadership Forum, 1989; past chair Nat. Assn. Attys. Gen. Environ. Com.; co-chair Nat. Policy Forum Environ. Coun.; candidate for 1996 election to U.S. Senate, 1995—. Named Young Career Woman Bus. and Profl. Wome, 1981, Young Lawyer of Yr., 1991. Mem. Federalist Soc., Colo. Women's Forum, Order of St. Ives. Republican. Methodist. Office: Colo Dept of Law 1525 Sherman St Fl 5 Denver CO 80203-1714

NORTON, JOAN JENNINGS, English language educator; b. Starke, Fla., Oct. 21, 1931; d. Thomas Joseph and Marie Louise (Wade) Jennings; m. James T. Norton (div. 1972); 1 child, Jeanne Marie. BS in edn., U. Ala., 1953; MEd, U. Fla., 1963. Cert. Tchr., Fla. Tchr. soc. studies Reinhold Jr. High, Green Cove Springs, Fla., 1958-61, tchr. soc. studies, English, 1961-67; tchr. English tchr., dept head Clay Jr., Sr. High, Greencove Springs, 1967-71, Clay H.S., Green Cove Springs, 1971-83; ret., 1993; sec. Clay County Tchrs. Assoc.,1954, mem. nom. com. FEA, Clay County, 1968, nom. com. Fla. P-R-I-D-E Writing Awards, 1979-80. Mem. Clay County Dem. Com., 1958-59, Sunday Sch. & Bible Sch. Tchr. 1st Presbyterian Green Cove Springs, 1940, 60. Recipient Clay's County Outstanding Young Tchr. award C. of C., Green Cove Springs, 1958. Mem. Clay COunty Retired Tchrs. Assoc., Clay County Historical Soc. Democratic. Presbyterian. Home: PO Box 372 Green Cove Springs FL 32043

NORTON, KAREN ANN, accountant; b. Paynesville, Minn., Nov. 1, 1950; d. Dale Francis and Ruby Grace (Gehlhar) N. BA, U. Minn., 1972; postgrad. U. Md., 1978; cert. acctg. U.S. Dept. Agr. Grad. Sch., 1978; MBA, Calif. State Poly. U.-Pomona, 1989. CPA, Md. Securities transactions analyst Bur. of Pub. Debt., Washington, 1972-79, internal auditor, 1979-81; internal auditor IRS, Washington, 1981; sr. acct. World Vision Internat., Monrovia, Calif., 1981-83, acctg. supr., 1983-87; sr. systems liaison coord., Home Savs. Am., 1987—; cons. (vol.) info. systems John M. Perkins Found., Pasadena, Calif., 1985-86. Author (poetry): Ode to Joyce, 1985 (Golden Poet award 1985). Second v.p. chpt. Nat. Treasury Employees Union, Washington, 1978, editor chpt. newsletter; mem. M-2 Prisoners Sponsorship Program, Chino, Calif., 1984-86. Recipient Spl. Achievement award Dept. Treasury, 1976, Superior Performance award, 1977-78; Charles and Ellora Alliss scholar, 1968. Mem. Angel Flight, Flying Samaritans. Avocations: flying, chess, racquetball, whitewater rafting.

NORTON, VIRGINIA SKEEN (MRS. JOHN H. NORTON, JR.), civic worker; b. Atlanta, June 1, 1907; d. Lola Percy and Rebecca (Baldwin) Skeen; A.B., Agnes Scott Coll., 1928; student Columbia U., 1934-35; m. John Hughes Norton, Jr., Dec. 16, 1938; children—Virginia Skeen Norton Kraft, John Hughes III. With personnel dept. Retail Credit Co., Atlanta, 1929-31, sec. to v.p., gen. mgr. Davison-Paxon, Co., Atlanta, 1931-34; with Aluminium Ltd., N.Y.C., 1935-41, sec. to pres., 1937-41; sec. to pres. Colonial Williamsburg, Inc., N.Y.C., 1943-44. Bd. dirs. North Shore Assos. Chgo. Commons, 1951-54, Infant Welfare Soc. Chgo., 1953-54, Catherine Morrill Day Nursery, Portland, Maine, 1956-59. Mem. Loch Haven Arts Soc., Winter Park Meml. Hosp. Aux., Morse Art Gallery Assocs. (dir. 1982-84), Nat. Soc. Colonial Dames Am. Episcopalian. Address: 1620 Mayflower Ct Apt A-606 Winter Park FL 32792-2500

NORVILLE, DEBORAH, news correspondent; b. Aug. 8, 1958; m. Karl Wellner; 2 children: Karl Nikolai, Kyle Maximilian. BJ, U. Ga., 1979. Reporter Sta. WAGA-TV, Atlanta, 1978-79, anchor, reporter, 1979-81; anchor, reporter Sta. WMAQ-TV, Chgo., 1982-86; anchor NBC News, N.Y.C., 1987-89; news anchor Today Show, NBC, N.Y.C., 1989, co-anchor, 1990-92; corr. Street Stories, CBS, N.Y.C., 1992-94; co-anchor America Tonight, CBS, N.Y.C., 1994; anchor Inside Edition, King World Prodns., 1994—; contbg. editor McCall's, N.Y.C. Bd. dirs. Greater N.Y. coun. Girl Scouts U.S. Recipient Outstanding Young Alumni award Sch. Journalism, U. Ga., Emmy award, 1985-86, 89; named Person of Yr., Chgo. Broadcast Advt. Club, 1989, Anchor of Yr. 2000, Washington Journalism Rev., 1989. Mem. Soc. Profl. Journalists. Office: Inside Edition 402 E 76th St New York NY 10021-3104*

NORWOOD, CAROLE GENE, middle school educator; b. Odessa, Tex., Feb. 27, 1943; d. Perry Eugene and Jeffie Lynn (Stephens) Knowles; m. James Ralph Norwood, Aug. 4, 1973. BA, U. Tex., 1966; MA, U. North Tex., 1975; cert. ESL, Our Lady of the Lake U., San Antonio, 1988. Cert. Sec. Edn. English, Spanish, ESL. Student intern Dept. of the Interior, Washington, 1962; receptionist Senate Chambers, Austin, Tex., 1965; English instr. Universidade Mackenzie, Sao Paulo, Brazil, 1966-67, Uniao Cultural Brasil-Estados Unidos, Sao Paulo, 1966-67; tchr. Terrell (Tex.) Jr. Sr. High Sch., 1967-68, Agnew Jr. High Sch., Mesquite, Tex., 1968-70; teaching asst. U. North Tex. Denton, Tex., 1970-71; sec. to pres. The Village Bank, Dallas, 1971-72; tchr. Plano (Tex.) High Sch., 1972-74; ESL adult edn. tchr. Dallas, 1972-73; tchr., yearbook sponsor Brentwood Middle Sch., San Antonio, 1975-90; instructional specialist Gus Garcia Jr. High Sch., San Antonio, 1990—, interdisciplinary team leader, 1992-93, 96—; yearbook and newspaper sponsor, Agnew Jr. High Sch., 1969-70. Contbr. articles to profl. jours. Mem. World Wildlife Fund, Audubon Soc., Nat. Wildlife Fedn., Nature Conservancy, San Antonio Museum Assn., San Antonio Zoological Soc., Los Padrinos (Mission Rd. Devel. Ctr.); U.I.L. coach 1976-87, 92-93. Named Outstanding Young Woman of Am., 1972. Mem. AAUE, NEA, ADCD, Nat. Coun. Tchrs. of English, San Antonio Area Coun. Tchrs. English, Tex. State Tchrs. Assn., Edgewood Classroom Tchrs. Assn. (faculty rep. 1991-94), Longhorn Singers Alumni Assn., Tex. Exes Alumni Assn., Delta Kappa Gamma (chpt. pres. 1990-92, San Antonio coord. coun. chair 1995—, state program com. mem. 1995—). Presbyterian. Office: Edgewood Ind Sch Dist Gus Garcia Jr School 3306 Ruiz San Antonio TX 78228

NORWOOD, CAROLYN VIRGINIA, business educator; b. Florence, S.C., Dec. 11; d. James Henry and Mildred (Jones) N. BS, N.C. A&T State U., 1956; MA, Columbia U., 1959; postgrad., Seton Hall U., Temple U.; cert. scholarly distinction, Nat. Acad. Paralegal Studies, 1991. Instr. Gibbs. Jr. Coll., St. Petersburg, Fla., Fayetteville State Coll., N.C.; asst. prof. Community Coll. Phila.; prof. Essex County Coll., Newark, 1968—; cons. Mercer County Coll., Trenton, N.J.; mem. assessment team Mid.-States Commn., Phila., 1980—. Co-author: Alphabetic Indexing, 1989. Recipient Eddy award Gregg/McGraw-Hill Co., N.Y.C., 1986, Who's Who in N.J. Bus. Edn. award N.J. Dept. Edn. Divsn. Vocat. Edn., 1990, Cert. of Recognition of Outstanding and Dedicated Svc., Mid. States Assn. Colls. and Schs., Commn. on Higher Edn., 1994; profiled in NBEA Yearbook chpt. on Leadership in Bus. Edn., 1993; doctoral fellow Temple U., Phila., 1977-78. Mem. AAUW, NAFE, NAACP, Nat. Bus. Edn. Assn. (bd. dirs. 1982-85), Ea. Bus. Edn. Assn. (pres. 1986-87, membership dir. 1976-85, Educator of the Yr. 1994), Nat. Coun. Negro Women, N.J. Bus. Edn. Assn., Alpha Kappa Alpha, Phi Delta Kappa, Delta Pi Epsilon. Office: Essex County Coll 303 University Ave Newark NJ 07102-1719

NORWOOD, DEBORAH ANNE, law librarian; b. Honolulu, Nov. 12, 1950; d. Alfred Freeman and Helen G. (Papsch) N.; 1 child, Nicholas. BA, U. Wash., 1972; JD, Willamette U., 1974; M in Law Librarianship, U. Wash., 1979. Bar: Wash., U.S. Dist. Ct. (we. dist.) 1975, U.S. Ct. Appeals (9th cir.) 1980. Ptnr. Evans and Norwood, Seattle, 1975-79; law librarian U.S. Courts Library, Seattle, 1980-89; state law librarian Wash. State Law Libr., Olympia, 1989—, reporter of decisions, 1994—. Mem. ALA, Am. Assn. Law Librs. (chmn. state, ct. and county spl. interest section 1995-96). Office: Wash State Law Libr PO Box 40751 Temple of Justice Olympia WA 98504-0751

NORWOOD, JANET LIPPE, economist; b. Newark, Dec. 11, 1923; d. M. Turner and Thelma (Levinson) Lippe; m. Bernard Norwood, June 25, 1943; children—Stephen Harlan, Peter Carlton. BA, Douglass Coll., 1945; MA, Tufts U., 1946; PhD, Fletcher Sch. Law and Diplomacy, 1949; LLD (hon.), Fla. Internat. U., 1979; LL.D. (hon.), Carnegie Mellon U., 1984. Instr. Wellesley Coll., 1948-49; economist William L. Clayton Ctr., Tufts U., 1953-58; with Bur. Labor Stats., U.S. Dept. Labor, Washington, 1963-91; dep. commr., then acting commr. Bur. Labor Stats. Dept. Labor, Washington, 1975-79, commr. labor stats., 1979-92; sr. fellow The Urban Inst., Washington, 1992—; dir. Republic Nat. Bank, Consortium for Internat. Earth Scis. Info. Network, Nat. Opinion Rsch. Ctr., chair adv. coun. unemployment compensation, 1993-96; mem. com. on nat. stats. NAS. Author papers, reports in field. Recipient Disting. Achievement award Dept. Labor, 1972, Spl. Commendation award, 1977, Philip Arnow award, 1979, Elmer Staats award, 1982, Pub. Svc. award, 1984; named to Hall Disting. Alumni, Rutgers U., 1987; recipient Presdl. Disting. Exec. rank, 1988. Fellow AAAS, Am. Statis. Assn. (pres. 1989), Royal Statis. Soc., Nat. Assn. Bus. Economists; mem. Am. Econ. Assn., Indsl. Rels. Rsch. Assn., Women's Caucus in Stats., Com. Status Women Econs. Profession, Internat. Statis. Inst., Internat. Assn. Ofcls. Stats., Nat. Acad. Pub. Adminstrn., Nat. Inst. Statis. Sci. (bd. trustees); mem. Cosmos Club (pres. 1995-96), Douglas Coll. Soc. Disting. Achievement. Home: Apt PH 21-D 5610 Wisconsin Ave Chevy Chase MD 20815-4415 Office: The Urban Inst 2100 M St NW Washington DC 20037

NORWOOD, JOY JANELL, real estate executive; b. Barnes, Kans., Aug. 25, 1936; d. Howard Clayton and Gladys Melveno (Wells) Cook; divorced; 1 child, Rebecca. Student, U. Colo., 1958-63; grad., Realtors Inst. Ohio State U., 1977. Lic. real estate broker, Ohio. Registered rep. First Investors Corp., Boston, 1966-68; area supr. Wohl Shoe Co., Boston, 1968-70; residential real estate broker Coldwell Banker, Cin., 1970-78, comml. real estate broker, 1978-80; comml. real estate broker Rubloff, Cin., 1980-82; real estate rep. Ky. Fried Chicken/Zantigo, Louisville, 1982-86; v.p. Otto Realty Corp., Cin., 1987-89; pres. Joy Norwood & Assocs., Westchester, Ohio, 1989—. Jr. high sch. tchr. Mason (Ohio) Ch. Christ, 1986—, mem. choir., 1986—. Served with U.S. Army, 1955-58. Mem. Nat. Assn. Corp. Real Estate Execs., Internat. Council Shopping Ctrs., Cin. Bd. Realtors (polit. affairs com. 1974, Million Dollar Club award, 1972-79, 93-95), Cin. Hist. Soc. Republican. Office: Joy Norwood & Assocs 8547 Ashwood Dr West Chester OH 45069-3035

NORWOOD, PAULA KING, medical biostatistics professional; b. Coco Solo, Panama, Aug. 28, 1946; came to U.S., 1946; d. Paul Alfred and Laura Merle (Smith) King; m. Thomas Edward Norwood, Mar. 18, 1972 (div. Aug. 1990); 1 child, David Thomas. BA in Math., Hendrix Coll., 1968; MS in Biometrics, U. Ark., 1970; PhD in Stats., Va. Polytechnic Inst./State U., 1974. Instr. Va. Polytechnic Inst./State U., 1973-74; sr. biometrician Norwich (N.Y.) Pharm. Corp., 1974-77; sr. biometrician Ortho Pharm. Corp., Raritan, N.J., 1977-78, mgr., med. biostats., 1978-81, dir., med. biostats. and data ops., 1981-88, exec. dir., med. biostats. and data ops., 1988-90; v.p., med. biostats. and data ops. worldwide RWJ Pharm. Rsch. Inst., Raritan, 1990-92, v.p. biostatistics and rsch. data svcs., 1992-96, v.p. global stats. and clin. data processing, 1996—. Fellow Am. Statis. Assn.; mem. Biometric Soc., Internat. Biometric Soc. (coun. mem.), Drug Info. Assn., Caucus for Women in Stats., Am. Statis. Assn., Sigma Xi. Home: 106 Moore St Princeton NJ 08540-9999 Office: RWJ Pharm Rsch Inst PO Box 300 Raritan NJ 08869-0602

NORWOOD, VIRGINIA TOWER, retired engineer; b. Ft. Totten, N.Y., Jan. 8, 1927; d. John Vogler and Eleanor (Monroe) Tower; m. Lawrence Norwood, June 5, 1947; children: Naomi, Peter, David; m. Maurice Schaeffer, Dec. 29, 1982. BS, MIT, 1947. Physicist Signal Corps Engring. Labs., Belmar, N.J., 1948-53; sr. engr. Sylvania Electronic Def. Lab., Sunnyvale, Calif., 1953-54; lab. scientist Hughes Aircraft Co., Culver City, Calif., 1954-90; cons. Aerospace Corp., El Segundo, Calif., 1992-93; ret., 1993. Patentee in field; contbr. articles to profl. publs., chpt. to book. Mem. corp. vis. com. MIT, Cambridge, 1976-78. Recipient William Pecora award U.S. Dept. Interior and NASA, 1979, Woman of Yr. in Sci. award YWCA, L.A., 1980. Mem. IEEE (life, sr., profl. group sec.), Sigma Xi (emeritus). Home: 1289 Old Topanga Canyon Rd Topanga CA 90290

NOTHERN, MARJORIE CAROL, nursing administrator; b. Bonners Ferry, Idaho, June 23, 1936; d. Carl John and Ione Faye (Hobson) Frank; m. Abbott Burton Squire, Dec. 15, 1956 (div. Aug. 5, 1972); m. William Thomas Nothern, Aug. 5, 1972. Diploma, Deaconess Hosp. Sch. Nursing, Spokane, Wash., 1956, BA, Stephens Coll., Columbia, Mo., 1981; MBA, Golden Gate U., San Francisco, 1987. Relief head nurse Deaconess Hosp., Spokane, Wash., 1956-57; staff nurse Kadlec Meth. Hosp., Richland, Wash., 1957-58, Southern Pacific Hosp., San Francisco, 1958-59; relief evening supr. The Gen. Hosp., Eureka, Calif., 1959-60; med. office nurse Eley & Davis, Eureka, Calif., 1960-66; head nurse Redbud Cmty. Hosp., Clear Lake, Calif., 1968-72, dir. nurses, 1972-77; supr. Hosp. Nursing Kaiser Found. Hosp., Martinez, Calif., 1977-78; dir. med. ctr. nursing Kaiser Permanente Med. Ctr., Richmond, Calif., 1978-80; asst. hosp. adminstr. Kaiser Found. Hosp., Hayward, Calif., 1980-94; assoc. M2, Inc., San Francisco, 1996—. Mem. health sci. adv. commn. Ohlone Coll., Fremont, Calif., 1980-94; mem. med. aux. and nursing adv. com. Chabot Coll., Hayward, Calif., 1980-94; mem. Grad. Coll. Nursing adv. bd. San Francisco State U., 1986—. Recipient Leadership award Sigma Theta Tau, Alpha Gamma, San Jose State U., 1990. Mem. ANA-Calif., Orgn. Nurse Execs.-Calif., East Bay Orgn. Nurse Execs., Assistance League Diablo Valley, Blackhawk Country Club, Blackhawk Bus. Women, Blackhawk Garden Club, Sigma Theta Tau., Alpha Gamma, Nu Xi. Republican. Office: 363 Jacaranda Dr Danville CA 94506-2124

NOTTI, DONNA BETTS, special education educator; b. Manassas, Va., Sept. 4, 1968; d. William Jackson and Christine Joan (Fant) B.; m. David L. Notti, Oct. 14, 1995. BS in Spl. Edn., Old Dominion U., 1990. Tchr., counselor Southeastern Cooperative Ednl. Programs, Norfolk, Va., 1991—; vol. tutor Tonelson Teaching and Learning Ctr., Norfolk, Va., 1989. Mem. Coun. for Exceptional Children (v.p. 1989-90), Coun. for Children With Behavior Disorders, Coun. for Exceptional Children-Mental Retardation, Am. Re-ED Assn. Lutheran. Home: 402 Surf Scoter Ct Virginia Beach VA 23462-5110 Office: Circle E Bldg Ste 140 861 Glenrock Rd Norfolk VA 23502

NOUN, LOUISE ROSENFIELD, community activist; b. Des Moines, Mar. 7, 1908; d. Meyer and Rose (Frankel) Rosenfield; m. Maurice Henry Noun, Dec. 19, 1936 (div. May 1968); 1 child, Susan Noun Flora. BA, Grinnell Coll., 1929, DHL (hon.), 1973; MA, Radcliffe/Harvard, 1933; DHL (hon.), Cornell Coll., Mt. Vernon, Iowa, 1985, Drake U., 1991. Curator exhbns. Des Moines Art Ctr., 1980, 94, rsch. asst., 1971, bd. dirs., 1956-63; founder, bd. dirs. LWV, Des Moines, 1944-60; pres. Iowa Civil Liberties Union, 1964-72; founder, bd. dirs. NOW, Des Moines, 1971-76, Young Women's Resource Ctr., Des Moines, 1975-82; founder, pres. Chrysalis Found., Des Moines, 1989-96; founder Iowa Women's Archives, Iowa City, 1991. Author: (books) Strong-Minded Women, 1969, Journey to Autonomy, 1996, More Strong-Minded Women, 1992; editor: (catalog) 3 Berlin Women of the Weimar Era, 1994. Recipient Disting. Citizen's award Nat. Mcpl. League, N.Y., 1956, award for dedication to art, Nat. Caucus for Art, 1992, Philanthropic Vision award MS Found. for Women, N.Y., 1995; named to Iowa Women's Hall of Fame, Iowa Com. on Status of Women, 1981. Mem. Consortium Club. Democrat. Jewish. Home: 3131 Fleur Dr Des Moines IA 50321

NOVAK, BARBARA, art history educator; b. N.Y.C.; d. Joseph and Sadie (Kaufman) N.; m. Brian O'Doherty, July 5, 1960. B.A., Barnard Coll., 1951; M.A., Radcliffe Coll., 1953, Ph.D., 1957. TV instr. Mus. Fine Arts, Boston, 1957-58; mem. faculty Barnard Coll., U. N.Y.C., 1958—; prof. art history Barnard Coll., Columbia U., 1970—, Helen G. Altschul prof., 1984—; adv. council Archives of Am. Art, NAD. Author: American Painting of the 19th Century, 1969, Nature and Culture, 1980, The Thyssen-Bornemisza Collection 19th Century American Painting, 1986, Alice's Neck, 1987, The Ape and the Whale, 1995, (play) The Ape and the Whale: Darwin and Melville in Their Own Words, 1987 (performed at Symphony Space 1987), Dreams and Shadows: Thomas H. Hotchkiss in 19th Century Italy, 1993; co-editor: Next to Nature, 1980; mem. editorial bd. Am. Art Jour. Commr. Nat. Portrait Gallery; trustee N.Y. Hist. Soc. Fulbright fellow Belgium, 1953-54; Guggenheim fellow, 1974; Nat. Book Critics nominee, 1980; Los Angeles Times Book Award nominee, 1980; Am. Book Award paperback nominee, 1981. Fellow Soc. Am. Historians, Phila. Atheneum;

mem. Soc. Am. Historians, Am. Antiquarian Soc., Coll. Art Assn. (dir. 1974-77), N.Y. Hist. Soc. (trustee), PEN. Office: Barnard Coll Art History Dept 606 W 120th St New York NY 10027-5706

NOVAK, JAUNITA KATHYL, retired teacher; b. Iberia, Mo., May 3, 1928; d. Arthur Hobert and Clarice (Gardner) Perkins; m. Joseph Thomas Novak, Aug. 7, 1965. BS in Edn., Central Mo State U., 1954, BS in Music, 1960, postgrad., 1966. Tchr. Iberia (Mo.) Pub. Sch., 1948-55, elem., h.s. music tchr., 1955-59; tchr. Cons Sch. Dist. #2, Raytown, Mo., 1959-80; sec. Farm Bureau & Midwest Mgmt., Liberty, Mo., 1980-82; bank teller Centerre Bank, Liberty, Mo., 1982-83; office mgr. Bedingers Ethan Allen Gallery, Liberty, Mo., 1983-84; Fashion Coordinator Donly & Co., Liberty, Mo., 1984-92; substitute tchr. Iberia R.V. Schs., 1992-96. Dir. Girls Scouts, Iberia, 1948-49; PTA pres. Iberia H.S., 1956; bd. dirs., sec. Iberia City Cemetery, 1990-96. Valedictorian scholarship Drury Coll., 1946. Mem. AAUW (life), Am. Bus. Women's Assn. Liberty Belles (life), Mo. State Tchrs. Assn. (life), Raytown Ret. Tchrs. (life), Music Edn. Assn. (life), Iberia Garden Club (pres. 1994-95), Iberia Cmty. Betterment Assn. (bd. dirs. 1995—), Iberia Acad.-Jr. Coll. Alumni Assn. (pres. 1994-96), Kappa Kappa Iota. Republican. Baptist. Home: PO Box 201 Iberia MO 65486

NOVAK, JO-ANN STOUT, chemical engineer; b. Glen Ridge, N.J., June 25, 1956; d. Herbert Austin and Anna (Messina) Stout; m. John Robert Novak Jr., Oct. 30, 1976; B. in Chem. Engring., Ga. Inst. Tech., 1977; MBA, Oakland U., 1984. Cert. engr.-in-tng., Ga.; registered profl. engr., Mich. Trainee AC Spark Plug div. GM, Flint, Mich., 1977-78, chemist, 1978-79, exptl. chemist, 1979-81, mfg. engr., 1981-84, sr. mfg. engr., 1984-87; sr. mfg. project engr., 1987-89, mgr. bus. and engring. processes, 1989-90, program planning mgr., 1990-92; supr. engring.-info. & sys., 1992-94, staff engr. chemical and metall. processes, 1994—. Mem. AIChE, Engring. Soc. Detroit, Nat. Soc. Profl. Engrs., Am. Electroplaters Soc. (dir. Saginaw Valley br. 1981-83, ednl. chmn. 1984-85, sec.-treas. 1985-86, 2d v.p. 1986-87, 1st v.p. 1987-88, pres. 1988-89), Soc. Mfg. Engrs. Office: Delphi Auto Sys GMC 1300 N Dort Hwy Flint MI 48506-3956

NOVAK, JULIE COWAN, nursing educator, researcher, clinician; b. Peoria, Ill., Oct. 2, 1950; m. Robert E. Novak, 1972; children: Andrew, Christopher, Nicholas. BS in Nursing, U. Iowa, 1972, MA in Nursing of Children, 1976; D.N.Sc., U. San Diego, 1989. RN, Va., Calif. Charge nurse surg. and med. ICU U. Iowa Hosp. and Clinics, 1972-73; instr. med. sur. nursing St. Luke's Sch. Nursing, Cedar Rapids, Iowa, 1973-74; instr. family and cmty. health U. Iowa Coll. of Nursing, 1974-75; perinatal nurse clinician U. Iowa Hosps., 1976-77; pediatric nurse practitioner Chicano Cmty. Health Ctr., 1978-80; lectr., asst. prof. child health nursing and physical assesstment San Diego State U., 1977-79; child health nurse practitioner program coord. U. Calif., San Diego, 1978-82; pediatric nurse practitioner San Diego City Schs., 1980-82; coord. infant spl. care ctr. follow-up program U. Calif., San Diego, 1982-83, assoc. clin. prof. intercampus grad. studies, 1983-90, dir. health promotion divsn. cmty. and family medicine, 1985-90; assoc. clin. prof. dept. cmty. family medicine U. Calif. Divsn. Health Care Sci., San Diego, 1990-94; assoc. prof. San Diego State U. Sch. Nursing, 1990-94, Calif. Nursing Students Assn. faculty advisor, 1992-94; pediatric nurse practitioner Naval Hosp., 1990-92, Comp. Health Clinic, 1990-94; prof., dir. Master's in Primary Care/ Family Nurse Practitioner, Pediatric Nurse Practitioner, Women's Health Practitioner programs U. Va. Schs., Charlottesville, 1994—; cons. child health San Diego State U. Child Study Ctr.; mem. accident prevention com. Am. Acad. Pediats.; mem. adv. bd. Albemarle County Sch Health, 1995—, Camp Holiday Trails, 1995—. Contbr. numerous articles to profl. jours. and book chpts. to 7 texts; co-author: Ingall's & Salerno's Maternal Child Nursing, 1995, Mosby Year Book; mem. editl. bd. Jour. Perinatal and Neonatal Nursing, 1986-93, Children's Nurse, 1982-88, ; mem. editl. bd., reviewer Jour. Pediatric Health Care, 1987-93; speaker in field. Chair Ann. Refugee Clothing Drive, East San Diego, ESL Program, Car Seat Roundup U. Calif., San Diego, 1983-85; mem. telethon March of Dimes; mem. steering com. Healthy Mothers/ Healthy Babies Coalition; chair ways and means com. Benchley-Weinberger Elem. Sch. PTA, 1985-87, pres., 1988-90; v.p., pres. Friends Jamul Schs. Found.; co-chair teen outreach program Jr. League San Diego, 1987-88, chair, 1989-90, bd. dirs., 1990-92; educator presch. health San Carlos Meth. Ch.; mem. Head Start Policy Coun., 1992-94, San Diego County Dropout Prevention Roundtable, 1991-93, Western Albemarle H.S. Planning Team, 1994—. Recipient Svc. award Benchley-Weinberger Elem. Sch. PTA, 1988, Hon. Youth Svc. award Calif. Congress Parents and Tchrs., Loretta C. Ford Award for excellence as an nurse practitioner in edn. U. Colo., 1990, March of Dimes Svc. commendation, 1983, Project Hope Svc. commendation, 1983,Hon. Svc. award Calif. Congress of Parents, Tchrs. & Students, 1988, Doctoral Student fellowship U. San Diego, 1986, and numerous others. Mem. ANA, Nat. Assn. Pediat. Nurse Practioners Assoc. (chpt. pres., program com., coord. legis. field, nat. cert. chair 1992—), Calif. Nurse Assn., Pi Lamda Theta, Sigma Theta Tau (mem. nominations com. 1990-91, pres. elect Gamma Gamma chpt. 1993-94, Beta Kappa 1995—, Media award, 1992). Home: 2415 Harmony Dr Charlottesville VA 22901-8990

NOVAK, KIM (MARILYN NOVAK), actress; b. Chgo., Feb. 13, 1933; d. Joseph A. and Blanche (Kral) N.; m. Richard Johnson, April 1965 (div.); m. Robert Malloy, Jan. 1977. Student, Wright Jr. College, Chgo.; A.A., Los Angeles City College, 1958. appeared in: (films) The French Line, 1953, Pushover, 1954, Phffft, 1954, Five Against the House, 1955, Son of Sinbad, 1955, Picnic, 1955, The Man with the Golden Arm, 1956, The Eddie Duchin Story, 1956, Jeanne Eagles, 1957, Pal Joey, 1958, Vertigo, 1958, Bell, Book and Candle, 1958, Middle of the Night, 1959, Strangers When We Meet, 1960, Pépé, 1960, Boys' Night Out, 1962, The Notorious Landlady, 1962, Of Human Bondage, 1964, Kiss Me Stupid, 1964, The Amorous Adventures of Moll Flanders, 1965, The Legend of Lylah Clare, 1968, The Great Bank Robbery, 1969, Tales That Witness Madness, 1973, The White Buffalo, 1977, Just a Gigolo, 1979, The Mirror Crack'd, 1980, The Children, 1990, Liebestraum, 1991; (TV movies) Third Girl from the Left, 1974, Satan's Triangle, 1975, Malibu, 1983; (TV series) Falcon Crest, 1986-87, Alfred Hitchcock Presents, 1985. Named one of 10 most popular movie stars by Box-Office mag. 1956, All-Am. Favorite 1961, Brussels World Fair poll as favorite all-time actress in world 1958. Office: William Morris Agency 151 El Camino Dr Beverly Hills CA 90212*

NOVAK, MARLENA, artist, educator, writer; b. Brownsville, Pa., Mar. 6, 1957; d. Anthony Edward and Mary Margaret (Shader) N.; m. Jay Alan Yim, June 28, 1990. BFA in Painting, Carnegie-Mellon U., 1982; MFA in Art Theory and Practice (Painting), Northwestern U., 1986. tchr. art, Northwestern U., Evanston, Ill., 1985, 89, 96, De Paul U., Chgo., 1986-92, 94, 96, Amsterdams Inst. voor Schilderkunst, The Netherlands, 1996; asst. prof. U. N.Mex., Albuquerque, 1992-93. One person shows include Handled With Care Gallery, Provincetown, Mass., 1983, Dittmar Gallery, Evanston, 1986, Carson Street Gallery, Pitts., 1989, C.G. Jung Inst. Chgo., Evanston, 1990, Wabash Coll., Crawfordsville, Ind., 1990, Esther Saks Gallery, Chgo., 1991, MC Gallery, Mpls., 1992, Ruschman Gallery, Indpls., 1993, Kay Garvey Gallery, Chgo., 1994, 95, Three Ill. Ctr., Chgo., 1994, Galerie Vromans, Amsterdam, 1995; exhibited in group shows at Harrisburg (Pa.) Mus., 1984, Govt. Ctr., Boston, 1984, Univ. Kobe (Japan), 1985, Union Art Gallery, Milw., 1986, Rockford (Ill.) Mus., 1986, Gracie Mansion Gallery Mus. Store, N.Y.C., 1987, George Walter Vincent Smith Art Mus., Springfield, Mass., 1988, East West Contemporary Art Gallery, Chgo., 1989, Provincetown Art Assn. and Mus., 1989, 94, Eve Mannes Gallery, Atlanta, 1990, Mary and Leigh Block Gallery, Northwestern U., Ill., 1990, Desonn-Saunders Gallery, Chgo., 1990, Chgo. Cultural Ctr., 1990, Art Inst. Chgo., 1990, Esther Saks Fine Art, Chgo., 1991, 92, DePaul U. Art Gallery, Chgo., 1992, Ruschman Gallery, 1992, 94, MC Gallery, 1992, Lowe Gallery, Atlanta, 1992, Kay Garvey Gallery, 1992, 93, 95, Charlotte Jackson Fine Art, Santa Fe, 1993, John Sommers Gallery, 1993, CWCA, Chgo., 1993, Klein Art Works, 1993, Greenpeace Fund Benefit, Chgo., 1994, Bethany Coll. Fine Art Ctr., Mankato, Minn., 1994, Galerie Vromans, 1994, 95, Wabash Coll., 1994, Global Focus, Beijing, 1995, Stichting Amazone, Amsterdam, 1995, Galerie Beeld & Ambeeld, Enschede, The Netherlands, 1996, Galerie Waszkowiak, Berlin, 1996; contbr. articles to various publs. Home: 835 N Wood St # 102 Chicago IL 60622

NOVAKOV, ANNA, art historian, art critic; b. Belgrade, Yugoslavia, Oct. 2, 1959; d. Tihomir and Marcia (Cvetkovic) N.; m. Rik Ritchey; 1 child, Christina. BA, U. Calif., Berkeley, 1981; MA, U. Calif., Davis, 1983; PhD, NYU, 1992. Vis. prof. Mills Coll., Oakland, Calif., 1991-92; instr. U. Calif., Berkeley, 1992-95; lectr. U. San Francisco, 1992-95; vis. prof. U. Calif., Davis, 1994, Calif. Coll. Arts & Crafts, Oakland, 1995; asst. prof. San Francisco AA Inst., 1992—. Author: (books) Markers: The Gender of Urban Space, 1994, Time Capsule: A Concise Encyclopedia of Women Artists, 1995, Global Focus: Women in Art and Culture, 1995, Veiled Histories, 1996. Reva and David Logan grantee Boston U., 1987, Beatrice Bain scholar U. Calif., Berkeley, 1995; named Inventer 89 Com. Bicentenaire, Paris, 1988. Office: San Francisco AA Inst 800 Chestnut St San Francisco CA 94133

NOVARA MURPHY, AMY, court reporter; b. Murphysboro, Ill., Jan. 24, 1962; d. Andrew C. and Alice Jane (Arbeiter) Novara; m. James R. Murphy, Dec. 31, 1993. AA, So. Ill. U., 1983, BS, 1985. Cert. shorthand reporter, Ill. Ct. reporter Amy A. Novara Reporting Svc., Murphysboro, 1991—. Interviewer: When the Whole World Changed, 1993. Sec. BPW, Murphysboro, 1991-93; vol. So. Ill. Hosp. Assn., Murphysboro, 1995—; mem. Murphysboro H.S. Booster Club, 1995—; sec. Murphysboro Pride Group, 1991—. Mem. Nat. Ct. Reporters Assn., Ill. Shorthand Reporters Assn., Ill. Ofcl. Ct. Reporters Assn., So. Ill. U. Alumni Club, Alpha Gamma Delta (pres. BH Alumnae chpt. 1995—, adviser undergrad. chpt. 1990—, bd. dirs. house assn. 1992—). Roman Catholic. Home: 7 Candy Ln Murphysboro IL 62966 Office: Amy A Novara Reporting Svc 2110 Rainbow Dr Murphysboro IL 62966

NOVELLO, ANTONIA COELLO, United Nations official, former U.S. surgeon general; b. Fajardo, P.R., Aug. 23, 1944; d. Antonio and Ana D. (Flores) Coello; m. Joseph R. Novello, May 30, 1970. BS, U. P.R., Rio Piedras, 1965; MD, U. P.R., San Juan, 1970; MPH, Johns Hopkins Sch. Hygiene, 1982; DSc (hon.), Med. Coll. Ohio, 1990, U. Ctrl. Caribe, Cayey, P.R., 1990, Lehigh U., 1992, Hood Coll., 1992, U. Notre Dame, Ind., 1991, N.Y. Med. Coll., 1992, U. Mass., 1992, Fla. Internat. U., 1992, Cath. U., 1993, Washington Coll., 1993, St. Mary's Coll., 1993, Ea. Va. Med. Sch., 1993, Ctrl. Conn. State U., 1993, Georgetown U., 1993, U. Mich., 1994, Mt. Sinai Sch. Medicine, 1995. Diplomate Am. Bd. Pediatrics. Intern in pediatrics U. Mich. Med. Ctr., Ann Arbor, 1970-71, resident in pediatrics, 1971-73, pediatric nephrology fellow, 1973-74; pediatric nephrology fellow Georgetown U. Hosp., Washington, 1974-75; project officer Nat. Inst. Arthritis, Metabolism and Digestive Diseases NIH, Bethesda, Md., 1978-79, staff physician, 1979-80; exec. sec. gen. medicine B study sect., div. of rsch. grants NIH, Bethesda, 1981-86; dep. dir. Nat. Inst. Child Health & Human Devel., NIH, Bethesda, 1986-90; surgeon gen. HHS, Washington, 1990-93; spl. rep. for health and nutrition UNICEF, N.Y.C., 1993—; clin. prof. pediatrics Georgetown U. Hosp., Washington, 1986, 89, Uniformed Svcs. U. of Health Scis., 1989; adj. prof. pediatrics and communicable diseases U. Mich. Med. Sch., 1993; adj. prof. internat. health Sch. Hygiene and Pub. Health, Johns Hopkins U., Balt.; mem. Georgetown Med. Ctr. Interdepartmental Rsch. Group, 1984—; legis. fellow U.S. Senate Com. on Labor and Human Resources, Washington, 1982-83; mem. Com. on Rsch. in Pediatric Nephrology, Washington, 1981—; participant grants assoc. program seminars Nat. Inst. Arthritis, Diabetes and Digestive and Kidney Diseases, NIH, Bethesda, 1980-81; pediatric cons. Adolescent Medicine Svc., Psychiat. Inst., Washington, 1979-83; nephrology cons. Met. Washington Renal Dialysis Ctr. affiliate Georgetown U. Hosp., Washington, 1975-78; phys. diagnosis class instr. U. Mich. Med. Ctr., Ann Arbor, 1973-74; chair Sec.'s Work Group on Pediatric HIV Infection and Diseases, DHHS, 1988; cons. WHO, Geneva, 1989; mem. Johns Hopkins Soc. Scholars, 1991. Contbr. numerous articles to profl. jours. and chpts. to books in field; mem. editorial bd. Internat. Jour Artificial Organs, Jour. Mexican Nephrology. Served to capt. USPHS, 1978—. Recipient Intern of Yr. award U. Mich. Dept. Pediatrics, 1971, Woman of Yr. award Disting. Grads. Pub. Sch. Systems, San Juan, 1980, PHS Commendation medal HHS, 1983, PHS Citation award HHS, 1984, Cert. of Recognition, Divsn. Rsch. Grants, NIH, 1985, PHS Outstanding medal HHS, 1988, PHS Unit Commendation, 1988, PHS Surgeon Gen.'s Exemplary Svc. medal, 1989, PHS Outstanding Unit citation, 1989, DHHS Asst. Sec. for Health Cert. of Commendation, 1989, Surgeon Gen. Medallion award, 1990, Alumni award U. Mich. Med. Ctr., 1991, Elizabeth Blackwell award, 1991, Woodrow Wilson award for disting. govt. svc., 1991, Congl. Hispanic Caucus medal, 1991, Order of Mil. Med. Merit, 1992, Washington Times Freedom award, 1992, Charles C. Shepard Sci. award, 1992, Golden Plate award, 1992, Elizabeth Ann Seton award, 1992, Ellis Island Congl. Medal of Honor, 1993, Legion of Merit medal, 1993, Athena award Alumnae Coun., 1993, Nat. Citation award Mortar Bd., 1993, Disting. Pub. Svc. award, 1993, Healthy Am. Fitness Leaders award, 1994, Pub. Leadership Edn. Network Mentor award, 1994, Disting. Svc. award Nat. Coun. Cath. Women, 1995, James E. Van Zandt Citizenship award, 1995, Ronald McDonald Children's Charities Excellence award, 1995; named Health Leader of Yr., COA, 1992; inductee Nat. Women's Hall of Fame, 1994. Fellow Am. Acad. Pediatrics (Excellence Pub. Svc. award 1993); mem. AMA (Nathan Davis award 1993, Meritorious Svc. award 1993), Internat. Soc. Nephrology, Am. Soc. Nephrology, Latin Am. Soc. Nephrology, Soc. for Pediatric Rsch., Am. Pediatric Soc., Assn. Mil. Surgeons U.S., Am. Soc. Pediatric Nephrology, Pan Am. Med. and Dental Soc. (pres.-elect, sec. 1984), D.C. Med. Soc. (assoc.), Johns Hopkins U. Soc. Scholars, Alpha Omega Alpha. Home: 1315 31st St NW Washington DC 20007-3334 Office: UNICEF 1315 31st St NW Washington DC 20007

NOVETZKE, SALLY JOHNSON, former ambassador; b. Stillwater, Minn., Jan. 12, 1932; married; 4 children. Student, Carlton Coll., 1950-52; HHD (hon.), Mt. Mercy Coll., 1991. Amb. to Malta, Am. Embassy, Valletta, 1989-93. Past mem., legis. rep. Nat. Coun. on Vocat. Edn.; past mem. adv. coun. for career edn., past mem. planning coun. Kirkwood C.C.; bd. dirs., life trustee Cedar Rapids (Iowa) Cmty. Theater; bd. dirs. James Baker III Pub. Policy Inst., Rice U.; trustee Shattuck-St. Mary's Sch., Faribault, Minn., Mt. Mercy Coll., Cedar Rapids; vice chmn., life trustee, mem. exec. com. Hoover Presdl. Libr., 1982-85; state chmn. Iowa Rep. Com., 1985-87; chmn. Linn County Rep. Com., 1980-83; mem. adv. bd. Iowa Fedn. Rep. Women, 1987-89; vice chmn. campaign adv. bd. Nat. Fedn. Rep. Women, 1987-89; co-chmn. V.P. Bush Inauguration, 1980; Iowa co-chmn. George Bush for Pres., 1988; bd. dirs. Greater Cedar Rapids Found., also chmn. grants com.; mem. Coun. Am. Ambs.; bd. dirs. Ambs. Forum; mem. nat. bd. New Designs for Two Yr. Insts. Higher Edn. Decorated dame Order of Knights of Malta; recipient Disting. Alumnus award Stillwater High Sch., 1991; Disting. Alumni award for outstanding achievement Carleton Coll., 1994. Home: 4747 Mount Vernon Rd SE Cedar Rapids IA 52403-3941

NOVINGER, CATHY BLACKBURN, utility company executive; b. Portsmouth, Ohio, Apr. 7, 1949; d. Donald E. and Leona (Collingsworth) Blackburn; m. Robert L. Novinger, June 8, 1968; 1 child, Travis Andrew. Diploma, Portsmouth Bus. coll., 1968; cert. sec., U. S.C., 1977; student, Limestone Coll., 1980-81. Edison Electric Inst., 1984. Adminstrv. asst. to pres. S.C. Electric and Gas Co., Columbia, 1979-81, exec. asst. to pres., 1981-82, v.p. corp. services, 1982-83, v.p., group exec. adminstrn., 1983, sr. v.p. adminstrn. and mktg., 1984-88; sr. vp. administn. govt. and public affairs SCANA Corp., 1988—; sem. instr. U. S.C., Columbia, 1982—. Bd. dirs. Nat. Soc. Prevent Blindness, Columbia, pres., 1986; adv. bd. Salvation Army, Columbia, 1986—; personel relations com. Edison Electric Inst.; bd. dirs. Jr. Achievement, Columbia, 1981—; bd. dirs. exec. com. Community Relations Council, Columbia, 1984—. Recipient Tribute to Women in Industry award YWCA, 1982; Ind. Bus. Women award, 1984; named Career Woman of Yr., Nat. Fedn. Bus. and Profl. Women, 1983; named to Tribute to Women in Industry Acad., YWCA, 1987. Mem. SE Electric Exchange (employee relations com.). Republican. Baptist. Office: SCANA Corp 1426 Main St Box 764 Columbia SC 29202*

NOVOGROD, NANCY ELLEN, editor; b. N.Y.C., Jan. 30, 1949; d. Max and Hilda (Kirschbaum) Gerstein; m. John Campner Novogrod, Nov. 7, 1976; children: James Campner, Caroline Anne. AB, Mt. Holyoke Coll., 1971. Sec. fiction dept. The New Yorker, N.Y.C., 1971-73, reader, 1973-76; asst. editor Clarkson N. Potter, Inc., N.Y.C., 1977-78, assoc. editor, 1978-80, editor, 1980-83, sr. editor, 1984-86, exec. editor, 1987; sr. editor HG (formerly House and Garden mag.), N.Y.C., 1987-88, editor-in-chief, 1988-93; editor-in-chief Travel & Leisure, N.Y.C., 1993—. Bd. dirs. N.Y. Bot. Garden, 1991, Mount Holyoke Coll., 1992—. Office: Travel & Leisure 1120 Avenue Of The Americas New York NY 10036-6700

NOVOTNY, DEBORAH ANN, management consultant; b. Oak Lawn, Ill., Sept. 23, 1964; d. Russell Anthony and Barbara J. (Doran) N. BA in Econs., Northwestern U., 1986; postgrad., U. Minn., 1988-91. Lic. mutual fund mktg. analyst; cert. PowerBuilder developer-profl., instr., Powersoft Corp., 1993—. Mgr. lab., cons. Northwestern U., Evanston, Ill., 1983-86; asst. mgr. microcomputer services Sara Lee Corp., Chgo., 1986; sr. cons. Lante Corp., Chgo., 1987-88; fin. exec. IDS Fin. Svcs., Inc., Mpls., 1988-91; fin. system coord. Met. Water Reclamation Dist. of Greater Chgo., Chgo., 1991-92; mgmt. systems cons., pres., CEO Deborah A. Novotny, Inc., Chgo., 1992—; sr. cons., profl. developer Powersoft Corp., Concord, Mass., 1993—; invited spkr., instr. Ann. Powersoft User Conf., Comdex Trade Show. Active teen retreat team St. Michael's Ch., Orland Park, Ill., 1978-84. Ill. State scholar. Mem. MacIntosh Users Group, Chi Omega Rho (charter, chmn. housing assn. 1986-91).

NOVOTNY, PATRICIA SUSAN, lawyer, educator; b. Omaha, Nov. 22, 1953; d. John Albert and Lauretta Lee (Waters) N. BA, Reed Coll., 1976; JD, U. Wash., 1983. Bar: Wash. 1983, U.S. Supreme Ct. 1995. Staff atty. Wash. Appellate Defender Assn., Seattle, 1989-91, 92-95, asst. dir., 1994-95; spl. counsel Wash. Defender Assn., Seattle, 1991-92; pvt. practice, Seattle, 1986-89, 95—; lectr. U. Wash. Sch. Law, U. Wash. Women Studies, Seattle, 1996—; mem. legal com. N.W. Women's Law Ctr., Seattle, 1990—, chmn., 1995—. Recipient individual artist award Seattle Arts Commn., 1990. Mem. Wash. Assn. Criminal Def. Lawyers. Office: Ste 398 4756 U Village Pl NE Seattle WA 98105

NOWAK, CAROL ANN, city official; b. Buffalo, Mar. 5, 1950; d. Walter S. and Stella M. (Gurowski) N. AAS in Bus. Adminstrn., Erie Community Coll., Buffalo, 1986; BS in Bus. Mgmt., SUNY, Buffalo, 1991. With Liberty Nat. Bank/Norstar, Buffalo, 1968-70; with City of Buffalo, 1970-74, asst. adminstrn. and fin., 1974-82, pension clk., adminstr. city police and fire pension fund, city clk., 1982-90, sr. coun. clk., city clk., 1990—. Artist, designer holiday greeting cards, 1984—. Mem. Nat. Notary Assn., SUNY Alumni Assn., Golden Key, Alpha Sigma Lambda. Home: 422 Dingens St Buffalo NY 14206-2321 Office: City of Buffalo City Clerk's Office 1308 City Hall Buffalo NY 14202-3313

NOWAK, CAROL LEE, art educator; b. Bryan, Ohio, Aug. 31, 1946; d. Otho Byron and Martha Lee (Hall) Stockman; children: Lisa Michelle, Travis Christian, Matthew Jay. BS in Art Edn., Bowling Green State U., 1968. Spl. cert. in art, K-12, Ohio. Art tchr. North Central (N.Y.) H.S., 1968-69, Hilltop H.S., West Unity, Ohio, 1972-74, Bryan (Ohio) City Schs., 1987—; adminstr., head tchr. Headstart, Bryan, 1970-71; LD tutor Bryan City Schs., 1974-75, LD tutor, tchr. K-5, 1975-77; tchr. Edgerton (Ohio) Elem. Schs., 1977-83, Edgerton and Bryan City Schs., 1984-87; hot glass asst. Sauder FarmCraft Village, Archbold, Ohio, 1989—; insight facilitator Williams County Probation Schs., Bryan, 1988-94; adv. Hi Art Assn., 1987—. V.p. Tri State Artists Club, Angola, Ind., 1994—. Jennings scholar, 1991. Mem. NEA, Ohio Edn. Assn., Bryan Edn. Assn., Ohio Art Edn. Assn., Art to Art, Tri State Artists Assn., Toledo Glass Collectors Club, Toledo Sculptors Guild, Toledo Art Mus. Home: 315 N Walnut Bryan OH 43506

NOWAK, JACQUELYN LOUISE, administrative officer, realtor, consultant; b. Harrisburg, Pa., Sept. 2, 1937; d. John Henry and Irene Louise (Clark) Snyder; children: Andrew Alfred, IV, Deirdre Anne. Student, Pa. State U., 1973-74; BA, Lycoming Coll., 1975. Editorial writer Patriot News Co., Harrisburg, Pa., 1957-58; dir. West Shore Sr. Citizens Ctr., New Cumberland, Pa., 1969-72; exec. dir. Cumberland County Office Aging, Carlisle, Pa., 1972-80, bur. dir. Bur. Advocacy, Pa. Dept. Aging, Harrisburg, 1980-88; exec. asst. to Pa. Senator John D. Hopper, Senate Com. on Aging and Youth, 1989; owner D&J Prodns., Art and Handcrafted Teddy Bears 1986, Ted E. Bear's Emporium, Harrisburg, 1988-92; assoc. Century 21 Piscioneri Realty, Inc., Camp Hill, Pa.; spl. projects coord. Pa. div. Am. Trauma Soc., 1991-93; adminstr. Country Meadows of West Shore II, Mechanicsburg, Pa., 1993-94; admininstrv. officer Am. Trama Soc., 1994—; recorder Pa. Gov.'s. Coun. Aging Cen. Region, 1972-74; chmn. pub. rels., 1973-74; mem. state planning com. Pa. State Conf. Aging, 1974, panelist, 1975-78; mem. state bd. Pa. Coun. Homemakers-Home Health Aide Svcs., 1972-80, v.p., 1975, chmn. ann. meeting, 1973-75; sr. citizens subcom. chmn. Pa. Atty. Gens. Commn. to Prevent Shoplifting, 1983; mem. adv. com. Tri-County Ret. Sr. Vol. Program, 1972-74; bd. dirs. Coun. Human Svcs. Cumberland, Dauphin, and Perry Counties, 1973-74; mem. svc. com. Family and Children's Svc. Harrisburg, 1970-74, mem. policy com., 1973-74, bd. dirs. Cumberland County unit Am. Cancer Soc., 1964-76, state del., 1964-66, chmn. county pub. rels., 1965-66, cancer crusade chmn., 1964. Recipient Herman Melitzer award, Pa. Conf. Aging, 1978; named Woman of the Yr. Sta. WIOO Radio, Carlisle, Pa., 1979. Mem. Nat. Assn. Area Ags. on Aging (bd. dir. 1975-80, pres. 1976-77; sec. 1978-79), Nat. Soc. Decorative Painters (bd. dirs. Penns Woods painters chpt. 1995—), Pa. Watercolor Soc., Harrisburg Art Assn., Mechanicsburg Art Ctr. (pres. 1987-90, bd. dirs. 1984-95), Gerontol Soc. Am., Am. Trauma Soc. (Pa. div. state bd. 1985-88), Older Women's League (founder chpt.), Lycoming Coll. Alumni Assn. (exec. bd. 1987-89), Pa. Fedn. of Women's Club (div. chmn. 1972-76), Torch Club (pres. 1987-88, 2d v.p. 1985-86), Zonta Internat. (sec. 1986-89). Home: 15 Paddock Ln Camp Hill PA 17011-1268

NOWAK, JUDITH ANN, psychiatrist; b. Albany, N.Y., Feb. 18, 1948; d. Jacob Frank and Anne Patricia (Romanowski) N. BA, Cornell U., Ithaca, N.Y., 1970, MD, 1974. Bd. cert. Psychiatry. Resident Univ. Va. Hosp., Charlottesville, 1974-77; fellow in psychiatry Cornell U. Med. Coll. Westchester Div., White Plains, N.Y., 1977-78, clin. affiliate, 1k978-79; staff psychiatrist Chestnut Lodge Hosp., Rockville, Md., 1979-81; med. officer psychiatry St. Elizabeth's Hosp., Washington, 1981; pvt. practice Washington, 1981—; clin. asst. prof. of psychiatry, George Washington U., Washington, 1981-89; clin. assoc. prof. psychiatry, George Washington U. 1989-94, clin. prof. psychiatry, 1994—. Mem. Am. Psychiat. Soc. (pub. affairs rep. 1995), Am. Psychoanalytic Soc., Washington Psychiat. Soc. (sec. 1989-90, pres. 1991-92),. Office: 908 New Hampshire Ave NW Washington DC 20037-2346

NOWAK, MARY LEONARDA, school administrator, principal; b. Springfield, Ill., Apr. 25, 1942; d. Leonard Louis and Agnes Bridget (Kowalski) N. BS in Edn., U. Akron, 1971; MS in Edn., Boston Coll., 1987; postgrad., Marquette U., 1990-91, Marquette U., 1992-93. Cert. adminstr., Wis. Religious edn. tchr. Mary Queen of Heaven Sch., Greensburg, Ohio, 1976-78; tchr. Christ the King Sch., Akron, Ohio, 1976-78; dir. religious edn., tutor, organist Visitation of BVM, Pitts., 1978-79; 1st and 2d grade tchr. St. Anthony Sch., Sharon, Pa., 1979-85, Sacred Heart Sch., Milw., 1985-87; 5th and 6th grade tchr. St. Augustine Sch., West Allis, Wis., 1987-89, adminstr., prin., 1989-93; adminstr., prin. St. Mary of good Counsel Sch., Mayville, Wis., 1993—; ch. musician, organist St. Adalbert Ch., Milw., 1987—; sec. Sch. Task Force East West Allis, 1990-93; chair Polit. Action Task Force of Region VI Prins., Milw., 1991-92; regional rep. Nat. Regional Congress of Cath. Schs., Mpls., 1991. Grantee, Youth Gardens for All, 1984, Milw. Found., 1986, Marquette U., 1991-92, 93-94; Reading Disability scholar Marquette U., 1987; recipient Exemplary award Cath. Mission Archdiocese Milw., 1990. Mem. ASCD, Nat. Cath. Edn. Assn., Assn. Liturgical Musicians of Archdiocese of Milw., Milw. Archdiocesan Elem. Prin.'s Assn. (dist. chair 1990-91), Milw. Art Mus., Diabetes Assn. Roman Catholic. Home: 116 Bridge St Mayville WI 53050-1634 Office: St Mary Sch 28 Naber St Mayville WI 53050-1735

NOWAK, NANCY STEIN, judge; b. Des Moines, Sept. 17, 1952; d. Russell D. and Christine (Evanoka) Stein; m. Raymond A. Nowak, May 26, 1973. BA, Drake Univ., Iowa, 1974, MA, 1976; JD, George Washington Univ., D.C., 1980. Bar: D.C. 1980, Iowa 1982, Tex. 1986. Briefing atty. Judge Jamie Boyd, 1983-84, Judge Edward Prado, 1984-87; asst. U.S. atty., 1987-88, asst. U.S. trustee, 1988-89; magistrate judge U.S. Dist. Ct. (Tex. we. dist.), 5th circuit, San Antonio, 1989—. Office: US Courthouse 655 E Durango Blvd San Antonio TX 78206-1102

NOWELL, GLENNA GREELY, librarian, consultant; b. Gardiner, Maine, Apr. 15, 1937; d. Bion Mellon and Faith Louise (Hutchings) Greely; m. Dana Richard Nowell, Sept. 1, 1956 (div. 1971); children: Dana A., Mark R., Dean E. BA in English, U. Maine, 1986. Dir. Gardiner Pub. Libr.,

1974—; bd. dirs. Gardiner Bd. Trade; mem. Maine Libr. Commn., 1980-88, Gov.'s Commn. Employment of Handicapped, 1978-81; mem. adv. bd. Gardiner Savs. Bank, 1986—; trustee J. Walter Robinson Welfare Trust, 1986—. Creator, editor Who Reads What publ., 1988—. Mem. Gardiner Econ. Devel. Com., 1989—; interim city mgr. City of Gardiner, 1991; bd. dirs. Kennebec Valley Mental Health, 1995—; mem. State Ct. Libr. com., 1996—. Recipient Hugh Hefner 1st Amendment award Playboy Found., 1987, Outstanding Libr. award Maine Libr. Assn., 1993, Cmty. Svc. award Kennebec Valley C. of C., 1993. Mem. Rotary (pres. Gardiner chpt. 1993-94). Office: Gardiner Pub Libr 152 Water St Gardiner ME 04345-2195

NOWIK, DOROTHY ADAM, medical equipment company executive; b. Chgo., July 25, 1944; d. Adam Harry and Helen (Kichkaylo) Wanaski; m. Eugene Nicholas Nowik, Aug. 9, 1978; children: George Eugene, Helen Eugene. A.A., Columbia Coll., 1980. Cert. lactation counselor, lactation educator, lactation cons. Sec., adminstrv. asst. to pres. Zenco Engring Corp., Chgo., 1970-71; sales rep. Medizenco USA Ltd., Chgo., 1971-73; ptnr. Pacific Med. Systems, Inc., Bellevue, Wash., 1973-76, pres., 1976—. Mem. NAFE, Pacific Mothers Support, Inc. (pres. 1991), Wash. Assn. Lactation Cons. (treas. 1994—). Mem. Orthodox Ch. Am. Home: 303 126th Ave NE Bellevue WA 98005-3217 Office: 1407 132nd Ave NE # 10 Bellevue WA 98005-2259

NOXON, MARGARET WALTERS, community volunteer; b. Detroit, Dec. 16, 1903; d. George Alexander and Ethelwyn (Taylor) Walters; grad., Liggett Sch. for Girls, Det., 1922; life teaching certificate Wayne State U., 1925; student Columbia Tchrs. Coll., 1939-40; m. Herbert Richards Noxon, July 15, 1926 (dec. Aug. 4, 1971). Bd. dirs. Coll. Club, Detroit, 1925-30; mem. Salvation Army Aux., Detroit, 1926—; mem. Coll. Club, Summit N.J., 1941-—; historian D.A.R., N.Y.C., 1943-46, vice regent, 1946-49; dir. New Eng., Women, 1961-64; dir. Woodycrest-Five Points Child Care, 1961-77; bd. dirs. ARC, Summit, N.J., service com. chmn. uniforms and insignias, 1943-45; v.p. N.Y. Infirmary Aux., N.Y.C., 1948-58, bd. dirs., 1959-80. Recipient award for meritorious personal service ARC, 1945. Mem. Nat. Inst. Social Scis., Grand Jury Assn. N.Y. County, D.A.R. (dir. 1950-70), St. David's Soc. State N.Y., English-Speaking Union, Daus. Am. Colonists, AAUW, Southampton Colonial Soc., Nat. Woman's Farm and Garden Assn. (dir. met. br. 1975—, dir. N.Y. State div. 1978-80, mem. nat. council 1978-80), Ch. Women's League for Patriotic Service, Women's Bible Soc. N.Y., Alpha Sigma Tau. Republican. Presbyterian. Clubs: Southampton (N.Y.) Bath and Tennis, City Gardens (dir. 1963-68, mem. adv. com. 1968-74, dir. 1974-80, adv. bd. 1980-83), York (bd. govs. 1965-66, 73-77), Barnard (trustee 1979-81), Sorosis (v.p. 1979-81), Regency (N.Y.C.). Home: care Virginia W Rider 634 Silvermine Rd New Canaan CT 06840-4324

NOYES, JUDITH GIBSON, library director; b. N.Y.C., Apr. 19, 1941; d. Charles II and Alice (Klauss) Gibson; m. Paul V. Noyes, June 1, 1991; children from previous marriage: Andrea Elizabeth Green, Michael Charles Green. BA, Carleton Coll., 1962; MLS, U. Western Ont., London, Can., 1972. Librarian edn. U. New Brunswick, 1972-86; libr. Can. Inst. Sci. and Tech. Info., Ottawa, Ont., Can., 1975-86; univ. librarian Colgate U., Hamilton, N.Y., 1986—; mem. OCLC Adv. Com. on Coll. and Univ. Librs., 1991-94; pres. bd. trustees Ctrl. N.Y. Libr. Resources Coun., 1992-96. Mem. ALA, Am. Coll. and Rsch. Librs. (nominating com. 1988-89, 92-93, legis. com. coll. libr. sect. liaison 1989-91, chair task force on intellectual freedom, 1992-94), Internat. Standards Orgn. (tech. com. 46, 1981-89). Office: Colgate U Everett Needham Case Libr 13 Oak Dr Hamilton NY 13346-1338

NOZERO, ELIZABETH CATHERINE, lawyer; b. Detroit, June 13, 1953; d. Peter J. and Pauline R. (Reeves) N.; m. Stephen A. Catalano, May 23, 1981 (div. May 1993); 1 child: Alexandra L. BA in history, U. Calif., 1975; JD, U. San Diego, 1978. Bar: Calif. 1979, Nev. 1980. Counsel State Industrial Ins. System, Las Vegas, 1980-81; sr. legal counsel Reynolds Elec. & Engring. CO., Las Vegas, 1981-85; asst. gen. counsel U. Nev., Las Vegas, 1985-89; v.p., gen. counsel Harrah's Casino Hotels, Las Vegas, 1989-95; sr. legal counsel Sierra Health Svcs., Inc., 1996—; mem. exec. bd. Nev. Bar Assn. Fee Dispute com. 1982-88, Nev. Law Found., 1980-88. Chairperson S. Nev. Area Health Edn. Ctr., Las Vegas, 1990-94; former chair Nev. Adv. Com. U.S. Commn. on Civil Rights, Nev., 1989-94; gov.'s com. Infrastructive Financing, 1994-95. Recipient Woman of Achievement award Las Vegas C. of C., 1992, Silver State Citizen award Nev. Atty. Gen., 1992. Mem. Nev. Gaming Attys. (v.p. 1994-95), Nev. Resort Assn. (chairperson, regulations com. 1993-95). Office: Sierra Health Svcs Inc PO Box 15645 2724 N Tenaya Way Las Vegas NV 89114-5645

NOZIGLIA, CARLA MILLER, forensic scientist; b. Erie, Pa., Oct. 11, 1941; d. Earnest Carl and Eileen (Murphy) Miller; m. Keith William Noziglia, Nov. 21, 1969; children: Pama Noziglia Cook, Kathryn Noziglia Volpi. BS, Villa Maria Coll., 1963; MS, Lindenwood Coll., 1984. Cert. med. technologist, Am. Soc. Clin. Pathologists. Med. technologist Monmouth (N.J.) Gen. Hosp., 1963-64; spl. chem. med. technologist Hamot Hosp. Med. Ctr., Erie, Pa., 1965-69; pathologist's assoc. Galion (Ohio) Comm. Hosp., 1969-75; dir. crime lab. Mansfield (Ohio) Police Dept., Richland County Crime Lab., 1978-81; crime lab. supr. St. Louis County Police, Clayton, Mo., 1981-84; dir. crime lab. Las Vegas (Nev.) Met. Police, 1984-88, dir. lab. svcs., 1988-93, dir., cons. forensic scis., 1993-95; lab. dir. Tulsa Police Dept., 1995—. Tech. abstracts editor Jour. Police Sci. and Adminstrn., 1983-91; editorial bd. Jour. Forensic Identification, 1988—; contbr. to (book) Journal of Police Science, 1989, Encyclopedia of Police Science, 1989. Mem. Gov.'s Com. on Testing for Intoxication, Las Vegas, 1984-93; mem. adv. bd. Nev. Bd. Pharmacy, 1988-93; recruiter United Blood Svcs., Las Vegas, 1986-93; bd. dirs., pres. Cmty. Action Against Rape, Las Vegas, 1987-94; co-founder So. Nev. Sexual Assault Protocol, 1986. Recipient award Ohio Ho. of Reps., 1981, Alumni of Yr. award Villa Maria Coll., 1981; named Outstanding Cath. Erie Diocese N.W. Pa., 1988, Woman of Achievement Las Vegas C. of C., 1989. Fellow Am. Acad. Forensic Sci. (bd. dirs. 1988-91, sec. Criminalistics sect. 1986, sect. chmn. 1987, Sect. award 1995); mem. Am. Soc. Crime Lab Dirs. (emeritus, bd. dirs. 1980-87, treas. 1981-82, 88-91, pres. 1986-87), Internat. Police Assn., Internat. Assn. for Identification (emeritus), S.W. Assn. Forensic Scientists, Am. Bus. Women's Assn. (Woman of Yr. 1988, one of Nat. Top Bus. Women 1993). Republican. Roman Catholic. Office: Tulsa Police Dept 600 Civic Ctr Tulsa OK 74103

NUCKLOS, SHIRLEY, medical administrator, consultant; b. Canton, Ohio, Aug. 30, 1949; D. Boyd Alexander and Julia Lillian (Hood) Curtis; m. William W. Nucklos, Mar. 11, 1972; children: Tuere Tene, Tiombé Nigina, Khari Oji-Lee. BS in Edn., Cen. State U., Wilberforce, Ohio, 1970; MA, Ohio State U., 1971. Cert. elem. tchr., guidance counselor. Guidance counselor Scioto Village High Sch., Powell, Ohio, 1973-78; acad. advisor Franklin U., Columbus, Ohio, 1980-82, acting asst. dir. records, 1982-83, asst. registrar, 1983-90; registrar Ohio Dominican Coll., Columbus, 1990-93; dir. human resources Mid-Am. Phys. Medicine & Exec. Med., Inc., Columbus, Ohio, 1994—; adminstrv. advisor to Black Student Union, Franklin U., 1982-85; human resource cons. Mid-Am. Phys. Medicine, Exec. Med., Inc., Westerville, Ohio, 1989-93, dir. human resources/bus. mgr., 1994—. Vol. tchr. Umoja Sasa Shule, Columbus, 1971-74; booster Mid-west Gymnastic and Cheerleading, Dublin, Ohio, 1988-93; active various com. for minority concerns. Mem. Ohio Assn. Collegiate Registrars and Admissions Officers (sec. 1991-93, Cert. Appreciation 1985, 93), Am. Assn. Collegiate Registrars and Admissions Officers, Nat. Assn. Coll. Deans, Registrars and Admissions Officers, Ohio Assn. Women Deans, Adminstrs. and Counselors, Nat. Assn. Women Deans, Adminstrs. and Counselors, Am. Assn. Univ. Adminstrn., Va. Admissions Counselors for Black Concerns, Ohio Health Info. Mgmt. Assn. Democrat. Mem. Church of God in Christ. Office: Mid Am Phys Medicine & Exec Med Inc 254 Woodland Ave Ste 105 Columbus OH 43203-1782

NUCKOLS, GAIL HODKINSON, legislative staff member; b. Bklyn., July 6, 1941; d. F. Roy and Gertrude E. (Myers) Hodkinson; m. Caswell G. Nuckols Jr., June 22, 1963; children: Andrew, Sharon. BA in History, U. Mich., 1963. Ind. rsch. asst. Arlington, Va., 1988-90; legis. asst. Va. Ho. Dels., Arlington, 1991—. Mem., chairperson Arlington County Sch. Bd., 1983-91; bd. dirs. No. Va. C.C., Annandale, 1995—, United Way, Arlington, 1996—; mem. Va. Ext. Leadership Coun., Arlington, 1995—; chairperson Va. Investment Partnership, 1995—. Named Outstanding Citizen, Arlington Sch. Bd., 1982. Mem. AAUW, LWV. Democrat. Mem. United Ch. of Christ. Home and Office: 5517 Yorktown Blvd Arlington VA 22207

NUGENT, CONSTANCE MARIE JULIE, health facility administrator; b. Lewiston, Maine, July 3, 1933; d. Joseph E.W. Sr. and Beatrice M.J. (Levasseur) Lessard; m. John Thomas Nugent Sr., Jan. 2, 1954 (dec. Feb. 27, 1982); children: John Thomas Jr., Michael Joseph. Diploma in nursing, Maine Gen. Hosp., 1953; BA, St. Joseph's Coll., Windham, Maine, 1974; family nurse practitioner cert., U. Maine Sch. of Nursing, 1976; M in Health Svc. Adminstrn., St. Joseph's Coll., Windham, Maine, 1995. RNNP, Maine, Calif., Ariz. Staff nurse med. surg., peds., gyn. Maine Med. Ctr., Portland, 1953-57; staff nurse ob-gyn. Mercy Hosp., Portland, Maine, 1957-59; emergency rm. nurse Huntington Meml. Hosp., Pasadena, Calif., 1959-63; supr. critical care unit Osteopathic Hosp. of Maine, Portland, 1963-69; clin. instr. sch. nursing Mercy Hosp., Portland, 1969; supr. ICU Dallas (Tex.) Osteopathic Hosp., 1970; adminstr. Nat. Med. Care of Portland, 1970-80; dir. nursing svcs. Lassen Cmty. Hosp., Susanville, Calif., 1980-87, Hospice of Monterey Peninsula, Carmel Valley, Calif., 1987; adminstr. Ukiah (Calif.) Convalescent Hosp., 1988—; cons. Office of Alcohol Drug Abuse Prevention, Augusta, Maine, 1975-77; mem. adv. com. Home Health Care, Portland, 1974-76, adv. coun. Bur. of Elderly, Portland, 1975-80, Provider Health Forum, Susanville, 1983-87. Sec. Lassen County Mental Health Bd., Susanville, 1980-81; co-facilitator Diabetic Clinic, Susanville, 1983-87; vice-chair Lassen County Health Human Svcs. Bd., Susanville, 1985-87. Mem. Bus. and Profl. Women (treas., v.p. 1990-94), Calif. Assn. Health Facilities, Coun. of Long Term Care Nurses of Calif. (pres. Redwood Empire chpt. 1989-92). Republican. Roman Catholic. Office: Ukiah Convalescent Hosp 1349 S Dora St Ukiah CA 95482-6512

NUGENT, JANE KAY, utility executive; b. Detroit, Aug. 31, 1925; d. Albert A. and Celia (Betzing) Kay; m. Robert L. Nugent, Apr.3, 1991. BS, U. Detroit, 1948; MA, Wayne State U., 1952; MBA, U. Mich., 1963. Sr. personnel interviewer employment Detroit Edison Co., 1948-60, personnel coord. for women, 1960-65, office employment adminstr., 1965-70, gen. employment adminstr., 1970-71, dir. personnel svcs., 1971-72, mgr. employee rels., 1972-77, asst. v.p. employee rels., 1977-78, v.p. employee rels., 1978-82, v.p. adminstrn., 1982-90, ret., 1990; bd. dirs. First Am. Bank-SE Mich., 1986-90, Bon Secours of Mich. Healthcare System, Inc., 1984-93, Detroit Exec. Svc. Corp., 1990—; tchr. U. Detroit Evening Coll. Bus. and Adminstrn., 1963-75; seminar leader div. mgmt. edn. U. Mich., 1968-74, Waterloo Mgmt. Edn. Centre, 1972-77. Mem. Mich. Employment Security Adv. Coun., 1967-81; chmn. bd. dirs. Detroit Inst. Commerce, 1976-79; exec. bd. NCCJ, 1980-91, nat. trustee, 1984-88; bd. dirs. Childrens Home Detroit, 1991—, 1st v.p. 1994-96, pres. 1996—. Recipient Alumni Tower award U. Detroit, 1967, Headliner award Women Wayne State U., 1970, Wayne State U. Alumni Achievement award, 1974, Career Achievement award Profl. Panhellenic Assn., 1973, Bus. Achievement award Assn. Bus. Deans, 1989; named one of Top Ten Working Women of Detroit, 1970, Alumnus of Yr., U. Detroit, 1981, Woman of Yr. Am. Lung Assn., 1991, Sr. Profl. in Human Resources Soc. Human Resource Mgmt.; cert. Adminstrv. Mgr. Am. Mgmt. Soc.; inducted in Mich. Women's Hall of Fame, 1988. Mem. Internat. Assn. Personnel Women (pres. 1969-70), Women's Econ. Club (v.p. 1971-72, pres. 1972-73), Am. Soc. Employees (bd. dirs. 1979-90), Personnel Women Detroit (pres. 1960-61), U. Detroit Alumni Assn. (pres. 1964-66), Phi Gamma Nu (nat. v.p. 1955-57), Boys and Girls Club S.E. Mich. (pres. 1987-89), Econ. Club Detroit (v.p. 1981-90), Internat. Womens Forum.

NUGENT, MARY KATHERINE, elementary education educator; b. Terre Haute, Ind., Aug. 15, 1953; d. Thomas Patrick and Jeanne (Butts) N. BS, Ind. State U., Terre Haute, 1975, MS, 1978. Cert. in elem. edn., spl. edn., Ind. Tchr. 6th grade Cloverdale (Ind.) Sch. Corp., 1976-79; tchr. 4th-6th grades Glenwood Sch., Richardson, Tex., 1986-88; tchr. intermediate mentally handicapped class Meadows Elem. Sch., Terre Haute, 1988-89, tchr. 5th grade, 1989-90, tchr. 4th grade, 1990-93; tchr. 6th grade lang. arts and reading Woodrow Wilson Mid. Sch., Terre Haute, 1993—; mem. steering com. Tchr. Applying Whole Lang., Terre Haute, 1989-91. Office: Vigo County Sch Corp 961 Lafayette Ave Terre Haute IN 47804-2929

NUGENT, WANDA E., occupational health nurse, consultant; b. Concord, Mass., May 9, 1956; d. Ernest S. and Dorothy B. Stevenson; m. James A. Nugent (div. May, 1994). BS, Fitchburg State Coll., 1981. Cert. occupl. health nurse specialist. Staff nurse Nashoba Cmty. Hosp., Ayer, Mass., 1981-83; supr. Health Stop Med. Mgmt., Cambridge, Mass., 1983-84; sr. acct. exec. Health Stop Med. Mgmt., Wellesley, Mass., 1985-92; nat. mkt. specialist Lynch, Ryan & Assoc., Westborough, Mass., 1992-93; occupl. health cons. Omni Health Resources, Natick, Mass., 1993-94; prin., founder, specialist program design, new bus. devel., patient resls. Carlisle (Mass.) Consulting Group, 1994—; faculty Harvard Sch. Pub. Health Ednl. Resource Ctr., 1995—. Vol. Coun. on Aging, Carlisle, Mass., 1995—. Mem. Am. Soc. Quality Control (chairperson health care divsn. Boston sect. 1994-95, 96—), Carlisle (Mass.) Bus. Assn. (pres. 1995-96), Toastmasters Internat. Home and Office: P O Box 363 Carlisle MA 01741-0363

NUMANN, PATRICIA JOY, surgeon, educator; b. Bronx, N.Y., Apr. 6, 1941. BA, U. Rochester, 1962; MD, SUNY Health Sci. Ctr., Syracuse, 1965. Intern, resident SUNY Health Sci. Ctr., Syracuse, 1970, from asst. prof. to assoc. prof. surgery, 1970-89, assoc. dean Coll. Medicine, 1978-84, assoc. dean Coll. Medicine Clin. Affairs, prof. surgery, 1989—; dir. breast care program SUNY Health Sci. Ctr., Syracuse, 1986—; presenter in field. Contbr. chpts. to books, articles to profl. jours. Found. bd. dirs. Vera House, Syracuse, 1993-94; hon. bd. dirs. F.A.C.T., Syracuse, 1994. Named one of Women of Distinction, N.Y. State Gov. Mario Cuomo, 1994, Disting. Tchg. Prof. SUNY, 1994; recipient Disting. Surgeon award Assn. Women Surgeons, 1991. Mem. AMA (coun. sci. affairs), ACS (com. on cancer grad. med. edn. com.), Am. Bd. Surgeons (bd. dirs. 1994—), Am. Assn. Endocrine Surgeons (v.p. 1992, pres. 1985), Assn. for Surg. Edn., Corinthian Club. Office: SUNY Health Sci Ctr 750 E Adams St Syracuse NY 13210-2306

NUÑEZ DE VILLAVICENCIO, MARIA IRENE, small business owner, consultant; b. Caibarien, Cuba, Jan. 19, 1940; came to U.S., 1956; d. Candido Gregorio and Sofia Irene Diaz; m. Antonio Luis Nuñez de Villavicencio, July 15, 1960; children; Ana Maria, Jacqueline, Mark Allan, Paul Anthony, Jennifer Susan. Student, Marsh Bus. Sch., Atlanta, 1960, Bentley Coll., 1989. With accounts receivable dept. GE Credit Corp., Atlanta, 1960-62; cashier Digital Equipment Corp., Marlboro, Mass., 1981-83, auditor, 1983-87; with profit and loss statements dept. Digital Equipment Corp., Maynard, Mass., 1987-92; owner, v.p. ops., cons. AMN Assocs., Westboro, Mass., 1991—. Roman Catholic. Home and Office: 22 Byard Ln Westborough MA 01581

NUNLEY, MALINDA VAUGHN, retired elementary school educator; d. William D. and Callie (Ross) Vaughn; m. Harry H. Nunley, Dec. 24, 1940 (dec.); chidlren: Jerry Michael, Sally Coleen. BS in Edn., Mid. Tenn. State U., 1961; MEd in Psychology, Middle Tenn. State U., 1972; postgrad., U. Tenn., Chattanooga, 1974-80, Mid. Tenn. State U. Cert. art tchr., spl. edn. tchr., guidance counselor and cons., individual testing and diagnostics in spl. edn. Tenn. Tchr. Panama Canal Co, Balboa, Panama Canal Zone, 1954-56; adult tchr. U.S. Army, Ft. Davis, Panama Canal Zone, 1956-60; elem. tchr. Ancon Elem. Panama Canal Zone Sch., Tenn., 1961-64; tchr. South Pitts. High Sch., 1964-66, Normal Park Elem. Sch., Chattanooga, Tenn., 1966-71; spl. edn. tchr. Griffith Creek Elem. Sch., Tenn., 1971-83; ret. Tenn.; tutor, substitute tchr., speaker to groups, Tenn., 1994—; homebound tchr. for alcohol and drug abuse adolescents, 1989-90; spl. speaker to class groups 4th-7th, 1993-94. Mem. NEA, Tenn. Edn. Assn., Marion County Tchrs. Assn., Tenn. Ret. Tchrs. Assn., Chattanooga Edn. Assn. (past faculty rep.). Home: 6555 Highway 27 Chattanooga TN 37405-7288

NUNNALLY, DOLORES BURNS, retired physical education educator; b. Strong, Ark., Jan. 2, 1932; d. Marion Saunders Burns and Emma Jo (Burns) Baca; m. Curtis Jerome Nunnally, Apr. 16, 1954; 1 child, Jo Lynn Nunnally Blair. BSE, Ark. State Tchrs. Coll., 1953; MSE, State Coll. Ark., 1964; EdD, U. Sarasota, 1981. Phys. edn. tchr. El Dorado (Ark.) Pub. Schs., 1953-72; real estate salesman Continental Real Estate, Downers Grove, Ill., 1972-74; phys. edn. instr. Triton Coll., River Grove, Ill., 1973-74; substitute tchr. DuPage and Kane County Schs., Ill., 1972-74; phys. edn. tchr. Wheeling (Ill.) Sch. Dist. 21, 1974-91; tennis coach El Dorado Pub. Schs., 1953-73; tennis pro El Dorado Racquet Club, City of El Dorado, summers 1965-72. Contbr. articles to profl. jours. Pres. Ark. Sq. Dance Fedn., Little Rock, 1971-72, Progressive Sunday Sch., El Dorado, 1994—. Recipient All Star Coaches Clinic award Ark. H.S. Coaches Assn., 1971. Mem. NEA, AAHPERD (pres. 1969-70, State Honor award 1972), Ark. Assn. Health, Phys. Edn., Recreation and Dance (life), Ill. Assn. Health, Phys. Edn., Recreation and Dance (Quarter Century award 1981, Svc. award 1991), U.S. Tennis Assn., Order Eastern Star, Delta Phi Kappa. Methodist. Home: PO Box 641 1415 Huttig Hwy Strong AR 71765

NUNNARI, JULIE, cable television executive. V.p. program scheduling Showtime Networks, Inc., N.Y.C. Office: Showtime Networks Inc 1633 Broadway 17th Fl New York NY 10019*

NUSBACHER, AILENE COHEN, sociologist; b. Bklyn., Feb. 23, 1943; m. Noel Nusbacher, Sept. 16, 1967; children: Joseph, Ora, Ahuva. BA, Bklyn. Coll., 1964, MA, 1977; MSW, Boston U., 1966; PhD, NYU, 1987. Lic. social worker, N.Y. Social worker Maimonides Hosp., Bklyn., 1966-68; instr. Touro Coll., N.Y.C., 1979, Adelphi U., Garden City, N.Y., 1987; adj./asst. prof. Kingsborough C.C./CUNY, Bklyn., 1990—; adj. asst. prof. Stern Coll., N.Y.C., 1990-91. Mem. NOW, NASW, Am. Sociol. Assn., Sociologists for Women in Soc. Office: Kinsborough CC Dept Behavioral Sci Oriental Blvd Brooklyn NY 11235

NUSBACHER, GLORIA WEINBERG, lawyer; b. N.Y.C., July 22, 1951; d. Murray and Doris (Togman) Weinberg; m. Burton Nusbacher, Aug. 4, 1974; 1 child, Shoshana. BA, Barnard Coll., 1972; JD, Columbia U., 1975. Bar: N.Y. 1976. Assoc. Hughes Hubbard & Reed, N.Y.C., 1975-83, counsel, 1983-91, ptnr., 1991—; atty. specializing in exec. compensation and employee benefits; lectr. in field. Contbr. articles to profl. jours. Troop leader, leader trainer Girl Scouts USA. Mem. ABA (employee benefits and exec. compensation com. 1987—, fed. regulation securities com., subcom. employee benefits and exec. compensation 1983—, task force Sect. 16, 1983—, chmn. subcom. fed. and state securities laws of com. employee benefits and exec. compensation 1994—, task force exec. compensation 1992-94), Phi Beta Kappa. Office: Hughes Hubbard & Reed 1 Battery Park Plz New York NY 10004-1405

NUSBAUM, MARLENE ACKERMAN, marketing professional; b. Portsmouth, Va., June 13, 1949; d. Martin and Betsy Freda (Katz) Ackerman; m. Robert Collier Nusbaum Jr., June 27, 1971; 1 child, Jessica Lynn. Deuxième Degré, Université d'Orléans Tours, 1970; BA magna cum laude, Rutgers U., 1971; MA, Brown U., 1973, PhD with distinction, 1980. Tchr. French Dana Hall Sch., Wellesley, Mass., 1974-75; master French and German Groton (Mass.) Sch., 1975-80; French instr. dept. humanities MIT, Cambridge, 1981; assoc., product mgr. Digital Equipment Corp., Maynard, Mass., 1981-83; mktg. mgr. interactive video Digital Equipment Corp., Bedford, Mass., 1983-85; pvt. practice mktg. cons. Newton, Mass., 1985-91; bus. devel. dir. Giga Info. Group, Norwell, Mass., 1991-95, dir. confs., 1995-96, worldwide dir. confs., 1996—; mem. mktg. adv. com. GlobalSports Ltd., Boston, 1989-90; cons. editor Heinle & Heinle Pub., Boston, 1981. Author: (with Verdier) Parlez Sans Peur!, 1983, (with Holden-Avard and Verdier) Le Français Sans Peur, 1991, (with Beyer) Beth Israel Hosp. Children's Doctor's Kit for Good Health, 1990. Organizer class size PTA Com., Newton, 1986-88, chairperson roundtable exec. com., 1987-88. Chairperson roundtable, exec. com. Newton PTA Coun., 1987-88. Mem. N.E. Conf. Tchrs. of Fgn. Langs., Am. Coun. Tchrs. Fng. Langs., Mass. Fgn. Lang. Assn. Office: Giga Info Group 1 Longwater Cir Norwell MA 02061-1616

NUSIM, ROBERTA, publisher; b. N.Y.C., Dec. 1, 1943; d. Seymour and Rae (Weiner) N.; m. Stephen Jablonsky, 1965. BA in English, CCNY, 1964; MA, CUNY, 1966. Tchr. N.Y.C. Bd. Edn., 1964-73; v.p. program devel. Mind, Inc., Westport, Conn., 1973-76; pres. Mind Media, 1976-78; founder, pres. Lifetime Learning Systems, Fairfield, Conn., 1978-90; founder dir. The Film Study Guild, 1979-90; founder, pres. The Work & Family Pub. Group, Inc., 1991-94; founder, pres. Youth Mktg. Internat., Ltd., 1995—. Editor: Let's Talk About Health, 1980. Mem. ASCD, NAFE, Am. Film Inst., Women in Comm., Ednl. Press Assn. Am., Ptnrs. for Global Edn. (founder). Avocations: reading, painting. Office: Youth Mktg Internat Ltd PO Box 305 Easton CT 06612-0305

NUSS, BARBARA GOUGH, artist; b. Washington, Apr. 11, 1939; d. Gaines Homer Gough and Edwerta Barbara (Beyer) Barber; m. Frederick A. Johnson, Sept. 30, 1968 (div. 1975); 1 child, Mark Eugene; m. Fred Dean Nuss, Dec. 18, 1982. BFA, Syracuse U., 1960; postgrad., Schuler Sch. Fine Arts, Balt., 1986-87. Art dir. Chappell's Dept. Store, Syracuse, N.Y., 1960-62, 66; mgr., illustrator Holman Anderson & Moore, Washington, 1967-70; art dir., advt. mgr. Ad-Media & Howard Advt. Assocs., Columbia, Md., 1970-75; acct. exec. Graphic Arts Inc., Alexandria, Va., 1975-77; sales mgr. The Jour. Newspapers, Washington, 1977-82; tchr., adult edn. Montgomery Coll., Rockville, Md., 1984-85; pvt. tchr. fine arts, Woodbine, Md., 1982—; chmn. Montgomery County Juried Art Exhibit, Rockville, 1988; pres. Nuss Fine Arts, Inc., 1992—. One person shows include Pa. State U., 1986, NIH, Bethesda, Md., 1989, 90, Md. Nat. Capital Park and Planning Commn., 1991, Art League Gallery, Alexandria, Va., 1992; exhibited in group shows at Art League at the Torpedo Factory, 1987-92, Heritage Gallery Classical Realism, 1989-90, Art Barn Gallery, Washington, 1990, Carmen's Gallery, 1991—, Art Showcase 100 Md. Artists, 1991-92, Assn. pour la Promotion du Patrimoine Artistique Francais, Galerie Jean Lammelin, Argenteuil, France, 1991, Salmagundi Club 14th Ann. Exhbn., 1991, 18th Ann. Exhbn., 1995, Atrium Gallery Georgetown U., Washington, 1991, Strathmore Hall, Bethesda, Md., 1995, Mid-Atlantic Regional Watercolor Exhbn., 1989, 90, 96; represented in permanent collections including Nat. Park Found., NIH, Am. Coun. Edn., Bell Atlantic, Kiplinger Washington Editors. Recipient 1st prize for watercolor C&O Canal Show, 1987, 1st prize for oil painting Rockville Art League, 1987, Montgomery County Art Assn., 1983, 89, Gaithersburg Fine Arts Assn., 1983, 89, Gaithersburg Fine Arts Assn., 1988, grand champion award for oil painting Howard County Fair, 1989, One of Top 100 award for oil painting Nat. Arts for Parks, 1989, 91, 92 (two images selected), image selected for notecard Nat. Parks and Conservation Assn.; images selected for Owen Co., Ind. phone book, U.S. Dept. State Art in Embassies Program, 1994-96. Mem. Nat. League Am. Pen Women (sec. Bethesda, Md. 1989), Balt. Watercolor Soc., Art League Torpedo Factory. Home: 3132 Cabin Run Woodbine MD 21797-7933

NUSS, SHIRLEY ANN, computer coordinator, educator; b. Madison, Min., Oct. 22, 1946; d. Woodland Henry and Aileen Thelma (Mattox) Cover; m. Sheldon Edward Nuss, May 29, 1970; 1 child, Melissa Ann. BEd, Trinity U., Washburn U., 1969; MA, Mich. State U., 1982, PhD, 1990. 3d grade tchr. Topeka Pub. Schs. System, 1969-70; 6th grade tchr. McCune (Kans.) Middle Sch., 1970-72; 7th grade English tchr. Muskego (Wis.) Norway Sch. Dist., 1972-78; intermediate level. tchr. Gibson Sch. for Gifted Children, Redford, Mich., 1979-82; 3d grade tchr. Cranbrook Edn. Community, Bloomfield Hills, Mich., 1982-89, computer coord., instr., 1989—; ednl. adv. bd. Henry Ford Mus. and Greenfield Village, Dearborn, 1988-91; Renaissance Outreach for Detroit Area Schs; task force Mich. Coun. for the Humanities, Lansing, 1991-92; speaker, presenter on tech. Mich. Sci. Tchr. Assn., Lansing, 1992-96, Mich. Assn. Computer Users in Learning, Ind. Sch. Assn. Ctrl. States; tchr. adv. bd. Teaching and Computer Magazine, 1988-90; developer grades 1-5 curriculum Brookside Sch., Cranbrook, 1995-96. Author: (museum activities) Henry Ford Museum, Greenfield Village, 1991. Space camp fellowship Mary Bramson award Huntsville, Ala., 1992; Detroit Edison Conservation grantee Detroit Edison, 1992, ROADS Mimi grant Mich. Coun. for Humanities, Lansing, 1993. Mem. Assoc. Supervision Curriculum Development, Cranbrook Schs. Faculty Coun. (pres., v.p. 1993-95). Republican. Presbyterian. Home: 32671 Eleven Mile Rd Farmington Hills MI 48336 Office: Cranbrook Schs Brookside 550 Cranbrook Rd # 801 Bloomfield Hills MI 48304-2715

NUSSBAUM, KAREN, federal agency administrator; b. Chgo., Apr. 25, 1950; d. Myron G. and Annette (Brenner) N.; m. Ira Arlook; children: Gene, Jack, Eleanor. BA, Goddard Coll., 1973. Exec. dir. 9 to 5 Nat. Assn. of Working Women, 1973-93; pres. dist. 925 Svc. Employees Internat. Union, 1975-93; dir. Women's Bur. U.S. Dept. Labor, Washington, 1993—. Co-author: Solutions for the New Work Force: Policies for a New Social Contract, 9 to 5: The Working Woman's Guide to Office Survival. Named to

Ohio Women's Hall of Fame, 1984. Office: Dept of Labor Women's Bur 200 Constitution Ave NW Washington DC 20210-0001

NUSSBAUM, MARTHA CRAVEN, philosophy and classics educator; b. N.Y.C., May 6, 1947; d. George and Betty (Warren) Craven; m. Alan Jeffrey Nussbaum, Aug., 1969 (div. 1987); 1 child, Rachel Emily. BA, NYU, 1969; MA, Harvard U., 1971, PhD, 1975; LHD (hon.), Kalamazoo Coll., 1988, Grinnell Coll., 1993. Asst. prof. philosophy and classics Harvard U., Cambridge, 1975-80, assoc. prof., 1980-83; vis. prof. philosophy, Greek and Latin Wellesley (Mass.) Coll., 1983-84; assoc. prof. philosophy and classics Brown U., Providence, R.I., 1984-85, prof. philosophy, classics and comparative lit., 1985-87, David Benedict prof. philosophy, classics and comparative lit., 1987-89, prof., 1989-95; prof. law and ethics U. Chgo., 1995—; rsch. advisor World Inst. Devel. Econs. Rsch., Helsinki, Finland, 1986-93; vis. prof. law U. Chgo., 1994. Author: Aristotle's De Motu Animalium, 1978, The Fragility of Goodness, 1986, Loe's Knowledge, 1990, The Therapy of Desire, 1994, Poetic Justice: The Literary Imagination and Public Life, 1996; editor: Language and Logos, 1983; (with A. Rorty) Essays on Aristotle's De Anima, 1992, (with A. Sen) The Quality of Life, 1993, (with J. Brunschwig) Passions and Perceptions, 1993, (with J. Glover) Women, Culture and Development, 1995. Soc. Fellows Harvard U. jr. fellow, 1972-75, Humanities fellow Princeton U., 1977-78, Guggenheim Found. fellow, 1983, NIH fellow, vis. fellow All Souls Coll., Oxford, Eng., 1986-87; recipient Brandeis Creative Arts award, 1990, Spielvogel-Diamondstein award, 1991; Gifford lectr. U. Edinburgh, 1993. Fellow Am. Acad. Arts and Scis. (membership com. 1991-93, coun. 1992—), Am. Philos. Soc.; mem. Am. Philos. Assn. (exec. com. Ea. divsn. 1985-87, chair com. internat. coop., ex-officio mem. nat. bd. 1989-92, chair com. on status of women 1994—), Am. Philol. Assn., PEN. Office: U Chicago The Law Sch 1111 E 60th St Chicago IL 60637

NUSZ, PHYLLIS JANE, fundraising consultant, meeting planner; b. Lodi, Calif., Dec. 16, 1941; d. Fred Henry and Esther Emma (Enzminger) N. BA, U. Pacific, 1963, MA, 1965; EdD, Nova Southwestern U., 1987. Cert. fund raising exec. Prof. speech comm. Bakersfield (Calif.) Coll., 1965-86; from asst. dir. student activites to found. exec. dir. Bakersfield (Calif) Coll., 1965-86; mgmt. seminar dir. Delta Kappa Gamma Soc. Internat., Austin, Tex., 1983-86; loaned exec. United Way San Joaquin County, Stockton, Calif., 1990; fund raising cons. PJ Enterprises, Lodi, Calif., 1987—. Bd. dirs. U. Calif. Sch. Medicine Surg. Found., San Francisco, 1989—; mem. Heritage Circle and Chancellor's Assn., U. Calif. San Francisco, 1987—. Recipient archives award of merit Evang. Luth. Ch. in Am., 1988; fellow Calif. Luth. U., 1985—. Mem. Nat. Soc. Fund Raising Execs. (chmn. mentor program Calif. Capital chpt. 1991, bd. dirs. 1988-91, chmn. acad. fund raising 1991, chmn. mentor program Golden Gate chpt. 1991, founding, pres. San Joaquin chpt. 1992-93, Pres.'s award for Meritorious Svc., Golden Gate chpt. 1991), U. Pacific Alumni Assn. (bd. dirs. 1974-82), Calif. Tchrs. Assn., Nat. Assn. Parliamentarians, Rotary (North Stockton bd. dirs. 1993—, treas. 1994-96, found. treas. 1994-96, pres.-elect 1996-97), Delta Kappa Gamma (internat. scholar 1986). Republican. Lutheran. Office: PJ Enterprises 1300 W Lodi Ave Ste A11 Lodi CA 95242-3000

NUTT, LINDA MARSDEN, administrator, consultant; b. Detroit, Oct. 4, 1952; d. Francis H. and Rita J. (Phillips) Marsden; m. Craig L. Nutt. BS in Spl. Edn., U. Ala., 1977, MA in Spl. Edn., 1978, PhD in Social Work, 1996. Tchr. Hale County Bd. Edn., Greensboro, Ala., 1977-84; adminstr. Ala. Dept. Mental Health/Mental Retardation, Tuscaloosa, Ala., 1984-89; tchr. secondary sch. Hale County Bd. Edn., 1987-89; transition specialist U. Ga. SPE Dept., Athens, 1989-90; rsch. asst. U. Ala., Tuscaloosa, 1990-92; adminstr., project dir. Futures Unlimited, CSP of West Ala., Inc., Tuscaloosa, 1992-96; cons. LMN Enterprises, Inc., Northport, Ala., 1995—; staff trainer transition Ala. Dept. Mental Health, 1994; presenter in field. Author: (with others) Developmental Disabilities: A Handbook for Best Practices, 1992, Mental Retardation and Developmental Disabilities, 1995. Rsch. grantee U. Ala., 1991. Mem. Am. Assn. Mental Retardation, Coun. Exceptional Children. Office: LMN Enterprises Inc PO Box 1451 Northport AL 35476-6451

NUTTER, ZOE DELL LANTIS, retired public relations executive; b. Yamhill, Oreg., June 14, 1915; d. Arthur Lee Lantis and Olive Adelaide (Reed) Lantis-Hilton; m. Richard S. West, Apr. 30, 1941 (div. Nov. 1964); m. Ervin John Nutter, Dec. 30, 1965. Assoc. in Bus., Santa Ana Jr. Coll., 1944. Cert. gen. secondary sch. tchr., Calif.; FAA cert. lic. commercial, instrument, single/multi engine land airplanes pilot. Promoter World's Fair & Comml. Airlines Golden Gate Internat. Expn., San Francisco, 1937-39; pirate theme girl, official hostess Treasure Island's World Fair, San Francisco, 1939-40; prin. dancer San Francisco Ballet, 1937-41; artist, 1941-45; program dir. Glenn County High Sch., Willows, Calif., 1952-58; pub. rels. Monarch Piper Aviation Co., Monterey, Calif., 1963-65; pilot, pub. rels. Elano Corp., Xenia, Ohio, 1968-85; bd. dirs. Nat. Aviation Hall of Fame, Dayton, Ohio, pres., chmn., 1989-92, bd. trustees, 1976—, chmn. bd. nominations, 1992—; bd. trustees Ford's Theatre, Washington, Treasure Island Mus., San Francisco; charter mem. Friends of First Ladies, Smithsonian, Washington, 1990-93. Assoc. editor KYH mag. of Shikar Safari Internat., 1985-87; contbg. columnist Scripps Howard San Francisco News, 1938. Bd. dirs. Cin. May Festival, 1976-80; cen. com. Glenn County Rep. Party, Willows, 1960-64; state cen. com. Rep. Party, 1962-64; adv. bd. Women's Air & Space Mus., Dayton, 1987-94. Warrant officer, Civil Air Patrol, 1967-69. Recipient Civic Contbn. Honor award Big Brothers/Big Sisters, 1991, John Collier Nat. award Camp Fire Girls & Boys, 1988, Tambourine award Salvation Army, 1982, State of Ohio Gov.'s award for Volunteerism, 1992; named Most Photographed Girl in World, News Burs. & Clipping Svcs., 1938-39. Fellow Pres.'s Club U. Ky., Ohio State U., Wright State U.; mem. 99's Internat. Women Pilots Orgn. (life, hospitality chmn. 1968), Monterey Bay Chapter 99's (mem. chmn. 1964-65), Walnut Grove Country Club, Lost Tree Country Club, Windstar County Club (Naples, Fla.), Rotary (Paul Harris fellow 1987), Old Port Yacht Club, Shikar Safari Internat. (host com. 1976), Country Club of the North. Home: 986 Trebein Rd Xenia OH 45385-9534

NWEKE, WINIFRED CHINWENDU, education educator; b. Ogbunike, Anambra, Nigeria, Dec. 8, 1947; came to U.S., 1980; d. Gabriel Abanobi and Grace Nonyem (Ezeani) Ejeckam; m. Ernest Ekeneme Nweke, Oct. 25, 1980; children: Jennifer, Jeffrey, Nkiruka, Chukwuma. BSc in Edn., U. Nigeria, 1974; MA, U. Ottawa, Ont., Can., 1977; PhD, U. Ottawa, 1980; MBA, Ea. Mich. U., 1984. Tchr. high sch. Govt. Coll., Ikorodu, Lagos, Nigeria, 1974-75; fed. edn. officer Women Tchrs' Coll., Aba, Nigeria, 1975-76; lectr. II U. Benin, Benin City, Nigeria, 1980; postdoctoral fellow U. Mich., Ann Arbor, 1984-85; asst. prof. Tuskegee (Ala.) U., 1987-89, assoc. prof., 1989—. Author chpt. to book; contbr. articles to profl. jours. Tech. adv. bd. State of Ala. Dept. Edn., Montgomery, 1991—; measurement and evaluation specialist Al Consortium for Minority Tchr. Edn., Tuskegee, Ala., 1989-94; fund raiser Girl Scouts Am., Auburn, 1992-93. Faculty fellow U. Ottawa, 1978-79; Dept. Def. Dep. Schs. grantee, 1990-92. Mem. Am. ednl. Rsch. Assn., nat. Coun. Measurement in edn., Midsouth edn. Rsch. Assn. (membership com. 1990, program com. 1995), Phi Delta Kappa. Episcopalian. Office: Tuskegee U 306 Thrasher Hall Tuskegee AL 36088

NYBERG, PAMELA JEAN, product development engineer; b. Anderson, Ind., Oct. 3, 1968; d. William Alan and Carol Marie Nyberg. BA in Math., DePauw U., 1990; postgrad., Stanford U., 1992-93; MS in Indsl. Engring., U. Mich., 1994. Biomed. engr. intern Meth. Hosp., Indpls., 1988; systems cons. intern Eli Lilly, Indpls., 1989; systems cons. Anderson Consulting, Indpls., 1990-92; product design engr. Whirlpool Corp., Benton Harbor, Mich., 1994-95. Inventor children's puzzle board, others. Vol. Cmty. Assn. Retarded, Palo Alto, Calif., 1994, Juvenile Diabetes Found., Greencastle, Ind., 1986-90. Nat. Inst. Orgnl. Safety & Health fellow, 1994; Rector scholar DePauw U., 1986-90, Hoosier scholar, 1986. Mem. AAUW, (assoc.) Human Factors and Ergonomics Soc. Republican. Office: Whirlpool Rsch & Engring 750 Monte Rd Maildrop 5210 Benton Harbor MI 49022

NYCUM, SUSAN HUBBELL, lawyer. B.A., Ohio Wesleyan U., 1956; J.D., Duquesne U., 1960; postgrad., Stanford U. Bar: Pa. 1962, U.S. Supreme Ct. 1967, Calif. 1974. Sole practice law Pitts., 1962-65; designer, adminstr. legal research system U. Pitts., Aspen Systems Corp., Pitts., 1965-68; mgr. ops. Computer Ctr., Carnegie Mellon U., Pitts., 1968-69; dir. computer facility Computer Ctr., Stanford U., Calif., 1969-72, Stanford Law and Computer fellow, 1972-73; cons. in computers and law, 1973-74; sr. assoc. MacLeod, Fuller, Muir & Godwin, Los Altos, Los Angeles and London, 1974-75; ptnr. Chickering & Gregory, San Francisco, 1975-80; ptnr.-in-charge high tech. group Gaston Snow & Ely Bartlett, Boston, NYC, Phoenix, San Francisco, Calif., 1980-86; mng. ptnr. Palo Alto office Kadison, Pfaelzer, Woodard, Quinn & Rossi, Los Angeles, Washington, Newport Beach, Palo Alto, Calif., 1986-87; sr. ptnr. Baker & McKenzie, Palo Alto, 1987—; trustee EDUCOM, 1978-81; mem. adv. com. for high tech. Ariz. State U. Law Sch., Santa Clara U. Law Sch., Stanford Law Sch., U. So. Calif. Law Ctr., law sch. Harvard U., U. Calif.; U.S. State Dept. del. OECD Conf. on Nat. Vulnerabilities, Spain, 1981; invited speaker Telecom, Geneva, 1983; lectr. N.Y. Law Jour., 1975—, Law & Bus., 1975—, Practicing Law Inst., 1975—; chmn. Office of Tech. Assessment Task Force on Nat. Info. Systems, 1979-80. Author:(with Bigelow) Your Computer and the Law, 1975, (with Bosworth) Legal Protection for Software, 1985, (with Collins and Gilbert) Women Leading, 1987; contbr. monographs, articles to profl. publs. Mem. Town of Portola Valley Open Space Acquisition Com., Calif., 1977; mem. Jr. League of Palo Alto, chmn. evening div., 1975-76. NSF and Dept. Justice grantee for studies on computer abuse, 1972—. Mem. ABA (sect. on sci. and tech. chmn. 1979-80, chmn. elect 1978-79), Internat. Bar Assn. (U.S. mem. computer com. of corps. sect.), Assn. Computing Machinery (mem. at large of council 1976-80, nat. lectr. 1977—, chmn. standing com. on legal issues 1975—, blue ribbon com. on rationalization of internat. proprietary rights protection on info. processing devel. in the '90s, 1990—), Computer Law Assn. (v.p. 1983-85, pres. 1986—, bd. dirs. 1975—), Calif. State Bar Assn. (founder first chmn. econs. of law sect., vice chmn. law and computers com.), Nat. Conf. Lawyers and Scientists (rep. ABA), Strategic Forum on Intellectual Property Issues in Software of NAS. Home: 35 Granada Ct Portola Valley CA 94028 Office: Baker & McKenzie PO Box 60309 Palo Alto CA 94306

NYE, MIRIAM MAURINE BAKER, writer; b. Castana, Iowa, June 14, 1918; d. Horace Boies and Hazel Dean (Waples) Hawthorn; B.A., Morningside Coll., 1939, postgrad., 1957-58; postgrad. U. Ariz., 1973, U. S.D., 1975-77, New Coll., U. Edinburgh (Scotland), 1974; m. Carl E. Baker, June 21, 1941 (dec. 1970); children: Kent Alfred, Dale Hawthorn; m. 2d, John Arthur Nye, Dec. 25, 1973 (dec. 1991). Tchr. jr. h.s., Rock Falls, Ill., 1939-41, Moville (Iowa) Cmty. Sch., 1957-62, Woodbury Central Cmty. Sch., Climbing Hill, Iowa, 1962-64; homemaking columnist Sioux City (Iowa) Jour.'s Farm Weekly, 1953-81; author: Recipes and Ideas From the Kitchen Window, 1973; But I Never Thought He'd Die: Practical Help for Widows, 1978; contbg. author Between the Rivers: A History of the United Methodist Ch. in Iowa, 1986; speaker, Iowa, Nebr., Minn., S.D. Counselor, Iowa State U., 1972—; county adv. Iowa Children's and Family Svcs., 1980-84; mem. pub. rels. com. Farm Bur., Woodbury County, 1980-82; advisor nat. orgn. for help to widows THEOS, Sioux City chpt., 1981-90; lay del. Iowa United Meth. Conf., 1981-83; mem. Archives History Commission of Iowa Methodist Ch., 1991—. Recipient Alumni award Morningside Coll., 1969, Svc. award Woodbury County Fair, 1969, Friend of Extension award Iowa State U., 1981. Mem. AAUW, Iowa Fedn. Women's Clubs (dist. creative writing chmn. 1978-80), Alpha Kappa Delta, Sigma Tau Delta. Methodist. Home and Office: PO Box 419 Moville IA 51039-0419

NYKIEL, KAREN ANN, retirement facility administrator, religious studies instructor; b. Chgo., July 27, 1945; d. John Marion and Dorothy Ann (Lasko) N. BA, Coll. St. Benedict, St. Joseph, Minn., 1969; MSNS, Seattle U., 1975; MA, Mundelein Coll., Chgo., 1989. Tchr. science Benet Acad., Lisle, Ill., 1969-73; adult edn. coord. St. Joan of Arc Ch., Lisle, 1973-77; adj. faculty chemistry Coll. DuPage, Glen Ellyn, Ill., 1975-92; campus min. Diocese of Joliet, Ill., 1982-92; adminstr. Queen of Peace Ctr., Lisle, 1992—; cons. Nat. Fusion Co., Plainfield, Ill., 1980-82; mem. Benedictine Sisters Sacred Heart, Lisle, 1965—, bd. dirs., 1980-92; state coord. Pax Christi Ill., 1994—; pres. Queen of Peace Ctr., Inc., Lisle, 1992—; adj. faculty religious studies Coll. DuPage, Benedictine U., Coll. St. Francis. Mem. C. of C., Lisle, 1992—. Grantee NSF, 1971, 72, 73, 74. Mem. Am. Chemical Soc., Assn. Sr. Svc. Providers, Rotary Internat. (Lisle chpt. chair internat. com.). Democrat. Roman Catholic. Home: 1910 Maple Ave Lisle IL 60532-2184 Office: Queen of Peace Retirement Ctr 1910 Maple Ave Lisle IL 60532-2184

NYLANDER, JANE LOUISE, museum director; b. Cleve., Jan. 27, 1938; d. James Merritt and Jeannette (Crosby) Cayford; m. Daniel Harris Giffen, Nov. 30, 1963 (div. 1970); children: Sarah Louise, Thomas Harris; m. Richard Conrad Nylander, July 8, 1972: 1 child, Timothy Frost. AB, Brown U., 1959; MA, U. Del., 1961; postgrad., Attingham (Eng.) Summer Sch., 1970; PhD (hon.), New England Coll., 1994. Curator Hist. Soc. York (Pa.) County, 1961-62, N.H. Hist. Soc., Concord, 1962-69; instr. New England Coll., Henniker, N.H., 1964-65, Monadnock Community Coll., Peterborough, N.H., 1966-69; curator of textiles and ceramics Old Sturbridge (Mass.) Village, 1969-85; adj. assoc. prof. Boston U., 1978-85; sr. curator Old Sturbridge Vill., 1985-86; dir. Strawbery Banke Mus., Portsmouth, N.H., 1986-92, Soc. Preservation New England Antiquities, Boston, 1992-93; pres. Soc. for Preservation of New Eng. Antiquities, 1993—; adj. asst. prof. U. N.H., Durham, 1987-92; adj. prof. art history and Am. studies Boston U., 1993—; trustee Worcester (Mass.) Hist. Mus., 1978-84, Hist. Deerfield (Mass.), Inc., 1981-94, Hist. Mass. Inc., 1991-93, Decorative Arts Trust, 1991—, Portsmouth Athenaeum, 1988-90, Japan Soc. N.H., 1988-92; mem. adv. bd. Concord (Mass.) Mus., 1986-94, Wentworth-Coolidge Commn., 1991-96, John Nicholas Brown Ctr. for Am. Studies, Providence, 1995—; mem. adv. bd. dept. Am. decorative arts Mus. Fine Arts, Boston, 1971—; mem. coun. Colonial Soc. Mass., 1993—; cons. in field. Author: Fabrics for Historic Buildings, 4th edit., 1990, Our Own Snug Fireside: Images of the New England Home 1760-1860, 1993, paperback edit., 1994; mem. editorial bd. Hist. New Hampshire; 1993—, The Dublin Seminar, 1984—; contbr. numerous articles to profl. jours. Mem. adv. bd. New Eng. Heritage Ctr., 1993—; active State House Adv. Com., Boston, 1984-85, Gov.'s Coun. for Wentworth Coolidge Mansion, Concord, 1964-66; mem. Com. for Preservation of N.H. State Flags, 1989-92; mem. H.F. duPont award com. Winterthur Mus., 1993—, Mt. Vernon adv. com. for 1999, 1996—, collections com. N.J. Hist. Soc., 1996—. Recipient Charles F. Montgomery Prize Decorative Arts Soc., 1985, (with Richard C. Nylander) The Anne and Roger Webb award Historic Massachusetts, Inc., 1996. Mem. Am. Antiquarian Soc., Am. Assn. for State and Local History, Nat. Trust Hist. Preservation, Royal Oak Assn., Portsmouth Athenaeum, New Eng. Mus. Assn., Trustees of Reservations, Soc. Winterthur Fellows, Hist. Mass., Soc. Preservation of N.H. Forests, N.H. Audubon Soc., N.H. Humanities Coun., New Eng. Hist. Genealogical Soc., Hist. Houses Trust NSW, Costume Soc. Am. (bd. dirs. 1977-83), Dublin Seminar, Nat. Soc. Colonial Dames in N.H. (bd. dirs. 1967-73), Colonial Soc. of Mass., The Garden Conservancy, N.H. Hist. Soc., Friends of Hist. Deerfield, Nat. Soc. Colonial Dames in Mass. (courtesy), Brown Club N.H. (trustee 1988-93). Episcopalian. Home: 17 Franklin St Portsmouth NH 03801-4501 Office: Soc Preservation New England Antiquities 141 Cambridge St Boston MA 02114-2702

NYMAN, GEORGIANNA BEATRICE, painter; b. Arlington, Mass., June 11, 1930; d. Daniel Eugene Nyman and Irene Krans (Müller) Lombardi; m. David Aronson, June 10, 1956; children: Judith, Benjamin, Abigail. Diploma, Boston Mus. Sch. Art., 1952, student, 1952-54; postgrad., Longy Sch. Music, Cambridge, Mass., 1965-73. Portraits displayed in Brookline (Mass.) Hosp., Inst. Critical Care Medicine, U. Pitts., McClosky Inst. Voice Therapy, Boston, U.S. Supreme Ct., Washington, New Eng. Sch. of Law, Boston, 1991, Milton (Mass.) Acad., Boston Acad. Music; group exhbns. include Shore Studio Gallery, Boston, 1960,61, Lee Nordness Gallery, N.Y.C., 1963, Copley Soc., Boston, 1980, Nat. Acad. Design, N.Y.C., 1990; solo exhbns. include Nancy Lincoln Gallery, Brookline, 1990; represented in permanent collections Rose Art Mus., Brandeis U., U. Pitts. Sch. Medicine; commd. portraits include Justice Sandra Day O'Connor, Mr. and Mrs. Pieh--headmaster Milton Acad., 1992, Justice Harry A. Blackmun, 1993, Julie Harris Am. actress, 1994, Hon. James R. Lawton, 1994, Richard Conrad, opera singer, dir. Boston Acad. Music, 1994, Justice Clarence Thomas, 1995, David Leisner, 1995. Jurist Art and Mental Illness--An Itinerary Boston U., 1989; active in LeMoyne Found., Fla., 1989. Recipient Boit prize, 1951, cert. of merit NAD, 1992; Kate Morse fellow Boston Mus. Fine Arts, 1953. Mem. Women's Indsl. Inst. (life), Mass. Soc. Mayflower Descendants. Home and Studio: 137 Brimstone Ln Sudbury MA 01776-3203 also: RR 2, Cornwall, PE Canada C0A 1H0

NYQUIST, KATHLEEN A., publishing executive; b. Biloxi, Miss., May 14, 1955; d. Clarence and Marianne M. (Mahoney) Boehm; m. John D. Nyquist, Nov. 5, 1983; children: Lindsay, Eric. BS in Edn., Miami U., Oxford, Ohio, 1977. High sch. biology tchr. Ill., 1978-79; home tutor Fed. Homebound Program, Ill., 1980; from sci. editor to editorial v.p. Scott Foresman & Co., Glenview, Ill., 1981-89, creative dir., 1990, pub., 1992, pres., 1993-95; author, ednl. cons., 1996—. Parent rev. com. mem. Sch. Dist. 96, Buffalo Grove, Ill., 1991-92. Mem. ASCD, Nat. Coun. Tchrs. Math., Nat. Sci. Tchrs. Assn., Chgo. Book Clinic.

NYSETH, ELIZABETH ANN, middle school educator; b. St. Paul, Nov. 4, 1948; d. Herbert John and Dagna Mabel (Eimon) Borgert; m. Gary Lynn Nyseth, Dec. 7, 1988; children: Robert, Catherine, Mark; stepchildren: Jeff, Amy, Pete, Christopher. BS in Home Econs. Edn., U. Wis.-Stout, Menomonie, 1970, MS in Clothing, Textiles and Related Art, 1984. Cert. home econs. tchr., Wis. Tchr. Chippewa Falls (Wis.) Schs., 1970—, student tchr. supr. with U. Wis.-Stout, 1973—, curriculum asst. for family/consumer edn., bus. and mktg., 1990—; advisor Future Hmemakers of Am., 1972—; mem. curriculum devel. pilot project Wis. Dept. Pub. Instrn., Madison, 1983-91, workshop facilitator, 1985-91; curriculum cons., 1989-91. Contbg. mem. Wis. Middle School Curriculum Guide for Family and Consumer Education, 1983-91. Recipient Cert. of Appreciation Wis. Dept. Pub. Instrn., 1991, U. Wis.-Stout, 1992, 93. Mem. ASCD, N.W. Wis. Edn. Assn., Wis. Home Economist in Elem. and Secondary Edn., Chippewa Falls Fedn. Tchrs. (v.p. 1993—, bldg. steward). Methodist. Home: N7890 555th St Menomonie WI 54751 Office: Chippewa Falls Mid Sch 750 Tropicana Blvd Chippewa Falls WI 54729-2010

OAK, CLAIRE MORISSET, artist, educator; b. St. Georges, Quebec, Can., May 31, 1921; came to U.S., 1945; d. Louis and Bernadette (Coulombe) Morisset; m. Alan Ben Oak, July 2, 1947. Student, Ecole des Beaux Arts, 1938-42, Parsons Sch. Design, N.Y.C., 1945, Art Students League, N.Y.C., 1945-46. Staff artist Henry Morgan & R. Simpson, Montreal, 1942-45; artist illustrator W.B. Golovin Advt. Agy., N.Y.C., 1947-49; freelance illustrator Arnold Constable & Advt. Agy., N.Y.C., 1948-50, Le Jardin des Modes, Paris, 1950-51, May & Co., L.A., 1956, Katten & Marengo Advt., Stockton, Calif., 1962-84; pvt. practice illustrator, designer San Joaquin Valley, Calif., 1984-92; art instr. San Joaquin Delta Coll., Stockton, 1973—; owner Fashion Illustrator's Workshop, N.Y.C., 1953-54; instr. Bauder Coll., Sacramento, 1975-76; painting workshop leader Lodi Art Ctr., 1991—; watercolor workshop leader D'Pharr Painting Adventures, Virginia City, Nev., 1992; ongoing watercolor workshop Galerie Iona, Stockton, Calif., 1993—. Named S.B. Anthony Woman of Achievement in the Arts, U. Pacific, 1982. Mem. Stockton Art League, Lodi Art Ctr., Ctrl. Calif. Art League, The League of Carmichael Artists, Delta Watercolor Soc. (bd. mem. 1988—). Home: 2140 Waudman Ave Stockton CA 95209-1755

OAKBRAE, CHRISTINE CATE, elementary education educator; b. Washington, Oct. 31, 1939; d. Phillip Harding and Catharine Gartland (Watson) Cate; m. E.L. Tucker Jr., June 10, 1966 (div. Oct. 1987); children: Thomas Matthew, Jeffrey Michael. AB in Edn., George Washington U., Washington D.C., 1962. Cert. tchr. Va., Calif. Tchr. Francis Hammond H.S., Alexandria, Va., 1962-64, DOD Dependent's Sch., Bermuda, 1964-66, Alisal H.S., Salinas, Calif., 1978, Alisal Elem. Sch. Dist., Salinas, 1978—; rep. Alisal Tchrs. Assn., Salinas, 1980-91. Mem. bd. dirs. NOW, Calif., 1978-80; treas. Lesbian Alliance of Monterey Peninsula, Calif., 1990-94. Mem. NEA, Calif. Edn. Assn., Alisal Tchrs. Assn. Democrat. Home: 619 St Augustine Dr Salinas CA 93905

OAKES, ELLEN RUTH, psychotherapist, health institute administrator; b. Bartlesville, Okla., Aug. 19, 1919; d. John Isaac and Eva Ruth (Engle) Harboldt; m. Paul Otis Oakes Sr., June 12, 1937 (div. April 1974); children: Paul Otis Jr., Deborah Ellen, Nancy Elaine Masters; m. Siegmar Johann Knopp, Nov. 24, 1975. BA in Sociology, Psychology summa cum laude, Oklahoma City U., 1961; MS in Clin. Psychology, U. Okla., 1963, PhD, 1967. Lic. clin. psychologist, Okla. Chief psychometrist Okla. U. Guidance Ctr., Norman, 1962; psychology trainee VA Hosp., Oklahoma City, 1962-64, Cerebral Palsy Ctr., Norman, Okla., 1964-65; psychology intern Guidance Service, Norman, 1965-66, staff psychologist, 1966-67; asst. prof. psychology Okla. U. Med. Sch., Oklahoma City, 1967-70; supr. psychology interns Okla. Univ. Health Scis. Ctr., 1967-80; founder, dir. Timberridge Inst., Oklahoma City, 1970-90, pres., 1980-90; pvt. practice clin. psychologist Oklahoma City, 1970-92; instr. Okla. U. extension course, Tinker AFB, Oklahoma City, 1963, U. Okla., 1965-66; discussion leader Inst. for Tchrs. of Disadvantaged Child Oklahoma City Sch. System, 1966; leader group therapy sessions Asbury Meth. and Westminster Presbyn. Chs., Oklahoma City, 1966; mem. psychology team confs. for hearing disorders, Okla. U. Med. Sch., 1967-70; cons. Oklahoma City Pub. Schs., 1970-72; cons., group leader halfway house, 1972; lectr. chs., PTAs, hosps.; reviewer Am. Psychol. Assn. Civilian Health and Med. Program of the Uniformed Svcs., 1978-89. Workshop conductor on Shame & Sexuality, Zurick Jungian Inst. winter seminar, 1992; attended Européen Congrès de Gestalt Thérapie in Paris, 1992; contbr. articles to profl. jours. Speaker Okla. County Mental Health Assn. Annual Worry Clinic, St. Luke's Ch., Oklahoma City, 1968-92, psychology dept. Sorosis Club, St. Luke's Ch.. Mem. Am. Psychol. Assn. (pres. rev. project with CHAMPUS, 1978-89), Okla. Psychol. Assn. (pres. 1975-76). Address: 18 Basore Dr Bella Vista AR 72714-5544

OAKES, MARIA SPACHNER, nurse; b. Cinn., Mar. 27, 1947; d. A. William and Roberta Mae (Linville) Stephens; m. John Cullwell Oakes, Nov. 27, 1976; children: John Cullwell II, Laura Suzann. Diploma Sch. Nursing, King's Daughters' Hosp., 1968. Cert. med./surg. nurse. Staff nurse Ohio State U. Hosp., Columbus, Lawrence County, Ironton; head nurse, neonatal intensive care King's Daughters' Med. Ctr., Ashland, Ky., staff nurse; staff nurse neonatal IC, Huntington Hosp. Behavioral Medicine. Bd. dirs. Am. Cancer Soc.; deacon bd. sessions, pres. Women's Assn. First Presbyn. Ch.; v.p. West Ironton Parent-Tchr. Group; pres. Kingsbury Parents for Better Schs.; past pres. Kings Daus. Hosp. Sch. Nursing Alumni Assn.; mem. strategic planning com. Ironton City Sch. Dist., Acad. Boosers Assn., H.S. Band Boosters mem., band nurse. Mem. ANA, Ky. Nurses Assn. (state offices nursing practice comm., legis. com., state nominating com., nurse practice commn., past pres., v.p., treas. Dist. 4, former v.p., program chmn., seminar planner, continuing edn. coord., current v.p. Dist. 4, mem. ad hoc com. health care reform). Home: 2210 N 3rd Ave Ironton OH 45638-1068

OAKLEY, CAROLYN LE, state legislator, small business owner; b. Portland, Oreg., June 28, 1942; d. George Thomas and Ruth Alveta Victoria (Engberg) Penketh; m. Donald Keith Oakley, June 27, 1965; children: Christine, Michelle. BS in Edn., Oreg. State U., 1965. Educator Linn County (Oreg.) Schs., 1965-76; owner Linn County Tractor, 1965-90; mem. Oreg. Legis. Assembly, Salem, 1989—, asst. majority leader, 1993—, majority whip, 1994; mem. exec. bd. Oreg. Retail Coun., 1987-90. Chmn. Linn County Rep. Ctrl. Com., 1982-84; chmn. bd. dirs. North Albany Svc. Dist., 1988-90; chair Salvation Army, Linn and Benton Counties, 1987—; vice chmn. bd. trustees Linn-Benton C.C. Found., 1987—; pres. Women for Agr., Linn and Benton Counties, 1984-86; mem. STRIDE Leadership Round Table, 1991—; state chair Am. Legis. Exch. Coun., 1991-96; nat. bd. dirs., exec. com., nat. sec.; mem. Edn. Commn. of the States, 1991—, com. policies and priorities, 1993—; mem. Leadership Coun. on State Rules in Higher Edn., 1995—; mem. nat. policy bd. Danforth Found., 1995—; state dir., Women in Govt., 1996; state dir., Nat. Order Women Legislators, 1993—; hon. mem. Linn-Benton Compact Bd., 1993—; active Linn County Criminal Justice Coun., 1994—. Named Woman of Yr. Albany chpt. Beta Sigma Phi, 1970. Mem. Nat Conf. State Legislators (chmn. edn. com. 1992—), Albany C. of C. (bd. dirs. 1986-93), Linn County Rep. women (legis. chmn. 1982-91). Republican. Methodist. Home: 3197 NW Crest Loop Albany OR 97321-9627 Office: Oreg Legis Assembly State Capital Salem OR 97310

OAKLEY, DEBORAH JANE, researcher, educator; b. Detroit, Jan. 31, 1937; d. George F. and Kathryn (Willson) Hacker; m. Bruce Oakley, June 16, 1958; children: Ingrid Andrea, Brian Benjamin. BA, Swarthmore Coll., 1958; MA, Brown U., 1960; MPH, U. Mich., 1969, PhD, 1977. Dir. teenage and adult programs YWCA, Providence, 1959-63; editorial asst. Stockholm U., 1963-64; rsch. investigator, lectr. dept. population planning U. Mich., 1971-77; asst. prof. community health programs U. Mich., Ann Arbor, 1977-79, asst. prof. nursing rsch., 1979-81, assoc. prof., 1981-89, prof., 1989—, interim dir. Ctr. Nursing Rsch., 1988-90; prin. investigator NIH-funded Rsch. grants on family planning and women's health, mem. nat. adv. com. nursing rsch., 1993—; co-chair Mich. Initiative for Women's Health, 1993—. Author: (with Leslie Corsa) Population Planning, 1979; contbr. articles to profl. jours. Bd. dirs. Planned Parenthood Fedn. Am., 1975-80. Recipient Margaret Sanger award Washtenaw County Planned Parenthood, 1975; Outstanding Young Woman of Ann Arbor award by Jaycees, 1970, Dist. Faculty award, Mich. Assn. Gov. Bds., 1992. Mem. Am. Pub. Health Assn. (chmn. population sect. council), Internat. Union Sci. Study Population, Midwest Nursing Rsch. Soc., Population Assn. Am., Nat. Family Planning and Reproductive Health Assn. (nat. comms.), Delta Omega, Sigma Theta Tau (hon.). Democrat. Home: 5200 S Lake Dr Chelsea MI 48118-9481 Office: U Mich Sch Nursing Ann Arbor MI 48109-0482

OAKLEY, LUCY ALICE, art historian; b. L.A., Aug. 19, 1951; d. John Peirce and Mary Virginia (Whitaker) O.; m. Joshua Louis Perl, Dec. 29, 1979; 1 child, Samuel John. BA, U. Calif., Berkeley, 1973; MA, Columbia U., 1977, M in Philosophy, 1980, PhD, 1995. Rsch. asst. Met. Mus. of Art, N.Y.C., 1975-86, rsch. assoc., 1986-87; lectr. Mus. of Modern Art, N.Y.C., 1977-78; guest curator Wallach Art Gallery Columbia U., N.Y.C., 1987-95, Rare Book and Manuscript Collection Columbia U., N.Y.C., 1994; adj. lectr. Hunter Coll., CUNY, 1994-95; mem. chancellors' adv. com. on art mus. U. Calif., Berkeley, 1972-73. Author: (books) Pierre Auguste Renoir, 1980, Edouard Vuillard, 1981, Unfaded Pageant: Edwin Austin Abbey's Shakespearean Subjects, 1994; also many articles, revs. and catalog entries. A.S. Johnston scholar U. Calif., Berkeley, 1972-73, P.A. Hearst scholar, 1973; Pres.'s fellow Columbia U., 1974-77, Wallach Art Gallery fellow, 1987-89. Mem. Coll. Art Assn., Am. Assn. Mus., Historians of Brit. Art, Historians of Am. Art, Assn. of Historians of 19th-Century Art. Home: 560 Riverside Dr Apt 15P New York NY 10027

OAKLEY, MARY ANN BRYANT, lawyer; b. Buckhannon, W.Va., June 22, 1940; d. Hubert Herndon and Mary F. (Deeds) Bryant; m. Godfrey P. Oakley, Jr., Sept. 2, 1961; children: Martha, Susan, Robert. AB, Duke U., 1962; MA, Emory U., 1970, JD, 1974. Tchr., Winston-Salem/Forsyth County Schs., N.C., 1961-65; assoc. Margie Pitts Hames, Atlanta, 1974-80; ptnr. Stagg Hoy & Oakley, Atlanta, 1980-83, Oakley & Bonner, Atlanta, 1984-90; pvt. practice, 1990-96; ptnr. Holland & Knight, Atlanta, 1996—; adj. prof. trial practice Ga. State U., 1986-95; adj. prof. pretrial practice Emory U. Law Sch., 1991, 95—; bd. dirs. Nat. Employment Lawyers Assn., 1989-94; founding coodr. NELA, Ga.; mem. Ga. Supreme Ct. Commn. on Racial and Ethnic Bias. Contbr. articles to law jours. Notes and Comments editor Emory Law Jour., 1973-74. Author: Elizabeth Cady Stanton, 1972; Bd. dirs. Atlanta Met. YWCA, 1975-79, lst v.p., 1978-79; mem. Leadership Atlanta, 1979; bd. dirs. Ga. chpt. ACLU, 1981-83; trustee Unitarian Universalist Congregation Atlanta, 1977-80, pres., 1979-80, mem. Unitarian Universalist Commn. Appraisal, 1980-85; bd. dirs. Unitarian Universalist Service Com., 1984-90, v.p., 1986-88, pres. 1988-90. Nat. Merit scholar, 1958. Mem. ABA, Am. Judicature Soc., State Bar Ga. (chmn. individual rights sect. 1979-81), Atlanta Bar Assn., Lawyers Club Atlanta, No. Dist. Bar Council, 1982-86, Ga. Assn. Women Lawyers, Ga. State Bar Disciplinary Bd. (investigative panel 1985-88, chmn., 1987-88), Bleckley Inn of Ct. (pres. 1996—), Gate City Bar Assn., Ga. Legal Svcs. Program Bd., LWV, Phi Beta Kappa, Order of Coif. Home: 2224 Kodiak Dr NE Atlanta GA 30345-4152 Office: 1201 W Peachtree St 1 Atlantic Ctr Ste 2000 Atlanta GA 30309-3400

OAKS, DONNA RAE, medical laboratory technician; b. Johnstown, Pa., Jan. 12, 1944; d. Carl Clark and Helene Marie (Schnurr) Haigh; m. John Samuel Oaks, May 22, 1971; children: Jennife Marie, Rebecca Catherine. BS magna cum laude, U. Pitts., 1967, MEd, 1968. Cert. med. lab. technician. Social svc. dir. Lee Hosp., Johnstown, Pa., 1969-73; phlebotomist Conemaugh Valley Meml. Hosp., Johnstown, Pa., 1982-83; med. lab. technician Good Samaritan Med. Ctr., 1983—. Minority inspector Cambria County Bd. Elections, 1984, majority inspector, 1993, judge of elections, 1994. Mem. Phi Beta Kappa. Democrat. Lutheran. Home: 109 DuPont St Johnstown PA 15902-2324 Office: Good Samaritan Med Ctr 1020 Franklin St Johnstown PA 15905

OAKS, LAURA MARY, anthropology educator; b. Pontiac, Mich., Dec. 31, 1967; d. David E. Oaks and Mary Kay (Lanktree) Sheldon; m. J. Douglas English, Dec. 30, 1993. BA in Anthropology summa cum laude, U. Ill., 1990; MA in Anthropology, Johns Hopkins U., 1994, postgrad. Copy editor Japan Orgn. Cooperation Family Planning, Tokyo, 1991; acad. advisor Johns Hopkins U., Balt., 1992-93, women's studies newsletter editor, 1992-94, rsch. asst., 1991-92, 94-96, teaching asst., 1993, tutor Tutorial Pilot Project, 1995, instr., 1996; instr. Towson (Md.) State U., 1995; instr. ESL, Tokyo, 1990-91. Co-author: Cyborgs and Citadels, 1996, Reproducing Reproduction, 1996. Pre-dissertation grantee Culture's Soc. & Women's Studies Program, 1992, Coun. European Studies, 1993, dissertation & coursework grantee Mellon Found., 1994—, Dean's Tchg. Fellowship grantee, dissertation grantee Woodrow Wilson-Johnson & Johnson, 1996. Fellow Edmund J. James Scholar Program; mem. Am. Anthropol. Assn., Population Assn. Am., Phi Beta Kappa. Office: Johns Hopkins U Dept Anthropology 3400 N Charles St Baltimore MD 21218

OAKS, LUCY MOBERLEY, social worker; b. Lexington, Ky., May 10, 1935; d. Shelton Neville Moberley and Jane Emison (Roberts) Meadors; m. William Bryant Oaks, Nov. 10, 1956; children: Bryant, Michael, Kevin, Richard, Deborah. BA in Social Work, U. Ky., 1957; MA in Counseling Psychology, Bowie (Md.) State Coll., 1979. Cert. mental health counselor, Wash. Youth dir. Calvary Bapt. Ch., Renton, Wash., 1960-64, ch. tng. dir., 1980-87; youth dir. Temple Bapt. Ch., Redlands, Calif., 1965-68, Calvary Bapt. Ch., Morgantown, W.Va., 1971-73; cmty. coll. parent educator Bellevue (Wash.) Cmty. Coll., 1980-89; pvt. counselor Renton, 1980-90; Christians social svcs. dir. Puget Sound Bapt. Assn., Federal Way, Wash., 1984-87; program dir. ACAP Child and Family Svcs., Auburn, Wash., 1989-93; assoc. dir. ACAP Child and Family Svcs., Auburn, 1994—; parent instr. APPLE Parenting, Auburn, 1990-92; seminar presenter, Puget Sound, Wash., 1980-95. Bd. trustee Valley Cmty. Players, Renton, 1995; bd. dirs. Calvary Bapt. Ch., Renton, 1981-87. Mem. Puget Sound Adlerian Soc. (bd. dirs. 1981-83), Nat. Assn. Adlerian Pscyhologists (assoc. mem.), Wash. Counseling Assn., Kiwanis (chmn. Internet com., membership chmn. 1994-95). Democrat. Baptist. Home: 2218 177th Pl NE Redmond WA 98052

OAKS, M(ARGARET) MARLENE, minister; b. Grove City, Pa., Mar. 30, 1940; d. Allen Roy and Alberta Bell (Pinner) Eakin; m. Lowell B. Chaney, July 30, 1963 (dec. Jan. 1977); children: Christopher Allen, Linda Michelle; m. Harold G. Younger, Aug. 1978 (div. 1986); m. Gilbert E. Oaks, Aug. 3, 1987. BA, Calif. State U., L.A., 1972; religious sci. studies with several instrs. Ordained to ministry Cmty. Ch., 1978. Tchr. Whittier (Calif.) Sch. Dists., 1972-74, Garden Grove (Calif.) Sch. Dist., 1974-78; instr. Fullerton Coll., 1974-75; founding min. Community Ch. of the Islands (now Ch. of Religious Sci.), Honolulu, 1978-80; min. Ch. of Divine Sci., Pueblo, Colo., 1980-83; founding min. Ch. Religious Sci., Palo Alto, Calif., 1983-86; min. First ch. Religious Sci., Fullerton, Calif., 1986-94, min. emeritus, 1994—; 2d v.p., chmn., corp. sec. VCC Internat., Anaheim, Calif., 1994—; founder, pres. LaVida Inst., Inc., 1994—; pres. Lavida Inst.; sr. pastor Lavida A Ch. for Today's World; 2nd v.p., vorp. sec. VCC Internat.; workshop leader Religious Sci. Dist. Conv., San Jose, Calif., 1985, Internat. New Thought Alliance Conf., Las Vegas, 1984, 92, Calgary, Alta., Can., 1985, Washington, 1988, Denver, 1989, Anaheim, Calif., 1990, Golden Valley Unity Women's Advance, Mpls., 1986, 87, Qume Corp., San Jose, 1985; presenter SANTI Conf., 1992-94; guest workshop leader Ctr. for Life Enrichment, 1990-92; speaker to cmty. of Tartarstan, 1993. Author: The Christmas in You, 1983, rev. edit., 1994, Ki Aikido the Inner Martial Art, 1984, Old Time Religion Is a Cult, 1985, 2d rev. edit., 1992, Service the Sure Path to Enlightenment, 1985, Stretch Marks on My Aura, 1987, rev. edit., 1995, Beyond Addiction, 1990, 10 Core Concepts of Science of Mind, 1991, Forgiveness and Beyond, 1992, rev. edit. Christmas for All Seasons, 1994, 21 Seeds, Miracle Grow For the Soul, 1995, Values Remembered, 1995, 21 Seeds-Miracle Grow for Your Soul, Values Remembered, Forgiveness and Beyond, The Alsone in English and in Russian. Del. Soviet and Am. Citizens Summit Conf., 1988, 89; pres. Soviet-Am. New Thought Initiatives, 1991, chmn. conf. St. Petersburg, 1992, Moscow, 1992, weekly radio program Radio Moscow, The Philippines, 1992—; founder Operation K.I.D.S., La Vida Inst., 1994; founder, bd. dirs. Awakening Oaks Found., 1990; pres. SANTI, 1991-94, founder and pres. La Vida Inst., 1994. Named Outstanding Businesswoman, Am. Businesswomen's Assn., 1989. Mem. Fullerton Interfaith Ministerial Assn. (sec.-treas. 1987-89, pres. 1991-92), United Clergy of Religious Sci. (treas. 1991-92, sec. 1992-93, treas. So. Calif. chpt. 1991-92, v.p. 1993-94, pres. 1994-95), Internat. New Thought Alliance (O.C. chpt. pres. 1990), Soroptomists (chair com. internat. coop. and goodwill 1987-88), Kappa Delta Pi. Republican. Office: LaVida Inst Awakening Oaks Press 1775 E Lincoln Ave Ste 101 Anaheim CA 92805-4300

OATES, JOYCE CAROL, author; b. Lockport, N.Y., June 16, 1938; d. Frederic James and Caroline (Bush) O.; m. Raymond Joseph Smith, Jan. 23, 1961. BA, Syracuse U., 1960; MA, U. Wis., 1961. Instr. English U. Detroit, 1961-65, asst. prof., 1965-67; prof. English U. Windsor, Ont., Can., 1967-87; writer-in-residence Princeton (N.J.) U., 1978-81, prof., 1987—. Author: (short story collections) By the North Gate, 1963, Upon the Sweeping Flood, 1966, The Wheel of Love, 1970, Marriages and Infidelities, 1972, The Hungry Ghosts, 1974, The Goddess and Other Women, 1974, Where Are You Going, Where Have You Been?: Stories of Young America, 1974, The Poisoned Kiss and Other Stories From the Portuguese, 1975, The Seduction and Other Stories, 1975, Crossing the Border, 1976, Night-Side, 1977, All the Good People I've Left Behind, 1978, The Lamb of Abyssalia, 1980, A Sentimental Education: Stories, 1981, Last Days: Stories, 1984, Wild Nights, 1985, Raven's Wing: Stories, 1986, The Assignation, 1988, Heat: And Other Stories, 1991, Where is Here?, 1992, Haunted: Tales of the Grotesque, 1994, Will You Always Love Me? and Other Stories, 1995; (novels) With Shuddering Fall, 1964, A Garden of Earthly Delights, 1967 (Nat. Book award nomination 1968), Expensive People, 1967 (Nat. Book award nomination 1969), them, 1969 (Nat. Book award for fiction 1970), Wonderland, 1971, Do With Me What You Will, 1973, The Assassins, 1975, Childwold, 1976, The Triumph of the Spider Monkey, 1976, Son of the Morning, 1978, Unholy Loves, 1979, Cybele, 1979, Bellefleur, 1980 (L.A. Times Book award nomination 1980), A Sentimental Education, 1981, Angel of Light, 1981, A Bloodsmoor Romance, 1982, Mysteries of Winterthorn, 1984, Solstice, 1985, Marya, 1986, You Must Remember This, 1987, (as Rosamond Smith) The Lives of the Twins, 1987, American Appetites, 1989, (as Rosamond Smith) Soul-Mate, 1989, Because It Is Bitter, and Because It Is My Heart, 1990, (as Rosamond Smith) Nemesis, 1990, I Lock My Door Upon Myself, 1990, The Rise of Life on Earth, 1991, Black Water, 1992, (as Rosamond Smith) Snake Eyes, 1992, Foxfire: Confessions of a Girl Gang, 1993, What I Lived For, 1994 (PEN/Faulkner award nomination 1995); (poetry collections) Women in Love, 1968, Expensive People, 1968, Anonymous Sins, 1969, Love and Its Derangements, 1970, Angel Fire, 1973, Dreaming America, 1973, The Fabulous Beasts, 1975, Season of Peril, 1977, Women Whose Lives are Food, Men Whose Lives are Money: Poems, 1978, The Stepfather, 1978, Celestial Timepiece, 1981, Invisible Women: New and Selected Poems, 1970-1972, 1982, Luxury of Sin, 1983, The Time Traveller, 1987; (plays) The Sweet Enemy, 1965, Sunday Dinner, 1970, Ontological Proof of My Existence, 1970, Miracle Play, 1974, Three Plays, 1980, Daisy, 1980, Presque Isle, 1984, Triumph of the Spider Monkey, 1985, In Darkest America, 1990, I Stand Before You Naked, 1990, The Perfectionist and Other Plays, 1995; (essays) The Edge of Impossibility, 1972, The Hostile Sun: The Poetry of D.H. Lawrence, 1973, New Heaven, New Earth, 1974, Contraries: Essays, 1981, The Profane Art, 1984, On Boxing, 1987, (Woman) Writer: Occasions and Opportunities, 1988; editor, compiler: Scenes from American Life: Contemporary Short Fiction, 1973, (with Shannon Ravenel) Best American Short Stories of 1979, 1979, Night Walks, 1982, First Person Singular: Writer's on Their Craft, 1983, (with Boyd Litzinger) Story: Fictions Past and Present, 1985, (with Daniel Halpern) Reading and Fights, 1988, The Oxford Book of American Short Stories, 1992, The Sophisticated Cat: An Anthology, 1992; editor (with Raymond Smith) Ontario Rev.; contbr. to nat. mags. including N.Y. Times Book Rev., Mich. Quarterly Rev., Mademoiselle, Vogue, North Am. Rev., Hudson Rev., Paris Rev., Grand Street, Atlantic, Poetry, Esquire. Recipient O. Henry award, 1967, 73, Rosenthal award Nat. Inst. Arts and Letters, 1968, O. Henry Spl. award continuing achievement, 1970, 86, Award of Merit Lotos Club, 1975, St. Louis Lit. award, 1988, Rea award for the Short Story, 1990, Alan Swallow award for fiction, 1990, Nobel Prize in Lit. nomination, 1993; Guggenheim fellow, 1967-68, Nat. Endowment for the Arts grantee, 1966, 68. Mem. Am. Acad. and Inst. Arts and Letters. Office: care John Hawkins 71 W 23rd St Ste 1600 New York NY 10010*

OATES, SHERRY CHARLENE, portraitist; b. Houston, Sept. 11, 1946; d. Charles Emil and Berniece Faye (Lohse) O. Student, North Tex. State U., 1965-66; student under Martin Kellogg; BA in English, Health and Phys. Edn., Houston Bapt. U., 1968. Cert. art tchr., Tex. Tchr. Jackson Jr. High Sch., Houston, 1968-69, Percy Priest Sch., Nashville, 1969-70, Franklin (Tenn.) High Sch., 1970-84; freelance illustrator Bapt. Sunday Sch. Bd., Nashville, 1978-85, United Meth. Pub. House, Nashville, 1980-85; portraitist in oils, owner Portraits, Ltd., Nashville, 1984—. Portraits include corp. leaders, educators, politicians, hist. and equestrian subjects, society figures and children; participated in various exhbns. at Bapt. Sunday Sch. Bd. and All State and Ctr. South Exhibits at the Parthenon. Recipient 3d place in graphics Ctrl. South Exhbn. at The Parthenon-Tenn. Art League, 1986. Mem. Tenn. Art League. Republican. Baptist. Studio: 816 Kirkwood Ave Nashville TN 37204-2602

OATIS-SKINNER, CHRISTINE, career counselor, college program administrator. BA, U. Dayton, 1968; MA, Assumption Coll., 1977; EdD, U. Mass., 1987. Cert. career counselor. Career counselor Northern Sessex Cmty. Coll., Naverhill, Mass., 1976-77; coord. career devel. U. Mass., Lowell, 1977-91; asst. dir. career ctr. Kennedy Sch., Harvard U., Cambridge, Mass., 1991-93; asst. dir. regional career devel. The Giampa Group, Andover, Mass., 1993-94; dir. career ctr. Carleton Coll., Northfield, Minn., 1994—. Mem. AAUW (co-chair membership, bd. dirs. 1995—, pres. elect 1996).

OATMAN, TAMRA-SHAE, advocate; b. San Antonio, Feb. 24, 1952; d. William Arthur and Audrea Lynne (Cox) O.; m. Mark Stanford, Mar. 13, 1981; children: Hunter Oatman-Stanford, Dashiell Oatman-Stanford. BBA, U. Tex., 1974. Dir. pers. and staff devel. Tex. State Treasury, Austin, 1983-85; owner Oatman-Pilney Consulting, Austin, 1985-92; small bus. advocate Tex. Nat. Resources Com., Austin, 1992—. Author, editor: Lone Star Baby, 1988. Vice-chair Exec. Women in State Govt., Austin, 1983-84, Tex. Abortion Rights Action League, 1984-86, Tex. Women's Polit. Caucus, Austin, 1985-87; chair Permian Basin Women's Polit. Caucus, Odessa, Tex., 1982-83. Methodist. Office: Tex Natural Resources CC PO Box 13087 Austin TX 78711-3087

O'BANION, BONITA ROSALYNDE, assistant principal; b. Chgo., Sept. 1; d. Robert Benjamin and Estella (Foote) Dixson; children: Dana Keone, Dathon Katrell. BA, Fisk U., Nashville, 1961; MEd, DePaul U., Chgo., 1982; MA, Gov. State U., Chgo., 1990. Tchr., dept. chair Hyde Park Career Acad., Chgo., 1969-94; asst. prin. Libby Elem., Chgo., 1994-95, Urban Youth H.S., Chgo., 1995—. Office: Urban Youth HS 65 E Wacker Pl Chicago IL 60601

O'BANNION, MINDY MARTHA MARTIN, nurse; b. Cushing, Okla., Aug. 19, 1953; d. John William and Martha Florence (Vineyard) Martin; student Okla. State U., 1971-73, Oscar Rose Jr. Coll., 1973; grad. St. Anthony Sch. Nursing, 1975; RN, Tex.; m. William Neal O'Bannion, Oct. 9, 1976; children: Mindi Martha Mae, William Neale Aaron. Med. clk. Martin Clinic, Cushing, Okla., 1968-72; nursing asst. Cushing Mcpl. Hosp., 1973-75, head nurse surg. fl., 1975-76, charge nurse med. unit, 1978-79, 82-83; staff nurse Met. Hosp., Dallas, 1985; staff nurse med. unit Mesquite (Tex.) Community Hosp., 1985-87; nurse post partum unit and discharge edn. post partum unit Trinity Med. Ctr., Carrollton, Tex., 1987—. ind. beauty cons. Mary Kay Cosmetics, Dallas, Tex., 1993—. Mem. social com. Royal Haven Bapt. Ch. Women's Missionary Union, Dallas, 1977-78; mem. extension dept. nursery First Bapt. Ch., Cushing, 1979-82, extension dept. presch., 1982-84; mem. extension dept presch. Royal Haven Bapt. Ch., Dallas, 1986-87; mem. Montgomery Elem. Sch. PTA, Farmers Branch, Tex., 1986-94, Vivian Field Jr. H.S. PTA, Farmers Branch, 1993—, R.L. Turner High Sch. PTA, Farmers Branch/Carrollton, 1995—; treas., mem. nominating com. Joyce Harms group Women's Missionary Union; clk., charter mem. Brookhaven Bapt. Ch., Farmers Br., 1989-92; mem. Valwood Park Baptist Ch., Farmers Br., 1994—. Mem. Am., Tex., Okla. State Nurses Assns., St. Anthony Hosp. Sch. Nursing Alumnae, Bluebonnet Shelties (founder), Tau Beta Sigma, Alpha Xi Delta (corr. sec. 1973). Baptist. Home: 13505 Onyx Ln Dallas TX 75234-4912

OBASEKI, LOVETTE I., consulting company executive, systems analyst; b. July 4, 1953; d. Samson O. Amba A. (Okai) O. BS, Fla. A&M U., 1979, MEd, 1984; diploma in systems analysis, NYU, 1989; cert. in small bus. program, Baruch Coll., 1995. Cert. Novell netware engr. Supr. systems adminstrn. Buccellati Ltd., N.Y.C.; systems mgr. JCCA, N.Y.C., 1988-95; cons. Binam Cons. Svcs., 1995—; sr. sys. analyst cons. Paragon, N.J., 1996—. Active numerous ch. groups. Recipient Honors awards Fla. A&M U. Mem. NAFE, NOW, AAUW, Assn. Sys. Mgmt. (bd. dirs. 1989—, v.p. 1992-93, Excellence in Sys. Mgmt. award 1994, Outstanding Svc. award 1992-93, Appreciation cert. 1990-91, Honors award), Data Processing Mgmt. Assn., Am. Mgmt. Assn., DAV Comdrs. Club (Bronze Leader 1995). Democrat. Address: PO Box 901026 Far Rockaway NY 11690-1026

OBENDORF, MARGARET DAWSON, preschool educator; b. Princeton, N.J., Jan. 18, 1961; d. John Myrick and Nancy Louise (Wildes) Dawson; m. Bruce Randall Obendorf; children: Mirra Elizabeth, Charles Avery. BA in Philosophy, U. Denver, 1984; MS in Parapsychology, John F. Kennedy U., Orinda, Calif., 1990. Housekeeper Orinda, Walnut Creek, Calif., 1984-87; desktop pub. Walnut Creek, Calif., 1988-91; managerial asst. Pro Bus. Ctr., Danville, Calif., 1989-90; Mac expert, engr.'s asst. Chevron, Richmond, Calif., 1990; daycare worker YMCA, Pinole, Calif., 1991; presch. tchr. The White Pony, Lafayette, Calif., 1991—. Editor: The Eclectic Jour., 1996—. Mem. Union of Concerned Scientists, Diablo Valley Mothers of Multiples, Sierra Club. Home: 1271 Bonita Ln Walnut Creek CA 94595

OBERHAUSEN, JOYCE ANN WYNN, aircraft company executive, artist; b. Plain Dealing, La., Nov. 12, 1941; d. George Dewey and Jettie Cleo (Farrington) Wynn; m. James J. Oberhausen, Oct. 15, 1966; children: Georgann, Darla Renee Estein Oberhausen Christopher, Dale Henry Estein Oberhausen. Student Ayers Bus. Sch., Shreveport, 1962-63, U. Ala., 1964-65. Stenographer, sec. Lincoln Nat. Life Co., Shreveport, 1965-66; sec. Baifield Industries, Shreveport, 1975-86; internat. art tchr., Huntsville, Ala., 1974—; co-owner Precision Splty. Co., Huntsville, 1966—, Mil. Aircraft, Huntsville, 1979—; pres., owner Wynnson Enterprises, Huntsville, 1983—; owner, artist, designer Wynnson Galleries Pvt. Collections, Florist, Meridianville, 1987; owner North Ala. Wholesale Flowers, 1988—, Wynnson Enterprises Mil. Packaging Co., 1988—. Co-founder Nat. Mus. Women in Arts; active Nat. Mus. Women in Arts. Mem. NAFE, Internat. Porcelain Guild, People to People, Porcelain Portrait Soc., United Artists Assn., Am. Soc. of Profl. and Executive Women Hist. Soc., Nat. Trust Hist. Preservation, Internat. Platform Assn., Met. Mus. Art., Smithsonian Assn., Assn. Community Artists, Rep. Senatorial Inner Circle, Ala. Sheriffs Assn., C. of C., Better Bus. Bur., Huntsville Art League and Mus. Assocs., Avocations: oil painting, antiques, handcrafts, gourmet cooking, horseback riding. Home: 156 Spencer Dr Meridianville AL 35759-2023 Office: Wynnson Enterprises Inc 12043 Highway 231 431 N Meridianville AL 35759-1201

OBERLY, KATHRYN ANNE, lawyer; b. Chgo., May 22, 1950; d. James Richard and Lucille Mary (Kraus) O.; m. Daniel Lee Goelzer, July 13, 1974 (div. Aug. 1987); 1 child, Michael W. Student, Vassar Coll., 1967-69; BA, U. Wis., 1971, JD, 1973. Bar: Wis. 1973, D.C. 1981, N.Y. 1995. Law clk. U.S. Ct. Appeals, Omaha, 1973-74; trial atty. U.S. Dept. Justice, Washington, 1974-77, spl. asst., 1977-81, spl. litigation counsel, 1981-82, asst. to Solicitor Gen., 1982-86; ptnr. Mayer, Brown & Platt, Washington, 1986-91; assoc. gen. counsel Ernst & Young LLP, Washington, 1991-94; vice chair, gen. counsel Ernst & Young LLP, N.Y.C., 1994—. Mem. ABA, Am. Law Inst., Wis. State Bar Assn., D.C. Bar Assn. Democrat. Office: Ernst & Young LLP 787 7th Ave New York NY 10019

OBERMEYER, THERESA NANGLE, sociology educator; b. St. Louis, July 25, 1945; d. James Francis and Harriet Clare (Shafer) Nangle; m. Thomas S. Obermeyer, Dec. 23, 1977; children: Thomas Jr., James, Margaret and Matthew (twins). BA, Maryville U., St. Louis, 1967; MEd, St. Louis U., 1970, PhD, 1975. Lic. real estate broker. Dir. student activities Lindenwood Colls., St. Charles, Mo., 1969-70; asst. dean of students Loyola Coll., Balt., 1972-73; asst. dir. student activities St. Louis Community Coll., 1973-78; dir. student activities U. Alaska, Anchorage, 1978-79; instr. sociology Chapman U., Anchorage, 1980-93; secondary tchr. McLaughlin Youth Ctr. for Juvenile Delinquents, 1984-90; elected Anchorage Sch. Bd., 1990-94. Contbr. articles to profl. jours. Mem. Anchorage Mcpl. Health Commn., 1980-81; elected coun. urban bds. edn. Nat. Sch. Bds. Assn., 1994; founder, mem. Alaska Women's Polit. Caucus. Recipient NDEA scholarship, 1970-72, Title I Grant U. Md. and Loyola Coll., 1972-73, Fed. Women's Equity Act U.S. Dept. Edn. U. Alaska, 1978-79; named Fulbright fellow Project India, 1974, Project Jordan, 1977. Mem. DAR (bd. dirs. Anchorage chpt. 1979—), AAUW (bd. dirs Anchorage br. 1980-81), Am. Soc. Pub Adminstrn. (pres., bd. dirs. south cen. chpt. 1981). Home: 3000 Dartmouth Dr Anchorage AK 99508-4413

OBERNDORF, MEYERA E., mayor; m. Roger L. Oberndorf; children: Marcie, Heide. BS in Elem. Edn., Old Dominion U., 1964. Broadcaster Sta. WNIS, Norfolk, Va.; mem. city coun. City of Virginia Beach, Va., 1976—, vice-mayor, 1986, mayor, 1988—. Mem. exec. bd. Tidewater coun. Boys Scouts Am.; bd. dirs. Virginia Beach Pub. Libr., 1966-76, chmn. bd., 1967-76. Mem. AAUW, U.S. Conf. Mayors, Va. Mcpl. League (exec. bd.), Nat. League Cities (vice-chmn.), Princess Anne Women's Club. Jewish. Home: 5404 Challedon Dr Virginia Beach VA 23462-4112 Office: Office of the Mayor Municipal Ctr City Hall Bldg Virginia Beach VA 23456*

OBERNE, SHARON BROWN, elementary education educator; b. Lakeland, Fla., Sept. 2, 1955; d. Morris C. and Amy (Beecroft) Brown; m. Ronald Allan Oberne, Mar. 29, 1980; children: Laura, Aaron, Kelley. AA in Pretchg., Hillsborough C.C., Tampa, Fla., 1975; BA in Elem. Edn., U. South Fla., 1976, cert., 1980, AA in Acctg., Fla., 1980. Cert. tchr. K-8. 3rd grade tchr. Zolfo Springs Elem., Wauchula, Fla., 1976-77, 2nd grade tchr., 1977-79; 1st grade tchr. Westgate Christian Sch., Tampa, Fla., 1979-80; 5th grade tchr. Pasoc Elem., Dade City, Fla., 1980-81; 3rd grade tchr. San Antonio Elem., Dade City, 1981-86; temporary reading tchr. Chesterfield Heights Elem., Norfolk, Va., 1986-87; 2nd grade tchr. Ocean View Elem., Norfolk, 1987—; dir. Ocean View Writing Club, Norfolk, 1992—. Author: Pink Monkey, 1994, Space Traveler, 1995, Daisy Dolphin (Spelling in Context). Pres. USS Guam's Wife's Club, Norfolk Naval Base, 1990-91; amb. of goodwill USS Guam, 1990-91; founder AmeriKids of Ocean View, Norfolk, 1991-93; liaison Adopt-A-Sch. Program, Norfolk, 1991—. Recipient Good Neighbor award NEA, 1994. Mem. Norfolk Reading Coun., Nat. Autism Soc., CHADD. Home: 8243 Briarwood Cir Norfolk VA 23518-2862

OBERSTAR, HELEN ELIZABETH, retired cosmetics company executive; b. Ottawa, Ill.; d. Milton Edward and Helen (Herrick) Weiss; m. Edward Charles Oberstar, Feb. 3, 1945 (dec. 1984). BS in Chemistry, Monmouth (Ill.) Coll., 1943; postgrad., Northwestern U., Chgo., 1947-49; LLD (hon.), Monmouth Coll., 1987. Asst. food technologist Standard Brands, Inc., Bklyn., 1943-45; chemist Miner Labs., Midwest div., Arthur D. Little, Chgo., 1946-50; rsch. chemist/rsch. supr. Toni Co., div. Gillette Co., Chgo., 1951-65; group leader rsch. and devel. Shulton, Inc., Clifton, N.J., 1965-72; sect. leader rsch. and devel. Am. Cyanamid, Clifton, 1972-75; mgr. rsch. and devel. Clairol Bristol Myers Internat., Stamford, Conn., 1975-82; dir. tech. Clairol Bristol Myers Squibb Consumer Products Group Internat., Stamford, 1982-93; dir. technology internat. group Clairol, Inc. divsn. Bristol-Myers Squibb, Stamford, 1993-95; ret. Wilton, Conn., 1995. Patentee in field. Recipient Disting. Alumni award Monmouth Coll., 1986, Hall of Achievement award Monmouth Coll., 1995. Mem. Soc. Cosmetic Chemists (house chmn. 1963-64), Cosmetic Toiletries Fragrance Assn. (internat. com. 1985-95). Episcopalian. Home and Office: 512 Belden Hill Rd Wilton CT 06897-4221

OBERSTEIN, MARYDALE, geriatric specialist; b. Red Wing, Minn., Dec. 30; d. Dale Robert and Jean Ebba-Marie (Holmquist) Johnson; children: Kirk Robert, Mark Paul, MaryJean. Student, U. Oreg., 1961-62, Portland State U., 1962-64, Long Beach State U., 1974-76. Cert. geriatric specialist, Calif. Florist, owner Sunshine Flowers, Santa Ana, Calif., 1982—; pvt. duty nurse Aides in Action, Costa Mesa, Calif., 1985-87; owner, activity dir., adminstr. Lovelight Christian Home for the Elderly, Santa Ana, 1987—; activity dir. Bristol Care Nursing Home, Santa Ana, 1985-88; evangelist, speaker radio show Sta. KPRZ-FM, Anaheim, Calif., 1985-88; adminstr. Leisure Lodge Resort Care for Elderly in Lake Forest, Lake Forest, Calif., 1996—; nursing home activist in reforming laws to eliminate bad homes, 1984-90; founder, tchr. hugging classes/laughter therapy terminally ill patients, 1987—; founder healing and touch therapy laughter Therapy, 1991-93; bd. dirs. Performing Arts Ctr.; speaker for enlightenment and healing. Author (rewrite) Title 22 Nursing Home Reform Law, Little Hoover Commn.; model, actress and voiceovers. Bd. dirs. Orange County Coun. on Aging, 1984—; chairperson Helping Hands, 1985—, Pat Robertson Com., 1988, George Bush Presdl. Campaign, Orange County, 1988; bd. dirs., v.p. Women Aglow Orange County, 1985—; evangelist, pub. spkr., v.p. Women Aglow Huntington Beach; active with laughter therapy and hugging classes for terminally ill. Recipient Carnation Silver Bowl, Carnation Svc. Co., 1984-85, Gold medal Pres. Clinton; named Woman of Yr., Kiwanis, 1985, ABI, 1990, Am. Biog. Soc., Woman of Decade; honored AM L.A. TV Show, Lt. Gov. McCarthy, 1984. Mem. Calif. Assn. Residential Care Homes, Orange County Epilepsy Soc. (bd. dirs. 1986—), Calif. Assn. Long Term Facilities. Home: 2722 S Diamond St Santa Ana CA 92704-6013

O'BRIAN, BONNIE JEAN, library services supervisor; b. Great Bend, Kans., Oct. 19, 1940; d. Claude Marion and Mildred Geraldine (Schmaider) Baker; m. Patrick Gilbert Gibson (div.); 1 child, Debra Kathleen; m. John Robinson O'Brian, Nov. 2, 1968. BS, UCLA, 1961; MS, Calif. State U., Northridge, 1977; Credential in Libr. Media Svcs., Calif. State U., Long Beach, 1978. Libr. L.A. Unified Sch. Dist., Northridge, 1978-84; supr. chpt. 2 L.A. Unified Sch. Dist., L.A., 1984, coord. field libr., 1984-87, supr. libr. svcs., 1987—; asst. prof. libr. sci. Calif. State U., L.A.; condr. workshops in field. Recipient N.W. Valley Parent Tchr. Student award 1978, San Fernando Valley Reading Assn. Myrtle Shirley Reading Motivation award 1986. Mem. ALA, Am. Assn. Sch. Librs., Calif. Sch. Libr. Assn. (pres.), So. Calif. Coun. on Lit. for Children and Young People, White House Conf. on Libr. and Info. Svcs. Republican. Office: Los Angeles Unifed Sch Dist 1320 W 3rd St Los Angeles CA 90017-1410

O'BRIEN, AMY JOY, electrical engineer; b. Smithtown, N.Y., June 22, 1964; d. Morgan Leo and Dorothea Helen (Carelli) O'B. BSEE, U. Del., 1987; MSEE, Loyola Coll., Balt., 1991. Rsch. asst. U. Del., Newark, 1987; cons. engr. Henry Adams, Inc., Balt., 1987-89; software design engr. Tex. Instruments, Inc., Hunt Valley, Md., 1989-90; elec. engr. Ques Tech, Inc., Falls Church, Va., 1990-91, Naval Rsch. Lab., Washington, 1991—; bd. dirs., chair project rev. Vol. for Med. Engring., Balt., 1988-92. Mem. IEEE. Roman Catholic. Office: Naval Rsch Lab Code 5344 4555 Overlook Ave SW Washington DC 20375-5336

O'BRIEN, ANNE J., lawyer; b. Winfield, Kans., July 24, 1945. BA, U. N.Mex., 1967; MBA, George Washington U., 1976; JD magna cum laude, Am. U., 1988. Bar: Md. 1988, D.C. 1989. Ptnr. Arnold & Porter, Washington. Vice chmn. Tax Mgmt. Estates, Gifts and Trusts Jour., 1989—. Mem. ABA (mem. sects. on taxation, estate and gift tax com., real property, probate and trust law books, others), Md. State Bar Assn., D.C. Bar (mem. steering com. estates, trusts and probate law sects.), D.C. Planning Coun. Office: Arnold & Porter 555 12th St NW Washington DC 20004*

O'BRIEN, CATHERINE LOUISE, museum administrator; b. N.Y.C., July 21, 1930; d. Edward Denmark and Catherine Louise (Browne) O'B.; m. Philip R. James (div.); m. Sterling Noel (div.). B.A., Finch Coll., N.Y.C.; postgrad. Williams Coll., Williamstown, Mass., Marymount Coll. Reprodn. mgr. Met. Mus. Art, N.Y.C., 1975—; dir. sales Simon Pearce Gallery, N.Y.C. Exhibited in group shows at Parrish Art Mus., Southampton, N.Y., 1965-70, Met. Mus. Art, N.Y.C., 1975-85, Guild Hall Exhibit, East Hampton, N.Y., 1965-85. Mem. aux. Southampton Hosp., 1970-85; founder East Hampton Horse Show, Ladies Village Improvement Soc., East Hampton, 1970—; mem. fair coms St. James Ch., N.Y.C., St. Luke's Ch., East Hampton, 1970-85; mem. alumnae adv. bd. Marymount Coll., N.Y.C., 1984-86, chmn. alumnae event, 1994; mem. Women's Nat. Rep. Club, N.Y.C.; chmn. Landmark and Tree Planting Com. For Madison Ave. Assn., N.Y.C., 1994—. Mem. DAR (vice regent East Hampton chpt. 1974-85), Colonial Dames Am. (archives com. 1980-85), Daus. Brit. Empire (historian 1978-85), United Daus. Confederacy (state historian 1970-85), Daus. Colonial Wars (corr. sec. 1983-85), Sons and Daus. of the Pilgrims (corr. sec. 1983-85), Victorian Soc., Soc. Mayflower Descs. (life), English Speaking Union, New Eng. Soc. (mem. ball com. 1983-86), Daus. of Cin. (historian 1979-85), Squadron "A". Republican. Episcopalian. Clubs: Devon Yacht, Maidstone (East Hampton, N.Y.); Southampton Yacht (N.Y.); Metropolitan (N.Y.C.) (women's com., chmn. debutante ball 1980-84); Reciprocal/India House, St. Anthony Union League (N.Y.C.). Avocations: show horses; dogs. Home: 605 Park Ave New York NY 10021-7016 also: Box 1488 Seacote Lily Pond Ln East Hampton NY 11937 Office: Met Mus Art Fifth Ave New York NY 10028 also: Simon Pearce Gallery 500 Park Ave New York NY 10022-1606

O'BRIEN, DELLANNA W., religious organization administrator; b. Wichita Falls, Tex.; d. Paul H. and M. West; m. William R. O'Brien; children: Denise O'Brien Basden, Erin O'Brien Puryear, William Ross. BS, Hardin Simmons U., 1953; MEd, Tex. Christian U., 1972; EdD, Va. Tech. and State U., 1983; LHD (hon.), Judson Coll., 1992; D in Social Svc. (hon.), U. Richmond, 1993. Tchr. elem. schs., Tex., 1953-63; missionary So. Baptist Conv., Indonesia, 1963-71; tchr. elem. schs., Va., 1972-88; pres. Internat. Family and Children's Ednl. Svcs., Richmond, Va., 1988-89; exec. dir., treas. Women's Missionary Union, Birmingham, Ala., 1989—; exec. com Bapt. World Alliance, budget and fin. com., Bapt. world aid com., global resource panel for women in evangelism; bd. dirs. AD 2000 Movement and Beyond; mem. N. Am. Bapt. Fellowship. Contbr. articles to religious mags.: The Commission, The Student, Baptist Heritage Update, Pioneer, Open Windows, In Christ's Name. Past mem. Henrico County (Va.) Sch. Bd. Recipient Disting. Alumni award Hardin Simmons U., Abilene, Tex., 1990. Office: Woman's Missionary Union PO Box 830010 Birmingham AL 35283-0010

O'BRIEN, DORENE FRANCES, journalist, educator; b. Hamtramck, Mich., Nov. 21, 1960; d. Bert and Maria Emma (Myten) Paluszczak; m. Patrick Brendon O'Brien, June 13, 1992; 1 child, Hadley Elise. AA, Oakland C.C., Bloomfield Hills, Mich., 1989; BA in English and Journalism summa cum laude, Wayne State U., 1994. Tchr. U.S. Postal Svc., Birmingham, Mich., 1982—; reporter Macomb Daily, Mt. Clemens, Mich., 1993—; freelance writer, journalist, 1990—; seminar conductor U.S. Postal Svc., Royal Oak, Mich., 1988—. Merit scholar Wayne State U., 1989, Lenore Upton scholar, 1993, Loughead-Eldridge Creative Writing scholar, 1996. Mem. Wayne State U. Alumni Assn., Women of Wayne.

O'BRIEN, HELEN ANDERSON, health services administrator; b. Worcester, Mass., Apr. 19, 1934; d. Albert and Mary Ellen (Connor) Anderson; m. Charles Gerald O'Brien, Jan. 24, 1955 (div. Apr. 1977); children: Mark, Karen O'Brien Tomko. Diploma in nursing, Mass. Gen. Hosp., Boston, 1956; BSN, Western Conn. State U., 1977; MPH with acad. honors, Yale U., 1979. RN, N.Y., Ohio, Mass., Conn. Nurse, charge nurse various locations, 1960-64; chmn. publicity and community edn. Wausau (Wis.) Hosp., 1966-69; adminstrv. resident Danbury (Conn.) Health Dept., 1978; health svcs. cons., Darien, 1979; pres., CEO, Stratford (Conn.) Vis. Nurse Assn., Inc., 1980—; presenter in field. Bd. dirs. Women's Leadership Coun., Bridgeport (Conn.) Regional Bus. Coun., 1995—; active Needs of Elderly Commn., Stratford, 1980-87; founder Hospice Program Greater Bridgeport, Conn., 1981—; vol. domestic violence and rape counselor YWCA, Bridgeport, 1990—. Fellow Yale U., 1977-79. Mem. APHA, Am. Mgmt. Assn., Conn. Pub. Health Assn. (bd. dirs. 1980-86), Yale Hosp. Adminstrv. Alumni Assn., Nat. League for Nursing, Assn. Yale Alumni in Pub. Health. Home: 129 Gallows Hill Rd Redding CT 06896-1408 Office: Stratford Vis Nurse Assn 88 Ryders Ln Stratford CT 06497-1666

O'BRIEN, JANET W., state legislator; m. John F. O'Brien; 4 children. BA, Tufts U.; MPA, Harvard U. Mem. Mass. Ho. of Reps., 1991—; team mediator Mass. joint labor mgmt. com., 1976-79; mem. Munic adv. bd. Mass. Dept. Personnel Adminstrn., 1984-90; coord. Cleanup North and South Rivers, 1985-89; mem. spl. legis. com. on collective bargaining and dispute resolution, 1985-90, cert. dist. ct. mediator, 1989—. Mem. Hanover Planning Bd., 1974-77; chair Hanover Growth Policy Com., 1976-79, Hanover Bd. Selectmen, 1977-79. Democrat. Home: 128 Washington St Hanover MA 02339-2340 Office: Mass Ho of Reps State Capitol Boston MA 02133*

OBRIEN, JEAN ANN, art appraiser; b. Woodward, Okla., Dec. 7, 1949; d. Alfred Harry and Dorthy Jean (Allen) Barby; m. Lawrence Patrick OBrien, Apr. 4, 1970 (div. Mar. 1987); children: Timothy Michael, Brenna Colleen, Lara Kathleen. BA in Fine Art, U. Mo., Kansas City, 1989; Diplomas, Royal Soc. Art/Christie's, London, 1990-92. Regional v.p. Hardy & Halpern, Inc., Nashville, 1992-93; owner J.A. OBrien Appraisals, Kansas City, 1993—. Mem. Am. Soc. Appraisers, Soc. of Fellows Nelson-Atkins Mus. Office: J A OBrien 5100 W 95 St Ste 200 Prairie Village KS 66207

O'BRIEN, KAREN MARIE, lawyer; b. Syracuse, N.Y., Dec. 7, 1958; d. Nathan Anthony and Barbara Ann (Smith) Marra; m. Michael Dennis O'Brien, Oct. 15, 1983; children: Michael Dennis, John Nathan, Adam James. BA in Polit. Sci. and Econs., SUNY, Geneseo, 1980; JD, Syracuse U., 1982. Bar: N.Y. 1984, Md. 1985, D.C. 1985, U.S. Supreme Ct. 1994. Assoc. Dibble & Wright, Rochester, N.Y., 1982-84, Joseph, Greenwald & Laake, Hyattsville, Md., 1984-86; supervising atty. SEC, Washington, 1986-90; gen. counsel N.Am. Securities Adminstrs. Assn., Washington, 1990—. Mem. ABA (subcom. state regulation of securities, com. non-pub. and small bus. offerings). Office: NAm Securities Adminstrs Assn 1 Massachusetts Ave NW Ste 310 Washington DC 20001-1401

O'BRIEN, MARGARET HOFFMAN, educational administrator; b. Melrose, Mass., Aug. 22, 1947; d. John Francis and Margaret Mary (Colbert) Hoffman; m. Edward Lee O'Brien, June 13, 1970 (div. Sept. 1988); children: John Hoffman, Elizabeth Lee; m. Michael Ellis-Tolaydo, Mar. 9, 1991. AB, Trinity Coll., Washington, 1969; LHD (hon.), Trinity Coll., 1994; MA, Cath. U., 1971; LHD (hon.), Georgetown U., 1991; PhD, Am. U., 1993. English tchr. D.C. Pub. Schs., Washington, 1969-73; edn. coord. Street Law, Georgetown Law Ctr., Washington, 1973-75; owner, mgr. Man in the Green Hat Restaurant, Washington, 1976-81; head of edn. Folger Shakespeare Libr., Washington, 1981-94; dir. Teaching Shakespeare Inst., Washington, 1983-94; v.p. edn. Corp. for Pub. Broadcasting, Washington, 1994—; mem. faculty Prince of Wales Shakespeare Sch., Stratford on Avon, Eng., 1993; edn. dir. Fairfax (Va.) Family Theatre, 1988-93, Md. Shakespeare Festival, St. Mary's City, 1988-91; head of faculty Atlantic Shakespeare Inst., Wroxton, U.K., 1985-90. Gen. editor: Shakespeare Set Free, 1993-95. Bd. dirs. Edmund Burke Sch., Washington, 1993—, Capitol Hill Day Sch., 1994—, Fillmore Arts Ctr., Washington, 1991-93, Capitol Hill Arts Workshop, Washington, 1989-91, Horizons Theatre, 1991, Janice F. Delaney Found., 1991—; site visitor U.S. Dept. Edn., Washington, 1990; mem. nat. adv. bd. Orlando Shakespeare Festival, 1990-93. Mem. Shakespeare Assn. Am., Nat. Coun. Tchrs. English. Office: Corp for Pub Broadcasting 901 E St NW Washington DC 20004-2037

O'BRIEN, MARGARET JOSEPHINE, retired community health nurse; b. N.Y.C., Dec. 5, 1918; d. John J. and Nellie (Coyle) O'B. BS, St.John's U., 1954, MS, 1962; MPH, Columbia U., 1964. With Health Dept., City of New York, 1943-81, assoc. dir. Bur. Pub. Health Nursing, dir. Pub. Health Nursing Svc., asst. commr. pub. health nursing; retired. Contbr. articles to profl. jours. Recipient Outstanding Alumnus of Columbia U. Sch. of Pub. Health award, 1994. Mem. ANA, APHA, NLN, N.Y. State Nurses Assn., N.Y.C. Pub. Health Assn. Home: 11055 72nd Rd Forest Hills NY 11375-5472

O'BRIEN, MARY DEVON, communications executive, consultant; b. Buenos Aires, Argentina, Feb. 13, 1944; came to U.S., 1949, naturalized, 1962; d. George Earle and Margaret Frances (Richards) Owen; m. Gordon Covert O'Brien, Feb. 16, 1962 (div. Aug. 1982); children: Christopher Covert, Devon Elizabeth; m. Christopher Gerard Smith, May 28, 1983. BA, Rutgers U., 1975, MBA, 1976. Project mgmt. cert., 1989. Contr. manpower Def. Comm. divsn. ITT, Nutley, N.J., 1977-80, adminstr. program, 1977-78, mgr. cost, schedule control, 1978-79, voice processing project, 1979-80; mgr. project Avionics divsn. ITT, Nutley, 1980-81, sr. mgr. projects, 1981-93, cons. strategic planning, 1983-95; pres. Anamex, Inc., 1995—; bd. trustees South Mountain Counseling Ctr., 1987—, chmn. bd. trustees, 1994—; bd. dirs. N.J. Eye Inst.; session leader Internet Conf., Florence, Italy, 1992; session moderator, panel mem. MES Conf., Cairo, Egypt, 1993, spkr., session leader Vancouver, 1994, keynote spkr. New Zealand, 1995; lectr. in field;. Author: Pace: System Manual, 1979, Voices, 1982; contbr. articles to profl. jours. and Maplewood Community calendar. Chmn. Citizens Budget Adv. Com., Maplewood, N.J., 1984-87, chmn. recreation, libr., pub. svcs., 1982-83, 94-96, chmn. pub. safety, emergency svcs., 1983-84, chmn. schs. and edn., 1984-85; first v.p. Maplewood Civic Assn., 1987-89, pres., 1989-91, sec. 1993-94, bd. dirs., officer, 1984—; chmn. Maple Leaf Svc. award Com., 1987-89, 94—, Community Svc. Coun. of Oranges and Maplewood Homelessness, Affordable Housing, Shelter Com., 1988—; chmn. speaker's bur. United Way, 1989-93; bd. trustees United Way Essex and West Hudson Cmty. Svc. Coun., 1988-; v.p. mktg. United Way Community Svc. Coun. of Oranges and Maplewood, 1990-93, v.p. 1994; mem. Maplewood Zoning Bd. of Adjustment, 1983—; officer, mem. exec. bd. N.J. Project Mgmt. Inst., 1985—, pres., 1987-88, 95—, v.p. adminstrn., 1994—; bd. dirs. Performance Mgmt. Assn.; chmn. Charter Com.; chmn. Internat. Project Mgmt. Inst. Jour. and Membership survey, 1986-87, mktg. com., 1986-89, long range planning and steering com., 1987—; bd. dirs., vice chmn. Coun. Chpt. Pres. Interaction Com., 1986-90, chmn., 1991—, pres. Internat. Project Mgmt. Inst., 1991, chmn., 1992, v.p. Region II, 1989-90; adv. bd. Project Mgmt. Jour., 1987-90, N.J. PMI Ednl., 1987—; liaison officer, PMI internat. liaison to Australian Inst. of Project Mgmt. and Western Australia Project Mgmt. Assn.; apptd. fellow Leadership N.J., 1993—, Internat. Project Mgmt. Inst. and Performance Mgmt. Assocs.; mem. MCA/N.J. Blood Bank Drive; chmn. Maplewood Community Calendar, 1990—; trustee community svc. coun. and edn. program United Way Essex and West Hudson, 1988—, also, chmn. leadership div., chmn. speakers bur., 1991— and mem. communications com.; pres. N.J. Project Mgmt. Inst., 1995—; chmn. Maplewood Republican County Com., 1996. Recipient Spl. commendation for Community Svc. Twp. Maplewood, 1987; First Place award Anti-Shoplifting Program for Distributive Edn. Club Am., 1981, N.J. Fedn. of Women's Clubs, 1981, 82, Retail Mchts. Assn., 1981, 82; Commendation and Merit awards Air Force Inst. Tech., 1981; Pres.'s Safety award ITT, 1983; State award 1st Pl. N.J. Fedn. of Women's Clubs Garden Show, 1982, Outstanding Pres. award Internat. Project Mgmt. Inst., 1988, Outstanding Svc. and Contbrn. award 1986-87; Cert. Spl. Merit award N.J. Fedn. of Women's Clubs, 1982, Disting. Contbn. award United Way, 1990, Pursuit of Exellence Cost Savings Achievement award ITT Avionics, 1990, Meritorious Svc. Recognition award Internat. Project Mgmt. Inst., 1989-90, Maple Leaf award for outstanding community svc., 1992, Phoebe and Benjamin Shackelford award United Way, 1992, U.S. Ho. Reps. citation, 1992, N.H. Gen. Assembly Senate resolution for Community Leadership and Svc., 1992, resolution of Appreciation Township of Maplewood; N.J. Leadership fellow, 1993, awarded fellow of Internat. Project Mgmt. Inst., 1995. Mem. Internat. Platform Speakers Assn., Grand Jury Assn., Telecommunications Group and Aerospace Industries Assn., Women's Career Network Assn., Nat. Security Indsl. Assn., Assn. for Info. and Image Mgmt., Internat. Project Mgmt. Inst. (liaison officer, pres. 1991—), Performance Mgmt. Assn., Indsl. Rels. Rsch. Assn., ITT Mgmt. Assn., NAFE, Rutger's Grad. Sch. Bus. Mgmt. Alumni Assn., Maplewood LWV (chair women and family issues com., voter registration bd. dirs.), Maplewood Women's Evening Membership Div. (pres. 1980-82), Lions (Maplewood dir. 1992-95, program chmn. 1991-92, treas. 1994-95, N.J. dist. 16E zone chmn. 1992-93, 95-96, cabinet sec. internat. dist., region chmn. 1993-94, 96—, trustee Eye Bank N.J., internat. dist. 16-E cabinet sec. 1994-95, dist. 16-E chmn. peace poster contest 1995—, pres. Newark 1995—, N.J. State chmn. youth outreach and quest 1995—). Home: 594 Valley St Maplewood NJ 07040-2616 Office: 21 Madison Plz Ste 152 Madison NJ 07940-2354

O'BRIEN, MARY ELLEN CHRISTINA, artist, educator; b. Caribou, Maine, Nov. 15, 1928; d. Richard Stephen and Caroline Elizabeth (McGuire) Sullivan; m. John Michael O'Brien, May 15, 1965; children: Maureen-Caroline, Kathleen. Cert. in arts, Cambridge Sch. of Design; student, Crafts Students League, 1958, Paul Puzinas Art Studio, 1959, Penland Sch. of Crafts, 1994. Freelance designer MIT and Harvard U., Cambridge, Mass., 1954-55; arts and crafts dir. Cambridge coun. Girl Scouts U.S., 1955; arts and crafts dir. Spl. Svcs., U.S. Army, Ft. Devens, Mass., 1956-57, Ft. Totten, N.Y., 1957-61, Europe, 1961-64; art tchr. Red Feather Agys., Boston, 1955-56; freelance comml. artist Jordon March, Boston, 1955-56; art tchr. Most Holy Redeemer Sch., Tampa, Fla., 1971-78, Acad. of Holy Names, Tampa, 1986-94; art specialist City of Tampa, 1979-81; pvt. tchr., 1981-86; creative art dir. polit. campaign Dem. Party, Tampa. 1970's. Cover design artist The Patron Sts., 1959; one-woman shows include Methodist Adminstrn. Bldg., Realistic Artist Gallery, Fed. Bank Bldg.; exhibitions include Busch-Reisinger Mus., Cambridge, Mass., 1955, Portland Art Mus., Maine, Art League L.I. Gallery Puzinas Studio, Gt. Neck, N.Y., Living Design Studio, Manchester, N.H., N.Y. Pub. Libr. Sys. Bayside Br., L.I., The Studio Gallery, L.I., N.Y., First Presbyn. Ch. Temple Terrace, Stewart Art Show, Gasparilla Outdoor Art Show, Lowry Park Outdoor Art Show, Vets. Adminstrn. Hosp., Fla., St. Joseph's Art Gallery, Fla., 1978, Rental Gallery of Tampa Bay Art Ctr., Fla., 1973, Mus. of Art., Fla., Performing Art Ctr., Fla., Fla. Craftsmen Gallery, St. Petersburg, and numerous others. Mem. delegation to Japan to observe art in schs. People to People Delegation, 1995; docent Mus. Art, 1974-85, 94—; vol. Performing Arts Ctr. Mem. Nat. League Am. Pen Women (pres. 1984-85, chair nat. art competition), Alpha Delta Kappa. Roman Catholic. Home: 10801 N Edison Ave Tampa FL 33612

O'BRIEN, MARYELLEN, state agency administrator, art educator; b. No. Attleboro, Mass., July 8, 1955; d. William Christopher and Alice Margaret O.; m. Robert Lane Latulippe, Aug. 14, 1976 (div. Oct. 1981); children: Paul Michael O'Brien Latulippe, Jeffrey Joseph O'Brien Latulippe. MFA, Lesley Coll., 1996. Med. sec. Univ. Hosp., Boston, 1984-85; adminstrv. sec. Boston Univ. Med. Ctr., 1985-88; asst. office mgr. Dept. of Employment and Tng., Boston, 1988—; adj. art instr. Quincy (Mass.) Coll., 1993—; performance recognition com. mem. Dept. of Employment and Tng., Boston, 1990, notary public, Boston, 1989—. Executed mural interior bathroom wall, Paradise Lane, Milton, Mass., 1992; represented in pvt. collections. Spkr. Gov. Dukakis Job Fair Bayside Expn. Ctr., Dorchester, Mass., 1985; vol. South Shore Art Assn., Cohasset, Maine, 1994, vol. instr. residential home, Chepachet, R.I., 1995. Recipient cert. of proficiency Boston Tech. Ctr., 1985. Mem. Nat. Mus. of Women in the Arts, South Shore Art Assn. Home: 85 Hollis Ave North Quincy MA 02171

O'BRIEN, PATRICIA NEVIN, computer scientist; b. Hanover, Pa., June 13, 1957; d. Malcolm Hugh and Lida Mae (Smith) Nevin; m. Thomas Gerard O'Brien, May 2, 1981; children: Thomas Joseph, Karen Louise. BS in Psychology, Towson State U., 1978, MA, 1980. Rsch. asst. Johns Hopkins U., Balt., 1980-82; programmer-analyst Johns Hopkins U., Towson, Md., 1982; ops. rsch. analyst U.S. Army, Aberdeen, Md., 1983-84, 86-87; officer BDM Corp., Albuquerque, 1984-85; pres. Maverick, Inc., Albuquerque, 1985-86; chief analysis div. Def. Test and Evaluation Support Agy., Albuquerque, 1987-89; ops. rsch. analyst Operational Test and Evaluation Ctr. USAF, Albuquerque, 1989—. Mem. Am. Soc. for Quality Control. Office: HQ AFOTEC/SAN 8500 Gibson Blvd SE Kirtland AFB NM 87117-5558

O'BRIEN, SANDRA CHRISTINE, county auditor, educator; b. Cleve., Sept. 30, 1951; d. Angelo and Evelyn (Wikowski) Citro; m. Patrick O'Brien, May 11, 1973; children: Casey, Colleen, Connor, Corey. BS in Elem. Edn., Bowling Green State U., 1973; M in Adminstrn., Edinboro U., 1983. Cert. elem. edn., Ohio. Tchr. St. Joan of Arc Sch., Chagrin Falls, Ohio, 1973-75; tchr. adult edn. Ashtabula (Ohio) County, 1984-85, tchr. elem. edn. Ashtabula Area City Schs., 1986-95; auditor Ashtabula County, Jefferson, Ohio, 1995—. Mem. NEA, Ohio Edn. Assn., Ohio Auditors Assn., Henderson Meml. Libr. Assn., Ashtabula Arts Ctr., Jefferson C. of C., Rep. Clubs. Roman Catholic. Home: 3434 Stumpville Rd Rome OH 44085 Office: Ashtabula County Auditor 25 W Jefferson St Ashtabula OH 44044

OBRINSKI, ROBYN RENEE, township official, assessor, accountant; b. Albion, Mich., Oct. 26, 1959; d. Stanley and Nancy Zoe (Fenley) Kulikowski; m. Duncan McLeod, July 3, 1984 (div. 1990), m. Walter Dean Obrinski, Aug. 8, 1992; children: Daniel, Dean, Slone. AAS in Acctg. with highest honors, Kellogg Cmty. Coll., 1992, AAS in Bus. Mgmt. with highest honors, 1992; BA in Acctg., Siena Heights Coll., 1994. Accounts payable clk. Kellogg Cmty. Coll., Battle Creek, Mich., 1991-92; deputy assessor Clarence Twp., Albion, 1992—; level II assessor Marengo Twp., Convis Twp., Sheridan Twp., 1994—; tech. cons. Sheridan Twp., Albion, 1994. Vol. Albion Vol. Agy., 1993. Mem. AICPA, Inst. Mgmt. Accts. Home: 25071 T Dr N Olivet MI 49076 Office: Marengo Twp 13395 23 Mile Albion MI 49224

O'BRYON, LINDA ELIZABETH, television station executive; b. Washington, Sept. 1, 1949; d. Walter Mason Ormes and Iva Genevieve (Batrus) Ranney; m. Dennis Michael O'Bryon, Sept. 8, 1973; 1 child, Jennifer Elizabeth. BA in Journalism cum laude, U. Miami, Coral Gables, Fla. News reporter Sta. KCPX, Salt Lake City, 1971-73; documentary and pub. affairs producer Sta. WPLG-TV, Miami, Fla., 1974-76; producer, reporter, anchor, news dir. then v.p. for news and pub. affairs, exec. editor, sr. v.p. The Nightly Business Report Sta. WPBT-TV (PBS), Miami, 1976—. Recipient award Fla. Bar, Tallahasse, 1977, 2 awards Ohio State U., 1976, 79, local Emmy award So. Fla. chpt. Nat. Acad. TV Arts and Scis., 1978, award Corp. for Pub. Broadcasting, 1978, Econ. Understanding award Amos Tuck Sch. Bus. Dartmouth Coll., Hanover, N.H., 1980, award Fla. AP, 1981, 1st prize Nat. Assn. Rea Hors, 1986, Bus. News Luminary award Bus. journalism Rev., 1990, Am. Women in Radio and TV award, 1995. Mem. Nat. Acad. TV Arts and Scis. (former So. Fla. bd. dirs.), Radio-TV News Dirs. Assn., Sigma Delta Chi. Republican. Roman Catholic. Office: Sta WPBT 14901 NE 20th Ave Miami FL 33181-1121

O'CALLAGHAN, KARIN CYNTHIA, marketing professional, textile designer; b. Oxford, Eng., May 15, 1962; came to U.S., 1964; d. Gerald Ray and Claire Ellen (Holtzen) Miller; m. Michael Thomas O'Callaghan, May 27, 1989 (div. Oct., 1992). BS in Textile Design, Phila. Coll. Textiles & Sci., 1984; postgrad. studies in Bus. Adminstrn., Pepperdine U., 1994—. Asst. textile stylist J.P. Stevens & Co., N.Y.C., 1984-85; women's wear designer Phillips Van Heusen, N.Y.C., 1985-86; textile stylist Delta-Woodside Industries, N.Y.C., 1986-88; mktg. mgr. Del Mar Window Coverings, Westminster, Calif., 1988-94, Cecil Saydah Co., L.A., 1994—. Mem. Color Mktg. Group (chair holder), Textile Inst. (Eng.). Home: 5400 The Toledo #607 Long Beach CA 90803

O'CALLAGHAN, ZINA B., sales manager; b. Chgo., Oct. 30, 1967; d. Santo and Gina (Conte) Barbaro; m. Michael O'Callaghan, July 10, 1994. BBA, Roosevelt U., 1991. Staffing mgr. Accountemps divs. Robert Half Internat., Inc., Hoffman Estates, Ill., 1992-95, dir. Accountemps divsn., 1995—, br. mgr., 1996—. Mem. Inst. Mgmt. Accts., Am. Inst. Profl. Bookkeepers. Roman Catholic.

OCHMAN, B. L., public relations executive, writer; b. N.Y.C., Mar. 13, 1949; d. Reuben and Dorothy (Bussel) Friedman. BA in Journalism, U. Bridgeport (Conn.), 1968. Account exec. Leo Miller Assocs., Westport, Conn., 1968-74; pub. rels. dir. M. Hohner Inc., L.I., N.Y., 1974-76; editorial dir. Ruder & Finn Pub. Rels., N.Y.C., 1976-78; account supr. Ben Kubasik Pub. Relations, N.Y.C., 1978-79; pres. Rent-A-Kvetch, Inc., N.Y.C., 1979—; pres. B.L. Ochman Pub. Relations, N.Y.C., 1979—. Mem. N.Y. C. of C., N.Y. New Media Assn. Office: 594 Broadway Rm 809 New York NY 10012-3257

OCHS, JOAN G., lawyer; b. Pitts., July 22, 1956. BA in History with honors, Northwestern U., 1978; JD, George Washington U., 1981. Bar: D.C. 1981. Ptnr. Arnold & Porter, Washington. Mem. ABA, D.C. Bar Assn. Office: Arnold & Porter 555 12th St NW Washington DC 20004*

OCKO, STEPHANIE, writer, journalist; b. Newport, R.I.; d. Howard Webster and Irma Coffin (Richardson) Goss; m. Stephen Ocko (div. 1993); 1 child, Peter Jeffrey. BA in Anthropology, Boston U., 1972; grad. degree in comm., Simmons Coll., 1978; MA in Fine Arts, Harvard U., 1986. English instr. Inst. Pedagogique Nat., Kinshasa, Zaire, 1965-66, Stonehill Coll.,

North Easton, Mass., 1985-89. Author: Environmental Vacations, 1990, 2d edit., 1991 (Best Travel Book, Am. Book Assn. 1990-91), Water, Almost Enough for Everyone, 1995 (1st Pl. award N.Y. Book Show 1995), Adventure Vacations, 1995. Mem. Nat. Writers Union, Internat. Sci. Writers Assn., Soc. Environ. Journalists. Home: PO Box 1959 Boston MA 02205

O'CONNELL, BARBARA KATHRYN, university administrator; b. Manhasset, N.Y., Apr. 17, 1963; d. John Joseph and Joan Amelia (McCorkell) O'C. BA, Westminster Coll., 1985. Admissions counselor Westminster Coll., Fulton, Mo., 1985-86, asst. dean admissions, 1986-87; assoc. univ. dir. admissions Fairleigh Dickinson U., Rutherford, N.J., 1987-90; campus dir. admissions Fairleigh Dickinson U., Teaneck, N.J., 1988-90; exec. dir. enrollment svcs. Rockhurst Coll., Kansas City, Mo., 1990-94; v.p. enrollment mgmt. Bryant Coll., Smithfield, R.I., 1995—; dir. "Tools of the Trade" workshop Mo. Assn. Coll. Admission Counselors, 1992. Bd. dirs. N.W. Cmty. Health Orgn.; mem. scholarship com. Children's Crusade, R.I.; mem. Alliance for Women's Awareness, R.I.; sponsor St. Ann's Ch. Sr. H.S. Youth Group, Mo.; tchr. Jr. Achievement Program, Mo. Named Dist. Leader of the Yr. Omicron Delta Kappa, 1985; named to Outstanding Young Women of Am., 1985. Mem. AAUW, Am. Assn. Collegiate Registrars and Admission Officers, Am. Mktg. Assn., Coun. for Advancement and Support of Edn., Greater Providence C. of C., Nat. Assn. Coll. Admission Counselors, Nat. Assn. Fin. Aid Adminstrs., Nat. Assn. Fgn. Student Advisors, Consortium of Jesuit Admission Dirs. (chair-elect 1994), Greater Providence C. of C. (mem. phone-a-thon). Roman Catholic. Office: Bryant College 1150 Douglas Pike Smithfield RI 02917

O'CONNELL, SISTER COLMAN, college president, nun. BA in English, Speech, Coll. St. Benedict, St. Joseph, Minn., 1950; MFA in Theater, English, Cath. U., 1954; PhD in Higher Edn. Adminstrn., U. Mich., 1979; student, Northwestern U., Birmingham U., Stratford, Eng., Denver U., Stanford U., Sophia U., Tokyo. Entered Order of St. Benedict. Tchr. English Pierz (Minn.) Meml. High Sch., 1950-53, Cathedral High Sch., St. Cloud, Minn., 1950-53; chairperson theater and dance dept. then prof. theater Coll. of St. Benedict, St. Joseph, 1954-74, dir. alumnae, parent relations, ann. fund, 1974-77, dir. planning, 1979-84, exec. v.p., 1984-86, pres., 1986-96; cons. Augsburg Coll., Mpls., 1983-85, Assn. Cath. Coll. and Univs., 1982, Minn. Pvt. Coll. Council, 1982, SW (Minn.) State U., Marshall, 1980-82, Wilmar (Minn.) Community Coll., 1980-82, Worthington (Minn.) Community Coll., 1980-82, U. Minn., Morris, 1980-82; bd. dirs. Minn. Publ Radio. Chair bd. dirs. Minn. Pvt. Coll. Coun., 1991-92; bd. dirs. St. Cloud Cmty. Found., 1991-94. Mem. Nat. Assn. Ind. Colls. and Univs. (bd. dirs. 1993), St. Cloud Area C. of C. (bd. dirs. 1987-90). Office: Coll Saint Benedict 37 College Ave S Saint Joseph MN 56374-2001

O'CONNELL, KATIE, film company executive. Sr. v.p. bus. and legal affairs The Walt Disney Motion Pictures Group, Burbank, Calif. Office: Walt Disney Pictures-Touchstone 500 S Buena Vista St Burbank CA 91521-0001*

O'CONNELL, KRISTIN ROSE, preschool educator; b. Ashland, Pa., Feb. 20, 1971; d. Francis Xavier and Roseann (Wolfgang) O'C. BS in Elem. Edn., Coll. Misericordia, 1993. Cert. early childhood tchr., Pa.; cert. elem. tchr., Pa. Asst. dir. Graham Rd. Child Devel. Ctr., Falls Church, Va., 1994-96, presch. tchr., 1994-96; presch. tchr. Tender Yr. Child Devel., Inc., Hershey, Pa., 1996—. Mem. ASCD.

O'CONNELL, MARGARET ELLEN, editor, writer; b. N.Y.C., May 2, 1947; d. Daniel Gregory O'Connell and Anastasia Marie Crowley. BA, Hunter Coll., 1969; std. cert., Am. Inst. Banking, 1974; postgrad., Pace U., 1995. Circulation dir., book reviewer, office mgr. Emmanuel Mag., N.Y.C., 1984-85; assoc. editor The Christophers, Inc., N.Y.C., 1985—. Editor: Christopher Book, Calendar, Pocket Planner, 1986—; book reviewer Cath. News Svc.; contbr. book revs. and articles to periodicals. Bd. dirs. Brewster-Carver Coop. Apts., Bronxville, N.Y., 1987-88, pres. bd. dirs., 1988-89; lay min. of the Eucharist, lector St. Francis of Assisi Ch., 1987—. Mem. AAUW, Internat. Union of Cath. Press, Cath. Press Assn., St. Benedict the Moor Fraternity (gov. coun., rec. sec. 1982-88, 91-95), Secular Franciscan Order N.Y.C. Office: The Christophers Inc 12 E 48th St New York NY 10017

O'CONNELL, MARY ANN, state senator, business owner; b. Albuquerque, Aug. 3, 1934; d. James Aubrey and Dorothy Nell (Batsel) Gray; m. Robert Emmett O'Connell, Feb. 21, 1977; children: Jeffery Crampton, Gray Crampton. Student, U. N.Mex., Internat. Coun. Shopping Ctrs. Exec. dir. Blvd. Shopping Ctr., Las Vegas, Nev., 1968-76, Citizen Pvt. Enterprise, Las Vegas, 1976; media supr. Southwest Advt., Las Vegas, 1977—; owner, operator Meadows Inn, Las Vegas, 1985—, 3 Christian bookstores, Las Vegas, 1985—; state senator Nev. Senate, 1985—; chmn. govtl. affairs; vice chmn. commerce and labor; mem. taxation com.; vice chmn. Legis. Commn., 1985-86, 95-96; mem., 1987-88, 91-93; commr. Edn. Commn. States; rep. Nat. Conf. State Legislators; past vice chair State Mental Hygiene & Mental Retardation Adv. Bd. Pres. explorer div. Boulder Dam Area coun. Boy Scouts Am., Las Vegas, 1979-80, former mem. exec. bd.; mem. adv. bd. Boy Scouts Am.; pres., bd. dirs. Citizens Pvt. Enterprise, Las Vegas, 1982-84, Secret Witness, Las Vegas, 1081-82; vice chmn. Gov.'s Mental Health-Mental Retardation, Nev., 1983—; past mem. community adv. bd. Care Unit Hosp., Las Vegas; past mem. adv. bd. Kidney Found., Milligan Coll., Charter Hosp.; tchr. Young Adult Sunday Sch. Recipient Commendation award Mayor O. Grayson, Las Vegas, 1975, Outstanding Citizenship award Bd. Realtors, 1975, Silver Beaver award Boy Scouts Am., 1980, Free Enterprise award Greater Las Vegas C. of C., Federated Employers Assn., Downtwon Breakfast Exch., 1988, Award of Excellence for Women in Politics, 1989, Legislator of Yr. award Bldg. and Trades, 1991, Legislator of Yr. award Nat. ASA Trade Assn., 1991, 94, Guardian of Liberty award Nev. Coalition of Conservative Citizens, 1991, Internat. Maxi Awards Promotional Excellence; named Legislator of Yr., Nev. Retail Assn., 1992. Mem. Retail Mchts. Assn. (former pres., bd. dirs.), Taxpayers Assn. (bd. dirs.), Greater Las Vegas C. of C. (past pres., bd. dirs., Woman of Achievement Politics women's coun. 1988). Republican. Mem. Christian Ch. Home: 7225 Montecito Cir Las Vegas NV 89120-3118 Office: Nev Legislature Senate 401 S Carson St Carson City NV 89701-4747

O'CONNELL, MARY ITA, psychotherapist; b. Balt., July 3, 1929; d. Richard Charles and Ona (Buchness) O'C.; m. Leon Jack Greenbaum, Dec. 28, 1962 (div. Jan. 1986); children: Jessie A., Elizabeth K. BA, U. Md., 1956; postgrad., Am. U., 1960—; M in Creative Arts in Therapy, Hahnemann Med. Coll., 1978. Registered Acad. Dance Therapists. Tchr. Robert Cohan Sch. Dance, Boston, 1958-61; instr., choreographer Wheaton Coll., Norton, Mass., 1959-60, Harvard/Radcliffe Colls., Boston, 1960-62; tchr., performer, choreographer Profl. Studios, Washington, 1962-69; asst. prof., adminstr. Fed. City Coll., Washington, 1969-74; movement psychotherapist Woodburn Ctr. for Community Mental Health, Fairfax, Va., 1975-76, Gundry Hosp., Balt., 1976-77, Prince Georges' Community Mental Health Dept., Capitol Heights, Md., 1978-80; lectr. George Washington U., D.C., 1981-85; pvt. practice psychotherapy Silver Spring, Md., 1977—; sr. movement psychotherapist Regional Inst. for Children and Adolescents, Rockville, Md., 1980-82; movement cons. Ctr. for Youth Svcs., Washington, 1981-83; movement psychotherapist D.C. Mental Health Ctrs., Washington, 1985-87, 90—, Community for Creative Non-Violence Women's Shelter, Washington, 1986, LICSW, Washington, 1989. Choreographer, soloist (dance performance) The Artist: A Theatre Happening, 1963; choreographer, co-dir. (outdoor dance event) Tree Sculpting, 1974; choreographer (dance performance) Excitations, 1967, A Dance Event, 1974; soloist, New England Opera, 1961; performer, choreographer WGBM TV/Laboratory Concert Series, 1961; performer, CBS-TV/Erika Thimey Dance Theatre, 1965; guest artist, Harford Coll. Art Festival, 1967. U. Md. scholar, 1955-56. Mem. Dance Circle of Boston (life, pres. 1959-61), Modern Dance Council of Washington (exec. bd dirs., editor 1965-69), Am. Dance Therapy Assn. (treas. metro chpt. 1977-81), Assn. Humanistic Psychology, Family Therapy Network, Am. Dance Guild, NIH (movement specialist 1978-79). Democrat. Home and Office: 16 Sussex Rd Silver Spring MD 20910-5435

O'CONNOR, BARBARA ANNE, circulation manager; b. Roslyn, N.Y., Sept. 29, 1962; d. Thomas Ronald and Barbara Jane (Bolina) O'C.; m. Stephen LaMantia, July 1, 1988. BA, SUNY, Stony Brook, 1984. Circulation asst. Equal Opportunity Publs., Inc., Greenlawn, N.Y., 1986-87; circulation coord. E.O.P., Inc., Greenlawn, N.Y., 1987-88, circulation mgr., 1988—. Contbr. articles to profl. publs. Vol. Family Svc. League of Suffold County, N.Y., 1991, Friends for Long Island's Heritage, 1996; exhibit organizer West Islip (N.Y.) Pub. Libr., 1991. Mem. NAFE, SUNY Stony Brook Alumni Assn., Heritage Treasures Collectors Club (libr.). Office: Equal Opportunity Publs Inc 1160 E Jericho Tpk Ste 200 Huntington NY 11743

O'CONNOR, BARBARA CASSIDY, middle school educator; b. Oceanside, Calif., Dec. 17, 1947; d. Kyle Zeigler and Genevieve Ruth (Clark) Cassidy; children: Kevin Christopher, Ryan Michael. BA in History, Whittier (Calif.) Coll., 1970; MA in Ednl. Adminstrn., U.S. Internat. U., San Diego, 1994. Tchr., chmn. jr. high dept. Sts. Simon and Jude Sch., Huntington Beach, Calif., 1981-89; learning specialist, dept. chmn., lang. arts/history tchr. McAuliffe Mid. Sch./Los Alamitos (Calif.) Unified Sch. Dist., 1989—; scorer Nat. Bd. for Profl. Tchg. Stds., Calif. Learning Assessment Sys., Sacramento. Mem. Nat. Coun. for the Social Studies, Nat. Coun. Tchrs. English. Roman Catholic. Office: McAuliffe Mid Sch 4112 Cerritos Ave Los Alamitos CA 90720-2577

O'CONNOR, BETTY LOU, service executive; b. Phoenix, Oct. 29, 1927; d. Georg Eliot and Tillie Edith (Miller) Miller; m. William Spoeri O'Connor, Oct. 10, 1948 (dec. Feb. 1994); children: Thomas W., William K., Kelli Anne. Student, U. So. Calif., 1946-48, Calif. State U., Los Angeles, 1949-50. V.p. O'Connor Food Svcs., Inc., Jack in the Box Restaurants, Granada Hills, Calif., 1983-93; pres. O'Connor Food Svcs., Inc., Granada Hills, Calif., 1994—, Western Restaurant Mgmt. Co., Granada Hills, 1986—; mem. adv. bd. Bank of Granada Hills. Recipient Frannie award Foodmaker, Inc., Northridge, Calif., 1984, First Rate award, 1992. Mem. Jack in the Box Franchisee Assn., Spurs Hon. (sec. U. So. Calif. 1947-48), Associated Women Students (sec. U. So. Calif. 1946-47), Gamma Alpha Chi (v.p. 1947-48), Chi Omega. Republican. Roman Catholic. Office: Western Restaurant Mgmt Co 17545 Chatsworth St Granada Hills CA 91344-5720

O'CONNOR, DENISE LYNN, marketing communications executive; b. West Palm Beach, Fla., Oct. 29, 1958; d. Joseph John and Ada Colleen (Doyle) Fields; m. William York O'Connor, May 31, 1985. BS in Bus., Fla. State U., 1979; MBA, Fla. Inst. Tech., 1983, postgrad. in elec. engring., 1984-86. Cons. Small Bus. Inst., Tallahassee, 1979; mgr. select accts. Burroughs, West Palm Beach, 1980-81; mgr. mktg. communications Harris-Satellite Communications, Melbourne, Fla., 1981-84; sect. mgr. mktg. communications Gen. Electric Info. Svcs., Rockville, Md., 1984-86; mgr. pub. rels. Mgmt. Sci. Am., Atlanta, 1986-88; pres., owner Mktg. Comms. Cons., Atlanta, 1988—, Saddle River, N.J., 1995—; cons. Sci.-Atlanta (Ga.), Inc., 1988—. Author (brochure) Genie, 1986 (Disting. award Soc. for Tech. Communications); editor (brochure) Electronic Data Interchange, 1986 (Excellence Soc. for Tech. Communications). Vol. Atlanta (Ga.) Humane Soc., 1988, (mem. auxiliary, 1989—). Recipient Ross Systems Pres. award, 1991. Mem. AAUW, PEO (v.p. reciprocity 1990-91, pres. evening and weekend reciprocity coun. 1991-92, chmn. Internat. Peace scholarship 1990), Soc. Tech. Comm., Atlanta Lawn and Tennis Assn.(pres. B-5 team 1989), Country Club South, Delta Zeta. Republican. Methodist. Home and Office: Mktg Comms 8 Denison Dr E Saddle River NJ 07458-2807

O'CONNOR, ELIZABETH PATRICIA, publishing executive; b. Chgo.; d. Michael John and Ann O'C. BA, U. Ill., 1983, MBA, 1986. Fin. trainee Sears Roebuck and Co., Chgo., 1984-86; fin. analyst Ency. Britannica, Chgo., 1986-88, mgr., 1989-91, dir. fin. opers., 1991-93, exec. dir. fin., 1993-95, v.p. fin. and adminstrn., 1995—; bd. dirs. Chgo. Book Clinic, program chair, 1995—. Mem. Chgo. Athletic Assn. (entertainment com. 1995-96). Office: Ency Britannica Inc 310 S Michigan Ave Chicago IL 60604

O'CONNOR, GAYLE MCCORMICK, law librarian; b. Rome, N.Y., July 8, 1956; d. John Joseph and Barbara Jane (Molyneaux) McC. Head libr. Bolling, Walter & Gawthrop, Sacramento, 1987-88, Weintraub, Genshlea & Sproul, Sacramento, 1988-93, Brobeck, Phleger & Harrison, San Diego, 1993-96; legal cons., author, 1996—; instr. law Lincoln U., Sacramento. Contbr. articles to profl. jours. Mem. ABA, No. Calif. Assn. Law Librs., So. Calif. Assn. Law Librs., Am. Assn. Law Librs., Spl. Librs. Assn. (chair-elect legal divsn. 1996—).

O'CONNOR, SISTER GEORGE AQUIN (MARGARET M. O'CONNOR), college president, sociology educator; b. Astoria, N.Y., Mar. 5, 1921; d. George M. and Joana T. (Loughlin) O'C. B.A., Hunter Coll., 1943; M.A., Catholic U. Am., 1947; Ph.D. (NIMH fellow), NYU, 1964; LL.D. Manhattan Coll., 1983. Mem. faculty St. Joseph's Coll., Bklyn., 1946—; prof. sociology and anthropology St. Joseph's Coll., 1966—, chmn. social sci. dept., 1966-69, pres., 1969—; Fellow African Studies Assn., Am. Anthrop. Assn.; Bklyn. C. of C. (dir. 1973—), Alpha Kappa Delta, Delta Epsilon Sigma. Author: The Status and Role of West African Women: A Study in Cultural Change, 1964. Office: Saint Joseph's Coll Office of Pres 245 Clinton Ave Brooklyn NY 11205-3602

O'CONNOR, GINGER HOBBA, speech pathologist; b. Poynette, Wis., Apr. 20, 1951; d. Walter Leslie and Mary Elizabeth (Krause) Hobba; m. William Scott Elliott, Dec. 27, 1973 (div. 1984); children: Todd C., William Trent, Tiffany Paige; m. Michael Robert O'Connor, Aug. 11, 1990; 1 child, Tanner Michael O'Connor. BA, Marietta Coll., 1973; MA, Ohio State U., 1974. Speech pathologist Del. (Ohio) Speech/Hearing Ctr., 1974-75; speech pathologist Washington County Bd. Mental Retardation Devel. Disabilities, Marietta, Ohio, 1975—, supr. dept. communications, 1985—; speech pathologist ancillary staff Marietta Hosp., 1975—; cons., lectr. Ohio U., Athens, 1980—; lectr. South Eastern Ohio Spl. Edn. Resource Ctr., Athens, 1975—; pres., co-founder MR/DD Speech-Lang.-Hearing Network of Ohio, 1992-94. Bd. dirs. Child Devel. Ctr., Marietta, 1977-80, Washington County ARC; mem. med. adv. bd. Headstart, Marietta, 1984—; dist. program chairperson Boy Scouts Am., Parkersburg, W.Va., 1989-92; mem. Ohio Safe Kids Coalition; speech pathologist Operation Smile mission to Russia, 1995, 96; co-chair YMCA com. for Internat. Awareness, 1992—. Mem. Am. Speech Lang. Hearing Assn. (spkr. 1979—), Ohio Speech Lang. Hearing Assn. (legis. coun. rep. 1990-94, pres.-elect 1995-96, pres. 1996-97), Southeastern Ohio Speech Hearing Assn. (v.p. 1982-83, pres. 1983-84), Profl. Assn. for Retarded Adults, Southeastern Ohio Soc. for Augmentative and Alternative Communication. Methodist. Home: 124 Keyser St Marietta OH 45750-1019 Office: Wash Cty Bd Men Ret Devel PO Box 702 Marietta OH 45750-0702

O'CONNOR, KAREN LENDE, Olympic athlete; b. Feb. 17, 1958; m. David O'Connor, 1993. Mem. US Equestrian Olympic Team, Seoul, Korea, 1988, Atlanta, 1996. Winner CCI, Boekelo (Holland), 1984, CCI, Chesterland (Pa.), 1985, placed 1st Role/Kentucky Internat. CCI Three Day Event, 1991, 1st Tetbury (Eng.) Horse Trials, 1991, 1st Fair Hill (Md.) Horse Trials, 1991, 3rd Burghley Three Day Event CCI (Eng.), 1991, 6th World Three Day Event Rider Rankings L'Annee Hippique, 1991, 3rd CCI, Loughanmore (Ireland), 1992, 6th Blenheim Audi Internat. Horse Trials (Eng.), 1993, 1st CCI, Punchestown (Ireland), 1993, 10th CCI Internat. de Saumur, 1994; recipient Silver medal, Olympic Games, Atlanta, 1996; named U.S. Combined Tng. Assn. Lady Rider of the Year, 1989, 90, 91, Female Equestrian Athlete of the Year Olympic Com., 1993; grantee USET, 1991. Office: care Am Horse Shows Assn 220 E 72nd St Ste 409 New York NY 10017*

O'CONNOR, KATHLEEN ANNE, office manager; b. Elmhurst, N.Y., Aug. 31, 1963; d. John J. and Virginia G. (Waldvogel) Uster; m. Terence O'Connor, May 12, 1985 (div. 1987). BA in Poly. Sci., CAS, CUNY, 1996. Legal sec. Stuart R. Kramer, P.C., Rego Park, N.Y., 1982-85, James S. Falletta Esq., Forest Hill, N.Y., 1985-87, Resnicoff, Samanowitz, Endzweig & Brawer, Great Neck, N.Y., 1987-89; office mgr. Mark E. Weinberger P.C., Great Neck, 1989—. Mem. Nat. Honor Soc., Pi Sigma Alpha. Democrat. Roman Catholic. Home: 1 Wooleys Ln #3L Great Neck NY 11023 Office: Mark E Weinberger PC 185 Great Neck Rd #350 Great Neck NY 11021

O'CONNOR, KATHLEEN MARIE, marketing and public relations executive; b. Kansas City, Mo., July 27, 1961; d. Thomas D. and Cecelia A. (O'Donnell) O'C. BA in Advt., Marquette U., 1983; M.J. in Journalism, U. N. Tex., 1985. Grad. teaching asst. dept. journalism U. N. Tex., Denton, 1983-85; constrn. news rep. F.W. Dodge Reports, Dallas, 1985-86; editor Boeing Aerospace & Electronics, Irving, Tex., 1986-88; editor (newsletter) Transmitter, 1987-89; with communications/pub. rels. Boeing Aerospace & Electronics, Irving, 1988-90; sr. mktg. writer 1st Gilbraltar Bank, Dallas, 1990-91; mgr. marketing comm. Waddell & Reed Inc., Overland Park, Kans., 1992—. Editor (newsletter) Transmitter, 1987-89. Mem. bd. dirs. Arthritis Found. Kans. chpt. 1993— (exec. com, 1993-95), rep., mem. Irving C. of C., 1988-89, mem. pub. relations com., 1989. Mem. Women in Communication, Inc., Internat. Assn. Bus. Communicators, Pub. Relations Soc. Am. Home: 2900 W 94th Ter Leawood KS 66206

O'CONNOR, KATHRYN MACVEAN, elementary educator; b. Middletown, N.Y., Aug. 9, 1960; d. Kenneth Alpin and Anna Margaret (Daley) MacVean; m. Shawn Richard O'Connor, Oct. 15, 1988; children: Andrew Kenneth, Matthew John. BS, Syracuse U., 1982; MA, SUNY, New Paltz, 1984. Educator Mt. Carmel Sch., Middletown, 1982-85; asst. prof. SUNY, New Paltz, 1985-90; tchr. Minisink Valley Ctrl. Sch., Slate Hill, N.Y., 1987—. Mem. Jr. League of Orange County, Middletown, 1985—; bd. dirs. People for People, Middletown, 1989—. Mem. Nat. Coun. Tchrs. Math., Phi Delta Kappa. Office: Minisink Valley Elem Sch Rt 6 PO Box 217 Slate Hill NY 10973

O'CONNOR, KAY, state legislator; b. Everett, Wash., Nov. 28, 1941; d. Ernest S. and Dena (Lampers) Wells; m. Arthur J. O'Connor, Sept. 1, 1959; 6 children. Diploma, Lathrop H.S., Fairbanks, Alaska, 1959. Office mgr. Blaylock Chemicals, Bucyrus, Kans., 1981-84; store mgr. Copies Plus, Olathe, Kans., 1984-86; acct. Advance Concrete Inc., Spring Hill, Kans., 1986-92; mem. Kansas Ho. of Reps., 1993—; bd. dirs. Hometel Ltd.; author sch. voucher legis. for State of Kans., 1994, 95, 96. Republican. Roman Catholic. Home: 1101 N Curtis St Olathe KS 66061-2709 Office: PO Box 2232 Olathe KS 66051-2232

O'CONNOR, KIM CLAIRE, chemical engineering and biotechnology educator; b. N.Y.C., Nov. 18, 1960; d. Gerard Timothy and Doris Julia (Bisagni) O'C. BS magna cum laude, Rice U., Houston, 1982; PhD, Calif. Inst. Tech., Pasadena, 1987. Postdoctoral rsch. fellow chemistry dept. Calif. Inst. Tech., Pasadena, 1987-88; postdoctoral rsch. fellow chem. engring., biochemistry, molecular biology, and cell biology depts. Northwestern U., Evanston, Ill., 1988-90; asst. prof. chem. engring. Tulane U., New Orleans, 1990-96, assoc. prof. chem. engring., 1996—, faculty molecular and cellular biology grad. program, Newcomb fellow, 1991—; co-dir. molecular and cellular biology grad. program Tulane U., 1993-96; mem. Tulane Cancer Ctr., 1994—; cons. in field. Reviewer of profl. jours. Mem. Am. Chem. Soc., Am. Inst. Chem. Engrs., Am. Soc. Engring. Edn., European Soc. Animal Cell Tech., Soc. In Vitro Biology, Assn. for Women in Sci., Sigma Xi, Tau Beta Pi, Phi Lambda Upsilon. Office: Tulane U Dept Chem Engring Lindy Boggs Ctr Rm 300 New Orleans LA 70118

O'CONNOR, MARY GUILMARTIN, elementary school educator; b. Hartford, Conn., Oct. 28, 1931; d. Joseph Thomas and Helen (Cominsky) Guilmartin; m. John A. O'Connor, July 16, 1955; children: Mark Alan, Ellen Mary Shugart, Jenifer Mary Fanaza. BS in History and Polit. Sci., St. Joseph Coll., West Hartford, Conn., 1953; MEd, Sacred Heart U., 1989. Cert. tchr., Conn. Tchr. grade 2 High Street Sch., S. Glastonbury, Conn., 1953-55; tchr. specialized reading and math., grades 1-3 Race Brook Sch., Orange, Conn., 1973-79; tchr. Grade 1 St. Lawrence Sch., Huntington, Conn., 1979—; Mem. Student Assistance Team, 1990—, Tchrs. Inst. Com., 1993-96. Vol. Hospice. Mem. Nat. Cath. Edn. Assn. Democrat. Roman Catholic. Home: 3 Rock Ridge Rd Huntington CT 06484

O'CONNOR, MAUREEN, public relations executive; b. Plainfield, N.J., Sept. 24, 1948; d. John Vincent and Etta Mary (North) O'C.; m. Stephen Priest, May 28, 1981; children: Danielle C. Priest, Margaret E. Priest. BSBA, Rider Coll., 1971; postgrad., Rutgers U., 1971-73. East and west coast dir. publicist Capital Records, N.Y.C., L.A., 1973-87; sr. v.p. Solters/Roskin/Friedman, L.A., 1987-92; exec. v.p. entertainment Rogers & Cowan, L.A., 1992—. Active Hollywood's Rock Walk, PTA. Mem. NARAS, Publicist Guild. Office: Rogers & Cowan 1888 Century Park East Los Angeles CA 90067

O'CONNOR, PATRICIA ERYL, telecommunications consultant; b. Kansas City, Mo., Oct. 16, 1945; d. Jesse Edwin O'Connor and Olive Mae (Geagan) Brooks; m. James Harrie Reed, Dec. 18, 1964 (div. July 1972); 1 child, Jana Diann Reed; m. John Robert Morgan, Sept. 27, 1985. AAS, Pima Community Coll., Tucson, 1982. Cert. Nat. Assn. Broadcast Engrs. Radio, radio-telephone lic. gen. class FCC. Communications technician AT&T, Kansas City, Mo., 1972-79, Tucson, 1979-85, San Francisco, 1985-92, Denver, 1992—; chief exec. officer, cons. Profl. Forum Mgmt./MacCircles, Tucson, 1985, Pleasanton, Calif., 1985-92, Denver, 1992-96; co-adminstr. Mac Symposium, Cupertino, Calif., 1987-93. Editor: (electronic mag.) Handshake, 1985-96. Election judge, Tucson, 1979-81; area v.p. CWA Local 8150, Ariz., N.Mex., 1984-84, exec. v.p., 1984-85. Home: 24949 Montane Dr W Golden CO 80401-9192

O'CONNOR, PEGGY LEE, communications manager; b. Chgo., Apr. 20, 1953; d. William Stanley and Eleanor Sopie (Levandowski) Czaska; m. Charles B. O'Connor, III, Feb. 14, 1978. BS in Biology, Northeastern Ill. U., 1982; MBA, No. Ill. U., 1985. Emergency med. technologist, 1976-82; instr. Chgo. City Wide Colls., 1976-81; program dir. U. Ill. Hosp. 1979-81; program dir. Fermilab, Roselle, 1978-82; dist. adminstrv. mgr. Decision Data Svc., Schaumburg, Ill., 1981-89; gen. mgr. sales svc. Putman Pub., 1989-91; mgr. fin. and adminstrn. Weyerhaeuser, 1992—; ops. mgr. Ameritech Cellular, 1993—. Program dir. Am. Cellular Women's Adv. Panel. Recipient award Summit Club 1987, 88, 89. Mem. NAFE, NWAAR, Women in Bus., Pres's. Club, BPA (chairperson bd. dirs.), Chgo. Credit Mgrs. Assn. Avocation: computers. Office: Ameritech Cellular 2365 N Hicks Rd Palatine IL 60074-1806

O'CONNOR, RUTH SUSAN, physician, educator; b. Augusta, Ga., Apr. 23, 1952; d. Henry and Margaret Adeline (Schneider) Wynstra; m. Thomas Joseph O'Connor, Apr. 23, 1977; children: Samuel, Grace, Anna, Rhoda, Daniel. Student, Wheaton Coll., 1970-73; MD, Med. Coll. Wis., 1977; cert. family practice, Caraway Meth. Med. Ctr., 1980. Diplomate Am. Bd. Family Practice. Intern Carraway Meth. Med. Ctr., Birmingham, Ala., 1977-78, resident in family practice, 1978-80; fellow family practice Caraway Meth. Med. Ctr., Birmingham, Ala., 1980-81, instr. family practice, 1981-85; pvt. practice Greenville, Ill., 1986-88; instr. family practice Sch. Medicine So. Ill. U., Belleville, 1986-88; staff physician Student Health Ctr. Purdue U., West Lafayette, Ind., 1989—; instr. family medicine Ind. U., Indpls., 1989—; clin. asst. prof. family medicine. Recipient Achievement citation Am. Women's Med. Soc., 1977. Mem. Christian Med. Soc. Baptist. Home: 714 Kossuth St Lafayette IN 47905-1447 Office: Purdue U 1826 Student Health Ctr West Lafayette IN 47907

O'CONNOR, SANDRA DAY, United States supreme court justice; b. El Paso, Tex., Mar. 26, 1930; d. Harry A. and Ada Mae (Wilkey) Day; m. John Jay O'Connor, III, Dec. 1952; children: Scott, Brian, Jay. AB in Econs. with great distinction, Stanford U., 1950, LLB, 1952. Bar: Calif. Dep. county atty. San Mateo, Calif., 1952-53; civil atty. Q.M. Market Ctr., Frankfurt am Main, Fed. Republic of Germany, 1954-57; pvt. practice Phoenix, 1958-65; asst. atty. gen. State of Ariz., 1965-69; Ariz. state senator, 1969-75, chmn. com. on state, county and mcpl. affairs, 1972-73, majority leader, 1973-74; judge Maricopa County Superior Ct., 1975-79, Ariz. Ct. Appeals, 1979-81; assoc. justice U.S. Supreme Ct., 1981—; referee juvenile ct., 1962-64; chmn. vis. bd. Maricopa County Juvenile Detention Home, 1963-64; mem. Maricopa County Bd. Adjustments and Appeals, 1963-64, Anglo-Am. Legal Exchange, 1980, Maricopa County Superior Ct. Judges Tng. and Edn. Com., Maricopa Ct. Study Com.; chmn. com. to reorganize lower cts. Ariz. Supreme Ct., 1974-75; faculty Robert A. Taft Inst. Govt.; vice chmn. Select Law Enforcement Rev. Commn., 1979-80. Mem. bd. editors Stanford (Calif.) U. Law Rev. Mem. Ariz. Pers. Commn., 1968-69, Nat. Def. Adv. Com. on Women in Svcs., 1974-76; trustee Heard Mus., Phoenix, 1968-74, 76-81, pres., 1980-81; mem. adv. bd. Phoenix Salvation Army, 1975-81; trustee Stanford U., 1976-81, Phoenix County Day Sch.; mem. citizens adv.

bd. Blood Svcs., 1975-77; nat. bd. dirs. Smithsonian Assocs., 1981—; past Rep. dist. chmn.; bd. dirs. Phoenix Cmty. Coun., Ariz. Acad., 1969-75, Jr. Achievement Ariz., 1975-79, Blue Cross/Blue Shield Ariz., 1975-79, Channel 8, 1975-79, Phoenix Hist. Soc., 1974-78, Maricopa County YMCA, 1978-81, Golden Gate Settlement. Recipient Ann. award NCCJ, 1975, Disting. Achievement award Ariz. State U., 1980; named Woman of Yr., Phoenix Advt. Club, 1972; inducted, National Women's Hall of Fame, 1995. Lodge: Soroptimists. Office: US Supreme Ct Supreme Ct Bldg 1 First St NE Washington DC 20543

O'CONNOR, SHEILA ANNE, freelance writer; b. Paisley, Scotland, Jan. 20, 1960; came to the U.S., 1988; d. Brian Aubrey Witham and Margaret Kirk (Reid) Davies; m. Frank Donal O'Connor, Aug. 9, 1986; children: David Michael, Andrew James, Christine Charlotte. BA in French and German, Strathclyde U., 1980, postgrad. diploma in office studies, 1981, MBA, 1992. Office asst. BBC, London, 1982-83; asst. to mng. dir. Unimatic Engrs. Ltd., London, 1983-84; freelance word processing operator London, 1984-88; staff asst. Internat. Monetary Fund, Washington, 1988-94; prin. Internat. Media Assn., Washington, 1988—. Contbr. numerous articles to various publs. Mem. Am. Mktg. Assn., Bay Area Travel Writers Assn., Calif. Writers Club. Home and Office: 2531 39th Ave San Francisco CA 94116-2752

O'CONNOR, SUSAN J., environmentalist, international development consultant; b. San Diego, Nov. 3, 1954; d. Thomas F. O'Connor and Ann Surrey. Cert. nutrition cons., Nassau C.C., New Hyde Park, N.Y., 1981; BA in Environmental Studies, SUNY, Stony Brook, 1996. Fisheries cons. Norwegion Orgn. R & D, Nairobi, Kenya, 1979; UN cons. econ. devel. UN Devel. Program, Kampala, Uganda, 1980; nutrition cons. World Vision, Las Dhure, Somalia, 1981; program dir., office of econ. devel. Mercants Assn.-City of N.Y., 1991—; adv. bd. Lamu (Kenya) Mus., 1993—. Southern Arts Found. Artists fellow, 1992; artist-in-residence, Ecole Nat. de Photographie, Arles, France, 1992. Mem. Ctr. for Sci. in Pub. Interest. Home and Office: Many Moons #1K 135 Eastern Pkwy Brooklyn NY 11238

O'DAY, ANITA BELLE COLTON, entertainer, singer; b. Chgo., Oct. 18, 1919; d. James and Gladys (Gill) C. Student, Chgo. public schs. Singer and entertainer various Chgo. Music Clubs, 1939-41; singer with Gene Krupa's Orch., 1941-45, Stan Kenton Orch., 1944, Woody Herman Orch., 1945, Benny Goodman Orch., 1959; singing tours in U.S. and abroad, 1947—; rec. artist Polygram, Capitol, Emily Records, Verve, GNP Crescendo, Columbia, London, Signature, DRG, Pablo; million-seller songs include Let Me Off Uptown, 1941, And Her Tears Flowed Like Wine, 1944, Boogie Blues, 1945; appeared in films Gene Krupa Stody, 1959, Jazz on a Summer's Day, 1960, Zigzag, 1970, Outfit, 1974; TV shows 60 Minutes, 1980; Tonight Show, Dick Cavett Show, Today Show, Big Band Bash, CBS Sunday Morning, CNN Showbiz Today, others. Author: High Times, Hard Times, 1981, rev. edit., 1989; performed 50 yr. anniversary concert Carnegie Hall, 1985, Avery Fisher Hall, 1989, Tanglewood, 1990, Town Hall, 1993, Rainbow and Stars, 1995, currently touring worldwide; albums include Drummer Man, Kenton Era, Anita, Anita Sings The Most, Pick Yourself Up, Lady is a Tramp, An Evening with Anita O'Day, At Mr. Kelly's, Swings Cole Porter, Travelin' Light, All the Sad Young Men, Waiter Make Mine Blues, With the Three Sounds, I Told Ya I Love Ya Now Get Out, Uptown, My Ship, Live in Tokyo, Anita Sings the Winners, Incomparable, Anita 1975, Live at Mingos, Anita O'Day/The Big Band Sessions, Swings Rodgers and Hart, Time for Two, Tea for Two, In a Mellowtone, At Vine St. Live, Mello'Day, Live at the City, Angel Eyes, The Night Has a Thousand Eyes, The Rules of the Road, Jazz Masters, others. Mem. AFTRA, Screen Actors Guild, BMI. Office: 1824 Vista Del Mar Ave Los Angeles CA 90028-5208

O'DELL, CHARLENE ANNE AUDREY, lawyer; b. Warwick, N.Y., Feb. 27, 1963; d. Charles Edward and Stella Ruth (Brazil) O'D. Student, Fordham U., 1981-83; BA summa cum laude with distinction, Boston U., 1985; JD, NYU, 1988. Bar: N.Y. 1989, U.S. Dist. Ct. (so. and ea. dists.) N.Y. 1989, D.C. 1990. Assoc. Winston & Strawn (previously Cole & Deitz), N.Y.C., 1988-90, Graham & James, N.Y.C., 1990—. Editor Moot Ct., NYU, 1987-88. Recipient Moot Ct. Advocacy award NYU, 1987. Mem. ABA, N.Y. State Bar Assn. Office: Graham & James 885 3rd Ave New York NY 10022-4834

O'DELL, LYNN MARIE LUEGGE (MRS. NORMAN D. O'DELL), librarian; b. Berwyn, Ill., Feb. 24, 1938; d. George Emil and Helen Marie (Pesek) Luegge; student Lyons Twp. Jr. Coll., La Grange, Ill., 1957; student No. Ill. U., Elgin Community Coll., U. Ill., Coll. of DuPage; m. Norman D. O'Dell, Dec. 14, 1957; children—Jeffrey, Jerry. Sec., Martin Co., Chgo., 1957-59; dir. Carol Stream (Ill.) Pub. Library, 1964—; chmn. automation governing com. DuPage Library System, v.p., 1982-85, pres. exec. com. adminstrv. librarians, 1985-86, chair automation search com., 1991-92. Named Woman of Yr., Wheaton Bus. and Profl. Woman's Club, 1968. Mem. ALA, Ill. Library Assn., Library Adminstrs. Conf. No. Ill. Lutheran. Home: 182 Yuma Ln Carol Stream IL 60188-1917 Office: 616 Hiawatha Dr Carol Stream IL 60188-1616

ODELL, MARY JANE, former state official; b. Algona, Iowa, July 28, 1923; d. Eugene and Madge (Lewis) Neville; m. Garry Chinn, 1945 (dec.); m. Jonn Odell, Mar. 3, 1967 (dec.); m. Ralph Sigler, Nov. 22, 1987; children: Brad, Chris. B.A., U. Iowa, 1945; hon. doctorate, Simpson Coll., 1982. Host public affairs TV programs Des Moines and Chgo., 1953-79; with Iowa Public Broadcasting Network, 1975-79, host Assignment Iowa, 1975-78, host Mary Jane Odell Program, 1975-79; sec. of state State of Iowa, 1980-87; ret., 1987—; tchr. grad. classes in communications Roosevelt U., Chgo., Drake U., Des Moines. Chmn. Iowa Easter Seals campaign, 1979-83; mem. Midwest Com. Future Options; bd. dirs. Iowa Shares; mem. exec. bd. Iowa Peace Inst., 1985-92. Recipient Emmy award, 1972, 75; George Washington Carver award, 1978; named to Iowa Women's Hall of Fame, 1979. Republican. Address: Apt 206 6129 Meadow Crest Dr Johnston IA 50131

ODEM, JOYCE MARIE, human resources specialist; b. Des Moines, Mar. 21, 1936; d. Robert Gibson and Minnie Anna (Godown) Hague; m. Phillip Wayne Odem, May 23, 1954; children: Vickie, Phillip, Beth, Amy, Keith. Student, Merced C.C., 1976-78. Legal sec. C. Ray Robinson, Merced, Calif., 1959-60; office mgr., legal aid Kane & Canelo, Merced, Calif., 1960-65; recorder disciplinary control bd. U.S. Army Civil Svc., Okinawa, Japan, 1965-69; legal aid, office mgr. Courtney & Sharrow, Merced, 1969-72; adminstr. USAF Civil Svc., Okinawa, 1972-75; asst. indsl. rels. mgr. Maracay Mills Divsn. Mohasco, Merced, 1975-78; safety dir., personnel mgr. Keller Industries, Merced, 1978-83; mgr. employee rels. McLane Pacific, Merced, 1983-85; corp. dir. human resources McLane Co., Inc., Temple, Tex., 1983—; mem. adv. bd. Pvt. Industry Coun., Merced, 1980-85. Mem. Temple Human Resource Mgrs. Assn., Soc. Human Resource Mgrs. Office: McLane Co Inc 4747 McLane Pky Temple TX 76503

ODEN, GLORIA, English educator, poet; b. Yonkers, N.Y., Oct. 30, 1923; d. Redmond Stanley and Ethel (Kincaid) Oden. BA in History, Howard U., 1944, JD, 1948. Faculty New Sch. for Social Rsch., N.Y.C., 1966; vis. lectr. dept. English SUNY, Stony Brook, 1969-70; asst. prof. English U. Md., Balt., 1971-75, assoc. prof., 1975-83, prof., 1983—; sr. editor IEEE Proc. and tech. mags., 1966-67; supr. math./sci. books Appleton-Century-Crofts, 1967-68; project dir. lang. arts books Holt, Rinehart and Winston, 1968-72, sr. editor coll. dept., 1968-71; editor Am. Inst. Physics/Am. Jour. Physics, 1961-66; lectr. in field; condr. numerous poetry readings; juror fiction panel Mass. Cultural Coun., 1994, poetry panel N.J. State Coun., 1993, 94, numerous others; cons. Reel Deal Prodns. Co., NEH, 1984, 87. Author: (books of poetry) The Tie that Binds, 1980, Resurrections, 1978; contbr. numerous poetry to mags., newspapers, audio, anthologies; contbr. numerous articles to profl. jours. Recipient Disting. Black women's award Towson U., 1984; NEH summer stipend, 1974; Breadloaf Writers scholar, 1960; John Hay Whitney Found. Creative Writing fellow, 1955-56; Yaddo fellow, 1956. Mem. Poetry Soc.. Am. (bd. givs. 1981-82, v.p. 1983-84), Soc. for Study of the Multi-Ethnic Lit. of U.S., Coll. English Assn., PEN Am. Ctr. Home: Sutton Pl #521 1111 Park Ave Baltimore MD 21201 Office: Univ of Maryland Dept of English Baltimore MD 21228

ODGERS-SCOFIELD, BRENDA LEA, secondary school educator; b. Belleville, Kans., Feb. 20, 1963; d. Joseph James and Alice Elaine (Norgard) Odgers; m. Jayme Lynn Scofield, July 19, 1986. BS in Edn., Emporia State U., 1985. French tchr. Newton (Kans.) H.S., 1985-88; English and French tchr. Mpls. H.S., 1988—; participant Folger Libr.'s Tchg. Shakespeare Inst., NEH, Washington, 1993. Recipient H.S. Tchr. Recognition award Bartlesville Wesleyan Coll., 1994. Mem. NEA, Kans. Edn. Assn., North Ottawa County Tchrs.' Assn. (pres. 1993-94, sec. 1994-95, mem. negotiations team 1992, 93, 94), Nat. Coun. Tchrs. English. Republican. Home: 122 E Jewell Ave Salina KS 67401-6122 Office: Mpls HS 602 Woodland Ave Minneapolis KS 67467-2036

O'DONNELL, KATHLEEN MARIE, lawyer; b. San Diego, Jan. 2, 1952; d. James Joseph and Patricia Ann (Dunne) O'D. AB, Boston Coll., 1974; JD, U. Miami, 1977. Bar: Mass. 1978. Title atty. Lawyers Title Ins. Corp., Boston, 1979-85; assoc. Hay & Dailey, Boston, 1985-86, DiCara, Selig, Sawyer & Holt, Boston, 1986-87, Ropes & Gray, Boston, 1987-92; ptnr. Dillingham & O'Donnell, Boston, 1992—; adj. prof. Boston U., 1995—. Editor: Residential Real Estate, 1996. Mem., asst. treas. Dedham (Mass.) Choral Soc. Mem. Boston Bar Assn., New Eng. Women in Real Estate, Mass. Conveyancers Assn. (bd. dirs. 1995—), Larchmont Yacht Club. Republican. Roman Catholic. Home: 12 Belcher Cir Milton MA 02186 Office: Dillingham & O'Donnell 100 Franklin St Boston MA 02110

O'DONNELL, PATRICIA, lawyer; b. Cleve., Dec. 17, 1948. BA summa cum laude, Cleve. State U., 1979; JD, Clevel. Marshall Coll. Law, 1982. Bar: Ohio 1982. Ptnr. Baker & Hostetler, Cleve. Mem. ABA, Ohio State Bar Assn., Cleve. Bar Assn. Office: Baker & Hostetler 3200 National City Ctr 1900 E 9th St Cleveland OH 44114-3485*

O'DONNELL, TERESA HOHOL, software development engineer, antennas engineer; b. Springfield, Mass., Nov. 25, 1963; d. Marion Henry and Lena Ann (Zajchowski) Hohol. BS in Computer Engring., MIT, 1985, BSEE, 1985, MSEE, MS in Computer Sci., 1986. Rsch. asst. MIT Rsch. Lab for Electronics, Cambridge, 1985-86; lead VHSIC insertion engr. USAF Electronic Systems Div., Hanscom AFB, Mass., 1986-88; intelligent antennas engr. USAF Rome Lab., Hanscom AFB, Mass., 1988-91; software devel. engr. Arcon Corp., Waltham, Mass., 1991-95; network cons. Arcon Sys., 1995—. Composer: (choral mass setting) Mass of Rejoicing, 1989; patentee in field. Performer Zbeide's Harem, Tewksbury, Mass., 1986-93; organist/composer St. Theresa's Choir, Billerica, Mass., 1987-95. Capt. USAF and USAFR, 1986—. Decorated Commendation medal (2), Joint Svc. Achievement medal. Mem. IEEE, Nat. Assn. Pastoral Musicians, Am. Guild Organists, Assn. for Computing Machinery, Res. Officers Assn., Sigma Xi, Eta Kappa Nu (v.p. 1985-86). Roman Catholic. Office: Arcon Corp 260 Bear Hill Rd Waltham MA 02154-1018

O'DONNELL, VICTORIA J., communication educator; b. Greensburg, Pa., Feb. 12, 1938; d. Victor C. and Helen A. (Detar) O'D.; children from previous marriage: Christopher O'Donnell Stupp, Browning William Stupp; m. Paul M. Monaco, Apr. 9, 1993. BA, Pa. State U., 1959, MA, 1961, PhD, 1968. Asst. prof. comm. Midwestern State U., Wichita Falls, Tex., 1965-67; prof. dept. chair comm. U. No. Tex., Denton, 1967-89; prof., dept. chair comms. Ore. State U., Corvallis, 1989-91; prof. comm., basic course dir. Mont. State U., Bozeman, 1991-93, prof. comm., dir. honors program, 1993—; prof. Am. Inst. Fgn. Studies, London, 1988; cons. Arco Oil & Gas, Dallas, 1983-86, Federal Emergency Mgrs. Agy., Salt Lake City, 1986; speechwriter Sen. Mae Yih, Salem, Ore., 1989-91; steering com. Ore. Alliance Film & TV Educators, 1990-91. Author: Introduction to Public Communication, 1992, 2d edit., 1993; co-author: Persuasion, 1982, Propaganda and Persuasion, 1986, 2d edit., 1992; producer: (video) Women, War and Work, 1994. Bd. dirs. Friends of the Family, Denton, 1987-89, Bozeman Film Festival, 1991—; del. Tex. Dem. Convention, Denton, 1976. Grantee Mont. Com. or the Humanities, 1993, Oreg. Coun. for the Humanities, 1991, NEH, 1977. Mem. Nat. Collegiate Honors Coun., Speech Comm. Assn., Internat. Comm. Assn., Univ. Film & Video Assn. (nom. com. 1995, 96, conf. v.p. 1989-91, bd. dirs. 1978-80), Western States Comm. Assn. Home: 290 Low Bench Rd Gallatin Gateway MT 59730-9741 Office: Univ Honors Program Mont State U Bozeman MT 39717

O'DORISIO, JENNIFER LYNN, educator; b. Key West, Fla., Nov. 7, 1946; d. Jack Daniel and Vecelia May (Jones) Trombla; m. Joseph Bernard O'Dorisio, Aug. 21, 1971; children: Steven Joseph, Amy Kathleen. BS in Edn., U. Nebr., 1968. Cert. type A tchr., Colo. Tchr., reading specialist Jefferson County Pub. Schs., Lakewood, Colo., 1968-73; tchr., coord. life edn. Shrine of St. Anne Sch., Archdiocese of Denver, Arvada, Colo., 1986—; tchr. Catechetical Sch., Archdiocese of Denver, 1992—; cons., spkr. edn. programs Denver area, 1991—; spkr. Cath. Schs. Conf., Denver, 1994; mem. Drug-Free Schs. Task Force, Cath. Schs. and Jefferson County Pub. Schs., 1988-94. Mem. speakers bur. subcom. Jefferson County HIV-AIDS Task Force, 1994-95. Classroom Connection Adaptor grantee, 1994-95, Classroom Connection Disseminator grantee, 1995-96. Mem. ASCD, CCIRA, Colo. Geog. Alliance, Impact II. Democrat. Home: 8554 W 84th Cir Arvada CO 80005-2314

ODOY, ANN MARIE, counselor; b. Derby, Conn., Aug. 22, 1966; d. Bernard William and Mary (Hartigan) O. BA in English/Theology, Boston Coll., 1988; MS in Edn./Counseling, Duquesne U., 1995. Lic. social worker. Profl. womens basketball player Alvest (Sweden) Club, 1990-91; women's asst. basketball coach Duquesne U., Pitts., 1991-93; therapeutic support staff Pressley Ridge Schs., Pitts., 1993-95; program dir., social worker Crisis and Stabilization Ctr., Christiansted, V.I., 1996—. Author/spkr. (workshop) Discovering Roots of Self-Intimacy. Vol. St. Croix Environ., Christiansted, 1996—, Triatholon com., Christiansted, 1996—. Mem. ACA, Am. Sch. Counseling Assn., NOW, Chi Sigma Iota.

ODUOLA, KAREN ANN, geriatrics nurse; b. Anna, Ill., Mar. 5, 1947; d. Edward Everett and Kathern Marie (Powell) Newton; m. Muyideen M. Oduola, May 11, 1988; children: Jonathon C. Newton, Shane L. Laminack, Christopher A. Oduola. Prac. Nurse Cert., Shawnee C.C., Ullin, Ill., 1978; BSN, OUHSC, Oklahoma City, 1993. Charge nurse, LPN Jonesboro (Ill.) Nursing Ctr., 1978-87, Carbondale (Ill.) Manor, 1987-88; flr. nurse, LPN Marion County Nursing Ctr., Indpls., 1988-89; charge nurse, LPN Cedar Crest Manor, Lawton, Okla., 1990-92; support svcs. coord., quality control coord., primary care coord. Okla. Christian Home, Edmond, 1992—; mem. CCRC accreditation com., Okla. Christian Home, 1994, quality assurance com., 1994-95, infection control com., 1994-95, pharmacy com., 1994-95. Mem. Sigma Theta Tau. Lutheran. Home: 1006 Swan Lake Ct Edmond OK 73003 Office: Oklahoma Christian Home 906 N Blvd Edmond OK 73034

O'DWYER, JOAN, judge; b. N.Y.C., Sept. 26, 1926; d. James and Mildred (Gantz) O'D.; m. John P. O'Neill, Nov. 24, 1959 (div. July 1973); children: Shane O'Neill, Liam O'Neill, Kelly O'Neill; m. Anthony P. Savarese, Aug. 24, 1973. BA, Beaver Coll., Jenkintown, Pa., 1947; LLB, Columbia U., 1950. Atty. O'Dwyer and Bernstein, N.Y.C., 1950-60; magistrate City of N.Y., 1960-96, criminal ct. judge, 1960-96; acting Supreme Ct. judge State of N.Y., N.Y.C., 1960-96, judge Ct. of Claims, 1996—; pres. Bronx Womens Bar Assn., 1960. Home: 59 Kenwood Rd Garden City NY 11530-3137

OERTEL, YOLANDA CASTILLO, pathologist, educator, diagnostician; b. Lima, Peru, Dec. 14, 1938; came to U.S., 1966; d. Leonardo A. and Dalila (Ramirez) C.; m. James E. Oertel, Sept. 24, 1969. MD, Cayetano Heredia, Lima, 1964. Diplomate Am. Bd. Pathology (mem. test com. for cytopathology 1989-94). Internat. postdoctoral fellowship NIH, Bethesda, Md., 1966-68; asst. prof. pathology Sch. Medicine George Washington U., Washington, 1975-78, assoc. prof., 1978-84, prof., 1984—; cons. Registry Cytology Armed Forces Inst. Pathology, Washington, 1981—. Author: Fine Needle Aspiration of the Breast, 1987; contbr. chpts. to books and articles to profl. jours. Recipient Francisco A. Camino prize Peruvian Med. Assn., 1965, cert. Meritorious Svc. Armed Forces Inst. Pathology, 1974; named Disting. Alumna Cayetano Heredia Med. Sch., 1989. Mem Internat. Acad. Cytology, Assn. Mil. Surgeons (hon), Colombian Soc. Pathology (hon.), Argentinian Soc. Pathology (hon.), Peruvian Soc. Pathologists (hon.), Argentinian Soc. Cytology, (hon.), Am. Soc. Cytology, Internat. Acad. Pathology, Soc. Latinoamericana Patologia, Am. Soc. Clin. Pathologists (coun. on cytopathology 1982-88). Office: George Washington U Med Ctr 901 23rd St NW Washington DC 20037-2377

OETTING, MILDRED KATHERINE See **SQUAZZO, MILDRED KATHERINE**

OFFEN, GAIL, advertising executive. Sr. v.p., creative dir. W.B. Doner & Co., Southfield, Mich. Office: WB Doner & Co 25900 Northwestern Hwy Southfield MI 48075*

OFFEN, KAREN MARIE, historian, educator; b. Pocatello, Idaho, Oct. 10, 1939; d. Norman V. and Ella Mae (McAlister) Stedtfeld; m. George R. Offen, Dec. 30, 1965; children: Catherine, Stephanie. BA, U. Idaho, 1961; AM, Stanford U., 1963, PhD, 1971. Lectr. History U. Santa Clara, Calif., 1973, U. San Francisco, 1975-76, Stanford (Calif.) U., 1978, 82, 84, 86, 89, 92; ind. scholar affiliated with Inst. Rsch. Women & Gender, Stanford U., 1978—; dir. summer seminar NEH, 1984, 86, 89, 92; founding mem., sec.-treas. Internat. Fedn. Rsch. Women's History, 1987-95; pres. Western Assn. Women Historians, 1991-93. Mem. editl. adv. bd. French Hist. Studies, Arenal, L'Homme, Jour. Women's History, History European Ideas, Hist. Reflections; contbr. articles to profl. jours. Recipient Disting. Alumni Achievement award U. Idaho, 1994, Sr. Scholar award, 1995; NEH Ind. Study & Rsch. fellow, 1980-81, Rockefeller Found. Humanities fellow, 1985-86, J.S. Guggenheim fellow, 1995-96. Mem. Am. Hist. Assn. (com. women historians 1983-86, chair com. internat. hist. activities 1986-90), Soc. French Hist. Studies (exec. com. 1983-86), P.E.O., Kappa Kappa Gamma. Democrat. Office: Stanford U Inst Rsch Women & Gender Stanford CA 94305-8640

OFFERLE, JUDITH A., transportation company executive; b. Ft. Wayne, Ind., Nov. 13, 1951; d. William J. and June (Pepe) O. BSME, BS in Aerospace Engring., U. Notre Dame, 1974; MS in Indsl. Adminstrn., Carnegie Mellon U., 1976. With Corning (NY.), Inc., 1976-77, Allied Signal Corp., N.Y.C., 1977-82, Ciba-Ceigy Corp., Ardsley, N.Y., 1982-91; v.p. fin. Schering-Plough Corp., Madison, N.J., 1992-94; sr. v.p., CFO, Vancom, Inc., Oakbrook Terrace, Ill., 1994—; v.p., bd. dirs. Women's Transp. seminar, 1994—. Mem. fin. com. S.W. Pa. coun. Girl Scouts U.S.A., 1975-76; mem. regional bd. dirs. Am. Youth Soccer Orgn. Mem. Fin. Execs. Inst., Soc. Women Engrs., Chgo. Fin. Exch. (bd. dirs. 1993—), Fin. Women's Assn. N.Y. Office: Vancom Inc 1 Mid Am Plz Ste 401 Oakbrook Terrace IL 60181-7320

OFFHOLTER, JEAN MARY, management consultant; b. Berkeley, Calif., Sept. 14, 1932; d. Clarence Ballard Hills and Frances Desire (Ramsay) Hanna; divorced; children: Cheryl Diane McKibbin, Sally Lynn Hillman. BA, San Jose State Coll., 1954. Tech. exec. U.S. Gen. Svcs. Adminstrn., San Francisco, 1966-70; inventory mgmt. specialist U.S. Gen. Svcs. Adminstrn., Washington, 1971-75, supervisory inventory mgmt. specialist, 1975-76, spl. asst., regional commr., 1977-78, dir. retail svcs. div., 1979-83; dir. supply and contracting divs. U.S. Gen. Svcs. Adminstrn., Kansas City, Mo., 1984-86; ret., 1986; cons. in procurement tng. and course devel. Washington, 1986—. Home: 11566 Rolling Green Ct # 200 Reston VA 22091-2243

OFFNER, ROXANE, social worker; b. N.Y.C., Nov. 22, 1930; d. Monroe Marc and Dorothy (Leopold) O.; m. Jules Brody, July 26, 1953 (div. June 1978); children: Rachel, David, Jonathan. BA, Oberlin Coll., 1951; MSW, Columbia U., 1953. Editor, dept. head United Synagogue of Am., N.Y.C., 1954-63; health educator The Arthritis Found., White Plains, N.Y., 1970-73; cmty. liaison Rusk Inst., NYU Med. Ctr., N.Y.C., 1973-78; dep. adv. N.Y. State Office of Adv. for the Disabled, N.Y.C., 1978-92; cons. Ams. with Disabilities Act The Lighthouse, Inc., N.Y.C., 1992—. Author: The InSights Manual, 1995, (booklet) ADA Accessibility Provisions for People with Impaired Vision, 1994; editor (newsletters and assorted publs.) United Synagogue of Am., 1954-63. em. profl. adv. com. Nat. Easter Seal Soc., Chgo., 1980's, Lighthouse Nat. Ctr. for Vision and Aging, N.Y.C., 1985-92; state accesibility officer Nat. Conf. States/Bldg. Codes and Stds., 1988-92. Mem. APHA (mem. governing coun. 1980's), NASW, P-Flag, Planned Parenthood, Phi Beta Kappa. Home: # 624 21 Fairview Ave Tuckahoe NY 10707 Office: The Lighthouse Inc 111 East 59th St New York NY 10022

OFFUTT, SUSAN ELIZABETH, economist; b. Newport, R.I., Apr. 17, 1954; d. William Franklin and Carol Dorothy (Chieves) O. BS, Allegheny Coll., 1976; MS, Cornell U., 1980, PhD, 1982. Asst. prof. agrl. econs. U. Ill., Urbana, 1982-87; sect. leader Econ. Rsch. Svc. USDA, Washington, 1987-88; chief agr. br. U.S. Office Mgmt. and Budget, Washington, 1988-92; exec. dir., bd. agr. Nat. Rsch. Coun., Washington, 1992-96; adminstr. U.S. Dept. Agrl./Econ. Rsch. Svc., Washington, 1996—. Office: Econ Rsch Svc 1301 New York Ave NW Washington DC 20005

O'GARA, BARBARA ANN, soap company executive; b. Newark, Aug. 8, 1953; d. Frank Percy and Rose (Giordano) Stevens. AA, Keystone Jr. Coll., 1973; BS, U. Ariz., 1976. Media buyer Wells, Rich, Green/Townsend, Irvine, Calif., 1977-80; dist. sales mgr. Dial Corp., Phoenix, 1980-82; regional sales mgr. Guest Supply, Inc., North Brunswick, N.J., 1982-85; dir. hotel mktg. and sales Neutrogena Corp., L.A., 1985-92, v.p. hotel mktg. and sales, 1992-96; cons. Bath and Body Works, 1996—. Keystone Jr. Coll. scholar, 1972, Morris County scholar, 1971, recipient Outstanding Sales Accomplishment award Armour-Dial, 1981. Mem. Am. Mktg. Assn., Am. Mgmt. Assn., Am. Hotel and Motel Assn., Network Exec. Women in Hospitality. Republican. Roman Catholic. Avocations: tennis, aerobics, running, skiing, photography. Home and Office: Penthouse A 2218 Main St Santa Monica CA 90405-2273

OGDEN, ANN, editor; b. Kansas City, Mo.; d. Audley W. and Leona R. (Locke) Porter; m. Alvin C. Ogden, Apr. 20, 1954; 1 child, Karen. BS in Tech. Journalism, Kans. State U., 1954; MA in Sec. Edn., U. Mo., Kansas City, 1968. Society editor Lyons (Kans.) Daily News, 1954-56; asst. editor Rose Pubs., Shawnee Mission, Kans., 1962-63; instr. developmental reading U. Mo., Kansas City, 1964-67; journalism tchr. Bishop Miege High Sch., Shawnee Mission, 1966-67; asst. editor Kans. Alumni, Lawrence, 1967-68, Vol. Leader and Trustee of Am. Hosp. Assn., Chgo., 1969-72; asst. editor, directory editor Barks Pubs., Chgo., 1975-81; adj. instr. bus. English Triton Coll., River Grove, Ill., 1981-84; freelance writer, editor, 1973-94. Bd. dirs. 2000 Found., Overland Park, Kans., 1991—, Strang hist. display com., 1991—. U. Mo. Kansas City fellow, 1964-65, 65-66. Mem. AAUW (chmn. Shawnee Mission chpt. money matters group 1987-89, chmn. Shawnee Mission chpt. Women Investing Now interest group 1993-94), Women in Comms. (pres. Chgo. chpt. 1973-74, historian-archivist Chgo. chpt. 1971-72, procedures manual com. 1971-72, career conf. com. 1971, vol. bur. com. 1971), Alpha Chi Omega (editor Lyre chpt. 1989-91, historian 1991-93, chaplain 1993-95).

OGDEN, JOANNE, real estate executive; b. Cumming, Ga., Apr. 9, 1941; d. Crafton Kemp Sr. and Mary Evelyn (Willis) Brooks; m. William Rush Williams, Jan. 3, 1961 (div. 1966); 1 child, Paul Rush Williams; m. Cecil Leavern Ogden, Sr.; stepchildren: Cecil Laverne Jr., Michael Vann. Grad. high sch., Cumming. Prin. Ogden & Ogden, Milledgeville, Ga., 1966—. Candidate Baldwin County Commnr., Milledgeville, 1984. Mem. Nat. Geog. Soc., Better World Soc., Cousteau Soc., Audubon Soc., Smithsonian Inst., U.S. C. of C., 700 Club (Virginia Beach). Republican. Methodist. Home: 402 Allen Memorial Dr SW Milledgeville GA 31061-4608 Office: Ogden & Ogden 2600 Irwinton Rd Milledgeville GA 31061-9762

OGDEN, LOUANN MARIE, dietitian, consultant; b. Enid, Okla., Dec. 16, 1952; d. Raymond Michael Schiltz and Donna Mae Stuever; m. Wendell Edwin Ogden, Jan. 5, 1979; 1 child, Gregory Jacob Jeremiah. BS in Home Econs., Okla. State U., 1974, MS, 1977. Registered dietitian; lic. dietitian, Tex. Dietetic intern Ind. U. Med. Ctr., Indpls., 1974; therapeutic dietitian-clin. svcs. and trayline ops. Bapt. Med. Ctr. Okla., Oklahoma City, 1975-76; grad. teaching asst. lower and upper level food preparation Okla. State U., Stillwater, 1976-77, teaching assoc. lower and upper level food preparation, 1977; chief clin. dietitian adminstrv. and clin. coordination Borgess Hosp., Kalamazoo, 1978; dietary cons. nutrition program Iowa Commn. on Aging, Des Moines, 1979-80; asst. food svc. dir., adminstrv. dietitian Timberlawn Psych. Hosp., Dallas, 1980-92; rep. group one purchasing program, mem. student tng. program Zale Lipshy U. Hosp., Dallas, 1992-93, food svc. cons., 1993—. Mem. Am. Dietetic Assn., Am. Soc. Hosp. Food Svc. Adminstrn.

(nat. nominating com. 1990-91, Disting. Health Care Food Svc. Adminstr. 1992, North ctrl. Tex. chpt.: corr. sec. 1985-86, comms. chair 1986-87, rec. sec. 1987-89, pres.-elect 1989-90, pres. 1990-91, nominating com. chair, health care food svc. week com. chair 1991-92, Outstanding Mem. award 1992), Tex. Dietetic Assn., Dallas Dietetic Assn. Democrat. Roman Catholic. Home and Office: 3302 Oxford Dr Rowlett TX 75088-5936

OGDEN, LYDIA LEE, strategic communications and policy analyst; b. Murfreesboro, Tenn., July 17, 1960; d. Alfred Edwin and June (McCarter) O.; m. Kenneth Roland Askew, Nov. 15, 1986 (div. Dec. 1994). BS, Middle Tenn. State U., 1981; MA, Vanderbilt U., 1984. Editor Am. Health Cons., Atlanta, 1984-86; strategic comms. cons. Words' Worth, Atlanta, 1986-89; account exec. Pringle Dixon Pringle, Atlanta, 1988; cmty. liaison Agy. for Toxic Substances & Disease Registry, Atlanta, 1989-92; comms. specialist Divsn. of HIV/AIDS Prevention Ctrs. for Disease Control & Prevention, Atlanta, 1992—; Mem. Atlanta Episcopal Diocese Commn. on AIDS, 1995—. Author: Applying Prevention Marketing, 1995; editor: Hosp. Risk Mgmt., 1984-86, The Public Health Implications of Medical Waste: A Report to Congress, 1989, Environmental Issues: Today's Challenge for the Future, 1990. Vol. cook Cafe 458, Atlanta, 1987-90. Recipient Spl. Act award USPHS, 1991. Democrat. Episcopalian. Office: Ctrs for Disease Control & Prevention 1600 Clifton Rd NE E25 Atlanta GA 30333

OGDEN, MAUREEN BLACK, retired state legislator; b. Vancouver, B.C., Nov. 1, 1928; came to U.S., 1930; d. William Moore and Margaret Hunter (Leitch) Black; m. Robert Moore Ogden, June 23, 1956; children: Thomas, Henry, Peter. BA, Smith Coll., 1950; MA, Columbia U., 1963; M in City and Regional Planning, Rutgers U., 1977. Researcher, staff asst. Ford Found., N.Y.C., 1951-56; staff assoc. Fgn. Policy Assn., N.Y.C., 1956-58; mem. Millburn (N.J.) Twp. Com., 1976-81; mayor Twp. of Millburn, N.J., 1979-81; mem. N.J. Gen. Assembly, Trenton, 1982—; chmn. Assembly Environment Com., N.J. Gen. Assembly; chmn. Energy and Pub. Utilities Com., Coun. State Govts., 1991-92; mem. adv. bd. Sch. Policy and Planning, Rutgers Univ., New Brunswick, N.J., 1992—. Author: Natural Resources Inventory, Township of Millburn, 1974. Bd. govs. N.J. Hist. Soc., Newark, 1990—; trustee N.J. chpt. The Nature Conservancy; hon. trustee Paper Mill Playhouse, Millburn, 1990—; former trustee St. Barnabas Med. Ctr., Livingston, N.J.; former pres. N.J. Drug Abuse Adv. Coun.; chair Gov.'s Coun. on N.J. Outdoors, 1996—; mem. Palisades Interstate Park Commn., 1996—. Recipient citation Nat. Assn. State Outdoors Recreation Liaison Officers, 1987, cert. appreciation John F. Kennedy Ctr. for the Performing Arts, The Alliance for Art Edn., 1987, disting. svc. award Art Educators N.J., 1987, ann. environ. quality award EPA Region II, 1988, citation Humane Soc. U.S., 1989, award N.J. Hist. Sites Coun., 1989, N.J. Sch. Conservation, 1990, pres.'s award The Nature Conservancy, 1995, pub. policy award Nat. Trust for Hist. Preservation, 1995. Republican. Episcopalian. Home: 59 Lakeview Ave Short Hills NJ 07078-2240

OGDEN, PEGGY A., personnel director; b. N.Y.C., Mar. 21, 1932; d. Stephen Arnold and Margaret (Stern) O. BA with honors, Brown U., 1953; MA, Trinity Coll., Hartford, Conn., 1955. Asst. dir. YMCA Counseling Svc., Hartford, 1953-55; employment interviewer R.H. Macy & Co., N.Y.C., 1955; asst. pers. dir. Inst. Internat. Edn., N.Y.C., 1956-59; pers. advisor Girl Scouts U.S.A., N.Y.C., 1959-61; store and pers. mgr. Ohrbachs, Inc., N.Y.C., 1961-74; dir. pers. N.Y.C. Tech. Coll. CUNY, Bkyn., 1974—; arbitrator Better Bus. Bur., N.Y.C., 1988—; cons. Girl Scout Coun. N.Y., N.Y.C., 1988-89. Mem APA, Am. Assn. U. Adminstrs., Women in Human Resources, N.Y. Pers. Mgmt. Assn. Home: 1100 Park Ave New York NY 10128-1202 Office: NYC Tech Coll 300 Jay St Brooklyn NY 11201-2902

OGDEN, VALERIA JUAN, management consultant, state representative; b. Okanogan, Wash., Feb. 11, 1924; d. Ivan Bodwell and Pearle (Wilson) Munson; m. Daniel Miller Ogden Jr., Dec. 28, 1946; children: Janeth Lee Ogden Martin, Patricia Jo Ogden Hunter, Daniel Munson Ogden. BA magna cum laude, Wash. State U., 1946. Exec. dir. Potomac Coun. Camp Fire, Washington, 1964-68, Ft. Collins (Colo.) United Way, 1969-73, Designing Tomorrow Today, Ft. Collins, 1973-74, Poudre Valley Community Edn. Assn., Ft. Collins, 1977-78; pres. Valeria M. Ogden, Inc., Kensington, Md., 1978-81; nat. field cons. Camp Fire, Inc., Kansas City, Mo., 1980-81; exec. dir. Nat. Capital Area YWCA, Washington, 1981-84, Clark County YWCA, Vancouver, Wash., 1985-89; pvt. practice mgmt. cons. Vancouver, 1989—; mem. Wash. Ho. of Reps., 1991—; mem. adj. faculty pub. adminstrn. program Lewis and Clark Coll., Portland (Oreg.) State U., 1979-94; mem. Pvt. Industry Coun., Vancouver, 1986-95; mem. regional Svcs. Network Bd., 1993—. Author: Camp Fire Membership, 1980. County vice chmn. Larimer County Dems., Ft. Collins, 1974-75; mem. precinct com. Clark County Dems., Vancouver, 1986-88; mem. Wash. State Coun. Vol. Action, Olympia, 1986-90; treas. Mortar Bd. Nat. Found., Vancouver, 1987-96; bd. dirs. Clark County Coun. for Homeless, Vancouver, 1989—, chmn., 1994; bd. dirs. Wash. Wildlife and Recreation Coalition, 1995—, Human Svcs. Coun., 1996—. Named Citizen of Yr. Ft. Collins Bd. of Realtors, 1975; recipient Gulick award Camp Fire Inc., 1956, Alumna Achievement award Wash. State U. Alumni Assn., 1988. Mem. Internat. Assn. Vol. Adminstrs. (pres. Boulder 1989-90), Nat. Assn. YWCA Exec. Dirs. (nat. bd. nominating com. 1988-90), Sci. and Society Assn. (bd. dirs. 1993—), Women in Action, Philanthropic and Ednl. Orgn., Phi Beta Kappa. Democrat. Home: 3118 NE Royal Oak Dr Vancouver WA 98662-7435 Office: John L O'Brien Bldg Rm 342 State Ave NE Olympia WA 98504-1134

OGLE, RICHELLE KATHLEEN, fund raising administrator, consultant; b. Fairbury, Nebr., May 18, 1954; d. Richard Eugene Ogle and Phyllis Imogene (Bard) Nelson; 1 child, Josiah Ferris. BA, LaSalle U., 1981; MA, Temple U., 1984. Writer OTC Review, Oreland, Pa., 1984-87; coord., pub. rels. and publs. William Penn Charter Sch., Phila., 1987-89; dir. devel. rsch. and comms. The Wharton Sch., U. Pa., Phila., 1989-93; prin., cons. Funding Works, Phila., 1994—; bd. mem. The Poetry Ctr., Phila., 1992-94. Mem. Nat. Soc. Fund Raising Execs., Coun. for the Advancement Secondary Edn. Office: Funding Works 335 W School House Ln Philadelphia PA 19144-3846

OGLE, ROBBIN SUE, criminal justice educator; b. North Kansas City, Mo., Aug. 28, 1960; d. Robert Lee and Carol Sue (Gray) O. BS, Ctrl. Mo. State U., 1982; MS, U. Mo., 1990; PhD, Pa. State U., 1995. State probation and parole officer Mo. Dept. Corrections, Kansas City, 1982-92; collector J.C. Penney Co., Mission, Kans., 1990-92; instr. U. Mo., Kansas City, 1990-92; grad. lectr. Pa. State U., University Park, 1992-95; prof. criminal justice dept. U. Nebr., Omaha, 1995—. Contbr. articles to profl. jours. Athletic scholar Ctrl. Mo. State U., Warrensburg, 1978-82. Mem. AAUW, ACLU, NOW, Am. Soc. Criminology, Acad. Criminal Justice Scis., Am. Correctional Assn., Phi Kappa Phi. Home: 9535 Western Circle # 4 Omaha NE 68114 Office: Univ Nebr 1100 Neihardt Criminal Justice Dept Lincoln NE 68588-0630

OGLESBY, JERRI BURDETTE, elementary education educator; b. Olney, Md., Oct. 13, 1953; d. Herbert M. and Ellen (Miller) Burdette; m. Albert C. Oglesby Jr., Nov. 18, 1978; children: Matthew Jacob, Nathan Bryan. BA in Elem. Edn., Shepherd Coll., 1975; MEd, Johns Hopkins U., 1995. Cert. elem. tchr. Tchr. elem. Montgomery County Pub. Schs., Rockville, Md., 1987—; assoc. faculty mem. Johns Hopkins U., 1995—. Deacon Boyds (Md.) Presbyn. Ch., 1980—. Mem. NEA, Nat. Coun. Tchrs. Math., Montgomery County Edn. Assn.

O'GORMAN, ANNETTE, nurse practitioner; b. Huntington, N.Y., Sept. 28, 1962; d. Walter Alexander and Mary Ann (Lombardi) Bilski; m. Jeffrey David O'Gorman, May 2, 1992; 1 child, John Thomas O'Gorman. BSN, U. South Fla., 1984; MSN, SUNY, Stony Brook, 1987. Cert. family nurse practitioner ANCC; cert. sign lang. interpreter, Wis. Nurse practitioner Johns Hopkins Hosp., Balt., 1987-90, Tampa (Fla.) Gen. Hosp., 1990-91; sign lang. interpreter Milw., 1993-96; nurse practitioner EmCare, S.C., Milw., 1991—; clin. instr. U. Wis., Milw., 1992-96, Marquette U., Milw., 1992-96; lectr. Metro Milw. Nurse Practitioners, Milw., 1995-96, mem. orgn. com., 1994-96; lectr. Wis. Nurses Assn., Milw., 1996. Contbr.: (textbook) Diagnostic Testing, 1996. Mem. ANA. Office: EmCare SC Rm C-244 945 N 12th St Milwaukee WI 53201

O'GRADY, BEVERLY TROXLER, investment executive, counselor; b. Greensboro, N.C., Nov. 26, 1941; d. Robert Andrew and Beverly Beam (Barrier) Troxler; m. Robert Edward O'Grady, Aug. 6, 1966. BA, St. Mary's Coll., 1963; MA, Columbia U., 1965. Exec. v.p. Wilkinson & Hottinger Inc., N.Y.C., 1973-94, Helvetia Capital Corp., N.Y.C., 1987-94; pres. Wilkinson O'Grady & Co., Inc., N.Y.C., 1994—; mem. adv. bd. Charles Schwab Fin., San Francisco, 1991-93. Active Women's Nat. Rep. Club, N.Y.C., 1991-94. Mem. Assn. Investment Mgrs., N.Y. Soc. Security Analysts, Women's Bond Club (pres. 1992-94), Univ. Club. Roman Catholic. Office: Wilkinson O'Grady & Co Inc 520 Madison Ave New York NY 10022-4213

O'GRADY, GAIL, actress. Appeared in (films) Blackout, 1989, Nobody's Perfect, 1990, Spellcaster, 1991; appeared in (TV series) NYPD Blue. Office: care Steven Bochco Prodns PO Box 900 Beverly Hills CA 90213*

O'GRADY, MARY J., editor, foundation consultant; b. Chgo., Sept. 25, 1951; d. Valentine Michael and Lillian Mary (Quinlan) O'G. Student, St. Mary's Coll., Rome, Italy, 1970-71; BFA, Manhattanville Coll., 1973. Assoc. editor Magnum Photos, N.Y.C., 1973-76; asst. picture editor Modern Photography Mag., N.Y.C., 1976-78; freelance photographer N.Y.C., 1978-80; sr. producer Trans-Atlantic Enterprises, N.Y.C., L.A., 1981-82; dir. pub. info. World Wildlife Fund, Washington, 1983-84; sr. analyst Mead Data Cen., Washington, 1985-87; editor photos U.S. News and World Report, Washington, 1987-90; program dir. Sacharuna Found., 1990-92; adminstr. Roland Films, 1991-92; assoc. dir. AIDS Control and Prevention Project Family Health Internat., 1994—; cons. Time, Inc., N.Y.C., 1981, Exxon Corp., N.Y.C., 1981-82, U.S. News and World Report, Washington, 1987, The German Marshall Fund of U.S., Conservation Internat., Washington, 1992, W. Alton Jones Found., 1993-94. Asst. editor: The Family of Woman, 1978; producer (TV shows) A Conversation With..., 1982, The Helen Gurley Brown Show, 1982, Outrageous Opinions, 1982; photo editor America's Best Colleges, 1989, 90, Great Vacation Drives, 1989. Recipient Editorial Excellence award Natural Resources Coun. Am., 1984. Mem. Soc. Environ. Journalists, Worldwide Women in Environment and Devel., Status and Trends of HIV/AIDS Epidemics in Africa Working Group.

O'HALLORAN, DEB, bank executive. Sr. v.p. br. support group First Bank Sys., Mpls. Office: First Bank Sys First Bank Pl 601 2nd Ave S Minneapolis MN 55402-4302*

O'HARA, CATHERINE, actress, comedienne; b. Toronto, Mar. 4, 1954; m. Bo Welch, 1992. Actress, writer with Second City, Toronto, 1974; cofounder of SCTV, 1976 (Emmy award); films include After Hours, 1985, Heartburn, 1986, Beetlejuice, 1988, Dick Tracy, 1990, Betsy's Wedding, 1990, Home Alone, 1990, Little Vegas, 1990, There Goes The Neighborhood, 1992, Home Alone II: Lost In New York, 1992, The Nightmare Before Christmas, 1993 (voice), The Paper, 1994, Wyatt Earp, 1994, A Simple Twist of Fate, 1994, Tall Tale, 1995; TV, SCTV, Comic Relief, Dream On (dir.); co-writer SCTV, Cinemax, 1984, Really Weird Tales, HBO, 1986. Office: care ICM 8942 Wilshire Blvd Beverly Hills CA 90211-1934*

O'HARA, JEAN METZGER, elementary education educator; b. Covington, Ky., Mar. 24, 1961; d. Ferdinand Joseph and Audrey Marie (Henke) Metzger; m. Eugene H. O'Hara, Jr., Mar. 2, 1961; children: Nicole, Cody, Kyle. BA, No. Ky. U., 1985; MA, Georgetown U., 1989. Tchr. St. Henry Mid. Sch., Erlanger, Ky., 1985-86, Conner Mid. Sch., Hebron, Ky., 1986-88, Ockerman Elem., Florence, Ky., 1988-91, Stephens Elem., Burlington, Ky., 1991—; sci. fair chmn. of elem. schs., Burlington, 1988-95. Pre-sch. tchr. St. Timothy Ch., Union, Ky., 1992-95. Recipient KEA award for Inspiring Creative Writing, Frankfort, Ky., 1992-93, Outstanding Educator award Jaycees, Louisville, 1994-95. Democrat. Roman Catholic. Home: 59 Harness Ln Florence KY 41042 Office: Stephens Elem Sch 5687 Hwy 237 Burlington KY 41005

O'HARE, MARILYNN RYAN, artist; b. Berkeley, Calif., Aug. 6, 1926; d. Lawrence and Linnie Marie (Ryan) Atkins; m. Lawrence Bernard O'Hare, Sept. 20, 1947; children: Timothy Lawrence, Kevin Roy, Shannon John, Kacey Sophia, Kelly Katherine. Student, Jean Turner Art Sch., San Francisco, 1944, 45, 46. Artist Cherubs children's dept. store, San Francisco, 1946, 47, Emporium Art Dept., San Francisco, 1947-54; freelance artist Capwells-Emporium, Liberty House, San Francisco, Oakland, civ4-64; artist-in-residence, coord. art program Childrens Fairyland USA, Oakland, 1962—; commissioned painting for Moffit Hosp., San Francisco, 1970, Havens Sch. Libr., Piedmont, Calif., 1975. Painter children's portraits; designer greeting cards; executed murals Children's Fairyland, Oakland, 1965, 66, 73, Kaiser Hosp., Martinez, Calif., 1974. Vol. art tchr. Oakland Pub. Schs., 1958-62; vol. Oak Mus., 1965—, Convelescant Hosp., Berkeley, Calif., 1975—. Named Mother of Yr., City of Oakland, 1993. Mem. Oakland Art Assn. Democrat. Home: 3361 Burdeck Dr Oakland CA 94602

O'HARE, SANDRA FERNANDEZ, secondary education educator; b. N.Y.C., Mar. 19, 1941; d. Ricardo Enrique and Rosario de Los Angeles (Arenas) Fernandez; m. S. James O'Hare, Oct. 12, 1963; children: James, Richard, Michael, Christopher. BA, Marymount Coll., 1962; MA, U. San Francisco, 1980. Cert. elem. and coll. tchr.; bilingual and lang. devel. specialist. Instr. adult edn. Guam, 1964-66, Spanish Speaking Ctr., Harrisburg, Pa., 1977-79; tchr. Colegio Salesiano, Rota, Spain, 1973, 84, Alisal Sch. Dist., Salinas, Calif., 1979-81, Liberty Sch., Petaluma, Calif., 1981-85, Cinnabar Sch., Petaluma, 1985—; instr. Chapman U., 1994—; also summer migrant edn. programs Cinnabar Sch., Petaluma, 1990, 91; instr. Santa Rosa (Calif.) Jr. Coll., 1982-83; mem. math. curriculum com. Sonoma County Office Edn., Santa Rosa, 1988; mem. Summer Sci. Connections Inst., Sonoma State U., 1994, Redwood Empire Math. Acad., summer 1995; mem. Sonoma County Math Project, 1995-96; summer '96 NEH stipend to Harvard U. Translator: Isabel la Catolica, 1962. Mem. Asian relief com. ARC, Harrisburg, 1975, Boy Scouts Am., Petaluma, 1983, Mechanicsburg, Pa., 1974, Monterey, Calif., 1971. Sarah D. Barder fellow Johns Hopkins U., 1990. Mem. NEA, AAUW (chair edn. founds. com. 1985-86), Calif. Assn. Bilingual Educators, Cinnabar Tchrs. Assn., Club Hispano-Americano Petaluma (pres. 1987-89). Roman Catholic. Home: 1289 Glenwood Dr Petaluma CA 94954-4326

O'HARE, VIRGINIA LEWIS, legal administrator; b. Pitts., May 2, 1951; d. Robert Edward and Ellen Marie (Saylor) Lewis; m. John Francis O'Hare, Sept. 17, 1994; 1 child, Merit Elisabeth. BS in Edn., U. Pitts., 1973; MS in Human Resources Mgmt., Laroche Coll., 1984. Legal asst. Meyer, Darragh, Buckler, Bebenek & Eck, Pitts., 1973-85; legal office mgr. Rockwell Internat., Pitts., 1985-86; pers. mgr. Rose, Schmidt, Hasley & DiSalle, Pitts., 1986-88; legal adminstr. Duquesne Light Co., Pitts., 1988—. Mem. Assn. Legal Adminstrs., Pitts. Legal Adminstrn. Assn. (sec. 1989-93, membership chair 1993—), Pa. Bar Assn., Allegheny Bar Assn., Pitts. Pers. Assn. Republican. Office: Duquesne Light Co 411 7th Ave 16-006 Pittsburgh PA 15219

O'HERN, CAROL ANN, publishing company executive; b. Chgo., Jan. 13, 1960; d. Elsie Helene (Ebert) Schiemann; m. Patrick Edward O'Hern, Aug. 13, 1982; 1 child, Patrick Edward II. BA, Northwestern U., 1981; postgrad., Nat. Coll. Edn., Evanston, Ill., 1989—. Radio announcer/pub. affairs dir. WSBW-FM, Sturgeon Bay, Wis., 1981; dir. mktg. Nat. Data Resources, Sturgeon Bay, 1981-83; corp. sec. MicroSearch Inc., Sturgeon Bay, 1983-85; product mgr. Nat. Safety Coun., Chgo., 1985-88, Macmillan Directory Div., Wilmette, Ill., 1988—; cons. computer applications Nat. Safety Coun., 1988—.

O'HICKEY, EILEEN LOUISE, military officer, chaplain; b. Boston, Aug. 10, 1947; d. James William and Doris Violet (Smith) Hickey; m. Dennis Bartley Kelly, Sept. 4, 1965 (div. Apr. 1971); children: Sean Patrick, Brian Scott; m. Giles Roderick Norrington, July 9, 1988; stepchildren: Keeley Norrington Hunt, Giles Roderick Jr. BA magna cum laude, U. N.H., 1974; MDiv, Andover Newton Theol. Sch., 1978. Commd. lt. (j.g.) USN, 1978, advanced through grades to capt., 1996; chaplain Naval Tng. Ctr., Orlando, Fla., 1978-80; chaplain, retreat facilitator Chaplains Relig. Enrichment Devel. Orgn., Norfolk, Va., 1980-82; pastoral counseling resident Portsmouth Naval Hosp., Va., 1982-83; chaplain Naval Air Sta., Norfolk, Va., 1983-85, Naval Support Facility, Diego Garcia, 1985-86, Marine Corps Base, Camp Pendleton, Calif., 1986-88; command chaplain Naval Submarine Sch., Groton, Conn., 1989-92, USS Emory S. Land, 1992-94; policy br. head chief chaplains office Bus. Naval Personnel, Washington, 1994-96; staff chaplain Naval Security Group Command, Ft. Meade, Md., 1996—. Named Outstanding Young Women of Am., 1982, Mil. Woman of the Yr. Naval Air Sta., Norfolk, Va., 1983, Marine Corps Base Camp Pendleton, Oceanside, Calif., 1987, Mil. Mem. of Yr., Naval Submarine Base, Groton, Conn., 1990. Mem. AAUW, LWV, Internat. Assn. Women Mins., Women Officers Profl. Assn. Democrat. Mem. United Church of Christ. Home: 3803 Elbert Ave Alexandria VA 22305 Office: Chief of Chaplains 2 Navy Annex Washington DC 20370

OHIRA, AKEMI, art educator, artist; b. Tokyo, May 7, 1967; came to U.S., 1980; d. Takeo and Michi (Wang) O. BFA, Cornell U., 1990; MFA, Carnegie Mellon U., 1992. Asst. prof. art U. Va., Charlottesville, 1993—. One-woman shows include Galerie Voyage, San Francisco, 1990, Santensho Gallery, Kumamoto, Japan, 1990, Collective Ctr. for the Arts, Jackson, Mich., 1994, St. Mary's Coll., Notre Dame, Ind., 1995, Piedmont Va. C.C., Charlottesville, 1995, Western Mich. U., Kalamazoo, 1996; exhibited in group show at Laguna Gloria Art Mus., Austin, Tex., 1994, U. Ala., Tuscaloosa, 1995, Ohio State U., Mansfield, 1995. Admissions amb. Cornell U., 1992-93. Recipient prize and grants John Kip Brady Found., Annapolis, Md., 1989, Francis Weatherspoon Printmakers award, Dome Gallery, 1991, Purchase award Rembrandt Graphics/Print Club, 1994; Visual Arts grantee Southeastern Coll. Arts Conf. Mem. Soc. Am. Graphic Artists, Coll. Art Assn., Print Club (Phila.). Office: University of Virginia McIntire Dept Art Fayerweather Hall Charlottesville VA 22903

OHMAN, DIANA J., state official, former school system administrator; b. Sheridan, Wyo., Oct. 3, 1950; d. Arden and Doris Marie (Carstens) Mahin. AA, Casper Coll., 1970; BA, U. Wyo., 1972, MEd, 1977, postgrad., 1979—. Tchr. kindergarten Natrona County Sch. Dist., Casper, Wyo., 1971-72; tchr. rural sch. K-8 Campbell County Sch. Dist., Gillette, Wyo., 1972-80, rural prin. K-8, 1980-82, prin. K-6, 1982-84, assoc. dir. instrn., 1984-87; dir. K-12 Goshen County Migrant Program, Torrington, Wyo., 1988-89; prin. K-2 Goshen County Sch. Dist., Torrington, Wyo., 1987-90; state supt. pub. instrn. State of Wyo., Cheyenne, 1991-94, secretary of state, 1995—; chmn. Campbell County Mental Health Task Force, 1986-87; mem. Legis. Task Force on Edn. of Handicapped 3-5 Yr. Olds, 1988-89. State Committeewoman Wyo. Rep. Party, 1985-88. Recipient Wyo. Elem. Prin. of Yr. award, 1990; named Campbell County Tchr. of Yr. 1980, Campbell County Profl. Bus. Woman of Yr. 1984, Outstanding Young Woman in Am., 1983. Mem. Coun. of Chief of State Sch. Officers (Washington chpt.), Internat. Reading Assn., Wyo. Assn. of Sch. Adminstrs., Kappa Delta Pi, Phi Kappa Phi, Phi Delta Kappa. Republican. Lutheran. Office: Sec State Office State Capitol Cheyenne WY 82002-0020*

O'KEEFE, BEVERLY DISBROW, state official, federal official; b. Wilton, Conn., Sept. 1, 1946; d. Harry Harbs and Jane Corrine (Young) Disbrow; children: Marcia Corrine, Jennifer Lynn; m. John Patrick O'Keefe, Aug. 1981 (div. 1985). AA, Berkshire Community Coll., 1973; BA in Psychology, U. Mass., 1975; MPA, U. S.C., 1979. Lic. social worker, S.C. Statis. clk. U. S.C., Columbia, 1976-78; pub. adminstr. employment and tng. Office of Gov., State of S.C., Columbia, 1976-78, 88—; project coord. Trident Tech. Coll., Charleston, S.C., 1981-82; office mgr. Med. U. S.C., Charleston, 1983-85; coord. bus. svcs. AMI East Cooper Community Hosp., Mt. Pleasant, S.C., 1985-87; mktg. rep. R.L. Bryan Co., Columbia, 1987; pub. adminstr. S.C. Dept. Social Svcs., Columbia, 1988; pub. adminstr., employment and tng. Office Gov. State S.C., Columbia, 1988-89; mem. employment and tng. staff City of Norfolk (Va.) Div. Soc. Svcs., 1990-91; social sci. analyst Naval Edn. and Tng. Ctr. Family Svc. Ctr., Newport, R.I., 1992-96; program coord. Naval Edn. and Tng. Ctr. Family Svc. Ctr., Newport, R.I., 1996—. Editor newsletter Friends of Library, 1982-84. Sec. Friends of Charleston County Libr., 1981-82, pres. 1982-84; bd. dirs. Wando High Sch. Local Adv. Coun., Mt. Pleasant, 1981-84; pres. Wando High Sch. PTA, 1982-83, editor newsletter, 1982-85; vol. Navy-Marine Corps Relief Soc., 1993—. Mem. Am. Counseling Assn., R.I. Counseling Assn., Am. Soc. Pub. Adminstrs., APA, Am. Pub. Welfare Assn., Southeastern Employment and Tng. Assn., Phi Theta Kappa. Democrat. Roman Catholic. Home: 472 Gardiner Rd West Kingston RI 02892-1068 Office: US Dept Def USN Family Svc Ctr Naval Edn and Tng Ctr Newport RI 02841

O'KEEFE, CAROL A., bank executive; b. Martinsville, Ind.; m. Brian T. O'Keefe, Aug. 30, 1980; children: Heather, Christine Marie. Student, U. Wash., 1977-79; BS in Fin., Calif. State U., Hayward, 1984. Cert. gen. real estate appraiser, Calif. Sr. appraiser Sanwa Bank Calif., San Francisco, 1987-90; owner, appraiser O'Keefe Valuations, Walnut Creek, Calif., 1990-92; chief adminstrv. officer, sr. v.p. Tracy Fed. Savings Bank, Concord, Calif., 1992—; western regional rep. Appraisal Inst., San Francisco, 1992-93. Mem. Western Savs. League (compliance com. 1995—), Sigma Kappa. Home: 3225 Caravelle Ct Walnut Creek CA 94598 Office: Tracy Fed Bank FSB 1003 Central Ave Tracy CA 95376

O'KEEFE, KATHERINE PATRICIA, account coordinator; b. Long Beach, N.Y., Mar. 6, 1971; d. Raymond John and Therese Marie (Lederman) O'K. Student, U. Fribourg (Switzerland), 1991-92; BA, Providence College, 1993. Lic. FCC. Journalist Merrick (N.Y.) Life, 1993; adminstrv. asst. Grey Entertainment, N.Y.C., 1994-95, acct. coord., 1995—; prodn., script and continuity asst. Piccoli and Piccoli Prodns., N.Y.C., 1995. Roman Catholic. Home: 1992 Debra Ct North Merrick NY 11566 Office: Grey Entertainment 875 Third Ave New York NY 10022

O'KEEFE, KATHLEEN MARY, state government official; b. Butte, Mont., Mar. 25, 1933; d. Hugh I. and Kathleen Mary (Harris) O'Keefe; B.A. in Communications, St. Mary Coll., Xavier, Kans., 1954; m. Nick B. Baker, Sept. 18, 1954 (div. 1970); children—Patrick, Susan, Michael, Cynthia, Hugh, Mardeen. Profl. singer, mem. Kathie Baker Quartet, 1962-72; research cons. Wash. Ho. of Reps., Olympia, 1972-73; info. officer Wash. Employment Security Commn., Seattle, 1973-81, dir. public affairs, 1981-90, video dir., 1990-95, ret., 1995; freelance writer, composer, producer, 1973—. Founder, pres. bd. Eden, Inc., visual and performing arts, 1975—; public relations chmn. Nat. Women's Democratic Conv., Seattle, 1979, Wash. Dem. Women, 1976-85; bd. dirs., composer, prodr., dir. N.Y. Film Festival, 1979; Dem. candidate Wash. State Senate, 1968. Recipient Silver medal Seattle Creative Awards Show for composing, directing and producing Rent A Kid, TV pub. svc. spot, 1979. Mem. Wash. Press Women. Democrat. Roman Catholic. Author: Job Finding In the Nineties, The Third Alternative, handbook on TV prodn., (children) So You Want to be President, 1995; composer numerous songs, also writer, dir., producer Job Service spots, Immigration & Naturalization Svc. spots, U.S. Dept. Labor spots, Dept. VA spots. Home: 4426 147th Pl NE # 12 Bellevue WA 98007-3162

O'KEEFE, NANCY JEAN, real estate company executive; b. Mpls., Jan. 26, 1926; d. Dana Charles and Bonnie Theresa (Lane) Eckenbeck; m. John Robert O'Keefe, Sept. 11, 1946 (div. June 1977); children: Teresa O'Keefe Ankeny, J. Patrick, Leslie O'Keefe Kelly, Bridget O'Keefe Gidley, Elizabeth O'Keefe Skrivseth, Peter C. BS in Social Welfare, U. Minn., 1973. Cert. real estate specialist, Minn., real estate appraiser, Minn.; grad. Real Estate Inst. Sales agt. Harvey Hansen Realty, Edina, Minn., 1976-87; pres., mgr., agt. 1st Mpls. Realty, Edina, 1987-90. Mem. 5th Dist. Rep. Com., Mpls., 1951-52, Minn. Rep. Cen. Com., 1951-52; dist. chmn. fund drive ARC, Mpls., 1956; city chmn. fund drive March of Dimes, Mpls., 1957, 58; bd. dirs. St. Barnabas Hosp., Mpls., 1960-61; pres. Mpls. League Cath. Women, 1974-75. Mem. Minn. Assn. Realtors (bd. dirs. 1990-92), Greater Mpls. Assn. Realtors (bd. dirs. 1986-89, chmn. arbitration bd. 1988, Super Sales Agt. award 1982), Profl. Women's Appraisal Assn., Am. Arbitration Assn. (panel), Pi Beta Phi. Roman Catholic. Home: 6400 York Ave S Apt 602 Minneapolis MN 55435-2339 Office: Great Mpls Real Estate 5357 Penn Ave S Minneapolis MN 55419-1056

O'KEEFE, SHANNON LEIGHTON, secondary school educator; b. Hattiesburg, Miss., Sept. 13, 1969; d. Jerry Joseph and Annette (Longeway) O'K. BS in Math. and Psychology, La. State U., 1992, MEd, 1993. Cert. secondary sch. math. tchr., La. Math. and computer sci. tchr. Andrew Jackson Magnet H.S., Chalmette, La., 1993—. Sponsor Key Club Svc. Orgn., Chalmette, 1994. Home: 222 Mehle Ave Arabi LA 70032 Office: Andrew Jackson HS 201 Eighth St Arabi LA 70032

OKIN, CAROL J., federal agency administrator; b. Calif., June 16, 1946; m. Robert J. Okin. Student, Trinity Coll. Dir. human resources devel. group Office of Personnel Mgmt., dep. dir. Washington area svc. ctr.; dir. Merit Syss. and Oversight, Washington. Mem. ASPA, Exec. Women in Govt. Office: Merit Syss and Oversight 1900 E St NW Rm 7470 Washington DC 20415-0001

OKIN, SUSAN MOLLER, political science educator; b. Auckland, New Zealand, July 19, 1946; came to U.S., 1970; d. Erling Leth and Kathleen Marion (Morton) Moller; m. Robert L. Okin, July 29, 1972; children: Laura, Justin. BA, U. Auckland, New Zealand, 1966; MPhil, Oxford U., Eng., 1970; PhD, Harvard U., 1975; PhD (hon.), Mt. Vernon Coll., 1991. Asst. prof. Brandeis U., Waltham, Mass., 1976-81, assoc. prof., 1981-89, prof., 1989-90; Marta Sutton Weeks prof. of ethics in soc., dir. ethics in soc. program Stanford U., Calif., 1990—. Author: Women in Western Political Thought, 1979, Justice, Gender and the Family, 1989; contbr. articles to profl. jours. and chpts. to books. Recipient Bing Tchg. fellowship Stanford U., 1995. Mem. Am. Polit. Sci. Assn. (Victoria Schuck prize 1990), Am. Soc. for Legal and Polit. Philosophy, Conf. for Polit. Thought. Democrat. Office: Stanford U Dept Polit Sci Stanford CA 94305

OKOLSKI, CYNTHIA ANTONIA, psychotherapist, social worker; b. N.Y.C., July 26, 1954; d. Augusto and Valerie (Toffolo) Zaccari; m. Andrzej L. Okolski, Jan. 8, 1983; children: Gabriel, Christian. BA, Hofstra U., 1976; MA, Columbia U., 1978, MSW, 1983; cert. psychoanalytic psychotherapy, Advanced Ctr. Analytic Therapy, 1986. Counselor, instr. Hofstra U., Hempstead, N.Y., 1975-76; recreational dir. Residence for Young Adults Hostel, Hempstead, 1976-78; rsch. asst. Ctr. Policy Rsch., N.Y.C., 1978-79, Ctr. Psychosocial Studies, N.Y.C., 1979-81; group leader Fidel Sch., Glen Cove, N.Y., 1981; rsch. asst. Assn. of Jr. League, N.Y.C., 1982; social worker Children's Aid Soc., N.Y.C., 1983-84, Manhattan Psychiat. Ctr., N.Y.C., 1984-85; psychotherapist Advanced Inst. Analytic Psychotherapy, Jamaica, N.Y., 1986—; supervising psychotherapist in therapeutic foster care program St. Christopher-Ottillie, 1994—. Mem. NASW, Acad. Cert. Social Workers, Alpha Kappa Delta.

OKOSHI, SUMIYE, artist; b. Seattle; d. Masanari and Riyoko (Fukuda) Ushiyama; m. George Mukai, Mar. 21, 1976. Grad. Rikkyo Jogakuin U., Futabakai; postgrad., Seattle U., Henry Fry Mus. Modern Art, Seattle, 1957-59. One-woman shows include Gallery Internat., N.Y.C., 1970, Miami Mus. Modern Art, 1972, NAS, Washington, Galerie Saison, Tokyo, 1982, St. Peter's Ch. Living Room Gallery, N.Y.C., 1987, Viridian Gallery, N.Y.C., 1987, 92, 96, Port Washington Pub. Libr., 1989, NAS, Washington, 1991-92; exhibited in group shows Met. Mus. Art, N.Y.C., 1977, World Trade Center, N.Y.C., 1979, Tokyo Nat. Mus., 1979, Pace U. Gallery, Briarcliff, N.Y., 1981, Joslyn Center Arts, Torrance, Calif., Newark Mus., 1983, Bergen Mus. Art and Scis., 1983, Am. Acad. Arts and Scis., 1984, Nassau C.C., 1985-86, Port Washington Pub. Library, L.I., N.Y., 1985, Hudson River Mus., 1985, NAWA Ann. Javits Fed. Bldg., 1986, São Paulo and N.Y. Culture Exchange, 1988, Hyndai Gallery, Pusan, Korea, 1988; represented in permanent collection at Steve Hasegawa Bank of Alaska, Kaplan Fund., N.Y., Mr. & Mrs. K. Yoshikawa, N.Y., Mr. & Mrs Haruo Yoshida, Conn., Nobart Pub. Co. Inc., The Mitsui & Co., N.Y., Hotel Nikko, Atlanta, Bank of Nagoya, N.Y., Palace Hotel, Guam Island, 1991, Port Washington (N.Y.) Pub. Libr., 1989, Lowe Gallery-U. Miami, Miami Mus. of Modern Art, Nat. Women's Edn. Ctr., Saitama-ken, Japan, NAS, Washington, 1992, Hammond Mus., N. Salem, N.Y., 1993, The Jane Voorhees Zimmerli Art Mus., N.J., 1994, Permanent Collection NAWA. Mem. Japanese Artists Assn. N.Y., Nat. Women Artists Assn. (Belle Cramer award, Ziuta and Joseph Fund. award, Ralph Mayer Meml. award), Nat. Mus. Women in the Arts (charter mem. 1994). Episcopalian. Office: 55 Bethune St # 226G New York NY 10014-1703

OLCHOWSKI, DEBORAH LYNN, interior designer; b. Suffern, N.Y., Aug. 26, 1962; d. Ferdinand Mark and Jeanette Ann (Radowicz) O. BA in Art History, Skidmore Coll., 1984; MS in Interior Design, U. Mass., 1991. Mus. sec. Mus. Fine Arts, Boston, 1985-87; interior designer housing svcs. U. Mass., Amherst, 1991; interior designer Rosalyn Cama Interior Design, New Haven, Conn., 1992-94, Barbara Marcus Design, Madison, Conn., 1993-94, Haverson Arch. and Design, Greenwich, Conn., 1994-95, Silvester Tafuro Design, Inc., South Norwalk, Conn., 1995—. Mem. Ski Bears Conn. Roman Catholic.

OLDDEN, JANE BURLING, psychiatrist, author; b. Jersey City, Nov. 27, 1916; d. Stanley Kenworthy and Ethen Anna (Brown) O.; m. Irving Robinson, May 20, 1942; m. John Marvin Prutting, June 20, 1946; children: Sandra, Maliga, Robert. BA, Cornell U., 1938; MD, Woman's Med. Coll., 1941. Diplomate Am. Bd. Psychiatry. Attending physician internal medicine staff Bellevue Hosp., N.Y.C., 1944-60; internist So. Calif. Perm Med. Group, Fontana, 1960-63; resident psychiatry U. So. Calif., L.A., 1963-65, Harvard U., Boston, 1965-66; psychiatrist, chief teaching staff U. So. Calif., 1966-68; psychiatrist, Langley ptnr. U. San Francisco, 1968-78; asst. prof. psychiatry U. Ala., Huntskill, 1979; exec. sec. psychiat. edn. NIMH, Washington, 1979-80; forensic psychiatrist; staff psychiatrist Student Health U. Calif., Berkeley, 1969-72; chief direct svcs. San Mateo Mental Health, Daly City, Calif., 1968-69. Mem. Assn. Women Psychiatrists. Home: 3509 Nyland Way Lafayette CO 80026

OLDHAM, ELAINE DOROTHEA, retired elementary and middle school educator; b. Coalinga, Calif., June 29, 1931; d. Claude Smith Oldham and Dorothy Elaine (Hill) Wilkins. AB in History, U. Calif., Berkeley, 1953; MS in Sch. Adminstrn., Calif. State U., Hayward, 1976; postgrad. U. Calif., Berkeley, Harvard U., Mills Coll. Tchr. Piedmont Unified Sch. Dist., Calif., 1956-94, ret., 1994. Pres., bd. dirs. Camron-Stanford House Preservation Assn., 1979-86, adminstrv. v.p., bd. dirs., 1976-79, 86—; mem. various civic and community support groups; bd. dirs. Anne Martin Children's Ctr., Lincoln Child Ctr., Acacia br. Children's Hosp. Med. Ctr., No. Light Sch. Aux., East Bay League II of San Francisco Symphony, Piedmont Hist. Soc. (bd. dirs.), Mem. Am. Assn. Museums, Am. Assn. Mus. Trustees, Internat. Council Museums, Inst. Internat. Edn., Am. Assn. State and Local History, Am. Decorative Arts Forum, Oakland Mus. Assn. (women's bd.), DAR (vice regent, Outstanding Tchr. Am. History award), Colonial Dames Am., Magna Charta Dames, Daus. of Confederacy (bd. dirs.), Hugeunot Soc. (bd. dirs.), Plantagenet Soc., Order of Washington, Colonial Order of Crown, Americans of Royal Descent, Order St. George and Descs. of Knights of Garter, San Francisco Antiques Show (com. mem.), U. Calif. Alumni Assn. (co-chmn. and chmn. of 10th and 25th yr. class reunion coms.), Internat. Diplomacy Coun. (San Francisco chpt.), Internat. Churchill Soc., English Speaking Union, Pacific Mus. Soc., Prytanean Alumnae Assn. (bd. dirs.), Phi Delta Kappa, Delta Kappa Gamma. Republican. Episcopalian. Clubs: Harvard (San Francisco), Bellevue.

OLDHAM, MAXINE JERNIGAN, real estate broker; b. Whittier, Calif., Oct. 13, 1923; d. John K. and Lela Hessie (Mears) Jernigan; m. Laurance Montgomery Oldham, Oct. 28, 1941; 1 child, John Laurence. AA, San Diego City Coll., 1973; student Western State U. Law, San Diego, 1976-77, LaSalle U., 1977-78; grad. Realtors Inst., Sacramento, 1978. Mgr. Edin Harig Realty, LaMesa, Calif., 1966-70; tchr. Bd. Edn., San Diego, 1959-66; mgr. Julia Cave Real Estate, San Diego, 1970-73; salesman Computer Realty, San Diego, 1973-74; owner Shelter Island Realty, San Diego, 1974—. Author: Jernigan History, 1982, Mears Geneology, 1985, Fustons of Colonial America, 1988, Sissoms. Mem. Civil Svc. Commn., San Diego, 1957-58. Recipient Outstanding Speaker award Dale Carnegie. Mem. Nat. Assn. Realtors, Calif. Assn. Realtors, San Diego Bd. Realtors, San Diego Apt. Assn., Internationale des Professions Immobilieres (internat. platform speaker), DAR (vice regent Linares chpt.), Colonial Dames 17th Century, Internat. Fedn. Univ. Women. Republican. Roman Catholic. Avocations: music, theater, painting, geneology, continuing edn. Home: 3348 Lowell St San Diego CA 92106-1713 Office: Shelter Island Realty 2810 Lytton St San Diego CA 92110-4810

OLDMAN, MARILYN, psychologist; b. N.Y., June 11, 1936; d. Barnett and Shirley (Kaplan) Binkowitz; m. Elliott Oldman, Sept. 15, 1962 (div. May 1989); children: Elizabeth Sue, Mark Stanford. BS, NYU, 1958; MEd, Trenton State Coll., 1979; postgrad., Rutgers U., 1979-81; EdD, Fairleigh Dickinson U., 1987. Lic. psychologist, N.J. Counselor East Brunswick (N.J.) Adult and Continuing Edn. Program, 1980-91; instr. Fairleigh Dickinson U., Rutherford, N.J., 1982-83; post doctoral externship Union County Psychiat. Clinic, Plainfield, N.J., 1987-89; pvt. practice Watchung, N.J., 1987—; assoc. mem. Group Psychotherapy Assocs., Cranbury, N.J., 1987-94. Assoc. fellow Inst. for Rational-Emotive Therapy; mem. APA, Soc. Psychologists in Pvt. Practice, N.J. Assn. Cognitive-Behavioral Therapists, N.J. Psychol. Assn., N.J. Assn. Women Therapists, N.J. Acad. Psychology. Office: Shawnee Profl Bldg 10 Shawnee Dr Ste 7A Watchung NJ 07060-5803

OLDS, JACQUELINE, psychiatrist, educator; b. Springfield, Mass., Jan. 4, 1947; d. James and Marianne (Ejier) O.; m. Richard Stanton Schwartz, Aug. 26, 1978; children: Nathaniel Leland, Sarah Elizabeth. BA, Radcliffe Coll., 1967; MD, Tufts U., 1971. Diplomate Am. Bd. Psychiatry and Neurology. Resident in adult psychiatry Mass. Mental Health Ctr., Boston, 1974; resident in child psychiatry McLean Hosp., Belmont, Mass., 1976, asst. attending child psychiatrist, 1979—; psychiatrist-in-charge inpatient unit McLean Hall-Mercer Children's Ctr., Belmont, 1976-79; assoc. child psychiatry Beth Israel Hosp., Boston, 1979—; cons. in child psychiatry Mass. Gen. Hosp., Boston, 1994—; instr. psychiatry Harvard U. Med. Sch, Boston, 1976-86; asst. prof. clin. psychiatry, 1986—; cons. North Shore Mental Health Ctr., Salem, 1981-82. Contbr. articles to profl. jours. Sec. Cambridge (Mass.) Nursery Sch. Bd., 1982-84. Fellow Am. Psychiat. Assn.; mem. Mass. Psychiat. Soc. (ethics com. 1988-93, mem. pub. affairs com. 1992—), Am. Acad. Child Psychiatry, Am. Psychoanalytic Assn., New England Coun. Child and Adolescent Psychiatry (bd. dirs.), Cambridge Skating Club (bd. dirs. 1989). Democrat.

O'LEARY, HAZEL R., federal official, former power company executive, lawyer; b. Newport News, Va., May 17, 1937; d. Russell E. and Hazel (Palleman) Reid; m. John F. O'Leary, Apr. 23, 1980 (dec.); 1 child, Carl G. Rollins. BA, Fisk U., Nashville, 1959; JD, Rutgers U., Newark, 1966. Bar: N.J. 1967, D.C. 1985; cert. fin. planner. V.p., gen. counsel O'Leary Assocs., Inc., Washington, 1981-89; exec. v.p. corp. affairs No. States Power Co., Mpls., 1989-93, pres., 1993; sec. U.S. Dept. Energy, Washington, 1993—. Mem. Phi Beta Kappa. Office: US Dept Energy Office Sec 1000 Independence Ave SW Washington DC 20585-0001

O'LEARY, PEGGY RENÉ, accountant; b. Billings, Mont., Dec. 6, 1951; d. Paul Eugene and Norma Dean (Metcalf) O'L.; m. Kim Patric Johnson, Mar. 19, 1983. BS, Mont. State U., 1976. CPA, Mont. Staff acct. Peat Marwick Main, Billings, 1976-80; dir. fin. Billings Clinic, 1980-95; chief ops. officer Billings Sch. Dist. 2, 1996—. Div. leader youth support campaign YMCA, Billings, 1987-88, 92-93, bd. dirs., 1988-94, sec. bd., 1989-94; vol. Big Brother and Sister, 1995—. Mem. Billings C. of C. (sch. tax com. 1982-88), Pink Chips Investment Club (treas. 1987-88). Republican. Roman Catholic. Home: 4565 Pine Cove Rd Billings MT 59106-1332 Office: Billings Sch Dist 2 415 N 30th St Billings MT 59101

O'LEARY, ROSEMARY, law educator; b. Kansas City, Mo., Jan. 26, 1955; d. Franklin Hayes and Mary Jane (Kelly) O'L; m. Larry Dale Schroeder; 1 child, Meghan Schroeder O'Leary. BA, U. Kans., 1978, JD, 1981, MPA, 1982; PhD, Syracuse U., 1988. Bar: Kans. 1981. Gov.'s fellow Office of Gov., Topeka, 1981-82; asst. gen. counsel kans. Corp. Com., Topeka, 1982-83; dir. policy, lawyer Kans. Dept. Health and Environment, Topeka, 1983-85; asst. prof. Ind. u., Bloomington, 1988-90; assoc. prof. Ind. U., Bloomington, 1994—; asst. prof. Syracuse (N.Y.) U., 1990-94. Author: Environmental Change: Federal Courts and the EPA, 1993, Public Administration and the Law, 2d edit., 1996; contbr. more than 50 articles to profl. jours. Bd. govs. U. Kans. Sch. Law, Lawrence, 1980-82, devel. bd., 1981-85; bd. dirs. League Women Voters Syracuse, 1986-88; vol. Habitat for Humanity, Mex., 1990; cons. NSF, 1990; panel mem. Nat. Acad. Scis., Washington, 1990-96. Recipient Outstanding Rsch. award Lily Found., 1992, Best Article award PAR, 1993, 94, Prof. of Yr. award NASPAA, 1996. Mem. ABA (editorial bd. Natural Resources and Environment jour. 1989-95, Award for Excellence 1981), ASPA (exec. com. law and environ. sects., chair environ. ment sect., Rsch. award 1991, Best Cont. Paper award 1991), Am. Polit. Sci. Assn. (nat. chair pub. adminstrn. sect., exec. com. sect. publ.), Acad. Mgmt., Law and Soc. Assn., Assn. Pub. Policy Analysis and Mgmt. Office: Ind U SPEA 410J Bloomington IN 47405

OLEKSEY, VICKY JOYCE, business owner; b. Glasgow, Mont., Dec. 12, 1952; d. Frank Smith Jr. and Mary Helen (Smith) McIntyre; m. John Peter Oleksey, Jr., Aug. 7, 1976 (div. May 1984); 1 child, Kathryn Elizabeth. Student, U. Colo., 1973-76, U. Md., Fed. Republic Germany, 1977-81; BSBA, U. Phoenix, 1984; MBA, Boise State U., 1988. Cert. quality analyst, quality award examiner, Minn.; cert. Myers Briggs Personality Typing and ISO 9000 auditor. Keytape operator lst Security Bank, Glasgow, 1968-71; programmer analyst Baldwin Data Svcs., Denver, 1973-76; acctg. technician dept. non-appropriated funds U.S. Govt., Ramstein, Fed. Republic Germany, 1977-79, systems operator dept. non-appropriated funds, 1979-80; programmer analyst II, United Banks Colo., Denver, 1982-85; programmer analyst Moore Fin. Group, Boise, Idaho, 1985-87, career developer, 1987-88; mgr. quality assurance West One Bancorp, Boise, 1988-90; mgr. quality assurance software products Bankers Systems, Inc., St. Cloud, Minn., 1991-93, sr. bus. analyst, 1993-95; owner Applied Bus. Strategies, St. Cloud, Minn., 1995—. Mem. pers. com., leader single parents group 1st Presbyn. Ch., Boise, 1988-89; bd. dirs. St. Cloud All-City H.S. Marching Band, 1995-96, Forum of Exec. Women, 1996. Recipient Outstanding Project Chmn. award, Jaycee of Month award U.S. Jaycees-Idaho, 1989, Staff Officer of Yr., 1991, Project Chmn. of Yr. 1991, Ambassador, 1993; named Statesman Minn. Jaycees, 1993, Single Parent of the Yr., 1994. Mem. Am. Bus. Women's Assn. (v.p. Boise chpt. 1987-88, Woman of Yr. award 1987), Capitol Jaycees (v.p. for mgmt. devel. 1989), Sartell Jaycees (pres. 1992-93, state del. 1993-94). Republican. Episcopalian. Home: 2808 21st Ave S Saint Cloud MN 56301-9063 Office: Applied Bus Strategies PO Box 7614 Saint Cloud MN 56302

OLENICK, SANDRA LEIGH, elementary education educator; b. Pitts., Sept. 4, 1950; d. Christopher Richard and Theresa Mary Kosor; m. Gerald James Olenick, Apr. 26, 1975; children: Terrilyn, Lindsay. BS in Elem. Edn., Calif. State U. Pa., 1971; MA in Elem. Edn., W.Va. U., 1973; postgrad., U. Pitts., 1977-80. Tchr. elem. grades 5 and 6 Greater Latrobe (Pa.) Sch. Dist., 1971-74, tchr. elem. and mid. sch., 1974-81, tchr. elem. grade 6, 1981—. Mem. St. Mary Ch. Coun., Forbes Road, Pa., Aquinas Acad. PTA; mem. athletic com. Aquinas Acad.; chair swim team Greensburg (Pa.) YMCA; tchr. rep. Mt. View PTO. Mem. ASCD, Nat. Coun. Tchrs. Math., Math. Coun. Western Pa., Pa. State Edn. Assn., Smithsonian Assocs., W.Va. U. Alumni Assn., Nat. Coun. Tchrs. English. Democrat. Roman Catholic. Office: Mt View Elem Sch 3110 Mt View Dr Greensburg PA 15601

OLESKOWICZ, JEANETTE, physician; b. N.Y.C., Oct. 10, 1956; d. John Francis and Helen (Zielinski) O. BA, NYU, 1977; D of Chiropractic, N.Y. Chiropractic Coll., 1982; MS, U. Bridgeport, 1984; MD, U. Medicine & Dentistry N.J., 1990. U.S. immigration officer U.S. Dept. Justice, N.Y.C., 1977; commd. med. officer USAR, 1983; advanced through grades to maj. HPSP, 1990; resident and intern Eisenhower Army Med. Ctr., Ft. Gordon, Ga., 1990-94; chief psychiatry U.S. Army Hosp., Vicenza, Italy, 1994-95; cons.- liaison psychiatrist Brooke Army Med. Ctr., Tex., 1995—. Am. sponsor for a cripples child's health care in Mid. East. Mem. AMA, Am. Psychiat. Assn. Home: 4000 Horizon Hill # 607 San Antonio TX 78229

OLEVSKY, KATHY KILMARTIN, owner, instructor karate school; b. Utica, N.Y., Nov. 17, 1957; d. Arthur F. and Mary Ellen (Benson) Kilmartin; m. Albert Robinson Olevsky, Sept. 27, 1980; children: Joshua, Casey. Grad. H. S., Raleigh, N.C., 1975; student, E. Carolina U., 1975-79; A in mgmt., Am. Martial Arts Inst., 1983. Instr., gen. mgr. Karate Internat., Raleigh, 1979—; physical edn. instr. Meredith Coll., Raleigh, 1990-95; dist. mgr. Nature's Sunshine Products, 1993-96; dir. karate divsn. N.C. Amateur Sports, Raleigh, 1987-92, dir. Am. Martial Arts Assn., Raleigh, 1988—. Author: Practical Self Defense Awareness, 1989, Real Estate Self Protection, 1994, Healthy People/Fit Kid 2000, 1995; editor: Essentials of American Karate Work Book, 1991. Chair Wake County Coun. on Fitness & Health, Raleigh, 1993—, bd. mem. Wake County Sch. Health Advisory Coun., 1995, 96, Youth Fitness Task Force, Raleigh, 1995, 96. Recipient Gold medals (3) N.C. Amateur Sports, Durham, N.C., 1993, award of Excellence Gov. Coun. Fitness & Health, 1994. Mem. Am. Martial Arts Assoc., Shodan, Nidan. Roman Catholic. Office: Karate Internat 2431 Spring Forest Rd # 157 Raleigh NC 27615

OLIAN, JOANNE CONSTANCE, curator, art historian; b. N.Y.C., d. Richard Edward and Dorothy (Singer) Wahrman; m. Howard Olian; children: Jane Wendy, Patricia Ann. Student, Syracuse U.; BA, Hofstra U., 1969; MA, NYU/Inst. Fine Arts, 1972. Grad. internship Met. Mus., N.Y.C., 1973; asst. curator Mus. of City of N.Y., 1974, curator costume collection, 1975-91; cons. curator Costume Collection, 1992-95, curator emeritus, 1995—; lectr. Parsons Sch. Design; vis. lectr. Musée des Arts Decoratifs, Paris, summer 1983, 84, 85. Author: The House of Worth: The Gilded Age, 1860-1918, 1982; editor: Authentic French Fashions of the Twenties, 1990, Everyday Fashions of the Forties, 1992, Children's Fashions from Mode Illustre 1860-1912, 1994, Wedding Fashions, 1862-1912, 1994, Everyday Fashions, 1909-1920, 1995; contbr. articles to profl. jours., chpts. to books. Mem. Internat. Council Mus. (costume com.), Costume Soc. Am. (dir. 1976-79, 83-86), Fashion Group (bd. dirs. 1985-86), Centre Internat. d'Etude des Textiles Anciens. Club: Cosmopolitan (N.Y.C.). Home: Shepherds Ln Port Washington NY 11050 Office: Shepherds Ln Sands Point NY 11050

OLIM, DOROTHY, theater administrator; b. Bronx, N.Y., Oct. 14, 1933; divorced;. Student, Julliard Sch. Music, 1949-50; BFA, Columbia Univ., 1955, MFA, 1956. Owner, operator, pres. Dorothy Olim Assocs., Inc., 1960-87; pres. Krone-Olim Advt. Inc., 1967-87. produced 6 plays; managed over 80 productions. Spl. drama adv. com. to pres. Carnegie-Mellon Univ., Pitts., 1992—. Mem. Assn. Theatrical Press Agents and Mgrs. (bd. govs. 1978-87, sec.-treas. 1987-91), League of Broadway Theatres and Producers (sec./treas. 1961-86), League of Advtsg. Agys. (pres. 1975), League of Profl. Theatre Women (bd. dirs. 1993—), N.Y. Coalition of Profl. Women in the Arts (spl. adv. 1993—, mem. Tony Awards nom. com. 1996—). Office: 588 West End Ave New York NY 10024

OLIN, SAMANTHA DEBRAH, writer; b. N.Y.C., Apr. 22, 1953; d. Roboret and Arline (Rosenberg) O.; 1 child, Sasha Blue. Writer, photographer Cirus mag., 1967-70; head chef Alive Kitchen, 1972-75; mgr. 42 5th Ave, 1972-75; founder, booking and promoter Sting Ray Prodns., 1976; with Sting Ray Rock Promotions, N.Y., 1973-76. Singer, songwriter, 70's and 80's; contbr. articles and photographs to various publs., 1963-96. Vol. chef area soup kitchen Chips, Bklyn., 1977-79. Democrat. Home: 5436 Nurge Ave Flushing NY 11378-3336

OLINGER, CARLA D(RAGAN), medical advertising executive; b. Cin., Oct. 8, 1947; d. Carl Edward and Selene Ethel (Neal) Dragan; m. Chauncey Greene Olinger, Jr., May 30, 1981. B.A., Douglass Coll., 1975. Mgr. info. retrieval services Frank J. Corbett, Inc., N.Y.C., 1976-77; editor, proofreader, prodn. asst. Rolf W. Rosenthal, Inc., N.Y.C., 1977-78, copywriter, 1978-80, copy supr., 1980-82, v.p. copy dept., 1982-83; v.p., group copy supr., adminstrv. copy supr. Rolf W. Rosenthal, Inc., div. Ogilvy & Mather, 1984-89, v.p., assoc. creative dir. RWR Advt., 1989; v.p., copy supr. Barnum & Souza, N.Y.C., 1990-92; v.p., copy supr. Botto, Roessner, Horne & Messinger, Ketchum Comm., N.Y.C., 1992-95, Lyons Lavey Nickel Swift, N.Y.C., 1995—. Editor: Antimicrobial Prescribing (Harold Neu), 1979. Mem. Am. Med. Writers Assn., Ch. Club N.Y., St. George's Soc. N.Y. Office: Lyons Lavey Nickel Swift 488 Madison Ave New York NY 10022

OLIPHANT, ERNIE L., safety educator, public relations executive, consultant; b. Richmond, Ind., Oct. 25, 1934; d. Ernest E. and Beulah A. (Jones) Reid; m. George B. Oliphant, Sept. 25, 1955; children: David, Wendell, Rebecca. Student, Earlham Coll., 1953-55, Ariz. State U., 1974, Phoenix Coll., 1974-78. Planner, organizer, moderator confs., programs for various women's clubs, safety assns., 1971-86; nat. field coordinator Operation Lifesaver, Inc., 1986-94; assoc. dir. Operation Lifesaver Nat. Safety Council, Phoenix, 1978-86; cons. Fed. R.R. Adminstrn.; prin. Highway and Rail Cons. Svcs., Phoenix, 1995—. lectr. in field.; adviser Am. Ry. Engring. Assn., Calif. Assn. Women Hwy. Safety Leaders, numerous others. Mem. R.R./Hwy. grade crossing com. Ariz. Corp. Commn.; mem. transp. and system com. Ariz. Gov.'s Commn. on Environment; mem. Ariz. Gov.'s Council Women for Hwy. Safety; mem. motor vehicle traffic safety at hwy.-r.r. grade crossings com., roadway environment com., women's div. com. Nat. Safety Council; mem. Phoenix Traffic Accident Reduction Program; task force mem. U.S. Dept. Transp. on Grade Crossing Safety. Recipient Safety award SW Safety Congress, 1973; citation of Merit Adv. Commn. on Ariz. Environment, 1974; Gov.'s award for hwy. safety, 1978; Gov.'s Merit of Recognition Outstanding Service in Hwy. Safety, 1980. Mem. Assn. R.R. Editors, NAFE, Inc., Pub. Relations Soc. Am., R.R. Pub. Relations Assn., committees Nat. Acad. Scis. (dir. transp. research, planning, adminstrn. of transp. safety com., r.r.-hwy. grade crossing safety com.), Women's Transp. Seminar, Ariz. Fedn. Women's Clubs (named pres. of yr. 1968), Ariz. Safety Assn. (safety recognition award 1975), Gen. Fedn. Women's Clubs (internat. bd. dirs.), Nat. Assn. Women Hwy. Safety Leaders, Soc. Govt. Planners, Inc., Phi Theta Kappa. Republican. Quaker. Author of tech. publs.

OLIVARIUS-IMLAH, MARYPAT, sales, advertising and marketing executive; b. Bklyn., Oct. 25, 1957; d. Kenneth William Joseph and Ann Marie (Beekley) Olivarius; m. Craig Alexander Olivarius-Imlah, Sept. 18, 1982; children: Christopher Edward, Jamison Robert, Meghan Patricia. BS in Mktg. and Communications, Ramapo State Coll. N.J., 1979; MBA in Mktg. and Mgmt., Fairleigh Dickinson U., 1985. Researcher, pub. rels. MacNeil/Lehrer Report, WNET-TV, N.Y.C., 1977; salesperson Terrace Realty, Montvale, N.J., 1977-79; direct mail advt. copywriter Prentice-Hall, Inc., Englewood Cliffs, N.J., 1979-81; editor, promotional designer Beauty & Barber Supply Inst., Englewood, N.J., 1981-83; nat. dir. advt. and pub. rels. Emerson Radio Corp., North Bergen, N.J., 1983-85; founder, pres. Imagery Print & Advt., Print Brokerage Design Agy.

OLIVEIRA, MARY JOYCE, middle school education educator; b. Oakland, Calif., Feb. 16, 1954; d. Joseph and Vivian (Perry) O. BA, U. Calif., Berkeley, 1978; student, Holy Names Coll., Oakland, 1992; grad. in math., Calif. State U., Hayward, 1994. Cert. tchr., Calif.; cert. single subject math. credential, Hawaii. Recreation specialist Oakland Parks and Recreation, 1977-89; substitute tchr. Diocese of Oakland, 1989-90; tutor Oakland Pub. Schs., 1991; substitute tchr. Alameda (Calif.) Unified Sch. Dist., 1991—, Piedmont (Calif.) Unified Sch. Dist., 1993-96; tchr. summer program Wood Mid. Sch., Alameda, 1993, 96, Chipman Mid. Sch., Alameda, 1994, Encinal H.S., Alameda, 1995; math. tutor Calif. State U., Hayward, 1996—. Creator children's sock toys Oliveira Originals, 1985. Vol. in art therapy oncology ward Children's Hosp., Oakland, 1985; vol. Berkeley Unified Sch. Dist., 1990-91. Mem. Nat. Coun. Tchrs. Math., Calif. Math. Coun., Math. Assn. Am. Home: 3903 Mera St Oakland CA 94601-4222

OLIVER, AMIE, artist, educator; b. Vaiden, Miss., Mar. 14, 1960; d. William Randolph III and Mable Sue (Vowell) O.; m. Harry Kollatz, Jr., June 20, 1996. BA, Miss. State U., 1982; MFA, Bowling Green State U., 1984. Tchg. asst. Bowling Green (Ohio) State U., 1982-84; assoc. prof. art Longwood Coll., Farmville, Va., 1986—; summer faculty Tyler Sch. Art, Temple U., Phila., 1990; juror Scholastic Art Awards, Richmond, Va., 1996; bd. dirs. 1708 Gallery, Richmond. Art dir. (catalogues) Making a Mark, 1995, Artists of the Cite Internationale Des Arts, 1996, Gala 96, 1996; contbg. artist Soho 20, N.Y.C., Virginia Beach Ctr. for the Arts, Longwood Ctr. for the Visual Arts, Heart of Virginia, Farmville, Va., 1986-90, Artists for Life, Richmond, 1988, Mental Health Assn., Richmond, 1995. Named One of 8 Rising Art Stars WRIC-TV, 1996. Mem. Coll. Art Assn., Richmond Women's Caucus for Art. Office: Longwood Coll Art Dept 201 High St Farmville VA 23909

OLIVER, ELIZABETH KIMBALL, writer, historian; b. Saginaw, Mich., May 21, 1918; d. Chester Benjamin and Margaret Eva (Allison) Kimball; m. James Arthur Oliver, May 3, 1941 (div. July 1967); children: Patricia Allison, Dexter Kimball. BA, U. Mich., 1940. Tchr. Dexter (Mich.) High Sch., 1940-41; libr. Sherman (Conn.) Libr. Assn., 1966-75; pres. Sherman (Conn.) Libr. Assn., 1983-84; writer, historian, 1976—; reporter Sherman Sentinel, 1965-70; editor newsletter Sherman Hist. Soc., 1977-78; columnist Citizen News, Fairfield County, Conn., 1981-83; guest columnist Mandarin News. Author: History of Staff Wives-AMNH, 1961, Background and History of the Palisades Nature Association, 1964, History and Architecture of Grace United Methodist Church, 1990, Legacy to St. Augustine, 1993. Vol. N.Y.

Hist. Soc., N.Y.C., 1961-65; treas. Coburn Cemetery Assn., Sherman, 1976-82; historian Greenbrook-Palisades Nature Assn., Tenafly, N.J., 1962-64, Wesley Manor/Wesley Village Retirement Cmty., 1995—; mem. St. Augustine Hist. Soc., Naromi Land Trust (life), Cedar Key Hist. Soc. Mem. AAUW, Friends of Libr. (life), Inst. Am. Indian Studies, Marjorie Kinnan Rawlings Co. (charter), St. Augustine Woman's Club (cert. of appreciation 1990), Sherman Hist. Soc., Mandarin Hist. Soc. Republican. Congregationalist. Home: 1500 Bishop Estates Rd Apt 12 B Jacksonville FL 32259-4250

OLIVER, GILDA MARIA, sculptor, artist; b. Manhattan, N.Y., Nov. 16, 1961; d. Thomas Tobin and Francoise Marie (Bonamy) Krampf; m. Shawn James Francis McLean, Aug. 1, 1983 (div. Dec. 1986); 1 child, Cory Shawn McLean; m. Marc Scott Oliver. BFA cum laude, Wells Coll., Aurora, N.Y., 1984; BFA, N.Y.S. Coll. of Ceramics at Alfred U., 1994; attending, Cranbrook Art Acad. dir. corp. sales and rentals Cambridge (Mass.) Art Assn., 1988-92; tchrs. asst. art dept. Wells Coll., Aurora, 1980-84. Commissioned sculptures include Heather, 1984, Mark Phillips, 1987, Dr. Cutler-West, 1987, George Orwell, 1988, B.F. Skinner, 1988, Margaret Gibson, 1993 (nom. Pulitzer Prize award 1995), David McKain, 1992 (nom. Pulitzer Prize award 1995); shows include U. Pitts., Bradford, Hanley Gallery, 1995; represented in collections Wells Coll., Aurora, 1984, Lillian Hellman, N.Y.C., 1984, Victoria and Richard MacKenzie-Childs, Ltd., Aurora, 1988, B.F. Skinner, Cambridge, 1989, Robert and Jane Saltonstall, Jr., Concord, Mass., 1989, David McKain and Margaret Gibson, Providence, R.I., 1995; represented in galleries including Copley Soc., Boston, 1985-89, Cambridge Art Assn., 1988-90, Bella Luna Gallery, Boston, 1992-93, Brickbottom Gallery, Somerville, Mass., 1989-95. Office: Unit 35 2945 Woodward Ave Bloomfield Hills MI 48304

OLIVER, JOYCE ANNE, journalist, editorial consultant, columnist; b. Coral Gables, Fla., Sept. 19, 1958; d. John Joseph and Rosalie Cecile (Mack) O. BA in Communications, Calif. State U., Fullerton, 1980, MBA, 1990. Corp. editor Norris Industries Inc., Huntington Beach, Calif., 1979-82; pres. J.A. Oliver Assocs., La Habra Heights, Calif., 1982—; corp. editorial cons. Norris Industries, 1982, Better Methods Cons., Huntington Harbour, Calif., 1982-83, Summit Group, Orange, Calif., 1982-83, UDS, Encinitas, Calif., 1983-84, MacroMarketing, Costa Mesa, Calif., 1985-86, PM Software, Huntington Beach, Calif., 1985-86, CompuQuote, Canoga Park, Calif., 1985-86, Nat. Semicondr. Can. Ltd., Mississauga, Ont., Can., 1986, Maclean Hunter Ltd., Toronto, Ont., 1986-90; Frame Inc., Fullerton, Calif., 1987-88, The Johnson-Layton Co., L.A., 1988-89, Corp. Rsch. Inc., Chgo., 1988, Axon Group, Horsham, Pa., 1990-91, Am. Mktg. Assn., Chgo., 1990-92, Kenzaikai Co., Ltd., Tokyo, 1991, Penton Pub., Cleve., 1991, Bus. Computer Pub., Inc., Peterborough, N.H., 1991-92, Helmers Pub., Inc., Peterborough, 1992, Schnell Pub., Co., Inc., N.Y.C., 1992-93, Diversified Pub. Group, Carol Stream, Ill., 1993; mem. Rsch. Coun. of Scripps Clinic and Rsch. Found., 1987-92. Contbg. editor Computer Merchandising/Resell, 1982-85, Computer Reselling, 1985, Reseller Mgmt., 1987-89; contbg. editor Can. Electronics Engring., 1986-90, west coast editor, 1990, Chem. Bus. mag., 1992-93; spl. feature editor Cleve. Inst. Electronics publ. The Electron, 1986-89; bus. columnist Mktg. News, 1990-92; contbr. articles to profl. jours. and mags. Bd. dirs. Action Comms., 1993—. Mem. IEEE, Internat. Platform Assn., Soc. Photo-optical Instrumentation Engrs., Inst. Mgmt. Scis., Nat. Writers Club (profl.), Internat. Mktg. Assn., Soc. Profl. Journalists, L.A. World Affairs Coun. Republican. Roman Catholic. Office: 2045 Fullerton Rd La Habra CA 90631-8213

OLIVER, K. RENÉE, sales representative; b. Cedartown, Ga., June 3, 1958; d. Cecil Dewey and Martha Elizabeth (Wooten) O.; m. Ronald Clyde Tuck, Feb. 14, 1981 (div. Dec. 1988); 1 child, Scott Anthony McDurmon. A in Bus., Floyd Coll., 1994. Mgr. First Franklin Fin. Savings, Cedartown, Ga., 1978-81; purchasing agt. Trinity Industries, Cedartown, Ga., 1981-83; assoc. realtor Jane Wyatt Realty, Cedartown, Ga., 1985-92; sales svc. mgr. Jefferson Smurfit Corp., Cedartown, Ga., 1986-95; sales rep. Smurfit Pallet Sys., Rancho Cucamonga, Calif., 1995-96, Jefferson Smurfit Corp., L.A., 1996—. Baptist. Home: 412 N Kenwood St # 304 Glenwood CA 91206 Office: Jefferson Smurfit Corp 2106 S Malt Ave Los Angeles CA 90040

OLIVER, LISA ANDREA, school psychologist; b. Savannah, Ga., Aug. 31, 1968; d. Joe Brantley and Peggy Ann (Wood) Oliver. BA, Ga. So. U., Statesboro, 1990, MEd, 1994, EdS, 1996. Social worker Chatham County Dept. Family and Children Svcs., Savannah, 1990-93; psychometrist Ga. Neurol. Inst., Savannah, 1993-95; sch. psychologist Beaufort County Schs., Beaufort, S.C., 1995-96, St. Mary's County Schs., Leonardtown, Md., 1996—. Recipient French award Fgn. Lang. Assn., 1987. Mem. ACA, Nat. Assn. Sch. Psychologists, Am. Epilepsy Soc., Assn. for Adult Devel. and Aging.

OLIVER, MARY, poet; b. Maple Heights, Ohio, Sept. 10, 1935; d. Edward William and Helen Mary (Vlasak) O. Student, Ohio State U., 1955-56, Vassar Coll., 1956-57. Chmn. writing dept. Fine Arts Work Ctr., Provincetown, 1972-73, mem. writing com., 1984; Banister poet in residence Sweet Briar Coll., 1991-95; William Blackburn vis. prof. creative writing Duke U., 1995; Catharine Osborn Foster prof. Bennington Coll., 1996—. Author: No Voyage and Other Poems, 1963, enlarged edit., 1965, The River Styx, Ohio, 1972, The Night Traveler, 1978, Twelve Moons, 1979, American Primitive, 1983, Dream Work, 1986, House of Light, 1990, new and Selected Poems, 1992, A Poetry Handbook, 1994, White Pine, 1994, Blue Pastures, 1995; contbr. to Yale U. Rev., Kenyon Rev., Poetry, Atlantic, Harvard mag., others. Recipient Shelley Meml. award, 1970, Alice Fay di Castagnola award, 1973; Cleve. Arts prize for lits., 1979; Achievement award Am. Acad. and Inst. Arts and Letters, 1983; Pulitzer prize for poetry, 1984; Christopher award, 1991, L.L. Winship award, 1991, Nat. Book award, 1992; Nat. Endowment fellow, 1972-73; Guggenheim fellow, 1980-81. Mem. PEN, Authors Guild. Home: care Molly Malone Cook Lit Agy PO Box 338 Provincetown MA 02657

OLIVER, MARY ANNE MCPHERSON, religion educator; b. Montgomery, Ala., Nov. 21, 1935; d. James Curtis and Margaret Sinclair (Miller) McPherson; m. Raymond Davies Oliver, Aug. 28, 1959; children: Kathryn Sinclair, Nathan McPherson. BA, U. Ala., Tuscaloosa, 1956; cert., Sorbonne, Paris, 1958; MA, U. Wis., 1959; PhD, Grad. Theol. Union, Berkeley, Calif., 1972. Vol. tchr., preacher, counselor, 1972—; instr. U. Calif., Berkeley, St. Mary's Coll., Moraga, Calif., 1973; adj. faculty San Francisco Theol. Sem., San Anselmo, 1977-81; lectr. San Jose (Calif.) State U., 1980-81, San Francisco State U., 1985-86; adj. prof. dept. liberal arts John F. Kennedy U., Orinda, Calif., 1987-95; vis. prof. Gen. Theol. Sem., N.Y.C., 1995. Author: History of Good Shepherd Episcopal Mission, 1978, Conjugal Spirituality: The Primacy of Mutual Love in Christian Tradition, 1994; contbr. articles to profl. jours. Rep. Ala. Coun. on Human Rels., Mobile, 1958; active deanery, conv. Good Shepherd Episc. Ch., Berkeley, Calif., 1970-75; rep. U. Calif. Fgn. Student Hospitality, Berkeley, 1965-70; vol. tchr. Berkeley pub. schs., 1965-73; bd. dirs. Canterbury Found., Berkeley, 1972-75; chmn. bd. dirs. West Berkeley Parish, Berkeley, 1976-78, adult edn. program St. Mark's Episc. Ch., 1992-93; mentor Edn. for Ministry, Univ. of the South, 1993—. Recipient award French Consulate, New Orleans, 1956; Fulbright grantee, 1956, grantee Mabelle McLeod Lewis Found., 1969. Mem. Am. Acad. Religion, Conf. on Christianity and Lit. Democrat. Home: 1632 Grant St Berkeley CA 94703-1356

OLIVER, MARY WILHELMINA, law librarian, educator; b. Cumberland, Md., May 4, 1919; d. John Arlington and Sophia (Lear) O. AB, Western Md. Coll., 1940; BS in Library Sci, Drexel Inst. Tech., 1943; JD, U. N.C., 1951. Bar: N.C. 1951. Asst. circulation librarian N.J. Coll. Women, 1943-45; asst. in law library U. Va., 1945-47; asst. reference, social sci. librarian Drake U., 1947-49; rsch. asst. Inst. Govt., U. N.C., Chapel Hill, 1951-52, asst. law librarian, 1952-55, asst. prof. law, law librarian, 1955-59, assoc. prof. law librarian, 1959-69, prof. law, law librarian, 1969-84, prof. law and law librarian emeritus, 1984—. Mem. ABA, N.C. Bar Assn., Am. Assn. Law Librs. (pres. 1972-73, Marian Gould Gallagher Disting. Svc. award 1992), Assn. Am. Law Schs. (exec. com. 1979-81), Law Alumni Assn. U. N.C., Order of Coif. Home: 157 Carol Woods Chapel Hill NC 27514 Office: U NC Law Libr Van Hecke Wettach Hall # 064A Chapel Hill NC 27514

OLIVER, NANCY LEBKICHER, artist, retired elementary education educator; b. Stockton, Calif., 1939; d. John B. and Marjorie Lebkicher; m. Douglas C. Oliver, 1963; children: Charles, Elaine. BA with honors, San Jose State U., 1961. Summer playground dir. Recreation Dept., Redwood City, Calif., 1956-61; 1st grade tchr. Redwood City (Calif.) Elem. Sch. Dist., 1961-63; kindergarten tchr. Ukiah (Calif.) Unified Sch. Dist., 1963-67; assoc. tchr. kindergarten San Carlos (Calif.) Elem. Sch. Dist., 1976-81; shopper for dept. store Macy's, San Francisco, 1975-82. Sunday sch. dir. St. Peter's Episcopal Ch., Redwood City, 1973-78; active White Oaks PTA, San Carlos, 1973-81, newsletter editor, 1978-81; leader Girl Scouts U.S.A., San Carlos, 1978-81. Mem. AAUW (San Carlos br. newsletter editor 1972-74, editor historic tour booklet 1981, editor historic resources booklet 1989, chmn. historic preservation sect. 1979—, pres. Willits br. 1966-67), San Carlos Hist./Heritage Assn. (founder, dir. 1995—), Sequoia H.S. Alumni Assn. (founding sec., membership chmn., centennial coord., pres. 1996—), Internat. Order Rainbow Girls (grand officer Calif. 1957-58, mother advisor Redwood City 1987-89). Democrat. Episcopalian. Home: 147 Belvedere Ave San Carlos CA 94070

OLIVER, SUZANNE KATHRYN, dancer, educator; b. Orange, N.J., Sept. 16, 1951; d. Chester Henry and Marybelle (Littell) O.; m. Mark William Replogle, May 21, 1986 (div. Dec. 1989); m. Paul Vernon McDonald, Jan. 18, 1991; children: Mathew Gregory, Alexandra Suzanne. BA, Adelphi U., Garden City, 1973; MFA, U. Ill., Urbana-Champaign, 1986, PhD in kinesiology, 1994. Dancer Contemporary Dancers, Winnipeg, Canada, 1974-78, Mathews/Masters Dance, N.Y.C., 1978-79; co-artistic dir., dancer One Plus One..., Champaign, Ill., 1980-83; grad. tchg. asst. U. Ill. Dance Dept., Urbana, Ill., 1981-85; artistic dir., choreographer The Dance Collective, Urbana, 1987-89; grad. tchg. asst. U. Ill. Kinesiology, Urbana, 1990-93; instr. San Jacinto Coll., Houston, 1994—; presenter Nat. Coll. Dance Festival, Huntsville, Tex., 1994, Soc. for the Study of Symbolic Interaction, Champaign, 1994, Nat. Athletic Trainers' Assn. Conf., Dallas, 1994. Choreographer (dances) various performances venues throughout career; contbr. articles to profl. jours. Mem. Sierra Club, Calif., PTA, Houston. Mem. AAUW, NOW, Tex. Assn. of Health, PE, Recreation & Dance, Tex. Junior Coll. Tchrs. Assn., Houston Dance Coalition, DiverseWorks. Democrat. Office: San Jacinto Coll 15735 Beamer Rd Houston TX 77089

OLIVER, VERNA MARIE, retired financial administrator; b. Twp. Genoa, Wis., Mar. 30, 1924; d. Fay and Hazel Marie (Taylor) West; m. Orbin Earle Oliver, Jan. 26, 1946; 1 chld, Anton. AD in Acctg., Wis. Tech. Coll., La Crosse, 1957. Cert. acctg. adminstrv. dir. Bookkeeper Vernon Electric Coop., Westby, Wis., 1957-61, asst. acctg.supr., 1961-66, acctg. supr., 1966-78, dir. office ops., 1978-87, dir. office ops.-fin., 1987-89. Contbr. to poetry anthologies. V.p. coun. Our Saviours Luth. Ch., Westby, 1992, pres., 1993, Sunday sch. supt., 1980-84, ch. del. to convs., 1973-93; sec.-treas. Westby Area Hist. Soc., 1990-94; mem. Dem. Nat. Com., 1992-95; mem. Pres. Clinton's Steering Com., 1995-96. Home: R 2 Box 120A Cadott WI 54727

OLIVERIO, CATHERINE ADORADIO, special education educator; b. San Jose, Calif., Nov. 22, 1958; d. Emery Eugene and Edwina Irene (Scilacci) Adoradio. BA in Speech and Hearing, U. Calif., Santa Barbara, 1982, MEd in Spl. Edn., 1987. Spl. edn. tchr. Moorpark (Calif.) H.S., 1985-87, Ventura (Calif.) Unified Sch. Dist., 1989—; rsch. assoc., supr. student tchrs. U. Calif., Santa Barbara, 1987-88. Mem. Coun. for Exceptional Children (divsn. for early childhood). Office: Blanche Reynolds Sch 450 Valmore Ave Ventura CA 93003-4752

OLIVER-WARREN, MARY ELIZABETH, retired library science educator; b. Hamlet, N.C., Feb. 23, 1924; d. Washington and Carolyn Belle (Middlebrooks) Terry; m. David Oliver, 1947 (div. 1971); children: Donald D., Carolyn L.; m. Arthur Warren, Sept. 14, 1990. BS, Bluefield State U., 1948; MS, South Conn. State U., 1958; student, U. Conn., 1977. Cert. tchr., adminstr. and supr., Conn. Media specialist Hartford (Conn.) Pub. Schs., 1952-86; with So. Conn. State U., New Haven, 1972—, asst. prof. Sch. Libr. Sci. and Instructional Tech., 1987-95, ret., 1995; mem. dept. curriculum com. So. Conn. State U., 1987-95, adj. prof., 1995—. Author: My Golden Moments, 1988, The Elementary School Media Center, 1990, Text Book Elementary School Media Center, 1991, I Must Fight Alone, 1991, (textbook) I Must Fight Alone, 1994. Mem. ALA, Conn. Ednl. Media Assn., Black Librs. Network N.J. Inc., Assn. Ret. Tchrs. Conn., Black and Hispanic Consortium, So. Conn. State U. Women's Assn., Cicuso Club (v.p.), Friends Club (v.p.), Delta Kappa Gamma, Alpha Kappa Alpha. Home: 6 Freeman Rd Somerset NJ 08873-2925 Office: So Conn State U 501 Crescent St New Haven CT 06515-1330

OLIVETI, SUSAN GAIL, sales promotion and public relations executive; b. Bklyn., Nov. 1, 1938; d. Peter and Nancy Jane (Wolk) Randolph; m. Fosco Anthony Oliveti, Sept. 18, 1970 (div. 1990); children by previous marriage: Lois, Peter, Elizabeth, Ruben. BBA, CCNY, 1967; student, NYU, 1968-69; diploma in nursing, Jewish Hosp. Sch. Nursing, 1960. Estimator, media rsch. Ogilvy & Mather, N.Y.C., 1966-68; TV rep. Adam Young, Inc., N.Y.C., 1968-69; exec. asst. Paramount Pictures, N.Y.C., 1969-80; mgr. conv. and media events Warner Amex Satellite Enterprise Co. (now MTV Networks), N.Y.C., 1980-83; exhibits and pub. rels. specialist Siemens Med. Systems, Iselin, N.J., 1983-85; meetings and pub. rels. mgr. U.S. Trademark Assn., N.Y.C., 1985; v.p. corp. communications J.R. Heimbaugh, Inc., 1986; mgr. sales promotions, pub. relations meetings, convs. Lightolier, Inc., Secaucus, N.J., 1986-90; exec. v.p. Globefern USA, Inc., 1990-95; sales & mktg. exec. marriott Sr. Living Svcs., 1995—. Recipient spl. honors United Airlines, 1978. Mem. Meeting Profls. Internat. (reception com., edn. com.), Pub. Rels. Soc. Am. Democrat. Jewish. Avocations: knitting, gardening, designing jewelry. Office: PO Box 4110 Vero Beach FL 32964

OLLANKETO, MARILYN WESALA, computer science educator; b. Hancock, Mich., Aug. 9, 1947; d. Wilbert Absolom and Martha Marie (Lampinen) Wesala; m. Arlen Matt Ollanketo, July 10, 1976; 1 child, Brandon. BA, No. Mich. U., 1969. Programmer/analyst Consumers Power Co., Jackson, Mich., 1969-74; office mgr. Ultramatic Data Processing, Hancock, 1976-78; instr. Suomi Coll., Hancock, 1980—; presenter Copper County Intermediate Sch., Hancock, 1988—. Mem. Am. Legion Aux. (pres.), Hancock Sports Booster Club (purchaser 1994—). Lutheran.

OLLIE, PEARL LYNN, artist, singer, songwriter; b. Highland Park, Mich., Oct. 15, 1953; d. Sam and Estelle Theresa (Wasielewska) O.; m. Christopher John Keyes, Nov. 29, 1975 (div. Nov. 1978); 1 child, Shane Michael Fiondella. Student, Henry Ford C.C., Dearborn, Mich., 1988-89, Soc. Arts and Crafts Coll., 1970-74, Ctr. for Creative Study, 1980-81. Tchr. ceramics Detroit Head Start, Mt. Zion, Mich., 1973; logo designer, platemaker, printer and painter Island Art Ctr., St. Simons Island, Ga., 1976-79; sec., receptionist High Performance Tube Inc., St. Simons Island, 1976-79; personal legal sec. State Senator Bill Littlefield, St. Simons Island, 1979; art coord., booking agt. Club Savoy Tivoli, San Francisco, 1979; tchr. art Redmond Hall, Squamakawa, Wash., 1980; artist Hollywood Costumes, Dearborn, Mich., 1980-90; account mgr. ins. Dr. Sheryl A. Ollie, Lynn, Mass., 1990; staff artist, acting, costumes Creative Currents, Ferndale, Mich., 1990—; art tchr. Art in Nahant, Mass., 1991-96; make-up artist Paramount Costumes (was Hollywood Costumes), Dearborn; art tchr. music St. Lukes Montessori Sch., Detroit; artist Mich. Art and Design, Detroit, Dearborn Awnings, Lincoln Park, Mich. make-up artist TV commls. and shows, movies. Co-pres. Nahant PTO, Johnson Sch., 1991-92. Roman Catholic. Home and Office: POP Prodns Art in Nahant 141 Nahant Rd Nahant MA 01908-1633

OLMSTED, AUDREY JUNE, communications educator; b. Sioux Falls, S.D., June 5, 1940; d. Leslie Thomas and Dorothy Lucille (Else) Perryman; m. Richard Raymond Olmsted; 1 child, Quenby Anne. BA, U. No. Iowa, 1961, MA, 1963; PhD, Ind. U., 1971. Comm. instr. Boston U., 1964-71, acting chair comm., 1972-73, asst. prof. comm., 1971-74; debate coach R.I. Coll., Providence, 1978-92, asst. prof. comm., 1987—, internat. student advisor, 1980—; text editor Prentice-Hall Pub., 1986-88. Recipient Faculty award R.I. Coll. Alumni Assn., 1987. Mem. Nat. Assn. Fgn. Student Advisors, Internat. Comm. Assn. Democrat. Office: RI Coll Dept Comm 600 Mount Pleasant Ave Providence RI 02908-1924

OLMSTED, RUTH MARTIN, editor; b. Albany, N.Y., Oct. 26, 1950; d. Sterling Pitkin and Barbara (Starr) O.; m. Lawrence Daniel Syzdek, Oct. 27, 1990. Student, Oberlin Coll., 1968-69; AB in Lit. and Lang./History and Govt., Wilmington Coll., 1972; MA in Comparative Lit., U. Wis., 1973, PhD in Comparative Lit., 1976. Cert. tchr., Iowa, N.Y. Adj. faculty mem. in sociology Chatfield Coll., St. Martin, Ohio, 1974-75; adj. faculty mem. in writing and phys. edn. Wilmington (Ohio) Coll., 1975-77; adj. faculty mem. in writing, speech and adult basic edn. So. State Coll., Wilmington, 1975-77; asst. prof. English, drama and speech William Penn Coll., Oskaloosa, Iowa, 1977-82; substitute tchr. 10 sch. dists., So. Iowa, 1982-83; instr. in English and humanities Emma Willard Sch., Troy, N.Y., 1983-89; asst. prof. speech Sage Jr. Coll. of Albany, N.Y., 1989-93; mng. editor assessment Regents Coll., Albany, 1993—; mem. workshops in medieval music-drama NEH, 1979, 81. Editor, desktop music pub. Theatre Wagon, 1994—; editor, translator: (plays) Crown Light Editions: Ordo Prophetarum, 1982, Iconia Sancti Nicolai, 1986. Life mem. Girl Scouts U.S., 1959—; mem. policy, pers. com., ann. meeting and gen. coms. Friends Com. on Nat. Legislation, Washington, 1979—. Ind. Study in Humanities fellow NIH, 1988. Mem. MLA, Nat. Coun. Tchrs. English, Tchrs. and Writers Collaborative, Country Dance and Song Soc. Am., Internat. Boethius Soc., Pokingbrook Morris Dancers (foreman, treas. 1984—). Office: Regents Coll Assessment 7 Columbia Cir Albany NY 12203

OLNESS, KAREN NORMA, pediatrics and international health educator; b. Rushford, Minn., Aug. 28, 1936; d. Norman Theodore and Karen Agnes (Gunderson) O.; m. Hakon Daniel Torjesen, 1962. BA, U. Minn., 1958, BS, MD, 1961. Diplomate Am. Bd. Pediatrics, Am. Bd. Med. Hypnosis. Intern Harbor Gen. Hosp., Torrance, Calif.; resident Nat. Children's Hosp. Med. Ctr., Washington; asst. prof. George Washington U., Washington, 1970-74; assoc. prof. U. Minn., Mpls., 1974-87; prof. pediatrics, family medicine and internat. health Case Western Res. U., Cleve., 1987—. Named Outstanding Woman Physician, Minn. Assn. Women Physicians, 1987. Fellow Am. Acad. Pediatrics, Am. Acad. Family Physicians, Am. Soc. Clin. Hypnosis (pres. 1984-86), Soc. Clin. and Exptl. Hypnosis (pres. 1991-93); mem. Soc. for Behavioral Pediatrics (pres. 1991-92), Northwestern Pediatric Soc. (pres. 1977). Office: Case Western Res U 11100 Euclid Ave Cleveland OH 44106-1736

O'LOONEY, PATRICIA ANNE, medical program administrator; b. Bridgeport, Conn., Dec. 2, 1954; d. John Joseph and Marjorie Ellen (Curran) O'L. BA in Molecular Biology, Regis Coll., 1976; MS in Biochemistry, George Washington U., 1978, PhD in Biochemistry, 1982. Rsch. asst. biochemistry dept. George Washington Med. Sch., Washington, 1976-82, teaching asst., 1978-81, rsch. assoc., 1982-84, sr. rsch. scientist, 1984-86, asst. prof. medicine and biochemistry, 1986-88; asst. dir. The Nat. Multiple Sclerosis Soc., N.Y.C., 1988-90, assoc. dir. rsch. and med. programs, 1990-91, dir. rsch. and med. programs, 1991—; vis. lectr. George Washington Med. Sch., 1988—. Author: Lipoprotein Lipase, 1987; contbr. articles to profl. jours. Recipient New Investigator Rsch. award NIH, 1985. Mem. Am. Soc. for Biochemistry and Molecular Biology, N.Y. Acad. Scis., Assn. for Women in Sci., The Mid-Atlantic Lipid Soc., Sigma Xi, Beta Beta Beta. Republican. Roman Catholic. Office: Nat Multiple Sclerosis Soc 733 3rd Ave New York NY 10017-3204

OLSEN, BARBARA ANN, mathematics educator; b. Ann Arbor, Mich., Sept. 25, 1949; d. Bruce Christian and Jean Bernice (Tuin) O. BS, Mich. State U., 1971; MEd, Wayne State U., 1976. Secondary edn. tchr. Math. tchr. Lake Shore Pub. Schs., St. Clair Shores, Mich., 1971—; chmn. math. curriculum com. Lake Shore Pub. Schs., 1988-92, mem. mfg. acad. curriculum com., 1993—, faculty coun. Nat. Honor Soc., 1987—, sr. class advisor, 1995—. Recipient Citation of merit for Outstanding Professionalism in Influencing The Lives of Students, Northwood Inst., Midland, Mich., 1990. Mem. Nat. Coun. Tchrs. of Math., Mich. Coun. Tchrs. Math.

OLSEN, DEBORAH LYNN, therapist; b. Great Falls, Mont., Feb. 27, 1955; d. Robert Matthew Asich and Dorothy Viola (Smith) Vukasin; m. Carl Nels Olsen, July 31, 1982; children: Matthew Nels, Lindsey Marie. BS, No. State U., Aberdeen, S.D., 1992, MS in Edn., 1994. Nat. cert. counselor. Child/family therapist North Ea. Mental Health Ctr., Aberdeen, S.D., 1992—; casemgr. North Ea. Mental Health Ctr., Aberdeen, 1992—, facilitator H.O.P.E. parent support group, 1992—, wrap around coord., 1994—, co-chair family support & preservation grant, 1995—. Mem. Am. Counseling Assn., North Ctrl. Counseling Assn., Zonta, Psi Chi, Pi Gamma Mu,. Democrat. Lutheran. Office: North Ea Mental Health Ctr Box 550 Aberdeen SD 57401

OLSEN, INGER ANNA, psychologist; b. Copper Mountain, B.C, Can., Dec. 25, 1926; d. Dagmar O.; B.S., Wash. State U., 1954, M.S., 1956, Ph.D., 1962. Psychiat. nurse Provincial Mental Health Services B.C., 1947-51, psychologist, 1956-58; psychologist Vancouver (B.C.) City Met. Health Services, 1958-60, Wash. State U. Student Counseling Center, Pullman, 1960-62; sr. psychologist Met. Health Services, Vancouver, 1962-66; instr. psychology Vancouver Community Coll., 1966-87; docent Vancouver Aquarium Assn. Bd. dirs. Second Mile Soc., 1975-89. Contbr. articles to profl. jours. Mem. Am. Psychol. Assn., Gerontol. Soc. Am., Can. Assn. Gerontology, Phi Beta Kappa, Sigma Xi, Alpha Kappa Delta. Home: 1255 Bidwell St Apt 1910, Vancouver, BC Canada V6G 2K8

OLSEN, LYNN MARIE, speech and language pathologist; b. Warren, Pa., July 12, 1966; d. Robert M. and Bonnie K. (Littlefield) O. BS cum laude, Clairon U. Pa., 1989, MS, 1991. Cert. clin. speech-lang. pathologist, cert. clin. competence. Speech-lang. pathologist Berkeley County Bd. Edn., Martinsburg, W.Va., 1991—; del. Berkeley County Coun., Martinsburg, 1994-95; del., mem. PTA, Hedgesville, W.Va., 1992-95; mem. sch. improvement com. Tomahawk Elem. Sch., Hedgesville, 1993-95, co-chair 1994-95. Mem. Am. Speech-Lang.-Hearing Assn., W.Va. Speech-Lang.-Hearing Assn., Phi Delta Kappa, Kappa Delta Pi. Home: PO Box 1584 Hedgesville WV 25427-1584 Office: Tomahawk Elem Sch Box 610 School Ln Hedgesville WV 25427

OLSEN, TILLIE, author; b. Omaha, Nebr., Jan. 14, 1912; d. Samuel and Ida (Beber) Lerner; m. Jack Olsen; children: Karla, Julie, Kathie, Laurie. LittD (hon.), U. Nebr., 1979, Knox Coll., 1982, Hobart and William Smith Coll., 1984, Clark U., 1985, Albright Coll., 1986, Wooster Coll., 1991, Mills Coll., 1995. Writer-in-residence Amherst Coll., 1969-70; vis. faculty Stanford U., 1972; Writer-in-residence, vis. faculty English M.I.T., 1973-74, U. Mass., Boston, 1974; internat. vis. scholar Norway, 1980; Hill prof. U. Minn., spring 1986; writer-in-residence Kenyon Coll., 1987—; Regents lectr. U. Calif. at San Diego, 1977—, UCLA, 1987; commencement spkr. English dept. U. Calif., Berkeley, 1983, Hobart and William Smith Coll., 1984 Bennington Coll., 1986. Author: Tell Me A Riddle, 1961 (title story received First prize O'Henry award 1961), Rebecca Harding Davis: Life in the Iron Mills, 1972, Yonnondio: From the Thirties, 1974, Silences, 1978, The Word Made Flesh, 1984; editor: Mother to Daughter, Daughter to Mother, 1984; Preface Mothers and Daughters, That Special Quality: A Exploration in Photographs, 1989; short fiction published in over 200 anthologies; books translated in 11 langs. Recipient Am. Acad. and Nat. Inst. of Arts and Letters award, 1975, Ministry to Women award Unitarian Universalist Fedn., 1980, Brit. Post Office and B.P.W. award, 1980, Mari Sandoz award Nebr. Libr. Assn., 1991, REA award Dungannon Found., 1994, Disting. Achievement award Western Lit. Assn., 1996; Grantee Ford Found., 1959, NEA, 1968; Stanford Univ. Creative Writing fellow, 1962-64, Guggenheim fellow, 1975-76, Bunting Inst. Radcliffe Coll. fellow, 1985; Tillie Olsen Day designated in San Francisco, 1981. Mem. Authors Guild, PEN, Writers Union. Home: 1435 Laguna St Apt 6 San Francisco CA 94115-3742

OLSEN-ESTIE, JEANNE LINDELL, golf course owner; b. Everett, Wash., July 17, 1946; d. Carmen David Lindell and Violet Louise (Harris) Johnson; m. Wayne William Olsen, Dec. 22, 1984 (dec. Apr. 1993); children: Kenda, Justin; m. John Gary Estie, Nov. 5, 1994. Grad., Lee Sch. Cosmetology, 1966, Everett Beauty Sch., 1968, Everett Plz. Sch. Cosmetology, 1987. With Marysville (Wash.) Police Dept., 1967-72, Durham Transp., 1979-87; owner, mgr. Riverside Golf Course and Olsons Golf Equipment, 1987—. Active Maryfest, Marysville, 1976-78. Mem. Nat. Granite Ware Collectors, Everett Antique Club, Hummel Club Collectors. Home and Office: 7612 Beverly Blvd Everett WA 98203

OLSHAN, KAREN, advertising agency executive. Former v.p., then sr. v.p. Batten Barton Durstine & Osborn (now BBDO), N.Y.C.; exec. v.p., dir. rsch. svcs. BBDO, Inc., N.Y.C., 1989—. Office: BBDO NY 1285 Avenue Of The Americas New York NY 10019-6028

OLSOE, LINDA ANN, retired real estate agent; b. Seattle, Mar. 9, 1941; d. Bjarne Oliver and Nancy Claire (Reynolds) Olsoe; m. Millard Ferdinand Schewe, Jr., Dec. 22, 1961 (div. Oct. 1993); children: Millard Ferdinand Schewe III, Mary Helen Schewe Fernstrom. BA, San Jose State U., 1974. Cert. property mgr. V.p. Commerce Communities Corp., Santa Clara, Calif., 1984-94; founder Humanitarian Orgn. for Minor to Excell. Clk., County of Santa Clara Registrar of Voters, 1995. Mem. Inst. Real Estate Mgmt. (v.p. 1993-94, program chair, candidate advisor). Republican.

OLSON, BARBARA FORD, physician; b. Iowa City, June 15, 1935; d. Leonard A. and Anne (Swanson) Ford; m. Robert Eric Olson, 1959 (div. 1973); children: Katherine Gee, Eric Ford, Julie Marie. BA, Gustavus Adolphus Coll., 1956; MD, U. Minn., 1960. Diplomate Am. Bd. Family Practice (cert. added qualifications geriatric medicine). Intern St. Paul-Ramsy Med. Ctr., 1960-61; resident in anesthesiology U. Hosp. Cleve., 1961-62, U. Minn. Hosp., Mpls., 1962-63; pvt. practice anesthesiology St. Johns Hosp. and Devine Redeemer Hosp., St. Paul, 1963-67, Mercy Hosp., Coon Rapids, Minn., 1967-74; staff physician Oak Terrace Nursing Home, Minnetonka, Minn., 1974-88; med. dir. nursing home care unit VA Med. Ctr., St. Cloud, Minn., 1988—. Pres., bd. dirs. Alpha Epsilon Iota Med. Found., Mpls., 1980-86. Mem. Minn. Med. Assn., Minn. Women Physicians (pres. 1981-82), Minn. Nursing Home Med. Dirs. Home: PO Box 7306 Saint Cloud MN 56302-7306 Office: VA Med Ctr 4801 8th St N Saint Cloud MN 56303-2014

OLSON, BETTYE JOHNSON, artist, educator; b. Mpls., Jan. 16, 1923; d. Emil Antonious and Irene Irina (Wandtke) J.; m. Howard Einar Olson, July 16, 1949; children: Martha, Jeffrey, Barbara, Virginia. BS in Art Edn., U. Minn., 1945, MEd in Art Edn., 1949; student, U. N.Mex., 1947, Cranbrook Acad. Art, Mich., 1948. Tchr. art grades 3-12 Summit Sch. for Girls, St. Paul, 1945-47; instr. art U. Minn., Mpls., 1947-49; instr. painting and design Concordia Coll., St. Paul, 1975-78, 83-84; instr. painting prints Augsburg Coll., Mpls., 1983-88; lectr. art Augsburg Coll. of 3rd Age, Mpls., 1984-96, dir., 1993—; mem. staff Walker Art Ctr., summer 1947; instr. Grunewald Guild, Wash., summer 1990; lectr. women in liturgical arts Luther Northwestern Sem., 1985, lectr. theology and the arts, 1987, 89; lectr. art and lit. series AAUW, 1986-89; artist-in-residence Holden Village Luth. Retreat Ctr., Chelan, Wash., summers 1967-68, 70-71, 73, 78-79, 86-90. One-woman shows include Met. Med. Ctr., Mpls., 1974, Concordia Coll., St. Paul, 1974-75, St. Olaf Coll., Northfield, Minn., 1977, West Lake Gallery, 1964, 67, 71, 75, 78, 82, Inver Hills Coll., Inver Grove Heights, Minn., 1978, House of Hope Ch., St. Paul, 1978, Plymouth Congl. Ch., Mpls., 1978, Fan Winer Gallery, Two Harbors, Minn., 1978, Jerome Gallery, Aspen, Colo., 1978, Osborn Gallery, St. Paul, 1979, Augsburg Coll., 1979, 96, Luther Coll., Decorah, Iowa, 1980, Wilson Libr., U. Minn., 1981, St. Paul Campus Gallery, U. Minn., 1981, Lake Harriet Meth. Ch., 1982, Am. Swedish Inst., 1982, Smaland Mus., Vaxjo, Sweden, 1982, Luth. Brotherhood Co., 1983, Phipps Gallery, Hudson, Wis., 1985, Sons. of Norway Gallery, 1990, Berge Gallery, Stillwater, Minn., 1995, Augsburg Coll., 1996; participant juried exhbns., including Walker Art Ctr., 1947, Mpls. Art Inst., 1947, St. Paul Gallery, 1961, Sky Gallery, 1975, Minn. Arts Assn., 1975 (Merit award 1975, 76), 76, Minn. Mus. Art, 1976, Watercolor U.S.A., Springfield, Mo., 1977, Minn. State Fair, 1947, 64, 66-68, 74-79, 90, 93 (Merit award 1976, 3rd prize 1977, 93), Lakewood Coll., White Bear Lake, Minn., 1974-79, 81 (Grand prize 1977, Purchase prize 1977), Butler Inst. Am. Art, Youngstown, Ohio, 1977, Warm Gallery, Mpls., 1977, Calif. Women's Conf., Pasadena, Calif., 1978, AAUW, 1981; exhibited in group shows at Friends of Art Inst., 1979, West Lake Gallery, 1964-83, Kuopio Art Mus., Finland, 1982, St. Paul Co., 1983, Augsburg Coll., 1988, 89, Minn. Mus. Art, 1988, Macalester Coll., 1992, Nash Gallery, U. Minn., 1994, Hill Mansion-History Soc., 1995, 96, others; represented in permanent collections: 3M Co., Minn. History Soc., Minn. Mus. Am. Arts, Employers Ins. Co. of Wausau, Concordia Coll., Nothern States Power Co., Cray Rsch., Pillsbury World Headquaters, Luther Coll., Kuopio Art Mus. Finland, Am. Swedish Inst., Smaland Mus. Sweden, Augsburg Coll. and many others. Mem. bd. congl. life Evang. Luth. Ch. Am., St. Paul, 1989-91; coop. mem. West Lake Gallery, Mpls., 1963-83; mem. Mpls. Art Inst., 1945—, Minn. Mus. Am. Art, Walker Art Ctr. Mentor tchg. scholar Met. Arts Coun. to Woman's Art Registry Minn., St. Paul, 1992-94; grantee liberal arts programs Minn. Humanities Commn., St. Paul, 1995-96. Mem. AAUW (bd. dirs. 1992-94), Woman's Art Registry Minn. (bd. dirs. 1992-95). Home: 1721 Fulham St Apt H Saint Paul MN 55113-5251 Studio: 2242 University Ave Saint Paul MN 55414 Office: Coll of 3rd Age Augsburg Cl 2211 Riverside Ave Minneapolis MN 55454

OLSON, BETTY-JEAN, elementary education educator; b. Camas, Wash., Apr. 26, 1934; d. Earl Raymond and Mabel Anna (Burden) Clemons; m. Arthur H. Geda, Dec. 31, 1957; children: Ann C. Geda, Scott A. Geda; m. Conrad A. Olson, June 14, 1980. AA, Clark Coll., 1954; BA in Edn., Cen. Wash. Coll. Edn., 1956; MEd, No. Mont. Coll., 1975. Cert. elem. tchr. class I, Mont., supr. K-9 class III. Supervising tchr., demo. teaching No. Mont. Coll.; kindergarten, 1st grade instr. Glasgow, Mont.; supervisor, head tchr. Reading Lab, Glasgow AFB, Mont., 1st grade instr., kindergarten tchr., elem. adminstr. K-7 Medicine Lake (Mont.) Dist. 7; certification stds. and practices Adv. Coun. to the State Bd. Pub. Edn.; mem. bd. examiners Nat. Coun. for Accred. of Tchr. Edn., adv. com. Western Mont. Coll., U. Mont.; workshop leader and presenter in field. Mem. Sheridan County Community Protective Svcs. Com., Med-Lake Scholarship Com. Mem. NEA, ASCD, Internat. Reading Assn., Nat. Coun. Social Studies, Nat. Elem. Prin. Assn., Medicine Lake Edn. Assn. (past pres.), Mont. Edn. Assn. (rev. bd., officerships), Mont. Elem. Prin., N.E. Mont. Reading Coun. (v.p.), Delta Kappa Gamma (state pres., chpt. pres., exec. bd., committeeships, mem. internat. exec. bd.). Home: 108 E Antelope Rd Antelope MT 59211-9607

OLSON, CAROL LEA, lithographer, educator, photographer; b. Anderson, Ind., June 10, 1929; d. Daniel Ackerman and Marguerite Louise Olson. AB, Anderson Coll., 1952; MA, Ball State U., 1976. Pasteup artist Warner Press, Inc., Anderson, 1952-53, apprentice lithographer stripper, 1953-57, journeyman, 1957-63, lithographic dot etcher, color corrector, 1959-73, prepres coord. art dept., 1973-81, prepres tech. specialist, 1981-83, color film assembler, 1983-96; part-time photography instr. Anderson Univ.; tchr. photography Anderson Fine Arts Ctr., 1976-79; instr. photography, photographics Anderson U., 1979—; mag. photographer Bd. Christian Edn. of Ch. of God, Anderson, 1973-86; freelance photographer. One person show Anderson U., 1979; exhibited in group shows Anderson U., 1980-93, Purdue U., 1982. Instr. 1st aide ARC, Anderson, 1969-79; sec. volleyball Anderson Sunday Sch. Athletic Assn., 1973—. Recipient Hon. mention, Ann Arbor, Mich., 1977, Anderson Fine Arts Ctr., 1977, 78, 83, 1st Pl., 1983, Hon. Mention, 1983, 2d Pl., 1988, Hon. Mention, 1988, 93, Best of Show, 1983, 91, 92, Best Nature Catagory Anderson Fine Arts Ctr., 1994. Mem. AAUW, Associated Photographer Internat., Nat. Inst. Exploration, Profl. Photographers Am. Mem. Ch. of God. Home: 2604 E 6th St Anderson IN 46012-3725

OLSON, CATHERINA, state legislator, farmer; b. Rock Rapids, Iowa, Oct. 24, 1928; d. Corneluis and Cornelia (Bakker) Gaalswyk; m. Robert R. Olson, Nov. 13, 1948; children: Cynthia, Shirley, Roberta, Kent, Amy. Student, Luther Coll., Mankato State U. Bd. mem. PTA Minn. State, 1968-84; mem. Trimont Sch. Bd., Minn., 1976-86; bd. mem. Edn. Coop. Svc. Unit, Mankato, Minn., 1980-86; commr. Region 9 Devel. Commn., 1982-86; rep. Minn. State Govt., St. Paul, 1986-94; vice chair Edn. Com. in House, St. Paul, 1986-94; asst. maj. leader Minn. House of Reps., 1992-94; ret., 1994; cons., lobbyist Minn. Rural Edn. Assn.; bd. dirs. Southeastern Minn. Initiative Fund, Heron Lake Environ. Learning Ctr. Home: RR 2 Box 115 Sherburn MN 56171-9747 Office: Minn State Office Rm 523 Saint Paul MN 55155-1606

OLSON, CYNTHIA JANE, speech therapist, educational administrator; b. DeKalb, Ill., Mar. 17, 1969; d. Ralph H. and Helen L. (Jones) Hannon; m. Matthew F. Olson, Apr. 18, 1992. Student, Kishwaukee Coll., 1987-89; BS in Comm. Disorders, Ea. Ill. U., 1991; postgrad., Tex. A&M, Kingsville, 1993-95. Cert. speech-lang. pathologist, elem. educator, spl. educator, Tex. Qualified mental retardation profl. Genesis House, Genoa, Ill., 1991; speech therapist Tex. Dept. Mental Health and Mental Retardation, Corpus Christi, Tex., 1992-95; spl. edn. tchr. 3d grade Mardon Ednl. Therapy Sch., 1996—. Habiltation therapy rep. State Employee Charitable Campaign, Corpus Christi, 1994. Mem. Coun. for Exceptional Children, Tex. A&M Kingsville Spl. Edn. Educators (program coord. 1993-94), Costal Bend Speech Lang. and Hearing Assn., Tex. Speech-Lang. Hearing Assn. Home: 25295 Vista Linda Lake Forest CA 92630 Office: Mardan Ednl Therapy Sch 1 Osborn Irvine CA 92714

OLSON, DIANA CRAFT, image and etiquette consultant; b. Langley, Va., May 5, 1941; d. Winfred O. and Joyce (Clark) Craft; m. Robert J. Olson, May 30, 1976; stepchildren: Stacey Anr, Kirsten Lowry. BA, U. Tex., 1963; MA, San Francisco State U., 1970; cert. image cons., Fashion Acad., Costa Mesa, Calif., 1979. Tchr. USAF, P.R., 1963-64, Long Beach (Calif.) Unified Sch. Dist., 1964-68, South San Francisco (Calif.) Unified Sch. Dist., 1968-79; pres. Diana's Color Collage & Color Collage Inst., Pasadena, Calif., 1979—; etiquette affiliates Dorthea Johnson and Marjabelle Stewart, Washington, 1988—; cons. Weight Watchers Internat., L.A., Ventura, Calif., 1987-90, Marriott Hotels, Long Beach, 1989, 1st Interstate Bank, L.A., 1990, Ritz Carlton Hotels, 1995. Contbr. articles to mags. Mem. Assn. Image Cons. Internat. (sec. 1989-90, v.p. 1990-92). Republican. Presbyterian. Office: Diana's Color Collage 465 E Union St # 100 Pasadena CA 91101-2417

OLSON, GEORGANN, elementary education educator; b. Woodstock, Ill., Feb. 21, 1941; d. George B. and Anna May (Coarson) Sandman; m. Allan Gage Olson Jr., May 28, 1971; children: Kristofor, Gage, Erik. BA, U. No. Colo., 1962, MA, 1967; MA, Calif. Luth. U., 1993. Tchr. Greeley (Colo.) Sch. Dist., 1963-67, Ventura (Calif.) Sch. Dist., 1974-96, Pierpont Sch., Ventura, 1994-96; presenter in field. Bd. dirs. Ventura High PTA, 1991-95; active Pierpont Sch. PTA, 1982-96. Named Outstanding Tchr. Ventura County Assn. Edn. Young Children, 1991, Outstanding Tchr. of Month Ventura C. of C., 1995; recipient Golden Wings award Ventura Ednl. Found., 1994. Mem. NEA, Nat. Assn. Edn. Young Children, Calif. Edn. Assn., Calif. Kindergarten Assn. (bd. dirs. 1993—), Calif. Tchrs. Assn., Assn. Childhood Edn. Internat. Home: 308 N Catalina St Ventura CA 93001-2432 Office: Pierpont Sch 1254 Marthas Vineyard Ct Ventura CA 93001-4014

OLSON, JEAN A., psychotherapist; b. Homewood, Ill., Sept. 9, 1956; d. John W. and Florence Mae (Anderson) Olson; m. Paul Duncan, May 27, 1990. ASN, Cuyahoga C.C., Parma Heights, Ohio, 1977; BSN, Case Western Res. U., 1980; MSN, Kent State U., 1985. Lic. profl. clin. mental health counselor, N.Mex.; approved clin. cons. in hypnosis; clin. specialist adult psychiat. nursing. Staff nurse critical care various hosps. Tucson, Cleve., 1977-80; nursing supr., staff devel. St. Alexis Hosp., Cleve., 1980-83; staff devel., clin. specialist Akron (Ohio) Gen. Med. Ctr., 1983-85; tchr.-practitioner Rush-Presbyn. St. Luke's Hosp., Chgo., 1985-88; psychotherapist, clin. coord. Assoc. Mental Health Svcs., Chgo., 1986-90; facult, program cons. Coll. Nursing, Divsn. Continuing Edn., U. N.Mex., Albuquerque, 1990—; psychotherapist, cons., educator Catalyst...Facilitating Change, Albuquerque, 1990—; coord. S.W. regional conf. on dissociative disorders Divsn. Continuing Edn., U. N.Mex., 1991-95; lectr. in field. Contbr. articles to profl. jours., chpts. to books. Recipient Linnea Henderson award for scholastic excellence Delta Xi chpt. Sigma Theta Tau, 1985. Mem. ANA, N.Mex. Nurses Assn. (clin. nurse specialist coun.), Am. Soc. Clin. Hypnosis (workshop and ann. meeting faculty 1992—, exec. com. 1992-94, Presdl. award 1996), Internat. Soc. for Study of Dissociation (co-chair women's issues com. 1991-94, workshop, ann. meeting presenter 1987—), Internat. Soc. Hypnosis. Office: Ste 222 2201 San Pedro Blvd NE Albuquerque NM 87110

OLSON, JEANNE INNIS, technology/technical management; b. South Bend, Ind., May 10, 1960; d. Francis Bedford and Mary Ann (Szachnia) Innis; m. Thomas Hilton Olson, Apr. 12, 1992. Student, Purdue U., 1978-80; BS in Tech. & Mgmt. summa cum laude, U. Md., 1986; MS in Sys. Mgmt. with honors, U. So. Calif., 1991. Analyst Potomac Rsch., Inc., Alexandria, Va., 1980-82; staff specialist SWL, Inc., McLean, Va., 1982-87; sr. staff Advanced Tech., Inc., El Segundo, Calif., 1987-89; prin. staff/section mgr. PRC, Inc., El Segundo, Calif., 1989-95, deputy dir. space sys. acquisition support, 1995—. Mem. South Bay Friends Planned Parenthood, Calif., 1992—, v.p. fund raising, 1994. Recipient Vol. Recognition award Planned Parenthood L.A., 1994. Mem. Innes Clan Soc. (v.p. 1984-91, pres. 1991-92), Innes Clan Ctr. Assn. (bd. dirs. 1993—), Phi Kappa Phi. Office: PRC Inc Ste 1310 222 N Sepulveda Blvd El Segundo CA 90245

OLSON, JEANNE M., real estate broker; b. Manitowoc, Wis., Aug. 31, 1947; d. Arthur J. and Grace M. (Schuh) Kolbe; m. Harlen C. Olson, Dec. 27, 1968; children; Kara, Ryan. BS, Stout State Univ., 1970. Tchr. Cudahy (Wis.) Schs., 1970, West Bend (Wis.) Schs., 1970-80, Madison Area Tech Schs., Reedsburg, Wis., 1980-85; realtor, broker Check Realty, Reedsburg, 1986-89; realtor, broker, owner Evergreen Realty, Reedsburg, 1989—; adv. bd. Madison Area Tech. Coll. Chmn. residental United Way, Reedsburg, 1989; mem. Positive Experiences and Activities for Kids, 1990-94. Mem. Saul/Columbia Bd. Realtors (treas. 1994-95), Wis. Realtors Assn., Nat. Realtors Assn., Mid-Wis. Builders Assn., Reedsburg C. of C. (bd. dirs., pres. 1989-94). Roman Catholic. Office: Evergreen Realty Inc 1733 E Main St Reedsburg WI 53959

OLSON, JEANNINE EVELYN, history educator; b. Caledonia, Minn.; d. Aloysius and Evelyn Hazel (Ellingson) Fahsl; children: Karen, Daniel, Rebecca. BA, St. Olaf Coll., Northfield, Minn., 1961; MA, Stanford U., 1962, PhD, 1981. Teaching asst. U. Minn., Mpls., 1972-76; asst. prof. San Francisco Theol. Sem., San Anselmo, Calif., 1979-86; mem. doctoral faculty Grad. Theol. Union, Berkeley, Calif., 1979-86; asst. prof. history R.I. Coll., Providence, 1986-90, assoc. prof., 1990—; mem. Internat. Congress for Luther Rsch., Erfurt, Germany, Norway, Mpls., 1983, 88, 93, Heidelbern, Calvio Rsch., Grand Rapids, 1990, Edinburgh; mem. Task Force on the Confessional Nature of the Ch., Presbyn. Ch., 1983-86, com. Theol. edn., 1991-93. Author: Histoire de L'Eglise, 1972, Calvin and Social Welfare, 1989, Deacons and Deaconesses Through Twenty Centuries, 1992; contbr. articles to profl. jours. Danforth Found. fellow, 1976-81; grantee Govt. of France rsch., 1978-79, Am. Coun. Learned Socs., 1982, 95, NEH, Geneva, 1985, 88-92, 96, Am. Acad. Religion, 1990-92, 94-95, Am. Philosophical Soc., 1994-95. Mem. AAUW, Renaissance Soc. Am., 16th Century Studies Soc., Calvin Studies Soc. (exec. com.), Am. Soc. Reformatin Rsch., Am. Soc. Ch. History (instl. liaison com.), R.I. Hist. Assn., New Eng. Master Swim Club, Rinconada Master Swim Club, Phi Beta Kappa. Home: 48 Lauriston St Providence RI 02906 Office: RI Coll Dept History Providence RI 02908

OLSON, JULIE ANN, systems consultant, educator; b. Oklahoma City, May 14, 1957; d. Willard Alton and Ruth Harriet (Ehlers) O.; m. Kevin Peter McAuliffe, Oct. 12, 1985; children: Scott Andrew, Shannon Elizabeth, Kathryn Victoria. BA in History, Augustana Coll., 1979; MBA, Keller Grad. Sch. Mgmt., Chgo., 1989. Systems analyst Continental Bank, Chgo., 1979-82; prin., adminstrv. mgr. Computer Scis. Corp. (formerly Computer Ptnrs.), Oakbrook, Ill., 1982—; instr. data processing Oakton Community Coll., Des Plaines, 1982—, faculty coord. accelerated data processing cert. program, 1983-92. Exec. dir., chmn. scholarship Miss N.W. Communities Inc., Des Plaines, 1984-88; bd. dirs. Mt. Prospect Hist. Soc., 1994—, Am. Cancer Soc., Mt. Prospect chpt. Mem. ASTD, NAFE, Data Processing Mgmt. Assn. (asst. faculty coord. Student chpt. 1985-87). Lutheran. Avocations: classical pianist, reading, flamenco dancing, snow skiing, cross stitch. Home: 401 S Pine St Mount Prospect IL 60056-3723 Office: Computer Sci Corp 2021 Spring Rd Ste 200 Oak Brook IL 60521-1854

OLSON, KATHRYN LAFOY, obstetrician, gynecologist; b. Santa Monica, Calif., Sept. 2, 1953; d. Byron Wesley and LaFoy Mae (Coblenz) O.; children: Daniel Byron Alberts and Nicholas Wesley Alberts (twins). BS in Biol. Scis., U. Calif., Irvine, 1984, BA in Psychology, 1984, MD, 1994. Diplomate Am. Bd. Ob-Gyn. Intern, resident Mass. Gen. Hosp./Brigham & Women's Hosp., Boston, 1988-92; physician Sts. Meml. Woman Health, Chelmsford, Mass., 1993—, dir. prenatal clinic, 1993—. Fellow Am. Coll. Ob-Gyn.; mem. AMA, Mass. Med. Assn., Alpha Omega Alpha. Office: Sts Meml Woman Health 2 Courthouse Sq Chelmsford MA 01824

OLSON, KAY MELCHISEDECH, magazine editor; b. Mpls., Nov. 16, 1948; d. John William and Carol Louise (Born) Melchisedech; m. John Addison Olson, Sept. 5, 1970 (div. 1988); children: Jennifer Marie, Nathan John. BA, U. Minn., 1971. News editor New Hope-Plymouth Post, Crystal, Minn., 1971-73; features editor Sun Newspapers, Bloomington, Minn., 1973-75; with pub. rels. dept. Nat. Car Rental, Bloomington, Minn., 1975-77; free-lance pub. rels. profl. Mpls., 1977-82; mag. editor Miller Pub., Minnetonka, Minn., 1982-90; exec. editor Flower & Garden mag., Workbasket mag. Easy-Does-It Needework & Crafts mag. KC Pub. Inc., Kansas City, Mo., 1990—. Mem. Garden Writers Assn. Am. Roman Catholic. Home: 4726 W 78th Ter Shawnee Mission KS 66208-4413 Office: KC Pub Inc 700 W 47th St Ste 310 Kansas City MO 64112-1805

OLSON, MARIAN EDNA, nursing consultant, social psychologist; b. Newman Grove, Nebr., July 20, 1923; d. Edward and Ethel Thelma (Hougland) Olson; diploma U. Nebr., 1944, BS in Nursing, 1953; MA, State U. Iowa, 1961, MA in Psychlogy, 1962; PhD in Psychology, UCLA, 1966. Staff nurse, supr. U. Tex. Med. Br., Galveston, 1944-49; with U. Iowa, Iowa City, 1949-59, supr. 1953-55, asst. dir. 1955-59; asst. prof. nursing UCLA, 1965-67; prof. nursing U. Hawaii, 1967-70, 78-82; dir. nursing Wilcox Hosp. and Health Center, Lihue, 1970-77; chmn. Hawaii Bd. Nursing, 1974-80; prof. nursing No. Mich. U., 1984-88; cons., ind. nursing svcs. adminstr. practice & curriculum, 1988—. Bd. trustees Bay de Noc C.C., 1988—. Mem. Am. Nurses Assn. (mem. nat. accreditation bd. continuing edn. 1975-78), Nat. League Nursing, Am. Hosp. Assn., Am. Public Health Assn., LWV. Democrat. Roman Catholic. Home and Office: 6223 County 513 T Rd Rapid River MI 49878-9595

OLSON, MARIAN KATHERINE, emergency management executive, consultant, publisher, information broker; b. Tulsa, Oct. 15, 1933; d. Sherwood Joseph and Katherine M. (Miller) Lahman; m. Ronald Keith Olson, Oct 27, 1956, (dec. May 1991). BA in Polit. Sci., U. Colo., 1954, MA in Elem. Edn., 1962; EdD in Ednl. Adminstrn., U. Tulsa, 1969. Tchr. public schs., Wyo., Colo., Mont., 1958-67; teaching fellow, adj. instr. edn. U. Tulsa, 1968-69; asst. prof. edn. Eastern Mont. State Coll., 1970; program assoc. research adminstrn. Mont. State U., 1970-75; on leave with Energy Policy Office of White House, then with Fed. Energy Adminstrn., 1973-74; with Dept. Energy, and predecessor, 1975—, program analyst, 1975-79, chief planning and environ. compliance br., 1979-83; regional dir. Region VIII Fed. Emergency Mgmt. Agy., 1987-93; exec. dir., Search and Rescue Dogs of the U.S., 1993—; pres. Western Healthclaims, Inc., Golden, Co.; pres. Marian Olson Assocs., Bannack Pub. Co.; mem. Colo. Nat. Hazards Mitigation Coun., Colo. Urban Search and Rescue Task Force. Contbr. articles in field. Grantee Okla. Consortium Higher Edn., 1969, NIMH, 1974. Mem. Am. Soc. for Info. Sci., Am. Assn. Budget and Program Analysis, Assn. of Contingency Planners, Internat. Assn. Ind. Pubs., Assn. of Contingency Planners, Nat. Inst. Urban Search and Rescue (bd. dirs.), Nat. Assn. for Search and Rescue, Colo. Search and Rescue, Search and Rescue Dogs of U.S., Colo. Emergency Mgmt. Assn., Front Range Rescue Dogs, Colo. State Fire Chiefs Assn., Kappa Delta Pi, Phi Alpha Theta, Kappa Alpha Theta. Republican. Home: 203 Iowa Dr Golden CO 80403-1337 Office: Western Healthclaims Inc 203 Iowa Dr Ste B Golden CO 80403-1337

OLSON, MAXINE LOUISE, artist, lecturer; b. Kingsburg, Calif., June 29, 1931; d. Alfred and Lena A. Marshall; divorced; children: Todd Olson, Terry Olson. BA, Calif. State U., Fresno, 1973, MA, 1975. Asst. prof. U. Ga., Athens, 1986-89; lectr. Coll. of Sequoias, Visalia, Calif., 1973-96; lectr. Fresno City Coll., 1990, Calif. State U., Fresno, intermittently 1973-96; tchr. U. Ga., Contona, Italy, 1987, 93.. Exhibited works at Oakland Mus., Palazzo Casali, Venice, Italy, Forum Gallery, N.Y.C., Soho 20, N.Y., The World's Women on-line/UN 4th World Conf. on Women, Beijing, China, William Sawyer Gallery, Palm Springs Mus., Calif. Recipient Gold award Art of Calif. Mag., 1992. Mem. Coll. Art Assn. Roman Catholic. Home: 1555 Lincoln Kingsburg CA 93631

OLSON, MICHELE SCHARFF, kinesiology/physical education educator; b. McMinnville, Oreg., Nov. 29, 1960; d. Harold Alfred and Ellen Marcella Scharff; m. Brian Astor Olson, Dec. 22, 1986. BA, Huntingdon Coll., Montgomery, Ala., 1986; MEd, Auburn U., 1987, PhD, 1991. Grad. rsch. asst. Auburn U., Montgomery, 1986-87; dir. preventive cardiology Montgomery Cardiovascular Assocs., 1987-89; asst. prof. kinesiology Huntingdon Coll., Montgomery, 1990-95; assoc. prof. phys. edn. Auburn U., Montgomery, 1995—; founder, exec. dir. Aerobic Leadership Tng. and Seminars (ALTS), Montgomery, 1985—; cons. Studio Workout, Montgomery, 1987—, Montgomery Athletic Club, 1990—; continuing edn. provider Am. Coun. on Exercise, San Diego, 1989—, Aerobic and Fitness Assn. Am., 1989; lectr. in field. Author various rsch. studies; contbr. articles to profl. jours. Mem. Jr. League of Montgomery, 1992—. Auburn U. grantee, 1990. Mem. AAHPERD, Ala. Assn. Health, Phys. Edn., Recreation and Dance (rsch. pres. 1990, v.p. elect dance div. 1996—), Am. Coll. Sports Medicine, Assn. Fitness Excellence (hon. bd. 1990), Am. Heart Assn. (cert.), Women's Sports Found. Home: 2272 Rosemont Dr Montgomery AL 36111-1009

OLSON, PAMELA JANE, mathematics educator; b. Price, Utah, Jan. 15, 1964; d. Robert Parley and Darlene (Wall) O. BS, Southern Utah U., 1986. Sci. tchr. Kennedy Jr. High, West Valley, Utah, 1987; math. tchr. Jefferson Jr. High, West Valley, Utah, 1987-90, Hunter H.S., West Valley, Utah, 1990—; varsity volleyball coach Hunter High, 1990—, varsity softball coach, 1990—. Mem. Nat. Honor Soc. Home: 3905 Hawkeye Dr Salt Lake City UT 84120-4110 Office: Hunter H S 4200 S 5600 W Salt Lake City UT 84120-4634

OLSON, PAMELA JOYCE, insurance company executive; b. Newark, Apr. 6, 1946; d. Richard Charles and Phyllis Hazel (Horton) Richter; m. William K. Olson, Apr. 5, 1969; 1 child, Stephanie Ann. BA, Ind. U., 1969. CPCU. Dir. product devel., mgr. regulatory compliance Crum & Forster Ins., Morristown, N.J., 1987—; instr. CPCU courses Seton Hall U. and N.J. chpt. Am. Inst. CPCU., 1983-93. Mem. NAFE, Am. Inst. CPCU. Home: 66 Alexandria Rd Morristown NJ 07960 Office: Crum & Forster Ins Co 6 Sylvan Way Parsippany NJ 07054

OLSON, PATRICIA JOANNE, artist, educator; b. Chgo., Aug. 22, 1927; d. Fred William and Fern Leslie (Shaffer) Kohler; m. Paul J. Olson, Jan. 21, 1950 (dec. July 1968); adopted children: Paulette, Dominic; stepchildren: Cindy, Katie, Larry, Daniel. BA, Northeastern Ill. U., 1976; MA, Loyola U., 1981. Advt. art dir. Chas. A. Stevens Dept. Store, Chgo., 1950-55; art dir. McCann, Erickson Advt. Agy., Chgo., 1955-57; pres. Olson Studio, Chgo., 1957-75; dept. chair, mem. faculty Chgo. Acad. Fine Art, 1974-78; exhibiting artist Chicago and Santa Barbara, Calif., 1981—; instr. Old Town Triangle Art Ctr., Chgo., 1978—, Bernard Horwich Ctr., Chgo., 1982-86, Art Inst. Chgo., 1987; prof. Columbia Coll., Chgo., 1978—; panelist Chgo. Cultural Ctr.; spkr., demonstrator Skokie Cultural Ctr., 1992, Joliet Art Ctr., 1992; guest spkr. AAUW, Evanston, Ill., 1991, Columbia Coll. Humanities, Chgo., 1992. Author: Women of Different Sizes, 1981; contbr. poetry to mags.; one woman shows include Artemesia Gallery, 1985, Highland Park H.S., 1987, One Ill. Ctr., 1987, Gallery 6000, 1988, Countryside Gallery of New Work, 1991, Old Town Triangle Gallery, 1991, Loyola U. Gallery, 1991; exhibited in group shows New Horizons, Art Inst. Gallery, 1975, 90, Beverly Art Ctr., 1978, 79, 82, 87, 89, 90, Beacon St. Gallery, 1984, 89, Art Inst. Chgo., 1984, Galex 19 Internat., Galesburg, Ill., 1985, Suburban Art League, 1986, Natalini Gallery, 1987, Societe des Pastellistes de France, 1987, Campanile Gallery, 1987, Artemsia Gallery, 1987, Delora Cultural Ctr., 1988, Alexandrian Mus., 1988, Gallery Genesis, 1988, 89, Adler Cultural Ctr., 1989, Post Rd. Gallery, 1989, Evanston Co-op Gallery, 1990, Pilsen Gallery, 1991, Old Town Triangle Gallery, 1991, Loyola U. Gallery, 1991, Chgo. Soc. Artists, 1992, R.H. Love Gallery, 1992, Chgo. Cultural Ctr., 1992, Wood St. Gallery, 1994, North Lakeside Cultural Ctr., 1994, State of Ill. Bldg. Chgo. Sr. Citizen Art Network (award), others. Hostess Rogers Park (Ill.) Hist. Soc., 1993. Named to Sr. Hall of Fame, Mayor Daley, Chgo., 1991, Womens Mus., Washington. Mem. Chgo. Soc. Artists, Chgo. Womens Caucus for Art (curator 1989-90), North Lakeside Cultural Ctr. (mem. art adv. bd. 1990—), Am. Jewish Art Club (juror, curator, speaker 1991), Wizo (juror 1989), Sr. Citizens Art Network. Democrat. Home: 1955 W Morse Ave Chicago IL 60626-3111

OLSON, SANDRA DITTMAN, medical and surgical nurse; b. Duluth, Minn., Mar. 27, 1953; d. Donald Gene and Evelyn Mae (Wilson) Dittman; m. Douglas Bruce Olson, Aug. 10, 1974; 1 child, Perryn Douglas. BSN, S.D. State U., 1974. Cert ACLS; cert. PALS. Staff nurse U.S. Army Hosp., Nurnberg, Fed. Republic Germany, 1975-79; dir. staff devel. Oak Ridge Care Ctr., Mpls., 1979-81; staff nurse med.-surg. Profl. Nursing, Metairie, La., 1982-83; staff nurse, weekend spl. Tulane Med. Ctr., New Orleans, 1982-83; charge nurse Meadowcrest Hosp., Gretna, La., 1983, house supr., 1983-95; utilization rev. and infection control nurse Advance Care Ctr., Marrero, La., 1995—; employee activity com. bd. mem. Pharmacy-Nursing Task Force; active numerous workshops on edn., staff devel., coronary and intensive care, infection control, long term care, mgmt. Bd. dirs., sec. Bon Temps Homeowners Assn.; chair ct. of honor Boy Scout Troop #378. Named Spink County Wheat Queen; recipient 1989 LA Great 100 Nurses award; S.D. Gov.'s scholar. Mem. Assn. of Women's Students (chmn. social-publicity), U. Women's Svc. Orgn. (Guidon historian), Sigma Theta Tau, Alpha Xi Delta (chmn. philathropy). Home: 2144 Lasalle Ave Terrytown LA 70056-4515

OLSON-HELLERUD, LINDA KATHRYN, elementary school educator; b. Wisconsin Rapids, Wis., Aug. 26, 1947; d. Samuel Ellsworth and Lillian (Dvorak) Olson; m. H. A. Hellerud, 1979; 1 adopted child, Sarah Kathryn. BS, U. Wis.-Stevens Point, 1969, teaching cert., 1970, MST, 1972; postgrad. U. Wis. at Madison, 1969-70; MS, U. Wis. Whitewater, 1975; EdS, U. Wis.-Stout, 1978; cert. k-12 reading tchr. and specialist. Clk., Univ. Counseling Ctr., U. Wis., Stevens Point, 1965-69; elementary sch. tchr., Wisconsin Rapids, 1970-76, sch. counselor, 1976-79, dist. elem. guidance dir., 1979-82, elem. and reading tchr., 1982—, also cons.; advocate Moravian Ch. Sunday sch. Mem. NEA, Wisconsin Rapids Edn. Assn., Internat. Reading Assn., Wis. Reading Assn., Ctrl. Wis. Reading Assn., Wis. State Hist. Soc., Wood County Hist. Soc., Wood County Literacy Coun. (cons.). Mem. United Ch. of Christ.Avocations: gardening, piano. Home: 1011 16th St S Wisconsin Rapids WI 54494-4548 Office: Howe Elem Sch Wisconsin Rapids WI 54494

OLVEY, CINDY LOU DEVANEY, human services planner; b. Tucson, May 3, 1954; d. Jesse Ulysses and Betty Jo (Coffey) DeVaney; m. James Michael Olvey, Jan. 24, 1976; children: James Michael II, Christopher Anderson. AA, Ea. Ariz. Coll., 1974; BA in Behavioral Sci., Grand Canyon U., 1976; MA in Edn., Guidance and Counseling, No. Ariz. U., 1980. Health and human svcs. planner Ctrl. Ariz. Assn. Govts., Florence, 1981-83; human svcs. planner Ariz. Dept. Econ. Security, Phoenix, 1983-85, exec. asst., 1985-87, program/project specialist, 1987-89, policy unit mgr., 1990-91, exec. asst. to the dir., 1992—; quality svc. exec. Office of the Gov., Phoenix, 1991-92; bd. dirs. Ariz. State Bd. on Geog. and Historic Names, Phoenix, 1994—; steering com. mem. Tempe (Ariz.) Cmtys. in Schs., 1995. Fellow Dept. Behavioral Sci., Grand Canyon U., Phoenix, 1975. Mem. Ea. Ariz. Coll. Alumni Assn. (bd. dirs. 1992—), Alpha Chi, Phi Kappa Phi. Office: Ariz Dept Econ Security 1717 W Jefferson Phoenix AZ 85007

O'MALLEY, BRIGID ANNE, language educator; b. Doughmakeon, Mayo, Ireland, Oct. 8, 1934; came to U.S., 1951; d. Anthony Joseph and Jane Agnes (Burke) O'M. BA, Mary Manse Coll., 1964, MA, 1970; M. in Edn. and Human Devel., George Washington U., 1994. Cert. master graphoanalyst. Tchr. English parochial schs., Toledo, 1955-75; tchr. Irish lang. various schs., 1974—; tchr. English Montgomery County C.C., Takoma Park, Md., 1983-84, Cath. U., Washington, 1983-85, D.C. Pub. Schs., Washington, 1986—, Sch. Without Walls, Washington, 1991-96. Mem. AAUW, Am. Conf. for Irish Studies, Irish Am. Cultural Inst., Nat. Coun. Tchrs. English. Democrat. Roman Catholic. Home: 3636 16th St NW # 1264 B Washington DC 20010

O'MALLEY, MARGARET PARLIN, marketing administrator; b. Cin., Jan. 20, 1940; d. John Andrew and Agnes Sophia (Tietig) Parlin; m. Daniel L. Hutchinson, Nov. 6, 1965 (div. 1986); children: Daniel L., Jr., Agnes Alexina; m. John Patrick O'Malley, June 24, 1989. BA, Bryn Mawr Coll., 1961, postgrad., 1963-65; MBA, Villanova U., 1989. Tchr. The Shipley Sch., Bryn Mawr, Pa., 1961-63; adminstrv. asst. Bryn Mawr Coll., 1963-67, Villanova (Pa.) U., 1976-90; v.p. Winsor Assocs., 1990-91; mgr. mktg. and support svcs. Normandeau Assocs., Inc., Spring City, Pa., 1992—. Mem. women's commn. Univ. Mus., U. Pa., Phila., 1969-76; bd. dirs. Phila. Child Guidance Clinic, Phila., 1970-76, The Agnes Irwin Sch., Rosemont, Pa., 1982-85, Strings for Schs., Villanova, 1982-89, The West Hill Sch., Rosemont, 1970-87, The Schuylkill River Greenway Assn., 1993-96. Mem. The Weeders Club. Republican. Episcopalian. Office: Normandeau Assocs Inc 3450 Schuylkill Rd Spring City PA 19087

OMALLEY, MARIE KIERNAN, healthcare products company professional; b. Sayre, Pa., May 1, 1964; d. James Joseph and Karin Margreta (Ottergren) Kiernan; m. James Sean O'Malley, Apr. 25, 1992. BS in Fin. summa cum laude, SUNY, Binghamton, 1990; MBA, Bentley Coll., 1992. Cert. mgmt. acct., Mass. Corp. staff acct. M/A-Com, Inc., Burlington, Mass., 1986-89; fin. analyst Bull Worldwide Info. Sys., Billerica, Mass., 1989-91, sr. fin. and operational auditor, 1991-93, sr. fin. planning analyst, 1993-94; sr. fin. analyst Bard Vascular Sys. divsn. C.R. Bard, Haverhill, Mass., 1994-95; mgr. sales and contracts adminstrn. Bard VAscular Sys. divsn. C.R. Bard, Haverhill, Mass., 1995—. Mem. strategic planning com. Town of North Andover, Mass., 1994—. Mem. Inst. Cert. Mgmt. Accts. (cert., Robert Beyer silver medal 1994). Home: 18 Lacy St North Andover MA 01845 Office: Bard Vascular Sys 25 Computer Dr Haverhill MA 01832

O'MALLEY, MARY NETTLETON, nurse practitioner; b. Nampa, Idaho, Oct. 24, 1946; d. Hubert and Helen (Zaehringer) Nettleton; m. Robert O'Malley, May 13, 1967; children: Rob, Maggie, May. AS, Boise State Coll., 1969. Staff nurse Mercy Hosp., Nampa, Idaho, 1969-73; nurse practitioner Terry Reilly Health Svcs., Nampa, Idaho, 1973—; bd. dirs. Idaho Region III Health and Welfare, Caldwell, Idaho Rural Health Coalition. Co-author: Health of Agricultural Workers, 1979; columnist: Idaho Statesman, 1994. Mem. Nurse Practitioners Conf. Groups (conf. chmn. 1994—), Idaho Acad. Physician Assts. (assoc.), Owyhee County Hist. Soc., Silver City Taxpayers Assn., Owyhee County Cattlemans Assn., Idaho Cattle Assn. Home: HC79 14 Propeller Dr Murphy ID 83650

O'MALLEY, PATRICIA, critical care nurse; b. Boston, May 13, 1955; d. Peter and Catherine (Dwyer) O'M. BSN, Coll. Mt. St. Joseph, Cin., 1977; MS, Ohio State U., 1984, postgrad., 1990—. Cert. critical care nurse. Primary nurse critical care unit Miami Valley Hosp., Dayton, Ohio, nurse educator, clin. nurse specialist, cons.; adj. faculty Wright State U., Dayton. Contbr. articles to profl. jours., textbooks. Recipient honors Dayton Area Heart Assn., Ohio Ho. of Reps., 1994, Ohio Dept. Health, 1996. Mem. AACN (bd. dirs. Dayton-Miami Valley), Soc. Critical Care Medicine, Sigma Theta Tau. Office: Miami Valley Hosp 1 Wyoming St Dayton OH 45409-2722

OMAN, DEBORAH SUE, health science facility administrator; b. North Platte, Nebr., Aug. 26, 1948; d. Rex Ardell and Opale Louise (Smith) O. BS, Kearney State Coll., 1970; MA in Journalism and Mass Comm., U. Nebr., 1993. Med. technologist Physicians Pathology Labs., Lincoln, Nebr., 1970-71; med. technologist student health Colo. State U., Ft. Collins, 1971-72; supr. hematology lab. Bryan Meml. Hosp., Lincoln, 1972-76; sect. supr. hematology, hemostasis Lincoln N.E. br. Corning Clin. Labs., divsn. Corning Life Scis., 1976—; hemostasis cons. Dade Diagnostics Internat., Inc., Miami Fla., 1991—; clin. cons. Med. Lab. Automation, Inc., Pleasantville, N.Y., 1990—; adj. prof. Sch. Med. Tech., Nebr. Wesleyan U., Lincoln, 1979-85; clin. instr. Sch. Med. Tech., U. Nebr. Med. Ctr., Omaha, 1990-95. Contbr. articles to profl. jours. Mem. Am. Soc. Clin. Pathologists (cert., affiliate, recognition award 1986), Lancaster Soc. Med. Technologists, Fastbreaker's for Nebr. Women's Basketball (sec. 1995—), Cornhusker Ski Club (pres. 1982-83), Kappa Tau Alpha. Republican. Mem. Christian Ch. Office: Corning Clin Labs Plz Mall South 1919 S 40th St Ste 333 Lincoln NE 68506-5243

OMAR, AMEENAH E.P., college dean; b. Laurel, Miss., Apr. 3, 1941; d. Denothras (Pickens) Pierce; m. Abdul Aziz Omar, Apr. 28, 1979 (dec.); children: Lakisha, Cheryl. BA in English, U. Detroit, MA in Curriculum Devel., EdS; EdD candidate, Wayne State U. Human resource specialist, personnel specialist U.S. Women Army Corps, 1965-70; tchr. Detroit Pub. Sch., 1972-77; mid. sch. tchr., spl. asst. to supt. Highland Pk. (Mich.) Pub. Schs., 1977-86; dir. coll. placement coop. edn. Highland Park Community Coll., 1986-88, dean student svcs.; sec. H.P. Bldg. Authority. Vice chairperson City of Highland Park Planning Commn.; mem. Highland Park Mothers Club, Parent Adv. Coun. for Gifted and Talented, Highland Park Caucus Club; bd. dirs. Reggie McKenzie Found.; mem. Ferris Sch. PTA; sec. Highland Park Bus. Authority; councilwoman Highland Park, 1996—. Recipient Outstanding Svc. to PTA award, 1978, Svc. Beyond Duty award Highland Park Sch. Dist., 1980, Outstanding Svc. award Black History Celebration, 1980, Outstanding Svc. award Mich. Week Celebration, 1980-85, Outstanding Svc. to Class awrd, 1986, Spirit of Detroit award, 1993, Achievement award Black Men Inc., 1993, Outstanding Leadership award City of Highland Park, 1994, Enstooled Queen Mother Village of Akwakrom, Ghana, 1994; named Outstanding Recruiter in State of Mich., 1970. Mem. Mich. Assn. Collegiate Registrars and Admissions Officers, Mich. Coun. Coll. Placement Officers, United Negro Coll. Fund (grad. landmark edn. forum, forum celebration 50th anniversary), Coun. Coll. Placement Officers, C.C. Employment Network, Coop. Edn. Assn., Nat. Assn. Sch. Execs., Nat. Alliance Black Sch. Educators, Alpha Kappa Alpha (outstanding soror Lambda Pi Omega chpt. 1994), Phi Delta Kappa. Home: 30 Farrand Park Highland Park MI 48203-3350 Office: Highland Pk C of C Glendale and Third Aves Highland Park MI 48203

O'MEALLIE, KITTY, artist; b. Bennettsville, S.C., Oct. 24, 1916; d. Earle and Rosa Estelle (Bethea) Chamness; m. John Ryan O'Meallie, June 27, 1939 (dec. Apr. 26, 1974); children—Sue Ryan, Kathryn Bethea; m. Lee Harnie Johnson, Aug. 21, 1976. BFA Tulane U., 1937; postgrad., 1954-59. One-woman shows include Masur Mus., Monroe, La., 1979, Marlboro County Mus. of S.C., 1975, Meridian Mus. Art, Miss., 1981, 85; exhibited in group shows at New Orleans Mus. Art, Contemporary Art Ctr., Meadows Mus., Cushing Gallery, SE Ctr. of Contemporary Art, Art 80, Art Expo West, Art Expo 81. Represented in permanent collections New Orleans Mus. Art, Tulane U. Pan-Am. Life Ctr., Masur Mus. Art, Meridian Mus. Art. Nat. officer Newcomb Coll. Alumnae Assn., 1964-66; lectr. exhibitor for many charitable orgns. Recipient award WYES-TV, 1979, Hon. Invitational New Orleans Women's Caucus, 1986, numerous awards and prizes in competitive exhibitions; grant St. Charles Ave. Presbyn. Ch., New Orleans, 1995-96. Mem. Womens Caucus for Art, New Orleans Womens Caucus for Art, Chi Omega Alumnae Assn. (pres. mothers' club 1964), Town and Country Garden Guild (pres. 1970, 1986). Avocations: bird-watching; bridge. Home and Office: 211 Fairway Dr New Orleans LA 70124-1018

O'MEARA, ANNA M., lawyer; b. Chgo., Aug. 11, 1947. BS cum laude, Loyola U., 1969, JD cum laude, 1984. Bar: Ill. 1984, U.S. Dist. Ct. (no. dist.) Ill. 1984. Ptnr. Mayer, Brown & Platt, Chgo., 1984—. Mem. ABA, Ill. Bar Assn. Office: Mayer Brown & Platt 190 S La Salle St Chicago IL 60603-3410*

OMELENCHUK, JEANNE, mayor, owner; b. Detroit, Mar. 25, 1931; d. Harry Douglas and Blanche (George) Robinson; m. George Omelenchuk (dec.); 1 child, Kristin. BA in Fine Arts, Wayne State U., 1954, M in Art Edn., 1962, postgrad. Art tchr., English tchr. grades 1-9 Detroit Pub. Schs., 1955-74; mem. U.S. Olympic Team Speed Skating, Squaw Valley, Calif., 1960, Grenoble, France, 1968, Sapporo, Japan, 1972; mem. World Championship Teams, Oostersund, Sweden, 1960, Edmonton, Can., 1963, West Allis, Wis., 1965, Flint, Mich., 1967, Helsinki, 1968, Grenoble, France, 1969, St. Paul, 1970; owner Grandfather Clock Headquarters, 1976-91; mem. Warren City Coun., 1985-91, pres., mayor pro tem, 1991-95; owner Metro Bus, Inc., 1980-95; ret., 1995. Coach, sponsorship Macomb Bicycle Racing Club, 1965-86; sponsorship, meet dir. Detroit Speed Skating Clubs Ann. Gold & Silver Skates Meet, 1974-83; vol. instr., coach Mich. Spl. Olympics, Traverse City, 1986-93; originator Warren's Thanksgiving Day Parade, 1986. Recipient Nat. Bicycle Racing Championship Titles, 1951, 55, 57-59, Nat. Speed Skating Championship Titles, St. Paul, 1954, 57-72, Nat. Bicycle Racing Championship, Antwerp, Belgium, 1957; inducted into Athletic Hall of Fame, Wayne State U., 1979, Mich. Amateur Athletic Hall of Fame, 1981, U.S. Amateur Skating Union Hall of Fame, Chgo., 1984, Mich. Sports Hall of Fame, Cobo Hall, Detroit, 1984, Mich. Women's Hall of Fame, Lansing, Mich., 1994; recognized by YWCA for outstanding contbns. to world of sports on Nat. Women's Sports Day, 1996. Mem. Southern Mich. Athletic Assn. (founding mem., sponsor). Home: 27544 Sutherland Warren MI 48093 Office: City Warren Coun Office 29500 Van Dyke Warren MI 48093

OMER, LAURA DIANE (LAURA DIANE PACE), military career officer, educator, nurse; b. Minden, La., Jan. 24, 1946; d. Floyd Curtis and Noble Celestial (Garrett) Pace; m. Lewis M. Omer III, July 26, 1986 (dec.). Diploma in nursing, Ga. Bapt. Hosp. Sch. Nursing, 1968; BSN, Am. U., 1983; MA in Edn. and Human Resource Devel., George Washington U., 1987. Various nursing positions, 1968-77; commd. lt. jr. grade USN, 1977, advanced through grades to comdr.; staff nurse Nat. Naval med. ctr., Bethesda, Md., 1977-81; staff charge nurse Naval Hosp., Guantanamo Bay, Cuba, 1981-82; head edn. and tng. Naval Med. Clinic, Quantico, Va., 1983-86, Naval Med. Command NEREG, Great Lakes, Ill., 1987-89; div. officer edn. and tng. Nat. Naval Med. Ctr., Bethesda, 1989-92, head edn. and tng. dept., 1992-95, dept. head edn. and tng., 1992-95; dir. continuing edn. for health profls. Uniformed Svc. U. of Health Scis., Rockville, Md., 1995—. Mem. ASTD, AACN, Assn. Mil. Surgeons of U.S., Sigma Theta Tau, Phi Kappa Phi. Home: 8329 Stockade Dr Alexandria VA 22308-1647 Office: Uniformed Svcs U Health Svcs Ste 400 11426 Rockville Pike Rockville MD 20852

O'MORCHOE, PATRICIA JEAN, pathologist, educator; b. Halifax, Eng., Sept. 15, 1930; came to U.S., 1968; d. Alfred Eric and Florence Patricia (Pearson) Richardson; m. Charles Christopher Creagh O'Morchoe, Sept. 15, 1955; children: Charles E.C., David J.C. BA, Dublin U., Ireland, 1953, MB, Bch., BAO, 1955, MA, 1966, MD. Intern Halifax (Yorkshire) Gen. Hosp., Eng., 1955-57; instr., lectr. physiology Dublin U., 1957-61, 63-68; instr. pathology Johns Hopkins U., Balt., 1961-62, 68-72, asst. prof. pathology, 1972-74; rsch. assoc. surgery, pathology Harvard U., Boston, 1962-63; asst. prof. anatomy U. Md., 1970-74; assoc.prof., prof. pathology, anatomy Loyola U. Chgo., 1974-84; prof. pathology, cell and structural biology U. Ill., Urbana, 1984—; head dept. pathology coll. medicine U. Ill., Urbana-Champaign, 1994—; staff pathologist VA Hosp., Danville, Ill., 1989—; assoc. head dept. pathology U. Ill., 1991-95; courtesy staff pathologist Covenant Hosp., Urbana, 1984—, Carle Clinic, Urbana, 1990—. Contbr. numerous articles to profl. jours. Recipient Excellence in Teaching award U. Ill., 1996. Mem. Internat. Acad. Cytology, Internat. Soc. Lymphology (auditor 1989-91, exec. com. 1991-93), N.Am. Soc. Lymphology (sec. 1988-90, treas. 1990-92, v.p. 1992-94, pres. 1994—), Am. Soc. Cytology, Am. Assn. Anatomists, Ill. Soc. Cytology. Home: 2709 Holcomb Dr Urbana IL 61801-7724 Office: U Ill Coll Med 506 S Mathews Ave Urbana IL 61801-3618

ONA-SARINO, MILAGROS FELIX, physician, pathologist; b. Manila, May 8, 1940; came to U.S., 1965, naturalized, 1983; d. Venancio Vale Ona and Fidela Torres Felix; m. Edgardo Formantes Sarino, June 11, 1966; children: Edith Melanie, Edgar Michael, Edenn Michele. AA, U. Santo Tomas, Manila, 1959, MD meritissimus cum laude 1964. Diplomate Am. Bd. Pathology; med. licensure N.Y., N.J., W.Va. Rotating intern N.Y. Infirmary, pediatrics, Roosevelt Hosp., N.Y.C., 1965-66; resident in anatomic and clin. pathology Lenox Hill Hosp., N.Y.C., 1966-71, asst. adj. pathologist, 1972-74; assoc. pathologist St. Francis Med. Ctr., Trenton, N.J., 1974-84, Hamilton Hosp., N.J., 1974-84; pathologist, chief pathology and lab. medicine svc. Louis A. Johnson VA Med. Ctr., Clarksburg, W.Va., 1984—; clin. instr. pathology Columbia U. Coll. Physicians and Surgeons, N.Y.C., 1973-85; clin. assoc. prof. pathology, W.Va. U. Sch. Medicine. Fellow Am. Soc. Clin. Pathologists, Coll. of Am. Pathologists; mem. Internat. Acad. Pathology, N.Y. Acad. Scis. (life). Office: Louis A Johnson VA Med Ctr Dept Pathology Clarksburg WV 26301

ONCLEY, LOUISE, civil rights manager; b. East Liverpool, Ohio, Sept. 22, 1940; m. Lawrence A. Oncley, 1959 (div. Feb. 1974); 1 child, Steven P. BA, U. Puget Sound, 1963; MA, Ind. U., 1967. Teaching assoc. Ind. U., Bloomington, 1963-67; instr. philosophy Ind. State U., Terre Haute, 1967-68; budget analyst edn. Pa. Gov.'s Budget Office, Harrisburg, 1969-71; asst. dir. planning & rsch. Pa. Human Rels. Commn., Harrisburg, 1971-76; chief planning, rsch. & evaluation Pa. Bur. Affirmative Action, Harrisburg, 1976-80; spl. asst. to exec. dir. Pa. Human Rels. Commn., Harrisburg, 1980—; v.p. 1st Pa. Feminist Credit Union, Harrisburg, 1975-77; sec. Keystone Assn. Hu an Rights Agys., Pa., 1982-84; v.p. Pennsylvanians for Women's Rights, 1972-75; speaker in field. Del. UN 4th World Conf. on Women, Beijing, 1995. Mem. NOW, NAACP, U.S. Network for Beijing & Beyond, Older Women's League. Office: Pa Human Rels Commn PO Box 3145 Harrisburg PA 17105-3145

O'NEAL, HARRIET ROBERTS, psychologist, psycholegal consultant; b. Covington, Ky., Dec. 28, 1952; d. Nelson E. and Georgia H. (Roberts) O'N. Student, U. Paris Sorbonne, 1972; BA in Psychology, Hollins Coll., 1974; JD, U. Nebr., 1978, MA in Psychology, 1980, PhD in Psychology, 1982. Therapist Richmond Maxi Ctr., San Francisco, 1979-81; clin. coord., therapist Pacifica (Calif.) Youth Svc. Bur., 1981-83; staff psychologist Kaiser Permanente Med. Ctr., Walnut Creek, Calif., 1983-91; pvt. practice psychotherapy Pleasant Hill, Calif., 1985—, San Francisco, 1995—; psycholegal cons., Nebr., 1975-79, Calif., 1979—; oral exam commr. Calif. Bd. Behavioral Sci. Examiners, Sacramento, 1982—; pvt. practice psychotherapy, Pleasant Hill, Calif., 1985—; psycholegal cons., presenter San Francisco State U., 1980, U. Calif., San Francisco, 1980, VA Med. Ctr., San Francisco, 1983. Cons. Nebr. Gov.'s Commn. on Status of Women, 1975, 78; vol. Make-A-Wish Found., 1992—. NIMH fellow, 1974-79. Mem. APA, Employee Assistance Profls. Assn., Phi Beta Kappa, Psi Chi.

O'NEAL, NELL SELF, retired principal; b. Glenwood, Ark., Feb. 19, 1925; d. Jewell Calvin and Nannie May (Bankston) Self; m. Billie Kenneth O'Neal, Apr. 1, 1943 (div. Jan. 1976); children: Kenneth Dan O'Neal, Rikki Devin O'Neal, Teresa Lynn Severson. BA, Little Rock U., 1964; MS in Edn., Ark. State Tchrs. Coll., 1965. Cert. tchr. mentally retarded, blind; cert. elem. sch. prin. Spl. edn. tchr. Little Rock Pub. Schs., 1961-65; prin. exceptional unit Ark. Sch. for the Blind, Little Rock, 1965-95; retired, 1995. Mem. NOW, NEA, AAUW, Assn. for the Edn., and Rehab. of Blind and Visually Impaired (J. Max Woolly Superior Svc. award 1990), Ark. Edn. Assn., Sierra Club, Alpha Delta Kappa. Democrat. Methodist. Home: 6513 Cantrell Rd Little Rock AR 72207-4218

O'NEIL, CHARLOTTE COOPER, environmental education administrator; b. Chgo., Sept. 21, 1949; d. Adolph H. and Charlotte Waters (Edman) Cooper; m. William Randolph O'Neil, Nov. 18, 1972; children: Sean, Megan. BA in Polit. Sci., Okla. State U., 1969; BS in Edn., U. Tenn., 1988. Cert. tchr., Tenn. Intern Senator Charles H. Percy, Washington, 1969; state treas., state hdqrs. office mgr. Jed Johnson for U.S. Senate, Okla., 1972; mem. acct. staff Pacific Architects & Engrs., Barrow, Alaska, 1973; tchr. social studies Jefferson Jr. High Sch., Oak Ridge, Tenn., 1988; edn. specialist Sci. Applications Internat. Corp., Oak Ridge, Tenn., 1988-94, mgr. environ. edn. and info. tech. sect., 1994-95, mgr. comm. edn. and pub. info. sect., 1995—; edn. strategies com. U.S. Dept. of Transp./FHWA/ITS Edn. 1995—. Author: Science, Society and America's Nuclear Waste, 1992, 2d edit., 1995, Technical Career Opportunities in High-Level Waste Management, 1993, The Environmental History of the Tonawanda Site, 1994, FAA Community Involvement Training: Better Decisions through Consensus, 1996; contbr. articles to profl. jours. Publicity chair, mem. steering com. Am. Mus. Sci. & Energy Tribute to Tech. Mem. ASCD, AAUW, Triangle Coalition, Tenn. Geography Alliance, Nat. Coun. for Social Studies (culture, sci. and tech. com., sci. and society com., sec.-treas. 1991—), Earthwatch, Internat. Alliance for High-Level Radioactive Waste Mgmt., Golden Key, Atomic City Aquatic Club (chair constl. rev. com. 1991—). Office: Sci Applications Internat PO Box 2502 Oak Ridge TN 37831-2502

O'NEIL, CHLOE ANN, state legislator; m. John G.A. O'Neil (dec.); children: Beth Ann Rice, John A.S. BS in Psychology, SUNY, Potsdam, 1967, MS in Edn. Tchr. Hermon-DeKalb Ctr. Sch.; tchr. SUNY, Canton, N.Y., Potsdam; elem. tchr. Parishville (N.Y.)-Hopkinton Ctrl. Sch.; mem. N.Y. State Assembly, 1993—. Past mem. St. Mary's Sch. Bd. Edn.; active St. Michael's Ch. in Parishville, N.Y. Mem. N.Y. State United Tchrs. Home: Cassidy Rd Hopkinton NY 12940 Office: NY State Assembly State Capitol Albany NY 12224*

O'NEIL, MICHELE CHRISTINE, special education educator; b. Skokie, Ill., June 13, 1970; d. Charles James and Alana Michele (Rachofsky) O'N. BA in Spl. Edn., Western Ill. U., 1992. Camp counselor Northwest Spl. Recreation Assn., Rolling Meadows, Ill., 1989, 90 summer; asst. camp dir. Northwest Spl. Recreation Assn., Rolling Meadows, 1991 summer; habilitation technician Blair House Group Home, Hoffman Estates, Ill., 1992—; case mgr. Elgin (Ill.) Comty. Living Facility, 1992—; devel. tng. supr. United Cerebral Palsy, Joliet, Ill., 1993—. Vol. Marklund Home Inc., Bloomingdale, Ill., 1988, Mc Donough County Rehabilitation Ctr., 1991. Mem. Coun. for Exceptional Children (v.p. student br. Western Ill. U. 1991-92), Phi Sigma Sorority (founding mem., chair philanthropy com. 1989-90, alumnae com. 1990-91). Home: 2512 Crystal Ct Apt 103 Woodridge IL 60517

O'NEIL, MURIEL, publishing executive; b. La Grange, Ill., Sept. 3, 1923; d. John Wallace and Olive (Andersen) Hight; m. Francis Raymond O'Neil, Oct. 3, 1959 (dec. Nov., 1981). BA, Northwestern U., 1949. Exec. sec. MacFadden Publs., Chgo., 1942-51; adminstrv. sec. Better Living (McCall's), N.Y.C., 1951-54; adminstrv. asst. to pres. Am. Heritage and Horizon Mags., N.Y.C., 1954-78; advt. mgr. Americana Mag., N.Y.C., 1979-80; advt. svc. mgr. PBS The Dial, N.Y.C., 1981-83; office mgr. N.Y. Times Found., 1984-93. Author: Monthly Letter to advertisers in Americana and Horizon Mags. Vol. Dem. Nat. Com., N.Y.C., 1956-93; vol. advisor Roundabout Theater, N.Y.C., 1976-93, Old Merchants House, N.Y.C., 1980-93, Big Apple Circus, 1988-93, Bryant Park Restoration, 1991-93; others. Mem. AAUW, Long Beach Island Women's Club. Home: 11 Meade Ave Brant Beach NJ 08008

O'NEIL, SUSAN M., public relations professional. BA in Comms., U. Dayton, 1989. Media asst. The Kountz Group, Cin., 1989-90; prodn. asst. Martiny & Co., Cin., 1990-91, pub. rels. asst. account exec., 1991-92, pub. rels. account exec., 1992-94; account mgr. pub. rels. Rourke & Co., San Jose, Calif., 1994-95; mgr. pub. rels. Polycom, Inc., San Jose, 1995—. Vol. Opera San Jose, 1995—, San Jose Downtown Assn., 1995—, Multiple Sclerosis Soc., San Jose, 1996—. Mem. NAFE, Pub. Rels. Soc. Am., Women in Comms., Inc., Nat. Investor Rels., Inc.

O'NEILL, ALICE See LICHT, ALICE VESS

O'NEILL, ALICE JANE, lawyer; b. Houston, May 14, 1951; d. Edward John Sr. and Martha Elisabeth (Alford) O'N. BA in Polit. Sci., U. St. Thomas, Houston, 1972, MBA, 1982; MEd in Ednl. Psychology, Tex. A&M U., 1974; JD, South Tex. Coll. Law, 1992. Bar: Tex. 1993, U.S. Dist. Ct. (so. dist.) Tex. 1993, U.S. Dist. Ct. Ariz. 1994. Therapist, supr. Family Svc. Ctr., Houston, 1978-81; personnel coord. Guest Quarters Hotel, Houston, 1981-84; therapist in pvt. practice Houston, 1984-90; law clk. Abraham Watkins Nichols Ballard & Friend, Houston, 1991-93; contract atty. Nelson & Zeidman, Houston, 1994, O'Quinn Kerensky McAninich & Laminack, Houston, 1994; assoc. Rosen & Newey, Houston, 1994—; mem. adv. bd. Juvenile Justice, Houston, Harris County Detention Ctr., Houston, 1986-93. Mem. ABA, Houston Bar Assn., Assn. for Women Attys., Houston Young Lawyers Assn. Republican. Methodist. Home: 403 Euclid St Houston TX 77009-7222 Office: Rosen & Newey 440 Louisiana St Ste 1800 Houston TX 77002-1636

O'NEILL, BEVERLY LEWIS, mayor, former college president; b. Long Beach, Calif., Sept. 8, 1930; d. Clarence John and Flossie Rachel (Nicholson) Lewis; m. William F. O'Neill, Dec. 21, 1952. AA, Long Beach City Coll., 1950; BA, Calif. State U., Long Beach, 1952, MA, 1956; EdD, U. So. Calif., 1977. Elem. tchr. Long Beach Unified Sch. Dist., 1952-57; instr., counsellor Compton (Calif.) Coll., 1957-60; curriculum supr. Little Lake Sch. Dist., Santa Fe Springs, Calif., 1960-62; women's advisor, campus dean Long Beach City Coll., 1962-71, dir. Continuing Edn. Ctr. for Women, 1969-75, dean student affairs, 1971-77, v.p. student svcs., 1977-88, supt.-pres., 1988—, exec. dir. Found., 1983—; mayor City of Long Beach, Calif. Advisor Jr. League, Long Beach, 1976—, Nat. Coun. on Alcoholism, Long Beach,

1979—, Assistance League, Long Beach, 1982—; bd. dirs. NCCJ, Long Beach, 1976—, Meml. Hosp. Found., Long Beach, 1984-92, Met. YMCA, Long Beach, 1986-92, United Way, Long Beach, 1986-92. Named Woman of Yr., Long Beach Human Rels. Commn., 1976, to Hall of Fame, Long Beach City Coll., 1977, Disting. Alumni of Yr., Calif. State U., Long Beach, 1985, Long Beach Woman of Yr. Rick Rackers, 1987, Assistance League Aux., 1987; recipient Hannah Solomon award Nat. Coun. Jewish Women, 1984, Outstanding Colleague award Long Beach City Coll., 1985, NCCJ Humanitarian award, 1991, Woman of Excellence award YWCA, 1990, Community Svc. award Community Svcs. Devel. Corp., 1991, Citizen of Yr. award Exch. Club, 1992, Pacific Regional CEO award Assn. Community Coll. Trustees, 1992. Mem. Assn. Calif. Community Coll. Adminstrs. (pres. 1988-90, Harry Buttimer award 1991), Calif. Community Colls. Chief Exec. Officers Assn., Rotary, Soroptomists (Women Helping Women award 1981, Hall of Fame award 1984). Democrat. Office: Office of the Mayor 333 W Ocean Blvd Long Beach CA 90802*

O'NEILL, ELIZABETH STERLING, trade association administrator; b. N.Y.C., May 30, 1938; d. Theodore and Pauline (Green) Sterling: m. W.B. Smith, June 18, 1968 (div. Aug., 1978); 1 child, Elizabeth S. Kroese; m. Francis James O'Neill, May 19, 1984. BA, Cornell U., 1958; postgrad. studies, Northwestern U., 1959-60. Social sec. Perle Mesta Ambassador Luxembourg, N.Y.C.; spl. asst. Vivian Beaumont Allen, philanthropist, N.Y.C.; rep. Prentice-Hall Pub. Co., Eastern Europe; exec. dir. New Caanan (Conn.) C. of C., 1986—; speaker various orgns. including Lions Club, Exchange Club, Kiwanis, Rotary, Poinsettia Club; apptd. Commn. Small Bus. State of Conn., 1996. Pres. Newcomers, New Caanan, Conn.; pub. rels. rep. Girl Scouts of U.S., Fairfield County; bd. dirs. Young Women's Rep. Club; mem. Gov. Weicker's Com. for Curriculum Reform; mem. community bd. Waveny Care Ctr., New Caanan; apptd. mem. Gov. John Roland's Commn. on Small Bus., Conn., 1996—. Recipient Service awards New Caanan YMCA, N.Y. ASPCA, certs. of appreciation New Caanan Lions Club, President Bush. Mem. AAUW (bd. dirs. New Canaan chpt.), Kiwanis. Christian Scientist. Home: Indian Waters Dr New Caanan CT 06840 Office: New Caanan C of C 111 Elm St New Caanan CT 06840-5419

O'NEILL, HOLLY MARGARET, marketing professional; b. Pottstown, Pa., Dec. 11, 1963. BS with high distinction, Penn State U., 1985; MBA, UCLA, 1991. Project dir. Info. Resources, Darien, Conn., 1985-87; sr. rsch. analyst SAMI/Burke, San Ramon, Calif., 1987-89; mktg. cons. pvt. practice, L.A., 1991-93; sr. mktg. mgr. Sebastian Internat., Woodland Hills, Calif., 1993-94; product mgr. Hunt-Wesson, Fullerton, Calif., 1994-96; v.p. mktg. Natural Body Bath/Aroma Art, Santa Ana, Calif., 1996—. Host, producer: Talking Business, 1993—. Advisor: Explorers, Fullerton, Calif., 1995, Jr. Achievement, Stamford, Conn., 1986-88. Mem. Literary Club of Orange County (chief libr.), Penn State U. Alumni Assn., Club 552. Office: Talking Business PO Box 1743 Newport Beach CA 92659

O'NEILL, MARGARET E., psychological counselor; b. Youngstown, Ohio, Jan. 23, 1935; d. Julius and Anna (Zakel) Huegel; children: Paul McCann, Kathleen McCann, Kevin McCann; m. Thomas B. O'Neill, Oct. 21, 1971 (div. 1979). BSN, UCLA, 1961, MS in Nursing, 1963; MA in Counseling, Calif. Luth. Coll., Thousand Oaks, 1974; PhD in Psychology, U.S. Internat. U., San Diego, 1986. Cert. hypnotherapist, Calif. Instr. Ventura Coll., Calif., 1965-69, dept. chair, 1969-74, coordinator Women's Ctr., 1974-79, counselor, 1979-91; marriage, family and child psychologist, Ventura, 1981-92, Morro Bay and San Luis Obispo, 1992—; trainer, cons. County of Ventura, 1984-90, County of San Luis Obispo, 1991—. Mem. NAFE, San Luis Obispo Psychol. Assn., Rotary Morro Bay, New Comers Club San Luis Obispo. Democrat. Avocations: reading, dancing, hiking, walking, travel. Office: 895 Napa Ave Ste A4 Morro Bay CA 93442-1945

O'NEILL, MARY JANE, health agency executive; b. Detroit, Feb. 24, 1923; d. Frank Roger and Kathryn (Rice) Kilcoyne; Ph.B. summa cum laude, U. Detroit, 1944; postgrad. U. Wis., 1949-50; m. Michael James O'Neill, May 31, 1948; children: Michael, Maureen, Kevin, John (dec.), Kathryn. Editor, East Side Shopper, Detroit, 1939-45; club editor Detroit Free Press, 1945-48; reporter UP, Milw. and Madison, Wis., 1949; dir. pub. rels. Fairfax-Falls Church (Va.) Cmty. Chest, 1955-60; copy editor Falls Ch. Sun-Echo, 1958-60; free-lance writer, Washington, 1960-63; assoc. editor Med. World News, Washington, 1963-66; dir. public relations Westchester Lighthouse, N.Y. Assn. for Blind, 1967-71; dir. public edn. The Lighthouse, N.Y.C., 1971-73, dir. pub. rels., 1973-80; exec. dir. Eye-Bank for Sight Restoration, Inc., 1980—. Mem. N.Y. State Transplant Coun., 1991—; bd. dirs. N.Y. Regional Transplant Program, 1987-91, 94—. Mem. Women in Communications (pres. N.Y. chpt. 1980-81), Eye Bank Assn. Am. (lay adv. bd. 1981-83, dir. 1983-86, pres. N.E. Region, 1993-96, exec. com. 1994-96), Pub. Rels. Soc. Am., Women Execs. in Pub. Rels. (dir. 1982-88, pres. 1986-87), N.Y. Acad. Scis., Cosmopolitan Club. Office: Eye-Bank for Sight Restoration 210 E 64th St New York NY 10021-7480

O'NEILL, PAMELA BLISS, secondary foreign language educator; b. Detroit, Sept. 26, 1949; d. William Everard and Susan Huntington (Blanchard) Bliss; m. Peter Joseph O'Neill, May 10, 1980; children: Jennifer, Katherine, Terence, Eleanor, Claire, Brendan. BA in English and French, So. Ill. U., 1973; level I tchg. cert., Shippensburg U., 1994. Tchg. cert., Pa. Tchr. English as a Fgn. Lang. Peace Corps, Ivory Coast, West Africa, 1973-75; human rels. rep. Pa. Human Rels. Com., Harrisburg, 1977-80; tchr. French and Spanish Big Spring Middle Sch., Newville, Pa., 1994—. Mem. Nat. Coun. Tchrs. English. Home: 3213 N 2nd St Harrisburg PA 17110-1304

O'NEILL, PATRICIA L., elementary educator; b. Chgo., Jan. 16, 1934; d. Francesco and Mary Phillipe (Scavo) Donati; m. William Bennett O'Neill, Dec. 29, 1956; children: Robin, Gail, William, Robert. BA in Edn., St. Xavier U., 1973; MS in Edn., Chgo. State U., 1985. Tchr. 1st grade Northwest Elem. Sch., Evergreen Park, Ill., 1973-94, head tchr., 1985-92; retired. Mem. Ill. Retired Tchrs. Assn., Phi Delta Kappa. Home: 8242 W 160th Pl Tinley Park IL 60477

O'NEILL, PEGGY K., secondary education educator; b. Manhattan, Kans., Dec. 12, 1943; d. Thomas R. and Fauneal R. (Colbert) O'N. BA, Marymount Coll., 1965; MS, Kans. State U., 1970. Instr., head of art dept. Bishop Miege H.S., Shawnee Mission, Kans., 1965—. Designed cartoons for hwy. patrol safety inks, 1965, bumper stickers for high schs., 1993—. Artist/photographer exhibit at Antioch Libr. and Kansas City, Kans.Libr., 1980—. Named Outstanding Young Educator Jaycees, Overland Park, Kans., 1973. Mem. Nat. Art Edn. Assn., Women Photographers of Kansas City (treas. 1980). Office: Bishop Miege H S 5041 Reinhardt Dr Shawnee Mission KS 66205-1508

O'NEILL, SHEILA, principal. Prin. Cor Jesu Acad., St. Louis. Recipient Blue Ribbon award U.S. Dept. Edn., 1990-91. Office: Cor Jesu Acad 10230 Gravois Rd Saint Louis MO 63123-4030

O'NEILL-MEJIA, DOLLY MARIE, retired bilingual educator; b. Holyoke, Mass., Feb. 21, 1936; d. James C. and Louise M. (Cianfichi) O'Neill; m. Marco A. Mejia. BA in Edn., St. Joseph Coll., 1958; MA in Edn., Manhattanville Coll., 1976; PhD in Adminstrn., Fordham U., 1989. Cert. ESL tchr., N.Y., bilingual edn. tchr., N.Y. Elem. tchr. Diocese of Conn., 1958-71; bilingual edn. tchr. Port Chester (N.Y.) Pub. Sch., 1971-81, 84-87, ESL tchr./coord., 1981-84, N.Y. state coord. of bilingual grant, 1984-95, dist. coord. bilingual edn., 1990-95, ret., 1995; tchr. mentor Port Chester Pub. Sch., 1982-95. Mem. Native Am. Rights Assn., N.Y., 1991-95, Am. Indian Relief Coun., 1992-95. Recipient Ednl. Program grant Westchester Tchr. Ctr., 1987, Dual Lang. grant N.Y. State Bilingual Edn. Office, 1983-95. Mem. N.Y. State Assn. for Bilingual Educators (conf./workshop presenter 1980-95, regional dir. for assn. 1992-95, Tchr. of Yr. 1991), N.Y. State Tchrs. ESL (sec. 1980-82), Hispanic Profl. Assn., Westchester Hispanic Edn. Assn. Democrat. Episcopalian. Home: 351 Garcia Moreno y Roca, Otavalo Ecuador

ONET, VIRGINIA C(ONSTANTINESCU), research scientist, educator, writer; b. Sarmasag, Salaj, Romania, Mar. 17, 1939; came to U.S., 1986; naturalized, 1991.; d. Virgil and Eugenia (Marinescu) Constantinescu; m. Gheorghe Emil Onet, Sept. 3, 1981. DVM, U. Agriculture Scis., Cluj-Napoca, Romania, 1966; PhD, Coll. Vet. Med., Bucharest, Romania, 1974. Asst. prof., then assoc. prof. Coll. Vet. Medicine, Cluj-Napoca, 1966-81, lectr., 1981-85; pvt. rschr. Germany, 1985-86; ind. cons. Detroit, 1986-88; rsch. group leader Grand Labs., Inc., Larchwood, Iowa, 1988-92, mgr. R&D dept. parasitology, 1992-95, mgr. R & D dept. spl. rsch. projects, 1995—; mem. profl. bd. Coll. Vet. Medicine, Cluj-Napoca, 1970-72, mem. faculty com., 1980-81; mem. Exam. Bd. for Screening Vet. Medicine Candidates, Cluj-Napoca, 1974-85. Author: Diagnosis Guide for Parasitic Disease, 1983; co-author: Laboratory Diagnosis in Veterinary Medicine, 1978; author 7 textbooks; contbr. over 45 articles to profl. jours. Merit scholar Coll. Vet. Medicine, Bucharest, 1964. Mem. AAAS, Am. Soc. Parasitologists, Am. Vet. Med. Assn., Am. Assn. Vet. Parasitologists, World Vet. Poultry Assn., World Assn. for Advancement Vet. Parasitology, Romanian Vet. Medicine Soc., Romanian Soc. Biologists, World Assn. Buiatrics, N.Y. Acad. Scis. Home: 4509 Mountain Ash Dr Sioux Falls SD 57103-4959 Office: Grand Labs Inc PO Box 193 Larchwood IA 51241-0193

ONGAS, SHARON ANNA, elementary education educator; b. Franklin, N.J., Mar. 6, 1948; d. Joseph J. and Maria (Lacika) Regavich; m. Kaljo Ongas, July 26, 1980. BA, William Paterson Coll., Wayne, N.J., 1972, MA in Spl. Edn., 1981. Tchr. Vernon (N.J.) Bd. Edn., 1972—; learning disability tchr. cons. William Paterson Coll., 1981. Named Vernon Twp. Tchr. of Yr., Vernon Bd. Edn., 1982-83.

ONGLEY, LOIS KATHE, geology educator; b. Kalamazoo, Mich.; d. George Henry Ongley, Jr. and Constance Rhea Danneberg; m. William Edward Todd-Brown, Jr.; children: Katherine, Margaret, Jesica. BA, Middlebury Coll., 1973; MS, Tex. A&M U., 1977; M in Environ. Sci., Rice U., 1988, PhD, 1993. Cert. profl. geologist. Exploration geologist Houston Oil & Minerals, 1977-81, The Anschutz Corp., Oklahoma City, 1981-82; cons. geologist Houston and Norman, Okla., 1982-88; instr. Bates Coll., Lewiston, Maine, 1992-93, asst. prof., 1993—. Mem. Assn. Women Geoscientists Found. (pres. 1983-85, 93—). Office: Bates Coll Geology Dept 44 Campus Ave Lewiston ME 04240

OPARIL, SUZANNE, cardiologist, educator, researcher; b. Elmira, N.Y., Apr. 10, 1941; d. Stanley and Anna (Penkova) O. AB, Cornell U., 1961; MD, Columbia U., 1965. Diplomate Am. Bd. Internal Medicine. Intern in medicine Presbyn. Hosp., N.Y.C., 1965-66; sr. asst. resident in medicine Mass. Gen. Hosp., Boston, 1967-68, clin. and rsch. fellow in medicine, cardiac unit, 1968-71; asst. prof. medicine Med. Sch., U. Chgo., 1971-75, assoc. prof., 1975-77; assoc. prof. dept. medicine U. Ala., Birmingham, 1977-81, asst. prof. physiology and biophysics, 1980-81, assoc. prof., 1981—, prof. medicine, 1981—, dir. vascular biology and hypertension program, 1985—; mem. vis. faculty Nat. High Blood Pressure Edn. Program, 1974—, Joint Nat. Com. on Detection, Evaluation and Treatment High Blood Pressure, 1991; mem. bd. sci. advisors Sterling Drug, Inc., 1988-91; lectr. in field; Selkurt lectr. Ind. U. Sch. Medicine, 1994; hon. prof. Peking Union Med. Coll., 1994. Author books on hypertension; editor Am. Jour. Med. Scis., 1984-94; assoc. editor Hypertension, 1979-83, mem. editl. bd., 1984—; assoc. editor Am. Jour. Physiology-Renal, 1989-91; mem. editl. bd. Jour. Hypertensioin, 1989—; contbr. over 300 articles to profl. jours., chpts. to books. Recipient Young Investigator award Internat. Soc. Hypertension, 1979, ann. award Med. Coll. Pa., 1984; fellow Am. Coll. Cardiology, 1992. Fellow Am. Coll. Cardiology; mem. Inst. Medicine of NAS (corr. com. on human rights 1992, chmn. com. advise Dept. Def. 1993 Breast Cancer Rsch. Program), AAAS, Endocrine Soc., Inter-Am. Soc. Hypertension, Am. Soc. Hypertension (pub. policy com. 1990—, sci. program com. 1990-92), Assn. for Women in Sci., Am. Heart Assn. (coun. for high blood pressure rsch., 1973—, exec. com. 1985-90, vice chmn. 1986, coun. on basic scis. 1978—, mem.-at-large, exec. com. 1979-81, mem.-at-large bd. dirs. 1992, chmn. Louis B. Katz Prize com. 1984-86, chmn., 1988-90, chmn. budget com. 1990-91, v.p. Ala. affiliate 1986-87, pres.-elect Ala. affiliate 1987-88, 93-94, pres. Ala. affiliate 1988-89, nat. pres.-elect 1993-94, nat. pres. 1994—, Lewis K. Dahl Meml. Lectr. 1993), Am. Physiol. Soc. (clin. physiology adv. com. 1992—), Am. Soc. for Clin. Investigation (sec.-treas. 1983-86), Soc. Exptl. Biology and Medicine (councillor 1993—), So. Soc. for Clin. Investigation (Founder's award 1995), Assn. Am. Physicians, Am. Fedn. for Clin. Rsch. (midwest councillor 1974-75, nat. councillor 1975-78, sec.-treas. 1978-80, pres. 1981-82), Phi Beta Kappa, Sigma Xi, Alpha Omega Alpha (mem. nat. bd. dirs., dir.-at-large 1991, treas. 1993). Office: U Ala Sch Medicine 1034 Zeigler Research Bldg Birmingham AL 35294*

OPATOW, LORNA, marketing research company executive, consultant; b. Phila.; d. Elias Opatow and Frances Blatt Schoenfeld. BA, U. Pa., 1952; MBA, Temple U., 1955. Rsch. assoc. Cluett Peabody, N.Y.C., 1955-57; rsch. dir. Hearst Mags., N.Y.C., 1957; pres. Opatow Assocs., N.Y.C., 1991-92, Market Rsch. Coun., N.Y.C., 1995—; bd. dirs. Advt. Rsch. Found. Contbr. articles to Progressive Grocer, Beverage Industry, Bankers Mag., Jour. Product Innovation Mgmt., Mobius, others. Bd. dirs. Caravan Inst., N.Y.C., 1993—. Fellow Inst. Packaging Profls. (bd. dirs. 1986-89, 94—), Am. Mktg. Assn. (bd. dirs. N.Y. 1991—), Cosmopolitan Club, Penn Club. Office: Opatow Assocs One Dag Hammarskjold Plz New York NY 10017

OPENSHAW, HELENA MARIE, investment company executive, portfolio manager; b. Beirut, July 30, 1953; d. Hubert J. and Lucile Openshaw. BA, U. South Fla., 1975, MA, 1977; PhD, SUNY, Buffalo, 1986. CFA. Tchg. asst. instr. SUNY, 1977-83; analyst specialist ValueLine, Inc., N.Y.C., 1986-88, sr. analyst, mem. portfolio mgmt. team, 1988-93; equity portfolio mgr. Ganz Capital Mgmt., Miami, Fla., 1993-94; v.p., sr. portfolio mgr. Comerica FSB, Ft. Lauderdale, Fla., 1994-95, Comerica Inc., Detroit, 1995—. Mem. Assn. for Investment Mgmt. and Rsch., Fin. Analysts Soc. Detroit. Office: Comerica Inc One Detroit Ctr 500 Woodward Ave Detroit MI 48226

OPENSHAW, JANICE AMELIA, special education educator; b. Phoenix, Nov. 24, 1962; d. Joseph Allen and Helen Doris (Morris) Beatty; m. Timothy Troy Openshaw, July 11, 1987; children: Nickolas, Tyler, Max. BS in Edn., No. Ariz. U., 1984. Tchr. spl. edn. Oak Creek Boarding Sch., Cottonwood, Ariz., 1984-85; tchr. Maryland Sch., Phoenix, 1985-87; tchr. spl. edn. Success (Mo.) Sch., 1987—; coord. Success Sch. Substance Abuse Prevention Program, 1987—. Mem. Mo. State Tchrs. Assn., Coun. Exceptional Children. Mem. LDS Ch. Home: 10360 Highway AE Plato MO 65552-8815

OPLINGER, KATHRYN RUTH, computer specialist; b. Wadsworth, Ohio, Apr. 18, 1951; d. Herman Carl and Blanche Ruth (White) Simshauser; m. Douglas E. Oplinger, July 26, 1986; children: Raymond, Karla, Kathleen, Laura Dawn. Student, Washington Coll., 1969-71, Kennesaw (Ga.) State Coll., 1988-89. Pres., chief exec. officer Dawn Enterprises, Inc., CMAS, Tiller Stewart & Co. LLC, Atlanta, 1981—; cons. mgmt. info. systems Procter & Gamble, Atlanta, 1989—, Arthur Andersen, USA, Peat Marwick, Guam, others; software expert, programmer Novell Network & Acctg.; spokesperson, designer Saks Fifth Ave, nationwide, 1981-86. Firestone Found. scholar, 1969. Mem. NAFE, Am. Bus. Women's Assn., Lions Internat. (pres. Woodstock, Ga. chpt. 1986-87). Republican. Methodist. Office: Dawn Enterprises care CMAS Tiller Stewart & Co LLC 780 Johnson Ferry Rd NE Ste 325 Atlanta GA 30342-1434

OPPENHEIM, LOIS HECHT, political science educator; b. N.Y.C., Feb. 15, 1948; d. Milton and Ruth (Berman) Hecht; m. Michael Oppenheim, June, 1970 (div. Jan. 1991); children: Amy Barbara, Benjamin Aaron. BA with highest honors, U. Rochester, 1969; MA, Washington U., St. Louis, 1972, PhD, 1980. Instr. polit. sci. Washington U., 1972; vis. rschr. Facultad Latinoamericana de las Ciencias Sociales, Santiago, Chile, 1972-73; rsch. asst. U. Iowa, Iowa City, 1975-76; instr. Whittier (Calif.) Coll., 1976-80, asst. prof., 1980-84, assoc. prof., 1984-88, prof. polit. sci., 1988-93; prof. polit. sci. U. Judaism, L.A., 1993—; vis. rschr. Program in Labor Econs., Santiago, 1987; dept. head Whittier Coll., 1987-88; head Latin Am. Studies Com., 1985-91; dir.-in-residence Danish Internat. Studies Program U. Copenhagen, 1988; vis. prof. U. Judaism, 1991-93, dept. head, 1991—, head Com. on Acad. Pers., 1994-95; head Latin Am. Studies Com. So. Calif. Consortium on Internat. Studies, 1989—; field work in Spain, Cuba, Mex., Nicaragua, El Salvador, Brazil, Denmark. Author: Politics in Chile: Democracy, Authoritarianism, and the Search for Development, 1993 (Outstanding Acad. Book Choice mag., 1995); editor book on cross-nat. gender strategies for representation, 1996; coordinating editor L.Am. Perspectives, 1984-89, issue editor, 1991; issue editor Rev. Latin Am. Studies, 1988; contbr. articles to profl. jours. Grace and Henry Doherty fellow L.Am., 1972-73, John and Dora Haynes fellow, 1981, 82; grantee NEH, 1983, 95, grantee NSF, 1987-89; Fulbright rschr., Brazil, 1984. Mem. Internat. Studies Assn., Am. Polit. Sci. Assn., Assn. Third World Studies, Brazilian Studies Assn., L.Am. Jewish Studies Assn., L.Am. Studies Assn., Asociacion Chilena de Ciencia Politica, Western Polit. Sci. Assn., Pacific Coast Coun. on L.Am. Studies (v.p. 1985, pres. 1986, exec. com. 1987, 90—, bd. govs. 1990—), Phi Beta Kappa, Pi Sigma Alpha. Jewish. Office: Dept Polit Sci Sunny and Isadore Familian Campus U Judaism Coll Arts and Scs 15600 Mulholland Dr Los Angeles CA 90077*

OPPENHEIMER, SONYA, advertising agency executive, graphic designer; b. Linden, N.J., Sept. 4, 1936; d. George and Lydia (Clark) Wein; m. Alfred Oppenheimer, Nov. 21, 1965; children: John Jacob, Simone Ayna. Student, Boston U., 1954-56, Thomas Edison State Coll., 1991; BA in Humanities, 1996. Disc jockey, copywriter Sta. WAUG, Augusta, Ga., 1956-57; copy and continuity writer Sta. WQXI, Atlanta, 1957-58; columnist, feature writer Fair Lawn (N.J.) News Beacon, 1962-63; copy and pub. rels. writer Park Advt., Elizabeth, N.J., 1963-65; copy chief Botany Industries, N.Y.C., 1965-67; freelance feature and copy writer A&S, Boston Globe, Cranford Chronicle, 1967-69; pres. Sonya Oppenheimer Advt., Randolph, N.J., 1969—. Bd. dirs. Holistic Alliance Internat., Denville, N.J., 1991—; mem. Sisterhood, Morristown Jewish Cmty. Ctr. Recipient 3 gold awards Advt. and Pub. Rels. Assn. N.J., 1991, 92. Mem. NOW, Internat. Women's Writing Guild, N.J. Advt. Club, Hadassah. Home and Office: 100 Radtke Rd Randolph NJ 07869

OPPENHEIMER, SUZI, state senator; b. N.Y.C., Dec. 13, 1934; d. Alfred Elihu Rosenhirsch and Blanche (Schoen) O.; m. Martin J. Oppenheimer, July 3, 1960; children: Marcy, Evan, Josh, Alexandra. BA in Econs., Conn. Coll. for Women, 1956; MBA, Columbia U., 1958. Security analyst McDonnell & Co., N.Y.C., 1958-60, L.F. Rothschild Co., N.Y.C., 1960-63; mayor Village of Mamaroneck, N.Y., 1977-85; mem. N.Y. State Senate, Albany, 1985—; ranking mem. transp. com., mem. fin., edn., environ. conservation, consumer protection and drugs com., chmn. Senate Dem. Task Force on Women's Issues, treas. Legis. Women's Caucus, pres. Senate Club. Former pres. Mamaroneck LWV, Westchester County Mcpl. Ofcls. Assn., Westchester Mcpl. Planning Fedn. Recipient Humanitarian Svc. award Am. Jewish Com., 1988, Legis. Leadership award Young Adult Inst., 1988, Legis. award Westchester Irish Com., 1988, Hon. Svc. award Vis. Nurses Svcs., 1989, Humanitarian Svc. award Project Family, 1990, Meritorious Svc. award N.Y. State Assn. Counties, 1990, Friend of Edn. award N.Y. State United Tchrs., 1991; honoree Windward Sch. Ann. Dinner, 1992; named Legislator of Yr., N.Y. State Women's Press Club. Democrat. Jewish. Dist Office: 16 School St Rye NY 10580

OPPENHEIM-SCHREINER, ELISSA, composer; b. N.Y.C., July 12, 1934; d. Gustave Denny and Birdie (Horn) Oppenheim; m. Leslie Marvin Schreiner, Jan. 22, 1956; children: Gary Nevin Schreiner, Robin Schreiner-Kroll. BS in Music, Hunter Coll., 1956. pvt. music tchr., Crestwood, N.Y., 1960—. Composer: (TV special) Sneakers, 1987-88 (Emmy award 1988); composer, producer: Let's Celebrate Hanukkah, 1991, Let's Celebrate Passover, 1993, Let's Celebrate Christmas, 1993. Tchr. music YWCA, Ridgewood, N.J., 1995, 96; composer music Temple Emanuel, 1996. Mem. ASCAP (awards 1978-95), NAATAS, Dramatists Guild, NARAS.

OPPLIGER, PEARL LAVIOLETTE, alcohol and drug abuse services professional; b. Barre, Vt., Aug. 16, 1942; d. Roland Bernard Sr. and Mae C. (Bouley) Laviolette; m. William Gregory Wotschak, Sept. 8, 1962 (div. Feb. 1983); children: Robin Lee Hillier, Rene Beth Greff, Rana Mae Wotschak; m. Edward Lee Oppliger, Aug. 16, 1988. BSW, Bowling Green State U., 1986; MSW, Ohio State U., 1995, Ohio State U., 1995. Lic. social worker, Ohio, CCDC III, Ohio. Sec. Ohio State U., Columbus, 1964-66; hostess Welcome Wagon, Bowling Green, Ohio, 1975-76; owner, mgr. children's clothing store Rhymes 'n' Reasons, Bowling Green, 1976-84; bookkeeper Friendly Ice Cream Inc., Bowling Green, 1979-80; sales clk. Wilson's Shoe Store, Bowling Green, 1984-85; alcoholism counselor Wood County Coun. on Alcoholism and Drug Abuse, Inc., Bowling Green, 1985-86, family counselor, 1986, supr., 1986-90, dir. recovery svcs., 1990—; adj. instr. in social work Bowling Green State U., 1988—; co-facilitator Parents Helping Parents, Bowling Green, 1990-95. Coun. mem.-at-large City of Bowling Green, 1990-93, mem. planning commn., 1988-89, asst. chmn. Bowling Green Rep. Club, 1989-91, chmn. 1991-92; co-founder Downtown Bus. Assn., Bowling Green, 1980-82; sec. Bowling Green Housing Agy., 1994—. Am. Bus. Women's Assn. scholar. Mem. AAUW (v.p. mem. com. Bowling Green br. 1991-93, Outstanding Woman in Cmty. Work 1990, 96), NASW, Phi Kappa Phi. Roman Catholic. Home: 505 Donbar Bowling Green OH 43402-1819 Office: Wood County Coun Alcoholism 320 W Gypsy Lane Rd Bowling Green OH 43402-4506

O'QUIN, BRENDA GAIL, juvenile advocate; b. Brownwood, Tex., Dec. 2, 1947; d. Pat O'Nell and Othell E. (Cantwell) Dutton; m. Alex McEachern, Aug. 5, 1969 (div. 1979); children: Jason, Michael; m. William O'Quin, June 7, 1985; children: Shannon, David. BA, North Tex. State U., 1969. Adv. for at-risk youth Tarrant County, Ft. Worth, Tex., 1992—. Prodr.: (video) Face to Face (Addy award, Cmty. Edn. award LWV). V.p. Violence Intervention/Prevention Coalition; co-chpt. leader Parents of Murdered Children; founder Katy & Mike Found.; active gang task force com. Citizen's Crime Commn.; pres. Nolan Jr. H.S. Parent Club, Ft. Worth, 1988; pres. bd. trustees, chairperson substance abuse task force Nolan H.S., 1990. Home: 7601 Willowood Ct Fort Worth TX 76112-5434 Office: Tarrant County Advocate Program 2826 E Rosedale St Fort Worth TX 76105-1431

ORAN, ELAINE SURICK, physicist, engineer; b. Rome, Ga.; d. Herman E. and Bessye R. (Kolker) Surick; m. Daniel Hirsh Oran, Feb. 1, 1969. AB, Bryn Mawr Coll., 1966; MPh, Yale U., 1968, PhD, 1972. Rsch. physicist Naval Rsch. Lab., Washington, 1972-76, supervisory rsch. physicist, 1976-88, sr. scientist reactive flow physics, 1988—; head Ctr. for Reactive Flow and Dynamical Systems, 1985-87; mem. adv. bd. NSF; cons. to U.S. govt., agys., NATO. Author: Numerical Simulation of Reactive Flow, 1987, Numerical Approaches to Combustion Modeling, 1991. Assoc. editor Jour. Computational Physics; mem. adv. bd. Computers in Physics; editl. bd. Prog. Ener. Comb. Sci., Combustion and Flame; contbr. numerous articles to profl. jours., chpts. to books. Recipient Arthur S. Flemming award, 1979, Women in Sci. and Engring. award, 1988; grantee USN, NASA, USAF, Advanced Rsch. Projects Agy. Mem. Aero. Adv. Coun. NASA, 1995—. Fellow AIAA (pubs. com. 1986—, v.p. publs. 1993—), Am. Phys. Soc. (exec. com. fluid dynamics divsn. 1986, 88, exec. com. computational physics 1989—, chair 1991-92); mem. AAAS, Am. Inst. Aeronautics and Astronautics, Am. Phys. Soc., Am. Geophys. Union, Combustion Inst. (bd. dirs. 1990—), Internat. Colloquium Dynamic Energy Systems (bd. dirs. 1989—), Sigma Xi. Office: Naval Rsch Lab Code 6404 # 6004 Washington DC 20011

ORAN, GILDA M., education educator; b. Miami, May 21, 1955; d. Marshall C. and Anita (Miller) O.; m. Bradley H. Saperstein, June 18, 1992; children: Daniel, Naomi, Gabriel. BA, U. Toronto, Ont., 1975; MEd, U. Miami, 1976, EdD, 1990. Cert. lang. profl., Fla., Pa. Early childhood educator Hebrew Acad. of Greater Miami, Miami Beach, Fla., 1977-85; Judaica tchr. Hebrew H.S., Ft. Lauderdale, Fla., 1984-85; prin., Sunday Sch. tchr. Beth Shalom Sunday Sch., Hollywood, Fla., 1981-89; fgn. lang. tchr. Hollywood Hills H.S., Hollywood, 1984-88; instr. U. Miami, 1988-90; asst. prof. Bloomsburg (Pa.) U., 1990—; polit. action chmn. Nat. Network of Early Lang. Learning, Washington, 1993-95. Contbr. articles to profl. jours. Active children's libr. program Dauphin County Libr., Harrisburg, Pa., 1995, Dynamic Learning/FLES Meteorology Fgn. Lang. Assocs., 1991—, All About Chanukah, Harrisburg Area Schs., 1993—, All Around the Jewish Yr., 1993—; bd. dirs. Kesher Israel Synagogue, 1995—, United Hebrew Inst., 1991-94; v.p. Kesher Israel Sisterhood, 1995—; pres. chpt. B'nai Brith Women, 1982-84, pres. dist. 1984-86. Grantee Ctr. for Rural Studies, Harrisburg, 1994, 95, Pa. Campus Compact, Harrisburg, 1994, Bloomsburg Found., Pa., 1993-95. Democrat. Jewish. Home: 3540 Green St Harrisburg PA 17110 Office: Bloomsburg Univ McCormick 2125 Bloomsburg PA 17815

ORAV, HELLE REISSAR, retired dentist; b. Tartu, Estonia, July 10, 1925; came to U.S., 1949, naturalized, 1954; d. Johan and Adele Johanna (Minski)

Reissar; m. Arnold Orav, May 30, 1952; children: Ilmar Erik, Hillar Thomas. Student Friedrich Alexander U., Erlangen, West Germany, 1946-49; DDS, NYU, 1952. Practice dentistry, N.Y.C., 1952, 60, 62, 68, Valencia, Venezuela, 1953-68. Counselor, Red Cross, Valencia, 1954-55; past mem. Rotary Ladies Republican. Lutheran. Clubs: Country of Maracaibo (Venezuela); Palm Beach Polo and Country (Fla.); Korp Filiae Patriae (N.Y.C.). Avocations: Pre-Colombian art, bridge, travel, swimming, reading. Address: 44 Cocoanut Row Palm Beach FL 33480-4005

ORBACH, EVELYN, artistic director; b. N.Y.C., July 25, 1932; d. Jacob and Esther (Schiller) Leisner; m. Harold Orbach, June 24, 1951; children: Richard, Sharon, Judith, Lila. Student, Bklyn. Coll., 1949-52. Freelance actress, dir. theatres, film and TV N.Y.C., 1951-56, 84-85, Detroit, 1962-90; dir. Group Theatre, Tulsa, 1958-62; dir. broadcasting Jewish Cmty. Coun., Detroit, 1965-76; v.p., film dir. Station 12, Detroit, 1977-81; artistic dir. Jewish Ensemble Theatre, Detroit, 1989—; chair women's com. AFTRA/SAG, Detroit, 1980-90; bd. dirs. AFTRA, Detroit, 1986-96; chair Nat. Coun. Jewish Theatres, N.Y., 1995-96; v.p. Mich. Allied Profl. Theatres, 1996. Recipient Gabriel award Cath. Broadcasters of Am., 1970, Lee Hills award for Disting. Career Svc., Detroit Free Press, 1995; named for Best Yr. Round Broadcasting, Coun. Jewish Fedns. and Welfare Funds, N.Y., 1974, 75, Excellence in a Major Market, Nat. Assn. TV Program Execs., 1976. Office: Jewish Ensemble Theatre 6600 W Maple Rd West Bloomfield MI 48322-3003

ORD, LINDA BANKS, artist; b. Provo, Utah, May 24, 1947; d. Willis Merrill and Phyllis (Clark) Banks; m. Kenneth Stephen Ord, Sept. 3, 1971; children: Jason, Justin, Kristin. BS, Brigham Young U., 1970; BFA, U. Mich., 1987; MA, Wayne State U., 1990. Asst. prof. Sch. Art U. Mich., Ann Arbor, 1994—; juror Southeastern Mich. Scholastic Art Award Competition, Pontiac, 1992, Scarab Club Watercolor Exhbn., Detroit, 1991, Women in Art Nat. Exhbn., Farmington Hills, Mich., 1991, U. Mich. Alumni Exhbn., 1989-90. One-woman shows Atrium Gallery, Mich., 1990, 91; group shows include Am. Coll., Bryn Mawr, Pa., Riverside (Calif.) Art Mus., Kirkpatrick Mus., Oklahoma City, Montgomery (Ala.) Mus. Fine Arts, Columbus (Ga.) Mus., Brigham Young U., Provo, Utah, Kresge Art Mus., Lansing, Mich., U. Mich., Ann Arbor, Detroit Inst. Arts, Kirkpatrick Ctr. Mus. Complex, Oklahoma City, 1994, Riverside (Calif.) Art Mus., 1995, San Bernadino County Mus., Redlands, Calif., 1996; works in many pvt. and pub. collections including Kelly Svcs., Troy, Mich., FHP Internat., Fountain Valley, Calif., Swords Into Plowshares Gallery, Detroit; work included in book The Artistic Touch, 1995. Chairperson nat. giving fund Sch. Art, U. Mich., 1993; Sch. Art rep. Coun. Alumni Socs., U. Mich., 1992—. Recipient 1st Pl. award Swords Into Plowshares Internat. Exhbn., Detroit, 1989, Silver award Ga. Watercolor Soc. Internat. Exhbn., 1991, Pres.'s award Watercolor Okla. Nat. Exhbn., Oklahoma City, 1992, Flint Jour. award Buckham Gallery Nat. Exhbn., 1993, Ochs Meml. award N.E. Watercolor Soc. Nat. Exhbn., Goshen, N.Y., 1993, Color Q award Ga. Watercolor Soc., 1994, St. Cuthberts award Tex. Watercolor Soc., 1996, many state and nat. painting awards. Mem. U. Mich. Alumni Assn. (bd. dirs. 1992—, Sch. Art rep.), U. Mich. Sch. Art Alumni Soc. (bd. dirs. 1989-91, pres.), Mich. Watercolor Soc. (chairperson 1992-93, bd. dirs. adv. 1993-94).

ORDWAY, ELLEN, biology educator, entomology researcher; b. N.Y.C., Nov. 8, 1927; d. Samuel Hanson and Anna (Wheatland) O. B.A., Wheaton Coll., Mass., 1950; M.S., Cornell U., 1955; Ph.D., U. Kans., 1965. Field asst. N.Y. Zool. Soc., N.Y.C., 1950-52; research asst. Am. Mus. Natural History, N.Y.C., 1955-57; teaching asst. U. Kans., Lawrence, 1957-61, research asst., 1959-65; asst. prof. U. Minn., Morris, 1965-70, assoc. prof. biology, 1970-85, prof., 1986—; cooperator and cons. U.S. Dept. Agr. Bee Research Lab., Tucson, Ariz., 1971, 1983. Contbr. articles to sci. jours. Mgr. preserves Nature Conservancy, Mpls., 1975—; lectr. Morris area service clubs, 1972—. Mem. Ecol. Soc. Am., Entomol. Soc. Am., Soc. Systematic Biology, Soc. Study Evolution, Kans. Entomol. Soc., Internat. Bee Research Assn., AAAS, AAUP (v.p. 1975-76, sec.-treas. 1971-73 Morris chpt.), Sigma Xi, Sigma Delta Epsilon. Episcopalian. Avocations: travel, photography, raquetball, exploring natural environments, wilderness, areas, etc. Office: U Minn Div Sci And Math Morris MN 56267

O'REILLY, FRANCES LOUISE, academic administrator; b. Great Falls, Mont., Feb. 20, 1947; d. Francis Joseph and Bernadine Madeline (DeRose) O'R. BA in Sociology and English, Carroll Coll., 1969; MBA, U. Mont., 1977. Head Start tchr. Rocky Mountain Devel. Coun., Helena, Mont., 1969, social svc. dir. Head Start, 1970-76; rsch. asst. U. Mont., Missoula, 1976, teaching asst., 1976-77; broker, owner Manning & O'Reilly Realty Inc., Great Falls, 1977-81; dir. residence hall Carroll Coll., Helena, 1981—; dir. residential life Carroll Coll., 1992—, coord. residential life, 1991-92, adj. faculty mem. dept. bus. acctg. & econs., 1982-86, dept. communications, 1991—, dir. summer programs, 1983—, mem. adv. bd. student affairs com., 1983—; social work cons. Office Children Devel. Region #8, Denver, 1970-76; supr. social work practicums Head Start Rocky Mountain Devel. Coun., 1970-76. Vol. Diabetes Found., Helena, 1993-94, various polit. campaigns, Helena, 1993-94. Mem. Mont. Assn. Student Affairs, Beta Gamma Sigma. Office: Carroll Coll Box 64 OConnell Hall Helena MT 59625

ORENS, ELAINE FRANCES, artist, printmaker; b. N.Y.C., July 18, 1929; d. Louis and Jennie (Diamond) Cohen; m. Perry Arnold Orens, Dec. 26, 1953; children: Matthew, Jonathan, Emily. BA, Hunter Coll., 1951; MA, C. W. Post Coll., 1978. Dir. printmaking workshop Elaine Orens Studio, Great Neck, N.Y., 1975—; illustrator: (textbook) Intaglio Printmaking Techniques. Exhibited in group shows U. Ark., Palazzo Vecchio, Florence, Italy, Hunterdon Mus., Lever House, N.Y., Jacob Javits Fed. Bldg., N.Y., Guild Hall, N.Y., Viridian Gallery, N.Y., Queens Mus., N.Y., Adelphi U., N.Y., Parrish Art Mus., N.Y., Nassau C.C., N.Y., Nat. Acad. Galleries, N.Y., Nat. Arts Club, N.Y., Hunter Coll., N.Y.; included in permanent collection Jane Voorhees Zimmerli Mus., Hunter Coll., N.Y., Adelphi U., N.Y., Queensboro C.C., N.Y., Juley Photographic Collections, Smithsonian Instn., Washington. Recipient Bronze award in graphics Fine Arts Mus., Roslyn, N.Y., 1989, St. Gaudens award for fine draftsmanship Art Students League, Pratt Inst. prize for graphics; William Graf scholar in fine arts. Mem. Audubon Artists (Silver medal 1973, Louis Lozowick award 1995), Nat. Assn. Women Artists Inc. (travel printmaking chair 1991-96, Medal of Honor Printmaking 1982, 8 other awards for graphics 1971-95).

ORESKES, SUSAN, private school educator; b. N.Y.C., May 24, 1930; d. Morris and Sarah (Rudner) Nagin; m. Irwin Oreskes, June 19, 1949; children: Michael, Daniel, Naomi, Rebecca. BA, Queens Coll., 1952; dance student, Eddie Torres Sch., Manhattan, N.Y., 1984-90. Organizer Strycker's Bay Neighborhood Coun., N.Y.C., 1961-75; dir. weekly column cmty. newspaper Enlightenment Press, N.Y.C., 1975-85; assoc. tchr. Riverside Ch. Weekday Sch., N.Y.C., 1985-95. Organizer, v.p. F.D.R.-Woodrow Wilson Polit. Club, Manhattan, 1961-71; organizer Hey Brother Coffee House, 1968—. Democrat. Jewish. Home: 670 W End Ave New York NY 10025-7313

ORGAN, JOAN E., education educator, school counselor, historian; b. Youngstown, Ohio, May 13, 1951; d. Richard Crosby and Mary Helen (Cooper) O.; m. Thomas Joseph Fleming, Dec. 27, 1976 (div. July 1989); children: Julie Patricia, Geoffrey Thomas. BA in English Lit., St. Mary's Coll., Notre Dame, Ind., 1973; MS in Edn. in Guidance and Counseling, Youngstown State U., 1987, MA in Am. History, 1989; PhD in History, Case Western Res. U., 1996. Cert. 7-12 English tchr., Ohio; registered profl. sch. counselor; nat. cert. counselor. Admissions counselor St. Mary's Coll., 1973-76; tchr. English, Boardman (Ohio) H.S., 1976-79; tchr. English, dir. admissions Villa Maria (Pa.) H.S., 1979-85; sch. counselor Cardinal Mooney H.S., Youngstown, 1986-89; instr. edn. John Carroll U., Cleve., 1992-94; instr. founds. of edn. Cleve. State U., 1993—; sch. counselor Cleveland Heights-University Heights (Ohio) H.S., 1996—; vis. instr. history Oberlin (Ohio) Coll., 1996—; mem. cmty. adv. bd. Western Res. Hist. Soc., Cleve., 1994—. Democrat. Mem. United Ch. of Christ. Home: 16050 Henley Rd East Cleveland OH 44112

ORITSKY, MIMI, artist, educator; b. Reading, Pa., Aug. 14, 1950; d. Herbert and Marcia (Sarna) O. Student, Phila. Coll. Art, 1968-70; BFA, Md. Inst. Coll. Art, 1975; MFA, U. Pa., 1979. Artist, supr. subway mural projects Crisis Intervention Network, Phila., 1978-83; instr. painting U. Arts, Phila., 1984, 89-93, Abington Art Ctr., Jenkintown, Pa., 1989—, Main Line Art Ctr., Haverford, Pa., 1993—. One-woman shows include Gross McCleaf Gallery, 1980-82, Callowhill Art Gallery, Reading, Pa., Amos Eno Gallery, N.Y.C., 1986, 89, 91, 94, 96, Hahnemann U. Gallery, Phila.,1 988, Kaufmann Gallery, Shippensburg, Pa., 1989, Kimberton (Pa.) Gallery, 1990, Rittenhouse Galleries, Phila., 1992-94; group exhbns. include Current Representational Painting in Phila., 1980, Gross McCleaf Gallery, 1980-82. Recipient Purchase award Pa. Coun. Arts/Beaver Coll., 1983, Reading Pub. Mus., 1984; fellow Artists for Environment Found., 1980, Millay Colony for Arts, 1983. Mem. Coll. Art Assn.

ORLECK, ANNELISE, historian, educator; b. Bklyn., Jan. 22, 1959; d. Norman and Thelma O.; life ptnr. Alexis Jetter. BA, Evergreen State Coll., 1979; PhD, NYU, 1989. Lectr. history Princeton (N.J.) Univ., 1989-90; asst. prof. history Dartmouth Coll., Hanover, N.H., 1990—. Author: Common Sense and a Little Fire: Women and Working-Class Politics in the United States, 1900-1965, 1995; co-editor: (with Alexis Jetter and Diana Taylor) Radicalizing Motherhood: Activist Voices From Left to Right, 1996. Coord. Mayor's Task Force on Holocaust, N.Y.C., 1981. Mem. Orgn. Am. Historians, Berkshire Conf. Women Historians (mem. coordinating com. on women in hist. profession). Home: HCR 73 Box 33 Thetford Center VT 05075*

ORLIK, CHRISTINA BEAR, music educator; b. Detroit, Nov. 10, 1945; d. Robert William and Olive Marie (Evans) Bear; m. Peter Blythe Orlik, Aug. 18, 1967; children: Darcy Anne, Blaine Truen. BS in Edn., Wayne State U., 1967, MS in Edn., 1969. Tchr. clarinet pvt. practice, Detroit, 1961-69; elem. band dir. City Recreation Dept., Troy, Mich, 1964-67; dir. bands Crary Jr. High Sch., Waterford, Mich, 1967-69; instr. woodwind pvt. practice, Mt. Pleasant, Mich, 1970-84; dir. bands Montabella Jr. High Sch., Blanchard, Mich, 1974-76; substitute tchr. Mt. Pleasant Schs., 1976-84, libr. media profl., 1984-85, tchr. gen. music, 1985—, orch. dir., 1987—; part-time instr. Cen. Mich. U. Tchr. Edn., 1989-91; organizing mem., mgr. Cen. Mich. Cmty. Band, Mt. Pleasant, 1973-75; clarinetist/bassoonist Alma (Mich.) Symphony Orch., 1973-86, Eddy Concert Band, Saginaw, Mich., 1973—. Tchr. Sunday sch. St. Andrew's Episcopal Ch., Clawson, Mich., 1966-67; treas., mem. chair LWV, Mt. Pleasant, 1972-73; chair Child Care Adv. Com., Mt. Pleasant, 1973-74. Mem. Am. String Tchrs. Assn. (program review grantee 1990), Mich. Edn. Assn., Mich. Sch. Band & Orch. Assn., Music Educator's Nat. Conf.. Home: 613 Kane St Mount Pleasant MI 48858-1949 Office: West Intermediate Sch 440 S Bradley Rd Mount Pleasant MI 48858-3052

ORME, MELISSA EMILY, mechanical engineering educator; b. Glendale, Calif., Mar. 12, 1961; d. Myrl Eugene and Geraldine Irene (Schmuck) O.; m. Vasilis Zissis Marmarelis, Mar. 12, 1989. BS, U. So. Calif., L.A., 1984, MS, 1985, PhD, 1989. Rsch. asst. prof. U. So. Calif., 1990-93; asst. prof. U. Calif., Irvine, 1993—; panel reviewer NSF, Arlington, Va., 1993—; cons. MPM Corp., Boston, 1993—. Contbr. articles to profl. jours. Recipient Young Investigator award NSF, 1994, Arch T. Colwell Merit award SAE, 1994. Mem. AAUW, AIAA, ASME, Am. Phys. Soc., Minerals, Metals and Materials Soc. Office: U Calif Irvine CA 92717-3975

ORNDOFF, ELIZABETH CARLSON, retired reference librarian, educator; b. Spearville, Kans., Mar. 28, 1918; d. Carl Edward and Laura Rebecca (Pine) Carlson; m. John Delbert Orndoff, Dec. 26, 1942; children: Barbara Kay Orndoff Fazal, David Keith, Richard Lee. BA in Sociology, U. Colo., 1940, BEd, 1940; postgrad., U. So. Calif., 1941. Lic. pvt. pilot; cert. tchr. sociology. Head coll. librarian Trinidad (Colo.) State Jr. Coll., 1940-42, tchr. sociology, 1941-42; reference librarian Los Alamos (N.Mex.) Pub. Libr., 1963-73. Editor: (non-fiction book) All of These Things, 1974. Tchr. Sunday sch. Meth. Ch., Trinidad, 1940-41; den mother Boy Scouts Am., Los Alamos, 1953-55; leader Girl Scouts U.S.A., Los Alamos, 1955-56; charter mem. United Ch. Los Alamos, 1947—, historian, 1994, 95; active Friends Los Alamos Pub. Libr., 1989-90, 94—, Habitat for Humanity, 1994—; active Los Alamos Retirement Ctr., Inc., Blood Mobile, Meals on Wheels, Svcs. and Aid for the Relief of the Poor, Inc., 1993—. Mem. AAUW (life), ALA, United Ostomy Assn., U. Colo. Alumni Assn., Sr. Citizens, Los Alamos Ski Club, Crohn's Colitis Found. Am., Am. Assn. Ret. Tchrs. Democrat. Home: 997-B 48th St Los Alamos NM 87544-1831

O'ROURKE, JOANNE A., state legislator; b. Manchester, N.H., Sept. 4, 1939; m. Thomas F. O'Rourke; 3 children. Attended, N.H. Coll. Formerly with New Eng. Telephone and Telegraph Co.; mem. N.H. Ho. of Reps., 1983—; asst. minority leader, 1985-90; Dem. whip N.H. Ho. of Reps., 1990-95, mem. appropriations com.; mem. rules com.; mem. state-fed. rels. com., mem. fin. com., legis. orientation com., performance audit & oversight com., 1995—, asst. dep. Dem. leader, 1995. Selectman ward three City of Manchester, 1972-77; bd. dirs. Greater Manchester Mental Health, 1985-91, So. N.H. Svcs., 1985—; co-chmn. State Dem. Policy Coun., 1985-87; chmn. Manchester Legis. Del., 1986-92, Dem. City Com., 1992—; mem. exec. com. Hillsborough County, 1986; vice chmn. Coun. State Govt. Intergovtl. Affairs, 1988, chmn., 1989. Democrat. Roman Catholic. Home: 91 Harrison St Manchester NH 03104-3611 Office: NH Ho of Reps State House Concord NH 03301*

O'ROURKE, MARGARET MARY, lawyer, political activist; b. East Orange, N.J., Dec. 20, 1947; d. Henry George and Mary Margaret (Walsh) Buckwalter; children: Richard A. Falkenrath, Mary Frances Falkenrath, Emma O'Rourke-Powell. BA in Econs. and Journalism, Calif. State U., Hayward, 1975; JD, Golden Gate U., 1980. Tchg. and mediator credential. Bookkeeper, asst. mgr. R and J Liquors, Hayward, 1976-78; paralegal Legal Svcs. Alameda County, Hayward, 1978-80; tchr. Coll. of Redwoods, Ft. Bragg, Calif., 1981-82; pvt. practice Mendocino, Calif., 1981—. Chair Mendocino Ctr. Bias Commn., 1990—; bd. dirs., mem. Mendocino Land Trust, 1996. Mem. NOW, Nat. Women's Polit. Caucus, Calif. Women's Lawyers, Mendocino Women's Bar Assn. (pres., founder). Office: 45160 Main St Mendocino CA 95460-0283

O'ROURKE, SUZAN MARIE, secondary education educator; b. Evergreen Park, Ill., Sept. 19, 1951. BA in English, St. Joseph's Coll., Rensselaer, Ind., 1972. Cert. 6-12 lang. arts tchr., Ill. Substitute tchr. Mother McAuley H.S., Chgo., 1972; tchr. St. Margaret of Scotland Sch., Chgo., 1973-75; tchr. lang. arts Park Jr. H.S., La Grange, Ill., 1975-77, St. Barnabas Grammar Sch., Chgo., 1977-80, St. Thomas More Grammar Sch., Chgo., 1980—. Recipient Heart of Sch. award St. Thomas More Grammar Sch.-Archdiocese of Chgo., 1993. Mem. ASCD, Nat. Coun. Tchrs. English, Nat. Cath. Edn. Assn. (tchr. assoc.). Roman Catholic. Office: St Thomas More Grammar Sch 8130 S California Ave Chicago IL 60652-2716

ORPHANIDES, NORA CHARLOTTE, ballet educator; b. N.Y.C., June 4, 1951; d. M.T. and Mary Elsie (Tilly) Feffer; m. James Mark Orphanides, July 1, 1972; children: Mark, Elaine, Jennine. BA, CUNY, 1973; student, Joffrey Ballet Sch., N.Y.C., 1970-75; postgrad., Princeton Ballet Sch., 1976-86. Cert. speech and hearing handicapped tchr. Sr. sales assoc. Met. Mus. Art, N.Y.C., 1970-86; membership asst. Patrons Lounge, M.M.A., N.Y.C., 1987—; mem. faculty Princeton (N.J.) Ballet Sch., 1983—, trustee emeritus, 1992—. Mem. cast Princeton Ballet ann. Nutcracker, 1985-90, now Am. Repertory Ballet Co., 1993—; appeared in Romeo & Juliet, 1995-96. Fundraising gala chmn. Princeton Ballet, 1985, 86, 91-92, chmn. spl. events, 1987—, trustee, 1986—, chmn. Nutcracker benefit, 1990—, Dracula benefit, 1991; vol. libr. Plainsboro (N.J.) Free Libr., 1985; program solicitation chmn. to benefit Princeton Med. Ctr., 1988, T-shirt chmn. benefit, 1990-91, 96, publicity chmn. ann. June Fete, 1992; mem. worship and arts commn. Nassau Presbyn. Ch., 1989, 90, dinner chmn. Bach Music Festival, 1989, Cambridge Singers, 1990; vol. Nat. Hdqrs. Recording for the Blind, 1991-93; trustee Princeton Youth Fund, 1991-92; dinner chmn. Nassau Ch. Music Festival, 1992, Handel Festival, Nassau Ch., 1993, Princeton Chamber Symphony, 1993; vol. Cmty. Park Sch. Libr., 1992-93; hon. chmn. Princeton Ballet Gala, 1993; chmn. Christmas Boutique, Princeton Med. Ctr., 1993; trustee, Princeton Med. Ctr. Auxilary Bd., 1992—, pres. 1997—, trustee 1995—. Democrat. Home: 35 Brearly Rd Princeton NJ 08540-6767 Office: 301 N Harrison St Princeton NJ 08540

ORR, ADRIANA PANNEVIS, retired librarian; b. Albertson, N.Y., Sept. 30, 1923; d. Adrian Jacobus and Clara (Edgar) Pannevis; m. Oliver Hamilton Orr Jr., Feb. 15, 1956. AB, Elmira Coll., 1944; MSLS, U. N.C., 1958; postgrad., U Md., 1967-68. Tchr. Wisner (Nebr.) H.S., 1944-45; tchr., libr. Downsville (N.Y.) Ctrl. H.S., 1945-48, Lago Cmty. Sch., Aruba, 1948-53; reference libr. U. N.C., Chapel Hill, 1953-58; Latin tchr. Josephus Daniels Jr. H.S., Raleigh, N.C., 1958-59; textiles libr. N.C. State U., Raleigh, 1959-65; reference libr. U.S. Dept. Transportation, Washington, 1966-70; libr. rschr. Oxford English Dictionary, Washington, 1966-90; ret. Active Chapel Hill Hist. Soc., 1991—, Chapel Hill Preservation Soc., 1991—. Methodist. Home: 434 W Cameron Ave Chapel Hill NC 27516

ORR, CAROL WALLACE, book publishing executive; b. Newton, Mass., Dec. 17, 1933; d. Barton Stuart Wallace and Mary (Blanthorne) Stigler; children: Brett Amanda, Ross Wallace. Student, Boston U., 1951-53; BA, Douglass Coll., 1966. Successively permissions mgr., paperback editor, reprint editor, asst. to assoc. dir. Princeton (N.J.) U. Press, 1966-75, exec. asst. to dir. then asst. dir., 1975-78; dir. U. Tenn. Press., Knoxville, 1978-91; aerobics instr., freelance editor, 1992—. Mem. editorial bd. Book Rsch. Quar., 1988-92; contbr. articles to Scholarly Pub. jour., 1974-86. Recipient Book Woman award Women's Nat. Book Assn., 1987, Disting. Career award Needham (Mass.) H.S., 1995. Mem. Assn. Am. Univ. Presses (pres. 1987-88), Internat. Assn. Scholarly Pubs. (sec.-gen. 1980-83), Women in Scholarly Pub. (first pres. 1980-81), AAUP Lang. Task Force (chair 1989-91), AAUP Golden Fluke Award Com. (chair 1984-91), Phi Beta Kappa, Phi Kappa Phi.

ORR, DOROTHY ANN, elementary physical education educator; b. Mattoon, Ill., May 2, 1953; d. William Vance and Doris Francis (Moore) O. BA, U. Mont., 1975; MA, U. Iowa, 1986. Cert. tchr. Tchr. in phys. edn. Paxson and Washington Schs., Missoula, Mont., 1976-81, Mountain View Elem. Sch., Anchorage, 1981-84, Abbott Loop Elem. Sch., Anchorage, 1985-87; tchr. expert Anchorage Sch. Dist., 1987-91; phys. edn. tchr. Ptarmigan Elem. Sch., Anchorage, 1991-92, Inlet View Elem. Sch., Anchorage, 1991-92; tchr. phys. edn. Sand Lake Elem., Anchorage, 1992-96, Kasuun Elem., Anchorage, 1996—; mem. curriculum com., Anchorage, 1981-94; sch. dist. rep. Sports Assn., Anchorage, 1978-91; mem. Seward Wellness Health Conf. Planning Team, Anchorage, 1987—; area rep. Phys. Edn. Adv. Bd., Anchorage, 1991-93. Mem. NEA, AAHPERD, Alaska Assn. Health, Phys. Edn., Recreation and Dance (pres. 1993-94, award 1994), N.W. Dist. AAHPERD (Elem. Phys. Edn. Tchr. of Yr. 1995), Anchorage Edn. Assn. (award 1994), Phi Delta Kappa, Delta Kappa Gamma (pres. 1988-92). Home: 4340 Ambler Cir Anchorage AK 99504-4697 Office: Kasuun Elem Sch 4000 E 68th Ave Anchorage AK 99504

ORR, SANDRA JANE, civic worker, pharmacist; b. Marion, Ohio, June 27, 1930; d. Lawrence Edward and Wanita Izell (Noyes) Schneider; m. Ross Moore Orr, Jr., Aug. 12, 1951; children: Sandra K. Orr Whiston, Sara L. Orr Cochrane. BS in Pharmacy, Med. Coll. Va., 1952. Pharmacist Atkiinson & Howard, Richmond, Va., 1952-54, Schneider's Walgreen Agy., Kenton, Ohio, 1954-73; part-time pharmacist Drug Svc., Bethlehem, Pa., 1954-57, Fastchnacts' Drug, Bethlehem, 1954-57. One-woman shows in oils, pastels and watercolors. Chmn. ball St. Luke's Hosp., Bethlehem, 1985, 87; bd. dirs. Hist. Bethlehem, 1988—; dir. liturgical dance 1st Presbyn. Ch., 1968, 78; instr. needlework YMCA, 1980-81; instr. movement Orff tchrs.; instr. ballet Lehigh U. football team, 1966; docent Allentown Art Mus., 1956-68, Art Goes to Sch., 1960-62. Mem. Jr. League Lehigh Valley. Republican. Presbyterian. Home: 405 High St Bethlehem PA 18018-6103

ORR, TRISHA, artist; b. Paterson, N.J., May 12, 1951; d. Robert and Elaine Winer; m. Gregory Orr, Mar. 3, 1973; children: Eliza, Sophia. Student, Sarah Lawrence Coll., 1969-71, RISD, 1971-72; BA, U. Mich., 1974; postgrad., N.Y. Studio Sch., 1978. Solo exhibits include Katharina Rich Perlow Gallery, N.Y., Main St. Gallery, Nantucket, Mass., Parkesberg (W.Va.) Art Ctr., Fayerweather Gallery U. Va. Individual Artists's Project grantee Va. Commn. Arts, 1994; Mid-Atlantic/NEA Regional Painting fellow, 1994. Mem. Phi Beta Kappa.

ORR-CAHALL, CHRISTINA, art gallery director, art historian; b. Wilkes-Barre, Pa., June 12, 1947; d. William R.A. and Anona (Snyder) Boben; m. Richard Cahall. BA magna cum laude, Mt. Holyoke Coll., 1969; MA, Yale U., 1974, MPhil, 1975, PhD, 1979. Curator of collections Norton Gallery Art, West Palm Beach, Fla., 1975-77; asst. prof. Calif. Poly. State U., San Luis Obispo, 1978-81, Disting. prof., 1981; dir. art div., chief curator Oakland (Calif.) Mus., 1981-88; chief exec. officer Corcoran Gallery Art, Washington, 1988-90; dir. Norton Mus. Art, West Palm Beach, 1990—. Author: Addison Mizner: Architect of Dreams and Realities, 1974, 2d printing, 1993, Gordon Cook, 1987, Claude Monet: Am Impression, 1993; editor: The Art of California, 1984, The American Collection at the Norton Museum of Art, 1995. Office: Norton Gallery of Art 1451 S Olive Ave West Palm Beach FL 33401-7162

ORSCHELN, SHERYL JANE, elementary school educator, art educator; b. Moberly, Mo., Nov. 21, 1948; d. Roy Allen Noel and MaryJane Ruddell Kline; m. Edward Gary Orscheln, Sept. 6, 1969; children: Eric, Karl, Emily. BAE, U. Kans., Lawrence, 1970; postgrad., U. Mo., 1990-96. Art tchr. Moberly Pub. Schs., 1970-71, Moberly Area Jr. Coll., 1978; sec. Beaufort Transfer Co., Moberly, 1983-85; art tchr. Middle Grove (Mo.) C-1 Sch., 1980-81, 87-94, St. Pius X Cath. Sch., Moberly, 1978-83, 88—. Art merit badge councilor Troop 14, Boy Scout Am., Moberly, 1986—, commr. sci. Gt. Rivers coun., 1986. Mem. Nat. Art Edn. Assn., Mo. Art Edn. Assn., Little Dixie Art Assn. (speaker 1994). Roman Catholic.

ORSINI, MYRNA J., sculptor, educator; b. Spokane, Wash., Apr. 19, 1943; d. William Joseph Finch and Barbara Jean (Hilby) Hickenbottom; m. Donald Wayne Lundquist, Mar. 31, 1962 (div. Mar. 1987); children: Laurie Jeanine Winter, Stephanie Lynne Lundquist. BA, U. Puget Sound, 1969, MA, 1974; postgrad., U. Ga., 1987. Tchr. Tacoma (Wash.) Pub. Schs., 1969-78; owner, pres. Contemporary Print Collectors, Lakewood, Wash., 1978-81, Orsini Studio, Tacoma, 1985—. Sculptor: works include Vartai symbolic gate for Ctrl. Europas Park, Vilnius, Lithuania, 1994; Menat steel and neon corp. commn. completed in Tacoma, Wash. 1995. Chair Supt.'s Supervisory Com., Tacoma, 1978-79; lobbyist Citizens for Fair Sch. Funding, Seattle, 1979; art chair Women's Pres. Coun., Tacoma, 1987-88; founder, bd. dirs. Monarch Contemporary Art Ctr., Wash. Recipient 1st pl. sculpture award Pleinair Symposium Com., Ukraine, 1992, Peron Symposium Com., Kiev, Ukraine, 1993; recognized 1st Am. sculptor to exhibit work in Ukraine, 1993; prin. works include seven monumental sculptures worldwide. Mem. N.W. Stone Sculptors Assn. (coun. leader 1989—), Pacific Gallery Artists, Internat. Sculpture Ctr., Tacoma City Club. Office: Orsini Studio 8431 Waldrick Rd Tenino WA 98589

ORSON, BARBARA TUSCHNER, actress; b. N.Y.C., May 19, 1929; d. Jonah Tuschner and Rebecca Traceman; m. Jay M. Orson, June 24, 1956; children: Beth-Diane, Theodore. Student, Dramatic Workshop, N.Y.C., 1948-50. Singer Am. Savoyards, N.Y.C., 1950-51, 53-55; actress Trinity Repertory, Providence, R.I., 1964—; founding mem. Trinity Sq. Repertory Co., Providence, 1964—. Actress Edinburgh Festival, Scotland, 1968, Am. Repertory Theatre, Cambridge, Mass., 1981-85, Williamstown (Mass.) Theatre, 1985-89, Yale Repertory Co., New Haven, Conn., 1991; appeared in: (film) Mission Hill, (TV) Theatre in America, Feating with Panthers, Life Among the Lowly and House of Mirth, (Am. premiere) The Suicide, 1980, (world premiere) Grown Ups, 1981, God's Heart, 1995; appeared in over 100 prodns. Trinity Sq. Repertory Co., Providence, 1964—. Mem. Am. Fedn. Radio and TV Artists, Screen Actors Guild, Actor's Equity Assn., Trinity Rep. Co. (founding). Home: 281 Hillside Ave Pawtucket RI 02860

ORTEGA, KAREN SUE, elementary school educator; b. Biloxi, Miss., Apr. 5, 1958; d. Paul John and Jean Frances (Hoh) Krycho; m. Frank Lee Ortega, May 23, 1987; children: Frances, Jasmin, Desiree, Alexia. BS in Edn., U. N.Mex., 1983, MA in Elem. Edn., 1988. Tchr. grade 5 Adobe Acres Elem. Sch., Albuquerque, 1984—; mem. Sch. Restructuring Coun., Albuquerque, 1991—; presenter Action Rsch. Conf., Ctr. for Tchg. Excellence, Taos, N.Mex., 1994. Action Rsch. grantee Ctr. for Tchg. Excellence, Ea. N.Mex. U., 1994. Republican. Lutheran. Home: 4308 Amherst Dr NE Albuquerque NM 87107-4840 Office: Adobe Acres Elem Sch 1724 Camino Del Valle SW Albuquerque NM 87105-6003

ORTEGA, LORRAINE G., state land office commissioner; b. Santa Fe, Apr. 4, 1940; d. Lorin A. and Aurelia (Rodriguez) Gonzales; m. Cecil R. Ortega Jr., June 17, 1961; children: Carl Michael, Nadine Ortega Wells, Carolyn L., Marilyn D. Student in bus. adminstrn., Coll. of Santa Fe, 1959, Santa Fe Bus. Coll., 1966. Various positions State of N.Mex. Health and Edn. Depts., 1958-78; dep. state dir. gov.'s svc. ctrs. Gov. King's Office, Santa Fe, 1978-82; personnel bur. chief N.Mex. State Land Office, Santa Fe, 1983-87; constituent svc. dir. Gov. King's Office, 1990-93; exec. asst. commr. N.Mex. State Land Office, 1993—. Mem. Santa Fe County steering com. for Bruce King for Gov., 1989-90, mgr. Santa Fe County office King Campaign 1989-90; N.Mex. State sec./treas. Nat. League of Postmasters Aux., 1990-93; Santa Fe County Dem. ctrl. com. mem., 1976—, State of N.Mex. Dem. ctrl. com. mem. 1976-91; dep. registrar voter registration Santa Fe County, 1975—; Santa Fe County Dem. ward chmn., Ward 48-A, precincts 24, 25, 27, 3d congrl. dist.; mem. Gov. Bruce King Inauguration Ceremonies com., 1978, 91; del. N.Mex. State Dem. Convs., 1976—; alternate del. Nat. Dem. Conv., N.Y.C., 1980; state coord. N.Mex. Queen's Pageant, Am. GI Forum, 1985. Recognized top-level position Hispanic employee in gov.'s adminstrn. by Albuquerque Hispano C. of C. and Hispanic Mag., 1991. Mem. Elks, Eagles. Democrat. Roman Catholic. Office: NMex State Land Office PO Box 1148 310 Old Santa Fe Trail Santa Fe NM 87504-1148

ORTEGO, GILDA BAEZA, librarian, information professional; b. El Paso, Tex., Mar. 29, 1952; d. Efren and Bertha (Singh) Baeza; m. Felipe de Ortego y Gasca, Dec. 21, 1986. BA, Tex. Woman's U., 1974, graduate, 1974-75; MLS, U. Tex., 1976, postgrad., 1990-93; cert., Hispanic Leadership Inst., 1988. Stack maintenance supr. El Paso Libr. U. Tex., 1974-75; pub. svcs. libr. El Paso Community Coll., 1976-77; ethnic studies libr. U. N.Mex., Albuquerque, 1977-81; br. head El Paso Pub. Libr., 1981-82; dep. head Mex.-Am. Svcs., El Paso Pub. Libr., 1982-84; libr. Mex.-Am. Studies U. Tex. Libr., Austin, 1984-87; libr. Phoenix Pub. Libr., 1987-89; assoc. libr., west campus Ariz. State U., Phoenix, 1989-90; Proyecto Leer libr. Tex. Woman's U., Denton, 1991-92; dir. div. learning resources Sul Ross State U., Alpine, Tex., 1992—; speaker and cons. in field. Founding editor jour. La Lista, 1983-84; founding indexer Chicano Periodical Index, 1981-86; reviewer jour. Voices of Youth Advocates, 1988-90; contbr. poetry and articles to books and jours. Mem. ALA (com. on standing of women in profession, com. on profl. edn.), MLA, Assn. for Libr. and Info. Sci. Edn., Tex. Libr. Assn., Ariz. State Libr. Assn. (pres. svcs. Spanish speaking Roundtable 1988-90), Reforma (pres. El Paso chpt. 1983, pres. Ariz. chpt. 1989-90, nat. v.p. 1993-94, pres. 1994-95), Unltd. Potential, Inc. (treas. 1988-89), Hispanic Leadership Inst. AQlumni Assn.

ORTENBERG, ELISABETH CLAIBORNE See CLAIBORNE, LIZ

ORTH-AIKMUS, GAIL MARIE, police chief; b. Kansas City, Dec. 31, 1956; d. Ben Roy and Janet Ferrell (Buckner) O.; m. Frank Henry Aikmus Jr., Oct. 5, 1980 (div. Oct. 1990); 1 child, Brian Russell. Cert. law enforcement officer, Mo.; cert. drug canine handler; cert. vanner. Patrol officer Parkville (Mo.) Police Dept., 1977-78; deputy Platte County Sheriff, Platte City, Mo., 1978-79; patrol officer, sgt., lt. Pleasant Valley (Mo.) Police Dept., 1979-85, police chief, 1985-95; police chief Avondale (Mo) Police Dept., 1995-96; dep. sheriff Clay County Police Dept., Liberty, Mo., 1996—; bd. dirs. Clay County Investigative, pres. bd. dirs., 1991-93; guest spkr. Clay County Mcpl. Judges Conf.; testified before House Com. with Mo. Ho. of Reps., 1994. Appeared in fraud investigation on ABC 20/20 mag., 1980. Named Officer of Yr. Vets. Fgn. Wars Aux., Kansas City, 1991; recipient Key to Manor Pleasant Valley Manor, 1990, Puppy Trucker award Heart of Am. Van Club, 1994, Lifesaving award ribbon, 1996, Unit citation ribbon, 1996. Mem. Mo. Police Chief's Assn., Mo. Peace Officer's Assn., Kansas City Police Chief's Assn., Kansas City Major Case Squad, Kansas City Women in Law Enforcement, Nat. Assn. Chief's of Police, NRA, Weimaraner Club Am., Weimaraner Club Greater Kansas City (pres. 1991—), World Wide Race Fans. Home: 8405 Kaill Rd Pleasant Valley MO 64068 Office: Clay County Sheriffs Liberty MO 64068

ORTHMANN, ROSEMARY A., editor; b. Ridgewood, N.J., Oct. 10, 1952. BA, Washington Coll., 1974; MA, U. Minn., 1977; PhD, Ind. U., 1987. Editl. asst. Am. Historical Review, Bloomington, Ind., 1977-80; asst. book editor 21st Century Books, Frederick, Md., 1987-88; mng. editor U. Publ. of Am., Frederick, 1987-88, editor, 1988—. Author: Out of Necessity, 1991; contbr. articles to profl. jours. Mem. steering com. Commn. for Women, Frederick, 1991-92; mem. Frederick County Commn. for Women, 1992—. Internat. Rsch. and Exch. Bd. fellow, 1980-81, Social Sci. Rsch. Coun. fellow, 1981-82; Fulbright-Hays scholar, 1981-82, German Acad. Exch. Svc. scholar, 1974-75. Mem. AAUW, ACLU, Nat. Mus. Women in Arts, Nat. Abortion Rights Action League. Democrat. Office: U Publ of Am 4520 East-West Hwy Bethesda MD 20814

ORTIZ, KATHLEEN LUCILLE, travel consultant; b. Las Vegas, N.Mex., Feb. 8, 1942; d. Arthur L. and Anna (Lopez) O. BA, Loretto Hghts. Coll., 1963; MA, Georgetown U., 1966; cert. tchg., Highlands U., 1980; cert. travel, ABQ Travel Sch., 1984. Mgr. Montezuma Sq., Las Vegas, 1966-70; office mgr. Arts Food Market, Las Vegas, 1971-75; tchr. Robertson H.S., Las Vegas, 1976-80; registered rep. IDS Fin. Svcs., N.Mex., 1980-84; travel cons. VIP Travel & Tours, Albuquerque, 1985-86, New Horizons Travel, Albuquerque, 1986-87, All World Travel, Albuquerque, 1987-90, Premium Travel Svcs., Albuquerque, 1990-91; travel cons., group tours Going Places Travel, Albuquerque, 1991—. Contbr. 100 articles to newspapers. Founding mem. Citizens Com. for Hist. Preservation, Las Vegas, 1977-79; fund raiser St. Anthony's Hosp., Las Vegas, 1969-75. Mem. LWV (numerous positions), Internat. Airlines Travel Agent Network, Airlines Reporting Corp. Agent, Georgetown Club of N.Mex. (bd. dirs. at large 1991-94). Home: 7600 Adele Pl NE Albuquerque NM 87109-5362 Office: Going Places Travel 6400 Uptown Blvd NE Ste 429E Albuquerque NM 87110-4203

ORTIZ, LOIDA A., communications executive; b. Vega Baja, P.R.; d. Luis and Alicia Ortiz. AA in Computer Scis., U. P.R., 1979; BA in Comm., U. Sacred Heart, 1985. From field prodr. to news dir. Sta. WSJN-TV, Hato Rey, P.R., 1987-90; news editor Stas. WIPR-Radio and WKAQ-Radio, Hato Rey, 1989-90; announcer Sta. WMDO Radio Mundo, Tampa, Fla., 1990-91; media cons. Am. Region United Bible Socs., Miami, Fla., 1991—. Office: United Bible Socs 1989 NW 88th Ct Miami FL 33172-2641

ORTIZ-BUTTON, OLGA, social worker; b. Chgo., July 12, 1953; d. Luis Antonio and Pura (Acevedo) Ortiz; m. Dennis Vesley, Aug. 11, 1973 (div. 1976); m. Randall Russell Button, Nov. 3, 1984 (div. Oct. 1993); children: Joshua, Jordan, Elijah. BA, U. Ill., 1975; MSW, Western Mich. U., 1981. Cert. social worker, sch. social worker. Social svcs. dir. Champaign County Nursing Home, Urbana, Ill., 1976; social svcs. and activity dir. Lawton (Mich.) Nursing Home, 1977; job developer Southwestern Mich. Indian Ctr., Watervliet, 1977-78; staff asst. New Directions Alcohol Treatment Ctr., Kalamazoo, 1978; counselor, instr. Alcohol Hwy. Safety, Kalamazoo, 1978-79; clin. social worker Mecosta County Community Mental Health, Big Rapids, Mich., 1981-84; program dir. substance abuse Sr. Svcs., Inc., Kalamazoo, 1984-85; sch. social worker Martin (Mich.) Pub. Schs., 1985-96; owner, therapist Plainwell (Mich.) Counseling Ctr., 1989—; S.W. cons. Med. Pers. Pool, 1993-94, G.L. Network Mktg., 1993—. Vol. social worker Hospice-Wings of Hope, Plainwell, 1984-85, mem. CQI bd., 1993—; supporter Students Against Aparteid South Africa, Kalamazoo, 1979-81; mem. World Vision and Countertop Ptnr., 1984—; sponsor, vol. People for Ethical Treatment of Animals, 1986-91; vol. helper Sparkies for Awana Club Ch., 1989-95; consortium mem. Mich. Post Adoption Svc. System, 1994—. NIMH Rural Mental Health grantee, 1979-81. Mem. NASW, Mich. Assn. Sch. Social Workers, Am. Assn. Christian Counselors. Office: Plainwell Counseling Ctr 211 E Bannister St Ste K Plainwell MI 49080-1372

ORTLIP, MARY KRUEGER, artist; b. Scranton, Pa.; d. John A. and Ida Mae (Phillips) Smale; m. Emmanuel Krueger, June, 1940 (dec. Nov. 1979); children: Diane, Keith; m. Paul D. Ortlip, June 26, 1981. Student, New Sch. Social Rsch., N.Y.C., 1957-59, Margarita Madrigal Langs., N.Y.C., Montclair (N.J.) Art Mus. Sch., 1978-79; Nomina Accademico Conferita, Accademia Italia, Italy, 1986; DFA (hon.), Houghton Coll., 1988. Dancer, dance instr. Fleischer Dance Studio, Scranton, Pa., 1934-38. One-woman shows include Curzon Gallery of Boca Raton, Fla. and London, 1986-93, Galerie Les Amis des Arts, Aix-en-Provence, France, 1987; group exhbns.: Salmagundi Club, N.Y.C., 1980, James Hunt Barker Galleries, Nantucket, Mass. and N.Y.C., 1983, Salon Internationale Musée Parc Rochteau à Revin, France, 1985, 90, Accademia Italia, Milan, 1986, many others in Europe and Am.; permanent collections Musée de parc Rocheteau, Revin, France, Pinacothèque Arduinna, Charleville-Meziéres, France. Named Invité d'Honneur, Le Salon des Nations a Retenu L'oeuvre, Paris, 1983, Artist of the Year, La Cote des Arts, France, 1986; recipient La Medaille d'Or, Du 13ème Salon Internationale al du Parc Rocheau au Revin, France, 1985, Medaille d' Honneur Ville de Marseille, France, 1987, Targo D'Oro, Accademia Italia Premio D'Italia, 1986; Trophy Arts Internationale Exposition de Peinture Marseille, Plaquette d' Honneur, Palais des Arts, 1987, Grand Prix Salon de Automne Club Internationale, 1987, Connaissance de Notre Europa Ardennes Eifel, Revin, France, 1990. Mem. Nat. Mus. Women in Arts, Accademia Italia (charter), Instituo D'Art Contemporanea Di Milano, Nat. Soc. Arts and Letters, Gov.'s Club, Salmagundi Club. Home (winter): 2917 S Ocean Blvd #703 Highland Beach FL 33487-1876 Home (summer): 588 Summit Ave Hackensack NJ 07601 Office: The Curzon Gallery 501 E Camino Real Boca Raton FL 33432-6127

ORTNER, TONI, English language educator; b. Bklyn., Mar. 11, 1941; d. Melvin and Sylvia (Klein) O.; m. Stephen Michael Zimmerman, May 27, 1962 (div. 1988); 1 child, Lisa Zimmerman. BA, Hofstra U., 1962; MA in English, Western Conn. State Coll., 1979. Tchr. English dept. Monroe Coll., Bronx; tchr. Mercy Coll., Bronx C.C., Coll. New Rochelle. Author: Woman in Search of Herself, 1971, To an Imaginary Lover, 1975, Never Stop Dancing, 1976, Entering Another Country, 1976, I Dream Now of the Sun, 1976, Stones, 1976, As If Anything Could Grow Back Perfect, 1979, Requiem, 1991; contbr. to anthologies and jours. Mem. Poets & Writers. Home: 213 Bell Hollow Rd Putnam Valley NY 10579

ORTON, EVA DOROTHY, volunteer; b. San Jose, Calif., Aug. 21, 1921; d. George Alfred and Marguerite Carolyn (Del Ponte) Prudhomme. AB in Dietitics, San Jose State Coll., 1943. Intern Highland-Alameda Hosp., Oakland, Calif., 1944; dietitian Providence Hosp., Oakland, 1944-46; relief dietitian Santa Clara Valley Med. Ctr., San Jose, 1949-51, 52-53, sr. dietitian, 1953-63; food adminstr., dir. nutrition and food svc. Santa Clara Valley Ctr., San Jose, 1963-86; ret., 1986—. Bd. dirs., vol. YWCA, San Jose, 1984-93; adv. legis. com. chair Adv. Coun. to Coun. on Agy., San Jose, 1987-95; fin. com. Cmty. Kids to Camp, San Jose, 1987-93, adv. bd., current; active Hunger Coalition, 1992—. Named Disting. Alumni, San Jose State U., 1982, Vol. of Yr. Silicon Valley Charity Ball Found., 1991-92; recipient disting. citizen award Exch. Club and City Coun. San José. Mem. LWV (exec. com., v.p., pres. 1993-95), Am. Dietitic Assn. (registered dietitian), State and Local Dietitic Assn. (chmn. various coms.), Interagency Nutrition Coun. (various coms.). Roman Catholic. Home: 4925 Bel Escou Dr San Jose CA 95124-5441

ORULLIAN, B. LARAE, bank executive; b. Salt Lake City, May 15, 1933; d. Alma and Bessie (Bacon) O.; cert. Am. Inst. Banking, 1961, 63, 67; grad. Nat. Real Estate Banking Sch., Ohio State U., 1969-71. With Tracy Collins Trust Co., Salt Lake City, 1951-54, Union Nat. Bank, Denver, 1954-57; exec. sec. Guaranty Bank, Denver, 1957-64, asst. cashier, 1964-67, asst. v.p., 1967-70, v.p., 1970-75, exec. v.p., 1975-77, also bd. dirs.; chair, CEO, dir. The Women's Bank N.A., Denver, 1989—, Colo. Bus. Bankshares, Inc., 1980—; vice chmn. Colo. Bus. Bank Littleton; chmn. bd., dir. Colo. Blue Cross/Blue Shield; bd. dirs. Rocky Mountain Life Ins. Co., Pro-Card, Inc., Holladay (Utah) Bank; chmn. bd. dirs. Frontier Airlines. Treas. Girl Scouts U.S.A., 1981-87, 1st. nat. v.p., chair exec. com., 1987-90, nat. pres., 1990—; bd. dirs., chair Rocky Mountain Health Care Corp.; bd. dirs. Ams. Clean Water Found., Denver Improvement Assn.; bd. dirs. Commn. Savings in Am. Recipient Woman Who Made a Difference award Internat. Women's Forum, 1994; named to Colo. Women Hall of Fame, 1988, Colo. Entrepreneur of Yr., Inc. Mag. and Arthur Young and Co., 1989, Woman of the Yr., YWCA, 1989, EMC Lion Club (citizen of the year, 1995). Mem. Bus. and Profl. Women Colo. (3d Century award 1977), Colo. State Ethics Bd., Denver C. of C., Am. Inst. Banking, Am. Bankers Assn. (adv. bd. edn. found.), Nat. Assn. Bank Women, Internat. Women's Forum (Woman Who Makes a Difference award 1994), Com. of 200. Republican. Mormon. Home: 10 S Ammons St Lakewood CO 80226-1331

ORY, MARCIA GAIL, social science researcher; b. Dallas, Feb. 8, 1950; d. Marvin Gilbert and Esther (Levine) O.; m. Raymond James Carroll, Aug. 13, 1972. BA magna cum laude, U. Tex., 1971; MA, Ind. U., 1972; PhD, Purdue U., 1976; MPH, Johns Hopkins U., 1981. Rsch. asst. prof. U. N.C., Chapel Hill, 1976-77; from adj. asst. prof. to assoc. prof. sch. pub. health U. N.C., 1978-88; rsch. fellow U. Minn., Mpls., 1977-78; asst. prof. Sch. Pub. Health U. Ala., Bham, 1978-80; program dir. biosocial aging and health Nat. Inst. on Aging, Bethesda, Md., 1981-86; chief social sci. rsch. on aging Nat. Inst. on Aging, Bethesda, 1987—. Contbr. articles, editor vols. profl. jours. Mem. several nat. task forces on aging and health issues. Recipient Dept. of Health and Human Svcs. award, 1984, 85, 88, Am. Men and Women of Sci., 1989-90, Nat. Inst. of Health Dir.'s award, 1995; named Disting. Alumna by Purdue U. Fellow Gerontol. Soc. Am.; mem. APHA (gov. coun. 1986-88, program chmn. 1986, chmn.-elect 1989-91, chmn. 1992-93), Am. Sociol. Assn. (regional reporter 1984—, program com. 1986, nominations com. 1987, councilor-at-large 1992-93), Soc. Behavioral Medicine (program chmn. pub. health track 1988-89, program com. 1991-92), Phi Kappa Phi, Omicron Nu. Office: Nat Inst Aging Gateway Bldg Ste 533 7201 Wisconsin Ave # 9205 Bethesda MD 20892-9205

ORZECH, RITA URSULA, nursing administrator; b. Chgo., Mar. 31, 1942; d. Joseph F. and Viola (Chodorski) O. BA in English Lit., Rosary Coll., 1964. RN, Ill., Fla. Tchr. Notre Dame H.S., Chgo., 1964-74; head nurse Ravenswood Hosp., Chgo., 1977-83; nursing adminstr. Ambcor-Ravenswood Hosp. Med. Ctr., Chgo., 1983-95; nurse Naples (Fla.) Cmty. Hosp., 1995—; bd. dirs. Seko Eye Care, Inc., Chgo. Mem. Ill. Nurses Assn. Roman Catholic.

ORZECHOWSKI, ALICE LOUISE, accountant; b. Washington, Jan. 14, 1952; d. Casimir T. and Frances (Zemaites) O.; m. Scott Mitchell Hoyman Jr. BS in Econs., U. Md., 1973, BS in Acctg., 1976; MS in Adminstrn. and Mgmt., Hood Coll., 1983. CPA, Md.; cert. mgmt. acct. Mgr. Gen. Bus. Svcs., Rockville, Md., 1972-78, Ross Assocs., Alexandria, Va., 1978-87; owner Alice L. Orzechowski, CPA, Cert. Mgmt. Acct., Frederick, Md., 1987—; adj. faculty Frederick (Md.) C.C., 1990-92, Montgomery Coll., Rockville, Md., 1992-96; spkr. in field. Named Outstanding Young Marylander, Md. Jaycees, 1991. Mem. AICPA, Am. Women's Soc. CPAs, Md. Assn. CPAs, Nat. Assn. Accts., Nat. Assn. Tax Practitioners, Downtowne Frederick Toastmasters (pres. 1991, Toastmaster of Yr. 1990), Frederick C. of C. (chair small bus. coun. 1990-91, dir. 1992—, Entrepreneur of Yr. 1992). Office: 529 N Market St Frederick MD 21701-5242

OSBAND, MARLA SUE, nursery school administrator; b. Santa Monica, Calif., Aug. 3, 1945; d. Murray Laurence and Fay (Herman) Haselkorn; m. Ronald Gary Osband, June 25, 1966; children: Lynn, Scott. BA, MA, UCLA, 1968, postgrad. Various positions Adat Shalom Synagogue, L.A., 1973-80; dir. nursery sch., day sch. B'nai Tikvah Nursery Sch./Kindergarten, L.A., 1980—; mentor tchr. Santa Monica Coll., 1984—; cons. Didi Hirsch Mental Health, Culver City, Calif., 1988—. Author: In Celebration of ..., 1986; contbr. articles to profl. jours. Active local PTA, Culver City, 1973—. Recipient Life Achievement award L.A. City Coun., 1986, Honorary Svc. award Culver City Coun. PTA, 1980, Continuing Svc. award, 1988. Mem. Nat. Assn. for Edn. Young Children (validator 1994), Assn. for Early Jewish Edn. (pres. 1994—), Nat. Jewish Early Childhood Network (v.p. 1992—), Culver City Edn. Found. (trustee), Bd. Jewish Edn. L.A. (chair accreditation project), Child Care Info. Exch. (mem. adv. panel). Office: Bnai Tikvah Nursery Sch 5820 W Manchester Ave Los Angeles CA 90045-4428

OSBERG, SUSAN E., dancer, choreographer, performance artist, educator, writer; b. Belefonte, Pa., Nov. 30, 1951; d. Philip H. and Priscilla (Hallam) O.; m. Winston Roeth. Diploma, Interlochen (Mich.) Arts Acad., 1970; BFA, Juilliard Sch., N.Y.C., 1975; MA Tchrs. Coll., Columbia U., N.Y.C., 1979. Cert. kundalini yoga, yogi bahjah. Dancer Helen McGehee, Kazuko Hirabayashi, Paul Sanasardo, Manuel Alum, Lucinda Childs, N.Y.C., 1975-79; choregorapher and artistic dir. Workwith Dancers Co., N.Y.C., 1979—; assoc. prof. Bard Coll., Annandale-on-Hudson, 1984—; asst. prof. Simon Fraser U., Vancouver, B.C., 1980-83; tchg. artist Lincoln Ctr. Inst., N.Y.C., 1984-92; co-curator Salon Project Dia Ctr. for Arts, N.Y.C., 1986-96; mem. artist adv. bd. Danspace Project St. Mark's Ch., 1990-96; co-founder and mem. steering com. Dance Across Borders (Internat.), 1995; instr. dance theatre workshops The Suitcase Fund, 1996—. Choreographer numerous works in internat. contemporary dance/theater. Grantee Simon Fraser U., 1982, Consol. Edison, 1979-95, N.Y. State Coun. for Arts, 1988, Lower Manhattan Cmty. Arts Fund, 1988, 90, N.Y. State Coun. Decentralization Fund, 1993, Joyce Mertz-Gillmore Found., 1990-91, Abraham and Lillian Rosenberg Found., 1994-95, Dia Ctr. for the Arts, 1986-95, Rockefellar Found. and Trust for Mutual Understanding, N.Y.C., 1996.

OSBORN, ANN GEORGE, retired chemist; b. Nowata, Okla., Aug. 1, 1933; d. David Thomas and Alice Audrey (Giles) George; m. Charles Wesley Osborn, Nov. 8, 1958 (dec. Dec. 1977); 1 child, Charles David. BA in Chemistry, Okla. Coll. Women, 1955. Rsch. chemist thermodynamics rsch. lab. Bartlesville (Okla.) Energy Rsch. Ctr., U.S. Dept. Energy, 1957—; ret., 1983. Contbr. articles to profl. jours. Mem. AAAS (emeritus), Am. Chem. Soc. Republican. Mem. Christian Ch. (Disciples of Christ). Home: 647 S Pecan St Nowata OK 74048-4015

OSBORN, FLORENCE CHERYL, special education educator; b. Albuquerque; d. Clinton Leon and Bertha Florence (Custer) McMath; m. Ruben Leslie Osborn, Aug. 11, 1967 (div. Oct. 1988); children: Tami Renea, Brian Clinton, Shonda Leigh. Degree in vocat. home econs., U. Okla., 1976, M of Spl. Edn., 1990, postgrad. spl. edn. Adminstrv. asst. U. Okla., Norman, 1967-72; dir. Free Meth. Day Care Ctr., Norman, 1974-76; vocat. edn. tchr. Moore (Okla.) Pub. Schs., 1976-77; piano tchr. Norman, 1977-80; dir. sheltered workshop Goodwill Industries, Oklahoma City, 1985-88; tchr. emotionally disturbed Norman Pub. Schs., 1988-90, lifeskills specialist, 1990—; homebound tchr. Norman Pub. Schs., 1980—; pres. FLOCO Land & Energy, Inc., Norman, 1985—. Author: The Business of Living, 1994. Chpt. officer various state and dist. levels Epsilon Sigma Alpha, 1978-84; grad. senate U. Okla., 1994—. IDEA-B grantee Okla. Dept. Spl. Edn., 1992, 94, Transitional Living grantee, 1990, Gardening grantee Nat. Gardening Assn., 1994. Mem. Coun. for Exceptional Children, Student Coun. for Exceptional Children (faculty advisor 1994—). Baptist. Home: 1603 Barwick Dr Norman OK 73072-3225 Office: Norman Pub Schs 1120 E Main St Norman OK 73071-5300

OSBORN, JUNE ELAINE, pediatrician, microbiologist, educator; b. Endicott, N.Y., May 28, 1937; d. Leslie A. and Dora W. (Wright) O.; divorced; children: Philip I. Levy, Ellen D. and Laura A. Levy (twins). BA, Oberlin (Ohio) Coll., 1957; MD, Western Res. U., 1961; DSc (hon.), U. Med. Dental Sch. N.J., 1990; DMS (hon.), Yale U., 1992; DSc (hon.), Emory U., 1993, Oberlin Coll., 1993; LHD (hon.), Med. Coll. Pa., 1994; DSc (hon.), Rutgers U., 1994. Intern, then resident in pediatrics Harvard U. Hosp., 1961-64; postdoctoral fellow Johns Hopkins, 1964-65, U. Pitts., 1965-66; mem. faculty, prof. med. microbiology and pediat. U. Wis. Med. Sch., Madison, Wis., 1966-84; prof. pediat. and microbiology U. Wis. Med. Sch., 1975-84, assoc. dean Grad. Sch., 1975-84; dean Sch. Pub. Health U. Mich., 1984-93; prof. epidemiology, pediat. and communicable diseases U. Mich., Sch. Pub. Health and Med. Sch., 1984—; mem. rev. panel viral vaccine efficacy FDA, 1973-79, mem. vaccines and related biol. products adv. com., 1981-85; mem. exptl. virology study sect. Divsn. Rsch. Grants, NIH, 1975-79; mem. med. affairs com. Yale U. Coun., 1981-86; chmn. life scis. associateships rev. panel NRC, 1981-84; mem. U.S. Army Med. R&D Adv. Com., 1983-85; chmn. working group on AIDS and the Nation's Blood Supply, NHLBI, 1984-89; chmn. WHO Planning Group on AIDS and the Internat. Blood Supply, 1985-86. Contbr. articles to med. jours. Mem. task force on AIDS, Inst. of Medicine, 1986; mem. adv. com. Robert Wood Johnson Found. Health Svcs. Program, 1986-91; mem. nat. adv. com. on health of pub. program Pew and Rockefeller Founds.; mem. health promotion and disease prevention bd. IOM, 1987-90, Global Commn. on AIDS, WHO, 1988-92; chmn. Nat. Commn. on AIDS, 1989 93; trustee Kaiser Found., 1990 ; trustee Case Western Res. U., Cleve., 1993—; mem. coun. Inst. Medicine, 1995—; mem. Nat. Vaccine Adv. Cte., HHS, 1995—. Grantee NIH, 1969, 72, 74-75, Nat. Multiple Sclerosis Soc., 1971; Scientific Freedom and Responsibility Award AAAS, 1994. Fellow Am. Acad. Arts and Scis., Am. Acad. Pediat., Am. Acad. Microbiology, Infectious Diseases Soc. Am.; mem. Am. Assn. Immunologists, Soc. Pediat. Rsch., Inst. Medicine. Office: U Mich Dept Epidemiology Sch Pub Health Ann Arbor MI 48109

OSBORN, KAYE ELLEN, special education educator; b. St. Louis, Sept. 15, 1952; d. John Ellsworth and Jean Mae (Kamp) Higgins; m. Jerry Ray Osborn, June 27, 1976; children: Amanda, Megan. BA, Calif. State U., Fresno, 1974, MA, 1975. Lifetime teacing credential. Tchr. deaf and hard of hearing Calif. Sch. for Deaf, Riverside, 1975-76, Modesto (Calif.) City Schs., 1976—; 2nd grade social studies mentor Modesto City Schs., 1992-93, phys. edn. mentor tchr., 1988; writing cons. Great Valley Writing Project, Modesto, 1989—, coord. young writers workshop, 1990—. Author: Albert and Annette's Amazing Alphabetical Adventure, 1993. Leader Girl Scouts U.S.A., Modesto, 1986—; Mem. Lakewood PTA/Sch. Improvement Program, La Loma Jr. High PTA/Sch. Improvement Program. Named Outstanding Tchr. Modesto Rotary Club, 1993-94, County Ambassador of Edn. Stanislaus County, Modesto, 1994, tchr. of Yr., 1995, P.E. Mastor Tchr., 1995; recipient World of the Arts award Girl Scouts U.S., 1994, Hon. Svc. award Lakewood PTA/Sch. Improvement Program. Mem. Coun. Exceptional Children (pres. 1983-84). Democrat. Home: 804 Hedgestone Way Modesto CA 95355-4559

OSBORN, MARY JANE MERTEN, biochemist; b. Colorado Springs, Colo., Sept. 24, 1927; d. Arthur John and Vivien Naomi (Morgan) Merten; m. Ralph Kenneth Osborn, Oct. 26, 1950. B.A., U. Calif., Berkeley, 1948; Ph.D., U. Wash., 1958. Postdoctoral fellow, dept. microbiology N.Y. U. Sch. Medicine, N.Y.C., 1959-61; instr. N.Y. U. Sch. Medicine, 1961-62, asst. prof., 1962-63; asst. prof. dept. molecular biology Albert Einstein Coll. Medicine, Bronx, N.Y., 1963-66; asso. prof. Albert Einstein Coll. Medicine, 1966-68; prof. dept. microbiology U. Conn. Health Center, Farmington, 1968—; dept. head U. Conn. Health Center, 1980—; mem. bd. sci. counselors Nat. Heart, Lung and Blood Inst., 1975-79; mem. Nat. Sci. Bd., 1980-86; adv. coun. Nat. Inst. Gen. Med. Sci., 1983-86, divsn. rsch. grants NIH, 1989-94, chair, 1992-94; trustee Biosci. Info. Systems, 1986-91; mem. German Am. Acad. Coun., 1994—; mem. space scis. bd. NRC, 1994—, chair com. space biology and medicine, 1994—. Assoc. editor Jour. Biol. Chemistry, 1978-80; contbr. articles in field of biochemistry and molecular biology to profl. jours. Mem. rsch. com. Am. Heart Assn., 1972-77, chair, 1976-77. NIH fellow, 1959-61; NIH grantee, 1962—; NSF grantee, 1965-68; Am. Heart Assn. grantee, 1968-71. Fellow Am. Acad. Arts and Scis. (coun. 1988-91), NAS (coun. 1990-93, com. sci. engring. and pub. policy 1993-96); mem. Am. Chem. Soc. (chmn. divsn. biol. chemistry 1975-76), Am. Fedn. Soc. Exptl. Biology (pres. 1982-83), Am. Soc. Biol. Chemists (pres. 1981-82), Am. Soc. Microbiology. Democrat. Office: U Conn Health Ctr Dept Microbiology Farmington CT 06030

OSBORN, SUSAN JEAN, artist; b. Huntington Park, Calif., May 16, 1946; d. James McLaughlin and Ramona Ruth (Mecey) Adcock; m. Gary Michael Osborn, July 1, 1966; children: Darla Lin, Nicole Jean. MA in Edn., Calif. State U., 1983, MA in Visual Art, 1971. Art instr. Chula Vista (Calif.) Adult Sch., 1973-75; instructional designer Courseware, Inc., San Diego, Calif., 1983-84, Olympus Ednl. Software, San Diego, 1984-86, Intelligent Images, San Diego, 1986-87; part-time art instr. Southwestern C.C., Chula Vista, Calif., 1975-87; art instr. The Bishop's Sch., LaJolla, Calif., 1987—; coord., curriculum devel. Fine Arts Cultural Experience, San Diego Mus. of Art, 1981-82; lectr. in field. One/two people shows including Southwestern C.C., Chula Vista, 1995, The Art Store Gallery, 1993, San Diego Art Inst., 1992, B St. Gallery, 1990, Perspectives Gallery, 1988, Jewish Cmty. Ctr., 1980, Seneca Falls Gallery, 1979, Foothill Coll., 1978; exhibited in group shows at Word Works Gallery, San Jose, Calif., 1980, San Diego Mus. of Art, 1981, Santa Monica Coll. Art Gallery, Santa Monica, 1981, Southwestern Coll., Faculty Exhibit, 1981, Harbor Coll. Gallery, 1987, San Diego Art Inst., 1989, Long Beach Arts, 1989, Brushworks Gallery, San Diego, 1989, Peter Hall Gallery, 1990, Clairemont Art Guild, 1990, Lyceum Theatre Gallery, 1991, Long Beach Arts, 1991, So. Calif. Expo, Del Mar, 1992, San Diego Art Inst., 1988, Gallery 21, 1993, San Diego Home and Gardens

Expo, 1994, Aztec Lounge, San Diego State U., 1994, Simply Devine Group Show, 1995, Art Union Bldg., 1995, San Diego Mus. of Art, 1995; represented in permanent collections Museo Internacional de Electrografia, U. Castilla-LaMancha, Cuenca, Spain, 1990. High sch. youth dir. St. Mark's Luth. Ch., Chula Vista, 1975-83. Recipient 1st Prize Mixed media So. Calif. Expo, 1978. Mem. San Diego Mus. of Art (past pres.), Combined Orgn. for Visual Arts, Calif. Arts Educators. Democrat. Lutheran. Studio: 903 K St San Diego CA 92101

OSBORN, SUSAN TITUS, editor; b. Fresno, Calif., July 11, 1944; d. Clifford Leland Feldt and Jane (Taylor) Cousins; m. Richard G. Titus, Aug. 28, 1965 (div. Dec. 1990); children: Richard David, Michael Craig; m. Richard A. Osborn, Aug. 22, 1992. BA in Religious Studies, Calif. State U., Fullerton, 1988, MA in Comm., 1993. Svc. rep. Mountain Bell Tel., Colorado Springs, Colo., 1965-67; free-lance writer Fullerton, Calif., 1978—; assoc. dir. Biola U. Writers Inst., La Mirada, Calif., 1986-92; co-dir. Christian Communicators Conf. The Master's Coll., Santa Clarita, Calif., 1993-95, adj. prof., 1993-96; adj. prof. Pacific Christian Coll., 1996; mem. adv. bd. Christian Writers Fellowship, Huntington Beach, Calif., 1987-93; mem. adv. bd. Christian Communicator, San Juan Capistrano, Calif., 1989-94, mng. editor, 1991-92, editor, 1992—; pub. cons. Ednl. Ministries, Brea, Calif., 1989-91; conf. spkr. numerous cities, 1987—; tchr. India Comm. Inst., Bombay; bd. dirs. Moscow Christian Sch. Psychology, 1992-95. Author: Parables for Young Teens, 1986, You Start With One, 1990, Meeting Jesus, 1990, Eyes Beyond the Horizon, 1991, Children Around the World Celebrate Christmas, 1993, The Complete Guide to Christian Writing and Speaking, 1994, Rest Stops for Single Mothers, 1995, Potpourri of Praise, 1995; editor The Christian Communicator. Bd. dirs. Jr. Ebell Club, Fullerton, 1969-75, Youth Sci. Ctr., Fullerton, 1970-75, YMCA Swim Club, Fullerton, 1976-82; pres. Troy Swim Boosters, Fullerton, 1982-88, Moscow Christian Sch. Psychology, 1992-95. Recipient Spl. Recognition award Troy Swim Boosters, 1986. Mem. Presbyn. Writers Guild., Spiritual Overseers Svc. Republican. Evangelical.

OSBORNE, GAYLA MARLENE, sales executive; b. Owenton, Ky., Aug. 9, 1956; d. Frederick Clay and Helen Beatrice (Mason) O. AAS, No. Ky. U., 1982, BS, 1986; cert. in Chinese Mandarin, Def. Lang. Inst., 1975. Pers. clk. Dept. Edn. State Ky., Frankfort, 1974; sec. Dept. Health, Edn., Welfare Nat. Inst. Occupational Safety Health, Cin., 1977-79; specialist sales promotion U.S. Postal Svc., Cin., 1980, coord. customer liaison, task force pub. image, account rep., 1986-87, with stamp distbn. task force, 1993—; reservation sale agt. Delta Airlines, 1987-89. Councilmember Florence City Coun., Ky. 1984-87; vol. Children's Home, Covington, 1982, 87. With USAF, 1974-76. Named to Hon. Order Ky. Cols. Mem. Disabled Am. Veterans, No. Ky. U. Alumni Assn., Nat. Assn. Postmasters U.S., Boone County Fraternal Order Police, Ky. Assn. Realtors, Nat. Bd. Realtors, Women in Mil. Svc. for Am. (charter). Democrat. Baptist. Club: Fraternal Order Police. Home: 8395 Juniper Ln Florence KY 41042-9279

OSBORNE, LAUREN GARDNER, oncological nurse; b. Ft. Worth, Dec. 25, 1959; d. Lawrence Gale Gardner and Ann Bailey (Zehner) Reed; married. BA in Art History, Smith Coll., 1982; BSN, U. Tenn., 1987. RN, oncology cert. nurse. Patient care asst. Meth. Hosp., Memphis, 1986, staff nurse gyn. med.-surg., 1987-89; staff nurse gyn. oncology U. N.C. Hosps., Chapel Hill, N.C., 1989-90; nurse edn. clinician gyn. oncology U. N.C. Hosps., Chapel Hill, 1990-92, U. N.C., Chapel Hill, 1992—. Pres. Orange County chpt. Am. Cancer Soc., Durham, N.C., 1994-95. Mem. ANA, Soc. Gynecologic Nurse Oncologists, Oncology Nursing Soc. (bd. dirs., sect. N.C. Triangle chpt. 1992-94), Sigma Theta Tau. Office: U NC Dept Ob-Gyn Divsn Oncology 5017 Old Clinic Bldg Chapel Hill NC 27599

OSBORNE, NANCY SEALE, librarian, archivist, educator; b. San Angelo, Tex., Mar. 5, 1936; d. Henry Herbert and Mamie Alberta (Moses) Seale; m. Vance Arlen Osborne, June 12, 1954 (div. 1976); cildren: Jean Ellen, Kevin Vance. BS in Edn., SUNY, Oswego, 1970, MS in Edn., 1971; MLS, Syracuse U., 1977. Cert. pub. libr., N.Y., cert. elem. edn., N.Y. Tchr. 3d grade Elm St. Sch., Phoenix, 1971-72; coordinating tchr., specialist lang. arts Children's Sch., Syracuse, N.Y., 1972-74; info. specialist Metro. Commn. on Aging, Syracuse, 1977-78; reference libr. SUNY, Cortland, 1978-79; reference/instrn. libr., archivist SUNY, Oswego, 1980—. Co-author: (with Joan Loveridge-Sanbonmatsu) Feminism and Woman's Life, 1995; contbr. articles to profl. jours. Bd. dirs. Oswego County Hist. Soc., 1983-85, Aux. Svcs., SUNY, Oswego, 1990—. Mem. Soc. Am. Archivists (cert.), Nat. Women's Studies Assn. (editor NWSA Perspectives 1985-87, chair archives com. 1986—), SUNY Librs. Assn., N.Y. Librs. Assn. Democrat. Unitarian. Home: 139 Valley View Dr Oswego NY 13126 Office: Penfield Libr SUNY Coll at Oswego Oswego NY 13126

OSBORNE-POPP, GLENNA JEAN, health services administrator; b. East Rainelle, W.Va., Jan. 5, 1945; d. B.J. and Jean Ann (Haranac) Osborne; m. Thomas Joseph Ferrante Jr., June 11, 1966 (div. Nov. 1987); 1 child, Thomas Joseph Osborne; m. Brian Mark Popp, Aug. 13, 1988. BA cum laude, U. Tampa, 1966; MA, Fairleigh Dickinson U., 1982; cert., Kean Coll., 1983. Cert. English, speech, dramatic arts tchr., prin./supr.; cert. nursing child assessment feeding scale and nursing child assessment tchg. scale, 1996. Tchr. Raritan High Sch., Hazlet, N.J., 1966; tchr. Keyport (N.J.) Pub. Schs., 1968-86, coord. elem. reading and lang. arts, 1980-84, supr. curriculum and instrn., 1984-86; prin. Weston Sch., Manville, N.J., 1986-88, The Bartle Sch., Highland Park, N.J., 1988-91, Orange Ave. Sch., Cranford, N.J., 1991-92; dir. The Open Door Youth Shelter, Binghamton, N.Y., 1992-94; child protective investigator supr. Dept. Health and Rehab. Svcs., Orlando, Fla., 1994-95; program supr. Children's Home Soc., Sanford, Fla., 1995; clin. supr. Healthy Families-Orange, Orlando, Fla., 1995—; regional trainer Individualized Lang. Arts, Weehawken, N.J., 1976-86; cons. McDougal/Little Pubs., Evanston, Ill., 1982-83; chair adv. bd. women's residential program Ctr. for Drug Free Living, Orlando, 1996. Contbr. chpt.: A Resource Guide of Differentiated Learning Experiences for Gifted Elementary Students, 1981. Sunday sch. tchr. Reformed Ch., Keyport, 1975-80, supt. Sunday sch., 1982-84. Mem. Order Ea. Star (Tampa, Fla.), Phi Delta Kappa. Republican. Methodist. Office: Healthy Families 623 S Texas Ave Orlando FL 32805

OSCARSON, KATHLEEN DALE, writing assessment coordinator, educator; b. Hollywood, Calif., Sept. 16, 1928; d. Chauncey Dale and Hermine Marie Rulison; m. David Knowles Leslie, June 16, 1957 (div. Aug. 1970); m. William Randolph Oscarson, Apr. 27, 1974. AB, UCLA, 1950, MA, 1952; Cert. Advanced Study, Harvard U., 1965; Diplomé Elementaire, Le Cordon Bleu U. Paris, 1972. Gen. secondary life credential, Calif. Cons. Advanced Placement English Calif. Dept. Edn., Sacramento, 1968-70; reader Calif. Assessment Program, Sacramento, 1989—; instr. individual study U. Calif. Extension, Berkeley, 1979-92; reader, leader Ednl. Testing Svc., Princeton, N.J. and Emeryville, Calif., 1967—; reader San Jose (Calif.) State U., 1991—; tchr. English, counselor Palo Alto (Calif.) Unified Sch. Dist., 1954-90, H.S. writing assessment coord., 1987—; adj. lectr. English Santa Clara (Calif.) U., 1990-91; commr. Curriculum Study Commn., San Francisco Bay Area, 1978—; chair tchrs. English Spring Asilomar Conf., Pacific Grove, Calif., 1992, Asilomar 44, Pacific Grove, 1994; presenter Conf. on English Leadership, Chgo., 1996. Mem. lang. arts assessment adv. com. Calif. State Dept. Edn., Sacramento, 1975-90; mem.-at-large exec bd. Ctrl. Calif. Coun. Tchrs. English, Bay Area, 1969-71; mem. Medallion Soc. San Francisco Opera, 1984—; mem. ann. summer event com., membership com. Internat. Diplomacy Coun. Mem. MLA, Nat. Coun. Tchrs. English (group leader conf. San Francisco), Calif. Assn. Tchrs. English, Internat. Diplomacy Coun. San Francisco (membership and events coms. 1996), Harvard Club San Francisco, Christopher Marlowe Soc. Home: 230 Durazno Way Portola Valley CA 94028

O'SCOTT, KATHRYN LINDSEY, middle school educator; b. Mt. Clements, Mich., Aug. 4, 1966; d. James Russell and Nellie Sue (Daniel) Lindsey; m. Patrick M. O'Scott, June 23, 1990. BS in Edn., Ga. So. Coll., 1988; MEd in Middle Grades, Valdosta State U. Cert. tchr., Ga. Tchr. math. Ben Hill Mid. Sch., Fitzgerald, Ga., 1988—, dept. coord. math., 1993-94; adult literacy instr. Ben Hill-Irwin Tech., Fitzgerald, 1993-94, faculty advisor yearbook staff, 1992-96. Sec. Episcopal Ch. Women, 1992-94. Recipient Hope Scholarship for Tchrs., 1995. Mem. Nat. Coun. Tchrs. Math. Democrat. Episcopalian.

OSEGUERA, PALMA MARIE, marine corps officer, reservist; b. Kansas City, Mo., Dec. 29, 1946; d. Joseph Edmund and Palma Louise (Utke) O'Donnell; m. Alfonso Oseguera, Jan. 1, 1977; stepchildren: Kristie M. Daniels, Michelle L. Nielson, Lori A. Kelley. BA in Phys. Edn., Marycrest Coll., 1969. Commd. 2d lt. USMC, 1969, advanced through grades to col., 1991; asst. marine corps exch. officer Hdqs. and Hdqs. Squadron, Marine Corps Air Sta., Beaufort, S.C., 1969-71; classified material control officer Hdqs. and Svcs. Battalion, Camp S.D. Butler, Okinawa, 1971-73; adminstrv. officer, asst. Marine Corps exch. officer Marine Corps Air Sta., El Toro, Santa Ana, Calif., 1973-76; Marine Corps exch. officer Marine Corps Air Sta., Yuma, Ariz., 1976-77; asst. marine corps exch. officer Hdqrs. and Support Bat., Marine Corps Devel. & Edn. Command, Quantico, Va., 1977-79; marine corps exch. officer Hqrs. Marine Corps, Washington, 1979-80; adminstrv. officer Marine Air Base Squadon 46, Marine Air Group 46, Marine Corps Air Sta., Santa Ana, 1981-83, Hdqs. and Maintanence Squadron 46, Marine Air Group 46, Marine Corps Air Sta., Santa Ana, 1983-85, Mobilization Tng. Unit Calif. 53, Landing Force Tng. Command, Pacific, San Diego, 1985-89, 3d Civil Affairs Group, L.A., 1989; dep. asst. chief of staff G-1 I Marine Expeditionary Force, Individual Mobilization Augumentaee Detachment, Camp Pendleton, Calif., 1990-91; assoc. mem. Mobilization Tng. Unit Del. 01, Del., 1992-94; adminstrn. officer Mobilization Tng. Unit, CA-53, EWTG Pac, NAB, Coronado, San Diego, 1994-96; exch. officer MWRSPT ACT IMA Det MCB, Camp Pendleton, Calif., 1996—. Mem. choir St. Elizabeth Seaton, Woodbridge, Va., 1978-80, St. Patricks, Arroyo Grande, Calif., 1990—; vol. Hospice, San Luis Obispo, 1995—; mem. Los Osos (Calif.) veteran's events com. Mem. AAUW (past libr.), Marine Corps Assn., Marine Corps Res. Officer Assn., Marine Corps Aviation Assn. (12 dist. dir. 1987), Women in Mil. Svc. for Am. Republican. Roman Catholic. Home: 728 Scenic Cir Arroyo Grande CA 93420-1617

OSGOOD, BARBARA TRAVIS, conservationist, sociologist; b. Nyack, N.Y., Nov. 10, 1934; d. Donald Lovatt and Dorothy Catherine (Hammond) Travis; m. William Milne Osgood, Dec. 26, 1955 (div. 1985); children: Stephen Milne, Donald William. BS, Cornell U., 1956, PhD, 1980; MS, Lehman Coll., 1972. Lectr. Herbert H. Lehman Coll., Bronx, 1972-75; asst. prof. Cornell U., Ithaca, N.Y., 1978; staff scientist Coop. State Rsch. Svc., Washington, 1979; with Soil Conservation Svc., 1980—; asst. div. dir. Soil Conservation Svc., Washington, 1985-88; state conservationist Soil Conservation Svc., Somerset, N.J., 1988-91; liaison to EPA Soil Conservation Soc., Washington, 1991-92, assoc. dir. strategic planning and policy analysis, 1992-94, asst. chief, 1994, spl. asst., 1994—. Co-author: (book chpt.) Yearbook of Agriculture, 1986, Conserving Soil, 1986. Flora Rose fellow Cornell U., 1977. Mem. Rural Sociol. Soc., Soil and Water Conservation Soc., Phi Kappa Phi, Omicron Nu. Methodist. Office: Natural Resources Cons Svc PO Box 2890 Washington DC 20013-2890

O'SHAUGHNESSY, ELLEN CASSELS, writer; b. Columbia, S.C., Oct. 1, 1937; d. Melvin O. and Grace Ellen (Cassels) Hemphill; m. John H. Sloan (dec.); children: John H., Anne H.; m. John F. O'Shaughnessy, Dec. 8, 1979 (div. Mar. 1990). BA, Internat. Coll., L.A., 1977; MA in Counseling Psychology, Fielding Inst., Santa Barbara, Calif., 1980. Tchr.'s aide, art instr. Monterey Peninsula (Calif.) Unified Sch. Dist., 1968-74; tchr. adult sch. Pacific Grove (Calif.) Unified Sch. Dist., 1974-82, spl. edn. cons., 1984-85; sustitute tchr. Monterey County Office Edn., Salinas, Calif., 1983-84; owner, writer, pub. Synthesis, Pacific Grove, Calif., 1984—. Author: Teaching Art to Children, 1974, Synthesis, 1981, You Love to Cook Book, 1983, I Could Ride on the Carousel Longer, 1989, Somebody Called Me A Retard Today...And My Heart Felt Sad, 1992, Walker & Co., N.Y.C. Episcopalian. Home: PO Box 51063 Pacific Grove CA 93950-6063

O'SHEA, CATHERINE LARGE, marketing and public relations consultant; b. Asheville, N.C., Feb. 27, 1944; d. Edwin Kirk Jr. and Mary Mitchell (Westall) Large; m. Roger Dean Lower, Dec. 19, 1970 (dec. Sept. 1977); children: Thaddeus Kirk Lower and David Alexander Lower (twins, dec.); m. Michael Joseph O'Shea, Dec. 29, 1980. BA in History magna cum laude, Emory U., 1966. Mktg. staff mem. Time Inc., N.Y.C., 1966-69; mktg. adminstr. Collier-Macmillan Internat., N.Y.C., 1970-71; circulation mgr. Coll. Entrance Exam. Bd., N.Y.C., 1971-73; spl. asst. to pres. Wayne Dressel Assocs. Exec. Search, N.Y.C., 1973-75; freelance writer, editor, pub. rels. Princeton, N.J., 1975-78; dir. constituency rels. Emory U., Atlanta, 1978-80; devel. assoc. U. Del., Newark, 1981-83; asst. to pres. Elizabethtown (Pa.) Coll., 1983-85; assoc. v.p. Beaver Coll., Glenside, Pa., 1985; cons. mktg. and pub. rels. Phila., S.C., 1985—. Co-author: 50 Secrets of Highly Successful Cats, 1994; editor Elizabethtown mag., 1983-85; contbr. articles to nat. mags. and profl. jours. Founder Helping Hands Internat.; trustee Large Found., Newberry Opera House Found; v.p. pub. rels. Phi Mu Found. Mem. Pub. Rels. Soc. Am. (accredited), Mortar Bd., Phi Beta Kappa, Phi Mu.

O'SHEA, LYNNE EDEEN, marketing executive, educator; b. Chgo., Oct. 18, 1945; d. Edward Fisk and Mildred (Lessner) O'S. B.A., B.J. in Polit. Sci. and Advt, U. Mo., 1968, M.A. in Communications and Mktg. Research, 1971; PhD in Consumer Cultures, Northwestern U., 1977; postgrad., Sch. Mgmt. and Strategic Studies, U. Calif., 1988. Pres. O'Shea Advt. Agy., Dallas, 1968-69; congl. asst. Washington, 1969-70; brand mgr. Procter & Gamble Co., Cin., 1971-73; v.p. Foote, Cone & Belding, Inc., Chgo., 1973-79; v.p. corp. communications Internat. Harvester Co., Chgo., 1979-82; dir. communications Arthur Andersen & Co., Chgo., 1983-86; v.p. strategic planning Campbell-Ewald, Detroit and Los Angeles, 1986; v.p. bus. devel. Gannett Co., Inc., Chgo., 1987-94; group strategic planning dir. DDB Needham Worldwide, Inc., Chgo., 1995-96; pres., chief oper. officer Shalit Place L.L.C., 1995—; exec. v.p. Mus. Broadcast Comm., Chgo., 1996—; prof. mktg. U. Chgo. Grad. Sch. Bus., 1979-80, Kellogg Grad. Sch. Mgmt., 1983-94; disting. vis. prof. Syracuse U., 1982—. Bd. dirs. Off-the-Street Club, Chgo., 1977-86; mem. adv. bd. U. Ill. Coll. Commerce, 1980—, Girl Scouts Am., 1985—, Chgo. Crime Commn., 1987—, Stephenson Rsch. Ctr., 1987—, DePaul U., 1989—, Roosevelt U., 1994—. Recipient numerous Eagle Fin. Advt. awards, Silver medalist Am. Advt. Fedn., 1989; named Advt. Woman of Yr. Chgo. Advt. Club, 1989; named Glass Ceiling Commn., 1991-95, Com. 21st Century, 1992—. Mem. Internat. Women's Forum (v.p. devel., v.p. communications, exec. com., bd. dir.), Chgo. Network, Women's Forum Chgo., Women's Forum Mich., Tarrytown Group, Social Venture Network, Execs. Club Chgo., Mid-Am. Club (bd. govs. 1990—), Women's Athletic Club Chgo. Office: Nat Investment Svcs The John Hancock Ctr 875 N Michigan Ave Ste 3060 Chicago IL 60611-1901

O'SHEA, PATRICIA A., physician, educator; b. Syracuse, N.Y., June 14, 1944; d. John Daniel and Mildred (Olbeter) Allen; m. John S. O'Shea, July 5, 1969. BS summa cum laude, Le Moyne Coll., 1966; MD, Johns Hopkins U., 1970. Diplomate Am. Bd. Pathology, Am. Bd. Anatomic, Clin. and Pediat. Pathology. From intern to resident Duke U. Med. Ctr., Durham, N.C., 1970-74; from asst. to assoc. prof. pathology Brown U., Providence, 1974-90; assoc. prof. pathology Emory U., Atlanta, 1990—; mem. faculty Armed Forces Inst., Washington, 1989; short-course faculty U.S. and Can. Acad. Pathology, Augusta, Ga., 1992—. Contbr. articles to profl. jours. Fellow Am. Acad. Pediats., Coll. Am. Pathologists; m. Soc. Pediat. Pathology (mem. coun.). Office: Egleston Children's Hosp Emory U 1405 Clifton Rd NE Atlanta GA 30322-1060

OSHEROW, JACQUELINE SUE, poet, English language educator; b. Phila., Aug. 15, 1956; d. Aaron and Evelyn Hilda (Victor) O.; m. Saul Korewa, June 16, 1985; children: Magda, Dora, Mollie. AB Magna cum laude, Radcliffe Coll., Harvard U., 1978; postgrad., Trinity Coll., Cambridge U., 1978-79; PhD in English and Am. Lit., Princeton U., 1990. Asst. prof. English U. Utah, Salt Lake City, 1989—. Author: (poetry) Looking for Angels in New York, 1988, Conversations with Survivors, 1994. Recipient Witter Bynner prize Am. Acad. and Inst. Arts and Letters, 1990, Lucille Medwick Meml. award, 1995; Ingram Merrill Found. grantee, 1990. Mem. Poetry Soc. Am. (John Masefield Meml. award 1993). Jewish. Home: 1148 E 100 S Salt Lake City UT 84102-1640 Office: U Utah Dept English 3500 LNCO Salt Lake City UT 84112

OSKEY, D. BETH, banker; b. Red Wing, Minn., Dec. 23, 1921; d. Alvin E. and Effie D. (Thompson) Feldman; m. Warren B. Oskey, Sept. 27, 1941; children: Jo Cheryl, Warren A., Peter (dec.), Jeffery L.; student U. Wis., River Falls, 1939-41; B.A., Met. State U., Minn., 1975; grad. degree in banking, U. Wis., 1973, M in banking, 1977; student in interior decorating LaSalle Extension U., Chgo., 1970. Officer Hiawatha Nat. Bank, Hager City, Wis., 1959-91, cashier, 1978-79, pres., 1979, chmn. bd., 1984—, exec. v.p., dir., sec. bd. dirs., 1959—, sec., mem. discount com.; with First Nat. Bank of Glenwood, Glenwood City, Wis., 1965—, pres., exec. v.p., 1979—, dir., sec. bd., 1965—, chmn. bd., 1984—, sec., mem. discount com.; ret., 1991; speaker on women in banking. Mem. banking com. Vo-Tech Sch., Red Wing; former officer civic orgns.; mem. Leisurettes, L.W. Barbershop Belles. Mem. AAUW, Ind. Bankers Am., Wis. Bankers Assn., Am. Bankers Assn., Gen. Fedn. Women's Clubs Internat., Inc. (bd. dirs., pres. 1988-90), Minn. Fedn. Women's Clubs (v.p. 1983-85, pres. dist. III 1988-90, pres. elect 1986-88, pres. 1988-90; Leisure World (in charge of comm., mem. mixed chorus), Mesa, Ariz. (pres. Wis. Club, 1991-92). Republican. Lutheran. Home: 1022 Hallstrom Dr Red Wing MN 55066-3819 also: 1561 Leisure World Mesa AZ 85206-2312 Office: Hiawatha Nat Bank Hager City WI 54014

OSLER, DOROTHY K., state legislator; b. Dayton, Ohio, Aug. 19, 1923; d. Carl M. and Pearl A. (Tobias) Karstaedt; BS cum laude in Bus. Adminstrn., Miami U., Oxford, Ohio, 1945; m. David K. Osler, Oct. 26, 1946; children: Scott C., David D. Mem. Conn. Ho. of Reps., 1973-92. Mem. Greenwich (Conn.) Rep. Town Meeting, 1968—, Eastern Greenwich Women's Rep. Club, 1970—; sec. Conn. Student Loan Found., 1973-83, v.p., 1983-84; mem. Spl. Edn. Cost Commn., 1976-77, Sch. Fin. Adv. Panel, 1977-78, Edn. Equity Study Com., 1980-81, Commn. on Goals for U. Conn. Health Ctr., 1975-76; bd. dirs. ARC, 1975. Mem. Nat. Order Women Legislators (sec. 1987-89), Conn. Order of Women Legislators (sec. 1983-84, pres. 1985-86), LWV (pres. Greenwich chpt. 1965-67, sec. Conn. chpt. 1967-72), AAUW (dir. 1971-73, 95-96), Mortar Board, Phi Beta Kappa, Alpha Omicron Pi. Republican. Christian Scientist. Bi-weekly columnist local newspaper, 1973-83.

OSMAN, EDITH GABRIELLA, lawyer; b. N.Y.C., Mar. 18, 1949; d. Arthur Abraham and Judith (Goldman) Udem; children: Jacqueline, Daniel. BA in Spanish, SUNY, Stony Brook, 1970; JD cum laude, U. Miami, 1983. Bar: Fla. 1983, U.S. Dist. Ct. (so. dist.) Fla. 1984, U.S. Dist. Ct. (mid. dist.) Fla. 1988, U.S. Ct. Appeals (11th cir.) 1985, U.S. Supreme Ct. 1987, U.S. Ct. Mil. Appeals 1990. Assoc. Kimbrell & Hamann, P.A., Miami, 1984-90, Dunn & Lodish, P.A., Miami, 1990-93; pvt. practice in law Miami, 1993—; spkr. in field. Mem. adv. com. for Implementation of the Victor Posner Judgement to Aid the Homeless, 1986-89; spkr. small firm and solo practitioner Town Hall Meetings, 1993; spkr. Bridge the Gap Seminar, Comml. Litigation, 1994. Mem. ABA (product liability com., corp. counsel com.), Fla. Bar Assn. (budget com. 1989-92, voluntary bar liaison com. 1989-90, spl. com. on formation of All-Bar Conf. 1988-89, chmn. mid-yr. conv. 1989, mem. long range planning com. 1988-90, bd. govs. 1991—, spl. commn. on delivery of legal svcs. to the indigent 1990-92, chair program evaluation com. bd. govs., 96—, mem. exec. com. 1992-93, 96—, rules and bylaws com. 1993-94, disciplinary rev. com. 1994—, investment com. 1994—, vice chair rules com. 1994—, Outstanding Past Voluntary Bar Pres. award 1996), Dade County Bar Assn. (fed. ct. rules com. 1985-86, chmn. program com. 1988-89, 90-91, exec. com. 1987-88, bus. law cert. com. 1995-96, practice law mgmt. com. 1995-96), Fla. Assn. Bar Assn. Pres. (bd. dirs. 1988-89, treas. 1989-90, v.p. 1990-91, pres. 1991-92), Fla. Assn. Women Lawyers (bd. dirs. 1985-86, v.p. Dade County chpt. 1986-87, pres. 1987-88, pres.-elect Fla. chpt. 1988-89, pres. 1989-90), Nat. Coun. Women's Bar Assn. (dir. nat. conf. 1990-91), Dade County Trial Lawyers Assn. Office: Edith G Osman PA Internat Place 100 SE 2nd St Ste 3920 Miami FL 33131-2148

OSMAN, MARY ELLA WILLIAMS, journal editor; b. Honea Path, S.C.; d. Humphrey Bates and Jennie Louise (Williams) Williams; student Coll. William and Mary, Ga. State Coll. for Women; A.B., Presbyn. Coll., 1939; B.S. in L.S., U. N.C., 1944; m. John Osman, Oct. 22, 1936. Asst. libr. Presbyn. Coll., Clinton, S.C., 1936-38, Union Theol. Sem., Richmond, Va., 1938-44; sr. cataloger, asst. libr. Rhodes Coll., Memphis, 1944-52; asst. test cities project Ford Found. Fund for Adult Edn., N.Y.C., 1952-57, assoc. dir. office of info., 1957-61, exec. asst. to pres., sec. to bd. dirs., 1960-61; asst. libr. AIA, Washington, 1962-68, asst. editor AIA Jour., 1969-72, assoc. editor, 1972-77, sr. editor, 1978-87. Mem. AIA (hon.), Chi Delta Phi, Kappa Delta. Presbyn. Contbr. to various mags. Home: 3600 Chateau Dr Apt 244 Columbia SC 29204-3971

OSMER-MCQUADE, MARGARET, business executive, broadcast journalist; b. N.Y.C.; d. Herbert Bernard and Margaret Normann (Brunjes) O.; m. Lawrence Carroll McQuade, Mar. 15, 1980; 1 son, Andrew. B.A., Cornell U., 1960. Assoc. producer UN Bur., CBS News, N.Y.C., 1962-69; producer 60 Minutes, N.Y.C., 1969-72; reporter, producer Bill Moyer's Jour., Pub. Broadcasting Service, N.Y.C., 1972-73, Reasoner Report, ABC News, N.Y.C., 1973-75; corr., anchor person Good Morning Am., ABC Morning News, Washington, 1975-77; corr. ABC TV News, Washington, 1977-79; v.p., dir. programs Council on Fgn. Relations, 1979-93; pres., CEO Qualitas Internat., N.Y.C., 1994—; dir. Dime Savs. Bank, 1980—; cons. pub. broadcasting; mem. program com. Ditchley Found. Producer, reporter: TV news shows Come Fly A Kite (Nat. Press Photographer's award 1974), Kissinger, 1970, No Tears for Rachel, 1972, Calder: Master of Mobiles, 1975; moderator, producer World in Focus, publ. TV series for Coun. Fgn. Relations/Sta. WNYC, PBS, Worldnet, 1988-93. Mem. U.S. delegation World Conf. on Cambodian Refugees, Geneva, 1980; mem. Def. Adv. Com. on Women in the Service, 1978-82; trustee Cornell U.; mem. bd. overseers Cornell U. Med. Coll., pres.'s coun. Cornell Women; mem. program com. The Ritchley Found., 1994—, task force N.Y. Sch. Vols., 1994—; vol. Nat. Svc. Learning, 1994—. Recipient Peabody award Staff of 60 Minutes, 1970. Mem. NATAS, Coun. Fgn. Relations, program comm. The Mitching Found., Task Force N.Y. Sch. Vol., Nat. Press Club, Mid. Atlantic Club., vol. Nat. Svc. Learning. Club: Cosmopolitan, Century. •

OSMON, CAROLINE NESBITT, media relations coordinator; b. Corpus Christi, Tex., Aug. 3, 1960; d. Earl Johnson Jr. and Kay (Zitzman) N.; m. Stephen Lee Osmon, Sept. 18, 1993. BJ, U. Tex., 1982. News producer KSAT-TV, San Antonio, 1982-84, WJZ-TV, Balt., 1984-88, KTRK-TV, Houston, 1988-94; media rels. coord. Meml. Healthcare Sys., Houston, 1994—. Adv. coun. Sam Houston Coun. Boy Scouts Am., Houston, 1994. Mem. Women in Comm., Gamma Phi Beta. Democrat. Episcopalian. Office: Meml Healthcare Sys 7737 SW Freeway Ste 240 Houston TX 77074

OSNES, PAMELA GRACE, special education educator; b. Burke, S.D., Sept. 10, 1955; d. John Ruben and Dortha Grace (Wilson) O.; children: Jocelyn Fern, Logan John. BS in Spl. Edn., U. S.D., 1977, BS in Elem. Edn., 1977; MA in Clin. Psychology, W.Va. U., 1981. Spl. edn. tchr. Sioux Falls (S.D.) Sch. Dist., 1977-79; instr. psychology dept. W.Va. U., Morgantown, 1982-85; dir. Carousel Preschool Program, Morgantown, 1982-85; assoc. prof. U. South Fla., Tampa, 1986-93, adminstrv. coord. advanced grad. programs dept. spl. edn., 1994—. Mem. Assn. for Behavior Analysis, Coun. for Exceptional Children (div. early childhood, div. rsch., tchr. edn. div.), Coun. Adminstrs. Spl. Edn., Coun. for Children with Behavior Disorders.

OSOWIEC, DARLENE ANN, clinical psychologist, educator, consultant; b. Chgo., Feb. 16, 1951; d. Stephen Raymond and Estelle Marie Osowiec; m. Barry A. Leska. BS, Loyola U., Chgo., 1973; MA with honors, Roosevelt U., 1980; postgrad. in psychology, Saybrook Inst., San Francisco, 1985-88; PhD in Clin. Psychology, Calif. Inst. Integral Studies, 1992. Lic. clin. psychologist, Mo., Ill. Mental health therapist Ridgeway Hosp., Chgo., 1978; mem. faculty psychology dept. Coll. Lake County, Grayslake, Ill., 1981; counselor, supr. MA-level interns, chmn. pub. rels. com. Integral Counseling Ctr., San Francisco, 1983-84; clin. psychology intern Chgo.-Read Mental Health Ctr. Ill. Dept. Mental Health, 1985-86; mem. faculty dept. psychology Moraine Valley C.C., Palos Hills, Ill., 1988-89; lectr. psychology Daley Coll., Chgo., 1988-90; cons. Gordon & Assocs., Oak Lawn, Ill., 1989—; adolescent, child and family therapist Orland Twp. Youth Svcs., Orland Park, Ill., 1993; psychology fellow Sch. Medicine, St. Louis U., 1994-95; clin. psychologist in pvt. practice Chgo., 1996—. Ill. State scholar, 1969-73; Calif. Inst. Integral Studies scholar, 1983. Mem. APA, Am. Psychol. Soc., Am. Women in Psychology, Am. Statis. Assn., Ill. Psychol. Assn., Calif. Psychol. Assn., Mo. Psychol. Assn., Gerontol. Soc. Am., Am. Soc. Clin. Hypnosis, Internat. Platform Assn., Chgo. Soc. Clin. Hypnosis, NOW (chair legal adv. corps, Chgo. 1974-76). Home: 6608 S Whipple St Chicago IL 60629-2916

OSSEIRAN-HANNA, KHATMEH AZIZ, advocate; b. Sidon, Lebanon, Jan. 28, 1961; came to the U.S., 1972; d. Aziz and Souhaila Adib (Al-Taqi) Osseiran; m. Ibrahim Aziz Hanna, Aziz Ibrahim Hanna. BA in Internat. Affairs, George Washington U., 1982; postgrad., McGill U., 1982-86. Student aid officer Save Lebanon, Inc., Washington, 1982, nat. coord., 1985, exec. dir., 1987-94; organizer, researcher Am.-Arab Anti-Discrimination Com., Washington, 1984; assr. dir. Nat. Coun. on Canada Arab Rels., Ottawa, Canada, 1986-87; maj. gifts assoc. Greenpeace, 1994-95; chair Save Lebanon, 1994-96; exec. dir. Am. U. of Beirut Alumni Assn. N.Am., 1995—; founder, co-chmn. Am.-Lebanese Pub. Affairs Com., Washington, 1989-91; coord. InterFuture, Washington, 1981-82. Editor, author: (newsletter) Our Hope For Children and Peace, 1989—. Del. Va. Dem. Cen. Com., Arlington, 1988, 89; pres. W&L Beautification Com., Arlington, 1977-78. Scholar InterFuture, 1981. Fellow Inst. Islamic Studies; mem. Pi Delta Phi. Home: 477 Walnut St Ridgefield NJ 07657 Office: AUB AANA 850 3rd Ave 18 Flr New York NY 10022

OSSENBERG, HELLA SVETLANA, psychoanalyst; b. Kiev, Russia, June 10, 1930; came to U.S., 1957, naturalized, 1964; d. Anatole E. and Tatiana N. (Dombrovski) Donath; diploma langs. and psychology, U. Heidelberg, Germany, 1953; MS, Columbia U., 1968; cert. Nat. Psychol. Assn. Psychoanalysis, 1977, diplomate Am. Bd. Examiners; m. Carl H. Ossenberg, June 7, 1958. Sr. psychiat. social worker VA Mental Hygiene Clinic, N.Y.C., 1968-80, pvt. practice psychoanalysis, N.Y.C., 1975—; mem. Theodor Reik Cons. Center, 1978—; field instr. Columbia U., Fordham U. schs. social work. Mem. NASW, Acad. Cert. Social Workers, Nat. Psychol. Assn. Psychoanalysis, Nat. Assn. Advancement Phychoanalysis (Am. Bds. Accreditation and Certification), Am. Group Psychotheraphy Assn. (founder), Coun. Psychoanalytic Psychotherapists. Home: 820 W End Ave New York NY 10025-5371 Office: 345 W 58th St New York NY 10019-1145

OSSEWAARDE, ANNE WINKLER, real estate developer; b. Dallas, June 2, 1957; d. Lowell Graves and Ruth Lenore (Lind) Winkler; m. Kirk L Ossewaarde, Apr. 27, 1991. BBA in Fin. with honors, Emory U., 1979; MBA in Acctg. and Fin. with honors, U. Tex., 1983; MS in Real Estate Devel., MIT, 1988. Mgmt. trainee Citizens & So. Nat. Bank, Atlanta, 1979-81; banking assoc. Continental Ill. Nat. Bank, Chgo. and Dallas, 1983-85; asst. v.p., devel. assoc. Trammell Crow Residential, Dallas, 1985-87, Seattle, 1988-91; devel. mgr. Blackhawk Port Blakeley Cmtys., Seattle, 1991-93; real estate portfolio mgr. Aegon U.S.A. Realty, Atlanta, 1994—. Charles Harritt Jr. Presdl. scholar U. Tex., 1982, Alexander Grant scholar, 1982. Mem. Jr. League of Atlanta, Comml. Real Estate Women, MIT Ctr. for Real Estate Alumni Assn., Alpha Epsilon Upsilon. Methodist. Home: 5510 Mount Vernon Pky NW Atlanta GA 30327-4739

OSSOLA, LUCINDA ANN, secondary school educator; b. Torrington, Conn., Apr. 17, 1947; d. George Andrew and Ida (Fainelli) O. BS, Plymouth State Coll., 1971. Varsity softball coach Laconia (N.H.) H.S., 1971-76, varsity field hockey coach, 1971-79, phys. edn. tchr., 1971—, varsity basketball coach, 1971-86, jr. varsity field hockey coach, 1974-76, dir. phys. edn. and health, 1976—, jr. varsity basketball coach, 1993—. Bd. dirs. Lakes Region Cmty. Svc. Coun., Region III, Laconia, 1988-91. Named to Athletic Hall of Fame, Plymouth State Coll., 1987. Mem. NEA (budget com. N.H. chpt. 1993-94, del. rep. 1991-95), Laconia Edn. Assn. (N.H. health care coalition 1993-95, bldg. rep. 1991-93, sec. 1993-94, negotiation team 1991-94, Lakes region health care coalition 1993-95, wellness task force 1995—). Home: Straits Rd RR 1 Box 321 D Ashland NH 03217 Office: Laconia HS Union Ave Laconia NH 03246

OSTEN, JANICE ANNE, education coordinator; b. Oil City, Pa., Sept. 20, 1956; d. John Joseph and Betty Ruth (Brandon) Ward; m. Dale Lee Osten, Feb. 11, 1978. Assoc. Degree, Clarion State U., Pa., 1976; BSN, Slippery Rock State U., Pa., 1985. Staff nurse Oil City (Pa.) Hosp., 1976-82, charge nurse, 1982-89; staff nurse Ind. Nurses Assn., Oil City, Pa., 1984-86, St. Vincent Health Ctr., Erie, Pa., 1989; staff nurse Med. Ctr. for Fed. Prisoners, Springfield, Mo., 1989-91, nurse educator, 1991-96; nat. continuing profl. edn. coord. Washington, 1996—; asst. prof. Southwest Bapt. U., Springfield, Mo., 1994-95. Contbr. articles to profl. jours. Planning com. Cmty. Work Group Springfield, Mo., 1993-94. Recipient Nat. Excellence in Clin. Practice award Bur. Prisons, Washington, 1993. Mem. AACN (Disting. Leadership award Ozarks chpt. 1995), Heart of the Ozarks, Sigma Theta Tau. Methodist. Home: 15461 Ambergate Dr Woodbridge VA 22191 Office: Fed Bur Prisons Health Svcs Divsn 320 1st St NW Washington DC 20534

OSTENDORF, JOAN DONAHUE, fund raiser, volunteer; b. Boston, Dec. 9, 1933; d. John Stanley and Genevieve Catherine (Morrissey) Donahue; m. Edgar Louis Ostendorf, Feb. 10, 1962; 1 child, Mary Elizabeth. BA, Marymount Coll., Tarrytown, N.Y., 1956; postgrad., Boston U., 1956. Tchr. Boston pub. schs., 1956-57, Waltham (Mass.) pub. schs., 1957-62. Trustee Cleve. Inst. Music, 1984—, mem. trustees coordianting coun., 1989; mem. Jr. League Cleve., 1964, 1st v.p. 1972-73; founder adv. coun. pub. rels. com. Cleve. Orch., 1974, 1st v.p., 1975-76; mem. del. assembly United Way, 1977-87; chmn. benefits Vis. Nurse Assn., 1987-88, March Dimes, 1982; trustee women's com. U. Hosps. Case Western Res. U. Med. Sch., 1974—; mem. nominating com. Inst. Music, 1990-91; 2d v.p. Music and Drama Club, 1991-93, corresponding sec., 1993-95; chair Lyric Opera, 1992, Platform Assn., 1992—; pres. bd. trustees Cleve. Inst. Music, 1980-82, pres. women's com., 1980-82; mem. adv. bd. Women's Community Found., 1991—; v.p. Cleve. Internat. Piano Competition, 1994—. Mem. Internat. Platform Assn., Longwood Cricket Club, Intown Club, Chagrin Valley Hunt Club. Republican. Roman Catholic. Address: 3425 Roundwood Rd Chagrin Falls OH 44022-6634

OSTERHOUT, ANNALISA, dance educator; b. Geneva, N.Y., Nov. 19, 1968; d. Donald Joseph and Ruth Carter (Bowers) Furano; m. David Lee Osterhout, Oct. 10, 1992. Student, Syracuse U., 1993—. Dance tchr. Dance Arts Studio, Syracuse, N.Y., 1991-94, Syracuse U., 1993—; founder, artistic dir. Carmellia Dance Troupe, Syracuse, 1993—; tchg. dance artist Cultural Resources Coun. for Arts in Edn., Syracuse, 1994—; tchr. modern dance Dance Ctr. North, Syracuse, 1994—, Syracuse Sch. Dance, 1995—; owner, artistic dir. The Conservatory of Dance, 1996—; bd. dirs. Decentralization Grants Program for Arts, Syracuse; guest choreographer Syracuse Contemporary Dance, Dance Arts Ensemble, Syracuse, 1991-94. Home: # K9 7300 Cedarpost Rd Liverpool NY 13088

OSTERKAMP, DALENE MAY, psychology educator, artist; b. Davenport, Iowa, Dec. 1, 1932; d. James Hiram and Bernice Grace (La Grange) Simmons; m. Donald Edwin Osterkamp, Feb. 11, 1951 (dec. Sept. 1951). BA, San Jose State U., 1959, MA, 1962; PhD, Saybrook Inst., 1989. Lectr. San Jose (Calif.) State U., 1960-61, U. Santa Barbara (Calif.) Ext., 1970-76; prof. Bakersfield (Calif.) Coll., 1961-87, emeritus, 1987—; adj. faculty, counselor Calif. State U., Bakersfield, 1990—; gallery dir. Bakersfield Coll., 1964-72. Exhibited in group shows at Berkeley (Calif.) Art, Ctr., 1975, Libr. of Congress, 1961, Seattle Art Mus., 1962. Founder Kern Art Edn. Assn., Bakersfield, 1962, Bakersfield Printmakers, 1976. Staff sgt. USAF, 1952-55. Recipient 1st Ann. Svc. to Women award Am. Assn. Women in C.C., 1989. Mem. APA, Assn. for Women in Psychology, Assn. for Humanistic Psychology, Calif. Soc. Printmakers. Home: PO Box 387 Glennville CA 93226-0387 Office: Calif State Univ Stockdale Ave Bakersfield CA 93309

OSTOLAZA, YVETTE, lawyer; b. Miami, Fla., Nov. 21, 1964; d. Oscar J. and Carmen (Astiazarain) O.; m. Peter B. Dewar, Nov. 10, 1991. BA, U. Miami, 1985, JD, 1992. Bar: Tex. 1992. Various mktg. positions Ea. Airlines, Ft. Lauderdale, Fla., Gainesville, Fla.; various mktg. positions Continental Airlines, Orlando, Fla.; internat. sales mgr. Continental/Ea. Sales, Inc., Miami; assoc. Weil, Gotshal & Manges LLP, Dallas, 1992—. Mem. U. Miami Law Rev., 1991-92; articles and comments editor Bus. Law Jour., 1991-92. Mem. ABA, Attys. Serving Cmty., Soc. Bar and Gavel, Golden Key. Office: Weil Ootshal & Marges 100 Crescent Ct Ste 1300 Dallas TX 75201-6950

OSTROVSKY, CYD CAROL, lawyer, consultant; b. Bklyn., Sept. 14, 1943; d. George and Helen Bell (Wiseman) Rosenberg; m. Marvin Carl Ostrovsky, June 14, 1964; children: Daniel Allen, Ellen Beth. BA, Bklyn. Coll., 1965; JD, Mass. Sch. Law, 1995. Bar: Mass. 1995. Social worker Divsn. of Child Guardianship, Boston, 1965-69, child welfare specialist, 1969-70; ind. contr. office mgmt. Southborough, Mass., 1986-91; adminstrv. asst. Health Info. Referral Svc., Marlborough, Mass., 1982-85, 91-92; cons. Southborough, 1991-95, pvt. practice law, 1996—; mem. human rights com. Wayside Programs, Inc., Framingham, 1995—; mediator Consumer Assistance Office, Natick, Mass., 1995—. Chmn. Sch. Com., Southborough, 1986-87, mem., 1984-87; mem. Southborough Adv. Com., 1980-82, chmn., 1983. Co-recipient Citizen of Yr. award (with spouse) Southborough Orgn. for Schs., 1981-82. Mem. Mass. Bar Assn., Worcester Bar Assn., Jewish Workshop for Edn. and Culture. Jewish. Home and Office: 1 Tara Rd Southborough MA 01772

OSTROW, RONA LYNN, librarian, educator; b. N.Y.C., Oct. 21, 1948; d. Morty and Jeane Goldberg; m. Steven A. Ostrow, June 25, 1972; 1 child, Ciné Justine. BA, CCNY, 1969; MS in LS, Columbia U., 1970; MA, Hunter Coll., 1975; postgrad., Rutgers U., 1990—. Cert. libr., N.Y. Br. adult and reference libr. N.Y. Pub. Libr., N.Y.C., 1970-73, rsch. libr., 1973-78; asst. libr. Fashion Inst. Tech., N.Y.C., 1978-80; assoc. dir. Grad. Bus. Resource Ctr., Baruch Coll., CUNY, 1980-90, assoc. prof., 1980-90; assoc. dean of librs. for pub. svcs. Adelphi U., Garden City, N.Y., 1990-94; chief libr. Marymount Manhattan Coll., N.Y.C., 1994—. Author: Dictionary of Retailing, 1984, Dictionary of Marketing, 1987; co-author: Cross Reference Index, 1989. Mem. ALA, AAUW, Libr. Info. and Tech. Assn., Assn. Coll. and Rsch. Librs. (chair N.Y.C. sect.). Office: Shanahan Libr Marymount Manhattan Coll 221 E 71st St New York NY 10021

OSTROWSKI, PAMELA LEE, secondary educator; b. Milw., Feb. 13, 1949; d. Earl George and Doris Ann (Radaszewski) Leigeb; m. James Allan Ostrowski, Jan. 13, 1973; 1 child, Jonathan James. BS, U. Wis., Whitewater, 1971; student, West Tex. A&M U., 1984, 87, 92. Cert. tchr., Tex., Wis. Tchr. Mac Arthur Elem. Sch., Green Bay, Wis., 1971-80, Onalaska (Wis.) Mid. Sch., 1980-83, Canyon (Tex.) Jr. H.S., 1983-84; tchr. Valleyview Jr. H.S., Amarillo, Tex., 1984—, advisor nat. jr. honor soc., 1985-87, 96—, advisor student coun., 1989-94, dept. chair, 1986—; dept. chair Onalaska Mid. Sch., 1982-83. Bd. dirs. cmty. edn. adv. coun. Canyon Ind. Sch. Dist., 1985-88; bd. dirs. PTA exec. bd. Valleyview Jr. H.S., Amarillo, 1987—; region social studies steering com. XVI Edn. Svc. Ctr., 1996—. Mem. NEA, ASCD, Tex. Coun. for Social Studies, Tex. State Tchrs. Assn., Tex. PTA (hon. life mem.). Lutheran. Home: 3407 Harmony St Amarillo TX 79109-4124 Office: Valleyview Jr HS 9000 Valleyview Dr Amarillo TX 79118

OSTWALT, PEGGY CATHERINE, mathematics educator; b. Billings, Mont., Sept. 25, 1956; d. John Clarence and Dorothy (Frank) O.; 1 child, Allison Marie Hanson. BS in Secondary Edn., Ea. Mont. Coll., 1978. Math. tchr. Belfry (Mont.) Pub. Schs., 1978-82, Columbus (Mont.) Pub. Schs., 1982—. Mem. NEA, Mont. Edn. Assn., Mont. Coun. Tchrs. Math. Home: RR 1 Box 206 Columbus MT 59019-9707

O'SULLIVAN, EILEEN ANN, banker; b. Phila., May 7, 1956; d. Thomas and Elisabeth (Kiehl) O'S. Student, Ctr. for Fin. Studies, Fairfield, Conn., 1988, U. Pa., 1994—. Teller trainee Beneficial Savs. Bank, Phila., 1974-75, jr. teller, 1975-80, teller #2, 1980-81, teller #3, 1981-82, head teller, 1982-84, mgmt. trainee, 1984-85, asst. mgr., 1975-87, mgr., 1987-96. Co-chmn. Widener Day com. Widener Meml. Sch., 1987—; mem., speaker community workshops 35th Police Dist., 1986—, chmn. holiday meals program, 1988—; sec. Greater Broad and Olney Bus. Assn., 1984-88; assoc. mem. Phila. Orch. Soc., 1987-91, 94—; mem. Smithsonian Inst., 1988—, Univ. Mus. Univ. Pa., 1991, neighborhood improvement coun. Phila. Neighborhood Housing Svcs., 1989, Earthwatch, 1990, Pa. Soc. for Prevention of Cruelty to Animals, 1990. Recipient Community Svc. award Phila. Police Dept., 1987, 88, 89, 91. Mem. Nat. Space-L5 Soc. (life). Democrat. Roman Catholic. Office: Beneficial Savs Bank 2 Penn Center Plz Philadelphia PA 19102-1721

O'SULLIVAN, JUDITH ROBERTA, government official, author; b. Pitts., Jan. 6, 1942; d. Robert Howard and Mary Olive (O'Donnell) Gallick; m. James Paul O'Sullivan, Feb. 1, 1964; children: Kathryn, James. BA, Carlow Coll., 1963; MA, U. Md., 1969, PhD, 1976; postgrad. in law, Georgetown U., 1992—. Editor Am. Film Inst., Washington, 1974-77; assoc. program coord. Smithsonian Resident Assocs., Washington, 1977-78; dir. instl. devel. Nat. Archives, Washington, 1978-79; exec. dir. Md. State Humanities Coun., Balt., 1979-81, 82-84, Ctr. for the Book, Libr. of Congress, Washington, 1981-82; dep. asst. dir. Nat. Mus. Am. Art, Washington, 1984-87, acting asst. dir., 1987-89; pres., CEO The Mus. at Stony Brook, N.Y., 1989-92; exec. dir. Nat. Assn. Women Judges, Washington, 1993; clk. Office Legal Adviser U.S. Dept. State, Washington, 1994-96; summer assoc. Piper & Marbury, Balt., 1995; with atty. gen.'s honors program U.S. Dept. Justice, 1996—; chair Smithsonian Women's Coun., Washington, 1988-89; mem. editorial advisory bd. Am. Film Inst., 1979—. Author: The Art of the Comic Strip, 1971 (Gen. Excellence award Printing Industry Am.), Workers and Allies, 1975, (with Alan Fern) The Complete Prints of Leonard Baskin, 1984, The Great American Comic Strip, 1991; editor Am. Film Inst. Catalogue: Feature Films, 1961-70, 1974-77. Trustee Child Life Ctr., U. Md., College Pk., 1971-74; chair Smithsonian Women's Coun., 1988-89. Univ. fellow U. Md., 1967-70, Mus. fellow, 1970-71; Smithsonian fellow Nat. Collection Fine Arts, Washington, 1972-73. Mem. Assn. Assn. Art Mus. Dirs., Am. Assn. Mus., Mid-Atlantic Mus. Conf., AAUW. Home: 17 F Ridge Rd Greenbelt MD 20770-1749 Office: US Dept Justice Exec Office Immigration Rev Falls Church VA 22041

O'SULLIVAN, MARY J., physician, maternal fetal medicine educator; b. Bklyn., Mar. 22, 1938; d. Michael and Annie (O'Donnell) Sullivan. BS, St. John's U., Bklyn., 1959; MD, Women's Med. Coll., Phila., 1963. Resident Hosp. Women's Med. Ctr., Phila., 1964-68; instr. ob-gyn. N.Y. Med. Coll., 1968-73, asst. prof., 1973-77, chief obstetrics and maternal fetal medicine, 1973-77, assoc. dean, 1975-77; assoc. prof. ob-gyn. U. Miami, Fla., 1977-80, prof., 1980—, dir. ob-gyn. svcs., 1982, chief obstetrics svcs. and reumatology, dept. ob-gyn., 1982—, chief maternal fetal medicine, 1987—. Col. USAR, 1981—. Rsch. grantee U. Miami, 1980, 83, 88. Fellow Am. Coll. Ob-Gyn. (sec. 1989—); mem. Soc. Perinatal Obstetricians, So. Atlantic Ob-Gyn. Soc. (membership com. 1988—), Miami Ob-Gyn. Soc. (sec. 1988—). Roman Catholic. Office: U Miami Dept Ob-Gyn PO Box 16960 Miami FL 33101-6960*

OSWALD, EVA SUE ADEN, insurance executive; b. Ft. Dodge, Iowa, Feb. 2, 1949; d. Warren Dale Aden and Alice Rae (Gingerich) Aspeslet; m. Bruce Elliott Oswald, Nov. 27, 1976. BBS, U. Iowa, 1972. With Great Am. Ins. Co., 1975—; v.p. mktg. div. Great Am. Ins. Co., Orange, Calif., 1987, v.p. profit ctr., 1988-90; pres. Garden of Eva, Inc., 1990—; mem. Snelling-Selby Bus. Coun. Mem. Nat. Assn. Ins. Women, State Guarantee Fund (bd. dirs. 1986-87), Exec. Women St. Paul, Midway C. of C., White Bear Lake C. of C. Methodist. Office: 1585 Marshall Ave Saint Paul MN 55104-6222

OTERO-SMART, INGRID AMARILLYS, advertising executive; b. Santurce, P.R., Jan. 9, 1959; d. Angel Miguel and Carmen (Prann) Otero; m. Dean Edward Smart, May 4, 1991; 1 child, Jordan. BA in Comm., U. P.R., 1981. Traffic mgr. McCann-Erickson Corp., San Juan, P.R., 1981-82, media analyst, 1982, asst. account exec., 1982-83, account exec., 1983-84, sr. account exec., 1984-85, account dir., 1985-87; account supr. Mendoza-Dillon & Assocs., Newport Beach, Calif., 1987-89, sr. v.p. client svcs., 1989—, exec. v.p., dir. client svcs. Mem. Youth Motivation Task Force, Santa Ana, Calif., 1989—; bd. dirs. Orange County Hispanic C. of C., Santa Ana, 1989-90, U.S. Hispanic Family of Yr.; mem. Santa Ana Project P.R.I.D.E., 1993. Office: Mendoza-Dillon & Assocs Ste 600 4100 Newport Place Dr Newport Beach CA 92660-2451

OTHELLO, MARYANN CECILIA, quality assurance professional; b. N.Y.C., Oct. 23, 1946; d. Alphonse Reasum and Edith (Atwater) O. BS, St. Paul's Coll., Lawrenceville, Va., 1968; MS, Columbia U., 1972. Cert. adoption specialist. Family therapist crisis intervention Dept. Social Svcs., N.Y.C., 1968-72; dir. treatment team Abbott House, Irvington, N.Y., 1972-73; unit chief Manhattan State Psychiat. Facility, N.Y.C., 1973-75; asst. dir., dir. social svcs. St. Peter's Sch., Peekskill, N.Y., 1975-77; dir. Patchwork Svcs. for Children, Santa Ana, Calif., 1977-78; dir. adult and geriatric svcs. Cen. City Community Mental Health, L.A., 1978-79; trainer, facilitator Lifespring, Inc., San Rafael, Calif., 1978-80; sr. mgmt. cons. Nelson Cons. Group, Inc., Mpls., 1980-92; dep. dir. Div. Family Svcs. Dept. of Svcs. to Children, Youth and Their Families, Wilmington, Del., 1992-93; dir. planning and quality assurance Episcopal Community Svcs./Diocese of Pa., Phila., 1993-94; dep. exec. dir. Episcopal Cmty. Svcs./Diocese of Pa., Phila., 1994—; cons. Calif. Dept. Edn., 1977; field instr. casework Hunter Coll. Sch. Social Work, N.Y.C., 1975-77; adj. instr. U. So. Calif., L.A., 1977-78; specialist career devel. Goal for It, L.A., 1977-82; mgmt. devel. cons. Mgmt. Dynamics, Irvine, Calif., 1980-82; treas. Images of Sisterhood, Crofton, Md., 1994. Contbr. articles to profl. jours.; was interviewed twice on radio talk show As It Is, U. Calif., Irvine. Bd. dirs., presenter humanitarian awards L.A. Commn. on Assaults Against Women, 1985-87, Lettye's Sisters In Session, Wilmington, 1993—; facilitator Ch. of Religious Scis., Huntington Beach, Calif., 1981-83, NAACP, Urban League; founding mem. Kinship Alliance, Pacific Grove and Tustin, Calif., 1992—; mem. Afro-Am. Mus., Phila., 1993—; mem. nat. adv. com. on managed care Child Welfare League Am., 1995—. Named one of Outstanding Young Women of Am., 1976, 81; N.Y. State Regent scholar, 1968; Marie Antoinette Canon fellow Columbia U., 1972. Fellow Child Welfare League Am. (Adoption Specialist plaque 1976-89); mem. NAFE, Smithsonian Instn., Nat. Soc. for Historic Preservation, Wadsworth Antheneum, Nat. Trust for Hist. Preservation, Assn. for Female Execs. Office: Episcopal Community Svcs Diocese of Pa 225 S 3rd St Philadelphia PA 19106-3910

OTHERSEN, CHERYL LEE, insurance broker, realtor; b. Bay City, Mich., Aug. 17, 1948; d. Andrew Julius and Ruth Emma (Jacoby) Houthoofd; m. Wayne Korte Othersen, Sept. 5, 1964; 1 child, Angela. Lic. ins., Mich. State U., 1980, lic. realtor, 1981. Owner, operator Glad Rags Boutique, Unionville, Mich., 1976-79; dept. mgr. Gantos, Saginaw, Mich., 1979-80; agt., bookkeeper Othersen Ins. Agy., Inc., Unionville, 1979-81, v.p., 1981—; realtor Osentoski Realty Corp., Unionville, 1981—. Active Mich chpt. Nat. Head Injury Found., Mich. chpt. Crohn's and Colitis Found. Am., Inc., Nat. Mus. In the Arts, Nat. Trust for Hist. Preservation; vol. local Rep. campaigns, 1982, 84, 86; assoc. mem. Am. Mus. Natural History; charter supporter U.S. Holocaust Meml. Mus. Fellow (hon.) John F. Kennedy Libr. Found.; mem. Profl. Ins. Agts., Unionville Bus. Assn., Nat. Mus. Women in the Arts (charter). Mem. Moravian Ch. Club: Sherwood-on-the-Hill Country (Gagetown, Mich.). Home: 3315 Christy Way Saginaw MI 48603 Office: Othersen Ins Agy Inc 6639 Center St Unionville MI 48767-9482

OTIS, DENISE MARIE, editor, writer; b. Detroit, July 25, 1927; d. J. Hawley and Florence Ruth O. AB cum laude, Radcliffe Coll., Cambridge, Mass., 1949. English tchr. Cambridge Sch., Weston, Mass., 1949-50; asst. to feature editor House and Garden, N.Y.C., 1952-53, assoc. decorating editor, 1953-56, editor, entertaining dept., 1956-66, assoc. editor, 1966-80, deputy editor, 1980-87; sr. editor and cons. Conde Nast Publs., N.Y.C., 1987-93; consulting editor Vogue Decoration, Paris, 1989-91. Author: Decorating with Flowers, 1978; contbr. articles to profl. jours. Fulbright scholar Inst. Internat. Edn., France, 1950-51. mem. Internat. Dendrology Soc., Decorators Club, Phi Beta Kappa. Episcopalian.

OTIS, KAREN LAURA, museum official; b. Brockton, Mass., Jan. 19, 1959; d. Loring Bert and Barbara F. (Gibbs) O. Cert. with merit, Katharine Gibbs, 1977; BA in Art History, U. Mass., 1988. Admissions asst. Stonehill Coll., North Easton, Mass., 1977-82; black & white photo adminstr. Mus. Fine Arts, Boston, 1988—; contbr. photographs to The Sunday Standard Times Mag., New Bedford, Mass., 1989. Author: At the Vanishing Point, 1993; author of poems.

OTIS, LEE LIBERMAN, lawyer, educator; b. N.Y.C., Aug. 19, 1956; d. James Benjamin and Deen (Freed) L.; m. William Graham Otis, Oct. 24, 1993. BA, Yale U., 1979; JD, U. Chgo., 1983. Bar: N.Y. 1985, D.C. 1994. Law clk. U.S. Ct. Appeals (D.C. cir.), Washington, 1983-84; spl. asst. to asst atty. gen., civil div. U.S. Dept. Justice, Washington, 1984-86; dep. assoc. atty. gen. U.S. Dept. Justice, 1986, assoc. dep. atty. gen., 1986; law clk. to Justice Antonin Scalia U.S. Supreme Ct., Washington, 1986-87; asst. prof. law George Mason U., Arlington, Va., 1987-89; assoc. counsel to the Pres. Exec. Office of the Pres., Washington, 1989-92; assoc. Jones, Day, Reavis & Pogue, Washington, 1993-94; chief judiciary coun. U.S. Sen. Spence Abraham, 1995—; adj. prof. law Georgetown Law Sch., 1995, 96. Mem. Federalist Soc. for Law & Pub. Policy (founder, dir., nat. co-chmn.). Republican. Jewish.

O'TOOLE, PATRICIA ELLEN, writer, educator; b. Alpena, Mich., Oct. 10, 1946; d. Gordon Roy and Gertrude T. (McKenna) O'T. BA, U. Mich., 1968. Writer on bus. and social issues, L.A. and Norwalk, Conn., 1976—; adj. prof. Columbia U. Sch. Arts, N.Y.C., 1995—. Author: Corporate Messiah: The Hiring and Firing of Million-Dollar Managers, 1984, The Five of Hearts: An Intimate Portrait of Henry Adams and His Friends, 1880-1918, 1990; guest curator Nat. Portrait Gallery, Washington, 1990; contbr. essays, articles and revs. to nat. publs. MacDowell Colony fellow. Mem. PEN, LWV, Am. Hist. Assn., Am. Studies Assn., Internat. Assn. for Feminist Econs. Democrat. Office: PO Box 239 Norwalk CT 06856

O'TOOLE, TARA J., federal official; b. Harold J. and Jeanne (Whalen) O'T. BA, Vassar Coll., 1974; MD, George Washington U., 1981; MPH, Johns Hopkins U., 1988. Diplomate Am. Bd. Internal Medicine, Am. Bd. Preventive/Occupational Medicine. Rsch. asst. Sloan-Kettering Cancer Inst., N.Y.C., 1974-77; resident in internal medicine Yale New Haven (Conn.) Hosp., 1981-84; physician Balt. Cmty. Health Ctrs., 1984-87; fellow in occupational medicine Johns Hopkins U., Balt., 1987-89; sr. analyst Office Tech. Assessment, Washington, 1989-93; asst. sec. energy for environ., safety and health Dept. Energy, Washington, 1993—. Democrat. Office: Dept of Energy Environ Safety & Health 1000 Independence Ave SW Washington DC 20585-0001*

OTT, MARY DIEDERICH, artist; b. Cleve., Aug. 31, 1944; d. Norman Frank and Agnes Marie (Gaertner) Diederich; m. Edward Ott, Jan. 5, 1974; children: William Louis, Susan Marie. BA in Physics, Seton Hill Coll., 1965; SM in Physics, U. Chgo., 1967, PhD in Edn., 1971; student, U. Md., 1991-96, Art League Sch., Alexandria, Va., 1991-95. Lectr. Sch. Applied & Engring. Physics Cornell U., Ithaca, N.Y., 1971-74, rsch. assoc. Ctr. Improvement Undergrad. Edn., 1973-74, lectr. dept. physics, 1974-75, rsch. assoc. Coll. Engring., 1974-78, rsch. assoc. Inst. Occupl. Edn., 1978-79; statistician Nat. Ctr. Edn. Stats. HEW, Washington, 1976; sr. rsch. analyst Office Instnl. Studies U. Md., College Park, 1982-90; artist Silver Spring, Md., 1995—; ednl. cons., Silver Spring, 1980-82, 91-94. Contbr. articles to profl. jours. Chair Women's Caucus Cornell U., 1978. Recipient Disting. Alumna award Seton Hill Coll., 1995; NSF fellow, 1965-66, U. Chgo. fellow, 1966-71; Nat. Merit scholar, 1961-65. Mem. AAAS, Art League of Alexandria, Va., Rockville Arts Place. Home: 12421 Borges Ave Silver Spring MD 20904-2940

OTTENHEIMER, HARRIET JOSEPH, anthropologist, educator; b. N.Y.C., June 11, 1941; m. Martin Ottenheimer, June 15, 1962. BA, Bennington Coll., 1962; PhD, Tulane U., 1973. Asst. prof. anthropology Kans. State U., Manhattan, 1969-80, assoc. prof., 1980-86, prof., 1986—, dir. Am. ethnic studies, 1988—. Book rev. editor Nat. Assn. for Ethnic Studies; co-author: Cousin Joe: Blues From New Orleans, 1987; (recording) Music of the Comoro Islands, 1982, Historical Dictionary of the Comoro Islands, 1994; author: Shinzwani-English Dictionary (disk data set), 1986; contbr. articles to profl. jours. Office: AMETH Leasure Hall Kans State U Manhattan KS 66506

OTTO, BARBARA Z., banker; b. N.Y.C.. BA magna cum laude, NYU, postgrad. From credit adminstr. to corp. planning unit head Citibank, N.Y.C.; sr. v.p., mgr. portfolio sr. mgmt. info. systems Crocker Nat. Bank, San Francisco; sr. v.p. credit policy Bank of Am., San Francisco, 1986-90, exec. v.p., dir. credit examination svcs. dept., 1990-93, group exec. v.p., Latin Am. and Can. Group, 1993—. Mem. Inst. Ams. (bd. dirs.), Commonwealth Club (bd. govs.), Phi Beta Kappa. Office: BankAmerica 555 California St San Francisco CA 94104-1502

OTTO, JEAN HAMMOND, journalist; b. Kenosha, Wis., Aug. 27, 1925; d. Laurence Cyril and Beatrice Jane (Slater) Hammond; m. John A. Otto, Aug. 22, 1946; children: Jane L. Rahman, Mary Ellen Takayama, Peter J. Otto; m. Lee W. Baker, Nov. 23, 1973. Student, Ripon Coll., 1944-46. Women's editor Appleton (Wis.) Post-Crescent, 1960-68; reporter Milw. Jour., 1968-

72, editorial writer, 1972-77, editor Op Ed page, 1977-83; editorial page editor Rocky Mountain News, Denver, 1983-89, assoc. editor, 1989-92, reader rep., 1992—; Endowed chair U. Denver, 1992—. Founder, chmn. bd. trustees First Amendment Congress, 1979-85, chmn. exec. com., 1985-88, 89-91, pres. 1991—, mem. bd. trustees, 1979—; founding mem. Wis. Freedom of Info. Council. Recipient Headliner award Wis. Women in Communications, 1974; Outstanding Woman in Journalism award YWCA, Milw., 1977; Knight of Golden Quill Milw. Presss Club, 1979; spl. citation in Journalism Ball State U., 1980; James Madison award Nat. Broadcast Editorial Assn., 1981; spl. citation for contbn. to journalism Nat. Press Photographers Assn., 1981; Ralph D. Casey award, 1984; U. Colo. Regents award, 1985; John Peter Zenger award U. Ariz., 1988; Paul Miller Medallion award Okla. State U., 1990; Colo. SPJ Lowell Thomas award, 1990, Disting. Alumna award Ripon Coll., 1992, Hugh M. Hefner First Amendment Lifetime Achievement award Playboy Found., 1994. Mem. Colo. Press Assn. (chmn. freedom of info. com. 1983-89), Assn. Edn. in Journalism and Mass Communications (Disting. Svc. award 1984), Am. Soc. Newspaper Editors (bd. dirs. 1987-92), Soc. Profl. Journalists (nat. treas. 1975, nat. sec. 1977, pres.-elect 1978, pres. 1979-80, First Amendment award 1981, Wells Key 1984, pres. Sigma Delta Chi Found. 1989-92, chair Found. 1992-94), Milw. Press Club (mem. Hall of Fame 1993). Office: Rocky Mountain News 400 W Colfax Ave Denver CO 80204-2607

OTTO, MARGARET AMELIA, librarian; b. Boston, Oct. 22, 1937; d. Henry Earlen and Mary (McLennan) O.; children—Christopher, Peter. A.B., Boston U., 1960; M.S., Simmons Coll., 1963, M.A., 1970; M.A. (hon.), Dartmouth Coll., 1981. Asst. sci. librarian M.I.T., Cambridge, 1963; Lindgren librarian M.I.T., 1964-67, acting sci. librarian, 1967-69, asst. dir., 1969-75, asso. dir., 1976-79; librarian of coll. Dartmouth Coll., Hanover, N.H., 1979—; pres., chmn. bd. Universal Serials and Book Exch., Inc., 1980-81; bd. dirs. Rsch. Libr. Group; trustee Howe Libr., Hanover, 1988—, chmn., 1992—; mem. Brown Libr. Com., rsch. lbirs. adv. com. OCLC, 1991—, ARL; editl. com. Univ. Press New Eng., 1993—. Council on Library Resources fellow, 1974; elected to Collegium of Disting. Alumnus Boston U., 1980. Mem. ALA (task force on assn. membership issues 1993—, ad hoc working group on copyright issues), Assn. Rsch. Librs. (chair preservation com. 1983-85, bd. dirs. 1985-88, mem. stats. com., chair membership com. 1992—), Coun. on Libr. Resources (proposal rev. com. 1992—), Dartmouth Club (N.Y.C.), St. Botolph Club (Boston), Sloane Club (London). Home: 2 Berrill Farms Ln Hanover NH 03755-3205 Office: Dartmouth Coll 115 Baker Meml Libr Hanover NH 03755

OTTO, WENDY HALSEY, public health nurse; b. Greenwich, Conn., June 15, 1947; d. Bates and Bettyjane (Ruwe) Halsey; m. Charles Edward Otto, June 26, 1971; children: Eric, Halsey, Robert. AA, Green Mountain Coll., 1967; BSN, Columbia U., 1969. RN, Conn., Pa. Staff nurse Mass. Gen. Hosp., Boston, 1969-71, Chestnut Hill Hosp., Phila., 1972, Abington (Pa.) Meml. Hosp., 1972-73; sch. nurse Greenwich Health Dept., 1989—. Mem. Nat. Assn. Sch. Nurses, Assn. of Sch. Nurses of Conn., Pocky Point Club. Episcopalian. Home: 12 Lake Dr S Riverside CT 06878

OUGH, MARCIA GWEN, primary school teacher; b. Hebron, Nebr., June 13, 1951; d. John Gerald and Lois Alene (Carter) O. BS in Health Edn., U. Nebr., 1979, MS in Spl. Edn., 1983. Cert. tchr., Nebr. Tchr. behaviorally impaired Beatrice (Nebr.) Pub. Sch., 1984; chptr., resource tchr. Edn. Svc. Unit #9, Hastings, Nebr., 1984-85; chptr. tchr. Henderson (Nebr.) Cmty. Sch., 1985-93; resource tchr. Henderson Com. Sch., 1994—; Eng., math. tchr. Internat. Found. for Edn. and Self-Help, Banjul, The Gambia, West Africa, 1993-94. Organist Aurora (Nebr.) United Meth. Ch., 1968-70, 92—, accompanist chancel choir, 1992—. Barkley scholar, 1982, 83. Mem. Am. Assn. Univ. Women (program chair 1995), Nat. & State Edn. Assn., Henderson Edn. Assn. (treas. 1991-93, pres.-elect 1996), Delta Kappa Gamma (recording sec. 1996), Eta Sigma Gamma. Democrat. Home: 2409 E 12th Rd Hampton NE 68843 Office: Henderson Com Sch Box 626 Henderson NE 68371

OUREDNIK, PATRICIA ANN, accountant; b. Balt., Oct. 5, 1962; d. John Matthew and Patricia Ann (Ruzicka) O. BS in Acctg., U. Balt., 1984; MS in Mgmt. Info. Sys., Fla. Inst. Tech., 1991. CPA, Md. Acctg. clk. Cello Corp., Havre de Grace, Md., 1981-84; staff acct. KPMG Peat Marwick, Balt., 1984-85; audit supv. Coughlin & Mann, Chartered, Bel Air, Md., 1985-88, 89-92; CFO Kidde Sys., White Marsh, Md., 1988-89, FAMIC Corp., Columbia, Md., 1994—, Top Tools Automation Sys., Timonium, Md., 1992-93; contr. CRMA, Balt., 1995—. Cons. Shepherd's Clinic, Balt., 1992—. Mem. Md. Assn. CPAs, Assn. Retarded Citizens. Republican. Methodist. Home: 1618 Bramble Ct Bel Air MD 21015-1560 Office: CRMA 100 E Pratt St Baltimore MD 21202

OUTHWAITE, LUCILLE CONRAD, ballerina, educator; b. Peoria, Ill., Feb. 26, 1909; d. Frederick Albert and Della (Cornett) Conrad; m. Leonard Outhwaite, Mar. 1, 1936 (dec. 1978); children—Ann Outhwaite Maurer, Lynn Outhwaite Pulsifer. Student, U. Nebr., 1929-30, Mills Coll., 1931-32; student piano, Paris, 1933-35, Legat Sch., London, 1934, N.Y.C. Ballet, N.Y.C., 1936-41, Royal Ballet Sch., London, 1957-59. Tchr. ballet Perry Mansfield, Steamboat Springs, Colo., 1932, Cape Playhouse, Dennis, Mass., 1937-41, Jr. League, N.Y.C., 1937-41, King Coit Sch., N.Y.C., 1937-41; toured with Am. Ambassador Ballet, Europe and S. Am., 1933-35; owner, tchr. dance sch., Oyster Bay, N.Y., 1949-57. Producer, choreographer ballets Alice in Wonderland, 1951, Pied Piper of Hamlin, 1952. Author: Birds in Flight, 1992, Flowers in the Wind, 1994. Mem. English Speaking Union, Preservation Soc., Alliance Française, Delta Gamma. Republican. Methodist. Clubs: Mills Coll., Spouting Rock Beach, Clambake (Newport, R.I.). Office: Beachmound Bellevue Ave Newport RI 02840

OUTZEN, TINA LOUISE, health care administrator; b. West Covina, Calif., Aug. 9, 1965; d. John Dern and Phyllis Ann (Pratt) O. AA, Coll. San Mateo, Calif., 1985; BA, Calif. State U., Hayward, 1988; MA in Pub. Health Adminstrn., Coll. Notre Dame, Belmont, Calif., 1995. Adminstrv. asst. Sequoia Capital, Menlo Park, Calif., 1988-89; provider rels. coord. Maxicare, Burlingame, Calif., 1988-92; dir. managed care Pacific Health Alliance, Burlingame, Calif., 1992—. Mem. Health Care Fin. Mgmt. (scholarship 1994), Delta Epsilon Sigma. Roman Catholic. Home: 212 Eaton Rd #2 San Mateo CA 94402

OVENS, MARI CAMILLE, school system administrator, dietitian; b. Spokane, Wash., June 18, 1954; d. Harold Chester and May Eloise (Gundry) Chapman; m. Dana Preston Ovens, Dec. 18, 1985; children: Dylan Preston, Delaney Camille. BS in Dietetics, Ea. Wash. U., 1976; MS in Home Econs., Wash. State U., 1979. Registered dietitian, Wash. Dietary coord. City of Vancouver, Wash., 1978-83; clin. dietitian Eastmoreland Gen. Hosp., Portland, Oreg., 1983; supr. child nutrition Vancouver Sch. Dist. 37, 1983—; mem. culinary arts adv. bd. Clark Coll., Vancouver, 1983—; mem. task force Am. Heart Assns., Seattle, 1988—. Mem. Am. Sch. Food Svc. Assn., (registered dir., adminstr. III), Am. Dietetic Assn. (Recognized Young Dietitian of Yr. Wash. State 1983), Wash. Sch. Food Svc. Assn. (treas. 1989-91, trainer 1993—), Wash. State Dietetic Assn., Soroptimists (pres. Vancouver 1990-92). Office: Vancouver Sch Dist 37 PO Box 8937 Vancouver WA 98668-8937

OVERBY, MONESSA MARY, clinical supervisor, counselor; b. Staples, Minn., Sept. 7, 1932; d. Joseph Melvin Overby and Marie Frances (Fellman) Vollstedt. BS, Coll. of St. Teresa, 1964; MS, Winona State U., 1978. Entered Franciscan Sisters, Roman Cath. Ch., 1953; nat. cert. counselor, Gestalt therapist, trainer. Elem. and jr. high tchr. Cath. Sch. System, Austin, Tracy, Lake City, Minn., 1955-67; sch. adminstr. McCahill Inst., Lake City, 1964-70; pastoral counselor and adult educator St. Edward's, Austin, Minn., 1970-76; adj. faculty and campus minister Winona (Minn.) State U., 1976-84; psychotherapist Family & Children's Ctr. and Human Devel. Assocs., La Crosse, Wis., 1978-84; family counselor Betty Ford Ctr., Rancho Mirage, Calif., 1987-89, clin. mgr. family and outpatient svcs., 1990—; workshop presenter in field. Mem. Am. Counseling Assn., Assn. for Specialists in Group Work, Minn. Assn. Specialists in Group Work (founding pres.). Democrat. Roman Catholic. Office: Betty Ford Ctr 39000 Bob Hope Dr Rancho Mirage CA 92270-3221

OVERDEER, BARBARA SUE, elementary education educator; b. Ind., Ind., July 18, 1946; d. Ralph Herbert and Bernice (Markley) Baker; m. Roger F. Bockelman, July 18, 1971 (div. Mar. 1985); children: Brent Alan, Lori Ann; m. William N. Overdeer, Mar. 28, 1987; stepchildren: Michael, Mark N., Matthew G. BS Elem. Edn., Manchester Coll., 1968; MS Elem. Edn., Ind. U., 1972. Cert. (life) elem. tchr., Ind. Elem. tchr. Union Twp. Schs., Columbia City, Ind., 1968-72, Columbia City Schs. (now Whitley County Consold. Schs.), 1979—. Mem. Whitley County Ext. Bd., Columbia City, 1989-91; club leader 4-H of Whitley County, 1989-94; mem. Whitley County Reps. Recipient Friends of Extension award Purdue U. Coop. Ext. Svc., West Lafayette, Ind., 1993. Mem. Internat. Reading Assn., NEA, Ind. state Tchrs. Assn., Whitley County Tcchrs. Assn. (bldg. rep. 1992-94), Extension Homemakers (pres., tres., sec. 1974—), Order Ea. Star, Delta Kappa Gamma, Tri-Kappa/Alpha Iota. Lutheran. Home: 3285 E Cider Mill Rd Columbia City IN 46725-9064 Office: Thorncreek Elem 3931 N Airport Rd Columbia City IN 46725

OVERDORFF, MARJORIE EILEEN, music educator; b. Connellsville, Pa., Dec. 20, 1943; d. Melvin Jacob and Beatrice Vance Keller; m. Gary Paul Overdorff, July 18, 1964; children: Jeffrey Alan, Wendy Lane. BS, Indiana U. Pa., 1965. Elem. music supr. Lock Haven (Pa.) Area Schs., 1965-68; music tchr. Livingston (Tex.) Ind. Sch. Dist., 1969-73; music specialist Maysville Local Schs., Zanesville, Ohio, 1973—. Vol. Hospice Care of Bethesda, Zanesville, 1994—. Grantee: Martha Holden Jennings Found., 1993-94. Mem. NEA, Ohio Edn. Assn., Maysville Edn. Assn., Music Educators Nat. Conf., Ohio Music Educators Assn. (past treas., dist. IX rep. 25 Yr. award 1992), Thursday Music Club (treas. 1981-91), Am. Orff Schulwerk Assn., Delta Kappa Gamma (music coord. 1991—), Delta Omicron. Republican. Methodist. Home: 3150 Nob Hill Zanesville OH 43701 Office: Maysville Local Schs 5500 Maysville Pike Zanesville OH 43701

OVERSTREET, KAREN A., judge. BA cum laude, Univ. of Wash., 1977; JD, Univ. of Oregon, 1982. Assoc. Duane, Morris & Heckscher, Phila., 1983-86; ptnr. Davis Wright Tremaine, Seattle, 1986-93; bankruptcy judge U.S. Bankruptcy Ct. (we. dist.) Wash., Seattle, 1994—; assoc. editor Oregon Law Review; dir. People's Law Sch.; mem. advisory com. U.S. Bankruptcy Ct. (we. dist.) Wash. Mem. Nat. Conf. of Bankruptcy Judges, Wash. State Bar Assn. (creditor-debtor sec.), Seattle-King County Bar Assn. (bankruptcy sec.), Am. Bar Assn., Wash. Women Lawyers Assn. Office: US Bankruptcy Ct Park Place Bldg 1200 6th Ave Ste 406 Seattle WA 98101-1128

OVERTON, JANE VINCENT HARPER, biology educator; b. Chgo., Jan. 17, 1919; d. Paul Vincent and Isabel (Vincent) Harper; m. George W. Overton, Jr., Sept. 1, 1941; children: Samuel, Peter, Ann. AB, Bryn Mawr Coll., 1941; PhD, U. Chgo., 1950. Rsch. asst. U. Chgo., 1950-52, mem. faculty, 1952-89, prof. biology, 1972-89; prof. emeritus, 1989. Author articles embryology, cell biology. NIH, NSF research grantee, 1965-87. Home: 1700 E 56th St Apt 2901 Chicago IL 60637-1935 Office: U Chgo 1103 E 57th St Chicago IL 60637-1503

OVERTON, ROSILYN GAY HOFFMAN, financial services executive; b. Corsicana, Tex., July 10, 1942; d. Billy Clarence and Ima Elise (Gay) Hoffman; m. Aaron Lewis Overton, Jr., July 2, 1960 (div. Mar. 1975); children: Aaron Lewis III, Adam Jerome; m. Mardiros Hatsakorzian, 1991. BS in Math., Wright State U., Dayton, Ohio, 1972, MS in Applied Econs. (fellow), 1973; postgrad. N.Y. U. Grad. Sch. Bus., 1974-76; Cert. Coll. Fin. Planning, 1987. CFP. Research analyst Nat. Security Agy., Dept. Def., 1962-67; bus. reporter Dayton Jour.-Herald, 1973-74; economist First Nat. City Bank, N.Y.C., 1974, A.T. & T. Co., 1974-75; broker Merrill Lynch, N.Y.C., 1975-80; asst. v.p. E.F. Hutton & Co., N.Y.C., 1980-84; v.p., nat. mktg. dir. investment products Manhattan Nat. Corp., 1984-86; pres. R.H. Overton Co., N.Y.C., 1986—; ptnr. Brown & Overton Fin. Svcs., 1987—. Named Businesswoman of Yr., N.Y.C., 1976. Mem. Inst. Cert. Planners, Internat. Assn. Fin. Planning (exec. v.p. N.Y. chpt.), Gotham Bus. and Profl. Womens Club, Rotary Internat., Wright State U. Alumni Assn., Mensa, Zonta. Methodist. Office: 142-05 Roosevelt Ave Ste 603 Flushing NY 11354-6007

OVERTON, SHARON FAYE, elementary education educator; b. Tell City, Ind., Oct. 20, 1949; d. Albert John Dauby and Anna Catherine Harpenau; m. Ron Overton, Apr. 14, 1973; children: Jennifer, Jeff. BS cum laude, Ind. State U., 1970, MS, 1972. Cert. elem. tchr., middle sch. endorsement math. 3d grade tchr. Tell City-Troy Twp. Sch. Corp., 1970-73; 2d grade tchr. E.V.S.C., Evansville, Ind., 1973-74; math. tchr. E.V.S.C., Evansville, Ill., 1974-84, 5th grade math. and sci. tchr., 1984—. Sunday sch. tchr. St. Benedict's Ch., Evansville, 1989—, mem.; debate judge North H.S. Debate Team, Evansville, 1994—; mem. PTA. Mem. Gamma Phi Beta (rituals chairperson). Roman Catholic. Home: 3725 Aspen Dr Evansville IN 47711 Office: Fairlawn Sch 2021 S Alvord Evansville IN 47714

OVERTON-ADKINS, BETTY JEAN, foundation administrator; b. Jacksonville, Fla., Oct. 10, 1949; d. Henry and Miriam (Gordon) Crawford; children from previous marriage: Joseph Alonzo III, Jermaine Lamar; m. Eugene Adkins, Apr. 24, 1992. BA in English, Tenn. State U., 1970, MA in English, 1974; PhD in English, Vanderbilt U., 1980; student Inst. Ednl. Mgmt., Harvard U., 1990. Reporter Race Rels. Reporter Mag., Nashville, 1970-71; tchr. Met. Nashville Sch. System, 1971-72; instr., project dir. Tenn. State U., Nashville, 1972-76; asst. prof. Nashville State Tech. Inst., 1976-78, Fisk U., Nashville, 1978-83; assoc. dean. grad. sch. U. Ark., Little Rock, 1983-85, dean grad. sch., 1985-91; program dir. Kellogg Found., Battle Creek, Mich., 1991—; asst. dir. Kellogg Nat. Fellowship Program, Battle Creek, Mich., 1991-94; coord. higher edn. programs Kellogg Found., Battle Creek, 1994—; instr. U. Tenn., Nashville, 1976-82; dir. rsch. sponsored programs U. Ark., 1986-88; bd. dirs. Ark. Sci. and Info. Liaison Office, 1984-91. Bd. dirs. Ark. Sci. and Tech. Authority, Little Rock, 1989—, Women's Project, 1986—, Ark. Pub. Policy Panel, 1988-91, No. Bank Women's Adv. Bd., 1988-91, Nashville Panel, 1974-83, Ctrl. Ark. Libr. Sys., 1990-91, Ark. coun. NCCJ, 1990-92, Bread for World, 1990-95; mem. Commn. on Edn. Credits and Credentials, Am. Coun. on Edn., 1989-95; chmn. bi-racial adv. com. Little Rock Sch. Dist., 1987—. Fellow Am. Coun. Edn., 1981-82, W.K. Kellogg Found., 1988-93. Mem. Nat. Coun. Tchrs. of English, Coun. Grad. Schs., Coun. So. Grad. Schs., Women Color United Against Domestic Violence (pres.), An. Assn. High Edn., Rotary, Alpha Kappa Alpha. Democrat. Roman Catholic. Office: W K Kellogg Found One Michigan Ave E Battle Creek MI 49017

OVIDIAH, JANICE, educational institute administrator; m. Isaac Ovidiah. BA, Washington U., St. Louis, 1965; MA, Columbia U., 1967, PhD, 1978. Dir. profl. study tours Am. Odysseys, Inc., 1973-84; escort, interpreter in French U.S. Dept. State, 1978-84; asst. to exec. dir. Meml. Found. for Jewish Culture, 1984-87; exec. dir. Congregation Shearith Israel/The Spanish & Portuguese Syn., N.Y.C., 1987-92; Sephardic House, N.Y.C., 1987—; instr. French Rutgers U., New Brunswick, N.J., 1972; asst. to dir. of The Maison Franclase, Columbia U., 1970-72; instr. French Columbia U., 1968-70; lectr. in field. Author: (books) Toward a Concept of Cinematic Literature: An Analysis of Hiroshima, Mon Amour, 1983, The Far Away Island of the Grey Lady, 1979, others; contbr. articles to profl. jours. Office: Sephardic House 2112 Broadway New York NY 10023

OWEN, CAROL THOMPSON, artist, educator; b. Pasadena, Calif., May 10, 1944; d. Sumner Comer and Cordelia (Whittemore) Thompson; m. James Eugene Owen, July 19, 1975; children: Kevin Christopher, Christine Celese. Student, Pasadena City Coll., 1963; BA with distinction, U. Redlands, 1966; MA, Calif. State U., L.A., 1967; MFA, Claremont Grad. Sch., 1969. Cert. community coll. instr., Calif. Head resident Pitzer Coll., Claremont, Calif., 1967-70; instr. art Mt. San Antonio Coll., Walnut, Calif., 1968-96, prof., dir. coll. art gallery, 1972-73. Group shows include Covina Pub. Libr., 1971, U. Redlands, 1964, 65, 66, 70, 78, 88, 92, Am. Ceramic Soc., 1969, Mt. San Antonio Coll., 1991, The Aesthetic Process, 1993, Separate Realities, 1995, San Bernardino County Mus., 1996, others; ceramic mural commd. and installed U. Redlands, 1991. Recipient award San Bernardino County Mus., 1996. Mem. Calif. Scholarship Fedn., Faculty Assn. Mt. San Antonio Coll., Coll. Art Assn. Am., Calif. Tchrs. Assn., Friends of Huntington Library, L.A. County Mus. Art, Redlands Art Assn., Heard Mus. Assn., Sigma Tau Delta. Republican. Presbyterian. Home: 534 S Hepner Ave Covina CA 91723-2921 Office: Mt San Antonio Coll Grand Ave Walnut CA 91789

OWEN, CAROLYN SUTTON, educator; b. Shreveport, La., Jan. 7, 1932; d. S.T. and Kathleen Willard (Judkins) Sutton; m. Donald Curtiss Owen, Aug. 6, 1955; children: Judith Kathleen Owen Moen, Kyle Curtiss. BA, La. Tech., 1953; MA, Tex. Woman's U., 1988. Cert. Tchr., Tex. Tchr. Calcasieu Parish, Lake Charles, La., 1953-54, Calcasien Parish, Westlake, La., 1955-56, San Antonio Independent Sch. Dist., 1954-55, Dallas Independent Sch. Dist., 1968-94; ret. Recipient Carolyn Owen Patio dedication J.L. Long Middle Sch. Faculty, 1980. Mem. AAUW, NEA (life). Republican. Episcopalian. Home: 7737 El Santo Ln Dallas TX 75248

OWEN, CHRISTINA L., lawyer; b. Oakland, Calif., Sept. 22, 1946. BS, U. Calif., Berkeley, 1968; JD, U. So. Calif., 1971. Bar: Calif. 1972. Ptnr. Baker & Hostetler, Long Beach, Calif. Mem. State Bar Calif., Maritime Law Assn. U.S. Office: Baker & Hostetler 300 Oceangate Ste 620 Long Beach CA 90802-6801

OWEN, CYNTHIA CAROL, sales executive; b. Ft. Worth, Oct. 16, 1943; d. Charlie Bounds and Bernice Vera (Nunley) Rhoads; m. Franklin Earl Owen, Oct. 20, 1961 (div. Jan. 1987); children: Jeffrey Wayne, Valeria Ann, Carol Darlena, Pamela Kay; m. John Edward White, Jan. 1, 1988 (div. Sept. 1991). Cert. Keypuncher, Comml. Coll., 1963; student, Tarrant County Jr. Coll., 1974-77; BBA in Mgmt., U. Tex., Arlington, 1981. Keypunch operator Can-Tex. Industries, Mineral-Wells, 1966-67; sec. Electro-Midland Corp., Mineral-Wells, 1967-68; exec. sec. to v.p. sales Pangburn Co., Inc., Ft. Worth, 1972-78; bookkeeper, sec. CB Svc., Ft. Worth, 1978-82; project mgr. Square D Co., Ft. Worth, 1982—. Mem. NAFE, NOW, AAUW. Baptist. Home: 816 Lee Dr Bedford TX 76022-7311 Office: Square D Co 860 Airport Fwy Ste 101 Hurst TX 76054-3262

OWEN, MARGARET GOUDELOCK, artist; b. Greenville, S.C., Nov. 20, 1967; d. John Clifton Goudelock and Laura Lynn (McLemore) Kerner; m. Kenneth Whiteside Owen, Dec. 5, 1987. BFA, U. North Tex., 1991. Pres. Capital Designs, New Albany, Miss., 1992—. Active Art History Soc., Denton, Tex., 1989-91, Coll. Art Assn., New Albany Garden Club, publicity chair, 1993-94; active Union County Hist. Soc., 1994; mem. phys. infrastructure planning com. Union County (Miss.) Competitive Comty. Program, 1994-95. Mem. Phi Mu Fraternity (alumnae bd. 1991—), Golden Key. Methodist. Office: Capital Designs 409 East Main St New Albany MS 38652

OWEN, MARTHA ELIZABETH, nursing administrator; b. Weleetka, Okla., July 3, 1935; d. John Milburn and Florence Loretta (King) Rasberry; m. Robert Fleming Owen, June 18, 1961; children: Robert Fleming Jr., Elizabeth Leanne. BSN, Okla. Bapt. U., 1958; MS, Troy State U., 1972. RN. Staff nurse Bryan Whitfield Hosp., Demopolis, Ala., 1962-66; pub. health nurse Marengo County Health Dept., Linden, Ala., 1962-66; coord. LPN program Wallace C.C., Selma, Ala., 1966-72; dir. edn. Selma Med. Ctr., 1972-73; dir. nursing edn. Wallace C.C., 1973-92; dir. edn. Four Rivers Med. Ctr., Selma, 1993-95; pres. Diversified Nursing Svc., Selma, 1992—. Tchr., choir mem. 1st Bapt. Ch., Selma, 1966—. 1st lt. U.S. Army Nurse Corps, 1958-62. Mem. Am. Diabetes Assn., Sigma Theta Tau, Delta Kappa Gamma. Republican. Home: 81 County Rd 65 Selma AL 36701 Office: Diversified Nursing Svcs 2918 Citizens Pky Selma AL 36701

OWEN, PATRICIA COX, former government official; b. Cedar Rapids, Iowa, Mar. 31, 1924; d. Don Gardner and Frances Maye (Chambers) Cox; m. Claude Worthington Owen Jr., Feb. 24, 1946; children: C.W. Owen III, Vandelia Maye, Don Franklin. Student, N.C. State Coll., 1940, Ritchie Sch., 1940-41, Peace Jr. Coll., Raleigh, N.C., 1941-42, George Washington U., 1943. Adminstrv. asst. to legal advisor Corps of Engrs. Manhattan Project-Atomic Bomb, Washington, 1942-47; bd. dirs., corp. sec. Polytronic Rsch., Inc., Rockville, Md., 1960-61; office mgr. Masonry Inst., Washington, 1963-66, Compackager Corp., Washington, 1969-75; program specialist health resources & svcs. adminstrn. HHS, Washington, 1976-92. Pres. Kiwanis Wives, Bethesda, Md., 1956; 1st v.p. Town Club, Bethesda, 1960; mem. Peggy Pledger Cir., Florence Cirttenton Home. Mem. Town Club, Congrl. Country Club, Kappa Bridge Club. Republican. Episcopalian. Home: 9200 Persimmon Tree Rd Potomac MD 20854

OWEN, PRISCILLA RICHMAN, judge. BA, Baylor U., JD, 1977. Bar: Tex. 1977, U.S. Ct. Appeals (5th, 8th and 11th cirs.). Former ptnr. Andrews & Kurth, L.L.P., Houston; justice Supreme Ct. Tex., Austin, 1995—; liaison to pro bono task force Supreme Ct. Tex., gender bias reform implementation com. Named Young Lawyer of Yr., Outstanding Young Alumna, Baylor U. Office: Supreme Ct Tex PO Box 12248 Austin TX 78711*

OWEN, SUZANNE, retired savings and loan executive; b. Lincoln, Nebr., Oct. 6, 1926; d. Arthur C. and Hazel E. (Edwards) O. BSBA, U. Nebr., Lincoln, 1948. With G.F. Lessenhop & Sons, Inc., Lincoln, 1948-57; with First Fed. Lincoln, 1963-91; v.p., dir. personnel, 1975-81, 1st v.p., 1981-87, sr. v.p., 1987-91, ret., 1991; mem. pers. bd. City of Lincoln, 1989-96. Mem. Lincoln Human Resources Mgmt. Assn., Lincoln Mgmt. Soc., Phi Chi Theta. Republican. Christian Scientist. Clubs: Wooden Spoon, Exec. Women's Breakfast Group, Community Women's, Lincoln Symphony Guild. Lodges: Pi Beta Phi Alumnae, Order of Eastern Star (Lincoln).

OWENS, ALEXANDRA CANTOR, professional society administrator; b. N.Y.C., Nov. 22, 1961; d. Murray A. and Lois (Van Arsdel) C.; m. Michael R. Owens. BA, William Smith Coll., 1983. Exec. sec. Nissel & Nissel, CPAs, N.Y.C., 1983-85, Am. Soc. Journalists and Authors Charitable Trust, N.Y.C., 1986—; exec. dir. Am. Soc. Journalists and Authors, N.Y.C., 1985—. Contbg. author: Tools of the Writer's Trade, 1990; editor Sitzmark newsletter of High Life Ski Club, Rockaway, N.J., 1994—. Office: Am Soc of Journalists 1501 Broadway Ste 302 New York NY 10036-5501

OWENS, ANN MARIE, social worker; b. Coaldale, Pa., Apr. 26, 1969; d. William Richard and Marie Ann (Neuroth) O. BS, Phila. Coll. Pharmacy and Sci., 1991; MA, Kutztown U., 1995. Lab. technician Ashland Chem., Easton, Pa., 1992-95; clin. social worker Kids Peace, Orefield, Pa., 1995—. Mem. ACA (profl. mem.), Am. Mental Health Assn. (profl.), Sigma Xi. Office: Kids Peace Nat Ctrs 5300 Kispeace Dr Orefield PA 18069

OWENS, BARBARA ANN, English educator; b. Muskogee, Okla., Jan. 11, 1947; d. Carl Howard Fullbright and Iris Oleta (Staffan) Evans; m. David Warren Owens, Jr., Feb. 28, 1964; children: Shelia DeLynn, Katherine Elizabeth, David Warren III. BS, Northeastern Okla. State U., 1976; MEd, U. Okla., 1990. Cert. reading specialist. Tchr. Muldrow (Okla.) Pub. Schs., 1976-77, Stafford (Mo.) Pub. Schs., 1977-79, Oklahoma City C.C., 1991—, Moore (Okla.) Pub. Schs., 1979—; sponsor, state pres. Moore West Nat. Jr. Honor Soc., 1996-97. Bd. dirs. Moore Parks & Recreation, 1988-89. Mem. NEA, Oklahoma Edn. Assn., Okla. Reading Coun., Okla. Romance Writers Am.)v.p.), Romance Writers Am., Moore Assn. Classroom Tchrs. Office: Moore Pub Schs 9400 S Pennsylvania Oklahoma City OK 73159

OWENS, CAROL ANN, counselor, consultant; b. Ft. Wayne, Ind., Feb. 13, 1939; d. Russell R. and Ruth E. (Shannon) O. B in Edn., St. Francis, 1974; M in Counseling, U. San Francisco, 1988. Tchr. K-12 Ft. Wayne Sch. Dist., 1974-79; legal asst., mgr. for various attys. and law firms San Francisco/Sonoma Co., Calif., 1979-85; dir., co-founder Face to Face/Sonoma County AIDS Network, Sonoma County, 1985-88; counselr, HIV specialist Sonoma County, 1988—. Vol. Home Hospice of Sonoma County, 1979, 80, 81, Face to Face, 1983-88; mem. Nat. Wildlife Fedn., 1995-96. With USN, 1957-61. Named YWCA's Woman of Achievement, 1988, Counseling Woman of Yr. Sonoma State U., 1988; recipient Russian River Chamber's Citizen award, 1988, Comty. Torchbearer award U.S. Olympic Com., 1996. Mem. Women in Mil. Meml. (Hon. Dis. award 1961), Women in Arts. Home and Office: PO Box 1334 Forestville CA 95436

OWENS, CAROLE EHRLICH, therapist; b. Mpls., Dec. 7, 1942; d. Jerome D. and Amy Ann (Scott) Schein; B.A., U. Md., 1970; M.A., Cath. U. Am., 1977; D of Social Work Yeshiva U., 1987; children: Todd Frederick, Joseph Eric. Lic. Social Worker, Mass. Youth advocate, leader Montgomery (Md.) County Recreation Dept., 1970-72, counselor, supr. preadjudication diversion program, Crisis Home Program, Family Service, 1972-74, adminstr. Karma House (residential drug treatment), 1974-75; program devel. dir.

Jewish Social Service Agy., Montgomery County, 1975-77, United Jewish Appeal Fedn. of Montgomery County, 1977-79; therapist, educator, writer, cons. in field, Englewood, N.J., 1979—; instr. Cath. U. Cons. to Montgomery County Exec. candidate, 1974; appointee Gov.'s Task Force, Md., 1978; bd. dirs. Jewish Community Center, 1981—, Temple Sinai Sisterhood, Bergen County, N.J., 1981—; pres. chpt. LWV, 1983. Mem. Internat. Platform Assn., AAUW, Am. Personnel & Guidance Assn. (cert.), Am. Assn. Marriage and Family Therapy (clin.), Am. Assn. Jewish Communal Workers, Nat. Assn. Social Workers, LWV (pres. 1983-84), N.Y. Acad. Scis. Author: The Berkshire Cottages: A Vanishing Era, 1984, Clinical Vs. Psychometric Judgement of Alcohol Use, 1987, Bellefontaine, 1989; Stockbridge, 1989; author: The Lost Days of Agatha Christie, 1995; author, editor: The Stockbridge Story; editor: Fund-Raising (Elton J. Kernes); reviewer Kirkus Revs.; contbr. articles in field to profl. jours. Home: PO Box 1207 Stockbridge MA 01262-1207

OWENS, DANA (QUEEN LATIFA), recording artist, actress; b. N.J, Mar. 18, 1970; d. Lance and Rita O. Student, Borough of Manhattan C.C. CEO Flavor Unit Entertainment. TV appearances include Living Single, Fresh Prince of Bel Air, In Living Color, The Arsenio Hall Show; film appearances in Jungle Fever, 1991, Juice, 1992, House Party 2, 1992; albums include All Hail the Queen, 1990, The Nature of Sista, 1991, X-tra Naked, 1992, Black Reign, 1994. Named Best New Artist, New Music Seminar, 1990, Best Female Rapper, Rolling Stone Readers' Poll, 1990; recipient Grammy award nomination, 1990, Soul Train Music award, 1995, Sammy Davis Jr. award, 1995, Entertainer of Yr. award, 1995. Office: care Tommy Boy Records 1747 1st Ave New York NY 10128*

OWENS, DEBRA ANN, chiropractor; b. Poplar Bluff, Mo., Dec. 21, 1953; d. James Alva and Veleta Frances (Pierce) Stutts; 1 child from previous marriage, Jacqueline. BS in Edn., S.E. Mo. State U., 1975; DC, Logan Coll. of Chiropractic, 1991. Chiropractor Albers Chiropractic, Washington, 1991-92, Owens Chiropractic Ctr., P.C., Dexter, Mo., 1992—. Mem. Am. Chiropractic Assn., Internat. Chiropractors Assn., Mo. Chiropractors Assn., World Congress of Women Chiropractors, Logan Coll. Alumni Assn. (alumni rsch. award 1991), Dexter C. of C. (2d v.p. 1993, 1st v.p. 1994, pres. 1995, sec. devel. corp. 1996, econ. devel. com. 1996), Kiwanis (bd. mem. 1994-96). Office: Owens Chiropractic Ctr PC 1013 Bus Hwy 60 W PO Box 678 Dexter MO 63841

OWENS, DORIS JERKINS, insurance underwriter; b. Range, Ala., June 16, 1940; d. Arthur Charles and Jennie (Lee) Jerkins; m. Gilbert Landers Owens, Jan. 29, 1959; 1 child, Alan Dale. Student Massey Draughon Bus. Coll., 1958-59, Auburn U., Montgomery, 1980, 81, 82. Cert. ins. counselor, profl. ins. woman. Exec. sec. Henry C. Barnet, Gen. Agt., Montgomery, Ala., 1959-66; sr. underwriter personal lines So. Guaranty Ins. Co., Montgomery, 1966—. Author: Bike Safety, 1976. Instr. Coop. State Dept. Defensive Driver Instr., 1975, 78; instr. ins. classes; v.p. Montgomery Citizens Fire Safety, 1981; panelist Gov.'s Safety Conf., Montgomery, 1975—; mem., panelist Women Annual Hwy. Safety Leaders, Montgomery, 1976, 78, 80; apptd. mem. Alliance Against Drugs, 1989. Recipient Able Toastmaster award Dist. 48 Toastmasters, 1979, Outstanding Lt. Gov. award, 1981, Outstanding Area Gov. award, 1980; named Ins. Woman of Year, 1979. Mem. Ins. Women Montgomery (pres. 1961, 85-86), Internat. Platform Assn., Blue-Gray Civitan Club. Office: So Guaranty Ins Co 2545 Taylor Rd Montgomery AL 36117-4706

OWENS, HELEN DAWN, elementary school educator, reading consultant; b. Eastman, Ga., Oct. 9, 1949; d. Eli B. and Irene (Harrell) Branch; m. Bobby Lee Owens, Dec. 9, 1967; children: Leslie Owens-McDonald, Monica Dawn. AA, Miami (Fla.) Dade Jr. Coll., 1969; BS, Fla. Internat. U., 1978; MEd, Mercer U., 1986, EdS, 1991. Cert. presch.-12th grade, reading specialist, early childhood edn. specialist, Ga. Youth ctr. dir. Dept. Def., Clark AFB, Philippines, 1969 70; English lang. instr. Chinese Mil. Acad., Feng Shan, Taiwan, 1973-75; tchr., music instr. ABC Presch., Miami, 1976-78; kindergarten and music tchr. Berkshire Sch., Homestead, Fla., 1978-79; tchr., reading specialist Perdue Elem. Sch. Houston County Bd. Edn., Warner Robins, Ga., 1979—; mem. nominating com. mem. Ga. picture book of yr. U. Ga., Athens, 1990-91; reading cons. for schs., county edn. bds., regional reading ctrs., Ctrl. Ga., 1990—. Author: With Loving Hands and Tender Hearts, 1975. Exec. bd. dirs. Ladies Ministries, Ch. of God., Warner Robins, 1990-94; dir. Internat. City Girls' Club, Warner Robins, 1990—. Recipient 25-Yr. Bible Tchr. Svc. award Internat. City Ch. of God., 1991; named Fla. State Family Tng. Dir. of Yr., Fla. Ch. of God, 1979, Ga. Girls' Club Coord. of the Year, 1995. Mem. Internat. Reading Assn. (mem. Ga. coun. 1979-96, dir. mem. devel. 1993-96, v.p. 1996-97, past pres. HOPE coun. 1990-92), Profl. Assn. Ga. Edn. Republican. Home: 111 Crestwood Rd Warner Robins GA 31093-6803 Office: Perdue Elem Sch 856 Highway 96 Warner Robins GA 31088-2222

OWENS, HILDA FAYE, management and leadership development consultant, human resource trainer; b. Fountain, N.C., Mar. 23, 1939; d. Floyd Curtis and Essie Lee (Gay) O. BS in Edn. and Psychology, East Carolina U., 1961, MA in Edn., 1965; PhD in Higher Edn., Fla. State U., 1973; postgrad., Western Carolina U., 1962, U. Louisville, 1967, U. N.C., 1968. Tchr. New Bern (N.C.) City Schs., 1961-65; dir. counseling svcs., prof. Mt. Olive (N.C.) Coll., 1965-71, dean students, prof., 1973-77; coord. student affairs, rsch. assoc. bd. regents State Univ. System Fla., Tallahassee, 1971-73; assoc. prof. higher edn. U. S.C., Columbia, 1977-83; v.p. acad. affairs, prof. Spartanburg (S.C.) Meth. Coll., 1985-90; exec. asst. to pres. for planning and rsch., cons. Spartanburg (S.C.) Meth. Coll., 1990-91; pres. Excel Resource Assocs., Spartanburg, 1991—; mem. bd. dirs. The Haven; numerous presentations in field; speaker bus., ednl., civic and ch. meetings, confs. and workshops. Editor: Risk Management and the Student Affairs Professional, 1984, (with Witten and Bailey) College Student Personnel Administration: An Anthology, 1982; mem. editl. bd. Jour. Staff, Orgn. and Program Devel., Assn. Student Pers. Adminstrs. Jour., Nat. Assn. Student Pers. Adminstrs. Monograph Bd., Coll. Student Affairs Jour.; contbr. articles to profl. jours., over 40 chpts. to books. Grad. Leadership Spartanburg, 1987; adminstrv. bd. Bethel United Meth. Ch.; mem. exec. bd. Tuscarora coun. Boy Scouts Am. S.C. Coll. Pers. Assn. named Rsch. and Writing award in her honor, 1995; named One of 45 Outstanding S.C. Women, 1980, Disting. Grad. award Fla. State U., 1981, Outstanding Bus. and Profl. Woman of Yr. Spartanburg Bus. and Profl. Women, 1986, Capital Bus. and Profl. Women, 1982, Mt. Olive Bus. and Profl. Women, 1977; recipient Meritorious Svc. award S.C. Coll. Pers. Assn., 1990. Mem. NAFE, ASTD, Am. Mgmt. Assn., Nat. Assn. Student Pers. Adminstrs. (adv. bd. region III, Disting. Svc. award), Am. Assn. Higher Edn., Carolinas Soc. Tng. and Devel., Nat. Orgn. on Legal Problems in Edn., S.C. Pers. Assn. (pres., award named in honor 1994), Bus. and Profl. Women S.C. (pres., bd. dirs. Ednl. Found.), Internat. Platform Assn., Spartan West Rotary Club (bd. dirs.), Pi Delta Kappa (pres. U. S.C. chpt.). Democrat. Home: 230 Old Towne Rd Spartanburg SC 29301-3555 Office: Excel Resource Assocs PO Box 17248 Spartanburg SC 29301-0103

OWENS, JANA JAE, entertainer; b. Great Falls, Mont., Aug. 30, 1943; d. Jacob G. Meyer and Bette P. (Sprague) Hopper; m. Sidney Greif (div.); children: Matthew N., Sydni C.; m. Buck Owens. Student, Interlochen Music Camp, 1959, Internat. String Congress, 1960, Vienna (Austria) Acad. Music, 1963-64; BA magna cum laude, Colo. Womens Coll., 1965, MusB magna cum laude, 1965. Tchr. music Ontario (Oreg.) Pub. Schs., 1965-67, Redding (Calif.) Pub. Schs., 1969-74; entertainer Buck Owens Enterprises, Bakersfield, Calif., 1974-78, Tulsa, 1979—; concertmistress Boise (Idaho) Philharm., 1965-67, Shasta Symphony, Redding, 1969-74. Rec. artist (violinist, vocalist) Lark Records, 1978—. Office: Jana Jae Enterprises Lake Record Prodns Inc PO Box 35726 Tulsa OK 74153

OWENS, LAURA LEWIS, lawyer; b. Atlanta, Sept. 27, 1965. BA cum laude, Furman U., 1982; JD cum laude, U. Ga., 1985. Bar: Ga. 1985. Ptnr. Alston & Bird, Atlanta. Mem. editl. bd. Ga. Jour. Internat. and Comparative Law, 1983-85, editor-in-chief, 1984-85; author: Annual Survey of Developments in International Trade Law, 1983. Mem. Atlantic Bar Assn., State Bar of Ga. Office: Alston & Bird 1 Atlantic Ctr 1201 W Peachtree St Atlanta GA 30309-3424*

OWENS, LUVIE MOORE, association executive; b. Cleve., July 26, 1933; d. Dan Tyler and Elizabeth (Oakes) Moore; m. Lloyd Owens, Jan. 1, 1955; children: Luvie Owens Myers, Elizabeth, Lloyd H. Student, Smith Coll., Northampton, Mass., 1956. Tchr. Howard Jr. High Sch., Wilmette, Ill., 1971-75; U.S. ops. mgr. Frank T. Ross & Co., Evanston, Ill., 1976-86; dir. Internat. Platform Assn., Winnetka, Ill., 1972—, chief exec. officer, 1986—. Treas., mem. jr. coun. Cleve. Mus. Art, 1964-65; commr. Police and Fire Commn., Winnetka, 1980-86; chmn. bd. Lake Shore Unitarian Ch., Winnetka, 1986-87; mem. alumnae bd. Madeira Sch., Greenway, Va., 1984-88. Mem. Jr. League Club (Chgo.), Rotary. Office: Internat Platform Assn PO Box 250 Winnetka IL 60093-0250

OWENS, MARY JO, electronic guidance services company executive; b. Asheville, N.C., Nov. 26, 1936; d. William James and Mamie Laura (Simms) O.; children: Lolita Omaria, Ionita. BS, N.C. State U., 1963; MS in Edn., Iona Coll., 1973; DLitt, Knightsbridge U., Copenhagen, 1995; PhD (hon.), World Acad., Germany, England, 1995, Australian Inst. Coord. Rsch., 1995, London Inst. Applied Rsch., 1995. Prof. English N.C. State U., Greensboro, 1961-62, prof. French, 1962-63; instr. French Phillips Sr. High Sch., Battleboro, N.C., 1963-64, Farmville (N.C.) Sr. High Sch., 1964-65; instr. French, English Jordan Sellars Sr. High Sch., Burlington, N.C., 1965-66; program coord. Project Aware, Fed. Grant Program, Greensboro, 1966-67; instr. French, English Westchester County Schs., Mt. Vernon, N.Y., 1967-88; instr. Spanish evening sch. Bedford Park Acad., Bronx, N.Y., 1976-79; realty broker, owner M.J. Howell and Co. Inc., Stanfordville, N.Y., 1982—; founder, owner Electronic Guidance Svcs. Corp., Hunns Lake, N.Y., 1988—; dep. Internat. Parliament for Safety and Peace, Palermo, Italy. Author: An No Clouds Over My Sun, 1973 (Demale Writers award 1975), Native American Images and Resipes, 1991, Through the Glass, Clearly a Character Study of the "Half-Breed" in America, 1992. Founder Children of Profls. Orgn., Westchester County, N.Y., 1991—; pres. New Rochelle (N.Y.) Assn. Women Voters, 1981-89. Recipient Ludwig von Beethoven Medal of Honor, 1995, Albert Einstein Medal of Honor, 1995, Henri Dunant Medal of Honor, 1995; Am. Sch. Honors scholar, 1959; City of Mt. Vernon grantee, 1982-84. Mem. Internat. Culture Club (pres. 1982—), N.Y. Profl. Women (pres. 1990-92), N.Y. State Tchrs. Fedn., N.Y. State Retired Tchrs. Assn., Westchester County Minority Bus. Assn. (pres. 1982—), Westchester County Minority Real Estate Bd. (bd. dirs. 1982—), Cherokee Child Orgn. (chmn. 1988-92, Native Am. Visionary award 1992, Inner Man award 1991). Home: PO Box 310 Stanfordville NY 12581-0310 Office: Electronic Guidance Svcs PO Box 27 Stanfordville NY 12581-0027

OWENS, SANDRA LOUISE, software consultant; b. June 1; d. Charles and Manola Bradley; m. Greg Owens; 1 child, Kimani. BS in Bus. Adminstrn., Ctrl. Conn. State U. Sys. coord., fin. analyst Westinghouse-Group W, Encino, Calif., 1980-85; bus. sys. trainer Whittaker, Simi Valley, Calif., 1985-88; software applications mgr. Tekelec, Calabasas, Calif., 1988-94; bus. owner Keman Comm., Chatsworth, Calif., 1994—; mem. Global Bus. Incubator Loyola Marmont, El Segundo, Calif., 1996. Mem. U. So. Calif. FasTrack, L.A., 1994. Mem. NOW, NAFE, NAACP (vol. tchr., banquet chairperson), Ind. Computer Cons. Assn., Black Data Processing Assn., Internat. Interactive Comms. Soc., Nat. Coun. Negro Women, Nat. Women Bus. Owners, World Future Soc., HTML Guild, Simi Valley C. of C.

OWENS, SUE GASTON, middle school educator; b. Greenville, S.C., Nov. 6, 1955; d. Dearman Samuel and Harriet (Gaston) O. BS, Winthrop U., 1976; MEd, Converse Coll., 1981. Tchr. Whitlock Jr. H.S., Spartanburg, S.C., 1977—. Bd. dirs. Bethlehem Comty. Ctr., Spartanburg, 1991—; dist. rep. Wallace (S.C.) Family Life Ctr., 1992—; cert. lay spkr. S.C. conf. United Meth. Ch., 1991—; pres. Spartanburg dist. United Meth. Women, 1993-96, coord. membership, nurture and outreach of S.C. conf., 1996—. Mem. AAHPERD, NEA, S.C. Alliance for Health, Phys. Edn., Recreation and Dance, S.C. Edn. Assn.

OWEN-TOWLE, CAROLYN SHEETS, clergywoman; b. Upland, Calif., July 27, 1935; d. Millard Owen and Mary (Baskerville) Sheets; m. Charles Russell Chapman, June 29, 1957 (div. 1973); children: Christopher Charles, Jennifer Anne, Russell Owen; m. Thomas Allan Owen-Towle, Nov. 16, 1973. BS in Art and Art History, Scripps Coll., 1957; postgrad. in religion, U. Iowa, 1977; DD, Meadville/Lombard Theol. Sch., 1994. Ordained to ministry Unitarian-Universalist Ch., 1978. Minister 1st Unitarian Universalist Ch., San Diego, 1978—; pres. Ministerial Sisterhood, Unitarian Universalist Ch., 1980-82; mem. Unitarian Universalist Svc. Com., 1979-85, pres., 1983-85. Bd. dirs. Planned Parenthood, San Diego, 1980-86; mem. clergy adv. com. to Hospice, San Diego, 1980-83; mem. U.S. Rep. Jim Bates Hunger Adv. Com., San Diego, 1983-87; chaplain Interfaith AIDS Task Force, San Diego, 1988—. Mem. Unitarian Universalist Ministers Assn. (exec. com. 1988, pres. 1989-91). Office: 1st Unitarian Universalist Ch 4190 Front St San Diego CA 92103-2030

OWINGS, ANNETTE RENEÉ, archacologist, artist; b. Leadville, Colo., Jan. 14, 1960; d. Edwin Merl and Louise Eleanor (Hanna) Pugh; m. James Randolph Carver, Aug. 6, 1978 (div. Mar. 1991); 1 child, Christopher Randall; m. Eric Richard Owings, June 20, 1992; children: Jeanette Sierra, Autumn Fawn. BA, S.W. Tex. State U., 1988. Pvt. practice archaeologist, 1989—; rschr. in field. Arist (album cover) Strage World Full of Twisted Fruit, 1985. Mem. Colo. Coun. Profl. Archaeology (voting mem. 1994-96), Smithsonian.

OWINGS, MARGARET WENTWORTH, conservationist, artist; b. Berkeley, Calif., Apr. 29, 1913; d. Frank W. and Jean (Pond) Wentworth; m. Malcolm Millard, 1937; 1 child, Wendy Millard Benjamin; m. Nathaniel Alexander Owings, Dec. 30, 1953. A.B., Mills Coll., 1934; postgrad., Radcliffe Coll., 1935; LHD (hon.), Mills Coll., 1993. One-woman shows include Santa Barbara (Calif.) Mus. Art, 1940, Stanford Art Gallery, 1951, stitchery exhbns. at M.H. De Young Mus., San Francisco, 1963, Internat. Folk Art Mus., Santa Fe, 1965. Commr. Calif. Parks, 1963-69, mem., Nat. Parks Found. Bd. 1968-69; bd. dirs. African Wildlife Leadership Found., 1968-80, Defenders of Wildlife, 1969-74; founder, pres. Friends of the Sea Otter, 1969-90; chair Calif. Mountain Lion Preservation Found., 1987; trustee Environmental Def. Fund, 1972-83; Regional trustee Mills Coll., 1962-68. Recipient Gold medal, Conservation Svc. award U.S. Dept. Interior, 1975, Converation award Calif. Acad. Scis., 1979, Am. Motors Conservation award, 1980, Joseph Wood Krutch medal Humane Soc. U.S., Nat. Audubon Soc. medal, 1983, A. Starker Leopole award Calif. Nature Conservancy, 1986, Gold medal UN Environment Program, 1988, Conservation award DAR, 1990, Disting. Svc. award Sierra Club, 1991. Home: Grimes Point Big Sur CA 93920

OWINGS, SUZANN M., consultant, educator; b. L.A., Jan. 26, 1947; d. Theodore Raymond and Elizabeth Marie O'Malley. BA, Calif. State Coll., L.A., 1969; MAT, Ind. U., 1971; PhD, U. N.Mex., 1978. Adminstr. Ind. U., Bloomington, 1970-71; tchr. Compton (Calif.) Sr. High Sch., 1971-75; cons. Owings, Albuquerque, 1975-78; assoc. dir. Energy Consumers of N.Mex., Albuquerque, 1978-79; statewide comprehensive planner CES, N.Mex. State U., Albuquerque, 1979; strategic planner Bechtel Inc., San Francisco, 1979-83; dean Golden Gate U., San Francisco, 1983-84; cons. Bitn Assocs., Corrales, N.Mex. and L.A., 1984—; coord. Albuquerque Pub. Schs., 1992—; instr. mgmt. Troy State U., U. Phoenix, Chapman U.. Co-author, co-editor: Southwest Images and Trends: Factors in Community Development, 1979, numerous others. Co-organizer Rio Rancho 2000, 1992-93; mem., chmn. Sandoval County Intergovtl./Bus. Adv. Coun., Bernalillo, N.Mex., 1993—; mem. Sandoval County Econ. Devel. Com., 1991—. Mem. ASTD (pres.-elect, v.p., bd. dirs.), Am. Soc. for Pub. Adminstrn. (pres.-elect, chairperson Pub. Policy Inst.), Optimist (bd. dirs., pres. N.W. Albuquerque club). Home: PO Box 872 Placitas NM 87043-0872

OWNBY, CHARLOTTE LEDBETTER, anatomy educator; b. Amory, Miss., July 27, 1947; d. William Moss and Anna Faye (Long) Ledbetter; m. James Donald Ownby, Sept. 6, 1969; children: Holly Ruth, Mary Faye. BS in Zoology, U. Tenn., 1969, MS in Zoology, 1971; PhD in Anatomy, Colo. State U., 1975. Instr. Okla. State U., Stillwater, 1974-75, asst. prof., 1975-80, assoc. prof., 1980-84, prof., 1984—; dir. electron microscope lab. Okla. State U., Stillwater, 1977—, head dept., 1990-95. Editor Proc. 9th World Congress Internat. Soc. Toxicology, 1989; editorial bd. Toxion, 1984—. Recipient SmithKline-Beecham award for rsch. excellence, 1992; NIH, USPHS grantee, 1979-92. Mem. Okla. Soc. Electron Microscopy (pres. 1977-78), Pan Am. Soc. Toxinology (pres. 1994—), Internat. Soc. of Toxinology (pres. 1994-97), Phi Beta Kappa, Sigma Xi, Phi Kappa Phi. Office: Okla State U Anatomy Pathology and Pharmacology Dept Physiol Scis 264 Vet Medicine Stillwater OK 74078

OWSIA, NASRIN AKBARNIA, pediatrician; b. Babol, Iran, Dec. 5, 1940; came to U.S., 1968; d. Ahmad and Hoora O.; m. Behrooz A. Akbarnia, Mar. 19, 1968; children: Halleh, Ladan, Ramin. MD, Tehran (Iran) U., 1966. Intern in pediatrics Berkshire Med. Ctr. Hosp., Pittsfield, Mass., 1968-69; resident in pediatrics Albany (N.Y.) Med. Ctr. Hosp., 1969-72; pediatric gastroenterologist St. Christopher Hosp. for Children, Phila., 1972-73; asst. prof. Albany Med. Coll., 1973-76, Tehran U., 1976-80; asst. prof. St. Louis U. Med. Ctr., 1981-89, clin. assoc. prof., 1989-90; pvt. practice San Diego, 1990—. Bd. mem. Persian Cultural Ctr., San Diego, 1993—. Recipient award AMA. Fellow Am. Acad. Pediatrics; mem. Allergy and Asthma Found., Calif. Med. Soc., San Diego Med. Soc. Office: 8010 Frost St Ste 414 San Diego CA 92123-4284

OXELL, LOIE GWENDOLYN, fashion and beauty educator, consultant, columnist; b. Sioux City, Iowa, Nov. 17, 1917; d. Lyman Stanley and Loie Erma (Crill) Barton; m. Eugene Edwin Eschenbrenner, Aug. 8, 1936 (dec. 1954); children: Patricia Gene, Eugene Edward (dec. Feb. 1994); m. Henry J. Oxell, Nov. 3, 1956 (dec. July 1994). AS in Fashion Merchandising, Broward C.C., Davie, Fla., 1978. Fashion rep. Crestmoor Suit & Coat Co., St. Louis, 1951-56; with "To the Ladies" weekly TV show KSD-TV, St. Louis, 1950's; cons./instr. Miami-Herald Newspaper Glamor Clinic, Miami, Fla., 1957-71; pres./owner Loie's (Loy's) Inc., Miami, Fla., 1958-71; owner West Coast East Talent Agy.; pres./owner W. Coast E. Talent Agy.; instr./lectr. Charron-Williams Coll., Miami, 1973-77; instr. Fashion Inst. Ft. Lauderdale, Fla., 1977-86; pres./owner Image Power Unltd., Plantation, Fla., 1992—; lectr. in field; columnist Sr. Life News, Fla., Sr. Beacon, Tex., 1995—, Sr. Life and Boomer Times, Fla., 1995—, others. Author: I'd Like You to Meet My Wife, 1964; appeared on weekly TV show To the Ladies, 1950s, Del Russo Beauty Show, 1960s, Red Skelton TV show, also fashion commentary, TV commls. Vol. The Work Force, lectr., instr. The AARP Sr. Cmty. Svc. Employment Program (SCSEP), Ft. Lauderdale, Hollywood, Fla., 1987—, SCSEP Product Dirs., Charlestown, S.C., 1986; life mem. women's com. Miami Children's Hosp.; faculty advisor Nu Tau Sigma sorority Charron Williams Coll., 1973-77; pres. Venice of Am. chpt. Am. Bus. Women's Assn., 1975-76. Recipient Cert. of Appreciation Dade County Welfare Dept. Youth Hall, Miami, 1966, Community TV Found., Miami, 1966, 71, Woman of the Yr. award Am. Bus. Women's Assn. (Venice of Am. chpt.), 1976-77, Award for Svc. AARP Sr. Community Svc. Program, 1993. Mem. The Fashion Group Internat. (life, womens com. Miami Childrens Hosp.). Office: Image Power Unltd 1859 N Pine Island Rd # 339 Plantation FL 33322-5224

OXENDORF, SUSAN BARBARA, educator family and consumer science; b. Milw., Apr. 13, 1942; d. Joseph F. and Lorraine E. (Huber) Banovich; m. Kenneth Oxendorf, Nov. 4, 1972. BS in Home Econs. Edn., U. Wis.-Stout, 1964, MS in Home Econs. Edn., 1968. Tchr. home econs. Longfellow Jr. High Sch., Wauwatosa, Wis., 1964-69, Whitman Jr. High Sch., Wauwatosa, 1969-73, Maine South H.S., Park Ridge, Ill., 1973-79, Hernando H.S., Brooksville, Fla., 1979—; mem. state curriculum revision and test writing team Fla. State Dept. Edn., 1982-94. Mem. Fla. League Tchrs., Hernando County Edn. Found. (sec. 1993-94), Fla. Vocat. Home Econs. Assn. (treas. 1992-94), Hernando county Tchrs. Acad. (chmn. 1993-94). Roman Catholic. Home: 13460 Pia Ct Spring Hill FL 34609-8920 Office: Hernando HS 700 Bell Ave Brooksville FL 34601-2240

OXENREIDER, LAURA ELIZABETH, special education educator; b. Bronx, Dec. 18, 1964; d. Salvatore Emile and Mary Ellen (Giglio) Sorrillo; m. David Alan Oxenreider, Oct. 16, 1993. BS in Psychology cum laude, East Stroudsburg U., 1990; MA in Sch. Counseling, U. Ctrl. Fla., 1996. Mental health tech. Meadows Psychiat. Ctr., Centre Hall, Pa., 1990-91; case mgr. Osceola County Mental Health, Kissimmee, Fla., 1991-93; tchr. emotionally handicapped Orange County Schs., Orlando, Fla., 1993-96; guidance counselor Orange County Pub. Schs., 1996. Mem. ACA, Orange County Counseling Assn. Home: 231 Baywest Neighbors Cir Orlando FL 32835

OXLEY, ANN, television executive; b. Canton, Ohio, Aug. 3, 1924; d. Edward and Dorothy (Duffy) Adang. B.A. with distinction, Ind. U., 1974, M.P.A., 1982; m. Jack Raymond Oxley, Aug. 10, 1946; children: Kathleen Oxley Wiggins, Maureen Oxley Gaff, Joseph, Jeffrey, Christeen Oxley Rhodes, Daniel, Sister Julie Marie Oxley, Jamie, Kevin, Valerie Oxley Fouch, Amy. Advt. account salesperson Ft. Wayne (Ind.) Jour. Gazette, 1945-47; office mgr. Ind. Equestrian Assn., Ft. Wayne, 1971-73; rsch. dir. Taxpayers Rsch. Assn., Ft. Wayne, 1974-76; exec. dir. Ft. Wayne Pub. TV Inc., 1976-86; founder, owner Akin Assocs., 1987—. Active Bicentennial Com., 1976; adviser Media Arts Panel Ind. Arts Commn. Mem. AAUW, Svc. Corp Retired Execs. (publicity chair., 1986nat. mktg. dir. 1989-90), Mensa Internat., C. of C. (cultural com.), Phi Alpha Alpha. Roman Catholic. Home: 4305 Arlington Ave Fort Wayne IN 46807-2635 Office: SCORE 1300 S Harrison Federal Bldg Fort Wayne IN 46807

OXLEY, MARGARET CAROLYN STEWART, elementary education educator; b. Petaluma, Calif., Apr. 1, 1930; d. James Calhoun Stewart and Clara Thornton (Whiting) Bomboy; m. Joseph Hubbard Oxley, Aug. 25, 1951; children: Linda Margaret, Carolyn Blair Oxley Greiner, Joan Claire Oxley Willis, Joseph Stewart, James Harmon, Laura Marie Oxley Brechbill. Student, U. Calif., Berkeley, 1949-51; BS summa cum laude, Ohio State U., 1973, MA, 1984, postgrad., 1985, 88, 92. Cert. tchr., Ohio. 2d grade tchr. St. Paul Sch., Westerville, Ohio, 1973—; presenter in field. Editl. adv. bd. Reading Tchr., vol. 47-48, 1993—; editl. rev. bd. Children's Literature Jour., 1996—; co-author: Reading and Writing, Where it All Begins, 1991, Teaching with Children's Books: Path to Literature-Based Instruction, 1995. Active Akita Child Conservation League, Columbus, Ohio, 1968-70. Named Columbus Diocesan Tchr. of Yr., 1988; Phoebe A. Hearst scholar, 1951, Rose Sterheim Meml. scholar, 1951; recipient Mary Karrer award Ohio State U., 1994. Mem. Nat. Coun. Tchrs. English (Notable Trade Books in the Lang. Arts com. 1993-94, chair 1995-96), Internat. Reading Assn. (Exemplary Svc. in Promotion of Literacy award 1991), Literacy Connection (pres.), Children's Lit. Assembly, Ohio Coun. Tchrs. English Lang. Arts (Outstanding Educator 1990), Phi Kappa Phi, Pi Lambda Theta (hon.). Democrat. Roman Catholic. Home: 298 Brevoort Rd Columbus OH 43214-3826

OYEN, MARY JO, ophthalmologist; b. Dubuque, Iowa, Nov. 18, 1959; d. James Albert and Geraldine Mae (Bertram) Kay; m. Thomas Joseph Oyen, June 23, 1979; Daniel, Stephen, Brian, Sara. BSME summa cum laude, U. Wis., Platteville, 1982; MD, U. Wis., 1993. Diplomate Nat. Bd. Med. Examiners. Project engr., team mgr. P&G Paper Products Divsn.), Green Bay, Wis., 1982-87; maintenance mgr. Oscar Mayer & Co., Madison, Wis., 1987-88; intern internal medicine U. Wis. Hosp. & Clinics, Madison, 1993-94; ophthalmology resident U. Wis. Hosp. and Clinics, Madison, 1994—. Participant Resident Clinic for the Indigent, U. Wis., Madison, 1995—. Recipient numerous scholarships based on acad. excellence including, Ernie Guenther Meml. scholarship, Elgie Ward scholarship and Alumni Assn. Scholarship U. Wis. Platteville, Jackson Found. Med. Sch. scholarship, 1989-91, Evan and Marian Helfaer scholarship, 1992; grantee AAUW Found., 1988. Mem. AMA, Am. Med. Women's Assn., Am. Acad. Ophthalmology, Wis.-Upper Mich. Soc. Ophthalmology, Am. Soc. Cataract and Refractive Surgeons, U.Wis. Med. Alumni Assn., Phi Kappa Phi, Alpha Lambda Delta, Alpha Omega Alpha. Home: 3330 Siggelkow Rd McFarland WI 53558 Office: U Wis Dept Ophthalmology 2880 University Ave Madison WI 53705

OYLER, BERTHA JEANNE, educator; b. Columbus, Ind., Feb. 3, 1943; d. Jean Hamilton and Julia Louise (Koch) LaSell; m. Michael Paul Oyler, Aug. 8, 1965 (dec. Mar. 1984); children: David, Joanthon, Sarah, Samantha. BS in Edn., Concordia Tchrs. Coll., 1965, MEd, 1988. Tchr. St. Peter's Luth. Sch., Hampton, Nebr., 1965-66, Mt. Calvary Luth. Sch., Milw., 1966-68, NAzareth Luth Sch., Milw., 1969-70, Luth. Children's Friend Soc., Wauwatosa, Wis., 1971, Trinity Luth. Sch., Sheboygan, Wis., 1985—; advisor Student Coun. Trinity, Sheboygan, 1991—, Trinity Scholastic Olympics, Sheboygan, 1986—. Advisor Sheboygan Area Luth Singles,

19866, Widow's Brunch, Sheboygan, 1987—; resource adminstr. Internat. Luth Singles, 1989—. Mem. Wis. Assn. Student Coun. (advisor), Luth. Edn. Assn. Office: Trinity Luth Sch 824 Wisconsin Ave Sheboygan WI 53081

OZAKI, NANCY JUNKO, performance artist, former educator; b. Denver, Feb. 14, 1951; d. Joe Motoichi and Tamiye (Saki) O.; m. Nathan Jeoffrey Inouye, May 25, 1980 (div. Aug. 1985); m. Gary Steven Tsujimoto, Nov. 12, 1989. BS in Edn., U. Colo., 1973; postgrad., U. Colo., Denver, 1977, Metro State Coll., 1982, Red Rocks C.C., 1982-83, U. No. Colo., 1982, U. N.Mex., 1985, U. No. Colo., 1988. Elem. tchr. Bur. Indian Affairs, Bloomfield, N.Mex., 1973-75, Aurora (Colo.) Pub. Schs., 1977-83, Albuquerque Pub. Schs., 1983-84, Denver Pub. Schs., 1984-87, Oak Grove Sch. Dist., San Jose, Calif., 1988-89, San Mateo (Calif.) City Elem. Dist., 1990-92; performing artist Japanese drums Young Audiences, San Francisco, 1992-93, Denver, 1994—; performing artist Japanese drums Walt Disney World, Epcot Ctr., Orlando, Fla., 1993—. Vol. worker with young Navajo children; co-sponsor girl's sewing and camping groups. Mem. Kappa Delta Pi (Theta chpt.). Home: PO Box 22777 Lake Buena Vista FL 32830 Office: One World Taiko PO Box 22777 Lake Buena Vista FL 32830

OZAWA, MARTHA NAOKO, social work educator; b. Ashikaga, Tochigi, Japan, Sept. 30, 1933; came to U.S., 1963; d. Tokuichi and Fumi (Kawashima) O.; m. May 1959 (div. May 1966). BA in Econs., Aoyama Gakuin U., 1956; MS in Social Work, U. Wis., 1966, PhD in Social Welfare, 1969. Asst. prof. social work Portland (Oreg.) State U., 1969-70, assoc. prof. social work, 1970-72; assoc. rsch. prof. social work NYU, 1972-75; assoc. prof. social work Portland State U., 1975-76; prof. social work Washington U., St. Louis, 1976-85, Bettie Bofinger Brown prof. social policy, 1985—. Author: Income Maintenance and Work Incentives, 1982; editor: Women's Life Cycle: Japan-U.S. Comparison in Income Maintenance, 1989, Women's Life Cycle and Economic Insecurity: Problems and Proposals, 1989; editl. bd. Social Work, Silver Spring, Md., 1972-75, 85-88, New Eng. Jour. Human Svcs., Boston, 1987—, Ency. of Social Work, Silver Spring, 1974-77, 91-95, Jour. Social Svc. Rsch., 1977—, Children and Youth Svcs. Rev., 1991—, Social Work Rsch., 1994—, Jour. Poverty. Grantee Adminstrn. on Aging, Washington, 1979, 84, NIMH, 1990-93, Assn. for Pub. Policy Analysis and Mgmt. Mem. Nat. Assn. Social Workers, Nat. Acad. Social Ins., Nat. Conf. on Social Welfare (bd. dirs. 1981-87), The Gerontol. Soc. Am., Coun. Social Work Edn., Washington U. Faculty Club (bd. dirs. 1986-91), Soc. for Social Work and Rsch. Home: 13018 Tiger Lily Ct Saint Louis MO 63146-4339 Office: Washington U Campus PO Box 1196 Saint Louis MO 63130-4899

OZEREKO-DECOEN, MARY THERESE, therapeutic recreation specialist and therapist; b. Salem, Mass., Oct. 4, 1961; d. Domenic S. and Monica M. (Gesek) Ozereko; m. Jeffrey G. deCoen, Nov. 21, 1987. BS, U. Mass., 1982; MEd, Springfield Coll., 1987. Cert. therapeutic recreation specialist, Pa.; cert. golf club maker. Dir. promotions and ops. Wheat Thins mayors cup race Nabisco, Salem, 1984-86; conf. planner Pioneer Valley Conv. and Visitors Bur., Springfield, Mass., 1986-87; dir. tennis and recreation Village of Smugglers Notch, Vt., 1987-88; mental health profl., therapeutic recreation specialist Hoffman Homes for Youth, Gettysburg, Pa., 1988-89; therapeutic recreation aide Chambersburg (Pa.) Hosp., 1990; caseworker, therapeutic recreation specialist Tressler Wilderness Sch., Boiling Springs, Pa., 1989-92; intake dir. Mentor Clin. Care, Harrisburg, Pa., 1993—; owner GolfAugusta Pro Shops, Hershey, Pa., 1995—; cons. clin. seminars on recreational therapy for mental health profls. Mem. Hershey Partnership, 1995—, Pa. Children's Panel, Harrisburg, 1992—. Mem. NAFE, Nat. Recreation and Parks Assn., Pa. Mental Health Providers Assn., Pa. Parks and Recreation Assn., Ctrl. Pa. C. of C. (golf planner ea. amputee spl. olympics 1996—), U.S. Golf Assn., Cert. Golfmakers Assn., Nat. Coun. for Therapeutic Recreation Cert., U. Mass.-Keystone Alumni Assn. (pres. 1994—), Harrisburg Exec. Womens Com. Democrat. Roman Catholic. Office: 2090 Linglestown Rd Harrisburg PA 17110

OZI, ELIZABETH, private school administrator; b. São Paulo, Brazil, Aug. 5, 1959; d. Heni and Firmina O. BA in Psychology, U. Las Vegas, 1987; postgrad., NOVA U., Fla., 1989—; cert. of continuing profl. edn., U. Nev., 1988. Cert. tchr. Tchr. Clark County Sch. Dist., Las Vegas, Nev., 1990-94; owner, sch. dir. Parent's Choice, Las Vegas, Nev., 1993—; dir. Home Base Bus., Las Vegas, Nev., 1993—. Interviewer (Radio Show Series) Recognizing Signs to Prevent Suicide, 1990. Counselor Suicide Prevention, Nev., 1988-90. Recipient Cert. of Leadership award Nat. U., Las Vegas, 1990. Mem. Psi Chi. Home: 4646 Grasshopper Dr Las Vegas NV 89122

OZICK, CYNTHIA, author; b. N.Y.C., Apr. 17, 1928; d. William and Celia (Regelson) O.; m. Bernard Hallote, Sept. 7, 1952; 1 dau., Rachel Sarah. BA cum laude with honors in English, NYU, 1949; MA, Ohio State U., 1950; LHD (hon.), Yeshiva U., 1984, Hebrew Union Coll., 1984, Williams Coll., 1986, Hunter Coll., 1987, Jewish Theol. Sem. Am., 1988, Adelphi U., 1988, SUNY, 1989, Brandeis U., 1990, Bard Coll., 1991, Spertus Coll., 1991, Skidmore Coll., 1992. Author: Trust, 1966, The Pagan Rabbi and Other Stories, 1971, Bloodshed and Three Novellas, 1976, Levitation: Five Fictions, 1982, Art and Ardor: Essays, 1983, The Cannibal Galaxy, 1983, The Messiah of Stockholm, 1987, Metaphor and Memory: Essays, 1989, The Shawl, 1989, Epodes: First Poems, 1992, What Henry James Knew, and Other Essays on Writers, 1994, The Cynthia Ozick Reader, 1996, Fame and Folly, 1996; (plays) Blue Light, 1994, The Shawl, 1996; also poetry, criticism, revs., transls., essays and fictions in numerous periodicals and anthologies. Phi Beta Kappa orator, Harvard U., 1985. Recipient Mildred and Harold Strauss Living award Am. Acad. Arts and Letters, 1983, Rea award for short story, 1986; Lucy Martin Donnelly fellow, Bryn Mawr Coll., 1992, Guggenheim fellow, 1982. Mem. PEN, Authors League, Am. Acad. of Arts and Scis., Am. Acad. of Arts and Letters, Dramatists Guild, Académie Universelle des Cultures (Paris), Phi Beta Kappa. Office: care Alfred A Knopf Co 201 E 50th St New York NY 10022-7703

PABON-PEREZ, HEIDI, physicist; b. San Juan, Oct. 6, 1939; d. José Antonio Pabon-Rivera and Tomasa D. (Pérez) Pabon. BS, U. Puerto Rico, 1960; MS, U. Rochester, 1961. Health physicist U. P.R. Nuclear Ctr., 1961-69, Dr. I. Gonzalez Martinez Hosp., San Juan, 1965-69; physicist State Dept. P.R., 1964-77; radiological physicist P.R. Med. Ctr., San Juan, 1969-77; instr. Radiological Scis. U. P.R., 1976-77; cons. Med. Physicist Caguas (P.R.) Nuclear Medicine Lab., 1977; lt. Med. Svc. Corps. USN, 1977-80; acting program dir. U. P.R., 1981-84, asst. prof., 1980-84, 1984—; health physicist VA Med. Ctr., San Juan, 1984—. Mem., treas. P.R. YL Club, San Juan, 1977-96. Lt. USN, 1977-80. Home: BC9 Yagrumo St Valle Arriba Heights PR 00983 Office: VA Medical Center One Veterans Pla San Juan PR 00927-5800

PACCHION, DONNA M., bank executive. Sr. v.p. corp. acctg. Nat. City Corp., Cleve. Office: Nat City Corp Nat City Ctr 1900 E 9th St Cleveland OH 44114-3484*

PACE, ANN CATHERINE, youth worker; b. Borger, Tex., May 5, 1969; d. Marion Carroll and Rosa Jane (White) P. BA in Math. Scis., Art and Art History, Rice U., 1991. High sch. youth worker, speaker Campus Crusade for Christ, Phoenix, 1991—.

PACE, BILLIE JEAN, gynecologist. MD, Howard U., 1975. Resident Martin Luther King Jr. Gen. Hosp., L.A.; pvt. practice ob-gyn. Sacramento, 1981-85, Orlando, Fla., 1985—; co-founder Altamonte Womens Ctr., Altamonte Springs, Fla., 1996—; co-funder, med. dir. Teenage Clinic Martin Luther King Jr. Gen. Hosp.; chair coun. concerns women physicians Nat. Med. Assn., 1993-95; vice chair Reproductive Health Tech. Project, Washington, 1993—; pub. spkr. women's health Fla.; co-founder Internat. Coalition Women Physicians. Office: Altamonte Womens Ctr 707 Ballard St Ste 1000 Altamonte Springs FL 32701

PACE, CAROLINA JOLLIFF, communications executive, commercial real estate investor; b. Dallas, Apr. 12, 1938; d. Lindsay Gafford and Carolina (Juden) Jolliff; student Holton-Arms Jr. Coll., 1956-57; BA in Comparative Lit., So. Meth. U., 1960; m. John McIver Pace, Oct. 7, 1961. Promotional asst., Dallas, dir. season ticket sales Dallas Theatre Ctr., 1960-61; exec. sec. Dallas Book and Author Luncheon, 1959-63; promotional and instl. cons. Henry Regnery-Reilly & Lee Pub. Co., Chgo., 1962-65; pub. trade rep. various cos., instl. rep. Don R. Phillips Co., Southeastern area, 1965-67; Southwestern rep. Ednl. Reading Svc., Inc.-Troll Assocs., Mahwah, N.J., 1967-72; v.p., dir. multimedia div. Melton Book Co., Dallas, 1972-79; v.p. mktg. Webster's Internat., Inc., Nashville, 1980-82; pres. Carolina Pace, Inc., 1982—; mem. adv. bd. Nat. Info. Ctr. of Spl. Edn. Materials; mem. materials rev. panel Nat. Media Ctr. for Materials of Severely-Profoundly Handicapped, 1981; mem. mktg. product rev. bd. LINC Resources, 1982, 83, 84, mktg. task force, 1983, adv. bd, 1987; reviewer spl. edn. U.S. Dept. Edn., 1975-79, 85; rev. cons. Health and Humas Svcs., 1982, 83, 84, 86; product rev. task force CEC, 1984, 85, 86; cons. Ednl. Cable Consortium, Summit, N.J., 1982-87. Mem. adv. coun. Grad. System Sch. Libr. and Info. Sci. Found., U. Tex., 1987—; co-vice chair Friends Highland Park Libr., 1989; mem. focus group City Dallas Growth Policy Plan; mem. art and design com. West Downtown Ctrs.; active Dallas City Wide Parking Task Force, Ctrl. Transp. Forum Ctrl. Bus. Dist., Union Sta. Art & Design Com., Downtown Transfer Ctrs., Art and Design Com., West End Task Force, Ctrl. Bus. Dist. Task Force; co-founder Operation TexRec, 1990-91; bd. dirs. Transp. Mgmt. Assn., 1995—; chair Vanpool Use Study, 1995; budget chmn. Dallas County Sesquicentennial com., 1996; bd. mem. Friends of Old Red Courthouse. Mem. Ctrl. Dallas Assn. (transportation com.), Dallas Plan (focus com.), Nat. Audio Visual Assn. (conf. panelist 1979), Internat. Comm. Industries Assn., Assn. Ednl. and Comm. Tech., Assn. Spl. Edn. Tech. (nat. dir., v.p. publicity 1980-82), Women's Nat. Book Assn, Women in Comm., Dallas Founders, Ctrl. Dallas Assn., Friends of the West End (pres. 1988—), West End Assn. Dallas (chmn. subcom. on traffic and parking 1986-87, com. demographic study 1987-88), Pub. Rels. Soc. Am., Coun. Exceptional Children (dir. exhibitors com., chmn. publ. com. 1979 conf., conf. speaker 1981), Downtown Transp. Mgmt. Assn. (adv. bd., chmn. vanpools subcom.), DAR (Jane Douglas chpt.), Dallas Zool. Soc., Dallas West End Hist. Dist. Assn., Dallas Mus. of Art, Dallas Southern Meml. Tex. Parking Assn., Kimball Art Mus., Alpha Delta Pi. Presbyterian. Producer ednl. videos; contbr. articles to profl. jours. Home: 4524 Lorraine Ave Dallas TX 75205-3613

PACE, KAREN YVONNE, mathematics and computer science educator; b. Jefferson City, Mo., Dec. 29, 1957; d. William John and Georgia (Loesch) Sippel; m. Charles Edward Pace, Dec. 27, 1982. EdB, Mo. State U., 1980; EdM, Drury U., 1985. Cert. secondary tchr. Tchr. Salem (Mo.) Sch. Dist., 1980—, Southwest Bapt. U., Boliver, Mo., 1985—; dist. chair Career Ladder Com., Salem, 1991-92; treas. Cmty. Tchrs. Orgn., Salem, 1992-93; assessment expert Salem Sch. Dist., 1993-94; sr. leader Mo. Assessment Project 2000, 1994. Pres. Community Cause Club, Salem, 1994. Mem. Salem Tchrs. Assn. (budget com. chair 1992-94). Democrat. Home: PO Box 795 Salem MO 65560-0795 Office: Salem Sch Dist 1400 W 3rd St Salem MO 65560-2730

PACE, LAURA DIANE See OMER, LAURA DIANE

PACE, ROSA WHITE, lawyer; b. Borger, Tex., Nov. 5, 1932; d. John Herron and Anna Mae (Caldwell) White; m. M. Carroll Pace, Jan. 3, 1968; children: Ann Catherine, Virginia Gale, Mary Jane. BA, William Jewell Coll., 1953; JD, U. Tex., 1956. Bar: Tex. 1956. Ptnr. White & White Attys., Borger, 1956-62, White, White & White Attys., Borger, 1962-65; pvt. practice Borger, 1966—. Co-author: Borger, a History, Hutchinson County History, 1983. Chmn. Hutchinson County Hist. Commn., 1985-94. Recipient Professionalism award Coll. of State Bar of Tex., 1996. Mem. ABA, State Bar Assn. Tex., Borger Bar Assn., DAR (local regent 1975-76), Beta Sigma Phi (women of yr. 1978). Office: 431 Deahl St Borger TX 79007-4113

PACE, SALLY MAE, student services dean; b. Tehachappi, Calif., Mar. 22, 1946; d. Ben Franklin Jr. and Mary Elizabeth (Miller) Stinson; m. Michael D. Pace, June 15, 1969; children: Ryan Seth, Natalie Michelle. BA in Home Econs., San Jose State U., 1969; MEd, Fresno Pacific, 1990. Home econs. tchr. Homestead H.S., San Jose, Calif., 1970, Visalia (Calif.) Unified, 1970-71; home econs. tchr. Woodlake (Calif.) H.S., 1971-86, counselor, 1986-90, dean student svcs., 1990—. Active Woodlake Meml. Dist., 1986-89. Named Calif. Home Econs. Tchr. of Yr., Calif. Home Econs. Assn., 1983, Woodlake Woman of the Yr., Woodlake C. of C., 1994. Mem. Woodlake Kiwanis (charter sec./treas. 1989-92, Kiwanian of Yr. 1995). Home: 19524 Ave 364 Woodlake CA 93286 Office: Woodlake HS 400 W Whitney Woodlake CA 93286

PACHECO, MARGARET MARY, marketing executive; b. Waterville, Maine, June 9, 1962; d. Louis E. and Jeannine F. (Guguere) DeRosby; m. Joseph Pacheco III, Sept. 1, 1989; 1 child, Kathryn Reagan. BJ, U. Mo., 1984. Staff writer, photographer Gannett Newspapers Corp., Waterville, 1976-79; asst. news dir. Kennebec Broadcasting Co., Waterville, 1979-80; staff writer McClatchy Newspapers Corp., Sacramento, Calif., 1982-84; mktg. dir. Leatherby Mktg. Inc., Sacramento, 1984-85; sr. market rsch. analyst Electronic Data Systems, Dallas, 1985-90; dir. mktg. Power Computing Co., Dallas, 1990-93; pres. Daniel Group, Dallas, 1993-94, dir. corp. mktg. and comm., 1994—. Jacob Stein Meml. scholar U. Mo., 1984. Mem. Internat. Assn. Bus. Communicators, Soc. Competitive Intelligence Profls., Am. Mktg. Assn. Office: 14180 Dallas Pky Ste 600 Dallas TX 75240-4341

PACHEPSKY, LUDMILA BAUDINOVNA, ecologist; b. Ukhta, Komi, Russia, Mar. 19, 1946; d. Baudin Nuraddin Islamov and Valentina Grigorievna (Tyrina) Islamova; m. Yakov Aronovich Pachepsky, June 8, 1978; children: Anna, Elizaveta. Diploma, Moscow State U., Russia, 1969, postgrad., 1969-72. Engr. Inst. Agrochemistry and Soil Sci. of Soviet Acad. Scis., Pushchino/Moscow, 1972-74, minor rsch. scientist, 1974-80, rsch. scientist, 1980-92; rsch. asst. U. Md., College Park, 1993-94; sr. rsch. scholar Duke U., Durham, N.C., 1994—; invited lectr. Moscow State U., 1990-91, U. Ekaterinburgh, Russia, 1990. Editor: Institute of Soil Science and Photosynthesis, 1983-86; author: Computer Modeling of Water and Salt Movement in Soils, 1973, Modeling of Soil Salinization and Alkalinization Processes, 1979, 86, Stable Characteristics and a Model of Ecosystems in Northern Prikaspy, 1982, Dynamic Model of the Tea Plantations Productivity, 1985, Photosynthetic Apparatus and Productivity of Triticale, 1991; contbr. articles to profl. jours. Recipient Spl. award for Efficient Sci. Govt. of Reg. of Georgia, USSR, 1985; rsch. grantee Terrestial Ecosystems Regional Rsch. and Analysis, USA, 1994, others. Mem. Am. Soc. Plant Physiologists, Am. Soc. for Gravitational and Space Biology, Am. Soc. Agronomy, Nat. Geographic Soc. Russian Orthodox. Home: 10403 Snowden Rd Laurel MD 20708 Office: USDA:ARS:Systems Rsch Lab Bldg 007 Rm 008 BARC-W 10300 Baltimore Ave Beltsville MD 20705

PACHNER, JOAN, art historian, curator; b. N.Y.C., Oct. 14, 1956; d. Charles W. and Janice F. (Frenkel) P.; m. Richard A. Newman, Sept. 24, 1989; 1 child, David. BA in Art History cum laude, Conn. Coll., New London, 1978; MA, NYU, 1982, PhD, 1993. Guest curator Cooper-Hewitt Mus., N.Y.C., 1982; organizer, cataloger Estate of Theodore Roszak, N.Y.C., 1983-84; cataloger Hans Namuth, N.Y.C., 1984; rsch. asst. NYU Inst. Fine Arts, N.Y.C., 1983-85, Stuart Davis Catalogue Raisonné, N.Y.C., 1985-86; guest co-curator Vestfälisches Landesmuseum, Münster, Germany, 1988; photo rschr., editl. prodr. Mus. Modern Art, N.Y.C., 1990, curatorial asst., 1995; rsch. cons. Storm King Art Ctr., Mountainville, N.Y., 1993—; cons. archivits, curator Estate of David Smith, N.Y.C., 1994—; lect. various galleris, colls. and art ctrs.; cons. co-curator Mus. Modern Art, N.Y.C. 1998 exhibit. Contbr. articles to profl. jours. Mem. Coll. Art Assn., Am. Assn. Museums. Democrat. Jewish. Home: 245 W 107th St New York NY 10025

PACIFICO, DIANE ALANE, ophthalmic nurse; b. Bethlehem, Pa., Sept. 23, 1952; d. William Edward and Martha Lou (Bradford) Reichard; m. Ronald L. Pacificio, Sept. 25, 1982. Diploma, Abington (Pa.) Meml. Hosp., 1973. Cert. RN in ophthalmology. Med.-surg. nurse St. Luke's Hosp., Bethlehem, 1973-76; ophthalmic nurse physician's office, Pitts., 1976-77, Everett & Hurite Ophthalmic Assocs., Pitts., 1977-80; dir. ops. and quality control Assocs. in Ophthalmology, Inc., Pitts., 1980—; speaker in field. Contbr. articles to profl. jours. Mem. NAFE, Founders Soc., Am. Soc. Ophthalmic Registered Nurses, Abington Nurses Alumnae, Am. Soc. Ophthalmic Adminstrs. Office: 500 Lewis Run Rd Ste 218 Pittsburgh PA 15236 also: 125 Daugherty Dr Ste 320 Monroeville PA 15146 also: Town Centre Bldg 10475 Perry Hwy Ste 315 Wexford PA 15090 Address: 4140 Brownsville Rd Ste 237 Pittsburgh PA 15227

PACK, ELIZABETH ELAINE, special education educator, program administrator; b. Portsmouth, Ohio, Sept. 9, 1957; d. Carl T. and Macie G. (Conley) Parsons; m. Douglas James Pack, Oct. 18, 1974; children: Kimberly Dawn Pack Ramey, Douglas James Pack Jr. B of Elem. Edn., Ohio U., 1980, M of Spl. Edn., 1989. Spl. edn. tchr. Minford (Ohio) Local Schs., 1981—; exch. tchr. to Eng., Hands Across the Water, summer 1995. Club adv. Scioto County 4-H, 1988—. Mem. NEA, Ohio Edn. Assn. Mem. Ch. of Christ. Home: 1515 Kinker Rd Minford OH 45653 Office: Minford Mid Sch Box 204 Minford OH 45653

PACK, PHOEBE KATHERINE FINLEY, civic worker; b. Portland, Oreg., Feb. 2, 1907; d. William Lovell and Irene (Barnhart) Finley; student U. Calif., Berkeley, 1926-27; B.A., U. Oreg., 1930; m. Arthur Newton Pack, June 11, 1936; children: Charles Lathrop, Phoebe Irene. Layman referee Pima County Juvenile Ct., Tucson, 1958-71; mem. pres.'s council Menninger Found., Topeka; mem. Alcoholism Council So. Ariz., 1960—; bd. dirs. Kress Nursing Sch., Tucson, 1957-67, Pima County Assn. for Mental Health, 1958-—, Ariz. Assn. for Mental Health, Phoenix, 1963—, U. Ariz. Found., Casa de los Niños Crisis Nursery; co-founder Ariz.-Sonora Desert Mus., Tucson, 1975—, Ghost Ranch Found., N.Mex.; bd. dirs. Tucson Urban League, Tucson YMCA Youth Found. Mem. Mt. Vernon Ladies Assn. Union (state vice regent, 1962-84),Mt. Vernon One Hundred (founder), Nature Conservancy (life), Alpha Phi. Home: Villa Compana 6653 E Carondelet Dr Apt 415 Tucson AZ 85710-2153

PACK, SUSAN JOAN, art consultant; b. N.Y.C., June 15, 1951; d. Howard Meade and Nancy (Buckley) P. BA summa cum laude, Princeton U., 1973. Copywriter Laurence Charles & Free, N.Y.C., 1978-83, Warwick Advt., N.Y.C., 1983-85; sr. copywriter Saatchi & Saatchi Compton, N.Y.C., 1985-88; pres. The Pack Collection, 1989—. Author: Film Posters of the Russian Avant-Garde, 1995. Mem. Princeton (N.J.) U. Libr. Coun., 1985-93; trustee Pack Found. for Med. Rsch., N.Y., 1983—; bd. dirs. The Poster Soc., N.Y., 1985-87. Recipient 4 Clio awards, 1981, 1 Clio award, 1982; named one of top art collectors under 40 Art and Antiques Mag., 1985, one of top 100 collectors in U.S., 1996. Mem. Phi Beta Kappa.

PACKARD, BARBARA BAUGH, science institute administrator, physician, physiologist; b. Uniontown, Pa., Mar. 10, 1938; d. Walter Ray and Yolande (Ciarlo) Baugh; m. Lawrence Arthur Krames, Nov. 24, 1963 (div. 1971); m. John E. Packard III, July 14, 1979. B.S., Waynesburg Coll., 1960; M.S., W. Va. U., 1961, Ph.D., 1964; M.D., U. Ala.-Birmingham, 1974. Rsch. assoc. Boston U., 1966; instr. biology, rsch. assoc. in medicine U. Chgo., 1966-67; physiologist myocardial infarction br. Nat. Heart Inst., Bethesda, Md., 1967-71; rsch. assoc. U. Ala., Birmingham, 1971-74; Osler med. intern Johns Hopkins Hosp., Balt., 1974-75; sr. med. scientist adminstr. cardiac disease br. div. heart and vascular disease Nat. Heart, Lung, and Blood Inst., Bethesda, Md., 1975-79, assoc. dir. cardiology, 1979-82, dir. div. heart and vascular diseases, 1980-86, assoc. dir. for sci. program operation, 1986—. Trustee Waynesburg Coll., 1991—. Asst. surgeon gen. USPHS, 1975—. Recipient Commendation medal USPHS, 1978, Outstanding Svc. medal, 1987, Meritorious Svc. medal, 1988, Disting. Svc. medal, 1991; Disting. Pa. Coll. Alumni citation, 1991, Disting. Alumna of Yr. award Waynesburg Coll., 1996. Fellow Am. Coll. Cardiology (bd. govs. 1992-95); mem. Am. Physiol. Soc., Am. Heart Assn., Johns Hopkins Med. and Surg. Soc., Assn. Mil. Surgeons, Sigma Xi. Office: Nat Heart Lung & Blood Inst Bldg 31 Rm 5A03 9000 Rockville Pike Bethesda MD 20892-0001

PACKARD, BONNIE BENNETT, state legislator; b. Concord, N.H., Nov. 9, 1946; d. James Oliver and Caro Lucia (Arsenault) Bennett; m. David Bartlett Packard, Oct. 1, 1983. Mem. N.H. Ho. of Reps., Concord, 1981-82, 85—, vice chair ho. econ. devel. com., 1992, chair ho. commerce com., 1993—; v.p., treas. Dodd Ins. Agy., Contoocook, N.H., 1984-85; bd. dirs. Bus. Fin. Authority. State pres. N.H. Fedn. Rep. Women, 1982-83; chmn. Merrimack County (N.H.) Rep. Com., 1979-80; mem. Hillsborough County Rep. Com., 1995, chair Hillsborough County Del., 1995—; mem. Bd. Selectmen, New Ipswich, N.H., 1989-90; nat. del. trustee Nat. Kidney Found., 1990-91, 1st v.p. N.H. chpt., 1990-91. Recipient Spirit of Independence award N.H. Health Underwriter's Assn., 1996. Mem. New Ipswich Hist. Soc., Greenville Women's Club. Episcopalian. Home: 6 Joy Ln New Ipswich NH 03071-3610 Office: NH Ho of Reps Legis Office Building Rm 302 Concord NH 03301

PACKARD, LINDA LEE, elementary education educator; b. Columbus, Ohio, July 28, 1955; d. Paul Richard and Wilma Laverta (Miller) P.; m. Earl Russell Schaeffer, Nov. 1, 1986; children: Michael Keller, Amanda Keller. BS summa cum laude, Ohio State U., 1992. Tchr. Hilliard (Ohio) City Schs., 1992—. Recipient Meritorious Svc. award Columbus State C.C., 1983; named Woman of Woodcraft, Woodmen of the World, Columbus, 1983. Mem. NEA, Nat. Coun. Tchrs. of Math., Golden Key, Phi Kappa Phi, Pi Lambda Theta. Republican. Methodist. Home: 1568 Buck Trail Ln Worthington OH 43085 Office: Britton Elem Sch 4501 Britton Rd Hilliard OH 43026-9446

PACKARD, PAMELA S., mathematics educator; b. Saginaw, Mich., Aug. 30, 1948; d. Richard A. and Marjorie M. (Morrison) Leidlein; children: Michelle Marie, Elyse Renee. BS Elem. Edn., Cen. Mich. U., 1970, MA Elem. Edn., 1977. Tchr. fifth, sixth and eighth grades Frankenmuth (Mich.) Pub. Schs., 1970-72; tchr. adult edn. Wiley Edn. Ctr., Neu Ulm, Germany, 1972-74; kindergarten tchr. Cleveland Elem., Lawton, Okla., 1974; tchr. eighth grade math. Alma (Mich.) Pub. Schs., 1974-75; off-campus instr. Cen. Mich. U., Mt. Pleasant, 1978, 94; elem. tchr. sixth, seventh and eighth grade Oscoda (Mich.) Area Schs., 1974-93, math. coord. K-9, 1993—; cons. UCMP/Everyday Maths., Evanston, Ill., 1994—; regional dir. Mich. Coun. Tchrs. Math., Lansing, 1990-94; cert. trainer Mich. Math. Insvc. Project, WMU, Kalamazoo, 1990—, New Directions in Math., MDE, Lansing, Mich., 1989-92. Campaign worker Thomas Huck for Probate Judge, Iosco County, Mich., 1994; day camp leader Mitten Bay Girl Scouts, 1991. 1st runner-up award math. coord., Mich. Assn. Sch. Bds., 1994. Mem. Mich. Coun. Tchrs. Math. (regional dir. 1984-94), Nat. Coun. Tchrs. Math. Home: 1609 Media Dr East Tawas MI 48730-9443 Office: Richardson Elem Sch Oscoda Elem Sch 3556 W River Rd Oscoda MI 48750-1459

PACKARD, ROCHELLE SYBIL, elementary school educator; b. June 25, 1951; d. Dave Wallace and Jeanette (Goddy) P. BA in Early Childhood Edn., Point Park Coll., 1973; MEd in Elem. Edn., U. Pitts., 1975. Instrnl. II permanent tchg. cert., Pa. Substitute tchr. Pitts. Pub. Bd. Edn., 1973-77, tchr. kindergarted, 1st grade, 2d grade, 1977—. Chair Israel Day Parade, Pitts., 1981; mem. Hadassah, Pitts., 1983—, Pioneer Women, Pitts., 1982—, ORT, Pitts., 1975—. Mem. Pitts. Fedn. Tchrs., Pitts. State Edn. Agy. Democrat. Jewish. Home: 4100 Lydia St Pittsburgh PA 15207

PACKER, DIANA, reference librarian; b. Cleve., Sept. 4; d. Herman and Sabina (Hochman) Reich; m. Herbert Packer, June 21, 1964 (dec.); children: Cynthia, Jeremy, Todd. BA, Case Western Res. U., 1951, MLS, 1952. Libr. Horizons Rsch. Inc., Cleve., 1952-64, Cleveland Heights (Ohio) University Heights Pub. Libr., 1969—. Officer Cleveland Heights PTA, 1971-84; bd. dirs. LWV, Cleveland Heights, 1974—; officer Spl. Librs. Assn., 1952-64. Mem. Ohio Libr. Assn. Home: 2201 Acacia Park Dr Apt 522 Lyndhurst OH 44124-3841

PACKER, KATHY, computer company executive. Sr. v.p., mktg. devel. CUC Internat. Inc., Stamford, Conn. Office: CUC Internat Inc 707 Summer St Stamford CT 06901*

PACTWA, THERESE ELLEN, finance educator, researcher; b. Chgo., Aug. 13, 1963; d. Robert Joseph and Catherine Cecilia (Tenzi) Pactwa. BBA in Econs., U. Iowa, Iowa City, 1985; MS in Finance, Drexel U., Phila., 1990; postgrad, Fla. Internat. U., Miami, 1993—. Comml. credit analyst Princeton Bank, Camden, N.J., 1986-88; mgr. comml. credit dept. Princeton Bank, Princeton, N.J., 1988; comml. banking officer Chemical Bank, Camden, 1988-90; comml. portfolio analyst Chemical Bank, East Brunswick, N.J., 1990; chief credit officer Regent Nat. Bank, Phila., 1990-92; instr., rschr. Fla. Internat. U., Miami, 1993—. Co-author: (book) The Return Generating Models in Finance: A Synthesis, 1996; contbr. articles to profl. jours. Ofcl. for basketball, volleyball and softball Fla. H.S. Activities Assn., Gainesville,

Fla., 1994—; ofcl. Nat. Fedn. Interscholastic Ofcls. Assn., Kansas City., Mo., 1994—; youth fastpitch umpire Nat. Softball Assn., Lexington, Ky., 1995—. Mem. Fin. Mgmt. Assn. Home: 9374 SW 172 Terr Miami FL 33157

PADBERG, HARRIET ANN, mathematics educator; b. St. Louis, Nov. 13, 1922; d. Harry J. and Marie L. (Kilgen) P. AB with honors, Maryville Coll., St. Louis, 1943; MMus, U. Cin., 1949; MA, St. Louis U., 1956, PhD, 1964. Registered music therapist; cert. tchr. math. and music, La., Mo. Tchr. elem. math. and music Kenwood Acad., Albany, N.Y., 1944-46; tchr. secondary math. Acad. of Sacred Heart, Cin., 1946-47; instr. math. and music Acad. and Coll. of Sacred Heart, Grand Coteau, La., 1947-48; secondary tchr. music Acad. Sacred Heart, St. Charles, Mo., 1948-50; instr. math. and music Acad. and Coll. Sacred Heart, Grand Coteau, 1950-55, Maryville Coll., St. Louis, 1955-56; tchr. elem. and secondary math. and music Acad. Sacred Heart, St. Louis, 1956-57; asst. prof. Maryville Coll., St. Louis, 1957-64, assoc. prof., 1964-68, prof. math., 1968-92, prof. emeritus, 1992—; music therapist Emmaus Homes, Marthasville, Mo., 1992—. Recipient Alumni Centennial award Maryville Coll., St. Louis, 1986; grantee Danforth Found., Colorado Springs, 1970, Tallahassee, 1970, Edn. Devel. Ctr., Mass., 1975, U. Kans., 1980. Mem. Assn. Women in Math., Am. Math. Soc., Math. Assn. Am., Nat. Coun. Tchr. Math., Mo. Acad. Sci., Delta Epsilon Sigma (sec. local chpt. 1962), Pi Mu Epsilon (sec. local chpt. 1958), Sigma Xi.

PADEN, KATHERINE ANNE, psychologist, educator; b. Modesto, Calif.; d. Thomas Ross and Hazel Ada (Johanson) P.; children: Kendra E. Thornbury, Clare P. Thornbury. BS in Edn., Lewis & Clark Coll., 1964; MS in Cmty. Counseling, St. Cloud State U., 1982; postgrad., U. St. Thomas, St. Paul, 1993—. Lic. psychologist, Minn. Elem. tchr. Anchorage (Alaska) Pub. Schs., 1964-65, Knoxville (Tenn.) Pub. Schs., 1966-68; elem. tchr., remedial tchr. Frankfurt (Germany) Internat. Sch., 1968-72; remedial tchr. Leicestershire, Eng., 1973-74; coord. wellness program Coll. St. Benedict, St. Joseph, Minn., 1980-87; coord. eating disorders program St. Cloud (Minn.) Hosp., 1987-93, staff psychotherapist, 1994—; adj. prof. Hamline U., St. Paul, 1995—. Mem. Minn. Psychol. Assn., Minn. Women Psychologists (vice chair 1995—). Office: St Cloud Hosp Behavioral Health Clinic 1406 Sixth Ave N Saint Cloud MN 56303

PADGETT, BECKY M., secondary school educator; b. Booneville, Miss., June 29, 1970; d. Kenneth Lee and Barbara (Brooks) M.; m. Bruce Padgett; children: Colby Jordan, Connor Bruce. BS, Blue Mountain (Miss.) Coll., 1992. Tchr. Kossuth (Miss.) H.S., summer 1992, Anderson Elem. Sch., Booneville, Miss., 1992-93; tchr. math and physics Jumpertown H.S., 1993—. Choir dir. Jumpertown (Miss.) United Meth. Ch., 1988—. Mem. NEA, Miss. Edn. Assn. Methodist. Office: Jumperton Sch Rt 3 Box 140 Booneville MS 38829

PADGETT, GAIL BLANCHARD, lawyer; b. Douglasville, Ga., Aug. 20, 1949; d. William David and Dorothy Rose (Bennett) P. BA, Ga. State U., 1971, MD, 1974; JD, Georgetown U., 1981. Bar: Va., Ga., D.C., U.S. Supreme Ct. Tchr. Clayton Co. Bd. Edn., Jonesboro, Ga., 1971-77; spl. asst. to dir. Community Rels Svc., Chevy Chase, Md., 1977-81, gen. counsel, 1981-89, assoc. dir., 1989-96; asst. chief immigration judge U.S. Dept. Justice, Falls Church, Va., 1996—. chmn. community bd. Countryside, Va., 1983-85; chmn. adminstrn. bd. Galilee Methodist Ch., Sterling, Va., 1985-87. Recipient Disting. Svc. award Atty. Gen. of the U.S., 1992. Mem. Soc. Profls. in Dispute (officer 1988-90). Home: 12 Carrollton Rd Sterling VA 20165-5627

PADILLA, BENITA RACHEL, engineering executive; b. Pensacola, Fla., Dec. 24, 1965; d. Ben Charles Sr. and Catherine Rachel (Paulk) P. Degree in Computer Science, Pensacola Jr. Coll., 1985; degree in Systems Science, U. West Fla., Pensacola, 1989; MBA, U. West Fla., 1993. Cert. in orgnl. devel. and leadership. Printer, clerk Good Neighbor Gift Shop, Pensacola, 1983-85; customer svc. TG&Y, Pensacola, 1984-85; clerk, carrier U.S. Postal Svc., Pensacola, 1985; sec. Carpet Master, Pensacola, 1985-86; sec. Gulf Power Co., Pensacola, 1986-90, engr. rep., 1990—; cons. Comfort Maker Heating & Cooling, Pensacola, 1990. Active caretaker program Humane Soc., Pensacola, 1995—. Recipient J.D. Carroll Scholarship award Pensacola Jr. Coll., 1984-85, Fellowship Scholarship award U. West Fla., 1992-93. Mem. NOW (clinic escort 1994—), Northwest Fla. Jr. Achievement (v.p. operational bd. 1995-96). Democrat. Mem. Unity Ch. of Christianity.

PADILLA, ELSA NORMA, special education educator, administrator; b. Guines, Havana, Cuba, Feb. 25, 1947; came to U.S., 1962; d. Regulo and Esther (Beato) Cuesta; m. Pedro Manuel Padilla, June 10, 1967; children: Jorge Alberto, Alejandro Manuel. BA, U. Ariz., 1970, MEd, 1972, cert. administration, 1982. Cert. elem. tchr. bilingual endorsement, spl. edn., adminstrn., Ariz. Spl. edn. tchr. Tucson Unified Sch. Dist., 1970, 1972-76, spl. edn. program specialist, 1976-78, spl. edn. tchr., 1978-81, bilingual diagnostician, 1981-84, asst dir. spl. edn., 1984-89; principal Ochoa Elem. Sch. Tucson Unified Sch. Dist., 1989-96, compliance coord., 1996—; part time instr. Ariz. Dept. Edn., 1980-87, No. Ariz. U., 1983-89, U. Ariz., Tucson, 1983-88; mem. Bilingual Diagnostic Team, Tucson Sch. Dist., 1978, author Bilingual Spl. Edn. Program, 1980; prin. in restructuring of sch. project funded by Charles Stewart Mott Found.; cons. in field. Co-author: Courage to Change. Bd. dirs. TETRA Corp., Tucson, 1988-94, Vista Adv. Coun., Tucson, 1990-93; mem. City of South Tucson Econ. Devel. Adv. Bd. Grantee: U.S. Dept. Edn., Tucson, 1984; recipient NEA Excellence award, 1994. Mem. ASCD, Tucson Assn. for Bilingual Edn., Tucson Adminstrs. Inc., Nat. Assn. for Bilingual Edn., Assn. Cubana de Tucson. Democrat. Office: Morrow Edn Ctr 1010 E 10th St Tucson AZ 85719

PADRON-FRAGETTA, AMELI, lawyer; b. Artemisa, Pinar Del Rio, Cuba, May 30, 1957; Came to the U.S., 1962; d. Ernesto and Ameli (Antunez) Padron; m. William Andrew Fragetta, Oct. 26, 1985; children: Erin Elizabeth, Christine Jeanette. AA, U. S. Fla., Tampa, 1977, BA, 1979; JD, Boston Coll. Law Sch., Newton Centre, Mass., 1982. Bar: Fla. 1985, U.S. Claims Ct. 1986, U.S. Dist. Ct. (so. dist.) Fla., 1985. Law clerk Anthony Dieguez, P.A., Hialeah, Fla., 1982-84; freelance law clerk, rschr. various law firms, Dade County, Fla., 1984-85; assoc. atty. Herrick & Larsen, Miami, 1985-87, Villalobos & Ramos, Miami, 1987-88; traffic magistrate Dade County Courts, Fla., 1993; atty., sole practitioner Law Office of Ameli Padron-Fragetta, Miami, 1988—; mem. profl. ethics com. Fla. Bar, Tallahassee, 1988—, mem. grievance com., Miami, 1992-95, mem. unlicensed practice of law com., Miami, 1995—; mem. supervisory com. Lawyers Credit Union, Miami, 1995-96. Rep. project steering com. Put Something Back Pro Bono, Miami, 1993-94; dir. Resourcemobile, Inc., Miami, 1992-96. Recipient Pedro Luis Boitel award of Merit Municipality of Artemisa in Exile, 1982, Exceptional Participation Pro Bono Svc. award Put Something Back Pro Bono Svc. Project, 1995. Mem. AAUW (dir., diversity chair 1995-96), Fla. Assn. Women Lawyers (hon. bd. mem., pres. 1992-93), Dade County Bar Assn., Concerned Citizens of N.E. Dade, Loch Ness Homeowners Assn. (v.p. 1993-96), U. S. Fla. Alumni Assn. (pres. Miami chpt. 1993-96). Office: Law Office of Ameli Padron-Fragetta 780 NW Le Jeune Rd Ste 421 Miami FL 33126

PADULA, MARJORIE ANN, psychologist, consultant, researcher; b. San Antonio, June 25, 1948; d. Gregory Joseph an Marjorie Pearl (Goodenough) P. BA, Northwestern U., 1970; MA, La. Tech. U., 1972, Edn. Specialist, 1985; PhD, U. Nebr., 1994. Licensed clin. psychologist, mental health practitioner; cert. rehab. counselor, secondary sch. counselor. Counselor Dept. Employment Security, Shreveport, La., 1970-73; caseworker Office of Family Security, Shreveport, La., 1973-76, 79-80, caseworker supr., 1980-83; rehab. couselor Dept. Rehab. Svcs., Shreveport, La., 1983-86; counselor Vicenza (Italy) Am. H.S., 1987-88; counselor, testing specialist edn. office Ghedi AFB, Italy, 1987-88; rehab. counselor, supr. Quality Rehab., Omaha, Nebr., 1989-94; instr. U. Nebr., Lincoln, 1990-91, 92-93; clin. psychologist, rschr. U. Nebr. Med. Ctr., Omaha, 1994—; rschr. U. Nebr., Lincoln, 1990-94, adj. faculty, 1995—; psychology intern Nebr. Internship Consortium in Profl. Psychology, Lincoln, 1993-94. Contbr. chpts. to books and articles to profl. jours. Mem. Am. Psychol. Assn., Am. Rehab. Counseling Assn., Am. Counseling Assn., Nat. Acad. Neuropsychology, Nebr. Psychol. Assn., Phi Kappa Phi, Alpha Lambda Delta (pres.), Kappa Delta Pi. Office: Univ Nebr Med Ctr Psychology Dept 600 S 42nd St Omaha NE 68198-5577

PAGANO, ALICIA I., education educator; b. Sidney, N.Y., June 29, 1929; d. Neil Gadsby Leonard and Norma (Carr) Collins; m. LeRoy Pagano, Feb. 26, 1963 (div. Oct. 1985); children: Janice, Daniel. BA in Music, Barrington Coll., 1952; MAT in Music, Rollins Coll., 1964; EdD in Edn. Adminstrn., Am. U., 1972. Tchr. music Prince Georges County Pub. Schs., Beltsville, Md., 1966-69; asst. prof. Medgar Evers Coll., Bklyn., 1973-78; nat. program dir. Girl Scouts USA, N.Y.C., 1978-83; nat. dir. vol. development U.S. Com. UNICEF, N.Y.C., 1983-84; pres. Pagano Consulting Internat., Jersey City, 1984—; asst. prof. mgmt. Coll. Staten Island, CUNY, 1985-89; adj. prof. museum studies NYU, N.Y.C., 1986-91; assoc. exec. dir. Louis August Jonas Found., Red Hook, N.Y., 1988-89; asst. prof. edn. Jersey City State Coll., 1990—; chair Wingspread Nat. Conf./Nat. Collaboration for Youth, Washington, 1982; adv. bd. dirs. Early Childhood Ctr., Jersey City State Coll., 1994—. Author, editor: Social Studies in Early Childhood, 1979; author: The Future of American Business, 1985, (with others) Learning Opportunities Beyond School, 1987; contbr. articles to profl. jours. Judge annual awards Girls, Inc., N.Y.C., 1985-90; reader Jersey City Spelling Bee, 1991; vol. Girl Scouts USA, Essex/Hudson Counties, N.J., 1995—, Boys & Girls Clubs, Hudson County, N.J., 1995—. Mem. ASCD, AAUW, Am. Ednl. Rsch. Assn., Nat. Assn. Early Childhood Tchr. Edn. (bd. dirs. 1995—), N.J. Assn. Early Childhood Tchr. Educators (v.p. 1994—), Orgn. Mondiale pour l'Edn. Prescolaire (N.J. regional dir. 1996—). Home: 227 Warren St Jersey City NJ 07302

PAGE, ANNE RUTH, gifted education educator, education specialist; b. Norfolk, Va., Apr. 13, 1949; d. Amos Purnell and Ruth Martin (Hill) Bailey; m. Peter Smith Page, Apr. 24, 1971; children: Edgar Bailey, Emmett McBrannon. BA, N.C. Wesleyan Coll.; student, Fgn. Lang. League; postgrad., N.C. State U.; student, Overseas Linguistic Studies, France, Spain, Eng., 1978, 85, 86. Cert. tchr., N.C. Tchr. Cary (N.C.) Sr. High Sch., 1971-72; tchr., head dept. Daniels Mid. Sch., Raleigh, N.C., 1978-83; chmn. fgn. lang. dept. Martin Mid. Gifted and Talented, Raleigh, N.C., 1983—; leadership team Senate Bill 2 Core co-chair; dir. student group Overseas Studies, Am. Coun. for Internat. Studies, France, Spain, Eng., 1982, 84, 86, 88; bd. dirs. N.T.H., Inc., Washington; cert. mentor tchr. Wake County Pub. Schs., 1989; dir. student exchs. between Martin Mid. Sch. and Sevigné Inst. of Compiegne, France. Sunday sch. tchr. Fairmont United Meth. Ch., Raleigh, 1983-85. Mem. Alpha Delta Kappa. Democrat. Home: 349 Wilmot Dr Raleigh NC 27606-1232 Office: Martin Mid Sch GT 1701 Ridge Rd Raleigh NC 27607-6737

PAGE, BERNADETTE RYAN, emergency physician; b. Chgo., Feb. 10, 1946; d. Frank James and Bernadette Rosamund (Halm) Ryan; m. Jack R. Page, Dec. 23, 1967; children: Jeremy, Sara, Alex, Rachel. MD, Loyola U., 1970. Diplomate Am. Bd. Emergency Medicine. Rotating O intern San Bernardino (Calif.) Hosp., 1970-71; resident in pediat. Orange County Med. Ctr., Anaheim, Calif., 1971-72; staff physician emergency rm. Kaiser Permanente, Bellflower, Calif., 1972-73, St. Mary's Hosp./Long Beach (Calif.) Cmty., 1973-76, Appalachian Regional Hosp., Beckley, W.Va., 1976-78, Charleston (W.Va.) Area Med. Ctr., 1978-82; staff physician, owner Doctors Urgent Care, Charleston, 1982-88; staff physician Orange Chatham Comp. Health, Carrboro, N.C., 1988-91; attending physician emergency dept. Duke U. Med. Ctr., Durham, N.C., 1991—; chair violance prevention com. Am. Assn. Women Emergency Physicians, Durham, 1994—; mem. adv. coun. family violence AMA, 1994—; mem. nat. faculty ACLS Am. Heart Assn., 1976-82. Active Durham City-County Violence Prevention Com., 1993—, North Carolians for Prevention of Gun Violence, 1993—. Fellow Am. Coll. Emergency Physicians. Democrat. Roman Catholic. Office: Duke U Med Ctr PO Box 3096 Durham NC 27715-3096

PAGE, CYNTHIA LYNN, public relations executive; b. York, Pa., Apr. 7, 1967; d. Harry MacDonald and Helen Gay (Landis) P. BA in Comms., Elizabethtown Coll., 1989. Pub. rels. dir. Boscov's Dept. Store, York, Pa., 1989-91; pub. rels. specialist Handi-Crafters, Inc., Thorndale, Pa., 1991-93; pub. rels. dir. Penn Laurel Girl Scout Coun., York, Pa., 1993—; mktg. com. mem. Pa. Assn. Rehab. Facilities, Harrisburg, 1992-93. Co-author: Enhancing Your Public Image Through Marketing and Public Relations, 1992. Educator Planned Parenthood of Lancaster, Pa., 1993; South Ctrl. Pa. coord. Take Our Daughters to Work, York, Pa., 1996. Mem. Women in Comms., Inc. Democrat. Methodist. Home: 263 Point Cir York PA 17402 Office: Penn Laurel Girl Scout Coun 1600 Mt Zion Rd York PA 17402

PAGE, LINDA KAY, banking executive; b. Wadsworth, Ohio, Oct. 4, 1943; s. Frederick Meredith and Martha Irene (Vance) P. Student Sch. Banking, Ohio U., 1976-77; cert. Nat. Pers. Sch., U. Md.-Am. Bankers Assn., 1981; grad. banking program U. Wis., Madison, 1982-84; BA Capital U. Asst. v.p., gen. mgr. Bancohio Corp., Columbus, Ohio, 1975-78, v.p., dist. mgr., 1979-80, v.p., mgr. employee rels., 1980-81, v.p., divsn. mgr., 1982-83; commr. of banks State of Ohio, Columbus, 1983-87, dir. Commerce, 1988-90; pres., CEO Star Bank Cen. Ohio, Columbus, 1990-92; state dir. FMHA-USDA, 1993—. Bd. dirs. Clark County Mental Health Bd., Springfield, Ohio, 1982-83, Springfield Met. Housing, 1982-83; bd. advisers Orgn. Indsl. Standards, Springfield, 1982-83; trustee League Against Child Abuse, 1986-90; treas. Ohio Housing Fin. Agy., 1988-90; vice chair Fed. Reserve Bd.-Consumer Adv. Coun., 1989-91. Bd. dirs. Pvt. Industry Coun. Franklin County, 1990—, Ohio Higher Edn. Facilities Commn., 1990-93, Ohio Devel. Corp., 1995—; trustee, treas. Columbus State Community Coll. Found., 1990—; bd. dirs. Columbus Urban League, 1992—. Recipient Leadership Columbus award Sta. WTVN and Columbus Leadership Program, 1975, 82, Outstanding Svc. award Clark County Mental Health Bd., 1983, Giles Mitchell Housing award, 1996. Mem. Nat. Assn. Bank Women (pres. 1980-81), Am. Bankers Assn. (govt. rels. coun. 1990-92), Women Execs. in State Govt., LWV (treas. edn. fund 1992—), Conf. State Bank Suprs. (bd. dirs., sec./treas. 1985-90), dist. chmn. 1984-85), Ohio Bankers Assn. (bd. dirs. 1982-83, 91-92), Internat. Womens Forum, Zonta. Democrat. Avocations: tennis, animal protection, reading, golf. Home: 641 Mirandy Pl Reynoldsburg OH 43068-1602 Office: 200 N High St Columbus OH 43215-2408

PAGE, PATRICIA HICKS, insurance agent; b. Athens, Tenn., Mar. 19, 1937; d. Edward Aldine and Mary Elizabeth (Jaco) Hicks; m. Hershel Gordon Gray, Dec. 27, 1962 (dec. Jan. 1971); children: Gregory Gordon Gray, Rebekah Elizabeth Gray Reeves; m. Douglass Page Jr., Oct. 15, 1978. BA in History and Polit. Sci., Carson Newman Coll., 1959; postgrad., U. Tenn., Chattanooga, 1965-67. Tchr. Chattanooga City Schs., 1959-63; tchr. Walker County Bd. Edn., Lafayette, Ga., 1963-74, head dept. grades 4-6 Mt. View Elem. Sch., 1968-74; ins. owner Allstate ins. Co., Chattanooga, 1974-94; agy. owner Page Agy./Allstate Ins. Co., Chattanooga, 1994—. Fundraiser Am. Cancer Soc., Chattanooga, 1986—; sec. No. Ga. Dem. Women, Catoosa, Ga., 1993—; sec. Catoosa County Dem. Party, 1993-94; county commr. Catoosa County, Ga., 1994—; mem. exec. com. Walker County Edn., Assn., Lafayette, 1970-74; mem. adv. bd. Catoosa County Farm Bur., Ringgold, Ga., 1995—. Mem. Dixieland Am. Bus. Women (pres. 1989, Woman of Yr. 1989), Brainerd/E. Hamilton C. of C. (bd. dirs. 1985—, pres. 1993), Chattanooga Area C. of C. (bd. dris. 1996—), Catoosa County C. of C. (bd. dirs. 1995—, Disting. Svc. award 1994), Rotary (pres. Ringgold club 1996-97). Baptist. Home: 319 Loach Dr Rossville GA 30741 Office: Page Agy/Allstate Ins Co 8174-B E Brainerd Rd Chattanooga TN 37421

PAGE, REBECCA LYNN JOHNSON, librarian; b. Ft. Payne, Ala., June 11, 1952; d. Elvin Laudry Johnson and Bobbie Jean (Ott Johnson) Broyles; m. Roger Dale Page, Dec. 28, 1973; 1 child, Allison Nicole. AS, N.E. Ala. State Jr. Coll., 1971; BS, U. North Ala., 1974; MA, U. Ala., 1982; postgrad., Jacksonville U., 1992. Cert. libr., media specialist, Ala. Tchr., media specialist Jackson County Bd. Edn., Scottsboro, Ala., 1974—; mem. exec. com. P.R.I.D.E., Higdon, Ala., 1993—; co-sponsor SADD Club, 1996—; sponson sch. newspaper News Sports and More, Higdon, 1992-95. Active Fine Arts Coun. Jackson County, Scottsboro, 1994—. Mem. Jackson County Edn. Assn. (faculty rep. 1994-95, chmn. SACS steering com. 1995-96), Alpha Delta Kappa (Historian, membership chmn., chaplain 1987—). Mem. Primitive Baptist Ch.

PAGE, SALLY JACQUELYN, university official; b. Saginaw, Mich., July, 1943; d. William Henry and Doris Effie (Knippel) P.; BA, U. Iowa, 1965; MBA, So. Ill. U., 1973. Copy editor, C.V. Mosby Co., St. Louis, 1965-69; edit. cons. Edit. Assos., Edwardsville, Ill., 1969-70; research adminstr. So. Ill. U., 1970-74, asst. to pres., affirmative action officer, 1974-77; officer of instn. U. N.D., Grand Forks, 1977—, lectr. mgmt., 1978—; polit. commentator Sta. KFJM, Nat. Public Radio affiliate, 1981-90; bd. dirs. Agassiz Enterprises, 1990-91, mayor's com. Employment of People With Disabilities, 1980—. Contbr. to profl. jours. Chairperson N.D. Equal Opportunity Affirmative Action Officers, 1987-96; pres., Pine to Prairie council Girl Scouts U.S., 1980-85; mem. employment com. Ill. Commn. on Status of Women, 1976-77; mem. Bicentennial Com. Edwardsville, 1976, Bikeway Task Force Edwardsville, 1975-77, Grand Forks Homes, 1986—, chair 1996—; mem. Civil Service Rev. Task Force, Grand Forks, 1982, civil service commr., 1983, chmn., 1984, 86, 88, 92, 96; ruling elder 1st Presbyn. Mem. AAUW (dir. Ill. 1975-77), PEO, Coll. and Univ. Personnel Assn. (research and publs. bd. 1982-84) Am. Assn. Affirmative Actiative Action, Soc. Research Adminstrs. Republican. Presbyterian. Home: 3121 Cherry St Grand Forks ND 58201-7461 Office: U ND Grand Forks ND 58202

PAGENKOPF, ANDREA LESUER, university official; b. Hamilton, Mont., July 28, 1942; d. Andrew and Martha Gail (Thompson) LeSuer; m. Gordon Kyle Pagenkopf, June 12, 1964 (dec. Feb. 1987); 1 child, Sarah Lynn. BA, U. Mont., 1964; PhD, Purdue U., 1968. Registered dietitian; lic. nutritionist. Asst. prof. Purdue U., West Lafayette, Ind., 1968, U. Ill., Champaign, 1968-69; asst. prof. Mont. State U., Bozeman, 1969-76, assoc. prof., 1976-86, prof. nutrition, 1986-91, dir. extension, 1991—, vice provost for outreach, 1993—. Author: (with others) Grow Healthy Kids, 1980. Worship commn. chair United Meth. Ch., Bozeman, 1989-90; cons. Gallatin Hospice, Bozeman, 1986-91. Recipient Excellence in Nutrition Edn. award Western Dairy Coun., 1987, Silver Buffalo award Mont. Extension, 1989, Mid-Career award Extension Hon., 1988; named Home Econs. Leader, Mont. Home Econs. Assn., 1990. Mem. Am. Dietetic Assn., Soc. Nutrition Edn. (interest group chair 1990-91), Am. Home Econs. Assn. Office: Mont State U Extension 211 N Montana Hall Bozeman MT 59717

PAGLIA, CAMILLE, writer, humanities educator; b. Endicott, N.Y., 1947; d. Pasquale John and Lydia (Colapietro) P. BA in English summa cum laude with highest honors, SUNY, Binghamton, 1968; MPhil, Yale U., 1971, PhD in English, 1974. Mem. faculty Bennington (Vt.) Coll., 1972-80; vis. lectr. Wesleyan U., 1980, Yale U., New Haven, 1980-84; prof. humanities U. Arts, Phila., 1984—. Author: Sexual Personae: Art and Decadence from Nefertiti to Emily Dickinson, 1990, Sex, Art, and American Culture, 1992, Vamps and Tramps: New Essays, 1994. Office: Univ Arts 320 S Broad St Philadelphia PA 19102-4901

PAGOTTO, LOUISE, English language educator; b. Montreal, June 22, 1950; came to U.S., 1980; d. Albert and Elena (Tibi) P. BA, Marianopolis Coll., Montreal, 1971; TESL Diploma, U. Papua New Guinea, 1975; MA, McGill U., 1980; PhD, U. Hawaii at Manoa, Honolulu, 1987. Tchr. Yarapos High Sch., Wewak, Papua New Guinea, 1971-73, Electricity Commn. Tng. Coll., Port Moresby, Papua New Guinea, 1975-76, Coll. of the Marshall Islands, Majuro, summers 1983-91, Leeward C.C., Pearl City, Hawaii, 1988-89, Kapiolani C.C., Honolulu, 1989—; presenter at confs. Contbr. articles to profl. jours. McConnell fellow McGill U., 1979, Can. Coun. fellow, 1980-83; recipient Excellence in Teaching award Bd. of Regents, 1993. Mem. AAUW, Linguistic Soc. Am., Nat. Coun. Tchrs. English, Hawaii Coun. Tchrs. English. Office: Kapiolani CC 4303 Diamond Head Rd Honolulu HI 96816-4421

PAI, SHIRLEY SHIN SIL, controller; b. Honolulu, Aug. 29, 1960; d. Harry M. H. and Sook Ja (Lee) Pai. BBA, U. Hawaii-Manoa, Honolulu, 1983, MA, 1992. CPA, Hawaii. Acct. GA Pacific Holdings, Honolulu, 1986-87; contr. ASE Enterprises, Honolulu, 1987—. Mem. fundraising com. Ronald McDonald House, Honolulu, 1992-94; dir., treas., v.p. Honolulu Chinese Jaycees, 1991-95, pres., 1995-96; dir. United Chinese Soc., Honolulu, 1996-98; treas. Orgn. Chinese Ams., Honolulu, 1996-97. Recipient Miyamura Meml. award Hawaii Jaycees, 1992, Akaka award, 1994, Nakano award, 1995. Home: 3722 Keanu St Honolulu HI 96816 Office: ASE Enterprises Ste 490 1001 Bishop Honolulu HI 96813

PAIGE, ANITA PARKER, retired English language educator; b. Valparaiso, Ind., Feb. 5, 1908; d. Eugene Mark and Grace Agnes (Noon) Parker; m. Robert Myron Paige, Aug. 12, 1933 (dec. 1965); children: Susan Marlowe Paige Morrison, Amy Woods Paige Dunker, Caroline Parker Paige McClennan. AB, Vassar Coll., 1929; MA, U. Chgo., 1930, postgrad., 1931-32. Instr. English Hillsdale (Mich.) Coll., 1930-31, asst. prof., 1931-33; bd. edn. Anglo-Am. Schs., Athens, Greece, 1948-51; tchr. secondary sch. Am. Sch., Teheran, Iran, 1957-58; instr. English Republic of China Mil. Cartographic Sec. group, Taipei, Taiwan, 1960-61; instr. dept. English Nat. Taiwan U., Taipei, 1961-62; intermittent lectr., 1988—; bd. dirs. Ginling Girls Mid. Sch., Taipei, 1960-62. Bd. dirs. (Presbyn.) Cmty. Ch., Teheran, 1957-58. Mem. LWV (chmn. Cook County, Ill. child welfare dept. 1933-36, mem. bd. Overseas Edn. Fund 1966-68), Diplomatic and Consular Officers Ret., Assn. Am. Fgn. Svc. Women, Asian Am. Forum (founding mem.), Friends of Soochow U., Phi Beta Kappa. Democrat.

PAIGE, NANCY LOUISE, genealogist; b. Waterloo, Ont., Can., Oct. 18, 1931; d. Ernest Bertram and Elva Estella (Turner) P. BA, U. Western Ont., London, 1959; BSW, U. Toronto, 1962; MLS, UCLA, 1967. Social worker Children's Aid Soc., London, 1958-64; libr. County of L.A., 1967-92; genealogist Family Finder Five-O, San Dimas, Calif., 1993—. Mem. San Dimas Coord. Coun., 1971-75; com. mem. San Dimas Woman's Club, 1972-80; fin. sec. San Dimas Hosp. Aux., 1972-73; vol. Pomona (Calif.) Pub. Libr., 1994—, German Geneal. Soc. of Am., LaVerne, Calif., 1995—. Named Woman of the Yr. San Dimas Bus. and Profl. Women's Club, 1974. Mem. Nat. Geneal. Soc., Assn. of Profl. Genealogists, Pomona Valley Geneal. Soc. (dir. 1992-96). Democrat. Unitarian. Home and Office: Family Finder Five-O 1418 Badillo St San Dimas CA 91773

PAIGE, NORMA, lawyer, corporate executive; b. Lomza, Poland, Oct. 11, 1922; came to U.S., 1927; d. Morris and Edith (Kachourek) Zelaso; children: Holly Paige Russek, Madelyn Paige Givant. BA, NYU, 1944, JD, 1946; postgrad. in bus. adminstrn., CCNY, 1953, NYU, 1969. Bar: N.Y. 1946, U.S. Supreme Ct. 1951. Ptnr. Paige and Paige, N.Y.C., 1948—; v.p., bd. dirs. Astronautics Corp. Am., Milw., 1959—, chmn. bd., 1984—; exec. v.p., bd. dirs. Kearfott Guidance & Navigation Corp., Wayne, N.J., 1988—; bd. dirs. Astronautics C.A., Ltd., Israel. Recipient Jabotinsky Centennial medal Prime Minister of Israel, 1980, Tribute to Women in Indsl. Industry Twin II award YWCA, 1981, NYU Sch. Law Outstanding Alumnus of Yr. award, 1991, Judge Edward Weinfeld award, 1996. Mem. N.Y. Women's Bar Assn. (pres. 1958-59). Office: Astronautics Corp Am 4115 N Teutonia Ave Milwaukee WI 53209-6731

PAIGE, SUSANNE LYNN, financial consultant; b. Bklyn., Feb. 25, 1950; d. Abraham and Florence Roslyn (Rosenfeld) P.; divorced. BA cum laude, C.W. Post Coll., 1972, postgrad., 1975. Lic. mortgage broker, N.Y. Buyer B. Gertz and Sons, Inc., Jamaica, N.Y., 1973-76; nat. field sales mgr. LeVison Care Products, Inc., New City, N.Y., 1976-82, Am. Vitamin Products, Inc., Lakewood, N.J., 1984-85; prin. Paige & Assocs., Scarsdale, 1982-87; loan officer and fin. cons. Bayside Fed. Savs. and Loan, Jericho, N.Y., 1987-88; prin. Paige Capital Enterprises, Inc., Rye, N.Y., 1988—; mem. Comml. Investment Divsn./Westchester Bd. Realtors, White Plains, N.Y.; pub. spkr. and lectr. in field. Author: Closing the Deal in Today's Volatile Market, 1994; satarist/polit. cartoonist C.W. Post Coll. News and Editorial, Brookville, N.Y., 1968-72; contbr. articles to profl. jours. Recipient award for Best Original Essay, Newsday Harry F. Guggenheim award, Garden City, N.Y., 1967, Hon. Mention award C.W. Post Coll. Gallery, 1982, Hon. Mention (sculpture) Fresh Meadows (N.Y.) Merchant's Assn., 1971, meritorious notation Real Estate Weekly, 1991-93; selected as Comml. Deal-Maker of Yr., N.Y. Real Estate Jour., 1992, Real Estate Personality, 1993, Northeast Fin. Work-Out Specialist N.Y. and New Eng. Real Estate Jours., 1990-93, also meritorious notation, 1990-93. Mem. Alumni Assn. C.W. Post Coll., 60's East Realty Club, Westchester Bd. Realtors, White Plains, N.Y., Assn. Commercial Real Estate. Office: Paige Capital Enterprises Inc PO Box 1234 Scarsdale NY 10583-9234

PAILLETTE, BEVERLY IRENE, secondary school educator; b. Colorado Springs, Colo., Nov. 11, 1949; d. Edward Irving and Irene Clara (Goodsell) Bryant; m. Phillip Bruce Paillette, June 26, 1971; 1 child, Gwendolyn Ann. BA, U. No. Colo., 1971; MEd, U. Wash., 1992. Cert. tchr. Tchr.

grade 9-12 Franklin Pierce Sch. Dist., Tacoma, 1971—; treas. Franklin Pierce Edn. Assn., Tacoma, 1973-74. Recipient Outstanding Tchr. award Wash. State U. Math. Dept., 1992; named Class Act Tchr., KSTW TV Sta., Seattle, 1994. Mem. Wash. State Math. Coun. (regional dir. 1990-95, treas. 1995—), Delta Kappa Gamma (Epsilon chpt. 1st v.p. 1992-94, scholarship 1990, 91, treas. 1996—). Home: 8307 116th St E Puyallup WA 98373-7849

PAIN, BETSY M., lawyer; b. Albertville, Ala., Aug. 29, 1950; d. Charles Riley and Jean Faye (Rains) Stone; m. William F. Pain, Nov. 18, 1977; children: Taylor Holland, Emily Anne Pain. AA, Northeastern Okla. A&M, Miami, Okla., 1970; BA, U. Okla., 1974, JD, 1976. Bar: Okla. 1977; U.S. Dist. Ct. (we. dist.) 1979. Staff atty. Okla. Dept. Corrections, Oklahoma City, 1978-79; gen. counsel Okla. Pardon and Parole Bd., Oklahoma City, 1979-84, exec. dir., 1984-88; corp. counsel Roberts, Schornick & Assocs., Inc., Norman, Okla., 1990—. Editor: (newsletter) RSA Environmental Report, 1991—. With extended family program Juvenile Svcs., Inc. Cleveland County, Okla., 1983-91. Mem. Okla. Bar Assn. (environ. law sect. 1977—), Am. Corp. Counsel Assn. Democrat. Methodist. Office: Roberts Schornick & Assoc Inc 3700 W Robinson St Ste 200 Norman OK 73072-3639

PAINE, HARRIETT JANE, home economist, educator; b. Lime Springs, Iowa, May 8, 1921; d. Royal A. and Bessie Joanna (Alink) Vanderbie; m. Eugene L. Smith, June 17, 1944 (dec. July 1958); children: Peter, Susan; m. Birwinn W. Paine, Feb. 18, 1960; 1 child, Darlene. BA in Home Econs. Edn., Cornell Coll., Mt. Vernon, Iowa, 1943. Cert. home economist; cert. in family and consumer svcs.; life adult edn. credential, life C.C. credential. Tchr. home econs. Maquoketa (Iowa) H.S., 1943-44; sr. home economist So. Calif. Gas Co., L.A., 1946-52; food instr. Norwalk & Downey (Calif.) Adult Schs., 1953-87; foods instr. Cerritos Coll., Norwalk, 1974-81; food editor Downey S.E. News and Sr. Life Mag., 1972—; tour dir., resource educator Downey Adult Sch., 1985—; owner Creative Home Econs. Co., Downey, 1983. Author: Home Canning, Freezing and Drying, 1976, Cook for the Health of It!, 1983, The Homestyle Cookbook, 1990; co-author: Modern Food Preservation, 1977, How to Survive an Earthquake, 1979; dir., author audiovisual prodns. for tchg. food preservation and healthful cooking. Chmn. bd. trustees Downey Meth. Ch., 1990. Named Outstanding Tchr. of Yr. Calif. Coun. Adult Edn., 1973, Master Tchr. State of Calif. Adult Edn., 1979, Bus. Home Economist of Yr., L.A., 1986. Mem. AAUW, Home Economists in Bus. (chmn. 1993). Republican. Home: 8818 Tweedy Ln Downey CA 90140 Office: Downey Adult Sch 12340 Woodruff Ave Downey CA 90241

PAINTER, DIANA JEAN, urban designer, consultant; b. Seattle, Dec. 29, 1953; d. Robert Cook and Nancy Marie (Chivers) P.; m. John Hazen McKean, Aug. 10, 1973 (div. Feb. 1975). BA, Western Wash. U., 1977; MUP, U. Wash., 1984; postgrad., U. Pa., 1987; PhD, Sheffield U., England, 1990. Cert. planner. Designer Cope Linder Assn., Phila., 1987-88, Dagit-Saylor Architects, Phila., 1988; urban designer WRT, Phila., 1989; designer Edwin Schlossberg Inc., N.Y.C., 1989-90; urban designer The SWA Group, Laguna Beach, Calif., 1990-91; assoc. planner City of Tukwila, Wash., 1993—; cons. Diana J. Painter Archtl. & Cmty. History, Seattle, 1982—; instr. U. Wash., Seattle, 1986. Contbr. articles to profl. jours.; presenter in field. Mem. Allied Arts of Seattle Downtown Com., 1984-85; bd. dirs. Greystone Found., Pullman, Wash., 1992-93. Fellow Northwest Inst. Architecture & Urban Studies in Italy; mem. Am. Inst. Cert. Planners, Am. Assn. Planning (head mentoring program 1995—, vice-chmn. urban design divsn.), Am. Inst. Architects (mem. urban design com. 1990-91). Studio: 712 N 34th # 205 Seattle WA 98103

PAINTER, MARY E. (MARY PAINTER YARBROUGH), editor; b. Tulsa, July 15, 1920; d. Ernest Balf Parker and Maggie Mae (Renaud) P.; BA, Oklahoma City U., 1943; postgrad. Columbia U., 1944; m. Charles J. Yarbrough, Apr. 7, 1946; children: Kirby John, Kevin Lee. Editorial asst., feature writer Office War Info., 1943-46; feature writer, news editor Dept. State, 1946-53; with USIA, Washington, 1953-78, editor USIA World, 1967-78; with U.S. Internat. Communication Agy., 1978-80, editor USICA World, 1978-80; with Food Policy Center, Washington, 1981-84, mng. editor Food Policy Center News/Views, 1981-84; with World Hunger Year, N.Y.C., 1981—; assoc. editor Food Monitor, 1981-83, editor, 1986-88; editor WHY Mag., 1989—. Editor USIAAA Newsletter, Washington, 1980-88, Reston (Va.) Interfaith Newsletter, 1982-90. Recipient Meritorious Service award USIA, 1964, Spl. Commendation, 1974; Dir.'s award for Outstanding Creativity, U.S. Internat. Communication Agy., 1980. Mem. NOW, Women's Action Orgn., Assn. Am. Fgn. Svc. Women, Am. Fgn. Svc. Assn. Democrat. Baptist. Home: 12232 Quorn Ln Reston VA 21091-2635 Office: World Hunger Yr 505 8th Ave Fl 21 New York NY 10018-6582

PAIVA WEED, M(ARIE) TERESA, state legislator; b. Newport, R.I., Nov. 5, 1959. B.A., magna cum laude, Providence Coll., 1981; J.D., Catholic Univ. of America, 1984. Bar: R.I., 1984. Former asst. city solicitor city of Newport; now mem. R.I. State Sen., 1992—. Mem. Newport County Bar Assn., Rhode Island Bar Assn., ABA. Office: RI State Senate State House Providence RI 02903*

PAIVIO, HEIDI SUSAN, sales executive; b. Newton, N.J., Sept. 25, 1958; d. Wayne A. and Joan (Crysler) Danielsen; m. Eric O. Paivio, Aug. 28, 1992. Student, Utah State U., Logan, 1976-78, U. Alaska, Anchorage, 1992-93. Sales rep., purchasing agt. Alaska Explosives Ltd., Anchorage, 1984-90; sales rep., purchasing agt.,office mgr. Alaska-Pacific/Dyno Nobel, Anchorage, 1990-93; sales rep., ops. mgr. Atlas Alaska/ICI Explosives, Anchorage, 1993—; pres. Alaska Crane & Lift Inspection, Anchorage, 1990—. Mem. Alaska Miners Assn., Alaska Women in Mining (v.p. 1987-95), Alaska Women in Timber, Women of the Moose. Republican. Home: PO Box 111951 Anchorage AK 99511 Office: Alaska Crane & Lift Inspection PO Box 111951 Anchorage AK 99511

PAJUNEN, GRAZYNA ANNA, electrical engineer, educator; b. Warsaw, Poland, Dec. 15, 1951; d. Romuald and Danuta (Trzaskowska) Pyffel; m. Veikko J. Pajunen (div. 1990); children: Tony, Thomas, Sebastian. MSc, Warsaw Tech. U., 1975; PhD in Elec. Engring., Helsinki (Finland) U., 1984. Grad. engr. Oy Stromberg Ab, Helsinki, 1974; design engr. Oy Stromberg Ab, 1975-79; teaching/rsch. asst. Helsinki U. Tech., 1979-85; vis. asst. prof. dept. elec. and computer engring. Fla. Atlantic U., 1985-86, asst. prof. elec. and computer engring., 1986-90, assoc. prof. elec. engring., 1990—; vis. asst. prof. dept elec. engring. UCLA, 1988-89; cons. in field; lectr. in field. Author: Adaptive Systems - Identification and Control, 1986; contbr. articles to profl. jours. Grantee Found. Tech. in Finland, Ahlstrom Found., 1982, Wihuri Found., 1982, Found.d Tech. in Finland, 1983, Acad. Finland, 1984, EIES Seed grantee, 1986, Finnish Ministry Edn., 1985, NSF, 1988-89, 93-94, State of Fla. High Tech. and Industry Coun., 1989. Mem. IEEE, Control Sys. Soci., N.Y. Acad. Sci., AAUW, SIAM, Control and Sys. Theory Group. Roman Catholic. Office: Florida Atlantic Univ Dept Elec Engring Boca Raton FL 33431

PAL, CHERYL LYNN, music teacher; b. Punxsutawney, Pa., July 11, 1954; d. Elvin Dale and Lois Jeanne (Geist) Depp; m. Dulal Pal, Mar. 11, 1978; children: Timothy Ranjan, Monica Suniti. BS in Music Edn., Rutgers U., 1976; MS, L.I. Univ., 1983. Cert. music educator K-12, N.J., N.Y. Music tchr. Island Park (N.Y.) Union Free Sch. Dist., 1976—. Leader Altar Guild, St. Peter's Lutheran Ch., 1994—, mem. ch. choir, 1980—. Mem. Am. String Tchrs. Assn., Music Educators Nat. Conf., L.I. String Festival Assn. (exec. bd. 1985—, membership chair, librarian), Nassau Music Educators Assn. Republican. Lutheran. Home: 680 Lakeside Dr Baldwin NY 11510 Office: Island Park UFSD Trafalgar Blvd Island Park NY 11558

PALAC, JUDITH ANN, music educator; b. Evanston, Ill., Feb. 8, 1954; d. Kazimir and Phyllis Josephine (Bochat) P.; m. James Edward Lorenz, July 25, 1992; 1 child, Matthew Palac Lorenz. MusB, U. Mich., 1976, MusM, 1977; DMA, U. Tex., 1987. Acad. staff specialist U. Wis., Oshkosh, 1977-81; asst. dir. U. Tex. String Project, Austin, 1983-85; lectr. violin S.W. Tex. State U., San Marcos, 1983-85; assoc. prof. music edn. Mich. State U., East Lansing, 1985—; 2d violinist Collegium String Quartet, Oshkosh, 1977-80; violinist Austin Symphony, 1981-85, Lansing (Mich.) Symphony Orch., 1985—. Editor: (booklet) Community Resources and School Orchestras, 1992; author: (jours.) Am. String Tchr., 1995, Med. Problems of Performing Arts, 1992, (periodical) Suzuki World, 1986. All-Univ. rsch. grantee Mich. State U., 1995. Mem. Internat. Arts Medicine Assn., Am. String Tchrs. Assn. (pres. Mich. unit 1996-98), Music Educators Nat. Conf., Suzuki Assn. of the Ams. Office: Mich State U Sch of Music East Lansing MI 48823

PALACIO, JUNE ROSE PAYNE, nutritional science educator; b. Hove, Sussex, Eng., June 14, 1940; came to U.S., 1949; d. Alfred and Doris Winifred (Blanch) P.; m. Moki Moses Palacio, Nov. 30, 1968. AA, Orange Coast Coll., Costa Mesa, Calif., 1960; BS, U. Calif., Berkeley, 1963; PhD, Kans. State U., 1984. Registered dietitian. Asst. dir. food svc. and res. halls Mills Coll., Oakland, Calif., 1964-66; staff dietitian Servomation Bay Cities, Oakland, 1966-67; commissary mgr. Host Internat., Inc., Honolulu, 1967-73; dir. dietetics Straub Clinic and Hosp., Honolulu, 1973-80; instr. Kans. State U., Manhattan, 1980-84; prof. and program dir. Calif. State U., L.A., 1984-85; prof., program dir. Pepperdine U., Malibu, Calif., 1985—; instr. Kapiolani Community Coll., Honolulu, 1973-79, U. Hawaii, Honolulu, 1975-80, Ctr. for Dietetic Edn., Woodland Hills, Calif., 1986—; cons. Clevenger Nutritional Svcs., Calabasas, Calif., 1985—, Calif. Mus. Sci. and Industry, L.A., 1989—, Calif. State Dept. Edn., Sacramento, Calif., 1985—. Author: Foodservice in Institutions, 1988, Introduction to Foodservice, 1992. Mem. Am. Dietetic Assn. (del. 1977-80, 86-89, reviewer 1986—), Calif. Dietetic Assn. (pres. 1992-93), L.A. Dist. Dietetic Assn., Foodsvc. Systems Mgmt. Edn. Coun., Dietetic Educators of Practitioners, Gamma Sigma Delta, Omicron Nu, Phi Upsilon Omicron. Republican. Episcopalian. Home: 24319 Baxter Dr Malibu CA 90265-4728 Office: Pepperdine U 24255 Pacific Coast Hwy Malibu CA 90263-0001

PALACIOS, ALANA SUE, computer programmer; b. Taylor, Tex., June 21, 1950; d. Alphonse T. and Doris Marie (Speegle) Hanzelka; m. Roberto C. Palacios, Mar. 10, 1956. BBA, U. Tex., 1978; MPA, Calif. State U., 1993. Asst. staff mgr. Southwestern Bell Telephone, St. Louis, 1978-80; sr. analyst Mountain Bell Telephone, Denver, 1980-81; asst. staff mgr. Southwestern Bell Telephone, 1981-84; project leader Hughes Aircraft, Long Beach, Calif., 1984-86; programmer, analyst City of Long Beach, 1986—. Civil svc. commr. Signal Hill, Calif., 1994—. Mem. NAFE, Phi Kappa Phi, Pi Alpha Alpha. Democrat. Episcopalian. Office: City of Long Beach 333 W Ocean 12th Fl Long Beach CA 90802

PALACIOS, SARA, artist; b. Guaimaro, Camaguey, Cuba, Feb. 22, 1955; came to U.S., 1968; d. Jose Manuel and Ondina L. (Lastre) Alvarez; m. Rodrigo Palacios, June 26, 1974; children: Rodrigo Andres, Paula. AA, Cerrito Coll., Norwalk, Calif., 1980. One-woman show at Art Studio Gallery, Santa Monica, Calif., 1995; exhibited in group shows at L.A. Contemporary Exhbn., 1992, Phillis Diller Internat., Beverly Hills, Calif., 1992, Galeria Las America, 1993, 94, 95, Cabrillo Pavilion Art Ctr., Santa Barbara, Calif., 1994. Treas. Latin Am. Art Coun., Northridge, Calif., 1993-94. Recipient Bronze award Art of Calif. Mag., 1993. Democrat. Home: 755 Trotter Ct Walnut CA 91789

PALAST, GERI D., federal agency administrator. BA in Polit. Sci., Stanford U., 1972; JD, NYU, 1976. Atty., legis. program analyst Am. Fedn. State County and Mcpl. Employees, Washington, 1976-77; legal counsel, field rep. Nat. Treasury Employers Union, Washington, 1977-79; dir., supervising atty. Nat. Employment Law Project, Washington, 1979-81; dir. politics and legislation Svc. Employees Internat. Union, AFL-CIO, Washington, 1981-93; asst. sec. congrl. and intergovtl. affairs Dept. Labor, Washington, 1993—. Office: Dept Labor Congl & Intergovtl Affairs 200 Constitution Ave NW Washington DC 20210-0001

PALCHO, KAREN DEAN, secondary art educator, studio potter; b. Pitts., Aug. 6, 1960; d. Ralph John and Elizabeth Rodgers (Snyder) P. BS, Pa. State U., 1982; MEd, Kutztown (Pa.) U., 1990. Cert. in art edn. K-12, Pa. Artist-in-residence Kodiak (Alaska) Village Schs., 1980-81; instr. art Kodiak C.C., 1980-82; artist, printer Nu-Art Graphics, West Chester, Pa., 1983-85; resident mgr. Kelsch Assocs., West Chester, 1985-86; secondary art tchr. Wyomissing (Pa.) Area H.S., 1987—, Am. Internat. Sch. of Luxembourg, 1992-93; insvc. speaker Am. Internat. Sch., Luxembourg, 1993; Women in Arts panelist Pa. State U., Reading, 1994. Exhibited ceramic sculpture in shows at New Arts Invitational Salon, 1994, Berks Coun. on Arts, 1994; subject of 2 TV programs. Vol. for cultural exch. Potters for Peace, Nicaragua, 1994. Recipient award for voluntary svc. AAUW, Berks County, 1990; arts fellow Coun. for Basic Edn., Nat. Endowment for Arts, 1992; Pa. Coun. on Arts artist in residence, Wyomissing, 1994. Mem. NEA, Pa. Edn. Assn., Nat. Art Edn. Assn., Pa. Art Edn. Assn., Pa. Guild of Craftsmen, Berks Art Alliance. Office: Wyomissing Area Sch Dist 630 Evans Ave Wyomissing PA 19610-2636

PALCZEWSKI, CATHERINE HELEN, communications educator; b. Honolulu, Oct. 14, 1964; d. Edmund and Helen Mary (Finks) P.; life ptnr. Arnold James Madsen. BS/MA, Northwestern U., 1987, PhD, 1994. Asst. prof. comm. St. John's U., Collegeville, Minn., 1991-94; asst. prof. U. Northern Iowa, Cedar Falls, 1994-96, assoc. prof., 1996—. Contbr. articles to profl. jours., chpts. to books. Cmty. coun. mem. Planned Parenthood of Greater Iowa, Cedar Falls, 1993—. Mem. AAUW, Speech Comm. Assn., Nat. Women's Studies Assn., Am. Forensic Assn., Kenneth Burke Soc., Ctrl. Sates Comm. Assn. (Outstanding New Tchr. 1993). Office: Univ Northern Iowa CAC 257 Cedar Falls IA 50614-0357

PALERMO, CATHERINE JOSEPHINE, lawyer; b. Rochester, N.Y., Apr. 7, 1968; d. John Charles and Constantina (Noun) P. BA, St. Bonaventure U., Olean, N.Y., 1990; JD, Union U., 1993. Bar: N.Y. 1993. Of counsel Kinnie Law Firm, Watertown, N.Y., 1996—. Mem. NOW, ABA, N.Y. State Bar Assn., Jefferson County Bar Assn. Home: 389 Pawling St Watertown NY 13601 Office: 137 Mullin St Watertown NY 13601

PALERMO, JUDY HANCOCK, elementary school educator; b. Longview, Tex., Sept. 7, 1938; d. Joseph Curtis and Bennie Lee (Deason) Hancock; m. Donald Charles Palermo, Apr. 1, 1961; 1 child, Donald Charles Jr. (dec.). BS in Secondary Edn., 1960. Cert. secondary and elem. edn. tchr., Tex. Art tchr. Dallas Ind. Sch. Dist., 1960-62, 65-67; asst. dir. freshmen orientation program North Tex. State U., Denton, summer 1969, dormitory dir. Oak St. Hall, 1968-71, tchr. part-time, 1970-77; substitute tchr. Denton Ind. Sch. Dist., 1975-78, tchr. 5th grade, 1979-87, art tchr., 1987—; tchr. kindergarten Kiddie Korral Pre-Sch., Denton, 1978-79; trained gifted tchr. Woodrow Wilson Elem. Sch., Denton, 1980, grade level chmn., 1980; grade level chmn. Eva S. Hodge Elem. Sch., Denton, 1988-89, 92-93; mem. rsch. bd. advisors Am. Biog. Inst., 1991—. Active Denton Humane Soc., 1982—, Denton Educators Polit. Action Com., 1984-85; Eva S. Hodge historian PTA, 1992—. Mem. NEA, NAFE, Tex. State Tchrs. Assn., Denton Classroom Tchrs. Assn. (faculty rep. 1984-85), Denton Edn. Assn., Denton Area Art Edn. Assn. (program chmn. 1990-91), Greater Denton Arts Coun., Numismatic Assn. (sec. Greater Denton chpt.), Denton Sq. Athletic Club, Denton Greater Univ. Dames Club (treas. 1970), Bus. and Profl. Women's Assn. (treas. 1990-91, chair audit com. 1992-93, chmn. 1993—), Delta Kappa Gamma (treas. 1986-88, comms. com. 1994—). Democrat. Home: 1523 Pickwick Ln Denton TX 76201-1290

PALERMO-MANDRACCHIA, VIOLET ANN, psychotherapist, educator; b. N.Y.C.; d. Anthony and Anna (Yetto) Palermo; m. John J. Mandracchia (dec. 1979); children: Dona Williams, Anne Marino, Marisa, John, Matthew, Lisa. Student, Coll. St. Vincent, 1946-48; BA, St. John's U., 1950; MA, Bklyn. Coll., 1953; cert. in ednl. adminstrn. & supervision, Hofstra U., 1978; MSW, SUNY, Stony Brook, 1990; advanced study in psychotherapy, L.I. Gestalt Ctr., 1988-92. Cert. social worker, secondary sch. adminstr., supr., English and social studies. Tchr. English Bay Ridge H.S., Bklyn., 1951-55, Ctrl. Islip (N.Y.) H.S., 1967-68, Smithtown (N.Y.) H.S., 1968-77; asst. prin. Shoreham-Wading River (N.Y.) H.S., 1977-81; prin. West Islip (N.Y.) H.S., 1981-83; pvt. practice as psychotherapist Stony Brook and Manhattan, 1990—; satellite psychotherapist Health House, Islandia, N.Y., 1988—, supr., 1990—. Active Suffolk County (N.Y.) Human Rights Commn., 1979-84, 88-92; chair adv. bd. Office for Women, Suffolk County, 1986-89; treas. bd. dirs. Women's Ctr., SUNY, Farmingdale, N.Y., 1985-87; chair Women's Equal Rights Coalition, Suffolk County, 1979-84, 88-92; chair North Fork Task Force in Arts, Suffolk County, 1977-79. Recipient Woman of Yr. award Suffolk County Exec. Office for Women, 1989; named Citizen of Yr., Smithtown LWV, 1984, Educator of Yr., Suffolk County Exec. & Women's Equal Rights Coalition, 1982; practitioner writing grantee Harvard U. Grad. Sch. Edn., 1981. Mem. NASW, NOW, Nat. Assn. Secondary Sch. Prins. Home: 15 Shore Oaks Dr Stony Brook NY 11790 Office: 211 Thompson St New York NY 10012

PALEY, GRACE, author, educator; b. N.Y.C., Dec. 11, 1922; d. Isaac and Mary (Ridnyik) Goodside; m. Jess Paley, June 20, 1942; children: Nora, Dan.; m. Robert Nichols, 1972. Ed., Hunter Coll., NYU. Formerly tchr. Columbia, Syracuse U.; ret. mem. lit. faculty Sarah Lawrence Coll., Stanford, Johns Hopkins, Dartmouth. Author: The Little Disturbances of Man, 1959, Enormous Changes at the Last Minute, 1974, Leaning Forward, 1985, Later the Same Day, 1985, Long Walks and Intimate Talks, 1991, New and Collected Poems, 1992, The Collected Stories, 1994 (Nat. Book award nomination 1994); stories published in Atlantic, Esquire, Ikon, Genesis West, Accent, others. Sec. N.Y. Greenwich Village Peace Center. Recipient Literary award for short story writing Nat. Inst. Arts and Letters, 1970, Edith Wharton award N.Y. State, 1988, 89, Rea award for short story, 1993, Vt. Gov.'s award for Excellence in the Arts, 1993, award for contbn. to Jewish culture Nat. Found. Jewish Culture; Guggenheim fellow. Mem. Am. Acad. and Inst. Arts and Letters. Office: PO Box 620 Thetford VT 05074-0620

PALEY, MAGGIE, writer, editor; b. N.Y.C., Dec. 29, 1939; d. David and Sylvia (Leichtling) P. BA magna cum laude, Brandeis U., 1960. Assoc. editor The Paris Rev., N.Y.C., 1963-66; mng. editor Status, N.Y.C., 1966-67; assoc. editor The Saturday Evening Post, N.Y.C., 1967-69; asst. editor Life, N.Y.C., 1969-71; writer Time, N.Y.C., 1971-72; contbg. editor Vogue, N.Y.C., 1984-85, Elle, N.Y.C., 1988-89, Mirabella, N.Y.C., 1990-94; adv. editor The Paris Rev., N.Y.C., 1967—. Author: (novel) Bad Manners, 1986, (chapbook) Elephant, 1990, (play) In One Door, 1985; contbr. articles and book revs. to N.Y. Times Book Rev., Mirabella, Elle, Vogue, Harper's Bazaar, Connoisser, others. Mem. The Creative Coalition, N.Y.C. Mem. Authors Guild, Nat. Writers Union. Home: 14 Bedford St # 2 New York NY 10014

PALINSKY, CONSTANCE GENEVIEVE, hypnotherapist, educator; b. Flint, Mich., May 31, 1927; d. George and Genevieve Treasa (Pisarski) Ignace; m. Joseph Palinsky, July 3, 1947; children: Joseph II, Mark Robert. Art student, Flint Inst. Arts, Oriental Artists Sch., others; numerous hypnosis studies including, Ethical Tng. Hypnosis Ctr., N.J. and Fla., Mid-West Inst., Hypnodye Found, Ill. and Fla.; tng., Nat. Guild Hypnotherapists. Cert NLP practitioner, neuro linguistics programmer. Owner, operator Palinsky Gallery of Art and Antiques, Flint, 1970-80; art lectr. Genesee County Grade Sch. System Flint Inst. Arts, 1972-74; owner, hypnosis cons. Hypno-Tech. Ctr., Flint, 1975-80; asst. mgr. Wethered-Rice Fine Jewelry, Flint, 1982-83; hypnotherapist, sr. cons. Dailey Life Ctr., Flint, 1985-96; mem. Am. Bd. Hypnotherapy, Calif.; numerous radio and TV shows and guest appearances, Flint, 1957—, ABC Nat. Network, 1959, Flint Calbe TV, 1972, others. Author: Constructive Personality Development, 1987, Secrets Revealed for Hypnosis Scripting, 1989, Designing Hypnosis Scripts for Relief of Multiple Sclerosis, 1994, Substance Abuse Issues Revealed of Effective Hypnosis Interventions, 1994, Light Touch Therapy for Pain Relief of Stress-Headache and Back Pain Relief--A Form of Hypno-Acupressure, 1995; one-woman show Dell's Artcraft Gallery, 1958; group shows at Flint Inst. Arts, U. Mich., Purdue U., Lafayette, Inc., Flint Artist Market, Saginaw, Detroit and Grand Rapids, Mich., Japan, others; contbr. articles to profl. jours.; author scripts and software in hypnosis field. Bd. dirs. The Chapel of The Angles Bldg. Fund for Lapeer County, 1974-75; pub. speaker various civic orgns. Named Oil Colorist of Yr. Profl. Photographers of Mich., 1959; recipient Pub. Svc. award Genesee County Sheriff's Dept., 1974. Mem. Internat. Soc. Profl. Hypnosis (regional v.p. 1977-79), Internat. Soc. Profl. Hypnotists and Counselors, Internat. Med. and Dental Hypnotherapist Assn., Nat. Guild Hypnotherapists, Nat. Guild Hypnotists (rsch. award for hypnosis for relief of multiple sclerosis 1991), Questers Antique Study Group (various offices including pres. 1972-90), Internat. Psychic Arts Rsch. (founder, pres. 1974-75), Flint Artist Market Group (program dir., treas.), Flint Soc. Arts and Crafts (v.p., pres. 1958-59), Quota Club, others. Republican. Roman Catholic. Home: 2362 Nolen Dr Flint MI 48504-5201

PALLADINO-CRAIG, ALLYS, museum director; b. Pontiac, Mich., Mar. 23, 1947; d. Stephan Vincent and Mary (Anderson) Palladino; m. Malcolm Arnold Craig, Aug. 20, 1967; children—Ansel, Reed, Nicholas. BA in English, Fla. State U., 1967; grad., U. Toronto, Ont., Can., 1969; MFA, Fla. State U., 1978, PhD in Humanities, 1996. Editorial asst. project U. Va. Press, Charlottesville, 1970-76; instr. English Inst. Franco Americain, Rennes, France, 1974; adj. instr. Fla. State U., Tallahassee, 1978-79, dir. Four Arts Ctr., 1979-82, dir. U. Mus. of Fine Arts, 1982—. Curator, contbg. editor carious articles and exhbn. catalogues, 1982—, including Nocturnes and Nightmares, Monochrome/Polychrome and Chroma; gen. editor Athanor I-XV, 1980—; represented in permanent collections Fla. Ho. of Reps., Barnett Bank, IBM. Individual artist fellow Fla. Arts Coun., 1979. Mem. Am. Assn. Mus., Fla. Art Mus. Dirs. Assn. (sec. 1989-91), Phi Beta Kappa. Democrat. Home: 1410 Grape St Tallahassee FL 32303-5636 Office: Fla State U Mus of Fine Arts 250 Fine Arts Bldg Tallahassee FL 32306-2055

PALLAIS, MARY LUCINDA, real estate broker; b. Manhattan, Kans., June 9, 1941; d. Robert and Cleo Wadina (Jagger) Pfanenstiel; m. Steven Ralph Pallais, Oct. 6, 1986; children: Steven G. Miller, Robin L. Miller, Carrie Lynn Miller, Jason E. Miller; 1 stepchild, Allison. Student, El Camino Coll., 1961-63; BA, Florrissant Valley Coll., St. Louis, 1975; postgrad., Orange Coast Coll., Santa Ana, Calif., 1979-82. Lic. real estate broker, Calif. Broker Orange County, Calif., 1978-90; owner/broker Pallais & Assocs., Oxnard, Calif., 1990-94; sr. real estate broker Young Real Estate, Westlake Village, Calif., 1996—. Sr. assoc. editor Ventura County Newspaper Youth Advocate, 1992 (Disting. Svc. award 1993). Chmn. Neighborhood Coun., Oxnard, 1993-96. Recipient Civic Awareness award Neighborhood Coun., 1995. Mem. Nat. Assn. Realtors, Assn. Realtors Camarillo, Oxnard Assn. Realtors (com. mem. 1994), Calif. Assn. Realtors, Toastmasters. Office: Young Realtors 971 Westlake Blvd Westlake Village CA 91316

PALLMEYER, REBECCA RUTH, federal judge; b. Tokyo, Sept. 13, 1954; came to U.S., 1957; d. Paul Henry and Ruth (Schrieber) P.; m. Dan P. McAdams, Aug. 20, 1977; children: Ruth, Amanda. BA, Valparaiso (Ind.) U., 1976; JD, U. Chgo., 1979. Bar: Ill. 1980, U.S. Ct. Appeals (7th cir.) 1980, U.S. Ct. Appeals 11th and 5th cirs.) 1982. Jud. clk. Minn. Supreme Ct., St. Paul, 1979-80; assoc. Hopkins & Sutter, Chgo., 1980-85; judge adminstrv. law Ill. Human Rights Commn., Chgo., 1985-91; magistrate judge U.S. Dist. Ct., Chgo., 1991—; mem. jud. resources com. Jud. Conf. of U.S., 1994—. Bd. govs. Augustana Ctr., 1990-91. Mem. Fed. Bar Assn. (bd. mgrs. Chgo. chpt. 1995-96), Womens Bar Assn. Ill. (bd. mgrs. 1996—), Nat. Assn. Women Judges, Fed. Magistrate Judges Assn. (bd. dirs. 1994—), Chgo. Bar Assn. (chair devel. law com. 1992-93, David C. Hilliard award 1990-91), Valparaiso U. Alumni Assn. (bd. dirs. 1992-94). Lutheran. Office: US Dist Ct Rm 2402 219 S Dearborn St Chicago IL 60604-1802

PALLOTTI, MARIANNE MARGUERITE, foundation administrator; b. Hartford, Conn., Apr. 23, 1937; d. Rocco D. and Marguerite (Long) P. BA, NYU, 1968, MA, 1972. Asst. to pres. Wilson, Haight & Welch, Hartford, 1964-65; exec. asst. Ford Found., N.Y.C., 1965-77; corp. sec. Hewlett Found., Menlo Park, Calif., 1977-84, v.p., 1985—; bd. dirs. Overseas Devel. Network. Bd. dirs. N.Y. Theatre Ballet, N.Y.C., 1986—, Consortium for Global Devel., 1992, Miramonte Mental Health Svcs., Palo Alto, Calif., 1989, Austin Montessori Sch., 1993. Mem. Women in Founds., No. Calif. Grantmakers, Peninsula Grantmakers. Home: 532 Marine World Pky # 6203 Redwood Shores CA 94065 Office: William & Flora Hewlett Found 525 Middlefield Rd Ste 200 Menlo Park CA 94025-3447

PALLOWICK, NANCY ANN, special education educator; b. Milw., May 27, 1953; d. William Bower and Harriette Ann (Lozar) P.; m. Douglas Richard Pugh, Aug. 11, 1990. B of Edn., U. South Fla., 1978; postgrad., Fla. Atlantic U., 1988, Fla. Internat. U., 1996—. Tchr. emotionally handicapped Ramblewood Mid. Sch., Coral Springs, Fla., 1978-83; freelance artist Ft. Lauderdale, Fla., 1983-85; tchr. emotionally handicapped Hunt Elem. Sch., Coral Springs, 1985-86; tchr. learning disabled Rock Island Elem. Sch., Ft. Lauderdale, 1986-92; tchr. emotionally handicapped Margate (Fla.) Mid.

Sch., 1992-94, behavior specialist, 1994-95; behavior specialist North Area Exceptional Student Edn., 1995—; dept. head Margate Mid. Sch., 1992-95, peer tchr., 1988-95, insvc. facilitator, 1993-95. Steward Broward Tchrs. Union, 1994-95. Broward County Sch. Bd. grantee, 1989-90, 91-92, 93-94. Mem. ASCD, Am. Fedn. Tchrs., Am. Craft Coun., Mich. Artists Guild, Tchr. Edn. Alliance, Teams Project, Fla. Craftsment, S. Fla. Fiber Artists, Assn. Behavior Analyst. Democrat. Roman Catholic. Home: 1110 SW 15th St Boca Raton FL 33486 Office: North Area Supt.'s Office 1400 NE 6th St Pompano Beach FL 33060

PALM, LINDA J., psychology educator; b. Abington, Pa., Jan. 28, 1949; d. Arthur W. Palm and M. Jean (Stucky) P. BA, Rollins Coll., 1970; MA, Wake Forest U., 1972; PhD, U. South Fla., 1980. Planner, evaluator Fla. Mental Health Inst., Tampa, 1980-83; asst. prof. psychology U. Wis., Platteville, 1983-88; prof. psychology Edison C.C., Fort Myers, Fla., 1988-92; assoc. prof. psychology Coastal Carolina U., Conway, S.C., 1992—. Contbr. articles to profl. jours. Bd. dirs. Tara Hall, Georgetown, S.C., 1996—. Mem. APA, S.C. Psychol. Assn., Phi Kappa Phi. Office: Coastal Carolina U Conway SC 29526

PALMER, ANN THERESE DARIN, lawyer; b. Detroit, Apr. 25, 1951; d. Americo and Theresa (Del Favero) Darin; m. Robert Towne Palmer, Nov. 9, 1974; children: Justin Darin, Christian Darin. BA, U. Notre Dame, 1973, MBA, 1975; JD, Loyola U., Chgo., 1978. Bar: Ill. 1978, U.S. Supreme Ct. 1981. Reporter Wall Street Jour., Detroit, 1974; freelancer Time Inc. Fin. Publs., Chgo., 1975-77, extern, Midwest regional solicitor U.S. Dept. Labor, 1976-78; tax atty. Esmark Inc., 1978; counsel Chgo. United, 1978-81; ind. contractor Legal Tax Rsch., 1981-89; fin. and legal news contbr. The Chgo. Tribune, 1991—, Bus. Week Chgo. Bur., 1991—, Automotive News, 1993—, Crain's Chgo. Bus., 1994—. Mem. Saddle and Cycle Club of Chgo., Detroit Golf Club. Roman Catholic. Home: 873 Forest Hill Rd Lake Forest IL 60045-3905

PALMER, BEVERLY BLAZEY, psychologist, educator; b. Cleve., Nov. 22, 1945; d. Lawrence E. and Mildred M. Blazey; m. Richard C. Palmer, June 24, 1967; 1 child, Ryan Richard. PhD in Counseling Psychology, Ohio State U., 1972. Lic. clinical psychologist, Calif. Adminstrv. assoc. Ohio State U., Columbus, 1969-70; rsch. psychologist Health Svcs. Rsch. Ctr. UCLA, 1971-77; commr. pub. health L.A. County, 1978-81; pvt. practice clin. psychology Torrance, Calif., 1985—; prof. psychology Calif. State U., Dominguez Hills, 1973—. Reviewer manuscripts for numerous textbook pubs; contbr. numerous articles to profl. jours. Recipient Proclamation County of L.A., 1972, Proclamation County of L.A., 1981. Mem. Am. Psychol. Assn. Office: Calif State U Dominguez Hills Dept Psychology Carson CA 90747

PALMER, FAITH BARBARA, real estate broker; b. Pawtucket, R.I., Nov. 1, 1919; d. Matthew Wilmot and Irene Luvia (Handy) Kenney; m. Charles Joseph Palmer, Jan. 25, 1986 (dec. July 1992); children: John Robert, Christopher Douglas. BA, Ohio State U., 1942; MEd, Salem State Coll., 1966. Cert. real estate broker, 1973. Sales assoc., mgr. Jack Conway & Co., Inc., Sandwich, Mass., 1973-86; regional v.p. Cape Cod office Jack Conway & Co., Inc., Sandwich, 1986—. Mem. Rep. Town Com., Sandwich, 1986—; del. Mass. Rep. Conv., Boston, 1990. Mem. Nat. Assn. Realtors (bd. dirs. 1989-91, 95, Omega Tau Rho), Mass. Assn. Realtors (bd. dirs. 1988-92, 94, regional v.p. 1995, Milton H. Shaw award 1993), Cape Cod and Islands Bd. Realtors (bd. dirs. 1985-86, 91-95, pres. 1990, Realtor of Yr. 1986), Opera New Eng. of Cape Cod (pres. 1988-90, 92-94, hospitality chair), Canal Region C. of C. Office: Jack Conway & Co Inc 128 Rte 6A Sandwich MA 02563

PALMER, JACQUELINE SUSAN, educational lab trainer; b. Arkansas City, Kans., June 9, 1950; d. Oscar John and Ileana Louise (Crawford) P.; m. Myrth Jimmie Killingsworth, July 12, 1985; 1 child, Myrth Ileana. BS, U. Mo., 1976; MS in Teaching, N.Mex. Tech. Coll., 1985; EdD, Memphis State U., 1992. Tchr. sci. Peace Corps/ACTION, Belize City, Belize, 1976-77, Kansas City (Mo.) Pub. Schs., 1978-79, Santa Fe (N.Mex.) Schs., 1979-80, St. Catherine's Indian Sch., Santa Fe, 1981-83, St. Michael's High Sch., Santa Fe, 1983-84; tcachng asst. N.Mex. Tech. Coll., 1984-86; instr. South Plains Coll., Lubbock, Tex., 1987-88, Memphis State U., 1988-90; rsch. asst. Tex. Alliance for Sci., Tech. & Math. Edn., College Station, 1990-91; sr. trainer Southwest Ednl. Devel. Lab., Austin, Tex., 1992—. Co-author: Ecospeak: Rhetoric and Environmental Politics in America, 1992, Alternative Assessment: A Toolkit for Professional Developers, 1994, addendum, 1995. Mem. local arrangements com. Conf. for the Advancement of Sci. Teaching. Mem. Nat. Sci. Edn. Leadership Assn., Nat. Sci. Tchrs. Assn., N.Am. Environ. Edn. Assn., Assn. for Edn. Tchrs. in Sci., Lab. Network Program. Office: Southwest Ednl Devel Lab 211 E 7th St Austin TX 78701

PALMER, LESLIE ELLEN, cardiovascular nurse clinician; b. Covington, Ky., Dec. 11, 1962; d. Ralph J. and Beth Edwards P. BSN, U. Ky., 1987. RN. Staff nurse U. Ky., Lexington, 1987-92; cardiovascular rsch. nurse Clinician Dorros-Feuer Interventional Cardiovascular Disease, Milw., 1992-93; cardiovascular nurse clinician Charleston (W.Va.) Cardiology Group, 1993-94; traveling nurse various orgns., 1994; cardiovascular nurse clinician Milw. Heart & Vascular Clinic, 1994-96; intra-aortic balloon pumping educator U. Ky., 1990-92; presenter profl. meetings. Contbr. articles to profl. jours. Named Primary Nurse of Yr. U. Ky., 1992, 90; recipient Golden Ear award U.Ky., 1991. Mem. Soc. Vascular Nursing, Am. Heart Assn., Am. Assn. Critical Care Nurses. Republican.

PALMER, MADELYN STEWART SILVER, family practice physician; b. Denver, July 18, 1964; d. Barnard Stewart and Cherry (Bushman) Silver; m. James Michael Palmer, Sept. 26, 1992; children: Adoniram Jacob, Benjamin Kern. BA cum laude, Wellesley (Mass.) Coll., 1986; MD, U. Utah, 1990. Family practice resident Mercy Med. Ctr., Denver, 1990-93; physician South Fed. Family Practice, Denver, 1993-95, South West Family Pracice, Littleton, Colo., 1995, Family Medicine Clinic, P.C., 1996—; staff St. Anthony Ctrl. Hosp., Denver, Porter Hosp., Denver, Swedish Hosp., Littleton Hosp. Ward Young Women's pres. LDS Ch., Littleton, ward primary sec., Englewood. Mem. AMA, Am. Acad. Family Practice, Colo. Acad. Family Practice, Colo. Med. Soc. Home: 543 E Maplewood Dr Littleton CO 80121 Office: 6169 S Balsam Way Littleton CO 80123

PALMER, MARTHA H., counseling educator; b. Chgo., Jan. 10, 1954; d. Thomas Manuel Sr. and Marie Louise (Cranford-Crawford) P.; m. Lewis A. Boahene, Mar. 1992; 1 child, Kwasi A. BA in Psychology, Ea. Ill. U., 1976, MS, 1977; cert. in cmty. law, John Marshall Law Sch., Chgo., 1981; student, U. Ill., Chgo., 1992; postgrad., No. Ill. U., 1995—. Med. asst. health svcs. Ea. Ill. U., Charleston, 1976-77; dir. sch. age and sr. citizen programs YMCA, Chgo., 1978-80; site dir., facilities mgr. Ctrs. for New Horizons, Chgo., 1980-85; counselor No. Ill. U., DeKalb, 1985-89; lectr. Malcolm X Coll., Chgo., 1989, recruitment coord., 1989-90; dir. Bethel Self Sufficiency Program, Chgo., 1989-90; asst. prof. counseling Harold Washington Coll. City Colls. Chgo., 1990—. Creator of character Marty The Clown; author poems; contbr. articles to profl. jours. Coord. Afrikan Cultural Pageant, Ea. Ill. U., Charleston and No. Ill. U., DeKalb, 1972-86; mem. polit. com. Chgo. Black United Comtys. and Black Ind. Polit. Orgns., Chgo., 1981—; program chair 500 Black Men and Women, Chgo., 1989-92; pres., mem. Sojourners United Polit. Action Commn., Chgo., 1993—; founder Harold Washington Coll., Black Women's Caucus, Chgo., 1991—; edn. rep. Task Force for Black Polit. Empowerment, Chgo., 1994—; coord. Coll. Support Groups for Self Help, 1991; co-founder Black Maleness Program, 1991; vol. La Rida Hosp., Chgo. Recipient Sharps and Flats Music Club Adv. award, 1994, BSU award, 1996. Mem. NOW, Nat. Assn. Black Psychologist, Ill. Assn. Black Psychologist, Delta Sigma Theta. Democrat. Roman Catholic. Office: City Coll Chgo Harold Washington Campus 30 E Lake St Chicago IL 60601

PALMER, PATRICIA, advertising professional, marketing consultant; b. Waltham, Mass., Jan. 29, 1954; d. Arthur C. and Edna (Matisse) P. BA in English and Art History, Rutgers U., 1976. Dir. mktg. G.K. Hall & Co., Boston, 1978; dir. mktg. and sales Dorison House, Inc., Boston, 1979-81, v.p. sales and mktg., 1982-85; office adminstr. Federated Dept. Stores, Cin., 1989-90; cons., 1990-91; advt. dir. The Green Co., Inc., Newton, Mass., 1991—; mktg. cons.; bd. dirs. Afiliated Investments, Inc., Wellesley, Mass. Democrat. Home: 52 Pickwick Way Wayland MA 01778 Office: The Green Co Inc 46 Glen Ave Newton MA 02159

PALMER, PATRICIA ANN TEXTER, English language educator; b. Detroit, June 10, 1932; d. Elmer Clinton and Helen (Rotchford) Texter; m. David Jean Palmer, June 4, 1955. BA, U. Mich., 1953; MEd, Nat.-Louis U., 1958; MA, Calif. State U.-San Francisco, 1966; postgrad. Stanford U., 1968, Calif. State U.-Hayward, 1968-69. Chmn. speech dept. Grosse Pointe (Mich.) Univ. Sch., 1953-55; tchr. South Margerita Sch., Panama, 1955-56, Kipling Sch., Deerfield, Ill., 1955-56; grade level chmn. Rio San Gabriel Sch., Downey, Calif., 1957-59; tchr. newswriting and devel. reading Roosevelt High Sch., Honolulu, 1959-62; tchr. English, speech and newswriting El Camino High Sch., South San Francisco, 1962-68; chmn. ESL dept. South San Francisco Unified Sch. Dist., 1968-81; dir. ESL Inst., Millbrae, Calif., 1978—; adj. faculty New Coll. Calif., 1981—, Skyline Coll., 1990—; Calif. master tchr. ESL Calif. Coun. Adult Edn., 1979-82; cons. in field. Past chair Sister City Com. Millbrae. Recipient Concours de Francais Prix, 1947; Jeanette M. Liggett Meml. award for excellence in history, 1949. Mem. AAUW, NAFE, TESOL, ASCD, Am. Assn. of Intensive English Programs, Internat. Platform Assn., Calif. Assn. TESOL, Nat. Assn. for Fgn. Student Affairs, Computer Using Educators, Speech Commn. Assn., Faculty Assn. of Calif. C.C., U. Mich. Alumnae Assn., Nat.-Louis U. Alumnae Assn., Ninety Nines (chmn. Golden West chpt.), Cum Laude Soc., Soroptimist Internat. (Millbrae-San Bruno Women Helping Women award 1993), Peninsula Lioness Club (pres.), Rotary Club (Millbrae), Chi Omega, Zeta Phi Eta. Home: 2917 Franciscan Ct San Carlos CA 94070-4304 Office: 450 Chadbourne Ave Millbrae CA 94030-2401

PALMER, PENNY KITT, finance manager; b. Centralia, Wash., Feb. 2, 1966; d. Ernest S. and Chloe M. (Arbogast) P. Student, Centralia Coll., 1984-86; BA, U. Wash., 1988. Sales sec. Boone Ford, Olympia, Wash., 1989-91, mgr. customer rels., 1991-92, fin. mgr., 1992—. Troop leader Girl Scouts USA, Centralia, 1980—. Recipient Crest award Pacific Peaks Girl Scouts Coun., 1991. Home: 8140 25th Ave SE Olympia WA 98503 Office: Boone Ford Sales Inc 3121 Pacific Ave Olympia WA 98501

PALMER, ROSEMARY GUDMUNDSON, elementary/secondary education educator; b. Logan, Utah, July 19, 1946; d. Melvin P. and Mary Mae (Jarvis) Gudmundson; m. Frederick W. Palmer, July 15, 1971; children: Christopher W., Melanie. BS, Utah State U., 1968, MEd, 1973; postgrad., U. Wyo., 1993—. Cert. elem. tchr. grades K-6, reading tchr. grades K-12, English tchr. grades K-12, remedial reading tchr. grades K-12, audio visual tchr. grades K-13. 5th grade tchr. Granite Sch. Dist., Granger, Utah, 1968-69; 6th grade tchr. Mesa (Ariz.) Pub. Schs., 1969-70, Davis Sch. Dist., Bountiful, Utah, 1970-71; supr. corrective reading grades 1-5 Spencer (Iowa) Cmty. Schs., 1973-74; jr. high reading, lang. arts tchr., study skills developer Sweetwater Sch. Dist. #1, Rock Springs, Wyo., 1981—; instr. reading in content area U. Wyo. Ext., Rock Springs, 1984-91; instr. children's lit. Western Syo. C.C., Rock Springs, 1992, 94, 96; crisis team adv. bd. mem. White Mt. Jr. High, Rock Springs, 1990—; presenter in field. Author (column) Sweetwater County Guide, 1987-91; contbr. articles to profl. jours. Story reader Nat. Libr. Week, Rock Springs (Wyo.) Pub. Libr., 1990—; bd. mem. Love Reading Com., Rock Springs, 1993—. Grad. assistantship U. Wyo., Laramie, 1993-94. Mem. Internat. Reading Assn. (state secondary sch. rep., secondary rep. on state bd. 1993—, del. People to People program 1992), Soc. Children's Book Writers and Illustrators, Nat. Coun. Tchrs. English (presenter confs.), Phi Delta Kappa, Phi Kappa Phi. Office: White Mountain Jr High PO Box 1089 Foothill Blvd Rock Springs WY 82902

PALMER, SUSAN MARIE, manufacturing company executive; b. Dennison, Ohio, Oct. 24, 1963; d. Vance Cy Smith and Agnes May (Moreland) Hursey; m. Paul Herbert Palmer Jr., July 7, 1990 (div. Oct. 1992). BS in Chemistry, Heidelberg Coll., 1986, BS in Math., 1986, BSBA in Econs., 1986. Hostess Atwood Lake Resort, Dellroy, Ohio, 1984-87; asst. mgr. Ponderosa, Canton, Ohio, 1987-89; chemist, metals Wadsworth/Alert Labs., North Canton, Ohio, 1989-91; sr. chemist, metals Enseco/Wadsworth/Alert Labs, North Canton, 1991-94; group leader metals Quanterra, Inc., North Canton, 1994—. Home: 2847 Miller Hill Rd NE Mineral City OH 44656

PALMER, THELMA JORGENSON, retired English educator, writer, publisher; b. Anacortes, Wash., Feb. 10, 1927; d. Alfred Kristian and Lilly Evangeline (Christenson) Jorgenson; m. Darrell W. Palmer (dec.); children: Dennis Wayne, Bradley Jorgen. AA, Sakgit Valley Coll., Mt. Vernon, Wash., 1961; BA in Edn., English, Western Wash. U., Bellingham, 1963, MA in Creative Writing, 1965. Cert. tchr., Wash.; cert. hypnotherapist, Wash. English tchr. Anacortes (Wash.) H.S., 1963-83; publisher, ptnr. Island Publishers, Anacortes, 1983—; hypnotherapist, owner Northwest Hypnotherapy, Anacortes, 1985—. Author: (books) The Sacred Round: Poems from an Island Garden, 1988, Long Journey to the Rose Garden, 1989; co-author (with Peter Moss) Enchantment of the World: France, 1986; contbr. articles and short stories to mags. and jours. including, Reader's Digest, Family Circle, The English Jour. and others. Recipient Benj. Franklin award, Publishers Mktg. Assn., 1989. Home and Office: Island Publishing Guemes Island 477 Secton Rd Anacortes WA 98221

PALMER, VIVIAN ROSE, physician assistant, chemist, biologist; b. Ft. Madison, Iowa, Sept. 24, 1957; d. James Lawrence and Rosalia Angeline (Rung) P. BS in Biology, Marycrest Coll., Davenport, Iowa, 1977-79; BS in Chemistry, Iowa Wesleyan U., 1988; BS in Physician Assistance, U. Osteo. Med & Health Scis, Des Moines, 1992. Cert. physician asst., Ill., Iowa. Physician asst. Horizons Ambulance Care Ctr., Carthage, Ill., 1992-93, Narvoo (Ill.) Med. Ctr., 1992-93, S.E. Iowa Med. Svcs., Ft. Madison, 1993-95. With U.S. Army, 1981-83. Fellow Am. Acad. Physician Assts.; mem. Lions (3d v.p. 1994).

PALMER-CARFORA, LINDA LOUISE, special education educator; b. Derby, Conn., Mar. 6, 1950; d. Robert Roy and Ruth Mae (Borcherding) Palmer; m. John Michael Carfora, July 22, 1972; 1 child, Rachel Ellen. BS, So. Conn. State U., 1972; M of Edn. of the Deaf, Smith Coll., 1987. Learning disabilities tchr. Melissa Jones Sch., Guilford, Conn., 1972-76; tchr. Nat. Soc. for Autistic Children, London, 1977-79; clinician The Developmental Ctr., London, 1979-80; tchr. The Benhaven Sch., New Haven, Conn., 1982-84, Woodstock (Vt.) Developmental Ctr., 1984-86, Willie Ross Sch. for the Deaf, Longmeadow, Mass., 1988—; writer, edn. cons. Bloomington, Ind., 1994—; spl. edn. cons. Dalton (Mass.) Pub. Schs., 1990. Vol. clinician Elmira (N.Y.) Coll. Speech Clinic, 1968-69; vol. tutor New Haven Regional Ctr. for Mentally Retarded, 1969-70. Mem. Coun. for Exceptional Children, Smith Coll. Alumnae Assn. Congregationalist. Office: Willie Ross Sch Deaf 32 Norway St Longmeadow MA 01106

PALMER-HASS, LISA MICHELLE, state official; b. Nashville, Sept. 4, 1953; d. Raymond Alonzo Palmer and Anne Michelle (Jones) Davies; m. Joseph Monroe Hass, Jr. BSBA, Belmont Coll., 1975; AA in Interior Design, Internat. Fine Arts Coll., 1977; postgrad., Tenn. State U., 1991—. Interior designer Lisa Palmer Interior Designs, Nashville, 1977-84; sec. to pres. Hermitage Elect. Supply Corp., Nashville, 1981-83; sec. to dir. Tenn. Dept. Mental Health and Mental Retardation, Nashville, 1984-86; transp. planner Tenn. Dept. Transp., Nashville, 1986—. Mem. Nat. Arbor Day Found. Recipient cert. of appreciation Tenn. Dept. Mental Health and Mental Retardation, 1986; named Hon. Mem. Tenn. Ho. of Reps., 1990. Mem. NAFE, Nat. Wildlife Fedn., Profl. Secs. Internat. (cert.), Nashville Striders Club, The Music City Bop Club, Music City Bop Club Dance and Exhibn. Team, Mensa. Republican. Mem. Disciples of Christ Ch. Office: Tenn Dept Transp Environ Planning Office 505 Deaderick St Ste 900 Nashville TN 37243-0334

PALMIERE, CATHERINE EMILIA, executive recruiter; b. Yonkers, N.Y., Apr. 4, 1959; d. Michael Anthony and Raffaela Theresa (Celentano) P. BS, Manhattan Coll., 1981, MBA, 1995. CPC, CTS, CIPC, CSS. V.P. Adam Pers. Inc., N.Y.C., 1981-92; dir. Advice Pers. Inc., N.Y.C., 1992—. Mem. Internat. Confedn. Pers. Svcs. Assns., Nat. Assn. Pers. Svcs., Delta Mu Delta. Home: 500 E 77th St # 1417 New York NY 10162

PALMORE, CAROL M., state government executive; b. Owensboro, Ky., Jan. 13, 1949; d. P.J. and Carrie Alice (Leonard) Pate; m. John Stanley Palmore Jr., Jan. 1, 1982. BS in History and Polit. Sci., Murray State U., 1971; JD, U. Ky., 1977. Social worker Dept. Human Resources, Frankfort, Ky., 1971-74; assoc. atty. Rummage, Kamuf, Yewell & Pace, Owensboro, 1977-81; hearing officer Ky. Bd. Claims, Frankfort, 1980-81; gen. counsel Ky. Labor Cabinet, Frankfort, 1982-83, dep. sec. labor, 1984, 1986-87, sec. labor, 1987-90, 91-94; ptnr. Palmore & Sheffer Attys., Henderson, Ky., 1984-86; dep. sec. Ky. Pers. Cabinet, Frankfort, 1996—; chmn. Ky. Safety & Health Stds. Bd., Frankfort, 1987-90, 91-94; co-chmn. Ky. Labor Mgmt. Adv. Coun., Frankfort, 1987-90, 91-94; bd. dirs. Ky. Workers' Comp Funding Commn., Frankfort, 1987-90, 91-94, Community Svc. Commn., Frankfort, 1993-94, Ky. Info. Resources Mgmt. Commn., Frankfort, 1994, Sch.-to-Work Partnership Coun., Frankfort, 1994; ex-officio bd. dirs. Pub. Employees Collective Bargaining Task Force, Frankfort, 1994, Ky. Workforce Partnership Coun., Frankfort, 1994. Labor liaison Jones for Gov., Lexington, 1990-91; del. Dem. Nat. Conv., N.Y.C., 1992; mem. inaugural class Ky. Women's Leadership Network, Frankfort, 1993; bd. dirs. Alliant Health Systems Adult Oper. Bd., Louisville, 1992-96, Ky. Commn. Homeless, Frankfort, 1993-94; candidate for Sec. State Commonwealth Ky., 1995; chair Dem. Women's Think Tank, 1995. Mem. Ky. Bar Assn. (del. ho. dels. 1985-86, chair law day/spkr. bur. 1985-86, mem. 1986-90), Ky. Bar Found. (bd. dirs. 1985-92, sec. 1986-89, pres. elect 1989-90, pres. 1990-91), Rotary (program chair Frankfort chpt. 1993-94). Episcopalian. Home: 2310 Peaks Mill Rd Frankfort KY 40601-9437 Office: Personnel Cabinet 200 Fair Oaks Dr Frankfort KY 40601-4000

PALMORE, JO NORRIS, English language/literature educator, consultant; b. Clarksville, Tenn., June 9, 1948; d. Ben Ed and Alma Ruth (Hunt) Norris; m. Bernard Hudgins Palmore, Jr. BA, U. Tenn., Knoxville, 1970, MS in English Edn., 1973. Cert. tchr. Tenn. Tchr. English and American history Clarksville H.S., Tenn., 1970-72; tchr. English Farragut H.S., Knoxville, Tenn., 1973-79; editl. asst. Cumberland mag., Clarksville, Tenn., 1980-81; tchr. English Montgomery Bell Acad., Nashville, Tenn., 1981-92, chmn. English dept., 1992—; essay reader advanced placement English lit., 1994—; essay reader SAT II, Ednl. Testing Svc., Princeton, N.J., 1995—, cons., 1996. Vol. Habitat For Humanity, Nashville, 1994, Mother's March of Dimes, Nashville; parent vol. Westminster Sch., Nashville, 1985-93. Recipient Stokely fellow U. Tenn., 1991, Summer Seminar grantee Nat. Endowment Humanities, Kenyon Coll., 1994. Mem. Nat. Coun. Tchrs. English, Tenn. Coun. Tchrs. English. Presbyterian. Home: 624 Royal Oaks Pl Nashville TN 37205 Office: Montgomery Bell Acad 4001 Harding Rd Nashville TN 37205

PALSHO, DOROTHEA COCCOLI, information services executive; b. Phila., June 9, 1947; d. John Charles and Dorothy Lucille (Decker) C.; m. Edward Robert Palsho; children: Christopher, Ryan, Erica (stepchild). BS, Villanova U., 1976; MBA, Temple U., 1977. V.p. info. svcs. Dow Jones & Co., Princeton, N.J., 1977—; now pres. bus. info. svcs. Named one of Class of Women Achievers YWCA Acad. of Women Achievers, 1985. Office: Dow Jones & Co Inc PO Box 300 Princeton NJ 08543-0300*

PALTROW, GWYNETH, actress. Appeared in (films) Shout, 1991, Hook, Malice, Flesh and Bone, Mrs. Parker and the Vicous Circle, Jefferson in Paris, Moonlight and Valentino, Seven, The Pallbearer, (TV movie) Cruel Doubt, (theatre) Picnic, The Adventures of Huck Finn, Sweet Bye and Bye, The Seagull. Office: care Screen Actors Guild 5757 Wilshire Blvd Los Angeles CA 90036*

PALUMBO, LOUISE COREY, fashion and special events administrator; b. Charleston, W.Va., Aug. 19, 1931; d. George N. and Bahia (George) Corey; m. Mario Joseph Palumbo, Apr. 13, 1933; children: Mario Joseph Jr., Corey Lee. BA, Morris Harvey Coll., 1955. Trainee Saks Fifth Ave., N.Y.C., 1956; asst. fashion coord. Ind. Retailers Syndicate, N.Y.C., 1956-59; corp. fashion and spl. events dir. Stone & Thomas, Charleston, W.Va., 1959—. State dir. Friendship Force, W.Va., 1983—; founder, chmn. River Lights, Charleston, 1982—; coord. Uniforms for Spl. Olympics, W.Va., 1992; chmn. Inaugural Balls for Gov. Rockefeller, W.Va., 1983, 87; mem. Preservation of Gov. Mansion, W.Va., 1992—, Women's Arts, W.Va., 1994—, Symphony League for Women, W.Va., 1994—; trustee Sunrise Mus., Charleston, 1983-89. Recipient Mayor's Award for the arts Fund for the Arts, 1992, Creative Achievement award Advt. Club Huntington, 1971, Cert. of Appreciation Nat. Coun. Jewish Women, 1992. Democrat. Ea. Orthodox. Home: 1838 Louden Heights Rd Charleston WV 25314 Office: Stone and Thomas Lee and Dickinson Sts Charleston WV 25326

PALVINO, NANCY MANGIN, librarian; b. Rochester, N.Y., Nov. 22, 1937; d. John Bernard and Miriam Lucille (Fox) Mangin; m. Lawrence Robert Palvino, July 2, 1960; children: Mark, Laurie, Lisa, Katharine, Thomas. BS, SUNY, Geneseo, 1959; MLS, U. Buffalo, 1993. Cert. libr., N.Y. Libr. Spencerport (N.Y.) Elem. Sch., 1959-60; tchr. East Greenbush (N.Y.) Elem. Sch., 1960-63; libr. # 41 Sch., Rochester, 1993—. Author: (bibliography) Autism, 1991. Fundraiser Rochester Philharm. Orgn., 1970; mem. women's bd. dirs. St. Mary's Hosp., Rochester, 1980—, giftshop chairperson, 1989-92, exec. coun., 1989-92, chmn. of ball, 1985, Imperial Ball Meml. Art Gallery, 1987, Holiday Open House, 1988; v.p. women's coun. Meml. Art Gallery, Rochester, 1989-91. Grantee DeWitt Wallace Reader's Digest Fund, 1994. Mem. N.Y. Libr. Assn. (scholarship 1992), Greater Rochester Areas Media Specialists (chmn. scholarship com. 1994-95, scholarship 1992). Home: 345 Kilbourn Rd Rochester NY 14618 Office: # 41 Sch 279 Ridge Rd W Rochester NY 14615-2927

PALZERE, EMMA LEONE, actress, producer, playwright; b. Manchester, Conn., June 15, 1962; d. Donald Edward and Jane (DiPietro) P. BFA, Emerson Coll., 1984; grad., Comml. Theater Inst., 1994. Prodr., actress Be Well Prodns., Newington, Conn., 1989—; exec. prodr. Womenkind Festival, N.Y.C., 1991—; mgr. Empire Theater, Block Island, R.I., 1994. Author: (juvenile) Peas Please, 1988; creator: I.C.U. - Improv Comedy Unit, 1990; writer, performer: Live from the Milky Way...It's Gilda Radner!, 1992. Winner One - Act Play contest Warner Ctr. Arts, Torrington, Conn., 1995. Mem. Actor's Equity Assn., AFTRA, SAG (vol. Book Pals, 1992-94), Dramatists Guild, Emerson Coll. Alumni Club Greater N.Y. (bd. dirs. 88—, sec. 90-92), Zeta Phi Eta (Marguerite Garden Jones award, 1991). Address: PO Box 310079 Newington CT 06131

PAM, CAROL SUE, college administrator, educator; b. N.Y.C., Jan. 30, 1939; d. Murray Jack and Lillian Shirley (Glatt) Hauser; m. Ronald Pam, Dec. 24, 1960; children: Tobi Cheryl, Stuart Evan, Lori Jo. BA, Hunter Coll., 1960; MA, Rider U., 1979; postgrad., Rutgers U., 1982-90. Cert. office automation profl. Tchr. h.s. N.Y.C. Bd. Edn., 1960-62; tchr. adult edn. East Brunswick (N.J.) Adult Sch., 1970-80; adj. tchr. Middlesex County Coll., Edison, N.J., 1975-79; instr. Middlesex County Coll., Edison, 1979-83, asst. prof., 1983-86, assoc. prof., 1986-91, prof., 1991—; dept. chair Middlesex County Coll., Edison, N.J., 1975—; acting chairperson Middlesex County Coll., Edison, 1993-94, chairperson, 1994—; mem. Inst. for Edn. Profl. Secs. Internat., Kansas City, 1990—. Contbr. articles to profl. jours. Mem. NAFE, Bus. Edn. Assn., Omicron Tau Theta. Office: Middlesex County Coll 155 Mill Rd Edison NJ 08818-3050

PAMMER, LESA GAIL, marketing professional; b. Chgo., Apr. 26, 1957; d. Frank James and Elene M. (Lieberman) Bobele; m. Fred Ross Pammer, May 7, 1978; children: David Ross, Daniel Matthew. AS, Prairie State Coll., 1977. Sportswear sales rep. Roselee, Matteson, Ill., 1975-80; editor market rsch. Bryles Survey, Crestwood, Ill., 1975-85; owner Pammer Rsch. Inc., Mokena, Ill., 1985—. Mem. Market Rsch. Assn. (chmn. arrangements 1994-95, chmn. PIP 1993-94). Jewish. Home: 18925 Meadow Creek Dr Mokena IL 60448-9110

PAN, LORETTA REN-QIU, retired educator; b. Changzhou, China, Oct. 1, 1917, came to U.S., 1951, naturalized, 1965; d. Ke-jun and Mei-ying (Xue) P.; B.A. in English Lit., Ginling Coll., 1940; cert. English Lit., Mt. Holyoke Coll., 1952. Instr. English, Nanking U., 1940-41; instr. English and Chinese, St. Mary's Girls Sch., Shanghai, 1941-44; instr. English, Ginling Coll., 1944-45; sr. translator info. dept. Brit. Embassy, Shanghai, 1945-48; Chinese editor U.S. Consulate Gen., Hong Kong, 1949-51; researcher, editorial asst. modern China project Columbia U., 1955-60, lectr. Chinese, 1960-67, sr. lectr., 1968-87. Methodist. Contbr. to various profl. publs. Home: 600 W 111th St New York NY 10025-1813

PAN, MARIA WEIYEI, company executive; b. Beijing, China, June 19, 1943; came to U.S., 1965; d. Po Han Liu and Lillian Shufen Lee; m. Ko-chang Casey Pan, Sept. 21, 1968; 1 child, Julie Marie. BSBA, Nat. Taiwan U., Tapei, Taiwan, Republic of China, 1965; MS in Math. Stats., U. Iowa, 1967. Biostatician U. Iowa, Iowa City, 1967-69; mathematician Modern Woodmen of Am., Rock Island, Ill., 1969-73; real estate agent Nelson Realty, Davenport, Iowa, 1974-77; math. U.S. Army, Picatinny Arsenal, N.J., 1978-83; real estate agent New Century Assocs., East Hanover, N.J., 1983—; dir. LPC Corp., Alhambra, Calif., 1987—; v.p. Handsome Enterprises of N.Y., N.Y.C., 1980-91; pres. BusinessPlus Corp. of N.J., Pine Brook, 1990—. Mem. NAFE, NOW, Am. Def. Preparedness Assn., Internat. Two Ten Found., N.J. Assn. Women Bus. Owners, Nat. Contract Mgmt. Assn. U.S. Army, Altrusa Internat. Republican. Office: Business Plus Corp NJ 400 Morris Ave Ste 233 Denville NJ 07834-1315

PANAYIRCI, SHARON LORRAINE, textiles executive, design engineer; b. San Diego, Nov. 11, 1957; d. Robert Vernon and Edna Ruth (Bayless) Reed; m. Mehmet Vefki Panayirci, Mar. 1, 1985; 1 child, Ruth Naile. AAS cum laude, Sinclair Coll., 1981; B in Tech. cum laude, U. Dayton, 1984. Designer Dayton (Ohio) Progress Corp., 1981-85; design engr. Hartzell Propeller Inc., Piqua, Ohio, 1987-88; v.p. Patex Exim Inc., Dayton, 1986-93, Aegean Apparel, Dayton, 1993—; cons. Cepateks A.S. Indsl. Engr., Denizli, Turkey, 1985-86; fin. cons. Aegean Apparel Inc., Dayton, 1991-93. Mem. NAFE, AAUW. Democrat. Office: Aegean Apparel Inc 4365 Lisa Dr Tipp City OH 45371

PANCAKE, EDWINA HOWARD, science librarian; b. Butte, Mont., Nov. 10, 1942; d. Robert Evan and Edwina Howard (Handfield) P. Student, Miami U., 1960-63; BS in Biology, Baylor U., 1967; MLS, U. Tex., 1969. Sci. info. specialist U. Va., Charlottesville, 1969-73, acting dir. sci. and tech. info. ctr., dir. sci. and engring libr., 1974-93, assoc. prof. emeritus, 1994—. NDEA fellow U. Tex., 1967-68. Fellow Spl. Libraries Assn. (bd. dirs. 1979-81, 83-84, 85-88, pres. 1994-95), Mensa. Episcopalian.

PANDAK, CAROL ANN, fraternal organization administrator; b. Park Ridge, Ill., Feb. 27, 1960; d. Theodore J. and Bette J. (Brune) P. BA, U. Ill., 1982; MA, Northeastern Ill., 1986; postgrad., No. Ill. U., 1996. Customer svc. rep. Baxter, Inc., Deerfield, Ill., 1984-87; sales mgr. Parke DeWatt Labs., Chgo., 1987-90; program. mgr. Soc. Actuaries, Schaumburg, Ill., 1990-92; coord. found. tng. Rotary Internat., Evanston, Ill., 1992-95, asst. mgr., 1995—. Recipient Achievement certs. Am. Soc. Assn. Execs., 1992; Paul Harris fellow Rotary Internat., 1993, Dissertation Completion fellow No. Ill. U., 1995-96. Mem. Literacy Vols. Am., Am. Assn. Adult & Continuing Edn., Internat. Soc. Third Sector Rsch., Rotary, Kappa Delta Pi. Home: 1926 Prairie Sq #131 Schaumburg IL 60173

PANDYA, DEANNA MEARS, mental health counselor; b. Norfolk, Va., Aug. 11, 1937; d. James Gordon Jr. and Sarah Talmadge (Johnson) Mears; m. David Luther Brinkley Jr. (div.); children: Kim Brinkley Hebebrand, David III, Jeffrey Lawrence Brinkley; m. Shirish Ramachandra Pandya, June 7, 1978 (dec.). AA, U. Akron, 1980; BA, Va. Wesleyan, 1983; MA, Antioch U., 1994. Dir. edn. svcs. Va. Coun. on Alcoholism, Drugs, Norfolk, 1985-87, exec. dir., 1990-93; outpatient program specialist Maryview Psychiat. Hosp., Portsmouth, Va., 1988-89; clin. therapist City of Portsmouth, 1988-89; educator, therapist City of Va. Beach, 1984-86, 93-95; mental health counselor Glasgow High Wellness Ctr., Newark, Del., 995; founder Survivors of Suicide, Virginia Beach, 1982-86, vol. educator AARP Bear, Del., 1995. Contbr. articles to profl. jours., various presentations. Bd. dirs. Hospice of Virginia Beach, 1983-85, Safe Place, 1988-90, Civitan Internat., 1990-92, comty. adv. coun. for curriculum Coll. of Edn., Old Dominion U., Norfolk, 1991-92. Named Rookie of Yr., Civitan Internat., 1991; recipient Disting. Svc. award Va. Alcohol and Drug Abuse Counselors, 1992. Mem. Nat. Coun. Sexual Addiction and Compulsivity, Nat. Assn. Alcohol and Drug Abuse Counselors, Am. Christian Counselors Assn., Obsessive Compulsive Disorders Found., Am. Counselors Assn., Nat. Assn. Cognitive Behavioral Therapists, Nat. Assembly Sch. Based Health Care, Parents and Friends of Lesbians and Gays, Lions Club Internat.

PANEPINTO, EILEEN SUSAN, artist; b. N.Y.C., Nov. 22, 1951; d. Louis and Lucy (Coniglio) P.; m. Michael Francis Bellacosa, June 10, 1989. BFA with honors, Sch. Visual Arts, N.Y.C., 1986. Type dir., computer graphic artist Sabine Press & Advt., N.Y.C., 1987-89; freelance computer artist N.Y.C., 1989; on-site cons. computer graphics/typography project Applied Graphics Techs., N.Y.C., 1989-90; type dir., computer graphic artist, typesetting mgr. Lintas: N.Y., N.Y.C., 1990-92; freelance computer graphics artist, typographer N.Y.C., 1992—; curator exhibits Jadite Galleries, N.Y.C., 1992., 67th Annual Conn. Women Artists Show, New Haven, 1996. One person show Jadite Galleries, N.Y.C., 1995; exhibited in group shows at Jadite Galleries, 1987, 88, 91, 92, Del Bello Gallery, Toronto, Can., 1987, Lamborghini Gallery, N.Y.C., 1988, Southwest Tex. State U., San Marcos, 1989, AIR Gallery, N.Y.C., 1992, 93, Real Art Ways, Hartford, Conn., 1995, Westport (Conn.) Arts Ctr., 1995. Home: 66 Lords Hwy Weston CT 06883

PANETTA, JANET, dancer, educator, choreographer; b. N.Y.C., Dec. 12, 1948; d. Vincent and Mary (Esposito) P.; m. Jeffrey Roth, Aug. 23, 1975; 1 child, Niles. Student, Met. Opera Ballet Sch., N.Y.C., 1958-70. Dancer Am. Ballet Theatre, N.Y.C., 1968-70; dir. White Street Ctr. for Movement and Bodywork, N.Y.C., 1991—; instr. ballet SUNY, Purchase, 1992-93; guest ballet tchr. various cos., Amsterdam, The Netherlands, Zurich Switzerland, Montpellier, France, Angers, France, 1985—, P.A.R.T.S., Brussels, 1991—, Rosas, Brussels, 1994—.

PANG, JOANNA See ATKINS, JOANNA PANG

PANG, MAYBELINE MIUSZE (CHAN), software and systems engineer, analyst; b. Shanghai, China, Sept. 9, 1945; came to U.S. from Hong Kong, 1964; d. Yee Sun and Margaret H. (Kong) Chan; m. Patrick Yewwah Pang, Aug. 4, 1968 (div. 1987); children: Elaine Weikay, Irene Weisum, George Siu-On. BS in Physics/Math, Lincoln U., 1967; postgrad, U. Mo., 1967-68, U. Ariz., 1984-86. Application programmer Ariz. Health Sci. Ctr., Physiology Lab., Tucson, 1984-85; software engr. System and Software Engring. Dalmo Victor, Singer, Tucson, 1985-88, McDonnell Douglas Helicopter Co., Mesa, Ariz., 1988-90, Sperry Marine, Charlottesville, Va., 1990—; cons., worked with Air Force (F111 Weather Simulation), Army (Advanced Apache Helicopter), Navy (Seawolf weapons, ship control, CNO-Automatic Depth Finder) projects; comml. (Integrated Software Analysis Sys.; Sperry's docking sys., Guardian Star) projects; familiar with sys. analysis and design; software devel. and testing; algorithms, pulse processing, sys. engr. and analyst for Marine Sensors; active in Sperry's New Tech. Group. Recipient Nat. Sci. Honor Soc. award, 1967, Teaching assistantship U. Mo., 1968. Home: 1517 Westfield Ct Charlottesville VA 22901-1602 Office: Sperry Marine Seminole Trail Charlottesville VA 22901

PANICCI, RAMONA JEAN, marketing professional; b. Fort Sill, Okla., Aug. 30, 1948; d. William Benedict and Ruby Isabele (DeLoach) Cooper; m. Lawrence Joseph Panicci, May 15, 1993 (div. Aug. 1995); children: Bryan William Hartman, Tanya Cheree Hartman. BSN, Ariz. State U., 1975. RN, Ariz. Girl Friday U.S. C. of C., Washington, 1969; sec. Army Emergency Relief, Washington, 1970; ICU/CCU Nurse Phoenix Registry, 1975-84; recovery room supr. Out Patient Surgery, Tempe, Ariz., 1984-85; staff nurse Chandler (Ariz.) Regional Hosp., 1985-87, Scottsdale (Ariz.) Mem. Out Patient, 1987-89; sales mgr. PCI Med., Inc., Phoenix, 1989-90; account mgr. NMC Homecare, Las Vegas, 1990-95; v.p. Women's Healthcare Coun., Las Vegas, 1994. Dir. Song and Dance, Lazy J's, Scottsdale, 1978; bd. dirs. Ariz. State U. Alumni Assn., Tempe, 1980; mem. Jr. League, Las Vegas, 1991. Mem. Ariz. State Nurses Alumni (pres.), So. Nev. Continuing Care (bd. dirs. 1995-96), NAFE, Nev. Orgn. Nurse Execs., Sigma Theta Tau. Republican. Home: 5316 N 78th Way Scottsdale AZ 85250 Office: Valley Home Health Svcs Ste A 7820 N 12th St Phoenix AZ 85020

PANICH, DANUTA BEMBENISTA, lawyer; b. East Chicago, Ind., Apr. 9, 1954; d. Fred and Ann Stephanie (Grabowski) B.; m. Nikola Panich, July 30, 1977; children: Jennifer Anne, Michael Alexei. A.B., Ind. U., 1975, J.D., 1978. Bar: Ill. 1978, U.S. Dist. Ct. (no. dist.) Ill. 1978, U.S. Dist. Ct. (cen. dist.) Ill. 1987, U.S. Ct. Appeals, 1987. Assoc. Mayer Brown & Platt, Chgo., 1978-86, ptnr., 1986—. Mem. ABA, Ill. State Bar Assn. Republican. Roman Catholic. Office: Mayer Brown & Platt 190 S La Salle St Chicago IL 60603-3410

PANIK, SHARON MCCLAIN, primary education educator, writer; b. Detroit, May 29, 1952; d. Robert and Phyllis L. McClain; m. Steven Panik, May 25, 1974; 1 child, Todd. BS, Ctrl. Mich. Univ., 1973; MA, U. No. Colo., 1978. Tchr. primary grades Tchr. Poudre R-1, Fort Collins, 1974—. Co-author: (with Marilyn Parke) A Quetzalcoatl Tale of Corn, 1992 (Parents' Choice Gold award paperback of yr. 1992), A Quetzalcoatl Tale of the Ball Game, 1992, A Quetzalcoatl Tale of Chocolate, 1994. Mem. Internat. Reading Assn., Soc. Children's Book Writers and Illustrators, Nat. Edn. Soc., Colo. Coun. Internat. Reading Assn. (membership dir.). Office: 1209 Parkwood Dr Fort Collins CO 80525*

PANKEY, DEBORAH SUE, critical care nurse; b. Wichita, Kans., Jan. 5, 1965; d. Bobby Frank and Barbara Alice (Brown) Benson; m. Donald Russell Pankey, Aug. 3, 1985 (div. Oct. 1991); m. Nov. 27, 1992. BSN, St. Mary of the Plains, 1989. RN, Kans.; cert. ACLS affiliate faculty, TNCC instr., ENPC instr., BLS, ENA. Nurse technician Via Christi Regional Med. Ctr./St. Joseph Campus, Wichita, 1988-90, staff nurse, relief charge nurse, chest pain ctr. coord., 1990—; presenter in field. Mem. Emergency Nurses Assn. (sec. local chpt. 1994). Home: 172 Champion St Haysville KS 67060-1901 Office: Via Christi Regional Med Ctr St Joseph Campus 3600 E Harry St Wichita KS 67218-3713

PANKIN, GLORIA SHAPIRO, small business owner; b. Kansas City, Mo., May 21, 1935; d. Samuel S. Shapiro and Dorothy Lillian (Eisberg) Shapiro Amdur; children: Sanford, Harris, David. AB, U. Mich., 1957. Cert. tchr., Mich., Calif. Owner, operator Alpha Buttons, Escondido, Calif., 1991—; substitute tchr. Vista (Calif.) Unified Schs., 1991-96. Membership chmn., ways and means com., regional officer comty svcs., children's programs Parents Without Ptnrs., St. Louis, 1974-81; v.p. ways and means Escondido Panhellenic, 1995-96; active Women in the Arts Mus., 1993. Mem. Hidden Valley Obedience Club (founder, dir. tng. 1986, treas. 1992), Therapy Dogs, NAFE, Sigma Delta Tau Alumni Assn. (pres. 1995). Jewish. Home: 211 N Citrus # 220 Escondido CA 92027

PANNELL, KIMBERLEY, magazine publishing administrator; b. Toronto, Nov. 10, 1966; d. Keith and Nancy (Pratt) P. BA, U. Tex., El Paso, 1990. Prodn. mgr. Twin Plant News, El Paso, 1991—; master cons. Mary Kay Cosmetics, El Paso, 1992—; owner mktg. co. Fresh Ideas, 1991—. Mem. Am. Advt. Fedn., Women In Action. Office: Twin Plant News 4110 Rio Bravo Ste 108 El Paso TX 79902

PANNELL-WOJAK, ANGELIA MARIE, artist, art educator; b. Springfield, Mo., June 22, 1968; d. Laurel Lester and Charlene (Caufield) P. BFA, Sch. Visual Arts, N.Y.C., 1990; MFA, U. Mo., 1992. Grad. instr. U. Mo., Columbia, 1990-95; adj. asst. prof. Lincoln U., Jefferson City, Mo., 1994; graphic design artist Mus. Art and Archaeology, Columbia, Mo., 1993. Exhibited in shows including North Valley Art League, Redding, Calif., 1993 (Gold medal), Berkeley (Calif.) Art Ctr Assn., 1993 (Juror's award), Nat. Oil and Acrylic Painters Soc. Exhibit '93, 1994, The Am. Drawing Biennial IV, 1994. Mem. Nat. Women's Caucus for Art, St. Louis Women's Caucus for Art. Democrat. Home: 2800 Tower Rd Lebanon MO 65536

PANNER, JEANNIE HARRIGAN, electrical engineer; b. Malone, N.Y., Jan. 4, 1948; d. Martin Thomas and Marjorie (Boyea) Harrigan; m. John Charles Panner, Aug. 17, 1974. BS summa cum laude, SUNY, Plattsburgh, 1970; MA in Math., U. Vt., 1974, MSEE, 1993. Programmer Microelectronics Divsn. IBM, Burlington, Vt., 1970-71, assoc. programmer, 1971-74, sr. assoc. programmer, 1974-79, staff engr., 1979-85, adv. engr., 1985-90, sr. engr., 1990—. Contbr. articles to engring. jours.; patentee in field. Mem. IEEE, ACM. Home: RR 1 Box 1310 Underhill VT 05489-9405

PANNIER, JUDITH MARIE SMITH, counselor; b. Little Rock, Mar. 20, 1947; d. John McCollough and Edith Marie (Angehr) Smith; m. Dan Henry Lee III, June 1, 1968 (div. Dec. 1981); 1 child, Susannah McCormick Lee; m. Robert Andrew Pannier, Feb. 18, 1991. BA, So. Methodist U., 1969; MA, Gallaudet U., 1976. Cert. profl. counselor; cert. advanced profl. guidance counselor, Md.; nat. bd. cert. counselors. Counselor, family services specialist Md. Sch. for the Deaf, Columbia, 1976—. Mem. Am. Counseling Assn. Home: 537 River Bend Rd Great Falls VA 22066 Office: Md Sch for the Deaf P O Box 894 Columbia MD 21044

PANNKE, PEGGY M., insurance agency executive; b. Chgo., Oct. 26; d. Victor E. and Leona (O'Leary) Stich; children: Thomas Scott, David Savonne, Heidi Mireille, Peter Helmut. Office mgr. DeHaan & Richter P.C., Chgo. and Des Plaines, Ill., 1983-86; v.p. long term care ins. Sales & Seminars, Des Plaines, 1986-90; pres., founder Nat. Consumer Oriented Agy., Des Plaines, 1990—; cons. on long-term care ins. The Travelers, Tchrs. Ins. & Annuity Assocs., and numerous other ins. cos., N.Y.C., Hartford, Conn. and throughout U.S.; speaker Exec. Enterprises, N.Y.C., 1988-93. Contbr. articles on long-term care ins. to profl. jours.; columnist Senior News. Sponsor Ill. Alliance for Aging, Chgo., 1990—, Ill. Assn. Homes for Aging, 1990-91; bd. govs. St. Matthew Luth. Home, Park Ridge, Ill., 1993-95. Recipient Speakers awards Health Ins. Assn. Am., Washington, 1990, Retired Officers Assn., Glenview, Ill., 1991, 93, Nat. Assn. Sr. Living Industries, Denver, 1992, Exec. Enterprises, N.Y.C., 1993. Mem. Nat. Assn. Sr. Living Industries, Nat. Assn. Long Term Care Profls. (charter), Ctr. for Applied Gerontology, Nat. Coun. on Aging, Mature Ams. (ad hoc com.), Am. Mensa of Ill. (program dir. 1983-85), Kiwanis (bd. dirs. Park Ridge 1992—, pres. 1996—), Am. Soc. on Aging, Internat. Soc. for Retirement Planning. Office: Nat Consumer Oriented Agy 2200 E Devon Ste 356 Des Plaines IL 60018-4503

PANNULLO, DEBORAH PAOLINO, manufacturing company executive; b. Providence, Apr. 2, 1953; d. Joseph and Lena (Wilde) Paolino; m. Michael J. Pannullo, Apr. 23, 1971 (div. 1973); 1 child, Melissa Jean. BA in Econs., R.I. Coll., 1977; cert. in mfg. mgmt., Bryant Coll., 1982, MBA, 1987; postgrad., Roger Williams U. Law Sch. Payroll analyst Bostitch/Textron, East Greenwich, R.I., 1977-79, cost analyst, 1979-80, U.S. mfg. coordinator, 1980-82, quality circles mgr., 1982-85; productivity mgr. Stanley Fastening Systems, East Greenwich, 1985-87; dir. quality assurance-productivity improvement Stanley-Bostitch, East Greenwich, 1987-91, plant mgr., 1991-95; pvt. mgmt. cons., trainer, 1995—; pres. Pannullo and Assocs.; adj. faculty R.I. Coll.; part-time instr. Bryant Coll.; cons. Small Bus. Devel. Ctr. Bd. dirs. R.I. Anti Drug Coalition. Named outstanding Woman of Yr. WMCA, 1985. Mem. NAFE, Am. Soc. Quality Assurance, Internat. Assn. Quality Circles (pres.1984-85, bd. dirs. R.I. chpt. 1985—), R.I. Tech. Coun. (chairperson quality assurance sub-com.), R.I. Coll. Alumni Assn. (exec. bd. dirs.), Delta Mu Delta. Roman Catholic. Home: 17 Hawkins St Greenville RI 02828-3103

PANTELAS, ANNE, accountant, finance specialist, consultant; b. Athienou, Cyprus, Australia, Dec. 16, 1957; d. Nick and Chrystalla (Papapetrou) P.; m. Oliver Andreas Hemmers, Nov. 22, 1992. B of Econs., U. Sydney, Australia, 1980; M of Commerce/Fin., U. NSW, Australia, 1992. CPA, Australia. Indsl. analyst The Prudential Assurance, Sydney, 1980-82; analyst Marshall's Reports, Sydney, 1983-84; mgr. corp. and internat. banking Nat. Mut. Royal Bank, Sydney, 1984-90; mgr. corp. banking State Bank of South Australia, Sydney, 1990-92; cons. Las Vegas, Nev., 1994-95; pres. FBA Las Vegas, 1995—; cons. Bus. Guide program Las Vegas C. of C., 1995—. Mem. Inst. Mgmt. Accts. (dir. 1995-96, dir. meetings 1996—), Securities Inst. Australia, Australian Soc. Accts. (assoc.), Nat. Soc. Pub. Accts. Home and Office: 5370 Angler Cir # 102 Las Vegas NV 89122

PANTER, TERRY EVE, accountant; b. Copperhill, Tenn., Apr. 30, 1957; d. Wallace Lloyd Panter and Lelia Louise (Burk) Baggett. BBA, Kennesaw (Ga.) Coll., 1983. CPA, Ga. Owner Panter Acctg. Svcs., Marietta, Ga. Mem. AICPA, Kennesaw Coll. Alumni Assn. Mem. Ch. of Christ. Home: 727 Bonnie Dell Dr Marietta GA 30062-3430 Office: Panter CPAs PO Box 7424 Marietta GA 30065

PAOLONI, VIRGINIA ANN, insurance company executive; b. Scranton, Pa., July 26, 1961; d. Edmund James and Virginia (Borick) P. BS in Mktg., King's Coll., 1983; MBA in Mktg., U. Scranton, 1995. Underwriter Reliance Ins., Phila., 1983-85; account exec. The Walsh Co., Phila., 1984-87; pres. Paoloni Ins. Agy., Olyphant, Pa., 1987—. Participant Leadership Lackawanna, Scranton, 1991—; bd. dirs. fin. planning Holy Name of Jesus Ch., Scranton, 1990-94; mem. allocation steering com. United Way, 1992-93; bd. dirs., chair corp. sponsorship Am. Heart Assn.; mem. pub. rels. com. Habitat for Humanity, 1993—. Mem. Greater Scranton Ins. Assn. (bd. dirs., chair edn. com. 1989—, 1st v.p.), Jr. League (chair strategic planning). Republican. Roman Catholic. Home: 1611 Wyoming Ave Scranton PA 18509-1960 Office: Paoloni Ins Agy 766 N Valley Ave Olyphant PA 18447-1716

PAOLUCCI, ANNE ATTURA, playwright, poet, English and comparative literature educator; b. Rome; d. Joseph and Lucy (Guidoni) Attura; m. Henry Paolucci. BA, Barnard Coll; MA, Columbia U., PhD, 1963; hon. degree, Lehman Coll., CUNY, 1995. Mem. faculty English dept. Brearley Sch., N.Y.C., 1957-59; asst. prof. English and comparative lit. CCNY, 1959-69; univ. research prof. St. John's U., Jamaica, N.Y., 1969—; prof. English St. John's U., 1975—, acting head dept. English, 1973-74, chmn. dept. English, 1982-91, dir. doctor of arts degree program in English, 1982—; Fulbright lectr. in Am. drama U. Naples, Italy, 1965-67; spl. lectr. U. Urbino, summers 1966-67, U. Bari, 1967, univs. Bologna, Catania, Messina, Palermo, Milan, Pisa, 1965-67; disting. adj. vis. prof. Queens Coll., CUNY; bd. dirs. World Centre for Shakespeare Studies, 1972—; spl. guest Yugoslavia Ministry of Culture, 1972; rep. U.S. at Internat. Poetry Festival, Yugoslavia, 1981; founder, exec. dir. Council on Nat. Lits., 1974—; mem. exec. com. Conf. Editors Learned Jours.-MLA, 1975—; del. to Fgn. Lang. Jours., 1977—; mem. adv. bd. Commn. on Tech. and Cultural Transformation, UNESCO, 1978—; vis. fellow Humanities Research Centre, Australian Nat. U., 1979; rep. U.S. woman playwright Inter-Am. Women Writers Congress, Ottawa, Ont., Can., 1978; organizer, chmn. profl. symposia, meetings; TV appearances; hostess Mags. in Focus, Channel 31, N.Y.C., 1971-72; mem. N.Am. Adv. Council Shakespeare Globe Theatre Center, 1981—; mem. Nat. Grad. Fellows Program Fellowship Bd., 1985—; mem. Nat. Garibaldi Centennial Com., 1981; mem. Nat. Grad. Fellows Program, 1985—; trustee Edn. Scholarship, Grants Com. of NIAF, 1990—; guest speaker with E. Albee Ohio No. State U., 1990. Author (with H. Paolucci) books, including: Hegel On Tragedy, 1962, From Tension to Tonic: The Plays of Edward Albee, 1972, Pirandello's Theater: The Recovery of the Modern Stage for Dramatic Art, 1974, Poems Written for Sbek's Mummies, Marie Menken, and Other Important Persons, Places, and Things, 1977, Eight Short Stories, 1977, Sepia Prints, 1985, 2nd edit., 1986; plays include: Minions of the Race (Medieval and Renaissance Conf. of Western Mich. U. Drama award 1972), Cipango!, 1985, pub. as book, 1985, 86, videotape excerpts, 1986, revision, 1990; performed N.Y.C. and Washington, 1987-88, Winterthur Mus., U. Del., 1990; The Actor in Search of His Mask, 1987, Italian translation and prodn., Genoa, 1987, The Short Season, Naples, 1967, Cubiculo, N.Y., 1973, German translation, Vienna, 1996, Three Short Plays, 1995; poems Riding the Mast Where It Swings, 1980, Gorbachev in Concert, 1991, Queensboro Bridge (and other Poems), 1995 (Pulitzer prize nominee 1995-96); contbr. numerous articles, rev. to profl. jours.; editor, author introduction to: Dante's Influence on American Writers, 1977; gen. editor tape-cassette series China, 1977, 78; founder Coun. on Nat. Lit.; gen. editor series Rev. Nat. Lits., 1970—, CNL/Quar. World Report, 1974-76, semi-ann., 1977-84, ann., 1985—; full-length TV tape of play Cipango! for pub. TV and ednl. TV with original music by Henry Paolucci, 1990. Bd. dirs. Italian Heritage and Culture City-wide com., 1986—; Pres. Reagan appointee Nat. Grad. Fellows Program Fellowship Bd., 1985-86, Nat. Coun. Humanities, 1986—, Ann. award, FIERI, 1990; pres. Columbus: Countdown, 1992 Fedn.; mem. Gov. Cuomo's Heritage Legacy Project for Schs., 1989—; bd. dirs. Am. Soc. Italian Legions of Merit (chmn. cultural com. 1990—); trustee CUNY, 1996—; mem. adv. com. on edn. N.Y. State Senate, 1996—. Named one of 10 Outstanding Italian Ams. in Washington, awarded medal by Amb. Rinaldo Petrignani, 1986; named Cavaliere Italian Republic, 1986, "Commendatore" of the Italian Republic Order of Merit, 1992; recipient Notable Rating for Mags. in Focus series N.Y. Times, 1972, Woman of Yr. award Dr. Herman Henry Scholarship Found., 1973, Amita award, 1970, award Women's Press Club N.Y., 1974, Order Merit, Italian Republic, 1986, Gold medal for Quincentenary Can. trustee NIIAF, 1990, ann. awards Consortium of Italian-Am. Assns., 1991, Am.-Italian Hist. Assn., 1991, 1st Columbus award Cath. Charities, 1991, Leone di San Marco award Italian Heritage Coun. of Bronx and Westchester Counties, 1992, Children of Columbus award Order of Sons of Italy in Am., 1993, 1st Nat. Elena Cornaro award Order of Sons of Italy, 1993; Columbia U. Woodbridge hon. fellow, 1961-62; Am. Council Learned Socs. grantee Internat. Pirandello Congress, Agrigento, Italy, 1978. Mem. Internat. Shakespeare Assn., Shakespeare Assn. Am., Renaissance Soc. Am., Renaissance Inst. Japan, Internat. Comparative Lit. Assn., Am. Comparative Lit. Assn., MLA, Am. PEN, Hegel Soc. Am., Dante Soc. Am. (v.p. 1976-77), Am. Found. Italian Arts and Letters (founder, pres.), Pirandello Soc. (pres. 1978—), Nat. Soc. Lit. and Arts, Nat. Book Critics Circle, Am. Soc. Italian Legions of Merit (bd. dirs. 1990—). Office: St Johns U Dept English Jamaica NY 11439

PAPADAKOS, DOROTHY JEAN, composer, organist; b. Coral Gables, Fla., Oct. 22, 1960; d. Peter James Papadakos and Dorothy Mae Johnson. BA, Barnard Coll., 1982; MM, Juilliard Sch., 1986. Organist, choirmaster St. Mark's Ch., Islip, N.Y., 1980-85; asst. organist Cathedral of St. John the Divine, N.Y.C., 1987-89, cathedral organist, 1990—; artistic dir. Vespers Improvisation Series, Cathedral St. John the Divine, N.Y.C., 1995; mem. Paul Winter Consort, Litchfield, Conn., 1984—; project dir. Gt. Organ Restoration Fund, Cathedral St. John the Divine, N.Y.C., 1990—. Composer: (orch. works for ballet) Triantafilia, 1992, Overture and Variation in E flat, 1991; improviser, performer: (CD rec.) Dorothy Over the Rainbow, 1996. Mem. adv. bd. AIDS Action, Internat., N.Y.C., 1994—. Composition grantee Meet the Composer, 1991, 92. Mem. ASCAP, Am. Guild Organists (1st prize N.Y.C. chpt. 1983). Democrat. Episcopalian. Home: 1047 Amsterdam Ave New York NY 10025 Office: Cathedral St John Divine 1047 Amsterdam Ave New York NY 10025

PAPADOPOULOS, PATRICIA MARIE, healthcare professional. AAS, No. Va. Community Coll., 1970; BS, George Mason U., 1988; MS, Va. Poly. Inst., 1992. RN, Va.; cert. nursing adminstr. Staff nurse ICU, PACU Jefferson Meml. Hosp., Alexandria, Va.; dept. dir. PACU Nat. Hosp. for Orthopedics and Rehab., Arlington, Va., 1977-82; dir. med. surg. dept. Nat. Hosp. for Orthopedics and Rehab., 1982-85, house supr., 1985-89; dir. nursing ops. Nat. Hosp. for Orthopedics and Rehab., Arlington, Va., 1989-92; asst. dir. emergency svcs. Potomac Hosp., Woodbridge, Va., 1992-95; dir. ICU Nat. Hosp. Med. Ctr., Arlington, Va., 1995; dir. nursing resources and ops. Nat. Hosp. Med. Ctr., 1995—. Mem. Emergency Nurses Assn. Office: 2455 Army Navy Dr Arlington VA 22206-2905

PAPANO, SUSAN G., lawyer; b. N.Y.C., Dec. 18, 1957. BA summa cum laude, Bklyn Coll., 1978; JD cum laude, Bklyn. Law Sch., 1983. Bar: N.Y. 1984, U.S. Dist. Ct. (so. and ea. dists.) N.Y. 1984. Law clk. to judge U.S. Bankruptcy Ct. (so. dist.) N.Y., 1983-85; ptnr. Anderson Kill Olick & Oshinsky, N.Y.C. Mem. Assn. of Bar of City of N.Y. Office: Anderson Kill Olick & Oshinsky 1251 Ave of the Americas New York NY 10020-1182*

PAPE, SHARON BETH, occupational therapist; b. Milw., June 2, 1964; d. Henry John and Marianne Irene Pape. BS in Occupl. Therapy, U. Wis., Milw., 1987. Registered occupl. therapist, Ind. Occupl. therapist Meml. Hosp., South Bend, Ind., 1987-89, Deaconess Hosp., Evansville, Ind., 1989-91; instr. occupl. therapy Marshall U. Sch. Medicine, Huntington, W.Va., 1991-94, coord. field work program, 1992-94, cons. rural geriatric program dept. family-cmty. health, 1993-94; occupl. therapist NovaCare, Inc., Indpls., 1995—; clin. rep. occupl. therapy program Shawnee State U., Portsmouth, Ohio, 1993-94; presenter in field. Contbr. articles to profl. jours. Project coord. youth yellow pages text Deaconess Hosp.-United Way Assn., 1986-87. Recipient Sousa award Pulaski H.S., 1982. Mem. Am. Occupl. Therapy Assn. (Brittell COTA-OTR Partnership award 1995), Ind. Occupl. Therapy Assn. Office: NovaCare Inc 3351 N Meridian Ste 201 Indianapolis IN 46208

PAPENTHIEN, RUTH MARY, fiber artist, retired art educator; b. Milw., Aug. 30, 1924; d. Roy Oliver and Hazel Mary (Heyer) P. BA, U. Wis.,

1946; student, The Konstfackskolan, Stockholm, 1959-60, The Konst Facks Kolan, Stockholm, 1959-60; MFA, Cranbrook Acad. Art, Bloomfield Hills, Mich., 1965. Elem. sch. tchr. Milw. Pub. Schs., 1948-63; instr. fiber art Alverno Coll., Milw., 1966-67; vis. instr. fiber art Sch. Fine Arts Ohio State U., Columbus, 1967-72; fiber art instr. Arrowmont Sch. Arts and Crafts, Gatlinburg, Tenn., summer 1970; vis. artist fiber art Ball State U., Gatlinburg, Tenn., 1972; asst. prof. fiber art Tyler Sch. Art Temple U., Phila., summer 1973. One-woman shows include Alverno Coll., Milw., 1967, Ohio State U. Union, Columbus, 1968, The Liturgical Arts, St. Luke's Meth. Ch., Oklahoma City, 1974; exhibited in group shows in Wis. Designer Craftsmen exhbns. at Milw. Arts Ctr. (Anonymous Donor award 1963, 64, Court of Honor 1965, 66, 70, 71), Miss. River Craft Exhbn., Brooks Meml. Art Gallery, Memphis, 1963, Detroit Art Inst., 1964, Rockford (Ill.) Art Assn. Burpee Gallery of Art, 1964, 65 (1st pl. and hon. mention 1966), Rochester (Minn.) Art Ctr., 1967, Capital U., Columbus (Liturgical Art award 1967, 71, 73), Coll. Wooster, Ohio, 1970, Midland (Mich.) Art Ctr., 1972, Ball State U., Muncie, Ind., 1972, S.C. Johnson Collection Contemporary Crafts, 1970-72, Ohio State U., 1972, Huntington Nat. Bank and Trust Co., Columbus, 1972, Ozaukee Art Ctr., Cedarburg, Wis., 1976, West Bend (Wis.) Gallery Fine Arts, 1978, Peninsula Mus. Art, Newport News, Va., 1995; represented in permanent collections Alverno Coll., Milw., Ohio Hist. Ctr., Columbus, Ohio Med. Indemnity Inc., Columbus, Karlsberger and Assoc. AIA, Columbus, U. Rochester (N.Y.) Meml. Gallery, IBM Bldg., Columbus; represented in pvt. collections in Ohio, Wis., Fla., La., Calif., Va.; contbr. artwork to jours. Home: 208 Woodmere Dr Williamsburg VA 23185

PAPI, LIZA, artist, writer, educator; b. Malacacheta, Minas Gerais, Brazil, Jan. 19, 1949; came to U.S., 1978; d. Rivadavia and Lair Bronzon Papi; 1 child. BA, Inst. Fine Arts Rio de Janeiro, 1974; MFA, CUNY, 1992. Art instr. CUNY, Henry St. Settlement, N.Y.C., Third St. Music; illustrator Studio T. Graphics, N.Y.C.; artist in residence Mus. del Barrio, N.Y.C., 1994-95; dir. publicity Art Sphere Cultural Ctr., N.Y.C., 1990-91; coord. Americanos, N.Y.C., 1990-94. Author: The Vanishing Beetles, 1991, Carnavalia, African Brazilian Folklore and Crafts, 1994. Residency planning grantee N.Y. Found. Arts, 1994. Mem. Soka Gankai Internat., Art Coll. Assn., The Fgn. Press. Buddhist. Office: Papi Studio 231 W 25th St #3D New York NY 10001

PAPPALARDO-MURPHY, DEBRA MARIE, human resources specialist; b. New Rochelle, N.Y., Oct. 6, 1962; d. Anthony N. and Joan M. (Foti) Pappalardo; m. Robert Evans Murphy, Oct. 21, 1995; 1 child, Connor Murphy. BA, SUNY, Albany, 1984; MA, Columbia U., 1985. Human resources mgr. Pergamon Press, Elmsford, N.Y., 1985-91, Macmillan Pub., Greenwich, Conn., 1992-93, USF&G, Purchase, N.Y., 1992-95; v.p., human resources Kraft Foods Fed. Credit Union, White Plains, N.Y., 1995—. Mem. soc. for Human Resources Mgmt., CUNA Human Resources Coun. Office: Kraft Foods Fed Credit 77 Westchester Ave White Plains NY 10604-3528

PAPPAS, EFFIE VAMIS, English and business educator, writer; b. Cleve., Dec. 26, 1924; d. James Jacob and Helen Joy (Nicholson) Vamis; m. Leonard G. Pappas, Nov. 3, 1945; children: Karen Pappas Morabito, Leonard J., Ellen Pappas Daniels, David James. BBA, Western Res. U., 1948; MA in Edn., Case Western Res. U., 1964; MA in English Lit., Cleve. State U., 1986; postgrad., Indiana U. Pa., 1979-80, 81-86. Cert. elem. and secondary tchr., Ohio. Tchr. elem. schs., Ohio, 1963-70; office mgr. Cleve. State U., 1970-72, adminstr. pub. relations, 1972-73; med. adminstr. Brecksville (Ohio) VA Hosp., 1974-78; lectr. English, bus. mgmt., math., comm., composition Cuyahoga C.C., Cleve., 1978-92; tchg. asst. Case Western Reserve U., 1979-80; lectr. bus. comms. Cleve. State U., 1980; participant in Sci. and Cultural Exch. dels. Am. Inst. Chemists, to Peoples Republic of China, 1984 and to Soviet Union, 1989. Feature writer The Voice, 1970-78; editor, writer Cleve. State U. newsletter and mag., 1970-73. Cub scout den mother Boy Scouts Am., Brecksville, 1960; mem. local coun. PTA, 1965-70; sec. St. Paul's Coun., 1990-91; Sunday Sch. tchr., mem. choir Brecksville United Ch. of Christ, 1975-76, mem. bd. missions, 1966-67, membership com. 1993, St. Paul Ladies Philoptohos, 1990-96; mem. Women's Econ. Action League. Recipient Editor's Choice award for outstanding achievement in poetry, Nat. Libr. of Poetry, 1995; grantee Cuyahoga C.C., 1982; named to Nat. Women's Hall of Fame. Mem. NEA, NAFE, AAUW (legis. chair, del. Ohio meetings 1993, 94, del. Ohio Coalition for Change, 1993, 94, mem. Ohio and Cleve. br. del. Gt. Lakes regional meeting 1994, internat. co-chair Cleve. br. 1994, 96—, del. to Internat. Fedn. Univ. Women triennial meeting Stanford U. 1992), AARP, Ohio Edn. Assn. (rep. assembly Columbus 1994), Nat. Mus. Women in Arts (hon. roll mem.), Nat. Trust for Hist. Preservation, Case Western Res. U. Planning Com. for Edn. Forum, Greater Cleve. Learning Project, Nature Conservancy, Smithsonian Instn., Internat. Soc. Poets. Home: 8681 Brecksville Rd Cleveland OH 44141-1912

PAPPAS, MARIA ELENI, nurse; b. Encino, Calif., Oct. 1, 1960; d. Nicholas Constantine and Helen Cleo (Tannors) P. BSN, U. San Francisco, 1985; M in Nursing, UCLA, 1991. Cert. critical care nurse, pub. health nurse. Staff med./surg. nurse VA Med. Ctr., West L.A., 1985-87; staff nurse ICU VA Med. Ctr., San Francisco, 1987-88; staff nurse SICU St. Mary's Hosp., San Francisco, 1988-89; staff nurse ICU St. Joseph's Hosp., Burbank, Calif., 1989-91; clin. nurse specialist Northridge (Calif.) Hosp. Med. Ctr., 1991-95; asst. clin. prof. Sch. Nursing, UCLA, 1993—. Co-author: (manual) Brain Death Policy Manual, 1993. VA scholar U. San Francisco, 1984, Reynolds Estate scholar UCLA, 1991. Mem. Sigma Theta Tau (Outstanding Contbn. award 1989). Greek Orthodox. Home: 8012 Comanche Ave Winnetka CA 91306-1832 Office: Raytel Heart Ctr 10445 Balboa Blvd Granada Hills CA 91394-9400

PARADIS, VICTORIA MAY, financial analyst; b. Deerfield, Ill., Nov. 22, 1966; d. Lawrence Chester and Christine Adele (Becker) May; m. Michael Charles Paradis, Sept. 22, 1990. BA, Cornell U., 1988; MBA, Columbia U., 1992. CFA. Staff auditor pension investment Prudential Ins., South Plainfield, N.J., 1988-91; asst. v.p. Becker & Rooney divsn. Kwasha Lipton, Ft. Lee, N.J., 1992-96; product specialist Pacific Investment Mgmt. Co., Newport Beach, Calif., 1996—. Mem. Beta Gamma Sigma. Home: 33 Maplewood Ave Maplewood NJ 07040

PARAISO, JOHNNA KAYE, elementary education educator; b. Wyandotte, Mich., Nov. 17, 1961; d. John Calvin and Ruth (Hughes) Underwood; m. Normandy Paraiso, Oct. 6, 1984; children: Sophia Elisabeth, Abigail Mahalia, Genevieve Christine. BS, Bob Jones U., 1983. Cert. ACSI, educator K-8 (all subjects). Tchr. fifth grade Temple Christian Sch., Redford, Mich., 1983-86; music tchr. Fairlane Christian Sch., Dearborn Heights, Mich., 1986-90; tchr. 2d grade Internat. Christian Sch., San Francisco, 1992-93, dept. head primary childhood edn., 1992-93; freelance musician children's concerts; leader Curriculum Selection Com.; initiator Elem. Music Program; dir. several dramatic prodns.; tchr. piano, guitar. Children's minister 1st Bapt. Ch., San Francisco, 1991-94. Mem. Pi Lambda Theta. Home: 2024 Stonebrook Rd Murfreesboro TN 37129

PARALEZ, LINDA LEE, technology management consultant; b. Raton, N.Mex., Oct. 29, 1955. AS, Amarillo Coll., 1975; student West Tex. State U., 1975-77, BBA, Century U., Beverly Hills, Calif., 1984, MBA, 1987, PhD in Bus. Mgmt. and Econ. Century U. Teaching asst. Amarillo (Tex.) Coll., 1974-75; drafter natural gas div. Pioneer Corp., Amarillo, 1975-76, sr. drafter exploration div. Amarillo Oil Co. 1976-77; drafting supr., engring. svcs. supr., dir. speakers' bur. Thunder Basin Coal Co., Atlantic Richfield Co., Wright, Wyo., 1977-86; ptnr., tech. and adminstrv. cons. Rose Enterprises, 1986—; prof. U. Phoenix, Utah; adj. prof. Weber State U., Ogden, Utah; tech. writer Eaton Corp., Riverton, Wyo., 1986-88; cons. State Wyo. Office on Family Violence and Sexual Assault, Cheyenne, 1986-89; Diamond L Industries, Inc., Gillette, Wyo., 1986-88; tech. writer, pubs. cons. Thiokol Corp., Brigham City, Utah, 1987-89, design specialist space ops., 1989-90, mgr. total quality mgmt. ctr. space ops., 1990—, cons. organizational effectiveness and quality mgmt. principles; cons. incident investigation team NASA Solid Rocket Booster Program, Huntsville, Ala.; cons. process improvement Puget Power, Seattle, Wash., Pub. Svc. Co. of Colo., W.R. White Co.; cons. process design Microsoft Corp., Seattle. Author: (poetry) God was Here, But He Left Early, 1976, Gift of Wings, 1980, 89; columnist Wytech Digest; contbr. numerous articles to profl. jours. Vol. NASA Young Astronauts Program Adv. Com., 1991—; bd. dirs. Campbell County Drafting Adv. Coun., 1984-85; sec. bd. dir. exec. com. Am. Inst. Design and Drafting, 1984-85, tech. publ. chairperson, 1984-85; vol. educator, data specialist child abuse prevention coun. Ogden. Named Most Outstanding Woman, Beta Sigma Phi, 1980, 81; recipient Woman in the Industry recognition Internat. Reprographics Assn., 1980; grand prize winner Wyo. Art Show with painting titled Energy, 1976. Mem. AAUW, NAFE, NOW, Am. Soc. Quality Control, Am. Productivity and Quality Coun., Am. Legion Aux., Ocean Rsch. Edn. Soc., Gloucester, Mass. (grant proposal writer, 1984), Soc. Tech. Communications, 4-H Club. Home: 2888 N 1300 E Ogden UT 84414-2607

PARAS, SOFIA DIMITRIA, counselor, writer, editor; b. Delaware, Ohio, Dec. 31, 1943; d. James Peter and Fotini Dimitria (Dellios) Stoycheff; m. Nicholas Andrew Paras, Dec. 8, 1968; 1 child, Alexandra Nicholas. BA, Ohio Wesleyan U., 1965; cert., Adelphi U., 1987. Tchr. Upper Arlington Schs., Columbus, Ohio, 1966-68; asst. tng. coord. personnel dept. Ohio State U. Hosps., Columbus, 1968-69, art fair coord., 1969; asst. tng. coord. personnel dept. New Eng. Deaconess Hosp., Boston, 1969-70; tng. coord. nursing dept. Meml. Hosp. of Sloan Kettering, N.Y.C., 1970-71; real estate salesperson Gen. Devel. Corp., 1971-72; adminstrv. asst. Ippocampos Maritime and Internship Fin. and Investments, Piraeus, Greece, 1976-81; office mgr. Internapa Fin. Svcs., Athens, Greece, 1981-86; adminstrv. dir. lawyer's asst. program Adelphi U., West Hempstead, N.Y., 1987-88, admissions counselor lawyer's asst. program, 1988—; cons. interior decorator hotel complex Paramount Tourist and Devel. Ltd., Paralimni, Cyprus, 1981-84; nat. nursing conf. coord. Meml. Hosp. Sloan Kettering, St. Louis, 1971. Editor Women's Internat. Club, Athens, 1978-84; author: (poetry) Observations, 1990, (screenplays) Contract I, 1990, Contract II, 1991, Mindlock, 1995, Reasonable in Richmond, 1996, Shipping Wars, 1996; editor: Traditional Hellenic Tastes (in Greek and English langs.), 1994. Theatre dir. Am. Farm Sch., Salonica, Greece, 1974; program coord. choir recitals St. Nicholas Greek Orthodox, Babylon, N.Y., 1989—; v.p. Internat. Women's Orgn. of Greece, Salonica, 1973-74; sec. Christian Orthodox Fellowship, Inc. Mem. Kappa Kappa Gamma, Theta Alpha Phi.

PARATJE, MERCEDES, bank executive; b. Barcelona, Spain; m. Sergio Verdu; 1 child, Ariana Verdu. Grad. telecommunications engring., Poly. U. Barcelona, 1981; MA in Labor Rels., U. Ill., 1983, MBA in Fin., 1985. Lic. stockbroker. Engr. N.V. Philips, Barcelona, 1978-81; fin. analyst Ctr. Internat. Fin. Analysis, Princeton, N.J., 1985-87; rsch. mgr. Ctr. Internat. Fin. Analysis, 1987-88; 2nd v.p., investment strategist internat. pvt. bank Chase Manhattan Bank, N.Y.C., 1988-90, 2d v.p., internat. equity analyst, 1990-91; v.p., portfolio mgr. pvt. banking internat. The Chase Manhattan Pvt. Bank, N.Y.C., 1991-94; v.p., global product head equity adv. svcs. Citicorp Securities Pvt. Bank Divsn., 1994—. Co-editor: Worldscope, Industrial, 1988; contbg. researcher: Worldscope, Financial, 1988, International Accounting Trends, 1989; contbr. articles to profl. publs. Mem. European Register Tech. Professions, Nat. Assn. Tech. Engrs. (prize 1981), Sigma Iota Epsilon. Home: 6 Farrand Rd Princeton NJ 08540-6777 Office: Citicorp Securities Citicorp Ctr 15th Flr 153 E 53rd St New York NY 10022-4602

PARCH, GRACE DOLORES, librarian; b. Cleve., May ; d. Joseph Charles and Josephine Dorothy (Kumel) P. B.A., Case Western Res. U., 1946, postgrad., 1947-50; B.L.S., McGill U., 1951; M.L.S., Kent State U., 1983; postgrad., Newspaper Library Workshop, Kent State U., 1970, Cooper Sch. Art, 1971-72, API Newspaper Library Seminar, Columbia U., 1971, Coll. Librarianship, U. Wales, 1984, 85. Cert. literacy instr., Ohio. Publicity librarian Spl. Services U.S. Army, Germany, 1951; post librarian Spl. Services U.S. Army, Italy, 1952; USAF base librarian, 1953-54; br. librarian Cleveland Heights (Ohio) Pub. Library, 1954-63; asst. head reference div. Va. State Library, Richmond, 1964; dir. Twinsburg (Ohio) Pub. Library, 1965-70; dir. newspaper library Cleve. Plain Dealer, 1970-83; county librarian N.C., 1987-92; cons. Cath. Library Assn., 1961-64; mem. home econs. adv. com., Summit County, 1969, books/job com., 1968; mem. adv. com. Guide to Ohio Newspapers, 1793-1973, 1971-74; appointed to del. spl. libs. for People-to-People Program in Russia, 1995. Contbr. articles to Plain Dealer, N. Summit Times, Twinsburg Bull., Sun Press; author: Where In the World But in the Plain Dealer Library, 1971; Editor: Directory of Newspaper Libraries in the U.S. and Canada, 1976. Recipient MacArthur Found. award, 1988, Libr. of Am. award, 1988. Mem. McGill U. Alumnae Assn. (sec. 1973), Kent State U. Alumni Assn., ALA (rep. on joint com. with Cath. Library Assn. 1967-70), John Cotton Dana award 1967, Library Pub. Rels. Coun. award 1972), Cath. Library Assn. (co-chmn. 1960-63), Spl. Libraries Assn. (chmn. newspaper library directory com. 1974-76, chmn. pub. relations Cleve. chpt. 1973, chmn. edn. com. newspaper div. 1982-83, mem. edn. com. nominating com. 1984), Ohio Library Assn., Western Res. Hist. Soc., Am. Soc. Indexers, Cleve. Mus. Art Assn., Coll. and Research Librarians, Nat. Micrographic Assn., Women Space, Women's Nat. Book Com., Nat. Trust Hist. Preservation. Roman Catholic. Clubs: Cleve. Athletic, Cleve. Women's City. Home: 688 Jefferson St Bedford OH 44146-3711

PARDO, MARIAN URSULA, investment management company executive; b. Rockville Centre, N.Y., Sept. 23, 1946; d. Francis V. and Dorothy E. (Bellidora) P.; BA, Barnard Coll., 1968; m. Michael S. Toonkel. With J.P. Morgan Cos., N.Y.C., 1968—, v.p. investment group, 1980-95, mng. dir., 1995—. Former chmn. bd. dirs. Opportunity Resources for Arts. Mem. Columbus Citizens Found., Bank & Fin. Analysts Assn. Office: JP Morgan Investment 522 Fifth Ave New York NY 10036

PARDUE, KAREN REIKO, elementary education educator; b. Honolulu, June 13, 1947; d. Rex Shinzen and Ruth Fujiko (Arakawa) Ishiara; m. Jerry Thomas Pardue, Oct. 21, 1978 (dec. Sept. 1994); 1 child, Holly. BS, Western Ill. U., 1969; MA, U. No. Colo., 1971, 72. Tchr. home econs. Galesburg (Ill.) High Sch., 1969-70; tchr. spl. edn. Jefferson County Pub. Schs., Golden, Colo., 1973-85, 87-94; tchr. 3d & 3d grades Englewood (Colo.) Christian Sch., 1985-86; tchr. 2d grade Jefferson County Pub. Schs., 1994—; adj. instr. Colo. Christian U., Lakewood, 1989—; mem. recommended basic list com. Jefferson County Pub. Schs., 1993-95. Colo. Dept. Edn. Mini grantee, 1976, Jefferson Found. Venture grantee, 1988. Mem. ASCD, Colo. Coun. LEarning Disabilities, Jefferson County Ednl. Assn., Jefferson County Internat. Reading Assn., Delta Kappa Gamma (rec. sec. 1988-89, pres. 1990-92, treas. 1994—).

PARDUE, MARY LOU, biology educator; b. Lexington, Ky., Sept. 15, 1933; d. Louis Arthur and Mary Allie (Marshall) P. B.S., William and Mary Coll., 1955; M.S., U. Tenn., 1959; Ph.D., Yale U., 1970; D.Sc. (hon.), Bard Coll., 1985. Postdoctoral fellow Inst. Animal Genetics, Edinburgh, Scotland, 1970-72; assoc. prof. biology MIT, Cambridge, 1972-80; prof. MIT, 1980—, Boris Magasanik prof. biology, 1995—; summer course organizer Cold Spring Harbor Lab., N.Y., 1971-80; mem. rev. com. NIH, 1974-78, 80-84, nat. adv. gen. med. scis. coun., 1984-86, sci. adv. com. Wistar Inst., Phila, 1976—; mem. health and environ. rsch. adv. com. U.S. Dept. Energy, 1987-94; bd. trustees Associated Universities, Inc., 1995—; Burroughs Wellcome Adv. Com. on Career Awards in Biomed. Scis., 1996—. Mem. editorial bd. Chromosoma, Molecular and Cellular Biology, Biochemistry; contbr. articles to profl. jours. Mem. rev. com. Am. Cancer Soc., 1990-93, Howard Hughes Med. Inst. Adv. Bd., 1993—. Recipient Esther Langer award Langer Cancer Rsch. Found., 1977, Lucius Wilbur Cross medal Yale Grad. Sch., 1989; grantee NIH, NSF, Am. Cancer Soc. Fellow AAAS, NAS (chmn. genetics sect. 1991-94, coun. 1995—), Am. Acad. Arts and Sci. (coun. mem. 1992-96); mem. NRC (bd. on biology 1989-95), Genetics Soc. Am. (pres. 1982-83), Am. Soc. Cell Biology (coun. 1977-80, pres. 1985-86), Phi Beta Kappa, Phi Kappa Phi. Office: MIT Dept Biology 68-670 77 Massachusetts Ave Cambridge MA 02139-4301

PARENT, LOUISE MARIE, lawyer; b. San Francisco, Aug. 28, 1950; d. Jules D. and Mary Louise (Bartholomew) P.; m. John P. Casaly, Jan. 5, 1980. AB, Smith Coll., 1972; JD, Georgetown U., 1975. Bar: N.Y. 1976, U.S. Dist. Ct. (so. dist.) N.Y. 1976. Assoc. Donovan Leisure, N.Y.C., 1975-77; various positions, then gen. counsel Am. Express Info. Svcs. Corp., N.Y.C., 1977-92; dep. gen. counsel Am. Express Co., N.Y.C., 1992-93, exec. v.p., gen. counsel, 1993—; mem. legal adv. com. N.Y. Stock Exch. Bd. dirs. A Better Chance Inc., Cooke Found. Spl. Edn., YWCA of N.Y. Mem. ABA (com. depts. corp. law). Home: 1170 Fifth Ave New York NY 10029-6527 Office: Am Express Co Am Express Tower World Fin Ctr New York NY 10285

PARETSKY, SARA N., writer; b. Ames, Iowa, June 8, 1947; d. David Paretsky and Mary E. Edwards; m. S. Courtenay Wright, June 19, 1976; children: Kimball Courtenay, Timothy Charles, Philip William. BA, U. Kans., 1967; MBA, PhD, U. Chgo., 1977. Mgr. Urban Rsch Ctr., Chgo., 1971-74, CNA Ins. Co., Chgo., 1977-85; writer, 1985—. Author: (novels) Indemnity Only, 1982, Deadlock, 1984 (Friends of Am. Writers award 1985), Killing Orders, 1985, Bitter Medicine, 1987, Blood Shot, 1988 (Silver Dagger award Crime Writers Assn., 1988), Burn Marks, 1990, Guardian Angel, 1992, Tunnel Vision, 1994, also numerous articles and short stories. Pres. Sisters in Crime, Chgo., 1986-88; dir. Nat. Abortion Rights Action League Ill., 1987—. Named Woman of Yr. Ms mag., N.Y.C., 1987. Mem. Crime Writers Assn. (Silver Dagger award 1988), Mystery Writers Am. (v.p. 1989), Authors Guild, Chgo. Network. *

PARHAM, ANNETTE RELAFORD, librarian; b. Petersburg, Va., Dec. 13, 1954; d. William Rosley and Sarah Matthews (Pierce) Relaford; m. Keith Lionel Parham, June 14, 1975; children: Loretta Springfield, Alison Nicole. BSBA, Va. Union U., 1977. File clk. Va. Farm Bur. Mut. Ins., Richmond, Va., 1981-82, ins. rater, 1982-83; file clk. tech. svcs. dept. of libr. Colonial Williamsburg (Va.) Found., 1987-89, acquisitions libr., 1989—. Named to Outstanding Young Women of Am., 1981. Mem. Va. Libr. Assn., Ethnic Librs. Forum. Democrat. Baptist. Office: Colonial Williamsburg Found Dept of Libr 415 N Boundary St Williamsburg VA 23185-3614

PARHAM, BETTY ELY, credit bureau executive; b. Drumright, Okla., Aug. 14, 1928; d. Wayne Albert and Edith May (Ledgerwood) Bingamon; m. Richard D. Ely, Dec. 22, 1946 (dec. Jan. 1971); children: Richard Wayne, Stephen Wyatt; m. Billy S. Parham, Mar. 10, 1991. BS, East Cen. U., Ada, Okla., 1962, M Teaching, 1965. Office mgr. Louis M. Long, Loans, Ada, 1946-78; owner Credit Bur. Ada, 1956—, mgr., 1978—. Mem. Soc. Cert. Credit Bur. Execs., Assoc. Credit Burs. Okla. (bd. dirs. 1980—, pres. 1990), AAUW (cert. of achievement 1989), Ada Bus. and Profl. Women (chmn. YC, Pres.'s award 1991), Toastmasters (pres. Ada 1984, Presdl. Excellence award 1984), Kiwanis (bd. dirs. Ada 1990-92). Democrat. Home: PO Box 506 Ada OK 74821-0506 Office: Credit Bur Ada 304 E 12th St Ada OK 74820-6510

PARHAM, ELLEN SPEIDEN, nutrition educator; b. Mitchells, Va., July 15, 1938; d. Marion Coote and Rebecca Virginia (McNiel) Speiden; m. Arthur Robert Parham, Jr., Dec. 16, 1961; children: Katharine Alma, Cordelia Alyx. BS in Nutrition, Va. Poly. Inst., 1960; PhD in Nutrition, U. Tenn., 1967; MSEd in Counseling, No. Ill. U., 1994. Registered dietitian. Asst. prof. to prof. No. Ill. U., DeKalb, Ill., 1966—; coord. programs in dietetics No. Ill. U., DeKalb, 1981-86, 90—, coord. grad. faculty in Human and Family Resources, 1985-87; cons. on nutrition various hosps., clins. and bus., Ill., 1980—; founder, dir. Horizons Weight Control Program, DeKalb, 1983-91; founder, leader "Escaping the Tyranny of the Scale" Group, 1994—; co-chair Nutrition Coalition for Ill., 1989-90; ptnr., mgr. Design on Fabric, 1986—. Bd. editors Jour. Nutrition Edn., 1985-90, Jour. Am. Dietetic Assn., 1991—; contbr. articles to profl. jours. Mem. Am. Inst. Nutrition, Soc. Nutrition Edn., Am. Dietetic Assn., Am. Home Econs. Assn., Soc. Nutrition Edn. (treas. 1991-94, chair divsn. nutrition and weight realities 1995-96), N.Am. Assn. Study Obesity.

PARIS, KAREN MARIE, nurse, educator; b. Bloomington, Ind., Oct. 15, 1952; d. Robert Ross and Theresa (Hessig) McEllininey; m. David J. Paris; 1 child, Stephanie. BS in Nursing, U. Evansville, 1975; M in Nursing Adminstrn., U. Tex.-Austin, 1989. RN, Ind., Tex.; cert. med.-surg. nurse. Commd. 1st lt. U.S. Army, 1973, advanced through grades to lt. col., 1990, ret. 1994; nurse instr. Acad. Health Scis., Ft. Sam Houston, Tex., 1978-79, phase 2 coord., 1979-80, tng. officer, 1980-81, dep. program dir. satellite TV, 1981-82; asst. head nurse Madigan Army Med. Ctr., Tacoma, Wash., 1983, nurse instr., 1983-85; head nurse surg. unit, 1986, exec. officer Spl. Assistance Team, Liberia, 1985; head nurse orthopedic unit Brooke Army Med. Ctr., Ft. Sam Houston, Tex., 1989-90; head nurse Consol. Troop Med. Clinic, 1990-94; nurse mgr. orthopedic dept. Bapt. Med. Ctr., 1994-95; resource nurse, healthcare finder Found. Health Fed. Svcs., San Antonio, 1996—. Prodr. 18 videotapes/live TV programs for health providers, 1981-82. Treas. Fox Glen Homeowners Assn., Tacoma, 1984; bd. dirs. Olympia Hills Neighborhood Assn., 1988-90; bd. dirs. Valhaven, Inc. Decorated Legion of Merit Army Commendation medal with 2 bronze oak leaf clusters, Humanitarian Svc. medal. Mem. AMSUS, Nat. Assn. Orthopaedic Nurses, Nat. League Nurses, Assn. Fed. Nurses (pres. 1984-85), Phi Kappa Phi, Sigma Theta Tau. Republican. Lodge: Order Eastern Star. Home: 8315 Athenian Dr Universal City TX 78148-2515 Office: Found Health Fed Svcs 7800 I10 Ste 300 San Antonio TX 78230-2025

PARISEAU, SUZETTE MARIE, preschool educator; b. Royal Oak, Mich., June 4, 1965; d. Ford Bernard Jr. and Mary Jane (Belland) P. BA, Ctrl. Mich. U., 1988. Cert. tchr., N.J. Head tchr. Children's Choice Child Care Ctr., East Brunswick, N.J., 1990-92; pre-kindergarten tchr. Our Lady of Peace Sch., Fords, N.J., 1992—. Mem. ASCD, Women of the Moose. Roman Catholic. Home: 177 Ford Ave Perth Amboy NJ 08863 Office: Our Lady of Peace Sch Amboy Ave Fords NJ 08863

PARK, BEVERLY GOODMAN, public relations professional; b. Boston, Nov. 10, 1937; d. Morris and Mary (Keller) Goodman; divorced; children: Glynis Forcht, Seth, Elyse. BS, Simmons Coll., 1959; MS, Ea. Conn. State U., 1968; postgrad., Western N.E. Coll. Law, 1994—. Asst. dir. comty. svc. Hartford (Conn.) Courant, 1976-79; mayor Borough of Colchester, Conn., 1979-83; lifestyle editor Chronicle, Willimantic, Conn., 1980-82, suburban editor, 1982-84; officer mktg. & comm. U. Conn. Health Ctr., Farmington, 1984—; selected team mem. radiation exposure info. study Belorussia, 1993; mem. adv. bd. Hosp. News; mem. women's affairs com. U. Conn. Health Ctr. Women's Networking Task Force; mem. Univ. Adminstrv. Staff Coun.; mem. minority awards com. U. Conn. Health Ctr., mem. John N. Dempsey hosp. disaster plan com. Designer: (libr. studies curriculum) Classroom Instruction on the Use of Books and Libraries, 1972; pub.: (ednl. booklets) Have You Made Plans for the Future?, 1977-78; editor of edn. holiday and bridal supplements The Chronicle, 1980-84; editor: U. Conn. Health Ctr. Anniversary Mag., 1986, U. Conn. Health Ctr. Med. Catalog, 1986—, (ann. pub.) Salute, 1988—, U. Conn. Health Ctr. 30th Anniversary Supplement, 1991. Bd. dirs. Ea. Conn. Found. for Pub. Giving, Norwich, 1990—; women's club officer Dem. Town Com., Colchester, Conn., 1963-90; active Hadassah, Northampton/Amherst, 1996—, Women's League for Conservative Judaism. Recipient Lifestyle Page award New England Press Assn., 1980, Media Excellence in Covering Human Svcs. award Conn. chpt. NASW, 1982, Ragan Report Arnold's Admirables award for excellence in graphics and typography, 1985, Gold award Healthcare Mktg. Report, 1987, award for video ACS, 1990. Mem. NOW (membership com. Southea. chpt., mem. legis. task force, Meritorious Svc. award Southea. Conn. chpt. 1985), Am. Soc. for Hosp. Mktg. and Pub. Rels., Am. Mktg. Assn., Assn. Am. Med. Colls. (mem. group on pub. affairs), Conn. Hosp. Assn. (participant hosp. pub. rels. conf.), State of Conn. Pub. Info. Coun. (mem. steering com.), New England Hosp. Pub. Rels. and Mktg. Assn. (bd. dirs. 1987, 88). Home: 111 Rick Dr Florence MA 01060

PARK, CAROL A., management consultant, industrial engineer; b. Bellefonte, Pa., Aug. 21, 1958; d. William Harold and Ruth D. (Dorsey) P.; m. Scott Albert Saunders (div. 1989). BS in Indsl. Engring., Pa. State U., 1981. Staff scientific Goodyear Aerospace, Akron, Ohio, 1982-85; indsl. engr. St. Onge, Ruff & Assoc., York, Pa., 1985-91; project mgr. St. Onge Co., York, Pa., 1991-95; ptnr. Applied Solutions, Inc., York, Pa., 1995—; sec. Inst. Indsl. Engring., York, Pa., 1992-94; spkr., lectr. in field. Mem. allocation com. United Way, York, Pa., 1990. Home: 130 Calvary Church Rd Wrightsville PA 17368 Office: Applied Solutions Inc 55 S Richland Ave York PA 17404

PARK, CATHERINE VIRGINIA, hotel manager; b. Honolulu, June 8, 1969; d. Steven Seung Bin and Young Ja (Lea) P. Student, Brown U., 1985, Georgetown U., 1990; BS, Cornell U., 1990. Asst. cabana mgr. Four Seasons Resort, Wailea, Hawaii, 1990, asst. pacific grill mgr., 1991, asst. banquet mgr., 1992, cabana cafe mgr., 1993, pacific grill mgr., 1994, rm. svc.

mgr., 1995; club concierge mgr. Four Seasons Resort, Wailea, 1995; cons. and valuations analyst Hospitality valuation Svcs., San Francisco, 1994; project cost assoc. Rockwell Power Sys., Kihei, Hawaii, 1996—; pres. Park Computer Cons. and Sys. Analysis, Pukalani, Hawaii, 1996—. Vol. Kula (Hawaii) Hosp., 1995. Mem. Cornell Soc. Hoteliers. Home: 15 Kulanihakoi St # 14G Kihei HI 96753

PARK, DOROTHY GOODWIN DENT (MRS. ROY HAMPTON PARK), broadcasting and newspaper executive; b. Raleigh, N.C.; d. Walter Reed and Mildred (Goodwin) Dent; student Peace Jr. Coll., 1925-33; A.B., Meredith Coll., 1936; m. Roy Hampton Park, Oct. 3, 1936; children—Roy Hampton, Adelaide Hinton. Sec., dir. RHP, Inc., Ithaca, N.Y., 1945—, Park Communications, Inc., Ithaca, N.Y., 1983-95; pres. Park Found.Inc., Ithaca, 1994—. Bd. visitors Peace Coll., Raleigh, 1968—. Mem. DAR (1st vice regent 1955-57), Daus. Am. Colonists, Nat. Soc. Magna Charta Dames, Sovereign Colonial Soc. Ams. Royal Descent, Descs. Knights of Garter, Colonial Order of Crown, Service League Ithaca, LWV. Presbyterian. Clubs: Garden (Ithaca), Ithaca Woman's. Home: 205 Devon Rd Ithaca NY 14850-1409

PARK, FRANCES MIHEI, food products executive, author; b. Cambridge, Mass., Apr. 3, 1955; d. Sei-Young and Heisook Hong Park. BS in Psychology, Va. Poly. Inst. and State U., 1977. Supr. masters programs Sch. Govt. and Bus. Adminstrn. George Washington U., Washington, 1978-81; founder, co-owner Park Ltd. T/A Chocolate Chocolate, Washington, 1982—. Contbr. stories, poems to profl. publs. Bus. subject of various mag. and newspaper articles, including Washington Dossier, N.Y. Times, Victoria Mag., Washington Post, Gault Millau Guide, Washingtonian Mag., also featured on local, nat. and internat. cable TV, BBC and Nat. Pub. Radio; recipient Best Candy Store award Washingtonian Mag., 1986, 2d prize for fiction award Willow Rev., 1993, Rosebud Mag. award for contemporary writing for short story "Premonition", 1995. Office: Chocolate Chocolate 1050 Connecticut Ave NW Washington DC 20036-5303

PARK, IRIS YOUNG SOOK, dancer, choreographer; b. Seoul, Korea, May 17, 1945; came to U.S., 1973; d. Joon Chang and Ryu Kwon (Kim) P. BA, Kyung Hee U., Seoul, Korea, 1967, MA, 1969; MFA, NYU, 1979. Artistic dir. Dance Theatre Sounds, N.Y.C., 1978—, Iris Park & Dancers, N.Y.C., 1980—; various performances around the world, 1978—; rsch. and performance Visva-Bharati Santiniketan, West Bengal, India, 1990-94, Beijing (China) Dance Acad., 1992-93; involved in disabled ministry, Flushing, N.Y., 1995—, the Lamb's ministry, N.Y.C., 1995—. Author: (book) My Dance, My Soul, 1989. Home and Office: 745 9th Ave #4S New York NY 10019

PARK, MARY WOODFILL, information consultant; b. Nevada, Mo., Nov. 20, 1944; d. John Prossor and Elizabeth (Devine) Woodfill; m. Salil Kumar Banerjee, Dec. 29, 1967 (div. 1983); children: Stephen Kumar, Scott Kumar; m. Lee Crandall Park, Apr. 27, 1985; stepchildren: Thomas Joseph, Jeffrey Rawson. BA, Marywood Coll., 1966; postgrad., Johns Hopkins U., 1983, Goucher Coll., 1986. Asst. to dir. U. Pa. Librs., Phila., 1968-69; investment libr. Del. Funds, Phila., 1969-71; investment officer Investment Counselors Md., Balt., 1980-84, 1st Nat. Bank Md., Balt., 1984-85; founder Info. Consultancy, Balt., 1985—; lectr. Villa Julie Coll., Balt., 1989, Loyola Coll., Balt., 1991-92, Cath. U., 1993. Editor, contbr. to profl. publs. Vol. Internat. Visitors' Ctr., Balt., 1979-80, 91; del. White House Conf. on Librs.; v.p. bd. dirs. Friends of Goucher Libr., 1988-90; mem. industry applications com. Info. Tech. Bd., State of Md., 1993—; mem. info. tech. com. of the Tech. Coun., Greater Balt. Com., 1993—. Named One of Md.'s Top 100 Women, Warfield's Bus. Publn., 1996. Mem. Spl. Librs. Assn. (pres. Balt. chpt. 1991-92, mem. network coord. coun. Sailor project 1993-95), Am. Soc. Info. Sci., Assn. Ind. Info. Profls., Md. Libr. Assn., Info. Futures Inst., Hamilton St. Club (bd. dirs. 1989-92), Soc. Competetive Intelligence Profls. Office: The Info Consultancy 308 Tunbridge Rd Baltimore MD 21212-3803

PARK, ROBERTA J., educator; b. Oakland, Calif., July 15, 1931; d. Robert Donald and Grace E. (Faulkes) P. AB, U. Calif., Berkeley, 1953; MA, Ohio State U., 1955; PhD, U. Calif., 1970. Instr. Ohio State U., Columbus, 1955-56; tchr. Oakland (Calif.) Pub. Schs., 1956-59; supr, prof. U. Calif., Berkeley, 1959-94, prof. grad. sch., 1994—. Editor: (with Jack W. Berryman) Sport and Exercise Science: Essays in the History of Sports Medicine, 1993, (with J.A. Mangan) From Fair Sex to Feminism: Sports and the Socialization of Women in the Industrial and Post-Industrial Eras, 1987. (with J.C. Harris) Play Games and Sports in Cultural Contexts, 1983. Alliance scholar Am. Alliance Health Phys. Edn. Recreation & Dance, 1991-92; recipient Disting. Scholar award Nat. Assn. Phys. Edn. in Higher Edn., 1994. Office: U Calif Dept Human Biodynamics Berkeley CA 94720

PARK, VALERIE JEAN, avionics technician; b. Inglewood, Calif., Dec. 15, 1954; d. Maurice Everett and Dee B. (Austin) P. AA in Gen. Edn., Golden West Coll., 1975; BA in Women's Studies, Humboldt State U., 1979; AA in Electronics Comms. Tech., Am. River Coll., 1985; cert. in aircraft maintenance tech., Sacramento City Coll., 1995. Cert. FAA airframe and powerplant, Calif.; cert. FCC gen. radiotelephone, Calif. Mgmt. trainee Bank of Am., Arcata, Calif., 1979-80; electronics technician Hewlett Packard Corp., Santa Rosa, Calif., 1985-91; avionics technician Redwood Aviation Inc., Santa Rosa, 1991-93, Patterson Aircraft Corp., Sacramento, Calif., 1996—; avionics technician San Joaquin Helicopters, Rancho Cordova, Calif., 1995. Scholar Sacramento City Coll. Donors, 1994, 95. Mem. NOW, Profl. Aviation Maintenance Assn., Santa Rosa Ninety-Nines (scholar 1994). Democrat. Home: PO Box 221898 Sacramento CA 95822

PARK, VIRGINIA MAY, county official, newspaper columnist; b. Clyde, Ohio, Jan. 16, 1941; d. Dale Blair and Helen Naomi (Stoner) Allen; m. Dennis L. Park, Dec. 19, 1960 (div. 1982); 1 child, Jeffrey Howard. Student, U. Toledo, 1959-60. News writer News-Herald, Port Clinton, Ohio, 1981-83; columnist Beacon, Port Clinton, 1983—; recorder Ottawa County, Port Clinton, 1989—. Mem. Sarah Cir., Trinity United Meth. Ch.; sec. Ottawa County Bd. Social Concerns, 1987-88; sec., media specialist Ottawa County Dem. Ctrl. Com., 1990-94; mem. adv. bd. Ottawa County Extension Svc., 1990-96; sec. Keeper's House Restoration Com., 1990-96; del. Dem. Nat. Conv., 1996. Mem. Ohio Recorder's Assn. (book and page publ. com. 1994, 95, legis. pub. rels. com. 1996, edn. com. 1996), Ottawa County Hist. Soc., Elmore Hist. Soc., Port Clinton Heritage Found., Lakeside Heritage Assn., Farmer's Union, Women of Moose. Home: 900 S Schau Rd Port Clinton OH 43452 Office: Ottawa County Recorder 315 Madison St Port Clinton OH 43452

PARKAS, IVA RICHEY, educator, historian, curator, paralegal; b. Comanche County, Tex., June 28, 1907; d. Andrew J. Richey and Pearl Lucretia (Kennedy) Richey; grad. Wayland Coll., 1927; BA, Tex. Tech. U., 1935; MLitt, U. Pitts., 1950; postgrad. UCLA, 1960, Pa. State U., 1961, U. Calif., Berkeley, 1962, Duquesne U., 1963, Carnegie-Mellon U., 1968; m. George Eduardo Parkas, May 5, 1945. Curator, historian Fort Pitt Blockhouse, Pitts., 1946-52, asst. curator-historian, 1964-84; tchr. U.S. history Pitts. sr. high schs., 1953-72; paralegal Allegheny County (Pa.) Law Dept., 1977-82. Del., White House Conf. on Children and Youth, Washington, 1960, 70; World Food Conf., Rome, 1974; U.S. Congl. Sr. Citizens intern, Washington, 1984. Named Disting. Alumnae, U. Pitts., 1978; recipient Classroom Tchr.'s medal Freedoms Found. Valley Forge, 1960; Henry Clay Frick Ednl. fellow; NDEA grantee; Greater Pitts. Air Force Squadron scholar, Pitts. Press scholar, 1960. Mem. NEA (life), AAUW (pres. Pitts. br. 1974-76), Hist. Soc. Western Pa., Western Pa. Council Social Studies (pres. 1969-71), DAR (regent Pitts. chpt. 1986-89), U. Pitts. Alumnae Assn. (bd. dirs. 1978—, v.p. 1984), Pa. Retired Pub. Sch. Employees Assn. (chairperson Am. revolution bicentennial 1974-76), Western Pa. Hist. Soc., Allegheny County Bicentennial Commn., Greater Pitts. Commn. for Women, Delta Kappa Gamma, Phi Alpha Theta. Commonwealth editor: So Your Children Can Tell Their Children, 1976; contbr. articles on hist. subjects to newspapers, mags. Home: 5520 5th Ave Apt C5 Pittsburgh PA 15232-2342

PARKE, MARILYN NEILS, writer; b. Libby, Mont., June 5, 1928; d. Walter and Alma M. Neils; m. Robert V. Parke, Aug. 25, 1951; children: Robert, Richard, Gayle Crawford, Lynn Parke Castle. BA, U. Mont., 1950; MEd, Colo. State U., 1973. Tchr. Poudre R-1, Fort Collins, 1973—. Co-author: (with Sharon Panik) A Quetzalcoatl Tale of Corn, 1992, A Quetzalcoatl Tale of the Ball Game, 1992 (Parent's Choice Gold award paperback of yr. 1992), A Quetzalcoatl Tale of Chocolate, 1994. Mem. Internat. Reading Assn., Soc. Children's Book Writers and Illustrators, Nat. Edn. Assn., Colo. Coun. Internat. Reading Assn. *

PARKER, ADRIENNE NATALIE, art educator, art historian; b. N.Y., May 23, 1925; d. Benjamin and Bertha (Levine) Lefkowitz; m. Norman Richard Parker, July 22, 1945; children: Dennis, Jonathan W., Steven L. BA cum laude, Hunter Coll., 1945; MFA, Montclair Coll., 1975; postgrad., Instituto Des Artes, San Miguel, Mex., 1987. Instr. art, English Granby High Sch., Norfolk, Va., 1945-46; instr. art Mahwah (N.J.) Bd. Edn., 1970-75, Daus. of Miriam Home for the Aged, Clifton, N.J., Fedn. Home, Paterson, N.J.; instr. art, history Bergen C.C., Paramus, N.J., 1980—. One-woman show Bergen C.C.; exhibited in group shows N.J. Art Educators, Bergen County Art Educators, N.J. Tercentenary (1st place), Pine Libr., Sara Delano Roosevelt House, Hunter Coll., Woodstock Art Assn., 1990-95, Fair Lawn Art Assn., 1991 (award), Palisade Guild Spinners and Weavers, 1994, Bergen C.C., 1994, 95. Editor Fairlawn H.S. PTA, Thomas Jefferson Jr. H.S.; pres. The Comty. Sch., Fairlawn, 1983-86, bd. dirs.; mem. art adv. exhbn. com. Pine Libr., 1992, 93, 94, 95, 96. Mem. N.J. Art Educators, Bergen County Art Educators, Wood Stock Art Assn., Fairlaw Art Assn., Hunter Coll. Alumni Assn. (bd. dirs. no. N.J. chpt. 1970—, pres. 1977-79, program chmn./v.p. 1993-94), Palisade Guild Spinners and Weavers (founder, editor, charter) Phi Beta Kappa. Home: 3827 Fair Lawn Ave Fair Lawn NJ 07410-4325

PARKER, ALICE, composer, conductor; b. Boston, Dec. 16, 1925; d. Gordon and Mary (Stuart) P.; widowed; children: David, Timothy, Katharine, Mary, Elizabeth. BA, Smith Coll., Northampton, Mass., 1947; MS, Julliard Sch., N.Y.C., 1949; MusD (hon.), Hamilton U., Clinton, N.Y., Macalester Coll., St. Paul, Bluffton (Ohio) Coll., Westminster Choir Coll., Princeton, N.J. Arranger Robert Shaw Chorale, N.Y.C., 1948-66; freelance composer, condr. N.Y.C., 1960—; tchr., workshop leader Westminster Choir Coll., Princeton, N.J., summers 1972—; artistic dir. Melodious Accord, N.Y.C., 1985—. Composer 4 operas, 30 cantatas, 8 song cycles and numerous anthems and suites. Recipient composer's award ASCAP, 1968—, Barlow Endowment, 1992, spl. award Nat. Endowment Arts, 1976. Mem. Am. Choral Dirs. Assn., Am. Condrs. Guild, Chorus Am. (Founders award 1994), Am. Music ctr., Hymn Soc. Am., Sigma Alpha Iota. Office: Melodious Accord Inc 175 9th Ave New York NY 10011

PARKER, BARBARA, internist, educator; b. Oxford, N.Y., Nov. 28, 1914; d. Charles Joel and Florence (Van Wagenen) P.; m. Herbert Chasis, Jan. 19, 1943; children: Joel Ann, Sarah. BA, Vassar Coll., 1936; MD, NYU, 1941. Diplomate Am. Bd. Internal Medicine. Intern, resident Bellevue Hosp., N.Y.C., 1941-43, dir. med. svc. psychiat. divsn., 1945-68, founder geriatrics unit, 1968-79, attending physician in geriatrics, 1979—; John Wyckoff fellow in medicine NYU Sch. Medicine, N.Y.C., 1943-45, instr. medicine, 1945-50, asst. prof., 1950—; asst. attending in medicine Tisch Hosp.-NYU Med. Ctr., 1963—. Mem. Alpha Omega Alpha. Home: 465 W 23d St Apt 17A New York NY 10011-2120 Office: NYU Med Ctr Faculty Practice Office 530 1st Ave New York NY 10016

PARKER, BEVERLY RIGGINS, photographer; b. Clarksville, Tenn., Mar. 31, 1946; d. Frazier and Nell (Willson) Riggins; m. Douglas Barnet Parker; 3 children. BFA, Austin Peay State U., Clarksville, 1995. Audio-visual coord. New Providence Mid. Sch., Clarksville, 1968-70; profl. photographer Clarksville. Author, photographer (periodical) The Tower,1991. Mem. Mid Cumberland Arts League (bd. dirs. 1996—). Republican. Baptist. Home and Office: 2601 Memorial Ext Clarksville TN 37043-5344

PARKER, CAROL, retired educator, real estate broker; b. N.Y.C., Mar. 7, 1928; d. Louis Krown and Ann Krown Davidoff; m. Howard Roseman, Dec. 16, 1947 (div. July, 1978); children: Robin Kilheeney, Jamie Motley; m. Colin James Parker, Jan. 20, 1980. BS in Edn., NYU, 1949. Tchr. Rockville Ctr. (N.Y.) Schs., 1959-61, Half Hollow Hills Schs., Dix Hills, N.Y., 1962-87; real estate agent Brenner Realty, Duck Key, Fla., 1992—; v.p. Half Hollow Hills Tchrs. 1972-77, pres. 1978-87; dir. (at large) N.Y. State United Tchrs., 1978-87. Guardian ad litem Monroe County, Key West, Fla., 1988-9; pres. Guardian Ad Litem Guild, 1994-96; pres., bd. dirs. Domestic Abuse Shelter, Marathon, Fla., 1995- 96. Named Guardian of the Yr., Guardian Ad Litem, 1996. Mem. AAUW, NOW, Marathon Bus. and Profl. Women (legis. chair 1992-96). Democrat. Office: Brenner Realty Duck Key Dr Duck Key FL 33050

PARKER, CAROL JEAN, psychotherapist, consultant; b. Plant City, Fla., Sept. 4, 1946; d. Fennimore Blaine and Verna Melissa (Robinson) Bowman; m. Charles Bridges, June 1, 1968 (div. 1979); children: James, Nova. AA, Hillsborough C.C., Tampa, Fla., 1979; BA, Internat. Coll., L.A., 1981, MA, 1983. Asst. Dr. Clarke Weeks, Plant City, 1964-65; med. transcriber Tampa Gen. Hosp., 1965-71, St. Joseph's Hosp., Tampa, 1976-80; psychotherapist Discovery Inst., Tampa, 1980-85; owner, dir. Ananda Counseling Ctr., Tampa, 1985—; clinician Human Devel. Ctr., New Port Richey, Fla., 1979-81; exec. dir. women's program, The Manors Hosp., Tarpon Springs, Fla., 1992—; program dir. stress related disorders Daylight Corp., Tampa, 1996—. Participant Task Force on Prostitution and Female Offender Diversion Program, Tampa, 1988. Mem. ACA, Am. Assn. on Mental Health, Am. Assn. Clin. Hypnotists, Internat. Soc. for Study Multiple Personality Disorders and Disassociation (pres. 1996-97), Tampa Bay Assn. Women Therapists (bd. dirs.), Tampa Bay Study Group on Multiple Personality Disorders and Dissociation (chmn. bd. 1990—, Outstanding Mem. award 1991). Office: Ananda Counseling Ctr 420 W Platt St Tampa FL 33606-2244

PARKER, DIANA L., nurse, consultant; b. Vancouver, Wash., Feb. 7, 1947; d. Ernest Ellsworth and Barbara Eleanor (Weber) Abrahamson; m. James William Eggert, Feb., 1965 (div.); 1 child, Staci Marie Eggert; m. William Robert Parker, Nov. 9, 1985. LPN, Skagit Valley Coll., 1969; RN, Everett (Wash.) C.C., 1971; BSN, U. Wash., 1993. Cert. ACLS, PALS, gastroenterology RN. Staff RN Island Hosp., Anacortes, Wash., 1971-73; office RN Family Med. Assoc., Anacortes, 1973-74; asst. to med. dir. Whatcom Med. Bur., Bellingham, Wash., 1975-76; office nurse Richard Schwindt MD, Bellingham, 1976-78; nurse mgr. United Gen. Hosp., Sedro Woolley, Wash., 1978-79; nurse mgr. St. Joseph Hosp., Bellingham, 1979-87, staff nurse, 1987—; presenter, cons. in field. Billet coord. Bellingham Ice Hawks, 1993-94. Named Vol. of Yr. B.C. Jr. Hockey League, 1994. Mem. ANA (mem. PAC 1993-94), Ambulatory Care Unit (chair adv. coun. 1994), Soc. Gastroenterology Nurses and Assocs. (cert. gastroent. RN, pres. Pacific N.W. chpt. 1992, 94, vice spkr. H.O.D. 1992, spkr. 1994, ex-officio bd. dirs., mem. nominations com. 1993, mem. found. 1994, Disting. Svc. award Pacific N.W. chpt. 1994), Cert. Bd. for Gastroenterology Nurses, SIGNEA, Toastmasters. Home: 349 W Hemmi Rd Bellingham WA 98226-9653 Office: St Joseph Hosp 2901 Squalicum Pky Bellingham WA 98225-1851

PARKER, DIANA LYNNE, restaurant manager, special events director; b. Eureka, Calif., June 21, 1957; d. Carol Dean and Lynne Diane (Havemann) P. BA in English, Humboldt U., 1981, postgrad., 1982-84. Lic. real estate agent, Calif. Retail clk. Safeway, Inc., Eureka, 1977-84; caterer, owner TD Catering, Eureka, 1982-84; asst. buyer Macy's Calif., San Francisco, 1984-85; realtor Mason-McDuffie, Alameda, Calif., 1985-87; host, Rotunda Neiman Marcus, San Francisco, 1987-89, asst. mgr., rotunda, 1989—, dir. spl. events, 1989—. Mem. Mus. Modern Art, Calif. Restaurant Assn., San Francisco Visitor and Conv. Bur., Common Wealth Club Calif. Republican. Office: Rotunda at Neiman Marcus 150 Stockton St San Francisco CA 94108

PARKER, DIANE CECILE, librarian; b. San Francisco, Dec. 22, 1942; d. Cecil William and Dorothy Kirk Westman; m. Manfred Parker, May 12, 1972. BA in Comparative Lit., U. Calif., Berkeley, 1964; MLS, U. Wash., 1967; postgrad., Case Western Res. U., 1981-82. Libr. Seattle Pub. Libr., 1967-72; head West Seattle Pub. Libr., 1972; libr. SUNY, Buffalo, 1972-74, head reference & grad. libr., 1975-81, dir. sci. & engring. libr., 1982-84; dir. librs. Western Wash. U., Bellingham, 1984-94, info. tech. libr., 1995—. PRes., bd. dirs. Whatcom Counseling and Psychiatric Clinic, Bellingham, 1995—. Mem. ALA, Wash. Libr. Assn. (exec. bd. 1990-92, Merit award 1993), Seattle City Librs. Assn. (pres. 1971-72), SUNY Libr. Assn. (pres. 1976-77), Assn. Coll. & Rsch. Librs. (pres. Wash. state chpt. 1990-91). Office: Western Wash U Libr MS 9103 Bellingham WA 98225

PARKER, EDNA G., federal judge; b. Johnston County, N.C., 1930; 1 child, Douglas Benjamin. Student, N.J. Coll. for Women (now Douglass Coll.); B.A. with honors, U. Ariz., 1953; postgrad., U. Ariz. Law Sch.; LL.B., George Washington U., 1957. Bar: D.C. Law clk. U.S. Ct. Claims, 1957-59; atty.-advisor Office of Gen. Counsel, Dept. Navy, 1959-60; trial atty. civil and tax div. Dept. Justice, 1960-69; adminstrv. judge Contract Appeals Bd., Dept. Transp., 1969-77; spl. trial judge U.S. Tax Ct., 1977-80, judge, 1980—. Mem. ABA, Fed. Bar Assn., D.C. Bar, D.C. Bar Assn., Women's Bar Assn. of D.C., Nat. Assn. Women Lawyers, Nat. Assn. Women Judges. Office: US Tax Ct 400 2nd St NW Washington DC 20217-0001*

PARKER, EILEEN M., accountant; b. Hartford, Conn., Nov. 17, 1969; d. Arthur Thomas Parker and Marie Catherine Chlebicki. BSBA in Acctg., Bryant Coll., Smithfield, R.I., 1991. Jr. cost acct. Fisher Pierce, Weymouth, Mass., 1991-93; property acct. Claremont Corp., Quincy, Mass., 1993—. Vol. Medjugorje Appeal, Inc., North Smithfield, R.I., 1994. Mem. Inst. of Mgmt. Accts., Alpha Phi Alumni Assn. (Boston chpt.). Roman Catholic. Office: Claremont Corp Batterymarch Park III Quincy MA 02169

PARKER, EVA ANNETTE, librarian; b. North Island, Calif., Nov. 27, 1950; d. R.L. and Eva Mae (Helm) Peters; m. Darrell Dwight Parker, Nov. 9, 1970; children: Geoff, Jenny. BS, Okla. Christian Coll., 1974; MEd, Southwestern Okla. State U., 1984. Cert. libr. media specialist. Tchr. Summer Safari program Oklahoma City Zoo, 1973; libr., tchr. Leedey (Okla.) Pub. Sch., 1983-87; prof. Draughon Tng. Inst., Wichita Falls, Tex., 1988-89; tchr. Region IX Edn. Svc. Ctr., Wichita Falls, 1990; libr. media specialist Vernon (Tex.) Intermediate Sch., 1990—; tutor Vernon Intermediate Sch., 1993—; del. alt. to NEA, Leedey, 1987; storm spotter for City of Grandfield, Okla. Contbg. author: What America's Teachers Wish Parents Knew, 1993; contbr. article to profl. jour. Tchr. Bible sch. Ch. of Christ, Iowa Park, Tex., 1987-93, Grandfield, Okla., 1994—; vol. ARC, Wichita Falls, 1987-93; coach bowling Spl. Olympics, 1992-93; coach track and field Spl. Olympics, Vernon, 1993—. Libr. improvement grantee Okla. State Dept. Edn., Leedey, 1984. Mem. Tex. Libr. Assn., Assn. Tex. Profl. Educators. Home: 1303 W 1st St Grandfield OK 73546 Office: Vernon Intermediate Sch 2201 Yamparika St Vernon TX 76384-6183

PARKER, GRACE PATRICE, insurance specialist; b. Phila., July 11, 1958; d. Patrick Henry and Doris Clara (Mason) P. BS, Temple U., 1980. 4th grade tchr. Clara Muhammad Sch., Phila., 1980; policy svc. clk. Dept. Vet. Affairs, Phila., 1981-85, ins. specialist, 1985—, total quality mgmt. instr., 1990—. Pres. bd. dirs. Acad. for Early Learning, Phila., 1992-95, bd. dirs., 1995—; bd. dirs. VA Employees Assn., 1996—. Mem. NAFE, Fed. Women's Exec. Leadership Program (diploma 1994). Baptist. Home: 8244 Forrest Ave Philadelphia PA 19150 Office: Dept Vets Affairs 5000 Wissahickon Ave Philadelphia PA 19144-4867

PARKER, JACQUELINE KAY, social work educator; b. Yuba City, Calif., June 3, 1934; d. LeRoy George and Veda (Kuster) P. AB, U. Calif., Berkeley, 1959, MSW, 1961, PhD, 1972. Foster care worker Santa Clara County Welfare Dept., San Jose, Calif., 1961-64; adoptions worker Alameda County Welfare Dept., Oakland, Calif., 1968-70; asst. prof. social work Va. Commonwealth U., Richmond, 1973-80, U. Oreg., Eugene, 1983-86; assoc. prof. Cleve. State U., 1986-90; mem. grad. faculty N.Mex. State U., Las Cruces, 1990-94; assoc. prof., MSW program coord. Radford U., 1994—; cons. Social Research Assocs., Inc., Midlothian, Va., 1978-80. Author biographical sketches for reference books, bibliographic essays, 1986—, oral histories, 1973—, also articles. Mem. Coun. on Social Work Edn., Friends of the Schlesinger Libr., Cuyahoga (Ohio) County Human Svcs. Adv. Com., 1989-90; referee Radcliffe Rsch. Scholars Program, Cambridge, Mass., 1983-84; bd. dirs. Opportunities Industrialization Ctr., Richmond, 1978-80. Mem. NASW (state bd. dirs. Ohio and N.Mex. chpts.). Office: Radford U Sch Social Work Box 6958 Radford VA 24142

PARKER, JANET, entrepreneur; b. Boston, June 9, 1958; d. Theodore B. and Lucy T. P. BA, Cornell U., 1980. Lic. real estate. Sales rep. McGraw-Hill Co., 1981-82; office mgr. Chestnut Hill (Mass.) Psych. Assn., 1982-85; adminstrv. dir., internat. educator The Parker Acad., Sudbury, Mass., 1985-93; dir. pub. rels. IRG/Computer Tune-Up Ctr., Sitka, Alaska, 1994—; owner, mgr. gifts/exec. gifts UnCommon WhatNot, Needham, Mass., 1991-93. Cable TV prodr., host children's interactive storytime "Talking Story Time", Acton, Mass., 1987-90. Mem. Soc. for the Preservation of the Integrity of the Word "Unique". Office: PO Box 825 Shaw Island WA 98286

PARKER, JANET ELAINE, special education educator; b. Dumas, Tex., Feb. 18, 1961; d. George Donald and Wylma Marie (Veatch) Gracey; m. Larry Dale Parker, Sept. 5, 1992. BSEd, Nat. U. of North Tex., 1984; MSEd, Ea. N.Mex. U., 1994. Cert. elem. tchr. Tex. 4th grade tchr. N.W. Ind. Sch. Dist., Newark, Tex., 1985-87; kindergarten/8th grade reading Saint Jo (Tex.) Ind. Sch. Dist., 1987-88; 3-5th grade spl. edn. Muleshoe (Tex.) Ind. Sch. Dist., 1988-91, 6-8th grade spl. edn., 1991—; head coach Spl. Olympics, Muleshoe, 1989-92; mem. spl. edn. adv. bd. 1995—. Actress Muleplex Theatre, Inc., Muleshoe, 1989-93, sec., 1991-92, head membership com., 1994—. Mem. Phi Kappa Phi, Kappa Delta Pi, Kappa Kappa Iota (pres. 1993-94, sec. 1994-96). Home: 615 W Ave E Muleshoe TX 79347 Office: Muleshoe Ind Sch Dist 514 W Ave G Muleshoe TX 79347

PARKER, JOAN, public relations executive; b. N.Y.C., Oct. 13, 1935; d. Albert and Elizabeth (Durgin) P.; m. Francis Shea (div. 1964); 1 child, Sarah Young; m. Dale Coenen; children: Stephen, Alison. Student, Hood Coll., 1953-55, Tobé Coburn Sch., 1956. Asst. to pub. relations dir. Elizabeth Arden, N.Y.C., 1956-57; acct. exec. Rowland Co., N.Y.C., 1958-60; owner pub. relations firm N.Y.C., 1969-81; dir. consumer products pub. relations N.W. Ayer Pub. Relations Co., N.Y.C., 1981-82, dir. pub. relations, 1982—; EVP, dir. Ayer & Ptnrs., 1994—. Dir. House of Vision, Chgo., 1983-85, Wolverine Worldwide, Grand Rapids, Mich., 1983—. Recipient Director's Choice award NWEA, 1990. Mem. Pub. Relations Soc. Am. (acad. counselor), Tobé Coburn Alumni Assn. (Most Disting. Alumni 1980), Fashion Group, Women's Jewelry Assn. Office: Ayer Pub Rels 825 8th Ave New York NY 10019-7416

PARKER, JUDITH ELAINE, language educator; b. Fresno, Calif., July 3, 1938; d. John Harris and Dorothy Henrietta (Nielsen) Oates; m. Brad Hill, Feb. 14, 1959 (div. Feb. 1979); children: Scott, Mark. BA, Fresno State U., 1960, M, 1968. Tchr. lang. arts Fresno Unified Sch. Dist., 1960—. Mem. NEA, NOW, Nat. Coun. Tchrs. English, Nat. Mus. Women in Arts, Calif. Assn. Tchrs. English, Fresno Art Mus., Women's Internat. League for Peace and Freedom, Fresno Met. Mus. Democrat. Methodist. Home: 5912 E Hamilton Fresno CA 93727 Office: Roosevelt HS 4250 E Tulare Fresno CA 93702

PARKER, KATHLEEN ANNE, psychologist; b. Chgo., July 23, 1955; d. Norman Kenneth and Anne Mary (Malonis) P.; children: Heather Anne, Candice Michelle, Adam David, Kenneth Anthony. BMus summa cum laude, DePaul U., 1975; MA magna cum laude, U. Chgo., 1978; postgrad., Ill. Sch. Profl. Psychology, Chgo. Registered music therapist. Music therapist Billings Hosp., Chgo., 1975-79; activity therapist Galesburg (Ill.) Mental Health Ctr., 1979-83, Waukegan (Ill.) Devel. Ctr., 1983-85; psychologist Ann M. Kiley Ctr., Waukegan, 1985—; presenter in field. Vol. Pioneer Club for Children, Montrose Bapt. Ch., 1988-91, Child Abuse Prevention Svcs., Chgo., 1993-94. Mem. APA (student mem.), Nat. Acad. Neuropsychology (student mem.). Home: 4255 N Melvina Ave Chicago IL 60634 Office: Ann M Kiley Ctr 1401 W Dugdale Waukegan IL 60085

PARKER, LINDA EUGENIA, engineering executive; b. Syracuse, N.Y., July 8, 1957; d. Thornton Jenkins and Eugenia Eva (Loeber) P. Admissions officer Am. Univ., Washington, 1982; asst. dir. Office of Summer Session U. Va., Charlottesville, 1982-85, rsch. asst., 1986-87; analyst NSF, Washington, 1988-94; engring. program evaluation dir. NSF, Arlington, Va., 1994—; cons. The World Bank, Washington, 1992, 95. Author: (with others) Industry-University Collaboration in Developed and Developing Countries,

1992, Industry-University Research Collaboration: An Option for Generating Revenue, 1993, Basic Research in the States, 1992, Transposition of Technology-Transfer Mechanisms Between Nations, 1996; contbr. articles to profl. jours. Mem. Technology Transfer Soc., Soc. Social Studies Sci. Office: NSF 4201 Wilson Blvd Arlington VA 22230

PARKER, LINDA SUSAN DENNIS, nonprofit organization executive; b. Chgo., Mar. 26, 1948; d. William Evert and Edwina Louise (Franke) Dennis; m. William Raymond Parker, Feb. 15, 1969; children: Anthony Wade, Kathleen Louise, Elizabeth Irene, Sarah Miriam. AA, Kenai Peninsula Coll., 1992—. Founder, dir. Kenai Peninsula Food Bank, Soldotna, Alaska, 1987—; co-chmn. Kenai Healthy Start, Soldotna, 1991—. Bd. dirs. Bishop's Attic, Soldotna, 1993—, Fed. Emergency Mgmt. Agy., Soldotna, 1992—, Soldotna C. of C., 1996—; vol. Boy Scouts Am., Soldotna, 1980-93, Girl Scouts Am., Soldotna, 1980-87, Kenai Peninsula Sch. Dist., Soldotna, 1980-90; co-chair Alaska Nutrition Coalition, 1996. Recipient Vol. of the Yr. award State of Alaska, 1986, Points of Light award Points of Light Found., 1992, Gold award United Way, Kenai, 1990-95, Woman of Distinction award Soroptimist. Mem. NAFE, Am. Legion Aux., Phi Theta Kappa (treas.). Methodist. Office: Kenai Peninsula Food Bank PO Box 1267 Soldotna AK 99669-1267

PARKER, LYNDA MICHELE, psychiatrist; b. Phila., Sept. 28, 1947; d. Albert Francis and Dorothy Thomasinia (Herriott) P.; B.A., C. W. Post Coll., 1968; M.A. (Martin Luther King Jr. scholar 1968-70), N.Y.U., 1970; M.D., Cornell U., 1974; postgrad. N.Y. Psychoanalytic Inst., 1977-82. Intern, N.Y. Hosp., N.Y.C., 1975; resident in psychiatry Payne Whitney Clinic, N.Y.C., 1975-78; psychiatrist in charge day program Cabrini Med. Center, N.Y.C., 1978-79, attending psychiatrist, 1978-96; admitting psychiatrist inpatient psychiat. treatment Payne Whitney Clinic, N.Y.C., 1978-96, supr. psychiatry residents, 1978-96, supr. long-term psychotherapy, 1980-82; attending psychiatrist N.Y. Hosp., Cornell Med. Center, 1979-96; practice medicine specializing in psychiatry, N.Y.C., 1979-96; instr. psychiatry Cornell U. Med. Coll., 1979-86, asst. prof., 1986-96; instr. psychiatry, N.Y. Med. Coll., 1978-96; regional chair dept. psychiatry Tex. Tech. U. Health Scis. Ctr., Amarillo, 1996—; psychiat. cons. Bldg. Service 32BJ Health Fund, 1983-89, Inwood House, N.Y.C., 1983-86, Time-Life Inc., 1986-96, Ind. Med. Examiners, 1986-96, Epilepsy Inst., 1986-87, asst. med. dir., 1987-88, med. dir., 1988; ind. med. examiner Rep. Health Care Rev. Sys. Mem. adv. bd. St. Bartholomew Community Presch., N.Y.C., 1990-96. Mem. Am. Psychiat. Assn., Am. Womens Med. Assn. Episcopalian. Office: Tex Tech U Health Scis 1400 Wallace Blvd Amarillo TX 79106

PARKER, MARION DEAN HUGHES, home care service executive; b. Greenwich, Conn., July 21, 1911; d. Walter A. and Marion K. (Dean) Hughes; B.A., UCLA, 1932; m. Conkey P. Whitehead, Nov. 14, 1929 (div. Aug. 1933); m. Andrew Granville Pierce III, Oct. 21, 1933; m. Willard Parker, Oct. 5, 1939 (div. 1951); 1 child, Walter van Eps Parker. Actress appearing in Broadway prodns. New Faces, Three Waltzes, I Must Love Someone, on tour in The Women, The Man Who Came to Dinner, Lady in the Dark; various night club engagements; appeared in motion picture All About Eve; TV appearances; owner, mgr. Marion Parker's Guys & Dolls, Scottsdale, Ariz., 1951-59; mng. dir., purchasing agt. shipboard gift and accessory shops Am. Export Lines, 1960-64; dir. spl. events ITT, N.Y.C., 1965-66; exec. dir. Assn. Operating Room Nurses, N.Y.C., 1966-67; asst. to v.p. in charge devel. Bennett Coll., Millbrook, N.Y., 1967-68; staff Park East Real Estate, 1968-70; pres. Home Care-Ring Svc., N.Y.C., 1970—; actress for TV and Commls. Mem. Women's Nat. Republican Club, N.Y.C., Manhattan East Rep. Club, N.Y.C.; sustaining mem. Rep. Nat. Com., 1981—. Mem. SAG, Actors Equity. Address: 301 E 78th St Apt 18A New York NY 10021-1333

PARKER, MARION HAWKINS, librarian; b. Lawrenceville, Va., June 6, 1942; d. John Lee and Alice Louise (Pearson) Hawkins; m. Ammie Parker Jr., Dec. 6, 1959; children: Anthony, Johnnye, Kenneth. Student, Hampton Inst., 1958-59; AA cum laude, Orange County C.C., 1971; BS in Elem. Edn., SUNY, New Paltz, 1974; MLS, L.I. U., 1976. Cert. elem. tchr., pub. libr., sch. libr. media specialist, N.Y. From clk. to head children's dept. libr. Newburgh (N.Y.) Free Libr., 1964-86; libr. media specialist West St. Sch., Primary Sch., Newburgh, 1986-87, Vails Gate High Tech Magnet Sch., Newburgh, 1987—. Co-author: (with Stella Denton) 1776; A Bicentennial Bibliography, 1976. Bd. dirs. United Fund, Meals on Wheels, fundraising chmn.; past chmn. Bd. Christian Edn., Ebenezer Bapt. Ch. Mem. N.Y. Libr. Assn., Order Ea. Star (grand matron, Star of Hope), Royal and Exalted Order Amaranth (past supreme grand assoc. matron, past state dep.). Democrat. Home: RD # 1 414 Bingham Rd Marlboro NY 12542 Office: Vails Gate Hi Tech Magnet 320 Old Forge Hill Rd Newburgh NY 12553-8513

PARKER, MARTHA ANN, public relations specialist; b. Gainsville, Fla., Jan. 25, 1948; d. Morris Evans and Marian A. (Hickey) Paddick. BA in Comms., U. Ill., 1970; MA in History, U. R.I., 1988. Advt. asst., then advt. mgr. R.I. Host. Trust Nat. Bank, Providence, 1971-74; legis. asst. Congresswoman Pat Schroeder (D. Colo.), Washington, 1974-76; spl. asst. to dean Sch. Architecture U. New Haven, 1977-83; researcher Union Pacific Corp., Omaha, 1983-86; dir. pub. rels. Gorman & Assocs., Providence, 1986-88; account supr. pub. rels. FitzGerald & Co., Cranston, R.I., 1988-89, v.p. pub. rels., 1989-91, pres., CEO, 1996—; sr. v.p., dir account planning and svc., dir. environ. comms. group ptnr., lectr. Entex Environ Conf., Washington, 1992, pres., 1995—; sr. v.p., dir. New Eng. Environ. Expo, 1992-1996. Author book revs. for Master Plots, Groher Pub., 1979, 80, 81, 82. Mem. Pub. Rels. Soc. Am. (accredited, mem. Counselors Acad.), Am. Hist. Soc., Orgn. Am. Historians. Office: FitzGerald & Co 105 Sockanosset Cross Rd Cranston RI 02920-5549

PARKER, MARY-LOUISE, actress; b. Ft. Jackson, S.C., Aug. 2, 1964. Attended, Bard Coll. Actress: (theatre) Hay Fever, 1987, The Miser, 1988, The Art of Success, 1989, The Importance of Being Earnest, 1989, Prelude to a Kiss, Broadway, 1990-91 (Theatre World award 1990), Babylon Gardens, 1991, (films) Signs of Life, 1989, Longtime Companion, 1990, Grand Canyon, 1991, Fried Green Tomatoes, 1991, Mr. Wonderful, 1993, Naked in New York, 1994, The Client, 1994, Bullets Over Broadway, 1994, Boys on the Side, 1995, Sugartime, 1996; (TV movies) Too Young the Hero, 1988, A Place for Annie, 1994. Office: William Morris Agency 151 El Camino Beverly Hills CA 90212*

PARKER, REBECCA POLLACK, film company executive. BA in History, UCLA. Exec. v.p. motion picture prodn. United Artists/MGM Pictures, Santa Monica, Calif. Mem. Phi Beta Kappa. Office: United Artists/MGM Pictures 2500 Broadway St Santa Monica CA 90404*

PARKER, SARA ANN, librarian; b. Cassville, Mo., Feb. 19, 1939; d. Howard Franklin and Vera Irene (Thomas) P. B.A., Okla. State U., 1961; M.L.S., Emporia State U., Kans., 1968. Adult svcs. librarian Springfield Pub. Libr., Mo., 1972-75, bookmobile dir., 1975-76; coord. S.W. Mo. Libr. Network, Springfield, 1976-78; libr. developer Colo. State Libr., Denver, 1978-82; state librarian Mont. State Libr., Helena, 1982-88, State Libr. Pa., Harrisburg, 1988-90; Pa. commr. librs., dep. sec. edn. State of Pa., Harrisburg, 1990-95; state libr. State of Mo., Jefferson City, 1995—; cons. and lectr. in field. Author, editor, compiler in field; contbr. articles to profl. jours. Sec., Western Coun. State Librs., Reno, 1984-88, mem. Mont. State Data Adv. Coun., 1983-88, Mont. Telecommunications Coun., 1985-88, WLN Network Coun., 1984-87, Kellogg ICLIS Project Mgmt. Bd., 1986-88. Recipient President's award Nature Conservancy, 1989, Friends award Pa. Assn. Ednl. Communications and Techs., 1989; fellow Inst. Ednl. Leadership, 1982. Mem. ALA, Chief Officers State Libr. Agys. (chair N.E. 1991-92, v.p., pres. elect 1994—), Mont. Libr. Assn. (bd. dirs. 1982-88), Mountain Plains Libr. Assn. (sec. chmn. 1980, pres. 1987-88). Home: PO Box 554 Jefferson City MO 65102 Office: Mo State Libr PO Box 387 600 W Main St Jefferson City MO 65102

PARKER, SARAH ELIZABETH, associate justice; b. Charlotte, N.C., Aug. 23, 1942; d. Augustus and Zola Elizabeth (Smith) P. AB, U. N.C., 1964, JD, 1969. Bar: N.C. 1969, U.S. Dist. Ct. (mid., ea. and we. dists.) N.C. Vol. U.S. Peace Corps, Ankara, Turkey, 1964-66; pvt. practice Charlotte, 1969-84; former judge N.C. Ct. Appeals, Raleigh; now assoc. justice N. C. Supreme Ct., Raleigh. Bd. of visitors U. N.C., Chapel Hill, 1993—; bd. dirs. YWCA, Charlotte, 1982-85; pres. Mecklenburg County Dem. Women, Charlotte, 1973. Mem. ABA, Inst. Jud. Adminstrn., N.C. Bar Assn. (v.p. 1987-88), Mecklenburg County Bar (sec.-treas. 1982-84), Wake County Bar Assn., Charlotte City Club, Capital City Club. Episcopalian. Office: NC Supreme Ct PO Box 1841 Raleigh NC 27602*

PARKER, SARAH JESSICA, actress; b. Nelsonville, Ohio, Mar. 25, 1965. Actress: (theatre) The Innocents, 1976, The Sound of Music, 1977, Annie, 1978, The War Brides, 1981, The Death of a Miner, 1982, To Gillian on Her 37th Birthday, 1983, 84, Terry Neal's Future, 1986, The Heidi Chronicles, 1989, (films) Rich Kids, 1979, Somewhere Tomorrow, 1983, Firstborn, 1984, Footloose, 1984, Girls Just Want to Have Fun, 1985, Flight of the Navigator, 1986, L.A. Story, 1991, Honeymoon in Vegas, 1992, Hocus Pocus, 1993, Striking Distance, 1993, Ed Wood, 1994, Miami Rhapsody, 1995, If Lucy Fell, 1996; (TV movies) My Body, My Child, 1982, Going for the Gold: The Bill Johnson Story, 1985, A Year in the Life, 1986, The Room Upstairs, 1987, Dadah Is Death, 1988, The Ryan White Story, 1989, Twist of Fate, 1989, In the Best Interest of the Children, 1992, (TV series) Square Pegs, 1982-83, A Year in the Life, 1987-88, Equal Justice, 1990-91, (TV pilots) The Alan King Show, 1986. Office: CAA 9830 Wilshire Blvd Beverly Hills CA 90212*

PARKERTON, PATRICIA HOSTETTER, healthcare administrator; b. Sacramento, Calif., June 24, 1945; d. James Trexler Hostetter and Martha Anna (Bachli) Cohoon; m. William Louis Parkerton, Jan. 21, 1968 (dec. Apr. 1994); children: Melissa, Jesse. Student, Occidental Coll., 1962-64; BA in Psychology, U. Calif., 1966; MPH, U. Mich., 1972; cert., Stanford U., 1992; postgrad., U. Mich., 1995—. Diplomate Am. Coll. Healthcare Execs. Vol. Peace Corps, Haryana, India, 1966-68; cross cultural studies coord. UCLA Peace Corps-India tng. program, 1968; rsch. assoc. dept. behavioral sci. U. Ky. Med. Ctr., Lexington, 1969-70; adminstrv. resident Met. Hosp. and Clinics, Detroit, 1971; adminstrv. assoc. primary care/cmty. medicine program U. Mich. Med. Ctr., Ann Arbor, 1972-75; asst. adminstr., project dir. Harrington Meml. Hosp., Southbridge, Mass., 1975-76; v.p. adminstrn. Cmty. Health Care Plan, Inc. & Prepaid Health Plans Conn., New Haven, 1978-87; health and member svcs. dir. Partners Health Plan of So. New Eng. Inc., Hamden, Conn., 1987-89; mgr. ops. Kaiser Found. Health Plan Conn. Inc., Hartford, 1989-95; cons. Valley Health Plan, Amherst Med. Assocs., 1976; cons. field surveyor Joint Commn. on Accreditation of Healthcare Orgns., 1987-90; lectr., preceptor, alumni coun. rep. U. Mich. Sch. Pub. Health, Med. Care Orgn.; preceptor, fin. aide task force, project sponsor dept. epidemiology and pub. health Yale U.; co-chair Conn. State Health Plan and Status Coms.; pres., v.p., plan devel. com., rev. panels chair Health Systems Agy. South Ctrl. Conn.; mem. emergency med. svcs. task force Comprehensive Health Planning Coun. Ctrl. Mass.; mem. cmty. devel. health svcs. planning com. Washtenaw County Health Resources Task Force, Comprehensive Health Planning Coun. Southeastern Mich.; chair Forum on Cmty. Health Svcs., Yale-New Haven Med. Ctr.; bd. dirs. Family Planning Found. Ctrl. Mass.; organizer, sex edn. counselor Ann Arbor Free Clinic. Mem. APHA (med. care sect.), Conn. Hosp. Assn. (del.), Conn. Women in Health Care Mgmt. (membership com.), State Health Coordinating Coun. (com. co-chair), Group Health Assn. Am. (edn. com.). Democrat. Unitarian.

PARKHILL, MIRIAM MAY, retired librarian; b. Ada, Ohio, July 8, 1913; d. Thomas Jefferson Jr. and Cora Anita (Kemp) Smull; m. Edwin Hamilton Parkhill, Oct. 4, 1935 (div. July 1966); children: Diane Paget Parkhill Seils, Thomas Hamilton. AB, Ohio No. U., 1934; MA, Ohio State U., 1935; MA in Libr. Sci., U. Mich., 1963; student, Detroit Bus. Inst., 1937. Staff mem. Nat. Youth Adminstrn., Ada, 1937-38; asst. supr. Nat. Youth Adminstrn., Lima, Ohio, 1939-40; libr. staff mem. Ohio No. U., Ada, 1959-62, asst. libr., instr., 1963-68, catalog dept. head, asst. prof., 1969-72, catalog dept. head, assoc. prof., 1973-78, assoc. prof. emerita, 1980—. Vol. Ada Pub. Libr., 1980—. Mem. AAUW, DAR, Ohio Libr. Coun., Acad. Libr. Assn. of Ohio, Colonial Dames XVII Century, Hardin County Mus., Inc., Alpha Phi Gamma, Zeta Tau Alpha. Republican. Presbyterian. Home: 301 S Main St Ada OH 45810-1415

PARKHURST, CONNIE LOU, audiologist; b. Bay City, Mich., Mar. 15, 1953; d. John Anthony and Betty Lou (VanPopplen) Horner; m. Steven Michael Parkhurst, Dec. 21, 1974; children: Sean, David, James. Assoc., Delta C.C., University Center, Mich., 1973; BS summa cum laude, Western Mich. U., Kalamazoo, 1975; MA in Audiology, La. State U., 1982. Clin. cert. competence Am. Speech & Hearing Assn. Speech therapist Carrollton (Mich.) Pub. Schs., 1975-78, East Baton Rouge Parish Schs., Baton Rouge, La., 1978-81; audiologist, deaf educator State of La. and East Baton Rouge Schs., 1981-84; clin. supr. grad. students Ctrl. Mich. U., Mt. Pleasant, 1984-89; clin. audiologist/hearing aid dealer Mich. Ear Clinic, Saginaw, 1989-92; cons. audiology Midland (Mich.) Intermediate Sch. Dist., 1992—; clin. audiologist Narendra Kumar, M.D., Saginaw, Mich., 1992-95; clin. supr. in audiology Cen. Mich. U., Mt. Pleasant, 1995—; com. mem. Head Start Mid Mich., Mt. Pleasant, 1985-88; presenter state conv., 1983, state and nat. convs., 1987-89. Leader Campfire Assn., Midland, 1986-88; com. mem. Homer Twp. Govt. Wage Com., Midland, 1989—; pres. Chippewassee Parent-Tchr. Group, Midland, 1993-95; baseball coach Westown League, Midland, 1992. Dept. Edn. grantee Cen. Mich. U., 1988. Mem. Am. Speech and Hearing Assn. (award for continuing edn. 1989-92), Am. Acad. Audiology, Mich. Speech and Hearing Assn., La. Speech and Hearing Assn., Phi Delta Kappa. Republican. Home: 69 Seeley Dr Midland MI 48640 Office: Cen Mich U 425 Moore Hall Mount Pleasant MI 48859

PARKS, ARVA MOORE, historian; b. Miami, Fla., Jan. 19, 1939; d. Jack and Anne (Parker) Moore; m. Robert Lyle Parks, Aug. 19, 1959 (div. May 1986); children: Jacqueline Carey, Robert Downing, Gregory Moore; m. Robert Howard McCabe, June 20, 1992. Student, Fla. State U., 1956-58; BA, U. Fla., 1960; MA in History, U. Miami, Coral Gables, 1971; LLD (hon.), Barry U., 1996. Tchr. Rolling Crest Jr. High Sch., West Hyattsville, Md., 1960-63, Miami Edison Sr. High Sch., Fla., 1963-64; grad. asst. U. Miami, Coral Gables, 1964-65; tchr. Everglades Sch. for Girls, Miami, 1965-66; cons., 1966-70; free-lance research historian Miami, 1970-86; adj. prof. U. Miami, Coral Gables, 1986-87; pres. Arva Parks & Co., Miami, 1986—; cons. thematic and interpretive rsch. and design Harry S. Truman Little White House, Key West, Fla., 1989-91; pres. Centennial Press, 1991—. Author: Miami the Magic City, 1981, rev. edit., 1991, The Forgotten Frontier, 1977, Harry Truman and the Key West Little White House, 1991, Miami Then and Now, 1992; editor Tequesta Jour. Hist. Soc. Fla., 1986—; writer: (film) Our Miami: The Magic City, 1994. Bd. advs., Nat. Trust for Hist. Preservation, 1984-93, chmn. so. region, 1990-91, Adv. Coun. Hist. Preservation, 1995; trustee Miami-Dade C.C., 1984-90, U. Miami, 1994—; bd. dirs. Louis Wolfson Media History Ctr., Miami, 1985-90, Orange Bowl Com., 1989—, Bapt. Health Systems of Miami, Inc., 1992—; cmty. adv. Dade Heritage Trust, Miami, 1988—, mem. Bi-Racial Tri-Ethnic Adv. Bd., Miami, 1984—, New World Sch. Arts (exec. com.), Miami, 1986-90. Recipient Historic Preservation award AIA, 1993, Outstanding Women of History award Cuban Am. Women's Club, 1992, Women Helping Women award Soroptimists, 1992, Am. History award DAR, 1987, Pathfinder's award Women's Com. 100, 1985, Outstanding Citizen award Coral Gables C. of C., 1983, Outstanding Preservationist award Dade Heritage Trust, 1983, Good Faith award Black Archives and Research Found., 1981, Mus. of Sci. award, 1981, Community Headliner award Women in Communications, 1980, Humanitarian award Urban League Guild, 1980, award City of Coral Gables Historic Preservation Bd., 1978, Women of Impact award Cmty. Coalition for Women's History, 1996, Cmty. Star award Family Counseling Svcs. of Greater Miami, 1996; named to Alumni Hall of Fame Dade County Pub. Schs., 1985, Fla. Women's Hall of Fame, 1986, one of Women Who Made a Difference YWCA, 1988, Woman of Distinction award Soroptimist Internat. of Ams., Woman of Distinction award Girl Scouts Am. Mem. Internat. Women's Forum, Jr. League. Democrat. Methodist. Home and Office: 1601 S Miami Ave Miami FL 33129-1103

PARKS, JULIA ETTA, retired education educator; b. Kansas City, Kans., Apr. 5, 1923; d. Hays and Idella Long; BEd, Washburn U., 1959, MEd, 1965; EdD, U. Kans., 1980; m. James A. Parks, Aug. 10, 1941; 1 child, James Hays. Tchr., concert vocalist, tchr. Lowman Hill Elem. Sch., 1959-64; faculty Washburn U., Topeka, Kans., 1964-93, prof. edn. 1981-92, mem. pres.'s adv. council, 1981-84, chair edn., phys. edn., health and recreation div., multicultural com., dept. edn., 1986-92; insvc. lectr. reading instrns. Kans. Pub. Schs., 1960-93; lectr. Topeka Pub. Schs. Mem. acad. sabbatical com., Washburn U., 1987-90, vis. teams Nat. Council for Accreditation of Tchr. Edn., 1974-86, prof. emeritus, 1993. Bd. dirs. Children's Hour, 1981-84, Mulvane Art Ctr., 1974-78; judge, All Kans. Spelling Bees, 1982-86; sec. Brown Decision Sculpture Com., 1974-85; oral record account of experiences as a miniority student in integrated Topeka High Sch., 1984. Mem. multicultural non-sexist com. Topeka Pub. Sch., 1967—; apptd. to Kans. Equal Edn. Opportunities Adv. Com., 1988; marshall Washburn U. Commencements, 1980-92; mem. State of Kans. Task Force in Edn., 1991-92; presenter in field. Recipient Educator's award Living the Dream com., Local award for Excellence and Equity in Edn., The Brown Found.; named to Topeka High Sch. Hall of Fame, 1991; The Julia Etta Parks Honor Award created in her honor, Edn. Dept. Washburn Univ. Mem. Kans. Intergenerational Network, Washburn U. Alumni Assn. (contbr. alumni mag. 1989, recipient Teaching Excellence award 1983), Internat. Reading Assn., Kans. Inst. Higher Edn. (mem. pres. adv. council, 1981-83), Kans. Reading Assn., Kans. Reading Profls. Higher Edn., Topeka High Sch. Hist. Soc., Links Club (pres. 1982-84, chairperson scholarship com. 1984-93, Topeka Back Home Reunion Club (historian, v.p. 1991—), Delta Kappa Gamma, Phi Delta Kappa, NONOSO Women's Hon. Sorority. Methodist. Office: Washburn U Dept Edn 1700 SW College Ave Topeka KS 66621-0001

PARKS, KATHRYN ANN, administrative assistant; b. Martins Ferry, Ohio, July 23, 1943; d. James Harry Parks and Betty Imogene (Cline) Mallett; children: Todd W., Alisha Fawn. Sec. to Dr. Robert M. Zollinger, also editor med. publs. Ohio State U. Coll. Medicine, Columbus, 1961-72; mgr., clin. asst. Orthopedics Inc., Columbus, 1972-79; exec. corp. mgr., coord. internal affairs James C. Cameron, D.O., Inc., Columbus, 1979—. Adv. Bd. Mental Retardation and Devel. Disabled, 1967—; coord. Spl. Olympics, Columbus, 1985—. Mem. AAUW, NAFE, Ohio Osteo. Assocs. and Assts. Assn., Aid to Retarded Citizens, Order Ea. Star. Democrat. Mem. Ch. of Christ. Home: 5520 Brackenridge Ave Columbus OH 43228-2532

PARKS, LENORE YVONNE, pediatrician; b. Rochester, N.Y., Sept. 6, 1963; d. Norman Howard and Joan Ann (Horsey) P.; m. James Cecil Koon III, Oct. 29, 1994. BA in Biology, Emory U., 1985, BA in English, 1985; MD, East Carolina U., 1990. Cert. Am. Bd. Pediat. Pediatric resident U. Med. Ctr. Eastern N.C., Greenville, 1990-93, pediatric chief resident, 1993-94; clin. instr. East Carolina U. Sch. of Medicine, Greenville, 1994-96, asst. clin. prof., 1996—; physician advisor Pitt County Pediatric Asthma Project, Greenville, 1995. Mem. AMA, Am. Acad. Pediatrics. Republican. Office: East Carolina U Sch Medicine Dept Pediatrics Greenville NC 27834

PARKS, MADELYN N., nurse, retired army officer, university official; b. Jordan, Okla.. Diploma, Corpus Christi (Tex.) Sch. Nursing, 1943; B.S.N., Incarnate Word Coll., San Antonio, 1961; M.H.A. in Health Care Adminstrn, Baylor U., 1965. Commd. 2d lt. Army Nurse Corps, 1943, advanced through grades to brig. gen., 1975; basic tng. Fort Meade, Md., 1944; staff nurse eye ward Valley Forge (Pa.) Gen. Hosp., 1944; served in India, Iran, Italy, 1944-45; gen. duty staff nurse Fort Polk, La., 1951; nurse eye clinic Tripler Army Med. Center, Hawaii, 1951-54; staff nurse eye, ear, nose and throat ward Brooke Army Med. Center, San Antonio, 1954-57; ednl. coordinator Fort Dix, N.J., 1957-58; instr., supr. enlisted med. tng. U.S. Army Med. Tng. Center, Fort Sam Houston, Tex., 1959-61; chief nurse surg. field hosp. 62d Med. Group, Germany, 1961-62, sr. nurse coordinator, 1962-63; adminstrn. resident Letterman Gen. Hosp., San Francisco, 1964-65; dir. clin. specialist course Letterman Gen. Hosp., 1965-67; chief nurse 85th Evacuation Hosp., Qui Nhon, Vietnam, 1967-68; asst. chief nursing sci. div., asst. prof. Med. Field Service Sch., U.S. Army-Baylor U. Program in Health Care Adminstrn., 1968-72; chief nurse surgeons office Hdqrs. Continental Army Command, Fort Monroe, Va., 1972-73; chief dept. nursing Walter Reed Army Med. Center, Washington, 1973-75; chief Army Nurse Corps, Office of Surgeon Gen., Dept. Army, Washington, 1975-79; ret. Army Nurse Corps, Office of Surgeon Gen., Dept. Army, 1979; faculty assoc. adminstr. U. Md., 1974-78. Decorated D.S.M., Army Commendation medal with 2 oak leaf clusters, Legion of Merit, Meritorious Service medal; recipient Alumna of Distinction award Incarnate Word Coll., 1981. Mem. Ret. Officers Assn., AMEDD Mus. Found. Address: 5211 Mctcalf San Antonio TX 78239-1933

PARKS, PATRICIA JEAN, lawyer; b. Portland, Oreg., Apr. 2, 1945; d. Robert and Marion (Crosby) P.; m. David F. Jurca, Oct. 17, 1971 (div. 1976). BA in History, Stanford U., 1963-67; JD, U. Penn., Phila., 1967-70. Bar: N.Y. 1971, Wash. 1974. Assoc. Milbank, Tweed, Hadley & McCoy, N.Y.C., 1970-73; assoc. Shidler, McBroom, Gates & Lucas, Seattle, 1974-81, ptnr., 1981-90; ptnr. Preston, Thorgrimson, Shidler, Gates & Ellis, Seattle, 1990-93; pvt. practice Seattle, 1993—. Active Vashon Allied Arts, Mountaineers, N.W. Women's Law Ctr., Wash. State Women's Polit. Caucus. Mem. NOW, ABA, Wash. State Bar Assn. (past pres. tax sect., past chair gift and estate tax com.), Washington Women in Tax, Washington Women Lawyers, Seattle-King County Bar Assn., Employee Stock Ownership Plan Assn., Western Pension Conf., Pension Roundtable, Wash. Athletic Club. Office: 1301 5th Ave Ste 3800 Seattle WA 98101-2603

PARKS, SALLIE ANN, county official, public relations executive, marketing professional; b. Detroit, Sept. 5, 1936; d. Bert A. Rennie and Edna V. (Lampman) Moran; m. Donald K. Parks, Aug. 22, 1959 (div. 1983); children: Sheri Lynn, Steven Rennie; m. Alden Matthews, Apr. 6, 1996. BA, Cen. Mich. U., 1959; postgrad., Mich. State U., 1962. Cert. accredited pub. relations profl. Editor Pinellas Classroom Tchrs. Assn., Clearwater, Fla., 1967-73; sub. tchr. Pinellas County Schs., Fla., 1972-74; real estate mgmt. Clearwater, 1971-74, bus. mgr., 1974-76; exec. dir. Pinellas County Arts Coun., Clearwater, 1976-81; dir. community relations Mease Health Care, Dunedin, Fla., 1981-86; pub. relations cons., tchr. Tokyo, Japan, 1986-87; dir. pub. rels. and mktg. Mease Health Care, Dunedin, 1987-92; county commr. Pinellas County, Clearwater, Fla., 1992-96, chairwoman, 1996; chair long term care subcom. Nat. Assn. Counties; bd dirs. Fla. Assn. Counties; chair Dist. V Juvenile Justice Bd.; mem. Met. Planning Orgn. Pinellas County, Pinellas County Arts Coun., Juvenile Welfare Bd. Pinellas County, Cmty. Health Purchasing Alliance Dist. V, Tampa Bay Regional Planning Coun. Area Agy. on Aging and Long Term Care subcom., Pinellas County Juvenile Boot Camp Task Force, Success by Six Task Force. Pres. Am. Heart Assn., Suncoast chpt., Clearwater, 1990-92; vice chairperson Clearwater Pub. Libr. Found., 1989; pres. LWV, Clearwater, 1972, PEO Sisterhood, Clearwater, 1975; trustee Pinellas Marine Inst. Recipient Athena award, Women in Communications, 1983, Leadership in the Arts award, Soroptimist Internat., 1980. Mem. Nat. Press Women, Fla. Pub. Rels. Assn. (past pres.). Republican. Presbyterian. Office: Office Bd Commrs 315 Court St Clearwater FL 34616-5165

PARKS-MCKAY, JANE RAYE, publicist, marketing specialist; b. Atlanta, Sept. 15, 1952. AA in Liberal Arts, West Valley Coll., Saratoga, Calif.; student, San Jose State U., 1981-83; BA in Cmty. Studies, U. Calif., Santa Cruz, 1992. Formerly profl. model; image cons. San Franciso and Monterey Bay, Calif., 1974-93; spkr. in field; media interviewee. Author: The Make-Over--A Teen's Guide to Looking and Feeling Beautiful, 1985, William Morrow. Mem. adv. bd. Peninsula Outreach Programs, Inc., Cultural Coun. of Santa Cruz County. Pres.' Undergrad. fellow U. Calif., Santa Cruz; named hon. mem. Marine Detachment # 711. Democrat.

PARLER, ANNE HEMENWAY, elementary education educator, horse trainer; b. Rochelle, Ill., July 15, 1931; d. William Merwin and Edith Florence (Ranger) Hemenway; m. William Carlos Parler, Aug. 13, 1955; children: William Jr., Blair Hemenway, Bethanie Parler Detar, B. Carolyn. BS in Edn., No. Ill. U., 1953. Cert. tchr., Md. Tchr. Long Beach (Calif.) Sch. Dist., 1953-54, West Covina (Calif.) Sch. Dist., 1954-55, Columbia (S.C.) Sch. Sys., 1955-58, U. Md., College Park, 1970-71, St. Patrick's Episcopal Sch., Washington, 1971-73, Montgomery County Pub. Schs., Rockville, Md., 1973-95; ret., 1995; owner Sunny Meadows Horse Farm, Frankford, Del., 1994—. Contralto soloist Faith Meth. Ch., Rockville, 1975-90, dir. handbell choirs, 1985-95; pvt. voice and piano tchr., Rockville, 1960-90. Home: 7005 Old Stage Rd Rockville MD 20852 Office: Sunny Meadows Horse Farm RFD 1, Box 132F Frankford DE 19945

PARLOTZ, BARBARA ELLYN, social worker; b. Rolla, N.D., May 18, 1945; d. Lyle and Vivian Agnes (Hudson) Armstrong; m. Robert David Parlotz, Aug. 14, 1963; children: David Bryon, Tonya Reneé. AA with honors, N.W. Coll., Kirkland, Wash., 1982; BA, U. Wash., 1984, MSW, 1986. Cert. social worker, Wash. Rsch. asst. U. Wash., Seattle, 1984-85; mental health therapist Eastside Mental Health, Bellevue, Wash., 1985-88; social worker Harborview Med. Ctr., Seattle, 1988-94, social work supr., 1994—; clin. instr. Wash. U., 1994—; cons. Eastside Mental Health, Bellevue, 1985-88, Wash. State Head Injury Found., Bellevue, 1988—; com. mem. Nat. Resource Inst. on Children with Handicaps, Seattle, 1987; speaker in field. Youth leader Assemblies of God. Mem. NASW, Acad. Cert. Social Workers, Res. Officers Ladies Assn. (v.p. 1994-95, chaplain 1987—), U. Wash. Alumni Assn., Wash. Head Injury Found. (pres. profl. group 1989-93), Golden Key Honor Soc. Home: 1640 167th Ave NE Bellevue WA 98008 Office: Harborview Med Ctr 325 Ninth Ave ZA70 Seattle WA 98104

PARR, CAROLYN MILLER, federal court judge; b. Palatka, Fla., Apr. 17, 1937; d. Arthur Charles and Audrey Ellen (Dunklin) Miller; m. Jerry Studstill Parr, Oct. 12, 1959; children: Kimberly Parr Trapasso, Jennifer Parr Turek, Patricia Audrey. BA, Stetson U., 1959; MA, Vanderbilt U., 1960; JD, Georgetown U., 1977; LLD (hon.), Stetson U., 1986. Bar: Md. 1977, U.S. Tax Ct. 1977, D.C. 1979, U.S. Supreme Ct. 1983. Gen. trial atty. IRS, Washington, 1977-81, sr. trial atty. office of chief counsel, 1982; spl. counsel to asst. atty. gen. tax divsn. U.S. Dept. Justice, Washington, 1982-85; judge U.S. Tax Ct., Washington, 1985—. Nat. Def. fellow Vanderbilt U., 1959-60; fellow Georgetown U., 1975-76; recipient Spl. Achievement award U.S. Treasury, 1979. Mem. ABA, Md. Bar Assn., Nat. Assn. Women Judges, D.C. Bar Assn., Am. Judges Assn. Office: US Tax Ct 400 2nd St NW Washington DC 20217-0001

PARR, KAREN HANSEN, retail merchant, retired educator; b. Oakland, Calif., Aug. 29, 1931; d. Milton Lawrence and Vesta LaVerne (Stout) Hansen; m. Warren Hathaway Day, Aug. 27, 1950 (div. Jan. 1953); m. Charles Hubert Parr, Oct. 8, 1958; stepchildren: Charles L. and Chipper L. (twins), Patricia Perri Carlson. BA, U. Calif., Berkeley, 1953; BS in Elem. Edn., Oreg. Coll. Edn., 1956; MA in English, U. Alaska, 1966, Edn. Specialist in edn. adminstrn., 1974. Type B tchr. cert. with supt. endorsement, Alaska. Tchr. various schs., 1953-61, Fairbanks (Alaska) North Star Sch. Dist., 1962-76, 84-87; co-owner, mgr. Alaska House & Xanadu, 1976—; prin. Karen Parr and Assocs., 1979—; mem., chmn. standing coms. on profl. ethics, tchr. edn. and profl. stds. Fairbanks Edn. Assn., 1962-70; mem. Alaska Profl. Tchg. Practices Commn., 1968-71; lectr. in field. Contbr. articles to profl. jours. Founding bd. mem. Hillcrest Home for Boys, Fairbanks, 1956-63; mem. citizens adv. coun. Tanana Valley C.C., 1972-76; assembly mem. Fairbanks North Star Borough, , 1975-78, 1995—; bd. mem. Fairbanks Light Opera Theater, 1987-88; mem. Alaska State Reapportionment Bd., 1989-90; pres. U. Ctr. Merchants Assn., Fairbanks, 1994. Mem. Alaska Soc. for Tech. in Edn. (founder, past pres., chmn. annual conf. 1992-93, exec. dir. 1995—), Fairbanks C. of C. Episcopalian. Home: 909 John Kalinas Rd Fairbanks AK 99712 Office: Fairbanks North Star Borough PO Box 71267 Fairbanks AK 99707

PARRA, PAMELA ANN, physician, educator; b. New Orleans, La., Nov. 24, 1949; d. Morris Louis and Mary Elizabeth (Monaghan) P.; m. Garrett John Beadle, May 7, 1983; children: Erin Elizabeth, Ryan Garrett. BS, Loyola U., 1971; MD, Tulane U., 1975. Diplomate Am. Bd. Emergency Medicine. Emergency physician Lakewood Hosp., Morgan City, La., 1975-76, 81-86; resident Charity Hosp., New Orleans, 1976-79, staff physician, 1979-81; staff physician Baton Rouge (La.) Gen. Med. Ctr., 1986—; asst. prof. medicine La. State U., Med. Sch., New Orleans, 1989—. Fellow Am. Coll. Emergency Physicians (sec.-treas. La. chpt. 1993—); mem. La. State Med. Soc. Republican. Roman Catholic. Home: 1020 Pastureview Dr Baton Rouge LA 70810-4725 Office: Baton Rouge Gen Med Ctr 3600 Florida Blvd Baton Rouge LA 70806-3842

PARRAMORE, BARBARA MITCHELL, education educator; b. Guilford County, N.C., Aug. 29, 1932; d. Samuel Spencer and Nellie Gray (Glosson) Mitchell; m. Lyman Griffis Worthington, Dec. 23, 1956 (div. 1961); m. Thomas Custis Parramore, Jan. 22, 1966; children: Lisa Gray, Lynn Stuart. AB, U. N.C., Greensboro, 1954; MEd, N.C. State U., 1959; EdD, Duke U., 1968. Counselor, thcr. Raleigh City Schs., 1954-59, sch. prin., 1959-65; prof. dept. of curriculum and instrn. N.C. State U., 1970-96, prof. emeritus, 1996—; acad. specialist Office Internat. Edn., U.S. Info. Svcs., sec. sch. initative program, The Philippines, 1987. Author: The People of North Carolina, 1972, 3rd edit. 1983. Japan Inst. Social and Econ. Affairs fellow, 1980; N.C. AAUW award for juvenile lit., 1973, Holladay medal for excellence N.C. State U., 1994. Mem. ASCD, N.C. ASCD (pres. 1994-96), N.C. Coun. for Social Studies (pres. 1985-87), Assn. Tchr. Educators, Delta Kappa Gamma, Kappa Delta Pi. Home: 5012 Tanglewood Dr Raleigh NC 27612-3135

PARRENAS, CECILIA SALAZAR, secondary school educator; b. San Jose de Buenavista, Antique, Philippines, July 17, 1945; came to U.S., 1983; d. Angel Xavier Salazar and Lourdes Quibing (Jabile); m. Florante Y. Parrenas, Dec. 24, 1964; children: Rolf, Celine, Rhacel, Rhanee, Cerissa, Rheana, Margarita, Cecille. BS in Elem. Edn., Philippine Normal Coll., Manila, 1966; MA in Adminstrn., Nat. Tchrs. Coll., Manila, 1971, EdD in Edn. Mgmt., 1977; postgrad., Boston U., 1979. Faculty mem. Internat. Sch., Inc., Metro Manila, 1967-81; dept. head English and art Woodrose, Pvt. Sch. for Girls, Metro Manila, 1981-83; assoc. prof. De LaSalle U., Manila, 1983-84; program asst. sr. edn. programs MIT Sloan Sch., Cambridge, 1984-85; resource tchr. San Bernardino (Calif.) City Unified Sch. Dist., 1986-91; bilingual tchr., unit leader Pomona (Calif.) Unified Sch. Dist., 1991—; cons. Boston Pub. Schs. and Boston U. Bilingual Resource Tng. Ctr., 1978-79; presenter 20th Internat. Conf. on Bilingual/Bicultural Edn., 1991. One-woman painting and brushworks shows Brush, Ink and Color, Manila, 1981, Touchen and Calligrafen, Innsbruck, Austria, 1981, Seasons, Manila, 1982. Philippine Normal Coll. Alumni Assn. grantee, Manila, 1962-66, grantee Curso para profesores Agencia de Cooperacion Internacional, Madrid, 1991; postdoctoral fellow Boston U., 1978-79. Mem. Nat. Assn. Bilingual Edn. Home: 3784 Canyon Terrace Dr San Bernardino CA 92407 Office: Pomona Unified Sch Dist Vejar Elem Sch 1381 S White Ave Pomona CA 91766

PARRIGIN, ELIZABETH ELLINGTON, lawyer; b. Colon, Panama, May 23, 1932; d. Jesse Cox and Elizabeth (Roark) Ellington; m. Perry G. Parrigin, Oct. 8, 1975. BA, Agnes Scott Coll., 1954; JD, U. Va., 1959. Bar: Tex. 1959, Mo. 1980. Atty. San Antonio, 1960-69; law libr. U. Mo., Columbia, 1969-77, rsch. assoc., 1977-82; atty. pvt. practice, Columbia, 1982—. Elder, clk. of session First Presbyn. Ch., Columbia; mem. permanent jud. commn. Presbyn. Ch. U.S., 1977-83, mem. advisory com. on constitution, 1983-90. Mem. ABA, Mo. Bar Assn. (chmn. sub-com. revision of Mo. trsut law 1988-92). Democrat. Presbyterian. Home: 400 Conley Ave Columbia MO 65201-4219 Office: 224 N 8th St Columbia MO 65201-4844

PARRINO, CHERYL LYNN, state agency administrator; b. Wisconsin Rapids, Wis., Jan. 21, 1954; m. Jack J. Parrino, Sept. 1, 1990; 1 child, George. BBA in Acctg., U. Wis., 1976. Auditor Pub. Svc. Commn. Wis., Madison, 1976-82, dir. utility audits, 1982-86, exec. asst. to chmn., 1986-91, commr., 1991—, chmn., 1992—; mem. adv. bd. Bellcore, 1991; vice chmn. bd. dirs. Wis. Ctr. Demand Side Rsch., Madison, 1991-92; chmn. bd. dirs. Wis. Pub. Utility Inst., Madison, 1992-95. Mem. Gov.'s Task Force Gross Receipts Tax, Madison, 1991-92, Gov.'s Task Force Alternative Fuels, Madison, 1992—, Gov.'s Task Force Clean Air, Madison, 1992—, Gov.'s Task Force Telecom., Madison, 1993-94. Mem. Nat. Assn. Pub. Utility Commrs. (exec. com. 1991, chmn. comm. com. 1992—, pres. 1995—, pres. Gt. Lakes conf. 1996). Republican. Lutheran. Office: Pub Svc Commn Wis PO Box 7854 610 N Whitney Way Madison WI 53707-7854

PARRIS, REBECCA (RUTH BLAIR MACCLOSKEY), musician; b. Needham, Mass., Dec. 28, 1951; d. Edmund Myer and Shirley (Robinson) MacCloskey; m. Robert Louis DeGrassie, Sept. 28, 1980 (div. June 1985). Student, Boston Conservatory of Music, 1969-70. artist-in-residence Monterey (Calif.) Jazz Festival, 1995, Howard U., Washington, 1991; clinician U. N.H., 1991, U. Wash., 1994. Vocalist, prodr., arranger: (mus. rec.) Love Comes and Goes, 1991 (Boston Music award 1991); vocalist: (mus. rec.) A Beautiful Friendship, 1995, Spring, 1993 (Grammy award nomination 1993); vocalist, lyricist: (mus. rec.) It's Another Day, 1994 (Grammy award nomination 1994). Performer, fundraiser Poor People's United Fund, Boston, 1984-95, AIDS Benefit, 1988, Holiday Project, 1989, Starlight Found., 1991, Living with AIDS, 1991, Stuff for Kids, 1993, Child and Family Svcs., 1993, AIDS Action, boston, 1986-95, ABCD, Boston, 1995, numerous others. Named Outstanding Jazz Vocalist, Boston Music Awards, 1987-95, Outstanding Jazz Album, 1991; recipient Outstanding Svc. to Jazz Edn. award Internat. Assn. Jazz Educators, 1993. Mem. AFTRA, ASCAP. Democrat. Home: 53 Railroad Ave Duxbury MA 02332 Office: Entertainment Exclusives 403-5F Commonwealth Ave Boston MA 02215

PARRISH, ALETA DARLENE, accountant, auditor; b. Balt., Oct. 23, 1956; d. Walter Lee and Hazel Yvonne (Smith) Blackwell; m. Steven Edward Parrish, June 12, 1976 (div. June 1983); 1 child, Jeremy Blackwell Parrish. AA in Acctg., C.C. of Balt., 1985; cert. in voice, Johns Hopkins U. Peabody Inst., 1990. Asst. acct. Balt. City Pub. Schs., 1975-86; acct., auditor Balt. City C.C., 1986—. Acctg. mgr. AFRAM, Balt., 1996; acctg. dir. United Negro Coll. Fund, Balt., 1991—; pub. affairs chair Nat. Forum for Black Pub. Adminstrs., Balt., 1994-95; com. mem. Walters Art Gallery, Balt., 1996—. Mem. Nat. Assn. Black Accts. Inc. (1st v.p. 1995—), Women of the Arts, Balt. Mktg. Assn. (exec. sec. 1994-95). Home: 821 N Kenwood Ave Baltimore MD 21205-1715 Office: Baltimore City CC 2901 Liberty Heights Ave Baltimore MD 21215

PARRISH, ALMA ELLIS, elementary school educator; b. Peoria, Ill., Mar. 28, 1929; d. William Edward and Marie (Allton) Ellis; m. Clyde R. Parrish, Jr., Nov. 20, 1949; children: Clyde R. III, Charles, Donald, Royce, Christopher. BS, Bradley U., Peoria. Cert. elem. tchr., S.C., Ill. Tchr. Community Consol. Sch. Dist. 59, Elk Grove Village, Ill., Sipp Sch. Dist., Peoria, Kershaw County Sch. Dist., Camden, S.C. Mem. KCRA, S.C. Edn. Assn., Tchrs. Coun. Dist. 59 (pres., com.), Kershaw County Edn. Assn. (sec., PACE com.), Ill. Ret. Tchr.'s Assn., S.I. Coun.

PARRISH, CAROLINE VIDAL, entrepreneur; b. Dominican Republic, Dec. 28, 1960; came to U.S., 1962; d. Pedro E. and Mercedes (Medina) Vidal; m. Eugene D. Parrish, Aug. 21, 1982; children: Valerie Ann, Patrick Eugene. BA, Tex. Christian U., 1982. Underwriter AIU divsn. Am. Internat. Group, Houston, 1982-84; owner, operator Cuisine & Cream Café, Paducah, Ky., 1984-86; piano instr. Caroline Parrish Piano, Paducah, Ky., 1987-93; entrepreneur VIP Cleaners, 1992—, Parrish/Feezor Property, 1992—. Literacy tutor Adult Learning Ctr., Paducah, Ky., 1986-88; bd. dirs., corr. sec. The Charity League, Paducah, 1991-92; musician Rosary Chapel, Paducah, 1993—. Named Young Career Woman City of Paducah Paducah Bus. and Profl. Women, 1984.

PARRISH, DENISE KAY, regulatory accountant; b. Garden City, Mich., May 20, 1954; d. Lewis William and Carol Ruby (Doederlein) P.; m. Michael Joseph Krause, Oct. 10, 1986 (div. Apr. 1992). BA in Acctg., Mich. State U., 1976. Analyst Mich. Pub. Svc. Commn., Lansing, 1977-81; sr. fin. analyst Colo. Pub. Utilities Commn., Denver, 1981-85; chief rate analyst Ariz. Residential Utilities Consuemr Office, Phoenix, 1985-86, Ariz. Corps. Commn., Phoenix, 1986-91; mgr. rates and pricing Wyo. Pub. Svc. Commn., Cheyenne, 1991—. Mem. NOW, Nat. Assn. Regulatory Utility Commrs. (chair SEC/FASB Task Force 1992—, mem. oversight com. on joint telecomm. audits 1991-92, 96—). Lutheran. Office: Wyo Pub Svc Commn 5709 Education # 201 Cheyenne WY 82002

PARRISH, E. JEANNE, social worker; b. Independence, Pa.; d. James John and Elizabeth B. (Robison) Sella. BA in Sociology and Psychology, West Liberty State, 1969; MA in Polit. Sci. and Pub. Adminstrn., Ohio U., 1994. Registered profl. counsellor, Ohio. Social worker Dept. Human Svcs., Steubenville, Ohio, 1969-87, social svcs. supr., 1987-88, social program adminstr., 1988-93, dir., 1993—; mem. exec. com. Ohio Human Svcs. Dirs. Assn., 1994—; pres. Canton Dist. Dirs. Assn., 1994—; mem. bus. & industry bd. Jefferson C.C., Steubenville, 1990—; mem. family com. Ohio Supreme Ct.; bd. dirs. Franciscan U., Steubenville. Bd. dirs. United Way, Steubenville, 1995—. Mem. Ohio Human Svc. Dirs. Assn., Ohio Child Support Dirs. Assn., Bus. & Profl. Women (v.p. 1987-91). Office: Jefferson County Dept Human Svcs 125 S Fifth St Steubenville OH 43952

PARRISH, SHERRY DYE, elementary school educator; b. Birmingham, Ala., Oct. 18, 1957; d. Charles Max and Peggy Gail (Doss) Dye; m. James Wiley Parrish, June 13, 1987; 1 child, Taylor Austin Shaw. BS in Elem. Edn., Samford U., 1979; MS in Elem. Edn., U. Ala., 1995. Cert. tchr. Rank I, Class A., Ala. Tchr. Franklin Acad., Birmingham, Ala., 1979-83, Shades Cahaba Elem. Sch., Homewood, Ala., 1986-94, Trace Crossings Sch., Hoover, Ala., 1994-95, South Shades Crest Sch., Hoover, Ala., 1995—; chairperson sci. fair Shades Cahaba Elem. Sch., Homewood, 1990-94; mem. accreditation team, Warrior (Ala.) Sch., 1990; presenter Homewood City Schs., 1988, Constructivist Conf., Birmingham, 1994, 95, co-presenter NCTM regional conf., 1995, presenter Mid-South Whole Lang. Conf., Birmingham, 1995. Rsch. participant (book) Theme Immersion: Inquiry Based Curriculum in Elementary and Middle Schools, 1994. Founder, tchr. Women in Transition, Shades Mt. Baptist Ch., Birmingham, 1993—; presenter Festival of Marriage, Ridgecrest N.C, 1994, Dayspring Women's Conf., Birmingham, 1994. Mem. Nat. Coun. Teachers of Math., Am. Edn. Rsch. Assn., Educator's Forum. Office: South Shades Crest Elem 3770 South Shades Crest Rd Hoover AL 35244

PARR-JOHNSTON, ELIZABETH, academic administrator; b. N.Y.C., Aug. 15, 1939; d. Ferdinand Van Siclen and Helene Elizabeth (Ham) Parr; m. David E. Bond, Dec. 28, 1962 (div. July 1975); children: Peter, Kristina Aline; m. Archibald F. Johnston, Mar. 6, 1982; children: James, Heather, Alexandra, Margaret. BA, Wellesley Coll., 1961; MA, Yale U., 1962, PhD, 1973; postgrad., Harvard U., 1986. Various positions Govt. of Can., Ottawa, Ont., 1973-76, INCO Ltd., Toronto, 1976-79; chief of staff, sr. policy advisor Minstry of Employment and Immigration, Govt. of Can., 1979-80; various positions Shell Can. Ltd., Calgary, Alta., 1980-90; pres. Parr-Johnston & Assocs., Calgary, 1990-91; pres., vice chancellor Mt. St. Vincent U., Halifax, Nova Scotia, N.S., 1991-96; pres., vice-chancellor The U. New Brunswick, Fredericton, Can., 1996—; instr. U. Western Ont., London, Ont., 1964-67, U. B.C., Vancouver, 1967-71; vis. scholar Wesleyan U., Middletown, Conn., 1971-72; acad. rsch. assoc. Carleton U., Ottawa, 1972-73; bd. dirs. Nova Scotia Power, Bank of Nova Scotia, Fishery Products Internat., The Empire Co.; spkr. and presenter in field. Mem. editorial bd. Can. Econ. Jour., 1980-83; contbr. articles to profl. jours. Bd. dirs. Dellcrest Home, 1980-84, Calgary S.W. Fed. Riding Assn., 1985-91, The Learning Ctr., Calgary, 1989-91, Halifax United Way, 1991-92, North/South Inst., 1992—, Vol. Planning N.S., 1992-93; planning chmn. John Howard Soc., 1980-84; mem. policy adv. com. C.D. Howe, 1980-85; mem. Ont. Econ. Coun., 1981-84. Woodrow Wilson fellow, 1962. Mem. Assn. Atlantic Univs. (chair 1994—), Assn. Univs. and Colls. in Can. (bd. dirs., mem. exec. com. 1994—), Coun. for Can. Unity (bd. dirs.), Women in Acad. Adminstrn. (adv. bd. 1991-96), Calgary Coun. Advanced Tech. (exec. 1990-91), Can. Econs. Assn., Inst. Pub. Adminstrn. Can., Sr. Women Acad. Adminstrs. Can., Phi Beta Kappa. Anglican. Office: The Univ N B Office of Pres, PO Box 4400, Fredericton, NB Canada E3B 5A3

PARRY, BARBARA DREPPERD, educational administrator; b. Coral Gables, Fla., Sept. 6, 1935; d. Clarence Hartsel and Mildred (Orme) Drepperd; m. William J. Parry, Nov. 3, 1978; children: William H. Glassford, Robert K. Glassford. BEd, U. Miami, 1957; MS in Ednl. Leadership, Nova U., 1993. Cert POP observer, Fla. Tchr. Dade County Pub. Schs., Miami, Fla., Montpelier (Vt.) Pub. Schs.; tkchr. Longmeadow (Mass.) Pub. Schs.; prin. Lower Sch. Gulliver Acad., Coral Gables. Mem. ASCD, NAESP, Nat. Coun. Tchrs. Math., AAUW, Delta Kappa Gamma. Office: Gulliver Acad 12595 Red Rd Miami FL 33156-6397

PARSHALL VEHAR, PERSIS ANNE, composer, pianist, consultant, educator; b. New Salem, N.Y., Sept. 29, 1937; d. Earl LeRoy and Lena Belle (Race) Parshall; m. Robert Rodney Vehar, Aug. 26, 1961; children: Gabrielle Suzanne Vehar, Jonathan Robert Vehar. BMus, Ithaca Coll., 1959; MMus, U. Mich., 1961; studied piano with, Ada Kopetz-Korf, 1961-64; studied with, Warren Benson, Ross Lee Finney, Roberto Gerhard and Ned Rorem. Mem. piano faculty U. Bridgeport, Conn., 1961-63, New Eng. Music Camp, Oakland, Maine, 1962-66; composer, pianist Berta/Vehar Duo, Geneva, N.Y., 1979-83, Shanti Chamber Music Ensemble, Buffalo, 1981-85, Kuelm/Vehar Duo, Buffalo, 1986—, Buried Treasure Ensemble, Buffalo, 1988—; keyboardist Ars Nova Chamber Orch., Buffalo, 1978-79, 86-94; composer, pianist, lectr. Austin Peay State U., Clarksville, Tenn., 1993; keyboardist Chamber Orch. of No N.Y., Potsdam, N.Y., 1994-95; mem. music faculty SUNY, Potsdam, 1994-95; guest lectr. SUNY, Buffalo, Fredonia, Potsdam, N.Y., 1978, 81, 83, 87, 96; mem. awards panel N.Y. State Foun. for Arts, Arts Coun. in Erie County, N.Y., 1983, 87, 89; cons. N.Y. State Coun. on Arts, N.Y.C., 1989—; music lectr. in field. Compositions include: Four Pieces for alto saxophone and piano, Spring Things for SSA and piano, Lord Amherst March for trumpet and piano, Sounds of the Outdoors for alto saxophone, Foursquare for trumpet, Circles in Space for flute, In a Shine Tangent to the Planet at Evening for soprano, oboe/English horn, bassoon, and piano, Trois Renaissance Tableaux for high voice, oboe/flute/clarinet/violin/bassoon/cello, piano or harsichord, Promenade and Cakewalk for saxophone quartet, Sonata for saxophone quartet, Mourning Bird for SATB and piano, Lullaby for SATB, Sonata for Brass Quintet, A Canadian Boat Song, Swan of Avon for three-part voices, SATB, two trumpets, and piano, Zoo-Day for three-part voices and piano, guitar quartet North Country Suite, full orchestra Inevitable Dawn, Light/Lux/Svietlo, wind ensemble Winter Mountain, one-act opera A Hill of Bones; recs. with various orchs. and radios. Meet the Composer grantee, 1983, 87, 89, 90. Mem. ASCAP (Ann. award 1984—), Am. Fedn. Musicians, Am. Music Ctr., Composers' Alliance of Buffalo (v.p., bd. dirs.), Sigma Alpha Iota (v.p., Sword of Honor 1959).

PARSONS, ESTELLE, actress; b. Lynn, Mass., Nov. 20, 1927; d. Eben and Elinor (Mattson) P.; m. Richard Gehman, Dec. 19, 1953 (div. Aug. 1958); children: Martha and Abbie (twins); m. Peter L. Zimroth, Jan. 2, 1983; 1 child, Abraham. B.A. in Polit. Sci., Conn. Coll. Women, 1949; student, Boston U. Law Sch., 1949-50. Stage appearances include: Happy Hunting, 1957, Whoop Up, 1958, Beg, Borrow or Steal, 1960, Threepenny Opera, 1960, Mrs. Dally Has a Lover, 1962, Ready When You Are C.B, 1964, Malcolm, 1965, Seven Descents of Myrtle, 1968, And Miss Reardon Drinks a Little, 1971, Mert and Phil, 1974, The Norman Conquests, 1975-76, Ladies of the Alamo, 1977, Miss Margarida's Way, 1977-78, The Pirates of Penzance, 1981, The Shadow Box, 1994; adapted, dir., performer Orgasmo Adulto Escapes from the Zoo, 1983, The Unguided Missile, Baba Goya, 1989, Shimada, 1992; film appearances include: Bonnie and Clyde, 1966; Rachel, Rachel, 1967, I Never Sang for My Father, 1969, Dick Tracy, 1990, Boys On The Side, 1995; TV appearances include: Roseanne, 1990—; artistic dir. N.Y. Shakespeare Festival Players, 1986. Recipient Theatre World award, 1962-63, Obie award, 1964; recipient award Motion Picture Acad. Arts and Scis., 1967; Recipient Medal of Honor, Conn. Coll., 1969. Home: 505 W End Ave New York NY 10024-4305

PARSONS, HELGA LUND, writer; b. Seattle, Sept. 5, 1906; d. Gunnar and Marie Pauline (Vognild) Lund; m. Durwin David Algyer, June 6, 1937 (dec. 1971); children: Deanne Algyer Mathisen, Marilyn A. McIntosh; m. James Stewart Parsons, Sept. 30, 1972 (dec. 1988). Grad., Columbia Coll. Expression, Chgo., 1926. Lead actress Repertory Playhouse, Seattle, 1929-34; assoc. prof. drama U. Wash., 1931-32; dir. apprentice group Repertory Playhouse, Seattle 1932-34; writer, anchor radio programs Bon Marche Dept. Store, Seattle 1933-35; v.p. creative dir. Norwegian Am. Mus., Decorah, Iowa 1960-66. Author: Norway Travel Newspaper Series, Seattle, 1930, Concert Touring, Monodramas, 1936, (novelized version) Blondie and Dagwood King Features, 1946; script writer serials for WOR, CBS, NBC, N.Y.C.; appeared in Solid Gold Cadillac, I Remember Mama; editor Surfsedge Newsletter. Activities chmn. Glenview, Naples. Mem. Norwegian Am. Mus. (life), MIT (hon.). Republican.

PARSONS, JAYNE DARLENE, special education educator; b. Maynard, Iowa, May 16, 1956; d. David G. and June E. (Olson) P. BA, U. No. Iowa, 1981, MA in Edn., 1984. Tchr. spl. edn. Garwin (Iowa) Comty. Schs., 1981-83; multicategorical resources tchr. Oelwein (Iowa) Comty. Schs., 1984—. Republican. Methodist. Home: 4021 Southlawn Rd Cedar Falls IA 50613-6357 Office: Oelwein Comty Schs 300 12th Ave SE Oelwein IA 50662-2645

PARSONS, KATHRYN KUEHL, accounting executive; b. East St. Louis, Ill., Aug. 8, 1937; d. Harold W. and Ruby N. (Monaghan) Kuehl; m. Edward Brian Parsons; 4 children. Student, U. Calif., San Francisco, 1957-58; BA in History, McKendree Coll., Lebanon, Ill., 1972; postgrad, Webster U., St. Louis. Cert. sec. edn. educator, Ill. Area mgr. Southwestern Bell Telephone Co., St. Louis, 1977—. Asst. sec. Franklin Neighborhood Cmty. Assn., Belleville, Ill., 1994-95; past pres. Hexenbukel Neighborhood Assn., Belleville. Mem. AAUW, NAFE. Episcopalian.

PARSONS, MARCIA PHILLIPS, judge. Bankruptcy judge U.S. Bankruptcy Ct. (Tenn. ea. dist.), 6th circuit, Greeneville, 1993—. Office: US Courthouse 101 W Summer St Greeneville TN 37743-4944

PARSONS, MINDY (MINDY ENOS), magazine editor; b. Cin., May 18, 1962; d. Max Allen and Margery Ann (White) Enos; m. Judd Lewis Parsons, Sept. 4, 1993; children: Cody Robert and Savannah Anne (twins). AA in Liberal Arts, Brevard Community Coll., 1983; BSBA, Fla. Inst. Tech., 1986; MBA, N.Y. Inst., Boca Raton, Fla., 1992. Mem. adminstrv. support staff IBM, Boca Raton, 1980, 81; dir. mktg. Progressive Pub., Melbourne, Fla., 1986; owner, pub. Echelon Pub. Inc., Melbourne, 1986-87; editor Keuthan Communications Inc., Melbourne, 1987-89; staff writer First Mktg. Corp., Pompano Beach, Fla., 1989-90; assoc. editor Billboard Publs. Inc., Coral Springs, Fla., 1990-92, Caribbean Clipper, Inc., Clearwater, Fla., 1992-93; reporter South Fla. News Network, Coral Springs, 1993-94; owner Creative Communications, Delray Beach, Fla., 1993—. Author: How to Save for Your Child's Education, 1990; editor: Soccer for Children, 1988, History of Bahamas, 1990; contbr. articles to profl. publs. Vol. Humane Soc. of Broward County, Coral Springs, 1990-91. Recipient Best Defensive Player award Hotlanta Volleyball Classic III, 1991. Mem. NAFE, Soc. Am. Bus. Editors and Writers, NOW. Republican. Methodist. Home: 221 SE 34th Ave Boynton Beach FL 33435-8632

PARSONS-SALEM, DIANE LORA, lawyer; b. Arlington, Mass., Apr. 17, 1945; d. Hugh Crocker and Tryphena Grace (Reader) Parsons; 1 child, Nicole D. Salem. BA, Boston U., 1967; JD, Suffolk U., 1970. Bar: Mass. 1970, U.S. Dist. Ct. Mass. 1972, U.S. Supreme Ct. 1979. Atty. Allstate Ins. Co., Weston, Mass., 1970-72; assoc. Haig Der Manuelian, Boston, 1972-80; sr. assoc. Widett, Slater & Goldman, P.C., Boston, 1980-84; real estate atty. Friendly Ice Cream Corp., Wilbraham, Mass., 1984-87; asst. gen. counsel Hardee's Food Systems, Inc., Rocky Mount, N.C., 1987-90, dep. gen. counsel, 1990—. Mem. ABA, Mass. Bar Assn., N.C. Bar Assn. Home: 724 Eagles Ter Rocky Mount NC 27804-6404 Office: Hardees Food Systems Inc 1233 Hardees Blvd Rocky Mount NC 27804-2029

PARTEE, BARBARA HALL, linguist, educator; b. Englewood, N.J., June 23, 1940; d. David B. and Helen M. Hall; m. Morriss Henry Partee, 1966 (div. 1971); children: Morriss M., David M., Joel T.; m. Emmon Werner Bach, 1973 (div. 1996). BA with high honors in Math., Swarthmore Coll., 1961; PhD in Linguistics, MIT, 1965; DSc (hon.), Swarthmore Coll., 1989, Charles U., Prague, Czechoslovakia, 1992. Asst. prof. UCLA, 1965-69, assoc. prof., 1969-73; assoc. prof. linguistics and philosophy U. Mass., Amherst, 1972-73, prof., 1973-90, Disting. Univ. prof., 1990—, head dept. linguistics, 1987-93; fellow Ctr. for Advanced Study in Behavior Scis., 1976-77; mem. bd. mgrs. Swarthmore Coll., 1990—. Author: (with Stockwell and Schachter) The Major Syntactic Structures of English, 1972, Fundamentals of Mathematics for Linguists, 1979, (with ter Meulen and Wall) Mathematical Methods in Linguistics, 1990; editor: Montague Grammar, 1976; coeditor: (with Chierchia and Turner) Properties, Types and Meaning, Vol. I: Foundational Issues, Vol. II: Semantic Issues, 1989, (with Bach, Jelinek and Kratzer) Quantification in Natural Languages, 1995; mem. editoral bd: Language, 1967-73, Linguistic Inquiry, 1972-79, Theoretical Linguistics, 1974—, Linguistics and Philosophy, 1977—. Recipient Chancellor's medal U. Mass., 1977; NEH fellow, 1982-83; Internat. Rsch. and Exchanges Bd. fellow, 1989-90, 95. Mem. NAS (chair anthropology sect. 1993-96), Linguistic Soc. Am. (pres. 1986), Am. Philos. Assn., Assn. Computational Linguistics, Am. Acad. Arts and Scis., Sigma Xi. Home: 50 Hobart Ln

Amherst MA 01002-1321 Office: U Mass Dept Linguistics Amherst MA 01003

PARTHEMORE, JACQUELINE G., physician, educator; b. Harrisburg, Pa., Dec. 21, 1940; d. Philip Mark and Emily (Buvit) Parthemore; m. Alan Morton Blank, Jan. 8, 1967; children: Stephen Eliot, Laura Elise. BA, Wellesley Coll., 1962; MD, Cornell U., 1966. Rsch. edn. assoc. VA Hosp., San Diego, 1974-78; staff physician VA Med. Ctr., San Diego, 1978-79, asst. chief, med. svc., 1979-80, acting chief, med. svc., 1980-81, chief of staff, 1984—; rsch. edn. assoc. VA Hosp., San Diego, 1974-78; asst. prof. U. So. Calif. Sch. Medicine, San Diego, 1974-80; prof., assoc. dean U. Calif. Sch. Medicine, $D, 1985—; prof. medicine, assoc. dean U. Calif. Sch. Medicine, San Diego, 1985—; assoc. prof. U. So. Calif. Sch. Medicine, San Diego, 1980-85; staff physician VA Med. Ctr., San Diego, 1978-79, asst. chief med. svc., 1979-80, acting chief, 1980-81; $D $D, $D; mem. nat. rsch. resources coun. NIH, Bethesda, Md., 1990-94. Contbr. articles to profl. jours., chpts. to books. Bd. dirs. San Diego Vets. Med. Rsch. Found.; mem. adv. bd. San Diego Opera. Recipient Bullock's 1st Annual Portfolio award, 1985, San Diego Pres.'s Coun. Woman of Yr. award, 1985, YWCA Tribute to Women in Industry award, 1987. Fellow ACP; mem. Endocrine Soc., Am. Fedn. Clin. Rsch., Am. Bone and Mineral Soc., Nat. Assn. VA Chiefs Staff (pres. 1989-91), Am. Assn. Clin. Endocrinologists, Wellesley Coll. Alumnae Assn. (1st v.p. 1992-95). Office: VA Med Ctr 3350 La Jolla Village Dr San Diego CA 92161-0002

PARTLOW, SHARA SUE, nursing educator; b. Amarillo, Tex., Apr. 24, 1951; d. William Frank and Lillie Ruth (Chambers) Partlow; divorced; children: David Ray, Daniel Mathis. Diploma of Nursing, N.W. Tex. Hosp., Amarillo, 1972; AAS, Amarillo Jr. Coll., 1978; BSN, W. Tex. State U., 1979, MSN, 1980. RN, Tex. Operating room supr. S.W. Osteopathic Hosp., Amarillo, Tex., 1973-75; team leader High Plains Bapt. Hosp., Amarillo, 1976-79; chmn. nursing leadership dept. N.W. Tex. Hosp., Amarillo, 1979-81; part-time staff nurse Okla. Teaching Hosp., Oklahoma City, 1986-87; instr. Southwestern Okla. State U., Weatherford, 1986-87; instr. sch. nursing Meth. Hosp., Lubbock, Tex., 1987—; instr./trainer Am. Heart Assn., Amarillo, 1980-83. Recipient N.W. Tex. Hosp. Community Svc. award, 1982, Estelle Munn award Toastmistress, 1982, 83; named Outstanding Young Woman of Am., 1982; winner regional contest Toastmistress, 1982. Mem. ANA, ARC, Nursing Oncology Edn. Programs. Roman Catholic. Home: 5817 22nd St Apt 40 Lubbock TX 79407-1701 Office: Meth Hosp Sch Nursing 2002 Miami Ave Lubbock TX 79410-1010

PARTNOW, ELAINE T., author, actress, business owner; b. L.A., Oct. 28, 1941; d. Al and Jeanette (Bernstein) P.; m. Turner Browne, Aug. 6, 1974. Student, UCLA, 1959-62. Repertory theater dir. Liberty Farm Teenage Tng. Ctr., Antrim, N.H., 1984-85; dir. U.S.-China Friendship Camp, 1986; acting tchr. Contemporary Arts Ctr., New Orleans, 1983-87; theater & festival dir. Interlocken Internat. Summer Camp, Hillsboro, N.H., 1987; tchr. repertory theater Isidore Newman Sch., New Orleans, 1985; co-dir. Seattle Peace Theater Chorus, 1989. Author: The Quotable Woman: 1800-1975, 1977, Breaking the Age Barrier, 1981, The Quotable Woman: 1800-1981, 1983, The Quotable Woman: Eve-1799, 1985, The New Quotable Woman, From Eve to the Present Day, 1992, (play) Hispanic Women Speak, 1987, Hear Us Roar, A Woman's Connection; (performance piece) A Visit with Emily Dickinson; contbr. articles to profl. jours.; actress (stage) Born Yesterday, Last of the Red Hot Lovers, Witnesses, Miss Perkins, The Year Boston Won the Pennant, Goodbye Charlie, Passion, Pigeons, Hear Us Roar, Movers & Shakers, A Visit with Emily Dickinson, The Belle of Amherst, King Lear, others; (film) What's Up, Doc?, Targets, Busting, Cool Breeze, Whiskey Flats, Only Once in a Lifetime, Mother Tiger, Mother Tiger, Seconds, Hauser, I Dismember Mama, Terror in the Jungle, Marigold Man, Nickleodeon, Uncle Tom's Cabin. Recipient Best Actress award Pasadena Playhouse, MEG/Arts Living History award, 1987, S.W. Interdisciplinary award La. Divsn. of Arts, Wash. Commn. for Humanities, Wash. Divsn. Arts, King County Divsn. Arts; La. Commn. for Humanities grantee.

PARTRIDGE, CONNIE R., advertising executive; b. Bklyn., Apr. 10, 1941; d. Nicholas and Teresa (Monteleone) Sorrentino; m. Vincent Richard Partridge, Dec. 17, 1960 (div. Aug. 1983); children: Jean Marie, Marianne, James. Student, Coll. New Rochelle (N.Y.), 1958-60; BA, Coll. Old Westbury, 1979. Sr. account exec. Finesse Promotions, Queens Village, N.Y., 1979-84; pres. Partridge Promotions, Wheatley Heights, N.Y., 1984—; mem. pres.'s roundtable Suffolk C.C. Pres. Taukomas Sch. PTA, Wheatley Heights, N.Y., 1972-74; v.p. Half Hollow Hills Coun., Dix Hills, N.Y., 1974-76; campaign mgr. Half Hollow Hills Sch. Bd. Elections, 1978; dir. Suffolk County Women's Bus. Enterprise Coalition, 1989—; mem. program adv. bd. Sta. WLIW/Channel 21; bd. dirs. Suffolk C.C. Found. Recipient Jenkins Meml. award N.Y. State PTA, 1974, Small Bus. Advocate of Yr. SBA with L.I. Assn., 1996. Mem. NAFE, Nat. Assn. Women Bus. Owners (L.I. chpt. founder 1985, corr. sec. 1986, v.p. 1989, pres. 1994—), L.I. Assn./Small Bus. Coun., L.I. Advt. Club, L.I. Ctr. Bus. and Profl. Women, Splty. Advt. Assn. Internat. (cert. advt. specialist), Splty. Advt. Assn. Greater N.Y. (scholarship award), Pres.'s Roundtable. Democrat. Roman Catholic.

PASCAL, LAURA ELLEN, counselor; b. Passaic, N.J., July 6, 1967; d. Mondy C. and Miriam C. (Smith) P. BA, Trenton State Coll., 1989; MA in Counseling, NYU, 1993. Supplemental instrn. leader Trenton (N.J.) State Coll., 1988-89; residence counselor South Bergen Mental health, Lyndhurst, N.J., 1989-94; counselor North Essex Devel. Coun., Montclair, N.J., spring 1992, Fairleigh Dickinson U., Madison, N.J., spring 1993, Hudson County C.C., Jersey City, 1994—. Mem. Grad. Student Orgn. NYU, 1993; vol. N.J. Buddies, 1993—. Scholar NYU Sch. Edn., 1992-93, Grad. Student Orgn., 1993. Mem. ACA, N.J. Edn. Assn. (counselor rep. 1995-96), N.J. C.C. Counselors Assn., NYU Alumni Assn., Am. Coll. Counseling Assn., Hudson County Guidance Assn. Home: 128 E Broad St Apt # 1 Westfield NJ 07090 Office: Hudson CC 25 Pathside Jersey City NJ 07306

PASCHAL, BETH CUMMINGS, journalist, editor; b. Lohrville, Iowa, June 26, 1917; d. Harry Ross and Agnes (Baird) Cummings. m. George Washington Paschal Jr., Dec. 20, 1944 (dec. Feb. 1995); children: George Washington III, Laura Huston, Robert Cummings. BS, Iowa State U., 1939. Assoc. editor Farm Jour., Phila., 1939-45; bd. dirs. N.C. Art Soc., Raleigh, 1959-69, v.p., pres., 1961-68; bd. dirs. N.C. Mus. Art, Raleigh, 1964—, vice chmn. new bldg. campaign, 1977-78, mem. works of art com., 1983—, docent, 1955-87, donor, 1970, docent emeritus, 1987—, trustee emeritus, 1995—. Editor: A Celebration of Art and Cookery, 1976; columnist Trident Mag., 1940-43; editor State Med. Aux. Newsletter, 1955-63. Arch. selection com. Fine Arts Ctr. Wake Forest U., Winston-Salem, N.C., 1975; chmn. mus. com. Gov. Cultural Adv. Coun., Raleigh, 1980. Recipient honor, N.C. Mus. Art, Acquisition of Art, 1974, Alumni Merit award Iowa State U., 1980, Raleigh medal of arts, 1986, Phi Beta Kappa award. 1995; named Tarheel of Week Raleigh News & Observer, 1965; elected YWCA Acad. of Women, 1983. Mem. Jr. League Raleigh, Nat. Humanities Ctr. (dir. coun.), Carolina Country Club, Nine O'Clock Cotillion, Mortar Bd., Delta Delta Delta, Theta Sigma Phi. Home: 3334 Alamance Dr Raleigh NC 27609

PASCHALL, EVITA ARNEDA, lawyer; b. Augusta, Ga., May 18, 1951; d. Marion R. and Lucille (Turner) Paschall; m. Felix Bryan Andrews, May 5, 1990; 1 child by previous marriage, Evita Lucille Young; 1 child, Felix Bryan Andrews Jr. BA, Howard U., 1973; JD, U. Ga., 1976. Bar: Ga. 1976, U.S. Ct. Appeals (11th cir.) 1978, U.S. Bankruptcy Ct. (so. dist.) Ga. 1982. Asst. dist. atty. Richmond County Dist. Atty.'s Office, Augusta, 1976-79; assoc. Brown and Paschall, Augusta, 1979-81; pvt. practice, Augusta, 1981—; asst. solicitor Ga. State Ct., Augusta, 1984-85; solicitor Magistrate's Ct., Augusta, 1987-94; judge Mcpl. Ct., Augusta, 1994—. Pub., co-editor Augusta Today Mag. Bd. dirs. Bethlehem Community Ctr., Augusta, 1981-89, v.p., 1987-88; mem. Leadership Augusta, 1979, Jaycees. Mem. Augusta Bar Assn.

PASCHKE, BARBARA PHILIPPS, academic administrator; b. Orange, N.J., Aug. 12, 1946; d. Robert J. and Mary A. Philipps; m. William L. Paschke, June 22, 1968. BA, Drew U., 1968; MA, U. Oreg., 1969. Rsch. assoc. U. Kans., Lawrence, 1972-75, adminstr., 1975-77, prin. analyst, 1977-82; asst. dir. Capitol Complex Ctr., Topeka, 1982-83; spl. asst. for planning State Computer and Telecom., Topeka, 1983-84, asst. dir. mgmt., 1984-86; dir. rsch. and policy State Pers. Svcs., Topeka, 1986-88; assoc. dir. acad. affairs Kans. Bd. Regents, Topeka, 1988—; mem. Swarthout Bd., Lawrence, 1984-86, Assn. Instl. Rsch., 1981-85. Named Contbr. of Yr., Cause/Effect, 1984. Mem. AAUW, Kans. Libr. Network Bd.

PASCOE, GRETCHEN ELIZABETH, legal society administrator; b. Huntsville, Ala., May 28, 1967; d. Paul Howell Glenn and Peggy Lucile (Guffin) Trout; m. Thomas Clark Pascoe, Dec. 21, 1995. BSBA, Samford U., 1989; fgn. lang. program, Shanghai Normal U., 1990. Registrar HBJ/Bar Bri, Washington, 1990-93; adminstrv. asst. Christian Legal soc., Annandale, Va., 1993-94, devel. coord., 1994-95, devel. officer, 1995—. Mem. Nat. Soc. Fund Raising Execs. Republican. Office: Christian Legal Soc Ste 222 4208 Evergreen Ln Annandale VA 22003

PASCOE, PATRICIA HILL, state senator, writer; b. Sparta, Wis., June 1, 1935; d. Fred Kirk and Edith (Kilpatrick) Hill; m. D. Monte Pascoe, Aug. 3, 1957; children: Sarah, Ted, Will. BA, U. Colo., 1957; MA, U. Denver, 1968, PhD, 1982. Tchr. Sequoia Union High Sch. Dist., Redwood City, Calif. and Hayward (Calif.) Union High Sch. Dist., 1957-60; instr. Met. State Coll., Denver, 1969-75; instr. Denver U., 1975-77, 81, research asst. bur. ednl. research, 1981-82; tchr. Kent Denver Country Day, Englewood, Colo., 1982-84; freelance writer Denver, 1985—; mem. Colo. Senate, Denver, 1989-92, 95—; commr. Edn. Commn. of the States, Denver, 1975-82. Contbr. articles to numerous publs. and jours. Bd. dirs. Samaritan House, 1990-94, Cystic Fibrosis Found., 1989-93; pres. East High Sch. Parent, Tchr. and Student Assn., Denver, 1984-85; mem. Moore Budget Adv. Com., Denver, 1966-72; legis. chmn. alumni bd. U. Colo., Boulder, 1987-89; del. Dem. Nat. Conv., San Francisco, 1984, N.Y.C., 1992. Mem. Soc. Profl. Journalists, Common Cause (bd. dirs. Denver chpt. 1986-88), Colo. Endowment for Humanities, Phi Beta Kappa. Presbyterian.

PASKAWICZ, JEANNE FRANCES, anesthesiologist; b. Phila., Mar. 3, 1954; d. Alex and Lillian (Pyluck) P. BSc, Phila. Coll. Pharmacy; MA, Villanova U., 1973; postgrad., St. Joseph U., 1979; PhD, Kensington U., 1984. Mem. anesthesiology staff Einstein Med. Ctr., Phila., 1990-94, Temple U. Hosp., 1994—; mem. detox./rehab. staff Presbyn. Med. Ctr., Phila., 1984—; house officer MCD-Elkins Park (Pa.) Campus, 1990—; mem. psychiatry staff Hahnemann U. Hosp., Phila., 1984-90; hostage negotiator Office of Mental Health, Phila., 1984-90; mem. surgery/anesthesiology staff Mt. Sinai Hosp., Phila., 1989-91. Bd. dirs. Phila. Coll. Pharmacy, St. Joseph U. Mem. NAFE, Am. Pain Soc., Nat. Parks Conservation Assn., North Shore Animal League, Amvets, DAV Comdrs. Club, Lambda Kappa Sigma.

PASKEY, MONICA ANNE, dietitian; b. Pasadena, Calif., Aug. 18, 1960; d. Harold Lloyd and Gloria Dolores (Swanson) Macomber; m. Dennis J. Paskey, Nov. 11, 1995; 1 child, Brittany Anne. Student, Mills Coll., 1978-80; BS cum laude, U. Conn., 1983. Registered dietitian. Clin. dietitian Marriott Corp., Washington, 1983-84; food svc. mgr. Marriott Corp., Virginia Beach, 1984-86; food svc. dir. Marriott Corp., Balt., 1987-88; oncology nutrition supr. Johns Hopkins U., Balt., 1988-89; cons. dietitian Beverly Enterprises, Balt., 1989-91; corp. menu mgr. Beverly Enterprises, Ft. Smith, Ark., 1991—; cons. dietitian, Virginia Beach, 1985-86. Author: (pamphlet) Campus Weekend Cooking Simplified, 1983; contbr. Beverly Enterprises Diet Manual, 1993, Thickened Liquids Manual, 1994. Recipient Spkr.'s award Eli Lilly, Inc., 1985. Mem. Am. Dietetic Assn., Va. Dietetic Assn., Tidewater Dist. Dietetic Assn. (treas. 1985-86), Md. Dietetic Assn. (job referral coord. 1987-89), Ark. Dietetic Assn. (media rep. 1996), Ark. Cons. Dietitians (health care facilities liaison 1992—, chair 1995-96). Roman Catholic. Office: Beverly Enterprises 5111 Rogers Ave Fort Smith AR 72919-3700

PASMANICK, FRANCES VIRGINIA COHEN, admissions director; b. Portsmouth, Va., Jan. 24, 1923; d. Meyer and Lillian (Walker) Cohen; m. Kenneth Pasmanick, Dec. 22, 1946; children: Philip, Anne. Student, Am. Univ., 1941-46. Editl. analyst Army-Navy Electronics Prodn. Agy., Washington, 1941-48; adminstrv. asst. CIO Polit. Action Com., Washington, 1948-50, Nat. Farmers Union, Washington, 1950-52; adminstrv. asst. spl. project aging Com. Nat. Health, Washington, 1960-63; dir. admissions Georgetown Day Sch., Washington, 1963—. Writer, editor (newsletter) Georgetown Day Sch., 1971-73. Tchr. Reevaluation Counseling, 1975-85. Recipient Extraordinary Efforts award Black Student Fund, 1978. Mem. AAUW, Women's Action Nuc. Disarmament (founder Washington chpt. 1984). Democrat. Jewish. Address: 5227 Church Pky Washington DC 20015

PASNIK, JUDITH L. CROOT, physical therapist, consultant, author; b. Basking Ridge, N.J., Aug. 13, 1941; d. Edward James and Eleonore Ruth (Becker) Croot; m. Michael James Pasnik, Nov. 25, 1967; children: Michael, Melissa, Mark, David. BS, Tufts U., 1963. Cert. Mass. Bd. Phys. Therapy, N.J. Lic. Bd. Phys. Therapy. Staff, clin. instr. Brigham Hosp., Boston, 1963-64; dir. rehabilitation Am. Leprosy Mission, N.Y.C., 1964-69; dir. rehabilitation, cons. Govt. Philippines, 1964-67; supr. therapies, cons. utilization rev. & profl. adv. Vis. Nurses Assn., Bernardsville, N.J., 1970-95; pres., owner Somerset Hills Phys. Therapy P.C., Bedminster and Basking Ridge, N.J., 1978—; clin. instr. Fairleigh Dickinson U., 1988-96, Damien Coll., 1989-96, Ind. U., 1992-96, U. Medicine & Dentistry of N.J., 1994-96, Howard U., 1995-96. Author: (textbook) Instructional Textbook for Physical Therapy in Leprosy, 1966, 67, 69, 72; contbr. articles to profl. jours. Ruling elder, chair edn. Presbyn. Ch., Basking Ridge, 1973-76, chair personnel com., 1992-95; mem., chmn. com. on theological edn. United Presbyn. Ch./Presbyn. U.S., Louisville, 1982-88; founding trustee Somerset Hills Adult Care Ctr., Basking Ridge, 1988-95; bd. trustees Somerset Hills YMCA, 1996—. Recipient Woman of the Yr. Somerset Women's Bus. Club, 1968. Mem. Am. Phys. Therapy Assn. (mem. N.J. chpt. 1969—, mem. pvt. practice sect., mem. hand sect., mem. sports medicine/orthopedic sect.). Home: PO Box 363 Basking Ridge NJ 07920 Office: Somerset Hills Phys Therapy PC 150 N Finley Ave Basking Ridge NJ 07920

PASSIDOMO-KHAN, MARIAN ANDREA, academic administrator; b. Bronx, N.Y., Jan. 31, 1940; d. Andrew Ralph and Lucille (Campagnola) Passidomo; m. Tamkeen Naim Khan, Sept. 9, 1984. BA, Hunter Coll., 1960; MS, Lehman Coll., 1969; PhD, Fordham U., 1978. Cert. tchr., N.Y. Tchr. N.Y.C. Bd. Edn., Bronx, 1962-65, prin., 1967-69; tchr. N.Y.C. Bd. Edn., 1969-71; rschr., writer Appleton Century Croft Publ., N.Y.C., 1965-67; nat. reading cons. Prentice Hall Publ., Englewood Cliffs, N.J., 1971-74; dir. curriculum Sch. Dist. Haverstraw-Stony Pt. Cen. Sch. Dist., Garnerville, N.Y., 1974-82, dir. reading, early chldhood, fed. funds and testing, 1982—; cons., pres. Edn. Cons., Darien, Conn., 1991—; adv. bd. RIECO, Darien, 1987—. Contbr. articles to profl. jours. Mem. Assn. Supervisory and Curriculum Dirs., Nat. Assn. for Edn. Young Children, Internat. Reading Assn. Office: Haverstraw Stony Point Ctrl Sch Dist 65 Chapel St Garnerville NY 10923

PASSONS, DONNA JANELLE, academic administrator; b. Ft. Benning, Ga., Apr. 15, 1951; d. Robert James and Mary Anita (Morris) P.; m. Phillip Michael Holmes, Oct. 27, 1989. BA in Govt., U. Tex., 1980, MBA, 1989. Adminstrv. asst. Gov.'s Div. Planning Coord., Austin, Tex., 1972-74, Commn. on Pub. Edn., Tex. Ho. of Reps., Austin, 1975, Med. Profl. Liability Study Commn., Austin, 1975-77; adminstrv. asst. U. Tex. Sch. of Law, Austin, 1977-80, conf. coord. Office Continuing Legal Edn., 1980-84; asst. dir. U. Tex. Sch. Law, Austin, 1984-85, dir., 1985-89, asst. dean Office Continuing Legal Edn., 1989-94; exec. dir. Tex. Inst. Continuing Legal Edn., Austin, 1995—; pres. Specialized Profl. Insts., Inc., 1992—. Mem. ABA, Assn. CLE Adminstrs. (bd. dirs.-at-large 1984-85, treas. 1985-86, sec. 1986-87, pres.-elect 1987-88, pres. 1988-89), Meeting Planners Internat. (bd. dirs. Hill Country chpt. exec. com. 1985-86, 91), Am. Assn. Law Schs. (bd. dirs. CLE com. 1991-92, sec. CLE com. 1992-93, chmn.-elect 1993-94, chmn. 1994-95), Am. Soc. Assn. Execs., Tex. Soc. Assn. Execs. Office: PO Box 4646 Austin TX 78765-4646

PASSUS, JENNIFER ASHLEY, elementary school educator; b. Concord, Mass., Oct. 4, 1971; d. Edward Anthony and Catherine Anna (Donato) P. BS in Edn., Framingham State Coll., 1993. Cert. grade 1-6 tchr., Mass. Tchr. grade 5 Pleasant Street Sch., Athol, Mass., 1993—. Mem. Nat. Coun. Tchrs. of Math., Nat. Coun. Tchrs. of English, Mass. Reading Assn., Internat. Reading Assn., Kappa Delta Pi, Sigma Tau Delta. Democrat. Roman Catholic. Office: Pleasant St Sch 1060 Pleasant St Athol MA 01331

PASSWATER, BARBARA GAYHART, real estate broker; b. Phila., July 10, 1945; d. Clarence Leonard and Margaret Jamison; m. Richard Albert Passwater, June 2, 1964; children: Richard Alan, Michael Eric. AA, Goldey-Beacom Coll., 1963; BA, Salisbury State U., 1981. Notary pub., Md. Sec. DuPont, Wilmington, Del., 1963-65, Nuclear-Chgo., Silver Spring, Md., 1965-67; office mgr. Montgomery County Sch. System, Wheaton, Md., 1977-79; adminstrv. asst. Solgar Nutritional Rsch. Ctr., Berlin, Md., 1979-94, asst. to dir. rsch., 1995—; assoc. broker Prudential-Groff Realty, Berlin, Md., 1983-87, ReMax, Inc., Berlin, Md., 1987-88; broker, mgr., developers rep. River Run Sales Ctr., Berlin, Md., 1988-96; pvt. practice, broker Berlin, 1996—. Treas. Ocean Pines (Md.) Vol. Fire Dept. Aux., 1981-84; emergency med. tech. Ocean Pines (Md.) Vol. Fire Dept., 1983-95; sec. Ocean Pines (Md.) Fire Dept., 1990-95; mem. Foster Care Review Bd., Snow Hill, Md., 1984—; life mem. Ocean Pines Vol. Fire Dept., 1996—. Mem. Beta Sigma Phi, Phi Kappa Phi. Office: Solgar Nutritional Rsch Ctr 11017 Manklin Meadows Ln Berlin MD 21811

PASTER, JANICE D., lawyer, state legislator; b. St. Louis, Aug. 4, 1942. BA, Northwestern U., 1964; MA, Tufts U., 1967; JD, U. N.Mex., 1984. Atty. in pvt. practice, 1984—; mem. N.Mex. State Senate from 10th dist. Democrat. Home: 5553 Eakes Rd NW Albuquerque NM 87107-5529 Address: PO Box 1966 Albuquerque NM 87103

PASTERNAK, CYNTHIA F., lawyer; b. N.Y.C., May 14, 1952; d. Joseph M. and Lillian Rosen; m. David J. Pasternak. BA, UCLA, 1973; JD, Loyola U., L.A., 1976. Assoc. Law Offices Edward L. Marsy, 1977-78; ptnr. Irwin, Hale & Jacobs, 1978-90; of counsel Herman & Wallach, 1990-93; mng. ptnr. Appleton, Pasternak & Pasternak, L.A., 1993—. Contbr. articles to profl. jours. Recipient Disting. Svc. award Harriet Buhai Ctr. Family Law, 1991. Mem. ABA (family law sect., litigation sect., torts & ins. practice sect.), ATLA, NAFE, Calif. Women Lawyers, Barristers L.A. County Bar Assn. (chmn. artists and law 1983-84, co-chmn. econs. law practice 1982-83), Beverly Hills Bar Assn. (family law sect., litigation sect., real estate sect., bd. govs. 1996—, chair legis. com. 1996—, resolutions com. 1995, 96, del. State Bar Conf. Dels. 1995, 96, spkr. mentor program 1994, spkr. MCLE extravaganza 1995, 96), Consumer Attys. Assn. L.A., Century City Bar Assn. (co-chair tort litigation sect. 1996—), L.A. County Bar Assn. (labor and employment sect., family law sect., litigation sect.), Valley Associated Settlement Team (settlement officer 1995, 96), Women Lawyers Assn. L.A., Mensa, UCLA Alumni Assn. (life), UCLA Mortar Bd. Alumni Assn. Office: Appleton Pasternak & Pasternak 1925 Century Pk E Ste 2140 Los Angeles CA 90067

PASTERNAK, JOANNA MURRAY, special education and gifted and talented educator; b. Houston, Feb. 9, 1953; d. Lee Roy and Evelyn Mary (Kirmss) Murray; children: Sheila Ann Tanner, Lawrence Ross Tanner IV; m. Allen Pasternak, Jan. 9, 1993. BA in Liberal Arts with honors, Our Lady of the Lake, San Antonio, 1990. Acctg. clk. Houston Post, 1981-85; owner, art cons. Tanner Fine Art, Houston, 1985-92; spl. edn. tchr. Houston Ind. Sch. Dist., 1991-94, dept. chmn., 1994; art cons. Plz. Gallery, Houston, 1985; mem. benefits com. Houston Ind. Sch. Dist., 1992—; presenter Am. Fedn. Tchrs. Nat. Edn. Conf., 1994. Contrb. articles to profl. jours. Vol. legis com. nat. health care campaign AFL-CIO; bd. dirs. PTA, SDMC; mem., pres. Westlawn Terrace Civic Club; Dem. campaign worker, 1993—; precinct and state del. Dem. Senate, 1994; sec. Dist. 13 Dem. Com., 1996. Mem. Tex. Fedn. Tchrs. (bd. dirs. quality ednl. stds. in tchg. 1993), Houston Fedn. Tchrs. (chmn. legis. liaison com. 1993—, v.p. 1992—), Delta Mu Delta. Democrat. Home: 2141 Colquitt St Houston TX 77098-3310 Office: Houston Fedn Tchrs 3100 Weslayan St Ste 445 Houston TX 77027-5748

PASTINE, MAUREEN DIANE, university librarian; b. Hays, Kans., Nov. 21, 1944; d. Gerhard Walter and Ada Marie (Hillman) Hillman; m. Jerry Joel Pastine, Feb. 5, 1966. AB, in English, Ft. Hays State U., 1967; MLS, Emporia State U., 1970. Reference librarian U. Nebr.-Omaha, 1971-77; undergrad. libr. U. Ill., Urbana, 1977-79; reference librarian, 1979-80; univ. libr. San Jose State U.-Calif., 1980-85; dir. librs. Wash. State U., Pullman, 1985-89; ctrl. univ. libr. So. Meth. U., 1989—; mem. adv. bd. Foothill Coll. Libr. 1983-85; leader ednl. del. librs. to People's Republic of China, 1985, Australia/New Zealand, 1986, Soviet Union, 1988, East & West Germany, Czechoslovakia, Hungary, Austria, 1991, Brazil, 1993. Co-author: Library and Library Related Publications: A Directory of Publishing Opportunities, 1973; asst. compiler: Women's Work and Women's Studies, 1973-74, 1975; compiler procs. Teaching Bibliographic Instruction in Graduate Schools of Library Science, 1981; editor: Integrating Library Use Skills into the General Education Curriculum, 1989, Collection Development: Present and Future in Collection Management, 1996; co-editor: In the Spirit of 1991: Access to Western European Libraries and Literature, 1992; contbr. articles to profl. publs. Recipient Disting. Alumni Grad. award Emporia State U., 1986, Dudley Bibliog. Instruction Libr. of Yr. award, 1989. Mem. ALA (chmn. World Book-ALA Goal awards jury 1984-85), Assn. Coll. and Rsch. Librs. (editorial adv. bd. BIS Think Tank 1982-85, chmn. bibliographic instrn. sect. 1983-84, editorial bd. Choice 1983-85, chmn. Miriam Dudley Bibliographic Instrn. Libr. of Yr. award com. 1984-85, mem. task force on librarians as instrs. 1986-88, chair task force internat. rels. 1987-89, BIS Libr. of Yr. 1989, rep. to AAAS/CAIP, 1989-94, chair internat. rels. com. 1990-94, ALA pay equity com. 1994—, chmn. rsch. libr. of yr. award's com. 1995-96, acad. status com. 1996—), Libr. Adminstrn. and Mgmt. Assn. (chmn. stats. sect. com. on devel., orgn., planning and programming 1982-83, sec. stats. sect. exec. com. 1982-83, mem. at large 1986-88), ALA Library Instrn. Round Table (long range planning com. 1986-94), ALA Libr. Rsch. Round Table, Wash. Libr. Assn., Assn. Libr. Collections & Tech. Svcs. Divsn., Libr. and Info. Tech. Assn., Assn. Specialized and Coop. Libr. Agencies (chair multilincs internat. networking discussion group 1990-92), Libr. Rsch. Roundtable, Women's Studies Sect., Eng. and Am. Lit. Studies Discussion Group, Tex. Libr. Assn. (mentor Tall Texans Leadership Inst., 1995-96), Pacific N.W. Libr. Assn., Phi Kappa Phi, Beta Phi Mu. Home: 8720 Hanford Dr Dallas TX 75243-6416 Office: So Meth U Cen Univ Librs PO Box 750135 Dallas TX 75275-0135

PASTVA, PATRICIA FRANKLIN, controller, accountant; b. Abingdon, Pa., Nov. 27, 1962; d. J. Thomas and Patricia (Peyton) Franklin; m. David Anthony Pastva, Oct. 12, 1985 (div. Nov. 1993). BS, Va. Tech., 1985. CPA, Va. Sr. acct. Jarrett & Co., Alexandria, Va., 1985-88; mgr. Murphy & Deane, Fairfax, Va., 1988-94; contr. Sonix Inc., Springfield, Va., 1994—. Mem. AICPA, NAFE, Va. Soc. CPAs. Home: 12260 Wye Oak Commons Cir Burke VA 22015 Office: Sonix Inc 8700 Morrissette Dr Springfield VA 22152

PATANO, PATRICIA ANN, health and fitness professional, marketing and public relations specialist; b. Chgo., June 14, 1950; d. Thomas Vincent and Gladys Estelle (Olejniczak) P. Student, Los Angeles Pierce Coll., 1968-70, UCLA, 1974-84; BS in Bus. and Mgmt. summa cum laude, U. Redlands, 1995. Pub. relations mgr. Motel 6, Inc., Century City, Calif., 1974-77; mgr. corp. communications 1st Travel Corp., Van Nuys, Calif., 1977-79; mktg. pub. relations mgr. Unitours, Inc., Los Angeles, 1979-81; asst. v.p. pub. relations Los Angeles Olympic Com., 1981-84; pres., co-owner PaVage Fitness Innovations, Playa del Rey, Calif., 1984-88; dir. spl. projects J.D. Power and Assocs., Agoura Hills, Calif., 1988—; trustee Nat. Injury Prevention Found., San Diego, 1983—; cons. Dick Clark Productions, Burbank, Calif., 1985, Reebok USA Ltd., Boston, 1983—. Co-author: MuscleAerobics, 1985; contbr. articles to profl. jours. Vol. Motion Picture Hosp., Woodland Hills, Calif., 1968-70; bd. dirs. Los Angeles Boys and Girls Club, 1984—; mem. council San Fernando Natural History Mus., 1987-89; big sister Pride House, Van Nuys, 1987-89; active juvenile delinquent program Pride House. Recipient Corp. award Pres.'s Council Phys. Fitness, 1983; fellow Alfred North Whitehead Leaderships Soc.-U. Redlands, 1995. Mem. L.A. Advt. Club, Nat. Injury Prevention Found. (trustee 1984-87), Child Shelter Homes: A Rescue Effort (bd. dirs.), Mid Valley Athletic Club (Reseda, Calif.), Marina City (Marina del Rey, Calif.). Republican. Presbyterian. Clubs: Mid Valley Athletic (Reseda, Calif.); Marina City (Marina del Rey, Calif.). Office: JD Power & Assocs 30401 Agoura Rd Agoura Hills CA 91301-2084

PATCH, JENNIFER LYNN, biologist; b. Raleigh, N.C., Nov. 17, 1974; d. Charles Ephraim and Linda Jane (Oby) P. BS in Biology, William & Mary, Williamsburg, Va., 1996. Coach, swim instr. Seven Oaks Pool, Raleigh, 1990-92; swim instr. MacGregor Pool, Cary, N.C., 1992-94; vet. technician asst. Armadale Vet., Raleigh, 1995; vet. technician Colonial Vet., Williamsburg, 1995—. Author poems. Academic Booster's Club scholar, 1993, Dept. of Navy scholar, 1993—. Mem. Kappa Kappa Gamma. Home and Office: CS Box 3030 Williamsburg VA 23186

PATCHECK, GEORGIA ANN, educator; b. Ballinger, Tex., Mar. 13, 1939; d. Mitchell Lee and Marjorie (Bruton) Christy; m. Robert E. Patcheck, Dec. 4, 1954; children: Cathy Wilson, Cindy Morgan, Robert, Mike. BA, Ft. Lewis Coll., 1972; MA, Adams State Coll., 1986. Dir. Kid's Coll., 1989—; 6th grade tchr. Kemper Elem., Cortez, Colo., 1972-81, Bayfield (Colo.) Middle Sch., 1982-89, Ft. Lewis Mesa Elem., Durango, Colo., 1981-91, Smiley Middle Sch., 1991—; mem., pub. rels. cons. Colo. Assn. Pub. Employees, Durango, 1993-94; pres. Community Centered Bd., Cortez, Colo., 1973-75. Mem. Colo. Edn. Assn. (assn. rep., Lion award 1994). Democrat. Lutheran. Home: 14869 CR 105 Mancos CO 81328 Office: Escalante Mid Sch Baker Ln Durango CO 81301

PATE, BOBBIE JOYCE KOHLER, secondary school educator, elementary principal; b. Clayton, N. Mex., Feb. 17, 1953; d. Joe and Sarah Opal (Williams) Kohler; m. Curtis Doyle Pate, Dec. 17, 1976; children: Chad Jerome and Tamara Nicole. BA in English, Panhandle State U., 1977; MEd in Sch. Adminstrn., West Tex. A&M U., 1995. Tchr. Texline (Tex.) Ind. Sch. Dist., 1977-81, Boise City (Okla.) Schs., 1981-84, Channing (Tex.) Ind. Sch. Dist., 1984-90, Dumas (Tex.) Ind. Sch. Dist., 1990-91, Goodwell (Okla.) Schs., 1991-92, Yarborough Schs., Goodwell, 1993—; sponsor speech club, nat. honor soc., Yarbrough Schs., Goodwell, 1993—, bowling league 1994-95; mem. gifted talented com. Yarbrough Schs., Goodwell, 1994—. Instr. Conversational Spanish, Boise City, Okla., 1983; sponsor H.S. Rodeo Club, Goodwell, 1993-94. Champion IFCA Reserve Barrel Racing, 1977, Region X and XIV, champion team roper, 1977. Democrat. Mem. Ch. of Christ. Home: PO Box 771 Stratford TX 79084

PATE, JACQUELINE HAIL, retired data processing company manager; b. Amarillo, Tex., Apr. 7, 1930; d. Ewen and Virginia Smith (Crosland) Hail; student Southwestern U., Georgetown, Tex., 1947-48; children: Charles (dec.), John Durst, Virginia Pate Edgecomb, Christopher. Exec. sec. Western Gear Corp., Houston, 1974-76; adminstr., treas., dir. Aberrant Behavior Ctr., Personality Profiles, Inc., Corp. Procedures, Inc., Dallas, 1976-79; mgr. regional site svcs programs Digital Equipment Corp., Dallas, 1979-92, ret. 1992; realtor Keller Williams Realty, Austin, Tex., 1996—; mem. Austin Bd. Realtors. Active PTA, Dallas, 1958-73. Mem. Daus. Republic Tex. (treas. French legation state com. 1996). Methodist. Home: 5505-B Buffalo Pass Austin TX 78745

PATE, SHARON SHAMBURGER, secondary school educator; b. Kenosha, Wis., Mar. 30, 1954; d. Thomas Benjamin and Ruth (Penny) Shamburger; m. Johnny Lee Pate, July 23, 1976. BS, Miss. U. Women, 1975; MEd, Miss. State U., 1980; postgrad., Fla. State U., 1994—. Cert. tchr., Fla. Mgr. Cato Dept. Stores, West Point, Miss., 1975-76; area mgr. Wal-Mart Stores, West Point, 1976; tchr. home econs. South Sumter High Sch., Bushnell, Fla., 1977-78; instr. community edn. Riverdale (Fla.) High Sch., 1982-84; substitute tchr., asst. to dean North Ft. Myers (Fla.) High Sch., 1982-84, tchr. home econs., 1978-80, 84-92, instr. community edn., 1984-89; mktg. instr. Mosley High Sch., Panama City, Fla, 1992-94; interior design svcs. instr. Haney Tech. Ctr., Panama City; mgmt. trainee J.C. Penney Co., Ft. Myers, 1980-81; sponsor Future Homemakers Am., Cypress Lake H.S., Ft. Myers, 1984-90, instr. cmty. edn., interior decorating; tchr. mktg. edn., fashion mktg. Mariner H.S., Cape Coral, 1989-92; adj. prof. fashion mktg. Gulf Coast C.C., Panama City, 1993-94. Recipient Grad. scholarship, 1996. Mem. Fla. Vocat. Assn., Fla. Assn. Mktg. Educators, Distributive Edn. Clubs Am. (advisor 1989-94), Elite Modeling Club (advisor 1990-92), Dauphin Allure Modeling (advisor 1993-94), Internat. Textile and Apparel Assn., Fla. State U. Fashion, Inc., Am. Family and Consumer Scis., Fla. Family and Consumer Scis. Republican. Pentecostal. Home: 3515-7 W 19th St # 332 Panama City FL 32405

PATE, SUZANNE EVELYN, university fundraising administrator; b. Washington, June 25, 1953; d. James Irby and Evelyn Elizabeth (Counts) P. BSBA, Miami U., Oxford, Ohio, 1976; MBA, U. Dayton, 1983. Cert. fin. planner, cert. employee benefit specialist. Software analyst ADP, Cin., 1983-86; asst. sec./mgr. data processing Mayflower Mortgage, Inc., Dayton, Ohio, 1986-87; fin. analyst Stickelman and Assocs., Dayton, 1987-89; sales account mgr./employee benefits specialist Colonial Life and Ins. Co., Dayton, 1989-92; assoc. dir. major gifts and planned giving Wright State U., Dayton, 1992—; supr. savings adminstrn. Citizens Fed. Sav. and Loan, Dayton, 1977-83. Mem. Internat. Assn. Fin. Planners (nat. and Dayton chpts., sec. 1988—), Miami Valley Estate Planning Coun. (v.p. 1992—), Dayton Planned Giving Coun. (bd. dirs. 1995—), Dayton Trust Estate Planning Group (treas. 1992—). Home: 6649 Carinthia Dr Dayton OH 45459 Office: Wright State U 3640 Colonel Glenn Hwy Dayton OH 45435

PATEL, MARILYN HALL, federal judge; b. Amsterdam, N.Y., Sept. 2, 1938; d. Lloyd Manning and Nina J. (Thorpe) Hall; m. Magan C. Patel, Sept. 2, 1966; children: Brian, Gian. B.A., Wheaton Coll., 1959; J.D., Fordham U., 1963. Bar: N.Y. 1963, Calif. 1970. Mng. atty. Benson & Morris, Esq., N.Y.C., 1962-64; sole practice N.Y.C., 1964-67; atty. U.S. Immigration and Naturalization Svc., San Francisco, 1967-71; sole practice San Francisco, 1971-76; judge Alameda County Mcpl. Ct., Oakland, Calif., 1976-80, U.S. Dist. Ct. (no. dist.) Calif., San Francisco, 1980—; adj. prof. law Hastings Coll. of Law, San Francisco, 1974-76. Author: Immigration and Nationality Law, 1974; also numerous articles. Mem. bd. visitors Fordham U. Sch. Law. Mem. ABA (litigation sect., jud. adminstrn. sect.), ACLU (former bd. dirs.), NOW (former bd. dirs.), Am. law Inst., Am. Judicature Soc. (bd. dirs.), Calif Conf. Judges, Nat. Assn. Women Judges (founding mem.), Internat. Inst. (bd. dirs.), Advs. for Women (co-founder), Assn. Bus. Trial Lawyers (bd. dirs.). Democrat. Office: US Dist Ct PO Box 36060 450 Golden Gate Ave San Francisco CA 94102

PATERSON, EILEEN, radiation oncologist, educator; b. Bklyn., Oct. 16, 1939; d. John Alexander and Frances (Rabito) P.; m. Bruce Leroy Benedict, Jan. 2, 1981. BA, Wilson Coll., Chambersburg, Pa., 1961; MD, Woman's Med. Coll. Pa., 1965. Diplomate Am. Bd. Radiation Oncology, Am. Bd. Nuclear Medicine. Intern Highland Hosp., Rochester, N.Y., 1965-66; resident radiology (radiation therapy) U. Rochester, 1966-69; asst. prof. radiation oncology U. Rochester, N.Y., 1970-83, assoc. prof., 1983—; chief dept. radiation oncology Rochester Gen. Hosp., 1983—; cons. Arnot Ogden Hosp., Elmira, N.Y., 1970-74, Genesee Hosp., Rochester, 1983—. Contbr. articles to med. jours. Mem. Am. Coll. Radiology, Am. Soc. Therapeutic Radiology and Oncology. Office: Rochester Gen Hosp 1425 Portland Ave Rochester NY 14621-3001

PATERSON, KATHERINE WOMELDORF, writer; b. Qing Jiang, China, Oct. 31, 1932; came to U.S., 1940; d. George Raymond and Mary Elizabeth (Goetchius) Womeldorf; m. John Barstow Paterson, July 14, 1962; children: Elizabeth Polin, John Barstow, David Lord, Mary Katherine Nah-he-sah-pe-che-a. A.B., King Coll., Bristol, Tenn., 1954, Litt.D. (hon.), 1978; M.A., Presbyn. Sch. Christian Edn., 1957; postgrad., Kobe Sch. of Japanese Lang., 1957-60; M.R.E., Union Theol. Sem., 1962; hon. LHD, Otterbein Coll., 1979; hon. LittD, U. Md., 1982; hon. Litt.D, St. Mary's of the Woods, 1981; hon. LittD, Shenandoah Coll., 1982; hon. degree, Washington and Lee U.; hon. LHD, Norwich U., 1990, Mount St. Vincent U., Halifax, N.S., Can., 1994. Tchr. Lovettsville (Va.) Elementary Sch., 1954-55; missionary Presbyn. Ch., Japan, 1957-61; master sacred studies and English Pennington (N.J.) Sch. for Boys, 1963-65. Author: The Sign of the Chrysanthemum, 1973, Of Nightingales That Weep, 1974, The Master Puppeteer, 1976, Bridge to Terabithia, 1977, The Great Gilly Hopkins, 1978, Angels and Other Strangers, 1979, Jacob Have I Loved, 1980, Rebels of the Heavenly Kingdom, 1983, Come Sing, Jimmy Jo, 1985, (with John Paterson) Consider the Lilies, 1986, Park's Quest, 1988, The Tale of the Mandarin Ducks, 1990, The Smallest Cow in the World, 1991, Lyddie, 1991, The King's Equal, 1992, Who Am I?, 1992, Flip-Flop Girl, 1994, A Midnight Clear: Stories for the Christmas Season, 1995, A Sense of Wonder, 1995, The Angel and the Donkey, 1996, Jip: His Story, 1996; translator: The Crane Wife, 1981, The Tongue-Cut Sparrow, 1987. U.S. nominee for Hans Christian Andersen award, 1979, 89; recipient Nat. Book award, 1977, 79, Newbery medal, 1978, 91, Newbery honor, 1979, New Eng. Book award New Eng. Booksellers Assn., 1982, Union medal Union Theol. Sem., 1992. Mem. Authors Guild, PEN, Children's Book Guild Washington. Democrat. Office: Lodestar/Dutton 375 Hudson St New York NY 10014-3658

PATERSON, PATRICIA MCDONNOUGH, secondary school educator, sports official; b. Chgo., July 25, 1918; d. James Martin and Minnie (Gronseth) McDonnough; m. Andrew Allan Paterson, Apr. 26, 1941; children: Andrew Jr., John James, Margaret Murray. BA, Mundelein Coll., 1939; MEd, Concordia, 1976. Cert. primary physically handicapped tchr. Tchr. Chgo. Pub. Schs., 1950-83; coach women's swimming DePaul U., Chgo., 1956-59; coach synchronized swim team Oak Park, Ill., 1964-72; adminstrv. chmn. Ill. Synchronized Swim Assn., 1960—; chmn. awards & opening & closing ceremonies Pan Am Games, 1959, U.S. Olympic Com., Portage Park, Chgo., U.S. Swim Trials, Chgo., 1972; history chmn. U.S. Synchronized Swimming, Indpls., 1978-94. Contbr. articles to profl. jours. Judge Official Level 3 Synchronized Swim, 1988—. Found. Rsch. grantee, 1985—.

PATI, PATRICIA ANN, psychologist; b. Queens Village, N.Y., Feb. 15, 1949; d. Charles and Helen (Annis) P.; m. Carlson Andrews Theodore, Sept. 9, 1989; children: Christine Gulnara, Andrew Eugene. BA, Loyola U., L.A., 1972, MA, 1974; PhD, U.S. Internat. U., 1982. Counselor Careunit, Laguna Beach, Calif., 1978-83; psychologist Humanistic Therapy Inst., Irvine, Calif., 1981-85, Orange County Substance Abuse Agy., Santa Ana, Calif., 1984-85; pvt. practice psychology San Diego, 1985-87, Poway, Calif., 1987—. Mem. APA, San Diego Psychol. Assn., Nat. Register Health Svc. Providers, Employee Assistance Profls. Assn. (bd. dirs., editor newsletter 1991-92), Psi Chi. Office: 15706 Pomerado Rd Ste 210 Poway CA 92064-2033

PATIN, SALLY GAIL, art educator; b. Lake Charles, La., Oct. 14, 1965; d. George Allen and Rosa Juanita (Sutherland) Wilkinson; m. Pierre Moise Patin, July 5, 1988; children: Ryan Paul, Dooley Hunter. BA in Edn., McNeese State U., 1992. Art tchr. Calcasieu Parish Sch. Bd., Lake Charles, 1993; art. tchr. Ralph Wilson Elem. Sch., 1994-95, Fondel Elem. Sch./Ralph Wilson Elem., 1995-96, St. John Elem. Sch., Lake Charles, 1996—. Mem. La. Assn. Educators, Calcasieu Assn. Educators, Order of Ea. Star. Methodist. Home: 1004 Sutherland Lake Charles LA 70611

PATMAN, JEAN ELIZABETH, journalist; b. Lincolnshire, Eng., Dec. 12, 1946; came to U.S., 1955, naturalized, 1967; d. Donald Geoffrey and Regina (Iwanir) P. BA in English, CCNY, 1967. Stringer Newsweek mag., 1966-67; copygirl, then asst. to entertainment editor N.Y. Post, 1964-70; successively copy editor, spl. sects. editor, night city editor Reporter-Dispatch, White Plains, N.Y., 1970-74; assoc. editor United Feature Syndicate, 1974-75; successively copy editor, asst. news editor, news editor, Sunday editor, exec. news editor, fgn. editor Newsday, L.I., 1975-85; asst. view editor, view editor L.A. Times, 1985-89; owner, pub. Keystone Gazette Weekly, Bellefonte, Pa., 1989-92; asst. mng. editor Fla. Today, 1992-95; writing coach Gannett, 1996—. Dir. team that won 1985 Pulitzer prize for international reporting. Office: Gannett Suburban Newspapers 1 Gannett Dr Harrison NY 10528

PATRICK, CINDY, broadcast executive. V.p. ops. CNN, Atlanta. Office: CNN CNN Ctr Atlanta GA 30348-5366*

PATRICK, JANET CLINE, personnel company executive; b. San Francisco, June 30, 1934; d. John Wesley and Edith Bertha (Corde) Cline; m. Robert John Patrick Jr., June 13, 1959 (div. 1988); children: John McKinnon, Stewart McLellan, William Robert. BA with distinction, Stanford U., 1955; postgrad. U. Calif.-Berkeley, 1957, George Washington U., 1978-82. English tchr. George Washington H.S., San Francisco, 1957, K.D. Burke Sch., San Francisco, 1957-59, Berkeley Inst., Bklyn., 1959-63; placement counselor Washington Sch. Secs., Washington, 1976-78, asst. dir. placement, 1978-81; mgr. med. personnel service Med. Soc. D.C., 1981-89, pres. Med. Pers. Svcs. Inc., 1989— . Chmn. area 2 planning com. Montgomery County Pub. Schs. (Md.), 1974-75; mem. vestry, corr. sec., Christ Ch., Kensington, Md., 1982-84, vestry, sr. warden, 1984-85, vestry, chmn. ann. giving com., 1986-89; chmn. long-range planning com., 1989-92, sec., 1992-93, jr. warden, 1994, co-chair capital campaign, 1996; fin. com. Montgomery County Pvt. Industry Coun., 1994. Mem. Met. D.C. Med. Group Mgmt. Assn., Phi Beta Kappa. Republican. Episcopalian. Club: Jr. League (Washington). Home: 5206 Carlton St Bethesda MD 20816-2306 Office: Med Personnel Svcs Inc 1707 L St NW Ste 250 Washington DC 20036-4201

PATRICK, PAULINE MARGARET, secondary school educator; b. Mpls., Oct. 18, 1949; d. Melvin H. and Margaret P. (Calvelage) Boone; m. Mark H. Patrick, Dec. 18, 1971; children: Lance, Megan. BS, U. Mankato, 1971; MEd, St. Mary's Coll., Winona, Minn., 1993; MA (hon.), Minnetonka U., 1990. Cert. tchr., Minn. Tchr. Edina (Minn.) Sch., 1972-79, Minnetonka (Minn.) Schs., 1986—; adj. prof. U. St. Thomas, St. Paul, 1989—, mem. T.E.A.C.H., 1991—. Recipient Apple award Ashland Oil Co., 1989. mem. ASCd, Nat. Coun. Tchrs. English, Nat. Coun. Tchrs. Social Studies. Baptist.

PATRICK, SUE FORD, diplomat; b. Union Springs, Ala., Nov. 9, 1946; d. Oscar Ford and Mildred (Hunter) Ford Carter; m. Henderson M. Patrick, Dec. 24, 1973; 1 child, Lauren. BA, Coll. Notre Dame of Md., 1967; postgrad., U. Va., 1967-69, 70-72; MA, Boston U., 1982; postgrad., Nat. War Coll., Washington, 1991-92. Joined Fgn. Svc., Dept. State, 1972; vice-consul Am. Consulate, Udorn, Thailand, 1973-74; desk officer Dept. State, Washington, 1976-78, 2d sec., 1982-84, spl. asst. refugee programs, 1984-85; 2d sec. U.S. Embassy, Nairobi, Kenya, 1978-81; 1st sec. polit. affairs U.S. Embassy, Abidjan, Ivory Coast, 1985-88; dep. chief of mission U.S. Embassy, Kigali, Rwanda, 1988-91, Nat. War Coll., Washington, 1991-92; adv. on NATO policy Office of Sec. of Def., The Pentagon, Washington, 1992-93, dir. office of fgn. civil. mil. affairs, 1993-94; congl. affairs advisor Office Regional Policy Bur. East Asian Pacific Affairs, Dept. State, Washington, 1994—. Mem. Am. Fgn. Svc. Assn. Roman Catholic. Office: Regional Security Policy EAP/RSP Rm 4312 Dept State Washington DC 20520

PATRICK, TERESA TIDMORE, elementary education educator; b. Centre, Ala., Oct. 31, 1961; d. James E. and Jane E. Tidmore; m. David C. Patrick, June 7, 1986; children: Lauren Elizabeth, David Alexander. BS in Elem. Edn., Jacksonville State U., 1984; Master's degree, Ala. A&M U., 1988, AA, 1989. 4th grade tchr. Stevenson (Ala.) Elem. Sch., 1985—. Mem. Scottsboro chpt. Friends of the Libr., v.p., 1991-92. Mem. AAUW (ednl. found. chair 1992—), Jr. Progress Club (mem. Scottsboro chpt. 1993-94, sec.). Presbyterian. Home: 1001 Byron Rd Scottsboro AL 35769 Office: Stevenson Elem Sch 930 Old Mt Carmel Rd Stevenson AL 35772

PATRZYK, PAMELA THERESE, chemist; b. Garfield Heights, Ohio, Feb. 27, 1965; d. Chester John and Margaret Rose (Emrisko) P. BS in Chemistry, John Carroll U., 1992. X-ray technician St. Alexis Hosp., Cleve., 1985-86, Bedford (Ohio) Hosp., 1985-87, Kaiser Permanente, Bedford, 1987-92; rsch. chemist Lubrizol Corp., Wickliffe, Ohio, 1992—. Mem. Am. Chem. Soc. Home: 15224 Maple Park Dr # 17 Maple Heights OH 44137

PATTERSON, ALLISON LEE, writer, entrepreneur; b. Albany, Ga., Oct. 9, 1958; d. John Armpstead and Lois Jeanne (Evans) P.; m. James Hector Zoia, Mar. 25, 1989. AA in Liberal Arts, Ferrum (Va.) Coll., 1978; BS in Criminal Justice, Old Dominion U., 1980. Teller Bank of Virginia Beach, Va., 1981-82; mem. campaign staff Sisisky for Congress, Portsmouth, Va., 1982; staff asst., exec. asst. U.S. Congressman Norman Sisisky, Washington, 1983-87; real estate agy. Coldwell Banker Real Estate Co., Washington, 1987-89; govt. affairs specialist Alexander & Alexander, Inc., Washington, 1989; exec. asst. exec. offices Paralyzed Vets. Am., Washington, 1989-93; freelance writer, cons., entrepreneur, 1993—. Mem. Nat. Dem. Com., Nat. Dem. Campaign Com., Prince George's County Dem. Party; bd. dirs. The Mission of Love. Mem. AAUW, NOW (group leader anti-violence rally 1995), Tex. Freedom Alliance, Am. Assn. Home-Based Businesses, Women Bus. Owners of Prince George's County, The Writers Ctr., Common Cause. Lutheran.

PATTERSON, ANITA MATTIE, union administrator; b. Birmingham, Ala., Feb. 19, 1940; d. John Evans Patterson and Flora Ella (Paul) Patterson/Mitchell; m. LeRoy Harold Walden, Mar. 19, 1958 (dec. Apr. 1966); children: Christopher Ann, DeRoy, Chanita. Student, Wayne State U., 1968-72, 72-78, Wayne State U., 1976-79. Sr. counselor City of Detroit, 1965-79; area dir. AFSCME, Washington, 1979—; exec. bd. Coalition Labor Union Women, Washington, exec. dir., 1975-77; chair nat. women's com. Coalition Black Trade Unionists, Washington, 1985—; tchg. fellow AFL-CIO Organizing Inst., Washington, 1992—; ofcl. election observer South Africa Election, 1994. Active So. Regional Coun., Atlanta, 1992—; mem. social svcs. com. Salem Bapt. Ch., Atlanta, 1990—. Recipient Cmty. Svcs. award A. Philip Randolph Inst., 1990, Cmty. Svcs. award So. Christian Leadership Coun., 1991, Leadership award Ga. State Legislature Black Caucus, 1992, Disting. Recognition award City of Detroit, 1989, Sojourner Truth award Coalition of Black Trade Unionists, 1994, Labor award Operation PUSH, 1994; named Addie L. Wyatt Women of Yr., Coalition of Black Trade Unionists, 1990, Ga. Labor Hall of Fame, 1996. Mem. Nat. Coun. Negro Women (ad hoc labor com. 1986—, Recognition award 1989, Svc. award 1988), Marracci Ct. # 32. Democrat. Office: AFSCME Internat Area Office 1720 Peachtree St NW Ste 150B Atlanta GA 30309-2439

PATTERSON, BEVERLY ANN GROSS, fund raising consultant, social services administrator, poet; b. Pauls Valley, Okla., Aug. 5, 1938; d. Wilburn G. Jack and Mildred E. (Steward) Gross; m. Kenneth Dean Patterson, June 18, 1960 (div. 1976); children: Tracy Dean, Nancy Ann Patterson-McArthur, Beverly Jeanne Patterson-Wertman. AA, Modesto (Calif.) Jr. Coll., 1958; BA in Social Sci., Fresno (Calif.) State U., 1960; M in Community Counseling, Coll. Idaho; postgrad., Stanislaus State Coll., Turlock, Calif., U. Idaho, Boise (Idaho) State U. Cert. secondary tchr., Calif., Idaho, lic. real estate agt., Idaho. Secondary tchr. Ceres and Modesto Calif., Payette and Weiser Idaho, Ontario Oreg., 1960-67; dir. vol. svcs. mental retardation and child devel. State of Idaho, 1967-70, cons. dir. vol. svcs. health and welfare, 1970-72; dir. Ret. Sr. Vol. Program, Boise, 1972-74; exec. dir. Idaho Nurses Assn., Boise, 1974-76; community svcs. adminstr. City of Davis, Calif., 1976-78; devel. dir. and fundraising Mercy Med. Ctr., Nampa, Idaho, 1978-85; exec. dir. St. Alphonsus Med. Ctr. Found., Boise, 1985-87; dir. devel. and gift planning Idaho Youth Ranch, Boise, 1989-94; fund devel. cons. Mercy Housing, Nampa, Idaho, 1994-96, Pratt Ranch Boys Home, Emmett, Idaho, 1994-96, Northwest Childrens Home, Lewiston, Idaho, 1994-96, Idaho Spl. Olympics, Boise, 1994-95, Port of Hope Inc., Boise, 1994-95, Idaho Found. for Parks and Lands, Boise, 1994-95, St. Vincent de Paul, Inc., Boise, 1995—, Nampa Shelter Found., Inc., 1994-95, Turning Point Inc., Nampa, 1994-95, Port of Hope Treatment Ctr. Inc., Boise, 1995-96, Idaho Theater for Youth, Inc., Boise, 1995-96, Boise Tennis Coalition, Inc., 1995—, El Ada Cmty. Action Ctr., Boise, 1995; with Hemophilia Found. Idaho, 1995-96, Boise YMCA, 1996—, Melba (Idaho) Sch. Dist., 1996—; and many more; founder Fellowship Christian Adult Singles, Boise, 1974; cons., exec. dir. Boise Hotline, 1988-90; cons., fundraiser Cmty. Resources and Devel., 1980; co-dir. ACOA workshop leader Child Within Concepts, Inc., Boise, 1987—; cons. coord. Rural Hosp. Edn. Consortium, 1988; cons. hosp. fund devel. and cmty. resources Gritman Meml. Hosp., Moscow, Idaho, 1987-88; cons., conf. coord. State of Idaho, 1987-88; counsel Adult Children of Alcoholics, 1991; incorporator, pres. Nonprofit Solutions, Inc., Boise, 1995—; co-dir., incorporator Concepts, Inc., Meridian, 1996—; pres. Q&A Distbg. and Cons., Meridian, Idaho, 1994-95. Contbr. articles to profl. jours. Coord. Idaho Golf Angels Open Pro-Am Tournament, Boise, 1989-91; founding exec. v.p. Coll. Fund for Students Surviving Cancer, 1993—; bd. dirs. Arthritis Found., Idaho, 1984-86, Idaho Mental Health Assn., 1985-87, charitable fund raising coord., 1978—; founder Ctrl. Vol. Bur., Boise, 1971; mem. Idaho Devel. Network, 1990—. Named Idaho Statesman Disting. Citizen, 1985. Mem. Nat. Assn. for Hosp. Devel. (accredited, treas. 1980, accreditation chmn. 1984-86, conf. chmn. 1982, 85), Assn. Hosps. in Philanthrophy (accredited), Nat. Soc. Fund Raising Execs. Mem. Community Christian Ch. Home and Office: PO Box 213 Meridian ID 83680-0213 also: Child Within Concepts Rt 1 Box 1277A Homedale ID 83628

PATTERSON, CLAIRE ANN, vocational educator; b. Cin., Dec. 28, 1950; d. Lloyd E. and Ruth T. (Flaherty) Lachtrupp; m. Calvin Stanley Patterson, Jr., July 14, 1973; children: Christopher, Alicia. BS, U. Cin., 1973, MEd, 1980. Cert. elem. tchr., elem. supr., secondary math, secondary prin., asst. supt., Ohio, Va., P.R. Third grade tchr. Academia de Aguidilla, P.R., 1973-74; fifth grade tchr. Our Lady of the Rosary, Norfolk, Va., 1974-76; jr. high math and sci. tchr. Yavneh Hebrew Day Sch., Cin., 1976-79; math tchr. Winton Woods City Schs., Cin., 1979-80; math. coord. Great Oaks Inst. of Tech. and Career Devel., Cin., 1980-86, benefits coord./personnel profl., 1986-88, career devel. mgr., 1987-93, asst. dir., 1993—; ednl. cons. schs. in Ohio, 1988—. Author: Let's Celebrate Math, 1991; contbr. articles to profl. jours. Recipient Career Coord. award State of Ohio, 1993. Mem. Ohio Vocat. Assn. (com. chmn. 1990-93, OVA Pacesetter award 1991, 92, 93), Career Edn. Assn. (pres. 1992-93), Nat. Coun. Local Adminstrs., Southwest Career Coun. (pres. 1991-92). Republican. Roman Catholic. Office: Great Oaks Inst Tech and Career Devel 3254 E Kemper Rd Cincinnati OH 45241-1540

PATTERSON, DAWN MARIE, dean, consultant, writer; b. Gloversville, N.Y., July 30; d. Robert Morris and Dora Margaret (Perham) P.; m. Robert Henry Hollenbeck, Aug. 3, 1958 (div. 1976); children: Adrienne Lyn, Nathaniel Conrad. BS in Edn., SUNY, Geneseo, 1962; MA, Mich. State U., 1973, PhD, 1977; postgrad., U. So. Calif. and Inst. Ednl. Leadership. Librarian Brighton (N.Y.) Cen. Schs., 1962-67; asst. to regional dir. Mich. State U. Ctr., Bloomfield Hills, 1973-74; grad. asst. Mich. State U., East Lansing, 1975-77; cons. Mich. Efficiency Task Force, 1977; asst. dean Coll. Continuing Edn., U. So. Calif., L.A., 1978-84; dean, assoc. prof. continuing edn. Calif. State U., L.A., 1985-96; CEO Acclaims Enterprises Internat.; pres. Co-Pro Assocs. Mem. Air Univ. Bd. Visitors, 1986-90, Commn. on Extended Edn. Calif. State U. Calif., 1988-91; Hist. Soc., Los Angeles Town Hall, Los Angeles World Affairs Council. Dora Louden scholar, 1958-61; Langworthy fellow, 1961-62; Edn. Professions Devel. fellow, 1974-75; Ednl. Leadership Policy fellow, 1982-83; Leadership Calif., 1992, Leadership Am., 1994. Mem. AAUW (pres. Pasadena br. 1985-86), Am. Assn. Adult and Continuing Edn. (charter), Nat. Univ. Continuing Edn. Assn., Internat. Assn. Continuing Edn. and Tng. (bd. dirs. 1990—), Calif. Coll. and Mil. Educators Assn. (pres.), Los Angeles Airport Area Edn. Industry Assn. (pres. 1984), Rotary Club of Alhambra (bd. dirs.), Fine Arts (Pasadena), Zonta (pres. 1994-96), Women in Internat. Trade, Kappa Delta Pi, Phi Delta Kappa, Phi Beta Delta, Phi Kappa Phi. Republican. Unitarian. Office: PO Box 86 South Pasadena CA 91031-0086

PATTERSON, DEE ANN, newspaper editor; b. Lawton, Okla., Nov. 11, 1961; d. Bobby Wayne and Faye Dean (Watts) P. BA in Journalism, U. Okla., 1984. Reporter Chickasha (Okla.) Daily Express, 1984; sch. reporter Lawton Constn., 1984-87, area reporter, 1987-88, copy editor, 1988, wire editor, 1988-91, city editor, 1992—. Democrat. Baptist. Office: Lawton Constn 102 SW 3rd Lawton OK 73505

PATTERSON, DONNA E., lawyer; b. Greensboro, N.C., Mar. 4, 1949. BA cum laude, Yale U., 1971, JD, 1981. Bar: D.C. 1981. Ptnr. Arnold & Porter, Washington. Office: Arnold & Porter 555 12th St NW Washington DC 20004-1202*

PATTERSON, ELIZABETH JOHNSTON, former congresswoman; b. Columbia, SC, Nov. 18, 1939; d. Olin DeWitt and Gladys (Atkinson) Johnston; m. Dwight Fleming Patterson, Jr., Apr. 15, 1967; children: Dwight Fleming, Olin DeWitt, Catherine Leigh. BA, Columbia Coll., 1961; postgrad. in polit. sci., U. S.C., 1961, 62, 64; LLD (hon.), Columbia Coll., 1987; D Pub. Svc. (hon.), Converse Coll., 1989. Pub. affairs officer Peace Corps, Washington, 1962-64; postgrad. VISTA, OEO, Washington, 1965-66; D Pub. Svc. Head Start and VISTA, OEO, Columbia, 1966-67; tri-county dir. Head Start, Piedmont Community Actions, Spartanburg, S.C., 1967-68; mem. Spartanburg County Coun., 1975-76, S.C. State Senate, 1979-86, 100th-102nd Congress from 4th S.C. dist., 1987-93. Trustee Wofford Coll., 1975-81; bd. dirs. Charles Lea Ctr., 1978-90, Spartanburg Coun. on Aging; pres. Spartanburg Dem. Women, 1968; v.p. Spartanburg County Dem. party, 1968-70, sec., 1970-75; trustee Columbia Coll., 1991—. Mem. Bus. and Profl. Women's Club, Alpha Kappa Gamma. Methodist. Office: PO Box 5564 Spartanburg SC 29304-5564

PATTERSON, GRACE LIMERICK, library director; b. N.Y.C., Nov. 21, 1938; d. Robert and Frieda (Zeiontz) Limerick; m. Joseph Nathaniel Patterson (dec.); children: Lorrayne Carole, Joseph Nathaniel Jr. BA in Sociology, Edn., CUNY, 1971; MLS, Columbia U., 1975; MS in Comm., Coll. New Rochelle, 1989. Cert. libr. N.J. Exec. dir. Manhattanville Community Outreach, N.Y.C., 1971-74; br. and outreach svcs. Paterson (N.J.) Pub. Libr., 1975-79; media specialist II Passaic County C.C., Paterson, 1979-81; coord. outreach svcs. Irvington (N.J.) Pub. Libr., 1981-84; assoc. prof. libr. Rockland C.C., Suffern, N.Y., 1984-89; libr. dir. Hudson County C.C., Jersey City, 1989—. Editor jours. in field. Exec. bd. dirs. Essex-Hudson Region II, Orange, N.J., 1991; vol. Ridgewood (N.J.) Schs., 1981-83; Ridgewood Centennial Com. First Night, 1993. U.S. Dept. Edn. fellow, 1974-75. Mem. ALA (com., chairperson Black Caucus pub. rels. 1990-92), N.J. Libr. Assn. Office: Hudson County CC 25 Journal Square Jersey City NJ 07306-4300

PATTERSON, HEATHER DIANE, special education educator; b. Parkersburg, W.Va., July 21, 1962; d. Pete E. and Betty Ann (Harvey) P. BA in Elem. Edn., Marshall U., 1985, cert. in phys. handicapped K-12, 1985, cert. in mental retardation K-12, 1985; postgrad., W.Va. U. Tchr. intermediate pub. health Wood County, Parkersburg, W.Va., 1985-89, tchr. secondary severe/pro., 1989-90, tchr. pre-sch. severe/pro., 1990—; mem. sch. improvement coun. Martin Sch., Parkersburg, W.Va., 1993—. Chmn. Local Sch. Improvement Coun., 1994-96; vol. coach Spl. Olympics, Parkersburg, 1986-92. Edn. grantee Assn. for Retarded Citizens, 1992. Mem. Coun. for Exceptional Children (student mem. 1982-85, profl. mem. 1992—), W.Va. Edn. Assn., Marshall U. Alumni Assn. Baptist. Home: 4403 Butler St Parkersburg WV 26104 Office: Rayon/Martin Sch 1301 Hillcrest St Parkersburg WV 26101-7039

PATTERSON, HELEN CROSBY, clinical psychologist; b. Jackson, Miss., Nov. 12, 1947; d. Thomas Atkinson and Helen Elizabeth (Crosby) Patterson; m. Fred C. Craig, July 7, 1967 (div. July 1970); 1 child, Erin Crosby. BA in Psychology, Millsaps Coll., 1972; MS in Clin. Psychology, U. Wyo., 1976, PhD in Clin. Psychology, 1978. Lic. clin. psychologist, Miss., N.Mex., Del. Coord., supervision and internships Antioch N.E. Grad. Sch., Keene, N.H., 1979-80; sr. clinician Jackson (Miss.) Mental Health Ctr., 1980-82; pvt. practice in Miss. and N.Mex., 1981—; clin. dir. Pain Mgmt. Ctr. St. Vincent Hosp., Santa Fe, N.Mex., 1990-91; psychol. cons. Disability Determination Svcs., Jackson, 1983—, Albuquerque, 1988-90, 91-93, Wilmington, Del., 1993-95; EAP cons., So. Beverage Co., Jackson, 1986-91, clin. dir. Pain Mgmt. Ctr., St. Vincent Hosp., Santa Fe, 1990-91. Mem. Hinds County Assn. for Children with Learning Disabilities, Jackson, 1985-88, Hinds County Mental Health Assn., Jackson, 1980-83. Mem. APA. Office: 11 Northtown Dr Ste 205 Jackson MS 39211 also: 3817 Don Juan Ct NW Albuquerque NM 87107-2812

PATTERSON, JEAN SOMMERS, gifted education educator; b. Hattiesburg, Miss., June 2, 1951; d. Fredrick Arthur and Pauline Elizabeth (Rutland) Sommers; divorced; 1 child, Tara Leigh. BS in Edn., U. So. Miss., 1973, MEd, 1979. Cert. tchr. mid. grades, for gifted, learning disabled, and mentally retarded, cert. elem. and secondary sch. prin., cert. spl. edn. supr. Tchr. severe profound retardates Ellisville (Miss.) State Sch., 1973-74; tchr. mildly mentally handicapped Marion County Schs., Ocala, Fla., 1974-76; tchr. mildly mentally handicapped and gifted Gulfport (Miss.) City Schs., 1977-79; tchr. learning disabled Biloxi (Miss.) City Schs., 1979-81; tchr. gifted and learning disabled Harrison County Schs., Gulfport, 1982-85, Jackson County Schs., Pascagoula, Miss., 1985-87; tchr. mildly mentally handicapped Ocean Springs (Miss.) Schs., 1987-89; tchr. gifted Bay St. Louis (Miss.)/Waveland Schs., 1989-90; tchr. gifted, 6th grade lang. arts/sci., 8th grade social Clayton County Schs., Jonesboro, Ga., 1990-94; tchr. gifted Gwinnett County Schs., Lawrenceville, Ga., 1994—; mid. sch. rep. supt.'s adv. bd. Clayton County Schs., 1991-92. Co-author mid. grades study skills curriculum, career module for mildly hanicapped curriculum; author gifted edn. curriculum. Office: Snellville Mid Sch 3155 Pate Rd Snellville GA 30278-5028

PATTERSON, KATHERYN CLEWS, lawyer; b. Glen Cove, N.Y., Jan. 29, 1954. AB with distinction, Stanford U., 1974; JD cum laude, Harvard Law Sch., 1977. Bar: N.Y. 1978. Ptnr. Coudert Bros., N.Y.C. Co-editor, contbg. author: A Practical Guide to Letters of Credit, 1990. Mem. ABA, Phi Beta Kappa. Office: Coudert Bros 1114 Avenue Of The Americas New York NY 10036-7703*

PATTERSON, LUCILLE M., retired hotel executive; b. Newton, Kans., Nov. 1, 1924; David Elmer and Hattie Lois (Guinty) Lambert; m. Lloyd O'Leary Patterson, Sept. 8, 1950 (div. Jan. 1966); children: Scott Elliott, Kip O'Leary. Student, Eldorado Jr. Coll., 1942-43, Purdue U., 1943-44, Wichita State U., 1946-47; BS in Home Econs./Art, Kans. State U., 1948. Jr. engr. RCA Victor, Harrison, N.J., 1944-45; home economist extension Kans. State U. Extension Svc., Harper County, 1948-49; home economist Gas & Electric, Wichita, Kans., 1949-51, Nev. Power, Las Vegas, 1962-65; social case worker Nev. State Welfare, Las Vegas, 1966-68; asst. mgr., food & beverage cashier Caesars Palace Hotel, Las Vegas, 1970-90. Author, editor: Holiday Cook Book for Las Vegas Hotel Chefs, 1962, 2nd edit., 1963, 3rd edit., 1964. Active Las Vegas Art Mus., 1994—, Friends of the Libr., Las Vegas, 1995—. Mem. AAUW. Presbyterian. Home: 304 Orland St # 46 Las Vegas NV 89107

PATTERSON, LYDIA ROSS, industrial relations specialist, consulting company executive; b. Carrabelle, Fla., Sept. 3, 1936; d. Richard D. Ross and Johnnie Mae (Thomas) Kelley; m. Edgar A. Corley, Aug. 1, 1964 (div.); 1 child, Derek Kelley; m. Berman W. Patterson, Dec. 18, 1981. BA, Hunter Coll., 1958. Indsl. rels. specialist U.S. Dept. Energy, N.Y.C., 1966-68; regional dir./mgr. Div. Human Rights State of N.Y., N.Y.C., 1962-66, 68-76; v.p. Bankers Trust Co., N.Y.C., 1976-87; pres., CEO Lydia Patterson Comm., N.Y.C., 1985-95; CEO Lydia Patterson Comms., 1996—; v.p., mgr. Merrill Lynch and Co. Inc., N.Y.C., 1987-90; seminar speaker Columbia U., Wharton Sch. Bus., Harvard U., Duke U., Cornell U., 1976-85; mem. conf. bd. Cornell U., Bus. Policy Rev. Coun., Exec. Leadership Coun. Bd. dirs. Project Discovery Columbia U., 1988, CUNY, Vocat. Edn. Adv. Coun., 1990. Mem. Nat. Urban League, Employment Mgrs. Assn., Fin. Women's Assn. (govt. and cmty. affairs com. 1986-87), Women's Forum, Employment Dissemination of Info., Wellington Cmty. Edn. Found. (bd. dirs. 1992—). Office: 12689 Coral Breeze Dr Wellington FL 33414-8070

PATTERSON, MABEL SUE, small business owner; b. Elizabethtown, Ky., Dec. 28, 1957; d. H. and M. (Florence) Sloan; m. Paul Lee Patterson II, Dec. 17, 1978; 1 child, Paul Lee III. BS in Home Econs., Edn., U. Ky., 1978. With Educare-Childcare, 1978-89, Oakhaven Bapt. Acad., 1981-82; co-owner, office mgr. Patterson Eye Care Ctrs., Inc., Campbellsville, Ky., 1982—; bd. dirs. Patterson Eye Care Ctrs., Inc. Mem. NAFE, Ky. Optometric Auxillary (state pres. 1991-93), Kappa Delta Pi, Phi Upsilon Omicron. Democrat. Baptist.

PATTERSON, MADGE LENORE, elementary education educator; b. Vandergrift, Pa., Nov. 9, 1925; d. Paul Warren and Lucy Mae (Lemmon) Schaeffer; m. Stanley Clair Patterson, June 19, 1948 (dec.); 1 child, Stanley Kent. BS in Edn., Indiana State Tchrs. Coll., Pa., 1946, MEd, 1971. Elem. tchr. New Kensington (Pa.) Pub. Schs., 1946-49; elem. tchr. Armstrong Sch. Dist. Schs., Ford City, Pa., 1951-52, kindergarten tchr., 1967-93; kindergarten tchr. Rural Valley (Pa.) Presbyn. Ch., 1957-67; vol. tutor Adult Lit., Kittanning, Pa., 1993—; co-owner dairy farm. Sunday sch. tchr., choir mem., 1949—; sec. Rural Valley Presbyn. Ch. Women's Assn., 1988-92. Mem. NEA, Pa. Assn. Sch. Retirees, Clara Cockerille Reading Coun. (treas. 1994-96), Pa. State Edn. Assn., Internat. Reading Assn., Keystone Reading Assn., Assn. Early Childhood Edn., Rural Valley Bus. and Profl. Club, Women's Civic Club (Woman of Yr. 1994), Am. Assn. Ret. Persons, Rural Valley Grange (former lectr.). Democrat. Home: RR 2 Box 182 Dayton PA 16222-8813

PATTERSON, MARIA JEVITZ, microbiology-pediatric infectious disease educator; b. Berwyn, Ill., Oct. 23, 1944; d. Frank Jacob and Edna Frances (Costabile) Jevitz; m. Ronald James Patterson, Aug. 22, 1970; children: Kristin Lara, Kier Nicole. BS in Med. Tech. summa cum laude, Coll. St. Francis, Joliet, Ill., 1966; PhD in Microbiology, Northwestern U., Chgo., 1970; MD, Mich. State U., 1984. Diplomate Am. Bd. Med. Examiners, Am. Bd. Pediatrics Gen. Pediatrics, Am. Bd. Pediatrics Infectious Diseases. Lab. asst., instr. med. microbiology for student nurses Med. Sch. Northwestern U., Chgo., 1966-70; postdoctoral fellow in clin. microbiology affiliated hosps. U. Wash., Seattle, 1971-72; asst. prof. microbiology and pub. health Mich. State U., East Lansing, 1972-77, assoc. prof., 1977-82, assoc. prof. pathology, 1979-82, lectr. dept. microbiology and pub. health, 1982-87, resident in pediatrics affiliated hosps., 1984-85, 86-87, clin. instr. dept. pediatrics and human devel., 1984-87, assoc. prof. microbiology-pub. health-pediatrics-human devel., 1987-90, prof., 1990—; staff microbiologist dept. pathology Lansing Gen. Hosp., 1972-75; dir. clin. microbiology grad. program. Mich. State U., 1974-81, staff microbiologist, 1978-81; postdoctoral fellow in infectious diseases U. Mass. Med. Ctr., Worcester, 1985-86; asst. dir. pediatrics residency Grad. Med. Edn. Inc., Lansing, 1987-90; med. dir. Pediatrics Health Ctr. St. Lawrence Hosp., Lansing, Mich., 1987-90, Ingham Med. Ctr., 1990-94; cons. clin. microbiology Lansing Gen. Hosp., 1972-75, Mich. State U., 1976-82, Ingham County Health Dept., 1988—, Am. Health Cons., 1993; cons. to editorial bd. Infection and Immunity, 1977; presenter seminars. Contbg. author: Microbiology: Principles and Concepts, 1982, 3d edit., 1991, Pediatric Emergency Medicine, 1992; contbr. articles to profl. jours. and publs. Mem. hon. com. Lansing AIDS Meml. Quilt, 1993. Recipient award for teaching excellence Mich. State U. Coll. Osteo. Medicine, 1977, 78, 79, 80, 83, Disting. Faculty award Mich. State U., 1980, Woman Achiever award, 1985, excellence in pediatric residency teaching award, 1988, Alumni Profl. Achievement award Coll. of St. Francis, 1991; grantee renal disease divsn. Mich. Dept. Pub. Health 1976-82. Fellow Pediatric Infectious Diseases Soc., Am. Acad. Pediatrics; mem. Am. Coll. Physician Execs., Am. Soc. Microbiology, Am. Soc. Clin. Pathologists (affiliate, bd. registrant), South Ctrl. Assn. Clin. Microbiology, Infectious Diseases Soc. Am., Mich. Soc. Infectious Diseases, N.Y. Acad. Scis., Kappa Gamma Pi, Lambda Iota Tau. Roman Catholic. Home: 1520 River Ter East Lansing MI 48823-5314 Office: Mich State Univ Microbiology/Pub Health East Lansing MI 48824-1101

PATTERSON, MARION LOUISE, photographer, educator; b. San Francisco, Apr. 24, 1933; d. Morrie Leslie and Esther Elizabeth (Parker) P. BA, Stanford U., 1955; MA, Calif. State U., San Francisco, 1970. Clk. Best's Studio (Ansel Adams Gallery), Yosemite, Calif., 1958-61; asst. to photography editor Sunset Mag., Menlo Park, Calif., 1961-64; freelance photographer Oaxaca, Mex., 1964-66; communications cons. Projects to Advance Creative in Edn., San Mateo, Calif., 1966-68; instr. in photography, chair photography dept. Foothill Coll., Los Altos Hills, Calif., 1968—; instr. U. Calif., Santa Cruz, 1984—. One woman shows include West German Embassy in the Hague, Bayreuth, Republic of Germany, Kasteel Hoensbrueck, Netherlands, Daxaca, Mex., San Francisco Mus. of Modern Art, Focus Gallery, San Francisco, Oakland Mus., Monterey County Mus., Stanford U., Ansel Adams Gallery, Yosemite, and others; exhibited in group shows MIT, George Eastman House, Polaroid Corp., Art in the Embassies, Ind. U., U. of Ala., Critics Choice Traveling Exhibit, New Light, New Directions, Reclaiming Paradise, and others; contbr. photographs and articles in books and magazines. Mem. Soc. for Photog. Edn. Office: Foothill Coll 12345 El Monte Ave Los Altos CA 94022-4504

PATTERSON, MARTHA ELLEN, artist, art educator; b. Anderson, Ind., Mar. 12, 1914; d. Clarence and Corrine Ringwald; m. John Downey, Nov. 27, 1935 (div. 1946); 1 child, Linda Carol; m. Raymond George Patterson, May 6, 1947. Student, Dayton (Ohio) Art Inst., Bendell Art Sch., Bradenton, Fla. Beauty operator WRENS, Springfield, Ohio, 1932-40; co-owner Park Ave. Gallery, Dayton; window decorator, art tchr.; tchr. art; judge art shows. One-woman shows include N.C.R. Country Club, Bill Turner Interiors, U. Dayton, High Street Gallery, Trails End Club, The Designerie, Riverbend Park, Statesman Club, State Fidelity Bank, Wegerzyn Hort. Ctr., Pebble Springs, Backstreet, First City Fed. Bank, Bradenton, Fla., Alley Gallery, Merrill Lynch, Miami U., Gem. City Bank, Dayton, Ohio, Winters Bank, Dayton, Sherwin Williams, Howard Johnsons, Dayton Woman's Club, Bergamo, Dayton Meml. Hall, Bob and Arts, Del Park Med. Soc., The Dayton Country Club, Christ Methodist Ch., Unitarian Ch., The Metropolitan, Rikes, Dr. Pavey's, Dr. Chaney's, Dayton Convention Ctr., The Yum Yum, Jan Strunk Interiors, Park Avenue Gallery; artist: (water colors, oils, acylics, inks and pastels) group exhbns. include: Dayton Art Inst., Meml. Hall of Dayton, Dayton Country Club, Bergamo, Women's Club of Dayton, Am. Watercolor Soc., Riverbend Park, First City Fed., NCR Country Club, Springfield (Ohio) Mus., Longboat Key Art Ctr., others; in pvt. collections of Mr. and Mrs. Richard Nixon, Virginia Graham, Les Brown, Paul Lynde, Air Force Mus. at Wright Patterson, Mr. and Mrs. Charles Lange of NCR, U. Dayton-Ohio, Dr. Stephen Hoose, Doug Yeager and others. Vol. Christian Woman's Soc. of Am., Twig Children's Hosp., Dayton, The Utopians; mem. Tri Art Dayton, Long Boat Key Art Ctr., Fla. Recipient first prize Dayton Soc. Painters and Sculptors Show Rikes, First Prize, 1976, 77, First Prize, Best in Show, 1978, Beavercreek Art Assn. First Place, Best in Show, Artist and Sculpture Yearly Show, 1966, 68 2d place, Dayton Art Inst. 2d prize, Tri County Hon. Mention, Walker Motor Sales 2d place, Bendell Art Gallery 2d and 3d, Montgomery County Fair Best in Show. Mem. Art League of Manatee County (Fla.), Nat. Mus. Women in Art, Am. Watercolor Soc., Springfield Mus. Art, Dayton Soc. Painters, N.Y. Watercolor Soc., Long Boat Key Art League, Tri Art. Republican. Methodist. Home: 3853 Lawrenceville Dr Springfield OH 45504-4459 Winter Address: 5920 7th Ave W Bradenton FL 34209-3519

PATTERSON, MARY DIANE, public health administrator; b. Schenectady, N.Y., June 30, 1963; d. Allen James and Joan Mary (Tonks) Patterson; m. Jesus Renovato Aguillon, Jan. 15, 1994. BA in Human Biology, Stanford U., 1986; MPH, U. N.C., 1990. Asst. to pres. Internat. Ctr. for Devel. Policy, Washington, 1986-88; trainee USPHS, Chapel Hill, N.C., 1988-89; rschr. Stepping Stones Playsch., Greensboro, N.C., 1989; profl. staff mem. Nat. Commn. to Prevent Infant Mortality, Washington, 1990; tng. coord. Edn. Programs Assn., Campbell, Calif., 1991-93, program mgr., 1993—; coun. chair, clinic staff Rotacare Clinic, San Jose, 1992—; nurses' asst. Congress Hts. Neighborhood Health Ctr., Washington, 1990. Co-founder, exec. sec. So. African Twp. Health Fund, Washington, 1986-88; campaign vol. Dem. Party of Santa Clara County, San Jose, 1992. Fulbright fellow, 1990. Mem. APHA, Delta Omega. Democrat.

PATTERSON, MARY JANE, religious organization administrator; b. Marietta, Ohio. BA in Philosophy and Acctg., Ohio State U., MSW, 1950. Ordained elder Presbyn. Ch. U.S.A., 1960. Acct. IRS; fin. dir. Columbus (Ohio) YWCA, asst. dir. for teenage programs, 1964-66; career missionary, cmty. developer, social work cons. Commn. Ecumenical Mission-Rels. Presbyn. Ch. East Africa, Nairobi, Kenya, 1966-68; cmty. organizing specialist and ombudsman Protestant Cmty. Svcs. of L.A. Coun. Chs., 1969-71; assoc. dir. Washington Office United Presbyn. Ch. U.S.A., 1971-76, dir., 1976—; pres. World Conf. on Religion and Peace, U.S.A., N.Y.C.; participant crisis im the nation program Nat. Coun. Chs., Chgo., L.A., 1968; participant local, regional, nat. and internat. Presbyn. Ch. and interdenominational and ecumenical couns. Mem. nat. bd. UN Assn., PAX World Svc., Washington Office on Africa, Ams. United for Separation Ch. and State, Internat. Human Rights Internship Program.; former mem. bd. dirs. U.S. sect. Amnesty Internat.; past mem. Pres. Carter's Presdl. Adv. Bd. for Ambassadorial Appointments. Recipient numerous awards for civil and human rights, peace and justice issues. Mem. NASW, Nat. Assn. Black Social Workers. Office: World Conf Religion and Peace USA 777 United Nations Plz New York NY 10017

PATTERSON, MARY-MARGARET SHARP, writer, editor, media strategist; b. Fairmont, W.Va., July 12, 1944; d. H. Sutton Sharp and Columbia Strock; m. David Sands, June 15, 1968; 1 child, Scott Sutton. BA cum laude, Ohio State U., 1966, MA, 1967. Media coordinator Am. Hosp. Assn., Chgo., 1969; feature and mag. writer Chgo. Today newspaper, 1969-70; reporter Houston Chronicle, 1971-73; instr. journalism U. Houston, 1974-76; asst. prof. Utica (N.Y.) Coll. U. Syracuse, 1976-78; dir. undergrad. studies coll. journalism U. Md., College Park, 1978-82, editor, 1982; dir. information and devel. Audubon Naturalist Soc. Cen. Atlantic States, Inc., Chevy Chase, Md., 1982-89; dir. media rels. Defenders of Wildlife, Washington, 1989-90; resident Johns Hopkins-Nanjing U. Ctr. for Chinese and Am. Studies, Nanjing, China, 1990-91; writer, editor Am. Assn. Retired Persons, Washington, 1993-95; prin. Mary Margaret Patterson Writer, Editor, Media Cons., 1996—; cons. project Africa Carnegie Mellon U. Pitts., 1969; newspaper div. head summer journalism inst. Trinity U., San Antonio, 1979-81; columnist San Antonio Mag., 1976-79; cons. Callahan & Assoc., Washington, 1992—. Editor: Credit Unions On-Line, 1996—; contbr. numerous articles and book revs. to newspapers and mags. Mem. Chevy Chase Presbyn. Ch. Choir, Washington, 1980—, ruling elder, 1993-96. Recipient Reporting Excellence award The Newspaper Fund, Cleve., 1966; Univ. Grad. fellow Ohio State U., 1966, Nat. Grad. fellow Women in Communications, 1967. Mem. Soc. Profl. Journalists, Mortar Bd., Washington Ind. Writers, Inc., Nat.Press CLub Libr., Kappa Tau Alpha. Democrat.

PATTERSON, MILDRED LUCAS, teaching specialist; b. Winston-Salem, N.C., Jan. 24, 1937; d. James Arthur and Lula Mae (Smith) Lucas; m. James Harrison Patterson Jr., Mar. 31, 1961; children: James Harrison III, Roger Lindsay. BA, Talladega Coll., 1958; MEd, St. Louis U., 1969; postgrad., Webster U., 1970. Classroom tchr. St. Louis Bd. Edn., 1961-72, reading specialist, 1972-88, co-host radio reading show, 1988-91; tchr. specialist Reading to Achieve Motivational Program, St. Louis, 1991—; bd. dirs. Supt.'s Adv. Com., University City, Mo., 1994—; presenter Chpt. I Regional Conf. Co-author: Wearing Purple, 1996. Bd. dirs. Gateway Homes, St. Louis, 1989-93; mem. com. University City Sch. Bond Issue, 1994. Recipient Letter of Commendation, Chpt. I. Regional Conf., 1991, Founders' award Gamma Omega chpt. Alpha Kappa Alpha, 1985. Mem. Internat. Reading Assn. (Broadcast Media award for radio 1990, Bldg. Rep. award St. Louis chpt. 1990), St. Louis Alliance of Black Educators.

PATTERSON, SALLY JANE, government affairs consultant; b. Ontario, Calif., May 28, 1948; d. James Lowell and Barbara Verle (Griffin) Swain; 1 child, Robert Elias Sandoval. BA, Calif. State U., Fullerton, 1970, MA, 1974. Adminstrv. asst. Congressman Jerry Patterson, U.S. House of Reps., Washington, 1978-81; v.p. Pub. Response Assocs., Washington, 1981-87, Hamilton & Staff, Washington, 1987-90; v.p. pub. affairs Planned Parenthood Fedn. of Am., N.Y.C., 1990-93; internat. cons. Mgmt. Systems Internat., Washington, 1993—; prin. Winner/Wagner & Francis, L.A., N.Y.C., Washington, 1994—; cons. Nat. Dem. Inst., Washington, 1994—; mem. bd. Reproductive Health Techs. Project. Author: Supporting Democracy in The Newly Independent States of The Former Soviet Union, 1994, Women in Government Relations: 20 Years of Vision, Leadership, Education and Networking, 1995. Trainer Nat. Women's Campaign Fund, Phoenix, Ariz., Chgo., Washington, 1993—. Recipient Gold Key award PR Soc. Am., 1992; named one of 74 Women Shaping Am. Politics, Campaigns and Elections, 1993. Mem. Women in Govt. Rels., Inc. (disting. mem., chair leader found. 1985-87, v.p. 1987-88, pres. 1988-89), Coun. Excellence in Govt. (prin.). Democrat. Episcopalian. Office: Winner/Wagner & Francis 1000 Potomac St # 401 Washington DC 20007

PATTERSON, VIRGINIA CATHARINE, religious organization executive; b. N.Mex., Jan. 23, 1931; d. Edward Cecil and Edith Elizabeth (Roweton) P. BA, U. Tulsa, 1953; MA Bible/Missions, Columbia Bible Coll. (S.C.), 1956; MS Elem. Ed., Okla. State U., 1963; EdD, No. Ill. U., DeKalb, 1978. Tchr., recreation dir. Girls Indsl. Sch., Columbia, S.C., 1954-57; tchr., prin., Kent Acad., Nigeria, 1958-68; publ. dir. Pioneer Girls, Inc., Wheaton, Ill., 1969-70; pres. Pioneer Clubs, Wheaton, Ill., 1970—; adj. prof. Gordon-Conwell Sem. Presbyterian. Office: Pioneer Clubs 27W130 Saint Charles Rd Wheaton IL 60187

PATTERSON-DEHN, CATHLEEN ERIN, pediatric nurse practitioner; b. Akron, Feb. 25, 1958; d. James Edward and Doris Elizabeth (Boyd) P.; m. James Keith Dehn, June 27, 1981. BSN, U. Akron, 1980; MSN, Case Western Res. U., 1988; MA in Dance, Case Western Reserve U., 1992; MA Applied Psychology, NYU, 1995, postgrad., 1995—. RN, Ohio; cert. pediatric nurse practitioner ANCC. Nurse technician Children's Med. Ctr. Akron, 1978-80, staff nurse, 1980-81; pediatric and advanced clin. nurse, asst. head nurse, clin. nurse specialist Rainbow Babies and Children's Hosp., Cleve., 1981-91, edn. coord., 1991-93, project dir., 1989-91; coord., pediatric nurse practitioner The Child Health Ctr., Bklyn., 1994-96; with Beth Israel Med. Ctr., N.Y.C., 1996—; lectr. Frances Payne Bolton Sch. Nursing, Case Western Res. U., Cleve., 1990-93; project dir. Dance Cleve., 1990-91; regional instr. Neonatal Resuscitation Program, Am. Heart Assn., Am. Acad. Pediatrics; instr. Nursing Child Assessment Satellite Tng. U. of Washington, 1991—. Co-founder Sick Kids Need Involved People, Cleve., 1987; pres. Friends Footpath, Cleve., 1989-90; team-walk capt. March of Dimes, Cleve., 1989-92 (Edn. grantee 1991); mem. Nat. Mus. Women in Arts. Recipient Samuel E. and Rebecca Elliott award for Community Svc. Case Western Res. U., 1988; named One of Outstanding Young Women of Am., 1988; Fed. Profl. Nurse Trainee scholar, 1986-87. Mem. APA (divsn. 7 devel. psychology), Kappa Delta Pi, Sigma Theta Tau. Home: 1 University Pl Apt 10L New York NY 10003-6645

PATTISON, DELORIS JEAN, counselor, university official; b. Logansport, Ind., Oct. 3, 1931; d. John R. and Grace I. Gallagher (Yocum) Taylor; m. John A. Pattison, July 3, 1952; children: Traci (dec.), John A. II, Scott, Becky. BS in Secondary Edn., Goshen Coll., 1973; MA in Edn., Ball State U., 1977. Life cert. vocat. edn. tchr., Ind. Tchr. home econs. Marion (Ind.) H.S., 1973-78; dir. youth employment Logansport Cmty. Schs., 1979-83; substitute tchr. Ft. Wayne (Ind.) Cmty. Schs., 1983-87; employment counselor Ind. Dept. Employment, Marion, 1987-90, counselor, coord. adminstrv. career svcs. Ind. Wesleyan U., Marion, 1990—. Editor: A Teen Trace, 1971; also articles. Bd. dirs. Ind. Christian Coll. Consortium, 1990—. Named Outstanding Employee, Ind. Dept. Employment and Tng., 1989. Mem. Nat. Assn. Colls. and Employers, Midwest Coll. Placement Assn., Great Lake Assn. for Sch., Coll. and Univ. Staffing, Dist. Min. Spouse Assn. (sec. 1987-89), Am. Legion Aux. Methodist. Home: 801 N Huntington #47 Hippensteel Dr Warren IN 46792 Office: Ind Wesleyan U 4201 S Washington St Marion IN 46953-4974

PATTON, LEE ANN RICHARDS, educator; b. Charleston, W.Va., Mar. 25, 1957; d. Denver Ray and Evelyn Anice (Matson) Richards (dec.); 1 child, Erica Faith. BS in Elem. Edn., W.Va. State Coll., 1995. Mem. Pinnacle Honor Soc., Kappa Delta Pi (v.p. 1994-95), Alpha Gamma Mu, Phi Alpha Theta. Home: 505 Shaw St Charleston WV 25301

PATTON, NANCY MATTHEWS, elementary education educator; b. Pitts., Apr. 7, 1942; d. Thomas Joseph and Sara Theresa (Jocunskas) Matthews; m. Jack E. Patton, July 20, 1974; children: Susan, Steven. BS in Edn., Ind. U. of Pa., 1963; grad. student, U. Pitts. 4th grade tchr. Elroy Sch., Pitts., 1980-91; 6th grade tchr. Brentwood Middle Sch., Pitts., 1991—; sponsor Brentwood Middle Sch. newspaper; coach Brentwood Varsity Cheerleaders, 1981-93. Councilperson Brentwood Borough Coun., 1988—, v.p., 1994—; sec. Brentwood Dem. Com., 1989-95; bd. trustees Brentwood Libr. Bd., 1988—; mem. Brentwood Econ. Devel. Corp., 1995—. Mem. NEA, Nat. Sci. Tchrs. Assn., Pa. State Edn. Assn., Brentwood Century Club. Democrat. Roman Catholic. Home: 105 Hillson Ave Pittsburgh PA 15227-2941

PATTON, SHARLENE DARLAGE, nurse; b. Seymour, Ind., July 20, 1933; d. Alfred J. and Viora E. (Elkins) Darlage; children: Raye Ellen, Scott, Susan, Martha, Lisa, Elise. RN, Sch. Nursing Michael Reese Hosp., 1953; BA, Gov.'s State U., 1985. Head nurse Drug Abuse Program, Chgo.; nurse Tinley Park (Ill.) Mental Hosp. Mem. ANA. Address: 593 8th St Chicago Heights IL 60411-1926

PATTON, SUSAN OERTEL, clinical social worker, educator; b. Syracuse, N.Y., May 18, 1946; d. Robert William and Jane (VanWormer) Oertel; m. Joseph D. Patton, Jr., June 3, 1967; children: Jennifer, Joseph D. III. BA, SUNY, Geneseo, 1984; MSW, SUNY, Buffalo, 1987. Cert. social worker, N.Y.; lic. ind. social worker, S.C.; cert. employee assistance profl.; qualified clin. social worker; bd. cert. fellow in managed mental health care; diplomate in clin. social work. Counselor Profl. Counseling Svc., Gowanda, N.Y., 1987-88, Mental Health Mgmt., Rochester, N.Y., 1988-93; counselor The Health Assn., Rochester, 1988-89, sr. counselor, 1989-90, asst. dir. mktg. and tng., 1990-92; pvt. practice Rochester, 1988-93; employee assistance program dir. Recovery Ctr. EAP, Hilton Head, S.C., 1993-95; pres., dir. Employee Assistance Program, Inc., Hilton Head Island, S.C., 1995—; instr. Medaille Coll., Buffalo, 1990-93. Co-author: Treating Perpetrators of Sexual Abuse, 1990. Mem. NASW, Acad. Cert. Social Workers, Am. Bd. Cert. Managed Care Providers, S.C. Counselors Assn., Employee Assistance

Profls. Assn. Office: Employee Assistance Program Carolina Bldg Ste 110 10 Office Park Rd Hilton Head Island SC 29928-7541

PATTY, ANNA CHRISTINE, middle school educator; b. Atlanta, Aug. 25, 1937; d. Henry Richard and Gertrude (Smith) Johnson; children: Robert E., C. Wayne Jr., Christine E. BS in Math., U. Ga., 1959; MA in Edn., Va. Poly. Inst. and State U., 1991. Cert. tchr., Va. Mgr. Steak and Ale Restaurants, Inc., Dallas, 1982-84; bus. mgr. Nova Plaza Corp., Charlotte, N.C., 1984-86; asst. mgr. WoodLo, Inc., Charlotte, 1986-87; food activity mgr. Army and Air Force Exch. Svc., Schweinfurt, Fed. Republic Germany, 1987-89; substitute tchr. Montgomery County Schs., Christiansburg, Va., 1989-91; rsch. asst. Va. Poly. Inst. and State U., Blacksburg, 1990-91; math. and sci. middle sch. tchr. Hampton (Va.) City Schs., 1991—; mem. NSTA/APST Summer Inst., U.Md., 1992, NSTA Summer Inst., Sci. and Tech., SUNY, Stoney Brook, N.Y., 1995; EXCEL coach Christopher Newport U., 1993-95. With Operation Path Finders, Sandy Hook, N.J., 1994. Mem. NEA, Va. Educators Assn., Nat. Sci. Tchrs. Assn. (summer inst. participant 1992), Va. Middle Sch. Assn., Va. Sci. Tchrs., Nat. Coun. Tchrs. Math. Republican. Unitarian. Home: 811 Player Ln Newport News VA 23602

PAUGH, PATRICIA LOU, business consultant; b. Pitts., Oct. 30, 1948; d. Marshall Franklin and Helen Jeanne (Graham) P. BA in English, Columbia U., 1982. Adminstrv. asst. Katz, Robinson, Brog & Seymour, N.Y.C., 1972-75; office mgr. Michael D. Martocci, N.Y.C., 1975-80; adminstrv. mgr. O'Melveny & Myers, N.Y.C., 1982-85, Latham & Watkins, N.Y.C., 1985-88; mgr. Nationwide Legal Svcs., N.Y.C., 1988-89; mgr. legal adminstrn. Aluminum Co. of Am., Pitts., 1990-93; ptnr. Domestic & Overseas Countertrade and Consulting Svcs., Ltd., 1986—; pres. Domestic & Overseas Trading Corp., Pitts., 1993—; mng. dir. Gen. Comml. Svcs., Ltd., 1994—. Mem. Am. Mgmt. Assn., Pitts. C. of C. Republican. Episcopalian. Office: Gen Comml Svcs 239 4th Ave Ste 1703 Pittsburgh PA 15222

PAUL, CAROL ANN, academic administrator, biology educator; b. Brockton, Mass., Dec. 17, 1936; d. Joseph W. and Mary M. (DeMeulenaer) Bjork; m. Robert D. Paul, Dec. 21, 1957; children: Christine, Dana, Stephanie, Robert. BS, U. Mass., 1958; MAT, R.I. Coll., 1968, Brown U., 1970; EdD, Boston U., 1978. Tchr. biology Attleboro (Mass.) High Sch., 1965-68; asst. dean., mem. faculty biology North Shore Community Coll., Beverly, Mass., 1969-78; master planner N.J. Dept. for Higher Edn., Trenton, 1978-80; assoc. v.p. Fairleigh Dickinson U., Rutherford, N.J., 1980-86; v.p. acad. affairs Suffolk Community Coll., Selden, N.Y., 1986-94, assoc. prof. biology, 1994—; faculty devel. cons. various colls., 1979—, title III evaluator, 1985—. Author: (lab. manual and workbook) Minicourses and Labs for Biological Science, 1972 (rev. edit., 1975); (with others) Strategies and Attitudes, 1986; book reviewer, 1973-77. V.p. League of Women Voters, Beverly, 1970-74, Cranford, N.J., 1982-83; alumni rep. Brown U., Cranford, 1972—. Commonwealth Mass. scholar, 1958; recipient Acad. Yr. award NSF, 1968-69, Proclamation for Leadership award Suffolk County Exec., 1989. Mem. AAHE, AAWCC, Profls. and Orgn. Developers (planning com. 1977-79, nat. exec. bd. 1979-80), Nat. Coun. for Staff, Phi Beta Kappa, Pi Lambda Theta. Roman Catholic. Address: 75 Fairview Cir Middle Island NY 11953-2340 Office: Suffolk Community Coll 533 College Rd Selden NY 11784-2851

PAUL, CHARLOTTE P., nursing educator; b. Clarendon, Tex., Jan. 13, 1941; d. William Clyde Peggram and Sibyl (Rattan) Jones; m. Robert M. Paul, Apr. 4, 1964; children: Peter, Lauraine. Diploma, St. Anthony's Hosp. Sch. Nursing, Amarillo, Tex., 1961; student, Amarillo Coll., 1958-65; BS, Syracuse U., 1972, MS, 1973, PhD in Edn. Adminstrn., 1979; postgrad., Wright State U., 1977-79, U. Tex., El Paso, 1983-86, U. Pitts., 1992-94. Nurse St. Anthony's Hosp., Amarillo, Tex., 1961-65; evening charge nurse Upstate Med. Ctr. SUNY, Syracuse, 1966-68, VA Hosp. Gen. Hosp., Syracuse, 1965-66; asst. to head nurse Meml. Hosp., Syracuse, 1966-68; nurse IV therapy Community-Gen. Hosp., Syracuse, 1968-72; instr. Syracuse Cen. Sch. System, 1972; asst. dir. insvc. edn. House of Good Samaritan Hosp., Watertown, N.Y., 1973-74; instr. SUNY Sch. Nursing, Syracuse, 1974-75, Syracuse U. Sch. Nursing, 1975-76; asst. dean Wright State U., Dayton, Ohio, 1977-79; assoc. prof. Edinboro U. Pa., 1979-86, prof., 1986—, chairperson dept. grad. studies, 1980-82, chairperson dept. nursing, 1987-89; coord. quality assurance William Beaumont Army Med. Ctr., Ft. Bliss, Tex., 1982-85; adj. assoc. prof. U. Tex., El Paso, 1982-85; cons. in field. Contbr. articles to profl. jours., papers in field. Bd. dirs. ARC, Syracuse, 1970-77, Erie County Emergency Mgmt. Agy.; chairperson Lake Erie Higher Edn. Coun., 1972-74, cons., 1987—; mem. Coun. on Aging Com. on Long Term Care, Dayton, 1977-78. Lt. col. USAR. Recipient Unit Citation award CAP, 1968, Excellence in Nursing Edn. award, 1992, Commdr.'s Commendation award, 1995, Leadership and Svc. award Lake Area Health Edn. Ctr., 1994; Gladys Post scholar, 1958-61, Rodney Horle scholar, 1971-72, Nellie Hurly scholar, 1971-72; grantee HEW, 1977, Wright State U., 1977-78, William Beaumont Army Med. Ctr., 1986, Edinboro (Pa.) U., 1979-80, 91; Nightingale Soc. fellow, 1988; named to Internat. Profl. and Bus. Women's Hall of Fame, 1994. Mem. APHA, St. Anthony's Hosp. Sch. Nursing Alumni Assn., Syracuse U. Alumni Assn., N.Y. Acad. Sci., Assn. Mil. Surgeons, U.S. Nightengale Soc., Nat. Ski Patrol (life), Kiwwanis (bd. dirs. Edinboro club 1987-95, pres. 1988-89, v.p. 1987-88), Sigma Theta Tau (advisor 1987-94), Pi Lambda Theta (life, pres. local chpt. 1973-75). Republican. Office: Edinboro U Pa 139 Centennial Hall Edinboro PA 16412

PAUL, EVE W., lawyer; b. N.Y.C., June 16, 1930; d. Leo I. and Tamara (Sogolow) Weinschenker; m. Robert D. Paul, Apr. 9, 1952; children: Jeremy Ralph, Sarah Elizabeth. BA, Cornell U., 1950; JD, Columbia U., 1952. Bar: N.Y. 1952, Conn. 1960, U.S. Ct. Appeals (2nd cir.) 1975, U.S. Supreme Ct. 1977. Assoc. Botein, Hays, Sklar & Herzberg, N.Y.C., 1952-54; pvt. practice Stamford, Conn., 1960-70; staff atty. Legal Aid Soc., N.Y.C., 1970-71; assoc. Greenbaum, Wolff & Ernst, N.Y.C., 1972-78; v.p. legal affairs Planned Parenthood Fedn. Am., N.Y.C., 1979—, v.p., gen. counsel, 1991—. Contbr. articles to legal and health publs. Trustee Cornell U., Ithaca, N.Y., 1979-84; mem. Stamford Planning Bd., Conn., 1967-70; bd. mem. Stamford League Women Voters, 1960-62. Harlan Fiske Stone scholar Columbia Law Sch., 1952. Mem. ABA, Conn. Bar Assn., Assn. of Bar of City of N.Y., Stamford/Norwalk Regional Bar Assn., U.S. Trademark Assn. (chairperson dictionary listings com. 1988-90), Phi Beta Kappa, Phi Kappa Phi. Office: Planned Parenthood Fedn 810 7th Ave New York NY 10019-5818

PAUL, LINDA BAUM, geriatrics nurse, toy business owner; b. Syracuse, N.Y., Aug. 18, 1946; d. LeRoy Stanley and Evelyn Lucille (Miller) Baum; m. James Frederick Paul, Mar. 2, 1974; children: Patricia Ann, Sharon Joy, Sarah Leigh. LPN, Ctrl. Tech. Adult LPN Program, Syracuse, 1970; postgrad. in RN, Human Svc., Onondaga C.C., 1990-92, postgrad. in MSW/Counseling, 1996—. LPN, charge nurse Maple Lawn Nursing Home, Manlius, N.Y., 1970-73; nurse, foster parent, personal care provider Ofc. Mental Retardation & Devel. Disabilities/Sequin Cmty., Syracuse, 1974-87; LPN, charge nurse Cmty. Gen. Hosp., Syracuse, 1989-96; owner Wood-You Crafts, Manlius, 1987-92. Election insp. Dem. Com. Bd. Elections, Dewitt/Fayetteville, N.Y., 1986-87; mem. Jamesville-DeWitt PTG, 1974—; mem. ch. missions and ourtreach Manlius Meth. Ch., 1995—, choir dir., 1993; choir dir. Bridgeport Meth. Ch., 1974-76; soloist Syracuse Chorale; mem. ENABLE/United Cerebbral Palsy Ctr. Home: 219 Hobson Ave Fayetteville NY 13066-1616

PAUL, LOIS ANN, principal; b. Perth Amboy, N.J., July 6, 1951; d. Louis Harold and Margaret Elizabeth (Rausch) Mielenhausen; m. John Stephen Paul Jr., July 24, 1971; 1 child, Melissa Ayn. BS in Edn., Indiana U. Pa., 1976, cert. elem. prin., 1994. Presch. tchr. Lollipop Ranch Presch., Davenport, Iowa, 1972-73; permanent substitute tchr. Greater Johnstown (Pa.) Sch. Dist., 1978; kindergarten tchr. St. Patrick Sch., Johnstown, 1978-85; tchr. grade 7 West End Cath. Sch., Johnstown, 1985-88; tchr. grade 8 St. Patrick Sch., Johnstown, 1988-92; prin. All Saints Cath. Sch., Cresson, Pa., 1992—; chairperson, mem. verifying the vision teams edn. office Diocese of Altoona-Johnstown, Hollidaysburg, Pa., 1988-91, adv. bd. mem. parish self-study commn., 1992-94; mem. instrnl. support team All Saints Cath. Sch., Cresson, 1994—. Editor (newsletter for pastoral musicians of the Altoona-Johnstown Diocese) The Whole Note, 1993-95. Chair, mem. Marriage Encounter Team, Ebensburg, Pa., 1985-91; chairperson liturgy com. St. Rochus Ch., Johnstown, 1987-93, sec. parish coun., 1990-93; team mem. Teens Encounter Christ, Ebensburg, 1990-92. Mem. Nat. Cath. Edn. Assn., Pa. Assn. Elem. Sch. Prins. Democrat. Roman Catholic. Home: 719 Russell Ave Johnstown PA 15902-2861 Office: All Saints Cath Sch 220 Powell Ave Cresson PA 16630-1219

PAUL, MARY JOAN, physical education educator; b. Sulligent, Ala., Feb. 19, 1935; d. Victor C. and Pauline (Gilmer) P. BS, Samford U., Birmingham, Ala., 1957; MS, U. Ala., Tuscaloosa, 1963, EdD, 1966. Tchr. Hewitt-Trussville H.S., Trussville, Ala., 1957-63; grad. asst. U. Ala., Tuscaloosa, 1963-66; prof., head dept. phys. edn. Southeastern La. U., Hammond, 1966-87, U. Tenn., Knoxville, 1987—; vis. prof. Jacksonville (Ala.) State U., summer 1966. Recipient John Tunstall award U. Tenn., Knoxville, 1994, Svc. award Nat. Assn. for Sport and Phys. Edn., 1993. Mem. AAHPERD (chair history acad.), So. Assn. for Health, Phys. Edn., Recreation and Dance (pres. 1986-88), Tenn. Assn. for Health, Phys. Edn., Recreation and Dance (chair higher edn. 1991-92), N.Am. Soc. for Sport History (pres. 1993-95). Democrat. Office: U Tenn Cultural Studies 1518 Andy Holt Ave Knoxville TN 37916-3811

PAUL, MARY MELCHIOR, human resources professional; b. Tipton, Ind., Apr. 29, 1952; d. John A. and Inez Marie (Clark) Meyer; 1 child, Regina. BS, U. Evansville, 1974; MBA, So. Ill. U., 1987. Mgr. The Children's Shops, St. Louis, 1980-86; cons., trainer Edison Bros. Stores, St. Louis, 1987; program mgr. Anheuser-Busch Cos., 1988-94; human resources devel. mgr. Campbell Taggart, Inc. (divsn. Anheuser-Busch Cos. Inc.), St. Louis, 1994-96; sr. orgn. devel. cons. Harley Davidson, Inc., Milw., 1996—. Mem. Coro Found. Mem. ASTD, Profl. Woman Network, Profl. Dimensions, Women in Leadership Alumnae. Home: 8763 Parkview Ct Milwaukee WI 53226 Office: Harley Davidson Motor Co 11700 W Capitol Dr Milwaukee WI 53201

PAUL, RHONDA ELIZABETH, university program director, career development counselor; d. John and Vivian (Griffin) P. BA, Mich. State U., 1977; MA, Atlanta U., 1979; postgrad., Wayne State U., 1982—. Cert. counselor, Mich.; nat. cert. career counelor; lic. profl. counselor. Counselor, student affairs dept. Spelman Coll., Atlanta, 1978-79; life/career devel. specialist Wayne State U., Detroit, 1979-81, minority devel. counselor, 1981-83; prog. dir. recruitment dept. Wayne State Sch. of Medicine, Detroit, 1983—; cons./proprietor RP Career Assocs., Detroit, 1990—. Recipient Award of Pride, Mich. State U., Lansing, 1977, Spl. Recognition award Nat. Bd. for Cert. Counselors, 1993. Mem. NAACP, Am. Counseling Assn., Mich. Counseling Assn., Assn. Multicultural Counseling and Devel. (nat. stds. and cert. com.), Nat. Career Devel. Assn., Nat. Coalition of 100 Black Women (bd. dirs.), Alpha Kappa Alpha. Home: 4068 Cortland St Detroit MI 48204-1506 Office: Wayne State U Dept Recruitment Detroit MI 48202

PAULEY, JANE, television journalist; b. Indpls., Oct. 31, 1950; m. Garry Trudeau; 3 children. BA in Polit. Sci, Ind. U., 1971; D. Journalism (hon.), DePauw U., 1978. Reporter Sta. WISH-TV, Indpls., 1972-75; co-anchor WMAQ-TV News, Chgo., 1975-76, The Today Show, NBC, N.Y.C., 1976-90; corr. NBC News, N.Y.C., 1976—; prin. writer, reporter NBC Nightly News, 1980-82, substitute anchor, 1990—; co-anchor Early Today, NBC, 1982-83; prin. corr. Real Life With Jane Pauley, NBC, 1990; co-anchor Dateline NBC, 1992—. Office: NBC News 30 Rockefeller Plz New York NY 10112*

PAULEY, VICKI VANCE, adaptive physical education educator; b. Dayton, Ohio, Aug. 21, 1966; d. Richard Griffith Sr. and Joan Marcella (Bent) Vance; m. Tim Andrew Pauley, Apr. 11, 1992; 1 child, Lauren. BS in Edn., U. Dayton, 1988, MS in Edn., 1994. Cert. tchr. adaptive phys. edn., phys. edn., health and biology, Ohio. Tchr. phys. edn. Ascension Sch., Dayton, 1989-90; adaptive phys. edn. specialist Greene County Bd. Edn., Yellow Springs, Ohio, 1990-91, Hamilton County Bd. Mental Retardation and Devel. Disability, Cin., 1992—; mem. standards com. Adapted Phys. Edn. Nat. Standards Project, Charlottesville, Va., 1993—; alumni rep. dept. health, phys. edn. and sport sci. U. Dayton, 1993—. Coach Spl. Olympics, Cin., 1992—. Mem. AAHPERD, Ohio Adapted Phys. Edn. Consortium. Roman Catholic. Home: 5322 Leatherwood Dr West Chester OH 45069-1876 Office: Rost Sch 5858 Bridgetown Rd Cincinnati OH 45248-3106

PAULIN, AMY RUTH, civic activist, consultant; b. Bklyn., Nov. 29, 1955; d. Ben and Alice Lois (Roth) P.; m. Ira Schuman, May 25, 1980; children: Beth, Sarah, Joseph. BA, SUNY, Albany, 1977, MA, 1978, postgrad., 1979—. Instr. SUNY, Albany, 1978, Queens (N.Y.) House of Detention, 1979; fundraiser United Jewish Appeal Fedn., N.Y.C., 1979-83; dir. devel. Altro Health & Rehab., Bronx, N.Y., 1983-86; fundraising cons. N.Y.C., 1986-88; pres. LWV, Scarsdale, N.Y., 1990-92, Westchester, N.Y., 1992-95; trustee Scarsdale (N.Y.) Village, 1995—; bd. dirs. Westco Prodns. Mem. adv. coun. Family Ct.; chair county budget chair Westchester Womens Agenda; mem. adv. com. Fund for Women & Girls; bd. dirs. Mid. Sch. PTA, Westchester Coalition for Legal Abortion, Scarsdale Open Soc. Assn., 1992-95, United Jewish Appeal Fedn. Scarsdale Women's Campaign; v.p. Westchester Children's Assn.; troop leader Girl Scouts U.S.; mem. Town Club Edn. Com., 1983-89; mem. Scarsdale Bowl com., 1992—, chair, 1994-95; mem. Scarsdale Japanese Festival, 1992-93; mem. Westchester Women's Equality Day, 1987-92; mem. nominating com. Heathcote Neighborhood Assn., 1991-92; bd. dirs. Westchester Cmty. Found., 1994-95; mem. Scarsdale Village Youth Bd., 1992-95; mem. legislators task force on women and youth at risk Westchester County Bd., 1984—; mem. Updating Voting Equipment Com., 1994, chair, 1994-95; chair Cmtys. Tobacco Free Westchester; co-chair Parent Tchr. Coun. Sch. Budget Study, 1991-94; future planning chair Kids Base Bd., 1992-95; chair parking and traffic subcom. Village Downtown Devel. Com., 1994-95; mem. Westchester Commn. Campaign Fin. Reform, Westchester Commn. Child Abuse. Mem. LWV (bd. dirs. women and children's issues Westchester chpt., dir. devel. N.Y. state), N.Y. State Pub. Health Assn. (bd. dirs. Lower Hudson Valley chpt.). Home: 12 Burgess Rd Scarsdale NY 10583-4410

PAULINA, DIANA, alternative school educator; b. Detroit; d. Walter and Marie (Hrit) P.; m. Kevin Crawley, Aug. 23, 1981. BA in German and English Edn., U. Mich., 1969; MA in Edn. Alternative Sch., Ind. U., 1979. Cert. tchr., German, English and reading. Various tchg. positions USAF/Lang. Inst., Germany, 1970-74; instr. Marshalltown (Iowa) C.C., 1974-79; dir., counselor Unbound, Inc., Iowa City, Iowa, 1980-90; instr. Cmty. Edn. Ctr. Alternative Schs., Iowa City, 1984—; sponsor Iowa City (Iowa) Student Computer Club, 1993—; internat cons. Iowa City Cmty. schs., 1991—; v.p., bd. dirs. Response TV, Inc., Iowa City, 1992—; policy bd. chair Iowa Student Computer Assn. bull. Bd. Svc., 1992—. Mem. ASCD, ALA, AAUW, NEA, Iowa State Edn. Assn. (internet cons. 1992—, Mem. of Yr. East Ctrl. Uniserve unit 1996), Iowa City Edn. Assn. (pres., v.p., tech. chair, Mem. of Yr. 1996), Internat. Reading Assn., Nat. Coun. Tchrs. English, Iowa Coun. Tchrs. Lang. Arts, Iowa Assn. Alternative Educators (Educator of Yr. award 1996), Iowa City Ednl. Cable Consortium, Iowa City Pub. Access (cmty. cable prodr. 1983—), Iowa Student Computer Assn., Assn. Computing Machinery, U. Mich. Alumni Assn., Ind. U. Alumni Assn. Home: PO Box 1963 Iowa City IA 52244-1963 Office: CEC Alternative Schs 509 S Dubuque St Iowa City IA 52240-4228

PAULK, ANNA MARIE, office manager; b. Columbia, Tenn., Feb. 5, 1959; d. Earl Gaston Woodard, Sr. and Anna Genette (McCuin) Woodard Tison; m. John Eason Paulk III, June 6, 1982 (div. June 1992); children: Erica Marie, Aimee Renae, Janna Elizabeth. AAS, Abraham Baldwin Coll., 1988; BBA cum laude, Ga. Southwestern U., 1992; postgrad., Albany State U., 1996—. Office mgr. E.J. Tison, D.D.S., P.C., Ashburn, Ga., 1979—. Pres. PTO/Tiftarea Acad., 1993—. Mem. Gamma Beta Phi. Republican. Mem. Ch. of Christ. Home: 792 Cedar Dr Ashburn GA 31714 Office: EJ Tison DDS PC 372 E College Ave Ashburn GA 31714-1209

PAULK, TERRI LYN, elementary school educator; b. Atlanta, Sept. 13, 1970; d. Joe Columbus Underwood II and Polly (Ellis) Martin; m. Herschel Leverne Paulk Jr., Apr. 4, 1992. AA, Brewton Parker Coll., Mt. Vernon, Ga., 1989; BS in Edn., U. Ga., 1992; MEd in Mid. Grades, Ga. So. U., 1995. Cert. tchr., Ga. Elem. tchr. gifted Effingham County Bd. Edn., Springfield, Ga., 1992—. Mem. Profl. Assn. Ga. Educators, Golden Ky, Kappa delta Pi. Baptist. Home: PO Box 790 Guyton GA 31312-0790

PAULL, ELSIE BEHREND, editorial stylist, interpreter; b. Washington, Feb. 18, 1912; d. Edwin and Frances (Sanders) Behrend; m. Francis Swann, June 6, 1936 (div. July 1943); m. Joseph Paull, July 11, 1947; children: Kathryn P. Brown, Elizabeth Jane O'Connell. Diplomate, U. Nancy, France, 1930, U. Paris, 1931-32; BA, Barnard Coll., 1933. Intelligence analyst Fgn. Econs. Adminstrn., Washington, 1942-43; vol. tchr. of French lang. Washington, 1955; editl. stylist, interpreter E.J. Lieberman, Washington, 1990—. Democrat. Home: 4827 Nebraska Ave NW Washington DC 20016

PAULOS, CHRISTINE ANN, athletic director, academic counselor; b. St. Paul, Sept. 17, 1956; d. Peter and Linda Joy (Kastner) P. BS in Phys. Edn. and Sociology, U. Minn., 1981; MA in Psychology and Counseling, Liberty U., Lynchburg, Va., 1990. Coach U. St. Thomas, St. Paul, 1980-81, softball coach, 1985—; coach, instr. Macalaster Coll., St. Paul, 1981-85; cons. Facility Mgmt., Minn., 1984-86. Author (jour.) The Balancing Act-Athletics and Academics, 1992 (award of excellence for innovations in acad. support Athletic Mgmt. Mag. 1994). Named to Softball Hall of Fame, U. Minn., 1989; named Softball All-Am. Am. Softball Assn., 1980, Outstanding All-Time Athlete-Field Hockey, U. Minn., 1995. Mem. NCAA, Nat. Assn. Acad. Advisors for Athletes, Am. Counseling Assn. Home: 9409 Grand Ave S Minneapolis MN 55420 Office: U St Thomas 2115 Summit Ave Saint Paul MN 55105

PAULSHOCK, BERNADINE Z., medical educator, editor, writer; b. Bethlehem, Pa., Feb. 28, 1928; d. Louis Charles and Ruth (Meyers) Ziegler; m. Marvin Paulshock, June 17, 1951; children: Craig Louis, Dale R., Sharon B. BA, U. Pa., 1947, MD, 1951. Diplomate Am. Bd. Internal Medicine, Am. Bd. Family Practice. Pvt. practice Wilmington, 1955-90; attending physician Med. Ctr. Del., 1955-90, faculty, family practice residency, 1973-90; assoc. prof. Jefferson Med. Coll., 1975—. Editor: Del. Med. Jour.; mem. editl. bd. Patient Care, Family Practice Rsch.; contbr. articles to profl. jours. Mem. Coun. Del. Humanities Forum, 1992—; bd. Curative Workshop, Brown Vocat. High. Recipient Trailblazers award Del. Women, 1985. Fellow ACP; mem. AMA, Am. Assn. History Medicine, Med. Soc. Del. (v.p. 1980), Phi Beta Kappa. Home: 1306 Marsh Rd Wilmington DE 19803-3532

PAULSON, DIANE FINKEL, lawyer; b. Cambridge, Mass., Mar. 26, 1938; d. Oscar and Mae (Borkum) Finkel; m. Donald Erwin Paulson, Sept. 8, 1963; childern: Michael, Susan, David. AB, Bryn Mawr Coll., 1959; MEd, Boston U., 1967; JD, Northeastern U., 1978. Bar: Mass. 1978. Staff atty. Ctrl. Mass. Legal Svcs., Worcester, 1978-83; staff atty. Greater Boston Legal Svcs., 1983-86, mng. atty., 1986—. Mem. Boston Bar Assn. Office: Greater Boston Legal Svcs 197 Friend St Boston MA 02114

PAULSON, LORETTA NANCY, psychoanalyst; b. L.A., Nov. 5, 1943; d. Frank Morris and Rose (Kaufman) Fargo; m. Maurice Krasnow. BA, U. So. Calif., 1966; MS in Social Work, Columbia U., 1969; cert. psychoanalyst, C.G. Jung Inst., N.Y.C. Cert. clin. social worker, N.Y., Conn., N.J. Pvt. practice psychoanalysis N.Y.C. and Wilton, Conn., 1976—; faculty, supr., past vice chmn. Inst. Tng. Bd. Mem. NASW (diplomate in clin. social work), Internat. Assn. for Analytical Psychology (del., bd. dirs.), N.Y. Assn. for Analytic Psychology (pres., program com.), Conn. Soc. Clin. Social Work (com. on psychoanalysis). Democrat. Office: 6 Turtleback Rd Wilton CT 06897-1223 Office: 334 W 86th St Apt 1A New York NY 10024-3130

PAULSON-EHRHARDT, PATRICIA HELEN, laboratory administrator; b. Moses Lake, Wash., June 10, 1956; d. Luther Roanoke and Helen Jane (Baird) Paulson; m. Terry Lee Ehrhardt, Mar. 12, 1983. Student, Pacific Luth. U., 1974-76; BS in Med. Tech., U. Wash., 1976; BS in Biology, MS in Biology, Eastern Wash. U., 1982. Med. technologist Samaritan Hosp., Moses Lake, 1979-81; lab. supr. Moses Lake Clinic, Kalispell (Mont.) Regional Hosp., 1982-88; med. technologist Kalispell Regional Hosp., 1987; account exec. Pathology Assocs. Med. Lab., Spokane, Wash., 1988—; mem. med. lab. tech. adv. com. Wenatchee (Wash.) Valley Coll., 1984-85, chmn., 1985-86; spkr. in field. Mem. Flathead Valley Community Band, 1987-90. Mem. Am. Soc. Clin. Lab. Scientists, Clin. Lab. Mgmt. Assn. (pres. Inland N.W. chpt. 1993-94, bd. dirs. 1994-95), Am. Soc. Clin. Pathologists (cert.), Pan Players Flute Soc., Flathead Tennis Assn., Sigma Xi, Kappa Delta (pledge class pres. 1976). Republican. Lutheran. Home: 26 Cub Dr Great Falls MT 59404

PAULUS, ELEANOR BOCK, professional speaker, author; b. N.Y.C., Mar. 12, 1933; d. Charles William Bock and Borghild (Nelson) Garrick; m. Chester William Paulus Jr., Sept. 6, 1952; children: Chester W. III, Karl Derrick, Diane Paulus Henricks. Student, Smith Coll., 1952-53. Owner, founder Khan-Du Chinese Shar-Pei, Somerset, N.J., 1980—; dir. Pet Net, Santa Fe, N.Mex., 1992—; co-owner, CFO Am. Dream TV Prodns., Washington, 1993—; co-owner, exec. prodr. Capitol Ideas, 1995—; lectr., cons. on Chinese Shar-Pei and canine health, 1980—; internat. con., lectr. on pet care and health. Author: Health Care Handbook for Cats, Dogs and Birds, The Proper Care of Chinese Shar-Pei; contbr. articles to mags. and jours., chpts. to books. Dir. bd. trustees Rutgers Prep. Sch., Somerset, 1970-76, v.p. bd. trustees, 1976-81, pres. PTA, 1966-76; chmn. Raritan River Festival, New Brunswick, N.J., 1980-91. Named Woman of Yr., City of New Brunswick, 1982. Mem. Dog Writers Am. Assn., Dog Fanciers N.Y.C., Bonzai Clubs Internat., Koi Club N.Y., Raritan Valley Country Club, Chinese Shar-Pei Club of Am. (v.p. 1982-86, bd. dirs. east sect. 1980-82, Humanitarian award 1986). Home: 321 Skillmans Ln Somerset NJ 08873-5325 Office: E B Paulus 20 Sutton Pl S # 5A New York NY 10022-4165

PAUN, DOROTHY ANN, marketing educator; b. Chgo., Apr. 11, 1954; d. Joseph and Dorothy P.; m. Mark Zirpel. BS, U. Wis., 1982; MBA, U. Leuven, 1984; PhD, U. Oreg., 1993. Stockbroker Shearson/Am. Express, Fairbanks, Alaska, 1979-82; lectr. Tanana Valley Coll., Fairbanks, Alaska, 1984-86, U. San Francisco, 1987-89, U. Oreg., Eugene, 1989-92; asst. prof. U. Wash., Seattle, 1993—; affiliate prof. Helsinki (Finland) U., 1995—. Contbr. articles to profl. jours. Mem. Am. Mktg. Assn., Acad. Internat. Bus., Alpha Kappa Psi. Office: U Wash Box 352100 Seattle WA 98195-2100

PAUR, CYNTHIA C., retail executive. Exec. v.p. better apparel merchandising Nordstrom, Inc., Seattle, 1994—. Office: Nordstrom Inc 1501 5th Ave Seattle WA 98101-1603*

PAUSTIAN, BONITA JOYCE, school health administrator; b. Duluth, Minn., Apr. 17, 1935; d. Theodore Herald Oliver and Olga Magdalene (Bongey) Oliver-Spaulding; m. E. Earl Paustian, June 30 1956; children: Caprice, Lori, Leisa, Jodi, Jena. Diploma, Mercy Hosp. Sch. Nursing, 1956; BS, Colombia Pacific U., 1985. RN, Mich., Ind.; cert. Nat. Bd. for Cert. Sch. Nurses. Staff nurse Mercy Hosp., Benton Harbor, Mich., 1956-60; charge nurse rehab. unit Berrien Gen. Hosp., Berrien Center, Mich., 1960-61; charge nurse newborn nursery Meml. Hosp., St. Joseph, Mich., 1965-70; sch. nurse Berrien Springs Pub. Schs., 1970-88; in-svc. dir. Medco, South Bend, Ind., 1989; ins. examination nurse Exam Mgmt. Svcs., Kalamazoo, Mich., 1989—; health educator, 1989; supr. sch. health Buchanan (Mich.) Cmty. Schs., 1990—; lectr., presenter various programs in field; nurse cons., Mich., 1992—; OSHA/MIOSHA trainer, Mich., 1992—; pres. Sch. Nurse Consulting Svcs. Author: School Nurse Brochures, 1994; prodr., photographer slide show The Michigan School Nurse, 1988. Mem. choir Berrien Center Bible Ch., 1985—. Recipient Golden Nugget award Mich. Coun. for Exceptional Children, 1994, cert. of appreciation Optimist Club, Berrien County Day Program for Hearing Impaired Children, Ottawa Elem. Sch., Moccasin Elem. Sch. cert. of honor Am. Heart Assn.; named Mich. Sch. Nurse of Yr., 1987, One of Top 10 Nurses in Mich., Wayne State U. and Met. Woman's Mag., 1994. Mem. Mich. Assn. Sch. Nurses (pub. rels. chair 1993—, exec. bd., Pres. award 1993, Sch. Nurse of Yr. 1987), Nat. Assn. Sch. Nurses (exec. dir., state bd. dirs. 1994—, cert. recognition, 1995). Home: 5703 Windy Acres Ln Berrien Springs MI 49103 Office: Buchanan Cmty Schs 401 W Chicago St Buchanan MI 49107-1044

PAVA, ESTHER SHUB, artist, educator; b. Hartford, Conn., June 29, 1921; d. Jacob H. and Rose (Rietkop) Shub; m. Jacob Pava, June 16, 1946; children: David Lauren, Jonathan Michael, Daniel Seth, Nathaniel Alexander. BFA, R.I. Sch. of Design, 1944; MA, San Francisco State U., 1971. Artist New Eng. Roto Engraving Co., Holyoke, Mass., 1944-46, Wyckoff

Advt. Agy., San Francisco, 1947-48; tchr. San Francisco Unified Sch. Dist., 1963-66, Laguna Salada Sch. Dist., Pacifica, Calif., 1966-83; artist, educator Belmont, Calif., 1983—; tchr. pvt. students Manor House, Belmont, Caif. Recipient numerous awards for artwork. Mem. Burlingame Art Soc. (pres. 1983-84), Thirty and One Artists (pres. 1992-93), Peninsula Art Assn., Soc. Western Artists (signature mem., exhibited in many juried shows), Belmont Art Assn., others. Home: 2318 Hastings Dr Belmont CA 94002-3318 Studio: Manor House 1219 Ralston Ave Belmont CA 94002

PAVEK, BRYN CARPENTER, director arts administration; b. Phoenix, Mar. 7, 1955; d. John Leon and Lenore Maxine (Stapp) Carpenter; m. Charles Christopher Pavek, Dec. 18, 1977. BFA in Theatre magna cum laude, Ariz. State U., 1977; student, U. Ariz., 1973. Freelance designer Phoenix, 1973-77; box office mgr. Ariz. State U. Theatre, Tempe, 1976; creative drama specialist City of Phoenix, summer 1976; box office ticketing asst. U. So. Calif., L.A., 1977; co. and stage mgr. Hartford (Conn.) Stage Co. Youth Theatre, 1978, adminstrv. mgr., 1979-80; budget analyst U.S. Naval Mil. Command, Arlington, Va., 1981; prodn. supr. Arlington County Visual & Performing Arts, 1981-84; dep. dir. McLean (Va.) Community Ctr., 1984-87; exec. dir. Reston (Va.) Community Ctr., 1987—; prodn. chair Southeastern Theatre Conf., Arlington, 1984; mem. Drug Free Recreation for Youth Task Force, Fairfax, Va., 1988—, Dogwood Edn. Task Force, Reston, 1989—. Mem. com. Fairfax County Coun. of the Arts, 1987—, Purple Sage Cluster Assn. Social Commn., Reston, 1988; mem. organizing com. Fairfax County Summit Youth Issues, 1989. Recipient Human Rights award Fairfax County, Va., 1991, Leadership Fairfax Grad., 1996. Mem. Va. Assn. Female Execs., Cultural Alliance Greater Washington, Pk. and Recreation Assn. Democrat. Unitarian. Home: 2515 Fowlers Ln Reston VA 22091

PAVLICH, JACQUELINE LEE, emergency nurse; b. Flint, Mich., Sept. 25, 1952; d. Jack Carthon and Olga (Harrison) Garland; m. Richard Pavlich (div.); 1 child, Stephen. Diploma, Hurley Sch. Nursing, 1973; postgrad., U. Mich. CCRN; cert. emergency nurse, paramedic, BTLS, instr. ACLS/BCLS, legal nurse cons. Staff nurse ortho-trauma Hurley Hosp., Flint, Mich., 1973-74; staff and charge nurse pediat. Flint Osteopathic Hosp., 1974-75; staff and charge nurse neonatal ICU William Beaumont Hosp., Royal Oak, Mich., 1975-80, staff and charge nurse emergency ctr., 1980-86; float nurse, preceptor Burns Clinic, Petoskey, Mich., 1987-88; staff and charge nurse, preceptor emergency dept. Northern Mich. Hosp., Petoskey, 1988-94, staff nurse cardiovasc. unit., 1994-95, float team nurse, 1995—. Mem. Emergency Nursing Assn., Am. Assn. Critical Care Nurses. Home: 610 Grove St Petoskey MI 49770-2731 Office: Northern Mich Hosp 416 Connable Ave Petoskey MI 49770-2212

PAVLICK, PAMELA KAY, nurse, consultant; b. Topeka, Aug. 16, 1944; d. Cy Pavlick and June Lucille (Arnold) (dec.) Dull. Diploma nursing, St. Luke's Hosp., Kansas City, Mo., 1966; BA in Psychology magna cum laude, U. North Fla., 1982, MS in Health Adminstrn. summa cum laude, 1987. RN, Mo., Ill., Fla.; cert. ins. rehab. specialist; lic. rehab. providor, Fla. Clin. instr. St. Luke's Hosp., Kansas City, 1966-70; instr. lic. practical nursing Springfield (Ill.) Sch. Bd., 1970-72; nursing supr. Jacksonville Beach (Fla.) Hosp., 1972-74; pub. health nurse State of Fla., Ocala, 1974-76; dir. nursing Upjohn Health Care, Jacksonville, Fla., 1976-77, mem. adv. com.; med. rep. Travelers Ins. Co., Jacksonville, 1977-84; rehab. cons. Aetna Life & Casualty, Jacksonville, 1985—, rep. nurse cons. adv. coun., 1988-90. Mem. Am. Nurses Assn., Am. Assn. Rehab. Nurses, Nat. Assn. Rehab. Providers, Phi Kappa Phi. Republican. Episcopalian. Home: 14023 Tontine Rd Jacksonville FL 32225-2025 Office: Aetna Life & Casualty PO Box 2200 Jacksonville FL 32203-2200

PAVLIK, NANCY, convention services executive; b. Hamtramck, Mich., July 18, 1935; d. Frank and Helen (Vorobojoff) Phillips; m. G. Edward Pavlik, June 30, 1956; children: Kathleen, Christine, Laureen, Michael, Bonnie Jean. Student, U. Ariz., 1956-80. Exec. sec. Mich. Bell, Detroit, 1951-56, RCA, Camden, N.J., 1956-58; owner, pres. S.W. Events Etc., Scottsdale, Ariz., 1969—. Chmn. hospitality industry com. Scottsdale City Coun., 1989—; bd. dirs. Scottsdale Curatorial Bd., 1987-89. Mem. Soc. Incentive Travel Execs., Meeting Planners Internat., Am. Soc. Assn. Execs., Indian Arts and Crafts Assn., Scottsdale C. of C. (bd. dirs., tourism steering com. 1984-88), Contemporary Watercolorists Club. Democrat. Roman Catholic. Home: 15417 Richwood Fountain Hills AZ 85268 Office: SW Events Etc 3200 N Hayden Ste 100 Scottsdale AZ 85251

PAVLONS, JANET LEIGH, secondary school educator; b. Peoria, Ill., Apr. 13, 1949; d. Chesley C. and Arliss E. (Pierce) Jones; m. Brian Stanley Pavlons, Jr., Aug. 2, 1969; 1 child, Alisha d. BS, Bradley U., 1972; MA in Tchg., Aurora U., 1995. Tchr. pre-sch. Greenwood Country Day Sch., Peoria, 1973-74; dir. pre-sch. and kindergarten Richland Bapt. Day Care, East Peoria, Ill., 1974-75; elem. tchr. St. Joseph's Cath. Sch., Pekin, Ill., 1975-76; tchr. pre-sch. and kindergarten Children's Ctr. Tazewell County, Creve Coeur, Ill., 1976-78; tchr. social studies Pekin H.S., 1980—. Advisor, leader, tchr. St. Thomas Prayer Group, Peoria, 1988—. Mem. NEA, Ill. Edn. Assn. (welfare mem.), Pi Gamma Mu. Home: PO Box 204 Pekin IL 61555-0204 Office: Pekin HS 207 N 9th St Pekin IL 61554-3408

PAWELKO, KATHARINE ANN, recreation educator; b. N.Y.C., Mar. 26, 1952; d. Martin Anthony and Muriel Henrietta (Greenhagen) P. BSE, SUNY, College at Cortland, N.Y., 1974, MSE, 1978; PhD, U. Md., 1994. Cert. tchr. recreation edn. and phys. edn. K-12, N.Y. Instr. U. Maine, Presque Isle, 1979-84, U. Md., College Park, 1982-88; adj. assoc. prof. Prince Georges C.C., Largo, Md., 1986-94; asst. prof. Western Ill. U., Macomb, 1994—; rsch. asst. Nat. Park Svc., Washington, 1983, U. Md., College Park, 1984-86, 87-88, U.S. Forest Svc., 1985, 86; fitness instr., mgr. Healthpro, Inc., U.S. Dept. of Agriculture, Beltsville, Md., 1989-94. Author: Exploring the Nature of River Recreation Visitors and Their Recreational Experiences on The Delaware River, 1994, (with others) Issues in Therapeutic Recreation: A Profession in Transition, 2nd edit., 1996. Lifeguard ARC, 1977-94, water safety instr., 1977—; mem. Presque Isle Cmty. Adult Edn. Tri-Coun., 1981-82, Presque Isle YMCA Adv. Bd., 1981-83. Mem. AAHPERD (life), Nat. Recreation and Park Assn., Nat. Wildlife Assn. (life), N.Y. State Outdoor Edn. Assn. (life), Quebec-Labrador Found./Atlantic Ctr. for the Environment, Phi Kappa Phi, Kappa Delta Pi, Phi Alpha Epsilon, Omicron Delta Kappa. Republican. Episcopalian. Office: Western Ill U 400 Currens Hall Macomb IL 61455

PAXTON, ALEXANDRA, non-profit arts administrator; b. N.Y.C., June 27, 1963; d. Glenn G. and Leslie H. (Davis) P. BA, Yale U., 1985; MS, U. Coll. London, 1989; MFA, Yale U., 1993. From adminstrv. asst. to adminstr. nat. playwrights conf. Eugene O'Neill Theater Ctr., N.Y.C. and Waterford, Conn., 1989-90; mng. dir. Yale Summer Cabaret, New Haven, Conn., 1991; assoc. mktg. dir. Yale Repertory Theater, New Haven, Conn., 1992, assoc. mng. dir., 1992-93; mng. dir. The Wooster Group, N.Y.C., 1993—.

PAXTON, ALICE ADAMS, artist, architect and interior designer; b. Hagerstown, Md., May 19, 1914; d. William Albert and Josephine (Adams) Rosenberger; m. James Love Paxton Jr., June 26, 1942 (div.); 1 child, William Allen III (dec.). Student, Peabody Inst. Music, Balt., 1937-38; grad., Parson's Sch. Design, N.Y., 1940; studies with J. Laurie Wallace, 1944-46; studies with Augustus Dunbier, 1947-48, Sylvia Curtis, 1949, Milton Wolsky, 1950, Frank Sapousek, 1951. Freelance work archtl. renderings and interior design, N.Y., 1937-40; interior designer, designer spl. furnishings, muralist Orchard and Wilhelm, Omaha, 1940-42; tchr. art classes Alice Paxton Studio, Omaha, 1957-64; tchr. mech. drawing, archtl. rendering and mech. perspective Parson's Sch. Design, N.Y., 1937-40. Designer (interior) Chapel Boys' Town, Nebr., 1942; one-woman show of archtl. renderings Washington County Mus. Fine Arts, Hagerstown, 1944; exhibited group shows at Joslyn Mus., Omaha, 1943-44 (1st place), Ann. Exhbn. Cumberland Valley Artists, Hagerstown, 1945; represented in permanent collections at No. Natural Gas Co. Bldg., Omaha, Swanson Found., Omaha; also pvt. collections; vol. designer, decorator: recreation room Omaha Blood Bank, ARC, 1943, recreation room Creighton U., 1943, lounge psychiat. ward Lincoln (Nebr.) Army Hosp., 1944; planner, color coordinator Children's Hosp., Omaha, 1947, painted murals, 1948, decorated dental room, 1950; designed Candy Stripers' uniforms; painted and decorated straw elephant bag presented to Mrs. Richard Nixon, 1960; contbr. articles and photographs to Popular Home mag., 1958. Co-chair camp and hosp. coms. ARC, 1943-45, mem. county com. to select and send gifts to servicemen, 1943-46; mem. Ak-Sar-Ben Ball Com., Omaha, 1946-48, Nat. Mus. Women in the Arts, The Md. Hist. Soc.; judge select Easter Seal design, Joslyn Mus., 1946; mem. council Girl Scouts U.S., Omaha, 1943-47; spl. drs. chmn. Jr. League, Omaha, 1947-48, chair Jr. League Red Cross fund dr., 1947-48; bd. dirs., vol. worker Creche, Omaha, 1954-56; mem. Omaha Jr. League; chmn. Jr. League Community Chest Fund Dr., 1948-50; co-chair Infantile Paralysis Appeal, 1944; numerous vol. profl. activities for civic orgns., hosps., clubs, chs., community playhouse, and for establishing wildlife sanctuary. Recipient three teaching scholarships Parson's Sch. Design, 1937-40, presdl. citation ARC activities, 1946, 1st prize Ann. Midwest Show Joslyn Mus., 1943. Mem. Associated Artists Omaha (charter), Internat. Platform Assn., U.S. Hist. Soc., Nat. Mus. Women in Arts (charter), Md. Hist. Soc., Fountain Head Country Club. Republican. Episcopalian. Home: 19614 Meadowbrook Rd Hagerstown MD 21742-2519

PAXTON, J. WILLENE, retired university counseling director; b. Birmingham, Ala., Oct. 30, 1930; d. Will and Elizabeth (Davis) P. AB, Birmingham So. Coll., 1950; MA, Mich. State U., 1951; EdD, Ind. U., 1971. Nat. cert. counselor, lic. profl. counselor, Tenn. Dormitory dir. Tex. Tech U., Lubbock, 1951-53; counselor Mich. State U., East Lansing, summer 1951, 52; dir. univ. ctr. and housing SUNY, Fredonia, 1953-56, assoc. dean of students, 1956-57; asst. dean of women U. N.Mex., Albuquerque, 1957-63; dean of women East Tenn. State U., Johnson City, 1963-68, 70-78, dir. counseling ctr., 1978-92; ret., 1993. Sec. adminstrv. bd. Meth. Ch., 1983-86, vice chmn., 1993, chmn., 1994—, chmn. social concerns com., 1991-93, program chmn. Good Timers fellowship, 1994-95, pres. Sunday Sch. class, 1994, chmn. fin. campaign, 1995, chair promotion and publicity, bldg. com., 1996—, chair scholarship com., chair promotion and publicity sub-com. bldg. campaign, 1996—; tng. dir. Contact Teleministries, Inc., 1983-87, chmn., 1988, 95, vice chmn., 1993-95; bd. dirs. Asbury Ctrs., 1990—, policy com., 1991—, chmn. policy com., 1995-96, mem. fin. com., 1996. Mem. APA, AAUW (br. pres., mem. nominating com. 1993-96, fin. com. 1996), Am. Counseling Assn., Tenn. Psychol. Assn., Assn. Univ. and Coll. Counseling Ctr. Dirs. (conv. planning com. 1991), Am. Coll. Pers. Assn. (media bd., newsletter editor), Nat. Assn. Women Deans, Adminstrs. and Counselors, Tenn. Assn. Women Deans and Counselors (state pres., v.p., program chmn.), East Tenn. Edn. Assn. (chmn. guidance divsn.), East Tenn. State U. Retirees Assn. (bd. dirs. 1993—, program com. 1993—, chair program com. 1996, pres.-elect 1996), Gen. Federated Woman's Club (pres. 1980-81, 88-89, 95-96, 2d v.p. 1991-95), Univ. Women's Club (v.p. 1993-94, pres. 1994, 95), Delta Kappa Gamma (chpt. pres. 1974-76, state rec. sec. 1977-79, v.p. 1979-81, chmn. nominating com. 1981-83, internat. rsch. com. 1982-84, chmn. leadership devel. com. 1983-85, chmn. self-study com. 1985-87, com. to study exec. sec. 1987-89, state pres. 1989-91, parliamentarian 1991-93, internat. constn. com. 1992-94, awards com. 1993-95, chmn. internat. conv. meal functions com. 1994, state pers. com. 1995—, state achievement award 1987). Home: 1203 Lester Harris Rd Johnson City TN 37601-3335

PAXTON, LAURA BELLE-KENT, English language educator, management professional; b. Lake Charles, La., Feb. 8, 1942; d. George Ira and Gladys Lillian (Barrett) Kent.; m. Kenneth Robert Paxton Jr., Jan. 2, 1962. BA, McNeese U., Lake Charles, 1963, MA in English, 1972; EdD, East Tex. U., 1983. cert. English, social studies instr., prin., supt., ednl. adminstr., Ariz. Tchr. Darrington (Wash.) High Sch., 1966-70; English instr. Maricopa Community Coll., Phoenix, 1974-92; migrant program instr. Phoenix Union High Sch., 1984-88; English instr. Embry-Riddle Aeronautical U., Luke AFB, Ariz., 1985-87; sales rep. Merrill Lynch Realty, Phoenix, 1985-88; co-owner Paxton Mgmt. Co., Phoenix, 1985—; assoc. prof. Western Internat. U., Phoenix, 1992—; author Ariz. corr. courses, 1987-88; presenter migrant worker program confs., 1987—; reviewer Prentice-Hall, 1985. Author: Handbook for Middle Eastern Dancer, 1978, The Kent Family History From 1787-1981, 1981, A Handbook of Home Remedies, 1981, Elements of Effective Writing: A Composition Guidesheet, 1994, A Practical Guide to Writing Power, 1995, Documentation for Business Papers: A Guidesheet, 1995. Mem. Everett, Wash. Opera Guild, 1966-70, Ariz. State U. Opera Guild, Tempe, 1978-80; mem. City of Darrington Council, 1969-70; ESL instr. Friendly House, Phoenix, 1978-79. Mem. Ariz. English Assn., Phi Delta Kappa.

PAYNE, ALMA JEANETTE, English educator and author; b. Highland Park, Ill., Oct. 28, 1918; d. Frederick Hutton and Ruth Ann (Colle) P. BA, Wooster (Ohio) Coll., 1940; MA, Case Western Res. U., 1941, PhD, 1956. Tchr. English, history, Latin Ohio Pub. Schs., Bucyrus and Canton, 1941-46; from instr. to prof. English and Am. studies Bowling Green (Ohio) State U., 1946-79, dir. Am. studies program, 1957-79, chair Am. culture PhD program, 1978-79, prof. emerita English, Am. studies, 1979—; adj. prof. Am. studies U. South Fla., 1982—. Author: Critical Bibliography of Louisa May Alcott, 1980, Discovering the American Nations, 1981; contbr. articles to profl. jours.; editor Nat. Am. Studies Assn. Newsletter; contbr. articles to profl. jours. Nat. Coun. for Innovation in Edn. grantee, Norway, U.S. Embassy and Norwegian Dept. Ch. and State, 1978-79. Mem. AAUW (pres. 1982-84), Soc. Mayflower Descs in Fla. (state treas. 1985), Nat. Am. Studies Assn. (v.p. 1977-79), Zonta, Phi Beta Kappa, Phi Kappa Phi, Kappa Delta Pi, Alpha Lambda Delta. Republican. Presbyterian. Home and Office: 11077 Orangewood Dr Bonita Springs FL 34135-5720

PAYNE, ANITA HART, reproductive endocrinologist, researcher; b. Karlsruhe, Baden, Germany, Nov. 24, 1926; came to U.S., 1938; d. Frederick Michael and Erna Rose (Hirsch) Hart; widowed; children: Gregory Steven, Teresa Payne-Lyons. BA, U. Calif., Berkeley, 1949, PhD, 1952. Rsch. assoc. U. Mich., Ann Arbor, 1961-71, asst. prof., 1971-76, assoc. prof., 1976-81, prof., 1981—, assoc. dir. Ctr. for Study Reprodn., 1989-94; vis. scholar Stanford U., 1987-88; mem. reproductive biology study sect. NIH, Bethesda, Md., 1978-79, biochem. endocrinology study sect., 1979-83, population rsch. com. Nat. Inst. Child Health and Human Devel., 1989-93. Assoc. editor Steroids, 1987-93; contbr. book chpts., articles to profl. jours. Recipient award for cancer rsch. Calif. Inst. for Cancer Rsch., 1953, Acad. Women's Caucus award U. Mich., 1986. Mem. Endocrine Soc. (chmn. awards com. 1983-84, mem. nominating com. 1985-87, coun. 1988-91), Am. Soc. Andrology (exec. coun. 1980-83), Soc. for Study of Reprodn. (bd. dirs. 1982-85, sec. 1986-89, pres. 1990-91). Office: Stanford U Med Ctr Dept Gynecology/Obstetrics Div Reproductive Biology Stanford CA 94305-5317

PAYNE, BERNADETTE, graphic designer; b. Henderson, Ky., Aug. 2, 1955; d. William Thomas Payne and Helen Waide; m. Michael Blane Jeffrey, Sept. 20, 1983 (div. Oct. 1989); m. Eric Frank Johnson, June 18, 1994; 1 child, River Elle Johnson. BFA, Ringling Sch. Art, 1977. Designer, illustrator Brady Advt., Chattanooga, 1977-79; prodn. artist Encom Graphics, Houston, 1979-80; art dir. Gardner Comms., Houston, 1980-83; book designer Gulf Pub. Co., Houston, 1983-84; art dir. Lea Pub., Houston, 1984-85; pvt. practice as graphic designer Houston, 1985-89, 92—; art dir. Am. Masters, Houston, 1989-92. Mem. Art League of Houston. Office: 1315 Beverly St Houston TX 77008

PAYNE, DEBORAH ANNE, medical company officer; b. Norristown, Pa., Sept. 22, 1952; d. Kenneth Nathan Moser and Joan (Reese) Dewhurst; m. Randall Barry Payne, Mar. 8, 1975. AA, Northeastern Christian Jr. Coll., 1972; B in Music Edn., Va. Commonwealth U., 1979. Driver, social asst. Children's Aid Soc., Norristown, Pa., 1972-73; mgr. Boddie-Noell Enterprises, Richmond, Va., 1974-79; retail food saleswoman Hardee's Food Systems, Inc., Phila., 1979-81; supr., with tech. tng. and testing depts. Cardiac Datacorp., Phila., 1981-95; tng. supr. Raytel Cardiac Svcs., Forest Hills, N.Y., 1995—. Mem. bd. advisers Am. Biog. Inst., 1989. Mem. NAFE, Delta Omicron (pres. Alpha Xi chpt. 1978-79, pres. Epsilon province 1980-85, chmn. Eastern Pa. alumni 1986-88, Star award 1979), Am. Soc. Profl. and Exec. Women. Republican. Home: 4301 Chippendale St Philadelphia PA 19136-3628 Office: Raytel Cardiac Svcs 118-35 Queens Blvd Forest Hills NY 11375

PAYNE, ELIZABETH ELEANORE, surgeon, otolaryngologist; b. Detroit, Mar. 17, 1945; d. Richard Franklin and Eleanore Grace (Dieterich) P.; 1 child from previous marriage, Julia Elizabeth Komanecky. Student, St. Olaf Coll., 1962-64; MD, U. Iowa, 1968. Cert. Am. Bd. Otolaryngology, Am. Acad. Otolaryngic Allergy; lic. in medicine, Minn., Iowa. Intern Phila. Gen. Hosp., 1968-69; resident gen. surgery U. Minn., Mpls., 1969-70; resident otolaryngology U. Minn., 1970-74, clin. asst. prof. dept. otolaryngology, asst. clin. prof. dept. family practice and community health; pvt. practice, Mpls., 1974—; mem. med. staff North Meml. Med. Ctr., Mpls., Children's Med. Ctr., AbbottNorthwestern Hosp. Contbr. articles to profl. jours. Mem. AMA, Am. Acad. Otolaryngology Head and Neck Surgery, Am. Acad. Otolaryngic Allergy, Minn. State Med. Assn., Minn. Acad. Otolaryngology Head and Neck Surgery (coun. mem.), Minn. Acad. Medicine, Hennepin County Med. Assn. Office: Affiliated Otolaryngologists 3366 Oakdale Ave N Ste 307 Minneapolis MN 55422-2977

PAYNE, FLORA FERN, retired social service administrator; b. Carrollton, Mo., Sept. 25, 1932; d. George Earnest and Bernadine Alice (Schaefer) Chrisman; m. H.D. Matticks, Oct. 20, 1950 (div. Oct. 1959); children: Dennis Don, Kathi D.; m. S.L. Freeman, Nov. 25, 1960 (div. Jan. 1973); 1 child, Gary Mark; m. Vernon Ray Payne, Mar. 18, 1988. Student, S.E. C.C., Burlington, Iowa, 1976-77; cert. stenographer, Corr. Sch., Chgo., 1960-61. Social svc. designee Mo. League Nursing, 1991. Sec. to v.p. Moore Co., Marceline, Mo., 1973-75; steno to trainmaster A.T. & S.F. Rlwy. Co., Fort Madison, Iowa, 1975-88; with social svc. Brookfield (Mo.) Nursing Ctr., 1990-95; candidate for Linn County Pub. Adminstr., 1996. Mem. NAFE, Mo. Orgn. Social Svcs. Republican. Home: 205 W 6th St Bucklin MO 64631-9097

PAYNE, FRANCES ANNE, literature educator, researcher; b. Harrisonburg, Va., Aug. 28, 1932; d. Charles Franklin and Willie (Tarvin) P. B.A., Shorter Coll, 1953, B.Mus., 1953; M.A., Yale U., 1954, Ph.D., 1960. Instr. Conn. Coll., New London, 1955-56; instr. U. Buffalo, 1958-60, lectr., 1960, asst. prof., 1960-67; assoc. prof. SUNY, Buffalo, 1967-75; prof. English and medieval lit. SUNY, 1975—; adj. fellow St. Anne's Coll., Oxford, Eng., 1966-67, 68-69. Author: King Alfred and Boethius, 1968; Chaucer and Menippean Satire, 1981. Contbr. articles to scholarly publs. AAUW fellow, Oxford, 1966-67; Research Found. grantee SUNY Central, Oxford, 1967, 68, 71, 72; recipient Julian Park award SUNY-Buffalo, 1979. Mem. Medieval Acad. Am., Internat. Arthurian Soc., New Chaucer Soc., Internat. Soc. Anglo-Saxonists, Pi Kappa Lambda. Office: SUNY-Buffalo 306 Clemens Hall Buffalo NY 14260

PAYNE, LINDA COHEN, business owner; b. N.Y.C., Jan. 9, 1953; d. Gerald Theodore and Bianca (Joselson) Cohen; m. Stephen George Payne, Mar. 20, 1977; 1 child, Joshua Theodore Cohen. BA, Hunter Coll., 1981. Brokerage asst. Harris, Upham & Co., N.Y.C., 1974-75; dept. head cen. inquiry Standard & Poor's Corp., N.Y.C., 1976-87; owner, mgr. Payne Fin. Rsch., N.Y.C., 1988—. Mem. ALA, NOW, Spl. Libr. Assn., Libr. Mgmt. Assn., Exec. Females. Home and Office: Payne Fin Rsch 27 Norchester Dr Princeton Junction NJ 08550-1225

PAYNE, MARY ALICE MCGILL, mental health quality consultant; b. Centreville, Miss., Jan. 2, 1936; d. Robert Malcolm and Alice (Brannon) McGill; m. Donald Ray Payne, Aug. 8, 1958; children: Patricia Alice, Margaret Jean, Donald Paul. Diploma, So. Bapt. Hosp. Sch. Nursing, New Orleans, 1958; BSN, Northwestern State U., 1962, postgrad. Psychiat. nursing instr. McNeese U., Lake Charles, La., 1964-67; drug rsch. nurse dept. psychiatry Med. Sch., Tulane U., New Orleans, 1969-79; psychiat. nurse East La. State Hosp., Jackson, 1959-80; acting CEO Feliciana Forensic Facility, Jackson, 1989, quality assurance dir., 1984-91. Mem. ANA, NAFE, Am. Psychiat. Nurses Assn., Am. Coll. Healthcare Execs. (assoc.), La. State Nurses Assn., Nat. Assn. Healthcare Quality, La. Assn. Healthcare Quality, Bapt. Nursing Fellowship, Feliciana Dist. Nurses Assn., Am. Soc. Quality Control, Nat. League for Nursing. Home: PO Box 144 3226 E College St Jackson LA 70748-0144

PAYNE, NANCY SLOAN, visual arts educator; b. Johnstown, Pa., Aug. 5, 1937; d. Arthur J. and Esther Jenkins (Ashcom) Sloan; m. Randolph Allen Payne, Nov. 19, 1970; 1 child, Anna Sloan. BS in Art Edn., Pa. State U., 1959; MFA in Sculpture, George Washington U., 1981. Visual arts tchr. Alexandria (Va.) Schs., 1960-61; art tchr. sch. program Corcoran Gallery of Art, Washington, 1962; visual arts tchr. Montgomery County Schs., Rockville, Md., 1965-67; instr. No. Va. C.C., Alexandria, 1971-73, Mt. Vernon Coll., Washington, 1971-73; visual arts tchr. Arlington (Va.) County Schs., 1967-79; edn. coord. The Textile Mus., Washington, 1982-87; mid. sch. visual arts tchr., K-12 dept. chair St. Stephen's and St. Agnes Sch., Alexandria, 1988—; co-founder Fiber Art Study Group, Washington, 1988—; co-owner Art Gallery, Chincoteague Island, Va., 1989—. Exhibited in group shows at Craftsmen's Biennial Va. Commonwealth U. (Excellence in Textiles award), 1973, Va. Craftsmen Biennial The Va. Mus., 1980, Creative Crafts Coun. 15th Biennial, 1982, Alexandria's Sculpture Festival, 1983, 84, 13 Fiber Artists Exhbn. Foundry Gallery, Washington, 1985. Founding mem. Alexandria Soc. for Preservation Black Heritage, Alexandria, 1982—. Mem. Nat. Art Edn. Assn. Democrat. Home: 600 Johnston Pl Alexandria VA 22301-2512 Office: St Stephens and St Agnes Schs 4401 W Braddock Rd Alexandria VA 22304

PAYNE, PAULA MARIE, minister; b. Waukegan, Ill., Jan. 13, 1952; d. Percy Howard and Annie Maude (Canady) P. BA, U. Ill., 1976; MA, U. San Francisco, 1986; MDiv, Wesley Theol. Sem., 1991, student, 1995—. Ordained to ministry United Meth. Ch., 1990. Chaplain for minority affairs Am. U., Washington, 1988-89; chaplain, intern NIH, Bethesda, Md., 1989-90; pastor Asbury United Meth. Ch., Charles Town, W.Va., 1990—; supt. ch. sch. United Meth. Ch., Oxon Hill, Md., 1989-90; mem. AIDS task force Wesley Theol. Sem., Washington, 1988-89; mem. retreat. com. Balt. Conf., 1990—; chair scholarship com. Asbury United Meth. Ch., 1990—. Bd. dirs. AIDS Task Force Jefferson County, Charles Town, 1991—, Community Ministries, Charles Town, 1991—. Tech sgt. USAF, 1984-88; chaplain Army N.G., Md. Recipient Cert. of Recognition, Ill. Ho. of Reps., 1988, 20th Century award of Achievement Internat. Biog. Ctr., Cambridge, Eng., 1993, 1st Five Hundred, Cambridge, 1994, Citizen's citation, City of Balt., 1994, others; Ethnic Minority scholar United Meth. Ch., 1988-89, Brandenburg scholar, 1988-89, Tadlock scholar, 1989-90, Calvary Fellow scholar Calvary United Meth. ch., 1989-90. Mem. U. Ill. Alumni Assn. (bd. dirs. 1987-88), Alpha Kappa Alpha (pres. local chpt. 1974-76, v.p. 1973). Democrat. Home: 8005 Richard Dr Forestville MD 20747

PAYNE, SUSAN FRANTZ, fundraiser, artist; b. N.Y.C., Feb. 17, 1941; d. Frederick P. and Caroline (Campbell) Frantz; m. John H. Payne III, Aug. 24, 1963; children: John H. IV, Sarah S. BS, Simmons Coll., 1963. Dir. edn. Am. Indian Archaeol. Inst. (now Inst. Am. Indian Studies), Washington, Conn., 1976-83, exec. dir., 1983-85; devel. assoc. New Milford (Conn.) Hosp. Found., 1991—; mem. adv. coun. Women's Ctr. Greater Danbury, Conn., 1993—; trustee Steep Rock Assn., Washington, 1991—, chair of Land Preservation Com. Vol. Re-election Campaign Nanncy Johnson, 1996, Conservation Plan, Washington, 1995—, Hammond Mus., North Salem, N.Y., 1991—. Mem. Oriental Brush Artists Guild (pres. 1993-94).

PAYNTER, VESTA LUCAS, pharmacist; b. Aiken County, S.C., May 29, 1922; d. James Redmond and Annie Lurline (Stroman) Lucas; m. Maurice Alden Paynter, Dec. 23, 1945 (dec. 1971); children: Sharon Lucinda, Maurice A. Jr., Doyle Gregg. BS in Pharmacy, U. S.C., 1943. Lic. pharmacist. Owner, pharmacist Cayce Drug Store, S.C., 1944-52, Dutch Fork Drug Store, Columbia, S.C., 1955-60, The Drug Ctr., Cayce, 1963-81; pharmacist Lane-Rexall, Columbia, 1952-55; dist. pharmacist S.C. Dept. Health and Environ. Control, Columbia, 1983-90, ret., 1990. Named Preceptor of Yr., Syntex Co., student body U. S.C., 1981. Fellow, 5th Dist. Pharm. Assn., S.C. Pharm. Assn., S.C. Pub. Health Assn., Alpha Epsilon Delta; mem. China, India, Burma VA Assn. (assoc.), 14th Air Force Assn. (assoc.). Baptist. Lodges: Order of Eastern Star, Order of Amaranth, Sinclair Lodge, White Shrine of Jerusalem, Columbia Shrine #6. Avocations: travel, tennis, golf, art. Home: 2351 Vine St Cayce SC 29033-3000

PAYNTER-HARRISON, MICHELE LOUISE, social worker; b. Washington, Mar. 4, 1952; d. Milton J. and Isadora Olivia (Cooper) Paynter; m. Victor Lee Harrison, Sr., Feb. 5, 1995. BA in Sociology, U. Md., 1974; postgrad., U. Mo. Kansas City, 1985. Tchr. Genesis Alternative Sch., Kansas City, Mo., 1976-77, St. Joseph's Diocese, Kansas City, 1979-88; social worker Met. Orgn. to Counter Sexual Assault, Kansas City, 1989—;

facilitator Victim Assistance Orgn., Kansas City, 1989—. Mem. Human Rights Project Kansas City, 1995—. Mem. NAFE, Crime Prevention Agy. (ad hoc com.). Democrat. Roman Catholic. Home: 4217 Charlotte Kansas City MO 64110 Office: MOCSA 3217 Broadway Ste 500 Kansas City MO 64111

PAYSON, HERTA RUTH, psychotherapist, theatrical costumer, theater educator; b. Oak Park, Ill., Jan. 31, 1933; d. Joseph Hale and Lily Brush (Bagley) P.; m. Elliott Proctor Joslin, Oct. 12, 1961 (div. Oct., 1984); children: Allen Payson, Rachel Elizabeth, David Elliott. BA, Goddard Coll., 1979; MA, Vt. Coll., 1982; PhD, The Union Inst., 1996. Tchr., dir. Queens (N.Y.) Cmty. Dance Sch., 1954-63; theatrical costumer N.Y.C., 1955-69; costumer Nat. Theatre of the Deaf, Waterford, Conn., 1970-84; instr. theater dept. Conn. Coll., New London, 1970—; pvt. practice psychotherapy Norwich, Conn., 1980—; co-owner SYZYGY for little b., N.Y.C., 1964-69; coord. small groups Friends Conf. Religion and Psychology, Haverford, Pa., 1975-79, co-clk., 1978-83. Choreographer for As You Like It, Two Gentlemen of Verona and Romeo & Juliet for N.Y. Shakespeare Festival, Alice in Wonderland for The Little Orch. Soc., others. Mem. AAUW, Am. Counseling Assn., Conn. Assn. Jungian Psychology, Assn. Transpersonal Psychology, Nat. Guild Hypnotists. Office: 74 W Main St Norwich CT 06360

PAYTON, ANTOINETTE SHIELDS, retired realtor; b. Miles City, Mont., Mar. 9, 1926; d. Claude M. and Odie (Waddell) Shields; m. Robert J. Iholts, Mar. 30, 1946 (dec. Oct. 1957); children: Robert C., Marilyn Tracy; m. Donald Glen Payton, Dec. 5, 1959. BA, U. Mont., 1959; postgrad., U. Nev., 1960-71. Cert. tchr., libr., Nev.; lic. realtor, Nev. Tchr. Reno Pub. Schs., 1960-64; libr. Billinghurst Jr. High Sch., Pine Mid. Sch., Reno, 1964-85; realtor, co-owner, sec. Century 21 All Seasons, Reno, 1985-95, also bd. dirs. Recipient Disting. Svc. award Washoe County Tchrs. Assn., 1985. Mem. AAUW, PTA (life Reno), Nat. Assn. Realtors, Nev. Assn. Realtors, Reno/Sparks Assn. Realtors, DAR, Mayflower Descendants Soc., Order of the Crown of Charlemayne in the U.S.A., Alpha Delta Kappa (pres., treas. 1975-82), Beta Sigma Phi (life, officer 1950-95).

PAZANDAK, CAROL HENDRICKSON, liberal arts educator; b. Mpls.; d. Norman Everard and Ruth (Buckley) Hendrickson; m. Bruce B. Pazandak (dec. 1986); children: David, Bradford, Christopher, Eric, Paul, Ann; m. Joseph P. O'Shaughnessy, May 1991. PhD, U. Minn., 1970. Asst. dir. admissions U. Minn., Mpls., 1970-72, asst. dean liberal arts, 1972-79, asst. to pres., 1979-85, office of internat. edn., acting dir., 1985-87, asst. prof. to assoc. to prof. liberal arts, 1970-96, prof. emerita, 1996—; vis. prof. U. Iceland, Reykjavik, 1984, periods in 1983, 86, 87, 88, 89, 90-92, 93, 94, 96; vis. rsch. prof. U. Oulu, Finland, 1993; exec. sec. Minn.-Iceland Adv. Com., U. Minn., 1984—; cons. U. Iceland, 1983—; co-chair Reunion of Sisters-Minn. and Finland Confs., 1986—; sec. Icelandic Assn. of Minn., 1995—. Editor: Improving Undergraduate Education in Large Universities, 1989. Past pres. Minn. Mrs. Jaycees, Mpls. Mrs. Jaycees; formerly bd. govs. St. John's Preparatory Sch., Collegeville, Minn.; former bd. trustees Coll. of St. Teresa, Winona, Minn.. Recipient Partnership award for contbn. to advancing shared interests of Iceland and Am., 1994; named to Order of the Falcon, Govt. of Iceland, 1990, Coll. Liberal Arts Alumna Notable Achievement, 1995. Mem. Am. Psychol. Assn., Am. Coun. Edn. (former steering com. Nat. Identification Program for Women in Higher Edn. Adminstrn. 1983-86), Soc. Advancement of Scandinavian Studies. Home: 1361 Prior Ave S Saint Paul MN 55116-2656 Office: U Minn N 247 Elliott Hall 75 E River Rd Minneapolis MN 55455-0280

PEABODY, LAURA ANN BAILE, government official; b. Balt., Aug. 29, 1963; d. Merle Harrison Jr. and Gloria Ann Margaret (Kanely) B.; m. Jeffrey Lee Peabody, Oct. 17, 1990 (div. Sept. 1993); 1 child, Krystle Lee. A Gen. Sci., Essex C.C., Balt., 1985; student, Carroll C.C., Westminster, Md., 1987-89, Tex. A&M U., 1989, 91, Sch. Med. Transcription, Atlanta, 1995. Sales assoc. Montgomery Ward, Balt., 1982-85; lab. asst. Md. Dept. Health, Balt., 1985-87; agrl. inspection technician Md. Dept. Agr., Balt., 1987-91; food processing insp. for total quality control USDA Food Safety and Inspection Svc., Greenbelt, Md., 1990-94, food processing insp. for processed products, 1994—. Mem. Am. Fedn. Govt. Employees (sec. 1995—). Democrat. Roman Catholic. Home: 2300 Leeward Dr Westminster MD 21158 Office: USDA FSIS IO 6303 Ivy Ln Greenbelt MD 20770

PEACOCK, JUDITH ANN See ERWIN, JUDITH ANN

PEACOCK, MARY WILLA, magazine editor; b. Evanston, Ill., Oct. 23, 1942; d. William Gilbert and Mary Willa (Young) P. B.A., Vassar Coll., 1964. Assoc. lit. editor Harper's Bazaar mag., N.Y.C., 1964-69; staff editor Innovation mag., N.Y.C., 1969-70; editor in chief, co-founder, sec.-treas., pres. Rags mag., N.Y.C., San Francisco, 1970-71; co-founder, features editor Ms. mag., N.Y.C., 1971-77; pub., pres. Rags mag., N.Y.C., 1977-80; sr. editor Village Voice, N.Y.C., 1980-85, style editor, 1985-89; editor-in-chief Model mag., N.Y.C., 1989—, editorial cons., 1991—; fashion dir. Lear's Mag., N.Y.C., 1992-93; dep. editor In Style Mag., 1993-94, Mirabella mag., 1994-95; cons., 1995—.

PEACOCK, SUSAN KIRBY, pharmacist, artist; b. Hibbing, Minn., Jan. 17, 1951; d. Donald Robinson Kirby Jr. and Janet Marion (Spencer) MacMichael; m. David Frank Moynanhan, June 9, 1982 (div. Nov. 1994); children: Daniel, Marley. Student, Sweet Briar Coll., 1969-71; BA in Biology, Fla. State U., 1973, BS in Fine Arts, 1987; BS in Pharmacy, Fla. A&M U., 1976. Registered pharmacist, Ga., Fla. Freelance pharmacist numerous hosps. and pharmacies, Fla., Ga., 1977—; dir. pharmacy Neighborhood Health Svcs., Tallahassee, 1988—; pharmacology thcr. nursing sch., staff pharmacist Presbyn. Ch. of E. Africa-Tumu Tumu (Kenya) Hosp., 1982-83; pottery tchr. Fla. State U.-Ctr. for Participant Edn., Tallahassee, 1980-81, Magnolia Sch., Tallahassee; bd. dirs. 621 Gallery, Tallahassee. Paintings exhibited in shows and represented in permanent collections; solo and two-person shows include Havana, Fla., 1996, Chipola Jr. Coll., Mrianna, Fla., 1995, Old Capitol Bldg., Tallahassee, 1995; works exhibited in 1990-94 include City Hall, Tallahassee, Space Gallery, Old Brookville, N.Y., 620 Gallery, Tallahassee, Broome St. Gallery, N.y.C., Tallahassee Little Theatre, Fla. State U., Tallahassee, others. Recipient Merit awards Thomasville (Ga.) Cultural Ctr., 1989, 93, 95, City Hall, Tallahassee, 1993. Mem. Nat. Oil and Acrylic Painters Soc. (Charles Woods award 1991), Nat. Assn. Woman Artists (medal of honor 1996), Women's Caucus for Art, Leon County Pharm. Assn. Democrat. Home: 2964 Lake Bradford Rd Tallahassee FL 32310

PEACOCK, VALERIE LYNN, paralegal; b. Tallahassee, Nov. 6, 1962; d. William Stanley and Valerie Jo (Tate) P. AA with honors, Tallahassee C.C., 1982; BS in Bus. Communication, Fla. State U., 1986. Cert. legal asst., Ga. With Fla. House of Reps., Tallahassee, 1980-84; with office of registrar Fla. State U., Tallahassee, 1984-85; tchr. Leon County Sch. Bd., Tallahassee, 1986-87; legal asst. Dept. of Ins.-Receivership, Tallahassee, 1987-88, B.K. Roberts, Baggett, LaFace & Richard, Tallahassee, 1988; paralegal specialist criminal div. Fla. Atty. Gen., Tallahassee, 1988—; mem. adv. bd. Nat. Ctr. Paralegal Tng., Miami and Ft. Lauderdale, Fla., 1990—; with paralegal studies program Rollins Coll. Ctr. for Lifelong Edn., 1992—. Mem. Jr. League of Tallahassee, 1992—, bd. dirs. 1993—, cmty. pub. rels. chmn., 1993—, chmn. internat. pub. rels. com. 1992-93; vol. missionary local ch. to Port-au-Prince, Haiti, 1985, mem. adminstrv. bd. local ch., Tallahassee, 1988—; atty gen. rep. Ptnrs. in Excellence, Tallahassee, 1990; bd. dirs. Am. Heart Assn., 1992—, v.p., 1996—; chmn. Children's Miracle Network, 1993, mem. cmty. bd. 1994—; Olympic torchbearer, cmty. hero, 1996; pres. Call Care of Fla., 1996. Recipient Pres.'s award Am. Heart Assn., 1996; finalist Vol. of Yr., Tallahassee and Leon County, 1994; named Cmty. Hero and Olympic Torchbearer, 1996 Olympics in Atlanta. Mem. Fla. Supreme Ct. Hist. Soc., Friends of Maclay Gardens, Pi Kappa Phi, Phi Sigma Soc., Phi Theta Kappa. Republican. Office: Atty Gen Criminal Div The Capitol Tallahassee FL 32399-1050

PEAKE, CANDICE K. LOPER, data processing professional; b. Sublette, Kans., Oct. 29, 1953; d. Robert Franklin and Marion Joyce (Sooby) L.; m. Eugene E. Peake, Aug. 12, 1993. Student, McPherson (Kans.) Coll., 1971-72; lic. in cosmetology, Crums Beauty Sch., Manhattan, Kans., 1974; student, Garden City (Kans.) Community Coll., 1975-76, Diablo Valley Coll., 1988-89. ICCP cert. data processor. Owner, operator Candi's For Beautiful Hair, Garden City, 1974-78; systems project librarian Bank of Am., San Francisco, 1980, analyst, 1981, systems analyst, 1981-82, sr. systems analyst, 1982-83, cons., 1983-84, systems cons., team leader, 1984; project mgr. Wells Fargo Bank, Concord, Calif., 1984-86; systems analyst 1st Nationwide Bank, San Francisco, 1986-88; adv. systems engr. Bank Am., Concord, Calif., 1988-89; owner Candi's Visions, Independence, Mo., 1988—; sys. svcs. mgr. Continuum Co., Kansas City, Mo., 1989—. Home: 3419 S Home Ave Independence MO 64052-1239 Office: Continuum Co 2d Fl 301 W 11th St Kansas City MO 64105-1634

PEALE, RUTH STAFFORD (MRS. NORMAN VINCENT PEALE), religious leader; b. Fonda, Iowa, Sept. 10, 1906; d. Frank Burton and Anna Loretta (Crosby) Stafford; m. Norman Vincent Peale, June 20, 1930; children: Margaret Ann (Mrs. Paul F. Everett), John Stafford, Elizabeth Ruth (Mrs. John M. Allen). AB, Syracuse U., 1928, LLD, 1953; LittD, Hope Coll., 1962; LHD (hon.), Milw. Sch. Engring., 1985, Judson Coll., 1988; LHD, Milw. Sch. Engring., 1985. Tchr. math. Cen. High Sch., Syracuse, N.Y., 1928-31; nat. pres. women's bd. domestic missions Ref. Ch. Am., 1936-46; sec. Protestant Film Commn., 1946-51; chmn. Am. Mother's Com., 1948-49; pres., editor-in-chief, gen. sec., CEO, chmn. bd. dirs. Peale Ctr. for Christian Living, 1940—; nat. pres. bd. domestic missions Ref. Ch. in Am., 1955-56; mem. bd. N. Am. Missions, 1963-69, pres., 1967-69; mem. gen. program council Ref. Ch. in Am., 1968—; mem. com. of 24 for merger Ref. Ch. in Am. and Presbyn. Ch. U.S., 1966-69; v.p. Protestant Council N.Y.C., 1964-66; hon. chancellor Webber Coll., 1972—; co-founder, pub. Guideposts, N.Y.C., 1945—, pres., 1985-92, chmn. bd., 1992—; pres. Fleming H. Revell, Tarrytown, N.Y., 1985-92; founder Ruth Stafford Peale Ctr., Syracuse, 1989—. Appeared on: nat. TV program What's Your Trouble, 1952-68; Author: I Married a Minister, 1942, The Adventure of Being a Wife, 1971, Secrets of Staying in Love, 1984; founder, pub. (with Dr. Peale) Guidepost mag., 1957—; co-subject with husband: film One Man's Way, 1963. Trustee Hope Coll., Holland, Mich., Champlain Coll., Burlington, Vt., Stratford Coll., Danville, Va., Lenox Sch., N.Y.C., Interchurch Center Syracuse U., 1955-61; bd. dirs. Cook Christian Tng. Sch., Lord's Day Alliance U.S.; mem. bd. and exec. com. N.Y. Theol. Sem., N.Y.C.; sponsor Spafford Children's Convalescent Hosp., 1966—; bd. govs. Help Line Telephone Center, 1970—, Norman Vincent Peale Telephone Center, 1977; mem. nat. women's bd. Northwood Inst., 1981. Named N.Y. State Mother of Yr., 1963, Disting. Woman of Yr., Nat. Art Assn., Religious Heritage Am. Ch. Woman of Yr., 1969; recipient Cum Laude award Syracuse U. Alumni Assn. N.Y., 1965, Honor Iowans award Buena Vista Coll., 1966, Am. Mother's com. award for religion, 1970, Disting. Svc. award Coun. Chs., N.Y.C., 1973, Disting. Citizen award Champlain Coll., 1976, Disting. Svc. to Cmty. and Nation award Gen. Fedn. Women's Clubs, 1977, Horatio Alger award, 1977, Religious Heritage award, 1979, joint medallion with husband Soc. for Family of Man, 1981, Soc. Family of Man award, 1981, Alderson-Broaddus award, 1982, Marriage Achievement award Bride's mag., 1984, Gold Angel award Religion in Media, 1987, Adela Rogers St. John Roundtable award, 1987, Disting. Achievement award Am. Aging, 1987, Paul Harris award N.Y. Rotary, 1989, Leader's award Arthritis Found. Dutchess County, 1992, Dave Thomas Well Done! award, 1994, Norman Vincent Peale award for positive thinking, 1994, Master of Influence award Nat. Speakers Assn., 1995. Mem. Insts. Religion and Health (bd. exec. com.), Am. Bible Soc. (trustee 1948-93, hon. trustee 1993—), United Bible Soc. (v.p.), Interch. Ctr. (bd. dirs. 1957-92, chmn. 1982-90), Nat. Coun. Chs. (v.p. 1952-54, gen. bd.; treas. gen. dept. Uniteed Ch. Women, vice chmn. broadcasting and film commn. 1951-55, program chmn. gen. assembly 1966), N.Y. Fedn. Women's Clubs (chmn. religion 1951-53, 57-58), Home Missions Coun. N.A. (nat. pres. 1942-44, nat. chmn. migrant com. 1948-51), Internat. Platform Orgn. (bd. govs. 1994—, Norman Vincent Peale award 1994), PEO, Alpha Phi (Frances W. Willard award 1976). Republican. Office: Peale Ctr Christian Living 66 E Main St Pawling NY 12564-1409

PEARCE, BECKY ANN, administrative assistant; b. Palestine, Tex., Nov. 28, 1954; d. Charlie Welburn and Mae Jean (Richardson) Rogers; m. Randy Lee Pearce, Apr. 14, 1973; children: Chad Clint, Justin Clay, Brent Nathan. Clk. Bealls, Palestine, 1988-89; bookkeeper 1st State Bank, Frankston, Tex., 1990-91, teller, 1992-94, adminstrv. asst., 1994—. Mem. Am. Inst. Banking. Methodist. Home: Rt 2 Box 98A Frankston TX 75763 Office: First State Bank PO Box 277 Frankston TX 75763

PEARCE, CAROL ANN, writer, editor; b. Dubuque, Iowa, Dec. 25, 1947; d. Wallace Harry Pearce and Edna Louisa (Williams) Meyer; m. Robert Theodore Worthington, June 23, 1984. BA, Clarke Coll., 1972; MFA, Villanova U., 1974. Sr. editor Show Magazine, N.Y.C., 1971-73; assoc. editor Backstage Newspaper, N.Y.C., 1973-74; sr, editor Weight Watchers Magazine, N.Y.C., 1974-78; featured poetry reader at various readings, N.Y.C., 1995-96. Author: (books) Amelia Earhart, A Biography, 1988, Career Chic, 1990; co-author (with others) Making Love Again, 1992; contbr. articles to mags. and pocket books., 1981-91, short stories to Quarterly West, Oregon East, Greensboro Rev. and other literary mags; poetry published in Small Pond, Anemone, Dell Love Poems, Julian's Journal, N. Am. Mentor. Recipient Langston Hughes Poetry award YM-YWCA, N.Y.C., 1982, Annual Poetry award Poetry Soc. Am., 1985, Deer Valley Fiction award U. Utah, 1986; creative writing fellowships to Wesleyan U., Columbia U., Bennington Coll.; poetry selected for Cornell Med. Libr. Tri-institutional Art Show, 1994, 96; named artist in residence Millay Colony for the Arts. AAUW.

PEARCE, CHRISTINE REYES, elementary education educator; b. San Antonio, Oct. 3, 1964; d. Pedro G. Jr. and Consuelo (Perez) Reyes; m. James Lee Pearce, Oct. 23, 1993. BA, Trinity U., 1987. Educator Round Rock (Tex.) Ind. Sch. Dist., 1995-96; cons. San Antonio Ind. Sch. Dist., 1987-95. Singer San Antonio (Tex.) Symphony Mastersingers, 1986-95. Mem. Kappa Delta Pi.

PEARCE, DRUE, state legislator; b. Fairfield, Ill., Apr. 2, 1951; d. H. Phil and Julia Detroy (Bannister) P.; m. Michael F.G. Williams; 1 child, Tate Hanna. AB, Ind. U., 1973; MPA, Harvard U., 1984. Sch. tchr. Clark County, Ind., 1973-74; curator of edn. Louisville Zoo, 1974-77; dir. Summerscene, Louisville, 1974-77; asst. v.p. Alaska Nat. Bank of the North, 1977-82; legis. aide to Alaska State Rep. John Ringstad, 1983; mem. Alaska Ho. of Reps., 1984-88; state senator Alaska Senate, 1988—, pres. senate, 1995—. Mem. Alaska Resource Devel. Coun., Alaska Women's Polit. Caucus. Mem. DAR, Alaska C. of C. Republican. Home: 716 W 4th Ave Ste 500 Anchorage AK 99501 Office: Office of the State Senate State Capitol Juneau AK 99801

PEARCE, ELLEN, information consultant, writer, editor; b. N.Y.C., Aug. 28, 1946; d. Charles A. and Clara (Kent) P. BA in English, Lake Erie Coll., 1968; MA in Libr. and Info. Sci., U. Mo., 1991. Editl. asst. IEEE, N.Y.C., 1969-70; mng. editor Boulder (Colo.) Express, 1970; dir. Giraffics, Rolla, Mo., 1982-87; mng. editor Morning Jour., Rolla, Mo., 1982; freelance tech. copy editor, 1973-91; tech. transfer coord. Mo. Small Bus. Devel. Ctrs., Rolla, 1992—. Author: Life in (very) Minor Works, 1968; author essays, poems and short stories; featured artist (video) Chalk Up Another.

PEARCE, JEANNIE, writer, insurance administrator; b. Casa Grande, Ariz., Sept. 24, 1948; d. Johnnie E. and Barbara (Dismukes) Pearce; m. Bryce Hallice Storseth, Aug. 15, 1981; 1 child, Michael Scott. B.S., U. Ariz., 1979. Mktg. rep. Group Health Coop., Seattle, 1981-83; dist. mgr. Health Plus/Blue Cross, Seattle, 1983-84; mktg. dir. Personal Health, Seattle, 1984-85; sales dir. Cigna Health Plan, Seattle, 1985-88; real estate agent John L. Scott Real Estate, Seattle, 1988-92; freelance writer, 1992—; prin. Bus. Writers Northwest, Seattle, 1994—. Avocations: oil painting, writing. Office: Bus Writers Northwest PO Box 66003 Seattle WA 98166-0003

PEARCE, KRISTI LAHR, education educator, counselor; b. Aberdeen, S.D., June 24, 1952; d. Anthony James and Marilyn Maxine (Dinger) Lahr; m. Lee Ray Pearce, Apr. 1, 1981; children: Joshua Pearce, Joshua Geffre, Justin Pearce, Jessica Geffre. AS, Presentation Coll., Aberdeen, 1973; BS, No. State Coll., Aberdeen, 1975; MS, U. S.D., Vermillion, 1978, EdD, 1989. Nat. cert. counselor; cert. tchr., sch. counselor, S.D. Alternative sch. advisor Black Hills Svcs. Coop., Sturgis, S.D., 1985-90; sch.-cmty. liaison Belle Fourche (S.D.) Schs., 1990-92; elem. sch. counselor Spearfish (S.D.) Schs., 1992-93; MSCI program coord., asst. prof. Black Hills State U., Spearfish, 1993—, coord. faculty devel. program, 1996—. Authoractivity books for middle level students. Vol. Meals on Wheels, Spearfish, 1993—. Mem. AAUW, ASCD, Am. Counseling Assn. Office: Black Hills State U 1200 University USB 9110 Spearfish SD 57799-9110

PEARCE, MARY MCCALLUM (MRS. CLARENCE A. PEARCE), artist; b. Hesperia, Mich., Feb. 17, 1906; d. Archibald and Mabel (McNeil) McCallum; m. Clarence A Pearce, June 30, 1928 (dec.); children: Mary Martha (Mrs. William B. Robinson), Thomas McCallum. AB, Oberlin Coll., 1927; student John Huntington Inst., 1929-34, Cleve. Inst. Art, 1935-37, 54, Dayton Art Inst., 1946-49. One woman shows at Cleve. Women's City Club, 1959, 69, Plymouth Harbor, Sarasota Fla., 1989, 90, 94, Cleve. Orch., 1967, Cleve. Playhouse Gallery, 1968, 71, 76, 87, Van Wezel Hall, 1979, Sarasota (Fla.) Library, 1979, Hilton Leech Gallery, Sarasota, 1979, 80, 81, 86 Fed. Bank, Sarasota, 1980, Unity Gallery, Sarasota, 1993; exhibited in group shows at Oberlin Art Mus., Smithsonian Inst., Birmingham Mus. of Art, Am. Watercolor Soc., Cleve. Mus. Art, Foster Harmon Galleries, 1986, Fla. Watercolor Soc., Ala., 1973, 74, 75, 77, 78, 79, 80, 87, 88, 92, 96, Fla. Artist Group, 1980, 81, 83, 85, 90, 94, 95, 96, Southeastern Watercolorists, 1989, Friends of Arts and Scis., 1992, Fla. Watercolor Signature Group, 1992, Hilton Leech Gallery, 1992, Sarasota Ctr. Visual Arts (Best of Show 1994), 1994, many others: represented in pvt. collections: tchr. art, supr. pub. schs., Mayfield Heights, Ohio, 1927-28, Maple Heights, Ohio, 1928-30, Chagrin Falls, Ohio, 1938-39. Named best woman artist Ohio Watercolor Soc., 1955; recipient Bush Meml. award Columbus Gallery Fine Arts, 1962; nat. 1st prize for drawing Nat. League Am. Pen Women, 1966, 68, 96; Littlehouse award Ala. Watercolor Soc., 1967; Wolfe award Columbus Gallery Fine Arts, 1971; awards Longboat Key Art Center, 1973, 75, 79-86; Equal award Longboat Key, 1993; award Southeastern Art Soc., 1975; 2d prize Art League Manatee County, 1973, 90, 1st prize, 1988, Merit awards, 1975, 77, 88, 89, 93; 3d prize Sarasota Visual Art Ctr. (formerly Sarasota Art Assn.), 1977, 78, hon. mention, 1989, Merit award, 1981, 85, 90, 91, Best of Show, 1994, hon. merit award, 1996; 1st prize Venice (Fla.) Art League, 1979, 81, 82, 83, 86, 87, 2d prize, 1979, 80, 81, 89, 3d prize, 1978, 1992, merit award, 1985, 89, 92; 1st prize Hilton Leech Gallery, 1981, 85, 90, 1st prize Friends of Arts and Scis., 2d prize Suncoast Watercolor Soc., 1987, 90, 92, Best of Show, 1994, 96; hon. mention Fla. State Merit award; Fla. West Coast Parade of prize winners, 1990, 1st award Women's Resource Ctr., 1992, Grumbacher award Fla. Artists Group, 1994. Mem. Nat. League Am. Pen Women (treas. 1962), Am. (assoc.), Ala., Fla. Watercolor Soc. (signature). Republican. Congregationalist. Home: 5400 Ocean Blvd Apt 1401 Sarasota FL 34242 Office: Donn Roll Contemporary 1301 First St Sarasota FL 34236

PEARD, LAURIE ANN, lawyer; b. Ft. Worth, Mar. 25, 1960; d. James Clarence and Mary Elizabeth (Jones) P.; m. Fernando J. Soler, May 31, 1985; children: Wendy M., Robert J. BS, U. Ill., 1982; JD, Loyola U., Chgo., 1991. Bar: Ill. 1991. Asst. mgr. Conesco Merchandising Corp., Franklin Park, Ill., 1988-94; assoc. Masuda, Funai, Eifert & Mitchell, Ltd., Chgo., 1991—. Mem. ABA, Ill. State Bar Assn., Chgo. Bar Assn. Office: Masuda Funai Eifert & Mitchell Ltd Ste 3200 One East Wacker Dr Chicago IL 60601

PEARL, HELEN ZALKAN, lawyer; b. Washington, Sept. 12, 1938; d. George and Harriet (Libman) Zalkan; m. Jason E. Pearl, June 27, 1959; children: Gary M., Esther H., Lawrence J. BA with hons., Vassar Coll., 1959; JD, U. Conn., 1978. Bar: Conn. 1978, U.S. Dist. Ct. Conn. 1978. Mkt. rsch. analyst Landers, Frary & Clark, New Britain, Conn., 1960-61; managerial statistician Landers, Frary & Clark, 1961-62; real estate salesperson Denuzze Co., New Britain, 1966-70; property mgr. self-employed New Britain, 1970-75; legal asst. Atty. Gen. Office, State of Conn., Hartford, 1978; assoc. Weber & Marshall, New Britain, 1978-83; ptnr. Weber & Marshall, 1983—; hearing officer Commn. on Human Rights & Opportunities, State of Conn., 1980—; spl. master State of Conn. Judicial Dept., 1986—. New Britain rep. to Cen. Conn. Regional Planning Agy., 1973-75, 84—, chmn., 1990-92; mem. New Britain Bd. Fin. and Taxation, 1973-77; founder, mem. Conn. Permanent Commn. on Status of Women, 1975-82; also others. Recipient Women in Leadership award, YWCA of New Britain, 1988, Book award for torts, Am. Jurisprudence, 1976, Econs. prize, Vassar Coll., 1959. Mem. AAUW (pres. 1970-72), Conn. Bar Assn., New Britain Bar Assn., LWV (Conn. specialist 1987—, local pres. 1996—), Hartford Vassar Club, Phi Beta Kappa. Democrat. Jewish. Home: 206 Hickory Hill Rd New Britain CT 06052-1010 Office: Weber & Marshall PO Box 1568 New Britain CT 06050-1568

PEARLE, FRIEDA, artist; b. N.J., Oct. 30, 1916; d. Hugo and Esther (Haller) Bachenheimer; m. George Pearle, June 26, 1940; children: Harry, Karen, Judith. Student, Nat. Acad. Fine Arts, 1945. Legal sec. B.M. Halpern, Atty., N.Y.C., 1935-40; sec. May Co., N.Y.C., 1940-50, Mus. Modern Art, N.Y.C., 1950-60, Jewish Mus., N.Y.C., 1960-70, Am. Jewish Com., N.Y.C., 1970. One-woman shows in two L.I. Galleries; groups shows in Longboat Key Art Assn., Sarasota, Sarasota Art Assn., 1986-95. Docent Nassau County L.I. Mus., N.Y., 1975-88, Ringling Mus., Sarasota, Fla., 1985-95; mem. B'Nai Brith, Oceanside, N.Y., 1984-95, Hadassah, Sarasota, Fla., 1984-95. Mem. L.I. Art Assn., Sarasota (Fla.) Art Assn., Longboat Key (Fla.) Art Assn. Democrat. Jewish. Home: 4906 Hidden Oaks Tr Sarasota FL 34232

PEARLMAN, BARBARA, artist, educator; b. N.Y.C., Apr. 25, 1938; d. Henry and Edith (Stein) P.; m. Charles Yulish (div. 1980); 1 child, Alexandre Yulish. BA, Parsons Sch. Design, 1960. Illustrator Neiman Marcus, Dallas, 1960-61, Vogue, Marie Claire, France, Eng., Germany, 1961-65, Galey & Lord, N.Y.C., 1965-78, Vogue, Harpers, N.Y. Mag., Glamour, N.Y. Art, N.Y.C., 1965-78; tchr. Parsons Sch. Design, N.Y.C., 1975-79, Fashion Inst. Tech., N.Y.C., 1979-95, Nassau Fine Arts Mus., 1980-81; Spkr. NYU Phenomenology in the Arts. Exhbns. N.Y.C., Germany, 1978-95; featured in Russian and Polish mags.; works featured in History of Fashion (Eunic Sloane); contbr. articles to Gebracht Graphic mag. Recipient award Soc. Illustrators, 1976, 69, 70. Mem. Nat. Orgn. Women Artists. Home: 2259 Edsall Ave Bronx NY 10463

PEARLMAN, BARI F., film director, producer, writer; b. Bronxville, N.Y., N.Y., Mar. 26, 1966; d. Lawrence Ronald Pearlman and Lenore Sylvia (Buckalter) Kaufman. BA in English, SUNY, Binghamton, 1987; MA in Lit., Ind. U., 1994. Jr. assoc. Whelan Group, Inc., N.Y.C., 1989-91; devel. asst. Merce Cunningham Dance Co., N.Y.C., 1993-94; asst. to exec. dir. Grad. Ctr. Found. CUNY, N.Y.C., 1994-96; hospitality coord. Hamptons internat. Film Festival, East Hampton, N.Y., 1996—; pres. BTG Prodns., N.Y.C., 1996—. Translator: (novel) Wanna Go Home, 1995; asst. dir. feature film: The Cat, 1995; dir., prodr. documentary: Maj Jong-The Tiles That Bind, 1996; assoc. prodr. short film The Mission, 1996—. Vol. advisor Common Cause, N.Y.C., 1995—, Motherless Daus., N.Y.C., 1995—; mem. steering com., chair and founder younger women's task force NOW, Rockland County, 1988-90; spkr. NARAL, N.Y.C., 1990. Mem. Assn. Ind. Video and Filmmakers, Women Make Movies.

PEARLMAN, ELLEN LOIS, writer, photographer, computer consultant; b. Bklyn., May 22, 1952; d. Sol and Norma (Fischel) P. BA, Hofstra U., 1974; postgrad., Naropa Inst., 1977. asst. to Oleg Grabar dept. fine arts Harvard U., Cambridge, Mass., 1980; dir. photography Karme Choling, Barnet, Vt., 1982; photo/performance collaborator Internat. Sch. Ballet, Flex Dance Co., Berlin, 1983; teaching asst. Internat. Ctr. Photography, 1984; owner photo studio, Denver, 1985-87; freelance photojournalist Colo. Daily, 1985-87; editor Vajradhatu Sun, 1988; conservation & restoration painter Presevar, Inc., 1991; asst. to dir. mktg. LAN Systems, N.Y.C., 1987; software trainer Software Tng. Labs., 1988; computer tutor various cos., 1990; adj. faculty mem. Columbia U., Baruch Coll.; software trainer, cons. Chubb Inst., 1994; prof. CTA program Columbia U., 1996. Contbg. editor EAR Mag., 1988, 90; rsch. editor Journey Throuth the Wheel of Time-The Kalachakra Sand Madala, 1992; contbg. writer Tricycle Mag., 1992-95; writer Shambhala Sun, Halifax, N.S., 1992; contbr. articles to numerous jours.; shows include Photochronicles, New Photography, Artbreak Hotel, Studio C-13, N.Y.C., Inst. Creative Living, N.Y.C., Bklyn. Waterfront Mus. Grantee Am. Inst. Indian Studies, Harvard Med. Sch., 1981; non-fiction scholar Breadloaf

Writers Conf., 1994. Mem. Nine Gates Inst., Shambala Lodge. Buddhist. Home and Office: 57 Hope St Fl 2 Brooklyn NY 11211

PEARSON, APRIL VIRGINIA, lawyer; b. Martinsville, Ind., Aug. 11, 1960; d. Clare Grill and Sheila Rosemary (Finch) Rayner; m. Randall Keith Pearson, Dec. 10, 1988; children: Randall Kyle, Austin Finch, Autumn Virginia. BA, Calif. State U., Long Beach, 1982; JD, Pepperdine U., 1987. Bar: Calif. 1987, Idaho 1993, D.C. 1989. Assoc. counsel Union Oil of Calif., L.A., 1988—; v.p. Pa's Bier, Long Beach, Calif., 1988—; bd. dirs. Unocal Chems. Internat., The Hague, The Netherlands, 1993-95, Ammonia Safety Tng. Inst., 1995—. Mem. Women Lawyers of Long Beach (v.p. 1990-93), Orange County Bar Assn., Chem. Industry Coun. Calif. (chair regulatory affairs com. 1995). Office: Union Oil Co dba Unocal 376 S Valencia Brea CA 92823

PEARSON, KAREN LEITER, speech and language pathologist; b. Syracuse, N.Y., Sept. 1, 1947; d. Leo A. and Gladys Leiter; m. Jeffrey S. Pearson, Aug. 16, 1970; 1 child, Wendy Elizabeth. BS, Syracuse U., 1969; MA, U. Conn., 1971. Cert. speech and lang. pathologist. Speech and lang. pathologist New Britain (Conn.) Meml. Hosp., 1971-72, Gaylord Hosp., Wallingford, Conn., 1972-76, Wethersfield (Conn.) Bd. Edn., 1976-78, St. Francis Hosp. and Med. Ctr., Hartford, Conn., 1975-80, Marlborough (Conn.) Elem. Sch., 1980-94, Rham High Sch., Hebron, Conn., 1985-86, Rham Mid. Sch., Hebron, 1994—. Contbr. articles to profl. jours. Bd. dirs. Glastonbury (Conn.) Recreational Swimming, 1985; ofcl. U.S. Swimming Assn., 1986-88. Mem. NEA, Am. Speech and Hearing Assn. (Ace award 1994, 95), Conn. Speech and Hearing Assn., Conn. Edn. Assn., Rham Edn. Assn. Home: 180 Shoddy Mill Rd Glastonbury CT 06033-3519

PEARSON, MARGARET DONOVAN, former mayor; b. Nashville, Oct. 29, 1921; d. Timothy Graham and Nelle Ligon (Schmidt) Donovan; m. Jimmie Wilson Pearson, Aug. 2, 1946 (dec. Oct. 1978). BS, Vanderbilt U., 1944, MA, 1950; MS, U. Tenn., 1954. Cryptanalysist Army Signal Corps, Washington, 1944-45; phys. edn. tchr. Nashville Bd. Edn., 1945-46; tchr. English, phys. edn. White County Bd. Edn., Sparta, Tenn., 1946-57; spl. edn. supr. Tenn. Dept. Edn., Cookeville, 1957-65; staff devel. dir. Tenn. Dept. Edn., Nashville, 1965-84; ret., 1984; 1st woman alderman City of Sparta, 1987-91, 1st woman mayor, 1991-95. Mem. U.S. Ret. Sr. Vol. Program, 1985—; dist. dir. Tenn. Mcpl. League, 1987-94, 1st woman elected as v.p.; mem. Tenn. Gov.'s Com. Employment of Disabled, 1989—. Recipient Cmty. Leader award Wal-Mart; Am. Speech, Lang. and Hearing Assn. fellow, 1971; Ky. Col.; Tenn. Col. Mem. Sparta C. of C., Rotary (1st woman elected pres.). Methodist. Home: 114 Highland Dr PO Box 22 Sparta TN 38583-0022

PEARSON, PATRICIA KELLEY, marketing representative; b. Carrollton, Ga., Jan. 21, 1953; d. Ben and Edith (Kelley) Rhudy; m. Ray S. Pearson, June 4, 1976; children: Chad, Jonathan, Kelly. BA in Journalism, Ga. State U., 1974; BSN, West Ga. Coll., 1990. RN Fla. Pub. rels. asst. Grady Meml. Hosp., Atlanta, 1974-77; editorial asst. Childers & Sullivan, Huntsville, Ala., 1977-78; sales rep. AAA Employment Agy., Huntsville, 1978-80; editor Wright Pub. Co., Atlanta, 1980-82; elect./electronic drafter PRC Cons., Atlanta, 1980-87; researcher Dept. Nursing at West Ga. Coll., Carrollton, 1989-90; med./surg. nurse Tanner Med. Ctr., Carrollton, Ga., 1989-90, Delray Community Hosp., Delray Beach, Fla., 1990-91; sales rep. Innovative Med. Svcs., 1991-94; with staff devel., employee rels. Beverly Oaks Rehab. and Nursing Ctr., 1994-95; sales rep./ pub. rels. rep. Columbia HCA, Melbourne, Fla., 1996—. Vol. Project Response. All-Am. scholar U.S. Achievement Acad., 1990, recipient Nat. Coll. Nursing award, 1989. Mem. NOW, Space Coast Bus. Writer's Guild, Omicron Delta Kappa. Democrat. Home: 139 Jamaica Dr Cocoa Beach FL 32931-2825

PEARSON, SUSAN ROSE, psychotherapist, fine arts educator, artist; b. Elmhurst, Ill., June 14, 1950; d. Ernest Elliott and Helen Julia (Drogoi) P. BA in Psychology, Calif. State U., 1992, MS in Edn. Psychology & Counseling, 1995. Cert. pupil pers. svcs. Art tchr., master artist Susan Rose Fine Art Gallery, Reseda, Calif., 1979—; therapist Lifestyle with Dignity, Canoga Park, Calif., 1985-93. Mem. Am. Counseling Assn., Am. Sch. Counselor Assn., Calif. Assn. Marriage & Family Therapists, Nat. Honor Soc. in Psychology (life), Nat. Bd. for Cert. Clin. Hypnotherapists (cert. hypnotherapist), Internat. Soc. Speakers, Authors and Cons. Home: 8104 Garden Grove Ave Reseda CA 91335

PEASE, ELLA LOUISE, elementary education educator; b. Kokomo, Ind., May 31, 1928; d. James E. and Carrie Alice (Ringer) Earnest; m. Harold Edwin Pease, Aug. 10, 1985; children: Charles Miller, James Miller, Ricky Ensley, Wanda Cisna. BS, Ball State U., 1956, MA, 1959; postgrad., Ind. U., Ft. Wayne. Tchr. 1st grade Union Twp. (Ind.) Pub. Schs., 1953-56, Wells City (Ind.) Pub. Schs., Forest Park Sch., Ft. Wayne, Ind., 1956-93. Docent Ft. Wayne Art Mus.; libr. Simpson United Meth. Ch., Ft. Wayne, bd. dirs., mem. child care bd. Mem. NEA-Ret., Internat. Reading Assn., Ret. Ind. Tchrs. Assn., Ft. Wayne Ret. Tchrs. Assn. Home: 5108 E State Blvd Fort Wayne IN 46815-7467

PEASE, MARY HAIGHT, retired educator, college counselor; b. Seattle, Aug. 8, 1924; d. Gilbert Pierce and Ruth (Gazzam) Haight; m. Otis Arnold Pease, Aug. 4, 1949 (div. Sept., 1987); children: Jonathan, Catherine, Martha, Emily. BA, Smith Coll., 1945. Tchr. Prospect Hill Sch., New Haven, Conn., 1949-52, Crystal Springs Sch., Hillsborough, Calif., 1964-66; tchr. The Bush Sch., Seattle, 1946-49. 62-63; tchr. The Bush Sch., 1966-67, tchr., dir. upper sch., 1967-76, tchr., coll. counselor, 1976-91; coll. counselor, pvt. practice Seattle; mem. bd. trustees Hyla Middle Sch., Bainbridge Island, Wash., 1993—. Bd. trustees First Ch. of Christ, Scientist, Seattle, 1974-76, 85-87, 91-92. Recipient Disting. Alumna award The Bush Sch., Seattle, 1991. Mem. AAUW, LWV, Pacific N.W. Assn. Coll. Admissions Counseling, Nat. Assn. Coll. Admissions Counseling. Democrat. Home and Office: Coll & Acad Counseling 921 11th Ave E Apt 5 Seattle WA 98102

PEASLEE, JAYNE MARIE, computer scientist, educator; b. Corning, N.Y., Mar. 1, 1958; d. Frank and Alice Joyce (Thresher) Walters; m. Kenneth Stewart Peaslee, June 28, 1980; children: Mary Alice, Brent Kenneth. BA, SUNY, Geneseo, 1980, SUNY Genesceo, 1980; postgrad., SUNY Binghamton, 1984-86; MS, Elmira Coll., 1987. Tchg. asst. Corning-Painted Post (N.Y.) Sch. Dist., 1980-81; instr. computer sci. Corning C.C., 1981—. Leader Seven Lakes Girl Scouts U.S. Council, Corning, 1994—. Recipient Honor plaque Data Processing Mgmt. Assn., 1985. Mem. AAUW, Assn. Computer Machinery, Nat. Mus. Women in Arts, Nat. C.C. Chair Acad., Math. Assn., Corning Quilters Guild. Methodist. Office: Corning CC 1 Academic Dr Corning NY 14830

PEASLEE, MARGARET MAE HERMANEK, zoology educator; b. Chgo., June 15, 1935; d. Emil Frank and Magdalena Bessie (Cechota) Hermanek; m. David Raymond Peaslee, Dec. 6, 1957; 1 dau., Martha Magdelena Peaslee-Levine. A.A., Palm Beach Jr. Coll., 1956; B.S., Fla. So. Coll., 1959; med. technologist, Northwestern U., 1958, M.S., 1964, Ph.D., 1966. Med. technologist Passavant Hosp., Chgo., 1958-59; med. technologist St. James Hosp., Chicago Heights, Ill., 1960-63; asst. prof. biology Fla. So. Coll., Lakeland, 1966-68, U. S.D., Vermillion, 1968-71; assoc. prof. U. S.D., 1971-76, prof., 1976, acad. opportunity liaison, 1974-76; prof., head dept. zoology La. Tech. U., Ruston, 1976-90, assoc. dean, dir. grad. studies and rsch., prof. biol. scis. Coll. Life Scis., 1990-93; v.p. for acad. affairs U. Pitts. at Titusville, Pa., 1993—. Contbr. articles to profl. jours. Fellow AAAS; mem. AAUP, Am. Inst. Biol. Scis., Am. Soc. Zoologists, S.D. Acad. Sci. (sec.-treas. 1972-76), N.Y. Acad. Scis., Pa. Acad. Sci., La. Acad. Sci. (sec. 1979-81, pres. 1983), Sigma Xi, Phi Theta Kappa, Phi Rho Pi, Phi Sigma, Alpha Epsilon Delta. Office: U Pitts Office of Acad Affairs Titusville PA 16354-0287

PEAVLER, NANCY JEAN, editor; b. Kansas City, Mo., Dec. 19, 1951; d. Elmer Alfred and Ruth Lenoris (Peterson) Zimmerli; m. Craig Eugene Peavler, Dec. 6, 1975; 1 child, Matthew Dean. Assoc., Kansas City (Kans.) Community Coll., 1976; BS in Human Resources Mgmt., Friends U., Wichita, Kans., 1995. Staff writer The Kansas City Kansan, 1972-73; assoc. editor Capper's Stauffer Communications, Topeka, 1976-87, editor, 1987—. Precinct com.-woman Shawnee County Rep. Party, Topeka, 1985-87. Mem. Women in Communications, Soc. Profl. Journalists. United Methodist. Office: Cappers 1503 SW 42nd St Topeka KS 66609-1214

PECCHIA, LORRAINE SHIRE, school counselor, career counselor; b. Boston, Jan. 3, 1962; d. Edward George and Kathleen Theresa (McLaughlin) Shire; m. Robert John Pecchia, Aug. 20, 1983; children: John Robert, Brian Edward. BA, U. New England, 1984; MS in Edn., U. So. Maine, 1995. Cert. sch. counselor; nat. cert. counselor. Admissions counselor U. New England, Biddeford, Maine, 1984-86, asst. dir. summer and elderhostel programs, 1985, asst. dir. admissions, 1986-89, asst. registrar, 1989-91; interim guidance counselor Middle Sch., Kennebunk, Maine, 1994. V.p. Young Sch. Parent Tchr. Orgn., Saco, Maine, 1994—, sec., 1995—; mem. Dist. Wide Coms., Saco, 1993—. Mem. ACA, Am. Sch. Counselors Assn., MEACD, MESCA. Home: 72 Jenkins Rd Saco ME 04072

PECK, CAROL FAULKNER, poet, writer, publisher, educator; b. Detroit, June 20, 1934; d. Edward Carroll and Barbara Ann (Fite) Faulkner; m. Lawrence David Peck, Dec. 18, 1954; children: David Edward Peck, Wendy Carol Peck Webster. BA in English, U. Mich., 1958; MA in English, U. Md., 1964; postgrad. in Teaching Creative Writing, U. Denver, 1977. Artist-in-edn. Md. State Arts Coun., Balt., 1971—; lectr. in English U. Md. Univ. Coll., Coll. Park, Md., 1971—; writer in residence Sidwell Friends Sch., Washington, D.C., 1978-91; poetry workshop leader Montgomery County Pub. Schs. Alternative Programs, Rockville, Md., 1978—; leader numerous poetry and writing workshops for ednl. and other audiences, 1971—; editl. bd. Md. English Jour., 1968-84, 95—; editor novels and dissertations for writers of same; owner carolpeck prodns., pacem Press. Author: From Deep Within, 1989; contbr. numerous articles to ednl. jours., poems to poetry and literary mags. Vol. poetry workshop leader Bethesda Retirement and Nursing Ctr., Chevy Chase, Md., 1978-91; judge numerous sch. and lit. groups poetry and writing contests; vol. Hospice Caring, Inc., 1994—. Assembly scholar U. Mich., 1953; recipient Hopwood award, 1953, first prize sonnet div. Alexandria Br., Nat. League of Am. PEN Women, 1984, Disting. Achievement award Ednl. Press Assn. Am., 1989, Excellence in Teaching award U. Md./U. Coll., 1993. Mem. Writers Ctr., Md. Coun. Tchrs. of English Lang. Arts, Internat. Women's Writing Guild, Alpha Lambda Delta, Phi Beta Kappa, Phi Kappa Phi. Home and Office: 14910 Brownstone Dr Burtonsville MD 20866-1849

PECK, CLAUDIA JONES, associate dean; b. Ponca City, Okla., Feb. 1, 1943; d. Claude W. and Josephine Jones; children: Jody Athene, Cameron Guthrie. BS, U. Okla., 1972; MS, U. Mo., 1976; PhD, Iowa State U., 1981. Instr. econs. Iowa State U., Ames, 1980-81; asst. prof. consumer studies Okla. State U., Stillwater, 1981-85, assoc. prof., 1985-88, prof., 1988-89; assoc. dean for rsch. and grad. studies U. Ky., Lexington, 1989—, faculty assoc. Sanders-Brown Ctr. on Aging, 1991. Contbr. articles to profl. jours. Recipient Lela O'Toole Rsch. award Okla. Home Econs. Assn., 1988, Merrick Found. Teaching. award Okla. State U., 1987. Mem. Am. Assn. Family and Consumer Scientists (v.p. 1990-92), Am. Coun. on Consumer Interests (pres. 1994-95, Applied Rsch. award 1985), Missouri Valley Econ. Assn. (v.p. 1994-96), Sigma Xi (pres. 1993-94). Office: U Ky 102 Erikson Hall 0050 Lexington KY 40506-0050

PECK, DEANA S., lawyer; b. Wichita, Kans., Nov. 6, 1947; d. Richard Rector Williams and Elva Alene (Davis) Williams; m. Frederick Page Peck, June 16, 1967 (div. Nov. 1981); 1 child, Paige. BA, Wichita State U., 1970; JD, U. Kans., 1975. Bar: Ariz. 1975, U.S. Dist. Ct. Ariz. 1975, U.S. Ct. Appeals (9th cir.) 1981, U.S. Ct. Appeals (10th cir.) 1990, U.S. Ct. Appeals (fed. cir.) 1991. Assoc. Streich Lang, Phoenix, 1975-80, ptnr., 1980—; vis. lectr. U. Kans. Sch. of Law, Lawrence, 1985. Mem. Phoenix Arts Commn. Mem. ABA, State Bar Ariz., Maricopa County Bar Assn., Kans. U. Law Soc. (bd. govs. 1980-82).

PECK, DIANNE KAWECKI, architect; b. Jersey City, June 13, 1945; d. Thaddeus Walter and Harriet Ann (Zlotkowski) Kawecki; m. Gerald Paul Peck, Sept. 1, 1968; children: Samantha Gillian, Alexis Hilary. BArch, Carnegie-Mellon U., 1968. Architect, P.O.D. R & D , 1968, Kohler-Daniels & Assos., Vienna, Va., 1969-71, Beery Rio & Assocs., Annandale, Va., 1971-73; ptnr. Peck & Peck Architects, Occoquan, Va., 1973-74, Peck, Peck & Williams, Occoquan, 1974-81; corp. officer Peck Peck & Assoc., Inc., Woodbridge, Va., 1981—; CEO, interior design group Peck Peck & Assoc., 1988—. Work pub. in Am. Architecture, 1985. Vice pres. Vocat. Edn. Found., 1976; chairwoman architects and engrs. United Way; mem. Health Systems Agy. of No. Va., commendations, 1977; mem. Washington Profl. Women's Coop.; chairwoman Indsl. Devel. Authority of Prince William, 1976, vice chair, 1977, mem., 1975-79; mem. archtl. rev. bd. Prince William County, 1996—; developer research project Architecture for Adolescents, 1987-88; mem. inaugural class Leadership Am., 1988, Leadership Greater Washington; mem. D.C. Coun. Metrication, 1992—, D.C. Hist. Preservation League, Rep. Nat. Com.; mem. Prince William County Archtl. Review Bd., 1996—. Recipient commendation Prince William Bd. Suprs., 1976, State of Art award for Contel Hdqrs. design, 1985, Best Middle Sch. award Coun. of Ednl. Facilities Planners Internat., 1989, Creativity award Masonry Inst. Md., 1990, First award, 1990, Detailing award, 1990, Govt. Workplace award for renovations of Dept. of Labor Bldg., 1990, Creative Use of Materials award Inst. of Bus. Designers, 1991, 1st award Brick Inst. Md., 1993, award Brick Inst. Va., 1994, Bull Elephant award Prince William County Young Reps., 1995; named Best Instl. Project Nat. Comml. Builders Coun.; subject of PBS spl.: A Success in Howard Co. Mem. Soc. Am. Mil. Engrs., Prince William C. of C. (bd. dir.). Roman Catholic. Club: Soroptimist. Research on inner-city rehab., adolescents and the ednl. environ. Office: 2050 Old Bridge Rd Woodbridge VA 22192-2447

PECK, ELLIE ENRIQUEZ, retired state administrator; b. Sacramento, Oct. 21, 1934; d. Rafael Enriquez and Eloisa Garcia Rivera; m. Raymond Charles Peck, Sept. 5, 1957; children: Reginaldo, Enrico, Francisca Guerrero, Teresa, Linda, Margaret, Raymond Charles, Christina. Student polit. sci. Sacramento State U., 1974. Tng. services coord. Calif. Div. Hwys., Sacramento, 1963-67; tech. and mgmt. cons., Sacramento, 1968-78; expert examiner Calif. Pers. Bd., 1976-78; tng. cons. Calif. Pers. Devel. Ctr., Sacramento, 1978; spl. cons. Calif. Commn. on Fair Employment and Housing, 1978; cmty. svcs. rep. U.S. Bur. of Census, No. Calif. counties, 1978-80; spl. cons. Calif. Dept. Consumer Affairs, Sacramento, 1980-83, project dir. Golden State Sr. Discount Program, 1980-83; dir. spl. programs for Calif. Lt. Gov., 1983-90, ret., 1990; pvt. cons., 1990—; cons., project dir. nat. sr. health issues summit Congress Calif. Srs. Edn. and Rsch. Fund, 1995; project dir. various post-White House Conf. on Aging seminars and roundtables, 1995—; coord. Calif. Sr. LEgis., 1995—; project dir. SSI/QMB Outreach Project, 1993-94. Author Calif. Dept. Consumer Affairs publ., 1981, U.S. Office Consumer Edn. publ., 1982. Bd. dirs Sacramento/Sierra Am. Diabetes Assn., 1989-90. Author: Diabetes and Ethnic Minorities: A Community at Risk. Trustee, Stanford Settlement, Inc., Sacramento, 1975-79; bd. dirs. Sacramento Emergency Housing Ctr., 1974-77, Sacramento Cmty. Svcs. Planning Coun., 1987-90, Calif. Advs. for Nursing Home Reform, 1990—, Calif. Human Devel. Corp., 1995—; campaign workshop dir. Chicano/Latino Youth Leadership Conf., 1982-95; v.p. Comision Femenil Nacional, Inc., 1987-90; del. Dem. Nat. Conv., 1976; mem. exec. bd. Calif. Dem. Cen. Com., 1977-89; chairperson ethnic minority task force Am. Diabetes Assn., 1988-90; steering com. Calif. Self-Esteem Minority Task Force, 1990-93; del. White House Conf. Aging, 1995. Recipient numerous awards including Outstanding Cmty. Svc. award Comuicaciones Unidos de Norte Atzlan, 1975, 77, Outstanding Svc. award, Chicano/Hispanic Dem. Caucus, 1979, Vol. Svc. award Calif. Human Devel. Corp., 1981, Dem. of Yr. award Sacramento County Dem. Com., 1987, Outstanding Advocate award Calif. Sr. Legis., 1988, 89, Calif. Assn. of Homes for Aging, Advocacy award, 1989, Resolution of Advocacy award, League Latin-Ams. Citizens, 1989, Meritorious Svc. to Hispanic Cmty. award Comite Patriotico, 1989, Meritorious Svc. Resolution award Lt. Gov. of Calif., 1989, Cert. Recognition award Sacramento County Human Rights Commn., 1991, Tish Sommers award Older Women's League/Joint Resolution Calif. Legislature, 1993, Latino Eagle award in govt. Tomas Lopez Meml. Found., 1994. Mem. Hispanic C. of C., Older Women's League, CongressCalif. Srs., Sacramento Gray Panthers, Latino Dem. Club Sacramento County (v.p. 1982-83). Home and Office: 2667 Coleman Way Sacramento CA 95818-4459

PECK, MARIE JOHNSTON, Latin American area studies consultant; b. New Haven, Aug. 15, 1932; d. James Howard and Marie Anna Christina (Voigt) Johnston; m. Austin Monroe Peck, July 9, 1952 (div. 1959). AS, Larson-Quinnipiac, 1952; BA, U. N.Mex., 1968, PhD, 1974. Writer, coord. bilingual edn. coll. edn. U. N.Mex., Albuquerque, 1976-78; pres., owner Southwestern Images, Inc., Shawnee Mission, Kans., 1978—; lang. cons. The Warren Found., Seattle, 1990-93; Vis. scholar U. N.Mex., Albuquerque, 1983; vis. instr. Wofford Coll., Spartanburg, S.C., 1984; adj. instr. humanities Johnson County Community Coll., Overland Park, Kans., 1985-86, coord. Brown V. Topeka Conf., 1986; cons. Brown V. Topeka Project, Merriam, Kans., 1984-88; bd. dirs. Op. SER, Colorado Springs, Colo., Midcoast Radio, Inc., Kansas City; curriculum writer Albuquerque Pub. Schs., 1980-81. Contbr. articles to profl. jours. Fulbright scholar, 1981-82; Fgn. Lang. fellow HEW, 1967-71, Rsch. fellow Orng. Am. States, 1970. Mem. NAFE, Puget Sound Grants Writers Assn., Fulbright Alumni Assn., N.W. Translators and Interpreters Soc., Am. Translators Assn. Home and Office: 8300 Phillips Rd SW Apt 123 Tacoma WA 98498-6311

PECK, SUSAN NELL, pediatric nurse; b. Dayton, Ohio, July 21, 1951; d. D. Bradley and Helen Louise (DePree) P. BSN, Northeastern U., Boston, 1974; MSN, U. Va., 1981. Cert. registered nurse practitioner. Sr. staff nurse Tufts-New Eng. Med. Ctr., Boston, 1974-79; staff nurse U. Va. Med. Ctr., Charlottesville, 1980-81, grad. teaching asst., 1980-81; clin. nurse specialist in gastroenterology The Children's Hosp. of Phila., 1981—; v.p. profl. edn. Delaware Valley chpt. Crohn's and Colitis Found. Am., Phila., 1992—. Contbr. articles to profl. jours.; author videotape: Facts From Your Friends, 1991. Bd. dirs. Phila. chpt. Am. Liver Found., 1988—. Named Woman of the Yr., Crohn's and Colitis Found. of Am., 1995. Mem. ANA, Nat. Assn. Pediatric Nurse Practitioners and Assocs., Soc. Gasteroenterology Nurses and Assocs. (editl. bd. 1986-92), Assn. Pediatric Gastroenterology and Nutrition Nurses (founder, sec.-treas. 1989-94, sec. 1994-95, treas. 1996), Sigma Theta Tau. Office: Childrens Hosp of Phila 34th and Civic Center Blvd Philadelphia PA 19104

PECKHAM, JOYCE WEITZ, foundation administrator, former secondary education educator; b. Rochester, N.Y., Oct. 11, 1937; d. Clarence Christian and Mildred Emma (Knapp) Weitz; m. Lauren Augustus Peckham, Dec. 20, 1958; children: David, Kent. BS, Elmira Coll., 1959, MS, 1967. Tchr. science Horseheads (N.Y.) Cen. Sch., 1959-71; sec.-treas. Peckham Pipe Organs, Breesport, N.Y., 1971—. Trustee and sec. electronic coms. Antique Wireless Assn., Bloomfield, N.Y., 1986—, sec. and mem. sec. 1986—, mem. bd. dirs. 1981—. Mem. Horseheads Hist. Soc., Internat. Majolica Soc., First United Methodist Ch. (trustee, choir mem.). Home: 194 Ormiston Rd Breesport NY 14816

PECORARO, MARILYN B., accountant; b. Wilmington, N.C., May 3, 1956; d. Francis J. and Lula E. (Stevens) Brown; m. Marc J. Pecoraro; children: Leigh Ann, Marc. Assoc. degree in bus., Chowan Coll., 1984; BS, U. Wilmington, 1987. CPA, N.C., CIA. Staff acct. Clement E. Goodson, CPA, Wilmington, N.C., 1987-89; sr. acct. Vance T. Moore, Jr., CPA, Wilmington, 1989-90; contr. Signatures USA, Inc., Wilmington, 1990-92; corp. acct. Goodmark Foods, Inc., Raleigh, N.C., 1992-94; dir. accts. North Atlantic Trading Co., Raleigh, 1994—. Mem. AICPA, Inst. Mgmt. Accts., Inst. Internal Auditors. Republican. Roman Catholic. Home: 1009 W Saint Julian Pl Apex NC 27502 Office: North Atlantic Trading Co Inc 3200 Beech Leaf Ct Ste 920 Raleigh NC 27604

PEDDY, JULIE ANN, federal agent; b. Chicago Heights, Ill., Apr. 2, 1959; d. Ronald Ryno and Myra Jean (Clark) P. MPA, Ind. U., Gary, 1984. Benefit authorizer trainee U.S. HHS, Chgo., 1979-80; investigator U.S. Office of Personnel Mgmt., Chgo., 1980-81, Def. Investigative Svc., Chgo., 1981-83; investigator, sr. resident agt. Def. Investigative Svc., Hammond, Ind., 1983-84; supervisory investigator, team chief Def. Investigative Svc., Chgo., 1984-89; spl. agt. in charge Def. Investigative Svc., Seattle, 1989—; mem. Seattle Fed. Exec. Bd., 1990—, chairwoman, 1995-96. Bd. dirs. Civic Light Opera, Seattle, 1996—, Lynwood (Ill.) Terr. Condominium Assn., 1989. Mem. ASPA, Ind. U. Alumni Assn. (life), Pi Alpha Alpha. Methodist. Office: Def Investigative Svc PO Box 33520 Seattle WA 98133-0520

PEDERSEN, DARLENE DELCOURT, health science publishing consultant; b. Westbrook, Maine; 1 child, Jorgen David. BSN, U. Conn., 1967; postgrad., U. B.C., 1974-75; MSN, U. Pa., 1997. RN, Pa. Various nursing positions, psychiat.-comty health, 1967-79; assoc. editor JB Lippincott Co., Phila., 1979-84; acquisition editor WB Saunders Co., Phila., 1984-88, v.p., editor in chief, 1988-91, sr. v.p., editorial dir. books divsn., liaison to London office, 1991-95, cons., domestic and internat., 1995—. Author: (with others) Canadian Nurse, 1976; contbr. Basic Nursing Skills, 1977; oil painter. Mem. ANA, Am. Psychiat. Nurses Assn., Am. Med. Pubs. Assn., Assn. Am. Pubs., Internat. Soc. Psychiat. Consultation Liaison Nurses, Forum Exec. Women, The Manuscript Soc., Assn. Profl. Comm. Cons., Internat. Platform Assn., Soc. for Edn. and Rsch. in Psychiat. Mental Health Nursing, Emily's List, Am. Orthopsychiat. Assn., Emily's List, U.S. Dressage Fedn., Inc. Office: Ste 200 516 Gordon Ave Penn Valley PA 19072

PEDERSON, KATHRYN MARIE, center director; b. Minot, N.D., Apr. 28, 1958; d. Clifford Artine and Leona (Schlecht) Lang; m. Robert Norman Pederson, Oct. 11, 1986. BA, Minot State U., 1984; MA, U. Mary, 1989. Mgr. Answer Dakota Answering Svc., Minot, 1980-82; legal sec. Teevens, Johnson, Montgomery, Minot, 1982-86; acctg. clk. Interstate Brands Corp., Minot, 1986; data input operator N.D. Legis. Coun., Bismarck, N.D., 1986-87; asst. Bismarck Pub. Schs./Tech. Enabling Disabled Individuals, Bismarck, 1987-89; state tech. dir. Dept. Pub. Instrn., Bismarck, 1989-92; instructional tech. administr. Prairie Pub. Broadcasting, Fargo, 1992-95; ctr. dir. N.D. State Coll. of Sci., 1995-96; human resource officer First Am. Bank West, Minot, 1996—. Editor: (newsletter) CEC Newsletter, 1987-89, TEDIgram, 1987-89, Superintendent's Report, 1990-92; author: (newsletter) TecTalk, 1990-92. Fin. com. Faith United Meth. Ch., Minot, 1986. Mem. N.D. Edn. Assn., N.D. Libr. Assn., Assn. Instrnl. Tech., N.D. Ednl. Telecommunications Coun. (exec. dir. 1989-92), Okla. State U. Satellite Program (adv. coun. 1989-92), Satellite Ednl. Resources Consortium (adv. coun. 1989-92), Jaycees (Outstanding Fundraiser 1989, Jaycee of Month 1989, Outstanding Com. chmn. 1989, Project of Yr. 1989, Top Mem. Recruiter 1990). Methodist. Office: NDSCS 5MSS/DPE 210 Missile Ave Unit 2 Minot AFB ND 58705

PEDERSON, MAI, noncommissioned air force officer; b. Kuwait, May 27, 1960; d. Moheb Abbas-Helmy al Sadat and Amira. BS in Occupational Edn., Southern Ill. U., 1986; AAS in Pers. Adminstrn., Community Coll. Air Force, 1988; AAS in Comm. Applications Tech., C.C. USAF, 1993. Enlisted USAF; telecommunications specialist Air Force Cryptologic Support Ctr., Kelly AFB, 1980-81; traffic analysis, telecommunications ops. specialist Air Force Communications Squadron, Norton AFB, 1981-82; with USAF, Kalkar Air Station, Fed. Republic of Germany, 1983-85; info. systems ops. specialist Robins AFB, Ga., 1985-86, base career advisor, 1986-89; non-commd. officer-in-chg. re-enlistments USAF, Ga., 1990-91, non-commd. officer-in-chg. Separations, 1990-91, non-commd. officer-in-charge Outbound Assignments, 1991; non-commd. officer-in-charge Customer Support Ctr. USAF, Robins AFB, Ga., 1992; non-commd. officer-in-charge Quick Response Debriefing Team USAF, Vogelweh AFB, 1993-94, non-commd. officer-in-charge Formica ops., 1994-95, chief pers./info. mgmt., 1995—; sole translator Operation Restore Hope USAF, Cairo West Air Base, Egypt, 1993-94. Vol. tchr. ESL, Robins AFB, 1986; lay leader Baha'i Faith, Robins AFB, 1985-92; field rep. for Women in Mil. Svc. for Am. Meml., 1991-95. Mem. Air Force Assn. (life), Non-Commd. Officers Assn. (life), Rambling Robins Volksmarch Club (pres. 1987-91).

PEDRAM, MARILYN BETH, reference librarian; b. Brewster, Kans., Apr. 3, 1937; d. Edgar Roy and Elizabeth Catherine (Doubt) Crist; m. Manouchehr Pedram, Jan. 27, 1962 (Oct. 28, 1984); children: Jaleh Denise, Cyrus Andre. BS in Edn., Kans. State U., 1958; MLS, U. Denver, 1961. Cert secondary educator, Mo. 7th grade tchr. Clay Ctr. (Kans.) Pub. Schs., 1958-59, Colby (Kans.) Pub. Sch. System, 1959-60; reference libr. Topeka (Kans.) Pub. Libr., 1961-62, extension dept. head, 1963-64, reference libr., 1964-65; br. libr. asst. Denver Pub. Libr., 1965-67; reference libr. Kansas City (Mo.) Pub. Libr., Plaza Br., 1974-79, Kansas City (Mo.) Main Libr., 1979—. Mem. AARP, ALA, NAFE, Mo. Libr. Assn., Pub. Libr. Assn.,

Kansas City Assn. Law Librs., Gluten Intolerance Group N.Am., Celiac Sprue Assn., Kans. State U. Alumni Assn., Kansas City Online Users Group, Nat. Parks and Conservation Assn. Office: Kansas City Pub Libr 311 E 12th St Kansas City MO 64106-2412

PEDRICK, JEAN, poet; b. Salem, Mass.; d. Laurence Davis and Elfrieda Augusta (Virchow) P.; m. Frank John Kefferstan II, Feb. 8, 1948; children: Laurence Dick, John Pedrick. BA, Wheaton Coll., 1943. Sec. to editor Houghton Mifflin Co., Boston, 1944-47; staff writer Beacon Hill News Cmty. Press, Inc., Boston, 1965-95; founding mem. Alice James Books, Cambridge, Mass., 1974; pres. Rowan Tree Press, Boston, 1980; instr. poetry Northeastern U., Ext., Boston, 1967-70, Boston Ctr. Continuing Edn., 1972-76. Author: The Fascination, 1947, (Poetry) Wolf Moon, 1974, Pride & Splendor, 1976, Greenfellow, 1981. Democrat.

PEDRICK, SALLY DUNBAR, artist, fine arts consultant; b. Newport, R.I., May 12, 1931; d. Arthur Joseph and Lillian Emma (DeLorme) Arseneault; children: Yvette Maria Orsini, Jesse Robert Dunbar; m. Robert Gordon Pedrick, Jr., Aug. 28, 1986. BA, U. Maine, 1952. Owner, mgr. The Library Art Studio, Greenwich, N.J., 1989—; fine arts cons. to pvt. and corp. collectors, 1986—; juror for area art exhbns., 1986—; art resident Vt. Studio Ctr., Johnson, 1993. Author: Archaeology, An Interdisciplinary Approach, 1979; one woman shows include The Gallery, Wheaton Village, Millville, N.J., Thomas Moser Cabinetmakers, Phila., 1994, The Library Art Studio, Greenwich, 1995; group shows include Trenton (N.J.) Avant Garde, Inc., 1996; represented in permanent collections Newman Galleries, Phila., Citicorp., N.Y.C., Conway-Milliken Corp., Chgo., Del. Bay Schooner Project, Dorchester and Bilvalve, N.J. Mem. fundraising group and networking initiative for Del. Estuary Watershed Action Agenda, Delaware Bay Schooner Project, Bivalve, N.J., 1993—; grants rev. panelist Cumberland County Cultural and Heritage Commn., 1993—. Grantee Office Gifted and Talented, 1978, vis. artist grantee Westtown (Pa.) Sch., 1995; Midcoast Maine scholar Nat. Audubon Soc., 1979. Mem. AAUW, Art Alliance for Contemporary Glass, Artists Equity, Glass Rsch. Soc. N.J., Glass Art Soc., Jersey Arts Communicators South, Phi Mu. Mem. Soc. of Friends.

PEEBLES, BETTY LEA, secondary school educator; b. Schenectady, N.Y., Aug. 3, 1954; d. Allen Jackson and Jean S. (Sasseen) P. BA, Harding U., 1976; MEd, U. S.C., 1992, EdS, 1996. Tchr. Evans (Ga.) H.S., 1977—, dept. chmn., 1985—; cons. ednl. dept. North Augusta (S.C.) Ch. Christ. Mem. NSTA, ASCD, PAGE, Tech. Prep. Republican. Office: Evans HS 4550 Cox Rd Evans GA 30809

PEEBLES, LAURA HEBNER, accountant; b. Lancaster, Calif., Aug. 23, 1956; d. Edgar Foster Peebles and Barbara Louise Hebner. BS, U. New Orleans, 1987. CPA, La.; cert. personal fin. specialist. Acct. Doody & Doody, CPA's, New Orleans, 1979-87; sr. tax mgr. Deloitte & Touche, New Orleans, 1988—. Contbr. articles to newspapers and mags. Recipient Elijah Watt Sells award, 1979; U. New Orleans scholar, 1988, La. Land Co. scholar, 1987. Mem. Am. Soc. Women Accts., Nat. Assn. Bankruptcy Trustees, World Trade Ctr., Assn. Insolvency Accts., New Orleans Estate Planning Coun., Beta Gamma Sigma, Phi Kappa Phi, Delta Sigma Pi. Democrat. Office: Deloitte & Touche 701 Poydras St Ste 3700 New Orleans LA 70139-6001

PEEPAS, KATHERINE T., elementary education educator; b. Worcester, Mass., Aug. 21, 1945; d. Theofanis George and Euterpe (Komenos) P. BS in Edn., Worcester (Mass.) State Coll., 1966, MA in Edn., 1971. Cert. elem. tchr., reading tchr., supr./dir., elem. prin. Elem. tchr. Fall Brook Sch., Leominster, Mass., 1966-67, Pakachoag Sch., Auburn, Mass., 1967-81, Julia Bancroft Sch., Auburn, 1981-86, Mary D. Stone Sch., Auburn, 1986-87, Pakachoag Sch., Auburn, 1987—; curriculum coun. pres. Auburn Schs., 1988-92. Recipient Excellence in Edn. award Auburn C. of C., 1988; Mini Tchr. grantee Alliance for Education, Worcester, 1986, 89, 90. Mem. NEA, Mass. Tchrs. Assn. Auburn Edn. Assn. (sec., v.p.).

PEET, PHYLLIS IRENE, women's studies educator; b. Winnipeg, Man., Can., Mar. 3, 1943; came to the U.S., 1948; d. Harold Parsons and Gladys Mae (Riley) Harrison; m. Thomas Peter Richman, June 14, 1963 (div. 1969); m. Charles Francis Peet, Sept. 9, 1972. BA in Art, Calif. State U., Northridge, 1972; MA in Art History, U. Calif., L.A., 1976, PhD in Art History, 1987. Sec. L.A. County Supr. Kenneth Hahn, 1960-68; assoc. in art history L.A. County Mus. Art, 1974-75; asst. dir., curator Grunwald Ctr. for the Graphic Arts, U. Calif., L.A., 1975-78; Am. art scholar High Mus. Art, Atlanta, 1984-90; instr. women's studies Monterey (Calif.) Peninsula Coll., 1986—, dir., instr. women's programs/women's studies, 1989—; dirs.' adv. com. The Art Mus. of Santa Cruz County, 1981-84, 89-94; vis. lectr. Calif. State U., Fresno, fall 1984; program coord. conf. Inst. for Hist. Study, San Francisco, 1987; lectr. bd. studies in art U. Calif. Santa Cruz, 1991-94. Author, co-curator, editor, compiler: (book and exhbn.) The American Personality: The Artist Illustrator of Life in the United States, 1860-1930, 1976; author, curator: (book and exhbn.) American Women of the Etching Revival, 1988; co-author: American Paintings in the High Museum of Art, 1994; contbr. articles to profl. jours. Vol., activist Dem. Party, L.A., 1960-66, Peace and Freedom Party, L.A., 1967-71; vol. Dem. Party Candidates, Santa Cruz, Calif., 1979-96, Santa Cruz Action Network, 1980-85; mem. nominating com. Girl Scouts of Am., Monterey Bay, 1991-93. Rockefeller Found. fellow U. Calif. L.A., 1978-79, 79-80, Dickson grantee U. Calif. L.A., 1981-82; recipient Women Helping Women award Soroptimists, Monterey and Carmel, Calif., 1991, 95, Allen Griffin for Excellence in Edn. award Cmty. Found. of Monterey County, 1993, Quality of Life award Econ. Devel. Corp., Monterey, 1994. Mem. NOW, AAUW, Nat. Women's Studies Assn., Inst. for Hist. Study, Western Assn. Women Historians, Women's Internat. League for Peace and Freedom, Monterey Bay Women's Caucus for Art (founder, bd. dirs. 1988-93). Office: Womens Programs Monterey Peninsula Coll 980 Fremont St Monterey CA 93940

PEIRCE, GEORGIA WILSON, public relations executive; b. Newton, Mass., Jan. 6, 1960; d. Norris Ridgeway and Anne (McCusker) P. BA, Duke U., 1982. Intern to Speaker of Ho. of Reps., Washington, 1981; prin. PR, etc., Quincy, Mass., 1987-94; dir. media rels. The Mass. Gen. Hosp., Boston, 1994—; cons. Mass. Group Insur. Commn., 1985. Contbr. articles to profl. jours. Mem. community rels. com. Vis. Nurse Assn./Hospice of South Shore; mem. com. to elect Mondale-Ferraro, Mass., coord. speakers bur., 1984; mem. charitable trust com. Maj. John F. Regan; com. mem. City of Quincy Recycling Com.; del. Mass. Dem. Conv., 1982, 83; v.p. South Shore Ad Club, 1990-91, mem.-at-large, 1991-92. Recipient 9th Wave awards 1989, 1st pl. in Pub. Rels. award, 1989, merit awards, 1992. Mem. NAFE, South Shore C. of C., Small Bus. Assn. New England, Women's Golf Assn. Mass., Publicity Club New England (Merit Bell Ringer award), Rotary Internat., Eastward Ho! Country Club Chatham (club champion 1977-81, 83, 91, 93), Wollaston Golf Club. Democrat. Roman Catholic. Home: 71 Bayfield Rd N Quincy MA 02171-2005 Office: Mass Gen Hosp Office of Pub Affairs Fruit St Boston MA 02114

PEISEN, DEBORAH JEAN, engineer, aviation planner; b. L.A., May 11, 1947; d. Walter Lewis and Florence Isabel (Hinchcliff) Hall; m. Jan W. Pritchard, Nov. 8, 1969 (div. Oct. 1981); 1 child, Jennifer Pritchard. BS, Calif. State Poly. U., 1970; MA, Calif. State U., L.A., 1976. Lic. helicopter pilot. Mgr. catering svc. Marriott Hotels, L.A., 1977-79; mgr. Gulliver's Restaurant, San Diego, 1979-80; sec. Crocker Nat. Bank, L.A., 1980-83; aviation planner Hoyle, Tanner & Assocs., Bedford, N.H., 1985-87; sr. engr. Systems Control Tech., Inc., Arlington, Va., 1987-94, SAIC, 1994—; coord. Model Ordnance Working Group, Alexandria, Va. ,1987-92; mem. FAA/Industry, 1988-92, sec. vertiport/heliport working group, 1988-94; mem. steering group Civil Rotocraft Initiative, Washington, 1991-92; chmn. Heliport Tech. Planning Com., Alexandria, 1991-92. Contbr. articles to profl. publs. Mem. Am. Helicopter Soc., Helicopter Assn. Internat. (lectr. joint Ga. Tech. Coll. heliport planning course 1987-92), Internat. Women Helicopter Pilots (sec. 1987-88), Mid-Atlantic Helicopter Assn. (sec. 1991-92, bd. dirs. 1990—, chairperson heliport com., pres. 1994-95), Ninety-Nines (sec. 1986-87). Office: SAIC Ste 1500 1213 Jefferson Davis Hwy Arlington VA 22202-4304

PEJSA, JANE ELIZABETH, writer, retired computer scientist; b. Mpls., Aug. 12, 1929; d. Walter U. and Irene M. (Melgaard) Hauser; m. Franz J.F. Gayl, Dec. 19, 1951 (div. Jan. 1968); children: Ilse E. Gayl, Franz J. Gayl; m. Arthur J. Pejsa, May 26, 1975. BA, Carleton Coll., 1951. Computer engineer, researcher Honeywell, Mpls., 1971-86. Author: The Molineux Affair, 1984, 3d edit., 1988 (finalist Edgar Allen Poe Fact Crime award Mystery Writers Am. 1985), Matriarch of Conspiracy, Ruth von Kleist 1867-1945, 1991, German edit., 1996, Japanese edit., 1996 (Best Book Overall Midwest Ind. Pubs. 1992, Best Biography Minn. Book award Minn. Office Libr. Devel. and Svcs. 1992), Gratia Countryman, Her Life, Her Loves and Her Library, 1995 (finalist Best Biography Minn. Book award Minn. Office Libr. Devel. and Svcs. 1995), To Pomerania, In Search of Dietrich Bonhoeffer, a Traveler's Companion, 1995; patentee energy submetering sys., 1986; contbr. articles to profl. jours. Chair philanthropy The Woman's Club, Mpls., 1993-95. Recipient Disting. Achievement award Carleton Coll., 1988; Artist's Fellowship grantee The Bush Found., St. Paul, 1986. Mem. Phi Beta Kappa. Congregationalist. Home: 2120 Kenwood Pkwy Minneapolis MN 55405-2326

PEKELNICKY, PATRICIA DEANE, secondary education educator; b. Roseland, Ill., Dec. 23, 1951; d. Elvie June (Nelson) Kurucar; m. David George Pekelnicky, Mar. 20, 1976; children: Robert, Jonathan. BA, Coll. of St. Francis, Joliet, Ill., 1974. Sec., receptionist Dial Tube Co., Bedford Park, Ill., 1974-76, Independence Tube Co., Bedford Park, 1976-78; tutor Sch. Dist. 126, Worth and Alsip, Ill., 1983-94, instr. parenting, 1987-89, substitute tchr., 1992-94, mem. discipline bd., 1992—; substitute tchr. Sch. Dists 127 and 127 1/2, Chicago Ridge, Ill., 1992-94; tchr. Epiphany Sch., Chgo., 1994-96, Queen of Martyrs, Chgo., 1996—; tchr. Bobbie Noonan Child Care, Inc., Worth, 1990-91. Den leader pack 4611 Cub Scouts Am., Alsip and Worth, 1986-92. Named Den Leader of Yr., Sauk Trail dist. Boy Scouts Am., 1990. Mem. Nat. Coun. Tchrs. Math. Roman Catholic.

PELCYGER, ELAINE, school psychologist; b. Jersey City, N.J., Apr. 13, 1939; d. Maurice C. and Bessie (Schneider) Morley; m. Iran Pelcyger, June 4, 1956; children: Stuart Lawrence, Gwynne Ellice, Wayne Farrol. BA magna cum laude, L.I. U., 1983; MS, St. John's U., Flushing, N.Y., 1995. Cert. sch. psychologist N.Y., N.Y.C., nat. cert. sch. psychologist. Sch. psychologist N.Y.C. Bd. Edn., 1985—. Mem. Nat. Assn. Sch. Psychologists, N.Y. Assn. Sch. Psychologists, Psi Chi. Office: Woodside Intermediate Sch 46-02 47th Ave Woodside NY 11377

PELFREY, DEANNA KAYE WEDMORE, public relations and marketing executive, educator; b. Cin., June 9, 1941; d. Irvin John and Ann Lee (Barone) Wedmore; divorced; 1 child, Danielle Newland Wedmore Pelfrey. BA in English, Coll. of Mt. St. Joseph, Ohio, 1964; postgrad., U. Poitiers, LaRochelle, France, 1966; MA in English and Am. Lit., Xavier U., 1972; postgrad., U. Louisville, 1977. Tchr. world lit. Wyoming High Sch., Cin., 1964-66; youth fashion coord. H&S Pogue Co., Cin., 1966-69; dir. fashion program Internat. Sch. for Young Ams., Cin., Europe, 1969-71; pres. Pelfrey Assocs., Inc., Louisville, 1976—; chmn. bd dirs. Youth Arts Coun., Louisville, 1988-91; bd. dirs. Walden Theatre, Louisville, 1988-94; pres. alumni bd. dirs. Coll. of Mt. St. Joseph, Cin., 1991—; mem. Edn. and Workforce Inst., 1991—. Chair Louisville Zoo Commn., 1977-84; pres. Louisville Zoo Found., 1979-81, chair Metazoo Capital campaign, 1981, co-chair herpetarium/aquarium capital campaign, 1982-84; mem. arts in edn. task force Jefferson County Pub. Schs., 1981-83; founding mem. planning team Ky. Inst. for Arts in Edn., 1982, mem. adv. com. planning team, 1983-87; bd. trustees Louisville Collegiate Sch., 1983-84, pres. parent's coun., 1983-84, mem. long range planning adv. com., 1984, mem. internat. adv. com., 1989-90; bd. dirs. Louisville Internat. Cultural Ctr., 1992—; mem. priority programs fund com. Metro United Way, 1992. Recipient 4 Citizen Contribution awards Mayor of Louisivlle, 1981-91. Mem. Am. Assn. Zool. Pks. and Aquariums (conf. del. 1975-84, 91), Pub. Rels. Soc. Am. (bd. dirs. Bluegrass chpt. 1992—, exec. com. internat. sect. 1993—), Counselors Acad. (exec. com. 1996), Fashion Group Internat. Fashion I (founder 1976, pres. 1977-78, advisor 1978-79, chair fashion seminar 1978, Stanley Marcus event 1980, co-chair fall fashion event 1983), Jr. League of Louisville (bd. dirs. 1977-80), Crane House/China Inst. (bd. dirs. 1995—). Office: Pelfrey Assocs Inc 730 W Main St Louisville KY 40202-2653

PELHAM, JUDITH, hospital administrator; b. Bristol, Conn., July 23, 1945; d. Marvin Curtis and Muriel (Chodos) P.; m. Jon N. Coffee, Dec. 30, 1992; children: Rachel, Molly, Edward. BA, Smith Coll., 1967; MPA, Harvard U., 1975. Various govt. postions, 1968-72; prin. analyst Urban Systems, Cambridge, Mass., 1972-73; dir. devel. and planning Roxbury Dental and Med. Group, Boston, 1975-76; asst. to dir. for gen. medicine and ambulatory care Peter B. Brigham Hosp., Boston, 1976-77, asst. dir. ambulatory care, 1977-79; asst. v.p. Brigham and Women's Hosp., Boston, 1980-81; dir. planning and mktg. Seton Med. Ctr., Austin, Tex., 1980-82, pres., 1982-92, chief exec. officer, 1987-92; pres., chief exec. officer Daughters of Charity Health Services, Austin, 1987-92; pres. Mercy Health Svcs., Farmington Hills, Mich., 1993—; cons. Robert W. Johnson Found., 1979-80; bd. dirs. Mercy Health Svcs., Healthcare Forum, Amgen, Mercy Health Found.; mem. mgmt. bd. Inst. for Diversity in Health Mgmt., 1994—. Author: Financial Management of Ambulatory Care, 1985; contbr. articles to profl. jours. Trustee A. Shivers Radiation Therapy Ctr., Austin, 1982-92, Marywood Maternity and Adoption Agy., 1982-86; bd. dirs. Quality of Life Found., Austin, 1985, Austin Rape Crisis Ctr., adv. bd., 1986-88; bd. dirs., trustee League House, 1982-93, Seton Fund, 1982-93, Greater Detroit Area Haelth Coun., 1994—; mem. Gov's Job Tng. Coordinating Council, 1983-85; adv. council U. Tex. Social Work Found., 1983-85; charter mem. Leadership Tex., Austin, 1983-93. Recipient Leadership award YWCA, Austin, 1986. Mem. Am. Coll. Healthcare Execs., Am. Hosp. Assn., Tex. Hosp. Assn. (mem. various couns. 1982-87), Austin Area Rsch. Orgn., Tex. Conf. Health Facilities (bd. dirs. 1985-89, pres. 1988), Cath. Health Assn. (bd. dirs. 1987-95, com. on govt. rels. 1984-91, sec., treas. 1982-95, chair fin. com. 1992-95). Office: Mercy Health Svcs 34605 W 12 Mile Rd Farmington Hills MI 48331

PELL, JANE EILEEN, insurance executive; b. Canton, Ohio, July 23, 1946; d. Edward G. and Alice C. (Snyder) Psolla; m. Richard W. Pell, Feb. 18, 1986. Cert. gen. ins., Ins. Inst. Am., Phila., 1976; Assoc., Am. Ednl. Inst., N.J., 1980. Sec. Glouka Ins. Agy., Cleve., 1964-65; jr. underwriter Employers Group, Cleve., 1965; sec., adjuster Md. Casualty, Phila., 1967-70; claims supr. PMA Ins., Phila., 1970-77; tech. supt. and claims INA, Phila., 1977-86, asst. v.p. major claims, 1986-89, field ops. v.p., 1989-92, regional claims v.p., 1992—. Mem. NAFE. Office: CIGNA One Beaver Valley Rd 4 West Wilmington DE 19850

PELL, LINDA DIANE, stockbroker; b. Pittsfield, Mass., May 31, 1961; d. Richard Frederick and Judith Mae (Giegerich) P. BSEE, Ohio State U., 1983; postgrad., U. Cen. Fla., 1994, M of Applied Econs., 1994. Lic. series 7 and series 63 Nat. Assn. Securities Dealers. Sys. engr. GE Co., Utica, N.Y., 1983-88; tech. mgr. McDonnell Douglas Space Sys. Co., Kennedy Space Center, Fla., 1988-94; stockbroker Montano Securities, New Smyrna Beach, Fla., 1994; tax preparer H&R Block, New Smyrna Beach, 1995-96; stockbroker Olde Discount Stockbrokers, Vero Beach, Fla., 1995—; fin. cons. Raymond James & Assocs., Port St. Lucie, Fla., 1996—. Voter register Jaycees, Merritt Island, 1990. Mem. AAUW, Am. Bus. Women's Assn. (treas.), Vero Beach C. of C., Indian River Photo. Club. Home: 1015 36th Ct Vero Beach FL 32960 Office: Raymond James & Assocs Ste 103 Renar Ctr 1100 SW Saint Lucie West Blvd Port Saint Lucie FL 34986

PELL, MARY CHASE (CHASEY PELL), civic worker; b. Binghamton, N.Y., May 23, 1915; d. Charles Orlando and Mary (Lane) Chase; m. Wilbur F. Pell, Jr., Sept. 14, 1940; children: Wilbur F., Charles Chase. BA, Smith Coll., 1937. Case worker Binghamton State Hosp., 1937; sociology tchr. Charles W. Wilson Meml. Hosp., Johnson City, N.Y., 1938; commentator travel and industry, sta. WSVL, Shelbyville, Ind., 1962-67. Contbr. articles to publs. Chmn. Ind. Fund Raising Com. for Smith Coll., Indpls., 1961; bd. dirs. Nat. Mental Health Assn., 1961-79, pres. 1976-77; pres. Ind. Mental Health Meml. Found., Indpls., 1964-65, Mental Health Assn. Ind., Indpls., 1962-63, bd. dirs., 1951-70; commr. Ind. Mental Health Planning Commn., Indpls., 1964-65; mem. Central Ind. Task Force on Mental Health Planning, 1965-66; mem. Ind. Com. on Nursing, Indpls., 1965-66, Central Ind. Regional Mental Health Planning Com., 1968; chmn. Manpower Conf. on Mental Health, Washington, 1969; del. Ind. Republican Conv., 1951; vice chmn. Shelbyville Rep. Com., 1951; sec. Ind. Com. for Rockefeller, 1969-70; pres. Indpls. Smith Coll. Club, 1969-70; participant Nat. Health Forum of Nat. Health Council, N.Y.C., 1971; mem. adv. bd. Isaac Ray Ctr. Rush Presbyn. St. Luke Medical Ctr., 1978-91; mem. gov.'s Task Force on the Future Mental Health in Ill., 1986-87; mem. commn. to revise the mental health code of Ill., 1988; pres. Mental Health Assn. Ill., Springfield, 1975; mem. Gov.'s Commn. for Revision of Mental Health Code Ill., 1975-76; v.p. for N.Am., World Fedn. for Mental Health, 1977-87; bd. dirs. Vis. Nurse Assn. Evanston (Ill.), 1975-87, v.p. 1981-84, pres., 1984-86; community mental health adviser Jr. League of Chgo., 1979-83; mem. Ill. Guardianship and Advocacy Commn., 1978-86, chmn., 1981; gov. Task Force on Future of Mental Health in Ill., 1986-87; mem. gov. commn. to revise mental health code; mem. home health adv. com. to Dept. Pub. Health, State of Ill., 1982-87; adv. com. Ill. Mental Health Svcs. System, 1992-93; pres. Mental Health Assn. Greater Chgo., 1983-84, mem. pub. policy com., 1987-92; pres. Smith Coll. Alumni of Chgo., 1984-86 (alumni award medal) ; mem. Women's Bd. Northwestern U., Aux. of Evanston and Glenbrook Hosps., University Guild of Evanston, Jr. League Evanston, pres. Ind. Lawyers' Wives, Indpls., 1959-60; treas. Nat. Lawyers' Wives, 1961-62; mem. commn. to rev. and revise Ill. Mental Health Code, 1987-90. Recipient Outstanding Citizen award Shelby County C. of C., 1959-60, Outstanding Vol. of Yr. award Indpls. Jr. League, 1962, Leadership award Mental Health Assn. Ind., 1971, Arts and Humanities award, Shelbyville Rotary Club, 1981, alumnae medal Smith Coll., 1993; named One of Ten Most Newsworthy Women In Ind., Indpls. News, 1962, Disting. Leader in Vol. Mental Health Movement, Ill. Ho. of Reps., 1976, Miss. Col., 1976, Ala. Lt. Gov., 1980. Presbyterian. Clubs: Fortnightly (Chgo.); Garden of Evanston, Jr. League of Evanston. Died Feb. 6, 1996.

PELLATT, NANCY E., artist; b. Paterson, N.J., Nov. 2, 1942; d. Albert Joseph and Ruth Lydia (Schalk) Senegeto; m. Francis Peter Pellatt, May 16; children: Suzanne Elizabeth, Brian Anthony. instr. Art at the Park, Ky. Horse Park, 1993-95. Exhbns. include Am. Acad. of Equine Art Ann. Juried Exhibits, 1992-93, Catherine Lorillard Wolfe Art Club, Audubon Artists Ann. Juried Exhibits at Nat. Arts Clu in N.Y.C. and numerous sporting art shows; exhibited Mus. Hounds & Hunting Morven Park, Leesburg, Va.; artwork has appeared on the cover of The Chronicle of the Horse and American Trakehener Mag., as well as in limited-edit. print series. Donations to orgns. include Canine Companions for Independence, Foothills Humane Soc., Okla. Thoroughbred Assn., Tyron Hounds (N.C.). Mem. So. Watercolor Soc., Knickerbocker Artists, Nat. Mus. of Women in the Arts.

PELLECCHIA, EVE WASSALL, management consultant; b. Columbus, Ohio, Dec. 7, 1956; d. Robert Byron Wassall and Constance Leona (Windey) Moult; m. Dennis John Pellecchia, Oct. 29, 1983; children: Kevin Patrick, Kara René. BS, Lebanon Valley Coll., 1978; MBA, Lehigh U., 1983. CFP. Ops. rsch. analyst Air Products & Chems., Inc., Trexlertown, Pa., 1978-83; ops. rsch. mng. analyst Air Products & Chems., Inc., Trexlertown, 1984-87, ops. rsch. mgr. gas. div., 1987-88; pvt. practice Wyomissing, Pa., 1990—. Mem. Reading Hosp. Aux., Wyomissing, 1987—; fundraiser Am. Heart Assn., 1991—. Home: 102 Robert Rd Wyomissing PA 19610-3116

PELLER, MARCI TERRY, real estate executive; b. Upland, Pa., Nov. 5, 1949; d. Max Maclyn and Lucille Eugenia (Zucker) P. AA, Harcum Jr. Coll., Bryn Mawr, Pa., 1971; student, Villanova U., 1971-73. With sales dept. William H. Cartwright Real Estate, North Palm Beach, Fla., 1985-91; realtor-assoc. Fin. Realty Group, Lake Park, Fla., 1991—; owner, operator Atlas Bookkeeping Svcs., 1996—. Republican. Jewish. Office: Fin Realty Group 9498 Alternate A1A Lake Park FL 33403-1439

PELLETIER, MARSHA LYNN, state legislator, secondary school educator; b. Mt. Pleasant, Mich., July 29, 1950; d. Eugene Russell and Mary Ellen (Edde) Mingle; m. Arthur Joseph Pelletier, May 19, 1973; 1 child, John Frederick. BS in Home Econs. and Edn., Kans. State U., 1971, MS in Edn. Guidance and Counseling, 1972. Lic. rela estate broker, N.H. Conf. coord., guidance counselor Kans. State U., Manhattan, 1971-73; tchr. home econs. Franklin (Mass.) H.S., 1974, Exeter (N.H.) H.S., 1974-75, Barrington (N.H.) Mid. Sch., 1975-81, Pentucket Regional Jr. H.S., West Newbury, Mass., 1981-82; realtor assoc. Century 21 Ocean and Norword Realty, Portsmouth, N.H., 1983-86; tchr. interior design, cons. U. N.H., Durham, 1986-87; tchr. home econs. Dover Jr. H.S., 1983—; rep. Dist. 12 Dover N.H. Ho. of Reps., Concord, 1992-94; ind. real estate broker Dover, 1986—. Bd. dirs. Dover Adult Learning Ctr., 1995—; mem. Health Task Force, Dover and Concord, 1993-94; trustee St. John's Meth. Ch., 1995—; mem. Dover Friends of the Pub. Libr., 1996—. Mem. NEA (local pres. negotiator, membership chair, leadership exec. com., rep. 1979—), Nat. Coalition for Consumer Edn., Alpha Delta Kappa. (v.p. historian altruistic chmn. 1984-89). Democrat. Home: 94 Back River Rd Dover NH 03820-4411

PELLMAN, AMY MIRIAM, lawyer, mediator; b. N.Y.C., Oct. 27, 1960; d. Carl Meyers and Renee Grace (Greenberg) P. BA, Mount Holyoke Coll., 1982; JD, City U. N.Y., 1987. Bar: N.Y. 1988, Calif. 1992. Rep. Manhattan, ombudsman N.Y. State Gov.'s Office, N.Y.C., 1987-88; prose law clk. U.S. Ct. Appeals (2nd cir.), N.Y.C., 1989-90; assoc. Law Office Mark Scherzer, N.Y.C., 1990-92, Hedges & Caldwell, L.A., 1992-93; pvt. practice L.A., 1993; sr. atty. dependency ct. legal svcs. Law Office of Jo Kaplan, L.A., 1993—; bd. dirs. Ashay Comms., L.A.; mediator Dispute Resolution Svcs., L.A., 1992—; mediator, founder Cmty. Mediation Svc. N.Y., 1989-92; guest lectr. juvenile dependency sys., 1993—. Author: (manual) The ABC's of Dependency Laws; contbr. chpt. to book. Democrat. Jewish. Office: DCLS Law Office Joe Kaplan 201 Centre Plaza Dr Monterey Park CA 91754

PELOSI, NANCY, congresswoman; b. Balt., Mar. 26, 1941; d. Thomas J. D'Alesandro Jr.; m. Paul Pelosi; children: Nancy Corinne, Christine, Jacqueline, Paul, Alexandra. Grad., Trinity Coll. Former chmn. Calif. State Dem. Com., 1981; committeewoman Dem. Nat. Com., 1976, 80, 84; fin. chmn. Dem. Senatorial Campaign Com., 1987; mem. 99th-102d Congresses from 5th Calif. dist., 1987-1992, 103rd Congress from 8th Calif. dist., 1993—; mem. appropriations com., subcoms. labor, HHD & edn., fgn. ops., D.C.; intelligence (select) com., standard official conduct com. Office: US House of Rep 2457 Rayburn Washington DC 20515-0508*

PELPHREY, RUTH JANE, music educator; b. Paterson, N.J., Mar. 6, 1953; d. Peter and Jane (Brockhuizen) Everett; m. Philip Grandison Pelphrey, Aug. 2, 1975; 1 child, Christina Joy. BA summa cum laude, Montclair State U., 1975. Cert. vocal and instrumental music edn. K-12, N.J. Program dir. Camp Cherith, Corinth, N.Y., 1971-77; music tchr. Flemington (N.J.) Raritan Middle Sch., 1975-77; supr., tutor Faith Christian Sch., Locktown, N.J., 1977-78; head tchr. Good Shepherd Nursery Sch., Warwick, N.Y., 1979-80; music tchr. Birches Elem. Sch., Turnersville, N.J., 1990—; pvt. piano instr., Turnersville, 1980—; accompanist various local chs., Turnersville, 1980—; pianist, organist St. John's United Meth. Ch., Turnersville, 1988—. Trainer youth choir performing with Phila. Orch., 1995. Mem. N.J. Edn. Assn., Christian Missionary Tech. Svcs. (sec. 1984-93), PTO. Home: 502 Wayne Ave Pitman NJ 08071-1726 Office: Birches Elem Sch Westminster Blvd Turnersville NJ 08012

PELTZ, COLLEEN JUNE, educational administrator, educator; b. Fort Dodge, Iowa, May 15, 1951; d. Walter Delbert and Ellen Jane (Elsberry) Morgan; m. Randy Joel Peltz, June 4, 1972; children: Matthew, Emily. BS in Edn., U. Iowa, Iowa City, 1973; MA in Edn., U. No. Iowa, Cedar Falls, 1993. Elem. tchr. Wilton (Iowa) Cmty. Sch., 1973-74, Fort Dodge Cmty. Schs., 1974-79; learning ctr. instr., coord. Iowa Lakes Cmty. Coll., Emmetsburg, Iowa, 1986—; chair devel. studies adv. bd. Iowa Lakes C.C., Emmetsburg, 1995-96; leader Inst. for a New Century Iowa State U., Ames, 1995-96. choir mem. 1st Presbyn. Ch., Ringsted, Iowa, 1981-86, session mem., Estherville, Iowa, 1986-89, choir mem. 1986—; leader 4-H Emmet County, Ringsted, Iowa, 1991-95. Mem. AAUW, Nat. Devel. Edn. Assn, Iowa Devel. Edn. Assn. (bd. dirs. 1993-94, pres.-elect 1994-95, pres. 1995-96). Home: 5191 260th St Ringsted IA 50578 Office: Iowa Lakes CC 3200 College Dr Emmetsburg IA 50536

PELTZ, PAULETTE BEATRICE, corporate lawyer; b. Bklyn., May 30, 1954; d. Joseph and Margaret P. BA, SUNY, Binghamton, 1976; JD, Am. U., 1979. Bar: D.C. 1980, Va. 1982, Md. 1986. Atty. U.S. EPA, Washington, 1979-83; assoc. Mahn, Franklin & Goldenberg, Washington, 1983-85, Deso, Greenberg & Thomas, P.C., Washington, 1985-87; corp. gen. counsel Western Devel. Corp., Washington, 1987-91; v.p. and corp. gen. counsel

Mills Corp., 1992-94; sr. v.p., gen. counsel Charter Oak Ptnrs., 1994—. Home: 11012 Beach Mill Rd Great Falls VA 22066-3026 Office: Charter Oak Ptnrs 8000 Towers Crescent Dr Ste 950 Vienna VA 22182

PELUSE, CATHERINE GINA, artist; b. Nova Iguassu, Rio de Janeiro, Nov. 14, 1923; d. Pasquale and Maria Luisa (Battistoni) Lazzari; m. Giuseppe Bertolozzi, July 23, 1949 (dec. Mar. 1970); children: Maria Luisa Blume, Joseph; m. Vincent Peluse, Nov. 7, 1971. Student, Colegio Santo Antonio, Nova Iguassu, Rio de Janeiro. Chairperson "Angolo Artistico" Noi Italiani d'Oggi, Poughkeepsie, N.Y., 1992—; art coord. 500th Christopher Columbus Italian Ctr., 1991-92. Contbr. articles to profl. jours; exhibited in permanent collection at Mt. St. Mary's Coll., Newburgh, N.Y. Past pres. Victory Lodge, Poughkeepsie, 1980, Italian-Am. Cultural Found., 1985; mem. program com. Cuneen-Hacket Cultural Ctr., Poughkeepsie, 1992-96; active Italian Ctr., Ladies Aux., Poughkeepsie, 1996. Named Editor's Choice, Nat. Libr. of Poetry, 1994; recipient Merit award Internat. Soc. Poets, 1995. Mem. Allied Artists of Am., Kent Art Assn. (selection juror 1994), Catskill Art Assn., Dutchess County Art Coun., Dutchess County Art Assn. (panelist 1991-92). Roman Catholic. Home: 11 Balding Ave Poughkeepsie NY 12601

PENA, AMALIA GISELA, lawyer; b. Santo Domingo, Dominican Republic, May 12, 1954. BA, SUNY, Stony Brook, 1977; JD, U. Mich., 1985. Bar: N.Y. 1988, U.S. Dist. Ct. (so. dist.) N.Y. 1988. Ptnr. Anderson Kill Olick & Oshinsky, P.C., N.Y.C. Contbr. articles to profl. jours. Office: Anderson Kill Olick & Oshinsky PC 1251 Ave of the Americas New York NY 10020-1182*

PENA, ELIZABETH, actress; b. Elizabeth, N.J., Sept. 23, 1961; d. Mario Peña and Marguarita Toirac. Grad., Sch. of the Performing Arts; studies with Curt Dempster, Endre Hules. Actress: (stage prodns.) Dog Lady, 1984, Becoming Garcia, 1984, Bring on the Night, Shattered Image, La Morena, Romeo and Juliet, Night of the Assassins, Act One and Only, Italian-American Reconciliation, Cinderella, (feature films) El Super, 1979, Times Square, 1980, They All Laughed, 1981, Crossover Dreams, 1984, Down and Out in Beverly Hills, 1985, La Bamba, 1986, Batteries not Included, 1987, Vibes, 1988, Blue Steel, 1989, Jacob's Ladder, 1990, The Waterdance, 1991, Lone Star, 1996, It Came from Outer Space II, 1996; (TV episodes) Saturday Night Live, Feeling Good, As the World Turns, Hillstreet Blues, Cagney and Lacey; regular (TV series) I Married Dora, 1987—, Shannon's Deal, Tough Cookies. Mem. Actors' Equity Assn., Screen Actors Guild, AFTRA. Office: Paradigm care Joel Rudnick 10100 Santa Monica Blvd Fl 25 Los Angeles CA 90067*

PENA, MARIA GEGES, academic services administrator; b. Torrance, Calif., Nov. 27, 1964; d. Nicholas John and Dina Connie (Vengel) Geges; m. Vicente Gregorio Pena, June 22, 1991. AA, El Camino Coll., 1985; BA, U. Calif., San Diego, 1987; MS, San Diego State U., 1989; postgrad., Claremont Grad. Sch., 1990—, Western State U., 1995—. Peer counselor El Camino Coll., Torrance, Calif., 1982-85; peer advisor U. Calif., San Diego, 1985-87, vice chancellor student affirmative action rsch. intern, 1986-87, outreach asst. disabled student svcs., 1986-89; coord. student svcs. Mira Costa Coll., Oceanside, Calif., 1989—. Contbr. articles to profl. jours. Mem. Calif. Assn. Postsecondary Educators of Disabled. Democrat. Greek Orthodox. Office: Mira Costa Coll 1 Barnard Dr Oceanside CA 92056

PENALOZA, BETTY RAQUEL, international affairs consultant; b. Lima, Peru, Oct. 4, 1947; came to U.S., 1970; d. Hernan and America (Ortiz) P.; m. Ray D. Roy Sr., Mar. 23, 1974 (div. Feb. 1989). BBA, U. St. Thomas, 1992, postgrad., 1993-94. Adminstrv. asst. Petroperu, Lima, 1968-70; adminstrv. asst. Petroperu, Houston, 1970-74, buyer, 1974-88; petroleum attache Consulate of Peru, Houston, 1974-87; buyer Serpimpex, S.A., Houston, 1991-93; owner Am. Victoria Trading Co., Houston, 1994—. Vice-chair Loop Program, End Hunger Network, 1993; vol. Mayor's Office, NAFTA Liaison, 1993. Named First Woman Elected Sec. of the Consular Corps, Consular Corps Houston, 1987. Mem. Consular Corps (hon. life).

PENCE, MARJORIE LOUISE, retired secondary education educator; b. Milw., Dec. 6, 1939; d. Robert and Marguerite (Parnkopf) Raisch. BS, Wis. State Coll., 1962. Cert. secondary tchr. Spanish, English, acad. speech, libr. English tchr. Flathead County H.S., Kalispell, Mont., 1962-64; English tchr., libr. Cody (Wyo.) H.S., 1964-66; English and Spanish tchr., libr. White Lake (Wis.) Sch., 1968-96. 4-H leader Northwoods High Riders, Crandon, Wis., 1991.

PENCEK, CAROLYN CARLSON, treasurer, educator; b. Appleton, Wis., June 13, 1946; d. Arthur Edward and Mary George (Notaras) Carlson; m. Richard David Pencek, July 10, 1971; children: Richard Carlson, Mallory Barbara Rowlinds. BA in Polit. Sci., Western Coll., 1968; Ma in Polit. Sci., Syracuse U., 1975; postgrad., Temple U., 1991—. Investment analysts asst. Bankers Trust Co., N.Y.C., 1969-71; substitute tchr. Lackawanna Trail Sch. Dist., Factoryville, Pa., 1971-81; instr. polit. sci. Keystone Coll., La Plume, Pa., 1972-73; USGS coding supr. Richard Walsh Assocs., Scranton, Pa., 1975-76; instr. polit. sci. Pa. State U., Dunmore, 1976-77; treas. Creative Planning Ltd., Dunmore, 1988—; bd. trustees Lourdesmont Sch., Clarks Summit, Pa., 1989—. Bd. dirs. Lackawanna County Child and Youth Svcs., Scranton, 1981—, pres., 1988-90; founding mem., sec. Leadership Lackawanna, 1982-84; bd. dirs. N.E. Pa. Regional Tissue and Transplant Bank, Scranton, 1984-88, Vol. Action Ctr., Scranton, 1986-91; founding mem. Women's Resource Ctr. Assn., Scranton, 1986—, pres., 1986-87; v.p. sch. improvement coun. Lackawanna Trail Sch. Dist., 1995-96. Named Vol. of Yr. nominee, Vol. Action Ctr., 1985; Temple U. fellow, Phila., 1991-92. Mem. AAUW (sec. 1973-75, state sel. com. 1979-81), Assn. Jr. Leagues Internat. (area II coun. mem. 1978-79), Jr. League Scranton (v.p. 1980, pres. 1981-83, Margaret L. Richards award 1984), Philharmonic League (v.p. 1976, pres. 1977). Episcopalian. Home: RR 2 Box 2489 Factoryville PA 18419-9649 Office: Creative Planning Ltd 1100 Dunham Dr Dunmore PA 18512-2653

PENDELL, SUE DAVIS, speech communication educator; b. Baton Rouge, Dec. 16, 1946; d. Frank B. and Elizabeth (Young) Davis. BS, Fla. State U., 1966; MA, Auburn U., 1970; PhD, U. Utah, 1976. Instr. speech U. Wis., La Crosse, 1971-73; asst. prof. speech communication, dir. speech extension U. Mo., Columbia, 1976-79; asst. then assoc. prof. speech communication Colo. State U., Ft. Collins, 1979—; faculty rep. Colo. Bd. Agr., 1988-90; vice chair faculty coun., 1992-94, chair faculty coun., 1994-96. Author: (with others) Speech Coursebook, 1986; contbr. articles to profl. jours. Cons. Ft. Collins Area United Way, 1986-88, bd. dirs., 1988-94. Mem. Internat. Communication Assn., Speech Communication Assn., Western States Communication Assn., Phi Kappa Phi. Office: Colo State U Dept Speech Comm 209 Eddy Fort Collins CO 80523

PENDERGAST, PAULA BROWN, personnel consultant; b. Cin., Nov. 17, 1943; d. Everett Raymond and Gayle (Hosutt) Brown; m. Michael Stewart Colvin, July 1962 (div. Aug. 1972); children: Kimberly Elaine, Barbara Gayle; m. Joseph Barry Pendergast, Apr. 1975; 1 child, Patrick Alexander. AS, SUNY, Hartsdale, 1990. Office adminstr. Eastman Kodak, Washington, 1961-63; pers. cons. Weatherby Assocs., Stamford, Conn., 1972-76; pres. Human Resources, Inc., Stamford, 1980—; mem. adv. bd. Amity Bancorp; bd. dirs. Conn. Community Cares, Inc., Norwalk. Mem. Nat. Assn. Temp. Svcs. (pres. Conn. chpt. 1990-91, Nat. Assn. Pers. Women (v.p. Conn. chpt. publs. 1986-87), Nat. Assn. Pers. Cons. Republican. Congregationalist. Office: Human Resources Inc 2505 Main St Stratford CT 06497

PENDLETON, GAIL RUTH, newspaper editor, writer; b. Franklin, N.J., May 8, 1937; d. Waldo A. and Ruby (Bonnett) Rousset; m. John E. Tyler, Mar. 10, 1956 (div. 1978); children: Gwenneth, Victoria, Christine; m. Jeffrey P. Pendleton, Oct. 1, 1978 (dec. 1992). BA, Montclair (N.J.) State Coll., 1959; M in Div., Princeton (N.J.) Theol. Sem., 1973. Ordained minister Presbyn. Ch., 1974. Tchr. Epiphany Day Sch., Kaimuki, Oahu, Hawaii, 1956-58; editor Women's Sect. Daily Record, Morristown, N.J., 1959-62, reporter, 1963-65; tchr. Hardystown Twp. Sch., Franklin, 1968-69; asst. pastor First Presbyn. Ch., Sparta, N.J., 1973-74; reporter N.J. Herald, Newton, 1976-78, editor lifestyle sect., 1978-93, editor Friday entertainment sect., 1993-95, editor spl. sect., 1995—; pres. Crystal Palace Networking Inc., Newton, N.J., 1995—. Recipient Ruth Cheney Streeter award Planned Parenthood N.W. N.J., 1985. Mem. N.J. Press Assn. (family sect. layout award 1985, 87, 88, 89, 91, 2nd feature columns award 1986). Office: NJ Herald 2 Spring St Newton NJ 07860-2077

PENDLETON, JOAN MARIE, microprocessor designer; b. Cleve., July 7, 1954; d. Alvin Dial and Alta Beatrice (Brown) P. BS in Physics, Elec. Engring., MIT, 1976; MSEE, Stanford U., 1978; PhDEE, U. Calif., Berkeley, 1985. Sr. design engr. Fairchild Semiconductor, Palo Alto, Calif., 1978-82; staff engr. Sun Microsystems, Mountain View, Calif., 1986-87; CEO Harvest VLSI Design Ctr. Inc., Palo Alto, 1988—; dir. engring. Silicon Engring. Inc., Scotts Valley, Calif., 1994-95; cons., designer computer sci. dept. U. Calif., Berkeley, 1988-90. Contbr. articles to profl. jours.; inventor, patnetee serpentine charge transfer device. Recipient several 1st, 2d and 3d place awards U.S. Rowing Assn., Fairchild Tech. Achievement award, 1982, 1st place A award Fed. Internat. Soc Aviron, 1991. Mem. IEEE, Assn. for Computing Machinery, Lake Merritt Rowing Club, Stanford Rowing Club, U.S. Rowing Assn. Home: 1950 Montecito Ave Apt 22 Mountain View CA 94043-4334

PENDLETON, MARY CATHERINE, foreign service officer; b. Louisville, Ky., June 15, 1940; d. Joseph S. and Katherine R. (Toebbe) P. BA, Spalding Coll., 1962; MA, Ind. U., 1969; cert., Nat. Def. U., 1990; D (hon.), U. N. Testemitanu, Moldova, 1994. Cert. secondary tchr., Ky. Tchr. Presentation Acad., Louisville, 1962-66; vol. Peace Corps, Tunis, Tunisia, 1966-68; employment counselor Ky. Dept. for Human Resources, Louisville, 1969-75; gen. svcs. Am. Embassy, Khartoum, Sudan, 1975-77; counsular officer Am. Embassy, Manila, Philippines, 1978-79; adminstrv. officer Am. Embassy, Bangui, Cen. African Republic, 1979-82, Lusaka, Zambia, 1982-84; post mgmt. officer Dept. of State Bur. European and Can. Affairs, Washington, 1984-87; adminstrv. counselor Am. Embassy, Bucharest, Romania, 1987-89; dir. adminstrv. tng. divsn. Fgn. Svc. Inst., Arlington, Va., 1990-92; ambassador Am. Embassy, Chisinau, Moldova, 1992-95; adminstrv. counselor Am. Embassy, Brussels, 1995—. Bd. dirs. Am. Sch. of Bucharest, 1987-89. Named to Honorable Order of Ky. Cols., 1988. Democrat. Roman Catholic. Home and Office: Emb USA, Blvd du Regent 27, B-1000 Brussels Belgium

PENEPENT, DINA L., finance company executive; b. Batavia, N.Y., July 27, 1961. BBA in Acctg., St. Bonaventure U., 1983. CPA. Mgr. audit divsn. BDO Seidman, N.Y.C., 1983-92; CFO, exec. v.p., sec. The Aegis Consumer Funding Group, Inc., Jersey City, 1992—. Mem. AICPA, N.Y. State Soc. CPA's. Office: Aegis Consumer Funding Grp 525 Washington Blvd Jersey City NJ 07310

PENFIELD, CAROLE H. (KATE PENFIELD), minister, church official. Grad., Andover Newton Theol. Sch. Co-pastor Ctrl. Bapt. Ch., Providence, 1st Bapt. Ch. Am., Providence; exec. dir. Ministers Coun. of ABC USA; mem. regional and nat. mins. coun. and senate Am. Bapt. Chs., v.p., 1994—; mem. state Senate ethics com. R.I. Legislature; pres. R.I. State Coun. Chs., 1987-89. Editor Ministry, Am. Bapt. Chs. Office: ABC in the USA PO Box 851 Valley Forge PA 19482-0851

PENN, BARBARA A(NNE), artist, educator; b. Pitts., Jan. 10, 1952; d. John Newton III and Jean (Schlafer) P. BS in Art Edn., SUNY, New Paltz, 1973; BFA in Painting, San Francisco Art Inst., 1983; postgrad., Showhegan Sch. Painting, Maine, 1985; MFA in Painting, U. Calif., Berkeley, 1986. K-12 tchr. art Delaware Acad. and Ctrl. Sch., N.Y., 1974-77; mem. installation crew San Francisco Mus. Modern Art, 1987-89; instr. extended univ. studio program U. Calif., Berkeley, 1988; instr. San Francisco Art Inst., 1989; vis. resident artist, lectr. Middlebury (Vt.) Coll., 1990-91; asst. prof. painting and drawing U. Ariz., Tucson, 1991—, coord. 2D Founds., 1991-95; dean students Showkegan Sch. Painting and Sculpture, summers 1987, 89; juror Ctrl. Arts Collective, Tucson, 1995, Coop. Gallery, 1995; lectr. Tucson Mus. Art, 1994; conf. planner, panelist, lectr. Women and Creative Process, Tucson, 1994; artist resident Millay Colony for Arts, Inc., Austerlitz, N.Y., 1990, Yaddo, Saratoga Springs, N.Y., 1990. One-womn shows Gallery Paule Anglim, San Francisco, 1990-91, Galerie Nalepa, Berlin, 1991, Univ. Art Mus., Tucson, 1995, Artemisia Gallery, Chgo., 1996; exhibited in group show Galerie im Haus am Lutzowplatz, Berlin, 1992; represented in permanent collections Art Source, San Francisco, Merrill Lynch, Mary Zlot and Assocs., San Francisco, numerous pvt. collections. Recipient juror's award Galeria Mesa, Mesa Ctr. for Arts, 1995; Seymour H. Knox scholar Showhegan Sch. Painting and Sculpture, 1985; Regent's fellow U. Calif., 1985-86; rsch. grantee U. Ariz., 1995, 96. Mem. Coll. Art Assn., Emily Dickinson Internat. Soc.

PENN, DAWN TAMARA, entrepreneur; b. Knoxville, Tenn., July 22, 1965; d. Morton Hugh and Virginia Audra (Wilson) P. AS, Bauder Fashion Coll., Atlanta, 1984; postgrad., U. Tenn., 1986; grad., Rasnic Sch. Modeling, Knoxville, 1986. Gen. mgr. Merry-Go-Round, Knoxville, 1984-86; mgr., dancer Lady Adonis Inc. Performing Arts Dance Co., Knoxville, 1987-90; owner, pres. Lady Adonis, Inc. Performing Arts Dance Co., Knoxville, 1990—, also chmn.; owner/pres. Penn Mgmt. and Investment Co. Comml. Real Estate, Knoxville, 1989—; deputized bonded rep. Knox County Sheriff's Dept., Knoxville, 1989-90; fgn. dance tours include Aruba, Curacao, Caracas, Barbados, Ont., Que., Montreal, Nfld., Labrador, N.S., New Brunswick; cons. The John Reinhardt Agy., Winston-Salem, N.C., 1987—, Gen. Talent Agy., Monroeville, Pa., 1990—, Xanadu, Inc., Myrtle Beach, S.C., 1991—. Author, editor: Lady Adonis Performing Arts promotional mag., 1988; TV and motion picture credits include: Innocent Blood, 1992, The Phil Donahue Show, N.Y.C., 1989, 91. Coord. bridal fair Big. Bros./Big Sisters Knox County, Knoxville, 1985, 86; judge Southeastern Entertainer of Yr. Pageant, Knoxville, 1992—, Miss Knoxville U.S.A. Pageant, Knoxville, 1990—; active Knoxville Conv. and Visitors Bur., 1993-94. Recipient 1st Pl. award for swimsuit TV comml. and runway modeling Internat. Model's Hall of Fame, 1986, 1st Pl. award for media presentation Modeling Assn. Am. Internat., 1986; nominee The Pres.'s Commn. on White House Fellowships, U.S. Office Pers. Mgmt., 1994-95. Mem. Internat. Platform Assn., Profl. Assn. Diving Instrs. (cert.). Methodist. Home: 5109 Ridgemont Dr Knoxville TN 37918-4539 Office: Lady Adonis Inc/Penn Mgmt Ste 4 7320 Old Clinton Hwy Knoxville TN 37921-1064

PENN, LYNN SHARON, materials scientist; b. Iowa City, June 18, 1945; d. Robert Joseph and Dorothy Evelyn (Etsinger) Johnson; m. Arthur Leon Penn, June 24, 1968; 1 child, Ethan. AB, U. Pa., 1966; MA, Bryn Mawr Coll., 1970, PhD, 1974. Chemist Lawrence Livermore Nat. Lab., Livermore, Calif., 1974-78; sr. scientist Textile Rsch. Inst., Princeton, N.J., 1978-80, Ciba-Geigy Corp., Ardsley, N.Y., 1980-83; prin. scientist Midwest Rsch. Inst., Kansas City, Mo., 1983-86; rsch. prof. Polytechnic U., Bklyn., 1987-91; prof. U. Ky., Lexington, 1991—; chair Gordon Rsch. Conf. on Sci. of Adhesion, 1992. N.Am. editor Internat. Jour. Adhesion and Adhesives; contbr. articles to profl. jours. Mem. ASTM, Am. Chem. Soc., Soc. Adv. Materials and Process Engring., Fiber Soc., Adhesion Soc. (sec. 1982-90), Kappa Kappa Gamma. Jewish. Home: 96 Washington Spring Rd Palisades NY 10964

PENNEY, BETH, English educator, editor, writer; b. Carmel, Calif., Feb. 7, 1955; d. William Carroll Penney and Raylyn Thyrza (Crabbe) Moore. BA in Journalism and English, Calif. State U., Fresno, 1978, MA in English Lit., 1985. Mng. editor Paul Kagan Assoc., Inc., Carmel, Calif., 1980-89; tech. writer Computer Svcs. Corp., Monterey, Calif., 1989-90; English instr. Monterey (Calif.) Peninsula Coll., 1990—; publs. mgr. Data Rsch. Assoc., Inc., Monterey, 1990—; feature writer, reviewer Carmel Pine Cone/Monterey Times, 1994—. Newsletter editor Monterey Peninsula Dickens Fellowship, Pacific Grove, Calif., 1991—, Unitarian Universalist Ch. of the Monterey Peninsula, 1990—, The Dickens Project, U. Calif., Santa Cruz, 1995—; reviewer, editor Gothic Jour. mag., Hugo, Minn., 1994—. Pres. Pacific Grove (Calif.) Feast of Lanterns, 1995—, Friends of the Dickens Project, 1995—; founder, hon. sec. Monterey Peninsula Dickens Fellowship, 1991—. Recipient hon. mention award for short fiction Byline Mag, 1995. Mem. Romance Writers Am., Freelance Editl. Assn., Pacific Grove C. of C. (newsletter editor 1995—). Democrat. Home: PO Box 604 Pacific Grove CA 93950

PENNEY, SHERRY HOOD, university president, educator; b. Marlette, Mich., Sept. 4, 1937; d. Terrance and B. Jean (Stoutenburg) Hood; m. Carl Murray Penney, July 8, 1961 (div. 1978); children: Michael Murray, Jeffrey Hood; m. James Duane Livingston, Mar. 30, 1985. BA, Albion Coll., 1959, LLD (hon.), 1989; MA, U. Mich., 1961; PhD, SUNY, Albany, 1972. Vis. asst. prof. Union Coll., Schenectady, N.Y., 1972-73; assoc. higher edn. N.Y. State Edn. Dept., Albany, 1973-76; assoc. provost Yale U., New Haven, Conn., 1976-82; vice chancellor acad. programs, policy and planning SUNY System, Albany, 1982-88; acting pres. SUNY, Plattsburgh, 1986-87; chancellor U. Mass., Boston, 1988-95, pres., 1995, chancellor, 1996—; chmn., bd. dirs. Nat. Higher Edn. Mgmt. Sys., Boulder, Colo., 1985-87; mem. commn. on higher edn. New Eng. Assn. Schs. and Colls., Boston, 1979-82, Mid. States Assn. Schs. and Colls., Phila., 1986-88; mem. commn. on women Am. Coun. Edn., Washington, 1979-81, commn. on govt. rels., 1990-94; bd. dirs. Boston Edison Co., Am. Coun. on Edn., Carnegie Found. for Advancement of Teaching, The Boston Pvt. Industry Coun. Author: Patrician in Politics, 1974; editor: Women in Management in Higher Education, 1975; cons. editor Change mag. and Jour. Higher Edn. Mgmt.; contbr. articles to profl. jours. Mem. Internat. Trade Task Force, 1994—; mem. exec. com., Challenge to Leadership, 1988, chair, 1996; mem. Mid-Am. adv. bd. HERS, 1992—; trustee Berkeley Div. Sch., Yale U., 1978-82, John F. Kennedy Libr. Found.; bd. dirs. Albany Symphony Orch., 1982-88, U. Mass. Found., 1988—, Mcpl. Rsch. Bur., Boston, 1990—, New Eng. Coun., New Eng. Aquarium, Boston Plan for Excellence, Boston Pvt. Industry Coun., Greater Boston One to One Leadership Coun., Hers Mid Atlantic Adv. Bd., NASULGC Commn. Urban Affairs, The Ednl. Resource Inst., 1994, The Environ. Bus. Coun., 1991—; corp. mem. United Way, 1990—. Recipient Disting. Alumna award Albion Coll., 1978, Disting. Citizen award for racial harmony Black/White Boston, 1994, ACE/NIP Mass. Leadership award, 1995, New Eng. Women's Leadership award, 1996. Mem. Am. Coun. Edn. (bd. dirs.), Am. Assn. Higher Edn., Orgn. Am. Historians, Internat. Assn. Univ. Pres., Nat. Assn. State Univs. and Land Grant Colls., Greater Boston C. of C. (bd. dirs.), Yale Club (N.Y.C.) St. Botolph Club, Comml. Club (Boston). Unitarian. Office: U Mass Boston 100 Morrisey Blvd Boston MA 02125

PENNING, PATRICIA JEAN, elementary education educator; b. Springfield, Ill., Sept. 3, 1952; d. Howard Louis and Jean Lenore (Hartley) P. AA, Lincoln Land C.C., Springfield, 1972; BA, Millikin U., 1975. Cert. tchr. grades K-9. Receptionist Drs. Penning, Marty & Teich, Springfield, 1968-72; child care asst. La Petite Acad., Springfield, 1970-72; tchr. St. Agnes Sch., Springfield, 1975—; mail clk. St. John's Hosp., Springfield, 1977-88; mem. dir. instrnl. tv St. Agnes Sch., Springfield, 1981—, sec. primary level, 1993—, mem. reading com., 1994—, mem. social com., 1994—. Mem. St. Agnes Folk Choir, Springfield, 1976—; cantor, St. Agnes Ch., Springfield, 1976—. Recipient Outstanding Tchr. award Office Cath. Edn., Springfield, 1988, Golden Apple award Ch. 20 and Town and Country Bank, Springfield, 1993; named Apprentice Cathechist, Diocese of Springfield, Ill., 1992. Mem. Internat. Reading Assn., Nat. Coun. Math., Nat. Cath. Edn. Assn. (Grad. award 1991), Ill. State Assn. Curriculum and Devel. Roman Catholic. Home: 22 Westminster Rd Chatham IL 62629-1254 Office: St Agnes Sch 251 N Amos Ave Springfield IL 62702-4796

PENNINGER, FRIEDA ELAINE, retired English language educator; b. Marion, N.C., Apr. 11, 1927; d. Fred Hoyle and Lena Frances (Young) P. AB, U. N.C., Greensboro, 1948; MA, Duke U., 1950, PhD, 1961. Copywriter Sta. WSJS, Winston-Salem, N.C., 1948-49; asst. prof. English Flora Macdonald Coll., Red Springs, N.C., 1950-51; tchr. English Barnwell, S.C., 1951-52, Brunswick, Ga., 1952-53; instr. English U. Tenn., Knoxville, 1953-56; instr., asst. prof. Woman's Coll., U. N.C., Greensboro, 1956-58, 60-63; asst. prof., assoc. prof. U. Richmond (Va.), 1963-71; chair., dept. English Westhampton Coll., Richmond, 1971-78; prof. English U. Richmond, 1971-91, Bostwick prof. English, 1987-91; ret., 1991. Author: William Caxton, 1979, Chaucer's "Troilus and Criseyde" and "The Knight's Tale": Fictions Used, 1993, (novel) Look at Them, 1990; compiler, editor: English Drama to 1660, 1976; editor: Festschrift for Prof. Marguerite Roberts, 1976. Fellow Southeastern Inst. of Mediaeval and Renaissance Studies, 1965, 67, 69. Democrat. Presbyterian. Home: 2701 Camden Rd Greensboro NC 27403-1438

PENNINGER, UNA LEE, health facility administrator, educator, lawyer; b. Flushing, N.Y., Feb. 2, 1954; d. William Myers and Una Lee (Massey) McLeer; m. William Holt Penninger, Jr., Aug. 8, 1981; children: Una Lee, William Holt III. BS in Nursing, Hunter Coll., 1976; MPA, NYU, 1979; JD, Tulane U., 1983. Bar: Mo. 1989, N.Y. 1986. RN NYU Med. Ctr., N.Y.C., 1976-80; mgmt. cons. Touche Ross, Newark, 1983-85; atty. Epstein Becker Green, N.Y.C., 1985-86; v.p. Cox Health Sys., Springfield, Mo., 1986—. Office: Cox Health Systems 1423 N Jefferson Ave Springfield MO 65802

PENNINGTON, BEVERLY MELCHER, financial services company executive; b. Vermillion, SD, Feb. 8, 1931; d. Cecil Lloyd and Phyllis Cecelia (Walz) M.; m. Glen D., Sept. 1, 1965 (dec. Aug. 1986); 1 child, Terri Lynn. BS, U. S.D., Vermillion, 1952. Enrolled agt. cert. IRS 1989. Sec budget dept. Bur. of Indian Affairs, Aberdeen, S.D., 1952-53, pvt. sec., 1953-54; pvt. sec. U.S. P.H.S. Indian Health, Aberdeen, 1954-55; adminstr. asst. U.S. Pub. Health Svc., Anchorage, 1955-58, U.S. Pub. Health, Dental Pub. Health, Washington, 1958-61; grant adminstr. Dental Pub. Health, Washington, 1961-65; co-owner Penn Mel Marina, Platte, S.D, 1965-74; co-owner Pennington Tax Service, Platte, 1974-86, owner, 1986-93; pres., CEO, White Tiger Fin. Svc., Inc., Platte, 1994—. Contbr. articles to profl. jours. Mem. Platte Women's Club, sec., 1965-68, pres., 1968-70, 89-91; mem. Libr. Bd., Sec., 1982-85, treas., 1995—. Fellow Am. Soc. Tax Profls. (sec. 1989-91, 2d v.p. 1995, 1st v.p. 1996, pres. 1997); mem. NAFE, Platte C. of C. (v.p. 1989, pres. 1990), Lyric Theatre Mus. Soc. (pres. 1988-92), U.S. C. of C., Washington Dakota Cen. Com. Republican. Presbyterian. Office: White Tiger Fin Svc Inc 420 Main Platte SD 57369

PENNINGTON, HELEN JOAN, lawyer; b. Riverside, N.J., Feb. 4, 1933; d. Chester Clayton and Ethel Madeline (Andrews) Tolson; m. Robert Leroy Pennington, Sept. 22, 1951 (div. 1984); children: Robert David, Denise, Dale, Darlene, Donna, Diane. AA, Salem County Coll., 1975; BA, Glassboro State Coll., 1977; JD, Rutgers U., 1981. Bar: N.J., 1983; cert. tchr. handicapped, N.J.; cert. domestic violence specialist, N.J. Staff atty. N.J. Pub. Interest Rsch. Group, Camden, 1982-83, Legal Aid Soc. Mercer County, Trenton, N.J., 1983-89, Nat. Ctr. on Women and Family Law, Inc., N.Y.C., 1989-92; exec. dir. Nat. Ctr. for Protective Parents, Inc., Trenton, 1992—. Author: (autobiography) Left Hand of Justice, 1996. Founder Salem County Humane Soc., Penns Grove, N.J., 1975, Nat. Ctr. for Protective Parents, Trenton, 1992, Consumers United for Action, Carneys Point, N.J., 1975. Named Advocate of Yr., N.J. Coalition for Battered Women, 1995, Woman of Inspiration, Trenton YWCA, 1991. Mem. Am. Profl. Soc. on the Abuse of Children N.J. (bd. dirs. 1995—), N.J. Assn. Domestic Violence Profls. (bd. dirs. 1993—), Women's Fund of N.J. (bd. dirs. 1994—). Democrat.

PENNY, GRACE ERNESTINE, special education educator, artist, broadcasting, consultant; b. Hartford, Conn., Mar. 16, 1936; d. Ernest Ora and Cecil Sarah (Sloat) Hunt; m. Frank Edward Penny, July 15, 1961; children: Lance Gordon (dec.), Verna Lynne. BA, Denison U., 1965; MS in Edn., SUNY, Binghamton, 1979. Cert. tchr., N.Y. Adj. instr. Empire State Coll., 1978-96; continuing adult edn. tchr. Binghamton H.S., 1973-76, 84-92; tchr. Broome-Tioga Boces Alternative Learning Ctr., Apalachin, N.Y., 1984-96; bd. dirs. Samaritan Counseling Svc., Endicott/Owego, N.Y., 1988-94; mem. tech. com. Broome Tioga BOCES, Binghamton, 1992-96; co-owner Penny Broadcasting Consultancy, Owego, 1991—. Exhibited in group shows at Metro-Ctr. Fasst Gallery, Binghamton, 1988-93, The Human Touch Gift Gallery, Manitou Springs, Colo., 1991—. Mem. fin. com. United Fund Campaign, Owego, 1970-75; bd. dirs. fine arts com. Tioga Agrl. Soc. and County Fair, Owego, 1970-77. Recipient grant Federated Women's Club, 1955, grant Am. The Beautiful Fund, 1975, 76. Mem. Fine Arts Soc. So. Tier, Tioga County Coun. of Arts (founding mem.), Nat. Women's Art Mus. Soc. (charter), Am. Soc. Marine Artists, U.S. Power Squadrons (Outstanding Jr. Mem. 1993), Ea. Star. Home: PO Box 234 Gales Ferry CT 06335 also: Harrison Condo Apt 302 B St Friday Harbor WA 98250

PENNY, JOSEPHINE B., retired banker; b. N.Y.C., July 7, 1925; d. Charles and Delia (Fahey) Booy; student Columbia U., Am. Inst. Banking; grad. Sch. Bank Adminstrn. U. Wis., 1975; m. John T. Penny, July 15, 1950 (div.); children—John T., Charleen Penny DeMauro, Patricia Penny Paras. With Prentice-Hall, N.Y.C., 1942-43; with Trade Bank & Trust Co., 1943-52, 61-70; with Nat. Westminster Bank U.S.A., 1970-85, v.p., dep. auditor, 1978-85. Mem. Bank Adminstrn. Inst. (chpt. dir. 1983-85), Inst. Internal Auditing, Nat. Assn. Bank Women (chpt. chmn. 1980-81). Home: 221A Manchester Ln Jamesburg NJ 08831-1711

PENSMITH, SHARYN ELAINE, communications executive; b. Washington, Mar. 22, 1945; d. Alfred Munk and Helen Victoria (Sollers) Lawson; m. Charles Lee Pensmith, Oct. 18, 1986. BA in Psychology, U. Md., 1967. Sales/acct. rep. GE, Bethesda, Md., 1967-75; sr. sales Nat. CSS, Arlington, Va., 1975-79, Itel Corp., McLean, Va., 1978-80; br. mgr. On-Line Systems, McLean, Va., 1980-82; dist. sales support AT&T, Rosslyn, Va., 1982-84; dir. bus. devel. Govt. Systems Incorporated, Fairfax, Va., 1984—; pres. ARI Consulting Group, Fairfax, 1993—; cons. Mint Corp., Fairfax, 1993—. Founder Migration Methodology strategy. Annual recipient pres.'s award Infonet, 1986-96, Best of the Best Infonet award, 1992, 93, 94, 96. Mem. NAFE, Women in Tech., Inter Agy. Com., Armed Forces Comm. and Electronics Assn. Home: 775 Bon Haven Dr Annapolis MD 21401 Office: Govt Systems Inc 3040 Williams Dr Ste 500 Fairfax VA 22031

PENTONEY, KRISTY DIANE, sales and marketing coordinator; b. Riverside, Calif., Mar. 16, 1959; d. Kenneth William and Rita Yvonne (Cross) P. Student, Coll. of the Desert, Palm Springs, Calif., 1983, Chaffey Coll., Ontario, Calif., 1983. Stockbroker Paine Webber, Riverside, 1979-84, Charles Schwab & Co., Irvine, Calif., 1985-87; office mgr. Remax Real Estate, Corona, Calif., 1988-90; sales and mktg. Pagnet Paging, Ontario, 1990-93, Pac-Tel Paging, Ontario, 1993-94, Western Outdoor Advt., Las Vegas, Nev., 1994-95; sales and mktg. coord. United Title of Nev., Las Vegas, 1995—. Mem. Zonta Internat. (hon.). Home: 4547 Fairbanks Riverside CA 92509

PEPIN, YVONNE MARY, artist, writer; b. San Francisco, May 28, 1956; d. Arthur Henry and Mary Alice (Ratté) P. BA, Antioch U., 1982; postgrad., Fielding Inst., 1989—, MA in Human Orgn. and Devel., 1991, PhD in Human Orgn. and Devel., 1992. Arts adminstr. Mendocino (Calif.) Art Ctr., 1978-85; founder, dir. Port Townsend (Wash.) Art Edn. Ctr., 1986—; dir. Blue Heron Gallery, Port Hadlock, Wash., 1989-92; presenter Am. Inst. of Med. Edn. Confs., 1987, 89-94. Author: Cabin Journal, 1984, Three Summers, 1986. Mem. AAUW.

PEPLOWSKI, CELIA CESLAWA, librarian; b. Montreal, June 4, 1918; came to U.S., 1923; d. Stanley and Wladyslawa (Fabisiak) P. BA and BS with honors, Tex. Woman's U., 1953; MALS, U. Wis., 1955. Substitute libr. Shorewood (Wis.) Pub. Libr., 1955; cataloger, libr. periodical svcs. Arlington (Tex.) State Coll., 1955-56; head libr. English sect. U. of the Sacred Heart, Tokyo, 1956-57; base libr. Sioux City (Iowa) Air Base/USAF, 1957-59; substitute libr. Milw. Sch. Bd., 1959-61; head tech. svcs. Milw. Downer Coll., 1961-63; cataloger, reference libr. Sterling Mcpl. Pub. Libr., Baytown, Tex., 1964-67, acting city libr., 1964-65; asst. extension supr. Mobile (Ala.) Pub. Libr., 1967-68, adminstrv. asst., pers. officer, 1968-69, internat. trade ctr. libr., 1969-70, supr. main libr., 1970-87, substitute libr., 1995—. Mem. AAUW (historian Mobile br.), ALA (subscription books rev. com. 1973-75), Wis. U. Alumni Assn., Tex. Woman's U. Alumni Assn., Pi Lambda Theta, Beta Phi Mu. Home: 217 Berwyn Dr W Apt 209 Mobile AL 36608-2119

PEPPARD, JACQUELINE JEAN, artist; b. Lynwood, Calif., Feb. 12, 1954; children: Nicole Bianca Pedersen, Olivia Christine Pedersen. Student, Colo. U., 1979; AA, Colo. Inst. Art, 1981. watercolor tchr. Aha Sch. Art, Telluride, Colo., 1994—; cons. for cmty. edn. South Washington Sch. Dist., Cottage Grove, Minn., 1996; represented by Toh-Atin, Durango, Colo., Golden West Gallery, Telluride, Debra Hudgins Gallery, Santa Fe, N.Mex., Anasazi Gallery, Dallas, Bader-Melnick Gallery, Vail, Colo. Exhibited in group shows at U.S. Open, Taos, N.Mex., 1985 (Hon. mention, 5th Pl. Public's Choice), Brush and Palette Club, Grand Junction, Colo., 1986 (1st Pl. in Watercolor Landscapes), Telluride Watercolor Exhbn., 1986 (Best Regional Artist Purchase award), Riverside (Calif.) Art Mus., 1988, Nat. Arts Club, N.Y.C., 1988, N.Mex. Watercolor Soc., 1989, 90, Collectors Mart, Denver, 1989, Brea (Calif.) Cultural Ctr., 1990, 95, Jackson Hole (Wyo.) Rotary, 1990, El Cajon (Calif.) Performing Arts Ctr., 1990, Denver Mus., 1994, Riverside Mus., Calif., 1995, Nat. Watercolor Society's 75th Annual Exhbn. Brea Cultural Ctr., Calif., 1995; featured in various mags.; posters commd. for Jazz Festival, Telluride, 1987-88, Wine Festival, Telluride, 1988-89, Premier Fly Found., Telluride; represented in permanent collections at Mountain Village Metro Offices, Telluride, DuPont Collection, Telluride, Bank of Telluride, Telluride Arts and Humanities Gallery; contbr. articles to newspapers. Brownie leader Girl Scouts U.S., Telluride, 1995-96. Grantee Telluride Coun. of Arts and Humanities, 1987. Mem. Nat. Watercolor Soc., N.Mex. Watercolor Soc. (2d Pl. award 1990), Watercolor West. Democrat. Office: Dancing Deer Fine Art PO Box 1134 Telluride CO 81435

PEPPER, BARBARA IRENE, public relations professional; b. Olean, N.Y., Nov. 4, 1941; d. Joseph Aloysius Slavin and Anna Margaret Skroback; m. Raymond Lloyd Pepper, Oct. 22, 1961 (div. Dec. 1980); children: Cynthia Moran, Randall, Melissa. Proofreader Olean Times Herald, 1959-60; sec. Beneficial Fin. Co., Olean, 1960-61; stenographer F. C. Thomas, Olean, 1961-62; legal stenographer James Maxwell Esquire, Enid, Okla., 1967-70; office mgr., real estate broker Pepper and Crandall Co., Olean, 1974-83; telephone salesperson GTE Directories, Erie, Pa., 1984-87; mortgage originator Empire of Am. Bank, Olean, 1987-88; sr. supr. Kelly Svcs., Erie, 1988-93; specialist pub. rels. and planning and devel. Erie Homes for Children and Adults Inc., 1996—; assoc. mem. Pers. Assn. N.W. Pa., Erie, 1988-93. Co-chairperson St. Bonaventure Friends Dr., Olean, 1975-76; bd. dirs. St. Bonaventure Pres. Coun., Olean, 1977-78; bd. dirs. Muscular Dystrophy Assn., Erie, 1989—, pres., 1996—. Mem. Pa. Assn. for Vols., Nat. Soc. Fund Raising Execs. Office: Erie Homes Children and Adults 226 E 27th St Erie PA 16504

PEPPER, DOROTHY MAE, nurse; b. Merill, Maine, Oct. 16, 1932; d. Walter Edwin and Alva Lois (Leavitt) Stanley; m. Thomas Edward Pepper, July 1, 1960; children: Walter Frank, James Thomas. RN, Maine Med. Ctr. Sch. Nursing, Portland, 1954. RN, Calif. Pvt. duty nurse Lafayette, Calif.; staff nurse Maine Med. Ctr., Portland, 1954-56, Oakland (Calif.) VA Hosp., 1956-58; pvt. duty nurse, dir. RN's Alameda County, Oakland. Mem. Profl. Nurses Bur. Registry, Maine Writers and Pubs. Alliance.

PEPPER, JENNIFER, artist, educator; b. Toronto, Oct. 14, 1959; came to U.S., 1977; d. Gordon E. and Diane E. (Young) P. BFA, Md. Inst. Coll. Art, 1987; MFA, U. Conn., 1989. Tchr. art N.Y.C. Pub. Schs., 1990—; instr. L.I. U., N.Y.C., 1992—. One-woman show U. Calif., Santa Cruz, 1995, Conn. Coll., 1996; 2-person show Erector Square Gallery, Conn., 1995, Trahern Gallery, Austin Peay State U., Tenn.; exhibited in numerous reginal, nat. and internat. art shows, 1988—. Mem. Phi Kappa Phi. Home: 51-55 Nassau Ave Brooklyn NY 11222

PEPPER, MARY JANICE, educational consultant; b. Pearsall, Tex., Oct. 1, 1942; d. Muriel Newton and Jane (Harbour) Moore; m. Clifton Gail Pepper, Feb. 19, 1961; children: John David, James Newton, Jeffery Michael. Student, U. Tex., 1960, 65, 76. Bus. mgr. Natalia (Tex.) Independent Sch. Dist., 1967-71; statistician Tex. Edn. Agy., Austin, 1971-72; mgr. bookkeeping div. Tex. Ednl. Cons. Svc. Inc., Austin, 1972-76, adminstrv. v.p., 1976-82, v.p., COO, 1982-93, pres., 1993—; team tchr. edn. program. U. Tex., Austin, 1985; lectr. Tex. Assn. Secondary Sch. Prins., Austin, 1988. Editor: Sch. Fin. Newsletter, Update for Sch. Adminstrs. Sec. Community Indsl. Found., Natalia, 1969-71, Medina County Water Control and Improvement, Natalia, 1970-71; mem. adv. com. Tex. Edn. Agy. Mem. Tex. Assn. Sch. Bus. Ofcls. (instr. 1987-88, chair coord. task force on sch. acctg. Tex. Edn. Agy. 1991—), Mended Hearts (sec. 1989-90, newsletter editor 1990-91). Baptist. Home: 16048 Hamilton Pool Rd Austin TX 78738-7401 Office: Tex Ednl Consultative Svcs Inc PO Box 18898 Austin TX 78760-8898

PEPPER, NANETTE, educator; b. Lexington, Ky.; d. Nathan and Lori Pepper; m. Dennis Callahan, May 4, 1991. BSN, U. Tex., Galveston, 1972; postgrad., Tex. Woman's U., 1977; MEd, U. Houston, 1981. RN, Tex.; cert. audio/visual screener. Clin. nurse U. Tex. Med. Br., Galveston, 1971-76; instr. nursing Victoria Coll. and Galveston Coll., 1976-79; nurse practitioner/officer mgr. Dr. James Dunaway, 1978-81; exec. dir. Child Study Clinic, Victoria, Tex., 1981-88; dir. nurses Victoria Nursing and Rehab. Ctr., 1988; nurse cons. survey and cert. rev. br. Health Care Financing Adminstrn., Dallas, 1988-92; nurse cons., quality mgmt. coord. Fed. Bur. Prisons, Washington, 1992-94, nat. continuing profl. ednl. coord., 1994-95; with Maternal Child Health Bur. of Pub. Health Svc., Rockville, Md., 1995—; mem. profl. adv. com. on nursing USPHS; lectr. in field. Mem. Jr. League of Washington; mem. Appointment Bd. for Nursing for the Pub. Health Svc. Comdr. USPHS. Decorated USPHS Commendation medal, PHS citation, achievement medal. Mem. ANA, Res. Officers Assn., Commd. Officers Assn., Assn. Mil. Surgeons U.S., Anchor and Caduceus Soc., U. Tex. Nursing Sch. Alumni Assn., Am. Contract Bridge League, Am. African Violet Soc., Gamma Phi Beta Alumni. Episcopalian. Home: 1401 Templeton Pl Rockville MD 20852-1422 Office: PHS Maternal Child Hlth Bur Health Svcs Divsn 5600 Fishers Ln 18A-19 Rockville MD 20857

PEPPER, NORMA JEAN, mental health nurse; b. Ellington, Iowa, Nov. 7, 1931; d. Victor F. and Grace Mae (Tate) Shadle; m. Bob Joseph Pepper, Dec. 28, 1956 (dec. Oct. 4, 1985); children: Joseph Victor, Barbara Jean, Susan Claire (dec.). Diploma in Nursing, Broadlawns Polk County Hosp., 1950-53; BSN, U. Iowa, 1953-55; MSN, U. Colo., 1955-60. Cert. mental health nurse. Head nurse Colo. Psychiatric Hosp., Denver, 1956; head nurse, Psychiatry Denver General Hosp., 1958-60; with Nurses Official Registry, Denver, 1960-73; staff nurse VA Med. Ctr., Denver, 1974-94; counselor VA Hosp. Employee Assistance Com., Denver, 1987-94. Mem. Colo. Nurses Assn. Home: 4836 W Tennessee Ave Denver CO 80219-3130

PEPPIN, LINDA LOUISE LINTON, information management company executive; b. Chgo., Aug. 6, 1947; d. Fred Bennett and Ada Lillian (Lewzader) Linton; m. William Lee Peppin (div. 1972); 1 child, Brian Lee. Student, Kankakee Community Coll., 1974-76, Rock Valley Coll., 1980-81. Draft bd. clk. U.S. Govt. Selective Svc. System, 1965-73; mgr. order dept. Homewood (Ill.) Industries, 1973-74; office supr. Conn. Gen. Life Ins., Kankakee, Ill., 1974-76; claim processor Aetna Life & CAsulaty, Olympia Field, Ill., 1976-78; auditor Aetna Life & CAsulaty, Rockford, Ill., 1978-80; mgr. medicare unit Pioneer Life Ins. Co. Ill., 1980-81; asst. claim cons. Prudential Ins. Co. Am., Chgo., 1981-84; contract writer II CNA Ins. Cos., 1985; account mgr. Resource Info. Mgmt. Systems, Inc., Naperville, Ill., 1986-88; asst. opers. mgr. HMO Mobile (Mobile), 1989-90; ind. cons., 1992-94; project mgr. Suburban Healthcare Benefits, Inc., Bolingbrook, Ill., 1991-93, mgr. support svcs., 1993-94; plan adminstrn. mgr. Option Care, Inc., Bannockburn, Ill., 1994—. Mem. Nat. Asns. Female Execs. Roman Catholic.

PERDUE, BEVERLY MOORE, state legislator, geriatric consultant; b. Grundy, Va., Jan. 14, 1948; d. Alfred P. and Irene E. (Morefield) Moore; children: Garrett, Emmett. BA, U. Ky., 1969; MEd, U. Fla., 1974, PhD, 1976. Pvt. lectr., writer, cons., 1980-86; pres. The Perdue Co., New Bern, N.C., 1985—; rep. N.C. State Gen. Assembly, Raleigh, 1986-90; senator N.C. Gen. Assembly, Raleigh, 1990—; bd. dirs. Nations Bank, New Bern. Bd. dirs. N.C. United Way, Greensboro, 1990-92; exec. mem. N.C. Dem. Party, Raleigh, 1989—; mem. N.C. travel bd. Nat. Conf. State Legislators. Named Outstanding Legislator, N.C. Aging Network, 1989, 92, Toll fellow Nat. Conf. State Legislators, Lexington, Ky., 1992. Mem. Nat. Coun. on Aging, Bus. and Profl. Women, Rotary. Episcopalian. Home: 211 Wilson Point Rd New Bern NC 28562-7519 Office: Perdue & Co PO Box 991 507 Pollack St New Bern NC 28563 also: NC Senate Raleigh NC 27601

PERDUE, JILL FLOWERS, accountant; b. Bowling Green, Ky., Mar. 30, 1970; d. Jerry Dee and Judy Ann (Dinwiddie) Flowers; m. Tommy Joe Perdue, Oct. 10, 1992. BS, Western Ky. U., 1992. CPA, Ky. Internal auditor Mid-South Bancorp, Inc., Franklin, Ky., 1992-93; acctg., compliance officer Simpson County Bank, Franklin, 1994; internal auditor Franklin Bank & Trust Co., 1994—. Vol. Jr. Achievement, Franklin, 1996. Mem. AICPAs, Ky. Soc. CPAs. Home: 1359 Phillips Ln Franklin KY 42134 Office: Franklin Bank & Trust Co 317 N Main St Franklin KY 42135

PEREIRA, CELINA ANTONIETA, physician; b. Bombay, India, Dec. 21, 1941; came to U.S., 1967; d. João Costa and Adelina (DeSousa) P.; m. Donald Andrew McGowan; children: Malini, Meena. MD, Grant Med. Coll., Bombay, 1965. Resident in pediats. Boston City Hosp., 1967-69, R.I. Hosp., Providence, 1969-70; instr. in pediats. Brown U., Providence, 1973-75; staff physician U. R.I., Kingston, 1975—. Contbr. articles to profl. jours. Vol. hospice VNA, Wakefield, R.I., 1994; active World Spiritual U. Fellow Am. Acad. Pediats. (diplomate), R.I. Med. Soc., Washington County Med. Soc. Roman Catholic. Office: U RI Health Svcs Kingston RI 02881

PERELI, EVA MAYER, retired physician; b. Budapest, Hungary, June 1, 1919; Came to the U.S., 1958; d. Andras Karoly and Maria Jozefa (Haraszti) Mayer; m. Julius Imre Pereli, Sept. 20, 1955 (dec. Aug. 1991); children: Julius Richard Pereli, Sylvia Ann Pereli. MD, U. Budapest, 1950, Ednl. Coun. for Med. Grads., 1970. Intern Framingham (Mass.) Union, 1970-71; resident Worcester (Mass.) City Hosp., 1971-72, Boston Children's Hosp., 1974-75; physician Newton (Mass.) Welesley Hosp., 1975-94, Metrowest Med. Ctr., Framingham, 1975-94. Mem. Bd. of Health, Wayland, 1981-84, Arts Coun., 1981-85, Pesticide Com., 1981-85. Fellow Mass. Med. Soc. Home: 106 Main St # 314 Wayland MA 01778

PERELLA, MARIE LOUISE, lawyer; b. Akron, Ohio, Feb. 5, 1967; d. Manuel James and Jean Ann (Nalencz) P. BA in Spanish, John Carroll U., 1989; student, Univ. Ibero Americana, Mexico City, 1988; JD, Akron U., 1992. Bar: Ohio 1992, U.S. Dist. Ct. (no. dist.) Ohio 1993, U.S. Supreme Ct. 1996. Law clk. Akron Law Dept., 1990; legal intern Cuyahoga Falls (Ohio) Law Dept., 1990-92; law clk. Ticktin, Baron, Koepper & Co. LPA, Cleve., 1992, assoc. atty., 1992—. Guest spkr. Cleve. Legal Secs. Assn. meeting, 1995. Mem. ABA, ATLA, Ohio State Bar Assn., Cuyahoga County Bar Assn., Cleve. Bar Assn., Centro Cultural Hispano, Justinian Forum, Phi Alpha Delta (clk. law sch./grant chpt. 1991-92), Sigma Delta Pi. Office: Ticktin Baron Koepper & Co LPA 1621 Euclid Ave 1700 Keith Bldg Cleveland OH 44115-2107

PERELLA, SUSANNE BRENNAN, librarian; b. Providence, Mar. 19, 1936; d. Laurence J. and Harriet E. (Delaplane) Brennan. B.A., U. Conn., 1960; M.L.S., U. Mich., 1967. Head M.B.A. Library, Univ. Conn., Hartford, 1964-66; asst. librarian Cornell Univ. Grad. Sch. Bus., Ithaca, N.Y., 1967-72; head reader's services FTC Library, Washington, 1972-79; library dir. FTC Library, 1979-92; libr. dir. Libr. and Info. Svcs. U.S. Treasury, Washington, 1992—. Mem. Law Librarians Soc., Spl. Libraries Assn., Am. Assn. Law Libraries, Fed. Library and Info. Ctr. Com. Office: US Dept Treasury Libr 1500 Pennsylvania Ave NW Washington DC 20005-1007

PERES, JUDITH MAY, journalist; b. Chgo., June 30, 1946; d. Leonard H. and Eleanor (Seltzer) Zurakov; m. Michael Peres, June 27, 1972; children: Dana, Avital. BA, U. Ill., 1967. Acct. exec. Daniel J. Edelman Inc., Chgo., 1967-68; copy editor Jerusalem (Israel) Post, 1968-71, news editor, 1971-75, chief night editor, 1975-80, editor, style book, 1978-80; copy editor Chgo. Tribune, 1980-82, rewriter, 1982-84, assoc. fgn. editor, 1984-90, nat. editor, 1990-95, nat./fgn. editor, 1995—. Office: Chicago Tribune 435 N Michigan Ave Chicago IL 60611-4001

PERET, KAREN KRZYMINSKI, health service administrator; b. Springfield, Mass., Mar. 8, 1950; d. Edward S. and Doris L. (Beaudry) Krzyminski; m. Robert J. Peret, June 19, 1971; children: Heather, James, Kaitlin, Matthew. BS in Nursing, St. Anselm's, 1972; MS in Nursing Adminstrn., Boston U., 1980; EdD in Orgnl. Devel., U. Mass. Amherst, 1993. RN, Mass. Staff nurse Boston VA's Hosp., 1972-73; staff nurse pediatrics Harrington Meml. Hosp., Southbridge, Mass., 1973-74, instr. edn., 1974-75, relief day asst. dir. nursing, 1975; coordinator continuing edn. Cen. Maine Med. Ctr., Lewiston, 1975-76; asst. dir. nursing Monson Devel. Ctr., Palmer, Mass., 1977-83, dir. nursing, 1983-94; exec. nursing cons. Liberty Healthcare, Waltham, Mass., 1994—; dir. nursing W.E. Fernald Ctr., Waltham, 1994—; ind. mgmt. cons., 1993—; instr. Quinsigamond Cmty. Coll., Worcester, Mass., 1972-73. Contbr. articles to profl. jours. Mem. Sigma Theta Tau. Home: RR 2 Box 105 Holland MA 01521-9705 Office: Fernald Devel Ctr 200 Trapelo Rd Waltham MA 02154

PERETTI, MARILYN GAY WOERNER, human services professional; b. Indpls., July 30, 1935; d. Philip E. and Harriet E. (Meyer) Woerner; children: Thomas A., Christopher P. BS, Purdue U., 1957; postgrad., Coll. DuPage, 1980—, U. Wis., 1981—. Nursery sch. lab. asst. Mary Baldwin Coll., Staunton, Va., 1957-58; tchr. 1st grade, nursery sch. No. Ill. area schs., 1958-61; asst. tchr. of blind Glenbard E. H.S., Lombard, Ill., 1978-80; adminstrv. asst. Elmhurst Coll., 1980-81; dir. vol. svcs. DuPage Convalescent Ctr., Wheaton, 1981-95; dir. cmty. outreach Sr. Home Sharing, Inc., Lombard, Ill., 1996—; developer new vol. pos. for vis. the non-verbal handicapped, 1994; prodr. 4 ednl. slide programs on devel. countries, 1988-91; initiator used book collection for library project U. Zululand, S. Africa, 1993-94. Editor, designer newsletter Our Developing World's Voices, 1994—. Bd. dirs. Lombard YMCA, 1977-83, pres., 1980; vol. Chgo. Uptown Ministry, 1979; participant fact finding trips El Salvador, 1988, Honduras, 1989, Nicaragua, 1989, Republic of South Africa, 1991; mem. Nature Artists Guild of Morton Arboretum; vol. PADS, 1994—. Mem. Nature Artists Guild of Morton Arboretum. Office: Sr Home Sharing Inc 837 Westmore-Meyers Rd Lombard IL 60148

PERETZ, EILEEN, interior designer; b. N.Y.C., Oct. 29, 1934; d. Leo and Mary Miller; m. David Peretz, Aug. 28, 1955; children: Deborah, Adam. BA in Fine Art, CCNY, 1956; Cert. in Interior Design, N.Y. Sch. Interior Design, N.Y.C., 1964. Interior design asst. Narden & Radoszy, N.Y.C., 1956; assoc. interior designer Renee Ross Interiors, N.Y.C., 1964-70; chief interior designer Peretz & Marks Interiors, N.Y.C., 1972-82; sole propr. Eileen Peretz Interiors Inc., N.Y.C., 1970-72, pres., 1982—; cons., mentor, lectr. Marymount Coll., N.Y.C., 1980; lectr. Fashion Inst. Tech.; cons., Paris. Columnist for weekly newspaper Our Town, N.Y.C., 1976-79. Mem. ASID (assoc.), Allied Bd. Trade. Home and Office: 300 Central Park W New York NY 10024-1513 also: 32 Rue de Varenne, Paris 75007, France

PEREZ, BARBARA ALLEN, art teacher, artist; b. Chgo., Aug. 7, 1957; d. Robert Albert and Barbara Maire (Batchelder) Nueske; m. Alphonse Lara Perez, Mar. 15, 1980; 1 child, Maryah Michelle. BA in Arts, Loyola U., 1979. Cert. State Bd. Edn., 1990. Art tchr. St. Athanasius, Evanston, Ill., 1990—; grant cons., publicity chair St. Athanasius, Evanston, 1990—. Beat rep. Chgo. Police Dept., 1990—. Mem. Nat. Arts Edn. Assn., Nat. Cath. Edn. Assn., Ill. Art Edn. Assn., Ill. art Alliance for Edn., Am. Craft. Roman Catholic. Office: St Athanasius Sch 2510 Ashland Evanston IL 60201

PEREZ, JOSEPHINE, psychiatrist, educator; b. Tijuana, Mex., Feb. 10, 1941; came to U.S., 1960, naturalized, 1968. BS in Biology, U. Santiago de Compostela, Spain, 1971; MD, 1975. Clerkships in internal medicine, gen. surgery, otorhinolaryngology, dermatology and venereology Gen. Hosp. of Galicia (Spain), 1972-75; resident in gen. psychiatry U. Miami (Fla.), Jackson Meml. Hosp. and VA Hosp., Miami, 1976-78; practice medicine specializing in psychiatry, marital and family therapy, individual psychotherapy, Miami, Fla., 1979—; nuclear medicine technician, EEG technician, supr. Electrographic Labs., Encino, Calif., 1963-71; emergency room physician Miami Dade Hosp., 1975; attending psychiatrist Jackson Meml. Hosp., 1979—, asst. dir. adolescent psychiat. unit, 1979-83; mem. clin. faculty U. Miami Sch. Medicine, 1979—, clin. instr. psychiatry, 1979—. Mem. AMA (Physicians' Recognition award 1980, 83, 86, 89), Am. Assn. for Marital and Family Therapy (cert. clin. mem., treas. 1982-84, pres.-elect 1985-87, pres. 1987-89), Am. Psychiat. Assn., Am. Med. Women's Assn., Assn. Women Psychiatrists, South Fla. Psychiat. Soc. Office: 420 S Dixie Hwy Ste 4A Coral Gables FL 33146

PEREZ, JULIE ANNA, audio engineer; b. Miami, Fla., Sept. 2, 1961; d. Miguel Angel and Dorothy Elizabeth (Headford) P. Student, U. Miami, 1979-83. Audio engr. NBC, Inc., N.Y.C., 1984—; asst. music mixer (TV shows) Saturday Night Live, 1987-93, Late Night with David Letterman 7th Anniversary Spl., 1989; music mixer Late Night with David Letterman, summer 1989, Late Night with Conan O'Brien, 1993—; audio engr. Later with Bob Costas, Friday Night Videos, Brokaw Reports; co-founder TECHNET; sem. chair AES Women in Audio, 1991, Saturday Night Live. Editor: Music Engring. Tech. newsletter, 1983; audio engr. TV talk-show Donahue, 1985-87 (Emmy nomination). Contbr. Planned Parenthood Fedn. Am., 1986—, Women in the Arts. Recipient Down Beat award Down Beat mag., 1982, Best Engineered Live Performance award Down Beat mag. Mem. NARAS, NOW, ACLU, NATAS, (Emmy nomination for sound mixing 1986), Acad. TV Arts and Scis. (Emmy nomination for sound mixing 1993), Audio Engring. Soc., Nat. Assn. Broadcast Employees and Technicians, Women in Music. Democrat. Home: 18 Harriot Ave Harrington Park NJ 07640-1518 Office: NBC Inc 30 Rockefeller Plz Rm 240 New York NY 10112

PEREZ, KATHERINE ANN, police officer; b. Hartford, Conn., Jan. 4, 1962; d. Eleanor (Rolka) Pisiack. Student, Trinity Coll. Lic. police officer, Conn. Police officer Hartford Police Dept., 1983-91, sergeant, 1991-95, lt., 1995—. Bd. dirs. Hartford Region YWCA, 1993—. Mem. Police Benevolent Assn. Roman Catholic. Home: 9 Basswood Ct Bloomfield CT 06002 Office: Hartford Police Dept 50 Jennings Rd Hartford CT 06120

PEREZ, LUZ LILLIAN, psychologist; b. Ponce, P.R., Aug. 7, 1946; d. Emiliano and Maria D. (Torres) P.; children: Vantroi, Maireni. BA, Herbert H. Lehman Coll., 1974; PhD, NYU, 1989. Lic. psychologist, N.Y. Staff psychologist Soundview Throgs Neck Community Mental Health Ctr., Bronx, 1980-88; coord. early childhood program Crotona Park Cmty. Mental Health Ctr., Bronx, 1988-91; cons. psychologist Highbridge Adv. Coun. Presch. Program, Bronx, N.Y., 1991-93, Coalition for Hispanic Family Svcs., Bklyn., N.Y., 1991-95, Marathon Child Devel. Ctr., Queens, N.Y., 1993-94, Bronx Orgn. for Learning Disabled, 1993—, Village Child Devel. Ctr., N.Y.C., 1994—, Graham-Windham Svcs. to Families and Children, 1994-95. Grantee NIMH, 1974-77. Mem. Assn. Hispanic Mental Health Profls.

PEREZ, MICHELLE, lawyer; b. Rochester, N.Y., Aug. 22, 1962. BS, Georgetown U., 1984; JD, Fordham U., 1989. Bar: N.Y. 1990, N.J. 1990, U.S. Dist. Ct. (so. and ea. dists.) N.Y. 1990, U.S. Dist. Ct. N.J. 1990, D.C. 1992. Ptnr. Anderson Kill Olick & Oshinsky, N.Y.C. Contbr. articles to law jour. Mem. N.Y. State Bar Assn., ABA. Office: Anderson Kill Olick & Oshinsky 1251 Ave of the Americas New York NY 10020-1182*

PEREZ, ROSIE, actress; b. Bklyn.; d. Ismael Serrano and Lydia Perez. Dramatic appearances include: (T.V.) 21 Jump Street, WIOU, (film) Do the Right Thing, 1989, White Men Can't Jump, 1992, Night on Earth, 1992, Untamed Heart, 1993, Fearless, 1993 (Acad. award nom. Best Supporting Actress 1994), It Could Happen To You, 1994, Somebody to Love, 1995, (TV series) House of Buggin, 1995. Office: CAA 9830 Wilshire Blvd Beverly Hills CA 90212-1804*

PEREZ-CASTRO, ANA VERONICA, developmental biology researcher; b. Lima, Peru, Jan. 27, 1962; came to U.S., 1986; d. Cesar Antonio and Ines Gladys (Marquina) P.; m. Alonso Castro, June 11, 1988. BS, Cayetano Heredia U., Lima, 1984, licentiate in chemistry and biology, 1985; MA, Columbia U., 1988, MPhil, 1990, PhD in Microbiology, 1992. Jr. prof. dept. chemistry Cayetano Heredia U., 1985-86; teaching asst. dept. microbiology U. Ga., Athens, 1987, Columbia U., N.Y.C., 1989; postdoctoral fellow life scis. div. Los Alamos (N.Mex.) Nat. Lab., 1992-95; rsch. assoc. dept. biology U. N.Mex., Albuquerque, 1996—; speaker Fedn. Am. Socs. for Exptl. Biology, 1992, Baylor Coll. Medicine, Houston, 1992, Mexican Soc. Genetics, Guanajuato, 1993, Mexico City 1994. Contbr. articles to sci. jours. Recipient young scientist award Fedn. Am Socs. for Exptl. Biology, 1992; Nat. Coun. Sci. and Tech. grad. fellow Cayetano Heredia U., 1985-86; Fieger predoctoral scholar Norris Comprehensive Cancer Ctr., U. So. Calif., 1991-92. Mem. AAAS, Am. Soc. Microbiology, Am. Soc. Human Genetics.

Home: 2546 Camino San Patricio Santa Fe NM 87505 Office: Univ NMex Dept Biology Castetter Hall Albuquerque NM 87131

PERFETTO, LISA ANN, academic administrator; b. Erie, Pa., Aug. 19, 1969; d. Dan Anthony and Judith Ann (Meyer) P. BS in Human Devel., Pa. State U., 1992; MS in Higher Edn., West Chester U., 1996. Dir. of tutoring, Act 101 asst. dir. West Chester U., 1994-96; owner Pathfinder Consulting; academic coach for students with learning disabilities, attention deficit disorder coach; presenter in field. Mem. ACA, Am. Coll. Personnel Assn., Nat. Tutoring Assn. Democrat. Roman Catholic. Home: 12 Manor Dr West Chester PA 19380 Office: U Tutoring Ctr 105 Lawrence Hall West Chester PA 19380

PERGER, DONNA SPAGNOLI, secondary school mathematics educator; b. Portsmouth, Va., Apr. 24, 1951; d. Delmo John and Lurline M. (Smith) Spagnoli; m. Steve John Perger Jr., June 9, 1980; 1 stepchild, Stephanie Lee. BS in Secondary Edn., Old Dominion U., 1973. Tchr. math. Manor H.S., Portsmouth, Va., 1973-74, Bettie Williams Sch., Virginia Beach, Va., 1974-78, Virginia Beach Jr. H.S., 1978-80, Queens Lake Sch., York County, Va., 1980—; lead tchr. VQUEST. Named Mid. Sch. Tchr. of Yr. Daily Press Newspaper, Newport News, 1993. Mem. NEA, Nat. Coun. Tchrs. Math., Va. Edn. Assn., Va. Coun. Tchrs. Math., York County Edn. Assn., Alpha Delta Kappa. Office: Queens Lake Sch West Queens Dr Williamsburg VA 23185

PERHACS, MARYLOUISE HELEN, musician, educator; b. Teaneck, N.J., June 15, 1944; d. John Andrew and Helen Audrey (Hosage) P.; m. Robert Theodore Sirinek, Jan. 27, 1968 (div. Jan. 1975). Student, Ithaca (N.Y.) Coll., 1962-64; BS, Juilliard Sch., 1967, MS, 1968; postgrad., Hunter Coll., 1976, St. Peter's Coll., Jersey City, N.J., 1977. Cert. music tchr., N.Y., N.J. Instr. Carnegie Hall, N.Y.C., 1966-69; program developer, coord., instr. urban edn. program Newburgh (N.Y.) Pub. Sch. System, 1968-69; adj. prof. dept. edn. St. Peter's Coll., Jersey City, 1976-92; tchr. brass instruments Indian Hills High Sch., Oakland, N.J., 1976; tchr. Jersey City Pub. Schs., 1976-77, N.Y.C. Pub. Sch., Bronx, 1980-84; pvt. tchr. Cliffside Park, N.J., 1976—; vocal music tchr. East Rutherford, N.J., 1990; tchr. music Bergen County Spl. Svcs. Sch. Dist., 1990-91; tchr. gen. music Little Ferry (N.J.) Pub. Schs., 1991-92; tchr. mid. sch. instrumental Paramus (N.J.) Pub. Schs., 1993-94; tchr. vocal music West New York (N.J.) Pub Schs., 1995—; Park Ridge N.J. High Sch. Summer Instrumental Music Pgm., 1995, 96; tchr., singer, trumpeter Norwegian Caribbean Lines, 1981-82, Jimmy Dorsey Band, Paris and London, 1974; music and edn. lect. cir., 1992—. Singer with Original PDQ Bach Okay Chorale, 1966, Live from Carnegie Hall Recordings, 1970, St. Louis Mcpl. Opera, 1970, Ed Sullivan Show, 1970; singer, dancer, actress (Broadway shows) Promises, Promises, 1969-71, Sugar, 1971-72, Lysistrata, 1972; trumpeter (Broadway shows) Jesus Christ Superstar, 1973, Debbie!, 1976, Sarava!, 1979, Fiddler on the Roof, Lincoln Ctr., 1981, Sophisticated Ladies, 1982; writer, host series on women in music Columbia Cable/United Artists, 1984; recordings: Carnegie Hall Live, Avery Fisher Hall, Lincoln Ctr. Cons. to cadette troop Girl Scouts U.S., Jersey City, 1967-68, Bergen County N.J. Coun., 1995—. Mem. NEA, AFTRA, Actors Equity Assn., Am. Fedn. Musicians (mem. theatre com. local 802 N.Y.C. 1972—, chmn. 1973), AFM Local N.J. 248, Music Educators Nat. Conf., N.J. Music Educators Assn., N.J. Sch. Music Assn., N.J. Edn. Assn., Internat. Women's Brass Conf. (charter mem.), Internat. Trumpet Guild, Women of Accomplishment (charter mem. 1992), Mu Phi Epsilon. Democrat. Episcopalian. Home and Office: 23 Crescent Ave Cliffside Park NJ 07010-3003

PERICH, TONI ANNETTE, insurance representative; b. Galveston, Tex., Sept. 22, 1946; d. Daniel John Jr. and Adelaide Lucia (Lopez) Traverso; m. Thomas Joseph Perich, June 3, 1978; children: Matthew John, Stephen Christopher. Comml. svc. rep. various ins. agys., Houston, 1965-87; field rep., outside sales Old Republic Surety, Houston, 1987-90; owner Galerie d'Alexandria, Galveston, Tex., 1990-92; ins. cons. various law firms, Houston, 1990-91; comml. svc. rep. The Houston Agys., Inc., 1992-94; field rep., outside sales Universal Surety of Am., Houston, 1994-95; field rep., sales exec. RLI Ins. Co., Dallas, 1995—; tchr. piano pvt practice Sugarland, Tex., 1994—. Schoolsite liaison Am. Heart Assn., Upper Pinellas County, 1996-97. North Tex. State U. Music scholar, 1964; recipient Gold medal Internat. Piano Recording Festival, 1956, 1st Pl. Contestant, 1963, Paderweski Gold medal Nat. Guild Piano Tchrs., 1964. Mem. Am. Coll. Physicians, Nat. Assn. Ins. Women (mem.-at-large 1995-96), Ins. Women St. Petersburg. Roman Catholic. Office: RLI Surety 3010 LBJ Frwy #555 Dallas TX 75323

PERISHO, SALLY L., curator; b. Streator, Ill., Oct. 20, 1951; d. Donald Max and Mary Frances (Hopkins) Perisho. BA, Ill. State U., 1973; MA, U. Ill., 1977. Asst. curator Indpls. Mus. Art, Denver Art Mus., 1978-79; dir. Arapahoe Community Coll., Littleton, Colo., 1979-85; dir., curator U. Colo., Colorado Springs, 1985-91; dir. Ctr. for Visual Arts, Metro State Coll. Denver, 1991-96. Author: Mexican-American Artists of the Southwest, 1989, Clay: Beyond Function, 1985, The Thinking Eye, 1980. Recipient awards, Colo. Coun. for Arts and Humanities, Pres.'s Fund for Humanities grantee, Nat. Endowment for Arts grantee, NEH grantee. Mem. Am. Assn. Mus., Colo./Wyo. Assn. Mus., Assn. of Coll. and U. Mus., Colo. Fedn. Arts. Home: 511 E 3rd Ave Castle Rock CO 80104

PERITORE, LAURA, law librarian; b. San Francisco, Nov. 28, 1945; d. Attilio and Anita (Firenzi) Marcenaro; children: Victor Anthony, Phillip Michael. BA, U. Calif., Santa Barbara, 1967, MA, 1970; MLS, U. Mo., 1974. Asst. libr. Mo. Hist. Soc., Columbia, 1971-74, 77-79; asst. libr. Hastings Law Libr., San Francisco, 1980-86, assoc. libr., 1986—; part-time tchr. legal rsch. City Coll., San Francisco, 1990-91. Author: Guide to California County Probate and Vital Records, 1994; contbr. articles and monographs to profl. jours. Mem. Am. Assn. Law Librs., No. Calif. Assn. Law Librs. (asst. editor newsletter 1984-86, workshop com. 1988, advt. editor 1990-91, sec. 1993-94, grantee 1984). Office: Hastings Law Libr 200 Mcallister St San Francisco CA 94102-4707

PERKINS, DEBORAH ANNE, interior designer; b. Mineola, N.Y., Mar. 8, 1954; d. Arthur Cudner and Maria (Risko) P.; 1 child, Olivia Anne Perkins. AAS in Interior Design magne cum laude, Chamberlayne Sch., Boston, 1975. Cert. fitness instr. YMCA. Film admissions coord. Gen. Cinema Corp., Chestnut Hill, Mass., 1976-78; tchr. adult edn. Kennedy Community Sch., Cambridge, Mass., 1976; interior design cons. Jordan Marsh Co., Quincy, Mass., 1978-81; freelance interior designer Honduras, Central Am., 1981; sales rep. New Eng. territory LaFrance (S.C.) Fabrics, 1982-84; owner, designer The Design Studio, Watertown, Mass., 1985—. Mem. Boston Soc. Architects Task Force for Homeless, 1988-90; big sister YWCA, Boston, 1985—; participant Grace Chapel Nursing Home Ministry, Lexington, Mass., 1989-90; co-leader Daybreak Single Parent Support Group, 1992-93. Mem. NAFE, Women Entrepreneurs Homebased, Am. Soc. Interior Designers, Alpha Nu Omega. Home and Office: 68 Washington St Natick MA 01760

PERKINS, DONNA WILSON, music educator; b. High Point, N.C., Feb. 4, 1952; d. David Thomas and Blanche Lorene (Gallion) Wilson; m. A. Odie Perkins, Apr. 3, 1979; children: Kenny, Jay Beverly, Ted. B of Music Edn., Appalachian State U., 1974; M of Music Edn, U. N.C., Greensboro, 1989. Cert. K-12 music tchr., N.C. Pvt. music instr. Perkins Music Studio, High Point, N.C., 1975-88; tchr. gen. music Ledford Middle Sch., Thomasville, N.C., 1988—; dir. 12 music prodns. Organist, choir dir. local ch.; mem. Gideons Internat. Named Tchr. of Yr., Ledford Mid. Sch., 1994. Mem. Music Educators Nat. Conf. Home: PO Box 161 Wallburg NC 27373-0161 Office: Ledford Middle Sch 3954 N NC Hwy 109 Thomasville NC 27360

PERKINS, ELIZABETH ANN, actress; b. Queens, N.Y.. Grad., Goodman Theatre, Chgo., 1981. Films include: About Last Night, 1986, From the Hip, 1987, Sweet Hearts Dance, 1988, Big, 1988, Love at Large, 1990, Enid is Sleeping, 1990, Avalon, 1990, He Said/She Said, 1991, The Doctor, 1991, Indian Summer, 1993, The Flintstones, 1994, Miracle on 34th Street, 1994, Moonlight and Valentino, 1995; TV film: For Their Own Good, 1993; theater: Brighton Beach Memoirs, 1984, Playwrights' Horizon, Ensemble Studio Theater, N.Y. Shakespeare Festival, Four Dogs and a Bone, 1995. Office: care Susan Culley & Assocs 150 S Rodeo Dr Ste 220 Beverly Hills CA 90212-1825

PERKINS, ELIZABETH ANN, elementary school educator; b. Union City, Ind., Mar. 18, 1963; d. Gerald Neil and Dixie Lee (Miles) Marshall; m. Frank Henry Perkins, II, July 31, 1982; children: Frank Henry III, Kyle Alexander. BS, Ball State U., 1984, MA, 1988. Substitute tchr. Mississinawa Valley Schs., Union City, Ohio, 1984-85; 2d grade tchr. Randolph Ea. Sch., Union City, 1985-87, substitute tchr., 1987-88; 5th grade tchr. Arcanum (Ohio) Butler LSD, 1988—; asst. math. lab. Project Discovery, West Region Ohio, 1994, mem. coun., Dayton, Ohio, 1994; mem. standard setting com. State Dept Edn., 4th grade math. proficiency, Ohio, 1994; presenter tchr. workshops and meetings, 1990—. V.p. TWIG # 35 Arcanum, 1990—; treas. PTO, Arcanum, 1992—; math. coord. St. Jude's Mathathon, Arcanum, 1993—; coach Odyssey of the Mind Primary Team, Arcanum, 1994; mem. Criterion Lit. Club, 1995. Recipient Ednl. Rsch. grant Ball State U., 1993, Resource Tchr. grant, 1995, Timewarner Cable in Classroom award, 1996, Ashland Inc. Golden Apple Achiever award, 1996. Mem. NEA, Nat. Coun. Tchrs. of Math., Ohio Coun. Tchrs. of Math., Arcanum-Butler Classroom Tchrs. Assn. (bldg. rep. 1988—), Mississinawa Alumni Assn (bd. dirs. 1991—), Phi Delta Kappa (mem. math. video project com. western Ohio chpt. 1994). Roman Catholic. Office: Arcanum Butler LSD 310 N Main Arcanum OH 45304

PERKINS, GLADYS PATRICIA, retired aerospace engineer; b. Crenshaw, Miss., Oct. 30, 1921; d. Douglas and Zula Francis (Crenshaw) Franklin; m. Benjamin Franklin Walker, Sept. 26, 1952 (dec.); m. William Silas Perkins, Sept. 16, 1956 (dec.). BS in Math., Le Moyne Coll., 1943; postgrad., U. Mich., 1949, U. Calif., L.A., 1955-62. Mathematician Nat. Adv. Com. for Aeronatics (now NASA), Hampton, Va., 1944-49, Nat. Bur. of Standards, L.A., 1950-53, Aberdeen Bombing Mission, L.A., 1953-55; assoc. engr. Lockheed Missiles Systems Div., Van Nuys, Calif., 1955-57; staff engr. Hughes Aircraft Co., El Segundo, Calif., 1957-80; engring. specialist Rockwell Internat., Downey, Calif., 1980-87, ret., 1987. Contbr. articles to profl. publs. Named Alumnus of Yr. Le Moyne-Owen Coll., 1952; recipient Nat. Assn. for Equal Opportunity in Higher Edn. award Le Moyne-Owen Coll. Mem. Soc. of Women Engrs., Assn. of Computing Machinery, Le Moyne-Owen Alumni Assn. (pres. 1984), U. Mich. Alumni Club, Alpha Kappa Alpha. Democrat. Congregationalist. Home: 4001 W 22nd Pl Los Angeles CA 90018-1029

PERKINS, NANCY ANN, nurse; b. American Fork, Utah, Jan. 31, 1961; d. George Thorvald and Ann Elizabeth (Williamson) Gardner; m. Layne Todd Perkins, Sept. 6, 1986; children: Christian H., Nathaniel B. BSN, Westminster Coll., 1982. RN, BLS, AHA, Utah. LPN med./surg. unit staff nurse Holy Cross Hosp., Salt Lake City, 1980-81; RN staff nurse renal St. Marks Hosp., Salt Lake City, 1982-86, RN charge nurse diabetic unit, 1986-87, RN diabetic educator, 1986-87, RN, charge nurse med. psych. unit, 1987-93, RN, community educator, 1991-94; RN resource nurse IHC, Salt Lake City, 1992—. Author/educator: (class design syllabus) Adoptive Parenting, 1991. Active Prenatal Boarding Home, Children's Aid Soc., Ogden, Utah, 1992-94; jr. leader Girl Scouts U.S., Salt Lake City, 1984-86; charge first aid clinic Presbyn. USA Gen. Assembly, Salt Lake City, 1990. Mem. Utah Nurses Assn. (Clin. Nurse Practice award 1988). Democrat. Presbyterian. Home: 3682 S 2110 E Salt Lake City UT 84109-4320 Office: IHC Telehealthcare Svc. PO Box 25547 Salt Lake City UT 84125-0547

PERKINS, NANCY JANE, industrial designer; b. Phila., Nov. 5, 1949; d. Gordon Osborne and Martha Elizabeth (Keichline) P. Student, Ohio U., 1967-68; BFA, U. Ill., 1972. Indsl. designer Peterson Bednar Assocs., Evanston, Ill., 1972-74, Deschamps Mills Assos., Bartlett, Ill., 1974-75; dir. graphic design Cameo Container Corp., Chgo., 1975-76; indsl. design cons. Sears Roebuck & Co., Chgo., 1977-88; cons. indsl. design, 1988—; founder Perkins Design Ltd., Anna Wagner Keichline Gallery, Bellefonte, Pa.; adj. prof. grad. design seminar U. Ill. Chgo., 1982, 88, 91, 93, adj. instr. undergrad. design, 1984, 88, 91, 93; adj. instr. Ill. Inst. Tech., 1987, 91; vis. assoc. prof. Carnegie-Mellon U., 1991; juror annual design rev. Indsl. Design mag., 1986; mem. tech. rev. com. Ben Franklin Partnerships, 1991—; keynote speaker several major U.S. design groups; speaker Design in Am. symposium, Nagoya, Japan, 1989. Contbr. articles to profl. jours.; patentee marine, automotive and consumer products. Co-leader Cadette troop DuPage County coun. Girl Scouts U.S., 1978-79. Recipient Outstanding Alumni award U. Ill. Alumni Jour., 1981, Goldsmith award, 1992; profiled in Indsl. Design mag., 1986, Feminine Ingenuity (by Anne L. Macdonald), 1992, Dun & Bradstreet Reports, 1993; profiled The Phila. Inquirer Mag., 1994; featured in Chgo. Athenaeum "33 plus 20", 1993, Pratt Manhattan Gallery, N.Y.C., 1994. Fellow Indsl. Designers Soc. Am. (treas. Chgo. chpt. 1977-79, vice chmn. 1979-80, chmn. 1981, mem. dist. membership com. 1982, mem. ann. conf. com. 1983, mem. publs. com. 1985-86, dir.-at-large 1987-88, v.p. Midwest dist. 1989-90, nat. sec.-treas. 1991-92, del. Internat. Coun. of the Socs. Indsl. Design 1989, speaker Mideast Conf.). Home and Office: Perkins Design Ltd 111 W Maple St Apt 1002 Chicago IL 60610-5403

PERKINS, NANCY LEEDS, lawyer; b. Washington, June 19, 1956; d. Roswell Burchard and Joan (Titcomb) P. AB, Harvard U., 1979, M in Pub. Policy, 1987, JD, 1987. Bar: Pa. 1988, D.C. 1989, U.S. Dist. Ct. D.C. 1990. Jud. clk. U.S. Dist. Ct. (ea. dist.) N.Y., Bklyn., 1987-88; assoc. Arnold & Porter, Washington, 1988—. Contbr. articles to profl. jours. Recipient Pro Bono svc. award Internat. Human Rights Law Group, 1990. Democrat. Office: Arnold & Porter 1200 New Hampshire Ave NW Washington DC 20036-6802

PERKINS, NINA ROSALIE, social worker; b. Huntington, W.Va., July 17, 1953; d. Lloyd William and Violet Macil (Elkins) Fowler; m. Homer Chester Bartoe, Jan. 30, 1972 (div. Dec. 1979); m. Gary Michael Lovejoy, Aug. 9, 1982 (div. Mar. 1989); m. Raymond Wesley Perkins, Apr. 14, 1989 (div. Nov. 1989); 1 child, Homer David. BSW, Marshall U., 1982; postgrad., W.Va. U., 1989-95. Lic. social worker, W.Va.; cert. personal care provider. Child care worker Charles W. Cammack Children's Ctr., Huntington, 1983-84; ins. underwriter Mut. of Omaha, Shreveport, La., 1984-86; banquet mgr. Ramada Inn, Shreveport, 1986-87; ctr. coord. Cabell County Community Svcs. Orgn., Inc., Huntington, 1987-90, case mgr. sr. svcs., 1990-92; minority AIDS program coord. W.Va. Dept. Health, Charleston, 1988-90, cons. instr., 1990-92; social worker Marshall U. Sch. Medicine, Frank E. Hanshaw Geriatric Ctr., Huntington, 1990—; owner, adminstr. Sr. Care Mgmt. Svcs., Huntington, W.Va., 1991-92; dir. social svcs. Wayne Continuous Care Ctr., 1992—; charter mem. Cabell County Com. for Drug Info., Huntington, 1990—; mem. Huntington Area AIDS Task Force, 1988—; social work cons. for Region 2, Area Agy. on Aging Adv. Com.; cons. and guest lectr., 1991-96; mem. ethics com. W.Va. Dept. HHS Office Social Svcs., 1995—; mem. partial hospitilization adv. com. Prestera Ctr. Mental Health. Mem. Dem. Women's Club, Cabell County. Recipient Cert. for Concerned Citizenship, State of W.Va., 1982. Mem. W.Va. Assn. Dirs. Sr. Programs, NAFE, Internat. Plaform Assn., Inst. Noetic Scis. Democrat. Baptist. Office: Frank Hanshaw Geriatric Ctr 2900 1st Ave Huntington WV 25702-1271

PERKINS, RACHEL ANN, nurse; b. Waltham, Mass., Jan. 19, 1966; d. Fred J. and Carol M. (White) P. BSN, U. N.H., 1988; MS in Bus. Mgmt., U. Laverne, 1995. ACLS instr., CPR/BLS instr. Staff nurse USAF, Andrews AFB, Md., 1988-89, ICU/IMCU staff nurse, 1991-93; SCU staff nurse USAF, Anchorage, Alaska, 1993-95, nurse supr. emergency rm., 1994-96; nurse mgr. multi svc. unit 39th Med. Group, Incirlik AFB, Turkey, 1996—; mem. flying ambulance surg. team 39th Med. Group, Incirlik AFB, 1996—; CPR instr. Andrews AFB, 1991-93; CPR instr. Elmendorf AFB, 1993-94, ACLS coord., 1993-94; trauma nurse care course instr, Incirlik, 1996. Capt. USAF, 1992—. Mem. AACN, ENA, DAR, CEN.

PERKINS, SUE DENE, journalism educator; b. Wichita Falls, Tex., Jan. 12, 1946; d. Darrye Clayton and Josephine Marie (Hall) P. BA, North Tex. State U., 1968; MA, Stephen F. Austin State U., 1980; postgrad., Angelo State U., 1979. Cert. tchr., Tex. Mag. editor Haire Pubs., N.Y.C., 1968-69; women's editor Arlington (Tex.) Daily News, 1970, police reporter editor, 1972; mag. editor Tex. Assn. Bus., Houston, 1972-74; editor in ho. pubs. P.R. Am. Assn. Respiratory Therapy, Dallas, 1974-76; asst. employee pub. rels. Gen. Telephone, San Angelo, 1976-79; dir. student publs. Stephen F. Austin State U., Nacogdoches, Tex., 1980-83, founder Women in Comm. chpt., 1982; instr. journalism Tex. A&M Univ., College Station, 1983-84; owner photo supply Photo-Graphics Co., Lufkin, Tex., 1985-88; adv. student pubs. Diboll (Tex.) Ind. Sch. Dist., 1987—; computer cons. Deep East Tex. Coun. Govt., Lufkin, 1990, Region VII Edn. Svc. Ctr., Kilgore, Tex., 1994. Editor: (mags.) Handbags & Accessories, 1968-69, Tex. Industry, 1972-74, (newspaper) Arlington Daily News, 1970-72, (newsletter) Am. Assn. for Respiratory Therapy Bull., 1974-76. Pres. Wheeler Cemetery Assn., Corrigan, Tex., 1992, v.p., 1993; sec. Youth for Christ, Diboll, Tex., 1993-95. Named Outstanding Ex-Student, Electra (Tex.) Alumni Assn., 1981-82. Mem. Journalism Educators Am., Tex. Journalism Edn. Assn., Tex. Classroom Tchrs. Assn., Order Ea. Star. Baptist. Home: RR 1 Box 106 Corrigan TX 75939-9739 Office: Diboll High Sch 1000 Harris St Diboll TX 75941-9762

PERL, LINDA SUZANNE, secondary education educator; b. N.Y.C., Apr. 1, 1951; d. Edwin Stanley and Evaline Ada (Lipp) Newman; m. Craig Barnett Perl, May 27, 1973; children: Rosalind Francine, Gordon Lewis. BA, Ariz. State U., Tempe, 1973, MA, 1975. Cert. tchr., Ariz. Tchr. lang. arts and social studies, chair dept. social studies Gilbert (Ariz.) Jr. H.S., 1973-76; tchr. lang. arts and social studies Tonto Elem. Sch., Scottsdale, Ariz., 1977-78; tchr. social studies Saguaro H.S., Scottsdale, 1978—; sponsor Nat. Honor Soc., 1989—. Bus. mgr. Pop Warner Football, Tempe, 1992; Brownies/Girl Scout leader Girl Scouts U.S., Tempe, 1984-87; den leader Boy Scouts Am., Tempe, 1986-89. Recipient various awards. Mem. Nat. Coun. for Jewish Women, Ariz. State U. Alumni Assn., Delta Kappa Gamma (corr. sec. Chi chpt., chair curriculum and instrn. com.). Democrat. Home: 1434 E Palomino Dr Tempe AZ 85284-2451 Office: Saguaro HS 6250 N 82nd St Scottsdale AZ 85250-5609

PERLESS, ELLEN, advertising executive; b. N.Y.C., Sept. 9, 1941; d. Joseph B. and Bertha (Messinger) Kaplan; m. Robert L. Perless, July 2, 1965. Student, Smith Coll., 1958-59; BA, Bard Coll., 1962. Copywriter Doyle, Dane Bernbach, N.Y.C., 1964-70, Young & Rubicam, N.Y.C., 1970-74; creative supr. Young & Rubicam, 1974-76, v.p., creative supr., 1977, v.p., assoc, creative dir., 1978, sr. v.p., assoc. creative dir., 1979-84; v.p., assoc. creative dir. Leber Katz Ptnrs., 1984-85, sr. v.p., creative dir., 1986-87; sr. v.p., sr. creative dir. FCB/Leber Katz Ptnrs., N.Y.C., 1987-93, sr. v.p., group creative dir., 1994—. Recipient Clio awards, Andy awards, awards Art Dirs. Club N.Y., N.Y. Festivals, One Club. Home: 37 Langhorne Ln Greenwich CT 06831-2611 Office: FCB/Leber Katz Ptnrs 150 E 42 St New York NY 10017

PERLICK, LILLIAN, counselor, therapist; b. Bklyn., Mar. 19, 1928; d. Harry and Rose Kravitz; m. Wallace Perlick; children: Wendy, Wynn, David. BS, Bklyn. Coll., 1949; MS, Hunter Coll., 1962. Cert. guidance counselor, N.Y.C., 1963. Tchr. Pub. Sch. #83, Bklyn., 1949-58, acting asst. prin., 1958-59; guidance counselor Elmont (N.Y.) Meml. H.S., 1959-61; therapist, pvt. practice Great Neck, N.Y., 1970-87; career counselor Nassau (N.Y.) Pub. Librs., 1977-79; cons. parent edn. Great Neck Pub. Schs., 1980-81; asst. dir. Womanspace in Great Neck, 1980-84, dir., 1984-86; counselor, therapist Ctr. Group Counseling, Boca Raton, Fla., 1996—; empathic counselor, fed. grant to Hunter Coll., 1961; exec. dir. Discovery Seminars Assn., Syosset, N.Y., 1980-82. Co-author: Grown Up Children, Grown Up Parents, 1994. Bd. dirs. Copay-Cmty. Clinic, Great Neck, 1981-85. Recipient spl. recognition Town of North Hempstead, Nassau County, N.Y., 1994. Mem. NOW, Poverty Law Ctr., Edgar Cayce Inst., Planned Parenthood, Women in the Arts (charter), Sci. of Mind. Home: 19750 Sawgrass Dr Boca Raton FL 33434

PERLMAN, BELLA BEACH, elementary school educator; b. Chgo., Mar. 12, 1931; d. Samuel and Eula Pearl (Hicks) Beach; m. Noel B. Perlman, June 29, 1963; 1 child, Samuel B. BA, Ky. State Coll., 1954; MEd, Nat. Coll. Edn., 1982. Cert. tchr., Ill. Tchr. Posen-Robbins (Ill.) Pub. Schs., 1957-67; substitute tchr. Chgo. Pub. Schs., 1973-75, Faulkner Pvt. Sch., Chgo., 1973-76; tchr. Faulkner Pvt. Sch., 1976—. Mem. Phillips 49 (sec. reunion com. 1989-94). Democrat. Baptist. Home: 400 E 33rd St Apt 514 Chicago IL 60616-4039 Office: Faulkner Sch 7110 S Coles Ave Chicago IL 60649-2611

PERLMAN, SANDRA LEE, playwright, consultant; b. Phila., June 18, 1944; d. Sidney Henry and Betty (Lee) P.; m. Henry Lewis Halem, Sept. 10, 1969; 1 child, Jessica Ariel. BA, Am. U., 1966. Actress st. theatre Soc. Hill Theatre/Phila. Recreation, 1968; rsch. editor Prof. Harvey Littleton, Madison, Wis., 1968-69; speech and advt. writer Sta. WMTV-Channel 15, Madison, 1969; English tchr. Garfield High Sch., Akron, Ohio, 1969-72; producer, writer PBS Channels 45/49, Kent, Ohio, 1975-81; communications cons. Halem Studios, Inc., Kent, 1981—; chmn. bd. Halem Studios, Kent, 1988—; promotions dir. Stas. NPR/WKSU-FM, Kent, 1985-87; playwright in residence Cleve. State U., 1993; playwright, dir. Massillon (Ohio) Mus., 1988-89. Editor: Glassblowing: A Search for Form, 1968. Bd. dirs. Bicentennial Commn., Kent, 1976, Kent Hist. Soc., 1977-87. Ohio Arts Coun. fellow, 1983, 86, Ohio Arts Coun./OHC Joint Program fellow 1989. Mem. Ohio Theatre Alliance (bd. dirs., playwriting chair), Dramatists Guild , Ohio Arts Coun. (new works panel 1987-89), First Internat. Women Playwrights Conf. (ops. dir. 1988), The Cleve. Playhouse (playwrights unit mem. 1995). Home and Office: Halem Studios Inc 429 Carthage Ave Kent OH 44240-2303

PERLMAN, WILLA M., publishing executive; b. Bklyn., Nov. 18, 1959; d. Amir Eytan Cohen, Mar. 24, 1991; 1 child, Jonathan. BA in Arts and Scis., Barnard Coll., 1981. Dir. children's books Harcourt Brace, San Diego, 1987-91; editorial dir. Willa Perlman book Harper Collins, N.Y.C., 1991-93; pres., pub. children's divsn. Simon & Schuster, N.Y.C., 1993—. Jewish. Office: Simon & Schuster 1230 6th Ave New York NY 10020

PERLMUTTER, DAWN, art and philosophy educator, aesthetics researcher; b. Phila., Oct. 10, 1959; d. Abraham Perlmutter and Joan Rocco Sutton. BFA in Interior Archtl. Design, Moore Coll. Art, 1980; MFA in Painting, Am. U., Washington, 1988; PhD in Arts & Humanities, N.Y. U., 1993. Docent edn. dept. gen. and specialized collection tours Hirshhorn Mus. & Sculpture Garden, Washington, 1985-88; instr. dept. fine arts The Art League Sch., Alexandria, Va., 1988-89; adj. asst. prof. dept. art & art history Mercer County C.C., Trenton, N.J., 1993; adj. lectr. dept. arts & humanities Richard Stockton Coll. N.J., Pomona, 1994; instr. dept. graphic design Del. County C.C., Media, Pa., 1994-95; adj. asst. prof. dept. philosophy U. Del., Newark, 1994—; asst. prof. art and philosophy dept. fine arts Cheyney U. Pa., 1995—; mem. exec. bd. Assn. Pa. State Coll. & U. Facilities, Harrisburg, 1995—. One-woman shows include Embassy of Sweden, Washington, 1983, Galerie Triangle, Washington, 1984 (best painting for the theme of children cash award 1983), Lansburghs Cultural Ctr., Washington, 1984, Washington Project for the Arts, 1985, 86, 87, Newmans Gallery, Washington, 1986, 90, 92, 94; exhibited in group shows at Please Touch Children's Mus., Phila., 1977, Gallery West, Alexandria, Va., 1984, Long Beach Mus. Art, L.A., 1984, Circle Theatre Gallery, Washington, 1986, Washington Consulting Group Art Gallery, 1988, Watkins Gallery Am. U., 1986, 87, 88, Studio Gallery, Washington, 1988, The Art League Gallery, Alexandria, Va., 1983, 87, 88, 89 (equal award of excellence 1983), The Capitol Hill Art League Gallery, Washington, 1988, 89 (cash award fall arts festival 1988, 3rd place 1989), Art East Gallery N.Y. U., 1991, Del. County C.C. Art Gallery, Media, Pa., 1994, Richard Hall Art Gallery Dixon U. Ctr., Harrisburg, Pa., 1995; exhibited in permancent collections at Please Touch Children's Mus., Phila., Hope Village, Inc., Washington, also in pvt. collections. Recipient Smithsonian Resident Assoc. scholarship, 1986, Grad. fellowship Am. U., 1987-88, Campus Faculty Profl. Devel. grant, Cheyney U. Pa., 1995. Mem. Am. Soc. for Aesthetics, Coll. Art Assn., Am. Acad. Religion, Internat. Soc. for the Advancement of Living Traditions in Art, The Greater Phila. Philosophy Consortium. Office: Cheyney U Pa Dept Fine Arts Box 526 Cheyney PA 19319

PERLMUTTER, DIANE F., communications executive; b. N.Y.C., Aug. 31, 1945; d. Bert H. and Frances (Smith) P. Student, NYU Grad. Sch. of Bus., 1969-70; AB in English, Miami U., Oxford, Ohio, 1967. Writer sales promotion Equitable Life Assurance, N.Y.C., 1967-68; adminstrv. asst. de Garmo, Inc., N.Y.C., 1968-69, asst. account exec., 1969-70, account exec., 1970-74, v.p., account supr., 1974-76; mgr. corp. advt. Avon Products, Inc., N.Y.C., 1976-79, dir. communications Latin Am., Spain, Can., 1979-80, dir. brochures, 1980-81, dir. category merchandising, 1981-82, group dir. motivational communications, 1982-83, group dir. sales promotion, 1983-84, v.p. sales promotion, 1984, v.p. internat. bus. devel., 1984-85, area v.p. Latin Am., 1985, v.p. advtg. and campaign mktg., 1985-87, v.p. U.S. operational planning, 1987; cons. N.Y.C., 1987-88; sr. v.p. Burson-Marsteller, N.Y.C., 1988-90, exec. v.p., mng. dir. consumer products, 1991-93, bd. dirs., 1992—, co-chief operating officer, 1993-94, chief operating officer, 1994—; chmn. mktg. practice/U.S., 1996—; chairperson ann. meeting Direct Selling Assn., Washington, 1982; v.p. Nat. Home Fashions League, N.Y.C., 1975-76; adj. instr. SUNY/Fashion Inst. Tech., 1992—; bd. dirs. Double L.P. Industries, Inc. Founding bd. mem. Am. Red Magen David for Israel, N.Y.C., 1970-75; mem. adv. coun. Miami Sch. Bus., 1986—, Miami Sch. Applied Scis., 1978-81. Mem. Pub. Rels. Soc. Am., Advt. Women of N.Y., Women in Communications, Miami U. Alumni Assn. (pres., chair 1986), Publicity Club N.Y. (bd. dirs. 1994—), Beta Gamma Sigma. Office: Burson-Marsteller 230 Park Ave S New York NY 10003-1513

PERLMUTTER, DONNA, music and dance critic; b. Phila.; d. Myer and Bessie (Krasno) Stein; m. Jona Perlmutter, Mar. 21, 1964; children: Aaron, Matthew. BA, Pa. State U., 1958; MS, Yeshiva U., 1959. Music and dance critic L.A. Herald Examiner, 1975-84, L.A. Times, 1984-94, N.Y. Times Contbr., 1994—; dance critic Dance Mag., N.Y.C., 1980—; music critic Opera News, N.Y.C., 1981—, Ovation Mag., N.Y.C., 1983-89, N.Y. Mag., 1995—, L.A. Mag., 1996—, Daily News, L.A., 1996—; panelist, speaker various music and dance orgns. Author Shadowplay: The Life of Antony Tudor, 1991. Recipient Deems Taylor award for excellence in writing on music ASCAP, 1991. Mem. Music Critics Assn. Home: 10507 Le Conte Ave Los Angeles CA 90024-3305

PERLMUTTER, LYNN SUSAN, neuroscientist; b. N.Y.C., Oct. 12, 1954; d. David Louis and Audrey Marilyn (Cherkoss) P.; m. Howard Jay Deiner, May 30, 1976; 1 child, Jocelyn Rae Perldeiner. BA with highest honors, SUNY, Stony Brook, 1976; MA, Mich. State U., 1980, PhD, 1984. Postdoctoral fellow U. Calif., Irvine, 1984-87; asst. prof. neurology and pathology U. So. Calif., L.A., 1987-94, sec. med. faculty assembly, 1990-92, assoc. prof. neurology and pathology, 1994; sci. coord. U. So. Calif. Bravo Med. Magnet H.S. Partnership, 1993-94; staff scientist pharm. divsn. Inst. Dementia Rsch., Bayer Corp., West Haven, Conn., 1994—; ad hoc reviewer John Douglas French Found., L.A., 1988, 91, Calif. Dept. Alzheimer's Disease Program, Sacramento, 1990, 92; mem. neurology rev. panel NIH, 1993, 94; chmn. blood-brain barrier session Internat. Conf. Alzheimer's Disease, Italy, 1992; organizer internat. symposium at Soc. Neuroscientists Africa, 1995. Contbr. articles to sci. jours. Coach Conn. state champions problem I, divsn. I, Odyssey of the Mind program, 1996. Travel fellow Internat. Conf. on Alzheimer's Disease, 1990, 92. Mem. AAAS, Soc. Neurosci., Electron Microscopy Soc. Am., Internat. Platform Assn., N.Y. Acad. Scis., Med. Faculty Women's Assn. (chmn. membership 1989-91), Phi Kappa Phi. Democrat. Jewish. Office: Bayer Corp Pharm Divsn Inst Dementia Rsch 400 Morgan Ln West Haven CT 06516-4140

PERLOFF, MARJORIE GABRIELLE, English and comparative literature educator; b. Vienna, Austria, Sept. 28, 1931; d. Maximilian and Ilse (Schueller) Mintz; m. Joseph K. Perloff, July 31, 1953; children—Nancy Lynn, Carey Elizabeth. A.B., Barnard Coll., 1953; M.A., Cath. U., 1956, Ph.D., 1965. Asst. prof. English and comparative lit. Cath. U., Washington, 1966-68; asso. prof. Cath. U., 1969-71; asso. prof. U. Md., 1971-73, prof., 1973-76; Florence R. Scott prof. English U. So. Calif., Los Angeles, 1976—; prof. English and comparative lit. Stanford U., Calif., 1986—, Sadie Dernham prof. humanities, 1990—. Author: Rhyme and Meaning in the Poetry of Yeats, 1970, The Poetic Art of Robert Lowell, 1973, Frank O'Hara, Poet Among Painters, 1977, The Poetics of Indeterminacy: Rimbaud to Cage, 1981, The Dance of the Intellect: Studies in the Poetry of the Pound Tradition, 1985, 2d edit., 1996, The Futurist Moment: Avant-Garde, Avant-Guerre and the Language of Rupture, 1986, Poetic License: Essays in Modern and Postmodern Lyric, 1990, Radical Artifice: Writing Poetry in the Age of Media, 1991, Wittgenstein's Ladder: Poetic Language and the Strangeness of the Ordinary, 1996; editor: Postmodern Genres, 1990; co-editor: John Cage: Composed in America, 1994; contbg. editor: Columbia Literary History of the U.S., 1987; contbr. preface to Contemporary Poets, 1980, A John Cage Reader, 1983. Guggenheim fellow, 1981-82, NEA fellow, 1985; Phi Beta Kappa scholar, 1994-95. Mem. MLA (exec. coun. 1977-81, Am. lit. sect. 1993—), Comparative Lit. Assn. (pres. 1993-94), Lit. Studies Acad. Home: 1467 Amalfi Dr Pacific Palisades CA 90272-2752 Office: Stanford U Dept English Stanford CA 94305

PERRAUD, PAMELA BROOKS, human resources professional; b. Mpls., May 27, 1948; d. Wright William and Gladys Brooks; m. Jean-Marc Francois Perraud, Nov. 22, 1975; children: Marc Alexander, Andrea Elizabeth. BA, Conn. Coll., 1970; MA in Urban Studies, Occidental Coll., 1972; MA in Indsl. Rels., U. Minn., 1977. Cert. sr. profl. in human resources; cert. compensation profl. Dir. personnel Mpls. Housing and ReDevel. Authority, Mpls., 1973-75; dir. adminstrn. United Svcs. Orgn., Paris, 1976-78; dir. office svcs. Pechiney Ughine Kuhlmann, Greenwich, Conn., 1979-80; lectr., trainer Monodnock Internat., London, 1981-85; personnel recruiter IBM Europe, Paris, 1989; prof. bus. Am. Bus. Sch., Paris, 1988-92; pres. Women's Inst. for Continuing Edn., Paris, 1992-93; human resource cons. N.Y.C., 1994—; chair Women on the Move, Paris, 1990-93; v.p. Women's Inst. for Continuing Edn., Paris, 1988-93. Co-author: (books) Living in France, 1994. Co-founder Focus Info. and Referral, London, 1982, Women in Mgmt., Mpls., 1973; trustee Conn. Coll., New London, 1970. Fellow in Pub. Affairs, Coro Found., L.A., 1970. Mem. Friends of WICE, Am. Compensation Assn., Soc. for Human Resources Mgmt., Soc. for Intercultural, Edn., Tng. and Rsch., Women's Econs. Roundtable, NAFE. Home: Ste 21E 200 E 90th St New York NY 10128

PERREAULT, SISTER JEANNE, college president; b. Providence, Dec. 13, 1929; d. Alphonse and Malvina I. (Chevalier) P. BSEd, Cath. Tchrs. Coll., Providence, 1959; MS, Cath. U., Washington, 1968; EdD (hon.), Salve Regina U., 1990. Tchr. elem. sch. St. Ann Sch., West Warwick, R.I.; tchr. jr. high sch. St. John Jr. High Sch., West Warwick; tchr. high sch. Notre Dame High Sch., Berlin, N.H.; assoc. prof. Rivier Coll., Nashua, N.H., pres., 1980—; mem. Gov.'s Task Force for Edn. Mem. State of N.H. Post-Secondary Edn. Commn., Concord; bd. dirs. Ctr. for Econ. Devel. for Nashua Area, Bishop Guertin H.S., Nashua; commr. New Eng. Assn. Schs. & Colls.; provincial coun. Sisters of Presentation of Mary. Mem. AAUP, Am. Coun. Colls., Assn. Cath. Colls. and Univs., N.H. Coll. and Univ. Coun.

PERRI, DOROTHY G., school nurse; b. Balt., May 8, 1949; d. Charles Edwin Sr. and Dorothy Viola (Smith) Grimmel; m. Anthony Joseph Perri, May 31, 1975; children: Anthony J. III, Christopher M. BSN, Am. U., 1971; MS, Tex. Woman's U., 1989. Cert. sch. nurse, Tex. Staff nurse gen. surgery, ICU, recovery rm. Georgetown U. Hosp., Washington, 1971-75; utilization rev. coord. Hahnemann Hosp., Phila., 1975-77; office mgr., urological nurse Office of Anthony J. Perri, MD, Phila., 1979-82; vis. nurse Tex. Star Health Care/Vis. Nurses East Tex., Corsicana, 1984-86; sch. nurse Dallas Ind. Sch. Dist., 1989-90; health svcs. coord., sch. nurse Highland Park Ind. Sch. Dist., Dallas, 1990—; vol., CPR, 1st aid instr. ARC, Dallas, 1991—. Mem. Dallas Area Sch. Health Assn., Tex. Assn. Sch. Nurses, Region 10 Assn. Sch. Nurses, Nat. Assn. Sch. Nurses, Navarro County Med. Soc. Alliance, Sigma Theta Tau. Republican. Roman Catholic. Home: 2105 Dartmouth Ln Corsicana TX 75110-2211

PERRI, NANCY ANN, community development director; b. Carbondale, Pa., June 1, 1960; d. Thomas and Anne Conaboy Tolerico; m. Carmino P. Perri, Sept. 18, 1982; children: Carmino, Melissa. BSBA, Marywood Coll., 1982. Adminstrv. asst. Bremer Hof Resort, Uniondale, Pa., 1982-85; teller Penn Security Bank and Trust, Scranton, Pa., 1986-87; comty. devel. dir. City of Carbondale, 1987—; project mgr. Carbondale Indsl. Devel. Authority; coord. Carbondale Enterprise Zone. Mem. Carbondale Area C. of C. (treas.), Carbondale YMCA (sec.), Carbondale 2000 (sec.). Democrat. Roman Catholic. Office: City of Carbondale 1 N Main St Carbondale PA 18407

PERRICCI, ELLEN SMITH, physician, writer; b. Bethesda, MD, Apr. 26, 1955; d. John McCoach and Elizabeth Sherman (Sewell) Smith; m. Michael Anthony Perricci, Dec. 17, 1977; children: Anna Lucile, Joseph. BA magna cum laude, U. Utah, 1974, MD, 1978. Diplomate Am. Bd. Psychiatry & Neurology. Emergency staff physician Good Samaritan Hosp., Pottsville, Pa., 1980-83, Reading (Pa.) Hosp. and Med. Ctr., 1983-85; gen. physician Eastern Lebanon County Family Health Ctr., Myerstown, Pa., 1985-86; gen. physician, chmn. infection control com. Philhaven Psychiat. Hosp., Mt. Gretna, Pa., 1986-89; psychiatry resident Pa. State U., Hershey, 1989-94; chief of svc. Divsn. Med. Rev., Psychiatry Office of Med. Assistance Programs, Harrisburg, Pa., 1995; staff physician VA Hosp., Lebanon, Pa., 1995-96; med. dir. substance abuse treatment programs Lebanon VA Med. Ctr., 1996—; cons. physician Birthright, Reading, Pa., 1983-85; chief of svc. divsn. Psychiatry Med. Rev., Office of Med. Assistance Programs, Harrisburg, Pa., Jan.-June, 1995. Recipient scholarship Med. Assistance Program, Swaziland, Southern Africa, 1978; rsch. asst. grantee NIH, 1974. Mem. Christian Med. and Dental Soc. (nat. del. 1987-88), Christian Community Health Fellowship, Quentin Riding Club, Phi Beta Kappa.

PERRIN, GAIL, editor; b. Boston, Oct. 14, 1938; d. Hugh and Helen (Baxter) P. B.A., Wellesley Coll., 1960. Copy girl Washington Daily News, summers, 1954-57, reporter, 1958, 60-61, acting women's editor, food editor, 1961-62, rewrite reporter, 1963-65; reporter Honolulu Star Bull., 1959; women's editor Boston Globe, 1965-71, asst. met. editor, 1971-74, food editor, 1974-92; food cons., free-lance writer, 1992—. Mem. Assn. Food Journalists, Women's Culinary Guild.

PERRIN, SARAH ANN, lawyer; b. Neoga, Ill., Dec. 13, 1904; d. James Lee and Bertha Frances (Baker) Figenbaum; m. James Frank Perrin, Dec. 24, 1926. LLB, George Washington U., 1941, JD, 1964. Bar: D.C. 1942. Assoc. atty. Mabel Walker Willebrandt, law office, Washington, 1941-42; atty. various fed. housing agys., 1942-69, asst. gen. counsel FHA, Washington, 1959-60, asst. gen. counsel HUD, Washington, 1960-69; sec. Nat. Housing Conf., Washington, 1970-80; rsch. cons. housing and urban devel., Palmyra, Va., 1970-76; acting sec. Nat. Housing Rsch. Coun., Washington, 1973-80; bd. dirs. Nat. Housing Conf., 1972—. Mem. Rep. Presdl. Adv. Commn., 1991-92, Senatorial Com.; trustee Found. for Coop. Housing, 1975-80; mem. Blue Ridge Presbytery Div. Mission, Presbyn. Ch., 1979-80, Friends of Fluvanna County Libr. Mem. ABA, Fed. Bar Assn., Women's Bar Assn. D.C. (pres. 1959-60), Nat. Assn. Women Lawyers, George Washington Law Assn., Charlottesville Area Women's Bar Assn., Fluvanna County Bar Assn., Fluvanna County Hist. Soc. (pres. 1973-75, exec. com. 1985-89), Order Eastern Star, Presbyn. Women (pres. Fork Union chpt. 1972-80, sec. 1980-94), Phi Alpha Delta (internat. pres. 1955-57, internat. adv. bd.). Home: Solitude Plantation Palmyra VA 22963

PERRONE, RUTH ELLYN, university administrator; b. Hearne, Tex., July 2, 1951; d. John Paul Perrone and Ellen Gayle (Sullivan) Perrone-Robertson. BS, Stephen F. Austin State U., 1973; MPA, Tex. A&M U., 1986. Social worker Tex. Dept. Pub. Welfare, Nacogdoches, Tex., 1974-76; licensing rep. Tex. Dept. Human Resources, Bryan, 1976-85; spl. asst. to vice chancellor for state affairs Tex. A&M Univ. System, Austin, 1987-90; asst. to pres. Tex. A&M U., College Station, 1990-92, dir. external rels., 1992—; advisor legis. study group Tex. A&M U., 1992—; bd. dirs. Scott & White Hosp. Health Plan, 1995—. Chair governing bd. John Ben Shepperd Pub. Leadership Found., Odessa, Tex., 1993-94; bd. dirs. Tex. Lyceum, Austin, 1992—; assoc. mem. St. Joseph Hosp. Aux., Bryan, 1993—. Mem. Nat. Assn. State Univ. and Land Grant Coll. (coun. on govtl. affairs), Coun. for Advancement and Support of Edn., Bryan/College Station C. of C. (coun. on govtl. affairs). Office: Texas A&M University Office of President 805 Rudder Tower College Station TX 77843

PERRONI, CAROL, artist, painter; b. Boston, July 28, 1952; d. Michael John and Mary Agnes (Collett) P.; m. John Richard Mugford, May 23, 1987; 1 child, Jonathan Perroni. Student, Boston Mus. Sch., 1970-71; BA in Art, Bennington Coll., 1976; student, Skowhegan Sch. Painting and Sculpture, 1978; MFA in Art, Hunter Coll., 1983. Studio asst. for artist Isaac Witkin Bennington, Vt., 1973-74; libr. asst. Simmons Coll. Libr., Boston, 1977-78; studio asst. for artist Mel Bochner N.Y.C., 1979; bookkeeper Internat. House, N.Y.C., 1979-80; studio asst. for Lee Krasner East Hampton, N.Y., 1980; rsch. asst. Art News Mag., N.Y.C., 1981; intern Greenespace Gallery, N.Y.C., 1982-83; tech. asst. Avery Architectural and Fine Arts Libr. Columbia U., N.Y.C., 1981-83; libr., rechr. Kennedy Galleries, Inc., N.Y.C., 1984-86; program specialist, art tchr. Swinging Sixties Sr. Citizen Ctr., Bklyn., 1986-87; with Arts in Edn. Program, R.I., 1993—. One-woman shows include Boston City Hall, 1978, Hunter Coll. Gallery, N.Y.C., 1983, Ten Worlds Gallery, N.Y.C., 1986, Gallery X, New Bedford, Mass., 1993, 94, Hera Galley, Wakefield, R.I., 1995, AS220, Providence, R.I., 1996, C.C. of R.I., Lincoln, 1996; group shows include Salem State Coll., Mass., 1978, Fuller Mus. Art, Brockton, Mass., 1989,90, Danforth Mus. Ar., Framingham, Mass., 1989, Attleboro Mus., Mass., 1989, Gallery X, New Bedford, Mass., 1992, 93, 94, 95, 96, Bell St. Chapel, Providence, 1994, 95, AS220, Providence, 1994, Hera Gallery, Wakefield, R.I., 1993, 94, 95, 96, St. Andrew's Sch., Barrington, R.I., 1994, McKillop Gallery Salve Regina U., Newport, R.I., 1995, North River Arts Soc., Marshfield Hills Village, Mass., 1995, Providence Art Club, 1995, The Sarah Doyle Gallery Brown U., Providence, 1995, R.I. Watercolor Soc. Slater Meml. Park, Pawtucket, 1995, Fed. Reserve Bank, Boston, 1996, others; represented in permanent collection at R.I. Hosp. Art Collection and pvt. collections. Bd. dirs. Hera Ednl. Found., 1994—. Recipient grant Artists Space, 1986, grant Flintridge Found., 1993, fellowship Vt. Studio Ctr., Johnson, 1990. Mem. SOHO 20 Gallery (nat. affiliate mem.). Home: 154 Lancaster St Providence RI 02906

PERROTTY, P. SUE, bank executive. Exec. v.p. strategic mktg. and distbn. sys. devel. Meridian Bancorp., Inc., Wyomissing, Pa. Office: Meridian Bancorp Inc One Meridian Blvd Wyomissing PA 19610*

PERRY, BETH BENTLEY, writer, artist; b. Oklahoma City, Apr. 4, 1928; d. Warren Edward and Ollie Antoinette (Kerr) Bentley; m. Kenneth Alvin Perry, Dec. 23, 1925; children: Pamela Lynn, Scott Kenneth, Angela Beth. AA, Fla. Jr. Coll., 1976; BA, U. North Fla., 1978, BFA magna cum laude, 1983. pres. Univ. Art League, Jacksonville, 1980-81; sec. Jacksonville Coalition for Visual Arts, 1986-87. Author: From the Same Cloth, 1994, Eyes of the Osprey, 1991. Vol. Dem. Party, Jacksonville, 1991-94, Taylor Residences, Jacksonville, 1980-95, Pub. TV, Jacksonville, 1978-85; bd. dirs. Am. United, Jacksonville, 1995-96. Recipient Grumbacher award for best in show, 1984. Democrat. Home: 7926 Praver Dr W Jacksonville FL 32217

PERRY, BLANCHE BELLE, physical therapist; b. New Bedford, Mass., Sept. 2, 1929; d. Joseph Rudolph and Beatrice (Faria) Andrews; BS, Ithaca (N.Y.) Coll., 1951; MA, Assumption Coll., Worcester, Mass., 1978; m. Louis Perry, Nov. 26, 1953; (dec. 1980); children: Marcia, Susan, Tracey, Evelyn. Office and hosp. phys. therapist, Mass. and N.Y., 1961-65; dir. rehab. svcs. St. Luke's Hosp., New Bedford, 1967-89; ret, 1989; profl. adv. com. Vis. Nurse Assn. Wareham, 1980; mem. faculty continuing edn. Newbury Coll., 1986; corporator New Bedford Five Cents Savs. Bank, Compass Bank for Savs. Chmn. Mattapoisett Sch. Com., 1970; vice chmn. Mass. Sch. Commn. Area IV, 1972-75; sec. Old Colony Regional Vocat. Sch. Com., 1973—; trustee Abner Pease Scholarship Found.; chmn. com. opportunity ctr. CARF, New Bedford, 1987; pres. St. Luke's Hosp. Retirees, 1996. Grantee Elks Nat. Found., 1965. Mem. Am. Phys. Therapy Assn., Nat. Rehab. Adminstrs. Assn., Delta Kappa Gamma. Republican. Club: Mattapoisett Women's (pres. 1996). Home: 41 Aucoot Rd Mattapoisett MA 02739-2401

PERRY, CATHERINE D., judge; b. 1952. BA, Univ. of Okla., 1977; JS, Wash. Univ. Sch. of Law, 1980. Sec., law clk. Gillespie, Perry & Gentry, Sentinel, Okla., 1970, 77-78; with Armstrong, Teasdale, Kramer & Vaughn, St. Louis, 1980-90; magistrate judge U.S. Dist. Ct. (Mo. ea. dist.), 8th circuit, St. Louis, 1990-94, district judge, 1994—. Mem. Fed. Magistrate Judges Assn., Nat. Assn. of Women Judges, Am. Bar Assn., Mo. Bar Assn., Bar Assn. of Metropolitan St. Louis, Women Lawyers Assn. of Greater St. Louis. Office: US Courthouse 1114 Market St Rm 840 Saint Louis MO 63101-2034*

PERRY, CHRISTINE STEFANOU, beverage company manager; b. Rochester, N.Y., Jan. 31, 1963; d. Constantine and Florence (Geoca) Stefanou; m. Geoffrey O. Perry, Apr. 25, 1987; 1 child, Demetra Mary. BS, Cornell U., 1985. Prodn. team mgr. Procter and Gamble, Mehoopany, Pa., 1985-86, project mgr., 1986-87; quality assurance supr. Pepsi-Cola, Newport News, Va., 1987-88, maintenance supr., 1988-89; assoc. mgr. ops. tng. Pepsi-Cola, Somers, N.Y., 1989-90; sr. employee rels. rep. Pepsi-Cola, Newport News, Va., 1990-92; process improvement mgr. Pepsi-Cola, Somers, 1992-95; mktg. devel. rep. Pepsi-Cola, Denver, 1995—. Mem. NAFE, Cornell Assn. Alumni (amb. 1987—). Office: Pepsi-Cola 3801 Brighton Blvd Denver CO 80216

PERRY, E. ELIZABETH, social worker, real estate manager; b. Balt., Oct. 2, 1954; d. James Glenn and Pearl Elizabeth (Christopher) P.; 1 child, Linden Andrew. AA, C.C. of Balt., 1973; B in Art, Psychology, Social Work, U. Md., Balt., 1975, MSW, 1978. Asst. grant coord. Md. Conf. Social Concern, Balt., 1975; dir. social svcs. West Balt. Cmty. Health Care Corp., 1978-80; tng. counselor NutriSystem Inc. of Md., Balt., 1983-86; counselor/psychotherapist Switlik Elem. Sch., Marathon, Fla., 1988-89; program dir. emergency shelter Children's Home Soc., Miami, 1990-91; health educator, spokesperson Rape Treatment Ctr., Miami, 1991-94; CEO, pres. bd. Child Assault Prevention Project, Miami, 1993—; self-employed in real estate rehab. and mgmt., 1980—; pub. spkr. on women's and children's issues/sexual assault issues, 1990—. Bd. dirs. Partnership Way, 1993-95, ACHIEVE, 1995—; pub. citizen Dem. Nat. Com. Mem. AAUW, NOW (bd. dirs. Dade County 1994-95), Nat. Abortion Rights Action League, Amnesty Internat., People for the Am. Way, Psi Chi, Phi Theta Kappa. Democrat. Home: 5161 Alton Rd Miami Beach FL 33140 Office: Child Assault Prev Project Omni Mall Ste 1195 1601 Biscayne Blvd Miami FL 33132

PERRY, ELISABETH SCHERF, psychologist; b. Kasel-Trier, Germany, Aug. 24, 1952; came to U.S., 1976; d. Willibald and Brigitta (Jakobs) Scherf; m. R. T. Perry. AA in Maths., Columbia Basin Coll., Pasco, Wash., 1978; BS in Psychology with honors, U. Wis., 1982; MA in Psychology, Calif. Sch. Prof. Psychology, L.A., 1985, PhD in Clin. Psychology, 1988. Lic. psychologist, N.Mex.; cert. Am. Bd. Forensic Examiners. Psychologist Psychol. Health Inc., Albuquerque, 1988-91, Los Lunas (N.Mex.) Sch. Dist., 1990-91; psychologist, dir. S.W. Psychol. Svcs., Santa Fe, 1991—; police psychologist Gallup (N.Mex.) Police Dept., 1992—, McKinley County Sheriff's Dept., Gallup, 1992—; psychologist, supr. Mesilla Valley, Gallup, 1995; sch. psychologist Los Alamos Schs., 1995. V.p. Santa Fe Child abuse Coun., 1991. Mem. APA, N.Mex. Psychol. Assn., Phi Kappa Phi. Office: SW Psychol Svcs 125 E Palace Ave Ste 62 Santa Fe NM 87544 also: 800 Trinity Dr Ste I Los Alamos NM 87544

PERRY, EVELYN REIS, communications company executive; b. N.Y.C., Mar. 9; d. Lou L. and Bertl (Wolf) Reis; m. Charles G. Perry III, Jan. 7, 1968; children: Charles G. IV, David Reis. BA, Univ. Wis., 1963; student Am. Acad. Dramatic Arts, 1958-59, Univ. N.Mex., 1963-64. Lic. real estate broker, N.C. Vol. ETV project Peace Corps, 1963-65; program officer-radio/tv Peace Corps, Washington, 1965-68; dir. Vols. in Svc. to Am. (VISTA), Raleigh, N.C., 1977-80; exec. dir. CETA Program for Displaced Homemakers, Raleigh, 1980-81; cons. exec. dir. to Recycle Raleigh for Food and Fuel, Theater in the Park, 1981-83, Artspace, Inc., Raleigh, 1983-84; pres., chief exec. officer Carolina Sound Comm., MUZAK, Charleston, S.C. and 12 counties in S.C., 1984—; pub. rels. account exec. various cos., Washington, Syracuse, N.Y., 1969-71; cons. pub. rels. and orgn. Olympic Organizing Com., Mexico City, 1968; cons. pub. rels., fundraising, arts mgmt. pub. speaking, Ill., Pa., N.C., 1971-77; orgnl. and pub. speaking cons. Perry & Assocs., Raleigh, 1980—. Mem. adv. bd. Gov.'s Office Citizen Affairs, Raleigh, 1981-85; mem. Involvement Coun. of Wake County, N.C., Raleigh, 1981-84; mem. Adv. Coun. to Vols. in Svc. to Am., Raleigh, 1980-84; mem. Pres.'s adv. bd. Peace Corps, Washington, 1980-82; v.p., bd. dirs. Voluntary Action Ctr., Raleigh, 1980-84, bd. dirs., Charleston, 1988-94; sec. bd. dirs. Temple Kahil Kadosh Beth Elohim, 1987-89, sec. fin., 1989-90, v.p. programming, 1990-93, v.p. adminstrn. 1993-95; bd. dirs. Chopstik Theater, Charleston, 1989-90; del., chmn. S.C. Delegation to White House Conf. Small Bus., 1995. Mem. N.C. Coun. of Women's Orgns. (pres., v.p. 1982-84), Charleston Hotel and Motel Assn., N.C. Assn. Vol. Adminstrs. (bd. dirs. 1980-84), S.C. Restaurant Assn., Nat. Assn. Women Bus. Owners, Internat. Planned Music Assn. (bd. dirs. 1986—, newsletter editor), NAFE, Nat. Fedn. Ind. Businesses (mem. adv. bd. 1987—, chmn. guardian adv. coun. 1994—), Internat. Platform Assn., Theaterworks (bd. dirs. 1994—), Charleston C. of C. Office: Carolina Sound Comm Inc 1941 Savage Rd Ste 200G Charleston SC 29407

PERRY, JACQUELIN, orthopedic surgeon; b. Denver, May 31, 1918; d. John F. and Tirzah (Kuruptkat) P. B.E., U. Calif., Los Angeles, 1940; M.D., U. Calif., San Francisco, 1950. Intern Children's Hosp., San Francisco, 1950-57; resident in orthopedic surgery U. Calif., San Francisco, 1951-55; orthopedic surgeon Rancho Los Amigos Hosp., Downey, Calif., 1955—; chief pathokinesiology Rancho Los Amigos Med. Ctr., 1961—; chief stroke service Rancho Los Amigos Hosp., 1972-75; mem. faculty U. Calif. Med. Sch., San Francisco, 1966—; clin. prof. U. Calif. Med. Sch., 1973—; mem. faculty U. So. Calif. Med. Sch., 1969—, prof. orthopedic surgery, 1972—, dir. polio and gait clinic, 1972—; Disting. lectr. for hosp. for spl. surgery and Cornell U. Med. Coll., N.Y.C., 1977-78; Packard Meml. lectr. U. Colo. Med. Sch., 1970; Osgood lectr. Harvard Med. Sch., 1978; Summer lectr., Portland, 1977; Shands lectr.; cons. USAF; guest speaker symposia; cons. Biomechanics Lab. Centinela Hosp., 1979—. Served as phys. therapist U.S. Army, 1941-46. Recipient Disting. Svc. award Calif. Assn. Rehab. Facilities,1981, Pres.'s award, 1984, Milton Cohen award Nat. Assn. Rehab., 1993, Isabelle and Lenard Goldensen award for tech. United Cerebral Palsy Assn., 1981, Jow Dowling award, 1985, Profl. Achievement award UCLA, 1988, Armistad award Rancho Los Amigos Med. Ctr., Calif., 1990; named Woman of Yr. for Medicine in So. Calif., L.A. Times, 1959, Alumnus of Yr., U. Calif. Med. Sch., 1980, Physician of Yr. Calif. Employment Devel. Dept., 1994. Mem. AMA, Am. Acad. Orthop. Surgeons (Kappa Delta award for rsch. 1977), Am. Orthop. Assn. (Shands lectr. 1988), Western Orthop. Assn., Calif. Med. Soc., L.A. County Med. Soc., Am. Phys. Therapy Assn. (hon. Golden Pen award 1965), Am. Acad. Orthotists and Prosthetists (hon.), Scoliosis Rsch. Soc., LeRoy Abbott Soc., Am. Acad. Cerebral Palsy. Home: 12319 Brock Ave Downey CA 90242-3503 Office: Rancho Los Amigos Med Ctr 7601 Imperial Hwy Downey CA 90242-3456

PERRY, JANET MARGARET, education networking consultant; b. Pitts., Sept. 18, 1956; d. Henry John and Eleanor Garard (Helman) Ehrenberger; m. Stephen Francis Perry, June 28, 1980; children: Margaret, Thomas, Anna Catherine. BA, St. John's Coll., 1978; MLS, U. Pitts., 1979; cert. exec. devel. program, Northwestern U., 1993. Sales rep. No. Lights Computers, Berkeley, Calif., 1985-87; mgr. edn. sales Kinetics, Walnut Creek, Calif., 1988-89; mgr. higher edn. programs Novell, Provo, Utah, 1989-94; mgr. technology transfer ptnrs. Novell, Provo, 1994-95; ptnr. Vision Interactive, Napa, Calif., 1995—; sysop Novell List Server, Syracuse, N.Y., 1991-95. Contbg. editor On The Internet, 1995; editor View from Napa Valley, 1996; guest editor On the Internet, 1996. Librarian, vol. Trinity Grammar and Prep, Napa, 1995—. Recipient Grace Murrey Hopper award Women in Informative Processing, 1982. Mem. Internet soc. (adv. coun. 1992-95, program com. co-chair 1995—), HTML Writers Guild, Internet Entrepreneurs Forum. Republican. Roman Catholic. Home: 3354 Brittany Circle Napa CA 94558 Office: Vision Interactive 2532 Jefferson St Napa CA 94558

PERRY, JANICE ARIEL, principal; b. Bainbridge Island, Wash., Aug. 6, 1940; d. Sigvard C. and Ariel Wright (Henderson) Stranne; m. Harold O. Perry, Aug. 12, 1960; children: Steven, Ann. Student, U. Puget Sound, Tacoma, Wash., 1958-60; BEd, U. Wash., 1972; M. Ednl. Adminstrn., Western Wash. U., 1986. Tchr. Seattle Sch. Dist., 1972—, Kimball Elem. Sch., 1985-95; with mastery in learning restructuring project NEA, 1986—; prin. McGilvra Elem. Sch., Seattle, 1995—; adj. faculty Antioch U. Cons. editor Teaching and Change, 1992—; contbr. articles to profl. jours. Mem. pub. edn. adv. bd. Antioch U., Seattle, 1989-94, Woodring Coll., Western Wash. U., Seattle, 1989-94; mem. ednl. tech. adv. com. Office of Spt. Pub. Instrn., State of Wash., Olympia, 1991—. Named Christa McAuliffe Educator, Nat. Found. for Improvement of Edn., Washington, 1991. Mem. ASCD, NEA (del. gen. assembly 1993, 94), Wash. Edn. Assn., Seattle Edn. Assn., Consortium for Sch. Networking, New Horizons, Nat. Assn. Elem. Sch. Prins., Assn. of Wash. Sch. Prins. Home: 1106 NE 42nd St Apt 18 Seattle WA 98105-6348 Office: McGilvra Elem. Sch. 1617 38th Ave E Seattle WA 98112

PERRY, JEAN LOUISE, dean; b. Richland, Wash., May 13, 1950; d. Russell S. and Sue W. Perry. BS, Miami U., Oxford, Ohio, 1972; MS, U. Ill., Urbana, 1973, PhD, 1976. Cons. ednl. placement office U. Ill., 1973-75; adminstrv. intern Coll. Applied Life Studies, 1975-76, asst. dean, 1976-77, assoc. dean, 1978-81, asst. prof. dept. phys. edn., 1976-81; assoc. prof. phys. edn. San Francisco State U., 1981-84, prof., 1984-90, chair, 1981-90; dean Coll. of Human and Community Scis. U. Nev., Reno, 1990—. Named to excellent tchr. list U. Ill., 1973-79. Mem. AAHPERD (fellow research consortium, pres. 1988-89), Am. Assn. Higher Edn., Am. Ednl. Research Assn., Nat. Assn. Phys. Edn. in Higher Edn., Nat. Assn. Girls and Women in Sports (guide coordinator, pres.), Delta Psi Kappa, Phi Delta Kappa. Home: 3713 Ranchview Ct Reno NV 89509-7437 Office: U Nev Coll Human and Cmty Scis 136 Reno NV 89557

PERRY, MARGARET, librarian, writer; b. Cin., Nov. 15, 1933; d. Rufus Patterson and Elizabeth Munford (Anthony) P. AB, Western Mich. U., 1954; Cert. d'etudes Francaises, U. Paris, 1956; MSLS, Cath. U. Am., 1959. Young adult and reference libr. N.Y. Pub. Libr., N.Y.C., 1954-55, 57-58; libr. U.S. Army, France and Germany, 1959-63, 64-67; chief circulation U.S. Mil. Libr., West Point, N.Y., 1967-70; head edn. libr. U. Rochester, N.Y., 1970-75, asst. prof., 1973-75, assoc. prof., 1975-82, asst. dir. librs. for reader svcs., 1975-82, acting dir. librs., 1976-77, 80; univ. libr. Valparaiso U., Ind., 1982-93; ret., 1993; mem. Task Force on Coop. Edn., Rochester, 1972; freelance writer Mich. Land Use Inst., 1995—. Author: A Bio-bibliography of Countee P. Cullen, 1903-1946, 1971, Silence to the Drums: A Survey of the Literature of the Harlem Renaissance, 1976, The Harlem Renaissance, 1982, The Short Fiction of Rudolph Fisher, 1987; also numerous short stories; contbr. articles to profl. jours. Bd. dirs. Urban League, 1978-80. Recipient 1st prize short story contest Armed Forces Writers League, 1966; 2d prize Frances Steloff Fiction prze, 1968, 1st prize short story Arts Alive, 1990, 2d prize short story Willow Rev., 1990; seminar scholar Schloss Leopoldskron, Salzburg, Austria, 1956, 3d prize short story West Shore C.C., Scottville, Mich., 1995. Mem. ALA, NOW. Democrat. Roman Catholic. Home: 15050 Roaring Brook Rd Thompsonville MI 49683-9216

PERRY, MARION JUDITH HELZ, English educator; b. Takoma Park, Md., June 2, 1943; d. Armin Werner and Adah Hubbard (Porter) Helz; m. Franklyn Alfred Perry, Jr., July 17, 1971; children: Judith, Scott. BA, Ripon (Wis.) Coll., 1964; MA, U. Iowa, 1966; MFA, 1969; MA, U. Buffalo, 1979, PhD, 1986. Instr. West Liberty (W.Va.) State Coll., 1966-68, Albright Coll., Reading, Pa., 1968-70; lectr. SUNYAB-EOC, Buffalo, N.Y., 1970-74; mentor Empire State Coll., Buffalo, N.Y., 1978-81; prof. English Lit. Erie C.C., Orchard Park, N.Y., 1980—; dir. Women's Ctr. Erie C.C., Orchard Park, N.Y., 1989-95. Author: (poetry) Establishing Intimacy, 1982, Dishes, 1989, The Mirror's Image, 1981, Icarus, 1980. Mem., v.p. League of Women Voters, E. Aurora, N.Y., 1987-92; sec. bd. dirs. ECC Found., Buffalo, N.Y., 1989—. Recipient Woman of Yr. award Bus. and Profl. Women, Orchard Park, N.Y., 1994, All Nations Poetry Contest Triton Coll., River Grove, Ill., 1980, 81. Mem. Nat. Coun. Tchrs. English, Poetry Soc. Am., Phi Delta Kappa. Office: Erie Community College S 4041 SW Blvd Orchard Park NY 14127

PERRY, MARSHA GRATZ, legislator, professional skating coach; b. Niagara Falls, N.Y., Dec. 9, 1936; d. William Henry and Margarett Edna (Barr) Gratz; m. Robert X. Perry, Jr., Jan. 28, 1961; children: Robert, Margarett, David. Student, Elmira Coll., 1954-57; BILR, Cornell U., 1959. Coll. recruiter Inmont, N.Y.C., 1959-61; skating dir. City of Bowie (Md.), 1971-86; skating coach Benfield Pines Ice Rink, Millerville, Md., 1974—; mem. Md. Ho. of Dels.; mem. Md. Ho. of Dels.; summer hockey & skating coach Washington Capitals, Landover, Md., 1986—; co-dir. Prostart Hockey Programs; dir. U.S. Ice Forums. Dist. dir., v.p., planning zoning dir. Crofton (Md.) Civic Assn., 1974-86; pres. West County Fedn. Cmty. Assn.; mem. AACO Drug & Alcohol adv. coun.; bd. dirs. Am. Cancer Soc., Am. Heart Assn., Md. Hall Creative Arts. Named Citizen of Yr. Crofton Civic Assn., 1986. Mem. Women Legislators. Home: 1605 Edgerton Pl Crofton MD 21114-1504 Office: MD Ho of Dels State Capital Annapolis MD 21401

PERRY, MICHELLE DIANE, lawyer, educator; b. Alexandria, Va., Jan. 1, 1965; d. Joseph Henry and Eloise Ann (Johnson) P. BS with honors, U. San Francisco, 1986; CLA, U. Calif. Santa Barbara, 1988; JD, Monterey Coll., 1993. Bar: Calif. 1993, lic. real estate, Calif. 1988. Office adminstr., paralegal Wright, Peterson, Sanders, Atascadero, Calif., 1984-85; paralegal Hoge, Fenton, Jones & Appel, Inc., San Luis, Calif., 1985-88, 89-93, law clerk, 1992; paralegal Horan, Lloyd, Karachale, Horan, Monterey, Calif., 1988-89; paralegal, law clerk Coudert Brothers, San Francisco, 1993; atty. Haims, Johnson, MacGowan, Oakland, 1994—; vis. prof. advanced litigation U. Calif. Santa Cruz, 1992; libr. com. Oakland Law Libr., 1995. Co-author Litigation Paralegal, 1987. Chair Am. Heart Assoc., Oakland, 1995, steering com. Profl. Women East Bay, Oakland, 1995. Mem. ABA, Calif. State Bar (del. conf. of dels.), Alameda County Bar Assoc., Profl. Women E. Bay, Montery Coll. of Law Alumni Assoc., Women Lawyers of Alameda County (pres.-elect), Delta Theta Phi. Office: Haims Johnson MacGowan & McInerney 490 Grand Ave Oakland CA 94610

PERRY, NANCY ESTELLE, psychologist; b. Pitts., Oct. 30, 1934; d. Simon Warren and Estelle Cecelia (Zaluski) Reichard; children: Scott, Karen, Elaine. BS, Ohio State U., 1956, MA in Psychology, 1969, PhD in Psychology (EPDA fellow), 1973. Nurse, various locations, 1956-63; sch. psychologist Public Schs. Columbus (Ohio), 1970-72; human devel. specialist Madison County (Ohio) Schs., 1972-75; pvt. practice clin. psychology, cons. psychology, Worthington, Ohio, 1975-80; tchr. U. Wis. Sch. Nursing, Milw., 1980-88, Milw. Devel. Center, 1980-83; pvt. practice Assoc. Mental Health Services, 1983-87; pvt. practice Glendale Clinic for Stress Mgmt. and Mental Health Clinics, 1987—; faculty Wis. Profl. Schs.; adj. faculty U. Wis., Milw. Ohio Dept. Edn. grantee, 1973-76. Mem. APA, Wis. Psychol. Assn., Am. Soc. Clin. Hypnosis, Internat. Soc. Study of Dissociation, Am. Assn. Marriage and Family Therapists. Home: 2210 W Charter Mall Thiensville WI 53092-5451 Office: 5225 N Ironwood Ln Milwaukee WI 53217-4909

PERRY, NANCY TROTTER, former telecommunications company executive; b. Cleve., Jan. 1, 1935; d. Charles Hanley and Mable Dora (Lowry) Trotter; m. Robert Anthony Perry, Apr. 27, 1957. Student, Dunbarton Coll., 1952-53, W.Va. U., 1953-55. Svc. rep. C&P Telephone Co., Balt., 1956-60, adminstrv. asst., 1960-67, staff supr., 1967-69; staff mgr., 1969-79; mgr. consumer affairs C&P Telephone Co., Balt., 1979-91. Bd. dirs., founding dir. Balt. Mus. Industry, Md., Info. and Referral Providers Coun., Learning Ind. Through Computers, Inc., 1991—, pres., 1994-96; bd. dirs. Md. Gerontol. Assn., 1991; bd. dirs. Md. Consumer Coun., chair, 1994-96; bd. dirs. Fgn.-Born Info. and Referral Network, Hearing and Speech Agy., 1989-94, sec., 1995—; founding dir. Tele-Consumer Hotline, 1986-92; vice-chair United Way Survival Needs Allocation Panel, 1994—. Mem. Soc. Consumer Affairs Profls. in Bus., Md. Ctr. For Ind. Living, Nat. Fedn. of Blind, Alliance for Pub. Tech., Sons of Italy. Home: 3701 Chatham Rd Ellicott City MD 21042-5105

PERRY, SARAH BRINN, sculptor, author and illustrator, educator; b. Mexico City, Jan. 30, 1956; parents Am. citizens; d. Jesse Parker Jr. and Sarah (Brinn) P.; m. Edward Grant Fowler, Jan. 15, 1986. BFA, Otis Art Inst., L.A., 1983. Sculptor, assemblage instr. Otis Coll. Art and Design, L.A., 1988-94; head preparator, photo and art galleries Santa Monica (Calif.) Coll., 1986-94. Exhibited sculpture in solo exhbns. at Santa Monica Coll., 1987, The Art Store, L.A., 1988, Redlands U. Gallery, 1992, Koplin Gallery, Santa Monica, 1992, 95; exhibited in group shows at Joan Robey Gallery, Denver, Riverside (Calif.) Art Mus., Folk Tree Mus., Pasadena, Calif., Mt. St. Mary's Coll., L.A., Mus. Contemporary Art and Design, San Jose, Costa Rica, Mus. Am. Illustration, N.Y.C., Calif. State U., Fullerton, Occidental Coll., L.A., Irvine (Calif.) Fine Arts Ctr., others; work commd. by City of Albuquerque for The Albuquerque Libr., 1990; works in numerous collections; author, illustrator: (children's book) IF. . ., 1995. Recipient Creativity '95 award Creativity Mag., 1995. Home: 346 Victoria Pl Claremont CA 91711

PERRYMAN, RUTH ANN, financial director; b. Roseville, Calif., Dec. 23, 1965; d. Lynn Eugene Perryman and Linda Penny Wagner; m. John Anthony Kluge, Feb. 12, 1984 (div. Aug. 1995); children: Kevin Andrew Kluge, Brandon Stephen Kluge. BSBA, Calif. State U., Sacramento, 1988; MBA, U. La Verne, Calif., 1990, postgrad., 1990—. Cert. mgmt. acct. Fin. analyst City of Oxnard, Calif., 1989-92; investment banker Sutro and Co., Inc., San Francisco, 1992-93; pub. fin. advisor Bartle Wells Assocs., San Francisco, 1993-94; bus. mgr. Novadyne Computer Sys., Inc., Larkspur, Calif., 1994-95; dir. of fin. Irwin Meml. Blood Ctrs., San Francisco, 1995—; owner, cons. ProfitAbility Mgmt., San Rafael, Calif., 1995—. Bd. dirs. Marin Ct.-Apptd. Spl. Advocates, San Rafael, 1993-94, Vallecito PTA, San Rafael, 1993-94. Mem. Am. Assn. Blood Banks, Coun. Comty. Blood Ctrs. (fin. com. 1996—). Democrat. Home: 998 Las Pavadas Ave San Rafael CA 94903 Office: Irwin Meml Blood Ctrs 270 Masonic Ave San Francisco CA 94118

PERRY-WIDNEY, MARILYN (MARILYN PERRY), international finance and real estate executive, television producer; b. N.Y.C., Feb. 11, 1939; d. Henry William Patrick and Edna May (Bown) Perry; m. Charles Leonidas Widney (dec. Sept. 1981). BA, Mexico City Coll., 1957. Pres. Marilyn Perry TV Prodns., Inc., N.Y.C., 1970—, C.L. Widney Internat., Inc., N.Y.C., 1977—; mng. dir. Donerail Corp., N.Y.C., 1980-88, Lancer, N.Y.C., 1980-88, Assawata, N.Y.C., 1980-88. Prodr., host TV program Internat. Byline, series of more than 90 documentaries on the UN; host 39 radio series Internat. Byline-mem. nations UN for Nat. Pub. Radio satellite, PBS in S.C., N.C., Ga., Tenn., WNYE-FM, N.Y.C., 1996—. Bd. dirs. UN After Sch. Program; ambassadorial candidate Pres. Bush., 1989; mem. Gibbes Mus., S.C. Recipient U.S. Indsl. Film Festival award, CINE Golden Eagle award, Bronze medal Internat. Film & TV Festival of N.Y., Bronzenen Urkinde, Berlin, award for superior quality Intercom-Chgo. Internat. Film Festival, Knights of Malta Trophy award for superior programming from Min. of Tourism, Internationales Tourismus award Filmfestival, Vienna, Manhattan Cable Ten Year award for continuous programming, citations from former pres. Ford and Carter, King Hussein Jordan. Mem. Asia Soc., UN Corrs. Assn., Rep. Presdl. Task Force (charter mem.), Rep. Nat. Com., Harbour Club (S.C.), Gibbes Mus. (S.C.). Home: 211 E 70th St New York NY 10021-5205

PERSAD, MERLYN RENOIR ROMNEY, counselor; came to U.S., 1991; d. Hubert and Ethne Belinda (Brookes) Romney; m. Teeluck Persad, Mar. 10, 1988; children: Terhys, Teejae. BA, U. V.I., St. Thomas, 1991; MA in Edn., U. Akron, 1995. LPN, Cottage Hosp., Anguilla, 1980-83; airline clk. Kisco Travel & Tours, Saint Kitts and Nevis, 1983-86; office mgr. Mut. of Omaha Agy., St. Thomas, Saint Thomas, 1987-89; rsch. asst. V.I. Bur. Econ. Rsch., St. Thomas, 1989-91; teller Charter One Bank, Akron, Ohio, 1991-93; grad. asst. U. Akron, 1993-95, counselor clinic for child life and family therapy, 1994-95; children's counselor Spouse Abuse Inc., Orlando, Fla., 1995—; counselor Alpha, Orlando, Fla.; counselor-in-tng. Ellet H.S., Akron, 1994-95; mem. Homeless Youth Interagy., Orlando. Vol., mentor Birth, Edn. Tng. and Acceptance (BETA), Lake Underhill, Orlando. Mem. ACA, Am. Sch. Counseling Assn. Home: PO Box 934426 Winter Park FL 32793

PERSCHBACHER, DEBRA BASSETT, lawyer; b. Pleasanton, Calif., Oct. 28, 1956; d. James Arthur and Shirley Ann (Russell) Bassett; m. Rex Robert Perschbacher, June 4, 1989. BA, U. Vt., 1977; MS, San Diego State U., 1982; JD, U. Calif., Davis, 1987. Bar: Calif. 1987, D.C. 1990, U.S. Dist Ct. (no. and ea. dists.) Calif. 1988, U.S. Ct. Appeals (9th cir.), 1988, U.S. Supreme Ct., 1991. Guidance counselor Addison Cen. Supr. Union, Middlebury, Vt., 1982-83, Milton (Vt.) Elem. Sch., 1983-84; assoc. Morrison & Foerster, San Francisco, 1986; jud. clk. U.S. Ct. Appeals (9th cir.), Phoenix, 1987-88; assoc. Morrison & Foerster, San Francisco and Walnut Creek, Calif., 1988-92; sr. atty. Calif. Ct. Appeal (3d appellate dist.), Sacramento, 1992—; tutor civil procedure, rsch. asst. U. Calif., Davis, 1985-87; instr. U. Calif. at Davis Ext., 1995—; vis. prof. law U. Calif., Davis, 1996 . Sr. articles editor U. Calif. Law Rev., Davis, 1986-87; editor, 1985-86. Bd. dirs. Samaritan Counseling Ctr., 1994—. Mem. AAUW, ABA (vice chmn. ethics com. young lawyers divsn. 1989-91, exec. com. labor and employment law com. 1989-90), Sacramento County Bar Assn., Women Lawyers of Sacramento. Democrat. Home: 1438 41st St Sacramento CA 95819-4041 Office: Ct Appeal 914 Capitol Mall Sacramento CA 95814-4811

PERSINGER, C(LARA) SUSAN, elementary music educator; b. Covington, Va., July 22, 1956; d. Lee Humphries and Elizabeth Persinger. MusB, St. Andrews Presbyn. Coll., 1977; MusM, U. N.C., Greensboro, 1978; postgrad., N.C. Ctr. Advancement Tchg. Pvt. music tchr. Music Unltd., Inc., Covington, 1973-74, Hillsborough (N.C.) Music Studio, 1980-86; residence hall dir. U. N.C., Greensboro, 1977-79; music tchr. Orange County Schs., Hillsborough, 1985—; mem. leadership team Ctrl. Elem. Sch., Hillsborough, 1991-93, mem. sch. improvement team, chair discipline design team, 1991—, mem. tchr. acad. team, 1994, multi-cultural coord., 1993—, cultural arts coord., 1986—, chair prin. interview team, 1995; choir dir. First Bapt. Ch., Hillsborough, 1980-90. Published composer and poet. Active Ctrl. Elem. Sch. PTO, 1985—. Recipient Gov.'s award N.C. state Dept. Instrn., 1990. Mem. N.C. Assn. Educators, Orange County Assn. Educators. Home: 1000 Smith Level Rd Apt C-8 Carrboro NC 27510-2501 Office: Ctrl Elem Sch 154 Hayes St Hillsborough NC 27278-2319

PERSINGER, JUDITH EILEEN, management plan clerk; b. Weston, W.Va., Aug. 4, 1944; d. William Edward and Pearl Lenna (Blake) Skinner; m. Claude Calvin Persinger, Sept. 4, 1962; children: Lisa, Shawn. Grad. high sch., Burnsville, W.Va. Telephone operator Chesapeake and Potomac Telephone Co., Morgantown, W.Va., 1965-68, plant clk., 1969-71; RAAS clk. Bell Atlantic Va., Culpeper, 1978-79; assignment clk. Bell Atlantic Va., Fairfax, 1979-86; mgmt. plan clk. Bell Atlantic Va., Falls Church, 1987—. Pres. Home Owners Assn., Slidell, La., 1975, Cmty. Rel. Bell Atlantic, Warrenton, Va., 1982-89; v.p. Literacy Vol., Warrenton, 1994; pres. Bell Atlantic Pioneers, Richmond, 1995—. Recipient Govs. award, State of Va., 1994. Mem. Eta Sigma (pres. 1989-90). Home: 5647 Wilshire Dr Warrenton VA 22186 Office: Bell Atlantic Va 2980 Fairview Pk Dr Falls Church VA 22186

PERSON, RUTH JANSSEN, academic administrator; b. Washington, Aug. 27, 1945; d. Theodore Armin and Ruth Katherine (Mahoney) Janssen. BA, Gettysburg (Pa.) Coll., 1967; AMLS, U. Mich., 1969, PhD, 1980; MS in Adminstrn., George Washington U., 1974. Head of reference/asst. prof. Thomas Nelson C.C., Hampton, Va., 1971-74; lectr. U. Mich., Ann Arbor, 1975-79, coord. of continuing edn., 1977-79; asst. prof. Cath. U., Washington, 1979-85, assoc. prof., 1985-86, assoc. dean Sch. of Libr. and Info. Sci., 1983-86; dean Coll. Libr. Sci. Clarion (Pa.) U., 1986-88; assoc. vice chancellor U. Mo., St. Louis, 1988-93; v.p. for acad. affairs, prof. bus. adminstrn. Ashland (Ohio) U., 1993-95; v.p. acad. affairs Angelo State U., San Angelo, Tex., 1995—; reviewer U.S. Dept. Edn., Washington, 1987-89, 92; trustee Pitts. Regional Libr. Ctr., 1986-88; chair publs. com. Assn. of Coll. and Rsch. Librs., Chgo., 1986-90; cons. United Way, Alexandria, Va., 1985; cons.-evaluator North Ctrl. Assn., 1993-95. Co-editor: (book) Academic Libraries: Their Role and Rationale in Higher Education, 1995; editor: (book) The Management Process, 1983; editl. bd. Coll. & Rsch. Librs., 1990—; contr. articles to profl. jours. Mem. Strategic Planning Task Force, Ashland C. of C., 1994; bd. dirs. Alternatives for Living in Violent Environs., Inc., St. Louis, 1992-94; commr. Commn. for Women, Anne Arundel County, Md., 1984-86; mem. Citizens Adv. Bd., Clarion, Pa., 1986-88; mem. Olivette, Mo. Human Rels. Commn., 1992-94, San Angelo Bus. and Profl. Women's Club, 1995—, pres.-elect 1996—; mem. bldg. design oversight com. San Angelo Mus. Fine Arts, 1995—; mem. com. Cactus Jazz Festival, 1995—. Fellow Am. Coun. Edn., 1990, Harvard Inst. Ednl. Mgmt., 1989, Rackham fellow U. Mich., 1976; ACE fellow Ariz. Bd. Regents, 1990-91; recipient Washington Woman award Washington Woman mag., 1986. Mem. ALA (com. on accreditation 1993—), Am. Assn. Univ. Adminstrs. (bd. dirs. 1993—), Coun. for the Preservation of Anthropol. Records (bd. dirs.), Psi Chi, Beta Phi Mu, Pi Lambda Theta, Kappa Delta Pi, Phi Alpha Theta. Lutheran. Home: 5218 N Bentwood Dr San Angelo TX 76904 Office: Angelo State U Box 11008 ASU Station San Angelo TX 76909

PERSYN, MARY GERALDINE, law librarian, law educator; b. Elizabeth, N.J., Feb. 25, 1945; d. Henry Anthony and Geraldine (Sumption) P. AB, Creighton U., 1967; MLS, U. Oreg., 1969; JD, Notre Dame U., 1982. Bar: Ind. 1982, U.S. Dist. Ct. (no. and so. dists.) Ind. 1982, U.S. Supreme Ct. 1995. Social scis. librarian Miami U., Oxford, Ohio, 1969-78; staff law librarian Notre Dame (Ind.) Law Sch., 1982-84; dir. law library Valparaiso (Ind.) U., 1984-87, law librarian, assoc. prof. law, 1987—. Editor Journal of Legislation, 1981-82; mng. editor Third World Legal Studies, 1986—. Mem. ABA, Ind. State Bar Assn., Am. Assn. Law Libraries, Ohio Regopma; Assm. Law Libraries (pres. 1990-91), Ind. State Quilt Guild (pres. 1996-98). Roman Catholic. Home: 1308 Tuckahoe Park Dr Valparaiso IN 46383-4032 Office: Valparaiso U Law Libr Sch Law Valparaiso IN 46383

PERTHOU, ALISON CHANDLER, interior designer; b. Bremerton, Wash., July 22, 1945; d. Benson and Elizabeth (Holdsworth) Chandler; m. A.V. Perthou III, Sept. 9, 1967 (div. Dec. 1977); children: Peter T.R., Stewart A.C. BFA, Cornish Coll. Arts, 1972. Pres. Alison Perthou Interior Design, Seattle, 1972—, Optima Design, Inc., Seattle, 1986-89; treas. Framejoist Corp., Bellevue, Wash., 1973-90; pres. Classics: Interiors & Antiques, Inc., 1988—; cons. bldg. and interiors com. Children's Hosp., Seattle, 1976—; guest lectr. U. Wash., Seattle, 1980-81. Mem. bd. trustees Cornish Coll. Arts, Seattle, 1973-80, sec. exec. com., 1975-77; mem. procurement com. Patrons of N.W. Cultural and Charitable Orgn., 1985—, mem. antiques com., 1991—. Mem. Am. Soc. Interior Design, Seattle Tennis Club (mem. house and grounds com. 1974-75), City Club. Office: 1000 Lenora Ste 222 Seattle WA 98121

PERTILLAR-BREVARD, LISA ANN, researcher; b. Hartford, Conn., Mar. 9, 1968; d. Lawrence Sr. and Edna Pearl (Roberts) P. BA with honors, Smith Coll., 1991; PhD, Emory U., 1995. Apprentice dance anthropologist Artists' Collective, Hartford, 1982-85; asst. mgr. Galt Toys-Hartford Civic Ctr., 1985, 87; intern Smithsonian Instn., Washington, 1987, 88, 89; academic peer asst. Community Coll. Connections Smith Coll., Northampton, Mass., 1990; intern coord. Smithsonian Instn., Washington, 1992—; researcher Afro-Am. Studies dept., Smith Coll., Northampton, 1988-89, liaison, 1989—, peer counselor Fin. Aid Office, Smith Coll., 1989; instr. Emory U., 1993-94; vis. scholar Smithsonian Inst., 1993; presenter April in Paris: African-Am. Music and Europe Conf., Paris, 1996. Author: A Selected Annotated Bibliography on Black American Gospel Music and Related Subjects, 1992, Madame Emma Azalia Smith Hackley (1867-1922): Preserver and Transmitter of African-American Folk Music, 1994, Black Butterfly: Madame Hackley, the Spirituals and Social Change, 1996, Ain't Got Time To Die: Madame Azalia Hackley, Classicist of the Spirituals, 1996; co-author: Wade in the Water: African-American Sacred Music Traditions, 1994, also tchr.'s guide, 1994; prodr., dir., narrator video documentaries Common Games of Black Inner-City Girls, 1988, Portrait of a Black Family, 1988, My Soul Is a Witness: African-American Women's Spirituality, 1995. Pres. Smith Coll. Choir Omega, 1987-88; liaison fin. aid Smith Coll., 1987-88, career devel. Smith Coll., 1989-90. Named one of Glamour Mag.'s Top Ten Coll. Women, 1990, Maybelline Cosmetics Top Ten Coll. Women, 1991. Mem. Internat. Alumnae Orgn. Smithsonian Inst., Loomis Chaffee Alumnae Orgn.

PESCOSOLIDO, PAMELA JANE, legal research service owner, graphic designer; b. Chgo., Dec. 28, 1960; d. Carl Albert Jr. and Linda Clark (Austin) P.; m. Larry Carl Vangroningen, Mar. 5, 1994; 1 child, Harley Austin. BA, Scripps Coll., 1983; JD, Vt. Law Sch., 1990. Bar: Maine 1990. Office mgr., asst. chef The Elegant Picnic, Stockbridge, Mass., 1983; receptionist, sec. Sequoia Orange County, Exeter, Calif., 1983-84; A/R clk. Tropicana Energy Co., Euless, Tex., 1984-85; owner, calligrapher Calligraphic Arts, Great Barrington, Mass., 1986-87; legal intern Pine Tree Legal Assistance, Augusta, Maine, 1989, Office of the Juvenile Defender, Montpelier, Vt., 1990; bookkeeper Badger Farming Co., Exeter, 1991—; owner, legal drafter and researcher Legal Rsch. Svc., Visalia, Calif., 1990—; owner, graphc designer Hourglass Prodns., Visalia, 1995—; rsch. editor Vt. Law Rev., Vt. Law Sch., South Royalton, 1989-90. Designer, graphic artist polit. propaganda for Libertarian Party of Calif.; contbr. poetry to Nat. Coll. Poetry Rev. Mem. county cen. com., chair Valley Libertarians, Libertarian Party of Calif., Visalia, 1996—; candidate Libertarian Party Dist. 19, Calif. U.S. Congress, 1996. Chase scholar Vt. Law Sch., 1989. Mem. ACLU, AAUW (newsletter editor 1994—), ABA. Office: Sequoia Orange Co 150 W Pine St Exeter CA 93221

PESEK, DONNA JEAN, purchasing agent; b. Detroit, Feb. 21, 1942; d. Stanley Chester and Mary (Gach) Morenc; m. Hugh Ewald Judge II, Nov. 21, 1964 (div. Apr. 1978); children: Hugh Ewald III, Glen Darren, Janice Jean, Keith Alan; m. Lawrence Raymond Pesek, May 17, 1993. BS in Edn., Western Mich. U., 1963. Libr. Oak Park (Mich.) Libr., 1958-68, Oak Park High Sch. Libr., 1963-65; purchasing agt. Ingersoll Rand, Farmington Hills, Mich., 1978—. Office: Ingersoll Rand 23400 Halsted Farmington Hills MI 48335

PESIN, ELLA MICHELE, journalist, public relations professional; b. North Bergen, N.J., Aug. 29, 1956; d. Edward and Helene Sylvia (Rattner) P. BA, Sarah Lawrence Coll., 1978. Press rep. CBS-TV News and Entertainment, N.Y.C., 1978-80; publicist Newsweek Mag., N.Y.C., 1980-81; prin. Pesin Pub. Rels., N.Y.C., 1980-94; freelance journalist N.Y.C., 1981—; publicist Universal Studios MCA Inc., L.A., 1982-83; with publicity and mktg. NBC-TV News, N.Y.C., 1985-86; media exec. Burson Marsteller Pub. Rels.-Press/Media Execs., N.Y.C., 1986-87. Contbg. editor Cable Age mag., TV Radio Age mag., Advt. Forum, Facts Figures & Film, Advt. Compliance Svc.; syndicated newspaper columnist. Active Israel Bonds/United Jewish Appeal, N.Y.C., Rudolph Giuliani for N.Y.C. Mayor campaign. Mem. Pub. Rels. Soc. Am., Am. Soc. Journalists and Authors, N.Y. Fin. Writers Group, N.Y. Venture Group, Women Comm., Women Bus., Publicity Club N.Y. Home and Office: 401 E 80th St Apt 11J New York NY 10021-0649

PESKORZ, ADELA, librarian; b. Bronx, N.Y., July 25, 1954; d. Irving and Ida Zylber; m. Joseph John Peskorz, Feb. 16, 1981. BA in English, SUNY, Oswego, 1976; MLS, Syracuse U., 1977. Account rep. Bernard Hodes Advt., N.Y.C. and Boston, 1977-79; young adult and reference libr. Newark Pub. Libr., 1980-81; freelance proofreader, N.Y.C., 1981-90; proofreader Am. Stock Exch., N.Y.C., 1988-89; young adult libr. Libr. for Blind and Physically Handicapped N.Y. Pub. Libr., N.Y.C., 1989-90; substitute reference libr. Mpls. Pub. Libr., 1991-92, coord. young adult svcs., 1992—; host cable TV program The Book Scene, Mpls. Pub. Schs., 1993—; instr. Coll. of St. Catherine's, St. Paul; guest spkr., panel participant numerous ednl. and cmty. programs; developer, facilitator profl. devel. workshops. Compiler ann. annotated booklist The Book Scene...Especially for Teens, 1993—. Active Youth in Mpls. After Sch. Program; co-chmn. vol. com. Dancin' in the Streets, Youth Coordinating Bd., Mpls., 1994, 95. Recipient Excellence award Mpls. Youth Coordinating Bd., 1995. Mem. ALA (Quick Picks for Reluctant Young Adult Readers com. 1994—), Young Adult Libr. Svcs. Assn. (Quick Picks for Reluctant Young Adult Readers com. 1994—, grantee 1994), Minn. Libr. Assn. Democrat. Jewish. Office: Mpls Pub Libr 300 Nicollet Mall Minneapolis MN 55401

PESTERFIELD, LINDA CAROL, school administrator, educator; b. Pauls Valley, Okla., May 3, 1939; d. D.J. and Geneva Lewis (Sheegog) Butler; m. W.C. Peterfield, Aug. 30, 1958; children: Ginger Carol, Walt James, Jason Kent. Student, E. Cen. State U., Ada, Okla., 1957, 76, 79; BS, Okla. State U., 1961; postgrad., Ottawa U., Ottawa, Kans., 1970, Okla. U., 1979. Tchr. Sumner Elem. Sch., Perry, Okla., 1961-62; tchr. Whitebead D-16, Pauls Valley, Okla., 1964-65, Cen. Heights Unified, Ottawa, Kans., 1969-71; prin., tchr. Whitebead D-16, Pauls Valley, 1975-91; Pauls Valley Sch., P.V., 1991—; mem. profl. standard bd. State Dept. Edn., Okla., 1988—; presenter in field. Bd. dirs. Positively Pauls Valley, 1987-96; county chmn. Nat. and Okla. 4-H Fund Drive, Garvin County, Okla., 1987-88; mem. organizational com. C-CAP-Child Abuse Prevention Orgn., Pauls Valley, 1987—; mem. vision 2000 com. Garvin County Assn. Svcs. Named to Gov.'s Honor Roll Recognition & Appreciation for Community Activities, Pauls Valley, Okla., 1985-86. Mem. Cooperative Coun. Okla. Sch. Adminstrn., NEA, Okla. Ednl. Assn., Whitebead Ednl. Assn., Okla. Orgn. Dependent Sch., Okla. Assn. Elem. Sch. Prins., AAUW, All Sports Club (v.p. 1984-89, pres. 1985, 90), Rotary (bd. dirs. 1993-96), Delta Kappa Gamma (past local auditor, parliamentarian, v.p., pres. 1979-96), Phi Delta Kappa. Democrat. Mem. Ch. of Christ. Home: RR 3 Box 306 Pauls Valley OK 73075-9232 Office: Pauls Valley Sch Superintendents Office 301 N Chickasaw St Pauls Valley OK 73075-3428

PETERMAN, DONNA COLE, communications executive; b. St. Louis, Nov. 9, 1947; d. William H. Cole and Helen A. Morris; m. John A.

Peterman, Feb. 7, 1970. BA in Journalism, U. Mo., 1969; MBA, U. Chgo., 1984. Mgr. employee comm. Sears Merchandise Group, Chgo., 1975-80; dir. corp. comm. Sears, Roebuck and Co., Chgo., 1982-85; affairs and mktg. comm. Seraco Real Estate, Chgo., 1980-82; sr. v.p., dir. corp. comm. Dean Witter Fin. Svcs. Group, N.Y., 1985-88; sr. v.p., mng. dir. Hill and Knowlton, Inc., Chgo., 1988-94; exec. v.p. Hill and Knowlton, Inc., N.Y.C., 1994-96; sr. v.p., dir. corp. comm. Paine Webber Group, Inc., N.Y.C., 1996—; Media chmn. DeKalb County Comm., Ga., 1975; media dir., Mo. Atty. Gen., 1971, Rep. Govs. Conf., 1974; copywriter Govt. fo Mo., 1971. Trustee Met. Planning Coun. Mem. Internat. Assn. Bus. Communicators, Pub. Relations Soc. Am., City Midday Club, Univ. Club, Women Execs. in Pub. Rels. Republican. Catholic.

PETERS, ALICE, clinical psychologist, psychotherapist; b. Vienna, Austria; came to U.S., 1940; d. Robert and Ilona (Gerstl) Peterselka; m. Leo Gottesman, Aug. 16, 1936 (dec. Aug. 1984). BA, New Sch., 1946; MA, CCNY, 1950; PhD, NYU, 1959. Intern in psychology Jewish Hosp., N.Y.C., 1947; psychologist PCA Guidance Ctr., N.Y.C., 1948-50, Remedial Reading Clinic, CCNY, 1950-52; psychologist, supr., mem. faculty Orphanage, Alcoholic Clinic, Knickerbocker Hosp., N.Y.C., 1952-60; supr. group psychotherapy Albert Einstein Med. Sch., Bronx, N.Y., 1960-67; supr. faculty Postgrad. Ctr. for Mental Health Albert Einstein Med. Sch., N.Y.C., 1962-66; supr. N.Y. Clinic for Mental Health, 1962-64; pvt. practice N.Y.C., 1962—; mem. faculty, cons. Westchester Inst. for Tng. in Pastoral Counseling and Psychotherapy, Yonkers, N.Y., 1966-72. Author: (with others) TAT and CAT, 1954; co-author: (projective test) CAT, 1949; contbr. articles to profl. jours. Recipient Founders Day award NYU, 1961. Mem. APA, Am. Group Psychotherapy Assn., Internat. Psychol. Assn., N.Y. State Psychol. Assn., Ea. Psychol. Assn., World Fedn. for Mental Health. Home: 235 E 57th St New York NY 10022-2842

PETERS, ANN LOUISE, accounting manager; b. Knoxville, Tenn., Jan. 26, 1954; d. William Brown and Louise (Emerson) Nixon; m. Raymond Peters, July 11, 1975. BBA, Miami U., Oxford, Ohio, 1976; MBA, Xavier U., 1985. Cert. internal auditor. Acctg. officer Soc. Bank (formerly Citizens Bank), Hamilton, Ohio, 1977-85; internal auditor Procter & Gamble Co., Cin., 1985-86, audit sect. mgr., 1986-88, sr. cost analyst, beauty care, 1988-90; plant fin. mgr. Procter & Gamble Mfg. Co., Phoenix, 1990-92; sr. fin. analyst, beauty care Procter & Gamble Co., Cin., 1992-93, group mgr., gen. acctg., 1993-96, group mgr. R&D fin., 1996—. Mem. Inst. Internal Auditors, Inst. Mgmt. Accts. Republican. Congregationalist. Home: 7889 Ironwood Way West Chester OH 45069-1623 Office: Procter & Gamble Co Sharon Woods Tech Ctr Box 221 HB2J14A 11511 Reed Hartman Hwy Cincinnati OH 45241

PETERS, BARBARA AGNES, assistant principal; b. Lockport, N.Y., Aug. 11, 1952; d. Raymond Charles Betsch and Evelyn Mae (Ehmke) Soulvie; m. Victor Waldorf Baker, June 17, 1978 (div.); children: Alexander, Erik; m. Robert Emerson Peters, Nov. 3, 1990; children: Brian, Jennifer. BS in Edn., SUNY, Fredonia, 1974; MEd, U. Wales, Cardiff, 1979. Cert. tchr. N, K-6, secondary English, reading, CAS-sch. dist. adminstr., N.Y, CAS Ednl. Adminstrn., SAS, SDA. Tchr. English Emmet Belknap Jr. H.S., Lockport, N.Y., 1974-76; exec. dir. Dept. of Youth and Recreation Svcs., Lockport, 1978-89; instr. Empire State Coll., Lockport, 1983—; tchr. English Akron (N.Y.) Cen. Sch. Dist., 1989-95; asst. prin. West Seneca East Middle Sch., 1995—; mem. dist. planning team Akron Sch., 1990-95, mem. tech. long-range planning com., 1992-94. Team owner's mgr. Buffalo Bills Football Club, Orchard Park, N.Y., 1978—; mem. Bd. Performing and Visual Arts, Tonawanda, 1992. Recipient Erie County Youth Best award, 1995; honoree Internat. Women's Decade, 1985; named to Outstanding Young Women of Am., 1986; Western N.Y. Women in Adminstrn. Excellence in Ednl. Leadership award, 1996; Rotary grad. fellow, 1975. Mem. ASCD, N.Y. State Middle Sch. Assn., Swiftwater Power Squadron Advanced Pilot, LaSalle Yacht Club, Phi Delta Kappa (award innovative ednl. program 1996). Office: West Seneca East Middle Sch 1445 Center Rd West Seneca NY 14224

PETERS, BERNADETTE (BERNADETTE LAZZARA), actress; b. Queens, N.Y., Feb. 28, 1948; d. Peter and Marguerite (Maltese) Lazzara. Student, Quintano Sch. for Young Profls., N.Y.C. Ind. actress, entertainer, 1957—. Appeared on TV series All's Fair, 1976-77; frequent guest appearances on TV; films include The Longest Yard, 1974, Vigilant Force, 1975, W.C. Fields and Me, 1975, Silent Movie, 1976, The Jerk, 1979, Heart Beeps, 1981, Tulips, 1981, Pennies from Heaven, 1982 (Golden Globe Best Actress award), Annie, 1982, Slaves of NewYork, 1989, Pink Cadillac, 1989, Impromptu, 1990, Alice, 1990; stage appearances include This is Google, 1957, The Most Happy Fella, 1959, Gypsy, 1961, Riverwind, 1966, Curly McDimple, 1967, Johnny No-Trump, 1967, George M!, 1968, Dames at Sea, 1968, La Strada, 1969, On the Town, 1971, Tartuffe, 1972, Mack and Mabel, 1974, Sally and Marsha, 1982, Sunday in the Park with George, 1983-85 (Tony nomination 1983), Song and Dance, 1985-86, Into the Woods, 1987, The Goodbye Girl, 1992-93; TV films David, 1989, Fall From Grace, 1990, The Last Best Year, 1990; rec. artist: (MCA Records) Bernadette Peters, 1980, Now Playing, 1981. Recipient Drama Desk award for Dames and Sea, 1968; Drama Desk award nomination for Into The Woods, 1987, 88, Tony award nominee, 1971, 74, 83, 85, 92, Tony award for Best Actress in Song and Dance, 1986, Theatre World citation for George M!, 1968, Drama Desk award, 1968, 86, Hasty Pudding Theatrical award, 1987 woman of the Yr., Sara Siddons Actress of Yr. award, 1993-94. Office: Judy Katz PR 1790 Broadway Ste 1600 New York NY 10019-1412

PETERS, BRENDA IRENE, computer specialist; b. Bethesda, Md., Feb. 2, 1952; d. William Elbert and Helen Gertrude (Monroe) P.; m. James Wayne Bradley, Dec. 21, 1972 (div. May 1976). AA in Computer Sci., Bus., Montgomery Coll., 1972. Clk.-typist NIH, Bethesda, Md., 1972, HEW, Rockville, Md., 1972; card punch operator Pope AFB, Fayetteville, N.C., 1973-74; card punch operator David Taylor R & D Ctr., Bethesda, Md., 1974-75, computer operator, 1975-77; computer programmer, analyst Carderock div. Naval Surface Warfare Ctr., Bethesda, 1977-86, computer specialist, 1986—; cons. Kengla Flag Co., Washington, 1988-95, Mt. Airy (Md.) Vol. Fire Co., 1995. Sunday sch. tchr. Germantown (Md.) Bapt. Ch., 1981—, asst. pianist, chmn. mission outreach, rec. sec., 1989—. Bd. trustees grantee Montgomery Coll., Rockville, Md., 1970-72. Office: Naval Surface Warfare Ctr Carderock Div Bethesda MD 20084-5000

PETERS, CAROL ANN DUDYCHA, counselor; b. Ripon, Wis., Dec. 23, 1938; d. George John and Martha (Malek) Dudycha; m. Milton Eugene Peters, Aug. 27, 1960. AB, Wittenberg U., 1960, MEd, 1963; leadership devel. cert., Ctr. for Creative Leadership, Greensboro, N.C., 1986; postgrad., U. Toledo, 1973—. Lic. profl. counselor, Ohio; nat. cert. counselor, nat. cert. career counselor Nat. Bd. Cert. Counselors, Inc. Tchr. Springfield (Ohio) City Schs., 1960-62, Mad River-Green Local Schs., Springfield, 1962-63; counselor Napoleon (Ohio) Area Schs., 1963-70, Findlay (Ohio) City Schs., 1970—; field counselor Career Relocation Corp. Am., Armonk, N.Y., 1992-95; cons., prin. Peters and Peters, Findlay, 1979—; leader Creative Edn. Found., Buffalo, 1980-91, colleague, 1985—; founder ednl. corp. Career Info. Bur. Hancock County, 1974. Pres. Big Bros./Big Sisters Hancock County, 1982-83; bd. dirs. Citizens Opposing Drug Abuse (C.O.D.A.), Findlay, 1982—; advisor, leader Hahcock Addictions Prevention for Youth (H.A.P.P.Y.), 1985-91; mem. Hancock County Community Devel. Found. Edn. Com., 1990-93, Findlay/Hancock County Am. 2000 New Sch. Design Team, 1991-92; mem. Hancock County Crisis Response Team, 1991—. Named One of Outstanding Young Women of Am., 1967; named Outstanding Woman in Edn., Bus. and Profl. Women, 1983; recipient Outstanding Citizenship award The Lincoln Ctr., Findlay, 1989, Meritorious Svc. award Big Bros./Big Sisters Hancock County, 1988. Mem. ACA, AAUW (Findlay br.), NEA (life), Am. Sch. Counselor Assn., Nat. Career Devel. Assn., Ohio Edn. Assn., Ohio Counseling Assn., Ohio Sch. Counselor Assn., Findlay-Hancock County C. of C. (sec. edn. com. 1984-90). Lutheran. Office: Findlay City Schs 227 S West St Findlay OH 45840-3324

PETERS, CAROL BEATTIE TAYLOR (MRS. FRANK ALBERT PETERS), mathematician; b. Washington, May 10, 1932; d. Edwin Lucius and Lois (Beattie) Taylor; B.S., U. Md., 1954, M.A., 1958; m. Frank Albert Peters, Feb. 26, 1955; children—Thomas, June, Erick, Victor. Group mgr. Tech. Operations, Inc., Arlington, Va., 1957-62, sr. staff scientist, 1964-66; supervisory analyst Datatrol Corp., Silver Spring, Md., 1962; project dir. Computer Concept, Inc., Silver Spring, 1963-64; mem. tech. staff, then mem. sr. staff Informatics Inc., Bethesda, Md., 1966-70, mgr. systems projects, 1970-71, tech. dir., 1971-76; sr. tech. dir. Ocean Data Systems, Inc., Rockville, Md., 1976-83; dir. Informatics Gen. Co., 1983-89; pres. Carol Peters Assocs., 1989—. Mem. Assn. Computing Machinery, IEEE Computer Group. Home and Office: 12311 Glen Mill Rd Potomac MD 20854-1928

PETERS, CATHY J., nurse practitioner, education consultant; b. Niagara Falls, N.Y., Dec. 9, 1951; d. Walter Anthony and Phyllis (La Barber) P. BSEd, SUNY, Cortland, 1973; AAS, SUNY, Syracuse, 1975; MS in Nursing, U. Rochester, 1981. Cert. adult nurse practitioner, N.Y. Nursing instr. SUNY, Brockport, 1981-82; dir. health edn. Group Health of Blue Cross/Blue Shield, Rochester, N.Y., 1985-88; dir. edn. Health Psychology Assocs., Rochester, 1988-91; nurse practitioner AC Rochester/GM, 1991-92; condr. stress mgmt. workshops, Rochester; editor, grant writer, dept. women's health and ob-gyn. Rochester Gen. Hosp., 1991-93; cons. health edn. adv. bd. Monroe County Health Dept., Rochester, 1989-90; mem. med. team Inst. for Shipboard Edn., U. Pitts., 1993. Author (column in Rochester Bus. mag.) Mind/Body, 1996—. Vol. Blessed Sacrement Ch., Rochester, 1991—. Robert Wood Johnson grantee, 1979-81; Civil Svc. Employees' Assn. scholar, 1975. Mem. APHA, N.Y. State Coalition Nurse Practitioners, Internat. Patient Edn. Coun., Rochester Nurses' Registry. Home and Office: PO Box 18555 Rochester NY 14618-0555

PETERS, DOLORES YVONNE, neonatal clinical nurse specialist; b. Washington, Aug. 9, 1951; d. Lewis Bradford and Thelma Beatrice (Walker) P. BSN cum laude, U. Md., 1975; MSN in Nursing of Developing Families, Catholic U. Am., 1989; BA in Biology cum laude, Western Md. Coll., 1973. RN, Va., D.C., Md.; cert. neonatal nurse practitioner. Obstet. staff nurse Sibley Meml. Hosp., Washington, 1975-76; staff nurse Nat. Naval Med. Ctr., Bethesda, Md., 1976-80, nursery ednl. coord., 1980-82, neonatal clin. nursing specialist, 1982-90; neonatal clin. nurse specialist Washington Hosp. Ctr., 1990—; mem. Resource Applications faculty C.V. Mosby Co., 1990-93. Am. Lung Assn. of Md. nursing rsch. fellow, 1987-88. Mem. Nat. Assn. Neonatal Nurses, Assn. of Women's Health, Obstet. and Neonatal Nurses, Am. Holistic Nurses Assn., Sigma Theta Tau, Beta Beta Beta. Home: 2337 Massanutten Dr Silver Spring MD 20906-6178

PETERS, DOROTHY MARIE, writer, consultant; b. Sutton, Nebr., Oct. 23, 1913; d. Sylvester and Anna (Olander) Peters; AB with high distinction, Nebr. Wesleyan U., 1941; MA, Northwestern U., 1957; EdD, Ind. U., 1968. Tchr. Nebr. pub. schs., 1931-38; caseworker Douglas County Assistance Bur., Omaha, 1941; hosp. field dir., gen. field rep. ARC, 1941-50; social worker Urban League, Meth. Ch., Washington, 1951-53; asst. prin., dir. guidance, Manlius (Ill.) Community High Sch., 1953-58; dean of girls, guidance dir. Woodruff High Sch., Peoria, Ill., 1958-66; vis. prof. edn. Bradley U., Peoria, 1959-77; coord., dir. Title I programs Peoria Pub. Sch. System, 1966-68, dir. pupil services, 1968-72; dir. counseling and evaluation Title I Programs, 1972-73; vol. dir. youth service programs, vol. program cons. Cen. Ill. chpt. and Heart of Ill. div. ARC, Peoria, 1973-77; owner, operator Ability-Achievement Unlimited Cons. Services, Saratoga Springs, N.Y., 1978-81; spl. cons. Courage Center, Golden Valley, Minn., 1981-84, mem. pub. policy com., bd. dirs., 1985-87; mem. sr. adv. bd. F&M Marquette Nat. Bank, 1981-85; cons. Sister Kenny Inst., Mpls., 1984-86; free-lance writer, 1984—; prin. Dorothy M. Peters & Assocs., Roseville, Minn., 1985-87. Bd. dirs, home service com. disaster com. Peoria chpt. ARC, 1958-73; pres., bd. dirs. Ct. Counselor Program; mem. Mayor's Human Resources Coun., City of Peoria; chmn. met. adv. com. transp. for handicapped; ednl. dir., prin., bd. dirs. Catalyst High Sch., 1975-77; hon. life bd. mem. Am. Nat. Red Cross; mem. Saratoga Springs Hosp. Bldg. Rehab. Com.; founder, steering com. Open Sesame, Saratoga Springs, 1978-81; appointee N.Y. State Employment and Tng. Council, 1979-81, Saratoga County Employment and Tng. Com., 1979-81; bd. dirs. Unlimited Potential, 1979-81; mem. Metro Mobility Adv. Task Force, Mpls., 1981-85, mem. policy com., 1984-85 ; mem. vol. action com. United Way, Mpls., 1982-85 ; mem. Minn. State Planning Coun. for Developmentally Disabled and liason to U. Mo. Affiliated Program, 1983-89 (appreciation award 1990); mem. Gov.'s Task Force on Needs of Adults with Brain Impairment, 1985-87; chmn., bd. dirs. Met. Ctr. for Ind. Living, 1986— (svc. appreciation award 1989); mem. sr. ministries coun. United Meth. Ch., 1984-88; mem. dept. rehab. svcs. Minn. Coun. Ind. Living, 1989—; gov.'s appointee Minn. Bd. on Aging, 1989-94; mem. gov.'s sr. agenda for Ind. Living in the 1990's, 1989-94; mem. Nebr. Wesleyan U. Nat. Caucus, Mpls., 1989—; mem. United Way Older Adults Vision Coun., 1993—. Recipient Spl. Congl. Recognition cert., 1994. Mem. Peoria Edn. Assn. (v.p. 1962-64), Ill. Guidance and Pers. Assn. (v.p. Area 8, 1963-64), NEA, Ill. Edn. Assn. (del. 1962-64), Am. Pers. and Guidance Assn., Am. Sch. Counselors Assn., Nat. Assn. Women Deans and Counselors (K-12 task force chmn. 1974—, editorial bd. Jour.), Ill. Vocat. Guidance Assn. (dir.), Minn. Head Injury Found., Nat. Head Injury Found., Ill. Assn. Women Deans and Counselors, Phi Kappa Phi, Psi Chi, Pi Gamma Mu, Pi Lambda Theta, Delta Kappa Gamma, Alpha Gamma Delta. Home: 6100 Summit Dr N Apt 103 Brooklyn Center MN 55430

PETERS, ELEANOR WHITE, retired mental health nurse; b. Highland Park, Mich., Aug. 11, 1920; d. Alfred Mortimer and Jane Ann (Evans) White; m. William J. Peters, 1947 (div. 1953); children: Susannah J., William J. (dec.). RN, Christ Hosp. Sch. Nursing, Jersey City, 1941; BA, Jersey City State Coll., 1968; postgrad., U. Del., 1969-70; MS, SUNY, New Paltz, 1983. RN, N.J., N.Y. Mem. staff various area hosps. N.J., 1941-58; indsl. nurse Abex, Mahwah, N.J., 1958-68; sch. nurse Liberty (N.Y.) Ctrl. Sch., 1971-76; coord. practical nurse program Hudson County C.C., Jersey City, 1979-80; community mental health nurse Letchworth Village, Thiells, N.Y., 1981-96. Historian, Bishop House Found., Saddle River, N.J. Mem. AAUW (pres. Liberty-Monticello br. 1988-92), Am. Sch. Health Assn., Alpha Delta Kappa (sec. Mu chpt. 1973-75), Sigma Theta Tau (Kappa Eta chpt.). Republican. Lutheran. Home: PO Box 224 Saddle River NJ 07458-0224

PETERS, ELIZABETH ANN HAMPTON, nursing educator; b. Detroit, Sept. 27, 1934; d. Grinsfield Taylor and Ida Victoria (Jones) Hampton; m. James Marvin Peters, Dec. 1, 1956; children: Douglas Taylor, Sara Elizabeth. Diploma, Berea Coll. Hosp. Sch. Nursing, 1956; BS in Nursing, Wright State U., Dayton, Ohio, 1975; MS in Nursing, Ohio State U., Columbus, 1978. Therapist-RN Eastway, Inc., Dayton, Ohio, 1979-81; therapist family counseling svc. Good Samaritan-Community Mental Health Ctr., Dayton, Ohio, 1981-83; instr. Wright State U. Sch. Nursing, Dayton, 1983-84; clin. nurse specialist, pain mgmt. svcs., pain mgmt. program UPSA, Inc., Dayton, 1983-86; staff nurse Hospice of Dayton, Inc., 1985-86, dir. vol. svcs., 1986-89, dir. bereavement svcs., 1986-87; asst. prof. Community Hosp. Sch. Nursing, Springfield, Ohio, 1990-93, prof., 1993—. Author: (with others) Oncologic Pain, 1987. Mem. Clark County Mental Health Bd., Springfield, 1986-95; mem. New Carlisle (Ohio) Bd. Health, 1990—. Mem. ANA, Ohio Nurses Assn., Sigma Theta Tau. Home: 402 Flora Ave New Carlisle OH 45344-1329

PETERS, ELLEN ASH, state supreme court chief justice; b. Berlin, Mar. 21, 1930; came to U.S., 1939, naturalized, 1947; d. Ernest Edward and Hildegard (Simon) Ash; m. Phillip I. Blumberg; children: David Bryan Peters, James Douglas Peters, Julie Peters Haden. BA with honors, Swarthmore Coll., 1951, LLD (hon.), 1983; LLB cum laude, Yale U., 1954, MA (hon.), 1964, LLD (hon.), 1985; LLD (hon.), U. Hartford, 1983; Georgetown U., 1984; LLD (hon.), Yale U., 1985, Conn. Coll., 1985, N.Y. Law Sch., 1985; HLD (hon.), St. Joseph Coll., 1986; LLD (hon.), Colgate U., 1986, Trinity Coll., 1987, Bates Coll., 1987, Wesleyan U., 1987, DePaul U., 1988; HLD (hon.), Albertus Magnus Coll., 1990; LLD (hon.), U. Conn., 1992; LLD, U. Rochester, 1994. Bar: Conn. 1957. Law clk. to judge U.S. Circuit Ct., 1954-55; assoc. in law U. Calif., Berkeley, 1955-56; prof. law Yale U., New Haven, 1956-78, adj. prof. law, 1978-84; assoc. justice Conn. Supreme Ct., Hartford, 1978-84, chief justice, 1984-96, sr. justice com., 1996—. Author: Commercial Transactions: Cases, Texts, and Problems, 1971, Negotiable Instruments Primer, 1974; contbr. articles to profl. jours. Bd. mgrs. Swarthmore Coll., 1970-81; trustee Yale-New Haven Hosp., 1981-85, Yale Corp., 1986-92; mem. conf. Chief Justices, 1984—, pres., 1994; hon. chmn. U.S. Constl. Bicentennial Com., 1986-91; mem. Conn. Permanent Commn. on Status of Women, 1973-74, Conn. Bd. Pardons, 1978-80, Conn. Law Revision Commn., 1978-84; bd. dirs. Nat. Ctr. State Cts., 1992-96, chmn., 1994. Recipient Ella Grasso award, 1982, Jud. award Conn. Trial Lawyers Assn., 1982, citation of merit Yale Law Sch., 1983, Pioneer Woman award Hartford Coll. for Women, 1988, Disting. Svc. award U. Conn. Law Sch. Alumni Assn., 1993, Raymond E. Baldwin Pub. Svc. award Quinnipiac Coll. Law Sch., 1995, Disting. Svc. award Conn. Law Tribune, 1996. Mem. ABA, Conn. Bar Assn. (Jud. award 1992, Spl. award 1996), Am. Law Inst. (coun.), Am. Acad. Arts and Scis., Am. Philos. Soc. Office: Conn Supreme Ct Drawer N Sta A 231 Capitol Ave Hartford CT 06106-1537

PETERS, JEAN THERESA, sales executive; b. Boulder, Colo., July 22, 1944; d. Barney Clifford and Frances Kathrine (Tholen) Neff; m. Ford Gordon Peters Jr., Jan. 29, 1982; 1 child, Christopher Samuel. Student, U. Colo., 1962-63; lic., Brown Radio-TV Sch., 1975. Reception clk. first aide and water safety dept. Denver chpt. ARC, 1960-62; reception clk. Takcom Jewelry, N.Y.C., 1963-64; mem. promotion staff Calla Records, N.Y.C., 1965-67; detail sales rep. Alright Med. Labs., N.Y.C., and R.I., 1971-74; engr., tech. dir. WTNH-TV, New Haven, 1975-76, KWGN-TV, Denver, 1976-79; engr. KBTV (name now KUSA-TV), Denver, 1976; adminstrv. asst., v.p. sales broadcast equipment G.P. Enterprises, Inc., Arlington, Tex., 1980—. Mem. Bowie High Sch. PTSA, Arlington, 1991—. Mem. Soc. Motion Picture and TV Engrs., World Wildlife Fund, Humane Soc. U.S., Wilderness Soc., Arlington Herb and Garden Club. Office: G P Enterprises Inc PO Box 912 Arlington TX 76004-0912

PETERS, JUDITH GRIESSEL, foreign language educator; b. Albany, N.Y., Sept. 30, 1939; d. Edward Ernest and Miriam Anne (Schurman) Griessel; m. Howard Nevin Peters, Aug. 24, 1963; children: Elisabeth Anne, Nevin Edward. BA, Valparaiso (Ind.) U., 1961; PhD, U. Colo., 1968. Prof. fgn. langs. and lit. Valparaiso U., 1983—, internat. svc. program chair, 1993—, dept. fgn. langs. chair, 1995—. Faculty fellowship Lilly Endowment, 1989, NDEA Title IV fellowship U.S. Govt., 1961-64. Mem. Am. Assn. of Tchrs. of Spanish and Portuguese. Home: 860 N 500 E Valparaiso IN 46383

PETERS, KAREN RONELL, public administrator; b. Topeka, Kans., June 20, 1944; d. Ralph Keller and Mary Jean (Meyers) Keller Wynn; 1 child, Lisa Renee. BA, U. Okla., 1966; MA in Spanish, Wichita State U., 1970; postgrad., U. Calif., Irvine, 1971-74, cert. in hazardous materials mgmt., 1986; JD, Western State U., 1993. Adminstrv. analyst I program planning div. County of Orange, Calif., 1976, adminstrv. analyst II program coordination div., 1976-79, staff analyst III program coordination div., 1979-80, mgr. adminstrv. services div. environ. mgmt. agy., 1980-84; sr. staff analyst Hazardous Materials Program/CAO, 1984-86; administrv. mgr. I hazardous materials program Orange County Fire Dept., 1986-94, adminstrv. mgr. I property mgmt., 1994; guest lectr. U. Calif., 1989. Co-chmn. issue briefing com. North Orange County chpt. NOW, 1983-84, state pres. Calif. 1979-81, chmn. polit. action task force, 1983-85, treas., 1983, numerous offices; sec. ERA-Orange County, 1982-83, treas. 1977-79; chmn. Community Devel. Coun., Inc., 1977-78, vice-chmn., 1976-77, chmn. project rev. and program devel. com., 1976-77; v.p., bd. dirs. Chateau Orleans Homeowners Assn., 1983-84, pres., 1977-78, treas., 1994—; active numerous polit. campaigns, 1976-84, prevention week activities Child Abuse Coun. Recipient numerous civic awards including Woman of Distinction award Soroptimist Internat. of Orange, 1989, Progress for Women award Santa Ana Coll., 1986, Cert. of Achievement for Leadership award North Orange County YWCA, 1986, Woman of Achievement award Women in Communications, Inc., 1983, Golden Key award Dem. Women Orange County, 1983, and many others. Mem. NOW, Calif. Hazardous Waste Assn., Am. Soc. Pub. Adminstrn. (exec. coun. Orange County chpt. 1977-81, treas. 1978-79, chmn. task force 1976-77), U. Okla. Alumni Assn. (life), Wichita State U. Alumni Assn., Unitarian Soc. Orange County, Nat. Women's Polit. Caucus, Sigma Delta Pi. Home: 2525 N Bourbon St Apt 2M Orange CA 92665-3013 Office: Orange County Fire Dept 180 S Water St Orange CA 92866-2123

PETERS, KATHERINE JEAN, television director; b. Bethesda, Md., July 8, 1954; d. Thomas Graham and Katherine Louella (Spooner) P.; m. Thomas Paul Pfeiffer, Apr. 10, 1976 (div. May 1987); 1 child, Katherine Janet. BA in Comm. Arts magna cum laude, Salisbury State U., 1985. Instr. developmentally handicapped Dorchester Devel. Unit, Cambridge, Md., 1977-80; tv camera operator, editor, dir. WMDT-TV 47, Salisbury, Md., 1984-89; dir. t.v. WBOC-TV 16, Salisbury, 1989—. Bd. dirs. Cmty. Players of Salisbury. Mem. NOW, Phi Kappa Phi. Democrat. Mem. Soc. of Friends.

PETERS, LAURALEE MILBERG, diplomat; b. Monroe, N.C., Jan. 28, 1943; d. Arthur W. and Opal I. (Mueller) Milberg; m. Lee M. Peters, May 30, 1964; children: David, Evelyn, Edward, Matthew. BA with highest honors, U. Kans., 1964, postgrad., 1965-67; student, Fgn Svc. Inst., 1975. Asst. pub. info. officer NAS, Washington, 1967-69; joined Fgn. Svc., Dept. State, 1972, commd. sr. fgn. svc. officer, 1985; chief visa sect. Am. Embassy, Saigon, Vietnam, 1972-74; internat. fin. officer Dept. State, Washington, 1975-79; U.S. rep. to Econ. and Social Commn. for Asia and Pacific, UN, Bangkok, Thailand, 1979-81; devel. fin. officer Dept. State, Washington, 1981-82; econ. officer Israel, West Bank, Gaza, 1982-84; dir. Office Monetary Affairs Dept. State, Washington, 1984-86; econ. counselor Am. Embassy, Islamabad, Pakistan, 1986-88; career devel. officer Dept. State, Washington, 1988-89, dep. asst. sec. for personnel, 1989-91; mem. Sr. Seminar, 1991-92; U.S. Ambassador to Sierra Leone, 1992-95; internat. affairs adviser to pres. Naval War Coll., 1995—. Various leadership positions Boy Scouts Am., 1977-88. Recipient Disting. award of merit Nat. Capitol Area Coun. Boy Scouts Am., 1986. Mem. Am. Fgn. Svc. Protective Assn. (v.p. 1981-84), Consular Officer's Assn. (sec. 1974-75), Phi Beta Kappa. Home: 9 Jackson Rd Newport RI 02840 Office: Naval War Coll Code 002 686 Cushing Rd Newport RI 02841-1207

PETERS, MARIAN VIRGINIA, elementary education educator; b. Boston, Feb. 4, 1951; d. Israel Harris and Ernestine Yvonne (Pugh) Moyston; m. George Thomas Peters (separated Sept. 1987); children: Latiya Bernice, Damali Yvonne. BA in Elem. Edn., Boston Coll., 1972, M in Edn. Psychology, 1975; M in Edn. Mgmt., Lesley Coll., 1993; M in Spl. Edn. Tech., Emmanuel Coll., 1994; postgrad., Walden U. Cert. elem. educator, prin. N-6. Tchr. kindergarten Cooper Cmty. Ctr., Boston, 1972-73; reading specialist METCO & IDT, Boston, 1973-74; tchr. Boston Pub. Schs. Taft Sch., 1974-75, Baldwin Sch., 1975-77, Holmes Sch., 1977-79, Marshall Sch., 1980—; coord. before sch. program Boston Pub. Schs., 1992-93, mem. sch. based mgmt., 1992-96, ptnrs. in prevention, 1993-94; mem. Landmark Edn., Cambridge, Mass., 1994-95. Author: Women in Psychology, 1975, Before and After School Programs, 1993, The Five Senses-English & Spanish, 1994. Vol., asst. aerobics & swim team Dorchester (Mass.) YMCA, 1984-92; vol., treas.- trustee Cedar St. Condo Trust, Boston, 1988-93; vol., eucharistic min. St. John-St. Hugh Parish, Boston, 1989-96; vice grand lady St. Peter Claver, Boston, 1994-96; vol. U.S. Youth Games, Boston, 1991; active child care leadership Parents United for Child Care, Boston, 1995. Mem. NAFE, ASCD, Mass. Elem. Sch. Prin. Assn., Mass. Computer Using Educators. Democrat. Roman Catholic. Home: 46A Cedar St # 2 Roxbury MA 02119 Office: J Marshall-Boston Pub Schs 35 Westville St Dorchester MA 02124

PETERS, MERCEDES, psychoanalyst; b. N.Y.C. Student Columbia U., 1944-45; BS, L.I. U., 1945; MS, U. Conn., 1953; tng. in psychotherapy Am. Inst. Psychotherapy and Psychoanalysis, 1960-70; cert. in Psychoanalysis Postgrad. Ctr. For Mental Health, 1976; PhD in Psychoanalysis, Union Inst., 1989. Cert. psychoanalyst Am. Examining Bd. Psychoanalysis; cert. mental health cons. Sr. psychotherapist Cmty. Guidance Svc., 1960-75; staff affiliate Postgrad. Ctr. for Mental Health, 1974-76; pvt. practice psychoanalysis and psychotherapy, Bklyn., 1961—. Contbr. articles to profl. jours. Bd. dirs. Brookwood Child Care Assn.; mem. vestry Grace Ch., Brooklyn Heights. Fellow Am. Orthopsychiat. Assn.; mem. LWV, NAACP, NASW, Postgrad. Psychoanalytic Soc., Wednesday Club. Office: 142 Joralemon St Brooklyn NY 11201-4709

PETERS, PEGGY L.S., investment broker; b. Milw., Dec. 28, 1945; d. Carl Frederick and Bernice Ida (Schpatz) Schoenfeldt; m. Michael Harvey Peters, June 5, 1981; 1 child, Lee Michael Peters. BA in Psychology, U. Wis., Milw., 1970. Mgr. Solana Studios Outboard Marine Corp., Milw., 1970-74; real estate broker, salesperson Relocation Realty, Milw., 1973-74; investment broker Prudential Bache, Washington D.C., 1975-82; v.p. investments, retirement planning cons. Paine Webber, Vienna, Va., 1982—. Rep. dive team, mem. bd. dirs. Great Falls Swim & Tennis Club, 1995; chmn. PTA, 1995. Mem. Gamma Phi Beta (life). Republican. Home: 917 Golden Arrow St Great Falls VA 22066

PETERS, RITA HEIDI, academic administrator; b. Riverhead, N.Y.. Grad., Lycoming Coll.; MS, U. Calif., Davis, 1990. Cert. fund raising exec. Owner The Winning Edge, Stockton, Calif., 1984-92; dir. grants and founds. U. of the Pacific, Stockton, 1992—; mem. faculty rsch. com. U. of the Pacific, Stockton, 1992—. Contbr. articles to profl. jours. Travel/rsch. grantee Ind. U. and the Lilly Endowment, 1991. Mem. AAUW, Nat. Coun. Univ. Rsch. Adminstrs., Soc. Rsch. Adminstrs., Nat. Soc. Fund Raising Execs. (Capital chpt., program dir., bd. dirs. San Joaquin chpt. 1992, v.p. San Joaquin chpt. 1993), Stockton Rotary (membership com. 1993, charity allocations com. 1993, fund raising com., 1994). Office: Univ of the Pacific 3601 Pacific Ave Stockton CA 95211

PETERS, ROBERTA, soprano; b. N.Y.C., May 4, 1930; d. Sol and Ruth (Hirsch) P.; m. Bertram Fields, Apr. 10, 1955; children: Paul, Bruce. Ed. privately; Litt.D., Elmira Coll., 1967; Mus. D., Ithaca Coll., 1968, Colby Coll., 1980; L.H.D., Westminster Coll., 1974, Lehigh U., 1977; D.F.A., St. John's U., 1982; LittD, Coll. New Rochelle, 1989. Author: Debut at the Met; Met. Opera debut as Zerlina in Don Giovanni, 1950; recorded numerous operas; appeared motion pictures; frequent appearances radio and TV; sang at Royal Opera House, Covent Garden, London, Vienna State Opera, Munich Opera, West Berlin Opera, Salzburg Festival, debuts at festivals in Vienna and Munich; concert tours in U.S., Soviet Union, Scandinavian countries, Israel, China, Japan, Taiwan, South Korea, debut, Kirov Opera, Leningrad, USSR, sang at Bolshoi Opera, Moscow (1st Am. to receive Bolshoi medal). Trustee Carnegie Hall; dir. Met. Opera Guild; chmn. Nat. Inst. Music Theater, 1991—; apptd. by Pres. Bush to Nat. Coun. Arts, 1992. Named Woman of Yr. Fedn. Women's Clubs, 1964; honored spl. ceremony on 35th anniversary with the Met. Opera Co., 1985; was 1st Am. to receive Bolshoi medal, 1972. Office: ICM Artists Ltd 40 W 57th St New York NY 10019-4001

PETERS, SARAH WHITAKER, art historian, writer, lecturer; b. Kenosha, Wis., Aug. 17, 1924; d. Robert Burbank and Margaret Jebb (Allen) Whitaker; m. Arthur King Peters, Oct. 21, 1943; children: Robert Bruce, Margaret Allen, Michael Whitaker. BA, Sarah Lawrence Coll., 1954; MA, Columbia U., 1966; student, L'Ecole du Louvre, Paris, 1967-68; diplome, Ecole des Trois Gourmandes, Paris, 1968; PhD, CUNY, 1987. Freelance critic Art in Am., N.Y.C.; lectr.-in-residence Garrison Forest Sch., Owings Mills, Md.; adj. asst. prof. art history C.W. Post, U. L.I.; lectr. Bronxville (N.Y.) Adult Sch., Internat. Mus. Photography, 1979, Tufts U., 1979, Madison (Wis.) Art Ctr., 1984, Meml. Art Gallery, Rochester, N.Y., 1988, 91, Caramoor Mus., Katonah, N.Y., 1988, Yale U. Art Gallery, New Haven, Conn., 1989, The Cosmopolitan Club, N.Y.C., 1977, 91, Sarah Lawrence Coll., Bronxville, 1992, The Phillips Collection, Washington, 1993, Mpls. Inst. Arts, 1993, Whitney Mus. Am. Art, Champion, 1994, U. Wis., Parkside, 1994, Nat. Mus. Wildlife Art, Jackson Hole, Wyo., 1995. Author: Becoming O'Keeffee: The Early Years, 1991, The Dictionary of Art, 1996; contbr. articles to profl. jours. Mem. Coll. Art Assn., Bronxville Field Club, The Cosmopolitan Club. Home: 14 Village Ln Bronxville NY 10708-4806

PETERS, VIRGINIA, actress; b. Los Angeles, July 15, 1924; d. Peter and Tessie (Skiller) Stetzenko. Grad., Pasadena (Calif.) Playhouse, 1944; student, Los Angeles City Coll. Tchr. Burbank (Calif.) Little Theatre, 1978-80, Burbank Acad. Performing Arts, 1979—. TV appearances in Night Strangler, 1972, Love American Style, 1973, Rita Moreno Show, 1977, Laverne and Shirley, 1977, 78, Happy Days, 1977, Dallas, 1980, The Waltons, 1981, House Detective, 1985, Knight Rider, 1985, Murder She Wrote, 1986, Hunter, 1986, Hardcastle and McCormick, 1986, Cavanaughs, 1986, Paper Chase, 1986, also Days of Our Lives, Divorce Court, Grace Under Fire, 1993; film appearances include The Arrangement, 1968, The Cat People, 1981, Fast Times at Ridgemont High, 1982, Rat Boy, 1985, The Deacon Street Deer, 1985, My Demon Lover, Mr. President, The Judge, Stripped to Kill II, 1988, Hero, My Girl II; appeared in: TV movie The 11th Victim, 1979; TV pilot We Got It Made; also numerous commls. Mem. Masquers Club (past dir.), Pasadena Playhouse Alumni Assos. (past dir.). Democrat. Roman Catholic.

PETERS, VIRGINIA BERGMAN, educator, writer; b. Lac Qui Parle, Minn., May 13, 1918; d. Samuel Oscar and Ruth Caroline (Erlandson) Bergman; m. J. Shelton Peters, Apr. 27, 1946 (dec. 1978); 1 child, Emory Bergman Peters. BS in Eng., Journalism, U. Minn., 1941; MA in Anthropology, George Washington U., 1965. Eng. tchr. Appleton (Minn.) Pub. Sch. Sys., 1941-43; rsch. analyst Dept. of Def., Arlington, Va., 1951-55; elem. sch. tchr. Fairfax County (Va.) Pub. Sch. Sys., 1956-61, H.S. tchr., 1965-71; tchr. feminism, anthropology Learning in Retirement, Fairfax County, 1993-95; tchr. anthropology U. Va. ext., Fairfax County, 1965-67; tutor Belvedere Elem. Sch., 1992-93, Graham Rd. Elem. Sch., 1995; coord. archeology dig, Am. U. History Commn., 1973-75. Author: The Florida Wars, 1979 (Rembert W. Patrick Meml. Book award), Women of the Earth Lodges; past editor, contbr. (ch. paper) The Towne Crier; contbr. articles to books and publs. Assoc. Cmty. of Holy Spirit; vol. Sleepy Hollow Nursing Home, archaeology lab. Heritage Resources Office, Fairfax County, 1996; mem. Fairfax County History Commn., 1974—, chmn., 1982-84. With USNR, 1943-46. Mem. Women's Meml. Found. (charter), Nat. Mus. Women in Arts (charter), Hist. Soc. Fairfax County. Democrat. Episcopalian. Home and Office: 3320 Executive Ave Falls Church VA 22042

PETERSEN, ANN NEVIN, computer systems administrator, consultant; b. Mexico City, Aug. 7, 1937; parents Am. citizens; d. Thomas Marshall and Gerry (Cox) Nevin; m. Norman William Petersen, Aug. 24, 1956; children: Richard, Robert, Thomas, Anita, David. AS in Electronics, Monterey Peninsula Coll., Monterey, Calif., 1962; student, U. N.Mex., 1956, Las Positas Coll., Livermore, Calif., 1992. Cert. computer profl. CAD mgr. Naval Air Rework Facility, Alameda, Calif., 1979-80; computer systems analyst Space and Naval Warfare System Command, Washington, 1980-84, Facilities Computer Systems Office, Port Hueneme, Calif., 1984-86; systems mgr. Lawrence Livermore Nat. Lab., Livermore, 1986-89; data base mgr. Clayton Environ. Cons., Pleasanton, Calif., 1989-90; computer systems mgr. Waltrip & Assocs., Sacramento, 1990-94; dir. computer systems, CFO Innovative Techs. Inc., Pleasanton, 1992—. Author databases. Bd. dirs. Am. Field Svc., Port Hueneme, 1976-78; mem. various adv. bds. U.S. Navy, 1957-86; mem. adv. bd. Calif. Deaf/Blind Regional Ctr., Sacramento, 1976-80; bd. dirs. ARC Alameda County, Hayward, Calif., 1992—. Recipient Superior Performance award U.S. Navy, 1980, Speaker of Month award Toastmsters, 1985. Mem. Data Processing Mgmt. Assn., bd. dirs., sec.), Assn. for Computing Machinery, Tri Valley MacIntosh Users Group, Inst. for Cert. of Computer Profls. Office: Innovative Techs Inc 5238 Riverdale Ct Pleasanton CA 94588-3759

PETERSEN, ANNE C(HERYL), foundation administrator, educator; b. Little Falls, Minn., Sept. 11, 1944; d. Franklin Hanks and Rhoda Pauline (Sandwick) Studley; m. Douglas Lee Petersen, Dec. 27, 1967; children: Christine Anne, Benjamin Bradfield. BA, U. Chgo., 1966, MS, 1972, PhD, 1973. Asst. prof., rsch. assoc. Dept. Psychiatry U. Chgo., 1972-80, assoc. prof., rsch. assoc., 1980-82; prof. human devel., head Dept. Individual and Family Studies Pa. State U., University Park, 1982-87, dean Coll. Health and Human Devel., 1987-92; dean grad. sch., v.p. for rsch. throughout state U. Minn., Mpls., 1992-94, prof. adolescent devel. and pediatrics, 1992—; dep. dir. NSF, Arlington, Va., 1994—; vis. prof., fellow Coll. End. and Devel. Psychology, Roosevelt U., Chgo., 1973-74; cons. Ctr. for Health Adminstrn. Studies U. Chgo., 1976-78, Ctr. for New Schs., Chgo., 1974-78, Robert Wood Johnson Found. Mathtech, Inc., 1987-89; coord. clin. rsch. tng. program Michael Reese Hosp. and Med. Ctr., Chgo., 1976-80, dir. Lab. for Study of Adolescence, 1975-82; mem. faculty Ill. Sch. for Profl. Psychology, 1978-79; statis. cons. Coll. Nursing U. Ill. Med. Ctr., 1975-83; assoc. dir. health program MacArthur Found., 1980-82, also cons. health program, 1982-88; chair sr. adv. bd. NIMH, 1987-88. Reviewer Jour. of Youth and Adolescence, 1975-80, Devel. Psychology, 1979—, Sci., 1979—, Jour. of Edn. Psychology, 1979—, Child Devel., 1980—, Jour. Edn. Measurement, 1980, Ednl. Researcher, 1980, Am. Ednl. Rsch. Jour., 1981—, Jour. of Mental Imagery, 1982-92, Sex Roles, 1984—; cons. editor Psychology of Women Quar., 1978-82, assoc. editor, 1983-86; adv. editor Contemporary Psychology, 1985-86; editorial bd. various profl. jours. Bd. overseers Lewis Coll., Ill. Inst. Tech., 1980-82; mem. adv. bd. longitudinal data archive project Murray Ctr., Radcliffe Coll., 1985-91, mem. sci. adv. bd., 1983-91. Mem. NAS (nat. forum on future children and their families 1987-91, chmn. panel on child abuse and neglect 1991-93), fellow AAAS, APA (chmn. task force on reproductive freedom 1979-81, program chmn. 1981-82, chmn. task force on long range planning 1986-89, pres. div. 7 1992-93), Am. Ednl. Rsch. Assn. (various offices), Assn. Women in Sci., Behavior Genetics Assn., Psychometric Soc., Acad. Europaea, Soc. for Rsch. on Adolescence (pres. 1990-92, past pres., chmn. nominations com. 1992-94). Home: 11166 Harbor Ct Reston VA 22091

PETERSEN, BARBARA ANN, music association administrator, author; b. Evansville, Ind., June 14, 1945; d. Rudolph Conrad and Helen Mary Madeline (Ross) Ellingson; m. Geoffrey Ames Petersen, June 21, 1969 (div.); m. Roger Raymond Roloff, Mar. 19, 1982. BA in Music cum laude, Carleton Coll., 1967; MA in Musicology, NYU, 1971, PhD in Musicology, 1977. Rsch. asst. NYU, 1968-72, teaching asst., 1969-70, music instr., 1972-73; editor Broude Bros. Ltd., N.Y.C., 1973-77; coord. concert music activities BMI, N.Y.C., 1977-85, asst. v.p. concert music adminstrn., 1985—. Author: Ton und Wort: The Lieder of Richard Strauss, 1980, Ton und Wort: Die Lieder von Richard Strauss, 1986; contbr. articles to profl. jours., chpts. to books. Mezzo soprano Choir Ch. Ascension, N.Y.C., 1967-78. Ind. Fedn. Music Clubs fellow, 1960, NDEA Title IV fellow NYU, 1967-72. Mem. Am. Music Ctr. (bd. dirs. 1986—), N.Y. Women Composers (chmn. 1984—), Poné Ensemble New Music (bd. dirs. 1987—), New Music Young Ensembles (adv. bd. 1982—), Friends of the Shawangunks, Mohonk Preserve (life), Wallkill Valley Rail Trail, John Burroughs Soc. Democrat. Office: BMI 320 W 57th St New York NY 10019

PETERSEN, BRENDA CAROLE, nurse, social worker; b. Bethesda, Md., Oct. 5, 1952; d. Mary Jane (Padgett) Cable; m. Harry Daniel Petersen, Oct. 15, 1971 (div. May 1986); children: Daniel Wayne, Amy Carole; m. Stephen Charles Mockrin, July 18, 1987. AA in Nursing, Prince Georges C.C., Largo, Md., 1976; BA in Applied Behavioral Sci., Nat. Louis U., Fairfax, Va., 1989; MS in Social Work, U. Md., Balt., 1994. RN, Md.; lic. graduate social worker; cert. sexual assault nurse examiner. Staff med. and surg. nurse Leland Meml. Hosp., Riverdale, Md., 1975-79; staff nurse critical care unit So. Md. Hosp. Ctr., Clinton, 1979-80, Doctors Hosp., Lanham, Md., 1980-81, Prince Georges Gen. Hosp., Cheverley, Md., 1981-86; home health nurse Consumer Home Health, Prince Frederick, Md., 1984-87; staff nurse Ambulatory Cardiac Catherization, Takoma Park, Md., 1989-94; hosp. supr., critical care nurse Washington Adventist Hosp., Takoma Park, 1982-94; coord. sexual abuse program Govt. of Montgomery County, Rockville, Md., 1994—; co-chmn. adv. bd. Sexual Abuse and Assault Ctr., Rockville, 1994—. Mem. NASW, AACN (cert. critical care RN, 1989), Am. Profl. Soc. on Abuse of Children (legis. com. 1995—, Md. state chmn. membership com., chairperson Ct. Watch, 1996—), Stepfamily Assn. Am., Internat. Assn. Forensic Nurses (cert. sexual assault nurse examiner, 1995), Alzheimers Assn. (legis. com. 1994—), Hemlock Soc. (med. study group 1995—). Home: 13328 Hathaway Dr Silver Spring MD 20906 Office: Montgomery County Govt 401 Hungerford Dr 3d Fl Rockville MD 20850

PETERSEN, CATHERINE HOLLAND, lawyer; b. Norman, Okla., Apr. 24, 1951; d. John Hays and Helen Ann (Turner) Holland; m. James Frederick Petersen, June 26, 1973 (div.); children: T. Kyle, Lindsay Diane. B.A., Hastings Coll., 1973; J.D., Okla. U., 1976. Bar: Okla. 1976, U.S. Dist. Ct. (we. dist.) Okla. 1978. Legal intern, police legal advisor City of Norman, 1974-76; sole practice, Norman, 1976-81; ptnr. Williams Petersen & Denny, Norman, 1981-82; pres. Petersen Assocs., Inc., Norman, 1982—; adj. prof. Okla. City U. Coll. Law, 1982, U. Okla. Law Ctr., 1987; instr. continuing legal edn. U. Okla. Law Ctr., Norman, 1977, 79, 81, 83, 84, 86, 89-95. Bd. dirs. United Way, Norman, 1978-84, pres., 1981; bd. dirs. Women's Resource Ctr., Norman, 1975-77, 82-84; mem. Jr. League, Norman, 1980-83, Norman Hosp. Aux., Norman, 1982-84; trustee 1st Presbyn. Ch., 1986-87. Named to Outstanding Okla. Women of 1980's, Women's Polit. Caucus, 1980, Outstanding Women Am., 1981, 83. Fellow Am. Acad. Matrimonial Lawyers (pres. Okla. chpt. 1990-91, bd. govs. 1991-95); mem. ABA (seminar instr. 1993, 95, 96), Cleve. County Bar Assn., Okla. Bar Assn. (chmn. family law sect. 1987-88, seminar instr. 1986-93, 95), Phi Delta Phi. Republican. Home: 4716 Sundance Ct Norman OK 73072-3900 Office: PO Box 1243 314 E Comanche St Norman OK 73069-6009

PETERSEN, ELLEN ANNE, artist; b. N.Y.C., Dec. 18, 1930; d. William George and Dina (Bochmeier) Heinrich; m. Ralph Lamon Petersen, Dec. 14, 1952; children: William, Bryan. BS, NYU, 1968, MS, 1970. Art educator Paramus (N.J.) High Sch., 1969-85; tchng. artist William Carlos Williams Ctr. for Arts, Rutherford, N.J., 1989-91; studio artist Parrish Mus., Southampton, N.Y., 1988—; artist workshops Guild Hall Mus., East Hampton, N.Y., 1992—; Video interview "Women in the Arts", Fairleigh Dickinson U., Teaneck, N.J., 1977, LTV-local TV, East Hampton, 1991. Represented in permanent collection Guild Hall Mus., East Hampton. Bd. dirs. Jimmy Ernst Artists' Alliance, East Hampton, N.Y., 1985-92; mem. edn. com. Parrish Art Mus., Southampton, 1989—; curator Springs Invitational Art Exhbn., East Hampton, 1994, 95, 96. Recipient hon. mention Guild Hall Mus., 1994, 1st prize N.J. state Exhbn., East Orange, N.J., 1967, award Springs-Ashawagh Hall Invitational, East Hampton, 1993, Juried Exhbn., Parrish Mus., 1992. Mem. Nat. Women's Caucus of Art, Artists' Equity, Jimmy Ernst Artists' Alliance (treas. 1988-90, v.p. 1990-92), Art Students' League (life), Women's Caucus for Art (v.p. Dallas chpt. 1987-88). Home and Studio: 7 S Pond Rd East Hampton NY 11937-3719

PETERSEN, EVELYN ANN, education consultant; b. Gary, Ind., July 2, 1936; d. Eric Maxwell and Julia Ann (Kustron) Ivany; m. Ozzie G. Hebert, Feb. 27, 1957 (div. July 1963); children: Heather Lynn Petersen Hewett, Eric Dean Hebert; m. Jon Edwin Petersen, June 13, 1964; children: Karin Patricia, Kristin Shawn. BS, Purdue U., 1964; MA, Cen. Mich. U., 1977. Cert. tchr. elem. edn. with early childhood and vocat. edn. endorsements, Mich. Elem. tchr. Harford Day Sch., Bel Air, Md., 1958-62, Interlochen (Mich.) Elem. Sch., 1964-67; dir., tchr. Traverse City (Mich.) Coop. Presch., 1969-77; off-campus instr. grad. level Cen. Mich. U., Mt. Pleasant, 1977-92; Child Devel. Assoc. nat. rep. Coun. for Early Childhood Profl. Recognition, Washington, 1981—; instr. N.W. Mich. Coll., Traverse City, 1974-75, 78, U. Wis., Sheboygan, 1981-83; project dir., instr. West Shore C.C., Scotville, Mich., 1984-86, 89; ednl. cons., 1980—; parenting columnist Detroit Free Press, Knight Ridder Tribune Wire, 1984—; bd. mem. Children's Trust Fund, Lansing, Mich., 1983-85; mem. ad hoc adv. com. Bd. Edn. State of Mich., Lansing, 1985-86, child care provider trainer Dept. Social Svcs., 1988; chairperson adv. bd. Traverse Bay Vocat. Edn. Child Care Program, 1976-79; panelist Nat. Parenting Ctr., L.A., 1992—. Author: A Practical Guide to Early Childhood Planning, Methods and Materials: The What, Why and How of Lesson Plans, 1996; author, co-prodr. (audio and video cassette series) Parent Talk, 1990, Effective Home Visits: Video Training, 1994. County coord. Week of the Young Child, Traverse City, 1974-78; vol. probate ct. Traverse City, 1973-83; commr. Traverse City Human Rights Commn., 1981-82. Mem. AAUW (chairperson, coord. Touch & Do Exploratorium 1974-76), Nat. Fedn. Press Women, Nat. Assn. for Edn. of Young Children, Children's Trust Fund for Abuse Prevention, Mich. Assn. for Edn. of Young Children, Mich. Mental Health Assn., Assn. for Childhood Edn. Internat., Author's Guild. Home and Office: 843 S Long Lake Rd Traverse City MI 49684

PETERSEN, MAUREEN JEANETTE MILLER, management information consultant, former nurse; b. Evanston, Ill., Sept. 4, 1956; d. Maurice James and M. Joyce (Mielke) Miller; m. Gregory Eugene Petersen, July 7, 1984; 1 child, Trevor James. BS in Nursing cum laude, Vanderbilt U., 1978; MS in Biometry and Health Info. Systems, U. Minn., 1984. Nurse U. Iowa Hosps. and Clinics, Iowa City, 1978-82; research asst. Sch. Nursing, U. Minn., Mpls., 1982-83; mgr. Arthur Andersen/Andersen Cons., Mpls., 1984—. Mem. Minn. 100. Mem. Minn. 100, Women in Biocomputing, Mensa. Methodist. Home: 1050 County Rd C2 W Saint Paul MN 55113-1945 Office: Andersen Cons 45 S 7th St Minneapolis MN 55402-1614

PETERSON, BARBARA ANN BENNETT, history educator, television personality; b. Portland, Oreg., Sept. 6, 1942; d. George Wright and Hope (Chatfield) Bennett; m. Frank Lynn Peterson, July 1, 1967. BA, BS, Oreg. State U., 1964; MA, Stanford U., 1965; PhD, U. Hawaii, 1978; PhD (hon.), London Inst. Applied Rsch., 1991, Australian Inst. Coordinated R, 1995. Prof. history U. Hawaii, Honolulu, 1967-96; prof. emeritus history, 1996—; chmn. social scis. dept. U. Hawaii, Honolulu, 1971-73, 75-76, asst. dean, 1973-74; prof. Asian history and European colonial history and world problems Champman Coll. World Campus Afloat, 1974, European overseas exploration, expansion and colonialism U. Colo., Boulder, 1978; assoc. prof. U. Hawaii-Manoa Coll. Continuing Edn., 1981; Fulbright prof. history Wuhan (China) U., 1988-89; Fulbright rsch. prof. Sophia U., Japan, 1978; rsch. assoc. Bishop Mus., 1995—; lectr. Capital Spkrs., Washington, 1987—; tchr. Hawaii State Ednl. Channel, 1993—. Co-author: Women's Place is in the History Books, Her Story, 1962-1980: A Curriculum Guide for American History Teachers, 1980; author: America in British Eyes, 1988; editor: Notable Women of Hawaii, 1984, (with W. Solheim) The Pacific Region, 1990, 91, American History: 17th, 18th and 19th Centuries, 1993, America: 19th and 20th Centuries, 1993, John Bull's Eye on America, 1995; assoc. editor Am. Nat. Biography; contbr. articles to profl. publs. Participant People-to-People Program, Eng., 1964, Expt. in Internat. Living Program, Nigeria, 1966; chmn. 1st Nat. Women's History Week, Hawaii, 1982; pres. Bishop Mus. Coun., 1993-94; active Hawaii Commn. on Status of Women. Fulbright scholar, Japan, 1967, China, 1988-89; NEH-Woodrow Wilson fellow Princeton U., 1980; recipient state proclamations Gov. of Hawaii, 1982, City of Honolulu, 1982, Outstanding Tchr. of Yr. award Wuhan (China), U., 1988, Medallion of Excellence award Am. Biog. Assn., 1989, Woman of Yr. award, 1991; named Hawaii State Mixed Doubles Tennis Champion, 1985. Fellow World Literacy Acad. (Eng.), Internat. Biog. Assn. (Cambridge, Eng. chpt.); mem. AAUW, Am. Hist. Assn. (mem. numerous coms.), Am. Studies Assn., Am. Studies Assn. (pres. 1984-85), Fulbright Alumni Assn. (founding pres. Hawaii chpt. 1984-88, mem. nat. steering com. chairwomen Fulbright Assn. ann. conf. 1990), Am. Coun. on Edn., Maison Internat. des Intellectuals, France, Hawaii Found. History and Humanities (mem. editl. bd. 1972-73), Hawaii Found. Women's History, Hawaii Hist. Assn., Nat. League Am. Pen Women (contest chairperson 1986), Women in Acad. Adminstrn., Phi Beta Phi, Phi Kappa Phi.

PETERSON, BARBARA MAE BITTNER OWECKE, artist, nurse, realtor; b. Winona, Minn., Nov. 25, 1932; d. Adelbert Paul and Hermanda Gilda (Pellowski) Bittner; m. Jerome Francis Owecke, Nov. 28, 1953 (div. 1974); children: Paul Richard Owecke, Michael Jerome Owecke, Margaret Francis Owecke (dec.), Stacy Ann Owecke, Wendy Alane Owecke (dec.), James William Owecke, William Harold Owecke; m. Roy Eugene Peterson, May 28, 1983. RN, Viterbo Coll., 1953; B Individualized Study, George Mason U., 1994. RN, Va., Wis., Mich., Ill., Ohio. Staff nurse Commonwealth Hosp., Fairfax, Va., 1973-74; realtor Century 21 United, Fairfax, Va., 1974-91; telemetry nurse Fairfax Hosp., 1974-76; med. sales rep. CB Fleet Pharm., Lynchburg, Va., 1976-78; territory mgr. Bristol-Myers Squibb, Northern Va., Washington, 1978-92; ret., 1992; v.p. B&R Farm, Goldvein, Va., 1989—; artist Goldvein, Va., 1993—; bd. dirs. Fauquier Artists' Alliance, Warrenton, Va., pres., 1994-95. Exhibited in group shows at Alexandria Art League, 1994, Ctr. for Creative Art, 1994-95, George Mason U., 1994. RN Fauquier Free Clinic, Warrenton, 1993—; mem. Goldvein Vol. Fire Dept., 1989-94. Mem. Alexandria Art League, Va. Mus. Fine Arts, Nat. Artists' Equity Assn., Va. Thoroughbreed Assn., Va. Horseman's Assn. Roman Catholic. Home: 13483 Oakview Dr Goldvein VA 22720 Office: BaMaBi PO Box 100 Goldvein VA 22720

PETERSON, BIANCA LORRIANNE, secondary education educator; b. Manhattan, N.Y., Jan. 12, 1962; d. John Bruce Peterson and Catherine Maybeth (Carone) Heckart. BS, U. Toledo, 1987; Cert. secondary edn., Cleve. State U., 1990. Sci. tchr. Parma (Ohio) City Schs., 1991—, coach volleyball, basketball, track, 1991—, coach cross country team, 1992; participant Project Discovery Participant, Life Sci. Inst., Physics Inst. Jenings scholar Martha Holden-Jenings, Ohio, 1994. Mem. Ohio Mid. Sch. Assn., Am. Coll. Sports Medicine, Sci. Edn. Coun. of Ohio, Nat. Sci. Tchrs. Assn., Ohio Volleyball Coaches, Ohio Track and Cross Country Coaches. Roman Catholic. Home: 4265 Rocky River Dr Cleveland OH 44135

PETERSON, BONNIE LU, mathematics educator; b. Escanaba, Mich., Jan. 19, 1946; d. Herbert Erick and Ruth Albertha (Erickson) P. AA, Bay de Noc C.C., 1966; BS, No. Mich. U., 1968, MA in Math., 1969; EdD, Tenn. State U., 1989. Tchr. Lapeer (Mich.) High Sch., 1969-70, Nova High Sch., Ft. Lauderdale, Fla., 1970-79, Hendersonville (Tenn.) High Sch., 1979—; adj. faculty Vol. State C.C., Gallatin, Tenn., 1989—; chair Sumner County Schs. Tchrs. Insvc., Gallatin, 1990-92; mem. math. specialist team State of Tenn., 1991-93; spkr. in field. Mem. edn. com. Vision 2000-City of Hendersonville, 1993-94. Tenn. State Bd. grantee, 1989-92; Woodrow Wilson fellow, 1993; State-Level Presdl. awardee, 1994, 95, 96; Tandy Scholars award, 1995. Mem. ASCD, Nat. Coun. Tchrs. Math. (chair workshop support com. 1990), Tenn. Math. Tchrs. Assn., Mid. Tenn. Math. Tchrs. Assn. (pres.), Phi Delta Kappa (past pres.). Home: 1081 Coon Creek Rd Dickson TN 37055-4014

PETERSON, DOROTHY LULU, artist, writer; b. Venice, Calif., Mar. 10, 1932; d. Marvin Henry and Fay (Brown) Case; m. Leon Albert Peterson, June 21, 1955; 1 child, David. AD, Compton (Calif.) Coll., 1950. Artist Moran Printing Co., Lockport, N.Y., 1955-59; caricature artist West Seneca and Kenmore Creative Artist Socs., 1973-86; commd. artist in pvt. practice, 1986—; comml. artist Boulevard Mall, Kenmore (N.Y.) Arts Soc., 1974—. Works include portraits of Pres. and Mrs. Reagan in Presdl. Libr. Collection, also portraits of Geraldine Ferraro, Presidents Clinton, Bush, Nixon, Ford, also Bette Davis, Lucille Ball, Bing Crosby, Elizabeth Taylor, 1971-94; author articles. Recipient awards West Seneca Art Soc., 1975, Kenmore Art Soc., 1982, 86. Democrat. Baptist. Home: 247 Pryor Ave Tonawanda NY 14150

PETERSON, EILEEN M., state agency administrator; b. Trenton, N.J., Sept. 22, 1942; d. Leonard James and Mary (Soganic) Olschewski; m. Lars N. Peterson, Jr., 1970 (div. 1983); children: Leslie, Valerie, Erica. Student, Boise State U. Adminstrv. sec. State Ins. Fund, Boise, 1983-85; legal asst. Bd. Tax Appeals, Boise, 1985-87, exec. asst., 1987-92, dir., 1992—. Vol. Boise Art Mus., Idaho Refugee Svc. Recipient Gov's. Cert. of Recognition for Outstanding Achievement, 1995. Mem. Mensa, Investment Club (pres.), Mountains West Outdoor Club, Idaho Rivers United. Democrat. Home: 3317 Mountain View Dr Boise ID 83704-4638 Office: Idaho State Bd Tax Appeals 1109 Main St Boise ID 83702-5640

PETERSON, GLORIA DOLORES, artist, educator; b. Chgo., Oct. 13, 1924; d. Erick Leonard and Signe Evelyn (Magnuson) P.; m. Vincent Carroll Scully, June 5, 1948 (div. Nov. 1968); children: Joni Scully-Campbell, Kristen (dec. 1986), Kreg, Erik. Diploma, Chgo. Acad. Fine Arts, 1944; BFA, Carnegie-Mellon U., 1953. Freelance portraitist, painter, 1944—; fashion illustrator Hornes & Gimbels Dept. Stores, Pitts., 1968-70; art tchr., freelance Pitts. Bd. Edn., 1970-71; art dir., tchr., freelance Universal Art Acad., Pitts., 1971-73; pvt. practice Pitts., 1973-75; art tchr. Wauconda (Ill.) Sch. Dist., 1975-77; graphic artist and fine arts J.T.'s Gen. Store, Barrington, Ill., 1981-88; graphic artist, freelance Barrington, Ill., 1988-92; pvt. practice Pitts., 1992—. One woman shows include chgo. Cultural Ctr., 1979, Lawrence U., Appleton, Wis., 1980, Judson Coll., Elgin, Ill., 1982, Borders, Pitts., 1996, others; pvt. collections include Laura West Libr., Pitts., Notre Dame U., South Bend, Ind., State Capital, Springfield, Ill., Freyvogel Funeral Home, Pitts., numerous others. Recipient numerous prizes and honorable mentions. Mem. Nat. League Am. Pen Women (Chgo. chpt. v.p. 1990-92, rec. sec. 1993-96, Pitts. chpt. co-pres. 1996—), North Hills Art Ctr. Home: 20 Chapel Dr Pittsburgh PA 15237

PETERSON, HELEN LOUISE, elementary education educator; b. Three Forks, Mont., May 29, 1938; d. George Edwin and Edna Lucinda (Williams) Bellach; m. Eugene M. Peterson, Feb. 1, 1959 (dec. Apr. 1992); children: Shawn Dana, Misti Dawn. Tchg. cert., Ea. Mont. Coll., 1958; BS, Mont. State U., 1966. Tchr. elem. Lewistown (Mont.) Pub. Sch., 1958, Laurel (Mont.) Pub. Sch., 1959-60, Livingston (Mont.) Pub. Sch., 1960—. Mem. NEA, Nat. Coun. Tchrs. Math., Mont. Edn. Assn., Mont. Assn. Gifted and Talented Edn., Mus. Rockies, Nat. Sci. Tchrs. Assn. Republican. Methodist. Home: Rt 85 Box 4162 Livingston MT 59047 Office: School District 4 132 S B St Livingston MT 59047-2612

PETERSON, JANE WHITE, nursing educator, anthropologist; b. San Juan, P.R., Feb. 15, 1941; d. Jerome Sidney and Vera (Joseph) Peterson; 1 child, Claire Marie. BS, Boston U., 1968; M in Nursing, U. Wash., 1969, PhD, 1981. Staff nurse Visiting Nurse Assn., Boston, 1964-66; prof. Seattle U., 1969—, dir. nursing home project, 1990-92, chair pers. com., 1988-90; chair dept. Community Health and Psychiat. Mental Health Nursing, 1987-89; sec. Coun. on Nursing and Anthropology, 1984-86; pres. Wash. League Nursing, Seattle, 1988-90; pres. bd. Vis. Nurses Svcs., Seattle, 1988-90; contbg. cons. CSI Prodn., Okla., 1987; cons. in nursing WHo/U. Indonesia, Jakarta, fall 1989, Myanmar, winter 1995, Thailand, 1995, China, Beijing, 1995. Contbr. articles to profl. jours., chptrs. to books. Co-owner (with Robert Colley) North End Train Ctr., Seattle; mem. Seattle Art Mus., 1986—. Fellow: Soc. for Applied Anthropology; mem. Am. Anthropological Assn., Soc. for Med. Anthropology, Nat. League for Nursing, Am. Ethological Soc. Office: Seattle U Sch Nursing Broadway and Madison Seattle WA 98122

PETERSON, JANET ANNE, pharmaceutical executive; b. Jersey City, June 15, 1961; d. Arthur Conrad and Gail Lois (Flury) P.; m. Mark Edward Bell, May 26, 1984; children: Matthew, Thomas, Andrew. BS cum laude, U. Mass., 1983; MS, Rutgers U., 1988, PhD, 1992. Lab. technician N.Y. Blood Ctr., N.Y.C., 1984-85; adj. prof. Kean Coll., Union, N.J., 1990-91; assoc. med. dir. Roberts Pharmaceutical, Eatontown, NJ, 1992-93; assoc. dir. med. affairs Enzon, Inc., Piscataway, N.J., 1993-94; assoc. dir. safety evaluation and epidemiology Pfizer Inc., N.Y.C., 1994-96; assoc. dir. sci. affairs Pfizer Internat. Inc., N.Y.C., 1996—; freelance med. writer, Highlands, N.J., 1990-92. Recipient Nat. Rsch. Svc. award, NIH, 1986-91. Mem. AAAS, Drug Info. Assn., N.Y. Acad. Scis. Roman Catholic. Home: 33 Shrewsbury Ave Highlands NJ 07732-1740 Office: Pfizer Internat Inc 235 E 42nd St New York NY 10017-5703

PETERSON, JEANNINE DORSEY, healthcare consultant; b. Pitts., July 25, 1951; d. Cornelius H. and Clara M. (Walker) Dorsey; m. William F. Peterson, Nov. 6, 1976; 1 child, Kendra Rose. BA, Mich. State U., 1973; MPA, Pa. State U., 1978. Case worker St. Francis Hosp., Pitts., 1973-74; program analyst Gov. Coun. on Drug and Alcohol Abuse, Harrisburg, Pa., 1974-78, dir. divsn. planning, 1978-80; dir. divsn. intervention Office Drug and Alcohol Programs Dept. Health, Harrisburg, 1980-82, dir. Bur. Program Svcs., 1982-87, dep. sec., 1987-93, dep. sec. Office Health Promotion, Disease and Substance Abuse, 1993-95; prin. Johnson Bassing & Shaw Inc., 1995—; adj. prof. Lincoln (Pa.) U., 1983-84; med./legal adv. com. Pa. Atty. Gen., 1991-94; cons. CSAP, Washington, 1992, NYU, P.R., 1992, U.S. V.I., 1992, Hawaii, 1993, Birch and Davis, New Orleans, 1994, George Washington U., Tampa, Fla., 1994; active Nat. Adv. Coun. Health Human Svcs. CSAT, 1993—. Active Jack & Jill in Am., 1993—. Mem. Nat. Assn. State Alcohol and Drug Abuse Dirs. (bd. dirs. 1993-95), Alpha Kappa Alpha. Home: 114 Curvin Dr Harrisburg PA 17112-2912

PETERSON, MARGIT SUSAN, marketing administrator; b. Aberdeen, S.D., Dec. 16, 1963; d. Harlan Wayne and Maryanna (Melby) P. B of Individualized Studies, U. Minn., 1987; MBA, U. St. Thomas, 1994. Customer svc. rep. Deluxe Corp., Shoreview, Minn., 1987-88, tng. specialist, 1988-89, mktg. specialist, 1989-94; mktg. mgr. AppDev, Mpls., 1994—.

PETERSON, ROSEMARIE J., federal agent; b. Wichita, Kans., Dec. 12, 1958; d. Robert Olsen and Edna (Bird) Peterson. BA, U. Kans., 1987. Buyer Westlakes Hardware, Lawrence, Kans., 1980-86; ESL instr. USD #497, Lawrence, 1979-84; legalization adjudicator U.S. Immigration and Naturalization, Lubbock, Tex., 1987-88; Spanish instr. U.S. Immigration and Naturalization, Glynco, Ga., 1988-90; spl. agent U.S. Dept. of Labor, Newark, 1990-91, U.S. Dept. of Energy, Albuquerque, 1991—. Mem. Women in Law Enforcement. Office: Dept of Energy Office of Insp Gen PO Box 5657 Albuquerque NM 87185

PETERSON, SALLY LU, communications executive; b. Waukegan, Ill., July 23, 1942; d. George C. and Luella Alice (Flood) P. BA, Govs. State U., Park Forest, Ill., 1983; MA, Calif. Grad. Sch. Theology, 1994; grad., United Christian Bible Inst.; ThD, Internat. Seminary, 1995. Ordained to ministry United Christian Ch. Ministerial Assn., 1990. V.p. Cabac TV, Gurnee, Ill., pres.; producer, dir. WHKE Channel 55, Wis.; outreach to Moscow, Jerusalem, Europe and Africa; founder, organizer, pres. radio ministry Trumpet Ministries, 1991—. Evangelist, founder, organizer TV ministry Calling Revival, 1977—, producer, dir. TV programming for Northern Ill., 1983—; co-founder, co-organizer TV ministry Interfaith Community Svc. Prayer for Peace. Mem. Cabac Cable TV Producers of Lake County Ill. (pres. 1984, 88—), Order Ea. Star (Worthy Matron of Waukegan 209, 1968), Warren-Newport Woman's Afternoon Club of Gurnee (pres. 1982-84, 86-80). Home and Office: 33712 S Oplaine Rd Gurnee IL 60031-3416

PETERSON, SHIRLEY D., academic administrator; b. Holly, Colo., Sept. 3, 1941; m. Donald M. Peterson; children: Katharine Peterson Beers, Sarah Peterson Maxwell. AB cum laude, Bryn Mawr Coll., 1963; LLB cum laude, NYU, 1967. Ptnr. Steptoe & Johnson, Washington, 1969-89, 93-94; asst. atty. gen. tax divsn. U.S. Dept. Justice, 1989-92; commr. IRS, U.S. Dept. Treasury, Washington, 1992-93; pres. Hood Coll., Frederick, Md., 1995—; bd. dirs. Bethlehem Steel Corp.; ind. trustee Kemper Mut. funds; prin. Coun. on Excellence in Govt., Washington, 1993—; mem. exec. com. Fed. city Coun., Washington, 1993-94; mem. adv. coun. U.S. Ct. Fed. Claims, Washington, 1993-94, William & Mary Tax Conf., Williamsburg, Va., 1993-94. Mem. pres.'s adv. bd. St. John's Coll., Annapolis, 1994-95; trustee Bryn Mawr Coll., 1994—; bd. dirs. Nat. Legal Ctr. for Pub. Interest, Washington, 1995—. Fellow Am. Coll. Probate Counsel; mem. ABA, Internat. Fiscal Assn. Office: Hood Coll 401 Rosemont Ave Frederick MD 21701-8575

PETERSON, SOPHIA, international studies educator; b. Astoria, N.Y., Nov. 24, 1929; d. George Loizos and Caroline (Hofstetter) Yimoyines; m. Virgil Allison Peterson, Dec. 28, 1951; children: Mark Jeffrey, Lynn Marie. BA, Wellesley (Mass.) Coll., 1951; MA, UCLA, 1956, PhD, 1969. Instr. Miami U., Oxford, Ohio, 1961-63; with W.Va. U., Morgantown, 1966—, assoc. prof., 1972-79, prof., 1979—, dir., internat. studies maj., 1980-92; dir. W.Va. Consortium for Faculty & Course Devel. in Internat. Studies, Morgantown, 1980—. Author: monograph Monograph Series in World Affairs, 1979. Recipient gold medal semi-finalist CASE Prof. of Yr. award Coun. for Advancement and Support of Edn., 1987, Outstanding Tchr. award W.Va. U., W.Va. U. Coll. Arts and Scis., 1988, finalist Prof. of Yr. award W.Va. Faculty Merit Found., 1991. Mem. Internat. Studies Assn. (v.p. Mid-Atlantic chpt. 1978-86), W.Va. Polit. Sci. Assn. (pres. 1984-85), AAAUP (pres. W.Va. U. chpt. 1976-78). Democrat. Home: 849 Vandalia Dr Morgantown WV 26505-6247 Office: WVa U Dept Polit Sci Morgantown WV 26506

PETERSON, SUSAN HARNLY, artist, writer; b. McPherson, Kans., July 21, 1925; d. Paul Witmore and Iva Wilda (Curtis) Harnly; m. Jack L. Peterson, Oct. 8, 1949 (div. 1972); children: Jill Kristin, Jan Sigrid, Taäg Paul; life ptnr. Robert Schwarz Jr. AA, Monticello Coll., Alton, Ill., 1944; AB, Mills Coll., 1946; MFA, Alfred U., 1950. Cert. tchr. sec. schs. Head of ceramics Wichita Art Assn. Sch., 1947-49, Chouinard Art Inst., L.A., 1951-55; prof. of ceramics U. So. Calif., L.A., 1955-72; head of ceramics Idyllwild (Calif.) Sch. of Music and Art, 1957-1987; prof. of ceramics Hunter Coll. CUNY, 1972-1994. Author: Shoji Hamada, A Potter's Way and Work, 1974, The Living Tradition of Maria Martinez, 1978, Lucy M. Lewis, American Indian Potter, 1984, The Craft and Art of Clay, 1992, 2d edit., 1995; exhibited in nat. and internat. group shows, 1950—; 54 half-hour TV shows, Wheels, Kilns and Clay, 1969-70. Recipient Critics award Nat. Endowment for the Arts, Washington, 1985, Wrangler ward, Nat. Cowboy Hall of Fame, 1978. Fellow Am. Craft Coun.; mem. World Craft Coun., Nat. Ceramic Educators Coun. Am., Am. Ceramic Soc., PEO, Phi Beta Kappa. Home and Studio: 38800 Spanish Boot Rd Carefree AZ 85377

PETERSON, VERONICA MARIE (RONNIE PETERSON), nursing supervisor; b. Washington, Feb. 29, 1956. BA, U. Wis., Eau Claire, 1978; BSN, U. Wis., Madison, 1990, MS, 1993. Oncology staff nurse U. Wis. Hosp. and Clinics, Madison, 1990-93, nursing supr., 1993—. Author: Just the Facts: A Pocket Guide to Basic Nursing, 1994; author/dir. videos: Understanding Changes in Your Health After Cancer Treatment, 1993, Reflections on Nursing, 1994; contbr. articles to profl. jours.; compiled, dir., participant dinner theatre prodn.: Reflections on Nursing. Mem. Wis. Nurses Assn. (bd. dirs. 1993—, nurse liaison to Wis. State Med. Soc. 1994—, Image of Nursing award 1993, 95), Madison Dist. Nurses Assn. (2d v.p. 1993-94, pres. 1995-97), Oncology Nursing Soc., Pi Kappa Delta (nat. oratory champion 1978). Office: Univ of Wis Hosp & Clinics 600 Highland Ave # F6-169 Madison WI 53792-0001

PETERSON, VIRGINIA BETH, counselor; b. Oak Park, Ill., July 19, 1946; d. Edward Henry and Lorraine Minnie (Hermann) Schmidtke; m. Roger Alan Peterson, Aug. 20, 1966; children: Mark Alan, Ross Edward, Ryan David. BS, U. Wis., Stevens Point, 1972, M in Edn. Profl. Devel., 1984; cert. in Guidance and Counseling, U. Wis., Stout Menomonie, 1987, EdS in Guidance and Counseling, 1993. Cert. K-8 tchr., K-12 counselor, Wis. Tchr. elem. sch. Deerfield (Wis.) Community Schs., 1966-68; tchr. elem. sch. Nekoosa (Wis.) Pub. Schs., 1972-86, tchr. elem. sch., dir. alcohol and drug program, 1986-90, dir. dist. alcohol and drug program, elem. sch. counselor, 1990-91; dist. counselor for at risk dist. alcohol and drug dir., elem. sch. counselor Wausau (Wis.) Pub. Schs., 1991—; apptd. mem. Citizens Coun. on Alcohol and Other Drugs, Madison, Wis., 1989-94; trainer, cons The Wood Group, Port Edwards, Wis., 1990—; apptd. mem. State Coun. on Alcohol and Other Drugs Prevention Com., 1994—. Contbg. author: SOS (Study on Suicide), 1989. Chmn., vice-chmn., mem. Reaching Others on Alcohol and Drugs, Nekoosa, 1986-91; bd. dirs. Wood County Partnership, Wisconsin Rapids, Wis., 1988-91, Family Counseling Svcs., Wausau, 1992—, U. Wis. Clearinghouse, Madison, 1987—, reviser pamphlets and booklets, 1987—. Recipient Drug Buster for Wis. award USA Today, 1989, Drs. Community Leaders award FBI, 1990, Gov's. award for outstanding work in alcohol and other drug prevention, 1996, Resolution of Commendation award Wausau Sch. Dist. Bd. Edn., 1996. Mem. Wis. Sch. Counselor Assn., Wisconsin Rapids Area C. of C. (drug free task force 1989-91). Lutheran. Home: 802 E Lakeshore Dr Wausau WI 54401-6708 Office: GD Jones Elem Sch 1018 S 12th Ave Wausau WI 54401-5873

PETERSON-ARMSTRONG, SUE, social services administrator; b. Weston, W.Va., Dec. 12, 1946; d. Morgan Hepner and Edna Grace (Wimer) Peterson; m. A. James Armstrong, Dec. 10, 1988; children: Allison, Eve Marie Harper. BA, U. Cin., 1985; MDiv, Iliff Sch. Theology, 1989. Pastor Winton Pl. United Meth. Ch., Cin., 1982-85; assoc. min. Burns United Meth. Ch., Denver, 1987-89; exec. dir. Mothers Against Drunk Driving, Denver, 1989-91, Fla. Coalition Against Domestic Violence, Orlando, 1991-93, Planned Parenthood Greater Orlando, 1993—. Bd. dirs. Orange County Healthy Start Coalition, 1994—. Mem. Planned Parenthood Nat. Exec. Dirs., Women's Resource Ctr. Democrat. Home: 1166 Carmel Cir # 220 Casselberry FL 32707 Office: Planned Parenthood 1350 W Colonial Dr Orlando FL 32804

PETERSON-PRAUS, TAMARA JEAN, school counselor, beauty consultant; b. Dickinson, N.D., May 28, 1968; d. Ronald Wayne and Jean JoAnn (Johnson) Peterson; m. Galen Allen Praus, Aug. 5, 1994. BS, Dickinson State U., 1991; MS, S.D. State U., 1994. Cert. sch. counselor. Sch. counselor Taylor (N.D.)/Richardton Elem. Sch., 1993-95, New England (N.D.) Elem. Sch., 1994-95, Regent (N.D.) Elem. Sch., 1994-95; beauty cons. Mary Kay Cosmetics, Dickinson, N.D., 1995—. Mem. Am. Counselors Assn., Am. Sch. Counselors Assn., N.D. Counselors Assn. Roman Catholic. Home: Rt 4 Box 121C Dickinson ND 58601

PETITTO, BARBARA BUSCHELL, artist; b. Jersey City; d. John Edward and Anna (Barnaba) Buschell; m. Joseph Bruno Petitto, Feb. 1, 1964; children: Vincent John, Christopher Joseph. Student, Fairleigh Dickinson U., 1969-70; studio art cert., N.J. Ctr. Visual Arts, Summit, 1985; student, Art Students League, N.Y.C., 1980, 89-92, Montclair Art Mus., 1991-93. Represented by Ward-Nasse Gallery, N.Y.C.; Artist-in-resident art faculty Acad. St. Elizabeth, Convent Stations, N.J., 1989, 90, 91; art faculty Morris County Art Assn., Morristown, N.J., 1989; curator Olcott Studio Gallery Art Show, Bernardsville, N.J., 1985; curator Color/Divine Madness Ward-Nasse Gallery, N.Y.C., 1996; demonstrator Acad. St. Elizabeth Convent Station, 1989, 90, DuCret Sch. of the Arts Student Art Exhbn.; organizer for acad. students, 1989; dir. Student's Art Festival WNET/Thirteen, Acad. St. Elizabeth, 1989. One-woman shows include County Coll. Morris, 1989, Allied Corp., N.J., 1989, Ariel Gallery, N.Y.C., 1987, 88, Corner Gallery, World Trade Ctr., N.Y.C., 1989, 90, Montserrat Gallery, N.Y.C., 1992; internat. juried shows include N.J. Ctr. Visual Arts, Summit, 1985, 92, Nat. Assn. Women Artists, Meadowlands Cultural Ctr. for Arts, Rutherford, N.J., 1995; exhibited in group shows at Ward-Nasse Gallery, 1989-94, 95, 96, Artworks-Trenton, N.J., 1989, 92, N.J. Assn. Ind. Schs., Gill St. Bernard, 1989, Jain Gallery, N.Y.C., 1989, 91, Blackwell St. Gallery, Dover, N.J., 1993, Montclair Art Mus., Bloomfield Coll., 1990, Ben-Shahn Gallery, William Paterson Coll., 1992, 94, Jain-Marunouchi Gallery, N.Y.C., 1992, 93, Cmty. Arts Assn., Ridgewood, N.J., 1995, Nat. Assn. Women Artists, Inc., Soho, N.Y., 1995, 96, Nat. Soc. Painters in Casein and Acrylic, Salmagundi Gallery, 1996; represented in permanent collections Palisades Amusement Pk. Hist. Soc., Cliffside Pk. Libr., also pvt. collections; contbr. articles to profl. jours. Named Miss Livingston N.J., Livingston C. of C., 1956; recipient Rudolph A. Voelcker Meml. award Art Ctr. N.J., 1982, Excellence award Hunterdon Art Mus., 1988, award for excellence Artists League Ctrl. N.J., 1989, Cornelius Low House, Middlesex County Mus., Montclair Art Mus., 1990, award for mixed media Millburn-Short Hills Art Assn., 1989, 1st Pl. award N.E. Caldwell Arts Festival, 1989, award Nabisco Brands, Inc., East Hanover, N.J., 1990, Excellence award Ann. Tri-State Artists League Ctrl. N.J., 1991, 92, Winsor & Newton plaque, Visual Arts League, Edison, N.J., 1992, Excellence award Manhattan Arts Internat. Cover Art Competition, 1994, Hunterdon Art Ctr. award for mixed media, 1996. Mem. Nat. Soc. Painters in Casein and Acrylic, Nat. Assn. Women Artists, Inc., Artists Equity, N.J. Ctr. Visual Arts, Nat. Mus. Women in Arts, Jersey City Mus., Catherine Lorillaird Wolfe Art Club, World Wildlife Fedn. Office: PO Box 515 Whippany NJ 07981-0515

PETRE, DONNA MARIE, county judge; b. Joliet, Ill., Apr. 21, 1947; d. James Jacob and Catherine (Hedrick) P.; m. Dennis Michael Styne, Sept. 4, 1971; children: Rachel Catherine, Jonathan James, Juliana Claire, Aaron Coopersmith. BA, Clarke Coll., 1969; MA, Northwestern U., 1971; JD, U. Calif., San Francisco, 1976. Bar: Calif. 1976. Jud. clk. Calif. Ct. Appeals, San Francisco, 1976-77; instr. legal rsch. and writing Hastings Coll. Law, U. Calif., San Francisco, 1976; dep. atty. gen. criminal appeals dept. State of Calif., San Francisco, 1977-80, dep. atty. gen. consumer fraud dept., 1980-83; dep. atty. gen. med. fraud dept. State of Calif., Sacramento, 1983-86; judge Yolo County Mcpl. Ct., Woodland, Calif., 1986-89, Yolo County Superior Ct., 1990—; presiding judge Consolidated Superior/Mcpl. Ct., 1993; adj. prof. trial practice U. Calif., Davis; mem. criminal justice commn. Marin County Bd. Suprs., 1982; mem. adv. com. Jud. Coun. on Adminstrv. Justice in Rural Counties, 1988—; mem. adv. com. on ct. consolidation Judicial Coun. Mng. editor Hastings Constl. Law Quar., 1975-76. Bd. dirs. Woodland Literacy Coun., 1986. Mem. AAUW, Calif. Judges Assn. (mem. commn. on studying problems with driving under influence of alcohol and other drugs), Yolo County Bar Assn., Women Lawyers Calif., Sacramento Women Lawyers, Bus. and Profl. Women (co-chairperson legis. 1986—), Davis C. of C., Woodland C. of C. Republican. Office: Yolo County Superior Ct 725 Court St Woodland CA 95695-3436

PETRE, SUZANNE MARIE, librarian, information scientist; b. Detroit, Apr. 24, 1949; d. Edward Lawrence and Antoinette (Theisen) Ziegler; m. Marvin Arthur Petre, Nov. 28, 1975; 1 child, Marvin Arthur Jr. BA, Mercy Coll. Detroit, 1971; AMLS, U. Mich., 1975; postgrad., Walsh Coll. Bus. Asst. law libr. GM, Detroit, 1971-76, tax libr., 1976-78, libr. corp. hdqs., 1979-94, mgr. bus. rsch. libr., 1994—. Mem., bd. dirs. Friends Detroit Pub. Libr., 1990—; bd. trustees, treas. Grosse Ile (Mich.) Libr. Bd., 1996—. Mem. ALA, Am. Soc. Info. Sci., Spl. Librs. Assn. Office: GM 3044 W Grand Blvd Detroit MI 48202

PETREDEN, ANN ROSENBAUM, county treasurer; b. Bklyn., May 9, 1944; d. George and Helen (Wessel) Weinstein; m. Paul Rosenbaum, Aug. 22, 1965 (div. 1980); children: Russell, David; m. George Petredean, Oct. 2, 1987. BA, Hofstra U., 1965; MPA, Western Mich. U., 1980. Social studies tchr. Islip (N.Y.) Pub. Schs., 1964-65; survey analyst NSF, Battle Creek, Mich., 1978-79; dep. treas. Calhoun County, Marshall, Mich., 1979-80, treas., 1980—. Vol. Marshall Forward, 1991—, Homer (Mich.) Futuring Com., 1992-93; treas., pres., trustee Kellogg C.C., Battle Creek, 1979—; trustee Oaklawn Hosp. Bd., Marshall, 1995—; bd. dirs. Calhoun Area Sch. Bd. Assn., 1984—, Calhoun County Econ. Devel., 1995—. Mem. Mich. Assn. County Treasurers (past pres.), Fort Custer Tax Incremental Auth., Calhoun County Vis. & Conv. Bur., United County Officers Assn., Mich. Mcpl. Fin. Officers, Battle Creek Tax Incremental Fin. Auth. Home: 26290 M-60E Homer MI 49245 Office: Calhoun County 315 W Green St Marshall MI 49068

PETRELLA, SUSAN LOUISE, entrepreneur; b. Buffalo, Feb. 11, 1957; d. Donald Paul and Evelynn Jane Wolf Petrella. BA, Lehigh U., 1978; MBA, U. Ill., Chgo., 1988. Pres., owner Petrella Inc., Chgo., 1988-91, Susan Inc., Chgo., 1988-91, Dessert Arts, Buffalo, 1991-94, Susan L. Petrella and Assocs., Buffalo, 1994—; market and mgmt. svc. for profl. chefs and culinary bus.; guest lectr. Millard Fillmore Coll., SUNY, Buffalo, Lifelong Learning Ctr., Buffalo State Coll., 1995. Columnist: (newspaper) Women and Money, 1995. Bd. dirs. Women for Downtown, Buffalo, 1994-95. Mem. AAUW (chair Amherst br. 1995), Western N.Y. Lehigh Club (pres. 1991-95), Chgo. Lehigh Club (pres. 1985-90). Democrat. Office: 3411 Delaware Ave Buffalo NY 14217

PETRO, JANE A., plastic and reconstructive surgeon; b. Erie, Pa., Dec. 17, 1946; d. William Irwin and Virginia (Douglas) Arbuckle; m. Denis J Petro, Mar. 28, 1969 (div. 1982); 1 child, Noah Edward. BS, Eckerd Coll., St. Petersburg, Fla., 1968; MD, Pa. State U., 1972. Diplomate Am. Bd. Surgery, Am. Bd. Plastic and Reconstrv. Surgery. 0; gen. surg. resident U. Louisville, 1972-74, Harrisburg Hosp., Pa., 1974-76; plastic surgery resident Pa. State U., Hershey, 1977-79; burn/microsurg. fellow Albert Einstein Coll. Medicine, Bronx, 1979-80; asst. prof. surgery N.Y. Med. Coll., Valhalla, 1981—; assoc. prof. surgery N.Y. Med. Coll., 1981—; assoc. dir. burns Westchester County Med. Ctr., Valhalla, 1981—, chief surg. HIV svcs., 1991—; courtesy affiliate dept. surg. divsn. plastic surgery Phelps Meml. Hosp., 1989—; chief pediatric plastic surgery St. Agnes Hosp., 1992—; mem. plastic and reconstructive surgery device adv. panel FDA, 1993—. Contbr. articles to profl. jours. Recipient Physicians Recognition award AMA, 1977, 90, 92, McArthur Alumni award for disting. achievement Eckerd Coll., 1980, My Sister's Place Ann. Leadership awrad, 1991. Mem. ACS, AAAS, APHA, Am. Soc. Plastic and Reconstructive Surgeons (AIDS task force com. 1991—), Am. Assn. Physicians for Human Rights (chmn. women's issues com. 1992—), Am. Trauma Soc., Assn. Women Surgeons, Am. Burn Assn., Am. Cleft Palate Assn., Am. Med. Women's Assn. (Cmty. Svc. award 1993), Am. Soc. Law, Medicine and Ethics, N.Y. Acad. Scis., N.Y. Acad. Medicine, Acad. Compensation Medicine, Am. Fedn. Clin. Rsch., N.Y. Soc. Plastic and Reconstructive Surgery, N.Y. Regional Head and Neck Soc., Soc. Office Based Surgery, N.E. Soc. Plastic and Reconstructive Surgeons, Undersea and Hyperbaric Med. Soc., Westchester County Med. Soc. (chmn. plastic surgery sect. 1990—, com. on women 1992—), Alpha Omega Alpha. Democrat. Presbyterian. Office: Westchester County Med Ctr Burn Unit Valhalla NY 10595

PETRO, SUSAN BERNADINE, elementary education educator; b. Akron, Ohio, May 12, 1944; d. Carroll Peter and Irene Mary (Stadtmiller) Krupp; m. James Joseph Petro, Nov. 24, 1972; children: John Edward, Kristina Suzanne. BS in Edn., Ohio U., 1966. Cert. elem. educator. Elem. tchr. Wickliffe (Ohio) City Schs., 1967—, elem. math. curriculum specialist, 1990—. Sci. Materials grantee Partners in Sci. Excellence, 1992-93, 1993-94, Martha Holden Jennings Found., 1992-93. Mem. Ohio Edn. Assn. Wicklifee Tchrs. Assn. (treas. 1971-72, Nat. Coun. Tchrs. Math., N.E. Ohio Edn. Assn., Ohio Coun. Tchrs. Math., N.E. Ohio Coun. Tchrs. Math, Wickliffe Wlem. Parent Tchr. Assn. Home: 7069 Andover Dr Mentor OH 44060-4601 Office: Wickliffe Elem Sch 1821 Lincoln Rd Wickliffe OH 44092-2416

PETROSKY, REGINE, art educator; b. Ihlauschen, Germany, Oct. 28, 1937; came to U.S., 1951; d. Bruno Max and Hedwig Louise (Ambrosius) Mallwitz; m. Anthony William Petrosky, Feb. 2, 1957; children: Debora, Phylis (dec.). Grad., N.Y. Sch. Indsl. Art, 1956; postgrad., Queens (N.Y.) C.C., 1973, Columbia Greene C.C., Hudson, N.Y., 1989. Staff art and pattern making dept. Simplicity Patterns, N.Y.C., 1956-57; staff expediting Bucilla Co., L.I., N.Y., 1972-73; clk., dispatcher United Parcel Svc., Maspeth, N.Y., 1973-84; instr. art Columbia Greene C.C., Hudson, 1985—; dir. activities St. Joseph's Villa, Catskill, N.Y., 1995—; freelance designer numerous mags., 1977—. Recipient award Grumbacher/Koh-I-Noor, 1993, Winsor and Newton Co., 1989, 93. Mem. Bethlehem Art Assn. (chair prize and show 1996), Kent Art Assn., Hudson River Watercolor Soc., Hudson-Athens Lighthouse Preservation Soc. (cons. interior restoration), Greene County Photography Club (trustee, bd. dirs.), Greene County Arts and Crafts Guild, Inc. (trustee, pres., Art award 1993, 94, 95). Lutheran. Home: 356 Rte 385 Catskill NY 12414 Office: Saint Josephs Villa 38 Prospect Ave Catskill NY 12414

PETRU, SUZANNE MITTON, health care finance executive; b. Shawano, Wis., Sept. 26, 1947; d. William Wallace and Gertrude Priscilla (Humphrey) Mitton; m. W. James Petru, Jan. 2, 1987. BSBA, Northwestern U., 1970, MBA, 1971. CPA, Ill., Wis. Diplomate Am. Coll. Healthcare Execs. Sr. acct. Arthur Andersen & Co., Chgo., 1971-77; v.p. fin. Thorek Hosp. and Med. Ctr., Chgo., 1977-82; sec./treas. La Grange (Ill.) Meml. Health Sys., 1982-85; v.p. fin. La Grange Meml. Hosp., 1982-85; audit prin. Deloitte & Touche (formerly Touche Ross & Co.), Chgo., 1985-88; sr. v.p. fin., treas. SSM Health Care Sys., St. Louis, 1988-95; pres. healthcare divsn. Am. Home Assurance Co. (subs. Am. Internat. Group, Inc.), 1995—. Mem. investment com. Sisters of Charity Healthcare Sys., Cin., 1993—, mem. fin. com., 1994—; mem. assoc. bd. La Grange Meml. Hosp., 1988—; advisor Jr. Achievement, 1971-76. Fellow Healthcare Fin. Mgmt. Assn. (bd. dirs. 1989-91), principles and practices bd. 1992-95, nat. matrix 1985-86, 88-89, pres., pres.-elect, sec., bd. First Ill. chpt. 1979-86, Follmer Bronze award 1982, Reeves Silver award 1985, Muncie Gold ward 1988, Alice V. Runyan chpt. 1988); mem. Fin. Execs. Inst., Country Club at Legends (adv. bd. 1991-93), St. Louis Club (house com. 1991-95). Republican. Presbyterian. Home: 12033 Tindall Dr Saint Louis MO 63131-3135 Office: Am Home Assurance Co 70 Pine St New York NY 10270

PETRUSKA, MARTHA ANN (MARTI PETRUSKA), poet, educator; b. Louisville, Dec. 31; d. Charles Martin and Lida M. (Buck) Proffitt; m. John Andrew Petruska, Aug. 9, 1957; children: David Alexander, Mark Jonathan. BA, U. Eng.; postgrad., U. Chgo., 1953-54. mem. Ford funded jury project Harry Kalven, U. Chgo., 1956, 57; linguistics rschr. Bodleian Libr., Oxford, Eng., 1990—, Cambridge (Eng.) U. Libr., 1977—, Huntington Libr., 1977—. Author: (poetry books) Cambridge Collection I, 1991, II, 1995; contbr. poetry to anthologies, jours.; star of musical Empire Theatre, Sheffield, Eng., 1952; performer various theatre groups, 1953—; playwrite and performer various groups, 1962-69. Vol. Michael Reese Hosp., Chgo., 1953, Huntington Meml. Hosp., Pasadena, 1962-70; vol. spl. docent, spkr. Huntington Libr., Art Gallery, San Marino, Calif., 1977—; pres. Univ. Literary Soc., Eng., San Marino chpt. Am. Field Svc., 1976—, Pasaden (Blair) chpt. Am. Field Svc.; active numerous civic orgns. Recipient White Compassion and Courage award N.E. Chs. and Profls., Louisville, 1949, Recognition award Jackson Sch., Pasadena, 1972, Cert. of Appreciation Talent Bank, San Marino Schs., 1977; named Poet of Yr. Calif. Press Club, 1983. Mem. Oxford and Cambridge Univ. Club of L.A. (exec. bd. 1991—, program exec. bd. 1993—), Pasadena Poets (pres. 1970-71), Caltech Women's Club (bd. dirs. 1975—), U. Chgo. Mountain Climbing Club. Home: 2174 Melville Dr San Marino CA 91108 Office: care Huntington Library 1151 Oxford Rd San Marino CA 91108

PETRUSKI, JENNIFER ANDREA, speech and language pathologist; b. Kingston, N.Y., Jan. 28, 1968; d. Andrew Francis and Judith (Cruger) P. BS, SUNY, Buffalo, 1990; MSEd, SUNY, 1992. Cert. tchr. speech-hearing handicapped, N.Y.; cert. clin. competence; lic. speech-lang. pathology, N.Y. Speech-lang. pathologist Kingston (N.Y.) City Schs., 1992—; cooperating tchr. SUNY, New Paltz, 1995—, clinic supr., 1996—. Mem. Am. Speech and Hearing Assn., N.Y. State Speech-Lang. and Hearing Assn., Speech and Hearing Assn. Hudson Valley (corr. sec. 1995—, membership com. 1995—, editor newsletter 1995—). Home: 342 Hurley Ave # 10-64 Kingston NY 12401 Office: Kingston City Schs 61 Crown St Kingston NY 12401

PETTERCHAK, JANICE A., researcher, writer; b. Springfield, Ill., Sept. 15, 1942; d. Emil H. and Vera C. (Einhoff) Stukenberg; m. John J. Petterchak, Oct. 5, 1963; children: John A., Julie Gilmour, James. AA, Springfield Coll., 1962; BS, Sangamon State U., 1972, MA, 1982. Supr. hist. markers Ill. State Hist. Soc., Springfield, 1973-74, asst. exec. dir., 1985-87; curator photographs Ill. State Hist. Libr., Springfield, 1974-79, assoc. editor, 1979-83, rep. local history svcs., 1983-85, libr. dir., 1987-95; project dir. NEH/Ill. newspaper cataloging project. Author: Mapping a Life's Journey: The Legacy of Andrew McNally III, 1995, Jack Brickhouse: A Voice for All Seasons, 1996, (booklets) Researching and Writing Local History in Illinois: A Guide to the Sources, 1987; editor: Illinois History: An Annotated Bibliography, 1995; assoc. editor Illinois Historical Jour.; contbr. articles to profl. jours. Grantee NEH, 1987-95. Mem. Soc. Midland Authors, Ill. State History Soc., Abraham Lincoln Assn. (co-editor Papers Abraham Lincoln Assn. 1981-82), Stephen A. Douglas Assn., Sangamon County Hist. Soc. (bd. dirs. 1991-94, v.p. 1996-97, pres. 1995-96). Home: 11381 Mallard Dr Rochester IL 62563-9753

PETTEY, KATHLEEN ELEANOR, police officer, lighting consultant, investor; b. Danbury, Conn., Oct. 22, 1950; d. William John Bubenicek and Eleanor Doris (Freygang) Bubenicek; m. Bill Stevens Pettey, Apr. 17, 1971 (div. Oct. 1973); 1 child, Rachel Lyda; m. Dennis Michael Wiese, Oct. 13, 1988; children: Andrew William and Jennifer Kathleen (twins). Grad., Westchester County Police Acad., Valhalla, N.Y., 1983. Comm. officer, operator doppler radar, breathalyzer operator Kent Police Dept., Carmel, N.Y., 1983—, records officer, 1983-92, N.Y. State Police Info. Network supr., 1985—, N.Y. State Police Info. Network instr., 1988—; police rep. Putnam County Mcpl. Arrest Reporting Sys., Carmel, Assn. of Towns, N.Y.C., 1984-88. Mem. Putnam County Sexual Abuse Task Force, Carmel, 1993—. Recipient meritorious police duty award Police Fedn., 1986, meritorious duty award Town of Kent, 1986. Mem. NOW, Internat. Assn. Women Police, United Fedn. Police, Police Benevolent Assn. (bd. dirs. Carmel 1983—, sec. 1983—), Juvenile Officers Assn., Kent Hist. Soc., 9 to 5 Working Women, Patterson C. of C. Republican. Home: 35 South St Box 153 Patterson NY 12563

PETTIGREW, JOHNNIE DELONIA, educational diagnostician; b. Electra, Tex., July 2, 1948; d. John Drew and Dolly Marie (Watkins) Chester; divorced; 1 child, Jan Elise. B Elem. Edn., U. North Tex., 1970, MEd, 1982; postgrad., Tex. Woman's U., 1993—. Cert. elem., kindergarten, learning disabilities, spl. edn. early childhood, gifted edn. tchr., ednl. diagnostician, adminstr., Tex. 2d grade tchr. Azle (Tex.) Ind. Sch. Dist., 1969-70; 3d grade tchr. Decatur (Tex.) Ind. Sch. Dist., 1970-72; kindergarten, spl. edn. tchr. Boyd (Tex.) Ind. Sch. Dist., 1972-74, kindergarten, gifted edn., spl. edn. tchr., 1981-93; spl. edn. tchr. Springtown (Tex.) Ind. Sch. Dist., 1977-81; gifted edn. tchr. Denton (Tex.) Ind. Sch. Dist., 1993-94, ednl. diagnostician, 1994—; cons. in gifted edn., early childhood and drama to various sch. dists., Tex.; adj. prof. U. North Tex., Denton, 1993. Author: (play) The Monks Tale: Romeo and Juliet, 1990, also ednl. materials. Co-founder children's story hour Decatur Pub. Libr., 1970; dir. Wise County Little Theatre, Decatur; life mem. Boyd Ind. Sch. Dist. PTA, 1989, Tex. PTA. Mem. Am. Assn. for Tchg. and Curriculum, Assn. for Childhood Edn. Internat., Am. Edn. Rsch. Assn., Tex. Assn. for Gifted and Talented, Nat. Assn. for the Edn. of Young Children, So. Early Childhood Assn., Phi Delta Kappa, Phi Kappa Phi. Home: PO Box 91 Decatur TX 76234-0091 Office: Denton Ind Sch Spl Edn Svcs 1117 Riney Rd Denton TX 76208

PETTIGREW, L. EUDORA, academic administrator; b. Hopkinsville, Ky., Mar. 1, 1928; d. Warren Cicero and Corrye Lee (Newell) Williams; children: Peter W. Woodard, Jonathan R. (dec.). MusB, W.Va. State Coll., 1950; MA, So. Ill. U., 1964, PhD, 1966. Music/English instr. Swift Meml. Jr. Coll., Rogersville, Tenn., 1950-51; music instr., librarian Western Ky. Vocat. Sch., Paducah, 1951-52; music/English instr. Voorhees Coll., Denmark, S.C., 1954-55; dir. music and recreation therapy W.Ky. State Psychiatric Hosp., Hopkinsville, 1956-61; research fellow Rehab. Inst., So. Ill. U., Carbondale, 1961-63, instr., resident counselor, 1963-66, coordinator undergrad. ednl. psychology, 1963-66, acting chmn. ednl. psychology, tchr. corps instr., 1966; asst. prof. to assoc. prof. dept. psychology U. Bridgeport, Conn., 1966-70; prof., chmn. dept. urban and met. studies Coll. Urban Devel. Mich. State U., East Lansing, 1974-80; assoc. provost, prof. U. Del., Newark, 1981-86; pres. SUNY Coll. at Old Westbury, 1986—; cons. for rsch. and evaluation Hall Neighborhood House Day Care Tng. Project, Bridgeport, 1966-68, U.S. Ea. Regional Lab., Edn. Devel. Ctr., Newton, Mass., 1967-69; coordinator for edn. devel., 1968-69; cons. Bridgeport Public Schs. lang. devel. project, 1967-68, 70; Lansing Model Cities Agy., Day Care Program, 1971; U. Pitts., 1973, 74, Leadership Program, U. Mich. and Wayne State U., 1975, Wayne County Pub. Health Nurses Assn., 1976, Ill. State Bd. Edn., 1976-77; assoc. prof. U. Bridgeport, 1970, Ctr. for Urban Affairs and Coll. of Edn., Mich. State U., East Lansing, 1970-73; trustee L.I. Community Found.; program devel. specialist Lansing Public Schs. Tchr. Corps program, 1971-73; chair commn. SUNY Higher Edn. in Africa, 1994—; lectr. in field; condr. workshops in field; cons. in field. Tv/radio appearances on: Black Women in Edn, Channel 23, WKAR, East Lansing, 1973, Black Women and Equality, Channel 2, Detroit, 1974, Women and Careers, Channel 7, Detroit, 1974, Black Women and Work: Integration in Schools, WITL Radio, Lansing, 1974, others.; Contbr. articles to profl. jours. Recipient Diana award Lansing YWCA, 1977, Outstanding Profl. Achievement award, 1987, award L.I. Ctr. for Bus. and Profl. Women, 1988, Educator of Yr. 100 Black Men of L.I., 1988, Black Women's Agenda award, 1988, Woman of Yr. Nassau/Suffolk Coun. of Adminstrv. Women in Edn., 1989, Disting. Ednl. Leadership award L.I. Women's Coun. for Equal Edn. Tng. and Employment, 1989, L.I. Disting. Leadership award L.I. Bus. News, 1990, Disting. Black Women in Edn. award Nat. Coun. Negro Women, 1991; named Outstanding Black Educator, NAACP, 1968, Oustanding Woman Educator, Mich. Women's Lawyers Assn. and Mich. Trial Lawyers Assn., 1975, Disting. Alumna, Nat. Assn. for Equal Opportunity in Higher Edn., 1990, Woman of Yr., Nassau County League of Women Voters, 1991. Mem. AAAS, Nat. Assn. Acad. Affairs Adminstrs., Internat. Assn. Univ. Pres. (exec. com.), Phi Delta Kappa. Office: SUNY-Old Westbury PO Box 210 Old Westbury NY 11568-0210

PETTIGREW WELCH, DANA MARY, musician, insurance agent; b. Oklahoma City, Jan. 15, 1951; d. Richard Clester and Alice Butler (Sargent) Pettigrew; m. Douglas A. Welch, Aug. 4, 1994; children: Marilyn Yvonne Pettigrew-Davenport, Lonnie Dean Dupuis Pettigrew Jr. Student, Oklahoma City U., 1966-68. Cert. profl. ins. agt. Cert. Profl. Ins. Assn. Profl. performance musician Oklahoma City, 1965—, Seattle, 1989—; ind. agt. Pettigrew Ins. Agy., Oklahoma City, 1974-89, Protection Designs, Seattle, 1989—; owner Protection Designs Ins. Agy.; organist Rainier Beach Presbyn. Ch., Seattle, 1995—, Burien Free Meth. Ch., 1995—. Ch. organist Pa. Ave Christian Ch., 1979-89. Life Underwriter Tng. Council fellow, 1984. Mem. Am. Guild Organists, Oklahoma City Health Underwriters Assn. (bd. dirs., sec. 1986—, v.p. 1987, pres. 1989), Oklahoma City Life Underwriters Assn. (bd. dirs. 1984-85), Seattle Musicians Assn. (exec. bd. dirs. 1996—), Renton-Auburn Musicians Assn., Okla. Country Music Assn., Ind. Ins. Agts. Assn., Profl. Ins. Agts. Assn., Cascade Assn. Life Underwriters (sec. 1995-96, treas. 1996—), Renton C. of C., Kiwanis (sec. Renton chpt. 1988, 89, pianist 1987—). Republican. Mem. Christian Ch. Home and Office: 3511 NE 11th Pl Renton WA 98056-3442

PETTINE, LINDA FAYE, physical therapist; b. New London, Conn., Nov. 11, 1958; d. Robert Anderson and Pauline Priscilla (Johnson) Erwin; m. H. Louis Pettine Jr., Mar. 6, 1982. BS, U. Conn., 1980; student, Quinnipiac Coll., Hamden, Conn., 1989-91. Registered phys. therapist, Conn. Staff phys. therapist Worcester (Mass.) Hahneman Hosp., 1980, Newport (R.I.) Hosp., 1980-82, Middlebury Orthopaedic Group, Waterbury, Conn., 1982; staff phys. therapist Easter Seal Rehab. Ctr. of Cen. Conn., Meriden, 1982-84, hosp. and rehab. ctr. coord., 1984-86; co-founder Pettine & McDiarmid Phys. Therapy, Cheshire and Wallingford, Conn., 1986-88; pres. Keystone Phys. Therapy & Sports Medicine P.C., Cheshire and Wallingford, Conn., 1988—; lectr. Diabetes Edn. Program, Meriden, 1985; cons. Waterbury (Conn.) Nursing Ctr., 1986-87. Mem. adv. bd. Waterbury Continuing Edn. program, 1985; guest speaker Conn. chpt. Am. Diabetes Assn., Meriden, 1986, Arthritis Support Group, Meriden, 1986, Meriden Indsl. Mgr. Assn., 1986. Katherine Wyckoff and Margaret Wyckoff Moore Endowed scholar, 1991. Mem. Am. Phys. Therapy Assn. (pvt. practice sect.), Conn. Phys. Therapy Assn. (program com. chair 1991-92, qualified peer reviewer 1995—). Office: Keystone Phys Therapy & Sports Medicine PC 675 S Main St Cheshire CT 06410-3153 also: 850 N Main Street Ext Wallingford CT 06492-2400

PETTITT, BARBARA JEAN, pediatric surgeon; b. Niagara Falls, N.Y., Feb. 2, 1952; d. Robert Andrew and Joan Marilyn (Boore) P.; m. Richard Allen Schieber, May 24, 1981; children: Christine Pettitt Schieber, Lucy Pettitt Schieber, Brian Pettitt Schieber. BA in Chemistry magna cum laude, Cen. Coll., Pella, Iowa, 1972; D of Medicine, Northwestern U., Chgo., 1976. Diplomate Am. Bd. Surgery with certificates of spl. competence in pediatric surgery and surg. critical care; lic. pediatric surgeon, Calif., Pa., Ga. Student fellow in rehab. medicine Rehab. Inst. Chgo., spring 1974; intern in straight surgery Los Angeles County-U. So. Calif. Med. Ctr., 1976-77, resident in gen. surgery, 1977-81; resident in pediatric surgery Childrens' Hosp. Pitts., 1982-84; asst. prof. surgery and pediatrics dept. Sch. Medicine Emory U., Atlanta, 1985—; mem. staff Henrietta Egleston Hosp. for Children, Atlanta, 1985-86; mem. staff Grady Meml. Hosp., Atlanta, 1985—, chief pediatric surg. svc., 1990—; chief of surgery Hughes Spalding Children's Hosp., 1993—; instr. ATLS, PALS; active various coms. Henrietta Egleston Hosp. for Children, 1985-86, Grady Meml. Hosp., 1986—, Hughes Spalding Children's Hosp., 1992—; lectr., presenter many profl. and ednl. orgns., 1983—. Contbg. author: (with M. Rowe) Pediatric Surgery, 4th edit., 1986; contbr. articles to profl. publs. Bd. dirs., trustees DeKalb Choral Guild, Atlanta, 1988—; pres. Summit Cmty. Assn., 1992—; chairperson health and safety com. Arbor Montessori Sch. Rsch. grantee Rsch. Corp., summer 1971, NIH, 1983-84; Rollscreen full-tuition scholar, 1969-72, Ruth G. White scholar Calif. State P.E.O., 1974-75; recipient 1st prize Bernard Baruch Essay Contest, Am. Congress Rehab. Medicine, 1975; named Outstanding Young Woman of Yr., State pf Pa., 1984, State of Ga., 1986, Disting. Alumna Ctrl. Coll., 1990. Fellow ACS, Am. Acad. Pediatrics (surg. sect., critical care sect.); mem. AMA, Am. Med. Womens' Assn., Southeastern Surg. Congress, Am. Pediatric Surg. Assn., Assn. Women Surgeons, Am. Soc. Parental and Enteral Nutrition, La.A. County-U. So. Calif. Med. Ctr. Soc. Grad. Surgeons, Phi Delta Epsilon (pres. med. sch. chpt. 1974-75, undergrad. midwest regional coord. 1974-75, nat. exec. com. 1976-80, nat. intern-resident liaison com. 1980-85, nat. constn. and bylaws com. 1986—, Isadore Pilot award Chgo. chpt. 1975, nat. svc. award 1976), Soc. Critical Care Medicine, Ga. Surg. Soc., Assn. Surg. Edn. Democrat. Episcopalian. Office: Emory Univ Sch Medicine Dept of Surgery 69 Butler St SE Atlanta GA 30303-3033

PETTUS, SALLY LOCKHART, psychologist; b. N.Y.C., Aug. 17, 1937; d. Alfred Sherman and Jane Clay (Zevely) Foote; m. Charlton Messick Pettus, June 21, 1958 (div. 1974); children: Charlton, Cybele; m. William Frank Wyatt Jr., Sept. 10, 1989. Student, Vassar Coll., 1955-58; AB, Roger Williams Coll., 1972; EdD, Boston U., 1977. Lic. Psychologist. Psychol. cons. Ipswich (Mass.) Sch. System, 1975-77, Human Resource Inst., Brookline, Mass., 1975-77, New England Meml. Hosp., Stoneham, Mass., 1977-78; sr. psychologist Newton (Mass.) Guidance Clinic, 1978-82; clin. assoc. East Side Ctr., Providence, 1987-89; sr. psychologist Netrowest Youth Guidance, Framingham, Mass., 1982-91; clin. psychologist Providence, 1989—; clin. supr. Women's Protective Svcs., Framingham, 1987-90; reviewer in field. Mem. APA, Nat. Register Health Svc. Providers in Psychology, Mass. Psychol. Assn., R.I. Psychol. Assn., Am. Soc. Clin. Hypnosis.

PETTY, LORI, actress. Appeared in films including Cadillac Man, 1990, Point Break, 1991, A League of Their Own, 1992; TV appearances include Bates Motel, 1987, Perry Mason: The Case of the Musical Murder, 1989, San Berdoo, 1989, The Line, 1987, Monster Manor, 1988, The Thorns, 1988, Booker, 1989. Office: care Creative Artists Agency 9830 Wilshire Blvd Beverly Hills CA 90212-1804*

PETTY, SHARON MARIE, secondary education educator; b. Highland, Ill., Jan. 15, 1947; d. Theodore G. and Helen M. (Kapp) Mersinger. BS, So. Ill. U., 1969. Tchr., dept. chair Edwardsville (Ill.) Sch. Dist., 1969—, varsity field hockey coach, 1973—; mem. Health and Phys. Devel. Com., 1994—. Bd. mem. Maryville Zoning Com., 1989—. Mem. AAHPERD, Ill. Health Phys. Edn. Recreation and Dance. Office: Edwardsville High Sch 145 West Edwardsville IL 62025

PETTYJOHN, SHIRLEY ELLIS, lawyer, real estate executive; b. Liberty, Ky., Aug. 16, 1935; d. Wesley Barker and Ada Lou (Bryant) Ellis; m. Flem D. Pettyjohn, Sept. 24, 1955; children: Deena Renee, Ellisa Denise. BS in Commerce, U. Louisville, 1974, JD, 1977. Bar: Ky. 1978, Ind. 1988; lic. real estate broker, Ky., Ind.; cert. mediator. Pres. Universal Devel. Corp., Ky. and Fla., 1984—, Pettyjohn Inc., Ky. and Ind., 1967—, Ind. Mediation Svcs., Inc., 1990—, Ky. Mediation Svcs., Inc., 1991—; v.p. Continental Investments Corp., 1986—; sr. ptnr. Pettyjohn & Assocs., Attys., 1987—. Editor Law-Hers Jour. Vice chmn. Louisville and Jefferson County Planning Commn., 1971-75; mem. Gov.'s Conf. on Edn., 1977, jud. nominee, 1981, Met. Louisville Women's Polit. Caucus, Bluegrass State Skills Corp., 1992—, Ky. Opera Assn. Guild; elected mem. Ky. State Dem. Exec. Com., 1988-92; del. Nat. Dem. Conv. and Dem. Nat. Platform Com., 1988; bd. dirs. Ky. Dem. Hdqs., Inc., 1988-92, Pegasus Rising, Inc.; chmn. Okolona Libr. Task Force; mem. Clinton-Gore Nat. Steering Com., 1995. Recipient Mayor's Cert. Recognition, 1974, Mayor's Fleur de lis award, 1969-73, Excellence in Writing award Arts Club Louisville, 1986, 87, 93. Mem. ABA, NAFE, Nat. Assn. Adminstrv. Law Judges, Ky. Bar Assn., Louisville Bar Assn., Women Lawyers Assn. of Jefferson County, Am. Judicature Soc., Clark County Bar Assn., Ind. Bar Assn., Ind. Assn. Mediators, Am. Inst. Planners, Women's C. of C. of Ky. (past bd. dirs., chmn. legis. com.), Am. Legion (aux.), Fraternal Order Police Assn. (award 1982), Louisville Legal Secs. (past pres., editor Law-Hers Jour.), Coun. of Women Pres. (past pres., Woman of Achievement award 1974), Louisville Visual Arts Assn. (former bd. dirs.), Louisville Ballet Guild (chair audience devel. 1989-91), Dem. Leadership Coun., Jefferson County Dem. Women's Club (past v.p.), Nat. Fedn. Dem. Women's Clubs, Spirit of 46th Club, Mose Green Club, North End Club, 12th Ward Club, S. End Club, 3rd Ward Club, Highland Pk. Club, Grass Roots Club, Harry S. Truman Club, Beargrass Club, Arts Club of Louisville (past pres.), Sigma Delta Kappa, Chi Thi Theta, Century 2000 Democrat Club. Home: 6924 Norlynn Dr Louisville KY 40228-1471 Office: PO Box 787 600 E Court Ave Ste 102 Jeffersonville IN 47131-0787

PETYKIEWICZ, SANDRA DICKEY, editor; b. Detroit, Sept. 23, 1953; d. James Fulton and Alice Diane (Nowak) Dickey; m. Edward W. Petykiewicz, Oct. 17, 1981; 1 child, Kendall Lee. BA, Cen. Mich. U., Mt. Pleasant, 1975. Reporter Big Rapids (Mich.) Pioneer, 1975, Midland (Mich.) Daily News, 1975-77; reporter Saginaw (Mich.) News, 1977-79, feature editor, 1979-80, asst. metro editor, 1980-81; copy editor Washington Post, 1981-82; asst. city editor Balt. News Am., 1982-83; metro editor Jackson (Mich.) Citizen Patriot, 1983-87, editor, 1987—; bd. dirs. Mich. AP, 1987-93, pres., 1990, 1991-92; bd. dirs. Mid Am. Press Inst., 1992—; mem. alumni bd. Ctrl. Mich. U., 1992-96, mem. journalism adv. bd., 1992—. Pulitzer Prize juror, 1990-92. Mem. Jackson Area Quality Initiative, 1990—. Mem. Am. Soc. Newspaper Editors, Soc. Profl. Journalists, Bus. and Profl. Women's Club (editor newsletter 1985-86, Young Career Woman of Yr. award 1984), Rotary Club, Jackson Eocn. Club (chairwoman 1992), Sigma Delta Chi.

PETZEL, FLORENCE ELOISE, textiles educator; b. Crosbyton, Tex., Apr. 1, 1911; d. William D. and A. Eloise (Punchard) P. PhB, U. Chgo., 1931, AM, 1934; PhD, U. Minn., 1954. Instr., Judson Coll., 1936-38; asst. prof. textiles Ohio State U., 1938-48; assoc. prof. U. Ala., 1950-54; prof. Oreg. State U., 1954-61, 67-75, 77, prof. emeritus, 1975—, dept. head, 1954-61, 67-75; prof., div. head U. Tex., 1961-63; prof. Tex. Tech U., 1963-67; vis. instr. Tex. State Coll. for Women, 1937; vis. prof. Wash. State U., 1967. Effie I. Raitt fellow, 1949-50. Mem. Met. Opera Guild, High Mus. Art, Sigma Xi, Phi Kappa Phi, Omicron Nu, Iota Sigma Pi, Sigma Delta Epsilon. Author Textiles of Ancient Mesopotamia, Persia and Egypt, 1987; contbr. articles to profl. jours. Home: 150 Downs Blvd Apt D205 Clemson SC 29631-2049

PETZOLD, CAROL STOKER, state legislator; b. St. Louis, July 28; d. Harold William and Mabel Lucille (Wilson) Stoker; m. Walter John Petzold, June 27, 1959; children: Ann, Ruth, David. BS, Valparaiso U., 1959. Tchr. John Muir Elem. Sch., Alameda, Calif., 1959-60, Parkwood Elem. Sch., Kensington, Md., 1960-62; legis. aide Md. Gen. Assembly, Annapolis, 1975-79; legis. asst. Montgomery County Bd. Edn., Rockville, Md., 1980; cmty. sch. coord. Parkland Jr. H.S., Rockville, 1981-87; mem. Md. Ho. of Dels., Annapolis, 1987—, mem. consl. and adminstrv. law com., 1987-93, mem. judiciary com., 1994—, vice chair Montgomery County del., 1995—; mem. transp. planning bd. Nat. Capitol Region, 1989—; vice chair energy and transp. com. Nat. Conf. State Legislatures; exec. com. Montgomery United Way Coun., 1981—. Editor Child Care Sampler, 1974, Stoker Family Cookbook, 1976. Pres. Montgomery Child Care Assn., 1976-78; mem. Md. State Scholarship Bd., 1978-87, chmn. 1985-87; chmn. Legis. Com. Montgomery County Commn. for Children and Youth, 1979-84; mem., v.p. Luth. Social Services Nat. Capitol Area, Washington, 1980-86. Recipient Statewide award Gov.'s Adv. Bd. on Homelessness, 1994; recognized for outstanding commitment to children U.S. Dept. HEW, 1980. Mem. AAUW (honoree Kensington br. 1971, honoree Md. div. 1981), Women's Polit. Caucus (chmn. Montgomery County 1981-83), Md. Women Legislators Caucus. Democrat. Lutheran. Home: 14113 Chadwick Ln Rockville MD 20853-2103

PEYSER, ROXANE D., lawyer; b. Queens, N.Y., June 17, 1959; m. Ted Ross Peyser; children: Rachel Renee, Natasha Tovah, Samuel Aaron. BA in Middle Eastern Studies, George Washington U., 1981; JD, U. Houston, 1987. Bar: Tex., Ala., U.S. Dist. Ct. (so., no. dists.) Tex., U.S. Ct. Appeals (5th cir.). Intern Harris County Dist. Atty's. Office, Houston, 1987; atty. Saccomanno & Clegg, Houston, 1988-90, Graham, Bright & Smith, Dallas, 1990-92; sr. legal counsel Compass Bancshares, Inc., Birmingham, 1992-94; atty. Sirote & Permutt, P.C., Birmingham, Ala., 1994—; participant grad. Project Corp. Leadership, Birmingham, 1993-94. Contbr. numerous articles to profl. jours. Mem. bd. dirs. Am. Jewish Congress, Dallas, 1990-91; tchr. Temple Emanu El, Birmingham, 1993—; mem., contbr. Israel Bonds Bd., 1994—, Nat. Coun. Jewish Women, 1993—; mem. steering com. bus. & profl. women section Jewish Fedn., 1994—. Mem. ABA, Am. Corp. Counsel Assn., Tex. Bar Assn., Ala. Bar Assn., Tex. Assn. Bank Counsel, Internat. Platform Assn. Office: Sirote & Permutt PC 2222 Arlington Ave S Birmingham AL 35205-4004

PFAELZER, MARIANA R., federal judge; b. L.A., Feb. 4, 1926. AB, U. Calif., 1947; LLB, UCLA, 1957. Bar: Calif. 1958. Assoc. Wyman, Bautzer, Rothman & Kuchel, 1957-69, ptnr., 1969-78; judge U.S. Dist. Ct. (ctrl. dist.) Calif., 1978—; mem. Jud. Conf. Adv. Com. on Fed. Rules of Civil Procedure. pres., v.p., dir. Bd. Police Commrs. City of L.A., 1974-78; bd. vis. Loyola Law Sch. UCLA Alumnus award for Profl. Achievement, 1979, named Alumna of Yr., UCLA Law Sch., 1980, U. Calif. Santa Barbara Disting. Alumnus award, 1983. Mem. ABA, Calif. Bar Assn. (local adminstrv. com., spl. com. study rules procedure 1972, joint subcom. profl. ethics and computers and the law coms. 1972, profl. ethics com. 1972-74, spl. com. juvenile justice, women's rights subcom. human rights sect.), L.A. County Bar Assn. (spl. com. study rules procedure state bar 1974), mem. Judicial Conf. Advisory Comm. on Federal Rules of Civil Procedure. Office: US Dist Ct 312 N Spring St Los Angeles CA 90012-4701

PFAFFLIN, SHEILA MURPHY, psychologist; b. Pasadena, Calif., July 31, 1934; d. Leonard Anthony and Honora (Shields) Murphy; m. James Reid Pfafflin, Sept. 7, 1957. BA, Pomona Coll., 1956; MA, Johns Hopkins U., 1958, PhD, 1959. Mem. tech. staff AT&T Bell Labs., Murray Hill, N.J., 1959-75; dist. mgr. AT&T, Morristown, N.J., 1975—; Chair sub com. on Women-Com. on Equal Opportunities in Sci. and Tech., NSF, Washington, 1981-85; mem. adv. coun. Math/Sci. Tchr. Supply and Demand, N.J. Dept. Higher Edn., 1982-83; mem. adv. bd. for Maths., Sci. and Computer Sci. Teaching Improvement Grants, N.J. Dept. Higher Edn., 1984-89. Co-editor: Expanding the Role of Women in the Sciences, 1978, Scientific-Technological Change & the Role of Women in Development, 1981, Psychology & Educational Policy, 1987; contbr. articles to profl. jours. Trustee Ramapo Coll. of N.J., Mahwah, N.J., 1984—; adv. bd. Project "SMART", Girls Clubs of Am., N.Y.C., 1984—, Consortium for Ednl. Equity, Rutgers U., New Brunswick, N.Y., 1983—; pres. Assn. for Women in Sci. Ednl. Found., Washington, 1982—. Fellow AAAS, N.Y. Acad. Scis., Am. Psychol. Assn.; mem. Assn. for Women in Sci. (pres. 1980-81, Women Scientist award, Met. Chpt., 1987), Phi Beta Kappa, Sigma Xi. Home: 173 Gates Ave Gillette NJ 07933-1719 Office: AT&T 100 Southgate Pkwy Rm 3F07 Morristown NJ 07960-6441

PFEFFERKORN, SANDRA J., secondary school educator; b. St. Louis, Jan. 14, 1940; d. Albert A. and Alice C. (Lowell) Carter; m. Michael G. Pfefferkorn, June 15, 1963; children: Michael G. Jr., Patricia A. BS in Secondary Edn., SE Mo. State Coll., 1961; MEd, U. Mo., 1966. Cert. life English, Spanish, French, and reading tchr., Mo. Tchr. English, head English and fgn. lang. dept. St. Louis Bd. Edn.; English tchr. Cleveland Naval Jr. Res. Officer Tng. Corps High Sch., St. Louis. Asst. editor Mo. Jour. Numismatics. Regents scholar, 1957; fellow Mo. Writing Project, 1981. Mem. AAUW, Assn. Tchrs. Spanish and Portuguese, Nat. Coun. Tchrs. English, Internat. Reading Assn., Mo. Assn. Tchrs. English, Delta Kappa Gamma. Roman Catholic. Home: 6803 Leona St Saint Louis MO 63116-2833 Office: Cleve Naval Jr ROTC 4352 Louisiana Ave Saint Louis MO 63111-1046

PFEIFFER, CHERYL LYNN, horticulturist; b. Harbor City, Calif., June 10, 1959; d. Peter Washington and Mavis Jayne (Guttu) Pfeiffer. BA in Environ. Studies, U. Calif., Santa Cruz, 1981; BFA in Painting, U. Washington, 1991; MFA in Painting, Parsons/The New Sch., N.Y.C., 1995. Primary sch. tchr. Dept. Interior, Navajo Reservation, Ariz., 1981-82; naturalist tour guide Denali Nat. Pk., Alaska, 1982-87; elderhostel guide Denari Nat. Pk., 1986-87; tchg. asst. Parsons Sch. Design, N.Y.C., 1994-95; horticulturist Zimora Designs, N.Y.C., 1995—; vis. asst. prof. Sewanee U. of the South, Tenn., 1996. Illustrator: (book) One Long Summer Day, 1981. Mem. Gay Men's Health Crisis, N.Y.C., 1996. Recipient rsch. grant Colgate-Palmolive Alaska, 1980. Mem. Coll. Arts Assn., Nat. Mus. of Women (Washington). Democrat. Bhuddist. Home: 21 Lincoln Pl Apt 2 Brooklyn NY 11217-3514

PFEIFFER, JANE CAHILL, former broadcasting company executive, consultant; b. Washington, Sept. 29, 1932; d. John Joseph and Helen (Reilly) Cahill; B.A., U. Md., 1954; postgrad., Cath. U. Am., 1956-57; LHD (hon.), Pace Coll., 1978, U. Md., 1979, Manhattanville Coll., 1979, Amherst U., 1980, Babson Coll., 1981, U. Notre Dame, 1991; m. Ralph A. Pfeiffer, Jr., June 3, 1975. With IBM Corp., Armonk, N.Y., 1955-76, sec. mgmt. rev. com., 1970, dir. communications, 1971, v.p. communications and govt. relations, 1972-76, bus. cons., 1976-78; chmn. NBC, Inc., N.Y.C., 1978-80; bus. cons., 1980—; dir. Ashland Oil Co., Mony Fin. Svcs., Internat. Paper Co., J.C. Penney Co.; trustee The Conf. Bd., 1991. Mem. pres.'s adv. com. White House Fellows, 1966, Pres.'s Gen. Adv. Commn. on Arms Control and Disarmament, 1977-80, Pres.'s Commn. Mil. Compensation, trustee Rockefeller Found., U. Md., Carnegie Hall, U. Notre Dame. White House fellow, Washington, 1966; recipient Achievement award Kapppa Kappa Gamma, 1974-80, Eleanor Roosevelt Humanitarian award N.Y. League for Hard of Hearing, 1980. Disting. Alumna award U. Md., 1975, Humanitarian award NOW, 1980, Centennial Alumna Medallion U. Md., 1988. Mem. Council on Fgn. Relations, Overseas Devel. Council. Club: Econ. of N.Y. Office: 90 Field Point Cir Greenwich CT 06830-7011

PFEIFFER, SOPHIA DOUGLASS, state legislator, lawyer; b. N.Y.C., Aug. 10, 1918; d. Franklin Chamberlin and Sophie Douglass (White) Wells; m. Timothy Adams Pfeiffer, June 7, 1941; children: Timothy Franklin, Penelope Mersereau Keenan, Sophie Douglass. AB, Vassar Coll., 1939; JD, Northeastern U., 1975. Bar: R.I. 1975, U.S. Ct. Apls. (1st cir.) 1980, U.S. Supreme Ct. 1979. Editl. rschr. Time, Inc., N.Y.C., 1940-41; writer Office War Info., Washington, 1941-43, N.Y.C., 1943-45; editl. staff Nat. Geog. Mag., Washington, 1958-59, 68-70; editor Turkish Jour. Pediatrics, Ankara, 1961-63; staff atty. R.I. Supreme Ct., Providence, 1975-76, chief staff atty., 1977-86; mem. Maine Ho. Reps., 1990-94; lectr. U. So. Maine, 1995; bd. dirs. Death and Dying project. Chair bioethics study League Women Voters. Contbr. in field. Pres., Karachi Am. Sch. (Pakistan), 1955-56; chair, Brunswick Village Review Bd., 1986-89. Home: 15 Franklin St Brunswick ME 04011-2101

PFITZER, LINDA PHILLIPS, elementary education educator; b. Old Hickory, Tenn., Nov. 22, 1943; d. Wesley Thomas and Lillian Pauline (Layhew) Phillips; m. Kenneth Carl Pfitzer, Aug. 24, 1963 (div. Apr. 1988);

children: Jeffrey Carl, Frieda Lynn, James Michael, Rebecca Marie. AA, Martin Jr. Coll., Pulaski, Tenn., 1963; student, Tenn. Tech. U., Cookeville, 1963-64; BS, U. Tenn., Chattanooga, 1981, MEd, 1988. Cert. tchr., Tenn. Elem. tchr. Our Lady of Perpetual Help Cath. Sch., Chattanooga, 1981-85; reading specialist Chpt. I Reading program Hamilton County Schs., Chattanooga, 1985-91, elem. tchr., 1991—; chmn. McBrien Sch. Improvement Coun., Chattanooga, 1995-96. Author: Poetry Anthology, 1995. Pres. Self Help for Hard of Hearing People, Chattanooga, 1995—. Recipient award Dept. Edn., 1987-88, State Dept. Edn., 1994. Mem. Phi Delta Kappa. Baptist. Home: 712 Shady Dr Chattanooga TN 37412 Office: McBrien Elem Sch 1501 Tombras Ave Chattanooga TN 37412

PFLOMM, KIRSTEN NELSON, grant writer; b. Norwich, Conn., Sept. 26, 1970; d. Robert Eiriksson and Ruth Matilda (Nelson) P. Student, Three Rivers Coll., Norwich, Conn., 1991-95, Conn. Coll., New London, Conn., 1995—. Grantwriter Eastern Pequot Tribe, Stonington, Conn., 1994—; adminstr. Hubbel Engring., Stonington, Conn., 1995—; cons. Eastern Pequot Tribe, Stonington, 1994—. Mem. ACLU, Amnesty Internat.; activities coord. Winthrop Highrise Family Support Ctr., New London, 1995. Mem. NOW, AAUW, Libr. of Congress, Phi Theta Kappa. Democrat. Home and Office: Eastern Pequot Tribe 292 Pequot Ave Apt 2N New London CT 06320

PFLUEGER, M(ELBA) LEE COUNTS, academic administrator; b. St. Louis, Sept. 2, 1942; d. Pless and Edna Mae (Russell) Counts; m. Raymond Allen Pflueger, Sept. 14, 1963 (div. June 1972); children: Salem Allen, Russell Counts. BS in Home Econs., Univ. Mo., 1969; MEd in Guidance and Counseling, Washington Univ., St. Louis, 1973. Ednl. psychologist Ozark Regional Mental Health Ctr., Harrison, Ark., 1974-75; from account mgr. to mgr. pers. Enterprise Leasing Co., St. Louis, 1977-79; mgr. employee rels. Eaton Corp., Houston, 1979-80; owner Nature's Nuggets Fresh Granola, St. Louis, 1980-83; dir. corp. ednl. svcs. Maryville Coll., St. Louis, 1983-84; adminstr. mgmt. skills devel. McDonnell Douglas, St. Louis, 1984-85, mgr. employee involvement, 1985-86, prin. specialist human resources mgmt., 1988-89; mgr. human resources McDonnell Douglas, Houston, 1986-88; dir. devel. sch. engring. U. Mo., Rolla, 1989-93, dir. devel., corp. and found. rels., 1992-93; regional dir. devel., assoc. dir. maj. gifts and capital projects Washington U., St. Louis, 1994—; part-time leader trainer Maritz Motivation, St. Louis, 1984-89. Chair United Fund Campaign for U. Mo., Rolla, 1991. Mem. PEO. Office: Washington U Office Maj Gifts and Capital Projects Campus Box 1228 One Brookings Dr Saint Louis MO 63130-4899

PFLUM, BARBARA ANN, pediatric allergist; b. Cin., Jan. 10, 1943; d. James Frederick and Betty Mae (Doherty) P.; m. Makram I. Gobrail, Oct. 20, 1973; children: Christina, James. BS, Coll. Mt. St. Vincent, 1967; MD, Georgetown U., 1971; MS, Coll. Mt. St. Joseph, 1993. Cons. Children's Med. Ctr., Dayton, Ohio, 1975—, dir. allergy clinic, 1983-89. Fellow Am. Acad. Pediatrics, Am. Acad. Allergy and Immunology, Am. Coll. Allergy and Immunology; mem. Ohio Soc. Allergy and Immunology, Western Ohio Pediatric Soc. (pres. 1985-86). Roman Catholic. Home: 4502 Lytle Rd Waynesville OH 45068-9483 Office: 201 E Stroop Rd Dayton OH 45429-2825

PHAIR, LIZ, recording artist, pop vocalist; b. Cin., Apr. 17, 1967; d. John and Nancy Phair. Diploma, Oberlin Coll., 1990. Freelance artist, 1990, singer, songwriter, 1992—. Albums include: Exile in Guyville (name Album of Yr. Village Voice), 1993, Whip-Smart, 1994. Named Best New Female Vocalist Rolling Stone Critic's Poll. Office: Matador Records 676 Broadway 4th Fl New York NY 10012*

PHARES, LYNN LEVISAY, public relations communications executive; b. Brownwood, Tex., Aug. 6, 1947; m. C. Kirk Phares, Aug. 22, 1971; children: Laura, Margaret, Adele, Jessica. BA, La. State U., 1970; MA, U. Nebr., 1987. Asst. to advt. mgr. La. Nat. Bank, 1970-71; writer, producer, asst. v.p., account exec. Smith, Kaplan, Allen & Reynolds, Inc., Omaha, 1971-80; assoc. dir. pub. affairs U. Nebr. Med. Ctr., 1980-83; dir. pub. rels. ConAgra, Inc., Omaha, 1985-87, 1985-87, v.p. pub. rels., 1987-90, v.p. pub. rels. and cmty. affairs, 1990-96; v.p., corp. relatives ConAgra, Inc., 1996—; pres. ConAgra Found. Office: ConAgra Inc 1 Conagra Dr Omaha NE 68102-5094

PHEIFER, DENISE ANN, educational consultant; b. Milw., Jan. 23, 1952; d. Ervin F. and Louise B. (Majcher) Bartczak; m. Lawrence F. Pheifer, Dec. 27, 1974; children: Joanna, Monica. Student, U. Grenoble, France, 1973; BA, St. Norbert Coll., 1974; MA, Cardinal Stritch Coll., 1980. Cert. English tchr., reading tchr., reading specialist, French tchr., Wis. Lang. arts tchr. grades 6-8 St. Mary Grade Sch., 1974-79; reading specialist, English tchr. Cedarburg (Wis.) H.S., 1979-87; cons. Archdiocese of Milw., 1988—; ednl. cons. Chase/Pheifer and Assocs., Mequon, Wis., 1992—; assoc. prof. Cardinal Stritch Coll., Milw.; prin.'s adv. com. mem. Steffan Middle Sch., Mequon, 1994; parents adv. group mem. Wilson Sch., Mequon, 1995. Editor: Living the Spirit: A Parish Council Manual, 1991, Called to Serve Parish Leadership Development, 1992; mem. editl. bd. Wis. State Reading Assn., 1995—. Mem. ASCD, Internat. Reading Assn., Nat. Coun. Tchrs. English, Wis. Assn. Supervision and Curriculum Devel. Roman Catholic. Home: 10612 W Sunset Woods Ln Mequon WI 53097

PHEIL, ROBIN LYNN, obstetrics nurse; b. Hagerstown, Md., Oct. 6, 1957; d. Elmer Granville Ryan and Rosalie Ann (Rooney) Putman; m. David Charles Pheil, May 3, 1980; 1 child, Lindsay Allison. Associate degree, Hagerstown Jr. Coll., 1988. LPN, Washington County Career Studies Ctr.; RNC.; cert. in-patient obstetric nurse. Nursing asst. Avalon Manor Nursing Home, Hagerstown, Md., 1973-75, LPN, 1975-77; LPN Washington County Hosp., Hagerstown, 1977-88, RN, 1988—; instr. advanced fetal monitoring Washington County Hosp., Hagerstown, 1994—; cert. Inpatient Obstetries. Active campaign activities NOW, Hagerstown, 1992. Democrat. Methodist. Home: 1377 Outer Dr Hagerstown MD 21742-3039

PHELAN, ELLEN, artist; b. Detroit, Nov. 3, 1943; d. Thomas Edward and Katherine Louise (Gojlewicz) P; m. Joel Elias Shapiro, Nov. 22, 1978. BFA, Wayne State U., 1969, MFA, 1971. Instr. Wayne State U., Detroit, 1969-72, Fairleigh Dickinson U., 1974, Mich. State U., East Lansing, 1974-75, Calif. Inst. Arts, 1978-79, Bard Coll., 1980, NYU, 1981, Sch. of Visual Arts, 1981-83, Calif. Inst. Arts, 1983; prof. of practice of studio art Harvard U., Cambridge, Mass., 1995—; Milton Avery vis. lectr. Bard Coll., 1994. One-woman exhbns. include Willis Gallery, Detroit, 1972, 74, Artist's Space, N.Y.C., 1975, Susanne Hilberry Gallery, Birmingham, Mich., 1977, 79, 81, 82, 84, 86, 88, 90, 92, 94, Wadsworth Athenaeum, Hartford, Conn., 1979, Ruth Schaffner Gallery, L.A., 1979, The Clocktower, N.Y.C., 1980, Hansen-Fuller-Goldeen Gallery, San Francisco, 1980, 82, Dart Gallery, Chgo., 1981, Barbara Toll Fine Arts, N.Y.C., 1982, 85, 86, 87-88, 89, 90, 92, 93, Asher/Faure, L.A., 1989, 92, 94, Balt. Mus. Art, 1989, Albright-Knox Art Gallery, Buffalo, 1991, U. Mass. Amherst Fine Arts Ctr., 1992, Saidye Bronfman Ctr., Montreal, Que., 1993, Contemporary Mus., Honolulu, 1993, John Stoller, Inc., Mpls., 1993, Cin. Art Mus., 1994; exhibited in group shows at Detroit Inst. Arts, 1970, 80, Willis Gallery, Detroit, 1971, 79, J.L. Hudson Gallery, Detroit, 1972, Cranbrook Acad. Art, Bloomfield Hills, Mich., 1972, 79, 84, Grand Rapids (Mich.) Art Mus., 1974, Paula Cooper Gallery, N.Y.C., 1975, 76, 77, 78, 79, 90, Fine Arts Bldg., N.Y.C., 1976, Acad. der Kunste, Berlin, 1976, Susanne Hilberry Gallery, Birmingham, 1976-77, 83, 85, 91, Willard Gallery, N.Y.C., 1977, Kansas City (Mo.) Art Inst., 1977, N.A.M.E. Gallery, Chgo., 1977, Hallwalls, Buffalo, 1977, Mus. Modern Art, N.Y.C., 1978, 89, 92, Weatherspoon Art Gallery U. N.C., Greensboro, 1979, 92, Albright-Knox Art Gallery, Buffalo, 1979, Brown U., Providence, 1980, XIII Olympic Winter Games, Lake Placid, N.Y., 1980, Jeffrey Fuller Fine Art, Phila., 1980, Portland (Oreg.) Ctr. for Visual Arts, 1980, The Drawing Ctr., N.Y.C., 1980, 82, Brooke Alexander Gallery, N.Y.C., 1980, Mus. Contemporary Art, Chgo., 1980, 81, P.S. 1 Mus., N.Y.C., 1981, 92, Art Latitude Gallery, N.Y.C., 1981, Leo Castelli Gallery, N.Y.C., 1981, Sutton Place, Guildford, Eng., 1982, Gallerie d'Arte Moderna di Ca'Pesaro, Venice, Italy, 1982, Inst. Contemporary Art of Virgini Mus., Richmond, Va., 1982, Galerie Biedermann, Munich, 1982, Thomas Segal Gallery, Boston, 1983, Fuller-Goldeen Gallery, San Francisco, 1983, 86, William Paterson Coll., Wayne, N.J., 1983, 89, Artist's Space, N.Y.C., 1983, 84, Harborside Indsl. Ctr., Bklyn., 1983, Orgn. Ind. Artists, N.Y.C., 1984, Bernice Steinbaum Gallery, N.Y.C., 1984, Brentwood Gallery, St. Louis, 1984, U. Calif., Irvine, 1984, U. No. Iowa Gallery Art, Cedar Falls, 1984, Hudson River Mus., N.Y.C., 1984, Barbara Toll Fine Arts, N.Y.C., 1984, 85, 86, 87, Detroit Focus Gallery, 1984, Cable Gallery, N.Y.C., 1984, Wayne State U., Detroit, 1984, Matthews Hamilton Gallery, Phila., 1984, Barbara Krakow Gallery, Boston, 1984, BlumHelman Warehouse, N.Y.C., 1984, Pam Adler Gallery, N.Y.C., 1985, Daniel Weinberg Gallery, L.A., 1985, 89, Knight Gallery, Charlotte, N.C., 1985, Bank of Boston, 1986, Whitney Mus. Am. Art, Stamford, Conn., 1987, 89, Scott Hansen Gallery, N.Y.C., 1987, Saxon-Lee Gallery, L.A., 1987, Parrish Art Mus., East Hampton, N.Y., 1987, Curt Marcus Gallery, N.Y., 1988, Loughelton Gallery, N.Y.C., 1988, 90, Whitney Mus. Am. Art, N.Y.C., 1988, 91, Hillwood Art Gallery C.W. Post Campus, Brookville, N.Y., 1989, USIA traveling exbhn., 1989, Edward Thorp Gallery, N.Y.C., 1989, Pine Street Lobby Gallery, San Francisco, 1989, Fuller Gross Gallery, San Francisco, 1989, Solo Press/Soho Gallery, N.Y.C., 1989, Maxwell Davidson Gallery, N.Y.C., 1989, Blum Helman Gallery, N.Y.C., 1989, R.I.S.D., Providence, 1989, Graham Modern, N.Y.C., 1990, Hood Mus. Art Dartmouth Coll., Hanover, N.H., 1990, 92, New Britain Mus. Am. Art, Hartfor, Conn., 1991, Asher-Faure, L.A., 1991, Annina Nosei Gallery, N.Y.C., 1991, Lintas Worldwide, N.Y.C., 1991, Nina Fredenheim Gallery, Buffalo, 1991, Molica Guidarte Gallery, N.Y.C., 1991, Squibb Gallery, Princeton, N.J., 1991, Cleve. State U. Gallery, 1992, Ind. Curators Inc., N.Y.C., 1992, Wexner Ctr. for the Arts, Columbus, Ohio, 1992, Transamerica Corp., San Francisco, 1992, The Gallery Three Zero, N.Y.C., 1992, Haggerty Mus. Art, Milw., Barbara Methes Gallery, N.Y.C., Asher Fauve Gallery, L.A., Hillwood Art Mus., Brookville, N.Y., Pamela Auchincloss Gallery, N.Y.C., Leo Castelli Gallery, N.Y.C.; represented in permanent collections Mus. Modern Art, N.Y.C., Whitney Mus. Am. Art, N.Y.C., Bklyn. Mus., Walker Art Ctr., Mpls., Balt. Mus., Toledo Mus. Art, Hood Mus. Dartmouth Coll., High Mus. Art, Albright-Knox Art Gallery, Moderna Museet, Stockholm, Mus. Contemporary Art, Mexico City, Detroit Inst. Arts, MIT, Whitehead Inst., Philip Morris, Inc., Volvo Corp., Chase Manhattan Bank, Chem. Bank, BankAm., Bank of Am., Prudential Ins. Co., U.S. Trust & Co., Inter Metro Industries, Lannan Found., numerous pvt. collections. Nat. Endowment for Arts grantee, 1978-79; recipient Am. Acad. Arts and Letters award, 1995, Arts Achievement award Wayne State U., 1989.

PHELPS, CAROL JO, neuroendocrinologist; b. Sendai, Japan, Apr. 20, 1948; d. Harry J. and Helen I. (Davies) P.; m. James B. Turpen, June 13, 1969 (div. Apr. 1982); children: J. Matthew Turpen, John A. Turpen; m. David L. Hurley, Oct. 12, 1985. BS in Zoology, U. Denver, 1969; PhD in Anatomy, La. State U. Med. Ctr., 1974. Postdoctoral fellow NIH, U. Rochester, N.Y., 1974-76; rsch. assoc. Pa. State U., Univ. Park, 1976-77; instr. Pa. State U., 1977-80, postdoctoral scholar, 1980-82; asst. prof. neurobiology U. Rochester, 1982-90; assoc. prof. anatomy Tulane U. Sch. Medicine, New Orleans, 1990-94; prof., 1994—; nat. scientific adv. coun. Am. Fedn. Aging Rsch., N.Y.C., 1988—; rev. coms. Nat. Inst. on Aging, Bethesda, Md., 1993—; editl. bd. Neuroendocrinology, Paris, 1994—, Endocrinology, 1996—, Jour. of Andrology, 1996—. Com. sec., chair Otetiana Coun. Pack 10 Boy Scouts Am., Honeoye Falls, N.Y., 1987-89. NIH fellow, 1974-76; grantee NIH, 1983—. Mem. Am. Assn. Anatomists, Soc. Exptl. Biology and Medicine, Endocrine Soc., Soc. Neurosci. (chpt. pres. 1995-96). Office: Tulane U Sch Medicine Dept Anatomy 1430 Tulane Ave New Orleans LA 70112-2699

PHELPS, CARRIE LYNN, public relations executive; b. Ft. Wayne, Ind., June 18, 1964; d. Richard Clair and Judith Elaine (Potts) P. BA in Journalism/Criminal Justice, Ind. U., 1986. Dir. communications Ind. Mfrs. Assn., Indpls., 1987-89, Ind. Dept. Commerce, Indpls., 1989-90; dir. Gray, Miller & Mitsch, P.R., Indpls., 1990-91; dir. comm. and devel. Wapehani coun. Girl Scouts U.S., Daleville, Ind., 1991-94; account exec. Caldwell VanRiper Advt./Pub. Rels., Indpls., 1994—. Contbr. articles to profl. jours., mags., and newspapers. Recipient Addy award, 6th dist. Addy award, Epic award of merit Internat. Assn. Bus. Communicators, Comm. Arts Design Ann. # 36 award of excellence. Mem. Pub. Rels. Soc. Am. (Keystone award). Home: 12139 Suffolk Ln Indianapolis IN 46260 Office: Caldwell VanRiper Advt/Pub Rels 1314 N Meridian St Indianapolis IN 46202-2303

PHELPS, FLORA L(OUISE) LEWIS, editor, anthropologist, photographer; b. San Francisco, July 28, 1917; d. George Chase and Louise (Manning) Lewis; m. C(lement) Russell Phelps, Jan. 15, 1944; children: Andrew Russell, Carol Lewis, Gail Bransford. Student, U. Mich.; AB cum laude, Bryn Mawr Coll., 1938; AM, Columbia U., 1954. Acting dean Cape Cod Inst. Music, East Brewster, Mass., summer 1940; assoc. social sci. analyst U.S. Govt., 1942-44; co-adj. staff instr. anthropology Univ. Coll., Rutgers U., 1954-55; mem. editorial bd. Américas mag. OAS, Washington, 1960-82; mng. editor, 1974-82, contbg. editor, 1982-89; N.J. vice chmn. Ams. Dem. Action, 1950; mem. Dem. County Com. N.J., 1948-49. Author articles in fields of anthropology, art, architecture, edn., travel; contbr. Latin Am. newspapers. Mem. AAAS, Am. Anthrop. Assn., Archaeological Inst. Am., Latin Am. Studies Assn., Soc. for Am. Archaeology, Soc. Woman Geographers. Home: Collington # 2212 10450 Lottsford Rd Mitchellville MD 20721-2748

PHELPS, GERRY CHARLOTTE, economist, minister; b. Norman, Okla., Oct. 15, 1931; d. George and Charlotte LeNoir (Yowell) P.; 1 child, Scott. BA, U. Tex., 1963, MA, 1984; MDiv, San Francisco Theol. Seminary, 1981. Cert. tchr., Calif. Lectr. in econs. U. Houston, 1966-69; pastor United Meth. Ch., Kelseyville, Calif., 1980-82; sr. pastor Bethany United Methodist Ch., Bakersfield, Calif., 1982-84; exec. dir. Bethany Svc. Ctr., Bakersfield, 1982-84; pres., exec. dir. Concern for the Poor, Inc., San Jose, Calif., 1985-92; pastor United Meth. Ch., Flatonia, Tex., 1993—; exec. dir. Coun. Econ. Strategies, Austin, 1992—, CRISES, Austin, 1994—. Mem. Task Force on the Homeless, San Jose, 1987, Santa Clara County, 1991. Recipient commendation Mayor of Bakersfield, 1984, Santa Clara County Bd. Suprs., 1992. Office: CRISES PO Box 4676 Austin TX 78765-4676

PHELPS, JAYCIE, gymnast, Olympic athlete; b. Indpls., Sept. 26, 1979. Mem. U.S. Women's Gymnastics Team, 1994—, U.S. Olympic Team, Atlanta, 1996. Recipient Sagamore of the Wabash award State of Ind., 1995, Gold medal team competition Olympic Games, Atlanta, 1996; placed 3rd in all around U.S. Olympic Festival, St. Louis, 1994, 2d for team Team World Championships, Dortmund, Germany, 1994, 3rd in all around Coca-Cola Nat. Championships, New Orleans, 1995, 3rd for team World Championships, Sabae, Japan, 1995. Office: care USA Gymnastics Pan Am Plz 201 S Capitol Ave Ste 300 Indianapolis IN 46225*

PHELPS, KATHRYN ANNETTE, mental health counseling executive, consultant; b. Creswell, Oreg., Aug. 1, 1940; d. Henry Wilbur and Lake Ilene (Wall) M.; children: David Bryan (dec.), Derek Alan, Darla Ailene. BS in edn., Western Oreg. State Coll., 1962; MSW, Columbia State U., 1992, PhD, 1993. Tchr. Germany, Thailand, U.S., 1962-88; acct. exec. ins. industry; weight-loss counselor, alcohol/drug abuse prevention/intervention counselor teens, 1990-93; counselor Eugene, 1989-94; sr. exec. v.p., edn. dir. Light Streams, Inc., Eugene, 1993—; sr. exec. v.p., therapist Comprehensive Assessment Svcs./The Focus Inst., Inc., Eugene, 1994—; mental health counselor in pvt. practice; ednl. cons. specializing in learning disability testing Comprehensive Assessment Svcs., Eugene, 1996—; co-owner, co-founder Comprehensive Assessment Svcs., LLC, 1995—; cons. consumer edn.; mem. Am. Bd. Disability Analysts. Author: Easy Does It, books 1 & 2; hosted weekly TV cooking segment, Portland and U.S. Guardian Jobs Daughters, 1980-82; bd. dirs., den mother Cub Scouts, Boy Scouts, Kansas, Oreg., 1974-82; coach girls volleyball, 1974-80; vol. in orphanages, elderly nursing homes, Thailand, Germany, U.S., 1954-95; sunday sch. tchr., 1956-90; sponsored exchange student, 1984-88. Mem. Am. Bd. Disability Analysts, Eastern Star, Nat. Assn. Social Workers, Am. Counseling Assn., Columbia State U. Alumni Assn., Women's Internat. Bowling Conf. Home: 3838 Kendra St Eugene OR 97404 Office: Comprehensive Assessment Sv The Focus Inst Inc 400 E 2d St Ste 103 Eugene OR 97401

PHENIX, GLORIA GAYLE, educational association administrator; b. Dallas, Mar. 4, 1956; m. Douglas William Phenix, Aug. 8, 1987; children: David William, Duncan Kenneth. BA, U. North Tex., 1979, postgrad., 1979-81; PhD, ABD, U. Minn., 1981-89. Dean Jordan Coll., Benton Harbor, Mich., 1990; pres. Phenix & Assocs. Tng. Cons., St. Joseph, Mich., 1991—, Topeka, Kans., 1993—; bd. dirs. Cornerstone, Inc. Mem. allocation com. United Way, 1990-92, Literacy Coun., 1991-93; mem. Topeka Race Rels. Task Force, 1994; Mayor's Commn. Status Women, 1996—. Fulbright-Hayes fellow Africa, 1990; Hewlett Mellon Found. grantee, 1987, Benton Found. grantee, 1988. Mem. Am. Polit. Sci. Assn., Minn. Polit. Sci. Assn. (bd. dirs. 1989-90), Midwest Polit. Sci. Assn., Am. Assn. Trainers and Developers, Am. Soc. for Quality Control. Presbyterian. Office: Phenix & Assocs 505 Pleasant St # 200 Saint Joseph MI 49085-1269 also: Phenix Assocs 530 S Kansas Topeka KS 66604

PHILBIN, ANN MARGARET, brokerage house executive; b. Clinton, Mass., June 15, 1941; d. John J. and Angela J. (O'Flynn) P. AB, Trinity Coll., Washington, 1962. With Paine Webber, Boston, 1963—, v.p. adminstrn., 1985—; arbitrator N.Y. Stock Exchange, Boston, 1987—. Mem. Trinity Coll. Alumnae Assn. (1st v.p. 1989-92, pres., trustee 1992-95, Alumnae Achievement award 1995). Office: Paine Webber 265 Franklin St Boston MA 02110-3113

PHILIBOSIAN, DIANNE LOUISE, associate dean; b. San Diego, Aug. 26, 1946; d. Fred Froeble and Mary (Berberian) P.; m. Thomas Daryl Seifert, Apr. 20, 1991. BA, U. of Pacific, 1967; MS, So. Ill. U., 1971, PhD, 1978. Cert. elem. tchr., Calif. Kindergarten tchr. Stockton (Calif.) Unified Sch. Dist., 1968-70; instr. in elem. edn. So. Ill. U., Carbondale, 1970-72; lectr. in elem. edn. Calif. State U., Northridge, 1973-77, coord., prof. child devel., 1977-79, prof. speech comm., leisure studies and recreation, 1978-87, assoc. dean Coll. Health and Human Devel., 1987—; project dir. Warner Ctr. Inst. for Family Devel., Woodland Hills, Calif., 1984—; program dir. ECE masters degree consortium Calif. State Univ. and Colls., Northridge, 1975-79; tng. officer/dir. Head Start Leadership Devel. program So. Ill. U., 1970-72. Editor: Removing Barriers to Childcare, 1993; contbr. articles to profl. jours. Chair, mem. Calif. Child Devel. Programs Adv. Com., 1989—; mem. Mayor's Child Care Adv. Bd., L.A., 1987-95; mem. L.A. County Child Care Planning Bd., 1994—; mem. alumni bd. U. of The Pacific, 1993—. Recipient award for childhood creativity program U.S. Dept. Edn., 1986-89, Ahmanson, 1989-92, GTE, 1989-92, 100th Congress Child Care Challenge award Congl. Caucus for Women's Issues, 1988. Office: Calif State U Coll Health and Human Devel 1811 Nordhoff St Northridge CA 91330-8215

PHILIPP, ELIZABETH R., manufacturing company executive, lawyer. Grad., Harvard U., 1978, Harvard U., 1982. Exec. v.p., gen. counsel, sec. Collins & Aikman Products Co., N.Y.C. Office: Collins & Aikman Products Co 210 Madison Ave New York NY 10016

PHILLIPPS, STEPHANIE M., lawyer; b. Boston, Mar. 13, 1952. BA magna cum laude, Radcliffe Coll., 1973; JD, Harvard U., 1976. Bar: Mass. 1977, D.C. 1977. Ptnr. Arnold & Porter, Washington. Office: Arnold & Porter Thurman Arnold Bldg 555 12th St NW Washington DC 20004-1202*

PHILLIPS, BERNICE CECILE GOLDEN, retired vocational education educator; b. Galveston, Tex., June 30, 1920; d. Walter Lee and Minnie (Rothsprack) Golden; m. O. Phillips, Mar. 1950 (dec.); children: Dorian Lee, Loren Francis. BBA cum laude, U. Tex., 1945; MEd, U. Houston, 1968. cert. tchr., tchr. coord., vocat. tchr., Tex. Dir. Delphian Soc., Houston, 1955-60; bus. tchr. various private schs., Houston area, 1960-65; vocat. tchr. coord. office edn. program Pasadena (Tex.) Ind. Sch. Dist., 1965-68, Houston Ind. Sch. Dist., John H. Reagan High Sch., 1968-85. Bd. dirs. Regency House Condominium Assn., 1991-93. Recipient numerous awards and recognitions for vocat. bus. work at local and state levels. Mem. AAUW (life, Houston Br. v.p. ednl. found. 1987-90, pres. 1992-94, bd. dirs. 1987-96), NEA, Nat. Bus. Edn. Assn. Am. Vocat. Assn. (life), Tex. State Tchrs. Assn. (life), Tex. Classroom Tchrs. Assn. (life), Tex. Bus. Edn. Assn. (emeritus), Vocat. Office Edn. Tchrs. Assn. Tex. (past bd. dirs.), Greater Houston Bus. Edn. Assn. (reporter), Houston Assn. Ret. Tchrs., Tex. Assn. Ret. Tchrs., Delta Pi Epsilon (emeritus), Beta Gamma Sigma. Home: 2701 Westheimer Rd 8H Houston TX 77098-1235

PHILLIPS, BETTIE MAE, elementary school educator; b. Ft. Worth, May 2, 1941; d. Robert Sr. and Charittie Barnes; m. George Vernon Phillips Sr., Aug. 29, 1960 (div. Aug. 1985); 1 child, George Vernon Jr. BS in Elem. Edn., Bishop Coll., 1967; MEd in Early Childhood Edn., East Tex. State U., 1976. Tchr. Dallas Ind. Sch. Dist., 1968—. Author: The Whole Armor, 1979, Petals, 1988, Lights in the Shadows, 1993; composer children's songs Bettie's Songs, Vol. 1, 1987, God's Cloud and There's Love Everywhere, 1994 (recorded by Hilltop Records, included in album America), You and I Free Your Score (recorded by Hilltop Records, included in album Hilltop Country), 1995. Mem. Classroom Tchrs. Dallas. Baptist. Home: 1312 Mill Stream Dr Dallas TX 75232-4604 Office: Bayles Elem Sch 2444 Telegraph Ave Dallas TX 75228-5819

PHILLIPS, BETTY LOU (ELIZABETH LOUISE PHILLIPS), author, interior designer; b. Cleve.; d. Michael N. and Elizabeth D. (Materna) Suvak; m. John S. Phillips, Jan. 27, 1963 (div. Jan. 1981); children: Bruce, Bryce, Brian; m. John D.C. Roach, Aug. 28, 1982. BS, Syracuse U., 1960; postgrad. in English, Case Western Res. U., 1963-64. Cert. elem. and spl. edn. tchr., N.Y. Tchr. pub. schs. Shaker Heights, Ohio, 1960-66; sportswriter Cleve. Press, 1976-77; spl. features editor Pro Quarterback Mag., N.Y.C., 1976-79; freelance writer specializing in books for young people, 1976—; interior designer residential and comml.; bd. dirs. Cast Specialties Inc., Cleve. Author: Chris Evert: First Lady of Tennis, 1977; Picture Story of Dorothy Hamill (ALA Booklist selection), 1978; American Quarter Horse, 1979; Earl Campbell: Houston Oiler Superstar, 1979; Picture Story of Nancy Lopez, (ALA Notable book), 1980; Go! Fight! Win! The NCA Guide for Cheerleaders (ALA Booklist), 1981; Something for Nothing, 1981; Brush Up on Your Hair (ALA Booklist), 1981; Texas ... The Lone Star State, 1989, Who Needs Friends? We All Do!, 1989; also contbr. articles to young adult and sports mags. Bd. dirs. The Children's Mus., Denver; mem. Friends of Fine Arts Found., Denver Art Mus., Cen. City Opera Guild, Alameda County Cancer League. Mem. Soc. Children's Book Writers, Internat. Interior Design Assn. (profl. mem.), Am. Soc. Interior Designers (profl. mem., cert.),. Delta Delta Delta. Republican. Roman Catholic. Home: 4278 Bordeaux Ave Dallas TX 75205

PHILLIPS, CARLA, county official; b. Balt., Nov. 14, 1963; d. Paulo Pereira de Mendonca and June Ann (Lewis) Cortese; m. Wayne Shriver Phillips, Mar. 24, 1990. BS, East Carolina U., 1985; MPA, U. Balt., 1993. Program dir. YMCA of Met. Washington, Alexandria, Va., 1985-86; ctr. supr. Balt. County Govt., Towson, Md., 1986-90, community supr., 1990-92, sr. community supr., 1992-94, asst. therapeutic recreation coord., 1994—. Water safety instr. YMCA of Greater Balt., 1986—, Rosedale Recreation Coun., Balt., 1991, 93; asst. basketball coach Md. Spl. Olympics, Towson, 1994—, soccer coach, dir. track and field; mem. 6th Dist. Substance Abuse Adv. Coun., Towson, 1990-92, Villa Cresta PTA, Parkville, Md., 1988-92; ski instr. Ski Roundtop, Lewisberry, Pa., 1996—. Mem. ASPA, Nat. Recreation and Park Assn. (cert. leisure profl.), Md. Recreation and Parks Assn., Soc. for Pub. Affairs and Adminstrn., Kappa Delta Pi, Phi Sigma Pi, Pi Alpha Alpha. Home: 1000 Harris Mill Rd PO Box 306 Parkton MD 21120-0306 Office: Balt County Govt Parks and Recreation 301 Washington Ave Baltimore MD 21204-4715

PHILLIPS, CAROLYN KAE, marketing professional; b. Santa Rosa, Calif., May 27, 1958; d. John Harmon and Marlene Kae (Welsh) P. BA, U. Mich., 1980; MBA, Northwestern U., 1982. Asst. acct. exec. Leo Burnett, 1982-85; acct. exec. Foote, Cone & Belding, 1985-87; mktg. mgr. The Nutra Sweet Co., 1987-89, Coca-Cola, Irvine, Calif., 1989-91; dir. mktg. Intellivoice, Atlanta, 1991-92, One-On-One Sports, Chgo., 1993—. Roman Catholic. Office: One-On-One Sports 1935 Techny Ste 18 Northbrook IL 60062

PHILLIPS, DOROTHY KAY, lawyer; b. Camden, N.J., Nov. 2, 1945; d. Benjamin L. and Sadye (Levinsky) Phillips; children: Bethann P., David M. Schaffzin. BS in English Lit. magna cum laude, U. Pa., 1964; MA in Family Life and Marriage Counseling and Edn., NYU, 1975; JD, Villanova U., 1978. Bar: Pa. 1978, N.J. 1978, U.S. Dist. Ct. (ea. dist.) Pa. 1978, U.S. Dist. Ct. N.J., 1978, U.S. Ct. Appeals (3d cir.), 1984, U.S. Supreme Ct. 1984. Tchr., Haddon Twp. High Sch. (N.J.), and Haddon Heights High Sch. (N.J.), 1964-70; lectr., counselor Marriage Council of Phila.; lectr. U. Pa. and

Hahnemann Med. Schs., Phila., 1970-75; atty. Adler, Barish, Daniels, Levin & Creskoff, Phila., 1978-79, Astor, Weiss & Newman, Phila., 1979-80; ptnr. Romisher & Phillips, P.C., Phila., 1981-86; prin. Law Office of Dorothy K. Phillips, 1986—; faculty Sch. of Law Temple U. Guest speaker on domestic rels. issues on radio and TV shows; featured in newspaper and mag. articles; contbr. articles to profl. jours. Rosenbach Found., Philadanco, Fedn. Allied Jewish Appeal (lawyers. div.), World Affairs Coun.; bd. mem. Anti-Defamation League of B'nai B'rith, Nat. Mus. Jewish History, mem. friends' circle, Athenaeum, Phila., shareholder. Mem. ABA, ATLA (membership com. 1990-91, co-chair 1989-90), Pa. Trial Lawyers Assn. (chair membership com. family sect. 1989-90, presenter ann. update civil litigators-family law, author procedures practice of family law Phila. County Family Law Litigation Sect. County practiced database 1991), Pa. Bar Assn. (continuing legal edn. com. 1990-92, faculty, lectr. Pa. Bar Inst. Continuing Legal Edn. 1990, panel mem. summer meeting 1991), N.J. Bar Assn., Phila. Bar Assn. (chmn. early settlement program 1983-84, mem. custody rules drafting com. for Supreme Ct. Pa., spl. events speaker on pensions, counsel fees, written fee agreements 1989-91, co-chair and moderator of panel mandatory continuing legal edn. 1994), Phila. Trial Lawyers Assn., Montgomery County Bar Assn., Lawyers Club. Office: 1818 Market St Ste 35 Philadelphia PA 19103-3602

PHILLIPS, DOROTHY LOWE, nursing educator; b. Jacksonville, Fla., June 3, 1939; d. Clifford E. and Dorothy (MacFeeley) Lowe; m. Dale Bernard Phillips, Feb. 14, 1973; children: Francis D., Sean E., Dorothy F. AA in Nursing, Ventura Coll., 1969; BSN, Calif. State U. Consortium, San Diego, 1984; M. Nursing, UCLA, 1987; EdD, Nova Southeastern U., 1995. Cert. community colls. tchr., Calif.; RN, Calif., pub. health nurse, Calif., clin. nurse specialist maternal/child. Staff nurse Community Meml. Hosp., Ventura, Calif., 1969-70; charge nurse women and children's clinic Ventura County Regional Med. Ctr., Ventura, 1974-76; staff nurse, RN II Pleasant Valley Hosp., Camarillo, Calif., 1978-85; lead instr. cert. nursing asst. program div. adult edn. Oxnard (Calif.) Union High Sch. Dist., 1984-89; staff rsch. assoc. UCLA, 1988; clin. instr. Sch. of Nursing Ventura Community Coll., 1988, college nurse, 1989; lectr. Sch. of Nursing UCLA, 1989, lectr., coord. maternity nursing Sch. of Nursing, 1989-90, 90-91; vocat. nursing dir., health scis. coord. Oxnard Union High Sch. Dist., 1990—; vis. educator Health Careers unit Calif. Dept. Edn., 1992-94; cons. Oxnard Adult Sch.; mem. adv. com. nursing asst./home health aide program Ventura County Regional Occupational Program; presenter in field. Competitive events judge 1st Annual Leadership Conf., Health Occupations Students of Am., Anaheim, Calif.; active St. John's Regional Med. Ctr. Health Fair, 1991, Pleasant Valley Hosp. Health Fair, 1991; seminar leader "Babies and You", March of Dimes, 1988. Grad. Div. Rsch. grantee UCLA, 1986; Calif. State PTA scholar UCLA, 1986, Ventura County Med. Secs. scholar, 1967. Mem. Calif. Assn. Health Career Educators (pres. 1994), So. Calif. Dirs. Vocat. Nursing Programs (rec. sec. 1996—), So. Calif. Vocat. Nurse Educators, Sigma Theta Tau. Republican. Lutheran. Home: 321 Bayview Ave Ventura CA 93003-2052 Office: Oxnard Adult Sch 935 W 5th St Oxnard CA 93030-5271

PHILLIPS, DOROTHY REID, retired medical library technician; b. Hingham, Mass., Apr. 21, 1924; d. James Henry and Emma Louise (Davis) Reid; m. Earl Wendell Phillips, Apr. 22, 1944; children: Earl W., Jr., Betty Herrera, Carol Coe. Cert., Durham Vocat. Sch., 1952; B.S. in Comml. Edn., N.C. Central U., 1959; postgrad. U. Colo., 1969; M.Human Relations, Webster Coll., 1979; postgrad. Grad. Sch. Library Sci., U. Denver, 1983. Vocat. nurse Meml. Hosp., U. N.C., Chapel Hill, 1955-59; vol. work, Cairo, Egypt, 1965-67; library technician Base Library, Lowry AFB, Colo., 1960-65, Fitzsimons Med. Library, Aurora, Colo., 1976-93; ret. 1993; mem. Denver Mus. Natural History, Denver Art Mus., Mariners. Mem. AAUW (chpt. community rep. 1982-83, state chmn. edn. found. 1982-84, pres. Denver br. 1984-86), Altrusa Internat. (corr. sec. Denver 1982-83, bd. dirs. 1984-85, pres. Denver chpt. 1988), Friends of Library, Colo. Library Assn., Council Library Technicians, Federally Employed Women, Delta Sigma Theta (corr. sec. Denver 1964-66), Women's Assn. of Peoples Presbyn. Ch., League of Women Voters, Denver Urban League. Democrat. Presbyterian. Home: 3085 Fairfax St Denver CO 80207-2714

PHILLIPS, ELAINE LEE, psychologist, educator; b. Atlanta, Nov. 13, 1950; d. Irving and Norma Young; m. Douglas Chambers. BA summa cum laude, Western Mich. U., 1973, MA, 1975, PhD, 1986. Lic. psychologist, Mich. Sch. psychologist Eastern Svc. Dist., Galesburg, Mich., 1975-77; coord. Family and Children's Svcs. Barry County Mental Health, Hastings, Mich., 1977-82; psychologist Pheasant Ridge Ctr., Kalamazoo, 1982-83, Kalamazoo Regional Psychiat. Hosp., 1983-87; assoc. prof. Western Mich. U., Kalamazoo, 1987—; cons. in field; presenter on health beliefs and practices of Am. youth, physician psycho-social assessment adolescents. Contbr. articles to profl. jours. Bd. dirs. Hospice Greater Kalamazoo, 1987—, mem. clin. records evaluation and rev. com., 1987—, mem. program evaluation and adv. com., 1987—, chmn. bereavement evaluation com., 1989—; sec. Commn. on Status Women, 1989-90, pres., 1990-92. Kalamazoo Consortium Higher Edn. grantee, 1989. Mem. APA, Women in Psychology and Clin. Group Psychology. Office: Western Mich U Kalamazoo MI 49008

PHILLIPS, ELIZABETH JASON, lawyer; b. Boston, Sept. 3, 1936; d. Richard Eliot and Elizabeth Harding (McClure) Jason; m. William Morris Phillips Jr., Mar. 2, 1991; children: Meredith Rowe, William Morris Phillips III, Eleanor Anne, Robert J., Lee B. Stewart. BA in History, U. Mass., 1958; MEd, U. Hartford, 1969; JD, Western New Eng. Coll., Springfield, Mass., 1977. Bar: Mass. 1977, U.S. Dist. Ct. Mass. 1978, Va. 1981, U.S. Dist. Ct. (ea. dist.) Va. 1981, U.S. Dist. Ct. D.C. 1981, U.S. Dist. Ct. (we. dist.) Va. 1982, U.S. Ct. Appeals (4th cir.) 1982, U.S. Supreme Ct. 1984. Ptnr. firm Thompson & Stewart, Ludlow, Mass., 1977-80; adminstr. Office Atty. Gen., Commonwealth of Va., Richmond, 1980-82, asst. atty. gen., 1982-84; dep. Commr. Indsl. Commn. Va., 1984-91; dep. commr., mgr. dispute resolution divsn. Va. Workers' Compensation Commn., Richmond, 1991—. Trustee Ludlow Hosp., 1979-80. Mem. ABA, Richmond Bar Assn., Va. Bar Assn., Ludlow C. of C. (pres. 1980). Episcopalian. Home: Cedar Shade 7906 Brays Point Rd Hayes VA 23072-4620 Office: Va Workers Compensation Commn 1000 Dmv Dr Richmond VA 23220-2036

PHILLIPS, ELIZABETH VELLOM, social worker, educator; b. Visalia, Calif., Nov. 7, 1922; d. Ralph Cauble and Mary Amelia (Cole) Vellom; m. William Clayton Phillips, Sept. 10, 1950 (div. 1976); children: Peter Clayton, David Cole, Ann Harper. BA, UCLA, 1943; MSW, Columbia U., 1950; MPH, Yale U., 1970; PhD, Union Grad. Sch., 1980. Lic. clin. social worker; diplomate Am. Bd. Examiners Clin. Social Work. Psychiat. social worker Jewish Bd. Guardians, N.Y.C., 1950-51, Cmty. Svc. Soc. Family Camp, N.Y.C., 1955-57, Jewish Family Svc., New Haven, 1962-64, New Haven Family Counseling, 1964-68; ass. clin. prof. psychiatry Sch. Medicine Yale U., New Haven, 1973—; pvt. practice New Haven, 1981—; sr. social work supr. mental health dept. Hill Health Ctr., New Haven, 1973-81; prof. Sch. Social Work Smith Coll., Northampton, 1981-84; initiator teen pregnancy program Hill Health Ctr., 1977-81, cons., 1975-79. Found. Women's Health Svcs., New Haven, 1985, Inner City Co-op Farm, New Haven, 1978; organizer Big Brother/Big Sister program Yale U., 1976. Named Disting. Practitioner Nat. Acads. Practice, 1996. Mem. NASW, Am. Group Psychotherapy Assn., Nat. Fedn. Socs. Clin. Social Work (sec. 1988, v.p. 1993, pres.-elect 1994-96, pres. 1996-98), Conn. Soc. Clin. Social Work (pres. 1987-88). Democrat. Jewish. Home: 13 Cooper Rd North Haven CT 06473

PHILLIPS, GAIL, state legislator; b. Juneau, Alaska; m. Walt Phillips; children: Robin, Kim. BA in Bus. Edn., U. Alaska. Mem. Homer (Alaska) City Coun., 1981-84, Kenai Peninsula Borough Assembly, 1986-87; chmn. legis. com. Alaska Mcpl. League; mem. Alaska Ho. of Reps., 1990, 92, 94, house majority leader, 1993-94, speaker, 1995—; owner, mgr. Quiet Sporting Goods; ptnr. Lindphil Mining Co.; pub. rels. cons. Active Homer United Meth. Ch., Rep. Ctrl. Com. Alaska, Kenai Peninsula Coll. Coun.; past mem. com. bd. and race coord. Iditarod Trail Dog Sled Race. Mem. Western States Legis. Coun. (exec. com.), Am. Legis. Exch. Coun. (state chmn.), Resource Devel. Coun. Alaska, Western Legis. Conf. (exec. bd.), Western States Coalition (co-founder), The Energy Coun. Home: PO Box 3304 Homer AK 99603-3304 Office: 126 W Pioneer Ave Homer AK 99603-7564 also: Alaska House of Reps State Capitol Juneau AK 99801-1182

PHILLIPS, GENEVA FICKER, editor; b. Staunton, Ill., Aug. 1, 1920; d. Arthur Edwin and Lillian Agnes (Woods) Ficker; m. James Emerson Phillips, Jr., June 6, 1955 (dec. 1979). BS in Journalism, U. Ill., 1942; MA in English Lit., UCLA, 1953. Copy desk Chgo. Jour. Commerce, 1942-43; editl. asst. patents Radio Rsch. Lab., Harvard U., Cambridge, Mass., 1943-45; asst. editor adminstrv. publs. U. Ill., Urbana, 1946-47; editorial asst. Quar. of Film, Radio and TV, UCLA, 1952-53; mng. editor The Works of John Dryden, Dept. English, UCLA, 1964—. Bd. dirs. Univ. Religious Conf., L.A., 1979—. UCLA teaching fellow, 1950-53, grad. fellow 1954-55. Mem. Assn. Acad. Women UCLA, Dean's Coun., Coll. Letters and Scis. UCLA, Friends of Huntington Libr., Friends of UCLA Libr., Friends of Ctr. for Medieval and Renaissance Studies, Samuel Johnson Soc. of So. Calif., Assocs. of U. Calif. Press., Conf. Christianity and Lit., Soc. Mayflower Descs. Lutheran. Home: 213 1st Anita Dr Los Angeles CA 90049-3815 Office: UCLA Dept English 2225 Rolfe Hall Los Angeles CA 90024

PHILLIPS, GLYNDA ANN, editor; b. Riverside, Calif.; d. Henry Grady and Patricia (Loflin) P. BA in English, Millsaps Coll., 1977; MS in Comms., Miss. Coll. News editor The Magee (Miss.) Courier, 1981-84; editor Miss. Farm Bur. Country and Miss. Farm Bur. Producer Edition, Jackson, 1984—. Contbr. articles to profl. jours. Recipient first place personal column Nat. Fedn. Press Women, 1984, first place personal column Miss. Press Women's Assn., 1984, first place feature articles Miss. Press Women's Assn., 1984, Best Media Campaign award AFBF Info. Contest, 1996. Mem. Soc. Profl. Journalists.

PHILLIPS, GRETCHEN, clinical social worker; b. Erie, Pa., July 14, 1941; life ptnr. Beverly Campbell, June 10, 1989. BA, Mercyhurst Coll., 1966; MSW, Yeshiva U., 1972; postgrad., Advanced Ctr. Psychotherapy, 1972-73, Washington Sq. Inst., 1973-77. Bd. cert. diplomate clin. social work; cert. social worker, N.Y. Psychiat. social worker, forensic social worker Creedmoor Psychiat. Ctr., Queens Village, N.Y., 1972-80; Med. social worker Bellevue Hosp. Ctr., N.Y.C., 1980-83; intake probation officer N.Y.C. Probation, Family Court, Bklyn., 1983—. Mem. NASW, Am. Group Psychotherapy Assn., Internat. Soc. for Traumatic Stress Studies (N.Y. chpt.). Home: 125 Radford St # 3C Yonkers NY 10705-3049 Office: Probation Intake Kings Family Ct 283 Adams St Brooklyn NY 11201-2898

PHILLIPS, JANET COLLEEN, educational association executive, editor; b. Pittsfield, Ill., Apr. 29, 1933; d. Roy Lynn and Catherine Amelia (Wills) Barker; m. David Lee Phillips, Feb 7, 1954; children—Clay Cullen, Sean Vincent. B.S., U. Ill, 1954. Reporter Quincy (Ill.) Herald Whig, 1951, 52, soc. editor, 1953; editorial asst. Pub. Info. Office U. Ill.-Urbana, 1953-54, asst. editor libr., 1954-61; asst. editor Assn. for Libr. and Info. Sci. Edn., State College, Pa., 1960-61, mng. editor, 1961-89, exec. sec., 1970-89; adminstrv. dir. Interlibr. Delivery Svc. of Pa., 1990—. Mem. AAUW, Assn. for Libr. and Info. Sci. Edn., Embroiderer's Guild Am., Pa. State Blue Course Club, Pa. State U. Women's Club, Theta Sigma Phi, Delta Zeta. Presbyterian. Address: 471 Park Ln State College PA 16803-3208

PHILLIPS, JEANNETTE VERONICA, municipal administrator, consultant; b. Batesburg, S.C., Sept. 29, 1940; d. Katherine Louise (Ramey) Ray; s. William alfred Phillips, June 23, 1962; children: Veronica Lynn, Marguerite Kathleen. BA in Sociology, Ohio Wesleyan U., 1962; MA in Pub. Adminstrn., William Paterson Coll., 1980. Cert. vocat. rehab. counselor. Asst. teen program dir. YWCA, Toledo, 1962-66; recreation therapist Mo. Inst. Psychiatry, St. Louis, 1967-70, rehab. specialist, 1970-72; counselor, mgr. Vocat. Bur. of Rehab., Toledo, 1972-74; skills ctr. dir. Passaic County Bd. Tech. & Vocat. Edn., Wayne, N.J., 1974-76, personnel dir., 1976-81; asst. personnel dir. City of Stamford, Conn., 1981-87; sec., treas. Phillips Packaging, Inc., Orange, Conn., 1985—; exec. dir. commn. aging City of Stamford, 1987-92; exec. dir. social svcs., 1992—; mgmt. cons. pvt. practice, Orange, Conn., 1986—. Sec. Stamford United Way, 1991—; mem. Cystic Fibrosis Found., 1986—. Named Woman of Yr., Conn. Am. Assn. Univ. Women, 1990. Mem. AAUW (state v.p. membership 1995—), S.W. Conn. Agy. on Aging (pres. 1990-92), Lions Club Internat. Home: 520 Hundred Acre Rd Orange CT 06477-3705 Office: Stamford Dept City Soc Svcs PO Box 10152 888 Washington Blvd Stamford CT 06901-2902

PHILLIPS, JERYL G. ROSE, physical and environmental planner; b. Middletown, Ohio, June 21, 1968; d. Teresa Grande Rose. BA in Govt., Coll. of William and Mary, 1989; MA in Planning, U. Va., 1991. Prin. phys. and environ. planner Hampton Roads Planning Dist. Commn., Chesapeake, Va., 1991—. Author: (reference manual) Vegetative Practices Guide for Nonpoint Source Pollution, 1992 (Chesapeake Bay Adv. Com. Innovative Project award 1993), (citizen's guidebook) NPS Pollution...Be Part of the Solution (A Guide for Hampton Roads Citizens), 1993; co-author: (planning assistance manual) Model Environmental Assessment Procedure, 1991. Environmental ed. vol. Chesapeake Bay Youth Conservation Corps., 1991—, gen. ed. degree tutor Chesapeake Vol. in Youth Services, 1993, stranding team vol. Va. Marine Sci. Museum Stranding Team, Va. Beach, 1991—. Recipient Judicial award Chesapeake Vol. in Youth Services, 1993. Mem. Am. Planning Assn. (sect. dir. 1996—). Office: Hampton Rds Planning Dist Commn 723 Woodlake Dr Chesapeake VA 23320

PHILLIPS, JULIA MAE, physicist; b. Freeport, Ill., Aug. 17, 1954; d. Spencer Kleckner and Marjorie Ann (Figi) Phillips. BS, Coll. William and Mary, 1976; PhD, Yale U., 1981. Mem. tech. staff AT&T Bell Labs., Murray Hill, 1981-88, supr. thin film rsch. group, 1988-95; dept. mgr. sensor and surface-controlled processes dept. Sandia Nat. Labs., Albuquerque, 1995—; program mgr. Consortium Superconducting Elecs., 1989-92; mem. com. on condensed matter and materials physics NRC, 1996—. Editor: Heteroepitaxy on Silicon Technology, 1987, Epitaxial Oxide Thin Films and Heterostructures, 1994; prin. editor Jour. Materials Rsch., 1990—; mem. editorial bd. Applied Physics Letters and Jour. Applied Physics, 1992-94; contbr. articles to profl. jours. Fellow APS; mem. Materials Rsch. Soc. (sec. 1987-89, councillor 1991-93, 2d v.p. 1993, 1st v.p. 1994, pres. 1995), Sigma Xi, Phi Beta Kappa.

PHILLIPS, JULIA MILLER, film producer; b. N.Y.C., Apr. 7, 1944; d. Adolph and Tanya Miller; m. Michael Phillips (div.); 1 dau., Kate Elizabeth. B.A., Mt. Holyoke Coll., 1965. Former prodn. asst. McCall's Mag.; later advt. copywriter Macmillan Publs.; editorial asst. Ladies Home Journal, 1966-67; later assoc. editor; East Coast story editor Paramount Pictures, N.Y.C., 1969; head Mirisch Prodns., N.Y., 1970; creative exec. First Artists Prodns., N.Y.C., 1971; founded (with Tony Bill and Michael Phillips) Bill/Phillips Prodns., 1971; founder, producer Ruthless Prodns., Los Angeles, 1971—. Author: You'll Never Eat Lunch in This Town Again, 1991, Driving Under the Affluence, 1995; films include Steelyard Blues, 1972, The Sting, 1973 (Acad. award for Best Picture of Yr.), Taxi Driver, 1976 (Palme d'or for best picture), The Big Bus, 1976, Close Encounters of the Third Kind, 1977, The Beat, 1988; dir. The Estate of Billy Buckner, for Women Dirs. Workshop, Am. Film Inst., 1974. Recipient Katherine McFarland Short Story award, 1963, Short Story award Phi Beta Kappa, 1964. Mem. Acad. Motion Picture Arts and Scis., Writers Guild. Office: care Writers Guild 8955 Beverly Blvd Los Angeles CA 90048-2420

PHILLIPS, KAREN SUZANNE, psychologist; b. Jackson, Miss., Dec. 4, 1959; d. Lawrence and Betty Mae (Riberdy) P. Secretarial degree, Phillips Coll., Jackson, 1981; AA, Hinds C.C., 1986; BS, U. So. Miss., 1989; M of Comty. Counseling, Miss. Coll., 1992. Sec., treas. bd. dirs., exec. sec. Miss. Artificial Limb Co., Inc., Jackson, 1980-87; intern Hospice of Cen. Miss., Jackson, 1991-92; psychology technician Miss. State Hosp.-Oak Cir. Ctr. Adolescent Unit, Whitfield, 1992-94; psychologist assoc. Miss. State Hosp.-Jaquith Nursing Home Cons. Svc., Jackson, 1994—; ct.-apptd. spl. advocate for abused children Children First, Jackson, 1995—, Hattiesburg (Miss.) Youth Ct., 1988-89. Vol. counselor Hospice of Cen. Miss., Jackson, 1992—. Democrat. Episcopalian. Home: 159 Canton Club Cir Jackson MS 39211

PHILLIPS, KIMBERLY EILEEN, coordinator therapist; b. Somerville, N.J., Sept. 2, 1968; d. Francis Xavier Phillips and Jeanne Lois (Cramer) Slack; m. kristopher Don Hawk, Nov. 16, 1994. BA in Psychology, Rutgers U., 1990. Respite counselor Developmental Resources, Raritan, N.J., 1988-89; family support worker Alternatives Inc., Somerville, 1989-90; therapist Princeton (N.J.) Child Devel. Inst., 1990-95; coord. of parent support svcs., helpline asst. Ctr. for Outreach Svc. for Autism Cmty., Ewing, N.J., 1994—. Recipient Vol. Svc. award, Salvation Army, 1986. Mem. Ctr. for Outreach Svc. for Autism Cmty., Coun. for Exceptional Children, Alpha Phi Omega (historian 1988-90). Home: 1700 Prospect St Ewing NJ 08638

PHILLIPS, LINDA DARNELL ELAINE FREDRICKS, psychiatric and geriatrics nurse; b. Calgary, Alta., Can., July 23, 1940; came to U.S., 1964; d. Richard and Adeline Ruth (Kuch) Fredricks; m. Marion Rolley Phillips, June 25, 1960 (div. 1962). Cert. in nursing with honors, Broward C.C., Ft. Lauderdale, Fla., 1983. Exec. sec. Grandeur Motor Cars, Pompano Beach, Fla., 1975-80; charge nurse Las Olas Hosp., Ft. Lauderdale, 1983-85; nurse Med. Pers. Pool, Ft. Lauderdale, 1984-85; pvt. duty nurse, Ft. Lauderdale, 1985—; pres., v.p. L.P.R.N. Inc., 1992-93; cons. nurse Waterford Point Condo, Pompano Beach, Fla., 1980-90. Mem. Fla. Nurses Assn., Internat. Platform Assn. Address: 2910 NE 55th St Fort Lauderdale FL 33308-3452

PHILLIPS, LINDA GOLUCH, plastic surgeon, educator, researcher; b. Chgo., Nov. 11, 1951; d. Edward Walter and Rosemarie (Tomasek) Goluch; m. William Anthony Phillips, July 12, 1975; children: Cooper William, Nolan Edward, Spencer Geoffrey, Corinna Lee. BA, U. Chgo., 1974, MD, 1978. Diplomate Am. Bd. Surgery, Am. Bd. Plastic Surgery (mem. qualifying examination team 1993). Resident U. Chgo., 1978-80; intern in gen. surgery Northwestern U., Chgo., 1980-81, instr., surgeon, 1982-83; asst. prof. Wayne State U., Detroit, 1985-88; asst. prof. plastic surgery U. Tex. Med. Br., Galveston, 1988-91, assoc. prof. plastic surgery, 1991-95; prof. plastic surgery, 1995—; Truman G. Blocker Jr., MD, Disting. chairperson U. Tex. Med. Br., Galveston, chief divsn. plastic surgery, 1994—; mem. consulting med. staff Shriners Burns Inst., Galveston, Tex., 1988—; chmn. basic rsch. grants com. Plastic Surgery Edn. Found., Chgo., 1992—, mem. ednl. assessment com., mem. scholarship com., 1987-92, mem. plastic surgery-in-svc. exam. com., 1987-88, 89-93, mem. instrnl. course com., 1991-92, mem. rsch. fellowship com., mem. rsch. fund proposals com., 1993, 94; parliamentarian Plastic Surgery Rsch. Coun., 1991-93; Morestin lectr. Nat. Med. Assn., 1991; guest speaker Royal Coll. Surgeons, Eng., 1993; speaker in field. Co-author book chpts.; contbr. articles, abstracts to profl. jours. Pres. Blue Marlin Swim Team, Houston, 1993; active Clear Creek Ind. Sch. Dist., Houston, 1992. Grantee in field. Fellow Am. Coll. Surgeons; mem. AMA, Am. Assn. Plastic Surgeons, Am. Burn Assn. (mem. orgn. and delivery of burn care com. 1988-91, mem. edl. com., 1991-94), Am. Soc. Plastic and Reconstructive Surgeons (mem. program com. 1991-92, mem. exhibits com. 1992, 93, chair, 1993-94, mem. sci. program com. 1994), Am. Soc. Maxillofacial Surgeons (mem. news com. 1992, mem. membership com. 1992-93), Am. Assn. Surgery of Trauma (mem. search com. editor of Jour. Trauma 1992), Am. Soc. Aesthetic Plastic Surgery, Am. Assn. Hand Surgery, Am. Geriatric Soc., Am. Diabetes Assn., Plastic Surgery Rsch. Coun., Surgical Infection Soc., Assn. Women Surgeons (pres. 1992-94, v.p./pres.-elect 1990-92, chair program com. 1990-92, chair membership com. 1988-89, mem. nominating com. 1989-92), Blocker-Lewis Surgery Soc. (exec. sec. 1988-92), Assn. Acad. Chairmen of Plastic Surgery (mem. prerequisite com. 1990, 91), The Wound Healing Soc. (mem. honors and awards com. 1993), Singleton Surg. Soc. (sec.-treas. 1993—), Soc. Head and Neck Surgeons, Tex. Soc. Plastic Surgeons, Assn. Acad. Surgery, N.Y. Acad. Sci., Tex. Med. Assn., Galveston Med. Soc., Sigma Xi. Roman Catholic. Home: 15823 Sylvan Lake Dr Houston TX 77062-4795 Office: U Tex Med Br 6.124 McCullough Bldg Galveston TX 77555-0724

PHILLIPS, LINDA LOU, pharmacist; b. Mason City, Iowa, Sept. 3, 1952; d. Reece Webster and Bettye Frances (Martin) Phillips. BS in Polit. Sci., So. Meth. U., 1974; BS in Pharmacy, U. Ark., 1976; MS in Pharmacy, U. Houston, 1980. Registered pharmacist, Tex. Pharmacy intern Palace Drug Store, Forrest City, Ark., 1976-77; pharmacy resident Hermann Hosp., Houston, 1978-79; dir. pharmacy Alvin Cmty. Hosp., (Tex.), 1979-80; relief pharmacist Twelve Oaks Hosp., Houston, 1980; cons. pharmacist Health Facilities, Inc., Houston, 1980-81; pharmacy supr. Meth. Hosp., Houston, 1981—; sec. spl. interest group, IBAX Pharmacy, 1990-93; chmn. HBO and Co., Series 4000, materials mgmt. spl. interest group, 1994—. Mem. Am. Soc. Hosp. Pharmacists, So. Meth. U. Alumni Assn., Ark. Alumni Assn., Rho Chi, Pi Sigma Alpha. Republican. Methodist. Club: Girls' Cotillion (bd. dirs. 1983-85). Home: 7400 Bellerive Dr Apt 403 Houston TX 77036-3045 Office: Meth Hosp Pharmacy 6565 Fannin St Houston TX 77030-2704

PHILLIPS, LYDIA JEFFCOAT, internist; b. Columbia, S.C., Oct. 25, 1965; d. Bobby Ray Jeffcoat and Minnie (Bodie) Rawl. BS in Biology, U. S.C., 1987; MD, Med. U. of S.C., 1991. Lic. physician, Mass., 1995. Resident internal medicine U. S. Fla., Tampa, 1991-94; internist Seacoast Healthcare, Inc., Newburyport, Mass., 1995—. Mem. AMA, ACP (assoc.), Am. Soc. Internal Medicine, Mass. Med. Soc., Mass. Soc. Internal Medicine, Greater U. S.C. Alumni Assn. Baptist. Home: 126 Merrimac St #33 Newburyport MA 01950 Office: 257 Low St Newburyport MA 01950

PHILLIPS, LYN WALTERS, secondary education educator; b. Laurel, Miss., July 21, 1947; d. Troy Lee and Emily Lucille (Bush) Walters; m. Ronald Denman Phillips, Aug. 24, 1969; children: Kristen Leigh, Breckenridge Denman. AA, Jones Jr. Coll., 1967; BS in Journalism, U. So. Miss., 1970, BS in Secondary Edn., 1987; MS in English, William Carey Coll., 1996. Cert. secondary tchr., Miss. Tchr. Hattiesburg (Miss.) H.S., 1986-96, Oak Grove Mid. Sch., Hattiesburg, 1981-86. Editor: Snail Trails, 1989; pub., adviser newspaper Hi-Flashes, 1986—; cons. Am. Jour., 1990—; contbr. articles to profl. jours. Troop leader Girl Scouts U.S., Hattiesburg, 1978-84; vol. ARC, Salvation Army, Spl. Olympics, Hattiesburg, 1980—; v.p. N.E. Lamar Fire Dept., Hattiesburg, 1989—. Mem. Am. Fedn. Tchrs. (cons.), Lounge Lizzard Soc. (charter, pres. 1993-95), U. So. Miss. Alumni Assn. (bd. dirs. 1989-91), Scholastic Journalism Soc., Soc. Profl. Journalists, Journalism Edn. Assn. Baptist. Home: 106 Tall Pines Dr Hattiesburg MS 39402 Office: Hattiesburg H S 301 Hutchinson Ave Hattiesburg MS 39401

PHILLIPS, MARCY, bank executive. Sr. v.p. retail bank urban Calif. Fed. Bank, Monrovia. Office: Calif Fed Bank 237 S Myrtle Ave Monrovia CA 91016*

PHILLIPS, MARGARET EDITH, elementary school educator; b. Barre, Vt., Sept. 5, 1951; d. Abbott Warren and Elizabeth Lincoln (Hatch) White; m. Arlette Lincoln Phillips, Mar. 29, 1975; children: Jon, Debbie. BS, Ea. Conn. State Coll., 1973; postgrad., Longwood Coll., Farmville, Va., 1982, 83, Lynchburg (Va.) Coll., 1992, 93. Tchr. grade 2 Timberlake Christian Sch., Forest, Va., 1973-76, tchr. grade 3, 1981—. Sunday sch. tchr. Leesville Rd. Bapt. Ch., Evington, Va., 1980—; mem. Athletic Booster Club, Timberlake Christian Sch., 1991—. Office: Timberlake Christian Sch 300 Horizon Dr Forest VA 24551-1606

PHILLIPS, MARGARET GIBSON, secondary school educator, researcher; b. Montgomery, Ala., July 23, 1942; d. Amie Elizabeth (Bennett) Gibson; m. Terry Russell Phillips, Jan. 14, 1961; children: Helen Elizabeth Phillips Llewellyn, David Charles. BS in Edn., Jacksonville State U., 1970, MEd, Frostburg State U., 1976; EdD, U. Md., 1983. Instr. Allegany C.C., Cumberland, Md., 1982-84, 88-91; tchr. Etowah H.S., Attalla, Ala., 1970-72, Ridgeley (W. Va.) Mid. Sch., 1975-84; prof. U. Nat. Autonomo Mex., Mexico City, 1985-86; tchr. Mineral County Bd. Edn. Keyser (W. Va.) H.S., 1988—; team leader Ridgeley Middle Sch., 1977-84; chair Mineral County Curriculum Com., Keyser, 1981-84, Sch. Improvement Coun., 93-94. Author: (books) Vocational Grammar, 1971, Retention in the Middle Sch., 1983; co-author USA-USSR Study of Underachievers, 1994; contbr. articles to Middle Muddle, 1978-83. Pres. Carpendale Pub. Svc. Dist., Mineral County, W. Va., 1977-79, Mother's Caucus, Ridgeley, 1978-82; speaker Ch. of Christ, Cumberland, Md., 1988; co-chair Mineral County Edn. Assn., Keyser, 1993-94. Grantee Mineral County Bd. Edn., Ridgely, 1982. Mem. ASCD, DAR, Am. Fedn. Tchrs., Nat. Coun. Tchrs. of English, Phi Delta Kappa (treas., v.p. program v.p., membership v.p., pres. Frostburg, Md. 1992-93), Sigma Tau Delta, Kappa Delta Epsilon. Mem. Ch. of Christ. Home: RR 2 Box 70a1 Keyser WV 26726-9208 Office: Keyser HS 1 E Piedmont St Keyser WV 26726-3135

PHILLIPS, MARION GRUMMAN, writer, civic worker; b. N.Y.C., Feb. 11, 1922; d. Leroy Randle and Rose Marion (Werther) Grumman; m. Ellis Laurimore Phillips, Jr., June 13, 1942; children: Valerie Rose (Mrs. Adrian Parsegian), Elise Marion (Mrs. Edward E. Watts III), Ellis Laurimore III, Kathryn Noel (Mrs. Philip Zimmermann), Cynthia Louise. Student, Mt.

Holyoke Coll., 1940-42, BA, Adelphi U., 1981. Civic vol. Mary C. Wheeler Sch., 1964-68, Historic Ithaca, Inc., 1972-76, Ellis L. Phillips Found., 1960-91; bd. dirs. New Hist. Geneal. Soc., 1990-93; bd. dirs. North Shore Jr. League, 1960-61, 64-65, 68-69, Family Svc. Assn. Nassau County, 1963-69, Homemaker Svc. Assn. Nassau County, 1959-61. Author: (light verse) A Foot in the Door, 1965, The Whale-Going, Going, Gone, 1977, Doctors Make Me Sick (So I Cured Myself of Arthritis), 1979; editor: (with Valerie Phillips Parsegian) Richard and Rhoda, Letters from the Civil War, 1982, Wooden Shoes the story of my Grandfather's Grandfather (F. M. Sisson), 1990, Irish Eyes, family hist. of McTarsneys and Sissons, 1990; editor Jr. League Shore Lines, 1960-61, The Werthers in America-Four Generations and their Descendants, 1987; A B-Tour of Britain, 1986, (Fletcher M. Sisson) Wooden Shoes, Irish Eyes; contbr. articles on fund raising to mags. Mem. New Eng. Hist. Geneal. Soc. (bd. dirs.), N.Y. Geneal. Biographical Soc., Moorings Club, Creek Club, PEO Sisterhood. Congregationalist. Adresss: 1855 Bay Rd #302 Vero Beach FL 32963-4396

PHILLIPS, MARJORIE RUTH, educator; b. N.Y.C., Nov. 9, 1932; d. Leo and Molly (Ringel) Birnbach; m. Bernard S. Phillips, Jan. 30, 1955; children: David Peter, Michael Lee. BS, Cornell U., 1954; MS, Boston U., 1967. Tchr. Beacon Hill Nursery, Boston, 1969-73; coord. early childhood edn. Minuteman Tech High Sch., Lecington, Mass., 1973-82, Middlesex C.C., Bedford, Mass., 1973-93; tchr. sci. Bailey Internat. Sch., Lowell (Mass.) Pub. Schs., 1988—. Democrat. Office: Bailey Internat Sch Campbell Dr Lowell MA 01831

PHILLIPS, MARRISE MASON, clinical research coordinator; b. York, S.C., Sept. 28, 1946; d. George T.C. and Terether Ella Mae (Stowe) Mason; m. George Ray Phillips, Sept. 5, 1970; children: Adrian Masonray, Persephone Dionne. ADN, Ctrl. Piedmont C.C., 1969; BSN, Wingate Coll., 1988. RN, N.C.; cert. clin. rsch. coord. Staff nurse pediat. ICU Carolinas Med. Ctr., Charlotte, N.C., 1969-70, staff nurse gen. pediat., 1970-73, nurse mgr. gen. pediat., 1973-82, nurse mgr. adolescent unit, 1982-85, nurse mgr. adult med. surg., 1985-91, diagnostics and therapeutics, 1985-91, clin. rsch. coord., 1991—; Author: (manual) Diagnostics & Therapeutics Patient Education, 1990; co-author: (manual) CMC Nursing Quality Assurance Program, 1991. Mem. Dermatology Nurses Assn. (pres. N.C. chpt. S.E. region 1995—), Soc. for Clin. Trials, Rsch. Coords. Network, Assn. Clin. Pharmacology, HPC Support Group, Chi Eta Phi. Democrat. Baptist. Home: 5111 Caravel Ct Charlotte NC 28215-1501

PHILLIPS, MARY KATHLEEN ELIZABETH, counselor; b. Muskegon, Mich., July 29, 1968; d. Robert Charles and Mary June (Paauwe) Packer; m. Matthew Phillips, July 12, 1991. BS, Western Mich. U., 1990; MEd, The Citadel, 1993. Lic. profl. counselor, Mich.; credentialed clin. counselor, S.C. Counselor West Mich. Alcoholism Therapy Svcs., Muskegon, 1990-91; mental health counselor Charter Hosp. of Charleston, S.C., 1991-92; clin. counselor Berkeley County, Moncks Corner, S.C., 1992-94; assoc./pvt. practice Grand Rapids, Mich., 1994-96; vocat./social worker Novacare Outpatient Rehab., Grand Rapids, 1995-96; assoc./pvt. practice Therapy Ctr., Grand Rapids, 1996—; clin. dir./program dir. West Mich. Therapy Svcs., Muskegon, 1996—; cons./counselor Caladonia (Mich.) Mid. Sch., 1996—. Vol. Therapy Dogs Internat., Charleston, 1993-94, Kent County Humane Soc., Grand Rapids, 1994—, AIDS Resource Ctr., Grand Rapids, 1994, ARC, 1996—; bd. dirs. March of Dimes, Muskegon. Mem. ACA, Am. Mental Health Counselors Assn., Mich. Counseling Assn., Nat. Assn. Alcohol/Drug Abuse Counselors, Mich. Assn. Alcohol/Drug Abuse Counselors, Exch. Club (Muskegon). Office: Therapy Center 2851 Michigan NE Grand Rapids MI 49506 also: 130 East Apple Ave Muskegon MI 49442

PHILLIPS, MAXINE E., editor; b. Wilkes-Barre, Pa., May 25, 1947; d. William Cornelius and Mary Catherine (Savine) P.; m. Thomas W. Roderick, May 2, 1981; children: Emma Rose, Anne Marie. BA, Junita Coll., 1967; MA, Syracuse U., 1969. Asst. editor Mental Hygiene Nat. Assn. for Mental Health, N.Y.C., 1969-71; cons. pub. info. and conf. dept. Child Welfare League Am., N.Y.C., 1971-76, dir. pub. info. and conf. dept., 1976-78; mng. editor Dem. Left Dem. Socialist Organizing Com., N.Y.C., 1978-81; orgn. dir. Dem. Socialists of Am., N.Y.C., 1981-83, exec. dir., 1984-85; mng. editor Dissent Mag., N.Y.C., 1986—. Author: Crime and the Law, 1981, revised, 1994; mem. adv. editl. bd. Christianity and Crisis mag., 1984-94, Dem. Left, 1985—; contbr. articles to profl. jours. Organizer Village Friends of Welfare Rights, N.Y.C., 1970; active Dem. County Com., N.Y.C., 1970; co-chairperson Religion and Socialism Com. of N.Y. Dem. Socialist Assn., 1984; moderator Judson Meml. Ch., N.Y.C., 1993-95. Mem. ACLU, NOW, Nat. Writers Union. Baptist. Home and Office: 536 W 111 Apt 37 New York NY 10025

PHILLIPS, PAMELA KIM, lawyer; b. San Diego, Feb. 23, 1958; d. John Gerald and Nancy Kimiko (Tabuchi) Phillips; m. R. Richard Zanghetti, Sept. 16, 1989. BA cum laude, The Am. U., 1978; JD, Georgetown U., 1982. Bar: N.Y. 1983, U.S. Dist. Ct. (so. dist.) N.Y. 1983, Fla. 1994, U.S. Dist. Ct. (mid. dist.) Fla. 1994. Assoc. Curtis, Mallet-Prevost, Colt & Mosle, N.Y.C., 1982-84; assoc. LeBoeuf, Lamb, Greene & MacRae, N.Y.C., 1984-90, ptnr., 1991—. Mng. editor The Tax Lawyer, Georgetown U. Law Sch., Washington, 1980-81. Coun. mem. The Fresh Air Fund, 1991-94. Am. Univ. scholar, Washington, 1976-78. Mem. ABA, Women's Bar Assn., Bar Assn. of City of N.Y. (sec. young lawyers com. 1987-89, chmn. 1989-91, second century com. 1990-93, banking law com. 1991-94), N.Y. Athletic Club, Jacksonville Bar Assn., The River Club. Democrat. Roman Catholic. Home: 108 Putters Way Ponte Vedra Beach FL 32082-2580 Office: LeBoeuf Lamb Greene & MacRae 125 W 55th St New York NY 10019-5369 also: 50 N Laura St Ste 2800 Jacksonville FL 32202-3656

PHILLIPS, PATRICIA ANNA, educator; b. Hutchinson, Kans., Mar. 19, 1962; d. Hugh William and Mary Pauline (Smith) P. AA, Hutchinson C.C., 1982; BA, Sch. of the Ozarks, 1985; MEd, Drury Coll., 1994. Tchr. high sch. sci. Pierce City (Mo.) R-6 Sch. Dist., 1985-94, 95—, Purdy (Mo.) R-2 Sch. Dist., 1994-95; mem. adv. bd. Regional Profl. Devel. Com., Springfield, Mo., 1996—; chair Profl. Devel. Com., Pierce City, 1994—. Mem. AAUW, ASCD, NEA (local pres., dist. chair, state women's issues com., state by-laws com.), Nat. Sci. Tchrs. Assn., Mo. NEA (govt. rels. team 1996—), Pierce City C. of C. Democrat. Home: 1416 N Central Monett MO 65708 Office: Pierce City High Sch 300 Myrtle Pierce City MO 65723

PHILLIPS, PATRICIA JEANNE, retired school administrator, consultant; b. Amarillo, Miss., Jan. 13, 1935; d. William Macon and Mary Ann (Cawthon) Patrick; m. William Henry Phillips, June 22, 1962; 1 child, Mary Jeanne. BA, Millsaps Coll., 1954; MA, Vanderbilt/Peabody U., 1957; EdD, U. So. Miss., 1978. Tchr. Jackson (Miss.) Pub. Schs., 1954-73, prin., 1973-75, asst. prin., 1975-77; dir. ednl. program Eden Prairie (Minn.) # 272, 1977-80; dir. elem. edn. Meridian (Miss.) Pub. Schs., 1980-91, asst. supt. curriculum, 1991, ret., 1991; prof. Miss. Coll., Clinton, part-time 1977, Miss. State U., Meridian, 1981-95; ednl. cons. in field. Co-author: (testing practice) Test Taking Tactics, 1987; contbr. articles to profl. jours. pres. Meridian Symphony Orch., 1987; v.p. Meridian Coun. Arts, 1986; bd. dirs. Meridian Art Mus. Named Boss of Yr., Meridian Secretarial Assn., 1985, Arts Education of Yr., Meridian Coun. Arts, 1991; recipient Excellence award Pub. Edn. Form, 1993. Mem. ASCD, Miss. ASCD, Miss. Assn. Women (pres.), Rotary, Phi Kappa Alpha, Phi Delta Kappa (pres. 1986-87), Alpha Delta Kappa Gamma (pres. 1962). Republican. Methodist. Home: 322 51st St Meridian MS 39305-2013 Office: Miss State Univ Meridian Campus 1000 Highway 19 S Meridian MS 39301-8205

PHILLIPS, SANDRA ALLEN, primary school educator; b. Newport News, Va., Mar. 10, 1943; d. Cecil Lamar and Mary (Schenk) Allen. BS, Appalachian State U., Boone, N.C., 1965; MEd, U. N.C., Charlotte, 1990. Tchr. Rockwell (N.C.) Elem. Sch., 1964-65, Granite Quarry (N.C.) Elem. Sch., 1965-68, Lillian Black Elem. Sch., Spring Lake, N.C., 1970, Berryhill Elem. Sch., Charlotte, N.C., 1970-71, 77—; tchr. J.C. Roe Sch., Wilmington, N.C., 1974-76, mem. tchr. adv. coun., 1995-96; elected to tchr.'s adv. coun. Charlotte Mecklenburg Schs., 1995-96, 96-97. Named Tchr. of Yr., Berryhill Elem. Sch., 1989. Mem. Profl. Educators N.C., Classroom Tchrs. Assn. Office: Berryhill Elem Sch 10501 Walkers Ferry Rd Charlotte NC 28208-9721

PHILLIPS, SUSAN DIANE, secondary school educator; b. Shelbyville, Ky., Aug. 28, 1955; d. James William and Catherine Elizabeth (Jones) P. B of Music Edn., Eastern Ky. U., 1977; postgrad., U. Ky., 1987. Tchr. music Breckinridge County Schs., Hardinsburg, Ky., 1978, Perry County Schs., Hazard, Ky., 1980-83, Music on the Move, Louisville, 1985-86, Cooter (Mo.) R-4 Sch., 1987-90, Lewis County High Sch., Vanceburg, Ky., 1990—; staff-cavalcade of bands Ky. Derby Festival, Louisville, 1984-86. Dir. Simpsonville (Ky.) United Meth. Ch. Handbell Choirs, 1985-86. Named Ky. Colonel Gov. Commonwealth of Ky., 1979. Mem. Nat. Band Assn., Am. Choral Dirs. Assn., Ky. Educators Assn., Ky. Music Educators Assn., Music Educators Nat. Conf. Office: Lewis County High Sch Lions Ln Vanceburg KY 41179

PHILLIPS, SUSAN MEREDITH, financial economist, former university administrator; b. Richmond, Va., Dec. 23, 1944; d. William G. and Nancy (Meredith) P. BA in Math., Agnes Scott Coll., 1967; MS in Fin. and Ins., La. State U., 1971, PhD in Fin. and Economics, 1973. Asst. prof. La. State U., 1973-74, U. Iowa, 1974-78; Brookings Econ. Policy fellow, 1976-77; econ. fellow Directorate of Econ. and Policy Rsch., SEC, 1977-78; assoc. prof. fin. dept. U. Iowa, 1978-83, assoc. v.p. fin. and univ. svcs., 1979-81; commr. Commodity Futures Trading Commn., 1981-83, chmn., 1983-87; prof. fin. dept., v.p. fin. and univ. svcs. U. Iowa, Iowa City, 1987-91; bd. govs. Fed. Res. Bd., Washington, 1991—. Author (with J. Richard Zecher): The SEC and the Public Interest; contbr. articles in field to profl. jours. Office: Fed Res System 20th Constitution St NW Washington DC 20551

PHILLIPS, TERESA LEIGH, human resources professional; b. Roanoke, Va., Mar. 31, 1966; d. Thomas E. and Sheila A. (Muse) Brown. Student, Mary Baldwin Coll. Sales tng. developer MCI, Arlington, Va., 1992-93; tng. mgr. MCI, Memphis, 1993-94; HRD tng. mgr. HRD/MCI, Arlington, Va., 1994—; trainer Lifeskills, Memphis, 1995. With U.S. Army, 1984-86. Mem. ASTD, Delta Adult Literary Coun. Democrat. Baptist. Office: MCI 601 S 12th St Arlington VA 22204

PHILLIPS HUGHES, ANDREA JOAN, school administrator, sales consultant; b. East St. Louis, Ill.; d. Bennie Thomas Phillips and Eddie Mae (Cushman) Phillips Gueno; m. Willie G. Hughes, July 9, 1988. BSBA, So. Ill. U., 1973, MS in Bus. Edn., 1975; Vocat. Edn. Specialist, U. Ill., 1980. Cert. math. thcr., Ohio, Ill., Md., Mo.; cert. adminstr., Ill., Md.; cert. bus. tchr., Mo. Computer programmer Krey Packing Co., St. Louis, 1965-70; tchr. bus. edn. Sch. Dist. # 189, East St. Louis, 1970-75; program coord. Housing Authority, East St. Louis, 1975-79; tchr. math. Sch. Dist. # 189, East St. Louis, 1979-88; tchr. math. Prince George's County Pub. Schs., Upper Marlboro, Md., 1989-93, adminstr., 1993—. Vice chairperson Prince George's County Black Rep. Coun., 1990-92; chief election judge Bd. Election, Prince George's County, 1988—. Mem. NAACP (exec. bd. dirs.), ASCD, Nat. Assn. Secondary Prins., Nat. Coun. Math. Tchrs., Nat. Assn. Club Women, Boys and Girls (life, state membership chairperson), Md. Initiative for Leadership in Edn., Prin.'s Ctr. Harvard Grad. Sch. Edn., Alpha Delta Kappa (Md. dist. II sec.-treas. 1994—). Office: Bowie HS 15200 Annopolis Rd Bowie MD 20715

PHILLIS, MARILYN HUGHEY, artist; b. Kent, Ohio, Feb. 1, 1927; d. Paul Jones and Helen Margaret (Miller) Hughey; m. Richard Waring Phillis, Mar. 19, 1949; children: Diane E., Hugh R., Randall W. Student, Kent State U., 1945; BS, Ohio State U., 1949. Chemist Battelle Meml. Inst., Columbus, Ohio, 1949-53; sec. Lakewood Park Cemetery, Rocky River, Ohio, 1972-75; illustrator periodical Western Res. Hist. Mag., Garrettsville, Ohio, 1974-78; illustrator book AAUW, Piqua, Ohio, 1976; art instr. Edison State C.C., Piqua, 1976; watermedia instr. Springfield (Ohio) Mus. Art, 1976-84; juror art exhbns. state and nat. art group, 1980—; painting instr. state and nat. orgns., 1980—; dir. Nat. Creativity Seminars, Ohio Watercolor Soc., Fairborn, 1993-95, 97; lectr. art healing Wheeling (W.Va.) Jesuit Coll., 1994-96. Author: Watermedia Techniques for Releasing the Creative Spirit, 1992; contbr. articles and illustrations to profl. jours.; one-woman shows include Stifel Fine Art Ctr., Wheeling, W.Va., Springfield (Ohio) Art Mus., Zanesville (Ohio) ARt Ctr., Cleve. Inst. Music, Columbus Mus. Art, Cheekwood Mus. of Art, Bot. Hall, Nashville; exhibited in group shows at No. Ariz. U. Art Mus., Flagstaff, 1993, Taiwan Art Edn. Inst., Taipei, 1994; represented in permanent collections at Springfield Mus. Art, Ohio Watercolor Soc., also corp. collections. Gallery dir. Green St. United Meth. Ch., Piqua, 1972-75; pres. Rocky River (Ohio) H.S. PTA, 1971; chmn. Cmty. Health and Humor Program, Wheeling, 1992. Recipient First awards Watercolor West, riverside, Calif., 1990, Hudson Soc. award Nat. Collage Soc., 1995, Art Masters award Am. Artist Mag., 1996. Mem. Internat. Soc. Study of Subtle Energies and Energy Medicine (art cons. sci. jour. 1992-96, art and healing workshop 1995), Am. Watercolor Soc. (dir. 1991-93, newsletter editor 1992—, Osborne award 1975), Soc. Layerists in Multi-Media (nat. v.p. 1988-93), Ohio Watercolor Soc. (sec. 1979-82, v.p. 1982-89, pres. 1990-96, Gold medal, Best of Show 1993), Nat. Watercolor Soc., Int. Noetic Sci., West Ohio Watercolor Soc. (pres. 1979-80, 2d award 1982), Allied Artists N.Y., W.Va. Watercolor Soc. (First award 1993), Ky. Watercolor Soc., Ga. Watercolor Soc. Home and Office: Phillis Studio 72 Stamm Cir Wheeling WV 26003-5549

PHINNEY, JEAN SWIFT, psychology educator; b. Princeton, N.J., Mar. 12, 1933; d. Emerson H. and Anne (Davis) Swift; m. Bernard O. Phinney, Dec. 11, 1965; children: Peter, David. BA, Mass. Wellesley Coll., 1955; MA, UCLA, 1969, PhD, 1973. Asst. prof. psychology Calif. State U., L.A., 1977-81, assoc. prof. psychology, 1981-86, prof. psychology, 1986—. Editor: Children's Ethnic Socialization, 1987; asst. editor Jour. Adolescence; contbr. articles to profl. jours. NIH grantee. Mem. APA, Soc. for Rsch. in Child Devel., Soc. for Rsch. in Adolescence, Internat. Soc. for Study of Behavior Devel. Office: Calif State U Dept Psychology 5151 State University Dr Los Angeles CA 90032

PHIPPS, LYNNE BRYAN, interior architect, clergywoman, parent educator; b. Chapel Hill, N.C., Sept. 23, 1964; d. Floyd Talmadge and Sandra Patricia (McLester) Bryan; m. Thomas Otey Phipps, July 18, 1985. BFA, RISD, 1986, B Interior Architecture, 1987; cert. in parent edn., Wheelock Coll., Boston, 1989; postgrad., Andover Newton Theol. Sem., 1991—. Nat. cert. interior arch. Apprentice Thompson Ventulett Stainback, Atlanta, 1983-85; jr. designer Flansberg & Assocs., Boston, 1986-87; sr. designer, prin. Innovative Designs, Duxbury, Mass., 1986—; parent educator, pres. Parenting Puzzle, 1990—; parent educator Families First, Cambridge, Mass.; youth min. St. Andrew's Episcopal Ch., Hanover, Mass., 1992-95; youth and family min. St. Stephen's Episcopal Ch., Cohasset, Mass., 1993—; guest lectr., jurist Auburn (Ala.) U., 1988, RISD, Providence, 1990; assoc. prof. Mass. Bay C.C., Wellesley, 1987-88; guest jurist Wentworth U., Boston, 1988-89; guest lectr. Architectural and Family Issues; guest jurist U. Memphis, 1995. Designer furniture. Mem. Internat. Interior Design Assn., Assn. Parent Educators, Jr. League Boston. Office: Innovative Designs The Parenting Puzzle 18 Bayview Rd Duxbury MA 02332-5009

PIAZZA, MARGUERITE, opera singer, actress, entertainer; b. New Orleans, May 6, 1926; d. Albert William and Michaela (Piazza) Luft; m. William J. Condon, July 15, 1953 (dec. Mar. 1968); children: Gregory, James (dec.), Shirley, William J., Marguerite P., Anna Becky; m. Francis Harrison Bergtholdt, Nov. 8, 1970. MusB, Loyola U., New Orleans; MusM, La. State U.; MusD (hon.), Christian Bros. Coll., 1973; LHD honoris causa, Loyola U., Chgo., 1975. Singer N.Y.C. Ctr. Opera, 1948, Met. Opera Co., 1950; TV artist, regular singing star Your Show of Shows NBC, 1950-54; entertainer various supper clubs Cotillion Room, Hotel Pierre, N.Y.C., 1954, Las Vegas, Los Angeles, New Orleans, San Francisco, 1956—; ptnr. Sound Express Music Pub. Co., Memphis, 1987—; bd. dirs. Cemrel, Inc. Appeared as guest performer on numerous mus. TV shows. Nat. crusade chmn. Am. Cancer Soc., 1971; founder, bd. dirs. Marguerite Piazza Gala for the Benefit of St. Jude's Hosp., 1976; bd. dirs. Memphis Opera Co., World Literacy Found., NCCJ; v.p., life bd. dirs. Memphis Symphony Orch.; nat. chmn. Soc. for Cure Epilepsy. Decorated Mil. and Hospittaler Order of St. Lazarus of Jerusalem; recipient svc. award Chgo. Heart Assn., 1956, svc. award Fedn. Jewish Philanthropies of N.Y., 1956, Sesquicentennial medal Carnegie Hall, St. Martin De Porres award So. Dominicans, 1994; named Queen of Memphis, Memphis Cotton Carnival, 1973, Person of Yr., La. Coun. for Performing Arts, 1975, Woman of Yr., Nat. Am. Legion, Woman of Yr., Italian-Am. Soc. Mem. Nat. Speakers Assn., Woman's Exchange, Memphis Country Club, Memphis Hunt and Polo Club, New Orleans Country Club, Summit Club, Beta Sigma Omicron, Phi Beta. Roman Catholic. Home: #301 Park Pl 5400 Park Ave Apt 301 Memphis TN 38119-3639

PICA, MARISSA ANN, critical care nurse, administrator; b. Waterbury, Conn., Feb. 25, 1961; d. Vincent John and Jennie (Natale) P. BSN, Mount St. Mary Coll., 1983; MSN, Hunter Coll., 1991. RN, N.Y.; cert. CCRN, CNAA; cert. BCLS. Staff nurse The N.Y. Hosp. Medicine, N.Y.C., 1983-85; staff nurse, sr. staff nurse The N.Y. Hosp.-Med. ICU, N.Y.C., 1985-88, nurse mgr., 1988-92; asst. dir. nursing critical care The N.Y. Hosp., N.Y.C., 1992—. Author AACN Newsletter, 1993-94; poster presenter in field. Mem. AACN (corr. sec. N.Y.C. chpt. 1992-93, pres.-elect 1993-94, pres. 1994-95, dir. 1995—), Soc. Critical Care Medicine, Am. Orgn. Nurse Execs., MENSA. Office: The NY Hosp Cornell Med Ctr 525 E 68th St New York NY 10021-4873

PICCOLO, KATHLEEN ANN, language educator; b. Harrisburg, Pa., June 17, 1948; d. Charles Earl Brubaker and Marian Jeanette (Hoffman) Wolfe; m. Joseph Vincent Piccolo, Sept. 22, 1968; children: Julie Marie, Jodi Louise, Joseph Kim. BA in English, Elizabethtown Coll., 1981; MA in English, SUNY Albany, 1987. Tchr. elem., English Weare (N.H.) Sch. Dist., 1978-81; tchr. English St. John's Regional Sch., Concord, N.H., 1981-82; tchr. substitute Hoosic Valley (N.Y.) Sch. Dist., 1982-83; tchr. English Averill Park (N.Y.) H.S., 1983-86; tchr. English, social studies Jakarta (Indonesia) Internat. Sch., 1987-90; tchr. English Internat. Sch., Kuala Lumpur, Malaysia, 1990-92, Averill Park H.S., 1993—. Mem. Phi Delta Kappa. Roman Catholic. Home: 6 Cumo Rd Johnsonville NY 12094 Office: Averill Park HS Gettle Rd Averill Park NY 12018

PICKANDS, D. MORGAN, principal; b. Balt., Mar. 28, 1944; d. Richard Paul and Louise Helen (Thomas) Morgan; m. Harry E. Smith, Aug. 25, 1964 (dec. Sept. 1984); children: Jason Wesley Smith, Jill Lydia Smith Kahlenberg; m. James Pickands III, Mar. 9, 1991. BA, Moravian Coll., 1966; EdM, Temple U., 1990, postgrad., 1992. Cert. prin., Pa. Tchr. Cumberland Valley Sch. Dist., Mechanicsburg, Pa., 1966-71; tax preparer Beneficial Fin. Co., Carlisle, Pa., 1971-81; sr. sales cons. Mary Kay Cosmetics, Carlisle, Pa., 1981-88; fiscal asst. Cumberland County Mental Health, Carlisle, Pa., 1987-88; grad. asst. Temple U., Phila., 1989-92; elem. prin. Athens (Pa.) Area Sch. Dist., 1993-95. Foster parent Cumberland County, 1969-76; asst. dist. commr. Boy Scouts Am., Carlisle, 1974-85; auditor Tri-Valley United Way, Carlisle, 1985. Recipient Merit award Boy Scouts Am., 1982, Gift of Time award Am. Family Inst. and Athens Area Sch. Dist., 1994, 95. Mem. Nat. Elem. and Secondary Prin. Assn., Pa. Elem. and Secondary Prin. Assn., Phi Delta Kappa. Republican. Episcopalian.

PICKARD, AGNES LOUISE, small business executive; b. St. Albans, Maine, Feb. 25, 1933; d. Walter S. Stone and Louise Allen; m. James A. Pickard, Apr. 15, 1950 (dec. June 1971); children: Asa, Jamie, James. Grad., Milo High Sch., 1949. Mgr. Milo (Maine) Hotel, 1947-64; mgr., owner Milo Sport Shop, 1957-76; owner Pickard's Sport Shop, Brewer, Maine, 1976—; owner Dakin Sporting Goods, Brown Tackle Co. Recipient Grand Cross of Color, Rainbow for Girls, 1973, numerous sales awards Johnson Motors, Starcraft Boats, 1969-91. Mem. Order of Eastern Star (sec. Rebakah Lodge 1972, award 1976). Republican. Home and Office: 802 Wilson St Brewer ME 04412-1015

PICKARD, CAROLYN ROGERS, secondary school educator; b. Steubenville, Ohio, Dec. 13, 1945; d. Thomas Orlando and Alice Marie (Romick) Rogers; 1 child, Carri Alyce. BA, Fla. State U., 1967; AA, Stephens Coll., Columbia, Mo., 1965. Cert. English tchr., Fla. Tchr. English, chair dept. New World Sch. Arts, Dade County Pub. Schs., Miami, Fla., 1969—; sponsor jr. class; advisor yearbook; liason New World Sch. Arts. Vol. Shores Performing Arts Theater Soc. Recipient Tchr. of Yr. award North Miami Beach High Sch., 1982, Presdl. Scholars Tchr. of Excellence award, 1984. Mem. Nat. Coun. Tchrs. English, United Tchrs. Dade County, Delta Kappa Gamma. Home: 539 Catalonia Ave Coral Gables FL 33134-6532

PICKERING, SHELBIE JEAN, mortgage loan executive; b. Ellisville, Miss., Sept. 5, 1939; d. Robert Lee and Virgie Clyde (Shoemake) Smith; m. James Dale Pickering, Aug. 24, 1958; 1 child, James Stephen. BS in Bus. magna cum laude, William Carey Coll., 1990. Reg. mortgage underwriter; cert. appraisal reviewer. Bd. secretary Jones County Bd. Edn., Laurel, Miss., 1960-63; ins. underwriter Graves/Montgomery Ins. Agy., Laurel, 1963-65; office mgr. Kux Distributors, Laurel, 1965-66; adminstrv. asst. Gen. Electric, Bay St. Louis, Miss., 1966-71; mortgage loan officer Hancock Bank, Gulfport, Miss., 1971—; seminar leader Hancock Bank, Gulfport, 1988-92; panelist Miss. Mortgage Lenders, Jackson, 1988-91; cons. Equitrust Mortgage, Gulfport, 1987-88; Gulf Coast rep. Nat. Mortgage Lenders, Atlanta, 1978-91. Tutor Adult Literacy Progam of Gulfport, 1989-92; sponsor March of Dimes Walk-a-Thon, Gulfport, 1988-92. Mem. Miss. Gulf Coast Mortgage Lenders Assn. (bd. dirs. 1991-92), Nat. Assn. Reg. Mortgage Underwriters and Cert. Rev. Appraisers, Gulf Coast Bd. Realtors, Garden Park Hosp. Health Mgmt. Resources. Republican. Baptist. Office: Hancock Bank # 1 Hancock Plaza Gulfport MS 39501

PICKETT, BETTY HORENSTEIN, psychologist; b. Providence, R.I., Feb. 15, 1926; d. Isadore Samuel and Etta Lillian (Morrison) Horenstein; m. James McPherson Pickett, Mar. 10, 1952. A.B. magna cum laude, Brown U., 1945, Sc.M., 1947, Ph.D., 1949. Asst. prof. psychology U. Minn., Duluth, 1949-51; asst. prof. U. Nebr., 1951; lectr. U. Conn., 1952; profl. assoc. psychol. scis. Bio-Scis. Info. Exchange, Smithsonian Instn., Washington, 1953-58; exec. sec. behavioral scis. study sect. exptl. psychology study sect. div. research grants NIH, Washington, 1958-61; research cons. to mental health unit HEW, Boston, 1962-63; exec. sec. research career program NIMH, 1963-66, chief cognition and learning sect. div. extramural research program, 1966-68, dep. dir., 1968-74, dir. div. spl. mental health programs, 1974-75, acting dir. div. extramural research program, 1975-77; assoc. dir. for extramural and collaborative research program Nat. Inst. Aging, 1977-79; dep. dir. Nat. Inst. Child Health and Human Devel., Bethesda, Md., 1979-81; acting dir. Nat. Inst. Child Health and Human Devel., 1981-82, dir. Div. Rsch. Resources, 1982-88; mem. health scientist adminstr. panel CSC Bd. Examiners, 1970-76, 81-88; mem. coun. on grad. edn. Brown U. Grad. Sch., 1989-91. Contbr. articles to profl. jours. Mem. APA, Am. Psychol Soc., Psychonomic Soc., Assn. Women in Sci., AAAS, Phi Beta Kappa, Sigma Xi. Home: Morgan Bay Rd PO Box 198 Surry ME 04684-0198

PICKETT, CATHERINE, displaced women mentor, family therapist; b. Winslow, Ariz., May 30, 1953; d. Jack Roderick and Mary McLaws (Turley) P.; children: Rachael Kirsty Grogan, Ericka Edan Grogan. BA in Mgmt. of Human Resources, George Fox Coll., Newberg, Oreg., 1992; MA in Counseling Psychology, Western Evang. Sem., Tigard, Oreg., 1996. Pvt. practice mentoring displaced women, Portland, Oreg., 1996—. Democrat. Roman Catholic.

PICKLE BEATTIE, KATHERINE HAMNER, real estate agent; b. Henrico County, Va., Sept. 30, 1936; d. Laurance Davis and Susan (Mooers) Hamner; widowed 1969; children: Katherine Carter Beattie, Harry Canfield Beattie IV, Margaret Spotswood Beattie; m. Timothy L. Pickle, III, Dec. 29, 1989. Attended, Va. Commonwealth U. Pres. Varina Wood Products, Inc., Gloucester-Mathews County, 1969-75; real estate agt. Nat. Assn. Bd. Realtors, Gloucester-Mathews County, Richmond, Va., 1975—; pres. Varina Wood Products, Inc., 1969-75. Pres. George F. Baker PTA, 1970; v.p. Varina Women's Club, Henrico, Va., 1969-70; sec. Mathews Women's Club, 1992-94; mem. Rep. Women's Club; mem. Va. Mus. Fine Arts, Naples, Fla. Philharm. Ctr. for Arts com. of a thousand. Mem. DAR, Va. Lioins Club, King's Daus., Raleigh Tavern Soc., Colonial Williamsburg, Va. Mus. Fine Arts. Episcopalian. Home: PO Box 317 Gwynn VA 23066-0317

PICKOVER, BETTY ABRAVANEL, retired executive legal secretary, civic volunteer; b. N.Y.C., Apr. 20, 1920; d. Albert and Sultana (Rousso) Abravanel; m. Bernard Builder, Apr. 6, 1941 (div. 1962); children: Ronald, Stuart; m. William Pickover, Aug. 23, 1970 (dec. Nov. 1983). Student, Taft Evening Ctr., 1961-70. Sec. U.S. Treasury Dept., Washington, 1942-43; exec. legal sec. various attys., Bronx, N.Y., 1956-70; exec. legal sec. various attys., Yonkers, N.Y., 1971-83, ret., 1983. Chair Uniongram Sisterhood of Temple

Emanu-El, Yonkers, N.Y., 1975—, Honor Roll, 1975—, v.p. 1995-96; sr. citizen cmty. leader Yonkers Officer for Aging, 1984—, Westchester County Sr. Adv. Bd., White Plains, N.Y., 1989-92; v.p. Mayor's Cmty. Rels. Com. of Yonkers, 1985—, historian, photographer, 1988—; v.p. Mayor's cmty. Rels. com. Yonkers, 1995; mem. adv. coun. Westchester County Office Aging Sr., 1993—; bd. legislators task force sr. citizens Westchester County, 1995-96; Mayor Silver City Coun. Yonkers, 1989; mem. Mayor's adv. coun. sr. citizens, 1990. Recipient Appreciation cert. Westchester County, 1992, Pres. Coun., City of Yonkers, 1992, Merit cert., 1993, Cmty. Svc. award Mayor, City of Yonkers, 1995, 96, John E. Andrus Meml. Vol. award, 1995, Appreciation cert. Westchester County Exec., 1993, 94, Merit cert. N.Y. State Senator, 1995, Merit cert. N.Y. State Senator, 1994, Proclamation Mayor of Yonkers, 1985, 89, 92, (2) Awards U.S. Ho. of Reps., 1992, Woman of Excellence award Yonkers C. of C., 1993, Awards Mayors of Yonkers, 1985-96, awards N.Y. State Senator and Assemblyman 1987-96, Resolution City of Yonkers, 1993, Cert. of Appreciation Westchester County Bd. of Legislators, 1996; nominee Pres.'s Svc. award, 1995; named to Sr. Citizen Hall of Fame, 1992. Democrat. Jewish. Home: 200 Valentine Ln Yonkers NY 10705-3608

PIECH, MARGARET ANN, mathematics educator; b. Bridgewater, N.S., Can., Apr. 6, 1942; d. Frederick Cecil and Margaret Florence (Laschinger) Garrett; m. Kenneth Robert Piech, June 19, 1965; children: Garrett Andrew, Marjorie Ann. BA, Mt. Allison U., Sackville, N.B., Can., 1962; PhD, Cornell U., 1967. Asst. prof. SUNY, Buffalo, 1967-72, assoc. prof., 1972-78, prof. math., 1978—; cons. NSF, Washington, 1980-81, Aspen Analytics, Buffalo, 1986—; v.p. Seventy Niagara Svcs., 1990—. Contbr. articles to profl. jours. Woodrow Wilson fellow, 1962-63; grantee NSF, 1976-85, U.S. Army Rsch. Office, 1985-89. Mem. IEEE, Am. Math. Soc., Assn. Computing Machinery, Greater Yellowstone Coalition, Henry's Fork Found. Office: SUNY Diefendorf Hall Buffalo NY 14214

PIECH, MARY LOU ROHLING, medical psychotherapist, consultant; b. Elgin, Ill., Jan. 20, 1927; d. Louis Bernard and Charlotte (Wylie) Rohling; m. Raymond C. Piech, Feb. 12, 1950 (dec. Feb. 1985); 1 child, Christine Piech. BA, U. Ill., 1948, MA, 1953; postgrad., Ill. Inst. Tech., 1966-68, Union Inst., 1991-96. Cert. clin. psychologist, Ill.; diplomate Am. Bd. Med. Psychotherapy. Instr. psychology Elmhurst (Ill.) Coll., 1955-61; asst. prof. psychology North Cen. Coll., Naperville, Ill., 1961-67, Elmhurst (Ill.) Coll., 1968-81; med. psychotherapist Shealy Pain & Health Rehab. Ctr., LaCrosse, Wis., 1977-82, Shealy Inst. Comprehensive Health Care, Springfield, Mo., 1982—. Author, editor: (video series) Mental Health, 1982, (audio tape series) Holistic Mental Health, 1983. Recipient award Lilly Found., Elmhurst Coll., Shealy Inst., 1977. Fellow Am. Bd. Med. Psychotherapy; mem. APA, N.Am. Soc. Adlerian Psychology, Assn. Psychol. Type (life), Phi Beta Kappa, Phi Kappa Phi, Mortar Bd. Office: Shealy Inst 1328 E Evergreen St Springfield MO 65803-4400

PIECUCH, PAMELA GAYLE, systems operator/coordinator; b. Chgo., Aug. 1, 1954; d. Leon Benjamin and Loretta Mae (Skronz) P. BA magna cum laude, Northeastern U., Chgo., 1987. From pension benefit processor to adminstrv. asst. Structural Ironworkers Pension Fund, Chgo., 1976-89; computer systems operator, coord. SIW, Chgo., 1989—. Bd. dirs. Huntington Commons Assn., Mt. Prospect, Ill., 1989; outreach com. St. Michaels Orthodox Ch., Niles, Ill., 1993—. Mem. Phi Alpha Theta (historian 1987-89), Pi Gamma Mu, Alpha Chi. Orthodox Christian.

PIEL, CAROLYN FORMAN, pediatrician, educator; b. Birmingham, Ala., Oct. 18, 1918; d. James R. and Mary Elizabeth (Dortch) Forman; m. John Joseph Piel, Aug. 3, 1951; children: John Joseph, Mary Dortch, Elizabeth Forman, William Scott. BA, Agnes Scott Coll., 1940; MS, Emory U., 1943; MD, Washington U., St. Louis, 1946. Diplomate Am. Bd. Pediatrics (examiner 1973-88, pres. 1986-87); diplomate Am. Bd. Pediatric Nephrology. Intern Phila. Gen. Hosp., 1946-47; resident Phila. Children's Hosp., 1947-49; fellow Cornell U. Med. Sch., N.Y.C., 1949-51; from instr. to assoc. clin. prof. Stanford U. Sch. Medicine, San Francisco, 1951-59; from asst. prof. to prof. Sch. Medicine, U. Calif., San Francisco, 1959-89, emeritus prof., 1989—. Author, co-author research articles in field. Bd. mem. San Francisco Home Health Service, 1977-83. Emeritus mem. Soc. for Pediatric Research, Am. Pediatric Soc., Am. Soc. for Pediatric Nephrology, Am. Soc. Nephrology, Western Soc. for Pediatric Nephrology (pres. 1960). Democrat. Presbyterian. Home: 2164 Hyde St San Francisco CA 94109-1701 Office: U Calif PO Box 748 San Francisco CA 94143

PIERCE, CAROL JEAN, freelance writer, photographer; b. Allentown, Pa., July 7, 1946; d. Russel and Viola (Meck) Brewer; m. Wayne Thomas Pierce, June 15, 1972; children: Alan, Wendy, Russel, Benjamin. BS in Elem. Edn., Kutztown U., 1968; postgrad., Moravian Coll., 1977-81, Writers Dig Sch., Cin., 1985-87. Cert. elem. edn. tchr., Pa. Elem. sch. tchr. Souderton (Pa.) Area Sch. Dist., 1968-84; instr. Williamsport Area C.C., Wellsboro, Pa., 1984-85; ch. sec. Trinity United Presbyn. Ch., Tioga, Pa., 1985-88; crew leader U.S. Dept. Commerce, Wilkes-Barre, Pa., 1988-89; freelance writer various newspapers Tioga County, Pa., 1987-95; computer cons. New Covenant Acad., Mansfield, Pa., 1991—. Contbr. articles to newspapers, mags., and bus. jours. Bd. dirs. ARC, Wellsboro, 1991—; sec. Tioga Grange # 1223, 1988-91; publicity chairperson Pa. State Laurel Festival, Wellsboro, 1986-91; treas. Presbyn. Women of Presbyery Northumberland, 1994-96; sec. First Presbyn. Women Wellsboro, 1994-95. Home: RR 2 Box 5 Tioga PA 16946-9504

PIERCE, CATHERINE MAYNARD, history educator; b. York County, Va., Oct. 11, 1918; d. Edward Walker Jr. and Cassie Cooke (Sheppard) Maynard; m. Frank Marion Pierce Jr., Oct. 4, 1940 (dec. 1974); children: Frank Marion III, Bruce Maynard. BS in Sec. Edn., Longwood Coll., Farmville, Va., 1939; postgrad., Coll. William and Mary, Williamsburg, 1948, 58, 68. Tchr. York County Pub. Schs., Va., 1939-45; instr. Chesapeake (Va.) pub. schs., 1946-49, 57-74; cons. Vol. Svcs., Williamsburg, Va., 1975—. Author audio-visual hist. narratives for use in pub. schs., 1965-86. Organizer The Chapel at Kingsmill on the James, Williamsburg, 1987—, chmn. governing bd., 1987—. Mem. DAR (regent Williamsburg chpt. 1980-83). Baptist. Address: Kingsmill on the James 4 Bray Wood Rd Williamsburg VA 23185-5504

PIERCE, DEBORAH MARY, educational administrator; b. Charleston, W. Va.; d. Edward Ernest and Elizabeth Anne (Trent) P.; m. Henry M. Armetta, Sept. 1, 1967 (div. 1981); children: Rosse Matthew Armetta, Stacey Elizabeth Pierce. Student, U. Tenn., 1956-59, Broward Jr. Coll., 1968-69; BA, San Francisco State U., 1977. Cert. elem. tchr., Calif. Pub. relations assoc. San Francisco Internat. Film Festival, 1965-66; account exec. Stover & Assocs., San Francisco, 1966-67; tchr. San Francisco Archdiocese Office of Cath. Schs., 1980-87; part-time tchr. The Calif. Study, Inc. (formerly Tchr's Registry), Tiburon, Calif., 1988—; pvt. practice as paralegal San Francisco, 1989—; tchr. Jefferson Sch. Dist., Daly City, Calif., 1989-91. Author: (with Frances Spatz Leighton) I Prayed Myself Slim, 1960. Pres. Mothers Alone Working, San Francisco, 1966, PTA, San Francisco, 1979, Parent Tchr. Student Assn., San Francisco, 1984; apptd. Calif. State Bd. Welfare Cmty. Rels. Com., 1964-66; block organizer SAFE, 1996; active feminist movement. Named Model of the Yr. Modeling Assn. Am., 1962. Mem. People Med. Soc., Assn. for Rsch. and Enlightenment, A Course in Miracles, Commonwealth Club Calif, Angel Club San Francisco. Democrat. Mem. Unity Christ Ch. Home: 1479 48th Ave Apt 2 San Francisco CA 94122-2832

PIERCE, ELIZABETH GAY, civic worker; b. N.Y.C., Mar. 26, 1907; d. Martin and Julia (Stone) Gay; AB, Barnard Coll., 1929; m. William Curtis Pierce, June 19, 1929; children: Martin Gay, Elizabeth Gay Pierce Fuchs, Josiah. Vol. worker Boston City Hosp., 1929-30, Community Service Soc., N.Y.C., 1931-32; mem. dependent children's sect. Welfare Council, N.Y.C., 1939-40; chmn. house com. North Shore Holiday House, Huntington, L.I., 1944, pres., 1945; co-chmn. thrift shop com. Knickerbocker Hosp., N.Y.C., 1957-64; mem. exec. com. of women's com. Legal Aid Soc., N.Y.C., 1958-59; mem. Women's Aux. Knickerbocker Hosp. (exec. com. 1960-64); adv. trustee Maine Citizens for Hist. Preservation, 1983-87; trustee Jones Mus. Ceramics and Glass, 1985-89. Mem. Soc. Colonial Dames in State N.Y. (bd. mgrs., 1962-67, corr. sec. N.Y. 1965-67, pres. 1967-70), Nat. Soc. Colonial Dames Am. (pres. 1972-76, nat. pres.), Soc. for Preservation New Eng. Antiquities (Maine council, former chmn. Marrett House, exec. com.), Mayflower Soc. N.Y. (sec. 1985-88), Daus. Founders and Patriots, Nat. Grange (mem. exec. com.). Episcopalian. Club: Colony, Ch. (N.Y.C.). Home: R1 Box 5140 West Baldwin ME 04091

PIERCE, ELLEN IRENE, language educator; b. Battle Creek, Mich., Feb. 4, 1944; d. Robert James Pratley and Melma Caroline (Harvey) Rubel; m. Donald Eugene Pierce. BA, We. Mich. U., 1966, postgrad., 1967-72. Cert. tchr. secondary, English, German, math. Tchr. Climax(Mich.)-Scotts H.S., 1966—. Recipient Tchr. of Yr. award Climax-Scotts Edn. Assn., 1987-88, Tchr. Advanced Placement English Tng. Stipend winner Upjohn Found. Mem. NEA, Nat. Coun. Tchrs. English, Mich. Edn. Assn., Kalamazoo County Edn. Assn. Office: Climax-Scotts HS 372 S Main St Climax MI 49034

PIERCE, HILDA (HILDA HERTA HARMEL), painter; b. Vienna, Austria; came to U.S., 1940; 1 child, Diana Rubin Daly. Student, Art Inst. of Chgo.; studied with Oskar Kokoschka, Salzburg, Austria. Art tchr. Highland Park (Ill.) Art Ctr., Sandburg Village Art Workshop, Chgo., Old Town Art Center, Chgo.; owner, operator Hilda Pierce Art Gallery, Laguna Beach, Calif., 1981-85; guest lectr. major art mus. and Art Tours in France, Switzerland, Austria, Italy; guest lectr. Russian river cruise and major art mus. St. Petersburg and Moscow, 1994. One-woman shows include Fairweather Hardin Gallery, Chgo., Sherman Art Gallery, Chgo., Marshall Field Gallery, Chgo.; exhibited in group shows at Old Orchard Art Festival, Skokie, Ill., Union League Club (awards), North Shore Art League (awards), ARS Gallery of Art Inst. of Chgo.; represented in numerous private and corporate collections; commissioned for all art work including monoprints, oils, and murals for Carnival Cruise Lines megaliner M.S. Fantasy, 1990, 17 murals for megaliner M.S. Imagination, 1995, 49 paintings for megaliner M.S. Imagination, 1995; contbr. articles to Chgo. Tribune Mag., American Artist Mag., Southwest Art Mag., SRA publs., others. Recipient Outstanding Achievement award in Field of Art for Citizen Foreign Birth Chgo. Immigrant's Svc. League. Mem. Arts Club of Chgo. Studio: PO Box 7390 Laguna Niguel CA 92607-7390

PIERCE, JANIS VAUGHN, insurance executive, consultant; b. Memphis, Dec. 23, 1934; d. Jesse Wynne and Dorothy Arnette (Lloyd) Vaughn; m. Gerald Swetnam Pierce, May 27, 1956; children: Ann Elizabeth Swetnam, John Willard. BA, U. Miss., 1956, MA, 1964. High sch. tchr., 1957-58; mem. faculty Memphis Univ. Sch., 1964-66, Memphis State U., 1968-75; agt. Aetna Life Ins. Co., Memphis, 1977-80, career supr., 1980—, mgr., 1983, supr. prime/career, 1984, chmn. Aetna Women's Task Force, 1980-85; coord. agy. tng. Specialist Union Cen. Life Ins. Co., Memphis, 1985-88, agt.; v.p., dir. Cons. System, Inc., bus. cons., 1975-84, pres., 1984—. Pres. Women's Resources Ctr., Memphis, 1974-77; sec. Tenn. chpt. Women's Polit. Caucus, 1975-76; bd. dirs., treas., mem. exec. com. Memphis YWCA, 1979—; mem. Memphis Area Transit Authority, 1982—, chmn. fin. and adminstrn. com., 1983—, chmn. bd. commn., 1990—; pres., bd. dirs. The Support Ctr. Memphis, 1986—, Support Ctrs. Am., 1987—; mem. Tenn. adv. com. U.S. Civil Rights Commn., 1980-85, steering com. Big Break, 1978; mem. adv. bd. Porter Leath Children's Ctr., 1984—, bd. dirs. 1986—; mem. planned giving com. Girl Scouts U.S., 1990—; mem. citizens adv. bd. St. Joseph Hosp., 1991—. Unvi. scholar U. Miss., 1952-56; named Aetna Regionnaire, 1977-82, First Yr. Top Achiever, 1977; mem. Leadership Memphis, 1981. Mem. United Daughters of the Confederacy (pres. Albert Sidney Johnston chpt. 1961), Million Dollar Roundtable, 1978, 79, Women Leaders Roundtable, Nat. Assn. Life Underwriters, Tenn. Life Underwriters Assn., Am. Pub. Transp. Assn. (bd. dirs. 1991—, governing bds. com. 1985—, sec. 1987-88, v.p. 1988-90, mem. task force transp. for the handicapped, 1987, pres. 1989, legis. com. 1985—, region III rep. 1991—), Women's Life Underwriters Conf. (bd. dirs., pres. 1985), Memphis Life Underwriters Assn. (bd. dirs. 1982, edn. chmn. 1982, pub. svc. com. 1983, law and legis. chmn. 1984, pres. 1986), Memphis PTA (coun. 1971-72), Memphis Soc. CLUs, LWV, AAUW, Mortar Bd. (regional coord. 1972-78), Memphis CLU Assn., C. of C. (amb. 1980), Alpha Lambda Delta, Sigma Delta Pi, Le Bonheur Club (bd. dir.), Memphis State U. Women's Club (pres. 1978). Republican. Episcopalian. Home: 1613 Lyttleton St Camden SC 29020-2906

PIERCE, LISA MARGARET, lecturer, product and market development manager; b. Nyack, N.Y., June 2, 1957; d. William Twining and Elizabeth P. BA with honors, Gordon Coll., Wenham, Mass., 1978; MBA, Atkinson Sch., Salem, Oreg., 1982. Campaign mgr. Carter/Mondale, Manchester, Mass., 1976; investigator Dept. Social Svcs., Nyack, 1977-78; paralegal Beverly, Mass., 1978-79; campaign mgr. Reagan Presdl. Primary, Rockland County, N.Y., 1980; cons. Sidereal, Portland, Oreg., 1981-82; performance analyst Dept. Social Svcs., Pomona, N.Y., 1982; market analyst Momentum Techs., Parsippany, N.J., 1983; cons. Booz Allen & Hamilton, Florham Park, N.J., 1984, Deloitte-Touche, Morristown, N.J., 1985; market researcher, forecaster AT&T, Bedminster, N.J., 1985-87, asst. pvt. line product mgr., 1987-89, Integrated Svcs. Digital Network product mgr., 1989-93; dir. Telecomms. Rsch. Assocs., St. Marys, Kans., 1993—; panelist, contbr. TeleComms. Assn., San Diego, 1992, Internat. Comm. Assn., Atlanta, Ea. Comm. Forum, N.Y., Nat. Engring. Consortium, Chgo.; contbr. N.Y.C. ISDN/Internat User's Group. Tutor Literacy Vols. Am., Somerville, N.J., 1989-91; mem. Jr. League Am., Morristown, N.J., 1987-90; mem. Internat. Oceanographic Found., Washington. Grantee in field. Mem. Am. Mgmt. Assn. (profl.), Soc. Telecomm. Cons. (profl.), Humane Soc. U.S., Internat. Platform Assn., W. Wilson Internat. Ctr. for Scholars, Environ. Def. Fund, Nat. Audubon Soc., Wilderness Soc., Nature Conservancy. Republican.

PIERCE, MARTHA R., government agency administrator; b. Whitebore, Tex., Mar. 13, 1946; d. Homer Max and Opal Mozelle (Elvington) Graves; m. Paul Pels (div. 1981); children: Paul, Bart, Ginger, Bret; m. Gary Pierce (div. 1990). Student, Cooke Coll., 1974, Grayson Coll., 1976. Owner salon Pilot Point, Tex., Rivera Travel, Denton, Tex.; housing officer Fed. Emergency Mgmt. Agy., Denton, head housing dept., mem. adv. bd. Home: 320 W Liberty St Pilot Point TX 76258 Office: Fed Emergency Mgmt Agy 116 W University Denton TX 76201

PIERCE, MARY, professional tennis player; b. Montreal, Que., Can., Jan. 15, 1975; d. Jim and Yannick P. 8th ranked woman USTA. *

PIERCE, NANCY W., lawyer; b. Bklyn., Sept. 20, 1950. BA, Wellesley Coll., 1971; JD, U. Pa., 1974. Bar: N.Y. 1975. Ptnr. Chadbourne & Parke LLP, N.Y.C. Mem. ABA. Office: Chadbourne & Parke LLP 30 Rockefeller Plz New York NY 10112*

PIERCE, PONCHITTA ANNE, television host, producer, journalist; b. Chgo., Aug. 5, 1942; d. Alfred Leonard and Nora (Vincent) P. Student, Cambridge (Eng.) U., summer 1962; BA cum laude, U. So. Calif., 1964. Asst. editor Ebony mag., 1964-65, assoc. editor, 1965-67; editor Ebony mag. (N.Y.C. office), 1967-68; chief N.Y.C. editl. bur. Johnson Pub. Co., 1967-68; corr. news divsn. CBS, N.Y.C., 1968-71; contbg. editor McCall's mag., 1971-77; editl. cons. Phelps Stokes Fund, 1971-78; staff writer Reader's Digest, 1976-77, roving editor, 1977-80; co-prodr., host Today in New York, Sta. WNBC-TV, N.Y.C., 1982-87; freelance writer, TV broadcaster; bd. govs. Overseas Press Club. WNBC-TV co-host: Sunday, 1973-77, The Prime of Your Life, 1976-80; author: Status of American Women Journalists on Magazines, 1968, History of the Phelps Stokes Fund 1911-1972; contbg. editor: Parade mag., 1993. Del. to WHO Conf., Geneva, 1973; bd. dirs. Dance Theatre of Harlem, Voice Found., Third St. Music Sch. Settlement, Big Sisters, Inc., Unward, Inc., Inner-City Scholarship Fund, Sta. WNET-TV; mem. women's bd. Madison Sq. Boys and Girls Club; mem. Columbia U. Health Scis. Adv. Coun. Recipient Penney-Mo. mag. award excellence women's journalism, 1967; John Russwurm award N.Y.C. Urban League, 1968; AMITA Nat. Achievement award in communications, 1974. Mem. NATAS, Women in Comm. (Woman Behind the News award 1969, Nat. Headliner award 1970), Fgn. Policy Assn. (mem. bd. govs., bd. dirs.), Coun. on Fgn. Rels., Calif. Scholarship Fedn. (life), Econs. Club N.Y., Lotos Club, Nat. Honor Soc., Mortar Bd.

PIERCE, RHONDA YVETTE, criminologist; b. Tampa, Fla., Dec. 4, 1959; d. Howard Jr. and Olivia (Powell) P. AA in Criminal Justice, Hillsboro C.C., Tampa, 1979; BS in Criminology, Fla. State U., Tallahassee, 1981. Cert. mgr. of housing. With Tampa Housing Authority, 1982-96, mgmt. coord., 1988-90, lease enforcement officer, exec. asst., 1991, dir. ops., 1992-94, dir. human resources, 1994-95; exec. dir. Sarasota (Fla.) Housing Authority, 1996—. Area youth dir. 11th Episcopal dist. A.M.E. Ch., Tampa, 1991-95, dir. ops., 1992-94, dir. human rels., 1994-96; local youth dir. Mt. Olive A.M.E. Ch., Tampa, 1989-91; exec. dir. Sarasota Housing Authority, 1996—. Recipient Dedicated Christian Svc. award Mt. Olive A.M.E. Ch., 1983. Mem. Nat. Assn. Housing and Redevel. Ofcls. Methodist. Office: Sarasota Housing Authority 1300 6th St Sarasota FL 34236

PIERCE, SUSAN RESNECK, academic administrator, English educator; b. Janesville, Wis., Feb. 6, 1943; d. Elliott Jack and Dory (Block) Resneck; m. Kenneth H. Pierce; 1 child, Alexandra Parr. AB, Wellesley Coll., 1965; MA, U. Chgo., 1966; PhD, U. Wis., 1972. Lectr. U. Wis., Rock County, 1970-71; from asst. prof. to prof. English Ithaca (N.Y.) Coll., 1973-83, chmn. dept., 1976-79, 81-82; dean Henry Kendall Coll. Arts and Scis., prof. English U. Tulsa, 1984-90; v.p. acad. affairs, prof. English Lewis and Clark Coll., Portland, Oreg., 1990-92; pres. U. of Puget Sound, Tacoma, 1992—; vis. assoc. prof. Princeton (N.J.) U., 1979; program officer div. ednl. programs NEH, 1982-83, asst. dir., 1983-84; bd. dirs. Janet Elson Scholarship Fund, 1984-1990, Tulsa Edn. Fund, Phillips Petroleum Scholarship Fund, 1985-90, Okla. Math. & Sci. High Sch., 1984-90, Hillcrest Med. Ctr., 1988-90, Portland Opera, 1990-92, St. Joseph's Hosp., 1992—, Seattle Symphony, 1993—; cons. U. Oreg., 1985, Drury Coll., Springfield, Mo., 1986; mem. Middle States and N. Cen. Accreditation Bds.; mem. adv. com. Fed. Women's Program, NEH, 1982-83; participant Summit Meeting on Higher Edn., Dept. Edn., Washington, 1985; speaker, participant numerous ednl. meetings, sems., commencements; chair Frederick Ness Book Award Com. Assn. Am. Colls., 1986; mem. award selection com. Dana Found., 1986, 87; mem. Acad. Affairs Council, Univ. Senate, dir. tchr. edn., chmn. adv. group for tchr. preparation, ex-officio mem. all Coll. Arts and Scis. coms. and Faculty Council on Internat. Studies, all U. Tulsa; bd. dirs. Am. Conf. Acad. Deans; bd. trustees Hillcrest Med. Ctr. Author: The Moral of the Story, 1982, also numerous essays, jour. articles, book sects., book revs.; co-editor: Approaches to Teaching "Invisible Man"; reader profl. jours. Bd. dirs. Arts and Humanities Coun., Tulsa, 1984-90; trustee Hillcrest Hosp., Tulsa, 1986-90; mem. cultural series com., community rels. com. Jewish Fedn., Tulsa, 1986-90; bd. dirs. Tulsa chpt. NCCJ, 1986-90. Recipient Best Essay award Arix. Quar., 1979, Excellence in Teaching award N.Y. State Edn. Council, 1982, Superior Group Service award NEH, 1984, other teaching awards; Dana scholar, Ithaca Coll., 1980-81; Dana Research fellow, Ithaca Coll., 82-83; grantee Inst. for Ednl. Affairs, 1980, Ford Found., 1987, NEH, 1989. Mem. MLA (adv. com. on job market 1973-74), South Ctrl. MLA, Soc. for Values in Higher Edn., Assn. Am. Colls. (bd. dirs.), Am. Conf. Acad. Deans (bd. dirs. 1988-91), Coun. of Presidents, Assn. Governing Bds., Phi Beta Kappa, Phi Kappa Phi, Phi Gamma Kappa. Office: U of Puget Sound 1500 N Warner St Tacoma WA 98416-0005

PIERCY, MARGE, poet, novelist, essayist; b. Detroit, Mar. 31, 1936; d. Robert Douglas and Bert Bernice (Bunnin) P.; m. Ira Wood, 1982. AB, U. Mich., 1957; MA, Northwestern U., 1958. Instr. Gary extension Ind. U., 1960-62; poet-in-residence U. Kans., 1971; disting. vis. lectr. Thomas Jefferson Coll., Grand Valley State Colls., fall 1975, 76, 78, 80; vis. faculty Women's Writers Conf., Cazenovia (N.Y.) Coll.; Elliston poetry fellow U. Cin., 1986; DeRoy Disting. vis. prof. U. Mich., 1992. Author: Breaking Camp, 1968, Hard Loving, 1969, Going Down Fast, 1969, Dance the Eagle to Sleep, 1970, Small Changes, 1973, To Be of Use, 1973, Living in the Open, 1976, Woman on the Edge of Time, 1976, The High Cost of Living, 1978, Vida, 1980, The Moon is Always Female, 1980, Braided Lives, 1982, Circles on the Water, 1982, Stone, Paper, Knife, 1983, My Mother's Body, 1985, Gone to Soldiers, 1988, Available Light, 1988 (May Sarton award 1991), Summer People, 1989, He, She and It, 1991, Body of Glass, 1991 (Arthur C. Clarke award 1993), Mars and Her Children, 1992, The Longings of Women, 1994, Eight Chambers of the Heart, 1995. Cons. N.Y. State Coun. on Arts, 1971, Mass. Found. for Humanities and Coun. on Arts, 1974; mem. Writer Bd., 1985-86; bd. dirs. Transition House, Mass. Found. Humanities and Pub. Policy, 1978-85, Am. ha-Yam, 1988—, v.p., 1995-96; gov.'s appointee to Mass. Cultural Coun., 1990-91, Mass. Coun. on Arts and Humanities, 1986-89; artistic adv. bd. ALEPH Alliance for Jewish Renewal, Am. Poetry Ctr., 1988—; lit. adv. panel poetry NEA, 1989. Recipient Borenstone Mountain Poetry award, 1968, 74, Lit. award Gov. Mass. Commn. on Status of Women, 1974, Nat. Endowment of Arts award, 1978, Carolyn Kizer Poetry prize, 1986, 90, Shaeffer-Eaton-PEN New Eng. award, 1989, Golden Rose Poetry prize, 1990, Brit ha-Dorot award The Shalom Ctr., 1992. Mem. PEN, NOW, Authors Guild, Authors League, Writers Union, Am. Poetry Soc., Nat. Audubon Soc., Mass. Audubon Soc., New Eng. Poetry Club. Address: PO Box 1473 Wellfleet MA 02667-1473

PIERI, DIANE, artist, educator; b. Phila., June 10, 1947; d. Vincent and Ruth (Ochroch) P.; m. Frank Galuszka, Sept. 8, 1968; 1 child, Greta Gabriel. BFA in Painting, Temple U., Phila., 1969. Mem. faculty Fleisher Art Meml., Phila., 1983; instr. Moore Coll. Art & Design, Phila., 1985-91; adj. faculty Chestnut Hill Coll., Phila., 1991-92; field faculty-mentor MFA program Vt. Coll. of Norwich U., Montpelier, 1992-95; asst. prof. U. Calif., Santa Cruz, 1995—; vis. artist fellow Brandywine Workshop, Phila., 1993-94; artist in residence Perkins Ctr. for Arts, Moorestown, N.J., 1994; pub. art juror Southeastern Pa. Transp. Authority, Phila., 1995; artist-juror Challenge Competition, Fleisher Art Meml., Phila., 1993-94; guest critic fine arts dept. U. Del., 1992, photography dept. Moore Coll. Art and Design, 1992, sr. thesis panelist painting dept. U. Arts, 1989, 92; lectr. various univs. One-person shows at Noel Butcher Gallery, Phila., 1984, Phila. Art Alliance, 1986, Seton Hall U., South Orange, N.J., 1986, Swarthmore (Pa.) Coll., 1987, The More Gallery, Phila., 1990, 92, 94, 96, U. of the Arts, Phila., 1990, Lycoming Coll., Williamsport, Pa., 1992, others; exhibited in group shows at Mus. of Fine Arts, St. Petersburg, Fla., 1991-94, Huntsville (Ala.) Mus. of Art, 1992-94, Ark. Art Ctr., Little Rock, 1992-94, Farnsworth Mus., Rockport, Maine, 1992-94, Fine Arts Gallery, U. Arts, Phila., 1993, 95, Moore Coll. Art and Design, Phila., 1991, 92, 93, 94, Pa. State Mus., Harrisburg, 1991, 93-94, Sordoni Art Gallery, Wilkes-Barre, Pa., 1993-94, Nexus Gallery, Phila., 1991, 93-94, Wood St. Galleries, Pitts., 1993-94, Blair Art Mus., Hollidaysburg, Pa., 1993-94, Johnstown (Pa.) Art Mus., 1993-94, Steinbaum Krauss Gallery, N.Y.C., 1993, Populi Gallery, Phila., 1994, Marywood Coll., Scranton, Pa., 1994, Bryn Mawr (Pa.) Coll., 1994, Kamin Gallery, Van Pelt-Deitrich Libr., U. Pa., Phila., 1995, The More Gallery, Phila., 1992, 95, Nexus Found. for Today's Art, Phila., 1995, Printed Image Gallery, Phila., 1995, Smith Coll., Northampton, Mass., 1996, others; represented in permanent collections at State Com. for Culture and Art, Bucharest, Romania, Beaver Coll., Glenside, Pa., State Mus. Pa., Harrisburg, Bryn Mawr Coll., others; contbr. articles to profl. jours. Kitchen vol. Met. AIDS Neighborhood Nutrition Alliance, Phila., 1993-95; food bank vol. Santa Cruz AIDS Project, 1995. Recipient Indsl. Valley Bank award Mus. PHila. Civic Ctr., 1979, Best of Show awards State Mus. Pa., Harrisburg, 1990, 91, Socrates Sculpture Park fellowships, Long Island City, N.Y., 1990, MacDowell Colony fellowship, Peterborough, N.H., 1990, Yaddo fellowship Corp. of Yaddo, Saratoga Springs, N.Y., 1991, Pollock-Krasner Found. grant, N.Y.C., 1992, Pa. Coun. of Arts grant, 1992, PEW Disciplinary winner, 1993. Home: 110 Hagar Ct Santa Cruz CA 95064 Office: U Calif at Santa Cruz Baskin Visual Arts Studios Art Bd Office Baskin E104 Santa Cruz CA 95064

PIERIK, MARILYN ANNE, librarian; b. Bellingham, Wash., Nov. 12, 1939; d. Estell Leslie and Anna Margarethe (Onigkeit) Bowers; m. Robert Vincent Pierik, July 25, 1964; children: David Vincent, Donald Lesley. AA, Chaffey Jr. Coll., Ontario, Calif., 1959; BA, Upland (Calif.) Coll., 1962; cert. in teaching, Claremont (Calif.) Coll., 1963; MSLS, U. So. Calif., L.A., 1973. Tchr. elem. Christ Episcopal Day Sch., Ontario, 1959-60; tchr. Bonita High Sch., La Verne, Calif., 1962-63; tchr., libr. Kettle Valley Sch. Dist. 14, Greenwood, Can., 1963-64; libr. asst. Monrovia (Calif.) Pub. Libr., 1964-67; with Mt. Hood C.C., Gresham, Oreg., 1972—, reference libr., 1983—, chair faculty scholarship com., 1987—; campus archivist Mt. Hood C.C., Gresham, 1994—; mem. site selection com. Multnomah County (Oreg.) Libr., New Gresham br., 1987, adv. com. Multnomah County Libr., Portland, Oreg., 1988-89; bd. dirs. Oreg. Episcopal Conf. of Deaf, 1985-92. Bd. dirs. East County Arts Alliance, Gresham, 1987-91; vestry person, jr. warden St. Luke's Epis. Ch., 1989-92; founding pres. Mt. Hood Pops, 1983-88, orch. mgr., 1983-91, 93—, bd. dirs., 1983-88, 91—. Recipient Jeanette Parkhill Meml. award Chaffey Jr. Coll., 1959, Svc. award St. Luke's Episcopal Ch., 1983, 87, Edn. Svc. award Soroptimists, 1989. Mem. AAUW, NEA, Oreg. Edn. Assn., Oreg. Libr. Assn., ALA, Gresham Hist. Soc. Office: Mt Hood CC Libr 26000 SE Stark St Gresham OR 97030-3300

PIERPOINT, KAREN ANN, marriage, family and child therapist; b. Puyallup, Wash., Sept. 1, 1944; d. Peyton Randolph Winn and Jessie Mae (Kenoyer) Kalmen; m. Randall Dean Pierpoint, Mar. 19, 1966; children: Janet, Wendy, Elizabeth, Nathan. BA, U. Oreg., 1966; MS in Counseling, San Diego State U., 1988. Lic. marriage, family and child counseling, Calif. Elem. tchr. Lane County Dist. 4, Eugene, Oreg., 1966-67, Umatilla County Dist. 19-R, Weston, Oreg., 1967-70; internat. student ministry staff mem. Campus Crusade for Christ, Internat., San Bernardino, Calif., 1970-75; dir. Christian edn. Graeagle (Calif.) Community Ch., 1975-83; dir. women's ministries Pine Valley (Calif.) Community Ch., 1983-87; lectr. counselor edn. dept. San Diego State U., 1988-89; mental health cons. San Diego City Schs., 1988-89; staff therapist Heartland Bibl. Counseling, El Cajon, Calif., 1987-90, Shepperson Psychol. Assocs., Fullerton, Calif., 1990-91; pvt. practice family therapist Fullerton, 1992—; ednl. cons. New Life Acad. Home Edn., San Diego, 1984-90; allied profl. Coastal Communities Hosp., Costa Mesa, 1991; allied health profl. Yorba Hills Hosp., Yorba Linda, Calif., 1991, Calif. Psychiat. Ctr., Santa Ana, 1992-95; profl. provider Ocean Hills Med. Group, 1996—. Columnist Free Indeed Mag., 1976-78. 4-H club leader Mohawk Valley 4-H Club, Plumas County, Calif., 1976-83, Mt. Empire 4-H Club, San Diego County, Calif., 1984-87; 4-H club advisor Mohawk Valley 4-H Club, Plumas County, 1982-83. Named for 4-H Ten Yrs. of Leadership, Mt. Empire 4-H Club, 1986. Mem. Calif. Assn. Marriage and Family Therapists (clin.), Am. Assn. Marriage and Family Therapy (clin.), Christian Assn. for Psychol. Studies (clin.), Am. Assn. Christian Counselors, Internat. Platform Assn., Nat. Parenting Instrs. Assn., Phi Kappa Phi. Republican. Office: 749 S Brea Blvd Ste 43 Brea CA 92821

PIERRARD-MUTTON, MARY V., artist, educator; b. Steubenville, Ohio, Sept. 22, 1921; d. Frank David and Mary E. (Huffman) Nation; m. Charles Joseph Pierrard, Sept. 5, 1942 (dec. May 1979); children: Karen Marie, Charles Joseph; m. James Mutton, May 27, 1994. Grad., Midway (Pa.) H.S., 1940. Tchr. China painting home studio, Midway, 1979—, sr. citizen group, California, Pa., 1993; artist Krauses, Washington, Pa., 1980-85; demonstrator Midway Firemen's, 1981, Pitts. Ctr. of Arts, 1990, Woman's Club, McDonald, Pa., 1992, Garden Club, McDonald, 1992, Fireman's, Midway, 1991, Pitts. Dist. of Chs., Legonier, Pa., 1993. Exhibited in group shows at Washington County Woman's Club, 1981 (1st Pl. award), 90 (1st Pl. award), Pa. Fedn. Woman's Club, 1989 (1st Pl. award), 90, S.W. Dist. Woman's Clubs, 1983 (1st Pl. award); contbr. drawing to book: Years of Duncan, 1980, cover to Internat. Porcelain Artists. Mem. Internat. Porcelain Art Tchrs., Inc., Nat. Mus. Women in Arts, Pitts. Porcelain Artists (treas. 1994-96), Pa. Porcelain Artists (treas. 1985-87), McDonald Woman's Club, Pa. Woman's Club. Home: 102 Washington Ave Box 85 Midway PA 15060

PIERRI, MARY KATHRYN MADELINE, cardiologist, critical care physician, educator; b. N.Y.C., Aug. 12, 1948; d. Charles Daniel and Margaret Loyola (Pesce) P. BA, Manhattanville Coll., 1969; MD, Med. Coll. Pa., 1974. Med. resident Med. Coll. Pa., Phila., 1974-77; fellow in cardiology N.Y. Hosp., N.Y.C., 1977-79; asst. physician Meml. Hosp., N.Y.C., 1980-89, assoc. physician, 1989—, chief cardiology svc., 1991—; assoc. prof. medicine Cornell Med. Coll., N.Y.C., 1989—. Fellow Am. Coll. Cardiology, N.Y. Cardiological Soc.; mem. ACP, Soc. Critical Care Medicine, Alpha Omega Alpha. Office: Meml Hosp Sloan Kettering Cancer Ctr 1275 York Ave New York NY 10021-6007

PIERRO, LINDA P., mathematics educator; b. West Reading, Pa., Mar. 27, 1950; d. Carl B. and June (Sterner) Pfau; m. Norman L. Mogel, June 9, 1971 (div. May 1988); 1 child, Elissa Raye Mogel; m. Daniel A. Pierro, Apr. 7, 1990. BA, Millersville U., 1971; MEd, Lehigh U., 1972. Cert. tchr., Pa. Tchr. math. Chichester Sch. Dist., Boothwyn, Pa., 1971—. Asst. leader Girl Scout Troop 261, Woodlyn, Pa., 1994-96, leader, 1996—; asst. youth group leader Holy Trinity Luth. Ch., Wallingford, Pa., 1995—; co-pres. Chester County Craft Guild, West Chester, Pa., 1984-85. Mem. NEA, AAUW, Nat. Coun. Tchrs. Math., Pa. Edn. Assn., Pa. Guild of Craftsmen, Assn. Tchrs. Math. of Phila. Office: Chichester Sch Dist 3333 Chichester Ave Boothwyn PA 19061

PIERSOL, CATHERINE VOGT, lawyer; b. Sioux City, Iowa, Nov. 26, 1940; d. William Paul and Elizabeth Jane (Richards) Vogt; m. Lawrence L. Piersol, June 30, 1962; children: Leah, Piersol Crain, William Millette, Elizabeth Jane. Student, Coll. St. Catherine, 1958-60; BS, U. S.D., 1962, JD, 1985; postgrad., Augustana Coll., 1981-82. Speech therapist Sioux City (Iowa) Sch. Sys., 1962-64, Sioux Falls (S.D.) Sch. Sys., 1972; ptnr. PSC Consulting, Sioux Falls, 1978-82; mem. Swanson, Carlsen, Carter, Hoy & Anderson, Sioux Falls, 1985-87; ptnr. Rose & Piersol, Sioux Falls, 1987-94; owner, prin. Piersol & Delaney (formerly Piersol Law Firm), Sioux Falls, 1994—; speech therapist Sioux Falls Sch. Sys., summer 1969, 70; co-owner Perfect Attendants, Sioux Falls, 1991-93. Contbr. articles to S.D. Law Rev. Pres. Sioux Falls Panhellenic, 1970-71; chair, vice-chair Sioux Falls Planning/Zoning, 1970-82; bd. dirs. S.D. Symphony, Sioux Falls, 1971-82, 89-94, sec., bd. dirs., 1973-75, pres., bd. dirs., 1975-77; mem. Minn.- Iowa- Kota Girls Scouts Coun. Publicity Com., Sioux Falls, 1972-74; pres. All Saints Aux., Sioux Falls, 1973; mem. Advs. (Low/Moderate Income Support Group), Sioux Falls, 1973-75; bd. dirs. Vol. and Info. Ctr., Sioux Falls, 1975-79, 88-90; mem. St. Joan Guild, Sioux Falls, 1976-77, 77-78; bd. dirs. CENCOAD, Sioux Falls, 1977-79, Minn. Pub. Radio, Mpls., 1978-81, Environ. Access, Sioux Falls, 1979-82, Ctr. for Women, Sioux Falls, 1985-88, Threshold Youth Svcs., Sioux Falls, 1985-89, Kilian C.C., 1995—; dir. Sioux Falls United Way, 1985-91; pres., bd. dirs. Sioux Empire Arts Coun., Sioux Falls, 1986-88; bd. dirs. Children's Inn, Sioux Falls, 1986-88, 92—; bd. dirs. Am. Indian Svcs., Sioux Falls, 1986-94, 95; mem. Susan G. Komen Adv. Bd., Dallas, 1990-93; state pres. Very Spl. Arts/S.D., Sioux Falls, 1990-95, bd. dirs. USD Found., Vermillion, S.D., 1991—, CASA, Sioux Falls, 1994—, S.D. Hist. Preservation Found., Pierre, 1995. Recipient YWCA Leader Luncheon award, 1980; named Gunderson lectr. U. S.D. Sch. of Law, 1987, S.D. Woman Lawyer of Yr., 1996. Mem. ABA, ATLA, S.D. Bar Assn. (law sch. com. 1991—), S.D. Trial Lawyers Assn., Supreme Ct. Hist. Soc. (chair state membership 1995-96), Roy D. Burns Inns of Ct., 8th Cir. Gender Fairness Task Force (com. 1994—), Phi Delta Phi. Roman Catholic. Office: Piersol Law Firm 515 S Cliff # 200 Sioux Falls SD 57104

PIERSON, CARRIE LEE MICHELLE, artist, educator; b. New Orleans, Jan. 6, 1960; d. Edward Jon and Mary Emma (Dutreix) P. BFA in Sculpture and Glass, Tulane U., 1989; MFA, RISD, 1993. Studio asst. Newcomb Coll. Art Dept. Tulane U., New Orleans, 1986-89; asst. to Gene Koss Newcomb Coll. Glass Dept. Tulane U., New Orleans, 1987-89; asst. to Michael Scheiner to Michael Scheiner, Ctrl. Falls, R.I., 1992-93; studio asst. Dennis Oppenheim, N.Y.C., 1993; intern Fountainhead Prods., N.Y.C., 1993, Eve Andrea Laramee, Bklyn., 1993; instr., vol. Computer Mentors Entergy Arts Bus. Ctr., New Orleans, 1993-94; instr. New Orleans Sch. Glass, 1993-94; substitute art instr. grades 1-12 M.P. Country Day & McGehee's Sch., New Orleans, 1994; computer cons. Nat. Coun. Negro Women, New Orleans, 1994; computer graphics cons. Morton Golberg Auction Galleries, Inc., 1994; art instr. Jewish Cmty. Ctr., New Orleans, 1994-95; art instr. grades K-6 Hynes and Gentilly Terr. Elem. Schs., New Orleans, 1994-95; instr. Country Day Creative Camp, Metairie, La., 1994-95; art instr. McMain Magnet and Ben Franklin H.S., New Orleans, 1995; computer in the arts instr. New Orleans Ctr. for the Creative Arts, 1995; adj. asst. prof. fine arts dept. U. New Orleans, 1995. Author of poems; one-woman shows include Loyola U. Gallery, New Orleans, 1994, Arthur Roger Gallery, New Orleans, 1995; group shows include Foster White Gallery, 1990, 20th Ann. Internat. Glass Art Soc., 1990, Stanwood, Wash., 1990, New Orleans Sch. Glass, 1990, 91, Glass 90, Gallery I/O, New Orleans, 1990, Contemporary Art Ctr., New Orleans, 1991, Le Mieux Gallery, New Orleans, 1991, Toyama Internat. Crafts Festival, Japan, 1992, Christie's, N.Y.C., 1993, Serenity Gallery, Pass Christian, Miss., 1993, Hall-Barnett Gallery, New Orleans, 1993, 94, Loyola Gallery, New Orleans, 1993, Artists Against the Hungry and Homeless Reginelli's, New Orleans, 1994, New Orleans Botanical Gardens, 1995, Gallier Hall, New Orleans, 1995, Isaac Delgado Fine Arts Gallery, New Orleans, 1995, others; represented in permanent collections; scenic artist Tulane Summer Lyric Theater, 1989; set and costume designer Jr. Lyric Theater, New Orleans, 1989-90; set painter, designer's asst. Werner & Lowe Prodn., 1991, Tulane Summer Lyric theater, 1991; set painter, asst. Stamford Theater Works, Conn., 1991; designer Trinity Rep Conservatory, 1991. Recipient Mayor's cert. of Appreciation for contbn. to the City of New Orleans, 1995, Grad. award of Excellence R.I. Sch. Design, Mary L.S. Neil prize and Downman Found. award Newcomb Coll., Tulane U., Claudia Woolworth Watkins award, Rusty Collier Meml. award, Newcomb Coll. Mem. Nat. Mus. Women in the Arts, Smithsonian Instn. (nat. assoc.), Art Dirs. and Designers Assn. (30th Ann. award 1995), New Orleans Mus. Art, New Orleans Arts Coun., New Orleans Athletic Club, Camellia Club New Orleans. Office: PO Box 20246 New Orleans LA 70141-0246

PIERSON, HELEN HALE, educator; b. Lee County, Va., Aug. 5, 1941; d. James William and Genevieve (Dalrymple) Hale; widowed; children: Christine H., Michael B. BA, Westminster Coll., 1963; MEd, Indiana U. Pa., 1968; cert.community coll. tchr, Glendale Community Coll., 1983. Cert. tchr., Pa. Tchr. Sharon (Pa.) City Schs., 1963-66, York (Pa.) City Schs., 1966-67, Prince George's County Schs., Upper Marlboro, Md., 1967-81; office mgr. Creative Realty, Inc., Phoenix, 1983-85; tchr. Rio Salado Coll., Phoenix, 1983—, N.Am. Coll., Phoenix, 1985-91; dir. edn. N.Am. Coll., 1989—; tchr. Rio Salado Coll., 1990, speaker, dept. transp., 1989; tchr. Glendale Community Coll., 1990—; tchr. Ariz. Dept. Youth Treatment and Rehab., 1991, Ariz. Corrections Edn. Program, 1991-94; edn. dir. Columbia Coll., 1993-95; edn. coord. Acad. Bus. Coll., 1996—. Recipient Outstanding Tchr. award Rio Salado Community Coll., 1990, 92, Most Outstanding Tchr. award Ariz. Pvt. Sch. Assn., 1990. Mem. NCTE, Nat. Bus. Edn. Assn., Indiana U. Pa. Alumni Assn., Chi Omega Alumni Assn. Republican. Home: 2716 W Michelle Dr Phoenix AZ 85023-1727

PIERSON, JILL ANN, critical care nurse; b. Springfield, Ohio, Dec. 14, 1957; d. Robert Oliver and Flarna Esther (Zirkle) P. Diploma, Cmty. Hosp. Sch. Nursing, 1980; BSN summa cum laude, Capital U., 1994. Cert. critical care nurse, 1995. Staff critical care nurse Cmty. Hosp., Springfield, Ohio, 1980-95. Mem. Am. Assn. Critical Care Nurses, Nat. Assn. Orthopaedic Nurses, Sigma Theta Tau. Democrat. Lutheran. Home: 3454 Folk Ream Rd #267 Springfield OH 45502

PIERSON-STEIN, MARJORIE MAXINE GORDON, property management and investment administrator; b. Boston, Feb. 22, 1925; d. David A. and Fannie (Klevansky) Gordon; m. Melvin Pierson, Nov. 10, 1946 (dec. Jan. 1981); children: Frederick, Eric, Jon; m. Daniel Stein, Dec. 4, 1982. AB in Edn., UCLA, 1945. Dir. The Mel Piersons Rec. Club, L.A., Malibu, Calif., 1953-70; adminstr. Property Mgmt. & Investments, San Diego, Malibu, Mexico, Hawaii, 1970-96. Clk., judge precinct voting, Studio City, 1980-91, 94—; bd. dirs. Big Bros. L.A., TBH Crisis Ctr., North Hollywood, 1996—; v.p. membership Valley Cmty. Philharm. Assn., 1994-96, rec. sec., 1996—;. Mem. AAUW, Valley U. Women (v.p. 1994-95, pres. 1992-94), UCLA Women's Sports (bd. dirs.), Bruin Boosters Women's Sports, Jewish Big Bros., Jewish Fedn. Coun. Democrat.

PIETKA, JAN MARIE, gifted education educator; b. Chgo., Feb. 1, 1955; d. Eugene Edward and Jeroldine A. (Rogers) P. BA, Loyola U., Chgo., 1976; MA in Gifted Edn., Northeastern Ill. U., Chgo., 1996. Cert. tchr., Ill. Jr. high sch. tchr. Our Lady of Lourdes Sch., Chgo., 1977-79, St. Cornelius Sch., Chgo., 1979-87; field mgr. Girl Scouts of Chgo., 1987-88; sr. claim rep. Allstate Ins. Co., 1988-92; gifted edn. tchr. Hill Mid. Sch., Naperville, Ill., 1993—; dir. MSC Leadership Programs, Chgo., 1980-90. Mem. adult staff Cath. Assn. Student Couns., Chgo., 1978-80. Mem. Nat. Assn. for Gifted Children, Ill. Assn. for Gifted Children, Coun. for Exceptional Children: The Assn. for the Gifted, Nat. Sci. Tchrs. Assn. Home: 1324 Normantown Rd Naperville IL 60564 Office: Hill Mid Sch 1836 Brookdale Rd Naperville IL 60563-2013

PIETRANTUONO, MARIA DOMENICA MICHELINA, health care administration; b. Campodipietra, Italy, May 22, 1949; came to U.S., 1961; d. Michael and Lucia Francalangia. BA in Psychology, Cen. Conn. State U., 1976; BSN, Western Conn. State U., 1979; MA in Delivery of Nursing Svcs., NYU, 1981, postgrad. RN, Conn.; cert. profl. in healthcare quality, instr. skills for an empowered workforce. Staff nurse New Britain (Conn.) Gen. Hosp., 1972-74; clin. fellow in cardiovasc. nursing Tex. Med. Ctr., Houston, 1979-81; nursing edn. instr. spl. care units N.Y. VA Hosp., N.Y.C., 1981-82; asst. dir. skills update Sch. Continuing Edn. - Nursing, N.Y.C., 1982-83; instr. critical care St. Luke's-Roosevelt Hosp. Ctr., N.Y.C., 1983-84; instr. critical care edn. Heart Internat. Teaching Projects, Rome, 1984, adminstrv. coord. nursing quality improvement, spl. projects, 1985-92, mgr. nursing quality improvement, 1992-95; svc. line dir. Hosp. for Spl. Care, New Britain, Conn., 1995—; part-time clin. instr. critical care nursing various Conn. hosps., 1974-78; mem. practice and standards com. St. Lukes-Roosevelt Hosp. Ctr., N.Y.C., continuing edn. rev. team, chair quality improvement ops. com., coord. patient edn./discharge planning task force, cons./resource to nursing leadership practice and standards com., coord. devel., planning, implementation and evaluation Comprehensive Nursing Documentation Model. Contbr. articles to med. jours. Mem. Nat. Assn. Healthcare Quality, Am. Soc. Quality Control, N.Y. Assn. Healthcare Quality, Choice In Dying Soc., Sigma Theta Tau. Home: 395 Brittany Farms Rd New Britain CT 06053 Office: Hosp for Spl Care 2150 Corbin Ave New Britain CT 06053

PIETRUS, CAROL LYNN, corporation executive; b. Chgo., Sept. 15, 1948; d. Alfred E. and Nellie V. (Komperda) Cregier; m. Walter Nmn, May 4, 1968; 1 child, Tracey Aileen. High sch. grad., Chgo. Adminstrv. asst. Spector Freight System, Inc., Bensenville, Ill., 1969-80; pres.'s asst. Kidco, Inc., Bensenville, Ill., 1980-82, Lauer Sbarbaro Assocs., Chgo., 1982-83, Cas Co., Lisle, Ill., 1984; pres. The Office Extension, Inc., Chgo., 1985-89, Originals Only, Inc., Ill., 1985-89, Money Mailer Greater Woodfield, Willowbrook, Ill., 1990-94, The Mktg. Coaches, Elk Grove Village, Ill., 1995—; town planner of Greater Woodfield Wheaton, Ill., 1994—; spkr. on direct mail mktg., networking, word of mouth mktg. for cos., chambers and convs. Author: (office info. series) "If You Asked Me About..."; co-author of 5 cassette series: Bullseye Marketing. Mem. North Suburban Assn. Commerce and Industry (mem. mktg. com.), Hoffman Estates C. of C., Palatine C. of C., Profl. Spkrs. of Ill., Nat. Spkrs. Assn., Toastmasters Network Plus. Home: 26w471 Grand Ave Wheaton IL 60187-2963 Office: Town Planner 26w471 Grand Ave Wheaton IL 60187-2963

PIGNATELLI, DEBORA BECKER, state legislator; b. Weehawken, N.J., Oct. 25, 1947; d. Edward and Frances (Fishman) Becker; m. Michael Albert Pignatelli, Aug. 22, 1971; children: Adam Becker, Benjamin Becker. AA, Vt. Coll., 1967; BA, U. Denver, 1969. Exec. dir. Girl's Club Greater Nashua, N.H., 1975-77; dir. tenant svcs. Nashua Housing Authority, 1979-80; vocat. counselor Comprehensive Rehab. Assocs., Bedford, N.H., 1982-85; specialist job placement Crawford & Co., Bedford, 1985-87; mem. appropriations com. N.H. Ho. of Reps., Concord, 1986-91, asst. minority leader, 1989-92; mem. N.H. State Senate, 1992—; Senate Dem. Whip; mem. environ., vice chmn., econ. devel., judiciary coms., fish and game com., interstate coop. com.; del. Am. Coun. Young Polit. Leaders, Germany, 1987. Mem. Nashua Peace Ctr., 1980—; asst. coach Little League Baseball, Nashua, 1987-90; mem. steering com. Gephardt for Pres. Campaign, N.H., 1987-88; del. Dem. Nat. Conv., 1988; mem. Gov.'s Commn. on Domestic Violence. Named One of 10 Most Powerful Women in N.H., N.H. Editions mag., 1995. Mem. N.H. Children's Lobby, Women's Lobby. Jewish. Home: 22 Appletree Grn Nashua NH 03062-2252 Office: NH State Senate State House Rm 115 Concord NH 03301

PIGOTT, IRINA VSEVOLODOVNA, educational administrator; b. Blagoveschensk, Russia, Dec. 4, 1917; came to U.S., 1939, naturalized, 1947; d. Vsevolod V. and Sophia (Reprev) Obolianinoff; m. Nicholas Prischepenko, Feb. 1945 (dec. Nov. 1964); children: George, Helen. Grad. YMCA Jr. Coll., Manchuria, 1937; BA, Mills Coll., 1942; cert. social work U. Calif.-Berkeley, 1944; MA in Early Childhood Edn., NYU, 1951. Dir.-owner Parsons Nursery Sch., Flushing, N.Y., 1951-59; dir. Montessori Sch., N.Y.C., 1966-67; dir., tchr. Day Care Ctr., Harlem, 1967-68; founder, dir. East Manhattan Sch. for Bright and Gifted, N.Y.C., 1968—; dir.-founder The House for Bright and Gifted Children, Flushing, N.Y., 1988-93; organizer, pres., exec. dir. Non-Profl. Children's Performing Arts Guild, Inc., N.Y.C., 1961-65, 87—. Organizer Back Yard Theatre, Bayside, N.Y., 1959-61. Democrat. Greek Orthodox. Avocations: music, dance, theatre, art, sports. Home and Office: East Manhattan Sch 208-210 E 18th St New York NY 10003

PIGOTT, KAREN GRAY, community health nurse, geriatrics nurse; b. Utica, N.Y., May 15, 1956; d. Charles Philip and Pauline (Nelson) Gray; m. James H. Pigott, Apr. 30, 1977; children: William Charles, Christopher McCabe. Diploma, Albany Med. Ctr. Sch. Nursing, 1978; diploma nurse practitioner, SUNY, Syracuse, 1982. Cert. adult nurse practitioner. Staff nurse Albany (N.Y.) Med. Ctr., 1978-79, St. Elizabeth's Hosp., Utica, 1979-80; staff nurse RN Community Meml. Hosp., Hamilton, N.Y., 1980-81; nurse practitioner pvt. office, Waterville, N.Y., 1982-87, VA Med. Ctr., Gainesville, Fla., 1987-90; nurse practitioner pvt. office Balt., 1990—; cons. in field; preceptor for grad. students U. Fla., 1988-90, U. South Fla., 1989-90, U. Md., Johns Hopkins U. Vol. health care provider Salvation Army Homeless Clinic, Gainesville, 1989-90, Spl. Olympics Events, Gainesville, 1990. Mem. ANA, Fla. Nurses Assn. (Expert in Clin. Practice award 1990). Presbyterian. Home: 115 Wakely Ter Bel Air MD 21014-5439 Office: 301 St Paul Pl Baltimore MD 21202-2102

PIHLAJA, MAXINE MURIEL MEAD, orchestra executive; b. Windom, Minn., July 19, 1935; d. Julian Wright and Mildred Eleanor (Ray) Mead; m. Donald Francis Pihlaja, Jan. 4, 1963; children: Geoffrey Blake, Kirsten Louise, Jocelyn Erika. BA, Hamline U., 1957; postgrad., Columbia U., 1957-58. Group worker Fedn. of Chs., L.A., 1956; case worker St. John's Guild Floating Hosp. Ship, N.Y.C., 1957-59; Y-Teen program dir. YWCA, Elizabeth, N.J., 1957-60, Boulder, Colo., 1964-65; spl. svcs. program and club dir. U.S. Army, Ingrandes and Nancy, France, 1960-62; music buyer, salesperson Guinn's Music, Billings, Mont., 1977-78, N.W. Music, Billings, 1978-79; office adminstr. Am. Luth. Ch., Billings, 1979-84; gen. mgr. Billings Symphony Orchestra, 1984—; substitute tchr. Community Day Care and Enrichment Ctr., Billings, 1971-76. Dir. Handbell choir 1st Presybn. Ch., Billings, 1972—, Am. Luth. Ch., 1981-84, 1st English Luth. Ch., 1982—; mem. Billings Symphony Chorale, 1965-91, Bellissimo!, 1983-93, Cmty. Concerts Bd., 1967-96. Mem. Nat. Soc. Fund Raising Execs. (sec. Mont. 1988), Mont. Assn. Female Execs. (mem. membership com. 1994-96, retreat com. 1996—), Am. Guild English Handbell Ringers (state chmn. 1988-89, treas. Area X bd. dirs. 1990-94, membership chmn. 1994-96), Mont .Assn. Symphony Orchs. (treas. 1987-92, sec. 1995-96). Lutheran. Office: Billings Symphony Orch Box 7055 401 N 31st St Ste 530 Billings MT 59103

PIIRMA, IRJA, chemist, educator; b. Tallinn, Estonia, Feb. 4, 1920; came to U.S., 1949; d. Voldemar Juri and Meta Wilhelmine (Lister) Tiits; m. Aleksander Piirma, Mar. 10, 1943; children: Margit Ene, Silvia Ann. Diploma in chemistry, Tech. U., Darmstadt, Fed. Republic of Germany, 1949; MS, U. Akron, 1957, PhD, 1960. Rsch. chemist U. Akron, Ohio, 1952-67, asst. prof., 1967-76, assoc. prof., 1976-81, prof., 1981-90; prof. emerita U. Akron, Ohio, 1990—; dept. head U. Akron, Ohio, 1982-85. Author: Polymeric Surfactants, 1992; editor: Emulsion Polymerization, 1982; contbr. articles to profl. jours. Recipient Extra Mural Rsch. award BP Am., Inc., 1989. Mem. Am. Chem. Soc. Home: 3528 Adaline Dr Cuyahoga Falls OH 44224-3929 Office: U Akron Akron OH 44325-3909

PIKE, JENNIFER LYNN, educational consultant, educator; b. Albany, N.Y., Aug. 10, 1969; d. Howard and Arlene (Kwapinski) P. Student, Leningrad U., St. Petersburg, Russia, 1990; BA in History, SUNY, Binghamton, 1991; MA in History, SUNY, Albany, 1993. Clk. U.S. Geol. Survey, Albany, 1991-93; VISTA vol. Interstate Svc. Coalition, Hancock, Md., 1993-95; ednl. cons. Berkeley Springs (W.Va.) Wellness Ctr., 1996—; adj. prof. Lord Fairfax C.C., Middletown, Va., 1996—; mem. Md. Food Com., Balt., 1993-95; tutor, Hancock, 1994—. V.p. bd. dirs. Washington County Food Resources, Hagerstown, Md., 1995; coord., supr. Interstate Lit. Coun., Hancock, 1995; treas., coach Hancock Girls Softball League, 1995. Mem. NOW, Phi Theta Kappa. Democrat. Episcopalian.

PIKE, JUDITH ANN, elementary education educator; b. Norwich, N.Y., Oct. 3, 1945; d. Archie Dwight and Lucy Marion (Breed) Hall; m. Robert Lloyd Pike, June 29, 1968; children: Jennifer, Stephanie. BS in Elem. Edn., SUNY, Oswego, 1967. Tchr. Oxford (N.Y.) Ctrl. Schs., 1967-68, West Genesee Schs., Camillus, N.Y., 1968-70, Norwich Pub. Schs., 1970-71, Alamogordo (N.Mex.) Pub. Schs., 1983-84; tchr. reading Petersburg (Va.) Pub. Schs., 1971-73; tchr. Edmond (Okla.) Pub. Schs., 1984—. Treas. Edmond Assn. for Family and Cmty. Edn., 1987—; vol. Friends Met. Libr., Oklahoma City, 1991—, H.O.P.E. (Help Our People in Emergencies), Edmond, 1991—. Recipient Presdl. award for excellence in sci. and math. tchg. NSF, 1994. Mem. ASCD, NEA, Nat. Coun. Tchrs. Math., Soc. Elem. Presdl. Awardees, Coun. Presdl. Awardees in Maths., Okla. Coun. Tchrs. Math., Ctrl. Okla. Assn. Tchrs. Math. (editor newsletter 1994—), Delta Kappa Gamma. Home: 1305 Mary Lee Ln Edmond OK 73034-5430

PIKE, NANCY ANN, pediatric cardiothoracic surgery nurse; b. Rome, N.Y., July 13, 1963; d. Bruce Martin and Marie (Parent) Pike. BS, Pa. State U., 1985; M in Nursing, UCLA, 1993. CCRN; cert. pediatric cardiothoracic surgery clin. nurse specialist; cert. BLS, ACLS, BLS instr. Staff nurse ICU/CCU Aliquippa (Pa.) Hosp., 1985-86; staff nurse IMC/ICU Pa. State U., Hershey, 1986-90; staff nurse ICU UCLA Med. Ctr., 1990-93; CNS cardiothoracic surgery Children's Hosp. at Stanford, Calif., 1993—; part-time transplant coord. Stanford U., 1993—; teaching asst. undergrad. nursing UCLA Sch. Nursing, 1993—. Author: RN jour., 1994; article reviewer: Am. Jour. Critical Care, 1993—; contbr. chpt. to book. Mem. AACN, Am. Heart Assn., Soc. Pediat. Cardiovasc. Nursing, Sigma Theta Tau (Gamma Tau chpt.). Roman Catholic. Home: 725 Roble Ave Apt # 12 Menlo Park CA 94025

PIKE, NANCY DEVINE, real estate agent; b. Norwalk, Conn., Dec. 28, 1958; d. Joseph Edward and Nina Wisdom (Cave) Devine, m. F. Norris Pike, Jan. 5, 1985; children: Lily Mulvaney, Harold Winfield. BA, Barnard Coll., Columbia U., N.Y.C., 1976-80. Salesperson Tiffany & Co., N.Y.C., 1979-80; admin. asst. Metropolitan Museum of Art, N.Y.C., 1980-84; deputy town clerk Town of New Shoreham, Block Island, R.I., 1984-86; real estate agent Sullivan Real Estate, Block Island, 1985—; owner, operator The Dewey Cottage, Block Island, 1994—. Treas., bd. trustees Island Free Libr., Block Island, 1994—; sch. bd. (search com.) Block Island Sch., 1995—. Mem. Washington/Kent Bd. of Realtors. Democrat. Home and Office: Southwest Point Block Island RI 02807

PILBOROUGH, BARBARA JEAN, healthcare consultant; b. Phila., Nov. 2, 1944; d. Stanley Anthony Brokowski and Jean (Tomczyk) O'Brien; m. Christopher Pilborough, Dec. 28, 1974; children: Joy, Lotus. BA in Polit. Econs., Holy Family Coll., Phila., 1965; tchg. cert. (master's program), U. San Francisco, 1971. Adminstr. G.I. Assocs. of Grad. Hosp., Phila., 1983-87, Ctr. for Urol. Care, Haddon Heights, N.J., 1987-94; healthcare cons. Button Assocs., Moorestown, N.J., 1994-95, Parente Consulting, Phila., 1995—. Pres. Pennsauken (N.J.) H.S. PTA, 1994. Mem. NOW (pres. Alice Paul chpt. 1991-92, State of N.J. legis. coord. 1992-94), AAUW, ACLU, MGMA, Nat. Assn. Healthcare Consultants, Amnesty Internat. Democrat. Home: 3238 49th St Pennsauken NJ 08109 Office: Parente Consulting Curtis Ctr Ste 550 Philadelphia PA 19106

PILCHER, ELLEN LOUISE, rehabilitation counselor; b. Washington, Feb. 5, 1949; d. Donald Everett and Edna Lois (Walker) P.; m. Adam J. Buzon Jr., July 27, 1974 (div. Apr. 1991). BA in Psychology, So. Ill. U., 1971, MA in Rehab. Counseling, 1973. Social svcs. asst. Dept. Army, Ft. Huachuca, Ariz., 1973-74, New Ulm, Germany, 1974-75, Ft. Sill, Okla., 1977-87; counselor Goodwill Industries, Lawton, Okla., 1976-77; ind. living specialist Ariz. Bridge to Ind. Living, Phoenix, 1984-87; disability specialist Samaritan Rehab. Inst., Phoenix, 1987-89; disability cons. Peoria, Ariz., 1989—; founder Problems of Architecture and Transp. to Handicapped, Lawton, Okla., 1976-79; founder, past pres. Polio Echo Support Group, Phoenix, 1985—; co-founder, bd. mem. Disability Network of Ariz., Phoenix, 1986—; disability speaker Easter Seal Soc. and free lance, Phoenix, 1984—; producer, host Cable Community Svc. TV Show, Glendale, Ariz., 1987-91; mem. nat. adv. bd. Polio Support Groups, St. Louis, 1987. Named Ms. Wheelchair Ariz. Good Samaritan Med. Ctr., Phoenix, 1986, Second Runner-Up Ms. Wheelchair Am., Ms. Wheelchair Am. Assn., Richmond, Va., 1986, Outstanding Bus. Person Ariz. Parks/Recreation, 1987; recipient Celebration of Success award Impact for Enterprising Women, Phoenix, 1989, Extraordinary Personal Achievement award Lions Club Found., Phoenix, 1987. Mem. NOW (co-founder Lawton chpt. 1982, Glendale, Ariz. chpt. 1984), Nat. Rehab. Assn., Nat. Rehab. Counselors Assn., Ariz. Rehab. Assn., Ariz. Rehab. Counselors Assn. Democrat. Unitarian.

PILDES, SARA, artist; b. N.Y.C.; d. Isidore and Minnie (Friedlander) Philipson; m. Harry Pildes, Dec. 1930; children: Michael, Jane, Daniel, Robert. BS, CCNY, 1953. Mem. panel C.W. Post Coll., L.I. U.; lectr. Temple U., Phila. Represented in permanent collections Doane Coll. Mus., Crete, Nebr., Bismarck (N.D.) State Coll.; one-woman shows include Gov.'s Mansion, Lincoln, Nebr., Rotunda Gallery, Washington, Raymond Duncan Gallery, Paris, Nat. Arts Club, Gramercy Park, Gallery Internat., N.Y.C. Mem. Nat. Assn. Women Artists, Met. Painters and Sculptors (treas., lectr.), Burr Artists, N.Y. State Soc. Women Artists, Visual Individualists United, Nat. Mus. Women in Arts (charter). Home and Studio: 2 Franklin Town Blvd Philadelphia PA 19103

PILECKI, MICHELLE CHRISTINE, magazine editor; b. Pitts., Jan. 5, 1952; d. Michael Joseph and Lois Loretta (Christ) P. BA in Sociology, Duquesne U., 1973. Asst. inside editor Pitts. Suburban News, 1971-72; copy editor, writer Steel City Sports/Score, Pitts., 1973-75; editor, music and theater critic Market Square, Pitts., 1973-86; editor, theater critic Gateway Publs., Pitts., 1986-90; corr. Pitts. Post-Gazette, 1991-92; mng. editor Pitts. Mag., 1992—; mem. pub. rels. adv. bd. Allegheny County Health Dept., Pitts., 1988. Presenter New Works Festival, Pitts., 1991—, theater judge, 1992—. Recipient Golden Quill award Press Club Western Pa., Pitts., 1986-89, Feature Writing award Nat. Suburban Newspapers, 1989, News Writer of Yr. award Tri State Sports and News, Pitts., 1992. Mem. Women's Press Club Pitts. (sec. 1980-82), Women in Comm. (Matrix award 1988), Addison DeWitt Soc., Audubon Soc. Democrat. Roman Catholic. Office: Pitts Mag 4802 Fifth Ave Pittsburgh PA 15213

PILETTE, PATRICIA CHEHY, health care organizational/management consultant; b. Rutland, Vt., June 28, 1945; d. John Edward and Mary T. (McNamara) Chehy; m. Wilfrid Pilette, July 22, 1972; 1 child, Patrick John. Diploma, Jeanne Mance Sch. Nursing, 1966; BSN magna cum laude, St. Anselm Coll., 1971; MS summa cum laude, Boston U., 1974, EdD in Counseling and Human Svcs. Adminstrn. summa cum laude, 1984. RN, Mass. Clin. specialist adult psychiatry mgmt. and counseling practice Framingham, Mass.; employee assistance counselor St. Elizabeth's Med. Ctr., 1984—. Contbr. articles to profl. publs., chpts. to books. Mem. Mass. Soc. Nurse Execs., N.E. Assn. for Specialists in Group Work, N.E. Soc. Group Psychotherapists, Mass. Assn., Women Deans, Adminstrs. and Counselors, Assn. for Humanistic Psychologists, N.Am. Soc. Employee Assistance, Am. Mental Health Counselors Assn., Pi Lambda Theta, Sigma Theta Tau.

PILGRIM, DEBORAH ANNICE, psychotherapist; b. Bklyn., Sept. 18, 1956; d. Charles Montague and Nellian Claire (Holloway) P. AB, Smith Coll., 1978; EdM, Harvard U., 1979; EdD, George Washington U., 1986. Rsch. analyst/supr. Crown Hts. Community Corp., Bklyn., summers 1974, 76; supr. Urban League Tutorial Program, Bklyn., summers 1975,77; substitute tchr. Smith Coll. Lab. Campus Sch., Northampton, Mass., 1978; dir. Crown Hts. North Multi-Svc. Ctr. Tutorial Program, Bklyn., summer 1978; psychology extern Cath. U. Am., Washington, 1980-81; psychiat. teaching fellow Boston U. Sch. Medicine, 1981-82; clin. psychology intern Boston City Hosp., 1981-82; psychology teaching fellow Harvard U., Cambridge, Mass., 1987, staff psychologist, 1985—; lectr. and cons. in field. Artist original sculpture in King's Plaza Ctr. in Bklyn., 1971. Prodn. mem. Brookline (Mass.) Community Theater; resident mem. Concerned Black Citizens of Brookline; recruiter/interviewer Smith Coll.; mem. admissions com. Harvard U. Grad. Sch. Edn., 1978-79. NIMH grantee, 1981-82. Mem. APA, Assn. Black Psychologists, Am. Assn. for Counseling and Devel., Assn. for Multi-Cultural Counseling and Devel. (co-chair nat. conv. 1988-89), The Coalition of 100 Black Women (Boston chpt.), Phi Delta Kappa. Democrat. Episcopalian. Office: Harvard U Bur Study Counsel 5 Linden St Cambridge MA 02138-3004

PILGRIM, DIANNE HAUSERMAN, art museum director; b. Cleve., July 8, 1941; d. John Martin and Norma Hauserman; divorced. BA, Pa. State U., 1963; MA, Inst. Fine Arts, NYU, 1965; postgrad., CUNY, 1971-74; LHD (hon.), Amherst Coll., 1991, Pratt Inst., 1994. Chester Dale fellow Am. wing. Met. Mus. Art, N.Y.C., 1966-68, rsch. cons. Am. paintings and sculpture, 1971-73; asst. to dirs. Pyramid Galleries, Ltd., Washington, 1969-71, Finch Coll. Mus. Art, Washington, 1971; curator dept. decorative arts Bklyn. Mus., 1973-88, chmn. dept., 1988; dir. Cooper-Hewitt Nat. Design Mus., N.Y.C., 1988—; mem. adv. com. Gracie Mansion, N.Y.C., 1980; mem. design adv. com. Art Inst. Chgo., 1988; mem. Hist. House Trust N.Y.C., Mayor's Office, 1989-94. Co-author, curator: (book and exhbn. catalogue) Mr. and Mrs. Raymond Horowitz Collection of American Impressionist and Realist Paintings, 1973, The American Renaissance 1876-1917, 1979; (book) The Machine Age in America 1918-1941, 1986 (Charles F. Montgomery prize Decorative Arts Soc.). Bd. dirs. Nat. Multiple Sclerosis Soc., 1989. Recipient Disting. Alumni award Pa. State U., 1991. Mem. Decorative Arts Soc. (pres. 1977-79), Art Deco Soc., Victorian Soc., Art Table. Office: Smithsonian Instn Cooper-Hewitt Nat Design Mus 2 E 91st St New York NY 10128-0606

PILGRIM, GENEVA HANNA, retired English educator; b. Paynesville, Minn., Nov. 25, 1914; d. George and Regula (Figi) Hanna; m. Walter Niebuhr Pilgrim, July 3, 1965. BA, Hamline U., 1937; MA, Northwestern U., 1941, PhD, 1946. Cert. secondary tchg., Minn., Iowa, Ill. Secondary sch. tchr. Minn. Pub. Schs., 1937-40, Des Moines Pub. Schs., 1940-43; tchr. exptl. sch. Ohio State U., Columbus, 1945-47, 48-50, U. Hawaii, Honolulu, 1947-48; prof. English edn. U. Tex., Austin, 1950-78; tchr. educator William & Mary Coll., summers 1946, 47, U. Ga., summers 1948, 49, 50, Baylor U., Waco, Tex., summer 1950. Author: Books Young People and Reading Guidance, 1960, rev., 1968; contbr. articles to profl. jours. Bd. mem. Crisis Ctr., Alexandria, Minn., 1993—; mem. LWV, pres. 1991-92. Mem. AAUW, Woman's Club. Democrat. United Methodist. Home: 1415 Lake St Alexandria MN 56308

PILLAERT, E(DNA) ELIZABETH, museum curator; b. Baytown, Tex., Nov. 19, 1931; d. Albert Jacob and Nettie Roseline (Kelley) P. B.A., U. St. Thomas, 1953; M.A., U. Okla., 1963; postgrad., U. Wis., 1962-67, 70-73. Asst. curator archaeology Stovall Mus., Norman, Okla., 1959-60, ednl. liaison officer, 1960-62; research asst. U. Okla., Norman, Okla., 1962; research asst. U. Wis., Madison, 1962-65, cons. archaeol. faunal analysis, 1965—; curator osteology Zool. Mus., Madison, 1965—, chief curator, 1967-92, assoc. dir., 1992—. Bd. dirs. Lysistrata Feminist Coop., Madison, 1977-81, Univ. YMCA, Madison, 1974-77. Mem. Soc. Vertebrate Paleontology, Wis. Archaeol. Soc., Okla. Anthrop. Soc., Am. Assn. Mus., NOW, Stoughton Hist. Soc., Am. Ornithological Union, Friends of Stoughton Libr., Friends of Stoughton Auditorium. Home: 216 N Prairie St Stoughton WI 53589-1647 Office: U Wis Zool Mus 434 Noland Bldg 250 N Mills St Madison WI 53706-1708

PILLING-JOLLES, JANET KAVANAUGH, lawyer; b. Akron, Ohio, Sept. 5, 1951; d. Paul and Marjorie (Logue) Kavanaugh; m. Martin Jolles, Mar. 6, 1987; children: Madeleine Sloan Langdon Jolles, Jameson Samuel Rhys Jolles. BA, Ohio Wesleyan U., 1973; JD, U. Mo., 1976; LLM, Villanova U., 1985. Bar: Pa. 1976, U.S. Tax Ct. 1976, U.S. Dist. Ct. (ea. dist.) Pa. 1976, Ohio 1996. Atty. Schnader, Harrison, Segal & Lewis, Phila., 1976-83; gen. counsel Kistler-Tiffany Cos., Wayne, Pa., 1983-95; lawyer Janet Kavanaugh Pilling & Assocs., Berea, Ohio, 1996—. Mem. Phila. Estate Planning Coun., Montgomery County Estate Planning Coun., Delaware County Estate Planning Coun., Del. Valley Planned Giving Coun., Chester County Estate Planning Coun. Mem. ABA, Phila. Bar Assn. (probate sect., tax sect.), Pa. Bar Assn., Delaware Valley Planned Giving Coun., Phi Beta Kappa, Phi Delta Phi. Office: 43 E Bridge St Ste 101 Berea OH 44017

PILSNER, JOYCE MARION, health services administrator; b. N.Y.C., Jan. 30, 1925; d. Sol and Estelle (Schaffle) Mayersohn; m. Harry Pilsner, Dec. 20, 1947; 1 child, Toby Jane. AB, Hunter Coll., 1944; MA, Columbia U., 1946, cert. Inst. for Not-for-Profit Mgmt., 1977. Tchr. N.Y.C., 1945-67; rsch. assoc. Inst. Community Studies Sarah Lawrence Coll., Bronxville, N.Y., 1968-69, asst. to dean, 1968-70; rsch. assoc., field coordinator Consortium on Community Crises Cornell U., Ithaca, N.Y., 1970-71; exec. dir. Riverdale Mental Health Ctr., Bronx, N.Y., 1971—; sec. Citywide Behavioral Network, 1986—. Membership chmn. corr. sec. Riverdale Cmty. Coun.; mem. dist. bd. Comprehensive Health Planning Agy.; mem., sec. sub-regional com. Bronx Fedn. Mental Health and Mental Retardation Agys.; bd. dirs. Riverdale Sr. Ctr., 1974-82; bd. dirs. Coalition of Vol. Mental Health Agys., 1975—, v.p., 1975-90, sec., 1995—; mem. Cmty. Bd. B, Bronx, 1975—, chmn. health com., ethics com., youth com., 2d v.p., 1989-96, 96—, 1st v.p., 1990-93, chmn., 1993-95; mem. cmty. adv. bd. North Ctrl. Bronx Hosp., 1983-89, chmn. health, membership and nominating coms.; mem. Users Group,. Info. Scis. Divsn. Nathan Kline Inst., 1984-87, exec. com., sec., 1985-86; borough outreach com. Greater N.Y. Fund/United Way, 1985-89. Named Riverdalian of Yr., 1979; recipient Cert. of Meritorious Svc. N.Y.C. Mayor Edward I. Koch, 1986, Cmty. Svc. award Benjamin Franklin Dem. Club, 1992, Cleveland E. Dodge award, 1995. Fellow Am. Orthopsychiat. Assn.; mem. Riverdale Mental Health Assn. (dir. 1965-71, chmn. pub. rels., editor newsletter), UN Assn. (dir. Riverdale chpt., chmn. publicity), East Hampton House Owners Ltd. (bd. dirs., v.p. 1986, pres. 1988—), Alumni Assn. Inst. for Not-for-Profit Mgmt. (exec. com. 1987-89), Bronx Mental Health Coun. (chmn. legis. com. 1980-94). Home: 4721 Delafield Ave Bronx NY 10471-3311 Office: Riverdale Mental Health Assn 5676 Riverdale Ave Bronx NY 10471-2138

PIMENTAL, PATRICIA ANN, neuropsychologist, consulting company executive, author; b. Warwick, R.I., Feb. 2, 1956; d. Thomas Robert and Veronica Madeleine (Costa) P.; m. John V. O'Hara, Dec. 16, 1989; children: John Bernard, Padraic James. BS in Pre-Med, Speech Pathology, Northwestern U., 1978, MA in Speech Pathology with honors, 1980; PsyD in Clin. Psychology with honors, Chgo. Sch. Profl. Psychology, 1987. Lic. psychologist, speech pathologist, Ill.; diplomate Am. Bd. Vocat. Neuropsychology, Am. Acad. Pain Mgmt., Am. Bd. Prof. Disability Cons., Am. Bd. Profl. Neuropsychology. Clin. psychology extern child psychology clinic U. Ill., Chgo., 1984-85, dir. psychol. svcs. dept. phys. medicine and rehab., 1987-91, asst. prof. dept. phys. medicine and rehab., 1987-91; clin. psychology extern Filmore Mental Health Ctr., Berwyn-Cicero (Ill.) Sr. Svcs., 1985-86; clin. psychology intern St. Elizabeth's Hosp., Chgo., 1986-87; mem. faculty Chgo. Sch. Profl. Psychology, 1991—; pres. Neurobehavioral Medicine Cons., Ltd., Oak Brook, Ill., 1991—. Sr. author: Neuropsychological Aspects of Right Brain Injury, 1989, The Mini Inventory of Right Brain Injury, 1989; contbr. articles and revs. to profl. jours., chpts. to books; manuscript reviewer Archives Phys. Medicine and Rehab., 1990; book reviewer Contemporary Psychology, 1991. Vol. trainer ARC Disaster Stress Relief Program, 1991—; leader U. Ill. Stroke Club, 1988-91; bd. dirs. Older Adult Rehab. Svcs., Cicero, 1987-90; active Chgo. Anti-Cruelty Soc., Lincoln Park Zool. Soc. Named one of Outstanding Young Women Am., 1984, 92; Am. Cancer Soc. scholar, 1979; recipient Outstanding Manuscript of Yr. award Am. Jour. of Pain Mgmt., 1993. Fellow Am. Coll. Profl. Neuropsychology; mem. APA, Am. Pain Soc., Ill. Psychol. Assn. (adv. bd. 1989-93, chair-elect, chair health and rehab. sect. 1991-92, 92-93, chair prescription privilege task force 1992-95, continuing edn. chair/clin. practice sect. 1993-95, pres.-elect 1995-96, pres. 1996—), Nat. Brain Injury Rsch. Found. (med. adv. coun. 1992—), Internat. Neuropsychol. Soc., Nat. Acad. Neuropsychology, Am. Congress Rehab. Medicine, Soc. Clin. and Exptl. Hypnosis, Midwest Neuropsychology Group, Am. Speech and Hearing Assn. Office: Glen Oaks Hosp Med Ctr Neurobehavioral Medicine 701 Winthrop Ave Glendale Heights IL 60139

PIMLEY, KIM JENSEN, financial training consultant; b. Abington, Pa., Apr. 29, 1960; d. Alvin Christian Jensen and Helen Marie (Kairis) Meinken; m. Michael St. John Pimley, Nov. 10, 1988; 1 child, Oliver Jensen Pimley. BA, Emory U., 1982, MA magna cum laude, 1982; postgrad., U. Chgo., 1985—. Mgr. tng. ops. Continental Bank, Chgo., 1986-88, mgr. coll. rels., 1988-90; mgr. client svcs. The Globecon Group, N.Y.C., 1990-92; prin. Pimley & Pimley, Inc., Glencoe, Ill., 1992-93; pres. P&P Tng. Resources, Inc., Glencoe, 1993—. Contbr. poetry to various jours. Mem. Chgo. Coun. on Fgn. Affairs, 1990—. Scholarship U. Chgo., 1984. Mem. ACLU, NOW, Oxford and Cambridge Club, Poetry Soc. Am. Office: P&P Tng Resources Inc 117 Library Pl Princeton NJ 08540

PINATARO, JEAN ELEANOR, artist; b. L.A.; d. Pasqual and Anna (Maresca) P. Student, UCLA, 1960-70; BA in Fine Arts, Calif. State U., Long Beach, 1988. Tech. artist, designer, illustrator N.Am. Aviation Inc. (now Rockwell Internat.); designer Apollo/Soyuz Patch NASA, 1974; artist in residence Villa Montalvo Ctr. Arts, Saratoga, Calif., 1984. Author, editor: Pinataro, 1976, Live From the Pyramids, 1979, Names Have Been Changed to Protect the Guilty, 1989; exhibitions include Calif. State U., Long Beach, 1987, System M Gallery, Long Beach, 1988, Palos Verdes Art Ctr. (Calif.), 1990, Graham Horstman Gallery, Denton, Tex., 1990, The Gate Gallery, San Pedro, Calif., 1991, Sasama Gallery, Chgo., 1992, The Bridge Gallery, L.A., 1992, Muckenthaler Cultural Ctr., Fullerton, Calif., 1992, Artspace Gallery, Woodland Hills, Calif., 1993, Downey Mus. Art, 1993, 94, 96, Gallery 57, Fullerton, 1995 (Gallery Choice). Mem. Nat. Watercolor Soc., Artists Support Group.

PINCH, PATRICIA ANN, insurance agent; b. Port Hueneme, Calif., Oct. 8, 1947; d. William Claude and Lois (Monroe) Pinch; m. Vincent J. Lupo, Apr. 6, 1973 (dec. 1975). B.S. in Med. Tech., Med. Coll. Va., 1969. Human cytogenetic researcher Bklyn. Hosp., 1970-72; animal genetic researcher Mt. Sinai Hosp., N.Y.C., 1972-74; med. tech. supr., owner Vee-Jay Clin. Labs., Bklyn., 1974-86; supr. G.J.L. Clin. Lab., Amityville, N.Y., 1986-87; dist. agt. Prudential Ins., 1987-94; owner Aerie Unlimited, Patchogue, N.Y., 1996—. Mem. Am. Soc. Clin. Pathologists. Roman Catholic. Office: Aerie Unlimited One S Ocean Ave Dove Plz Patchogue NY 11772

PINCKLEY, FRANCES ANN, middle school language arts educator; b. Lawrenceburg, Tenn., Jan. 12, 1941; d. Henry Walter and Velma Lorene (Appleton) Mitchell; m. David Allen Pinckley, June 12, 1966. Postgrad., David Lipscomb U., 1959-61; BS, Mid. Tenn. State U., 1965, MS, 1984; MS, Tenn. State U., 1989. Cert. elem. tchr., music tchr., curriculum and instrn., Tenn. English, music tchr., band and choral dir. Summertown (Tenn.) H.S., 1965-78; 11th grade English, speech, drama tchr., band/choral dir. Lawrence County H.S., Lawrenceburg, 1978-80; history, lang. arts, choral, drama tchr. Coffman Mid. Sch., Lawrenceburg, 1980—; career ladder II tchr. Tenn. State Bd. Edn., Nashville, 1990—; tutor. Soloist, mem. Lawrence County Oratorical Soc., Lawrenceburg, 1988—; bd. dirs. Lawrenceburg Cmty. Theatre, 1976-82; Sunday sch. tchr. Pulaski St. Ch. of Christ, Lawrenceburg, 1952—, youth sponsor, 1990—; in-svc. tng. tchr. Lawrence County Bd. Edn. Mem. NEA, Tenn. Edn. Assn., Lawrence County Edn. Assn., Delta Kappa Gamma (treas. Phi chpt. 1981-91, 2d v.p. 1992-94, 1st v.p. 1994-96, pres. 1996—, State Music Dir. 1988-90, Outstanding Mem. 1991), Delta Omicron (life). Home: 1005 W Gaines Lawrenceburg TN 38464-3138

PINCUS, ANDREA J., lawyer; b. N.Y.C., June 20, 1965. BA magna cum laude, Yale U., 1987; JD, NYU, 1991. Bar: N.Y. 1992, U.S. Dist. Ct. (so. and ea. dists.) N.Y. 1995. Ptnr. Anderson Kill Olick & Oshinsky, P.C., N.Y.C. Root-Tilden-Snow scholar. Mem. N.Y. County Lawyers Assn. (women's rights com., young lawyers com., com. on law reform), N.Y. Women's Bar Assn. Office: Anderson Kill Olick & Oshinsky PC 1251 Ave of the Americas New York NY 10020-1182*

PINCUS, ANN TERRY, federal agency administrator; b. Little Rock, Sept. 12, 1937; d. Fred William and Cornelia (Witsell) Terry; m. Walter Haskell Pincus, May 1, 1965; children: Ward, Adam, Cornelia Battle. BA, Vassar Coll., 1959. Editorial asst., writer Glamour Mag., 1963; reporter Ridder Pubs., Washington, 1963-66; freelance writer Washington, 1966-76; dir. info. select com. on U.S. population U.S. Ho. Reps., Washington, 1977-79; nat. publicist Nat. Pub. Radio, Washington, 1979-83; press sec. U.S. Sen. Charles Mathias, Washington, 1983-87; profl. staff mem. Senate Com. on Rules, Washington, 1983-87; v.p. communications Stas. WETA-TV/Radio, Washington, 1987-93; dir. Office of Rsch., U.S. Info. Agy., Washington, 1993—; bd. dirs. Fgn. Student Svcs. Coun., Washington, Woodley House. Editor: Kennedy Center Cookbook, 1977; contbr. articles to profl. jours. Home: 3202 Klingle Rd NW Washington DC 20008-3403 Office: Office of Rsch US Info Agy 301 4th St SW Rm 352 Washington DC 20547-0009

PINCUS, JILLIAN RUTH, physician; b. Bklyn., May 26, 1947; d. William and Elsa Bronson Pincus. BA, Radcliffe Coll., 1969; MD, Med. Coll. Pa., 1974. Cert. Am. Bd. Internal Medicine, Am. Bd. Nephrology. Intern, resident U. Medicine and Dentistry of N.J.-Robert Wood Johnson Med. Sch., 1974-77, nephrology fellow, 1978-79; nephrology fellow U. Miami Sch. Medicine, 1977-78; attending physician Jewish Inst. Geriatric Care, New Hyde Park, N.Y., 1979-80, L.I. Jewish Hosp.-Hillside Med. Ctr., New Hyde Park, 1980-82; from asst. to assoc. med. dir. Sandoz Pharm., East Hanover, N.J., 1982-88; med. dir. CIBA-Geigy Corp., Summit, N.J., 1988-90, exec. med. dir., 1990-92, clin. head, 1992-93, head, 1993—. Active Nat. Kidney Found. Mem. AMA, Am. Soc. Nephrology, Am. Med. Women's Assn., Women in Nephrology. Home: 1 Plymouth Rd Chatham NJ 07928-1814 Office: CIBA-Geigy Corp 556 Morris Ave Summit NJ 07901-1330

PINCUS, PATRICIA HOGAN, nurse; b. Lockport, N.Y., Dec. 4, 1945; d. George W. and Theresa J. (Harrington) Wendel; children: Jennifer, Molly, Peter. RN, Mercy Hosp. Sch. Nursing, Buffalo, 1966; MPH, U. Rochester, 1985; BS, Empire State Coll., Rochester, N.Y., 1977. RN, N.Y.; cert. infection control nurse. Instr. Empire Nine Emergency Med. Tech. Program, Rochester, 1976; infection control practitioner dept. medicine U. Rochester Med. Ctr., 1975-79, asst. nursing practice coord. dept. nursing, 1979-80; tech. assoc. IDU Univ. Rochester, 1980-92, nurse mgr. Clin. Rsch. Ctr., 1992—. Contbr. numerous articles to profl. jours. Mem. ANA, AONE, Nat. Assn. Gen. Clin. Rsch. Ctr. Nurse Mgrs., Genesee Valley Nurses Assn., Assn. for Practitioners in Infection Control (bd. dirs.), Western N.Y. State Infection Control Officers (bd. dirs.). Home: 14 W Jefferson Rd Pittsford NY 14534-1902 Office: Univ Rochester Med Ctr Box 619-13 609 Elmwood Ave Rochester NY 14620-2913

PINCUS, RANDI, advertising executive; b. Bklyn., June 10, 1957. BS, Queens Coll., 1977; cert. in printing, Hofstra U., 1980. Asst. prodn. mgr. Brancy Design & Media, Hicksville, N.Y., 1979-81; asst. advt. mgr. Nature's Bounty Inc., Bohemia, N.Y., 1981-85; advt. mgr. Milgray Electronics Inc., Farmingdale, N.Y., 1985-90; community & profl. liaison New Medico Rehab. Svcs. of Nassau, Great Neck, N.Y., 1990-91; mktg. rep. Ctr. for Rehab., Hauppage, N.Y., 1991-92; advt. profl., dir. advt. Aid Auto Stores, Inc., Westbury, N.Y., 1992-95; dir. patient svcs. Lehneis Orthotics & Prosthetics Assocs., Ltd., Roslyn, N.Y., 1995—.

PINDER, JULIE ANN, mortgage banker; b. Wilmington, Del., Dec. 19, 1969; d. Clifton Tyrone and Jeanette Elizabeth (McCollum) Robinson. Mortgage processor Beneficial Mortgage, Newark, Del., 1991-93, Corestates Bank, Wilmington, Del., 1993-95; mortgage file mgr., team leader Soverign Bank, Glen Mills, Pa., 1995—; mem. IRS Vol. Income Tax Assistance, 1995. Mem. Am. Soc. Notaries (hon. mem.). Democrat. Office: Sovereign Bank 131 Wilmington West Chester Pike Glen Mills PA 19342 Office: 1515 Tower Rd Wilmington DE 19806

PINEDA, CECILE, novelist, creative writing educator; b. N.Y.C., Sept. 24, 1942; d. Emilio Rosendo Pineda-Galvan and Marthe-Alice (Henriod) P.; divorced; children: David Leneman, Michael Leneman. BA, Barnard Coll., 1954; MA, San Francisco State U., 1970. Founder, dir., prodr. Theater of Man, exptl. theater co., San Francisco, 1969-81; prof. creative writing San Jose (Calif.) State U., 1991-94, San Diego State U., 1995—. Author: (novels)) Face, 1984, Frieze, 1985, Love Queen of the Amazon, 1991, (novella) Fishlight, 1996. Recipient Gold medal Commonwealth Club Calif., 1985, Sue Kaufman 1st fiction award Am. Acad. and Inst. Arts and Letters, 1985; NEA fiction fellow, 1988. Mem. Nat. Writers Union. Office: San Diego State U English Dept 5500 Campanile Dr San Diego CA 92182

PINEDA, MARIANNA, sculptor, educator; b. Evanston, Ill., May 10, 1925; d. George and Marianna (Dickinson) Packard; m. Harold Tovish, Jan. 14, 1946; children: Margo, Aaron, Nina. Student, Cranbrook Acad. Art, summer 1942, Bennington Coll., 1942-43, U. Calif.-Berkeley, 1943-45, Columbia U., 1945-46, Ossip Zadkine Sch. Drawing and Sculpture, Paris, 1949-50. instr. sculpture Newton Coll. Sacred Heart, 1972-75, Boston Coll., 1975-77; vis. assoc. prof. Boston U., 1974, 78, annually 83-87, 89-90; vis. sculptor Sch. of Mus. Fine Arts, Boston, 1990-91; vis. critic Boston U., 1992. One-woman shows include Slaughter Gallery, San Francisco, 1951, Walker Art Ctr., Mpls., 1952, Currier Gallery, Manchester, N.H., 1954, De Cordova Mus., Lincoln, Mass., 1954, Premier Gallery, Mpls., 1963, Swetzoff Gallery, Boston, 1953, 56, 64, Honolulu Acad. Art, 1970, Alpha Gallery, Boston, 1972, Newton Coll., (Mass.), 1972, Bumpus Gallery, Duxbury, Mass., 1972, Contemporary Art Ctr., Honolulu, 1982, Hanalei Palace, Kona, Hawaii, 1982, Lyman House Mus., Hilo, Hawaii, 1982, Pine Manor Coll., Mass., 1984, Rotenberg Gallery, Boston, 1990, 93, 94, Coll. of William and Mary, 1992, Wiggin Gallery, Boston Libr., 1993 ; group shows include Oakland (Calif.) Civic Mus., 1944, Village Art Ctr., N.Y.C., 1944, Albright Art Gallery, Buffalo, 1947, Bklyn. Mus., 1947, Galerie 8 Paris, 1950, Met. Mus. Art, N.Y.C., 1951, Art Gallery U. Nebr., 1953, San Francisco Mus. of Art, 1955, Inst. Contemporary Art, Boston, 1958, 59, 61, Whitney Mus. Am. Art, N.Y.C., 1953, 54, 55, 57, 59, Boston Arts Festival, 1957, 58, 60, 62, 63, 65, 85, Silvermine Annual Exhibit, Conn., 1957, Art Inst. Chgo., 1957, 61, Pitts. Internat., 1958, Mus. Modern Art., N.Y.C., 1960 (traveling), Addison Gallery Am. Art, 1959, Dallas Mus. Art, 1961, Nat. Inst. Arts & Letters, 1961, N.Y. World's Fair, 1964, De Cordova Mus., 1963, 64, 1972, 75, 87, Sculptors Guild, N.Y.C., 1967-95, Pine Manor Coll., Mass., Pa. State U., 1974, The Women's Bldg., L.A., 1976, Simmons Coll., Mass., 1980, Helen Schlein Gallery, Boston, 1982, SUNY-Buffalo, 1983, Fitchburg Mus. Art, Mass., 1984, Newton Art Ctr., Mass., 1985, Boston U. Art Gallery, 1986, Shulman Sculpture Pk., White Plains, N.Y., 1986, 87, 88, Alchemie Gallery, Boston, 1987, 93, Nat. Acad. Design, N.Y.C., 1985-89, 91, 92, 93, 94-95, Boston Visual Artist Union Invitational, 1986, Bunting Inst., Fed. Reserve Gallery, Boston, 1986, Port of History, Phila., 1987, Brockton Art Ctr., Mass., 1987, Judi Rotenberg Gallery, Boston, ann. 1987—, A.I.R. Gallery, N.Y.C., 1988, Boston Pub. Libr., 1988, Nat. Sculpture Soc., N.Y.C., 1986-89, 90-95, Holyoke Mus., Mass., 1989, Washington Art Assn., Conn., 1989, Bumpus Art Gallery, Duxbury, 1989, Page St. Gallery, San Francisco, 1989, Louis Ross Gallery, N.Y.C., 1990, Shidoni Galleries, Santa Fe, N. Mex., 1990, The Contemporary Mus., Honolulu, 1990, Cast Iron Gallery, 1993, Kyoto (Japan) Civic Gallery, 1993, Walsh Art Gallery, Fairfield, Conn., 1991, Wingspread Gallery, Northeast Harbor, Maine, 1991, World Fin. Ctr. Gallery, 1992, Phila. Sculptors Guild, 1992, Kingsborough C.C., Bklyn., 1994, Womens Caucus for Arts, Staten Island, N.Y., 1995, FSS Gallery, N.Y.C., 1995, Danforth Mus., Framingham, Mass., 1995, Rose Art Mus. Brandeis U., Mass., George Washington U., 1996; represented permanent collections, Walker Art Ctr., Mus. Fine Arts, Boston Williams Coll., (Mass.), Dartmouth coll., Hanover, N.H., Addison Gallery, Andover, Mass., Munson-Williams-Proctor Inst., Ithaca, N.Y., Fogg Art Mus., Cambridge, Mass., Radcliff Coll., Boston Pub. Library, Wadsworth Athenaeum, Hartford, Conn. State of Hawaii, NAD, 1983, 84, 85, 87, 88, 90, 91, 92, 93, 94, Muscarelle Mus., Williamsburg, Va., Walker Art Ctr., Mpls., Bowdoin Coll., Lewiston, Me., U. Mass., Perseus Collection, Honolulu, Nat. Acad. Design, N.Y.C., Boston Conservatory Music, Boston U.; commd. work, Twirling, Bronze figure group, East Boston Housing for Elderly, The Spirit of Lili'uokalani bronze, Hawaii Stat Capitol. Recipient award Oakland Civic Mus., 1944, Mather prize Chgo. Art Inst., 1944, Best of Show award Minn. State Fair, 1954, Margaret Brown award Ins. Contemporary Art, Boston, 1957, Grand prize Boston Arts Festival, 1960, Lampston prize Nat. Sculpture Soc., N.Y.C., 1986, Gold medal Nat. Sculpture Soc., 1988, Herbert Adams Meml. medal, 1996, Taillex award, 1991, Lifetime Achievement award Nat. Womens Caucus Art, 1996; grantee Florsheim Art Fund, 1995, Mass. Found. for Humanities, 1995, Thanks to Grandmother Winnefred Found., 1995; Bunting Inst., Radcliffe Coll. fellow, 1962, 63. Fellow NAD (Gold medal 1987, Artists award 1988, 93). Home: 380 Marlborough St Boston MA 02115-1502 Office: care Judi Rotenberg 130 Newbury St Boston MA 02116-2904

PINEDO, MYRNA ELAINE, psychotherapist, educator; b. Riverton, Wyo., Apr. 28, 1944; d. Pedro Berumen and Ruth Jama (Kuriyama) P.; m. Alan P. Schiesel, Sept. 9, 1964 (div. July 1973); 1 child, Elaine Marie (Schiesel) Thompson; m. Wallace Vern Calkins, Aug. 31, 1990. BA in Psychology, Calif. State U., Northridge, 1980; MA in Cmty. Clin. Psychology, Calif. Sch. Profl. Psychology, 1982; PhD in Cmty. Clin. Psychology, Calif. Sch. Profl. Psychiatry, 1987. Lic. marriage, family and child counselor, Calif.; cert. mental health counselor, Wash.; cert. marriage and family therapist, Wash.

Pychiat. asst. William Newton, M.D., Marine del Rey, Calif., 1983-84; psychologist forensic svcs. dept. Kern County Mental Health, Bakersfield, Calif., 1984-88; alcohol counselor Spl. Treatment Edn. Program Svcs., Bakersfield, 1985-87; marriage and family therapist Jay Fisher & Assocs., Bakersfield, 1986-87; therapist program devel. Correctional Specialties, Bellevue, Wash., 1988-90; pvt. practice HAP Counseling Svcs., Bellevue, 1990—; adj. faculty Calif. State U., Bakersfield, 1986, Kern County Mental Health, 1987, Bellevue C.C., 1989, Antioch U., 1992, 93; instituted various treatment programs for adolescents, Spanish speaking adults and Spanish speaking sex offenders; spkr. in field; expert witness in ct. Panelist EastSide Domestic Violence Com., 1991-93; bd. dirs. Kern County Child Abuse Coun., 1986-88; mem. treatment com. Kern County Child Abuse Task Force, 1985-88; mem. Stop-Abuse by Counselors, 1993—. Mem. Am. Counseling Assn., Am. Assn. Christian Counselors, Assn. Orthopsychiatry, Wash. Assn. Mental Health Counselors, Assn. Marriage and Family Therapists. Office: HAP Counseling Svcs 515 116th Ave NE Ste 114 Bellevue WA 98004-5204

PINEGAR, PATRICIA P., denominational administrator; b. Cedar City, Utah; m. Ed Pinegar; 8 children. Mem. primary gen. bd. LDS Ch., Salt Lake City, 1991-94, gen. pres. of primary, 1994—. Missionary LDS Ch., London, 1985-88; with Provo (Utah) Missionary Tng. Ctr., 1988-90; former 2d counselor young women's gen. presidency LDS Ch., mem. children's sacrament meeting presentation, leadership and missionary tng. ctr. coms., 1995, former ward and stark primary pres. and tchr., pres., tchr. ward relief soc., ward young women pres. and tchr., stake young women adviser; past pres. PTA. Office: LDS Ch 15 East South Temple St Salt Lake City UT 84150

PINES, EUNICE KRUEGER, tax specialist; b. Onaway, Mich., June 17, 1923; d. Arthur Emil and Esther (Cordes) Krueger; m. I. Kurt Pines, Oct. 17, 1942; children: Kurt A., Mark A. (dec.) Brad E. BSBA, Ferris State Coll., 1980; postgrad. studies, Ctrl. Mich. U. Acct. U.S. Steel Corp., Rogers City, Mich., 1941-42; sec. civil svc. variousmil. facilities, 1942-47; sec., editor Scripps Howard Newspaper, Cleve., 1947-51; owner Computerized Tax & Bus. Svc., Treaverse City, Mich., 1981—. Editor Presque Isle County Cemetery, 1993-95; co-editor: Barnum Cemetery, 1986; editor (newsletter) Mich. PTA Bulletin, 1975-79; newspaper columnist 1972-79. Mem. gen. edn. adv. coun. Mich. Dept. Edn., Lansing, 1976-78, title IV adv. coun., 1978-80. Mem. AAUW, Mich. Genealogical Coun., Ikebana, Friendly Garden Club.

PINES, LOIS G., state legislator; b. Malden, Mass., 1940; m. Joseph Pines; 2 children. BA, Barnard Coll., 1960; JD, U. Cin. Law Sch., 1963. Corp. tax atty., 1964-72; alderman City of Newton, Mass., 1971-73; mem. Mass. Ho. of Reps., 1973-78; regional dir. New England Fed. Trade Commn., 1979-81; mem. Mass. State Senate, 1986—. Home: 40 Helene Rd Newton MA 02168-1025 Office: Mass State Senate State House Rm 504 Boston MA 02133*

PINES, NANCY FREITAG, psychotherapist; b. Teaneck, N.J., Nov. 29, 1943; d. Arthur and Miriam L. (Johnson) Freitag; m. Wayne L. Pines, Apr. 16, 1966; children: Noah Morris, Jesse Mireth. BA, Douglass Coll., 1965; MA, George Washington U., 1972; MSW, Cath. U. of Am., 1980. Diplomate Am. Bd. Esaminers in Clin. Social Work. Psychotherapist Family Svcs. of Montgomery County, Rockville, Md., 1981-84; team social worker Psychiat. Inst. of Montgomery County, Rockville, 1984-85; psychotherapist Met. Psychiat. Group, Rockville, 1985-87; pvt. practice Rockville, 1987-88; admissions coord. Chestnut Lodge Hosp., Rockville, 1988-90; mental health therapist Montgomery Gen. Hosp., Olney, Md., 1991—; pvt. practice Washington, 1991—. Mem. NASW, Am. Group Psychotherapy Assn., Greater Washington Soc. for Clin. Social Work. Home: 5821 Nevada Ave NW Washington DC 20015-2547 Office: Montgomery Gen Hosp 18101 Prince Philip Dr Olney MD 20832-1514

PINHEIRO, AILEEN FOLSON, secondary education educator; b. Park River, N.D., Oct. 24, 1921; d. Morris Bernard and Clara Christine (Olson) Folson; m. Eugene Arthur Pinheiro, Sept. 9, 1948. BA, Concordia Coll., 1942; MA, Whittier (Calif.) Coll., 1963. Cert. secondary edn. tchr. Tchr. Kiester (Minn.) High Sch., 1942-44, Wasco (Calif.) Jr. High Sch., 1944-45, Taylors Falls (Minn.) High Sch., 1945-47; tchr. Baldwin Park (Calif.) Unified Sch. Dist., 1947-52, 53-73, ret., 1973. Author: (handbook) The Heritage of Baldwin Park, 1981, (pamphlets) The Heritage of Baldwin Park, 1982-88. Volunteer mus. dir. City of Baldwin Park, 1983—. Recipient Older Am. Recognition award L.A. County Bd. Suprs., 1991. Mem. AAUW (pres. 1967-69), Baldwin Park Hist. Soc. (bd. dirs. 1981-91, Trophy 1983, chmn. 1985-94), Baldwin Park C. of C. (Golden Heritage award 1983, Citizen of Yr. award 1993), Baldwin Park Women's Club (program chmn. 1990-91, treas. 1991-92, internat. chmn. 1989-96, publicity chmn. 1992-96). Presbyterian. Home: 13009 Amar Rd Baldwin Park CA 91706-5702 Office: Baldwin Park Mus 14327 Ramona Blvd Baldwin Park CA 91706-3242

PINKHAM, ELEANOR HUMPHREY, retired university librarian; b. Chgo., May 7, 1926; d. Edward Lemuel and Grace Eleanor (Cushing) Humphrey; m. James Hansen Pinkham, July 10, 1948; children: Laurie Sue, Carol Lynn. AB, Kalamazoo Coll., 1948; MS in Library Sci. (Alice Louise LeFevre scholar), Western Mich. U., 1967. Pub. svcs. libr. Kalamazoo Coll., 1967-68, asst. libr., 1969-70, libr. dir., 1971-93, ret. 1993; vis. lectr. Western Mich. U. Sch. Librarianship, 1970-84; mem. adv. bd., 1977-81, also adv. bd. Inst. Cistercian Studies Libr., 1975-80. Mem. ALA, AAUP, ACRL (chmn. coll. libr. sect. 1988-89), Mich. Libr. Assn. (pres. 1983-84, chmn. acad. div. 1977-78), Mich. Libr. Consortium (exec. coun. 1974-82, chmn. 1977-78, Mich. Libr. of Yr 1986), OCLC Users Coun., Beta Phi Mu. Home: 2519 Glenwood Dr Kalamazoo MI 49008-2405

PINN, VIVIAN W., pathologist, federal agency administrator; b. Halifax, Va., 1941. BA, Wellesley Coll., 1963; MD, U. Va., 1967. Intern in pathology Mass. Gen. Hosp., Boston, 1967-68, rschr. in pathology, 1968-70; asst. pathologist Tufts U. New England Med. Ctr. Hosp., 1970-77, pathologist, 1977-82; from asst. to assoc. prof. pathology Tufts U., 1971-82, asst. dean student affairs, 1974-82; prof., dept. chair pathology Howard U., 1982-91; first dir. Office Rsch. on Women's Health, NIH, Bethesda, Md., 1991-94, assoc. dir. women's health rsch., 1994—. Office: NIH Office Rsch on Women's Health 9000 Rockville Pike Rm 201 Bethesda MD 20892-0001

PINSKER, PENNY COLLIAS (PANGEOTA PINSKER), television producer; b. Miami, Fla., Aug. 22, 1942; d. Theodore Peter and Agatha Madge (Bridgeman) Collias; m. Raymond Robert Elman , Feb. 19, 1962 (dec. 1967); 1 child, Alan; m. Lewis Harry Pinsker, Oct. 22, 1968. Grad. high sch., Miami, Fla. Operator So. Bell Telephone Co., Miami, 1960-67; asst. dir. pub. affairs Sta. WCKT-TV, Miami, 1968-70; dir. pub. affairs Sta. WOR-AM, N.Y.C., 1971-78; reporter documentary and consumer affairs Sta. WTFM, N.Y.C., 1978-81; dir. editorials and sta. svcs. Sta. WWOR-TV, N.Y.C. and Secaucus, N.J., 1981-87; mgr. community affairs and spl. projects Sta. WWOR-TV, Secaucus, 1987-91, dir. community affairs and spl. projects, 1991—. Author, editor: (resource directory) Sta. WOR on Crime, 1982 (recipient George Washington Medal Honor Freedom Found., Emmy award for Outstanding Editorial, 1981), The Changing Family, 1982 (recipient Broadcast Media award San Francisco State U., Emmy nominated), A Child is Missing, 1983 (recipient Broadcast Media award San Francisco State U., Emmy nominated), Taking the High Out of High School, 1984 (recipient Broadcast Media award San Francisco State U, Angel award Religion Media, Bronze medal Internat. TV and Film Soc.); project mgr. A+ For Kids (Emmy award 1989, also Emmy nomination, named 12th nat. Point of Light, 1989), At For Kids: Project Director National, (Emmy nominations 1989-91; N.Y. Emmy award 1989, 1991; Nat. Edn. Assn. award 1991). Media advisor N.J. Crime Prevention Officers Assn.; mem. comm. com. N.J. affiliation Am. Heart Assn., Am. Cancer Soc.; bd. dirs. Queensboro Soc. Prevention Cruelty to Children, 1978-83, Hoboken Chamber Orch., 1989-90, N.J. Edn. Found., 1991-92; pub. mem. N.J. Gov.'s Task Force on Child Abuse and Neglect, 1988—; trustee Assn. for Children of N.J., 1990—; mem. N.J. Coun. on Adult Edn. and Literacy, 1992-93. Recipient disting. svc. award N.J. Speech-Lang.-Hearing Assn., 1987, community svc. award Urban League Hudson County, 1986, media award for achievement in preventing child abuse N.J. Child Assault Prevention Project, 1993. Mem. NAFE, Nat. Broadcast Editl. Assn. (bd. dirs. 1986-87), Nat. Broadcast Assn. Cmty. Affairs, Advt. Coun. N.J. (bd. trustees 1986—), N.J. Broadcasters Assn. (bd. dirs. 1992), Meadowlands Regional C. of C. (bd. dirs. 1991-92). Home: Winterwood Farm 449 Kingwood-Locktown Rd Flemington NJ 08822 Office: Sta WWOR-TV 9 Broadcast Plz Secaucus NJ 07094-2913

PINSKY, ELIZABETH LEAR, social worker; b. N.Y.C., Mar. 22, 1940; d. Phillip E. and Dora (H.) Lear; m. Lawrence M. Pinsky, Sept. 9, 1973; children: Stacey F., Caroline R. BS, Simmons Coll., 1961; MSW, Columbia U., 1963. Cert. social worker, N.Y. Intake worker Dept. of Child and Family Welfare, Westchester, N.Y., 1963-64; med. social worker Mt. Sinai Hosp., N.Y.C., 1964-67; psychiatric social worker Epilepsy Found., Nassau County, N.Y., 1968-72; field instr. Hunter Coll. Sch. Social Work, N.Y.C., 1970-72; dir. social svcs. Margaret Teitz Ctr. Nursing Care, Queens, N.Y., 1972-75, Grace Plaza Long Term Care Facility, Great Neck, N.Y., 1982-87; field instr. Adelphi U. Sch. Social Work, Garden City, N.Y., 1982-87; dir. Home Based Counseling Svcs., Great Neck, 1991—; pvt. practice psychotherapist, elder care cons. Great Neck, 1991—. Mem. NASW (exec. dir. Nassau County div. 1979-82), Acad. Cert. Social Workers, Sr. Umbrella Network of Nassau County (co-chairperson).

PINSKY, JOANNA K., artist, artistic director; b. Bklyn., July 22, 1942; d. Arthur and Miriam (Kapit) Leff; m. Mark Allan Pinsky, Dec. 23, 1963; children: Seth, Jonathan, Lea. BFA, Cornell U., 1964. Co-artistic dir. Art Encounter, Evanston, Ill., 1979-94, artistic dir., 1994—. One-woman shows include Nancy Lurie Gallery, Chgo., 1978, 80, 82, Perimeter Gallery, Chgo., 1986, 90, 93, 96, Air Gallery, N.Y.C., 1991; group shows include Ill. State Mus., 1981, Charles Wustum Mus., Racine, Wis., 1988, Osaka (Japan) Triennial, 1990, Shidoni Galleries, Santa Fe, N.Mex., 1994. Grantee Ill. Arts Coun., 1980. Mem. Chgo. Artists Coalition. Home: 1223 Grant St Evanston IL 60201

PINSON, ARTIE FRANCES, elementary school educator; b. Rusk, Tex., June 20, 1933; d. Tom and Minerva (McDuff) Neeley; m. Robert H. Pinson, Dec. 14, 1963 (div. Nov. 1967); 1 child, Deidre R. BA magna cum laude, Tex. Coll., 1953; postgrad., U. Tex., 1956, North Tex. U., 1958, 63, New Eng. Conservatory, 1955, 57, 59, 62, Tex. So. U., 1971-72; MEd, U. Houston, 1970. Music tchr. Bullock High Sch., LaRue, Tex., 1953-59; music tchr., 9th grade English tchr. Story High Sch., Palestine, Tex., 1959-64; 3d to 6th grade gifted and talented math. tchr. Turner Elem. Sch., Houston, 1964-66; 3d, 5th and 6th grade tchr. Kay Elem. Sch., Houston, 1966-70; 6th grade tchr. Pilgrim Elem. Sch., Houston, 1970-75; 3d to 6th grade math. tchr. Pleasantville Elem. Sch., Houston, 1975-79; kindergarten to 5th grade computer/math. tchr. Betsy Ross Elem. Sch., Houston, 1979—, instrnl. coord., tchr. technologist; instrnl. coord.; lead tchr. math./sci. program Shell/Houston Ind. Sch. Dist., 1986-87, Say "Yes" program, 1988-89; math. tchr. summer potpourri St. Francis Xavier Cath. Ch., 1991; math. tchr. sci. and engring. awareness and coll. prep. program Tex. So. U., 1993, 94, 95, 96; presenter confs. in field; condr. tchr. tng. workshops. Author computer software in field; contbr. articles to mags. Musician New Hope Bapt. Ch., Houston, 1991—, Sunday sch. tchr.; pianist Buckner Bapt. Haven Nursing Home, Houston, 1990-91; mem. N.E. Concerned Citizens Civic League. Recipient Excellence in Math. Teaching award Exxon Corp., 1990. Mem. Assn. African Am. Math. Educators (Salute to Math. Tchrs. award 1991, treas. 1991-93, sec. 1993—), Nat. Coun. Tchrs. Math., Tex. Coun. Tchrs. Math. (Excellence in Math. Tchg. award 1988), Houston Coun. Tchrs. of Math. (Excellence in Math. Tchg. award 1993), Heoines of Jericho, Palestine Negro Bus. and Profl. Women (charter mem.). Home: 5524 Makeig St Houston TX 77026-4021 Office: Betsy Ross Elem Sch 2819 Bay St Houston TX 77026

PINTCHMAN, LISA, technical company executive; b. White Plains, N.Y., Feb. 3, 1959. BA in Psychology, Cornell U., 1981. Acct. exec. Creamer Dickson Basford, 1983-87; acct. exec. Weber Group, Cambridge, Mass., 1987-88, supr., 1988-90, v.p., 1990-92, sr. v.p., 1992—. Mem. IABC. Office: 101 Main St Cambridge MA 02142

PINTO, ANDREA, marketing executive; b. Bronx, N.Y., Sept. 8, 1967; d. Andrew and Winifred Pinto. BS in Mktg., Fordham U., 1989. Mktg. coord. Almor Corp., Congers, N.Y., 1990-92; dir. of mktg., asst. v.p., asst. CRA officer Bankers Fed. Savs., NYC, 1992—. Mem. Comml. Bankers Assn. of N.Y., Fin. Mktg. Forum. Office: Bankers Federal Savings FSB 110 William St New York NY 10038

PINTO, ROSALIND, retired educator, civic volunteer; b. N.Y.C.; d. Barney and Jenny Abrams; m. Jesse E. Pinto (dec.); children: Francine, Jerry, Evelyn. BA in Polit. Sci. cum laude, Hunter Coll.; MA in Polit. Sci., History, Columbia U.; postgrad., Queens Coll., LaGuardia Community Coll. Lic. social studies tchr. jr. high sch., N.Y., per diem lifetime substitute; cert. N.Y. State secondary sch. social studies grades 7-12. Substitute tchr., 1966-69, 90, 91—; tchr. social studies I.S. 126Q, L.I. City, N.Y., 1969-88, Jr. High Sch. 217 Briarwood, N.Y.C., 1988-89; ret., 1989; part-time cluster tchr. social studies and communication arts Pub. Sch. 140, Bronx, N.Y., 1990-91, 92; substitute tchr. I.S. 227Q, 1992-93; participant numerous personal and profl. devel. seminars and workshops. Author curriculum materials; contbr. study guide for regent's competency test, 1990; contbr. poems to anthologies; recorded poem for The Sound of Poetry, Nat. Libr. Poetry (Editor's Choice award 1993, 94). Enrollment asst. Insight Heart Team, 1989; vol. receptionist Whitney Mus., N.Y.C.; mem. com. on pub. transp. Cmty. Bd. 6, Queens, 1990-96, mem. com. on history, 1990—, chmn. beautification com., 1992—, mem. com. on planning and zoning, 1996—; active Great Smokies Song Chase Warren-Wilson Coll., N.C., 1992; vol. local polit. campaigns; mem. Queens Hist. Soc., Forest Hills Van Ct. Homeowners Assn., Ctrl. Queens Hist. Soc., bd. dirs.; mem. Rego Park Coalition Against Violence, Forest Hills Civic Assn., Neighbors Against Graffiti. Recipient cert. of appreciation for participation in workside sponsor program Dept. Probate Cmty. Svc. Project, 1993, for participation in Make a Difference Day, 1994, 95, Beautification Com., 1995, 96. Fellow Mcpl. Art Soc. (hon. mention design 2000 award); mem. NAFE, Internat. Soc. Poets (life mem. adv. panel, Internat. Poet of Merit award 1993), N.Y. Insight Alumni Assn., Columbia U. Grad. Sch. Arts and Scis. Alumni Assn., Hunter Coll. Alumni Assn., Robert F. Kennedy Dem. Assn. (bd. dirs.), Ctr. for Sci. in the Pub. Interest. Home: 97-04 70th Ave Forest Hills NY 11375-5808

PINZA, SUSAN KATHLEEN, secondary education educator; b. Santa Monica, Calif., Apr. 4, 1961; d. Roland Anthony and Eileen Anne (O'Loughlin) P. BA, Stanford U., 1984; MA, Calif. Polytechnic State U., 1995. Cert. tchr., Calif. Tchr. Coalinga (Calif.)-Huron Unified Sch. Dist., 1985—; fellow San Joaquin Valley Writing Project, Fresno, Calif., 1988—; instr. West Hills Coll., Coalinga, 1995. Bd. dirs. Los Niños, San Diego, 1993—. Office: Coalinga HS 750 Van Ness St Coalinga CA 93210

PIOTROWSKI, KIMBERLY, artist; b. Buffalo, N.Y., Aug. 27, 1965; d. Robert John and Patricia Arlene (Murawski) P.; m. James G. Lutes II, Jan. 15, 1994. Student, SUNY, 1983-84; BFA, Sch. Art Inst. Chgo., 1987. Mus. bookstore mgr. Mus. Contemporary Art, Chgo., 1984-90; gallery dir. Dart Gallery, Chgo., 1990-93; gallery mgr. Robert Henry Adams Fine Art, Chgo., 1993-95. Exhibits include Zoe Prodns., Chgo., 1990, Greensboro (N.C.) Artist's League, 1990, Amos Eno Gallery, N.Y., 1990, Randolph St. Gallery, Chgo., 1990, SPACE Gallery, Chgo., 1991, 92, 93, Zephyr Gallery, Louisville, 1991, The Printmakers Collaborative, Chgo., 1992, Davenport (Iowa) Mus. Art, 1992, NAME Gallery, Chgo., 1993, 94, Klein Art Works, Chgo., 1993, Hyde Park Art Ctr., Chgo., 1994, Evanston (Ill.) Art Ctr., 1995, A.R.C., Chgo., 1995, Design ARC, Santa Barbara, Calif., 1995, Prairie State Coll., Chicago Heights, Ill., 1996. Vol. Scotchwood Nursing Home, Bloomington, Ill., 1996. Mem. Nat. Mus. Women in the Arts, N.A.M.E. Gallery, Evanston Art Ctr., Mus. of Contemporary Art-Chgo, Hyde Park Art Ctr. Address: Leroy Opera House 212-214 E Ctr St Leroy IL 61752

PIOTROWSKI, NANCY ANN, psychological scientist; b. Jersey City, May 8, 1963; d. Anthony John Piotrowski and Barbara Jean (Drimones) Seriro. BA in Psychology, Rice U., 1985; MA in Clin. Psychology, U. Houston, 1989, PhD in Clin. Psychology, 1992. Rsch. technician, Health Sci. Ctr. U. Tex., Houston, 1986-88; rsch. asst., project dir., psychiatry Baylor Coll. Medicine, Houston, 1988-92; practicum trainee, psychology svc. Houston VA Med. Ctr., 1988-89, predoctoral intern, psychology svc., 1990-91; rsch. asst., psychology U. Houston, 1989-90; postdoctoral fellow U. Calif., San Francisco, 1992-94, Berkeley, 1994-96; reviewer Jour. Health Psychology, 1992—, Jour. Cmty. Psychology, 1993—, Cognitive Therapy and Rsch., 1994—, Addiction, 1995—. Vol. counselor, trainer, speaker, Crisis Intervention Hotline, Inc., Houston, 1983-92; vol. telephone counselor, Friendship Line, San Francisco, 1993-94; active Sierra Club, 1983—. Mem. APA, ACLU, Assn. for the Advancement of Behavior Therapy. Office: Alcohol Rsch Group U Calif Berkeley 2000 Hearst Ave #300 Berkeley CA 94709

PIPER, FREDESSA MARY, school system administrator; b. Monroe, La., June 19, 1945; d. Floyd Preston and Zona Mary (Jones) P.; m. Robert John Parks, Mar. 20, 1969 (div. 1980). BS, Ill. State U., 1964; MEd with distinction, DePaul U., 1972; EdD, Loyola U., Chgo., 1984. Cert. tchr., gen. adminstr., sch. supt., Ill. Tchr. secondary schs. Chgo. Pub. Schs., 1964-73, staff asst., 1974-76, coord., 1977-83, tchr., coord., 1984-87; asst. supt. Ednl. Svc. Region Cook County, Chgo., 1987-95; project coord. Malcolm X City Coll., Chgo., 1973-74; coord. Athletes for Better Edn., Chgo., 1975-77; cons. Community Reading is Rewarding Program, Chgo., 1989—; author radio scripts, speeches. Project coord. Local Ward Back to Sch. Fun-Fest, Chgo., 1983—; program coord. Pre-Thanksgiving Day Srs. Dinner, Chgo., 1983—; asst. to chmn. Re-election Campaign, Chgo., 1986, 88; promotional dir. Unity in Community Boat Cruise, Chgo., 1987—. Mem. ASCD, Nat. Alliance Black Sch. Educators, Am. Assn. Sch. Adminstrs., Phi Delta Kappa, Delta Epsilon Sigma. Democrat. Baptist.

PIPER, MARGARITA SHERERTZ, retired school administrator; b. Petersburg, Va., Dec. 20, 1926; d. Guy Lucas and Olga Doan (Akers) Sherertz; m. Glenn Clair Piper, Feb. 3, 1950; children: Mark Stephen, Susan Leslie Piper Weathersbee. BA in Edn., Mary Washington Coll. of Fredericksburg, 1948; MEd, U. Va., 1973, EdS, 1976. Svc. rep. C&P Telephone, Washington, 1948-55, adminstrv. asst., 1955-56, svc. supr., 1956-62; tchr. Culpeper (Va.) County Pub. Schs., 1970-75, reading lab dir., 1975-80; asst. prin. Rappahannock (Va.) County Pub. Schs., 1980-81, prin., 1981-88, dir. pupil pers., spl. programs, 1988-95; ret., 1995; chair PD 9 regional transition adv. bd. Culpeper, Fauquier, Madison, Orange and Rappahannock Counties, Va., 1991-94; vice chair Family Assessment and Planning Team, Washington, 1992-95. Recipient Va. Gov. Schs. Commendation cert. Commonwealth of Va., 1989-93. Mem. NEA, Va. Edn. Assn., Va. Coun. Adminstrs. Spl. Edn., Va. Assn. Edn. for Gifted, Rappahannock Edn. Assn. Democrat. Episcopalian.

PIPERNO, SHERRY LYNN, psychotherapist; b. La Crosse, Wis., Sept. 22, 1953; d. Morris and Leona Jennie (Shelmadine-Hanson) Piperno. BA in Fine Arts, U. N.Mex., 1982, MA in Counseling, 1989. Nat. cert. counselor; lic. clin. mental health counselor; cert. criminal justice specialist. Mental health counselor Bernalillo County Detention Ctr., Albuquerque, 1990—; group facilitator and youth authority Juveinile Probation dept. 2d Jud. Dist. Ct., Albuquerque, 1990-92; program therapist Heights Psychiatric Hosp., Albuquerque, 1990-91; cons. Albuquerque Fire Dept. Mem. ACA, Nat. Assn. Forensic Counselors, Am. Mental Health Counselors Assn., Internat. Assn. Addictions and Offender Counseling, Fraternal Order of Police. Democrat. Lutheran.

PIPIA, ROSARIA ANNA, publishing executive, consultant; b. Trapani, Sicily, Italy, Mar. 17, 1962; came to U.S., 1978; d. Gaspare and Gaetana (Nicolosi) P. AA, CUNY, 1985, MA in Italian Lit., 1990; BA in Italian Lang. and Lit., St. John's U., 1987; PhD, NYU. Mgr. book dept. Speedimpex U.S.A., Inc., N.Y.C., 1988-94; pres. Transglobal Books, Inc., 1995—; prof. Italian St. John's U., 1995—; adj. lectr. Italian CUNY, 1989-95; prof. Italian St. John's U., 1995—; Italian tchr. Holy Cross High Sch., 1987-88; Italian tutor Queensborough C.C., 1982-83; book reviewer. Contbr. articles to profl. jours. Mem. MLA, NAFE, Gamma Kappa Alpha. Roman Catholic. Home: 73-22 72nd St Glendale NY 11385-7352 Office: Transglobal Books Inc 73-22 72d St Glendale NY 11385

PIPITONE, GERALDINE, social services professional; b. N.Y.C., Jan. 22, 1951; d. Gilbert Gonazales and Mildred (Lind) Gary; divorced. AA, Broward C.C., Coconut Creek, Fla., 1982. Cert. forensic counselor, addictions counselor Bd. Addiction Profls., Fla. Adminstrv. asst. South Fla. Prestressed, Pompano Beach, 1983-85; addictions counselor House of Hope, Inc., Ft. Lauderdale, Fla., 1985-88, program coord., 1988-90, exec. dir., 1990—; adv. bd. SUB Com., 1994—; adv. mem. Health Care for Homeless, Ft. Lauderdale, 1992—. Fellow Nat. Assn. Alcoholism and Drug Abuse Counselor, Fla. Alcohol and Drug Abuse Assn., Appalachian Mountain Club. Democrat. Lutheran. Home: 2018 NE 17th Ct # 21 Fort Lauderdale FL 33305 Office: House of Hope Inc 908 SW 1st St Fort Lauderdale FL 33312

PIPPIN, KATHRYN ANN, state agency administrator; b. Wilmington, Del., July 12, 1947; d. Allen Davis and Mary T. (Thawley) P. BA, U. Del., 1968, MA, 1969; MA, U. N.C., 1972, PhD, 1977. Cert. tchr., Del. Instr. U. Del., Newark, 1969; teaching asst. U. N.C., Chapel Hill, 1972-73; dir. rsch. and info. devel. SOICC-Dept. Labor, Wilmington, 1979-81; adminstrv. asst. to commr. Del. Dept. Correction, Wilmington, 1982-83, rsch. analyst, 1983—; chairperson Deljis Bd. Mgrs., Dover, Del., 1983-84; mem. adj. faculty Wesley Coll., Dover, 1985-86, Wilmington Coll., 1987—; exec. dir. Mother and Child Reading Program, New Castle, Del., 1993—. Author: Chesapeake Lore, 1980, Teachers: Guardians of our Hopes and Dreams, 1992, (play) Chains of Glory, 1983; producer: (documentary film) A Secret Road North: Harriet Tubman & The Underground Railroad, 1993, Families in Transition: A Smyrna History, 1995, Living in Harmony with Nature, 1995. Del. Rep. State Conv., Lewes, Del., 1982; active Open Spaces Com., New Castle, 1982-83, Pacem in Terris, Wilmington, 1991—; bd. dirs. St. Patrick's Sr. Ctr., Wilmington, 1982-83. Mem. Am. Correctional Assn. (sec. 1988-90, pres. 1990-92, historian 1993-95), Fort Del. Soc. (historian 1983—), Ea. Evaluation Rsch. Soc., Duck Creek Hist. Soc., Leadership Del., Rotary Internat., Phi Beta Kappa. Roman Catholic. Home: 10 N Delaware St Smyrna DE 19977-1102 Office: Del Dept Correction 80 Monrovia Ave Smyrna DE 19977-1530

PIPPIN, LINDA SUE, pediatrics nurse, educator; b. Abingdon, Va., Sept. 10, 1954; d. James Robert and Mary (Reedy) P. ADN, Midlands Tech. Coll., 1988. Registered pediatric nurse, S.C.; RNC, ANCC. RNC Lexington Med. Ctr., West Columbia, S.C., 1988—; adj. faculty Midlands Tech. Coll., 1990-95; PALS instr. Lexington Med. Ctr., 1994, mem. various hosp. coms., 1992—. Super sibling tchr. Lexington Med. Ctr., 1994, hosp. adventure instr., 1993—; tchr. Sunday sch. Grace Chapel, West Columbia, 1982—, sponsor Pioneer Club, 1992—; vol. Spl. Olympics, 1995—. Mem. Soc. Pediatric Nurses.

PIRET, MARGUERITE ALICE, investment banker; b. St. Paul, May 10, 1948; d. E.L. and Alice P.; children: Andrew, Anne. AB, Radcliffe Coll., 1969; MBA, Harvard U., 1974. Comml. loan officer Bank New Eng. (now Fleet Bank), Boston, 1974-79; mng. dir. Kridel Securities, N.Y.C., 1979-81; pres., founder, dir. Newbury, Piret & Co., Inc., Boston, 1981—; trustee, chmn. audit com. Pioneer Mutual Funds, Boston. Vis. com. mem. Am. decorative arts and sculpture Mus. Fine Arts, Boston, 1982—; mem. nominating com. for candidates for overseer of Harvard U. and for candidates for dir. of Harvard Alumni Assn.; adv. com. on shareholder responsibility Harvard U., 1986-87; trustee, mem. exec. com. Boston U. Med. Ctr. Hosp., 1979—, chmn. fin. com.; trustee Mass. Hosp. Assn., 1983-86, Boston Ballet Ctr. for Dance Edn., 1989-93. Mem. Harvard Club. Office: Newbury Piret & Co Inc One Boston Pl Boston MA 02108

PIRNIE, ABBY J., federal agency administrator; b. N.Y.C., Dec. 17, 1949; d. Duncan and Esther (Lewis) P.; m. Abbott B. Lipsky, Jr., Aug. 20, 1971 (div. 1983); children: Leah M. Lipsky, Alyson B. Lipsky; m. Brian J. Maas, Sept. 22, 1984; children: Brittain M. Maas, Dana P. Maas. AB, Smith Coll., 1971, EdM, 1972. Tchr. Pinewood Sch., Los Altos, Calif., JFK Jr. H.S., Florence, Mass., 1971-75; market adminstr. MCI, Washington, 1976-77; cons. Booz, Allen and Hamilton, Bethesda, Md., 1977-78; spl. asst. to dir. Office of Enforcement and Office of Water EPA, Washington, 1978-84, chief environ. results br. Office Mgmt. Sys. and Evaluation, Office Policy, Planning and Evaluation, 1984-86, dir. info. mgmt. and svcs. divsn. Office Info. Resources Mgmt., Office Adminstrn. and Resources Mgmt., 1986-89, dir. program sys. divsn., 1989-91, dir. Office Coop. Environ. Mgmt., office dir., 1991—. Office: EPA 401 M St SW Rm 1601F Washington DC 20460-0001

PIRONTI, LAVONNE DE LAERE, developer, fundraiser; b. L.A., Jan. 11, 1946; d. Emil Joseph and Pearl Mary (Vilmur) De Laere; m. Aldo Pironti, May 21, 1977. BA in Internat. Rels., U. So. Calif., L.A., 1967. Commd. ensign USN, 1968-91, advanced through grades to comdr., 1979; pers. officer Lemoore (Calif.) Naval Air Sta., 1972-74; human rels. mgmt. specialist Human Resource Mgmt. Detachment, Naples, Italy, 1975-78; comms. staff officer Supreme Hdqrs. Allied Powers Europe, Shape, Belgium, 1979-83; dir. Navy Family Svc. Ctr. Sigonella Naval Air Sta., Sicily, 1983-85; exec. officer Naval Sta. Guam, Apra Harbor, 1985-87; comms. staff officer NATO Comm. and Info. Sys. Agy., Brussels, Belgium, 1987-89; polit. officer for Guam, trust Territories Pacific Islands Comdr. Naval Forces Marianas, Agana, Guam, 1989-91; store mgr. Sandal Tree, Lihue, Hawaii, 1991-92; CEO, exec. dir. YWCA of Kauai, Lihue, 1992—. Mem. Kauai Children's Justice com., Lihue, 1993—; co-chair Kauai Human Svcs. Coun., Lihue; bd. dirs. Hawaii Health and Human Svcs. Alliance, Lihue, 1993—; chair Kauai County Family Self Sufficiency Program Adv. Bd., Lihue, 1993—. Decorated Navy Commendation medal, Meritorious Svc. Medal with 1 star, Def. Meritorious Svc. Medal with 2 stars, others; named Fed. Woman of the Yr. Comdr. Naval Forces Marianas, 1986-87. Roman Catholic. Office: YWCA of Kauai 3094 Elua St Lihue HI 96766-1209

PIROVANO, DOROTHY OLIVER, communications executive. Student, Roosevelt U., 1978-83. Reporter, editor Daily Herald (Paddock Publs.), 1970-78; account exec. Pub. Comms. Inc., Chgo., 1981-84, account supr., 1984-85, v.p., dir. tng., 1985-90, sr. v.p., dir. tng., 1990—; mem. faculty, student advisor Harper C.C., 1978-82. Recipient Silver Feather award Women in Comms., 1973, UPI award, 1974-75, Jacob Scher award Sigma Delta Chi/Soc. Profl. Journalists, 1974-75, Charles Stewart Mott award, 1976, Gold Trumpet award Publicity Club Chgo., 1993, 94, 95, Quality of Life award Publicity Club Chgo., 1990, Disting. Achievement award Internat. Assn. Bus. Comms., 1991, 93, Am. Med. Writers Assn., 1993, Silver Anvil award Pub. Rels. Soc. Am., 1983, 85, 86, 95. Office: 35 E Wacker Dr # 1254 Chicago IL 60601*

PIRSCH, CAROL MCBRIDE, state senator, community relations administrator; b. Omaha, Dec. 27, 1936; d. Lyle Erwin and Hilfrie Louise (Lebeck) McBride; student U. Miami, Oxford, Ohio, U. Nebr., Omaha; m. Allen I. Pirsch, Mar. 28, 1954; children: Pennie Elizabeth, Pamela Elaine, Patrice Eileen, Phyllis Erika, Peter Allen, Perry Andrew. Former mem. data processing staff Omaha Public Schs.; former mem. wage practices dept. Western Electric Co., Omaha; former legal sec., Omaha; former office mgr. Pirsch Food Brokerage Co., Inc., Omaha; former employment supr. U.S. West Communications, Omaha, now mgr. pub. policy; mem. Nebr. Senate, 1979—. mem. Omaha Pers. Bd.; founder, past pres., bd. dirs. Nebr. Coalition for Victims of Crime. Recipient Golden Elephant award; Outstanding Legis. Efforts award YWCA, Breaking the Rule of Thumb award Nebr. Domestic Violence Sexual Assault Coalition, Cert. of Appreciation award U.S. Dept. Justice, Partnership award NE Credit Union League, 1995, Wings award League of Women Voters of Greater Omaha, 1995, NE VFW Spl. Recognition award for Exceptional Svc., 1995. Mem. VASA, Nat. Orgn. Victim Assistance (Outstanding Legis. Leadership award), Freedom Found., Orgn. U.S. West Women, Nat. Order Women Legislators, Tangier Women's Aux., Footprinters Internat., Nebr. Hist. Soc., Nebr. Taxpayers Assn., Gretna Optimists, Springfield Boosters, Keystone Citizen Patrol (Keystoner of the Month award), Audubon Soc., Rotary Internat., N.W. Community Club, Benson Rep. Women's Club, Bus. and Profl. Rep. Women Club. Office: State Capitol Lincoln NE 68509

PISCATELLI, NANCY MARIE, educator; b. Boston, Feb. 11, 1953; d. Joseph Murphy and Eleanor Elizabeth (Jeffers) Kelley; m. Thomas George Piscatelli, Apr. 17, 1976; 1 child, Thomas Joseph. BS, Bridgewater State Coll., 1975, MEd, 1979; MEd, Boston Coll., 1977; EdD, Northeastern U., 1989. With sales Wm. Filenes & Sons Co., Boston, 1969-76; lead tchr., computer specialist Boston Pub. Schs., 1975—; cons. Tchrs. Corp. Network, 1979-80. Author/editor: (handbook) The Paraprofessional Handbook, 1979; contbr. articles to profl. jours. Campaign worker Dem. Com., Quincy, Mass., 1975—; active sch. vol. pet project of Mrs. George Bush. Mem. Am. Fedn. Tchrs., Nat. Coun. Tchrs. Math., Internat. Reading Assn., Ea. Educators Rsch. Assn., Boston Tchrs. Union, Boston Computer Soc. Roman Catholic. Home: Pheasant Hill 10 Chickadee Dr Norfolk MA 02056-1741 Office: Boston Pub Schs 26 Court St Boston MA 02108-2505

PISCIOTTA, VIVIAN VIRGINIA, psychotherapist; b. Chgo., Dec. 7; d. Vito and Mary Lamia; m. Vincent Diago Pisciotta, Apr. 1, 1951; children: E. Christopher, Vittorio, V. Charles, Mary A. Pisciotta Higley, Thomas Sansone. BA in Clin. Psychology, Antioch U., 1974; MSW, George Williams Coll., 1984; postgrad., Erickson Inst. of No. Ill., 1990. Lic. clin. social worker; diplomate in clin. social work. Short-term therapist Woman Line, Dayton, Ohio, 1976-79; psychotherapist Cicero (Ill.) Family Svcs., 1982-83, Maywood (Ill.) - Proviso Family Svcs., 1983-84, Maple Ave. Med. Ctr., Brookfield, Ill., 1985-88, Met. Med. Clinic, Naperville, Ill., 1986-88; allied staff Riveredge Psychiat. Hosp., Forest Park, Ill., 1986—, Linden Oaks Hosp., Naperville, Ill., 1990—; psychotherapist, pvt. practice Oakbrook, Ill., 1988—; psychotherapist, co-founder Archer Austin Counseling Ctr., Chgo., 1988-89; psychotherapist, founder Archer Counseling Ctr., Chgo., 1989—; allied staff Linden Oaks Psychiat. Hosp., Naperville, 1990—; substitute tchr. Chgo. Pub. High Sch., 1981. Author treatment prog., workshops in field. Co-founder Co-op Nursery Sch., Rockford, Ill., 1956; leader Great Books of the Western World series, Piqua, Ohio, 1977, Rockford, 1960-65; leader Girl Scouts U.S., St. Bridget Sch., Rockford, 1968-71. Mem. Assn. Labor-Mgmt. and Cons. on Alcoholism, Soc. Clin. Exptl. Hypnosis, Nat. Assn. Social Workers, Acad. Cert. Social Workers, Nat. social Wk. Register, Antioch Univ. Alumnus Assn. Rockford Coll. Alumnae Orgn. (newsletter contbr. 1972-73), Soc. for Clin. and Exptl. Hypnosis (assoc. mem.), Internat. Soc. for Clin. and Exptl. Hypnosis (assoc. mem.). Republican. Roman Catholic. Office: Archer Counseling Ctr 7002 W Archer Ave Ste 2B Chicago IL 60638-2202

PISKOR, CHRYSTAL LEA, manufacturing company professional; b. San Diego, Feb. 1, 1963; d. Gilbert E. Chostner and Sheila I. Radley. BA, Lindenwood Coll., 1984. Sr. estimator Teledyne Ryan Aero., San Diego, 1985-89; sr. contract pricing adminstr. Sundstrand Power Systems, San Diego, 1989-91, sr. supplier cost analyst, 1991-93; contracts mgr. Photon Rsch. Assocs., Inc., San Diego, 1993—; cons. CLC Enterprises, San Diego, 1992—. Advisor Jr. Achievement, San Diego, 1985. Mem. Soc. Cost Estimating and Analysis (dir. edn. 1987, 88, v.p. 1989, treas. 1990), Nat. Contract Mgmt. Assn., Nat. Mgmt. Assn. (co-chair scholarship fund 1985). Republican. Seventh-day Adventist. Office: Photon Rsch Assocs Inc 5720 Oberlin Dr San Diego CA 92121-1723

PISTELLA, CHRISTINE LEY, public health educator; b. Pitts., July 11, 1949; d. David Adam and Mary Louise (Barrett) Ley; m. Frank Joseph Pistella; 1 child, Lauren Nicole. BA in Edn., U. Pitts., 1970, MSW, 1972, MPH, 1977, PhD with distinction, 1979. Lic. social worker, Pa. Program counselor/supr. Transitional Svcs., Inc., Pitts., 1972-74; mental health profl. St. Francis Med. Ctr., Pitts., 1974-75; sr. rsch. social worker Magee-Women's Hosp., Pitts., 1976-78; rsch. assoc. Sch. Pub. Health U. Pitts., 1976-80, rsch. coord. Sch. Social Wk., 1978-79; asst. prof. pub. health U. Pitts. Sch. Pub. Health, 1980—; rsch. cons. USPHS Region V, Chgo., 1985-88, Washington-Greens Human Svcs., 1982-84, Southwestern Pa. Area on Aging, Monessen, 1980-83; rsch. dir. Family Health Coun. of Western Pa., Pitts., 1982-87. Contbr. articles to profl. jours., chpts. to books; editor/co-editor more than 10 rsch. monographs on family health, social wk. Active Mayors Commn. on Families, Pitts., 1988-94, Infant Mortality Rev. Team, Pa. Perinatal Assn., Pitts., 1990-93, Injury Prevention Adv. Bd. Allegheny County, Pitts., 1989—, Venango-Forest Cmty. Health Action Com., 1992-95; steering com. Pa. Area Health Edn. Ctr., 1994—. Mem. NASW, APHA, Nat. Rural Health Assn., Pa. Forum for Primary Health Care, Pa. Pub. Health Assn., Assn. of Tchrs. of Maternal and Child Health, Assn. Cert. Social Workers, Greater Pitts. C. of C. (alumni bd. of leadership Pitts. 1991-94), Delta Omega. Democrat. Roman Catholic. Office: U Pitts Grad Sch Pub Health 216 Parran Hall Pittsburgh PA 15261

PITARRESI, FRANCES LOUISE, controller; b. N.Y.C., Mar. 8, 1948; d. Frank Stanley and Louise Alexandria (Turowska) Deptula; m. Simone Pitarresi, May 30, 1967; children: Frank, Gregory, Catherine, Christopher. BA, NYU, 1968. Acctg. supr., office mgr. Gen. Composition Service, N.Y.C., 1964-78; acctg. mgr. Mediterranean Importing Co., L.I., N.Y., 1978-85; asst. controller World Brands, Inc., L.I., 1985-88; fin. mgr., purchasing mgr., legal adminstr. Redmond, Pollio & Pittoni, PC, L.I., 1988—. Co-pres. Spl. Edn. Parent Tchrs. Assn., Sewanhaka Cen. Sch. Dist., 1988—. Recipient Silver GBPSAL award City of N.Y., 1962, 63, Gold GBPSAL award City of N.Y., 1964. Mem. Assn. Legal Adminstrs., Mensa, Internat. Platform Assn. Republican. Roman Catholic. Office: Redmond Pollio & Pittoni 1461 Franklin Ave Garden City NY 11530-1603

PITCHER, SUSAN INGRID, art consultant; b. Gloucestershire, Eng., Feb. 7, 1967; d. Clive Anthony and Judith (Chandler) P. BA in Art History, Kent (Ohio) State U., 1991. Gallery asst., slide libr. Sch. of Art Kent State U., 1989-91; prodn. artist Line Art Unltd., Chagrin Falls, Ohio, 1992; gallery dir. Michael Thompson Gallery, San Francisco, 1992-95; mktg. assoc. NRG Studio, San Francisco, 1995—; art cons. Mus. West, San Francisco, 1995—. Asst. coord. Camp Okizu Art Auction, San Francisco, 1995; mem. Cartoon Art Mus., San Francisco; vol. Sportsbridge. Mem. Sierra Club.

PITMAN, BARBARA J., environmental education consultant; b. Newark, Apr. 11, 1953; d. Harold F. and Mary M. (Evans) P. BA, Bridgewater Coll., 1975. Edn. coord. Indochinese Refugee Assistance Program, Arlington, Va., 1976-78; classroom tchr. Arlington County Pub. Schs., 1978-86; mktg. rep. Modern Curriculum Press, Va., Md., Washington, 1986-89; dir. environ. edn. Nat. Wildlife Fedn., Washington, 1989-94; cons. in field Washington, 1994—; adv. bd. D.C. Environ. Edn. Coun., 1993-95, Project Wild, Bethesda, Md., 1994-95. Fund raising com. vol. Arlington-Alexandria Coalition for the Homeless, 1992—. Mem. ASCD, North Am. Assn. Environ. Edn.

PITMAN, BONNIE LOUISE, museum director; b. Stamford, Conn., Apr. 24, 1946; d. Benjamin and Margaret (Hackett) P.; m. George Gelles (div. 1985); 1 child, David Gelles. AA, Pine Manor Coll., 1966; BA, Sweet Briar Coll., 1968; MA, Tulane U., 1972. Curator of edn. Winnipeg Art Gallery, Can., 1968-71, New Orleans Mus. Art, 1971-75; cons. NEA, NEH, Washington, 1976-80; assoc. dir. Seattle Art Mus., 1981-89, dir. acting, 1985-86; dep. dir. Univ. Art Mus. U. Calif., Berkeley, 1990-95; exec. dir. Bay Area Discovery Mus., Sausalito, Calif., 1995—; cons. Parker Bros. Games, Salem, Mass., 1980, Lincoln Ctr., N.Y.C., 1980-81; program dir. The Pew Charitable Trusts, Phila., 1994—; adv. com. San Francisco Art Inst., 1996. Author: Watermelon, 1972, Museums, Magic & Children, 1981, Taking a Closer Look: Evaluation in Art Museums, 1992, Excellence and Equity: Education & The Public Dimension of Museums. Recipient leadership tomorrow award United Way of King County, Seattle, 1984-85. Mem. Am. Assn. Mus. (chair nat. taskforce on edn. 1989-94, mus. educators award 1983, v.p. 1976-80, 88-92, chair accreditation com. 1985—), Sausalito C. of C., Nat. Hist. Trust, Western Mus. Assn. (dir.'s chair award 1992). Democrat. Episcopal. Office: Bay Area Discovery Mus 557 E Fort Baker Sausalito CA 94965

PITT, JANE, medical educator; b. Frankfurt, Fed. Republic Germany, Aug. 25, 1938; came to U.S., 1939.; d. Ludwig Friederich and Vera (Aberle) Ries; m. Martin Irwin Pitt, Aug. 12, 1962 (dec. 1980); children: Jennifer, Eric Jonathan; m. Robert Harry Socolow, May 25, 1986; stepchildren: David, Seth. BA, Radcliffe Coll., 1960; MD, Harvard U., 1964. Diplomate Am. Bd. Pediatrics. Resident Children's Hosp. Med. Ctr., Boston, 1964-66; fellow Tufts U. Med. Sch., Boston, 1966-67, Harvard U. Med. Sch., Boston, 1967-69; asst. prof. SUNY Downstate Sch. Medicine, N.Y.C., 1970-71; asst. prof. Coll. Physicians and Surgeons Columbia U., N.Y.C., 1971-75, assoc. prof. Coll. Physicians and Surgeons, 1975—; mem. instl. rev. bd. Columbia Health Scis. Campus, N.Y.C., 1982—. Reviewer Jour. of Infectious Diseases, New Eng. Jour. Medicine, 1976—; contbr. articles to profl. jours. NIH grantee, 1974—. Fellow Infectious Disease Soc.; mem. NIH (study sect.), Pediat. Infectious Disease Soc., Soc. Pediat. Rsch. Democrat. Jewish. Home: 34 Westcott Rd Princeton NJ 08540-3060 Office: Columbia U Coll Physicians Surgeons 630 W 168th St New York NY 10032 3702

PITTMAN, JACQUELYN, mental health nurse, nursing educator; b. Pensacola, Fla., Dec. 22, 1932; d. Edward Corry Sr. and Hettie Oean (Wilson) P. BS in Nursing Edn., Fla. State U., 1958; MA, Columbia U., 1959, EdD, 1974. Physician asst. Med. Ctr. Clinic, Pensacola, 1953-55; clin. instr., asst. dir. nursing svc. Sacred Heart Hosp., Pensacola, 1955-56; instr.psychiatric nurse Fla. State Hosp., Chattahoochee, 1958, Pensacola Community Coll., 1959-60, 62-63; chmn. div. nursing Gulf Coast Community Coll., Panama City, Fla., 1963-66; asst. prof. U. Tex., Austin, 1970-72, assoc. prof., 1972-80; prof. nursing, coord. curriculum and teaching Grad. Program La. State U. Med. Ctr. Sch. Nursing, New Orleans, 1980—; curriculum cons. Nicholls State U., Thibodaux, La., 1982, Our Lady of the Lake Sch. Nursing, Baton Rouge, 1983; rsch. liaison So. Bapt. Hosp., New Orleans, 1987-89, Med. Ctr. La., 1992—; mem. Sci. Misconduct Inquiry com. La. State U. Med. Ctr., 1992—; adv. bd. Sister Henrietta Guyot Professorship. Tchr. Christian edn. program for mentally retarded St. Ignatius Martyr Ch., 1979-80; tchr. initiation team Rite of Christian Initiation of Adults, Our Lady of the Lake Cath. Ch., Mandeville, La., 1983-86; ethics com., bd. trustees Hotel Dieu Hosp., New Orleans, 1987-91; v.p., bd. dirs. St. Tammany Guidance Ctr., Inc., Mandeville, 1987-91; mem. Dem. Nat. Comm., Presdl. Task Force, 1992, Ctr. for Study of Presidency; judge Internat. Sci. and Engring. Fair Assn., 1990, 92; del. La. State Nurses' Assn. State Conv., 1992, 94; assoc. Libr. of Congress, Smithsonian Instn. Mem. ANA, LWV, N.Y. Acad. Scis., Acad. Polit. Sci., Libr. of Congress Assocs., Nat. Trust for Hist. Preservation, La. Endowment for Humanities, La. Nurses Assn. (archivist 1987—, state task force com. to preserve hist. documents 1987—), So. Nursing Rsch. Soc., Nat. League Nursing, Boston U. Nursing Archives, Women's Inner Cir. Achievement N.Am. Cmtys., Internat. Order of Merit, World Found. Successful Women, Wilson Ctr. Assocs., Kappa Delta Pi, Sigma Theta Tau. Democrat. Roman Catholic. Address: 204 Woodridge Blvd Mandeville LA 70471-2604 Office: La State U Med Ctr 1900 Gravier St New Orleans LA 70112-2232

PITTMAN, LISA, lawyer; b. Limestone, Maine, Jan. 4, 1959; d. William Franklin and Rowena Paradis (Umphrey) P.; m. Edward Leon Pittman, May 26, 1984; 1 child, Graham Edward Paradis. BA, U. Fla., 1980, MA, 1981, JD, 1984; LLM, George Washington U., 1988. Bar: Fla. 1984, D.C. 1993, U.S Supreme Ct. 1993. Spl. asst. to gen. counsel Nat. Oceanic and Atmospheric Adminstrn., Washington, 1984-85, atty., advisor, 1985-87; minority counsel Com. on Mcht. Marine & Fisheries, Ho. of Reps., Washington, 1987-95; dep. chief counsel com. on resources U.S. Ho. of Reps., Washington, 1995—. Pres. Ho. of Reps. Child Care Ctr. Parents Assn., Washington. Home: 6123 Ramshorn Dr Mc Lean VA 22101-2333 Office: US House of Reps 1324 Longworth HOB Washington DC 20515

PITTMAN, MIRIAM LEE, dietician; b. Guntersville, Ala., May 11, 1965; d. Wynston Eugene and Oma Dell (May) P. BS, David Lipscomb U., 1987. Lic. registered dietician; cert. nutrition support dietician. Coord. dietary svcs. Beverlu Enterprises, Atlanta, 1988; clin. dietician U. Hosp., Birmingham, Ala., 1988-91; chief clin. dietician Bapt. Med. Ctr., Birmingham, Ala., 1991-95; clin. nutrition mgr. Brimingham Bapt. Med. Ctrs., 1995—. Mem. Birmingham Dist. Dietetic Assn. (bd. dirs., edn. and career devel. coord. 1995—). Republican. Mem. Ch. of Christ. Office: Birmingham Bapt Med Ctr 701 Princeton Ave Birmingham AL 35211

PITTMAN, NATALIE ANNE, paralegal; b. Detroit, Apr. 17, 1952; d. George Jack and Catherine Helen (Platusich) Ochenski; children: Erik Garrett Pittman, Jason Christopher Pittman; m. John Robert Pittman, Dec. 16, 1977; stepchildren: Mark Allen, David Robert. AS with highest honors, Cen. Tex. Coll., 1985. Bd. cert. legal asst. civil trial law, Tex. Owner, mgr. pet store, Killeen, Tex., 1977-85; paralegal Silverblatt Law Office, Killeen, 1985—; corp. sec. Am. Budgerigar Soc., Inc., Killeen, 1986—; also bd. dirs.; spkr. legal asst. program Ctrl. Tex. Coll., Killeen, 1986—, adv. com., 1989—, instr., 1991—; editorial adv. Office Mgmt. and Legal Ethics, 1995; bd. dirs. Heart of Tex. Hospice; show promoter Thunder in the Hills Drum Corps, 1993—; mem. show promoters task force Drum Corps Internat., 1994—. Editorial advisor Know Your Pet-Budgerigars, 1987. Spokesperson Concerned Citizens Quality Edn., Killeen, 1981; pres. Pebble Sch. PTA, Killeen, 1984; active Killeen H.S. Band Boosters, 1987—, pres., 1991-93; Help One Student To Succeed (HOSTS) tutor Killeen Ind. Sch. Dist., 1993-94; umpire state softball tournaments, 1976; active polit. and civic orgns. Mem. State Bar Tex., Heart of Tex. Assn. Legal Profls. (pres. 1996—), Nat. Notary Assn., Dallas-Ft. Worth Exhbn. Budgerigar Club (show sec. 1989), Heart 'O Tex. Exhbn. Budgerigar Club (founding). Republican. Roman Catholic. Home and Office: 1704 Kangaroo Ave Killeen TX 76543-3334

PITTONI, MARY JO, English educator; b. S.I., N.Y., Sept. 1, 1947; d. Francis Albert and Mary Helen (O'Grady) Rocque; m. Luke M. Pittoni, July 8, 1972; children: Elizabeth, Katherine, Ellen. AB in English, Coll. of New Rochelle, 1969; MA in Am. Studies, Fairfield U., 1976. Cert. secondary English tchr., Conn. 7th and 8th grade English tchr. Stamford (Conn.) Pub. Schs., 1969-76, 7th grade English, gifted/talented tchr., 1988-93, 8th grade English tchr., 1993—; moderator Improv Club for Mid. Schoolers, 1989—; mem. Coalition Sch. Cabinet, 1993-95; mentor to new tchrs., 1995—. Editor Sch. Yearbook, 1993-95. Mem. parent's bd. Stamford H.S., 1993—, Trinity H.S., Stamford; mem. LWV, Stamford, 1980—; mem. exec. bd. Stamford Jr. Women, 1977-87; mem. St. Joseph Hosp. Aux., 1976—. Mem. AAUW (bd. dirs. 1977-87), NCTE, CCTE, ASCD. Democrat. Roman Catholic. Office: Rippowam Magnet Mid Sch 381 High Ridge Rd Stamford CT 06903

PITTS, BARBARA TOWLE, accountant; b. St. Paul, Minn., Nov. 8, 1944; d. James Francis and Helen (Gorman) Towle; m. E.R. Pitts, Oct. 19, 1965; 1 child, Paris Tucker Pitts. BSBA, U. Ala., 1980. CPA, Wash., Tenn. Prin. Barbara M. Pitts Assocs., Fayetteville, Tenn., 1982-90, Barbara M. Pitts CPA, Seattle, 1990—. Bd. dirs. United Way Lincoln County, Fayetteville, 1989, Lincoln County Bd. Edn., Fayetteville, 1988-90; mem. planning com. Tenn. Hist. Soc., Nashville, 1989. Recipient Cert. of Recognition Tenn. Main St. Program, 1989; named Woman of Yr. Fayetteville Bus. and Profl. Women, 1988. Mem. AICPA, Wash. Soc. CPA, N.W. Watercolor Soc. (treas.), Group Health Coop. Puget Sound (ctrl. regional coun.). Home: 3515 E Marion St Seattle WA 98122-5258

PITTS, VIRGINIA M., human resources executive; b. Boston, Nov. 22, 1953; d. Harold Francis and Connie (Caico) Cummings; m. Daniel J. Pitts, Mar. 12, 1977. Student, Northeastern U., 1982-85, Lesley Coll. Adminstrv. asst. J. Baker Inc., Hyde Park, Mass., 1980-82, fin. adminstr., 1982-84, dir. human resources, 1984—, 1st sr. v.p., 1991—; trustee New Eng. Joint Bd. AFL-CIO, Quincy, Mass., 1984-89; guest lectr. Aquinas Jr. Coll.; mem. bd. dirs. Boston Crusaders, Drum & Bugle Corps. Instr. Boston Crusaders Drum and Bugle Corps, other marching bands, Mass., R.I., Maine, N.H., 1973-85; regional v.p. 210 Charitable Assn., Watertown, Mass., 1989-90; bd. dirs. Handi-Kids, Boston Crusaders Drum and Bugle Corps; guest lectr. Aquinas Jr. Coll., Milton, Mass. Mem. Am. Mgmt. Assn., Am. Compensation Assn. (cert. profl.), Soc. Human Resource Mgrs. Office: J Baker Inc 555 Turnpike St Canton MA 02021-2724

PIVER, SUSAN M., lawyer, insurance manager; b. Phila.; d. David and Rosalind (Nicholas) Myers; m. M. Steven Piver; children: Debra, Carolyn, Kenneth. AB, U. Pa.; postgrad., Temple U.; JD, SUNY, Buffalo, 1976. Bar: N.Y. 1977. Spl. counsel fraud and abuse Erie County (N.Y.) Medicaid, Buffalo, 1976-82, atty., dir. medicaid utilization rev., 1982-85; atty., v.p. legal affairs, counsel Children's Hosp. of Buffalo, 1985-95; pvt. practice Buffalo, 1995—; adj. faculty D'Youville Coll., 1991-95. Mem. Brylin Adv. Bd., D'Youville Health Svcs. Adv. Bd.; bd. dirs. Coordinated Care, 1989—, vice chair 1994-96, chair 1996—. Mem. Am. Acad. Hosp. Lawyers, Nat. Health Lawyers Assn., N.Y. State Bar Assn. (com. on health care law, 1988—), Erie County Bar Assn. (co-chair health care law com.). Office: 315 Lincoln Pky Buffalo NY 14216-3127

PIVIN, JEANETTE EVA, psychotherapist; b. Fall River, Mass., Feb. 24, 1932; d. Oscar and Ida Antoinette (Gauthier) P. B in Edn., Cath. Tchrs. Coll., 1956; MA in Theology, U. Notre Dame, 1967; cert. clin. pastoral edn., Worcester State Hosp., 1975; cert. interior design, Hall Inst. Tech., 1989; cert. divorce mediator, Roger Williams Univ, 1995. Tchr. St. Matthew Sch., Cranston, R.I., 1956-64; assoc. prof. religious studies Salve Regina U., Newport, R.I., 1967-74; staff counselor La Salette Counseling Svcs., Attleboro, Mass., 1975-80; pastoral counselor Interfaith Counseling Ctr., Providence, R.I., 1975—; pvt. practice Providence, 1980—. Home and Office: 139 Woodbine St Providence RI 02906-2543

PIZZAMIGLIO, NANCY ALICE, performing company executive; b. Oak Park, Ill., Aug. 22, 1936; d. Howard Joseph and Marian Louise (Henne) Gilman; m. Ernest George Lovas, May 17, 1957 (div. Nov. 1976); children: Lori Dianne, Randall Gilman; m. Albert Theodore Pizzamiglio, Mar. 27, 1978. Student, North Tex. State U., 1955-56. Stewardess North Cen. Airlines, Chgo., 1956-57; receptionist Leo Burnett Advt. Agy., Chgo., 1957-59; office mgr. Judy Stallons Employment Agy., Oak Brook, Ill., 1973-75; mgr. and escort Prestige Vacations, Inc., Oak Brook, Ill., 1975-76; corp. dir. Al Pierson Big Band U.S.A., Inc., Aubrey, Tex., 1976—, Al Pierson, Ltd., Aubrey, Tex., 1978—; corp. pres. Gilman, Inc. Artists Mgmt., Aubrey, Tex., 1982—; owner Dancing Horse Ranch, Aubrey, Tex., 1983—; bus. mgr. Guy Lombardo's Royal Canadians, Aubrey, Tex., 1989—. Editor: (newsletter) Property Owners Assn., 1972-73; contbr. articles to profl. jours. Recipient expert award NRA, 1952. Mem. U.S. Lipizzan Registry (bd. dirs. 1986-89), Dallas Dressage Club (bd. dirs. 1988-94), Am. Horse Shows Assn., Am. Quarter Horse Assn., U.S. Dressage Fedn. (qualified rider 1989, third/all breeds, first level 1989, first/all breeds, fourth level 1991, third Vintage Cup, fourth level 1991, third all-breeds first level 1992, third vintage cup first level 1992). Republican. Episcopalian. Address: Gilman Inc Artist Mgmt 34201 FM 428 East Aubrey TX 76227

PIZZORNO, LARA ELISE, writer, editor; b. N.Y.C., Oct. 5, 1948; d. Daniel A. and Elinor M. (Kugel) Udell; m. John James Leary Jr. (div. 1979); m. Joseph E. Pizzorno; children: Galen Udell. BA magna cum laude, Wheaton Coll., 1970; MAR in Philos. Theology, Yale U., 1973; MA in English Lit., U. Wash., 1986. Lic. massage therapist. Instr. philosophy Edmonds (Wash.) C.C., 1974-78; grants writer Seattle U., 1978-79, asst. dir. devel., 1979-81; devel. cons. Bastyr U., Seattle, 1981-83, copyeditor Textbook of Natural Medicine, 1986-89; instr. English North Seattle C.C., 1986-89; dir. publs. Trillium Health Products, Seattle, 1992-93; owner WordWorks, Seattle, 1993—; mem. adv. bd. Bastyr U., Seattle, 1989—. Author: The Complete Book of Bread Machine Baking, 1993; editor, contbg. writer: Choices, Natural Lifestyle and Nutrition mag.; editor, contbg. writer: Total Wellness, 1996contbr. numerous articles to popular mags. Mem. Phi Beta Kappa. Home: 4220 NE 135th St Seattle WA 98125 Office: WordWorks 4220 NE 135th St Seattle WA 98125

PIZZULLI, AMY, elementary education educator; b. N.Y.C., Oct. 30, 1956; d. Ralph and Christine (Modena) Villarola. BS, Trenton State U., 1978. Tchr. Holmdel (N.J.) Sch. Dist. Office: Holmdel Sch Dist 67 McCampbell Rd Holmdel NJ 07733

PLAAS, KRISTINA MARIA, neonatal nurse specialist; b. Salt Lake City, June 6, 1959; d. Hyrum and Johanna Emilie Maria (Westerduin) P. BSN, U. Tenn., 1981; MSN, Vanderbilt U., 1990. RN, Utah. Staff nurse intensive care nursery U. Tenn. Meml. Rsch. Ctr. and Hosp., Knoxville, 1981-84; staff nurse neonatal ICU Vanderbilt U. Hosp., Nashville, 1984-86; staff specialist newborn ICU U. Utah Hosp., Salt Lake City, 1986, staff nurse/clin. specialist newborn ICU, 1987—; mem. nursing purchasing coun. U. Hosp. Consortium, Oak Brook, Ill., 1993—; cons., product specialist Baxter Healthcare, Round Lake, Ill., 1994—. Author, editor: U. Utah Dept. Nursing Standards of Practice, 1986—, Nat. Assn. Neonatal Nurses Practice Guidelines, 1993—; editor: Perspective newsletter, 1994—. Mem. Nat. Assn. Neonatal Nurses (practice com. 1984—, Robyn Main Excellence in Clinical Practice award 1990), Utah Perinatal Assn. (edn. bd. 1994—), Utah Assn. Neonatal Nurses, Nat. Perinatal Assn., Sigma Theta Tau. Home: 2256 Foothill Dr # F 116 Salt Lake City UT 84109-3971 Office: U Utah Hosp Newborn ICU 50 N Medical Dr Salt Lake City UT 84132-0001

PLAHETKA, ROSE ANNE, elementary school teacher; b. Michigan City, Ind., Oct. 18, 1960; d. Joseph W. Jr. and Rose E. (May) P. BA, Purdue U., 1982; MEd, U. Houston, 1987. Cert. ednl. diagnostician, Tex. 1988; cert. elem. tchr. Tex, 1984, spl. edn. Tex., 1984. Resource room tchr. Dodson Elem. Sch., Houston, 1983-90, generic spl. edn. tchr., 1990-94; life skills tchr. Piney Point Elem. Sch., Houston, 1994—; mem. Reading is Fundamental

Com., Houston, 1988-94. Author: (computer software) What's the Weather?, 1983. Mem. Rite of Christian Initiation of Adults Team St. Francis de Sales, Houston, 1992-95, lector, 1994—; vol. income tax assistance IRS, Houston, 1994—. Roman Catholic. Home: 9201 Clarewood #99 Houston TX 77036 Office: Piney Point Elem Sch 8921 Pagewood Houston TX 77063

PLAIA, CAROL ANN, artist; b. Granite City, Ill., Oct. 10, 1945; d. Alan Arthur and Gertrude May (Marlow) Dale; m. Mark Edward Plaia, Sept. 8, 1984. mem. bd. dirs., newsletter editor Oreg. Women's Caucus For Art, Portland, 1992-94; del. 4th world conf. on women Nat. Women's Caucus for Art, Beijing, People's Republic of China, 1995. Author: (guest editl.) Progressive Woman, 1993, (book) Visages With A Voice, 1995. Arts commr. City of Redmond, Wash., 1995—. Mem. Seattle Women's Caucus For Art, Artist's Trust. Home: 11106 158th Ave NE Redmond WA 98052

PLAIN, BELVA, writer; b. N.Y.C., Oct. 9, 1919; d. Oscar and Eleanor Offenberg; m. Irving Plain, June 14, 1941 (dec. 1982); 3 children. Grad., Barnard Coll. Author: Evergreen, 1978, Random Winds, 1980, Eden Burning, 1982, Crescent City, 1984, The Golden Cup, 1987, Tapestry, 1988, Blessings, 1989, Harvest, 1990, Treasures, 1992, Whispers, 1993, Daybreak, 1994, The Carousel, 1995. Office: care Delacorte Press 1540 Broadway New York NY 10036-4039

PLAINE, LLOYD LEVA, lawyer; b. Washington, Nov. 3, 1947. BA, U. Pa., 1969; postgrad., Harvard U.; JD, Georgetown U., 1975. Bar: D.C. 1975. Legis. asst. to U.S. Rep. Sidney Yates, 1971-72; with Sutherland, Asbill & Brennan, Washington, 1975-82, ptnr., 1982—. Fellow Am. Bar Found., Am. Coll. Trust and Estate Counsel, Am. Coll. of Tax Counsel; mem. ABA (chmn. real property, probate and trust law sect.). Office: Sutherland Asbill & Brennan 1275 Pennsylvania Ave NW Washington DC 20004-2404

PLAISTED, CAROLE ANNE, elementary education educator; b. Meredith, N.H., Apr. 3, 1939; d. Morris Holman and Christina Martin (Dunn) P. BEd with honors, Plymouth (N.H.) Tchrs. Coll., 1960; MA, Columbia U., 1966; cert., N.Y. Inst. Photography, 1990. Cert. tchr., N.H. Tchr. Lang St. Sch., Meredith, 1960-61, Mechanic St. Sch., Laconia, N.H., 1961-62, Wheelock Lab. Sch., Keene, N.H., 1963-94; asst. prof. emeritus Keene State Coll.; summer tchr. Cheshire County Headstart, Hinsdale, N.H., 1965; tchr. children's lit. Keene State Coll., 1974, 75; classroom evaluator D.C. Heath Co., Lexington, Mass., 1985-86; dist. trainer for drug edn. supervisory unit, Keene, 1988-94. Author: The Graduates Speak, 1990; co-author curriculum materials; contbr. Kindergarten: A Sourcebook for School and Home, 1984. Trustee Reed Free Libr., Surry, N.H., 1988—; program chair Wheelock Sch. PTA, 1964-65. Named Outstanding Elem. Tchr. of Am., 1973. Mem. Cheshire County Ret. Tchrs. Assn., Delta Kappa Gamma (pres. Alpha chpt. 1996, corr. sec. Alpha chpt. 1972-76, state scholarship chmn. 1985—, Beta Alpha state scholarship 1989).

PLAISTED, JOAN M., diplomat; b. St. Peter, Minn., Aug. 29, 1945; d. Gerald A. and Lola May (Peters) P. Student, U. Grenoble, France, 1965-66, U. Calif., Berkeley, 1966; BA in Internat. Rels., Am. U., 1967, MA in Asian Studies, 1969; graduate, Nat. War Coll., 1988. Korea desk officer Commerce Dept., Washington, 1969-72, Japan desk officer, 1972-73; commercial officer Am. Embassy, Paris, 1973-78; internat. economist Orgn. Econ. Cooperation & Devel., Paris, 1978-80; econ. officer Am. Consulate Gen., Hong Kong, 1980-83; trade negotiator White House Office of Spl. Trade Rep., Geneva, 1983-85; deputy dir. China desk State Dept., Washington, 1985-87; acting dep. dir., chief econ./comml. sect. Am. Inst. in Taiwan, Taipei, 1988-91; chargé d'affaires, deputy chief of mission Am. Embassy, Rabat, Morocco, 1991-94; dir. Thai and Burma affairs Dept. of State, Washington, 1994-95; sr. advisor U.S. Mission to UN N.Y.C., 1995; amb. to Republic of Marshall Islands and Republic of Kiribati, 1996—. Recipient Lodestar award Am. U., 1993. Mem. Am. Fgn. Svc. Assn., Hong Kong Wine Soc. (founding). Address: PO Box 1379 Majuro MH 96960-1379

PLANCK, SUSAN HILGART, farmer; b. Chgo., Apr. 9, 1941; d. Arthur Alfred and Naomi (Nelson) Hilgart; m. Charles Robert Planck, Sept. 1962; children: Hilary (dec. 1977), Charles F., Nina. Student, Oberlin Coll., 1959-62; BA, SUNY, Buffalo, 1973. Vegetable farmer Potomac Vegetable Farms, Vienna, Va., 1973-77; technician Mountain Horticultural Crops Rsch. Sta., Fletcher, N.C., 1978; owner, operator Wheatland Vegetable Farms, Purcellville, Va., 1979—. Mem. Affordable Housing Com., Loudoun County, Va., 1988-92. Mem. Pa. Sustainable Agr. Assn., Piedmont Environmental Coun., Purple Martin Conservation Assn. Democrat. Home and Office: 38287 John Wolford Rd Purcellville VA 20132

PLANT, MARETTA MOORE, public relations and marketing executive; b. Washington, Sept. 4, 1937; d. Henry Edwards and Lucy (Connell) Moore; m. William Voorhees Plant, June 14, 1959; children: Scott Voorhees, Craig Culver, Suzannah Holliday. BS in Bus. Adminstrn., U. Ark., 1959. Owner, mgr. Handcrafts by Maretta, Westfield, N.J., 1966-73; photographer M-R Pictures, Inc., Allendale, N.J., 1973-77; communications asst. United Way-Union County, Elizabeth, N.J., 1977-79; pub. rels. cons. Creative Arts Workshop, Westfield, 1977-81, Coll. Adv. Cons., 1983-89; community rels. coord. Raritan Bay Health Svcs. Corp., Perth Amboy, N.J., 1979-81; dir. pub. rels. St. Elizabeth Hosp., Elizabeth, N.J., 1981-86; dir. mkgt./communications Somerset Med. Ctr., Somerville, N.J., 1986-90; v.p. mktg. and pub. rels. Somerset Med. Ctr., Somerville, 1990—. Trustee Bridgeway House, Elizabeth, 1982-86, Far Hills Race Meeting Assn., N.J., 1989—, pub. rels com. N.J. Hosp. Assn., Princeton, 1982-83, 89-92, coun. auxs., 1988-92, pub. rels. com., 1989-92; committeewoman Union County Rep. Com., Westfield, 1983-85; bd. dirs. pub. affairs com. Morris Mus., Morristown; bd. dirs. communications com. Somerset County United Way, 1992—. Mem. Pub. Rels. Soc. Am., Nat. Fedn. Press Women, N.J. Press Women (chmn. communications contest 1990-92), Am. Soc. Hosp. Mktg. and Pub. Rels. (coun. mem. Region II, membership com.), N.J. Hosp. Mktg. and Pub. Rels. Assn. (corr. sec. 1984-86, pres. 1986-88), Somerset County C. of C. (mag. com. 1988-93), U. Ark. Alumni Assn., Summit-Westfield Assn., Delta Gamma, Coll. Women's (Westfield) Club, Soroptomists (internat., charter). Home: 118 Effingham Pl Westfield NJ 07090-3926 Office: Somerset Med Ctr Rehill Ave Somerville NJ 08876-2546

PLANTIKOW, FRANCES KAY, human resources specialist; b. Lansing, Mich., Jan. 28, 1947; d. Charles Black and Vivian Jane (Francis) Leighton; m. John Steven Plantikow, Feb. 21, 1970 (div.); children: Jennifer Ann, Bertram Jay (dec.). BA, Mich. State U., 1969; MS in Edn., SUNY, Plattsburgh, 1980. Cert. nat. counselor. Program dir. Stop ctr. for domestic violence Clinton County Mental Health Assn., Plattsburgh, 1981-83, community residence supr. Breakthrough II, 1985-86, dir. employee assistance svcs., 1986-93; counselor/advocate, vol. coord. A Woman's Place, Merced, Calif., 1984-85; guest Gov.'s Task Force on Domestic Violence, Albany, N.Y., 1981-83, N.Y. State Coalition Against Domestic Violence, Albany, 1981-83; lectr., cons., trainer in field. Author manual: Domestic Violence Training Guide, 1984; editor manual: Management Training and Supervisors' Training Guide, 1987; author A Woman's Place Newsletter, 1984-85. Founder safe home network for battered women and battered women's support group STOP Domestic Violence, Plattsburg, 1981-83; founer safe home network for battered women A Woman's Place, 1984; founding mem. Ctrl. Calif. Coalition Against Domestic Violence, Merced, Calif., 1984-85; sec. Merced Zool. Soc., 1984-85; deacon, sec. bd. deacons 1st Presbyn. Ch., Plattsburg, 1987-90, sec., chmn. nurture coun., 1986-89, elder, 1993-95, chmn. outreach coun., 1992-95. With USAF, 1969-71. N.Y. State Dept. Social Svcs. grantee, 1982. Mem. NAFE, AACD, Am. Mental Health Counselors Assn., Soc. Human Resouce Profls. Home: 43 Set Pt Plattsburgh NY 12901-1771

PLASKET, DONNA JEAN, music educator; b. Camden, N.J., Sept. 22, 1949; d. John Thornton and Dorothy Unice (Rugg) P.; m. Chester Langdon Cable, Apr. 27, 1974 (div. Jan. 1988); m. David Worthy Breneman, Sept. 11, 1993. B of Music Edn., Westminster Choir Coll., 1971, MusM, 1983; MEd in Adminstrn. Planning, Harvard U., 1989, EdD in Adminstrn. Planning, 1992. Tchr. music Gov. Livingston Regional High Sch., Berkeley Heights, N.J., 1971-75, Cherry Hill (N.J.) High Sch., 1975-80; dir. alumnus Westminster Choir Coll., Princeton, N.J., 1981-87, faculty choral conducting, 1983-86, exec. dir. devel., 1987-88; faculty music edn. New Eng. Conservatory Music, Boston, 1992-95; project mgr., researcher Harvard U., Cambridge, Mass., 1988-93; project dir., rsch. assoc. Harvard U., Cambridge, 1993-96; devel. dir. Women's Ctr. U. Va., 1996—; mem. leadership coun. Westminster Choir Coll., 1994—; cons. in field; conductor Va. Women's Chorus U. Va., 1995—. Mem. AAUW, ASCD, Am. Choral Dirs. Assn., Phi Delta Kappa, Pi Kappa Lambda (pres. 1983). Republican. Presbyterian. Home: 209 Sprigg Ln Charlottesville VA 22903 Office: The Women's Ctr Univ Va Corner Bldg Univ Pl Charlottesville VA 22903

PLATOU, JOANNE (DODE), museum director; b. Mpls., Jan. 6, 1919; d. Wesley Richmond and Catherine Harriet (Fisher) Pierson; m. Ralph Victor Platou, Jan. 23, 1942 (dec. Sept. 1968); children: Peter Erling, Thomas Stoud, Mary Kirk Platou Marloff. BS, U. Minn., 1939; MFA, Tulane U., 1959. Columnist Mpls. Tribune, 1939-42; med. photographer Ochsner Clinic, New Orleans, 1943-46; tchr. photography Metairie (La.) Pk. Country Day Sch., 1946-51; free lance artist New Orleans, 1953-68; curator edn. New Orleans Mus. Art, 1969-75; chief curator Historic New Orleans Collection, 1976-86, dir., 1986-92, dir. emerita, 1992—; ret., 1992; bd. dirs. Arts Coun. New Orleans, 1972-88, Long Vue House and Gardens, New Orleans, 1982-88; tchr. mus. career course Tulane U., New Orleans, 1983-87. Curator exhbns. The Wit of It, 1972, The Art Works, 1972, The Camera, 1974; author catalogue, curator exhbn. Alfred R. Waud, 1979. NEH grantee, New Orleans Mus. Art, 1975. Mem. Am. Mus. Assn., Friends of the Cabildo, Coll. Art Assn., Am. Assn. State and Local History.

PLATT, JAN KAMINIS, former county official; b. St. Petersburg, Fla., Sept. 27, 1936; d. Peter Clifton and Adele (Diamond) Kaminis; m. William R. Platt, Feb. 8, 1962; 1 son, Kevin Peter. B.A., Fla. State U., 1958; postgrad. U. Fla. Law Sch., 1958-59, U. Va., 1962, Vanderbilt U., 1964. Pub. sch. tchr. Hillsborough County, Tampa, Fla., 1959-60; field dir. Girl Scouts Suncoast Coun., Tampa, 1960-62; city councilman Tampa City Council, 1974-78; county commr. Hillsborough County, 1978-94; chmn. Hillsborough County Bd. County commrs., 1980-81, 83-84, ret., 1994; chmn. Tampa Bay Regional Planning Council, 1982; chmn. West Coast Regional Water Supply Authority, Tampa, 1985; chmn. Hillsborough County Council of Govts., 1976, 79; chmn. Sunshine Amendment Drive 7th Congrl. Dist., Tampa, 1976; chmn. Community Action Agy., Tampa, 1980-81, 83-84; chmn. pro tem Tampa Charter Revision Commn., 1975; chmn. Prison Sitting Task Force, Tampa, 1983, Tampa Housing Study Com., 1983, Met. Planning Orgn., Tampa, 1984, Bd. Tax Adjustment, Tampa, 1984; appointee Constitution Revision Commn., Fla., 1977, HRS Dist. IV Adv. Council, Fla.; mem. Hillsborough County Expressway Authority, Taxicab Commn.; vice chmn. steering com. Nat. Assn. Counties Environ. Task Force; Bd. dirs. March of Dimes, Tampa, The Fla. Orchestra, Tampa; trustee Hillsborough County Hosp. Authority, Tampa, 1984-94; pres. Suncoast Girl Scout Council, Citizens Alert, Tampa, Bay View Garden Club; v.p. Hillsborough County Bar Aux.; mem. adv. bd. Northside Community Mental Health Ctr.: Access House, Tampa; active mem. Arts Council of Tampa-Hillsborough County, 1983-85, Drug Abuse Coordinating Council Orgn., Tampa, Bd. Criminal Justice, Tampa, Fla. Council on Aging, Inebriate Task Force, Tampa, Tampa Downtown Devel. Authority Task Force, Tampa Sports Authority, Tampa Area Mental Health Bd., Children's Study Comm., Manahill Area Agy. on Aging, Tampa, Athena Soc., Tampa Area Com. Fgn. Affairs, LWV. Recipient Athena award Women in Comm., 1976, First Annual Humanitarian award Nat. Orgn. for Prevention of Animal Suffering, 1981, Spessard Holland Meml. award Tampa Bay Com. for Good Govt., 1979, First Lady of Yr. award Beta Sigma Phi, 1980, Women Helping Women award Soroptimist Internat. Tampa, 1983, Eliza Wolff award Tampa United Methodist Ctrs., 1982, Good Govt. award Tampa Jaycees, 1983, Good Govt. award League of Women Voters, 1983. Mem. Am. Judicature Soc., State Assn. County Commrs. Fla. (at-large dir.), AAUW (bd. dirs.), Mortar Bd., Garnet Key, Phi Beta Kappa, Phi Kappa Phi. Democrat. Episcopalian. Home and Office: 3531 Village Way Tampa FL 33629-8950

PLATT, KAREN MARIE, artist, curator; b. Grand Forks, N.D., Oct. 9, 1962; d. Arthur Frederick and Jutta Kaethe (Mueller) P. BFA, Washington U., St. Louis, 1986; MFA, U. N.D., 1994. bd. dirs. No Name Exhbns., Mpls., spl. projects dir., 1992-93, curator, 1992-95, Hair Police Gallery, Mpls., 1992-93; guest curator Walker Art Ctr., Mpls., 1994, North Valley Arts Coun., Grand Forks, N.D., 1995. One woman shows include Knitting Factory, N.Y.C., 1992, De Media Gallery, Belgium, 1992, Speedboat Gallery, St. Paul, 1993, De Effenaar Gallery, Eindhoven, Netherlands, 1993, Novy Horizont Gallery, Prague, Czechoslovakia, 1993, Rogue's Gallery, Mpls., 1994, Hughes Fine Arts Ctr., U. N.D., Grand Forks, 1994, Fontbonne Coll., St. Louis, 1995, Knitting Factory, N.Y.C., 1996, Gallery Rebolloso, Mpls., 1996; exhibited in group shows at Wexner Ctr. for the Arts, Ohio State U., Columbus, 1991, L.A. Contemporary Exhbns., 1992, N.D. Mus. of Art, Grand Forks, 1994, Katherine Nash Gallery, U. Minn., Mpls., 1994, San Diego Art Inst., 1994, Esperanza Peace and Justice Ctr., San Antonio, 1995, Thomas Barry Fine Arts, Mpls., 1995, Mpls. Coll. Art & Design, 1995, Walker Art Ctr., Mpls., 1995, Ctr. Contemporary Art, Seattle, 1995, Vide Cultura, Haarlem, The Netherlands, 1996, Tweed Mus., Duluth, Minn., 1996; represented in permanent book collections Walker Art Ctr., Wexner Ctr. for the Arts; author/artist: (comic book) Dolo Romy, 1990; editor/artist: (comic book/anthology) Oubliette, 1992; contbg. artist Deadline Mag., 1993, Evergreen Chronicles, 1995. Encouragement grantee Film in the Cities, 1992; Jerome Found. fellow MCAD, 1994-95. Office: PO Box 80023 Minneapolis MN 55408-8023

PLATT, MARCIA ELLIN, gerontologist; b. Astoria, N.Y., Jan. 20, 1947; d. Benjamin and Ethel (Glassberg) Berman; m. Leslie A. Platt, Aug. 10, 1969; 1 child, Bill Lawrence. BS, NYU, 1968, MA, 1972; MA, George Mason U., 1986. Cert. activity cons. Nat. Certification Coun. of Activity Profls. Sr. adult program dir. Reston (Va.) Community Ctr., 1991-92. Mem. No. Va. Assn. of Activity Profls., Am. Psychol. Assn. (assoc.), Psi Chi. Home: 11901 Triple Crown Rd Reston VA 22091-3015

PLATT, MARY CATHERINE, elementary educations educator; b. St. Paul, Aug. 16, 1950; d. John Wesley and Catherine Marie (Zander) Gibler; m. Charles Phillip Rudin, May 1970 (div. 1982); children: Paul Rudin, Valerie Rudin. BA, Fla. Atlantic U., 1973, MEd, 1976. Cert. tchr. early childhood, elem., English speakers of other lang. Tchr. Palm Beach County (Fla.) Sch. Bd., 1973—. Recipient Master Tchrs. award State of Fla., 1984. Mem. Classroom Tchrs. Assoc., Phi Kappa Phi. Home: 486 81st Ave West Palm Beach FL 33411

PLATTI, RITA JANE, educator, draftsman, author, inventor; b. Stockton, Calif., Aug. 29, 1925; d. Umbert Ferdinand and Concettina Maria (Natoli) Strangio; m. Elvin Carl Platti, July 27, 1955; 1 child, Kimberley Jane. Student, Dominican Coll., 1943-45; AB in Math, U. Pacific, 1947, postgrad., 1947-52, 68. Cert. sec. tchr., Calif.; lic. real estate agt., Calif. Farmer Escalon, Calif., 1943—; tchr. math St. Mary's High Sch., Stockton, 1947-49, 52, 54; chem. analyst Petri Winery, Escalon, 1949; draftsman Kyle Steel Co., Stockton, 1950-52; pvt. practice as draftsman Stockton, 1952-66; tchr. math Montezuma Sch., Stockton, 1956-57, Davis Elem. Sch., Stockton, 1957-58; with rental bus., 1958-81; tchr. math Amos Alonzo Stagg High Sch., 1961-80, Humphreys Coll., 1981-83, Hamilton Jr. High Sch., 1984-90; owner, involved in prodn. and mktg. R.J. Creations, 1991—; spkr. workshops Stanislaus State U., 1992, Calif. Math. Coun., Fresno State U., 1992, Nat. Sci. Found. Conf., 1993; spkr. math./sci. conf. Calif. State U., Bakersfield, 1994, 95, 96; evaluator Math. Framework (K-12) Calif. State Dept. Edn. Author: Math Proficiency Plateaus, 1979, Preparing Fundamentals of The Use of Sound in the Teaching of Mathematics, 1994; author, pub. series, 1979-86; 3 patents in field. Mem. NEA, Calif. Tchrs. Assn. Democrat. Roman Catholic.

PLAVINSKAYA, ANNA DMITRIEVNA, artist; b. Moscow, Nov. 26, 1960; came to U.S., 1989; d. Dmitri and Nina (Tihomirova) P.; m. Gennady Ioffe, Jan 9, 1988 (div. July 1993). Diploma in Costume Design, Theatrical Art Coll., Moscow, 1976-80. Costume designer Evgeny Vahtangov Theater, Moscow, 1980-82; artist freelance Moscow, 1983-89; art restorator pvt. studio, N.Y.C., 1990-93; artist freelance N.Y.C., 1993—. Recipient 2nd prize 11th Cleveland Internat. Drawing Biennale, Middlesbrough, Eng., 1993. Russian Orthodox. Home: 815 W 181 St Apt 3E New York NY 10033

PLAWECKI, JUDITH ANN, nursing educator; b. East Chicago, Ind., June 5, 1943; d. Joseph Lawrence and Anne Marilyn (Hamnik) Curosh; m. Henry Martin Plawecki, June 10, 1967; children: Martin H., Lawrence H. BS, St. Xavier Coll., Chgo., 1965; MA, U. Iowa, 1971; PhD, 1974. Asst. prof. Mt. Mercy Coll., Cedar Rapids, Iowa, 1971-73; asst. dept. chmn., assoc. prof., 1974-75; assoc. prof. U. Iowa, 1975-76; asst. dean, assoc. prof. U. Minn., 1976-81; acting dean, assoc. dean and prof. U. N.D., Grand Forks, 1981-82, dean and prof. nursing, 1982-83; dean and prof. nursing Lewis U., Romeoville, Ill., 1983-87; dean U. South Fla., Tampa, 1987-95, prof. nursing, 1987—. Univ. Iowa Fellow, 1973. Mem. ANA, AHNA, Nat. League for Nursing, Older Women's League, Sigma Xi, Sigma Phi Omega, Sigma Theta Tau, Phi Lambda Theta. Office: U South Fla Coll Nursing MDC 22 12901 Bruce B Downs Blvd Tampa FL 33612-4742

PLAYER, GERALDINE (JERI PLAYER), small business executive; b. Cleve., Mar. 26, 1952; d. Cornelius Millsape and Ola Mae (Maxie) Fisher; m. Van O. Player, Aug. 27, 1970 (dec. Mar. 1975); children—Ricardo T., Van O., Michelle. Student Sawyer Coll. Bus., Mayfield, Ohio, Virginia Marti Sch. Design, Lakewood, Ohio, Inst. Children's Lit., Conn., Case Western Res. U., Fall 1988. Owner, Jeri's Designs, Inc., Cleve., 1970—, Success Writers, Cleve., 1986—; freelance scriptwriter, 1990—; fashion cons. Active adoptive parenting orgn. Mem. Nat. Assn. Female Execs. Club: Back Wall (Beachwood, Ohio). Lodge: Brotherhood (Bklyn.). Avocations: aerobics; photography; theatre; speech. Home: PO Box 12471 Cleveland OH 44112-0471 Office: 1605 N Cahuenga Blvd Ste 211 Los Angeles CA 90028-6276

PLAYER, THELMA B., librarian; b. Owosso, Mich.; d. Walter B. and Grace (Willoughby) Player; B.A., Western Mich. U., 1954. Reference asst. USAF Aero. Chart & Info. Center, Washington, 1954-57; reference librarian U.S. Navy Hydrographic Office, Suitland, Md., 1957-58; asst. librarian, 1958-59; tech. library br. head U.S. Navy Spl. Project Office, Washington, 1959-68, Strategic Systems Project Office, 1969-76. Mem. ALA, Spl. Libraries Assn., D.C. Library Assn., AAUW, Canterbury Cathedral Trust in Am., Nat. Geneal. Soc., Internat. Soc. Brit. Genealogy and Family History, Ohio Geneal. Soc., Royal Oak Found., Daus. of Union Vets. of Civil War. Episcopalian. Home: 730 24th St NW Washington DC 20037-2543

PLEDGER, MARY S., secondary school educator; b. Jamestown, Ark., Mar. 3, 1938; d. William Abner Clinic Steward and Hollis Landrum; m. Reuben Marco Oxner, Oct. 14, 1961 (div. June 1978); 1 child, Gregory; m. Van H. Pledger, Sept. 21, 1985. BA, Lyons Coll., 1958; MS, U. Ark., Fayetteville, 1980. Cert. secondary math., biology and gen. sci., Ark. Tchr. Vanndale (Ark.) Sch. Dist., 1958-59, North Little Rock (Ark.) Sch. Dist., 1959-61, Marianna (Ark.) Sch. Dist., 1966-70; interviewer Ark. Employment Security Divsn., Harrison, 1970-74; tchr. Harrison Sch. Dist., 1974—. Mem. NEA, Ark. Edn. Assn., Ark. Coun. Tchrs. Math., Nat. Coun. Tchrs. Math., Harrison Edn. Assn., Order Eastern Star.

PLEFKA-WEIR, MARY ANNE, financial consultant; b. Barberton, Ohio, Mar. 20, 1947; d. Joseph and Anna (Hlivka) Plefka; m. William Francis Weir, Sept. 8, 1974. BA in Arts and Scis., Ohio U., 1969; MA in Pers. and Mgmt., Cen. Mich. U., Honolulu, 1977. Tchr. Vinton County H.S., McArthur, Ohio, 1969-70, West Jr. H.S., Akron, Ohio, 1970-74; instr. St. Louis H.S., Honolulu, 1975-77; v.p. Merrill Lynch, Sacramento, 1977—. Treas., bd. dirs. YWCA, Sacramento, 1987-90; bd. trustees St. Tikhon's Seminary, South Canaan, Pa., 1990—. Democrat. Eastern Orthodox.

PLEIN, KATHRYN ANNE, secondary educator; b. Ashland, Wis., Jan. 28, 1945; d. Donald and Frances (Tankersly) Smith; m. Arvid Arthur Plein, Dec. 19, 1970; children: Marty, Michelle. BS in Broadfield Sci., Northland Coll., 1967; MS in Teaching, U. Wis., Superior, 1973. Cert. secondary science tchr., Wis. 7th grade sci. tchr. Wausau (Wis.) Sch. Dist., 1967-73; tchr. John Muir Middle Sch., Wausau, 1977—. Mem. Wis. Soc. Sci. Tchrs., Nat. Sci. Tchr. Assn., AAUW (program v.p. 1995-97, past v.p. membership). Roman Catholic. Home: R 8800 Hwy J Schofield WI 54476 Office: John Muir Middle Sch 1400 W Stewart Ave Wausau WI 54401

PLESHETTE, SUZANNE, actress, writer; b. N.Y.C., Jan. 31; d. Eugene and Geraldine; m. Thomas Joseph Gallagher III, Mar. 16, 1968. Student, Sch. Performing Arts, Syracuse U., Finch Coll., Neighborhood Playhouse Sch. of Theatre. Founder, prin. The Bedside Manor (later div. of J.P. Stevens). Theatre debut in Truckline Cafe; star in Broadway prodns. Compulsion, The Cold Wind and the Warm, The Golden Fleecing, The Miracle Worker, Special Occasions; star TV series Bob Newhart Show, 1972-78, Suzanne Pleshette is Maggie Briggs, 1984; starred in TV series Bridges to Cross, 1986-87, Nightingales, 1988-89, The Boys Are Back, 1994-95; star 30 feature films including The Birds, Forty Pounds of Trouble, If It's Tuesday This Must Be Belgium, Nevada Smith, Support Your Local Gunfighter, Hot Stuff, Oh God! Book II; TV movies include Flesh and Blood, Starmaker, Fantasies, If Things Were Different, Help-Wanted Male, Dixie Changing Habits, One Cooks, The Other Doesn't, For Love or Money, Kojak, The Belarus File, A Stranger Waits, Alone In The Neon Jungle, Leona Helmsley: The Queen of Mean, 1990, Battling for Baby, 1991-92, A Twist of the Knife, 1993; writer, co-creator, producer two TV series; published author.

PLESS, VERA, mathematics and computer science educator; b. Chgo., Mar. 5, 1931; d. Lyman and Helen (Blinder) Stepen; m. Irwin Pless, June 15, 1952 (div. 1980); children: Naomi, Benjamin, Daniel. PhD, U. Chgo., 1949, MS, 1952; PhD, Northwestern U., 1957. Mathematician USAF, Lincoln, Mass., 1962-72; rsch. assoc. MIT, Cambridge, Mass., 1972-75; prof. math. U. Ill., Chgo., 1975—. Author: The Theory of Error Correcting Codes, 1989; contbr. articles to profl. publs. U. Ill. scholar, 1989-92; recipient Tempo All-Professor Team, Sciences, Chicago Tribune, 1993. Mem. Am. Math. Soc. (chair nominating com. 1984), Math. Assn. Am., IEEE (bd. govs. 1985-89), Assn. Women in Math. Office: UIC MSCS (M/C 249) 851 S Morgan 322 SEO Chicago IL 60607-7045

PLESTER, JUDITH ELIZABETH CARNES, music educator; b. Detroit, Sept. 9, 1946; d. Harry Earle and Mary Glen (Snow) Carnes; 1 child, Tracy Michelle Plester. MusB, Eastern Mich. U., Ypsilanti, 1969; MusM, 1979. String tchr. Jackson (Mich.) Pub. Schs., 1969-70; substitute tchr. 5 local dists., Ypsilanti, Mich., 1974; permanent music substitute Adrian (Mich.) Schs., 1975; string Plymouth (Mich.) /Canton Pub. Schs., 1976-80; vocal music, 1981-94; pvt. tchr. Harp, Dulcimer, Fiddle, Violin, Piano, 1969—; Gittfiddler Music Store tchr. Northville, Mich., 1981-96; So. Dulcimer Festival workshop, 1981-94; Lima (Ohio) Black Swamp Festival workshop, 1981-94. Author, arranger: Fiddle Tune Books, 1992. Violist Jackson (Mich.) Civic Orch., 1964-68, No. Civic Orch., 1967-79, Eastern Civic Orch., Ypsilanti, Mich., 1967-79; faculty string quartet at No. and Ea. U., 1964-79. Recipient scholarship Bd. Regents to Ea. Mich. U., 1966-69. Mich. Edn. Assn., Music Educators Nat. Conf., Am. String Tchrs. Assn. Office: Plymouth/Canton Schs 1000 S Haggerty Rd Plymouth MI 48188

PLETCHER, BARBARA, lawyer; b. L.A., Nov. 18, 1945. AB cum laude, Smith Coll., 1967; JD, U. Calif. Ptnr. Brobeck, Phleger & Harrison, San Francisco. Mem. Calif. Law Rev., 1983-84. Mem. Order of the Coif. Office: Brobeck Phleger & Harrison Spear St 1 Market Plz San Francisco CA 94105*

PLISKOW, VITA SARI, anesthesiologist; b. Tel Aviv, Israel, Sept. 13, 1942; arrived in Can., 1951; came to U.S., 1967; d. Henry Norman and Renee (Mushkatel) Stahl; m. Raymond Joel Pliskow, June 30, 1968; children: Tia, Kami. MD, U. B.C., Vancouver, 1967. Diplomate Am. Bd. Anesthesiology. Ptnr. Olympic Anesthesia, Bremerton, Wash., 1971-74, pres., anesthesiologist, 1974-84; co-founder Olympic Ambulatory Surgery Ctr., Bremerton, 1977-83; ptnr., anesthesiologist Allenmore Anesthesia Assocs., Tacoma, 1983—; staff anesthesiologist Harrison Meml. Hosp., Bremerton, 1971-95, Allenmore Hosp., Tacoma, 1983—. Trustee Tacoma Youth Symphony Assn., 1994—; active Nat. Coun. Jewish Women, 1972—. Fellow Am. Coll. Anesthesiologists, Am. Coll. Chest Physicians; mem. Am. Soc. Anesthesiologists (del. Wash. State 1987—), Wash. State Med. Assn. (del. Pierce County 1993-94), Wash. State Soc. Anesthesiologists (pres. 1985-87), Pierce County Med. Soc. (sec.-treas. 1992). Office: # 109 900 Sheridan Rd Bremerton WA 98310-2701

PLITT, DORIS SMITH, elementary education educator; b. Clarksdale, Miss., Feb. 15, 1949; d. Eldrew Polk and Mavis Melissa (Bates) Smith; m. Milton Christian Plitt, Feb. 7, 1971; children: Matthew, Laren. BS in Elem. Edn., Delta State U., Cleveland, Miss., 1970, MEd, 1972; cert. in gifted and talented edn., U. North Tex., 1994. Tchr. Claibourne Edn. Found., Port Gibson, Miss., 1971-72, Coun. Manhattan Sch., Jackson, Miss., 1972-75, Madison (Miss.) Ridgeland Acad., 1975-77, Jackson (La.) Elem. Sch., 1977-78, Walker (La.) Elem. Sch., 1978-80, St. Thomas More Sch., Baton Rouge, 1980-88; tchr., team leader Christie Elem. Sch., Plano, Tex., 1988—; insvc. facilitator Plano Ind. Sch. Dist. Neighborhood capt. United Way, March of Dimes, Am. Heart Assn. Named Tchr. of Yr., Christie Elem. Sch., 1994; recipient Excellence in Tchg. award Plano Ind. Sch. Dist., 1994. Mem. Delta Kappa Gamma, Delta Delta Delta. Baptist. Home: 2604 Micarta Dr Plano TX 75025-2418 Office: Christie Elem Sch 3801 Rainier Rd Plano TX 75023-7220

PLOENER, MARGARET, artist; b. Wilmington, Del., Aug. 19, 1959; d. Arthur J. and Florence Patricia (Wainger) P. BA, Earlham Coll., 1981; cert., Pa. Acad. Fine Arts, 1985; postgrad., Naropa Inst., 1989, 90. vis. artist Moravian Coll., Bethlehem, 1994; instr. Viewing Program: The Drawing Ctr., N.Y.C., 1994-96, Outreach Program: No. Westchester Ctr. for the Arts, Mt. Kisco, 1994—; art dir. Norwest Day Camp for Disabled Children, Cortlandt, N.Y., 1995. One-woman shows include Zone One Gallery, Phila., 1991, 94, 95, BAG: Boulder Artists Gallery, 1992, Moravian Coll., Bethlehem, Pa., 1994; group exhibits include Woodmere Art Mus., Germantown, Pa., 1984, 88, 89, Zone One Gallery, Phila., 1989-95, Boulder Art Gallery, 1990-91, Art at the Armory, Phila., 1990, Boulder Art Ctr., 1991, Pirate Gallery, Denver, 1991, Port of History Mus., Phila., 1991, No. Westchester Ctr. for the Arts, Mt. Kisco, N.Y., 1995. Recipient Huldah Bender Kerner prize Pa. Acad. Fine Arts, 1985, 1st prize Woodmere Art Mus. Endowment Fund, 1989. Mem. Tara Dhatu (East Coast rep.). Democrat. Buddhist. Home: 33 Old Locust Ave Peekskill NY 10566

PLOTTEL, JEANINE PARISIER, foreign language educator; b. Paris, Sept. 21, 1934; came to U.S., 1943; m. Roland Plottel, 1956; children: Claudia S., Michael E., Philip B. Baccalauréat lettres, Lycée Français de N.Y., 1952; BA with honors, Barnard Coll., 1954; MA, Columbia U., 1955, PhD with distinction, 1959. Lectr. dept. French and Romance philology Columbia U., N.Y.C., 1955-59; rsch. assoc. fgn. lang. program MLA of Am., N.Y.C., 1959-60; lectr. dept. romance langs. CUNY, N.Y.C., 1960; asst. prof. div. humanities Julliard Sch. Music, N.Y.C., 1960-65; dir. lang. labs. Hunter Coll. CUNY, N.Y.C., 1965-69; asst. prof. dept. romance langs. Hunter Coll. CUNY, N.Y.C., 1965-69, assoc. prof. dept. romance langs., 1969-81, prof. dept. romance langs., 1981—, assoc. prof. French doctoral program grad. sch., univ. ctr., 1980-81, prof. French doctoral program grad. sch., univ. ctr., 1981—; extensive adminstrv. experience in CUNY including chairperson Dept. Romance Langs. Author: Les Dialogues de Paul Valéry, 1960; pub., editor N.Y. Literary Forum, 1978-88; contbr. articles to profl. jours., chpts. to books. Pres. Maurice I. Parisier Found., Inc. Named Chevalier des Palmes Acad., 1982; recipient NEH fellowship, 1979; grantee N.Y. Coun. for the Humanities, 1986, Helena Rubenstein Found., 1986, Florence J. Gould Found., 1986, N.Y. Times Found., 1986. Mem. Maison Française (bd. dirs. Columbia U.). Home: 50 E 77th St Apt 14a New York NY 10021-1836

PLOZIZKA, JEANETTE LOUISE, elementary education educator, curriculum coordinator; b. Litchfield, Ill., Mar. 6, 1947; d. August John and Pauline Louise (Fedder) P. BS in Edn., Concordia Coll., 1969, MS in Edn., 1984. Cert. elem. tchr., Iowa, Mo., Ill. Elem. tchr. Nazareth Luth. Sch., Milw., 1969-70, Mt. Olive Luth. Sch., Des Moines, Iowa, 1970-86, Trinity Luth. Sch., Springfield, Ill., 1986—; Sec. Luth. Ch.-Mo. Synod Ongoing Ambs. for Christ, Des Moines, 1971-75; title IV adv. com. Des Moines Pub. Sch., 1976-81; treas. Iowa West Tchrs. Conf., Western Iowa, 1982, sec., 1983. Mem. Administers and Reading Specialists Interest Coun. (Ill.), Luth. Edn. Assn., Internat. Reading Assn., Ill. Reading Coun., Early Chilhood Coun. Ill. Lutheran. Home: 1021 W Governor St Apt 3 Springfield IL 62704-1767 Office: Trinity Luth Sch 515 S Macarthur Blvd Springfield IL 62704-1744

PLUMLEY, DANIELLE L., social worker; b. Rochester, N.Y., Nov. 10, 1967; d. Michael Pratt and Barbara Janet (Sautter) LaGrange; m. James Donald Plumley, Aug. 22, 1992. BA magna cum laude, Hamilton Coll., 1990; MSW, Syracuse U., 1994. Cert. social worker, N.Y. Residence counselor Catholic Charities, Utica, N.Y., 1990-91, social worker I, 1991-92; social worker I Ctrl. N.Y. Devel. Svcs. Office, Rome, 1994—. Vol. adv. Ctrl. N.Y. D.S.O., Verona, 1992—; active Camden (N.Y.) Substance Abuse Adv. Coun., 1993—. Mem. NASW, Acad. Cert. Social Workers, Phi Beta Kappa. Democrat. Home: 13 6th St Camden NY 13316 Office: Ctrl NY DSO WOC I Unit 6545 State Rt 26 Rome NY 13440

PLUMMER, MARCIE STERN, real estate broker; b. Plymouth, Mass., Oct. 28, 1950; d. Jacob and Rosalie (Adelman) Stern; m. John Dillon McHugh II, Oct. 8, 1974 (div.); 1 child, Joshua Stern; m. Louis Freeman Plummer Jr., Sept. 25, 1982; children: Jessica Price, Denelle Boothe. BA, Am. Internat. Coll., 1972, MAT in English, 1973, postgrad., 1974; postgrad., U. Conn., 1974; lic. real estate broker, Anthony Sch. Real Estate, Walnut Creek, Calif., 1985. Educator, chair dept. Windsor Locks (Conn.) Sch. Dist., 1972-74; educator, placement dir. Heald Bus. Coll., San Francisco, 1974-77; educator evening and day divs. Diablo Valley Coll., Pleasant Hill, Calif., 1975-77; real estate agt. Morrison Homes, Pleasant Hill, Calif., 1977-78; real estate agt., tract mgr. Dividend Devel., Santa Clara, Calif., 1978-81; real estate agt. Valley Realty, 1981-84; broker, owner Better Homes Realty, 1984-89; real estate broker, owner The Presád Co. Inc. subs. Better Homes Realty, Danville, Calif., 1984-90; owner The Mktg. Group, 1989—; v.p., treas. Realty Resource Group, 1996. Better Homes Realty rep. for orgn. of Danville 4th of July Parade, City of Danville, 1984-88; publicist San Ramon Valley Little League, Alamo, Calif., 1986—; active Battered Women's Found., Contra Costa County, Calif., 1986—, Yosemite Fund, 1992—, Safe Home Teen Program, 1991—; active rep. voter registration, Walnut Creek, Calif., 1987—; mem. Civic Arts Coun., Walnut Creek, 1988—; drama coach, dir. Advanced Drama Ensemble, 1993-94. Recipient numerous nat., state and regional awards in field, $400 million closed vol. in real estate sales achievement award, 1991. Mem. AAUW, Bldg. Industry Assn. (Sales vol. award 1978-89), Sales & Mktg. Coun. (sponsor MAME awards banquet 1978-89, Gold sponsor 1986-88), Calif. Assn. Realtors, Contra Costa Bd. Realtors. Jewish. Home: 123 Erselia Trl Alamo CA 94507-1311 Office: Better Homes Realty PO Box 939 Danville CA 94526-0939

PLUMMER, ORA BEATRICE, nursing educator, trainer; b. Mexia, Tex., May 25, 1940; d. Macie Idella (Echols); B.S. in Nursing, U. N.Mex., 1961; M.S. in Nursing Edn., UCLA, 1966; children—Kimberly, Kevin, Cheryl. Nurses aide Bataan Meml. Meth. Hosp., Albuquerque, 1958-60, staff nurse, 1961-62, 67-68; staff nurse, charge nurse, relief supr. Hollywood (Calif.) Community Hosp., 1962-64; instr. U. N.Mex. Coll. of Nursing, Albuquerque, 1968-69; sr. instr. U. Colo. Sch. Nursing, Denver, 1971-74; asst. prof. U. Colo. Sch. Nursing, Denver, 1974-76; staff assoc. III Western Interstate Commn. for Higher Edn., Boulder, Colo., 1976-78; dir. nursing Garden Manor Nursing Home, Lakewood, Colo., 1978-79; ednl. coordination Colo. Dept. Health, Denver, 1987—. Active Colo. Cluster of Schs.-faculty devel.; mem. adv. bd. Affiliated Children's and Family Services, 1977; mem. state instl. child abuse and neglect adv. com., 1984—; mem. bd. trustee Colo. Acad., 1990—; mem. planning com. State Wide Conf. on Black Health Concerns, 1977; mem. staff devel. com. Western Interstate Commn. for Higher Edn., 1978, minority affairs com., 1978, coordinating com. for baccalaureate program, 1971-76; active minority affairs U. Colo. Med. Center, 1971-72; mem. ednl. resources com. public relations com., rev. com. for reappointment, promotion, and tenure U. Colo. Sch. Nursing, 1971-76; regulatory tng. com., 1989—, gerontol. adv. com., Met. State Coll., 1989-93; expert panel mem. Long Term Care Training Manual, HCFA, Balt., 1989; mem. EDAC com. Colo. Dept. of Health, 1989-96. Mem. NAFE, Am. Soc. Tng. and Devel., Am. Nurses Assn., Colo. Nurses Assn. (affirmative action comm. 1977, 78, 79, 93-96), Phi Delta Kappa. Avocation: pub. speaking, training. Contbr. articles in field to profl. jours. Office: 4300 Cherry Creek South Dr Denver CO 80222-1523

PLUMMER, PATRICIA LYNNE MOORE, chemistry and physics educator; b. Tyler, Tex., Feb. 26; d. Robert Lee and Jewell Ovelia (Jones) Moore; m. Otho Raymond Plummer, Apr. 10, 1965; children: Patrick William Otho, Christina Elisa Lynne. BA, Tex. Christian U., Ft. Worth, Tex., 1960; postgrad., U. N.C., 1960-61; PhD, U. Tex., 1964; grad., Bryn Mawr Summer Inst., 1992. Instr., Welch postdoctoral fellow U. Tex., Austin, 1964-66; postdoctoral fellow Dept. Chemistry, U. Ark., Fayetteville, 1966-68; rsch. assoc. Grad. Ctr., Cloud Phys. Rsch., Rolla, Mo., 1968-73; asst. prof. physics U. Mo., Rolla, 1973-77; assoc. dir. Grad. Ctr. Cloud Phys. Rsch., 1977-79, sr. investigator, 1980-85; assoc. prof. physics U. Mo., 1977-85; prof. dept. chemistry and physics U. Mo., Columbia, 1986—; internat. sci. advisor Symposium on Chemistry and Physics of Ice, 1982—, chair of Faculty Sen., 1995—, pres. U. of Mo. Intercampo Fac. Sen., 1994-95. Assoc. editor Jour. of Colloid and Interface Sci., 1980-83; contbr. articles to profl. jours., chpts. to books. Rsch. grantee IBM, 1990-92, Air Force Office Rsch., 1989-91, NSF, 1976-86, NASA, 1973-78; Air Force Office Rsch. summer fellow, 1988, Bryn Mawr Summer Inst., 1992. Mem. Am. Chem. Soc., Am. Phys. Soc., Am. Geophys. Union, Sigma Xi (past pres.). Democrat. Baptist. Office: Univ of Missouri 314 Physics Bldg Columbia MO 65211

PLUNKERT, DONNA MAE, business owner; b. Pa., Apr. 26, 1951; d. Norman Francis and Rada Mae (Snyder) Dickensheets; m. Bruce Herbert Plunkert, Nov. 2, 1975; 1 child, Gabriel Bruce. Grad., Littlestown (Pa.) H.S., 1969. Sales clk. Colonial Fair, Hanover, Pa., 1970-72, sec., 1972-75; full-time sec., Norm's Auction, Hanover, 1975-79, part-time sec., 1979-84; owner Old Buttermould Patterns Products, Littlestown, 1989—. Reproduced antique buttermolds for gift shops Carroll County Farm Mus., Westminster, Md., Historic Michie Tavern, Charlottesville, Va. Mem. U.S. C. of C., Mus. Store Assn. (assoc.). Mem. Brethren Ch. Home: 315 N Queen St Littlestown PA 17340-1221

PLUNKETT, MELBA KATHLEEN, manufacturing company executive; b. Marietta, Ill., Mar. 20, 1929; d. Lester George and Florence Marie (Hutchins) Bonnett; m. James P. Plunkett, Aug. 18, 1951; children: Julie Marie Plunkett Hayden, Gregory James. Educated pub. schs. Co-founder, 1961, since sec.-treas., dir. Coils, Inc., Huntley, Ill. Mem. U.S. C. of C., U.S. Mfg. Assn., Ill. C. of C., Ill. Notary Assn. Roman Catholic. Home: 15N 170 Sleepy Hollow Rd West Dundee IL 60118 Office: 11716 Algonquin Rd Huntley IL 60142

PLUSKER, ELLEN, advertising executive. Sr. v.p., strategic planning dir. Bayer Bess Vanderwarker, Inc., Chgo. Office: Bayer Bess Vanderwarker 225 N Michigan Ave Ste 1900 Chicago IL 60601-7601*

POBLETE, RITA MARIA BAUTISTA, physician, educator; b. Manila, May 19, 1954; came to U.S., 1980; d. Juan Gonzalez and Rizalina (Bautista) Poblete. BS, U. Philippines, 1974, MD, 1978. Diplomate Am. Bd. Internal Medicine and Infectious Disease. Intern, resident Wayne State U./Detroit Med. Ctr., 1982-85, fellow in infectious disease, 1986-87; fellow in infectious disease Chgo. Med. Sch./VA Hosp., North Chicago, Ill., 1985-86; fellow in spl. immunology U. Miami (Fla.)-Jackson Meml. Hosp., 1987-89; adj. clin. instr. dept. of medicine U. Miami, 1989-90, asst. prof. medicine, 1990-94; infectious disease cons. Cedars Med. Ctr. and Mercy Hosp., Miami, 1994—. Contbr. articles to med. jours. Mem. Am. Soc. for Microbiology, Am. Soc. Internal Medicine, World Found. Successful Women. Office: Cedars Med Ctr 1295 NW 14th St Ste E Miami FL 33125-1600

POCHOWSKI, ALEXA EMILY, educational administrator; b. Two Rivers, Wis., Mar. 24, 1952; d. Louis Joseph and Virginia Ruth (Strope) Posny; m. Donald Anthony Pochowski, June 11; 1 child, Alek. BS, U. Wis., Stevens Point, 1974; MS, U. Wis., Madison, 1976, PhD, 1988. Cert. adminstr., Wis., Kans., Ill. Learning disabled tchr. Middleton (Wis.) Pub. Schs., 1976-79; emotionally disturbed tchr. Neenah (Wis.) Pub. Schs., 1979-80; human rels. instr. Fox Valley Tech. Inst., Appleton, Wis., 1980; coord. Coop. Edn. Svc. Agy., Stevens Point, 1980-81; dir. spl. edn. Coop. Edn. Svc. Agy., Gillett, Wis., 1981-85, regional svc. network coord., 1983-85; staff devel. coord., spl. edn. supr. S.W. Cook County Coop., Oak Forest, Ill., 1985-88; sr. rsch. assoc. Rsch. and Tng. Assoc. Inc., Overland Park, Kans., 1988-91, dir. curriculum and instrn. specialty option, 1991—; chmn. Oak Hill Sch.-Based Leadership, Overland Park, 1992-95, Enrichment Design Team Coun., Overland Park, 1992-94; mem. adv. coun. Blue Valley Sch. Bd., Overland Park, 1994-96; mem. Oak Hill Quality Performance Accreditation Design Team, Overland Park, 1992-94; participant Nat. Policy Forum on Early Childhood, Washington, 1992, Nat. Chpt. 1 Spl. Edn. Forum, Washington, 1992 presenter St. Louis Pub. Schs., 1993, Chgo. Grantback 1993, Forest Ridge Sch. Dist., Oak Forest, Ill., 1986, Chgo. Spl. Project, 1994, Minn. Pilot Project, 1994, 11th Ann. Rural Families Conf., Manhattan, Kans., 1991, Ill. Bd. Edn., Chgo., 1993, Nat. Conf. State Chpt. 1 Coords., Washington, 1992, Minn. Assn. Adminstrs. State and Fedn. Edn. Programs, Mpls., 1991, Ill. Coun. for Exceptional Children Conv., Chgo., 1988, Nat. Coun. for Exceptional Children Conv., San Francisco, 1989, Internat. Rural Conf., Bismarck, N.D., 1990, also others. Contbr. articles to profl. publs. Chairperson YMCA Child Care Adv. Coun., Johnson County, Kans., 1990-92; bd. dirs. Johnson County YMCA Bd., 1990-92; mem. Christian bd. edn. Colonial Ch., Prarie Village, Kans., 1992-94, mem. Christian youth adv. bd., 1992-93. Recipient scholarship Portage County Assn. for Mental Health, 1974, Elks, 1970, Wis. Honor Scholarship, 1970. Mem. ASTD, Coun. Adminstrs. Spl. Edn., Ill. Coun. Adminstrs. Spl. Edn. (program com. 1987-88), Nat. Coun. Tchrs. English, Coun. for Exceptional Children, Coun. Adminstrs. Spl. Edn., Phi Delta Kappa (life), Pi Lambda Theta (life), Alpha Delta Kappa. Democrat. Home: 12434 Mastin St Overland Park KS 66213-1820 Office: Rsch and Tng Assocs Inc 9209 W 110th St Overland Park KS 66210-1401

PODARIL, CINDY LOU, critical care educator; b. Muscatine, Iowa, July 26, 1958; d. James Lee and Betty Louise (Yoder) P. LPN, Scott C.C., Davenport, Iowa, 1977; ADN, Des Moines Area C.C., 1981; BSN, Marycrest Coll., 1989. RN, Iowa, Ill.; cert. ACLS instr., Am. Heart Assn., BCLS instr., Am. Heart Assn., emergency pediat. nursing course provider, Emergency Nurse Assn., trauma nursing core course instr., Emergency Nurse Assn., emergency nurse, Emergency Nurse Assn., nursing staff devel., ANA Credential Ctr., emergency pediatric nurse course instr. LPN, staff nurse Muscatine (Iowa) Gen. Hosp., 1977-79; staff/charge nurse St. Luke's Hosp. (now Genesis Med. Ctr.), Davenport, Iowa, 1981-89, critical care educator, 1989-94; nurse cons. Iowa Bd. Nursing, Des Moines, 1994. Mem. Am. Heart Assn. Mem. AACN, Am. Assn. of Nurses, Am. Heart Assn., Nat. Nursing Staff Devel. Orgn., Emergency Nurses Assn., Soc. Trauma Nurses, Sigma Theta Tau. Presbyterian. Home: 2323 N Myrtle St Davenport IA 52804-1816 Office: Genesis Med Ctr 1227 E Rusholme St Davenport IA 52803-2459

PODLES, ELEANOR PAULINE, state senator; b. Dudley, Mass., June 6, 1920; d. Francis and Pauline Magiera; student U. N.H.; m. Francis J. Podles, June 28, 1941; children: L. Patricia Podles Barrett Fogleman, Elizabeth Lee Podles Keegan. Mem. N.H. Ho. of Reps., Concord, 1976-80; selectman City of Manchester, N.H., 1976-81, v.p., 1978—; mem. N.H. State Senate, Concord, 1980—; asst. majority whip, mem. fin. com., chmn. public affairs com., public instns. health and welfare com. Del., N.H. Republican Conv., 1976, 78, N.H. Constl. Conv., 1984; pres. pro tem N.H. Senate, 1986—, chair jud. com., vice chair exec. com., senate fin. com., senate edn. com., health and human services for pub. insts. com.; pres. Manchester Rep. Women's Club, 1979—; bd. dirs. St. Joseph's Community Service, Manchester Vis. Nurse Assn., Mental Health Ctr. Manchester, Senate Edn. Com.; state chmn. Am. Legis. Exchange Council; mem. sen. fin. com., 1995—; sen. pres. pro tem, 1995—. Bd. dirs. Mental Health Ctr. Greater Manchester; mem. N.H. Childrens Trust Fund, 1986—. Mem. Am. Legis. Exch. Coun. (state chmn.), Orgn. Women Legislators, Manchester Vis. Nurse Assn., Manchester Country Club. Club: Manchester Country. Home: 185 Walnut Hill Ave Manchester NH 03104-2136 Office: N H State Senate State Capitol Concord NH 03301

PODMOKLY, PATRICIA GAYLE, typesetting company professional; b. Chgo., May 15, 1940; d. Edwin Paul Baker and Frances (Williams) Popiela. Grad., Jones Comml. Sch., Chgo. Bookkeeper, sec. William C. Douglas & Ralph Falk II, Lake Forest, Ill., 1958—; owner Global Graphics, Inc., Elmhurst, Ill., 1987—. Roman Catholic.

PODOLSKY, ANDREA G., lawyer; b. Phila., 1951. BA, U. Pa., 1972; JD, Columbia U., 1977. Bar: N.Y. 1978. Ptnr. Cleary, Gottlieb, Steen & Hamilton, N.Y.C. Editor Columbia Law Rev., 1976-77. Kent scholar. Mem. ABA, N.Y. State Bar Assn., Phi Beta Kappa. Office: Cleary Gottlieb Steen & Hamilton One Liberty Plz New York NY 10006*

PODOS-UNTERMEYER, SALLE, lawyer; b. Bklyn., Oct. 1, 1938; d. David Meyer and Rose (Ifshin) Garber; m. Steven Maurice Podos, June 20, 1959 (div. Dec. 1978); children: Richard Lance Podos, Lisa Beth Podos; m. Walter Untermeyer, Jr., May 2, 1982. BA, Vassar Coll., 1959; MA, Brandeis U., 1960; JD, Columbia U., 1977. Bar: N.Y. 1978. Assoc. Paul, Weiss, Rifkind, Wharton & Garrison, N.Y.C., 1977-79; gen. counsel, v.p., sec. MacAndrews & Forbes Group, Inc., N.Y.C., 1979-81; sr. assoc. Sage Gray Todd & Sims, N.Y.C., 1981-84, Proskauer Rose Goetz & Mendelsohn, N.Y.C., 1984-87; pres., gen. counsel Untermeyer Mace Ptnrs., 1987-89; of counsel Mazur Carp & Rubin, 1989-91; mem. fin. com. Congresswoman Carolyn Maloney, 1994-96; founder, bd. dirs. Hamptons Music Festival, 1995—. Class fund-raising chmn. Vassar Coll., 1977-80; bd. dirs. Vassar Club N.Y., 1978-80; chmn. women's div. U.S. Senate Campaign, 1970; regional chmn. U.S. Presdl. Campaign, 1972; chmn. State Rep.'s Campaign, 1973; del.-elect Interim Dem. Conv., 1974, Lawyers Com. for Gov. Carey, 1978; chmn. Mo. state legis. Nat. Coun. Jewish Women, 1969-75, mem. nat. affairs com., 1969-77, chmn. Mo. juvenile justice project, 1970-75, mem. legis. coordinating com. Midwestern region, 1971-75, mem. nat. task force on constl. rights, 1974-77; v.p., bd. dirs. St. Louis Jewish Community Rels. Coun., 1970-75, chmn. ch.-state and Black Jack Amicus Curiae coms.; v.p., bd. dirs. St. Louis chpt. Am. Jewish Com., 1969-75, chmn. urban affairs and placement for ex-offenders coms., mem. com. on status of women, 1974-77; mem. legis. liaison Coalition for Environment, St. Louis, 1970-74; bd. dirs. St. Louis Jewish Community Ctrs. Assn., 1970-74, chmn. urban affairs and legis. affairs coms.; bd. dirs. St. Louis Jewish Family and Children's Svc., 1972-74, chmn. welfare rights and health svcs. coms.; bd. dirs. Glaucoma Found., 1986—; vol. coord. Poor People's Campaign, 1968; founder, bd. dirs. Consumer's Assn., 1967-69; founder, chmn. Urban Corps program St. Louis Mayor's Com. on Youth, 1969-72; panelist White House Conf. on Children and Youth, 1970, 72, White House Conf. on Aging, 1974; founder, bd. dirs. Mo. chpt. PEARL (Pub. Edn. and Religious Liberty), 1972-75; fundraising chmn. N.Y. Found. Arts, 1992-94; bd. dirs. N.Y. Found. Sr. Citizens. Woodrow Wilson Found. fellow, 1959, NDEA fellow, 1959. Mem. ABA, Assn. of Bar of City of N.Y. (mem. continuing legal edn. com., com. on lecture), N.Y. State Bar Assn., Womens Prison Assn. (bd. dirs.). Home: 950 Park Ave New York NY 10028-0320

PODWALL, KATHRYN STANLEY, biology educator; b. Chgo., Oct. 14; d. Frank and Marie C. Stanley. BS, U. Ill.; MA, NYU. Prof. biology Nassau C.C., Garden City, N.Y.; developmental reviewer West Ednl. Pub., Amesbury, Mass. and Highland Park, Ill., 1989, 91-92; reviewer AAAS, Washington, 1970-96; exec. bd., advisor Women's Faculty Assn., Nassau C.C., 1990—; lectr. in field. Author: Tested Studies for Laboratory Teaching, vol. 5, 1993; editor: (books and cassettes) Rhyming Simon Books and Cassettes, 1990. Mem. AAUW, Nat. Assn. Biology Tchrs., Nat. Sci. Tchrs. Assn., Soc. for Coll. Sci. Tchrs., Am. Women in Sci., Met. Assn. Coll. and Univ. Biologists, Southampton Colonial Soc., LaSalle County Hist. Soc. (life), Garden City Hist. Soc. (life), Soroptimist Internat. (Dist. 1 dir. 1994-96, club pres. 1992-94). Office: Nassau Community College One Education Dr Garden City NY 11530

POE, LENORA MADISON, psychotherapist and author; b. New Bern, Ala., Jan. 3, 1934; d. Tommy and Carrie (Norfleet) Madison; m. Levi Mathis Poe, June 21, 1957; children: Michael DeWayne, Michaelle DaNita Burke. BS, Stillman Coll., Tuscaloosa, Ala., 1956; MA, Calif. State U., Hayward, 1972, MS, 1980; PhD, Ctr. for Psychol. Studies, Albany, Calif., 1991. Lic. marriage, family and child therapist. Classroom tchr. Perry County Schs., Uniontown, Ala., 1956-59, Richmond (Calif.) Unified Schs., 1962-69; guidance counselor Berkeley (Calif.) Unified Schs., 1969-79; psychotherapist in pvt. practice Berkeley, 1982—, West Coast Children's Ctr., El Cerrito, Calif., 1982—; lectr. Grandparents as Parents, 1992—; part-time prof. J.F.K. U., Orinda, Calif., 1993; del. White House Conf. on Aging, Washington, 1995; cons. in field; staff cons. Cmty. Adult Day Health Svcs., Highland Gen. Hosp., Oakland. Author: Black Grandparents as Parents, 1992. Pres. nat. bd. dirs. Stillman Coll., 1992—; mentor cons. Black Women Organized for Ednl. Devel., Oakland, Calif., 1994—; mem. adv. bd. Nat. Black Aging Network, Oakland, 1992—; founding mem., advisor Realmindcas Civic Club, Richmond, 1976—; mem. Families United Against Crack Cocaine, Oakland; bd. dirs. Ctr. for Elders for Independence, Oakland; trustee Ctr. for Psychol. Studies, Albany; chairperson Grandparents Caregivers Advocacy Task Force, Oakland, Calif.; mem. bd. edn. Ministry of Ch. by Side of Road, Berkeley; also others. Recipient cert. of Appreciation African Am. Hist. and Cultural Soc., San Francisco, 1992, President's citation for Excellence Nat. Assn. for Equal Opportunity in Higher Edn., 1993, award Excellence in Edn. Nat. Coun. Negro Women, 1993, S award Stillman Coll., Appreciation award for Excellence Nystrom Elem. Sch., Richmond, 1994, Outstanding Alumna of the Yr. award Ctr. for Psychological Studies, 1995. Mem. Nat. Coalition Grandparents as Parents (adv. com. 1992—), No. Coalition Grandparents as Parents (co-chmn. 1991-93), Stillman Coll. Nat. Alumni Assn. (pres.), Calif. Coalition Grandparent/Relative Caregivers (co-chair), Nat. Coalition Grandparent/Relative Caregivers (advisor). Home: 940 Arlington Ave Berkeley CA 94707-1929 Office: 2034 Blake St Ste 1 Berkeley CA 94704-2604

POEHLMANN, JOANNA, artist, illustrator, designer; b. Milw., Sept. 5, 1932; d. Herbert Emil and Lucille (Conover) P. Attended, Layton Sch. Art, 1950-54, K.C. (Mo.) Art Inst., 1954, Marquette U., 1958, U. Wis., 1965, 1985. Solo exhbns. include St. James Gallery, Milw., 1963, (retrospective) Milw. Art Mus., 1966, Bradley Galleries, Milw., 1982, Signature Gallery, John Michael Kohler Art Ctr., Sheboygan, Wis., 1979, 84, Woodland Pattern Book Ctr., Milw., 1988, The Cell Gallery, Rochester, N.Y., 1988, 89, Charles Allis Art Mus., Milw., 1991, Layton Gallery at Cardinal Stritch Coll, Milw., 1993, Univ. Meml. Libr., Madison, Wis., 1993, Wustum Mus. Fine Arts, Racine, Wis., 1994; two-man shows include Bradley Galleries, 1964, 69, 80, 91, Cardinal Stritch Coll., Milw., 1980; invitational group shows include Cudahy Gallery of Wis. Art, Milw. Art Mus., 1962-85, 92, Bradley Galleries, 1967-79, Lakefront Festival of Art, Milw. Art Mus., 1962-63, 70-72, 76-79, Country Art Gallery, Long Island, N.Y., 1963-71, Mount Mary Coll., Milw., 1979, 83, Chosy Gallery, 1980, 81, 86, U. Dallas, 1987, Frick Gallery, Germany, 1991, Spertus Mus. Judaica, Chgo., 1986, World Fin. Ctr., N.Y.C., 1992, Istvan Kiraly Muzeum, Budapest, Hungary, 1992, Artspace, Richmond, Va., 1994, Va. Ctr. For Craft Arts, Richmond, 1994, many others; juried group shows include Milw. Art Mus., 1963, 75, 78, Chgo. Art Inst., 1978, 81, Milw. Fine Arts Gallery, 1980, U. Wis. Fine Arts Gallery, Milw., 1980, The West Pub. Co., St. Paul, 1982, Auburn U., 1983, Zaner Gallery, Rochester, N.Y., 1984, Pratt Graphics Ctr., N.Y.C., 1985, Art 54 Gallery, N.Y.C., 1987, Boston Art Inst., 1987, Bradley U., Peoria, Ill., 1989, Wustum Mus. Fine Arts, 1989, 1992, Trenton State Coll., 1991, numerous others, represented in collections including Victoria & Albert Mus., London, N.Y. Pub. Libr., Mus. Kunsthandwerk, Frankfurt, Germany, Milw. Art Mus., Milw. Pub. Libr., U. Dallas, Orchard Corp. Am., St. Louis, McDonald's Corp., GE Med. Systems Bldgs., Waukesha, Goldhirsh Group, Boston, Marquette U.-Haggerty Mus. Art, others; subject of articles; author: Love Letters, Food for Thought, Cancelling Out. Recipient Merit award Art Dir.'s Club, Milw., 1962, 100 Best award, 1967, 100 Best award Milw. Soc. Communicating Arts, 1973, 76, MGIC award Wis. Painters & Sculptors, 1981, Merit award Illustration Milw. Advt. Club, 1983, 2d award Wustum Mus. Fine Arts, 1983, 4th Purchase Prize award McDonald's Fine Art Collection Competition, 1983, Juror's award Zaner Gallery, 1984, Hopper/Koch award Wustum Mus. Fine Arts, 1985, spl. mention, Purchase award Bradley U., 1985, Purchase award Moravian Coll., 1985, Jack Richeson award Wustum Mus. Fine Arts, 1985, Purchase award U. Del., 1986, Strathmore Paper Co. award Wustum Mus. Fine Arts, 1986, Purchase award U. N.Dak., 1987, Award of Excellence miniature art Metro Internat. Competition, N.Y.C., 1987, 3d award Wustum Mus. Fine Arts, 1987, Purchase award U. Dallas, 1988, Award of Excellence Wustum Mus. Fine Arts, 1992, Individual Art fellowship Milw. County, 1993; Arts Midwest/NEA Regional Visual Artist fellow, 1994—. Roman Catholic. Home and Studio: 1231 N Prospect Ave Milwaukee WI 53202-3013

POE-JACKSON, GERTIE LAVERNE, sales executive; b. Chgo., Feb. 7, 1949; d. L.C. and Gertrude (Winfrey) Poe. BSBA, Roosevelt U., 1978, MBA, 1984. Policy analyst Continental Bank, Chgo., 1971-87; fin. planner

IDS/Am. Express, Merrillville, Ind., 1987-89; sales rep. Valic, Chgo., 1990-94, Invest Fin. Svcs., Bridgeview, IL, 1994—. Mem. Sigma Gamma Rho. Baptist. Home: PO Box 19201 Chicago IL 60619-0201 Office: Invest Fin Svcs Bridgeview Bank & Trust 7940 S Harlem Ave Bridgeview IL 60455-1500

POETHIG, EUNICE BLANCHARD, clergywoman; b. Hempstead, N.Y., Jan. 16, 1930; d. Werner J. and Juliet (Stroh) Blanchard; m. Richard Paul Poethig, June 7, 1952; children: Richard Scott, Kathryn Aileen, Johanna Klare, Margaret Juliet, Erika Christy. BA, De Pauw U., 1951; MA, Union Theol. Seminary, 1952; MDiv, McCormick Theol. Sem., 1975, STM, 1977; PhD, Union Theol. Seminary, 1985. Ordained to ministry Presbyterian Ch., 1979; missionary United Presbyn. Ch. USA to United Ch. of Christ in Philippines, 1956-72; mem. faculty Ellinwood Coll. Christian Edn., Manila, 1957-61; mem. faculty, campus ministry Philippine Women's U., Manila, 1962-68; bd. dirs. Jane Addams Conf., Journey's End Refugee Resettlement Agy., Coun. of Bishops and Execs. of Buffalo Area Met. Ministries; trustee Presbyn. Found., 1991-94, Gen. Bd. Nat. Coun. Chs. Christ, 1995—; editor New Day Pubs., Manila, 1969-72; curriculum editor Nat. Council Chs., Manila, 1962-72; assoc. exec. Presbytery Chgo., 1979-85; exec. Presbytery of Western N.Y., 1986-93; dir. congl. ministries divsn. gen. assembly Presbyn. Ch. U.S.A., 1994—; speaker Presbyn. Women, 1973, 76, 79, 81, 85, 88, 94; mem. Council Execs., Ill. Council Chs., 1980-85. Author: Bible Studies in Concern, Response, A.D., 1975, (book) Good News Women, 1987, Sing, Shout, and Clap for Joy: Psalms in Worship, 1989, Friendship Press Study on Philippines, 1989, Liturgy 9:1, 1990, Hunger Program Workbook, 1991; editor Hymn book-series: Everybody, I Love You, 1971-72, 150 Plus Tomorrow: Churches Plan for the Future, 1982, 85, Our Living Tradition, 1994. Mem. organizing bd. Asian Center Theology and Strategy, Chgo., 1974; bd. dirs. Ch. Women United, Chgo., 1974-79; mem. Environ. Def. Fund, Women's Ordination Conf. Nat. Presbyn. Ch. Com., planning com. Celebrate Adult Curriculum, 1987-93, Presbyn. Gen. Assembly Challenge to the Ch. Fund., 1989; trustee McCormick Theol. Sem., Chgo., 1974-75; mem. Erie County (N.Y.) Environ. Mgmt. Coun., 1990-93; mem. NGO Forum UN Fourth World Conf. Women, Beijing, 1995. Recipient Walker Cup, DePauw U., 1951. Nettie F. McCormick fellow in Old Testament Hebrew, McCormick Sem., Chgo., 1975. Mem. Soc. Bibl. Lit., Soc. Ethnomusicology, Assn. of Exec. Presbyters (bd. dirs., chairperson, 1991-93), Am. Schs. Oriental Research, Witherspoon Soc., Nat. Assn. Religious Women, Internat. Assn. Women Mins., Nat. Assn. Presbyn. Clergywomen. Home: 3606 Trail Ridge Rd Louisville KY 40241 Office: Presbyn Ch USA Divsn Congl Ministries 100 Witherspoon St Louisville KY 40202-1396

POGGI, CHRISTINE, art historian, educator; b. Oakland, Calif., July 11, 1953; d. Thomas Francis and Marisa Poggi; m. Bernard M. Elliot, Aug. 3, 1985; children: Peter, Sophia and Claire (twins). AB, U. Calif., Santa Cruz, 1975; MA, U. Chgo., 1979; PhD, Yale U., 1988. Instr. Yale U., New Haven, 1987; asst. prof. U. Pa., Phila., 1987-93, assoc. prof., 1993—; lectr. Phila. Mus. Art, Nat. Gallery Art, Washington, 1992, Smithsonian Instn., Washington, 1993, and many others; cons. Inst. Contemporary Art, Phila., 1988—, Smart Gallery, U. Chgo., 1991, Phila. Mus. Art, 1994. Author: In Defiance of Painting: Cubism, Futurism and the Invention of Collage, 1992; contbr. articles to profl. jours. Curatorial fellow NEA Guggenheim Mus., 1979-80, Fulbright fellow, 1983-84; Georges Lurcy grantee Yale U., 1985-86. Mem. Coll. Art Assn. Office: U Pa Dept History of Art 3405 Woodland Walk # 6208 Philadelphia PA 19104

POGREBIN, LETTY COTTIN, writer, lecturer; b. N.Y.C., June 9, 1939; d. Jacob and Cyral (Halpern) Cottin; m. Bertrand B. Pogrebin, Dec. 8, 1963; children: Abigail and Robin (twins), David. A.B. cum laude with spl. distinction in English and Am. Lit, Brandeis U., 1959. V.p. Bernard Geis Assocs. (book pubs.), N.Y.C., 1960-70; columnist The Working Woman column Ladies Home Jour., 1971-81; editor Ms mag., N.Y.C., 1971-87, columnist, editor at large, 1987-89, contbg. editor, 1990—; columnist The N.Y. Times, Newsday, Washington Post, Moment Mag., Washington, 1990—, Moment Mag., Washington, 1990—; contbg. editor Family Circle, Ms. mag., Tikkun mag.; cons. Free to Be, You and Me projects, 1972—; lectr. women's issues and family politics, changing roles of men and women, friendship in Am., non-sexist child rearing and edn., Judaism and feminism, Mid-East politics. Author: How to Make It in a Man's World, 1970, Getting Yours: How to Make the System Work for the Working Woman, 1975, Growing Up Free, 1980, Stories for Free Children, 1982, Family Politics, 1983, Among Friends, 1986, Deborah, Golda, and Me: Being Female and Jewish in America, 1991, Getting Over Getting Older: An Intimate Journey, 1996; mem. editl. bd. Tikkun Mag.; contbr. articles to N.Y. Times, Washington Post, Boston Globe, The Nation, TV Guide, also other mags., newspapers. Sec. bd. Author's Guild; bd. dirs. Ms. Found., Ams. for Peace Now, New Israel Fund, Jewish Fund for Justice, Commn. on Women's Equality, Am. Jewish Congress, PEN Am.; mem. Task Force on Women Fedn. Jewish Philanthropies, Women's Forum. Pointer fellow Yale U., 1982, MacDowell Colony fellow, 1979, 89, 94, Cummington Colony Arts fellow 1985, Edna St. Vincent Millay Colony fellow, 1985; named one of Foremost Women of 20th Century; recipient Gloria Steinem Women of Vision award, Matrix award Women in Comm., Abram L. Sachar medal Brandeis U. Address: 33 W 67th St New York NY 10023-6224

POGUE, MARY ELLEN E. (MRS. L. WELCH POGUE), youth and community worker; b. Fremont, Nebr., Oct. 27, 1904; d. Frank E. and Mary (Coe) Edgerton; m. L. Welch Pogue, Sept. 8, 1926; children: Richard Welch, William Lloyd, John Marshall. BFA, U. Nebr., 1926; studied violin with Harrison Keller, Boston, 1926-28, Kemp Stillings Master Class, N.Y.C., 1935-37. Mem. Potomac String Ensemble, 1939-80. Historian, Gov. William Bradford Compact, 1966—; vice chmn. Montgomery County (Md.) Victory Garden Ctr., 1946-47; pres. Bethesda Community Garden Club, 1947-48; founder Montgomery County YWCA, bd. dirs., 1946-50, 52-55; founder Welcome to Washington Music Group, 1947—; co-founder Group Piano in Montgomery County, Md. schs., 1954. Recipient Outstanding Service award Bethesda United Meth. Ch., 1984, Bethesda Cmty. Garden Club, 1985, 93, Devoted Svc. award D.C. Mayflower Soc., 1985, 89, Welcome to Washington Internat. Club award, 1986. Mem. Soc. Mayflower Descs. D.C. (dir. D.C. 1954—, elder 1971-91, elder emeritus), PEO Sisterhood (pres. 1957-59, charter mem. chpt. R, PEO), Mortar Bd. Alumnae (pres. 1965-67, Mortar Bd. award, 1986), Nat. Cap. Area Fedn. Garden Clubs, Bethesda United Meth. Women, Nat. Geneal. Soc., New Eng. Historic Geneal. Soc. (life), Ohio Geneal. Soc. (life), Md. Geneal. Soc., Md. Hist. Soc., Conn. Soc. Genealogists, Pilgrim Soc. (life), Plimoth Plantation, Hereditary Order of Descs. Colonial Govs., Nat. Soc. Magna Charta Dames, Colonial Order of Crown, Sovereign Colonial Soc. Ams. Royal Descent, Order of Descs. Colonial Physicians and Chirurgiens, Nat. Soc. Women Descs. Ancient and Hon. Arty. Co., First Families of Ohio, Sons and Daughters of the Colonial and Antebellum Bench and Bar 1565-1861 (charter mem.), Welcome to Washington Internat. Club, Ind. Agy. Women (assoc.), Capital Speakers Club, The Plantagenet Soc., Soc. Descs. of Knights of the Most Noble Order of the Garter, DAR, Order Ams. Armorial Ancestry, Saybrook Colony Founders Assn., Soc. Founders of Norwich, Conn., Kenwood Country Club, Delta Omicron Music (life). Methodist. Compiler, editor: Favorite Menus and Recipes of Mary Edgerton of Aurora, Nebraska, 1963, Edgerton-Coe History, 1965. Home: 5204 Kenwood Ave Bethesda MD 20815-6604

POGUE, RHONDA FAY, secondary school science educator; b. Orange County, Calif., July 25, 1956; d. William Kenneth and Elizabeth Ann (Johnson) Renfrow; m. Jerome Bedford Pogue, June 14, 1974; children: Valerie, Kimberly, Thomas. BS, Western Ky. U., 1991. Cert. tchr., Ky. Tchr. Greenwood H.S., Bowling Green, Ky., 1992-93, Earl C. Clements Job Corp., Greenville, Ky., 1994—. Asst. editor (video) Lab Safety, 1992. Mem. SNEA. Home: 5139 US Hwy 431 S Belton KY 42324-9802

POHLER, DANNA GARDNER, accountant, consultant; b. Ft. Worth, Aug. 4, 1959; d. Joe Dell and Gypsy Adair (Blalock) Gardner; m. Steven Anthony Pohler, Sept. 5, 1981; children: Evan Gardner, Kendall Erin. BBA, Tex. Tech U., 1981. CPA, Tex. Auditor, compliance officer MONCOR, Hobbs, N.Mex., 1982-85; comml. loan officer BancHome, Midland, Tex., 1986-88; auditor Tex. Nat. Bank, Midland, 1991-92, mortgage bank mgr., 1992-93; CPA P.S. Enterprises, Midland, 1993—. Treas. Compassionate Friends, Midland, 1994-95; mem. First Bapt. Ch., 1990—. Republican. Home: 5011 Polo Pky Midland TX 79705

POHLMAN, CONSTANCE, artist, educator; b. Cin.; d. G.S. and D.L. Pohlman. BFA with honors, Art Ctr. Coll. Design, Pasadena, Calif., 1993; MFA, Claremont Grad. Sch., 1996. Slide rsch. asst. Art Ctr. Coll. Design, Pasadena, 1992-93; program coord. DA Gallery, Pomona, Calif., 1995; gallery/office asst. Claremont (Calif.) Grad. Sch., 1994-96; art tchr. Armory Ctr. for Art, Pasadena, 1995—. One-woman show Dillingham Caples Gallery, Claremont Grad. Sch., 1995, East Gallery, 1996; exhibited in group shows Moorpark (Calif.) C.C., 1989, Conejo Valley Art Mus., Thousand Oaks, Calif., 1994, Claremont West Gallery, 1994, Roark, L.A., 1995, The Haven, Pomona, Calif., 1995, Calif. Mus. Art Luther Burbank Ctr. for Arts, Santa Rosa, 1995, West Gallery, Claremont Grad. Sch., 1995, East Gallery, 1995; represented in pvt. collections; represented by The Loft, Laguna Beach, Calif. Karl and Bev Benjamin fellow, 1995-96, Lester M. Bonar fellow Art Ctr. Coll., 1992, 93. Mem. Western Assn. for Art Conservation. Home: PO Box 2972 Rancho Cucamonga CA 91729 Office: The Loft 2091 Laguna Canyon Rd Laguna Beach CA 92651

POIANI, EILEEN LOUISE, mathematics educator, college administrator, higher education planner; b. Newark, Dec. 17, 1943; d. Hugo Francis and Eileen Louise (Crecca) P. BA in Math., Douglass Coll., 1965; MS in Math., Rutgers U., 1967, PhD in Math., 1971. Teaching asst., grad. preceptor Rutgers U., New Brunswick, N.J., 1966-67; asst. counselor Douglass Coll., New Brunswick, 1967, 69-70; instr. math. St. Peter's Coll., Jersey City, 1967-70, asst. prof., 1970-74, dir. of self-study, 1974-76, assoc. prof., 1974-80, prof., 1980—, asst. to pres., 1976-80; asst. to pres. for planning St. Peter's Coll., 1980—; chairwoman U.S. Commn. on Math. Instrn., NRC of NAS, Washington, 1983-90; founding nat. dir. Women and Math. Lectureship Program, Washington, 1975-81, mem. adv. bd., 1981—; project dir. Consortium for Advancement of Pvt. Higher Edn., Washington, 1986-88; mem. N.J. Math. Coalition, 1991—, Nat. Seminar on Jesuit Higher Edn., 1990-94, mem. strategic planning com. N.J. Assn. Ind. Colls. and Univs., 1990-92; charter trustee Rutgers U., 1992—. Author: (with others) Mathematics Tomorrow, 1981; contbr. articles to profl. jours. Mem. Newark Mus., Nutley (N.J.) Hist. Soc., Friends of Newark Libr.; trustee Nutley Free Pub. Libr., 1974-77, St. Peter's Prep. Sch., Jersey City, 1986-92; active fee arbitration commn. N.J. Supreme Ct., 1983-86, ct. ethics com., 1986-90; U.S. nat. rep. Internat. Congress Math. Edn., Budapest, Hungary, 1988; mem. statewide planning com. NCCJ, 1988-92; chair evaluation teams Mid. States Assn. Coll. and Schs.; mem. U.S. delegation to Internat. Congress on Math; trustee The Cath. Advocate, 1993—. Recipient Douglass Soc. award Douglass Coll., 1982, Outstanding Cmty. Svc. award Christopher Columbus Found., N.J., 1994, Outstanding Svc. award Middle States Assn. Colls. and Schs., 1994, Cert. of Appreciation in Reconition of Outstanding Contbns. as Nat. Dir. of Women and Math. Program, 1993; named Danforth Assoc., Danforth Found., 1972-86. Mem. AAUP, Math. Assn. Am. (bd. dirs. lectureship program, gov. N.J. chpt. 1972-79, chair human resources coun. 1991—, Outstanding Coll. Tchg. award 1993), Am. Math. Soc., Nat. Coun. Tchrs. Math. (spkr. 1974—), Soc. Coll. and Univ. Planning (program com. 1989—, spkr. nat. conf. 1986, 88, 89, 90, judge grad. paper competition), Pi Mu Epsilon (1st woman pres. in 75 yrs. 1987-90, C.C. MacDuffee award for disting. svc. and to math. 1995). Roman Catholic. Office: St Peter's Coll 2641 Kennedy Blvd Jersey City NJ 07306

POINDEXTER, BARBARA GLENNON, secondary school educator; b. Dallas, Oct. 19, 1937; d. Victor and Ruth (Gaskins) Ward; m. Noble Turner Poindexter, Aug. 2, 1994; 1 child, Victoria Angela Glennon Betts. BS, Tex. Woman's U., 1958; postgrad., Kans. State U., 1969-70. Cert. tchr. S.C., Kans., N.Mex., Tex. Drama and English tchr. Linn (Kans.) High Sch., 1968-69; tchr. Mosquero (N.Mex.) High Sch., 1973-74, Sumter (S.C.) Sch. Dist., Maywood Sch., 1974-76, Harleyville (S.C.) High Sch., 1976-78, Hampton (S.C.) High Sch., 1978-79, Centerville Sch., Cottageville, S.C., 1979-80; tchr. English Scurry-Rosser Sch., Scurry, Tex., 1981-82; tchr. French and Spanish Christ the King, Dallas, 1982-83; tchr. French and English, chmn. fgn. lang. dept. Wilmer-Hutchins High Sch., Dallas, 1983—. Mem. Theta Alpha Phi. Democrat. Methodist. Home: 5315 Maple Springs Blvd Dallas TX 75235 Office: Wilmer-Hutchins High Sch 5520 Langdon Rd Dallas TX 75241-7148

POINDEXTER, BEVERLY KAY, media and communications professional; b. Noblesville, Ind., Nov. 12, 1949; d. Wayne Francis and Rosalie Christine (Nightenhelser) Hunter; m. Jerry Roger Poindexter, Dec. 7, 1969; children: Nick Ashley, Tracy Lynne, Wendy Dawn, Cory Matthew. Student, Purdue U. Editor Tri Town Topics Newspaper, 1965-69; reporter, photographer Noblesville Daily Ledger, 1969-70; asst. mgr., sales mgr., sports dir. Sta. WHYT Radio, Noblesville, Ind., 1973-79; sales mgr., music dir., DJ, news Sta. WBMP Radio, Elwood, Ind., 1979-88; acct. exec. Sta. WAXT-WHBU Radio, Anderson, Ind., 1988-89; gen. mgr., sales mgr. Sta. WEWZ, Elwood, Ind., 1989-90; now news stringer Sta. WRTV-6, Indpls., Sta. WTHR TV-13, Indpls.; acct. exec. Sta. WLHN Radio, Elwood, Ind.; real estate broker Booker Realty, Cicero, Ind., 1990—. Area rep. Am. Field Svc.. Hamilton County, Ind.; pres. bd. dirs. Hamilton Heights Elem. Football, Arcadia, Ind., 1981-83; founder, chmn. Hamilton Heights Elem. Cheerleaders, Arcadia, 1981-87; youth leader, counselor Ch. of the Brethren, Arcadia, 1991-94; active Ch. of Brethren Women's Fellowship. Mem. Nat. Assn. Realtors, Ind. Assn. Realtors, Met. Indpls. Bd. Realtors. Republican. Home: 14645 E 281st St Atlanta IN 46031-9722 Office: Booker Realty PO Box 437 99 S Peru Cicero IN 46034

POINDEXTER, KATHLEEN A. KRAUSE, nursing educator, critical care nurse; b. Platteville, Wis., Aug. 30, 1956; d. Gene A. and Catherine E. (Boyle) Gilbertson; m. David L. Poindexter, July 20, 1990; children: Nicholas, Brendon, Ashley, Anna, Steve. BA in Nursing, Coll. of St. Scholastica, Duluth, Minn., 1978; MSN, No. Mich. U., Marquette, 1990. RN, Minn., Mich.; cert. ACLS, BCLS instr.; PALS. Staff nurse pediatrics ICU St. Mary's Med. Ctr., Duluth, 1978-83, head nurse pediatrics/pediatric ICU, 1983-85; clin. III staff nurse ICU/critical care unit Marquette Gen. Hosp., 1985-88; staff nurse critical care unit Bell Meml. Hosp., Ishpeming, Mich., 19909—; assoc. prof. No. Mich. U. Sch. Nursing, Marquette, 1988-96, 1996—; researcher in field. Mem. coll. adv. coun., mem. faculty grante com. No. Mich. U.; advisor, founder No. Mich. U. Practical Nurses Assn. Recipient Excellence in Edn. award; Exemplary Citizen award, 1995. Mem. AACN (edn. advisor), AAUP (staff coun.), ANA, Am. Heart Assn., Hursing Honor Soc. (sec.), Sigma Theta Tau. Home: 1806 Gray St Marquette MI 49855-1546

POINSETT-WHITE, SADIE RUTH, elementary education educator; b. Chgo., May 11, 1934; d. Alexander Abraham and Adele Marie (Prindle) Poinsett; m. Robert Eli White, Sept. 11, 1955; children: Susan Murray, Michael L. White. BS in elem. edn., U. Ill., 1954; MA in early childhood edn., U. Md., 1980. Cert. elem. edn. tchr., Md. Head start tchr. San Bernadino (Calif.) Pub. Sch., 1966, kindergarten tchr., 1967; day care tchr. Kensington (Md.) Day Care, 1970; head start tchr. Montgomery County Pub. Sch., Rockville, Md., 1972-84; kindergarten tchr. Montgomery County Pub. Sch., Silver Spring, Md., 1984—; mem. tchr. evaluation adv. task force Montgomery County Pub. Sch., 1996-97; presenter confs. in field. Mem. adv. bd. Noyes Libr., Kensington, 1980-84, 90-93; mem. NAACP Nat. Black Child Devel. Inc. Rsch. fellow U. Md., College Park, 1980. Mem. Nat. Sci. Tchrs. Assn. (conf. presenter 1991-96), Md. State Dept. Edn. (conf. presenter 1991-96), Md. Assn. Sci. Tchrs. (conf. presenter 1991-96), Montgomery County Edn. Assn. (poll vol. 1986—, precinct capt. 1994—), Nat. Coun. Negro Women, Zeta Phi Beta (Basileus 1996). Office: Broad Acres Elem Sch 710 Beacon Rd Silver Spring MD 20903

POIRIER, HELEN VIRGINIA LEONARD, elementary education educator; b. Worcester, Mass., Oct. 2, 1954; d. Robert O'Donnell and Rose C. (Pepper) Leonard; m. Paul Nelson Poirier, Aug. 3, 1985. BS, Worcester State Coll., 1976. Cert. tchr. K-6, reading supr. K-12, adminstrn. K-8. Tchr. grade 5-6 reading and social studies Quabbin Regional Sch. Dist., Oakham, Mass., 1980—. Sec. Local Cable Access Com., Auburn, 1985-92. NEH grantee, 1986; town history grantee Oakham Hist. Soc., 1986, Oakham Hist. Commn., 1986. Mem. Cen. Mass. Coun. Social Studies (bd. dirs., sec. 1986-90, treas. 1990—), Hodges Village Environ. Edn. Assn., Tanheath Hunt Club (pres. 1995—, sec./newsletter editor 1988-95). Office: Oakham Center Sch Deacon Allen Dr Oakham MA 01068

POKRAS, SHEILA FRANCES, judge; b. Newark, Aug. 5, 1935; m. Norman M. Pokras, 1954; children: Allison, Andrea, Larry. Student, Beaver Coll., 1953-54; BS in Edn., Temple U., 1957; JD cum laude, Pepperdine U., 1969. Bar: Calif. 1970, U.S. Dist. Ct. D.C. 1970, U.S. Dist. Ct. Calif. 1970, U.S. Supreme Ct. 1975. Tchr. elem. and secondary schs. Phila. and Newark, 1957-59; pvt. practice law Long Beach, Calif., 1970-78; city councilwoman Lakewood, Calif., 1972-76; judge Long Beach Mcpl. Ct., 1978-80, L.A. Superior Ct., 1980—; supervising judge, 1986; del. Calif. State Dem. Cen. Com., 1975, Calif. State Conv., 1975; mem. Com. on Gender Bias in Calif. Courts, 1986-89. Advisor Jr. League, 1980-85; mem. early childhood adv. bd. Long Beach City Coll.; bd. dirs. Long Beach Alcoholism Coun., 1979-80, Boys and Girls Club Am., 1981-89, Long Beach Symphony, 1985, Jewish Community Fedn., 1982-86, past mem. community rels. com.; active Nat. Women's Polit. Caucus, LWV. Named Woman of Yr. NOW, Long Beach, 1984; recipient Torch of Liberty award B'nai B'rith Anti-Defamation League, 1974; honoree Nat. Conf. Christians and Jews, 1986. Mem. ABA, AAUW, Nat. Assn. Women Judges (dist. supr. 1986), Calif. Bar Assn. (judges div.), Calif. Judges Assn. (mem. ann. seminar com. 1981-89), Mcpl. Cts. Judges Assn. (mem. Marshall com. 1979-80), L.A. County Bar Assn. (judges div., mem. arbitration com.), Women Lawyers Assn., L.A. (judges sect.), Women Lawyers Assn. Long Beach, Long Beach Legal Aid Found. (v.p. 1976-78), Long Beach Bar Assn. (active various coms., bd. govs. 1977-78, Judge of Yr. 1987), Long Beach C. of C. (bd. dirs.). Office: So Dist Superior Ct 415 W Ocean Blvd Long Beach CA 90802-4512

POL, ANNE, operations executive; b. Cavan, Ireland, Sept. 10, 1947; came to U.S., 1960; d. Patrick John and Margaret (Rahill) McN.; m. Richard Stephen Pol, Dec. 2, 1967; 1 child, Anne Cristin. BA, CCNY, 1971, MA, 1977. Tchr. St. Jude's Sch., N.Y.C., 1971-73; mgmt. intern N.Y.C. Fire Dept., 1973, labor rels. officer, 1974-75, dep. dir. Office of Mgmt. Planning, 1975-77, pers. dir., 1977-78; mgr. labor and employee rels. Becton Dickinson & Co., Franklin Lakes, N.J., 1978-80; mgr. employee rels. planning Ingersoll Rand Co., Woodcliff Lakes, N.J., 1980-81, mgr. manpower and orgn. planning, 1981-82; cons. Oakland, N.J., 1982-84; dir. orgn. planning and exec. staffing Pitney Bowes, Stamford, Conn., 1984-85, dir. of mfg. components, 1985-86, dir. of mfg. assembly, 1986-87, v.p. pers., 1987-90, v.p. mfg. ops., 1990-91; v.p. new product devel. Pitney Bowes, Inc., Stamford, 1991-93, pres. shipping and weighing systems divsn., 1993—; bd. dirs. VGI, Valley Forge, Pa., Arrow Electronics, Inc., Melville, N.Y., Allegheny Ludlum Corp., Pitts. Bd. dirs. St. Joseph's Hosp., Stamford, 1988-95. Regents scholar N.Y. State, 1966-71. Office: Pitney Bowes Inc 27 Waterview Dr Shelton CT 06484-4733

POLACCO, PATRICIA, children's author, illustrator. Works include (juevniles) Meteor!, 1987, Rechenka's Eggs, 1988, The Keeping Quilt, 1988, Uncle Vova's Tree, 1989, Boatride with Lillian Two-Blossom, 1989, Thunder Cake, 1990, Just Plain Fancy, 1990, Babushka's Doll, 1990, Some Birthday!, 1991, Appelemando's Dreams, 1991, Picnic at Mudsock Meadow, 1992, Mrs. Katz & Tush, 1992, Chicken Sunday, 1992, The Bee Tree, 1993, Babushka Baba Yaga, 1993, Tikvah Means Hope, 1994, Pink & Say, 1994, My Rotten Readheaded, Older Brother, 1994, Firetalking, 1994, My Ol' Man, 1995, Babushka's Mother Goose, Aunt Chip and the Great Triple Creek Dam Affair, 1995; illustrator: Casey at the Bat, 1992. Office: Putnam Pub Group 200 Madison Ave New York NY 10016-3903*

POLAK, VIVIAN LOUISE, lawyer; b. N.Y.C., Nov. 1, 1952; d. Henri and Greta Etty (Querido) P. BA, Barnard Coll., 1974; JD, Harvard U., 1977. Bar: N.Y. 1978, D.C. 1978, U.S. Dist. Ct. (ea. and so. dists.) N.Y. 1978. Assoc. Donovan, Leisure, Newton and Irvine, N.Y.C., 1977-86; ptnr. LeBoeuf, Lamb, Greene & MacRae, N.Y.C., 1986—. Mem. N.Y. Bar Assn. (sec. antitrust sect. 1991-92, mem. exec. com. 1993-95, chmn. internat. trade com. 1985-90). Office: LeBoeuf Lamb Greene and MacRae 125 W 55th St New York NY 10019-5369

POLAKOFF, EILEEN, genealogist; b. Cambridge, Mass., June 27, 1947; d. John E. Lyons and Marion G. (Stickney) Cousins; m. Jack A. Polakoff, Oct. 10, 1981 (div. Dec. 1991). BA, Coll. New Rochelle, 1976. Adminstrv. asst. to dep. mayor City of N.Y., 1976-81; profl. genealogist N.Y.C., 1985—. Contbr. articles to profl. jours. Mem. Assn. Profl. Genealogists (Grahame T. Smallwood Merit award 1991), Geneal. Spkrs. Guild. Home: 240 West End Ave #15-A New York NY 10023-3613

POLAN, ADELE KARP, biostatistician; b. Carteret, N.J., July 16, 1917; d. Samuel Max and Goldie Blossom (Minsky) Karp; m. Isadore Polan, Sept. 3, 1944 (dec. 1980); children: Judith S. and Steven M. BA cum laude, Bklyn. Coll., 1938; MA, Columbia U., 1940; postgrad., Yale U., 1965. Supr. U.S. Census Bur., Washington, 1940-41; biostatistician N.Y. State Dept. of Health, Albany, N.Y., 1941-81, rsch. sci. epidemiology, 1981-91; ret., 1991; mem. task force on women's issues N.Y. State Dept. of Health, Albany, 1983-91. Contbr. articles to profl. jours. registered vol. N.Y. State Dept. of Health, Albany, N.Y., 1991—. jewish. Home: 59 Orchard St Delmar NY 12054 Office: NY State Dept of Health 2 University Pl Albany NY 12203-3313

POLAN, ANNETTE LEWIS, artist, educator; b. Huntington, W.Va., Dec. 8, 1944; d. Lake and Dorothy (Lewis) P.; m. Arthur Lowell Fox Jr., Aug. 31, 1969 (div. 1994); children: Courtney Van Winkle Fox, Arthur Lowell Fox III. 1st degree, Inst. des Profs. de Francaise, Paris, 1965; BA, Hollins Coll., 1967; postgrad., Corcoran Sch. Art, 1968-69. Vis. artist Art Therapy Italia, Vignale, Italy, 1986; dir. summer program La Napoule Art Found., Chateau de la Napoule, France, 1987, 88, 90; guest lectr. China, Japan, 1989, Australia, 1996; prof. Corcoran Sch. Art, Washington, 1974—; chmn. painting dept. Corcoran Coll. Art, Washington, 1991—; dir. Washington Project for the Arts. Illustrator: Say What I Am, 1989, Relearning the Dark, 1991; cover designer Doers of the Word, 1995; portrait commns. include Sandra Day O'Connor, Va. Gov. Gaston Caperton. Bd. dirs. Washington Project for the Arts, 1994—. Mem. Corcoran Faculty Assn. (pres. 1988-89). Office: Corcoran Sch Art 1680 Wisconsin Ave NW Washington DC 20007-2707

POLAN, NANCY MOORE, artist; b. Newark, Ohio; d. William Tracy and Francis (Flesher) Moore; m. Lincoln Milton Polan, Mar. 28, 1934; children: Charles Edwin, William Joseph Marion. AB, Marshall U., 1936. One-man shows include Charleston Art Gallery, 1961, 67, 73, Greenbrier, 1963, Huntington Mus. Art, 1963, 66, 71, N.Y. World's Fair, 1965, W.Va. U., 1966, Carroll Reese Mus., 1967; exhibited in group shows Am. Watercolor Soc., Allied Artists of Am., Nat. Arts Club, 1968-74, 76-77, 86, 87, 91-95, Pa. Acad. Fine Arts, Opening of Creative Arts Center W.Va. U., 1969, Internat. Platform Assn. Art Exhibit, 1968-69, 72-74, 74, 79, 85-86, 88-90, (Gold medal Best of Show 1991, 2d award painting 1994, 1st award watercolor), Allied Artists W.Va., 1968-69, 86, Joan Miro Graphic Traveling Exhbn., Barcelona, Spain, 1970-71, XXI Exhibit Contemporary Art, La Scala, Florence, Italy, 1971, Rassegna Internazionale d'Arte Grafica, Siena, Italy, 1973, 79, 82, Opening of Parkersburg (W.Va.) Art Center, 1975, Art Club Washington, 1992, Pen & Brush, 1992-93, others. Hon. v.p. Centro Studie Scambi Internazionale, Rome, Italy, 1977. Recipient Acad. of Italy with Gold medal, 1979, 86, Norton Meml. award 3d Nat. Jury Show Am. Art, Chautauqua, N.Y., 1960; Purchase prize, Jurors award, Watercolor award Huntington Galleries, 1960, 61; Nat. Arts Club for watercolor, 1969; Gold medal Masters of Modern Art exhbn., La Scala Gallery, Florence, 1975, gold medal Accademia Italia, 1984, 1986, diploma Internat. Com. for World Culture and Arts, 1987, Philip Isenberg Watercolor award Pen & Brush, 1995, many others. Mem. AAUW, DAR, Nat. Mus. Women Artists (charter), Allied Artists W.Va., Internat. Platform Assn. (3rd award-painting in ann. art exhbn. 1977, Gold medal for Best of Show 1991, 1st award for painting 1994), Huntington Mus. Fine Arts (life), Tri-State Arts Assn. (Equal Merit award 1978), Sunrise Found., Composers, Authors, Artists Am., Inc., Pen and Brush, Inc. (Watercolor exhbn. 1993, Grumbacher golden palette mem., Grumbacher award 1978), W.Va. Watercolor Soc. (charter mem.), Nat. Arts Club, Leonardo da Vinci Acad. (Rome), Accademia Italia, Vero Beach Arts Club, Riomar Bay Yacht Club, Guyan Golf and Country Club, Huntington Cotillion (charter mem.), Mass. Hist. Soc. (hon.), Sigma Kappa. Episcopalian. Address: 2106 Club Dr Vero Beach FL 32963 also: 2 Prospect Dr Huntington WV 25701

POLAND, CAROL JOANNE, counselor; b. Sargent, Nebr., May 31, 1939; d. STeven L. and Agnes E. (Kamarad) Gruber; m. Larry L. Poland, Dec. 27,

1962; children: Lauri, Lisa, Cari, Katrina. BS in Edn., Marymount Coll., Salina, Kans., 1960; M. in Counseling and Psychology, Kearney State U., 1988. Nat. cert. profl. counselor; lic. practical counselor Nebr. Sch. counselor Anselmo Merna (Nebr.) Sch., 1988-92, Sargent Pub. Sch., 1992—. Mem. ACA, Nebr. Counselor Assn. (bd. dirs. 1993-95), Am. Sch. Counseling Assn., Nebr. Sch. Counselor Assn. (pres.-elect 1992-93, pres. 1993-94). Roman Catholic. Home: Box 396 Semler St Sargent NE 68874

POLAND, PHYLLIS ELAINE, secondary school educator, consultant; b. Norwood, Mass., May 10, 1941; d. Kenneth Gould Vale and Mildred Eloise (Fisk) Arnold; m. Thomas Charles Poland, June 6, 1968 (div. Nov. 1991); 1 child, Sherilyn Ann Poland Colon. AB in Math., Ea. Nazarene Coll., 1963; BS in Math., Nova U., 1986. Cert. secondary tchr., Fla. H.S. math. tchr. Burrillville, R.I., 1963-64; jr. H.S. math. tchr. Quincy, Mass., 1964-65; math. tchr. Seekonk (Mass.) H.S., 1965-68, Howard Jr. H.S., Orlando, Fla., 1968-74, Lake Highland Prep. Sch., Orlando, Fla., 1977-81, Lake Brantley H.S., Altamonte Springs, Fla., 1981—. Mem. coun. Joy Club Ctrl. Nazarene Ch., 1988—, adult edn. sec., 1990—, mem. choir, 1986—. Grantee NSF, 1969, 70, 71, 72. Mem. NEA. Home: 401 Navarre Way Altamonte Springs FL 32714-2224

POLASCIK, MARY ANN, ophthalmologist; b. Elkhorn, W.Va., Dec. 28, 1940; d. Michael and Elizabeth (Halko) Polascik; BA, Rutgers U., 1967; MD, Pritzker Sch. Medicine, 1971; m. Joseph Elie, Oct. 2, 1973; 1 dau., Laura Elizabeth Polascik. Jr. pharmacologist Ciba Pharm. Co., Summit, N.J., 1961-67; intern Billings Hosp., Chgo., 1971-72; resident in ophthalmology U. Chgo. Hosp., 1972-75; practice medicine specializing in ophthalmology, Dixon, Ill., 1975—; pres. McNichols Clinic, Ltd.; cons. ophthalmology, Jack Mabley Devel. Ctr., 1976-93; mem. staff Katherine Shaw Bethea Hosp. Bd. dirs. Sinnossippi Mental Healh Ctr., 1977-82, Dixon Cmty. Trust Mental Health Ctr., 1989—. Mem. AMA, Ill. Med. Soc., Ill. Assn. Ophthalmology, Am. Assn. Ophthalmology, Alpha Sigma Lambda. Roman Catholic. Club: Galena Territory. Office: 1700 S Galena Ave Dixon IL 61021-9600

POLASEK, PATRICIA ANN CATHERINE, small business owner; b. Houston, Nov. 4, 1947; d. John and Ann Polasek. Student, U. Houston, U. Ind., S.W. Tex. State U. With W-K-M Valves, Missouri City, Tex., 1969-71, Exxon Co. U.S.A., Houston, 1973-76; owner SCI Resources, Internat., Houston. Author: Space Drama, 1992, City Odyssey, 1992 (films). Mem. Toastmistress Club, St. Michael's Club (sec. 1973-76), Gathering Place Club (sec. 1996). Democrat. Roman Catholic. Home and Office: 11730 Kathy Ave Houston TX 77071-3406

POLASKI, ANNE SPENCER, lawyer; b. Pittsfield, Mass., Nov. 13, 1952; d. John Harold and Marjorie Ruth (Hackett) Spencer; m. James Joseph Polaski, Sept. 14, 1985. BA in Psychology, Allegheny Coll., 1974; MSW, U. Pa., 1976; JD, George Washington U., 1979. Bar: D.C. 1979, U.S. Dist. Ct. (D.C. dist.) 1980, U.S. Ct. Appeals (D.C. cir.) 1980, Ill. 1982, U.S. Dist. Ct. (no. dist.) Ill. 1982, U.S. Ct. Appeals (7th cir.) 1982. Law clk. to assoc. judge D.C. Ct., Washington, 1979-80; trial atty. Commodity Futures Trading Commn., Chgo., 1980-84, sr. trial atty., 1984, dep. regional counsel, 1984-88; assoc. Gottlieb and Schwartz, Chgo., 1988-91; staff atty. Chgo. Bd. of Trade, 1991-92, sr. atty., 1992-94, asst. gen. counsel, 1994—. Mem. ABA, Chgo. Bar Assn. Office: Chgo Bd of Trade 141 W Jackson Blvd Chicago IL 60604-2904

POLEMITOU, OLGA ANDREA, accountant; b. Nicosia, Cyprus, June 28, 1950; d. Takis and Georgia (Nicolaou) Chrysanthou. BA with honors, U. London, 1971; PhD, Ind. U., Bloomington, 1981. CPA, Ind. Asst. productivity officer Internat. Labor Office/Cyprus Productivity Ctr., Nicosia, 1971-74; cons. Arthur Young & Co., N.Y.C., 1981; mgr. Coopers & Lybrand, Newark, 1981-83; dir. Bell Atlantic, Reston, Va., 1983—; chairperson adv. coun. Extended Day Care Community Edn., West Windsor Plainsboro, 1987-88. Contbr. articles to profl. jours. Bus. cons. project bus. Jr. Achievement, Indpls., 1984-85. Mem. NAFE, AICPAs, Nat. Trust for Hist. Preservation, Ind. CPA Soc., N.J. Soc. CPAs (sec. mems. in industry com.), Princeton Network of Profl. Women. Home: PO Box 2744 Reston VA 22090-0744 Office: Bell Atlantic Video Svcs Co 1880 Campus Commons Dr Reston VA 22091-1512

POLEN, RITA, principal; b. Lawton, Okla., Apr. 11, 1946; d. Wilburn Eugene and Almareeta (Willis) Billington; m. Jerry Wayne Polen, Nov. 24, 1967; 1 child, Jeremy Blake. BS in Edn., U. Okla., 1970; MA in Edn., U. Tex., San Antonio, 1985; postgrad., Tex. A&I U., 1989-92. Tchr. Live Oak Elem. Sch., San Antonio, 1971-74, Crestview Elem. Sch., San Antonio, 1974-82, 84-86, Crestview/Live Oak Elem. Schs., 1982-84; instructional supr. Randolph Field. Ind. Sch. Dist., Randolph AFB, Tex., 1986-92, dir. curriculum, 1986-95, interim elem. prin., dir. curriculum, 1995—; mem. adv. bd. Tex. Student Vol. Program, 1989-91, Kindergarten Program, San Antonio, 1988-90; mem. planning bd. Tex. Assn. Adminstrs. and Suprs., 1990-92. Mem. ASCD, Tex. Assn. Supervision and Curriculum Devel., Alamo Area Assn. Supervision and Curriculum Devel. (pres. 1994-95, sec. 1993-94). Office: Randolph Field Ind Sch Dist Bldg #1225 Randolph AFB TX 78148

POLEN-DORN, LINDA FRANCES, communications executive; b. Cleve., Mar. 23, 1945; d. Stanley and Mildred (Kain) Neuger; m. Samuel O. Dorn; children: Lanelle, Brian, Adam, Dawn. BA cum laude, U. Miami, 1967; MBA, Nova Southeastern U., 1993. Reporter Miami (Fla.) News, 1966-67; writer Miamian Mag., 1967-68; dir. pub. rels. Muscular Dystrophy Assn., Miami, 1968-72; cons., adv. and pub. rels. Ft. Lauderdale, 1974-77; pub. rels. writer J. Cory and Assocs., Ft. Lauderdale, Fla., 1978-79; account supr. Maizner & Franklin, Fla., 1979-86; v.p. mktg., communications mgr. Glendale Fed. Bank, Fla., 1986-95; prod. mktg. mgr. Ryder Sys., Inc., Miami, 1995—. Sustaining mem. Mus. Art., Ft. Lauderdale, 1986—, Philharmonic Soc., Ft. Lauderdale, 1987—. Mem. Internat. Assn. Bus. Communicators, Pub. Rels. Soc. Am., Am. Mktg. Assn., Broward C. of C. (vice chmn. govt. affairs 1984-85). Office: Ryder System Inc 3600 NW 82 Ave Miami FL 33166

POLENZ, JOANNA MAGDA, psychiatrist; b. Cracow, Poland, Oct. 20, 1936; came to U.S., 1961; d. Mieczyslaw and Nusia (Goldberger) Uberall; m. Daryl Louis Polenz, July 8, 1962 (div. 1991); children: Teresa Ann, Daryl Philip, Elizabeth Sophia. MD, U. Sydney, Australia, 1960; MPH, Columbia U., 1992. Diplomate Am. Bd. Psychiatry and Neurology. Intern Bklyn. Hosp., 1961-62; resident Mt. Sinai Med. Ctr., N.Y.C., 1962-65; ednl. fellow Mt. Sinai Med. Ctr., 1965-66, rsch. assoc., 1966-67; med. dir. Tappan Zee clin. Phelps Meml. Hosp., Tarrytown, N.Y., 1968-71, dir. dept. psychiatry, 1972-77; sr. attending psychiatrist Meml. Hosp. Ctr., 1972-93; pvt. practice Briarcliff Manor, N.Y., 1971-91; physician Joint Commn. Accreditation of Healthcare Orgns., Oakbrook Terrace, Ill., 1993—; lectr. in field. Author: In Defense of marriage, 1981; (with other) Test Your Marriage IQ, 1984, Test Your Success IQ, 1985; contbr. articles to profl. jours.; numerous TV appearances including Phil Donahue, 1988, Oprah Winfrey 1984. Grant Found. grantee, 1970. Fellow Am. psychiatric Assn., Royal Soc. for Health; mem. AMA, N.Y. Acad. Scis., Pan Am. Med. Assn., Westchester Psychiatric Assn. (sec. 1982-85, chair person fellowship com. 1989). Home: 1755 York Ave Apt 31E New York NY 10128

POLEVOY, NANCY TALLY, lawyer, social worker, genealogist; b. N.Y.C., May 27, 1944; d. Charles H. and Bernice M. (Gang) Tally; m. Martin D. Polevoy, Mar. 19, 1967; children: Jason Tally, John Gerald. Student, Mt. Holyoke Coll., 1962-64; BA, Barnard Coll., 1966; MS in Social Work, Columbia U., 1968, JD, 1986. Bar: N.Y. 1987. Caseworker unmarried mothers' svc. Louise Wise Svcs., N.Y.C., 1967, caseworker adoption dept., 1969-71; caseworker Youth Consultation Svc., N.Y.C., 1968-69; asst. rsch. scientist, psychiat. social worker dept. child psychiatry NYU Med. Ctr., N.Y.C., 1973-81; adv. ct. apptd. spl. advs. Manhattan Family Ct., N.Y.C., 1981-82; cons. social work, 1981-86; matrimonial assoc. Ballon, Stoll & Itzler, 1987, Herzfeld & Rubin, P.C., 1987-88; pvt. practice, N.Y.C. Contbr. articles on early infantile autism and genealogy to profl. jours. Mem. Parents' Adv. Bd. Riverdale Country Sch., 1988-93; mem. outreach bd. Manhattan divsn. United Jewish Appeal Fedn., 1990-94, exec. bd. Manhattan divsn., 1992-94, mem. met. campaign cabinet, 1994-95; mem. archives com. Cen. Synagogue, 1991—, chmn. 1994—; trustee Am. Jewish Hist. Soc., 1992—, asst. treas., 1995—; trustee Jewish Assn. for Svcs. for the Aged, 1996—; bd. dirs. Ctr. for Jewish History. 1996—. Recipient French Govt. prize, 1963. Mem. NASW, Bar Assn. of City of N.Y., N.Y. State Bar Assn., Acad. Cert. Social Workers, Barnard Coll. Alumni Assn. (v.p. 1966, class pres. of 1966 1996—). Home and Office: 1155 Park Ave New York NY 10128-1209

POLIKOWSKY, MARY ELIZABETH, retired English educator; b. St. Louis, June 2, 1938; d. James Franklin and Elizabeth Arminda (Durham) Heaton; m. Lawrence Burdette Cobb, Jr., Dec. 23, 1958 (wid. Aug. 1971); 1 child, Stephen Lawrence; m. John Hughes Polikowsky, June 25, 1993. AB, Okla. Bapt. U., 1959; MA, U. Wash., 1969, PhD, 1984. Tchr., English North Kansas City, Mo. Sch. Dist., 1960; thcr., lang. arts and social studies, jr. high Seattle Sch. Dist., 1961-67, tchr., lang. arts and social studies, h.s., 1967-87; lectr. in English Western Wash. U., Bellingham, 1987-89, asst. prof. English, 1989-94; dept. head English, Ingraham H.S., Seattle, 1977-83; co-dir. Puget Sound Writing Project, U. Wash., 1989-90, Fourth Corner Writing Project, Western Wash. U., 1991-94. Bd. dirs. ACLU, Bellingham, 1989-90; tutor Snohomish County Literacy Coalition, Everett, Wash., 1995-96. Recipient Spl. Commendation, Citizen Com. for Acad. Excellence, Seattle Pub. Schs., 1981; summer rsch. grantee Western Wash. U., 1990; grantee U.S. Dept. Edn., Berkeley, Calif., 1992-94. Democrat. Home: 9205 Olympic View Dr Edmonds WA 98020

POLIMENI, ANNA MARIA, actuary; b. Canandaigua, N.Y., Dec. 3, 1969; d. John F. and Ellen M. (Goggin) P. BS, Cornell U., 1992. Actuarial trainee Kwasha Lipton, Ft. Lee, N.J., 1992, actuarial analyst, 1993-95, asst. actuary, 1995—. Mem. AAUW. Democrat. Roman Catholic. Home: 64 Willow Terr # 2 Hoboken NJ 07030 Office: Kwasha Lipton 2100 N Central Rd Fort Lee NJ 07024

POLIN, JANE LOUISE, foundation official; b. N.Y.C., Sept. 30, 1958; d. Raymond and Constance F. (Caplan) P. BA, Wesleyan U., Middletown, Conn., 1980; MBA, Columbia U., 1988. Asst. dir. ann. giving Wesleyan U., 1980-82; centennial fund assoc. Met. Opera Assn., N.Y.C., 1982-84; devel. officer Columbia U., N.Y.C., 1984-88; program mgr., compt. GE Founds., Fairfield, Conn., 1988—. Panelist arts-in-edn. Nat. Endowment for Arts, Washington, 1989-90, 94; adv. bd. mem. Carnegie Hall, N.Y.C., 1992—, Nat. Corp. Theatre Fund, N.Y.C., 1991—, Young Audiences, N.Y.C., 1991—. Mem. Alpha Delta Phi. Office: General Electric Fund 3135 Easton Tpke Fairfield CT 06431-0002

POLINGER, IRIS SANDRA, dermatologist; b. N.Y.C., Feb. 10, 1943; m. Harvey I. Hyman, Feb. 6, 1972. AB, Barnard Coll., 1964; PhD, Johns Hopkins U., 1969; MD, SUNY Downstate, Bklyn., 1975. Diplomate Am. Bd. Dermatology. Teaching positions various schs. including NYU Coll. Dentistry and Harvard Med. Sch., 1969-73; med. intern Baylor Coll. Medicine, 1975-76, resident in dermatology, 1976-79; pvt. practice dermatology Houston, 1979—. Bd. dirs. Ft. Bend County Women's Ctr., Richmond, Tex., 1993—. Mem. Am. Bus. Women's Assn. (chair scholarship com. 1992, 96, chair scholarship event com. 1993—). Office: 4915 S Main St Ste 104 Stafford TX 77477-4601

POLINSKY, JANET NABOICHECK, state official, former state legislator; b. Hartford, Conn., Dec. 6, 1930; d. Louis H. and Lillian S. Naboicheck; BA, U. Conn., 1953; postgrad. Harvard U., 1954; m. Hubert N. Polinsky, Sept. 21, 1958; children: Gerald, David, Beth. Mem. Waterford 2d Charter Commn. (Conn.), 1967-68, Waterford Conservation Commn., 1968-69; Waterford rep. Town Meeting, 1969-71, SE Conn. Regional Planning Agy., 1971-73; mem. Waterford Planning and Zoning Commn., 1970-76, chmn., 1973-76; mem. Waterford Dem. Town Com., 1976-92, del. State Dem. Conv., 1976, 78, 80, 82, 84, 86, 90, 92; mem. Conn. Ho. of Reps. from 38th Dist., 1977-92, asst. majority leader, 1981-83, chmn. appropriations com., 1983-85, 87-89, ranking mem., 1985-87, minority whip, 1985-86, dep. speaker, 1989-92; dep. commr. dept. adminstrv. svcs., State of Conn., 1993-94, commr., 1994-95, asst. sec. of state, 1995; commr. utilities ctrl. auth. State of Conn., 1995—. Trustee Eugene O'Neill Meml. Theatre Ctr., 1973-76, 81-92; corporator, Lawrence and Meml. Hosps., 1987—; mem. New Eng. Bd. Higher Edn., 1981-83; mem. fiscal affairs com. Eastern Conf. Council of State Govts., 1983-88. Named Woman of Yr., Waterford Jr. Women's Club, 1977, Nehantic Women's Bus. and Profl. Club, 1979, Legislator of Yr., Conn. Library Assn., 1980. Mem. Order Women Legislators, Delta Kappa Gamma (hon.). Home: 15 Gardner Cir New London CT 06320-4314 Office: 10 Franklin Sq New Britain CT 06051-1629

POLITE, EDMONIA ALLEN, consultant; b. Washington, June 22, 1922; d. Thomas Samuel and Narcissus Bertha (Porter) Allen-Sylvester; m. George Frederick Polite, Jan. 5, 1941; 1 child, Frederick Gartrell. BA, Roosevelt U., 1958; MEd, Loyola U., Chgo., 1966; PhD in Adminstrn. and Supervision, Purdue U., 1973; DDiv, Ea. U., Tampa, Fla., 1971, DEd in Psychology, 1972. Dir. Media Ctr., Chgo., 1958-69, 73-81; instr. media scis. Purdue U., West Lafayette, Ind., 1969-73; pres. Cons. Inc., Chgo. and Orlando, Fla., 1974—; dir. Community Tutoring Ctr., Chgo., 1974-80; dir. workshop U. Cen. Fla., 1987; cons. Lake Region Conf., Detroit, 1966, Librarians, Inc., Chgo., 1970-71. Author: In Passing, 1970, People Who Help Us, 1982. Founder South End Parents Council, Chgo., 1960, Humanitarian Profls., Chgo., 1974, Orlando, 1983—; bd. dirs. Salem House, Chgo., 1980—. Recipient Outstanding Service award Lions Club, Chgo., 1975, Outstanding Educator award Fla. Agrl. and Mech. U. Alumni Assn. Mem. Nat. Assn. Club Women (dir. archives 1980—), Ill. Audio Visual Assn., Phi Delta Kappa. Club: Successful Progressors (Orlando) (pres. 1983—). Avocations: writing, community service, counseling. Home and Office: PO Box 580459 Orlando FL 32858-0459

POLITY, LEDDY SMITH, retired preschool administrator; b. Wrightsville, Pa., Nov. 6, 1936; d. Michael Kenneth and Vivian Lentz (Birnstock) Smith; m. Richard Milton Polity, Sept. 15, 1956; children: Karen, Bruce, Jennifer. Student, Gettysburg (Pa.) Coll., 1954-56, Kean Coll., 1966-74. Cert. early childhood edn. Tchr. Little Folks Nursery Sch., Woodbridge, N.J., 1966-67; co-founder, tchr. Presbyn. Nursery Sch., Matawan, 1967; dir. Presbyn. Nursery Sch., 1982-95; cons. community services bd. Brookdale Community Coll., 1977-82; workshop presentor, various community groups statewide. Contbr. articles to profl. jours.; appeared as TV panelist on N.Y. and N.J. talk shows. Mem. Sch. Aged Child Care Task Force, N.J. Dept. Human Services, 1983; ad hoc citizens adv. bd., N.J. Bur. of Licensing, 1981, 85, 86-87; Sunday sch. tchr., Cross of Glory Luth. Ch., Aberdeen, 1963-73, Sunday Sch. supt., 1974-76, vacation sch. dir., 1976-78; coordinator, Girl Scouts of U.S., Matawan, 1976-79; apptd. to Gov's. Child Care Adv. Council of N.J., 1984—. Mem. N.J. Shore Chpt. Assn. for Edn. of Young Children (pres. 1976-78), N.J. Assn. for Edn. of Young Children (lit. chmn. 1978-80, 1st v.p. 1980-82, state pres. 1982-84, exec. bd. advisor 1984-86), Assn. for Edn. of Young Children (state conf. planner, 1980, 81, 82). Home: 509 Periwinkle Way Southport NC 28465

POLK, CONSTANCE CHRISTINE, educator; b. Madera, Calif., Dec. 8, 1934; d. Joe Coronado and Belle R. (Gonzalez) Contreras; m. Arthur Clayton Polk, Oct. 16, 1960 (div. Aug. 1965); children: Susan Polk-Hoffses, Lance Arthur. BA, U. Calif., Berkeley, 1972, MA, 1973, postgrad., 1976; postgrad., U. San Francisco, 1994—. Multiple subject credential, 1991, single subject credential Spanish, 1991, adminstrv. credential, 1995. Prin., dir. New World Univ. H.S., San Francisco, 1978-85; tchr. Oakland (Calif.) Unified Sch. Dist., 1985-90; instr. Sch. of Edn. Wash. U., Pullman, 1996—; presenter in field. Merit scholar U. San Francisco, 1994-95. Mem. AAUW, NEA, Nat. Assn. Bilingual Edn. (editor of column), Calif. Assn. Bilingual Edn., Am. Assn. Sch. Adminstrs., Calif. Assn. Sch. Adminstrs., U. Calif. Berkeley Alumni Assn. Democrat. Home: 21 Crescent Ave San Francisco CA 94110

POLKINGHORNE, PATRICIA ANN, hotel executive; b. Galveston, Tex., Aug. 17, 1948; d. C.L. and Barbara Ann (Rathke) Hughes; children: Pamela, Christopher. Student, Sam Houston State Tchrs. Coll., Huntville, Tex. Catering mgr. Rodeway Inn, Denver; office mgr. sales dept. Hyatt Regency, Phoenix; asst. to v.p., treas., controller Continental Drilling, Okla. City; asst. to v.p. resort food and beverage The Pointe Resorts Inc., Phoenix; dir. adminstrn. S.W. Audio Visual, Inc.; asst. to dir. and mgr. catering Phoenician Resort, 1991-92, asst. to dir. of travel industry sales, 1992-93, exec. adminstrv. asst. to dir. of food and beverage divsn., 1993—. Mem. NAFE. Republican. Episcopalian. Office: 6000 E Camelback Rd Scottsdale AZ 85251-1949

POLK-MATTHEWS, JOSEPHINE ELSEY, school psychologist; b. Roselle, N.J., Sept. 24, 1930; d. Charles Carrington and Olive Mae (Bond) Polk; m. Donald Roger Matthews, Aug. 29, 1959 (div. 1974); children: John Roger, Alison Olivia; m. William Y. Delaney, Sept. 17, 1994. AB, Mt. Holyoke Coll., 1952; credential in occupational therapy, Columbia U., 1954; MA, U. So. Calif., L.A., 1957; Cert. Advanced Study, Harvard U., 1979, MS, 1980; postgrad., Coll. William & Mary, 1995-96. Cert. elem. edn. life teaching credential, Calif; cert. ednl. adminstrn. life credential, Calif.; cert. pupil personnel svcs., counseling life credential, sch. psychology credential, Calif.; sch. psychology credential, Nev. Occupational therapist VA Hosp., Northport, N.Y., 1953-55, L.A., 1955-57; health svcs. adminstr. John Wesley County Hosp., L.A., 1957-59; elem. tchr. L.A. (Calif.) City Schs., 1959-60, Santa Clara (Calif.) Unified Sch. Dist., 1960-65, 71-74; asst. prof. Sch. Edn., San Jose (Calif.) State U., 1971; asst. prin. Berryessa Union Sch. Dist., San Jose, Calif., 1974-77, 85-86; ednl. cons. Boston (Mass.) U. Sch. Medicine, 1981-83; asst. prin. Inglewood (Calif.) Unified Sch. Dist., 1986-90; sch. psychologist Clark County Sch. Dist., Las Vegas, 1990-94; contract sch. psychologist Newport News (Va.) Sch. Dist., 1995—; med. facility developer Commonwealth Mass., Dept. Mental Health, Boston, 1980-81, ednl. liaison, Roxbury Juvenile Ct., 1979. Author: (with others) The New Our Bodies Ourselves, 1983; prodr.: (video) Individualized Rsch., 1971. Commr. Commn. on the Status of Women, Cambridge, Mass., 1981-83; hostess Ctr. for Internat. Visitors, Boston, 1983-84; pers. recruiter L.A. (Calif.) Olympic Organizing Com., 1984; vol. tutor Las Vegas (Nev.) Libr., 1992. Mem. Nat. Assn. Sch. Psychologists, Calif. Assn. Sch. Psychologists, Nev. Assn. Sch. Psychologists, Clark County Assn. Sch. Psychologists, Assn. Black Psychologists, Phi Delta Kappa, Alpha Kappa Alpha. Office: Sch Edn Spl Edn PO Box 8795 Williamsburg VA 23187-8795

POLLACK, FLORENCE K.Z., management consultant; b. Washington, Pa.; d. Charles and Ruth (Isaacson) Zaks; divorced; children: Melissa, Stephanie. BA, Flora Stone Mather Coll., Western Res. U., 1961. Pres., CEO Exec. Arrangements, Inc., Cleve., 1978—. Lobbyist Ohio Citizens Com. for Arts, Columbus, 1975-83; mem. Leadership Cleve., 1978-79; trustee jr. com. Cleve. Orch., mem. pub. rels. adv. com.; trustee Great Lakes Theatre Festival, 1989-90; mem. pub. rels. adv. com., Cleve. Ballet, Dance Cleve., Jr. Com. of No. Ohio Opera Assn., Cleve. Opera, Shakers Lakes Regional Nature Ctr., Cleve. Music Sch. Settlement, Playhouse Sq. Cabinet, Cleve. Ctr. Econ. Edn., ARC, Cleve. Conv. and Visitors Bur., domed stadium adv. com. Named Idea Woman of Yr. Cleve. Plain Dealer, 1975, to Au Courrant list Cleve. Mag., 1979, one of Cleve.'s 100 Most Influential Women, 1985, one of 1988 Trendsetters Cleve. Woman mag. Mem. Cleve. Area Meeting Planning, Skating Club, Univ. Club, Women's City Club, Playhouse Club, Shoreby Club. Avocations: arts, travel, reading. Office: Exec Arrangements Inc 13221 Shaker Sq Cleveland OH 44120

POLLACK, PHYLLIS ADDISON, ballerina; b. Victoria, B.C., Can., Aug. 31, 1919; d. Horace Nowell and Claire Melanie (Morris) Addison; m. Robert Seymour Pollack, Sept. 6, 1941; children: Robert Addison, Gwenda Joyce, Victoria Jean, Phyllis Anne. Student, SUNY, 1941-42, San Mateo Tech. Coll., 1958-62, U. Calif., San Francisco, 1962. Owner, dir. Phyllis Addison Dance Studio, Victoria, 1936-38; ballerina Taynton Dancers/Marcus Show Ballet Troupe, 1939-41, Ballet Russe, 1941; x-ray therapy tech. Meml. Hosp., N.Y.C., 1943-45; corr. fgn. tellers dept. N.C.B., N.Y.C., 1945-46; owner, designer The Dancing Branch Studio, Sonoma, Calif., 1988—; floral designer J. Noblett Gallery, Sonoma, 1988-94. Pres. PTA, 1955-56, 62-63; mem. Assistance League San Mateo, Calif., 1960-70. Mem. Metro. Club. Democrat. Unitarian. Home: 384 Avenida Barbera Sonoma CA 95476-8069

POLLACK, SYLVIA BYRNE, educator, researcher, counselor; b. Ithaca, N.Y., Oct. 18, 1940; d. Raymond Tandy and Elsie Frances (Snell) Byrne; divorced; children: Seth Benjamin, Ethan David. BA, Syracuse U., 1962; PhD, U. Pa., 1967; MA, Antioch U., 1993. Instr. Women's Med. Coll. Pa., Phila., 1967-68; rsch. assoc. U. Wash., Seattle, 1968-73, rsch. asst. prof., 1973-77, rsch. assoc. prof., 1977-85, rsch. prof., 1985—, counselor Sch. Nursing, 1993—; asst. mem. Fred Hutchinson Cancer Ctr., Seattle, 1975-79, assoc. mem., 1979-81; mem. study sect. NIH, Washington, 1978-79, 83-85. Contbr. numerous articles to profl. jours.; reviewer for profl. jours. Recipient rsch. grants Am. Cancer Soc., 1969-79, Nat. Cancer Inst., 1973—, Chugai Pharm. Co., Japan, 1985-91. Mem. Am. Counsel Assn., Am. Assn. Immunologists, Soc. Devel. Biology. Office: U Wash Box 357261 Seattle WA 98195-7261

POLLAK, ELLEN MARGARET, literary critic; b. N.Y.C., Sept. 21, 1948; d. John Paul Pollak and Tania (Lewin) Pollak-Schreiber-Milicevic; m. Nigel Sefton Paneth, Dec. 16, 1973; children: Rachel, Tessa. BA, Bennington Coll., 1970; MA, Columbia U., 1971, PhD in English Lit., 1979. Asst. prof. English U. Pa., Phila., 1980-88; Mellon faculty fellow Harvard U., Cambridge, Mass., 1988-89; assoc. prof. English Mich. State U., East Lansing, 1989—. Author: The Poetics of Sexual Myth, 1985; contbr. articles to lit. jours. Woodrow Wilson Found. fellow, 1970-71, Danforth Found. fellow, 1970-75. Mem. MLA (Florence Howe award Women's Caucus 1982), Am. Soc. for 18th Century Studies. Office: Mich State U 201 Morrill Hall East Lansing MI 48824

POLLAK, JOANNE E., lawyer; b. Cleve., July 16, 1944. BA magna cum laude, Dickinson Coll., 1965; JD with honors, U. Md., 1976. Bar: Md. 1976. V.p., gen. counsel The Johns Hopkins Health System Corp., Balt. Office: Johns Hopkins Health System Corp 600 N Wolfe St Baltimore MD 21205-2110

POLLAN, CAROLYN JOAN, state legislator; b. Houston, July 12, 1937; d. Rex and Faith (Basye) Clark; B.S. in Radio and TV, John Brown U., 1959; postgrad. NYU, 1959; PhD in Edn., Walden U., 1993. m. George A. Pollan, Jan. 6, 1962; children—Cee Cee, Todd (dec.), Robert. Mem. Ark. Ho. of Reps., 1974—, now sr. Republican mem., asst. speaker pro-tempore, 1993; apptd. by Gov. numerous coms., commns.; ex-officio mem. Workplace Literacy Project Adv. Bd. U.S. Dept. Labor & Ednl. Testing Svc., 1990-93, Nat. Adult Literacy Survey, 1990-93; del. Am. Soviet Seminar, Am. Council Young Polit. Leaders, Exeter, N.H., 1976; co-developer Total Touch Test; owner Patent Model Mus.. Vice chmn. Ark. Rep. Com., 1972-76; del. Rep. Nat. Conv., 1976; bd. dirs. Ark. Cancer Soc., Ark. Easter Seals Soc.; bd. dirs. Greg Kistler Treatment Center for Physically Handicapped, Ark. Found. Assoc. Colls., 4-H Found. for Sebastian County; trustee John Brown U.; mem. legis. adv. com. So. Regional Edn. Bd. Recipient Conservation Legislator of Yr. award Ark. Wildlife Fedn., Nat. Wildlife Fedn., Sears Roebuck & Co., 1976, Outstanding State Legislator of Yr. award Ark. Pub. Employees Assn., 1979, Lifetime Mem. award Ark. PTA, 1994, many others; named 1 of 10 Outstanding Legislators, Assembly of Govtl. Employees, 1980, Legislator of Yr., Ark. Human Service Providers Assn., 1982, Citizen of Yr. by Ark. Social Workers, 1993, Outstanding Women in Ark. Politics by Ark. Dem., 1990, One of 10 Top Legislators in 1993 Ark. Dem. Gazette, 1993, one of Top 100 Women in Ark., Ark. Bus. Publ., 1995, 96; voted 1 of Ft. Smith's 10 Most Influential Citizens, S.W. Times Record Readers, 1979. Mem. Ark. Internat. Woman's Forum (founding mem.), Ft. Smith Car Restoration Assn. Baptist. Office: 2201 S 40TH Fort Smith AR 72903

POLLAN-COHEN, SHIRLEY, poet; b. N.Y.C., June 6, 1924; d. Benjamin and Anna (Flatow) Pollan; children: Robert, Linda. Student, CUNY, 1967. Editor newsletter Bronx C.C., CUNY, 1974-76, adminstrv. asst., 1980—; coll. students ESL tutor, 1993—; cons. Bronx Coun. on Arts, 1983-90. Performer poetry Bronx Mus. Arts, Acd. Gerontol. Edn. and Devel., Bronx C.C., Coll. of Mt. St. Vincent, Fordham U., Kingsbridge Heights C.C., Hostos C.C., CUNY, Lehman Coll., CUNY, also others; contbr. poetry to Bronx Roots I, II and III, Connections, Grub Street, Jewish Currents, Heiroglyphics Press, Garland, also others. Mem. Poets and Writers (grantee 1986-91), Bronx Poets and Writers Alliance (bd. dirs. 1983-90), Internat. Women's Writing Guild, Phi Theta Kappa.

POLLARD, BETTE MARLENE, computer scientist; b. Knoxville, Iowa, July 24, 1943. BA in History, U. Calif., Berkeley; MS, U. Chgo. Cert. in Data Comm. (Am. Inst.), Client Server Computing (Learning Tree Inst.), Computer Programming (Prince Georges Coll.). Computer scientist NIH,

Bethesda, Md., 1983—. Pres. Fox Hills Civic Assn., Potomac, Md., 1979-82; v.p. Area III adv. bd., Bethesda, 1979-82; treas. U. Chgo. Alumni Assn., Washington, 1982. Recipient 4 meritorious svc. awards NIH, 1985, 87, 89, 93. Mem. Internet Soc. Office: NIH DHHS 9600 Rockville Pike Bethesda MD 20892

POLLARD, DIANNE RENÉ, business consultant; b. Downey, Ill., Oct. 6, 1956; d. Alvin Lee and Mary Alice (DuVaul) P. AAS, Coll. St. Catherine, St. Mary's Campus, Mpls., 1991. Word processing operator Debbie Temporaries, Naperville, Ill., 1985-86, Word Processors Personnel-ADIA, Mpls., 1986-88; computer lab. asst. Coll. St. Catherine, St. Mary's Campus, Mpls., 1989-91; adminstrv. asst. First Trust Ctr., St. Paul, 1992-93, Dolphin Temporaries, Mpls., 1993-94; receptionist, adminstrv. asst. Dain Bosworth, Mpls., 1994—. Recipient Dirs. award Minn. Inst. Med. & Dental Careers, 1988, Women's Leadership award Abigail Quigley Women's Ctr., 1991, Minority Leadership award U.S. Achievement Acad., 1991, Judson Bemis Visionary award United Negro Coll. Fund, 1995. Mem. NAACP, Nat. Wildlife Fedn., Library of Congress Assocs., Minority Employee Assn. (sec. 1995-96), Smithsonian Assocs. Home: 1611 W York Ln Wheaton IL 60187

POLLARD, MARGARET LOUISE, association administrator; b. Leominster, Mass., Nov. 15, 1934; d. Edward Francis and AliceMary (Sosvielle) Sasseville; m. Walter Howard Pollard III, Mar. 10, 1957 (dec. Oct. 1974); children: Caroline Pray, Walter Howard IV, Margaret Peirce, Melissa Anne; m. James L. Baird Jr., Jan. 9, 1993. BS, Simmons Coll., 1956; MS, Boston U., 1983. Editor Hist. Soc. Western Pa., Pitts., 1971-75; mgr. advtr. and promotions F.W. Faxon Co., Westwood, Mass., 1976-80; owner, mgr. Peg Pollard Communications, Boston, 1981-84; dir. comms. Mass. Dental Soc., Natick, 1984-93; coord. vols. Lyman Allyn Art Mus., New London, Conn., 1993-96; exec. dir. Norwich (Conn.) Heritage Trrust, 1994-96. Editor LWV, Westwood, 1966, pres., Greensburg, Pa., 1968-71; bd. dirs. First Night, Inc., Boston, 1982-89, Friends Boston Ctr. for Arts, 1985-88. Mem. Am. Soc. Assn. Execs., Am. Soc. Med. Writers, New Eng. Soc. Assn. Execs., Publicity Club New Eng. (Bellringer award 1984). Home: 48 Misty View Ave Mystic CT 06355-2210 Office: 54 Arkansas Ave Nantucket MA 02554

POLLARD, SHIRLEY, employment training director, consultant; b. Brunswick City, Va., July 8, 1939; 1 child, Darryl. Degree in bus. adminstrn., Upper Iowa U., 1978. Adminstr. East. Balt. Community Corp.; tng. coord. Balt. County Concentrated Employment Tng. Program; exec. dir. Park Heights Community Corp., Balt.; dir. Linkages, Inc., Balt.; mem. women's and children's adv. coun. Sinai Hosp. Contbr. articles to Afro Am. newspaper. Pres. Park Hts. Cmty. Devel. Corp., United Black Fund, Balt., 1989—, Presdl. Task Force, 1992; active Balt. Urban League, Balt. Welfare Rights Orgn.; founder, pres. Balt. County Polit. Action Coalition, 1982—; founder, dir. Linkages, Inc., 1980; founder, dir. Tng. and Placement Svcs., 1989; active United Svc. Orgn., Md. Minority Contractors Assn., U.S. Civil Rights Mus. and Hall of Fame, Smithsonian Instn.; founder African Am. Culture Ctr.; co-founder Project Lou, Inc.; founder The Afro Fund, Inc.; active Fund for a Free South Africa's Founding Assocs. Leadership Coun., Nat. Women's Hall of Fame, Nat. Abortion Rights Action League, Srs. Coalition, Md. Edn. Coalition, CORE, So. Christian Leadership Conf., Nat. Trust for Hist. Preservation; presdl. appointment Md. Selective Svc. Bd., 1993, Exec. Com. of Am. Friends Svc. Com.; mem. women's adv. coun. Sinai Hosp., 1994—. Recipient Outstanding Achievement award Md. Minority Contractors Assn., Mayor's Citation, Martin Luther King Civil Rights award, 1987, Md. State Dept. Edn. award, 1987, congl. Achievement award, Kool Achiever awards, 1990, Nat. Black Caucus Spl. award, 1990, Congressional Achievement award, 1988, Svc. award The Writers Club, 1991, USO Meritorious Svc. award, 1991, Gov.'s Vol. award, 1992, Acad. of Excellence award, 1992, Signs of Hope award, 1995, Mayor's citation, 1984, Gov.'s citation, 1995, Senatorial award, 1995; recipient Bud Achiever award 1996. Mem. Am. Soc. Pers. Adminstrn., Am. Soc. Health/Manpower/Edn./Tng., Assn. for Providers Employment and Tng., NAACP (founder, pres. Randallstown chpt. 1988-95, Signs of Hope award), Balt. Coun. on Fgn. Affairs, Transafrica, USO, Md. Minority Contractors Assn. (Achievement award 1986, bd. dirs. 1984-89), Smithsonian Assoc., Md. C. of C. (greater Balt. com. 1985). Office: PO Box 32051 Baltimore MD 21208-8051

POLLER, LEAH, art activist, sculptor; b. Blakely, Pa., May 6, 1942; d. Louis and Rose (Goodman) P.; m. Alan M. Kornbluh, Oct. 15, 1960 (div. 1974); children: Kenneth, Laura K., Michelle. AA, Dade Jr. Coll., 1972. Pres., founder Kornbluh Assocs., Miami, Fla., 1962-72; prodn. sec. Free Lance Film Industry, Paris, 1974-78; editor, founder Editions Ouskokata, Paris, 1982-86; assoc. editor Editions J.M. Place, Paris, 1982-84; pres., founder WCIC, Washington, Paris, 1985—, The Art Alliance, N.Y.C., 1991—; cons. Avanstar, Cleve., 1995—. Exhibited regularly as artist, sculptor, 1974—. Recipient various sculpture prizes. Mem. Women's Caucus for the Arts, Pen Club, Nat. Sculpture Assn. Jewish. Office: Art Alliance 98 Greene St New York NY 10012-3804

POLLINA, JENNIFER, secondary school educator; b. Bklyn., Aug. 30, 1971; d. Robert Joseph and Margie (Napolitono) P. BA in Math., Trenton State Coll., 1993. Cert. secondary sch. math. tchr., N.J., Pa. Math. tchr. Toms River (N.J.) Regional Sch. Dist., 1993—; tutor Trenton State Coll. Math./Sci. Lab., Ewing, N.J., 1990-92, Huntington Learning Ctr., Manalapan, N.J., 1993; freshman class advisor Toms River H.S. South, 1994—. Vol. Head Start, Trenton, N.J., 1992. Named N.J. Disting. scholar State of N.J., 1989; Paul Douglas Tchg. scholar State of N.J., 1989, Meml. scholar Trenton State Coll., 1992. Mem. NEA, Nat. Coun. Tchrs. of Math., Assn. Math. Tchrs. N.J., Pi Mu Epsilon, Phi Kappa Phi. Home: 13 Homestead Rd Sea Girt NJ 08750 Office: Toms River HS South Hyers Street Toms River NJ 08753

POLLITT, PHOEBE ANN, school nurse; b. Washington, Mar. 29, 1954; d. Daniel Hubbard and Jean Ann (Rutledge) P.; m. David Randolph Paletta, July 1, 1977 (div. Dec. 1989); children: Douglas, Andrew. BS in Nursing, U. N.C., 1977; MA in Edn., Appalachian State U., 1989; PhD in Curriculum and Instrn., U. N.C., Greensboro, 1994. Pub. health nurse Durham County Health Dept., Durham, N.C., 1977-80; disability devel. specialist Appalachian Devel. Evaluation Ctr., Boone, N.C., 1980-81; home health nurse Watauga County Health Dept., Boone, 1981-82; nursing instr. Caldwell C.C., Lenoir, N.C., 1989-91; adj. prof. nursing Winston-Salem (N.C.) State U., 1990—; sch. nurse, health edn. coord. Watauga County Schs., Boone, 1991—; sec. Watauga County Adolescent Pregnancy Coalition, Boone, 1991—; mem. exec. com. Watauga County Healthy Carolinas 2000, Boone, 1993—; mem. statewide exec. com. Smoke Free 2000, Raleigh, 1994; mem. exec. bd. Watauga County Alcohol and Other Drugs Coun., Boone, 1993. Contbr. articles to profl. jours. Alumni fellow Appalachian State U., 1988, 89; recipient Certs. of Appreciation, Am. Heart Assn., 1992, 93, Hospitality House, 1987, 88, 89, Outstanding Vol. award N.C. Gov. Jim Hunt, 1989, Plaque of Appreciation, OASIS, 1992, Hist. Article award N.C. Hist. Soc., 1994; grantee Arts Coun., 1982, Appalachian State U., 1989, U. N.C., Greensboro, 1991, Healthful Living Sect., Dept. Pub. Instrn., 1992, 93, Janirve Corp., Asheville, N.C., 1992, Project Assist, 1996, N.C. Dept. Pub. Instrn., 1996, Watauga Ednl. Found., 1996. Mem. ANA, N.C. Nurse Assn. (named Great 100 Nurses 1995), Sch. Nurse Assn. N.C. (mem. exec. com., membership chair 1994), Dist. 23 Nurse assn., Sigma Theta Tau. Democrat. Unitarian-Universalist. Home: 116 Ann Marie Dr Boone NC 28607 Office: Watauga County Bd Edn Box 1790 Hwy 194 Boone NC 28607

POLLOCK, KAREN ANNE, computer analyst; b. Elmhurst, Ill., Sept. 6, 1961; d. Michael Paul and Dorothy Rosella (Foskett) P. BS, Elmhurst Coll., 1984; MS, North Cen. Coll., 1993. Formatter Nat. Data Corp., Lombard, Ill., 1985; computer specialist Dept. VA, Hines, Ill., 1985—. Lutheran.

POLLOCK, MARY CATHERINE, education educator, consultant; b. Grand Haven, Mich., July 6, 1955; d. Donald Kenneth and Gloria Mary Schanz; m. William E. Pollock, Aug. 23, 1976; children: Emily Elizabeth, Joseph William. BA, Grand Valley State U., 1976, MA, 1980. Tchr. Holland Pub. Schs., 1976-90, tchr., cons., 1990—; instr. Hope Coll., Holland, 1993—; co-chair Spl. Edn. Tech. Ctr., Holland, Outcomes Driven Edn. Project, Holland; regional facilitator Outcomes Tng. Project, Hollad. Mem. Alexander Graham Bell Assn. for the Deaf. Office: Holland Pub Schs 372 S River Ave Holland MI 49423-3356

POLLOCK, SANDRA SUE, retired elementary educator; b. South Lyon, Mich., Mar. 12, 1941; d. Robert Wesley Pollock and Erma Eylene (Westerman) Keating. BS, Ea. Mich. U., 1965. 4th grade tchr. Huron Sch. Dist., New Boston, Mich., 1965-95; ret., 1995. Mem. choir First Congl. United Ch. of Christ, Ypsilanti, Mich., 1985—, Ypsilanti Cmty. Choir, 1995—; vol. patient rels. St. Joseph Mercy Hosp., Ann Arbor, Mich., 1995—; tutor basic lang. skills Washtenaw Literacy, Ann Arbor, 1995—; block capt. Neighborhood Watch, Ypsilanti, 1994—. Recipient Favorite Tchr. award Detroit News, 1968. Mem. AARP, Mich. Assn. Ret. Sch. Personnel. Home: 1515 Ridge Lot 311 Ypsilanti MI 48198

POLLY, DIANNE KAMMERER, dietitian, lawyer; b. Omaha, Dec. 10, 1951; d. Clyde Albert and Dorothy Marie (Argabright) K.; m. Stuart McGrath Polly, June 27, 1980; children: Alexandra, Samantha. BS cum laude, U. Nebr., 1974, MS, 1980; JD, U. Memphis., 1996. Registered and lic. dietitian, Tex. Adminstrv. dietitian U. Nebr. Med. Ctr., Omaha, 1976-78; clin. dietitian St. Joseph Hosp., Omaha, 1978-80; dir. food and nutrition svc. Thomason Gen. Hosp., El Paso, Tex., 1980-90; workshop instr. Tex. Dept. Human Svcs., El Paso, 1983-90; dietitian Met. Inter-Faith Assn., Memphis, 1990-92, dir. sr. citizen nutrition program, 1992—. Author: Effective Food Service Supervisor, 1989; contbr. articles to profl. jours. Participant Leadership El Paso, 1985-86; bd. dirs., com. chmn. YMCA East Br., El Paso, 1986-89; cons. Am. Cancer Soc., El Paso, 1988-89. Mem. Memphis Dietetic Assn., Am. Dietetic Assn., Tex. Dietetic Assn. (v.p. 1990-91), El Paso Dietetic Assn. (bd. dirs., pres. 1981-88), Am. Soc. Hosp. Food Svc. Adminstrs. (bd. dirs., pres., treas 1983-90, Accomplished Health Care award 1986, Disting. Health Care award 1990), Tex. Soc. Hosp. Food Svc. Dirs. (pres., bd. dirs. 1986-89), Phi Kappa Phi. Lutheran. Home: 6751 Sunburst Cv Memphis TN 38119-6711 Office: Met Inter Faith Assn 910 Vance Ave Memphis TN 38126-2911

POLOS, IRIS STEPHANIE, artist, art educator; b. Oakland, Calif., Feb. 14, 1947; d. Theodore C. and Catherine (Pappas) P.; 1 child Apollo Papafrangou. BFA, Calif. Coll. Arts and Crafts, Oakland, 1968, MFA, 1971. Instr. figure drawing Am. Sch. of Art, Athens, Greece, 1969-71 summers; instr. advanced drawing U. Calif. Extension Open Exchange, San Francisco, 1978-79; artist in residence Chabot Elem. Sch., Oakland, Calif., 1986-92, Mus. of Children's Art, Oakland, 1988—; instr. children's hosp. MOCHA, 1995—; art tchr. Arrowsmith U. Acad., Berkeley, 1991—. Artist: selected exhibitions include: San Francisco Mus. of Modern Art, 1971, Richmond (Calif.) Art Ctr., 1973, Calif. Coll. of Arts and Crafts, Oakland, 1973, Art for Art Sake Gallery, San Francisco, 1977, Jehu Wong Gallery, San Francisco, 1979, Triangle Gallery, San Francisco, 1981, Bond Gallery, N.Y.C., 1985, 86, Berkeley (Calif.) Art Ctr., 1987, 88, Emanuel Radnitzky, San Francisco, 1990 (2 shows), San Francisco Art Commn. Gallery, 1991, Fine Arts Ctr., Irvine, Calif., 1991, Trojanowska Gallery, San Francisco, 1991, Nelson Morales Gallery, San Francisco, 1992, Morphos Gallery, L.A., 1993, 94, Morphos Gallery, San Francisco, 1994, 95, Hotel Triton Art Fair with Morphos Gallery, San Francisco, 1995, Moreau Galeries, Notre Dame, Ind., 1995, Fort Mason Found., San Francisco, 1995, Magic Theater Lobby, San Francisco, 1995 and others; permanent collections include the Oakland Mus., Catharine Clark, Gary Noguera, Helen Salz, Daniel Soto, Caroline Zecca, and others; her works also include book illustration and theatre set design. Grantee: Arts in Edn. grant Cultural Arts Divsn., Oakland, 1991-96, Berkeley Repertory Theater, 1995. Democrat. Home: 5801 Broadway Oakland CA 94618 Office: Arrowsmith Acad. Art Dept Berkeley CA 94704

POLSTER, EDYTHE MAY, art consultant; b. Columbus, Ohio, May 10, 1911; d. Morris and Leah (Niebloom) P. BA, Ohio State U., 1930; postgrad., U. So. Calif., 1943-44; MA, New Sch. for Social Rsch., 1951; postgrad., Columbia U., 1960-67. Freelance editl. work Am. Lending Libr., Inc., 1935-41; copy and prodn. chief W. Kastor Agy., L.A., 1941-44; freelance, 1944-50, owner agy., 1950-58, freelance, 1958-62. Author: Surimono, 1980. Mem. Japan Soc. N.Y.C., Asia Soc. N.Y.C., Haiku Soc. Am. (Best Am. haiko 1976). Jewish. Home and Office: RR 2 Box 266 Deming NM 88030

POMPA, CHRISTINE ANN, quality engineer; b. Poughkeepsie, N.Y., Feb. 14, 1969; d. Edward A. and Phyllis J. (Eryasha) Carbone; m. Marian Pompa, Jr., Nov. 23, 1991. BS in Math., Niagara U., 1990; MS in Stats., Rochester Inst. Tech., 1991. Cert. quality engr.; cert. quality auditor. Quality engr. Chemprene, Inc., Beacon, N.Y., 1992—. Rochester Inst. Tech. scholar, 1990-91. Mem. Am. Soc. for Quality Control. Home: 29-U Scenic Dr Croton-on-Hudson NY 10520 Office: Chemprene Inc 570 Fishkill Ave Beacon NY 12508

POMPER, CATHERINE JANICE, health care administrator; b. Peckville, Pa., Jan. 29, 1940; d. Joseph Aloysius and Catherine Helen (Purcell) Hart; m. Frank Joseph Pomper, July 20, 1963; children: Patricia Ann, Robert Francis. RN, St. Joseph Hosp. Sch. Nursing, Paterson, N.J., 1960; BS in Nursing, Winston-Salem (N.C.) State U., 1980. Cert. rehab. nurse; cert. case mgr.; cert. Calif. pub. health nurse. Work compensation case mgr. Resource Opportunities, Charlottesville, Va., 1981-82; rehab. nurse, clinician A U. Va. Hosp., Charlottesville, 1982-86; work compensation case mgr. Am. Internat. Adjustmment Co., Lafayette, Calif., 1986-88; work compensation dist. mgr. Mirfak Assocs., Oakland, Calif., 1988-90; case mgr., U/R supr. Lincoln Nat. Life, Pleasanton, Calif., 1990-92; dist. mgr. Resource Opportunities, Walnut Creek, Calif., 1992-93; dist. managed care case mgr. Hillhaven, Concord, Calif., 1993-94; Medicare case mgr. Good Samaritan Med. Found., San Jose, Calif., 1994-95; Medicare case mgr., coord. Cigna for Srs., Oakland, Calif., 1995—; mem. task force Calif. HMO, Oakland, 1996—; mem. rehab. adv. bd. Stanford U. Hosp., Palo Alto, Calif., 1992-94; mem. Nurse Practice Act Adv. Study, 1985; mem. Task Force Drafting Case Mgmt. Guidelines and Definition ARN and AETNA Task Force, 1986, 93. Book reviewer ARN mag., 1984-90. Mem. ICMA, CMSA (mem. legis. com. 1991-94), RING, ARN, Continuity of Care. Home: 120 Pebble Pl San Ramon CA 94583 Office: Cigna Health Care No Calif 1999 Harrison St Ste 1000 Oakland CA 94612

POMPETTI-SZUL, IRENE CATHERINE, language educator; b. Phila., Jan. 4, 1948; d. Joseph and Catherine (Sortino) Pompetti; children: Sonya, Steven; m. Andrij V.R. Szul, Mar. 26, 1988. BA in Spanish, Beloit (Wis.) Coll., 1968; MA in Internat. Rels., U. Pa., 1971, CAS in Ednl. Linguistics, 1989; MEd in English Edn., Temple U., 1977; postgrad., SUNY, Albany, 1992—. Cert. tchr. Spanish, English as second lang., and social studies, N.Y. Tchr. Spanish and Latin Am. history Solebury Sch., New Hope, Pa., 1970-71; tchr. English as second lang. Sch. Dist. Phila., 1972-78, bilingual curriculum developer, 1980-84, English as second lang. coord., 1984-85; instr. English and speech communication Penn State Ogontz, Abington, Pa., 1985-87; Spanish tchr. Liberty (N.Y.) High Sch., 1988-89; tchr. English as second lang. Middletown (N.Y.) Jr. High Sch., 1989-91; link program coord., instr. Spanish Orange County Community Coll., Middletown, 1991-92; instr. English as second lang. Sullivan County C.C., Loch Sheldrake, N.Y., 1990; asst. prof. ESL and bilingual edn. SUNY, New Paltz, 1990-92; cons. Abington Meml. Hosp., 1987; ESL cons. N.Y. State Edn. Dept., 1993; cons., clin. trainer US AID Egyptian Inspectors Program U. Albany, 1994-96; assoc. prof., dir. clin. tng. U. Albany, SUNY, 1995-96; supr., clin. lab. instr. MAT program Union Coll., 1996—. Author: English: Your Second Language: Readings in ESOL for Secondary Students, 1981; asst. editor Inclusion: Buzzword or Hope for the Future, 1994; contbr. articles to profl. jours. Vol. organizer Clean Air Coun., Phila., 1981; testifier Pa. Govs. Energy Coun., Phila., 1981; active Sullivan County Planning Bd., Monticello, N.Y., 1990; vice chmn. Environ. Mgmt. Coun., Lumberland, N.Y., 1988-89; active Lumberland Fire Dept., 1989-90. Recipient Book prize Columbia Tchrs. Coll., 1968. Mem. Am. Ednl. Rsch. Assn., Am. Assn. Applied Linguistics, N.Y. Tchrs. English as 2d Lang. (asst. coord. Mid-Hudson region 1992), Phi Sigma Iota. Republican. Roman Catholic. Home: PO Box 3712 Albany NY 12203-0899

POMPEY, CYNTHIA D., nursing educator; b. N.Y.C., Oct. 30, 1954; d. James and Mable (Black) Best; m. Douglas Pompey, Aug. 25, 1978; 1 child, Jennifer Marie. ADN, Bellevue (Wash.) C.C., 1982. Cert. Med./Surg. Nurse. Mem. RN com. Virginia Mason Hosp., Seattle, 1987-95, mem. profl. recognition com., 1987-92; mem. sch. commn. St. Paul Sch., Seattle, 1990-94; basic life support provider, instr. Am. Heart Assn., Seattle, 1994—, instr. ACLS, 1995. Editor: Profl. Recognition Program packet, 1991. Mem. ANA. Home: 9716 57th Ave S Seattle WA 98118-5804 Office: Virginia Mason Hosp Med Ctr 925 Seneca St Seattle WA 98101-2742

POMROY, NANCY ELIZABETH, physical education educator; b. Hartford, Conn., Dec. 8, 1966; d. Harold Richard and Betty Mae Pomroy. BS, Springfield (Mass.) Coll., 1989. Cert. tchr., Conn., Mass. Gross motor instr. Benhaven Sch. of Autism, Yalesville, Conn., 1985-88; residential case worker Hamden Assn. for Mentally Retarded, Springfield, 1987-90; coach Mass. Spl. Olympics, Springfield, 1987-90; instr. phys. edn., athletic dir. St. Croix (U.S. V.I.) Country Day Sch., 1990—; mem. prof. growth com. St. Croix Country Day Sch., 1992—; mem. vis. com. Mid. States Assn. Colls. and Schs., St. Croix, 1994. Mem. AAHPERD, Nat. Assn. for Girls and Women in Sport, St. Croix Interscholastic Athletic Assn. (sec.). Office: St Croix Country Day Sch RR 1 Box 6199 Kingshill VI 00850-9807

POND, LINDA RAE, senior research scientist, administrator; b. Flint, Mich., Aug. 22, 1944; d. Frederick Lewis and Orle Darlene (Fairbanks) Smith; m. Joseph M. Wood, Aug. 31, 1964 (div. 1979); children: Timothy Joseph, Melissa Jill; m. Daniel James Pond, June 18, 1983; children: David Alan, Steven Douglas. BS in Orgnl. Comm., U. Ctrl. Fla., 1983; MS in Human Resource Mgmt., Fla. Inst. Tech., 1985. System engrng. specialist Harris Corp., Melbourne, Fla., 1984-90; sr. rsch. scientist Pacific N.W. Lab., Richland, Wash., 1990-94, mgr. operational effectiveness, 1994—. Mem. Acad. Mgmt., Phi Kappa Phi. Home: RR 3 Box 3885 Prosser WA 99350-9541 Office: Battelle Pacific NW Lab Battelle Blvd Richland WA 99352

POND, PATRICIA BROWN, library science educator, university administrator; b. Mankato, Minn., Jan. 17, 1930; d. Patrick H. and Florence M. (Ruehle) Brown; m. Judson S. Pond, Aug. 24, 1959. BA, Coll. St. Catherine, St. Paul, 1952; MA, U. Minn., 1955; PhD, U. Chgo., 1982. Sch. libr. Minn., N.Y., 1952-62; asst. prof. libr. sci. U. Minn., 1962-63; reference libr. U. Mont., 1963-65; asst. prof. U. Oreg., 1967-72, assoc. prof., 1972-77; prof., dept. chair, assoc. dean Sch. Libr. and Info. Sci. U. Pitts., 1977-85. Mem. ALA (life), Phi Beta Kappa, Beta Phi Mu, Delta Phi Lambda, Kappa Gamma Pi. Home: 14740 SW Forest Dr Beaverton OR 97007-5117

POND, PHYLLIS JOAN, state legislator; b. Warren, Ind., Oct. 25, 1930; d. Clifford E. and Rosa E. (Hunnicutt) Ruble; m. George W. Pond, June 10, 1951; children: William, Douglas, Jean Ann. BS, Ball State U., Muncie, Ind., 1951; MS, Ind. U., 1963. Tchr. home econs., 1951-54; kindergarten tchr., 1961—; mem. Ind. Ho. of Reps. from 15th dist., 1978-82, from 20th dist., 1982-92, from 85th dist., 1992—, majority asst. caucus chmn., vice chmn. ways and means com., 1995. Del. Ind. State Rep. Conv., 1976, 80, 84, del., 1986, 88; alt. del. Rep. Nat. Conv., 1980. Mem. AAUW, New Haven Woman's Club. Lutheran.

PONKO, VERA, artist, museum intrepreter; b. Lysander, N.Y., Aug. 1, 1931; d. Amos W. and Myrtle (Brown) Vest; m. Charles W. Ponko, Mar. 1956 (div. June 1979); children: Velton, John, Ronald, Terry, Stephen. Mus. intrepretor Frederic Remington Art Mus., Ogdensburg, N.Y. Exhibited stained glass in art exhbn., Heuvelton; masonry and glass designer; build of custom designed windows. Home: PO Box 322 Heuvelton NY 13654

PONTIUS, LISA MARGARET, lawyer, business manager; b. Royal Oak, Mich., Aug. 8, 1964; d. James Roscoe and Norma Jean (Theis) P. AB in Econs., U. Chgo., 1985; JD, U. Mich., 1989. Bar: Calif. 1989, U.S. Dist. Ct. (ctrl. dist.) Calif. 1989, U.S. Dist. Ct. (ea. dist.) Calif. 1993, U.S. Ct. Appeals (9th cir.) 1993. Atty. Paul, Hastings, Janofsky & Walker, L.A., 1989-92, Jencks & Hunt, San Luis Obispo, Calif., 1992-93; CFO Advanced Legal Svcs., San Luis Obispo, 1993—; account rep. West Publishing, San Francisco, 1994—. Vol., advocate Battered Women's Shelter of San Luis Obispo, 1993. Named Pro Bono Assoc. of Yr., Legal Aid Found. L.A., 1992. Mem. ABA. Office: West Pub Co 505 Montgomery St Ste 1250 San Francisco CA 94111

PONTORIERO, ROSA CHRISTINA, secondary school educator; b. Newark, Oct. 12, 1970; d. Giuseppe and Annunziata Pontoriero. BS, Montclair State Coll., 1993. Math. tchr. Roosevelt Middle Sch., Elizabeth, N.J., 1993—; tchr. of Italian, St. Vianney Elem. Sch., Colonia, N.J., 1992-93. Mem. Nat. Coun. Tchrs. of Math., N.J. Edn. Assn.

PONTRELLI, ANNIE MARIE, public relations and marketing professional; b. Missoula, Mont., Dec. 28, 1960; d. Alphonse Dante and Mary Claire (Anderson) P. BA in Journalism, U. Oreg., 1983. Sales rep. McCaw Telepage, Bellevue, Wash., 1984; tour dir. Princess Tours, Seattle, 1984-85; promotions rep. Expo '86 World's Fair, Seattle, 1986; svc. coord., recruiting supr. Manus Temporary Svcs., Seattle, 1986-88; pers. mgr. Western Distbn. Svcs., Kent, Wash., 1988-89; mktg. mgr. Express Pers. Svcs., Missoula, Mont., 1989-90; Centennial coord. U. Mont., Missoula, 1990-93, coord. cmty. rels. and outreach, 1993—; bd. dirs. Camp-Mak-A-Dream, Missoula, 1993—; chair mktg. coun. U. Mont., Missoula, 1994—. Mem. Leadership Missoula, 1992; conf. coord. Missoula Businesswomen's Network, 1990-91; facilitator Nat. Student Leadership Forum on Faith and Values, Washington, 1995; coord. Mont. State Student Leadership Forum on Faith and Values, Helena, 1995-96. Recipient YWCA Salute to Excellence award YWCA, 1993; CASE scholar, 1992. Mem. C. of C. (bd. dirs.), Mo. Conv. and Visitors Bur., Missoula Sunrise Rotary. Christian. Home: 420 Burlington Ave Missoula MT 59801 Office: U Mont Brantly Hall Missoula MT 59812

PONZI KAY, MARYLOU, human resources specialist; b. N.Y.C., Oct. 14, 1950; d. Bruno and Constance Louise (DeLuca) P.; m. William J. Kay, Jr., Oct. 24, 1993. BA, SUNY, Geneseo, 1972; MA, U. Iowa, 1974, SUNY, Buffalo, 1979; cert. in advanced study in labor rels., N.Y. Inst. Tech., 1995. Pers. adminstr. Michelin Tire Corp., Lake Success, N.Y., 1978-83; tech. recruiter 1st Data Resources, Lake Success, N.Y., 1983-84; mgr. human resources Chem. Bank, Jericho, N.Y., 1984-87; pers. officer J.P. Morgan Inc., N.Y.C., 1987-89; mgr. employment Am. Express Inc., N.Y.C., 1989-92; dir. human resources RockBottom Stores, Inc., 1992-95; asst. dir. human resources Canon U.S.A., Lake Success, N.Y., 1995—; instr. French and Spanish Amityville H.S. Adult Edn., 1986—. Editor: (guidebook) New England Guide, 1982, Canada Guide, 1982. Pres. LeBourget Alliance, Amityville, N.Y., 1995—; pres. bus. adv. coun. Adults and Children with Learning Disabilities, 1994—. Mem. Soc. Human Resources Mgmt. Roman Catholic. Office: 1 Canon Plz New Hyde Park NY 11042-1119

POOL, MARY JANE, design consultant, writer; d. Earl Lee Pool and Dorothy (Matthews) Evans. Grad., St. de Chantal Acad., 1942; BA in Art with honors, Drury Coll., 1946. Mem. staff Vogue mag., N.Y.C., 1946-68; assoc. merchandising editor Vogue mag., 1948-57, promotion dir., 1958-66, exec. editor, 1966-68; editor House and Garden mag., 1969, editor-in-chief, 1970-80; cons. Baker Furniture Co., 1981-94, Aves Advt., Inc., 1981-94, bd. dirs.; mem. bd. govs. Decorative Arts Trust; past mem. bd. govs. Fashion Group, Inc., N.Y.C. Co-author: The Angel Tree, 1984, The Gardens of Venice, 1989, The Gardens of Florence, 1992, The Angel Tree-A Christmas Celebration, 1993; editor: 20th Century Decorating, Architecture, Gardens, Billy Baldwin Decorates, 26 Easy Little Gardens. Mem. bus. com. N.Y. Zool. Soc., 1979-86; trustee Drury Coll., 1971—; bd. dirs. Isabel O'Neil Found., 1978—. Recipient award Nat. Soc. Interior Designers, Disting. Alumni award Drury Coll., 1961. Address: 1 E 66th St New York NY 10021-5852

POOLE, EVA DURAINE, librarian; b. Farrell, Pa., Dec. 20, 1952; d. Leonard Milton and Polly Mae (Flint) Harris; m. Tommy Lynn Cole, May 15, 1970 (div. Sept. 1984); 1 child, Tommy Lynn Cole; m. Earnest Theodore Poole, Sept. 22, 1990; 1 child, Aleece Remelle Poole. BA in LS, Tex. Woman's U., 1974, MLS, 1976; postgrad., U. Houston, 1989. Libr. asst. Emily Fowler Pub. Libr., Denton, Tex., 1970-74; children's libr. Houston Pub. Libr., 1974-75, 1st asst. libr., 1976-77; children's libr. Ector County Libr., Odessa, Tex., 1977-80; head pub. svcs. Lee Davis Libr. San Jacinto Coll., Pasadena, Tex., 1980-84; libr. dir. San Jacinto Coll. South, Houston, 1984-90; libr. svcs. mgr. Emily Fowler Pub. Libr., Denton, 1990-93, interim dir., 1993; dir. libr. svcs. Denton Pub. Librs., Denton, 1993—. Named to Outstanding Young Women of Am., 1991. Mem. ALA (conf. program com. 1994-96), Pub. Libr. Assn., Libr. Adminstrn. and Mgmt. Assn. (program com. 1994—), Tex. Libr. assn. (pub. libr. divsn. sec. 1995-96, leadership devel. com. 1995—, ad hoc leadership inst. com. 1995, alumnae 1st class Tex. Accelerated Libr. Leaders 1994, chair-elect pub. libr. divsn. 1996—), Pub. Libr. Adminstrs. North Tex. (vice chair 1994-95, chair 1995-96), Tex. Mcpl. Libr. Dirs. Assn. (pres. 1995-96, grantee 1993), Denton Rotary Club. Office: Denton Pub Libr 502 Oakland St Denton TX 76201-3102

POOLE, LISA LYN, photographer; b. Beverly, Mass., Mar. 11, 1967; d. Stanley Barker and Ruth Eleanor (Bacon) P.; m. Matthew John Putaansuu, Sept. 11, 1993. AS, Endicott Coll., 1988, BS, 1992. Photographer Poole Photography, Gloucester, Mass., 1988—; photographer rsch. cruise and Alvin dive Woods Hole Oceanographic Instn., 1991. Photographer Exploring Iceland, 1995, Around and About in Albuquerque, 1993, Soviet Union-The Grip of Winter, 1988, (cover photo) Oceanus Mag., 1991. Mem. Rockport Art Assn. (photography mem. 1994—, First Color Photography award 1994), Alpha Chi. Office: Poole Photography 10 Stanwood Ave Gloucester MA 01930

POOLE, SANDRA LAWRENCE, nurse practitioner; b. Statesboro, Ga., June 20, 1953; d. Maywood Outland and Frances (White) Lawrence; m. Robert Mitchell Poole, Mar. 20, 1976; 1 child, Zachary. AD, Columbus Coll., 1974; NNP, U. Ariz., 1979. RN, Ga.; CNP, neonatal nurse practitioner, NCC. Clin. supr. Regional Newborn and Pediatric Medicine, Columbus, 1987-92; staff nurse The Med. Ctr., Columbus, 1974-79, neonatal nurse practitioner, 1979-87, 92—. Baptist. Home: 109 Emerling Ln Peachtree City GA 30269 Office: The Med Ctr 710 Center St Columbus GA 31995

POOLEY, BONNIE INGRAM, language educator; b. Wilmington, Del., Sept. 7, 1944; d. Albert L. and Margaret S. (Smith) Ingram; 1 child, Kenneth Thomas. BA, U. Del., 1970; MEd, U. So. Maine, 1985. Registered Maine guide. Tchr. English Mt. Pleasant H.S., Wilmington, Del., 1970-73; tchr. English, counselor Gould Acad., Bethel, Maine, 1973—; instr. Hurricane Island Outward Bound Sch., Newry, Maine, 1987—; trip leader Maine Explorations, Bethel, 1996. Bd. dirs. Mahoosue Land Trust, Bethel; officer Bethel Conservation Com., 1990—. Mem. New Eng. Assn. Coll. Admissions Counselors. Home: 7 Summer St Bethel ME 04217 Office: Gould Academy Church St Bethel ME 04217

POOR, ANNE, artist; b. N.Y.C., Jan. 2, 1918; d. Henry Varnum and Bessie (Breuer) P. Student, Bennington Coll., 1936, 38, Art Students League, 1935, Acad. Julien, Paris. trustee, gov. Skowhegan Sch. Painting and Sculpture, 1947-61, 89, 96; artist corr. WAC, 1943-45. Illustrator: Greece, 1964; works exhibited Am. Brit. Art Ctr., 1944, 45, 48, Maynard Walker Gallery, 1950, Graham Gallery, 1957-59, 62, 68-71, 85, Rockland Ctr. for Arts, West Nyack, N.Y., 1982, 83, Terry Dintefass Gallery, N.Y.C.; executed murals, P.O., Gleason, Tenn., DePew, N.Y., South Solon, Maine, Free Mtg. House, 1957, others; represented permanent collections Whitney Mus., Bklyn. Mus., Wichita Mus., Art Inst. Chgo. Edwin Austin Abbey Meml. fellow, 1948; grantee Nat. Inst. Arts and Letters, 1957; recipient Benjamin Altman 1st prize landscape painting N.A.D., 1971, 86, Childe Hassam award, 1972, 77. Mem. Artists Equity Assn., Nat. Inst. Arts and Letters. Office: Terry Dintenfass Gallery 20 E 79th St New York NY 10021

POOR, JANET MEAKIN, landscape designer; b. Cin., Nov. 27, 1929; d. Cyrus Lee and Helen Keats (Meakin) Lee-Hofer; m. Edward King Poor III, June 23, 1951; children: Edward King IV, Thomas Meakin. Student, Stephens Coll., 1947-48, U. Cinn., 1949-51, Triton Coll., 1973-76. Pres. Janet Meakin Poor Landscape Design, Winnetka, Ill., 1975—; chmn. bd. dirs. Cgho. Horticultural Soc., Chgo. Botanic Garden. Author, editor: Plants That Merit Attention Vol. I: Trees, 1984; contbr. articles to profl. jours. Participant in longe range planning City of Winnetka, 1978-82, archtl. and environ. bd., 1980-84, beautification commn., 1978-84, garden coun., 1978-82; adv. coun., sec. of agr. Nat. Arboretum, Washington; nat. adv. bd. Filoli, San Francisco; trustee Ctr. Plant Conservation at Mo. Botanical Garden, St. Louis, also mem. exec. com., mem. adv. coun. The Garden Conservancy, 1989—; trustee Winnetka Congl. Ch., 1978-80. Recipient merit award Hadley Sch. Blind, 1972; named Vol. of Yr. Hadley Sch. Blind. Mem. Chgo. Hort. Soc. (chmn. bd. dirs. 1987-93, medal 1984, gold medal garden design, exec. com., chmn. rsch. com., women's bd., designer herb garden Farwell Gardens at Chgo. Botanic Garden, Hutchinson medal 1994), Am. Hort. Soc. (bd. dirs., Catherine H. Sweeney award 1985), Garden Club Am. (chmn. nat. plant exchange 1980-81, chmn. hort. com. 1981-83, bd. dirs., 1983-85, corresponding sec. 1985-87, Horticulture award Zone X1 1981, Creative Leadership award 1986), Fortnightly Club, Garden Guild (bd. dirs.), Garden Club Am. (v.p. 1987-89, medal awards chmn. 1991-93, Honor medal 1994). Republican.

POOR, VIRGINIA HARDIN, piano teacher; b. Selma, Ala., Oct. 31, 1925; d. John Luther and Lovie (Edwards) Hardin; m. Harold Edgar Poor, Jr., Sept. 12, 1947; children: Ann Victoria, Harold Vincent, John Geoffrey. AB, Bob Jones Univ., 1946; MMus, Columbus Coll., 1992. Cert. Music Tchrs. Nat. Assn. Dir. Christian edn. Trinity United Meth. Ch., Phenix City, Ala., 1946-48; tchr. Phenix City Bd. Edn., 1960-67; English, choral tchr. Russell County (Ala.) Bd. Edn., 1969-71; child welfare caseworker Dept. Child & Family Svcs., Muscogee County, Ga., 1971-77; organist, choir dir. St. Mary Magdalene Episcopal, Columbus, Ga., 1980—; pvt. piano tchr., Columbus, Ga., 1992—, Phenix City, 1988—; organist, choir dir. St. Mary Magdalene Episcopal Ch., Columbus, 1980—. Pres. Mental Health Assn., Russell County, 1985—; vol. tutor Adult Literacy Program, Russell County, 1992—. Mem. Music Tchr.'s Nat. Assn., Mensa, Am. Guild Organists, Alliance Francaise Columbus, Columbus Women's Symphony Guild, Columbus Mus. Guild, Columbus Music Tchr. Assn. (v.p., program chair 1988-90, corr. sec. 1990-93), Orpheus Music Club (v.p., program chair 1991-93). Democrat. Home: 1509 45th St Phenix City AL 36867

POPE, CONSTANCE WALL, massage therapist; b. Wilmington, Del., Sept. 17, 1952; d. Eugene and Claire P. Wall; m. John Peyton Pope, Jr. Student, Strayer Coll., 1970-71, No. Va. C.C., 1980, 92, 96. Cert. massage therapist, Nat. Cert. Bd. of Massage Therapists and Bodyworkers. Sec. to sales/mktg. v.p. Pulte Homes, Vienna, Va., 1980-85; v.p. Westwood Homes, Inc., Fairfax, Va., 1985-87; sec. to constrn. v.p. Dekar Homes, Clifton, Va., 1987-89; chiropractic asst. Culbertson Chiropractic Clinic, Vienna, 1990-91; massage therapist Harrison Chiropractic Clinic, Vienna, 1991-94, No. Va. Massage Ctr., Herndon, Va., 1994—. Mem. Va. Bus. Connection, Oakton, 1995. Mem. Am. Massage Therapy Assn., Herndon C. of C. Office: No Va Massage Ctr 1037 Sterling Rd # 202 Herndon VA 22070

POPE, DEBORAH, English language educator, poet; b. Cin.; d. Charles Foster and Barbara Myrtle (Buxton) P.; children: Nicholas, Matthew. BA in History and English, Denison U.; MA in English, U. Wis., PhD in English. Co-dir. Duke Writers' Conf., Durham, N.C., 1982-89; assoc. prof. dept. English Duke U., Durham. Assoc. editor SIGNS: A Jour. of Women and Soc., 1984-89; author: A Separate Vision, 1984, Fanatic Heart, Mortal World; editor: (essay collection) Ties That Bind, 1990; author of poems. Mem. Phi Beta Kappa, Phi Gamma Kappa. Office: Dept English Duke Univ Durham NC 27708

POPE, INGRID BLOOMQUIST, sculptor, lecturer, poet; b. Arvika, Sweden, Apr. 2, 1918; came to U.S., 1928; became U.S. citizen.; d. Oscar Emanuel and Gerda (Henningson) Brostrom; m. Howard Richard Bloomquist, Feb. 14, 1941 (dec. Nov. 1982); children: Dennis Howard, Diane Cecile Connelly, Laurel Ann Shields; m. Marvin Hoyle Pope, Mar. 9, 1985. BA cum laude, Manhattanville Coll., 1979, MA in Humanities, 1981; MA in Religion, Yale Div. Sch. Yale U., 1984. lectr. Nat. Assn. Am. Pen Women, Greenwich, Soroptimist Club, Greenwich, Greenwich Travel Club, Ch. Women United Greenwich, 1st Congl. Ch., Scarsdale, N.Y., 2d Congl. Ch., Greenwich, 1st Congl. Ch., Stamford, Conn., 1st Ch. of Round Hill, St. Mary Ch., Greenwich. Exhbns. include Manhattanville Coll., Purchase, N.Y., Yale Div. Sch., Ch. of Sweden in N.Y.C., Greenwich Arts Coun., Greenwich Arts Soc., First Ch. of Round Hill; author: (poems) Musings, 1994. Past bd. dirs. N.Y.C. Mission Soc., Greenwich YWCA, Greenwich Acad. Mother's Assn.; past trustee First Ch. Round Hill, Greenwich, mem.; pres. Ch. Women United, Greenwich, 1989-91; bd. dirs. Greenwich Chaplaincy. Mem. AAUW, Nat. Assn. Pen Women, English Speaking Union, Yale Club N.Y.C. and Greenwich, Stanwich Club, Acad. Am. Poets, Nat. Mus. of Women in the Arts. Home: 538 Round Hill Rd Greenwich CT 06831 also: 538 Round Hill Rd Greenwich CT 06831

POPE, JANICE JEAN, educator; b. Saginaw, Mich., June 29, 1944; d. Eugene William and Lila Margarite (Rigg) Butler; m. Richard John Pope, May 18, 1968. BA, Alma (Mich.) Coll., 1966; MEd, Saginaw Valley State, 1979, postgrad., 1991. 3rd grade Bridgeport (Mich.)-Spaulding Community Sch., 1966—. Mem. NEA, Bridgeport Edn. Assn. (co-sec. 1991-92), Mich. Edn. Assn. Home: 6440 Baker Rd Bridgeport MI 48722

POPE, SARAH ANN, elementary education educator; b. Granite City, Ill., Dec. 4, 1938; d. Vance Guy and Lily Lovinia (Fischer) Morgan; m. Thomas E. Pope; children: Robert, Susan, James, John, William. BS in Edn., So. Ill. U., Edwardsville, 1970, MS in Edn., 1976. Lang. arts, humanities, sci., English, reading, math. tchr. Madison (Ill.) Community Sch. Dist., 1970—. Co-founder libr. Harris Elem. Sch., 1990. Fellow Old Six Mile Hist. Soc.; mem. Am. Hemerocallis Soc. Office: Madison Community Unit Sch 1707 4th St Madison IL 62060-1505

POPE, STEPHANIE ANNE ORR, accountant; b. Nashville, Aug. 19, 1969; d. Robert Alvin and Helen Jean (Freeman) Orr; m. Jeffrey Thomas Pope, June 12, 1993. BS in Bus. Adminstrn., Samford U., 1991. Pub. acct. Dale A. Sitton and Assocs. CPAs, Birmingham, Ala., 1991-93; staff acct. HealthSouth Corp., Birmingham, Ala., 1993-95, asst. group leader, 1995-96. Mem. choir, youth leadership staff Garywood Assembly of God, Hueytown, Ala., 1991—. Recipient Loren F. Fitch scholarship in Accounting Samford U., 1990. Mem. Inst. Mgmt. Accts., Omicron Delta Kappa, Phi Mu (scholarship chmn. 1990-91). Mem. Assembly of God.

POPKIN, ELIZABETH DINSMORE, artist, musician, fashion designer; b. N.Y.C., July 19, 1968; d. Mark Anthony and Elsie (Dinsmore) P.; m. Daniel Van Allen, Sept. 28, 1952. Student, Glasgow (Scotland) Sch. Art, 1989; BFA, Md. Inst. Coll. Art, 1990. Owner Spoon!? hats and clothes, Balt., 1989—; antique furniture restorer Danny's Svc., Balt., 1990-93; musician, art designer Women of Destruction, Balt., 1990-95, Estrojet, Balt., 1995—; booking agt. Estrojet/W.O.D., Balt., 1990—. Artist (book): Fine Art of the Tin Can, 1996. Recipient Visual Arts award Nat. Found. for Advancement of Arts, 1987, Individual Arts New Genre award Md. State Arts Coun., 1992, Individual Artist Visual Arts award City Arts, 1992. Democrat. Home: 118 S Arlington Ave Baltimore MD 21223

POPKIN, JOYCE GAIL, psychologist; b. Bklyn., Nov. 18, 1947; d. Gilbert and Fally (Mardex) P.; m. Theodore William Hilgeman, July 19, 1987; 1 child, Alexandra Elaine. BA, Queens Coll., 1968; EdM, Temple U., 1970, PhD, 1984. Licensed psychologist, N.Y.; cert. sch. psychologist, N.Y., N.J., Pa. Sch. psychologist Comsewogue Sch. Dist., Port Jefferson Station, N.Y., 1971—. Mem. APA, Suffolk County Psychol. Assn. (sch. psychology com. 1990—), Nat. Assn. Sch. Psychologists. Home: 22 Paul Revere Ln Centerport NY 11721-1610

POPLER, BOBBY JEAN, association administrator, consultant; b. Richmond, Va., Dec. 24, 1946; d. George T. and Betty Mae (Preston) Penn; m. Clarence Jackson, Oct. 12, 1968 (div. Aug. 1985); children: Brian Jackson, Jeanine Jackson; m. Gary L. Popler, Apr. 7, 1990. BA in Psychology, W.Va. State U., 1974; MS in Dispute Resolution, Nova Southeastern U., 1994. Cert. family mediator, Fla. Probation & parole officer State of Fla., Fort Lauderdale, 1974-76; occupl. specialist Sch. Bd. Broward, Fort Lauderdale, 1976-78, peer mediation coord., 1987-95; learning lab. coord. Broward C.C., Fort Lauderdale, 1978-87; pres., founder, conflict resolution trainer, family mediator Global Peace & Assocs., Fort Lauderdale, 1995—; peace cons., trainer Peace Edn. Found., Miami, Fla., 1991-95, PALS, Jamaica, 1994—; cons., trainer Peoples Empowerment Program, Lakeland, Fla., 1996; mem. Blueprint 2000 Legis. Workgroup Fla. Legis., Talahassee, 1992. Mem. Fla. Acad. Family Mediators, Delta Sigma Theta. Democrat. Baptist. Home: 153 Granada Ave Fort Lauderdale FL 33326 Office: Global Peace & Assocs Inc 13730 State Rd 84 Ste M Fort Lauderdale FL 33326

POPOFSKY, LINDA S., university official; b. Cambridge, Mass.; m. M. Laurence Popofsky; children: Mark, Kaye. BA, Wellesley Coll.; MA, U. Calif., Berkeley, PhD, 1970. Asst. prof. history Mills Coll., Oakland, Calif., 1975-82; assoc. prof. history Mills Coll., Oakland, 1982-88; asst. dir. fin. aid U. Calif., Berkeley, 1989-95; mgr. Chancellor's Office U. Calif., San Francisco, 1995—. Mem. Am. Hist. Assn., Conf. on Brit. Studies, Phi Beta Kappa. Office: U Calif San Francisco Office of Chancellor 513 Parnassus Ave # 126 San Francisco CA 94143-0402

POPP, CHARLOTTE LOUISE, health development center administrator, nurse; b. Vineland, N.J., July 26, 1946; d. William Henry and Elfriede Marie (Zickler) P. Diploma in Nursing, Luth. Hosp. of Md., Balt., 1967; BA in Health Edn., Glassboro (N.J.) State Coll., 1972; MA in Human Devel., Fairleigh-Dickinson U., 1981. Cert. Sch. Nurse, N.J., Health Educator, N.J. Charge nurse Newcomb Hosp., Vineland, N.J., 1967-71; supr. Vineland Rehab. Ctr., 1971-72; charge nurse Bridgeton (N.J.) Hosp., 1972-73; dir. insvc. edn. Millville (N.J.) Hosp., 1973-76; dir. hosp. insvc. edn. Vineland Devel. Ctr. State of N.J., 1976-78, program asst. Vineland Devel. Ctr., 1978-87; dir. habilitation planning services State of N.J., Vineland Devel. Ctr., 1987—, lead program coord. Vineland Devel. Ctr., 1981—; exam proctor State of N.J. Bd. Nursing, Newark, 1973-91. Editorial rev. bd. (jour.) Nursing Update, 1973-77. Instr. basic life support, Am. Heart Assn., bd. dirs. Tri-county chpt., 1979-83, South Jersey chpt., 1983-90. Mem. ANA, N.J. State Nurses Assn., Am. Assn. Mental Retardation, South Jersey Insvc. Exch. (life), Smithsonian Assn., Luth. Hosp. of Md. Alumni Assn., Glassboro State Coll. Alumni Assn., Fairleigh-Dickinson U. Alumni Assn. Lutheran. Office: Vineland Devel Ctr 1676 E Landis Ave Vineland NJ 08360-2901

POPP, LILIAN MUSTAKI, writer, educator; b. N.Y.C.; d. Peter and Mae Claire (Cary) Mustaki; m. Robert J. Popp, Dec. 27, 1941. BA, Notre Dame Coll., 1939; postgrad Columbia U., 1939-40; MS in Edn., Hunter Coll., 1960. Tchr. English, McKee Vocat. and Tech. High Sch., S.I., N.Y., 1946-63, chmn. acad. studies, 1963-71; prin. William Howard Taft High Sch., Bronx, N.Y., 1971-79; adj. prof. Wagner Coll., S.I., 1960-85; instr. Richmond Coll., CUNY, 1968-70, chmn. curriculum com., 1990-91; prof. St. John's U., 1991—; mem. Community Sch. Bd., 1980-93, chmn. 1989-90, chmn. legis. com., 1981-86, chmn. substance abuse and adolescent issues com., 1986—, chmn. pupil pers. svcs. com., 1991-93; asst. examiner N.Y.C. Bd. Edn., 1960-85. Books include: Journeys in Science Fiction, 1961; Four Complete World Novels, 1961; Gertrude Lawrence as Mrs. A., 1961; Four Complete Modern Novels, 1962, Four Complete Heritage Novels, 1963; Four Complete Novels of Character and Courage, 1964; contbr. articles to profl. jours. Bd. dirs. S.I. Mental Health Soc.; chmn. vols. N.Y.C. Child Abuse Prevention Program, 1984-86; regional dir., mem. exec. bd. March of Dimes; book discussion leader Snug Harbor Cultural Ctr., 1981—; pres. Com. for a Nuclear-Free Island, 1986-91; v.p. Staten Islanders Against Nuclear Weapons, 1991—; pres. Brandeis Univ. Nat. Wommen's Com. (Staten Island chpt.), 1996, pres. Coalition of Staten Island Women's Orgns., 1996, mem. edn. com. S.I. Cmty. TV; mem. libr. com. S.I. Hist. Richmondtown. Recipient Women Helping Women award Soroptimists, 1985, Thomas Wilson award for Substance Abuse Prevention, S.I. Advance Woman of Achievement award, 1994. Mem. Belles Lettres Lit. Soc. (pres.), S.I. Hist. Soc., N.Y.C. Assn. Tchrs. English (pres. 1967-71), Nat. Council Tchrs. English (bd. dirs. 1968-69), Acad. Pub. Edn., McKee Tchrs. Assn. (pres. 1969), High Sch. Prins Assn. (exec. bd.), Council Suprs. and Adminstrs., Arista Honor Soc. (hon.), Delta Kappa Gamma (pres.), Phi Delta Kappa (v.p. 1990—), Am. Assn. Univ. Women. Avocations: travel, reading, photography, jewelry making. Home: 40 Flagg Pl Staten Island NY 10304-1119

POPPE, DONNA, music educator; b. Newton, Kans., Feb. 25, 1953; d. Louis Gustav and Dorothy Elizabeth (VanDenBrand) P. Student, Hastings Coll., 1970-72; BA in Music Edn., U. North Colo., 1974; cert. Orff-Schulwerk, U. Denver, 1977; MEd in Curriculum, Seattle Pacific U., 1990, MA in Integrated Arts, 1990. Band, music, orch. tchr. Weld County Sch. Dist., Greeley, Colo., 1974-79; spl. edn. tchr. Franklin Pierce Sch. Dist., Tacoma, Wash., 1979-84; music tchr. Sumner (Wash.) Sch. Dist., 1984—; cons. Seattle Pacific U., 1982; cons., prof. Fla. State U., Tallahassee, 1985-89, U. Ga., Athens, 1988-89; mem. adj. faculty Pacific Luth. U., Tacoma, 1995—; clinician/presenter U. Nebr., Lincoln, 1991; clinician N.W. Orff Conf., 1994, Orff 100 Conf., Melbourne, Australia, 1995; chair Nat. Orff Conf., Seattle, 1997. Contbr. articles to profl. jours. Mem. Tacoma Symphony, 1983-85; coord. team Wash. State Tchrs. Strike, 1991; chair dist. Valuing Diversity, 1993-95; drama clinician N.W. Orff Conf., 1994; condr. children's performance 20th Anniv. Wash. Orff chpt., 1994. Am. Orff-Schulwerk Assn. grantee, 1991. Mem. NEA, Nat. Audubon Soc. (newsletter editor 1974-79, field trip leader Seattle 1992), Am. Orff-Schulwerk Assn. (nat. bd. trustees 1987-90, editorial bd. 1984-87, clinician and presenter Cleve. 1983, Denver, 1990), Music Educators Nat. Conf. (rep. 1983-85, rsch. session Olympia, Wash. 1990), Drum Corps Internat. Democrat. Home: 11609 Marine View Dr SW Seattle WA 98146-1825 Office: Sumner Sch Dist 230 Wood Ave Sumner WA 98390-1279

POPPE, MARIA IRENE, physical therapist; b. Cin., May 29, 1969; d. Chatrchai and Eleanor Irene (Good) Watanakunakorn; m. Ty Lane Poppe, July 18, 1992. BS in Phys. Therapy, Bowling Green State U., 1991. Lic. phys. therapist, Pa., Ohio. Phys. therapist Western Reserve Care Sys., Youngstown, Ohio, 1992, Milton S. Hershey Med. Ctr., Hershey, Pa., 1992—. Mem. Am. Phys. Therapy Assn.

POPPE, PAMELA ELIZABETH, mathematics educator; b. N.Y.C., July 2, 1947; d. Jack William and Gladys (Haas) Herman; m. Paul Odin Poppe, Dec. 21, 1968; children: Michael Christopher, David William. BS Math., U. Nebr., 1969; MS Math., Tulane U., 1986; EdS Math. Edn., U. Ga., 1988; Phd, Ga. State U., 1993. Cert. tcchr. math., 7-12. Math. tchr. Grand Island (Nebr.) Pub. Schs., 1969-74, Mentor (Ohio) Pub. Schs., 1978-79, Jefferson County Pub. Schs., Birmingham, Ala., 1980-81; math. tchr. and computer technologist Long Beach (Calif.) Unified Schs., 1981-84; math. tchr. and dept. chair Gwinnett County Pub. Schs., Lawrenceville, Ga., 1986—; com. mem. restructuring com., Lawrenceville, 1992-94, curriculum com., 1992—, textbook com., 1994—; presenter in field. Co-author: (curriculum) Computer Literacy, 1983. Den mother Boy Scouts Am., Huntington Beach, Calif., 1982-83; vol. Gwinnett Soc. Assn., Lilburn, Ga., 1986-89; edn. com. mem. United Meth. Ch., Hungtington Beach, 1982-84. Recipient Outstanding Achievement in Edn. award Ga. High Tech. Month, 1993, Tchr.-leader award Tchrs. as Leaders, Inc., 1994, Tex. Instrument grantee, 1996; named Outstanding Math. Tchr., Math.-Sci. Roundtable, 1994. Mem. ASCD, Nat. Coun. Tchrs. Math., Ga. Coun. Tchrs. Math., Math. Assn. Am., Ga. Assn. Supervision and Curriculum, Ga. Assn. Advanced Placement Math. Tchrs., Phi Delta Kappa. Home: 2658 Colony Cir Snellville GA 30278 Office: Gwinnett County Pub Schs 52 Gwinnett Dr Lawrenceville GA 30245

POPPER, VIRGINIA SOWELL, education educator; b. Macon, Ga., Sept. 10, 1945; d. Clifford E. and Hazel (Lewis) Sowell; m. James Clarence Sikes, June 24, 1967 (div. 1989); children: Zachary Andrew, Cristen Elizabeth; m. Joseph W. Popper, Jr., Dec. 28, 1992. AB, Wesleyan Coll., Macon, 1967; MEd, U. North Fla., 1973; PhD, Ga. State U., 1991. Tchr. 6th grade Jones County Schs., Gray, Ga., 1966-67; tchr. 12th grade Richmond County Schs., Augusta, Ga., 1967-68; guidance counselor Aiken County Schs., North Augusta, S.C., 1968-69, asst. prin., 1969-71; dir. Durham (N.C.) campus Kings Coll., 1974-77; rsch. asst. Ga. Dept. Edn., Atlanta, 1983-85; assoc. prof. Mercer U., Macon, 1989—; tchr. cultural studies exch. program Seinanto Gakuin Coll. of Kitakusha, Japan-Mercer U. Contbg. author: Business in Literature, 1986; contbr. articles, reports to profl. publs. Chmn. Mid. Ga. Regional Libr. System, Macon, 1989-91; bd. dirs. Jr. League Macon, Macon YWCA, Macon Intown, Macon Heritage Found., Bibb County Am. Cancer Soc., March of Dimes, Macon Ballet, Friends of Libr., Gladys Lasky Weller Scholarship Found., Mayor's Lit. Task Force. Mem. ASCD, Assn. Tchr. Educators, Ga. Coun. Social Studies, Ga. Assn. Ind. Coll. Tchr. Edn., Kappa Delta Lambda, Pi Lambda Theta. Republican. Episcopalian. Home: 798 Saint Andrews Dr Macon GA 31210-4769 Office: Univ Coll Mercer Tift College Dr Forsyth GA 31029

POPPLER, DORIS SWORDS, lawyer; b. Billings, Mont., Nov. 10, 1924; d. Lloyd William and Edna (Mowre) Swords; m. Louis E. Poppler, June 11, 1949; children: Louis William, Kristine, Mark J., Blaine, Claire, Arminda. Student, U. Minn., 1942-44; JD, Mont. State U., 1948. Bar: Mont. 1948, U.S. Dist. Ct. Mont. 1948, U.S. Ct. Appeals (9th cir.) 1990. Pvt. practice law Billings, 1948-49; sec., treas. Wonderpark Corp., Billings, 1959-62; atty. Yellowstone County Attys. Office, Billings, 1972-75; ptnr. Poppler and Barz, Billings, 1972-79, Davidson, Veeder, Baugh, Broeder and Poppler, Billings, 1979-84, Davidson and Poppler, P.C., Billings, 1984-90; U.S. atty. Dist. of Mont., Billings, 1990-93; field rep. Nat. Indian Gaming Commn., Washington, 1993—. Pres. Jr. League, 1964-65; bd. dirs., pres. Yellowstone County Metre Bd., 1982; trustee Rocky Mt. Coll., 1984-90, mem. nat. adv. bd., 1993—; mem. Mont. Human Rights Commn., 1988-90; bd. dirs. Miss Mont. Pageant, 1995—. Recipient Mont. Salute to Women award, Mont. Woman of Achievent award, 1975, Disting. Svc. award Rocky Mt. Coll., 1990. Mem. AAUW, Mont. Bar Assn., Nat. Assn. Former U.S. Attys., Nat. Rep. Lawyers Assn., Internat. Women's Forum, Yellowstone County Bar Assn. (pres. 1990), Alpha Chi Omega. Republican. Office: Nat Indian Gaming Commn 1441 L St NW 9th Fl Washington DC 20005

PORCHÉ-BURKE, LISA MARIE, chancellor; b. L.A., Nov. 9, 1954; d. Ralph Antoine and June Yvonne (James) P.; m. Peter A. Burke, Oct. 27, 1984; children: Mallory, Dominique, Lauren. BA in Psychology magna cum laude, U. So. Calif., 1976; MA in Counseling Psychology, U. Notre Dame, 1981, PhD in Psychology, 1983; LLD (hon.), Chgo. Sch. Profl. Psychology, 1994. Tchr. Spanish Pius X High Sch., Downey, Calif., 1976-77; assoc. AVENUES of South Bend (Ind.), Inc., 1981-82; clin. psychology intern Boston U. Sch. Medicine, 1983-84; sch. psychologist Pierce Sch., Brookline, Mass., 1983-84; asst. prof., profl. tng. faculty Calif. Sch. Profl. Psychology, L.A., 1985-87, asst. prof., 1987-90, coord. ethnic minority mental health proficiency, 1987-90, assoc. prof., 1987-90, coord. multicultural cmty./ proficiency clin. psychology, 1990-91, chancellor, 1992—; guest lectr. Ind. U., South Bend, 1981; adj. faculty Calif. Sch. Profl. Psychology, 1985, acting provost, 1991-92; cons. Clarke-Porche Constrn. Co., Inc., 1981, Adolscent Sch. Health Program Boston City Hosp., 1983-84, Calif. State Dept. Edn., 1987, The Feilding Inst., Santa Barbara, Calif., 1991; workshop leader Personnel Dept. City of South Bend, 1979; rsch. asst. U. Notre Dame, 1980-81; presenter in field. Contbr. articles to profl. jours. Minority fellow U. Notre Dame, 1977; grad. scholar U. Notre Dame, 1979; recipient Outstanding Young Women Am. award, 1983, Exemplary Profl. Svc. award, 1991. Fellow APA (pub. info. com., 1993-95, mem.-at-large 1987-90, 92-95, treas. 1990—, chair 1985-86, chair fundraising com. 1988-90, midwinter program com. 1989-93, bd. ethnic minority affairs 1987-88, Jack B. Krasner award 1991); mem. Nat. Coun. Sch. Profl. Psychology (nominating com. 1989-90, chair nominating subcom. 1989-90, chair ethnic racial diversity com. 1990-92), Calif. Psuchol. Assn. Found. (bd. dirs. 1992, treas./CEO 1993—), Women Psychology for Legislative Action (bd. dirs. 1992—), Assn. Black Psychologists. Office: Calif Sch Profl Psychology 1000 S Fremont Ave Alhambra CA 91803-1360

PORITZ, DEBORAH T., former state attorney general, state judge. Atty. gen. State of N.J., 1994-96; chief justice Supreme Ct. N.J., Trenton, 1996—. Office: Supreme Ct NJ Hughes Justice Complex CN 970 Trenton NJ 08625*

POROBIC, NORA, engineer; b. Mar. 19, 1953; came to U.S., 1979; d. Srdjan and Maria (Rizova) P. BAS, U. Toronto, 1977. Cert. state contractor. Field engr. Kaiser Transit Group, Miami, 1980-81, Metro Dade County Transp. Adminstrn., Miami, 1981-84; pres. Aztec Roofing & Fence, Miami, 1985—; Mem. Constrn. Trades Qualifying Bd., Miami, 1994—. Mem. South Fla. Roofing and Sheet Metal Contractors Assn. Office: Aztec Roofing & Fence 12950 SW 189th St Miami FL 33177

PORTELA, ANA MARIA DE, artist; b. San Antonio, Jan. 19, 1962; d. Adolph de la Pena Portela and Martha (Valencia Rivas) Funicella. Student, Md. Inst. Coll. Art, 1989. Artist Tex. sculpture symposium U. Tex., San Antonio, 1987; curator video exhbn. Palais des Beaux Arts, Brussels, 1993, Americana Haus, Leipzig, 1993, Dogenhaus, Berlin, 1993. Exhibited in group shows at Dooley Le Chappallaine Gallery, N.Y.C., 1992, Biz Art, Copenhagen, 1992, Flamingo East, N.Y.C., 1992, John Post Lee, N.Y.C., Jack Tilton Gallery, N.Y.C., 1993, 303 Gallery, N.Y.C., Mus. Contemporain, Martigne, Switzerland, 1993, Esther Schipper Gallery, Cologne, Germany, 1993, P.S. 1, Long Island City, N.Y., 1993, Elizabeth Koury Gallery, N.Y.C., 1994, Goethe Inst., N.Y.C., 1994, Andrea Rosen, N.Y.C., 1994, Am. Fine Art fundraising benefit, N.Y.C., 1995, Biennale di Venezia, Italy, 11995, Museumsquartier, Vienna, Austria, 1995, P.S. 1, 1995, U. Tex., 1995others; editor video mag. New Observations, 1994, Virnal, 1992, mag. Jabberwocky, 1980; contbg. editor Artists Literary Mab., 1991-93. Recipient awards and grants from BWFK, Vienna, Amerikahaus, Leipzig, Germany, Change Inc., N.Y.C., Nicaragua Arts and Letters, San Antonio Coll., Tex. Sculpture Symposium, Trinity U. Creative Writing. Home: PO Box 1722 Canal Sta New York NY 10013-0871 Office: 8615 Norwich San Antonio TX 78217

PORTER, ALECIA M., accountant; b. Chgo., Aug. 28, 1962; d. William S. and Ethel R. (Steed) P. BS, Roosevelt U., Chgo., 1992. Notary pub., Ill., 1993—. Acct Jewish Coun. Youth Svcs., Chgo., 1989-93; v.p. Acctg. & Tax Source, Inc., East Hazel Crest, Ill., 1993—. Vol. Literacy Vol. Am., 1990-92. Recipient cert. Miss Black Am. Pageant, West Palm Beach, Fla., 1987. Mem. Nat. Assn. Female Execs., Nat. Assn. Self-Employed.

PORTER, DIANE M., religious organization administrator. AB in Am. Govt. and Politics, Purdue U.; M in Urban Planning, U. Ill.; sr. mgrs. in govt. program, Harvard U.; LHD (hon.), St. Augustine Coll., 1994. Chief planner Roosevelt Island Devel. Corp., N.Y.C.; regional adminstr. Region II U.S. Dept. HUD, Washington; sr. v.p. N.Y. State Mortgage Loan Enforcement and Adminstrn. Corp., Albany; chief of staff Congressman Edolphus Towns 11th Congl. Dist., N.Y.; dir. pub. ministries Episcopal Ch. in U.S., N.Y.C., 1988-92; sr. exec. for program Episcopal Ch. Ctr., N.Y.C., 1992—; vis. prof. Urban League's Black Exec. Exchange Program. Mem. planning adv. coun. Dept. Urban and Regional Planning U. Ill.; bd. trustees Gen. Theol. Sem., N.Y.C.; bd. dirs. Bklyn. Econ. Devel. Program; trustee, mem. standing com. Estate Diocese of Long Island. Office: Episcopal Church Center 815 2nd Ave New York NY 10017-4503

PORTER, DONNA JEAN, genealogist; b. Monte Vista, Colo., Aug. 20, 1931; d. George W. and Alma R. (Kile) Bishop; m. Earl Edwin Carmack, Nov. 14, 1949 (div. 1955); m. Paul W. Porter, June 4, 1955; children: LeiLonia Virginia, Paul Benjamin, Rebecca Ann. Registered profl. genealogist. Genealogist Denver, 1969—; owner Stagecoach Libr. for Geneal. Rsch., Denver; instr., lectr. in field. Co-author: Welding Link, An Introduction to Genealogy, 1968; editor Colo. Genealogist mag., 1970-75; contbr. articles to profl. jours. and mags. Asst. libr. Family History Ctr. Libr., LDS Ch., Denver, 1966-76, mem. acquisition com., instr. spl. geneal. instrn. com.; v.p. Colo. chpt. Palatines to Am., Denver, 1985-86, pres., 1986-87, exhibitor's chair Nat. Conf., 1988. Mem. West Palm Beach Geneal. Soc. (founder, pres. 1964-66), Colo. Geneal. Soc. (corr. sec. 1968-69, pres. 1969-70, 2nd v.p., program chairperson 1971-73, seminar chairperson 1974, chairperson, judge Black Sheep contest 1988), Foothills Geneal. Soc. (pres. 1996—, genealogist 1983-88, ednl. dir. 1992—, staff genealogist Foothills Inquirere mag. 1983—, Genie of Yr. award 1992), Colo. Coun. Geneal. Socs. (v.p. 1986-87, pres. 1987-90, chairperson Colo. State Archives Ednl. Gift Fund 1991—), Nat. Soc. DAR (Peace Pipe chpt. state lineage chairperson 1970-73, registrar 1971-77), Ind. Hist. Soc., Ind. Geneal. Soc., Nat. Geneal. Soc., Internat. Soc. for Brit. Genealogy and Family History, Ohio Geneal. Soc. (life, Colo. chpt., Champaign County chpt., Madison County chpt., Ross County chpt., Monroe County chpt.), Mo. Geneal. Soc. (life), Md. Geneal. Soc. (life), St. Andrew Soc. (life), Inst. Heraldic and Geneal. Studies, Assn. Profl. Genealogists, Assn. for Gravestone Studies, Palatines of Am. (Colo. chpt.), Lower Delmara Geneal. Soc., Baltimore County Geneal. Soc., Shockey Family Meml. Fellowship. Home: 1840 S Wolcott Ct Denver CO 80219-4309

PORTER, EDITH PRISCILLA, elementary school educator; b. Aberdeen, Wash., Mar. 1, 1941; d. Robert M. and June J. (Crown) Crawford; m. Lawrence A. Porter, June 12, 1963; children: Melanie S., Jeffrey L., Michael A. BA in Edn., Ctrl. Wash. State U., 1963; MA in Edn., Lesley Coll., 1991. Cert. tchr. Wash. 1st grade tchr. Hoquiam (Wash.) Sch. Dist., 1962-63; 1st grade tchr. Oak Harbor (Wash.) Sch. Dist., 1963-66, 3d grade tchr., 1967-68, 90—, 2d grade tchr., 1977-86, 88-90, kindergarten tchr., 1986-88. Co-author, narrator Famous Black Women of Song, 1994. Elder Whidbey Presbyn. Ch., Oak Harbor, 1995—. Recipient 2 May Carvell awards Venture Clubs Am. Mem. NEA, AAUW, Wash. Edn. Assn., Oak Harbor Edn. Assn. (rec. sec. 1994—), Delta Kappa Gamma (chpt. pres. 1977-80, state rec. sec. 1981-83, state area liaison 1983-87, state corr. sec. 1985-87). Democrat. Office: Oak Harbor Schs 1250 Midway Blvd Oak Harbor WA 98277

PORTER, ELSA ALLGOOD, writer, lecturer; b. Amoy, China, Dec. 19, 1928; d. Roy and Petra (Johnsen) Allgood; m. Raeford B. Liles, Mar. 19, 1949 (div. 1959); children: Barbara, Janet; m. G. Hinckley Porter, Nov. 22, 1962; children: David, Brian, Wendy. BA, Birmingham-So. Coll., 1949; MA, U. Ala., 1959; M in Pub. Adminstrn., Harvard U., 1971; LHD (hon.), U. Ala., 1986. With HEW, Washington, 1960-73; with U.S. CSC, Washington, 1973-77; asst. sec. Dept. Commerce, Washington, 1977-81; disting. practitioner in residence Washington Pub. Affairs Ctr., U. So. Calif., Washington, 1982-84; sr. mgmt. assoc. The Prodn. Group, Alexandria, Va., 1985-87; project dir. Cathedral Coll. of the Laity, Washington, 1987-89; v.p. R & D The Maccoby Group, Washington, 1990-96. Bd. dirs. Delphi Internat. Group, 1981—. Fellow Nat. Acad. Pub. Adminstrs.; mem. Women's Nat. Dem. Club. Home: # 742 2309 S W First Ave Portland OR 97201

PORTER, HELEN VINEY (MRS. LEWIS M. PORTER, JR.), lawyer; b. Logansport, Ind., Sept. 7, 1935; d. Charles Lowry Viney and Florence Helen (Kunkel) V.; m. Lewis Morgan Porter, Jr., Dec. 26, 1966; children: Alicia Michelle, Andrew Morgan. A.B., Ind. U., 1957; J.D., U. Louisville, 1961. Bar: Ind. and Ill. 1961, U.S. Supreme Ct. 1971. Atty. office chief counsel Midwest regional office IRS, Chgo., 1961-73; assoc. regional atty. litigation center Equal Employment Opportunity Commn., Chgo., 1973-74; practice in Northbrook, Ill., 1974-79, 80-86; ptnr. Porter & Andersen, Chgo., 1979-80, Porter & Porter, Northfield, Ill., 1986—; lectr. Law in Am. Found., Chgo., summer, 1973, 74; assoc. prof. No Ill Coll Law (formerly Lewis U. Coll. Law), Glen Ellyn, Ill., 1975-79. Lectr. women's rights and fed. taxation to bar assns., civic groups. Recipient Disting. Alumni award U. Louisville Sch. of Law, 1986, President's award Nat. Assn. of Women Lawyers, 1985. Fellow Am. Bar Found., Ill. State Bar Found.; mem. Women's Bar Assn. Ill. (pres. 1972-73), ABA (chmn. standing com. gavel awards 1983-85, bd. editors jour. 1984-90, mem. standing com. assn. comm. 1990-93), Fed. Bar Assn. (pres. Chgo. chpt. 1974-75), Ill. Bar Assn. (assembly del. 1972-78), Nat. Assn. Women Lawyers (pres. 1973-74). Home and Office: 225 Maple Row Northfield IL 60093-1037

PORTER, JEANNE SMITH, civic worker; b. Hammond, Ind., Feb. 27, 1930; d. Cyril Augustus and Mary (Mabley) Smith; m. William Harry Porter, Apr. 1, 1953; children: Wendy Alice, David William, Mary Elizabeth, Audrey Jeanne. Student, Hanover Coll., 1948-50; BA in Lit. with honors, Ind. U., 1953. Developer, area leader Recovery, Inc., Mont., 1971-82; mem. adv. bd. Mont. House Day Treatment Ctr., Helena, 1980-93; bd. dirs., libr. chmn., Mont. Alliance for Mentally Ill, Helena, 1979—; organizer, planner Columbarium garden, Episcopal Ch., Helena, 1988—; organizer T-House project Mental Health Svcs., 1983-88; developer Social Club-Mentally Ill., 1968—. Recipient Disting. Svc. award Jaycees Helena, 1974, svc. to cmty. award Carroll Coll., 1986, Electrum award Helena Arts Coun., 1988, award for long term svc. Mont. Alliance for Mentally Ill., 1989, Vol. of Yr. award Mental Health Assn. Mont., 1989. Mem. P.E.O. (philanthropic com. chpt. O 1994—). Home: 1425 Winne Ave Helena MT 59601

PORTER, JEANNETTE UPTON, elementary education educator; b. Mpls., Mar. 5, 1938; d. Robert Livingston and Ruby Jeannette (Thomas) Upton; divorced; children: Steven, Fritz, Susan Porter Powell. BS, U. Minn., 1960, Mankato State U., 1968; postgrad., St. Thomas U., 1991. Camp dir. St. Paul's Episcopal Ch., Mpls., 1956-66; tchr. elem. sch. Bloomington (Minn.) Pub. Schs., 1967—, dir. title I, 1975-82, tchr. spl. assignment of rsch. and devel., 1990-91; team cons. Hillcrest Cmty. Sch., Bloomington, 1990-95. Tutor Telephone Hot Line Minn. Fedn. Tchrs., Mpls., 1988-92; crisis counselor Neighborhood Improvement Programs, Mpls., 1988-93; adult literacy counselor Right to Read, Mpls., 1987-89; vol. Abbott Northwestern Hosp. Recipient 1st Bank award Mpls., Red Apple award, Mpls., 1988; named Minn. Tchr. of Excellence, 1988, 89. Mem. Assn. Early Childhood Edn. (treas. 1990-94), Bloomington Edn. Found., Delta Kappa Gamma (1st v.p. 1992-93), PEO (past pres. A.C. chpt.). Home: 4400 West 44th St Saint Louis Park MN 55424

PORTER, JENNIFER MADELEINE, producer, director; b. Milw., Oct. 3, 1962; d. John Hamlin and Helen Meak (Smith) P. BA in Comm., Bowling Green State U., 1984. Audio visual supr. Liberty Mutual Ins. Group, Berwyn, Pa., 1985-88; sr. prodr. audio visual Prudential Ins. Co., Mpls., 1988-93; proprietor Shoot The Moon Prodns., Mound, Minn., 1993—. Prodr., dir., writer: (audio visual program) Phantom Lake... A Lifetime of Memories, 1991 (Best of Show 1991, Script award Assn. for Multi-Image, Internat. 1991), Vision... The Gamma Phi Beta Foundation, 1992 (First Place award 1993). Mentor U. Minn., Mpls., 1989—; fund raiser Gamma Phi Beta Found. Philanthropy-Spl. Camping for Girls, Minn., Wis., 1991—; chairperson 100th Celebration, Phantom Lake YMCA Camp, Mukwonago, Wis., 1994—. Mem. Assn. for Multi-Image Internat. (exec. bd. local 1986-88), Gamma Phi Beta (internat. officer, pub. rels. speaker/prodr. 1991—). Home and Office: Shoot The Moon Prodns 4105 Upton Ave S Minneapolis MN 55410

PORTER, JILL, journalist; b. Phila., Aug. 5, 1946; d. Sidney and Mae (Merion) Chalfin; m. Eric Porter, Mar. 7, 1970 (div. 1975); m. Fred Hamilton, Oct. 28, 1983; 1 child, Zachary. BA, Temple U., 1968. Pub. rels. Manning Smith P.R., Phila., 1968-69; reporter Norristown Times Herald, Norristown, Pa., 1969-72, The Trentonian, Trenton, N.J., 1972-75; reporter The Phila. Daily News, Phila., 1975-79, columnist, 1979—; instr. Temple U., 1976-80. Contbr. articles to numerous mags. Vol. Phila. Futures, 1994, 95, 96. Recipient numerous journalism awards. Home: 134 Rolling Rd Bala Cynwyd PA 19004-2113 Office: Phila Newspapers Inc Phila Daily News 400 N Broad St Philadelphia PA 19130-4015

PORTER, JOAN MARGARET, elementary education educator; b. Vernon, Tex., Dec. 25, 1937; d. Elton Lonnie and Clara Pearl (Yeager) Smith; m. Claude Walker Porter, Feb. 13, 1960; children: Jolene Porter Mohindroo, Richard Euin, Vonda Sue, Darla Ailese Porter Blomquist. BA, Wayland Bapt. U., 1960; M in Elem. Edn., Ea. N.Mex. U., 1981, bilingual endorsement, 1982. cert. classroom tchr., N.Mex. ESL tchr. Jefferson Elem. Sch., Lovington, N.Mex., 1979-81, tchr. first grade, 1981-82; tchr. bilingual first grade Jefferson Elem. Sch., Lovington, 1982-89; tchr. bilingual first grade Highland Elem. Sch., Plainview, Tex., 1989-91, 1992—, tchr. first grade, 1991-92, tchr. bilingual first grade, 1992-95, tchr. bilingual second grade, 1995-96; vol. tchr. Cert. Adult Literacy, Lovington. Mem. PTA, Assn. Tex. Profl. Educators, Delta Kappa Gamma (profl. affairs com. chmn. 1991), Phi Kappa Phi. Southern Baptist. Home: 101 Juanita St Plainview TX 79072-7625 Office: Highland Elem Sch 1707 W 11th St Plainview TX 79072-6439

PORTER, JOYCE KLOWDEN, theatre educator and director; b. Chgo., Dec. 21, 1949; d. LeRoy and Esther (Siegel) Klowden; m. Paul Wayne Porter, June 8, 1980; 1 child, David Benjamin. BA in Speech Edn., U. Ill., 1971; MA in Theatre, Northwestern U., 1972; postgrad., Northeastern U., Chgo., 1980, 89, Ill. State U., 1985-90. Prof. theatre, play dir. Moraine Valley C.C., Palos Hills, Ill., 1972—, acting theatre coord., 1986-87; adj. faculty Columbia Coll., 1988-92; co-owner, tour organizer Chgo. Theatre Arts Tours, Calumet City, Ill., 1988-93; co-owner Porter Video Prodns.; actress, 1972—. Author: (textbook) Humanities on the Go, 1992. Mem. adv. bd. Oak Park (Ill.) Park Dist., 1983; co-chmn. Moraine chpt. Chgo. Area Faculty for nuclear Freeze, Palos Hills, 1985-87; announcer for blind Chgo. Radio Info. Svc., 1982-83; bd. dirs. Festival Theatre, Oak Park, 1989—; mem. play selection com. Village Players of Oak Park. Mem. Assn. for Theatre in Higher Edn., Ill. Theatre Assn., C.C. Humanities Assn (presenter midwest conf. 1993), Ill. Fedn. Tchrs., Nature Conservancy, Zeta Phi Eta. Office: Moraine Valley CC 10900 S 88th Ave Palos Hills IL 60465-2175

PORTER, KAREN SUE, counselor; b. Elkton, Md., Aug. 11, 1959; d. Frank and Hazel May (Childres) P. BA in Psychology, Salisbury State U., 1981; MEd in Guidance/Counseling, Loyola U., Balt., 1994. Cert. guidance counselor. Program coord. Wicomico-Teen Adult, Mardela Springs, Md., 1985-86; counselor, evaluator Benedictine Ctr., Ridgely, Md., 1986—; cons., counselor Dorchester Devel. Unit, Cambridge, Md., 1992-94. Mem. ASCA, ACA. Home: 29595 Dutchmans Ln # 402 Easton MD 21601

PORTER, LAEL FRANCES, communication consultant, educator; b. N.Y.C., July 30, 1932; d. Ronald William Carpenter and Frances Veneranda Fernandez; m. Ralph Emmett Porter, June 9, 1954; children: Paula Lee Porter Leggett, Sandra Lynn Livermore. BA in Comm. and Theater, U. Colo., Denver, 1982, MA in Comm. and Theater, 1986. Speech instr. Moultrie, Ga., 1954-55; owner, distributor Lael's Cosmetics & Wigs, Alexandria, Va., 1966-69; sales dept. mgr. May D & F, Denver, 1974-80; instr. comm. U. Colo., Denver, 1987-89, Red Rocks Cmty. Coll., Lakewood, Colo., 1989—; mem. coord. com. Nat. Hispana Roundtable, Denver, 1985; mem. diversity coun. and internat. dimensions Red Rocks C.C., Lakewood, Colo., 1994-96. Mem. bd. dirs. Girls Count, Denver, 1991—, Colo. Statewide Systemic In., Denver, 1994—; mem. adv. bd. Cmty. Liberal Arts & Sci. U. Colo., Denver, 1988-93; mem. utility consumers adv. bd. State of Colo., Denver, 1989-91. Recipient Founding Star award Girls Count, Cert. of Appreciation USAF, 1974, Mack Easton award U. Colo., Denver, 1990. Mem. AAUW (numerous coms. and positions including state pres. 1992-94, named gift award 1991, branch named gift award 1988, branch continuing svc. award 1994), Colo. Speech Comm. Assn., Internat. Soc. Edn., Tng. and Rsch., Latin Am. Rsch. and Svc. Orgn., Western Speech Comm. Assn., Speech Comm. Assn., Leadership Lakewood. Episcopalian. Home: 2613 S Wadsworth Cir Lakewood CO 80227

PORTER, LEAH LEEARLE, biological researcher; b. Remington, Va., Sept. 19, 1963; d. James Wallace and Earline Yvonne (Moore) P. BS, U. Md., 1985; MS, Cornell U., 1990, PhD, 1993. Biol. technician U.S. Dept. Agr., Beltsville, Md., 1981-85; agrl. cons. Md. Dept. Agr., College Park, 1985; cons., office mgr. Carpigraphics, Inc., Beltsville, 1985-86; grad. rsch. asst. Cornell U., Ithaca, N.Y., 1986-94; cons., mktg. asst. LeEarle Enterprises, Ithaca, 1988-94; mgr. internat. project Glahe Cons. Group, Washington, 1994-95; rsch. mgr. Chem. Mfrs. Assn., Washington, 1995—; cons., mktg. asst. Le Earle Enterprises, Ithaca, 1988-93. Md. State Senate scholar, 1984-85; faculty grad. fellow Cornell U., 1986-87. Fellow N.Y. Acad. Scis.; mem. Am. Phytopathological Soc., Assn. Women in Sci., Black Grad. and Profl. Students, Alpha Chi Sigma, Zeta Phi Beta. Democrat. Baptist. Office: 1300 Wilson Blvd Arlington VA 22209

PORTER, LISA ANN, psychotherapist, educator; b. Davenport, Iowa, Feb. 25, 1956; d. J. Darnell and Gladys G. (Nelson) Hattam; m. Charles Garey Heider, June 12, 1976 (div. Dec. 1987); children; Whitney Heider, Kelley Heider; m. Douglas Brent Porter, Aug. 4, 1988. BS, U. Nebr., 1977, MS, 1995. Nat. cert. counselor. Educator Vocat.-Tech. Coll., Helena, Mont., 1984-85, Nebr. Coll. Bus., Omaha, 1985-88; health and major med. claim auditor World Ins., Omaha, 1988-89; vocat. rehab. counselor Heartland, Omaha, 1989-91; substitute tchr. Omaha, 1991-94; psychotherapist Arbor Family Counseling, Omaha, 1995. Contbr. articles to profl. jours. Vol. Salvation Army, Omaha, 1994, ARC Disaster Relief World Wide, 1995. Mem. Am. Counseling Assn., Am. Mental Health Counselors Assn., Nebr. Counseling Assn., Chi Sigma Iota. Republican. Lutheran. Home: 5011 S 171st Cir Omaha NE 68135-1407

PORTER, LYNNE KATHLEEN, theatre educator, scenic designer; b. Colorado Springs, Colo., Oct. 20, 1960; d. David Leo and Lovena Lu (Hutson) P. BA, Western State Coll., Gunnison, Colo., 1981; MFA, Ind. U., 1985. Instr., resident designer Susquehanna U., Selinsgrove, Pa., 1985-89; v.p. ops. MLR Theatrical Studio, Bridgeport, Pa., 1989-91; props master artisan Alliance Theatre Co., Atlanta, 1991-93; adj. instr. Mars Hill (N.C.) Coll., 1991-93; asst. prof. U. North Tex., Denton, 1993-95, Fairfield (Conn.) U., 1995—; scenic/lighting designer So. Appalachian Repertory Theatre, Mars Hill, 1986-93; scenic designer Horizon Theatre Co., Atlanta, 1991-93, Arden Theatre Co., Phila., 1989-91; scenographer Harrisburg (Pa.) Shakespeare Festival, 1995—. Scenic designer (theatre prodn.) An Enemy of the People, 1986, (theatre prodn.) Man of La Mancha, 1987, (opera prodn.) Postcard from Morocco, 1995; scenographer (theatre prodn.) Julius Caesar, 1995. Faculty advisor SAYSO and 10% Gay/Straight Alliance, Fairfield U., 1995—. Humanities Inst. grantee Fairfield U., 1996. Mem. U.S. Inst. Theatre Tech., Southeastern Theatre Conf., Northeastern Theatre Conf., Alpha Psi Omega.

PORTER, MARIE ANN, neonatal nurse; b. St. Paul, June 29, 1961; d. Theodore J. Morrison and Betty Ann Verdick; 1 child, Angela. ADN, Columbia Basin Coll., 1988. RN, Wash.; cert. neonatal resusitation, Neonatal Resuscitation Program instr. Staff RN Kennewick (Wash.) Gen. Hosp., 1988-95; legal nurse cons. Richland, Wash., 1995—; owner, pres. Porter Med. Conss. Active March of Dimes. Mem. ANA, Nat. Assn. Neonatal Nurses, Tri-Cities Coun. Nursing, Wash Med. Case Mgmt. Assn., Richland C. of C.(amb.).

PORTER, MARSHA KAY, Language professional and educator, English; b. Sacramento, Feb. 7, 1954; d. Charles H. and Eileen J. (Miller) P. BA in English and Edn., Calif. State U., Sacramento, 1976, traffic safety credential, 1979, MA in Ednl. Adminstrn., 1982. Cert. lang. devel. specialist, Calif.; cert. first aid instr. ARC. Bookkeeper Chuck's Parts House, Sacramento, 1969-76; substitute tchr. Sacramento City Unified Sch. Dist., 1976-78; coord. Title I, Joaquin Miller Mid. Sch., Sacramento, 1978-81; tchr. ESL and driver's edn. Hiram Johnson H.S., Sacramento, 1981-85, C.K. McClatchy H.S., Sacramento, 1985—; freelance editor, 1981-87; guest lectr. Nat. U., Sacramento, 1992-93. Co-author film reference book Video Movie Guide, pub. annually; contbr. movie revs., short stories and articles to publs. Vol. instr. CPR and first aid ARC, Sacramento, 1986-92; guest writer United We Stand Calif., Sacramento, 1993-94. Gov.'s scholar State of Calif., 1972. Mem. NEA, Calif. Tchrs. Assn., Calif. Assn. Safety Educators, Calif. Writers, Calif. Writers Assn. (sec. 1987-94, pres. 1996), Delta Kappa Gamma. Roman Catholic.

PORTER, PAULA LEE, editor, writer; b. Council Bluffs, Iowa, Mar. 2, 1954; d. Paul George and Liane Luree (Bettcher) Bintz; m. James Joseph Porter, Jr., June 8, 1974 (dec. Dec. 1987). AA in Journalism, Iowa Western C.C., Council Bluffs, 1974; BA in Journalism, U. Nebr., 1976; BA in Elem. Edn., Buena Vista Coll., 1988; MA in English, Iowa State U., 1993. Tchg. cert. and reading cert., Iowa, Nebr. Darkroom technician Council Bluffs (Iowa) Nonpareil, 1976; editl. asst., affiliates editor Mutual of Omaha, Nebr., 1977-82; info./edn. specialist Papio-Missouri River Natural Resources Dist., Omaha, 1983-91; tchg. asst. English Iowa State U., Ames, 1991-92; dir. publs. Soil and Water Conservation Soc., Ankeny, Iowa, 1992-93; editor Environ. Health and Engring. Inc., Newton, Mass., 1993-96; web editor Cahner's Pub., Newton, 1996—; mem. v.p., treas., spl. svcs. v.p., Internat. Assn. Bus. Communicators, Omaha, 1977-91; mem. program com. Nebr. Groundwater Found., Lincoln, 1989-93. Pub. affairs staff Am. Cancer Soc., Omaha, 1978-85; mem. newsletter editor Omaha Jaycees, 1978-82; organizer Great Am. Smokeout Campaign, Pub. Rels. Soc. Am., 1979; active Big Bros./Big Sisters, Omaha, 1988-91; explorer post leader Boy Scouts Am., Omaha, 1989-91; mem., pres. Pottawattamie County Conservation Bd., Council Bluffs, 1989-91; vol. grief support U. Nebr. Med. Ctr., 1990; con. com. Town of Ashland (Mass.) Conservation Commn., 1994—. Named one of Ten Outstanding Young Omahans, Omaha Jaycees, 1989, Outstanding Environ. Edn. Program, Nat. Assn. Conservation Dists., 1989, 91; recipient award of excellence jour. Am. Soc. Assn. Execs., 1992, Assn. Trends, 1993. Mem. Soil and Water Conservation Soc. (bd. rep. 1989—). Home: 368 Chestnut St Ashland MA 01721 Office: Cahners Pub 275 Washington St Newton MA 02158-1630

PORTER, PRISCILLA MANNING, artist; b. Balt., Feb. 1, 1917; d. William Hamilton and Amy Russell (Manning) P. BA in Sci., Bennington Coll., 1940. Lab. technician Coll. of Physicians and Surgeons, N.Y.C., 1940-43; sci. tchr. The Brearley Sch., N.Y.C., 1943-45, The Chapin Sch., N.Y.C., 1946-52; ceramic tchr. Mus. Modern Art, N.Y.C., 1952-61; owner fused glass studio, Washington, Conn., 1960—. Contbr. articles to profl. publs. Trustee Steep Rock Assn., Washington, 1993—. Mem. Soc. Conn. Craftsmem, Washington Art Assn. Episcopalian. Home and Office: 24 Plumb Hill Rd Washington CT 06793

PORTER, RHONDA DAVIS, critical care, emergency nurse; b. Cabarrus County, N.C., July 31, 1956; d. Donald Matthew and Margaret Louise (Cauble) Davis; m. Allen Lovejoy Porter, Dec. 15, 1979; children: Jeffrey Allen, Matthew Glenn. Diploma, Mercy Sch. Nursing, Charlotte, N.C., 1977; BSN, U. N.C., Charlotte, 1979. Cert. mobile intensive care nurse, trauma nurse, ACLS. Staff nurse Wesley Long Community Hosp., Greensboro, N.C.; nurse cons. Aetna Life Ins., 1990-92, clin. nurse specialist, 1992—; case mgr. Aetna Health Plans, 1992—, trainer, auditor, 1995—. Mem. Boy Scouts Am., coord. Tiger Cub, 1994-95, asst. den leader pack 17, Greensboro, N.C., 1995-96. Home: 5506 Cobble Glen Ct Greensboro NC 27407-6351

PORTER, ROBERTA ANN, counselor, educator, school system administrator; b. Oregon City, Oreg., May 28, 1949; d. Charles Paul and Verle Maxine (Zimmerman) Zacur; m. Vernon Louis Porter, Dec. 27, 1975. B in Bus. Edn., So. Oreg. Coll., 1971, M in Bus. Edn., 1977; cert. in counseling, Western Oreg. Coll., 1986; cert. adminstrn., Lewis and Clark Coll., 1995. Cert. in leadership Nat. Seminars, 1991. Tchr. Klamath Union H.S., Klamath Falls, Oreg., 1971-73, Mazama Mid./H.S., Klamath Falls, Oreg., 1973-83; instr. Oreg. Inst. Tech., Klamath Falls, Oreg., 1975-92; counselor Mazama H.S., Klamath Falls, 1983-93, mem. site based mgmt. steering com., 1991-95; vice prin. Bonanza (Oreg.) Schs., 1993-95; counselor Klamath County Sch. Dist., Oreg., 1995—; site com. chair Lost River Jr./Sr. H.S., 1995—; presenter Oreg. and Nat. Assn. Student Coun., 1989-92, Oreg. Sch. Bds. Assn., Sch. Counselor Assn., 1995, state mini workshops counselors/adminstrs.; mem. task force for ednl. reform in Oreg., 1993-94; trainer asst. Leadership Devel. Am. Sch. Counselor Assn. Mem. editl. bd. dirs. Eldorado Wellness, 1996—, Turning Points, 1996—. Trainer U.S. Army and Marines Recruiters, Portland and Medford, Oreg., 1988-89; master trainer Armed Svcs. Vocat. Aptitude Battery/Career Exploration Program, 1992—; candidate Klamath County Sch. Bd., Klamath Falls. Recipient Promising, Innovative Practices award Oreg. Sch. Counselors, 1990. Mem. NEA, ACA, COSA, ASCD, ASCA, Oreg. Sch. Counseling Assn. (presenter, v.p. h.s. 1988-91, membership com. 1991-93, pres. 1992-95, pres.'s award), Oreg. Edn. Assn., Oreg. Counseling Assn. (Pres. award 1995, parliamentarian 1994-95, area 8 rep. 1995—), Oreg. Assn. Student Couns. (bd. dirs. activity advisors 1989-91), Nat. Assn. Student Couns., Klamath Falls Edn. Assn. (bldg. rep. 1990-93, sec. 1991-92, negotiations team 1992-93), Delta Kappa Gamma (exec. bd. Alpha chpt. 1985-94, pres. 1990-92, state conv. chmn. 1992, state legis. com. 1991-93, chmn. 1993-95, state expansion com.). Home: 3131 Derby St Klamath Falls OR 97603-7313 Office: Cost River Jr/Sr High Sch 23330 Hwy 50 Merrill OR 97633

PORTER, VERNA LOUISE, lawyer; b. L.A., May 31, 1941. B.A., Calif. State U., 1963; JD, Southwestern U., 1977. Bar: Calif. 1977, U.S. Dist. Ct. (cen. dist.) Calif. 1978, U.S. Ct. Appeals (9th cir.) 1978. Ptnr. Eisler & Porter, L.A., 1978-79, mng. ptnr., 1979-86, pvt. practice law, 1986—; judge pro-tempore L.A. Mcpl. Ct., 1983—, L.A. Superior Ct., 1989—, Beverly Hills Mcpl. Ct., 1992—; mem. state of Calif. subcom. on landlord tenant law, panelist conv., mem. real property law sect. Calif. State Bar, 1983; speaker on landlord-tenant law to real estate profls., including San Fernando Bd. Realtors; vol. atty. L.A. County Bar Dispute Resolution, mem. client rels. panel, fee arbitrator. Mem. adv. coun. Freddie Mac Vendor, 1995—. Editl. asst., contbr. Apt. Owner Builder; contbr. to Apt. Bus. Outlook, Real Property News, Apt. Age; mem. World Affairs Coun. Fre Mem. ABA, L.A. County Bar Assn. (client-rels. vol. dispute resolution and fee arbitration, 1981—), L.A. Trial Lawyers Assn., Wilshire Bar Assn., Women Lawyer's Assn., Landlord Trial Lawyers Assn. (founding mem., pres.), Freddie Mac Vendor Adv. Coun., da Camera Soc. Republican. Office: 2500 Wilshire Blvd Fl 1226 Los Angeles CA 90057-4317

PORTER, WILMA JEAN, university director; b. Sylacauga, Ala., May 30, 1931; d. Harrison Samuel and Blanche Leonard Butcher; m. Douglas Taylor Porter, Apr. 18, 1953; children: Daria Cecile, Blanche Evette, Douglas Vincent. BS, Tuskegee U., 1951; MS, Mich. State U., 1966; PhD, Iowa State U., 1980. Asst. dietitian Miss. State Tb Sanatorium, 1951-52; therapeutic dietitian dept. of hosp. City of N.Y., S.I., 1952-53; libr. asst. Mississippi Valley State Coll., Itta Bena, Miss., 1963-65; asst. prof. Grambling (La.)

State U., 1966-75, Howard U., Washington, 1976-80; country dir. U.S. Peace Corps, Tonga, 1980-82; asst. dir. internat. programs Ft. Valley (Ga.) Coll., 1983-84, dir. Inst. Advancement, 1984-88; dir. Sch. Home Econs., Tenn. Technol. U., Cookeville, 1989—; project dir. Capitol Hill Health and Homemaker, Washington, 1982-83; interim dir. Inst. Advancement Alcorn State U., Lorman, Miss., 1988-89. Author lab. manual for quantity foods, 1977; editor: (cookbook) Some Christmas Foods and Their Origins from Around the World, 1983. Convenor Nat. Issues Forums, Ga. and Tenn., 1985—; citizen participant Nat. Issues Forums Soviet Dialogue, Newport Beach, Calif., 1988; bd. dirs. Leadership Putnam, Cookeville, 1990-94; chmn. Tenn. Technol. U. campaign United Way, 1989; mem. devel. and planning com. Peach County Ft. Valley, 1985-87; mem. Peach County Heart Fund Dr., 1986-88; participant People to People Citizens Amb. program U.S./China Women's Issues Program, 1995. Title III grantee U.S. Dept. Edn., 1986, 87; Tenn. Dept. Human Svcs. grantee, 1993, 94. Mem. AAUW (program chair 1991-92, pres. Cookeville br. 1993-94), Am. Home Econs. Assn., Am. Dietetic Assn., Nat. Coun. Adminstrs. Home Econs., Tenn. Home Econs. Assn., Tenn. Dietetic Assn. Democrat. Roman Catholic. Home: 512 Fisk Rd Cookeville TN 38501-2925

PORTMAN, NANCY ANN, artist, art educator; b. Bath, N.Y., Dec. 10, 1936; d. Lewis Menzo Peck and Neva Irene (Keeler) Wheeler; m. Warren Conrad Portman, Apr. 1, 1961; children: Lorraine Jean Portman Irelan, Errol Lawrence. BA with honors, SUNY, New Paltz, 1958; MA with honors, NYU, 1965; postgrad., Coll. New Rochelle, 1982-86, SUNY, Purchase, 1985-90, Pace U., 1990. Permanent tchg. cert., N.Y. Art tchr. Yorktown Ctrl. Schs., Yorktown Heights, N.Y., 1958-60, 61-65, Yorktown Heights, 1971-91; art tchr. Pearl River (N.Y.) Schs., 1960-61. Group shows include NYU and Jacksonville Watercolor Soc. Campaigner for Steve Alexander, State Dist. Atty. Fla., St. Augustine, 1992. Mem. Fla. Watercolor Soc., Jacksonville Watercolor Soc. (chair fall show 1994, co-chair fall show 1995), St. Augustine Art Assn., Jacksonville Mus., Cummen Mus. Republican. Methodist. Home: 3497 Lone Wolf Trail Saint Augustine FL 32086

POSEN, SUSAN ORZACK, lawyer; b. N.Y.C., Nov. 5, 1945. BA, Sarah Lawrence Coll., 1967; JD, Bklyn. Law Sch., 1978. Bar: N.Y. 1979. Assoc. Stroock & Stroock & Lavan, N.Y.C., 1978-83, 84-86; ptnr. Stroock, Stroock & Lavan, N.Y.C., 1987—; asst. gen. counsel Cablevision Systems Corp., Woodbury, N.Y., 1983-84. Office: Stroock & Stroock & Lavan 7 Hanover Sq New York NY 10004-2616

POSNER, KATHY ROBIN, communications executive; b. Oceanside, N.Y., Nov. 3, 1952; d. Melvyn and Davonne Hope (Hansen) P. BA in Journalism, Econs., Manhattanville Coll., 1974. Fin. planner John Dreyfus Corp., Purchase, N.Y., 1974-80; corp. liaison Gulf States Mortgage, Atlanta, 1980-82; dir. promotion Gammon's of Chgo., 1982-83; coordinator trade show mktg. Destron, Chgo., 1983-84; pres. Postronics, Chgo., 1984-87; v.p. Martin E. Janis & Co., Inc., Chgo., 1987-90; pres., CEO Comm 2 Inc., Chgo., 1990—. Editor: How to Maximize Your Profits, 1983; contbg. editor Internat. Backgammon Guide, 1974-84, Backgammon Times, 1981-84, Chgo. Advt. and Media; columnist Food Industry News. Bd. dirs. Chgo. Beautification Com., 1987, Concerned Citizens for Action, Chgo., 1987; mem. steering com. Better Boys Found.; campaign mgr. Brown for Alderman, Chgo., 1987; mem. bd. cons. Little City Found. Mem. NATAS, NOW, Women in Comm., Am. Soc. Profl. and Exec. Women, Women in Film-Chgo. (bd. dirs.), Mensa, Acad. Arts (v.p.), Ill. Restaurant Assn. (mem. adv. bd.), Chgo. Area Pub. Affairs Group, Baderbrau Beer Drinking Soc. (v.p. pub. rels.), Gammon's Chgo. (bd. dirs. 1980-83, editor newsletter 1982-83), Little City Found. (bd. dirs.), City Club Chgo. (bd. dirs.), Cavendish North Club (bd. dirs. 1984-87), Met. Club, Plaza Club, Monroe Club, 410 Club. Republican. Jewish. Office: Comm 2 Inc 921 W Van Buren St Ste 240 Chicago IL 60607

POSNER, LINDA IRENE, government official; b. Balt., Feb. 6, 1939; d. Morris and Rosabelle (Hankin) Rosen; m. Allan Bernard Posner, Dec. 29, 1957; children: Larry Gregg, Michael Glenn, Robert Ira. BA summa cum laude, Coll. of Notre Dame, 1989. Dir., lectr. Montgomery Ward's Fashion, Modeling and Charm Sch., Md., 1962-66; fashion and pub. rels. dir. Montgomery Ward, Md., 1966-75; freelance writer Balt., 1975-76; pres., co-owner Designer's Circle Ltd., Balt., 1976-78; TV writer, producer Dept. of Def., Ft. Meade, Md., 1979-87; TV mgr. Dept. Def., Ft. Meade, Md., 1980-87, sr. edn. and tng. mgr., 1987-91, performance technologist, 1991-94, multi-media ops. mgr., 1994—; regional dir. The Fashion Group, Balt., 1972-74. Mem. com. March of Dimes, Balt., 1976-78; chairperson Combined Fed. Campaign Com., 1987, U.S. Savs. Bonds, 1989. Dept. of Def. scholar, 1987-88. Mem. Women in Communications, Human Resources Mgmt. Assn., AFTRA. Jewish. Home: 11008 Valley Heights Dr Owings Mills MD 21117-3055

POSPISIL, JOANN, historian, archivist; b. Schulenburg, Tex., Dec. 10, 1947; d. Edwin James and Jossie Annie (Mica) Krametbauer; m. Gerald Joseph Pospisil, Nov. 19, 1966; 1 child, Ryan Joseph. BA summa cum laude, U. Houston, 1992, MA, 1994. Sec. to v.p. Bohler Bros. of Am., Inc., Houston, 1972-75, asst. to corp. sec., 1975-77; archival intern Sul Ross State U. Archives of the Big Bend, Alpine, Tex., 1993; rsch. asst. U. Houston Recovering U.S.-Hispanic Literary Heritage, 1993-94; archive technician Houston Acad. Medicine-Tex. Med. Ctr. Jesse H. Jones Libr., 1995—; task force mem., rsch. cons. Houston Urban Coun., 1993; mem. adv. bd. Tex. Hist. Records, Austin, 1996. Contbr. articles to profl. jours. Sec. handbook com. Clay Road Bapt. Parent-Tchr. Orgn., Houston, 1980-81; coord. Houston Police Dept., Houstonians on Watch, 1982-91; sec., membership chair, libr. aide Spring Branch Ind. Sch. Dist. Parent-Tchr. Assn., Houston, 1983-89; presenter geographical and cultural topics to classrooms in Spring Br. Elem. Sch., Northbrook H.S., Houston, 1985-95. Recipient Spanish award Houston C.C., 1985, Josephine Del Barto scholarship in history U. Houston, 1989, 90, Helen M. Douthitt scholarship in history, 1990, 91;named Sadie Iola Daniels scholar Assn. for Study of African Am. Life and History, Washington, 1990. Mem. Ctr. for Big Bend Studies, Soc. Southwest Archivists, Tex. Hist. Assn., Tex. Cath. History Assn., West Tex. Hist. Assn., Tex. Oral History Assn., Phi Kappa Phi, Phi Alpha Theta. Home: 9418 Railton Houston TX 77080 Office: HAM/TMC Jesse H Jones Libr Hist Rsch Ctr 1133 M D Anderson Blvd Houston TX 77030

POST, BARBARA JOAN, elementary education educator; b. Passaic, N.J., June 29, 1930; d. John Ward and Florence Barbara (Barnum) Post; m. Edward Wayne Poppele, Apr. 10, 1954 (dec. Mar. 1978); children: E. Scott Poppele, Sara Elizabeth Poppele, Andrew John Poppele. BSE, William Paterson Coll., 1953; cert. in counseling, Rutgers U., 1981; postgrad., Columbia U., 1983, Northeastern U., 1983. Cert. tchr., N.J. Elem. tchr. Cen. Sch., Glen Ridge, N.J., 1953-55, Middletown (N.J.) Village Sch., 1956, Our Lady of Perpetual Help, Highlands, N.J., 1981-85; reading tchr. Monmouth Reading Ctr., Long Branch, N.J., 1985; tchr. gifted/talented Harmony Sch., Middletown, 1987-88; edn. coord. for Monmouth County Nat. Coun. on Alcoholism, Freehold, N.J., 1988-89; coord. math./sci. consortium Brookdale Community Coll., Lincroft, N.J., 1989-90; tchr., owner Learning Post and Creative Garden of Art for Children, Middletown, 1991—; dir. art Hillel Sch., Ocean, N.J., 1991—; dir.-owner Learning Post, Middletown, 1986—; art tchr. Art Alliance of Monmouth County, Red Bank, N.J., 1986-88. Author: (poem) The Lift, 1988 (short story) Sarah-Grand, 1984, Hooked on the Classics, 1988; artist (program cover) Country Christmas, 1990, 91. Demonstrator Family Reading Fair, Lincroft, 1989; participant Muscular Dystrophy Telethon, Eatontown, N.J., 1986. Mem. AAUW (tchr., mentor for teen women 1989-92, Appreciation award 1989-90), Nat. Soc. DAR (chairperson 1961-62), N.J. Shore Rose Soc. (exhibitor, 2d and 3d prize for roses 1986). Republican. Presbyterian. Home: 14 Oakland St Red Bank NJ 07701-1102

POST, CLAUDIA, messenger service executive; b. Phila., May 17, 1947; d. Alexander Michael and Florence (Sidransky) P.; m. Claude Gabay, May 1972 (div. Mar. 1982); children: Philippe, Nicholas. BS in Edn., Athens Coll., 1969; postgrad., Temple U., 1969. Sr. acct. exec. Purolator Courier, Phila., 1983-86; regional sales mgr. TNT Skypak, Phila., 1986-88; gen. mgr. Heaven Sent Courier, Phila., 1988-89; pres. Diamond Courier Svc., Phila., 1990—; pres. CP & Co., Phila., 1993—; spkr. in field. Mentor womens Enterprise Resource Ctr.; appointee Mayors Task Force on Bicycle Safety, Phila.; bd. dirs. Small Bus. Coun. Greater Phila. C. of C.; exec. dir. Kensington H.S. Hospitality Charter; active Phila. Convention and Visitors Bur. Named Small Bus. Person of Yr., U.S. Small Bus. Adminstrn., Phila., 1994, Women to Watch, Working Women Mag. and Bus. Phila., 1994. Mem. Nat. Assn. Women Bus. Owners, Messenger Courier Assn. the Americas (bd. dirs., chair spl. projects and awards, co-chair membership com., editl. com.), Mail Systems Mgmt. Assn. (pres.), forum Exec. Women, Del. Valley Bicycle Coalition, PhilaPride, Ctr. City Proprietors. Home: 253 Croyden Rd Cheltenham PA 19012 Office: Diamond Courier Svc Inc 417 N 4th St Philadelphia PA 19123

POST, EMILY (ELIZABETH LINDLEY POST), author; b. Englewood, N.J., May 7, 1920; d. Allen L. and Elizabeth (Ellsworth) Lindley; m. George E. Cookman, 1941 (dec. 1943); 1 child, Allen C.; m. William G. Post, Aug. 5, 1944; children: William G., Lucinda Post Senning, Peter L. Grad. high sch. Dir. Emily Post Inst., 1965—. Author: Emily Post's Book of Etiquette for Young People, 1968, Wonderful World of Weddings, 1970, Please Say Please, 1972, Emily Post's Etiquette, 1965, rev. edit. 1992, The Complete Book of Entertaining, 1981, Emily Post's Complete Book of Wedding Etiquette, 1982, rev. edit., 1991, Emily Post Talks with Teens about Manners and Etiquette, 1986, Emily Post on Weddings, 1987, Emily Post on Entertaining, 1987, Emily Post on Etiquette, 1987, Emily Post on Invitations and Letters, 1990, Emily Post on Business Etiquette, 1990, Emily Post on Second Weddings, 1991, Emily Post's Wedding Planner, rev. edit., 1991, Emily Post's Table Manners For Today: Advice For Every Dining Occasion, 1994, Emily Post on Guests and Hosts, 1994; contbg. editor: Good Housekeeping Mag. Republican. Episcopalian. Office: Good Housekeeping Hearst Corp 959 8th Ave New York NY 10019-3767

POST, MARKIE, actress; b. Palo Alto, Calif., Nov. 4, 1950; d. Richard and Marylee Post; m. Michael Ross; 1 child, Kate. BA, Lewis and Clark Coll. Researcher TV game show Split Second; assoc. producer game show Double Dare, 1976-77; actress, 1977—. Actress: (stage prodns.) Joe Egg, The Fantastiks, The Hairy Ape, Guys and Dolls, (TV shows) Masquerade Party, Frankie and Annette - the Second Time Around, (TV series) Semi-Tough, 1980, The Gangster Chronicles, 1981, The Fall Guy, 1982-85, Night Court, 1985-92, Hearts Afire, 1992-95, (TV movies) Not Just Another Affair, 1982, Triple Cross, 1986, Glitz, 1988, Tricks of the Trade, 1988. Mem. AFTRA, Screen Actors Guild. *

POST, ROSE ELIZABETH, retired elementary education educator; b. New Kensington, Pa., Aug. 26, 1925; d. Vincent Capo and Josephine Elizabeth (Demio) Capo-Dickson; m. Francis V. Post, Mar. 4, 1947 (dec. Oct. 1982); children: Bradley, David, Claudia Jo, James C., Laura Rose. BS in Edn. cum laude, U. Pitts., 1963, MEd cum laude, 1965. Cert. tchr.; metric system specialist. Lectr. Pa. State U., 1966-90; tchr. New Kensington-Arnold Schs., 1967-96; elem. math. chairperson, head dept. New Kensington, 1978-93. Author Elem. Metric Course of Study, 1978. Mem. Bus. and Profl. Women's Club, New Kensington, 1989—, sec.; mem., del. Quota Club New Kensington, 1987—. Mem. NEA, Pa. State Edn. Assn., New Kensington Edn. Assn., Pi Lamba Theta.

POST, ROSE ZIMMERMAN, newspaper columnist; b. Morganton, N.C., Oct. 2, 1926; d. Samuel Sinai and Anna (Pliskin) Zimmerman; m. Edward Martin Post, July 8, 1947; children: David Bruce, Phyllis Post Lebowitz, Samuel Michael, Jonathan Alan, Anna Susan. BA, U. N.C., Greensboro, 1948; postgrad., U. N.C., 1972-74; LittD (hon.), Catawba Coll., 1981. Reporter Salisbury (N.C.) Post, 1951-83, columnist, 1983—; adj. prof. journalism Catawba Coll., Salisbury, 1988-89. Mem. Temple Israel PTA, Salisbury, 1950-80s; bd. dirs. Nat. Coun. Jewish Women; various offices numerous orgns. Recipient Ernie Pyle award Scripps Howard News, 1989, O Henry award N.C. AP News Coun., 1991, 92, 95, N.C. Working Press Excellence in Writing award, 1988, 89, 90, 93; named Citizen of Yr. Salisbury Civitan Club, 1976, Woman of Achievement Salisbury B&PW, 1971, N.C. Journalism Hall of Fame, 1996. Mem. AAUW, NCCJ, Nat. Assn. Newspaper Columnists (1st pl. for gen. columns 1994), N.C. Press Women (sec. 1983, 2d v.p. 1984, 1st v.p. 1983, pres. 1986), N.C. Press Club. Democrat. Jewish. Home: 125 E Corriher Ave Salisbury NC 28144-2427 Office: Salisbury Post 131 W Innes St Salisbury NC 28144-4338

POSTON, ANN GENEVIEVE, psychotherapist, nurse; b. Sioux City, Iowa, July 28, 1936; d. Frank Earl and Ella Marie (Stanton) Gales; m. Gerald Connell Poston, June 27, 1959; children: Gregory, Mary Ann, Susan. BSN, Briar Cliff Coll., 1958; MA, U. Mo., 1978; postgrad., Family Inst. of Kansas City, Inc., 1989-91. RN, Kans., Mo.; lic. counselor, Mo. Staff nurse, sr. team leader St. Joseph Mercy Hosp., Sioux City, 1958-59; head nurse St. Anthony's Hosp., Rock Island, Ill., 1960, charge nurse, 1966-69; charge nurse St. Mary's Hosp., Mpls., 1970-71, North Kansas City (Mo.) Hosp., 1972-73, Tri-County Mental Health Ctr., North Kansas City, 1973-79; psychotherapist VA Med. Ctr., Kansas City, 1979-84, Leavenworth, Kans., 1984-85; psychotherapist The Kans. Inst., Olathe, 1985-95; psychotherapist, marriage and family therapist Psychiatry Assocs., Chartered, Overland Park, Kans., 1994—; cons. Synergy House, Parkville, Mo., 1974-75, North Kansas City Hosp., 1978-79, VA Hosps., Kansas City and Leavenworth, 1979-85, Cath. Charities, Kansas City, 1983-87, Olathe Med. Ctr., 1985-95, Humana Med. Ctr. Overland Park, Kans., 1986-95, St. Joseph Med. Ctr., Kansas City, Mo., 1990-95; psychotherapist, marriage & famiy therapist Cath. Charities, Kansas City, Mo., 1996—, Shawnee Mission (Kans.) Med. Ctr., 1996—. Author, presenter (video) Depression & Suicide, 1980. Third officer King's Daus., Moline, Ill., 1960-69; campaign worker Rep. Party, Moline, 1963-68; community asst. New Mark Community Affairs, Kansas City, 1972-76; nursing rep. Combined Fed. Campaign, Kansas City, 1982; coord. mental health program com. Midwest Health Congress, Kansas City, 1981. Mem. ACA, ANA (cert.), Internat. Assn. for Marriage and Family Counselors, Am. Assn. Marriage and Family Therapy (clinical), Nat. Bd. Cert. Counselors, Mo. Assn. Marriage and Family Therapy, Sigma Theta Tau. Roman Catholic.

POSTON, IONA, nursing educator; b. Charleston, S.C., Sept. 11, 1951; d. Fulton C. and Laura M. (Wolfe) P. BSN, Med. U. of S.C., 1973; MSN, Med. Coll. of Ga., 1979; PhD, U. Fla., 1988. Instr. Clemson (S.C.) U., 1979-81; asst. prof. U. N.C., Greensboro, 1981-85; assoc. in nursing Fla. State U., Tallahassee, 1989; assoc. prof. East Carolina U., Greenville, N.C., 1989—. Contbr. articles to profl. jours. Alden B. Dow Creativity Ctr. fellow, 1993; HBO & Co. nurse scholar, 1995. Mem. So. Nursing Rsch. Soc., NLN, Soc. Pediat. Nurses, AAUP, Sigma Theta Tau.

POSTON, MARTHA ANNE, author, researcher; b. Eden, N.C., Feb. 6, 1936; d. Charlie and Cornelia (Leisure) Hopper. BS in Human Resources, N.C. A&T State U., 1972; AS in Computer Sci., Rutledge Coll., 1985. Monogramist dept. store, Winston-Salem, N.C., 1966-72; ext. officer Peace Corps, Jamaica, 1972-74; vol. Peace Corps, Liberia, 1974-78; edn. material specialist Liberian Ministry Agr., 1978-81. Author: In the Service of My God, 1991, editor Human Resource Newsletter, 1979-81. Active Save the Children, Westport, Conn., 1989—; primary tchr. LDS Ch., Atlanta, 1993—. Recipient award Beyond War, Atlanta, 1987. Mem. NAFE, AAUW, Internat. Congress on Arts and Comm. (del. 1994—). Home: 6455 Glenridge Dr Apt 106 Atlanta GA 30328

POSUNKO, BARBARA, retired elementary education educator; b. Newark, July 17, 1938; d. Joseph and Mary (Prystauk) P. BA, Rutgers U., Newark, 1960; MA, Kean Coll., Union, N.J., 1973; teaching cert., Seton Hall U., Newark, 1966. Cert. elem. tchr., reading specialist, N.J. Social case worker Newark City Hosp., 1960-65; elem. tchr. Plainfield (N.J.) Bd. Edn., 1966; elem., jr. and sr. high sch. tchr. minimum basic skills and reading Sayreville (N.J.) Bd. Edn., 1966-82; tchr. Chpt. I and minimum basic skills Sayreville (N.J.) Bd. Edn., Parlin, 1982-95, cooperating tchr. to student tchrs., 1983-95, coord. testing, 1984-95; ret., 1995; sch. coord. for congressionally mandated study of ednl. growth and opportunity, 1991-95; mem. numerous reading coms. Recipient Outstanding Tchr. award N.J. Gov.'s Tchr. Recognition Program, 1988. Mem. NEA, Internat. Reading Assn., N.J. Reading Assn., N.J. Edn. Assn. Home: 17 Drake Rd Mendham NJ 07945-1805

POSUNKO, LINDA MARY, retired elementary education educator; b. Newark, Dec. 24, 1942; d. Joseph and Mary (Prystauk) P. BA, Newark State Coll., Union, N.J., 1964; MA, Kean Coll., Union, 1974. Cert. permanent elem. tchr., supr., prin., N.J. Elem. tchr. Roselle (N.J.) Bd. Edn., 1964-65; elem. tchr. Garwood (N.J.) Bd. Edn., 1965-92, head tchr., 1974-76, 79-81, head tchr. elem. and early childhood edn., tchr. 1st grade, 1992-95; ret., 1995; cooperating tchr. to student tchrs.; instr. non-English speaking students and children with learning problems; mem. affirmative action, sch. resource coms.; conductor in-svc. workshops on early childhood devel. practices, 1993. Recipient honor cert. Union County Conf. Tchrs. Assn., 1972-73, The Garwood award N.J. Gov.'s Tchr. Recognition Program, 1983, 88, Outstanding Tchr. award N.J. Gov.'s Tchr. Recognition Program, 1988; nominee N.J. Gov.'s Tchr. Recognition award, 1993-94. Mem. ASCD, NEA, Internat. Reading Assn. (bd. dirs. suburban coun.), N.J. Edn. Assn., Garwood Tchrs. Assn. (sec., v.p., pres.), High/Scope Ednl. Found. Home: 17 Drake Rd Mendham NJ 07945-1805

POTASH, JANE, artist; b. Phila., May 3, 1937; d. Norval and Mary (Fox) Levy; m. Charles Potash, Jan. 21, 1962; children: Andrew Samuel, Dorothy Frances. BA, U. Pa., 1959. One-woman shows include Storelli Gallery, Phila., 1979, Langman Gallery, Jenkintown, Pa., 1979, 81, Phoenix Gallery, N.Y., 1981, A.R.T. Beasley Gallery, San Diego, 1986, Vorpal, N.Y., 1987; exhibited in group shows at Wayne Art Ctr., 1971, Lancaster Summer Arts Festival, 1971, 72, 74, Cooperstown (N.Y.) Nat. Juried Show, 1971, Abington Art Ctr., 1972-74, Phila. Art Alliance, 1975, Allentown Art Mus., 1976, Pa. Acad. Fine Arts, 1978, 80, Butcher and More Gallery, Phila., 1981, Wachs Davis Gallery, Washington, Shayne Gallery, Montreal, Can., 1982, Montreal Mus. Fine Arts, 1982, Source Gallery, San Francisco, 1983, Langman Gallery, 1987, Virginia Miller Gallery, Coral Gables, Fla., 1990; represented in collections at Fox Companies, Blue Cross, Blue Shield of Pa., Subaru, N.J., Nordstrom Stores, Calif., Beaver Ins. Co., San Francisco; represented in pvt. collections in U.S. and Can. Recipient Best of Show award Old York Rd. Studio: 220 Old York Rd Jenkintown PA 19046-3244

POTASH, JEREMY WARNER, public relations executive; b. Monrovia, Calif., June 30, 1946; d. Fenwick Bryson and Joan Antony (Blair) Warner; m. Stephen Jon Potash, Oct. 19, 1969; 1 child, Aaron Warner. AA, Citrus Coll., 1965; BA, Pomona Coll., 1967. With Forbes Mag., N.Y.C., 1967-69, Japan External Trade Orgn., San Francisco, 1970-75; v.p., co-founder Potash & Co. Pub. Rels., Oakland, Calif., 1980-87; pres. Potash & Co. Pub. Rels., San Francisco, 1987—; founding exec. dir. Calif.-S.E. Asia Bus. Coun., Oakland, 1991—; exec. dir. Customs Brokers and Forwarders Assn., San Francisco, 1990—. Editor: Southeast Asia Environmental Directory, 1994; editor: Southeast Asia Infrastructure Directory, 1995-96. Bd. dirs. Judah L. Magnes Mus., Berkeley, 1981-94, co-founder docent program, 1980, pres. Women's Guild, 1980-81; bd. dirs. Temple Sinai, Oakland, 1984-86; pres. East Bay region Women's Am. Orgn. for Rehab. Through Tng., 1985-86. Mem. Am. Soc. Assn. Execs., World Trade Club San Francisco, Oakland Women's Lit. Soc., Book Club Calif. Office: Potash & Co Pub Rels 1946 Embarcadero Oakland CA 94606-5213

POTASH, VELLA ROSENTHAL, lawyer, educator; b. Balt., Oct. 3, 1937; d. Joseph and Rona (Glasner) Rosenthal; m. Michael Donald Potash, June 20, 1957 (div. Aug., 1982); children: James Bennet, John Lawrence. BA in Edn., Goucher Coll., 1959; JD, U. Balt., 1974. Bar: Md. 1975, Pa. 1975, Family Mediation Fla., 1992. Tchr. Balt. Sch. System, 1959-62; pub. rels. dir. Citizens Planning & Housing Assn., Balt., 1968-69; asst. pub. defender Pub. Defender's Office, Balt., 1975-78; lawyer pvt. practice, Balt., 1978-82, Guardian Ad Litem Program Family Law Sect., Broward County, Fla., 1987—; family mediator pvt. practice, Broward County, 1992—. Mem. NOW (bd. dirs., chairperson women's ctr. Boca Raton), Md. Bar, Pa. Bar, Broward County Bar Assn. (assoc.), So. Fla. Goucher Alumnae Assn. Home: 2900 N Palmaire Dr Apt 301 Pompano Beach FL 33069

POTEET, MARY JANE, computer scientist; b. Raleigh, N.C., May 26, 1946; d. Charles William and Geraldine Lucile (Adams) Hampton; m. William Walter Schubert, Dec. 30, 1967 (div. June 1979); children: Kristen, Stephen, Betsy, Kathryn; m. H. Wesley Poteet, Mar. 21, 1991 (div. Mar. 1996). BA in Math., Park Coll., 1967. Programmer U. Mo. Med. Ctr., Columbia, 1968-72, City and County of Denver, 1979-80; sr. sys. programmer Citicorp Person to Person, Denver, 1980-82; sys. support rep. Software AG, NA, Denver, 1982-83; prin. info. sysm. specialist Idaho Nat. Engring. Lab., EG&G, Idaho Falls, 1983-89; adv. svcs. specialist IBM Profl. Svcs., Albuquerque, 1989-91; field mgr. IBM Svc., Boulder, Colo., 1991-93; project mgr. IBM Cons. & Svcs. SW, Denver, 1993—; presenter career workshop for girls No. Colo. U., Greeley, 1993. Leader Girl Scout Am., Pocatello, Idaho, Columbia, Mo., 1969-79, Idaho Falls, 1986-89, cluster leader, Rigby, Idaho, 1988-89; active Albuquerque Civic Chorus, 1990-91, Luth. Ch. Coun., 1994-96; bd. dirs. LWV, Pocatello, 1977-79, 84-85, pres., 1978-79; bd. dirs. Luth. Ch. Women, Pocatello, 1978-79; youth advisor Luth. Ch., Idaho Falls, 1984-89; tchr. Sunday sch. local ch., Albuquerque, 1990-91; youth com. chair local ch., Boulder, Colo., 1994-96; tchr. 7th and 8th grade Sunday sch., 1993-96, mem. ch. choir, 1995-96. Mem. AAUW. Lutheran. Home: 3916 W 104th Pl Westminster CO 80030-2402

POTOKER, ELAINE SHARON, international trade services company executive, business educator; b. Bklyn.; children: Kristen Aimee, Beth Anne. BA cum laude, SUNY, Potsdam, 1965; MAT in Spanish Lang. and Lit., U. Chgo., 1968; PhD, Ohio State U., 1994. Cert. tchr., Pa., Ill., N.Y. Tchr. New Trier H.S., Northfield, Ill., Commack (N.Y.) H.S.; itinerant instr. ESL program Edinboro (Pa.) State Coll., 1976-78; coord. internat. sales divsn., area mgr. Ctrl. Am. Reed Mfg. Co., Erie, 1978-84; instr./advisor mktg. Gannon U., Erie, Pa., 1987-89; lectr./advisor Spanish, Level III Pa. State U., Erie, 1988-91; mgr. import/export agy. svcs. Interloqui, Erie, 1984—; chair divsn. bus. Ohio Dominican Coll., Columbus, 1994-95; judge moot court competition Case Western Reserve U.; lectr. in field; condr. workshops in field. Asst. editor Comparative Edn. Rev., 1991-93; contbr. articles to profl. jours. Mem. Multicultural Task Force, Ohio State U., Columbus, 1993-94; mem. internat. bus. edn. com. Cleve. World Trade Assn., exec. bd., 1989-91; bd. dirs. Hispanic Coun., Erie, 1985-88. Mem. Am. Assn. Internat. Execs. in Export Mgmt., Rotary (chair pub. rels. com., sch. liaison person 1991-92), Phi Kappa Phi. Office: Ohio Cominican College Divsn of Bus 1216 Sunbury Rd Columbus OH 43219-2086

POTOPE, HEATHER ANN, elementary school educator; b. Easton, Pa., Mar. 25, 1970; d. Francis Nicholas and Wilhelmina Jean (Richebacher) Donnelly; m. Michael James Potope, June 26, 1993. AA in Elem. Edn., Northampton C.C., Bethlehem, Pa., 1990; BE, Kutztown U., 1992. Cert. elem. tchr., Pa. Coiler Martin Guitar, Nazareth, Pa., 1992; assoc. tchr. Nazareth Sch. Dist., 1992-94, long term substitute, 1995—, substitute tchr., 1995—; mem. Strategic Planning Com., Nazareth, 1994—. Social mem. Bushkill Fire Co., Nazareth, 1992-94. Mem. ASCD. Republican.

POTT, SANDRA KAY, finance company executive; b. Denver, Apr. 1, 1946; d. Sanford N. and Mary Helen (Davis) Groendyke; m. Joel Frederic Pott, Mar. 7, 1970; children: Eric Christopher, Jessica Elizabeth. BA in English, Ea. Mich. U., 1969. CFP, Mich. Account exec. Dean Witter Reynolds, Troy, Mich., 1984-93, assoc. v.p., 1993—. Mem. AAUW (bd. dirs. 1977-83), Nat. Assn. Women Bus. Owners (bd. dirs. 1994—), econ. devel. com. 1991—), Royal Oak League Women Voters (bd. dirs. 1977-83). Office: Dean Witter Reynolds 100 W Big Beaver Ste 500 Troy MI 48099

POTTER, ALICE CATHERINE, clinical laboratory scientist; b. Oil City, Pa., June 24, 1928; d. Howard Taylor and Hilda Marian (Lewis) P. BA, U. Findlay, 1949; postgrad., Springfield (Ohio) City Hosp., 1949-50. Cert. med. technician Am. Soc. Clin. Pathologists; cert. clin. lab. scientist. Med. technologist Mercy Hosp., Springfield, 1950-54, Oil City Hosp., 1954-67; staff med. technologist Thomas Jefferson U. Hosp., Phila., 1968-83, sr. med. technologist, 1983—. Vol. Acad. Natural Scis., Phila., 1995—. Mem. Am. Soc. Clin. Lab. Scientists, Pa. Soc. Clin. Lab. Scientists (membership chmn. Delaware Valley chpt. 1977-78, chmn. pub. rels. 1982-94, bd. dirs. 1989-91, pres.-elect 1991-92, pres. 1992-93, Scrimshaw award 1992). Republican. Home: 1701 Wallace St Philadelphia PA 19130-3312

POTTER, DEBORAH ANN, news correspondent, educator; b. Hagerstown, Md., June 10, 1951; d. Peter R. and H. Louise (McDevitt) P.; m. Robert H. Witten, May 1, 1982; children: Cameron, Evan. BA, U. N.C., 1972; MA, Am. U., 1977. Assignment editor Sta. WMAL-TV, Washington, 1972-73, prodr., 1973-74; reporter Voice of Am., Washington, 1974-77; anchor Sta. KYW, Phila., 1977-78, CBS Radio, N.Y.C., 1978-81; White House corr. CBS

News, Washington, 1981-85, state dept. corr., 1985-87, congl. corr., 1987-89, environ. corr., 1989-91; contbg. corr. 48 Hours, 1989-90; host Nightwatch CBS News, Washington, 1991; Washington corr. Cable News Network, Washington, 1991-94; asst. prof. Sch. Comm. Am. U., Washington, 1994-95; dir. Poynter Election Project, St. Petersburg, Fla., 1995—; faculty mem. Poynter Inst. Media Studies. Co-author: Poynter Election Handbook; host (video prodn.) Beyond the Spotted Owl, 1993, Health Beat, 1994, Risk Reporting, 1995. Mem. adv. coun. Environ. Journalism Ctr., Radio and TV News Dirs. Found., Washington, 1994—; lay reader St. Alban's Episc. Ch., Washington, 1988-89. Mem. Radio TV News Dirs. Assn., Soc. of Environ. Journalists, Investigative Reporters and Editors, Assn. for Edn. in Journalism and Mass Comm., U. N.C. Alumni Assn. (bd. dirs. 1990-93, Disting. Young Alumna award 1990). Office: Poynter Institute 801 3rd St S Saint Petersburg FL 33701

POTTER, ELIZABETH STONE, academic administrator; b. Mount Kisco, N.Y., Oct. 18, 1931; d. Ralph Emerson and Elizabeth (Fleming) Stone; m. Harold David Potter, Aug. 1, 1953; children: David Stone, Nicholas Fleming. BA, Wellesley Coll., 1953. Tchr. Spence Sch., N.Y.C., 1960-62; from audiovisual head to asst. to mid. sch. head Chapin Sch., N.Y.C., 1970—, sci. tchr., sci. coord., 1970—; evaluator NYSAIS, N.Y.C., 1994-95. Mem. NSTA, ATIS. Home: 1160 Fifth Ave New York NY 10029-6936 Office: Chapin Sch 100 E End Ave New York NY 10028

POTTER, EMMA JOSEPHINE HILL, language educator; b. Hackensack, N.J., July 18, 1921; d. James Silas and Martha Loretta (Pyle) Hill; m. James H. Potter, Mar. 26, 1949. AB cum laude with honors in Classics (scholar), Alfred (N.Y.) U., 1943; AM, Johns Hopkins U., 1946. Tchr. Latin, Balt. County Pub. Schs., 1943-44; instr. French, Spanish, Balt. Poly. Inst., 1950-83; instr. Spanish adult edn. classes, 1946-48; treas. Bruno-Potter Inc., acctg. Trustee James Harry Potter Gold Medal, ASME, Martha Pyle Hill Commemorative Plaque at Chenango County Coun. Arts, Norwich, N.Y. Donor Commemorative plaque in honor of Martha Pyle Hill to Chenango County Coun. Arts, 1996. Mem. Johns Hopkins U., Alfred U. alumni assns., Internat. Platform Assn., Johns Hopkins U. Faculty Club. Democrat. Home: 419 3rd Ave Avon By The Sea NJ 07717-1244

POTTER, JUNE ANITA, small business owner; b. La Crosse, Wis., Jan. 22, 1938; d. Christian John and Ethel Marie (Stafslien) Stefferud; m. James Oscar Potter, June 18, 1961; children: Jill Potter Rutlin, Todd. BA in Home Econs., St. Olaf Coll., Northfield, Minn., 1960; postgrad., N.Y. Sch. Interior Design, 1964; MS in Edn., U. Wis., Menomonie, 1977. Sr. high home econs. tchr., FHA advisor Tomah (Wis.) High Sch., 1960-64, Black River Falls (Wis.) High Sch., 1971-83; freelance interior designer Warrens, Wis., 1964—; ptnr., mgr. James Potter Cranberry Marsh, Inc., Warrens, 1968—. Co-pubr.: Warrens Centennial Book, 1968, Cranberry Centennial Book, 1989. Active various charitable and church orgns.; bd. dirs. Warrens Cranberry Festival, 1984—; mem. Warrens Area Bus. Assn., 1990—; sec. Wis. Cranberry Bd., Inc., 1990—; sec. Warren Mills Cemetery Assn., 1993—; mem. com. Wis. Alice in Dairyland Finale, 1993—; mem. Jellystone Campground and Ministry; found. bd. Wis. Exec. Residence, 1994—. Mem. AAUW (v.p. 1989—), NAFE, Wis. State Cranberry Growers Assn. (pub. rels. com. 1994—, mem. centennial com. 1988—), Tomah Pky. Garden Club, Beta Sigma Phi (officer, com. mem. 1962—, Nat. Order or Rose 1983, Silver Cir. award 1985, Girl of Yr.). Lutheran. Home and Office: RR 2 Box 12 Warrens WI 54666-9501

POTTER, LILLIAN FLORENCE, business executive secretary; b. Montreal, Que., Can., Oct. 19, 1912; came to U.S., 1934; naturalized citizen.; d. Thomas Joseph and Lily Rose (Robertson) Quirk; m. Theodore Edward Potter, July 20, 1932 (dec. Apr. 1980); children: Peter Edward, Stephen Thomas. Grad. high sch., Montreal, 1929, grad., 1931. Sr. sec. S.D. Warren div. Scott Paper Co., Westbrook, Maine, 1955-69, editor indsl. publ. S.D. Warren div., 1969-72; editor Nat. Antiques Rev. mag., Portland, Maine, 1972-77; exec. sec. Humboldt Portland Litho div. Humboldt Nat. Graphics, Inc., Fortuna, Calif., 1977—; free lance writer Guy Gannett Pub. Co., Portland, 1960-64. Author: (children's book) Once Upon an Autumn, 1984 (state 1st pl. award, nat. 3d pl. award), (antiques and collectibles) A Re-Introduction to Silver Overlay on Glass and Ceramics, 1992; co-author: (textbook, tchrs. manual) Foundations of Patient Care, 1981; asst. editor, N.E. dist. The Secretary mag., Profl. Secs. Internat., 1960-62; editor Maine Chpt. Bull., 1963-64. Recipient George Washington Honors medal Freedoms Found., Valley Forge, Pa., 1964, Sec. of Yr. award Portland chpt. Profl. Secs. Internat., 1967, Outstanding Svc. award State of Maine Sesquicentennial, 1970, Outstanding Svc. award Island Pond (Vt.) Hist. Soc. 1978. Mem. Maine Media Women (pres. 1970-71, Woman of Yr. 1973, Communicator of Achievement plaque and prize 1991), Maine Writers and Pubs. Alliance, Woman's Lit. Union, Portland Lyric Theater, Island Pond Hist. Soc., Jones Mus. Glass and Ceramics, Westbrook Woman's Club, OES (past matron, past pres.). Republican. Episcopalian. Home: 80 Payson St Portland ME 04102-2851

POTTICARY, ANN LOUISE, secondary school educator; b. Breckenbridge, Minn., Oct. 11, 1943; d. Herman and Ann Louise (Solmonson) Nordin; m. James F. Potticary; children: Billie Potticary-Thorne, Richard Dean, Heidi Potticary Pickerill. BS, S.D. State U., 1965; M in Liberal Arts, So. Meth. U., 1990; postgrad., U. Tex., Dallas, 1996—. Cert. tchr., Tex. Math. tchr. Watertown (S.D.) Jr. H.S., 1965-66, Hopkins (Minn.) North Jr. H.S., 1979-80, John Ireland Parochial Sch., Hopkins, 1980-82, Bishop Lynch H.S., Dallas, 1983—. Master lector Diocese of Dallas, 1992—; mem. Dallas Arborteum, 1995—. Mem. Nat. Coun. Tchrs. Math., GDCTM, NTA3PMT. Republican. Roman Catholic. Home: 10122 Bridgegate Ct Dallas TX 75243-5014

POTTORFF, JO ANN, state legislator; b. Wichita, Kans., Mar. 7, 1936; d. John Edward McCluggage and Helen Elizabeth (Alexander) Ryan; m. Gary Nial Pottorff; children: Michael Lee, Gregory Nial. BA, Kansas State U., 1957; MA, St. Louis U., 1969. Elem. tchr. Pub. Sch., Keats and St. George, 1957-59; cons., elem. specialist Mid Continent Regional Edn. Lab., Kansas City, Mo., 1971-73; cons. Poindexter Assocs., Wichita, 1975; campaign mgr. Garner Shriver Congl. Camp, Wichita, 1976; interim dir. Wichita Area Rape Ctr., 1977; conf. coord. Biomedical Synergistics Inst., Wichita, 1977-79; real estate sales asst. Chester Kappelman Group, Wichita, 1979—; state rep. State of Kans., Topeka, 1985—. Mem. sch. bd. Wichita Pub. Schs., 1977-85; bd. dirs. Edn. Consol. and Improvement Act Adv. com., Kans. Found. for the Handicapped; mem. Children and Youth Adv. com. (bd. dirs.); active Leadership Kans.; chairperson women's network Nat. Conf., State Legislators; mem. Wichita Children's Home Bd. Recipient Disting. Svc. award Kans. Assn. Sch. Bds., 1983, Outstanding Svc. to Sch. Children of Nation award Coun. Urban Bds., 1984, awards Gov.'s Conf. for Prevention of Child Abuse and Neglect, Kans. Assn. Reading. Mem. Leadership Am. Alumnae (bd. dirs., sec.), Found. for Agr. in Classroom (bd. dirs.), Jr. League, Vet. Aux. (pres.), Bd. Nat. State Art Agys., Rotary, Ky. Assn. Rehab. Facilities (Ann. award), Nat. Order Women in Legislature (past bd. dirs.), Rotary, Chi Omega (pres.). Office: Chester Kappelman Group PO Box 8036 Wichita KS 67208-0036

POTTS, ANNIE, actress; b. Nashville, Oct. 28, 1952. Student, Calif. Inst. of Arts; BFA, Stephens Coll. Appeared in films including Corvette Summer, 1978, King of the Gypsies, 1978, Heartaches, 1982, Crime of Passion, 1984, Ghostbusters, 1984, Stick, 1985, Pretty in Pink, 1986, Jumpin' Jack Flash, 1986, Pass the Ammo, 1988, Who's Harry Crumb, 1989, Ghostbusters II, 1989, Texasville, 1990, Breaking the Rules, 1992, Toy Story (voice only) 1995; plays include Richard III, Charley's Aunt, Cymbeline; TV appearances include Black Market Baby, 1977, Flatbed Annie and Sweetie Pie: Lady Truckers, 1979, Cowboy, 1983, Why Me?, 1984, Ladies in Waiting; TV series include Goodtime Girls, 1980, Designing Women, 1986-1993, Love and War, 1993-95 (Emmy nomination, Lead Actress - Comedy Series, 1994), Dangerous Minds, 1996. Spokesperson Women for the Arthritis Found.; mem. aux. bd. MADD. *

POTTS, BARBARA JOYCE, historical society executive; b. L.A., Feb. 18, 1932; d. Theodore Thomas and Helen Mae (Kelley) Elledge; m. Donald A. Potts, Dec. 27, 1953; children: Tedd, Douglas, Dwight, Laura. AA, Graceland Coll., 1951; grad., Radiol. Tech. Sch., 1953; grad. program for sr. execs. in state and local govt., Harvard U., 1989. Radiol. technician Independence (Mo.) Sanitarium and Hosp., 1953, 58-59, Mercy Hosp., Balt., 1954-55; city coun. mem.-at-large City of Independence, 1978-82, mayor, 1982-90; exec. dir. Jackson County Hist. Soc., 1991—; chmn. Mid-Am. Regional Coun., Kansas City, Mo., 1984-85; bd. dirs. Mo. Mcpl. League, Jefferson City, 1982-90, v.p., 1986-87, pres., 1987, 88; chmn. Mo. Commn. on Local Govt. Cooperation, 1985-90. Author: Independence, 1985. Mem. Mo. Gov.'s Conf. Edn., 1976, Independence Charter Rev. Bd., 1977; bd. dirs. Hope House Shelter Abused Women, Independence, 1982—, Vis. Nurses Assn., 1990-93, Mid-Continent Coun. U.S. Girl Scouts, 1991-95; pres. Child Placement Svcs., Independence, 1972-89, Greater Kansas City region NCCJ, 1990—; trustee Independence Regional Health Ctr., 1982-90, 94—, Park Coll., 1989—, chmn. bd. trustees, 1995—; mem. Nat. Women's Polit. Caucus, 1978—; mem. adv. bd. Greater Mo. Focus on Leadership, mem. steering com., 1989—; bd. mem. Independence Cmty. Found., 1990—; bd. mem. Harry S. Truman Libr. Inst., 1995—. Recipient George Lehr Meml. award for community svc., 1989, Woman of Achievement award Mid-Continent coun. Girl Scouts U.S.A., 1983, 75th Anniversary Women of Achievement award Mid-Continent coun. Girl Scouts, 1987, Jane Adams award Hope House, 1984, Community Leadership award Comprehensive Mental Health Svcs., Inc., 1984, 90, Graceland Coll. Alumni Disting. Svc. award 1991, Disting. Citizen award Independence C. of C., 1993, Outstanding Community Svc. award Jackson County Inter-Agy. Coun., 1994; named Friend of Edn. Indpendence NEA, 1990. Mem. LWV (Community Svc. award 1990), Am. Inst. Pub. Svc. (mem. bd. nominators), Nat. Trust for Hist. Preservation. Mem. Reorganized LDS Ch. Home: 18508 E 30th Ter S Independence MO 64057-1904

POTWIN, JUANITA R., marketing professional, dental hygienist; b. St. Albans, Vt., Oct. 15, 1957; d. Gerald Albert Potwin and Beatrice Julia (Blake) Lamica. Cert. chemistry, N.H. Vo-Tech., Claremont, 1982; AS in Dental Assisting, Champlain Coll., 1984; AS in Dental Hygiene, N.H. Tech. Inst., 1986. Registered dental hygienist ADA. Freelance dental hygienist N.H., 1986—; New Eng. sales dir. Oxyfresh, USA, Spokane, Wash., 1993; exec. sales dir. Oxyfresh, USA, Spokane, 1994-95; N.E. sales dir. Life Sci. Products, St. George, Utah, 1995—. Mem., supporter Am. Humane Assn., Wold Wildlife Fund, The Wilderness Soc. Scholar Dr. David S. Faigel Meml. Found., 1982. Mem. NAFE, VFW, Am. Legion Aux. Home: 263406 Camino de Vista San Juan Capistrano CA 92675 Office: Life Sci Products 321 N Mall Dr Saint George UT 84790

POU, LINDA ALICE, interior designer, architectural designer; b. Huntsville, Ala., Oct. 26, 1942; d. Louis and Lillian Maurice (Garvin) Grabensteder; m. Robert LeRoy Pou, Aug. 27, 1965; children: Susan Caroline, Stephanie Lynn. B of Interior Design, Auburn U., 1964; postgrad., Ecoles D'Art Americaines, 1964. Interior designer Martin Interiors, Huntsville, Ala., 1963, Blance Reeves Interiors, Atlanta, 1964-65, Militare, Atlanta, 1965, Loveman's Dept. Store, Huntsville, Ala., 1966, Southeastern Galleries, Charleston, S.C., 1967; draftsman Brown Engring., Huntsville, Ala., 1967-68, Naval Electronics Systems Command, S.C., 1968, Leland Engrs., Charleston, S.C., 1968-69; owner Drafting Svc., Mobile, Ala., 1977-78, The Design Svc., Prattville, Ala., 1980-92; The Design Svc., Savannah, Ga., 1992—. Composer songs including (adult anthems), Sing for Joy, 1983, Sing Hallelujah to the Lord, He's the Rainbow in My Life, 1984, (children's)ûLord of Harvest, 1984, Sing a Song to the Lord of Earth, 1985, (children's musical) Six Myths of Christmas, 1986; compiler and editor book of poetry, Nana's Legacy. Mem. jr. bd. Florence Crittendon Home for Unwed Mothers, Mobile, Ala., 1977-79, Prattville Planning Commn., 1980-92, chmn., 1985-88, vice-chmn., 1988-92; mem. Prattville Hist. Re-devel. Authority, 1988-89; children's choir dir. 1st United MEth. Ch., 1979-83, 87-89, adminstrv. bd., 1987-89, bldg. commn., 1987-89, trustee, 1990-92; mem. Savannah Symphony Women's Guild, 1993—. Mem. ASCAP, Spinners (treas. 1982-83), Prattville C. of C., Garden Club of Savannah (2nd v.p. 1995-97), Alpha Gamma Delta. Home and Office: 202 E 45th St Savannah GA 31405-2216

POULIN, MARIE-PAULE, Canadian government official; b. Sudbury, Ont., Can., June 21, 1945; d. Alphonse-Emile and Lucille (Ménard) Charette; m. Bernard A. Poulin, May 21, 1977; children: Elaine, Valérie. BA, Laurentian U., Sudbury, 1966; MSW, U. Montréal, Que., Can., 1969; PhD (hon.), Laurentian U., Sudbury, 1995. Lectr. U. Montreal, 1969-70, Coll. of Gen. and Profl. Instrn., Hull, Que., 1972-73; rschr. Ctr. Social Svcs., Hull, 1972-73; interviewer, rschr. French Radio and TV, Ottawa, Ont., 1973-74; prodr. Sta. CBOF-CBC, Ottawa, 1974-78; founder and dir. svcs. in N.E. and N.W. Ont. Sta. CBON (French Network-CBC), Sudbury, 1978-83; exec. dir. regional programming CBC, Ottawa, 1983-84, assoc. v.p. regional broadcasting, 1984-88, sec. gen., 1988-90, v.p. human resources, 1990-92; dep. sec. for comm. and consultation The Privy Coun. Govt. of Can., Ottawa, 1992-93; chmn. Can. Artists and Prodrs. Profl. Rels. Tribunal, Ottawa, 1993—; senator Can. Govt., Ottawa; mem. Senate Standing com. Internal Economy, Budgets and Adminstrn., Nat. Fin., Transport and Comm.; bd. dirs. Cité Collégiale, Ottawa, 1988-91. Commr. for French lang. svcs. Province of Ont., 1986-89; regent U. Sudbury, 1981-83; bd. dirs. Laurentian Hosp., Sudbury, 1980-88, Cambrian Coll.Found., Sudbury, 1983-88; v.p. Art Ctr., Ottawa, 1988-90; pres. Regroupement gens d'affaires, Ottawa, 1991-92. Recipient medal for contbn. to Can. Culture, Coun. of French-Am. Life, 1987, Prix Marcel-Blouin for best morning program in Can., 1983, Profl. Woman of Yr. award Réseau des femmes d'affaires professionnelles, 1990; named Chevalier Ordre de la Pléiade, 1995. Mem. Can.-U.S. Inter-Parliamentary Group, Can.-Japan Inter-Parliamentary Group, Can.-Europe Parliamentary Assn., Can.-France Inter-Parliamentary Assn., Can.-Israel Friendship Group, Can.-Korea Friendship Group, Can.-Italy Friendship Guide, Assn. Grads. of U. Montréal, Can. Circle (exec.). Home: 100 Pretoria Ave, Ottawa, ON Canada K1S 1W9 Office: Senate Can, Ottawa, ON Canada K1A 0A4

POULIOT, ASSUNTA GALLUCCI, retired business school owner and director; b. West Warwick, R.I., Aug. 14, 1937; d. Michael and Angelina (DeCesare) Gallucci; m. Joseph F. Pouliot Jr., July 4, 1961; children: Brenda, Mark, Jill, Michele. BS, U. R.I., 1959, MS, 1971. Bus. tchr. Cranston High Sch., R.I., 1959-61; bus. dept. chmn. Chariho Regional High Sch., Wood River Junction, R.I., 1961-73; instr. U. R.I., Kingston, 1973-78; founder, dir. Ocean State Bus. Inst., Wakefield, R.I., 1977-95; fin. aid cons., 1995—; dir. Fleet Nat. Bank, 1985-91; bd. mgrs. Bank of New Eng., 1984-85; commr. Accrediting Coun. Ind. Colls. and Schs., 1995—; speaker in field. Pres. St. Francis Women's Club, Wakefield, 1975; sec. St. Francis Parish Coun., Wakefield, 1980; mem. Econ. Devel. Commn., Wakefield, 1981-85; mem. South County Hosp. Corp., Wakefield, 1978—; fin. dir. Bus and Profl. Women's Club, Wakefield, 1982-84; chmn. Ladies Golf Charity, 1985-91; mem. Computer Info. Systems Com., Chariho Regional Career and Tech. Ctr.; mem. Galilee Beach Club Assn., R.I. Bus. Edn. Assn. (newsletter editor 1979-81), New Eng. Bus. Coll. Assn. (sec. 1984-86, pres. 1985-87), R.I. Assn. Career and Tech. Schs. (treas., bd. dirs. 1979—), Eastern Bus. Edn. Assn. (conf. leader), Nat. Bus. Edn. Assn. (conf. leader), Career Coll. Assn. (conv. speaker, pub. rels. com., govt. rels. com., membership com., key mem., nominating com., evaluator), Assn. Colls. and Schs. (commr. commn. on postsecondary schs. accreditation 1994—, ednl. cons. 1995—), R.I. Women's Golf Assn., Am. Cancer Soc., U. R.I. Alumi Assn. (Excellence Bus. award 1992), Phi Kappa Phi, Delta Pi Epsilon (pres., newsletter editor). Roman Catholic. Club: Point Judith Country (past ladies golf chmn.). Avocations: golf, gardening. Home: 137 Kenyon Ave Wakefield RI 02879-4242 Office: Ocean State Bus Inst Mariner Sq 140 Point Judith Rd Boxes 1 & 2 Narragansett RI 02882

POULOS-WOOLLEY, PAIGE M., public relations executive; b. Woodland, Calif., Apr. 26, 1958; d. Paul William Jr. and Frances Marie (Gibson) Poulos; m. John Stuart Woolley, Feb. 3, 1990. Student, U. Calif., Davis, 1977-80. Mgr. pub. rels. Somerset Wine Co., N.Y.C. and San Martin, Calif., 1982-88; dir. comm. The Beverage Source, San Francisco, 1988-89, Rutherford (Calif.) Hill Winery, 1989-90; pres. Paige Poulos Comm., Berkeley, Calif., 1990—; founder, chmn. WINECOM, 1992—. Pub. rels. editor: Practical Winery & Vineyards, 1994—; wine editor Focus Mag. Mem. Pub. Rels. Soc. Am. (bd. dirs. 1993—, sec. 1994, pres. East Bay chpt. 1994-96, editor newsletter food and beverage sect. 1993-95, chmn. food and beverage sect.), Women in Comm., Acad. Wine Comm. (program chair 1994), Internat. Assn. Bus. Communicators. Republican. Episcopalian. Office: Paige Poulos Comm PO Box 8087 Berkeley CA 94707-8087

POUND, E. JEANNE, school psychologist, consultant; b. N.Y.C., Oct. 19, 1949; adopted d. W. James and Thelma (Rendall) P.; div.; 1 child, Courtney Jason Pound. BA in English cum laude, U. Mass., 1971; MS in Social Work, U. Wis., 1973; EdS in Sch. Psychology, U. Ga., 1977. Cert. sch. psychologist, Ga., Mass.; cert. sch. social worker, N.Y. Psychiat. social worker White Mountain Community Mental Health Svcs., Littleton, N.H., 1974; sch. social worker Lake Placid (N.Y.) Ctrl. Schs., 1974-75; sch. psychologist Wilbraham (Mass.) Pub. Schs., 1977-80, Stoneham (Mass). Pub. Schs., 1980-81, Richmond County (Ga.) Pub. Schs., 1981-83, Griffin (Ga.) Regional Ednl. Svc. Agy., 1984-87, Atlanta Pub. Schs., 1987—; evaluator of innovative program grants Ga. State Dept. Edn., Atlanta, 1987—; supr. sch. psychology interns Ga. State U., Atlanta, 1994—; mem. Ga. Adv. Panel Spl. Edn., 1995—. Author: (chpt.) Children's Needs-Psychological Perspectives ("Children and Prematurity"), 1987. Mem. APA, Nat. Assn. Sch. Psychologists (cert.), Ga. Assn. Sch. Psychologists (regional rep. 1991-93, chmn. GASP/NASP conv. com. 1995-96), Humane Soc. U.S., World Wildlife Fedn., Kappa Delta Pi, Phi Kappa Phi, Phi Delta Kappa. Home: 150 Bryson Ln Fayetteville GA 30215-5478 Office: Atlanta Pub Schs Office Youth Svcs 978 North Ave NE Atlanta GA 30306-4456

POUR-EL, MARIAN BOYKAN, mathematician, educator; b. N.Y.C.; d. Joseph and Mattie (Caspe) Boykan; m. Akiva Pour-El; 1 dau., Ina. A.B., Hunter Coll.; A.M., Harvard U., 1951, Ph.D., 1958. Asst. prof. math. Pa. State U., 1958-62, assoc. prof., 1962-64; mem. faculty U. Minn., Mpls., 1964—; prof. math. U. Minn., 1968—; mem. Inst. Advanced Study, Princeton, N.J., 1962-64; mem. coun. Conf. Bd. Math. Scis., 1977-82, trustee, 1978-81, mem. nominating com., 1980-82, chmn., 1981-82; lectr. internat. congresses in logic and computer sci., Eng., 1971, Hungary, 1967, Czechoslovakia, 1973, Germany, 1983, 96, Japan, 1985, 88, China, 1987; lectr. Polish Acad. Sci., 1974; lecture series throughout Fed. Republic of Germany, 1980, 87, 89, 91, Japan, 1985, 87, 90, 93, China, 1987, Sweden, 1983, 94, Finland, 1991, Estonia, 1991, Moscow, 1992, Amsterdam, 1992; mem. Fulbright Com. on Maths., 1986-89. Author: (with I. Richards) Computability in Analysis and Physics, 1989; author numerous articles on mathematical logic (theoretical computer sci.) and applications to mathematical and physical theory. Named to Hunter Coll. Hall of Fame, 1975; NAS grantee, 1966. Fellow AAAS, Japan Soc. for Promotion of Sci.; mem. Am. Math. Soc. (coun. 1980-88, numerous coms., lectr. nat. meeting 1976, also spl. sessions 1971, 78, 82, 84, chmn. spl. sessions on recursion theory 1975, 84), Assn. Symbolic Logic, Math. Assn. Am. (nat. panel vis. lectrs. 1977—, lectr. nat. meetings 1982, 89), Phi Beta Kappa, Sigma Xi, Pi Mu Epsilon, Sigma Pi Sigma. Office: U Minn Sch Math Vincent Hall Minneapolis MN 55455-0488

POWELL, ANICE CARPENTER, librarian; b. Moorhead, Miss., Dec. 2, 1928; d. Horace Aubrey and Celeste (Brian) Carpenter; student Sunflower Jr. Coll., 1945-47, Miss. State Coll. Women, 1947-48; B.S., Delta State Coll., 1961, M.L.S., 1974; m. Robert Wainwright Powell, July 19, 1948 (dec. 1979); children: Penelope Elizabeth, Deborah Alma. Librarian, Sunflower (Miss.) Pub. Library, 1958-61; tchr. English, Isola (Miss.) High Sch., 1961-62; dir. Sunflower County Library, Indianola, Miss., 1962—; mem. adv. coun. State Instl. Library Services, 1967-71; mem. adv. bd. library services and constrn. act com. Miss. Library Commn., 1978-80, mem. pub. library task force, 1986—; mem. Pub. Library Standards Com., 1988—; mem. state adv. coun. adult edn., 1988-92; mem. steering com. NASA community involvement program Miss. Delta Community Coll., 1990, adult edn. adv. com.; mem. Dist. Workforce Coun., 1994—, Mid Delta Enpowerment Zone Alliance, 1995—; commn. mem. Mid-Delta Empowerment Zone Alliance. Mem. AAUW, NOW, ALA (speaker senate subcom. on illiteracy 1989, honoree ALA 50th Anniversary 1996), Miss. Library Assn. (exec. dir. Nat. Library Week 1975, steering com. 1976, chmn. Right to Read com. 1976, co-chmn., 1987, chmn. legis. com. 1979, chmn. intellectual freedom com. 1975, 80, mem. legis. com. 1973-86, 96, chmn. membership com. 1982, pres. 1984, chmn. nominating com. 1986, chmn. election com. 1989, mem. registration com. 1991—, mem. membership com., mem. nominating com. 1994, mem. publicity com. 1996, mem. fiscal mgmt. com. 1996, mem. awards com. 1996, Peggy May award 1981), Sunflower County Hist. Soc. (pres. 1983-87), Delta Coun. Methodist. Home: PO Box 310 Sunflower MS 38778-0310 Office: Sunflower County Libr 201 Cypress Dr Indianola MS 38751-2415

POWELL, ANNE ELIZABETH, editor; b. Cheverly, Md., Nov. 11, 1951; d. Arthur Gorman and Barbara Anne (MacAran) P.; m. John Alan Ebeling Jr., 1972 (div. 1983). BS, U. Md., 1972. Reporter Fayetteville (N.C.) Times, 1973-75; home editor Columbus (Ga.) Ledger-Enquirer, 1976; assoc. editor Builder mag., Washington, 1977-78; architecture editor House Beautiful's Spl. Publs., N.Y.C., 1979-81; editor Traditional Home mag., Des Moines, 1982-87, Mid-Atlantic Country mag., Alexandria, Va., 1987-89; editor in chief publs. Nat. Trust for Hist. Preservation, Washington, 1989-95; editor-in-chief Landscape Architecture Mag., Washington, 1995—. Author: The New England Colonial, 1988. Mem. Nat. Press Club, Am. Soc. Mag. Editors. Home: 707 S Royal St Alexandria VA 22314-4309 Office: Am Soc Landscape Arch 4401 Connecticut Ave NW Washington DC 20008

POWELL, CAROL ANN, accountant; b. Bklyn., Dec. 5, 1954; d. William Preston and Adelaide Hertha (Sohl) Batty; m. Michael Robert Powell, Jan. 17, 1976; children: Michael David, David Jason. AAS, Delhi Agrl. and Tech. Coll., 1974; BS, Syracuse U., 1975. CPA, N.Y. Sr. acct. Hall & Yann, CPAs, Fayetteville, N.Y., 1975-78; pvt. practice acct. Cold Spring, N.Y., 1979—; adj. tchr. acctg. Onondaga C.C., Syracuse, N.Y., 1977, Dutchess C.C., Poughkeepsie, N.Y., 1982. Den leader Philipstown Pack 137 Boy Scouts Am., Cold Spring, N.Y., 1987-96; treas. Philipstown Little League, Cold Spring, 1990—, Philipstown Babe Ruth League, Cold Spring, 1994. Mem. AICPA, N.Y. State Soc. CPAs. Methodist. Home: PO Box 312 Cold Spring NY 10516-0312 Office: 159 Main St Cold Spring NY 10516-2818

POWELL, CAROL SUE, pediatric special education educator, nursing consultant; b. Phoenix, Nov. 15, 1944; d. Leonard Newson and Rebecca Jane (Housh) Stephens; m. Howard Powell Jr., Aug. 26, 1967; children: Jim, Howard III, Nicole. LPN, Champaign (Ill.) Sch. Practical Nursing, 1965; BA, Ea. Ill. U., 1975, MS in Edn., 1979; ADN, Lincolnland C.C., 1986. RN, Ill.; lic. EMT; cert. elem. and secondary edn. tchr., Ill.; qualified mental retardation profl., Ill. Nurse Pattie A. Clay Infirmary, Richmond, Ky., 1966-68, Clark County Hosp., Winchester, Ky., 1968-69, Mattoon (Ill.) Hosp., 1970-77; substitute tchr. Mattoon, Charleston, Findlay, Arcola Schs., 1978-79; spl. edn. and kindergarten tchr. Buda (Ill.) Sch. Dist., 1979-81; staff nurse St. John's Hosp., Springfield, Ill., 1981-87; health svc. supr. Assn. for Retarded Citizens, Springfield, 1987-88; staff nurse St. Vincent's Hosp., Taylorville, Ill., 1988-89; spl. edn. tchr., asst. dir. edn., mental retardation profl. Luth. Social Svcs., Beardstown, Ill., 1989—. Nurse Shrine Clinics, Springfield, 1989-96, nurse, EMT first aid meets Boy Scouts Am., Springfield, 1988-96. Methodist. Home: 834 Evergreen Dr Chatham IL 62629-1118 Office: St Luke Health Care Ctr RR3 Box 446 Beardstown IL 62618

POWELL, CAROLYN WILKERSON, music educator; b. Hamburg, Ark., Oct. 9, 1920; d. Claude Kelly and Mildred (Hall) Wilkerson; m. Charles Luke Powell, Dec. 12, 1923; children: Charles Luke Jr., James Davis, Mark Wilkerson, Robert Hall. AB, Cen. Methodist, Fayette, Mo., 1942; MAT, U. N.C., Chapel Hill, 1970. Life Teaching Cert. Mo. Teaching Cert. N.C. Choral dir. Maplewood Richmond Heights Sch., St. Louis, 1943-45; pvt. piano tchr. Greensboro N.C. Area, Greensboro, 1951-63; organist Presbyterian and Methodist Ch., Greensboro, 1950-61; dir. Ch. Youth Choirs, Greensboro, 1958-61; choral and humanities tchr. Page High Sch., Greensboro, 1963-67; choral dir. Githens Jr. High Sch., Durham, N.C., 1967-80; organist St. Peter's Episcopal Ch., Altavista, Va., 1981-83; chmn. Dist. Choral Festival N.C. Dist., 1968-78; accompanist and music dir. Altavista Little Theatre Altavista, Va., 1981-83. Sunday and vacation schs. tchr., organist Grace Meth. Ch., Greensboro; den mother Boy Scouts Am., Greensboro, 1951-57; mem. Chapel Hill Preservation Soc., 1985—; vol., chapel organist, pediat. tutor U. N.C. Hosps., Chapel Hill, 1984-89. Mem. NEA, AAUW, Music Educators Nat. Conf., Am. Organists Guild, Classroom Tchrs. Assn., Ackland Art Mus. Assn., Chapel Hill Preservation Soc., Nat. Federated Music Club Euterpe, Chapel Hill Country Club, U. Woman's Club, The Carolina Club, Delta Kappa Gamma. Avocations: reading, golf, needlework, gardening, travel and antiques. Home: 2446 Honeysuckle Rd Chapel Hill NC 27514-6821

POWELL, ELAINE MARIE, writer; b. St. Louis, Nov. 25, 1946; d. Edsel Arthur and Jessie Louise (Whitelaw) Hatfield; m. David Eugene Powell; children: Steven, Bryan. Grad. H.S., Florissant, 1964. Sec. U. Mo., Columbia, 1969-71, Francis Howell Sch. Dist., St. Charles County, Mo., 1985-93; free-lance writer Orlando, Fla., 1994—; mng. rep. Excel Telecom., 1996—. Coun. tng. staff Boy Scouts Am., 1980-85, dist. tng. chmn., 1982-85; mem. long range planning coun. Francis Howell Sch. Dist., 1989-93, others. Recipient Dist. award of merit Boy Scouts Am., 1983, Howell of Fame award, 1987, Silver Beaver award Boy Scouts Am., 1991. Mem. numerous geneal. socs. Republican. Presbyterian. Home and Office: 4620 Saddleworth Cir Orlando FL 32826-4126

POWELL, ENID LEVINGER, writer, educator; b. Bklyn., Nov. 24, 1931; d. Herbert Roosevelt and Selma Esther (Sherman) Levinger; m. Bert Powell, Nov. 5, 1950; children: Pip Irene, Jon Lawrence. BA in English, Barat Coll., 1974; MA in English and Creative Writing, U. Ill., Chgo., 1978. Staff writer The Young and the Restless, L.A., 1983-94; tchr. Columbia Coll., Chgo., 1993-95, Newberry Libr., Chgo., 1994—; freelance writer Chgo. Co-author: The Big Steal, 1980, The Divorce Handbook, 1982; contbr. short stories and poetry to popular mags. Nominee for Best Writing award NATAS, 1986, 87, 90-91, 91-92. Mem. NATAS, NOW, ACLU. Home: 1300 N Lake Shore Dr # 21B Chicago IL 60610

POWELL, JEANNE MARIE, accountant; b. N.Y.C., Sept. 5, 1947; d. Vincent and Genevieve (Josephs) Calabretta; children: Lisa M., Roger J. Jr. Student, CUNY, 1968. Owner, pres. Jeanne Powell Assocs., Howard Beach, N.Y., 1972—; bd. dirs. Putnam Investment Co., Boston, 1987-90, bd. govs., 1990-95, mem. adv. bd., 1993-95. Fundraiser for Geraldine Ferraro, Queens, N.Y., 1991. Mem. Nat. Soc. Pub. Accts., Nat. Assn. Tax Profls., Nat. Soc. Tax Profls., N.Y. Soc. Ind. Accts. (pres. Queens chpt. 1995-96, state sec.). Roman Catholic. Office: 155-52 101st St Howard Beach NY 11414

POWELL, JUDITH E., nursing administrator; b. Wheeling, W.Va., Aug. 12, 1939; d. James Paul and Alice Jean (Lisk) Cummins; m. William Allen Powell, Nov. 23, 1984; children: Kimberly, David, Brad, Carrie, Shaun. Diploma, Ohio Valley Gen. Hosp., Wheeling, 1960; BNA, Columbia Pacific U., Mill Valley, Calif., 1981, MBA, M in Nursing Adminstrn., 1983. Cert. in nursing adminstrn. DON Med. Found. of Bellaire, Ohio, dir. health svcs.; v.p. patient care svcs. DON Meml. Hosp. of Union County, Marysville, Ohio. Mem. adv. bd. Ohio Hi Point Joint Vocat. Sch., Tri-Rivers Sch. Practical Nursing, Marion Tech. Coll. Mem. Am. Acad. Ambulatory Nursing Adminstrn. (charter), Am. Hosp. Assn., Ohio Soc. for Nurse Execs.

POWELL, KARAN HINMAN, university program administrator, consultant; b. Great Lakes, Ill., May 25, 1953; d. David Daniel and Mary Anne (Buretz) Hinman; m. David Leonidas Powell, Feb. 14, 1987; children: Meloni (dec.), Erik. BS, We. Ill. U., 1975; MDiv, Loyola U., Chgo., 1981, B Sacred Theology (hon.), 1981; postgrad., George Mason U., 1994—. Cert. tchr., Ill., Va.; cert. orgn. devel. profl. Tchr. St. Hugh Cath. Sch., Lyons, Ill., 1975-77; tchr. Lay Ministry Tng. Program, Chgo., 1980-81, Jackson, Miss., 1981-83; adminstr. Inst. Creation Centered Spirituality Mundelein Coll., Chgo., 1978-79; exec. dir. North Am. Forum Catechumenate, Washington, 1983-88; dir. Profl. Devel. Program, tchr. theol. studies, tng. cons., exec. devel., direct contact tng. Georgetown U., Washington, 1988-94, dir. organization devel. program, 1991-95, mng. acad. dir., 1995—; assoc. pastor Annunciation Cath. Ch., Columbus, Miss., 1981-83; cons. dioceses in U.S., Can., 1983—; cons. to fed. govt., profit and non-profit corps.; ptnr. Wahl & Powell Cons. Resources, 1994—. Author: How to Form a Catechumenate Team, 1985; editor: Breaking Open the Word of God series, 1986-88, The Ninety Days, 1989; contbr. articles Cath. mags.; speaker Religious Edn. Congress, L.A., 1987-88, 90. Active on Blessed Sacrament RCIA Team, Alexandria, Va., 1984-86; apptd. to Va. State Child Fatality Review Team, 1995—. Recipient tchr.'s scholarship State of Ill., 1971-75, cert. recognition KC, Columbus, Miss., 1982. Mem. ASTD, Acad. of Mgmt., Assn. Psychol. Type, N.Am. Forum Catechumenate (cons. 1982—), Cath. Edn. Future's Project (mem. com. 1985-88, Va. SIDS Alliance, 1991—, state steering com. 1993-94, bd. dirs., 1993-94, pres. 1994-96), Orgn. Devel. Network. Democrat. Office: 21351 Sweet Clover Pl Ashburn VA 20147-5431

POWELL, KIMBERLEY KAY, mathematician, educator; b. Oklahoma City, Dec. 2, 1965; d. Rockie Leo Smith and Alice Faye Bancroft; m. William Joseph Powell, Dec. 22, 1990; 1 child, Brett Maxwell. BS in Math., Okla. State U., 1989, BS in Edn., 1989; MEd in Counseling, U. Ctrl. Okla., 1994. Tchr. math. Carney (Okla.) Pub. Schs., 1989-91, Perry (Okla.) Jr. H.S., 1991-92, Bethany (Okla.) Pub. Schs., 1992—. Leadership Bethany com. C. of C., 1994-95. Mem. Nat. Coun. Tchrs. Math., Okla. Coun. Tchrs. Math., Okla. Counseling Assn., Chi Sigma Iota (pres. 1994-95). Democrat. Baptist. Office: Bethany Schs 6721 NW 42nd St Bethany OK 73008-2664

POWELL, LINDA, state education official. Commr. of edn. Minn. Dept. Edn. Office: Edn Dept 712 Capitol Sq Bldg 550 Cedar St Saint Paul MN 55101-2233*

POWELL, MARGARET ANN SIMMONS, computer scientist; b. Gulfport, Miss., May 26, 1952; d. William Robert and Nancy Rita (Schloegel) Simmons; m. Mark Thomas Powell, Sept. 11, 1983. AS in Math., N.W. Miss. Jr. Coll., 1972; BS in Edn., Memphis State U., 1977; BS in Computer Sci., U. Md., 1988; MS in Computer Sci., Johns Hopkins U., 1991. Tchr. Sacred Heart Sch., Walls, Miss., 1973-80; office mgr. Hyman Builders Supply, Memphis, 1980-84; tech. instr. Bendix Field Engring. Corp., Greenbelt, Md., 1985-87; software engr. Assurance Technology Corp., Alexandria, Va., 1987-89, Naval Rsch. Lab., Washington, 1989-93; computer scientist Naval Info. Systems Mgmt. Ctr., Washington, 1993—. Bd. dirs. Greenbrook Village Homeowners Assn., 1992-96; sec. Greenbelt East Adv. Com., 1994, chair, 1995-96. Named one of Outstanding Young Women Am., 1977. Mem. IEEE Computer Soc., Assn. for Computing Machinery, Phi Kappa Phi, Kappa Delta Pi, Phi Theta Kappa, Mu Alpha Theta. Roman Catholic. Home: 4652 Kell Ln Alexandria VA 22311 Office: NISMC 1225 Jefferson Davis Hwy Ste 1500 Arlington VA 22202-4311

POWELL, MARY ARTHUR, adult and family nurse practitioner, administrator; b. Greenport, N.Y., Mar. 12, 1950; d. Francis and Mary (Hill) Arthur; divorced; 1 child, Patrick Joseph. Student, Pace U., 1977; BS in Healthcare Scis., George Washington U., 1978; student, Johns Hopkins U., 1980; MPA, Pa. State U., 1995. RN, Pa.; cert. family nurse practitioner, adult nurse practitioenr. Staff nurse emergency dept. Norwalk (Conn.) Hosp., 1970-77; staff nurse Group Health Assn. (HMO), Washington, 1977-78; adult nurse practitioner Johns Hopkins Hosp., Balt., 1978-82; dir. student health svcs. Dickinson Coll., Carlisle, Pa., 1982—; chair health and safety com. Dickinson Coll., Carlisle; part-time nurse practitioner family practice Graham Med. Clinic, Newville, Pa., 1994—; chair program com. South Cen. Pa. Nurse Practitioner Spl. Interest Group, 1987-88; instr. EMT course Norwalk Hosp., 1976-77; instr. phys. assessment Johns Hopkins U. Grad. Sch. midwifery program, 1979; lectr. Johns Hopkins Phys. Assessment Workshop, 1983; speaker CHAP Nat. Nurse Practitioner Conf., 1986, 90;. Author column Jour. Am. Acad. Nurse Practitioners, 1989-93. Co-founder CH.A.D.D. (Children with Attention Deficit Disorders) of Capital area, pres., 1989-91, 93-94, exec. bd. dirs., sec., 1989-94. Recipient Cert. of Appreciation CHADD Nat. Orgn., 1993, U. Pa. Primary Care Program. Mem. Am. Coll. Health Assn. (com. legis. and regulatory initiatives 1992—, presenter ann. conf. Boston 1991, mem. editl. bd. com. standards 1991, sect. del. 1984-87), Am. Acad. Nurse Practitioners (writer 1st nat. certifying exam. for nurse practitioners 1993, presenter 3d ann. conf. Portland, Oreg. 1991, exec. bd. dirs., rec. sec. 1987-90, conf. program com. 1989, cert. of appreciation 1991). Office: Dickinson Coll PO Box 1773 Carlisle PA 17013-2896

POWELL, NANCY EGAN, elementary education educator; b. Galesburg, Ill., Nov. 5, 1944; d. Robert Matthew and Eva (Fullerton) Egan; m. Dennis Lynn Powell, May 26, 1973; children: Matthew, Susan. BE, Washburn U., 1968; postgrad., Emporia State U., 1973-78, Ottawa U., 1979-85, Avilia U., 1985-89, Portland State U., 1987-88. Cert. K-8, Kans. Tchr. grade 2, permanent substitute tchr. Kansas City Dist. 500, Kans., 1968-69; kindergarten tchr. Kansas City (Kans.) Dist. 500, 1969-91, collaborative kindergarten tchr., 1991—; instr. Math Learning Ctr., Portland State U., 1989—; tchr.'s adv. bd. Kans. Children's Mus., Kansas City, 1988—; presenter S.W. Regional Conf. Kans. Assn. Tchrs. Math., 1989, 90, 92, mem. Kindergarten Curriculum Guide Com., 1988, Math Curriculum Guide Com., 1990, U.S. Russian Joint Conf. Math. Edn., Moscow, 1993, Scope Sequence Writing Team, 1993, Kansas City Math Cadre; mem. Hartcourt Brace Math Tchrs. Adv. Bd., 1995. Mem. Harcourt Brace Math. Tchrs. Adv. Bd., 1995. Troop leader, trainer Santa Fe Trail coun. Girl Scouts U.S., 1982—; troop leader Mid Am. coun. Boy Scouts Am., 1983-90. Grantee Kansas City, Kans. Profl. Devel. Coun. Spl. Edn. Dept., 1990, N.E. Kans. Elem. Sch. Math. Dissemination Project, 1993, 94. Mem. NEA, Internat. Reading Assn., Assn. Childhood Edn. Internat., Nat. Coun. PTA, Nat. Assn. Tchrs. Math., Nat. Assn. Edn. Young Children, Profl. Devel. Coun. Kansas City, Alpha Delta Kappa (v.p. 1986-88, pres. 1988-90, state courtesy chmn. 1992-94). Republican. Methodist. Home: 7924 Armstrong Ave Kansas City KS 66112-2547 also: Kansas City Pub Schs Libr Bldg 625 Minnesota Ave Kansas City KS 66101-2805

POWELL, NANCY NOREM, secondary school educator; b. Ottawa, Ill., Jan. 12, 1952; d. Robert Ellyot and Mary Elizabeth (Sharpnack) Norem; m. Kalley Ray Powell, July 1, 1978; children: Kalley Robert, Nicholas Andrew, Jonathon Ellyot. BS in Math. Edn., Ill. State U., 1974, BS in Ednl. Adminstrn., 1990. Math. tchr. Danville (Ill.) H.S., 1974-78; math. and computer tchr. Bloomington (Ill.) H.S., 1979—; adult edn. programming tchr. Bloomington-Normal Adult Edn., 1981-83; basic programming tchr. Coll. for Youth, Ill. State U., Normal, summers 1982, 83; math. and computer tchr. Summer Enrichment Program for Acad. Talented Minorities, Normal, 1986—; cons. Ill. State Bd. Edn., Springfield, 1988—, Impact II Nat. Office, N.Y.C., 1993—, del. to visions of edn. conf., 1992, 94. Author, editor: The Teacher's Guide to Cyberspace, 1996. Fair judge 4-H, Bloomington, 1986—; scorer Odyssey of the Mind Competition, Bloomington, 1991—; mem. adv. bd. Jerry Keiper Ctr. Tchr. Devel. Sci., Math. & Tech., 1994—. Grantee Pioneering Ptnrs. in Tech., State of Ill./GTE, 1992. Mem. ASCD, Nat. Coun. Tchrs. Math., Ill. Coun. Tchrs. Math. (dir.-at-large 1993-96, Presdl. Excellence in Secondary Math. Teaching award 1992, Tandy scholar 1995), Bd. Christian Edn. (sec. 1990-95), Delta Kappa Gamma (state literacy com., rules chmn. 1992-94), Phi Delta Kappa. Lutheran. Home: 1221 Cadwell Dr Bloomington IL 61704-3683 Office: Bloomington HS 1202 E Locust St Bloomington IL 61701-3363

POWELL, PATRICIA ANN, secondary education educator; b. Covington, Ga., Apr. 6, 1956; d. John Doyle Sr. and Pauline Josephine (Thompson) Dunn; m. Jackie Lee Powell, May 10, 1980; 1 child, Jackie Lee II. BS, Lee Coll., 1978; MEd in Adminstrn. and Supervision, U. Tenn., 1993. Br. loan officer Am. Nat. Bank and Trust, Chattanooga, 1979-81; tchr. math. Hamilton County Schs., Chattanooga, 1983-85; customer svc. rep. First Union Nat. Bank, Atlanta, 1986-88; instr. tech. bus., typing DeKalb County Schs., Decatur, Ga., 1989; grad. asst. U. Tenn., Chattanooga, 1991-93; tchr. math. Hamilton County Sch. Sys., 1993—; instr. English, bus. math. and bus. skills Urban League Bus. Skills Tng. Ctr., Chattanooga; mem. adj. faculty Chattanooga State Tech. C.C., 1991-92; joint stds. rep. for sch. consolidation, 1995-96. Co-author: Career Orientation-Grade 8, 1985 (monetary award 1984-85); singer African Americans Against Blood Disorders Benefit, Atlanta, 1994. Singer, Mayor's Office Performing Artists Against Drugs, Atlanta, 1990; vol. Chattanooga Comty. Kitchen, 1990—; tutor, coord. math., reading United Way's Adult Reading Program, Chattanooga, 1991—; instr. aerobics Am. Heart Assn., Chattanooga, 1991—; vol. Warner Park Zoo, Chattanooga; treas. Looking to the Word Ministries, Inc., 1985-94; v.p. parents group 1st Cumberland Child Devel. Ctr., 1992-94; sch. rep. Joint Stds. Com. for Consol., 1995-96, Diversity Com. for Consol., 1996-97. Outstanding Classroom Tchr. nominee, 1993-94; recipient Black Grad. fellowship U. Tenn., Chattanooga, 1992, 93; named Woman of Yr. and Mrs. Congeniality, Mrs. Chattanooga-Am. Pageant, 1990; Endowment scholar, 1977-78. Mem. NAFE, AAUW, Hamilton County Edn. Assn. (chmn. minority affairs com. 1995-97), Chattanooga Area Math. Assn. (v.p. mid. schs. 1996-97), Friends of Zoo Preservation Group, Delta Sigma Theta, Kappa Delta Pi (pres., v.p. 1993-95). Home: PO Box 24912 Chattanooga TN 37422-4912

POWELL, R. JEAN, editor; b. Livingston, Mont., Sept. 7, 1935; d. Richard Henry Robinson and Gertrude Mary (Cook) Bauer; m. Donald Robert Powell, May 7, 1960; children: Tamala Jo, David Michael, Leslie Anne. Attended, U. Mont., Missoula, 1956-59, Ea. Mont. Coll., Billings, 1964-66, Mont. State U., Bozeman, 1971-72. Photo finisher Sax & Fryer's, Livingston, Mont., 1950-55, Oatis Photography, Phoenix, 1955-56; prodn. mgr. darkroom and printing Big Timber (Mont.) Pioneer Newspaper & Print Shop, 1974-79; co-founder Mont. Celiac Soc., Bozeman, 1995; resource chmn. Celiac Soc. Am., Omaha, Nebr., 1991—; editor Gluten-Free Friends Newsletter Mont. Celiac Soc., Bozeman, 1995—; adminstr. Mont. Celiac Soc., 1995—, resources pub. editor, 1995—. Photographer: Abstracts in Photography, 1982. Funding and donations coord. Mont. Celiac Soc., Bozeman, 1996—. Recipient 2d Place Photography award Enjoy mag., 1982. Democrat. Unitarian. Home and Office: 1019 S Bozeman Ave # 3 Bozeman MT 59715

POWELL, SHARON LEE, social welfare organization administrator; b. Portland, Oreg., July 25, 1940; d. James Edward Carson and Betty Jane (Singleton) Powell. BS, Oreg. State U., 1962; MEd, Seattle U., 1971. Dir. outdoor edn. Mapleton (Oreg.) Pub. Schs., 1962-63; field dir. Totem Girl Scout Council, Seattle, 1963-68, asst. dir. field services, 1968-70, dir. field services, 1970-72; dir. pub. rels. and program Girl Scout Council of Tropical Fla., Miami, 1972-74; exec. dir. Homestead Girl Scout Council, Lincoln, Nebr., 1974-78, Moingona Girl Scout Coun., Des Moines, 1978—. Pres. agy. dirs. assn. United Way Cen. Iowa, Des Moines, 1987-88, mem. priorities com., 1986-90, chairperson agy. rels., 1994—, chairperson agy. issues, 1989-90; mem. priority goals task group United Way Found., Des Moines, 1985-92; capt. Drake U. Basketball Ticket Drive, Des Moines, 1983-87; sec. Urbandale Citizens Scholarship Found., 1989-93; mem. ad hoc long-range planning com. Urbandale Schs., 1989, mem. budget rev. task group, mem. year-round sch. task group, 1992-93; mem. gender equity task force State of Iowa, 1993—. Mem. AAUW, Assn. Girl Scouts Execs. (chair nat. conv. 1985-90, nat. bd. dirs. 1985-87, nat. nominating com. 1982-84, nat. treas. 1987-90, nat. pres. 1991—), Urbandale C. of C. (bd. dirs., chair edn. com.), Animal Rescue League of Iowa (bd. dirs. 1992—, shelter chair 1992—), Des Moines Obedience Tng. Club (pres. 1987-89), Des. Moines Golden Retriever Club (bd. dirs., pres. 1992-94), Rotary, Altrusa (treas. Des Moines chpt. 1983-85, cmty. svc. chair 1986-87), Des Moines Kennel Club. Office: Moingona Girl Scout Coun 10715 Hickman Rd Des Moines IA 50322-3733

POWELL, STEPHANIE, visual effects director, supervisor; b. Dayton, Ohio, Sept. 27, 1946; d. Harley Franklin and Evelyn Luella Pence. Pres., CEO Video Assist Systems, Inc., North Hollywood, Calif., 1979—, Out of the Blue Visual Effects, 1989. Cons.: (motion pictures) Jurassic Park, 1993, Flintstones, 1994, Waterworld, 1995, Get Shorty, 1995; visual effects supr.: Blown Away, 1994, My Brother's Keeper, 1994, Powder, 1995, various commls.; co-visual effects supr. Quantum Leap (TV); developer using 3/4-inch videotape for broadcast; co-developer color videotape for motion picture work. Mem. Acad. TV Arts and Scis., Acad. Magical Arts and Scis. Office: Video Assist Systems Inc 11030 Weddington St North Hollywood CA 91601-3212

POWELL, SUSAN LYNN, middle school educator; b. Hayti, Mo., Oct. 26, 1970; d. Lynn Banks III and Nina R. (Sanders) P. BA, Baldwin-Wallace Coll., 1992. Athletic trainer Baldwin-Wallace Coll., Berea, Ohio, 1990-92, women's intercollegiate volleyball coach, 1993-95; tchr. North Olmstead (Ohio) Mid. Sch., 1992—. Mem. Ohio Edn. Assn., Ohio Mid. Sch. Assn., Nat. PTA, Ohio PTA. Roman Catholic. Home: 23380 Wainwright Ter Olmsted Falls OH 44138 Office: North Olmsted Mid Sch 27351 Butternut Ridge Rd North Olmsted OH 44070

POWELL HILL, ELIZABETH T., singer, small business owner; b. San Antonio, Feb. 5, 1954; d. Elijah and Mattie B. Tyler; m. Frederick Powell, Apr. 16, 1977 (div.); children: Frederick Powell, Michael Powell; m. James LaRue Hill, Mar. 10, 1989; 1 child, Victoria Hill. Degree in Applied Science, St. Philip's Coll., 1987, AA, 1989. Lic. fin. broker, real estate investor. Sec. San Antonio Light Newspaper, 1979-80; bus. owner T. Powell Express Co., San Antonio, 1982—; singer pop rock various locations, 1985—; owner Queen Elizabeth Enterprise Global Wealth Builder, San Antonio, 1996—. Author: (song) Just Seeing You, 1985, (book) The Elizabeth Powell Letters, 1992; designer curio dress, 1989; copyright original works as author, 1992. Founder Perfect Abundant Life Mockulisaphen Ch., San Antonio, 1996. Recipient Trophy award for Best Performer Inner City Prodns., 1986, 1st Runner up trophy for performance Elks Lodge, 1990. Mem. Am. Fedn. Musicians, Internat. Platform Assn. Office: T Powell Express Co PO Box 200643 San Antonio TX 78220-0643

POWELSON, MARY VOLIVA, golf course and banquet facility executive; b. Evansville, Ind., Sept. 10, 1954; d. Edward Jr. and Norma Elaine (Koenig) Voliva; m. Kent Howard Powelson, Aug. 4, 1979 (div. 1988); 1 child, Nicholas H. BS, Purdue U., 1976, postgrad., 1979-80; postgrad., U. Evansville, 1977-79, 80-85. Asst. mgr. Paul Harris, Evansville, Ind., 1977-79; speech therapist Dr. Tom Logan, Henderson, Ky., 1979; gen. mgr. Clearcrest Pines, Evansville, 1987—. Exhibited in group shows Evansville Mus. Fine Art, 1983, Ind. Heritage Arts, Nashville, 1984, Brown County Art Guild, Nashville, 1984, Catherine Lorillard Wolfe Art Club, N.Y.C., 1984, Pastel Soc. of Am., N.Y.C., 1984, Oak Meadow Country Club, Evansville, 1991. Mem. Am. Culinary Fedn., Tri-State Chef and Cook's Assn., U.S. Golf Assn., Pastel Soc. of Am., Women in Arts, Gun Club (treas. 1990—). Office: Clearcrest Pines 10521 Darmstadt Evansville IN 47710-5095

POWER, ELIZABETH HENRY, consultant; b. Hickory, N.C., Sept. 28, 1953; d. William Henry Power and Katheryn Otis (Smith) Nelson. Cert. in creative writing, N.C. Sch. Arts, 1971; BA in Sociology, U. N.C., Greensboro, 1977; MEd in Human Resources Devel., Vanderbilt U. With adoption and foster home recruitment Davidson County Dept. Human Svcs., Nashville, 1980-81; behavioral cons. Nutri-System Weight Loss Ctr., Nashville, 1982-84; corp. sec., cons. Quantum Leap Cons., Inc., Nashville, 1984-86; pres., owner EPower & Assocs., Brentwood, Tenn., 1980-84, 86—; owner MPD/DD Resource & Edn. Ctr., Nashville, 1991-93; cons. GM/Saturn, 1988-96. Author: Getting the Fat Out of Your Head So It Stays Off Your Body, 1987, If Change Is All There Is, Choice Is All You've Got, 1990, Managing Our Selves: Building a Community of Caring, 1992; co-author, editor: Circle of Love: Child Personal Safety, 1984; contbg. author: Nonprofit Policies and Procedures, 1992, More than Survivors: Conversations with Multiple Personality Clients, 1992, also articles. Vol. West Chester (Pa.) Women's Resource Ctr., 1977; vol. instr. theology Lay Acad. Episc. Diocese Western N.C., Asheville, 1976-77; mem. Burke County Coun. Status Women, Morganton, N.C., 1977-79, sec., 1978; vol. Western N.C. Flood Com., 1977-78; exec. dir. N.C. Rape Crisis Assn., Raleigh, 1979, Foothills Mental Health Ctr., Morganton, 1978-79; mem. task force, writer, convener, facilitator N.C. Gov.'s Conf. Mental Health, 1979; trainer, vol. Rape House Crisis Ctr., Nashville, 1979-81; vol., trainer Rape and Sexual Abuse Ctr., Nashville, 1981-82, bd. dirs., 1981-82; mem. quality circles steering com. Tenn. Dept. Human Svcs., 1980-81; program cons. Women's Resource and Assistance Program, Jackson, Tenn., 1988-92; bd. dirs. Life Challenge Tenn., 1989-91. Recipient numerous awards N.C. Dept. Mental Health/Mental Retardation, 1979, State of N.C., 1979, Central Nashville Optimist Club, 1982, Waco YWCA, Waco, Tex., 1985. Mem. NAFE, Internat. Soc. for Study of Multiple Personality and Dissociation. Democrat. Home and Office: PO Box 2346 Brentwood TN 37024-2346

POWERS, BRENDA AURETTA, social worker; b. Memphis, Dec. 15, 1949; d. George Ellis and Mattie Joe (Boyd) Harris; m. William Lawrence Powers, Sept. 29, 1978 (dec.); children: Brandy Allison, Brittany Jo. BA, Memphis State U., 1971, MEd, 1976. Cert. secondary sch. guidance counselor. Welfare worker State of Tenn., 1971-73; cirriculum coord. Fayette County Schs., Somerville, Tenn., 1973-74; career edn. counselor Tipton County Schs., Covington, Tenn., 1974-75; human svcs. supr. State Tenn., Memphis, 1975-76, elibility supr., 1976-77, cmty. svcs. rep., 1977-91, program evaluator, 1991—. Bd. dirs. com. adminstrn. YWCA, 1981-83; nominating com. Mertie Buckman YWCA, 1989-92; chmn. com. ch. and soc. United Meth. Memphis Asbury Dist., 1987-94. Democrat. Home: 7541 Olivia Hill Dr Memphis TN 38133 Office: Dept Fin & Adminstrn 3230 Jackson Ave Memphis TN 38122

POWERS, CLAUDIA MCKENNA, state government official; b. Key West, Fla., May 28, 1950; d. James Edward and Claudia (Antrim) McKenna; m. Richard Garland Powers, Dec. 27, 1971; children: Gregory, Theodore, Matthew, Thurston. BA in Edn., U. Hawaii, 1972; MA, Columbia U., 1975. Cert. tchr., N.Y. Rep. Greenwich (Conn.) Rep. Town Meeting, 1979-93, sec. bldg. com., 1982-84, sec. legis. com., 1986-88, 90-93; mem. Conn. Ho. of Reps., 1993—, ranking mem. govt. adminstrn. and elections com., 1995—. Mem. editorial bd. Greenwich Mag., 1995—. Campaign chmn. Greenwich Rep. Town Com., 1984, 85, chmn., 1986-90; sec. Rep. Round Table, Greenwich, 1988-90; bd. govs. Riverside Assn., Greenwich, 1987-91, sec., 1991-92; class mother Riverside Sch., Greenwich, 1984-90; mem. altar guild Christ Ch., Greenwich, 1990—; adminstrv. coord. Greenwich Teen Ctr., 1990-91; alt. del. Rep. Nat. Conv., New Orleans, 1984—; v.p. LWV of Greenwich, 1990-91. Episcopalian. Home and Office: 15 Hendrie Ave Riverside CT 06878-1808

POWERS, DORIS HURT, retired engineering company executive; b. Indpls., Jan. 17, 1927; d. James Wallace Hurt Sr. and Mildred (Johnson) Devine; m. Patrick W. Powers, Nov. 12, 1950 (dec. 1989); children: Robert W. Powers, Jaye P., Laura S. Powers. Student, So. Meth. U., 1944-45; BS in Engring., Purdue U., 1949; postgrad., U. Tex., W. Tex., 1952-53, Ecole Normale Du Musique, Paris, 1965-68; grad., Harford County Leadership Acad., 1991. Flight instr. Red Leg Flying Club, El Paso, Lawton, Okla., 1951-57; check pilot Civil Air Patrol, El Paso, Lawton, Okla., 1952-57; ground instr. Civil Air Patrol, Washington, Tex., Okla, 1957-61; exec. v.p. T&E Internat., Inc., Bel Air, Md., 1979-88, pres., 1989-91; exec. v.p. T.E.I.S., Inc., Bel Air, 1979-88, pres., 1989-91; pres. Shielding Technologies, Inc., Bel Air, 1987-95; retired, 1995. Mem. Northeastern Md. Tech. Coun., 1991—; bd. dirs. Leadership Acad., 1991-94. Recipient Svc. award U.S. Army, 1978, Cert. of Appreciation U.S. Army Test and Evaluation Command, 1988, Woman of Distinction award Soroptomist Club, 1996; selected as Old Master Purdue U., 1995. Mem. CAP (lt. maj. 1951-58), Soc. of Women Engrs. (sr., v.p. 1977, treas. 1979, sec. rep. 1986-88, mentor 1986—, speaker 1978—, selected to Coll. of Fellows 1993), Engring. Soc. Balt. (speaker 1980—), 99's (pres. 1951-53), Am. Soc. Indsl. Security, Am. Def. Preparedness Assn., Hartford County Econ. Devel. Coun., Assn. of U.S. Army, Northeastern Md. Tech. Coun. Home: 11 Glen Gate Ct Bel Air MD 21014

POWERS, ESTHER SAFIR, organization design consultant; b. Tel Aviv, Sept. 1, 1948; arrived in Can., 1953, came to U.S., 1977; d. Nisan and Batia (Epstein) Safir; children: Jared Barnet, Eliott Robert. MusB, McGill U., Montreal, Que., Can., 1969; MusM, Ga. State U., 1982, PhD, 1985. Music tchr. North York Bd. Edn., Toronto, Ont., 1969-77; pres. Ested Mgmt., 1975-77, Mescon Group, Atlanta, 1985-95; cons. PeopleTech, 1995—. Contbr. articles to profl. jours., chpt. to book. Pres. bd. dirs. Montessori Sch., Atlanta, 1978; vol. Nat. Coun. Jewish Women, Atlanta, 1990; mem. Ga. Exec. Womens Network; bd. dirs. Coun. Battered Women, 1994—. Mem. Nat. Assn. Sch. Karate, Nat. Soc. for Performance and Instrn. (pres. Atlanta chpt. 1984-85, conf. mgr. 1983-84, internat. v.p. 1988-90, internat. pres. 1991-92, presdl. citation 1988, presdl. award 1989, leadership award 1990). Office: PeopleTech 1040 Crown Pointe Pky # 570 Atlanta GA 30338-4777

POWERS, EVELYN MAE, education educator; b. Norfolk, Va., Aug. 4, 1946; d. Albert Earl and Dorothy Mae (Weller) P.; m. Curtis Grubb Fitzhugh, June 21, 1969 (div. 1981). BA in Spanish, James Madison U., 1968; MEd in Curriculum & Instrn., Fgn. Langs., U. Va., 1976, PhD in Social Founds. of Edn., 1985. Spanish teacher pub. high schs., Va., 1969-77; grad. instr., instr. U. Va., Charlottesville, 1977-85; adj. and part-time faculty Va. Commonwealth U., Richmond, 1985-88; asst. prof. edn. Lycoming Coll., Williamsport, Pa., 1988-91; asst. prof. social founds. of edn. E. Carolina U., Greenville, N.C., 1991—. Mem. Am. Ednl. Studies Assn., N.C. Founds. of Edn. Profs., So. Atlantic Philosophy of Edn. Soc. (yearbook editor 1994-98, archivist 1993-96), Phi Delta Kappa. Home: 307 Joseph St Greenville NC 27858-9242

POWERS, KATHY ELAINE, accountant; b. Marietta, Ohio, Aug. 28, 1957; d. Donald L. and Donna J. (Edington) Hendershot; m. Jack L.

Powers, Jr., Sept. 15, 1990; 1 child, Jack L. III. Cert. in Bookkeeping, Belmont Tech. Sch., St. Clairsville, Ohio, 1975-76; student, Ohio U., St. Clairsville, Ohio, 1976-77; BS in Acctg., Franklin U., 1991. CPA, Ohio. Confidential sec. N.Am. Coal Co., Powhatan Point, Ohio, 1978-84; cost acct./payroll supr. Proler Internat., Houston, 1984-87; fin. analyst Gates McDonald Co., Columbus, Ohio, 1987-88; plan ledger acct. Nationwide Ins., Columbus, 1988-92; sr. acct. Motorists Ins., Columbus, 1992-95; acctg. mgr. ASC Columbus Sunroof, Columbus, 1995—. Bd. dirs., pheresis donor ARC, 1987—; vol. Columbus Marathon, 1990-91, Multiple Sclerosis, Columbus, 1990-92. Franklin U. scholar, 1990, 92, Ohio Soc. CPAs, 1991. Mem. Ohio Soc. CPAs, Inst. Mgmt. Accts., Tau Pi Phi. Home: 1931 Willow Run Rd Grove City OH 43123 Office: ASC Columbus Sunroof 5200 Crosswinds Dr Columbus OH 43228

POWERS, MARTHA MARY, nursing consultant, education specialist; b. Medford, Mass., Jan. 8, 1940; d. John Francis and Mary (Denning) P. BS, Boston Coll., 1962; MS in Nursing, Boston U., 1978, EdD in Health Edn., 1985. Mem. faculty Boston Coll. Sch. Nursing; asst. prof. nursing Regis Coll., Weston, Mass.; nursing cons., edn. specialist NIH, Bethesda, Md.; cons. health care NATO, Belgium; coord. curriculum Somerville (Mass.) Hosp. Sch. Nursing; researcher medications, cardiac rehab., interaction analysis and leadership. Author: Health Promotion in Home Nursing: A Teaching Manual, 1986; contbr. articles to profl. jours. Chair nominating com. ARC Boston and Massachussetts Bay, past chmn. nursing and health, specialist home nursing, bd. dirs.; vol. Mass. Assn. Blind. Mem. AAUP, ANA, AACN, Mass. Nurses Assn., Nat. League Nursing, Mass. and R.I. League Nursing , N.Y. Acad. Sci., Assn. Nurse Researchers, Phi Lambda Theta.

POWERS, PAULINE SMITH, psychiatrist, educator, researcher; b. Sept. 23, 1941; m. Henry P. Powers; children: Jessica, Samantha. AB in Math., Washington U., 1963; MD, U. Iowa, 1971. Med. intern Emanuel Hosp., Portland, Oreg., 1971-72; psychiatry resident U. Iowa, Iowa City, 1972-74, U. Calif., Santa Barbara, 1974-75; from asst. prof. to assoc. prof. psychiatry Coll. Medicine U. So. Fla., Tampa, 1975-85, prof., 1985—, dir. eating disorder program, 1979—, dir. psychosomatic medicine divsn., 1979—. Author: Obesity: The Regulation of Weight, 1980; editor: The Current Treatment of Anorexia Nervosa and Bulimia, 1984. Fellow Am. Psychiat. Assn. (Dorfman Jour. Paper award 1987, Rush Gold Outstanding Exhibit medal 1976); Founding Pres. Acad. Eating Disorders. Office: U So Fla Coll Medicine Dept Psychiatry 3515 E Fletcher Ave Tampa FL 33613

POWERS, RUNA SKÖTTE, artist; b. Anderstorp, Sweden, Oct. 29, 1940; d. Gösta Nils Folke and Kristina Torborg (Andersson) S.; m. David Britton Powers, Mar. 13, 1965; children: Kristina, Davis. Student, Art Inst. So. Calif., 1976-83; BMA, U. So. Calif., 1986. Exhbns. include Newport Festival Arts, Newport Beach, 1980, Costa Mesa Art League, 1980, Orange County Fair, Costa Mesa, 1980, Art Inst. So. Calif., Laguna Beach, 1976-83, Studio Sem Ghelardini, Pietrasanta, Italy, 1983, Design House, Laguna, 1984, Vorpal Gallery, 1983-84, Laguna Beach Mus. Art, 1984, Gallery Sokolov, Laguna Beach, 1985-93, Margareta Sjödin Gallery, Malibu, 1988, Ana Izax Gallery, Beverly Hills, 1988, Envision Art, 1991, Gallery Slottet, Hörle, Sweden, 1990-92, J.F. Kennedy Performing Arts Ctr., Washington, 1991, Internat. Art Expn., L.A., 1985, N.Y., 1986-87, San Bernardino County Mus., 1993. Founder Found. Hörle Manor House, Värnamo, Sweden, 1987—. Home: 1831 Ocean Way Laguna Beach CA 92651 Address: PO Box 2080, S 334 00 Anderstorp Sweden

POWERS, RUTH L., lawyer; b. Niagara Falls, N.Y., June 30, 1950; d. Charles W. and Helen (Pile) Pinches; m. Stephen B. Finch, Jr., Aug. 9, 1975 (div. 1982). BA, Wheaton Coll., 1972; JD, George Washington U., 1976. Bar: N.Y. 1977. From counsel to v.p. Chem. Bank, N.Y.C., 1977-85; v.p., counsel for credit cards Citibank, N.Y.C., 1985-86, v.p., group gen. counsel consumer-internat. group, 1986-87, v.p./gen. counsel pvt. banking group, global asset mgmt., 1988—. Pres. Water's Edge Property Owner's Assn., Plainsboro, N.J., 1987—; elder Nassau Presbyn. Ch., Princeton, N.J., 1989-91; mem. Women's Campaign Fund Leadership Cir. Mem. ABA, Fin. Women's Assn. (bd. dirs. 1989—, pres. 1993-94), Internat. Alliance (bd. dirs.). Republican. Office: Citibank 153 E 53rd St New York NY 10022-4602*

POWERS, SHIRLEY MARIE, retired banker; b. Miles City, Mont., Feb. 27, 1930; d. Emil Henry and Karen Elizabeth (Topp) Swanson; m. William Howard Powers Jr., Apr. 5,1952; children: Michael Howard, Thomas Mark. AAS, Coastal Carolina Community Coll, 1969; cert. Sch. Banking, U. N.C., Chapel Hill, 1978. Lic. real estate broker, N.C. Adminstrv. asst. Bank of N.C., Jacksonville, 1974-77; mortgage loan officer Bank of N.C., Raleigh, 1977-82; real estate lending officer N.C. Nat. Bank, Raleigh, 1983; asst. v.p. So. Nat. Bank N.C., Raleigh and Charlotte, 1983-86; v.p. So. Nat. Bank N.C., Charlotte, 1987-95. Mem. Home Builders Assn. Charlotte (treas. women's coun. 1988). Democrat. Lutheran.

POWERS, STEFANIE (STEFANIE FEDERKIEWICZ), actress; b. Hollywood, Calif., Nov. 2, 1945; m. Patrick de la Chenais, April 1, 1993. Film appearances include Among the Thorns, Experiment in Terror, 1962, McClintock, 1963, Fanatic, 1964, Warning Shot, 1967, Herbie Rides Again, 1973, Escape to Athena, 1979, Invisible Stranger, 1984, Mother's Day, 1984; TV movie appearances include Five Desperate Women, 1971, Sweet Sweet Rachel, 1971, Paper Man, 1971, Ellery Queen: Don't Look Behind You, 1971, Hardcase, 1972, Sky Heist, 1975, Return to Earth, 1976, Washington: Behind Closed Doors, 1977, Nowhere to Run, 1978, A Death in Canaan, 1978, Family Secrets, 1984, Mistral's Daughter, 1984, Hollywood Wives, 1985, Deceptions, 1985, At Mother's Request, 1987, (co-producer) Beryl Markham: A Shadow on the Sun, 1988, She Was Marked for Murder, 1988, Love and Betrayal, 1989, When Will I Be Loved?, 1990, The Burden of Proff, 1992, Survive The Night, 1993, Hart to Hart: Old Friends Never Die, 1994; TV series The Girl from U.N.C.L.E., 1966, The Feather and the Father Gang, 1977, Hart to Hart, 1979-84. Office: care Internat Creative Mgmt 8942 Wilshire Blvd Beverly Hills CA 90211-1934*

POWERS, SUSAN JOAN, special education educator; b. Flushing, N.Y., Dec. 29, 1948; d. Patrick Sylvester and Virginia Lulu (Kleber) Hannigan; m. Bruce Edward Powers, June 19, 1971 (div. Feb. 1981); children: Michelle, Danielle. BS, U. Conn., 1970; postgrad., U. Western Conn., 1970-71, 71-74. Tchr. Wassaic (N.Y.) Devel. Ctr., 1970-74; rehab. asst. Harlem Valley Psychiat. Ctr., Wingdale, N.Y., 1983-85; tchr. Webutuck Ctrl. Sch., Amenia, N.Y., 1985—; tchr. adult edn. BOCES, Salt Point, N.Y., 1987-94; instruction coord. Webutuck Ctrl. Sch., Amenia, N.Y., 1994-95, network systems operator, 1994—. Pres. Gaylordsville (Conn.) Fire Dept. Aux., 1978-81, Gaylordsville Civic Assn., 1981-83; treas. Webutuck Tchrs. Assn., 1994, bldg. rep., 1987-94. Mem. Nat. Learning Differences Network, Danbury Music Ctr. Roman Catholic. Home: RR 1 Box 123B Wassaic NY 12592-9710 Office: Webutuck Elem Sch Haight Rd Amenia NY 12501

POWLEY, ELIZABETH ANN, health facility administrator; b. Massillon, Ohio, June 26, 1950; d. William Julius and Marilyn Helen (McDermott) Maier; m. Donald S. Powley Jr., June 16, 1984. Diploma, Mercy Hosp. Sch. Nursing, 1971; BS, U. Cin., 1988; postgrad., St. Joseph's Coll., Windham, Maine. RN, Ohio. Staff nurse ICU Good Samaritan Hosp., Cin., 1977-80; critical care pool Good Samaritan Hosp., 1980-81; asst. head nurse intermediate critical care unit Good Samaritan Hosp., Cin., 1981-82, nurse mgr. intermediate critical care unit, 1982-89, dir. diagnostic studies, 1989-93; adminstrv. dir. diagnostic and radiology svcs. Good Samaritan Hosp., 1993-95; adminstrv. dir. Diagnostic Imaging Svcs., TriHealth, Cin., 1995—, Diagnostic Imaging Svcs./Trihealth, 1995—. Contbr. articles to profl. publs. Bd. dirs. Mental Health Svcs. Agy. Mem. AACN, Am. Coll. Cardiovascular Adminstrn., Am. Coll. Med. Adminstrs., Am. Healthcare Radiology Adminstrs., Delta Tau Kappa. Home: 2576 Little Dry Run Rd Cincinnati OH 45244-2850 Office: Bethesda Oak Hosp 619 Oak St Cincinnati OH 45206

POZNIAKOFF, RITA OPPENHEIM, education software consultant; b. Munich, Nov. 19, 1949; (parents Am. citizens); d. Lester and Pearl Tobia (Waldman) Oppenheim; m. Theodore A. Pozniakoff, Dec. 29, 1985. BS, Cen. Mo. State U., 1973. Dept. mgr. Venture Dept. Stores div. May Co., St. Louis, 1973-75; dist. sales mgr. Seven Up Co., St. Louis, 1975-76; account exec. Christmas Club A Corp., Easton, Pa., 1976-83, Bankers Systems Inc., St. Cloud, Minn., 1983-85; edn. svcs. rep. Control Data Corp., Mpls., 1985-86; edn. specialist Radio Shack bus. products Tandy Corp., Ft. Worth, 1986-87, dist. govt. and edn. mktg. mgr., 1987-88, area edn. mktg. mgr., 1988-89; mgr. govt. accounts Grid Systems Corp. div. Tandy Corp., Parsippany, N.J., 1989; sr. account rep. N.Y.C. schs. Unisys Corp., White Plains, N.Y., 1989-90; mktg. mgr. N.Y. schs. Jostens Learning Corp., Phoenix, 1990-92, TRO Learning, Inc., Edina, Minn., 1993—. Republican. Home and Office: 7004 Boulevard East 3 1-C Guttenberg NJ 07093-5029

PRABHAKAR, ARATI, federal administration research director, electrical engineer; b. New Delhi, Feb. 2, 1959; came to U.S., 1962; d. Jagdish Chandra and Raj (Madan) P. BSEE, Tex. Tech U., 1979; MSEE, Calif. Inst. Tech., 1980, PhD in Applied Physics, 1984; DEng (hon.), Rensselaer Poly. Inst., 1995. Congl. fellow Office Tech. Assessment U.S. Cong., Washington, 1984-86; program mgr. electronic sci. divsn. DARPA, Arlington, Va., 1986-90, dep. dir. defense sci. office, 1990-91, dir. microelectronics tech. office, 1991-93; dir. Nat. Inst. Standards & Tech., Gaithersburg, Md., 1993—. Contbr. articles to profl. jours. Rsch. fellow Calif. Inst. Tech., 1979-84, grad. rsch. program for women Bell Labs., 1979, 80; named Disting. Engr. of 1994, Tex. Tech. U.; elected to Tex. Tech. Elec. Engring. Acad., 1994; recipient Disting. Alumni award Calif. Inst. Tech., 1995. Mem. IEEE, Eta Kappa Nu, Tau Beta Pi. Office: Nat Inst Stds & Tech US Dept of Commerce Rte 270 Bldg 101 Rm A1134 Gaithersburg MD 20899

PRACHT, DRENDA KAY, psychologist; b. Carrollton, Mo., Jan. 15, 1952; d. Ethan Lyle Pracht and Wilma Esteleen (Henderson) Lucas; 1 child, Matthew Kent. BA in Psychology, William Jewell Coll., 1974; MS in Clinical Psychology, Cen. Mo. State U., 1976; postgrad. in clin. psychology, Fielding Inst., Santa Barbara, Calif., 1987—. Lic. psychologist, marriage and family therapist, Minn., Kans.; lic. psychologist, Mo., Minn. Therapist Briscoe Carr Cons., Kansas City, Mo., 1978-79; psychologist Crittenton Ctr., Kansas City, 1979-81, Cen. Minn. Mental Health Ctr., St. Cloud, 1981-85, St. Cloud Hosp., 1985-87; gen. practice psychology St. Cloud, 1985-92, Kansas City, 1992—; cons. St. Benedicts Ctr., Country Manor, 1986-92. Mem. Cen. Minn. Child Abuse Team, St. Cloud, 1981-85; bd. dirs. Cen. Minn. Child Care Assn., St. Cloud, 1982-83. Mem. Am. Psychol. Assn., Cen. Minn. Psychol. Assn. (pres. 1984-85), Minn. Lic. Psychologists, Minn. Psychol. Assn., Alpha Delta Pi Aumni Assn. Presbyterian. Office: Ste 110 4500 College Blvd Overland Park KS 66211

PRADA, GLORIA INES, mathematics and Spanish language educator; b. San Vicente de Chucuri, Colombia, Dec. 2, 1954; came to U.S., 1985; d. Roberto Gomez and Maria Celina (Serrano) Duran; m. Luis Eduardo Prada, June 19, 1975; children: Luis Ricardo, Nicholas. BS in Math., U. Indsl., Santander, Colombia, 1978. Tchr. h.s. math. Santander Sch. Dist., Bucaramanga, 1973-84; tchr. mid. sch. math., mentor tchr. Hayward (Calif.) Unified Sch. Dist., 1989—; pres. Bilingual Adv. Com., Hayward, 1986-89; mem. Gate Task Force, Hayward, 1990-93, Spanish for Educators Alameda County Office Edn., 1995—. Author: Prada's Spanish Course, 1992, Family Math, 1992, Stations on Probabilities, 1994, (math. replacement unit) Success, 1994. Office: Hayward Unified Sch Dist Winton Intermediate Sch 119 Winton Ave Hayward CA 94544-1413

PRAGER, SHARON LEE, paralegal; b. Brookline, Mass., June 25, 1960; d. Sidney and Wendy (Edleson) P. Cert., Blaine Hair Inst., Boston, 1980, Lee Inst. Real Estate, Boston, 1983; BS, Newbury Coll., Brookline, Mass., 1991. Credit mgr. Frye Boot, Marlboro, Mass., 1983-86, Eaton Fin., Framingham, Mass., 1986-89; ops. mgr. Vector Fin., Marlboro, Mass., 1989-90; office mgr., paralegal Garrahan & Assocs., Framingham, Mass., 1986-90; paralegal Gargiulo Rudnick & Gargiulo, Boston, 1990-92; sr. paralegal Feinberg, Charnas & Birmingham, Boston, 1992-94; paralegal Law Office of William Griset, Boston, 1994-95; case adminstr. JAMS/Endispute, Boston, 1995—. Vol. Spl. Olympics, Boston, 1988, AIDS Walk, Boston, 1995, Horizons for Youth, Canton, Mass., 1995; big bro./big sister Jewish Big Bro./Big Sister, Newton, Mass., 1990-94. Mem. Paralegal Assocs. Democrat. Jewish. Home: 35 Wait St Boston MA 02120 Office: JAMS/ENDISPUTE 73 Tremont St Boston MA 02108

PRAGER, SUSAN WESTERBERG, dean, law educator; b. Sacramento, Dec. 14, 1942; d. Percy Foster Westerberg and Aileen M. (McKinley) P.; m. James Martin Prager, Dec. 14, 1973; children: McKinley Ann, Case Mahone. AB, Stanford U., 1964, MA, 1967; JD, UCLA, 1971. Bar: N.C. 1971, Calif. 1972. Atty. Powe, Porter & Alphin, Durham, N.C., 1971-72; acting prof. law UCLA, 1972-77, prof. Sch. Law, 1977—, Arjay and Frances Fearing Miller prof. of law, 1992—, assoc. dean Sch. Law, 1979-82, dean, 1982—; bd. dirs. Pacific Mut. Life Ins. Co., Newport Beach, Calif. Editor-in-chief, UCLA Law Rev., 1970-71. Trustee Stanford U., 1976-80, 87—. Mem. ABA (council of sect. on legal edn. and admissions to the bar 1983-85), Assn. Am. Law Schs. (pres. 1986), Order of Coif. Office: UCLA Sch Law Box 951476 Los Angeles CA 90095-1476

PRAKUP, BARBARA LYNN, communications executive; b. Cleve., Oct. 6, 1957; d. Edward Vincent and Carol Marie (O'Hara) Reese; m. Gary M. Prakup, July 2, 1977; 1 child, Sarah Ellen. BA, Cleve. State U., 1979; MA, Cleve. State U., Ohio, 1981. Cert. Clinical Competence, Ohio. Speech therapist Keystone Local Sch. Dist., LaGrange, Ohio, 1981-82; lang. devel. spl. Cuyahoga County Bd. M.R., Cleve., 1982-86; sr. clinician InSpeech, Inc., Valley Forge, Pa., 1987-88; speech pathologist Middleburg Heights, Ohio; dir. speech pathologists Litchfield Rehab. Ctr., Akron Gen. Med. Ctr., 1988-90; owner Comprehensive Communication Specialists, Medina, Ohio, 1990—. Mem. Am. Sph. & Hrng. Assn., Aphasiology Assn. Ohio, Akron Regional Sph & Hrng Assn. Democrat. Mennonite. Office: Comprehensive Comm Specialists 750 E Washington St # A-6 Medina OH 44256-2137

PRANSKY, JOAN E., lawyer, community organizer; b. N.Y.C., Apr. 26, 1946; d. John and Sharon (Harris) P.; 1 child, Leah. BS, Syracuse U., 1967; JD, Seton Hall U., 1974. Bar: n.J. 1974, U.S. Dist. Ct. N.J. 1974. Social worker Dept. Social Svcs., N.Y.C., 1967; elem. sch. tchr. V.I. Bd. Edn., St. Thomas, 1968; lawyer Essex-Newark Legal Svcs., 1974-83; supervising trial atty. Urban Legal Clinic, prof. Rutgers U. Sch. Law, Newark, 1983-86; atty. in pvt. practice Montclair, N.J., 1986—; atty., N.J. State Bar fellow Seton Hall Law Sch. Ctr. for Social Justice, Newark, 1992-94; legal counsel N.J. Tenant Orgn., 1984—; legal counsel, advisor City-wide Tenant Orgns., East Orange, Newark, Paterson, Elizabeth, Orange, Jersey City, 1976-90; adv. mem. N.J. State Com. on Rent Control, , N.J. State Com. on Multifamily Dwellings, 1983-85. Editor, co-founder Shelterforce, 1976-85; contbr. articles to N.Y. Times, others. Bd. dirs. N.J. Citizen Action, 1990-94; mem. budget adv. com. Montclair Bd. Edn., 1996; co-founder Support Integrated Pub. Edn., Montclair, 1996. Recipient Equal Justice medal Legal Svcs. of N.J., 1989, Ronald B. Atlas Meml. award N.J. Tenant Assn., 1988. Mem. N.J. State Bar, N.J. Nat. Lawyers Guild, N.J. Rainbow Coalition (Fannie Lou Hamer br.). Home: 11 Stephen St Montclair NJ 07042 Office: 460 Bloomfield Ave Montclair NJ 07042

PRASAD-HINCHEY, SHEILA, electrical engineering educator; b. Bangalore, India, Jan. 3, 1934; came to U.S., 1953; d. Ram and Manik (Kosambi) Prasad; m. Fred Alvin Hinchey; 1 child, Manik Tara. BSc, U. Mysore, Bangalore, India, 1953; SM, Harvard U., 1955, PhD, 1959. From asst. prof. electrical engring. to assoc. prof. electrical engring. N.Mex. State U., Las Cruces, 1961-67; prof. applied physics Am. U., Cairo, 1970-72; assoc. prof. electrical engring. Birla Inst. Tech. & Sci., Pilani, India, 1972-75; assoc. prof. physics King Saud U., Riyad, Saudi Arabia, 1976-78; assoc. prof. electrical engring. Northeastern U., Boston, 1979-91, prof. electrical engring., 1991—; cons. Indian Space Rsch. Orgn., Ahmedabad, 1973, 74, C.E. Smith Engrs., Cleve., 1970, Stolar Inc., Raton, N.Mex., 1979-80, UN Devel. Programme UNDP-Tokten, 1994. Co-author: (with R.W.P. King) Fundamental Electromagnetic Theory & Applications, 1986; contbr. articles to profl. jours.; rev. on several panels, ad hoc rev. NSF, Washington, 1989—. Mem. IEEE (sr. mem.), Sigma Xi. Home: 250 Cambridge St # 301 Boston MA 02114 Office: Northeastern U ECE Dept DANA 409 360 Huntington Ave Boston MA 02115

PRASIL, LINDA ANN, lawyer, writer; b. Chgo., July 27, 1947; d. Joseph J. and Helen Marie (Palucki) P.; m. John T. Rank, July 25, 1970; 1 child, Sean Patrick Prasil Rank. BA in Interdisciplinary Studies, Am. U., Washington, 1974, JD, 1977; MALS, Mundelein Coll., Chgo., 1992. Bar: Ill. 1977. Ind. contractor Baker & McKenzie, Chgo., 1977-78; atty. Pretzel, Stouffer, Nolan & Rooney, Chgo., 1978-79; sole practitioner Lincolnshire, Ill., 1979—; atty. Leonard M. Ring, Chgo., 1982; grader Ill. State Bar Examiners, Chgo., 1978-90; organizer Kennedy for Pres., Chgo., 1979-80, NOW-ERA Ill., Chgo., 1980, Ill. Polit. Action Com., Chgo., 1981. Legal advisor Holy Cross Talk of Town, Deerfield, Ill., 1992-96; tchr. Holy Cross Drug Awareness Program, Deerfield, 1993-94; religious tchr. Holy Cross, Deerfield, 1983-86. Mem. Ill. State Bar Assn., Internat. Alliance of Holistic Lawyers. Office: 35 Keswick Ct Lincolnshire IL 60069-3425

PRATHER, LENORE LOVING, state supreme court presiding justice; b. West Point, Miss., Sept. 17, 1931; d. Byron Herald and Hattie Hearn (Morris) Loving; m. Robert Brooks Prather, May 30, 1957; children: Pamela, Valerie Jo, Malinda Wayne. B.S., Miss. State Coll. Women, 1953; JD, U. Miss., 1955. Bar: Miss. 1955. Practice with B. H. Loving, West Point, 1955-60, sole practice, 1960-62, 65-71, assoc. practice, 1962-65; mcpl. judge City of West Point, 1965-71; chancery ct. judge 14th dist. State of Miss., Columbus, 1971-82; supreme ct. justice State of Miss., Jackson, 1982-92; presiding justice State of Miss., 1993—; v.p. Conf. Local Bar Assn., 1956-58; sec. Clay County Bar Assn., 1956-71. 1st woman in Miss. to become chancery judge, 1971, and supreme ct. justice, 1982. Mem. ABA, Miss. State Bar Assn., Miss. Conf. Judges, DAR, Rotary, Pilot Club, Jr. Aux. Columbus Club. Episcopalian. Office: Miss Supreme Ct PO Box 117 Jackson MS 39205-0117 also: PO Box 903 Columbus MS 39703-0903

PRATHER, SUSAN LYNN, public relations executive; b. Melrose Park, Ill.; d. Horace Charles and Ruth Anna Paula (Backus) P.; divorced. BS, Ind. U., 1973, MS, 1975. Arts administr. Lyric Opera Chgo., 1975; jr. account exec. Morton H. Kaplan Assocs., Chgo., 1976-78, sr. account exec., 1978-81; account supr. Ketchum Pub. Relations, Chgo., 1981-83, v.p., 1983-87, v.p., group mgr., 1985-87; v.p., dir. pub. relations Cramer-Krasselt, Chgo., 1987-95; sr. v.p., dir. pub. rels. Cramer-Krasselt, 1996—; cons. Velamints, S.W. Airlines, Beechnut Nutrition Corps., Foster Wheeler, Diners Club, Reading Energy, Kellogg Co., Battle Creek, Mich., 1985—, Village of Rosemont, Ill., Air Jamaica, Humana, Inland Steel, AMP, Cracker Barrel Old Country Stores, Rust-Oleum, 1977—. Singer various recitals; founder, dir. Chgo. Sports Hall of Fame, 1978-81. Mem. archives com. Chgo. Symphony Orch., 1986—, mem. long term planning com., 1987-89; mem. press advance team Papal Visit to Chgo., 1978; mem. White House Press Advance Team, Chgo., 1976-80. Mem. Pub. Rels. Soc. Am. (bd. dirs. Chgo. chpt. 1987—), Internat. Pub. Rels. Assn., Publicity Club (bd. dirs. 1986—, Merit award 1982, Golden Trumpet awards, Silver Trumpet awards), Bus. and Profl. Assn. Lutheran. Home: 155 N Harbor Dr Apt 2212 Chicago IL 60601

PRATT, ALICE REYNOLDS, retired educational administrator; b. Marietta, Ohio, Oct. 5, 1922; d. Thurman J. and Vera L. (Holdren) Reynolds. BA, U. Okla., 1943. Reporter, high sch. tchr., 1944-50; asst. dir. Houston office Inst. Internat. Edn., 1952-58, dir. office, 1958-87, v.p., 1976-87, ret. 1987. Decorated Palmes Academiques (France), 1966; Order of Merit (Fed. Republic Germany), 1972; knight Order of Leopold II (Belgium), 1973; named Woman of Yr., Houston Bus. and Profl. Women, 1958; recipient Matrix award Theta Sigma Phi, 1961; Nat. Carnation award Gamma Phi Beta, 1976. Mem. Houston Com. Fgn. Rels., Japan Am. Soc. (Houston), Houston Philos. Soc., Houston-Taipei Soc. (founding mem., pres. 1989-92), Houston-Galveston/Stavanger Sister City Assn. (founding mem.), Sister Cities Internat. (past nat. bd. dirs.), Nat. Coun. Internat. Visitors (past nat. bd. dirs.), Pan Am. Roundtable (bd. dirs.), Inst. Internat. Edn. (bd. dirs. so. regional office),. Houston Forum (past bd. govs.). Republican. Episcopalian.

PRATT, CAROLYN KAY, language arts/mathematics educator; b. Madison, W.Va., Apr. 30, 1943; d. Lonnie Clifford and Patty (Hicks) Miller; m. Michael Pratt, Dec. 23, 1967 (div. June 1989). BS in Elem. Edn., Concord Coll., Athens, W.Va., 1964; MA in Edn., Salem-Teykyo U., 1995. Cert. elem. educator. Tchr. Boone County Schs., Madison, W.Va., 1964-69; tchr. title I lang. arts/math. Mercer County Schs., Princeton, W.Va., 1969—; presenter W.Va. State Reading Conf., White Sulphur Springs, W.Va., 1991, 93, Nat. Coun. Tchrs. Math. Conf., Charleston, W.Va., 1994, W. Va. State Math. Conf., 1995. Author, editor: (booklet) Math Can Be Fun, 1991; author: (poems) The New American Poetry Anthology, 1991 (cert. of merit 1991), Treasured Poems of America, 1993; contbr. poems to The Coming of Dawn, 1995, Best Poems of 1996, articles to profl. jours. Grantee Greater Kanawha Valley Found., 1988, Kellog Co., 1993, 94, Cynthia Lorentz-Cook Found., 1995. Mem. Internat. Reading Assn., Nat. Coun. Tchrs. Math., W.Va. State Reading Coun. (pub. info. com. chair 1989-90, citations and awards com. chair 1991-95, mem. exec. bd. 1991—, Eddie C. Kennedy Tchr. of Yr. 1990), W.Va. Coun. Tchrs. Math., Mercer County Reading Coun. (corr. sec. 1987-90, Reading Tchr. of Yr. 1989, recording sec. 1995-96), Mercer County Writer's Workshop, W.Va. Writers', Inc., Delta Kappa Gamma (com. chair Zeta chpt. 1994-96). Home: 124 Valley View St Princeton WV 24740-2314 Office: Spanishburg Sch PO Box Drawer 7 Spanishburg WV 25922

PRATT, ELAINE ANN, language educator; b. Cleve., Oct. 22, 1938; d. Raymond Frank and Jessie (Prokopowicz) Kaminski; m. Lawrence Anthony Pratt, Aug. 19, 1961; children: Kenneth, Dennis, Benjamin, Jennifer. BA, Ohio U., 1961. Tchr. Hamilton Jr. H.S., Cleve., 1961, Monfort Heights (Ohio) Sch., 1961; from learning disabilities aide to ESL tutor Loudoun County Schs., Leesburg, Sterling, Va., 1979-90; tchr. ESL Loudoun County Schs., Sterling, 1990—. Tng. chmn. Boy Scouts Am., Silver Beaver award 1983, adult leader Cath. com. Grantee Washington Post, 1988, 90. Mem. Washington Area Tchrs. of English to Spkrs. of Other Langs., Alpha Delta Kappa. Home: 205 Fletcher Rd Sterling VA 20164-3009 Office: Park View HS 400 W Laurel Ave Sterling VA 20164

PRATT, KAREN MAE, mathematician, educator; b. Ticonderoga, N.Y., Feb. 17, 1959; d. Gerald E. and Wilma Mae (Hayford) Ryan; m. Steven Eric Pratt, Aug. 24, 1985; children: Ryan Anthony, Zachary Steven. BS, SUNY, Plattsburgh, 1981; MS, Castleton State Coll., 1985. Cert. tchr. math. (permanent), N.Y. Tchr. gifted and talented Ticonderoga (N.Y.) Elem. Sch., 1981-83; tchr. math. Corps de la Paix, Zaire, Africa, 1983; tchr. mid. sch. math. Ticonderoga Ctrl. Sch., 1983—. Mem. Nat. Coun. Tchrs. Math. Home: 5 Battery St Ticonderoga NY 12883-1402 Office: Ticonderoga Ctrl Sch Ticonderoga NY 12883

PRATT, KATHERINE MERRICK, environmental consulting company executive; b. Alexandria, Egypt, July 4, 1951; d. Theodore and Bettie (Curland) R.; m. Harry Kenneth Todd (div.); 1 child, Kirsten Todd-Pratt. BBA in Mgmt. Systems, U. Iowa, 1980; postgrad., U. Tex., 1985-87. Program data mgr. Rockwell Internat., Dallas, 1981-85; support coord. GTE Govt. Systems, Taunton, Mass., 1987-89, support engr., 1989-93; pres. Enviro-Logistics Inc., Jamestown, R.I., 1993—. Mem. Soc. Logistics Engrs. (officer, mem. standing com. environ. applications, bd. dirs. New Eng. dist., dir. New Eng. dist., nat. chpt. newsletter judge), U.S. Pony Club (Ctrl. New Eng. championship chairwoman).

PRATT, MARY, retired baseball player, retired educator; b. Bridgeport, Conn., Nov. 30, 1918; d. William Young Pratt and Daisy Edna Gore. BS, Boston U., 1940; MS, U. Mass. Tchr. Quincy (Mass.) Sch. Dept., 1941-65, 68-86; profl. baseball player All Am. League, Chgo., 1943-47; recreation supr. Quincy, 1948-68; assoc. prof. Salem (Mass.) State U., 1965-68; tchr. Braintree (Mass.) Sch. Dept., 1986-88, ret., 1988; mem., archivist Mass. Assn. Health, Phys. Edn., Recreation and Dance, 1941-88. Named Hon. Aux., Sargent Coll., Boston, 1939, Twiness, 1940. Mem. Mass. Interscholastic Athletic Assn., Boston U. Alumni Assn., Sargent Coll. Alumni Assn., Boston U. Hall of Fame (Moose Washburn award 1990), Weymouth Tennis and Fitness Club. Home: 1428 Quincy Shore Dr Quincy MA 02169

PRATT, RENEE GILL, state legislator. BA, Dillard U.; MEd, U. New Orleans. Mem. La. Ho. of Reps. Named Spl. Educator of Yr. Mem. Nat. Honor Soc., Alpha Kappa Mu. Democrat. Roman Catholic. Office: La Ho of Reps State Capitol Baton Rouge LA 70804 Address: 1636 Toledano St Ste 304 New Orleans LA 70115-4526

PRATT, SUSAN G., architect; b. Kansas City, Mo., Sept. 24, 1951; d. John Bohman and Alice Marguerite (Harris) Grow; m. W. Scott Pratt; children: David, Alice; stepchildren: David, Laura. BArch, Kans. State U., 1973. Registered architect, Mich., Wis. Project arch. Skidmore Owings & Merrill, Chgo., 1973-78, 83-85; project arch. Murphy/Jahn, Inc., Chgo., 1978-82, 86—, now v.p.; sr. project arch. Froelich & Marik, L.A., 1982-83, Marshall & Brown, Kansas City, 1985-86. Prin. works include New World Ctr., Hong Kong, Group Repertory Theatre, North Hollywood, Calif., Bi State Indsl. Park, Kansas City, Mo., State of Ill. Ctr., Chgo., John Deere Harvester Works Office Facility, Moline, Ill., Two Liberty Pl., Phila., Livingston Pla., Bklyn., North Loop Block 37, Chgo., 1st and Broadway, L.A., Kudamm 119, Berlin, Cologne/Bonn Airport, Cologne, Jeddah Airport, Saudi Arabia, Sony European Hdqs., Berlin, Munich Airport Ctr., 21st Century Tower, Shanghai, China. Mem. First Presbyn. Ch., Evanston, Ill. Mem. AIA (corp. mem.). Presbyterian. Office: Murphy/Jahn 35 E Wacker Dr Chicago IL 60601

PRAY, MERLE EVELYN, nurse psychotherapist, educator; b. Washington, Vt., Apr. 19, 1931; d. Clifton Clough and Dorothy (Wadleigh) P. Diploma in nursing, N.H. Sch. Nursing, Concord, 1952; BSN, Loyola U., Chgo., 1977; MS, U. Ill., Chgo., 1983. RN, Ill.; cert. in addictions nursing Nat. Nurses Soc. on Addictions; cert. clin. specialist in adult psychiat. and mental health nursing ANA. Community placement coord. Ill. Dept. Mental Health and Devel. Disability, Chgo., 1977, mental health adminstr., planning area coord., 1978-81; head nurse VA West Side Med. Ctr., Chgo., 1984, clin. specialist, 1985—; adj. clin. instr. psychiat. nursing U. Ill., 1986—. Mem. ANA, Nat. Nurses Soc. on Addictions, Am. Psychiat. Nurses Assn., Ill. Nurses Assn. Home: 175 E Delaware Pl Chicago IL 60611-1756 Office: VA West Side Med Ctr 820 S Damen Ave Chicago IL 60612-3728

PREBISH, LISA MARIE (PATTERSON), primary school educator; b. Altoona, Pa., June 24, 1967; d. Francis Eugene and Ruth Ann (Shultz) Patterson; m. John Joseph Prebish Jr., June 22, 1991; 1 child, Tyler John. BS in Elem. Edn., St. Francis Coll., 1989; postgrad., U. Pitts., Johnstown, Pa., 1992-94, Indiana U. Pa., 1995—. Tchr., catechism instr. St. Brigid's Ch., Lilly, Pa., 1987-91; 1st grade tchr. St. Joseph Sch., Portage, Pa., 1989-96, Penn Cambria Sch. Dist., Lilly, Pa., 1996—. Lector St. Brigid's Ch., 1993—; active St. Francis Edn. Club, Loretto, Pa., 1985-89, St. Joseph Home-Sch. Assn., Portage, 1989-96; student tutor; sch. fundraiser. Mem. Nat. Coun. Tchrs. Math., Laurel Highlands Math. Alliance. Democrat. Roman Catholic. Home: 536 Willow St Lilly PA 15938-1036 Office: Penn Cambria Primary Main St Lilly PA 15938

PREBLE, SARAH HAMILTON, art librarian, author; b. N.Y.C., Sept. 19, 1939; d. John Leonard and Elizabeth (Collier) Hamilton; m. Duane Preble, Mar. 13, 1961; children: Jeffrey Hamilton, Kristen Malia. BA in Psychology, U. Hawaii, 1962, MLS, 1980. Reference libr. U. Hawaii, Honolulu, 1981-89; libr. Manoa Pub. Libr., Honolulu, 1989-90; art libr. Hawaii State Libr., Honolulu, 1990—. Co-author: Artforms, 2nd edit., 1978, 3rd edit., 1984, 4th edit., 1989, 5th edit., 1994. Bd. dirs. Life of the Land, Honolulu, 1972. Mem. Honolulu Acad. Arts, The Contemporary Mus., The Authors Guild. Home: 3347 Anoai Pl Honolulu HI 96822 Office: Hawaii State Libr 478 S King St Honolulu HI 96813

PREER, JEAN LYON, associate dean, information science educator; b. Rochester, N.Y., June 25, 1944; d. Henry Gould and Helen Corinne (McTarnaghan) Lyon; m. James Randolph Preer, June 24, 1967; children: Genevieve, Stephen. BA in History with honors, Swarthmore Coll., 1966; MLS, U. Calif., Berkeley, 1967; JD with highest honors, George Washington U., 1974, PhD, 1980. Bar: D.C. 1975. With Henry E. Huntington Libr., San Marino, Calif., 1967-69; Woodrow Wilson Found. teaching intrn Fed. City Coll., Washington, 1969-70; cons. Inst. for Svcs. to Edn., Silver Spring, Md., 1981-82; vol. edn. divsn. Nat. Archives, Washington, 1981-89; adj. prof. U. D.C., 1984-85; adj. prof. Cath. U. Am., Washington, 1985-87, asst. prof. sch. libr. and info. sci., 1987-92, assoc. prof., 1993—, assoc. dean., 1991-93, 94—, acting dean, 1993-94; adj. assoc. prof. George Washington U., 1985-87. Contbr. articles to profl. jours. Mem. governing bd. Nat. Cathedral Sch., Washington, 1987-91. Fellow Nat. Acad. Edn., 1984-85; grantee Nat. Endowment for Humanities. Mem. Order of Coif, Beta Phi Mu. Home: 2900 Rittenhouse St NW Washington DC 20015-1524 Office: Cath U Am Sch Libr and Info Sci Washington DC 20064

PREESHL, ARTEMIS SUSAN, choreographer, actor; b. St. Paul, Apr. 15, 1962; d. F. Warren Preeshl and Marcelaine Evelyn (Preeshl) Westergren. BA in French-Psychology with high honors, Bates Coll., 1984; MA in Dance, Ohio State U., 1988; MFA in Drama, U. Ariz., 1989; cert. movement analyst, Laban Inst. Movement Studies, N.Y.C., 1992; cert. Labanotation tchr., Dance Notation Bur., N.Y.C., 1994. Lic. series 7 and 63 Nat. Assn. Securities Dealers. Dancer Pooh Rye & Eccentric Motions, N.Y.C., 1992; a% Avodah Dance Ensemble, N.Y.C., 1992-94, Elizabeth Strebl/Ringside, N.Y.C., 1993-94; asst. choreographer Caesar's, Atlantic City, 1994; broker The Wellington Group, N.Y.C., 1994; choreographer, treas. Artemis and The Wild Things, N.Y.C., 1987—; actor, dance capt. Creative Faires, N.Y.C., 1994—; media asst. Young & Rubicam, N.Y.C., 1995—; personal trainer Peninsula Spa, N.Y.C., 1996—; trainer Aline Fitness, N.Y.C., 1995, In High Form, N.Y.C., 1995; mem. Dance Theater Workshop, 1994-96. Actor Fall Prodns., N.Y.C., 1996; choreographer Bond, Grendel, Owl, Iroquois Dreams, Daphne and Apollo. Dana scholar Bates Coll., 1981-84; fellow U. Ariz., 1988-89; grantee Lehman Bros., Manhattan Cmty. Arts Fund, Field's Emerging Artist Challenge, Freed of London, Ltd. Mem. Cum Laude Soc., Phi Beta Kappa. Office: Young & Rubicam 285 Madison Ave New York NY 10017

PREGO, MAYDA, lawyer; b. N.Y.C., Oct. 21, 1966. BA, Yale U., 1988; JD, U. Mich., 1992. Bar: N.Y. 1993, Mass. 1993, U.S. Dist. Ct. (so. and ea. dists.) N.Y. 1993. Ptnr. Anderson Kill Olick & Oshinsky, P.C., N.Y.C. Contbg. editor: U. Mich. Jour. Law Reform, 1990-92. Mem. ABA, Hispanic Nat. Bar Assn., Phi Delta Phi. Office: Anderson Kill Olick & Oshinsky PC 1251 Ave of the Americas New York NY 10020-1182*

PREHEIM, PEGGY S., artist; b. Yankton, S.D., May 7, 1963; d. Rodney G. and Joan Kay (Senner) P.; m. Lawrence Allen Horn, Oct. 22, 1984. Student, Mpls. Coll. Art and Design, 1981-83. One-woman shows include Thread Waxing Space gallery, N.Y.C., 1995, Caren Golden Fine Art gallery, N.Y.C., 1995, Tanya Bonakdar Gallery, N.Y.C., 1996; exhibited in group shows at Pa. State U., 1995, Weatherspoon Art Gellary, Greensboro, N.C., 1995—. Home and Office: 160 E 48th St # PHC New York NY 10017

PREHLE, TRICIA A., accountant; b. Queens, N.Y., Oct. 17, 1970; d. William G. and Dolores (Cameron) P. BBA in Acctg., CUNY, Baruch Coll., 1992. CPA, N.Y.; cert. mgmt. acct. Fin. analyst Gruntal & Co., Inc., N.Y.C., 1992—. Mgr. Community Tax Aid, Inc., N.Y.C., 1992—. Mem. Inst. Cert. Mgmt. Accts., Sigma Alpha (Delta chpt.). Home: 60-48 69th Ave Flushing NY 11385-5140 Office: Gruntal & Co Inc 14 Wall St New York NY 10005-2101

PREISS, PATRICIA ELLEN, musician, educator; b. N.Y.C., May 19, 1950; d. Fredric H. and Madeline (Robbins) P.; m. Eric A. Lerner, Nov. 1970 (div. 1975); m. William H. Harris, Aug. 13, 1995. BA, Harvard U., 1973; MFA, Calif. Inst. Arts, 1987. Performer, bassist Carla Bley Band, Willow, N.Y., 1977-78; instr. piano, composition The Hall Sch., Pittsfield, Mass., 1983-84; instr. music Santa Monica (Calif.) C.C., 1989; tchr. piano The Hackley Sch., Tarrytown, N.Y., 1991; tchr. piano and composition Fraioli Sch. of Music, Greenwich, Conn., 1991—; accompanist SUNY, Purchase, N.Y., 1991-95; pvt. piano tchr., N.Y., Conn., Mass., 1980—; pianist Greenwich Hyatt Hotel, 1995—. Author: Musical Materials, 1987; composer, performer Jamaica's Album, 1984; composer Complete Enlightenment, 1986. Performance grantee Cambridge (Mass.) Arts Coun., 1977, Artists grantee No. Berkshire Coun. on Arts, 1983. Home: 162 Toms Rd Stamford CT 06906

PREJEAN, JOHNETTE MARIE, pension administrator; b. Lafayette, La., June 20, 1967; d. John Allen and Carolyn Agnes (Mouton) P. BS in bus. adminstrn. (hons.), U. Southwestern La., 1989; MS in Accountancy, U. Houston, 1996. Adminstrv. asst. Cullen Bank, Houston, 1990-93; fin. analyst Southshore Harbour Devel., Houston, 1993-95; trust acctg. supr. Pension Benefit Adminstrs., Houston, 1995—. Mem. Phi Kappa Phi, Pi Sigma Epsilon (v.p.). Home: 2010 Winrock Blvd Apt 613 Houston TX 77057 Office: Pension Benefit Adminstrs 5251 Westheimer Ste 370 Houston TX 77056

PRENTICE, ANN ETHELYND, academic administrator; b. Grafton, Vt., July 19, 1933; d. Homer Orville and Helen (Cooke) Hurlbut; divorced; children: David, Melody, Holly, Wayne. AB, U. Rochester, 1954; MLS, SUNY, Albany, 1964; DLS, Columbia U., 1972; LittD (hon.), Keuka Coll., 1979. Lectr. sch. info. sci. and policy SUNY, Albany, 1971-72, asst. prof., 1972-78; prof., dir. grad. sch. library and info. sci. U. Tenn., Knoxville, 1978-88; assoc. v.p. info. resources U. South Fla., Tampa, 1988-93; dean Coll. of Libr. and Info. Svcs. U. Md., 1993—. Author: Strategies for Survival, Library Financial Management Today, 1979, The Library Trustee, 1973, Public Library Finance, 1977, Financial Planning for Libraries, 1983, 2d edit., 1996, Professional Ethics for Librarians, 1985; editor Pub. Literary Quar., 1978-81; co-editor: Info. Sci. in its Disciplinary Context, 1990; assoc. editor Library and Info. Sci. Ann., 1987-90. Cons. long-range planning and pers. Knox County Libr. System, 1980, 85-86, Richland County S.C. Libr. System, 1981, Upper Hudson Libr. Fedn., N.Y., State Libr. Ohio, 1986; trustee Hyde Park (N.Y.) Free Libr., treas., 1973-75, pres., 1976; trustee Mid-Hudson Libr. System, Poughkeepsie, N.Y., 1975-78; trustee adv. bd. Hillsborough County Libr., 1991-93. Recipient Disting. Alumni award SUNY, Albany, 1987, Columbia U., 1991. Mem. ALA, Am. Soc. Info. Sci. (exec. bd. 1986-89, conf. chmn. 1989, pres. 1992-93, chmn. info. policy com. 1994-96), Assn. for Libr. and Info. Sci. Edn. (pres. 1986). Office: Univ Md Coll Libr and Info Svcs 4105 Hornbake Bldg College Park MD 20742

PRENTICE, MARGARET HAUGH, fine art educator, artist; b. Indpls., Jan. 25, 1944; d. Charles Egenhart and Grace (Ferguson) Haugh; m. Glenn David Prentice, 1976 (div. Jan. 1980). BFA, U. Ariz., 1966; MFA, U. Colo., 1980. Co-founder Twinrocker Handmade Paper, Inc., Brookston, Ind., 1972-74; instr. art dept. Purdue U., West Lafayette, Ind., 1972-74, vis. asst. prof., 1980-81; assoc. Twinrocker Handmade Paper, Inc., Brookston, 1981-83; vis. asst. prof. U. Wis., Milw., 1984-85; assoc. prof. fine arts U. Oreg., Eugene, 1986—. Triptych etching exhibited Portland Art Mus. (Jurors prize 1991); contbr. articles to art jours.; permanent collections include Nelson Atkins Mus. Art, Portland Art Mus., Alaska State Art Mus., Brit. Mus. & Libr., Yale U. Spl. Collections, Getty Mus. Collection. Japan Found. fellow, 1994. Mem. N.W. Print Coun. (pres. 1990-92), Coll. Art Assn., Friends of Dard Hunter Mus. Democrat. Office: Univ of Oreg Dept Fine and Applied Arts Eugene OR 97403

PRESCOTT, CARMELLA MARIA, mental health counselor; b. Chgo., Jan. 14, 1966; d. Lawrence David and Dianna Jean (Barker) P. BA, Mercer U., 1988; MA, Coll. William and Mary, 1990; advanced cert., U. North Fla., 1995. Cert. hypnosis counselor. Psychology asst. Ea. State Hosp., Williamsburg, Va., 1988-90; case mgr. Mental Health Resource Ctr., Jacksonville, Fla., 1990-91; intake counselor St. Johns River Hosp., Jacksonville, 1991-92; program mgr. Nassau County Comty. Svcs., Fernandina Beach, Fla., 1992-94, program dir., 1994-95; program dir. Henry & Rilla White Found., Jacksonville, 1995—; sec. Nassau county Wellness Alliance, Fernandina Beach, 1992—, Nassau County Alliance for Mentally Ill, Fernandina Beach, 1993-95; chair Am. Heart Assn. Heart Walk, Fernandina Beach, 1994-95. Contbr. articles to profl. jours. Mem. Young Dems., Fernandina Beach, 1995. Recipient Chairperson award Am. Heart Assn., 1994, Free Food Program award Dept. Edn., 1993-95. Mem. ACA, Am. Mental Health Counselors Assn. Roman Catholic. Office: Henry & Rilla White Found 6112 Arlington Rd Jacksonville FL 32211

PRESCOTT, DIANA LEE, psychologist; b. Tipton, Ind., Nov. 25, 1961; d. Dallas Franklin and Marilyn (Cotton) Etchison; m. David Lloyd Prescott, June 25, 1988; 1 child, Rachel Ann Prescott. BA in Psychology & Spanish, Butler U., Indpls., 1983; MA in Psychology, U. Nebr., Lincoln, 1986; intern, Ind. U. Sch. Medicine, Indpls., 1990; PhD in Psychology, U. Nebr., Lincoln, 1992. Lic. psychologist; cert. health svc. provider in psychology. Clin. psychologist St. Mary's Med. Ctr., Evansville, Ind., 1992-94; cons. Ea. Maine Med. Ctr., Bangor, Maine, 1994—; pvt. practice 6 State St. Ste 612, Bangor, 1996—; chief psychology intern Ind. U. Sch. Medicine, Indpls., 1989-90; ex-officio mem. Child Devel. Ctr. Adv. Bd. St. Mary's Med. Ctr., Evansville, 1992-94; mem. St. Mary's Comm. Action Coun., Evansville, 1992-93. Mem. Junior League, Bangor, 1996—. Recipient Regents Tuition fellow UNL, 1983-84, Rural Tng. fellow NIMH, 1984-86, Spencer fellow Tipton H.S., 1987, Rsch. fellow UNL, 1987, 88, 91. Mem. APA (divsn. 12 clin. psychology, divsn. 42 ind. practice), Alpha Chi Omega (Claudia Steele Baker fellow 1985). Democrat. Home: 307M Husson Ave Bangor ME 04401 Office: 6 State St Ste 612 Bangor ME 04401

PRESCOTT, PEGGY COLLINS, school principal; b. Laurens, S.C., Mar. 8, 1955; d. Gordon Byron and Mary Hughes (Lanford) Collins; m. Edwin William Prescott II, June 5, 1976; children: Edwin William III, Byron Collins, Tyson Brett. BS, Winthrop Coll., Rock Hill, S.C., 1976, MEd, 1978; EdS, Clemson U., 1984. Cert. tchr., S.C. Tchr. Edgewood Elem. Sch., Rock Hill, 1976-78; tchr., asst. prin. Sanders Elem. Sch., Laurens, 1978-87; asst. prin. Ford Sch., Laurens, 1987-91, prin., 1991-95; prin. E.B. Morse Elem. Sch., Laurens, 1995—. Dir. children's choir First Bapt. Ch., Laurens, 1992-93. Named Young Career Woman of Yr., Bus. and Profl. Women, 1984. Mem. Kiwanis Club (bd. dirs. 1993-96), Delta Kappa Gamma (treas.). Baptist. Home: 114 Sherwood Frst Laurens SC 29360-2642 Office: EB Morse Elem Sch 200 Parkview Dr Laurens SC 29360-2148

PRESIDENT, TONI ELIZABETH, guidance counselor; b. Charleston, S.C., Aug. 23, 1954; d. Sam and Margaret (Shokes) P.; 1 child, Kayla Javonne. BS cum laude, S.C. State Coll., 1976; MEd, The Citadel, 1984; postgrad., Coll. of Charleston, 1993. Tchr., grade 5 Berkeley Elem. Sch., Moncks Corner, S.C., 1976-77; tchr., grade 2 Ben Tillman Elem. Sch., Charleston, 1977-85; guidance counselor Ronald E. McNair Elem. Sch., Charleston, 1985-92, Jennie Moore Elem. Sch., Mt. Pleasant, 1992-94, Orange Grove Elem. Sch., Charleston, S.C., 1994—. Mem. Ebenezer A.M.E. Ch., Charleston, Charleston PTA. Recipient bd. mem. awards Charleston (S.C.) Actors Theatre Soc., 1987, 88, Young Women's Christian Assn., Charleston, 1988; named Best Supporting Actress, Charleston (S.C.) Actors Theatre Soc., 1988. Mem. NEA, Am. Sch. Counselors Assn., S.C. Sch. Counselors Assn., S.C. Edn. Assn., Charleston County Edn. Assn., Phi Delta Kappa, Alpha Kappa Alpha, S.C. State U. Alumni Assn. Office: Orange Grove Elem Sch 1225 Orange Branch Rd Charleston SC 29407-3336

PRESKA, LORETTA A., federal judge; b. 1949. BA, Coll. St. Rose, 1970; JD, Fordham U., 1973; LLM, NYU, 1978. Assoc. Cahill, Gordon & Reindel, N.Y.C., 1973-82; ptnr. Herzog, Calamari & Gleason, N.Y.C., 1982-92; fed. judge U.S. Dist. Ct. (so. dist.) N.Y., N.Y.C., 1992—. Mem. ABA, N.Y. State Bar Assn., N.Y. County Lawyers Assn., Assn. Bar City N.Y., Fed. Bar Coun., Fordham Law Alumni Assn. (v.p.). Office: US Courthouse Rm 1320 500 Pearl St New York NY 10007

PRESKA, MARGARET LOUISE ROBINSON, education educator, district service professional; b. Parma, N.Y., Jan. 23, 1938; d. Ralph Craven and Ellen Elvira (Niemi) Robinson; m. Daniel C. Preska, Jan. 24, 1959; children: Robert, William, Ellen Preska Steck. B.S. summa cum laude, SUNY, 1957; M.A., Pa. State U., 1961; Ph.D., Claremont Grad. Sch., 1969; postgrad., Manchester Coll., Oxford U., 1973. Instr. LaVerne (Calif.) Coll., 1968-75, asst. prof., asso. prof., acad. dean, 1972-75; instr. Starr King Sch. for Ministry, Berkeley, Calif., summer, 1975; v.p. acad. affairs, equal opportunity officer Mankato (Minn.) State U., 1975-79, pres., 1979-92; project dir. Kaliningrad (Russia) Mil. Re-Tng., 1992—; Disting. svc. prof. Minn. State U., Winona, 1993—, pres. Inst. for Effective Tchg., 1993—; bd. dirs. No. States Power Co., Norwest Corp., Mankato, Minn. Pres. Pomona Valley chpt. UN Assn., 1968-69, Unitarian Soc. Pomona Valley, 1968-69, PTA Lincoln Elem. Sch., Pomona, 1973-74, Campfire Boys and Girls, 1986-88; mem. Pomona City Charter Revision Commn., 1972; chmn. The Fielding Inst., Santa Barbara, 1983-86; bd. dirs. Elderhostel Internat., 1983-87, Minn. Agrl. Interpretive Ctr. (Farmam.), 1983-92, Am. Assn. State Colls. and Univs., Moscow on the Mississippi - Minn. Meets the Soviet Union; nat. pres. Campfire, Inc., 1985-87; chmn. Gov.'s Coun. on Youth, Minn., 1983-86, Minn. Edn. Forum, 1984; mem. Gov.'s Commn. on Econ. Future of Minn., 1985—, NCAA Pres. Commn., 1986-92, NCAA Cost Cutting Commn., Minn. Brainpower Compact, 1985; commr. Great Lakes Govs.' Econ. Devel. Coun., 1986, Minn Gov.'s Commn. on Forestry. Carnegie Found. grantee Am. Coun. Edn. Deans Inst., 1974; recipient Outstanding Alumni award Pa. State, Outstanding Alumni award Claremont Grad. Sch., YWCA Leader award 1982, Exch. Club Book of Golden Deeds award, 1987; named one of top 100 alumni, SUNY, 1985, Hall of Heritage award, 1988, Wohelo Camp Fire award, 1989. Mem. AAUW (pres. Mankato 1990-92), LWV, Women's Econ. Roundtable, St. Paul/Mpls. Com. on Fgn. Rels., Am. Coun. on Edn., Am. Assn. Univ. Adminstrs., Zonta, Rotary, Benedicts Dance Club. Unitarian. Home: 476 W Broadway St Winona MN 55987-5218 Office: Minn State Univ Inst for Effective Teaching 1125 W Wabasha St Winona MN 55987-2452

PRESLEY, EVA LUISE, counselor, writer; b. Jamestown, Md., Mar. 3, 1955; d. Armin Ernst and Elizabeth Louise (White) Graber; children: Melissa, Jason, Christopher. BA, Ft. Hays State U., 1974; Tchr. Cert., U. Colo., 1976; AS, Pikes Peak C.C., 1979; MA, U. No. Colo., 1995. Mgr. Fontasia Heisley Advt., Colorado Springs, Colo., 1982-85; bus. owner Design-Tech, Colorado Springs, Colo., 1985-90; freelance writer, 1990—; residential adolescent counselor Chins Up, Colorado Springs, 1993; counselor/clinician Pikes Peak Mental Health Ctr., Colorado Springs, 1993-94; counselor Parkview Episcopal Med. Ctr., Pueblo, Colo., 1995—; team clinician So. Colo. CISM Team, Colorado Springs, 1995—; vol. Child Abuse Prevention Project, El Paso County Health Dept., Colorado Springs, 1992-93. Mem. bd. United We Stand Women's Svcs., Colorado Springs, 1992-92; co-founder Youth Employment Svc., Colorado Springs, 1992; chair parent steering com. Dare to Be You Parenting Program, Colorado Springs, 1993. Recipient scholarship NCADD, 1992, scholarship AAUW, 1993. Mem. ACA, IAOCC, IATP. Republican. Roman Catholic. Office: Parkview Chem Dependency 58 Club Manor Dr Pueblo CO 81008

PRESLEY, PRISCILLA, actress; b. Bklyn., May 24, 1945; m. Elvis Presley, 1967 (div. 1973). Studies with Milton Katselas; student, Steven Peck Theatre Art Sch., Chuck Norris Karate Sch. Prin. Bis and Beau; co-executor Graceland, Memphis. Appearances include (films) The Naked Gun, 1988, The Adventures of Ford Fairlaine, 1990, The Naked Gun 2 1/2, 1991, The Naked Gun 33 1/3, 1994, (TV series) Those Amazing Animals, 1980-81, Dallas, 1983-88, (TV movie) Love Is Forever, 1983; prodr. (TV movie) Elvis and Me, 1988. Office: William Morris 151 El Camino Dr Beverly Hills CA 90212*

PRESNELL, JENNY LYNN, librarian; b. Cin., Jan. 24, 1961; d. Joseph Hobart and Carmen Jeanne (Thomas) P. BA in History, Miami U., 1983; MLS, Ind. U., 1984; MA in History, Xavier U., 1992. Libr. Xavier U., Cin., 1984-88, Miami U., Oxford, Ohio, 1988—. Contbr. articles to profl. jours. Mem. Greater Cin. Libr. Consortium. Methodist. Office: Miami U King Libr Oxford OH 45056

PRESNELL, SHARON JUNE, counselor; b. Bloomington, Ind., June 11, 1940; d. Robert Hugh and Roxie Emma (Baugh) Marlin; m. Lewis Owen Presnell, Sept. 5, 1959; children: Kevin Lane, Kyle Evan. Student, Ind. Bapt. Coll., 1976-79, Liberty U., 1987-90; BA, Trinity Coll., Deerfield, Ill., 1990; postgrad. in counseling, Liberty U., 1990—. Gen. office worker St. Joe Paper Co., Port St. Joe, Fla., 1959-60; free-lance writer, 1982—; counselor unwed mothers Jeremiah Agy. and Wheeler Crisis Maternity Home, 1985-89; counselor Greenwood (Ind.) Counseling Assocs., Inc., 1988-90; counselor Cmty. Counseling Ctr. Cmty. Ch. Greenwood, 1986—, dir. counseling Ctr. for Bibl. Counseling, 1991—. Contbr. articles to profl. jours. Dir. Vacation Bible Sch., Southport (Ind.) Nazarene Ch., 1965; tchr. jr. age Greenwood Nazarene Ch., 1971-74, ladies' Bible study tchr., 1972-84; ladies' Bible study tchr. Emmanuel Bapt. Ch., Greenwood, 1972-84, dir. women's ministries, 1980-84; leader Bible study fellowship dir. Southport Presbyn. Ch., 1983-86; workshop leader Cmty. Ch. Greenwood, 1986—, lay counselor coord., 1987—. Mem. ASCD, Christian Writers Guild. Home: 5501 Travis Rd Greenwood IN 46143-9019

PRESS, AIDA KABATZNICK, former editor, writer; b. Boston, Nov. 18, 1926; m. Newton Press, June 5, 1947; children: David, Dina Press Weber, Benjamin Presskreischer. BA, Radcliffe Coll., 1948. Reporter Waltham (Mass.) News-Tribune, 1960-63; freelance writer, 1960-63; editl. cons. Mass. Dept. Mental Health, Boston, 1966-72; Waltham/Watertown reporter Boston Herald Traveler, 1963-70; dir. news and publs. Harvard Grad. Sch. Design, Cambridge, Mass., 1972-78; publs. editor Radcliffe Coll., Cambridge, 1978-81, dir., editor of publs., 1981-83, editor Radcliffe Quar., 1971-93, dir. pub. info., 1983-93; cons. editor Regis Coll. Alumnae Mag., Weston, Mass., 1994. Editor emerita Radcliffe Quar., 1993—; contbr. articles to newspapers and mags. Recipient Publs. Distinction award Am. Alumni Coun., 1974, Top 5 coll. Mag., Coun. for Advancement and Support of Edn., 1984, Top 10 Univ Mags., 1991, Gold medal Coll. Mags., 1991, Alumnae Achievement award Radcliffe Coll., 1994.

PRESS, MICHELLE, editor; b. Memphis, Nov. 22, 1940; d. Sam and Rana (Cohen) Appelbaum; m. Robert Press, June 18, 1960 (div. 1965). B.A., New Sch. for Social Research, 1967. Tchr. U.S. Peace Corps, Malawi, Africa, 1962-64; copy editor Japan Quar., Tokyo, 1967-71; asst. editor Am. Scientist, New Haven, 1971-78, mng. editor, 1978-80, editor, 1981-90; mng. editor Scientific American, N.Y.C., 1990—. Office: Scientific American 415 Madison Ave New York NY 10017

PRESSER, HARRIET BETTY, sociology educator; b. Bklyn., Aug. 29, 1936; d. Phillip Rubinoff and Rose (Gudowitz) Jabish; m. Neil Nathan Presser, Dec. 16, 1956 (div.); 1 child, Sheryl Lynn. BA, George Washington U., 1959; MA, U. N.C., 1962; PhD, U. Calif., Berkeley, 1969. Statistician Bur. Census, Washington, 1959; research assoc. Inst. Life Ins., N.Y.C., 1962-64; lectr. demography U. Sussex, Brighton, England, 1967-68; staff assoc. Population Council, N.Y.C., 1968-69; asst. prof. sociomed. scis. Columbia U., N.Y.C., 1969-73, assoc. prof. sociomed. scis., 1973-76; prof. sociology U. Md., College Park, 1976—, dir. Ctr. on Population, Gender, and Social Inequality,, 1988—, disting. faculty rsch. fellow, 1993-94; fellow in residence Netherlands Inst. for Advanced Study in Humanities & Social Sci., Wassenaar, The Netherlands, 1994-95; fellow Ctr. for Advanced Study in the Behavioral Scis., Stanford, Calif., 1986-87, 91-92; bd. dirs. Population Reference Bur., 1993—; cons. Nat. Inst. for Child Health and Human Devel., 1975—. Editl. bd. Time and Soc., 1991-95, Special Forces, 1984-87, Signs, 1975-85; assoc. editor Jour. Health and Social Behavior, 1975-78. Nat. Inst. for Child Health and Devel. grantee, 1972-78, 83-88, Population Coun. grantee, 1976-79, NSF grantee, 1982-83, 90-94, Rockefeller Found. grantee, 1983-85, 88-94, William and Flora Hewlett Found. grantee, 1989—, Andrew W. Mellon Found. grantee, 1994-95, W. T. Grant Found., 1996—. Mem. Population Assn. Am. (bd. dirs. 1972-75, 2nd v.p. 1983, 1st v.p. 1985, pres.-elect 1988, pres. 1989), Am. Pub. Health Assn. (council mem. population sect. 1976-79), Am. Sociological Assn. (coun. mem. at large 1990-93, chmn., coun. mem. population sect. 1978-83), Sociological Research Assn. (elected). Office: U Md Dept Sociology College Park MD 20742

PRESTAGE, JEWEL LIMAR, political science educator; b. Hutton, La., Aug. 12, 1931; d. Brudis L. and Sallie Bell (Johnson) Limar; m. James J. Prestage, Aug. 12, 1953; children—Terri, James, Eric, Karen, Jay. B.A., So. U., Baton Rouge, 1951; M.A., U. Iowa, 1952, Ph.D., 1954; LHD (hon.), U. D.C., 1994. Assoc. prof. polit. sci. Prairie View (Tex.) Coll., 1954-55, 56; assoc. prof. polit. sci. So. U., 1956-57, 58-62, prof., 1962—, chairperson dept., 1965-83, dean pub. policy and urban affairs, 1983-89; Honors prof. polit. sci. Banneker Honors Coll., Prairie View U., 1989—, dean, 1990—; chmn. La. adv. com. to U.S. Commn. on Civil Rights, 1975-85; mem., chmn. nat. adv. coun. on women's edn. programs U.S. Dept. Edn., 1980-82; vis. prof. U. Iowa, 1987-88. Author: (with M. Githens) A Portrait of Marginality: Political Behavior of the American Woman, 1976; contbr. articles to profl. jours. Rockefeller fellow, 1951-52; NSF fellow, 1964; Ford Found. postdoctoral fellow, 1969-70. Mem. Am. Polit. Sci. Assn. (v.p. 1974-75), So. Polit. Sci. Assn. (pres. 1975-76), Nat. Conf. Black Polit. Scientists (pres. 1976-77), Nat. Assn. African Am. Honors Programs (pres. 1993-94), Am. Soc. for Pub. Adminstrn. (pres. La. chpt. 1988-89, mem. nat. exec. coun. 1989-90), Links Inc., Alpha Kappa Alpha. Home: 2145 77th Ave Baton

Rouge LA 70807-5508 Office: So Univ PO Box 125 Prairie View TX 77446-0125

PRESTERA, LAURETTA ANNE, newspaper executive; b. Newark, Dec. 15, 1947; d. George Anthony and Carmela (Sallustro) P. BA in Communications, Bridgewater State Coll., 1976; MBA in Mgmt., Fairleigh Dickinson U., 1981. Advt. sales rep. The N.Y. Times, N.Y.C., 1980-81, circulation sales rep., 1981-82, asst. mgr. circulation, 1982-83; home delivery mgr. The N.Y. Times, Torrance, Calif., 1983-84; S.W. mgr. The N.Y. Times, Dallas, 1984-85; west coast mgr. The N.Y. Times, Torrance, 1985-87; nat. sales dir. The N.Y. Times, N.Y., 1987-92; home delivery dir. The N.Y. Times, N.Y.C., 1992-93, group dir. distbn., 1992-95; v.p. circulation, 1995—; treas. The N.Y. Times Distbn. Corp., N.Y. and Calif., 1984-89. Recipient Pub. award The N.Y. Time, 1984. Mem. People for Ethical Treatment of Animals, San Francisco SPCA, L.A. SPCA, Am. Newspaper Pubs. Assn. Roman Catholic.

PRESTON, CAROL ANN, special education educator; b. Buffalo, Aug. 11, 1953; m. Robert George Preston, June 7, 1980; children: Nicole, Amy. Student, Keuka Coll., 1971-73; BS, SUNY, Plattsburg, 1975; MS, Russell Sage Coll., 1992. Cert. elem., spl. edn. tchr., N.Y. Program analyst N.Y. State Higher Edn. Svcs. Corp., Albany, 1977-82; tchr. spl. edn. Saratoga Springs (N.Y.) City Sch. System, 1992-94, Schuylerville (N.Y.) Jr./Sr. H.S., 1994—. Daisy Girl Scout leader, 1989-90, Brownie leader Girl Scouts U.S., Clifton Park, N.Y., 1990-93, jr. leader, 1993-94; substance abuse chmn. N.Y. State PTA, Albany, 1992-93, spl. edn. chmn., 1993-97; mem. sch. bd. Shenendehowa Ctrl. Sch. Dist., Clifton Park, 1989-92. Named Honorary Life mem. Shenendehowa PTA Coun., 1990. Mem. Phi Kappa Phi. Home: 15 Turnberry Ln Clifton Park NY 12065-1104

PRESTON, DEBRA SUE, counselor, educator; b. Lansing, Mich., Mar. 28, 1964; d. Thomas Michael and Nancy Jean (Dickenson) P. BSW, East Carolina U., 1986, MA in Edn., 1989; CAGS, Va. Tech., 1994, PhD, 1995. Lic. sch. counselor; lic. profl. counselor; nat. cert. counselor; nat. cert. career counselor; cert. social worker. Sch. counselor Roanoke Rapids Schs., Roanoke, N.C., 1989-91, social worker, 1992-93; pub. rels. specialist Va. Tech., Blacksburg, 1993-95; adj. prof. W.Va. Grad. Sch., Beckley, 1994-95; asst. prof. U. N.C., Pembroke, 1995—; mem. state tng. team State Occupl. Info. Coordinating Com., Raleigh, N.C., 1995—. Author monthly letter Counselor's Corner, 1993-95. Mem. ACA, Chi Sigma Iota (pres., sec., faculty advisor). Home: 4730-C Dunrobin Dr Hope Mills NC 28348 Office: U NC-Pembroke 1 University Dr Pembroke NC 28372

PRESTON, ELIZABETH FLORENCE, government official; b. Athens Twp., Mich., Apr. 2, 1932; d. Aaron Elsworth and Mary Ann Katherine (Lutz) Munn. BS, Columbia Pacific U., 1981, MBA, 1982. Adminstrv./staff asst. Regional Office of Mich. State Farm Ins. Cos., Marshall, 1962-68, U.S. Army Communications Command, Okinawa, Japan, 1968-74; indsl. liaison specialist (TILO)/U.S. Army Material Devel./Readiness Command, Alexandria, Va., 1975-77; adminstrv. and mgmt. officer DPCA/U.S. Army HQ, Ft. Huachuca, Ariz., 1977-79, Shasta Dam/U.S. Dept. Interior, Bur. Reclamation, Redding, Calif., 1979-81; bus. mgr., chief NAF div. U.S. Army Support Group, Bremerhaven, Germany, 1981-83; dir. personnel and community activities DPCA/USMC The Netherlands, Schinnen, The Netherlands, 1983-92; ind. rep., area coord. EXCEL Comm., Inc., Ocala, Fla., 1996—. Methodist.

PRESTON, ELODIA H., health facility administrator; b. Miami, Fla.; d. Sumner and Hannah Elizabeth (Cash) Hutcheson; m. Charles Andrew Preston, Nov. 14, 1945 (dec. Feb. 1985); children: Charlene, Clyde. RN, Hampton U., 1945; student, Barry U., 1981-84. RN, Va., Ill., Fla. Head nurse labor and delivery Christian Hosp., Miami, 1947-48; nurse labor and delivery rm. Cook County Hosp., Chgo., 1948-50; nurse pediatric and premature Jackson Meml. Hosp., Miami, 1952-54; nurse labor and delivery Mt. Siani Hosp., Miami Beach, Fla., 1954-56; nursing supr. Christian Hosp., Miami, 1956-59, DON, 1959-61, adminstr., 1964-68; psychiat. head nurse South Fla. State Hosp., Hollywood, 1961-63, adminstr. supr., 1968-78; owner, mgr. Hannah Boarding Home Adult Congreate Living Facility, Miami, 1968—. Dir. Red Cir. and Sunshine band 1st Bapt. Ch. Bunche Pk., Opa Locka, Fla., 1955-89; pres. Choir and Nurses Guild, Opa Locka. Mem. Fla. State Ch. Nurses Guild, Fla. Nat. Ch. Nurses Guild, 1st Bapt. Nurses Guild (pres. 1981-91). Democrat. Home: 2135 NW 158th St Opa Locka FL 33054-2017

PRESTON, FAITH, college president; b. Boston, Sept. 14, 1921; d. Howard Knowlton and Edith Smith (Wilson) P.; m. Winthrop Wadleigh, Dec. 19, 1970. B.A., Boston U., 1944; M.A., 1945; Ed.D., Columbia U. Tchrs. Coll., 1964. Tchr. Georgetown (Mass.) High Sch., 1945-47; tchr. Stoneham (Mass.) High Sch., 1947-50, Endicott Jr. Coll., Beverly, Mass., 1950-53; dir. research P.R. Jr. Coll., 1953-55; dean adminstrn., 1955-63, v.p., 1963-65; pres. White Pines Coll., 1965-91, pres. emerita, 1991—, also life trustee. Author: David and the Handcar, 1950, Jose's Miracle, 1955, The Silver Box, 1979, A Gift of Love, 1994. Mem. bd. incorporators Cath. Med. Ctr., Manchester, N.H., 1978-89; bd. dirs. Caregivers; pres. bd. dirs. N.H. Assn. for Blind; trustee funds Chester Congl. Bapt. Ch., deacon, 1988—. Kellogg fellow, 1964. Mem. Am. Assn. Jr. Colls., Phi Lambda Theta, Kappa Delta Pi, Delta Kappa Gamma. Republican. Clubs: Univ. Women's (London); The College (Boston); Fortnightly. Home: PO Box 25 Chester NH 03036-0025 Office: White Pines Coll Office of the Pres 40 Chester St Chester NH 03036-4305

PRESZLER, SHARON MARIE, psychiatric home health nurse; b. L.A.; d. Rudolph Edward Wirth and Bertha Marie (Thornton) Paddock; m. Alan Preszler, Aug. 31, 1966; children: Brent, Alison. BS in Nursing, Loma Linda (Calif.) U., 1963, MS in Marriage and Family Counseling, 1978. RN, Calif., Idaho; cert. pub. health nurse. Team leader med. fl. Loma Linda U. Hosp., 1963-64; office nurse Dr. Lowell Johnson, Redlands, Calif., 1964-65, Dr. H. Glenn Stevens, Loma Linda, 1965-72; team leader women's oncology Loma Linda U. Hosp., 1974-75; pub. health nurse Riverside County Pub. Health, Hemet, Calif., 1975-78; nurse, staff psychologist Dept. Health and Welfare, Idaho Falls, Idaho, 1989-91, Boise, Idaho, 1991-92; psychiat. nurse Cmty. Home Health, Boise, 1992-94, Mercy Home Health & Hospice, Nampa, Idaho, 1995—; hospice nurse, home health nurse Mercy Med. Ctr., 1995—; instr. YWCA, Bartlesville, Okla., 1984-88; tchr. Bartlesville Pub. Sch., 1984-88, Heritage Retirement, Boise, 1994. Contbr. to Focus, 1986. Mem. Am. Assn. Marriage and Family Therapy, Sigma Theta Tau.

PREVE, ROBERTA JEAN, librarian, researcher; b. Wilmington, Del., Feb. 27, 1954; d. Burton Hugo Sanders and Betsy (Kan) Klein; m. Thomas Alan Preve, Sept. 23, 1978; children: Stephanie Jean, Melanie Marie. BA, U. N.H., 1975; MLS, Simmons Coll., 1985. Rschr. U. N.H., Durham, 1974-75; rsch. asst. Eikonix Corp., Burlington, Mass., 1976-79; asst. cashier, credit dept. mgr. Dania (Fla.) Bank, 1980-83; rsch. assoc. Ctr. for Strategy Rsch., Cambridge, Mass., 1984-86; info. svcs. Braxton Assocs., Boston, 1986-87; mktg. adminstr. Summit Tech., Waltham, Mass., 1987-91; mgr. market rsch. AT&T Capital Corp., Framingham, Mass., 1991-95; mgr. Bus. Info. Ctr. Raytheon Co., Lexington, Mass., 1995—; co-owner T&R Pest Mgmt., Attleboro, Mass., 1988-95. Mem. Spl. Librs. Assn., New England Online (dir., logistics chair 1986-90), Beta Phi Mu. Office: Raytheon Co Bus Info Ctr 141 Spring St Lexington MA 02173

PREVOR, RUTH CLAIRE, psychologist; b. N.Y.C., June 20, 1944; d. Gustav and Greta (Dreifuss) Strauss; m. Sydney Joseph P., July 4, 1963; children: Joy, Grant, Jed. BA, U. P.R., 1966; PhD, Caribbean Ctr. of Postgrad., Studies, San Juan, 1988. Cert. forensic psychologist, critical incident stress debriefing. Asst. dean Caribbean Ctr. of Postgrad. Studies, 1986-87; dir. prenatal edn. Ashford Meml. Hosp., San Juan, 1987; pvt. practice San Juan, 1984—; advisor, field faculty Vt. Coll., Norwich U., 1990-91; trustee Caribbean Ctr. for Advanced Studies, San Juan, Miami, Fla., 1990—. Bd. dirs. Jewish Community Ctr., Miramar, P.R., 1986—, bd. dirs. pre-sch., 1990—; pres. Home and Sch./St. John's Prep., San Juan, 1980-81, P.R. chpt. Hadassah Sch., 1972-74; presdl. adv. com., 1990-92. Mem. Am. Psychol. Assn., Assn. of Psychology of P.R. (hon. award 1984), Caribbean Counselors Assn., Caribe Hilton Club, Nat. Assn. Children with Learning Disabilities, Nat. Register Health Svc. Providers in Psychology. Jewish. Office: Ashford Med Ctr San Juan PR 00907

PREW, DIANE SCHMIDT, information systems executive; b. Orange, N.J., Jan. 21, 1945; d. Herman and Elfriede (Witt) Schmidt; m. Jonathan Prew, Jan. 27, 1968; 1 child, Heather Diane. BSBA, U. N.H., 1967. Cert. systems profl. Programmer analyst Eastman Kodak Co., Rochester, N.Y., 1967-70; program and system mgr. Nat. Acad. Scis., Washington, 1970-72; owner Active Info. Systems, Nashua, N.H., 1974-79; dir. info. svcs. City of Manchester, N.H., 1980—; bd. dirs. Manchester Mcpl. Employees Credit Union, v.p., 1993—. Mem. Data Processing Mgmt. Assn. (sec. 1982-84, exec. v.p., 1984-85, pres. 1985-86, treas. 1986—, Bronze award 1988, Silver award 1991), Rotary Club. Office: City of Manchester Info Systems Dept 100 Merrimack St Manchester NH 03101-2210

PREY, BARBARA ERNST, artist; b. Jamaica, N.Y., Apr. 17, 1957; d. Herbert Henry and Margaret (Joubert) Ernst; m. Jeffrey Drew Prey, Jan. 11, 1986; children: Austin William Ernst Prey, Emily Elizabeth Prey. BA with honors, Williams Coll., 1979; MDiv, Harvard U., 1986. Sales staff Tiffany and Co., N.Y.C., summer 1977; summer intern Met. Mus. Art, N.Y.C., summer 1979; personal asst. Prince Albrecht Castell, Castell, Germany, 1980-81; with modern painting dept. Sotheby's Auction House, N.Y.C., 1981-82; sales asst. Marlborough Gallery, N.Y.C., 1982; teaching asst. Boston Coll., 1984, Harvard U., Cambridge, Mass., 1984-85; vis. lectr. Tainan (Taiwan) Coll. and Sem., 1986-87; artist Prosperity, Pa., 1987—; art juror Washington and Jefferson Coll., Washington, Pa., 1990; presenter in field. Illustrator: (book) Boys Harbor Cookbook, 1988, A Dream Became You, (4 book series) A City Grows Up, 1991, (cover) Am. Artist Mag., summer 1994; exhibited paintings in group shows including Mus. of Fine Arts, Nassau County, N.Y., 1988, Nat. Arts Club N.Y.C., 1988, Gallery One, Rockland, Maine, 1992, Williams Coll., Williamstown, Mass., 1993, Johnstown (Pa.) Art Mus., 1993, Blair Art Mus., Hollidaysburg, Pa., 1993, Phila. Mus. of Art Gallery, 1995; exhibited in one-woman shows including Harvard-Yale-Princeton Club, Pitts., 1991; represented in many pvt. collections including Pres. and Mrs. George Bush Farnsworth Mus. Art. Class agt. Williams Coll., Williamstown, Mass., 1981-91; bd. mem. Citizens Libr., Washington, 1992-93; active Bethel Presbyn. Ch. Recipient Fulbright scholarship Fulbright Assn., Germany, 1979-80, grant Roothbert Fund, Chataugua, N.Y., 1982-84, Ch. History award Gordan-Conwell Sem., S. Hamilton, Mass., 1984, Henry Luce Found. grant Henry Luce Found., Taiwan, 1986-87. Mem. Pitts. Watercolor Soc. (Jean Thoburn award 1994), Nat. Mus. Women in the Arts. Republican.

PRICE, BETTY JEANNE, choirchime soloist, writer; b. Long Beach, Calif., June 12, 1942; d. Grant E. and Miriam A. (Francis) Sickles; m. Harvey H. price, Aug. 6, 1975; 1 child, Thomas Neil Gering. Degree in Acctg., Northland Pioneer Coll., Show Low, Ariz., 1977. Youth missionary Open Bible Standard Missions, Trinidad, 1958-59; typographer Joel H. Weldon & Assocs., Scottsdale, Ariz., 1980-89; exec. chief acct. Pubs. Devel. Corp., San Diego, 1991-93. Author: 101 Ways to Fix Broccoli, 1994; ABC's of Abundant Living, 1995; (with others) God's Vitamin C for the Spirit, 1995. Coord. choirchime soloist Coll. Ave Bapt. Ch., San Diego, 1986—, coord. music, worship, 1994-95. Mem. Christian Writers Guild, Nat. Assn. Factoring Specialists, Nat. Entrepreneurs Assn., Bus. Incubator Alliance, Econ. Devel. Coun., Internat. Platform Assn., Soroptimist Internat. Home: PO Box 151115 San Diego CA 92175-1115

PRICE, CAROLE RUNYAN, hospital administrator; b. Covina, Calif., Feb. 3, 1937; d. Willard Ahab and Maude H. (Brubaker) Runyan; divorced; children: Devin, Jennifer. BA, Pomona Coll., 1958; JD, U. Santa Clara, 1977. Tchr. West Covina (Calif.) Sch. Dist., 1958-61, Mill Valley (Calif.) Sch. Dist., 1961-62, San Carlos (Calif.) Elem. Sch. Dist., 1962-63; sec. Stanford (Calif.) U., 1969-71, legal asst., 1973-79, assoc. staff counsel, 1979-81; asst., then assoc. dir. Stanford U. Hosp., 1981-88; dir. physician svcs. and risk mgmt. Stanford U. Hosp., 1988-93; dir. risk mgmt. and asst. prof.dept. surgery Pa. State Hershey Med. Ctr., 1993-94, exec. dir. risk mgmt. and adminstrn., asst. prof. dept. surgery, 1994—; lectr. Stanford U. Sch. Medicine, 1983-93. Contbr. articles to profl. publs. Mem. Am. Soc. Healthcare Risk Mgmt., Univ. Healthcare Consortium (risk mgmt. sect.). Democrat. Office: Pa State Hershey Med Ctr 500 University Dr Hershey PA 17033

PRICE, DEBBIE MITCHELL, journalist, newspaper editor; b. Littlefield, Tex., June 3, 1959; d. Horace A. and Diane (Hall) Mitchell; m. Larry C. Price, May 2, 1981. BFA, So. Meth. U., 1980. Reporter Ft. Worth Star-Telegram, 1980-83, 91, Phila. Daily News, 1983-87, Washington Post, 1988-91; columnist Ft. Worth Star-Telegram, 1991-93, exec. editor, 1993—, v.p., 1994—; free-lance writer, Phila., 1987-88. Recipient 1st place Gen. Column Writing award Tex. AP Mng. Editors, 1991, 1st place Mag. Writing award Women's Sports Journalism, 1989, 1st place award Chesapeake Bay AP Mng. Editors, 1990. Mem. Am. Soc. Newspaper Editors, Soc. Profl. Journalists (Ft. Worth chpt.). Office: Ft Worth Star-Telegram Inc PO Box 1870 400 W 7th St Fort Worth TX 76102

PRICE, GAIL A., mathematics/computer science educator; b. Boston, Aug. 29, 1952; d. Lauren W. and C.A. Virginia (Wenstrom) Young; divorced; children: Erik, Jason, Nicole. BS in Computer Sci., Bridgewater State Coll., 1983; MS in Computer Sci., W.Va. U., 1985. Palms tng. specialist. Assoc. prof. math. and computer sci. Bridgewater (Mass.) State Coll., 1985—, chair math. and computer sci., 1995—; math. cons. Fall River Sch. Dist., Mass., 1993—; adv. bd. Mass. Environ. Trust, Boston, 1993—; presenter Conf. workshops on gender equity in math and sci., 1990—. Adv. bd. Town of Bridgewater, 1991—. Grant dir. Sci-Ma Connection Grant, Nat. Sci. Foudn. Young Scholars, 1992-94, 1994-96, Project Palms Grant, Mass. Dept. Edn., 1992-94. Mem. ASCD, AAUW, Assn. Computing Machinery. Democrat. Episcopalian. Office: Bridgewater State Coll Hart Hall Bridgewater MA 02325

PRICE, GAYE DENISE, languages educator; b. Montclair, N.J., July 31, 1949; d. Christopher Edward and Lucie Hensla (Coleman) Walton; m. Belgacem Ben Salem, Oct. 20, 1978 (div. July 1987); m. James Kenneth Price, Jan. 24, 1988; children: Jason Wali, Elizabeth Amal. AB, Bucknell U., 1971; MA, Yale U. Divinity Sch., 1975; MS, Georgetown U., 1980, PhD, 1990. Subject and lang. specialist Yale Divinity Sch. Libr., New Haven, 1971-72; adminstrv. asst. Religious Edn. Assn., New Haven, 1974-75; dir. membership svcs. TESOL, Washington, 1979-80; adminstrv. officer Ctr. for Contemporary Arab Studies, Washington, 1980-83; instr. modern standard Arabic U. D.C., Washington, 1990-91, Mid. East Inst., Washington, 1991; instr. conversational Arabic Calif. State, Sacramento, 1993—; bilingual tchg. assoc. Elk Grove Unified Sch. Dist., 1996—; cons. Children's Internat. Summer Villages, Washington, 1991. Del. Citizenship Inst., New Brunswick, N.J., 1966. U.S. Dept. Edn. fellow, 1983-84. Mem. AAUW, Am. Assn. Tchrs. Arabic, Mid. East Inst.

PRICE, GAYL BAADER, residential construction company administrator; b. Gothenburg, Sweden, Mar. 1, 1949; came to U.S., 1951; d. Harold Edgar Anderson and Jeanette Helen (Hallberg) Akeson; m. Daniel J. Baader, Nov. 27, 1971 (div. Sept. 1980); m. Leigh C. Price, Feb. 28, 1983; foster children: Heidi, Heather. BA in Fgn. Lang., U. Ill., 1971. Asst. buyer The Denver, 1971-73, buyer, 1973-75; escrow sec. Transam. Title, Evergreen, Colo., 1975-76, escrow officer, 1976-78, sr. escrow officer, 1978-79, br. mgr., 1979-84; sr. account mgr. Transam. Title, Denver, 1984-87, sales mgr., 1987-91, v.p., 1989-94; cmty. mgr. Village Homes of Colo., Littleton, Colo., 1994—. Vol. Safehouse for Battered Women, Denver, 1986—, Spl. Olympics, 1986—, Adult Learning Source, 1993—, Kids Cure for Cancer, 1994—. Mem. Home Builders Assn. Met. Denver (bd. dirs. 1989-93, exec. com. 1991, assoc. mem. coun. 1988-93, co-chair 1990, chair 1991, Arthur Gaeth Assoc. of Yr. 1989), Sales and Mktg. Coun. Met. Denver (bd. 1986-92, 95—), Mame (chair 1989-90, Most Profl. award 1989, Sales Master award 1995, Silver Mame award 1996), Douglas County Econ. Devel., Zonta Club Denver II (charter, pres. 1990, Zontian of Yr. 1988), Colo. Assn. Homebuilders (Assoc. of Yr. 1992). Home: 1975 Linda Ln Evergreen CO 80439 Office: Village Homes 6 W Dry Creek Cir Ste 200 Littleton CO 80120-8031

PRICE, HELEN (LOIS) BURDON, artist, retired nurse educator; b. St. Louis, Sept. 23, 1926; d. Kenneth Livingston and Estelle Lois (Pemberton) Burdon; m. John Bryan Price, Jr.; children: Diane Price Baker, Jeannette B., John Bryan III. BS, La. State U., 1946; BS, RN, Johns Hopkins U., 1949; postgrad., Boston U., 1951-52. Head nurse in pediatrics Johns Hopkins Hosp., Balt., 1949-51; instr. nursing sch. Boston Children's Hosp., 1951-52; physician's aide, sec. U.S. Army-Osaka (Japan) Hosp., 1952-54; instr. pediat. nursing Holy Name Hosp., Teaneck, N.J., 1965-67; primary nurse, office nurse mgr. Englewood (N.J.) Hosp., 1974-79; dir.- curator Vineyard Theatre Gallery, N.Y.C., 1980-90; bd. mem., coord. pub. lecture series Ward Nasse Gallery, N.Y.C., 1987-92; program planner, judge, panel participant, curator Salute to Women in the Arts, Bergen County, N.J., 1977-95. Fund raiser Women's Aux., Presbyn. Med. Ctr., N.Y. Hosp. Fund, N.Y.C., 1982-90. Mem. Nat. Assn. Women Artists (past sec., v.p., pres., permanent advisor, Akston Found. award 1987, Blake award 1991, Bronze medal 1995). Home: 151 Tweed Blvd Nyack NY 10960 Office: Burdon Price Studio 151 Tweed Blvd Nyack NY 10960

PRICE, ILENE ROSENBERG, lawyer; b. Jersey City, July 2, 1951; d. Irwin Daniel and Mildred (Riesberg) Rosenberg; m. Jeffrey Paul Price, Feb. 18, 1973. AB, U. Mich., 1972; JD, U. Pa., 1977. Bar: Pa. 1977, D.C. 1978, U.S. Dist. Ct. D.C. 1979, U.S. Ct. Appeals (D.C. cir.) 1979. Assoc. Haley, Bader & Potts, Washington, 1977-80; staff atty. Mut. Broadcasting System Inc., Arlington, Va., 1980-82, asst. gen. counsel, 1982-85; gen. counsel MultiComm Telecommunications Corp., Arlington, 1985-88; east coast counsel Westwood One, Inc., Arlington, 1988-91; gen. counsel Resource Dynamics Corp., Vienna, Va., 1991—. Mem. ABA, Fed. Communications Bar Assn., Wash. Met. Area Corp. Counsel Assn., Women's Bar Assn. D.C. (bd. dirs. 1984-87). Office: Resource Dynamics Corp 8605 Westwood Center Dr Vienna VA 22182-2231

PRICE, JEANNINE ALLEENICA, clinical psychologist, computer consultant; b. Cleve., Oct. 29, 1949; d. Q. Q. and Lisa Denise (Wilson) Ewing; m. T. R. Price, Sept. 2, 1976. BS, Western Res. U., 1969; MS, Vanderbilt U., 1974; MBA, Stanford U., 1985. Cert. alcoholism counselor, Calif. Health Service coordinator Am. Profile, Nashville, 1970-72; exec. dir. Awareness Concept, San Jose, Calif., 1977-80, counselor, 1989—, exec. dir., 1989-90, v.p. Image Makers (formerly Awareness Concepts), 1994—; mgr. employee assistance program Nat. Semiconductor, Santa Clara, Calif., 1980-81; mgmt. cons. employee assistant programs. Mem. Gov.'s Adv. Council Child Devel. Programs. Mem. Am. Bus. Women's Assn., NAFE, AAUW, Coalition Labor Women, Calif. Assn. Alcohol counselors, Almaca. Author: Smile a Little, Cry a Lot, Gifts of Love, Reflection in the Mirror, The Light at the Top of the Mountain, The Dreamer, The Girl I Never Knew, An Act of Love, Walk Toward the Light.

PRICE, LEONTYNE, concert and opera singer, soprano; b. Laurel, Miss., Feb. 10, 1927; d. James A. and Kate (Baker) P.; m. William Warfield, Aug. 31, 1952 (div. 1973). BA, Central State Coll., Wilberforce, Ohio, 1949, DMus, 1968; student, Juilliard Sch. Music, 1949-52; pupil, Florence Page Kimball; LHD, Dartmouth Coll., 1962, Fordham U., 1969, Yale U., 1979; MusD, Howard U., 1962; Dr. Humanities, Rust Coll., 1968. Profl. opera debut in 4 Saints in 3 Acts, 1952; appeared as Bess in Porgy and Bess, Vienna, Berlin, Paris, London, under auspices U.S. State Dept., also N.Y.C. and U.S. tour, 1952-54; recitalist, soloist with symphonies, U.S., Can., Australia, Europe, 1954—; appeared concerts in India, 1956, 64; soloist, Hollywood Bowl, 1955-59, 66, Berlin Festival, 1960; role as Mme. Lidoine in Dialogues des Carmelites, San Francisco Opera, 1957; opera singer, NBC-TV, 1955-58, 60, 62, 64, San Francisco Opera Co., 1957-59, 60-61, 63, 65, 67, 68, 71, as Aida at La Scala, Milan, 1957, Vienna Staatsoper, 1958, 59-60, 61, Berlin Opera, 1964, Rome Opera, 1966, Paris Opera, 1968, recital, Brussels Internat. Fair, auspices State Dept., 1958, Verona Opera Arena, 1958-59, recitals in Yugoslavia for, State Dept., 1958; rec. artist, RCA-Victor, 1958—, appeared Covent Garden, London, 1958-59, 70, Chgo. Lyric Theatre, 1959, 60, 65, Oakland (Calif.) Symphony, 1980, soloist, Salzburg Festival, 1959-63, Tetro alla Scala, Milano, 1960-61, 63, 67, appeared Met. Opera, N.Y.C., 1961-62, 64, 66, 75, 76; since resident mem., until 1985; soloist, Salzburg Festival, 1950, 60, debut, Teatre Dell'Opera, Rome, 1967, Teatro Colon, Buenos Aires, Argentina, 1969, Hamburg Opera, 1970; recordings include A Christmas Offering with Karajani, God Bless America with Charles Gerhardt, Arias from Don Giovanni, Turandot, Aida, Emani, Messa di Requiem, Trovatore, Live at Ordway, The Prima Donna Collection, A Program of Song with D. Garvey, Right as the Rain with André Previn. Hon. bd. dirs. Campfire Girls; hon. vice-chmn. U.S. com. UNESCO; co-chmn. Rust Coll. Upward Thrust Campaign; trustee Internat. House. Decorated Order at Ment Italy; recipient Merit award for role of Tosca in NBC-TV Opera, Mademoiselle mag., 1955, 20 Grammy awards for classical vocal recs. Nat. Acad. Rec. Arts and Scis., citation YWCA, 1961, Spirit of Achievement award Albert Einstein Coll. Medicine, 1962, Presdl. medal of freedom, 1964, Springarn medal NAACP, 1965, Schwann Catalog award, 1968, Nat. Medal of Arts, 1985, Essence award, 1991, others; named Musician of Year, Mus. Am. mag., 1961. Fellow Am. Acad. Arts and Sci.; mem. AFTRA, Am. Guild Mus. Artists, Actors Equity Assn., Sigma Alpha Iota, Delta Sigma Theta. Office: Columbia Artists Mgmt Inc Walter Divsn 165 W 57th St New York NY 10019-2201 also: 1133 Broadway New York NY 10010-7903*

PRICE, LINDA RICE, community development administrator; b. Norman, Okla., Sept. 17, 1948; d. Elroy Leon and Esther May (Wilson) Rice; m. Michael Allen Price, May 17, 1970; children: Justin R, Mathew Lyon. BA in Am. History, U. Okla., 1970, M. Regional and City Planning, 1975. Dir. U. Okla. Crisis Ctr., Norman, 1969-70; cardio-pulmonary technician Bethany Med. Ctr., Kansas City, Kans., 1970-72; mgr. congressional campaign Barsotti for Congress, Kansas City, 1972; planning intern City of Seminole (Okla.), 1973-74, City of Tecumseh (Okla.), 1974-75; planner I City of Norman, 1975-76, planner II, 1975-80, community devel. coord., 1980-96, asst. dir. planning and cmty. devel. for revitalization, 1996—; adj. prof. U. Okla., Norman, 1986-93; cons. in field, Norman, 1980—. Past pres., mem. LWV Norman, 1979—; chmn. Norman Arts & Humanities Coun., 1983-86; bd. dirs. Women's Resource Ctr., Norman, 1991-92; v.p. Oakhurst Neighborhood Assn., Norman, 1991-94; mem., past pres. bd. Thunderbird Clubhouse, 1992-95. Named to Leadership Norman, Norman C. of C., 1992, for Exemplary Mgmt. Practice, The Urban Inst., 1989, for Outstanding Performance, HUD, 1988; recipient Citation of Merit, Okla. State Hist. Preservation, 1991, Spl. Recognition, Okla. Hist. Soc., 1991. Mem. Am. Inst. Cert. Planners (cert.), Am. Planning Assn. (sec. Okla. chpt. 1980-82), Planning and Women (regional coord. 1987-90), Assn. Cen. Okla. Govt. (areawide planning and tech. adv. com. 1979—), Nat. Community Devel. Assn., (state whip 1988—, chair nat. membership 1994-96), Homeless Here Coalition, Social Svcs. Coordinating Coun. Democrat. Presbyterian. Office: City of Norman PO Box 370 Norman OK 73070-0370

PRICE, PATRICIA KAREN, elementary education educator, minister; b. Dallas, Mar. 31, 1943; d. Warren Anotole and Sarrina Elizabeth (Wilson) P.; m. Charles Michael McInteer, May 28, 1962 (div. Sept. 1986); children: Teri Elaine Rodriguez, Debbi Michelle, Marc Stephen, Ronnye Marie; m. Aubrey John Price, July 1, 1989. BS in Edn., S.W. Tex. State Coll., 1966; MEd, S.W. Tex. State U., 1972. Elem. tchr. McAllen (Tex.) Ind. Sch. Dist., 1971-84, Am. Sch. Guadalajara, Mexico, 1984-85, Unified Sch. Dist. #480, Liberal, Kans., 1986-94; PTA sec.-translator McAllen (Tex.) Ind. Sch. Dist., 1982-84. Vol. Reorganized Ch. of Jesus Christ of Latter Day Saints, Guadalajara, 1984-85, Liberal, Kans., 1986-94, Scranton, Pa., 1994—, minister, elder, 1996. Democrat. Home: 207 Birch Dr Tunkhannock PA 18657

PRICE, RITA FLEISCHMANN, artist, educator; b. N.Y.C.; d. John and Rae (Warschaw) Fleischmann; m. Irving M. Price; children: Allyson Lou, Louis Evan, Jolan Sue. BFA, Sch. of Art Inst. of Chgo., 1982; postgrad., U. Ill., 1984. Asst. dir. admissions Sch. of Art Inst. of Chgo., 1984, asst. dir. non degree, 1985, dir. alumni affairs, 1985-93, mem. faculty, 1990-91; mem. faculty North Shore Art League, Winnetka, Ill., 1983—, Suburban Fine Arts Ctr., Highland Park, Ill., 1995; bd. trustee Evanston (Ill.) Art Ctr., 1991—, cons. Sch. of Art Inst. of Chgo., 1992—. Vol. Am. Cancer Soc., Deerfield, Ill., 1985-87, pres. N. Shore Art League, Winnetka, Ill., 1995—. Recipient award of excellence Mcpl. Art, 1988, Am. Jewish Arts Club, Chgo., 1988-93. Mem. North Shore Art League (pres.), Art Inst. Chgo., Evanston Art Ctr., Alumni Assn. Home and Studio: 1665 Dartmouth Ln Deerfield IL 60015

PRICE, ROSALIE PETTUS, artist; b. Birmingham, Ala.; d. Erle and Ellelee (Chapman) Pettus; AB, Birmingham-So. Coll., 1935; MA, U. Ala.,

Tuscaloosa, 1967; m. William Archer Price, Oct. 3, 1936. Instr. Birmingham (Ala.) Mus. Art, 1967-70, Samford U., 1969-70. Painter in watercolors, casein, oil and acrylic; One-man shows include Samford U., 1964, Birmingham Mus. of Art, 1966, 73, 82-83, Town Hall Gallery, 1968, 75, South Central Bell, 1977, Birmingham Southern Coll., 1992; represented in permanent collections Birmingham Mus. Art, Springfield (Mo.) Art Mus., U. Ala. Moody Gallery of Art, many others. Bd. dirs. Birmingham Mus. of Art, 1950-54, vice chmn., 1950-51; bd. trustees Birmingham Music Club, 1956-66, rec. sec., 1958-62. Recipient purchase award Watercolor USA, 1972; named to Watercolor USA Honor Soc., 1986. Mem. Nat. Watercolor Soc., Nat. Soc. Painters in Casein and Acrylic (W. Alden Brown Meml. award 1970, Joseph A. Cain Meml. award 1983), Birmingham Art Assn. (pres. 1947-49, Best Watercolor award 1950, Little House on Linden purchase award 1968), So. Watercolor Soc., Watercolor Soc. Ala. (sec. 1948-49), La. Watercolor Soc., Pi Beta Phi. Episcopalian. Clubs: Jr. League of Birmingham (chmn. art com. 1947-50), Window Box Garden. Home: 2831 Highland Ave S # 616 Birmingham AL 35205-1843 Office: 2132 20th Ave S Birmingham AL 35223-1002

PRICE, SANDRA HOFFMAN, secondary school educator; b. Emden, Ill., July 24, 1935; d. William Frederick and Grace May (Randolph) Hoffman; m. Arthur Elliott Price, Jr., Dec. 27, 1957; 1 child, Anne Marie Price Powell. BS in Math. Tchg., U. Ill., 1957, MA in Math., 1962. Tchr. Ill. Pub. Schs., 1957-69, Libertyville (Ill.) Pub. Sch. Dist. #70, 1970—; adj. staff Coll. Lake County, Grayslake, Ill., 1972-81, Nat.-Louis U., Evanston, Ill., 1996; interdisciplinary team leader Highland Sch., Libertyville, 1979—. Contbr. articles to profl. jours. Pres. Litchfield (Ill.) Women's Club, 1964, Libertyville (Ill.) Edn. Assn., 1979. Univ. scholar-bronze tablet U. Ill., Urbana, 1957; Acad. Yr. fellow NSF, 1961. Mem. Nat. Coun. Tchrs. Math., Phi Beta Kappa, Phi Kappa Phi. Methodist. Office: Libertyville Pub Schs Dist 70 310 W Rockland Rd Libertyville IL 60048-2739

PRICE, THEODORA HADZISTELIOU, individual and family therapist; b. Athens, Greece, Oct. 1, 1938; came to U.S. 1967; d. Ioannis and Evangelia (Emmanuel) Hadzisteliou; m. David C. Long Price, Dec. 26, 1966 (div. 1989); children: Morgan N., Alkes D.L. BA in History/Archaeology, U. Athens, 1961; DPhil, U. Oxford, Eng., 1966; MA in Clin. Social Work, U. Chgo., 1988; Diploma in Piano Teaching, Nat. Conservatory, Athens, 1958. Lic. clin. social worker; bd. cert. diplomate in clin. social work. Mus. asst. and resident tutor U. Sydney, Australia, 1966-67; instr. anthropology Adelphi U., N.Y.C., 1967-68; archaeologist Hebrew Union Coll., Gezer, Israel, 1968; asst. prof. classical archaeology/art U. Chgo., 1968-70; jr. rsch. fellow Harvard Ctr. Hellenic Studies, Washington, 1970-71; clin. social worker Harbor Light Ctr., Salvation Army, Chgo., 1988-89; therapist Inst. Motivational Devel., Lombard, Ill., 1989-90; caseworker Jewish Family & Community Svc., Chgo., 1989-90; staff therapist Family Svc. Ctrs. of South Cook County, Chicago Heights, 1990-91; pvt. practice child, adolescent, family therapy Bolingbrook, Ill., 1991—; dir. counseling svcs., clin. supr., psychotherapist The Family Link, Inc., Chgo., 1993; therapist children, adolescents and families dept. foster care Catholic Charities, Chgo., 1993-94; individual and family therapist South Ctrl. Cmty. Svcs. Individual-Family Counseling Svcs., Chgo., 1994—; staff therapist Cen. Bapt. Family Svcs., Chgo., 1991, Gracell Rehab., Chgo., 1991-92; casework supr., counselor Epilepsy Found. Greater Chgo., 1992-93; lectr. in field; bd. mem., counselor Naperville Sch. for Gifted and Talented, 1982-84. Author: (monograph) Kourotrophos, Cults and Representations of the Greek Nursing Deities, 1978; contbr. articles to profl. jours. Meyerstein Traveling awardee, Oxford, Eng., 1963, 64; Sophocles Venizelos scholar, 1962-65; nominated Internat. Woman of Yr. for 1995-96 Internat. Biog. Ctr., 20th Century Achievement award, 1996. Mem. NASW, Nat. Acad. Clin. Social Workers, Ill. Clin. Social Workers. Home and Office: 10 Pebble Ct Bolingbrook IL 60440-1557

PRICE BODAY, MARY KATHRYN, choreographer, small business owner, educator; b. Fort Bragg, N.C., May 20, 1945; d. Max Edward and Katharine (Jordan) P.; m. Les Boday (div. 1982); children: Shawn Leon Boday, Irmali Ferecho Boday; m. Richard A. Weil, May 1, 1986. BFA, U. Okla., 1968, MFA, 1970; studies with David Howard, 1972-74. Soloist dancer Mary Anthony Dance Co., N.Y.C., 1971-74, Larry Richardson Dance Co., N.Y.C., 1971-73; dancer Pearl Lang Dance Co., N.Y.C., 1971-73, Gaku Dance Theater, N.Y.C., 1972-74; ballet mistress and soloist dancer St. Gallen Ballet, Switzerland, 1974-75; dancer, tchr. Zurich Ballet, Switzerland, 1975-76; asst. prof. U. Ill., Champaign-Urbana, 1976-79; artist-in-residence Cornish Inst., Seattle, 1979-80; pres. The Dance Works, Inc., Seattle, 1981-90; dir. Seahurst Ballet, 1982-84; pres. The Dance Works, Inc., Erie, Pa., 1990—; dir. dance dept., asst. prof. Mercyhurst Coll., Erie, Pa., 1990-94; dir. Peoria Ballet, 1994—; asst. prof. Bradley U., Peoria, 1994—; tchr. Harkness Ballet N.Y., Mary Anthony Dance Sch., Zurich Ballet, Nat. Acad. Arts Ill., Jefferson High Sch. Performing Arts Portland, also choreographer; tchr. Summer Dance Lab.; choreographer Mary K. Price Dance Co., U. Ill., Nat. Acad. Arts, Cornish Inst., Seahurst Ballet; tchr. Kneeland Workshops, Port Townsend, Wash., 1988; tchr., co-dir. Kneeland Seminars, Las Vegas, Nev., Port Townsend, summers 1989, 90, Oklahoma City U., summer 1990, Am. Coll. Dance Festival, 1991, 92, 93; tchr. Pa. Gov's. Sch. of the Arts, 1991, 92, 94, David Howard summer seminar Mercyhurst Coll., summer 1992, David Howard Summer Workshop with Tulsa Ballet Theatre, 1993, 94; guest artist, asst. prof. Slippery Rock U., 1994. Choreographer 3 ballets Ballet Co. St. Gallen, 1988, dance concert Mary & Friends, Seattle, 1990, The Nutcracker for Warner Theatre Erie; co-choreographer The Nutcracker Ballet, 1991-93, Coppelia, 1993, The Little Mermaid of Lake Erie at the Warner Theater, 1994. Outstanding Dancer award U. Okla., 1968; named one of Outstanding Young Women of Am., 1977. Office: Mary Price Boday Dance Bradley Univ Communications/Fine Arts Peoria IL 61625

PRICE JONES, TONYA DIANTHA, educational and marketing consultant; b. Dayton, Ohio, Sept. 3, 1954; d. Leonard Raymond and Helen Eileen (Freyermuth) Price; m. Kent A. Jones, May 21, 1977; children: Ana-Lisa, Diantha Clara. AB in Polit. Sci., Oberlin Coll., 1976; MBA, Cornell U., 1981. Sales devel. mgr. Hewlett-Packard Corp., Andover, Md., 1982-84; customer support mgr. Think Techs., Inc., Bedford, Mass., 1987-88; mktg. mgr. Nat. Mgmt. Sys., Vienna, Va., 1988-90; v.p. sales and mktg. Bowers Devel. Corp., Concord, Mass., 1990-93; ind. ednl. cons. Franklin, Mass., 1984-86, 93—; product tester various ednl. software cos., Franklin, 1992-95; customer svcs. mgr. UltraNet Comms., Inc., Marlboro, Mass., 1995-96; pres. StrategicIdeas.com, Franklin, Mass. Editor newsletter for parents and tchrs. CLUE—Computer Learning, Understanding and Enhancement, 1993—. Chairperson computer com. Oak St. Elem. Sch., Franklin, 1992—; mem. tech. com. Franklin Sch. Sys., 1994—. Mem. Boston Computer Soc. (mem. ednl. planning com. 1994—), United C. of C. (bus./edn. partnership com. 1995—). Home: 24 Daniels St Franklin MA 02038-1104

PRICE-SHARPS, JANA L., English as second language educator; b. Denver, Dec. 7, 1961; d. Gordon Alexander and Betty Jane (Brookins) Price; m. Matthew Joseph Sharps, Aug. 6, 1994; 1 child, Tina Dawn Kipp. AA, Laramie County C.C., Cheyenne, Wyo., 1982; BA, Calif. State U., Fresno, 1992, MS, 1994; postgrad., U. of Pacific, 1995—. Cert. rehab. counselor. Rsch. asst. Calif. State U., Fresno, 1991-94, instr. Sch. Edn., 1995—; instr. continuing edn. Fresno (Calif.) Pacific Coll., 1995; project cons. SRI-Healthy Start, Fresno, 1994-95; v.p. QED Inc., Clovis, Calif., 1995—; group counselor, facilitator Drug Rehab., Fresno, 1995. Contbr. articles to profl. jours. With Upward Bound Assessment, Fresno, 1993-95. Mem. ACA, APA, Nat. Rehab. Assn. Republican. Office: Calif State U Sch Edn 5005 N Maple MS # 1 Fresno CA 93740-0001

PRICHARD, LINDA LOUISE, lawyer; b. Seattle, Mar. 6, 1953; d. William Everett Miller and Joan Louise Villa (Arata) Prichard. BA in Philosophy, U. North Tex., 1986; JD, Tex. Wesleyan U., 1995. Bar: Tex., 1995, U.S. Dist. Ct. (no. dist.) 1995; lic. social worker, Tex. Dept. Health, 1988. Law clerk, office mgr. Law Offices of Sylvia Cantu, Irving, Tex., 1988-95; lawyer, ptnr. Cantu & Prichard, Irving, 1995—. Contbr. poetry to various jours. Specialist 4 AUS, 1976-78, U.S./Germany. Recipient Key Scholarship award for acad. excellence, Delta Theta Phi, 1995. Mem. Disabled Am. Vets. (life; svc. officer 1987), Am. Legion.

PRIDE, MIRIAM R., academic administrator; b. Canton, China, June 6, 1948; d. Richard E. and Martha W. Pride; divorced. Grad., Berea College Found. Sch., 1966, College of Wooster, 1970; MBA, U. Ky., 1989. With sales room Boone Tavern Hotel Berea Coll., Berea, Ky., 1963-70; intern in administrn. in higher edn., head resident College of Wooster, Wooster, Ohio, 1970-72; accounts payable clerk, dir. Boone Tavern Hotel, head resident, dir. student activities Berea Coll., 1972-88; eligibility worker dept. human resources State of Ky., 1975-76; assistantship undergrad. advising coll. bus. U. Ky., 1987-89; asst. to pres. for campus life, v.p. for administrn., pres. Blackburn Coll., Carlinville, Ill., 1989—. Chair United Way Berea, Carlinville, 1989-92; mem. Berea Tourism Commn., Blue Grass Area Devel. Dist., United Way Macoupin Allocation Com., 1989-92; bd. dirs. Girl Scouts, Land of Lincoln, 1993—, fin. chair, 1995—; bd. dirs. Carlinville Area Hosp., 1993—, Assn. Presbyn. Colls. and Univs., Fedn. Ind. Ill. Colls. and Univs., 1993—, Fedn. Ch., 1996—; fin. chair Carlinville Hosp., 1995—. Mem. Carlinville C. of C. (bd. dirs.), Rotary (bd. dirs. 1996—). Mem. Federated Ch. Office: Blackburn Coll Office of the President Carlinville IL 62626

PRIDGEN, CYNTHIA LAYNE, distribution performance analyst; b. Sarasota, Fla., May 18, 1956; d. G. Cleveland Jr. and Helen Jane (Taylor) P. BA, U. South Fla., 1984; MBA, Nova Southeastern U., Ft. Lauderdale, Fla., 1994. Computer specialist Fla. Power & Light Co., Sarasota, 1984-88; distbn. designer Fla. Power & Light Co., Punta Gorda, 1989; plant mgmt. specialist Fla. Power & Light Co., Ft. Myers, 1990-91; sr. performance analyst Fla. Power & Light Co., Plantation, 1992—; mem. transmissiant distbn. com. Electric Utility Cost Group, 1995—. Mentor Riverview H.S., Sarasota, Fla., 1992-93. Mem. NAFE, Am. Bus. Women's Assn. (hospitality chair 1992-93), Christian Bus. Women (program chair 1988-91), Am. U of Women, 1996—. Office: Fla Power & Light Co 7200 NW 4th Ave Plantation FL 33317

PRIEBE, MARSHA L., counselor; b. Pierre, S.D., Sept. 23, 1952; d. Herbert and Kathryn (Buechler) Auch; m. Glenn D. Priebe, Nov. 9, 1974 (div. Feb. 1982), remarried Nov. 9, 1987; children: Andrew D., Christa L. ADN, Presentation Coll., Aberdeen, S.D., 1972; BS in Psychology, St. Joseph's Coll., North Windham, Maine, 1984; MEd in Counseling, S.D. State U., Brookings, 1990. Lic. prof. counselor, S.D.; nat. cert. counselor. Staff nurse Cmty. Bailey Hosp., Chamberlain, S.D., 1972-73; surg. nurse Sioux Valley Hosp., Sioux Falls, S.D., 1973-74; health/nutrition/mental health coord. South Ctrl. Child Devel., Lake Andes, S.D., 1975-85; program specialist, med. svcs. Dept. Social Svcs., Pierre, 1985; alternative care/home base provider Dept. Social Svcs., Chamberlain, 1986-91; family svc. counselor St. Joseph's Indian Sch., Chamberlain, 1991—; health care specialist Westinghouse Health Systems, Denver, 1979-81, Am. Heritage Alliance, Denver, 1985; faculty trainer dept. social svcs. U. S.D., Vermillion, 1990-91. Mem. Brule County Child Protection Team, Chamberlain, 1988—; facilitator Cmty. Parenting Classes, Chamberlain, 1989-93. Recipient Outstanding Svc. award Child Welfare Tng. Inst., 1991, Head Start Program, 1985. Mem. ACA, S.D. Counseling Assn. Office: St Joseph Indian Sch Box 89 Chamberlain SD 57235

PRIESAND, SALLY JANE, rabbi; b. Cleve., June 27, 1946; d. Irving Theodore and Rosetta Elizabeth (Welch) P. B.A. in English, U. Cin., 1968; B.Hebrew Letters, Hebrew Union Coll.-Jewish Inst. Religion, 1971, M.A. in Hebrew Letters, 1972; D.H.L. (hon.), Fla. Internat. U., 1973. Ordained rabbi, 1972. Student rabbi Sinai Temple, Champaign, Ill., 1968, Congregation B'nai Israel, Hattiesburg, Miss., 1969-70, Congregation Shalom, Milw., 1970, Temple Beth Israel, Jackson, Mich., 1970-71; rabbinic intern Isaac M. Wise Temple, Cin., 1971-72; asst. rabbi Stephen Wise Free Synagogue, N.Y.C., 1972-77; assoc. rabbi Stephen Wise Free Synagogue, 1977-79; rabbi Temple Beth El, Elizabeth, N.J., 1979-81, Monmouth Reform Temple, Tinton Falls, N.J., 1981—; chaplain Lenox Hill Hosp., N.Y.C., 1979-81. Author: Judaism and the New Woman, 1975. Mem. commn. on synagogue rels. Fedn. Jewish Philanthropies N.Y., 1972-79, mem. com. on aged commn. synagogue rels., 1972-75; mem. task force on equality of women in Judaism pub. affairs com. N.Y. Fedn. Reform Synagogues, 1972-75; mem. com. on resolutions Ctrl. Conf. Am. Rabbis, 1975-77, com. on cults, 1976-78, admissions com., 1983-89; chmn. Task Force on Women in Rabbinate, 1977-83, chmn. 1977-79, mem. exec. bd., 1977-79, com. on resolutions, 1989-92, chmn. com. conv. program, 1993-96; mem. joint commn. on Jewish edn. Ctrl. Conf. Am. Rabbis-Union Am. Hebrew Congregations, 1974-77; mem. task force on Jewish singles Commn. Synagogue Rels., 1975-77; mem. N.Y. Bd. Rabbis, 1975—, Shore Area Bd. Rabbis, 1981—; mem. interim steering com. Clergy and Laity Concerned, 1979-81; bd. dirs. NCCJ, N.Y.C., 1980-82, Jewish Fedn. Greater Monmouth County, trustee, 1988—; trustee Planned Parenthood of Monmouth County, 1982-90; chair religious affairs com. Brookdale Ctr. for Holocaust Studies, 1983-88; v.p. Interfaith Neighbors, 1988—; mem. UAHC-CCAR Joint Commn. on Unaffiliated, 1992—; bd. govs. Hebrew Union Coll.-Jewish Inst. Religion, 1993—; trustee Union Am. Hebrew Congregations, 1994—. Cited by B'nai Brith Women, 1971; named Woman of Yr. Temple Israel, Columbus, Ohio, 1972, Woman of Yr. Ladies Aux. N.Y. chpt. Jewish War Vets., 1973, Woman for All Seasons N. L.I. region Women's Am. ORT, 1973, Extraordinary Women of Achievement NCCJ, 1978, Woman of Achievement Monmouth County Adv. Commn. on Status Women, 1988; recipient Quality of Life award Dist. One chpt. B'nai B'rith Women, 1973, Medallion Judaic Heritage Soc., 1978, Eleanor Roosevelt Humanities award Women's div. State of Israel Bonds, 1980, Rabbinical award Coun. Jewish Fedn., 1988, Woman of Leadership award Monmouth Coun. Girl Scouts U.S., 1991, The Woman Who Dares award Nat. Coun. Jewish Women, 1993. Mem. Hadassah (life), Ctrl. Conf. Am. Rabbis, NOW, Am. Jewish Congress, Am. Jewish Com., Assn. Reform Zionists Am., Jewish Women Internat. (life), Jewish Peace Fellowship, Women's Rabbinic Network, Nat. Breast Cancer Coalition. Home: 10 Wedgewood Cir Eatontown NJ 07724-1203 Office: 332 Hance Ave Tinton Falls NJ 07724-2730

PRIESMAN, ELINOR LEE SOLL, family dynamics administrator, mediator, educator; b. Mpls., Jan. 19, 1938; d. Arthur and Harriet Lucille (Premack) Soll; m. Ira Morton Priesman, Mar. 30, 1958; children: Phillip Sherman, Artyce-Joy Erin. PhD, Union Inst., 1993. Cert. mediator, Va.; cert. family life educator. Nursery sch. tchr. Jewish Comty. Ctr., Santa Monica, Calif., 1958-59; head tchr. Altrusa Day Nursery, Battle Creek, Mich., 1959-60; prin. Arlington/Fairfax Jewish Ctr., Arlington, Va., 1966-67; tchr. grades 1-10 Congregation Olam Tikvah, Fairfax, Va., 1970-75; dir. Creative Play Nursery Sch., Fairfax, Va., 1970-71; tchr. high sch. Temple Sinai, Washington, Va., 1976-78; prin. Congregation Olam Tikvah, Fairfax, Va., 1975-76; asst. to pres.-emeritus Coun. for Advancement and Support of Edn., McLean, Va., 1987-90; cons. to univ. Union for Experimenting Colls. and Univs., McLean, Va., 1988-90; dir. family dynamics inst. Fairfax; mem. doctoral com. Union Inst., Cin., 1991-92, 92—; faculty mentor Ea. U., Albuquerque, 1993—. Author: The Empowered Parent, 1993, A New Perspective on Parenting, 1994 (Spanish, Korean translations 1996), A New Perspective on Parenting for Attorneys and Mediators, 1995; editor: Empowered Parenting newsletter, 1991-92. Pres. No. Va. Artistic Skating Club, Manassas, 1983-85; chair edn. com. Olam Tikvah Synagogue, Fairfax. Recipient Pres.'s award Olam Tikvah Synagogue, 1976. Mem. N.Am. Soc. Adlerian Psychology, Nat. Coun. on Family Rels., Children's Rights Coun., Acad. Family Mediators, No. Va. Mediation Svc. (mediator), Hadassah (life, Alexandria chpt. pres. 1966-67, Esther award 1965). Jewish. Office: Family Dynamics Inst 9302 Swinburne Ct Fairfax VA 22031-3027

PRIEST, HARTWELL WYSE, artist; b. Brantford, Ont., Can., Jan. 1, 1901; d. John Frank Henry and Rachel Thayer (Gavet) Wyse; m. A.J. Gustin Priest, Aug. 4, 1927; children: Paul Lambert, Marianna Thayer. BA, Smith Coll. Former tchr. graphic art Va. Art Inst., Charlottesville; former lectr. on prints and lithography; juror art exhbn. Unitarian Ch., 1993. One-woman shows include Argent Gallery, N.Y.C., 1955, 58, 60, 73, 77, 81, Va., 1969, 71, Nantucket, Mass., 1956, Ft. Lauderdale, Fla. Art Ctr., 1956; Pen & Brush, N.Y.C., 1973, 91, invitational retrospective exhbn. McGuffey Art Ctr., Charlottesville, Va., 1984, Va., N.Y., 1984, 88; work represented in permanent collections Library of Congress Washington, Norton Gallery, Palm Beach, Fla., Soc. Am. Graphic Artists, Hunterdon County Art Ctr., Longwood Coll., Smith Coll., Va. Mus., Richmond, Carnegie Mellon U. and numerous others; solo exhbn. of prints McGuffey Art Ctr., Charlottesville, Va., 1988, 90, 93, Woodstock Artist Gallery, 1990, Soc. Am. Graphic Artists, 1988-89, 92, Bombay, 1989, U. Va. Hosp., 1989, Bergen Mus. Art and Sci., 1991; represented in group shows McGuffey Gallery, 1988, 94, Gallery Show, Richmond, Va., 1988, Nat. Assn. Women Artists, Florence, Italy, 1972, N.Y.C., 1989, 96, ann. show Ojibway Hotel Club, Pointe au Baril, Georgian Bay, Ont., Can., 1991, Soc. Am. Graphic Srts, N.Y.C., 1989, 92, Woodstock, N.Y. Art Assoc., 1990, McGuffey Art Ctr., Charlottesville, Va., 1990, 94, Pen and Brush ann. Graphic Show, N.Y.C., 1991 (award for etching Spring, Ada Rosario Cecere Meml. award), Bergen Mus., N.J., 1991, Ojibway Club, Ont., Can., 1991; Pen and Brush Christmas exhbn., 1994-95, Showing of a Video, Harrisonburg, Va.; represented in traveling group shows Nat. Assn. Women Artists, Puerto Rico, 1987, India, 1989, N.Y.C., 1994; pvt. collection U. Va. Hosp., Charlottesville, 1989; subject of TV documentary Hartwell Priest: Printmaker, 1995. Recipient awards for lithograph Field Flowers, Longwood Coll., 1965, Nat. Assn. Woman Artists, 1965, lithograph West Wind, A Buell award, 1961, print Streets of Silence, T. Giorgi Meml. award, 1973, lithograph Blue Lichen, Pen & Brush, 1984, award for collage, 1985; 1st award for graphics Blue Ridge Art Show, 1985, Gene A. Walker award for print Glacial Rocks, 1986, award for print Blue Ridge Show, 1987, Philip Isenburg award for graphic PreCambrian Rock Pattern, 1988, Ada R. Cecere Meml. award Pen and Brush, 1991, Art award Piedmont Coun. Arts, 1993. Mem. Nat. Assn. Women Artists (Travelling Printmaking Exhbn. 1987-89), Pen and Brush, Soc. Am. Graphic Artists, Washington Print Club, 2d St. Gallery, Charlottesville, McGuffey Art Ctr. Home: 41 Old Farm Rd Charlottesville VA 22903-4725

PRIEST, RUTH EMILY, music minister, choir director, composer arranger; b. Detroit, Nov. 7, 1933; d. William and Gertrude Hilda (Stockley) P. Student, Keyboard Studios, Detroit, 1949-52, Wayne State U., Detroit, 1953, 57, Ea. Pentecostal Bible Coll., Peterborough, Ont., Can., 1954-55, Art Ctr. Music Sch., Detroit Inst. Mus. Arts, 1953-54. Legal sec., 1951-90; organist, pianist, vocalist Berea Tabernacle, Detroit, 1943-61; organist Bethany Presbyn. Ch., Ft. Lauderdale, Fla., 1961-67, 69-72; choir dir., organist Bethany Drive-in Ch., Ft. Lauderdale, Fla.; organist First Bapt. Ch., Pompano Beach, Fla., 1967-68, St. Ambrose Episcopal Ch., Ft. Lauderdale, 1969-72; music dir., organist Grace Brethren Ch., Ft. Lauderdale, 1972-75; organist Boca Raton (Fla.) Community Ch., Bibletown, 1975-85; min. music, organist Warrendale Community Ch., Dearborn, Mich., 1985—; ptnr. Miracle Music Enterprises; concert and ch. organist/pianist; organist numerous weddings, city-wide rallies of Detroit and Miami Youth for Christ, Christ for Labor and Mgmt., Holiness Youth Crusade, numerous other civic and religious events; featured weekly as piano soloist and accompanist on Crusade for Christ Telecast, Detroit, 1950-60, CBC-TV, Windsor, Ont., Can.; staff organist Enquire Hotel, Galt Ocean Mile, Ft. Lauderdale, Fla., 1962-67; tchr. piano adult edn. evening sch. program Southfield (Mich.) Pub. Sch. System, 1991—. Ongoing educator in pvt. piano, organ, music theory; Recording artist: Ruth Priest at the Organ, Love Notes from the Heart, Christmas with Ruth. Mem. Am. Guild Organists (past mem. exec. bd. Detroit chpt.). Office: Miracle Music Enterprises care Warrendale Cmty Ch 19700 Ford Rd Dearborn MI 48128

PRIEST, SHARON DEVLIN, state official; b. Montreal, Quebec, Can.; m. Bill Priest; 1 child, Adam. Tax preparer, instr. H & R Block, Little Rock, 1976-78; account exec. Greater Little Rock C. of C.; owner, founder Devlin Co.; mem. Little Rock Bd. Dirs., 1986—; vice mayor Little Rock, 1989-91, mayor, 1991-93; Sec. of State State of Arkansas, 1994—; bd. dirs. Invesco Inc., New Futures. Bd. dirs., past pres. Metroplan (Environ. Svc. award 1982), YMCA, Southwest Hosp.; mem. Advt. and Promotion commn., Ark. Internat. Visitors Coun., Pulaski Are Transp. Svc. Policy Com., St. Theresa's Parish Coun., Exec. com. for Ark. Mcpl. League, Nat. League of Cities Trans. and Communications Steering Com. and Policy Com., adv. bd. M.M. Cohn., Little Rock City Beautiful Commn., 1980-86; former bd. dirs. Downtown Partnership, Southwest YMCA, 1984, 86, sec.; former mem. Community Housing Resource Bd., 1984-86, Pub. Facilities Bd. Southwest Hosp., 1985-86, Southwest Merchants' Assn., 1985—, 2d v.p., 1985; chmn. Little Rock Arts and Humanities Promotion Commn.; led petition dr. for appropriation for Fourche Creek Plan 7A. Mem. Leadership Inst. Alumni Assn. (4 Bernard de la Harpe awards). Office: Office of Secretary of State State Capitol Bldg 256 Little Rock AR 72201*

PRIGMORE, MARALEE SANDS, inn owner; b. Kansas City, Mo., July 22, 1930; d. Virgil J. and Edith (Plimmer) Sands; m. Edward Parks Prigmore, Oct. 28, 1949; children: Suzette Rexford, Margaret Michele Prigmore Van Cleave. Projects mgr. Rad Daniel Corp., Memphis, 1963-67; pres. Maralee Prigmore, Contractor, Memphis, 1967-76, Maralee Prigmore, Inc., Gen. Contractor, Memphis, 1974-76; constrn. engr. McDonald's Corp., New Orleans, 1977-84; pres., owner Heritage Hist. Homes, 1984—; owner Sully Mansion Bed and Breakfast Inn, New Orleans. Bd. dirs. Symphony League, Fine Arts Festival, Birmingham, Ala., 1956-58, Needs Children's Lunch Program, Memphis, 1968-70; mem. Air. Svc. Commn. Memphis, 1972-77; bd. dirs. Family Svc. Assn. Memphis, 1972-75; del. Rep. Conv., 1972, 76; pres. Rep. Women, Memphis, 1974; mem. fin. com. Election Sen. Bill Brock, Tenn., 1976; mem. Nat. Civic Affairs Com., Washington, 1973-76. Mem. Nat. Home Builders. Presbyterian. Home: 2631 Prytania St New Orleans LA 70130-5962

PRIMO, JOAN ERWINA, retail and real estate consulting business owner; b. Detroit, Aug. 28, 1959; d. Joseph Carmen and Marie Ann (Nash) P. BA, Wellesley Coll., 1981; MBA, Harvard U., 1985. Acct. exec. Michigan Bell, Detroit, 1981-82, AT&T Info. Sys., Southfield, Mich., 1983; planning analyst Gen. Motors, Detroit, 1984; v.p. Howard L. Green & Assocs., Troy, Mich., 1985-89; prin., founder The Strategic Edge, Inc., Southfield, 1989—. Contbr. articles to profl. jours. Founders soc. mem. Detroit Inst. Arts, 1989—. Mem. Internat. Coun. Shpping Ctrs. (faculty, seminar leader 1987-), Wellesley Club Southeastern Mich. (pres. 1994—), Harvard Bus. Sch. Club Detroit (bd. dirs. 1994—, v.p. 1995—, exec. v.p. 1996), Ivy Club Detroit (bd. dirs. 1994—, sec. 1995—). Republican. Roman Catholic. Home: 1185 Stonecrest Dr Bloomfield Hills MI 48302-2841 Office: The Strategic Edge 24333 Southfield Rd Ste 211 Southfield MI 48075-2849

PRINCE, DONNA JEAN, artist; b. L.A., Feb. 3, 1954; d. Robert Henry and Anna Marie (Estatico) P.; m. Donald James Molyneux, Sept. 2, 1989. BA with honors, Art Ctr. Coll. of Design, 1989. Key background painter Queen of the Universe Prodn., L.A., 1990, Disney TV Animation, N. Hollywood, 1995—; background painter Turner Publ., Hollywood, Calif., 1991, Hanna Barbera, Hollywood, 1991-92, Rich Animation, Burbank, Calif., 1993-94. Mem. neighborhood activist Friends of Washington Park, Pasadena, 1991-96, workshop presenter Neighborhoods USA Conf. Pasadena, 1994. Recipient Vol. award City of Pasadena Parks & Recs., 1995. Mem. Motion Picture Screen Cartoonists Guild, Friends of Washington Park (pres. 1991-94), Soc. of Illustrators (v.p. 1991). Democrat. Home: 1277 N El Molino Pasadena CA 91104 Office: Disney TV Animation Ste 600 5200 Lankershim Blvd North Hollywood CA 91601

PRINCE, FRANCES ANNE KIELY, civic worker; b. Toledo, Dec. 20, 1923; d. John Thomas and Frances (Pusteoska) Kiely; m. Richard Edward Prince, Jr., Aug. 27, 1951; children: Anne, Richard III (dec.). Student U. Louisville, 1947-49; AB, Berea Coll., 1951; postgrad., Kent Sch. Social Work, 1951, Creighton U., 1969; MPA, U. Nebr., Omaha, 1978. Instr. flower arranging Western Wyo. Jr. Coll., 1965, 66; editor Nebr. Garden News, 1979-81, 83-90, emeritus, 1990. Author poems. Chmn. Lone Troop coun. Girl Scouts U.S.A., 1954-57, trainer leaders, 1954-68, mem. state camping com., 1959-61, bd. dirs. Wyo. state coun., 1966-69; chmn. Cmty. Improvement, Green River, Wyo., 1959, 63-65, Wyo. Fedn. Women's Clubs State Libr. Svcs., 1966-69; mem. Wyo. State Adv. Bd. on Libr. Inter-Co-op., 1965-69, state libr. bd., 1965-69, Nat. sub com. Commn. on the Bicentennial of the U.S. Constitution, 1986-91; bd. dirs. Sweetwater County Libr. System, 1962-69, pres. bd., 1967-68; adv. coun. Sch. Dist. 66, 1970-79; bd. dirs. Opera Angels, 1971, fund raising chmn., 1971-72, v.p., 1974-80; bd. dirs. Morning Musicale, 1971-82; bazaar com. Children's Hosp., 1970-75; docent Joslyn Art Mus., 1970—; mem. Nebr. Forestry Adv. Bd., 1976—; citizens adv. bd. Met. Area Planning Agy., 1979—; mem. Nebr. Tree-Planting Commn., 1980—; bd. dirs. U.S. Constn. Bicentennial Commn. Nebr., 1986-92, Omaha Commn. on the Bicentennial, 1987-92, Nat. commn. on Bicentennial of U.S. Constitution, 1986-92; bd. dirs. United Ch. Christ, Intermountain, 1963-69, mem. exec. com., 1966-69. Recipient Libr. Svc. award Sweetwater County Library, 1968; Girl Scout Svcs. award, 1967; Conservation award U.S. Forest Service, 1981; Plant Two Trees award, 1981; Nat. Arbor Day award, 1982; Pres. award Nat. coun. of State Garden Clubs, 1986, 87, 89, Joyce Kilmer award Nat. Arbor Day Found., 1990; awards U.S. Constn. Bicentennial Commn. Nebr., 1987, 91, Omaha Commn. on the

Bicentennial, 1987, Nat. Bicentennial Leadership award Coun. for Advancement of Citizenship, 1989, Nat. Conservation medal DAR, 1991, George Washington silver award Nat. commn. on Bicentennial of U.S. Constitution, 1992, Mighty Oak award Garden Clubs of Nebr., 1992. Mem. ALA, AAUW (Vol. of Yr. Omaha br. 1989), New Neighbors League (dir. 1969-71), Ikebana Internat., Symphony Guild, Assistance League Omaha, Omaha Playhouse Guild, Nebr. Libr. Assn., Omaha Coun. Garden Clubs (1st v.p. 1972, pres. 1973-75, state bd. dirs. 1979—, mem. nat. council bd. dirs. 1979—, pres. award 1988, 89, 90), Internat. Platform Assn., Internat. Poets Soc. (Disting. mem. 1996), Nat. Trust for Hist. Preservation, Nebr. Flower Show Judges Coun. (chmn. 1995—), Nat. Coun. State Garden Clubs (chmn. arboriculture 1985-90, 93—, chmn. nature conservancy 1991-93), Nebr. Fedn. Garden Clubs (pres. 1978-81), Garden Club (dir. 1970-72, pres. 1972-75). Home: 8909 Broadmoor Dr Omaha NE 68114-4248

PRINCE, LEAH FANCHON, art educator and research institute administrator; b. Hartford, Conn., Aug. 12, 1939; d. Meyer and Annie (Forman) Berman; m. Herbert N. Prince, Jan. 30, 1955; children: Daniel L., Richard N., Robert G. Student, U. Conn., 1957-59, Rutgers U., Newark, 1962; BFA, Fairleigh Dickinson U., 1970; postgrad., Caldwell Coll. for Women, 1973-75, Parsons Sch. of Design, N.Y.C., 1978. Cert. tchr. art, N.J. Tchr. art Caldwell-West Caldwell (N.J.) Pub. Schs., 1970-75; pres. Britannia Imports Ltd., Fairfield, N.J., 1979-89; tchr. religious studies Bohrer-Kaufman Hebrew Acad., Randolph, N.J., 1981-82; co-founder and corp. sec. Gibraltar Biol. Labs., Inc., Fairfield, 1970—; dir., co-founder Gibraltar Inst. for Rsch. and Tng., Fairfield, 1984—; cons. Internat. Antiques and Fine Arts Industries, U.K., 1979-89; cons. in art exhibitry Passaic County Coll., Paterson, N.J., 1989-93; art curator Fairleigh Dickinson U., Rutherford, N.J., 1972-74; curator history of design Bloomfield (N.J.) Coll., 1990-91; lectr. nat. meeting Am. Soc. Microbiology, New Orleans, 1989; spkr. in field. Exhibited in group shows at Bloomfield (N.J.) Coll., 1990, Caldwell Women's Club, N.J., 1991, State Fedn. Women's Clubs Ann. Show, 1992 (1st pl. award 1992), Newark Art Mus., 1992, West (N.J.) Essex Art Assn., 1990, Somerset (N.J.) Art Assn. Ann. Juried Show, 1994, Mortimer Gallery, Gladstone, N.J., 1994, Tewksbury His. Soc. (1st pl. award 1994); one-woman shows include Passaic County Coll., N.J., 1990, Caldwell Coll., N.J., 1990. Chair ann. juried art awards Arts Coun. of Essex Bd. Trustees, Montclair, N.J., 1984-90; chair fundraising Arts Coun. Essex County, N.J., 1989. Recipient 1st place award N.J. Tewksbury Hist. Soc., 1994. Mem. AAUW, Somerset Art Assn., Nat. Mus. of Women in the Arts, Barnegat Light Yacht Club. Republican. Home: 5 Standish Dr Morristown NJ 07960-3224

PRINCE, LEANA MARIE, secondary school educator; b. Lancaster, Calif., Nov. 26, 1954; d. Hector and Leoma Jean (Brown) Solares; m. David Edward Prince, July 14, 1972; children: Brenden Lee, Jared Edward. BS in English summa cum laude, BS in Secondary Edn. summa cum laude, So. Oreg. State Coll., 1988, MS in Secondary Edn. summa cum laude, 1992. Cert. lang. arts tchr., Oreg. Tchr. English and Spanish North Valley H.S., Grants Pass, Oreg., 1988—, lang. arts dept. coord., 1995—. Mem. NEA, ASCD, MLA, Nat. Coun. Tchrs. of English (regional judge achievement awards on writing 1992-95), Oreg. Edn. Assn., Phi Kappa Phi. Office: North Valley HS 6741 Monument Dr Grants Pass OR 97526-8536

PRINCE, MARTHA, botanic illustrator, writer, photographer; b. Birmingham, Ala., Aug. 8, 1925; d. Frank Hartley and Martha (Fort) Anderson; m. Jordan Herbert Prince, June 20, 1946. BA, Piedmont Coll., 1944; postgrad., Art Students League, N.Y.C., 1944-46, N.Y. State Coll. Ceramics, 1949. Artist, illustrator U.S. Army, Bklyn., 1945-46; art dir. Mears Advt., N.Y.C., 1946-48; freelance artist, writer, photographer, Locust Valley, N.Y., 1949—; notecards artist George Caspari, Inc., 1978, Doehla, Inc., 1978, Arboretum Press, 1979; porcelain plate artist Royal Hort. Soc., 1981. One-woman shows include U.S. Nat. Arboretum, Washington, 1978, Am. Hort. Soc. Hdqrs., Va., 1978, Callaway Gardens, Ga., 1974; exhibited in group shows Hunt Inst. Bot. Documentation, 1978; represented in permanent collections Hunt Inst. Bot. Documentation, Carnegie Mellon U., Pitts., Mus. of Garden History, London, Planting Fields Arboretory Libr., Oyster Bay, N.Y., Seaford Libr., N.Y.; writer, designer: (booklet) Native Azaleas, 1975; contbr. illustrations and articles to Gourmet mag., Am. Horticulturist, Wilderness, Horticulture, Rock Garden Quar., Jour. Am. Rhododendron Soc., numerous others. Bd. dirs. Planting Fields Arboretum, Oyster Bay, N.Y., 1991-95. Fellow Royal Hort. Soc.; mem. Am. Rhododendron Soc. (bd. dirs. N.Y. chpt. 1988-91, bronze medal 1991), Art Students League (life). Home and Office: 9 Winding Way Locust Valley NY 11560

PRINCE, NANCY L., finance company executive. BA, Bowdoin Coll.; MBA with highest honors, Boston U. Mem. corp. banking mgmt. tng. program Bay Bank, 1980, various positions including spl. asst. to the chmn., corp. account relationship mgr. and team leader, dir. corp. product mgmt., dir. corp. svcs., trust and pvt. banking, sr. v.p., head corp. projects dept. Office: Baybanks Inc 175 Federal St Boston MA 02110

PRINCINSKY, JULIANNE T., academic administrator. BS in Mktg., Ferris State U., 1967; MBA in Mgmt., U. Mich., 1976; EdD in Curriculum and Instrn., Wayne State U., 1992. Buyer fashion mdse. divsn. Dayton-Hudson Corp., Detroit, 1967-70; tchr. bus. edn. Mott Adult H.S., Flint, Mich., 1975-76; instr. bus. adminstrn. and tech. divsn. Baker Coll., Flint, 1976-86, assoc. dean bus. adminstrn. and tech. divsns., 1987; owner, ptnr. MPACT Assocs., Flint, 1983-89; campus dir., dean, v.p. Baker Coll. Ea. Mich., Clinton Twp., Mich., 1994-95; dean bus. adminstrn. and office adminstrn. divsns. Baker Coll., 1987-94, pres., 1995—; presenter in field; mem. profl. devel. com. Greater Flint EdnL Consortium, 1991—, chmn., 1992-93, bd. dirs., 1996—; v.p. Inst. for Cert. Profls. Edn. Found., 1987, pres., 1988-89. Elder, Sunday sch. tchr. St. Andrews Presbyn. Ch., 1974—; program chmn., sec., h.s. football and girls' booster Kearsley Sch. Dist. PTO, 1977-93; bd. dirs., v.p., sec., dir. Flint Falcons swim team YMCA, 1986-89; fundraider Jr. Achievement, 1989; bd. dirs. Genesee and Flint Area Econ. Growth Alliance, 1995—; hon. chmn. World's Greatest Office Party, Whaley Children's Home, 1996—; chmn. high potentials com. United Way Genesee and Lapeer Counties, 1995—, campaign vice chmn., 1996; chmn. Baden Powell dist. Friends of Scouting, 1996—. Mem. ASCD, Nat. Staff Devel. Coun., Ednl. Spl. Interest Group (bd. dirs. 1983-84, pres. 1985, past pres. 1986), Data Processing Mgmt. Assn. (bd. dirs. Flint area 1980, 83-88, v.p. 1981, pres. 1982, 94, sec. 1983, edn. chmn. region 9 1984, sec. 1985-86, v.p. 1987-88, pres. 1989-90, internat. chmn. curriculum com. 1988-89, long-range planning com. 1992, nominating com. 1993, bronze individual performance award 1986, gold individual performance award 1987, emerald individual performance award 1991), Rotary (student leadership com. 1994, student scholarship com. 1995—). Office: Baker Coll of Flint 1050 W Bristol Rd Flint MI 48507

PRINCIPAL, VICTORIA, actress; b. Fukuoka, Japan, Jan. 3, 1950; d. Victor and Ree (Veal) P.; m. Harry Glassman, 1985. Attended, Miami-Dade Community Coll.; studied acting with Max Croft, Al Sacks and Estelle Harman, Jean Scott, Royal Acad. Dramatic Arts. Worked as model, including TV commls.; appearences include (film) The Life and Times of Judge Roy Bean, 1972, The Naked Ape, 1973, Earthquake, 1974, I Will I Will For Now, 1976, Vigilante Force, 1976; (TV movies) Last Hours Before Morning, 1975, Fantasy Island, 1977, The Night They Stole Miss Beautiful, 1977, Pleasure Palace, 1980, Not Just Another Affair, 1982, Mistress, 1987, The Burden of Proof, 1990, Just Life, 1992, Beyond Obsession, 1994; exec. prodr., actress Naked Lie, 1989, Blind Witness, 1989, Sparks: The Price of Passion, 1990, Don't Touch My Daughter, 1991, Seduction: Three Tales from the Inner Sanctum, 1993, River of Rage: The Taking of Maggie Keene, 1993; exec. prodr. Midnight's Child, 1992; (TV series) Dallas, 1978-87; (theatre) Love Letters, 1990; author: The Body Principal, 1983, The Beauty Principal, 1984, The Diet Principal, 1987. Office: ICM 8942 Wilshire Blvd Beverly Hills CA 90211*

PRINGLE, BARBARA CARROLL, state legislator; b. N.Y.C., Apr. 4, 1939; d. Nicholas Robert and Anna Joan (Woloshinovich) Terlesky; m. Richard D. Pringle, Nov. 28, 1959; children: Christopher, Rhonda. Student, Cuyahoga C.C. With Dunn & Bradstreet, 1957-60; precinct committeewoman City of Cleve., 1976-77; elected mem. Cleve. City Coun., 1977-81; mem. Ohio Ho. of Reps., Columbus, 1982—; 20th dist. state ctrl. committeewoman, 1982-92; mem. family svcs. com., ranking mem. children and youth subcom., pub. utilities com.; mem. Ohio Children's Trust Fund, Supreme Ct. Domestic Violence Task Force. Vol. Cleve. Lupus Steering Com., various community orgns.; charter mem. Statue of Liberty Ellis Island Found. Recipient cert. of appreciation Cleve. Mcpl. Ct., 1977, Exch. Club Bklyn., 1978, Cmty. Recreation Appreciation award City of Cleve., 1978, Key to City of Cleve., 1979, Cleve. Area Soapbox Derby cert., 1976, 77, 81, cert. of appreciation Ward 9 Youth League, 1979-82, No. Ohio Patrolman's Benevolent Assn. award, 1983, Cuyahoga County Firefighters award, 1983, Outstanding Pub. Servant award for Outstanding Svc. to Hispanic Cmty., 1985, Nat. Sr. Citizen Hall of Fame award, 1987, cert. of appreciation Cleve. Coun. Unemployed Workers, 1987, Ohio Farmers Union award, 1990, award of appreciation United Labor Agy., 1993, Susan B. Anthony award, 1995. Mem. Nat. Order Women Legislators, Fedn. Dem. Women of Ohio, Nat. Alliance Czech Catholics, St. Michael Ch. Altar and Rosary Soc., Ward 15 Dem. Club, Polish Falcons. Democrat. Home: 708 Timothy Ln Cleveland OH 44109-3733

PRINGLE, KATHLEEN SANTOS, nurse midwife; b. Lakeville, Mass., June 12, 1967; d. David and Pauline Doris (Bothelo) Santos; m. James L. Pringle, Dec. 18, 1992. BSN, R.I. Coll., 1989; postgrad., Boston Coll., 1991-92, SUNY, 1995-96; cert. nurse midwife, Baystate Med. Ctr., Springfield, Mass., 1993. Staff RN Women and Infants Hosp., Providence, 1989-92; nurse midwife Goddard Med. Assocs., Brockton, Mass., 1994-95, Ptnrs. in Ob-Gyn., Providence, 1995—; dir. nurse midwifery svcs. Good Samaritan Med. Ctr., Stoughton, Mass., 1994—. Scholar Baystate Med. Ctr., 1993. Mem. Am. Coll. Nurse-Midwives, Midwives' Alliance of N.Am. Home: 104 Pierce Ave Lakeville MA 02347 Office: Ptnrs in Ob-Gyn 655 Broad St Providence RI 02907

PRINISKI, MARY, religious center administrator. BA in Theology, U. Detroit, 1972; PhD in Theology, Union Inst., 1992. Joined Adrian Dominican Sisters, Roman Cath. Ch., 1968. Dir. Glenmary Rsch. Ctr., Decatur, Ga., 1993—; master tchr. So. Rural Ministry Inst., Brescia Coll. Founding coord. Connective Ministries; vol. Cath. Com. of South. Office: Glenmary Rsch Ctr Ste 226 235 E Ponce de Leon Ave Decatur GA 30030

PRINS-GROSE, LAVONNE KAY, software engineer; b. Sibley, Iowa, Feb. 28, 1957; d. Henry Simon and Katherine (Schram) Prins; m. Dan Matthew Grose, Feb. 6, 1993. BA, S.W. State U., Marshall, Minn., 1982; postgrad., Mankato (Minn.) State U., 1982-84. Instr. math. Mankato State U., 1982-84; computer operator Sathers, Round Lake, Minn., 1985; law records analyst ITT Consumer Fin. Corp., St. Louis Park, Minn., 1985-86; systems programmer Metaphor, Eden Prairie, Minn., 1987-89; pres. Ablazon Unltd. Inc., Ramsey, Minn., 1990—; sr. systems programmer Health Risk Mgmt., Edina, Minn., 1989-91; software engr. Dimensional Medicine, Inc., Minnetonka, Minn., 1992-95; programmer/analyst DynaMark Inc., Arden Hills, Minn., 1995—. Sgt. U.S. Army, 1975-79. Republican. Mem. Reformed Ch. in Am. Home and Office: 5631 164th Ln NW Ramsey MN 55303-5828

PRINTZ, JILLIAN KREUGER, college program administrator; b. Chgo., Sept. 16, 1942; d. Joseph Davis and Shirley Ann (Sondel) K.; children: Warren Davis, Joseph Granville, Allison Heather. BA in Lit., Bennington Coll., 1964. Asst. curator exhbns. Mus. Art, Ft. Lauderdale, Fla., 1985-86; mktg. coord. Broward C.C., Ft. Lauderdale, Fla., 1986-88, dir. coll. rels., 1988—. Former bd. mem., current assoc. Beaux Arts of the Mus. of Art, Ft. Lauderdale, 1980—; past bd. chair, various coms., Kids in Distress, Ft. Lauderdale, 1982—; former bd. mem. Women's Polit. Caucus, Ft. Lauderdale, 1990—; media ctr. adminstr. and press liaison, Whitbread Round-the-World Race, Ft. Lauderdale, 1994. Leadership Enhancement and Advancement Program grad., Fla. Dept. Edn. Mem. Nat. Coun. Mktg. and Pub. Rels. (conf. presenter 1992, 96, Gold Medallion Achievement 1995, Silver Medallion Achievement 1994), Women in Comm., Inc. (former bd. com. chair), Fla. Assn. C.Cs. (commn. chair 1988—, Jim Mulcahey award 1993). Office: Broward CC 225 E Las Olas Blvd Fort Lauderdale FL 33301

PRISBELL, KATHLEEN FRANCES, middle education educator, language arts; b. Rahway, N.J., Aug. 9, 1950; d. William Joseph and Helen Frances (Kowaleski) Wolfe; m. Fred Prisbell, Mar. 1, 1973; children: Eric S., Sandra L., Andrew F. BA in English, Kean Coll., 1972. Cert. secondary educator in English, elem. educator, N.J. Tchr. lang. arts Twp. of Ocean (N.J.) Intermediate Sch., 1972-82, Lakewood (N.J.) Middle Sch., 1986-90, Russell O. Brackman Middle Sch., Barnegat, N.J., 1990—; site-based mgmt. team Lakewood Middle Sch., 1987-90, com. mem. curriculum devel., 1988; site-based mgmt. core team Russell O. Brackman Middle Sch., Barnegat, 1991—, curriculum coun. chair, 1992—. Writer: (curriculums) MAX (Gifted and Talented) Curriculum, 1994, Core Curriculum Stds.-Social Studies. Tchr. Christian Doctrine St. Mary's Cath. Ch., Barnegat, 1989-93. Mem. Nat. Coun. Tchrs. English, N.J. Coun. Tchrs. English, Nat. Arbour Day Found. Democrat. Roman Catholic. Home: 6 Maplewood Ct Barnegat NJ 08005-2008

PRISSEL, BARBARA ANN, paralegal, law educator; b. Plum City, Wis., July 7, 1946; d. John Henry and Mary Ann Louise (Dankers) Seipel; m. Stephen Joseph Prissel, Dec. 16, 1967; children: Angela, Benjamin. Graduate with honors, Mpls. Bus. Coll., 1966; student, Moraine Park Tech. Coll., 1983—. Cert. adult edn. instr. Legal sec. Mott, Grose, Von Holtum & Hefferan, Mpls., 1966-67, Whelan, Morey & Morey Attys. at Law, Durand, Wis., 1967-70, Murry Law Office, River Falls, Wis., 1968-70, Potter, Wefel & Nettesheim, Wisconsin Rapids, Wis., 1970-71; sec. to adminstr. Moraine Park Tech. Coll., Fond du Lac, Wis., 1971-72, instr., 1972—; paralegal Kilgore Law Office, Ripon, Wis., 1985—; chmn. legal adv. com. Moraine Park Tech. Coll., Fond du Lac, Wis., 1985—, mem. adminstrv. assts. adv. com., 1984-86. Contbr. poems to newspapers. Ch. rep. Ch. Women United, Ripon, Wis., 1984-87; pianist Christian Women's Orgn., Ripon, Wis., 1985-95; pianist, organist Our Lady of the Lake Ch., Green Lake, Wis., 1987—; mem. sr. class night parent com. Ripon H.S., 1992-96; mem. parent bd. Young Life Christian Orgn., Ripon, Wis., 1994. Mem. Fond du Lac (Wis.) County Legal Secs. Assn. (pres. 1994-95, Legal award of Excellence 1995-96), Legal Secs. Assn. (sec. 1995-96). Roman Catholic. Home: 129 Wolverton Ave Ripon WI 54971

PRITCHARD, KATHLEEN JO, not-for-profit association administrator; b. Milw., Feb. 6, 1951; d. Owen J. and Madelon (Coogan) P.; m. William A. Durkin Jr., Oct. 22, 1982; children: Elizabeth Durkin, Christine Durkin, W. Ryan Durkin. BA in Anthropology, U. Wis., Oshkosh, 1973; MA in Pub. Adminstrn., U. Wis., 1980; PhD in Polit. Sci., U. Wis., Milw., 1986. Rsch. analyst Wis. Coun. on Criminal Justice, Madison, 1974-77; planning analyst Wis. Dept. Health and Social Svcs., Madison, 1977-80; assoc. lectr. U. Wis., Milw., 1980-89; vis. asst. prof. Marquette U., Milw., 1986, 90-91; policy cons. dept. adminstrn. City of Milw., 1992; Outcomes Project dir. United Way of Greater Milw., 1992—; faculty advisor Model OAS, UN advisor, Milw., 1986-91; campus rep. spkr. Wis. Inst. for Study of War, Peace and Global Cooperation, Milw., 1989-90; mem. United Way Am. Task Force on Impact, 1995—; instr. Nat. Acad. Volunteerism, 1996. Contbr. articles to profl. jours. Recipient Alice Paul Dissertation award Women's Caucus for Polit. Sci., 1984; Grad. Sch. fellow U. Wis., Milw., 1983, fellow Kenyon Coll. Summer Inst., 1983. Mem. Am. Polit. Sci. Assn., Internat. Polit. Sci. Assn., Phi Kappa Phi (chpt. officer 1989).

PRITCHARD, MARJORIE JEAN, editor; b. Norwood, Mass., Oct. 30, 1959; d. John William and Lynn Eva (Herron) P.; m. Gregory Edward Fayne, Oct. 19, 1991; children: Hannah Mae Fayne, Zachary Andrew Fayne. BA, Northeastern U., 1982. Editor op-ed page Boston Globe, 1985—. Mem. Assn. Opinion Page Editors (Gold award 1991). Office: Boston Globe Box 2378 Boston MA 02562

PRITT, JUDITH KAY, service executive, nurse; b. Arthurdale, W.Va., Aug. 14, 1945; d. Ralph Norman and Eleanor Collins B.; m. Jimmie Martin Pritt, June 12, 1965; children: James Scott, Tammyra Renee. BS in Nursing, W. Va. U., 1967; MA in Counseling, Ball State U., 1973; Postgrad., Ga. State U., 1978. Cert. Nurse Adminstr. Advanced, Am. Nursing Assn. 1988. Insvc. instr./supr. Singing River Hosp., Pascagoula, Miss., 1968; staff nurse in neurosurg. W. Va. U. Med. Ctr., Morgantown, W.Va., 1971-72; curriculum coord./instr. Darmstadt (Germany) Career Ctr., 1972-73; sch. nurse Aukamn Elem. Sch., Weisbaden, Germany, 1973-75; dir. of Edn. Svcs. Med. Ctr. of Cen. Ga., Macon, Ga., 1976-78; dir. of Clinical Nursing Marysvale Samaritan, Phoenix, 1979-80; patient care coord. Albert Einstein Med. Ctr., Phila., 1981-82; asst. dir. nursing Fox Chase Cancer Ctr., Phila., 1983-84; coord. of Edn. Mercy Med. Ctr., Springfield, Ohio, 1984—; v.p. Madison County Hosp., London, Ohio, 1985—; Instr. trainer, CPR, Am. Heart Assn., Ga. and Ariz., Am. Red Cross, Ohio; cons. speaker and organizer for various orgns. including counseling employees and patients, crisis intervention, the nursing process; presenter Oncology Nurse's Soc., San Diego 1982. Tchr. Ch. of Christ, Springfield, Ohio, 1988-87. Recipient Faculty Award, Convocation, W. Va. U., Morgantown, W.Va., 1967. Fellow Am. Acad. Med. Adminstrs. (pres. 1989-91, Disting. Svc. award 1991, diplomate in health care 1992, state dir. 1992-95, region IV dir. 1995—); mem. Ohio Nurse Exec. Assn., Sigma Theta Tau. Democrat. Office: Madison County Hosp Inc 210 N Main St London OH 43140-1115

PRITZKER, ELISA, painter, sculptor, educator, theater director; b. Rio Cuarto, Cordoba, Argentina, Dec. 10, 1955; came to US, 1993; d. Samuel and Esther (Maladetsky) P.; m. Leonardo Fabio Castria, Sept. 22, 1986 (div. Apr. 1994); 1 child, Jimena Castria; m. Enrique Rob Lunski, June 14, 1994. BA in Ceramic Arts, Sch. of Ceramics, Mar del Plata, Argentina, 1976; student in Theater Direction, Body Expression, Acting, Siembra Group, Mar del Plata, Argentina, 1983; MA in Visual Arts, Superior Inst. Visual Arts, Mar del Plata, Argentina, 1986. Prof. pottery, sculpture Superior Inst. Visual Arts, Mar del Plata, Argentina, 1983-88, prof. drawing, 1987-88; prof. drawing, visual arts Sch. Ceramics, Mar del Plata, Argentina, 1986-88; graphic art designer Alzamora S.A., Palma de Mallorca, Spain, 1991-93; prof. painting, pottery Ulster BOCES, Port Ewen, N.Y., 1995—; artistic dir. Internat. Club YWCA, Kingston, N.Y.; founder, artistic dir. Highland (N.Y.) Cultural Ctr., curator, juror Nat. Juried Art Exhbn., 1994, juror of selection, 1995, co-chair creation peace park and monument, 1995; organizer, curator Ann. Juried Exhbn. UNISON, New Paltz, N.Y., 1994, prof. ceramics Arts & Learning Ctr.; curator Latin Am. show Latin Am. Studies SUNY, New Paltz, 1994; curator Global Sisters in Peace photography show SUNY, New Paltz, 1995. One woman exhbns. include Agora Art Gallery, Palma de Mallorca, Spain, 1989, Casa Argentina, Jerusalem, 1995, Lynn Prince Gallery, Poughkeepsie, N.Y., 1995; group exhbns. include 28th Pollensa Internat. Festival of Sculpture and Painting, Baleares, Spain, 1989, Colonya Art Gallery, Pollensa, Baleares, Spain, 1990, Es Cafeti, Palma de Mallorca, Spain, 1992, Manzana 50 Art Gallery, Palma de Mallorca, Spain, 1993, Middletown (N.Y.) Art Ctr. Arts Coun. Orange County, 1993, Putnam Arts Coun. Levine Art Ctr., Mahopac, N.Y., 1993-94, Mamaroneck Artists Guild, Inc. Westbeth Gallery, N.Y.C., 1994, Lynn Prince Gallery, Poughkeepsie, N.Y., 1994, Heritage Art Gallery, Poughkeepsie, N.Y., 1994, Fitton Ctr. Creative Arts, Hamilton, Ohio, 1995, Nassau Coliseum, 1995; represented in permanent collections La Pruna Art Gallery, Manzana 50 Art Gallery, La Luna Art Gallery, numerous pub. and pvt. collections; dir. Urban Theater, Palma de Mallorca, Spain, 1990-92. Mem. reflections program com. PTA, Highland, N.Y., 1994-95, 150th Anniversary com. Town of Lloyd, Highland, N.Y., 1995. Recipient Best Original Painting, Ecol. Soc., 1987, First award Galeria Praxis, 1988, award of Excellence Manattan Arts Internat. Cover Arts Competition, 1994, 2nd Place logo contest, Railroad Bridge Co., Inc., 1994, 4th prize ReviewArt Contest Columbia Pacific U., 1994, 1st prize, 1994, 2nd prize 1995. Mem. Nat. Mus. Women in the Arts. Office: Highland Cultural Ctr PO Box 851 Highland NY 12528

PRITZKER, PENNY, investor; b. Chgo., May 2, 1959; d. Donald N. and Sue Ann (Sandel) P.; m. Bryan Traubert, Sept. 10, 1988; children: Donald Pritzker Traubert, Rose Pritzker Traubert. B in Econs., Harvard U., 1981; JD, Stanford U., 1985, MBA, 1985. Bar: Ill. 1985. Mgr. Hyatt Devel. Corp., Chgo., 1985-87; pres. Classic Residence by Hyatt, Chgo., 1987—; ptnr. Pritzker & Pritzker, Chgo., 1987—; pres. Penguin Group, L.P., Chgo., 1990—; corp. adv. bd. mem. Mayor Daley's Exec. Fellows Program, Chgo., U.S. Cmty. Adjustment & Investment Program, Washington; bd. dirs. William Wrigley, Jr. Co., Chgo., Coast-to-Coast Fin. Corp., N.Y.C. Vice chmn. Mus. Contemporary Art, Chgo.; adv. bd. dirs. Chgo. Cares; mng. trustee Democratic Nat. Com., Washington, 1991—; mem. Women's Issues Network, Chgo., 1991—, The Chgo. Network, 1992—, Internat. Women's Forum, Chgo. Recipient Brick & Mortar award Chgo. Equity Fund, 1991, Disting. Svc. award REIA Kellogg, 1995. Mem. Nat. Assn. Sr. Living Industries (bd. dirs. 1989-91), Urban Land Inst., Young Pres.'s Orgn. Office: Classic Residence by Hyatt 200 W Madison St 38th Fl Chicago IL 60606-3414

PRIVETTE, NANCY ANNETTE, newspaper editor; b. Fayetteville, N.C., Sept. 20, 1967; d. Grady Lee and Nancy Carol (Shatley) P. BA, U. N.C., 1989. Reporter Statesville (N.C.) Record & Landmark, 1990-94, audio-text coord., 1994-95; mng. editor Mooresville (N.C.) Tribune, 1995—. Active Woods Tech. Adv. Com., Mooresville, Chamber Edn. Com., Mooresville, Mitchell C.C. Adv. Bd., Mooresville, Young Dems., Statesville, centennial fundraising com. U. N.C., Greensboro. Mem. N.C. Press Assn., Mooresville/South Iredell C. of C., U. N.C. Greensboro Alumni Assn., Mooresville Civitan Club. Democrat. Baptist. Office: Mooresville Tribune 147 E Center Ave Mooresville NC 28115

PROACH, SISTER JOHN ANN, secondary education principal; b. Wilkes-Barre, Pa., May 10, 1948. BS in Biology, Alvernia Coll., 1974; MS in Sci., Villanova U., 1985, MA in Ednl. Adminstrn., 1987. Cert. tchr. biology, physics, supr. sci., secondary sch. principal, Pa. Sci. tchr., 5-8 grades Sacred Heart Elem. Sch., Clifton Heights, Pa., 1969-70; biology and IPS tchr. grades 9-10 Little Flower H.S., Phila., 1970-72; biology tchr. grades 9-12 Bishop Hoban H.S., Wilkes Barre, Pa., 1972-77; sci. tchr. grades 9-12 Bishop Conwell H.S., Levttown, Pa., 1977-93; biology tchr. Cowell-Egan Catholic H.S., Fairless Hills, Pa., 1993-94; principal Bishop McDevitt H.S., Wyncote, Pa., 1994—; mem. sci. curriculum com. Archdiocese Phila., 1977—, chair, 1984—; sci. cons. The Coll. Bd., N.Y.C., 1984-92; book reviewer for biology Prentice Hall Publ. Co., Englewoods, N.J., 1990, book reviewer for chemistry Glencoe Publ. Co., 1995. Recipient fellowship GTE Corp., Boston, Washington, 1990, Tech. Scholar award, Tandy Corp., Tex., 1991, Presidential award NSF, Washington, 1992. Mem. ASCD, Nat. Cath. Educators Assn., Nat. Assn. Biology Tchrs. (Outstanding Biology Tchr. 1988), Nat. Assn. Sci. Tchrs., Am. Assn. Physics Tchrs., Pa. Jr. Acad. of Sci. (judge). Office: Bishop McDevitt HS 125 Royal Ave Wyncote PA 19095-1111

PROBST, CAROL JEAN, mathematics educator; b. Freeburg, Ill., June 13, 1948; d. Lorraine William and Virginia Eloise (Nichols) Baumgarte; m. Dale Elmer Probst, June 6, 1970; children: Jason Dale, Corey Lorraine. EdB, Ea. Ill. U., 1970; MEd, So. Ill. U., 1974, Specialist in Edn., 1994. Math. tchr. Highland (Ill.) Jr. H.S., 1970-76, Highland H.S., 1970—; computer instr. Belleville (Ill.) Area Coll., 1983-89; computer camp instr. So. Ill. U., Edwardsville, 1984-92; dist. math. curriculum chair Highland Comty. Schs. # 5, 1986—; math. dept. chair Highland H.S., 1994—, ednl. mgmt. ptnr., 1994—; mem. secondary adv. bd. Greenville Coll., 1990—; mem. steering com. strategic planning team Highland Comty. Schs., 1993—, chmn. Blue Ribbon Schs. Application, 1989, 91, 93; conv. spkr. Ill. Coun. Tchrs. Math. Contbr.: The Experienced Teacher Handbook, 1993. Mem. Granite City (Ill.) Hockey Assn., 1991-94; mem., 1st lady Collinsville (Ill.) Soccer Assn., 1981-91; mem. Collinsville Baseball and Softball League, 1981-91. Recipient Presdl. award Ill. Coun. Tchrs. Math., Those Who Excel award Ill. State Bd. Edn. Mem. ASCD, Nat. Coun. Tchrs. Math. (regional conv. com. 1993-94), Ill. Prins. Assn., Ill. Coun. Tchrs. Math., Ill. Assn. H.S. Republican. United Ch. of Christ. Home: 702 Peachtree Trl Collinsville IL 62234-5230 Office: Highland Community Schs 1800 Lindenthal St Highland IL 62249-2206

PROCACCIO, GINA, track and field athlete. Student, Villanova U. Long distance runner. Office: USA Track and Field PO Box 120 Indianapolis IN 46206-0120

PROCTOR, BARBARA GARDNER, advertising agency executive, writer; b. Asheville, N.C.; d. William and Bernice (Baxter) Gardner; B.A. Talladega Coll., 1954; m. Carl L. Proctor, July 20, 1961 (div. Nov. 1963); 1 son, Morgan Eugene. Music critic, contbg. editor Down Beat Mag., Chgo., from 1958; internat. dir. Vee Jay Records, Chgo., 1961-64; copy supr. Post-Keyes-Gardner Advt., Inc., 1965-68, Gene Taylor Assos., 1968-69, North Advt. Agy., 1969-70; contbr. to gen. periodicals, from 1952; founder Proctor &

Gardner Advt., Chgo., 1970—, now pres., chief exec. officer. Mem. Chgo. Urban League, Chgo. Econ. Devel. Corp. Bd. dirs. People United to Save Humanity, Better Bus. Bur. Cons. pub. relations and promotion, record industry. Recipient Armstrong Creative Writing award, 1954; awards Chgo. Fedn. Advt. Clubs, N.Y. Art Dirs. Club. Woman's Day; Frederick Douglas Humanitarian award, 1975; named Chgo. Advt. Woman of Year, 1974. Mem. Chgo. Media Women, Nat. Assn. Radio Arts and Sci., Women's Advt. Club, Cosmopolitan C. of C. (dir.), Female Execs. Assn., Internat. Platform Assn., Smithsonian Instn. Assos. Author TV documentary Blues for a Gardenia, 1963. Office: Proctor & Gardner Advt Inc 111 E Wacker Dr Ste 321 Chicago IL 60601-4208*

PROCTOR, BETTY JANE, English language and literature educator; b. Houston, June 10, 1952; d. H.D. and Opal Jimmie (Givens) P.; m. Frank Roberts, Dec. 15, 1990. BA, U. Houston, 1973, MA, 1974; PhD, Tex. A&M U., 1978. Instr. English, Tex. A&M U., College Station, 1977-78; instr. English, U. Houston, 1978-80, dir. devel. English, 1980-82; instr. English, Houston C.C., 1982—; v.p. Cavalier-Houston Resources, ind. oil and gas co., 1990—; creative cons. Am. Cascade Industries, oil and gas co., Houston and L.A., 1992—. Editor: Southwestern Studies, 1993—, Tchg. English in C.C., 1993—. Vol. Harris County Rep. Com., Houston, 1988-95. Mem. South Cen. MLA, Coll. English Assn., Houston Athletic Club, Phi Kappa Phi.

PROFET, MARGIE, biomedical researcher; b. Berkeley, Calif., Aug. 7, 1958. BA in Polit. Philosophy, Harvard U., 1980; BA in Physics, U. Calif., Berkeley, 1985. comupter programmer, Munich, Germany, 1980-81. Author: (with others) The Adapted Mind, 1992; contbr. articles to Quarterly Review of Biology. MacArthur fellow John D. and Catherine T. MacArthur Found., 1993.

PROFICE, ROSENA MAYBERRY, elementary school educator; b. Natchez, Miss., Oct. 8, 1953; d. Alex Jr. and Louise V. (Fuller) Mayberry; m. Willie Lee Profice, Feb. 12, 1977; children: Jamie Martez, Alesha Shermille. BS in History, Jackson State U., 1974, MS in Elem. Edn., 1975, Edn. Splty. in Elem. Edn., 1977. Cert. elem. reading and social studies tchr., Miss. Tchr. reading Ackerman (Miss.) H.S., 1975-76, North Hazlehurst (Miss.) Elem. Sch., 1976-79; tchr. reading and elem. edn. Natchez-Adams Sch. Sys., Natchez, 1979—. Mem. NEA, Miss. Assn. Educators, Concerned Educators of Black Students, Internat. Reading Assn., Nat. Alliance Black Sch. Educators, Natchez Assn. for the Preservation of Afro-Am. Culture (bd. dirs. 1996-97), Linwood Circle Ruritan Club (bd. dirs. 1992-93, sec. 1994-95), Jackson State U. Alumni Assn., 100 Black Women, Zion Hill #1 Bapt. Ch. Democrat. Baptist. Home: 11 Elbow Ln Natchez MS 39120-5346

PROFIT, VERA BARBARA, German language and literature educator; b. Vienna, Austria; came to U.S., 1957; d. Franz Johann and Edith E. (Kratochwil) P. Student, Inst. European Studies, Paris, 1965-66; BA in French and German, Alverno Coll., 1967; postgrad., U. Vienna, 1968-69; MA in Comparative Lit., U. Rochester, 1969, PhD in Comparative Lit., 1974. Instr. St. Olaf Coll., Northfield, Minn., 1974-75; asst. prof. U. Notre Dame, Ind., 1975-81, assoc. prof., 1981-96, prof., 1996—; vis. scholar Harvard U., Cambridge, Mass., 1979-80, Northwestern U., Evanston, Ill., 1984; lectr. in field. Author: Interpretations of Iwan Goll's Late Poetry with a Comprehensive and Annotated Bibliography of the Writings by and about Iwan Goll, 1977, Ein Porträt meiner Selbst: Karl Krolow's Autobiographical Poems (1945-58) and Their French Sources, 1991, Menschlich: Gespräche mit Karl Krolow, 1996. Office: U Notre Dame Dept German Russian Notre Dame IN 46635

PROIETTI, ROSE MARIE, nursing educator; b. Woonsocket, R.I., Jan. 19, 1948; d. Vincent and Filomena (Gesualdi) P.; m. Mark Savory, Feb. 5, 1988. Diploma, R.I. Hosp. Sch. Nursing, 1968; BA in Psychology, U. Hartford, 1979; MBA in Health Care, U. Conn., 1982. With State Exam. for RN, Providence, 1968—. Patron The Morris Mus., Morristown, N.J., 1991. Mem. Assn. Oper. Rm. Nursing, Assn. for Advancement of Med. Instruments, Assn. Practitioners of Infection Control. Home: 26 Vom Eigen Dr Morristown NJ 07960-4747

PROPP, GAIL DANE GOMBERG, computer consulting company executive; b. N.Y.C., Mar. 22, 1944; d. Oscar and Goody (Rosenburgh) Dane; BA in Econs., Barnard Coll., 1965; m. Ephraim Propp; children: Eric Wesley, David Marc, Anna Michelle. Instr., programmer IBM Corp., N.Y.C., 1965-66; systems and programmer analyst R.S. Topas Co., N.Y.C., 1966-67; dir. systems and programming Abercrombie & Fitch Co., N.Y.C., 1967-69; dir. corp. data processing and MIS, 1969-77; founder, 1977, pres. Met Data Systems, Inc., N.Y.C., 1977—; founder, pres. Datatype Internat. Inc, 1982—; sr. v.p./CIO Slim-Fast Foods Co., 1991—. Bd. overseers Bar-Ilan U., Israel; mem. adv. bd. KIRUV. Mem. Internat. Coun. Computers in Edn., Women in Info. Processing, Assn. Systems Mgmt., Data Processing Mgmt. Assn., Assn. Systems Mgmt., Assn. Inst. Cert. Systems Profls., Photog. History Soc. Am., Photog. Historic Soc. N.Y. Contbr. articles to profl. jours. Office: 919 3rd Ave New York NY 10022

PROTOS, AMY REED, secondary school educator; b. Rochester, N.Y., Sept. 14, 1965; d. Robert C. and Helen M. (Foos) Reed; m. Paul T. Protos, Mar. 5, 1994; 1 child, Sarah Ann. BS, U. Dayton, 1987, MS, 1992. Cert. tchr., Ohio. Math. tchr. Archbishop Alter H.S., Kettering, Ohio, 1987-88, basketball coach, 1987-88, 91-94; math. tchr. Kettering Jr. H.S., 1989—, softball coach, 1989-94. Office: Kettering Jr HS 3000 Glengarry Dr Kettering OH 45420-1227

PROULX, EDNA ANNIE, writer; b. Norwich, Conn., Aug. 22, 1935; d. George Napolean and Lois Nelly (Gill) Proulx; m. James Hamilton Lang, June 22, 1969 (div. 1990); children: Jonathan Edward Lang, Gillis Crowell Lang, Morgan Hamilton Lang. BA cum laude, U. Vt., 1969; MA, Sir George Williams U., Montreal, Can., 1973; DHL (hon.), U. Maine, 1994. Author: Heart Songs and Other Stories, 1988, Postcards, 1992 (PEN/Faulkner award 1993), The Shipping News, 1993 (Nat. Book award for fiction 1993, Chgo. Tribune Heartland award 1993, Irish Times Internat. Fiction award 1993, Pulitzer Prize for fiction 1994), Accordian Crimes, 1996; contbr. more than 50 articles to mags. and jours. Kress fellow Harvard U., 1974, fellow Vt. Coun. Arts, 1989, NEA, 1991, Guggenheim Found., 1992; rsch. grantee Inter.-U. Ctr., 1975; resident Ucross Found., 1990-92. Mem. PEN Am. Ctr., Phi Beta Kappa, Phi Alpha Theta. Office: care Darhansoff Verrill Agy 179 Franklin St New York NY 10013*

PROULX, MARIA ANTOINETTE, retired psychologist; b. Newark, Nov. 9, 1921; d. Anthony Paul and Pasqualina Mary (Salerno) Iannarone; widowed; 1 child, Barbara Elaine Chandler. BA, U. Cin., 1962, MA, 1963; postgrad., Rutgers U. Diplomate Am. Coll. Forensic Examiners; cert. pub. mgmt., N.J. Psychologist State of N.J. Human Svcs., Marlboro, 1968-80, State of N.J. Corrections Dept., Jamesburg, 1980-92; ret., 1992; cons. psychologist Arthur Brisbane Sch. Dist., Allaire, N.J., Hunterdon (N.J.) State Sch.; cons. in retardation New Lisbon (N.J.) State Sch., Brookdale C.C., Lincroft, N.J., 1970-72; tchr. in psychology Monmouth Coll., West Long Beach, N.J., 1970-71; adj. prof. Middlesex (N.J.) Coll.; instr., presenter at numerous seminars in field; lectr. on preretirement. Vol. Monmouth Park Charity Fund, Oceanport, N.J., 1994, 95, 96,; mem. Friends of Monmouth County Libr., 1992—; sec. Deborah Heart Found., Browns Mills, N.J., 1994-96. Fellow Am. Acad. Pain Mgmt, Am. Psychol. Assn. (assoc.), Internat. Platform Assn., Phi Beta Kappa, Psi Chi.

PROUTY, JILL, psychodramatist, psychotherapist; b. Chgo., Oct. 22, 1939; d. Nathan Alfred and Beverly (Bramson) Berkson; m. Robert Howard Winer, July 30, 1961 (div. 1987); children: Garry, Marc, Richard; m. Garry Franklyn Prouty, May 26, 1990. BA, Lake Forest Coll., 1961; MA, Gov. State U., 1973. Cert. trainer, educator, practitioner in psychodrama sociometry and group psychotherapy. Pres. Illiana Psychodrama Inst., Flossmoor, Ill., 1980-90, Fedn. Trainers and Tng. Programs in Psychodrama, 1982-83; psychodramatist Four Winds Hosp., Lemont, Ill., 1990-93, Charter Hosp., Hobart, Ind., 1990-93, Chgo. Osteo. Health Sys., Olympia Fields, Ill., 1995—; adj. prof. Govs. State U., University Park, Ill., 1975-88; internat. cons. Pre-Therapy, Ghent, Belgium, 1988—. Fellow Am. Soc. Group Psychotherapy and Psychodrama; mem. ACA, Nat. Assn. Dual Diagnosed, Nat. Coun. Jewish Women (life). Home: 6015 Lakeside Pl Tinley Park IL 60477

PROVENCHER, JEANNE STANSFIELD, secondary education educator; b. Methuen, Mass., June 30, 1948; d. Ernest Daniel and Rita Marie (Vayo) Stansfield; m. Richard Leonard Provencher, Dec. 15, 1978; children: Matthew, Ryan. BA, Newton Coll., 1970; MA, Rivier Coll., Nashua, N.H., 1990. Cert. tchr., Mass.; cert. experienced educator, N.H. Tchr. St. Francis Acad., Nevada, Mo., 1970-71, Salem (N.H.) H.S., 1971-72, Pelham (N.H.) Meml. Sch., 1983-87; tchr. English and women's studies Nashua Sr. H.S., 1987—; critical reader Grammar Workshop, 1994; contbg. reader Adventures in Appreciation, 1994. Lector St. Kathryn Ch., Hudson, N.H., 1988—. Mem. Nat. Coun. Tchrs. English (state judge for student lit. mags. 1994—), New Eng. Coun. Tchrs. English, N.H. Coun. Tchrs. English. Office: Nashua Sr HS 36 Riverside Dr Nashua NH 03062

PROVENSEN, ALICE ROSE TWITCHELL, artist, author; b. Chgo.; d. Jay Horace and Kathryn (Zelanis) Twitchell; m. Martin Provensen, Apr. 17, 1944; 1 child, Karen Anna. Student, Art Inst. of Chgo., 1930-31, U. Calif., L.A., 1939, Art Student League, N.Y., 1940-41; D.H.L. (hon.), Marist Coll., 1986. With Walter Lanz Studios, Los Angeles, 1942-43; OSS, 1944-45. Exhibited (with Martin Provensen) Balt. Mus., 1954, Am. Inst. Graphic Arts, N.Y., 1959, Botolph Group, Boston, 1964; exhibited one person shows: Henry Feiwel Gallery, N.Y.C., 1991, Children's Mus., Washington, 1991, Moscarelle Mus. Art, Williamsburg, Va., 1991; books represented in Fifty Books of Yr. Selections, Am. Inst. Graphic Arts, 1947, 48, 52 (The Charge of the Light Brigade named Best Illustrated Children's Book of the Yr. N.Y. Times 1964, co-recipient Gold medal Soc. Illustrators 1960); author/illustrator: books including Karen's Opposites, 1963, Karen's Curiosity, 1963, What is a Color?, 1967, (with Martin Provensen) Who's In the Egg, 1970, The Provensen Book of Fairy Tales, 1971, Play on Words, 1972, My Little Hen, 1973, Roses are Red, 1973, Our Animal Friends, 1974, The Year at Maple Hill Farm, 1978, A Horse and a Hound, A Goat and a Gander, 1979, An Owl and Three Pussycats, 1981, Town and Country, 1984, Shaker Lane, 1987, The Buck Stops Here, 1990, Punch in New York, 1991 (Best Books N.Y. Times 1991), My Fellow Americans, 1995; illustrator: (with Martin Provensen) children's books including Mother Goose Book, 1976, Old Mother Hubbard, 1977, A Peaceable Kingdom, 1978, The Golden Serpent, 1980, A Visit to William Blake's Inn, 1981, Birds, Beasts and the Third Thing, 1982, The Glorious Flight, 1984 (Caldecott medal 1984), The Voyage of the Ludgate Hill, 1987; also textbooks.

PROVINE, LORRAINE, mathematics educator; b. Altus, Okla., Oct. 6, 1944; d. Claud Edward and Emmie Lorraine (Gasper) Allmon; m. Joe A. Provine, Aug. 14, 1966; children: Sharon Kay, John David. BS, U. Okla., 1966; MS, Okla. State U., 1988. Tchr. math. U.S. Grant High Sch., Oklahoma City Schs., 1966-69; tchr. East Jr. High Sch., Ponca City (Okla.) Schs., 1969-70; tchr. Ponca City High Sch., 1978-79, 81-96; lectr. math. Okla. State U., Stillwater, 1996—. Mem. NEA, Coun. for Exceptional Children, Internat. Soc. Tchrs. in Edn., Math. Assn. Am., Nat. Coun. Tchrs. Math., Sch. Sci. and Math. Assn., Okla. Edn. Assn., Okla. Coun. Tchrs. Math., Assn. Women in Math., Ponca City Assn. Classroom Tchrs. (treas. 1983-86, 91-96), Okla. Assn. Mothers Clubs (life, state bd. dirs. 1977-87, pres. 1984-85), Delta Kappa Gamma (treas. 1996—). Republican. Baptist. Home: 1915 Meadowbrook St Ponca City OK 74604-3012 Office: Okla State U Dept Math MS 408 Stillwater OK 74078-1058

PROVIS, DOROTHY L(OUISE), artist, sculptor; b. Chgo., Apr. 26, 1926; d. George Kenneth Smith and Ann Hart (Day) Smith Guest; m. William H. Provis Sr., July 28, 1945; children: Timothy A., William H. Jr. Student Sch. Art Inst., Chgo., 1953-56, U. Wis.-Milw., 1967-68, 69-70. Sculptor Port Washington, Wis., 1963—; pres. bd. dirs. West Bend Gallery of Fine Arts, Wis., 1984-86, bd. dirs., 1987-89; speaker, presenter in field. Author, lobbyist Wis. Consignment Bill, Madison, 1979; presenter Art of Bead Making Charles Allis Art Mus., Milw., 1991, Fimo, polymer clay jewlry techniques Moraine valley Commumity Coll., Palos Hills, Ill., 1992; panelist Women's Caucus for Art Conf., Phila., 1983, Coalition Women's Art Orgn. at Coll. Art Assn. Conf., Seattle, 1993; mem. adv. bd. Percent for Art Pro., 1985-87; mem. adv. bd. Wis. Arts Bd., salary assistance program, 1991; pres. workshop Milw. Art Mus., 1990.; conf. panelist Coll. Art Assn., N.Y.C., 1990. Co-curated exhbn. West Bend Gallery of Fine Arts, 1992; Wis. Arts Bd. Designer-Craftsmen grantee, NEA, 1981. Mem. Coalition of Women's Art Orgns. (del. to continuing com. Nat. Women's Conf. 1979, panelist conf. 1981, v.p. for membership/nominations, 1981-83, pres. 1983-85, nat. pres. 1985-87, 89-91, 91-93, 93—, v.p. communications 1987-89, editor CWAO newsletter 1985—, rep. CWAO at Am. Coun. for Arts Advocacy Day, Washington 1993, panelist Southeastern Coll. Art Conf. 1995), Wis. Painters and Sculptors (pres. 1982-84, editor newsletter 1982-85), Wis. Women in Arts (legis. liaison 1978-80), Nat. Women's Studies Assn. (conf. presenter 1988), Artists for Ednl. Action (corr. 1979-85), Wis. Designer Crafts Coun. (membership chair 1991-93, editor newsletter 1993-95), Women's Caucus for Art (panelist 1981, 83, 86, 87, conf. com. panelist 1987, presenter 1989), Chgo. Artists Coalition. Home and Studio: 123 E Beutel Rd Port Washington WI 53074-1103

PROVOST, LUCY SAVIDGE, government relations specialist; b. Harrisburg, Pa., Aug. 7, 1962; d. Dalton William and Mary (Mitchell) Savidge; m. Vincent Raoul Provost, June 22, 1991; children: William George, Marjorie Coderre. BA, Pa. State U., 1984. Legis. corr. U.S. Senate Spl. Com. on Aging, Washington, 1984-86; rsch. asst. U.S. Senate Fin. Com., Washington, 1986-87; govt. rels. specialist U. Pa., Phila., 1987-89; from asst. dir. to assoc. dir. corp & found. rels. U. Pa., 1989-92; from devel. officer to dir. govt. rels. Elwyn (Pa.), Inc., 1992—. Mem. Pa. State Alumni Assn., Chi Omega, Phi Kappa Psi. Republican. Lutheran. Home: 228 Moria Pl Aston PA 19014 Office: Elwyn Inc 111 Elwyn Rd Elwyn PA 19063

PRUDEN, ANN LORETTE, chemical engineer, researcher; b. Norfolk, Va., Sept. 3, 1948; d. James Otis and Elora Maie (Bagwell) P.; m. Alan Todd Royer, Aug. 13, 1983; children: James Sebastian Royer, Annabelle Grace Royer. BS in Chemistry, Maryville (Tenn.) Coll., 1970; MA in Chem. Engring., Princeton (N.J.) U., 1978; PhD, 1981. Chemist Mobil Rsch. and Devel. Corp., Princeton, N.J., 1970-73, rsch. chemist, 1973-76, rsch. engr., 1980-86; sr. rsch. engr. Mobil Chem. Co., Princeton, N.J., 1986-92, supr., 1992—; mem. Quality Director's Network, Indsl. Rsch. Inst., Washington, 1992—. Contbg. author: Photocatalytic Purification and Treatment of Water and Air, 1993; contbr. articles to profl. jours. Fellow Mobil R&D Corp., Princeton, N.J., 1976-79. Mem. ASTM, AIChE, Am. Chemical Soc. Office: Mobil Chemical Co Rte 27 and Vineyard Rd PO Box 3029 Edison NJ 08818-3029

PRUD'HOMME, CINDY JO, controller; b. Milw., June 3, 1959; d. James Frederick and Patricia Sharon (Kennedy) P.; m. William Lee Clifton, May 17, 1978 (div. 1982); 1 child, Erica Laine Clifton. Student in bus. mgmt., Santa Monica (Calif.) Coll., 1976, West LA Coll., 1977-80. Acctg. coord. Mega Ins. Agy./Midland Ins., Menlo Park, Calif., 1980-82; prodn. mgr. Corp. Graphics, L.A., 1982-84; acct., adminstv. mgr. Thomson Consumer Products Corp., Culver City, Calif., 1984-87; mgr. acctg. and pers. Hogg Robinson, Inc., L.A., 1987-90; contr. Hogg Robinson, Inc., Saginaw, Mich., 1990-94, Acordia, Inc., Saginaw, 1995—. Contbr. articles to profl. jours. Site leader Clinic Def. Alliance/L.A., 1989-90; active Calif. Abortion Rights Action League, L.A., 1989-90, Amnesty Internat., 1989-90; bd. dirs. Underground Railroad, Inc., Saginaw, Mich., 1995—. Named Young Careerist, Glendale (Calif.) Bus. and Profl. Women, 1989. Mem. Calif. Fedn. Bus. and Profl. Women (cert., instr.; Wilshire Bus. and Profl. Women treas.-fin. chair 1988, rec. sec.-treas. 1989); L.A. Sunset Dist. chair PEP/PAC 1989 (rec. sec. 1990, Dist. Individual Devel. winner 1988), Saginaw Bus. and Profl. Women (2d v.p., chair issues mgmt. Dist. II Mich. Fedn. 1991). Democrat. Lutheran. Office: Acordia Inc 5090 State St Bldg C Saginaw MI 48603-7705

PRUETT, GRETA JOYCE, elementary education educator; b. West Plains, Mo., Aug. 28, 1936; d. Burk and Ilene Marguerite (Bridges) Hopkins; m. William Moses, oct. 8, 1955; children: Keith Alvin, Paul Alan. BS Edn., Southwest Mo. State U., 1970, MS Edn., 1981. Elem. tchr. Richards Elem. Sch., West Plains, 1967-95. Mem. Mo. Nat. Ednl. Assn., Internat. Reading Assn. Democrat. Baptist. Home: 7835 County Rd 5090 West Plains MO 65775

PRUITT, ALICE FAY, mathematician, engineer; b. Montgomery, Ala., Dec. 17, 1943; d. Virgil Edwin and Ocie Victoria (Mobley) Maye; m. Mickey Don Pruitt, Nov. 5, 1967; children: Derrell Gene, Christine Marie. BS in Math., U. Ala., Huntsville, 1977; postgrad. in engring., Calif. State U., Northridge, 1978-79. Instr. math. Antelope Valley Coll., Quartz Hill, Calif., 1977-78; space shuttle engr. Rockwell Internat., Palmdale, Calif., 1979-81; programmer, analyst Sci. Support Svcs. Combat Devel. and Experimentation Ctr., Ft. Hunter-Liggett, Calif., 1982-85; sr. engring. specialist Loral Vought Systems Corp., Dallas, 1985-92; mgr. new concepts devel. army tactical sys. and tech. Nichols Rsch. Corp., Huntsville, Ala., 1992—. Mem. DeSoto (Tex.) Coun. Cultural Arts, 1987-89. Mem. AAUW (sch. bd. rep. 1982, legal advocacy fund chairperson 1989-91), Toastmasters Internat., Phi Kappa Phi. Republican. Methodist. Office: Nichols Rsch Corp PO Box 40002 4040 S Memorial Pkwy Huntsville AL 35815-1502

PRUITT, SHERI DIANE, clinical psychologist; b. Ada, Okla., Feb. 21, 1960; d. Dexter Alvin and Betty Yvonne (Ballard) P. BS in psychology, Univ. Okla., 1982, MEd in counseling psychology, 1984; MS in psychology, Univ. New Mex., 1988, PhD in psychology, 1990. Lic. clinical psychologist. Psychologist Health South Rehabilitation Hosp., Albuquerque, N.Mex., 1991-93; asst. adj. prof. dept. psychiatry Univ. Calif., San Diego, 1993—. Co-author: (book chpt.) Handbook of Child Clinical Psychology, 1992, Stress and Medical Procedures, 1990; contbr. articles to profl. jours. Vol. Am. Cancer Soc., 1988-89. Recipient Trainee Rsch. award Am. Soc. Psychosomatic 1988, B.F. Haught Rsch. award Univ. N.Mex., 1989. Mem. Soc. Behavioral Medicine, Am. Psychological Assn., N. Mex. Soc. Biofeedback & Behavioral Medicine (sec., treas.), Phi Kappa Phi. Office: VA Medical Ctr 116B 3350 La Jolla Village Dr San Diego CA 92161

PRUSSING, LAUREL LUNT, state official, economist; b. N.Y.C., Feb. 21, 1941; d. Richard Valentine and Maria (Rinaldi) Lunt; m. John Edward Prussing, May 29, 1965; children: Heidi Elizabeth, Erica Stephanie, Victoria Nicole Johanna. AB, Wellesley Coll., 1962; MA, Boston U., 1964; postgrad., U. Calif., San Diego, 1968-69, U. Ill., 1970-76. Economist Arthur D. Little, Cambridge, Mass., 1963-67, U. Ill., Urbana, 1971-72; mem. county bd. Champaign County, Urbana, 1972-76, county auditor, 1976-92; mem. local audit adv. bd. Office Ill. Compt., Chgo., 1984-92. Contbr. to Illinois Local Government: A Handbook, 1990. Founder Com. for Intelligent Tax Reform, Urbana, 1982—, Com. for Elected County Exec., Urbana, 1986—; state rep. 103d dist. Ill. Gen. Assembly, 1993-95; dem. cand. Ill. 15th dist. U.S. Congress, 1996. Named Best Freshman Legislator Ind. Voters Ill., 1994; recipient Friend of Agriculture award Ill. Farm Bur., 1994; named to Legis. Honor Roll Ill. Environ. Coun., 1994. Mem. LWV, Govt. Fin. Officers Assn., U.S. and Can. (com. on acctg., auditing and fin. reporting 1980-88, Fin. Reporting award 1981-91, Disting. Budget award 1986), Nat. Assn. Local Govt. Auditors (charter), Ill. Assn. County Auditors (pres. 1984-85). Democrat. Home: 2106 Grange Dr Urbana IL 61801-6609

PRUTER, MARGARET FRANSON, encyclopedia editor; b. Oak Park, Ill., Jan. 16; d. Frederick G. and Margaret K. (Svoboda) Franson; m. Robert D. Pruter, July 22, 1972; 1 child, Robin. AB, Rosary Coll., 1961; MA, Northwestern U., 1965. Asst. editor Am. People's Ency., Chgo., 1961-62; rsch. assoc. AMA, Chgo., 1962-63; asst. editor New Standard Ency., Chgo., 1964-66, assoc. editor, 1966-75, sr. editor, 1975—; exec. dir. Militaria Archives, Elmhurst, Ill., 1972—. Co-author: DuPage Roots, 1985 (Ill. State Hist. Publ. award 1986). Mem. Elmhurst Hist. Commn., 1981—, v.p., 1995—; bd. dirs. DuPage County Hist. Soc., Wheaton, Ill., 1982—, Dupage County Sesquicentennial Com., 1988-89; mem. Friends of Elmhurst Pub. Libr., Elmhurst Art Mus. Found.; bd. dirs. North Ctrl. Coll. Parents Assn., 1995—. Mem. AAUW (bd. dirs. Elmhurst br. 1995—), Orgn. Am. Historians, Nat. Trust Historic Preservation, Am. Studies Assn., Ill. Hist. Soc., Elmhurst Hist. Soc., Chgo. Hist. Soc., Chgo. Architecture Found., Byrd's Nest Chapel Questers (pres. 1992-94), Sisters in Crime, Pi Gamma Mu. Office: Standard Ednl Corp 200 W Madison St Chicago IL 60606-5015

PRUZAN, IRENE, arts administrator, music educator, flutist, marketing and public relations specialist; b. Watertown, N.Y., Jan. 3, 1949; d. John Edward and Esther (Coahn) P.; m. Charles G. Ullery, Jan. 30, 1972 (div. 1978); m. Charles Robert Freeman, May 20, 1988. Student, U. Ariz., 1966-68; MusB, U. So. Calif., 1971; postgrad., San Francisco State U., 1972-74, U. Minn., 1976-80. Tchr. flute, coach chamber music MacPhail Ctr. for Arts, U. Minn., Mpls., 1976-85, coordinator instrumental music, 1978-81, program dir. instrumental music, 1982-85, div. head of programs, 1985-86; regional dir. Music On The Move, Inc., Valley Cottage, N.Y., 1986-87; pres. Music On the Move Minn., Inc., St. Paul, 1987—; founding mem. Crocus Hill Trio, 1976—; pub. rels. cons. Sch. of Music, U. Minn., 1991; faculty Nat. Music Camp, Interlochen, Mich., 1983, 84; cons. edn. and festival Ordway Music Theatre, St. Paul, 1985-87; mgr. Sartory String Quartet, Mpls., 1986-93; developer numerous master classes. Writer teaching materials for flute. Mem. Ariz. Chamber Orch., Tucson, 1967, San Gabriel (Calif.) Symphony, 1968-71; extra player St. Paul Chamber Orch., 1977-91; bd. dirs. Twin Cities Friends of Chamber Music, 1982-89; organizer German jazz residency USIA, Minn. and Wis., 1986; cons., program dir. Young Audiences Minn., Mpls., 1986-88. Mem. Nat. Flute Assn. (dir. mktg. 1987-90), Minn. Alliance for Arts in Edn., Twin Cities Musicians Union. Office: Music On The Move Minn Inc PO Box 4125 Saint Paul MN 55104-0125

PRYCE, DEBORAH D., congresswoman; b. Warren, Ohio, July 29, 1951. BA cum laude, Ohio State U., 1973; JD with honors, Capital U., 1976. Bar: Ohio 1976. Former asst. city prosecutor, asst. city atty., first asst. city prosecutor Columbus, Ohio; former judge Franklin County Mcpl. Ct., Columbus; mem. 103rd Congress from 15th Ohio dist., Washington, D.C., 1993—; mem. coms. rules. Republican. Presbyterian.

PRYE, ELLEN ROSS, graphic designer; b. Waynesboro, Va., Mar. 12, 1947; d. John Dewey and Betty Lou (Hardman) Ross; m. Warren Douglas Drumheller, June 7, 1969 (div. 1987); children: Amy Heather Drumheller, Warren Daniel Drumheller; m. John Paul Prye, July 24, 1993. BS, James Madison U., 1990. Cert. tchr. art K-12, Va/. Graphic artist The News-Virginian, Waynesboro, 1990-92, advt. prodn./composing mgr., 1992-94; graphic designer The Humphries Press, Inc., Waynesboro, Va., 1994—. Recipient Distinction award Shenandoah Valley Art Ctr., 1989, 1st pl. award for design of newsletter Printing Industries of Va., 995, 1st pl. for design of brochure, 1995. Mem. Va. Press Assn. (1st pl. color automotive advt. merit cert. 1991, 1st pl. color health, profl. svcs. advt. merit cert. 1991, 1st pl. color food and drugs, variety advt. merit cert. 1993). Presbyterian. Home: 1830 S Talbott Pl Waynesboro VA 22980-2252 Office: The Humphries Press Inc 1400 Hopeman Pkwy Waynesboro VA 22980

PRYGA, SUZANNE MARIE, gender equity consultant, sociology educator; b. Chgo., Apr. 19, 1969; d. John Michael and Rosemarie Jean (Weldin) Pryga. BA in Sociology, DePaul U., 1992, MA in Sociology, 1992. Gender equity cons. Ill. State Bd. of Edn., Springfield, 1993—; adj. faculty Joliet (Ill.) Jr. Coll., 1995—. Vol. advocate Northwest Action Against Rape, Schaumburg, Ill., 1993. Mem. AAUW (co-chair of initiative for ednl. equity, 1995—), Am. Sociol. Assn. Democrat. Roman Catholic. Office: Illinois Bd Education 301 South Swift Addison IL 60101

PRYOR, CAROL GRAHAM, obstetrician, gynecologist; b. Savannah, Ga.; m. Louis O.J. Manganiello, June 11, 1950; children: Carol Helen, Victoria Manganiello Mudano. AB, Ga. Coll., 1943; MD, Med. Coll. Ga., 1947. Rotating intern City Hosps., Balt., 1947-48; asst. resident pathology Baroness Erlanger Hosp., Chattanooga, 1948; intern. obstetrics City Colls., Balt., 1949; coll. physician Ga. State Coll. for Women, Milledgeville, Ga., 1949-50; resident obstetrics City Hosps., Balt., 1950-51; asst. resident gynecology Univ. Hosp., Balt., 1951-52; sr. resident ob-gyn. Univ. Hosp., Augusta, Ga., 1952; pvt. practice ob-gyn. Augusta, 1952—. Mem., former pres. Iris Garden Club, Augusta; mem. coun. on maternal and infant health State of Ga., Atlanta, 1981-90; mem. edn. found. AAUW, 1961-63, state v.p., br. pres., 1963-65. Recipient Cert. of Achievement-Community Leadersip, Ga. div. AAUW, 1982; named Med. Woman of Yr., Ga. br. 51 Am. Med. Women's Assn., 1961. Fellow Am. Coll. Surgeons (1st woman mem. Ga. chpt. 1956), Am. Coll. Ob-Gyn.; mem. AMA, Richmond County Med. Soc., So. Med. Assn., So. Surg. Congress, Delta Kappa Gamma. Democrat. Methodist. Office: 2316 Wrightsboro Rd Augusta GA 30904-6220

PRYOR, DIXIE DARLENE, elementary education educator; b. Anderson, Ind., May 22, 1938; d. Thurman Earle and Alice D. (Watson) Rinker; m. Charles Lee Pryor, Mar. 13, 1958; children: Charles A., Deborah Lee Pryor Evans, Laurinda Ann Pryor Owen. BS, Ball State U., 1967, MEd, 1974. Tchr. Anderson (Ind.) Pub. Schs., 1967-72, Wawasee Cmty. Sch. Corp., Syracuse, Ind., 1972—; bd. dirs. Internat. Palace Sports-Scholarship, North Webster, Ind. Bd. dirs. North Webster Day Care, Cardinal Ctr., Inc., Warsaw, Ind. Named Outstanding Mem. Tippkee Reading Coun., 1995, Outstanding Educator Honor Srs., 1995; recipient Ind. State Reading Assn., 1995. Mem. Ind. State Reading Assn.(pres. 1994-95, Outstanding Mem. award 1996), Kiwanis (com. chair North Webster 1988—, sec. 1996-97). Republican. Methodist. Home: 4630 E Armstrong Rd Leesburg IN 46538-9588

PRZELOMSKI, ANASTASIA NEMENYI, retired newspaper editor; b. Cleve., Dec. 11, 1918; d. Ernest Nicholas and Anna (Ress) Nemenyi; m. Edward Adrian Przelomski, July 4, 1946 (dec. July 1995). A.B., Youngstown State U., 1939; M.Ed., U. Pitts., 1942. Tchr. Youngstown Pub. Sch., Ohio, 1939-42; reporter Vindicator, Youngstown, 1942-57, asst. city editor, 1957-73, city editor, 1973-76, mng. editor, 1976-88, ret., 1988. Named Woman of Yr., Youngstown Bus. and Profl. Women's Club, 1977, bus. category Woman of Yr., YWCA, 1986; recipient Community Service award Youngstown Fedn. Women's Clubs, 1981, Woman of Yr. award YWCA, 1983; named to Ohio Woman's Hall of Fame, 1986. Mem. AP Mng. Editors Assn., UPI Ohio Editors Assn. (bd. dirs. 1984-88), Ohio Assn. AP, Ohio Soc. Newspaper Editors, Youngstown State U. Alumni Assn. (trustee 1978-83), Catholic Collegiate Assn., Phi Kappa Phi. Republican. Roman Catholic. Home: 4000 Logan Gate Rd Youngstown OH 44505-1773

PRZYBYZEWSKI, LESLIE CAMILLE, mathematics educator; b. Big Spring, Tex., June 18, 1955; d. Joseph Mac Montgomery and Emily Reese Dann; m. Joseph Stanaslous Przybyzewski, June 20, 1992; children: Jocelyn, Keely, Danny Eagan. AA, Mt. Wachusett C.C., Gardner, Mass., 1980; BS in Math. Edn. magna cum laude, Columbus Coll., 1989; M in Applied Math., Auburn U., 1991, postgrad., 1991-92. Grad. asst. Auburn (Ala.) U., 1991-92; math. instr. Tuskegee (Ala.) U., 1992-96. Mem. Collegiate Curriculum Reform and Cmty. Action, Greensboro, N.C., 1994-95, 95-96. Recipient scholarship Ga. Bd. Regents, 1975, Columbus Coll., 1987-88, 88-89. Mem. AAUP, MAA, Pi Mu Epsilon, Kappa Delta Pi. Methodist. Home: 465 Lee Rd 227 Smiths AL 36877

PSILLOS, SUSAN ROSE, artist, educator; b. Bethpage, N.Y., Feb. 15, 1960; d. Reginald and Gloria Barbara Psillos; 1 child, Jennifer Rose. Student, Alfred U., 1978-80; Teaching Degree in Art, L.I. U., Southampton, 1996. Substitute tchr. art Shoreham-Wading River Schs., Shoreham, N.Y., 1992—; tchr. arts and crafts Round-out S.W.R. Sch., Shoreham, 1995-96; guest speaker in field. Exhibited sculpture at Smithtown (N.Y.) Mus., 1995, Bellemeade Gallery, 1992; exhibited paintings at Ambiente Gallery, 1991-92, Smithtown Twsp. Art Mus., 1995, 96. Advisor Partnership for Survival, Smithtown, 1991—; bd. dirs., pub. rels. person Sexual Abuse Survivors, Smithtown,1991—. Recipient Art Judge's award Parrish Art Mus., 1976, Outstanding award Sch. Visual Arts, 1976, Profl. Recognition Day award, 1996, Child Abuse & Neglect Family Violence Vol. award Town of Brookhaven. Mem. NOW, Artist Support Group.

PUCKETT, ELIZABETH ANN, law librarian, law educator; b. Evansville, Ind., Nov. 10, 1943; d. Buell Charles and Lula Ruth (Gray) P.; m. Joel E. Hendricks, June 1, 1964 (div. June 1973); 1 child, Andrew Charles; m. Thomas A. Wilson, July 19, 1985. BS in Edn., Eastern Ill. U., 1964; JD, U. Ill., 1977, MS in L.S., 1977. Bar: Kans. 1978, Ill. 1979. Acquisitions/reader services librarian U. Kans. Law Library, Lawrence, 1978-79; asst. reader services librarian So. Ill. U. Law Library, Carbondale, 1979-81, reader services librarian, 1981-83; assoc. dir. Northwestern U. Law Library, Chgo., 1983-86, co-acting dir., 1986-87; dir./assoc. prof. South Tex. Coll. Law Library, Houston, 1987-89; dir./prof. South Tex. Coll. Law Libr., Houston, 1990-94, U. Ga. Law Libr., Athens, 1994—. Co-author: Evaluation of System-Provided Library Services to State Correctional Centers in Illinois, 1983; co-editor Uniform Commercial Code: Confidential Drafts, 1993. Mem. ABA, Am. Assn. Law Librs. (mem. exec. bd. 1993-96). Office: U Georgia Law Libr Athens GA 30602-6018

PUCKETT, GENA LIVINGSTON, paralegal; b. Phila., Nov. 3, 1958; d. Edward Eugene and Dawn Janet (Brown) Livingston; m. Steven Eugene Puckett, Oct. 4, 1984. BA, Atlantic Christian Coll., 1981; cert., Nat. Ctr. Paralegal Tng., 1982. Collector Intregratec, Atlanta, 1989-91; paralegal Wallace & DeMayo, Atlanta, 1991-93, Citizens Trust Bank, Atlanta, 1995—; dep. clk. Eleventh Cir. Ct. Appeals, Atlanta, 1993-94. Mem. Native Am. Rights, Washington, 1994—. Episcopalian. Home: 346 Carpenter Dr Apt 37 Atlanta GA 30328 Office: Citizens Trust Bank 75 Piedmont Ave Atlanta GA 30303

PUCKETT, HELEN LOUISE, tax consulting company executive; b. Ripley, Ohio, Oct. 29, 1934; d. Joseph and Gladys Muriel (Madden) Haney; grad. Columbus Bus. U., 1971; m. Marvin R. Puckett, May 26, 1953 (dec.); children: Steven W., Thomas J. Office mgr. Al-Win Tng., Inc., West Jefferson, Ohio, 1971—, sec.-treas., 1971—, agt., 1977-79; owner, operator HLP Bus. Enterprises, bookkeeping and tax service; notary public, 1975—. Sunday Sch. tchr. London (Ohio) Ch. of Christ, 1975—, pres. Women's Fellowship, 1979-81. Mem. London Bus. and Profl. Women (pres.), Coover Soc., Loving Care Hospice, Madison County Hosp. Corp. Office: 485 Glade Run Rd SE Jefferson OH 43162-9601

PUCKO, DIANE BOWLES, public relations executive; b. Wyndotte, Mich., Aug. 15, 1940; d. Mervin Arthur and Bernice Letitia (Shelly) Bowles; m. Raymond J. Pucko, May 22, 1965; children: Todd Anthony, Gregory Bowles. BA in Sociology, Bucknell U., Lewisburg, Pa., 1962. Accredited in pub. rels. Asst. to pub. rels. dir. Edward C. Michener Assocs., Inc., Harrisburg, Pa., 1962-65; advt./pub. rels. coord. Superior Switchboard & Devices, Canton, Ohio, 1965-66; editorial dir. women's svc. Hutchins Advt. Co., Inc., Rochester, N.Y., 1966-71; pres. Editorial Communications, Rochester and Elyria, Ohio, 1971-77; mgr. advt. and sales promotion Tappan Air Conditioning, Elyria, 1977-80; mgr. pub. affairs Kaiser Permanente Med. Care Program, Cleve., 1980-85; corp. dir. pub. affairs Keystone Health Plans, Inc., Camp Hill, Pa., 1985-86; v.p., dir. client planning Young-Liggett-Stashower, Cleve., 1986; v.p., dir. pub. rels. Marcus Pub. Rels., Cleve., 1987-91; sr. v.p. Proconsul, Cleve., 1991-95, also bd. dirs.; sr. ptnr. pub. rels. Poppe Tyson, Cleve., 1995—; mgr., role model Women in Mgmt. Field Placement program, Cleve. State U., 1983-92; prof. advisor, pub. rels. adv. bd. Pub. Rels. Student Soc. Am., Kent State U., 1988—. Bd. trustees, mem. exec. com., chmn. pub. rels. adv. com. Ronald MacDonald House of Cleve., 1993—; bd. dirs., chmn. pub. rels. com. Assn. Retarded Citizens, Cleve., 1987-91; mem. pub. rels.-mktg. com. Beech Brook, 1996—. Recipient Woman Profl. Excellence award YMCA, 1984, MacEachern award Acad. Hosp. Pub. Rels., 1985, Bell Ringer award Cmty. Rels. Report, 1985, Bronze Quill Excellence award Internat. Assn. Bus. Communicators, 1992, 93, Cleve. Comms. award Women in Comms. Internat., 1993, 95, Tower award Bus./Profl. Advt. Assn., 1993, 95, Creativity in Pub. Rels. award, 1994, Silver Screen award U.S. Internat. Film & Video Festival, 1995. Fellow Pub. Rels. Soc. Am. (bd. dirs. 1983-85, 86-94, officer 1991-95, mem. counselors acad. 1986—, Silver Anvil award 1985, Mktg./Consumer Rels. award East Ctrl. dist. 1992, 95, Lighthouse award 1995); mem. Press Club Cleve. (bd. dirs. 1989-96, v.p. 1990-96), Cleve. Advt. Club, Women's City Club Cleve. Republican. Methodist. Home: 656 University Ave Elyria OH 44035-7239 Office: Erieview Tower 1301 E 9th St Cleveland OH 44114

PUDICK, DONNA EASTMAN, adult education educator; b. Milford, Mass., Sept. 7, 1939; d. Walter Smith and Theodora Elsa (DeAmicis) Eastman; m. Sheldon Pudick, Jan. 26, 1964; children: Jill Teddie, Glenn Eastman. BS, Simmons Coll., 1961. Writer Allyn & Bacon, Inc., Boston, 1961-62; editor Allergy Found., Boston, 1962, Little/Brown, Inc., Boston, 1963-64; writer, editor McGraw-Hill Book Co., N.Y.C., 1964-65; instr., model Barbizon Schs., Highland Park, N.J., 1972-75; writer, agy. dir. Barbizon Agy., Montclair, N.J., 1975-85; editor Howmark Pub., Elizabeth, N.J., 1985-92; instr., cons. adult edn. Flagler County Schs., Palm Coast, Fla., 1995—. Columnist (newspapers) Mirror-Mirror, 1972-78; contbr.: Inkslingers, 1995; editor, contbr.: Scribblings, 1993, The Brass Ring, 1996. Mem. AAUW (program chair 1995—), DAR (publicity chair 1994—), Am. Pen Women, Ormond Writers League, Poets and Writers Soc., Scribblers (sec.-treas.).

PUDLES, LYNNE, art historian; b. Pitts., July 30, 1951; d. Saul B. and Claire (Marcus) P.; m. Martin Davis, July, 1974 (div. 1978); m. R.B. Duncan, June 10, 1989. BA summa cum laude, U. Pitts., 1973; MA, U. Calif., Berkeley, 1977, PhD, 1987. Vis. instr. art history Humboldt State U., Arcata, Calif., 1977-78, U. Chgo., 1985-86; instr. art history Cleve. State U., 1986-87, asst. prof. art history, 1987; asst. prof. art history Lake Forest (Ill.) Coll., 1987-93, assoc. prof. art history, 1993—; exec. adv. com. Interdisciplinary Nineteenth Century Studies, 1988-91; commr. Winnetka (Ill.) Archtl. Landmarks Preservation, 1992—; advisor Ill. Acad. Fine Arts; cons. in field. Author: (exhbn. catalogue) Roger Snakkers Retrospective Exhbn., 1991, Michael Croydon, "The Love Poems" Exhbn., 1988; contbr. articles to profl. jours. Founder The Pitts. Women's Ctr., 1970-73, Pitts. Rape Crisis Ctr., 1970-73; coord. Letter Drive to Support Reauthorization of NEA, Lake Forest, 1990. Fellow Samuel Kress Found., 1975, U. Calif., Berkeley, Found. and Alumni Assn., 1979-80, Danforth Found., 1974-79, 1981-82, Theodore Rousseau Met. Mus. Art, 1981-82, Belgian Ministry of Edn. and Culture, 1981-82, U. Calif., Berkeley, Grad. Humanities Rsch., 1981-82. Mem. AAUP, Am. Assn. Museums, Soc. for Values in Higher Edn., Midwest Art History Soc., Coll. Art Assn. Am., Phi Beta Kappa (U. Calif. Berkeley fellow 1985, No. Calif. Assn. fellow 1985), Mortar Board Nat. Hon. Soc. Home & Office: Lake Forest Coll Art Dept 555 N Sheridan Rd Lake Forest IL 60045-2338

PUDLIN, HELEN POMERANTZ, lawyer; b. N.Y.C., June 26, 1949; d. George and Claire Pomerantz; m. David B. Pudlin, Dec. 23, 1973; children: Alexander R., Julia H. BA cum laude, U. Pa., 1970, MS, 1971, JD, 1974. Bar: Pa. 1974. Lectr. U. Pa. Law Sch., 1983-87; asssoc. Ballard, Spahr, Andreas & Ingersoll, Phila., 1974-81, ptnr., 1981-89; gen. counsel Provident Nat. Bank, Phila., 1989-93; sr. v.p., dep. gen. counsel PNC Fin. Corp., Pitts., 1992-93; sr. v.p., mng. gen. counsel PNC Bank Corp., Pitts., 1993, sr. v.p., gen. counsel, 1993—; speaker in field. Author: (with others) Review of Antitrust Laws and Procedures, 1983, Criminal Antitrust Litigation Manual, 1983, Pennsylvania Medical Society Handbook, 1989; co-author: Joint Ventures in Healthcare. Active mem. Bd. of Ethics City of Phila.; bd. dirs. Phila. Facilities Mgmt. Corp.; bd. advisors Pub. Interest Law Ctr. Phila. Mem. ABA (antitrust sect., litigation sect., bus. law sect.), Pa. Bar Assn. (former mem. ho. of dels., judiciary com.), Phila. Bar Assn. (bd. govs. 1989-91, fed. cts. com., bus. law sect.), Forum Exec. Women, Acad. Natural Scis. (bd. dirs., trustee), Duquesne Club. Office: PNC Bank Corp 249 Fifth Ave Pittsburgh PA 15222-2707

PUDLO, VIRGINIA MARY, medical surgical nurse; b. Hartford, Conn., Jan. 22, 1951; d. Alexander and Eve Antoinette (Paczkowski) P. AS in Secretarial Sci., U. Hartford, 1974; BSN, St. Joseph Coll., 1988. RN, Conn.; cert. med.-surg. nursing ANCC. Exec. sec. Pratt & Whitney Aircraft divsn. United Techs. Corp., East Hartford, Conn., 1969-85; clin. nurse I med.-surg. orthopedic/rehab. unit Hartford Hosp., 1988-93, clin. nurse II surg. unit, 1993-96, with preadmission testing ctr., 1996—; staff nurse coun. Hartford Hosp., rep., 1989—, sec., 1993—. Tchr. calligraphy East Hartford Adult Edn., 1983—. Recipient Linda Richards-June Long Nursing award for Leadership Excellence Hartfield Hosp., 1994. Mem. Nat. Assn. Orthopedic Nurses, Conn. Nurses Assn., Conn. Valley Calligraphers (libr. 1993—), Sigma Theta Tau (Upsilon chpt., mem.-at-large 1992). Home: 63 Lafayette Ave East Hartford CT 06118-2628

PUETZ, PAMELA ANN, human resources executive; b. Lawrence, Mass., Aug. 17, 1949; d. Gregory and Eleanor Christine (Stull) Bedrosian; m. Tracy Barnum Braun, Jan. 26, 1974 (div. 1985); 1 child, Susannah Barnum; m. Dan Lee Puetz, May 31, 1986. AS, Fisher Jr. Coll., Boston, 1969; BS in Mgmt. with high distinction, Babson Coll., Wellesley, Mass., 1973. Br. mgr. First Security Bank of Utah, N.A., Salt Lake City, 1974-76; bus. mgr. U.S. Ski Team, Inc., Park City, Utah, 1976-77; banking specialist Tracy Collins Bank, Salt Lake City, 1980-83; instr. Fitness Inst., LDS Hosp., Salt Lake City, 1983-85; owner/operator Grapevine Svcs., Redondo Beach, Calif., 1987-88; human resources adminstr. PacifiCare Health Systems, Inc., Cypress, Calif., 1988-89, human resources analyst, 1989-91, human resources project mgr., 1991—, human resources info. systems mgr., 1992—; assoc. DLP Constrn. & Devel., Garden Grove, Calif., 1992-94; sr. mgr. human resources systems Mattel, Inc., El Segundo, Calif., 1994-95; sr. cons., HRIS mgr. PacifiCare Health Systems, Inc., Cypress, Calif., 1995—. Mem. Am. Compensation Assn., Internat. Human Resources Info. Mgmt. Assn., Soc. for Human Resources Mgmt.

PUFFER, SHARON KAYE, residential loan officer; b. Portland, Oreg., June 23, 1944; d. Henry and Linda Katherine (Olsen) Clearwater; m. Arleigh Rocco Puffer, Feb. 5, 1965; children: Michele Lynn, Heidi Leigh. Student, Portland State U., 1962-64. Lic. real estate salesperson. Real estate sales agt. Valley Realty, Dublin, Calif., 1979-82; with real estate sales The Ryness Co., Danville, Calif., 1982-83; sales coord. spl. projects Coldwell Banker, San Ramon, Calif., 1983-86; residential loan officer Coldwell Banker Mortgage, Danville, 1986-87, Glenfed Mortgage, San Ramon, 1987-89; sr. real estate loan officer Bank of America Residential Loan Ctr., Walnut Creek, Calif., 1989—. Membership chmn. Livermore (Calif.) Jr. Women affiliate Nat. Fedn. of Women, 1974-75, pres., 1975-76. Mem. Contra Costa Bd. Realtors. Republican. Home: 330 Mccloud Pl Danville CA 94526-5017

PUGH, DOROTHY GUNTHER, ballet company executive. Grad. magna cum laude, Vanderbilt U., 1973; studied with Raymond Clay, studied with Donna Carver, studied with David Howard; student, Royal Acad. Dancing, London. Founder, artistic dir. Ballet Memphis (formerly Memphis Concert Ballet). Mem. AIDS Consortium Com.; mem. fine arts com. St. Agnes Acad. Recipient Woman of Achievement award for Initiative, 1987; featured as one of city's influential citizens in Memphis Mag. Office: Memphis Concert Ballet PO Box 11136 Memphis TN 38111

PUGH, JOYE JEFFRIES, educational administrator; b. Ocilla, Ga., Jan. 23, 1957; d. Claude Bert and Stella Elizabeth (Paulk) Jeffries; m. Melville Eugene Pugh, Sept. 21, 1985. AS in Pre-law, S. Ga. Coll., 1978; BS in Edn., Valdosta State Coll., 1980, MEd in Psychology, Guidance and Counseling, 1981; EdD in Adminstrn., Nova U., Ft. Lauderdale, Fla., 1992. Cert. tchr., adminstr., supr., Ga. Personnel adminstr. TRW, Inc., Douglas, Ga., 1981-83; recreation dir. Ocilla (Ga.), Irwin Recreation Dept., 1983-84; exec. dir. Sunny Dale Tng. Ctr., Inc., Ocilla, 1984—; pres. and registered agt. Irwin County Resources, Inc., Ocilla, 1988—, Camelot Ct., Inc., 1994—. Contbr. articles on handicapped achievements to newspapers, mags. (Ga. Spl. Olympics News Media award, 1987, Assn. for Retarded Citizens News Media award, 1988). Adv. bd. Area 12 Spl. Olympics, Douglas, Ga., 1984-88; pres. Irwin County Spl. Olympics, 1984—, mem. adv. task force Spl. Olympics Internat. for 6-7 yr. olds, 1995—, elected to Ga. Spl. Olympics bd. dirs., 1995-98, serve on the comm. and mktg. com. for Ga. Spl. Olympics, 1995-96; exec. dir., fund raising chmn. Irwin Assn. for Retarded Citizens, Ocilla, 1984—; arts and crafts chmn. Ga. Sweet Tater Trot 5k/1 Mile Rd. Races, 1993—; bd. dirs., com. mem., mktg. com. Ga. Spl. Olympics, 1995—; founder, chmn. Joseph Mascolo Celebrity Events, 1985—. Recipient Spirit of Spl. Olympics award Ga. Spl. Olymics, Atlanta, 1986, Cmty. Svc. award Ga. Assn. for Retarded Citizens, Atlanta, 1987, Govs.' Vol. award Ga. Vol. Awards, Atlanta, 1988, Presdl. Sports award AAU, Indpls., 1988, Humanitarian award Sunny Dale Tng. Ctr., Inc., Ocilla, 1988, Golden Poet award New Am. Poetry Anthology, 1988, Outstanding Coach-Athlete Choice award Sunny Dale Spl. Olympics, Ocilla, 1992, Dist. Coach award, 1993, Outstanding Unified Sports Ptnr. of Yr. award, 1995, Coach of Yr. award, 1996; carried Olympic Torch, Ocilla, Ga., 1996. Mem. DAR, Mut. Unidentified Flying Object Network (Ga. state sect. dir., asst. state dir.), Ga. State Assn. for Retarded Citizens, Ctrs. Dirs. Ga., Ocilla Rotary Club (program dir. 1995—, bd. dirs. 1995—, sec. 1996—), Sunny Dale Unified Track Club (founder 1991—), Sunny Dale Unified Track Club (founder 1991—), Sunny Dale Ensemble (founder), Ocilla/Irwin County C. of C. Baptist. Home: 201 Lakeside Cir Douglas GA 31533-9656 Office: Sunny Dale Tng Ctr Inc Mascolo Dr Box 512 Ocilla GA 31774-9801

PUGH, MARION STIRLING, archaeologist, author; b. Middletown, N.Y., May 12, 1911; d. Louis and Lena May (Randall) Illig; m. Matthew Williams Sirling, Dec. 11, 1933 (dec. 1975); children: Matthew Williams, Jr. (dec.), Ariana Stirling Withers; m. John Ramsey Pugh, Aug. 7, 1977 (dec. Mar. 1994). BS, Rider Coll., 1930; postgrad. George Washington U., 1931-33. Office sec. Bur. Am. Ethnology, Smithsonian Instn., Washington, 1931-33; archaeologist with Matthew W. Stirling, Fla., 1934-38, Smithsonian Instn.-Nat. Geog. Soc. archeol. expdn. Mex., 1939-46, Panama, 1948-53, Ecuador, 1957, Costa Rica, 1962. Author: (with Matthew Stirling) Tarqui, an Early Site in Manabi, Ecuador, 1962, El Limon, an Early Tomb Site in Cocle Province, Panama, 1963, Archaeological Notes on Almirante Bay, Bocas del Toro, Panama, 1963, The Archeology of Taboga, Uraba and Taboguilla Islands, Panama, 1963; contbr. articles to Nat. Geog. mag. and Ames. mag. Trustee The Textile Mus., Washington, 1968—, pres. 1984-87. Co-recipient Franklyn L. Burr award Nat. Geog. Soc., 1941, Disting. Svc. medal Peruvian Embassy, 1985. Fellow Am. Anthrop. Assn., Gen. Div. Anthropology; mem. Am. Ethnol. Soc., Soc. Latin Am. Anthropology, Washington Anthrop. Soc., Washington Acad. Sci., Soc. Woman Geographers (pres. 1960-63, 69-72, mem. exec. council 1954-74, Gold medal 1975). Avocations: swimming, textiles. Home: 20351 Airmont Rd Round Hill VA 20141

PUGH, PHYLLIS CHERI, neuroscientist; b. Perry, Ohio, Feb. 12, 1966; d. Olen Wright and Amy Katharine (Anderson) P. BS, Calif. Inst. Tech., 1988; PhD, U. Calif., 1995. Grad. tchg. asst. U. Calif., San Diego, 1989-94, grad. rsch. asst., 1989-94; mentor in genetics Minority Scientists Program San Diego State U., 1994; postdoctoral fellow, rsch. assoc. U. Pitts., 1995—. Singer Sewickley (Pa.) Choir Inst., 1995-96. NIMH fellow, 1995, USPHS fellow, 1995. Mem. AAWU, Soc. for Neurosci., Am. Contract Bridge League, Sigma Xi. Office: U Pitts Dept Neurobiology E1440 BST Pittsburgh PA 15261

PUGH, SHANNON MICHELLE, secondary education educator; b. Wichita Falls, Tex., Sept. 18, 1970; d. Thomas William and E. Diane (Fischer) P.; BA, Midwestern State U., 1992, MA, 1995. Cert. tchr., Miss. Vol. tutor Tex. Adult Literacy Coun., Wichita Falls, 1990-94; office intern to Rep. Sarpalius U.S. House Reps., Washington, 1991; UIL coord. Midwestern State U., Wichita Falls, 1992-94, lectr., 1993-94; tchr. secondary edn. Teach for Am., Tunica, Miss., 1994—; mem. adv. bd. Miss. TRI-HI-Y, Jackson, 1994—. Active Dem. Com., 1989—; pres. North/Midwest Tex. Young Dems., Wichita Falls, 1990-92; mem. Laubach Literacy Coun., Tex., 1990-94; mem. com. Young Texans for Ann, Austin, 1993-94; bd. dirs. Miss. Ind. YMCA, Jackson, 1995—. Mem. NEA, LWV, Americorps Nat. Svc. Corps, Teach for Am. Nat. Tchr. Corp., Rural Advocacy Edn. Coun., Tunica Edn. Assn. (curriculum bd.). Methodist.

PUGH-MARZI, SHERRIE, daycare center administrator; b. Atlanta, July 16, 1955; d. Joseph Grey and Mary Elizabeth (Gregory) Pugh; divorced; children: Michael, Mari. BS, Jacksonville U., 1977. Cert. early childhood tchr., N.J. Tchr. Beth Torah Nursery Sch., Willingboro, N.J., 1976-79; kindergarten tchr. Fox Learning Ctr., Hainesport, N.J., 1979-84, Indian Mills (N.J.) Preschool, 1984-85; co-dir. Excel Learning Ctr., Marlton, N.J., 1985-87; owner, dir. Day Bear Care Learning Ctr., Medford Lakes, N.J., 1987—; cons. energy program Phila. Electric Co., 1989-90. V.p. recreation Medford Lakes Colony, 1990—; co-chair Medford Lakes Canoe Carnival, 1994, zoning bd., 1993; mem. Medford Lakes Zoning Bd. Adjustment, 1991—; mem. review bd. Burlington County Child Placement, 1993—; active Child Support Recovery, 1992; chair canoe carnival event Mcpl. Alliance Medford Lakes, 1994—. Mem. Medford Lakes Home and Sch. Assn. (exec. bd. 1987—, pres. 1995, Vol. of Yr. award 1990). Democrat. Baptist. Home and Office: Day Bear Care Learning Ctr 177 Stokes Rd Medford Lakes NJ 08055-1522

PUGLIESE, KAREN OLSEN, freelance public relations counsel; b. S.I., N.Y., Aug. 20, 1963; d. Harold Birger and Janet Mildred (Cronk) Olsen; m. John Michael Pugliese Jr., Oct. 21, 1989; 1 child, Emily Olsen. BA in Polit. Sci., Union Coll., 1985. Asst. editor Food Mgmt. mag., N.Y.C., 1985-86; account exec. Edelman Pub. Rels., N.Y.C., 1986-87; account exec., sr. v.p., group dir. Creamer Dickson Basford, N.Y.C., 1987-96; freelance pub. rels. counsel, Darien, Conn., 1996—. Recipient Gold Quill, Internat. Assn. Bus. Communicators, 1991, award Internat. Pub. Rels. Soc., 1993, Creativity in Pub. Rels., Inside PR, 1993. Republican.

PUGLIESE, MARIA ALESSANDRA, psychiatrist; b. Phila., Sept. 16, 1948; d. Peter Francis and Ida Agnes (Rosa) P.; m. J. Paul Hieble, Sept. 14, 1985; children: Helen Elisa Hieble, Jesse Paul Hieble. BS, Chestnut Hill Coll., 1970; MD, U. Pa., 1974. Diplomate Am. Bd. Psychiatry and Neurology; with added qualifications in addiction psychiatry. Intern in pediatrics Children's Hosp. of Phila., 1974-75; resident in psychiatry Inst. Pa. Hosp., Phila., 1975-78, attending psychiatrist, 1978—; attending psychiatrist Malvern (Pa.) Inst., 1982—. Office: 111 N 49th St Philadelphia PA 19139-2718

PUIG-SOS, MONICA ANDREA, public relations executive; b. Barcelona, Spain, July 18, 1964; came to U.S., 1975; m. Sam Stier, Nov. 24, 1986; 1 child, Joshua. BS in Legal Studies, Nova Southeastern U., 1993. V.p. mktg. L.Am. divsn. USP Products, Inc., Pompano Beach, Fla., 1983-90; free lance writer The Cambridge Exch., Pompano Beach, 1990-93; dir. pub. rels. Legal Club of Am., Ft. Lauderdale, Fla., 1993-96; v.p. pub. rels. Med. Rsch. Industries Inc., Davie, Fla., 1996—. Mem. Nat. Dem. Com., Washington, People for Ethical Treatment of Animals, Washington, Animal Rights Found. of Fla., Ft. Lauderdale. Mem. NOW, Phi Alpha Delta Internat. Democrat. Office: Medical Rsch Ind Inc 6200 Stirling Rd Davie FL 33314

PUJOLAS, ELIZABETH MARIE, chamber of commerce administrator; b. Buffalo, Mar. 2, 1964; d. William James and Elizabeth (Taylor) P. BA in Polit. Sci., SUNY, Cortland, 1986; MPA in Pub. Policy Analysis, SUNY, Binghamton, 1987. Grad. fellow N.Y. State Senate, Albany, 1987-88, legis. dir., 1988-93, spl. legis. analyst, 1993-94; dir. govt. rels. Greater Buffalo Partnership, 1994—. Active Women for Downtown, Buffalo, 1995, Women TAP Fund, Buffalo, 1995, Frontier Polit. Club, Buffalo, 1996, Allentown Homeowners Assn., 1995; mem. com. Vision for Tomorrow Project, Buffalo, 1995—; vol. United Way Success By 6, Buffalo, 1995—. Mem. Profl. Skaters Assn., Cortland Coll. Alumni Reunion (chair 1996), Cortland Coll. Alumni Bd. Home: 65 Mariner St Buffalo NY 14201 Office: Greater Buffalo Partnership 300 Main Place Tower Buffalo NY 14202

PULANCO, TONYA BETH, special education educator; b. Portland, Oreg., Apr. 17, 1933; d. Anthony Lorenzo and Adelfa Elizabeth (Dewey) P. BA, San Jose State U., 1955; MA, Columbia U., 1966. Occupl. therapist Langley Porter Hosp., San Francisco, 1958-60; writer ednl. sub-contracts Columbia U., N.Y.C., 1961-64; from tchr. to dir. edn. Gateway Sch. N.Y., N.Y.C., 1965—. Mem. Assn. for Children with Learning Disabilities, Am. Occupl. Therapy Assn., Japanese Am. Citizens League. Office: Gateway Sch NY 921 Madison Ave New York NY 10021

PULASKI, LISA VALERIA, graphic designer; b. Guatemala City, Guatemala, Feb. 12, 1973; d. Stephen John and Valerie A. (Karolkiewicz) P. BA in Art, Va. Polytechnic Inst. and State U., Blacksburg, 1995. Graphic designer The New Virginians, Blacksburg, 1992-95; graphics and prodn. mgr. Laszlo & Assocs., Inc., Washington, D.C., 1996—; chair pub. rels. Chi Delta Svc. Sorority, Blacksburg, 1994-95. Recipient 1st Place award BIC Pen Corp., 1995. Mem. Women in Comms., Inc. Office: Laszlo & Assocs Inc 1823 Jefferson Pl NW Washington DC 20036

PULASKI, LORI JAYE, career officer; b. Madison, Wis., June 22, 1962; d. Stanley Harold and Phyllis Mabel (Block) P.; m. Joseph Kawika Kim, Sept. 14, 1986 (div. Aug. 1991). BS, USAF Acad., 1984; MA in Aero. Sci., Embry Riddle Aero. U., 1995. Commd. 2d lt. USAF, 1984, advanced through grades to capt., 1988; evaluator/instr. pilot USAF, Carswell AFB, Tex., 1986-92; flight safety officer USAF, Edwards AFB, Calif., 1992-95, evaluator/instr. pilot, 1992-95; command flight safety officer Hqrs. Air Combat Command USAF, Langley AFB, Va., 1995—. Home: 106 Derosa Dr Hampton VA 23666

PULHAMUS, MARLENE LOUISE, elementary school educator; b. Paterson, N.J., Sept. 11, 1937; d. David Weeder and Elfrieda (Ehler) Wemmell; m. Aaron R. Pulhamus, Aug. 20, 1960; children: Steven, Thomas, Nancy. Student, Trenton State U., 1957; BS, William Paterson U., 1959;

postgrad., Rutgers U., 1992. Cert. elem. tchr., N.J. Kindergarten tchr. Wayne (N.J.) Bd. Edn., 1959-63; kindergarten tchr. Paterson Bd. Edn., 1974-75, 2d grade tchr., 1975-81; basic skills instr. Paterson Pub. Schs., 1981—, tchr. accelerated program 1st grade, 1992—; trainer for insvc. groups of learning ctrs. and math. with manipulatives for local pub. schs., trainer for local pub. schs. Contbr. Lessons 4Mat in Action, 3d edit. Pres. Friends of Eisenhower Libr., Totowa, N.J., 1975-77; coord. ch. sch. Preakness Reformed Ch., Wayne, 1990—. Recipient Gov.'s award for tchg. excellence State of N.J. Commn. Edn., 1991, 4Mation program award, 1994. Mem. ASCD, NEA, AAUW, Nat. Coun. Tchrs. Math., Nat. Assn. for Edn. Young Children, N.J. Edn. Assn., Passaic County Edn. Assn., Paterson Edn. Assn. (mem. exec. bd., 1985-89, legis. chmn. 1986-89). Home: 47 Easedale Rd Wayne NJ 07470-2486 Office: Paterson Pub. Sch # 3 448 Main St Paterson NJ 07501-2818

PULITZER, EMILY S. RAUH (MRS. JOSEPH PULITZER, JR.), art consultant; b. Cin., July 23, 1933; d. Frederick and Harriet (Frank) Rauh. AB, Bryn Mawr Coll., 1955; student, Ecole du Louvre, Paris, France, 1955-56; MA, Harvard U., 1963. Mem. staff Cin. Art Mus., 1956-57; asst. curator drawings Fogg Art Mus., Harvard, 1957-64, asst. to dir., 1962-63; curator City Art Mus., St. Louis, 1964-73; mem. painting and sculpture com. Mus. Modern Art, 1975—; chmn. visual arts com. Mo. Arts Council, 1976-81; co-chmn. fellows Fogg Art Mus., 1978—; mem. bd. Inst. Mus. Services, 1979-84; commr. St. Louis Art Mus., 1981-88, vice chmn., 1988; chair collections com. Harvard U. Arts Museums, 1992—; bd. dirs. Pulitzer Pub. Co. Bd. dirs. Forum, St. Louis, 1980—, pres., 1990-94; bd. dirs. Mark Rothko Found., 1976-88, Grand Ctr., 1993-95, St. Louis Symphony Orch., 1994—; bd. dirs. arts in transit com. Bi-State Devel. Agy., vice-chmn., 1987—; mem. Leadership St. Louis, 1990-91; mem. overseers com. to visit Harvard Art Mus., 1990—; trustee Mus. Modern Art, 1994—. Mem. Am. Fedn. Arts (dir. 1976-89), St. Louis Mercantile Libr. Assn. (bd. dirs. 1987-93), Women's Forum of Mo. Home: 4903 Pershing Ave Saint Louis MO 63108-1201

PULITZER, ROSLYN K., social worker, psychotherapist; b. Bronx, N.Y., Apr. 25, 1930; d. George and Laura Eleanor (Holtz) P. BS in Human Devel. and Life Cycle, SUNY, N.Y.C., 1983; MSW, Fordham U., 1987; postgrad., Masterson Inst., N.Y.C., 1991. cert. in psychoanalytic psychotherapy of the personality disorders, Masterson Inst., N.Y.C.; lic. clin. social worker, N.Y. Clinic dir. Resources Counseling and Psychotherapy Ctr., N.Y.C., 1985-89; social worker, clin. supr. methadone maintenance treatment program Beth Israel Med. Ctr., N.Y.C., 1989—; cons. therapist, clin. supr. Identity House, N.Y.C., 1980—, exec. dir., 1985, clin. dir., 1993-94. Mem. regional adv. coun. N.Y. State Div. Human Rights, N.Y.C., 1975-76; mem. Community Bd. 6, N.Y.C., 1978-81; founder, legis. chmn. N.Y. State Women's Polit. Caucus, 1978-80. Mem. NASW, Acad. Cert. Social Workers, Soc. Masterson Inst., N.Y. Milton Erickson Soc. for Psychotherapy and Hypnosis (cert.). Home: 110 Bank St Apt 5F New York NY 10014-2171

PULLEN, JANE ANN ARNOLD, mental health educator; b. Massena, N.Y., June 4, 1922; d. Benjamin Harrison and Jessie Maud (Emmons) Arnold; m. Charles Ralph Pullen, Sept. 1, 1940 (div. Jan. 1975); children: Charles, Jennifer. BA cum laude, UCLA, 1944; MA, Goddard Coll., 1972. Cert. mental health counselor State Wash. Counseling psychologist UCLA, 1967; dir. counseling, tchr. Everett (Wash.) C.C., 1977-86; dir., tchr. human svcs. Western Wash. U., Bellingham, 1986-95; cons., tchr. Cancer Lifeline, Seattle, 1995—; adv. bd. Counterpoint, Edmonds, Wash., 1981-84. Precinct worker Bd. Elections, L.A., 1955-66; recorder Ration Bd., L.A., 1941-43; vol. nurse Culver City (Calif.) Hosp., 1942-46; charter mem. Nat. Mus. Women in the Arts, Washington. Named outstanding leader Camp Fire Girls, 1962, 65. Mem. Nat. Orgn. Human Svcs. Orgn. (v.p. 1991), Northwest Health Found. (v.p. 1990). Democrat. Methodist. Home: 4838 88th Pl SE Mercer Island WA 98040

PULLEN, PENNY LYNNE, non-profit administrator, former state legislator; b. Buffalo, Mar. 2, 1947; d. John William and Alice Nettie (McConkey) P.; BA in Speech, U. Ill., 1969. TV technician Office Instructional Resources, U. Ill., 1966-68; community newspaper reporter Des Plaines (Ill.) Pub. Co., 1967-72; legislative asst. to Ill. legislators, 1968-77; mem. Ill. Ho. of Reps., 1977-93, chmn. ho. exec. com., 1981-82, minority whip, 1983-87, asst. minority leader, 1987-93; pres., founder Life Advocacy Resource Project, 1992—; exec. dir. Ill. Family Inst., 1993-94; dir. Legal Svcs. Corp., 1989-93; mem. Pres.'s Commn. on AIDS Epidemic, 1987-88; mem. Ill. Goodwill Del. to Republic of China, 1987. Del. Atlantic Alliance Young Polit. Leaders, Brussels, 1977, Rep. Nat. Conv, 1984; mem. Republican Nat. Com., 1984-88; summit conf. observer as mem. adhoc Women for SDI, Geneva, 1985; former mem. Maine Twp. Mental Health Assn.; active Nat. Coun. Ednl. Rsch., 1983-88. Recipient George Washington Honor medal Freedoms Found., 1978, Dwight Eisenhower Freedom medal Chgo. Captive Nations Com., 1977, Outstanding Legislator awards Ill. Press Assn., Ill. Podiatry Soc., Ill. Coroners Assn., Ill. County Clks. Assn., Ill. Hosp. Assn., Ill. Health Care Assn.; named Ill. Young Republican, 1968, Outstanding Young Person, Park Ridge Jaycees, 1981, One of 10 Outstanding Young Persons, Ill. Jaycees, 1981. Mem. Am. Legis. Exchange Council (dir. 1977-91, exec. com. 1978-83, 2d vice chmn. 1980-83), DAR. Lodge: Kiwanis.

PULLEY, BETTY CHRIS, special education educator; b. Detroit, Sept. 25, 1939, d. Doyle Hudson and Allie Sue (Bell) Richmond; m. Robert Edward Pulley Sr., June 7, 1959; children: Robert Edward Jr., Pamela Gayle Pulley Brown. BS, Memphis State U., 1985, MS, 1989. Exec. sec. Memphis (Tenn.) Acad. for Learning Disabilities, 1980-86, tchr., prin., 1985-86; spl. edn./math tchr. Memphis (Tenn.) City Schs., 1986—; presenter math. workshops Memphis City Schs., 1993—, instr. profl. devel., 1994—; mentor AT&T Tchrs. and Tech., 1995; presenter Tenn. Ednl. Tech. Conf., 1996; team mem. ConncTEN, 1996. Presenter in field. Gov.'s fellow AT&T, 1994. Mem. Nat. Coun. Tchrs. Math., Coun. for Exceptional Children, Assn. for Suprs. and Adminstrs., Kappa Delta Pi. Mem. Church of Christ. Home: 1522 Stonegate Pass Memphis TN 38138 Office: Shrine/MCS 4259 Forestview Memphis TN 38118

PULLIAM, BRENDA JANE, secondary school educator; b. Griffin, Ga., Jan. 28, 1941; d. Delmus Lawton and Eva Jane (Cobb) P. BA, Mercer U., 1963; MA in Teaching, Converse Coll., 1972; EdD, Nova U., 1993; postgrad., U. Toulouse, France. Cert. secondary tchr., Ga. Tchr. French Jonesboro (Ga.) H.S., 1963—, chair fgn. lang. dept., 1970—; co-founder KPS Leadership Specialists, 1993—; correlator Harcourt Brace Jovanovich, 1989; speaker So. Conf. Lang. Teaching, 1993, adv. bd. Contbr. articles to profl. jours.; contbr. ednl. papers to ERIC. Chair citizen exchs. Atlanta-Toulouse Sister Cities, 1987—, tour leader, 1989, 94; interpreter Travelers Aid Met. Atlanta, 1989—. Grantee NDEA, 1963; recipient STAR Tchr. award, 1983. Mem. NEA, Am. Coun. Teaching Fgn. Langs., Am. Assn. Tchrs. French, Ga. Assn. Educators, Fgn. Lang. Assn. Ga., Clayton County Edn. Assn., So. Conf. Lang. Teaching. Baptist. Home: 9261 Brave Ct Jonesboro GA 30236-5110 Office: Jonesboro High School 7728 Mount Zion Blvd Jonesboro GA 30236-5110

PUMARIEGA, JOANNE BUTTACAVOLI, mathematics educator; b. Coral Gables, Fla., May 27, 1952; d. Ciro Charles and Rosaria Frances (Calabrese) Buttacavoli; m. Andres Julio Pumariega, Dec. 26, 1975; children: Christina Marie, Nicole Marie. BA in Math. and Edn. magna cum laude, U. Miami, 1973, MA in Math., 1974; postgrad., U. Houston, 1991-92. Cert. secondary math. tchr., Tex., Fla., Tenn., N.C. Grad. tchg. asst. U. Miami, Coral Gables, 1973-74; substitute tchr. Dade County Pub. Schs., Miami, 1975; math. instr. Miami Dade C.C., 1975-76; math. and G.E.D. instr. Durham (N.C.) Tech. Inst., 1976-77; math. instr. Durham H.S., 1977-78, Durham Acad., 1978-80, Univ. Sch. of Nashville, 1980-83; pvt. practice math. instr. Houston, 1984-86; tutor Clear Lake Tutoring Svc., Houston, 1987-90; pvt. practice, S.A.T, lang. instr. League City, Tex., 1990-92; pvt. practice math. and S.A.T. instr. Columbia, S.C., 1992—; instr. lang. Nelson Elem. Sch., Columbia, 1993-96; instr. fgn. langs. and math. Lonnie B. Nelson Elem. Sch., Columbia, S.C. Chair bd. edn. St. Mary Parish, League City, 1988-90, lector, 1992; C.C.E. tchr. St. John Neumann Cath. Ch., Columbia, S.C., 1993-95, lector, 1992—; treas. St. Thomas More Women's Club, Houston, 1985-86; v.p., then pres. housestaff med. wives Duke U., Durham, N.C., 1978-80. Mem. Newcomers of Greater Columbia (chair pub. rels. chpt. 1993, 95), Newcomers of Greater Colo. (com. chair coord. 1994-95), Welcome Neighbors of Bay Area (v.p., program chmn. 1991-92), Tex. Med. Aux., Bay Area Med. Wives, Phi Kappa Phi, Kappa Delta Pi, Alpha Lambda Delta (Woman of Yr. 1972), U. S.C. Faculty Women's Club (v.p. 1993-94, pres. 1994-95, parliamentarian/advisor 1995-96). Roman Catholic. Home and Office: 2 Roundtree Ct Johnson City TN 37604

PUMPHREY, JANET KAY, editor; b. Balt., June 18, 1946; d. John Henry and Elsie May (Keefer) P. AA in Secondary Edn., Anne Arundel C.C., Arnold, Md., 1967, AA in Bus. and Pub. Adminstrn., 1976. Office mgr. Anne Arundel C.C., 1964—; mng. editor Am. Polygraph Assn., Severna Park, Md., 1973—; archives dir. Am. Polygraph Assn., Severna Park, 1973—; owner JKP Publ. Svcs., 1990—; dir. Am. Polygraph Assn. Reference Svc., 1995—. Editor: (with Albert D. Snyder) Ten Years of Polygraph, 1984, (with Norman Ansley) Justice and the Polygraph, 1985, 2d edit., 1996, A House Full of Love, 1990, Mama, There's A Mouse in My House, 1996. Mem. Rep. Nat. Sustaining Com. Mem. NAFE, Am. Polygraph Assn. (hon.), Md. Polygraph Assn. (affiliate), Anne Arundel County Hist. Soc., Alumni Assn. Anne Arundel Community Coll. Republican. Methodist. Home: 3 Kimberly Ct Severna Park MD 21146-3703 Office: JKP Pub Svcs PO Box 1535 Severna Park MD 21146-8535

PUMPHREY, JEAN, English language educator; b. Dayton, Ohio, Dec. 3, 1931; d. Robert E. and Audrey Pumphrey. BA, Denison U., 1953; MA, San Francisco State U., 1967. Prof. English Coll. of San Mateo, Calif., 1967—; founding dir. Poetry Ctr., Coll. of San Mateo, 1970-93. Author: Poetry: The Way Through Language, 1975, (book of poetry) Sheltered at the Edge, 1982; contbr. numerous articles to periodicals and anthologies. Nat. Endowment for Arts grantee for funding Poetry Ctr., Coll. of San Mateo. Mem. PEN, Poetry Soc. Am., Calif. Writer's Club (co-pres.), Marin Poetry Ctr. (pres.). Home: 650 Main St Sausalito CA 94965

PURCELL, ANN RUSHING, state legislator, office manager medical business; b. Reidsville, Ga., May 12, 1945; d. William Robert and Katie (Dasher) Rushing; m. Dent Wiley Purcell, May 26, 1966; children: Edwin Wiley, Mieke Ann, Mikki Marie. BS in Edn., Ga. So. Coll., 1966. Cert. secondary tchr. Tchr. math. Evans (Ga.) High Sch., 1966-68; tchr. math., earth and sci. Beaumont Jr. High Sch., Lexington, Ky., 1969-70; substitute tchr. Tallahassee, Fla., 1970's; agt. Noblin Realty, Tallahassee, 1970's; office mgr. Radiation Therapy Assocs., PC, Savannah, Ga., 1979—; state legislator Ho. of Reps. Ga. Gen. Assembly, Atlanta, 1991—. Author: Purcells of South Georgia and Other Related Families, 1976. Bd. dirs. Med. Assn. Ga. Polit. Action Com., Atlanta, 1988-89, Girl Scout Coun. Savannah, 1991—, Ga. So. U. Found., 1992—; mem. adv. com. Effingham County Extension Svc., 1992—; fin. chmn. State YMCA, 1991—; bd. adv. Claxton Youth Detnetion Ctr. Recipient Friend of Medicine award Med. Assn. Ga., 1991, 93, 94, Guardian of Small Bus. award Nat. Fedn. Ind. Bus., 1992, 94, Commendation cert. Ga. Emergency Mgmt. Agy., 1995. Mem. Aux. to the Med. Assn. Ga. (pres. 1985), Aux. to the Ga. Med. Soc. (pres. 1981-82), Ga. Salzburger Soc., Effingham County Pub. Officials Assn., Rotary Internat. Democrat. Methodist. Home: 410 Willowpeg Way Rincon GA 31326-9111 Office: State Capitol SW Ste 401 Atlanta GA 30334-1600

PURCELL, JANICE RUTH, social worker; b. Ludington, Mich., Feb. 18, 1936; d. Frank Richard and Hilde (Kronlein) Shilander; m. James A. Purcell, Nov. 19, 1960; children: Kristine Ruth, Karen Rebecca, Kimberly Ann, Kevin Allen. BA, Western Mich. U., 1956; postgrad., Moody Bible Inst., 1959-60, 83, U. Wis., 1981-83, Milw. Area Tech. Coll., 1991-93. Cert. social worker, Wis. Nursing asst. Jackson County Hosp., Maquoketa, Iowa, 1969-70, Bradley Convelescent Ctr., Milw., 1980-84; elem. tchr. VCY Christian Schs., Milw., 1984-86; QMRP Hearthside Rehab. Ctr., Milw., 1986-93; QMRP/cert. social worker Marian Franciscan Ctr., Milw., 1993—. Vol., guardian Assn. of Retarded Citizens, Milw., 1995—; vol. Spl. Olympics, Milw., 1995—, Wis.-Right to Life, Milw., 1990—; vestry mem. St. Frances Episcopal Ch., Menomonee Falls, Wis., 1993-95; mem. Chgo. Art Mus., 1995—; ch. organist St. Francis Episcopal Ch., 1993-96, N.W. Bapt. Ch., 1996—. Baptist. Home: 6975 W Glenbrook Milwaukee WI 53223 Office: Marian Franciscan Ctr 9632 W Appleton Ave Milwaukee WI 53225

PURCELL, LEE, actress; b. N.C., June 15, 1953; m. Gary A. Lowe, 1 child, Gary, 1 stepchild. Student, Royal Acad. Dramatic Art; studies with Margot Lister, Milton Katselas, Jeff Corey, Robert F. Lyons. Appeared in (films) Adam at 6 A.M., 1970, The Toy Factory, 1971, Dirty Little Billy, 1972, Kid Blue, 1973, Mr. Majestyk, 1974, Almost Summer, 1978, Stir Crazy, 1980, Valley Girl, Eddie Macon's Run, 1983, Laura's Dream, 1986, (TV) Highjack, 1973, Stranger in Our House, 1978, Kenny Rogers as the Gambler, 1980, Killing at Hell's Gate, 1981, Magnum P.I., Murder, She Wrote, 1985, My Wicked Wicked Ways: The Legend of Errol Flynn, 1986, Secret Sins of the Father, 1994 (Emmy nomination, Supporting Actress - Special, 1994), (stage) Richard III, A Streetcar Named Desire, The Taming of the Shrew, A Midsummer Night's Dream. Recipient Bronze Halo Career Achievement award So. Calif. Motion Picture Council, 1985. Mem. Actors' Equity Assn., Screen Actors Guild, AFTRA, Acad. Motion Picture Arts and Scis., Acad. TV Arts And Scis. Office: Artists Agency 1000 Santa Monica Blvd Ste 305 Los Angeles CA 90067*

PURCELL, MARY HAMILTON, speech educator; b. Ft. Worth; d. Joseph Hants and Letha (Gibson) Hamilton; m. William Paxson Purcell, Jr., Dec. 28, 1950; children: William Paxson III, David Hamilton. BA, Mary Hardin-Baylor Coll., 1947; MA, La. State U., 1948; HHD (hon.), Mary Hardin-Baylor Coll., 1986. Instr., dept. speech and dramatic arts Temple U., Phila., 1948-53, 60-61; part-time instr. speech Cushing Jr. Coll., Bryn Mawr, Pa., 1966-78. Pres., Pa. Program for Women and Girl Offenders, 1968-73; pres. Nether Providence Parent Tchr. Orgn., 1975-76; treas. Virginia Gildersleeve Internat. Fund Univ. Women, 1975-81, bd. dirs., 1987-93; bd. dirs. Citizens Crime Commn. of Phila., 1976—; mem. Wallingford-Swarthmore Dist. Sch. Bd., 1977-83; bd. dirs. Nat. Peace Inst. Found., 1983-86, Big Bros./Big Sisters of Am., 1985-90, Pa. Women's Campaign Fund, 1985-88; bd. dirs. Ministers and Missionaries Fund Am. Bapt. Conv., 1985-94, pres., 1995—, Internat. Devel. Conf., 1986—; mem. U.S. Del. to 40th Session, UN Commn. on Status of Women, 1996. Named Outstanding Alumna Mary Hardin-Baylor Coll., 1972, Disting. Dau. Pa., 1982, v.p., 1994-95, pres. 1996—; recipient Zeta Phi Eta award excellence in communications, 1983. Mem. AAUW (Pa. div. pres. 1968-70, v.p. middle Atlantic region 1973-77, program v.p. 1979-81, pres. 1981-85, rep. to UN, 1985-89), Internat. Fedn. Univ. Women (1st v.p. 1986-89, pres. 1989-92, rep. to UN 1992—; pres. UN Dept. Pub. Info. Non Govt. Orgn. ann. conf. 1993), Speech Assn. Am., Pi Kappa Delta, Pi Gamma Mu, Delta Sigma Rho, Alpha Psi Omega, Alpha Chi. Democrat. Baptist. Home: 9 Oak Knolls Dr Wallingford PA 19086-6315

PURCELL, MARY LOUISE GERLINGER, educator; b. Thief River Falls, Minn., July 17, 1923; d. Charles and Lajla (Dale) Gerlinger; student Yankton Coll., 1941-45, Yale Div. Sch., 1949-50, NYU, summer 1949; MA (alumni fellow), Tchrs. Coll. Columbia, 1959, EdD, 1963; m. Walter A. Kuyawski, June 9, 1950 (dec. July 1954); children: Amelia Allerton, Jon Allerton; m. 2d, Dale Purcell, Aug. 26, 1962. Teen-age program dir., YWCA, New Haven, 1945-52; dir. program in family rels., asst. prof. sociology and psychology Earlham Coll., Richmond, Ind., 1959-62, conf. coord. undergrad. edn. for women, 1962; chmn. div. home and community Stephens Coll., Columbia, Mo., 1962-73, chmn. family and community studies, 1962-78, dir. Learning Unltd., continuing edn. for women, 1974-78, developer course The Contemporary Am. Woman, 1962, cons., 1962; prof., Auburn (Ala.) U., 1978-88, prof. emerita, 1988—, head dept. family and child devel., 1978-84, spl. asst. to v.p. acad. affairs, 1985-86. chmn. search com. for v.p. acad. affairs, 1984; vis. prof. Ind. U. Summer Sch., 1970. Cons. student personnel svcs., Trenton (N.J.) State Coll., 1958-59, 61. Recipient Alumni Achievement award Yankton Coll., 1975. Mem. AAUW, Am. Home Econs. Assn. (bd. dirs. 1967-69, chair 1st subject matter unit 1969, family relations and child devel. sect. 1986-89), Groves Conf. on Family, Nat. Council Family Relations (dir., chmn.-elect affiliated councils, 1981-82, chmn., 1982-84, nat. program chmn. 1977, chmn. film awards com., chmn. spl. emphases sect., bd. dirs., Ernest G. Osborne award for excellence in teaching 1979), Delta Kappa Gamma. Presbyterian. Contbr. articles to coll. bulls., jours. Home: 120 Belden St Falls Village CT 06031-1112

PURDES, ALICE MARIE, adult education educator; b. St. Louis, Jan. 8, 1931; d. Joseph Louis and Angeline Cecilia (Mozier) P. AA, Belleville Area Coll., 1951; BS, Ill. State U., Normal, 1953, MS, 1954; cert., Sorbonne U., Paris, 1964; PhD, Fla. State U., Tallahassee, 1976. Cert. in music edn., elem. edn., secondary edn., adult edn. Teaching/grad. asst. Ill. State U., 1953-54; music supr. Princeton (Ill.) Pub. Schs., 1954-55; music dir. Venice (Ill.) Pub. Schs., 1955-72, secondary vocal music dir., 1955-72; coord. literacy program Venice-Lincoln Tech. Ctr., 1983-86, chair lang. arts dept., 1983—; tchr. in space candidate, 1985. Mem. St. Louis chpt. World Affairs Coun., UN Assn., Nat. Mus. of Women in the Arts, Humane Soc. of Am.; charter mem. St. Louis Sci. Ctr., Harry S. Truman Inst.; contbr. Old Six Mile Mus., 1981, Midland Repertory Players, Alton, Ill., 1991; chair Cystic Fibrosis Spring Bike-A-Thon, Madison, Ill., 1981, Granite City, Ill., 1985. Recipient gold medal Nat Senior Olympics, 1989, Senior World Games, 1992, several scholarships. Mem. AAUW, Music Educators Nat. Conf., Ill. Music Educators Assn., Am. Choral Dirs. Assn., Fla. State Alumni Assn., Ill. Adult and Continuing Educators Assn., Am. Fedn. Tchrs. (pres. 1957-58), Western Cath. Union, Croation Fraternal Union, Nat. Space Soc., Travelers Abroad (pres. 1966-68, 89—), Internat. Platform Assn., Archaeol. Inst. Am., Friends St. Louis Art Mus., St. Louis Numis. Assn. Madison Rotary Club (internat. amb., Humanitarian award 1975), Slavic and East European Friends (life), Lovejoy Libr. Friends, Ill. State U. Alumnia Assn. Roman Catholic. Home: PO Box 274 Madison IL 62060-0274 Office: Venice-Lincoln Tech Ctr S 4th St Venice IL 62090-1063

PURDY, LAUREL MILLS, accountant; b. Toledo, Ohio, Nov. 16, 1968; d. Charles Edward Mills and Karen Lea Wangberg; m. David C. Purdy, June 9, 1995. BS, Ohio State U., 1991. Staff acct. Expersoft, San Diego, 1992-94; acct. River Medical/IVAC, San Diego, 1994-95; sr. acct. "A" Co. Orthodontics, San Diego, 1995—. Vol. Big Brothers/Big Sisters, Columbus, Ohio, 1989-91. Mem. Inst. Mgmt. Accts. (bd. dirs. 1993-94), Treasury Mgmt. Assn., Phi Eta Sigma, Alpha Lambda Delta. Office: "A" Co Orthodontics 9900 Old Grove Rd San Diego CA 92121-1683

PURDY, SHERRY MARIE, lawyer; b. Billings, Mont., Mar. 12, 1960. Student, U. Mont., 1978-80; BS, Mont. State U., Billings, 1983; JD, Willamette U., 1987. Bar: Colo. 1987, U.S. Dist. Ct. Colo. 1987. Assoc. Holland & Hart, Denver, 1987-90; sr. atty. Atlantic Richfield Co., Denver, 1990—. Contbr. articles to profl. jours. Mem. ABA, Colo. Bar Assn., Colo. Women's Bar Assn., Colo. Hazardous Waste Mgmt. Soc. (program com. chair 1989-90, v.p. 1990-91), Denver Bar Assn. Office: Atlantic Richfield Co 555 17th St Ste 1600 Denver CO 80202-3941

PURITZ, HOLLY SUZANNE, obstetrician-gynecologist; b. N.Y.C., Feb. 10, 1957; d. Sheldon and Rubie (Meyers) P.; m. Stephen D. Wohlgemuth, June 26, 1982; children: Zachary, Leah. BS, Tufts U., 1979, MD, 1983. Diplomate Am. Bd. Ob-Gyn. Chief resident Eastern Va. Sch. of Medicine, Norfolk, Va., 1986-87; ptnr. The Group for Women, Norfolk, 1987—; chief Dept. Ob-Gyn., Sentara Hosps., Norfolk, 1993—. Mem. bd. dirs. Jewish Family Svcs., Norfolk, 1992—, spkrs. bur. March of Dimes Campaign for Health Babies, 1992-93. Mem. Phi Beta Kappa, Alpha Omega Alpha. Jewish. Office: The Group for Women 880 Kempsville Rd Norfolk VA 23502

PURKERSON, MABEL LOUISE, physician, physiologist, educator; b. Goldville, S.C., Apr. 3, 1931; d. James Clifton and Louise (Smith) P. AB, Erskine Coll., 1951; MD, U. S.C., Charleston, 1956. Diplomate Am. Bd. Pediat. Instr. pediat. Washington U. Sch. Med., St. Louis, 1961-67, instr. medicine, 1966-67, asst. prof. pediat., 1967—, asst. prof. medicine, 1967-76, assoc. prof. medicine, 1976-89, prof., 1989—, assoc. dean curriculum, 1976-94; assoc. dean acad. projects, 1994—; cons. in field. Editl. bd. Jour. Am. Kidney Diseases, 1981-87 ; contbr. articles to profl. jours. USPHS spl. fellow, 1971-72. Bd. counselors Erskine Coll., 1971—. Mem. Am. Heart Assn. (exec. com. 1973-81), Coun. on the Kidney, Am. Physiol. Soc., Am. Soc. Nephrology, Internat. Soc. Nephrology, Central Soc. Clin. Rsch., Am. Soc. Renal Biochemistry and Metabolism, Sigma Xi (chpt. sec. 1974-76). Avocations: traveling; gardening; photography. Home: 20 Haven View Dr Saint Louis MO 63141-7902 Office: Washington U Sch Medicine Renal Div Dept 660 S Euclid Ave St Box 8132 Saint Louis MO 63110

PURNELL, FLORIE ELIZABETH, adult education educator; b. Winston-Salem, N.C., Mar. 29, 1955; d. Bernard Owen and Mary Elizabeth (Thompkins) Taylor; m. Rodney James Roundtree, Mar. 9, 1973 (div. Apr. 1978); 1 child, Rodney James; m. Fason Anderson, May 28, 1988; children: Rachel, Jasmin. AAS in Bus. Adminstrn., Forsyth Tech. Coll., Winston-Salem, 1981; BS in Bus. Adminstrn., High Point Coll., Winston-Salem, 1985; MS in Human Resource Counseling, N.C. A&T State U., Greensboro, 1992. Supr. Piedmont Airlines, Winston-Salem, 1974-88; counselor Tokyo English Life Line, Tokyo, 1990-91; trainer Oak Assocs., Tokyo, 1991-92; program dir. Am. C. of C., Tokyo, 1993-94; adult edn. coord. Internat. Sch. Kuala Lumpur, Malaysia, 1995—; aerobics instr. Pres. Girl Talk, Tokyo, 1991-92. Mem. Am. Counseling Assn. Democrat. Baptist. Home: Apt 8 191 Condominium, 191 Jalan Ampang, 50450 Kuala Lumpur Malaysia

PURRINGTON, LINDA DECKER, civil rights worker; b. Wareham, Mass., Nov. 16, 1942; d. Philip Foster and Margarete Wilhelmina (Becker) P.; 1 child, Cheyenne Dexter Purrington. BA in Edn., U. Mich., 1967; MA in English, Wayne State U., 1969. Co-founder Parents for Title IX, Petaluma, Calif., 1992—. Mem. Feminist Majority Found. (leader), Coalition for Title IX, Sonoma Consortium.

PURSGLOVE, BETTY MERLE, small business owner, technical writer, quality assurance tester; b. Pitts., Sept. 15, 1923; d. Earle E. and Merle A. (Smith) Baer; m. Larry A. Pursglove, June 30, 1944; children: Diana, Kathleen, Merry, Tanya, Yvonne. BS in Physics, U. Pitts., 1944; postgrad., Minn. U., 1945-47, Carnegie-Mellon U., 1947-49, W.Va. U., 1949-51, Mich. State U., 1968-69. Micro-pilot plant operator Minn. Mining and Mfg., St. Paul, 1944-46; cons. rsch. chemist Food Mach Co., Pitts., 1947-49; computer coder Dow Chem. Co., Midland, Minn., 1954; asst. entomologist pvt. collections, Midland, 1955-56; instr. chemistry Cen. Mich. U., Midland, 1958; head chem. dept. Midland Hosp., 1958-64; tchr. chemistry and physics parochial schs., Bay City, Mich., 1964; prin., chief exec. officer Crypticlear, Inc., Applegate, Oreg., 1965—. Leader Midland troup Girl Scout U.S., 1953-63. Mem. AAUW, Sigma Xi, Sigma Pi Sigma. Home and Office: PO Box 3125 Applegate OR 97530-3125

PURSLEY, CAROL COX, psychologist; b. Chattanooga, Dec. 7, 1951; d. George Edwin and M. Sue (Clarke) Cox; m. James V. Pursley; 1 child, Drew Vinson; stepchildren: Nancy, John. BS, U. Tenn., 1973, MS, 1975; PhD, U. Ky., 1983. Registered rehab. supplier, Ga.; cert. rehab. counselor; lic. psychologist, Ky., Ga.; lic. profl. counselor, Ga.; diplomate Am. Bd. Forensic Examiners. Dir. rehab. Goodwill Industries, Knoxville, Tenn., 1975-77; rsch. and evaluation asst. region IV rehab. continuing edn. U. Tenn., Knoxville, 1977; crisis intervention cons., job placement counselor KACRC, Knoxville, 1977-78; instr., cons. region IV rehab. continuing edn. program U. Tenn., Knoxville, 1978-79; teaching/rsch. asst. U. Ky., Lexington, 1979-80; rehab. specialist Internat. Rehab. Assocs., Louisville, 1980; psychologist and assoc. clin. staff Ea. State Hosp., Lexington, 1981-84; rehab. cons. Southeastern Transitions, Atlanta, 1985-86; pvt. practice rehab. cons. Marietta, Ga., 1986—; rehab. counselor U.S. Dept. of Labor OWCP Program, 1987—; pvt. practice psychotherapy and testing Marietta and Atlanta, 1994—; allied health profl. Ridgeview Inst., 1994-95, clin. psychology staff mem., 1995—; assessments/group therapy, allied health profl. for Rehab. Evaluation and Comprehensive Treatment Program Kennestone Hosp. at Windy Hill, Marietta, 1988-92; clin. assoc. Am. Bd. Med. Psychotherapists, 1986—; strategy meeting cons. Sony Music Entertainment, N.Y.; cons. ADA; expert witness Ga. Composite Bd. Profl. Counselors, Social Workers and Marriage and Family Therapists, 1991—; cons. to Gov.'s Rehab. Adv. Com., 1990. Chairperson-elect Vol. State Rehab. Counseling Assn., Knoxville, 1976; mem. Mayor's Adv. Com. for Handicapped, Knoxville, 1974-76. Facility Improvement grantee s.e. region Rehab. Svcs. Adminstrn., 1975-77, Facility Establishment grantee United Cerebral Palsy, 1977. Mem. APA, Am. Coll. Forensic Examiners, Ga. Psychol. Assn., Ky. Psychol. Assn., Nat. Assn. Rehab. Providers in Pvt. Sector (rsch. and tng. com. 1988-94), Pvt. Rehab. Suppliers of Ga. (chairperson ethics com. 1989-91, named person of distinction state PRSG chpt. newsletter 1990, ethics com. 1986-92), Phi Kappa Phi. Office: 2520 E Piedmont Rd Ste F Marietta GA 30062-1700

PURYEAR, JOAN COPELAND, English language educator; b. Columbus, Miss., May 10, 1944; d. John Thomas and Mamie (Cunningham) Copeland.; m. James Burton Puryear, June 13, 1965; children: John James, Jeffrey Burton, Joel Harry. BA summa cum laude, Miss. State U., Starkville, 1965; MA, Fla. State U., 1969; EdD, U. Ga., 1987. Cert. tchr., Ga. English instr. Fla. State U., Tallahassee, 1965-69, Augusta (Ga.) Coll., 1987-88; head English dept. Augusta Tech. Inst., 1989-93; chairperson gen. edn. and devel. studies, 1993—, mem. dean's coun., mgmt. team and grant proposal team, 1994—; chmn. State Exec. Bd. English, Ga., 1990-92, East Ctrl. Consortium English, Ga.,1990-92; mem. Augusta Tech. Inst. Tech. Com., 1990—; chmn. Capital Funds Raising Family Campaign, Augusta Tech. Inst., vice chmn. Capital Fund Raising Cmty. Campaign; mem. and co-chmn. Continuous Improvement Coun., 1996—, Augusta Tech. Inst.; facilitator Total Quality Mgmt. Tech. Tng.; mem. exec. steering com. Continuous Improvement Coun.; chmn. editing com. Augusta Tech. Inst. Self Study, 1992-93, chmn. long range planning goals and objectives com., 1994. Mem. Cmtys. in Schs., 1996—; trustee Augusta Tech. Inst. Found. Bd., 1996—; co-pres. Davidson Fine Arts Sch. PTA, 1995, co-pres. bd. boosters, 1996; pres. Med. Coll. Spouse's Club, Augusta, 1972; dir. Women's Mission Orgn., First Bapt. Ch., Augusta, 1982, dir. Youth Sunday Sch., 1992—, chmn. 175th Anniversary, 1992, deacon, 1996—, mem. ministerial adv. com. Mem. Modern Lang. Assn., Nat. Coun. Tchrs., Am. Vocat. Assn., Ga. Vocat. Assn., So. Assn. Colls. (accreditation team 1994), Phi Theta Kappa (adv. 1992—). Baptist. Office: Augusta Tech Inst 3116 Deans Bridge Rd Augusta GA 30906-3375

PUSEY, ELLEN PRATT, home economist; b. Milford, Del., Aug. 27, 1928; d. Algeo Newell and Ruby Newton (Boorman) Pratt; m. William W. Pusey, June 12, 1950; children: William W., Patricia A., Cynthia L., Daniel N. BS, U. Md., 1950, MS, 1951, PhD in Home Econs. Edn., 1990. Camp dietitian N.Y. Herald Tribune Fresh Air Fund Camps, 1947; supr. cafeteria Roosevelt Hosp., N.Y.C., 1948; supt. sch. cafeterias, Seaford, Del., 1964; field faculty home economist Md. Coop. Ext. Svc., Wicomico County, Md., 1967-92, Worcester County, Md., 1992-94. Chmn. lower shore coun. Am. Lung Assn., Md., 1978-79; pres. U. Md. Coll. Human Ecology Alumni Bd., 1988-89. Named one of 10 Outstanding Women Wicomico County, Commn. for Women, 1989. Mem. Internat. Fedn. Home Econs.,Am. Home Econs. Assn., Asian Regional Assn. Home Econs., Md. Home Econs. Assn., Nat. Assn. Extension Home Economists, Md. Assn. Extension Home Economists, Tri-County Home Econs. Assn. (chmn. 1973), Nutrition Jour. Club of Eastern Shore, Phi Kappa Phi, Alpha Xi Delta, Soroptimists Club (pres. 1978, 2d v.p. 1989, South Atlantic region Women Helping Women award 1989). Presbyterian. Home: 301 W Federal St Snow Hill MD 21863-1116 Office: Pusey's Country Store PO Box 265 Snow Hill MD 21863-0265

PUSEY, MAVIS, artist, educator. Student, Art Students League, 1961-65, Birgit Sch. Workshop, London, 1967-68, Robert Blackburn Workshop, 1969-72, New Sch. for Social Rsch., 1974, 76, 87. instr. painting New Sch. for Social Rsch., N.Y.C., 1973-88; asst. prof. painting and printmaking SUNY, Stony Brook, 1974-77; instr. intermediate painting Pa. Acad. Fine Arts, Phila., 1974-86; instr. printmaking and painting N.Y. State Summer Sch. of the ARts, 1978-79; instr. etching and painting Drew U., Madison, N.J., 1980-81; instr. studio art, art history and art appreciation Woodberry Forest (Va.) Sch., 1993—; lectr. in field. One-woman shows include Rainbow Art Found., N.Y., 1977, Franklin and Marshall Coll., Pa., 1979, New Sch. Assocs., N.Y.C., 1980, Korn Gallery, Drew U., Madison, 1980, Piedmont Va. C.C., 1993, St. Catherine's Sch., 1995; group exhbns. include Douglas Coll. Art Gallery, Rutgers U., New Brunswick, 1980, William Penn Meml. Mus., Harrisburg, Pa., 1983, City Gallery/2 Dept. Cultural Affairs, City of N.Y., 1983, Art Students League, 1986, 93, Lamar Dodd Art Ctr., LaGrange, Ga., 1991, Nat. Arts Club, 1993, others; traveling group exhbns. include Greenville (S.C.) Mus. Art, 1984, Metro-Dade Cultural Ctr., Miami-Dade Pub. Libr., 1988, The Artmobile, Miami-Dade Pub. Libr. Sys., 1991, Bronx (N.Y.) Art Ctr. and Gallery, 1992, Hillwood Art Mus., L.I. U., Bronxville, N.Y., 1992, others; represented in permanent collections Citibank, N.Y.C., First Nat. Bank Chgo., Chem. Bank, Tougaloo Coll., Miss., Mus. Modern Art, N.Y.C., numerous pvt. collections. Recipient Bryon Browne Meml. award Art Students League, 1963, Ford Found. Tuition award Art Students League, N.Y., 1964, Louis Comfort Tiffany Found. award, 1972, Louis Comfort Tiffany Found. Purchase award, 1974, Majors Travel Tour award S.I. Mus., 1975, Internat. Woman's Yr. award in recognition of outstanding cultural contbn. and dedication to women and art, 1976. Home: 20305 Gum Tree Rd Orange VA 22960

PUTMAN, DEBORAH, elementary educator; b. Madisonville, Ky., Oct. 10, 1950; d. Charles Crittenden and Doris Virginia (Major) Herring; m. Larry Hight Putman; children: Christel, Candius, Clarissa, Larry Michael. BA, Western Ky. U., 1979, MA, 1987, postgrad., 1992. Cert. elem. tchr., Ky. Math. tchr. Hopkins County Sch. Dist., Madisonville, 1979—; cons. Badgett Regional Ctr. for Ednl. Enhancement, Madisonville, 1991-95; presenter in field. Named Educator of Yr., Hopkins County C. of C., 1990-91. Mem. NEA, Nat. Coun. Tchrs. Math., Internat. Reading Assn., Ky. Coun. Tchrs. Math., Ky. Edn. Assn., Hopkins County Reading Assn. Democrat. Presbyterian. Home: 1319 Mt Carmel Rd White Plains KY 42464 Office: West Broadway Elem 127 W Broadway Madisonville KY 42431

PUTNAM, JOANNE WHITE, college financial aid administrator, bookkeeper; b. Chattanooga, Nov. 27, 1945; d. Joseph Mitchel and Virginia (Spencer) White; m. Richard Worcester Putnam, Dec. 23, 1967; children: Joseph Worcester, Charles Jason. BS, Emory U., 1967. Sci. programmer Lockheed Ga. Co., Marietta, Ga., 1967-71; bookkeeper Dr. Richard Worcester Putnam, Blairsville, Ga., 1973—; admissions staff Young Harris (Ga.) Coll., 1984-86, dir. fin. aid, 1986—. Contbr. articles to profl. jours. Mem. Union County Hist. Soc., 1980—, Creative Study Club, Atlanta, 1976—; youth advisor Sharp Meml. United Meth. Ch., 1991-93. Mem. Ga. Student Fin. Aid Adminstrs. (program com. 1989-90, nominating com. 1988-89), So. Assn. Student Fin. Aid Adminstrs., Nat. Assn. Student Fin. Aid Adminstrs., Garden Club of Ga. Inc. (chmn. hydroponics 1979-81, chmn. horticulture 1981-83, dir. laurel dist. 1983-85, chmn., advisor laurel dist. 1985—), Nat. Coun. State Garden Club Inc. (master flower show judge 1989—, landscape design critic 1985—, gardening cons. 1985—), Blairsville Garden Club (pres. 1977-79, awards and legislation chmn. 1989-93). Home: PO Box 2059 Blairsville GA 30514 Office: Young Harris Coll PO Box 247 Young Harris GA 30582-0247

PUTNAM, LINDA LEE, communication educator, researcher; b. Frederick, Okla., Aug. 10, 1945; d. Allard Warren and Etta Wanona (Tucker) Loutherback; m. Thomas Milton Putnam III, Mar. 28, 1970; 1 child, Ashley Ann. BA, Hardin-Simmons U., 1967; MA, U. Wis., 1968; PhD, U. Minn., 1977. Instr. U. Mass., Amherst, 1968-69; instr., chair dept. speech-theatre Normandale Community Coll., Bloomington, Minn., 1969-77; prof. communication Purdue U., West Lafayette, Ind., 1977-93; dept. head Tex. A & M Univ., 1993—; vis. scholar Stanford U., U. Calif.-Berkeley, San Francisco, 1984, Harvard U.-Harvard Negotiation Project, 1992. Editor: Communication and Organization, 1983(Best Publ. award 1985), Handbook of Organizational Communication, 1987 (Best Publ. award 1988), Communication and Negotiation, 1992. Del. Dem. State Conv., Mpls., 1972-74; treas. local dist. Dem. Farm Labor Party, Mpls., 1973-74, co-chairperson, 1974-75; block chair Am. Can. Soc. Fund Raiser, West Lafayette, 1986-87. Recipient AMOCO Teaching award Purdue U., 1986, Andersch award Ohio U., 1991, Disting. Alumni award Hardin-Simmons U., 1991, Charles H. Woolbert Rsch. award Speech Comm. Assn., 1993. Fellow Internat. Comm. Assn. (chair 1986-88, orgn. com. divsn. 1995); mem. Acad. Mgmt. (chair power negotiation, conflict mgmt. com. 1989-91), Speech Comm. Assn. (mem. at large 1984-87), Ctrl. States Speech Assn. (sec. comm. theory com. 1978-79, Scholar Showcase award 1989), Internat. Assn. for Conflict Mgmt. (bd. dirs. 1990-92, pres. 1994).

PUTNEY, MARY ENGLER, federal auditor; b. Overland, Mo., May 1, 1933; d. Bernard J. and Marie (Kunkler) Engler; children: Glennon (dec.), Pat Michael, Michelle. Student Fontbonne Coll., 1951-52; AA, Sacramento City Coll., 1975; BS in Bus., Calif. State U., 1981; CPA, Calif; cert. fraud examiner; cert. govt. fin. mgr. From asst. to acct. Mo. Rsch. Labs., Inc., St. Louis, 1953-55, adminstrv. asst., 1955-60; sec. western region fin. office Gen. Electric Co., St. Louis, 1960-62, credit analyst Crocker Nat. Bank, Sacramento, 1962-72 ; student tchr. Sacramento County Dept. Edn., 1979-81; acctg. technician East Yolo Community Services Dist., 1983; mgmt. specialist USAF Logistics Command, 1984; staff auditor Office Insp. Gen., U.S. Dept. Transp., 1984-92; staff auditor Adminstrn. for Children and Families U.S. Dept Health and Human Svcs., 1992—. Mem. Sacramento Community Commn. for Women, 1978-81, bd. dirs., 1980—; mem. planning bd. Golden Empire Health Systems Agy. Mem. AARP (tax counselor for the elderly), AAUW (fin. officer 1983—), AICPA, Nat. Assn. Accts. (dir., newsletter editor), Fontbonne Coll. Alumni Assn., Calif. State Alumni Assn., Assn. Govt. Accts. (chpt. officer), Calif. Soc. CPAs, German Geneological Soc. (bd. dirs. 1990—, publicity dir. 1994—), Rio Del Oro Racquet Club, Beta Gamma Sigma, Beta Alpha Psi. Roman Catholic. Home: 2616 Point Reyes Way Sacramento CA 95826-2416 Office: US Dept Health & Human Svcs ACF/OCSE Div of Audits 801 I St Ste 214 Sacramento CA 95814

PUTTERMAN, FLORENCE GRACE, artist, printmaker; b. N.Y.C., Apr. 14, 1927; d. Nathan and Jean (Feldman) Hirsch; m. Saul Putterman, Dec. 19, 1947. BS, NYU, 1947; MFA, Pa. State U., 1973. Founder, pres. Arts Unlimited, Selinsgrove, Pa., 1969—; curator Milton Shoe Collection, 1970—; artist in residence Title III Program Cultural Enrichment in Schs. Program, 1969-70; instr. Lycoming Coll., Williamsport, Pa., 1972-74, Susquehanna U., Selinsgrove, PA, 1984—. Exhibited one-woman shows, Everson Mus., Syracuse, N.Y., 1976, Hagerstown, Md., 1978, Stuhr Mus., Grand Island, N.B., 1979, Muhlenburg Ctr. for the Arts, Pa., 1985, Harmon Gallery, Fla., 1985, The State Mus. of Pa., 1985-86, Segal Gallery, N.Y., 1986, Canton Inst. Fine Arts, Ohio, 1986, Fla. Biennial Polk Mus., Lakeland, Fla., 1987, 89, Artists Choose Artists, Tampa Mus., 1987, Auburn Works on Paper, 1987, Ala., Ruth Volid Gallery, Chgo., 1989, Polk Mus. Art, Lakeland, Fla., 1989, Lowe Gallery, Atlanta, 1990, Mickelson Gallery, Washington, 1990, Palmer Mus., Pa. State U., 1990, Payne Gallery, Moravian Coll., 1991, Everhart Mus., Scranton, Pa., 1991, Lowe Gallery, L.A., 1992, Center Gallery, Bucknell U., Pa., 1993, Lore Degenstein Gallery, Susquehanna U., Selinsgrove, Pa., 1993, Lowe Gallery, Atlanta, 1993, Down Roll Gallery, Sarasota, Fla., Gallery 10, Washington, Donn Roll Contemporary, Sarasota, Fla., 1996; group shows include Libr. Congress, Soc. Am. Graphic Artists, Ball State Drawing Ann., Muncie, Ind., Arts Club N.Y., Colorprint, U.S.A., Smithsonian Traveling Exhbn., Boston Printmakers, N.C. Print & Drawing, Chautauqua Nat., U. Dallas Nat. Print Invitational, Segal Gallery, Rutgers Drawing, Polk Mus., Tampa Mus., Sichaun Fine Art Inst., Mickelson Gallery, Harmon Gallery, Mus. Art U. Ariz., 1988, U. Del., Newark, 1988 Mid Am. Biennial, Owensboro Mus. Art, VCCA Exhbn. Mcpl. Gallery, Regensburg, Federal Republic of Germany, 1989, Erie (Pa.) Art Mus., 1990, 1990 twenty year survey Palmer Mus., Pa. State U., Univ. Park, Payne Gallery Moravian Coll., Bethlehem, Pa., 1991, Everhart Mus., Scranton, Pa., 1991, U. Del. Biennial, Phila. Watercolor Soc., Noyes Mus., N.J., 1992, Erie (Pa.) Mus., 1991, Mus. Fine Arts, Hanoi, 1991, Spanish Embassy, Madrid, 1992, Anita Shapolsky Gallery, N.Y., 1990, American Women's Artists, Foster Harman Gallery Sarasota, Fla., 1993, Humphrey Gallery, N.Y., 1992, Anita Shapolsky Gallery, N.Y., 1993, Fla. Printmakers, Miami, 1993, Fla. Artists Ringling Mus., 1994, Walter Wickiser Gallery, N.Y., 1995. Recipient award Silvermine Guild Conn. Appalachian Corridors, Arena, 1976, Gold medal of honor Audubon Artists ann. competition, Whitehead award Boston Printmakers, 1985, Shellenberg award Artists Equity, 1985, award N.C. Print & Drawing, 1985, award Chautauqua Nat., 1985, Johnson & Johnson award 3rd Ann. Nat. Printmaking Coun. of N.J., 1985, Purchase award N.J. State Mus., 1987, Disting. Alumni award Pa. State U. Sch. Arts & Architecture, 1988, Ethel Klassen Meml. award Fla. Artists Group, 1992, Earl Horter award Phila. Watercolor Club, 1992, award of excellence, 1995, Stella Drabkin Meml. award Colorprint Soc.; Va. Ctr. for the Creative Arts fellow, 1983-84; Nat. Endowment Arts grantee. Mem. Soc. Am. Graphic Artists (v.p.), Nat. Assn. of Women Artists (Nat. Medal of Honor, Elizabeth Blake award). Home: 220 Morningside Dr Sarasota FL 34236-1113

PUTZEL, CONSTANCE KELLNER, lawyer; b. Balt., Sept. 5, 1922; d. William Stummer and Corinne (Strauss) Kellner; m. William L. Putzel, Aug. 28, 1945; 1 son, Arthur William. A.B., Goucher Coll., 1942; LL.B., U. Md., 1945, J.D., 1969. Bar: Md. 1945. Social worker Balt. Dept. Pub. Welfare, 1945-46; atty. New Amsterdam Casualty Co., Balt., 1947; staff atty. Legal Aid Bur., Balt., 1947-49; mem. Putzel & Putzel, P.A., Balt., 1950-89; sole practitioner Balt., 1989—; instr. U. Balt. Sch. Law, 1975-77, Goucher Coll., 1976-77; chmn. character com. Ct. Appeals for 3d Cir., 1976—. Author: Divorce Organization System, 1984, 3d edit., 1993, Representing the Older Client in Divorce, 1992. Mem. Md. Com. on Status of Women, 1972-76; mem. Com. to Implement ERA, 1973-76; Pres. U. Md. Law Alumni Assn., 1978; bd. dirs. Legal Aid Bur., 1951-52, 71-73. Fellow Am. Acad. Matrimonial Lawyers, Internat. Acad. Matrimonial Lawyers; mem. ABA, Md. Bar Assn. (bd. govs. 1972-73, chmn. family law sect. 1978-79). Home: 8207 Spring Bottom Way Baltimore MD 21208-1859 Office: 29 W Susquehanna Ave Baltimore MD 21204-5201

PYDYNKOWSKY, JOAN ANNE, journalist; b. Ft. Riley, Kans., Oct. 2, 1951; d. Fredrick Albert and Mary Elizabeth (O'Connor) Gadwell; m. Michael Stanley Pydyknowsky, Mar. 14, 1981; children: Deborah Findley, Alexandra Pydyknowsky, Royce. BA in Journalism, U. Ctrl. Okla., 1991, MEd in Journalism, 1993. Trust clk. Ill. Nat. Bank, Rockford, 1974-75; engring. aide Barber Colman, Rockford, 1976-77; draftsperson Gen. Web, Rockford, 1979-80, Keeson, Ltd., Rockford, 1981; editor Oklahoma City Marriage Encounter, 1988-89, 94-95; humor columnist UCO Vista, Edmond, Okla., 1990-91; city editor Guthrie (Okla.) Daily Leader, 1991-92; substitute tchr. Edmond (Okla.) Pub. Schs., 1993-94; with N.W. News, Piedmont, Okla., 1994-95, South Oklahoma City Leader, 1995-96; staff writer, columnist, reporter, photographer N.W. News Piedmont-Surrey Gazette, Okarche Chieftain, Edmond, 1996—; city editor Okarche Chieftain, Edmond, 1996—; copywriter, cons., Edmond, 1991—, photographer, 1990—, cartoonist, 1984—, humorist, 1990—; columnist, contbg. writer N.W. News, Piedmont, Okla., 1994-95; reporter and assoc. editor: All About Kids/South Oklahoma City Leader, 1995-96. Asst. leader Boy Scouts Am., Edmond, 1993-95; league coach Young Am. Bowling Alliance, Edmond, 1993—; counselor Oklahoma City YWCA Rape Crisis, 1986-88; mem. Tiaras Jr. Women's Honor Soc., 1990-91; mem. selection com. Okla. Journalism Hall of Fame, 1990. Recipient awards State Fair of Okla., 1983-95, Feature Writing award Okla. chpt. Soc. Profl. Journalists, 1994, six awards, 1995; first place Feature Writing award, State Fair of Okla. Better Newspaper Contest, 1995. Mem. Soc. Profl. Journalists (pres. U. Ctrl. Okla. chpt. 1990, treas. 1989, 91), Kappa Tau Alpha. Roman Catholic. Home: 301 Reynolds Rd Edmond OK 73013-5121

PYLE, CAROL L. HORSLEY, choral music educator; b. Dallas, Mar. 29, 1946; d. John Otis and Flora Eileen Horsley; m. Michael R. Pyle (dec. 1995). B Music Edn., East Tex. State U., 1970, MusM, 1972. Cert. music and English tchr., Tex. Choral dir. Dumas (Tex.) Jr. H.S., 1970-72, Haltom H.S., Birdville, Tex., 1981-84, Glen Rose (Tex.) Jr. and Sr. H.S., 1986-88, Springtown (Tex.) H.S., 1988-91, Azle (Tex.) H.S., 1991—; choral dir., vocal coord. Weatherford (Tex.) H.S. and Mid. Schs., 1972-81; English reading tchr. Aledo (Tex.) H.S., 1984-86; mem. adv. bd. Tex. Girls' Choir, Ft. Worth; founder, mus. dir. Parker County Choral Soc., Weatherford, 1984-86. Contbr. articles to profl. jours. Founder, bd. dirs., 1st pres. Weatherford Assn. Performing Arts, 1974-77; pres. Weatherford Classroom Tchrs. Assn., Weatherford, 1979-80; soloist, guest condr. various civic, ch. and cmty. choirs, Tex., 1970—; tchr. Azle Ch. of Christ, 1980—; vol. Tarrant County Fine Arts Coun., Parker County Cancer Soc. Named Tchr. of Yr. Weatherford Ind. Sch. Dist./VFW Aux., 1980, Nat. Finalist Tchr. of Yr., Nat. VFW Aux., 1980. Mem. Tex. Music Educators Assn. (chair region VII 1987-88, region V 1991-92), Tex. Choral Dirs. Assn. (state sec. 1980-81), Assn. Tex. Pub. Educators, Renaissance Consort of Ft. Worth, Schola Cantorum of Tex., Inc. (bd. dirs. 1974-75, Mem. of Yr. 1992), Mu Phi Epsilon, Alpha Chi, Alpha Lambda Delta. Home: 1515 Oliver St Weatherford TX 76086 Office: Azle HS 1200 Boyd Rd Azle TX 76020

PYLE, JOANNE LINDEN, administrative aide; b. Arlington, Va., Sept. 19, 1954; d. Joseph M. and Joyce P. (Sterling) Linden; m. Harlen Pyle, Mar. 13, 1982; children: Bryce, Cassie. BA in Environ. and Urban Sus., Va. Poly. Inst. and State U., 1977, M of Urban Affairs and Mgmt., 1978. Assoc. A.T. Kearney, Inc., Alexandria, Va., 1979-82; sr. health policy analyst AMA, Chgo., 1982-87; adminstrv. aide to vice mayor City of Alexandria/City Coun., 1994—; campaign chair City Councilwoman Del Pepper, Alexandria, 1994; mem. adv. bd. Ho Ho Ho, Alexandria, 1995—; bd. dirs. Alexandria Network Preschool, 1993-95. Co-author: (training manual) Program Budgeting: Techniques and Procedures, 1978. Mem. Alexandria Commn. for Women, 1990-93, chair, 1992-93. Recipient Women Helping Women award Soroptimist Internat., 1993. Mem. Alexandria LWV (membership chair 1989-92,96—), Hopkins House, Friends of Campagna Ctr. Democrat.

PYLE, KATHERINE ANN, geriatric nurse; b. Maryville, Mo., Oct. 1, 1954; d. Richard Leonard Martin and Velda Fae (Myers) Mantano; m. Steven Glen Pyle, June 5, 1976; 1 child, Kevin. BSN, Avila Coll., 1976. Cert. in gerontol. nursing ANA, 1994. Nursing asst. Kans. City Coll. of Osteo. Medicine, Kansas City, Mo., 1975-76; staff nurse med.-surg. KCCOM, Kansas City, 1976-79, continuing edn. instr., 1979-80; staff nurse med.-surg. Park Lane Med. Ctr., Kansas City, 1980-83, charge nurse skilled nursing unit, 1989—; claims investigator Equifax Svcs., Inc., Overland Park, Kans., 1986-89; part time fac. instr. nursing Sanford Brown Coll., 1995—. Mem. Mo. League Nursing (mem. planning com.). Baptist. Home: 4719 Northern Ave Kansas City MO 64133-2219 Office: Park Lane Med Ctr 5151 Raytown Rd Kansas City MO 64133

PYLES, CAROL DELONG, dean, consultant, educator; b. Oil City, Pa., Apr. 6, 1948; d. William J. and Doris (Gresh) DeLong; m. Richard Pyles, Mar. 26, 1980; 1 child, Whitney Dawn. BS, Alderson-Broaddus Coll., Philippi, W.Va., 1966-70; MS in Nursing, Tex. Woman's U., 1982-85; MA, W. Va. U., 1972-73, EdD, 1974-80. RN, W.Va., Tex., Fla.; cert. health edn. specialist; lic. profl. counselor, Tex., Okla.; nat. cert. counselor. Instr. nursing Fairmont (W.Va.) State Coll., 1971-73, asst. prof. nursing edn., 1973-76, asst. dean Com. Coll., 1976-78, prof. nursing, chmn. divsn. health careers, 1978-81; cons., adj. faculty Salem Coll., Clarksburg, W.Va., 1978-81; officer Allied Health Houston Com. Coll. System, 1981-83, chmn. divsn. sales, mktg. & mgmt., 1983-85; dean Coll. Spl. Arts & Scis., prof. health edn. adminstrn. Cen. State U., Edmond, Okla., 1985-87; dean Coll. of Health, Phys. Edn. & Recreation Ea. Ill. U., Charleston, 1987-91, prof. health studies, 1987-91; dean, prof. med. ctr. campus Miami-Dade (Fla.) C.C., 1991—; bd. dirs. Dade County Area Health Edn. Ctr., Inc.; treas. bd. dirs. Nat. Network for Health Career Programs in Two Yr. Colls.; pres. cons. seminar devel., P & P Assoc., Inc., Houston; coun. pvt. practice for marriage, life crises, behavior & image problems. Author: articles for Issues in Higher Edn. Mem. South Fla. Health Planning Coun., Indigent Health Care Task Force, Met. Dade County, Fla., Dade County Area Health Edn. Ctr., Inc.; chmn. Indsl. Commn., Charleston (Ill.) Recreation Ctr., 1989; bd. dirs. ARC, East Coles County chpt., Reg. United Way, Coalition Against Domestic Violence, Am. Cancer Soc. Named Personality of Am. 1986, Outstanding Young Leader in Allied Health, 1984, Most Outstanding Young Women of Am., 1983; recipient Svc. award Am. Cancer Soc., 1984. Mem. Am. Coun. Edn., Nat. Identification Program, Am. Cancer Soc., Am. Assn. Coll. for Tchrs. Edn. Inst. Rep., Assn. Schs. Allied Health Professions, Fla. Assn. Community Colls., Alliance of 100 (Fla. Hosp. Assn.), Rotary Internat., Sigma Theta Tau. Office: Miami Dade Community Coll Med Ctr Campus 950 NW 20th Med Ctr Miami FL 33127-4693

PYLES, DEBRA KAY, elementary education educator; b. Parkersburg, W.Va.. BA, Glenville State Coll., 1979; MA in Spl. Edn., W.Va. U., 1995. Cert. elem. tchr., Ohio; cert. elem. and spl. edn. (learning disabilities) W.Va. Tchr. Warren Local Sch. Dist., Vincent, Ohio, 1981—; elem. coord. drug-free schs. com. Warren Local Schs., 1987—. Soprano chancel choir Meml. Ch. of Good Shepherd, Parkersburg, W.Va., 1994—, lector, 1994—, vacation ch. sch. tchr., 1984—. Social sci. scholar Parkersburg C.C., 1975-77, Martha Holden Jennings scholar, 1982. Mem. NEA, Phi Delta Kappa. Episcopalian. Office: Warren Local Sch Dist RR 1 Vincent OH 45784-9801

PYNN, KATHLEEN ANN, accounting manager; b. Sioux City, Iowa, Mar. 28, 1950; d. Clarence John and Yvette Ida (DeMers) Backer; m. Gordon Edwin Pynn Jr., Mar. 15, 1969; children: Teresa, Marce. Student, Augustana Coll., Sioux Falls, S.D., 1979-80, C.C. Sioux Falls, 1982, Wayne State Coll., South Sioux City, Nebr., 1989-91, Morningside Coll., Sioux City, Idaho, 1991-94. Acct. Fiscal Control Office, Karamursel AFB, Turkey, 1970-72, Williams & Co., Sioux City, 1976-78, Jerald B. Davis Co., Sioux Falls, 1981-82; contr. Warren Supply Co., Sioux Falls, S.D., 1982-84; ops. mgr. Designers Ltd., Sioux Falls, 1984-85; co-owner, operator LaVentura Ltd., Sioux City, 1986-89; customer acctg. mgr. Gateway 2000, North Sioux City, S.D., 1989-90; contr. Network Comm., Sioux City, 1990; acct. Terry Lockie, CPA, Sioux City, 1991-93; acctg. mgr. Mid Bell Music Inc., Sioux City, 1993—; v.p. comm. Inst. Mgmt. Accts., 1996—; cons. Minnikota Girl Scouts, Sioux Falls, 1986, fin. chair, 1985; presenter in field. Bd. dirs. Women Aware, Sioux City, 1989-91. Mem. Nat. Assn. for Women in Careers (advisor, pres. 1986-89, treas. 1986-87, Woman of Achievement 1988, Woman of Yr. 1984), Women of Excellence Program (nomination com. 1989, co-chair 1990, 91), Tri-State Women Bus. Conf. (planning com. 1987-88), Sioux City C of C, PEO, Quota. Roman Catholic. Home: 3813 Douglas Ct Sioux City IA 51104-1405 Office: Mid Bell Music Inc Sioux City IA 51106

PYZOW, SUSAN VICTORIA, artist, educator; b. Bronx, Oct. 27, 1955; d. John and Helen Pyzow; m. Paul Marcus. BFA, Cooper Union, 1976; MFA, Buffalo U., 1978. instr. painting and drawing Parsons Sch. Design, N.Y.C., 1984—. One person shows include Caldwell (N.J.) Coll., 1994; exhibited in group shows N.Y. Pub. Libr., N.Y.C., 1981, P.P.O.W. Gallery, N.Y.C., 1984, The Print Club, Phila., 1987, Mus. Modern Art, N.Y.C., 1988, Ann. Juried Exhbn., N.Y.C., 1992, Gallery Three-Zero, N.Y.C., 1993, Butler Inst. Am. Art, Youngstown, Ohio, 1993. Recipient Mervin Honig Meml. award in painting Audubon Artists, Nat. Arts Club, 1992, Ava award for works on paper Assn. for Visual Artists, 1992, Labutis Klue award in painting Am. Artists Profl. League, Salamagundi Club, 1992; grantee in oil painting Ludwig Vogelstein Found., 1993.

QUACKENBUSH, AUDREY M., trucking executive; b. Troy, N.Y., Sept. 2, 1947; d. Ernest David and Vera Emeline (Church) Yerke; m. Ralph Gilbert Quackenbush III, Jan. 2, 1983 (div. Sept. 1986); 1 child, Earle Francis Pierce. AA in Bus. Mgmt., So. Vt. Coll., 1976. Owner operator Prefab Transit, Farmer City, Ill., 1979-80; traffic mgr., exec. sec. Am. Elec., Jacksonville, Fla., 1981; dispatcher Versatile Trucking, Jacksonville, Fla., 1981; asst. mgr. local Bowman Trans., Jacksonville, Fla., 1981-83; office mgr. Lumber Transport, Jacksonville, Fla., 1983; pres. White Line Trucking, Inc., Jacksonville, Fla., 1983—. Mem. Jacksonville C. of C. (bd. dirs. West coun. 1994-95, Growing Bus. of Yr. 1993), Women Bus. Owners of N.E. Fla. (Woman Bus. Owner of Yr. 1995). Office: White Line Trucking Inc 9800 Normandy Blvd Jacksonville FL 32221

QUADE, CYNTHIA, real estate broker, sales and marketing executive; b. Albany, N.Y., Feb. 5, 1962; d. Alfred R. and Rosemarie Quade. Student, Siena Coll., Londonville, N.Y., 1986. Dir. sales and mktg. The Michaels Devel. Group, Latham, N.Y., 1988—; broker, owner Signature Homes Realty, Latham, 1992—; dual broker assoc. The Michaels Realty Group, Latham, 1990—. Mem. Albany C. of C., Greater Capital Region Bd. Realtors, Nat. Assn. Homebuilders, Capital Regiona New Home Sales and Mktg. Home: PO Box 41 Latham NY 12110 Office: Signature Homes Realty PO Box 41 Latham NY 12110

QUADER, PATRICIA ANN, elementary education educator; b. Pitts., Sept. 9, 1941; d. Andrew and Julia Supira; m. Walter Anthony Quader, Jan. 15, 1966. BA, Carlow Coll., 1963; MEd, U. Pitts., 1967. Cert. elem. tchr., supt., Pa. Tchr. Diocese of Pitts., 1963-64; tutor Pitts. Tchrs. Tutoring Svc., 1964-65; intern tchr. Burrell Sch. Dist., Lower Burrell, Pa., 1966; tchr. Kiski Area Sch. Dist., Vandergrift, Pa., 1966-91; computer, libr. skills tchr. Vandergrift Elem. Sch., 1991—; instr. Pa. State U., New Kensington, 1970-72; in-svc. instr. in computer literacy Kiski Area Sch. Dist., 1985-91, 95, edited K-3 computer skills curriculum. Co-author: 4th and 5th grade computer literacy curricula for Kiski Sch. Dist.; editor Kiski Area K-6 Computer Skills Curriculum, 1991—. Chmn. Bell-Avon PTA, Salina, Pa., 1988-91. Recipient scholarship Carlow Coll., 1959. Mem. NEA, ASCD, Pa. State Edn. Assn., Kiski Area Edn. Assn., Phi Delta Kappa. Democrat. Roman Catholic. Office: Vandergrift Elem Sch 420 Franklin Ave Vandergrift PA 15690-1311

QUAIFE, MARJORIE CLIFT, nursing educator; b. Syracuse, N.Y., Aug. 21. Diploma in Nursing with honors, Auburn Meml. Hosp; BS, Columbia U., 1962, MA, 1978. Cert. orthopaedic nurse; cert. in nursing continuing edn. and staff devel.; BLS instr. Staff instr. Columbia Presbyn. Hosp., N.Y.C.; content expert for computer assisted instrn. program-ctrl. venous catheters. Contbr. articles to numerous profl. publs. Mem. ANA, N.Y. State Nurses Assn., Nat. Assn. Orthopaedic Nurses, Nat. Assn. Nursing Staff Devel., Nat. Assn. Vascular Access Networks, Intravenous Nurses Soc., Sigma Theta Tau.

QUALLS, ROXANNE, mayor of Cincinnati. Former exec. dir. Women Helping Women; former dir. No. Ky. Rape Crisis Ctr.; former dir. Cin. office Ohio Citizen Action; councilwoman City of Cin., 1991-93, mayor, 1993—; former chairperson Cin. City Council's Intergovtl. Affairs and Environment Com.; former vice chairperson Community Devel., Housing and Zoning Com.; 2d v.p. OKI Regional Coun. Govts.; mem. Gov.'s Commn. on Storage and Use of Toxic and Hazardous Materials, Solid Waste Adv. Com. of State of Ohio, Gov.'s Waste Minimization Task Force; former chair bd. commrs. Cin. Met. Housing Authority; bd. dirs. Shuttlesworth Housing Found. Hon. chair Friends of Women's Studies; mem. Jr. League Adv. Coun. Recipient Woman of Distinction award Girl Scouts U.S., 1992, Woman of Distinction award Soroptimists, 1993, Outstanding Achievement award Cin. Woman's Polit. Caucus, 1993. Office: City Hall 801 Plum St Ste 150 Cincinnati OH 45202-5704*

QUAN, SUSAN, dental hygienist; b. San Antonio, Dec. 16, 1968; d. Stewart and Judy (Leung) Q.; m. Mark Chan, Oct. 3, 1992. BS, U. Tex. Health Sci. Ctr., 1990; postgrad., San Jose State U., 1994—. Registered dental hygienist, Calif. Dental hygienist Sacramento County Job Corps., 1992, Dr. Ed Sims, DDS, Sacramento, 1991-93, Dental Placements, Saratoga, Calif., 1992-93, Dr. Robert Rutner, DDS, Sunnyvale, Calif., 1993-94, Dr. Dennis Macaulay, DDS, Sunnyvale, 1994—. Counselor First Chinese Bapt. Ch., San Antonio, 1984-90, Sunday sch. tchr., 1984-90, bible study leader, 1984-90; youth group counselor, Bible study coord. Sacramento Chinese Bapt. Ch., 1991-92. Named Dean's scholar San Jose State U., 1996. Mem. Am. Dental Hygienists Assn. (scholarship 1989). Baptist. Home: 401-17 Camille Circle San Jose CA 95134 Office: Dr Dennis Macaulay DDS 584 S Mathilda #1 Sunnyvale CA 94086

QUATTRO-HUNT, CARMELLA MARIE, school counselor; b. Balt., July 16, 1949; d. Cosmos Damien and Antoinette (Brocato) Qauttro; m. Alan Louis Hunt, Aug. 27, 1988; 1 child, Lauren Genevieve. AA, Villa Julie Coll., Stevenson, Md., 1969; BS in Elem. Edn., Towson State U., 1971; MS in Guidance and Counseling, Johns Hopkins U., 1977; MA in Art History, Hunter Coll., N.Y.C., 1987. Cert. ESOL tchr., Md.; cert. profl. counselor, Md. Tchr. 3d grade Balt. City Pub. Schs., 1971-74; receptionist admissions office Johns Hopkins U., Balt., 1974-77; dir. student activities and housing, asst. dean students Md. Inst., Coll. of Art, Balt., 1977-81; receptionist Drawing Ctr., N.Y.C., 1981-84; tchr. ESL Superior Career Inst., N.Y.C., 1984-85; tchr. ESL Kent County Pub. Schs., Chestertown, Md., 1987-93, counselor, 1988—; tchr. Kent County Adult Edn., Chestertown, 1987-88. Curator show Space Telescope Sci. Inst., balt., 1986. Recipient Monetary award Md. Arts Coun., 1988. Mem. ACA, Md. ASsn. Counseling. Home: 9261 Upper Creek Ln Chestertown MD 21620-4162 Office: Kent County Pub Schs Washington Ave Chestertown MD 21620

QUATTRONE-CARROLL, DIANE ROSE, clinical social worker; b. N.Y.C., July 18, 1949; d. Mario Anthony and Filomena (Serpico) Quattrone; m. Rene Eugene Carroll Jr., June 7, 1980; children: Jenna Cristine, Jonathan Rene. BA cum laude, Bklyn. Coll., 1971; MSW, Rutgers U., 1974. Lic. marriage and family counselor, lic. clin. social worker, N.J.; bd. cert. diplomate in clin. social work. Clin. social worker, field instr. Essex County Guidance Ctr., East Orange, N.J., 1974-82; exec. dir. Psychotherapy Info. and Referral Svc., Madison, N.J., 1982-87; pvt. practice Sparta, N.J., 1982—. Nat. Assn. Social Workers.

QUAYLE, MARILYN TUCKER, lawyer, wife of former vice president of United States; b. 1949; d. Warren and Mary Alice Tucker; m. J. Danforth Quayle, Nov. 18, 1972; children: Tucker, Benjamin, Corinne. BA in Polit. Sci., Purdue U., 1971; JD, Ind. U., 1974. Pvt. practice atty. Huntington, Ind., 1974-77; ptnr. Krieg, DeVault, Alexander & Capehart, Indpls., 1993—. Author: (with Nancy T. Northcott) Embrace the Serpent, 1992, The Campaign, 1996.

QUEEN, EVELYN E. CRAWFORD, judge, law educator; b. Albany, N.Y., Apr. 6, 1945; d. Iris (Jackson) Crawford; m. Charles A. Queen, Mar. 6, 1971; children: Angelia, George. BS, Howard U., 1968, JD, 1975. Bar: N.Y. 1976, D.C. 1977, U.S. Ct. Appeals (D.C. cir.) 1977, U.S. Dist. Ct. (D.C. dist.) 1978, U.S. Supreme Ct. 1980. Park ranger Nat. Park Svc., Washington, 1968-69; pers. specialist NIH, Bethesda, Md., 1969-75; staff atty. Met. Life Ins. Co., N.Y.C., 1975-76; atty. advisor Maritime Adminstrn.-U.S., Washington, 1976-78; att. U.S. atty.-D.C. Justice Dept., Washington, 1978-81; hearing commr. D.C. Superior Ct., Washington, 1981-86, judge, 1986—; adj. law prof. Howard U., 1988, D.C. Sch. Law, 1993, 94. Recipient spl. achievement awards HEW, 1975, certs. of appreciation and placques Dept. Justice, 1981, Trefoil award Hudson Valley coun. Girl Scouts U.S.A., 1988. Mem. ABA, Nat. Bar Assn., Nat. Assn. Women Judges, Washington Bar Assn. Office: DC Superior Ct 500 Indiana Ave NW Washington DC 20001-2131

QUEEN, SALLY ANN CRANNELL, business consultant; b. Dallas, Feb. 25, 1949; d. Kenlen Bates and Eleanor (Owens) Crannell; m. Bruce Fielding Queen, Apr. 20, 1968; children: Heather Leigh Queen Dennis, Christopher Dyer Queen. BS in Home Econs., U Ariz., 1983. Mgr. Wicker Rocker, Panama City, Fla., 1973-75, House of Fabrics, Alamogordo, N.Mex., 1984-86, Colonial Williamsburg (Va.) Found., 1987-95; owner Calico Queen, Fla., Ariz., Germany, 1975-83, Sally Queen & Assocs., Arlington, Va., 1995—. Creator: (video) Costuming at Colonial Williamsburg, 1995. Fund raiser various wive's clubs, 1972—; dist. commr. Girl Scouts U.S., Germany, 1978-80; active Arlington Ridge Civic Assn., 1996—. Named Outstanding new member Panama City C. of C., 1975. Mem. Peninsula Women's Network, Costume Soc. Am. (regional bd. dirs. 1992-96, nat. bd. dirs. 1993—, long range planning coord. 1994-96, regional v.p. 1996—), Kappa Omicron Nu. Republican. Disciples of Christ. Home and Office: 2801 S Joyce St Arlington VA 22202

QUEEN, SANDY (SANDRA JANE QUEEN), psychologist, trainer, small business owner; b. Washington, Jan. 25, 1946; d. Ralph Edward and Nettie Mae (Peeler) Bort; m. Roy Queen (div. 1973); children: David Brice, Lara Renee, Wendy Joy. BS in Psychology summa cum laude, Towson State U., 1975. Mem. staff social svc. dept. St. Joseph Hosp., Towson, Md., 1973-76; outreach dir. St. Joseph Hosp., Towson, 1980-82; legal rsch. aide, office mgr. Ellin and Assocs., Balt., 1976-77; mkt. mgr. east coast Nat. Med. Cons., Kansas City, Mo., 1977-80; owner, dir. Lifeworks, Columbia, Md., 1982—; wellness coord. St. Anthony Sch., Balt., 1975—, Goucher Coll., 1981-87, Nat. Wellness Conf., Stevens Point, Wis., 1982—, Nat. Humor Conf., 1996; adv. coun. Gov.'s Coun. on Physical Fitness, Balt. 1990—; cons.Ministry of Sport and Recreation, Australia, 1991—, Singpore Kidney Found. Author: Wellness for Children, 1982, Wellness for Youth, 1992, vol. II, 1993; (curriculi) Well and Wonderful, 1982, Child Abuse Resistance, 1985. Chmn. edn. com. Nat. Cancer Soc., Towson, 1981-83, pub. info. com. Am. Heart Assn., Balt., 1982-83; race dir. Am. Heart Assn., Balt., 1982-84; commr. Gov's Coun. on Physical Fitness, Balt., 1984-90; mem. Md. Wellness Com., Balt., 1991—; owner Lifeline Publs., 1993. Recipient Spl. Svc. award, Jaycees of Md., 1982, Am. Heart Assn., 1983. Democrat. Baptist. Office: Lifeworks PO Box 2668 Columbia MD 21045-1668

QUEEN LATIFA See OWENS, DANA

QUELER, EVE, conductor; b. N.Y.C.. Student, Mannes Coll. Music, CCNY. Music dir. Opera Orchestra of N.Y. Music staff N.Y.C. Opera, 1958-70; assoc. condr. Ft. Wayne (Ind.) Philharm., 1970-71; founder, music dir. Opera Orch., N.Y., 1968; condr. Lake George Opera Festival, Glen Falls, N.Y., 1971-72, Oberlin (Ohio) Music Festival, 1972, Romantic Festival, Indpls., 1972, Mostly Mozart Festival, Lincoln Center, 1972, New Philharmonia, London, 1974, Teatro Liceu, Barcelona, 1974, 77, San Antonio Symphony, 1975; guest condr. Paris Radio Orch., 1972, P.R. Symphony Orch., 1975, 77, Mich. Chamber Orch., 1975, Phila. Orch., 1976, Montreal Symphony, 1977, Cleve. Orch., 1977 (Recipient Martha Baird Rockefeller Fund for Music award 1968, named Musician of Month Mus. Am. Mag. 1972), N.Y.C. Opera, 1978, Opera Las Palmas, 1978, Opera de Nice, 1979, Nat. Theatre of Prague, 1980, Opera Caracas, Venezuela, 1981, San Diego Opera, 1984, Australian Opera, Sydney, 1985, Kirov Opera, St, Petersburg, Russia, 1993, Hamburg Opera, Germany, 1994, Pretoria, South Africa, 1995, Hamilton, Ont., 1995; recording CBS Masterworks, 1974, 76, Hungaroton Records, 1982-85. Office: care Alix Barthelmes Manager Opera Orchestra NY 239 W 72nd St #2R New York NY 10023-2734*

QUENNEVILLE, KATHLEEN, lawyer; b. Mt. Clemens, Mich., July 31, 1953; d. Marcel J. and Patricia (Armstrong) Q.;. BA, Mich. State U., 1975; JD, Golden Gate U., 1979. Bar: Calif. 1980. Atty. Wells Fargo Bank, San Francisco, 1980-81; staff counsel Calif. State Banking Dept., San Francisco, 1981-83; assoc. Manatt, Phelps, Rothenburg & Tunney, Los Angeles, 1983-84; v.p., assoc. gen. counsel Bank of Calif., San Francisco, 1984-96; gen. counsel The Mechanics Bank, Richmond, Calif., 1996—. Asst treas. AIDS Legal Referral Panel of the San Francisco Bay Area, 1986-92. Mem. Calif. State Bar Assn. (bus. law sect. corp. law depts. com. 1988-90), Calif. Bankers Assn. (chair regulatory compliance com. 1994-96, legal affairs com. 1996—). Office: The Mechanics Bank 3170 Hilltop Mall Rd Richmond CA 94806-0047

QUESADA, FRANCINE BARBARA, social services administrator, therapist, educator; b. N.Y.C., Nov. 21, 1942; d. Samuel David and Rose (Feiner) Weiss; m. Joseph R. Quesada, Nov. 25, 1979 (dec. Aug. 1988); children: Sherifa, Samora. BS in Human Svcs., Empire State Coll., N.Y.C., 1991; MS in Rehab. Counseling, U. Scranton, 1994. Cert. rehab. counselor, Pa.; cert. addiction counselor, Pa. Office mgr. Dr. David Richter, N.Y.C., 1973-91; exec. dir. Vision House, Inc., Scranton, Pa., 1992—; intensive outpatient counselor, couples therapist A Better Today, Inc., Scranton, 1996—; adj. prof. Marywood Coll., Scranton, 1994—. Dist. leader Ind. Dem. Club, N.Y.C., 1987-87; sec. exec. bd. Village East Towers, Inc., N.Y.C., 1986-88; mem. Housing Coalition for Scranton Families, 1995—. Office: A Better Today Inc 1339 N Main Ave Scranton PA 18508

QUESINBERRY, TERRI LYNNE, educator; b. San Francisco, Sept. 17, 1964; d. Murray Edwin and Gladys Marie (Van Hook) Randleman; m. Peter Dean Quesinberry, July 27, 1991; children: Parker Dalton, Brooke Lynne. BA, UCLA, 1987. Tchr. 4th grade New Haven Unified Schs., Union City, Calif., 1988-90, 91—, tchr. 6th grade, 1990-91, adminstr. summer sch., 1994, 95, ptnr. tchr., 1994—, dept. head., tech. trainer, after sch. club coord., 1995—; facilitator assessment group New Haven Unified Schs., 1994-95, mentor, 1994—, mem. writing com., 1990-93. Mem. NEA, Calif. Tchrs. Assn., New Haven Tchrs. Assn., Alameda County Reading (rec. sec., rsch. chmn.), Internat. Reading Assn. Home: 3349 Hudson Pl Fremont CA 94536 Office: Alvarado Elem Sch 31100 Fredi St Union City CA 94587

QUESTEL, MAE, actress; b. Bronx, N.Y., Sept. 13, 1908; d. Simon and Frieda (Glauberman) Q.; m. Leo Balkin, Dec. 22, 1930 (dec.); children: Robert (dec.), Richard; m. Jack E. Shelby, Nov. 19, 1970. Student in drama, J.G. Geiger, N.Y.C., 1916-24; scholar, Theatre Guild, N.Y.C., 1923, Columbia U., 1949, Theatre Wing, 1951. Appeared in vaudeville at, Palace Theatre, 1930, on RKO theater circuit, 1931-38; radio shows include Betty Boops Frolics, NBC, 1932; cartoon voices Betty Boop, 1931—, Olive Oyl, 1933—, Mr. Bugs Goes to Town, 1934, Little Audrey, 1946; TV cartoon Winky Dink and You, 1956-60, Popeye (as Olive Oyl), 1981; stage appearances include Dr. Social, 1948, A Majority of One, 1959-61, Come Blow Your Horn, 1963, Enter Laughing, 1963, Bajour, 1964, The Warm Peninsula, 1966, Walk Like A Lion, 1969, Barrel Full of Pennies, 1970, Where Have You Been, Billy Boy, 1969, Betty Boop—60 Yrs., N.Y.C., 1990, Betty Boop (Olive Oyl), U. Nebr., Lincoln, 1990; appeared: films A Majority of One, 1961, It's Only Money, 1962, Funny Girl, 1967, Move, 1969, Zelig, 1983, Hot Resorts, 1984, Who Framed Roger Rabbit?, 1988, New York Stories: A Trilogy, 1988-89, Christmas Vacation, 1989; TV spokeswoman for Scott Paper Co. as Aunt Bluebell films, 1971-78; other commls. include Playtex, 1970-72, Romilar, 1970-72, Folger's Coffee, 1970-72, Speidel Watch Bands, 1980, S.O.S, 1981, Parker Bros. video game Popeye, 1983-84; soap opera Somerset, 1976-77, All My Children, 1983; other TV appearances include Good Morning America, 1980, Good Day Show, 1980, Picture Pages, 1981, Entertainment Tonight, Joan Rivers and Her Friends; also numerous recs. including Good Ship Lollipop; (Troupers award for outstanding contbn. to entertainment 1979, Annie award Internat. Animated Film Soc. 1979). Named Living Legend NYU Sch. Social Work, 1979. Mem. Screen Actors Guild, AFTRA, Actors Equity Assn., Nat. Acad. TV Arts and Scis. (award 1978), Hadassah. Clubs: Troupers (award 1963), Variety. Home: 27 E 65th St Apt 7C New York NY 10021-6556

QUICK, ABBIE JEAN, retired personnel director; b. Hartford, Conn., Aug. 22, 1910; d. George Hand and Mary (Ritzenthaler) Q. BS, U. Conn., 1932. Asst. alumni sec. U. Conn., Storrs, 1934-37; indsl. rels. staff U.S. Rubber Co., Naugatuck, Conn., 1937-44; pers. cons. Kurt Salmon Assoc., Inc., Washington, 1944-75; pers. dir. Atlanta.

QUICK, LISA R., accountant; b. Baytown, Tex., Aug. 14, 1964; d. Bob R. Allen and H. Ruth (Reeder) Allen; m. Terry K. Quick, Oct. 5, 1991. AA in Bus. Adminstrn., Lee Coll., 1985; BBA in Gen. Bus., U. Houston-Clear Lake, 1987, BS in Finance, 1994. Accounts receivable supr. D.E. Harvey Builders, Inc., Houston, 1988-89; document controller Brown & Root, Inc., Houston, 1989-90, cost engr., 1990-94, internal auditor, 1994-95, acct., 1996—. Mem. NAFE, Inst. Internal Auditors. Methodist. Office: Brown & Root Inc PO Box 3 Houston TX 77001

QUICK, VALERIE ANNE, sonographer; b. Alta., Can., Feb. 14, 1952; came to U.S., 1953; d. Kenneth Conrad and Kathryn (Maller) Bjorge. Grad. high sch., Salinas, Calif. Registered adult and pediatric echocardiographer, abdomen, small parts and ob-gyn sonographer; registered cardiovasc. technician, registered diagnostic cardiac sonographer. Chief EKG technician Natividad Med. Ctr., Salinas, 1978-81, chief ultrasound dept., 1981-94, chief cardiac echo lab., 1995—. Mem. Am. Inst. Ultrasound in Medicine, Am. Soc. Echocardiography, Nat. Soc. for Cardiopulmonary Technicians, Soc. Pediat. ECHO, Soc. Diagnostic Med. Sonographers, Am. Heart Assn., Am. Registry Diagnostic Med. Sonographers. Office: PO Box 6694 Salinas CA 93912-6694

QUIGLEY, SUSAN HAREN, sales executive; b. Pitts., Oct. 9, 1958; d. Edward Arthur and Marilyn (Wolber) Haren; m. Robert Eugene Quigley; children: Jon Robert, Lauren Marie. Bachelor's degree, Pa. State U.; paralegal cert., Assoc. degree, Harrisburg Area C.C. Paralegal Comm. of Pa., Dept. Labor and Industry, Harrisburg, 1977-81; analyst, cons. Martin Urling Co., Camp Hill, Pa., 1981-83; sales exec. Digital Equipment Corp., Harrisburg, 1983-95. Vol. St. Joseph Ch., Mechanicsburg, Pa., 1976-95. Democrat. Roman Catholic. Home: 63 Honeysuckle Dr Mechanicsburg PA 17055

QUILLEN, MARY ANN, university administrator, consultant; b. Md., Dec. 10, 1947; 1 child, Jessica. BS, Del. State U., 1977; Cert. Spl. Edn., Pa. State U., 1981; MS, U. Pa., 1991. Spl. edn. tchr. Wordsworth Acad., Ft. Washington, Pa., 1979-82; tchr. specialist Rens, Inc., Langhorne, Pa., 1982-83; area rep. Pa. State U., King of Prussia, 1983-85; dir. continuing edn. Ea. Montgomery County AVTS, Willow Grove, Pa., 1985-93; mgr. Drexel U., Phila., 1993—; con. in field. Vice chair Montgomery County Commn. on Women and Families, Norristown, Pa., 1992—; coord. Domestic Violence Forum for Montgomery County, Norristown, 1994—. Mem. ASTD, AAUW, Pa. Assn. for Adult and Continuing Edn., U. Pa. Alumni Assn. (dir. comm. com. 1993—). Home: 1000 Valley Forge Cir #1103 King Of Prussia PA 19406

QUILLIAN, LINDA, English language educator; b. Atlanta, Sept. 13, 1950; d. Lloyd A. and Merian H. Q.; m. Bobby Melvin Jr.; children: Bobby Melvin III,Quillian Carrington Melvin. BA, Spelman Coll., 1972; MA in English, Howard U., 1978, PhD, 1983. Tchr. English, dir. drama and speech South Mountain High Sch., Phoenix, 1973-76; adj. prof. dept. English U. D.C., Washington, 1979-81; instr. dept. English Howard U., Washington, 1977-82; prof. dept. English and linguistics Morehouse Coll., Atlanta, 1983-84; adminstrv. adjutant D.C. Pub. Schs., Office of the Supt., 1985-87; coord. incentive programs for tchrs. D.C. Pub. Schs. Office of the Supt., 1987-88; spl. asst. D.C. Pub. Schs., Office of the Supt., 1988-90; asst. prof. dept. English studies U. D.C., Washington, 1990—. Contbr. articles and poetry to profl. jours. and anthologies. Bd. dirs. Black Theatre Troup, Phoenix, 1974-76; oratorical advisor Optimist Internat. Club Contests, Phoenix, 1974-76. Recipient scholarship Spelman Coll., 1968, Virginia Chase award in English Edn., Spelman Coll., 1972, scholarship Exch. Program, U. West Indies and Spelman Coll., 1972, Grad. grant Howard U., 1976-77, Doctoral Terminal fellowship Howard U., 1982-83, Outstanding Young Woman of Am. award, 1982-83. Mem. NEA, NAFE, ASCD, Nat. Coun. Tchrs. English, Coll. English Assn., Mid-Atlantic Group. Home: 856 Yuma St SE Washington DC 20032-3972 Office: U DC Dept of English 4200 Connecticut Ave NW Washington DC 20008-1174

QUILTER, DEBORAH, writer, consultant, educator; b. San Diego, June 24, 1950; d. Edward Sinon and Mary Ann (Murray) Q. BA, San Francisco State U., 1973; student, MIT, 1994. Consumer reporter, columnist San Francisco Bay Guardian, 1981-82; legal correspondent Andrews Litigation Reporter, Westtown, Pa., 1982-85; travel and entertainment editor Better Health and Living, N.Y.C., 1985-87; columnist UDT News, N.Y.C., 1995; contbg. editor Am. Cheerleader, N.Y.C., 1995—; cons. and speaker, N.Y.C., 1994—; tchr. Marymount Manhattan Coll., N.Y.C., 1996—. Co-author: Repetitive Strain Injury: A Computer User's Guide, 1994; contbg. writer: Total Health for Women, 1995. Recipient Honorable Mention award for best non-daily newspaper story San Francisco Press Club, 1983. Mem. Authors Guild. Home: 108 W 73d St # 2 New York NY 10023

QUINDLEN, ANNA, journalist, author; b. Phila., July 8, 1953; d. Robert V. and Prudence Quindlen; m. Gerald Krovatin; children: Quin, Christopher, Maria. BA, Barnard Coll., 1974. Reporter New York Post, N.Y.C., 1974-77; gen. assignment, city hall reporter New York Times, N.Y.C., 1977-81, columnist About New York, 1981-83, dep. met. editor, 1983-85, columnist Life in the 30's syndicated, 1986-89, columnist Public and Private, 1990-94. Author: Living Out Loud, 1988, (novel) Object Lessons, 1991, The Tree That Came to Stay, 1992, Thinking Out Loud, 1993, One True Thing, 1994. Recipient Mike Berger award for Disting. Reporting, 1983, Pulitzer Prize for commentary, 1992; named Woman of Yr., Glamour mag., 1991. *

QUINLAN, DIANA SMITH, nurse anesthetist, consultant, lecturer; b. Balt., Feb. 10, 1947; d. Clayton Paul and Shirley Mae (Babington) Smith; m. Arthur Fred Banné, Feb. 24, 1968 (div. Aug. 1975); m. Raymond William Quinlan, May 20, 1977; 1 child, Kristen Leigh. AA, Catonsville C.C., Balt., 1971; BA, Ottawa U., Kansas City, Mo., 1982; MA, U. Ala., Birmingham, 1985. RN, Fla.; cert. RNA, advanced RN practitioner. Head nurse CCGH, Westminster, Md., 1971-73; mem. clin. faculty Pa. Hosp., Phila., 1973-78; dir. nurse anesthesia program U. Fla., Gainesville, 1978-83; mem. didactic faculty U. Ala., Birmingham, 1983-86; dept. mgr. Nemours Children's Clinic, Jacksonville, Fla., 1986-94; chair peer assistance Am. Assn. Nurse Anesthetists, Park Ridge, Ill., 1994—; cons. DPR, Fla., 1986. Elder, mem. choir, Sunday sch. tchr., lay min. Presbyn. Ch.; vol., fundraiser various polit. candidates, Jacksonville, 1993, 94; vol. Habitat for Humanity, Jacksonville, 1992-95; fundraiser Am. Cancer Soc., Jacksonville, 1994; chair pub. rels. Duval County Med. Soc., Jacksonville, 1995-96; bd. dirs. Fla. Assn. Nurse Anesthetists, 1987-89; mem. task force Fla. Nurses Assn., 1988. Recipient Plaques of Appreciation, Fla. Assn. Nurse Anesthetists, 1986-96, Plaque Presbyn. Ch., Birmingham, 1986, Sustained Contbns. in Peer Assistance award Nat. Nurse's Soc. on Addictions, 1996. Mem. Am. Assn. Nurse Anesthetists (mem. coms. 1975—, edn. cons. 1986—,), Anesthesia History Assn., Nat. Nurses Soc. Addiction. Home and Office: 6644 Epping Forest Way N Jacksonville FL 32217

QUINLAN, KATHLEEN, actress; b. Pasadena, Calif., Nov. 19, 1954. Actress: (theatre) Taken in Marriage, 1979 (Theatre World award 1979), Accent on Youth, 1983, Les Liaisons Dangereuses, 1988, (feature films) One is a Lonely Number, 1972, American Graffiti, 1973, Lifeguard, 1976, Airport '77, 1977, I Never Promised You a Rose Garden, 1977, The Promise, 1979, The Runner Stumbles, 1979, Sunday Lovers, 1981, Hanky Panky, 1982, Independence Day, 1982, Twilight Zone: The Movie, 1983, The Last Winter, 1983, Warning Sign, 1985, Wild Thing, 1987, Sunset, 1988, Clara's Heart, 1988, The Doors, 1991, Trial by Jury, 1994, Apollo 13, 1995 (Acad. award nominee for best actress 1996); (TV movies) Can Ellen Be Saved?, 1974, Lucas Tanner, 1974, Where Have All the People Gone?, 1974, The Missing Are Deadly, 1975, The Turning Point of Jim Malloy, 1975, The Abduction of Saint Anne, 1975, Little Ladies of the Night, 1977, She's in the Army Now, 1981, When She Says No, 1984, Blackout, 1985, Children of the Night, 1985, Dreams Lost, Dreams Found, 1987, Trapped, 1989, The Operation, 1990, Strays, 1991, An American Story, 1992, Stolen Babies, 1993, Last Light, 1993, Perfect Alibi, 1994, Breakdown, 1996. Mem. Actors' Equity Assn., Screen Actors Guild. *

QUINLAN, MARY LOU, advertising executive. CEO, pres. N.Y.C. office N.W. Ayers & Ptnrs., N.Y.C. Office: NW Ayer & Ptnrs 825 8th Ave New York NY 10019*

QUINN, AMBER MCLAIN, telecommunications executive; b. Jacksonville, Fla., June 13, 1962; d. Nicholas Edward and Maureen (O'Leary) McLain. BA, Wells Coll., 1984. Fin. advisor John Hancock, Amsterdam, N.Y., 1984-85; sucessively sales rep., account exec., sales mgr., account mgr. RCI Corp., Albany, N.Y., 1985-88; account exec. Computer Telephone Co., Albany, 1988-89; account cons. State Govt. div. U.S. Sprint, Albany, 1989-91, sr. account mgr. State Govt. div., 1994—; innkeeper, owner Inn At Rutland, Vt., 1991-94. Recipient Gold medals at Empire State Games, N.Y., 1984, 85. Mem. Nat. Assn. Female Execs., Capital Area Telecommunications Assn. Republican. Club: Schenectady Winter Sports. Office: US Sprint III Winners Cir. Albany NY 12205

QUINN, BARBARA ANN, writer; b. Bronx, N.Y., June 10, 1950; d. Anthony Joseph and Alice Rita (Sacchetti) Ferrara; m. Thomas Gerard Quinn, June 30, 1973; 1 child, Bret Thomas. BA, SUNY, Stony Brook, 1972; JD, Pace U., 1979. Bar: N.Y. 1979, U.S. Dist. Ct. (ea. dist.) N.Y. 1979, U.S. Supreme Ct. 1984. Mgr. contracts Matrix Leasing, San Francisco, 1973-76; asst. West. Co. Atty., White Plains, N.Y., 1979-85; town atty. North Salem, N.Y., 1986-87; writer The Scarsdale (N.Y.) Inquirer, 1992; features editor Strictly Scarsdale (N.Y.)/Garrido Assn., 1993-96; mgr. PROSE bd. and contest judge AOL Sixty Second Novelist Cyberspace Area, 1995-96; legal adviser Lake Katonah Club, Lewisboro, N.Y., 1982-85. Author of short stories. Bd. mem. Friends of the Scarsdale (N.Y.) Libr., 1993-95. Mem. The Fiction Co. (founder, spokeswoman).

QUINN, CHRISTINE MARIE (JENSEN), elementary education educator; b. Ottawa, Ill., Oct. 5, 1969; d. Laurie Ann (Marta) Clifford; m. Jason R. Quinn. AA, Illinois Valley C.C., Oglesby, Ill., 1989; BS in Edn., We. Ill. U., Macomb, 1992; MS in Edn., Ill. State U., 1995. Tchr. 5th grade McKinley Grade Sch., Ottawa Elem. Dist. 141, 1992—. Mem. Trinity Luth. Ch. Choir. Mem. ASCD, Ottawa Jr. Women's Club. Lutheran. Home: 1543 W Jefferson St Ottawa IL 61350 Office: McKinley Grade Sch 1320 State St Ottawa IL 61350

QUINN, JANE, journalist; b. San Antonio, Tex., Oct. 5, 1916; d. James Edward and Willie Stell (Mitchell) Q. BA, Fla. State U., 1938; MS in Social Work, Cath. U. of Am., 1945. Reporter St. Augustine (Fla.) Record, 1938-41; journalist, editl. staff The Fla. Cath. for Diocese of St. Augustine, 1940-68, The Fla. Cath., St. Augustine, 1940—, The Fla. Cath. for Diocese of Orlando, Fla., 1968—; archivist Diocese of Orlando, 1988—. Author: Minorcans in Florida, 1975, Story of a Nun: Jeanie Gordon Brown, 1979, others; contbr. articles to profl. jours. Recipient Papal award Pro Ecclesia et Pontifice, 1979, citation Cath. Press Assn. of U.S. and Can., 1994. Fellow Orlando Interfaith Sponsoring Com.; mem. Assocs. of Josephite Nuns, Assocs. of Cath. Diocesan Archivists, St. Joseph Alumni Assn., Alpha Xi Delta. Roman Catholic. Office: Diocese of Orlando 421 E Robinson St Orlando FL 32801

QUINN, JANE BRYANT, journalist, writer; b. Niagara Falls, N.Y., Feb. 5, 1939; d. Frank Leonard and Ada (Laurie) Bryant; m. David Conrad Quinn, June 10, 1967; children—Matthew Alexander, Justin Bryant. B.A. magna cum laude, Middlebury Coll., 1960. Assoc. editor Insiders Newsletter, N.Y.C., 1962-65, co-editor, 1966-67; sr. editor Cowles Book Co., N.Y.C., 1968; editor-in-chief Bus. Week Letter, N.Y.C., 1969-73, gen. mgr., 1973-74; syndicated financial columnist Washington Post Writers Group, 1974—; contbr. fin. column to Women's Day mag., 1974-95; contbr. fin. column Good Housekeeping, 1995—; contbr. NBC News and Info. Service, 1976-77; bus. corr. WCBS-TV, N.Y.C., 1979, CBS-TV News, 1980-87, ABC-TV Home Show, 1991-93; contbg. editor Newsweek mag., 1978—. Author: Everyone's Money Book, 1979, 2d edit., 1980, Making the Most of Your Money, 1991, A Hole in the Market, 1994. Mem. Phi Beta Kappa. Office: Newsweek Inc 251 W 57th St New York NY 10019-1802

QUINN, JANITA SUE, city secretary; b. Breckenridge, Tex., Apr. 14, 1950; d. Doyle Dean and Peggy Joyce (Melton) Allen; m. John Lloyd Rippy, June 27, 1969 (div. Mar. 1976); children: Johna DeAnn, Jason Allen; m. Ervel Royce Quinn, Jan. 31, 1987; stepchildren: Amy Talitha, Jason Ervel. Student, Odessa (Tex.) Jr. Coll., 1968-70, U. Tex. of Permian Basin, Odessa, 1978-79, 85-86. New accts. clk. State Nat. Bank, Odessa, Tex., 1975-76; accts. receivable clk. Woolley Tool Corp., Odessa, Tex., 1976-78; data entry operator M-Bank, Odessa, Tex., 1978-79; asst. county treas. Ector County, Odessa, Tex., 1979-83, county treas., 1983-88; office mgr., co-owner Nat. Filter Svc., Inc., San Antonio, 1988-91; temporary employment Kelly Temporary Svcs., Abilene, Tex., 1991; sec. Pride Refining, Inc., Abilene, Tex., 1991-93; city sec. City of Eastland, Tex., 1993—. Mem., treas., bd. dirs. Family Outreach Svc. Taylor County; vol. tchr. Parenting for Parents and Adolescents; recorder, del. West Tex. Corridor II Com., Eastland and Dallas, 1993; county del. Taylor County dem. Party, Abilene, 1992; state del. Tex. Dem. Party, Dallas, 1991; pres., charter mem. Bluebonnet chpt. City Secs. Region 6 Group, 1994-96. Named Outstanding Mcpl. Clk., Bluebonnet Chpt. Mcpl. Clks./Sec., 1994. Mem. Tex. Mcpl. Clks. Assn., Bluebonnett Chpt. Mcpl. Clks. (founder, pres. 1995—), County Treas. Alumni Assn. (recorder 1991-93), Rotary Internat. Democrat. Ch. of Christ. Office: City of Eastland 416 S Seaman St Eastland TX 76448-2750

QUINN, JOAN K., writer, small business owner; b. Evanston, Ill., Oct. 9, 1952; d. Raymond Adolph and Rhoda Joan (Anderson) Kliphardt; m. Thomas C. Quinn, Sept. 22, 1973; children: Bryan, Sean, Andrew, Katherine. DDH, Northwestern U., 1972; BA, SUNY, Albany, 1976; MEd, Johns Hopkins U., 1989. Dental hygienist Roland K. Meyer, Jr. DDS, Evanston, 1972-74; tchr. Robin Child Care Ctr., Albany, 1975-76; prin., writer, cons. Joan K. Quinn, Inc., Balt., 1993—. Vol. libr. asst. Ch. of Redeemer Parish Day Sch., Balt., 1983-94; vol. Sch. of Cathedral, Balt., 1983—, picture parent educator, 1991—; active Homeland Archtl. com., Balt., 1992-95, Aux. Family and Children's Svcs., Balt., 1995—. Mem. AAUW, Nat. Mus. Women of Arts, Am. Counseling Assn., Assn. Humanistic Edn. and Devel., Md. Hist. Soc., Gibson Island Club. Home and Office: 5304 St Albans Way Baltimore MD 21212

QUINN, LORA, accountant; b. Kinston, N.C., July 21, 1959; d. Alfonzo and Beatrice Jewel (Lanier) Q. BSBA in Acctg., East Carolina U., 1979. CPA, N.C. Staff acct. Barry L. Gutfeld & Assocs., P.A., Washington, N.C., 1980-82, mgr., shareholder, 1984-86; staff acct. Carrington & Hughes, CPAs, Raleigh, N.C., 1982; asst. contr. Carolina Leaf Tobacco Co., Inc., Greenville, N.C., 1982-84; ptnr., prin. Bryant & Quinn, CPAs, Greenville, 1986-92; acctg. cons. B. Humienny CFP, New Bern, N.C., 1992-94; acctg. mgr. Coastal Physician Group, Inc., Durham, N.C., 1995; acct., owner Lora Quinn CPA, Raleigh, 1995—. Treas., v.p., then pres. Greenville Bus. and Profl. Women's Club, 1990-93. Fellow AICPA, N.C. Assn. CPAs. Home and Office: 1521 Creekwood Ct Unit 201 Raleigh NC 27603

QUINN, MARY ANN, English language educator; b. Santa Barbara, Calif., Sept. 24, 1946; d. William Morris and Marion (Wilson) Q.; m. Peter Lee (div. 1973); m. Steven L. Allaback. BA, Simmons Coll., 1969, MA in English, 1981; MA in English, U. Calif., 1981, Phd in English, 1984. Tchg. asst. U. Calif., Santa Barbara, 1978-82, vis. lectr., 1982-83, dir. south coast writing project, 1983-84; asst. prof. U. San Diego, 1984-88, assoc. prof., 1989-95, prof., 1996—; dir. writing ctr. U. San Diego, 1993-96. Author: The Mask of Anarchy Draft Notebook, 1990, Shelley's 1819-1821 Huntington Notebook, 1994, Shelley's 1821-22 Huntington Notebook, 1996; contbr. articles to profl. jours. Huntington Library grantee, 1987, Am. Philosophical Soc., 1989. Mem. Nat. Coun. Tchrs. English, Am. Assoc. of U. Women, Modern Lang. Assn. Office: U San Diego 5998 Alcala Park San Diego CA 92110-2429

QUINN, PATRICIA ANNE, university official; b. Rochester, N.Y., Sept. 25, 1948; d. Harold Joseph and Marion Elizabeth (Loucks) Q.; m. Martin Finkenstaedt, July 10, 1982. BA in History, BA in English with honors, U. Rochester, 1970; MA, SUNY, Binghamton, 1972, PhD, 1985. Instr. Broome Community Coll., Binghamton, 1975-78; acad. advisor SUNY, Binghamton, 1976-78, dir. continuing edn. for women ctr., 1978-82; coordinator adult opportunity U. of Wis., Eau Claire, 1982-94; chmn. senate U. Wis., Eau Claire, 1991-93; dir. U. Wis. Ednl. Opportunity Ctr., Eau Claire, 1994—. Author: Better Than The Sons of Kings, 1989; contbr. articles to profl. jours. Program coord. Wis. Humanities Com., Eau Claire, 1987. Fulbright-Hays fellow, Fed. Republic Germany, 1973-74. Mem. AAUW (corp. rep. 1985-87, reader, cons. 1986-87, bd. internat. fellows 1987—), Am. Hist. Assn., Internat. Ctr. Medieval Art, Inst. Internat. Forecastors, World Future Soc., Eau Claire C. of C. (Ptnrs. in Edn. award 1986). Democrat. Office: U Wis Ednl Opportunity Ctr Eau Claire WI 54702

QUINN, SALLY, journalist; b. Savannah, Ga., July 1, 1941; d. William Wilson and Bette (Williams) Q.; m. Benjamin Crowninshield Bradlee, Oct. 20, 1978; 1 child, Josiah Quinn Crowninshield Bradlee. Grad., Smith Coll. Reporter, Washington Post, 1969-73, 74-80; co-anchorperson CBS Morning News, N.Y.C., 1973-74. Author: We're Going to Make You a Star, 1975, (novels) Regrets Only, 1986, Happy Endings, 1991. Address: 3014 N St NW Washington DC 20007-3404

QUINN, YVONNE SUSAN, lawyer; b. Spring Valley, Ill., May 13, 1951; d. Robert Leslie and Shirley Eilene (Morse) Q.; m. Ronald S. Rolfe, Sept. 1, 1979. BA, U. Ill., 1973; JD, U. Mich., 1976, MA in Econs., 1977. Bar: N.Y. 1978, U.S. Dist. Ct. (ea. and so. dists.) N.Y. 1978, U.S. Ct. Appeals (3d, 5th, 9th, 10th and D.C. cirs.) 1982, U.S. Ct. Appeals (2d cir.) 1992, U.S. Ct. Appeals (4th cir.) 1994, U.S. Supreme Ct. 1982. Assoc. Cravath, Swaine & Moore, N.Y.C., 1977-80; assoc. Sullivan & Cromwell, N.Y.C., 1980-84, ptnr., 1984—. Mem. ABA, Assn. of Bar of City of N.Y., India House Club. Office: Sullivan & Cromwell 125 Broad St New York NY 10004-2400

QUINN-TEMPLETON, JOANNA, advertising executive. Sr. v.p., creative dir. DDB Needham N.Y., N.Y.C. Office: DDB Needham NY 437 Madison Ave New York NY 10022*

QUIRK, ANITA MARIE, lawyer; b. Spokane, Wash., Dec. 7, 1955; d. Guy Brown and Delores Rae (Wessling) Davis; m. Matthew Thomas Quirk, Aug. 26, 1979. AA, Spokane Falls C.C., Wash., 1976; student, Colegio Adventista de Sagunto, Spain, 1977-78; BA, Walla Walla Coll., 1979; JD, Lewis and Clark Coll., 1990. Bar: Wash. 1991. Presch. tchr. King's Child Devel. Ctr., Longview, Wash., 1987-88; law clk. Daggy Legal Svcs., Longview, Wash., 1989-91; assoc. Daggy & Anagnostou, P.S., Longview, Wash., 1991-96; solo practice atty. Longview, Wash., 1996—. Mem. bd. ARC of Cowlitz County, Longview, 1994-95. Mem. Amnesty Internat., People for the Ethical Treatment of Animals. Office: 1128 Broadway Longview WA 98632

QUIRK, DONNA HAWKINS, financial analyst; b. Chgo., Sept. 29, 1955; d. Martin Francis and Monica Mae (Hesslau) Hawkins; m. John James Quirk, Dec. 5, 1981; children: Martin Patrick, Mary Kathleen, Colleen Monica. BS in Commerce, DePaul U., 1977, M.B.A., 1982. With Jewel Food Stores, Melrose Park, Ill., 1977—, acctg. mgr., 1980-85, fin. analyst, 1985—. V.p. St. Tarcissus Sch. Bd. Mem. Assn. M.B.A. Execs., Nat. Assn. Female Execs., Twice as Nice Mothers of Multiples, Beta Gamma Sigma, Delta Mu Delta. Roman Catholic. Home: 5046 N Mason Ave Chicago IL 60630-1947 Office: Jewel Food Stores 1955 W North Ave Melrose Park IL 60160-1101

QUISENBERRY, NANCY LOU, university administrator, educator; b. Washington, Ind., Jan. 29, 1938; d. Joseph Franklin and Maud Helen (Fitch) Forbes; m. James D. Quisenberry, Feb. 6, 1960; 1 child, James Paul. BS in Home Econs., Ind. State Tchrs. Coll., 1960, MS in Home Econs., 1962; EdD, Ind. U., 1971. Cert. tchr., Ind. Home economics tchr. Honey Creek High Sch., Terre Haute, Ind., 1961-62; third grade tchr. Indpls. Pub. Sch., 1962-64; sustitute tchr. Dep. of Def., Baumholder, Fed. Republic Germany, 1964-65; first grade tchr. Wayne Twp. Schs., Indpls., 1966-67; assoc. faculty lang. arts Purdue U., Ind. U., Indpls., spring 1970; prof. curriculum and instruction So. Ill. U., Carbondale, 1971—, assoc. dean Coll. of Edn., 1976—; cons. U. N.C., Durham, 1977, Ministry Edn., Bangkok, Thailand, 1980, 84, DePaul U., 1990; dir. tech. and tng. assistance grant Head Start-OCD, Carbondale, 1972-74, Cameroon project USAID, Carbondale, 1984-86; mem. Ill. State Tchr. Certification Bd., 1981-84, 84-87. Co-author: Early Childhood Education Programs: Developmental Objectives and Their Use, 1975, Play as Development, 1978. Chair candidacy com. Ctrl. So. Ill. Synod Evang. Luth. Ch. Am., Springfield, 1987-90, sec. multisynodical com., Chgo., 1987-90, synod coun., 1992-95; pres. Epiphany Luth. Ch. Coun., Carbondale, 1984-85, 89-92, 94—; bd. dirs. Jackson County YMCA, 1988. Recipient Dare To Be Great award Ill. Women Adminstrs. and So. Ill. Region Ill. Women Adminstrs., 1989, Woman of Distinction award, So. Ill. U., 1992; grantee Bur. Educationally Handicapped, 1979-82, 90-95. Mem. Internat. Coun. on Edn. for Teaching (bd. dirs. 1988—, N.Am. v.p. 1992-94), Assn. Childhood Edn. Internat. (chair tchr. edn. com. 1989-93, folio rev. coord. elem. edn. 1989—), Nat. Coun. for Accreditation Tchr. Edn. (bd. examiners 1987—), Am. Assn. Colls. for Tchr. Edn. (chair adv. coun. state reps. 1987-88, bd. dirs. 1986-88, 91-94), Ill. Assn. Colls. for Tchr. Edn. (pres. 1984-86), Assn. Tchr. Educators (chairperson com. racism from a healing perspective, 1995—). Home: 3208 W Kent Dr Carbondale IL 62901-1917 Office: So Ill U Coll Edn Carbondale IL 62901-4624

QUISGARD, LIZ WHITNEY, artist, sculptor; b. Phila., Oct. 23, 1929; d. Kenneth E. and Elizabeth (Warwick) Whitney; children: Kristin, Berit. Grad. night sch., Md. Inst. Coll. Art, 1947, grad. day sch., 1949; student, Johns Hopkins U., evenings 1952-58; pupil of, Morris Louis, 1958-60; BFA in Painting, Md. Inst., 1966, MFA in Sculpture, 1966. Pvt. tchr. painting Balt., 1955-65; tchr. Balt. Hebrew Congregation, 1962-80; mem. faculty Md. Inst. Coll. Art, 1965-76, Goucher Coll., 1966-68, Balt. Jewish Community Ctr., 1974-78, Villa Julie Coll., Stevenson, Md., 1978-80; art critic Balt. Sun, 1969-71, Craft Horizons, 1969-72, The Paper, 1971-72; designer prodns. Center Stage, Goucher Coll., Johns Hopkins U.; lectr. in Md., Va., W.Va., Pa., Ark., Ohio, N.Y., N.J. One-woman exhbns. include Jefferson Pl. Gallery, Washington, 1960, Emmerich Gallery, N.Y.C., 1962, Goucher Coll., Balt., 1966, U. Md., 1969, Gallery, 707, Los Angeles, 1974, Arts and Sci. Center, Nashua, N.H., 1975, Mechanic Gallery, Balt., 1978, Marymount Manhatten Coll., N.Y.C., 1983, Tiffany's windows, N.Y.C., 1984, Starkman Gallery, N.Y.C., 1984, Fordham U., N.Y.C., 1985, Henri Gallery, Washington, 1987, Artemisia Gallery, Chgo., 1987, Savannah (Ga.) Coll. Art and Design, 1987, Life of Maryland Gallery, Balt., 1988, Franz Bader Gallery, Washington, 1989, Fairleigh Dickinson U., N.J., 1990, Herr-Chambliss Gallery, Hot Springs, Ark., 1990, Huntington (Ind.) Coll., 1991, Bergdorf Goodman Windows, 1991, Coll. of New Rochelle, N.Y., 1992, Broadway windows, N.Y.C., 1992, Nexus Found., Phila., 1993, Carnegie Arts Ctr., Leavenworth, Kans., 1994, Asheville (N.C.) Mus., 1995; group exhbns. include, Balt. Mus., 1951-53, 58, Corcoran Gallery Area Show, 1956, 64, Corcoran Biennial Show, 1963, Peale Mus., Balt., 1947, 56, Butler Inst. Am. Art, Youngstown, Ohio, 1957, Provincetown (Mass.) Art Assn., 1955, Pa. Acad. Am. Art ann., 1964, Chgo. Art Inst., 1965, Gallery 707, 1973, S. Houston St. Gallery, N.Y.C., 1974, Balt. Mus. travelling show, 1978, Mus. of Hudson Highlands, Cornwall, N.Y., 1983; represented in permanent collections U. Ariz., U. Md., U. Balt., Johns Hopkins U., Lever House, N.Y.C., Center Club, Balt., Libyan Mission to UN, Englewood, N.J., Datalogix Corp., Valhalla, N.Y., Gt. Northern Nekoosa Corp., Norwalk, Conn., Quality Inns, Newark, Can. Imperial Bank of Commerce, N.Y.C., Rosenberg Diamond Co., N.Y.C., Marsh, Inc., Indpls., Kirkpatrick and Lockhart, Pitts., Fordham U., N.Y.C., Atlantic Realty, Atlanta, Miss. Mus. Art, Jackson, St. Joseph Health Ctr., Hot Springs, Ark., Dermatology Assocs., Pitts., Scudder, Stevens & Clark, Boston, also pvt. collections; executed mural William Fell Elem. Sch., Balt., 1980, Urban Wall, Atlanta, 1990, floor painting Vet.'s Stadium, Phila., 1992, mural Med. Coll. Va., Richmond, 1994. Recipient Best in Show award Loyola Coll. Invitational, Balt., 1966, Florsheim Purchase Grant, 1991; scholar Md. Inst., 1947-49; Rinehart fellow in sculpture, 1964-66. Address: 145 Reade St New York NY 10013-3833

QUIST, JEANETTE FITZGERALD, television production educator, choreographer; b. Provo, Utah, July 4, 1948; d. Sherman Kirkham and Bula Janet (Anderson) Fitzgerald; m. G. Steven Quist; children: Ryan, Amy, Michelle, Jeremy. Student, U. Redlands, Calif., 1970; BA, Brigham Young U., 1971; postgrad., Calif. State U., Riverside, 1972, Calif. State U., San Bernardino, 1973. Host, co-producer children's show PBS Sta. KBYU-TV, Provo, 1968-69; buyer ready to wear J.C. Penney & Co., Redlands, 1969-71; tchr. spl. reading program Fontana (Calif.) Elem. Sch. Dist., 1971-73; owner, choreographer Jeanette Quist Creative Dance, Tri Cities, Wash., 1975-79; owner, tchr. Dance Studio, Gridley, Calif., 1979-81; producer, instr. Butte Coll., Oroville, Calif., 1986—; asst. producer Kate Knight Prodn. Co., Chico, Calif., 1987; video producer Gridley Sch. Dist., 1987-88. Prodr., editor promotional video Police Acad., 1986, commls. for Butte Coll., 1987—; prodr., dir. telecourse Interior Designer, 1988—; prodr., hostess TV talk shows Crossroads, 1988—, NVCA Today, BCTV Forum, 1991—; prodr. orientation video Butte Coll., 1989, 90, video series Intro to Telecommunications, video series on Recycling for Butte Environ. Coun., 1995, Early Alert video for Butte Coll., 1995, promotion video City of Chico, 1995, video Sports Events for Butte Coll., 1995—, video series on Small Bus. Devel. Ctr., 1996, video Work Tng. Ctr., 1996, Project Maestros, 1996; choreographer Kaleidoscope, 1988, South Pacific, 1989, Fantasticks, 1990, Amahl and the Night Visitors, 1990, An Evening of Song and Dance, Butte Coll., 1991, Kiss Me Kate, Butte Coll., 1992, Hello Dolly, Chico Stake, 1992; chmn. 3D Expo-Fine Arts Festival, 1991; prodr. 2 videos; choreographer Tumbleweeds, Butte Theatre, 1994. State judge Miss. Am. Contest, Provo, 1968; 1st v.p. Friends of Libr., Gridley, 1988; chmn. Regional Fine Arts Festival Tri Cities, 1978; v.p. Gridley High Sch. Parent Club, 1990; chmn. 3D Expo Fine Arts Festival for Oroville, Gridley, and Butte Coll., 1991. Recipient Acad. Excellence award Butte Coll., 1993-94; Mask club scholar Brigham Young U., 1967; Project Maestro grantee, 1994. Mem. AAUW (membership v.p. 1989—, com. for gender equity for Gridley br.), Butte County Arts Coun. (spl. com. 1986), Kaleidoscope Arts Coun., Am. Assn. Women in Community Jr. Colls. Republican., Ch. of Jesus Christ Latter-day Saints.

QUIVERS, ROBIN, radio personality; b. 1953; d. Charles and Louise Quivers. Student, U. Md. Radio personality WXRK-FM, N.Y.C. Co-author: Quivers, 1995. With USAF. Office: WXRK-FM 600 Madison Ave New York NY 10022-1615*

QURESHI, NILOFER, biochemist; b. Karachi, Pakistan, July 31, 1947; came to U.S., 1970; d. Ahmed Hussain A. and Ayesha Kazi; m. Asaf A. Qureshi, Nov. 26, 1970; 1 child, Arif A. BS, St. Joseph's Coll., Karachi, Pakistan, 1967; MS, Karachi U., 1969; PhD in Physiol. Chemistry, U. Wis., 1975. Sr. exec. ops. rsch. Sui Gas Transmission Co., Karachi, 1975-76; rsch. assoc. VA Hosp. and U. Wis., Madison, 1976-77, project assoc., 1977-81; rsch. biochemist VA Hosp., Madison, 1981—; adj. assoc. prof. dept. bacteriology U. Wis., 1993—. Contbr. over 85 articles to profl. jours. NIH grantee. Mem. Am. Soc. Biochemistry and Molecular Biology (congl. liaison com.), Internat. Endotoxin Soc. (charter mem.), Am. Soc. Microbiology, Am. Chem. Soc. Home: 8251 Raymond Rd Madison WI 53719-5045 Office: VA Hosp 2500 Overlook Ter Madison WI 53705-2254

QURESHI, SARAH Q., accountant; b. Pakistan, Dec. 4, 1969; came to U.S., 1970; d. Naeem and Afsar Qureshi. BBA, So. Meth. U., 1991; MBA, U. Tex., Dallas, 1993. CPA, Tex. Auditor Deloitte & Touche, Dallas, 1991-92; gen. ledger acct. First Equipment Co., Dallas, 1992-94; asst. contr. Colonial Casualty Ins., Dallas, 1994—; cons. in field, 1991—. Home: #3123 6528 Shady Brook Ln Dallas TX 75206 Office: Colonial Casualty Ins. #125 4230 LBJ Freeway Dallas TX 75244

RAABE, SUSAN E., lawyer; b. Euclid, Ohio, June 23, 1955. BA, Capital U., 1977; JD, Ohio State U., 1983. Bar: Ohio 1983. Ptnr. Arter & Hadden, Cleve. Mem. ABA, Nat. Health Lawyers Assn., Ohio State Bar Assn., Ohio Hosp. Assn., Cleve. Bar Assn. (health care law sect., health care law coun.), Tau Pi Phi, Kappa Alpha Pi, Phi Delta Phi. Office: Arter & Hadden 1100 Huntington Bldg 925 Euclid Ave Cleveland OH 44115-1475*

RAASH, KATHLEEN FORECKI, artist; b. Milw., Sept. 12, 1950; d. Harry and Marion Matilda (Schwabe) Forecki; m. Gary John Raash, June 13, 1987. BS, U. Wis., Eau Claire, 1972; MFA, U. Wis., Milw., 1978. One-, two- and three-person shows include Sight 225 Gallery, Milw., 1979, 81, Nicolet Coll., Phinelander, Wis., 1981, Messing Gallery, St. Louis, 1982, Arts Consortium, Cin., 1982, Ctr. Gallery, Madiwon, Wis., 1982, Otteson Theatre Gallery, Waukesha, Wis., 1982, Foster Gallery, Eau Claire, 1984, Duluth (Minn.) Art Inst., 1984, West Bend (Wis.) Gallery of Fine Arts, 1987, U. Wis.-Waukesha Fine Arts Gallery, 1988, Marion Art Gallery, Milw., 1990, Layton Honor Gallery, Milw., 1991, West Bend Art Mus., 1995, Gwenda Jay Gallery, Chgo., 1995, Wis. Acad., Madison, 1996; exhibited in group shows at River Edge Galleries, Wis., 1990, 91, 94, 95, Peltz Gallery, Milw., 1990, 91, 92, 93, 94, 95, Minnetonka Ctr. Arts, Wazata, Minn., 1996; represented in permanent collections United Bank and trust of Madison, Fine Arts Gallery U. Wis., Miller Brewing Co., Independence Bank Waukesha, U. Wis. Home and Studio: W 1630 Bear Trail Rd Gleason WI 54435

RABB, HARRIET SCHAFFER, lawyer, educator; b. Houston, Sept. 12, 1941; d. Samuel S. and Helen G. Schaffer; m. Bruce Rabb, Jan. 4, 1970; children: Alexander, Katherine. BA in Govt., Barnard Coll., 1963; JD, Columbia U., 1966. Bar: N.Y. 1966, U.S. Supreme Ct. 1969, D.C. 1970. Instr. seminar on constl. litigation Rutgers Law Sch., 1966-67; staff atty. Center for Constl. Rights, 1966-69; spl. counsel to commr. consumer affairs N.Y.C. Dept. Consumer Affairs, 1969-70; sr. staff atty. Stern Community Law Firm, Washington, 1970-71; asst. dean urban affairs Law Sch., Columbia U., N.Y.C., 1971-84, prof. law, dir. clin. edn., 1984—; George M. Jaffen prof. law and social responsibility Law Sch., Columbia U., 1991—, vice dean, 1992—; gen. counsel Dept. Health and Human Svcs., Washington, 1993—; mem. faculty employment and tng. policy Harvard Summer Inst., Cambridge, Mass., 1975-79. Author: (with Agid, Cooper and Rubin) Fair Employment Litigation Manual, 1975, (with Cooper and Rubin) Fair Employment Litigation, 1975. Bd. dirs. Ford Found., 1977-89, N.Y. Civil Liberties Union, 1972-83, Lawyers Com. for Civil Rights Under Law, 1978-86, Legal Def. Fund NAACP, 1978-93, Mex. Am. Legal Def. and Edn. Fund, 1986-90, Legal Aid Soc., 1990-93; mem. exec. com. Human Rights Watch, 1991-93; trustee Trinity Episcopal Sch. Corp., 1991-93. Office: Dept Health and Human Svcs 200 Independence Ave SW Rm 722A Washington DC 20201-0004

RABE, ELIZABETH ROZINA, hair stylist, horse breeder; b. Granby, Quebec, Canada, Sept. 28, 1953; d. John J. and Christina Maria (De Vaal) Gluck; m. Oct. 21, 1972 (div. 1981); children: Diana Marie Claire, Michelle Diane. Diploma in hairstyling, Art Inst. Film hairstylist Internat. Alliance Theatrical, Stage Employees and Moving Pictures Machine Operators Local 706, L.A., 1977-94. Recipient Design Patent hock support horse brace U.S. Design Patent Office, Washington, 1994. Home: 522 W Stocker St Apt 1 Glendale CA 91202-2299

RABE, LAURA MAE, mathematician, educator; b. Cin., May 28, 1945; d. Howard Lawrence and Alberta Catherine (Held) R. BS, U. Cin., 1967, MS, 1972, supr. cert., 1982. Tchr. Colerain H.S., Cin., 1967—, chairperson math. dept., 1980—; presenter grant writing workshop Miami U., Oxford, Ohio, 1994; pressenter in field. Named Hixon Tchr. of Yr., 1996; grantee GTE, 1994-95, NSF, 1980, Dartmouth Univ., 1995, 96. Mem. NEA, Nat. Coun. Tchrs. Math., Ohio Coun. Tchrs. Math., Greater Cin. Coun. Tchrs. Math. Roman Catholic. Office: Colerain HS 8801 Cheviot Rd Cincinnati OH 45251-5907

RABEN, NINA, molecular biologist, biochemist; b. Moscow, Russia, Jan. 13, 1945; came to the U.S., 1987; d. Anatoly S. and Liza M. (Vinogradsky) R.; m. Mark Belenky, Sept. 23, 1966; 1 child, Masha Belenky. MD, 1st Moscow (Russia) Med. Inst., 1967; PhD in Biochemistry, USSR Acad. Med. Sci., Moscow, 1973. Rschr. USSR Surgery Ctr., Moscow, 1968-73, sr. investigator, 1973-79; vis. assoc. Nat. Inst. of Diabetes, Digestive and Kidney Diseases, Bethesda, Md., 1987-90; vis. scientist Nat. Inst. of Arthritis and Musculoskeletal Diseases, Bethesda, 1990-94; rsch. chemist NIAMS, NIH, Bethesda, 1994—; translator of English lang. books and articles Moscow Pub., Houses Mags., 1968—. Contbr. articles to profl. jours.; patentee in field. Mem. AAAS. Jewish. Home: 5455 Grove Ridge Way Rockville MD 20852 Office: NIAMS NIH 9000 Rockville Pike Bethesda MD 20892

RABIDEAU, MARGARET CATHERINE, media center director; b. Chgo., Nov. 24, 1930; d. Nicholas and Mary Agnes (Burke) Oberle; m. Gerald Thomas Rabideau, Nov. 27, 1954; children: Mary, Margaret, Michelle, Gregory, Marsha, Grant. BA cum laude, U. Toledo, 1952, MA in Ednl. Media Tech., 1978. Cert. tchr. K-12 media tech., supr. ednl. media, tchr. English and journalism. Asst. dir. pub. rels. U. Toledo, 1952-55; publicity writer United Way, Toledo, 1974-75; tchr. Toledo Pub. Schs., 1975-80, libr., media specialist, 1980-90; dir. media svcs. Sylvania (Ohio) Schs., 1990—; task force to evaluate coll. programs Ohio Dept. Edn., 1987; on-site evaluation team, Hiram Coll., Ohio, 1991; north ctrl. evaluation team Northwestern Ohio, 1985—. Citizen task force Toledo/Lucas County Libr., Ohio, 1991, mem. friends of the libr., 1990—; task force Sta. WGTE-TV PBS Sta., Toledo, 1993; instr. U. Toledo, 1990. Mem. ALA, U. Toledo Alumni Assn., Ohio Ednl. Libr. Media Assn. (N.W. dir. 1993—, vocat. dir. 1985-89, Libr. Media Specialist of Yr. 1993), Am. Ednl. Comm. and Tech., Maumee Valley Computer Assn. (task force), Phi Delta Kappa (Outstanding Newsletter Nat. award 1990, pres. Toledo chpt.). Home: 1038 Olson St Toledo OH 43612-2828 Office: Sylvania Schs 6850 Monroe St Sylvania OH 43560-1922

RABII, PATRICIA BERG, church administrator; b. Lynn, Mass., Nov. 7, 1942; d. Clarence Oscar and Naomi Ruth (MacHugh) B.; m. S. Rabii, Oct. 26, 1966 (div. 1988); children: Susan M., Elizabeth L. AA, Green Mtn. Coll., Poultney, Vt., 1962; BA cum laude, U. Pa., 1978. Cons. City of Phila., 1981; fin. svcs. officer U. Pa., Phila., 1981-90; asst. to exec. dir. Psi Upsilon Found., Paoli, Pa., 1990-92; parish adminstr. St. David's (Radnor) Episcopal Ch., Wayne, Pa., 1992—; co-dir. career planning/pub. rels. Resources for Women, Phila., 1978-81. Counselor direct patient and care ARC, St. Louis, 1967-69; bd. dirs. Upper Merion PTA, 1976-78, Dental Clinic, King of Prussia, 1976-78; leader Girl Scouts U.S.A., King of Prussia, 1976-77, 80-81. Recipient ACT 101 Svc. award, Penn Cap, 1989. Mem. AAUW, U. Pa. Women's Club (bd. dirs. 1975-80, v.p. 1979-80). Home: 5 Drummers Ln Wayne PA 19087-1503 Office: St Davids Radnor Episcopal 763 Valley Forge Rd Wayne PA 19087-4724

RABINER, SUSAN, editor; b. Bklyn., May 5, 1948; d. Nathan M. and Gloria (Bodinger) R.; m. Alfred G. Fortunato, Mar. 27, 1974; children: Anna, Matthew. B.A. cum laude, Goucher Coll., 1969. Asst. editor Random House, N.Y.C., 1969-72; editor Oxford U. Press, N.Y.C., 1973-79, sr. editor, 1980-86; sr. editor St. Martin's Press, N.Y.C., 1986-87, Pantheon Books, N.Y.C., 1987-90; sr. editor Basic Books, Inc., N.Y.C., 1990—, editl. dir., 1995—, v.p., 1996—; vis. lectr. Yale U., New Haven, 1983, 84. Home: 1009 Brent Dr Wantagh NY 11793-1043 Office: Basic Books Inc 10 E 53rd St New York NY 10022-5244

RABINOVICH, RAQUEL, painter, sculptor; b. Buenos Aires, Argentina, Mar. 30, 1929; came to U.S., 1967, naturalized, 1973; d. Enrique Rabinovich and Julia Dinitz; m. Jose Luis Reissig, Feb. 14, 1956 (div. 1981); children—Celia Karen, Pedro Dario, Nora Vivian. Student U. Córdoba, Argentina, 1950-53, Sorbonne, Paris, 1957, U. Edinburgh, Scotland, 1958-59; lectr. Whitney Mus., 1983-86, Marymount Manhattan Coll., 1984-90. Exhbns. include Hecksher Mus., Huntington, N.Y., 1974, Susan Caldwell Gallery, N.Y.C., 1975, CUNY Grad. Ctr., 1978, The Jewish Mus. Sculpture Ct., N.Y.C., 1979, Ctr. Inter-Am. Rels., 1983, Bronx Mus. Arts, N.Y.C., 1986, Fordham U. Lincoln Ctr., N.Y.C., 1985, Ams. Soc., 1990, Erik Stark Gallery, 1991, Montgomery Ctr., 1992, Trans-Hudson Gallery, 1993, Noyes Mus., 1994, Nelson Atkins Mus. Art, 1995, Intar Gallery, N.Y.C., 1996, others; represented in collections World Bank Fine Art Collection, Washington, Univ. Art Mus., Austin, Cin. Art Mus., Walker Art Ctr., others. NEA fellow, 1991-92; grantee N.Y. State Coun. Arts, 1995—.

Avocations: travel, music. Home and Studio: 141 Lamoree Rd Rhinebeck NY 12572-3013

RABOLD, JEANETTE WADE, artist, researcher; b. Franklin, Ky., July 30, 1924; d. Avery and Chloe (James) Wade; m. Stanley Joseph Rabold; children: Alan L., J. Gregory, Mark B. Student, Art Students League, N.Y.C., 1969; BS in Art, Vanderbilt U., 1978, postgrad. in Art, 1978-79. Sub. tchr. Nashville Met. Schs., 1963-64; pvt. art tchr. Nashville, 1964-66, printmaker, photographer, 1966—. Exhibited in 10 one-woman shows; group juried shows include Brooks Mus. Art, Memphis, 1965, 75, 84, 86, 88, The Parthenon, Nashville, Cheekwood Mus. Art, Nashville (numerous awards) and other juried exhbns.; illustrator (stereo album) The Winner, 1965, (book cover) Prayer and Our Bodies, 1987; printmaking and figure drawing Internat. Miniature Exhbn., Clearwater, Fla., 1985, Madison, N.J., 1983; exhibitor, mem. Mus. Women in Arts, Washington, 1993. Activist Bringing Urban Recycling to Nashville Today, 1990-93, Against Landfill and Dumping on Native Am. Sacred Grounds, Nashville, 1991; activist, spkr. Oak Ridge Nuclear Protest, 1992; activist, mem. Sierra Club, 1980-96. Mem. Nashville Artist Guild (v.p. 1983-84, publicity dir. 1983-85, hospitality chmn. 1992-93), Inst. Noetic Scis., Tenn. Environ. Coun. Democrat. Home: 248 Cargile Ln Nashville TN 37205

RABSON, ANN, musician, songwriter; b. N.Y.C., Apr. 12, 1945; d. Gustave and Alice (Brand) R.; m. James Aaron Morford, 1965 (div.); 1 child, Elizabeth; m. George Lindsay Newman, July 5, 1981. Grad. high sch., Yellow Springs, Ohio. Solo guitar player, vocalist, 1962-82; piano and guitar player, vocalist with Saffire-The Uppity Blues Women, also others, 1982—; tchr. Augusta Heritage Workshops, Elkins, W.Va., 1987—. Albums include (with Queen Bee and The Blue Hornet Band) Dealin' the Blues, Harder Than a Freight Train, (with SAFFIRE-The Uppity Blues Women) Middle Aged Blues, SAFFIRE-The Uppity Blues Women, Hot Flash, Broadcasting, Old New Borrowed and Blue, (with Skeeter Brandon) High Test Blues, (with Deborah Coleman) Takin' A Stand, (with Ani De Franco) Puddle Dive, (with Niles Hokkanen) On Fire and Ready, (with Carla Sciaky) Awakening, (with Noble "Thin Man" Watts) King of the Boggie Sax. Home and Office: PO Box 167 Hartwood VA 22471

RABUCK, DONNA FONTANAROSE, English educator; b. Edison, N.J., Aug. 2, 1954; d. Arthur Thomas and Shirley Gertrude (Golub) Fontanarose; m. John Frederick Rabuck, July, 28, 1973; 1 child, Miranda Rose. BA in Eng., Rutgers U., 1976, MA in Eng. Lit., 1980, PhD in Eng. Lit., 1990. Prof. writing Pima C. C., Tucson, 1981-86; asst. dir. writing skills program U. Ariz., Tucson, 1983—; asst. dir. summer inst. writing U. Ariz., Tucson, 1985—; adj. faculty Pima C. C., Tucson, 1992-95. Author: The Other Side of Silence: Performing Heroinism in the Victorian Novel, 1990, Writing Ctr. Perspectives, 1995; editor: Writing is Thinking: Collected Writings of the Summer Inst., 1985—. Founder, pres. Miles East-West Neighborhood Assn., Tucson, 1983—; dir. Ctr. for Sacred Feminine, Tucson, 1995—; program coord. U. Ariz. Arts and Scis. Minority Retention Program, 1988-93. Rutgers Alumni scholar, 1972-76; Bevier fellow Rutgers U., 1976-78. Mem. Intercollegiate Writing Com. (task force), Commn. Cultural Thinking (task force), Nat. Coun. Tchrs. Eng. Home: 345 S Cherry Ave Tucson AZ 85719 Office: Univ Ariz Writing Skills Program 1201 E Helen St Tucson AZ 85719

RABUSKA, MICHÈLE JOANNE, financial analyst; b. Waterbury, Conn., Dec. 6, 1963; d. Peter Constantine and Joan Elfreida (Bergstrom) R. BA in Govt., Wesleyan U., 1995; postgrad., Trinity Coll., Hartford, Conn., 1995—. With bus. office St. Francis Hosp. and Med. Ctr., Hartford, Conn., 1990-93; customer rels. specialist St. Francis Hosp. and Med. Ctr., Hartford, 1993-96; fin. analyst VSM & Co., P.C., Farmington, Conn., 1996—; adminstrv. support, personal computer trainer, cons. The 1000 Corp., Hartford, 1993-94; cons. St. Francis Hosp. Profl. Svcs., 1995. Election pollwatcher Hartford Courant newspaper, 1992—; mem. Pub. Concern Found., Washington, 1993-94, Amnesty Internat., 1989—. Grantee State of Conn., 1993, 94; scholar Wesleyan U., 1993, 94, Etherington scholar Wesleyan U., 1993, 94. Mem. St. Francis Hosp. Women's Aux., We Adopt Greyhounds, Phi Theta Kappa, Alpha Zeta Psi. Democrat. Russian Orthodox. Home: 47-C Congress St Hartford CT 06114-1025 Office: VSM & Co., P.C. 231 Farmington Ave Farmington CT 06032-1922

RACHAL, DONNA KATHLEEN, elementary education educator; b. Wichita Falls, Tex., Oct. 5, 1961; d. John Robert and Donna Eileen (Flinn) Fraser m. Woody Wilson Rachal, Nov. 17, 1990; 1 child. BS, Centenary Coll. of La., 1983, MEd, 1988; postgrad., Centenary & La. State U., 1991. Cert. elem. tchr., La. Kindergarten tchr. Caddo Parish Schs., Shreveport, La., 1983-88, tchr. 4th grade, 1988—; reading specialist The Reading Ctr. Inc., Shreveport, 1988-92. Mem., edn. com. Broadmoor Presbyn. Ch., Shreveport, 1988. Caddo Pub. Edn. Found., grantee, 1994. Mem. Internat. Reading Assn., N.W. Reading Coun., La. Reading Assn., Phi Delta Kappa. Home: 185 Stuart Ave Shreveport LA 71105-3529

RACINE, LINDA JEAN, college health nurse; b. Chester, Pa., Dec. 8, 1948; d. Charles D. and Marion E. (Clark) Malloy; m. Eugene F. Racine, Oct. 19, 1968; children: Valerie, Danielle. A in Applied Sci., Delaware County C.C., Marple, Pa., 1971. RN; cert. coll. health nurse, Pa. Coll. health nurse Lincoln U., Pa. Mem. Am. Coll. Health Assn (mid-Atlantic chpt.), Md. Coll. Health Nurses Assn., Southeastern Pa. Coll. Health Nurses Assn. (v.p. 1994, pres.). Lutheran. Office: Lincoln Univ Lincoln University PA 19352

RACLE, LORRAINE LOUISE, secondary education educator; b. Buffalo, June 16, 1946; d. Elliott Irving and Angelita Marina (Castillo) Jaquays; m. Robert Michael Racle, Aug. 23, 1969; 1 child, Karen Louise. BS in Edn., SUNY, Buffalo, 1968, MS in Secondary Edn., 1973. Social studies tchr. North Tonawanda (N.Y.) City Sch. Dist., 1968-94, gifted programming tchr., 1994—. Mem., past sec. North Tonawanda United Tchrs., 1968; mem. Variety Club Tent # 7, Buffalo, 1994—. Mem. ASCD, AAUW, N.Y. State Mid. Schs. Assn. (conf. com. 1991), North Tonawanda Staff Devel. Team. Republican. Roman Catholic. Home: 84 Wendover Ave Buffalo NY 14223 Office: North Tonawanda City Sch 175 Humphrey St North Tonawanda NY 14120

RADABAUGH, MICHELE JO, sales executive; b. Ashland, Ohio, May 1, 1961; d. James L. and Natalie J. (Barnhart) Sonnett; m. Brett L. Radabaugh, Sept. 22, 1990; 1 child, Natalie M. Assoc. in Advt., Northwood Inst., 1983, BA, 1984. Xerox operator Nolan, Norton, Inc., Lexington, Mass., 1984-85; instr. Stautzenberger Coll., Findlay, Ohio, 1986-88; acad. coord. Stautzenberger Coll., Findlay, 1988-90, acad. dean, 1990-93; sales rep. Glencoe divsn. McGraw-Hill, 1993—. With USN, 1986. Recipient Golden Eagle award, 1994, 95, 96; named Outstanding Educator, C. of C., Findlay, 1988. Mem. Nat. Bus. Edn. Assn. Republican. Office: 1701 Wendell Ave Lima OH 45805-3158

RADCLIFF, MELINDA SUE, language arts teacher; b. Weston, W.Va., Jan. 16, 1972; d. Herbert Gary and Iela Grace (Beall) R. BEd, Glenville State Coll., 1995. Fin. adi asst. Glenville (W.Va.) State Coll., 1991-94. pvt. tutor Glenville, 1991, 93. Sec. Gilmer County FFA Alumni, Glenville, 1995-97; project leader Cox's Mill Tailtwisters 4-H Club, W.Va., 1994-95; mem. Mt. Earnest United Meth. Ch., Conings, W.Va., 1994-95. Am. FFA Degree, Nat. FFA Orgn., Kansas City, Mo., 1993. Mem. Kappa Delta Pi. Democrat. Home: Rt 1 Box 132 New Milton WV 26411

RADER, DIANE CECILE, lawyer; b. San Francisco, Sept. 8, 1949; d. Dale A. and Genevieve A. (Couture) R. BA, Portland State U., 1987; JD, Lewis and Clark Coll., 1990. Bar: Oreg. 1990, Idaho 1992, U.S. Dist. Ct. Idaho, U.S. Dist. Ct. Oreg. Founder, cons. D.C. Rader & Assocs., Portland, 1972-88; real estate broker Rader Realty, Portland, 1982—; pvt. practice law Boise, 1992—; with Rader and Rader, Ontario, Oreg., 1990—; bd. dirs. Criminal Justice Adv. Bd., Malheur County, Oreg. Asst. mng. editor: Internat. Legal Perspectives, 1989-90. Polit. cons. and fundraiser various parties and campaigns, Oreg., 1972-88; fundraiser, cons. charitable orgns., Oreg., 1972—, others. Mem. ABA, ATLA, Nat. Assn. Criminal Def. Lawyers, Oreg. Trial Lawyers Assn., Oreg. Criminal Def. Lawyers Assn., Oreg. State Bar (pub. svc. and info. com. 1994-97, chmn. pub. rels. subcom. 1994—), Phi Alpha Delta. Office: Rader & Rader 381 W Idaho Ontario OR 97914

RADER, ELLA JANE See **ASHLEY, ELLA JANE**

RADER, HANNELORE, library director, consultant; b. Berlin, Germany, Dec. 19, 1937; d. Henry H. and Talia E. (Tramontin) Busch; widowed; 1 child, Ingrid M. BA in Russian, U. Mich., 1960, MA in Libr. Sci., 1968, MA in German Lit., 1971; Degree in Ednl. Leadership, Eastern Mich. U., 1978. Children's librarian Washington D.C. Pub. Libr., 1960-62; asst. humanities librarian Eastern Mich. U., Ypsilanti, 1968-70, orientation librarian, 1970-76, coord. edn., psychology div., 1976-80; libr. dir. learning ctr. U. Wis.-Parkside, Kenosha, 1980-87; dir. univ. libr. Cleve. State U., 1987—; evaluator, libr. instr. Ball State U., Muncie, Ind., 1983; evaluator for self study Calif. State U.-L.A. Libr., 1989, CCNY Libr., 1989. Contbr. articles to numerous jours. Recipient Walter H. Kaiser award Mich. Libr. assn., 1977, Disting. Alumnus award U. Mich. Libr. Sch., 1984; fellow Coun. Libr. Resources, 1975-76; USIA and West German Libr. grantee, 1987, Disting. Edn. and Behavioral Scis. Libr. award ACRL/EBSS, 1995. Mem. ALA (mem. coun. 1980-84, 84-92, 92—), AAUW (pres. Cleve. chpt. 1993-95, Edn. Found. honoree 1994), Assn. Coll. and Rsch. Librs. (pres., bd. dirs. 1985-88, Miriam Dudley Libr. Instrn. award 1993, Disting. Edn. and Behavioral Scis. Libr. award 1995), Spl. Libr. Assn., Ohio Libr. Assn., Rotary. Office: Cleve State U Libr 1860 E 22nd St Cleveland OH 44114-4435

RADER, TINA LOUISE, pathology technologist; b. Allentown, Pa., Apr. 9, 1959; d. Marlin Robert and Gioconda Maria (Alpago) R. BS in Med. Tech., Bloomsburg U., 1981; M Health Sci., Quinnipiac Coll., 1987. Med. technologist Lehigh Valley Hosp. Ctr., Allentown, Pa., 1981-84, Brigham & Womens Hosp., Boston, 1984-85; pathologists' asst. Dartmouth-Hitchcock Med. Ctr., Lebanon, N.H., 1987-89, New Eng. Med. Ctr., Boston, 1989-91, R.I. Hosp., Providence, 1991-94, Fox Chase Cancer Ctr., Phila., 1994—. Fellow Am. Assn. Pathologists' Assts. (edn. com. chairperson 1990-96, v.p. 1996—). Office: Fox Chase Cancer Ctr Dept Pathology 7701 Burholme Ave Philadelphia PA 19111-2412

RADFORD, DEBORAH BYRD, newspaper editor; b. Marietta, Ga., Sept. 13, 1952; d. Luther McCrary and Olive Lorraine (Tisdale) Byrd; m. George Davis Radford Jr., Nov. 25, 1972. BA in English, Tift Coll., Forsyth, Ga., 1975. Lifestyles editor The Beaufort (S.C.) Gazette, 1975—. Body double for Sharon Stone in Last Dance. Recipient 2d place award for page design, S.C. Press Assn., 1990, 1st place for best Gulf War human interest story, 1991, 2d place column, 1995. Methodist. Home: 2427 Pigeon Point Rd Beaufort SC 29902 Office: The Beaufort Gazette 1556 Salem Rd Beaufort SC 29902

RADFORD, DIANE MARY, surgeon, surgical oncologist; b. Irvine, Ayrshire, Scotland, Nov. 14, 1957; came to U.S., 1985; d. Sidney and Mary Margery (Parr) R. BSc with honors, Glasgow U., Scotland, 1978, MBChB, 1981; MD, Glasgow U., 1991. Jr. house officer Gartravel Gen. Hosp., Glasgow, 1981-82, Monklands Dist. Gen. Hosp., Airdrie, Scotland, 1982; sr. house officer Western Infirmary, Glasgow, 1982-83, Royal Infirmary, Edinburgh, Scotland, 1983-84; registrar Crosshouse Hosp., Kilmarnock, Scotland, 1984-85; fellow in surg. oncology Roswell Park Meml. Inst., Buffalo, 1985-87; resident in surg. St. Louis U. Hosp., 1987-91; instr. in surgery Wash. U., St. Louis, 1991-92; asst. prof. surgery Washington U., St. Louis, 1992-96; mem. Parkcrest Surg. Assocs., St. Louis, 1996—. Contbr. articles to profl. jours. Recipient 1st prize residents competition Mo. chpt. ACS, 1989. Fellow Am. Coll. Surgeons (bd. cert. gen. surgery), Royal Coll. Surgeons (Edinburgh); mem. Brit. Assn. Surg. Oncology, Am. Assn. Cancer Rsch., Assn. Acad. Surgery, Mo. State Med. Assn., Mo. Acad. Sci., St. Louis Met. Med. Soc., Roswell Pk. Surg. Soc. Office: 675 Old Ballas Rd Saint Louis MO 63141

RADFORD, MARTHA JO, physician, educator; b. Boston, June 21, 1948; d. Edward Parish and Nettie (Garrison) R.; m. Louis George Graff IV, May 10, 1980; children: Louis George Graff V, Alice Elizabeth Graff. BS, U. Calif., Berkeley, 1970, MA, 1973; MD, Harvard U., 1978. Resident in internal medicine Brigham and Women's Hosp., Boston, 1978-81; fellow in cardiovascular disease Duke U. Med. Ctr., Durham, N.C., 1981-84; asst. prof. medicine U. Conn., Farmington, 1984-93, assoc. prof. medicine, 1993—; cons. Conn. Peer Rev. Orgn., Middletown, 1993—. Fellow Am. Coll. Cardiology. Office: U Conn Health Ctr 263 Farmington Ave Farmington CT 06030-1305

RADICE, ANNE-IMELDA, museum director; b. Buffalo, Feb. 29, 1948; d. Lawrence and Anne (Marino) R. AB, Wheaton Coll., 1969; MA, Villa SchiFanoia, Florence, Italy, 1971; PhD, U. N.C., 1976; MBA, Am. U., 1984. Asst. curator Nat. Gallery of Art, Washington, 1972-76; archtl. historian U.S. Capitol, Washington, 1976-80, curator Office of Architect, 1980-85; dir. Nat. Mus. Women in the Arts, 1985-89; chief div. of creative arts USIA, 1989-91; sr. dep. chmn. Nat. Endowment for Arts, Washington, 1991-92; acting chmn., 1992-93; exec. v.p. Gray & Co. II, Miami, Fla., 1993; prodr. World Affairs TV Prodn., 1994; assoc. producer Think Tank, 1994; chief spl. projects, confidential adviser Courtney Sale Ross, 1994-96; v.p., COO ICL Internat., 1996—; cons. in pub. rels. and TV, 1994—. Contbr. articles to profl. jours.

RADICE, SHIRLEY ROSALIND, education educator; b. Newark, June 2, 1935; d. Gerald Alexander and Pauline Deborah (Baitz) Deitz; m. Richard Charles Radice, Dec. 17, 1955; children: Carol, Richard Neil. BA, Kean Coll., Union, N.J., 1960, MA, 1963; EdD, Rutgers U., 1985. Tchr. Edison (N.J.) Bd. Edn., 1960-64, 70—, trainer, 1990—; instr. grad. sch. edn. Rutgers U., 1992—; mem. grant com. N.J. Dept. Higher Edn., 1988-90; lectr. Rutgers U., 1989—, instr. in edn., 1992—; staff devel. specialist Edison, 1994—; ednl. cons. in field; presenter Rutgers U. Ann. Reading Conf., 1996. Contbr. articles to profl. jours. Recipient N.J. Gov.'s Recognition award for outstanding contbn. to edn., 1991; grantee Ford Found., 1966, State of N.J., 1973, NSF/Smithsonian Inst., 1995. Mem. AAUP, ASCD, Nat. Assn. Sci. Tchrs., N.J. Sci. Tchrs. Assn., Nat. Assn. Math. Tchrs., Nat. Tchrs. Assn. (del. 1980-87), N.J. Tchrs. Assn., Edison Tchrs. Assn. (co-chmn. legis. com. 1975-76), Kappa Delta Phi.

RADIN, CECILE HOROWITZ, artist; b. Worcester, Mass., June 10, 1904; d. Jacob and Jeanne (Bloch) Horowitz; m. Morris J. Radin, Apr. 10, 1932; children: Harley, Robert. Student, Worcester Art Mus., 1922-23, Boston Mus. Sch. Fine Arts, 1923-27. One-woman show U. Hartford (Conn.) Lincoln Theater, 1994; exhibited in group shows Wadsworth Atheneum, Hartford,1930, Conn. Acad. Fine Arts, Hartford, 1931, Grand Central Galleries, N.Y.C., 1931, Ind. Artists Boston, 1931, Worcester Mus. Fine Arts, 1933, New Britain (Conn.) Mus., 1962 (portrait prize), West Hartford Art League, 1972, 75, Essex (Conn.) Art Assn. Gallery, 1976, John Slade Mus., New Haven, 1977, Slater Meml. Mus., Norwich, Conn., 1979, 83, Temple Beth-El, West Hartford, 1984, Conn. Art Festival, Hartford, Northwestern C.C., Winsted, Atria Gallery, Hartford, 1987. Mem. Conn. Acad. Fine Arts, Women in Art (charter), West Hartford Art League. Home and Studio: 781 Farmington Ave West Hartford CT 06119

RADKE, MARGARET HOFFMAN, retired secondary school educator; b. Rochester, Minn., Nov. 22, 1923; d. Roy John and Lucille Hoffman; m. Frederick H. Radke, Sept. 4, 1946 (dec. Nov. 1977); children: Kathryn, Frederick R., Lori Radke Bessette, Eileen Radke Nokes, Sharon E. BS summa cum laude, Hamline U., 1945; MA in Zoology, U. Calif., Berkeley, 1947; postgrad., U. Maine, 1964-67. Technician bacteriology lab. Mayo Clinic, Rochester, 1943, 44; teaching asst. in zoology U. Calif., 1945-46; instr. chemistry and microbiology Hamline U., St. Paul, 1946-47, 48; instr. zoology Iowa State U., Ames, 1947-49; pvt. techr. piano, voice and clarinet, Orono, Maine, 1960-74; tchr. sci. Old Town (Maine) High Sch., 1968-70; tchr. sci. Bangor (Maine) Sch. System, 1970-88, head dept., 1979-86; ret., 1988; instr., biochemistry U. Maine, Orono, 1964-66, technician zoology, summer 1967; asst. music dir. Penobscot Valley Children's Theater, Orono. Author: (poems) Soul Love, 1969. Condr. children's choir United Meth. Ch., Orono, 1964-78; mem. oratoria U. Maine, 1953—, donated Hudson Mus., 1992—; bd. dirs. Maine Noetic Studies, 1993-95. New sci. wing dedicated in her honor Bangor High Sch., 1988. Mem. AAUW, NEA, Nat. Sci. Tchrs. Assn., Maine Sci. Tchrs. Assn., Maine Tchrs. Assn., New Eng. Assn. Chemistry Tchrs., Order Eastern Star (soloist 1964-67), Alpha Delta Kappa (coms.). Republican. Methodist. Home: 17 Mainwood Ave Orono ME 04473-1326

RADKOWSKY, KAREN, advertising/marketing research executive; b. Washington, Nov. 8, 1957; d. Alvin and Florence (Kramer) R. BA, Columbia U., 1979. Rsch. analyst Cosmair, Inc., N.Y.C., 1979-82, sr. rsch. analyst, 1982-84; asst. rsch. mgr. Am. Express Co., N.Y.C., 1984-85; account rsch. mgr. BBDO, Inc., N.Y.C., 1985-88, v.p., assoc. rsch. dir., 1988-94, sr. v.p., assoc. rsch. dir., 1994-95; sr. v.p., rsch. dir. BBDO N.Y., N.Y.C., 1995—.

RADLEY, VIRGINIA LOUISE, humanities educator; b. Marion, N.Y., Aug. 12, 1927; d. Howard James and Lula (Ferris) R. B.A., Russell Sage Coll., 1949, L.H.D., 1981; M.A., U. Rochester, 1952; M.S., Syracuse U., 1957, Ph.D., 1958. Instr. English Chatham (Va.) Hall, 1952-55; asst. dean students, asst. prof. English Goucher Coll., 1957-59; dean freshmen, asst. prof. English Russell Sage Coll., 1959-60, assoc. dean, assoc. prof. English, 1960-61, prof. chmn. dept., 1961-69; dean coll., prof. English Nazareth Coll., Rochester, N.Y., 1969-73; provost for undergrad. edn., central adminstrn. SUNY, Albany, 1973-74; exec. v.p., provost Coll. Arts and Scis., SUNY, Oswego, 1974-76; acting pres. Coll. Arts and Scis., SUNY, 1976-78; pres. SUNY, Oswego, 1978-88; prof. English and Humanities SUNY, 1988-93; scholar-in-residence Russell Sage Coll., 1993—; vis. prof. Syracuse U., summer 1957-59, Nazareth Coll., summer 1965; cons. N.Y. State Dept. Edn.; chmn. commn. on women Am. Coun. on Edn., 1978-81, sr. assoc. Office of Women, 1990—; trustee Marymount Manhattan Coll., 1988-90; mem. commn. on higher edn. Middle States Assn., 1979-86; disting vis. prof. Russell Sage Coll., 1994-95. Author: Samuel Taylor Coleridge, 1966, Elizabeth Barrett Browning, 1972, also articles. Mem. MLA (chmn. regional sect. Romanticism 1969), English Inst., Pi Lambda Theta. Republican. Home: 75 Plank Rd Poestenkill NY 12140-1706

RADNOFSKY, BARBARA A., lawyer, mediator/arbitrator; b. Broomall, Pa., July 8, 1956; m. Daniel Edward Supkis Jr.; children: Danielle Esther, Max David, Michaela Sarah. BA magna cum laude, U. Houston, 1976; JD with honors, U. Tex., 1979. Bar: Tex. Assoc. Vinson & Elkins, L.L.P., Houston, 1979-87, ptnr., 1987—; mem. faculty intensive trial advocacy programs U. Tex. Sch. Law, Internat. Acad. Trial Lawyers; spkr. in field; mediator/arbitrator in field; mem. Disting. Panel of Neutrals of Ctr. for Pub. Resources. Contbr. articles to profl. jours. Albert Jones scholar U. Tex. Sch. Law; named Outstanding Young Lawyer Houston, Houston Young Lawyers Assn., 1988-89. Mem. ABA (chmn. Nat. Trial Competition 1983), Tex. Young Lawyers Assn. (Outstanding Young Lawyer Tex. 1988-89), Nat. Health Lawyers Assn. Office: Vinson & Elkins 3300 First City Tower 1001 Fannin St Houston TX 77002

RADO, KIM MARIE, elementary school educator; b. Akron, Ohio, Apr. 3, 1963; d. Norman Lance and Sandra Jean (Fenwick) R. BS in Edn., U. Akron, 1985, MS in Edn., 1990; postgrad., Baldwin-Wallace Coll., 1995. Cert. tchr., Ohio. Tchr. Akron Parochial Schs., 1985-88, Bedford (Ohio) Pub. Schs., 1988—; stratetic planning-environ. com. Bedford City Schs., 1992, sci. coord., 1993—. Tchr. rep. Aurora Sch. PTA, Bedford, 1994; mem. bldg. leadership team, 1995-96. Recipient Tchr. at Sea award NOAA, 1993, Field Geology Rsch. award Miami U., Ohio, 1992. Mem. Sci. Edn. Coun. Ohio, Ohio Edn. Assn., Bedford Edn. Assn., Alpha Delta Kappa. Democrat. Home: 2819 Vincent St Cuyahoga Falls OH 44221-1910

RADO HARTE, AVA LIVIA, artist; b. Budapest, Hungary, Feb. 1, 1941; came to U.S., 1956; d. Rado Istvan. Visual artist, arts adminstr. Art World, N.Y.C.; owner Rado Gallery, Miami, Fla., 1991—; founder, exec. dir. Ctr. for Emerging Art. One-woman shows at One Stop Art, N.Y.C., East Village, N.Y.C., Nonson Gallery, N.Y.C., SoHo Gallery, N.Y.C., Herald Sq., N.Y.C., Little Carnegie Art Gallery, N.Y.C., Global Art Gallery, Brisbane, Australia; exhibited in group shows at Fourth All-Florida Biennial, 1993. Mem. Juvenile Justice Com., 1991—, Environ. Working Group. Winner Design for Wynwood Project Competition, City of Miami Devel. Office. Office: The Rado Gallery 800 West Ave Miami FL 33139-5542

RADOJCSICS, ANNE PARSONS, librarian; b. Mansfield, Ohio, Mar. 23, 1929; d. Richard Walbridge Parsons and Iva Pearl (Ruth) Kemp; m. Joseph Michael Radojcsics, July 8, 1950; children: Kurt Joseph, Jo Anne Radojcsics Kent. Diploma, Bethel Woman's Coll., Hopkinsville, Ky., 1949; BS, Miss. State U., 1972, MEd, 1974. Cert. secondary tchr., Miss. Chemist Humphries Borg-Warner Co., Mansfield, 1950-53; asst. reference libr. Mansfield Pub. Libr., 1953-59; libr. media specialist Verona (Miss.) Sch., 1970-92, supr. Verona computer lab., 1985-92; libr. media specialist Pierce St. Elem. Sch., Miss., 1992-95; ret., 1995; libr. Saints Libr., Miss., 1995—; supr. libr. Guntown (Miss.) Sch., 1988-90, Shannon (Miss.) Sch., 1988-92; chmn. assessment project Miss. Libr.-Miss. Dept. Edn., Jackson, 1986-92; coord. region I Miss. Conf. on Libr. and Info. Svc., 1990; mem. Miss. Edn. TV Adv. Coun., 1985—; cons. content instrnl. prodn.-libr. rsch. skills Miss. Ednl. Tv., 1995. Author: Clay Tablets to Media Centers: Library Development from Ancient to Modern Times, 1975; (tchr. guide) Media Mania, 1996 Mississippi Educational TV. Bd. dirs., past pres. SAFE, Inc., Tupelo, Miss., 1978-92, bd. dirs. emeritus, 1992—; mem. Lee County Adult Lit. Task Force, Tupelo, 1987-90; sch. chmn. Target Tupelo, 1981-85. Recipient Ed Ransdell Instructional TV award, 1991. Mem. AECT, DSMS, AAUW (pres. Tupelo chpt. 1977-81, 1993—, Miss. divsn. 1984-86)), Miss. Profl. Educators, Mississippians for Ednl. Broadcasting, Miss. Ednl. Computer Assn., Miss. Libr. Assn. (project chmn. com. on sch. librs. 1989, awards chmn. 1987-88, ednl. comml. and tech. roundtable chair 1993), Miss. Profl. Educators Tupelo/Lee County (treas. 1993-95, pres. 1995—), Apple Computer User Group (co-organizer). Democrat. Episcopalian. Home: Carr Vista 105 Michael St Tupelo MS 38801-8608

RADTKE, KAREN DOROTHY, school nurse; b. Chgo., Jan. 16, 1951; d. John Mansfield and Dorothy Lena (Kleinau) Byrne; m. Richard F. Radtke, Nov. 18, 1978; children: Erin, Gretchen, R. Eric. BSN, Pacific Luth. U., 1974, AA, Tacoma C.C., 1976; Ma in Human Resource Devel., Redlands U., 1986. RN, Calif.; cert. health svcs., San Diego State U. Patient care liaison St. Josephs Hosp., Tacoma, Wash., 1975-77; educator, interim dir. Mark E. Reed Meml. Hosp., Tacoma, Wash., 1977-78; clin. dir. Home Health Svcs., San Bernardino, Calif., 1979-80; head nurse, orthopaedics Riverside (Calif.) Cmty. Hosp., 1980-85, educator, 1985-89; sch. nurse Riverside County Office Edn., 1989—; adminstrv. liaison Riverside Cmty. Hosp., 1990—. Named Outstanding Achievement Parent Tchr. Assn., Riverside, 1990. Mem. Nat. Assn. Sch. Nurses, Calif. Sch. Nurse Assn. (spl. edn. rep. 1993, mktg. chmn. 1995). Office: Riverside County Office Edn 3939 13th St Riverside CA 92501-3505

RADYCKI, DIANE JOSEPHINE, art historian, writer; b. Chgo., Dec. 4, 1946; d. Casimir Constantine and Sophie Jeanette (Wilczynski) R. BA, U. Ill., 1969; MA, Hunter Coll., 1975; MA, Harvard U., 1983, PhD, 1993. Rsch. assoc. Met. Mus. Art, N.Y.C., 1980-81; tchg. fellow Harvard U., Cambridge, Mass., 1984-92; intern Busch-Reisinger Mus., Cambridge, 1984-85; guest-curator Fogg Mus., Cambridge, 1983, 87, 88; instr. U. Houston, 1992-93, asst. prof., 1993-96. Transl. editor: Letters and Journals of Paula Modersohn-Becker, 1980. Agnes Mongan fellow, 1982-84, Fulbright fellow, 1989-91, AAUW fellow, 1991. Mem. Coll. Art Assn. Office: U Houston Dept Of Art Houston TX 77204

RAEBEL-HEWSON, CATHRYN SUE, secondary education educator, mathematician; b. Yuma, Ariz., Aug. 5, 1964; d. Martin G. and Janice K. (Shipp) Raebel; m. Daniel Todd Hewson, Apr. 9, 1994. BS in Edn., No. Ariz. U., 1987; MA, Calif. Luth. U., 1995. Tchr. math., asst. swim/diving coach, asst. gymnastics coach Kofa H.S., Yuma, Ariz., 1988-89; tchr. math. Anacapa Mid. Sch., Ventura, Calif., 1989-90, Camarillo (Calif.) H.S., 1990-91, Moorpark (Calif.) H.S., 1991-92; tchr. math., diving coach Rio Mesa H.S., Oxnard, Calif., 1992—. Mem. Internat. Soc. Tech. Edn., Am. Fedn. Tchrs., Nat. Coun. Tchrs. Math., No. Ariz. Univ. Alumni Assn., Ventura County Math. Coun., Rio Mesa H.S. Vanguard and Tech Prep. Com.

RAEBURN, NICOLE C., sociologist; b. Warren, Ohio, June 18, 1967; d. Duane F. and Mary G. (Girard) R.; life ptnr. Kerri Jo Griffin. BS, Miami U., 1989; MA, Ohio State U., 1992, PhD, 1997. Elem. educator Lakewood

(Ohio) City Schs., 1989-90; grad. tchg. assoc. Ohio State U., Columbus, 1990—. Mem. Am. Sociol. Assn., North Ctrl. Sociol. Assn., Soc. for Study of Social Problems, Sociologists for Women in Soc., Sociologists' Lesbian and Gay Caucus, Phi Kappa Phi, Kappa Delta Pi. Office: Ohio State U 300 Bricker Hall Columbus OH 43210

RAEBURN, SUSAN DELANEY, clinical psychologist; b. N.Y.C., Dec. 1, 1950; d. Boyd Raeburn and Ginnie Powell; m. William Phillip Delaney, May 25, 1991. BA in Psychology, UCLA, 1972; MA in Rsch. Psychology, San Francisco State U., 1974; PhD in Social-Clin. Psychology, The Wright Inst., 1984. Lic. psychologist, Calif. Asst. faculty San Francisco State U., 1973-74; evaluation specialist Model Cities Agy., Office of Mayor, San Francisco, 1975-76; spl. studies coord. Alameda County Health Care Scis. Agy., Oakland, Calif., 1977-78; pub. health planner Alameda County Health Care Svcs. Agy., Oakland, 1980-87; staff psychologist Behavioral Medicine Clinic Dept. Psychiatry Stanford U. Med. Ctr., 1986-92; clin. psychologist pvt. practice Berkeley, Calif., 1987—; clin. assoc. U. Calif., San Francisco, Health Program for Performance Artists, 1988—; psychologist Kaiser Permanente, 1992—. Contbr. articles to profl. jours. Mem. NOW, 1991—, Amnesty Internat., 1991—. Named Calif. State scholar, 1968-72. Mem. APA, Calif. Psychol. Assn., Alameda County Psychol. Assn., Performing Arts Medicine Assn. Democrat. Office: 2576 Shattuck Ave Berkeley CA 94704-2724

RAEDER, MYRNA SHARON, lawyer, educator; b. N.Y.C., Feb. 4, 1947; d. Samuel and Estelle (Auslander) R.; m. Terry Oliver Kelly, July 13, 1975; children: Thomas Oliver, Michael Lawrence. BA, Hunter Coll., 1968; JD, NYU, 1971; LLM, Georgetown U., 1975. Bar: N.Y. 1972, D.C. 1972, Calif. 1972. Spl. asst. U.S. atty. U.S. Atty.'s Office, Washington, 1972-73; asst. prof. U. San Francisco Sch. Law, 1973-75; assoc. O'Melveny & Myers, L.A., 1975-79; assoc. prof. Southwestern U. Sch. Law, L.A., 1979-82, prof., 1983—, Irwin R. Buchalter prof. law, 1990; mem. faculty Nat. Judicial Coll., 1993—; advisor drafting com. to revise uniform rules of evidence Nat. Conf. Commrs. on Uniform State Laws, 1996. Prettyman fellow Georgetown Law Ctr., Washington, 1971-73. Author: Federal Pretrial Practice, 2d edit., 1995, ALI, 1989. Fellow Am. Bar Found.; mem. ABA (chmn. com. on fed. rules and criminal procedure criminal justice sect. 1987-93, vice-chair pubs. criminal justice sect. 1994—, trial evidence com. litigation sect. 1980—, adv. to nat. conf. commrs. unform state laws drafting com. uniform rules of evidence 1996), Assn. Am. Law Schs. (chair elect evidence sects. 1996, com. on sects. 1984-87, chairperson women in legal edn. sect. 1982), Nat. Assn. Women Lawyers (bd. dirs. 1991—, pres.-elect 1993, pres. 1994—), Women Lawyers Assn. L.A. (bd. dirs., coord. mothers support group 1987—), Order of Coif, Phi Beta Kappa. Office: Southwestern U Sch Law 675 S Westmoreland Ave Los Angeles CA 90005-3905

RAFAEL, RUTH KELSON, archivist, librarian, consultant; b. Wilmington, N.C., Oct. 28, 1929; d. Benjamin and Jeanette (Spicer) Kelson; m. Richard Vernon Rafael, Aug. 26, 1951; children: Barbara Martinez Yates, Brenda Elaine. BA, San Francisco State U., 1953, MA, 1954; MLS, U. Calif.-Berkeley, 1968. Cert. archivist, 1989. Tchr. San Francisco Unified Sch. Dist., 1956-57; libr. Congregation Beth Sholom, San Francisco, 1965-83; archivist Western Jewish History Ctr. of Judah L. Magnes Mus., Berkeley, Calif., 1968, head archivist, libr., curator of exhibits, 1969-94; cons. NEH, Washington, NHPRC, Congregation Sherith Israel, San Francisco, Mount Zion Hosp., San Francisco, Benjamin Swig archives project, San Francisco, Koret Found., Camp Swig, Saratoga, Calif.; project dir. Ethnicity in Calif. Agriculture, 1989, San Francisco Jews of European Origin, 1880-1940, an oral history project, 1976; curator exhibits Western U.S. Jewry. Author: Continuum, San Francisco Jews of Eastern European Origin, 1880-1940, 1976, rev. edit., 1977; (with Davies and Woogmaster) poetry book Relatively Speaking, 1981; Western Jewish History Center: Archival and Oral History Collections, Judah L. Magnes Meml. Mus., 1987; contbg. editor Western States Jewish History, 1979—. Mem. exec. bd. Bay Area Library Info. Network, 1986-88. Bur. Jewish Edn. scholar, San Francisco, 1983; NEH grantee, 1985. Mem. Calif. Libr. Assn., Soc. Am. Archivists, Soc. Calif. Archivists, No. Calif. Assn. Jewish Librs. (pres. 1975-76), Jewish Arts Coun. of the Bay (bd. dirs. 1981-83)

RAFFA, JEAN BENEDICT, author, educator; b. Lansing, Mich., Apr. 23, 1943; d. Ernest Raymond and Verna Lois (Borst) Benedict; m. Frederick Anthony Raffa, June 15, 1964; children: Juliette Louise, Matthew. BS, Fla. State U., 1964, MS, 1968; EdD, U. Fla., 1982. Tchr. Leon County Sch. Sys., Tallahassee, Fla., 1964-69; coord. children's programming WFTV, Orlando, Fla., 1978-80; cons. edn. Tchr. Edn. Ctr. U. Ctrl. Fla., Orlando, 1980-89; writer Orlando, Fla., 1989—; instr. Disney Inst., Orlando, Fla., 1996; adj. instr. U. Cen. Fla., 1977-85; vis. asst. prof. Stetson U., DeLand, Fla., 1988-89; cons. Lang. Arts Curriculum Com. Orange County Sch. Sys., 1983; CEO Inner World Encounters, Orlando, 1995—. Author: Introduction to Television Literacy, 1989, The Bridge to Wholeness: A Feminine Alternative to the Hero Myth, 1992, Dream Theatres of the Soul: Empowering the Feminine Through Jungian Dreamwork, 1994; contbr. articles to profl. jours., articles and meditations to religious jours. Mistress of ceremonies Young Authors' Conf., Orange and Volusia County Sch. Sys., 1984-85; cons. Young Authors' Conf. Orange and Seminole County Sch. Sys., 1985-89; judge Volusia County Pub. Schs. Poetry Contest, 1983, 84, Seminole County Pub. Schs. Lit. Mag., 1985-89; pres. Maitland (Fla.) Jr. H.S. PTA, 1986-87; pres., bd. dirs. Canterbury Retreat and Conf. Ctr. Episcopal Diocese Ctrl. Fla., 1988-90; chair edn. commn. Episcopal Ch. of the Good Shepherd, 1986-89; sr. warden Vestry of Episcopal Ch. of the Good Shepherd, 1988. Mem. Kappa Delta Pi, Phi Delta Kappa. Democrat. Office: 17 S Osceola Ave Ste 200 Orlando FL 32801

RAFFAELE, HEIDI ANN, elementary education educator; b. Pittsburgh, Oct. 15, 1961; d. Robert and Melanie (Carr) R. BS in Edn., Lock Haven State Coll., 1983; MEd, Ga. State U., 1988. Cert. tchr. spl. edn. Tchr. spl. edn. Roswell (Ga.) H.S., 1983-89, Topeka (Ga.) Bd. Edn., 1989-90, Conyers (Ga.) Mid. Sch., 1990-93; tchr. spl. edn., inclusion cons. Blatchley Mid. Sch., Sitka, Alaska, 1993-94; tchr. elem. Baranof Elem. Sch., Sitka, 1994—; pres., CEO Success Tutoring and Consulting Svcs., Inc., Conyers, 1991—; cons. Atlanta, 1990—, Sitka, 1990—. Mem. NCTM, NEA, ASCD, AAUW, Phi Delta Kappa. Home: PO Box 1346 Sitka AK 99835

RAFFERTY, NANCY SCHWARZ, anatomy educator; b. Jamaica, N.Y., June 11, 1930; d. Franklin and Louise (Barry) Schwarz; m. Keen Alexander Rafferty, Aug. 7, 1953; children: Burns Arthur, Katherine Louisa. B.S., Queens Coll., 1952; M.S., U. Ill., 1953, Ph.D., 1958. Instr. anatomy Johns Hopkins U., 1963-66, asst. prof., 1966-70; asst. prof. anatomy Northwestern U., Chgo., 1970-72; asso. prof. Northwestern U., 1972-76, prof., 1976-94, prof. emeritus, 1994—; corp. mem., gen. libr. reader Marine Biol. Lab., Woods Hole, Mass. Contbr. articles on cell biology of the crystalline lens to profl. jours. USPHS fellow, 1958-63; USPHS grantee. Mem. Assn. Research in Vision and Ophthalmology, Internat. Soc. for Eye Research, Am. Assn. Anatomists, AAAS, Am. Soc. Cell Biology, Visual Scis. (study sect. of NIH), Sigma Xi, Phi Sigma. Home: 59 Harbor Hill Rd Woods Hole MA 02543-1219 Office: Marine Biol Lab Woods Hole MA 02543

RAFFO, SUSAN HENNEY, elementary education educator; b. Kendallville, Ind., Feb. 14, 1945; d. Gordon Theron and Sue (Kizer) Henney; m. Lawrence Albert Raffo, Feb. 19, 1977; children: Timothy, Kathleen. BS in Elem. Edn., Ball State U., 1967; M in Spl. Edn., San Francisco State U., 1972. Cert. elem. tchr., Calif. Tchr. East Noble Sch. Corp., Kendallville, Ind., 1967-68, Burlingame (Calif.) Sch. Dist., 1968—; master tchr. San Francisco State U., 1970-95, Coll. Notre Dame, Belmont, Calif., 1980-95. Registrar AYSO, Burlingame, 1987-94; bd. dirs. Burlingame Cmty. Edn. Found., 1989-95, sec., 1992-94. Recipient Svc. award PTA, 1989, J. Russell Kent award for innovative programs San Mateo County Sch. Bds. Assn., 1993; named Tchr. of Yr., Lions Club, 1993. Mem. Calif. Reading Assn., Alpha Delta Kappa. Office: Franklin Sch 2385 Trousdale Burlingame CA 94010

RAFTER, ROSALIE, secondary school educator; b. N.Y.C., Oct. 22, 1942; d. Francis Joseph and Lena (Colonnelli) R.; m. Gerald H. Osterberg, Dec. 20, 1974. BA in Latin, Seat of Wisdom Coll., 1967; MA in English, St. John's U., 1972, diploma in ednl. adminstrn., 1977. Latin tchr. Our Lady of Wisdom Acad., Ozone Park, N.Y., 1964-67; reading tchr. Ind. Sch. 271, Bklyn., 1968-69; English tchr., dept. chair Westbury (N.Y.) H.S., 1969-87; reading and lang. arts/ESL coord. Westbury (N.Y.) Pub. Schs., 1987—. Author: RCT Writing Revised, 1990; editor N.Y. State English Coun. newsletter, 1989-91. Grantee NEH, 1986-87. Mem. ASCD, TESOL, Nat. Coun. Tchrs. English, N.Y. State English Coun. (news editor 1989-91, pres. elect., pres. 1992-94, monograph editor 1995, FELLOWS award 1996), Internat. Reading Assn. Office: Westbury Pub Schs. 2 Hitchcock Ln Westbury NY 11568-1615

RAGAN, BETTY SAPP, artist, educator; b. Birmingham, Ala., Mar. 15, 1937; d. Robert William and Emma Mildred (O'Neal) Sapp; m. Thaxton Drew Ragan, Apr. 1958 (div. Aug. 1986); 1 child, Robert McClearan. BA cum laude, Birmingham-So. Coll., 1958; student, Allegheny Coll., 1971-72, Auburn U., 1980-83; MFA, Pratt Inst., 1985. Teachng asst. Pratt Inst., Bklyn., 1985; vis. asst. prof. dept. art Auburn U., 1985-89; asst. prof. dept. art U. Puget Sound, 1989-91, assoc. prof. photography and printmaking, dept. art, 1992—; panel moderator Soc. for Photo Edn. N.W., Tacoma, 1993; co-curator But Is It Art, Tacoma, 1993. Exhibited photography in solo shows at Maude Kerns Gallery, Eugene, Oreg., 1995, Helen Smith Gallery, Green River C.C., Auburn, Wash., 1996, others; group shows include Hanson Gallery, New Orleans, 1980, Montgomery (Ala.) Mus. Fine Arts, 1981, Ga. State U., Atlanta, 1981, Park Ave Atrium, N.Y.C., 1985, Carnegie Art Ctr., Walla Walla, Wash., 1990, Definitive Image Gallery, Seattle, 1992, Seattle Ctr. Pavilion, 1993, San Diego Art Inst., 1993, Eagle Gallery, Murray, Ky., 1994, B St. Pier Gallery, San Diego, 1995, numerous others; artist/photographer various collage series; co-curator But Is It Art?, Tacoma, 1993. Recipient numerous awards for art including Merit award Fine Arts Mus. of the South, Mobile, 1983, Dirk Andrew Phibbs Rsch. award U. Puget Sound, Tacoma, 1994. Mem. Soc. for Photog. Edn., Soc. Photog. Edn./N.W. (sec. 1990-93), Artist Trust, Women's Caucus for Art, Coll. Art Assn., Seattle Women's Caucus for Art. Unitarian. Office: U Puget Sound Dept Art 1500 N Warner Tacoma WA 98416

RAGAN, LISA CAROL, magazine editor; b. Muncie, Ind., Oct. 30, 1967; d. Jack Ray and Elizabeth (McDowell) R. BS, Ball State U., 1990. Editor Vanderbilt U., Nashville, 1991-93, Ideals mag., Nashville, 1993—. Mem. ACLU. Democrat. Office: Ideals Mag 535 Metroplex Dr Ste 250 Nashville TN 37211

RAGEAS, SUE A., bank executive. Sr. v.p. pub. rels. No. Trust Corp., Chgo. Office: No Trust Corp 50 S LaSalle St Chicago IL 60675*

RAGER, KATHLEEN BYRNE, academic administrator; b. Port Chester, N.Y., Oct. 5, 1943; d. Lawrence Sylvester Jr. and Mary Josephine (Matthews) Byrne; m. James J. DeFilippo, July 16, 1966 (div.); children: Elizabeth Anne, Sharon Marie, Kristen Leigh; m. Ira S. Rager, July 2, 1994. BA in English, Coll. Mt. St. Vincent, 1965; MS in Edn., SUNY, New Paltz, 1976. Tchr., television instr. Wappingers Ctrl. Sch. Dist., Wappingers Falls, N.Y., 1965-68; owner, mgr. Silver Apple, Inc., Hopewell Junction, N.Y., 1980-83; freelance comm. cons., 1983-88; dir. corp. and profl. edn. Marist Coll., Poughkeepsie, N.Y., 1988-93; dir. Downtown Ctr. and contract tng. svcs. Wichita (Kans.) State U., 1993—; cons. leadership tng. edn. com. So. Dutchess C. of C., Wappingers Falls, 1988-93, Poughkeepsie C. of C., 1991-93. Sunday sch. tchr. Hopewell Reform Ch., 1974-85, youth adviser, 1985-88; bd. dirs. Poughkeepsie YWCA, 1992-93. Mem. N.Y. State Assn. Women in Higher Edn., Am. Coun. Edn., N.Y. Assn. Continuing Community Edn. Republican. Home: 818 Whippoorwill Rd Derby KS 67037 Office: Wichita State U Downtown Ctr 127 N Market Wichita KS 67202-1801

RAGGI, REENA, federal judge; b. Jersey City, May 11, 1951. BA, Wellesley Coll., 1973; JD, Harvard U., 1976. Bar: N.Y. 1977. U.S. atty. Dept. Justice, Bklyn., 1986; ptnr. Windels, Marx, Davies & Ives, N.Y.C., 1987; judge U.S. Dist. Ct. (ea. dist.) N.Y., Bklyn., 1987—. Office: US Courthouse 225 Cadman Plz E Brooklyn NY 11201-1818

RAGGIO, LOUISE BALLERSTEDT, lawyer; b. Austin, Tex., June 15, 1919; d. Louis F. and Hilma (Lindgren) Ballerstedt; m. Grier H. Raggio, Apr. 19, 1941; children: Grier, Thomas, Kenneth. B.A., U. Tex., 1939; student, Am. U. Washington, 1939-40; J.D., So. Methodist U., 1952. Bar: Tex. 1952, U.S. Dist. Ct. (no. dist.) Tex. 1958. Intern Nat. Inst. Pub. Affairs, Washington, 1939-40; asst. dist. atty. Dallas County, Tex., 1954-56; shareholder Raggio and Raggio, 1956—. Sec. Gov.'s Commn. on Status of Women, 1970-71; trustee Tex. Bar Found., 1982-86, chmn., 1984-85, chmn. fellows, 1993—, Dallas Women's Found., 1993—, Nat. Conf. Bar Founds., 1986-92. Recipient Zonta award, Bus. and Profl. Women's Club award, So. Meth. U. Alumni award, Woman of Yr. award Tex. Fedn. Bus. and Profl. Women's Clubs, 1985, award Internat. Women's Forum, 1990, Disting. Law Alumni award So. Meth. U., 1992; Disting. Trial Lawyer award, 1993, Outstanding Trial Lawyer award Dallas Bar Assn., 1993, Pacemaker award Nat. Bus. Women Owners Assn., 1994, Thomas Jefferson award ACLU, 1994, Courage award Women Journalists North Tex., 1995; inducted into Tex. Women's Hall of Fame, 1985. Fellow Am. Bar Found.; mem. ABA (chmn. family sect. 1975-76, Best Woman Lawyer award 1995), LWV (pres. Austin 1945-46), State Bar Tex. (chmn. family law sect. 1965-67, dir. 1979-82, citation for law reform 1967, Pres.'s award 1987, Sarah T. Hughes award 1993), Dallas Bar Found. (pres. fellow com. 1991), Am. Acad. Matrimonial Lawyers (gov. 1973-81, trustee found. 1992—), Bus. and Profl. Women's Club (pres. Town North 1958-59), Phi Beta Kappa (pres. Dallas chpt. 1970-71, 90-92). Unitarian. Home: 3561 Colgate Ave Dallas TX 75225-5010 Office: Raggio and Raggio 3316 Oak Grove Ave Dallas TX 75204-2365

RAGLAND, CARROLL ANN, law educator; b. New Orleans, Nov. 28, 1946; d. Herbert Eugene Watson and Mary May (LeCompte) Leathers; children: Robert A. Sinex, Jr., Stacie Bateman, Joy Montgomery. JD, San Francisco Law Sch., 1980. Bar: Calif. 1980. Pvt. practice Santa Rosa, Calif., 1980-85; child custody mediator Sonoma County Superior Ct., Santa Rosa, 1985-86; chief dep. county counsel Butte County Counsel, Oroville, Calif., 1986-87; chief dep. dist. atty. Butte County Dist. Atty., Oroville, 1987-94; referee Shasta County Superior Ct., Redding, Calif., 1995-96; commr. Shasta County Superior Ct., Redding, 1996—; dean faculty, law prof. Calif. No. Sch. of Law, Chico, 1987—; instr. Shasta Coll., 1996—. Commr. Yuba County Juvenile Justice and Delinquency Prevention Commn., Marysville, Calif., 1993-94. Fellow Lawyers in Mensa. Office: Shasta County Superior Ct 1431 Market St Redding CA 96001

RAGLAND, INES COLOM, principal; b. Washington, Mar. 12, 1947; d. Jose Luis Sr. and Frances Yerby (Pannill) Colom; m. Banjamin Michael Ragland, Dec. 17, 1977 (div. May 1991); children: Michelle Elizabeth, Rachael Christine. BA in Secondary Edn., Longwood Coll., 1969, MS in Secondary Adminstrn., 1992. Clk. Va. State Water Control Bd., Richmond, 1969; tchr. Spanish Richmond City Pub. Schs., 1969-74; planning supr. Va. State Water Control Bd., 1974-78; asst. prin., tchr., prin. Grove Ave. Bapt. Christian Sch., Richmond, 1978-83; guidance tchr., asst. prin. Victory Christian Acad., Richmond, 1990—; cons. in field. Mission participant, El Salvador, 1992. Mem. ASCD. Office: Victory Christian Acad 8491 Chamberlayne Rd Richmond VA 23227-1550

RAGLE, GEORGE ANN, accountant; b. Detroit, Dec. 21, 1946; d. Joseph Theodore and Josephine Theresa (Mastrogiovanni) Gibson; m. James Albert, Sept. 3, 1976; children: Gina Ann, Jeffrey Allen. Assoc. Bus., Oakland C.C., Farmington Hills, Mich., 1974; B Accountancy, Walsh Coll., Troy, Mich., 1975; MBA, Ctrl. Mich. U., 1981. Cert. sch. bus. adminstr., Mich. Tax analyst Burroughs Corp., Detroit, 1976, Robillard & Joyce, St. Clair Shores, Mich., 1977-78; acctg. mgr. Baker Driveaway, Bloomfield Hills, Mich., 1978-79; staff acct. Macomb County Contr., Mt. Clemens, Mich., 1979-80; sr. acct. Macomb Intermediate Sch. Dist., Mt. Clemens, 1980-86; dir. bus. Mt. Clemens Community Schs., 1986-88, Pinconning (Mich.) Area Sch., 1988-90; dir. bus. and pers. St. Clair Intermediate Sch. Dist., Port Huron, Mich., 1990—. Bd. officer, treas. Fraser (Mich.) Pub. Schs. Bd. Edn., 1984-88; mem. Anchor Bay Schs. Bd. Edn., New Baltimore, Mich., 1991-95, treas., 1991-92, 94-95. Mem. Assn. Sch. Bus. Ofcls., Mich. Sch. Bus. Ofcls., Mich. Assn. Sch. Pers. Adminstrs., Macomb/St. Clair Sch. Bus. Ofcls. Home: 52134 Charleston Ln New Baltimore MI 48047-1191 Office: St Clair Intermediate Sch Dist 499 Range Rd Port Huron MI 48061

RAGNO, NANCY NICKELL, educational writer; b. Phila., Sept. 2, 1938; d. Paul Eugene and Sara Jane (Mensch) Nickell; m. Joseph Diego Ragno, Aug. 25, 1961; 1 child, Michelle Angela. BA, Lebanon Valley Coll., 1960; MA, NYU, 1968. Cert. tchr., N.J. Tchr. N.J. pub. schs., 1961-68; project editor Prentice-Hall, Inc., Englewood Cliffs, N.J., 1968-70, Harcourt Brace Jovanovich, N.Y.C, 1970-72; sr. editor Silver Burdett Co., Morristown, N.J., 1972-76; editor, writer Houghton Mifflin Co., Boston, 1976-77; sr. editor J.B. Lippincott Co., Phila., 1977-79; sr. author Silver Burdett Ginn, Morristown, 1984—. Author: (textbook series) Silver Burdett English, 1984, World of Language, 1992, (sound filmstrip) The City and the Modern Writer, 1970, Buying on the Installment Plan, 1974. Bassoonist Harrisburg (Pa.) Symphony Orch., 1959, Plainfield (N.J.) Symphony Orch., 1976, Somerset (N.J.) County Orch., 1989, Princeton (N.J.) Community Orch., 1992. Mem. ASCD, Nat. Coun. Tchrs. English, Internat. Reading Assn., Am. Soc. Journalists and Authors, Textbook Authors Assn., Authors Guild, U.S. Power Squadron. Democrat. Mem. Ch. of Christ. Home: 38 Tortoise Ln Tequesta FL 33469

RAGO-MCNAMARA, JULIET MAGGIO, artist; b. Chgo., Mar. 21, 1927; d. Henry Clifford and Grace (Canadeo) Maggio; m. Henry A. Rago, Oct. 7, 1950 (dec. 1969); m. Robert J. McNamara, Aug. 14, 1973 (dec. 1995); children: Christina, Carmela, Anthony, Martha. BFA, Sch. of Art Inst., Chgo., 1950; MFA, Sch. of Art Inst., 1973; postgrad., Accademia di Belli Arti, Florence, Italy, 1960-61, Vt. Studio Sch., 1988, Putney Painting Intensive, Vt., 1990. Prof. fine arts Loyola U. Chgo., 1969—; art instr. Barat Coll. of Sacred Heart, Lake Forest, Ill., 1970-71. Solo sculpture shows include U. Ill. Med. Ctr., 1978, Loyola U., Chgo., 1979; group sculpture shows include Evanston Art Ctr., 1987, Nina Owen Gallery, Chgo., 1987; solo painting exhbns. include Kerrigan-Hendricks Gallery, Chgo., 1954, Devorah-Sherman Gallery, Chgo., 1963, 65, Rosary Coll., River Forest, Ill., 1970, Wabash Transit Gallery, Sch. Art Inst., Chgo., 1973, Evanston Art Ctr., 1977, Cloud Hands Gallery, Chgo., 1978, Northwestern U., Chgo., 1983, 84, Sykes Gallery, Lancaster, Pa., 1987, Lawrence Perrin Gallery, Chgo., 1989, Space 900, Chgo., 1992, Chgo. Cultural Ctr., 1993, Gallery 1933, 1994, Lincoln Pub. Libr., 1995, many others; group painting shows include Renaissance Soc. Christmas Shows, 1953-69, Old Orchard Art Fair, Skokie, Ill., 1979, Chgo. Bot. Gardens, Glencoe, Ill., 1985, Ill. Arts Coun. Gallery, Chgo., 1986, Assisi, Italy, 1989, Gallery 1933, 1990, 90, Lincoln Pub. Libr., 1994, many others; and pvt. collections. Fellow Yaddo Found., 1971, Skowhegan Sch. Painting, 1972, Va. Ctr. Creative Arts, 1986, Vt. Studio Found., 1987, Ragdale Found., 1987, The Ucross Found., 1988, Byrdcliffe Art Colony, 1991, 92; grantee Ill. Arts Coun., 1979. Mem. Coll. Art Assn. (mem. women's caucus). Home: 1555 Sherman Ave # 231 Evanston IL 60201 Office: Loyola U Chgo 6525 Sheridan Rd Chicago IL 60626

RAGSDALE, BERTHA MAE See KOLB, BERTHA MAE

RAGSDALE, CHRISTINA ANN, public relations executive, consultant; b. Long Beach, Calif., July 27, 1956; d. David Neal and Mary Lou (Kaiser) Webber; m. Joel Gordon Ragsdale, Mar. 14, 1987. BA in Creative Writing, Lone Mountain Coll., 1978; MA in Communication Studies, Calif. State U., Sacramento, 1983. Instr. comm. studies Calif. State U., Sacramento, 1981-84; prodn. mgr. Videomedia, Inc., Sunnyvale, Calif., 1984-85; comm. specialist Mercy Gen. Hosp., Sacramento, 1985-88, community rels. mgr., 1988; owner Ragsdale Comm., Sacramento, 1988-93; water quality info. mgr. County of Sacramento, 1993—; cons. Cablevision of Sacramento, 1982; presenter Ideas Unltd. workshop Soc. Healthcare Pub. Rels. and Mktg., 1985, Calif. Water Pollution Control Assn. Conv., 1994, Water Environment Fedn. Internat. Conf., 1996. Mem. exec. com. Harry S. Truman Dem. Club, Sacramento, 1990-94; active comm. com. Am. Lung Assn., Sacramento, 1988-94, chair Clean Air Week, 1993-94, bd. dirs. Mem. Sacramento Pub. Rels. Assn. (bd. dirs. and sec. 1989-91, numerous awards), Natomas Optimist (charter), Nat. Assn. Profl. Environ. Communicators. Home: 14887 Trinidad Dr Rancho Murieta CA 95683

RAHE, PEGGY ANN, realtor; b. Cin., Oct. 5, 1951; d. William Thomas and Shirley Lee (Court) Sheff; m. Charles Albert Rahe, Sept. 11, 1970; children: Julie Ann, Jennifer Lynn. Office mgr. Creative Promotions, Cin., 1970-80; photographer proprietorship Cin., 1977-85; realtor Keyes Gateway, Inc., Dayton, Ohio, 1985—. Mem. T.W.I.G.-Terrific Women in Giving Children's Med. Ctr., Dayton, Ohio, 1984-95. Mem. Dayton Area (Ohio) Bd. Realtors, Keyes Gateway, Inc. Circle of Excellence Club, Keyes Gateway Pres. Club. Home: 10483 Streampark Ct Dayton OH 45458 Office: Keyes Gateway Inc 7265 Far Hill Ave Dayton OH 45459

RAHILL, MARGARET FISH, retired museum curator; b. Milw., Feb. 21, 1919; d. Joseph Benedict and Margaret (Scherdan) Schmidt; m. William James Fish, Nov. 14, 1941 (dec. 1945); 1 child, Mary Fish Arcuri; m. Frank M. Rahill, Mar. 14, 1951 (dec. Oct. 1986); children: Marguerite, Laura Rahill Maramba. BA, U. Wis., 1958; student, Mt. Mary Coll., 1958. With pub. rels. Blackland Army Air Base, Waco, Tex., 1942-43; reporter, art critic Milw. Sentinel, 1945-62; with pub. rels. dept. Milw. Art Mus., 1962-63, Layton Sch. Art, Milw., 1965-68, Bel Canto Chorus, Milw., 1965-68; curator in charge Charles Allis Art Mus., Milw., 1968-91; prin. Book Bay, Milw., 1962-72; vis. instr. journalism Marquette U., Milw., 1972-73; mem. organizing com. Florentine Opera Club, 1962, with pub. rels. dept. 1962-65, Bel Canto Chorus, 1966-68; mem. organizing com. Wis. Chamber Orch., Milw., 1975-76; v.p. art, councillor-at-large Wis. Acad. Sci. Arts and Letters, Madison, 1981-85; juror numerous art competitions, Wis., 1962-91. Contbr. articles to profl. jours. Active City of Milw. Art Commn., 1982-90, pres., 1984-85. Recipient Gridirm award Milw. Press Club, 1955, 57, 59, 60, Community Svc. award Milw. Art Commn., 1976, Ann. Bookfellows award Milw. Pub. Libr., 1977, Devel. award Milw. County Hist. Soc., 1982, Promotion of Hispanic Culture award Centro de la Communidad Unida, 1988. Mem. Wis. Painters and Sculptors (hon.), Wis. Crafts Coun. (hon.). Roman Catholic. Home: 4801 Connecticut Ave NW Apt 302 Washington DC 20008-2203

RAHL, LESLIE LYNN, risk advisor, entrepreneur; b. N.Y.C., May 16, 1950; d. Myron and Esther (Botwin) Horwitz; m. Jeffrey Mark Lynn, Dec. 20, 1969 (div. 1981); m. J. Andrew Rahl Jr., Apr. 30, 1989; 1 child, Kevin; stepchildren: Kaitlin, Stephen. SB, MIT, 1971, MBA, 1972. V.p. swaps and derivatives Citibank, N.Y.C., 1972-91; pres. Leslie Rahl Assocs., N.Y.C., 1991-94; co-prin. Capital Market Risk Advisors, N.Y.C., 1994—; presenter in field. Contbr. articles to profl. jours. Recipient On the Rise award Fortune. Mem. Internat. Assn. Fin. Engrs. (bd. dirs. 1993—), Madison Beach Club. Office: Capital Market Risk Advisors 565 Fifth Ave New York NY 10017

RAHM, DIANNE, government and international affairs educator; b. N.Y.C., Sept. 27, 1951; d. Olaf Lennart and Jeanne (Todd) R.; m. Richard R. Valdes, Apr. 23, 1971 (div. 1982); 1 child, Anastasia Rahm Valdes. BA in Liberal Arts, Wichita State U., 1975, MA in Am. History, 1976; MS in Computer Sci., Fitchburg State Coll., 1985; PhD in Pub. Adminstrn., Syracuse U., 1989. Computer sci. instr. Cen. New Eng. Coll., Worcester, Mass., 1979-82; assoc. prof. computer mgmt. Becker Jr. Coll., Worcester, Mass., 1982-86; adj. prof. pub. adminstrn. Syracuse (N.Y.) U., 1987; asst. prof. pub. adminstrn. Pa. State U., 1988-90; assoc. prof. govt. and internat. affairs U. South Fla., Tampa, 1990-95, dir. computing, 1991-92, 1991-92; programmer, analyst Data Gen. Corp., Westboro, 1978-79; sr. rsch. assoc. tech. and info. policy program Syracuse U., 1986-88; cons.Mtmg. Info. Systmes and Computer Systems, Worcester, 1980-86, U.S. Gen. Acctg. Office, Washington, 1989, Fla. Dept. Labor and Employment, Tampa, 1991, City of Clearwater, Fla., 1991, City of Pinellas Park, Fla., 1991. Contbr. articles to profl. jours. Mem. Am. Soc. Pub. Adminstrn., Assn. Pub. Policy Mgmt., Policy Studies Orgn., Sci. and Tech. in Govt., So. Polit. Scis. Assn., Union Concerned Scientists. Unitarian. Office: Dept Political Science Iowa State U Ames IA 50014

RAHM, MARY ELLEN, educator; b. Middletown, Ohio, Apr. 15, 1940; d. John Russel and Evelyn Brockamp McDermott; m. Herbert William Rahm Jr., Dec. 28, 1963; children: Evala Rahm Bailey, Herbert William III, John Anthony, Edward Joseph. BA, Ursuline Coll., 1962; MEd, U. Louisville, 1969. Primary tchr. Jefferson County Bd. Edn., 1962-66, substitute tchr., 1966-79; owner, operator J. H. Brockamp Advt. Specialties, 1966-70; with

Stevens Rsch., 1979-88; office mgr. Janet McIntyre DMD, 1988-89; statistical clk. U.S. Census Bur., 1989—; part time owner, outside sales rep. Travel Profl. Internat. Mem. Meadow Heights Womens Club, Ascension Cath. Ch. in Louisville, Ascension Womens Club, Ascension PTA, tchr. Confraternity of Christian Doctrine, 1969-72; brownie and jr. leader Girl Scouts Kentuckiana Coun., 1972-76; active Boy Scouts, Old Ky. Home Coun.; coach Upper Highlands Swim Club; dem. judge, 1992; leader parent group 12 step program, 1988-90; aerobic tchr. Walking Program for Sr. Citizens, 1987—; vol. usher Ky. Ctr. for the Arts, 1989—; fund raiser for Booklawn A Substance Treatment Ctr. for Teens, 1985. Mem. AAUW (pres. 1977-81, many other offices state and br. divsn.), Meadow Heights Women Club, Kentuckiana Swim Offls. Home: 2404 Sir Johns Ct Louisville KY 40220-1055

RAHM, SUSAN BERKMAN, lawyer; b. Pitts., June 25, 1943; d. Allen Hugh and Selma (Wiener) Berkman; m. David Alan Rahm, Nov. 23, 1972; children: Katherine, William. BA with honors, Wellesley Coll., 1965; postgrad., Harvard U., 1966-68; JD, NYU, 1973. Bar: N.Y. 1974, D.C. 1988. Assoc. Marshall, Bratter, Greene, Allison & Tucker, N.Y.C., 1973-81, ptnr., 1981-82; ptnr. Kaye, Scholer, Fierman, Hays & Handler, N.Y.C., 1982—, chair real estate dept., 1993—; N.Y. adv. bd., Chgo. Title Ins. Co., 1995. Editor: New York Real Property Service, 1987. Bd. dirs. Girls Inc., 1989-93; mem. aux. bd. Mt. Sinai Hosp., N.Y.C., 1976-78. Recipient cert. of outstanding svc. D.C. Redevel. Land Agy., 1969, She Knows Where She's Going award Girls' Clubs of Am., 1987. Mem. ABA, Assn. of Bar of City of N.Y., N.Y. Bar Assn. (real property law com., co-chmn. real-estate devel. . 1987-91), Am. Coll. Real Estate Lawwyers, Comml. Real Estate Women N.Y. (bd. dirs. 1988-94), v.p. 1988-91, pres. 1991-93). Office: Kaye Scholer Fierman Hays & Handler 425 Park Ave New York NY 10022-3506

RAHMANI, LORETTA HARDIE, university administrator; b. Burbank, Calif., Dec. 9, 1955; d. Alexander Simpson and Marie Virginia (Kaczmaryn) Hardie; m. Ali Mossaver Rahmani, Oct. 28, 1989. BA, San Diego State U., 1979, MS, 1982; EdD, U. LaVerne, 1994. Coord. residential life Calif. State U., Northridge, 1983-87, asst. dir. housing, 1987-88; asst. mgr. housing UCLA, 1988-89; asst. dean of students U. LaVerne, Calif., 1989-94, assoc. dean of students, 1994-95, dean of student affairs, 1995—; co-founder Kaleidoscope Leadership Cons., LaVerne, 1995; small coll. network chair NASPA, 1994-95; sec. Cacuho, 1987-88, v.p. 1988-89. Office: U LaVerne 1950 Third St LaVerne CA 91750

RAIDL, MARTHA ANNE, nutrition and dietetics educator, dietitian; b. Chgo., Aug. 28, 1951; d. Frank Karel and Martha (Brodsky) R. BS, U. Ill., 1973, MS, 1983; BS, U. Ill., Chgo., 1975; PhD, Purdue U., 1993. Clin. dietitian Hammersmith Hosp., London, 1975-77; lectr. nutrition Flour Adv. Bur., London, 1977-78; clin. dietitian Loretto Hosp., Chgo., 1978-80; grad. asst. U. Ill., Urbana, 1980-83; clin. dietitian Lakeland (Fla.) Regional Med. Ctr., 1983-85; food technologist Coca-Cola Foods, Plymouth, Fla., 1985-88; grad. asst. Purdue U., West Lafayette, Ind., 1988-93; asst. prof. East Tenn. State U., Johnson City, 1993—; spkr. weight control classes Franklin Wellness Ctr., Elizabethton, Tenn., 1995; participant radio show WKPT, Kingsport, Tenn., 1995-96. Contbr. articles to profl. jours. including Jour. Am. Dietetics Assn., Nutrition Rsch., Cereal Chemists. Rschr., cons. Jr. League Cookbook, Johnson City, 1995. Mem. Am. Dietetic Assn., Tenn. Dietetic Assn. (planning com. 1994-95), Tri-Cities Dist. Dietetic Assn. (bd. dirs., edn. and rsch. com. 1993-96). Office: E Tenn State U PO Box 70671 Johnson City TN 37614-0671

RAIKEN, ESTHER CAGEN, librarian; b. Cleve., Dec. 22, 1907; d. Charles and Ida (Kaufman) Hirsch; m. Samuel Lawrence Cagen, June 18, 1934 (dec. Jan. 1982); children: Lenore, Barbara (dec.), Robert; m. Oscar Harris Raiken, Sept. 18, 1988. BS, Western Res. U., 1962, MLS, 1963. Head children's rm. Lee Br. Libr., Cleveland Heights, Ohio, 1953-57; head Fairfax Sch. libr. Cleveland Heights Sch. Libr. System, 1957-69; instr. children's lit. Case Western Res. U., Cleve., 1964-67, Cleve. State U., 1967-69; dir. pilot media ctr. Belvoir Elem. Sch., Cleveland Heights, 1969-74; libr. Convent of Sacred Heart, San Francisco, 1974-76, Congregation Sherith Israel, San Francisco, 1980—. NDEA scholar Kent (Ohio) U., 1964. Mem. Assn. Jewish Librs. (award presenter 1991, Best Book of Yr. award 1991), AAUW, Beta Phi Mu. Democrat. Jewish. Home: 1900 Jackson St San Francisco CA 94109-2860

RAILSBACK, SHERRIE L., adoption search/reunion consultant; b. Phila., Mar. 12, 1942; children: Ricky, Cindy. BBA, U. Ky., 1981. Sales mgr. Marjo Cosmetics, Ft. Wayne, Ind.; asst. dir. patient fin. svcs. Riverside Meth. Hosp., Columbus, Ohio; cons. Railsback and Assocs., Long Beach, Calif.; adoption search/reunion cons. L.A. Mem. NAFE, ASTD, Book Publicists of So. Calif., Toastmasters.

RAIN, CHERYL ANN, underwriter; b. Alton, Ill., Aug. 22, 1950; d. Robert E. and Mary F. (Miller) Gill; m. William A. Rain Jr., Mar. 31, 1973; children: Nathan A. Rain, Jeremy S. Rain. BA, So. Ill. U., Edwardsville, 1972, MBA, 1992. Tng. mgr. Germania Fed. Savs., Alton, Ill., 1983-86; with St. Louis Commerce Mortage Corp., St. Louis, 1986—, asst. v.p., 1992—; regional underwriting mgr. Commerce Mortgage Corp., St. Louis, 1994—; mortage loan officer Commerce Banks of St. Louis, Peoria, Bloomington & S.E. Mo., 1992—. Asst. treas. Jr. League of Greater Alton, 1984-85, treas., 1985-86; pres., bd. dirs. Evang. Sch. for Young, Godfrey, Ill, 1982-83; moderator for bd. deacons Elm St. Presbyn. Ch., Alton, 1981-82. Republican. Methodist. Home: 32 Frontenac Pl Godfrey IL 62035-1635 Office: Commerce Mortgage Corp 8000 Forsyth Blvd # 1010 Clayton MO 63105-1707

RAIN, RHONDA L., performing arts executive, counselor, educator; b. Grinnell, Iowa, Feb. 28, 1952; d. Henry Garrett and Anne Lucille (Roberts) Rook. B in Univ. Studies, U. N.Mex., 1984, MA in Counseling, 1993. Lic. profl. counsel, N.Mex.; nat. cert. counselor. Tchr./counselor Rough Rock (Ariz.) Demo. Sch., 1973; acad. support staff U. N.Mex. Med. Sch., Albuquerque, 1974-84, U. N.Mex. Main Campus, Albuquerque, 1988-91; intern counselor Manzanita Ctr. U. N.Mex., Albuquerque, 1993; intern counselor Career Ctr. and Albuquerque Tech.-Vocat. Inst., 1993, career counselor, 1993—; acad. advisor and counselor, coord. advisement and testing U. N.Mex.-Valencia, Los Lunas, 1994-96, chief examiner GED, 1994-96; CEO Raindrops, 1996—; vocat. adv. com. New Futures H.S., Albuquerque, 1988-93; peer counselor U. N.Mex. Main Campus, Albuquerque, 1988-93; grad. asst. counseling dept. U. N.Mex., Albuquerque, 1991-92; vol. counselor Youth Diagnostic and Detention Ctr., Albuquerque, 1992. Neighborhood Watch capt. Crime Prevention Program, N.Mex., 1986-94; vol. musician Albuquerque Civic Light Opera Assn., 1978-83; mem. Valley cultural com. U. N.Mex.-Valencia, 1994-96. Recipient Fine Arts award Bank of Am., Huntington Beach, Calif., 1970; No. Ariz. U. music scholar, 1970-73. Mem. ACA, Nat. Acad. Advising Assn., Nat. Career Devel. Assn., N.Mex. Career Devel. Assn., Nat. Bd. Cert. Counselors (nat. cert. counselor), Internat. Platform Assn., Golden Key Internat. Honor Soc. (life), Pi Lambda Theta (v.p. 1986).

RAINES, CHARLOTTE AUSTINE BUTLER, artist, poet; b. Sullivan, Ill., July 1, 1922; d. Donald Malone and Charlotte (Wimp) Butler; m. Irving Isaack Raines, Sept. 26, 1941; children: Robin Raines Collison, Kerry Raines Lydon. BA in Studio Arts magna cum laude, U. Md., 1966. One-woman show at Castle Theatre, 1988, C.T.V. Awards Hall, Md., 1993; exhbd. in numerous group shows including Corcoran Gallery, 1980, Md.'s Best Exhbn., 1986, Md. State House, 1990, four-artist video documentary, 1992, U. Md. Univ.-Coll. Gallery, 1996; represented in various pvt. collections and permanent collection at U. Md. Univ.-Coll.; selected works in U.S. Dept. State Arts in Embassies Program; contbr. poems to lit. publs. Mem. Artists Equity Assn., Writers' Ctr., Phi Kappa Phi. Studio: 4103 Longfellow St Hyattsville MD 20781-1748

RAINEY, JEAN OSGOOD, public relations executive; b. Lansing, Mich., Apr. 5, 1925; d. Earle Victor and Blanche Mae (Eberly) Osgood; m. John Larimer Rainey, Nov. 29, 1957 (dec. Oct. 1991); children: Cynthia, John Larimer, Ruth. Grad., Lansing Bus. U., 1942. Pub. rels. dir. Nat. Assn. Food Chains, Washington, 1954-59; v.p. pub. rels. Manchester Orgns., Washington, 1959-61; ptnr. Rainey, McEnroe & Manning, Washington, 1962-73; v.p. Manning, Selvage & Lee, Washington, 1973-79, pres. Washington div., 1979-84, sr. counsellor, 1985—; owner Jean Rainey Assocs., Washington, 1986-87; sr. v.p. Daniel J. Edelman Inc., 1987-96; owner Sean Raney Assocs., Washington. Author: How to Shop for Food, 1972. Pres. Hyde Home and Sch. Assn., Washington, 1969-71; co-chmn. Nat. Com. for Reelection of the Pres., 1972. Mem. Pub. Rels. Soc. Am. (accredited), Am. Women in Radio and TV (pres. Washington chpt. 1962-63, mem. nat. bd. 1963-65), Am. News Women's Club (pres. 1973-75). Republican. Episcopalian. Club: City Tavern. Home: Apt 250B 4000 Cathedral Ave NW Washington DC 20016-5249 Office: PO Box 251 Main Lobby W 4000 Cathedral Ave NW Washington DC 20016-5249

RAINS, JOANNE WARNER, nursing educator; b. Sioux Falls, S.D., June 27, 1950; d. Arnold D. and Arlene M. (Lawrence) W.; m. Daniel P. Rains, Dec. 13, 1975; children: David Warner, Isaac Daniel. BA, Augustana Coll., 1972; MA, U. Iowa, 1976; D of Nursing Sci., Ind. U., 1990. Vis. nurse Delaware County Vis. Nurse Assn., Muncie, Ind., 1976-77; cons. Ind. State Bd. Health, Indpls., 1977-78; instr. Briar Cliff Coll., Sioux Falls, 1981-82; adj. faculty Okla. Bapt. U., Shawnee, 1985; asst. prof. Ind. U., Indpls., 1990—; mem. policy com. Friends Com. on Nat. Legis., Washington, 1992—; fellow Primary Health Care Policy, Washington, 1996. Campaign mgr. Doug Kinser for State Rep. Ind. House Dist. 54, 1988-94; exec. com., mem. New Castle (Ind.) Healthy City Com., 1989—; chair residential drive Am. Cancer Soc., New Castle, 1989. Mem. ANA, Assn. Cmty. Health Nurse Educators (bd. dirs.), Ind. Polit. Sci. Assn. (v.p. 1993-94,. pres. 1994-95). Quaker. Office: Ind U E 2325 Chester Blvd Richmond IN 47374

RAINS, MURIEL BARNES, retired educator, real estate agent; b. Atlanta, Feb. 6, 1916; d. George Washington and Nancy Blodgett (Enos) Barnes; m. David Dean Rains (dec.); children: Rose Muriel, David Dean II. BS, Wilberforce (Ohio) U., 1937; MA, Tex. So. U., 1955; postgrad., Temple U., 1956-81. Cert. tchr., N.J., Tex., Del., Pa.; cert. news reporter, Ohio. News reporter Ohio State News, Columbus, 1937-40; tchr. Houston Pub. Schs., 1950-56, Camden (N.J.) Pub. Schs., 1956-63, various schs., Wilmington, Del., 1963-78; various schs., Claymont, Del., 1978-81; real estate agt., Phila., 1980—; former mem. city profl. growth com. Wilmington Pub. Schs., 1963-67; instr. in physics Brandywine Coll., Wilmington; co-author WOMP (Wilmington Occupational Project). Poetry author; contbr. articles to profl. jours. Active Houston Interracial Commn., 1950-56, State Reception Com., Houston, 1949. Mem. AAUW, Am. Assn. Math. Tchrs., Nat. Hist. Soc., Germantown Civic League (rec. sec., 1986-91), Alpha Kappa Alpha (life). Episcopalian. Home and Office: 6909 Boyer St Philadelphia PA 19119-1908

RAINWATER, RITA RENEER, county official; b. Barberton, Ohio, Mar. 1, 1948; d. Marlin Howard Reneer and Charlotte Ann (Brown) Michael; m. Raymond Thomas Rainwater Sr., July 29, 1972; children: Raymond Thomas Jr., Rustin Ashley. Grad. high sch., Akron, Ohio. Owner Rainwater Employment Svc., Douglasville, Ga., 1977-93, Sunshine Temps, Douglasville, Ga., 1983-93; chmn. bd. commrs. Douglas County, Douglasville, Ga., 1993—. Mem. Regional Leadership Inst. Republican. Baptist. Home: 4059 Lakeland Hills Dr Douglasville GA 30134

RAIT, SUZANNE GRACE, publishing executive; b. Detroit, Sept. 13, 1950; d. Robert James and Beverly June (Geisler) Kilpatrick; m. Charles Rait, Feb. 14, 1981. RN, Harper Hosp. With circulation dept. Neonatal Network, Petaluma, Calif., 1981-86, editor, 1986-90, mng. editor, 1990—. Mem. Nat. Assn. Neonatal Nurses (office mgr. 1984-90). Office: Neonatal Network 1304 Southpoint Blvd Ste 280 Petaluma CA 94954-6861

RAITT, BONNIE LYNN, blues singer, guitarist; b. Burbank, Calif., Nov. 8, 1949. Student, Radcliffe Coll. Performer blues clubs, East Coast; concert tours in Britain, 1976, 77; albums include Bonnie Raitt, 1971, Give It Up, 1972, Takin' My Time, 1973, Streetlights, 1974, Home Plate, 1975, Sweet Forgiveness, 1977, The Glow, 1979, Green Light, 1982, Nine Lives, 1986, Nick of Time, 1989 (Grammys 1990, Rock-Best Vocal Performance, Female, Pop-Best Vocal Performance, Female, Album of Yr.), I'm in the Mood (with John Lee Hooker) (Grammy 1990, Blues-Best Traditional Record), The Bonnie Raitt Collection, 1990, Luck of the Draw, 1991 (Grammy 1992, Rock-Best Vocal Performance, Female, Grammy for Best Duet with Delbert McClinton), Longing In Their Hearts, 1994 (Grammy award Best Pop Album), Road Tested, 1996; songs include Something to Talk About (Grammy 1992, Best Pop Vocal Performance, Female), Good Man, Good Woman (with Delbert McClinton) (Grammy 1992, Rock-Best Vocal by a Duo or Group). Recipient numerous Grammy nominations, four Grammy awards 1990, three Grammy awards 1992. Office: PO Box 626 Los Angeles CA 90078*

RAJESH, JODY ANNE, violinist; b. Vancouver, Wash., Jan. 29, 1965; d. John Blythe and Judith Ann (packard) McComb; m. Srinivasan Rajesh. MusB, U. Pacific, 1987; MusM, U. So. Calif., 1989. Stockton (Calif.) symphony, 1983-87; with L.A. Baroque Orch., 1988-94, L.A. Mozart Orch., 1990-94; freelance violinist L.A., 1987-94, Phila., 1994—; tchr. L.A., 1987-94, Princeton, N.J., 1994—. Home: 2703 Pheasant Run Monmouth Junction NJ 08852

RAJSKI, PEGGY, film director, film producer; b. Stevens Point, Wis.. Attended, U. Wis. Films include: (prodn. mgr.): Lianna, 1982, Almost You, 1984; (prodr., prodn. mgr.) The Brother From Another Planet, 1984, Matewan, 1987, Eight Men Out, 1988; (prodr.) The Grifters, 1990, Little Man Tate, 1991 (also 2nd. unit dir.), Used People, 1992; (prodr. video) Bruce Springstein's Glory Days; (dir.) Trevor, 1994 (Acad. award for Best Live Action Short Film). Office: 140 Riverside Dr Ste 5E New York NY 10024-2605*

RAK, CHRISTINA MARIE, technical writer, producer; b. Columbus, Ohio, Dec. 27, 1964; d. William H. and Frances M. (Hampton) P.; Michael W. Rak, Aug. 4, 1990. BS, Ohio State U., 1988. Cert. tchr. English and Reading, Ohio. Civil svc. clk. II ob. gyn. dept. Ohio State U. Hosp., Columbus, 1985-87; substitute tchr. Ctrl. Ohio Schs., 1988-89; tchr. English Washington Sr. H.S., 1989-91; asst. dir. devel. Columbus Sch. for Girls, Bexley, Ohio, 1991-95; tech. writer Metatec Corp., Dublin, Ohio, 1995-96, tech. writer, prodr., 1996—; mktg. and sales rep. Black Forest Pines, Johnstown, Ohio, 1988—; bus. asst. Michael Rak, Columbus, 1990—. Contbr. articles to profl. jours. Vol. Columbus Sch. for Girls, Bexley, 1995-96, N.A.H.S. Alumni Assn., New Albany, Ohio, 1989-91. Disting. scholarship Ohio State U., 1982, Lucy Lelila scholarship, 1984. Mem. NAFE, Women in Comm., Inc., Ohio State U. Alumnae Scholarship House (ho. sec. 1984-85, cultural chairperson 1984-85). Office: Metatec Corp 7001 Metatec Blvd Dublin OH 43017

RAKER, IRMA STEINBERG, judge; b. Bklyn., Apr. 28, 1938; d. Manuel J. and Fannie (Rakov) Steinberg; m. Samuel K. Raker, Apr. 3, 1960; 1 child, Mark Stefanie Leslie. BA, Syracuse U., 1959; cert. of attendance (hon.), Hague (The Netherlands) Acad. Internat. Law, 1959; JD, Am. U., 1972. Bar: Md. 1973, D.C. 1974, U.S. Dist. Ct. Md. 1977, U.S. Ct. Appeals (4th cir.) 1977. Asst. state's atty. State's Atty.'s Office of Montgomery County, Md., 1973-79; ptnr. Sachs, Greenebaum & Tayler, Washington, 1979-80; judge U.S. Dist. Ct. Md., Rockville, 1980-82, Cir. Ct. for Montgomery County, Md., 1982-94, Ct. of Appeals of Md., Rockville, 1994—; adj. prof. Washington Coll. Law, Am. U., 1980—; faculty seminar leader child abuse course Nat. Coll. Dist. Attys. at U. Mass., 1977; mem. faculty Md. Jud. Inst., Nat. Criminal Def. Inst., 1980, 81, 82; instr. litigation program Georgetown Law Ctr.-Nat. Inst. Trial Advocacy; mem. legis. com. Md. Jud. Conf., mem. exec. com., 1985-89, mem. commn. to study bail bond and surety industry in Md.; mem. spl. com. to revise article on crimes and punishment State of Md., 1991—; mem. inquiry com. atty. Grievance Commn. Md., 1978-81; chair com. on criminal law and traffic U.S. Dist. Ct. Md., 1981. Past editor Am. U. Law Rev. Treas., v.p. West Bradley Citizens Assn., 1964-68; mem. adv. com. to county exec. on child abuse Montgomery County, 1976-77, mem. adv. com. to county exec. on battered spouses, 1977-78, mem. adv. com. on environ. protection, 1980; mem. citizens adv. bd. Montgomery County Crisis Ctr., 1980. Recipient Outstanding Contbn. awards (2) Montgomery County Govt. Fellow Md. Bar Found.; mem. ABA (del. nat. conf. state trial judges, active various coms.), Md. State Bar Assn. (chairperson coun. criminal law and practice sect., mem. bd. govs. 1981, 82, 85, 86, 90, mem. coun. litigation sect., active coms.), Nat. Assn. Women Judges, Internat. Acad. Trial Judges, Montgomery County Bar Assn. (chairperson criminal law sect. 1978-79, mem. exec. com. 1979-80, active other coms.), Montgomery County Bar Leaders, Women's Bar Assn. Md., Women's Bar Assn. D.C., Hadassah Women's Orgn. (life), Pioneer Women Na'amat (hon. life, Celebration of Women award 1985), Pi Sigma Alpha. Office: Ct of Appeals of Md Judicial Ctr # 50 Rockville MD 20850*

RAKES, RANDI LEE, elementary school educator, test developer; b. Edison, N.J., June 24, 1969; d. Edward Eli and Florence (Yatrofsky) Leviten; m. Randy Ray Rakes, June 27, 1992; 1 stepchild, Laura M.; 1 child, Allyson B. BA in Psychology, Rutgers U., 1991; postgrad, Trenton State Coll., 1995. Cert. spl. edn., elem. edn., N.J. Substitute tchr. Woodbridge (N.J.) Bd. Edn., 1989-91; substitute tchr. Pemberton Twp. Schs., Browns Mills, N.J., 1991-92, tchr., 1992-93; test developer N.J. DOP, Trenton, 1993-95; tchr. Pemberton Twp. Schs., Browns Mills, N.J., 1995—. Gov.'s Teaching scholar State of N.J., 1987. Mem. N.J. Edn. Assn. Roman Catholic. Home: 412 Pardee Blvd Browns Mills NJ 08015-1137

RAKOV, BARBARA STREEM, marketing executive; b. Bklyn., Jan. 4, 1946; d. Harold B. and Claire (Colbert) Streem; m. Harris J. Rakov, Nov. 20, 1970 (div. Mar. 1972). BS, Boston U., 1967; postgrad. NYU, 1972-74. Market rsch. analyst, product mgr., mktg. mgr. J.B. Williams, N.Y.C., 1967-77; mktg. mgr. Del Labs., Farmingdale, N.Y., 1977-78; product mgr., sr. product mgr., asst. to office of pres., dir. mktg. and sales Benelux countries, v.p. group mktg., dir., dir. new products, v.p. bus. devel. Joseph E. Seagram & Sons, 1978-90; pres. BSR Assocs., N.Y.C., 1990-92; v.p. mktg. Del Labs., 1992-94; v.p. mktg. Tsumura Internat., Secaucus, N.J., 1994-96; v.p. Disneymktg. Franco Mfg. Co., Inc., Metuchen, N.J., 1996—. Mem. L'Ordre des Coteaux de Champagne, Les Gastronomes de la Mer, Am. Mgmt. Assn. Avocations: tennis, skiing, squash, reading, water skiing. Office: Franco Mfg Co Inc 555 Prospect St Metuchen NJ 08840

RAKOWICZ-SZULCZYNSKA, EVA MARIA, molecular oncologist; b. Poznan, Poland, Nov. 22, 1951; came to U.S., 1984; d. Tadeusz and Wieslawa Maria (Hankiewicz) Rakowicz; divorced; 1 child, Adriana Maria. MS in Biochemistry, A. Mickiewicz U., Poznan, 1974; PhD in Biochemistry, Acad. Medicine, Poznan, 1977, DMS in Human Genetics & Molecular Biol., 1981. Asst. prof. Inst. Human Genetics, Poznan, 1978-82, assoc. dir., 1982-86, assoc. prof., 1982-89; assoc. scientist, lab. head Wistar Inst., Phila., 1984-90, rsch. asst. prof., 1991-92; assoc. prof. ob/gyn. U. Nebr. Med. Ctr., Omaha, 1992—, assoc. prof. Eppley Inst., 1993—, assoc. prof. biochemistry, 1995—; mem. Eppley Cancer Ctr., Omaha, 1995—. Author: Nuclear Localization of Growth Factors and of Monoclonal Antibodies, 1993; contbr. articles to Am. Jour. Pathology, Carcinogenesis, others. Grantee Nebr. Dept. Health, 1993—, Elson U. Pardee Found., 1993-94, Olson Ctr. for Women's Health, 1993—. Grantee Nebr. Dept. of Health, 1993—, Elas U. Pardee Found., 1993-94, Olson Ctr. for Women's Health, 1993—. Mem. AAAS, Am. Assn. Cancer Rsch., N.Y. Acad. Scis. Roman Catholic. Office: U Nebr Med Ctr Dept Ob/Gyn 600 S 42d St Omaha NE 68198-3255

RALLIS, HELEN, geography educator; b. Johannesburg, South Africa, Mar. 20, 1960; came to U.S., 1984; d. Costa John and Edna Isabel R. BA in Phys. Edn., Rhodes U., Grahamstown, South Africa, 1980; BA Honours, U. Witwatersrand, Johannesburg, South Africa, 1981; MA, U. Miami, 1985; PhD, Pa. State U., 1989. Tchr. phys. edn., geography St. Andrews Sch., Johannesburg, 1982; tchr. geography Jeppe Girls H.S., Johannesburg, 1982-83; tchr. phys. edn. St. Mary's Sch., Johannesburg, 1982-83; grad. asst. dept. geography U. Miami, Coral Gables, Fla., 1984; grad. asst. dept. curriculum and instrn. Pa. State U., State Coll., 1986-89; assoc. prof. U. Minn., Duluth, 1989—; mem. steering com. Minn. Alliance for Geog. Edn., St. Paul, 1990—; mem. com. Minn. State U. H.S. Geography Project, St. Paul, 1991-93; mem. Vice Chancellor's Commn. on Lesbianism, Gay, Bisexual Diversity Issues, Duluth, 1990—; reviewer Nat. Assn. for Multicultural Edn., Kans., 1994-95. Co-author: (handbook) High School Preparation Competencies, 1993; coach internat. invitational case study competition, 1994, 95. Mem. com. Safari for Sci. Tchrs., Duluth, 1994—; vol. Life House, Duluth, 1992-93; mem. African Nat. Congress, South Africa, 1993—. Recipient Horace T. Morse award for outstanding contbns. to undergrad. edn. U. Minn. Alumni Assn., 1995. Mem. ASCD, AAUW, Am. Ednl. Rsch. Assn., Phi Delta Kappa. Office: Univ Minn 120 Montague Hall Duluth MN 55812

RALPH, JEAN DOLORES, education educator; b. Detroit, Sept. 6, 1923; d. Alfred Heath and Genevieve (Taber) Smith; m. Fred A. Ralph, May 4, 1946 (dec. June 1979); children: Nancy Jean, Ellen Sue, Marty. BA, Ea. Mich. U., 1946; MA, Wayne State U., 1961; edn. specialist, U. Mich., 1973; EdD, Nova U., 1981. Cert. gifted elem. and secondary English tchr., adminstr., supr., reading specialist, Mich., Ariz., Fla. Elem. tchr. pub. schs., Harper Woods, Farmington, Mich., 1954-61; elem. prin. Farmington Pub. Schs., 1961-73; curriculum writer Nogales (Ariz.) Pub. Schs., 1973-74; elem. prin. Miami (Ariz.) Pub. Schs., 1974-75; adminstr. Tucson Hebrew Acad., 1975-76; adminstr., tchr. Santa Cruz Sch. Dist. 28, Nogales, 1976-77; dir. edn. Eckerd Wilderness Camps, Brooksville, Fla., 1977-78; prof. edn. Eckerd Coll., St. Petersburg, Fla., 1978-79; adminstr. edn. program Nova U., Orlando, Fla., 1981-86, prof. edn., 1986-89; prof. edn. Kennesaw State Coll., Marietta, Ga., 1989-96; adj. prof. Ea. Ariz. Coll., Gila County, 1974-75; tchr. gifted Orange County Schs., Orlando, 1979-83, tchr. lang. lab. for migrant children, 1983-86, Chpt. I coord., tchr. reading, 1986-89; edn. cons. Ency. Brit., 1969-73, Ariz. Dept. Edn., Phoenix, 1973-77; reading cons. Holt Winston Rinehart, 1973-75. Mem. Nat. Coun. Tchrs. English, Internat. English Reading Assn., Coun. Exceptional Children, Assn. Supervision and Curriculum Devel. Home: 4774 Colony Dr Acworth GA 30102-2820

RALSTIN, JEANICE DIANE, artist, poet; b. Kingfisher, Okla., Nov. 4, 1954; d. Jimmie Lee and Ramona Lee Ralstin. Student, Oxnard Coll., Ventura Coll. Exhibited paintings at various shows; painting in collection at Disneyland, Anaheim, Calif.; wrote and recorded country songs; poetry included in Today's Greatest Poems, 1983, New Voices in Am. Poetry, 1980, 81. Home: 83379 Parkway Dr Florence OR 97439

RALSTON, JOANNE SMOOT, public relations counseling firm executive; b. Phoenix, May 13, 1939; d. A. Glen and Virginia (Lee) Smoot; m. W. Hamilton Weigelt, Aug. 15, 1991. B.A. in Journalism, Ariz. State U., 1960. Reporter, The Ariz. Republic, Phoenix, 1960-62; co-owner, pub. relations dir. The Patton Agy., Phoenix, 1962-71; founder, pres., owner Joanne Ralston & Assocs., Inc., Phoenix, 1971-87, 92—; pres. Nelson Ralston Robb Comm., Phoenix, 1987-91; pres. Joanne Ralston & Assoc., Inc., Scottsdale, Ariz., 1992—. Contbr. articles to profl. jours. Bd. dirs. Ariz. Parklands Found., 1984-86, Gov.'s Council on Health, Phys. Fitness and Sports, 1984-86; task force mem. Water and Natural Resources Council, Phoenix, 1984-86; mem. Ariz. Republican Caucus, 1984—, others. Recipient Lulu' awards (36) Los Angeles Advt. Women, 1964—, Gold Quill (2) Internat. Assn. Bus. Communicators, Excellence awards Fin. World mag., 1982-93, others; named to Walter Cronkite Sch. Journalism Hall of Fame, Coll. Pub. Programs Ariz. State U., 1987; name one of 25 Most Influential Arizonians, Phoenix Mag., 1991. Mem. Pub. Relations Soc. Am. (counselor sect.), Internat. Assn. Bus. Communicators, Phoenix Press Club (pres. bd.), Investor Rels. Inst., Phoenix Met. C. of C. (bd. dirs. 1977-84, 85-91), Phoenix Country Club. Republican. Avocations: horses, skiing.

RALSTON, LUCY VIRGINIA GORDON, artist; b. Washington, Sept. 9, 1926; d. Byron Brown and Lucy (Virginia (Gordon) R. Grad., Finch Jr. Coll., 1942; student, Parsons Sch. Design; studied with, Leon Kroll. Freelance artist Tiffany and Co., 1947-48; designer U.S.S. Constution book Am. Bible Soc. and John Jay and Eliza Jane Watson Found. for presentation Bibles to grads. U.S. Naval Acad., USCG Acad., Marchant Marine Acad., 1953—; art tchr. Sr. Citizens of Pelham, 1948-50. One-woman show Pelham (N.Y.) Meml. High Sch., 1939; exhibited in group shows Westchester Fedn. Women's Clubs, Bronxville, N.Y., 1954, Mt. Vernon (N.Y.) Art Assn., 1955, Allied Artists Am., N.Y.C., 1955, others; represented in permanent collections Assn. Jr. Leagues Am., N.Y.C. and tour U.S. and Can., John Jay and Eliza Jane Watson Found., Elizabeth, N.J.; executed mural at Westchester Restaurant, Mamaroneck, N.Y.; commd. portraits of Princess Anne and Prince Charles of Eng., Brit. Am. Soc. Vol. numerous civic orgns., 1942-45. Recipient Popular prize Manor Club, 1947, 48, 2d prize, 1958, 1st prize for graphic art, 1957; Popular prize Westchester Assn. Women's Clubs, 1951, Mt. Vernon Art Assn., 1954, 2d prize Met. Mus., Pelham, 1969. Mem. DAR (registrar Knapp chpt. 1961-63, rec. sec. Anne Hutchinson chpt. 1989—), Jr. League Pelham, Daus. of Cin. (registrar 1973-78), Colonial Soc.

Ams. Royal Descent, Nat. Soc. Magna Carta Dames, Colonial Soc. Descs. Knights of Garter, Colonial Order Crown, Huguenot Soc. Am., Welcome to Washington Internat. Club. Republican. Episcopalian. Home and Studio: 4784 Boston Post Rd Pelham NY 10803

RALSTON, PAULA JANE, nurse; b. Cedar Rapids, Iowa, Feb. 2, 1960; d. Paul Raymond and Martha Jane (Salato) R. BSN, Morningside Coll., Sioux City, Iowa, 1982; MA in Human Resource Devel., Webster U., 1994. Cert. med.-surg. nurse; cert. EMT. Commd. 2d lt. USAF, 1984, advanced through grades to maj., 1995; staff nurse Cass County Meml. Hosp., Atlantic, Iowa, 1982-84; staff nurse male med. USAF, Scott AFB, Ill., 1984-85, staff nurse female surg., 1985-86, staff nurse 1st Aeromed. Staging Flight, 1986-88, flight nurse, flight nurse instr, quality improvement coord. 57AES/37SAES, 1991-95; officer in charge nursing staff devel. 10TFW Clinic USAF, RAF, Alconbury, 1988-90, charge nurse acute care clinic and 24 hour ambulance svc., 1988-90; ob-gyn. asst. charge nurse 50 TFW Hosp. USAF, Hahn AB, Fed. Republic Germany, 1990-91; nurse mgr. multi-svc. unit, officer in charge hosp. dietary dept, USAF, Misawa AB, Japan, 1995-96, exercise evaluation team chief, 1995—; group edn., tng. coord. USAF, 1996—; mem. coord Air Tatto USAF Air Show, RAF Alconbury, 1990; air festival coord. Misawa AFB, Japan, 1995, 96; mem. hyperbaric med. team USAF, 1988-90, 10 T.F.W. Hosp. Desert Storm USAF, Incirlik, Turkey, 1991; instr. ARC, Preparation for Parenthood, Health Baby, Health Pregnancy, Cmty. First Aid & Safety, CPR, ACLS, PALS. USAF rep. for hosp. Fete Hinchingbrooke Hosp., Huntington, U.K., 1988-90; mem. Bury Ch. Eng. Band, U.K., 1988-90, Belleville (Ill.) Philharm. Orch., 1984-88, 91-95; bd. govs. Nebr.-Iowa Circle K Dist., 1981-82, sec.-treas., 1980-81; 35th med. group change of command coord., USAF, 1995. Decorated Achievement medal, 1995, Commendation medal with two oak leaf clusters, Meritorious medal, Joint Svc. medal, 1991-1994, 15th Air Force Air Crew Excellence award, 1994. Mem. Assn. Women's Health, Obstetrics & Neonatal Nurses, AACN, Morningside Coll. Circle K Club (v.p. 1979-80), Sigma Theta Tau. Methodist. Home: 8952 Audubon Ct Longmont CO 80503-8668 Office: USAF, 35th Med Group, Misawa AFB Japan

RALSTON, RUTH ANNE, women's health nurse; b. Staunton, Va., May 15, 1958; d. Thomas Edward and Betty Lee (King) Graham; m. Daniel Thomas Ralston, Aug. 15, 1981; children: Anne Katherine, Adam Thomas, Alison Brooke Rebecca. BS in Biology, Longwood Coll., 1981; ADN, Piedmont Va. C.C., 1985. RN, Va. Med./surg. staff nurse Montgomery County Hosp., Blacksburg, Va., 1985-86; staff/charge nurse obstetrics and nursery Martha Johnson Hosp., Charlottesville, Va., 1986-88; office nurse mgr. Bruce D. Campbell MD, med. office, Free Union, Va., 1988-94, William B. Freedman, M.D., Cardiologist, Charlottesville, 1995—; childbirth instr., labor coach Martha Jefferson Hosp., 1991—. Mem. Internat. Childbirth Edn. Assn. (cert. childbirth educator). Democrat. Home: 4235 Viewmont Rd Earlysville VA 22936-9722

RALSTON, SARAH LUCILLE, veterinarian, educator; b. Elyria, Ohio, Apr. 11, 1951; d. James Vickroy and Lucille Shrum Ralston. BA, U. Pa., Phila., 1973, VMD, 1980, PhD, 1983; MS, Colo. State U., 1976. Diplomate Am. Coll. Vet. Nutrition. Asst. prof. Colo. State U., Ft. Collins, 1983-89; asst. prof. Rutgers U., New Brunswick, N.J., 1989-95, assoc. prof., 1995—; chmn. NRC-136 Equine Rsch. Com., 1993-94. Co-editor, author: Large Animal Clnical Nutrition, 1991; sect. editor, author: Current Therapy in Equine Medicine, 1991; editl. bd. Jour. Equine Vet. Sci., 1992—, Jour. Vet. Clin. Nutrition, 1994—; ad hoc reviewer 8 jours., 1991—. Bd. dirs. Spl. People United to Ride, Red Bank, N.J., 1994—. Recipient Rsch. awards Purina Mills, Inc., 1990-93, Church & Dwight Inc., Princeton, N.J., 1992-94, Chr. Hansen Labs., St. Louis, 1993-94, Am. Cyanamid, 1995-96. Mem. Am. Coll. Vet. Nutrition (v.p. 1995-96, pres.-elect 1996-97), Am. Vet. Med. Assn. (Samuel F. Scheidy award 1991), Am. Assn. Equine Practitioners, N.J. Assn. Equine Practitioners, Equine Nutrition and Physiology Soc., Am. Soc. Animal Sci. Office: Rutgers U Dept Animal Sci Bartlett Hall Lipman Dr New Brunswick NJ 08903

RAMALEY, JUDITH AITKEN, academic administrator, endocrinologist; b. Vincennes, Ind., Jan. 11, 1941; d. Robert Henry and Mary Krebs (McCullough) Aitken; m. Robert Folk Ramaley, Mar. 1966 (div. 1976); children: Alan Aitken, Andrew Folk. BA, Swarthmore Coll., 1963; PhD, UCLA, 1966; postgrad., Ind. U., 1967-69. Rsch. assoc., lectr. Ind. U., Bloomington, 1967-68, asst. prof. dept. anatomy and physiology, 1969-72; asst. prof. dept. physiology and biophysics U. Nebr. Med. Ctr., Omaha, 1972-74, assoc. prof., 1974-78, prof., 1978-82, assoc. dean for rsch. and devel., 1979-81; asst. v.p. for acad. affairs U. Nebr., Lincoln, 1980-82; prof. biol. scis. SUNY, Albany, N.Y., 1982-87, v.p. for acad. affairs, 1982-85, acting pres., 1984, exec. v.p. for acad. affairs, 1985-87; exec. vice chancellor U. Kans., Lawrence, 1987-90; pres. Portland (Oreg.) State U., 1990—; bd. dirs. Bank of Am.; mem. endocrinology study sect. NIH, 1981-84; cons.-evaluator North Cen. Accreditation, 1978-82, 89-90; mem. regulatory panel NSF, 1979-82; mem. Ill. Commn. Scholars, 1980—. Co-author: Progesterone Function: Molecular and Biochemical Aspects, 1972; Essentials of Histology, 8th edit., 1979; editor: Covert Discrimination, Women in the Sciences, 1978; contbr. articles to profl. jours. Bd. dirs. Family Svc. of Omaha, 1979-82, Albany Symphony Orch., 1984-87, mem. exec. com., 1986-87, Urban League Albany, 1984-87, 2d v.p., mem. exec. com., 1986-87, Upper Hudson Planned Parenthood, 1984-87, Capital Repertory Co., 1986-89, Assn. Portland Progress, 1990—, City Club of Portland, 1991-92, Metro Family Svcs., 1993—, Campbell Inst. for Children, Portland Met. Sports Authority, 1994; bd. dirs. NCAA Pres. Commn., 1991, chair divsn. II sub-com., 1994, mem. joint policy bd., 1994; chmn. bd. dirs. Albany Water Fin. Authority, 1987; mem. exec. com. United Way Douglas County, 1989-90; mem. adv. bd. Emily Taylor Women's Resource Ctr., U. Kans., 1988-90; mem. Silicon Prarie Tech. Assn., 1989-90, Portland Opera Bd., 1991-92, Portland Leaders Roundtable, 1991—; mem. bd. devel. com. United Way of Columbia-Williamette, 1991—; active Oreg. Women's Forum, 1991—, Portland Met. Sports Authority; progress bd. Portland-Multinomah County, 1993—. NSF grantee, 1969-71, 71-77, 75-82, 77-80, 80-83. Fellow AAAS; mem. Nat. Assn. State Univs. and Land Grant Colls. (exec. com., mem. senate 1986-88, vice chair commn. urban agenda 1992—), Assn. Am. Colls. and Univs. (bd. dirs. 1995—), Endocrine Soc. (chmn. edn. com. 1980-85), Soc. Study Reprodn. (treas. 1983-85), Soc. for Neuroscis., Am. Physiol. Soc., Am. Coun. on Edn. (chmn. commn. on women in higher edn. 1987-88), Assn. Portland Progress (bd. dirs.), Portland C. of C. (bd. dirs. 1995), Western Assn. of Schs. and Colls. (commr. 1994). Office: Portland State U Office of the President PO Box 751 Portland OR 97207-0751

RAMAZZINI, JUDITH WILLIAMS, curator, artist; b. Milw., Nov. 13, 1945; d. Bruno Bernard and Verna Marie (Williams) R.; m. Jack Allen Porter, Mar. 15, 1975 (div. Oct. 1981); m. Lawrence Anthony Baldassaro, Feb. 26, 1995. BA, U. Wis., Milw., 1978. Gallery mgr. Milw. Art Mus., 1968-78, spkr., 1988—; freelance artist, 1980-92; curator Quad Graphics, Pewaukee, Wis., 1992—; instr. U. Wis., Milw., 1980-85. One-woman show includes Charles Allis Art Mus., 1989; exhibited in group show Bradley Gallery, 1991; creator Sacajawea award design, 1986; author: The Guild: A Sourcebook of American Craft Artists, 1986. Active Jr. League, Milw., 1976-78; bd. dirs. Wis. Arts Alliance, Madison, 1995—, co-chair creative ticket for student success, 1996; bd. dirs. Milw. Mus. Art, 1995, Print Forum Milw. Art Mus., 1995—, v.p., 1996-97; mem. adv. bd. Jazz Series at the Pabst, Milw., 1994-95, 96. Recipient 1st place award Wis. Women in the Arts, 1982, award Art and the Law, 1982, award Wis. Designer Crafts Coun., 1976; grantee Amoco Prodn. Co., 1987. Mem. Print Forum (bd. dirs.), Contemporary Art Soc. Office: Quad Graphics Duplainville Rd Pewaukee WI 53072

RAMBANA, ANDREA MARIE, nursing educator; b. Kingston, Jamaica, Dec. 29, 1961; d. George Albert and Lilieth Theresa (Watts) Russell; m. Richard Craig Rambana, Dec. 7, 1986; children: Michelle, Andrew. Nursing Diploma, Jackson Meml. Hosp. Sch. of, Nursing, Miami, 1984; BSN, Barry U., 1991. RNC. Med. unit staff nurse Jackson Meml. Hosp., Miami, 1984, staff nurse labor and delivery unit, 1985-88; newborn spl. care unit staff nurse Jackson North Maternity Ctr., Opa-Locak, Fla., 1989-92; nursing clin. educator Jackson North Maternity Ctr., Opa-Locak, 1993—; neonatal resuscitation program instr. Am. Acd. Pediatrics, Miami, 1991—; coord./instr. babysitting course, Jackson North Maternity Ctr., 1993—; CPR instr., 1993; coord. sibling and parent safety courses class, 1996. Participant: (TV series) Healthy Babies, Happy Parents, 1994. Mem. AWHOON, Sigma Theta Tau. Roman Catholic. Office: Jackson North Maternity Ctr 14701 NW 27th Ave Opa Locka FL 33054-3350

RAMBERG, LAURA LOUISE, sculptor; b. Hannibal, Mo., Jan. 22, 1956; d. David Freeman and Joanne (Anderson) R.; m. Charles Alan Seibel, Aug. 28, 1977 (div. 1996); children: Jonah Seibel, Ella Seibel, Julia Seibel, Katy Seibel, Copper. BFA, U. Kans., 1981. vis. artist Kansas City area, 1989—. Prin. works include lifesized carved wooden Crucifix, St. Johns The Evangelist, 1995, carved limestone relief falcon Riley County H.S., 1994, original tilework Wheatfields Bakery, 1995, Paradise Cafe, 1992. Vol. Wildcare, Inc., Lawrence, Kans. Recipient Amsden Book award Kress Found., 1988, Burgess award N.Am. Sculpture Exhbn., 1985; Fine Arts grantee Alpha Delta Kappa, 1981; Fine Arts scholar U. Kans., 1980. Mem. Internat. Sculpture Ctr., Nat. Mus. Women in the Arts. Home and Office: Rt 12 Box 162 AA Lawrence KS 66044-9165

RAMBERG, PATRICIA LYNN, training director; b. Melrose Park, Ill., June 15, 1951; d. Roy Andrew and Elsie Elaine (Lossau) Fricke; m. Richard Lynn Ramberg, May 31, 1980; children: Richard Lynn II, Caitlyn Elizabeth. BS in Bus. Adminstrn. magna cum laude, Elmhurst Coll., 1976; MA in Edn., U. St. Thomas, 1989. Lic. broker. Assoc. dir. ops. Bank Mktg. Assn., Chgo., 1972-75; exec. dir. Soc. Tchrs. Family Medicine, Kansas City, Mo., 1975-78, Minn. Assn. Children with Learning Disabilities, St. Paul, 1979-80; sr. instrnl. designer Applied Learning Systems, Mpls., 1989-90; dir. Upper Midwest Conservation Assn., Mpls., 1990-92; account exec. Dean Witter Reynolds, Inc., Bloomington, Minn., 1992-94; investment specialist FBS Investment Svcs., Inc., Mpls., 1994; mgr. retail investments tng. First Bank Sys., Mpls., 1994—; adj. faculty U. St. Thomas, St. Paul, 1990. Developer curriculum materials; contbr. to profl. publs. Lutheran. Home: 10049 Johnson Ave S Bloomington MN 55437-2443 Office: First Bank System 601 2d Ave S Minneapolis MN 55402 Office: First Bank Sys 601 2nd Ave S Minneapolis MN 55402

RAMBO, SYLVIA H., federal judge; b. Royersford, Pa., Apr. 17, 1936; d. Granville A. and Hilda E. (Leonhardt) R.; m. George F. Douglas, Jr., Aug. 1, 1970. BA, Dickinson Coll., 1958; JD, Dickinson Sch Law, 1962; LLD (hon.), Wilson Coll., 1980, Dickinson Sch. Law, 1993, Dickinson Coll., 1994, Shippensburg U., 1996. Bar: Pa. 1962. Atty. trust dept. Bank of Del., Wilmington, 1962-63; pvt. practice Carlisle, 1963-76; public defender, then chief public defender Cumberland County, Pa., 1974-76; judge Ct. Common Pleas, Cumberland County, 1976-78, U.S. Dist. Ct. (mid. dist.) Pa., Harrisburg, 1979-92; chief judge Pa. & Md., 1992—; asst. prof., adj. prof. law Dickinson Sch. Law, 1974-76. Mem. Nat. Assn. Women Judges, Phi Alpha Delta. Democrat. Presbyterian. Office: US Dist Ct Federal Bldg PO Box 868 Harrisburg PA 17108-0868

RAMEY, JUDY PHARR, nursing administrator; b. Booneville, Miss., Apr. 18, 1948; d. Ross Brooks and Edna (Parks) Pharr; m. Jimmy Dale Ramey, Oct. 27, 1967; children: Michael, Martha Gail, Jason. ADN, Northeast Miss. C.C., Booneville, 1975; BSN, U. N. Ala., 1982; MA in Bus. Adminstrn., Crescent City Christian Coll., New Orleans, 1989. RN, Miss. Staff nurse Northeast Miss. Hosp., Booneville, 1975-77, house supr., 1977-78; critical care coord. Baptist Meml. Hosp., Booneville, 1978-89, asst. dir. nursing svc., 1989-90, dir. nursing svc., 1990—; mem. adv. bd. practical nurse program Northeast C.C., Booneville, 1990—, ADN adv. com., 1990—. Vol. leader Coop. Extension Svc., Booneville, 1991—; sec. Prentiss County Dems., Booneville, 1992; mem. Prentiss County ARC, 1993—, Prentiss County Devel. Assn. Mem. ANA, Miss. Nurses Assn., Miss. Orgn. of Nurse Execs. (bd. dirs. 1993—), N.E. Miss. Coun. Nurse Execs. (pres. 1994). Mem. Ch. of Christ. Office: Bapt Meml Hosp 100 Hospital St Booneville MS 38829-3354

RAMEY, PATRICIA ANN, elementary education educator; b. Maries County, Mo., Sept. 5, 1939; d. John Wesely and Ethel Editha (Prewett) Perkins; m. George Grover Ramey, June 7, 1959; children: Jonathan Edward, Steven Wesely. BA in Edn., William Jewell Coll., 1961; MA in Edn., Union Coll., 1981; postgrad., U. Conn., 1985, Purdue U., 1994. Cert. elem. edn. grades 1-8. Tchr. No. Kansas City (Mo.) Pub. Sch. Dist., 1961-63, Jefferson County Pub. Sch. Dist., Louisville, 1963-65; edn. dir. First Bapt. Ch., Williamsburg, Ky., 1974-77; tchr. Williamsburg Ind. Sch. Dist., Williamsburg, 1979—; Ky. tchr. intern program Williamsburg (Ky.) Ind. Sch., 1987-91, leader numerous profl. devel. activities, 1985—; guest lectr., student tchr. supr. Cumberland Coll., 1979—. Active First Bapt. Ch., Williamsburg, 1968—; den leader Boy Scouts Am., Williamsburg, 1974-82; mem., sec. Laural Lake Camp Bd., Corbin, Ky., 1988-91; active Cultural/Humanitarian Exch., U.S. and Kazakhstan, Almata, Kazakhstan, 1991; bd. dirs. Cleft Rock Retreat Ctr., Mt. Vernon, Ky., 1992—. Recipient State prize Presdl. award for Excellence in Sci. Teaching, 1994. Mem. NEA, Ky. Edn. Assn., Williamsburg Edn. Assn., Nat. Sci. Tchrs. Assn. (presenter nat. meeting 1995, 96), Ky. Sci. Tchrs. Assn. (presenter 1995), Nat. Coun. Tchrs. Math. (presenter ctrl. regional conf. 1991), Ky. Coun. Tchrs. Math., Coun. for Elem. Sci. Internat., Phi Delta Kappa (chpt. v.p.), Delta Kapa Gamma (Alpha Lamda Gamma chpt. sec. 1990-96). Home: 75 Hemlock St Williamsburg KY 40769-1793

RAMIREZ, GLORIA MARIA, physician; b. Mayagüez, P.R., Apr. 14, 1953; d. Jose Ramirez and Gloria E. (Baez-Murphy) Ruiz; m. Bruce William Konrad, Mar. 31, 1951. BS, U. P.R., Mayaguez, 1973; MT, Inst. Health Labs., Rio Piedras, P.R., 1974; MD, San Juan Bautista Med. Sch., 1981. Lic. physician, N.Y., Va. Med. technologist Inst. Health Labs., Rio Piedras, 1974-77; intern Bronx-Lebanon Hosp., 1981-82; resident in internal medicine Barnabas Hosp., Bronx, 1982-84; chief resident Bronx-Lebanon Hosp., 1984-85, fellow in hematology, 1985-86; fellow in hematology/oncology L.I. Coll. Hosp., Bklyn., 1986-88, attending physician in ambulatory surgery/med., 1988-89; internist Family Care Group Practice/St. Luke's Roosevelt Hosp., N.Y.C., 1989-94; hematologist Sickle Cell program/St. Luke's Roosevelt Hosp., 1989—. Contbr. articles to profl. jours. Vol. counselor Hole in the Wall Gang Camp, Ashford, Conn., 1989-96. Mem. AMA, Am. Women's Med. Assn., Spanish Am. Med. Soc., P.R. Coll. Med. Technologists. Office: St Lukes-Roosevelt Hosp Sickle Cell Program 1111 Amsterdam Ave New York NY 10025

RAMIREZ, MARIA C(ONCEPCIÓN), educational administrator; d. Ines and Carlota (Cruz) R. BA, Incarnate Word Coll., San Antonio, 1966; MEd, U. Tex., Austin, 1979; postgrad., S.W. Tex. State U., San Marcos, 1980. Cert. elem. tchr., bilingual tchr., supr. Elem. tchr. regular and bilingual Edgewood Ind. Sch. Dist., San Antonio, 1966-69; elem tchr. regular and bilingual Austin (Tex.) Ind. Sch. Dist., 1969-74, bilingual program coord., 1974-89; instructional coord. Austin Ind. Sch. Dist., 1989-91, helping tchr., 1991—. Mem. NAFE, ASCD, Tex. Assn. for Bilingual Edn., Austin Area Assn. for Bilingual Edn., Austin Assn. for Pub. Sch. Adminstrs., Hispanic Pub. Sch. Adminstrs.

RAMIREZ, SUSAN ELIZABETH, Latin-American history educator; b. Toledo, Ohio, Oct. 11, 1946; d. Eduardo Salvador and Helen Elizabeth (McCartney) R. BA, U. Ill., 1968; MA, U. Wis., 1973, PhD, 1977. Asst. prof. Ohio U., Athens, 1977-82; asst. prof. DePaul U., Chgo., 1982-84, assoc. prof., 1984-89, dir. Latin-Am. studies, 1988-95, prof., 1989—. Author: Provincial Patriarchs: Land Tenure...Peru, 1986, The World Upside Down, 1996; editor: Indian-Religious Relations in Colonial Spanish America, 1989. Named Fulbright-Hayes fellow, 1978-79, NEH fellow 1987, 92, Ford Found. fellow 1987-88; grantee De Paul U. 1992—; recipient Fulbright fellowship, 1993-94. Mem. Am. Hist. Assn. (coms.), Am. Cath. Hist. Assn. (program com. 1986, exec. com. 1992—), Conf. on Latin-Am. History (sec. colonial studies com. 1987-88, gen. com. 1987-90, chair program com. 1989-90), Ill. Congress Latin-Ams. (pres., 1988-89). Office: DePaul Univ Dept History Dept History 2320 N Kenmore Ave Chicago IL 60614-3210

RAMIREZ, TINA, artistic director; b. Caracas, Venezuela; d. Gloria Maria Cestero and Jose Ramirez Gaonita. Studied dance with Lola Bravo, Alexandra Danilova, Anna Sokolow. Toured with Federico Rey Dance Co.; founder, artistic dir. Ballet Hispanico, N.Y.C., 1970—; panelist NEA, N.Y. Sate Coun. on Arts; mem. advisory panel N.Y.C. Dept. Cultural Affairs; bd. dirs. Dance Theater Workshop. Appearances include (Broadway) Kismet, Lute Song, (TV) Man of La Mancha. Recipient Arts and Culture Honor award Mayor of N.Y.C., 1983, Ethnic New Yorker award N.Y.C., 1986, Gov.'s Arts award N.Y. State Gov. Mario Cuomo, 1987; honoree Nat. Puerto Rican Forum, Hispanic Inst. for Performing Arts. Office: Ballet Hispanico 167 W 89th St New York NY 10024-1901*

RAMIREZ-GARNICA, GABRIELA, epidemiologist, translator; b. Chihuahua, Mex., Nov. 2, 1964; Came to the U.S., 1978; d. Roberto and Manuela (Garnica) Ramirez; m. Gabriel E. Noboa, Mar. 20, 1992. BA in French Lang. and Lit., Ariz. State U., 1988, BS in Health Sci., 1988; MPH in Epidemiology, Fla. Internat. U., 1991; PhD, U. South Fla., 1991—. Tchg. asst. Ariz. State U., Tempe, spring 1989; translation editor Profl. Translating Svcs., Miami, Fla., 1989-91; rsch. asst. Fla. Internat. U., Miami, 1990-91; site coord. Orange Count Pub. Health Unit, Orlando, Fla., 1992; cons. RAND Corp., Orlando, 1992-95; rsch. asst. U. South Fla., Tampa, 1989—; freelance translator, Orlando, 1989—; project mgr. CODA/CRC, Inc., 1996—. Vol. Orlando Humane Soc., 1996. Student scholar Ariz. State U., 1983-88, Fla. Internat. U., 1990-91. Mem. APHA, Soc. for Epidemiol. Rsch., Coll. Pub. Health Student Assn., (sec. 1990-91), Latin Am. Student Assn. (founder, v.p. 1984-86). Home: 12613 Lysterfield Ct Orlando FL 32837 Office: Dept Epidemiology & Biostatistics Coll Public Health Univ So Fla Tampa FL 33602

RAMO, ROBERTA COOPER, lawyer; b. Denver, Aug. 8, 1942; d. David D. and Martha L. (Rosenblum) Cooper; m. Barry W. Ramo, June 17, 1964. BA magna cum laude, U. Colo., 1964, LHD (hon.), 1995; JD, U. Chgo., 1967; LLD (hon.) U. Mo., 1995, U. Denver, 1995. Bar: N.Mex., 1967, Tex. 1971. With N.C. Fund, Durham, N.C., 1967-68; nat. teaching fellow Shaw U., Raleigh, N.C., 1968-70; mem. Sawtelle, Goode, Davidson & Troilo, San Antonio, 1970-72, Rodey, Dickason, Sloan, Akin & Robb, Albuquerque, 1972-74; sole practice law, Albuquerque, 1974-77; dir., shareholder Poole, Kelly & Ramo, Albuquerque, 1977-93; shareholder Modrall, Sperling, Roehl, Harris & Sisk, 1993—; bd. dirs. United N.Mex. Bank of Albuquerque, 1983-88; lectr. in field. Bd. dirs., past pres. N.Mex. Symphony Orch., 1977-86; bd. dirs. Albuquerque Cmty. Found., N.Mex. First, 1987-90, Coll. of Law Practice Mgmt.; trustee Manzano Day Sch., 1975-77; bd. regents U. N.Mex., 1989-94, pres. 1991-93, chmn. presdl. search com. 1990; mem. vis. com. U. Chgo. Law Sch., 1987-90; mem. adv. bd. N.Mex. Performing ARts Ctr. 1987-90, others. Recipient Disting. Pub. Svc. award Gov. of N.Mex., 1993. Fellow Am. Bar Found.; mem. Albuquerque Bar Assn. (bd. dirs., pres. 1980-81), N.Mex. Bar Assn. (chmn. bus., banking and corp. sect. 1979-80, Outstanding Contbn. award 1981, 84), ABA (pres. 1995, bd. govs. 1994—, vice chmn. 1981-82, chmn. law practice sect. 1984, ALI/ABA com., chmn. select com. of the ho. 1991, mem. coun. law practice mgmt. sect. 1974—, chmn. coun. of sect. officers 1984-86, chmn. legal tech. adv. commn. 1984-88, chmn. coord. coun. on legal tech. 1989-94, chmn. ABA celebration of bicentennial of constitution at ann. meeting 1986-87, past mem. tax sect. com. on employee benefits, past mem. tax sect. com. on profl. svc. corps., others), Am. Bar Retirement Assn. (bd. dirs. 1990-94), Am. Judicature Soc. (bd. dirs. 1988-91), Greater Albuquerque C. of C. (bd. dirs. exec. com. 1987-91). Co-author: New Mexico State Administration System, 1980; contbr. articles to profl. jours. and chpts. to books; editor: How to Create a System for the Law Office, 1975; contbg. editor: Tex. Probate Sys., 1974. Address: Modrall Sperling Roehl Harris & Sisk PO Box 2168 Albuquerque NM 87103-2168

RAMO, VIRGINIA M. SMITH, civic worker; b. Yonkers, N.Y.; d. Abraham Harold and Freda (Kasnetz) Smith; B.S. in Edn., U. So. Calif., DHL (hon.), 1978; m. Simon Ramo; children—James Brian, Alan Martin. Nat. co-chmn. ann. giving U. So. Calif., 1968-70, vice chmn., trustee, 1971—, co-chmn. bd. councilors Sch. Performing Arts, 1975-76, co-chmn. bd. councillors Schs. Med. and Engring.; vice-chmn. bd. overseers Hebrew Union Coll., 1972-75; bd. dirs. The Muses of Calif. Mus. Sci. and industry, UCLA Affiliates, Estelle Doheny Eye Found., U. So. Calif. Sch. Medicine; adv. council Los Angeles County Heart Assn., chmn. com. to endow Chair in cardiology at U. So. Calif.; vice-chmn., bd. dirs. Friends of Library U. So. Calif.; bd. dirs., nat. pres. Achievement Rewards for Coll. Scientists Found., 1975-77; bd. dirs. Les Dames Los Angeles, Community TV So. Calif.; bd. dirs., v.p. Founders Los Angeles Music Center; v.p. Los Angeles Music Center Opera Assn.; v.p. corp. bd. United Way; v.p. Blue Ribbon-400 Performing Arts Council; chmn. com. to endow chair in gerontology U. So. Calif.; vice chmn. campaign Doheny Eye Inst., 1986. Recipient Service award Friends of Libraries, 1974, Nat. Community Service award Alpha Epsilon Phi, 1975, Disting. Service award Am. Heart Assn. 1978, Service award U. So. Calif., Spl. award U. So. Calif. Music Alumni Assn., 1979, Life Achievement award Mannequins of Los Angeles Assistance League, 1979, Woman of Yr. award PanHellenic Assn., 1981, Disting. Service award U. So. Calif. Sch. Medicine, 1981, U. So. Calif. Town and Gown Recognition award, 1986, Asa V. Call Achievement award U. So. Calif., 1986, Phi Kappa Phi scholarship award U. So. Calif., 1986, Vision award Luminaires of Doheny Eye Inst., 1994. Mem. UCLA Med. Aux., U. So. Calif. Pres.'s Circle, Commerce Assos. U. So. Calif., Cedars of Lebanon Hosp. Women's Guild (dir. 1967-68), Blue Key, Skull and Dagger.

RAMON, ALICIA, day care center director; b. Buenos Aires, Mar. 6, 1942; came to U.S., 1967; BS in Sociology, Mercy Coll., 1984; MEd, SUNY, New Paltz, 1987. Cert. nursery and elem. sch. tchr., N.Y. Co-founder, dir. Montebello (Calif.) Day Care, 1967-74; founder, dir. Anne Sullivan Nursery Sch., Wildomar, Calif., 1975-79, Seed Day Care Ctr., Yorktown, N.Y., 1980—. Co-founder, co-dir. Spiritual Cmty. of CAFH Order, 1967-74, Montebello, 1967-74, founder, dir., Wildomar, 1974-79, Yorktown, 1979—; treas. CAFH Found., N.Y.C., 1977-85. Mem. Nat. Assn. for Edn. of Young Children, Internat. Reading Assn. Office: Seed Day Care Ctr 2084 Baldwin Rd Yorktown Heights NY 10598

RAMOS, DOROTHY JO, information resource manager; b. Little Rock, July 8, 1949; d. Otis Joe and Dorothy Juanita (Graham) Green; m. Eddmond Virgil Mann (dec. Dec. 1979); children: Brian Eddmond, Jeremy Earl; m. Francisco Ramos Jr., Oct. 24, 1987. Student, St. Mary's Coll., 1995—. Computer specialist Naval Supply Ctr., Oakland, Calif., 1973-91, USAF, McClellan AFB, Calif., 1991-93; mgr. Defense Info. Sys. Agy., McClellan AFB, Calif., 1993-95, U.S. Treasury, San Francisco, 1995—. Mem. Greater Vallejo Lioness Club (pres. 1985). Home: 130 Suncrest Way Vacaville CA 95688 Office: US Treasury 390 Main St San Francisco CA 94119

RAMOS, ELEANOR LACSON, internist; b. Quezon City, The Philippines, Mar. 26, 1956; d. Pol and Evelyn (Manahan) Ramos. BS, Tufts U., 1977; MD, Tufts Med. Sch., Boston, 1981. Diplomate Am. Bd. Internal Medicine, Am. Bd. Nephrology. Resident in internal medicine New Eng. Med. Ctr., Boston, 1981-84; fellow in nephrology Brigham and Women's Hosp., Boston, 1984-88, med. dir. renal transplant svc., 1988-90; med. dir. renal transplant svc. U. Fla., Gainesville, 1990-94; assoc. dir. immunology clin. rsch. Bristol-Myers Squibb Pharm. Rsch. Inst., Wallingford, Conn., 1994-96; asst. clin. prof. medicine Yale U., 1995-96; dir. med. rsch. Roche Global Devel., Palo Alto, Calif., 1996—. Mem. Am. Soc. Transplant Physicans (chairperson patient care and edn. com. 1994-95, Young Investigator award 1988), Am. Soc. Nephrology, Internat. Soc. Nephrology, Alpha Omega Alpha. Office: Roche Golbal Devel 3401 Hillview Ave Palo Alto CA 94304-1397

RAMOS, MARY GASSETT, editor; b. Raymondville, Tex., Jan. 10, 1937; d. Wilson E. and Esther (Koger) Gassett; m. Joe W. Crawford, 1961 (div. 1987); 1 child, Wade W.; m. Charles Ramos, July 23, 1994. BFA, U. Tex., 1958. Mgr. group & tour desk reservations dept. Braniff Internat., Dallas, 1958-68; freelance writer, editor, photographer Dallas, 1970—; editor, compiler indexes Southwestern Legal Found., Dallas, 1972-85; editorial asst. Tex. Almanac-Dallas Morning News, 1985-86, assoc. editor, 1986-94, editor, 1994—. Bd. trustees Preservation Dallas (formerly Historic Preservation League), 1984-90, 93-95. Recipient Historic Preservation award for News Media Tex. Hist. Commn., 1986, News Media award, 1990, Lantern Svc. award Historic Preservation League, Dallas, 1986. Mem. Tex. State Hist. Assn., Nature Conservancy Tex. Office: Tex Almanac PO Box 655237 Dallas TX 75265

RAMOS-CANO, HAZEL BALATERO, social worker, early childhood educator, food service director, executive chef; b. Davao City, Mindanao, Philippines, Sept. 2, 1936; came to U. S., 1960.; d. Mauricio C. and Felicidad (Balatero) Ramos; m. William Harold Snyder, Feb. 17, 1964 (div. 1981);

children: John Byron, Snyder, Jennifer Ruth; m. Nelson Allen Blue, May 30, 1986 (div. 1990); m. A. Richard Cano, June 25, 1994. BA in Social Work, U. Philippines, Quezon City, 1958; MA in Sociology, Pa. State U., 1963, postgrad., 1966-67. Cert. exec. chef, Am. Culinary Fedn. Faculty, tng. staff Peace Corps Philippine Project, University Park, Pa., 1961-63; sociology instr. Albright Coll. Sociology Dept., Reading, Pa., 1963-64; research asst. Meth. Ch. U.S.A., State College, Pa., 1965-66; research asst. dept. child devel. & family relations Pa. State U., University Park, Pa., 1966-67; exec. dir. Presbyn. Urban Coun. Raleigh Halifax Ct. Child Care and Family Svc. Ctr., 1973-79; early childhood educator Learning Together, Inc., Raleigh, 1982-83; loan mortgage specialist Raleigh Savings & Loan, 1983-84; restaurant owner, mgr. Hazel's on Hargett, Raleigh, 1985-86; admissions coord., social worker Brian Corp. Nursing Home, Raleigh, 1986-88, food svc. dir., 1989-90; regional dir. La Petite Acad., Raleigh, 1989-90; asst. food svc. mgr. Granville Towers, Chapel Hill, N.C., 1990-92; mgr. trainee Child Nutrition Svcs. Wake County Pub. Sch. System, Raleigh, N.C., 1993-94; food svc. dir. S.W. Va. 4-H Ednl. Conf. Ctr., Abingdon, 1994-95; caterer, owner The Eclectic Chef's Catering, 1995—; innkeeper, owner Love House Bed and Breakfast, 1996—; cooking instr. Wake Cmty. Tech. Coll., Raleigh, 1986-92; freelance caterer, 1964-95; chair Internat. Cooking Demonstrations Raleigh Internat. Festival, 1990-93. Pres. Wake County Day Care United Coun., 1974-75, N.C. Assn. Edn. Young Children (Raleigh Chpt.), 1975-76; bd. mem. Project Enlightenment Wake County Pub. Schs., 1976-77; various positions Pines of Carolina Girl Scout Council, 1976-85; chmn. Philippine Health and Medical Aid Com., Phil-Am Assn. Raleigh 1985-88 (publicity chmn.); elder Trinity Presbyn. Ch., Raleigh, 1979-81, bd. deacons, 1993-94. Recipient Juliette Low Girl Scout Internat. award, 1953, Rockefeller grant Rockefeller Found., 1958-59, Ramon Magsaysay Presidential award, Philippine Leadership Youth Movement, 1957; Gov.'s Cert. Appreciation State N.C., 1990, Raleigh Mayor's award Quality Childcare Svcs., 1990. Mem. Am. Culinary Fedn., Presby. Women, Raleigh, (historian 1975-76), Penn State Dames (pres. 1968-69). Democrat. Office: Love House Bed & Breakfast 210 E Valley St Abingdon VA 24210

RAMPERSAD, PEGGY A. SNELLINGS, sociologist; b. Fredericksburg, Va., Jan. 12, 1933; d. George Daniel and Virginia Riley (Bowler) Snellings; m. Oliver Ronald Rampersad, Mar. 19, 1955; 1 child, Gita. BA, Mary Washington Coll., Fredericksburg, 1953; student, Sch. of Art Inst. of Chgo., 1953-55; MA, U. Chgo., 1965, PhD, 1978. Grad. admissions counselor U. Chgo., 1954-57, adviser to fgn. students, 1958, dir. admissions Grad. Sch. Bus., 1959-63, rsch. project specialist Grad. Sch. Bus., 1970-78, pers. mgr. Grad. Sch. Bus., 1979-80, mgr. organizational devel. Grad. Sch. Bus., 1980-82, adminstr. dept. econs., 1983-95; cons. PSR Consulting, Chgo., 1995—; cons. North Ctrl. Assn. Colls. and Secondary Schs., Chgo.,1964-70, Orchestral Assn. of Chgo. Symphony Orch., 1982, Chgo. Ctr. for Decision Rsch., 1982, Harvard U., 1993—. Exhibited paintings in juried shows at Va. Mus. Fine Arts, Art Inst. Chgo., others; editor North Cen. Assn. Quar., 1972; contbr. articles to profl. jours. U. Chgo. grad. fellow, 1963-67. Mem. AAUW, Am. Econ. Assn., Am. Acad. Polit. and Social Sci., Art Inst. Chgo. (museum assoc.), Pi Lambda Theta (past pres.). Episcopalian. Home and Office: 5531 S Kenwood Ave Chicago IL 60637-1755

RAMSAY, JANE PATTERSON, executive secretary; b. Seattle, Feb. 23, 1941; d. Gerland Ramsay and Vida Gwendolyn (Nelson) Patterson; m. Pater A. Formuzis, Dec. 28, 1965 (div. May 1976); children: Katie Cassandra Formuzis and Alexander Peter Formuzis (twins). BA, Wash. State U., 1963. Exec. asst. Lake Washington Sch. Dist., Kirkland, Wash.; office mgr. Wash. Rsch. Found., Seattle; corp. sec. Fed. Home Loan Bank Seattle, 1988—. Active parents club Overlake Sch., Redmond, Wash., 1984-90; fin. com. March of Dimes, Seattle, 1995; bd. dirs. Toastmasters, Seattle, 1994-95. Office: Fed Home Loan Bank 1501 4th Ave # 1900 Seattle WA 98101

RAMSAY, KARIN KINSEY, publisher, educator; b. Brownwood, Tex., Aug. 10, 1930; d. Kirby Luther and Ina Rebecca (Wood) Kinsey; m. Jack Cummins Ramsay Jr., Aug. 31, 1951; children: Annetta Jean, Robin Andrew. BA, Trinity U., 1951. Cert. assoc. ch. edn., 1980. Youth coord. Covenant Presbyn. Ch., Carrollton, Tex., 1961-76; dir. ch. edn. Northminster Presbyn. Ch., Dallas, 1976-80, Univ. Presbyn. Ch., Chapel Hill, N.C., 1987-90, Oak Grove Presbyn. Ch., Bloomington, Minn., 1990-93; coord. ecum. ministry Flood Relief for Iowa, Des Moines, 1993; program coord. 1st Presbyn. Ch., Green Bay, Wis., 1994-95; publicity & tour dir. Hist. Resources Press, Green Bay, 1994—; mem. Presbytery Candidates Com., Dallas, 1977-82, Presbytery Exams. Com. Dallas, 1979-81; clk. coun. New Hope Presbytery, Rocky Mount, N.C., 1989-90; creator, dir. Thee Holy Fools and This Is Me retreats. Author: Ramsay's Resources, 1983—; contbr. articles to jours. in field. Design cons. Brookhaven Hosp. Chapel, Dallas, 1977-78; elder Presbyn. Ch. U.S.A., 1982—; coord. Lifeline Emergency Response, Dallas, 1982-84. Mem. Internat. Platform Assn., Assn. Presbyn. Ch. Educators.

RAMSDEN, LINDA GISELE, lawyer; b. Lewiston, Maine, July 19, 1969; d. Donald Jean and Rita Lorraine (Lemieux) Rossignol; m. Matthew Edmund Ramsden, Aug. 13, 1994. Student, Bristol (Eng.) U., 1989-90; BA cum laude, Colby Coll., 1991; JD cum laude, U. Maine, 1994. Bar: Mass. 1995, U.S. Dist. Ct. Mass. 1995. Prearraignment screening vol. Maine Pretrial Svcs., Portland, 1991-92; law clk. U.S. Atty., Dist. of Maine, 1993; legal intern Gardner, Gardner and Murphy, Saco, Maine, 1993-94; ptnr. Hoffman and Ramsden, Boston, 1995—. Mem. ACLU, ABA, Mass. Bar Assn., Boston Bar Assn., Phi Beta Kappa, Nat. Polit. Honor Soc. Democrat. Roman Catholic. Home: 15 Howitt Rd Boston MA 02132 Office: Hoffman & Ramsden Ste 632 294 Washington St Boston MA 02108

RAMSDEN, NORMA LA VONNE HUBER, nurse; b. Lewiston, Idaho, Aug. 1, 1921; d. Lawrence Henry and Gertrude Melissa (Ryder) Huber; m. John Burton Wormell, Nov. 18, 1942 (div. 1950); m. Everett Glenn Ramsden, Dec. 25, 1957; 1 child, Valerie Ann Ramsden Brooks. Diploma in nursing, St. Joseph's Hosp., Lewiston, 1952. Psychiatric nurse Oreg. State Hosp., Salem, 1952-57; clin. instr. Idaho State Hosp., Orofino, Idaho, 1957-58; night nurse ICU Tri State Hosp., Clarkston, Wash., 1969-94; adv. bd. Rogers Counseling Ctr., Clarkston, 1969—; ret., 1994. Leader Camp Fire Girls Am., 1958-61, 69-71; Episcopalian vestry, 1992-94, fellowship chmn., 1994—; vol. Interlink, 1994—. Recipient Woman Achievement award Altrusa Club, 1985. Mem. Am. Nurses Assn., Anatone Grange, Pollyette (pres., sec., treas.). Home: 817 Highland Ave Clarkston WA 99403

RAMSEY, BETTY JANE, elementary school educator; b. Marshall, N.C., Nov. 29, 1948; d. Ernest and Mary Marjorie (Presley) Chandler; m. Quentin Ramsey, Jan. 23, 1967; children: Melissa Quentina Ramsey Chandler, Angela Quenette. BA in Edn., Mars Hill Coll., 1978; MA in Edn., Western Carolina U., 1988; degree in ednl. media for librs., Appalachian U., 1995; PhD in Edn., Columbia Pacific U., 1996. Cert. tchr. k-5, reading k-12, media coord., N.C. Reading and math. tchr. Laurel Elem. Sch., Marshall, N.C., 1978-80; kindergarten tchr. Laurel Elem. Sch., Marshall, 1980-92; media coord. Marshall Elem. Sch., 1994, Walnut and Laurel Elem. Schs., 1995—; mem. OBE CORE team Madison County Ctrl. Office, 1993. Author: (poetry) Great Am. Poetry Anthology, 1989 (Golden Poet award), 1990 (Silver Poet award). V.p. Revere-Rice Cove Comty. Devel., Marshall, N.C., 1990, pres., 1993, 94. Named Tchr. of Yr., TOY Com., Madison County, N.C., 1989-90, Woman of Yr., Revere-Rice Cove Comty. Devel., 1993, 95. Mem. ASCD, N.C. Assn. Edn. (rep., NCAE award 1989), N.C. Assn. Sch. Librs., Kappa Delta Pi. Republican. Baptist. Home: 4771 Revere Rd Marshall NC 28753-9207 Office: 1255 Hwy 212 Marshall NC 28753

RAMSEY, BONNIE JEANNE, mental health facility administrator, psychiatrist; b. Tucson, Dec. 9, 1952; d. William Arnold Jr. and Doris Marie (Gaines) R. BS cum laude, U. S.C., 1971-75, MD, 1981. Diplomate Am. Bd. Psychiatry and Neurology; lic. child and adult psychiatrist S.C., N.C., Ga. Chief resident in psychiatry William S. Hall Psychiat. Inst., Columbia, S.C., 1983, unit dir. adolescent girls, 1986-89; chief child and adolescent inpatient program William S. Hall Psychiat. Inst., Columbia, 1989—, interim dir. child and adolescent div., 1989-92; interim chmn. child and adolescent div. dept. neuropsychiatry U. S.C., Columbia, 1989-92; instr. Sch. of Medicine U. S.C., Columbia, 1986-89, asst. prof. Sch. of Medicine, 1989—. Mem. choir Trinity Meth. Ch., West Columbia, 1981—, vice chmn. bd. trustees, 1989—, trustee, 1990—, mem. at large adminstrn. bd., 1993—; adv. coun. Habitat for Humanity. Named one of Outstanding Young Women of Am., 1985. Mem. AMA (del. residents physician sect. 1983, 84, 86, housing staff sect. 1988—), Am. Psychiat. Assn. (local sec.-treas., pres. 1981—), Am. Acad. Child Psychiatry, S.C. Med. Soc., Columbia Med. Soc., Palmetto Soc. United Way. Methodist. Office: William S Hall Psychiat Inst PO Box 202 Columbia SC 29202-0202

RAMSEY, ELEANORE EDWARDS, design bookbinder; d. Arthur Decatur Jr. and Eleanore Virginia (Edwards) R.; m. Andrew Thomas Nadell, July 24, 1993. BA, Coe Coll. Bookbindings exhibited in N.Am., Eng., Scotland, France, Belgium and Germany; permanent collections include of Libs. of Stanford U., Book Club of Calif., U. Tex., U. Chgo. and Manchester U., Eng. Recipient Wollenberg Internat. Prize for Art Bookbinding Stanford U., 1992. Mem. Hand Bookbinders of Calif. (v.p. 1994—), Designer Bookbinders (London), Roxburghe Club of San Francisco, Colophon Club (San Francisco). Episcopalian. Office: 366 Thirty-First Ave San Francisco CA 94121

RAMSEY, INEZ LINN, librarian, educator; b. Martins Ferry, Ohio, Apr. 25, 1938; d. George and Leona (Smith) Linn; m. Jackson Euguene Ramsey, Apr. 22, 1961; children: John Earl, James Leonard. B.A. in Hist. SUNY-Buffalo, 1971; M.L.S., 1972; Ed.D. in Audiovisual Edn., U. Va., 1980. Librarian Iroquois Central High Sch., Elma, N.Y., 1971-73, Lucy Simms Elem. Sch., Harrisonburg, Va., 1973-75; instr. James Madison U., Harrisonburg, 1975-80, asst. prof., 1980-85; assoc. prof. 1985-91, prof. 1991—; mem. Va. State Library Bd., Richmond, 1975-80; cons. Contr. to Enclopedia, articles to profl. jours.; author (with Jackson E. Ramsey): Budgeting Basics, Library Planning and Budgeting; project dir. Oral (tape) History Black Community in Harrisonburg, 1977-78; storyteller, puppeteer. Rsch. grantee James Madison U., Harrisonburg, 1981, Commonwealth Ctr. State Va., 1989. Mem. ALA, Am. Assn. Sch. Librarians, Assn. Edn. Communications Tech. (exec. bd. DSMS 1989—), Higher Edn. Media Assn. (sec., treas. 1989—), Children's Lit. Assn., Puppeteers Am., Nat. Assn. Preservation and Perpetuation of Storytelling, Va. Ednl. Media Assn. (sec. 1981-83, citation 1983 pres. 1985-86, Educator of Yr. award 1984-85, Meritorious Service award 1987-88), Phi Beta Kappa (pres. Shenandoah chpt. 1980-81), Higher Edn. Media Assn. (sec. treas., 1989—), Beta Phi Mu. Home: 282 Franklin St Harrisonburg VA 22801-4019 Office: James Madison U Dept Secondary Edn Sci Harrisonburg VA 22807

RAMSEY, LUCIE AVRA, small business owner; b. N.Y., Mar. 3, 1942; d. Albert and Mazie (Gordon) Miller; m. Charles Allen Ramsey, Feb. 3, 1968; children: Aaron Ramsey (dec.), Jacqueline Hartigan. BS, U. San Francisco, 1986. Office mgr. Quicksilver Products Inc., San Francisco, 1962-66; exec. sec. Far West Lab. for Educ. Rsch. and Devel., San Francisco and Berkeley, Calif., 1966-68; office mgr. The Ark Pub. Co., Tiburon, Calif., 1973-75; adminstrv. asst. Nat. Coun. Jewish Women, San Francisco, 1979-80; asst. to the chief Tiburon Fire Protection Dist., 1980; exec. dir. Zionist Orgn. Am., San Francisco, 1980-87; asst. dir. Bay Area Coun. for Soviet Jews, San Francisco, 1987-89; exec. dir. Jewish Community Rels. Coun., Oakland, Calif., 1989-91; pres. Ramsey Cons., Mill Valley, Calif., 1991—; leader first ever interreligious task force to the USSR. Author: Concerns of the Jewish Community 1930's/1970's. Civic organizer, planner, chairperson Marin County Clergy Group, San Rafael, Calif., 1975-79; asst. area dir. Am. Jewish Com., San Francisco Bay Area chpt., 1994—. Democratic. Jewish.

RAMSEY, LYNN ALLISON, public relations executive; b. Phila., July 31, 1944; d. Charles Edward and Edna Berry (Whetstone) R. Student, Inst. European Studies, Vienna, Austria, 1964-65; BA, Boston U., 1967. Copy editor Am. Heritage Pub. Co., N.Y.C., 1969-71; prodr., writer Rick Carrier Film Prodns., N.Y.C., 1971-72; mng. editor New Ingenue mag., N.Y.C., 1973-75; freelance writer N.Y.C., 1975-80; mgr. pub. rels. Cunningham and Walsh (acquired by Ayer Pub. Rels. 1987), N.Y.C., 1981—; v.p., mgr. Ayer Pub. Rels., N.Y.C., 1988-95; pres., CEO Jewelry Info. Ctr., N.Y.C., 1995—. Author: Gigolos; The World's Best-Kept Men, 1978; photographer: FLY: The Complete Book of Sky Sailing, 1974; contbr. articles to profl. jours. Mem. Fgn. Policy Assn. 1982-87; sec. U.S.A. Bald Eagle Command, 1975—. Mem. Pub. Rels. Soc. Am. (accredited, bd. dirs. N.Y. chpt. 1993-95), The Fashion Group, Women's Jewelry Assn. (bd. dirs. 1993—, Award for Excellence 1993).

RAMSEY, SANDRA LYNN, psychotherapist; b. Camp LeJeune, N.C., Feb. 7, 1951; d. Robert A. and Lola J. (Hann) R.; m. Edward G. Schmidt, July 9, 1988; children: Seth, Sarah, Anna, Rachel. Student, U. Calif., Long Beach, 1969-70, Orange Coast Coll., Costa Mesa, Calif., 1971-72; BA in Psychology with distinction, U. Nebr., 1987, MA in Counseling Psychology, 1989. Vol. coord., client adv. Rape/Spouse Abuse Crisis Ctr., Lincoln, 1989-90; mental health therapist Health Am., HMO, Lincoln, 1991-94; pvt. practice, Lincoln, 1994—; adj. faculty S.E. Cmty. Coll; contract therapist Lincoln Pediatric Group, 1990-91, Family Svc. Assn., Lincoln, 1990-91, Cmty. Preservation Assocs., Lincoln, 1991-94. Mem. Nebr. Domestic Violence Sexual Assault Coalition; vol. ARC Disaster Mental Health Svcs.; mem., vol. Nebr. Critical Incident Stress Debriefing team. Portenier scholar U. Nebr., 1986-87. Mem. APA (assoc., divsn. 50 addictions), Am. Assn. Sex Educators, Counselors and Therapists, Assn. Pvt. Practice Therapists, Nebr. Assn. for Counseling and Devel., Sex Info. and Edn. Coun. of the U.S., Am. Mental Health Counselors Assn. (clin.), Golden Key, Psi Chi.

RAMSEY-GOLDMAN, ROSALIND, physician; b. N.Y.C., Mar. 22, 1954; d. Abraham L. and Miriam (Colen) Goldman; m. Glenn Ramsey, June 29,1 975; children: Ethan Ramsey, Caitlin Ramsey. BA, Case Western Res. U., 1975, MD, 1978; MPH, U. Pitts., 1988, DPH, 1992. Med. resident U. Rochester (N.Y.), 1978-81; chief resident Rochester Gen. Hosp., 1981-82; staff physician Univ. Health Svc., Rochester, 1982-83; rheumatology fellow U. Pitts., 1983-86, instr. medicine, 1986-87, asst. prof., 1987-91, co-dir. Lupus Treatment and Diagnostic Ctr., 1987-91; asst. prof. medicine Northwestern U., Chgo., 1991-96; assoc. prof. medicine Northwestern U., 1996—; dir. Chgo. Lupus Registry, Northwestern U., Chgo., 1991—. Contbr. rsch. articles to profl. jours. Recipient Finkelstein award Hershey (Pa.) Med. Ctr., 1986. Fellow Am. Coll. Rheumatology; mem. Am. Coll. Physicians, Soc. for Epidemiologic Rsch., Ctrl. Soc. Clin. Rsch. Office: Northwestern U Ward 3-315 303 E Chicago Ave Chicago IL 60611-3008

RAN, SHULAMIT, composer; b. Tel Aviv, Oct. 21, 1949; came to U.S., 1963; m. Abraham Lotan, 1986. Studied composition with, Paul Ben-Haim, Norman Dello, Joio, Ralph Shapey; student, Mannes Coll. Music, N.Y.C., 1963-67. With dept. music U. Chgo., 1973—, William H. Colvin prof. music; composer-in-residence Chgo. Symphony Orch., 1990—, Lyric Opera of Chgo., 1994—. Compositions include 10 Children's Scenes, 1967, Structures,1 968, 7 Japanese Love Poems, 1968, Hatzvi Israel Eulogy, 1969, O the Chimneys, 1969, Concert Piece for piano and orch., 1970, 3 Fantasy Pieces for Cello and Piano, 1972, Ensembles for 17, 1975, Double Vision, 1976, Hyperbolae for Piano, 1976, For an Actor: Monologue for Clarinet, 1978, Apprehensions, 1979, Private Game, 1979, Fantasy-Variations for Cello, 1980, A Prayer, 1982, Verticals for piano, 1982, String Quartet No. 1, 1984, (for woodwind quintet) Concerto da Camera I, 1985, Amichai Songs, 1985, Amichai Songs, 1985, Concerto for Orchestra, 1986, (for clarinet, string quartet and piano) Concerto da Camera II, 1987, East Wind, 1987, String Quartet No. 2, 1988-89, Symphony, 1989-90, Mirage, 1990, Inscriptions for solo violin, 1991, Chicago Skyline for brass and percussion, 1991, Legends for Orch., 1992-93, Invocation, 1994, Yearning for violin and string orch.; commd. pieces include for Am. Composers Orch., Phila. Orch., Chgo. Symphony, Chamber Soc. of Lincoln Ctr., Mendelssohn String quartet, Da Capo Chamber Players, Sta. WFMT; composer and soloist for 1st performances Capriccio, 1963, Symphonic Poem, 1967, Concert Piece, 1971. Recipient Acad. Inst. Arts and Letters award, 1989, Pulitzer prize for music, 1991, Friedheim award for orchestral music Kennedy Ctr., 1992; Guggenheim fellow, 1977, 90. Office: U Chgo Dept Music 1010 E 59th St Chicago IL 60637-1404

RANCK, STACEY STELTS, elementary education educator; b. Savannah, Ga., Apr. 8, 1964; d. Frederick Wahl and Judith (Zipperer) Stelts; m. Robert William Ranck, Aug. 26, 1989; 1 child, William Mason. BS, Coll. Charleston, 1987; MEd, Kenensaw State Coll., 1995. Tchr. elem. sch. Charleston (S.C.) Sch. System, 1987-88, Cobb County Sch. System, Marietta, Ga., 1988—; pilot tchr. multiage program Cobb County, 1993-95, mem. textbook adoption com., 1993-95, mem. visitation com., 1994-95, workshop presenter, 1989—. Mem. Cobb Area Internat. Reading Assn. (pres.-elect 1994-95, pres. 1995-96), Jr. League Cobb. Republican. Methodist. Home: 466 Hascall Rd Atlanta GA 30309 Office: Clay Elem Sch 730 Boggs Rd Mableton GA 30059-4206

RAND, JOELLA MAE, nursing educator, counselor; b. Akron, Ohio, July 9, 1932; d. Harry S. and Elizabeth May (Miller) Halberg; m. Martin Rand; children: Craig, Debbi Stark. BSN, U. Akron, 1961, MEd in Guidance, 1968; PhD in Higher Edn. Adminstrn., Syracuse U., 1981. Staff nurse Akron Gen. Hosp., 1953-54; staff-head nurse-instr. Summit County Receiving, Cuyahoga Falls, Ohio, 1954-56; head nurse psychiat. unit Akron Gen. Hosp., 1956-57; instr. psychiatric nursing Summit County Receiving, Cuyahoga Falls, 1957-61; head nurse, in-service instr. Willard (N.Y.) State Hosp., 1961-62; asst. prof. Alfred (N.Y.) U., 1962-76, assoc. prof., assoc. dean, 1976-78, acting dean, 1978-79, dean, 1979-90, dean coll. profl. studies, 1990-91, prof. counseling, 1991—; cons. N.Y. State Regents Program for Non-Collegiate Sponsored Instrn., 1984; cons. collegiate programs N.Y. State Dept. Edn., 1985, Elmira Coll., 1991, U. Rochester, 1992-93; accreditation visitor Nat. League for Nursing, 1984-92; ednl. cons. Willard Psychiat. Hosp., 1992-93; mem. profl. practice exam. subcom. Regents Coll., 1990-95. Recipient Teaching Excellence award Alfred U., 1977, Mary E. Gladwin Outstanding Alumni award Akron U. Coll. Nursing, 1983, Alfred Alumni Friends award, 1989, Grand Marshall commencement Alfred U., 1993. Mem. Am. Counseling Assn., N.Y. State Counseling Assn. (v.p. elect profl. svcs.), N.Y. State Coun. of Deans (treas. 1984-88), Genesee Regional Consortium (v.p.), Western N.Y. League Nursing (bd. dirs. 1991-93), Genesee Valley Edn. Com. (chair 1984-86), Sigma Theta Tau (treas. Alfred chpt. 1984-85). Office: Alfred U 343 Myers Hall Alfred NY 14802

RAND, KATHY SUE, public relations executive; b. Miami Beach, Fla., Feb. 24, 1945; d. William R. and Rose (Lasser) R.; m. Peter C. Ritsos, Feb. 19, 1982. BA, Mich. State U., 1965; M in Mgmt., Northwestern U., 1980. Asst. editor Lyons & Carnahan, Chgo., 1967-68; mng. editor Cahners Pub. Co., Chgo., 1968-71; pub. rels. writer Super Market Inst., Chgo., 1972-73; account supr. Pub. Communications Inc., Chgo., 1973-77; divisional mgr. pub. rels. Quaker Oats Co., Chgo., 1977-82; exec. v.p., dep. gen. mgr. Golin/Harris Communications, Chgo., 1982-90; exec. v.p. Lesnik Pub. Rels., Northbrook, Ill., 1990-91; mng. dir. Manning, Selvage & Lee, Chgo., 1991—. Dir. midwest region NOW, 1972-74; mem. Kellogg Alumni Adv. Bd.; bd. dirs. Jr. Achievement of Chgo. Mem. Pub. Rels. Soc. Am. (Silver Anvil award 1986, 87), Pub. Club Chgo. (Golden Trumpet awards 1982-87, 90, 94, 95), Northwestern Club Chgo., Kellogg Alumni Club, Beta Gamma Sigma. Home: 400 Riverwoods Rd Lake Forest IL 60045-2547

RAND, PAMELA STEWART, physician; b. Dunn, N.C., Aug. 18, 1949; d. Edwin Byrd and Mary Frances (Wood) Stewart; m. Edward Gordon Pell, Apr. 10, 1983; 1 child, Hannah Kathryn. BA in Chemistry, U. N.C., 1971, MD, 1975. Diplomate Am. Bd. Pathology, Am. Bd. Dermatology. Intern anatomic pathology UCLA Med. Ctr., 1979-81, resident in dermatology, 1981-83; pvt. practice Santa Monica, Calif., 1983—; staff Santa Monica-UCLA Med. Ctr., St. Johns Med. Ctr. Mem. L.A. County Med. Assn. Office: 1260 15th St #1109 Santa Monica CA 90404

RAND, VENESSA AUSTIN, artist; b. Columbia, S.C., Apr. 27, 1969; d. Henry Alan Miller and Nancy Ellen (Jones) Carver; m. Mark Andrew Rand, Nov. 26, 1988. BFA, Savannah Coll. Art & Design, 1991. Graphic designer S.C.A.D., Savannah, Ga., 1988-90, mgr., 1990—. Illustrator (game) RomantiCards, 1992. Recipient Spl. Judges' award Savannah Advt. Club, 1993, Addy award, 1994, 95, 96, resolution from Ga. Ho. of Reps., 1990, Celebrate Savannah award, 1995. Mem. NOW, Nat. Mus. Women in the Arts. Democrat.

RANDA, LAURA ELIZABETH, educational administrator; b. Phila., Oct. 5, 1965; d. Stuart K. and Sally A. (Finanger) R. BS in Econs. and Edn., Ohio State U., 1988; postgrad., U. Del. Cert. secondary edn. social studies, Del. Tchr. social studies Phoenix Acad., Wilmington, Del., 1989, Seaford (Del.) Sch. Dist., 1989-91; lead tchr. social studies Sussex County Vocat. Tech. Sch. Dist., Georgetown, Del., 1991-92; exec. dir. Del. Tchr.'s Acad. for Svc. Learning, Wilmington, Del., 1992—; rsch. com., bd. dirs. Nat. Coun. Social Studies, Washington; mem. rural assistance coun. Rsch. for Better Schs., Phila.; com. mem. Domestic Violence Coord. Coun.-Pub. Info., Wilmington. Author: Structured Controversy Through Critical Thinking: The Death Penalty, 1993, How Can an Individual Make a Difference in Our Society?, 1994, Domestic Violence Service Learning Curriculum, 1994. Vol. Police Athletic League, Wilmington, 1994; mem. adv. bd., bd. dirs. New Castle County Vocat. Sch. Dist., 1993—, Polytech. Sch. Dist., 1992—; mem. Del. 2000, 1991-92, Culture of Study Team, 1991-92. Mem. ASCD, NCSS. Office: Del Tchrs Acad Svc Learning 105 Banbury Dr Wilmington DE 19803

RANDALL, CARLA ELIZABETH, nurse educator; b. Calif., Dec. 28, 1958; d. Lester Lee and Carrie Allen (Helm) R. Diploma, Luth. Hosp. Sch. Nursing, Ft. Wayne, Ind., 1979; BSN, Coe Coll., 1981; MSN, U. Dubuque, 1987; postgrad., U. B.C., Vancouver, Can., 1996—. RN, Mont. Staff nurse CCU U. Iowa, Iowa City, 1982-84; faculty U. Iowa, 1985-90, Kirkwood C.C., Cedar Rapids, Iowa, 1983-85, Salish Kootenai Coll., Pablo, Mont., 1990-93; nurse supr. West Mont., Polson, Mont., 1991-96; dir., counselor Earth Unbound, 1987—. Contbr. articles to profl. jours. Bd. dirs. Montana Pride, Helena, 1995—, Mont. Human Rights Network, Helena, 1994—, Flathead Reservation Human Rights Coalition, Ronan, Mont., 1990-96, Mont. PFLAG, St. Regis, Mont., 1994-96. Rsch. grantee Sigma Theta Tau, U. Iowa, 1988. Mem. ANA. Home: 1127 Barclay St Apt 201, Vancouver, BC Canada V6E 4C6

RANDALL, CAROLYN MAYO, chemical company executive; b. Atlanta, June 11, 1939; d. Frank and Winifred (Layton) Mayo; m. James Allen Hall, Dec. 28, 1960 (dec. 1973); children: James Allen Hall Jr., Christopher Mayo Hall, Charlotte Ann Hall O'Neal. BA, U. Ga., 1959. Ptnr. Mayo Chem. Co., Marietta, Ga., 1989—. Bd. dirs. Mayo Edn. Found; active Alliance Theater Atlanta, Salvation Army Aux., Voters Guild Met. Atlanta, Friendship Force Atlanta, Kennestone Hosp. Cancer Group, Am. Cancer Soc. Mem. Cobb County Gem & Mineral Soc. (trustee), S.E. Fedn. Mineralogical Soc. (historian), Atlanta Preservation Soc., Nat. Trust Historic Preservation, Ga. Trust Hist. Preservation, Nat. Meml. Day Assn., Better Films Assn. Met. Atlanta (bd. dirs.), Ret. Officers Assn. (ladies aux. bd. dirs.), Ga. Mineral Soc., Native Atlantians Club, 100 Club (pres.), The Frogg Club, Terrell Mill Estates Women's Club (bd. dirs.), Dobbins AFB OFficers Wives Club (bd. dirs.), Alpha Chi Omega, Atlanta Steinway Soc. (bd. dirs.), French-Am. Ch. of C., Raban Gap Nacoochee Guild, Freedoms Found. of Valley Forge, Atlanta Butterfly Club, Make A Wish Found., The Etowah Found., The Civil War Trust. Republican. Episcopal. Home: 3244 Beechwood Dr Marietta GA 30067-5420

RANDALL, CLAIRE, church executive; b. Dallas, Oct. 15, 1919; d. Arthur Godfrey and Annie Laura (Fulton) R. A.A., Schreiner Coll., 1948; BA, Scarritt Coll., 1950; DD (hon.), Berkeley Sem., Yale U., 1974; LHD (hon.), Austin Coll., 1982; LLD, Notre Dame U., 1984. Assoc. missionary edn. Bd. World Missions Presbyterian Ch., U.S., Nashville, 1949-57; dir. art Gen. Council Presbyterian Ch., U.S., Atlanta, 1957-61; dir. Christian World Mission, program dir., assoc. dir. Ch. Women United, N.Y.C., 1962-73; gen. sec. Nat. Council Ch. of Christ in U.S.A., N.Y.C., 1974-84; nat. pres. Ch. Women United, N.Y.C., 1988-92; ret., 1992—. Mem. Nat. Commn. on Internat. Women's Yr., 1975-77, Martin Luther King Jr. Fed. Holiday Commn., 1985. Recipient Woman of Yr. in Religion award Heritage Soc., 1977; Empire State Woman of Yr. in Religion award State of N.Y., 1984; medal Order of St. Vladimir, Russian Orthodox Ch., 1984. Democrat. Episcopalian. Home: 13427 W Countryside Dr Sun City West AZ 85375-4711

RANDALL, ELIZABETH ELLEN, press clippings company executive; b. Maple Hill, Kans., Mar. 21, 1915; d. Edwin and Ann (Scott) Sage; m. George Albert Randall, May 29, 1941; children: Cheryl Ann, Rebecca Lynn. Student, Kans. State U., 1932-34. Tchr. elem. sch Maple Hill, Kans., 1932-34, Dover, Kans., 1934-46; reader Luce Press Clippings, Topeka, 1959-63, supr., 1964, office mgr., 1964—. Tchr. Jr. High Ch. Sch., 1949-61; mem. pastoral com. Dover Federated Ch., 1991—. Mem. Dover 4-H Club (leader

1960-62), Dover Rebekah Lodge, Eastern Star, Am. Leg. Aux., Disabled Am. Vets. Aux., 14th Armored Divsn. Aux. Democrat. Home: 5731 SW 22nd Ter Topeka KS 66614-1831 Office: Luce Press Clippings 912 S Kansas Ave Topeka KS 66612-1211

RANDALL, HERMINE MARIA, retired power plant engineer; b. Vienna, Austria, July 22, 1927; came to U.S., 1948; d. Heinrich Georg Adametz and Maria Antonia (Paul) Safranek; m. May 25, 1948 (div. 1975); children: George Eugene, Dorothy Maria. Lic. 1st class stationary engr., Mass. Shift supr. Stony Brook Generating Sta. Mass. Mcpl. Wholesale Electric Co., Ludlow, 1980-82; chief engr. power plant U. Mass., Amherst, 1982-87, mgr. utility generation and distbn., 1987-90, acting dir. engring., 1990-91; dir. engring., 1991-95, ret., 1995. Recipient spl. achievement award Region I, U.S. Dept. Labor, 1980, Chancellor's Citation U. Mass., 1990, Citation for Outstanding Performance, Commonwealth of Mass., 1990. Mem. Nat. Assn. Power Engrs. (pres. Springfield chpt. 1989-90), Assn. Energy Engrs., Am. Inst. Plant Engrs. Republican. Home: 4 Popes Way Hadley MA 01035-9749

RANDALL, LINDA LEA, biochemist, educator; b. Montclair, N.J., Aug. 7, 1946; d. Lowell Neal and Helen (Watts) R.; m. Gerald Lee Hazelbauer, Aug. 29, 1970. BS, Colo. State U., 1968; PhD, U. Wis., 1971. Postdoctoral fellow Inst. Pasteur, Paris, 1971-73; asst. prof. Uppsala (Sweden) U., 1975-81; assoc. prof. Washington State U., Pullman, 1981-83, prof. biochemistry, 1983—; guest scientist Wallenberg Lab., Uppsala U., 1973-75; study section NIH, 1984-88. Editorial bd. Jour. of Bacteriology, 1982—; co-editor: Virus Receptors Part I, 1980; contbr. articles to profl. jours. Recipient Eli Lilly Award in Microbiology and Immunology, Am. Soc. Microbiology, Am. Assn. Immunologists, Am. Soc. Exptl. Pathology, 1984, Faculty Excellence Award in Rsch., Washington State U., 1988, Disting. Faculty Address, 1990, Parke-Davis award, 1995. Fellow Am. Acad. Microbiology; mem. AAAS, Am. Microbiol. Soc., Am. Soc. Biol. Chemists, Protein Soc. Office: Washington State U. Biochemistry Biophysic Dept PO Box 644660 Pullman WA 99164-4660

RANDALL, LYNN ELLEN, librarian; b. Chgo., Oct. 10, 1946; d. Ward W. and Hazel A. (Nettles) R. BA, King's Coll., 1970; MA, Seton Hall U., 1973; MLS, Rutgers U., 1978. Libr. N.J. Inst. Tech., Newark, 1970-75; libr. dir. N.E. Bible Coll., Essex Fells, N.J., 1975-81; reference libr. Seton Hall U., South Orange, N.J., 1983-85; dir. libr. svc. Berkeley Coll. Bus., West Paterson, N.J., 1985-89, libr. dir. Caldwell Coll., 1989—; reference libr., instr. Morris (N.J.) County Coll., 1981-83. Co-author: N.J. Online Directory, 1983; editor N.J. Librs., fall 1984, spring 1986, winters 1990, 91; chair N.J. region III resource sharing com. Mem. Union County (N.J.) Heritage Commn., 1975-76. Mem. ALA (treas. Libr. Instrn. Round Table 1989-90, chair libr. instrn. roundtable, Libr. Sch. Task Force 1992—), Assn. Coll. and Resource Librs. (chair evaluation Bl Handbook task force 1991-95), Middle States Assn., Am. Assn. Bible Colls. (evaluator 1977, 79, 84, 92, 95), N.J. Libr. Assn. (chair automated libr. svcs. sect. 1986-88, conf. program editor 1987-89, chair exhibits com. 1989-91, 94-95, chair adminstrv. sect. 1990-92, chair coll. & univ. sect. 1990-91, conf. chair 1991-94, editor coll. and univ. sect. newsletter 1982-84, 87-92, 2d v.p. 1992-94, v.p., pres. elect 1995-96, pres. 1996-97), N.J. Libr. Network (pres. Region II 1987-89, chair resource sharing com. 1993, info. svcs. com. 1994), Lib. Network (mem. review bd. 1995—). Office: Jennings Libr Caldwell Coll 9 Ryerson Ave Caldwell NJ 07006-6109

RANDALL, PATRICIA MARY, consulting firm executive; b. Boston, June 12, 1948; d. Alfred Earl Randall and Evangeline A. (McHugh) Blackwell; m. Richard Paul James, June 26, 1982 (div. 1989); children: David, Jennifer; m. Scott Darren Graff, Jan. 1, 1990. BA in Philosophy, Bridgewater (Mass.)State Coll., 1980. Owner, mgr. The Indoor Garden, Brockton, Mass., 1972-78; dining room mgr. Red Coach Grill Cambridge, Mass., 1981-82, Boston Ramada, Allston, Mass., 1982-85; br. mgr. The Resource Group, Cambridge, 1985-90; sr. tech. specialist Brandon Systems Corp., Boston, 1990-95; account exec. Analysts Internat. Corp., Boston, 1995—. Roman Catholic. Home: 62 Lake Shore Dr S Westford MA 01886 Office: Analysts Internat Corp 67 S Bedford St Ste 400W Burlington MA 01803

RANDALL, PRISCILLA RICHMOND, travel executive; b. Arlington, Mass., Mar. 19, 1926; d. Harold Bours and Florence (Hoefler) Richmond; m. Raymond Victor Randall, Mar. 2, 1946; children: Raymond Richmond, Priscilla Randall Middleton, Susan Randall Geery. Student, Wellesley Coll., 1943-44; Assoc., Garland Coll., 1946; student, Winona State U., 1977-81. Pub. relations dir. Rochester Meth. Hosp., Rochester, Minn., 1960-69; dir. pub relations Sheraton Rochester, 1969-71; pres. Med. Charters, Rochester, 1970-75, Ideas Unltd., Rochester, 1969-77; chief exec. officer Randall Travel, Rochester, 1977-89; pres. Randall Travel Delray, Delray Beach, Fla., 1989—; pres. Bar Harbour Apts. Inc., Delray Beach, 1989. Editor, Inside Story, 1960-69, Rochester Meth. Hosp. News, 1960-69; producer Priscilla's World, 1972-75. Pres. Rochester Meth. Hosp. Aux., 1957-59, Downtown Bus. Assn., Rochester, 1985. Recipient Woman of Achievement Bus. YWCA, Rochester, 1983, Golden Door Knob, Bus. and Prfl. Women, Rochester, 1979. Mem. Inst. Cert. Travel Agts. (life), Assn. Retail Travel Agts. (life, nat. bd. 1988-90, sec. to bd. 1988-90, sec.-treas. Arlington, Va. nat. bd. 1990), Am. Soc. Travel Agts., Pacific Area Travel Agts., Minn. Exec. Women in Travel, Cruise Line Internat. Assn. (master cruise counselor), Women's Golf Com. Little Club (Gulfstream, Fla.) (sec.), Hibiscus Garden Club (Delray Beach, Fla.) (pres.). Home: 86 Macfarlane Dr Apt 2C Delray Beach FL 33483-6901 Office: Randall Travel Delray Inc 1118 E Atlantic Ave Delray Beach FL 33483-6936

RANDALL, SHERRI LEE, accountant; b. Burlington, Vt., Dec. 21, 1959; d. Robert Dale and Carolyn Sue (Ferguson) Schaffner; m. Cleve Hadley Randall, Feb. 11, 1981 (div. Mar. 1992); 1 child, Clayton James. BBA with high honors, Idaho State U., 1985. CPA, Idaho. Staff acct. Price Waterhouse, Anchorage, 1985-87; acct. Little-Morris, Boise, Idaho, 1987-95; comptroller Comml. Lending Corp., 1995—; mem. acctg. alumni adv. panel Idaho State U., Pocatello, 1989-90. Vol. coord. Caribou Nat. Forest, Pocatello, 1984; treas. Assn. for Retarded Citizens Ada County, Boise, Idaho, 1989-91, mem. fin. com., 1989-92; treas. Eagle Citizens Alliance, 1995—; mem. downtown devel. task force City of Eagle. Scholar Idaho State U., 1983-84, Crawford-Moore Found., 1984. Mem. AICPA, Idaho Soc. CPAs, Inst. Mgmt. Accts. (bd. dirs. acad. resl. ednl. projects 1992-94, v.p. and edn. & profl. devel. 1994-95, v.p. mem. & mktg. 1995-96), Phi Kappa Phi, Beta Gamma Sigma, Beta Alpha Psi. Office: Comml Lending Corp 565 W Myrtle # 410 Boise ID 83702-5469

RANDALL, VICKY, sculptor, jeweler; b. Selmer, Tenn., May 3, 1953; d. R.B. and Mary Helen (Farrell) Randall; m. Carl Jacob Schreiner III, Nov. 22, 1994. BFA, Mid. Tenn. State U., Murfreesboro, 1975; MFA, So. Ill. U., 1979. Asst. prof. art Bethany Coll., Lindsborg, Kans., 1980-85; owner, operator, creator Vicky Randall Studios, Sarasota, Fla., 1980—; faculty Ringling Sch. of Art and Design, Sarasota, Fla., 1996—. Exhibited in shows at Sandzen Gallery, Lindsborg, Kans., 1983, Trostberger Sculpture Park, Poesch, West Germany, 1985, Joan Hodgell Gallery, Sarasota, 1989, 90, 91, Sarasota Arts Assn., 1991, numerous others; represented in pvt. collections, including Home Fed. Bank, Nashville, Mid. Tenn. State U.; works include metal sculpture, painted steel wall reliefs, metal furniture; 1st art in Arts and Theater Dist., Sarasota County; represented in over 50 pvt. collections. Mem. exhbn. com. Arts Coun., Sarasota, 1993—; bd. dirs. Sarasota Visual Arts Ctr., 1990—. Recipient grant to study Henry Moore and Barbara Hepworth in Eng., 1983; named Artist of Yr. for Sarasota County, 1993; Bildhauer Symposium grantee, Mertigen, West Germany, 1983; commn. Women's Resource Ctr. for Monumental Garden Sculpture. Mem. Sculptors Internat. Home: 727 Hand Ave Sarasota FL 34232 Office: Vicky Randall Studios 1216 Central Ave Sarasota FL 34232

RANDAZZO, REBECCA ANN, nursing administrator; b. Bellevue, Pa., May 20, 1950; d. David E. and Mary Anna (Braham) Bickett; m. Andrew M. Randazzo, Nov. 10, 1973; children: Gwen, Janet. BSN, U. Evansville, 1972; MPA, Ind. U., Gary, 1991. RN, Ind., Ill. Staff nurse Good Samaritan Hosp., Vincennes, Ind., 1972-73, Clark County Hosp., Clarksville, Ind., 1973-75; staff nurse, shift coord. St. Anthony Med. Ctr., Crown Point, Ind., 1975-91; assoc. dir. nursing St. Anthony Home, Crown Point, Ind., 1991-96, DON, 1996—; cons. Vale Hops., Valparaiso, Ind., 1990; mem. rehab. adv. bd. St. Anthony Med. Ctr., Crown Point, 1993-94. Mem. Am. Coll. Healthcare Execs., Ind. Assn. Health Care Quality (edn. com. 1991). Home: 10408 W 173rd Ave Lowell IN 46356-9575 Office: St Anthony Home Inc 203 W Franciscan Dr Crown Point IN 46307-4802

RANDINELLI, TRACEY ANNE, magazine editor; b. Morristown, N.J., Apr. 6, 1963; d. Andrew R. and Patricia Ann (Brenner) R. BA in Comm., U. Del., 1985. Copywriter Macy's N.J., Newark, 1985-86; edit. asst. Globe Comms. Corp., N.Y.C., 1986-87; from asst. editor to assoc. editor Scholastic Math and DynaMath Mags. Scholastic, Inc., N.Y.C., 1987-89, editor Scholastic Math Mag., 1989-95; mng. editor Zig Zag Mag. Games Pub. Group, N.Y.C., 1995; sr. editor 321 Contact Mag. Children's Television Workshop, N.Y.C., 1996—. Mem. Soc. Children's Book Writers, Ednl. Press Assn. Am. (Disting. Achievement award feature articles divsn. 1991, 95, cover design 1996).

RANDISI, ELAINE MARIE, law corporation executive, educator; b. Racine, Wis., Dec 19, 1926; d. John Dewey and Alveta Irene (Raffety) Fehd; AA, Pasadena Jr. Coll., 1946; BS cum laude (Giannini scholar), Golden Gate U., 1978; m. John Paul Randisi, Oct. 12, 1946 (div. July 1972); children: Jeanine Randisi Manson, Martha Randisi Chaney (dec.), Joseph, Paula, Catherine Randisi Carvalho, George, Anthony (dec.); m. John R. Woodfin, June 18, 1994. With Raymond Kaiser Engrs., Inc., Oakland, Calif., 1969-75, 77-86, corp. acct., 1978-79, sr. corp. acct., 1979-82, sr. payroll acct., 1983-86, acctg. mgr., Lilli Ann Corp., San Francisco, 1986-89, Crosby, Heafey, Roach & May, Oakland, Calif., 1990—; corp. buyer Kaiser Industries Corp., Oakland, 1975-77; lectr. on astrology Theosophical Soc., San Francisco, 1979—; mem. faculty Am. Fedn. Astrologers Internat. Conv., Chgo., 1982, 84. Mem. Speakers Bur., Calif. Assn. for Neurologically Handicapped Children, 1964-70, v.p. 1969; bd. dirs. Ravenwood Homeowners Assn., 1979-82, v.p., 1979-80, sec., 1980-81; mem. organizing com. Minority Bus. Fair, San Francisco, 1976; pres., bd. dirs. Lakewood Condominium Assn., 1984-87; mem., trustee Ch. of Religious Sci., 1992-95; treas. First Ch. Religious Sci., 1994—. Mem. Am. Fedn. Astrologers, Nat. Assn. Female Execs., Calif. Scholarship Fedn. (life), Alpha Gamma Sigma (life). Mem. Ch. of Religious Science (lic. practioner pres. 1990-91, sec. 1989-90). Initiated Minority Vendor Purchasing Program for Kaiser Engrs., Inc., 1975-76. Home: 742 Wesley Way Apt 1C Oakland CA 94610-2339 Office: Crosby Heafey Roach & May 1999 Harrison St Oakland CA 94612-3517

RANDLE, ELLEN EUGENIA FOSTER, opera and classical singer, educator; b. New Haven, Conn., Oct. 2, 1948; d. Richard A.G. and Thelma Lousie (Brooks) Foster; m. Ira James William, 1967 (div. 1972); m. John Willis Randle. Student, Calif. State Coll., Sonoma, 1970; studied with Boris Goldovsky, 1970; student, Grad. Sch. Fine Arts, Florence, Italy, 1974; studied with Tito Gobbi, Florence, 1974; student, U. Calif., Berkeley, 1977; BA in World History, Lone Mountain Coll., 1976, MA in Performing Arts, 1978; studied with Madam Eleanor Steber, Graz, Austria, 1979; studied with Patricia Goehl, Munich, Fed. Republic Germany, 1979; MA in Counseling and Psychology, U. San Francisco, 1990, MA in Marital Family Therapy, 1994, postgrad., 1994—. instr. East Bay Performing Art Ctr., Richmond, Calif., 1986, Chapman Coll., 1986. Singer opera prodns. Porgy & Bess, Oakland, Calif., 1980-81, LaTraviata, Oakland, Calif., 1981-82, Aida, Oakland, 1981-82, Madame Butterfly, Oakland, 1982-83, The Magic Flute, Oakland, 1984, numerous others; performances include TV specials, religous concerts, musicals; music dir. Natural Man, Berkeley, 1986; asst. artistic dir. Opera Piccola, Oakland, Calif., 1990—. Art commr. City of Richmond, Calif. Recipient Bk. Am. Achievement award. Mem. Music Tchrs. Assn., Internat. Black Writers and Artists Inc. (life mem., local #5), Nat. Coun. Negro Women, Nat. Assn. Negro Musicians, Calif. Arts Fedn., Calif. Assn. for Counseling and Devel. (mem. black caucus), Nat. Black Child Devel. Inst., The Calif.-Nebraskan Orgn., Inc., Calif. Marital & Family Therapist Assn. (San Francisco chpt.), Black Psychotherpist of San Francisco and East Bay Area, San Francisco Commonwealth Club, Gamma Phi Delta. Democrat. Mem. A.M.E. Zion Ch. Home: 5314 Boyd Ave Oakland CA 94618-1112

RANDLE, ROLINDA CAROL, elementary education educator; b. Fort Worth, Nov. 3, 1959; d. John Arthur and Ann Junette (Jones) Richards; m. Joseph L. Randle, June 12, 1982; children: Joseph Jr., Jennifer Michelle, Ja'Lissa Maurnice. BS in Edn., Tex. Christian U., 1982; postgrad., Tarleton State U. Cert. elem. edn., English, mid-mgmt., Tex. 2d grade tchr. Sunset Valley Elem. Sch., Austin, Tex., 1982-84; 6th grade tchr. Rosemont Middle Sch., Fort Worth, 1985-87; 6th grade tchr., adminstrv. intern Meadowbrook Middle Sch., Fort Worth, 1987—; pres./ceo Triple "J" Enterprises, Ft. Worth, 1996—; mem. site-based decision making team Rosemont Middle Sch., 1985-87, Meadowbrook Middle Sch., 1987-90, mem. leadership team, 1994—, mem. tech. com., 1991—; indsl. tech. trainer Fort Worth Ind. Sch. Dist., 1994—; owner, pres., CEO Triple J Enterprises. Fellow Summer Writing Inst; mem. United Educators Assn., NEA, Jack-n-Jill of Am. Inc., ASCD, Delta Sigma Theta. Methodist. Home: 4733 Leonard St Fort Worth TX 76119-7540

RANDOLPH, BEVERLEY, production stage manager; b. Norristown, Pa., Aug. 26, 1951; d. Robert Lyman Kratz and Sarah Randolph (McDonnell) DaCosta. BFA magna cum laude, Ithaca Coll., 1973. Prodn. supr. Time and Again Old Globe, N.Y.C., 1996. Prodn. supr. Follies in Concert, Lincoln Ctr., 1985, Uptown It's Hot, Phila., 1985, Queenie Pie, Duke Ellington Mus., Phila. and Washington, 1987, Jerome Robbins Broadway, Nat. Tour, Japan, L.A., 1990-91, Tony Awards, 1992, Sansho the Bailiff, Bklyn. Acad. Music, 1993, Time and Again, Old Globe, 1996; prodn. stage mgr. Merrily We Roll Along, N.Y.C., 1981, A Doll's Life, L.A., N.Y.C., 1982, Gala Opening of Ky. Ctr. of Performing Arts, Louisville, 1983, End of the World, Washington and N.Y.C., 1984, Grind, 1985, Cabaret, N.Y.C., 1988, Jerome Robbin's Broadway, 1989-90, Kiss of the Spider Woman, Purchase, 1990, N.Y., 1993, Metro, N.Y.C., 1992, Falsettos, N.Y.C., 1992, Kiss of the Spider Woman, 1993, Passion, 1994; stage mgr. Chapter Two, 1979. Stage mgr. Nat. Inst. of Music Theatre, N.Y.C., 1986-87; participant Broadway Cares. Mem. Actors Fund (life), Actor's Equity Assn.

RANDOLPH, LILLIAN LARSON, medical association executive; b. Spokane, Wash., May 3, 1932; d. Charles P. and Juanita S. (Parrish) Larson; m. Philip L. Randolph, Nov. 12, 1952; children: Marcus, Andrew. BA, U. Wash., 1954, MA, 1956; PhD, U. Calif., Berkeley, 1966; EdD, N.Mex. State U., 1979. Researcher U. Wash., Seattle, 1954-59; asst. prof. Calif. State U., Hayward, 1964-68, U. Tex., El Paso, 1972-74; dir. S.W. Conservatory of Music, El Paso, 1972-74; adj. prof. Loyola U. and DePaul U., Chgo., 1974-78; asst. prof. DeVry Inst. Tech., Lombard, Ill., 1982-84; mgr. AMA, Chgo., 1985—; cons. Weber Co., Chgo., 1979-85. Author: Fundamentals of Government Organizations, 1971, Third Party Settlement of Disputes, 1973. Mem. AAUP, Phi Beta Kappa. Home: 408 W Wilshire Dr Wilmette IL 60091-3154

RANDOLPH, LYNN MOORE, artist; b. N.Y.C., Dec. 19, 1938; d. Cecil Howard and Dorothy (Didenhover) M.; m. Robert Raymond Randolph, June 5, 1959 (div. June, 1975); children: Robert Cean, Grayson Moore; m. William Simon, July 22, 1986. BFA, U. Tex., 1961. pres. Houston chpt. Nat. Women's Caucus for Art, 1979-80. regional v.p., 1982-85, nat. adv. bd. 1986-88, co-chair ann. 1988 ann. conf.; lectr. and conf. participant to art and women's groups, 1980—; set designer, Space, Dance Theater, Houston, 1977, Main St. Theater, 1982; coord. Art Under Duress, El Salvador, Lawndale Art and Performance Ctr., Houston. Artist: solo exhibitions include Graham Gallery, Houston, 1984, 86, 91, Mary Ingraham Bunting Inst., Cambridge, Mass., 1990, Lynn Goode Gallery, Houston, 1995; group shows: Contemporary Arts Mus., Houston, 1978, 79, 90. 500 Exposition Gallery, Dallas, 1980, Ga. State U. Gallery, 1982, Mus. Fine Arts, Houston, 1986, Aspen (Colo.) Art Mus., 1987, Nat. Mus. of Women in Art, Washington, 1988, San Antonio Mus. of Art, 1989, Sewell Gallery, Rice U., 1993, Diverse Works, Houston, 1994; works in pub. collections at Ariz. State U., Tempe, The Menil Collection, Houston, San Antonio Mus. of Art, Mary Ingraham Bunting Inst., Cambridge, Houston Mus. Fine Arts, others. Organizer Houston Area Artist's Call Against U.S. Intervention in Ctrl. Am., 1984. Recipient summer fellowship Yaddo, Saratoga Springs, N.Y., 1987, fellowship Mary Ingraham Bunting Inst., Radcliffe Coll., 1989-90. Mem. The Ilusas (women's drum corps), Artists Bd. Lawndale Art and Performance Ctr., Houston. Home: 1803 Banks Houston TX 77098

RANDOLPH, SUZANNE MARIE, psychology educator; b. New Orleans, Aug. 4, 1953; d. Alfred Joseph and Mildred (Hambrick) R. BS, Howard U., 1974; MS, U. Mich., 1977, PhD, 1981. Rsch. coord. Howard U., Washington, 1981-86, asst. prof. pediatrics, 1983-86; project dir., evaluator Am. Nat. Red Cross, Washington, 1986-88, 91-92; asst. prof. family studies U. Md., College Park, 1988-95, assoc. prof., 1995—; sr. rsch. assoc. Maya Tech. Corp., Silver Spring, Md., 1981—. Author: (poem) When You Hear the Children Cry, 1990; co-editor Jour. Black Psychology, 1993. Evaluator HIV/AIDS Jamaica Red Cross, ARC, 1994—, Kingston and Washington; evaln. project dir. Robert Wood Johnson Opening Doors Program, 1994-96; pres. bd. dirs. YWCA Nat. Capitol Area, Washington; task force mem. Washington Aids Partnership, 1994—; class IV mem. Leadership Washington. Kellogg fellow W.K. Kellogg Found., 1985-88. Mem. APA (newsletter editor Devel. Psychology 1992-95, minority fellow adv. com.), Assn. Black Psychologists (nat. pres. 1989-90, Cmty. Svc. award 1994), Soc. Rsch. in Child Devel. (chair com. ethnic and racial issues 1993-95), Nat. Coun. Family Rels., Delta Sigma Theta. Office: U Md Family Studies 1204 Marie Mount Hall College Park MD 20742

RANEY, MIRIAM DAY, actress; b. Florence, S.C., Sept. 30, 1922; d. Lewie Griffith and Iola Lewis (Edwards) Day; m. Robert William Raney, Mar. 31, 1946 (div. Sept. 1976); children: Robert William Jr., Miriam, Kevin Paige, Megan. BSM in Voice, Music Edn., U. N.C., Greensboro, 1939-43; student (summers), Julliard Sch. Music, 1942-43; BA in Music History, U. Ark., Little Rock, 1978-81; Certificate, Adam Roarke Film Actors Lab., Irving, Tex., 1989. Singing chorus N.Y.C. Ctr. Opera Co., 1943-44; understudy, singing chorus Oklahoma, Theater Guild, N.Y.C., 1944-45; ingenue lead Connecticut Yankee, Geosan Subway Cir., N.Y.C., 1945; understudy, singing chorus Up In Central Park, Michael Todd, N.Y.C., 1945-46; beauty cons. Mary Kay Cosmetics, Inc., Dallas, 1993-96. Author: slide sound synchronized show Ark. Women in Music, 1982; composer, lyricist: The Bend and the Willows, 1982, Ballad of Petit Jean, 1983; recent stage appearances include Hedda Gabler (Reponde de Capite repertory), 1990, Time of Your Life (Cmty. Theatre of Little Rock), 1991, Our Town, 1991, Evening with Women II (Regional Theatre of Ctrl. Ark.), 1991, 1988; appeared in TV program Unsolved Mysteries, 1988; film Killing Time with Aunt Olene, 1988; also commercials tng. films, 1987-96; print model, Little Rock, Memphis, Ft. Worth, 1988-95. Ch. soloist, various protestant chs., Little Rock, 1946-55; music dir., leader Ouachita Girl Scout Coun., Little Rock, 1963-70; choir mem. adminstrv. bd., adult ch. sch. tchr. Pulaski Heights United Meth. Ch., Little Rock, 1970-76; mem. Speakers Bur. Coalition of Womens Clubs for ERA, Little Rock, 1974-75; bd. dirs. Local 266, AFM, Little Rock, 1980-83. Named Illustrious Alumna, U. N.C. at Greensboro, 1965. Mem. AAUW (Little Rock legis. com. 1973-79, program com. 1973-79, state rep. for cultural interests 1976-79), Musical Coterie (Little Rock), Cen. Ark. Guild of Organists (pres. student chpt. 1977-80). Democrat. Home: 25 Valley Forge Dr Little Rock AR 72212-2613

RANEY-DEWITT, VICKIE LYNN, art educator; b. Clarksburg, W.Va., Sept. 13, 1959; d. Kenneth Glenn and Dixie Shirlene (Phillips) Raney; m. Gregory Dean Wright, Aug. 9, 1980 (div. 1986); m. Gregory Dean DeWitt, June 23, 1989. BFA, U. Evansville, 1982; MEd, Ind. U. SE., 1988; postgrad., Ind. U./Purdue U., 1993. Cert. tchr., Ind. Legal sec. R. Wood Turrentine, Louisville, 1982-83, Morgan & Pottinger, Louisville, 1983-84; legal asst. Brown, Todd & Heyburn, Louisville, 1985; art educator Clarksville (Ind.) Sch. Corp., 1985—; illustrator J.V. Reed & Co., Louisville, 1982-85; art instr. Louisville Visual Art Assn., 1988-91, Clarksville Adult Edn., 1988-89; mem. performance based accreditation com. Clarksville Sch., 1992-93; prin. selection com. chairperson Clarksville Middle Sch., 1993, volleyball coach, 1985-87. Exhibited works in numerous art shows including Louisville Visual Art Assn., 1990, Alumni Exhibit, 1994, Jefferson C.C., 1993. Chairperson Polit. Action Com., Clark and Floyd Counties, 1985-87. Grantee Ind. Dept. Edn., 1991-92, 92-93, 93-94. Mem. Clarksville Edn. Assn. (pres. 1989-90, v.p. 1988-90), Nat. Art Edn. Assn., Ind. Art Edn. Assn., Internat. Airbrush Assn., Ind. Middle Sch. Assn. Democrat. Methodist. Home: 7625 Pine Shore Dr SE Elizabeth IN 47117-7439 Office: Clarksville Middle Sch 101 Ettels Ln Clarksville IN 47129-1815

RANGEL, ANITA ARELLANO, bilingual educator; b. Taylor, Tex., Feb. 5, 1955; d. Gilberto and Crescencia (Garcia) A.; m. Rodolfo Rangel, July 25, 1981. BA, West Tex. State U., 1976; MEd, Wayland Bapt. U., 1994. Cert. mid-mgmt. adminstr. 3d grade tchr. Dimmitt (Tex.) Ind. Sch. Dist., 1976-80; kindergarten tchr. San Antonio Ind. Sch. Dist., 1979-80; 4th grade tchr. North East Ind. Sch. Dist., San Antonio, 1980-81; kindergarten tchr. Lubbock (Tex.) Ind. Sch. Dist., 1981-89, bilingual/ESL K-6th grade tchr., 1989-91, 3d grade tchr., 1991-92, 4th grade tchr., 1992—; mem. tchr. advisory Campus Performance Objectives Coun., Lubbock, 1989-96; mem. com. TEA TAAS Review, Lubbock, 1994-95. Sunday sch. tchr. St. Joseph's Cath. Ch., Lubbock, 1981—; mem. Meth. Hosp. Vol. Aux., Lubbock, 1993—; vol. Make a Wish Found., Lubbock, 1992-93. Mem. ASCD, Tex. Classroom Tchrs. Assn., Cath. Daus. of Am., Delta Kappa Gamma. Democrat. Home: 5209 44th St Lubbock TX 79414

RANKAITIS, SUSAN, artist; b. Cambridge, Mass., Sept. 10, 1949; d. Alfred Edward and Isabel (Shimkus) Rankaitis; m. Robbert Flick, June 5, 1976. B.F.A. in Painting, U. Ill., 1971; M.F.A. in Visual Arts, U. So. Calif., 1977. Rsch. asst., art dir. Plato Lab., U. Ill., Urbana, 1971-75; art instr. Orange Coast Coll., Costa Mesa, Calif., 1977-83; chair dept. art Chapman Coll., Orange, Calif., 1983-90; Fletcher Jones chair in art Scripps Coll., Claremont, Calif., 1990—; represented by Robert Mann Gallery, N.Y.C.; overview panelist visual arts Nat. Endowment for Arts, 1983, 84. One-woman shows include Los Angeles County Mus. Art, 1983, Internat. Mus. Photography, George Eastman House, 1983, Gallery Min. Tokyo, 1988, Ruth Bloom Gallery, Santa Monica, 1989, 90, 92, 95, Schneider Mus., Portland, Ore., 1990; Ctr. for Creative Photography, 1991, Robert Mann Gallery, N.Y.C., 1994, Mus. Contemporary Photography, Chgo., 1994; represented in permanent collections U. N.Mex. Art, Santa Monica Coll., Ctr. for Creative Photography, Mus. Modern Art, Santa Barbara Mus. Art, Los Angeles County Mus. Art, Mpls. Inst. Arts, San Francisco Mus. Modern Art, Mus. Modern Art, Lodz, Poland, Princeton U. Art Mus., Stanford U. Art Mus., Contemporary Art Mus., Honolulu, others. Active L.A. Ctr. for Photographic Studies, 1988—, mem. adv. bd. trustees. Nat. Endowment for Arts fellow, 1980, 88, U.S./France fellow, 1989, Agnes Bourne fellow in Painting and Photography, Djerassi Found., 1989; recipient Graves award in Humanities, 1985. Mem. Coll. Art Assn., L.A. Contemporary Exhbns. (adv. trustee L.A. Ctr. for Photographic Studies), L.A. County Mus. Art. Studio: Studio 5 1403 S Santa Fe Ave Los Angeles CA 90021-2500

RANKIN, BONNIE LEE, insurance executive; b. Lancaster, Pa., June 27, 1953; d. E. Lee and Mary Jane (Weaver) R. BA in Liberal Arts, Millersville (Pa.) U., 1975; postgrad., U. Pa., 1994—. Cert. ins. counselor, 1986; CPCU, 1981. Claim adjuster Nationwide Ins. Co., Phila., 1973-76; comml. underwriter Nationwide Ins. Co., Harrisburg, Pa., 1976-78; sr. comml. underwriter Harleysville (Pa.) Mut. Ins. Co., 1978-79, tng. coord., 1979-81, br. underwriting mgr., 1981-84; with Worcester (Mass.) Ins. Co. subs. HMIC, 1984-92, asst. v.p., 1987-89, v.p., 1989-92; asst. v.p. comml. underwriting group HMIC, Harleysville, Pa., 1992-95, v.p. comml. underwriting group, 1995-96; pres., COO N.Y. Casualty, Watertown, N.Y., 1996—. Mem. adv. bd. Mechs. Hall, Worcester, 1987-92; bd. dirs., mem. fin. com. Worcester Community Action Coun., 1991-92; bd. dirs. Harleysville Sr. Adult Activity Ctr., 1996—; active IIPLR Coun., 1995—, ISO Comml. Lines Panel, 1996—. Mem. Soc. CPCUs (dir. cand. devel. 1985-87), Greater Valley Forge Soc. CPCUs (founder, bd. dirs. 1983-94), Cen. Mass. Soc. CPCUs, Pa. Assn. Mut. Ins. Cos. (edn. com. chmn. 1980-82, mem. consumer and edn. com. 1994—), Ins. Soc. Phila. (mem. faculty 1980-84), Ins. Inst. Am. (mem. grading bd. Malvern, Pa. 1981—), Mensa. Republican. Methodist. Office: NY Casualty Ins Co 120 Washington St Watertown NY 13601-3352

RANKIN, DEBORAH MARIE, journalist; b. N.Y.C., Aug. 17, 1943; d. Ruth Rankin; m. Lawrence A. Heald, Feb. 10, 1974; children: David Heald, Michael Heald. BA, Mundelein Coll., 1968. Bus. writer, fgn. desk editor, reporter AP, N.Y.C. and Chgo., 1964-74; econs. editor Consumer Reports, N.Y.C., 1974-76; fin. reporter, columnist N.Y. Times, N.Y.C., 1977-81; freelance journalist N.Y. Times, others, 1982—. Author: Investing on Your

Own, 1994, also article series on fin. impact of divorce, 1986 (award N.Y. State Soc. CPAs 1986). Treas. Bronxville (N.Y.) PTA, 1987-89; 1st v.p. Lincoln H.S. PTA, Portland, Oreg., 1994; bd. dirs. Friends of the Library, Bronxville, 1991-92. Walter Bagehot fellow Columbia U., 1976-77. Mem. Reed Coll. Women's Com., City Club of Portland. Home: 2894 NW Ariel Ter Portland OR 97210-3138

RANKIN, ELIZABETH ANNE DESALVO, nurse, psychotherapist, educator, consultant; b. Wurtzburg, Germany, Sept. 30, 1948; d. William Joseph and Elizabeth Agnes (Faraci) DeSalvo; m. Richard Forrest Rankin, June 5, 1971; children: William Alvin, David Michael. BSN, U. Md., Balt., 1970, MS, 1972; PhD., U. Md., College Park, 1979. Cert. health edn. specialist, specialist stress mgmt. edn., master hypnotherapist, master practitioner neurolinguistic programmer, nonquatic exercise instrn.; cert. Nat. Bd. Cert. Clin. Hypnotherapists. Prof. U. Md.; mem. dept. psychiat. mental health/community health nursing U. Md. at Balt. Sch. Nursing, dir. div. bus. and industry; prof. U. Md.; cns. Ctr. for Alternative Medicine, Pain Rsch. and Evaluation; cons. various publs. Co-author of books; contbr. chpts. to books, articles to profl. jours.; editor: Network Independent Study; mem. editl. bd. Md. Nurse, Delmarva Found. Newsletter. Advisor U. Md. chpt. Nat. Student Nurses Assn. Recipient Twila Stinecker Leadership award, 1987, Leadership Excellence award Md. Assn. Nursing Students, 1990-92. Mem. ANA, Md. Nursing Assn. (bd. dirs., exec. com., 2d v.p., appointments mgr.), U. Md. Assn. Nursing Students (chpt. Nat. Student Nurses Assn. advisor), Nat. Coun. Family Rels., Coun. Nurse Rschrs., Nat. Assn. Cert. Health Educators (charter), Am. Assn. Profl. Hypnotherapists, Milton H. Erickson Found., Washington Soc. Clin. Hypnosis, Aquatic Exercise Assn., Capital Area Roundtable on Informatics in Nursing, Sigma Theta Tau, Phi Epsilon Alpha, Phi Kappa Phi, Alpha Xi Delta.

RANKIN, HELEN CROSS, cattle rancher, guest ranch executive; b. Mojave, Calif; d. John Whisman and Cleo Rebecca (Tilley) Cross; m. Leroy Rankin, Jan. 4, 1936 (dec. 1954); children—Julia Jane King Sharr, Patricia Helen Denvir, William John. A.B., Calif. State U.-Fresno, 1935. Owner, operator Rankin Cattle Ranch, Caliente, Calif., 1954—; founder, pres. Rankin Ranch, Inc., Guest Ranch, 1965—; mem. sect. 15, U.S. Bur. Land Mgmt.; mem. U.S. Food and Agrl. Leaders Tour China, 1983, Australia and N.Z., 1985; dir. U.S. Bur. Land Mgmt. sect. 15. Pres., Children's Home Soc. Calif., 1945; mem. adv. bd. Camp Ronald McDonald. Recipient award Calif. Hist. Soc., 1983, Kern River Valley Hist. Soc., 1983. Mem. Am. Nat. Cattlemen's Assn., Calif. Cattlemen's Assn., Kern County Cattlemen's Assn., Kern County Cowbelles (pres. 1949, Cattlewoman of Yr. 1988), Calif. Cowbelles, Nat. Cowbelles, Bakersfield Country Club, Bakersfield Raquet Club. Republican. Baptist. Office: Rankin Ranch Caliente CA 93518

RANKIN, JACQUELINE ANNETTE, communications expert, educator; b. Omaha, Nebr., May 19, 1925; d. Arthur C. and Virdie (Gillispie) R. BA, Calif. State U., L.A., 1964, MA, 1966; MS in Mgmt., Calif. State U., Fullerton, 1977; EdD, U. LaVerne, Calif., 1981. Tchr. Rowland High Sch., La Habra, Calif., 1964-66, Lowell High Sch., La Habra, Calif., 1966-69, Pomona (Calif.) High Sch., 1969-75; program asst. Pomona Adult Sch., 1975-82; dir. Child Abuse Prevention Program, 1985-86; faculty evening divsn. Mt. San Antonio C.C., 1966-72; asst. prof. speech Ball State U., Muncie, Ind., 1993; instr. No. Va. U., Alexandria, Annendale, Manassas, Woodbridge, 1995—; assoc. faculty dept. comm. and theatre, Ind. U., Purdue U., Indpls., 1993; trainer internat. convs., sales groups, staffs of hosps., others; lectr., cons. in field. Columnist, Jackie's World, Topics Newspapers, Indpls.; author: Body Language: First Impressions, Body Language in Negotiations and Sales; contbr. articles to profl. jours. Mem. Fairfax County Dem. Com. Mem. Pi Lambda Theta, Phi Delta Kappa. Home and Office: 7006 Elkton Dr Springfield VA 22152-3330

RANKIN, MARGIE ANN BOND, elementary school educator; b. Williams, Ariz., Mar. 15, 1939; d. Damon U. and Marie Elizabeth (London) Bond; m. Bobby Joe Rankin, Sept. 5, 1959; children: Catherine Rankin Davis, Amy Elizabeth Rankin. A. in Bus., Okla. State U., 1959; BS in Edn., N.Mex. StateU., 1971, MA in Edn., 1982. Cert. reading specialist. Sec. Poultry Sci. Dept., Okla. State U., Stillwater, 1959-61; tchr. Las Cruces (N.Mex.) Pub. Schs., 1976—, dist. trainer for N.Mex. social studies curriculum, 1992. Coord. for "Ag in Classroom", Dona Ana Farm and Livestock Bur., 1989—; sustainer Jr. Svc. League, 1993—. Named Outstanding Educator N.Mex. Farm and Livestock Bur., 1992, Tchr. of the Yr. N.Mex. Coun. for Social Studies Tchrs., 1993. Mem. Las Cruces Classroom Tchrs., Phi Kappa Phi, Phi Kappa Delta. Republican. Presbyterian. Home: 3007 Bowman St Las Cruces NM 88005

RANKIN, MARY ANNE, director; b. Hackettstown, N.J., Feb. 2, 1944; d. Joseph Edward and Barbara Jean (Cornish) Sekerke; m. John M. Rankin, June 10, 1966; children: Andrew M., Christopher J. BA, Albion Coll., 1966; MAT, George Washington U., 1968. Tchr. Redlands (Calif.) Ind. Sch. Dist., 1980-86, Colton (Calif.) Ind. Sch. Dist., 1986-88, Concord (Calif.) Ind. Sch. Dist., 1989-90; dir. RSVP, Shreveport, La., 1992—; chmn. Post Office Adv. Coun., Shreveport, 1992—. Pres. Altrusa Club, Shreveport, 1996—; v.p. H.S. Booster Club, Shreveport, 1991-93. Mem. AAUW, LAOAVPD, Local Vol. Coords. (sec./treas. 1993—), Nat. RSVP. Methodist. Home: 410 Dunmoreland Cir Shreveport LA 71106-6102 Office: Caddo Coun Aging RSVP 3719 Lakeshore Dr Shreveport LA 71109

RANKIN, TERESA P. FRONCEK, insurance educator, consultant, former state agency administrator; b. Camp Lejeune, N.C., May 5, 1952; d. Richard A. and Carol Ann (Leverenz) Froncek; m. Robert W. Rankin, Dec. 22, 1978. BA, Ariz. State U., 1974; JD, U. Ariz., 1979. Chartered property casualty underwriter. Atty. Smith & Gamble, Carson City, Nev., 1979-80; dep. legis. counsel Legis. Counsel Bur., Carson City, 1981-83; chief ins. asst. Nev. Ins. Divsn., Carson City, 1984-91, commr. ins., 1991-95. Recipient Recognition award U. Nev. Las Vegas-Inst. Ins. & Risk Mgmt., 1993. Mem. Nat. Assn. Ins. Commrs., Reno Jaquar Club (bd. dirs. 1986-95). Home and Office: 4221 Tara St Carson City NV 89706-1333

RANKIN-SMITH, PAMELA, photographer; b. Kansas City, Kans., Jan. 12, 1918; d. Dexter Leon and Ruth Dee (Millard) Rankin; m. George W. Witcher, 1943 (div. 1945); 1 child, Vann Leigh Witcher; m. A. Arthur Smith, 1968 (dec. 1968). Diploma, Dallas Little Theater, 1936; student, U. Tex., 1937-41; lic. in real estate, New Sch., N.Y.C., 1954; cert., Sogetsu Sch. Ikebana, N.Y.C., 1989-93. Real estate agt. N.Y.C., 1954-91; flower arranger Ikebana Flowers The Met. Mus. Art, Patrons Lounge, N.Y.C., 1989-96. Author: Perfectly Candid, 1994; one-woman photography shows include Soho/Stieglitz Gallery, N.Y.C., 1978, La Galerie, Paris, 1979, Donnell Libr., N.Y.C., 1979, Fed. Hall, N.Y.C., 1978, Nikon House, N.Y.C., 1980, Overseas Press Club, N.Y.C., 1980, Le Gallery, Kent, Conn., 1981, Camera Club N.Y., N.Y.C., 1985. Mem. PEN, Photographic Adminstrs., Inc., Actors Equity Assn., Am. Soc. Media Photographers Ikebana Internat., Nat. Guild Decoupeurs, Mcpl. Art Soc., Nat. Arts Club, Camera Club N.Y., Circle of Confusion. Home: 150 E 69th St New York NY 10021-5704

RANKS, ANNE ELIZABETH, retired elementary and secondary education educator; b. Omaha, June 10, 1916; d. Salvatore and Concetta (Turco) Scolla; m. Harold Eugene Ranks, Aug. 20, 1955 (dec.). B in Philosophy, Duchesne Coll., Omaha, 1937; MA, Creighton U., 1947. Tchr. Good Shepherd Parochial HighSch., Omaha, 1937-38, St. Benedicts High Sch., Omaha, 1938-39, Omaha Pub. Schs., 1939-81. Pres. women's divsn. Dem. Cen. Com., Nebr.; chmn. Gov.'s Profl. Practices Commn. Nebr., 1938-39; vol. Bergan-Mercy Hosp., Omaha, 1980-86, hosp. mem. aux. bd. dirs., 1985-86; vol. Saddleback Hosp., Laguna Hills, Calif., 1989-91; bd. dirs. Sylvia Tischhauser CRTA divsn. Scholarship Found., 1989-94; mem. bd. dirs. Saddleback Valley Ednl. Found., 1990-92. Mem. AAUW (v.p. Laguna Hills br. 1988-91), Womens Club, Cath. Daus. Regent Omaha Ct. (rec. sec. Lake Forest, Calif. Ct. 1988-90), Orange Diocesan Coun. Cath. Women Calif. (bd. dirs. 1989-90, 2d v.p. 1990-94). Coll. Club of Leisure World (v.p. 1990-95).

RANNEY, HELEN MARGARET, physician, educator; b. Summer Hill, N.Y., Apr. 12, 1920; d. Arthur C. and Alesia (Toolan) R. AB, Barnard Coll., 1941; MD, Columbia U., 1947; ScD, U. S.C., 1979. Diplomate: Am. Bd. Internal Medicine. Intern Presbyn. Hosp., N.Y.C., 1947-48, resident, 1948-50, asst. physician, 1954-60; practice medicine specializing in internal medicine, hematology N.Y.C., 1954-70; instr. Coll. Phys. and Surg. Columbia, N.Y.C., 1954-60; assoc. prof. medicine Albert Einstein Coll. Medicine, N.Y.C., 1960-64, prof. medicine, 1965-70; prof. medicine SUNY, Buffalo, 1970-73; prof. medicine U. Calif., San Diego, 1973-90, chmn. dept. medicine, 1973-86, Disting. physician vet. adminstr., 1986-91; mem. staff Alliance Pharm. Corp., San Diego, 1991—. Master ACP; fellow AAAS; mem. NAS, Inst. Medicine, Am. Soc. for Clin. Investigation, Am. Soc. Hematology, Harvey Soc., Am. Assn. Physicians, Am. Acad. Arts and Scis., Phi Beta Kappa, Sigma Xi, Alpha Omega Alpha. Office: Alliance Pharm Corp 3040 Science Park Rd San Diego CA 92121-1102

RANNEY, MARY ELIZABETH, business executive; b. Louisville, Nov. 10, 1928; d. James William and Erna Marie Katerina (Hansen) Connell; m. Glen Royal Ranney, July 26, 1947; children: Darleen Diane Ranney Bowie, Nancy Elizabeth Ranney Pieratt. Student, Monmouth Coll., 1946-47. Cert. profl. sec., nursing asst. Nursing asst. Monmouth (Ill.) Hosp., 1957-63; asst. in fin. Bd. Pub. Instrn. Collier County, Naples, Fla., 1964-68; sec. 1st Nat. Bank, Bonita Springs, Fla., 1969-71; founder, dir. Planned Parenthood, Naples, 1972-76; writer Am. Hibiscus Soc., 1977-82; owner Tree Gallery, Naples and Ft. Myers, 1983—; tchr., seedling judge Am. Hibiscus Soc., 1977-79. Author: (brochure) Abortion, 1976; solo performance Fiddler on the Roof, 1976. Chair Fla. Assn. for Repeal Abortion Laws, Lee and Collier County, 1972; founder Abortion Referral Svc. S.W. Fla., 1972-75; founder, dir. Accordion Band, Naples, 1974-79, Floridian Accordion Band, Ft. Myers, 1989-91; founding officer Naples Concert Band, 1972-79; sponsor Am. hibiscus shows, Naples, 1973-81. Recipient Prominent Woman of Cmty. award Naples Star, 1977, 78, 79, Mover of 70's award Naples NOW Mag., 1980, Shaker, Mover and Star award Naples NOW Mag., 1983, Life Work Feature award Naples Star, 1981, Great Achiever award Naples Star, 1982. Mem. NOW (charter nat. pres. 1975-77), Am. Hibiscus Soc. (life, founder Ranney chpt. 1973—, editor Show Chair Manual 1979, Judges Manual 1980, Pres. Svc. award 1979, Hibiscus of Yr. 1980, 82), Meml. Soc. S.W. Fla. (pres. 1975-77). Democrat. Home: 3164 Palm Beach Blvd Fort Myers FL 33916

RANNEY-MARINELLI, ALESIA, lawyer; b. Ithaca, N.Y., 1952. BA, Mich. State U., 1973; JD cum laude, Harvard U., 1977. Bar: Del. 1977, N.Y. 1986. Ptnr. Skadden Arps Slate Flom & Meagher, N.Y.C. Office: Skadden Arps Slate Meagher & Flom 919 3rd Ave New York NY 10022*

RANOUS, ELAINE, elementary education educator; b. Kenosha, Wis., Nov. 13, 1941; d. Walter and Johanne (Andreasen) Walton; m. John Garrison Ranous, Sept. 12, 1964; 1 child, Jeffrey Garrison. BS, Wis. State U., 1965. Cert. elem. tchr., Wis. Tchr. St. Joseph Ridge Sch., LaCrosse, Wis., 1964-65, Bangor (Wis.) Area Schs., 1965—; owner Treasure Chest Craft Shop, Bangor, Wis., 1975-78; pub. rels. co-chair Coulee Region United Educators, LaCrosse, Wis., 1985—. leader Girl Scouts Am., Bangor, Wis., 1967-70; cub master Boy Scouts Am., Bangor, 1970-80. Mem. Wis. Edn. Assn. Coun. (pub. rels. com. 1990—), Wis. Sch. Pub. Rels. Assn., Wis. State Reading Assn., Wis. State Math. Assn., Alpha Delta Kappa (pres. 1988-90). Republican. Home: N6012 Big Creek Rd Bangor WI 54614 Office: Bangor Area Schs 701-14 Ave S Bangor WI 54614

RANSIER, MARTHA ESTHER, social gerontologist; b. San Antonio, Oct. 3, 1951; d. Harry D. and Mary Elizabeth (Love) R.; divorced; children: Lydia Elizabeth Parkman, Priscilla Jerene Parkman. Cert., Med. and Dental Assts. Sch., San Antonio, 1976; BA in Psychology and Sociology, Our Lady of Lake U., San Antonio, 1991; MA in Social Gerontology and Adminstrn., U. of the Incarnate Word, San Antonio, 1996. Registered med. asst. With Dunhill Temp. Agy., San Antonio, 1984—; devel. sec. Patriot Heights Retirement Cmty., San Antonio, 1993-94; program asst. Goodwill Industries Rural Svcs., San Antonio, 1994-95; home health care asst. Outreach Home Health Primary Health Care, San Antonio, 1995-96; intern, activity coord. elder day care program Pueblo of Isleta, N.Mex., 1996; cons. Nat. Coun. on Elder Abuse, Albuquerque, 1995—; presenter in field. Vol. ARC, San Antonio, 1989—. Mem. AAUW, Sigma Phi Omega. Republican. Baptist. Home: 8512 Rockmoor Dr San Antonio TX 78230

RANSOM, CHRISTINA ROXANE, librarian; b. N.Y.C., Oct. 28, 1951; d. Roy Martin Palhof and Virginia O'Brien Starr; m. Eddie Darden (div.); 1 child, Shani Aisha Darden; m. Stanley Austin Ransom, Jr., Nov. 27, 1980; children: Sarah, Austin, Rebecca. BA in Chemistry, Bard Coll., 1973; MLS, Columbia U., 1974; postgrad., Sage Coll., 1994—. Libr. asst. Libr. of Bard Coll., Annandale-on-Hudson, N.Y., 1969-73, Columbia U. Law Libr. and Libr. Svc. Libr., N.Y.C., 1973-74, Winthrop, Stimson, Putnam & Roberts, N.Y.C., 1974-76; tax libr. White & Case, N.Y.C., 1976-78; libr. cons. Corning (N.Y.) Glass, 1978; info. scientist Wyeth-Ayerst Labs., Rouses Point, N.Y., 1979-84; med. libr. CVPH Med. Ctr., Plattsburgh, N.Y., 1984—; libr. skills instr. SUNY Plattsburgh, N.Y., 1981-82; trustee North Country Reference and Rsch. Resources, Canton, N.Y., 1982-83; mem. trres., sec., v.p., pres. No. N.Y. Health Info. Coop., 1979-89. Recipient North Country Regional Centennial Coms. Excellence in Librarianship award New York Libr. Assn., 1990. Mem. Med. Libr. Assn., Friends of the Nat. Libr. Medicine, No. Adirondack Libr. Assn. Home: 39 Broad St Plattsburgh NY 12901-3447 Office: CVPH Med Ctr 75 Beekman St Plattsburgh NY 12901

RANSOM, EVELYN NAILL, language educator, linguist; b. Memphis, Apr. 20, 1938; d. Charles Rhea and Evelyn (Goodlander) Naill Ransom; m. Gunter Heinz Hiller, June 7, 1960 (div. Mar. 1964). AA, Mt. Vernon Jr. Coll., 1958; BA, Newcomb Coll., 1960; MA, N.Mex. Highlands U., 1965; PhD, U. Ill., 1974. Cert. secondary tchr., N.Mex. Instr. Berlitz Sch. Langs., New Orleans, 1961; tchr. MillerWall Elem. Sch., Harvey, L.A., 1961-62; teaching asst. N.Mex. Highlands U., Las Vegas, 1963-64; instr. U. Wyo., Laramie, 1965-66; teaching asst. U. Ill., Urbana, 1966-70; prof. English lang. Ea. Ill. U., Charleston, 1970-93; vis. prof. in linguistics No. Ariz. U., Flagstaff, 1990-91, adj. faculty, 1993-94; adj. faculty Ariz. State U., Tempe, 1995—; referee Pretext: Jour. of Lang. and Lit., Ill., 1981; co-chair roundtable Internat. Congress of Linguistics, 1987; linguistics del. People to People, Moscow, St. Petersburg, Prague, 1993; dissertation reader SUNY, Buffalo, 1982; vis. scholar UCLA, 1977; conductor workshop LSA summer inst. Author: Complementation: Its Meanings and Forms, 1986; contbr. articles to profl. publs. Organizer Prairie Women's Cir., Champaign, 1981-83; mem. Women's Cir., Yavapai County, Ariz., 1993. Nat. Def. Fgn. Lang. fellow, 1969; grantee Ea. Ill. U., 1982, 87, 88, NSF, 1988. Mem. Linguistic Soc. Am., Linguistic Assn. S.W. Home: 201 E Southern Ave # 135 Apache Junction AZ 85219-3740

RANSOM, MARGARET PALMQUIST, public relations executive; b. Davenport, Iowa, Aug. 13, 1935; d. Herman Philip and Margaret (Burchell) Palmquist; m. David Duane Ransom, July 16, 1960; 1 child, David Burke. BA in Speech and English, Augustana Coll., 1957. Tchr. speech and English Beloit (Wis.) High Sch., 1957-59; tchr. English Lake Forest (Ill.) High Sch., 1959-60, Warren High Sch., Gurnee, Ill., 1960-62, 64-66; asst. to dean Grad. Sch. Bowling Green (Ohio) State U., 1963; freelance writer Coll. Bd. Examinations, 1966; market rsch. analyst Kitchens of Sara Lee, Deerfield, Ill., 1972-74; pub. affairs mgr. Sara Lee Bakery, Deerfield, 1975-89; sr. cons. Ransom Pub. Svc. Cons., Libertyville, Ill., 1990-94; cons. Olsten Staffing Svcs., Chgo., 1994-96; judge nat. competitions Pub. Rels. Soc. Am., 1986-89; spkr. on motivation and orgn.; chmn. employer coun. Ill. Dept. Employment Security, 1995-96. Bd. dirs. Early Childhood Adv. Coun., Northeastern Ill. State U., 1989-91; mem. Main St. Libertyville com., 1990-92; creator Job Market Place '96, Lake County. Recipient Ill. Citizens Svc. medal, 1993. Mem. AAUW, Bus. and Profl. Women Lake County, Mortar Bd. Office: 1037 Mayfair Dr Libertyville IL 60048-3548

RANSOM, NANCY ALDERMAN, sociology and women's studies educator, university administrator; b. New Haven, Feb. 25, 1929; d. Samuel Bennett and Florence (Opper) Alderman; m. Harry Howe Ransom, July 6, 1951; children—Jenny Alderman, Katherine Marie, William Henry Howe. B.A., Vassar Coll., 1950; postgrad. Columbia U., 1951, U. Leeds (Eng.), 1977-78; M.A., Vanderbilt U., 1971; EdD, Vanderbilt U., 1988. Lectr. sociology U. Tenn.-Nashville, 1971-76; grant writer Vanderbilt U., Nashville, 1976-77, dir. Women's Ctr., 1978—, instr. sociology, 1972, 74, lectr. sociology and women's studies, 1983, 90—; speaker profl. meetings. Vol. counselor family planning Planned Parenthood Assn. of Nashville, 1973-77, bd. dirs., 1978—, v.p., 1981—, pres., 1987-89; mem. planning com. ACE/ACE nat. identification program Women in Higher Edn., 1984-92. Recipient Woman of Achievement award Middle Tenn. State U., 1996; Columbia U. residential fellow, 1951; Vanderbilt U. fellow, 1971. Mem. AAUW, NOW, Am. Sociol. Assn., Nat. Women's Studies Assn., Southeastern Women's Studies Assn., Nat. Women's Polit. Caucus, LWV, Cable Club, Phi Beta Kappa (v.p. Alpha of Tenn. 1994-95, pres. 95—). Office: Vanderbilt U PO Box 1513 Nashville TN 37235

RANTA AHO, MARTHA HELEN, retired elementary education educator; b. Poplar, Wis., July 12, 1923; d. John and Aurora (Aho) Ranta; m. Wayne August Aho, Dec. 19, 1942 (dec. June 1978); children: Dennis Wayne, Marla Jane Thibodeau. BS in Elem. Edn. with honors, U. Wis., Superior, 1968, MS in Teaching, Elem. Edn., 1977, postgrad., 1979-86; postgrad., U. Minn., Superior, 1980-91, Coll. of St. Scholastica, 1978, Coll. St. Scholastica, Duluth, Minn, 1991. Cert. elem. tchr., Minn. Tchr. kindergarten Ind. Sch. Dist. #709, Duluth, 1968-75; tchr. first grade ISD #709, Duluth, 1975-89, master tchr., 1978-89, ret., 1989. Mem. St. Luke's Vol. Svc. Guild, tchr. leader insvc. sessions, 1972-80; docent St. Louis County Hist. Soc.-Depot Mus., Duluth, 1989—; mentor tchr. Kenwood Elem. Sch., 1987-89, vol. storyteller, 1989—, Chester Park Elem. Sch., 1993—; storyteller Rockridge Elem. Sch., 1995—, Congdon Park Elem. Sch., 1995—. Recipient trophy and award Wis. Indianhead Dist. of Garden Club, Superior, 1964. Mem. AAUW, Minn. Reading Assn., Arrowhead Reading Coun., Duluth Area Ret. Educators Assn., Am. Assn. Ret. Persons, Minn. Hist. Soc, Univ. for Srs. (vol. tchr. leader 1991), Parent Tchr. Student Assn. (hon. life), Finnish Am. Hist. Soc., Nat. Storytelling Assn., Minn. Gen. Fedn. Women's Clubs, Twentieth Century Club, Delta Kappa Gamma. Democrat. Lutheran. Home: 2722 E 1st St Duluth MN 55812-1907

RANTS, CAROLYN JEAN, college official; b. Hastings, Nebr., Oct. 3, 1936; d. John Leon and Christine (Helzer) Halloran; m. Marvin L. Rants, June 1, 1957 (div. July 1984); children: Christopher Charles, Douglas John. Student, Hastings Coll., 1954-56; BS, U. Omaha, 1960; MEd, U. Nebr., 1968; EdD, U. S.D., 1982. Tchr. elem. Ogallala (Nebr.) Community Sch., 1956-58, Omaha Pub. Schs., 1958-60, Hastings Pub. Schs., 1960-64, Grosse Pointe (Mich.) Community Schs., 1964-67; asst. prof., instr. Morningside Coll., Sioux City, Iowa, 1974-82, dean for student devel., 1982-84, v.p. for student affairs, 1984-94, interim v.p. for acad. affairs, 1992-94; v.p. enrollment and student svcs., 1994—. Mem. new agy. com., chmn. fund distbn. and resource deployment com. United Way, Sioux City, 1987-94, co-chair, United Way Day of Caring, 1996; mem. Iowa Civil Rights Commn., 1989—; bd. dirs. Leadership Sioux City, 1988-93, pres., 1992-93; bd. dirs. Siouxland Y, Sioux City, 1985-90, pres., 1988; bd. dirs. Girls, Inc., 1995—, Work Activity Co., 1996—; mem. Vision 2020 Cmty. Planning Task Force, 1990-92. Mem. Iowa Women in Ednl. Leadership (pres. Sioux City chpt. 1986), Nat. Assn. Student Pers. Adminstrs.(region IV-E adv. bd.), Nat. Assn. for Women Deans, Adminstrs. and Counselors, Iowa Student Pers. Adminstr. (chmn. profl. devel. Iowa chpt. 1988-89, pres. 1991-92, Disting. Svc. award 1995), AAUW (corp. rep., coll./univ. rep. 1994-96), P.E.O. (pres. Sioux City chpt., Tri-State Women's Bus. Conf. (treas., planning com. Sioux City chpt. 1987-89), Quota Club (com. chmn. Sioux City 1987-89, v.p. 1992-94, pres. 1994-95, Siouxland Woman of Yr. award 1988), Sertoma (officer, bd. govs., regional dir.), Omicron Delta Kappa, Delta Kappa Gamma (state 1st v.p. 1993—, state pres. 1995—). Republican. Methodist. Home: 2904 S Cedar St # 4 Sioux City IA 51106-4246 Office: Morningside Coll 1501 Morningside Ave Sioux City IA 51106-1717

RANUM, JANE BARNHARDT, lawyer; b. Charlotte, N.C., Aug. 21, 1947; d. John Robert and Gladys Rose (Swift) B.; m. James Harry Ranum, Mar. 29, 1972; 1 child, Elizabeth McBride. B.S., East Carolina U., 1969; J.D., Hamline U., 1979. Bar: Minn. 1979, U.S. Dist. Ct. Minn. 1979. Tchr. elem. sch. Durham County, Durham, N.C., 1969-70; tchr. Dept. Def., Baumholder, W.Ger., 1970-72, Dist. 196, Rosemount, Minn., 1972-76; law clk. Hennepin County Dist. Ct., Mpls., 1982; asst. county atty. Hennepin County, Mpls., 1982—. Mem. exec. com., lobbying coordinator DFL Feminist Caucus, St. Paul, 1980-84; bd. dirs. Project 13 for Reproductive Rights, Mpls., 1981-82; state del. Minn. Democratic Farmer Labor Party Conv., 1982, 84, precinct del., 1974—; mem. Minn. Sen., 1991—, chair legislature commn. on children, youth and their families, 1993—; senate rep. chemical abuse and prevention resource coun., 1993. Named Feminist of the Yr. Minn. NOW, 1994, Legis. of the Yr. Minn. Assn. for Retarded Citizens, 1994. Mem. Minn. Women's Lawyers, Minn. Family Support and Recovery Council, Hennepin County Bar Assn., Minn. Bar Assn. Democrat. Home: 5045 Aldrich Ave S Minneapolis MN 55419-1207 Office: County Govt Ctr A-2000 Hennepin Minneapolis MN 55487

RAPAPORT, RITA, artist, sculpture, painter; b. N.Y.C., May 25, 1918; d. Mandel E. and Birdie (Shapiro) Cohen; m. Alexander Rapaport, Oct. 13, 1940 (widowed June 1983); children: Anne, Marshall, Judith; m. Leon L. Wolfe, Mar. 15, 1986. BA, N.Y.U., 1940. artist-in-residence Westchester Holocaust Commn. Manhatanville Coll. Purchase N.Y., 1990—. Prin. works include Gate of Remembrance, 1992. Mem. Nat. Orgn. Women, Dem. Party, B'nai Brith Haddassah, Mamaroneck Artists Guild, Hudson River Mus., Metro. Mus., Hudson River Contemporary Artists, Jewish Mus. N.Y., Nat. Holocaust Mus. Jewish. Home: 15 Tompkins Rd Scarsdale NY 10583

RAPHAEL, BARBARA C., food products executive; b. San Diego, June 11, 1944; d. Benjamin F. and Constance M. (Benson) Howell; m. Barry S. Raphael, Dec. 14, 1968; children: Jonathan W., Jessica C. BS, Pa. State U., 1966, MS in Nutrition, 1969, PhD in Food Sci., 1972. Asst. prof. U. Del., Newark, 1974-76; food technologist to dir. Kraft Foods Corp., White Plains, N.Y., 1977-93; v.p. global confectionary R&D Warner Lambert, Morris Plains, N.J., 1993—. Mem. Inst. Food Technologists, Sigma Xi. Home: 14 Bradford Way Cedar Grove NJ 07009 Office: Warner Lambert 175 Tabor Rd Morris Plains NJ 07950

RAPHAEL, BONNIE NANETTE, voice, speech, text and dialect coach, educator; b. Bklyn., Mar. 27, 1944; d. David A. and Helen (Rutstein) Newmark; m. Jay E. Raphael, June 21, 1966 (div. Mar. 1988). BA in Speech Edn., Bklyn. Coll., 1964; MA in Theatre, U. Mich., 1965; PhD in Theatre, Mich. State U., 1973. Lectr. theater So. Ill. U., Carbondale, 1971-73; asst. prof. theater Northwestern U., Evanston, Ill., 1973-76; asst. prof. drama U. Va., Charlottesville, 1976-81; assoc. prof. theater U. Mo., Kansas City, 1981-82; voice and speech coach Colo. Shakespeare Festival, Boulder, summer 1979-83; voice and speech coach, tchr. Denver Ctr. Theater Co., 1982-86; rschr. Rec. and Rsch. Ctr. Denver Ctr. for Performing Arts, 1982-86; voice and speech coach, tchr. Am. Repertory Theatre, Cambridge, Mass., 1986—. Author: (chpts.) Professional Voice: The Science and Art of Clinical Care, 1991; mem. editl. bd. Jour. of Voice, 1987—; contbr. articles to profl. jours. Smoking cessation facilitator Am. Cancer Soc., Denver. Recipient Disting. Woman award Am. Theatre Assn., 1977; named one of Outstanding Young Women of Am., 1980. Mem. Voice and Speech Trainers Assn. (life, bd. dirs. 1985), Actors Equity Assn., Assn. for Theatre in Higher Edn. (charter mem.), Voice Found. (Sackler Awards com. 1992-94.). Office: Am Repertory Theatre & Inst 64 Brattle St Cambridge MA 02138

RAPHAEL, LOUISE ARAKELIAN, mathematician, educator; b. N.Y.C., Oct. 24, 1937; d. Aristakes and Antionette (Sudbeaz) Arakelian; m. Robert Barnett Raphael, June 12, 1966 (div. 1985); children: Therese Denise, Marc Philippe. BS in Math., St. John's U., 1959; MS in Math., Cath. U., Washington, 1962; PhD in Math, Cath. U., 1967. Asst. prof. math. Howard U., Washington, 1966-70, vis. prof., 1981-82, assoc. prof., 1982-86, prof., 1986—; assoc. prof. Clark Coll., Atlanta, 1971-79, prof., 1979-82; vis. assoc. prof. MIT, Cambridge, 1977-78, vis. prof., 1989-90. Contbr. over 35 rsch. articles to profl. jours. Program dir. NSF, Washington, 1986-88; acting adminstrv. officer Conf. Bd. Math. Scis., 1985-86. Grantee NSF, 1975-76, 79-81, 89-91, Army Rsch. Office, 1981-89, Air Force Sci. Rsch., 1981-82, 91-95, Nat. Security Agy., 1994—. Mem. AAAS, Am. Math. Soc. (com. mem.), Math. Assn. Am. (chmn. minorities in math. task force 1988, 1st v.p. 1996—), Soc. Indsl. and Applied Math., Sigma Xi. Democrat. Roman Catholic. Office: Howard U Dept Math Washington DC 20059

RAPHAEL, SALLY JESSY, talk-show host; b. Easton, Pa., Feb. 25, 1943; children: Allison (dec.), Andrea; m. Karl Soderlund; 2 step-daughters, 1 adopted son, also foster children. BFA, Columbia U. Anchored radio program Jr. High Sch. News Sta. WFAS-AM, White Plains, N.Y., 1955; host of cooking program WAPA-TV, San Juan, P.R., 1965-67; radio and television broadcaster Miami and Ft. Lauderdale, Fla., 1969-74; host Sta. WMCA-Radio, N.Y.C., 1976-81; talk show host NBC Talk-net, N.Y.C., 1982-88, ABC Talkradio, N.Y.C., 1988-91; syndicated TV talk-show host N.Y.C., 1983—; part-time owner of a perfume factory, 1964-68; owner of an art gallery, 1964-69; owner, The Wine Press, N.Y.C., 1979-83; ind. producer TV films, 1991;. Author: (with M.J. Boyer) Finding Love, 1984, (with Pam Proctor) Sally: Unconventional Success, 1980; film appearances include: Resident Alien, 1990, The Addams Family, 1991, The Associate, 1996, Meet Wally Sparks, 1996; TV appearances include: Murphy Brown, Dave's World, The Nanny, The Tonight Show, Nightline, Diagnosis Murder, Conspiracy of Silence, Touched By An Angel. Recipient Bronze medal, Internat. Film & Television Festival of NY, 1985; Emmy award as outstanding talk-show host, daytime, 1988, 89. Office: Multimedia Entertainment 515 W 57th St New York NY 10019-2901

RAPHAEL-HOWELL, FRANCES JAYNE, clinical psychologist; b. Alexandria, Va., Apr. 26, 1945; d. Robert Arthur and Isabelle Georgiana (Francis) Raphael; m. Frederick Alfred Howell, June 14, 1977; children: Robert, Carolyn, Cheryl. BS in Psychology, Howard U., 1971; MA in Clin. Psychology, Clark U., 1976, PhD, 1992; pre-doctoral intern, Children's Hosp. Med. Ctr., Boston, 1974-75. Cert. clin. psychologist; play therapist and supr. Assn. for Play Therapy. Spl. edn. tchr. Boston U. Mini Sch., 1975-76; instr. psychopathology U. Mass., Boston, 1976; psychologist Boston U. Med. Ctr., 1976-77; psychologist cons. Head Start, Boston, 1977; psychologist Montgomery County Pub. Schs., 1978; clin. psychologist D.C. Pub. Schs., Washington, 1978-91, supr. psychol. svcs., 1991-93; dir. Title I Pupil Pers. Svcs., Washington, 1993—; instr. urban edn. Grad. Sch. George Washington U., 1995-96; instr. play therapy Trinity U., 1996; presentations at confs. and workshops. Bd. dirs. Washington Humane Soc. Harvard U. fellow, 1974-75. Mem. APA (div. Clin. Psychology), Am. Bd. Forensic Examiners, Assn. for Play Therapy, Inc., D.C. Assn. for Sch. Psychologists. Democrat. Methodist. Home: 3010 W St SE Washington DC 20020-3361 Office: DC Pub Schs Winston Ednl Ctr 31st and Erie Sts SE Washington DC 20020

RAPHEL, ROBIN, federal official; b. Vancouver, Wash., Sept. 16, 1947; m. Leonard Arthur Ashton; 2 children. BA, U. Wash.; Diploma in Hist. Studies, Cambridge U., Eng.; MA, U. Md. Lectr. history Damavand Coll., Tehran, Iran; analyst CIA; with Fgn. Svc., 1977, Islamabad, Pakistan, 1977-78; with office investment affairs bur. econs. Dept. of State, 1978-80, staff asst. to asst. sec. Near East and South Asian affairs, 1980-81, econ. officer Israel desk, 1981-82, spl. asst. to under sec. polit. affairs, 1982-84; 1st sec. polit. affairs London, 1984-88; polit. counselor Pretoria, South Africa, 1988-91, New Delhi, 1991-93; asst. sec. South Asian affairs Dept. of State, Washington, 1993—. Mem. Am. Econ. Assn., Am. Fgn. Svc. Assn., Phi Beta Kappa. Office: S Asian Affairs 2201 C St NW Washington DC 20520-0001*

RAPIN, ISABELLE, physician; b. Lausanne, Switzerland, Dec. 4, 1927; d. Rene and Mary Coe (Reeves) R.; m. Harold Oaklander, Apr. 5, 1959; children: Anne Louise, Christine, Stephen, Peter. Physician's Diploma. Faculte de Medicine, U. Lausanne, 1952, Doctorate in Medicine, 1955. Diplomate Am. Bd. Psychiatry and Neurology. Intern in pediatrics N.Y. U. Bellevue Med. Center, 1953-54; resident in neurology Neurol. Inst. of N.Y., Columbia-Presbyn. Med. Center, 1954-57, fellow in child neurology, 1957-58; mem. faculty Albert Einstein Coll. Medicine, Bronx, N.Y., 1958—; prof. neurology and pediatrics Albert Einstein Coll. Medicine, 1972—; attending neurologist and child neurologist Einstein Affiliated Hosps., Bronx.; Mem. Nat. Adv. Neurol. and Communicative Disorders and Stroke Coun., NIH, 1984-88. Contbr. chpts. to books, articles to med. jours. Recipient award Conf. Ednl. Adminstrs. Serving the Deaf, 1988. Fellow Am. Acad. Neurology (exec. bd. 1995—); mem. AAAS, Internat. Child Neurology Assn. (sec.-gen. 1979-82, v.p. 1982-86, Frank R. Ford lectr. 1990), Am. Neurol. Assn. (v.p. 1982-83), Child Neurology Soc. (Hower award 1987), Internat. Neuropsychology Soc., N.Y. Acad. Scis., Assn. for Rsch. in Nervous and Mental Diseases (v.p. 1986). Office: Albert Einstein Coll Medicine 1410 Pelham Pky S Bronx NY 10461-1101

RAPOPORT, FLORENCE ROSENBERG, English language educator; b. N.Y.C., May 1, 1920; d. Samuel and Rebecca (Solomon) Rosenberg; m. Carl A. Rapoport, Sept. 11, 1941; children: Mark S., Miles S. BA magna cum laude, Hunter Coll., 1941; MA, Queens Coll., 1959; Cert. Comm. Theory, Fordham U., 1968. Cert. tchr. secondary English, N.Y. Script writer Emerson Yorke Prodns./Documentary Film Co., N.Y.C., 1941-43; rschr. and speech-writer U.S. Dept. Labor, N.Y.C., 1943-44; econ. analysis and writing U.S. War Labor Bd., N.Y.C., 1944-46; educator Great Neck (N.Y.) Pub. Schs., 1959-78; television talk show producer and host Cable Vision, Great Neck, 1983—; tchr., adminstr. Alternative Sch., Great Neck, 1973-78; founder, chmn. Task Force on Sexism, Great Neck Pub. Schs., 1974-76; creator/instr. in-svc. course for tchrs., Great nec, 1975; coord. Title 9, Great NecK Pub. Schs., 1976-78; dir. sr. values seminar program, Great Neck H.S., 1970-74. Founder, faculty sponsor: (literary mag.) Epiphany, 1965-69; founder, editor-in-chief: (literary mag.) More Womanspace, 1981-84; host TV talk show: Focus on Women, 1983—; contbr. articles to profl. publs. Active United Parent-Tchr. Coun., Great Neck, 1952-57; mem. Nat. Speaker's Bur., Women's Am. ORT, Great Neck, 1954-57; campaign chair United Jewish Appeal, Great Neck, 1955-57; co-founder, dir. Womanspace, 1978-85. Named Woman of the Yr., Women on the Job, L.I., 1988, Am. Jewish Congress, L.I., 1990, Crohn's and Colitis Found. of Am., 1994, Women's Honor Roll, Town of North Hempstead, L.I., 1994; inducted Hunter Coll. Hall of Fame, 1996. Mem. Vet. Feminists of Am., Womanspace (dir. emerita), Phi Beta Kappa. Democrat. Jewish. Home: 231 Kings Point Rd Great Neck/Long Isld NY 11024 Office: Cablevision Long Island 705 Middle Neck Rd Great Neck NY 11023

RAPOPORT, JUDITH, psychiatrist; b. N.Y.C., July 12, 1933; d. Louis and Minna (Enteen) Livant; m. Stanley Rapoport, June 25, 1961; children: Stuart, Erik. BA, Swarthmore Coll., 1955; MD, Harvard U., 1959. Lic. psychiatrist. Cons., child psychiatrist NIMH/St. Elizabeth's Hosp., Washington, 1969-72; clin. asst. prof. Georgetown U. Med. Sch., Washington, 1972-82, clin. assoc. prof., 1982-85, clin. prof. psychiat., 1985—; med. officer biol. psychiatry br. NIMH, Bethesda, Md., 1976-78, chief, child mental illness unit, biol. psychiat. br., 1979-82, chief, child psychiatry lab. of clin. scis., 1982-84, chief, child psychiatry div. intramural rsch. programs, 1984—; prof. psychiatry George Washington U. Sch. Med., Washington, 1979—; prof. pediatrics Georgetown U., Washington, 1985—; cons. in field. Author: (non-fiction) The Boy Who Couldn't Stop Washing, 1989 (best seller literary guild selection 1989), Childhood Obsessive Compulsive Disorder, 1989. Fellow Am. Psychiat. Assn., Am. Acad. Child Psychiat.; mem. D.C. Psychiat. Assn., Inst. Medicine. Home: 3010 44th Pl NW Washington DC 20016-3557 Office: NIMH Bldg 10 Rm 6N240 Bethesda MD 20892

RAPOPORT, SONYA, artist; b. Boston; d. Louis Aaron and Ida Tina (Axelrod) Goldberg; m. Henry Rapoport; children—Hava Rapoport de Fereres, David, Robert. Student Mass. Coll. Art, 1941-42; B.A., NYU, 1945; M.A., U. Calif.-Berkeley, 1949. One woman shows Calif. Palace of Legion of Honor, 1963, Peabody Mus., Harvard U., 1978, N.Y.C. Pub. Library, 1979, New Sch. Social Research, N.Y.C., 1981, NYU Grad. Sch. Bus. Adminstrn., 1982, Sarah Lawrence Coll., Bronxville, N.Y., 1984, Kuopio Mus., Finland, 1992; group shows include Union Gallery San Jose State U., Calif., 1979, Ctr. for Visual Arts, Oakland, Calif., 1979, Walker Art Ctr., Mpls., 1981, Nat. Library, Madrid, 1982, SUNY Library, Purchase, 1983, Otis Art Inst. of Parsons Sch. of Design, Los Angeles, 1984, Cleve. Inst. Art, 1984, FISEA93, 95, 96, Digital Salon, 1965, 66, Copenhagen Film Festival, 1996, 4th Internat. Symposium on Electronic Art, Mpls.also others; respresented in permanent collections Stedelijk Mus., Amsterdam, Indpls. Mus. Art, Grey Art Gallery, NYU, San Francisco Mus. Modern Art, San Jose State U. Found.-Union Gallery, Crocker Art Mus., Sacramento, Hall of Justice, Hayward, Calif.; book artist Shoe-Field, Chinese Connections, About Me, Objects on My Dresser, (interactive books) Gateway to Your Ka, Your Fate is in Your Feet, Digital Mudra2; producer A Shoe-In, Biorhythm, Coping with Sexual Jealousy, (computer assisted interactive installations) The Animated Soul, Digital Mudra, Transgenic Bagel; contbr. to profl. publs. Web Art Works for Internet, 1995, 96, Smell Your Destiny, Brutal Myths. Home: 6 Hillcrest Ct Berkeley CA 94705-2805

RAPP, NINA BEATRICE, financial company executive; b. Copenhagen, Denmark, Sept. 3, 1958; came to the U.S., 1984; d. Sven Ove Lars Larsen and Kirsten Rung Mechik; m. Steven Douglas Rapp, July 14, 1984; 1 child, Stepanie Beatrice. BA in Econs. and Polit. Sci., Danish Royal Mil. Acad., 1982; MBA in Fin., Harvard U., 1990. Cert. explosives expert; lic. ins. and securites rep. Cons. Mei & Assocs., Waltham, Mass., 1987-88; leasing mgr. Wright Runstad & Co., Seattle, 1990-92; regional v.p. Primerica Fin. Svcs., Seattle, 1992—; ptnr. R & R Assocs., Seattle, 1990-93. Author: International Terrorism, 1982. Capt. Danish Army, 1977-82, lt., 1982-84. Mem. NAFE. Home: 6516 163rd St SW Lynnwood WA 98037-2717 Office: Primerica Fin Svcs 21911 64th Ave W - C Mountlake Terrace WA 98043

RAPPACH, NORMA JEANNE, health occupations educator; b. Hastings, Pa., Mar. 7, 1938; d. James Eugene and Katherine Luella (Lear) Fairbanks; m. James Davis Mrus, June 30, 1959 (div. Aug. 1978); children: Timothy James, Susan Marie Mrus Hughes, Joseph Michael; m. Ronald Michael Rappach, Aug. 9, 1979; stepchildren: Kelley Rae, Lynn Rae Rappach Paris. Diploma, Trumbull Meml. Sch. Nursing, 1959; cert. EMT/paramedic, Cuyahoga C.C., 1978; AAS with honors, Kent State U., 1983, vocat. tchr. cert., 1996; BSN magna cum laude, Youngstown State U., 1986. RN, Ohio; cert. diversified health occupations instr., Ohio. Pediatric staff nurse Trumbull Meml. Hosp., Warren, Ohio, 1960-62, part-time pvt. duty nurse, 1969-71; geriatric staff nurse Meadows Manor, Terre Haute, Ind., 1965-66; Vocat. Tchr.; substitute sch. nurse Howland Local Schs., Warren, 1972-78; cert. emergency med. instr. Ohio Dept. Edn., Columbus, 1973-78; substitute indsl. nurse Packard Electric divsn. GM, Warren, 1974-76; sch. nurse Lordstown Local Schs., Warren, 1978-93; diversified health occupations instr. Gordon D. James Career Ctr., Lordstown Schs., Warren, 1993—; part-time nurse obstetrical office, Warren, 1961-73; part-time gen. office nurse, Warren, 1960-72; part-time geriatric nurse Gillette's Nursing, Warren, 1972-74; instr. nurse aid tng. Ohio Bd. Nursing, 1993—. Adviser Teen Inst. for Alcohol Abuse, Warren, 1981; county emergency med. coord. Trumbull County, Warren, 1976-77; pres. Trumbull County Emergency Med. Com., 1976-77; HIV/AIDS coord. Lordstown Local Schs., 1985-93, mem. diversified health adv. bd., 1990—; vol. nurse, 1st aid/CPR/HIV-AIDS instr., ARC, Warren, 1990—; parish nurse Blessed Sacrament Ch., Warren, 1992-94. Named Profl. Woman of Yr., Trumbull County Fair, 1977, Hon. Firewoman, Howland Twp. Fire Dept., 1978, Vocat. Citizenship award Omicron Tau Theta chpt. Kent State U., 1995; nursing scholar Warren Kiwanis Club, 1956. Mem. Am. Fedn. Tchrs., Ohio Vocat. Assn.

RAPPAPORT, ELLEN DIANE, library media specialist; b. Bklyn., Sept. 19, 1943. BA, Bklyn. Coll., 1965; MLS, Columbia U., 1966; MA, SUNY, Stony Brook, 1975. Sci. libr. Am. Cyanamid, Wayne, N.J., 1966-67; sch. libr. media specialist Freehold (N.J.) H.S., 1967-68, Patchogue (N.Y.)-Medford Schs., 1968—. Recipient Jenkins award N.Y. State PTA, 1982; grantee N.Y. Pub. TV., 1989-91. Mem. ALA, Internat. Assn. Sch. Librs., Internat. Reading Assn., N.Y. State Libr. Assn., Suffolk Sch. Libr. Media Assn. (program chmn. 1991—). Office: Barton Elem Sch Barton Ave Patchogue NY 11772

RAPPAPORT, NANCY SUE, psychotherapist; b. Elizabeth, N.J., Aug. 27, 1947; d. David George and Mary (Seidman) R.; m. Carl Peter Hemingway, Sept. 4, 1967 (div. June 1978); 1 child, Jonathan Adam. MEd, Harvard U., 1981. Cert. tchr. of co-counseling Re-evaluation Counseling Found. Program coord. Adolescent Parent Program Montachusett Opportunity Coun., Fitchburg, Mass., 1984-85; hospice vol. coord. Burbank Hosp., Fitchburg, Mass., 1984-86; clin. psychotherapist Monadnock Family Svcs., Keene, N.H., 1989-92, Charter Brookside Hosp., Nashua, N.H., 1992—; mem. crisis intervention allied staff Monadnock Hosp., Peterborough, N.H., 1989—, Chesire Hosp., Keene, N.H., 1990-92; adj. prof. Antioch New Eng. Coll., Keene, 1993—. Author: (manual/handbook) Thanotology-Processing Grief and Loss, 1985, Eating Disorder Protocol, 1992. Mem. Am. Counseling Assn., Am. Mental Health Counselor Assn., N.H. Mental Health Counselors Assn. (pres. 1996—). Jewish.

RAPS, GENA, pianist; b. Cleve., June 21, 1941; d. Louis Raps and Pola (Tannenbaum) Geier; divorced; 1 child, Symra Cohn. BA, Bklyn. Coll., 1964; MMA, MS, Juilliard Sch. Music, 1968. Mem. piano faculty Mannes Coll. Music, N.Y., 1970—; with Sarah Lawrence Coll., N.Y., 1984-85. Pianist recs./CDs of Dvorak Waltzes, Dvorak Slavonic Dances, Mozart, 1985, 94; author: The Bach Book, 1995; Mozart, Complete 4-Hand Music; author, prodr.: (CD) Play Bach!, 1996. Tchg. fellow Juilliard, 1968; writing grantee The New Sch., 1991, producing grantee, 1992. Home: 537 Manhattan Ave New York NY 10027

RASBERRY, JOHNEVA, education educator; b. Mancos, Colo., June 12, 1934; d. John R. and Eva Charlotte (Dyer) Pond; m. Howard Henry Rasberry, Aug. 3, 1968; children: Sean Price, Shannon H. BA, U. Oreg., 1956; MS, U. Houston Clear Lake, 1983. Tchr. C.E. Hughes Jr. H.S., Long Beach, Calif., 1956-59; tchr. Bret Harte Jr. H.S., Oakland, Calif., 1959-63, tchr., counselor, 1963-65; dean of students Albany (Calif.) H.S., 1965-69; adj. faculty U. Houston, Clear Lake, 1983-86; dir. tchr. ctr. U. Houston Clear Lake Sch. Edn., 1986—; cons. Parent Vol. Programs, Houston, 1982-83; advisor U. Houston Clear Lake Studen Edn. Assn., 1989—. Pres. Whitcomb Elem. Sch. PTA, Houston, 1980-81, Clear Lake Intermediate Sch. PTA, Houston, 1982-83, Clear Creek Area Coun. PTAs, Houston, 1983-84, Clear Lake H.S. PTA, 1984-86. Mem. Tex. Edn. Assn. (grantee), Assn. Tchr. Educators, Tex. Tchr. Educators (exec. bd. dirs. 1992-94, Tex. Dirs. of Field Experience (sec. 1993-95), Tex. Tchr. Ctr. Network (pres. 1994-95), Consortium State Orgns. for Tchr. Edn. (chair 1995-96). Home: 15602 Rill Ln Houston TX 77062 Office: U Houston Clear Lake Sch Edn 2700 Bay Area Blvd Box 30 Houston TX 77058

RASCH, ELLEN MYRBERG, cell biology educator; b. Chicago Heights, Ill., Jan. 31, 1927; d. Arthur August and Helen Catherine (Stelle) Myrberg; m. Robert W. E. Rasch, June 17, 1950; 1 son, Martin Karl. PhB with honors, U. Chgo., 1945, BS in Biol. Sci., 1947, MS in Botany, 1948, PhD, 1950. Asst. histologist Am. Meat Inst. Found., Chgo., 1950-51; USPHS postdoctoral fellow U. Chgo., 1951-53, rsch. assoc. dept. zoology, 1954-59; rsch. assoc. Marquette U., Milw., 1962-65, assoc. prof. biology, 1965-68, prof. biology, 1968-75, Wehr Disting. prof. biophysics, 1975-78; rsch. prof. biophysics East Tenn. State U., James H. Quillen Coll. Medicine, Johnson City, 1978-94, interim chmn. dept. cellular biophysics, 1986-94, prof. anatomy and cell biology, 1994—. Mem. Wis. Bd. Basic Sci. Examiners, 1971-75, sec. bd., 1973-75. Recipient Post-doctoral fellowship USPHS, 1951-53, Research Career Devel. award, 1967-72; Teaching Excellence and Disting. award Marquette U., 1975; Kreeger-Wolf vis. disting. prof. in biol. sci. Northwestern U., 1979. Mem. Royal Microscopic Soc., Am. Soc. Cell Biology, Am. Soc. Zoologists, Am. Soc. Ichthyologists and Herpetologists, The Histochem. Soc., Phi Beta Kappa, Sigma Xi. Contbr. articles to various publs. Home: 1504 Chickees St Johnson City TN 37604-7103 Office: East Tenn State U Dept Anatomy & Cell Biology PO Box 70 421 Johnson City TN 37614-0421

RASCO, CAROL HAMPTON, federal official; b. Columbia, S.C., Jan. 13, 1948; d. Frank Barnes and Mary Ruby (Dallas) Hampton; children: Howard Hampton, Mary-Margaret. Student, Hendrix Coll., 1965-66; BSE, U. Ark., 1969; MS, U. Ctrl. Ark., 1972. Elem. sch. tchr. Springdale and Fayetteville (Ark.) Pub. Schs., 1969-71; counselor Bryant (Ark.) Middle Sch., 1972-73; liaison to human svcs. and health agys. Gov. Bill Clinton, Little Rock, Ark., 1983-85; exec. asst. for govtl. ops. Gov. Bill Clinton, Little Rock, 1985-91, sr. exec. asst., 1991-92; liaison to Nat. Govs. Assn., 1985-92; asst. to President U.S. for domestic policy White House, Washington, 1993—. V.p., pres. Ark. Symphony Orch. Soc. Guild Bd., 1975-78, mem. exec. com., 1976-78; pres. Fullbright Elem. Sch. PTA, 1982-83; child advocate coord. Little Rock Conf. United Meth. Women's Bd., 1979-80; family life coord. Little Rock Conf. United Meth. Ch. Coun. Ministries, 1980-82; active Friends of Ark. Repertory Theatre Bd., 1977-79, First United Meth. Ch., 1973—, chmn. bd. stewards, 1981, chmn.coun. on ministries, 1980, lay leader, 1982, chmn. child devel. ctr. bd., 1982, bd. trustees, 1988-90, Ark. Devel. Disabilities Svcs. Bd., 1979-82; vol. Ark. Coalition for Handicapped, 1974-77, Little Rock Mcpl. Ct. Vols. in Probation, 1975-78, Gov. Task Force on Coordination of Svcs. Sch.-Aged Children, 1979, Little Rock Pub. Sch. Spl. Edn. Adv. Com., 1981-91, Pulaski County Coord. for Bill Clinton for Gov., 1982. Recipient Germaine Menteil Vol. Activist award, 1976, Community Svc. award Channel 4-GOVCP, 1979. Spl. Friend of Children award Ark. Advocates for Children and Families, 1985. Democrat. Office: The White House Office of Domestic Policy 1600 Pennsylvania Ave NW Washington DC 20502*

RASDAL, AMELIA JANE, systems engineer; b. Ogallala, N.C., Aug. 5, 1961; d. William Daniel and Karen Lea (Unger) R.; m. Christopher Faust, Apr. 1, 1993. BS in Computer Sci., BA French, Music, San Diego State U. cum laude, 1986; MBA, Dartmouth Coll., 1992; cert. in mfg. studies, Foothill Coll. Software engr. ASK Computer Systems, Inc., Mountain View, Calif., 1987-90; intern sales and profl. rels. Advanced Cardiovascular Systems, Inc., Santa Clara, Calif., 1991; from assoc. bus. devel. to sr. prin engr. IVAC Corp., San Diego, 1992—. Trustee Isaacs, McCaleb and Dancers. Mem. Am. Prodn. Inventory Control Soc. (cert.), Golden Key, Phi Eta Sigma, Upsilon Pi Epsilon. Office: IVAC Med Systems 10221 Wateridge Cir San Diego CA 92121

RASKIN, ROSE ESTHER, veterinary educator; b. Albany, N.Y., Mar. 4, 1950; d. Morris and Helen (Fishman) R.; m. Shengheng Lin, June 23, 1989 (div. Oct., 1994). BA, Rutgers U., Newark, 1971; DVM, Purdue U., 1976; PhD, Mich. State U., 1987. Diplomate Am. Coll. Vet. Pathologists. Associate vet. Cameron Animal Hosp., Montclair, N.J., 1976-82; resident, instr. vet. medicine Mich. State U., Lansing, 1982-85, sr. resident, instr., 1985-87; asst. prof. U. Fla., Gainesville, 1987-93, assoc. prof. and svc. chief of clin. pathology, 1993—; co-advisor Pre-veterinary Medicine Club, U. Fla., Gainesville, 1995—. Author: (text books) Textbook of Small Animal Surgery, 1993, Saunders Manual of Small Animal Practice, 1994; also contbr. articles to profl. jours. Named Tchr. of Yr., Class of 97 U. Fla., Gainesville, 1995, SCAVMA Tchr. of Yr. (clin. scis.), 1995. Mem. Am. Animal Hosp. Assn., Am. Vet. Med. Assn., Assn. for Women Veterinarians, Vet. Cancer Soc., Am. Coll. Vet. Pathologists, Am. Soc. for Vet. Clin. Pathology. Jewish. Office: Univ Fla PO Box 100144 Gainesville FL 32610

RASKIN, SARAH BLOOM, lawyer; b. Medford, Mass., Apr. 15, 1961; d. Herbert and Arlene (Perlis) Bloom; m. Jamin B. Raskin, Aug. 11, 1990; children: Hannah Grace, Thomas. BA in Econs., Amherst Coll., 1983; JD, Harvard U., 1986. Bar: N.Y. 1987, D.C. 1989, U.S. Dist. Ct. Md. Assoc. Mayer, Brown & Platt, N.Y.C., 1986-88, Arnold & Porter, N.Y.C. and Washington, 1989-93; counsel U.S. Senate Banking Com., Washington, 1993—. John Woodruff Simpson fellow Amherst Coll., 1983. Mem. Women Housing and Fin., Phi Beta Kappa. Home: 7209 Holly Ave Takoma Park MD 20912-4223 Office: US Senate Banking Com 534 Dirksen Senate Office Bldg Washington DC 20510

RASMUSSEN, ELLEN L., secondary school educator; b. Clark, S.D., Nov. 25, 1936; d. Lloyd R. and Zella Dollie (Fisk) Acker; m. Donald M. Rasmussen, Aug. 6, 1960; children: LaDonna, Diann, Curtis. BS, S.D. State U., 1963. Cert. secondary edn. tchr., S.D. Educator Strandburg (S.D.) Sch. Dist., 1956-61, Brookings (S.D.) Pub. Sch., 1963, Hurley (S.D.) Sch. Dist., 1963-64, Bridgewater (S.D.) Sch. Dist., 1964-65, Lakeview (Oreg.) High Sch., 1965-66; educator South Lane Sch. Dist. 45J3, Cottage Grove, Oreg., 1966-95, ret., 1995. Mem. NEA, Nat. Coun. Tchrs. Math., Oreg. Coun. Tchrs. Math., Oreg. Edn. Assn., Lane Unified Bargaining Coun. (sec.-treas. 1988-91), Three Rivers Edn. Coun. (treas. 1991-95), South Lane Edn. Assn. (treas. 1982-95). Lutheran. Home: 1218 W D St Springfield OR 97477-8111 Office: Lincoln Mid Sch 1565 S 4th St Cottage Grove OR 97424-2955

RASMUSSEN, TINA MARIE, organizational development consultant, writer; b. LaGrange, Ill., Oct. 17, 1963; d. William and Barbara Jean (Meyer) R. BA, No. Ill. U., 1985; MA, The Fielding Inst., 1995. Cert. Neurolinguistic Programming Practitioner. Tng. developer Gandalf Tech., Wheeling, Ill., 1981-87; advt. rep. MicroTimes, Hollywood, Calif., 1987-88; trainer Citizen Wristwatch, L.A., 1988-90; asst. v.p. Santa Barbara (Calif.) Bank & Trust, 1990-93; tng., orgn. devel. mgr. Nestle', San Francisco, 1993-94; founder Enteleky Assoc., San Francisco, 1994—; bd. dirs. Am. Red Cross, Santa Barbara, 1992-93. Author: Leadership in a New Era, 1994, Reflections on Leadership, 1995, In Action: Conducting Needs Assessments, 1995, The ASTD Trainer's Source Book: Diversity, 1995. Vol. Holiday Project, Santa Barbara, 1990-93, San Francisso Rescue Mission, 1995, pub. rels. Am. Red Cross, Santa Barbara, 1991-92,. Mem. Inst. of Noetic Scis., Bus. For Soc. Responsibilty, OD Network. Office: Enteleky PO Box 471377 San Francisco CA 94147-1377

RASOR, DINA LYNN, investigator, journalist; b. Downey, Calif., Mar. 21, 1956; d. Ned Shaurer and Genevieve Mercia (Eads) R.; m. Thomas Taylor Lawson, Oct. 4, 1980. BA in Polit. Sci., U. Calif., Berkeley, 1978. Editorial asst. ABC News, Washington, 1978-79; researcher Pres.'s Commn. on Coal, Washington, 1979; legis. asst. Nat. Taxpayers Union, Washington, 1979-81; founder, dir. Project on Mil. Procurement, Washington, 1981-89; investigative reporter Lawson-Rasor Assocs., El Cerrito, Calif., 1990-92; pres., CEO, investigator Bauman & Rasor Group, El Cerrito, Calif., 1993—. Author: The Pentagon Underground, 1985; editor: More Bucks, Less Bang, 1983; contbr. articles to profl. jours. Recipient Sigma Delta Chi Outstanding Leadership award Soc. Profl. Journalists, 1986; named to register Esquire Mag., 1986, Nat. Jour., 1986. Mem. United Ch. Christ.

RASOR, DORIS LEE, secondary education educator; b. Gonzales, Tex., June 25, 1929; d. Leroy and Ora (Power) DuBose; m. Jimmie E. Rasor, Dec. 27, 1947; children: Jimmy Lewis, Roy Lynn. BS, Abilene (Tex.) Christian U., 1949. Part-time sec. Abilene Christian Coll., 1946-50; sec. Radford Wholesale Grocery, Abilene, 1950-52; tchr. Odessa (Tex.) High Sch., 1967—. Author play: The Lost Pearl, 1946. Recipient Am. Legion award, 1946. Mem. AAUW, Classroom Tchrs. Assn., Tex. Tchrs. Assn., NEA, Tex. Bus. Educators Assn., Alpha Delta Kappa (pres. 1976-78). Ch. of Christ. Home: 3882 Kenwood Dr Odessa TX 79762-7018 Office: Odessa High School 1301 Dotsy Ave Odessa TX 79763-3576

RASSAI, RASSA, electrical engineering educator; b. Tehran, Oct. 15, 1951; d. Farjollah and Farideh (Mofakhami) R.; m. Mehdi Roustayi, Aug. 12, 1974 (separated). BSEE with high honors, U. Md., 1973, MSEE, 1975, PhD, 1985. Sr. engr. Traycor Electronics Co., Arlington, Va., 1975; project engr. Iran Electronics Industry, Tehran, 1977-79; lectr. U. Md., 1980, 81-91, George Washington U., Washington, 1980-82, George Mason U., Fairfax, Va., 1982; rschr. elec. engring. dept. U. md., 1986-92; prof. No. Va. C.C., Annandale, 1986—, program head engring./elec. engring. tranfer program, 1991. Contbr. articles to profl. jours.; patentee remote telephone links. Mem. NOW. Democrat. Home: 6612A Jupiter Hills Cir Alexandria VA 22312

RAST, HEATHER LYNN, advertising executive; b. Pensacola, Fla., Jan. 14, 1972; d. Robert Maynard and Sara Kathryn (Bush) Comander; m. Robert Scott Rast, Sept. 25, 1994. BA in English and Journalism, Fla. State U., 1993. Mktg. coord. Flash Tech. Corp., Brentwood, Tenn., 1993-94; account coord. The Buntin Group, Nashville, 1994-96; account supr. Teledigm Inc., 1996—. Contbr. articles to profl. jours. Mem. NAFE, Creative Forum. Methodist. Home: 620 Huntington St Brandon FL 33511

RATAJ, ELIZABETH ANN, artist; b. Flint, Mich., Oct. 3, 1943; d. Lloyd Milton Clem and Mildred (Lamrock) Clem-Taylor; m. David Henry Rataj, Oct. 17, 1970. BA, Bob Jones U., 1966; BFA, U. Iowa, 1987. Educator Oscoda (Mich.) Area Schs., 1966-71, 73-83, Ft. Wayne (Ind.) Pub. Schs., 1971-72, St. Louis Pub. Schs., 1983-85. Represented in permanent collections Mich. Edn. Assn., Lansing, 1978, Munson Williams Proctor Mus., Utica, N.Y., 1989, Jesse Besser Mus., Alpena, Mich., 1993; two-person shows include The Art Ctr., Mount Clemens, Mich., 1996; group shows include Mus. Modern Art Miami, 1993, San Bernardino County Mus., Redlands, Calif., 1995, 96, Austin Peay State U., Clarksville, Tenn., 1995, The Art Ctr., Mount Clemens, Mich., 1996. Mem. Delta Kappa Gamma (1978-82, 86-87, 76-87), Nat. Mus. of Women in the Arts (charter).

RATAJSKI, MAGDA ANNE, public relations executive; b. Hampshire, Farnborough, Eng., Dec. 20, 1950; came to U.S., 1957; d. James May and Halina K. (Podlewski) R. BA, Marquette U., 1972; MA, Georgetown U., 1979; grad. Advanced Mgmt. Program, Harvard U., 1992. Asst. to v.p. pub. affairs Norfolk and Western Ry. Co., Washington, 1976-77, rep. pub. affairs,

1977-80, asst. v.p. pub. affairs, 1980-82; asst. v.p. pub. affairs Norfolk So. Corp., Washington, 1982-84; v.p. pub. rels. Norfolk (Va.) So. Corp., 1984—; vice chmn. bd. dirs. exec. com. Sta. WHRO Pub. TV and Radio, Norfolk. Mem. exec. adv. coun. Coll. Bus. and Pub. Adminstrn., Old Dominion U., Norfolk, 1986—; chmn. Va. Waterfront Adv. Coun.; mem. Bus. Com. Arts, Inc., N.Y. Mem. R.R. Pub. Rels. Assn., Assn. R.R. Advt. and Mktg., Pub. Rels. Soc. Am., Hampton Roads C. of C. (bd. dirs. 1985, pub. info. com.), Am. Coun. R.R. Women, Arthur W. Page Soc., Mid-Atlantic Arts Found. (bd. dirs.), Pub. Rels. Seminar, Nat. Dem. Club (Washington), The Harbor Club, 116 Club (Washington). Office: Norfolk So Corp 3 Commercial Pl Norfolk VA 23510-2108

RATCLIFF, MARY CURTIS, artist, educator; b. Chgo., Dec. 3, 1942; d. Francis Kenneth and Marian Elizabeth (Carter) R. AA, Pine Manor Jr. Coll., Wellesley, Mass., 1963; BFA, RISD, 1967; postgrad., U. Calif., Berkeley, 1976-79. Cert. art tchr., Calif. Founding mem. and camera operator Videofreex, Inc., N.Y.C., 1969-71; video prodr. Everson Mus., Syracuse, N.Y., 1972; designer and fabricator, prop dept. Am. Conservatory Theater, San Francisco, 1974; artist in schs. Calif. Arts Coun., various cities, 1976-79; asst. model maker Lucasfilm, Ltd., San Rafael, Calif., 1985-86; visual arts instr. East Bay French Am. Sch., Berkeley, 1986-91; artist and sculptor pvt. studio, 1987—; instr. Women's Daytime Drop-in Ctr., Berkeley, 1996; mem. adv. bd. No. Calif. Women's Caucus for Art, San Francisco, 1992-93. One-woman shows include Meridian Gallery, San Francisco, 1994; exhibited in group shows at Snug Harbor Cultural Ctr., S.I., N.Y., 1995, Waitakare Arts Ctr., Titirangi, New Zealand, 1995, also numerous others. Mem. NOW, Nat. Abortion and Reproductive Rights Action League, Pacific Rim Sculptor's Group (exhbns. com. 1994—), No. Calif. ISD Alumni Club (mem. steering com. 1994—). Home: 630 Neilson St Berkeley CA 94707

RATH, MARY LOU, state senator; b. Buffalo, June 17; d. George Lewis and Margaret M. Whetzle; m. Edward A. Rath, Jan. 10, 1959; children—Allison, Melinda, Edward A., III. B.S., Buffalo State U., 1956; Ins. Broker's lic., U. Buffalo, 1965. Home service rep. Nat. Fuel Gas, Buffalo, 1958-61; communications affiliate Communications Affiliates of N.Y.C., 1961-67; legislator, Erie County, N.Y., 1978—, mem. N.Y. State Senate, chmn. Community Sentencing Task Force, 1982, Buffalo Better Bus. Found. Bur., 1983—, Adminstrv. Regulations Rev. Commn., mem. Alcohol & Drug Abuse, Children & Families, Civil Svc. & Pensions, Edn., Higher Edn. & Taxation, Investigations & Govt. Ops. Coms., various other legis. coms. 1979—. Vice pres. Research and Planning Council, Buffalo and Erie County, 1973-74; pres. Jr. League, 1973-74, mem. admissions com., 1974-78; chmn. Theodore Roosevelt Inaugural Site Restoration com., 1974-78; vol. WBEN "Call for Action", 1974-78; moderator candidates night Coalition for Better Edn., community adv. council SUNY-Buffalo, 1974—, arts adviser, 1981—; mem. Regan Dinner com., 1975; appointed Republican com. woman 8th Dist., Town of Amherst, N.Y., 1979—; trustee Buffalo Sem., 1975-79; bd. dirs. United Way of Buffalo and Erie County, 1977-78; pres. Landmark Soc. of Niagara Frontier, 1977-78; trustee, mem. vestry Calvary Episcopal Ch., Williamsville, N.Y., 1975-78; founding mem. Amherst "Lunch and Issues" program, 1980; bd. dirs. Daemen Coll. Assocs., 1980-81, Buffalo Better Bus. Bur., 1981—, Buffalo Soc. Natural Scis, 1984—; mem. commn. adv. com. State U. of N.Y. at Buffalo, 1985. Recipient Disting. Community Service award Crisis Services, 1984; named Pub. Servant of Yr., Erie County Fedn. Sportsmen's Clubs, 1981, Outstanding Women in Western N.Y., SUNY, 1984; Participant Am. Gas Assn. Lab. Tour, Cleve., 1982 (one of 8 persons invited-nationwide). Mem. Buffalo Philharm. Orchestra Soc., Buffalo Zool. Soc., Erie County Hist. Soc., Landmark Soc. Niagara Frontier, Williamsville Hist. Soc., Amherst C. of C., Buffalo C. of C., Alpha Hon. Soc. Home: 125 S Cayuga Rd Buffalo NY 14221-6732 Office: NY State Senate Legis Office Bldg Rm 817 Albany NY 12247

RATHBONE, SUSAN WU, social services administrator; b. Hofei, Anhwei, China, Oct. 29, 1922; came to U.S., 1946; d. Chung Liu and Jin Ban (Gung) Wu; m. Frank Harold Rathbone, Aug. 20, 1945; children: Frank, Edward George. BA, CUNY, 1984. Tchr. Second Sch., Chungking, China, 1941-42; founder Chinese-Am. Bus. Women's Assn., Flushing, N.Y., 1990; founder, chair Chinese Immigrants Soc. Inc., Flushing, N.Y., 1984—, Queens Chinese Woman's Assn., Flushing, N.Y., 1984—. Editor Women's Voice mag., 1995—. Recipient Susan B. Anthony award NOW, 1987, Ethnic New Yorker award City of N.Y., 1984, Cmty. Svc. award NAACP, 1994, Gov.'s Woman of Distinction award N.Y. State, 1994. Mem. Anhui Provincial Assn. (founder, hon. life pres.), Nat. Women's Polit. Caucus, Univ. Women. Home: 26-10 Union St Flushing NY 11354 Office: 135-17 40th Rd PO Box 1656 Flushing NY 11354

RATHER, LUCIA PORCHER JOHNSON, library administrator; b. Durham, N.C., Sept. 12, 1934; d. Cecil Slayton and Lucia Lockwood (Porcher) Johnson; m. John Carson Rather, July 11, 1964; children: Susan Wright, Bruce Carson. Student, Westhampton Coll., 1951-53; A.B. in History, U. N.C., 1955, M.S. in Library Sci., 1957; PhD in History, George Washington U., 1994. Cataloger Library of Congress, Washington, 1957-64; bibliographer Library of Congress, 1964-66, systems analyst, 1966-70; group head MARC Devel. Office, 1970-73, asst. chief, 1973-76, acting chief, 1976-77, dir. for cataloging, 1976-91; Chmn. standing com. on cataloguing Internat. Fedn. Library Assns., 1976-81; sec. Working Group on Content Designators, 1972-77; chmn. Working Group on Corp. Headings, 1978-79, Internat. ISBD Rev. Com., 1981-87. Co-author: the MARC II Format, 1968. Recipient Libr. Congress Disting. Svc. award, 1991, Disting. Alumnus award U. N.C. Sch. Libr. and Info. Sci., 1992. Mem. ALA (Margaret Mann award 1985, Melvil Dewey award 1991), Phi Beta Kappa. Democrat. Presbyterian. Home: 10308 Montgomery Ave Kensington MD 20895-3327

RATHKE, SHEILA WELLS, advertising and public relations executive; b. Columbia, S.C., Aug. 9, 1943; d. Walter John and Betty Marie (McLaughlin) Wells; m. David Bray Rathke, Sept. 1966 (div. Apr. 1977); 1 child, Erinn Michele. BA summa cum laude, U. Pitts., 1976, postgrad., 1976-77. Loan coord. Equibank, Pitts., 1961-65; office mgr. U.S. Steel Corp., Pitts., 1966-70; various account and mgmt. positions Burson-Marsteller, Pitts., 1977-87, exec. v.p., gen. mgr., 1987-94; CEO Can. ops. Burson-Marsteller, Toronto, Montreal, Ottawa, Vancouver, 1994-96; sr. v.p., dir. corp. devel. Young and Rubicam, Inc., N.Y.C., 1996—; bd. dirs. Y & R Group of Cos., Can., 1994-96; instr. Slippery Rock Coll., Pitts., 1984-85; adviser Exec. Report Mag., Pitts., 1986-88. Trustee U. Pitts., 1976-80; mem. alumni bd. dirs., trustee Robert Morris Coll., 1992-95; bd. dirs. Vocat. Rehab. Ctr., 1987-93, Freewheelers, 1989-92, Pitts. Hist. Soc., River City Brass Band. Named Disting. Alumnus, U. Pitts., 1992. Mem. Female Execs. Am., Am. Assn. Advt. Agys. (chair ea. region 1994-95), Pitts. Advt. Club (bd. dirs. 1988-91, pres. 1990), Alpha Sigma Lambda (charter). Home: 330 E 38th St New York NY 10016 Office: Young and Rubicam Inc 285 Madison Ave New York NY 10017-6486

RATHMANN, PEGGY, author, illustrator; b. St. Paul. BA in Psychology, U. Minn.; student, Am. Acad. Chgo., Atelier Lack, Mpls., Otis Parsons Sch. Design, L.A. Author: Ruby the Copycat (Most Promising New Author Cuffie award Pubs. Weekly 1991), Good Night, Gorilla (ALA Notalbe Children's Book 1994), Officer Buckle and Gloria (Caldecott medal 1996); illustrator: Bootsie Barker Bites, 1992. Office: Putnam Berkley Group 200 Madison Ave New York NY 10016*

RATHMELL, SANDRA LEE, women's health nurse; b. St. Louis, Apr. 3, 1944; d. Charles Chester and Estelle Lucille (Simon) Dunham; m. Thomas S. Rathmell, Sept. 17, 1965 (div. May 1990); children: John Thomas, Tamara Lynn. Diploma, St. Luke's Hosp., 1965. RN, Ariz., Mo., Del. Staff nurse Dover (Del.) AFB Hosp., 1966-68, Luth. Med. Ctr., St. Louis, 1975-82, Maricopa Med. Ctr., Phoenix, 1982-84, Chandler (Ariz.) Regional Hosp., 1984-96; instr. hosp. postpartum classes, St. Louis, Phoenix. Mem. St. Luke's Alumni Assn.

RATICAN, KATHLEEN LAMBERT, mental health counselor, educator, writer; b. Balt., Sept. 4, 1952; m. Thomas Francis Ratican, Aug. 28, 1976; 1 child, Jonathan Andrew. AA, Catonsville (Md.) C.C., 1972; BS, Johns Hopkins U., 1979; MS, Loyola Coll., Balt., 1987. Cert. profl. counselor, hypnotherapist. Various adminstrv. pos. in bus., 1977-83; mental health counselor pvt. practice, Balt., 1983—; presenter in field. Contbr. articles to profl. jours. Mem. Am. Counseling Assn., Am. Mental Health Counselors Assn.

RATLIFF, LEIGH ANN, pharmacist; b. Long Beach, Calif., May 20, 1961; d. Harry Warren and Verna Lee (Zwink) R. D in Pharmacy, U. Pacific, 1984. Registered pharmacist, Calif., Nev. Pharmacist intern Green Bros. Inc., Stockton, Calif., 1982-84, staff pharmacist Thrifty Corp., Long Beach, Calif., 1984-85, head pharmacist, 1986-87, pharm. buyer, 1987-92; pharmacy. mgr. Kmart Pharmacy, Long Beach, Calif., 1992—; mem. joint mktg. com. Calif. Pharmicist's Assn. Mem. Pacific Alumni Assocs., Nat. Trust for Hist. Preservation, Friends of Rancho Los Cerritos; treas. Bixby Knolls Ter. Homeowners Assn., 1988-92, pres. 1992-96; vol. Docent Rancho Los Cerritos Hist. Site, 1988—; vol. preceptor U. So. Calif. Sch. Pharmacy; vol. Fairfield YMCA, Long Beach. Mem. Am. Pharm. Assn., Am. Inst. History Pharmacy, Calif. Pharmacist Assn., Lambda Kappa Sigma. Republican. Methodist. Avocations: raising African cichlids, growing herbs, collecting Hull pottery, antiquing. Home: 3913 N Virginia Rd Unit 301 Long Beach CA 90807-2670 Office: Kmart Pharmacy 5450 Cherry Ave Long Beach CA 90805-5502

RATLIFF DENNY, MYRTLE LEE, educator; b. Morven, N.C., Aug. 14, 1952; d. Walter Alexander and Corine (Streater) Ratliff; divorced; children: Shaun Alexander, Chewan Anglice. BA in Edn., Belmont Abbey, 1989; MEd, U. N.C., Charlotte, 1992. Tchr. Gaston County Schs., Gastonia, N.C., 1989-90; tchr., asst. prin. Charlotte (N.C.) Meck Schs., 1990—. Mem. ASCD, NEA, NAt. Assn. Young Children, Nat. Reading Assn., Nat. Teaching Assn. Charlotte, Alpha Kappa ALpha, Alpha Lambda Omega. Home: 7708 Beatties Ford Rd Charlotte NC 28216 Office: Winterfield Elem Sch 3100 Winterfield Pl Charlotte NC 28216

RATNER-GANTSHAR, BARBARA GRACE, organization administrator; b. Phila.; d. Jules and Samuella (Isadora) Ratner; m. Martin Gantshar, June 1961 (div. 1984); children: Judith Susan Claire, Lois Nichole Merraine, David Joseph. MS, Simmons Coll., 1985. Project dir. Boston Family Inst., Brookline, Mass., 1982-84; exec. dir. Summer's World Ctr. for the Arts, Worcester, Mass., 1985-87; assoc. dir. of devel. Am. U., Washington, 1987-88; dir. devel. Harford Day Sch., Bel Air, Md., 1988-90, Balch Inst. for Ethnic Studies, Phila., 1991-92; exec. dir. Temple Beth Hillel/Beth El, Wynnewood, Pa., 1993-95, Jewish Cmty. Fedn., Utica, N.Y., 1996—; fair coord. Mass. and R.I. Antiquarian Booksellrs Assn., 1978, 79; cons. Alzheimer's Disease Ctr., Falls Ch., Va., 1988, The Galleries, Wellesley, Mass., 1984-85, The Etz Chaim Ctr., Balt., 1990. Author: A Beacon Was Hoisted in Boston, 1975, Philadelphia: The City and the Bell, 1976. Mem. N.Am. Assn. Synagogue Execs., Antiquarian Booksellers Assn. Am. (emeritus), Nat. Soc. Fundraising Execs., Am. Prospect Rsch. Asn., Rotary. Democrat. Office: Jewish Cmty Fedn 2310 Oneida St Utica NY 13501

RATNOFF, SUSAN R., secondary school administrator; b. Queens, N.Y., Feb. 14, 1952; d. Philip and Malka (Rose) R. BA, George Washington U., 1974; MS, Coll. New Rochelle, 1978; MEd, Notre Dame Coll., 1996. Cert. tchr., N.Y., N.H., Mass., cert. prin., N.H. Tchr. Eagle Hill Sch., Hardwick, Mass., 1974-77; tchr. Concord (N.H.) H.S., 1978-82, spl. edn. cons., 1982-83, spl. edn. coord., 1983-90, alternative educator, 1990-92, asst. prin., 1993-96; prin. Exeter (N.H.) Area H.S., 1996—; mem. task force for diversion Concord Dist. Ct., 1995. Coord., editor: The Directory for Internships, 1992. Vice-chair fund raising United Way, Concord, 1995. Mem. ASCD, Nat. Assn. Secondary Sch. Prins., N.H. Assn. Sch. Prins., Concord C. of C. (mem. com. for edn. 1990—). Office: Exeter HS 30 Linden St Exeter NH 03833

RATTAZZI, SERENA, art museum and association administrator; b. Taranto, Italy, Aug. 20, 1935; came to U.S., 1969; d. Umberto and Ligetta (Maresca) Bardelli; m. Mario Cristiano Rattazzi, Jan. 15, 1962; 1 child, Claudia. BA, Liceo Umberto I, Naples. Italy, 1953; MSW, U. Naples, 1958; postgrad. in legal problems of mus. adminstrn., Am. Legal Inst., ABA, 1985, 86, 87, 89. Pub. rels., publs. asst. Albright-Knox Art Gallery, Buffalo, 1974-76, coord. pub. rels., 1976-82, asst. dir. for adminstrn., 1982-84; asst. dir. for adminstrn. The Bklyn. Mus., 1984-85, vice dir. for adminstrn., 1985-89, assoc. dir., 1989-90; dir. Am. Fedn. Arts, N.Y.C., 1990—; adv. bd. The Pitts. Ctr. for Arts, 1989-92, A.I.R. Gallery, N.Y.C., 1990-93; field reviewer Inst. Mus. Svcs., Washington, 1990; adv. coun. dept. art history and archaeology Columbia Univ., 1992—. Mem. ArtTable Inc. (bd. dirs. 1986-88, pres. 1986-88), Am. Assn. Museums (standing profl. com. on pub. rels. mgmt. 1978-82, bd. 1990—). Office: Am Fedn Arts 41 E 65th St New York NY 10021-6508

RATTLEY, JESSIE MENIFIELD, former mayor, educator; b. Birmingham, Ala., May 4, 1929; d. Alonzo and Altona (Cochran) Menifield; m. Robert L. Rattley; children: Florence, Robin. BS in Bus. Edn.with hons., Hampton U., 1951; postgrad., Hampton Inst., 1962, IBM Data Processing Sch., 1960, LaSalle Extension U., 1955. Tchr. Huntington High Sch., Newport News, Va., 1951-52; owner, operator Peninsula Bus. Coll., Newport News, 1952-85; hosp. adminstr. Newport News Gen. Hosp., from 1986; fellow Inst. Politics John F. Kennedy Sch. Govt. Harvard U., 1990; sr. lectr. polit. sci. Hampton U.; elected mayor of Newport News, 1986-90. Mem. Nat. League Cities, bd. dirs., 1975, 2d v.p., 1977, 1st v.p., 1978, pres., 1979-90, active various coms. and task forces; active on adv. bds. and coms. State Dem. Party; mem. exec. com. Va. Mcpl. League, 1974, 2d v.p., 1976, 1st v.p., 1977, pres., 1979; chair state adv. com. U.S. Civil Rights Commn.; apptd. trustee Va. Vet. Care Facility. Recipient Cert. of Merit Daus. of Isis, 2d annual Martin Luther King, Jr. Meml. award Old Dominion U., Sojourner Truth award Nat. Assn. of Negro Bus. and Profl. Women's Clubs, Cert. of Appreciation NAACP, Hampton Inst. Presdl. award for Outstanding Citizenship.

RATTLEY-LEWIS, SANDRA, radio executive. Former media cons.; former corr., editor, news dir., specials prodr., talk show host WHUR-FM, Washington; with Nat. Pub. Radio, Washington, 1980—, adminstr. satellite program devel. fund, 1983-87, sr. prodr. Hothouse Project, 1992, v.p. cultural programming, 1994—. Exec. prodr. Wade in the Water: African American Sacred Music Traditions (Peabody award), Making the Music (Peabody award); prodr. numerous live concerts and performance events. Mem. Blacks in Pub. Radio (founding). Office: Nat Pub Radio 635 Massachusetts Ave NW Washington DC 20001-3752*

RATTO, CAROLYN ELIZABETH, educator; b. Oakland, Calif., July 16, 1951; d. Frederick McLean and Elizabeth Ellen (Geers) Cranston; m. Michael Peter Ratto, June 24, 1973; children: Rebecca, Luke, Jessica. BA in English cum laude, Holy Names Coll., 1973. Cert. tchr., Calif. Tchr. Our Lady of the Rosary Sch., Union City, Calif., 1973, St. Brendan's Sch., San Francisco, 1973-75, Turlock (Calif.) Unified Sch. Dist., 1986-88. Commr. Parks and Recreation, City of Turlock, 1984-88, planning commr., 1988-90; mem. Turlock City Coun., 1990—; chair leadership tng. coun. Nat. League of Cities, 1996—, mem. adv. coun. 1995—, mem. bd. dirs. 1993-95; mem. bd. dirs. Emmanuel Hosp., 1996—, League of Calif. Cities, 1993, 95, pres. mayor's and coun. mems. dept. 1994-95. Named Tchr. of the Year Julien PTA, 1988. Mem. Statesman Club (past bd. dirs., pres. 1984-88). Roman Catholic.

RATZER, MARY BOYD, secondary education educator, librarian; b. Troy, N.Y., Sept. 6, 1945; d. John Leo and Katherine M. (Van Derpool) Boyd; m. Philip J. Ratzer, July 30, 1972; children: Joseph, David. BA cum laude, Coll. of St. Rose, Albany, N.Y., 1967; MA, SUNY, Albany, 1968, MLS, 1981. Cert. secondary tchr., sch. libr. media specialist, N.Y. Secondary tchr. English, Shenendehowa Cen. Sch., Clifton Park, N.Y., 1968-85; sch. libr. media specialist Shendehowa Cen. Sch., Clifton Park, N.Y., 1985—; coord., mentor tchr. intern program; lectr. SUNY Grad. Sch. Info. Sci. and Policy, Albany; frequent speaker at state-level confs., 1986—. Contbr. articles to profl. jours. Recipient grants. Mem. ALA, N.Y. Libr. Assn., Nat. Coun. Tchrs. English, N.Y. Assn. for Supervision and Curriculum Devel., BIRT, LUERT (past pres.). Home: 433 County Route 68 Saratoga Springs NY 12866-6636

RAUAM, NAIMA, artist, photographer, writer; b. Hanau, Fed. Republic of Germany, Feb. 26, 1946; d. Walter and Naadi (Tombak) R. Student, Art Students League N.Y., 1964-69. Freelance fine artist N.Y.C., 1964—. Exhibited in solo and group shows, U.S. and abroad; contbr. articles to profl. jours. Recipient Popular prize Artists Assn., 1985. Mem. Nat. Arts Club (Pres.'s award 1990, Grumbacher award 1985, Popular award 1986, House of Heydenryk award 1985, 92), Artists' Fellowship, Art Students League, Artists Equity. Office: Art in the Afternoon 146 Beekman St New York NY 10038-2003

RAUCCI, FRANCES LUCILLE, secondary education educator; b. Mt. Vernon, N.Y., Aug. 22, 1944; d. Charles G. and Theresa (Pastore) Servidio; m. Basil E. Raucci, Apr. 1, 1966; children: Michael C., Michelle T. BA, SUNY, Albany, 1966; MS, SUNY, New Paltz, 1980, CAS, 1982. Cert. secondary Spanish tchr., sch. dist. adminstr. Spanish tchr. Nanuet H.S., New City, N.Y., 1966-68, Highland (N.Y.) H.S., 1970-96; proprietor Letter Perfect Translation, Hyde Park, 1993—; curriculum cons. Ulster Boces, New Paltz, 1987; chair Mid-Hudson Regional, New Paltz, 1970-88; moderator, panelist N.Y. State Confs., 1970-88. Editor Modern Lang. Curriculum Guide, 1987. Fund raiser PTA Scholarship Dance. Recipient Leadership award N.Y. State Fgn. Lang. Tchrs., 1985. Mem. Am. Translators Assn., Hyde Park C. of C. Republican. Roman Catholic. Office: Presdl Homes NY 730 Violet Ave Hyde Park NY 12538

RAUCH, CATHERINE KERKES, secondary school educator; b. Ill., Nov. 12, 1951; d. Michael and Catherine (Dornik) Kerkes; m. Peter J. Rauch, Aug. 2, 1974; children: Katie, Elizabeth. BS, Northeastern Ill. U., 1972; MS, U. Ill., Chgo., 1975. Cert. tchr., Ill. Math. tchr. Notre Dame H.S., Chgo., 1973-76, Marillac H.S., Northfield, Ill., 1976-79, Oakton C.C., Des Plaines, Ill., 1979-85; math. tchr., math. team coach Adlai Stevenson H.S., Lincolnshire, Ill., 1985—; co-dir. North Suburban Math. League, Evanston, Ill., 1991—. Mem. AAUW, Nat. Coun. Tchrs. of Math. (Presdl. Excellence state award 1993), Ill. Coun. Tchrs. of Math. Office: 1 Stevenson Dr Lincolnshire IL 60069-2824

RAUCH, IRMENGARD, linguist, educator; b. Dayton, Ohio, Apr. 17, 1933; d. Konrad and Elsa (Knott) R.; m. Gerald F. Carr, June 12, 1965; children: Christopher, Gregory. Student, Nat. U. Mex., summer 1954; B.S. with honors, U. Dayton, 1955; M.A., Ohio State U., 1957; postgrad. (Fulbright fellow), U. Munich, Fed. Republic Germany, 1957-58; Ph.D., U. Mich., 1962. Instr., German and linguistics U. Wis., Madison, 1962-63, asst. prof., 1963-66; assoc. prof. German U. Pitts., 1966-68; assoc. prof. German and linguistics U. Ill., Urbana, 1968-72, prof., 1972-79; prof. U. Calif., Berkeley, 1979—. Author: The Old High German Diphthongization: A Description of a Phonemic Change, 1967, The Old Saxon Language: Grammar, Epic Narrative, Linguistic Interference, 1992; editor: (with others) Approaches in Linguistic Methodology, 1967, Spanish edit., 1974, Der Heliand, 1974, Linguistic Method: Essays in Honor of Herbert Penzl, 1979, The Signifying Animal: The Grammar of Language and Experience, 1980, Language Change, 1983, The Semiotic Bridge: Trends From California, 1989, On Germanic Linguistics: Issues and Methods, 1992, Insights in Germanic Linguistics I: Methodology in Transition, 1995, Insights in Germanic Linguistics II: Classic and Contemporary, 1996; editor of three series: Berkeley Insights in Linguistics and Semiotics, Berkeley Models of Grammars, Studies in Old Germanic Languages and Literatures; contbr. articles to profl. jours. Named outstanding woman on campus U. Ill. Sta. WILL, 1975; recipient Disting. Alumnus award U. Dayton, 1985; research grantee U. Wis., summer 1966, U. Ill., 1975-79, Eastern Ill. U., 1976, Nat. Endowment Humanities, 1978, U. Calif., Berkeley, 1979—; travel grantee NSF, Linguistics Soc. Am., 1972; Guggenheim fellow, 1982-83; IBM Distributed Acad. Computing Environment, 1986; NEH grantee, 1988. Mem. Linguistics Soc. Am., MLA, Am. Assn. Tchrs. German, Society for Germanic Philogy, Philogical Assn. of the West Coast, Phonetics Assn., Semiotic Soc. Am. (pres. 1982-83), Semiotic Circle of Calif. (founder), Internat. Assn. for Semiotic Studies (pres., dir. 5th congress 1994), Alpha Sigma Tau, Delta Phi Alpha. Home: 862 Camden Ct Benicia CA 94510-3633 Office: U Calif Dept German Berkeley CA 94720

RAUCH, KATHLEEN, computer executive; b. Franklin Square, N.Y., Oct. 30, 1951; d. William C. and Marian (Shull) R.; B.A., U. Rochester, 1973; M.A. in L.S., U. Mich., 1974; postgrad. N.Y. U., 1981-82. Media specialist Sutton (Mass.) Sch., 1974-76; program cons. Advanced Mgmt. Rsch. Internat., N.Y.C., 1976-79; pub. rels. cons., N.Y.C., 1979; pres. N.Y. chpt. NOW, N.Y.C., 1979-80; computer programmer Blue Cross/Blue Shield of Greater N.Y., N.Y.C., 1981-82; computer programmer analyst Fed. Res. Bank of N.Y., 1983-84; systems officer Citibank, N.A., 1984-85; systems analyst Fed. Res. Bank of N.Y., 1986-89; computer and children's libr. East Meadow (N.Y.) Pub. Libr., 1989-91; pres. Panorama Children's Videos, Inc., 1988-93; microcomputer specialist N.C. State U., 1992-93; prin., v.p. The Computer Lab., Inc., 1993—; v.p., The Computer Lab of Atlanta, Inc., 1994. Mem. ALA, NOW (dir. pub. rels. N.Y.C. chpt. 1978, v.p. programs 1978, chmn. bd. 1981, founding mem., sec. Svc. Fund NOW, N.Y.C. chpt. 1981), Assn. for Women in Computing (v.p. membership 1984, exec. v.p. 1985, treas. 1986, mem.-at-large 1987, pres. 1988), N.C. Libr. Assn., Triangle Bus. and Profl. Guild. Home and Office: The Computer Lab Inc PO Box 97682 Raleigh NC 27624-7682

RAULERSON, PHOEBE HODGES, school superintendent; b. Cin., Mar. 16, 1939; d. LeRoy Allen and Thelma A. (Stewart) Hodges; m. David Earl Raulerson, Dec. 26, 1959; children: Julie, Lynn, David Earl, Jr., Roy Allen. BA in Edn., U. Fla., 1963, MEd, 1964. Tchr. several schs., Okeechobee, Fla., 1964-79; asst. prin. Okeechobee Jr. H.S., 1979-81, prin., 1983-84; asst. prin. South Elem. Sch., Okeechobee, 1981-82; asst. prin. Okeechobee H.S., 1982-83, prin., 1984-96, asst. supt. for curriculum and instrn., 1996—; mem. Dept. Edn. Commr.'s Task Force on H.S. Preparation, 1993-94, chair Task Force Tchr. Preparation & Certification, 1995-96. Mem. Okeechobee Exchange Club. Recipient Outstanding Citizen award Okeechobee Rotary Club, 1986; week named in her honor, Okeechobee County Commrs., 1990. Mem. Am. Bus. Women's Assn., Fla. Assn. Secondary Sch. Prins. (pres. 1993-94, Fla. Prin. of Yr. award 1990), Fla. Assn. Sch. Adminstrs. (bd. dirs. 1992-95), Okeechobee Cattlewomen's Assn. Democrat. Episcopalian. Home: 3898 NW 144th Dr Okeechobee FL 34972-0930 Office: Okeechobee County Sch Dist 700 SW 2d Ave Okeechobee FL 34974

RAUSCH, JOAN MARY, art historian; b. Calmar, Iowa, Dec. 25, 1937; d. Bernard Joseph and Irene Sophia (Wieling) Menne; m. Gerald William Rausch, Sept. 3, 1960; children: John Thomas, Jennifer Nicole Rausch Goodhart. BS, Coll. St. Teresa, Winona, Minn., 1959; postgrad., U. Wis., LaCrosse, 1974-79; MA, U. Wis., Milw., 1982. Instr. nursing Mercy Hosp., Iowa City, Iowa, 1960-63, St. Francis Hosp./Viterbo Coll., LaCrosse, 1966-71; rsch. asst. dept. art U. Wis., LaCrosse, 1977-79; asst. dept. art history U. Wis., Milw., 1979-81; historic planner Southwest Regional Planning Commn., Platteville, Wis., 1982-83; pres. Archtl. Researches, Inc., LaCrosse, 1983—; cons. historic preservation divsn. State Hist. Soc. Wis., 1983—, Wis. Dept. of Transp., Dist. 5, 1991—. Author: A Catalog of the Oyen Collection, 1979, Historic LaCrosse Architectural and Historic Record, 1984, Chippewa Falls, 1985, Watertown, A Guide to Its Historic Architecture, 1987; (with Joyce Mckay) Richland Center Wisconsin, Architectural and Historical Survey Report, 1988; (with Carol Cartwright) City of Mineral Point, Architectural and Historic Survey Report, 1992, LaCrosse Wisconsin: Architectural and Historical Survey Report, 1996. Pres. Women's Polit. Caucus, 1972-78, coord., 1974-75. Recipienc Scholarship award Victorian Soc. in Am., 1981, Workshop award Ctr. for Art Criticism, Mpls., 1986. Mem. Soc. Archtl. Historians (pres. Wis. chpt. 1982-84), Nat. Trust Hist. Preservation (Preservation Forum(, Wis. Trust Hist. Preservation (charter, task force mem. 1986), Preservation Alliance of LaCrosse (bd. dirs. 1982-88, Heritage award 1989), LaCrosse County Hist. Soc. (hist. preservation com. 1992—, bd. dirs. 1994—). Home and Office: Archtl Researches Inc W5722 Sherwood Dr La Crosse WI 54601

RAUSCHENBERGER, BEVERLY ELIZABETH, school counselor; b. Rochester, Pa., Oct. 24, 1940; d. Lewis John Blistan and Olive Mae Tomer; m. John Lee Rauschenberger, June 13, 1964; children: Lori Lynn Wilhelmi, Norman Lewis. BA, Thiel Coll., 1962; MA in Edn., Western Carolina U., 1994. Cert. counselor Nat. Bd. Cert. Counselors, Inc., and N.C. Dept. Pub. Instrn. Tchr. Northwestern Jr./Sr. H.S., Darlington, Pa., 1962-64, Havre de Grace (Md.) Jr./Sr. H.S., 1964-65; co-owner Humpty Dumpty Shoes, Asheville, N.C., 1974-87; tchr. Groce Meth. Presch., Asheville, N.C., 1975-

78; admissions sec. Montreat-Anderson Coll., Montreat, N.C., 1983-87; adminstrv. asst. Highland Hosp., Asheville, N.C., 1987-93; sch. counselor, Juvenile Evaluation Ctr. N.C. Dept. Human Resources, Divsn. Youth Svcs., Swannanoa, N.C., 1994—. Choir mem., mem. coun. St. Mark's Luth. Ch., Asheville, 1968—; troop leader Brownie Girl Scout Troop, Swannanoa, 1972; Swannanoa Elem. Sch. PTA, 1979; mem. adv. com. Swannanoa Mid. Sch., 1981; meal preparer for homeless ABC Christian Ministry Shelter, Asheville, 1986. Mem. Am. Counseling Assn., Am. Sch. Counseling Assn., N.C. Counseling Assn., N.C. Sch. Counselor Assn., Pi Gamma Mu. Home: 16 Sunset Dr Swannanoa NC 28778 Office: NCDHR-DYS Juvenile Evaluation Ctr 741 Old Hwy 70 Swannanoa NC 28778

RAUSCHENBERGER, JANICE RUTH, environmental engineer; b. Selma, Ala., July 11, 1946; d. Henry Owen and Leeada Elizabeth (Trawick) Watkins; m. Willibald Rauschenberger, 1972 (div. 1982); children: Jessica, Karen. BSCE, U. South Fla., 1991, MCE, 1993. Registered profl. engr., Fla. Lab. technician Lever Bros., Edgewater, N.J., 1967-68; computer operator S. W. Barbanel Archtl. Engrs., Queens, N.Y., 1968-69; bookkeeper Clayco Corp., Marin County, Calif., 1980-81; civil engr. Apollo Environ., Inc., Gibsonton, Fla., 1991-95, City of Tampa Water Dept., 1995—. Home: 5227 Presidential St Seffner FL 33584 Office: Apollo Environ Inc 306 E Jackson St Tampa FL 33584

RAUSCHER, ELIZABETH ANN, physics educator, researcher; b. Berkeley, Calif., Mar. 18, 1943; d. Philip Jenkins and Claire Elsa (Soderblom) Webster; m. Warren Carleton Rauscher, Oct. 5, 1962 (div. June 1965); 1 child, Brent Allen; m. William Lloyd Van Bise, Mar. 1, 1995. BS in Chemistry and Physics, U. Calif., Berkeley, 1962, MS in Nuclear Engring., 1964, PhD in Nuclear Sci., 1979. Staff rschr. Lawrence Berkeley Lab. U. Calif., 1963-79; staff rschr. Lawrence Livermore Nat. Lab., Livermore, Calif., 1966-69; prof., instr. U. Calif., 1971-74; instr., rschr. Stanford (Calif.) Linear Accelerator Ctr., 1971-72; rschr. SRI Internat., Menlo Park, Calif., 1974-76; dir. Tecnic Rsch. Labs., San Leandro, Calif., 1979—; v.p. Magtek Labs, Inc., Reno, 1988-94; prof. physics U. Nev., Stanford, 1990-96; cons. McDonnell-Douglass, L.A., 1978, 80, Learned Soc. Can., Montreal, 1981, USN, Silver Spring, Md., 1983, NASA, Martin-Marietta, New Orleans, 1988-89; adviser Engring. Inst., Provo, Utah, 1979. Patentee in field. Del. UN, N.Y.C., 1979, mem. UN com., 1989; adviser Congress Office Tech. Assessment, Washington, 1979-81; adviser, cons. City Coun., Reno, 1993. Recipient Outstanding Contbn. award Am. Astron. Soc., 1978, Honor award Rosebridge Grad. Sch., 1988; grantee USN, 1970-74, 82-83, PF Found., 1978, 79, 81; Delta Delta Delta scholar, 1960; Iota Sigma Pi Woman's fellow, 1961. Mem. IEEE, Am. Phys. Soc. (chair), Am. Chem. Soc. (v.p.), Lawrence Berkeley Lab. Fundametal Physics (chair, pres.), Psychology Rsch. Group San Franciso (bd. dirs., pres.).

RAVEN, ABBE, broadcast executive; m. Martin Tackel; 1 child, David. BA in Theater, U. Buffalo; MA in Cinema and Theater, Hunter Coll. Prodn. mgr., stage mgr. Manhattan Theater Club, Bklyn. Acad. Music, N.Y.C.; mgr. prodn. Hearst/ABC Video Svcs.; dir. prodn. svcs. A&E TV Networks, 1984-88, sr. v.p. prodn., 1988—; sr. v.p. programming and prodn. The History Channel and HTV Prodns., 1995—; arts and media cons.; instr. various ednl. instns. Active Competition Com. CableACE Awards, chair 12 Ann. Ceremonies; active coms. focusing on violence in TV. Mem. NATAS, Women in Cable, Am. Women in Radio and TV, PROMAX, Nat. Acad. Cable Programming. Office: A&E TV Networks The Hearst Corp 235 E 45th St New York NY 10017

RAVEN, ARLENE, art historian, educator; b. Balt., July 12, 1944; d. Joseph and Annette (Latin) Rubin. AB, Hood Coll., 1965, HHD (hon.), 1979; MFA, George Washington U., 1967; MA, Johns Hopkins U., 1971; PhD, Internat. Coll., 1975. Founder, bd. dirs. The Woman's Bldg., Los Angeles, 1973-83; founder, exec. editor Chrysalis mag., Los Angeles, 1976-80; guest curator Long Beach Mus. Art, Calif., 1982-83; mem. faculty U. So. Calif., 1982-83, Otis/Parsons, Los Angeles, 1981-83; mem. faculty New Sch. Social Research, N.Y.C., 1983—; freelance art critic, N.Y. and Calif., 1983—; advisor arts com. Com. on the Observance of Internat. Women's Yr., 1977. Author: At Home, 1983, Crossing Over: Feminism and the Art of Social Concern, 1988, Feminist Criticism: An Anthology, 1988, Exposures: Women and Their Art, 1988, New Feminist Criticism, 1994, also monographs; contbr. articles, broadsheets and book introductions; author monographs. Founder, advisor Women's Caucus for Art, 1973, Calif. Commn. on Status of Women, 1977-83. Recipient Vesta award Woman's Bldg., 1983; NEA fellow, 1979, 85; Calif. Arts Commn. grantee, 1975, others. Mem. Coll. Art Assn., Art Critic's Internat. (Am. sect.), Nat. Writer's Union. Democrat.

RAVERT, APRIL ANDERSON, public health administrator; b. Oakland, Calif., Apr. 7, 1964; d. Max Glenn and Shirley June (Hardesty) Anderson; m. Russell Douglas Ravert, Jan. 16, 1993. AA, Eastfield Coll, 1984; BS in Bus. Adminstrn., U. Tex., 1986; MS in Family Studies, Tex. Woman's U., 1994. Acct. exec. MCI Comm. Corp., Colo. Springs, 1987-89; sr. acct. exec. MCI Comm. Corp., Dallas, 1989-92; prenatal and parenting educator Life Span program Parkland Hosp., Dallas, 1992-94; family planning and med. asst. counselor Planned Parenthood Fed., Dallas, 1993-94; program coord. better chance project The Johns Hopkins Hosp., Balt., 1995—; adv. counsel for Tex. Atty., Dallas, 1994, presenter Nat. Assn. for Perinatal Addication Rsch. and Edn., Balt., 1995. Mem. AAUW, NOW, Phi Kappa Phi. Democrat. Home: 2416 Briarwood Rd Baltimore MD 21209 Office: The Johns Hopkins Hosp Carnegie Bldg Rm 134 600 N Wolfe St Baltimore MD 21205

RAVET, LOREY, marketing professional; b. Detroit, Feb. 10, 1960; d. Emanuel and Shirley (Stein) R. BS, Mich. State U., 1982. Lic. real estate broker. Property mgr. San Diego, Calif., 1990; bus. broker Page Olson Real Estate, San Diego, 1990-92, San Diego, 1992-94; sales mgr., distbr. Life Ext. Internat., Dallas, 1994—. Mem. NAFE, Assn. Women in Sales and Mktg. Office: Ageless Living Inc 10226 Vista de la Cruz La Mesa CA 91941

RAVITCH, DIANE SILVERS, historian, educator, author, government official; b. Houston, July 1, 1938; d. Walter Cracker and Ann Celia (Katz) Silvers; m. Richard Ravitch, June 26, 1960 (div. 1986); children: Joseph, Steven (dec.), Michael. BA, Wellesley Coll., 1960; PhD, Columbia U., 1975; LHD (hon.), Williams Coll., 1984, Reed Coll., 1985, Amherst Coll., 1986, SUNY, 1988, Ramapo Coll., 1990, St. Joseph's Coll., N.Y., 1991. Adj. asst. prof. Tchrs. Coll., Columbia U., N.Y.C., 1975-78, assoc. prof., 1978-83, adj. prof., 1983-91; asst. sec. office ednl. rsch. and improvement U.S. Dept. Edn., Washington, 1991-93, counselor to the sec. edn., 1991-93; vis. fellow Brookings Instn., Washington, 1993-94, non-resident sr. fellow, 1994—; sr. rsch. scholar NYU, 1994—; adj. fellow Manhattan Inst., 1996—. Author: The Great School Wars, 1974, The Revisionists Revised, 1977, The Troubled Crusade, 1983, The Schools We Deserve, 1985, National Standards in American Education, A Citizens Guide, 1995, (with others) Educating an Urban People, 1981, The School and the City, 1983, Against Mediocrity, 1984, Challenges to the Humanities, 1985, What Do Our 17 Year Olds Know?, 1987, The American Reader, 1990; co-editor: The Democracy Reader, 1992; editor: Learning from the Past, 1995, Debating the Future of American Education, 1995. Chair Ednl. Excellence Network, 1988-91, 94—; trustee N.Y. Pub. Libr., N.Y.C., 1981-87, hon. life trustee, 1988—; trustee N.Y. Coun. on Humanities, 1996—; bd. dirs. Woodrow Wilson Nat. Fellowship Found., 1987-91, Coun. Basic Edn., 1989-91. Recipient Award for Disting. Svc., N.Y. Acad. Pub. Edn., 1994; Guggenheim fellow, 1977-78; Phi Beta Kappa vis. scholar. Mem. Nat. Acad. Edn., Am. Acad. Arts and Scis., Soc. Am. Historians, N.Y. Hist. Soc. (trustee 1995—). Office: NYU 82 Washington Sqare E New York NY 10003-6644

RAVIV, SHEILA, public relations executive. Degree, Ind. U., U. Wis. Faculty mem. Sch. Medicine and Health Sci. George Washington U.; dir. rsch. Ministry Social Welfare, Israel; dir. Nat. Vol. Orgns. for Ind. Living for the Aging; asst. dir. Nat. Coun. on the Aging; sr. v.p., dir. of constituency rels. Burson-Marsteller, 1988-91, mem. Am. bd. dirs., 1993, exec. v.p., dir. constituency rels., 1991-94; pres., CEO Burson-Marsteller/Washington, 1994—. Office: Burson-Marsteller 1850 M St NW Washington DC 20036-5803*

RAWDON, CHERYL ANN, elementary school educator; b. Dallas, June 13, 1957; d. Billy Wayne and Carol Ann (Murdock) R.; 1 child, Meagan. BS, East Tex. State U., 1979. Cert. kindergarten, elem., jr. high sch. reading and English tchr., Tex. Tchr. reading and spelling Canton (Tex.) Ind. Sch. Dist. Jr. High Sch.; tchr. pre 1st grade Midlothian (Tex.) Ind. Sch. Dist., tchr. kindergarten. Mem. First Bapt. Ch., Midlothian, tchr. Sunday sch., mem. choir, mission friends tchr., Awana leader; active numerous cmty. orgns. Recipient Golden Poet award, 1989, 90. Mem. Canton Tchrs. Assn. (pres.), Tex. State Tchrs. Assn., Canton Classroom Tchrs. Assn.

RAWLEY, ANN KEYSER, small business owner, picture framer; b. N.Y.C., July 11, 1923; d. Ernest Wise and Beatrice (Oberndorf) Keyser; m. James Albert Rawley, Apr. 7, 1945; children: John Franklin, James Albert. BA, Smith Coll., 1944. Owner Ann Rawley Custom Framing, Lincoln, Nebr., 1969—. Pres. Friends of Fairview, Lincoln, 1976, Lincoln City Ballet Co., 1983-84; bd. dirs. Lincoln Community Playhouse; mem. adv. bd. Nebr. Repertory Theatre. Mem. Nebr. Art Assn. (sec. 1976-77, life trustee). Republican. Episcopalian. Home and Office: 2300 Bretigne Dr Lincoln NE 68512-1910

RAWLINS, ELIZABETH B., education educator; b. Cambridge, Mass., Nov. 25, 1927; d. Archibald Fitz-Allen and Nellie Mae (Williams) Miller; m. Keith W. Rawlins Jr., Aug. 27, 1954; children: Paul Henry, Pattie Elizabeth. BS in Edn., Salem Tchr.'s Coll., 1950; MSEd in Urban Edn., Simmons Coll., 1967; EdD in Higher Edn. Adminstrn., U. Mass., 1991. Tchr. elem. edn. Springfield (Mass.) Pub. Schs., 1950-52, The Buckingham Sch., Cambridge, 1952-53, 54-62, Narimasu Elem. Sch., Tokyo, 1953-54; tchr. elem. edn. Hingham (Mass.) Pub. Schs., 1964, tchr. Title I program, 1964-67; lectr. Simmons Coll., Boston, 1967-69, instr., 1967-75, asst. prof. edn., 1975-79, assoc. dean, 1976-79, assoc. prof. edn., coord. human svcs. program, 1979-92, assoc. dean of the coll., 1984-92, prof. edn., 1992—; exec. sec. Cambridge Camping Assn., 1957-61; co-dir., dir. Williams Coll. Tchr. Tng. Inst., Williamstown, Mass., 1969-71; workshop leader Worcester Title I Project, HERS Project, Wellesley Coll. Editor: (coll. rev.) ABAFAZI, 1991—. Commr. from Mass., Edn. Commn. of the States, 1982-92; regent Mass. Bd. Regents-Pub. Higher Edn., Mass., 1980-91; pres., mem. Mass. Assn. Mental Health, Boston, 1970-90; mem. Nat. Assn. Mental Health, 1973-85; chair, mem. bd. trustees Salem State Coll., 1991—; bd. sec. Cambridge Family Soc.; incorporator, bd. dirs. St. John's Comty. Nursery Sch., Hingham, Mass.; bd. dirs. Friends of Nat. Ctr., Afro-Am. Artists, New Eng. Orgn. Human Svc. Educators, New Eng. Inst. for Health Care Svcs., 1983-85, United Way, 1979-80; bd. trustees Nathan Mayhew Seminars. Recipient E. T. Stewart award for alumni involvement Coun. for Advancement and Support of Edn., 1996, NAACP Edn. award, 1986, Tribute to Women award YWCA, 1988. Mem. AAUW (found. mem. 1995—), Nat. Assn. Women in Higher Edn. (KSP trustee-sec. 1991—), Black Women in Higher Edn., Greater Boston Inter-Univ. Coun., Corp. Bd. Resource, African Am. Alumnae Assn. (advisor 1989—, Crystal Stair award 1993), Phi Kappa Phi. Democrat. Episcopalian. Home: Box 135 Oak Bluffs MA 02557

RAWLINS, MARY L., broadcast executive; married; three children. BA in Speech Comm., Colo. State U., 1978. Agy. accounts rep. Continental Airlines, 1978-82; account exec. KPKE-FM Radio, Denver, 1982; nat. sales mgr. KBCO-FM Radio, 1988, gen. sales mgr.; gen. mgr. KBCO-FM & AM and KHIH-AM, 1994—. Office: Ste 315 2500 Pearl St Boulder CO 80302

RAWLINSON, HELEN ANN, librarian; b. Columbia, S.C., Mar. 30, 1948; d. Alfred Harris and Mary Taylor (Moon) R. BA, U. S.C., 1970; MLS, Emory U., 1972. Asst. children's librarian Greenville (S.C.) County Library, 1972-74, br. supr., 1974-76, asst. head extension div., 1976-78; children's room librarian Richland County Pub. Library, Columbia, 1978-81; sr. adult services librarian Richland County Pub. Library, 1981-82, chief adult services, 1982-85, dep. dir., 1985—; mem. adv. com. S.C. Pre-White House Conf. on Libr. and Info. Svcs., chmn. program com.; mem. tech. com. Columbia World Affairs Coun. Mem. ALA, S.E. Libr. Assn., S.C. Libr. Assn. (2d v.p. 1987-89, editl. com. 1993, chmn. pub. libr. sect. 1995), U. S.C. Thomas Cooper Soc. (bd. dirs.). Mem. ALA, S.E. Libr. Assn., S.C. Libr. Assn. (2d v.p. 1987-93, editl. com. 1993, chmn. pub. libr. sect. 1995). Baptist. Home: 1316 Guignard Ave West Columbia SC 29169-6137 Office: Richland County Pub Libr 1431 Assembly St Columbia SC 29201-3101

RAWLS, EUGENIA, actress; b. Macon, Ga.; d. Hubert Fields and Louise (Roberts) R.; m. Donald Ray Seawell, Apr. 5, 1941; children: Brook Ashley, Donald Brockman. Grad., Wesleyan Conservatory, Macon, 1932; student, U. N.C., 1933; L.H.D., U. No. Colo., Greeley, 1978; D.F.A., Wesleyan Coll., Macon, Ga., 1982. Participant 25th Anniversary of Lillian Smith Book Awards, Atlanta, 1993. Author: Tallulah—A Memory, 1979; Broadway appearances include The Children's Hour, 1934, Pride and Prejudice, 1936, The Little Foxes, 1939, 41, Guest in the House, 1942, Rebecca, 1945, The Second Mrs. Tanqueray, 1940, The Shrike, 1952, Private Lives, 1949, The Great Sebastians, 1956, First Love, 1961, The Glass Menagerie, 1964, 67, Our Town, 1967, Tallulah: A Memory; appeared at Lincoln Ctr., 1971, London, 1974, U.S. tour, 1979, Denver Ctr. Performing Arts, 1980, Theatre of Mus., N.Y.C., 1980, Four Arts Soc., Palm Beach, Fla., 1981, Herbst Theater, San Francisco, 1981, Kennedy Ctr. (cable TV), 1981, Nat. Theatre Great Britain, 1984, Queen Elizabeth II, 1984-86; one-woman show Affectionately Yours Fanny Kemble, London, 1974, U.S. tour, 1979, Nat. Portrait Gallery, Washington, 1983, Grolier Club Exhbn., N.Y.C., 1988; appeared in The Enchanted, 1973, Sweet Bird of Youth, 1975, 76, Daughter of the Regiment, 1978, Just the Immediate Family, 1978, Women of the West, U.S. tour, 1979, Am. Mus. in Britain, Bath, Eng., 1981, Kennedy Ctr. and Denver Ctr. Performing Arts, 1980; one-woman show Fanny Kemble, Arts Theatre, London, 1969, Queen's Hall, Edinburgh, 1980, St. Peter's Ch., N.Y.C., 1980, Internat. Theater Festival, Denver, 1982, also Kennedy Center; appeared as Emily, Denver, 1976; with Abbey Theatre, Dublin, Ireland, 1972; one-woman show tour of Europe, 1972; appeared as: Fanny Kemble, Shakespeare World Congress, Washington, 1976; TV appearances, U.S. Steel Hour, Love of Life, Women of the West; (for ednl. TV) Tallulah: A Memory (performed for presdl. inauguration), 1977; Memory of a Large Christmas, Folger Shakespeare Library, 1977; mem., Sarah Caldwell Opera Co., Boston, 1978; rec. talking books for blind; mem. com.: Plays for Living, 1964-67; Rockefeller Found. artist-in-residence, Denver U., 1967, 68, U. Tampa, Fla., 1970, artist-in-residence, U. No. Colo., 1971, 72, 73; artist Annenberg Theatre, Desert Art Mus., Palm Springs, Calif., 1988, 89, "Our Town" Pitts. Pub. Theatre, 1990; author: (poems) A Moment Ago, 1984; participant Edwin Forrest Day Celebrating Shakespeare's 427th Birthday The Actors' Fund of Am.'s Nursing and Retirement Home Lucille Lortel Theatre, 1991; appeared in Our Town, Pitts. Pub. Theater, 1990-91, Three Sisters, 1991—. Mem. Internat. Women's Forum, Vail, Colo., 1989. Recipient Alumna award U. N.C., 1969; Disting. Achievement award Wesleyan Coll., 1969; Gold Chair award Central City (Colo.) Opera House Assn., 1973; (with husband) Frederick H. Koch Drama award U. N.C., 1974; citation Smithsonian Instn., 1977. Address: care Donald Seawell 1050 13th St Denver CO 80204-2157

RAWSKI, EVELYN SAKAKIDA, history educator; b. Honolulu, Feb. 2, 1939; d. Evan T. and Teruko (Watase) Sakakida; m. Thomas G. Rawski, Dec. 16, 1967. B.A., Cornell U., 1961; M.A., Radcliffe Coll., 1962; Ph.D., Harvard U., 1968. Asst. prof. history U. Pitts., 1967-72, assoc. prof., 1973-79, prof. history, 1980—; univ. prof., 1996—. Author: Agricultural Change and the Peasant Economy of South China, 1972, Education and Popular Literacy in Ch'ing China, 1979; co-author: Chinese Society in the Eighteenth Century, 1987; co-editor: Popular Culture in Late Imperial and Modern China, 1985, Harmony and Counterpoint: Chinese Music in Ritual Context, 1996. Am. Coun. Learned Soc. grantee, 1973-74; NEH fellow, 1979-80, Chinese Studies fellow Am. Coun. Learned Soc./Sci. Rsch. Coun., 1989, Guggenheim Meml. Found. fellow, 1990, Woodrow Wilson Internat. Ctr. fellow 1992-93. Mem. Assn. Asian Studies (China-Inner Asia coun., bd. dirs. 1976-79, v.p. 1994-95, pres. 1995-96). Home: 5317 Westminster Pl Pittsburgh PA 15232-2120 Office: U Pitts Dept History Pittsburgh PA 15260

RAWSON, ELEANOR S., publishing company executive; m. Kennett Longley Rawson (dec.); children—Linda, Kennett Longley. V.p., exec. editor David McKay Co.; exec. v.p., editor-in-chief Rawson, Wade Publishers, Inc.; v.p. Scribner Book Cos.; pub. Rawson Assocs. divsn. Macmillan; v.p., chmn. Rawson Assocs. (divsn. Macmillan Pub. Co.); teaching staff Columbia U.; now pub. Rawson Assocs./Simon & Schuster; lectr. NYU, New Sch., N.Y.; organizer, panelist various writers' confs.; mem. exec. coun., nominating chair Am. Assn. Pubs., 1970-74. Former editorial staff writer Am. mag.; free-lance writer radio and mags., newspaper syndicates; fiction editor Collier's mag., Today's Woman. Trustee, past v.p. Museums at Stony Brook. Mem. Assn. Women's Nat. Book Assn., P.E.N., Am. Assn. Museums, Yale Club, Cosmopolitan Club, Old Field Club, Women's Forum, Women In Media, Women in Comms. Office: 1230 Ave of the Americas New York NY 10020-4941

RAWSON, PAMELA ANN, secondary school educator; b. Framingham, Mass., June 5, 1964; d. Francis Joseph and Anna G. (Riccio) Morin; m. David Rawson, Oct. 8, 1988. BS, U. Lowell, 1986; postgrad., U. Maine, 1986-88. Teaching asst. U. Maine, Orono, Maine, 1986-88; planetarium instr. U. Maine, Orono, 1987-88; tchr. Portland (Maine) H.S., 1988-90; dir. faculty So. Maine Sci. and Math. Acad., 1993-94; tchr. Cape Elizabeth (Maine) H.S., 1990-95; curriculum cons. Brunswick Sch. Adminstrv. Dist., 1995—. Office: Bowdoin Coll 203 Rhodes Hall Brunswick ME 04011

RAY, AMY, vocalist, guitarist; b. Atlanta, 1964. Attended, Vanderbilt U.; diploma, Emory U. Vocalist, guitarist Saliers & Ray, 1980-83, Indigo Girls, 1983—. Recordings include: Indigo Girls, 1986 (released under Saliers & Ray), Strange Fire, 1987, Indigo Girls, 1988, (Grammy award Best Contemporary Folk Recording 1990), Nomads * Indians * Saints, 1990, Back on the Bus Y'All, 1991 (Grammy award nomination Best Contemporay Folk Album 1991), Rites of Passage, 1992 (gold record after 12 weeks on Billboard's Top Pop Albums 1992), Swamp Ophelia, 1994; appeared in (movie) Boys on the Side, 1995. Recipient Grammy award nomination Best New Artist, 1990. *

RAY, ANNETTE D., business executive; b. Decatur, Ind., Mar. 24, 1950; d. Gilbert O. and Florence L. Hoffman; m. Richard M. Ray, Nov. 28, 1975; children: Michelle Ann, Ellen Marie, Laura Leigh, David Richard, Ruth Anne. AA, Concordia Jr. Coll., Ann Arbor, Mich., 1970; BS, Concordia Tchrs. Coll., Seward, Nebr., 1972; attended, Ctrl. Fla. C.C., Ocala, 1974. Lic. real estate, Ind.; lic. tchr., Ind., Fla. Elem. tchr. St. John's Luth., Ocala, 1972-74; mgr. apt. complex Victoria Sq. Apts., Ft. Wayne, Ind., 1974-75; substitute tchr. East Allen County Schs., Allen County, Ind., 1976-79, Circut A Luth. Schs., Adams and Allen County, Ind., 1977-81; corp. sec., treas., office mgr. Heritage Wire Die, Monroeville, Ind., 1987—. Co-author, co-editor: 1928-1988 A Rememberance, 1988. Vol. Monroeville C. of C., 1987—, Concerned Area Residents Quality Edn., Allen County, 1990—, Am. Cancer Soc., Allen County, 1991—, chairperson Celebrity Bagger Day, 1995, 96; bd. dirs. Hoagland (Ind.) Hist. Soc., 1985—. Lutheran. Home: 16901 Berning Rd Hoagland IN 46745-9753 Office: Heritage Wire Die Inc 19819 Monroeville Rd Monroeville IN 46773-9113

RAY, BETTY JEAN G., lawyer; b. New Orleans, June 7, 1943; d. William E. George and Iris U. (Berthold) Grizzell; m. Gerald L. Ray, June 9, 1962; children: Gerald L. Ray, Jr., Brian P. BS Psychology, La. State U., 1976, JD, 1980. Bar: La., 1980; U.S. Dist. Ct. (ea., mid. and we. dists.) La. 1981; U.S. Ct. Appeal (5th cir.) 1981. Jud. law clk. 19th Jud. Dist. Ct., Baton Rouge, 1980-81; atty. Jean G. Ray, Baton Rouge, 1981-83; counsel Gulf Stream, Inc., Baton Rouge, 1982-83; staff atty. La. Dept. Justice, Baton Rouge, 1983-84, asst. atty. gen., 1984-87; staff atty. FDIC, Shreveport, La., 1987-88, mng. atty., 1988-94; spl. dep. receiver Receivership Office, La. Dept. Ins., Baton Rouge, 1994-95; spl. counsel Brook, Pizza & van Loon, L.L.P., Baton Rouge, 1995—. Mem. La. Bar Assn., Baton Rouge Bar Assn., Baton Rouge Assn. Women Attys., Order of Coif, Phi Beta Kappa, Phi Delta Phi (scholar 1980). Episcopalian. Home: 1143 Oakley Dr Baton Rouge LA 70806 Office: Brook Pizza & van Loon Ste 402 9100 Bluebonnet Centre Blvd Baton Rouge LA 70809

RAY, EULA ZOLINE, broadcast executive. Motivational and directional speaker various cities, 1958-78; host, producer KHVN Radio, Anchorage, 1978-80; mgr. trainee Peck & Peck, Las Vegas, 1980-81; studio mgr. CPI Corp., 1981-82; station mgr. Roughrider Broadcasting, KPAH Radio, Tonopah, Nev., 1982—; guest lectr. Clark County C.C., Las Vegas, Nev., Miss Nev. Teen-USA, Official Preliminaries for Miss Universe 1992; pub. rels. com. Easy Living in Las Vegas, 1992. Bd. dirs. Pioneer Ter. for NYE County, State Job Tng., 1986—, Econ. Devel. and Tourism for Tonopah, Tonopah Conv. Ctr., 1985, Cen. Nev. Devel. Authority, 1987; mem. Town Bd. for Tonopah, 1991—; chmn. Jim Butler Celebration, Tonopah. Named Woman of Yr. for Tonopah, 1986. Mem. Tonopah C. of C. (pres. 1985). Home: 6700 E Russell Rd Trlr 122 Las Vegas NV 89122-8311

RAY, GAYLE ELROD, sheriff; b. Murfreesboro, Tenn., Oct. 22, 1945; d. Jesse Smith and Jennie Hare (McElroy) Elrod; m. Roy Norman Ray, Dec. 27, 1970; children: Molly Elizabeth, Austin Elrod. BA, Mid. Tenn. State U., 1967; MA, U. Ark., 1969; MBA, Belmont U., 1989. Instr. English La. State U., Baton Rouge, 1969-72, Tenn. State U., Nashville, 1972-76; program coord. Vanderbilt U., Nashville, 1992-94; sheriff Davidson County, Nashville, 1994—. Pres. LWV, Nashville, 1987-89; mem. Women's Polit. Caucus, Nashville, 1987—; mem. alumni bd. Leadership Nashville, 1993. Recipient Polit. Star award Davidson County Dem. Women, 1993.

RAY, JEAN JOHNSTONE See JOHNSTONE, JEAN

RAY, JEANNE CULLINAN, lawyer, insurance company executive; b. N.Y.C., May 5, 1943; d. Thomas Patrick and Agnes Joan (Buckley) C.; m. John Joseph Ray, Jan. 20, 1968 (dec. Mar. 1993); children: Christopher Lawrence, Douglas James. Student, Univ. Coll., Dublin, Ireland, 1963; AB, Coll. Mt. St. Vincent, Riverdale, N.Y., 1964; LLB, Fordham U., 1967. Bar: N.Y. 1967. Atty. Mut. Life Ins. Co. N.Y. (MONY), N.Y.C., 1967-68, asst. counsel, 1969-72, assoc. counsel, 1972-73, counsel, 1974-75, asst. gen. counsel, 1976-80, assoc. gen counsel, 1981-83, v.p. pension counsel, 1984-85, v.p. area counsel group and pension ops., 1985-87; v.p. sector counsel group and pension ops., 1988, v.p., chief counsel exec. and corp. affairs, 1988-89; v.p. law, sec. MONY Securities Corp., N.Y.C., 1980-85; v.p. law, sec. MONY Advisers, Inc., N.Y.C., 1980-88; sec. MONYCO, Inc., N.Y.C., 1980-85; v.p., counsel MONY Series Fund, Inc., Balt., 1984-87; v.p., assoc. gen. counsel Tchrs. Ins. and Annuity Assoc. Coll. Ret. Equities Fund (TIAA-CREF), N.Y.C., 1989-91, v.p., chief counsel ins., 1991—. Contbr. articles to legal jours. Cubmaster, den mother Greater N.Y. coun. Boy Scouts Am., N.Y.C., 1978-84, mem. bd. rev. and scouting com., 1985—. Mem. ABA (chmn employee benefits com. Tort and Ins. Practice sect. 1981-82, vice-chmn. 1983-96), Assn. Life Ins. Counsel (chmn. policyholders tax com. tax sect. 1982-91, chmn. tax sect. 1993), Assn. Bar City N.Y. (chmn. 1992-93), Investment Co. Inst. (mem. pension com. 1993), Am. Coun. Life Ins. (chmn. fiduciary task force of pension com. 1990—). Democrat. Roman Catholic.

RAY, LINDA DRIVER, clergyperson; b. Oak Ridge, Tenn., Apr. 8, 1959; d. George Wayne and Minnie Louise (Barclay) Green; m. David Lee Driver, Aug. 20, 1983 (dec. Apr. 1994); m. Bruce Wayne Ray, Feb. 11, 1995; children: Noah, Diana Driver Ray, Nathan. BA in Music Edn., Rhodes Coll., Memphis, 1980; M Choral Conducting and Music History, Scarritt Coll., Nashville, 1982; MDiv in Theology and Ch. History, Memphis Theol. Sem., 1992; postgrad., U. Ark., Little Rock, 1992—. Cert. ch. music, Christian Edn., high sch. tchr.; ordained to ministry Meth. U., 1990. Asst. mus. curator Scarritt-Towner Mus., Nashville, 1981-82; music tchr. St. Michaels Sch., West Memphis, Ark., 1992-93; consecrated clergy United Meth. Ch., Ark., 1983-90, ordained clergy, 1990—; chair Conf. Choir Festival, Little Rock, 1983—; mem. steering com. Ozark Mission Project, Conway, 1986—; mem. faculty Area Sch. at Christian Mission, Conway, 1993—; chair Bd. Diaconal Ministry, Little Rock, 1984-90. Vol. Habitat for Humanity, Ark., 1992-95. Recipient Liturgics award Memphis Theol. Sem., 1993. Mem. AAUW. Democrat. Home: PO Box 515 Des Arc AR 72040 Office: PO Box 277 Cotton Plant AR 72036

RAY, MARY VIRGINIA, retired federal government worker; b. Essex, Va., June 13, 1924; d. William Ernest and Mary Ida (Johnson) W.; m. Robert Edward Bates, Feb. 14, 1942 (div. 1947); children: Robert E., James A.; m. Frederick Lacey Ray, Oct. 23, 1947; children: Fredericka A., Natalia F. Mgmt. Devel. Program for Women, Nat. Sch. of Home Study, N.Y.C., 1984; Paralegal Study in Civil Litigation, The Sch. of Paralegal Studies, Atlanta, 1991. Display mgr. Lerner Shops, Arlington, Va., 1948-55; card punch operator USCG, Washington, 1955-56; card punch operator Interstate Commerce Commn., Washington, 1956-60, accident report reviewer, analyst,

1960-67; hwy. safety mgmt. specialist Fed. Hwy. Adminstrn., Washington, 1967-76, 76-78, 1978-80, 1980-85; ret., 1985; paralegal Banks & Assocs. Law Firm, Woodbridge, Va., 1990-92; spl. police crossing guard Prince William County Police Dept., Manassas, Va., 1990-92. Mem. Sr. Choir, 1947—, Gospel choir, 1952—; music coord. Starlighter Gospel Singers, 1982—; pastor's wife Mount Olive Bapt. Ch., Woodbridge, 1972—, pres. Mount Olive Bapt. Ch. Deaconess & Women's Aux., Woodbridge, 1978—; religious affairs chairwoman NAACP, Prince William County, Va., 1986—; committee chairwoman Woodbridge Dem. Magisterial Dist., 1992-95; sch. crossing guard Prince William Police Dept., 1989-91. Recipient Superior Achievement on the Job Performance award Dept. Transp., 1976, Superior Achievement award Freedom of Information, 1979, Afro-Am. Achievement award program Disting. Achievement in the field of pub. svc., 1994. Democrat. Baptist. Home: 2016 Horner Rd Woodbridge VA 22191

RAY, SANDRA LEE, secondary school educator; b. Cin., Mar. 12, 1948. BA, Baylor U., 1970; MEd, U. Mo., 1982; MA in Tchg., Webster U., 1996. Cert. grades 7-12 math tchr., prin., Mo. Math. tchr. Soldan H.S., St. Louis, 1971-76; math. instr. St. Louis C.C.-Meramec, 1982-94; math. instr. Mehlville Sr. H.S., St. Louis, 1976—, chair math. and computer sci. dept., 1993—. Mem. NEA, Nat. Coun. Tchrs. Math., Mo. Coun. Tchrs. Math.

RAY, SYLVIA GOODING, social services organization administrator; b. Kinston, N.C., June 1, 1941; d. Guy Vernon and Ella Naomi (Long) Gooding; m. Robert Glenn Ray, June 8, 1968; children: Theresa Nicole Gooding-Ray, Olivia Lauren Ray. Student, Salem Coll., 1959-61; BA, Fayetteville State U., 1984. Sec. Trust Co. of Ga., Atlanta, 1965-66; adminstrv. asst. N.C. State U., Raleigh, 1967-69; sec. Pan Am. World Airways, N.Y.C., 1969-72; sales rep. Suzanne Barlow Realtors, Fayetteville, N.C., 1985-89; exec. dir. Women's Ctr. of Fayetteville, 1990—. Bd. vis. Meth. Coll., Fayetteville; mem. Workforce Preparedness Commn.; bd. dirs. Old Fayetteville; activist for ERA; active Fayetteville Once and For All com. Mem. NOW (pres. Fayetteville chpt.). Democrat. Episcopalian. Home: 204 Hillside Ave Fayetteville NS 28301 Office: Women's Ctr Fayetteville 230 Hay St Fayetteville NC 28301

RAYBURN, CAROLE (MARY AIDA) ANN, psychologist, researcher, writer; b. Washington, Feb. 14, 1938; d. Carl Frederick and Mary Helen (Milkie) Miller; m. Ronald Allen Rayburn (dec. Apr. 1970). BA in Psychology, Am. U., 1961; MA in Clin. Psychology, George Washington U., 1965; PhD in Ednl. Psychology, Cath. U. Am., 1969; MDiv in Ministry, Andrews U., 1980. Lic. psychologist, Md., Mich. Psychometrician Columbian Prep. Sch., Washington, 1963; clin. psychologist Spring Grove State Hosp., Catonsville, Md., 1966-68; pvt. practice, 1969, 71—; staff clin. psychologist Instl. Care Svcs. Div. D.C. Children's Ctr., Laurel, Md., 1970-78; psychologist Md. Dept. Vocat. Rehab., 1973-74; psychometrician Montgomery County Pub. Schs., 1981-85; lectr. Strayer Coll., Washington, 1969-70; forensic psychology expert witness, 1973—; guest lectr. Andrews U., Berrien Springs, Mich., 1979, Hood Coll,, Frederick, Md., 1986-88; instr. Johns Hopkins U., 1986, 88-89; adj. faculty Profl. Sch. Psychology Studies, San Diego, 1987; adj. asst. prof. Loyola Coll., Columbia, Md., 1987; cons. Julia Brown Montessori Schs., 1972, 78, 82—, VA Ctr., 1978, 91-93. Editor: (with M.J. Meadow) A Time to Weep and a Time to Sing, 1985; contbg. author: Montessori: Her Method and the Movement (What You Need to Know), 1973, Drugs, Alcohol and Women: A National Forum Source Book, 1975, The Other Side of the Couch: Faith of thge Psychotherapist, 1981, Clinical Handbook of Pastoral Counseling, 1985, An Encyclopedic Dictionary of Pastoral Care and Counseling, 1990, Religion Personality and Mental Health, 1993; author copyrighted inventories Religious Occupationl and Stress Questionnaire, 1986, Religion and Stress Questionnaire, 1986, Organizational Relationships Survey, 1987, Attitudes Toward Children Inventory, 1987, State-Trait Morality Inventory, 1987, Body Awareness and Sexual Intimacy Comfort Scale (Basics), 1993; cons. editor Profl. Psychology, 1980-83; assoc. editor Jour. Pastoral Counseling, 1985-90, guest editor, 1988; contbr. numerous articles to profl. jours. Recipient Svc. award Coun. for Advancement Psychol. Professions and Scis., 1975, cert. D.C. Dept. Human Resources, 1975, 76, cert. recognition D.C. Psychol. Assn., 1976, 1985; AAUW rsch. grantee, 1983. Fellow APA (pres. divsn. psychology of religion 1995-96, psychology of women, clin. psychology, cons. psychology, psychotherapy, state assn. affairs, chair equal opportunity affirmative action divsn. clin. psychology 1980-82, mem. editl. bd. Jour. Child Clin. Psychology 1978-82, pres. clin psychology women's sect. 1984-86, program chair 1991-94, divsn. psychology women chair task force on women and religion 1980-81, divsn. psychology issues in grad. edn. and clin. tng. 198c —, pres. 1995-96), Am. Orthopsychiat. Assn., Md. Psychol. Assn. (editor newsletter 1975-76, chpt. recognition 1978, chair ins. com. 1981-83, pres. 1984-85, exec. adv. com. 1985—), Am. Assn. Applied & Preventive Psychology (sec. 1992-93, chair fellows com. 1992-93); mem. Assn. Practicing Psychologists Montgomery-Prince George's Counties (pres. 1986-88, editor newsletter 1990—), Balt Assn. Cons. Psychologists (pres. D.C. chpt. 1991-92), Psi Chi (hon.). Address: 1200 Morningside Dr Silver Spring MD 20904-3149

RAYL, INDIA, marketing executive; b. Chateauroux, France, May 1, 1956; d. Rommie Clarence and Peggeanne (Moore) Walker; m. Robert Richard Rayl, Jr., June 19, 1982; children: Brandon Joseph, Nelia Ashley. Student, Mesa Coll., San Diego, 1982-85, U. San Diego, 1988-89; cert. in direct mktg., San Diego State Univ., Univ. San Diego, 1990. Brand mgr. Undergear Catalog, San Diego, 1983; dir. customr relations Internat. Male, San Diego, 1977-86; catalog dir. ACA Joe, San Diego, 1986-87; media mgr. Internat. Male-Hanover House Ind., San Diego, 1988; gen. mgr. Petco-Animal City, San Diego, 1988-89; mktg. mgr. More Direct Health Products, 1989-90; dir. sales and mktg. Healy and Clark, San Diego, 1991-92; mktg. promotions mgr. Road Runner Sports, San Diego, 1992-93, dir. new bus., 1993-95; dir. product devel. Entrepreneur Mag. Group, 1995—; new bus. cons. Gift Baskets, Inc., San Diego, 1988. Editor various catalogs. Mem. Nat. Assn. Female Execs., San Diego Direct Mktg. Club, Catalog Coun., We. Fulfillment Assn., Nat. Coun. Mktg. Execs. (mem. bd.). Office: Entrepreneur Mag 2392 Morse Ave Irvine CA 92714

RAYMOND, ANTHEA, producer, educator; b. Plainfield, N.J., Mar. 10, 1959; d. Joseph Cicchino and Alyce Catherine R. BA, Wellesley Coll., 1981; JD, UCLA, 1987; postgrad., CCNY. Producer Nat. Pub. Radio/KCRW, Santa Monica, Calif., 1985-93; assoc. dir. UCLA Ctr. for Arts & Entertainment, L.A., 1989-93; ind. producer, cons. N.Y.C., 1993-95; journalist Wall St. Jour. Radio Network, N.Y.C., 1995—; cons. in field. Mem. Am. Women in Radio & TV, Acad. Television Arts & Scis., Wellesley Coll. Visual Artists Assn. (founding mem., orgn. com. 1996—), Wellesley Coll. Club Bd. (N.Y. chpt., sec.). Office: 511 6th Ave Ste 262 New York NY 10011

RAYMOND, DOROTHY GILL, lawyer; b. Greeley, Colo., June 2, 1954; d. Robert Marshall and Roberta (McClure) Gill; m. Peter J. Raymond, June 8, 1974. BA summa cum laude, U. Denver, 1975; JD, U. Colo., 1978. Bar: Conn. 1978, Colo. 1981. Assoc. Dworkin, Minogue & Bucci, Bridgeport, Conn., 1978-80; counsel Tele-Communications, Inc., Englewood, Colo., 1981-88; v.p., gen. counsel WestMarc Communications, Inc., Denver, 1988-91; v.p., gen. counsel Cable Television Labs., Inc., Boulder, Colo., 1991-96, sr. v.p., gen. counsel, 1996—. Mem. Am. Corp. Counsel Assn. (pres. 1990-91, Colo. chpt. dir. 1988-94), Colo. Assn. Corp. Counsel (pres. 1987), Sports Car Club Am. (nat. champion ladies stock competition 1981, 85, 86, 88). Office: Cable Television Labs Inc 400 Centennial Pky Louisville CO 80027-1266

RAYMOND, MARILYN PALMA, health care services executive; b. Niagara Falls, N.Y., Apr. 9, 1933; d. William Raymond and Grace (Crossley) Laffsa; children: Bryan, Matthieu. RN, St. Mary Hosp., Walla Walla, Wash., 1954; BSN, Hunter Coll., 1960; MA, NYU, 1962. Cert. RN; pub. health nurse supr. Drug counselor N.Y.C. Dept. Health, 1970-74; patient svc. mgr. Vis. Nurse Svc. N.Y., N.Y.C., 1974-80; dir. CHHA/LHHCP Montefiore Med. Ctr., Bronx, N.Y., 1980-85; corp. dir. N.Y.C. Health & Hosp. Corp., N.Y.C., 1986-88; adminstr. DPS VIP Health Svcs., Queens, N.Y., 1990-95; pres., chief cons. M-R Consultants, Yonkers, N.Y., 1984—; site visitor Nat. League Nursing, CHAP, 1995—. Founder Soho 20 Women's Cooperative Art Gallery, N.Y.C., 1973. Fed. Nursing Edn. scholar, 1960-62. Mem. Home Care Assn. of N.Y. State, Rotary Club (West Yonkers), Sigma Theta Tau. Democrat. Home: 120 Franklin Ave Yonkers NY 10705

RAYMOND, SUSAN GOLD, conference educator; b. Phila., Sept. 30, 1948; d. Walter and Lillian Lena (Zimmerman) Gold; m. Harry Raymond, Mar. 22, 1970; children: Kimberly Dawn, Aviva, Shayna, Leslie, Steven. Tchr. Howard County Jewish Cmty. Sch., Columbia, Md., 1971—; prin. Howard County Jewish Cmty. Sch., Columbia, 1974-77; asst. prin. Balt. Hebrew Congregation, 1993—; conf. educator, 1971—. Author: Aleph Through Tav-Chalkboard Games, 1989, Reading Hebrew is Just a Game, 1992; co-author: World of Difference, 1991, Jewish Handbook for Group Discussion I, 1988, Jewish Handbook for Group Discussion II, 1989. Recipient Samuel Glasner award Bd. of Jewish Edn., 1990; named Most Inspiring Tchr. Hebrew Tchrs. Assn., 1990. Home and Office: 9360 Dewlit Way Columbia MD 21045-5118

RAYMOND, VIRGINIA ANN, artist; b. Ft. Myers, Fla., May 14, 1932; d. Horace Raymond and Nona Langford Presson; m. Arthur James Valluzzi, July 20, 1948; children: Bruce, Laura, Mark. AA, Brevard C.C., Cocoa, Fla., 1973; BFA, U. Ctrl. Fla., Orlando, 1975; MFA, U. Guanajuto, Mex., 1982. Self-employed as artist Cocoa Beach, 1975—. Exhibited in solo show at Art Works, Orlando, 1996; exhibited in group shows at Brevard Art Ctr. and Mus., Melbourne, Fla., 1995, Fla. Inst. Tech., Melbourne, 1996, Dragon Point Gallery, Melbourne, 1996. Founder Space Coast Art Festival, Cocoa Beach, 1966, Surfside Theatre, Cocoa Beach, 1968; bd. dirs. Artist Forum, Brevard Art Mus., 199-95. Recipient more than 75 painting awards and honors from art festivals, museums and galleries, U.S. and Mex., 1975—. Mem. Art World Orlando, Art Students League (bd. dirs.), Wednesday Group. Studio: Surfside Studio 144 Bayshore Dr Cocoa Beach FL 32931

RAZOOK, STACIA ANN, bank officer; b. Wichita, Kans., May 24, 1956; d. Fred John and Jeanne E. (Howell) R. AS in Legal Assisting, Wichita State U., 1986; BS in Mgmt., Friends U., 1987. Trust sec. Bank IV Wichita, N.A., 1980-87; legal asst. Farm Credit Bank Wichita, 1987-93; compliance coord. Intrust Fin. Corp., Wichita, 1993—; adj. asst. prof. Wichita State U., 1987-94, faculty advisor legal asst. program, 1993-94. Mem. Big Bros. and Big Sisters Sedwick County, Wichita, 1986-88, Wichita Symphony Orch. Chorus, 1993—. Mem. Kans. Bankers Assn., Kans. Bar Assn. (assoc.). Office: Intrust Fin Corp 105 N Main St Wichita KS 67202

REA, ANN HADLEY KUEHN, social organization marketing administrator; b. Arlington, Va., Oct. 14, 1962; d. Alvin Henry Kuehn and Barbara Ann (Schmall) Schanzenbach; m. Burt Richard Rea, June 30, 1990; 2 children. BA in Communications, Va. Poly. Inst. & State U., Blacksburg, 1984; MA in Liberal Studies, Georgetown U., Washington, 1993. Desk asst., prodn. asst. ABC News, Washington, 1986-88; media/info. officer Embassy of Australia, Washington, 1988-90; mktg. and membership dir. YWCA, Summit, N.J., 1992—. Mem. LWV. Episcopalian. Home: 38 Minton Ave Chatham NJ 07928-2741 Office: Summit YWCA 79 Maple St Summit NJ 07901-2517

READ, ELEANOR MAY, financial analyst; b. Arcadia, N.Y., July 4, 1940; d. Henry and Lena May (Fagner) Van Koevering; 1 child, Robin Jo. Typist, clk., sec., credit corr. Sarah Coventry, Inc., Newark, N.Y., 1957-61; exec. sec. Mobil Chem. Co., Macedon, N.Y., 1961-68; bus. mgr. Henry's Hardware, Newark, 1968-72; with Xerox Corp., Fremont, Calif., 1973—, internat. clk. analyst, personnel adminstrv. asst., employment coordinator, exec. sec., cycle count analyst., acctg. specialist, tax preparer H&R Block, 1985-92. Mem. Xerox/Diablo Mgmt. Assn., Am. Mgmt. Assn., Profl. Businesswomen's Assn., NAFE. Office: Xerox AMTX 5450 Campus Dr Canandaigua NY 14425

READ, SISTER JOEL, academic administrator. BS in Edn., Alverno Coll., 1948; MA in History, Fordham U., 1951; hon. degrees, Lakeland Coll., 1972, Wittenburg U., 1976, Marymount Manhattan Coll., 1978, DePaul U., 1985, Northland Coll., 1986, SUNY, 1986. Former prof., dept. chmn. history dept. Alverno Coll., Milw., pres., 1968—; pres. Am. Assn. for Higher Edn., 1976-77; mem. coun. NEH, 1977-83; bd. dirs. Ednl. Testing Svc., 1987-93, Neylan Commn., 1985-90; past pres. Wis. Assn. Ind. Colls. and Univs.; mem. Commn. on Status of Edn. for Women, 1971 76, Am. Assn. Colls., 1971-77; mem. exec. com. Greater Milw. com. GMC Edn. Trust. Mem. exec. bd. Milw. YMCA. First recipient Anne Roe award Harvard U. Grad. Sch. Edn., 1980. Fellow Am. Acad. Arts and Scis.; mem. Found. for Higher Edn. Office: Alverno Coll Office of the President PO Box 343922 Milwaukee WI 53234-3922

READ, NANCY CAROL, project administrator; b. Maywood, Calif., Apr. 26, 1950; d. Harold Melvin and Juanita Christena (Hill) Campbell; divorced; 1 child, Stanley Edwards IV. Student, Humboldt State Coll., 1968-72. Instrnl. asst. Eureka (Calif.) City Schs., 1971-75; tchr., project mgr., grant writer Petaluma (Calif.) Children's Pk., 1975-76; co-owner, mgr. Shade Tree Automotive Svc., Petaluma, 1975-85; data processing dept. Santa Rosa City Schs., 1976-91; regional mktg. rep. Zurich Am. Life Ins. Co., Petaluma, 1991-94; project mgr. Design Architects, Inc., 1995—. Performer Humboldt Light Opera Co., Santa Rosa Players, Cinnabar Theater. City coun. mem., Petaluma, 1991—, planning commn., 1983-90, zoning ordinance update com., 1988—, pks. and recreation commn., 1977-83, vice mayor, 1993-94; mem. Bay Area Pks. and Recreation Commn., 1977-83, chmn., 1979, 82; mem. human svcs. com. County of Sonoma; mem. Petaluma Boy's and Girl's Club, 1985—; del. Dem. State Ctrl. com.; district schedular for Congresswoman Lynn Woolsey, 1991-94; bd. dir. Golden Gate Bridge, 1995—. Mem. Nat. Women's Polit. Caucus, Sonoma County Mayors and Councilmems. Assn., Santa Rosa Dem. Club. Home: 135 Acorn Dr Petaluma CA 94952

READ, PATRICIA BUTLER, entrepreneur, management consultant; b. San Diego, July 15, 1948; d. John Franklin and Evadele Jane (Monroe) Butler; m. Michael Clift Read, May 19, 1986 (div. Mar. 1994); children: Lisa Michelle, Jeffrey Clift. BA in History, Coll. William and Mary, Williamsburg, Va., 1970. Programmer, analyst Def. Logistics Agy., Alexandria, Va., 1970-75; mgmt. systems analyst Def. Contract Audit Agy., Alexandria, 1975-77; ctr. mgr., enrollment mgr. Werner Erhard & Assocs., Pitts., Balt., Atlanta, 1977-85; mgmt. cons. Smith Ross & Assocs., Arlington, Va., 1985-86; owner Errands & more, Danville, Calif., 1995—. Mem. Diablo Bonsai Club, Sierra Club, Kappa Alpha Theta. Democrat. Home: 517 Sycamore Circle Danville CA 94526

READ, PATRICIA ELLEN, administrator non-profit organization, editor; b. Indpls., Apr. 29, 1952; d. Horace Manson and Patricia Ramal (Downtain) R.; m. William A. Shunk, Jr., Dec. 29, 1995. BA in English cum laude, Rockford Coll., 1974; MS in Libr. Sci. with hons., Columbia U., 1978. Mng. editor Neal Schuman Publishers, N.Y.C., 1977-80; dir. publs. The Foundation Ctr., N.Y.C., 1980-84, v.p., sec., 1984-87; cons. N.Y.C., 1987—; exec. dir. Am. Reading Coun., N.Y.C., 1988-91; cons., mktg. dir. The Feminist Press, N.Y.C., 1991-93; exec. dir. Colo. Assn. Nonprofit Orgns., Denver, 1993—. Contbr. articles in field. Mem. Comm. Network in Philanthropy, Washington, 1981-87, rsch. adv. group Independent Sector, Washington, 1982-87, membership com., 1983-85, adv. com. Giving USA, N.Y.C., 1984-87, adv. com. Nat. Ctr. for Charitable Stats., Washington, 1986-87, task force in classification of non-profit sector, 1984-86; bd. dirs. Sports Ctr. of N.Y., 1990-93, Blue Hill Troupe (Gilbert and Sullivan Repertory Co.), N.Y.C., 1989-91, v.p. 1990-91; mem. Colo. Symphony Orch. Chorus, 1993-94. Finalist 1994 Women of Achievement, YWCA of Denver, 1994. Mem. Nat. Coun. Non-profit Orgns. (bd. dirs.), Metro Vols., Denver (bd. dirs. 1993—, mem. transition team for merger with vol. ctr. 1993, co-chair nominating com. 1994). Home: 679 S Reed Ct Apt 2-307 Lakewood CO 80226 Office: Colo Assn Nonprofit Orgns 22 E 16th Ave Ste 1060 Denver CO 80203

READE, BARBARA ASHLEY, counselor; b. Spokane, Wash., Apr. 25, 1951; d. Walter Henry Bramman and Eleanor Brice (Black) Bishop. BA, U. Md., 1973; teaching cert., Tex. Christian U., 1984; MS in Counseling Psychology, Tex. A&M U., 1991. Lic. profl. counselor, Tex. Documentary photographer State of Md., 1973-74; tech. cons. photography, computer, graphics Typographic Svcs., Inc., Washington, 1973-74; owner Bramman Advt. & Ednl. Pub., Fort Worth, 1975-84; crisis interventionist, tchr. Richardson (Tex.) Ind. Sch. Dist., 1984-89; counselor East Tex. State U., Commerce, 1990-91; counselor family violence Arlington (Tex.) Women's Shelter/Family Violence Outreach Ctr., 1991-92; counselor abused children, families, stress, trauma, addiction Dallas, 1992—; dir., founder Child Reach Found., Inc., Dallas, 1992—; cons. child abuse & recovery; mem. Mayor's Com. Status Women, Fort Worth, 1977-78. Pub. cons. Washington Post/Watergate Papers, 1974. Mem. Am. Counseling Assn., Dallas C. of C., Dallas Task Force Against Violence, North Dallas Counseling Assn., Dallas Metro Counseling Assn. Office: 6320 LBJ Fwy Ste 224 Dallas TX 75240

READE, CLAIRE ELIZABETH, lawyer; b. Waltham, Mass., June 2, 1952; d. Kemp Brownell and Suzanne Helen (Dorntge) R.; m. Earl Phillip Steinberg, Nov. 22, 1980; children: Evan Samuel, Emma Miriam. BA, Conn. Wesleyan U., 1973; JD, Harvard U., 1979; MA in Law and Diplomacy, Tufts U., 1979. Bar: Mass. 1980, D.C. 1983. Sheldon fellow Harvard U., Cambridge, Mass. and, Republic of China, 1979-80; assoc. Ropes & Gray, Boston, 1980-82; assoc. Arnold & Porter, Washington, 1982-86, ptnr., 1987—. Exec. editor: International Trade Policy: The Lawyer's Perspective, 1985; contbr. articles to profl. jours. Mem. ABA (co-chair internat. trade com.), D.C. Bar Assn., Fed. Bar Assn., Am. Soc. Internat. Law, Washington Coun. Lawyers, Women in Internat. Trade. Office: Arnold & Porter 555 12th St NW Washington DC 20004-1202

READE, KATHLEEN MARGARET, paralegal; b. Ft. Worth, Tex., Sept. 6, 1947; d. Ralph S. and Margaret Catherine (Stark) R.; m. John Mason Smith; 1 child, Kathryn Michelle Carter. BA in English and Polit. Sci., Tex. Christian U., postgrad.; postgrad., Tex. Tech, El Centro Coll., Dallas. Asst. land and legal dept. Am. Quasar Petroleum, Ft. Worth, 1971-74; paralegal and office mgr. Law Offices of George Sims, Ft. Worth, 1974-81; asst. criminal cts. #2 and #3 Tarrant County Dist. Atty., Ft. Worth, 1981; ind. paralegal Ft. Worth, 1982-84; paralegal Law Offices of Brent Burford, Ft. Worth, 1982-85; sr. paralegal/litigation Law Offices of Windle Turley, Dallas, 1985-90; major case supr. The Dent Law Firm, Ft. Worth, 1990-96, Michener, Larimore, Swindle, Whitaker, Flowers, Sawyer, Reynolds & Chalk, L.L.P., 1996—; instr. paralegal program, U. Tex., Arlington, 1996—; active Tex. Christian U. Writer's Continuous Workshop. Author: Plaintiff's Personal Injury Handbook, 1994, Dangerous Products, 1996; contbg. author: Legal Assistant's Letter Book, 1995; editl. com. Tex. Paralegal Jour.; contbr. articles to profl. jours. Recipient scholarship Tex. Christian U., Ft. Worth. Mem. AAUW, Am. Assn. Paralegal Edn., Assn. Trial Lawyers, State Bar of Tex. (Legal Asst. Divsn.), Nat. Assn. Legal Assts., Nat. Paralegal Assn., Ft. Worth Paralegal Assn., Freelance Writers' Network, Austin Writer's League, Okla. Writers' Fedn. Home: PO Box 101641 Fort Worth TX 76185

READING, SADIE ETHEL, retired public health nurse; b. Louisiana, Mo., Dec. 16, 1915; d. William M. Reading and Sadie E. Vasconcellos. BSN, Vanderbilt U., 1948; MA, Columbia U., 1956. RN, Mo., Tenn., Fla. Asst. supr. Children's Hosp., Chattanooga, Tenn., 1937-42; sr. staff nurse Chattanooga-Hamilton County Health Dept., Chattanooga, 1948-52; supr. pub. health nursing Gibson County Health Dept., Trenton, Tenn., 1952-55; asst. supr., ednl. dir. Chattanooga-Hamilton County Health Dept., Chattanooga, 1956-59; cons. pub. health nursing Fla. State Bd. Health, Jacksonville, 1959-64, asst. dir. pub. health nursing, 1964-75; pub. health nursing supr. health program office Dept. of Health, Tallahassee, 1975-80; adj. prof. U. Mich. Sch. Pub. Health, Ann Arbor, 1960-74; dist. pres. Tenn. Nurses Assn., 1953; v.p. Fla. Nurses Assn., 1971-72, pres., 1972-73. Author: Blue and Gray: Nursing Outlook, 1962. 1st female lobbyist Fla. State Bd. Health, Jacksonville and Tallahassee, 1974; mem. Common Cause, Hunter Mus., Friends of Chattanooga Pub. Libr., Friends of Signal Mountain Libr., Tenn. Aquarium, Chattanooga. Capt. USAF and Army Nurse Corps, 1942-46, ETO. Mem. AAUW, ANA (vice chair pub. health nursing sect. 1952), LWV, DAR, Fla. Pub. Health Assn. (life, Meritorious Svc. award 1975), Women in Mil. Svc. for Am. (charter), U.S. Golf Assn., Am. Assn. Ret. People, Fla. Sheriff's Assn., Signal Mountain Golf and Country Club, Vanderbilt Alumni Assn., Sigma Theta Tau. Democrat. Home: Apt S-313 100 James Blvd Signal Mountain TN 37377-1862

REAGAN, LARRY GAY, dean; b. Jackson, Tenn., Mar. 30, 1938; d. Larry Alfred and Ann Mabel (Welker) Lane. BA, Union U., 1959; MA, Tulane U., 1961; MS, Ea. Ky. U., 1971; EdD, Vanderbilt U., 1975. Instr. Ill. Coll., Jacksonville, 1961-63, Union Univ., Jackson, Tenn., 1963-64, Chipola Jr. Coll., Marianna, Fla., 1964-67; asst. prof. Campbellsville (Ky.) Coll., 1967-70; divsn. dir. arts and letters, dean acad. affairs Manatee C.C., Bradenton, Fla., 1972—; health educator Tenn. Dept. Pub. Health, Nashville, 1974-75; chair dept. Volunteer State C.C., Gallatin, Tenn., 1975-90, divsn. chair, prof., 1990-92; v.p. Shelby State C.C., Memphis, 1991-92; v.p. Nat. Inst. Leadership Devel., New Coll. Libr. Assn.; lectr. in China, England, and Mexico. Contbr. poems to profl. publs. Bd. dirs. Fla./Colombia Alliance, Marianna, 1964-67; trustee Christian Sr. Housing, Atlanta, 1990—; pres. Tenn. Assn. of Women in C.C.'s, Nashville, 1991-92; mem. Manatee Cultural Alliance, Bradenton, 1993—. Recipient citation award Mex. Sec. of Edn., 1983, award Nat. Inst. Leadership, 1989. Mem. AAUW, AAHPERD, LWV, Am. Assn. Women in C.C.'s (keynote speaker, regional dir.), Fla. Assn. Women in C.C.'s (bd. dirs. 1993—), Nat. Coun. Instrnl. Adminstrn., Rotary Club, Phi Kappa Iota. Home: 6605 Gulfside Rd Longboat Key FL 34228-1416 Office: Manatee CC 5840 26th St W Bradenton FL 34207-3522

REAGAN, NANCY DAVIS (ANNE FRANCIS ROBBINS), volunteer, wife of former President of United States; b. N.Y.C., July 6, 1923; d. Kenneth and Edith (Luckett) Robbins; step dau. Loyal Davis; m. Ronald Reagan, Mar. 4, 1952; children: Patricia Ann, Ronald Prescott; stepchildren: Maureen, Michael. BA, Smith Coll.; LLD (hon.), Pepperdine U., 1983; LHD (hon.), Georgetown U., 1987. Contract actress, MGM, 1949-56; films include The Next Voice You Hear, 1950, Donovan's Brain, 1953, Hellcats of the Navy, 1957; Author: Nancy, 1980; formerly author syndicated column on prisoner-of-war and missing-in-action soldiers and their families; author (with Jane Wilkie) To Love a Child, (with William Novak) My Turn: The Memoirs of Nancy Reagan, 1989. Civic worker, visited wounded Viet Nam vets., sr. citizens, hosps. and schs. for physically and emotionally handicapped children, active in furthering foster grandparents for handicapped children program; hon. nat. chmn. Aid to Adoption of Spl. Kids, 1977; spl interest in fighting alcohol and drug abuse among youth: hosted first ladies from around the world for 2d Internat. Drug Conf., 1985; hon. chmn. Just Say No Found., Nat. Fedn. of Parents for Drug-Free Youth, Nat. Child Watch Campaign, President's Com. on the Arts and Humanities, Wolf Trap Found. bd. of trustees, Nat. Trust for Historic Preservation, Cystic Fibrosis Found., Nat. Republican Women's Club; hon. pres. Girl Scouts of Am. Named one of Ten Most Admired Am. Women, Good Housekeeping mag. ranking #1 in poll, 1984, 85, 86; Woman of Yr. Los Angeles Times, 1977 permanent mem. Hall of Fame of Ten Best Dressed Women in U.S.; recipient humanitarian awards from Am. Camping Assn., Nat. Council on Alcoholism, United Cerebral Palsy Assn., Internat. Ctr. for Disabled; Boys Town Father Flanagan award; 1986 Kiwanis World Service medal; Variety Clubs Internat. Lifeline award; numerous awards for her role in fight against drug abuse. Address: Century City Fox Plaza 2121 Ave of the Stars 34th Fl Los Angeles CA 90024*

REAM, ANGELA MARIE, elementary education educator; b. Waukesha, Wis., July 27, 1970; d. Kenneth Richard Ream and Kathleen Kay (Meier) Fox. AAS, U. Wis.-Rock County, 1992; BS in Elem. Edn., U. Wis., Whitewater, 1995. Baker The Abbey on Lake Geneva, Fontana, Wis., 1986-90; lead tchr. Kids Korner, Evansville, Wis., summer 1990; supr. Pvt. Industry Coun., Janesville, Wis., summer 1992; child care supr. chpt. 1 Washington Elem., Janesville, 1992-95; Title I tchr. Janesville Sch. Dist., 1995—; supr. YWCA, Janesville, 1990-95, camp counsel, summers 1991-94, instr. early childhood cook class, 1991-92, instr. babysitting clinic, 1991-93, cmty. children's parade, 1993, chaperone for sleep-over, 1993, v.p. fundraiser, fall 1994, accreditation team mem., 1994-95; tchr. summer sch. Ft. Atkinson (Wis.) Sch. Dist., 1995. Author: Personal Portfolio, 1994. Scholar Grace Alvord, U. Wis., Whitewater, 1993-94, 95. Mem. ASCD, Nat. Assn. for Edn. Young Children, Golden Key Nat. Honors Soc. Home: 1314 Barham Ave Janesville WI 53545-1507

REAMER, SANDRA L., artist, art educator; b. Franklin Lakes, N.J., July 12, 1960; d. Bruce W. R. and Paula D. DiPietro; m. Philip M. Jacobson, Aug. 15, 1980. BFA, U. Denver, 1991; MFA in Painting and Computer Graphics, Pratt Inst. Art, 1996. Apprentice to Prof. Ernst Fuchs Vienna, Austria, 1983; art tchr. children's program U. No. Ariz., Flagstaff, 1988; professor art and humanities U. for Youth Bur. Ednl. Svcs. U. Denver, 1988-89; head printmaking dept. Overland H.S., Aurora, Colo., 1991-92; adj. faculty The Naropa inst., Boulder, Colo., 1992—; adj. prof. painting U.

Denver, summer 1991; ceramic tech. Pratt Inst. Art, Brooklyn, N.Y., 1993-94; designer Banyon Design, Boulder, Colo., 1990-92; gallery asst. U. Denver, 1988-91; art therapist divsn. youth N.Y. State Psychiatric Facility, Rochester, N.Y., 1985. Illustrations featured in Light of Consciousness mag., Quest mags. Mem. Holistic Source, Nat. Honor Soc. Home: P O Box 20381 Boulder CO 80308-3381

REAMER, SHIRLEY JEAN, minister; b. South Bend, Ind., Aug. 15, 1935; d. John Lewis and Vivian Leora (Hammer) Helvey; m. Thomas Charles Reamer, June 22, 1956; children: Thomas Darwin, Trent Alan, Terry Michael, Traci Sue, Tricia Ann. Grad. high sch., South Bend, 1953; ThD, Shalom Bible Coll. and Sem., West Des Moines, Iowa, 1992. Ordained to ministry Full Gospel Fellowship, 1974. Dir. children's ministry Calvary Temple, South Bend, 1972-73; evangelist Full Gospel Fellowship, 1976—; founder, pastor Maranatha Temple, South Bend, 1981-83; founder, pres. Women's Aglow Fellowship, Michiana, Ind., 1976-79; founder, dir. Prison Ministry-Aglow, Westville, Ind., 1976-77; founder, dir. Soup Kitchen/Care Ctr., Maranatha Temple, 1982—, Supplied Facilities for Ctr. for Homeless, 1984-87, dir. City March, 1989; mem. United Religious Community Task Force, South Bend, 1985. Author: Ministerial Ethics, 1984, Teaching Syllabus, 1985, Recruits for Christ, 1987, Teaching Syllabus, Genesis, The Beginning, 1994. Recipient Spirit of Am. Women award J.C. Penneys, South Bend, 1988; named one of 16 Best Pastors, Charisma Mag., 1988.

REAP, SISTER MARY MARGARET, college administrator; b. Carbondale, Pa., Sept. 8, 1941; d. Charles Vincent and Anna Rose (Ahern) R. BA, Marywood Coll., Scranton, Pa., 1965; MA, Assumption Coll., Worcester, Mass., 1972; PhD, Pa. State U., 1979. Elem. tchr. St. Ephrem's, Bklyn., 1966-67; secondary tchr. South Catholic High, Scranton, Pa., 1967-69, Maria Regina High Sch., Uniondale, N.Y., 1969-72; mem. faculty Marywood Coll., Scranton, Pa., 1972-86, dean, 1986-88, pres., 1988—; tchr. Mainland China, Wuhan, 1982, Marygrove Coll., Detroit, 1979; bd. dirs. Moses Taylor Hops., Scranton Prep. Sch.; bd. dirs., exec. com. Lourdesmont Sch. Contbr. articles to profl. jours. Recipient bilingual fellowship Pa. State U., 1976-79, Local Chpt. Svc. award UN, 1984, Woman of Yr. awrd Boy Scouts Am., 1993; named Northeast Woman, Scranton Times, 1986, Outstanding Alumna, Pa. State Coll. Edn., 1989. Mem. Pa. Assn. for Colls. and Univs. (exec. com.), Coun. for Ind. Colls. and Univs., Am. Assn. Cath. Colls., Phi Delta Kappa (Educator of Yr. award 1990). Office: Marywood Coll Office of the President Scranton PA 18509-1598

REARDEN, CAROLE ANN, clinical pathologist, educator; b. Belleville, Ont., Can., June 11, 1946; d. Joseph Brady and Honora Patricia (O'Halloran) R. BSc, McGill U., 1969, MSc, MDCM, 1971. Diplomate Am. Bd. Pathology, Am. Bd. Immunohematology and Blood Banking. Resident and fellow Children's Meml. Hosp., Chgo., 1971-73; resident in pediatrics U. Calif., San Diego, 1974, resident then fellow, 1975-79, asst. prof. pathology, 1979-86, dir. histocompatability and immunogenetics lab., 1979-94, assoc. prof., 1986-92, prof., 1992—, head divsn. lab. medicine, 1989-94; dir. med. ctr. U. Calif. Thornton Hosp. Clin. Labs., San Diego, 1993—; prin. investigator devel. monoclonal antibodies to erythroid antigens, recombinant autoantigens; dir. lab. exam. com. Am. Bd. Histocompatibility and Immunogenetics. Contbr. articles to profl. jours. Mem. Mayor's Task Force on AIDS, San Diego, 1983. Recipient Young Investigator Rsch. award NIH, 1979; grantee U. Calif. Cancer Rsch. Coordinating Com., 1982, NIH, 1983. Mem. Am. Soc. Investigative Pathology, Acad. Clin. Lab. Physicians and Scientists, Am. Soc. Hematology, Am. Assn. Blood Banks (com. organ transplantation and tissue typing 1982-87), Am. Soc. Histocompatibility and Immunogenetics. Office: U Calif San Diego Dept Pathology 0612 9500 Gilman Dr La Jolla CA 92093-5003

REARDON, ELAINE ANNE, early education education educator; b. Everett, Mass., Dec. 12, 1952; d. John Francis and Anna Ruth (Haroutunian) R.; m. Ronald D. DeHart, Feb. 25, 1989; 1 child, Jenny Etain. BA in Edn., U. Mass., 1992. Tchr. Associated Day Care Ctr., Chelsea, Mass., 1973-80; family day care adminstr. Orange (Mass.) Day Care Ctr., 1980-82; head tchr., adminstr. Head Start, Orange, 1982-90; early childhood tchr. Boston U./Chelsea Partnership Chelsea (Mass.) Pub. Schs., 1992—; pres., mem. PTO, Warwick, Mass., 1985-91; bilingual com. mem. Chelsea (Mass.) Pub. Sch., 1993—. Pres. Mass. Blast Everett, Mass., 1979-81; mem. Arts Coun., Warwick, 1989-93, Orange, 1990-92. Grantee Armenian Gen. Benelovent Soc., 1990, 91, Armenian Relief Soc., Amherst, 1991; scholar Hai Guin Scholarships, 1991, U. Mass. Scholarships, Amherst, 1992. Mem. Golden Key Honor Soc. Home: PO Box 64 Wendell Depot MA 01380-0064

REARDON, KATHLEEN KELLEY, communication educator, writer; b. Bridgeport, Conn., June 13, 1949; d. John Frances and Elizabeth Loretta (Kelley) R.; m. Christopher Thomas Noblet, Oct. 22, 1983; 3 children. BA with high honors, U. Conn., 1971; MA with highest honors, U. Mass., 1973, PhD with highest honors and distinction, 1978. English, comm. tchr. South Windsor (Conn.) H.S., Stratford (Conn.) H.S.; from. asst. to assoc. prof. U. Conn., Storrs, 1978-85; from assoc. prof. to prof. U. So. Calif., L.A., 1985—, full prof., 1996—; vis. scholar Stanford (Calif.) U., 1984-85; vis. acad. Trinity Coll., Dublin, Ireland, 1996; adv. bd. Grad. Women Bus., L.A., 1995-96, Eastern Comm. Assn., 1979-83, chair, 1982-83. Author: Persuasion in Practice, 1991, They Don't Get It, Do They?, 1995; prodr. (documentary) How Will I Survive?, 1994. Mem. rsch. adv. bd. Starbright Found., L.A., 1989-92; adv. coun. Cancer Info. Svc., L.A., 1990-93; mem. Pub. Edn. subcom. Am. Cancer Soc., 1982-86. Mem. AAUP, Women in Film, Internat. Comm. Assn. (bd. dirs. 1992-95), Acad. Mgmt., Speech Comm. Assn. (chair action caucus 1978-88), Phi Beta Kappa, Phi Kappa Phi. Office: U So Calif Sch Bus Bridge Hall 307H Los Angeles CA 90089-1421

REARDON, NANCY ANNE, human resource executive; b. Little Falls, N.Y., Sept. 19, 1952; d. Warren Joseph and Elizabeth Owen (Tiel) Reardon; m. Steven Jonathan Sayer, Aug. 28, 1976; children: Scott Jason, Kathryn Anne. BS in Psychology, Union Coll., Schenectady, N.Y., 1974; MS in Social Psychology, Syracuse U., 1978. With GE Co., N.Y.C., 1979-85, Avon Products Inc., N.Y.C., 1985-89, Am. Express, N.Y.C., 1989-91; sr. v.p. human resources Duracell Internat., Inc., Bethel, Conn., 1991—; adv. bd. mem. Catalyst, 1995. Mem. Human Resource Planning Soc. (bd. dirs. 1991-94, treas. 1992-93), N.Y. Human Resource Planners (bd. dirs., pres. 1989-91), Sr. Pers. Execs. Forum, Nat. Fgn. Trade Coun. (bd. dirs. 1995). Office: Duracell Internat Inc Berkshire Corporate Pk Bethel CT 60801

REARDON, PEARL RANCE, real estate executive, writer; b. Savanna La Mar, Westmoreland, Jamaica, Apr. 17, 1941; came to U.S., 1968; d. Hugh Lawrence Rance and Ada Louise (Mullings) Watson; m. Michael I. Phillips, June 9, 1962 (div. Sept. 1977); children: Karim Irving, Felita Alessandra; m. Michael John Reardon, May 24, 1980. Student, Howard Community Coll., 1974-77; MFA in Creative Writing, Am. U., 1996. Cert. real estate broker Grad. Real Estate Inst. Sr. sec. Nat. Coun. Cath. Men, Washington, 1968-69; exec. sec. Nat. Acad. Sci, Washington, 1969-71; sr. sec. Pres.'s Commn. on Population, Washington, 1971-72; exec. sec. Westinghouse Health System, Columbia, Md., 1972-76; adminstrv. group mgr. Price, Williams & Assocs., Silver Spring, Md., 1976-78; assoc. broker Merrill Lynch Realty, Silver Spring, 1977-81; pres. and CEO Pearl Properties, Silver Spring, 1982-93; v.p. Croton Mgmt. Svcs., Washington, D.C., 1994—. Organizer Peoples Nat. Party, Linstead, Jamaica, 1966; founding mem. Jamaica Nat. Assn., Washington, 1969, sec. 1969-73. Mem. Nat. Assn. Realtors, D.C. Bd. Realtors, Authors Guild, Dramatists Guild. Office: Croton Mgmt Svcs 110 Gallatin St NW # 1 Washington DC 20011-3270

REAS, CATHY MARIE AKINS, college administrator, educator; b. Hodgensville, Ky., Jan. 14, 1954; d. Marvin Ray and Charlene Reid (Lawson) Akins; m. Gary Lewis Reas; children: Kelly Marie Reas, Robert Aaron Reas. BA summa cum laude, U. Md., College Park, 1983; MS in Systems Mgmt., U. So. Calif., L.A., 1985. Asst. to dir. Lake County Housing Authority, Ill., 1978-80; field registrar U. Md., Heidelberg, West Germany, 1981-82; program coord. U. So. Calif., Heidelberg and Worms, West Germany, 1983-85, area coord., 1985-87; instr. City Coll. Chgo., Heidelberg and Worms, West Germany, 1984-87; instnl. data analyst Office of Planning & Budgets U. Ala., Huntsville, 1989-90, sr. staff officer, 1990-91, resource coord. Coll. Nursing, 1991—; mem. adv. bd. First Baptist Ch., Huntsville, 1991-94. Mem. Nat. Assn. Coll. & Univ. Bus. Officers, Univ. Women's Club (pres., 1st v.p., 2d v.p. 1989-96), Bus. Officers of Schs. of Nursing (co-chair spl. project 1993-96), Am. Assn. Coll. Nursing (benchmarking task force 1995-96), Phi Kappa Phi. Home: 1208 Siniard Dr Huntsville AL 35803 Office: Coll Nursing U Ala Huntsville AL 35899

REASOR, STACEY, librarian; b. St. Joseph, Mo., Oct. 15, 1963; d. Richard Smith and Rolande (Thompson) Pinkerton; m. Darrin Martin Reasor, Feb. 15, 1992; 1 child, Jordan; 2 stepchildren: Kristen, Joel. BS in Psychology, U. S.W. La., 1985; MLS, U. South Fla., 1991. Server Dave's Deli, Visalia, Calif., 1980-81; tour guide Cypress Gardens, Winter Haven, Fla., 1981; retail salesperson Scarboroughs Dept. Store, Austin, Tex., 1982-83, Selber Bros. Dept. Store, Lafayette, La., 1983-85; mental health technician, counselor Winter Haven Hosp., 1986-87, Charter Hosp. Tampa Bay, Tampa, Fla., 1987-89; med. asst. Tampa Womens Health Ctr., 1989-91; libr. ITT Tech. Inst., Tampa, 1991—; mem. student activities com. ITT Tech. Inst., Tampa, 1994—. Editor: (sch. newsletter) The Technogram, 1994—. Recipient Small Grant award ITT Ednl. Svcs., 1995. Mem. ALA, Fla. Libr. Assn., Spl. Librs. Assn., Suncoast Info. Specialists. Office: ITT Tech Inst 4809 Memorial Hwy Tampa FL 33634

REAVIS, LIZA ANNE, semiconductor executive; b. N.Y.C., July 27, 1959; d. William Ralph and Juliette (Bustillo y Zelaya) Bartlett; m. Paul H. Reavis, May 25, 1985. BA in Internat. Rels., Rice U., 1981; MBA, Georgetown U., 1988. Project asst. Latham, Watkins & Hills, Washington, 1982-83; assoc. mgr. countertrade Sears World Trade, Washington, 1983-85; export asst. Weadon, Dibble & Rehm, Washington, 1985-86; assoc. cons. Vanguard Comm. Corp., Palo Alto, Calif., 1988-90; bus. mgr. Teleport Comm. Corp., San Francisco, 1990-94; sr. fin. analyst Nat. Semicondr. Corp., 1995—. Contbr. Project Open Hand, San Francisco, Calif. Wheelchair Vets. Assn., Am. Assn. for AIDS Rsch., San Francisco, 1990—; mem. Golden Gate Nat. Recreation Area, San Francisco, 1990—. Recipient TCG Ann. Hero award; Presdl. scholar. Mem. Women in Tech., Acad. Polit. Sci., Club des Hiboux (sec. 1979-80), Commonwealth Club, Sierra Club, Cousteau Soc., Phi Beta Kappa, Beta Gamma Sigma, Pi Delta Phi. Home: 6931 Geary Blvd San Francisco CA 94121-1620 Office: Nat Semicondr Corp 2900 Semiconductor Dr Mail Stop C1245 Santa Clara CA 95052-8090

REBACK, JOYCE ELLEN, lawyer; b. Phila., July 11, 1948; d. William and Sue (Goldstein) R.; m. Itzhak Brook, Aug. 2, 1981; children: Jonathan Zev, Sara Jennie. BA magna cum laude, Brown U., 1970; JD with honors, George Washington U., 1976. Bar: D.C. 1976, U.S. Dist. Ct. D.C. 1976, U.S. Ct. Appeals (D.C. cir.) 1976, U.S. Ct. Appeals (3d cir.) 1983, U.S. Ct. Appeals (Fed. cir.) 1985. Assoc. Fulbright & Jaworski, Washington, 1976-84, ptnr., 1984-87; legal cons. IMF, Washington, 1987—. Contbr. articles to profl. jours. Mem. ABA, D.C. Bar Assn., Phi Beta Kappa. Jewish. Office: Internat Monetary Fund 700 19th St NW Washington DC 20431-0001

REBB, KAREN MARLENE, music educator; b. Columbus, Ga.; d. Glen Percival and Vivian Irene (Williams) Loken; 1 child, Michael John-Glen. BS in Music Edn., Elem. Edn., Grand Canyon U., 1981; MA in Music Edn., No. Ariz. U., 1986. Cert. tchr., Ariz.; cert. I, II, III Levels Orff cert. Tchr. Heatherbrae Elem. Sch., Phoenix, 1981-82, Park Meadows Elem. Sch., Phoenix, 1982-95, Arrowhead Elem. Sch., Glendale, Ariz., 1995—; mem. adj. faculty Ottawa U., 1989—. Author: project Science of Music: Integrating the Arts and Technology, 1995. Mem. 1st Hist. Presbyn. Ch.; mem. site-based mgmt. team Park Meadows Sch., 1994, 95; mem. Dist. Strategic Planning Com., 1994; mem. dist. fine arts coun. writing Fine Arts Curriculum for Dist., Phoenix, 1995, 96. Recipient Ray Maben Scholar award Grand Canyon U., 1980, Ariz.; artist-in-residence grantee, 1989. Mem. NEA, Am. Orff-Schulwerk Assn., Ariz. Edn. Assn., Ariz. Orff-Schulwerk Assn. (sec., bd. dirs. 1990-92), Ariz. Music Educators Assn., Music Educators Nat. Conf. Home: 10829 N 10th St Phoenix AZ 85020

REBE, BEVERLY GRUBBS, contracts administrator; b. Colorado City, Tex., Jan. 14, 1945; d. John Keaton and Lottie Mae (Saunders) Grubbs; m. Salomon Rebe, Apr. 8, 1968; children: Kelley, Rennie, Ryan. BA, U. Tex., 1968; MBA, U. Tex., El Paso, 1987. Adminstrv. asst. YWCA, El Paso, 1977-78, adminstrv. exec., 1978-81; full charge bookkeeper Guevara, Rebe, Baumann & Coldwell, El Paso, 1982-84; health, phys. edn. and recreation adminstr. YWCA, 1987; contracts and compliance adminstr., 1989—; mem. nat. resource tng. team YWCA, N.Y.C., 1979; compliance and acctg. cons. YWCA, El Paso, 1989; dir. slide prodns. YWCA-2001, 1981, El Paso Coun. on Aging, 1982. Editor: (handbook) YWCA Volunteer Handbook, 1980, (manual) YWCA Policies and Procedures Manual, 1978. Co-founder El Paso High Soccer Booster Club, 1989; v.p. YWCA Bd., El Paso, 1972, chair fin. com., 1986; pres. El Paso High PTA, 1987, sec., 1993, treas., 1994; treas. Goodwill Industries, Inc., El Paso, 1995; Tex. life mem. PTA, 1986, nat. life mem., 1993. Mem. U. Tex.-El Paso Alumni Assn., Delta Gamma Alumni Assn.

REBECCA, LAURA MARY, English educator; b. N.Y.C., June 9, 1964; d. Dominic Joseph and Maryann Steinhauer. BA, Hofstra U., 1986; MSEd, U. So. Calif., 1994. Cert. tchr. secondary English, N.Y., English, secondary lang. devel. specialist, Calif. Drama instr./coord. Levels Youth Ctr., Great Neck, N.Y., 1986-88; substitute tchr. L.A. Unified Sch. Dist., 1990-92; tchr. English, drama, ESL Berendo Mid. Sch., L.A., 1993-94; tchr. English, theater arts Garden City (N.Y.) High Sch., 1994—; mem. health awareness day com., Garden City H.S., 1994-96, sch. leadership coun. Berendo Mid. Sch., L.A., 1993-94, lang. assessment team, 1993-94. Edn. Alumni scholar U. So. Calif. Edn. Alumni Assn., 1993-94; drama dept. merit scholar Hofstra U., 1984-86. Mem. Nat. Coun. Tchrs. of English, Alpha Psi Omega. Office: Garden City High Sch 170 Rockaway Ave Garden City NY 11530

REBER, CHERYL ANN, consultant, social worker; b. Cin., Feb. 7, 1956; d. Randland John and Marcella Catherine (Hollstegge) R. AA, Xavier U., 1976, BA, 1980. Lic. social worker. Social worker Altercrest, Cin., 1977-79; social worker Hamilton County Dept. Human Svcs., Cin., 1979-85, adoption specialist, social worker, 1985-92; social worker, AIDS specialist Hospice of the Miami Valley, 1992-95; cons., spl. needs adoption specialist, program developer, 1995—; trainer, program developer Hamilton County Dept. Human Svcs., Cin., 1988-92. Mem. Cmty. Task Force on Adoption, Cin., 1989-91, 95—. Mem. S.W. Ohio Adoption Resource Exch. (pres. 1990-91, treas. 1991-92), Beechmont Players, Inc. (v.p. 1982-86, pres. 1990-92). Democrat. Roman Catholic.

RECAR, TERESA LYNN, real estate broker; b. Ark., July 29, 1961. BE of Secondary and Spl. Edn., S.W. Tex. State U., 1983. Tchr. spl. edn. Dallas Ind. Sch. Dist., 1983-86; pres., broker Recar & Assocs., Austin, 1986—; pres., dir. Austin Bd. Realtors Leasing Mgmt. Divsn., Austin, 1990-93. Mem. Nat. Assn. Residential Property Mgrs. (master property mgr., nat. dir. 1993-96). Office: Recar & Assocs 8400 N Mopac #200 Austin TX 78759

RECH, SUSAN ANITA, obstetrician, gynecologist; b. Summit, N.J., Nov. 5, 1957; d. William F. and Mary Jane (Crooks) R. BA in Biology, Swarthmore Coll., 1979; MD, U. Medicine Dentistry N.J., Newark, 1984. Diplomate Am. Bd. Ob-Gyn. Resident in ob-gyn. Temple U. Hosp., Phila., 1984-88; pvt. practice, Plattsburgh, N.Y., 1990—; asst. clin. prof. de. ob-gyn. U. Vt. Sch. Medicine, 1991—; mem. med. adv. bd. Planned Parenthood No. N.Y., Plattsburgh, 1989—, Clinton County Health Dept., Plattsburgh, 1989—; bd. dirs. Cmty. Providers, Inc., Plattsburgh, 1994—. Active Newman Ctr., John XXIII Cath. Parish, Plattsburgh, 1990—; mem. alumni coun. Swarthmore (Pa.) Coll., 1994-96; mem. Seton Cath. H.S. Sch. Bd., Plattsburgh, 1995—. Rsch. grantee U. Medicine and Dentistry N.J., summer 1980. Fellow ACOG; mem. AMA, Am. Med. Women's Assn. (founding pres. Champlain Valley chpt. 1991), No. N.Y. Ind. Practice Assn. (bd. dirs. 1994—), Champlain Valley Oratorio Soc. (soloist 1989—), Nat. Honor Soc. Home: 244 Smith Dr Plattsburgh NY 12901 Office: Assocs in Ob-Gyn PC 210 Cornelia St Ste 201 Plattsburgh NY 12901

RECK, ELIZABETH TORRE, social worker, educator; b. Winston-Salem, N.C., June 17, 1931; d. Vernon Clark and Mary (Pfohl) Lassiter; m. Mottram Peter Torre, Apr. 13, 1957 (dec.); m. Andrew Joseph Reck, June 17, 1987. student Wellesley (Mass.) Coll., 1948-49; BA, Duke U., 1952; MRE, Union Theol. Sem., 1957; MSW, Tulane U., 1966, PhD, 1972; cert. social worker, La. Field dir. undergrad. admissions Duke U., Durham, N.C., 1952-53; head tchr. primary dept. Riverside Ch., N.Y.C., 1957-60; instr. Sch. Social Work, Tulane U., New Orleans, 1966-72, assoc. prof., 1972—, coord. Indsl. Social Work Program, 1982-88; mem. faculty senate Tulane U., 1972-88. Non-govtl. orgn. rep. UNICEF, World Fedn. Mental Health, 1957-61; cons. to v.p. community affairs WETA, Washington, 1979; cons. Office Spl. Symposia and Seminars, Smithsonian Instn., Washington, 1979-86. Treas., N.Y. Jr. League, 1961-62, v.p., 1962-63; bd. dirs. Community Vol. Svcs., New Orleans, 1965-68; mem. profl. adv. com. Project Pre-Kindergarten, Orleans Parish Sch. Bd., New Orleans, 1967-69; mem. adv. bd. DePaul Community Mental Health Ctr., New Orleans, 1971-72; mem. citizens adv. com. Orleans Parish Juvenile Ct., New Orleans, 1970-73; mem. Coun. on Social Work Edn. Task Force on Prevention, 1981-87; mem. New Orleans Women's Coalition Task Force on Employers and Working Parents, 1985-90; mem. med. social svcs. subcom. Mayor's Adv. Com. on Domestic Violence, 1995-96. NIMH grantee; Summer Inst. grantee Nat. Endowment Humanities, 1982; Newcomb Coll. fellow, 1989—. Mem. AAUW (Tulane Corp. rep. 1990—), Coun. Social Work Edn., Nat. Assn. Social Workers (bd. dirs. La. chpt. 1987-89), Am. Orthopsychiat. Assn. (life), AAUP (treas. Tulane chpt. 1984-86, 88-91, exec. com. 1991-95, v.p. New Orleans chpt. 1996—), Tulane U. Women's Assn. (v.p. 1996—), Phi Beta Kappa (Tulane chpt. exec. com. 1990—, pres. Tulane chpt. 1991, regional sec. 1994—). Office: Tulane U Sch Social Work New Orleans LA 70118

RECKE, JUDITH GRACE, sales executive; b. Weymouth, Mass.; d. George Edgar and Catherine Greenwood (Kelly) R. BA, Dartmouth Coll., 1980. Dir. sales Merriam-Webster, Springfield, Mass., 1993—. Office: Merriam-Webster Inc 47 Federal St Springfield MA 01102

RECKER, JO ANN MARIE, foreign language educator; b. Cin., Oct. 26, 1942; d. Richard George and Angeline Marie (Peters) R. BA, Edgecliff Coll., 1965; MA, Ohio State U., 1972, PhD, 1982. Joined Sister of Notre Dame de Namur. Tchr. Summit Country Day Sch., Cin., 1965-70, St. Joseph Acad., Columbus, Ohio, 1970-77; grad. tchg. asst. Ohio State U., Columbus, 1977-82, program coord. dept. romance lang., 1982-87, asst. dir. fgn. lang. ctr., 1988; assoc. prof. Xavier U., Cin., 1988—, supr. student tchrs., 1988-92, chair dept. modern lang., 1991—, prof., 1996—; bd. trustees Summit Country Day Sch., Cin., 1991—; presenter in field.' Author: Appelle-Moi Pierrot: Wit and Irony in Letters of Madame de Sevigne, 1986; co-author (with H. Jay Siskin) Situations et Contextes, 1990; editor (Fgn. Lang. Ctr. newsletter Ohio State U.) Communique, 1988, (dept. newsletter Ohio State U.) Lingua Franca, 1983-87; editl. bd. mem. Cin. Romance Rev., 1988—; contbr. articles to profl. jours. Docent Cin. (Ohio) Art Mus., 1993—. Mem. MLA, Midwest MLA, Am. Assn. Tchrs. French, Am. Coun. Tchg. Fgn. Lang., Ohio Fgn. Lang. Assn. (v.p. 1991-93), Phi Kappa Phi. Roman Catholic. Home: 3455 Steeplechase Ln Apt 3D Loveland OH 45140-3282 Office: Xavier Univ Dept Modern Lang 3800 Victory Pky Cincinnati OH 45207-5784

RECTOR, MARGARET HAYDEN, writer; b. Azusa, Calif., May 23, 1916; d. Floyd Smith and Anna Martha (Miller) Hayden; m. Robert Wayman Rector, Aug. 25, 1940; children: Cleone Rector Grabowski Black, Robin Rector Krupp, Bruce Hayden. AA, Citrus Jr. Coll., 1936; BA, Pomona Coll., 1938; postgrad., Stanford U., 1938-40, Columbia U., 1942-46, St. John's Coll., Annapolis, Md., 1946-56, U. So. Calif., 1959-65, UCLA, 1959-66. Mem. advt. staff Curt Wagner, Redondo Beach, Calif., 1957-67; writer Am. Home Mag., N.Y.C., 1942-46, House Beautiful Mag., N.Y.C., 1942-46; author children's books Grossmont Press, San Diego, 1974-76. Author: Norton and Gus, 1976; Alva, That Vanderbilt-Belmont Woman, 1992; editor: History of Citrus, 1994; playwright, screenwriter. Dem. organizer, Annapolis, Md., 1946-56; mem. UCLA affiliates; bd. dirs. Friends of Rsch. Libr. Mem. AAUW (life), PEN, Women in Film, Women in Theatre, UCLA Faculty Wives Writers Group, Surfwriters Palos Verdes Peninsula, First Stage, The Audrey Skirball-Kenis Theatre, Dramatists Guild, Authors Guild, Womens Internat. Ctr. in San Diego, Pomona Coll. Alumni, Stanford U. Alumni. Home: 10700 Stradella Ct Los Angeles CA 90077-2604

RECTOR, MARY MARGARET, secondary school educator; b. Mpls., Apr. 30, 1946; d. Edmund James and Margaret Ruth (Schaber) Cain; m. William A. Rector, Aug. 4, 1973; children: Meghan, Brian. BS in Home Econs., U. Minn., 1969; MS in Spl. Edn., U. Las Vegas, 1974. Cert. tchr., Minn. Nev. Home econs. tchr. Jim Bridger Jr. H.S., Las Vegas, 1969-71, Rancho H.S., Las Vegas, 1971-73, Chaparral H.S., Las Vegas, 1973-85, Valley H.S., Las Vegas, 1985—; mem. adv. bd. South Nev. Ext. Nutrition Coun., Las Vegas, 1982-90; spkr. YMCA, Las Vegas, 1983; reader Nutrition Edn. Grants, Las Vegas, 1984; advisor FHA, Las Vegas, 1971—. Contbr. articles to profl. jours. Leader Girl Scouts USA, Las Vegas, 1984-90; voter registrar Clark County Election Dept., Las Vegas, 1976-78; mem. Clark County Dem. Ctrl. Com., Las Vegas, 1976-78. Grantee Clark County Sch. Dist., 1984-85. Mem. Am. Home Econs. Assn. (cert.), So. Nev. Home Econs. Assn. (pres. 1988-90), Clark County Vocat. Assn., Nev. Vocat. Assn. (Outstanding FHA/Hero adviser award 1993), Am. Fedn. Tchrs. (treas. 1974-78). Democrat. Roman Catholic. Office: Valley HS 2839 Burnham Ave Las Vegas NV 89109-1793

RECTOR, SHEILA DAWN, surgeon; b. Birmingham, Ala., Oct. 9, 1959; d. Rodney Roy and Katherine Ann (Logan) R.; m. Noel Thomas Nuckols III, Feb. 24, 1996. BA, Vanderbilt U., 1981; MD, Med. Coll. Ga., 1985. Diplomate Am. Bd. Surgery. Resident in gen. surgery U. Ky., 1985-90; assoc. gen. surgery practice St. Andrews Surg. Assocs., Columbia, S.C., 1990-92, Columbia Surg. Assocs., 1992-93; pvt. practice Bennettsville, S.C., 1995—. Fellow ACS (assoc.); mem. Assn. Women Surgeons. Office: PO Box 1174 Bennettsville SC 29512

REDA, ANN ELIZABETH, podiatrist; b. Elizabeth, N.J., Aug. 11, 1960; d. Peter R. and Marian D. (Rutz) R. BS, St. Bonaventure (N.Y.) U., 1982; D Podiatric Medicine, Pa. Coll. Podiatric Medicine, 1986. Resident Riverside Hosp., Wilmington, Del., 1987; pvt. practice N.J., 1988—. Roman Catholic.

REDD, J. DIANE, professional fund raiser and grants management executive; b. Beckley, W.Va., Apr. 10, 1945; d. Robert Fountain and Lillian (Fitts) Redd. B.S., W.Va. State Coll., 1967. Instr. bus. subjects Paterson (N.J.) Bus. Edn., 1967-68; with U. Medicine and Dentistry N.J., Newark, 1968-89, adminstrv. asst. research and sponsored programs, 1968-73, asst. dir. health edn., 1973-76, sr. devel. officer, 1976-79, asst. dir. devel., 1979-83, chief devel. and alumni affairs, 1983-89; dir. devel. Planned Parenthood Fedn. Am., Inc, N.Y.C., 1989—. Mem. priorities com., devel. com. United Way of Essex and West Hudson, Newark, 1983-85; chmn. human resources com. Community Adv. Bd., U. Medicine and Dentistry N.J., Newark, 1978-82; mem. rsch. bd. advisors Am. Biographical Inst., 1992—. Recipient Recognition of Achievement award Young Women of America, Inc., Montgomery, Ala., 1979, Black Achiever award YMWCA, 1986. Mem. Council Advancement and Support of Edn., Nat. Soc. Fund Raising Execs. Inc. (cert., trustee, v.p., parliamentarian, sec.), Assn. Am. Med. Colls., Exec. Women N.J. (trustee, chmn. scholarship com.), Women in Fin. Devel., Consortium of Devel. and Alumni Profls. of Greater N.Y. Democrat. Office: Planned Parenthood Fedn of Am 810 7th Ave New York NY 10019-5818

REDD, MARY DELENA, social service administrator; b. East Gulf, W.Va., Jan. 24, 1943; d. John D. and Bettie Elizabeth (Hubbard) R. BA in Sociology, W.Va. State Coll., 1963; MS in Social Casework, Fordham U., 1967. Caseworker Soc. for Seamen's Children, Staten Island, N.Y., 1963-68; dir. social svcs. Bronx River Neighborhood Ctr., 1968-72; dir. Manhattan ctr. The Wiltwyck Sch., N.Y.C., 1972-76, coord. cmty. mentel health svcs., 1976-78; exec. dir. Steinway Child & Family Svcs., Inc., L.I., N.Y., 1978—; cons. Bronx River Head Start Ctrs., 1977—; ajd. prof. Fordham U. Sch. Social Sci., N.Y.C., 1978-80. Dir. Riverbend Housing Co., Inc., 1993, pres., 1994; vice chair Multicultural Adv. Com., 1991; dir. UpperManhattan Empowerment Zone Devel. Corp., N.Y.C., 1995. Mem. N.Y. State Office Mental Health, Pan-Hellenic Coun. N.Y. (pres. 1980-84), Coalition of Vol. Mental Health Agys., W.Va. State Coll. Alumni Assn. (corr. sec. 1980-84), The Links, Delta Sigma Theta (N.Y. state coord. 1985-87). Democrat. Baptist. Home: 2333 5th Ave #1-HH New York NY 10037 Office: Steinway Child & Family Svc 41-36 27th St Long Island City NY 11101

REDDING, BARBARA J., nursing administrator, occupational health nurse; b. Youngstown, Ohio, Jan. 5, 1938; d. Richard Howard and Helen N. (Price) Sterling; m. Philip L. Redding, Nov. 7, 1957; children: Cheryl L.,

Jeffrey A., Scott P. Diploma in nursing, Miami Valley Hosp., Dayton, Ohio, 1959; AA in Sociology, Miami U., Oxford, Ohio, 1984; postgrad., U. Cin. RN, Ohio; cert. EMT, CPR, BLS. Office nurse Dr. Stewart Adam, Dayton; primary nurse Miami Valley Hosp; adminstr. employee health Armco Steel Co., L.P., Middletown, Ohio; v.p. Redding Ins. Agy., Inc., Middletown, Ohio, 1993—. Instr. CPR, ARC. Mem. NAFE, Am. Assn. Occupational Health Nurses, Ind. Ins. Agts. Am., Inc. Home: 4501 Riverview Ave Middletown OH 45042-2938

REDDING, JANET CAROL, academic administrator; b. Phila., Mar. 23, 1949; d. Arnold Hurxthal and Barbara Jean (Blundin) R.; m. Thomas Monet Richardson, June 27, 1970; children: Ross Monet. BA in Intellectual History, Scripps Coll., 1971; secondary edn. credential, San Jose State U., 1976. Cert. fund raising exec. Fund coord. Menlo Sch. and Coll., Atherton, Calif., 1974-76; substitute tchr. Santa Clara County, Calif., 1976-79; dir. devel. Castilleja Sch., Palo Alto, Calif., 1979-83; cons. No. Calif. Cancer Program, Palo Alto, 1983-85; exec. dir. San Jose State U. Alumni Assn., 1985-88; spl. asst. to the pres. San Jose State U., 1988-91, dir. univ. advancement, 1991-95, v.p. univ. advancement, 1996—; conf. chair Calif. State U. Advancement Conf., Long Beach, 1995. Treas. San Jose Conv. and Visitors Bur., 1994; fin. chair St. John the Divine Episcopal Ch., Morgan Hill, 1995. Mem. Nat. Soc. Fund Raising Execs., Nat. Com. on Planned Giving, Coun. for the Advancement and Support of Edn. (conf. com. dist VII conf. 1996). Home: 15030 Pear Tree Ct San Martin CA 95046 Office: San Jose State Univ One Washington Sq San Jose CA 95192-0256

REDDING-STEWART, DEBORAH LYNN, psychologist; b. Miami, Fla., Feb. 16, 1953; d. Sidney Douglas and Lois May (Tily) R.; m. John Thomas Stewart, Aug. 19, 1978; children: Garrett Lorne, Tyler Douglas, Kelly Lynn. BA in Psychology, San Diego State U., 1975; MA in Psychology, U. Calif., Santa Barbara, 1980. Instr. Allan Hancock Coll., Lompoc, Calif., 1980-86; adminstr., dir. clin. svcs. Mary Lou Stewart Learning Ctr., Lompoc, Calif., 1982—; prin. Pacific Health and Fitness, Lompoc, 1994—; owner Pacific Health and Fitness. Author: The Soft Voice of the Rain, 1993. State Coun. Devel. Disabilities PDF grantee, 1990, Instructional Deve. grantee U. Calif., 1979. Home: 1019 Onstott Rd Lompoc CA 93436-2342

REDENBACH, SANDRA IRENE, educational consultant; b. Boston, Nov. 18, 1940; d. David and Celia (Wish) Goldstein; m. Gunter L. Redenbach, Mar. 16, 1963 (div. 1980); 1 child, Cori-Lin; m. Kenneth L. Gelatt, June 25, 1989. BA, U. Calif., Davis, 1972; MEd in Ednl. Leadership, St. Mary's Coll., Moraga, Calif., 1995. Cert. tchr., Calif. Tchr. Solano County Juvenile Hall, Fairfield, Calif., 1968-70, St. Basil's Sch., Vallejo, Calif., 1970-73, St. Philomenes Sch., Sacramento, 1973; tchr., assoc. dean Vet.'s Spl. Edn. Program, U. Calif., Davis, 1973-75, Woodland (Calif.) Jr. High Sch., 1973-76, Lee Jr. High Sch., Woodland, 1976-79, Woodland High Sch., 1979-87; founder, coord., tchr. Ind. Learning Ctr., Woodland, 1987-94; dir. curriculum and instrn. Dixon (Calif.) Unified Sch. Dist., 1994—; teaching asst., lectr. U. Calif., Davis, 1985-86; pres., cons. Esteem Seminar Programs and Pubs., Davis, 1983—; cons., leader workshop. Author: Self-Esteem: The Necessary Ingredient for Success, 1991; author tng. manual: Self-Esteem: A Training Manual, 1990-91, Innovative Discipline: Managing Your Own Flight Plan, 1994, Autobiography of a Dropout: Dear Diary, 1996. Active Dem. Club of Davis, 1976-79; human rights chair Capitol Svc. Ctr., Sacramento, 1987-92. Martin Luther King scholar, 1986; Nat. Found. for Improvement of Edn. grantee, 1987-88. Mem. Assn. Calif. Sch. Adminstrs., Woodland Edn. Assn. (pres. 1980-83, Outstanding Educator 1992, 93), Phi Delta Kappa (pres. 1992-93). Jewish. Home: 313 Del Oro Ave Davis CA 95616-0416 Office: Esteem Seminar Programs & Publs 313 Del Oro Ave Davis CA 95616-0416

REDFERN, BERNICE IRENE, librarian; b. Rhinebeck, N.Y., Feb. 16, 1947; d. Charles Gordon and Irene Anna (Bogdanffy) R. BA in History, San Francisco State U., 1970; MS in Libr. Sci., U. So. Calif., L.A., 1972; MA in Social Sci., San Jose State U., 1979. Libr. San Jose (Calif.) State U., 1973—; mem. women's studies adv. bd. San Jose State U., 1985—. Compiler: (bibliography) Women of Color in the U.S., 1989. Mem. ALA, Assn. Coll. and Rsch. Librs., Calif. Acad. and Rsch. Librs. Office: San Jose State U 1 Washington Sq San Jose CA 95192

REDGRAVE, LYNN, actress; b. London, Mar. 8, 1943; d. Michael Scudemore and Rachel (Kempson) R.; m. John Clark, Apr. 2, 1967; children: Benjamin, Kelly, Annabel. Ed., Queensgate Sch., London, Central Sch. Speech and Drama, London. Stage debut as Helena in Midsummer Night's Dream, 1962; theatrical appearances include The Tulip Tree, Andorra, Hayfever, Much Ado About Nothing, Mother Courage, Love for Love, Zoo, Zoo, Widdershins Zoo, Edinburgh Festival, 1969, The Two of Us, London, 1970, Slag, London, 1971, A Better Place, Dublin, 1972, Born Yesterday, Greenwich, 1973, Hellzapoppin, N.Y., 1976, California Suite, 1977, Twelfth Night, Stratford Conn. Shakespeare Festival, 1978, The King and I, St. Louis, 1983, Les Liaisons Dangereuses, L.A., 1989, The Cherry Orchard, L.A., 1990, Three Sisters, London, 1990; Broadway appearances include Black Comedy, 1967, My Fat Friend, 1974, Mrs. Warren's Profession (Tony award nomination), 1975, Knock, Knock, 1976, St. Joan, 1977, Sister Mary Ignatius Explains It All, 1985, Aren't We All?, 1985, Sweet Sue, 1987, A Little Hotel on the Side, 1992, The Masterbuilder, 1992, Shakespeare For My Father (Tony and Drama Desk nominations, Elliot award 1993), 1993, also nat. tour, 1993; film appearances include Tom Jones, Girl With Green Eyes, Georgy Girl (Recipient N.Y. Film Critics award, Golden Globe award, Oscar nomination for best actress 1967), The Deadly Affair, Smashing Time, The Virgin Soldiers, Last of the Mobile Hotshots, Don't Turn the Other Cheek, Every Little Crook and Nanny, Everything You Always Wanted to Know About Sex, The National Health, The Happy Hooker, The Big Bus, Sunday Lovers, Morgan Stuart's Coming Home, Getting It Right, Shine, 1996; TV appearances include: The Turn of the Screw, Centennial, 1978, The Muppets, Gauguin the Savage, Beggarman Thief, The Seduction of Miss Leona, Rehearsal for Murder, 1982, Walking On Air, The Fainthearted Feminist (BBC-TV), 1984, My Two Loves, 1986, The Old Reliable, 1988, Jury Duty 1989, Whatever Happened to Baby Jane, 1990, Fighting Back (BBC-TV), 1992, Calling the Shots (Masterpiece Theatre), 1993; guest appearances include Carol Burnett Show, Evening at the Improv and Steve Martin's Best show Ever, Circus of the Stars; co-host nat. TV syndication Not for Women Only, 1977—; nat., TV spokesperson Weightwatchers, 1984-92; TV series include House Calls, 1981, Teachers Only, 1982, Chicken Soup, 1989; albums: Make Mine Manhattan, 1978, Cole Porter Revisited, 1979; video: (for children) Meet Your Animal Friends, Off We Go, Off We Go Again: audio book readings include, Pride and Prejudice, The Shell Seekers, The Blue Bedroom, The Anastasia Syndrome, The Women in His Life, Snow In April, Gone With The Wind, 1994; author: This is Living, 1990. Named Runner-up Actress, All Am. Favorites, Box Office Barometer 1975; recipient Sarah Siddons award as Chgo.'s best stage actress of 1976, 94. Mem. The Players (pres. 1994). Office: care John Clark PO Box 1207 Topanga CA 90290-1207*

REDGRAVE, VANESSA, actress; b. London, Jan. 30, 1937; d. Michael and Rachel (Kempson) R.; m. Tony Richardson, Apr. 28, 1962 (div.); children: Natasha Jane, Joely Kim, Carlo. Student, Central Sch. Speech and Drama, London, 1955-57. Prin. theatrical roles include Helena in Midsummer Night's Dream, 1959, Stella in Tiger and the Horse, 1960, Katerina in The Taming of the Shrew, 1961, Rosalind in As You Like It, 1961, Imogene in Cymbeline, 1962, Nina in The Seagull, 1964, Miss Brodie in The Prime of Miss Jean Brodie, 1966; other plays include Cato Street, 1971, Threepenny Opera, 1972, Twelfth Night, 1972, Antony and Cleopatra, 1973, Design for Living, 1973, Macbeth, 1975, Lady from the Sea, 1976, 78, 79, The Aspern Papers, 1984, The Seagull, 1985, Chekhov's Women, 1985, The Taming of the Shrew, Ghosts, 1986, Touch of the Poet, 1988, Orpheus Descending, 1989, A Madhouse in Goa, 1989, Three Sisters, 1990, When She Danced, 1991, Heartbreak House, 1991, Maybe, 1993, Brecht in Hollywood, 1994, Vita and Virginia, 1994—; film roles include Leonie in Morgan-A Suitable Case for Treatment, 1965 (Best Actress award Cannes Film Festival 1966), Sheila in Sailor from Gibraltar, 1965, Anne-Marie in La Musica, 1965, Jane in Blow-Up, 1967, Guinevere in Camelot, 1967, Isadora in Isadora Duncan, 1968 (Best Actress award Cannes Film Festival); other films include The Charge of the Light Brigade, 1968, The Seagull, 1968, A Quiet Place in the Country, 1968, Daniel Deronda, 1969, Dropout, 1969, The Trojan Women, 1970, The Devils, 1970, The Holiday, 1971, Mary, Queen of Scots, 1971, Murder on the Orient Express, 1974, Winter Rates, 1974, 7 per cent solution, 1975, Julia, 1977 (Academy award Best Supporting Actress, Golden Globe award), Agatha, 1978, Yanks, 1978, Bear Island, 1979, Playing for Time, 1980, My Body My Child, 1981, Wagner, 1982, The Bostonians, 1984 (Oscar nomination Best Actress, Golden Globe nomination), Wetherby, 1985, Steaming, 1985, Prick Up Your Ears, 1987, Comrades, 1987, Consuming Passions, 1988, Diceria dell'Untore, 1989, The Ballad of the Sad Café, 1990, Howard's End, 1992 (Oscar nomination Best Supporting Actress), Great Moments in Aviation, 1993, Crime and Punishment, 1993, The House of the Spirits, 1994, Mother's Boys, 1994, A Month by the Lake, 1995, Little Odessa, 1995; TV film and miniseries appearances include Snow White and the Seven Dwarfs, 1985, Three Sovereigns for Sarah, 1985, Peter the Great, 1986, Second Serve, 1986 (Emmy award, Golden Globe award), A Man for All Seasons, 1988, Young Catherine, 1990, Whatever Happened to Baby Jane, 1990, Playing for Time (Emmy award), The Wall, 1992, Down Came A Blackbird, 1994; Author: Pussies and Tigers, 1964, (autobiography) Vanessa, 1991, Vanessa Redgrave: An Autobiography, 1994. Bd. govs. Central Sch. Speech and Drama, 1963—. Decorated comdr. Order Brit. Empire; recipient 4 times Drama award Evening Standard, 1961-91, Best Actress award Variety Club Gt. Brit., 1961, 66, Best Actress award Brit. Guild TV Producers and Dirs., 1966, Laurence Olivier award Best Actress for The Aspern Papers, 1984, London Standard Drama award Best Actress for The Seagull, 1985, New York Film Critics Circle award Best Supporting Actress for Prick Up Your Ears, 1988, Evening Standard award Best Actress for When She Danced, 1991, Ace award Best Supporting Actress movie/mini-series for Young Catherine, 1992, Variety Club of Great Britain award, 1992, Best Actress Nat. Film Critics (USA) New Delhi Internat. Film Festival for The Bostonians, Laurence Olivier award Actress of the Yr. in a Revival for A Touch of the Poet; fellow Brit. Film Inst., 1988.

RED HAWK, VIRGINIA A. See LYNCH, VIRGINIA ANNE

REDMAN, HELEN CORNELLA, radiologist, educator; b. Newton, Mass., Oct. 17, 1935. MD, Columbia U., 1961. Diplomate Am. Bd. Radiology (trustee). Intern Stanford (Calif.) Med. Ctr., 1961-62, resident in diagnostic radiology, 1962-65; fellow in radiology U. Hosp., Lund, Sweden, 1965-66; prof. radiology Southwestern Med. Sch., Dallas, 1983—; current hosp. appts.; Parkland Meml. Hosp., Dallas, 1983—, Dallas VA Med. Ctr., 1983—, Zale Upshy Hosp., 1991—. Mem. AMA, Am. Coll. Radiologists, Assn. Univ. Radiologists, Radiology Soc. N. Am. (pres. 1994-95), Radiology Technologists Ednl. Fund (chmn. bd. trustees), Tex. Radiology Soc. (pres. 1995); Soc. Cardiovascular and Interventional Radiology. Office: U Tex SW Med Sch 5323 Harry Hines Blvd Dallas TX 75235-7200*

REDRUELLO, ROSA INCHAUSTEGUI, municipal department executive; b. Havana, Cuba, Dec. 6, 1951; came to U.S., 1961, naturalized, 1971; d. Julio Lorenzo and Laudelina (Vazquez) Inchaustegui; m. John Robert Redruello, Dec. 14, 1972; 1 child, Michelle. AA, Miami-Dade Community Coll., 1972; BS, Fla. Internat. U., 1974. Cert. systems profl. With Fla. Power & Light Co., Miami, 1975-81, records analyst, 1981-84, sr. records analyst, 1984-87, office mgr. Miami Beach Sanitation Dept., 1987—; exec. Mcpl. Dept., 1986-89; police officer patrol divsn. Miami Police Dept., 1989-91, narcotics divsn., 1991—; mem. spl. task force Drug Enforcement Adminstrn. HDTA Group 1, 1994-96; cons. United Bus. Records, Miami, 1985—. Editor South Fla. Record newsletter, 1983-86; editor, producer Files Mgmt. video tape, 1984-85. Rotary Club scholar, 1970. Mem. Assn. Records Mgrs. and Adminstrs. (chpt. chmn. bd. 1985—, chpt. mem. of yr. 1985), Assn. for Info. and Image Mgmt., Exec. Female, Nuclear Info. and Records Mgmt. Assn. (Appreciation award 1985). Republican. Roman Catholic. Avocations: swimming, jazzercise, reading. Office: Miami Beach Police Dept 1100 Washington Ave Miami FL 33139-4612

REEB, W. SUZANNE, middle school educator; b. Glascow, Ky., Jan. 14, 1932; d. Arthur Henry and Wilma (Kolb) R. BA, Asbury Coll., 1955; Assoc. BS, Henry Ford C.C., 1960. Tchr. ctrl. elem. sch. grade 2 Fairborn (Ohio) City Schs., 1960 61, tchr. south elem. grade 5, 1961-65; tchr. social studies Lake Wales (Fla.) H.S., Polk County Sch. Bd., 1965-67; tchr. phys. edn. Avon Park (Fla.) Elem. Sch., Highlands County Sch. Bd., 1967-68, tchr. 5th and 6th grades, 1968-71, tchr. 7th and 8th grade Avon Park Mid. Sch., 1971—; basketball coach Avon Park Mid. Sch., 1973-81, nat. jr. honor soc. peer tutor program, 1990-92, nat. geography bee coach, 1992-95, dept. chmn., team chmn., sch. improvement com. chmn., others, 1966—; mem. Polk coun. social studies Polk Edn. Assn., 1964-66. Vol. sch. nurse, 1971-93. Mem. NEA, Nat. Coun. for the Social Studies, Highlands County for the Social Studies, Highlands County Edn. Assn. Home: 2022 Scenic Hwy Babson Park FL 33827

REECE, BETH PAULEY, commodities broker; b. Warsaw, Ind., June 4, 1945; d. Lester Elden and Genevene (Walter) Pifer; m. Gyle Barry Reece, June 20, 1987. BA, Grace Coll., 1967; interior design degree, Harrington Inst. Design, Chgo., 1995. Grain trader, hedger Cen. Soya Inc., Ft. Wayne, Ind., 1973-82; account exec. ACLI Internat. Inc., Chgo., 1982-83; account exec., hedger Cen. States Enterprises, Ft.Wayne, 1983-84; account exec. Stotler & Co., Chgo., 1984-89, LaSalle Brokerage Inc., Chgo., 1989—. Mem. Nat. Futures Assn., Art Inst. of Chgo., Met. Club. Republican. Presbyterian. Home: 227 E Delaware Pl Apt 5C Chicago IL 60611-1713

REECE, KARYN LYNN, independent financial consultant; b. Niagara Falls, N.Y., Apr. 14, 1967; d. George John and Eleanor Roberta (O'Donnell) R. BS in Bus., Empire State Coll., 1996. Lic. stockbroker and fin. cons., N.Y. Stockbroker B.C. Fin., Buffalo, 1989; ins. agt. Mutual of Omaha, Buffalo, 1989-90; fin. cons. Cook Fin. Group, Buffalo, 1990—. Mem. Women Everywhere. Republican.

REECE MYRON, MONIQUE ELIZABETH, marketing, advertising and sales consultant; b. Eldora, Iowa, Jan. 12, 1960; d. Barry Lynne and Vera Marie (Powell) R.; m. Gordon Duane Myron, Mar. 14, 1992; 1 child, Morgan Reece. BSBA, Regis U., 1991. Mgr. regional advt. Silo, Inc., Denver, 1979-86; dir. mktg. LaserLand Corp., U.S.A., Denver, 1986-87; advt. mgr. King Soopers, Denver, 1987-90; supr. brand devel. Garrison-Lontine Advt., Denver, 1991; pres. Monique Myron and Assocs., Denver and La Jolla, Calif., 1991-94, MarketSmarter, Denver and San Diego, 1994—; chmn. bus. partnership com. Colo. Mktg. Tech. Advt. Com., Denver, 1987-91. Mem. publ. rels. com. Make-A-Wish Found., Denver, 1989. Recipient 1st Place Advt. award Nat. Frozen Food Assn., 1988, 89, 90, award Retail Advt. Coun., 1990. Mem. NAFE, Am. Soc. Tng. Devel., Nat. Assn. Women Bus. Owners (bd. dirs.), Nat. Assn. Profl. Saleswomen, Colo. Women's C. of C., Toastmasters, La Jolla C. of C. (bus. profl. com. 1992-93), Denver Met. C. of C. Home and Office: 430 S Garfield St Denver CO 80209-3505

REED, BERENICE ANNE, art historian, artist, government official; b. Memphis, Jan. 1, 1934; d. Glenn Andrew and Berenice Marie (Kallaher) R. BFA, St. Mary-of-the-Woods Coll., Ind., 1955; MFA in Painting and Art History, Istituto Pio XII, Villa Schifanoia, Florence, Italy, 1964. Cert. art tchr., Tenn. Comml. artist Memphis Pub. Co., 1955-56; arts adminstr., educator pub. and pvt. instns., Washington, Memphis, 1957-70; arts adminstr. Nat. Park Svc., 1970-73; mem. staff U.S. Dept. of Energy, Washington, 1973-81, U.S. Dept. Commerce, Washington, 1983-84, Exec. Office of the Pres., Office of Mgmt. and Budget, Washington, 1985; with fin. mgmt. svc. U.S. Treasury Dept., Washington, 1985—; cons. on art and architecture in recreation AIA, 1972-73; artist-in-residence St. Mary-of-the-Woods Coll., Ind., 1965; guest lectr. instr. Nat. Sch. Fine Arts, Tegucigalpa, Honduras, 1968; mem. exec. com. Parks, Arts and Leisure Project, Washington, 1972-73; researcher art projects, Washington, 1981-83. Developer (video) In Your Intere$t, 1992. Bd. dirs. Am. Irish Bicentennial Com., 1974-76; advisor Royal Oak Found. Recipient various awards for painting. Mem. Soc. Woman Geographers, Nat. Soc. Arts and Letters, Ctr. for Advanced Study in Visual Arts, Art Barn Assn. (bd. dirs. 1973-83). Roman Catholic. Home: PO Box 34253 Bethesda MD 20827-0253 Office: Dept Treasury Fin Mgmt Svc 401 14th St SW Washington DC 20227-0001

REED, CAROL LOUISE, designer; b. Pontiac, Ill., Apr. 16, 1938; d. Rollin Kenneth and Lucille Hortence (Myer) Snethen; m. Richard Willis Reed, Feb. 13, 1960; children: Rena Louise Davis, Ronda Lee Howle. BBA in Mktg. and Advt., Tex. Tech. U., 1959. Office mgr. Sappington Devel., Inc., Rociada, N.Mex., 1990-91; owner Designs by Carol, Rociada, 1988—. Elected state officer Tierra y Montes Soil and Water Conservation Dist., Las Vegas, 1990—; mem. Mora-San Miguel Water Planning Bd., 1991-94; treas. 1st Meth. Ch., Las Vegas, 1989-90; sec. Calvary Bapt. Ch., Las Vegas, 1991-92; treas. 1st Bapt. Ch., 1996. Recipient award of merit Goodyear Tire and Rubber Co., 1991; named Outstanding Supr. of Tierra y Montes Soil and Conservation Dist., 1992, 94, 95. Mem. N.Mex. Assn. Soil and Water Conservation Dists. (chair region IV 1994—), Phi Kappa Phi. Republican. Home and Office: PO Box 853 Rociada NM 87742-0853

REED, CONSTANCE LOUISE, materials management and purchasing consultant; b. Point Pleasant, W.Va.; d. John Melvin Supple and Garnet L. Tooley; m. James Wesley Reed Jr., Sept. 20, 1985. Student, Ohio State U., 1974-76, Capital U., 1984-85. Buyer Abex Corp., Columbus, Ohio, 1971-79; maj. component buyer Grumman Corp., Delaware, Ohio, 1979-81; purchasing mgr. Atlantic Richfield (ANATEC), Dublin, Ohio, 1981-85; purchasing agt. Columbus Lodging, Inc., 1986-87, Monitronix Corp., Westerville, Ohio, 1988-89; contracts adminstr. Cellular Communications Inc., Worthington, Ohio, 1989-90; dir. materials mgmt. Fibrebond Corp., Minden, La., 1991-92; v.p. C&P Mgmt. Cons., Powell, Ohio, 1985—. Mem. NAFE, Am. Mgmt. Assn., Nat. Assn. Purchasing Mgmt., Bus. and Profl. Women's Club. Republican. Roman Catholic. Home: 1166 Highland Dr Columbus OH 43220-4940 Office: C&P Mgmt PO Box 158 Powell OH 43065-0158

REED, CYNTHIA KAY, minister; b. Amarillo, Tex., July 10, 1952; d. Carlos Eugene and Marjorie Marie (Daughetee) R. B of Music Edn., McMurry Coll., Abilene, Tex., 1976; MDiv, Perkins Sch. Theol., Dallas, 1991. Ordained to ministry Meth. Ch., 1989; cert. dir. music. Dir. music and Christian edn. Oakwood United Meth. Ch., Lubbock, Tex., 1978-84; dir. music and Christian edn. 1st United Meth. Ch., Childress, Tex., 1976-78, Littlefield, Tex., 1984-86; intern min. 1st United Meth. Ch., Lubbock, 1989-90, assoc. min., 1990-91; min. Meadow and Ropesville United Meth. Chs., 1991-93, Earth (Tex.) United Meth. Ch., 1993—; extern chaplain Meth. Hosp., Lubbock, 1989—, Walk to Emmaus Renewal Movement, Lubbock, 1990—. Com. mem. Life Gift-Organ Donation, Lubbock, 1991; mem. Arthritis Found., Lubbock, 1991. Georgia Harkness scholar Div. Ordained Ministry, 1989. Mem. Christian Educators & Musicians Fellowship, Am. Guild Organists.

REED, DIANE GRAY, business information service company executive; b. Trion, Ga., Sept. 5, 1945; d. Harold and Frances (Parker) Gray; m. Harry Reed, Oct. 2, 1982. Student, Jacksonville U., 1963-64, Augusta Coll., 1972-74; BS, Ga. State U., 1981. Various mgmt. positions Equifax Svcs., Inc., Atlanta, 1964-72, field rep., 1972-74, tech. rep., 1974-79, mgr. systems and programs, 1979-84, dir. tech., 1984-86, asst. v.p., 1986—; v.p. info. tech. sector Equifax Svcs., Inc., 1989—; presdl. adv. council Equifax Svcs., Inc., Atlanta, 1984—; cons. Ga. Computer Programmer Project, Atlanta, 1984-86, spkr. Oglethorpe U. Career Workshop, Atlanta, 1986. Bd. dirs. Atlanta Mental Health Assn., 1985-89; bd dirs., pres. Atlanta Women's Network, 1990; bd. dirs. United Way Bd. Bank, Atlanta, 1984-86; chairperson EquiFax United Way Campaign, 1988-89; vol. Cobb County Spl. Olympics, Marietta, Ga., 1984-87; mem. adv. coun. Coll. Bus. Adminstrn. Ga. State U. mgmt. info. systems industry adv. bd. U. Ga.; mem. Leadership Atlanta Class of '92, Girl Scouts Friendship Circle, Friends of Spelman Coll.; vol. coord. Atlanta Partnership Bus. and Edn.; co-chair salute to women of achievement YWCA, 1992; mem. Leadership Am. Class 1994; tech. steering com. 1996 Olympic Games. Named Woman of Achievement, Atlanta YWCA, 1987; recipient Decca award as one of top 10 bus. women in Atlanta, 1992; named to Leadership Am. Class 1994. Mem. Women in Info. Processing, Inst. Computer Profls. (cert.), Soc. Info. Mgmt., Internat. Women's Alliance, Ga. State Alumni, LWV, Atlanta Yacht Club, Kiwanis Internat. (bd. dirs. Atlanta Buckhead chpt.). Office: Equifax Svcs Inc 1600 Peachtree St NW Atlanta GA 30309-2403

REED, DIANE MARIE, psychologist; b. Joplin, Mo., Jan. 11, 1934; d. William Marion and Olive Francis (Smith) Kinney; married; children: Wendy Robison, Douglas Funkhouser. Student, Art Ctr. Col., L.A., 1951-54; BS, U. Oreg., 1976, MS, 1977, PhD, 1981. Lic. psychologist. Illustrator J.L. Hudson Co., Detroit, 1954-56; designer, stylist N.Y.C., 1960-70; designer, owner Decor To You, Inc., Stamford, Conn., 1970-76; founder, exec. dir. Alcohol Counseling and Edn. Svcs., Inc., Eugene, Oreg., 1981-86, clin. supr., 1986; clin. supr. Christian Family Svcs., Eugene, 1986-87; pvt. practice Eugene, 1985-94; founder Reed Consulting, Bend, Oreg., 1995—. Evaluator Vocat. Rehab. Div., Eugene, 1982—; alcohol and drug evaluator and commitment examiner Oreg. Mental Health Div., 1981-86; life mem. Rep. Presdle. Task Force. Mem. APA, Oreg. Psychol. Assn., Lane County Psychol. Assn. (pres. 1989-90), Network of Entrepreneurial Women, Bend C. of C., Sunriver Area C. of C., Rotary Internat.

REED, ELIZABETH MAY MILLARD, mathematics and computer science educator, publisher; b. Shippensburg, Pa., July 1, 1919; d. Jacob Franklin and Isabelle Bernadine (Dorn) Millard; m. Jesse Floyd Reed, Aug. 5, 1961; 1 child, David Millard. BA, Shepherd Coll., 1941; MA, Columbia U., 1948; postgrad., W.Va. U., U. Hawaii, Columbia U., NSF Summer Insts., Oakland U., 1974-85. Cert. assoc. in tchr. edn., W.Va. Math. tchr. Hedgesville (W.Va.) High Sch., 1941-47, Martinsburg (W.Va.) High Sch., 1948-51, George Washington High Sch. and Territorial Coll. Guam, Agana, 1952-54, Valley Stream (N.Y.) Meml. Jr. High Sch., 1954-55, Rye (N.Y.) High Sch., 1955-57, Elkins (W.Va.) Jr. High Sch., 1971-87; dir. admissions Davis and Elkins Coll., 1957-67, asst. prof. math., 1968-71, adj. prof., 1987—, lectr. geography, 1971-73; pres. Three Reeds Studios, Elkins, 1989—; Vets. Upward Bound, 1989-94; statis. clk. Lord, Abbett & Co., N.Y.C., 1947-48; customer rep. Kay, Richards & Co., Winchester, Va., 1951-52; mem. adj. grad. faculty W.Va. U., Morgantown, 1984-89; mem. adj. faculty Evans Coll. U. Charleston, W.Va., 1989-90; presenter regional and state computer workshops, W.Va. Author: Computer Literacy at Elkins Junior High School, 1983; project dir. (video) Women: Professionally Speaking, 1988. Dir. pilot project Project Bus., Jr. Achievement, Elkins, 1972-78; organizer Randolph County Math. Field Day, Elkins, 1977; initiator Comprehensive Achievement Monitoring, Elkins, 1980; treas. Humanities Found. W.Va., Charleston, 1983-85, pres., 1985-87; vice-moderator quadrant II Presbytery of W.Va. Recipient Presdl. award for Excellence in Tchg. Math. in W.Va., NSF, 1985. Mem. AAUW (pres. W.Va. divsn. 1977-79, editor 1983—, pres. Elkins br. 1966-68, 1988-94), W. Va. Coun. Tchrs. of Math., Nat. Coun. Tchrs. of Math., W. Va. Item Writing Workshop-Math. 9-12 (writer 1985-86). Home & Office: 4 Lincoln Ave Elkins WV 26241-3669

REED, EVA SILVER STAR, chieftain; b. Vinita, Okla., Nov. 29, 1929; d. Robert Elbert Jones and Anna Mae (Campfield) Reed; m. Johnnie Silver Eagle Reed, June 10, 1946 (dec. Sept. 1982); children: Patty Deeanne, Lorrie Ann, Billy John. Sec. United Lumbee Nation of N.C. and Am., Fall River Mills, Calif., 1979-82; nat. head chieftain United Lumbee Nation of N.C. and Am., Fall River Mills, 1982—, also bd. dirs.; bd. dirs., sec. Chapel of Our Lord Jesus, Exeter, Calif., 1974—, Native Am. Wolf Clan, Calif., 1977—; tchr. Indian beading and crafts, Calif., 1977—. Author, compiler: Over the Cooking Fires, 1982, Lumbee Indian Ceremonies, 1982, United Lumbee Deer Clan Cook Book, 1988; editor: (newspaper) United Lumbee Nation Times, 1981—. Mem. parent com. Title IV & Johnson O'Malley Indian Edn. Program, Tulare/Kings County, 1976-80, Shasta County, Calif., 1982-84. Recipient United Lumbee Nation of N.C. and Am.'s Silver Eagle award, 1991, also various awards for beadwork Intermountain Fair, Shasta County, 1982-96. Office: United Lumbee Nation of NC & Am PO Box 512 Fall River Mills CA 96028

REED, KATHRYN E., artist, photographer; b. Warner Robins, Ga., July 16, 1964; d. John W. and Sally (Gillespie) R.; m. Boaz Sharon, Dec. 28, 1991; 1 child, Ethan Sidney. AB, Brown U., Providence, R.I., 1986; MFA, U. Fla., Gainesville, 1992. Workshop instr. Maine Photo Workshop, Rockport, 1993; vis. artist Albion (Mich.) Coll., 1995; asst. to Jerry Uelsmann, Gainesville, 1991-95; adj. asst. prof. U. Fla., Gainesville, 1995; curator Pixels to Paper Show, Ctr. for Creative Imaging, Camden, Maine, 1994; panel moderator Macworld Expo, Boston, 1994. Artist: solo exhbns. include Catholic U. Am., 1993, Steinway Hall, N.Y.C., 1993, Nat. Mus., Prague, Czech Rep., 1995, Tel Hai Mus. Photography, Israel, 1996. Recipient Juror's award Magic Silver Show Murray State U., Murray, Ky,

1992. Mem. Coll. Art Assn., 1993—. Home: 2135 NW 9th Ave Gainesville FL 32603

REED, NANCY BINNS, composer, poet, artist; b. Palo Alto, Calif., Dec. 11, 1924; d. Clyde Arthur and Mary Ella (Loder) Binns; m. Ogden Cartwright Reed, Jan. 17, 1948 (dec. Feb. 1980); children: Hayward C., Cartwright, Chris B., Amy Reed Geiger. BA, U. Calif., Davis and Berkeley, 1945; postgrad. in social work, U. Calif., Berkeley, 1946-47; AA in Fine Arts, No. Va. C.C., 1990. Composer, poet, artist, 1941—; social worker in Calif., Washington, 1947-50; tchr. art, music and poetry at Mildred Green Elem. Sch., Anacostia, Washington, 1981—. Composer: (songs) Oh Happy Day, 1952 (Nat. hit, three different recordings simultaneously on Hit Parade), Our Lions (march), 1971, Civilian March, 1974 (performed ann. at Pentagon Civilian award ceremonies), Tocqueville! (musical), 1976, Ali Baba, 1977, The Halloween Suite, 1978, The Duckling, 1981, Royalty Revisited, 1986, Frank Rowley's Rally, 1991, American Patchwork: The Star, The Eagle, The Parade, The Ring and The Rose, 1987, Vive Leche!, 1992, Dragon Divertimento, 1992, Concert Christmas Music, 1992, (opera) David, David Jesse's Son, 1993, others; author, illustrator: The Magic Gourds, 1969, The Sun and the Moon, 1969, A Tale of the Heidelberg Lion, 1974, Le Conte Du Lion De Heidelberg, 1983; music recorded by London Philharmonia Winds, 1984. Mem. ASCAP (recipient 18 awards for compositions, 1977-96).

REED, NANCY BOYD, English language and elementary education educator; b. Lodi, Calif., Oct. 10, 1946; d. Leo H. and Anna Gwen (Coombes) Boyd; m. Maurice Allen Reed, Dec. 22, 1966; 1 child, Scot Alastair. AA Recreational Adminstrn. with honors, Delta Coll., 1974; BA Recreational Adminstrn. with honors, Calif. State U., Sacramento, 1976, MA in Edn., English Lang. Devel., 1988; cert. computers in edn., U. Calif., Davis, 1984. Cert. multiple subject, phys. edn., computers in edn. teaching. Tchr. 4th grade Hagginwood Sch., Sacramento, 1980-81; tchr. 4th/5th grade impacted lang. Noralto Sch., Sacramento, 1981-88, bilingual resource tchr., 1988-91, tchr. English lang. devel., 1991-94, bilingual resource tchr., 1996—; mentor tchr. North Sacramento Sch. Dist., Sacramento, 1992-95, bilingual resource tchr., 1996—; fellow, tchr./cons. No. Calif. Math. Project, U. Calif., Davis, 1985—. Dir. Jasmine Flower Dancers, Sacramento, 1984—; comty. rep. Am. Host Found., Sacramento, 1976—. Named Outstanding Educator Capitol Svc. Ctr., 1992, Tchr. of Yr., Noralto Sch., North Sacramento Sch., 1996; scholar Fridtjof-Nansen-Akademie, Ingleheim, Germany, 1993, Adenauer Found., Berlin, 1982, 93. Mem. NEA, Nat. Vis. Tchrs. Assn. (bd. dirs. 1994—), Nat. Assn. Bilingual Edn., Nat. Coun. Tchrs. Math., Calif. Tchrs. Assn. (state coun. rep. 1995—), North Sacramento Edn. Assn. (sec. 1986-88, v.p. 1988-90, pres. 1990-92, outstanding educator 1992). Home: PO Box 246 Thornton CA 95686-0246 Office: Noralto Sch North Sacramento Sch Dist 477 Las Palmas Ave Sacramento CA 95815-3023

REED, NANCY ELLEN, educator; b. Mpls., Aug. 11, 1955; d. Jacob Alen and Mary Emeline (Howser) Lundgren; m. Todd Randall Reed, June 18, 1977. BS in Biology, U. Minn., 1977, MS in Computer Sci., 1988, PhD in Computer Sci., 1995. Rsch. lab. technician gastroenterology rsch. unit Mayo Clinic, Rochester, Minn., 1978-81; pys. sci. technician U.S. Environ. Hygiene Agy., Fitzsimmons Army Med. Ctr., Aurora, Colo., 1982-83; profl. rsch. asst. molecular, cellular, devel. biology dept. U. Colo., Boulder, 1983-84; teaching asst. U. Minn., 1985-86, rsch. asst., 1985-88; computer programmer Control Data Corp., Arden Hills, Minn., 1986; asst. Artificial Intelligence Lab. Swiss Fed. Inst. Tech., Lausanne, 1989-91; lectr. computer and info. sci. dept. Sonoma State U., Rohnert Park, Calif., 1993-94; lectr., rschr. computer sci. dept. U. Calif., Davis, 1994-96, asst. adj. prof. computer sci. dept., 1996—. Contbr. articles to profl. jours.; speaker in field. Am. Electronics Assn. Fellowship, 1985-89, Microelectronic and Info. Scis. Fellowship, 1984-85. Mem. IEEE, Am. Assn. for Artificial Intelligence (scholarship for travel nat. conf. on artificial intelligence 1992, 94), Assn. for Computing Machinery. Office: U Calif Computer Sci Dept Davis CA 95616-8562

REED, PAMELA, actress; b. Tacoma, Wash., Apr. 2, 1949; d. Vernie Reed; m. Sandy Smolar. BA in Drama, U. Wash. Prin. stage roles include Getting Through the Night, Ensemble Studio Theatre, N.Y.C., 1976, Curse of the Starving Class, N.Y. Shakespeare Festival, Pub. Theatre, 1978, The November People (Broadway debut), Billy Rose Theatre, 1978, All's Well That Ends Well, N.Y. Shakespeare Festival, Delacorte Theatre, 1978, Getting Out, Phoenix Theatre, Marymount Manhattan Theatre, N.Y.C., 1978, Seduced, Am. Place Theatre, N.Y.C., 1979, Sorrows of Stephen, N.Y. Shakespeare Festival, Pub. Theatre, 1979, Fools, Eugene O'Neill Theatre, N.Y.C., 1981, Criminal Minds, Theatre Guinevere, N.Y.C., 1984, Fen, N.Y. Shakespeare Festival, Pub. Theatre, 1984, Aunt Dan and Lemon, N.Y. Shakespeare Festival, Pub. Theatre, 1985, Mrs. Warren's Profession, Roundabout Theatre, N.Y.C., 1985, Haft Theatre, 1986; film appearances include The Long Riders, 1980, Melvin and Howard, 1980, Eyewitness, 1981, Young Doctors in Love, 1982, The Right Stuff, 1983, The Goodbye People, 1984, The Best of Times, 1986, The Clan of the Cave Bear, 1986, Rachel River, 1989, Chattahoochee, 1990, Cadillac Man, 1990, Kindergarten Cop, 1990, Passed Away, 1992, Junior, 1994; TV series appearances include The Andros Targets, 1977, Tanner, 1988, The Dark Horse (HBO), 1988, Grand, 1990, The Home Court, 1995—; TV films include Inmates: A Love Story, 1981, I Want to Live, 1983, Heart of Steel, 1983, Scandal Sheet, 1985, Born Too Soon, 1993, Mary Hemingway miniseries, 1988, Caroline? (Hallmark Hall of Fame), 1989. Office: ICM 8942 Wilshire Blvd Beverly Hills CA 90211-1934*

REED, PATSY BOSTICK, university administrator, nutrition educator; b. Holland, Tex., Dec. 1, 1936; d. William T. and Evelyn R. (Smith) Bostick; m. F. Dewitt Reed, Sept. 6, 1958. BS, U. Tex., 1959, MS, 1967, PhD, 1969. Tchr. pub. schs., Austin and Port Arthur, Tex., 1959-65; postdoctoral fellow U. Va., Charlottesville, 1969-70; research chemist U. Heidelberg, W.Ger., 1970-72; assoc. prof. nutrition Idaho State U., Pocatello, 1973-79; prof. nutrition, adminstr. No. Ariz. U., Flagstaff, 1979-94, dean Coll. Design and Tech., 1981-85; asst. v.p. acad. affairs U. N.C., Asheville, 1985-87, v.p. acad. affairs, 1987-94, chancellor, 1994—. Author: Nutrition: An Applied Science, 1980. Mem. AAAS, Am. Chem. Soc., Am. Dietetic Assn., Phi Kappa Phi, Sigma Xi. Office: U NC 1 University Hts Asheville NC 28804-3229

REED, PAULA ELAINE, realtor; b. Muncie, Ind., May 10, 1952; d. Kenneth Paul and Barbara Lucile (Wiesenauer) Tweedy; m. Richard Allan Reed, Oct. 7, 1978; children: Ryan Kenneth, Stephanie Kathryn. Student, Brigham Young U., 1975. Cert. residential specialist; grad. sr. appraiser; grad. Realtors' Inst. Social worker Delaware County Welfare Dept., Muncie, Ind., 1975-79; exec. asst. Social Sci. Cons., New Orleans, 1979-81; social worker Clinton County Childrens Svcs., Wilmington, Ohio, 1980-81; realtor Century 21 Lucien & Assocs., Rocky River, Ohio, 1983—; mem. designations com. Cleve. Area Bd. Realtors, 1993-94; trustee Harold R. Karreich Scholarship Found., Cleve., 1995—. Mem. citizens' adv. com. to Lakewood (Ohio) Bd. Edn. Exec. Com., 1995-96; del. Emerson Middle Sch. PTA, 1995; mem.-at-large Lakewood PTA Coun., 1995-96; mem., membership chair Jr. Bd. Lakewood Hist. Soc., 1995—. Recipient Pres.'s Club award Ohio Assn. Realtors, 1990-95, Sales Achievement award Cleve. Area Bd. Realtors, 1990-95, Century 21 Quality Svc. award, 1993-95. Office: Century 21 Lucien & Assocs 20680 Center Ridge Rocky River OH 44116

REED, SUE ELLEN, secondary education educator; b. South Hampton, N.Y., Oct. 23, 1954; d. Richard C.D. and Virginia Mae (McNair) Peper; m. Rickey D. Reed, June 29, 1974; children: Jonathan C., Stephen Nathanael. AA, Fla. Keys C.C., Key West, Fla., 1974; BA in Edn., Fla. Atlantic U., 1978; MS, Nova S.E. U., 1991. Cert. tchr. English, social studies, middle sch., Fla. Bookkeepper Zales Jewelers, Key West, Deerfield Beach, Fla., 1973-76; tchr. Moore Haven (Fla.) H.S., 1978-79; tchr. Bell (Fla.) Middle H.S., 1979—, tech. trainer, 1993—; state com. mem. Am. Fedn. Tchrs.-Ednl. R&D Team, 1988; vis. team mem. So. Assn. Colls. Schs., Middleburg, Fla., 1992; state com. chaiperson Fla. Bapt. Conv.-Bapt. Young Women Com., 1992-93. Exec. mem. Glades County Dem. Exec. Com., Moore Haven, Fla., 1977; mem. stewarship com., Women's Missionary Union leader Bethel Bapt. Ch., 1992—. Home: PO Box 186 Bell FL 32619-0186 Office: Trenton HS PO Box 7 Trenton FL 32693-0007

REED, VANESSA REGINA, secondary education educator; b. Grenada, Miss., Oct. 4, 1965; d. Willie Mann and Elma Lee (Finley) R. BS in Social Sci. Edn., Miss. Valley State U., 1987; MA in History, Jackson State U., 1988; postgrad., Miss. State U., Meridian, 1991, 92. Cert. tchr. social sci. History tchr. Jackson (Miss.) State U., 1987-88; social studies tchr. Magnolia Mid. Sch., Meridian, 1988-93; U.S. history tchr. Kate Griffin Jr. H.S., Meridian, 1993—. Sunday sch. tchr., dir. children's ch. Mt. Olive Bapt. Ch.; mem. Heroines of Jericho. Mem. Am. Fedn. Tchrs., Sigma Gamma Rho. Democrat. Office: Kate Griffin Jr HS 2814 Davis St Meridian MS 39301-5655

REED, VASTINA KATHRYN (TINA REED), child psychotherapist; b. Chgo., Mar. 5, 1960; d. Alvin Hillard and Ruth Gwendolyn (Thomas) R.; 1 child, Alvin J. BA in Human Svcs. magna cum laude, Nat.-Louis U., Chgo., 1988; MA, Ill. Sch. Profl. Psychology, 1991. Tchr. early childhood edn. Kendall Coll. Lab. Sch., Evanston, Ill., 1983-85, Rogers Park Children's Learning Ctr., Chgo., 1983-85; child life therapist Mt. Sinai Hosp., Chgo., 1988; child psychotherapist Nicholas Barnes Therapeutic Day Sch., Chgo., 1989-90. Den leader Boy Scouts Am., Chgo., 1989-92, scoutmaster troop 267, 1992—. Recipient Cub Scouter award Boy Scouts Am., 1990, Scoutmaster award of merit, 1993, 94, Scouters Vet. award, 1994, Scouters Tng. award, 1995, Scoutmasters Key award, 1996, Okpik Cold Weather Camping cert., 1994-95. Mem. APA, Nat. Orgn. for Human Svc. Edn., Order of the Arrow, Ea. Stars, Phi Theta Kappa, Kappa Delta Pi. Democrat. Roman Catholic. Home: 1872 S Millard Ave Chicago IL 60623-2542

REEDER, BETTY MCKENZIE, corporate executive, consultant; b. Balt., Feb. 26, 1939; d. George William and Margaret (Knox) McKenzie; m. Dexter Lee Reeder, June 18, 1961; children: Grant McKenzie, Tracy Elizabeth. BA, San Jose State U., 1960. Cert. tchr., 1960. Tchr. Saragota (Calif.) Schs., 1960-64; pres. Pioneer Underground, San Jose, Calif., 1979—; co-owner Pioneer Livestock, San Jose, 1989—; v.p. Zonta Sch., 1965-79; co-owner Rebedex Kennels, San Jose, 1968-79. Contbr. articles to profl. jours. Mem. Eastfield Jr. League, Gilroy (Calif.) Found., 1973-85; assoc. mem. Gilroy Assistance League, 1985—; active Sparatan Found. San Jose U., 1985—. Mem. Monterey Bay Panhellenic (treas. 1992-94), Women in Touch, Chi Omega (Ada Tallman award 1994, corp. bd. treas.), Iota Delta (advisor, Diamond Badge award). Republican. Home: 9030 El Matador Dr Gilroy CA 95020 Office: Pioneer Undeground Inc San Jose CA 95020

REEDY, CATHERINE IRENE, science and health educator, library/media specialist; b. Suffolk County, N.Y., Dec. 27, 1953; d. Edward and Catherine (Spindler) Grafenstein. AA, Suffolk C.C., Selden, N.Y., 1980; BA in Social Sci., summa cum laude, Dowling Coll., Oakdale, N.Y., 1983, MS in Edn., 1986. Media specialist, tchr. coord. for sci. and health St. Ignatius Sch., Hicksville, N.Y., 1983—, dir. sci. lab. and media ctr. Contbr. poetry to Beyond the Stars, 1996, Walk Through Paradise, 1995, Best Poems of 1996. Recipient Editor's Choice award Nat. Soc. Poetry, 1995, Nat. Lib. Poetry, 1995. Mem. ASCD, AAUW, N.Y. Acad. Scis., N.Y. Sci. Tchrs. Assn., Nat. Assn. Univ. Women, Nat. Poet Soc., Internat. Soc. Poets, Alpha Zeta Nu (1st sec.), Phi Theta Kappa, Phi Alpha Sigma, Kappa Delta Pi (pres. Xi Chi chpt. 1985-87). Home: 15 Nikia Dr Islip NY 11751-2630 Office: St Ignatius Sch 30 E Cherry St Hicksville NY 11801-4302

REEDY, SUSAN, painter; b. Buffalo, N.Y., June 1, 1956; d. John Oliver and Joan Carol (Kummer) Spragge; m. Charles Joseph Reedy, Aug. 20, 1982; 1 child, Erin. BFA, Daemen Coll., 1978; MFA, SUNY, Buffalo, 1981. Gallery dir. Niagara County Cmty. Coll., Sanborn, N.Y., 1984-88, instr., 1983-87; asst. prof. Daemen Coll., Amherst, 1992—. One woman show at Castellani Art Mus., Niagara Falls, 1993; exhibited in group exhibitions at Meml. Art Gallery, Rochester, N.Y., 1995, 96, Goldman-Greenfield Gallery, Amherst, N.Y., 1995, Albright-Knox Art Gallery, Buffalo, N.Y., 1993, 94, Butler Inst. of Am. Art, Youngstown, Ohio, 1990, 92, O.K. Harris Gallery, N.Y.C., 1988; permanent collections include Meml. Art Gallery, Castellani Art Mus., Std. Fed. Bank Hdqrs., Rich Products Corp., Hospice Found. of Western N.Y., Mobil Oil Corp. Recipient Dr. J. Warren Penny award Art Dialogue Gallery, 1995, Dirs. Choice award Meml. Art Gallery, 1995, Mfrs. and Traders Trust Co. award Albright Knox Art Gallery, 1980, Dorothy Cripps Salo Meml. award Meml. Art Gallery, 1996.

REEMELIN, ANGELA NORVILLE, dietitian consultant; b. Pitts., Apr. 28, 1945; d. Richard Gerow and Kathleen Taylor (Brannen) Norville; m. Philip Barrows Reemelin, Nov. 17, 1973; children: Richard Barrows, Kathleen Easson. BS, U. Tenn., 1967; dietetic intern, Emory U., 1968. Cert. water safety instr. Adminstr. dietitian Servomation of Atlanta, 1968-70; food svc. dir. ARA Food Svcs., Norfolk, Va., 1970-80; cons. Jacksonville, Fla., 1980—; cons. William T. Hall Convalescent Home, Portsmouth, Va., 1975-79. Recipient Outstanding Young Dietitian award Tidewater Dietetic Assn., 1974; Best of Show in sewing FFWC State Arts Festival, 1985, 86, 87. Mem. ARC (30 yr. Vol. award), ADA, Am. Soc. Hosp. Food Svc. Adminstrs., Jr. Womans Club Orange Park (pres. 1986-87, v.p., fundraiser, membership chair, Outstanding Dist. Pres. 1987), U. Tenn. Alumni Assn. (pres. 1982-84, bd. govs. 1984-85), Omicron Nu. Roman Catholic. Home: 601 Lorn Ct Orange Park FL 32073-4228

REENS, DENISE JUNG, educational association executive; b. Evanston, Ill., Nov. 12, 1947; d. John Peter and Dorothy Rose (May) Jung; m. Steven David Reens, June 6, 1970; children: Jon Robert, Jeffrey Thomas. BS in Edn., No. Ill. U., 1969. Tchr. elem. sch. St. Norbert, Northbrook, Ill., 1969-70, Dist. 150, South Holland, Ill., 1970-73; part-time promotions staff Southlake Mall, Merrillville, Ind., 1979-89; part-time reading specialist pub. schs., Porter Township, Ind., 1986-89; instr. adult edn. Hammond, Ind., 1990-93; meeting planner Alpha Phi, Evanston, Ill., 1989-93; assoc. exec. dir. Alpha Phi Internat., Evanston, Ill., 1993—; instr. Purdue U. Coop. Ext., Hammond, 1991-94. Mem. Am. Soc. Assn. Execs. Home: 2147 Greenvalley Dr Crown Point IN 46307 Office: Alpha Phi Internat 1930 Sherman Evanston IL 60201

REES, NORMA S., academic administrator; b. N.Y.C., Dec. 27, 1929; d. Benjamin and Lottie (Schwartz) D.; m. Raymond R. Rees, Mar. 19, 1960; children—Evan Lloyd, Raymond Arthur. B.A., Queens Coll., 1952; M.A., Bklyn. Coll., 1954; Ph.D., NYU, 1959. Cert. speech-language pathology, audiology. Prof. communicative disorders Hunter Coll., N.Y.C., 1967-72; exec. officer, speech and hearing scis. grad. sch. CUNY, N.Y.C., 1972-74, assoc. dean for grad. studies, 1974-76, dean grad. studies, 1976-82; vice chancellor for acad. affairs U. Wis., Milw., 1982-85, from 1986, acting chancellor, 1985-86; vice chancellor for acad. policy and planning Mass. Bd. Regent for Higher Edn., Boston, 1987-90; pres. Calif. State U., Hayward, 1990—; bd. dirs. Am. Assn. State Colls. and Univs., 1995—, Coun. of Postsecondary Accreditation, Washington, 1985-94; chmn. Commn. Recognition of Postsecondary Accreditation, 1994—. Contbr. articles to profl. jours. Trustee Citizens Govtl. Rsch. Bur., Milw., 1985-87; active Task Force on Wis. World Trade Ctr., 1985-87; bd. dirs. Greater Boston YWCA, 1987-90; mem. Mayor's Cabinet Ednl. Excellence, Oakland, Calif.; mem. steering com. Econ. Devel. Adv. Bd. Alameda County, 1995—. Fellow Am. Speech-Lang-Hearing Assn. (honors); mem. Am. Coun. Edn. (com. internat. edn. 1991-93), Am. Assn. Colls. and Univs. (chair task force on quality assessment 1991-92, mem. steering com. of coun. of urban met. colls. & univs. 1992—), Nat. Assn. State Univs. and Land Grant Colls. (exec. com. divsn. urban affairs 1985-87, com. accreditation 1987-90). Office: Calif State Univ-Hayward 25800 Carlos Bee Blvd Hayward CA 94542-3000

REES, PATRICIA GLINES, occupational health nurse, consultant, educator; b. Santa Maria, Calif., Aug. 28, 1945; d. Jack Holloway and Frances Ruth (Baril) Glines; m. Nov. 28, 1970 (div. July 1989); children: Eric Michael, Jennifer Lynne. BSN with honors, U. Calif., San Francisco, 1968; MSN, Clarkson Coll., Omaha, 1994. RN, Nebr., Calif.; cert. occupational health nurse; cert. BLS, CPR, first aid instr., hearing conservationist. Staff nurse Marin Gen. Hosp., Marin County, Calif., 1968-70; sch. health nurse Novato (Calif.) Unified Sch. Dist., 1968-70; obstetrics office nurse Oxon Hill, Md., 1971-72; vol. sch. health svcs. Sullivan Sch., Yokosuka, Japan, 1976-80; sch. health nurse, client svcs. rep. Vis. Nurse Assn., Omaha, 1987-89; occupational health nurse Armour Swift-Eckrich, Omaha, 1989-91; program mgr. Advantage Health Sys., Inc., Kansas City, Mo., 1991—; preceptor U. Nebr. Med. Ctr., Omaha, 1994-95; vol./instr. ARC, Omaha, 1989-96; presenter in field. Co-author: Cumulative Trauma Disorders, 1991, Case Management, 1994, Work Injury Management, 1996; contbr. articles to profl. jours. Mem. Nebr. Safety Coun., Omaha, 1989-91, U.S. Swimming, Omaha, 1981-89. Pres.'s scholar U. Calif., San Francisco, 1967-68. Mem. APHA, Am. Assn. Occupational Health Nurses, Nebr. Assn. Occupational Health Nurses (edn. com. 1995—), Clarkson Honor Soc. (pres. 1994-96), Sigma Theta Tau, Alpha Xi Delta. Home: 1311 Beechwood Ave Papillion NE 68133-2509

REES, TONI HEATHER, special education educator; b. Newquay, Cornwall, Eng., Feb. 24, 1946; d. Cecil and Daphne (Sollis) R. K-8 tchg. cert., Norwich Coll. of Edn., Eng., 1967; diploma deaf edn., Lady Spencer Churchill Coll., 1971; MA in Edn., Southampton U., 1977; PhD, Gallaudet U., 1983. Cert. tchr. of deaf children; cert. spl. edn. cons., Maine. H.s. tchr. V.S.O., Kenya, 1967-69; elem. sch. tchr. Longwill Sch. for Deaf Children, Eng., 1970-73; spl. edn. officer Ctr. Bur. for Ednl. Exchs., Eng., 1973-75; h.s. tchr. No. Counties Sch. for Deaf Children, Eng., 1975-76; dir. internat. student svcs. Gallaudet U., Washington, 1978-84; due process hearing officer Maine Dept. Edn., 1986—; assoc. prof. U. of So. Maine, Gorham, 1985—; co-chair bd. mem. Divsn. of Deafness, 1986-95, co-chair policy rev. bd. Gov. Bakter Sch. for the Deaf, Maine, 1993—. Co-author: (handbook) Interpreters for the Deaf: Rules and Responsibilities in Educational Settings, 1994. Bd. dirs. Rape Crisis Ctr., Brunswick, Maine, 1989-94; spkr. Maine Speakout for Equal Rights, 1995—; bd. dirs. Shellfish Conservation, South Harpswell, Maine, 1988-92. Fellowship for Tchrs. of the Handicapped Rotary Internat., 1977. Democrat. Home: RFD #1 Box 614 South Harpswell ME 04079 Office: Univ So Maine 218 Bailey Hall Gorham ME 04038

REESE, ANN N., financial executive. Formerly tres. Mobil Europe; asst. treas. ITT Corp., 1987-89, v.p., 1989-92, sr. v.p., treas., 1992—, exec. v.p., CFO. Office: ITT Corp 1330 Avenue Of The Americas New York NY 10019*

REESE, BARBARA SIMS, school system administrator; b. Birmingham, Ala., Aug. 16, 1958; d. John Edwin and Betty Lee (Wormley) Sims; m. George Reese II, Dec. 23, 1989; 1 child, Jasmine Celeste. BS, U. Ala., 1980, MA, 1984. Cert. sch. adminstr., Ala. Tchr. Valley Elem. Shelby County, Pelham, Ala., 1980-83, Inverness Elem. Shelby County, Inverness, Ala., 1983-91; asst. prin. Elvin Hill Elem., Columbiana, Ala., 1991—; supr. tchr. Univ. of Montevallo, Ala., 1983-91; participant Leader 123, Montgomery, 1994. Mem. Leadership Shelby County, 1994-95. Beeson fellow Samford U., Birmingham, 1988. Mem. NEA, Ala. Edn. Assn. (Emerging Leader award 1988), Shelby County Edn. Assn., Optimists (bd. dirs. v.p. Metro Shelby club 1992-93), Women in Edn. Network, South Shelby County C. of C. Baptist. Office: Elvin Hill Elem 201 Washington St Columbiana AL 35051

REESE, KRISTY RENEÉ, accountant; b. Newport News, Va., Oct. 21, 1971; d. Edwin Merril Jr. and Rita Kay (Kelso) R. Student, Christopher Newport U., 1994—. Accounts payable clk. Gloucester County Pub. Schs., Gloucester, Va., 1988-91, sec., bookkeeper, 1991—, claims and safety coord., 1991—. Sunday sch. tchr.'s asst. St. Luke's United Meth. Ch., Grafton, Va., 1995-96, Sunday sch. tchr., 1996. Mem. NOW, P. Buckley Moss Soc. Democrat. Home: PO Box 373 Ark VA 23003-0373 Office: Gloucester County Pub Schs 6097 TC Walker Rd Glouceser VA 23061

REESE, NORMA CAROL, psychologist; b. Biloxi, Miss., Oct. 26, 1946; d. Virgil Stephen and Lila Mae (Shelton) Tatom; m. John Jay Reese, June 5, 1965 (div. Mar. 1983); children: Cher LeAnne, James Steven. AA in Psychology, Dade County Jr. Coll., Kendall, Fla., 1971; BS in Psychology, U. Miami, 1973; MS and PhD in Psychology, U. So. Miss., 1976. Lic. psychologist, Minn., N.D. Rsch. asst. NASA Lang. Rsch. Lab., Coral Gables, Fla., 1971-73; psychology instr. U. So. Miss., Hattiesburg, 1975-76, Grambling (La.) State U., 1976-78; clin. psychologist II Lake Charles (La.) Mental Health Ctr., 1979-83; tng. cons. Human Rels. Cons., Lake Charles, 1983-86; clin. dir. Grafton (N.D.) State Sch., 1986-89; dir. psychol. svcs. State Devel. Ctr., Grafton, 1989-95; ind. contractor, cons. psychol. svcs. Harley Residential Svcs. (name changed to Applied Behavioral Cons., Inc. 1990), Roseville, Minn., 1990-91; pvt. practice MYNDAK Moblie Cons., Minn. and N.D., 1990-95; program dir. for spl. needs Saint Coletta Sch., Jefferson, Wis., 1995—, mem. human rights and sexual health curriculum coms., 1995—; dir. sexual health project for devel. disabled and mentally retarded N.D. Dept. Human Svcs., Grafton, 1989-95, dir. sex offender and treatment program devel. disabled offenders, 1986-87; mem. adj. faculty grad. clin. psychology dept. U. N.D., Grand Forks, 1994—. Author: The Bulletin of the Psychonomic Soc., 1975-76; author/cartoonist The Worm Runner's Digest, 1975-80. Freedom writer Amnesty Internat., Midwest, 1989; founding mem. Sexual Health Coalition Steel of N.D., 1990; nat. disaster mental health technician, chpt. family svc. worker Red River Valley chpt. ARC, 1993—; mentor Am. Assn. Mental Retardation, 1992—; vol. Red Cross Nat. Disaster Mental Health Team, 1993, Emilys List, 1993. Named Silver Knight candidate, art, Miami (Fla.) Herald News, 1965; nominated Profl. of the Yr., La. Assn. Retarded Citizens, Lake Charles, 1983. Mem. APA (Div. 10), N.D. Psychol. Assn. (legis. action com. 1990-91, mem. disaster action com. 1993-94, mem. women in psychology 1995), Am. Assn. Mental Retardation (sec.-treas. N.D. chpt. 1991), Women in Networking, Assn. for Advancement of Psychology, Assn. for Sexual Abuse Prevention, Assn. for Play Therapy, Century Club. Republican. Methodist. Office: St Coletta Sch Hwy 18 Jefferson WI 53719-2428

REESE, PATRICIA ANN, retired editor, columnist; b. Superior, Nebr., Mar. 14, 1954; d. Robert John and Billie Jo (Gooch) R. BS in Wildlife Ecology, Communications, Okla. State U., 1976. Proofreader Ada (Okla.) Evening News, 1976-77, reporter, 1977-81, wire editor, 1981-85, city editor, 1985-92, sects. editor, 1992, ret., 1992. Bd. dirs. Ada Arts and Humanities Coun., 1981-85, 92-95, 96—, historian, 1982-83, sec., 1983-85, 92-95, 96—; charter mem. Seekers dept. Tanti Study Club, Ada, 1982. Recipient Carl Rogan News Excellence award Associated Press/Okla. News Execs., 1986, 90, 91, 92, Best Column award Okla. Natural Gas, 1991. Mem. Am. Mus. Natural History, Archaeology Inst. Am., Okla. Lupus Assn., Ada Cmty. Theatre II, Okla. Press Assn., Internat. Ceramic Inst., Soc. Environ. Journalists. Democrat. Home: RR 4 Box 118 Ada OK 74820-9407

REESE-COUPLAND, JO, florist, interior decorating consultant; b. Warren, Ohio, Sept. 1, 1931; d. Carl Irwin and Anita May (Clark) Heitman; m. Norman James Reese, Oct. 7, 1950 (dec. June 11, 1954); children: Jackie Lynn Reese Dell, Norman James; m. Gary Robert Coupland, Sept. 2, 1990. Student, Kent State U., 1980. Cert. floral designer. Floral design apprentice Jensen Flowers, Niles, Ohio, 1949-53; owner Reese Floral Art, Niles, Ohio, 1954—. Floral designer Sambo chain, State of Ohio, 26 2d Nat. Banks, State of Ohio, Butler Art Inst., Youngstown, Ohio, Warren Chamber Orch., Kent State; artist (oil painting) Kent State, 1960-92 (numerous awards). Mem. Trumbull Geneol. Soc., Warren, 1990-95; bd. dirs. Warren Chamber Orch., 1991—; trustee Butler Art Inst., 1989—. Mem. Warren-Youngstown C. of C. Republican. Baptist. Home and Office: Reese Floral Art 49 Vienna Ave Niles OH 44446-2601

REESER, RACHEL ANNE EVERSON, graphic designer; b. Shreveport, La., Nov. 16, 1964; d. Robert Higgins and Marian Louise (Wimberly) Everson; m. Kirk Allen "Korky" Reeser, Feb. 1, 1994. BS, Okla. State U., 1986. Mgr. Fabric, Floors & Such, Oklahoma City, Okla., 1986-87; advt. dir. Pipkin Cameras & Video, Oklahoma City, 1987-88; asst. nat. advt. mgr. Morgan Bldgs. & Spas, Dallas, 1988-89; sr. art dir. Avrea/Pugliese, Coconut Grove, Dallas, 1989-91; pres., creative dir. Freestyle Studio, Dallas, 1991—. Mem. Dallas Soc. Illustrators (bd. dirs. 1992-96, Merit award 1993), Dallas Soc. Visual Comms. Office: Freestyle Studio PO Box 823554 Dallas TX 75382-3554

REETZ, RUTH ELAINE SANFORD, artist; b. Parkers Prairie, Minn., May 3, 1938; d. Robert Paul and Charlotte Belle (Roberts) S.; m. Gary Engelbert, May 27, 1960; children: Randall Robert, Ryan Sanford. BSc, N.D. State U., 1960. Textile lab. technician Munsingwear Inc., Mpls., 1960-62; asst. home economist Pillsbury, Mpls., 1962-65; promotional home economist Armo Co., N.Y.C., 1965-72; owner Creative Textiles, Mpls., 1966-83; owner, artist The Spell of the Shell, Mpls., 1978—; cons. in field; cons. Almark, Miami, 1987. Author: Quality Dressmaking, 1968, Flat Method of Sewing, 1976. Mem. Nat. Trust Hist. Preservation, Minn. Soc. of Conchologists (pres. 1980-81), Conchologists of Am., Sanibel-Captiva Shell Club (life mem.), Cousteau Soc. Home and Office: 40 Norman Ridge Dr Bloomington MN 55437

REEVE, LORRAINE ELLEN, biochemist, researcher; b. Cato, Wis., Aug. 12, 1951; d. Robert K. and Lila M. (Breneman) R.; m. Dennis L. Kiesling, July 21, 1990. BS, U. Wis., 1973, MS, 1978, PhD, 1981. Postdoctoral scholar U. Mich., Ann Arbor, 1981-86; project scientist Cleve. Clinic Found., 1986-88; sr. rsch. scientist R.P. Scherer Corp., Troy, Mich., 1988-89, Mediventures, Inc., Dearborn, Mich., 1989-92; prin. investigator Mediventures, Inc., Dearborn, 1992-94; project mgr. MDV Technologies, Inc. (formerly Mediventures, Inc.), Dearborn, 1994—. Contbr. articles to profl. jours. Mem. Founders Soc. Detroit Inst. Art, 1989—, Nat. Trust for Historic Preservation, 1991—. Mem. AAAS, N.Y. Acad. Sci. Home: PO Box 2962 Ann Arbor MI 48106-2962 Office: MDV Techs Inc 15250 Mercantile Dr Dearborn MI 48120-1207

REEVES, ALEXIS SCOTT, journalist; b. Atlanta, Feb. 4, 1949; d. William Alexander and Marian (Willis) Scott; m. Marc Anthony Lewis, Sept. 14, 1968 (div. 1973); m. David Leslie Reeves, Mar. 16, 1974; children: Cinque Scott, David Leslie, Jr. Student Barnard Coll., 1966-68; student Spelman Coll., 1989-90, Regional Leadership Inst., 1992. Reporter, asst. city editor, cable TV editor, mgr. video edit., v.p. community affairs Atlanta Jour. & Constn., Atlanta, 1974-93; dir. Diversity for Cox Enterprises Inc., 1993—; vis. instr. summer program for minority journalists, Berkeley, Calif., 1980, 81, 84, 85, 87 Grady High Sch., Atlanta, 1982-83; journalist-in-residence Clark Coll., Atlanta, 1983. Researcher, writer: The History of Atlanta NAACP, 1983 (NAACP award, 1984). Recipient Disting. Urban Journalism award Nat. Urban Coalition, 1980. Michele Clark fellow Columbia U. Sch. Journalism, 1974. Named one of 100 Top Black Bus. & Profl. Women, 1986; recipient Acad. Achievement award YWCA, 1989. Mem. Nat. Assn. Media Women (Media Woman of Yr. award, 1983, Media Woman of Yr. nat. award 1983, pres. Atlanta chpt. 1985-87), Atlanta Assn. Black Journalists (Commentary Print award 1983), Nat. Assn. Black Journalists, Sigma Delta Chi (bd. dirs. 1980-84, treas. 1985-88). Moderator, First Congl. Ch., 1982-92. Office: Cox Enterprises Inc PO Box 105357 1400 Lake Hearn Dr NE Atlanta GA 30348

REEVES, BARBARA ANN, lawyer; b. Buffalo, Mar. 29, 1949; d. Prentice W. and Doris Reeves; m. Richard C. Neal; children: Timothy R. Neal, Stephen S. Neal (dec.), Robert S. Neal, Richard R. Neal. Student, Wellesley Coll., 1967-68; B.A. (NSF fellow, Lehman fellow), New Coll., Sarasota, Fla., 1970; J.D. cum laude, Harvard U., 1973. Bar: Calif. 1973, D.C. 1977. Law clk. U.S. Ct. Appeals, 9th Circuit, Portland, Oreg., 1973-74; assoc. firm Munger, Tolles and Rickershauser, L.A., 1977-78; trial atty. spl. trial sect. Dept. Justice (Antitrust div.), 1974-75; spl. asst. to asst. atty. gen. Antitrust div. Dept. Justice, Washington, 1976-77; chief antitrust div. L.A. field office, 1978-81; ptnr. Morrison & Foerster, L.A., 1981-94, Fried, Frank, Harris, Shriver & Jacobson, L.A., 1995—; mem. exec. com. state bar conf. of dels. L.A. Delegation, 1982-91; del. 9th Cir. Jud. Conf., 1984-88; mem. Fed. Ct. Magistrate Selection Com., 1989; bd. dirs. Pub. Counsel, 1988-92, Western Ctr. Law and Poverty, 1992—; lectr. in field. Editor: Federal Criminal Litigation, 1994; contbg. author: International Antitrust, 1995; contbr. articles to profl. jours. Mem. ABA (litigation sect., antitrust sect.), Am. Arbitration Assn. (arbitrator, mediator, mem. adv. panel large complex case program), L.A. County Bar Assn. (antitrust sect. officer 1980-81, litigation sect. officer 1988-93 trustee 1990-92, chair alternative dispute resolution sec. 1992-95, L.A. County Ct. ADR com.). Home: 1410 Hillcrest Ave Pasadena CA 91106-4503 Office: Fried Frank Harris Shriver & Jacobson 725 S Figueroa St Ste 3890 Los Angeles CA 90017-5438

REEVES, CARLA MARIANNE, women's health, nurse midwife; b. San Francisco, June 25, 1949; d. Robert Dwight and Irma Marianne (Nelson) R. BS in Nursing, U. Md., Balt., 1971; MS in Nursing, U. Ky., 1975. RN, Ariz., Calif.; cert. nurse midwife, Ariz., Calif. Commd. officer U.S. Army, 1967-77; commd. officer USAF, 1978, advanced through grades to maj., 1971-83; nurse, midwife USAF Hosp. Luke, Luke AFB, Ariz., 1978-84, sr. nurse, midwife, 1985-88; sr. nurse, midwife Regional Med. Ctr., Clark Air Base, The Philippines, 1984-85; ret., 1988; nurse midwife S.W. Women's Health Svcs., Phoenix, 1988-94, Loma Vista Med. Group, San Jose, Calif., 1994-96, Palo Alto Med. Found., Fremont, Calif., 1996—; pvt. duty-clinic nurse Homemakers Upjohn, Santa Maria, Calif., 1978; ob-gyn nurse practitioner Planned Parenthood Santa Barbara (Calif.), Inc., 1978. Decorated Meritorious Svc. medal with oak leaf cluster; named Ariz. Outstanding Achievement-PMH Physician Office Nurse of Yr., 1992. Mem. Am. Coll. Nurse Midwifes (cert.), Assn. of Women's Health, Obstetric and Neonatal Nurses, Soc. of Retired Air Force Nurses, World Wildlife Fund, Ariz. Humane Soc., Doris Day Animal League, Cousteau Soc. Home: 882 Bedford St Fremont CA 94539 Office: Palo Alto Med Found 39500 Liberty St Fremont CA 94538-2211

REEVES, CATHY CLANTON, psychologist, consultant; b. St. Louis, Dec. 4, 1959; d. Wayne A. and Ora K. (King) Clanton; m. David H. Reeves, Jan. 22, 1983; children: Mari Catherine and Matthew Ryan Henry. BS in Psychology, U. Ark., Monticello, 1981; MS in Psychology, N.E. La. U., 1983, cert. specialist in sch. psychology, 1985; PhD in Psychology, Miss. State U., Starkville, 1988. Lic. psychologist, Ky.; registered play therapist. Clin. svcs. dir., supr. psychologist Rivendell Psychiat. Hosp., Bowling Green, Ky., 1989—; pvt. practice Bower, Starks, Reeves, and Assocs., Bowling Green, Ky., 1993—; adj. faculty Western Ky. U., Bowling Green, 1990—; cons. Head Start program, Ky., 1994—, cons. play therapist Mental Health Ctr., Bowling Green, 1996—, supr. psychologist Lifeskills Inc., Bowling Green, 1996—. Bd dirs. Child Protection Inc., Bowling Green, 1993—, chmn. bd. dirs., 1993-94, bd. dirs. regional Child Devel. Clinic, Bowling Green, 1995—. Mem. Ky. Psychol. Assn., Ky. Play Therapy Assn., Assn. Play Therapy, Beta Sigma Phi (pres. 1989). Republican. Baptist. Office: Bower, Starks, Reeves, and Assocs 1212 Ashley Cir Ste 3 Bowling Green KY 42104

REEVES, CONNIE LYNN, retired army officer, writer; b. Houston, Tex., Oct. 12, 1954; d. Calvin Arthur and Ineva Dorthene (Wilkinson) R.; m. Clifton Willey Lewis, Jr., May 19, 1979; children: Derek Alexander, Jessica Megan. BA in Sociology, U. Tex., 1975; MA in History, George Washington U., 1987; postgrad. Commd. 2d lt. U.S. Army, 1976, advanced through grades to lt. col., ret., 1994; ops. officer Davison Army Airfield, Ft. Belvoir, Va., 1985; instr. and course mgr. Def. Intelligence Coll., Washington, 1985-86; indications and warning intelligence analyst, polit./mil. intelligence analyst for Western Europe; div. chief Joint Intelligence Ctr., Directorate of Intelligence U.S. European Command, Stuttgart, Germany, 1988-91; defense fgn. lang. program U.S. Army, Washington, 1992-93; staff officer U.S. Army Counter Drug Program, 1993-94. Author: French Women During World War I: Their Contribution to the National Defense, 1987; contbr. articles to profl. jours. Univ. fellow George Washington Univ., 1995-96. Mem AAUW, Ret. Officer Assn., Women Mil. Aviators (editor newsletter 1994-95), Whirly-Girls: Internat. Women Helicopter Pilots. Republican. Office: PO Box 117 Dowell MD 20629-0117

REEVES, DIANNE L., artist; b. Milw., Apr. 8, 1948; d. John J. and Bernice M. (Hendricksen) Kleczka; m. Robert A. McCoy, Oct. 15, 1983 (div. June 1988). BFA, U. Wis., Milw., 1968; student, Mus. Fine Arts, Houston, 1974-77, 83, Glassell Sch. Art, Houston, 1980-83. Instr. papermaking Glassell Sch. Art, 1984-85. Exhibited in solo shows at Women and Their Work Gallery, Austin, Tex., 1988, Moreau Galleries/Hamms Gallery, Notre Dame, Ind., 1991, The Martin Mus. of Art, Waco, Tex., 1996; internat. exhibns. include Leopold-Hoesch Mus., Duren, Germany, 1991, 92, 93, galleries in Netherlands and Basel, Switzerland; exhibited in numerous group exhbns.; author: (ltd. edit.) From Fiber to Paper, 1991. Bd. dirs., sec. Friends of Dard Hunter, Inc., 1993-94. NEA/Tex. fellow Mid-Am. Arts Alliance/NEA, 1986; recipient awards for art work. Mem. Internat. Assn. Hand Papermakers and Paper Artists (co-chair nominating com. 1993-94), Women and Their Work, Inc., Sierra Club, Tex. Fine Arts Assn., Austin Visual Arts Assn. Home and Studio: 1103 S 3rd St Austin TX 78704

REEVES, JOANNE SHAW, marriage and family therapist; b. Colorado Springs, Colo.; d. Harry Earnest and Harriet Louise (Woolsey) Shaw; m. George Henry Reeves, May 13, 1959 (div. Sept. 1969); children: George Henry, Melissa Anne. AA, Mohegan C.C., Norwich, Conn., 1980; BA, So. Conn. State U., 1982, MS in Marriage and Family Therapy, 1985. Lic. marriage and family therapist, Conn. Marriage and family therapist Salutaris Cons., Niantic, Conn., 1983—; justice of peace, East Lyme, Conn., 1995—. Vol. Beechtree Medicine Circle, Conn. prisons, 1984—; vol. East Lyme (Conn.) Dem. Com., 1994—; sec. White Buffalo Soc., Conn., Fla., Maine, 1994—. With USAF, 1955-58. Fellow New Eng. Psych. Assn., 1982. Mem. AAUW, Am. Assn. Marriage and Family Therapists.

REEVES, LUCY MARY, retired secondary school educator; b. Pewamo, Mich., July 2, 1932; d. Lavaldin Edgar and Marian S. (Lee) Hull; m. Walter Emery Reeves, Jan. 21, 1922. BS, Western Mich. U., Kalamazoo, 1965; postgrad., Western Mich. U., 1965-75. Tchr. Country Sch. One Room, Matherton, Mich., 1956-57, Ionia, Mich., 1957-58, Belding, Mich., 1958-62, Saranac, Mich., Belding, Mich., 1965; tchr. Belding (Mich.) Area Schs., 1965-89; ret. Mem. NEA, Mich. Edn. Assn., Belding Area Edn., Profl. Businesswomen's Assn.

REEVES, PATRICIA RUTH, heavy machinery manufacturing company executive; b. Bklyn., Mar. 26, 1931; d. Maurice G. and Ethel Helen (Kessler) Der Brucke m. Cedric E. Reeves, June 22, 1952. BA, Adelphi U., 1952. Chief of records sect. Hydrocarbon Rsch., Inc., N.Y.C., 1952-65; lead sec. C.F. Braun & Co., Murray Hill, N.J., 1965-69; exec. sec. Wilputte Corp., Murray Hill, N.J., 1969-75, adminstrv. asst., 1975-79, sales coord., 1979-81, pers. adminstr., 1981-82; sales coord. Krupp Wilputte Corp., Murray Hill, N.J., 1982-84; pers. adminstr. Somerset Techs., Inc., N.J., 1984-85, pers. mgr., 1985-95; pres. Human Resources Svcs., Watchung, N.J., 1995—. Pres. Mountain Jewish Community Ctr., Warren, N.J., 1976-77, bd. dirs., 1972-81. Mem. NAFE, AAUW, Women's NetWork Ctrl. N.J. (v.p., editor newsletter 1981-83, coord. career assistance 1984-85, membership chair 1986-89), Am. Soc. Pers. Adminstrs. (membership chair 1986-88, sec. 1986-88), Soc. Human Resources Mgmt. (sec. Ctrl. N.J. chpt. 1986-88, v.p. 1988-89, pres. 1989-90, sec.-treas. N.J. State Coun. 1990-92, sec.-treas. Area I bd. 1993-95, dir mem. at large, 1996, co-chair N.J. Conf., 1994-95, chair chpt. awards 1996, sr. advisor 1996). Home and Office: Human Resources Svcs 89 Knollwood Dr Watchung NJ 07060-6245

REEVES, PEGGY LOIS ZEIGLER, accountant; b. Orangeburg, S.C., May 12, 1940; d. Joseph Harold and Lois Vivian (Stroman) Zeigler; m. Donald Preston Reeves, Sept. 9, 1961. Degree in Secretarial Sci., Coker Coll., 1960. Sec. Ladson Beach, CPA, Orangeburg, 1960-61; acctg. clk. Milliken & Co., Laurens, S.C., 1962-67, sec., 1967-73, mgmt. trainee, 1973, plant contr., 1973-74, 76-81; cost acctg. supr. Milliken & Co., Spartanburg, S.C., 1974-76, 81—. Chair bd. dirs. Enoree (S.C.)-Lanford Fire dist., 1982—, treas., 1988—; mem. alumni exec. bd. Coker Coll., 1996—. H.L. Jones scholar Coker Coll., 1959-60. Mem. Inst. Mgmt. Accts. (sec. 1991-94, v.p. membership 1994-95, v.p. adminstrn. and fin. 1995-96, pres.-elect 1996—), Profl. Secs. Internat. (v.p., rec. sec., Sec. of Yr. 1973). Baptist.

REFIOR, MICHELLE DAWN, accountant; b. Kearney, Nebr., Oct. 18, 1968; d. Richard Lloyd and Karla Kay (Daake) S. BS, Kearney State Coll., 1991. Acctg. adminstr. Bus. Men's Assurance, Kansas City, Mo., 1991—. Mem. Inst. Mgmt. Accts. (dir. ednl. seminars 1993-94, dir. News Notes 1994-95, dir. membership participation and retention 1995-96, sec. 1996—). Office: BMA Fin Svcs 1901 W 47th Pl Ste 210 Westwood KS 66205

REGA, FRANCES LOUISE, English educator; b. Revere, Mass., July 13, 1950; d. Leo and Marie Frances (Interrante) R. BA in English, Boston Coll., 1972, MEd in Reading, 1977; MEd in Integrated Studies, Cambridge Coll., 1996. Cert. English and Reading Specialist. Tchr. English and reading Abraham Lincoln Sch., Revere, Mass., 1972-90, Beachmont Middle Sch., Revere, Mass., 1990—; co-advisor Nat. Jr. Honor Soc., Revere, Mass., 1990-94, co-advisor The Aspirers Club, 1995. Contbr. articles to profl. jours. Mem. NEA, Nat. Coun. Tchrs. English, Internat. Reading Assn., Revere Tchrs. Assn., Mass. Tchrs. Assn., Alpha Upsilon Alpha. Home: 164 Ridge Rd Revere MA 02151-3825 Office: Beachmont Middle School 15 Everard Ave Revere MA 02151-5516

REGALMUTO, NANCY MARIE, small business owner, psychic consultant, therapist; b. Bay Shore, N.Y., Aug. 24, 1956; d. Antonio J. Jr. and Agnes C. (Dietz) R. Student, SUNY, Stony Brook. Sales mgr. Fire, Inc., Hempstead, N.Y.; sports handicapper Red Hot Sport, J. Dime Sports, Diamond Sports, Hicksville, N.Y.; small bus. owner, pres. Synergy (vitamin/nutritional product mfr. and distributor), Bellport, N.Y., 1989—; cons. on medicine, fin., past life, bus. readings, hypnosis, substance abuse, archeology, law enforcement investigations, family, counseling, inter-species comm., animal therapy, psychic surgery, healing; lectr. in field, specializing in holistic remedies and therapies. Columnist Daily Racing Form; appeared on numerous TV programs, worldwide radio, mags., newspapers. Lectr., seminar leader, written about in several books. Mem. NAFE, Horse Protection Assn., Am. Biog. Inst. (named Woman of Yr. 1994). Home and Office: 18 Woodland Park Dr Bellport NY 11713-2315

REGAN, ELLEN FRANCES (MRS. WALSTON SHEPARD BROWN), ophthalmologist; b. Boston, Feb. 1, 1919; d. Edward Francis and Margaret (Moynihan) R.; AB, Wellesley Coll., 1940; MD, Yale U., 1943; m. Walston Shepard Brown, Aug. 13, 1955. Intern, Boston City Hosp., 1944; asst. resident, resident Inst. Ophthalmology, Presbyn. Hosp., N.Y.C., 1944-47, asst. ophthalmologist, 1947-56, asst. attending ophthalmologist, 1956-84; instr. ophthalmology Columbia Coll. Physicians and Surgeons, 1947-55, asso. ophthalmology, 1955-67, asst. clin. prof., 1967-84. Mem. Am. Ophthal. Soc., AMA, Am. Acad. Ophthalmology, N.Y. Acad. Medicine, N.Y. State Med. Soc., Mass. Med. Soc., River Club. Office: PO Box 632 Tuxedo Park NY 10987-0632

REGAN, MARIE CHRISTINE, nursing educator; b. Wilmington, Del.; d. Jeremiah and Della Agnes (Kelly) R. Diploma in nursing, Wilmington Gen. Hosp., 1959; BSN, U. Md., Balt., 1965; MS in Health Edn., Nova Southeastern U., 1983; cert. Vietnamese langs. culture, U. Hawaii, 1967. RN, Fla.; cert. aerospace medicine, cert. tchr., Fla. Sr. pub. health nurse Balt. City Health Dept.; instr., comty. health nurse Church Home & Hosp. Sch. Nursing, Balt.; advisor to chief of pub. health U.S. Dept. State, Vietnam; nursing instr. Miami-Dade C.C., Miami, Fla.; nursing instr. psychiatry Jackson Meml. Hosp., Miami; nursing supr. Vis. Nurse Assn., Miami; instr. nursing Robert Morgan Inst., Miami; med. crew dir. USAFR, Charleston, S.C. Contbr. articles to med. jours. Bd. dirs. Greater Miami YMCA, Miami, 1973-80. Maj. USAFR, 1972-80. Mem. Nat. League Nursing, Fla. League Nursing, Res. Officers Assn., Fla. Vocat. Assn., Dade Assn. Vocat. Edn. Roman Catholic. Home: 6516 SW 112th Pl Miami FL 33173-1981

REGAN, MURIEL, librarian; b. N.Y.C., July 15, 1930; d. William and Matilda (Riebel) Blome; m. Robert Regan, 1966 (div. 1976); 1 child, Jeanne Booth. BA, Hunter Coll., N.Y.C., 1950; MLS, Columbia U., 1952; MBA, Pace U., N.Y.C., 1982. Post libr. US Army, Okinawa, 1952-53; researcher P.F. Collier, N.Y.C., 1953-57; asst. libr. to libr. Rockefeller Found., N.Y.C., 1957-67; dep. chief libr. Manhattan Community Coll., N.Y.C., 1967-68; libr. Booz Allen & Hamilton, N.Y.C., 1968-69, Rockefeller Found., N.Y.C., 1969-82; prin. Gossage Regan Assocs., Inc., N.Y.C., 1980-95; pub. svcs. libr. Carlsbad (N.Mex.) Pub. Libr., 1995—; dir. N.Y. Met. Reference and Rsch. Libr. Agy., 1988-95, Coun. Nat. Libr. and Info. Assns., 1991-95; cons. Librs. Info. Ctrs. Mem. SLA (pres. 1989-90), Archons of Colophon, Altrusa, N.Y. Libr. Club. Home: 604 N Lake St Carlsbad NM 88220 Office: Carlsbad Pub Libr 101 S Halagueno St Carlsbad NM 88220

REGAN, SYLVIA, playwright; b. N.Y.C., Apr. 15, 1908; d. Louis and Esther (Albert) Hoffenberg; m. James J. Regan, Feb. 11, 1931 (div. June 1936); m. 2d Abraham Ellstein, Nov. 7, 1940 (dec. Mar. 1963). Student pub. schs. Broadway actress N.Y.C., 1927-31; with pub. relations and promotion dept. Theratre Union and Orson Welles Mercury Theatre, N.Y.C., 1932-39; playwright, 1940—. Author: Morning Star, 1940, The Golden Door, 1951; musical Great to be Alive, 1951; The Fifth Season, 1953; libretto for grand opera The Golem, N.Y.C., 1962; Zelda, 1969. Sec. Sydney Epstein Meml. Fund for Strang Cancer Clinic, N.Y.C., 1948-68. Recipient cititon Fedn. Women Zionists of Gt. Britain and Ireland, 1953. Mem. Dramatists Guild, Authors League of Am., Am. Jewish Hist. Soc., Nat. Council Jewish Women (citation of merit 1953). Democrat. Home: 55 E 9th St New York NY 10003-6311

REGENTHAL, JEANINE A., immunologist, researcher; b. Elizabeth, N.J., Sept. 2, 1964; d. Joseph M. and Frances M. (Sullivan) Todaro; m. Mark A. Regenthal, June 27, 1992. BS in Biology, Cook Coll., Rutgers U., New Brunswick, N.J., 1986; MS in Cell Devel. Biology, U. Medicine and Dentistry of N.J. and Rutgers Grad. Sch. of Biomed. Scis., New Brunswick, 1995. Rsch. assoc. Human Immuology Found., Red Bank, N.J., 1987-89, Dept. Toxicology, Coll. Pharmacy, Rutgers U., New Brunswick, 1989-93; assoc. scientist Immunobiology Rsch. Inst. Johnson & Johnson, Annandale, N.J., 1993-94; assoc. immunologist Ortho Diagnostic Systems, Inc. Johnson & Johnson, Raritan, N.J., 1994-95, assoc. scientist Robert Wood Johnson Pharm. Rsch. Inst., 1995—. Contbr. numerous articles to sci. jours. including Jour. of Leukocyte Biology, Hepatology, chpts. to books. Vol. League of Women Voters, Ocean County, 1991, AIDS Resource Found. for Children, Neptune, 1995, Coalition for Peace Action, N.J., 1995. Mem. AAAS, NOW. Democrat. Roman Catholic. Home: 1310 Eisenhower St Lakewood NJ 08701 Office: Robert Wood Johnson Pharm Rsch Inst 1000 Rt 202 Raritan NJ 08869

REGES, MARIANNA ALICE, marketing executive; b. Budapest, Hungary, Mar. 23, 1947; came to U.S., 1956, naturalized, 1963; d. Otto H. and Alice M. R.; m. Charles P. Green, Feb. 15, 1975; children: Rebecca, Charles III. AAS with honors, Fashion Inst. Tech., N.Y.C., 1967; BBA magna cum laude, Baruch Coll., 1971, MBA in Stats., 1978. Media rsch. analyst Doyle, Dane, Bernbach Advt., N.Y.C., 1967-70; rsch. supr. Sta. WCBS-TV, N.Y.C., 1970-71; rsch. mgr. Woman's Day mag., N.Y.C., 1971-72; asst. media dir. Benton & Bowles Advt., N.Y.C., 1972-75; mgr. rsch. and sales devel. NBC Radio, N.Y.C., 1975-77; sr. rsch. mgr. Ziff-Davis Pub. Co., N.Y.C., 1977-84; media mgr. Bristol-Myers Squibb Co., 1984—; mem. Spanish Radio Adv. Coun., N.Y.C., 1986-88; mem. Pan-European TV Audience Rsch. Mgmt. Com., 1988—. Mem. Vt. Natural Resources Council, 1977—; advisor Baruch Coll. Advt. Soc., 1975—. Mem. Am. Mktg. Assn., Am. Advt. Fedn., Media Rsch. Dirs. Assn., Radio and TV Rsch. Coun., Advt. Rsch. Found., Nature Conservancy, Vt. Natural Resources Coun., World Future Soc., Beta Gamma Sigma. Home: 626 E 20th St New York NY 10009-1509 Office: Bristol-Myers Squibb Co 345 Park Ave New York NY 10154-0004

REGGIE, TINA KADLUBAR, nurse; b. Denison, Tex., Nov. 26, 1964; d. Bernard Daniel and Hattie Georgia (Hanzlicek) Kadlubar; m. Paul Peter Reggie, Apr. 24, 1993. BS, McNeese State U., Lake Charles, La., 1986. RN, La. Office nurse Dr. John Cocchiara, Lake Charles, 1986-88, nurse first asst., 1988—. Mem. ANA, La. State Nurses Assn., Assn. Oper. Rm. Nurses (sec. 1992-93). Democrat. Roman Catholic. Home: 702 Laurel St Lake Charles LA 70605 Office: 1739 Ryan St Lake Charles LA 70601

REGIER, MARY HANANIA, statistics educator; b. Beirut, Lebanon, July 10, 1926; came to U.S., 1953; d. Issa Habib and Emily (Matar) Hanania; m. Frank Arthur Regier, June 17, 1958; children: Terrance Philip, Christopher George. BA in Math., Am. U. Beirut, 1946, MA in Math., 1948; PhD in Stats., U. Calif., Berkeley, 1957. From. asst. prof. to prof. Am. U. Beirut, 1957-87; vis. prof. Case Western Res. U., Cleve., 1987-88, adj. prof., 1996—; cons. Mid. East Indsl. Rels. Co., Beirut, 1962-83; chair internat. com. Women in Stats., 1995—. Author: Biomedical Statistics with Computing, 1982; editl. bd. Statistical Education Encyclopedia; contbr. articles to profl. jours. Mem. Am. Statis. Assn. (com. mem. 1958—), Internat. Statis. Inst. (coun. mem., chair 1973—), Internat. Assn. Statis. Edn. (exec. com. 1991—). Republican. Home: 19577 Misty Lake Dr Cleveland OH 44136-7456 Office: Case Western Res U Dept Stats 10900 Euclid Ave Cleveland OH 44106-7054

REGIS, NINA, librarian, educator; b. Corinth, Miss., Oct. 19, 1928; d. W.C. and Mary Isabelle (Rushing) Hanner; m. George Regis, Sept. 5, 1949 (dec. Jan. 6, 1990); 1 child, Simonne Marie. BA, Bridgewater (Mass.) State U., 1971, MEd, 1975; MALS, U. South Fla., 1981. Cert. libr., tchr. Geneal. libr., asst. rschr. to curator New Bedford (Mass.) Pub. Libr., 1963-71; assoc. libr. New England Hist. Geneal. Soc., Boston, 1972-73; media specialist, libr. Brevard County Schs., Port Malabar Elem. Sch., Palm Bay, Fla., 1978-90; libr., faculty Brevard C.C., Palm Bay, 1990—. Developer and organizer libraries, 1968, 80, 91—. Mem. ALA, Fla. Assn. C.C.s, Libr. Assn. of Brevard County, Internat. Platform Assn., Phi Kappa Phi, Beta Phi Mu. Office: Brevard Community Coll Melbourne Campus Libr 3865 N Wickham Rd Melbourne FL 32935-2310

REGN FRAHER, BONNIE, educator; b. Neptune, N.J., Mar. 29, 1957; d. Alfred Wesley and Jennie Jeanette Regn; m. William James Fraher III. BA, U. Calif., Santa Cruz, 1978; EdS, Rutgers U., 1982, MA, 1983. Cert. tchr. of the handicapped, cert. elem. tchr. Tchr. Search Day Program, Wanamassa, N.J., 1978-87; v.p. Fin-Addict Charters, Wall, N.J., 1987-93, Archtl. Woodworking, Bradley Beach, N.J., 1994-95; v.p., dir. fin. William Cook Custom Homes, Wall, 1987-95; v.p. Archtl. Woodworking, 1993-95; tchr. Palm Beach County Sch. Dist., 1995-96, Elmcrest Hosp. Sch., 1996—. Mem. sisterhood Temple Beth Torah. Mem. Autism Soc. Am., Long Branch Ski Club.

REHART, MARGARET LEE, controller; b. Van Nuys, Calif., Apr. 11, 1961; d. Ross Leo and Carolyn Lee (Stewart) R.; m. Robert Leslie Putnam, June 13, 1981 (div. July 1988); 1 child, Sabrina Nicole. Degree in bus. mgmt., LaSalle U., 1996. Gen. acct. Whittaker, ERI, Inc., Simi Valley, Calif., 1988-89; acct. ASNA, Big Bear Lake, Calif., 1990; asst. controller Splendor Tile Co., Calabasas, Calif., 1990-95; controller Wesco Sales Corp., Chatsworth, Calif., 1995—; cons. Earth & Art Landscape, Van Nuys, 1993—. Author: Accounting Procedures for the Small Construction Company, 1994. Mem. Am. Mgmt. Assn. Republican. Mem. Reorganized Ch. Latter Day Saints. Home: 2006 N Cheam Ave Simi Valley CA 93063

REHBAUM, TABER SHIRLEY, social service administrator; b. Seattle, Apr. 23, 1952; d. Robert Bruce Shirley and Patricia Alden (Neff) Pearson; m. Robert William Rehbaum, May 15, 1981 (dec. May 1990). BA in English, Skidmore Coll., 1974. With Skidmore Coll., Saratoga Springs, N.Y., Saratoga Performing Arts Ctr., Saratoga Springs, Union Coll., Schenectady, N.Y., Richmor Aviation, Saratoga and Schenectady, Burnt Hills-Ballston Lake (N.Y.) Schs., Niskayvna Schs., Schenectady; asst. br. mgr. N.E. Savs., F.A., Scotia, N.Y., 1986-95; exec. dir. Big Bros./Big Sisters-Greater Fairbanks (Alaska) Area, 1995—; loaned exec., allocations com. United Way Schenectady, 1992; mem. spkrs. bur., loaned exec. trainer United Way of the Tanana Valley, Fairbanks, 1995; mem. nat. profl. staff coun. Big Bros./Big Sisters, 1995—, exec. dirs. assn., 1995—. V.p., pres. Zonta Club Schenectady, 1993-95; bd. treas. YWCA of Schenectady, 1993-95; co-founder Womens Issues Network-Schenectady, 1995; com. chair Clean Up Day, Fairbanks, 1996. Mem Arctic Alliance for People (past treas., current pres.). Democrat. Office: Big Bros Big Sisters Greater Fairbanks Area 1100 W Barnette Fairbanks AK 99701

REHNS, MARSHA LEE, magazine editor; b. Balt., Dec. 23, 1946; d. Fred and Ruth (Lieber) R.; m. Walter Richard Arnheim, Sept. 5, 1971; children: Ethan, Phillip. BS, U. Pitts., 1967; MPhil, Yale, 1970. editor Sci. Med. Pub., N.Y.C., 1972-75; editor Haymarket Pub., London, 1975-76; mng. editor Harcourt Brace Jovanovich, N.Y.C., 1977-79; editor Sta. WGBH-TV, Boston, 1979-80; columnist Weightwatchers Mag., N.Y.C., 1979-81; editor Am. Baby, N.Y.C., 1981—; cons. Cradle Pub., N.Y.C., 1990-94; writer Kids Discover, N.Y.C., 1991—, Nat. Mus. Natural History, 1994—; editor Educating Our Children, N.Y.C., 1996—. Docent Nat. Mus. Natural History, Washington, 1990—. Home: 10712 Barn Wood Ln Potomac MD 20854-1326

REHORN, LOIS M(ARIE), nursing administrator; b. Larned, Kans., Apr. 15, 1919; d. Charles and Ethel L. (Canaday) Williamson; m. C. Howard Smith, Feb. 15, 1946 (dec. Aug. 1980); 1 child, Cynthia A. Huddleston; m. Harlan W. Rehorn, Aug. 25, 1981. RN, Bethany Hosp. Sch. Nursing, Kansas City, Kans., 1943; BS, Ft. Hays Kans. State U., Hays, 1968, MS, 1970. RN, N.Mex. Office nurse, surg. asst. Dr. John H. Luke, Kansas City, Kans., 1943-47; supr. nursing unit Larned (Kans.) State Hosp., 1949-68, dir. nursing edn., 1968-71, dir. nursing, 1972-81, ret., 1981. Named Nurse of Yr. DNA-4, 1986. Mem. Am. Nurses Assn., Kans. Nurses Assn. (dist. treas.), N.Mex. Nurses Assn. (dist. pres. 1982-86, dist. bd. dirs. 1992-94). Home: 1436 Brentwood Dr Clovis NM 88101-4602

REHR, HELEN, social worker; b. N.Y.C., Dec. 16, 1919; d. Philip and Rose (Stern) R. BA, CUNY, 1940, DS (hon.), 1995; MS, Columbia U., 1943, DSW, 1970. Social worker, asst. dir. Sydenham Hosp., N.Y.C., 1943-45; supr. Grasslands Hosp., Valhalla, N.Y., 1945-47; asst. prof. medicine NYU Bellevue Med. Ctr., N.Y.C., 1947-51; med. soc. cons. Dept. Health, Maternal & Child Health, N.Y.C., 1951-52; assoc. dir. Mt. Sinai Med. Ctr., N.Y.C., 1954-89, dir., Edith S. Baerwald prof. cmty. medicine, prof. cmty. med. emerita; dir. Israel/Australia Leadership Project, 1986—; vis. prof. U. Flinders, U. Melbourne, Australia, 1990, Ben Gurion U., Israel, 1991; Kenneth Pray vis. prof. U. Pa., Phila., 1979-80; cons. Mt. Sinai, 1986—. Author, editor books, jour. and articles in field; mem. editl. bd. Social Work in Health Care, Health and Social Work. Bd. dirs. N.Y. Found., Ctr. for Study of Social Work Practice/Columbia U., Joint Commn. on Accreditation of Hosps.; mem. adv. bd. scholarship and welfare fund Hunter Coll. Named Disting. Practitioner, Nat. Acad. Practitioners; named to Hunter Coll. Hall of Fame. Home: 27 W 96th St # 6C New York NY 10025 Office: Mt Sinai Med Ctr 1 Gustave & Levy Pl New York NY 10029

REIBMAN, JEANETTE FICHMAN, retired state senator; b. Ft. Wayne, Ind., Aug. 18, 1915; d. Meir and Pearl (Schwartz) Fichman; m. Nathan L. Reibman, June 20, 1943; children: Joseph M. Edward D., James E. AB, Hunter Coll., 1937; LLB, U. Ind., 1940; LLD, Lafayette Coll., 1969; hon. degree, Lehigh U., 1986, Wilson Coll., 1974, Cedar Crest Coll., 1977, Moravian Coll., 1990. Bar: Ind., 1940, U.S. Supreme Ct. 1944. Pvt. practice law Ft. Wayne, 1940; atty. U.S. War Dept., Washington, 1940-42, U.S. War Prodn. Bd., Washington, 1942-44; mem. Pa. Ho. of Reps., 1956-66, Pa. State Senate, Harrisburg, 1966-94; chmn. com. on edn. Pa. State Senate, 1971-81, minority chmn., 1981-90, majority caucus adminstr., 1992-94; mem. Edn. Commn. of the States. Trustee emeritus Lafayette Coll.; bd. mem. Pa. Higher Edn. Assistance Agy., Pa. Coun. on Arts, Camphill Schs. Recipient Disting. Dau. of Pa. award and medal Gov. Pa., 1968, citation on naming of Jeanette F. Reibman Adminstrn. Bldg., East Stroudsburg State Coll., 1972, Early Childhood Learning Ctr. Northampton Community Coll., 1992, Pub. Svc. award Pa. Psychol. Assn., 1977, Jerusalem City of Peace award Govt. Israel, 1977; named to Hunter Coll. Alumni Hall of Fame, 1974; U. Ind. Law Alumni fellow, 1993. Mem. Hadassah (Myrtle Wreath award 1976), Sigma Delta Tau, Delta Kappa Gamma, Phi Delta Kappa, Order Ea. Star. Democrat. Jewish. Office: 711 Lehigh St Easton PA 18042-4325

REICE, SYLVIE, columnist, editor, author; b. N.Y.C.; d. Samuel and Dora (Weinstock) Wolshine; m. Albert Reice, July 15, 1962; children: Milo, Naomi, Seth, Andrew, Richard. BA cum laude, CUNY, 1939; postgrad., New Sch. for Social Rsch., N.Y.C., 1940. Mng. editor Co-ed mag. Scholastic Publs., N.Y.C., 1955-59; editor-in-chief Ingenue mag. Dell Pub. Co., N.Y.C., 1959-67; columnist The Swinging Set, Pubs. Hall Syndicate, 1965-70; sr. editor McCalls mag., N.Y.C., 1967-71; editor-in-chief Family Health mag., N.Y.C., 1971-74; exec. editor Newspaper books Chgo. Tribune-N.Y. News Syndicate, N.Y.C., 1975-76; sr. editor Grosset & Dunlap Books, N.Y.C., 1976-79; columnist United Features Syndicate, N.Y.C., 1980—; freelance writer, 1946—; adj. prof. mag. journalism SUNY-Stony Brook. Author: (short story collections) For Girls Only, 1957, Season of Love, 1962, (novel) Now or Never, 1994; contbr. articles to various publs., including McCalls, Health, Seventeen, Ladies Home Jour. Guest editor Taproot mag. for elder citizens, L.I., N.Y., 1986-87. Recipient Penney Missouri award for best article of yr., 1970, award for best short story Bur. of Intercultural Edn., 1952. Mem. PEN, Newswomens Club N.Y. (v.p. 1984—, pres. 1983-84), Phi Beta Kappa. Home: 401 E 81st St New York NY 10028-5811

REICH, NANCY BASSEN, musicologist, educator; b. N.Y.C., July 3, 1924; d. Hyman and Ida (Orland) Bassen; m. Haskell A. Reich, June 25, 1945 (dec. 1983); children: Matthew, Susanna. BA, Queens Coll., 1945; MA, Tchrs. Coll., 1947; PhD, N.Y.U., 1972. Lectr. Queens Coll., N.Y.C., 1957-61, Hunter Coll., N.Y.C., 1963-67; adj. asst. prof. N.Y.U., N.Y.C., 1967-75; asst. prof. Manhattanville Coll., Purchase, N.Y., 1975-81; vis. prof. Bard Coll., Annandale-on-Hudson, N.Y., 1991-92, Williams Coll., Williamstown, Mass., 1993; vis. scholar Stanford U., 1982-83. Author: Clara Schumann: The Artist and the Woman, 1985 (Deems Taylor award ASCAP, 1986); editor: An Annotated Bibliography of Writings on Women in Music, 1989; contbr. articles and essays to anthologies and jours. Recipient Robert Schumann prize, 1996; fellow NEA, 1982; grantee German academic exchange Am. Philosoph. Soc., 1978, 87. Mem. Internat. Musicol. Soc., Am. Musicol. Soc., Robert-Schumann-Gesellschaft, Authors Guild. Home: 121 Lincoln Ave Hastings-on-Hudson NY 10706

REICH, PAULA JUDY, nursing educator; b. Troy, N.Y., Jan. 27, 1942; d. Samuel and Dora (Luskin) Bendick; m. Lawrence W. Reich, Nov. 1, 1964; children: Ronna, Heather, Sheara. AAS in Nursing, Queens Coll., 1961; BSN, St. John's U., Queens, N.Y., 1964; MS in Curriculum and Instrn., SUNY, Albany, 1975; MS in Nursing, Adelphi U., 1982. RN, N.Y. Staff nurse obstetrics Flushing Hosp., Queens, 1962-63; staff nurse ob/gyn. Queens Gen. Hosp., 1963-64; sr. staff nurse pediatrics Mt. Sinai Hosp., N.Y.C., 1964-65; supr. ob-gyn. Nassau Hosp., Mineola, N.Y., 1965-67; staff nurse obstetrics St. Peters Hosp., Albany, 1968-73; dir. Tri Cities Childbirth Instrn., Albany, 1973-78; mem. faculty dept. nursing Adelphi U., Garden City, N.Y., 1978-79, SUNY, Farmingdale, 1978—; clin. instr. Albany Jr. Coll., 1977-78; cons. maternal/child continuing edn. Adelphi U., 1984; dir. nursing continuing edn. SUNY, Farmingdale, 1985-91, dir. LPN/ADN nursing ract, 1990-94. V.p. bd. dirs. Suffolk Network Adolescent Pregnancy, Suffolk County, N.Y., 1985-90. Mem. Suffolk Perinatal Coalition. Office: SUNY Farmingdale Dept Nursing Rt 110 Melville NY 11735

REICH, ROSE MARIE, retired art educator; b. Milw., Dec. 24, 1937; d. Valentine John and Mary Jane (Grochowski) Kosmatka; m. Kenneth Pierce Reich, July 13, 1968; 1 stepson, Lance Pierce. BA, Milw. Downer Coll., 1959; MA, U. Wyo., 1967. Art tchr. Oconomowoc (Wis.) Area Schs., 1959-93, ret., 1993. Mem. Oconomowoc Edn. Assn., NEA (life), Wis. Edn. Assn., AAUW (v.p. membership 1989—), Delta Kappa Gamma (past pres.). Roman Catholic. Home: 3717 N Golden Lake Rd Oconomowoc WI 53066-4104

REICHBLUM, AUDREY ROSENTHAL, public relations executive; b. Pitts., June 28, 1935; d. Emanuel Nathan and Willa (Handmacher) Rosenthal; m. M. Charles Reichblum, Jan. 25, 1956; children: Robert Nathan, William Mark. Student, Bennington Coll., 1952-53; BS, Carnegie Mellon U., 1956. Accredited Pub. Rels. Soc. Pitts. Founder, creator, chmn. Pitts. Children's Mus., 1970-73; mag. writer Pitts. Mag., 1978; dir. pub. rels. Pitts. Pub. Theater, 1978-79; pres. arPR audrey reichblum PUB. RELS. inc., Pitts., 1980—; pub. rels. cons., bd. mem. Pitts. Planned Parenthood, 1980—, United Jewish Fedn., Bus. and Profl. Women, Pitts., 1980-85, Pitts. City Theater, 1985-94, Pa. Coun. on Aging, 1996—; chmn. Villa de Marillac Nursing. Recipient Gold Cindy award Info. Film Producers Am., 1982, award of excellence Internat. Assn. Bus. Communicators, Pitts., 1986, Matrix award Three Rivers Arts Festival, Lifetime Achievement award NAWBD-YWCA. Mem. Publ. Rels. Soc. Am. (award of merit 1983, G. Victor Barkman award for excellence 1984, 1st place award Race For The Cure), Women in Comm. (Matrix-sales promotion award 1987), Nat. Assn. Women Bus. Owners (Life Time Achievement award 1995), Exec. Women's Coun., Am. Women in Radio and TV, Am. Mktg. Assn., Rotary. Office: 1420 Centre Ave Ste 2216 Pittsburgh PA 15219-3528

REICHENBACH, M. J. GERTRUDE, retired university program director, consultant; b. Heerlen, Limburg, The Netherlands, Aug. 18, 1912; came to U.S., 1946; d. Jan Hubert Emile and M.J. Gertruda (Cardaun) Consten; m. Joseph Winfield, May 7, 1946; children: Paul Joseph, Peter David, Miriam Johanna, Eric Emile, Ingrid Gertrude. MA in English, U. Utrecht, The Netherlands, 1936; postgrad., Post Grad. Sch., The Netherlands, 1942-43; MA in German, U. Pa., 1971. English tchr. St. Clara Coll., Heerlen, The Netherlands, 1940-46; coord., originator Dutch studies U. Pa., Phila., 1969-87, cons. Dutch programs, 1987—; cons. Dutch programs Syracuse (N.Y.) U., 1987—. Co-editor presentations and lectures, 1985. Recipient John Adams medal The Netherlands Govt., 1976; named Officer in the Order of Orange Nassau, The Netherlands Govt., 1986, Officer in the Crown Order of Belgium, Belgian Govt., 1987. Mem. Internat. Assn. Netherlandic Studies, Am. Assn. Netherlandic Studies, Netherlands Soc. Phila. (chmn. lectures, mem. exec. bd. 1988—), Netherland Am. Assn. Delaware Valley (exec. bd. 1988—), Assn. for Advancement Dutch Studies, Can. Assn. English Netherlandic Studies, Am. Translators Assn., Germantown Cricket Club, AAUW. Republican. Roman Catholic. Home: 3031 W Coulter St Philadelphia PA 19129-1021

REICHERT, CHERYL MCBROOM, pathologist, research consultant; b. Great Falls, Mont., Sept. 4, 1946; d. Harold and Arlyne (Cohn) R.; m. Sherwood McBroom Jr., 1964 (div. 1971); children: Scott, Cari. BS, Coll. of Great Falls, 1969; MS, U. Mich., 1971, PhD, 1974, MD, 1976. Diplomate Am. Bd. Med. Examiners, Am. Bd. Pathology. Tching fellow dept. biochemistry U. Mich., Ann Arbor, 1969-74; resident in anatomic pathology Nat. Cancer Inst., Bethesda, Md., 1977-79; resident in clin. pathology NIH, Bethesda, 1979-80, surgical pathologist, chief autopsy service, 1981-85; pathologist Sibley Meml. Hosp., Washington, 1985-86; cons. Digene Corp., College Park, Md., 1985-90, Nat. Cancer Inst., Bethesda, 1985-92; pathologist Columbus Hosp., Great Falls, 1987—, dir. labs., 1990-91, 94—; assoc. rsch. scientist McLaughlin Research Inst., Great Falls, 1987—; clin. assoc. prof. Uniformed Svcs. U. Health Scis., Bethesda, 1983-86; presenter President's Nat. Cancer Adv. Bd., Washington, 1983. Contbr. 50 articles to profl. jours. Trustee Coll. of Gt. Falls, 1991-94; mem. profl. edn. com. Am. Cancer Soc.; bd. dirs. Ann Arbor Child Care and Devel.; charter mem., bd. dirs. Project Heal Montana, 1993-96. Lt. comdr. USPHS, 1977-80. Named Outstanding Young Women of Yr., State of Mich., 1993, Great Falls Profl. Women of Yr., YMCA, 1991. Mem. U.S. Acad. Pathologists, Mont. Pathologists Soc. (pres. 1989-90, sec.-treas. 1990-91), Galens Med. Soc., Alpha Omega Alpha. Home: 51 Prospect Dr Great Falls MT 59405-4123

REICHERT, MARY GASSMANN, lawyer; b. N.D., 1944. BA, Coll. of St. Catherine, 1966; MA, U. Notre Dame, 1969; JD, Ill. Inst. Tech., 1975; LLM in Taxation, Washington U., 1981. Bar: Ill. 1975, U.S. Dist. Ct. (no. dist.) Mo. 1978, U.S. Tax Ct. 1980. Ptnr. Bryan Cave LLP, St. Louis. Mem. Chgo-Kent Law Rev., 1974-75. Office: Bryan Cave LLP 211 N Broadway One Metropolitan Sq Saint Louis MO 63102*

REICHGOTT JUNGE, EMBER D., state legislator, lawyer; b. Detroit, Aug. 22, 1953; d. Norbert Arnold and Diane (Pincich) R.; m. Michael Junge. BA summa cum laude, St. Olaf Coll., Minn., 1974; JD, Duke U., 1977; MBA, U. of St. Thomas, 1991. Bar: Minn. 1977, D.C. 1978. Assoc., Larkin, Hoffman, Daly & Lindgren, Bloomington, Minn., 1977-84; counsel Control Data Corp., Bloomington, Minn., 1984-86; atty. The Gen. Counsel, Ltd., 1987—; mem. Minn. State Senate, 1983—, chmn. legis. com. on econ. status of women, 1984-86, vice chmn. senate edn. com., 1987-88, senate majority whip, 1990-94, chmn. property tax div. senate tax com., 1991-92, chmn. senate judiciary com., 1993-94; senate asst. majority leader, 1995—, chmn. spl. subcom. on Ethical Conduct; instr. polit. sci. St. Olaf. Coll., Northfield, Minn., 1993; dir. Citizens Ind. Bank, St. Louis Park, Minn., 1993—. Host (cable TV monthly series) Legis. Report, 1985-92. Trustee, bd. dirs. N.W. YMCA, New Hope, Minn., 1983-88; Greater Mpls. Red Cross, 1988—, United Way Mpls., 1989—. Youngest woman ever elected to Minn. State Senate, 1983; recipient Woman of Yr. award North Hennepin Bus. and Prof. Women, 1983, Award for Contbn. to Human Svcs., Minn. Social Svcs. Assn., 1983, Clean Air award Minn. Lung Assn., 1988, Disting. Svc. award Mpls. Jaycees, 1984, Minn. Dept. Human Rights award, 1989, Myra Bradwell award Minn. Women Lawyers, 1993, Disting. Alumnae award Lake Conf. Schs., 1993; named One of Ten Outstanding Young Minnesotans, Minn. Jaycees, 1984, Policy Advocate of Yr. NAWBO, 1988, Woman of Achievement Twin West C. of C., 1989, Marvelous Minn. Woman, 1993. Mem. Minn. Bar Assn. (bd. govs. 1992—, Pro Bono Publico Atty. award 1990), Hennepin County Bar Assn., Corporate Counsel Assn. (v.p. 1989—), Minn. Dem. Farmer-Labor Party (state co-chair Clinton/Gore Presdl. Campaign 1992, 96, del. nat. Dem. conv. 1984, 92). Home: 7701 48th Ave N Minneapolis MN 55428-4515

REICHMAN, DAWN LESLIE, lawyer, educator, deputy sheriff; b. Portsmouth, Va., Feb. 15, 1951; d. Stanley J. and Ernestine Enid (Kaiserman) Greif; m. James Richard Smith, Apr. 27, 1975 (div. July 1978); m. Victor I. Reichman, Nov. 24, 1979; children: Mark Heath, Margo Ilene, Shelley Renee. BA, U. Calif., L.A., 1972; cert. dep. sheriff, Sheriff Acad., 1974; JD, Whittier Coll., 1988. Bar: Calif. 1988, U.S. Dist. Ct. (ea. and cen. dists.) Calif. 1988. Dep. sheriff L.A. County Sheriff's Dept., 1973-81; substitute tchr. Palmdale (Calif.) Sch. Dist., 1988-90; pvt. practice law Palmdale, 1988—; alt. def. counsel, 1990-91. Spokesperson Ana Verde Homeowners Assn., Palmdale, 1989-95; assoc. Alpha Charter Guild of Antelope Valley Hosp.; former bd. dirs. Palmdale Cmty. Assn.; bd. dir. Families Caring for Families; v.p. Desert Haven Enterprises; mem. strategic planning task force Antelope Valley Hosp. Med. Ctr.; mem. Career Prep Coun. Law and Govt. Adv. Com.; pres. Primary Source Profl. Referral Bd.; former mem. gala com. Antelope Valley Hosp. Gift Found. Mem. AAUW, Antelope Valley Bar Assn. (pres. 1995), Calif. Women Lawyers, High Desert Criminal Def. Bar Assn. (v.p. 1993, former sec.), Antelope Valley Bar Citizens Law Sch. (chmn.), Encouraging Potential in Children (co-chmn.), Palmdale & Quartz Hill C. of C., Phi Alpha Delta. Office: 1305 E Palmdale Blvd Ste 4 Palmdale CA 93550-4853

REICHMAN, NANCI SATIN, oil company owner; b. Tulsa, July 7, 1939; d. Jack Harold and Tybie Mary (Davis) Satin; m. Louis Reichman, Dec. 25, 1960 (dec. Feb. 1972); children: David Michael, Jill Satin; life ptnr. Phillip M. Citrin. Student, Sarah Lawrence Coll., Bronxville, N.Y., 1957-59; cert. Jungian psychology, C.G. Jung Inst., Evanston, Ill., 1988. Fashion model Miss Jackson's, Tulsa, 1969-70; pres. LIR Investments, Tulsa, 1972-78; pres., dir. devel. Tymar Oil Co., Tulsa and Santa Fe, N.Mex., 1990—; owner ind. oil prodn. Chgo., 1972—; audio tape lectr for various workshops. Pres. C.G. Jung Inst., Evanston, Ill., 1980-81, 81-82, 84-85, also mem. adv. bd.; v.p. Tulsa Jr. Philharm., 1968; sec. Tulsa Ballet, 1968; mem. Women's Forum N.Mex., 1996—; bd. dirs. Found. Santa Fe Cmty. Coll., 1995—. Home: 653 Canyon Rd # 4 Santa Fe NM 87501

REICHSTETTER, CRYSTAL PROCTOR, assistant principal; b. Greensboro, N.C., Jan. 22, 1969; d. Lawrence Darrell and Mary Trudi (Mooney) Proctor; m. Thomas Eugene Reichstetter, Aug. 3, 1991. BS in Spl. Edn., East Carolina U., 1991, postgrad., 1995—. Cert. in mentally handicapped edn., cross-categorical edn., sch. adminstrn., N.C. Cross-categorical tchr. 6th, 7th and 8th grades Southwestern Randolph Mid. Sch., Asheboro, N.C., 1991-94; tchr. learning disabled, educable mentally handipped Speight Mid. Sch., Wilson, N.C., 1994-95; asst. prin. Randleman Mid. Sch., N.C., 1995-96. N.C. Teaching fellow, Raleigh, 1987; N.C. Prin. Fellows scholar, 1995—. Mem. ASCD, Profl. Educators N.C. Baptist.

REID, DONNA JOYCE, small business owner; b. Springfield, Tenn., June 25, 1954; d. Leonard Earl Reid and Joyce (Robertson) Kirby; m. Kenneth Bruce Sadler, June 26, 1976 (div. Apr. 1980); m. John Christopher Moulton, Oct. 18, 1987 (div. Dec. 1992); m. Peter Leatherland, Apr. 3, 1993. Student, Austin Peay State U., Clarksville, Tenn., 1972-75. Show writer, producer WTVF-TV (CBS affiliate), Nashville, 1977-83, promotion producer, 1983-85, on-air promotion mgr., 1985-86; gen. mgr. Steadi-Film Corp., Nashville, 1986-90; co-owner Options Internat., Nashville, 1990—. Big sister Buddies of Nashville, 1981-87. Named to Honorable Order of Ky. Cols. John Y. Brown, Gov., 1980; recipient Significant Svc. award ARC, 1982, Clara Barton Communications award, 1983. Mem. NAFE, Nat. Assn. TV Arts and Scis., Nat. Film Inst., Nat. Assn. Broadcasters, Internat. Platform Assn. Methodist. Office: Options Internat Inc 913 18th Ave S Nashville TN 37212-2102

REID, FRANCES EVELYN KROLL, cinematographer, director, film company executive; b. Oakland, Calif., Mar. 25, 1944; d. William Farnham and Marion Storm (Teller) Kroll. BA, U. Oreg., 1966. Tchr. secondary sch., Los Angeles, 1968-69; sound recordist Churchill Films, Los Angeles, 1971; freelance sound recordist Los Angeles, 1972-75, freelance producer, dir., 1975-78; freelance cinematographer Berkeley, Calif., 1978—; pres. Iris Films, Berkeley, 1977—; vol. Peace Corps, Malawi, Africa, 1969-70. Dir. (film) In The Best Interests of the Children, 1977 (Blue Ribbon Am. Film Festival 1978), The Changer: A Record of the Times, 1991, Skin Deep, 1995, Talking About Race, 1994, Straight from the Heart, 1994 (Acad. award nominee 1995); cinematographer: (film) The Times of Harvey Milk, 1984 (Oscar 1985), Living with AIDS, 1986 (Student Acad. award 1987), Common Threads: Stories from the Quilt, 1989 (Oscar award 1990), Complaints of a Dutiful Daughter, 1994 (Acad. award nominee 1995). Mem. Film Arts Found., Assn. Ind. Video and Filmmakers, Acad. Motion Picture Arts and Scis. Office: Iris Films PO Box 5353 Berkeley CA 94705-0353

REID, INEZ SMITH, lawyer, educator; b. New Orleans, Apr. 7, 1937; d. Sidney Randall Dickerson and Beatrice Virginia (Bundy) Smith. BA, Tufts U., 1959; LLB, Yale U., 1962; MA, UCLA, 1963; PhD, Columbia U., 1968. Bar: Calif. 1963, N.Y. 1972, D.C. 1980. Assoc. prof. Barnard Coll. Columbia U., N.Y.C., 1972-76; gen. counsel youth div. State of N.Y., 1976-77; dep. gen. counsel HEW, Washington, 1977-79; inspector gen. EPA, Washington, 1979-81; chief legis. and opinions, dep. corp. counsel Office of Corp. Counsel, Washington, 1981-83; corp. counsel D.C., 1983-85; counsel Laxalt, Washington, Perito & Dubuc, Washington, 1986-90, ptnr., 1990-91; counsel Graham & James, 1991-93, Lewis, White & Clay, P.C., 1994-95; assoc. judge D.C. Ct. Appeals, 1995—. William J. Maier, Jr. vis. prof. law W.Va. U. Coll. Law, Morgantown, 1985-86. Author: Together Black Women, 1972; contbr. articles to profl. jours. and publs. Bd. dirs. Homeland Ministries Bd. United Ch. of Christ, N.Y.C., 1978-83, vice chmn., 1981-83; chmn. bd. govs. Antioch Law Sch., Washington, 1979-81; chmn. bd. trustees Antioch U., Yellow Springs, Ohio, 1981-82; bd. trustees Tufts U., Medford, Mass., 1988—, Lancaster (Pa.) Sem., 1988—; bd. govs. D.C. Sch. Law, 1990—, chmn., 1991-95. Recipient Emily Gregory award Barnard Coll., 1976, Arthur Morgan award Antioch U., 1982, Service award United Ch. of Christ, 1983, Disting. Service (Profl. Life) award Tufts U. Alumni Assn., 1988. Office: DC Ct Appeals 500 Indiana Ave NW 6th Fl Washington DC 20001-2131

REID, JOAN EVANGELINE, lawyer, stockbroker; b. Mich., Apr. 22, 1932; d. August W. and Evangeline R. (Brozeau) Rogers; m. Belmont M. Reid. AA in Bus., San Jose State U., 1951; JD, McGeorge Sch. Law, 1989. Bar: Nev.; lic. realtor, life, disability and annuity ins. Officer, dir. Lifetime Fin. Planning Corp., San Jose, Calif., 1967-77, Lifetime Realty Corp., San Jose, 1967-77; co-founder, officer, dir. Belmont Reid & Co., San Jose, 1960-77; officer, corp. counsel, dir. JOBEL Fin. Inc., Carson City, Nev., 1980—. Past sec., treas. Nev. Fedn. Rep. Women; charter pres. Santa Clara Valley Rep. Women Federated; past v.p. Carson City Rep. Women's Club. Paul Harris fellow Rotary. Mem. ABA, First Jud. Dist. Bar Assn., Washoe County Bar Assn., State Bar Nev., No. Nev. Women Lawyers Assn., Carson City C. of C., Soroptomist (past pres. Carson City club). Address: PO Box 3676 Carson City NV 89702-3676

REID, LISA RAE, program director; b. New Castle, Ind., Aug. 15, 1962; d. Ray and Sarah Catherine (Russ) Caudill; m. James Kenneth Reid; 1 child, Jeremy Kenneth. BS, Troy State U., 1985, MS in Counseling and Human Devel., 1995. Cert. tchr. Tchr. Socastee Middle Sch., Myrtle Beach, S.C., 1985-87; daycare dir. Ea. Hills Bapt. Ch., Montgomery, Ala., 1987; edn. supr. Coun. on Substance Abuse, Montgomery, 1988-92; program dir. info. and referral ministry Perry Hill United Meth. Ch., Montgomery, 1992—; youth dirs. coord. Montgomery (Ala.) United Meth. Dist., 1993—, young adult coord., 1994—, dist. presenter, 1995. Creator, editor The Beacon. Sec. Mental Health Assn., Montgomery, 1993-95, operation Santa Claus chairperson, 1993-95. Mem. ACA, Ala. Counseling Assn., Am. Christian Counseling Assn., Assn. Marriage and Family Counselors. Republican. Office: Perry Hill United Meth Ch 910 Perry Hill Rd Montgomery AL 36109

REID, LORENE FRANCES, middle school educator; b. St. Louis, May 28, 1946; d. Frank Bernard and Marcella Marie (Froechtenigt) Niemeyer; m. Patrick Joseph Reid, Aug. 11, 1967; 1 child, Christina Marie. BA in Spanish, Maryville U., 1968; MED in Secondary Edn., U. Mo., St. Louis, 1990; PhD in Edn., St. Louis U., 1995; MA in English, Southeast Mo. State U., 1996. Cert. Spanish, social studies, ESL tchr., Mo. Spanish tchr. Rosary H.S., Spanish Lake, Mo., 1968-69, Taylor Sch., Clayton, Mo., 1969-70, Roosevelt H.S., St. Louis, 1988-89, Cleve. Jr. Naval Acad., St. Louis, 1989-90, Thomas Dunn Meml. Adult Edn., St. Louis, 1992—; social studies tchr. St. Luke's Sch., Richmond Heights, Mo., 1981-88; ESL tchr. Grant Mid. Sch., St. Louis, 1990-92, Fanning Mid. Sch., St. Louis, 1992—; tutor Sylvan Learning Ctr., Crestwood, Mo., 1990-92; mem. St. Louis Ednl. Leadership Inst., 1994—. Mem. Cmty. Leadership Program for Tchrs., St. Louis, 1993-94. Recipient Emerson Electric Excellence in Teaching award, 1994; named Tchr. of Yr., St. Louis Pub. Schs., 1994-95; named as one of 60 tchrs. recognized by Disney Channel Salutes the Am. Tchr., 1995-96. Mem. ASCD, Am. Ednl. Rsch. Assn., Tchrs. English to Spkrs. of Other Langs., Nat. Coun. Tchrs. English, Midam. Tchs. English to Spkrs. of Other Langs., Phi Delta Kappa.

REID, LYNNE MCARTHUR, pathologist; b. Melbourne, Australia, Nov. 12, 1923; d. Robert Muir and Violet Annie (McArthur) R. M.D., U. Melbourne, 1946; M.D. (hon.), Harvard U., 1976. Reader in exptl. pathology London U., 1964-67, prof. exptl. pathology, 1967-76; dean Cardiothoracic Inst., 1973-76; pathologist-in-chief Children's Hosp., Boston, 1976-89, pathologist-in-chief emeritus, 1990—; S. Burt Wolbach prof. pathology Harvard Med. Sch., Boston, 1976—. Fellow Royal Coll. Physicians (U.K.), Royal Australian Coll. Physicians, Royal Coll. Pathologists, Royal Coll. Radiologists (hon.), Royal Soc. Medicine, Royal Inst. Gt. Britain, Pathol. Soc. Gt. Britain and Ireland, Thoracic Soc., Assn. Clin. Pathologists, Brit. Thoracic Soc., Fleischner Soc., Can. Thoracic Soc., Neonatal Soc., Am. Thoracic Soc., Am. Soc. Pathologists, Fedn. Am. Socs. Exptl. Biology. Office: 300 Longwood Ave Boston MA 02115-5724

REID, MARILYN JOANNE, state legislator, lawyer; b. Chgo., Aug. 14, 1941; d. Kermit and Newell Azile (Hahn) N.; m. M. David Reid, Nov. 26, 1966 (div. Mar. 1983); children: David, Nelson. Student, Miami U., 1959-61; BA, U. Ill, 1963; JD, Ohio No. U., 1966. Bar: Ohio 1966, Ark. 1967, U.S. Dist. Ct. 1967. Trust adminstr. First Nat. Bank, Dayton, Ohio, 1966-67; assoc. Sloan & Ragsdale, Little Rock, Ohio, 1967-69; ptnr. Reid and Reid, Dayton, 1969-76, Reid & Buckwalter, Dayton, 1975—; mem. Ohio Ho. of Reps., 1993—; mem. Judiciary and Criminal Justice com., vice chmn. ins. com., Vets. com., Pub. utilities com. Mem. Ohio adv. bd. U.S. Commn. Civil Rights; chmn., treas. various polit. campaigns, 1975—; trustee Friends Libr. Beavercreek (Ohio); bd. dirs. Beavercreek YMCA, 1985-88; active Mt. Zion United Ch. of Christ. Mem. ABA, Ohio Bar Assn., Greene County Bar Assn., Beavercreek C. of C. (pres. 1986-87), Dayton Panhellenic Assn. (pres. 1982), Altrusa (v.p. Greene County 1978-79, pres. 1979-80), Lioness (pres. Beavercreek 1975), Rotary, Kappa Beta Pi, Gamma Phi Beta (v.p. 1974-75). Republican. Mem. Ch. Christ. Office: Reid & Buckwalter 3866 Indian Ripple Rd Dayton OH 45440-3448

REID, REBECCA LOIS FARRIS, school system administrator, consultant; b. Montgomery, Ala., Nov. 4, 1938; d. Bernard Young and Mabel Dorothy (Peazant) Farris; m. Herman Edward Reid Jr., Aug. 19, 1963; children: Michael Edward, Michele Bernita, Mabel Rebecca, Maurice Herman. BA in Sociology, Bennett Coll., 1960; MSLS, Atlanta U., 1968; EdS, U. Ga., 1977. Cert. media specialist, Ga. Asst. libr. Langston (Okla.) U., 1960-62; circulation libr. Albany (Ga.) State Coll., 1962-64; grad. asst. Atlanta U., 1964-65; tchr., libr. Cedartown (Ga.) City Sch. Sys., 1965-66; elem. sch. libr. coord. Sylacauga (Ala.) City Bd. Edn., 1966; asst libr. Albany State Coll., 1988; libr., libr. media specialist Dougherty County Bd. Edn., Albany, 1967-91, dir. media svcs., 1991—. Mem. edn. guild Albany Symphony Guild, 1986-88; Christian edn. coord. St. Mark's Episcopal Ch., 1982—. Mem. ALA, ASCD, Ga. Libr. Media Assn., Inc. (chmn. intellectual freedom com. 1992—), Ga. ASCD. Democrat. Home: 2313 Bettys Dr Albany GA 31705-4301 Office: Dougherty County Sch Sys 1503 N Jefferson St Albany GA 31701-1607

REID, SARAH LAYFIELD, lawyer; b. Kansas City, Mo., Sept. 22, 1952; d. Jim Tom and Sarah Pauline (Clark) R.; m. David Harris Gikow, June 12, 1983; children: Stephen Nathaniel, Emily Pauline. AB, Bryn Mawr Coll., 1974; JD, Harvard U., 1977. Bar: N.Y. 1978, U.S. Dist. Ct. (so. and ea. dists.) N.Y. 1978, U.S. Ct. Appeals (11th cir.) 1981, U.S. Ct. Appeals (2d cir.) 1982, U.S. Supreme Ct. 1988, U.S. Ct. Appeals (3d cir.) 1990. Assoc. Kelley Drye & Warren, N.Y.C., 1977-85, ptnr., 1986—, co-head securities litigation practice group, 1995—. Mem. ABA, N.Y. State Bar Assn., Fed. Bar Coun., Assn. of Bar of City of N.Y. (mem. task force on women in the profession). Office: Kelley Drye & Warren 101 Park Ave New York NY 10178

REID, SHARON LEA, educational facilitator; b. Wheeler, Tex., Apr. 24, 1949; d. George S. and Arvazine (Deering) Robinson; m. Thomas Michael Reid, July 9, 1989. BS, McMurry Coll., 1970; MEd, Tarleton State U., 1979. Cert. tchr., edn. adminstr., supr., Tex. Tchr. Fleming Elem., San Antonio, Tex., 1971-72, Peebles Elem., Killeen, Tex., 1972-84; tchr. Sugar Loaf Elem., Killeen, 1984-85, facilitator, 1985—; trainer/dist. Marilyn Burns Problem Solving, Killeen, 1982-85, trainer/campus 4 MAT Lesson Design/ Excel, Inc., Killeen, 1994—. Mem. Heights Concert Band, Harker Heights, Tex. Recipient music scholarship McMurry Coll., Abilene, Tex., 1968. Mem. ASCD, Tex. State Tchrs. Assn., Phi Delta Kappa. Office: Sugar Loaf Elem Sch 1517 Barbara Ln Killeen TX 76542

REID, SUE TITUS, law educator; b. Bryan, Tex., Nov. 13, 1939; d. Andrew Jackson Jr. and Loraine (Wylie) Titus. BS with honors, Tex. Woman's U., 1960; MA, U. Mo., 1962, PhD, 1965; JD, U. Iowa, 1972. Bar: Iowa 1972, U.S. Ct. Appeals (D.C. cir.) 1978, U.S. Supreme Ct. 1978. From instr. to assoc. prof. sociology Cornell Coll., Mt. Vernon, Iowa, 1963-72; assoc. prof., chmn. dept. sociology Coe Coll., Cedar Rapids, Iowa, 1972-74; assoc. prof. law. U. Wash., Seattle, 1974-76; exec. assoc. Am. Sociol. Assn., Washington, 1976-77; prof. law U. Tulsa, 1978-88; dean, prof. Sch. Criminology, Fla. State U., Tallahassee, 1988-90; prof. pub. adminstrn. and policy Fla. State U., 1990—; acting chmn. dept. sociology Cornell Coll., 1965-66; vis. assoc. prof. sociology U. Nebr., Lincoln, 1970; vis. disting. prof. law and sociology U. Tulsa, 1977-78, assoc. dean 1979-81; vis. prof. law U. San Diego, 1981-82; mem. People-to-People Crime Prevention Del. to People's Republic of China, 1982; George Beto Vis. Prof. criminal justice Sam Houston U., Huntsville, Tex., 1984-85; lecture/study tour of Criminal Justice systems of 10 European countries, 1985; cons. Evaluation Policy Rsch. Assocs., Inc., Milw., 1976-77, Nat. Inst. Corrections, Idaho Dept. Corrections, 1984, Am. Correctional Inst., Price-Waterhouse. Author: (with others) Bibliographies on Role Methodology and Propositions Volume D - Studies in the Role of the Public School Teacher, 1962, The Correctional System: An Introduction, 1981, Crime and Criminology, 7th edit., 1994, Criminal Justice, 1987, 3d edit., 1993, 4th edit. Brown and Benchmark, 1996, Criminal Law, 1989, 3d edit., 1995; editor: (with David Lyon) Population Crisis: An Interdisciplinary Perspective, 1972; contbr. articles to profl. jours. Recipient Disting. Alumni award Tex. Woman's U., 1979; named One of Okla. Young Leaders of 80's Oklahoma Monthly, 1980. Mem. Am. Soc. Criminology, Acad. Criminal Justice Scis., Soc. Criminal Jus. Assn. Office: Fla State Univ Dept Pub Adminstrn Tallahassee FL 32306

REID, WENDY, performing company executive. Gen. dir. Les Grands Ballet Candiens, Montreal, Can. Office: Les Grands Ballets Canadiens, 4816 rue Rivard, Montreal, PQ Canada H2J 2N6*

REIDA-ALLEN, PAMELA ANNE, healthcare consultant and administrator; b. Fitchburg, Mass., June 8, 1944; d. Alvah Michael Reida and Sirkka Margaret (Anttila) Kao; m. Dennis Alan Joaquin, 1967 (div. 1973); children: Joshua, Amy, Sebastian; m. Yahya Radazar, Oct. 1983 (dec. Sept. 1987); m. Loyall C. Allen. BA in English, Philosophy, Calif. State U., Los Angeles, 1966; RN diploma with honors, Leominster (Mass.) Hosp., 1976; BS in Nursing cum laude, Fitchburg (Mass.) State Coll., 1982; MS magna cum laude, Lesley Coll., 1986. Substitute tchr. Fitchburg Pub. Schs., 1966-67; social worker N.Y.C. Dept. Social Services, N.Y.C., 1967-68; news correspondent The Lowell (Mass.) Sun, 1969-71; nurse lab., delivery Leominster Hosp., 1976-77A; inservice coordinator Birchwood Manor Nursing Home, Fitchburg, 1977, asst. dir. nursing, 1977-78, dir. nursing, 1978-80; dir. nursing Naukeag Hosp., Ashburnham, Mass., 1980-84; asst. dir. nursing Beech Hill Hosp., Dublin, N.H., 1984-87, dir nursing, 1987-90, chair utilization rev. com., 1985-95; clin. coord. Hospice of Cape Cod, Yarmouthport, Mass., 1995—; mem. adv. council allied health majors Mass. Regional Voc. Sch., Fitchburg, Mass., 1977-84; with Area Speakers Bur., Fitchburg, 1980-84, vice chair Quality Assurance Program, 1988; cons. Quality Healthcare Resources, Inc. subs. Joint Commn. on Accreditation of Hosps., 1988—, Joint Commn. on Accreditation of Healthcare Orgns., Chgo., 1988-95. Vol. Family Planning, Fitchburg, 1981-82; del. Intercity Mgmt. Council, Fitchburg, 1980-84; clin. coord. Hospice Cape Cod, 1995—. Mem. NAFE, Tri-City Nursing Home Assn. (pres. 1978-80), Nat. Nurses Assn., N.H. Nurses Assn. (program com. 1985—), Greater Fitchburg C. of C., N.H. Orgn. Exec. Nurses, N.H. Quality Assurance Assn. Office: Hospice of Cape Cod 962 Rt 6A Yarmouth Port MA 02675

REID-BILLS, MAE, editor, historian; b. Shreveport, La.; d. Dayton Taylor and Bessie Oline (Boles) Reid; m. Frederick Gurdon Bills (div.); children: Marjorie Reid, Nancy Hawkins, Frederick Taylor, Virginia Thomas, Elizabeth Sharples. AB, Stanford U., 1942, MA, 1965; PhD, U. Denver, 1977. Mng. editor Am. West mag., Tucson, Ariz., 1979-89; cons. editor, 1989—. Gen. Electric fellow, 1963, William Robertson Coe fellow, 1964. Mem. Orgn. Am. Historians, Am. Hist. Assn., Phi Beta Kappa, Phi Alpha Theta.

REID-CRISP, WENDY, publishing executive; m. Ewing Walker; 1 child, Max Crisp. BA in Eng., Whitman Coll., 1965. Editor-in-chief Savvy Mag.; founder, pub. New Chapter Press, N.Y.C.; editor-in-chief Small Press; dir National Association of Female Executives, New York, NY; nat. dir. Nat. Assn. Female Execs., founder, editor Profl. Libr. bus. books for women, liaison other women's orgns.; lectr. profl. women's issues, 1988—. Author: Give Me One Good Reason: Why Living Takes Up So Much Of Our Time, 1992. Bd. dirs. United Meth. Comms., 1984—. *

REIDER, BARBARA, school psychologist; b. Phila., Mar. 26, 1941; d. Charles G. and Mildred M. (Lessing) Grossman; m. Harry Reider, June 6, 1976; 1 child, Heather Blatt. BS Elem. Edn., Temple U., 1964, EdM Ednl. Psychology, 1971; PhD Human Devel., Bryn Mawr, 1989. Lic. sch. psychologist, N.Mex. Tchr. Phila. Pub. Sch. Systems, 1964-66; dir. of youth activities YMYWHA, Phila., 1966-69; program dir. Fedn. Day Care Svcs., Phila., 1969-76; ednl. cons. Reider Assocs., Phila., 1976-89; assoc. prof., edn. dept. chmn. Coll. of Santa Fe, N.Mex., 1989—; adj. prof. Temple U., Phila., Phila., 1980-87, Beaver Coll., Glenside, Pa., 1980-87. Author: The Integrated Elementary Classroom, 1994. Decorated Legion of Honor. Mem. Am. Ednl. Rsch. Assn., N.Mex. Assn. Sch. Psychologists, Phi Delta Kappa. Office: Coll of Santa Fe 1600 St Michaels Dr Santa Fe NM 87505-7634

REIDER, BARBARA POWELL, accounting educator; b. Alliance, Ohio, 1960; d. Charles and Gaye Powell; m. Robert M. Reider. BBA, Kent State U., 1983; MA, Ohio State U., 1986; PhD, Kent State U., 1991. CPA, Wash., CMA. Lectr. U. Akron, Ohio, 1989-90; assoc. prof. acctg. U. Alaska, Anchorage, 1990—; dir. Inst. Mgmt. Accts., Anchorage, 1990—; rep. Univ. Assembly, Anchorage, 1995-96. Contbr. articles to profl. jours. Dir. Alzheimer's Assn., Anchorage, 1991-96. Office: U Alaska-Anchorage Sch Bus 3211 Providence Dr Anchorage AK 99508

REIDER, CARROLL ANN, nutritionist, consultant; b. Phoenix, Feb. 28, 1960; d. John Jerome and Patricia Elaine (Heath) Reider. BS in Nutrition, Calif. State U., Long Beach, 1983; Advanced MS in Nutrition, Inst. Health Professions, Mass. Gen. Hosp., Boston, 1989. Registered dietitian, cert. nutrition support dietitian. Clin. dietetic technician Hoag Hosp., Newport Beach, Calif., 1982-84; dietetic intern U. Calif., San Francisco, 1984-85; chief clin. dietitian, nutrition support specialist St. Mary's Med. Ctr., San Francisco, 1986-88; nutrition support team dietitian, surg. rsch. dietitian Mass. Gen. Hosp., Brigham & Women's Hosp., Harvard U., Boston, 1988-89; critical care nutritionist UCLA Med. Ctr., 1989-92, associated faculty, instr., 1989-94; corp. mgr. nutritional support svcs. Salick Health Care/ INFUSX, Inc., Beverly Hills, 1992-95; cons., lectr., 1986—; home care nutrition cons. Am. Dietetic Assn., Chgo., 1993—. Contbr. articles to profl. jours. Mem. Am. Dietetic Assn. (excellence/leadership award 1993, 96, cert. of recognition 1992, 95, cabinet mem. dietitians in nutrition support practice group), Am. Soc. Parenteral and Enteral Nutrition. Home: 1521 Centinela Ave Apt A Santa Monica CA 90404-3206

REID FIGUEROA, MARCELLA INEZ, educator, minister; b. Jamaica, N.Y., Mar. 12, 1956; d. Marcellus Emanuel Reid and Elizabeth (Dean) Reid-Joseph; stepfather: Alpha Omega Joseph; m. Steven Figueroa, Oct. 25, 1980. BA in Liberal Arts and Scis., CCNY, 1979; postgrad. Health, Edn., Nursing, Arts., NYU, 1981-82; MDiv, New Brunswick Theol. Sem., 1995. Ordained to ministry, 1996; ministry lic., N.Y., New Jerusalem Bapt. Ch., 1992. Svc. rep. HEW Social Security Adminstrn., Jamaica, N.Y., 1977-78; social ins. rep. Social Security Adminstrn., Jamaica, 1979-81; dancing tchr. N.Y.C. Bd. Edn., 1983-84; coord., tchr. dance program N.Y.C. Bd. Edn. Aftersch., Jamaica, 1984-85; hosp. chaplain intern N.Y. Hosp. and Med. Ctr., Queens, N.Y., 1994; program design, coord. Assn. Black Seminarians, Queens, 1993-94; minister fine arts New Jerusalem Bapt. Ch., Jamaica, N.Y., 1991—; founder, exec. artistic dir. Dance Explosion Ltd., Laurelton, Queens, N.Y., 1973—; founder, CEO Gethsemane to Paradise Inc., 1996—; mentor: to coll. student Bernard M. Baruch Coll., Jamaica, 1982, to h.s. student Fiorello La Guardia Middle Coll. H.S., Jamaica, Queens, N.Y., 1983, to handicapped choreographer Deja Vu Dance Theatre, Queens, 1984; dance educator on tour Cultural Exchange Network, USSR, summer, 1991. Contbr. articles to N.J. Bapt. Ch. Messenger, 1994-95; choreographer liturgical dances New Brunswick Theol. Sem. Archives, 1992-95; design coord. Seminars Unity in the Comty. Koinonia, 1992-95 (AOBS 1992-95). Work sponsor Coalition of 100 Black Women & Hunter Coll., Jamaica, 1984, Dept. Employment, Summer Youth Employment, Jamaica 1985; advocate 20's and the 40's Civic Assn., Jamaica, 1994; hdgqtrs. hostess Com. to Re-elect Barbara Clark, N.Y. State Assembly, Jamaica, summer 1993. Recipient Benjamin E. Mays scholarship Fund for Theol. Edn., N.Y.C., 1994-95; grantee for spl. art svcs. N.Y. State Coun. on the Arts, 1978-96. Mem. Sacred Dance Guild, Assn. Black Seminarians (sec. 1992-93 Women in Ministry award 1992), New Brunswick Theol. Sem. Alumni,. Democrat. Baptist. Office: Dance Explosion Ltd PO Box 110417 Cambria Heights NY 11411 studio: 224-01 141 Ave Laurelton NY 11413

REID-MACNEVIN, SUSAN ALICE, criminologist, sociology educator; b. Hamilton, Ont., Can., Jan. 9, 1958; d. R. Bruce and Alice E. (Costigan) Reid; m. Ed T. MacNevin, July 8, 1989; children: Kyle and Jordan (twins); stepchildren, Jennifer, Lindsay. B Applied Sci., U. Guelph, Ont., 1981; MA in Criminology, U. Toronto, Ont., 1985, PhD, 1994. Rsch. asst. Addiction Rsch. Found., Toronto, 1981-84, rsch. cons., 1984; rsch. assoc. Ctr. Criminology U. Toronto, 1983-84, lectr. Woodsworth Coll., 1986-88; lectr. sociology U. Guelph, 1984-93, asst. prof., 1994—; rsch. cons. Portage Found., Montreal, Que., Can., 1993. Contbg. author: Young Offenders Act Revolution, 1991, Youth Injustice: Canadian Perspectives, 1993; contbr. articles to profl. jours. Named Prof. of Yr. U. Guelph Ctrl. Students Assn., 1991; recipient Outstanding Cmty. Svc. award Portage Found., 1993. Mem. John Howard Soc. Can. (v.p. issues 1994—), John Howard Soc. Ont. (v.p. 1994-96, pres. 1996—). Office: U Guelph, Dept Sociology-Anthropology, Guelph, ON Canada N1G 2W1

REID-ROBERTS, DAYL HELEN, mental health counselor; b. Rochester, N.Y., Oct. 15, 1941; d. Russell Harrison and Elizabeth Spencer (Page) Ferrey; m. David Alan Reid, July 16, 1960 (div. 1982); children: Deborah Elizabeth, Patricia Anne, David Alan Jr. (dec.), Matthew Stephen; m. David Gillies Roberts, Aug. 9, 1985. BA, Salisbury (Md.) State U., 1988, MEd, 1990. Lic. profl. counselor; cert. group psychotherapist. Clinician Community Svcs. Bd., Eastern Shore, Nassawadox, Va., 1990—; clinician substance abuse svc. Community Svcs. Bd., Eastern Shore, Onancock, Va., 1990—; clinican, mental social worker, psychiat. Northampton Accomack Meml. Hosp., Nassawadox, 1992-93; v.p. Humanitec, Inc., Accomac, Va., 1993—; instr. philosophy, psychology Ea. Shore Cmty. Coll., 1995—; asst. dir. Literacy Coun. of No. Va., Annandale, 1980-85. Contbr. articles to profl. jours. Treas., co-founder Ea. Shore Literacy Coun., 1986. Mem. Am. Counseling Assn., Am. Psychologists Assn. (student), Phi Sigma Tau, Kappa Delta Phi. Republican. Presbyterian. Home: The Oliver House Onancock VA 23417 Office: Humanitec Inc Front St PO Box 580 Accomac VA 23301-0580

REID-WALLACE, CAROLYN, broadcasting executive. PhD in English and Am. Lit., George Washington U. Instr. English Grinnell (Iowa) Coll., George Washington U., Washington, Howard U., Washington, Talladega (Ala.) Coll.; prof. English, dean coll., v.p. acad. affairs, acting chief exec. Bowie (Md.) State Coll.; dir. precollegiate edn., asst. dir. Divsn. Edn. Programs NEH, 1982-87; vice chancellor acad. affairs CUNY, 1987-91; asst. sec. postsecondary edn. U.S. Dept. Edn., Washington, 1991-93; sr. v.p. edn. and programming Corp. Pub. Broadcasting, Washington, 1995—; bd. dirs. Am. Coll. Testing, Carnegie Found. Advancement of Teaching. Rockefeller scholar; Ford fellow. Office: CPB 901 E Street NW Washington DC 20004-2037*

REIFF, DOVIE KATE, urban planner; b. Birmingham, Ala., Nov. 5, 1931; d. Roy Humes and Lou Ada (Erwin) Petty; married, Dec. 25, 1956 (div. Dec. 1977); children: Donna Lynn Reiff Jayanathan, Benjamin Lyle, Johanna Carol Davis. BArch, U. Pa., 1954, M in City Planning, 1969, postgrad. in city and regional planning, 1975. Registered architect, Pa. Architect Oskar Stonorov Architect, Phila., 1954-57; research asst. Inst. Environ. Studies, Phila., 1967-68; sr. planner Montgomery County Planning Commn., Norristown, Pa., 1969-71; urban planner Wallace McHarg Roberts & Todd, Phila., 1971-74; research analyst Del. Valley Regional Planning Commn., Phila., 1974-77; recreation planner U.S. Heritage Conservation and Recreation Service, Phila., 1977-80; community planner U.S. Gen. Services Adminstrn., Phila., 1980-85; vol., urban planner U.S. Peace Corps, Kathmandu, Nepal, 1986-87; program devel. planner Chattanooga Neighborhood Enterprise Inc., 1987-88; environ. planner dept. urban planning City of Birmingham, 1989-92; planning cons., 1992—; mem. exec. com. Phila. chpt. Am. Inst. Planners, 1970-75; bd. dirs. Phila. chpt. AIA, 1978-79, mem. architects in govt. com., Washington, 1984-85. Participant nat. conf. Pres.'s Com. on Employment of Handicapped, Washington, 1974-76; regional del. Gov.'s Coun. on Handicapped, Harrisburg, Pa., 1975, Birmingham Urban Forestry and Tree Commn., 1990-92, Tenn. Urban Forestry Coun., 1993—; vol. Laurel House Women's Shelter, Norristown, Pa., 1985, GSA Adopt-a-Sch. Program, Phila., 1985, Birmingham Ptnrs. in Edn., 1990; VISTA vol. East Tenn. Cmty. Design Ctr., 1994-95. Brunner grantee AIA, N.Y.C., 1974. Mem. Am. Inst. Cert. Planners, Am. Planning Assn., Nat. Trust for Hist. Preservation. Home: 212 Sunnybrook Trail Signal Mountain TN 37377-1859

REIGSTAD, RUTH ELAINE, lay worker, retired physical therapy consultant; b. Mpls., Apr. 26, 1923; d. Olin Spencer and Amanda Sophia (Fjelstad) R. BA, St. Olaf Coll., Northfield, Minn., 1945; cert., U. Minn., 1947. Lic. phys. therapist, Wash. Phys. therapist Crippled Childrens's Sch., Jamestown, N.D., 1948-52; phys. therapist, clin. instr. Shriners Hosp., U. Minn., Mpls., 1955-58; phys. therapist Rehab. Center, Albuquerque, N.M., 1958-60, Brit. Nat. Health Svc., London; phys. therapy cons. Wash. State Health Dept., Olympia, 1961-73, cons., 1961-74; lay worker Good Shepherd Luth. Ch., Olympia, 1972-75; mem. various coms. Christ Luth. Ch., Tacoma, 1980—; Vol. Children Health Svcs. and Pub. Health of Wash. 1974—; bd. dirs. Morningside Rehab. Orgn., Olympia, Wash., PAVE rehab. orgn. Bd. dirs. Wash. State Phys. Therapy Assn., 1965-68; mem. communiversity planning com. Pierce County Assoc. Ministries. With USCG, 1943-45. Recipient Fellowship award Nat. Easter Seal Soc. Chgo. 1949; Scholarship award US Pub. Health Service Wash. 1962-64. Mem. Am. Phys. Therapy Assn. (life), Am. Pub. Health Assn., Am. Acad. Religion, Luth. Brotherhood Fraternity and Benevolent Orgn. (bd. dirs. Pierce County), Air Force Assn. (exec. coun. Pierce County, 1985—). Mem. Evang. Luth. Ch. Am. Home: 7318 20th Ave E Tacoma WA 98438

REIK, RITA ANN FITZPATRICK, pathologist; b. Cleve., Mar. 9, 1951; d. Charles Robert Sr. and Rita Mae (Wilke) Fitzpatrick; m. Curtis A. Reik, Oct. 19, 1974. BA in Chemistry, Fla. Internat. U., 1985; MD, U. Miami, 1989. Diplomate Am. Bd. Anatomic and Clinical Pathology. Resident in pathology Jackson Meml. Hosp., Miami, Fla., 1989-95; mem. faculty dept. pathology U. Miami Sch. Medicine, 1995—; attending physician transfusion med. svcs. U. Miami/Jackson Meml. Hosp., 1996—; dir. immunogentics & cryopreservation lab. U. Miami Sch. Medicine/Jackson Meml. Hosp.; dir. lab. svcs. Jackson U. Maternity Ctr., Miami; dir. lab. svcs. North Dade Amb. Care Ctr. Fellow Coll. Am. Pathologists; mem. AMA, NOW, U. Miami Med. Women (pres. 1988-89), Am. Soc. Clin. Pathologists, Alpha Omega Alpha, Phi Kappa Phi. Office: U Miami Jackson Meml Hosp Dept Pathology 1611 NW 12th Ave Miami FL 33136-1015

REILLY, CAROLYN ANN, claims investigator; b. San Francisco, July 24, 1941. BA, Seattle U., 1963; paralegal cert., San Francisco State U., 1991; A in Claims, Ins. Inst. Am., 1995. Exam analyst Civil Svc. Commn. San Francisco, 1979-87; supr. dept. Social Svcs. San Francisco, 1987-92; claims investigator City and County of San Francisco, 1992—. Commr., v.p. San Francisco Commn. on Status of Women, 1977. Recipient Humanitarian award Smallwood Found., 1979, Outstanding Cmty. Svc. award Irish-Italian-Israeli Soc., 1982, Disting. Citizen award San Francisco Police Officer's Assn., 1984, Earthquake Heroism award Mayor of San Francisco, 1989. Democrat. Roman Catholic. Home: 1894 20th Ave San Francisco CA 94122 Office: Mcpl Claims Dept 949 Presidio Ave San Francisco CA 94115

REILLY, JEANETTE P., clinical psychologist; b. Denver, Oct. 19, 1908; d. George L. and Marie (Bloedorn) Parker; A.B., U. Colo., 1929; M.A., Columbia U., 1951, Ed.D., 1959; m. Peter C. Reilly, Sept. 15, 1932; children: Marie Reilly Heed, Sara Jean Reilly Wilhelm, Patricia Reilly Davis. Lectr. psychology Butler U., Indpls., 1957-58, 60-65; cons. child psychologist Mental Hygiene Clinic, Episcopal Community Services, Indpls., 1959-65; cons. clin. psychologist VA Hosp., Indpls., 1965-66; Christian Theol. Sem., 1968-70; pvt. practice clin. psychology, Indpls., 1967-89; cons. clin. psychologist St. Vincent's Hosp., 1973-86; adv. cons. middle mgmt. group Indpls. City Council, 1980-81. Mem. women's aux. council U. Notre Dame, 1953-65; trustee Hanover (Ind.) Coll., 1975-91; bd. dirs. Community Hosp. Found., Indpls., 1978-92, Regional Cancer Hosp. Bd., 1988-90, Indpls. Mus. Art, 1987-93; mem. Ind. Bd. Examiners in Psychology, 1969-73; mem. Com. for Future of Butler U., 1985-86. Mem. Am. Psychol. Assn., Am. Personnel and Guidance Assn., Am. Vocat. Assn., Ind. Psychol. Assn., Central Ind. Psychol. Assn., Ind. Personnel and Guidance Assn., Nat. Registry Psychologists in U.S.A. Office: 3777 Bay Road N Dr Indianapolis IN 46240-2973

REILLY, JOY HARRIMAN, theatre educator, playwright, actress/director; b. Dublin, Ireland, May 17, 1942; came to U.S., 1969; d. Rene William and Sybil Mary (MacGowan) Harriman; m. Lawrence W. Kieffer, Dec. 29, 1965 (div. Sept. 1974); m. Richard Reilly, June 23, 1978; 1 child, Patrick Harriman. BFA, Ohio State U., 1977, MA, 1979, PhD, 1984. Intern The Times, London, 1961-62; asst. radio-TV prodn. J. Walter Thompson Advt., Frankfurt and London, 1962-67; copy editor, journalist The Newark (Ohio) Adv., 1970-83, part-time, 1973-80; assoc. prof. Ohio State U., Columbus, 1985—; artistic dir. Grandparents Living Theatre, Columbus, 1984; theatre critic Sta. WOSU Radio, Columbus, 1979—; presenter papers Internat. Found. for Theatre Rsch., Stockholm, 1989, Dublin Eire, 1992, Assn. for Theater in Higher Edn., N.Y.C., 1989, 96, Chgo., 1990, 94, Seattle, 1991, Atlanta, 1992, Phila., 1993, San Francisco, 1995; presenter 1st Internat. Festival Sr. Adult Theater, Cologne, Germany, 1991, 1st Nat. Festival Sr. Theatre, 1993, numerous others. Author: (plays) A Grandparent's Scrapbook, 1986, Golden Age is All the Rage, 1989, I Was Young, Now I'm Wonderful!, 1991, A Picket Fence, Two Kids and a Dog Named Spot, 1993, Woman, 1995, (chpt.) Olga Nethersole's Sapho, 1989. Commr. Upper Arlington (Ohio) Arts Coun., 1987. Recipient Ohioana citation Ohioana Libr. Assn., 1989, Columbus Mayor's award for Vol. Svcs. in Arts, 1986, Woman of Achievement award YWCA, 1991, Outstanding Achievement in Theatre award Ohio Theatre Alliance, 1991, Living Faith awards Columbus Met. Area Ch. Coun., 1992, Disting. Teaching award Ohio State U., 1994; Battelle Endowment for Tech. and Human Affairs grantee, 1994. Mem. Am. Theatre Assn., Am. Soc. for Theatre Rsch., Internat. Fedn. for Theatre Rsch., Assn. for Theatre in Higher Edn., Ohio Theatre Alliance. Roman Catholic. Office: Ohio State U Dept Theatre Columbus OH 43210

REILLY, LOIS ANN PELCARSKY, middle school educator, consultant; b. Cleve., Feb. 25, 1941; d. William Paul and Eleanor (Mikulski) Pelcarsky; m. Anthony Eugene Reilly, June 19, 1980; 1 stepchild, David. BS in Edn., Baldwin-Wallace Coll., Berea, Ohio, 1962; MEd, Kent State U., 1970. Cert. reading specialist, permanent tchr., Ohio. Elem.-jr. high sch. tchr., reading specialist South Euclid-Lyndhurst (Ohio) Schs., 1962-74; ednl. cons. Scott, Foresman & Co., Glenview, Ill., 1974-75, Laidlaw Bros. Pubs., River Forest, Ill., 1978-80; reading cons. Pub. Schs. Cleveland Heights and University Heights, Ohio, 1975-76, Solon (Ohio) Schs., 1976-77; ednl. cons. Chgo. Sun-Times, 1981-84; clem. tchr. Solomon Schechter Day Sch., South Euclid, Ohio, 1984-87; jr. high sch. tchr. St. Joseph-Collinwood Sch., Cleve. Cath. Diocese, Cleve., 1988—; seminar presenter, 1974—; bd. dirs. South Euclid-Lyndhurst Tchrs. Credit Union, 1969-74. Contbr. articles to various publs. Pres. Women's Christian Fellowship League, Forest Hill Presbyn. Ch., Cleveland Heights, 1987-89, v.p., 1990-91. Mem. AAUW (v.p. 1976-78, sec. 1980-81, newsletter editor 1981-82, v.p 1988-90), Cleve. Coll. Club, Irish Am. Club East. Home: 343 Royal Oak Blvd Richmond Heights OH 44143

REILLY, MARGARET MARY, retired therapist; b. N.Y.C.; d. Thomas Michael and Margaret Mary (Lane) R. AB, Coll. of New Rochelle, 1933; MSW, Fordham U., 1966. Case worker, case supr., sr. case supr., dir. N.Y.C. Dept. Social Svcs., 1947-77; therapist Cath. Charities Counselling Svc., N.Y.C., 1980-94; ret. Mem. NASW, Acad. Cert. Social Workers. Roman Catholic. Home: 309 E Mosholu Pky N Bronx NY 10467-4840

REIMER, JUDY MILLS, pastor; m. George G. Reimer, 1964; children: Todd, Troy. BA, Emory and Henry Coll., 1962; MDiv, Bethany Theol. Sem., 1994. Ordained into Set Apart Ministry, Ch. of the Brethren, 1994. Vol. Brethren Vol. Svc. NIH, Bethesda, Md., 1962-64, Hessish Lichtenau, Germany, 1964-65; elem. sch. tchr. Pub. and Private Schs., various cities, 1965-76; deacon Ch. of the Brethren, 1966—; mem Virlina Dist. Bd., 1978-90; chair of nurture com. Ch. of the Brethren Virlina Dist., 1979-82, chair of outdoor ministry, 1983-84, conf. speaker, 1992; pastor Ch. of the Brethren, Smith Mountain Lake, Va., 1996—; owner, sr. v.p. Harris Office Furniture Co., Roanoke, Va., 1976—. Co-chair and vice-chair of two Virlina Fin. Campaigns, Ch. of the Brethren, 1980s, mem. Gen. Bd., Ch. of Brethren, 1977-90; mem. PTA, United Way Allocation Com., Roanoke Valley Women Owners Assn. (charter mem.); adult advisor Nat. Youth Cabinet. 1991, 92; worship coord. Nat. Youth Conf. 1994 numerous other coms. for Ch. of Brethren; official observer for Nat. Coun. of Chs. at Nicaraguan Election, Feb., 1990; rep. of Ch. of the Brethren, 1989, Atlanta, The Torch of Conscience Campaign to sensitize congregation to the campaign to abolish death penalty; workshop leader across the denomination on leadership devel., pastor/spouse retreats, women's rallies, etc.; ann. conf. moderator elect, 1993-94. Mem. Inst. Indsl. Comml. Chaplains (chmn. bd. dirs. local unit, asst. treas. nat. bd.). Office: Church of the Brethren General Offices 1451 Dundee Ave Elgin IL 60120-1674

REIN, CATHERINE AMELIA, financial services executive, lawyer; b. Lebanon, Pa., Feb. 7, 1943; d. John and Esther (Scott) Shultz. BA summa cum laude, Pa. State U., 1965; JD magna cum laude, NYU ., 1968. Bar: N.Y. 1968, U.S. Supreme Ct. 1971. Assoc. Dewey, Ballantine, Bushby, Palmer & Wood, N.Y.C., 1968-74; with Continental Group, Stamford, Conn., 1974-85, sec., sr. atty., 1976-77, v.p., gen. counsel, 1980-85; sec., asst. gen. counsel Continental Diversified Ops., 1978-80; v.p. human resources Met. Life Ins. Co., N.Y.C., 1985-88, sr. v.p. human resources, 1988-89, exec. v.p. corp. and profl. svcs. dept., 1989—; bd. dirs Bank of NY., Gen. Pub. Utilities, Corning Inc., Nat. Urban League, Inroads, N.Y.C. Trustee Nat. Urban League, NYU Sch. Law Found. Mem. ABA, Assn. of Bar of City of N.Y. Episcopalian. Home: 21 E 22nd St Apt 8B New York NY 10010-5335 Office: Met Life Ins Co 1 Madison Ave New York NY 10010-3603

REINARD, KATHLEEN ANN, elementary school educator; b. Rock Springs, Wyo., July 19, 1951; d. Louis Edward and Ruth Marie (Nalivka) Gaspar; m. James Henry Reinard, July 28, 1987; 1 child, Richard James. BA, U. Wyo., 1973. Tchr. 4th grade Rocky Boy (Mont.) Sch., 1973-75; tchr. Thoman Ranch Sch., Green River, Wyo., 1975-78; tchr. 2d grade Washington Sch., Green River, 1978-80, tchr. 3d grade, 1980-93, tchr. multiage 3d to 5th grades, 1993—. Mem. NEA, Wyo. Edn. Assn., Green River Edn. Assn., Wyo. Wildlife Assn., YWCA, Bus. and Profl. Christian Women's Orgn. (sec. 1983-87). Democrat. Episcopalian. Home: Star Rt 2 Box 210 Green River WY 82935 Office: Washington Elementary Sch 750 W 5th North Green River WY 82935

REINDOLLAR, SUE S., English educator, writer, editor; b. Cleve.; d. Preston Daniel and Evelyn Virginia (Brown) Somerville; children: Skip, Beth Ann Reindollar Page. BA in English, Slippery Rock U., 1972, MA in English, 1974; MA in Scandinavian Studies, U. Wis., 1989, PhD in Scandinavian Studies, 1992. Cert. English tchr., Wis. Tchr. English Oil City (Pa.) H.S., 1974-75, Slippery Rock (Pa.) H.S., 1975-78, Stoughton (Wis.)

H.S., 1978—; freelance editor and writer; writing cons. Wordsmithy, Madison, Wis. Recipient Torger Thompson fellowship in Scandinavian studies U. Wis., 1984, Fulbright Tchg. fellowship, 1987, Rsch. grant, 1989. Mem. NEA, Kettle Moraine Press Assn. (tchg. staff 1981-82, bd. dirs. 1982-83), Madison Area Freelance Writers and Editors, Women in Comm. Home: 3624 Gregory St Madison WI 53711-1730

REINERT, JOY ANN, elementary education educator; b. Des Moines, Iowa; d. Willie Earl and Ila Lucille (Aulman) Spoonholtz; m. Wilbert Dean Reinert Jr., May 27, 1961; 1 child, Debra. Student, Cornell Coll., 1956-57; diploma, Grand View Jr. Coll., 1958; BS in Edn., Drake U., 1965. Educator Hubbard (Iowa) Cmty. Sch., 1958-66, educator chpt. I, 1970-88; educator chpt. I Hubbard-Radcliffe Sch., Radcliffe, Iowa, 1988—; coord. chpt. I Hubbard Sch., 1973-88; coord. talented and gifted Hubbard Sch., 1983-88. Mem. Internat. Reading Assn., Iowa Reading Assn. (v.p. 1988-89, pres.-elect 1989-90, pres. 1990-91), Hardy Reading Coun. (pres. 1983-84, 93-94). Missouri Synod Lutheran. Home: 23877 270th St Hubbard IA 50122 Office: Hubbard-Radcliffe Sch 501 Isabella Radcliffe IA 50230

REINHARD, SISTER MARY MARTHE, educational organization administrator; b. McKeesport, Pa., Aug. 29, 1929; d. Regis C. and Leona (Reese) R. AB, Notre Dame Coll.; MA, U. Notre Dame. Asst. prin. Regina High Sch., Cleve., 1960-62, prin., 1963-64; prin. Notre Dame Acad., Chardon, Ohio, 1965-72; pres. Notre Dame Coll. of Ohio, Cleve., 1973-88; dir. devel. Sisters of Notre Dame Ednl. Ctr., Chardon, 1989—. Trustee, mem. exec. com. NCCJ, Cleve., 1987; bd. dirs. Centerior Energy; mem. coun. Geauga United Way Svcs., 1990—, vice-chair fund raising, 1991-94, vice-chair planning 1995—; mem. adv. bd. Kent State U., Geauga campus, 1991-94; trustee Leadership Geauga 1995—. Recipient Fidelia award Notre Dame Coll., 1989, Woman of Yr. award 1990; Humanitarian award Cleve. chpt. NCCJ, 1990; named one of 100 most influential women in Cleve. Women's City Club, 1983, one of 79 most interesting people in Cleve. The Cleve. mag., 1979. Roman Catholic. Home and Office: 13000 Auburn Rd Chardon OH 44024-9330

REINHARDT, LINDA LOU, medical and surgical nurse; b. Meadville, Pa., July 15, 1950; d. Kenneth A. and Dorothy M. (Hartman) Beers; m. John F. Reinhardt, May 15, 1979 (div. Sept. 1995); 1 child, Moses A. ADN, Clarion U., 1982, BSN, 1993. RN, Calif.; Cert. BLS, ACLS. Staff nurse Oil City (Pa.) Health Ctr., 1982-84; nursing supr. Beverly Enterprises, Oil City, 1984-88, 92-93, Snyder Meml. Hosp. Ctr., Marianville, Pa., 1988-90; staff nurse Titusville (Pa.) Hosp., 1990-92; commd. 1st lt. USAF, 1993, advanced through grades to capt., 1994; asst. officer in charge med.-surg. Vandenberg AFB 30 Med. Group, Lompoc, Calif., 1993—; tutor Lompoc Lit. Counsel (pub. svc. award), 1994. Author: (original care plan) Nursing Plan of Care for Homeless of Venango County According to Roy's Model of Nursing, 1992. Mem. Sigma Theta Tau. Home: 1002 Hazelnut St Vandenberg AFB CA 92437 Office: 30 Med Group South Dakota St Vandenberg AFB CA 93437

REINHARDT, SUSAN ELAINE GANTT, family resource center administrator, counselor; b. Newton, N.C., July 17, 1961; d. Charles Lenwood and Brenda Gail (McKee) Gantt; m. Albert Franklin Reinhardt, Dec. 18, 1983; children: Andrew Franklin, Adam Michael. BA in Psychology, U. N.C., 1983; MEd in Counseling, East Tenn. State U., 1985. Elem. sch. counselor Newton-Conover City Schs., Newton, N.C., 1985-86; counselor, educator Women's Health Edn. Ctr. Catawba Meml. Hosp., Hickory, N.C., 1992-95; instr. human resources Catawba Valley C.C., Hickory, N.C., 1995; dir. Footprints Family Learning & Creative Play Ctr., Hickory, 1995—. Mem. NAFE, Postpartum Support Internat., Catawba Valley Assn. Counselors and Therapists, Children's Protection Coun. (activities chmn. prevent child abuse group, 1994-95). Mem. United Ch. of Christ. Home: 1114 Sturnbridge Ct Newton NC 28658

REINHARDT, VICTORIA ANN, environmentalist; b. Hastings, Minn., June 30, 1953; d. LeRoy August and Florence Rose (Nogle) R.; m. James Patrick Barone, Oct. 25, 1991; children: Michael Shane Barone, Erich LeRoy Reinhardt. BA, Met. State U., St. Paul, 1996. Account clk. Hastings (Minn.) State Hosp., 1972-73; asst. cost analyst Sperry Univac, Roseville, Minn., 1973-77; office mgr. Erhart Law Office, Anoka, Minn., 1980-84; energy auditor No. States Power, White Bear Lake, Minn., 1980-84; prin. asst. Ramsey County Comm. Orth., St. Paul, 1984-86; lobbyist, cons. White Bear Lake, 1986-87; solid waste abatement specialist Anoka County, Anoka, 1987-88; abatement grants adminstr. Met. Coun., St. Paul, 1988-94; problem materials coord. Minn. Office of Environ. Assistance, St. Paul, 1994—; chair White Bear Lake Recycling Adv. Com., 1988—; mem. Ramsey County Capital Improvements Com., 1994—, Ramsey County Strategic Planning Com., 1994—. Contbr. articles to profl. jours. Bd. dirs., charter mem. White Bear Lake Counseling Ctr., 1984—; vol., spkr. on domestic abuse Law Explorers White Bear Lake Counseling Wilder Found., St. Paul, 1985—; bd. dirs. Recycling Assn. Minn., 1988-95, chair, 1990-93; pres., steward, co-chair PAC Am. Fedn. State County & Mcpl. Employees, 1990-94; senate dist. affirmative action State Ctrl. Com. Dem. Farm Labor party; pres. PTO Excellence in Edn. com. Sch. Dist. 624. Recipient Recognition of Svc. award Recycling Assn. Minn., 1993, Recognition of Svc. award Democrat Farmer Labor Party, 1995. Mem. Nat. Recycling Coalition (state recycling orgn. liaison, spkr. 1987—, recycling edn. excellence award 1994), Solid Waste Assn. N.Am., Minn. Assn. Profl. Employees (bd. dirs. polit. action com. 1994—), Assn. of Recycling Mgrs., Minn. Earth Day Network. Democrat. Lutheran. Home: 4995 Wood Ave White Bear Lake MN 55110-6645 Office: Minn Office of Environ Assistance 520 Lafayette Rd N Saint Paul MN 55155-4100

REINHART, MARY ANN, medical board executive; b. Jackson, Mich., Aug. 14, 1942; d. Herbert Martin and Josephine Marie (Keyes) Conway; m. David Lee Reinhart, Dec. 28, 1963; children: Stephen Paul, Michael David. MA, Mich. State U., 1983, PhD, 1985. Rsch. asst. Mich. State U., East Lansing, 1979-82, 85, teaching asst. dept psychology, 1982-84, asst. prof. Office Med. Edn. R&D, Coll. Human Medicine, 1985-88; assoc. exec. dir. Am. Bd. Emergency Medicine, East Lansing, 1988-95, dep. exec. dir., 1995—; cons. Am. Bd. Emergency Medicine, 1985-88; chairperson collegewide evaluation com. Coll. Human Medicine, Mich. State U., East Lansing, 1985-88; adj. asst. prof. Office Med. Edn. Rsch. and Devel., Coll. Human Medicine, 1988—. Reviewer Annals of Emergency Medicine, 1987-95, Acad. Emergency Medicine, 1995—. Bd. dirs. Neahtawanta Rsch. and Edn. Ctr., Traverse City, Mich., 1991—. Mem. APA (divsn. indsl./orgnl. psychology, health psychology), Phi Kappa Phi. Office: Am Bd Emergency Medicine 3000 Coolidge Rd East Lansing MI 48823-6319

REINING, BETH LAVERNE (BETTY REINING), public relations consultant, journalist; b. Fargo, N.D.; d. George and Grace (Twiford) Reimche; student N.D. State Coll., U. Minn., Glendale Community Coll., Calif. State Coll., Carson; 1 dau., Carolyn Ray Toohey Hiett; m. Jack Warren Reining, Oct. 3, 1976 (div. 1984). Originated self-worth seminars in Phoenix, 1970-76; owner Janzik Pub. Relations, 1971-76; talk show reporter-hostess What's Happening in Ariz., Sta. KPAZ-TV, 1970-73; writer syndicated column People Want to Know, Today newspaper, Phoenix, 1973; owner JB Communications, Phoenix, 1976-84; owner, pres. Media Communications, 1984—; freelance writer; tchr. How to Weigh Your Self-Worth courses Phoenix Coll., Rio Solado Community Coll., Phoenix, 1976-84; instr. pub. rels. Scottsdale (Ariz.) Community Coll., 1987; muralist, works include 25 figures in med. office. Founder Ariz. Call-A-Teen Youth Resources, Inc., pres., 1975-76, v.p., 1976-77, now bd. dirs. Recipient awards including 1st pl. in TV writing Nat. Fedn. Press Women, 1971-88, numerous state awards in journalism Ariz. Press Women, 1971-76, Good Citizen award Builders of Greater Ariz., 1961. Mem. Ariz. Press Women (1st place award 1988), No. Ariz. Press Women (pres. 1983), Nat. Fedn. Am. Press Women, Pub. Relations Soc. Am., Phoenix Pub. Relations Soc., Nat. Acad. TV Arts and Scis., Phoenix Valley of Sun Convention Bur., Verde Valley C. of C. (bd. dirs., tourism chmn. 1986-87, Best Chair of Yr. award 1986), Phoenix Metro C. of C. Cottonwood C. of C. (chmn. of Yr. award, 1986). Inventor stocking-tension twist footlet, 1962. Club: Phoenix Press. Office: PO Box 10509 Phoenix AZ 85064-0509

REINING, PRISCILLA COPELAND, anthropologist; b. Chgo., Mar. 11, 1923; d. Kenneth Bayard and Mary Elsie (Weser) Copeland; m. Conrad Copeland Reining, June 26, 1944 (dec. Oct. 1984); children: Robert Cushman, Anne Elizabeth, Conrad Copeland Schilling. AB, U. Chgo., 1945, AM, 1949, PhD, 1967. Lectr. U. Minn., Mpls., 1956-60, Howard U., Washington, 1960-65; rsch. assoc. Cath. U. Am., Washington, 1966-68; assoc. Smithsonian Instn., Washington, 1966, 68, 70; cons. The World Bank, 1972, USAID, 1973; cons. AAAS, Washington, 1971-73, project dir., 1974-81, program dir., 1982-90; vis. prof. African Studies U. Fla., Gainesville, 1994—; mem. bd. on sci. and tech. for internat. devel. NAS, Washington, 1976-80; mem. arid ecosys. interation Internat. Geosphere/Biosphere Program, Boulder, 1989—; mem. adv. bd. Population and Environ., N.Y.C., 1990—; bd. dirs. Renewable Natural Resources Found., Bethesda, Md., 1991—; mem. U.S. del. UN Conf. on Desertification, Nairobi, Kenya, 1977. Author: Challenging Desertification, 1980; author, editor: Village Women, 1977; editor: Village Viability, 1980, Resource Inventory, 1984. Mem. Peace Commn. Washington Cathedral, 1986-91. Grantee NIMH, 1966, NSF, 1967, Nat. Geographic Soc. Com. for Rsch. and Exploration, 1994. Fellow AAAS (sec. 1978-89), Am. Anthrop. Assn. (task force on AIDS, task force on environ., Disting. Svc. award 1990), African Studies Assn. (bd. dirs. 1978-80); mem. Anthrop. Soc. Washington (pres. 1976-77), Soc. Women Geographers. Home: 3601 Rittenhouse St NW Washington DC 20015-2413

REININGHAUS, RUTH, artist; b. N.Y.C., Oct. 4, 1922; d. Emil William and Pauline Rosa (Lazarik) R.; m. George H. Morales, Feb. 20, 1944; children: George James, Robert Charles; m. Allan Joseph Smith, May 28, 1960. Student, Hunter Coll., NYU, Nat. Acad. Sch. of Design, 1960-61, Frank Reilly Sch. of Art, 1963, Art Students League, 1968. Instr. art Banker's Trust, N.Y.C., 1971-77, 79—, Kittredge Club for Women, N.Y.C., 1967-77. Exhibited in group shows at Berkshire Art Mus., 1970s, Hammer Galleries, Inc., N.Y.C., 1974, Far Gallery, N.Y.C., 1974, Mufalli Gallery, N.Y. and Fla., 1983-90, Pen and Brush Club, 1985—, Petrucci Gallery, Saugerties, N.Y., 1988-94, Pastel Soc. Am., 1988—, John Lane Gallery, Rhinebeck, N.Y., 1992—, Regianni Gallery, N.Y.C., 1994, Catharine Lorillard Wolfe Club, Salmagundi Club, Allied Arts Am., Heidi Newhoff Gallery, N.Y.C., Hudson Valley Art Assn., Knickerbocker Artists, N.Y.C., Pastel Soc. Am., others. Recipient Robert Lehman award, 1960s, 3d prize in oils Murray Hill Art Show, 1968, Coun. Am. Artists award, 1985, Internat. award Oil Pastel Assn., 1987; scholar Nat. Acad., 1962, Frank Reilly Sch. Art, 1963, NYU, 1968; subject NBC TV show You Are an Artist, 1950s. Fellow Am. Artists Profl. League (Claude Parsons Meml. award 1974), Hudson Valley Art Assn.; mem. Pastel Soc. Am. (bd. dirs. 1988-90, J. Giffuni purchase award 1988, Flora B. Giffuni pres.' award 1990), Allied Artists Am. (assoc.), Soc. Illustrators (hon. 1983-87), Nat. Arts Club, Reciprocal, Artists Fellowship, Washington Sq. Outdoor Art Assn. (bd. dirs. 1983-90, Talens award 1963, Richtone Artists award 1968), Salmagundi Club N.Y. (pres. 1983-87, curator 1989—, Baker Brush award 1969, scholar 1969, Philip Isenberg award 1974, 89, 90, 92, 95, hon. mention 1983, 84, 96, Salmagundi Club prize 1985, Franklin B. Williams Fund prize 1987, Tom Picard award 1987, Mortimer E. Freehof award 1988, John N. Lewis award 1988, Salmagundi Club medal of honor 1989, John N. Lewis award 1989, Samuel T. Shaw award 1990, Thomas Moran award 1990, Helen S. Coes award 1990, hon. mention 1991, Alice B. McReynolds award 1991, Salmagundi award 1991, Alphaeus Cole Meml. award 1991), Catharine Lorillard Wolfe Art Club (bd. dirs. 1987—, Anna Hyatt Huntington award 1978), Coun. Am. Artists (award 1985, hon. mention 1991, Catharine Lorillard Wolfe award for pastel 1992, cash award 1993), Pen and Brush Club (Helen Slotman award 1986, OPA Internat. award 1987, Gene Alden Walker award 1988, Pen and Brush Solo award 1992, hon. mention 1991, Margaret Sussman award 1996), Knickerbocker Artists (Flora B. Giffuni PSA Pres.' award 1990), Oil Pastel Assn. (Pen and Brush award 1987, Strathmore award 1989, Salmagundi Club award 1991), Am. Artists Profl. League (Claude Parson's Meml. award 1974, 2nd prize in oils 1992, 3d prize oils 1993, Pres. award 1994), Alpha Delta Pi. Lutheran. Home: 222 E 93rd St Apt 26A New York NY 10128-3758

REINISCH, JUNE MACHOVER, psychologist, educator; b. N.Y.C., Feb. 2, 1943; d. Mann Barnett and Lillian (Machover) R. BS cum laude, NYU, 1966; MA, Columbia U., 1970, PhD with distinction, 1976. Asst. prof. psychology Rutgers U., New Brunswick, N.J., 1975-80; assoc. prof. psychology Rutgers U., New Brunswick, N.J., 1980-82, adj. assoc. prof. psychiatry, 1981-82; prof. psychology Ind. U., Bloomington, 1982-93, dir. Kinsey Inst. Rsch. in Sex, Gender, and Reprodn., 1982-93; prof. clin. psychology Sch. Medicine, Indpls., 1983-93; dir. emeritus Kinsey Inst., 1993—; dir., prin. investigator Prenatal Devel. Projects, Copenhagen, 1976—, sr. rsch. fellow, trustee The Kinsey Inst., 1993—; pres. R2 Sci. Comms., Inc., Ind., N.Y., 1985—; vis. sr. rschr. Inst. for Preventive Medicine, Copenhagen Health Svcs., Kommunehospitalet, Copenhagen, 1994—; cons. SUNY. Author: The Kinsey Institute New Report on Sex, 1990, pub. 8 fgn. edits.; editor books Kinsey Inst. series; syndicated newspaper columnist: The Kinsey Report; contbr. rsch. reports, revs., articles to profl. jours.; appeared on TV shows including PBS, Discovery, Oprah Winfrey, Sally Jessy Rafael, Good Morning Am., Today Show, CBS This Morning; guest host TV shows including CNBC Real Personal, TalkLive, also fgn. appearances. Founders day scholar NYU, 1966; NIMH trainee, 1971-74; NIMH grantee, 1978-80, Ford Found. grantee, 1973-75, Nat. Inst. Edn. grantee, 1973-74, Erikson Ednl. Found. grantee, 1973-74, grantee Nat. Inst. Child Health and Human Devel., 1981-88, Nat. Inst. on Drug Abuse, 1989-95; recipient Morton Prince award Am. Psychopath. Assn., 1976, medal for 9th Dr. S.T. Huang-Chan Meml. Lectr. in anatomy Hong Kong U., 1988, Dr. Richard J. Cross award Robert Wood Johnson Med. Sch., 1991, Award First Internat. Conf. on Orgasm, New Delhi, 1991, Disting. Alumnae award Tchrs. Coll. Columbia U., 1992. Fellow AAAS, APA, Am. Psychol. Soc., Soc. for Sci. Study Sex; mem. Internat. Acad. Sex Rsch. (charter), Internat. Women's Forum, Women's Forum. Inc., Internat. Soc. Psychoneuroendocrinology, Internat. Soc. Rsch. Aggression, Internat. Soc. Devel. Psychobiology, Am. Assn. Sex. Educators, Counselors and Therapists, Sigma Xi. Office: SUNY HSCB PBL Box 120 450 Clarkson Ave Brooklyn NY 11203-2012 also: The Kinsey Inst Prenatal Devel Project Ind U Bloomington IN 47405

REINKE, DARLENE SUSAN, management executive; b. Cook County, Ill., Sept. 29, 1965; d. Robert Charles and Darlene Carol (Strom) Reinke; m. Jeffrey P. Arndt, July 29, 1988. Student, Mt. Mary Coll., 1983-85; BBA, U. Milw., 1988. V.p. Classic Med. Products, Muskego, Wis., 1986-94; pres. Bouqhets of Lake Geneva, Wis., 1994—, New Age Resources; corp. sec. Classic Med. Group, Muskego, 1991—. Mem. NAFE, Assn. System Mgmt. Office: Bouquets of Lake Geneva 71 E Main St Lake Geneva WI 53147-1969

REINKE, DORIS MARIE, retired elementary education educator; b. Racine, Wis., Jan. 12, 1922; d. Otto William Reinke and Louise Amelia Goehring. BS, U. Wis., Milw., 1943; MS, U. Wis., Whitewater, 1967. Tchr. kindergarten Elkhorn (Wis.) Area Sch. Sys., 1943-69, bldg. prin., 1968-70, summer sch. dir., 1974-75, grade 2 tchr., 1970-84, primary dept. chmn., 1971-84, administrv. asst., supervising tchr., 1957-83, student tchr., 1984, ret., 1984; oriented experience tchr. Program Area Sch. Sys., Elkhorn, 1966; pres. Elkhorn Edn. Assn., 1949-50; rep. dist. State Kindergarten Conf., Oshkosh, Wis., 1966; participant early edn. conf. State Early Edn. Conf., Eagle River, Wis., 1968. Columnist Mature Life Styles newspaper; monthly columnist Beacon, 1994—; contbr. weekly newspaper column Webster Notes, 1989; Walworth County Diary Monthly column in The Week, 1991—; author Doris' Corner newsletter Walworth County Geneal. Soc., 1992—. Bd. dirs. Food Pantry, Elkhorn, 1985-88, 95—, RSVP Vol. Food Pantry, Elkhorn, 1985-95; del. dist. constn. conv. Evang. Luth. Ch. Am., Beloit, Wis., 1987; com. mem. Luth. Ch., Elkhorn, 1987; chmn. sch. centennial, Elkhorn, 1987; mem. Elkhorn Hist. Preservation Com., 1991—: archivist Sugar Creek Luth. Ch., 1992—, choir mem., 1995—; dir. Webster House Mus., 1991—. Recipient Wis. Edn. Research, West Bend, Wis., 1966, Outstanding Elem. Tchrs., Wash., 1973, Wis. Dept. Edn., Madison, 1980, Local History award State Hist. Soc. Wis., 1993. Mem. Nat. Ret. Tchrs. Assn., Walworth County Ret. Tchrs. Assn. (v.p. 1988, pres . 1991), Walworth County Hist. Soc. (treas. 1985-89, v.p. 1990-91, pres. 1991-96), Walworth County Geneal. Soc. (bd. dirs. 1991-92), Alpha Delta Kappa (state pres. 1968-70, 76-78). Home: 516 N Wisconsin St Elkhorn WI 53121-1119

REINKER, NANCY CLAYTON COOKE, artist; b. Owensboro, Ky., July 6, 1936; d. Billie Clayton and Barbara Jane (Mitchell) Cooke; m. Dale Bruce Reinker, Sept. 29, 1956; children: Shahn Elizabeth, Laura Beth, Karen Christian. Student, Kent State U., 1954-55, Cleve. Art Inst., 1956-57; studied sculpture with, Stanley Bleifeld, 1979-80; student, Silvermine Sch. of Art, 1988-89. Owner Nettle Creek Shops of Westport and Cos Cob, Conn., 1974-86, Cross River Design Studio, 1986-89. One woman shows at Hayes Gallery, 1992 Silvermine Guild Arts Ctr., 1992, Art Place, 1993, 95, Westport Art Ctr., 1994, also in numerous nat. and internat. exhbns. Chmn. Cultural Events Commn., Weston, Conn., 1993-94; pres. Inst. for Visual Artists, New Canaan, Conn., 1992-93; v.p., pres. Art Place Gallery, Southport, Conn., 1991-92, 94. Named to 1992 Cir. of Excellence, Soc. Nat. Art Patrons, 1992; recipient 1st prize Spectrum, 1992, 93, 94. Mem. ASID, Silvermine Guild of Artists (trustee 1994—), New Haven Paint and Clay (Merit award 1993), Nat. Assn. Women Artists, Conn. Women Artists (Painting award 1991), Greenwich Art Soc. (Randolph Chitwood award 1994), Women's Caucus for Art, Chi Omega. Home and Studio: 87 Valley Forge Rd Weston CT 06883-1913

REINSCHMIEDT, ANNE TIERNEY, nurse, lawyer, rancher; b. Washington, Mar. 6, 1932; d. Edward F. and Frances (Palmer) Tierney; m. Edwin Ruben Reinschmiedt, Sept. 20, 1959 (div. 1961); 1 child, Kathleen Frances Tierney. BS, Cen. State U., Edmond, Okla., 1975; JD, Oklahoma City U. Sch. Law, 1991. RN, Calif., Okla.; lic. residential care facility adminstr., nursing home adminstr. Nurse San Jose (Calif.) Hosp., 1952-55; owner, operator Hominy Studio, 1960-62; dir. nurses, lab and x-ray, technician, adminstr. Hominy (Okla.) City Hosp., 1961-63; nurse Jackson County Dept. Health, Altus, Okla., 1963-65; adminstr. Propp's Inc., Oklahoma City, 1965-80; nursing homes cons. Propps & Self, Oklahoma City, 1965—; pres. Shamrock Health Care Ctr., Bethany, Okla., 1981—; operator Lakeview Lodging Residential Care Facility, 1981—; adult edn. instr., med. aide technicians East Central U., Ada, Okla., 1987-89; cons. residential care facilities, 1985—. Author: Recovery Room Procedures, 1958. Mem. Jackson County (Okla.) Draft Bd., 1965-70. Lt. USN, 1955-60. Mem. ANA, Nat. Assn. Residential Care Facilities (sec., bd. dirs. 1983-85), Okla. Bar Assn., Okla. Assn. Residential Care Facilities (founding pres. 1981-87, bd. dirs. 1981—), Beta Sigma Phi, Phi Alpha Delta (vice justice, exec. bd. 1988-90). Republican. Roman Catholic. Office: Shamrock Health Care PO Box 848 Bethany OK 73008-0848

REIS, JEAN STEVENSON, administrative secretary; b. Wilburton, Okla., Nov. 30, 1914; d. Robert Emory and Ada (Ross) Stevenson; m. George William Reis, June 24, 1939 (dec. 1980). BA, U. Tex., El Paso, 1934; MA, So. Meth. U., 1935; postgrad., U. Chgo., summers 1937-38, U. Wash., 1948-49. Tchr. El Paso High Sch., 1935-39; safety engr., trainer Safety and Security Div., Office of Chief Ordnance, Chgo., 1942-45; tchr. Lovenberg Jr. High Sch., Galveston, Tex., 1946; parish sec. Trinity Parish Episcopal Ch., Seattle, 1950-65; adminstrv. sec., asst. Office Resident Bishop, United Meth. Ch., Seattle, 1965-94; observer Africa U. installation, Mutare, Zimbabwe, 1994; mem. com. on legislation for the 1996 gen. conf. Hist. Soc. of United Meth. Ch. Mem. AAUW, Beta Beta Beta. Home: 9310 42nd Ave NE Seattle WA 98115-3814

REISER, TRISTA ANN, alcohol and drug abuse services professional; b. Bronx, N.Y., Feb. 6, 1968; d. Michael Matthew Jr. and Elizabeth Cabrini (Murray) R. BA in Psychology, Glassboro (N.J.) State Coll., 1991. Cert. drug and alcohol counselor, aerobic instr., personal trainer, drug and alcohol prevention specialist. Substance abuse counselor Spectrum Health Care, Newark, 1991-93; coord. substance abuse prevention Covenant House, Atlantic City, 1993—; creator, advisor KIK IT! Peer education, Atlantic City; mem. Healthy Cities, Kathy's Atlantic City Cable Kids. Prodr. Beyond Pacific Ave. (video), 1993. Creator, advisor Atlantic City Youth Coun., 1994-95; mem. Atlantic County Alliance. Mem. Alpha Epsilon Phi. Office: Covenant House 3529 Pacific Ave Atlantic City NJ 08401

REISNER, ELENA MACKAY, retired educational administrator; b. Inverness, Scotland, June 1, 1922; came to U.S., 1932; d. John Alexander and Jane Logan (Wells) Mackay; m. Sherwood Hartman Reisner, June 1, 1946 (dec. 1990); children: Ruth Reisner Brock, James Sherwood. BA, Wellesley Coll., 1944; MA, Columbia U., 1945. Tchr. St. Margaret's Sch., Waterbury, Conn., 1945-46; missionary tchr. Presbyn. Ch. U.S.A., Mexico City, 1946-50; instr. Tex. A&I U., Kingsville, 1960-65; tchr. Presbyn. Pan Am. Sch., Kingsville, 1957-80, interim pres., 1990-91, asst. to pres., 1991-95; ret., 1995. Founder Amistad Vol. Coun., Kingsville, 1984; past pres. Laurel Home Extension Club; mem. Kleberg County Resource Coun.; chmn. Mission Presbytery's Hispanic Ministries Coun., Presbyn. Ch. U.S.A., 1993, 94, 95; elder Presbyn. Ch., 1976—. Named One of 10 Outstanding Women in Kingsville History, Zonta Club, 1975; recipient lifetime svc. award Kingsville C. of C., Bell-MacKay prize for mission Presbyns. for Renewal-Presbyn. Gen. Assembly, 1994. Mem. AAUW (pres. 1977-79), Downtown Mchts. Assn., Presbyn. Women (hon. life, pres. 1985-87), Phi Beta Kappa, Delta Kappa Gamma (hon.). Democrat. Home: 332 University Blvd Kingsville TX 78363-4239 Office: Presbyn Pan Am Sch PO Box 1578 Kingsville TX 78364-1578

REISNER, SUSAN L., public defender; b. Dec. 1, 1953; m. Paul H. Schneider. BA, Princeton U., 1975; JD, Rutgers U., Newark, 1978. Bar: N.J. 1978, U.S. Dist. Ct. N.J. 1978, U.S. Ct. Appeals (3d cir.) 1982, U.S. Ct. Appeals (D.C. cir.) 1990, U.S. Supreme Ct. 1982. Chief pub. utilities and civil rights sect. N.J. Dept. Law and Pub. Safety, Newark, 1988-91; chief environ. sect. N.J. Dept. Law and Pub. Safety, Trenton, 1991-92, dep. atty. gen. in charge of agy. advice, 1992; dir. divsn. rate counsel N.J. Dept. Pub. Advocate, Newark, 1992-94; acting commr. N.J. Dept. Pub. Advocate, Trenton, 1994; pub. defender N.J. Office Pub. Defender, Trenton, 1994—; commr. gov.'s study commn. on discrimination in pub. works, procurement and contrn. contracts, Trenton, 1992. Contbr. articles to profl. jours. Mem. N.J. Bar Assn. Office: Office Pub Defender Justice Complex CN 850 Trenton NJ 08625

REISS, SUSAN MARIE, editor, writer; b. Washington, Sept. 14, 1963; m. Paul L. Roney Jr., May 25, 1991. BA in English Lit., U. Va., 1985; MA in English, George Mason U., 1989. Editorial asst. Water Pollution Control Fedn., Alexandria, Va., 1985-87; freelance writer, editor Arlington, Va., 1987-90; staff writer George Mason U., Fairfax, Va., 1988-90; staff writer Optical Soc. Am., Washington, 1990-91, news editor, 1991-93, mng. editor, 1993—. Newsletter editor: Arlington County Tennis Assn., 1990-91; contbr. articles to profl. jours. and mags. Mem. Nat. Press Club, Washington Ind. Writers, D.C. Sci. Writers Assn., N.Y. Acad. Scis., Sigma Tau Delta (founding mem. U. Va. chpt.). Home: 6814 30th Rd N Arlington VA 22213-1602 Office: Optical Soc Am 2010 Massachusetts Ave NW Washington DC 20036-1023

REISSENWEBER, BETH RANDERSON, controller, small business owner; b. Berwyn, Ill., June 14, 1961; d. Robert M. and Gloria (Dallner) Randerson; m. Klaus Wolfgang Reissenweber, Feb. 14, 1991. BS, Elmhurst (Ill.) Coll., 1981; MBA, Ind. U., 1983. CPA, cert. mgmt. acct. Fin. analyst The Christian Sci. Monitor, Boston, 1984-85; assoc. prof. Massasoit Community Coll., Canton, Mass., 1985-86; sr. fin. analyst The 1st Ch. of Christ, Scientist, Boston, 1986-88, payroll mgr., 1988-89, income acctg. mgr., 1989; chief fin. officer Chgo. Jr. Sch., Elgin, Ill., 1990; controller Legal Assistance Found. Chgo., 1990—; owner K. R. Consulting, 1990—. With USN, 1985. Mem. Nat. Assn. Accts., Ind. U. Alumni Assn., Omicron Delta Kappa, Sigma Kappa (1st v.p. 1979). Office: Legal Assistance Found Chgo 343 S Dearborn St Ste 700 Chicago IL 60604-3805

REISTER, RUTH ALKEMA, lawyer, business executive; b. Grand Rapids, Mich., May 30, 1936; d. Henry and Lena (Land) Alkema; m. Raymond A. Reister, Oct. 7, 1967. B.A., U. Mich., 1958, J.D., 1964; grad. Program in Bus. Adminstrn., Harvard U., 1959, postgrad. Program in Mgmt. Devel., 1976. Bar: Minn., Mich. 1964, U.S. Supreme Ct. 1976. Trust officer Northwestern Nat. Bank, Mpls., 1964-70; asst. counsel, asst. v.p., sec. Fed. Res. Bank, Mpls., 1970-81; asst. sec., bd. govs. Fed. Res. System, 1977; dep. under sec. U.S. Dept. Agr., Washington, 1981-83; pres. First Bank Systems Agrl. Credit Corp., Mpls., 1983-84; pres. Groveland Corp., Mpls., 1986—; dir. Herman Miller, Inc., Zealand, Mich., 1984—. Bd. dirs. United Way, ARC, Jones Harrison Home, Mpls., Gustavus Adolfus Coll., 1995—; chmn. Jones-Harrison Found. Mem. Harvard Bus. Sch. Club Minn., Minn. Women's Econ. Round Table (pres. 1980-81). Republican.

REITER, CAROLYN MARIE PRILL, special education educator; b. Billings, Mont., Nov. 25, 1965; d. Thomas W. and Julie Ann P.; m. Rodney J.. Reiter, Aug. 17, 1985; children: Lindsey Marie, Adam James, Philip Alexander. BS in Edn., Ea. Mont. Coll., 1989; MS in Curriculum, Lesley Coll., 1993. Tchr. spl. edn. Chewelah (Wash.) Sch. Dist., 1989-93, Great Falls (Mont.) Sch. Dist., 1994—; drama dir. Dept. Human Svcs., Colville, Wash., 1990-92. Instr. religious edn. St. Mary of the Rosary, Chewelah, 1993-94. Mem. Alpha Chi Omega (rush chmn. 1985-87, rush advisor 1987-89). Roman Catholic. Home: 1005 Durango Ave Great Falls MT 59404

REITER, DAISY K., elementary education educator; b. Lewisburg, Pa., Aug. 25, 1936; d. Clark B. and Maude E. (Bensinger) Zimmerman; m. Edward P. Reiter, June 3, 1978; children: Edward, Amy, Russ, Elizabeth Sieber White, Katheryn Sieber Ellis, Ann Sieber Myers. BS in Elem. Edn., Pa. State U., 1957; postgrad., U. No. Colo., Greeley, Pa. State U. Cert. permanent elem. tchr., Pa.; lic. real estate agt. Tchr. grade 4 Hershey (Pa.) Sch. Dist., 1957-58; tchr. grades 4 and 5 Red Land Sch. Dist., New Cumberland, Pa., 1959-61; kindergarten tchr. Topeka City Schs., 1958-59; tchr. grade 5 Wallaceton-Boggs Elem. Sch. Philipsburg (Pa.)-Osceola Area Sch. Dist., 1975—; inservice leader transactional analysis and arts in edn.; researcher Civil War, newspapers, animals and habitats, body systems. Mem. choir lst Luth Ch. Recipient Arts in Edn. grants (4 yrs.). Mem. NEA, Pa. State Edn. Assn., Philipsburg-Osceola Edn. Assn, Toughlove Chpt. (founder). Home: PO Box 704 Philipsburg PA 16866-0704

REITER, EUNICE HARRIS, accountant; b. Dallas, Jan. 16, 1938; d. Thoedore and Pearl Ann (Baier) Harris; m. Karl H. Reiter, Dec. 29, 1957; children: Joseph, Sheila, Elaine. Student, U. Tex., 1955-56. Acct. White Petrov McHone CPAs, Houston, 1962-80; corp. treas. Perlite of Houston, Inc., 1980-84; owner EH Reiter Acctg. Svcs., Houston, 1984—; moderator Channel 13 TV Tax Show, Houston, 1986-87. Pres. Fondren Pk. Cmty. Inprovement Assn., Missouri City, Tex., 1972, 73, 87, 88, 89, 91, 92; commr. Planning and Zoning Commn., Missouri City, 1989-94; councilwoman Missouri City Coun., 1994—. Mem. Am. Soc. Women Accts. (pres. 1983, pres. meml. fund 1993—), Fedn. Houston Profl. Women (v.p. 1989), Hadassah (life, pres. 1979-81). Jewish. Home: 11723 N Perry Ave Houston TX 77071 Office: 4200 Westheimer Ste 210 Houston TX 77027

REITZ, BARBARA MAURER, poet, freelance writer; b. Teaneck, N.J., Dec. 26, 1931; d. William Ritschy and Ruth Gunhill (Noren) Maurer; m. William Stanley Reitz, Jr., Sept. 15, 1956; children: William Stanley III, David Stewart. BA in English, Bucknell U., 1953. Sec. UN, N.Y.C., 1953-54; sec. to pres. Charles Scribner's Sons, N.Y.C., 1954-56; freelance writer Chillicothe, Ohio, 1987—, poet, 1949—. Contbr. articles to local newspapers. Campaign mgr., creative dir. William S. Reitz, Jr. , Chillicothe City Coun. pres.; patron Bucknell Assn. for Arts, Columbus Symphony, Area Artist Series, Majestic Theatre; mem. Friends of WOSU-PBS, Pump House Art Gallery, Civic Theatre. Mem. AAUW (Chillicothe br. pres. 1988-90, v.p. Rockville, Md. bd. 1961-62), Acad. Am. Poets, Bucknell Alumni Assn. (sec.-treas. Chillicothe-Ross county chpt. 1973-82), Sigma Tau Delta (pres. 1952-53), Pi Delta Epsilon, Alpha Lambda Delta, Pi Beta Phi (treas. 1952-53). Republican. Presbyterian (elder 1981—). Home: 675 Hilltop Ct Chillicothe OH 45601-2928

REJENT, MARIAN MAGDALEN, pediatrician; b. Toledo, Aug. 12, 1920; d. Casimir Stanley and Magdalen (Szymanowski) R. BS, Mary Manse Coll., 1943; MD, Marquette U., 1946; MPH, U. Mich., 1960. Diplomate Am. Bd. Pediatrics. Intern St. Vincent Med. Ctr., Toledo, 1946-47; resident communicable diseases City Hosp., Cleve., 1947-48; resident pediatrics Childrens Hosp., Akron, Ohio, 1948-50; pvt. practice Toledo, 1950-54; chief div. maternal child health Toledo Bd. Health, 1953-64; dir. pediatrics Maumee Valley Hosp., Toledo, 1964-69; assoc. prof. pediatrics Med. Coll. Ohio, Toledo, 1969-76; med. dir. State Crippled Childrens Program, Columbus, Ohio, 1976-78; attendant pediatrician St. Vincent Med. Ctr., Toledo, 1978-80, 87—; chief pediatric svcs. Wake County Health Dept., Raleigh, N.C., 1980-87; clin. prof. pediatrics Med. Coll. Ohio, 1987—. Exec. com. March of Dimes, 1988-92. Mem. AMA, APHA, Am. Acad. Pediatrics, Am. Med. Women's Assn., Ohio PHA, Ohio State Med. Assn., NW Ohio Pediatric Assn., Acad. Medicine Toledo, Alpha Omega Alpha. Republican. Roman Catholic. Home: 2902 Evergreen Rd Toledo OH 43606-2724

REJMAN, DIANE LOUISE, industry analyst; b. Hartford, Conn., Jan. 14, 1956; d. Louis P. and Genevieve (Walukevich) R. BS in Aviation Adminstrn., Embry Riddle Aero. U., 1980; M in Internat. Mgmt., Am. Grad. Sch. Internat. Mgmt., 1991; cert. in cross cultural negotiation, Western Internat. Univ., 1994. Indsl. engr./planner Hamilton Aviation, Tucson, 1980-82; indsl. engr. assoc. Gates Learjet, Tucson, 1984; tech. writer, FAA coord. Dee Howard Co., San Antonio, 1984-86; indsl. engr. McDonnell Douglas Helicopter Systems, Mesa, Ariz., 1986-88; systems analyst McDonnell Douglas Helicopter Sys., Mesa, Ariz., 1988-95; sr. aerospace industry analyst Frost & Sullivan, Mountain View, Calif., 1995—; bd. dirs. McDonnell Douglas Helicopter Sys. Employee Community Fund., adminstr. 1992-95. Author: (reports) World Commercial Avionics Market, 1996, World Airport Ground Equipment Markets, 1996. Mem. Mesa Leadership Tng. Class of 1995. With U.S. Army, 1977-80. Home: 562 Kendall Ave #42 Palo Alto CA 94306

REKTORIK-SPRINKLE, PATRICIA JEAN, Latin language educator; b. Robstown, Tex., Feb. 19, 1941; d. Julius and Elizabeth Lollie (Ermis) Rektorik; m. Edgar Eugene Sprinkle, June 22, 1963; children: Julie Anne, Mark. BA in English and Latin, Our Lady of the Lake Coll., San Antonio, 1963, MA, 1967; doctoral student, Tex. A&M U., 1968-74, U. North Tex., 1987—. Cert. secondary tchr., Tex. Latin and English tchr. Ysleta Independent Sch. Dist., El Paso, Tex., 1963-64, El Paso Independent Sch. Dist., 1964-65; instr. Our Lady of the Lake Coll., 1965-66; rhetoric and composition instr. Tex. A&M U., College Station, 1968-69, 72-74, Harford Community Coll., Bel Aire, Md., 1970-71; Latin tchr. Denton (Tex.) Pub. Schs., 1974—; mem. residents adv. com. Tex. Acad. Math. and Sci., Denton, 1987-88; chmn. Latin reading competition Nat. Jr. Classical League, Miami, Ohio, 1988-93; mem. methodology com. Am. Classical League, 1993-95; dir. Tex. State Jr. Classical League Conv., 1996; presenter workshops in field; mem. Tex. State Textbook Adv. Com., 1989-90. Costume designer Denton Cmty. Theater, 1984; choir dir. Immaculate Conception Ch., Denton, 1985-87; chmn. costume competition Tex. State Jr. Classical League, 1987—, exec. bd. sponsor, 1981—. Arthur Patch McKinlay scholar, 1986, 91. Mem. Am. Classical Assn., Classical Assn. of the Mid-West and South, Metroplex Classics Assn. (constl. adv. com. 1988), Classics Assn. Southwestern U.S. (pres. 1987-88), Tex. Classics Assn., Tex. Fgn. Lang. Assn. (chmn. hon. mem. 1988-89, chmn. local arrangements 1977). Roman Catholic. Office: Billy Ryan High Sch 5101 E McKinney St Denton TX 76208-4630

RELL, M. JODI, state official; b. Norfolk, Va.. Student, Old Dominion U., Western Conn. State U. Mem., dep. minority leader Conn. Ho. Reps., 1984-94; lt. gov. State of Conn., 1995—. Past vice chmn. Brookfield Rep. Town Com.; trustee YMCA Western Conn. Mem. Nat. Order Women Legislators (past nat. pres., former v.p., treas., corr. sec.), Brookfield Rep. Women's Club (past pres.), Brookfield Bus. and Profl. Women's Club. Address: 125 Long Meadow Hill Rd Brookfield CT 06804-1339 Office: Office Lt Governor State Capitol Rm 304 Hartford CT 06106

REMAK, JEANNETTE ELIZABETH, quality control executive; b. Queens, N.Y., Nov. 23, 1952; d. Bela Alexander and Helen (Almassy) R. Student, N.Y. Inst. Photography, 1971-72; student, Sch. Visual Arts, N.Y.C., 1972-73, CUNY, 1973-76. Cert. photo finishing engr. Photo Mktg. Assn. Prodn. mgr. Rembrandt Color Labs., Jamaica, N.Y., 1976-80; builder, operator Fast Photo, N.Y.C., 1980-83; prodn. mgr. Jackson Photo, N.Y.C., 1983-86; quality control and prodn. mgr. Universal Photo, N.Y.C., 1986—. Paintings exhibited at Internat. Art Challenge Art Show, Calif., 1987; paintings included in (book) American Artists an Illustrated Survey, 1990, USAF Mus., Wright-Patterson AFB, Ohio, the Pentagon, Washington. Contbg. mem. USAF Art Program. Mem. Soc. Photofinishing Engrs., Am. Soc. Aviation Artists, Am. Soc. Sci. Fiction Fantasy Artists, Challenger Ctr. for Edn. (sponsor).

REMER, DEBORAH JANE, secondary education educator; b. Detroit, Dec. 10, 1953; d. Maynard William and Marie Josephine (Wells) R. BS, Mich. State U., 1976, MA in Tchg., 1977. Mich. secondary provisional tchg. cert., 1976, Mich. secondary continuing tchg. cert., 1981. Sci. tchr. grade 8 Walled Lake (Mich.) Middle Sch., 1977-81; substitute tchr. Utica (Mich) Cmty. Schs., 1981-85; sci. tchr. Kingsbury Sch., Oxford, Mich., 1985-86; sci. tchr. grade 8, sci. dept. chair Walled Lake (Mich.) Consol. Schs., 1986—; chair 8th grade sci. fair Walled Lake (Mich.) Middle Sch., 1987, 89—, coach sci. competition, 1987-94; mem. K-12 sci. com. Walled Lake (Mich.) Consol. Schs., 1990—. Author: The Joachim Ernest Theodore Remer Family in Michigan, 1980, revised, 1995; contbr. Environmental Conservation Program Design, 1976; author of various booklets and pamphlets. Archaeology program presenter, pianist Rochester Mills (Mich.) Mus. at Van Hoosen Farm, 1988—, co-dir. archaeology programs, 1989—. 4-H state winner in conservation Mich. 4-H Clubs, East Lansing, 1971; recipient 4-H Key Club award Mich. 4-H Clubs, Macomb County, Mich., 1972, Earl Borden Historic Preservation award City of Rochester Hills, Mich. Historic Dist. Commn., 1995. Mem. ASCD, NEA, Nat. Sci. Tchrs. Assn., Nat. Earth Sci. Tchrs. Assn., Mich. Edn. Assn., Walled Lake Edn. Assn., Mich. Earth Sci. Tchrs. Assn., Mich. Sci. Tchrs. Assn. (middle sch. program com. 1977-81, dir.-at-large 1981, conf. presenter 1993-95, finalist Middle Sch. Sci. Tchr. of Yr. 1995), Mich. Assn. Sci. Edn. Specialists, Met. Detroit Sci. Tchrs. Assn. (conf. presenter 1993-94), Nat. Audubon Soc., Mich. Audubon Soc., Macomb Audubon Soc., Cranbrook Inst. Sci., Smithsonian Assocs., Earthwatch, Hist. Soc. Mich., Rochester Avon (Mich.) Hist. Soc. (rec. sec. 1990), Suffolk County (N.Y.) Hist. and Geneal. Soc., New Eng. Historic Geneal. Soc., Founders Soc.-Detroit Inst. Arts, Bat Conservation Internat., Archaeol. Inst. Am., Mich. State U. Alumni Assn., Nat. Wildflower Rsch. Ctr., Colonial Williamsburg Found., Mich. Archaeol. Soc. (Clinton Valley chpt.), Detroit Zool. Soc., Oakland County Pioneer and Hist. Soc., Nat. Trust for Historic Preservation, Soc. for the Preservation of Old Mills (Great Lakes chpt.), Mich. Karst Conservancy, Archaeol. Conservancy, Am. Minor Breeds Conservancy, MADD, Alpha Zeta. Republican. Congregationalist. Office: Walled Lake Middle Sch 46720 N Pontiac Trail Walled Lake MI 48390

REMER, JANE TOBA, author, arts education consultant; b. Bklyn., Sept. 22, 1932; d. David Louis and Duds Rose (Schwarzbart) Weissman; m. Michael D. Remer, June 18, 1955 (div. Aug. 1967); children: Abby, Harry. BA, Oberlin Coll., 1954; MA, Yale U., 1957. Asst. dir. Young Audiences, N.Y.C., 1965-67, Lincoln Ctr. for Performing Arts/Edn., N.Y.C., 1967-72; program dir. N.Y.C. Bd. Edn.'s Learning Coop., N.Y.C., 1972-73; assoc. dir. John D. Rockefeller's 3d Fund, N.Y.C., 1973-79; dir. Capezio-Ballet Makers Dance Found., Totowa, N.J., 1985—; author, cons. N.Y.C., 1980—; dir. 440 West End Ave. Corp., N.Y.C., 1990—, New Dance Group, N.Y.C., 1970-85; advisor City Ctr. for Music/Dance, N.Y.C., 1993—, Manhattan Theater Club, N.Y.C., 1993—. Author: Changing Schools Through the Arts, 1982, rev. and expanded edit., 1990, Beyond Enrichment: Building Effective Arts Partnerships With Schools and Your Community, 1996.

REMETTA, JANET, pharmaceutical company executive, veterinarian; b. Camden, N.J., July 11, 1952; d. John Matthew and Marie Stella (Klemaszewski) R.; m. Neal Robert Frank, Oct. 19, 1974. BA, Trenton State Coll., 1974; MSW, Rutgers U., 1975; postgrad., Delaware Valley Coll., 1977-79; VMD, U. Pa., 1985. Lic. vet. medicine, Pa., N.J. Program specialist N.J. Dept. Health, Trenton, 1975-77, labor/mgmt. cons., 1977-79, supervising program specialist, 1979-81; clin. vet. Emerson Vet. Clinic, Buckingham, Pa., 1985-86, Ewing Vet. Hosp., Trenton, 1986-88; mgr. issues mgmt. Sandoz Pharm. Corp., East Hanover, N.J., 1988-90, assoc. dir. issues mgmt., 1990-91, dir. issues mgmt., 1992, interim dept. head sci. and external affairs, 1992-93, exec. dir. site ops., 1993-95; exec. dir. internat. pub. policy Rhône-Poulenc Rorer Pharms., Collegeville, Pa., 1995—. Mem. policy and legis. com. N.J. Chem. Industry Coun., Trenton, 1988-92, chairperson-biotech. com., 1989-91; legis. com. N.J. Bus. and Industry Assn., Trenton, 1988-92; apptd. mem. N.J. Commn. on Smoking and Health, 1991-92; exec. chairperson N.J. Lung Assn., 1994; mem. bus. adv. bd. Women in Govt., 1994—; mem. steering com. Ctr. for the Am. woman, 1995; bd. dirs. YWCA, 1994-95. Recipient Tribute to Women in Industry award, 1992. Mem. AVMA, European Women's Mgmt. Devel. Network, Pa. Vet. Med. Assn. (legis. com. 1990—, long range planning com. 1995), Am. Mgmt. Assn., Am. Lung Assn. (exec. chairperson 1994), Assn. Indsl. Vets. Healthcare Businesswomen's Assn., N.J. Health Products Coun. (chairperson elect 1989-91, chairperson 1991-93), Nat. Pharm. Coun. (pub. affairs com. 1988-91, sci. affairs com. 1989-90), Pharm. Rsch. and Mfrs. Assn. (govt. affairs com. 1989-93, internat. com. 1995, exec. com. internat. sect. 1995—, econ. policy task force 1995—), Greater Valley Forge Rhodesian Ridge Back Club (founding mem.), Internat. Pharm. Aerosol Consortium (corp. rep. 1996—), Internat. Bus. Coun. (corp. rep. 1996—). Home: 379 Sweetbriar Rd Perkasie PA 18944-3868

REMINGTON, FRANÇOISE, secondary school educator; b. Paris, Oct. 13, 1947; came to U.S., 1972; d. Andre Robert and Marie-Louise (Coignet) Granger; m. Michael J. Remington, June 24, 1972; children: Cecile, Elise, Christophe. D in French Lit., U. Sorbonne, 1981; M in Internat. Rels., Johns Hopkins U., 1985. French tchr. Coll. of Adzope, Ivory Coast, 1970-71, Washington Internat. Sch., 1975-79, 90—; lectr. in French, Sch. of Advanced Internat. Studies Johns Hopkins U., 1979-88; dir. India program Am. Adoption Agy., Washington, 1988-90; cons. World Bank, Washington, 1985-90, 91, Creative Assoc. Internat., Washington, 1993. Contbr. articles to profl. jours. Advocate for st. children, India, 1989—; exec. dir. Forgotten Children, Arlington, Va., 1994—. Recipient fellowship to conduct rsch. on bilingual edn. European Coun. of Internat. Schs., 1994. Mem. Alliance Francaise. Roman Catholic. Office: Washington Internat School 3100 Macomb St NW Washington DC 20008-3324

REMMO, TRACI MEREDITH, laboratory supervisor; b. Indpls., Jan. 15, 1971; d. William Francis and Marjorie Ann (Strange) R. BS, Ind. U., 1993. Environ. technician Metalworking Lubricants Co., Indpls., 1989-93, environ. coord., 1993-95, lab. supr., 1995—; site mgr. Environ. Products & Svcs., 1995—. Mem. Am. Chem. Soc. Office: Environmental Products & Svcs 100 Creasy Ct Lafayette IN 47903

RENARD, MEREDITH ANNE, marketing and advertising professional; b. Newark, Apr. 12, 1952; d. W. Edward and Lois E. (Velthoven) Young. BA, Caldwell Coll., 1974. Advt., pub. rels. asst. Congoleum Corp., Lawrenceville, N.J., 1974-77; account mgr. Saatchi & Saatchi Compton, N.Y.C., 1977-82; dir. advt., sales promotion Singer Sewing Co., Edison, N.J., 1982-86, dir. product mktg., 1986-88, dir. nat. accounts, 1988-90; sr. mktg. rep. Walt Disney World Co., Lake Buena Vista, Fla., 1990-91; div. mktg. rep. Vista Advt., Walt Disney World Co., Lake Buena Vista, Fla., 1991-92; mgr. advt. Walt Disney World Co., Lake Buena Vista, Fla., 1992-94, mgr. Fla. tourist mktg., 1994—. Contbr. articles to profl. jours. Vol. North Brunswick Dem. Orgn., 1985-87; pub. rels. mgr. Cultural Arts Com., North Brunswick, 1986-87; props chair Adult Drama Group, North Brunswick, 1986-87; mem. mktg. com. Vol. Ctr. Ctrl. Fla., 1993-94. Mem. Fla. Direct Mktg. Assn., Cen. Fla. Direct Mktg. Assn. (bd. dirs. 1990-92). Democrat. Episcopalian. Office: Walt Disney World Co PO Box 10000 Orlando FL 32830-1000

RENDER, ARLENE, ambassador. Joined Fgn. Svc., Dept. State, 1970; consular officer Fgn. Svc., Dept. State, Abidjan, Cote D'Ivoire, 1971-73, Tehran, Iran, 1973-76, Genoa, Italy, 1976-78; polit. officer Fgn. Svc., Dept. State, 1978-79, internat. rels. officer AF/C, 1979-81; dep. chief of mission Fgn. Svc., Dept. State, Brazzaville, Republic of the Congo, 1981-84; consul-gen. Fgn. Svc., Dept. State, Kingston, Jamaica, 1984-86; dep. chief of mission Fgn. Svc., Dept. State, Accra, Ghana, 1986-89; mem. sr. seminar Fgn. Svc., Dept. State, 1989-90, amb. to The Gambia, 1990-93; dir. Office of Ctrl. African Affairs Fgn. Svc., Dept. State, Washington, 1993—; amb. to Zambia, 1996—. Office: State Dept Office Ctrl African Affairs Washington DC 20520

RENDL-MARCUS, MILDRED, artist, economist; b. N.Y.C., May 30, 1928; d. Julius and Agnes (Hokr) Rendl. BS, NYU, 1948, MBA, 1950; PhD, Radcliffe Coll., 1954; m. Edward Marcus, Aug. 10, 1956. Economist, GE, 1953-56, Bigelow-Sanford Carpet Co., Inc., 1956-58; lectr. econs. evening sessions CCNY, 1953-58; rsch. investment problems in tropical Africa, 1958-59; instr. econs. Hunter Coll. CUNY, 1959-60; lectr. econs. Columbia U., 1960-61; rsch. econ. devel. Nigeria, West Africa, 1961-63; sr. economist Internat. div. Nat. Indsl. Conf. Bd., 1963-66; asst. prof. Grad. Sch. Bus. Adminstrn., Pace Coll., 1964-66; assoc. prof. Borough of Manhattan C.C., CUNY, 1966-71, prof., 1972-85; vis. prof. Fla. Internat. U., 1986; prin. MRM Assocs., Rendl Fine Art; corp. art econ. and contemporary art cons.; fine arts appraiser; artist Allied Social Sci. Assn. Conf., Boston, 1994; participant Internat. Econ. Meeting, Amsterdam, 1968, Prague, Czech Republic, 1993, Brussels, 1994, Econs. of Fine Arts in Age of Tech., 1984, Internat. Economic Assn. N.Am., Laredo, Tex., 1987-88, London, 1994, Soc. Southwestern Economists, San Antonio, 1988, New Orleans, 1989, Dallas, 1989, Houston, 1991, Dallas, 1994, S.W. Soc. Economists, San Antonio, 1992, Dallas, 1994, San Diego, 1990, 92, Reno, 1991, Western Econ. Assn. Internat., 1990, Ind. U. Pa., 1990, London, 1992-93, Ariz. Sr. Acad., Tucson, 1995. Exhibited New Canaan Art Show, 1982-85, Am. Soc. of Bus. and Behavioral Scis, Las Vegas, 1996, New Canaan Soc. for Arts Ann., 1983, 85, New Canaan Arts, 1985, Silvermine Galleries, 1986, Stamford Art Assn., 1987, Women in the Arts at Phoenix Gallery, Group Show, N.Y.C., 1988, Parkview Point Gallery, Miami Beach, Fla., 1982-89, Art Complex, New Canaan, Miami Beach, 1985—; group shows include Lever House, N.Y.C., 1990, Cork Gallery, Lincoln Ctr., N.Y.C., 1990, Women's Caucus for Art, San Antonio, 1990, Artist's Equity, Broome St. Gallery, N.Y.C., 1991, Greater Hartford Architecture Conservancy, 1991; symposium participant Sienna, Italy, 1988, South Fla. Art Ctr., Miami Beach, 1990, 92-93, Wadsworth Atheneum, Hartford, Conn., 1994-95, Annual Barnum Festival, 1995-96, Discovery Mus., Bridgeport, Conn., 1995. Bd. dirs. N.Y.C. Coun. on Econ. Edn., 1970—; mem. program planning com. Women's Econ. Roundtable, N.Y.C.; participant Eastern Econ. Assn., Boston, 1988, Art and Personal Property Appraisal, NYU, 1986-88. Recipient Disting. Svc. award CUNY, 1985; Dean Bernice Brown Cronkhite fellow Radcliffe Coll., 1950-51, Anne Radcliffe Econ. Rsch. Sub-Sahara Africa fellow, 1958-59. Fellow Gerontol. Assn.; mem. Internat. Schumpeter Econs. Soc. (founding), Comm. Internat. Internat., Am. (vice chmn. ann. meeting 1973), Met. (sec. 1954-56) econ. assns., Indsl. Rels. Rsch. Assn., Audubon Artists and Nat. Soc. Painters in Casein (assoc. 1987-88) Allied Social Sci. Assn. (vice chmn. conv. 1973, artist Boston nat. conv. 1994), AAUW, N.Y.C. Women in Arts, Allied Social Sci. Assn. (artist 1994), Women's Econ. Roundtable, Greater Hartford Architecture Conservancy, NYU Grad. Sch. Bus. Adminstrn. Alumni (sec. 1956-58), Radcliffe Club, Women's City Club (art and landmarks com.). Author: (with husband) Investment and Development of Tropical Africa, 1959, International Trade and Finance, 1965, Monetary and Banking Theory, 1965; Economics, 1969; (with husband) Principles of Economics, 1969; Economic Progress and the Developing World, 1970; Economics, 1978, Fine Art with Many Equilibrium Prices, 1995; also monographs and articles in field. Econ. and internat. rsch. on industrialization less developed areas, internat. debtor nations and workability of buffer stock schemes, pricing fine art; columnist economics of art, Art As An Investment, Money Substitute, or Consumer Durable Good Art Valuation; When Is A Price of Fine Art The Price?, Prices and Varied Appraisals, Fine Art with Many Equilibrium Prices: Price Distortion-A Segmented Market in Fine Art, Am. Soc. of Bus. and Behavioral Sci. (Las Vegas Ann. Meeting 1996); editor Women in the Arts Found. Newsletter, 1986-92; contbr. Coalition Women's Arts Orgns., 1986-92, other profl. publs. Home and Office: PO Box 814 New Canaan CT 06840-0814 also: 7441 Wayne Ave Miami FL 33141

RENDON-PELLERANO, MARTA INES, dermatologist; b. Sept. 19, 1957; d. Uriel and Rosa Rendon. BA and Scis., U. P.R., Mayaquez, 1977; postgrad., Autonoma U., Santo Domingo, Dominican Republic, 1977-79; MD, U. P.R., San Juan, 1982. Diplomate Am. Bd. Internal Medicine, Am. Bd. Dermatology; lic. physician, Fla., Tex., Pa., ACLS, Drug Enforcement Adminstrn. Intern and resident in internal medicine Albert Einstein Med. Ctr., Phila., 1982-85; resident in dermatology Parkland Meml. Hosp., Southwestern Med. Sch., Dallas, 1985-88; emergency rm. physician Pottsborough (Tex.) Med. Clinic, 1985-86; coord. dermatology clinic Kayser Permanente Med. Assn. Tex., Dallas, 1986-88; dermatology assoc. Dermatology Ctr., Dallas, 1988-89; staff physician Southwestern Med. Sch., Vets. Hosp., Dallas, 1988-89; clin. asst. prof. dept. deramtology U. Miami (Fla.) Sch. Medicine, 1989—; chief dept. dermatology Cleveland Clinic Fla., Ft. Lauderdale, 1989—; mem. adv. bd. South Fla. Vis. Lectureship Series, 1991-92; mem. rsch. bd. advisors Medecis Corp. Featured on TV shows and in popular mags.; contbr. articles to profl. jours., chpts. to books. Recipient Radio Klaridad award for best sci. work, Miami, 1990. Fellow Am. Acad. Dermatology; mem. ACP (assoc.), AAUW, Womens Med. Assn., Womens Dermatol. Soc., Cuban-Interam. Dermatol. Soc., Women of Spanish Origin, Tex. Med. Assn., Miami Dermatology Soc., Fla. Med. Assn., Broward Dermatology Soc., Broward County Med. Assn., Etta Gamma Delta. Roman Catholic. Office: Cleveland Clinic Fla 3000 W Cypress Creek Rd Fort Lauderdale FL 33309-1710

RENEE, LISABETH MARY, art educator, artist; b. Bklyn., July 28, 1952; d. Lino P. and Elizabeth M. (Dines) Rivano; m. John S. Witanowski, May 15, 1982. Student, U. Puget Sound, 1972-74; BA in Art, SUNY, Buffalo, 1977; MFA, L.I. U., 1982; EdD, U. Ctrl. Fla., 1996. Cert. art tchr., Fla. Adj. faculty L.I. U., Greenvale, N.Y., 1980-82, Rollins Coll., Winter Park, Fla., 1982; art tchr. Phyllis Wheatley Elem. Sch., Apopka, Fla., 1983-85, McCoy Elem. Sch., Orlando, Fla., 1985-86, Lake Howell H.S., Winter Park, Fla., 1986-93; adj. faculty U. Ctrl. Fla., 1994-95, vis. instr., 1995-96; gallery dir., instr. West Campus Valencia (Fla.) C.C., 1996—; adj. faculty Valencia C.C., 1995-96; dir. So. Artists Registry, Winter Park, 1984-87; cons. Fla. Dept. Edn., 1989-90, mem. curriculum writing team for arts edn. program; mem. com. Fla. Bd. Edn. Task Force for Subject Area Subtest of Fla. Tech. Cert. Exam.; visual arts dir. Very Spl. Arts Ctr. Fla. Fest, 1996; presenter at profl. confs. Author: The Phenomenological Significance of Aesthetic Communion, 1996; editor: Children and the Arts in Florida, 1990. Visual arts dir. Very Spl. Arts Ctrl. Fla. Festival, 1995; mem. local Sch. Adv. Coun., Winter Park, 1992. Grantee Found. for Advancement of Cmty. Throught Schs., 1991, Divsn. Blind Svcs. Invision, 1995, Tangelo Park Project, 1995; ACE scholar Arts Leadership Inst., 1993-96; recipient Tchr. Merit award Walt Disney World Co., 1990. Mem. NEA, ASCD, Nat. Art Edn. Assn., Fla. Art Edn. Assn. (regional rep. 1989-94), Seminole County Art Edn. Assn., Coll. Art Assn., Caucus on Social Theory and Art Edn., Women's Caucus for Art, Phi Kappa Phi, Kappa Delta Pi. Home: 20 Cobblestone Ct Casselberry FL 32707-5410 Office: Valencia CC West Campus Humanities Dept MC 4-11 Orlando FL 32802

RENEE, PAULA (PAULA RENEE WILK), artist; b. Hackensack, N.J., Mar. 3; d. Paul and Helen (Boyko) Wilk; m. Robert F. Handschuh, June 19, 1954 (div. Dec. 1968); children: Kim, Dawn; m. Thomas D. Murray, Jan. 4, 1969 (div. Dec. 1975); m. Samuel R. Hazlett, June 6, 1978 (div. Apr. 1986). Student, Fairleigh Dickenson U., 1973-77, Ramapo State Coll., 1973, Rockland Community Coll., 1970-71, Thomas A. Edison Coll., 1978; AS, Empire Coll., 1990. Artist self-employed, Tenafly, N.J., 1978-84; artist self-employed Palisades Park, N.J., 1984-87, Nyack, N.Y., 1987—; artist-in-residence Bergen Community Coll., Hackensack, 1978-79. Exhibited in group shows at New London (Conn.) Art Soc. Gallery, Hudson River Mus. Westchester, Yonkers, N.Y., Trenton City (N.J.) Mus., Long Beach Found. Art and Sic., Loveladies, N.J., Bergen Mus. Art and Sci., Paramus, N.J., and other galleries in U.S.; represented in permanent collections Nat. Inst. Design, Ahmedabad, India, IBM, Princeton, AT&T, N.J., N.Y. Telephone, N.Y.C., Olin Corp., Schlumberger-Doll Res., Conn., Touche Ross, Inc., N.Y.C., Calif., United Fed. Bank, Clearwater, Fla., Savs. and Loan, Fla., Stouffer's Resort, Palm Springs, West Point (N.Y.) Jewish Chapel, U.S. Army Mil. Acad., Sheraton Hotel, Chgo., Admiral Royale Hotel, Egg Harbor, N.J., The Wood Sch., N.Y.C., numerous others; photos exhibited in numerous mags. Home: Rivercrest 103 Gedney St Apt 1H Nyack NY 10960-2226

RENEKER, MAXINE HOHMAN, librarian; b. Chgo., Dec. 2, 1942; d. Roy Max and Helen Anna Christina (Anacker) Hohman; m. David Lee Reneker, June 20, 1964 (dec. Dec. 1979); children: Sarah Roeder, Amy Johannah, Benjamin Congdon. BA, Carleton Coll., 1964; MA, U. Chgo., 1970; DLS, Columbia U., 1992. Asst. reference libr. U. Chgo. Libraries, 1965-66; classics libr. U. Chgo. Libr., 1967-70, asst. head acquisitions, 1970-71, personnel libr., 1971-73; personnel/bus. libr. U. Colo. Libr., Boulder, 1978-80; asst. dir. sci. and engring. div. Columbia U., N.Y.C., 1981-85; assoc. dean of univ. librs. for pub. svcs. Ariz. State U. Libr., Tempe, 1985-89; dir. instrnl. and rsch. svcs. Stanford (Calif.) Univ. Librs., 1989-90; dir. info.

svcs., dir. Dudley Knox Libr. Naval Postgrad. Sch., Monterey, Calif., 1993—; acad. libr. mgmt. intern Coun. on Libr. Resources, 1980-81; chmn. univ. librs. sect. Assn. Coll. and Rsch. Librs., 1989-90. Contbr. articles to profl. jours. Rsch. grantee Coun. on Library Resources, Columbia U., 1970-71, fellow, 1990-92. Mem. ALA, Am. Soc. Info. Sci., Sherlockian Scion Soc., Phi Beta Kappa, Beta Phi Mu. Home: 740 Dry Creek Rd Monterey CA 93940-4208 Office: Naval Postgrad Sch Dudley Knox Libr 411 Dyer Rd Monterey CA 93943-5198

RÉNI See BROWN, ARLENE PATRICIA THERESA

RENICK, CAROL BISHOP, insurance planning company executive, consultant; b. Arlington, Mass., June 5, 1956; d. Francis Joseph and Mary Ruth (Robinson) Bishop; m. Lawrence A. Balboni, May 5, 1979 (div. 1982); m. Gary L. Renick, Jan. 31, 1986. Grad., Harvard U., 1991. Mgr. Larson Ins., Arlington, Mass., 1979-85; v.p. Larson Ins., Arlington, 1987-88; mgr. Merrill Lynch Realty Ins. Svcs., Boca Raton, Fla., 1985-87; pres. Essex Ins. Planners, Haverhill, Mass., 1988—; v.p. United Internat. Ins. Agy., Inc., Braintree, Mass., 1992-94. Vol. Mus. Sci., Boston, 1988, Mus. Sci., 1988—; vol., cultural cons., advisor Free Romania Found., Cambridge, Mass., 1990—; tutor Mass. Campaign for Literacy, 1988—. Mem. Profl. Ins. Agts., Inc. Democrat.

RENICK, NANCY ELIZABETH, museum educator; b. Bloomington, Ind., Sept. 28, 1965; d. Howard and Lynda Patricia (Bell) R.; m. Barry Jay Kornstein, Sept. 2, 1990. BA in Art History, Trinity U., San Antonio, 1987; MA in Art History, U. Minn., 1989. Assoc. pub. programs Mpls. Inst. Art, 1989-91; assoc. curator of edn. JB Speed Art Mus., Louisville, 1991—; mem. Sr. Cultural Connections, Louisville, 1992—; advisor Oldham County Hist. Mus., LaGrange, Ky., 1994-95; adv. coun. Multi-Cultural Ctr., U. Louisville, 1994—; adv. bd. Master of Liberal Studies, Bellarmine Coll., Louisville, 1994—; presenter in field. Social action chair Temple Shalom, Louisville, 1993-95, edn. com., 1994—, bd. mem., sec., 1994—; bd. mem. Ctrl. Agy. for Jewish Edn., Louisville, 1993-95; mem. adult edn. com. Jewish Cmty. Ctr., 1995—. Mem. Toonerville Neighborhood Assn., Phi Beta Kappa, Phi Alpha Theta. Democat. Office: JB Speed Art Mus 2035 S 3rd Louisville KY 40708

RENNE, LOUISE HORNBECK, lawyer; b. Pitts., Aug. 26, 1937; d. Lewis Alvin and Anne (Bartrem) Hornbeck; m. Paul A. Renne, July 11, 1959; Christine, Anne. BA, Mich. State U., 1958; postgrad. law, Harvard U., 1958-59, U. Pa., 1959-60; JD, Columbia U., 1961. Bar: Calif. 1964, D.C. 1961, U.S. Supreme Ct. 1969. With broadcast bur., office gen. counsel FCC, 1961-64; assoc. Peterson & Barr, San Francisco, 1964-66; dep. atty. gen. State of Calif., San Francisco, 1966-77; pres. Calif. Women Lawyers, San Francisco, 1977-78; mem. Bd. Suprs., San Francisco, 1978-86; city atty. San Francisco, 1986—. Office: Office of City Atty 1390 Market St 5th Fl San Francisco CA 94102

RENNINGER, MARY KAREN, librarian; b. Pitts., Apr. 30, 1945; d. Jack Burnell and Jane (Hammerly) Gunderman; m. Norman Christian Renninger, Sept. 3, 1965 (div. 1980); 1 child, David Christian. B.A., U. Md., 1969, M.A., 1972, M.L.S., 1975. Tchr. English West Carteret High Sch., Morehead City, N.C., 1969-70; instr. in English U. Md., College Park, 1970-72; head network services Nat. Libr. Svc., Libr. of Congress, Washington, 1974-78, asst. for network support, 1978-80; mem. fed. women's program com. Libr. of Congress, Washington, 1978-80; chief libr. divsn. Dept. Vets. Affairs, Washington, 1980-90; chief serial and govt. publs. divsn. Libr. of Congress, Washington, 1991—, mem. fed. libr. com., 1980-90, mem. exec. adv. bd., 1985-90; mem. USBE pers. subcom., 1982-84; bd. regents Nat. Libr. of Medicine, 1986-90, mem. outreach panel, 1988-89; fed. libr. task force for 1990 White House Conf. on Librs., 1986-90; liaison to The White House Conf. Med. Libr. Assn., 1989-90. Recipient Meritorious Svc. award Libr. of Congress, 1974, Spl. Achievement award, 1976, Performance award VA, ann. 1982-89, Adminstr.'s Commendation, 1985, Spl. Contbn. award, 1986. Mem. ALA (Govt. Documents Roundtable), Libr. Tech. Assn., Med. Libr. Assn. (govt. rels. com. 1985—), D.C. Libr. Assn., Soc. Applied Learning Tech., Med. Interactive Videodisc Consortium, Govt. Documents Roundtable, Knowledge Utilization Soc., Nat. Multimedia Assn. Am., U.S. Tennis Assn., Phi Beta Kappa, Alpha Lambda Delta, Beta Phi Mu. Home: 840 College Pky Rockville MD 20850-1931 Office: Libr of Congress Ser and Govt Pub Divsn LM 133 Washington DC 20540

RENO, JANET, federal official, lawyer; b. Miami, Fla., July 21, 1938; d. Henry and Jane (Wood) R. A.B. in Chemistry, Cornell U., 1960; LL.B., Harvard U., 1963. Bar: Fla. 1963. Assoc. Brigham & Brigham, 1963-67; ptnr. Lewis & Reno, 1967-71; staff dir. judiciary com. Fla. Ho. of Reps., Tallahassee, 1971-72; cons. Fla. Senate Criminal Justice Com. for Revision Fla.'s Criminal Code, spring 1973; adminstrv. asst. state atty. 11th Jud. Circuit Fla., Miami, 1973-76, state atty., 1978-93; ptnr. Steel Hector and Davis, Miami, 1976-78; atty. gen. Dept. Justice, Washington, 1993—; mem. jud. nominating commn. 11th Jud. Circuit Fla., 1976-78; chmn. Fla. Gov.'s Council for Prosecution Organized Crime, 1979-80. Recipient Women First award YWCA, 1993. Mem. ABA (Inst. Jud. Adminstrn. Juvenile Justice Standards Commn. 1973-76), Am. Law Inst., Am. Judicature Soc. (Herbert Harley award 1981), Dade County Bar Assn., Fla. Pros. Atty.'s Assn. (pres. 1984-86). Democrat. Office: Dept Justice 10th & Constitution Ave NW Washington DC 20530

RENSE, PAIGE, editor, publishing company executive; b. Iowa, May 4, 1929; m. Kenneth Noland, Apr. 10, 1994. Student, Calif. State U., L.A. Editor-in-chief Architectural Digest, L.A., 1970—. Recipient Nat. Headliner award Women in Communications, 1983, pacifica award So. Calif. Resources Coun., 1978, editl. award Dallas Market Ctr., 1978, golden award Chgo. Design Resources Svc., 12982, Agora award, 1982, outstanding profl. in comms. award, 1982, trailblazers award, 1983, disting. svcs. award Resources Coun., Inc., 1988; named woman of yr. L.A. Times, 1986, Muses, 1986, woman of internat. accomplishment, 1991; named to Interior Design Hall of Fame. Office: Architectural Digest 6300 Wilshire Blvd Fl 11 Los Angeles CA 90048-5202

RENSHAW, AMANDA FRANCES, retired physicist, nuclear engineer; b. Wheelwright, Ky., Dec. 10, 1934; d. Taft and Mamie Nell (Russell) Wilson; divorced; children: Linda, Michael, Billy. BS in Physics, Antioch Coll., 1972; MS in Physics, U. Tenn., 1982, MS in Nuclear Engring., 1991. Rsch. asst. U. Mich., Ann Arbor, 1970-71; teaching asst. Antioch Coll., Yellow Springs, Ohio, 1971-72; physicist GE, Schenectady, N.Y., 1972-74, Union Carbide Corp., Oak Ridge, Tenn., 1974-79; rsch. assoc. Oak Ridge Nat. Lab., 1979-91, mgr. strategic planning, 1991-92, liaison for environ. scis., 1993-96; ret., 1996; asst. to counselor for sci. and tech. Am. Embassy, Moscow, 1990; asst. to dir. nat. acid precipitation assessment program Office of Pres. U.S., 1993-94. Contbr. articles to profl. jours. Mem. AAUW, Am. Assn. Artificial Intelligence, Am. Nuclear Soc. (Oak Ridge chpt.), Soc. Black Physicists. Home: 1850 Cherokee Bluff Dr Knoxville TN 37920-2215

RENSHAW, JEAN REHKOP, management educator, consultant; b. Canoga Park, Calif., Oct. 15, 1936; d. Al H. and Ada E. (Heins) Rehkop; m. William B. Renshaw (div. 1985); children: Blair, Jeannine, Alan. BS, UCLA, 1959, MS, 1972, PhD, 1974. Economist The RAND Corp., Santa Monica, Calif.; prof. U. So. Pacific, Suva, Fiji, U. Hawaii, Honolulu; prof., chair bus. dept. Ea. Oreg. State Coll., La Grande; prof. mgmt. Pepperdine U., L.A.; cons. AJR Internat. Assocs., San Diego, 1979—; monitor New Zealand Qualification Auth., Wellington, 1989—. Author: Japanese Women Manager, 1996; contbr. chpt. to book, articles to profl. jours. Cons. Hawaii State, Honolulu, 1990-94. Fulbright sr. rsch. scholar Tokyo, 1990-93. Mem. Womencare, Assn. Asian Studies.

RENSHAW, PATRICIA KATHERINE, videographer; b. Barstow, Calif., Mar. 2, 1953; d. Joe Bell and Gloria Catherine R. Student, Pasadena City Coll. Graphic artist NBC-TV, Burbank, Calif., 1974-78, asst. editor news, 1978-80; tech. dir. KSBY-TV, San Luis Obispo, Calif., 1981-84; owner Alpha Video Prodns., San Luis Obispo, 1984—. Mem. NOW (pres. San Luis Obispo 1983-93). Office: Alpha Video Prodns 3436 Sacramento Dr Ste A San Luis Obispo CA 93401

RENT, CLYDA STOKES, academic administrator; b. Jacksonville, Fla., Mar. 1, 1942; d. Clyde Parker Stokes Sr. and Edna Mae (Edwards) Shuemake; m. George Seymour Rent, Aug. 12, 1966; 1 child, Cason Lynley Rent Helms. BA, Fla. State U., 1964, MA, 1966, PhD, 1968; LHD (hon.), Judson Coll., 1993. Asst. prof. Western Carolina U., Cullowhee, N.C., 1968-70; asst. prof. Queens Coll., Charlotte, N.C., 1972-74, dept. chair, 1974-78, dean Grad. Sch. and New Coll., 1979-84, v.p. for Grad. Sch. and New Coll., 1984-85, v.p. acad. affairs, 1985-87, v.p. community affairs, 1987-89; pres. Miss. U. for Women, Columbus, 1989—; bd. dirs. Trustmark Nat. Bank, Trustmark Corp.; cons. Coll. Bd. N.Y.C., 1983-89; sci. cons. N.C. Alcohol Rsch. Authority, Chapel Hill, 1976-89; bd. mem. So. Growth Policies Bd., 1992-94; mem. adv. bd. Nat. Women's Hall of Fame; rotating chair Miss. Instns. Higher Learning Pres.' Coun., 1990-91; commn. govtl. rels. Am. Coun. Edn., 1990-93; adv. bd. Miss. Power and Light, 1994—. Mem. editl. rev. bd. Planning for Higher Education, 1995; author rsch. articles in acad. jours.; speeches pub. in Vital Speeches; mem. editl. bds. acad. jours. Trustee N.C. Performing Arts Ctr., Charlotte, 1988-89, Charlotte County Day Sch., 1987-89; bd. visitors Johnson C. Smith U., Charlotte, 1985-89; exec. com. bd. dirs. United Way Allocations and Rev., Charlotte, 1982-88; bd. advisors Charlotte Mecklenburg Hosp. Authority, 1985-89; bd. dirs. Jr. Achievement, Charlotte, 1983-89, Miss. Humanities Coun., Miss. Inst. Arts and Letters, Miss. Symphony, Miss. Econ. Coun.; chair Leadership Miss. and Collegiate Miss.; chmn. bd. dirs. Charlotte/Mecklenburg Arts and Sci. Coun., 1987-88; Danforth assoc. Danforth Found., St. Louis, 1976-88, Leadership Am., 1989; golden triangle adv. bd. Bapt. Meml. Hosp.; pres. So. Univs. Conf., 1994-95; mem. commn. govt. rels. Am. Coun. Edn., 1990-93. Recipient Grad. Made Good award Fla. State U., 1990, medal of excellence Miss. U. for Women, 1995; named Prof. of Yr., Queens Coll., 1979, One of 10 Most Admired Women Mgrs. in Am., Working Women mag., 1993, One of 1000 Women of the 90's, Mirabella mag., 1994; Ford Found. grantee, 1981; Paul Harris fellow, 1992. Mem. Am. Assn. State Colls. and Univs. (bd. dirs. 1994-96), Sociol. Soc., So. Assn. Colls. and Schs. (mem. commn. on colls. 1996), N.C. Assn. Colls. and Univs. (exec. com. 1988-89), N.C. Assn. Acad. Officers (sec.-treas. 1987-88), Soc. Internat. Bus. Fellows, Miss. Assn. Colls. (pres. 1992), Newcomen Soc. U.S., Internat. Women's Forum, Univ. Club, Rotary. Office: Miss U Women Pres Office Box W 1600 Columbus MS 39701-9998

RENTELN, ALISON DUNDES, political science educator; b. Bloomington, Ind., Jan. 9, 1960; d. Alan and Carolyn (Browne) Dundes; m. Paul Alexander Renteln, June 9, 1985; children: David Alexander, Michael Alan. BA in History and Lit. cum laude, Harvard U., 1981; postgrad., London Sch. Econs., 1981-82; M of Jurisprudence, U. Calif., Berkeley, 1985, PhD in Jurisprudence and Social Policy, 1987; JD, U. So. Calif., 1991. Acting dir., vis. lectr. law and soc. U. Calif., Santa Barbara, 1986-87; asst. prof. polit. sci. U. So. Calif., L.A., 1987-93, assoc. prof. polit. sci., 1993—, acting dir. Unruh Inst. Pol., 1995-96, vice-chair dept. polit. sci., 1995—; lectr. Calif. State Judges Assn., Nat. Assn. Women Judges, UN Assn., Nat. Assn. Fgn. Student Affairs, L.A. Refugee Forum, Calif. Assn. of Adminstrn. of Justice Educators Delinquency Control Inst.; others; coord. Contemporary Issues in Law and Pub. Policy lectr. series Pasadena Sr. Citizens Ctr.; participant Hearing of U.S. Adv. Bd. on Child Abuse and Neglect. Author: International Human Rights: Universalism Versus Relativism, 1990; co-editor: (with Alan Dundes) Folk Law: Essays on the Theory and Practice of Lex Non Scripta, 1994; reviewer: Am. Anthropologist, Am. Jour. Comparative Law, Am. Jour. Polit. Sci., Human Rights Quar., others; contbr. numerous articles to profl. publs. Named Mentor of Distinction, Women's Caucus for Polit. Sci., 1993; Soroptomist Internat. Founder fellow, 1986; grantee Mark De Wolfe Howe Fund for rsch. in civil rights civil rights, civil liberties, and legal history Harvard U., 1985, Faculty Rsch. and Innovation Fund, 1988, Irvine Found. for diversity course devel., 1991, Faculty Fund for innovative tchg., 1993, Zumberge Faculty Rsch. and Innovation Fund, 1994. Mem. Am. Polit. Sci. Assn., Law and Soc. Assn., Commn. on Folk Law and Legal Pluralism, Am. Soc. Internat. Law, Internat. Law Assn. Office: U So Calif Dept Polit Sci VKC 327 Los Angeles CA 90089-0044

RENTERIA, CHERYL CHRISTINA, retired federal agency administrator; b. Corpus Christi, Tex., May 11, 1944; d. C.J. and Nazelle (Smart) Casey; m. Carlos Raymundo Renteria, Oct. 17, 1975; children: Crissa Cybele, Cori Renee. Grad. Inst. U.S. & World Affairs, Am. U., 1965; BA, Tex. Christian U., 1966. Inventory mgmt. specialist Tinker AFB, Oklahoma City, 1966-67; with U.S. Dept. HUD, 1967-94; resident initiatives coord., program mgr. region VI U.S. Dept. HUD, Ft. Worth, 1988-92; mgr. Office of Pub. Housing, 1993-94; ret., 1994; cons., 1995-96; co-chair Pointe Shoe Boutique, 1995-96. Pres. Dallas Office Orgn. Women, 1974-75; treas. Fed. Woman's Program Coun., Dallas, 1977-78; bd. dirs. Ballet Guild, Ft. Worth, 1984—, treas., 1985, v.p., 1986-88, programs chmn., 1990, 91, 92, 93, 94; bd. dirs. lectr. series U. Tex., Arlington, 1987-91, Dance Theatre, Arlington, 1987-91; bd. dirs. Planned Parenthood North Tex., 1986-90, Coun. Advisors, 1990-95; vol. Tex. Christian U. LINKS, Campfire, 30 yr. reunion com.; treas. Arlington Speech/Debate Booster Club, 1994; rec. sec. Ft. Worth Panhellenic Coun., 1994-96; permanent housing subcom. City of Arlinton Priority Home, 1995; co-chmn. Pointe Shoe Boutique, 1995-96; vol. Prevent Blindness. Smith scholar, 1966. Mem. Women in Govt., (pres. 1989-90), Fed. Bus. Assn., Women's Policy Forum, Theater Arlington Guild, Internat. Sister Cities, Opera Guild Ft. Worth, Friends Univ. Tex. Libr., Symphony Soc. Tarrant County (editor newsletter 1984), Jr. Woman's Club Decortique (v.p. 1977), Woman's Club Ft. Worth, Delta Gamma (pres. house corp. 1985, 86, bd. dirs. 1987—, chair Province leadership seminar 1987, corr. 1984). Home: 1115 Montreau Ct Arlington TX 76012-2737

RENTZ, TAMARA HOLMES, software consultant; b. Austin, Tex., Nov. 23, 1964; d. Thomas Michael and Elizabeth Dianne (Ames) Holmes; m. Christopher Michael Rentz, Sept. 21, 1991. BS in Speech/Orgnl. Comm., U. Tex., 1987. Cert. meeting facilitator; notary public State of Tex. Mgr. PC Sta., Inc., Austin, 1985-86; telecom. advisor Internat. Talent Network, Austin, 1986-87; mktg. rep. Wm. Ross & Co., Austin, 1987; life ins. rep. A.L. Williams, Austin, 1987-88; exec. sec. Adia Temporaries/SEMATECH, Austin, 1988; tng. adminstr. SEMATECH, Austin, 1988-89, data coord. equipment improvement program, 1989-90, user group program mgr., 1992-93; pres. Innovative Bus. Solutions, Austin, 1994—. Mem. Austin Software Coun. Home and Office: 4004 Love Bird Ln Austin TX 78730-3522

RENVILLE, DEBORAH ADAMS, English educator, writer; b. Come-by-Chance, Nfld., Can., July 10, 1965; came to U.S., 1967; m. Jeffery Todd Renville, Aug. 4, 1990; 1 child, Nicholas Adam. AA, Joliet (Ill.) Jr. Coll., 1991; BA in Media, Governors State U., 1992, MA in English, 1996. Customer svc. rep. Am. Cablesystems, Romeoville, Ill., 1986-87; store mgr. Brooks Fashion Stores, N.Y.C., 1985-90; area sales mgr. Cole Key Corp., Cleve., 1990-91; staff writer/photographer New Cath. Explorer, Romeoville, 1992; substitute tchr. Kankakee (Ill.) County Schs., 1992-93; freelance writer The Daily Jour., Kankakee, 1990—; adj. prof. English Kankakee C.C., 1993—. Campaign worker Paul Simon for Congress, Joliet, 1984; walker March of Dimes Walk-America, Kanakakee, 1993, 94, 96; mem. Jr. League of Kankakee County, 1996—. Recipient Am. Legion award, 1979; Governor's State U. tuition scholar, 1991-92, Rotary Club scholar, 1983. Mem. Nat. Coun. Tchrs. English, Joliet Jr. Coll. Alumni Assn. (bd. dirs. 1996—). Republican. Roman Catholic. Home: 1115 Armour Rd Bourbonnais IL 60914

REPLANSKY, NAOMI, poet; b. Bronx, N.Y., May 23, 1918; d. Sol and Fannie (Ginsberg) R. BA, UCLA, 1956. Author: (book of poems) Ring Song, 1952, Twenty-One Poems, Old and New, 1988, The Dangerous World: New and Selected Poems 1934-1994, 1994. Mem. PEN Am. Ctr., Poetry Soc. Am., Poets House. Home: # 8E 711 Amsterdam Ave New York NY 10025

REPPERT, NANCY LUE, former county official, legal consultant; b. Kansas City, Mo., June 17, 1933; d. James Everett and Iris R. (Moomey) Moore; m. James E. Cassidy, 1952 (div.); children: James E., II, Tracy C. Student Cen. Mo. State U., 1951-52, U. Mo., Kansas City, 1971-75; cert. legal asst., Rockhurst Coll., Kansas City, Mo., 1980; cert. risk mgr., 1979. With Kansas City (Mo.) chpt. ARC, 1952-54, N. Cen. region Boy Scouts Am., 1963-66, Clay County Health Dept., Liberty, Mo., 1966-71, City of Liberty, 1971-80; risk mgr. City of Ames (Iowa), 1980-82; risk mgr. City of Dallas, 1982-83; dir. Dept. Risk Mgmt., Pinellas County, Fla., 1984-94; ind. legal cons., Cedar Rapids, Iowa, 1994—; mem. faculty William Jewell Coll., Liberty, 1975-80; vis. prof. U. Kans., 1981; adj. prof. dept. polit. sci. masters program U. So. Fla., 1990; seminar leader, cons. in field. Lay min.r United Meth. Ch., 1965—; dir. youth devel. Hillside United Meth. Ch., Liberty; co-chmn. youth dir. Collegiate United Meth. Ch. scouting coord. Palm Lake Christian Ch., Exec. Fellow U. South Fla., mem. Coun. of Ministries; advancement chmn. Mid-Iowa Coun. Boy Scouts Am., membership chmn. White Rock Dist. coun., health and safety chmn. West Cen. Fla. coun., 1985—; scouting coord., chmn. youth dept., bd. dirs., pastor's cabinet, diaconate Palm Lake Christian Ch., 1987—; skipper Sea Explorer ship, 1986—; bd. dirs. Neighborly Sr. Svcs., Inc. Recipient Order of Merit, Boy Scouts Am., 1979, Living Sculpture award, 1978,79; Svc. award Rotary Internat., 1979; Internat. Award of Merit/Leadership Excellence, IBA, 1992; Exec. fellow U. South Fla., 1988. Mem. NAFE, Am. Mgmt. Assns., Internat Platform Assn., Risk Mgrs. Soc., Pub. Risk & Ins. Mgmt. Assn., Am. Soc. Profl. & Exec. Women, Am. Film Inst., U.S. Naval Inst., Nat. Inst. Mcpl. Law Officers. Author: Kids Are People, Too, 1975. Pearls of Potentiality, 1980; also articles. Home: 257 38th Street Dr SE Apt 8 Cedar Rapids IA 52403-1116

RESIDES, DIANE LOUISE, adult education counselor; b. Bellefonte, Pa., June 24, 1959; d. George Clair and Evelyn Louise (Immel) R. BS, Penn State U., 1981, MEd, 1989. Cert. rehab. counselor, Pa. Program mgr. Skills of Ctrl. Pa. Inc., Bellefonte, 1983-85; coord. student svcs. Ctr. Bus. Sch., Inc., State College, Pa., 1985-86; tng. coord. Pvt. Industry Coun. of Center Co., Pleasant Gap, Pa., 1986; coord. residence halls Penn State U., University Park, 1986-90, counselor Ctr. Adult Learner Svcs., 1990—; mem. steering com. State Coll. Job Svc., 1990—. Pres. Fredericksburg Homeowners Assn., State Coll., 1990—. Mem. Am. Assn. Adult Continuing Edn., Pa. Assn. Adult Continuing Edn., Phi Delta Kappa, Pi Lambda Theta, Phi Kappa Phi. Home: 20 Fredericksburg Ct State College PA 16803-1670 Office: Penn State U 323 Boucke Bldg University Park PA 16802-5901

RESNICK, ALICE ROBIE, state supreme court justice; b. Erie, Pa., Aug. 21, 1939; d. Adam Joseph and Alice Suzanne (Spizarny) Robie; m. Melvin L. Resnick, Mar. 20, 1970. PhB, Siena Heights Coll., 1961; JD, U. Detroit, 1964. Bar: Ohio 1964, Mich. 1965, U.S. Supreme Ct. 1970. Asst. county prosecutor Lucas County Prosecutor's Office, Toledo, 1964-75, trial atty., 1965-75; judge Toledo Mcpl. Ct., 1976-83, 6th Dist. Ct. Appeals, State of Ohio, Toledo, 1983-88; instr. U. Toledo, 1968-69; justice Ohio Supreme Ct., 1989—; co-chairperson Ohio State Gender Fairness Task Force. Trustee Siena Heights Coll., Adrian, Mich., 1982—; organizer Crime Stopper Inc., Toledo, 1981—; mem. Mayor's Drug Coun.; bd. dirs. Guest House Inc. Mem. ABA, Toledo Bar Assn., Lucas County Bar Assn., Nat. Assn. Women Judges, Am. Judicature Soc., Toledo Women's Bar Assn., Ohio State Women's Bar Assn. (organizer), Toledo Mus. Art, Internat. Inst. Toledo. Roman Catholic. Home: 2407 Edgehill Rd Toledo OH 43615-2321 Office: Supreme Ct Office 30 E Broad St Fl 3 Columbus OH 43215-3414

RESNICK, STEPHANIE, lawyer; b. N.Y.C., Nov. 12, 1959; d. Diane Gross. AB, Kenyon Coll., 1981; JD, Villanova U., 1984. Bar: Pa. 1984, N.J. 1984, U.S. Dist. Ct. (ea. dist.) Pa. 1984, U.S. Dist. Ct. N.J. 1984, N.Y. 1990, U.S. Ct. Appeals (3d cir.) 1993. Assoc. Cozen and O'Connor, Phila., 1984-87; assoc. Fox, Rothschild, O'Brien & Frankel, Phila., 1987-92, ptnr., 1992—. Mem. Vols. for Indigent Program, Phila., 1987-92. Mem. ABA, Pa. Bar Assn. (disciplinary bd. and study com. 1989-91, prof. liability com. 1991-92), Phila. Bar Assn. (profl. responsibility com. 1992—, profl. guidance com. 1992-96, investigative divsn. Commn. on Jud. Selection and Retention 1988-94, women's rights com. 1993—, co-chair 1995, 96, Comm. on Jud. Selection and Retention 1995, vice-chair 1996), N.J. Bar Assn., N.Y. Bar Assn. Home: 233 S 6th St Apt 2306 Philadelphia PA 19106-3756 Office: Fox Rothschild O'Brien & Frankel 2000 Market St Ste 10 Philadelphia PA 19103-3201

RESNIK, LINDA ILENE, marketing and information executive, consultant; b. Dallas, Oct. 26, 1950; d. Harold and Reatha (Gordon) R. BJ in Broadcast Journalism, U. Mo., 1971; MA in Journalism, U. North Tex., 1977, MBA in Mktg., 1980. News and documentary producer Sta. KDFW-TV, Dallas, 1971-73; mktg.-info. officer Dallas County Community Coll. Dist., 1973-79; dir. mktg. The Learning Channel, Washington, 1980-82; dir. Nat. Narrowcast Service, Pub. Broadcasting Service, Washington, 1982-85; exec. dir. Am. Soc. Info. Sci., Washington, 1985-89, White House Conf. on Libr. and Info. Svcs., Washington, 1990—; mem. adv. com. ALA Library/Book Fellows Project; fellow Ctr. for Info. and Communication Scis., Ball State U.; mem. U.S. exec. com. U. of the World; mktg., tng. and telecommunications cons. to ednl. assns., others. Writer and editor college-level study guides; scriptwriter college credit TV courses. Youth activities coordinator YMCA, Dallas, 1975-78; spl. event organizer Am. Cancer Soc., Dallas, 1976-77; com. leader Goals for Dallas, 1978-80. Recipient Best TV Feature Story award AP, Tex., 1973. Mem. Am. Soc. Assn. Execs., Am. Soc. Info. Sci. (pub. bull. 1985-89), Women in Cable, Info. Inst., Am. Mktg. Assn., Washington Met. Cable Club. Office: 3533 Piedmont Dr Plano TX 75075-6254

RESOR, PAMELA P., state legislator; b. Lincoln, Nebr., Feb. 26, 1942; d. Roland B. and Margaret L. (Flynn) Phillips; m. Griffith L. Resor III, July 6, 1963; children: Karen E. Resor Savage, Philip G., Kristen M. BA, Smith Coll., 1964. Exec. dir. Mass. Assn. Conservation Com., Belmont, 1986-88; mem. Mass. Ho. Reps., Boston, 1990—. Selectman Town of Acton, Mass., 1981-87. Mem. LWV (pres. 1978-80). Office: State Ho Reps State Ho 33 Boston MA 02133

RESTANI, JANE A., federal judge; b. San Francisco, Feb. 27, 1948; d. Roy J. and Emilia C. Restani. BA, U. Calif., Berkeley, 1969; JD, U. Calif., Davis, 1973. Bar: Calif., 1973. Trial atty. U.S. Dept. Justice, Washington, 1973-76, asst. chief comml. litigation sect., 1976-80, dir. comml. litigation sect., 1980-83; judge U.S. Ct. Internat. Trade, N.Y.C., 1983—. Mem. Order of Coif. Office: US Ct Internat Trade 1 Federal Plz New York NY 10278-0001*

RESTANTE, DELORES, small business owner, fundraiser; b. Herkimer, N.Y., Oct. 10, 1935; d. Anthony and Mary (Norod) Cirelli; m. Mario J. Restante, May 31, 1958; children: Sherry Lee, Paul. Grad., Mohawk Hairstyling and Beauty Sch., 1968, Bruno's Hairstyling Toronto, Can., 1970, Paul Mitchell Advanced Sch., 1972. Regional mgr. Jewelry Firm, Herkimer, 1965-68; asst. Ezio's Hair Salon, 1968-69; owner, operator Madrid Hair Fashions, 1969—; co-owner Cat's Meow, 1985; coord. fashion shows; lectr. makeover classes. Costume designer Make-A-Wish Found.; dir. cosumes Herkimer County 200 Year Celebration. Chair fundraiser Hosp. Guild, 1970-95; bd. trustees Mohawk Valley Ctr. Arts, 1991-95, pres., chair, 1992-95, chair spl. events; choir mem. Holy Family Parish; mem. Mohawk Valley Choral Soc. Roman Catholic.

RESTINE, LOIS NAN, education educator; b. Portales, N.Mex., Mar. 30, 1948; d. Thelma Lorraine (Risher) Daniel; m. Keith Alan Restine, Mar. 9, 1979. BS, Ea. N.Mex. U., 1971; MA, N.Mex. State U., 1980; cert. edn. specialist, U. N.Mex., 1990, PhD, 1990. Tchr., coach Loving (N.Mex.) Mcpl. Schs., 1971-75; tchr., coach Carlsbad (N.Mex.) Mcpl. Schs., 1975-79, tchr., dept. chmn., dean, 1979-87; asst. dir. coop. ednl. adminstrn. internship program U. N.Mex., Albuquerque, 1987-90; asst. prof., program dir. Western Ky. U., Bowling Green, 1990-92; asst. prof. Okla. State U., Stillwater, 1992—; cons. Ctr. for Industry and Tech./Western Ky. U., Bowling Green, 1990-92. Author: Administrative Internships, 1991, Taking Stock: A Study of the Danforth Programs, 1991, Women in Administration: Facilitators for Change, 1993; mem. editl. bd. People in Edn., 1991—. Coach, sponsor youth sports programs, Carlsbad, 1971-87; water safety instr. ARC, Carlsbad, 1971-85. Recipient Outstanding Achievement award Dept. Ednl. Adminstrn. U. N.Mex., 1990. Mem. ASCD, Am. Ednl. Rsch. Assn., Nat. Assn. for Secondary Sch. Prin., U. Coun. for Ednl. Adminstrn., Coop. Coun. for Okla. Sch. Adminstrs. (cons. new prin. assistance program 1994—), Phi Delta Kappa. Home: 2915 Black Oak Dr Stillwater OK 74074-2257 Office: Okla State Univ Dept Ednl Adminstrn Higher 309 Gundersen Stillwater OK 74078

RESWEBER, ELLEN CAMPBELL, retired mathematics educator; b. Scott, La., June 21, 1930; d. Milton George and Louise (Mouton) Campbell; m. Francis Thomas Resweber, Dec. 27, 1954; children: Paul Adolphe, Henrietta Louise, Milton George, Louis Joseph, Peter John. BS, U. So. La.,

1951; MEd, La. State U., 1957. Math. tchr. Youngsville (La.) High Sch., 1950-52, Lafayette (La.) High Sch., 1952-55, Northside High Sch., Lafayette, 1970-91; ret., 1991; head math. dept. Northside High Sch., 1986-91. Mem. Nat. Coun. Tchrs. Math., La. Ret. Tchrs. Assn., Lafayette Ret. Tchrs. Assn. (v.p. 1993). Roman Catholic. Home: 1010 Roper Dr Scott LA 70583

RETHEMEYER, KAY LYNN, secondary school educator; b. Nevada, Mo., Oct. 27, 1946; d. John Albert and Wanda Lee (Hill) Kinnamon; m. Robert J. Rethemeyer, Aug. 22, 1971; children: Robin, Rustin. BS in Edn., Ctrl. Mo. State U., Warrensburg, 1968, MA in History, 1971. Tchr. Lee's Summit (Mo.) Jr. High, 1968-73, Longview C.C., Lee's Summit, 1984-88, Pleasant Lea Jr. High, Lee's Summit, 1988-89, Lee's Summit H.S., 1989—. Mem. R-7 Adv. Com. Mem. NEA, Nat. Coun. Social Studies, Delta Kappa Gamma. Home: 1026 SE Timbercreek Ln Lees Summit MO 64081-3003 Office: Lees Summit HS 400 SE 8th St Lees Summit MO 64063-4214

RETZLAFF, LINDA JANE, elementary school educator; b. Lockport, N.Y., Oct. 17, 1943; d. Floyd William and Florence Lorraine (Campbell) Spencer; m. Arthur Kenneth Retzlaff, Apr. 13, 1968; children: Marc William, Kristina Lynn. BS in Edn., SUNY, Brockport, 1965, postgrad. Cert. tchr., N.Y. Kindergarten tchr. Roy-Hart Sch., Middleport, N.Y., 1965-71, 86-92, elem. tchr., 1973-86, 92—. Sec. Zion Luth. Ch. Coun., 1988-89; pres. Johnson Creekettes Home Bur., 1985-87; mem. Gasport-Middleport H.S. PTA. Mem. Delta Kappa Gamma. Republican. Home and Office: 8873 Ridge Rd Gasport NY 14067-9413

REUTER, CAROL JOAN, insurance company executive; b. Bklyn., June 1, 1941; d. Michael John and Elizabeth Lucille (Garmer) R. BA, St. John's U., 1962. Pres., CEO N.Y. Life Found., N.Y.C., 1979-89, sec., 1989-90, pres., 1990-96, CEO, 1996—; also bd. dirs.; asst. v.p. N.Y. Life Ins. Co., N.Y.C., 1984-89, corp. v.p., 1990-95, v.p., 1995—. Mem., former chmn. contbns. coun. Conf. Bd., N.Y. Contbns. Adv. Group; mem. corp. adv. coun. ARC; chmn. corp. assoc. United Way of Am. Named Acad. of Women's Achievers, YWCA, 1987. Republican. Roman Catholic. Office: NY Life Ins Co 51 Madison Ave New York NY 10010-1603

REUTERSHAN, MARY ELLA, gerontologist, consultant; b. Maryville, Tenn., Aug. 10, 1921; d. James Vincent Hopkins and Mamie (DeArmond) Hopkins Brooks; m. James Hall Reutershan, Aug. 12, 1958 (dec. Feb. 1971); m. Mark Gadd Richard, Nov. 28, 1974 (div. July 1981). PhB, U. Chgo., 1947; M.Gerontology, L.I. U., 1992. Lic. real estate salesperson, N.Y., 1972, real estate broker, N.Y., 1986, mortgage broker, 1987. Adminstrv. sec. Exec. Office of Pres., Washington, 1943-44; Spanish translator Container Corp. of Am., Chgo., 1945-47; adminstrv. sec. Time, Inc., N.Y.C., 1947-55; writer/rschr. U.S. Com. for UNICEF, N.Y.C., 1955-56; cons. divsn. aging Fedn. Protestant Welfare Agencies, Inc., N.Y.C., 1956-58; tchr. jr./sr. pub. schs. East Hampton, Southampton, N.Y., 1958-64; real estate salesperson, broker East Hampton, 1972-77; mortgage broker, mortgage cons. Riverhead/Am. Savs. Bank, Riverhead, N.Y., 1987-90; founder, owner Senior Svcs., Amagansett, N.Y., 1992—. Founder, pub. The Stony Hill Citizen newsletter, 1976. Treas. Suffolk County Inter-Agy. Coord. Coun., Riverhead, 1993—; corr. sec. Riverhead Health Ctr. Cmty. Adv. Bd., 1994—; bd. dirs. South Fork Cmty. Health Initiative, Inc., East Hampton, 1994—; mem. cmty. com. Southampton Hosp., 1993—; councilwoman (Dem.) Town of East Hampton, 1980-81; mem. East Hampton Town Bd. Ethics, 1995—, vice chair, 1996; founder Suffolk Women's Polit. Caucus, Amagansett, 1972; co-founder The Stony Hill Assn., Amagansett, 1962; mem. East End women's Network, South Fork Geriatric Network, RSVP Program, Nat. Women's Polit. Caucus/Suffolk. Recipient Vol. Svc. award Suffolk County Human Rights Commn., Hauppauge, N.Y., 1971. Mem. LWV of Hamptons, NOW, NAACP, Am. Assn. Ret. Persons, Gerontology Profls. of L.I., Baronial Order of Magna Charta (baroness of order), Order of First Families of Va., N.Y. State Coalition for the Aging, Inc., State Soc. on Aging of N.Y., Pi Beta Phi.

REUTHER, ROSANN WHITE, advertising agency executive; b. Nashville, Nov. 24, 1943; d. Wiley Butler and Mildred Elizabeth (Little) White; student George Peabody Coll., 1961-64; m. Peter Martin Reuther, Oct. 3, 1964. Advt. copywriter WHMA Radio, Anniston, Ala., 1964-65, Bapt. Sunday Sch. Bd., Nashville, 1965-72, Thomas Nelson Pubs., Nashville, 1972-73; account exec. Holder-Kennedy Pub. Relations, Nashville, 1973-74; pub. relations dir. T. Nelson, Nashville, 1974-75; pension adminstr. Wood, Bateman, Nord, Assos., Nashville, 1975-76; owner, pres. In-Vision Advt. and Pub. Relations, Nashville, 1976—; lectr. Tenn. State U., 1978-79; part-time instr. Nashville State Tech. Inst.; faculty Tenn. Entrepreneur Forum, 1984. Worker, Carter for Pres. campaign, Tenn., 1976; bd. dirs. Nat. Neighborhood Alliance, 1992. Recipient Paul M. Hinkhous award of excellence in advt., 1974. Mem. Nashville Advt. Fedn. (bd. dirs. 1986-88), Am. Women in Radio and TV (pres. Nashville chpt. 1981-82, dir. dist. B, 1982-83), Hist. Waverly Place Neighborhood Assn. (pres. 1988-89). Baptist. Home: 1908 Elliott Ave Nashville TN 37204-2004 Office: PO Box 41161 Nashville TN 37204-1161

REVEAL, ARLENE HADFIELD, librarian, consultant; b. Riverside, Utah, May 21, 1916; d. Job Oliver and Mabel Olive (Smith) Hadfield; children: James L., Jon A. BS with hons., Utah State U., 1938; grad. in librarianship San Diego State U., 1968; M in Libr. and Info. Sci., Brigham Young U., 1976. Social case worker Boxelder County Welfare, Brigham City, Utah, 1938-40; office mgr. Dodge Ridge Ski Corp., Long Barn, Calif., 1948-65, Strawberry Inn, Strawberry, Calif., 1950-65, Pinecrest Permittees Assn., 1955-66; adminstrv. asst. Mono County Office of Edn., Bridgeport, Calif., 1961-67; catalog libr. La Mesa-Spring Valley Sch. Dist., La Mesa, Calif., 1968-71; libr. Mono County Libr., Bridgeport, Calif., 1971—; chmn. Mountain Valley Library System, 1987-89. Author: Mono County Courthouse, 1980. Active Devel. Disabilities Area Bd. # 12, 1974—, chmn., 1990-92. Recipient John Cotton Dana award H.W. Wilson Co., 1974; named Bridgeport Citizen of Yr., 1993. Mem. Delta Kappa Gamma (pres. Epsilon Alpha chpt. 1984-88), Beta Sigma Phi (treas. Xi Omicron Epsilon chpt. 1981, 83-85, 91—, pres. 1982, 85, 89), Beta Phi Mu. Lodge: Rebekah (treas. 1973-90). Home: 185 Main St Bridgeport CA 93517-0532 Office: Mono County Free Libr 94 N School St Bridgeport CA 93517-0398

REVELLINO, JANE, lawyer; b. Nagoya, Japan, Oct. 6, 1948. BS, CUNY, 1969, MA, 1972; JD magna cum laude, St. John's U., N.Y.C., 1982. Bar: N.Y. 1983. Ptnr. Anderson, Kill, Olick & Oshinsky, P.C., N.Y.C. Mem. N.Y. State Bar Assn. (tax sect., trusts and estates law sect.), Assn. of Bar of City of N.Y. Office: Anderson Kill Olick & Oshinsky PC 1251 Avenue of the Americas New York NY 10020-1182*

REVERE, VIRGINIA LEHR, clinical psychologist; b. Long Branch, N.J.; d. Joseph and Essie Lehr; m. Robert B. Revere; children: Elspeth, Andrew, Lisa, Robert Jr. PhB, U. Chgo., 1949, MA, 1959, PhD, 1971. Lic. cons. clin. psychologist, Va. Intern, staff psychologist Ea. Mental Health Reception Ctr., Phila., 1959-61; instr. Trenton (N.J.) State Coll., 1962-63; staff psychologist Trenton State Hosp., 1964-65, Bucks County Psychiat. Ctr., Phila., 1965-67; assoc. prof. Mansfield (Pa.) State U., 1967-77; clin. rsch. psychologist St. Elizabeth Hosp., Washington, 1977-81, tng. psychology coord., 1981-83, staff psychologist, 1985-91; child psychologist Community Mental Health Ctr., Washington, 1983-85; pvt. practice Alexandria, Va., 1980—; cons., lectr. in field. Author: Applied Psychology for Criminal Justice Professionals, 1982; contbr. articles to profl. jours. Recipient Group Merit award St. Elizabeth's Hosp., 1983, Community Svc. award D.C. Psychol. Assn., 1978, Outstanding Educator award, 1972; traineeship NIH, USPHS, Chgo., 1963-65; fellow Family Svcs. Assn., 1958-59. Mem. APA, No. Va. Soc. Clin. Psychologists, Va. Acad. Clin. Psychologists. Home: 9012 Linton Ln Alexandria VA 22308-2733 Office: 5021 Seminary Rd Ste 110 Alexandria VA 22311-1923

REVIT, JENNIFER BETH, art consultant; b. N.Y.C., Sept. 18, 1972; d. Martin Burton and Susan Elizabeth (Turnbull) R. BA, U. Denver, 1994. In adminstrn. and mgmt. Closure Strapping Systems, Marina del Rey, Calif., 1994-95; art const. Gallery Galgano, L.A., 1995—. Active West Hollywood Homeless Orgn., 1995. Mem. Phi Beta Kappa. Home: 754 N Edinburgh Ave Los Angeles CA 90046 Office: Gallery Galgano 8642 Melrose Ave Los Angeles CA 90069

REX, ANNA JEAN, special education educator; b. Winamae, Ind., Mar. 19, 1939; d. Albert Leroy and Dora Carolina (Beaver) R.; m. Kenneth James Williams, July 4, 1964 (div. Jan. 1982); children: Christopher Scott, Timothy Kenneth (adopted); m. Eugene Lee Miltz, June 21, 1985. AA, Thornton C.C., South Holland, Ill., 1978; BA, Calumet Coll., 1981; MEd, S.W. Tex. State U., 1993. Educator Griffith (Ind.) Pub. Schs., 1981-82, Florence (Tex.) Ind. Sch. Dist., 1987-89, Del Valle (Tex.) Ind. Sch. Dist., 1989-92, Harlandale Ind. Sch. Dist., San Antonio, 1992—. Home: 1920 Bentwood Ave Floresville TX 78114-6715 Office: Harlandale Ind Sch Dist 743 Southcross San Antonio TX 78211

REXROAT, VICKI LYNN, occupational child development educator; b. Oklahoma City, Okla., June 12, 1957; d. Troy Bill and Opal Pauline (Flinn) Miller; m. David Edward Rexroat, Sept. 6, 1980; children: Jamie Lynn, Amber Donn, Emily Sue. BS, U. of Sci. and Arts, 1991; postgrad., U. Ctrl. Okla., 1991—. Presch. tchr. Caddo-Kiowa Vocat. Sch., Fort Cobb, Okla., 1981-84, child devel. dir., 1984-89; child devel. instr. Caddo-Kiowa Vocat. Sch., Fort Cobb, 1989—; rep., advisor Child Devel. Assoc., Washington, 1989—; mem. curriculum team Okla. Dept. of Vocat. Edn., Stillwater, Okla., 1991—; adv. bd. Child Care Careers, Oklahoma City, 1992—. Contbr. articles to profl. jours. Co-chair Reach Out, Inc. Homeless Shelter, Anadarko, Okla., 1992—; founder, vol. Caddo County Welfare Vols., 1989—; friends for life mem. Fort Cobb Sr. Citizens, 1990—; mem. Fort Cobb Booster Club, 1989—. Named Friend of Children Okla. Inst. of Child Advocacy, 1993, New Tchr. of Yr. Okla. Vocat. Assn., 1993. Mem. Friends in the Okla. Early Childhood Assn. (pres. 1989—), So. Early Childhood Assn., Okla. Assn. for the Edn. of Young Children, Nat. Assn. for the Edn. of Young Children, Am. Vocat. Assn. (dist. v.p. 1989—, New Tchr. of Yr. 1994). Democrat. Bapt. Office: Caddo-Kiowa Vocat Sch North 7th Fort Cobb OK 73038

REY, MARGRET ELIZABETH, writer; b. Hamburg, Germany, May 16, 1906; came to U.S., 1940; d. Felix and Gertrude (Rosenfeld) Waldstein; m. Hans A. Rey (dec. 1977). Art degree, Art Acad., Hamburg, Germany, 1929, Bauhaus, Dessau, Germany, 1931, Acad. Art, Dusseldorf, Germany, 1932. Children's author Houghton Mifflin Co., Boston, 1941—, Harper & Row, N.Y.C., 1945—; script cons. Curgeo, Montreal, Quebec, Can., 1977-83; adj. prof. Brandeis U., Waltham, Mass., 1978-84. Author: Pretzel, 1944, Spotty, 1945, Billy's Picture, 1948; co-author: Curious George, 1941, Curious George Takes a Job, 1947, Curious George Rides a Bike, 1952, Curious George Gets a Medal, 1957, Curious George Flies a Kite, 1958, Curious George Learns the Alphabet, 1963, Curious George Goes to the Hospital, 1966. Founder, trustee The Curious George Found., Cambridge, Mass., 1991—; bd. dirs. Phillips Brooks House, Harvard U., Cambridge, Mass., 1989—. Mem. World Wildlife, Smithsonian, Mus. Fine Arts, Audobon Soc., Defenders of Wildlife. Democrat. Home: 14 Hilliard St Cambridge MA 02138-4922

REYES, DELIA, consulting company executive; b. Habana, Cuba. Pres., owner Adrian Rsch. Group, Adrian Info. Strategies, Reyes Consulting Group; bd. dirs. H.F. Ahmanson & Co.; apptd. commr. Glass Ceiling Commn. Bd. dirs. YMCA of Met. Dallas, Dallas Mus. Art, Cuban Am. Nat. Coun., Inc., State Bar of Tex. Bd. Dirs. Named Woman of the Yr., Hispanic Am. C. of C., 1992. Mem. U.S. Hispanic C. of C. (chair 1991-92), Dallas Hispanic C. of C. (pres., Female Entrepreneur of the Yr. 1991). Office: Reyes Consulting Group Ste 201 14677 Midway Dallas TX 75244*

REYES, LINDA NELMS, lawyer; b. L.A., Jan. 21, 1957; d. Joseph Winston and Estela (Reyes) Nelms. BS in Law, Western State U., 1989, JD, 1991. Bar: Calif. 1992; cert. mediator, Calif. Supervising law clk. Orange County (Calif.) Dist. Atty.'s Office, 1989-91; atty. death penalty cases Riverside County (Calif.) Pub. Defender's Office, 1992-93; pvt. practice criminal appeals, domestic and corporate law, 1993—; adj. prof. IDRAC U., Paris, 1991; lay arbitrator Orange County Bar Assn., 1989-91. Mem. ACLU, Mex.-Am. Law Assn., Criminal Def. Trial Lawyers, Calif. Bar Assn., Amnesty Internat., Alpha Delta Phi. Democrat. Roman Catholic. Home and Office: 335 Paraiso Ave Spring Valley CA 91977

REYES, MARCIA STYGLES, medical technologist; b. Winchester, Mass., July 15, 1950; d. Bernard Francis and Eleanore Cecilia (Nicgorska) Stygles; B.S. in Med. Tech., Merrimack Coll., North Andover, Mass., 1972; M.S. in Health Scis. (Kellogg Found. grantee), SUNY, Buffalo, 1977; m. Carlos Reyes, Aug. 5, 1978. Sr. med. technologist Symmes Hosp., Arlington, Mass., 1970-73; sr. microbiologist and serologist Mt. Auburn Hosp., Cambridge, Mass., 1973-75; asst. prof., clin. coordinator Quinnipiac Coll., Hamden, Conn., 1976-81; lab. supr. Canberra Clin. Labs., Meriden, Conn., 1981-86; lab. supr. Hill Health Ctr, New Haven, Conn., 1984—; cons. in med. tech. mgmt., allied health edn. Mem. Am. Soc. Clin. Pathologists, Am. Soc. Med. Tech., Conn. Soc. Med. Tech. (Speaker awards), Am. Soc. Microbiology, Am. Soc. Allied Health Profls. Home: 199 Dover St New Haven CT 06513-4818

REYES, MARIA ELENA, academic program director; b. Eagle Pass, Tex.; d. Jorge Vargas and Maria Claudia (Cardona) R. BA in Sociology and English cum laude, Pan-Am. U., 1973; MA in Secondary Edn., Sul Ross U., 1988; PhD in Curriculum and Instrn., U. Tex., 1991. Part-time Spanish tutor lang. lab. U. Tex., Austin, 1968-70; state caseworker Tex. Welfare Dept., Pharr, 1971-75; tchr. English Eagle Pass H.S., 1978-88; supr. student tchrs. English edn. dept. U. Tex., Austin, 1988-90, rsch.-tchg. asst. to prof. emeritus Don Americo Paredes, 1990-91, cons. Grad. Sch., 1991-92, project dir. Hispanic Mother-Dau. Program, 1992—; vol. United Farm Workers, McAllen, Tex., 1970-73; intern in urban studies, Pan Am. U., 1971-72; rsch. asst. focus group series U. Tex. Sch. Nursing, 1990; developer Lang. Arts IV Course Eagle Pass H.S., 1986, mgr. migrant tutoring program; advisor, bd. dirs. SMART Student Orgn., U. Tex., Austin, cons. Mex. Am. Health Professions Orgn., pres. Chicana/o Grad. Students Assn., minority recruiter, mem. adv. bd. Ctr. for Mex.-Am. Studies; trainer Family Math program; presenter in field. Author: The 1995 Guide to the Top 25 Colleges for Hispanics, 1995; contbr. articles to Hispanic Mag. Mem. KLRU Cmty. Bd., 1995-96, 4-H Aerospace Task Force, Mendez Mid. Sch. PTA; bd. dirs. Found. for Women's Resources Conf., Austin; head Bilingual Students' Support Group Martin Jr. H.S. PTA; vol. tutoring program Bedichek Mid. Sch. Recipient Nat. Hispanic Achievement award, 1995, cert. appreciation Eagle Pass H.S. Student Coun., 1985; rsch. fellow U. Tex. at Austin Ctr. for Mex.-Am. Studies, 1991, Title VII fellow, 1990-91, Univ. Grad. fellow, 1988-91, Urban Studies fellow Pan Am. U., 1973. Mem. ASCD, AAUW (adv. panel, Internat. Fellowship Awards Panel 1995—), Am. Assn. Higher Edn., Exec. Women in Tex. Govt., Expanding Your Horizons (Austin chpt.), Hispanic Assn. Colls. and Univs., U. Tex. Latina Women's Caucus, Tex. Assn. Chicanos in Edn., Kappa Delta Pi (v.p. U. Tex., Austin), Phi Kappa Phi. *

REYES, SHIRLEY NORFLIN, computer learning center educator; b. New Orleans, Aug. 5, 1949; d. William Jr. and Annie (Stephens) Norflin; m. Vide Manuel Reyes, Oct. 2, 1972 (div. 1979); 1 child, Drew Haynes Reyes. BS, U. New Orleans, 1975, MA, 1990. Elem. tchr. Caddo Parish Pub. Sch. System, Shreveport, La., 1975-78; 4th grade tchr. St. Charles Parish Sch. System, Luling, La., 1979-80; elem. tchr. Jefferson Parish Sch. System, Gretna, La., 1980—; GED tchr. St. Bernard Community Bapt. Ch., New Orleans, 1991—; ranking tchr. Live Oak Manor Elem. Sch., Westwego, La., 1991—, dir. child care site, 1992-94, coord. testing and La. Edn. Assessment Program, 1992-94, La. Assessor for Intern Tchrs.: Field Test and Pilot, 1993-94; chmn. drug free schs. Jefferson Parish Pub. Sch. Sys., also instrnl. TV chmn.; pres. Edn. Network Agy., Inc. Writer/storyteller children's books and songs; writer gospel songs; producer, writer learning aids for children. Edn. program writer The Reading Literacy Project, 1991—; coord. reading literacy project St. Bernard Community Bapt. Ch., 1991—; den mother Boy Scouts Am., 1991—. Recipient Parent Adv. award Waggaman Kindergarten Ctr., 1985-86, New Music writer Gospel Music Workshop of Am., 1989. Mem. AAUW (chmn. community interest), Jefferson Fedn. of Tchrs., La. Edn. Assn., U. New Orleans Alumni Assn. Democrat. Home and Office: 131 Prairieview Ct Westwego LA 70094-2541

REYNA, VALERIE FRANCES, psychologist, educator, researcher; b. Miami Beach, Fla., Apr. 20, 1955; d. Benjamin Villa and Patricia Ruth (Wilson) R.; m. Charles J. Brainerd, Oct. 5, 1985; 1 child, Bertrand Reyna-Brainerd. BA, Clark U., 1976; PhD, Rockefeller U., 1981. Asst. prof. U. Tex., Dallas, 1981-87; adj. prof. U. Ariz., Tucson, 1987-88, asst. prof. dept. ednl. psychology, 1988-92, assoc. prof., 1992-1996, assoc. prof. depts. surgery and medicine, 1996—; vis. scientist Stanford (Calif.) U., 1982-83. Guest editor: Developmental Psychology, 1985, Development of Long-Term Retention, 1992; contbr. articles to profl. jours.; author books. Fellow AAAS; mem. APA, Am. Psychol. Soc., Ariz. Ednl. Rsch. Orgn., Soc. Advancement Chicanos and Native Ams. in Sci., Hispanic Profls. Action Com. Edn., Psychonomic Soc., Soc. for Rsch. in Child Devel., Sigma Xi. Democrat. Home: 6060 E Calle Ojos Verde Tucson AZ 85750 Office: U Ariz Health Scis Ctr 1501 N Campbell Ave Tucson AZ 85724-5066

REYNARD, MURIEL JOYCE, lawyer; b. Miami Beach, Fla., May 20, 1945; d. Hyman and Faye (Feinstein) Friedkin; m. Brian Patrick Delaney, Nov. 27, 1983; children: Kelly, Charlotte. BA, SUNY, Stony Brook, 1967, MS, 1973; JD cum laude, Yeshiva U., 1983. Bar: N.Y. 1984, U.S. Dist. Ct. (so. and ea. dists.) N.Y. 1984. Health planner Nassau-Suffolk RMP/CHP, Centereach, N.Y., 1972-74; adminstr. N.Y.C. Health and Hosps. Corp., 1974-75; health planner AFSCME Dist. Coun. 37, N.Y.C., 1975-76; adminstr. Inst. Emergency Medicine Albert Einstein Coll. Medicine, N.Y.C., 1977-80; asst. atty. U.S. Atty.'s Office (so. dist.) N.Y., N.Y.C., summer 1982; assoc. Skadden, Arps, Slate, Meagher & Flom, N.Y.C., 1983-85, Paskus, Gordon & Mandel, N.Y.C., 1985-86; v.p., sr. assoc. counsel The Chase Manhattan Bank, N.A., N.Y.C., 1986—. Notes and comments editor Cardozo Law Rev.; contbr. numerous articles to law jours. Mem. ABA, N.Y.C. Bar Assn., N.Y. State Bar Assn. Home: 607 Colonial Ave Pelham NY 10803-2201 Office: Chase Manhattan Bank NA 1 Chase Manhattan Plz Fl 25 New York NY 10005-1401

REYNOLDS, BEVERLY MAY, public relations executive; b. Calgary, Alberta, Can., Mar. 20, 1948; d. Roy George and Irene Muriel (Gilliham) R. Degree, Mt. Royal Coll., 1974, BA in Applied Comm. (hon.), 1996. Accredited pub. rels. Comm. asst. TransCan. Pipelines, Calgary, 1975-77; v.p., sr. counsel McKim, Baker, Lovick, Calgary, 1977-92; CEO, pres. BRPR, Inc., 1992-96; bd. dirs. Expo 2005 Corp. Bd. govs. Mt. Royal Coll., 1990-96; campaign cabinet YWCA, Calgary, 1992-93; media advisor Alta Progressive Conservatives, Alberta, 1977-92; bd. dirs. 1st Night Festival, 1993-96; judge Alta Internat. Edn. awards 1994-96, Oilweek Ann. Report awards 1990—, CPRS Nat. campaign awards 1994-95. Mem. Can. Pub. Rels. Soc. (bd. dirs. 1982-84, town crier 1991). Office: BRPR Inc, 3520-14A St SW, Calgary, AB Canada T2T 3X9

REYNOLDS, BILLIE ILES, financial representative and counselor, former association executive; b. Oakland, Calif., Mar. 26, 1929; d. Walter F. and Frances Olive (Blakesley) Iles; m. William V. Reynolds, June 23, 1950; children: Gilbert, Wendy Lee Bryant, Cynthia Lea Waple, Christy Dirren. Registered fin. rep.; registered fin. counselor; registered pension and retirement specialist. Ptnr. Reynolds Advt. Agy., 1963-70; asst. to exec. dir. Nat. Sch. Transp. Assn., Springfield, Va., 1964-76; exec. dir. Nat. Sch. Transp. Assn., 1976-83, Ariz. Landscape Contractors Assn., 1984-86; Registered life and health ins. agt. Freelance writer scripts for radio, TV, newspapers, nat. mags., 1953-70; author: Planning is the Key: Basics of Financial Understanding for Beginners, 1984. Methodist.

REYNOLDS, CAROLYN MARY, elementary education educator; b. Bklyn., May 17, 1936; d. Wesley and Christine (Cardieri) Russo; m. Richard Martin Reynolds, Apr. 12, 1958; children: Donna Marie Reynolds Dewey, Richard Edward. BS, Adelphi U., 1968; MA, SUNY, Stony Brook, 1971. Cert. tchr., N.Y. Tchr. Rocky Point (N.Y.) Sch., 1956-57, Little Flower Sch., Wading River, N.Y., 1957-59, Shoreham (N.Y.)-Wading River Sch. Dist., 1969—; mem. sch. consolidation task force Shoreham-Wading River Sch. Dist., 1992-93, mem. supt. search com., 1995, mem. dist. shared decision making team, 1995-96; supervising tchr. St. Joseph Coll., 1991, 95, Dowling Coll., Oakdale, N.Y., 1992, C.W. Post Coll., Southampton, N.Y., SUNY, Stonybrook; coord. constructivist course, Shoreham, N.Y., 1990—. Editor tchr. union publ. VOX, 1989-90 (award 1990). Leader Girl Scouts U.S., Rocky Point, N.Y., 1956. Noyes Found. fellow; NSF grantee. Mem. ASCD, Nat. Coun. Tchrs. English, N.Y. State United Tchrs., Shoreham-Wading River Tchrs. Assn. (co-pres., sec., negotiator tchrs. contract), United Fedn. Tchrs. (10 Yr. pin for leadership), Internat. Reading Assn. (coun. pres. 1980—). Home: 50 Highland Down Shoreham NY 11786-1122

REYNOLDS, DEBBIE (MARY FRANCES REYNOLDS), actress; b. El Paso, Tex., Apr. 1, 1932; m. Eddie Fisher, Sept. 26, 1955 (div. 1959); children—Carrie, Todd; m. Harry Karl, Nov., 1960 (div. 1973); m. Richard Hamlett (div. May 1996). Active high sch. plays; screen debut Daughter of Rosie O'Grady; motion pictures include: June Bride, 1948, The Daughter of Rosie O'Grady, 1950, Three Little Words, 1950, Two Weeks With Love, 1950, Mr. Imperium, 1951, Singin' in the Rain, 1952, Skirts Ahoy!, 1952, I Love Melvin, 1953, The Affairs of Dobie Gillis, 1953, Give a Girl a Break, 1953, Susan Slept Here, 1954, Athena, 1954, Hit the Deck, 1955, The Tender Trap, 1955, The Catered Affair, 1956, Bundle of Joy, 1956, Tammy and the Bachelor, 1957, This Happy Feeling, 1958, The Mating Game, 1959, Say One for Me, 1959, It Started With a Kiss, 1959, The Gazebo, 1959, The Rat Race, 1960, Pepe, 1960, The Pleasure of His Company, 1961, The Second Time Around, 1961, How the West Was Won, 1962, My Six Loves, 1963, Mary, Mary, 1963, The Unsinkable Molly Brown, 1964, Goodbye Charlie, 1964, The Singing Nun, 1966, Divorce American Style, 1967, How Sweet It Is!, 1968, What's the Matter with Helen?, 1971, Charlotte's Web, (voice only) 1973, That's Entertainment!, 1974, The Bodyguard, 1992, Heaven and Earth, 1993; star TV program The Debbie Reynolds Show, 1969; star Broadway show Irene, 1973-74, Annie Get Your Gun, Los Angeles, San Francisco, 1977, Woman of the Year, 1984, The Unsinkable Molly Brown, 1989-90 (nat. tour), (with Albert Brooks) Mother, 1996; author: If I Knew Then, 1963, Debbie-My Life, 1988; creator exercise video Do It Debbie's Way, 1984. Prin. Debbie Reynolds's Hotel/Casino and Hollywood Motion Picture Mus., Las Vegas, 1993—. Named Miss Burbank, 1948. Office: Debbie Reynolds Studios care Margie Duncan 6514 Lankershim Blvd North Hollywood CA 91606-2409

REYNOLDS, ELIZABETH MARIA, writer, lecturer; b. Kingston, Jamaica, Mar. 3, 1953; came to U.S., 1968; d. Mallica Reynolds and Caroline Lucilda Haynes Mitchell. m. Canute Donat Robinson, Dec. 12, 1978 (div. 1987); children: Michael, Andrew, Michelle, Clarissa Reynolds, Malesha Roberts. Student, NYU, 1977-80. Cert. real estate sales mgr., Pa. Letter carrier U.S. Postal Svc., Bklyn., 1990-92; day care dir. Nurturing Tree Child Care, Queens, N.Y., 1995-96; entrepreneur Circles of Time Enterprises, Queens, 1990—, pub., bd. dirs., 1986—; role model facilitator Sheltering Arms, N.Y.C., 1992—; performer, moderator Black Spectrum Theatre, Queens, 1992; producer African Poetry Theatre, Queens, 1993; motivational speaker; guest speaker. Author: Concepts of Building the Inner Self, 1996, (poetry) The Circles of Time Survive Where Memories Dwell, 1986, Spirit of the Age, 1996. Curator Black Heritage Reference Ctr., Langston Hughes Com. Libr. and Cultural Ctr., 1994. Recipient Editors Choice award Nat. Libr. Poetry, 1996. Mem. Internat. Soc. Poets (Disting. mem.), Kiwanis Club (poet laureate 1992-95), Bright Star. Office: Circle of Time Ent 144-47 224th St Laurelton NY 11413

REYNOLDS, GAIL SMITH, accountant; b. Detroit, May 11, 1945; d. Woodrow and Trannie (McCool) Smith; m. Robert Kenneth Reynolds, Mar. 21, 1975; children: Robert Kenneth Jr., Jonathan Colin. BS in Acctg., Miss. U. for Women, 1985. Acctg. operator First Nat. Bank, Waco, Tex., 1966-67; acctg. clk. Miss. U. for Women, Columbus, 1970-80, accounts payable specialist, 1980-85, head cashier office of comptroller, 1985-86, acctg. supr., 1986—. Bd. dirs., mem. Columbus Lowndes Assn. for Handicapped Citizens, 1993—. Mem. Am. Soc. Women Accts. (pres. 1989-90, bd. dirs. 1985—, Outstanding Woman Acct. of the Yr. Miss. Golden Triangle chpt. 1990), Inst. Mgmt. Accts. Office: Mississippi Univ for Women Box W1604 Columbus MS 39701

REYNOLDS, GENEVA B., special education educator; b. Saginaw, Mich., Nov. 2, 1953; d. Roger and Alrine (Braddock) Rucker; m. Montie Reynolds, Aug. 1, 1981; children: Monte, Marcus. BS, Chgo. State U., 1992. Cert. educable mental handicap and learning disability, social/emotional disturbed. Adminstrv. specialist USAF, 1973-77, command and control specialist, 1977-81; info. supt. USAFR, Chgo., 1981—; head tchr. South Ctrl. Cmty.

Svcs., Chgo., 1986—. SM sgt. USAF, 1973-81, USAFR, 1981—. Mem. Coun. for Exceptional Children, Kappa Delta Pi. Democrat. Baptist.

REYNOLDS, HELEN ELIZABETH, management services consultant; b. Minerva, N.Y., Aug. 30, 1925; d. Henry James and Margurite Catherine (Gallagher) McNally; m. Theodore Laurence Reynolds, Feb. 27, 1948; children: Laurence McBride, David Scott, William Herbert. BA, SUNY, Albany, 1967; MA, Union Coll., Schenectady, N.Y., 1971. Grad. Realtors Inst., N.Y. Owner, mgr. Schafer Studio, Schenectady, 1970-73; co-owner, v.p. Reynolds Chalmers Inc., Schenectady, 1971—; pres. HR Mgmt. Cons., Schenectady, 1994—; program coord. Schenectady County, 1980-81; adminstr. Wellspring House of Albany, N.Y., 1981-94; cons., examiner N.Y. State Civil Service, Albany, 1971-81; mem. adv. council SBA, Washington, 1978-80. Mem. planning bd. Town of Niskayuna, N.Y., 1977-81, town councilwoman, 1986-94; co-chair Gt. N.E. Festival on the Mohawk River, 1989, 90; bd. dirs. HAVEN, Schenectady YWCA; mem. Schenectady Indsl. Devel. Agy., N.Y. State Commn. on The Capital Region, 1994—, Acad. of Women of Achievement, Schenectady, 1994, Libr. of Congress, VNSA Coun. Schenectady. Named Woman Vision, 1986, 87, Today's Woman, 1987, Schenectady YWCA. Mem. Antique and Classic Boat Soc. (bd. dirs. 1974-89, Disting. Svc. award 1979, Founders award 1989), Assn. Adminstrs. Ind. Housing (pres. 1986-88, 92-94), Zonta (pres. 1981-82), Nat. Trust for Historic Preservation, Adirondack Mus., Antique Boat Mus., Schenectady Mus., League of Schenectady Symphony Orch., Union Coll. Alumni Assn., Charlotte Harbor Yacht Club, Charlotte County Art Guild. Home: 1365 Van Antwerp Rd Apt J104 Niskayuna NY 12309-4441 Office: 104 SW Leland St Port Charlotte FL 33952

REYNOLDS, KELLIE ANNE, administrator, visual artist; b. San Diego, Aug. 31, 1965; d. William Grey Reynolds and Roxanne marie (Douda) Reynolds-Cond. Cert., Experts Tng. Travel, 1985. Teller Met. Savings, Seattle, 1990-92; billing clk. Kaye-Smith, Renton, Wash., 1992-93; ASR clerk CCPCO Fin., Kirkland, Wash., 1993-95. Prin. works include Apples, 1985, Sun God, 1993, Cala-Lilly, 1994, The Dragon, 1995. Mem. Seattle Art Mus., 1993-94. Mem. Artist Trust. Democrat. Lutheran. Home: 12028 100th Ave NE A-201 Kirkland WA 98034

REYNOLDS, LAURA ANN, insurance company professional; b. Rahway, N.J., May 27, 1968; d. Paul Craig Dobbins and Susan Ward (Richmond) Valladao; m. Jeffrey Don Reynolds, Apr. 18, 1994. BBA, West Tex. State U., 1989. Buyer, mdse. mgr. J.C. Penney Co., San Francisco and Plano, Tex., 1989-93; personal lines underwriter, home inspector Safeco Ins. Co., Plano, 1993-95; benefits, account analyst Clark/Bardes, Inc., Dallas, 1995—. Republican. Methodist. Home: 1908 Jubilee Rd Plano TX 75092 Office: Clark Bardes Inc Ste 2200 2121 San Jacinto St Dallas TX 75201

REYNOLDS, LAUREAN WILSON, elementary education educator; b. Jackson, Miss., Nov. 10, 1946; d. Jack Gordon and Ann Louise (Smith) Wilson; m. Wallace Wayne Reynolds, Jan. 28, 1978; 1 child, Susannah Marguerite. BFA, Miss. U. for Women, 1968; MEd, U. New Orleans, 1990. Cert. tchr. art K-12, early childhood, La. Tchr. art, art history All Sts. Episc. Sch., Vicksburg, Miss., 1968-70; tchr. art J.F. Gauthier Elem. Sch., St. Bernard, La., 1970-85; tchr. kindergarten J.F. Gauthier Elem. Sch., St. Bernard, 1985—; master tchr. La. Assessment Program for Interns La. Dept. Edn., Baton Rouge, 1993-94. Exhibitor Jackson Mcpl. Art Gallery, 1982, Miss. Univ. for Women, 1981; graphics designer Jane Austen Soc. La., 1988. Named Tchr. of Yr. Internat. Reading Assn., 1990-91; recipient Excellence in Tchg. Math. award La. Assn. Math. Tchrs., 1991. Mem. NEA, Nat. Assn. Edn. Young Children, La. Assn. Educators, La. Reading Assn. Episcopalian. Home: 6410 General Haig St New Orleans LA 70124 Office: JF Gauthier Elem Sch 2214 Bobolink Dr Saint Bernard LA 70085

REYNOLDS, LOUISE MAXINE KRUSE, retired school nurse; b. Waynesboro, Va., May 28, 1935; d. Emil Herman and Cora Lee (Hammer) Kruse; m. Elbert B. Reynolds Jr., June 13, 1964; children: David Emil, Jane Marie. Diploma, Rockingham Meml. Hosp., 1956; student, Madison Coll., Tex. Tech U. RN, Tex., Va, cert. sch. nurse. Head nurse orthopedic, opthalmology dept. surgery Duke U., Durham, N.C., 1961-62; head nurse surg. fl. Waynesboro (Va.) Hosp., 1962-64; sch. nurse Lubbock (Tex.) Ind. Sch. Dist., 1974-94, ret., 1994. Mem. Va. Nurses Assn. (dist. sec., chair), Tex. Assn. Sch. Nurses (sec., treas. dist. 17, program chair 1989 state conv.).

REYNOLDS, MARGARET JENSEN, quality assurance professional; b. Miami, Fla., Nov. 15, 1950; d. Arden Edward Jensen and Elizabeth Emma (Stevenson) Galliher; m. Lawrence S. Stewart, Jr., June 2, 1969 (div. Aug. 1990); 1 child, Lawrence S. Stewart Jr.; m. Thomas L. Reynolds, July 17, 1993. BS, Auburn U., 1972; MS, U. So. Miss., 1991. Chemist Am. So. Dyeing & Finishing Corp., Opa Locka, Fla., 1972-74; sr. chemist Morton Internat., Moss Point, Miss., 1976-91, quality cert. coord., TQM facilitator, 1991—; treas. Dog River Fed. Credit Union, Moss Point, 1981-83. Vestry St. John's Episcopal Ch., Ocean Springs, Miss., 1989-91; mem. City/County Taxation Commn., Miss. Econ. Coun., Jackson, 1985-86. Mem. Am. Soc. Quality Control (cert., treas. 1994—, auditor 1993-94), AAUW (br. v.p. 1980-82, br. pres. 1984-87, Miss. state Edn. Found. chair 1984-86, crisis in higher edn. forum chair 1986). Home: 10805 Eagle Nest Rd Ocean Springs MS 39564-8339 Office: Morton Internat 5724 Elder Ferry Rd Moss Point MS 39563-9506

REYNOLDS, MARY TRACKETT, political scientist; b. Milw., Jan. 11, 1913; d. James P. and Mary (Nachtwey) Trackett; m. Lloyd G. Reynolds, June 12, 1937; children: Anne Reynolds Skinner, Priscilla Reynolds Roosevelt, Bruce; m. Yoke San Lee. BA, U. Wis., 1935, MA, 1935; postgrad. (Rebecca Green fellow), Radcliffe Coll., 1935-36; PhD (U. fellow, Barnard fellow), Columbia U., 1939. Rsch. asst. Littauer Sch. Harvard U., 1938-39; instr. Queens Coll., 1939-40; instr. Hunter Coll., 1941-42, lectr., 1945-47; assoc. in polit. sci. Johns Hopkins U., 1942-43; lectr. Conn. Coll., 1947-48, asst. prof., 1948-50; rsch. assoc. in econs. Yale U., 1961-67, vis. lectr. in English, 1973-82; meml. lectr. Joyce Centennial, 1982; assoc. fellow Berkeley Coll., 1982—. Author: Interdepartmental Committees in the National Administration, 1940, Joyce and Nora, 1964, Source Documents in Economic Development, 1966, Joyce and D'Annunzio, 1976, Joyce and Dante: The Shaping Imagination, 1982, Mr. Bloom and the Lost Vermeer, 1989, James Joyce: New Century Views, 1993; bd. editors James Joyce Quar., 1985—, James Joyce Studies Ann., 1990—. Rsch. asst. Pres.'s Com. Adminstrn. Mgmt., 1936; sr. economist Nat. Econ. Com., 1940; adminstrn. asst. Glenn L. Martin Aircraft Co., Balt., 1942-43; editorial asst. pub. adminstrn. com. Social Sci. Rsch. Coun., 1944-45; cons. Nat. Def. Adv. Commn., 1949, Nat. Mcpl. Assn., 1956, Orgn. Econ. Cooperation and Devel., Paris, 1964, U.S. State Dept.-AID 1965. Mem. MLA, AAUP, LWV, Am. Polit. Sci. Assn., Dante Soc. Am., Internat. James Joyce Found. (bd. trustees 1995—), Conn. Acad. Arts and Scis. (coun. 1988-89), Elizabethan Club (sec.-treas. 1984-89, bd. incorporators 1986-89), Sulgrave Club (Washington), Grolier Club, Appalachian Mountain Club, Phi Beta Kappa. Home: 4000 Cathedral Ave NW Apt 147B Washington DC 20016-5249 Office: Yale Sta PO Box 604 New Haven CT 06520

REYNOLDS, MEGAN BEAHM, primary and elementary education educator; b. Lima, Ohio, Aug. 29, 1955; d. Walter Clarence and Jo Ann (Wood) Beahm; m. Dale Myron Reynolds, Aug. 28, 1976 (div. July 1983); 1 child, Emily Jo Reynolds. BS, Tenn. Wesleyan Coll., 1977; postgrad., U. Tenn., 1986-88. Cert. elem. and early edn. tchr., Tenn. Tchr. adult basic edn. Athens (Tenn.) City Schs., 1977-78; asst. dir. Child Shelter Home, Cleveland, Tenn., 1978; tchr. kindergarten First Bapt. Presch./Kindergarten, Cleveland, 1978-80; teller, bookkeeper C & C Bank Monroe County, Sweetwater, Tenn., 1982-83; substitute elem. tchr. Knox County Schs., Knoxville, Tenn., 1983-85, elem. tchr., 1985-87, tchr. kindergarten, 1987—; career ladder III Knox County Schs., Knoxville, 1993; mem. adv. bd., grade-level chairperson Norwood Elem. Sch., Knox County Schs., 1990-93, mem. adopt a sch. com., 1992-93, S team rep., 1991-92. Editor Norwood Elem. Yearbook, 1989-90. Parent helper Girl Scouts U.S., 1986-90; neighborhood collector Am. Heart Assn., 1987—; v.p. Norwood Elem./Knox County Schs. PTO, 1991-92; Norwood rep. Ft. Kid, 1990-91; youth counselor Middlebrook Pike Meth. Ch., mem. Costa Rica missions team; active participant Vols. of Am. Mem. NEA, Tenn. Edn. Assn., Knox County Edn. Assn., Knox County Assn. Young Children, Children and Adults with Attention Deficit Disorder (presch. Summer intervention program, parent/sch. comms. program 1995—). Methodist. Home: 8525 Savannah Ct Knoxville TN 37923 Office: Norwood Elem Sch 1909 Merchants Dr Knoxville TN 37912-4714

REYNOLDS, NANCY BRADFORD DUPONT (MRS. WILLIAM GLASGOW REYNOLDS), sculptor; b. Greenville, Del., Dec. 28, 1919; d. Eugene Eleuthere and Catherine Dulcinea (Moxham) duPont; m. William Glasgow Reynolds, May 18, 1940; children: Kathrine Glasgow Reynolds, William Bradford, Mary Parminter Reynolds Savage, Cynthia duPont Reynolds Farris. Student, Goldey-Beacom Coll., Wilmington, Del., 1938. One-woman shows include Rehoboth (Del.) Art League, 1963, Del. Art Mus., Wilmington, Caldwell, Inc., 1975, Wilmington Art Mus., 1976; exhibited group shows Corcoran Gallery, Washington, 1943, Soc. Fine Arts, Wilmington, 1937, 38, 40, 41, 48, 50, 62, 65, NAD, N.Y.C., 1964, Pa. Mil. Coll., Chester, 1966, Del. Art Ctr., 1967, Met. Mus. Art, N.Y.C., 1977, Lever House, N.Y.C., 1979; sculpture work Brookgreen Gardens, S.C.; represented in permanent collections Wilmington Trust Co., E.I. duPont de Nemours & Co., Children's Home, Inc., Claymont, Del., Children's Bur., Wilmington, Stephenson Sci. Ctr., Nashville, Lutheran Towers Bldg., Travelers Aid and Family Soc. Bldg., Wilmington, bronze fountain head Longwood Gardens, Kennett Square, Pa., bronze statue Brookgreen Gardens, Murrells Inlet, S.C.; contbr. articles to profl. jours. Organizer vol. svc. Del. chpt. ARC, 1938-39; chmn. Com. for Revision Del. Child Adoption Law, 1950-52; pres., bd. dirs. Children Bur. Del.; pres., trustee Children's Home, Inc.; del., past regent Gunston Hall Plantation, Lorton, Va.; mem. adv. com. Longwood Gardens, Kennett Sq., Pa.; garden and grounds com. Winterthur (Del.) Mus.; mem. rsch. staff Henry Francis DuPont Winterthur Mus., 1955-63; mem. archtl. com. U. Del., Newark. Recipient Confrerie des Chevaliers du Tastevin Clos de Vougeot-Bourgogne France, 1960; Hort. award Garden Club Am., 1964, medal of Merit, 1976; Dorothy Platt award Garden Club of Phila., 1980; Alumni medal of merit Westover Sch., Middlebury, Conn. Mem. Pa. Hort. Soc., Wilmington Soc. Fine Arts, Mayflower Descs., Del. Hist. Soc., Colonial Dames, League Am. Pen Women, Nat. Trust Hist. Preservation. Garden Club of Wilmington (past pres.), Garden Club of Am. (past asst. zone 4 chmn.), Vicmead Hunt Club, Greenville Country Club, Chevy Chase Club (Washington), Colony Club (N.Y.C.). Episcopalian. Address: PO Box 3919 Greenville DE 19807-0919

REYNOLDS, NANCY HUBBARD, sociology educator; b. Norfolk, Va., Aug. 1, 1923; d. Francis Marion and Nancy Augustine (Bell) Jones; m. Lawrence James Hubbard, May 16, 1955 (dec. Nov. 1968); m. George Allen Reynolds, Feb. 19, 1970 (dec. Feb. 1971). AA, Longview Community Coll., 1974; BA, U. Mo., 1976, MA, 1979; PhD, Kans. State U., 1985. Clerical asst. U.S. Govt., 1942-67; rsch. asst., lectr. U. Mo., Kansas City, 1978-79; aging cons. North Cen.. Flint Hills Area Agy. on Aging, Manhattan, Kans., 1982-84; instr. Kans. State U., Manhattan, 1979-86, Emporia (Kans.) State U., 1986-92. Author: Older Volunteer Leaders in a Rural Community; contbr. articles to profl. jours. Bd. dirs. Hospice, 1989; hon. mem. Sr. Citizens of Marion County. Mem. Mental Health Assn. (bd. dirs. 1989), Am. Sociol. Assn., Midwest Sociol. Soc., Midwest Coun. for Social Rsch. in Aging, Nat. Assn. Retired Fed. Employees, Phi Kappa Phi, Mortar Bd.

REYNOLDS, NANCY REMICK, editor, writer; b. San Antonio, July 15, 1938; d. Donald Worthington and Edith (Remick) R.; m. Brian Rushton, June 25, 1983; 1 child, Ehren T. Park. Student, Sch. Am. Ballet, 1951, 53-61, Juilliard Sch. Music, 1957, Martha Graham Sch. Contemporary Dance, N.Y.C., 1959, U. Sorbonne, Paris, 1962; BA in Art History, Columbia U., 1965; postgrad., Goethe Inst., Prien, 1972, U. Chgo. and Sarah Lawrence Coll., 1974-77. Dancer N.Y.C. Ballet, 1956-61; editor Praeger Pubs., N.Y.C., 1965-71; dir. rsch. book Choreography by George Balanchine: A Catalogue of Works, N.Y., 1979-82 (pub. 1983); dir. rsch. pub. TV spl. Balanchine, N.Y., 1983-84; assoc. editor Internat. Ency. of Dance, 1982—; dir. rsch. The George Balanchine Found., N.Y.C., 1994—; co-pub. Twentieth-Century Dance in Slides, 1978-93. Author: Repertory in Review: Forty Years of the New York City Ballet, 1977 (De la Torre Bueno prize 1977), The Dance Catalog: A Complete Guide to Today's World of Dance, 1979, co-author: In Performance,1980, Dance Classics, 1991 (rec. for teen age N.Y. Pub Libr.); editor: Movement and Metaphor: Four Centuries of Ballet (Lincoln Kirstein), 1970, Dance as a Theatre Art: Source Readings in Dance History from 1581 to the Present (Selma Jeanne Cohen), 1974, School of Classical Dance (V. Kostrovitskaya and A. Pisarev), 1978; contbr. (book) Ballet: Bias and Belief, "Three Pamphlets Collected" and Other Dance Writings of Lincoln Kirstein, 1983, also numerous articles and revs. to Dancing Times, Ballet News, Playbill, ArtsLine, Dancemag., Town & Country, Connoisseur, N.Y. Times, Ency. Britannica., others. Ford Found. Travel and Study grantee, 1974; Mary Duke Biddle Found. grantee, 1990. Mem. Dance Critics Assn. (pres. 1986-87), Soc. Dance History Scholars, Soc. for Dance Rsch., Am. Soc. for Theatre Rsch., European Assn. Dance Historians, Internat. Fedn. for Theatre Rsch. in affiliation with Societe Internat. des Bibliotheques et Musees des Arts du Spectacle. Home: 9 Prospect Park W Brooklyn NY 11215-1758

REYNOLDS, PATRICIA REGINA, English studies educator; b. Phila., Sept. 24, 1946; d. John C. and Josephine (Lucas) Wolf; m. Christopher Thomas Reynolds, Nov. 22, 1972; children: David Christopher, Patricia Kathleen. BS in Secondary Edn., Temple U., 1968, MS in Psychology of Reading, 1975; PhD in English Composition and Literacy, U. Pa., 1995. English instr. Heritage Jr. Sch., Cherry Hill, N.J., 1969-76; homebound tutor Marple-Newtown Pub. Schs., Newtown Square, Pa., 1978-85; adult English grammar instr. Upper Darby Adult Sch., Drexel Hill, Pa., 1980-88; reading instr. Pa. State U., Lima, 1989-95; tutor Learning Ctr. Delaware County C.C., Media, Pa., 1985-86; reading and English composition instr. Neumann Coll., Aston, Pa., 1990-91; reading and English composition instr. Harcum Jr. Coll., Bryn Mawr, 1991—, reading instr., 1988-94, reading, writing, learning specialist, mentor, 1991-94, student spl. svcs. mentor, 1994—, English instr., 1985-95, asst. prof. English, 1995—; instr. grad. courses in reading Holy Family Coll., Phila., 1995—; reporter County Press, Newtown Square, 1990; adj. prof. English composition Drexel U., Phila. Former mem. exec. com. Dem. Party of Marple, Broomall, Pa., 1994-95. Grantee AAUW, 1993. Mem. Internat. Reading Assn., Phi Lambda Theta. Roman Catholic. Home: 211 Cornwall Dr Broomall PA 19008-3840

REYNOLDS, SALLIE BLACKBURN, artist, civic volunteer; b. Kansas City, Mo., Feb. 9, 1940; d. Anton and Sallie Churchill (Blackburn) Zajic; m. Jeffrey Calhoun Loker, Mar. 25, 1959 (div. May 1965); children: Toni Lynne, Michael David, Kathryn Lee Loker Simpson; m. Everett Lee Reynolds, Mar. 29, 1969 (dec. Sept. 1992). Student, William Jewell Coll., 1959, BA magna cum laude, 1977; student, U. Mo., Kansas City, 1966-67, Kansas City Art Inst., 1966-70; Cert., Famous Artists Sch., 1965. Cert. tchr., Mo. From clk. to sec. Hdqrs. Strategic Air Command, Offutt AFB, Omaha, 1960-62; sec., wage and hr. law enforcement asst. wage hr. div. U.S. Dept. of Labor, Kansas City, 1963-68, exec. sec. to regional manpower adminstr., 1968-71, spl. asst. to regional exec. com., 1971-72, mgmt. asst. Office of Regional Dir., 1972-73; from. clk. to sec. air carrier dist. office FAA, Kansas City, 1978-81; from clk. typist to sec. regional personnel officer Bur. of Reclamation, U.S. Dept. of Interior, Boulder City, Nev., 1982-84; editorial asst. div. of planning Bur. of Reclamation, Boulder City, 1984-86; owner, operator B-Bar-L Farms, 1990—. Editor newsletter Laurie Fine Art, 1989-90. Ofcl. commr., sec., corr. Clay County (Mo.) Bicentennial Commn., 1974-76; mem. Ozark Brush and Palette, Inc., Camdenton, Mo., 1987—, editor newsletter, 1988-89; v.p., sec. Clay County Hist. Soc., 1972—, active Nat. Wildlife Fedn. Recipient 1st Pl. award Nat. Soc. DAR Am. Heritage Contest in oil/acrylic painting, 1990, 3d pl., 1991, 1st pl. gold award 1992, 1st pl. award profl. photography Laurie Fine Art Show, 1991, miscellaneous local art show awards, 1988—. Mem. DAR (pub. rels. chmn., rec. sec., archives chmn., corr. sec. Niangua chpt. Camdenton 1987—), Nat. Oil and Acrylic Painters Soc., Phi Epsilon of Phi Beta Kappa, Versailles Saddle Club. Presbyterian. Home and Office: RR 1 Box 95A Versailles MO 65084-9724

REYNOLDS, SIDNEY RAE, marketing communications executive; b. Alliance, Nebr., June 27, 1956; d. Harold Edward and Dolores Jean (Bestol) James; m. Eddie Ellis Reynolds, May 27, 1975; children: Ashley Dawn, Tyler John. BAgr, Kans. State U., 1977. Asst. editor Harvest Pub. Co., Lansing, Mich., 1977-78, assoc. editor, 1978-80; assoc. editor Harvest Pub. Co., Topeka, 1980-82; editor Specialized Agrl. Publs., Raleigh, N.C., 1982-88, editorial dir., 1984-88; rep. NCH Corp., Raleigh, N.C., 1988-89; pres. Wordcraft, Inc., The Signature Agy., Raleigh, 1987—. Contbr. articles to profl. jours.; developed models for integrated mktg. agys. and pub. rels. measurement, 1987—. Advisor Episcopal Youth Group, Wake Forest, N.C., 1986-89, Raleigh, N.C., 1987—. Named Writer of Yr., Harvest Pub. Co., 1978. Mem. Am. Agrl. Editors Assn., Women in Comms. (bd. dirs. 1978-79), Soc. Profl. Journalists (reorgnl. chairperson 1985-88), Spurs Club (nat. v.p. 1976-78), Agrl. Communicators Club (pres. Manhattan Kans. chpt. 1976), Rotary (treas. Raleigh-Millbrook chpt. 19992-94, v.p. 1994-95, pres. 1995-96, dist. comms. com. chair 1996—), Am. Mktg. Assn., Coun. for Entrepreneurial Devel., Sigma Delta Chi, Gamma Sigma Delta, Alpha Zeta. Home: 512 Brookfield Rd Raleigh NC 27615-1510 Office: 6608 Six Forks Rd Ste 201 Raleigh NC 27615-6522

REYNOLDS, SUSAN, public relations executive. Spokesperson Frank Sinatra; exec. Solters/Roskin/Friedman, Inc., 1981-87; v.p., mgr. entertainment mktg. and publicity Burson-Marsteller, 1988-90; prin. Scoop Mktg., 1990—. Office: Scoop Marketing 3701 Wilshire Blvd Los Angeles CA 90010-2804

REYNOLDS, W. ANN, academic administrator. Chancellor Mount Sinai Sch. Medicine, N.Y.C. Office: One Gustave L Levy Pl New York NY 10029-6574*

REYNOLDS, W(YNETKA) ANN, academic administrator, educator; b. Coffeyville, Kans., Nov. 3, 1937; d. John Ethelbert and Glennie (Beanland) King; m. Thomas H. Kirschbaum; children—Rachel Rebecca, Rex King. BS in Biology-Chemistry, Kans. State Tchrs. Coll., Emporia, 1958; MS in Zoology, U. Iowa, Iowa City, 1960, PhD, 1962; DSc (hon.), Ind. State U., Evansville, 1980; LHD (hon.), McKendree Coll., 1984, U. N.C., Charlotte, 1988, U. Judaism, L.A., 1989, U. Nebr., Kearney, 1992; DSc (hon.), Ball State U., Muncie, Ind., 1985, Emporia (Kans.) State U., 1987; PhD (hon.), Fu Jen Cath. U., Republic of China, 1987; LHD (hon.), U. Nebr., Kearney, 1992, Colgate U., 1993; LHD, No. Mich. U., 1995. Asst. prof. biology Ball State U., Muncie, Ind., 1962-65; asst. prof. anatomy U. Ill. Coll. Medicine, Chgo., 1965-68, assoc. prof. anatomy, 1968-73, research prof. ob-gyn, from 1973, prof. anatomy, from 1973, acting assoc. dean acad. affairs Coll. Medicine, 1977, assoc. vice chancellor, dean grad. coll., 1977-79; provost, v.p. for acad. affairs, prof. ob-gyn. and anatomy Ohio State U., Columbus, 1979-82; chancellor Calif. State Univ. system, Long Beach, 1982-90, prof. biology, 1982-90; bd. dirs. Abbott Labs., Maytag, Owens-Corning, Humana, Inc.; clin. prof. ob/gyn. UCLA, 1985-90; chancellor CUNY, 1990—; mem. Nat. Rsch. Coun. Com. Undergrad. Sci. Edn., 1993—; co-chair Fed. Task Force on Women, Minorities and Handicapped in Sci. and Tech., 1987-90, Pacesetter Program Reform for Secondary Sch. Coll. Bd., 1992—; adv. bd. Congl. Black Caucus Inst. Sci., Space and Tech., 1987-91; Calif. Labor Employment and Tng. Corp., 1993—;. Contbr. chpts. to books, articles to profl. jours; assoc. editor Am. Biology Tchr., 1964-67. Active numerous civic activities involving edn. and the arts; mem. nat. adv. bd. Inst. Am. Indian Arts, 1992—; bd. dirs. Lincoln Ctr. Inst., 1993—, UAW Calif., Calif. Econ. Devel. Corp., 1984-90; trustee Internat. Life Scis. Inst.-Nutrition Found., 1987—, Southwest Mus., L.A. County High Sch. for Arts Found., 1985-90. Recipient Disting. Alumni award Kans. State Tchrs. Coll., 1972, Calif. Gov.'s Award for the Arts for an Outstanding Individual in Arts in Edn., 1989, Prize award Cen. Assn. Obstetricians and Gynecologists, 1968; NSF Predoctoral fellow, 1958-62, Woodrow Wilson Hon. fellow, 1958. Fellow ACOG; mem. AAAS, Perinatal Rsch. Soc., Soc. Gynecol. Investigation (sec./treas. 1980-83, pres. 1992-93), Nat. Assn. Systems Heads (pres. 1987-88), Sigma Xi. Office: CUNY Office of the Chancellor 535 E 80th St New York NY 10021-0767

REYNOLDS-SAKOWSKI, DANA RENEE, science educator; b. Centralia, Ill., June 28, 1968; d. David Lavern and Betty Lou (Shelton) Reynolds; m. Jason Bielas Sakowski, Oct. 8, 1994. BS in Edn., U. No. Colo., 1991, MEd in Middle Sch. Edn., 1996. Tchr. life sci. and math. Ken Caryl Mid. Sch., Littleton, Colo., 1991-92; tchr. sci. Moore Mid. Sch., Arvada, Colo., 1992-93; tchr. life sci. Moore Mid. Sch., Arvada, 1993—. Mem. Nat. Wildlife Fedn., Colo. Assn. Sci. Tchrs., Colo. Biology Tchrs. Assn., Sierra Club, World Wildlife Fund, Nat. Parks and Conservation Assn., Natural Resources Def. Coun., Audubon Soc., Nature Conservancy. Office: Moore Mid Sch 8455 W 88th Ave Arvada CO 80005-1620

REZAC, ROSELYN ANN, graphic designer, business owner; m. Martin R. Skoro, Mar. 4, 1984. BA, U. Minn., 1976, MA, 1978. Counselor, tchr. various orgns., 1971-78; art dir., graphic designer and supr. various cos., 1978-84; prin., owner, graphic designer MartinRoss Design, Mpls., 1984—. Mem. BrynMawr Transp. Com., Mpls., 1996. Recipient awards for 3M poster design Am. Graphic Design Awards, 1994, logo design, New Am. Logos, 1994, brochure design Best of Brochure Design, 1992, poster and packaging designs Computer Graphics II, 1995. Mem. Am. Inst. Graphic Arts.

RHAMY, JENNIFER FRANCES, marketing professional; b. Swindon, Eng., Nov. 14, 1954; d. Robert Keith and Evelyn Imel Rhamy. BS in Med. Tech., U. Ariz., 1977; postgrad., Vanderbilt U., 1979, U. Tex., Galveston, 1985; MBA, Colo. State U., 1994. Registered med. technologist. Med. technologist blood bank Vanderbilt U. Hosp., Nashville, 1979-84; tech. dir. United Blood Svcs., Tucson, 1985-87; supr. blood bank Park Plaza Hosp., Houston, 1987-88; mgr. transfusion svc. St. Luke's Episcopal Hosp., Houston, 1988-90; clin. application specialist blood component tech. COBE BCT, Inc., Lakewood, Colo., 1990-96, internal product tng. and comms. coord., 1996—; presenter in field; rotation faculty blood bank U. Ariz., 1986-87; faculty, adminstr., specialist in blood banking program St. Luke's Episcopal Hosp., 1988-90. Scholar Gulf Coast Regional Blood Ctr., Houston, 1985. Mem. Am. Soc. Clin. Pathology, South Cen. Assn. Blood Banks, Am. Assn. Blood Banks, Am. Soc. for Apheresis. Democrat. Office: COBE BCT Inc 1201 Oak St Lakewood CO 80215-4409

RHEA, CHERYL H., mathematics educator; b. Jeannette, Pa., Apr. 10, 1953; d. George Edward and Iliene (Ruschaupt) Hughes; m. Harry Allen Rhea, May 31, 1975; children: Allen, Neal. BA, Seton Hill Coll., 1975. Cert. tchr. secondary edn. Pvt. tutor, 1971—; homebound instr. Penn-Trafford Sch. Dist., Harrison City, Pa., 1983-96, TELS instr., 1985, 88-89; math. instr. Westmoreland County C.C., Youngwood, Pa., 1992—. Editor: (newsletter) First Thoughts, 1992—. Sunday Sch. tchr. First Presbyn. Ch., Jeannette, 1985—, Youth Club tchr., 1989—; vol. Jeannette Band Parents, 1993—, dir. Christian Edn., 1996—; dist. treas. Reading is Fundamental, 1989-91. Mem. Nat. Coun. Tchrs. Maths., Math. Assn. Am. Democrat. Presbyterian. Home: 448 Guy St Jeannette PA 15644-1816

RHEA, MARCIA CHANDLER, accountant; b. Columbia, S.C., Apr. 27, 1956; d. Foster Frazier and Virginia Elizabeth (Goude) Chandler; m. Randall W. Rhea, Aug. 23, 1980. AA, Bauder Coll., Atlanta, 1975; BA magna cum laude, Coll. of Charleston, S.C., 1981; postgrad., CPA studies. Cert. tax practice ptnr., notary pub., S.C., CPA, S.C. Writer, prodr. U.S. Army C.E., Charleston, 1984; mng. ptnr. Care/Share Prodns., Charleston, 1981—; ptnr. Chandler Rhea, CPA, Johns Island, S.C., 1987—; agt. Deering Lit. Agy.; media cons., roving reporter Worldfest-Charleston Internat. Film Festival. Author: Does It Have to Happen Again?, From Hell's Angel to Heaven's Saint; author (screenplays) The Carolina Storyteller, The Life Shift; contbr. articles to mags. and profl. jours.; prodr. various films. Adult tchr. Ashley Rivers Bapt. Ch.; mem. Tri-County Advocates for Women on Bds. and Commns. for S.C. Recipient Outstanding Acad. Achievement award Coll. of Charleston. Mem. AICPA, Am. Soc. Notaries, S.C. Assn. CPAs, S.C. Motion Picture TV Assn., Script Writers of S.C., Inc., Screenwriters Guild of Charleston (charter), Acctg. Assn., Coll. of Charleston Alumni, Film Soc. Coll. Charleston (bd. dirs.), Phi Kappa Phi, Phi Mu. Republican. Baptist. Office: 3226 Maybank Hwy Ste 1 PO Box 508 Johns Island SC 29455

RHEAMS, ANNIE ELIZABETH, education educator; b. Lake Providence, La.; d. Curtis Kleinpeter Sr. and Annie Augusta (Webb) Kleinpeter; 1 child, Darryl Jemall Rheams. BA, Grambling (La.) U., 1971; MS, Ala. A&M U., 1975; PhD, U. Wis., Milw., 1989. Cert. tchr. in exceptional edn., adminstrn. Tchr. Ala. A&M U., Normal, 1971-79, adminstr., 1977-79; acad. specialist U. Wis., Milw., 1979-82, Parkside, 1982-84; tchr. diagnostician, adminstr. Milw. Schs., 1984-89; asst. prof. dept. edn. Marquette U., Milw., 1989-96; career counselor Madison County Career Counseling Svcs., Huntsville, 1975; adj. prof. Oakwood (Ala.) SDA Coll., 1975-78; tchr. Gateway to Engring.

Program, Milw., 1984-88; cons. pub. schs./Wee Care Day Care, Milw., 1992-96. Author: P.A.C.E.: A Thematic Approach to Developing Essential Experiences, 1996. Voter registrar/poll watcher NAACP, Lake Providence, 1966; v.p. Work for Wis., Inc., Milw., 1993-94, Messmer H.S. Bd., Milw., 1990-94; com. chmn. Citizen's Rev. Bd., Milw., 1980-82, Met. Milw. Alliance Black Sch. Educators, 1994-95. Assoc. fellow Ctr. for Great Plains Studies, U. Nebr.-Lincoln, 1995; named Outstanding Tchr. Educator, Am. Assn. for Coll. Tchr. Educators Directory, 1995. Mem. Zonta Internat., Alpha Kappa Alpha, Phi Delta Kappa. Home: PO Box 09681 Milwaukee WI 53209

RHEINTGEN, LAURA DALE, research center official; b. Takoma Park, Md., July 13, 1962; d. Robert William and Ethel Frances (Snyder) Schiedel. BA in Internat. Studies and German, W.Va. U., 1984; MA in Internat. Affairs, Am. U., 1988. Rsch. asst. Brookings Instn., Washington, 1986; staff cons. Birch & Davis Assocs., Inc., Silver Spring, Md., 1988-89; devel. analyst Ctr. for Strategic and Internat. Studies, Washington, 1989-92, mgr. devel. rsch. and records, 1992-93; asst. dir. devel. Ctr. for Strategic and Internat. Studies, 1994-95, dir. found. rels., 1995—. Mem. Women in Internat. Security Studies, German Lang. Soc. Office: Ctr for Strategic & Internat Studies 1800 K St NW Ste 400 Washington DC 20006-2202

RHOADES, CATHIE JEAN, mathematics educator; b. Fostoria, Ohio, Apr. 20, 1949; d. Norman Ralph and Doris Mary (Roberts) Bolen; m. Russell Lee Rhoades, Aug. 22, 1971; children: Bethany Lyn, Robyn Brianne. BS Edn., Ohio U., 1971; MEd in Curriculum/Supervision, Ashland U., 1986, MED in Computer Edn., 1994; postgrad., Ohio State U., Bowling Green, State U., 1990-95. Tchr. Northmont Jr. High Sch., Clayton, Ohio, 1971-72; tchr., dept. chmn. Taft Mid. Sch./Marion (Ohio) City Schs., 1972-79; tchr., math and computer dept. chmn. River Valley High Sch., Marion, 1983—; dist. team mem. Ohio Model for Excellence in Math., Ohio, 1992—; core group River Valley Dist. Tech. Planning Com., Marion, 1993—, math. team Tech Prep Consortium, Marion, 1992—; insvc. instr. River Valley Local Schs., Marion, 1991—. Leader Troop 233, Girl Scouts U.S., Marion, 1988—. Jennings Scholar, Martha Holden Jennings Found., 1992-93. Mem. Phi Delta Kappa, Phi Kappa Phi. Methodist. Home: 2084 Crissinger Rd Marion OH 43302 Office: River Valley High Sch 1267 Columbus Sandusky R/N Marion OH 43302

RHOADES, MARCIA DIANE, career counselor; b. L.A., Sept. 17, 1937; d. Edward Owen Northbrook and Gladys Evelyn (Trano) Pigeon; m. Richard Allison Rhoades, Jan. 29, 1960 (div. 1993); children: Julie, Donald, James. BS in Bus. Edn., UCLA, 1960; MS in Counseling with distinction, Calif. State U., Northridge, 1989. Cert. marriage, family and child counselor, Calif.; cert. counselor; registered counselor, Wash. Counselor Woman at Work, Pasadena, Calif., 1988-91; tchr. U. Wash. Ext., Seattle, 1995—; career cons., Bellevue, 1991-95; career mgmt. and cons. Right Assoc., 1995—. Adv. bd. Wash. Cert. in Career Devel. Program, Seattle, 1995—, YWCA Eastside, Remond, Wash., 1992—; bd. dirs. Puget South Career Devel. Assn., Seattle, 1993-94. Mem. ACA, Nat. Career Devel. Assn.

RHOADES, MARYE FRANCES, paralegal; b. Ft. Defiance, Va., Jan. 29, 1937; d. Silas Caswell Sr. and Mary Ann Frances (James) Rhodes; m. Minter James Rowe, May 1964 (div. 1968); children: Margaret Frances Omar, James Robert; m. Robert Charles Rhoades Jr., July 25, 1980. Student, Coll. W.Va., 1956-58, 68, U. Charleston, 1962-63, 74, 89, Antioch U., 1972-73; grad., Mike Tyree Sch. Real Estate, 1984, Evans Coll. Legal Studies, 1990. Educator Nicholas County Sch. System, Summersville, W.Va., 1958-61; edit. staff, columnist, staff writer, reporter, photographer Beckley Newspapers Corp., 1962-76; Educator Raleigh County Bd. Edn., Beckley, W.Va., 1967-68; exec. editor, columnist Local News Jour., Whitesville, W.Va., 1976-77; libr. bookmobile, asst. ref. libr., outreach coord. Raleigh County Pub. Libr., Beckley, 1977-78; agt. Combined Ins. Co., Chgo., 1978-79; legal sec., paralegal W.Va. Legal Svcs. Inc., Beckley, 1979-82; paralegal Applachian Rsch and Defense Fund Inc., Beckley, 1982-83; exec. dir., owner Rhoades and Rowe, Beckley, 1983-85; paralegal patinet advocate Comty. Health Sys. Inc., Beckley, 1986-96; pvt. practice Mac Arthur, W. Va., 1996—. Contbr. articles to mags. State bd. dirs., pub. resl. LWV, Beckley; pub. rels., various coms. Raleigh County Dem. Women, Beckley; sec., pub. rels. Orchard Valley Women's Club, Crab Orchard, W.Va.; trustee Fraternal Order Ealges; pub. rels., various coms. Loyal Order Moose, Beckley, Beckley Profl. Bus. Women; com. mem. Nat. Coalition to Save the New River; sales rep. So. U.S. Rep. to U.S. Mil. Acad., West Point, N.Y.; mem. Am. Legion Aux., Mullens, W.Va. Mem. NEA, Classroom Tchrs. Assn., Nat. Paralegal Assn., Nat. Fedn. Paralegals Assn., Nat. Ind. Paralegals Assn., Nat. Com. Save Soc., Sec. Medicare, Nat. Legal Aid and Def. Assn., Nat. Orgn. Social Security Claimants Reps., State Soc. Sec. Task Force, Nat. Vets. Legal Svcs. Project Inc., W.Va. U. Alumni Assn., Community AIDS Edn. Com., W.Va. Edn. Assn. Democrat. Pentacostal Holiness. Home: PO Box 416 Mac Arthur WV 25873-0416 Office: Benefit Advocates PO Box 416 Mac Arthur WV 25873-0416

RHOADES, NANCY LYBARGER, retired librarian; b. Coshocton, Ohio, Sept. 17, 1915; d. Harry Swayne and Ethel (Finney) Lybarger; m. Rendell Rhoades, Feb. 7, 1953 (dec. Sept. 1976). BA, Westminster Coll., 1939; BS in Libr. Sci., Case-Western Res. U., 1943. Head reference dept., sch. libr. Warder Pub. Libr., Springfield, Ohio, 1939-45; reference asst. history divsn. Cleve. Pub. Libr., 1945-54; reference asst. Columbus (Ohio) Pub. Libr., 1954-56; libr. Starling Jr. High Columbus (Ohio) Pub. Schs., 1956-58; reference asst., serials cataloger Ohio State U. Librs., Columbus, 1968-62; libr. Ashland (Ohio) Theol. Sem., 1963-70; dir. cataloging Coll. of Wooster, Ohio, 1971-74; assoc. editor Atlanta Univ. Black Culture Collection Coll. of Wooster, 1971-74, head tech. svcs., 1974-76; libr. Ashland County Law Libr., 1977-90; libr. cons. Ohio Agrl. Rsch. and Devel. Ctr., Wooster, 1976; libr., cons. First Presbyn. Ch., Ashland, 1977-83. Author: Croquet: An Annotated Bibliography from the Rendell Rhoades Croquet Collection, 1992. Pres. Ashland Br., AAUW, 1972-73, Ohio State Divsn. Bd. Internat. Rels., 1973-75; Ashland County chmn. Martha Kinney Cooper Ohioana Libr., Columbus, 1974-90. Mem. Ch. and Syngague Libr. Assn. Republican. Presbyterian. Home: Apt B408 6000 Riverside Dr Dublin OH 43017

RHOADS, NANCY GLENN, lawyer; b. Washington, Oct. 15, 1957; d. Donald L. and Gerry R. R.; m. Robert A. Koons, June 23, 1984. BA, Gettysburg Coll., 1980; JD, Temple U., 1983. Bar: Pa., U.S. Dist. Ct. (ea. dist.) Pa. 1983. Rsch. asst. Prof. Mikochick, Phila., 1982-83; law clk. Phila. Ct. of Common Pleas, 1983-85; assoc. Post and Schell P.C., Phila., 1985-90, Sheller, Ludwig and Badey, Phila., 1990—. Co-author: Aging and the Aged: Problems, Opportunities, Challenges, 1980. Vol. Spl. Olympics. Mem. Phila. Bar Assn. (med. legal com.), Phi Beta Kappa, Phi Alpha Theta, Pi Delta Epsilon, Eta Sigma Phi. Home: Gwynedd Knoll 1374 Tanglewood Dr North Wales PA 19454-3671 Office: Sheller Ludwig and Badey 1528 Walnut St Third Fl Philadelphia PA 19102-3604

RHODARMER, LISA DENDY, elementary education educator; b. Franklin, N.C., July 30, 1968; d. Alton Clyde and Annie Ruth McCall Dendy; m. William Derek Rhodarmer, Dec. 19, 1992. BS in Edn., We. Carolina U., Cullowhee, N.C., 1990; MA in Edn., We. Carolina U., Cullowhee, N.C., 1992. Cert. elem. tchr. N.C., Pa. Coord. Student Literacy Corps Grant on Cherokee Reservation, Cullowhee, 1990-92; tchr. pre-K Haywood Co. Schs., Canton, N.C., 1992-95; tchr. 1st grade Colonial Sch. Dist., Conshohocken, Pa., 1995—; rep. Haywood Co. Reading Assn., Canton, N.C., 1993-94, pres. 1994-95; mem. Lang. Arts Com. Colonial Sch. Dist., Pa.; vol. Families and Schs. Together Colonial Sch. Dist., 1995. Presenter various workshops in field. Recipient 1st Yr. Tchr. award Sallie Mae Loan Corp., 1993. Mem. Nat. Assn. Edn. of Young Children, Pa. State Edn. Assn., , N.C. Coun. Tchrs. of Math., 1994—, Internat. Reading Assn., Phi Kappa Phi. Presbyn. Home: 231 N 3d St #320 Philadelphia PA 19106 Office: Conshohocken Elem 301 Harry St Conshohocken PA 19428

RHODE, DEBORAH LYNN, law educator; b. Jan. 29, 1952. BA, Yale U., 1974, JD, 1977. Bar: D.C. 1977, Calif. 1981. Law clk. to judge U.S. Ct. Appeals (2d cir.), N.Y.C., 1977-78; law clk. to Hon. Justice Thurgood Marshall U.S. Supreme Ct., D.C., 1978-79; asst. prof. law Stanford (Calif.) U., 1979-82, assoc. prof., 1982-85, prof., 1985—; dir. Inst. for Rsch. on Women and Gender, 1986-90, Keck Ctr. of Legal Ethics and The Legal Profession, 1994—; trustee Yale U., 1983-89; chmn. profl. responsibility sect. Am. Assn. Law Schs., co-chmn. ABA com. profl. responsibility. Author several books; contbr. articles to profl. jours. Office: Stanford U Law Sch Crain Quadrangle Stanford CA 94305

RHODE, KIM, Olympic athlete; b. July 16, 1979. Recipient Bronze medal in women's skeet 1994 USASNC, bronze medal women's double trap 1995 Seoul World Cup, team Gold medal skeet, team Bronze medal double trap 1995 World Shotgun Championships, Gold medal women's double trap 1995 U.S. Olympic Festival, Gold medal women's double trap Olympic Games, Atlanta, 1996. Mem. Safari Club Internat., Women's Sports Shooting Found. Office: care USA Shooting One Olympic Plz Colorado Springs CO 80909*

RHODEN, MARY NORRIS, educational center director; b. Greenville, S.C., Jan. 3, 1943; d. Tony and Carrie Thelma (Reuben) Norris; 1 adopted child, Scottie Brooks-Rhoden. BS in Biology, Allen U., Columbia, S.C., 1966; postgrad., Atlanta U., 1967-68. Dir., tchr. MSR Learning Ctr., Riverdale, Ga., 1989—. Author poetry. Vol. Buffalo Soldiers Monument Commn., Ft. Leavenworth, Kans., 1991—; developed letters for nat. campaign to petition Congress, Postmaster Gen. to issue Buffalo Soldiers Stamp. Recipient Cert. Appreciation NAACP, Greenville, S.C., 1979, Wheat St. Bapt. Ch., Atlanta, 1989. Mem. Alpha Kappa Alpha, Alpha Kappa Delta. Democrat. African Meth. Episcopal Ch. Office: MSR Learning Ctr 7037 Shangrila Trl Riverdale GA 30296-2138

RHODES, ALICE GRAHAM, lawyer; b. Phila., June 15, 1941; d. Peter Graham III and Fannie Isadora (Bennett) Graham; m. Charles Milton Rhodes, Oct. 14, 1971; children: Helen, Carla, Shauna. BS, East Stroudsburg U. Pa., 1962; MS, U. Pa., 1966, LLB, 1969, JD, 1970. Bar: N.Y. 1970, U.S. Dist. Ct. (so. and ea. dists.) N.Y. 1971, U.S. Ct. Appeals (2d cir.) 1971, Ky. 1983, U.S. Dist. Ct. (ea. dist.) Ky. 1985, 69-72. Staff atty. OEO, HAR, MFY, N.Y.C., 1969-70; coord. Cmty. Action Legal Svcs., N.Y.C., 1970-72; assoc. dir. HUD Model Cities Cmty. Law Offices, N.Y.C., 1972-73; resource assoc. Commn. on Women, N.C. Dept. Adminstrn., Raleigh, 1975-76; mgr. policies and procedures Div. for Youth, N.C. Dept. Human Resources, Raleigh, 1976; petroleum atty. Ashland (Ky.) Oil, Inc., 1980-82, corp. atty., 1985-87, 88-91; Ashland City Commn. Human Rights, 1993—; bd. regents Ea. Ky. U., 1994—; mem. task force on sex discrimination ins. N.C. Dept. Ins., 1976; mem. disciplinary appeals com. bd. regents Ea. Ky. U., 1994—; mem. Property Valuation Appeals Commn., 1994—; pub. mem. selection and performance review bd. Fgn. Svc., U.S. Dept. State, 1995. Mem. Usher bd. New Hope Bapt. Ch., Ashland, 1980-94; bd. dirs. YWCA Ashland, 1983-84; bd. dirs. Ashland Heritage Pk. Commn., 1983-85; bd. dirs., budget com. United Way, Greenup County, Ashland, 1988-92; driver Meals on Wheels, Ashland, 1983-91; vol. Am. Heart Assn., 1982-91; bd. dirs. Our Lady of Bellefonte Hosp. Found. (Franciscan Sisters of the Poor), 1996—. Recipient Community Svc. award Queens Community Corp., N.Y.C., 1972, Ashland Community Coll., 1986; NSF fellow, 1964, 65, Reginald Heber Smith fellow 1969; faculty friends of Pa. scholar U. Pa., 1966-69; named to Hon. Order of Ky. Cols. Fellow Ky. Bar Found.; mem. AMA, KMA, AAUW (bd. dirs. Phila. 1963-65), Nat. Bar Assn., N.Y. Bar, Ky. Bar Assn., Boyd County Bar Assn., Pilot Club (exec. bd. Ashland 1983), Links, Inc., Paramount Women's Assn., Penn Club Alliance, Aux. Our Lady of Bellefonte Hosp., Pub. Mems. Assn. of Fgn. Svc. Democrat. Home: 507 Country Club Dr Ashland KY 41101-2143

RHODES, ANN L., theatrical producer, invester; b. Ft. Worth, Oct. 17, 1941; d. Jon Knox and Carol Jane (Greene) R.; student Tex. Christian U., 1960-63. V.p. Rhodes Enterprises Inc., Ft. Worth, 1963-77; owner-mgr. Lucky R Ranch, Ft. Worth, 1969—, Ann L. Rhodes Investments, Ft. Worth, 1976—; pres., chmn. bd. ALR Enterprises, Inc., Ft. Worth, 1977-93; pres. ALR Prodns., Inc., 1993—. Bd. dirs. Tarrant Coun. Alcoholism, 1973-78, hon. bd. dirs., 1978—; bd. dirs. N.W. Tex. coun. Arthritis Found., 1977-84; adv. bd. Stage West, 1987—, Hip Pocket Theatre, 1994—; bd. dirs. Circle Theater, 1987-94, Arts Coun. of Ft. Worth and Tarrant County, 1991-94; bd. govs. Ft. Worth Theatre, 1989—; mem. pro-arts bd. TCU Coll. Fine Arts & Communications, 1994, exec. com. Tarrant County Rep. Party, 1964-69; bd. dirs. Live Theatre League Tarrant County, 1993—, Casa Mañana Theatre, 1993—, exec. com., 1995—. Recipient various svc. awards, including Patron of Yr. award Live Theatre League Tarrant County, 1992-93. Mem. Jr. League Ft. Worth, Addison and Randolph Clark Soc. Tex. Christian U., Alpha Psi Omega, Kappa Kappa Gamma. Episcopalian. Office: Ste 908 Ridglea Bank Bldg Fort Worth TX 76116

RHODES, BETTY MOORE, elementary education educator; b. Suffolk, Va., Aug. 23, 1963; d. Albert Eugene and Phyllis Imogene (Byrum) Moore; m. Robert Joseph Rhodes, Dec. 29, 1985. BA in Elem. Edn., Coll. William and Mary, 1985. Cert. tchr. 5th grade tchr. Virginia Beach (Va.) City Pub. Schs., 1985—; aerobics instr. Chesapeake (Va.) Gen. Hosp., 1987—. Mem. Suffolk Bus. and Profl. Women, 1990-92; chmn. women's fellowship Suffolk Christian Ch., 1993-95. Mem. NEA, Va. Edn. Assn., Virginia Beach Edn. Assn., Virginia Beach Reading Coun. Home: 4497 Chatham Rd Suffolk VA 23435-2830 Office: Kempsville Elem Sch Kempsville Rd Virginia Beach VA 23464

RHODES, HELEN MARY, real estate broker, educator; b. Ft. Branch, Ind., Jan. 12, 1921; d. Henry A. and Anna J. (Herr) Wirth; m. David A. I, May 3, 1952; children: David A. II and Brooke Anthony. Grad., Lockyear Coll., 1939, Real Estate Inst., 1981. Grad. Realtors Inst. Clk. War Dept., Washington, 1942-44; stenographer OSS, Washington (D.C.), 1944-45; clk. Dept. of Fgn. Svc., London, 1945-46; asst. sales mgr. printing and advt. Keller Crescent Co., Evansville, Ind., 1946-52; stenographer Indpls. Air Procurement, Evansville, 1952-53; asst. media dir. Grant Advt., 1953-56; freelance writer, 1955-70; prin. real estate Columbus, Ohio, 1970—; real estate instr. Columbus State Community Coll., 1977—. Author: Josie's Bedtime Stories, 1966; writer Chicago Heights Star, Ill., 1961-61; contbr. articles to profl. jours. Pub. rels. officer Sauk Village, Ill., 1962. Mem. Nat. Assn. Realtors, Ohio Assn. Realtors, Columbus Bd. Realtors, Nat. Real Estate Educators Assn. (charter), Ohio Real Estate Educators Assn.

RHODES, LINDA JANE, psychiatrist; b. San Antonio, May 23, 1950; d. George Vernon and Lucy Agnes (O'Dowd) R. BA, Trinity U., 1972; MD, U. Tex. Med. Br., 1975. Diplomate Am. Bd. Pediat. Resident in pediat. U. Tex. Med. Br., Galveston, 1975-78; fellow in ambulatory pediat. U. Tex. Health Sci. Ctr., Houston, 1978-80; asst. prof. psychiatry U. Tex. Health Sci. Ctr., San Antonio, 1995—, resident in psychiatry, 1990-92, child and adolescent psychiatrist, fellow in biol. psychiatry, 1992-95; pediatrician Kelsey Seybold Clinic, P.A., Houston, 1980-95; pediat. rep. Tex. Lay Midwifery Bd. Tex. Dept. Health, Austin, 1994—. Active San Antonio Conservation Soc., San Antonio Zool. Soc., San Antonio Mus. Assn., Trinity U. Assocs., 1992—, Witte Mus. Assn.; patron McNay Art Inst. Fellow Am. Acad. Pediat.; mem. Am. Psychiat. Assn., Ambulatory Pediat. Assn., Tex. Pediat. Soc., Tex. Soc. Psychiat. Physicians, Tex. Acad. Child and Adolescent Psychiatry, Am. Med. Women's Assn., Am. Soc. Clin. Psychopharmacology, Tex. Med. Assn., AMA, Bexar County Psychiat. Soc. Office: U Tex Health Sci Ctr-SA Dept Psychiatry/Divsn Biol 7703 Floyd Curl Dr San Antonio TX 78284-7792

RHODES, MARLENE RUTHERFORD, counseling educator, educational consultant; b. St. Louis; d. Odie Douglas and Helen (Ward) Rutherford; m. David L. Rhodes, Nob. 18, 1961; children: Jay David, Michael Stanford, John David, Mark Stanford. BS in Psychology cum laude, Washington U., St. Louis, 1973, MA in Counseling Edn., 1975; postgrad., St. Louis U., 1987—. Registered med. record libr. Caseworker I and II, Mo. Div. Family Svcs., St. Louis, 1961-65, supr. caseworker II's, 1965-70; personal effectiveness trainer women's program U. Mo., St. Louis, 1974-77; assoc. prof. counseling, chair counseling St. Louis C.C. at Forest Park, 1975—, chmn. dept., 1993—, dir. step up coll. program, 1990-93; developer, coord. crisis intervention facilitation tng. St. Louis Pub. Schs., 1987-88; ednl. project cons. Project Achievement, Ralston Purina Co., 1993-94; developer, presenter over 80 ednl. project consultations for area colls., profl. orgns. and bus. groups, 1975—. Author: Crisis Intervention Facilitation Training Manual, 1988. Chmn. Ft. Louis Friends of Arts, 1984—; coord. for coun. of elders for Better Family Life Orgn., 1995—; com. co-chmn. for black dance and unity ball Better Family Inc., St. Louis, 1990—; panelist for counseling support svcs. for families United Way Greater St. Louis, 1993—; mem. fin. com. St. Thomas Archdiocese, 1995—; bd. dirs. Bishop Hearly Cath. Sch. Recipient Disting. Svc. as Am. Educator award Alpha Zeta chpt. Iota Phi Lambda, 1990, role model award St. Louis Pub. Schs., 1993, cert. of achievement Nat. Orgn. for Victim Assistance, 1993. Mem. NEA (co-coord. polit. action com. St. Louis 1985-90, bargaining negotiator 1987—), ACA (nat. chair orgn., adminstrn. and mgmt. com. 1994-95), Assn. Multicultural Counseling and Devel. (nat. pres. 1994-95), Nat. Assn. for Multicultural Counseling and Devel. (rep. for 13 states 1990-92, pres. 1994-95, Exemplary Svc. award 1992, 94), Mo. Assn. Multicultural Counseling and Devel. (chpt. pres. 1977-78). Democrat. Roman Catholic. Home: 5935 Pershing Ave Saint Louis MO 63112-1513 Office: St Louis CC at Forest Park 5600 Oakland Ave Saint Louis MO 63110-1316

RHODES, RHODA ELLEN, gifted education educator; b. Chgo., Aug. 20, 1941; d. Nathan and Pearl (Wald) Krichilsky; m. Mitchell Lee Rhodes, Aug. 4, 1963; children: Steven, Dana, Jeffrey. BEd, Chgo. Tchrs. Coll., 1963; MEd in Curriculum and Instrn., Nat. Louis U., Evanston, Ill., 1989. Tchr. Harvey (Ill.) Sch. Dist. 152, 1963-66; tchr., curr. developer Indpls. Hebrew Congregation, 1982-84; tchr. gifted primary pilot program Indpls. Pub. Schs., 1984; coord./tchr. gifted edn. Highland Park-Highwood Sch. Dist. 111, Ill., 1986-89; project discovery tchr. gifted edn. Waukegan (Ill.) Community Sch. Dist. 60, 1989-90; gifted edn. tchr. Kildeer Countryside Sch. Dist. 96, Buffalo Grove, Ill., 1990—; bd. dir. Lake County Adv. Bd. Gifted Edn., Grayslake, Ill., 1992—; profl. adv. bd. Sycamore Sch. for Gifted, Indpls., 1984-85; lectr. Barat Coll., Ill., 1995. Plan comm. mem. Washington Twp. Pub. Schs., Indpls., 1984-85; bd. dir. Bur. Jewish Edn., Indpls., 1979-81. Mem. ASCD, Kildeer Edn. Assn., Ill. Assn. Gifted. Office: Kildeer Countryside SD 96 Willow Grove Sch 555 Checker Dr Buffalo Grove IL 60089-1645

RHODES, SUSAN E., pharmaceuticals executive; b. Springfield, Mo., Jan. 25, 1954; d. Alan Duryea and Joyce Elaine (Pine) Sutherland. AA, Santa Fe Community Coll., Gainesville, Fla., 1973; BA, U. of South Fla., 1976; attended mgmt. and supr. program, Wilmington Coll., 1983. Clin. rsch. asst. Janssen Pharms., Piscataway, N.J.; clin. rsch. assoc. DuPont Pharms., Wilmington, Del.; sr. clin. rsch. assoc. Schering Rsch Key Pharms., Miami; sr. clin. rsch. assoc. and asst. project mgr. Clin Rsch. Internat., Rsch. Triangle Park, N.C.; group leader, project mgr. Clin Rsch. Internat., Rsch. Triangle Park; asst. bus. devel. mgr., project mgr., GHBA/PACT Clin Rsch. Internat., Rsch Triangle Park, St. Davids, Pa.; sr. project mgr. Pharmaco LSD, Austin, Tex.; cons. Austin, Tex., Med. Trials, Dallas, Tex. Mem. NAFE, NOW, Psi Chi. Home: 301 N Marlborough Ave Dallas TX 75208

RHONE, SYLVIA, recording industry executive; b. Philadelphia, PA, Mar. 11, 1952; d. James and Marie (Christmas) R.; 1 daughter, Quinn. M.A., Wharton Sch. Bus. U. Pa., 1974. Dir. nat. black music promotion Atlantic Records, New York, N.Y., 1985-88; Sr. V.P. Atlantic Records, New York, N.Y., 1988-91; chair/CEO EastWest Records America, New York, N.Y., 1991—; chair Elektra Entertainment, N.Y.C., N.Y., 1994—. Mem., bd. dirs. Alvin Ailey Am. Dance Theatre, The RIAA, Rock n' Roll Hall of Fame, Jazz at Lincoln Ctr., R&B Found. Office: Elektra Enterntainment 75 Rockefeller Plz New York NY 10016

RIBBLE, ANNE HOERNER, communications representative; b. Balt., Oct. 30, 1932; B.A., Smith Coll., 1954; M.A., Harvard U., 1955; m. John C. Ribble, July 26, 1974; tech. asst. IBM, N.Y.C., 1958-63, editor, Armonk and White Plains, N.Y., 1969-75, mgr. editorial services data processing div., White Plains, 1976-77, program adminstr. systems communications div., N.Y.C., 1977-78, staff tech. edn., fed. systems div., Houston, 1978-80, info. rep., 1980-87, staff info. IBM Federal Systems Co., 1988-93; prin. Creative Commn., 1993—. Bd. dirs. Stanley Isaacs Community Center, N.Y.C., 1968-72; mem. United Way allocations com., Houston, 1989-94. Mem. Pub. Rels. Soc. Am. (accredited), Internat. Assn. Bus. Communicators (pres. Houston chpt. 1982, community rels. dir. 1989-92), Women In Communications Inc. (program v.p. 1994-95). Home: 6200 Willers Way Houston TX 77057-2808 Office: Creative Commn 6355 Westheimer Rd # 171 Houston TX 77057-5103

RIBBLE, KAREN LEIGH, telecommunications company official; b. Phoenix, Oct. 24, 1962; d. Leonard Dale and Bettye Ruth (Bentley) Hagan; m. David R. Ribble, Sept. 3, 1983; children: Ian Russel, Erika Leigh. BS in Mgmt. Info. Sys., U. Ariz., 1984. Network planning analyst GTE Calif., Long Beach, 1984-91; adminstr. GTE Calif., Huntington Beach, 1991-95. Mem. NAFE. Home: 4094 Quinn Dr Evans GA 30809

RIBEIRO, MICHELE DENISE, family therapist; b. Shirley, Mass., Nov. 7, 1969; d. Anthony Joseph and Anna-Marie (Scheirer) R. BS in Psychology, Appalachian State U., 1991; MS in Agy. Counseling, Ind. State U., 1994. Residential counselor Life Resources/Malta House, Brockton, Mass., 1994-95; staff therapist South Bay Mental Health, Plymouth, Mass., 1995—. Youth outdoor leader Appalachian Mt. Club Youth Opportunities Program, Boston, 1995—; vol. home support svcs. AIDS Action Com., Boston, 1995—. Mem. ACA, Internat. Assn. Marriage and Family Counselors, Specialists in Group Work, Mass. Counseling Assn.

RIDEN, MIRAH (MARSHA RIBEN), author, secretary; b. Bklyn., Jan. 26, 1945; d. Jack F. and Frances (Goldstein) Klein; m. Todd Riben, Nov. 29, 1971 (div. Dec. 1992); children: Adam, Matthew, Adira. Student, Rutgers U., 1994—. Assoc. mag. editor Volitant/Lopez Pub., N.Y.C., 1969-73; real estate assoc. ERA Designs for Living, Old Bridge, N.J., 1987-88; prin. sec. Rutgers U., New Brunswick, N.J., 1990—; substitue tchr. S.I. (N.Y.) C.C., 1990. Author: shedding light on...The Dark Side of Adoption, 1988; appeared in TV programs, including Morton Downey Jr., 1987, Joan Rivers, 1989, Rivera Live, 1994; contbr. articles to profl. jours.; revs., presenter in field. Co-founder, group leader, former newsletter editor of ORIGINS (nat. orgn. for women who have lost children to adoption, N.J. chpt.); v.p. Voorhees Sch. PTA, Old Bride, N.J., 1980. Recipient Author of the Year award People Searching News, 1989. Am. Adoption Congress (former dir.-at-large, event chmn.), La Leche League Internat. (former lactation cons., group leader, former editor of Garden Statements, N.J. State newsletter). Home: 43 Allison Ct Monmouth Junction NJ 08852 Office: Rutgers Univ Foran Hall Cook Campus New Brunswick NJ 08903

RICARDO-CAMPBELL, RITA, economist, educator; b. Boston, Mar. 16, 1920; d. David and Elizabeth (Jones) Ricardo; m. Wesley Glenn Campbell, Sept. 15, 1946; children: Barbara Lee, Diane Rita, Nancy Elizabeth. BS, Simmons Coll., 1941; MA, Harvard U., 1945, PhD, 1946. Instr. Harvard U., Cambridge, Mass., 1946-48; asst. prof. Tufts U., Medford, Mass., 1948-51; labor economist U.S. Wage Stabilization Bd., 1951-53; economist Ways and Means Com. U.S. Ho. of Reps., 1953; cons. economist, 1957-60; vis. prof. San Jose State Coll., 1960-61; sr. fellow Hoover Instn. on War, Revolution, and Peace, Stanford, Calif., 1968-95, sr. fellow emerita, 1995—; lectr. health svc. adminstrn. Stanford U. Med. Sch., 1973-78; bd. dirs. Watkins-Johnson Co., Palo Alto, Calif., Gillette Co., Boston; mgmt. bd. Samaritan Med. Ctr., San Jose, Calif. Author: Voluntary Health Insurance in the U.S., 1960, Economics of Health and Public Policy, 1971, Food Safety Regulation: Use and Limitations of Cost-Benefit Analysis, 1974, Drug Lag: Federal Government Decision Making, 1976, Social Security: Promise and Reality, 1977, The Economics and Politics of Health, 1982, 2d edit., 1985; co-editor: Below-Replacement Fertility in Industrial Societies, 1987, Issues in Contemporary Retirement, 1988; contbr. articles to profl. jours. Commr. Western Interstate Commn. for Higher Edn. Calif., 1967-75, chmn., 1970-71; mem. Pres. Nixon's Adv. Coun. on Status Women, 1969-76; mem. task force on taxation Pres.'s Coun. on Environ. Quality, 1970-72; mem. Pres.'s Com. Health Services Industry, 1971-73, FDA Nat. Adv. Drug Com., 1972-75; mem. Econ. Policy Adv. Bd., 1981-90, Pres. Reagan's Nat. Coun. on Humanities, 1982-89, Pres. Nat. Medal of Sci. com., 1988-94; bd. dirs. Ind. Colls. No. Calif., 1971-87; mem. com. assessment of safety, benefits, risks Citizens Commn. Sci., Law and Food Supply, Rockefeller U., 1973-75; mem. adv. com. Ctr. Health Policy Rsch., Am. Enterprise Inst. Pub. Policy Rsch., Washington, 1974-80; mem. adv. coun. on social security Social Security Adminstrn., 1974-75; bd. dirs. Simmons Coll. Corp., Boston, 1975-80; mem. adv. coun. bd. assocs. Stanford Librs., 1975-78; mem. coun. SRI Internat., Menlo Park, Calif., 1977-90. Mem. Am. Econ. Assn., Mont Pelerin Soc. (bd. dirs. 1988-92, v.p. 1992-94), Harvard Grad. Soc. (coun. 1991), Phi Beta Kappa. Home: 26915 Alejandro Dr Los Altos Hills CA 94022-1932 Office: Stanford U Hoover Instn Stanford CA 94305-6010

RICARTE, MARIA-CHRISTINA, lawyer; b. Havana, Sept. 28, 1965. AA, Miami Dade C.C., 1985; BA, U. Miami, 1989; JD, Fordham U., 1992. Bar: N.J. 1992, N.Y. 1993. Ptnr. Anderson Kill Olick & Oshinsky, N.Y.C. Mng. editor: Fordham Intellectual Property Media and Entertainment Law Jour. Mem. Assn. of Bar of City of N.Y., N.Y. State Bar Assn., ABA. Office: Anderson Kill Olick & Oshinsky 1251 Ave of the Americas New York NY 10020-1182*

RICCIARDI, CHRISTINE SECOLA, international trade consultant; b. New Haven, Apr. 19, 1963; d. Carl Albert and Marie Rose (Pupello) Secola; m. Carmine C. Ricciardi, Nov. 24, 1990. BA, Fairfield (Conn.) U., 1985. Editl. asst. Conn. Woman Mag., Fairfield, 1984-85; corr. internat. money transfer divsn. Chase Manhattan Bank, N.Y.C., 1985-86; editor employee comm. Port Authority of N.Y. & N.J., N.Y.C., 1986-88; internat. trade assn. adminstr. World Trade Ctrs. Assn., Inc., N.Y.C., 1988-95, dir. mem. svcs., 1990-95; ind. cons., 1995—. Editor, contbg. author Corporate Comm., 1986-95; contbg. writer newspaper and mag. articles and trade publs., 1988—. Vol. mem. Conn. Spl. Olympics Com., 1981-82; big sister Conn. Big Sister Program, Bridgeport, 1984-85. Recipient Good Citizenship award City of Hamden, Conn., 1981. Mem. Am. Soc. Assn. Execs., Internat. Assn. Bus. Communicators, Alpha Mu Gamma, Nat. Lang. Honor Soc.

RICE, (ETHEL) ANN, publishing executive, editor; b. South Bend, Ind., July 3, 1933; d. Walter A. and Ethylan Maude (Worden) R. A.B., Nazareth Coll., Kalamazoo, 1955. Editorial asst. Ave Maria mag., Notre Dame, Ind., 1955-63, asst. editor, 1963-64; asst. editor Today mag., Notre Dame, 1963-64, Scott, Foresman & Co., Chgo., 1964-67; editor U. Notre Dame Press, 1967-74, exec. editor, 1974—. Democrat. Roman Catholic. Office: U Notre Dame Press Notre Dame IN 46556

RICE, ANNE, author; b. New Orleans, Oct. 14, 1941; d. Howard and Katherine (Allen) O'Brien; m. Stan Rice, Oct. 14, 1961; children: Michele (dec.), Christopher. Student, Tex. Woman's U., 1959-60; BA, San Francisco State Coll., 1964, MA, 1971. Author: Interview with the Vampire, 1976, The Feast of all Saints, 1980, Cry to Heaven, 1982, The Vampire Lestat, 1985, The Queen of the Damned, 1988, The Mummy or Ramses the Damned, 1989, The Witching Hour, 1990, Tale of the Body Thief, 1992, Lasher, 1993, Taltos, 1994, Memnoch the Devil, 1995; (as A.N. Roquelaure) The Claiming of Sleeping Beauty, 1983, Beauty's Punishment, 1984, Beauty's Release: The Continued Erotic Adventures of Sleeping Beauty, 1985, Memnoch the Devil, Servant of the Bone, 1996; (as Anne Rampling) Exit to Eden, 1985, Belinda, 1986; screenwriter: Interview with a Vampire, 1994. Office: care Alfred A Knopf Inc 201 E 50th St New York NY 10022-7703*

RICE, ANNIE L. KEMPTON, medical, surgical and rehabilitation nurse; b. West Fairlee, Vt., Oct. 26, 1932; d. James Warren and Lena May (Bower); m. Abbott Eames Rice, Aug. 29, 1959; children: James W., Beverly A., Abbott Jr., David K. Diploma, Mary Hitchcock Sch. Nursing, Hanover, N.H., 1955; student, U. R.I., 1956-57; BSN, Boston U., 1959; postgrad., St. Anthlems Coll., Manchester, N.H. RN. Staff nurse spl. care unit R.I. Hosp., 1955; staff nurse New Eng. Deaconess Hosp., Boston, 1957; head nurse Jordan Hosp, Plymouth, Mass., 1960; staff nurse ICU/emergency Lakes Region Hosp., Laconia, N.H., 1968; staff nurse Pine Hill Nurses Registry, Nashua, N.H., 1976; charge nurse Greenbriar Terr., Nashua, 1985—. Past mem. Arthritis Found. Mem. Mary Hitchcock Sch. Nursing Alumnae, Boston U. Alumnae, Ea. Star, Grange, Women's Club. Home: 28 Sunland Dr Hudson NH 03051-3209

RICE, ARGYLL PRYOR, Hispanic studies and Spanish language educator; b. Va.; d. Theodorick Pryor and Argyll (Campbell) R. BA, Smith Coll., 1952; MA, Yale U., 1956, PhD, 1961. Spanish instr. Yale U., New Haven, 1959-60, 61-63; asst. prof. Spanish, Conn. Coll., New London, 1964-67, assoc. prof., 1967-72, prof., 1972—, chair dept. Hispanic Studies, 1971-74, 77-84. Author: Emilio Ballagas: poeta o poesia, 1967, Emilio Ballagas, Latin American Writers III; editor in chief Carlos A. Sole, Charles Scribner's Sons, 1989. Mem. MLA, Am. Assn. Tchrs. of Spanish and Portuguese, New Eng. Coun. Latin Am. Studies, U.S. Tennis Assn. (New England hall of fame), Phi Beta Kappa. Avocations: music, tennis. Home: 292 Pequot Ave New London CT 06320-4437

RICE, BARBARA LYNN, stage manager; b. Hartford, Conn., Nov. 9, 1955; d. Joe Roger and Betty Barbara (Baxter) R. BA in Theatre and French, Ind. U., 1978; MFA in Directing, U. Cin., 1982. Freelance stage mgr. N.Y.C.; dir. The Open Eye: New Stagings, N.Y.C., 1989; prodn. stage mgr. Belmont Italian-Am. Playhouse, N.Y.C., 1994, 95; prodn. asst. Silence, Cunning, Exile, N.Y.C., 1995; asst. stage mgr. The Merry Wives of Windsor, N.Y.C., 1995. Dir. The Open Eye: New Stagings, N.Y.C., 1989; stage mgr. 20 Years Ago Today, Cin., 1989, Fourscore & 7 Years Ago, Paramus, N.J., 1989-90, Hanging the President, N.Y.C., 1990; prodn. asst. Kiss of the Spiderwoman, Purchase, N.Y., 1990, (off-Broadway) Beau Jest, N.Y.C., 1992, Belmont Italian-Am. Playhouse, N.Y.C., 1994, 95. Mem. Actors' Equity Assn., Stage Mgrs. Assn. Presbyterian. Home: 412 W 56th St Apt 10 New York NY 10019-3647

RICE, CHARLENE RUSSELL, human resources professional, consultant; b. Knoxville, Tenn., May 25, 1952; d. Julian Frank and Elizabeth J. (Johnson) Russell; m. Barry L. Rice, Oct. 10, 1980 (div. Oct. 1990); 1 child, Brian C. BS in Bus. Adminstrn., U. Tenn., 1975, MS in Ednl. Psychology, 1985. Staff asst. U. Tenn. Office Human Resources, Knoxville, 1977-81, employment mgr., 1981-86, compensation mgr., 1986-94, rsch. mgr., 1995—; cons. Univ. Cons., Knoxville, Tenn., 1989-94. Bd. pres. Planned Parenthood of East Tenn., 1990-93; vice-chmn., mem. Affiliate Pres.'s Coun. Planned Parenthood Fedn. Am., 1992-95; vice-chmn. Southern Region Coun. Planned Parenthood Fedn. Am., 1995—; loaned exec. United Way of Greater Knoxville, Tenn., 1995. Recipient Vol. of Yr. award Planned Parenthood of East Tenn., Inc., 1989. Mem. Am. Compensation Assn. (cert. compensation profl.), East Tenn. Compensation Assn. (pres. 1994-95). Republican. Baptist. Home: 2319 Gorby Way Knoxville TN 37923

RICE, CONSTANCE ELIZABETH, quality assurance professional; b. Orange, N.J., Oct. 18, 1950; d. William Taylor and Joan Ruth Rice. BS in Chemistry, Hobart and William Smith Coll., Geneva, N.Y., 1972. Imaging devel. engr. Eastman Kodak Co., Rochester, N.Y., 1972-76, prodn. engr., 1976-79, quality engr., 1979-86, product staff supr., 1986-89, quality sys. mgr., 1989—. Mem. Am. Soc. Quality Control, Women's Forum Kodak Employees. Office: Eastman Kodak Co Kodak Park Rochester NY 14652-5667

RICE, DIANE S., lawyer; b. Pitts., Feb. 19, 1958. BA cum laude, U. Notre Dame, 1980, JD cum laude, 1983. Bar: Conn. 1983, Fla. 1984, Fla. 1985. Ptnr. Brobeck, Phleger & Harrison, San Francisco. White scholar White Ctr. for Law and Pub. Policy. Mem. ABA (rep. State of Calif. young lawyers divsn. 1988-90), Calif. Young Lawyers (bd. dirs. 1990-91), Notre Dame Assn. (bd. dirs. 1987—), Barristers Club of San Francisco (bd. dirs., sec. 1986-87, pres. 1987-88. Office: Brobeck Phleger & Harrison Spear St Tower 1 Market Plz San Francisco CA 94105*

RICE, DOROTHY PECHMAN (MRS. JOHN DONALD RICE), medical economist; b. Bklyn., June 11, 1922; d. Gershon and Lena (Schiff) Pechman; m. John Donald Rice, Apr. 3, 1943; children: Kenneth D., Donald B., Thomas H. Student, Bklyn. Coll., 1938-39; BA, U. Wis., 1941; DSc (hon.), Coll. Medicine and Dentistry N.J., 1979. With hosp., and med. facilities USPHS, Washington, 1960-61; med. econs. studies Social Security Adminstrn., 1962-63; health econs. br. Community Health Svc., USPHS, 1964-65; chief health ins. rsch. br. Social Security Adminstrn., 1966-72, dep. asst. commr. for rsch. and statistics, 1972-75; dir. Nat. Ctr. for Health Stats., Rockville, Md., 1976-82; prof. Inst. Health & Aging U. Calif., San Francisco, 1982-94, prof. emeritus, 1994—; developer, mgr. nationwide health info. svcs.; expert on aging, health care costs, disability, and cost-of-illness. Contbr. articles to profl. jours. Recipient Social Security Adminstrn. citation, 1968, Disting. Service medal HEW, 1974, Jack C. Massey Found. award, 1978. Fellow Am. Public Health Assn. (domestic award for excellence 1978, Sedgwick Meml. medal, 1988), Am. Statis. Assn.; mem. Inst. Medicine, Assn. Health Scvs. Rsch. (President's award 1988), Am. Econ. Assn., Population Assn. Am., LWV. Home: 13895 Campus Dr Oakland CA 94605-3831 Office: U Calif Sch Nursing Calif San Francisco CA 94143-0646

RICE, ELIZABETH JANE, lawyer; b. Ottawa, Ill., Oct. 5, 1949; d. John Evans and Mabel Jane (Peck) Jackson: m. Charles R. Rice, Dec. 12, 1979; 1 dau., Amy Elizabeth. BA, Ill. Wesleyan U., 1971; JD, Chgo. Kent Coll. Law, Ill. Inst. Tech., 1980. Bar: Ill. 1980, U.S. Dist. Ct. (no. dist.) Ill. 1980. Pub. aid caseworker Ill. Dept. Pub. Aid, Ottawa, Ill., 1974-78, casework supr., 1978-83; asst. state's atty. LaSalle County, Ill., 1983-89; atty. John L. Cantlin P.C. & Assocs. Attys. at Law, Ottawa, Ill., 1989—. Class of 1971 agt. Ill. Wesleyan Alumni Fund, Bloomington, 1978-83; mem. exec. bd. Parent Tchr. Orgn., Jefferson Sch., Ottawa, 1983-84; mem. exec. bd. Ottawa chpt. ARC, 1983-84. Mem. AAUW, LaSalle County Bar Assn., Ill. State Bar Assn., ABA, Am. Legion Auxilliary, Zonta, LaSalle County Geneal. Soc.. Presbyterian. Club: Roaming Wheeles Touring (bd. dirs. 1980-87) (Streator, Ill.). Home: 619 Adams St Ottawa IL 61350-3803 Office: John L Cantlin PC & Assoc 223 W Madison St Ottawa IL 61350

RICE, FERILL JEANE, writer, civic worker; b. Hemingford, Nebr., July 4, 1926; d. Derrick and Helen Agnes (Moffatt) Dalton; m. Otis LaVerne Rice, Mar. 7, 1946; children: LaVeria June McMichael, Larry L. Student, U. Omaha, 1961. Dir. jr. and sr. choir Congl. Ch., Tabor, Iowa, 1952-66; tchr. Fox Valley Tech. Inst., Appleton, Wis., 1970-77; activity dir. Family Heritage Nursing Home, Appleton, Wis., 1972-75; dir. activity Peabody Manor, Appleton, Wis., 1975-76. Editor: Moffatt and Related Families, 1981; asst. editor (mag.) Yester-Year, 1975-76; contbr. articles to profl jours. Chmn. edn. Am. Cancer Soc., Fremont County, 1962, 63, 64; founder, 1st pres. Mothers Club Nishna Valley chpt. Demolay for Boys. Mem. DAR, Internat. Carnival Glass Assn., Heart Am. Carnival Glass Assn., Nat. Cambridge Collectors, Heisey Collectors Am., Iowa Fedn. Women's Clubs (Fremont county chmn. 1964, 65, 66, 67, 7th dist. chmn. libr. svcs. 1966-67), Tabor Women's Club (pres. 1962, 63, 64), Jr. Legion Aux. (founder, 1st dir. 1951-52), Fenton Art Glass Collectors Am. (co-founder 1977, sec., editor newsletter 1976-86, editor/sec. 1988-93, pres./editor 1993-95, treas. 1995—), Mayflower Soc., John Howland Soc., Ross County Ohio Geneal. Soc., Iowa Geneal. Soc., Dallas County Mo. Geneal. Soc., Imperial Collectors Am., Clay County (Ind.) Geneal. Soc., Owen County (Ind.) Geneal. Soc., Fenton Finders of Wis. (chpt. #1 pres. 1988-90). Republican. Methodist: Lodges: Order Ea. Star (worthy matron 1956, 64), Rainbow for Girls (bd. dirs. 1964), Internat. Order Job's Daus. (honored queen 1945). Home: 302 Pheasant Run Kaukauna WI 54130-1802 Office: Rice Enterprises & Rice & Rice 1665 Lamers Dr # 305 Little Chute WI 54140-2519

RICE, FRANCES MAE, pediatrician; b. Oakland, Calif., Apr. 19, 1931; d. George Henry and Clare Evelyn (Youngman) Rice. AB cum laude, U. Calif., Berkeley, 1953, MPH, 1964; MD, U. Calif., San Francisco, 1957. Intern U. Calif. Hosp., San Francisco, 1957-58; pediatric resident U. Calif., San Francisco, 1959-61; pediatric and family physician HMO, Hanford, Calif., 1974-75; clin. pediatrician Kern County Health Dept., Bakersfield, Calif., 1975-76; physician Kern Med. Group, Inc., Bakersfield, 1976-83; pvt. practice Shafter, Calif., 1983-89; physician Kern County Health Dept., Bakersfield, 1989, Mercy Medicenter, Bakersfield, 1990-91, K.C.E.O.C. Family Clinic, Bakersfield, 1993—. USPHS fellow, 1963-64. Fellow Royal Soc. Medicine; mem. AMA, N.Y. Acad. Sci., Calif. Med. Assn. Home: 5909 Lindbrook Way Bakersfield CA 93309 Office: KCEOC Family Health Clinic 1611 1st St Bakersfield CA 93304

RICE, KATHRYN JANE, special education educator, reading specialist; b. Potsdam, N.Y., Aug. 4, 1965; d. Arthur and Dorothy (Peterson) Rivers; m. John F. Rice II. AS, Onondaga C.C., 1985; BS, Syracuse U., 1989, MS, 1993. Cert. reading and spl. edn. tchr., N.Y., N.H. Tchr.'s asst. St. Lawrence County BOCES, Canton, N.Y., 1985-87; spl. edn. tchr. Dansville (N.Y.) Primary Sch., 1990, Liverpool (N.Y.) H.S., 1990-91, Fayetteville-Manlius (N.Y.) Schs., 1991-92; grad. asst. Syracuse (N.Y.) U., 1992-93; spl. edn. tchr. Oswego County BOCES, Mexico, N.Y., 1993-95; learning specialist Lyme (N.H.) Elem. Sch. Editl. and rsch. asst. Learning Disabilities: The Interaction of Learner, Task and Setting, 3d edit., 1993. Pres. grad. student adv. coun. Syracuse U., 1992-93. Mem. Internat. Reading Assn., Nat. Head Injury Assn., Alpha Sigma Lambda. Home: 16 High St Lebanon NH 03766 Office: Lyme Sch SAU #22 Lyme NH 03768

RICE, LINDA JOHNSON, publishing executive; b. Chgo., Mar. 22, 1958; d. John J. and Eunice Johnson; m. Andre Rice, 1984. BA Journalism, Univ. Southern California, Los angeles, 1980; MBA, Northwestern Univ., Evanston, 1988. With Johnson Pub. Co., 1980—, past v.p. and asst. to pub., pres., 1987—, also chief oper. officer. *

RICE, LOIS DICKSON, former computer company executive; b. Portland, Maine, Feb. 28, 1933; d. David A. and Mary D. Dickson; m. Alfred B. Fitt, Jan. 7, 1978 (dec. 1992); children: Susan, John Rice. A.B. magna cum laude, Radcliffe Coll., 1954; postgrad. (Woodrow Wilson fellow), Columbia U., 1954-55; LL.D. (hon.), Brown U., 1981, Bowdoin Coll., 1984. Dir. counseling services Nat. Scholarship Service and Fund for Negro Students, N.Y.C., 1955-59; with The Coll. Bd., N.Y.C. and Washington, 1959-81; v.p. The Coll. Bd., Washington, 1973-81; sr. v.p. govt. affairs, bd. dirs. Control Data Corp., 1981-91; guest scholar The Brookings Inst., Washington, 1991—; bd. dirs. McGraw Hill Inc., Bell Atlantic, Washington, Hartford Steam Boiler Inspection and Ins. Co., Internat. Multifoods, Shawmut Nat. Corp., UNUM Corp.; overseer Tuck Sch. Mgmt. Dartmouth Coll., 1990-94; mem. Pres. Fgn. Intelligence adv. bd., 1993—; trustee George Washington U., 1992-94. Contbr. articles on edn. to profl. publs.; editor: Student Loans: Problems and Policy Alternatives, 1977. Mem. Gov.'s Commn. on Future of Postsecondary Edn. in N.Y. State, 1976-77; mem. Carnegie Coun. on Higher Edn., 1975-80; bd. dirs. Potomac Inst., 1977-92, German Marshall Fund, 1984-94, Joint Ctr. Polit. and Econ. Studies, 1991-94, Harry Frank Guggenheim Found., 1990—, Reading is Fundamental, 1991—; trustee Radcliffe Coll., 1969-75, Stephens Coll., Mo., 1976-78, Beauvoir Sch., Washington, 1970-76, Children's TV Workshop, 1970-73; chmn. adv. bd. to dir. NSF, 1981-89, chair 1986-89. Recipient Disting. Service award HEW, 1977. Mem. Cosmos Club, Phi Beta Kappa. Episcopalian. Home: 2332 Massachusetts Ave NW Washington DC 20008-2801 Office: The Brookings Instn 1775 Massachusetts Ave NW Washington DC 20036-2188

RICE, MARY ESTHER, biologist; b. Washington, Aug. 3, 1926; d. Daniel Gibbons and Florence Catharine (Pyles) R. AB, Drew U., 1947; MA, Oberlin Coll., 1949; PhD, U. Wash., 1966. Instr. biology Drew U., Madison, N.J., 1949-50; rsch. assoc. Columbia U., N.Y.C., 1950-53; rsch. asst. NIH, Bethesda, Md., 1953-61; curator invertebrate zoology and dir. Smithsonian Marine Sta., Smithsonian Instn., Washington, 1966—; mem. adv. panel on systematic biology NSF, Washington, 1977-78; mem. com. on marine invertebrates Nat. Acad. Sci., 1976-81; mem. overseers com. on biology Harvard U., Cambridge, Mass., 1982-88. Assoc. editor Jour. Morphology, Ann Arbor, Mich., 1985-91, Invertebrate Biology, 1995—; editor: (with M. Todorovic) Biology of Sipuncula and Echiura, 1975, 2nd vol., 1976, (with F.S. Chia) Settlement and Metamorphosis of Marine Invertebrate Larvae, 1978, (with F.W. Harrison) Microscopic Anatomy of Invertebrates, Vol. 12, 1993; contbr. articles to profl. jours. Recipient Drew U. Alumni Achievement award in sci., 1980. Fellow AAAS; mem. Am. Soc. Zoologists (pres. 1979), Phi Beta Kappa. Office: Smithsonian Marine Sta 5612 Old Dixie Hwy Fort Pierce FL 34946-7303

RICE, MELVA GENE, retired education educator; b. Celeste, Tex., July 24, 1918; d. Lilbum Miller and Mary Ruth (Green) Powell; m. Clarence Prather Rice, Feb. 6, 1944; 1 child, Anna Rice Cleary. BS, East Tex. U., 1955, MEd, 1958. Cert. elem. tchr. Elem. tchr. Tidwell Ind. Sch., Greenville, Tex., 1938-39; prin. Merrick Ind. Sch., Greenville, 1942-44, Ctr. Pt. Ind. Sch., Greenville, 1944-45; office mgr. S.H. Kress and Co., Greenville, 1945-55; tchr. Greenville Ind. Schs., 1955-84; adj. prof. East Tex. State U., Commerce, 1985-95; ret., 1995—; dir., instr. summer enrichment Greenville Ind. Sch., 1961-63; supr. student tchrs. East Tex. State U., 1985-95. Soliciter silent auction Hunt County Mus., Greenville, 1991; bd. dirs. YMCA, Greenville, 1987-88; bell ringer, register Salvation Army, Greenville, 1980—; fund collector Am. Heart Assn., 1987-89; lifetime mem. Travis Elem. Sch. PTA, Greenville, 1983—. Fellow Ret. Tchrs. Assn., Tex. State Tchrs. Assn., Nat. Educators; mem. Delta Kappa Gamma (pres. 1964-66, auditor). Democrat. Baptist. Home: 14 Mullaney Dr Greenville TX 75402-6914

RICE, PAMELA SUE, nurse, consultant; b. Bloomington, Ill., Aug. 5, 1958. Diploma in nursing, Mennonite Hosp. Sch. Nursing, 1979; BSN, Mennonite Coll. Nursing, 1989. Cert. gastroenterology nurse; lic. pharmacy technician. Staff nurse Mennonite Hosp., Bloomington, Ill., 1979-83; office nurse, office mgr. Phaosawasdi & Phaosawasdi, Ltd., Bloomington, 1983-89, Digestive Disease Cons., Ltd., Bloomington, 1989-95; owner, cons. Rice Med.-Legal Assocs., Bloomington, 1995—; v.p. Mennonite Coll. Nursing Alumni Adminstr. Bd., Bloomington, 1994-95; mem. Mennonite Coll. Nursing Alumni Exec. Bd., Bloomington, 1991-95. Contbr. articles to profl. jours. Mem. Am. Assn. Legal Nurse Cons., Soc. Gastrointestinal Nurses and Assocs., Ill. State Bar Assn., Mennonite Coll. Nursing Honor Soc., Sigma Theta Tau Internat.

RICE, PATRICIA, health executive. Sr. v.p. clin. ops. Continental Med. Sys., Inc., Mechanicsburg, Pa. Office: Continental Med Sys Inc PO Box 715 600 Wilson Ln Mechanicsburg PA 17055*

RICE, PATRICIA OPPENHEIM LEVIN, special education educator, consultant; b. Detroit, Apr. 5, 1932; d. Royal A. and Elsa (Freeman) Oppenheim; m. Charles L. Levin, Feb. 21, 1956 (div. Dec. 1981); children: Arthur David, Amy Ragen, Fredrick Stuart; m. Howard T. Rice, Dec. 16, 1990 (div. Apr. 1994). AB in History, U. Mich., 1954, PhD, 1981; MEd, Marygrove Coll., 1973. Tchr. reading and learning disabled, cons., Detroit, 1967-76, Marygrove Coll.; coord. spl. edn., Marygrove Coll., 1976-86; adj. prof. Oakland U., 1987-90, U. Miami, 1989-95; edn., curriculum cons. Lady Elizabeth Sch., Jávea (Alicante) Spain, 1988-91; dir. Oppenheim Tchr. Tng. Inst., Detroit; v.p. Mashpelah Cemetary Bd., Ferndale, Mich., 1978—; mem. adv. bd. Eton Acad., Birmingham, Mich., 1991-93; internat. conf. presenter; workshop presenter Dade City Schs., 1992—. Mem. Mich. regional bd. ORT, 1965-68, 86—; mem. youth svcs. adv. com. S.E. Mich. chpt. ARC Bd., 1973-79; mem. Met. Mus., N.Y.C., Seattle Art Mus., Detroit Art Mus., Smithsonian Instn.; v.p. women's aux. Children's Hosp. Mich.; bd. dirs. women's com. United Cmty. Svcs., 1968-73; judge Dade County Schs. for Tchr. Grants, 1996; women's com. Detroit Grand Opera Assn., 1970-75; mem. coms. Detroit Symphony Orch., Detroit Inst. Arts; torch drive area chmn. United Found., 1967-70; bd. dirs. Greater Miami Opera Guild, 1992, Miami City Ballet Dade Guild, 1996—, Opera Ball com., 1992, Lincoln Rd. Walk, chair, 1996, Diabetes Rsch. Inst. & Found. Love & Hope Com., Fla. Concert Assn. Cresendo Soc., 1993—, Villa Maria Angel, 1996—. Mem. NAACP, Navy League (mem. Miami Coun.), Internat. Reading Assn., Nat. Coun. Tchrs. of English, Assn. Supervision and Curriculum Devel., Nat. Assn. Edn. of Young Children, Mich. Assn. Children with Learning Disabilities (edn. v.p., exec. bd. 1976-80), Coun. Exceptional Children, Williams Island Club, Westview Country Club (mem. house com.), Turnberry Isle Clubs (signiture), Phi Delta Kappa, Pi Lambda Theta.

RICE, REBECCA KYNOCH, writer, consultant, educator; b. Pittsfield, Mass., June 13, 1954; d. John Hamilton and Nancy Anne (Kynoch) R.; m. Leonard Charles Feldstein, Oct. 17, 1981 (dec. Dec. 1984); m. Bradford Martin Smith, Aug. 14, 1993; 1 child, Oliver Van Santvoord Smith. BA, Sarah Lawrence Coll., 1977; MA, Fairleigh Dickinson U., 1980; MFA, George Mason U., 1996. English tchr. Newark Acad., Livingston, N.J., 1977-79; staff writer, editor Am. Internat. Group, N.Y.C., 1983-85; instr. English George Mason U., Fairfax, Va., 1990-92; mng. editor Green Mtns. Review, Johnson, Vt., 1993-94; freelance writer Johnson, 1994—; cons. Rebecca Rice Literary Svcs., Johnson, 1993-96. Author: A Time to Mourn: One Woman's Journey Through Widowhood, 1990; contbr. articles to pop. publs. Woodrow Wilson fellow, 1977. Mem. Authors Guild. Avocation: tennis. Home: PO Box 157 Ober Hill Rd Johnson VT 05656

RICE, REGINA KELLY, marketing executive; b. Yonkers, N.Y., July 11, 1955; d. Howard Adrian and Lucy Virginia (Butler) Kelly; m. Mark Christopher Rice, Sept. 11, 1981; children: Amanda Kelly, Jaime Brannen. BS in Community Nutrition, Cornell U., 1948. Account exec. J. Walter Thompson Co., N.Y.C., 1978-79; sr. account exec. Ketchum, MacLeod & Grove, N.Y.C., 1979-80; supr. Burson Marstellar, Hong Kong, 1981-83; v.p., dep. dir. food and beverage unit, creative dir. N.Y. office Hill and Knowlton, N.Y.C., 1983-91; mktg. cons. Rice & Rohr, N.Y.C., 1991-93; sr. v.p., dir. consumer mktg. practice Manning, Selvage & Lee, N.Y.C., 1993—. Writer Fast and Healthy Mag., 1991. Mem. Pub. Rels. Soc. Am., Women Execs. in Pub. Rels. Roman Catholic. Home: 18 Westminster Dr Croton On Hudson NY 10520-1008 Office: Manning Selvage & Lee 79 Madison Ave New York NY 10016-7802

RICE, SHARON MARGARET, clinical psychologist; b. Detroit, Sept. 4, 1943; d. William Christopher and Sylvia Lucille (Lawecki) R.; m. John Robert Speer, Aug. 14, 1977 (dec. Mar. 1994). AB, Oberlin Coll., 1965; MA, Boston U., 1968, PhD, 1977. Clin. psychologist Los Angeles County Juvenile Probation, L.A., 1969-75, Las Vegas (Nev.) Mental Health Ctr., 1976-81, Foothills Psychol. Assn., Upland, Calif., 1981—; pvt. cons., Claremont, Calif., 1984—. NIMH grantee, 1967-69; recipient Good Apple award Las Vegas Tchrs. Ctr., 1978-80. Mem. APA, Calif. Psychol. Assn., Internat. Soc. for Study of Dissociation, Inst. Noetic Scis., Sigma Xi. Office: Foothills Psychol Assn 715 N Mountain Ave # G Upland CA 91786-4364

RICE, SUE ANN, dean, industrial and organizational psychologist; b. Ponca City, Okla., Sept. 17, 1934; d. Alfred and Helen (Revard) R. BS in Edn., U. Okla., 1956; MA, Cath. U., 1979, PhD, 1988. Ensign USN, 1956, advanced through grades to comdr., 1973; ednl. svcs. officer 9th Naval Dist., Great Lakes, Ill., 1956-58; adminstr., asst. staff, comdr. in-chief Pacific Fleet, Honolulu, 1958-61; head edn. div. Naval Air Sta., Lemoore, Calif., 1961-63; instr., acad. dir. Women Officers' Sch., Newport, R.I., 1963-66; head. tng. div. Naval Command Systems Support Activity, Washington, 1966-70; head, ops. support sec., comdr.-in-chief Lant, Norfolk, Va., 1970-74; sr. U.S. rep. NATO, subgroup 5 orgn. JCS, Washington, 1974-77; ret. USN, 1977; head vocation office Archdiocese of Washington, 1977-78; con. Notre Dame Inst., Arlington, Va., 1989—, dean of students, 1990-95; lectr. Cath. U. Am., Washington, 1983-84; bd. dirs. Villa Cortona Apostolic Ctr., Bethesda, 1984-94. Tech. reviewer Personnel Administration, 1964; editor (newsletter) Vocation News, 1978. Conoco scholarship Continental Oil Co., 1952-56; recipient Meritorious Svc. medal Pres. of U.S., 1977, rsch. grant Cath. U., Sigma Xi, 1986. Mem. Washington Acad. Scis., Cath. War Vets. (nat. dir., chmn. nat. pub. rels. com., nat. youth act subcom., combined Nat. Vets. Assn. rep.), Lay Women's Assn. (nat. pres.), Potomac Ch. Human Factors Soc. (assoc.), Kappa Delta Pi, Gamma Phi Beta. Roman Catholic. Office: PO Box 1035 Falls Church VA 22041-0035

RICE, THERESA MARY, secondary school educator; b. Syracuse, N.Y., May 24, 1949; d. Dominick J. and Teresa A. (Gaffney) Riccardi; m. Harry Robert Rice, Aug. 11, 1973; children: Angela, Marc, Jeffrey, Anthony. BS in Secondary Math., SUNY, Oswego, 1971. Permanent cert. in secondary math. Math. tchr. Liverpool (N.Y.) H.S., 1971-82, Ctrl. City Bus. Inst., Syracuse, N.Y., 1980-85, Westhill H.S., Syracuse, 1985-91, Cicero (N.Y.) North Syracuse H.S., 1991—; advisor Acad. Decathlon, Cicero, 1991—; tchr., rep. Bldg. Planning Team, Cicero, 1993—; tchr., rschr. NSF, Cicero, 1994—. Coord. religious edn. grades 6-10 St. Vincent DePaul, Syracuse, 1991—; tchr. mem., rep. Cmty. Connections, Cicero, 1993—. Mem. Assn. Math. Tchrs. in N.Y. State, N.Y. State United Tchrs., North Syracuse United Tchrs., Onondaga County Math Tchrs. Assn. Democrat. Roman Catholic. Home: 424 Brattle Rd Syracuse NY 13203-1103 Office: Cicero HS Northstar Dr Cicero NY 13212

RICH, ADRIENNE, writer; b. Balt., May 16, 1929; d. Arnold Rice and Helen Elizabeth (Jones) R.; m. Alfred H. Conrad (dec. 1970); children: David, Paul, Jacob. AB, Radcliffe Coll., 1951; LittD (hon.), Wheaton Coll., 1967, Smith Coll., 1979, Brandeis U., 1987, Coll. Wooster, Ohio, 1988, CCNY, Harvard U., 1990, Swarthmore Coll., 1992. Tchr. workshop YM-WHA Poetry Ctr., N.Y.C., 1966-67; vis. lectr. Swarthmore Coll., 1967-69; adj. prof. writing divsn. Columbia U., 1967-69; lectr. CCNY, 1968-70, instr., 1970-71, asst. prof. English, 1971-72, 74-75; Fannie Hurst vis. prof. creative lit. Brandeis U., 1972-73; prof. English Douglass Coll., Rutgers U., 1976-79; Clark lectr., disting. vis. prof. Scripps Coll., 1983-84; A.D. White prof.-at-large Cornell U., 1981-87; disting. vis. prof. San Jose State U., 1984-85; prof. English and feminist studies Stanford U., 1986-93; Marjorie Kovler vis. lectr. U. Chgo., 1989. Author: (poetry) Collected Early Poems, 1950-1970, 1993, Diving into the Wreck, 1973, The Dream of a Common Language, 1978, A

Wild Patience Has Taken Me This Far, 1981, Your Native Land, Your Life, 1986, Time's Power, 1989, An Atlas of the Difficult World, 1991, Dark Fields of the Republic, 1995; (prose) Of Woman Born: Motherhood as Experience and Institution, 1976, 10th anniversary edit., 1986, On Lies, Secrets and Silence, 1979, Blood, Bread and Poetry, 1986, What Is Found There: Notebooks on Poetry and Politics, 1993. Mem. nat. adv. bd. Bridges, Boston Women's Fund, Sisterhood in Support of Sisters in South Africa, Nat. Writers Union. Recipient Yale Series of Younger Poets award, 1951, Ridgely Torrence Meml. award Poetry Soc. Am., 1955, Nat. Inst. Arts and letters award in poetry, 1961, Bess Hokin prize Poetry mag., 1963, Eunice Tietjens Meml. prize, 1968, Shelley Meml. award, 1971, Nat. Book award, 1974, Fund for Human Dignity award Nat. Gay Task Force, 1981, Ruth Lilly Poetry prize, 1986, Brandeis U. Creative Arts medal for Poetry, 1987, Nat. Poetry Assn. award, 1989, Elmer Holmes Bobst award arts and letters NYU, 1989, others. Mem. PEN, Am. Acad. Arts and Letters (dept. of lit. 1990—), Nat. Writers Union, Am. Acad. Arts and Scis. Office: care W W Norton Co 500 Fifth Ave New York NY 10110

RICH, KAREN MARY, secondary school educator; b. St. Albans, Vt., July 24, 1948; d. Robert Francis and Elaine Gloria (Cantell) St. Pierre; m. David James Rich, Apr. 17, 1971; children: Jason, Shawn, Adam, Aaron. BA in Math., U. Vt., Burlington, 1970, MEd in Tchr. Edn., 1982. Cert. secondary math. tchr., Vt. Secondary tchr. math. Essex Junction (Vt.) H.S., 1970-84, secondary tchr., chair dept. math., 1984—; SAT prep. tchr. Princeton (N.J.) Ednl. Testing Svcs., 1991—; adj. faculty U. Vt., 1995—. Named Tchr. of Yr., Essex Junction Sch. dist./U. Vt., 1982, Presdl. Recognition award 1987, others. Mem. NEA, Assn. Tchrs. of Math. New England, Vt. Edn. Assn., Essex Junction Edn. Assn., Vt. Coun. Tchrs. of Math., Alpha Delta Kappa. Home: 31 Greenbriar Dr Essex Junction VT 05452 Office: Essex Junction HS 2 Educational Dr Essex Junction VT 05452-3167

RICH, KERRY ANN, computer science and mathematics educator; b. Buffalo, N.Y., Oct. 11, 1968; d. Gary Lee and Marilyn Ann (Endress) R. BA in Math., SUNY, Buffalo, 1990, EdM in Psychology, 1992, PhD in Ednl. Psychology, 1996. Cert. secondary math. and K-6 tchr., N.Y. Computer cons. Buffalo, N.Y., 1988; rsch. asst. SUNY, Buffalo, N.Y., 1990-93; computer sci. and math. tchr. Frontier Ctrl. H.S., Hamburg, N.Y., 1993—. Tchr. Christian Edn., St. Matthews United Ch. of Christ, Hamburg, 1991, 1993-94. Mem. APA, Assn. Advancement of Computing in Edn., Nat. Coun. Tchrs. of Math., N.Y. State Computer and Tech. Educators. Republican. Protestant. Office: Frontier Central School 4432 Bayview Rd Hamburg NY 14075

RICH, S. JUDITH, public relations executive; b. Chgo., Apr. 14; d. Irwin M. and Sarah I. (Sandock) R. BA, U. Ill., 1960. Staff writer, reporter Economist Newspapers, Chgo., 1960-61; asst. dir. pub. rels. and communications Coun. Profit Sharing Industries, Chgo., 1961-62; dir. advt. and pub. rels. Chgo. Indsl. Dist., 1962-63; account exec., account supr., v.p., sr. v.p., exec. v.p. and nat. creative dir. Edelman Pub. Rels. Worldwide, Chgo., 1963-85; exec. v.p., dir. Ketchum Pub. Rels. Worldwide, Chgo., 1985-89, exec. v.p., exec. creative dir. USA, 1990—; frequent spkr. on creativity and brainstorming. workshop facilitator, spkr. in field. Mem. pub. rels. adv. bd. U. Chgo. Grad Sch. Bus., Roosevelt U., Chgo., DePaul U., Chgo., Gov.'s State U. Mem. Pub. Rels. Soc. Am. (Silver Anvil award, judge Silver Anvil awards), Counselors Acad. of Pub. Rels. Soc. Am. (exec. bd.), Chgo. Publicity Club (8 Golden Trumpet awards). Home: 2500 N Lakeview Ave Chicago IL 60614-1836 Office: Ketchum Pub Rels # 3400 205 N Michigan Ave Chicago IL 60601-5925

RICHARD, ALISON FETTES, anthropology educator; b. Great Britain, Mar. 1, 1948. BA, Cambridge U., 1969; PhD, London U., 1973. Asst. prof. anthropology Yale U., New Haven, 1972-76, assoc.prof. anthropology, 1976-85, prof. anthropology, 1985—, provost prof., 1994—; dir. Yale Peabody Mus. Natural History, 1990-94. Bd. dirs. Yale-New Haven Health Svcs., 1994—, World Wildlife Fund, 1995—. Mem. Am. Primatological Soc., Am. Assn. Phys. Anthropologists, Am. Anthrop. Assn., Brit. Ecol. Soc., Primate Soc. Gt. Britain, Zool. Soc. London, Cambridge Philosophical Soc. Office: Office of the Provost Yale U New Haven CT 06520-8118

RICHARD, CATHERINE MARIE, elementary education educator; b. Boston, Mar. 29, 1950; d. Ernest Amerigo and Melina (Belmonte) Caezza; m. Robert Joseph Richard, Aug. 30, 1970; 1 child, Robert. BS in Edn., Salem State Coll., 1971; M in Early Childhood Edn., Wheelock Coll., 1996. Tchr. jr. h.s. St. Charles Sch., Woburn, Mass., 1971-73; elem. art tchr. Malden (Mass.) Pub. Schs., 1974-85, tchr. 2d grade, 1985-91, tchr. 3d grade, 1991—; mem. bldg. integration team C.W. Holmes Sch., Malden, 1992—, mem. Gt. Book Found., 1990—; mem. sch. curriculum com. Austin Prep. Sch., Reading, Mass., 1992—, mem. Austin Athletic Assn., 1990—; tchr. religious edn. St. Theresa's Parish, North Reading, Mass., 1983-85. Mem. Malden Living Mus., 1981-84. Creative Arts and Lang. grantee Mass. Dept. Edn., 1987. Mem. ASCD, Nat. Assn. Edn. Young Children. Roman Catholic. Home: 236 Central St North Reading MA 01864-1361 Office: C W Holmes Sch 257 Mountain Ave Malden MA 02148-2711

RICHARD, MAXINE SANDRA, artist; b. Jersey City, Aug. 2, 1946; d. Harry Engel and Pauline Beatrice (Axel) Lewiskin; m. Thomas Grant Richard, Apr. 26, 1976 (div. 1985); 1 child, Sarah Mateel. Student, Pratt Inst., Bklyn., 1964-67; BA, Calif. State U., Hayward, 1975; MFA, U. Tulsa, 1987. Tchr. Floyd Sch. of Philbrook Mus., Tulsa, 1980—; owner, operator Mimosa Press, 1988—; part-time asst. prof. Oral Roberts U., Tulsa, 1993, Tulsa Jr. Coll., 1991; vis. asst. prof. Coll. of Wooster, Ohio, 1987-88; tchr. Cmty. Arts/Tulsa Arts and Humanities Coun., 1995-96. Illustrator: (book of poetry) Plain English, 1995, Nimrod, 1980, 82, 89, 94, 96; creator series of 10 etched plates for Huff Gallery exhibit Philbrook Mus., 1994; cons. (instrnl. book) Etching and Lithography, 1994, Monotypes, 1993. Mem. exbhn. rev. com. Tulsa Ctr. for Contemporary Art, 1989-91. Eben Demarest Trust grantee Mellon Bank/Demarest Found., 1993, Vogelstein grantee Ludwig Vogelstein Found., 1990; Vt. Studio Ctr. residency Mid-Am. Arts Alliance, 1994. Mem. Okla. Visual Arts Coalition (artist award of excellence 1994), Living Arts of Tulsa. Home and Office: Mimosa Press 1204 E 48th St N Tulsa OK 74126

RICHARD, PATRICIA ANTOINETTE, physician, dentist; b. Bridgeport, Conn., June 15, 1950; d. Mr. and Mrs. Richard. DMD, U. Conn., 1976; MD, Hahnemann U., 1980. Cert. sr. FAA med. examiner. Intern in internal medicine St. Vincents Med. Ctr., Bridgeport, Conn., 1980-81; resident in surgery U. Med. and Dentistry, Rutgers U., Camden, N.J., 1983-84; resident in internal medicine U. Hosp., Jacksonville, Fla., 1984-85; sr. resident in internal medicine Hartford (Conn.) Hosp., 1985-86; emergency medicine physician St. Francis Hosp., Hartford, 1985-87, U. Conn.-John Dempsey Hosp., Farmington, 1986-88, Bristol (Conn.) Hosp., 1986-87; pvt. practice in medicine and dentistry, biotech. R&D cons. Fairfield, Conn., 1987—; mem. medico-legal com. Fairfield County Med. Assn., 1994—, Fairfield County Ctr. for Trauma and Internal Medicine, Temporomandibular Joint Disorders, Aviation Medicine and Biotech., R&D, 1993—. Mem. Rep. Senatorial Inner Cir., Washington, 1992; perpetual mem. Franciscan Benefactors Assn., Mt. Vernon, N.Y., 1994; mem. Lourdes Prayer League, Shrine of Our Lady of Snows, Belleville, Ill., 1995. Recipient Rep. Presidential award Bd. of Govs.-Rep. Presidential Task Force, 1994. Mem. AIAA, AMA, ADA, Aerospace Med. Assn., Am. Bd. Forensic Examiners. Office: 1735 Post Rd PO Box 702 Fairfield CT 06430

RICHARD-AMATO, PATRICIA ABBOTT, language educator, author, consultant; b. Erskine, Minn., May 29, 1940; d. Wallace Marvin and Myrtle Lydia (Forsythe) Abbott; m. James Joseph Amato, May 16, 1983. BS, U. Minn., Duluth, 1962; MEd, U. Ariz., 1965; PhD, U. N.Mex., 1984. Cert. tchr., Colo., Ariz. Tchr. Pueblo High Sch. Tucson Pub. Schs.; tchr., dir. ESL Ctr. Jefferson County Pub. Schs., Lakewood, Colo.; coord. Tchrs. of Eng. to Speakers of Other Langs. Programs Calif. State U., L.A., prof. emeritus. Author: Making it Happen: Interaction in the Second Language Classroom, 1996, Reading in Content Areas, 1990, (with John Oller, Jr.) Methods that Work, 1983, (with Ann Snow) The Multicultural Classroom: Readings for Content-Area Teachers, 1992, Exploring Themes: An Interactive Approach to Literature, 1993, (with Wendy Hansen) Worlds Together: A Journey into Multicultural Literature, 1995, All Star English (levels 2, 3), 1996. Mem. Am. Assn. Applied Linguistics, Calif. Assn. Bilingual Educators, Tchrs. of Eng. to Speakers of Other Langs. Office: Calif State U EFIS/Sch Edn 5151 State University Dr Los Angeles CA 90032-4221

RICHARDS, ALETA WILLIAMS, marketing professional; b. Pitts., Nov. 16, 1965; d. John Quincy and Sara Ann (Dorman) Williams; m. Frank D. Richards III, Nov. 16, 1982; 1 child, Cassandra Nicolle. BSBA, U. Pitts., 1990. Asst. to exec. directory Allegheny County Pvt. Industry Coun., Pitts., 1984-90; co-owner Richards Properties, Pitts., 1991-93; tech. mktg. rep. II Miles, Inc., Pitts., 1990-94, bus. champion Miles re-engring. project, 1995; cons. AWR Comm., Pitts., 1994—; mgr. continuous improvement Bayer Corp., Pitts., 1996—; speaker employment Salem (W.Va.)-Teikyo U., 1991-92; communications graphic designer The Way, The Truth and Life Ministries, Pitts., 1989-91. mentor Mobay Corp. program Reizenstein Mid. Sch., 1990-91. Author, editor: (reference book) Funding Resources Guide, 1989. Speaker Pitts. in Partnership with Parents, 1988-90; bd. dirs. Ptnrs. in Self-Sufficiency, Pitts., 1986-90. Recipient Mayor's Recognition award City of Pitts., 1990. Mem. NAFE, Nat. Assn. Desktop Pubs., River City Elite Track Club (treas. 1995-96). Home: PO Box 2816 Pittsburgh PA 15230-2816

RICHARDS, ANN WILLIS, former governor; b. Lakeview, Tex., Sept. 1, 1933; d. Cecil and Ona Willis; children: Cecile, Daniel, Clark, Ellen. B.A., Baylor U., 1954; postgrad., U. Tex., 1954-55. Cert. tchr. Tex. Tchr. Austin Ind. Sch. Dist., Tex.; mgr. Sarah Weddington Campaign, Austin, Tex., 1972, adminstrv. asst., 1973-74; county commr. Travis County, Austin, 1976-82; treas. State of Tex., Austin, 1983-91; gov. State of Tex., 1991-95; sr. advisor Verner, Liipfert, Bernhard, McPherson & Hand, Austin, 1995—; chair Dem. Nat. Conv. 1992; Austin Transp. Study, Tex., 1977-82, Capital Indsl. Devel. Corp., Austin, Tex., 1980-81, Spl. Commn. Delivery Human Services in Tex., 1979-81; Dem. com. Southern Governor's Assn. Travis County Dem. com. Author (with Peter Knobler): Straight From the Heart, 1989. Mem. com. strategic planning Dem. Nat. Com., 1983; keynote speaker Dem. Nat. Conv., 1988. Named Woman of Yr. Tex. Women's Polit. Caucus, 1981, 83. Mem. Nat. Govs.' Assn. Office: care Verner, Liipfert, Bernhard, McPherson & Hand PO Box 684746 Austin TX 78768*

RICHARDS, CARMELEETE A., computer training executive, network administrator; b. Springport, Ind., Feb. 8, 1948; d. Gordon K. and Virginia Christine (New) Brown; 1 child, Annasheril. AA in Elem. Edn., No. Okla. Coll., 1969; BS in Edn., Southwestern State Coll., Weatherford, Okla., 1971; postgrad., Ashland (Ohio) Coll., 1981—; postgrad. in Edn., U. Phoenix, 1994—. Cert. tchr., Ohio. 6th grade tchr. Scott City, Kans., 1971; salesperson, customer svc. Jafra Cosmetics, 1979-81; br. asst. mgr. Barclays Am. Fin., Columbus, 1981-84; tng. mgr., ednl. dir. Computer Depot, Columbus, Ohio, 1984-85; corp. trainer, exec. sales Litel Telecommunications, Worthington, Ohio, 1985-87; communications cons. Telemarketing Communications of Columbus, Ohio, 1988-89; corp. computer tng. O/E Learning, Troy, Mich., 1989-94; corp. computer trainer ETOP Cols., Ohio, 1989—. Pres. PTA, 1981-82. Recipient Outstanding Participation award Dorothy Carnegie Pub. Speaking. Mem. NAFE, Am. Soc. for Tng. and Devel., Columbus Computer Soc., Kappa Delta Pi. Baptist.

RICHARDS, CHARLENE ANNA, computer manufacturing company executive; b. Muncie, Ind., May 10, 1963; d. Delmar Gene and Mary Catherine (O'Bryant) Coffman; m. Bruce Richards, Aug. 26, 1983; children: Shaun Michael, Shannon Michelle, Shayna Marie. Grad. high sch., Albuquerque. Dispatcher asst. Morgan Drive Agy., Albuquerque, 1979-80; account asst. Sta. KOB-TV, Albuquerque, 1980-81, TV copywriter, 1982-83; display advt. cons. Albuquerque Jour.-Tribune, 1981-82; mgr. TLC Svcs., Albuquerque, 1983-87; owner, mgr. The Computer Man, Beaufort, S.C., 1988-91; pres. Computer Techs. Systems, Inc., Beaufort, 1991—, East Coast Holdings, Ltd., Beaufort, 1994-95; mgr. Computer Outlet, Beaufort, 1995—; instr. Tech. Coll. Low Country, Beaufort, 1989. Designer mfg. computer systems. Mem. NAFE, Nat. Fedn. Ind. Bus., U.S. C. of C., Nat. Platform Assn. Republican. Baptist. Home: 10 Wiggins Rd Beaufort SC 29902-2630 Office: PO Box 2239 Beaufort SC 29901-2239

RICHARDS, CONSTANCE ELLEN, nursing school administrator, consultant; b. Exeter, N.H., June 21, 1941; d. Edward Nowell and Mary Isabel (Bean) R. RN diploma, Concord (N.H.) Hosp., 1964, BSN, U. Cin., 1971, MA in Pub. Adminstrn., 1973, MS in Comprehensive Health Planning, 1973. RN, Mass. Nurse ICU/Opening CCU Syracuse (N.Y.) Meml. Hosp., 1964; instr. ICU and CCU Crouse-Irving Meml. Hosp., Syracuse, 1967; instr. cardiovascular, orthopedic and surg. The Christ Hosp., Cin., 1973; instr. med.-surg. nursing Md. Gen. Hosp., Balt., 1978; night supr. Manor Care Ruxton, Towson, Md., 1980; adult health svcs. mgr. Exeter Vis. Nurses Assn., 1982; dir. insvc. edn. Bethany Hosp., Framingham, Mass., 1983; assoc. prof. nursing Mass. Bay C.C., 1985; instr. insvc. edn. Brockton-West Roxbury (Mass.) VA Hosp., 1986; staff nurse Charles River Hosp., Wellesley, Mass., 1987; night supr. Blair House, Milford, Mass., 1988; staff nurse psychogeriatrics Worcester State Hosp., 1989; with Agys. Internat. Health Talent Tree, Olsten Health Care Svcs., 1990; with indsl. svcs. program, CNA tng. program Northampton State Hosp., 1992; nursing asst., state tester ARC, 1992-93; pres. Caring Hands, Inc., 1993—; DON Excel Health Svcs., Inc., 1993—; instr. LPN evening program Greater Lowell Regional Vocat. Tech. Sch., 1992-94; adv. bd. Excel Health Svcs., Tewksbury, Mass., 1993-94; pres. Splitap Arts, Lowell, Mass., 1993-94. Author: Freddie the Foot, 1982. Mem. Lowell Hist. Soc., 1994, Women's Network, Lowell, 1994, Crime Watch Group Edn. Component, Lowell, 1994. Mem. ANA, Mass. Nurses Assn., Nat. League Nurses. Democrat. Roman Catholic. Home: 30 Hungton St Lowell MA 01852 Office: Caring Hands Inc 353 Lodes Pond Shutesbury MA 01072

RICHARDS, DIANA LYN, psychologist; b. Baton Rouge, Dec. 8, 1944; d. William Allen Richards and Julia Viola (Hamilton) Richards Hamilton. AA, Stephens Coll., 1964; BA, U. Colo., 1966; MA, Miami U., Oxford, Ohio, 1969, PhD, 1974. Lic. psychologist, Mo. Dir. community psychol. svcs. Malcolm Bliss Mental Health Ctr., St. Louis, 1975-77; mem. staff Women's Counseling Ctr., St. Louis, 1976-78; mem. faculty Gestalt Inst., St. Louis, 1977-80; instr. Washington U., St. Louis, 1977; dir. psychology Lindenwood Coll. for Individualized Edn., St. Louis, 1978-80, core faculty in psychology, 1984-94; psychologist in pvt. practice St. Louis, 1977—; career cons. Stephens Coll., Columbia, Mo., 1994—; mem. Psychoanalytic Study Group, St. Louis, 1980—; supr. psychology clinic, clin. doctoral program U. Mo., St. Louis, 1994—; facilitator Coun. of All Beings Workshops, 1995—; presenter in field. Contbr. articles to profl. jours. and conf. presentations. Mem. Operation Food Search, Defenders of Wildlife, Humane Soc., People for Ethical Treatment of Animals, Arts and Edn. Fund, Mo. Bot. Garden, Digit Fund, Earth Island Inst., World Wildlife Fund, Nature Conservancy, Audubon Soc., Humane Farming Assn.; founding mem. The Pleiades; vol. food ministry, chair fellowship dinners, edn. com. Trinity Episcopal Ch.; vol. Wildbird Rehab. Ctr. Mem. APA, Mo. Psychol. Assn., St. Louis Psychol. Assn. (program chair 1988-89, pres.-elect 1995-96, pres. 1996—), Network of Women Psychologists (program chair 1986), St. Louis Psychoanalytic Inst. Democrat. Home: 2014 S Mason Rd Saint Louis MO 63131-1619 Office: 7396 Pershing Ave Saint Louis MO 63130-4206

RICHARDS, HILDA, academic administrator; b. St. Joseph, Mo., Feb. 7, 1936; d. Togar and Rose Avalynne (Williams) Young-Ballard. Diploma nursing St. John's Sch. Nursing, St. Louis, 1956; BS cum laude, CUNY, 1961; MEd, Columbia U., 1965, EdD, 1976; MPA, NYU, 1971. Dep. chief dept. psychiatry Harlem Rehab. Ctr., N.Y.C., 1969-71; prof., dir. nursing Medgar Evers Coll., CUNY, N.Y.C., 1971-76, prof., assoc. dean, 1976-79; dean Coll. Health and Human Service, Ohio U., Athens, 1979-86; provost, v.p. for acad. affairs Indiana U., Pa., 1986-93; chancellor Ind. U. N.W., Gary, 1993—; bd. dirs. Sta. 56-TV; active N.W. Satir Inst., Execs. Coun. N.W. Ind., ACE Commn. on Minorities in Higher Edn., AASCU Com. on Diversity and Social Change. Author: (with others) Curriculum Development and People of Color: Strategies and Change, 1983; editor Black Conf. on Higher Edn. Jour., 1989-93. Bd. dirs. Avanta Network, 1984—, Urban League N.W. Ind., 1993, N.W. Ind. Forum, 1993, Bank One Regional Bd., Merrillville, Ind., 1994, The Meth. Hosps., Inc., Gary.Merrillville, 1994, Lake Area United Way, 1994, Boys and Girls Clubs N.W. Ind.; life mem. Gary chpt. NAACP; exec. com. Pa. Black Conf. on Higher Edn., 1988-93. Recipient Rockefeller Found. award Am. Council Edn., Washington, 1976-77, Black Achiever award Black Opinion Mag., 1989, Athena award Bus. and Profl. Women's Club Ind., 1991; Martin Luther King grantee NYU, N.Y.C., 1969-70, Gunt Found. grantee Harvard Inst. Ednl. Mgmt., Cambridge, Mass., 1981. Fellow Am. Acad. Nursing; mem. ANA (Outstanding Woman of Color award 1990), AAHE, AAUW, APHA, Am. Assn. State Colls. and Univs., Nat. Assn. Allied Health Profls., Am. Assn. Univ. Adminstrs., Assn. Black Nursing Faculty in Higher Edn. (bd. dirs. 1989—), Pa. Nurses Assn., Assn. Black Women in Higher Edn., Inc., Nat. Black Nurses Assn. (bd. dirs., 1st v.p. 1984—, editor jour. 1985—, Spl. Recognition award 1991, Disting. African-Am. Nurse Educator award Queens County chpt., 1991), Nat. Assn. Women in Edn., Am. Coun. Edn. (exec. com. coun. fellows), Internat. Assn. Univ. Pres., N.W. Rotary, N.W. Kiwanis, Phi Delta Kappa, Sigma Theta Tau, Zonta Club of Ind. County. Democrat. Avocations: needlepoint, travel. Home: 7807 Hemlock Ave Gary IN 46403-2164 Office: Ind U NW Office of Chancellor 3400 Broadway Gary IN 46408-1197

RICHARDS, LACLAIRE LISSETTA JONES (MRS. GEORGE A. RICHARDS), social worker; b. Pine Bluff, Ark.; d. Artie William and Geraldine (Adams) Jones; m. George Alvarez Richards, July 26, 1958; children: Leslie Rosario, Lia Mercedes, Jorge Ferguson. BA, Nat. Coll. Christian Workers, 1953; MSW, U. Kans., 1956; postgrad. Columbia U., 1960. Diplomate Clin. Social Work, Am. Bd. of Examiners in Clin. Social Work, Nat. Assn. Social Workers; cert. gerontologist. Psychiat. supervisory, teaching, community orgn., adminstrv. and consultative duties Hastings Regional Ctr., Ingleside, Nebr., 1956-60; supervisory, consultative and adminstrv. responsibilities for psychiat. and geriatric patients VA Hosp., Knoxville, Iowa, 1960-74, field instr. for grad. students from U. Mo., EEO counselor, 1969-74, 78-90, com. chmn., 1969-70, Fed. women's program coordinator, 1972-74; sr. social worker Mental Health Inst., Cherokee, Iowa, 1974-77; adj. asst. prof. dept. social behavior U. S.D.; instr. Dept. of Psychiatry U. S.D Sch. of Medicine, 1988-96, Augustana Coll., 1981-86; outpatient social worker VA Med. and Regional Office Center, Sioux Falls, S.D., 1978-96; med., surg. & intensive care social worker, 1990-92, surg. & intermediate care social worker, 1992-96; EEO counselor. Mem. Knoxville Juvenile Adv. Com., 1963-65, 68-70, sec., 1965-66, chmn., 1966-68; sec. Urban Renewal Citizens' Adv. Com., Knoxville, 1966-68; mem. United Methodist Ch. Task Force Exptl. Styles Ministry and Leadership, 1973-74, mem. adult choir, mem. ch. and society com.; counselor Knoxville Youth Line program; sec. exec. com. Vis. Nurse Assn., 1979-80; canvasser community fund drs., Knoxville; mem. Cherokee Civil Rights Commn.; bd. dirs., pub. relations, membership devel. and program devel. cons. YWCA, 1983-85; bd. dirs. Family Svc. Agy., 1989-90, Food Svcs. Ctr. Inc., 1992-96; mem. S.D. Symphonic Choir, 1991—; mem. Youth-At-Risk Task Force and Multicultural Ctr. Advocate. Named S.D. Social Worker of Yr., 1983. Mem. NAACP (chmn. edn. com. 1983-85), AAUW (sec. Hastings chpt. 1958-60), Nat. Assn. Social Workers (co-chmn. Nebr. chpt. profl. standards com. 1958-59), Acad. Cert. Social Workers, S.D. Assn. Social Workers (chmn. minority affairs com., v.p. S.E. region 1980, pres. 1980-82 exec. com. 1982-84, mem. social policy and action com.), Nebr. Assn. Social Workers (chmn. 1958-59), Seventh Dist. S.D. Med. Soc. Aux., Coalition on Aging., Nat. Assn. Social Workers (qualified clin. social worker 1991—), Methodist (Sunday sch. tchr. adult div.; mem. commn. on edn.; mem. Core com. for adult edn.; mem. Adult Choir; mem. Social Concerns Work Area); mem. 1st Evangelical Free Ch., 1995—. Home: 1701 E Ponderosa Dr Sioux Falls SD 57103-5019

RICHARDS, LYNN, company training executive, consultant; b. Kansas City, Mo., Sept. 2, 1949; d. Robert A. and Betty (Arnold) Nelson. BS in Edn., U. Kans., 1971; MA in Edn., San Diego State U., 1979. Prin. staff ORI, Inc., Silver Spring, Md., 1980-81; sr. corp. trainer Amerada Hess Corp., Woodbridge, N.J., 1981-83; tng. and devel. mgr. Kimberly-Clark Corp., Beech Island, S.C., 1983-85; orgn. devel. mgr. M&M Mars, Hackettstown, N.J., 1985-89; corp. tng. and devel. mgr. Rohr, Inc., Chula Vista, Calif., 1989-93; customer edn. mgr. ComputerVision, Corp., San Diego, 1993-95; leadership devel. cons. Children's Hosp., San Diego, 1995—; pvt. cons., San Diego, 1990—. Contbr. articles to profl. mags. Mem. Internat. Soc. for Performance and Instrn. (chmn. awards com. 1988, presdl. citations, achievement awards).

RICHARDS, RHODA ROOT WAGNER, civic worker; b. Phila., Oct. 2, 1917; d. Edward Stephen and Rhoda Earley (Root) Wagner; student U. Pa., 1937-39; A.A., Wildcliff Jr. Coll., 1938; m. J. Permar Richards, Jr., May 18, 1940; children: Patricia A.V. Richards Cosgrave, J. Permar III. Profl. artist; founder, chmn. Hosp. Corps, Navy League Service, 1941-43; chmn. ARC Nurses Aide Corps, Jacksonville, Fla., 1944-45, Long Beach, Calif., 1945-46; founder, chmn. Fiesta Benefits, Hahnemann Hosp., 1950-57; former chmn. jr. com. Met. Opera; bd. dirs. Phila. Lyric Opera Co.; chmn. Ring for Freedom Republican Campaign of S.E. Pa., 1960; pres. Emergency Aid of Pa., 1961-64; v.p. bd. dirs. Inglis House, Phila., 1977-82; pres. women's bd. Phila. div. Am. Cancer Soc., 1978-81, hon. life mem.; gen. chmn. 1st Ann. Washington Crossing Assembly, 1978; trustee Baldwin Sch.; co-chmn. fundraising com. Ambulatory Service Pavilion, Presbyn.-U. Pa. Med. Center; vice chmn. Women's Commn. for Bicentennial, 1976; bd. dirs., mem. Appleford Commn. Parsons-Banks Arboretum. Vol., chmn. women's bd. Phila. div. Am. Cancer Soc., 1978-86; vol. Phila. chpt. Lupus Found., 1980-81; mem. Delaware Valley women's bd. Freedoms Found. at Valley Forge; past v.p. women's assn., past chmn. fin. com., chmn. centennial spl. event and gen. com. for the celebration Bryn Mawr Presbyn. Ch.; hon. col. corps of cadets Valley Forge Mil. Acad. and Jr. Coll.; founder, chmn. Rittenhouse Preservation Coalition, 1982—; founder, v.p., asst. treas. Preservation Coalition of Greater Phila., 1984—; mem. Hospitality, Phila. Style; chmn. bd. dirs. Emergency Aid of Pa. Found., chmn. 75th anniversary celebration, fin., long range planning, investment coms.; liaison Fairmont Park Waterworks Com. Recipient Crusade award Am. Cancer Soc., 1976; spl. award for community service St. John's Settlement House, 1977; Florence A. Sanson award for patriotism, 1986; named Disting. Dau. of Pa., 1985. Mem. Phila. Mus. Art, Pa. Acad. Fine Arts, Hahnemann Hosp. Women's Assn. (Phila. chpt.), DAR, Daus. of the Cincinnati, Dames of Loyal Legion, Nat. Soc. Colonial Dames of XVII Century, Dames Sovereign Mil. Order Temple of Jerusalem, Honolulu Mus. Art, Geneal. Soc. Pa., Am. Hist. Soc., Nat. Trust for Historic Preservation, Smithsonian Instn., Friends of Independence Hall, Friends of Hist. Cliveden, Andalusia Friends. Clubs: Sedgeley, Cosmopolitan, Bald Peak Colony. Home: 1250 Lafayette Rd PO Box 608 Bryn Mawr PA 19010-0608

RICHARDS, RHONDA SUE, accountant; b. Shawano, Wisc., May 27, 1963; d. Thomas Lee and Betty Lou (Splitgerber) R. A in acctg., Northeast Wisc. Tech. Coll., Green Bay, 1988; BA, Lakeland Coll., Sheboygan, 1992. CMA, Wisc. Sr. acct. Oneida Tribe of Indians, Green Bay, Wis., 1995—; instr. Northeast Wisc. Tech. Coll., Green Bay, 1994—; acct. Paper Converting Machine Co., Green Bay, 1985-95. Mem. Institute of Mgmt. Accts. Home: 1110 Roscoe St Green Bay WI 54304

RICHARDS, ROXANNE, gallery exhibition coordinator; b. Jamaica, Mar. 5, 1963; came to U.S., 1966; d. Herbert Richards and Pearl Wilson Arbouin. Docent Whitney Mus., N.Y.C., 1993-96; exhbn. coord. Paul Kasmin Gallery, N.Y.C., 1996—. Democrat. Roman Catholic. Address: 425 E 25th St # 392 New York NY 10010

RICHARDS, SHIRLEY MASTIN, retired public housing executive; b. Osceola, Ark., Jan. 16, 1927; d. Gilbert Edward and Florence Wilma (Sangster) Mastin; m. Robert Herman Richards, Dec. 28, 1930; children: Roberta, Gilbert, Mary. Grad. high sch., Osceola. Cert. public housing mgr. Bank teller Mississippi County Bank, Osceola, 1945-53; mgmt. aide, dir. Osceola Housing Authority, 1961-78, asst. exec. dir., 1978-95, exec. dir., 1995, ret., 1995. Charter mem., sec.-treas. Mississippi County (Ark.) Hist. and Geneal. Soc., 1988—. Republican. Baptist. Home: 515 W Ford Ave Osceola AR 72370-2401 Office: Osceola Housing Authority 501 Cotton Ave Osceola AR 72370-3119

RICHARDS, SUSAN LYNNE, library director; b. Franklin, Pa., Dec. 4, 1956; d. L. Burton and Phyllis D. (Ditzenberger) R.; m. Rex C. Myers, Jan. 10, 1987; stepchildren: Gary Myers, Laura Myers. AB, Grove City Coll., 1978; MA in History, Clarion U., 1980; MLS, Kent State U., 1982. Profl. libr. Tech. svcs. libr. Morningside Coll., Sioux City, Iowa, 1983-85; head serials dept. Briggs Libr. S.D. State U., Brookings, 1986-88, head acquisitions dept. Briggs Libr., 1988-91; asst. dir. librs. U. Vt., Burlington, 1992-95; dir. libr. svcs. Western State Coll., Gunnison, Colo., 1995—; editor VLA News, Vt. Libr. Assn., 1992-94, Book Marks, S.D. Libr. Assn., 1989-91; gov. bd. dirs. Pathfinder Libr. Sys., Colo.; mem. Vt. Newspaper Project Adv. Bd., 1994-95. Contbr. articles to profl. jours. and mags. Mem. Cmty. Band Bd., Brookings, 1991, City Planning Commn., Brookings, 1989-91; judge Nat. History Day, S.D. and Iowa, 1984, 85, 88. Grantee NEH, 1984. Mem. AAUW (local and state officer 1990), ALA (com. mem. 1987—), Mountain Plains Libr. Assn. (com. chair, 1990, 91), Colo. Libr. Assn., Phi Alpha Theta, Beta Phi Mu. Office: Western State Coll Leslie J Savage Libr Gunnison CO 81231

RICHARDS, SUZANNE V., lawyer; b. Columbia, S.C., Sept. 7, 1927; d. Raymond E. and Elise C. (Gray) R. AB, George Washington U.,. 1948, JD with distinction, 1957, LLM, 1959. Bar: D.C., 1958. Sole practice, Washington, 1974—; lectr. in family and probate law. Recipient John Bell Larner award George Washington U., 1958; named Woman Lawyer of the Yr., Women's Bar Assn. D.C., 1977. Mem. Bar Assn. D.C. (pres. 1989-90), Women's Bar Assn. (pres. 1977-78), Trial Lawyers Assn. of D.C. (bd. govs. 1978-82, 85—, treas. 1982-85), D.C. Bar, Fed. Bar Assn., Nat. Assn. Women Lawyers, ABA (mem. ho. dels. 1988-90), D.C. Jud. Conf. Office: 1701 K St NW Washington DC 20006-1409

RICHARDS-KORTUM, REBECCA RAE, biomedical engineering educator; b. Grand Island, Nebr., Apr. 14, 1964; d. Larry Alan and Linda Mae (Hohnstein) Richards; m. Philip Ted Kortum, May 12, 1985; children: Alexander Scott, Maxwell James. BS, U. Nebr., 1985; MS, MIT, 1987, PhD, 1990. Assoc. U. Tex., Austin, 1990—. Named Presdl. Young Investigator NSF, Washington, 1991; NSF presdl. faculty fellow, Washington, 1992; recipient Career Achievement award Assn. Advancement Med. Instrumentation, 1992, Dow Outstanding Young Faculty awd., Am. Soc. for Engineering Education, 1992. Mem. AAAS, Am. Soc. Engrng. Edn. (Outstanding Young Faculty award 1992), Optical Soc. Am., Am. Soc. Photobiology. Office: U Tex Dept Elec & Computer Engrng Austin TX 78712

RICHARDSON, ALMA SUSAN, consultant; b. West Helena, Ark., Nov. 25, 1951; d. Alvin Young and Dorothy (Scott) Blue; m. Ernest R. Richardson, Dec. 28, 1974 (div. Oct. 1988); 1 child, Candace Ray. BS, Jackson State U., 1972. Sec., libr. asst., adminstrv. asst. AT&T, Atlanta and Washington, 1973-95; cons. KRA Corp., Silver Spring, Md., 1995—; rschr. U. Mich., Ann Arbor, 1996. Election judge Rep. Party, Landover, Md., 1996; mem. Akosua Visions Global Ministries, 1996—; mentor Nicholas Orem Mid. Sch., 1994-95; founder FGO-For Girls Only Program Series, 1996. Mem. Nat. Mus. for Women in Arts, Network Enhancement Self-Esteem. Home and Office: 1923 Dutch Village Dr Landover MD 20785

RICHARDSON, ARLINE ANNETTE, accountant, comptroller; b. N.Y.C., Aug. 20, 1939; d. Charles Sidney and Kathleen Gertrude (Sinclair) Hunt; m. David Edward Richardson, Sept. 13, 1958; children: Valerie-Jayne, LaVerne; stepchildren: James, David, Carl. AA, Bronx (N.Y.) C.C., 1976; BBA, CUNY, 1979, MPA, 1984. Mgr. patient accounts Jewish Home and Hosp. for Aged, N.Y.C., 1960-80; chief bookkeeper Edwin Gould Svcs. for Children, N.Y.C., 1980-81; staff acct. N.Y. Hosp., N.Y.C., 1981-84; mgr. Met. Transp. Authority, N.Y.C., 1984-92; compt. The Computer Lab., Morrisville, N.C., 1993—. Vol. cmty. tax aide, N.Y.C., 1979-83; tutor Henderson (N.C.) Mid. Sch., 1993-95; vol. Maria Parham Hosp., 1993—, mem. ethics com., 1996—; mem. Henderson-Vance County Human Rels. Commn., 1996—; active Leadership Vance, 1996. Recipient Mitchell-Titus award, 1979. Mem. Am. Assn. Ret. Persons (assoc. dist. coord., instr. tax-aide program North Ctrl. N.C. 1993—), Henderson Bus. and Profl. Women's Club (leadership vance 1996), Beta Gamma Sigma, Phi Theta Kappa (Mitchell-Titus award 1979). Home: 1614 Peace St Henderson NC 27536-3549 Office: The Computer Lab 2700 Gateway Centre Blvd Morrisville NC 27560-9137

RICHARDSON, BARBARA HULL, state legislator, social worker; b. Danville, Pa., Sept. 30, 1922; d. Robert Alonzo and Clara Lucille (Woodruff) H.; widowed; children: Barbara Follansbee, Lawrence, Christine, Lovel Pratt. BA, Bryn Mawr Coll., 1944; MSW, Smith Coll., 1973. Social worker child and family svcs. divsn. children and youth svcs. HHS, Keene, N.H., 1969-71; adminstr. child and family svcs. HHS, Concord, N.H., 1975-88, supr., policy writer, 1988-91; mem. N.H. Ho. Reps., Concord, 1992—. Trustee Meeting Sch., 1980—; bd. dirs. Cheshire Housing Trust, 1986-93, pres., 1993—; adv. bd. Casey Family Svcs. N.H., 1990—; vol. Hospice Monadnock Region, 1991—; mem. community coun. Luth. Social Svcs. New England, 1993—. Democrat. Home: 101 Morgan Rd Richmond NH 03470-4909 Office: NH Ho of Reps State Capitol Concord NH 03301

RICHARDSON, BETTY KEHL, nursing educator, administrator, counselor, resear; b. Jacksonville, Ill., Mar. 24, 1938; d. Alfred Jason and Hilda (Emmons) Kehl; m. Joseph Richardson, June 27, 1959 (div. 1980); children: Mark Joseph, Stephanie Elaine. BA in Nursing, Sangamon State U., 1975, MA in Adminstrn., 1977; MSN, Med. Coll. Ga., 1980; PhD in Nursing, U. Tex., 1985. Cert. advanced nursing adminstrn., clin. specialist child and adolescent psychiat. nursing ANCC; lic. profl. counselor, marriage and family counselor. Instr. nursing Lincoln Land Community Coll., Springfield, Ill., 1978-79; acting dir. nursing MacMurray Coll., Jacksonville, Ill., 1979-81; asst. prof. Sangamon State U., Springfield, 1981-82; adminstr. children and adolescent programs Shoal Creek Hosp., Austin, 1989-90; nursing dir. Austin State Hosp., 1983-89; therapist San Marcos (Tex.) Treatment Ctr., 1989-90; instr. Austin C.C., 1990—; pvt. practice psychotherapy, Austin, 1990—. Advising editor: Parenting in the 90s jour.; contbr. articles to profl. jours. Pres. PTA, 1968. Named Outstanding Nurse, Passavant Hosp., 1958, Nurse of Yr., Tex. Nurses Assn., 1994-95; recipient Plaque for Outstanding Leadership, Austin State Hosp., 1989, plaque for svc. to the poor people of Mexico and C.Am. Internat. Good Neighbor Coun. (Austin chpt.) and U. Area Rotary Club, 1995. Mem. ANA, DAR, Southwest Group Psychotherapy Assn., Tex. Counseling Assn., Assn. Play Therapy, Rotary (Good Neighbor Coun./Univ. award 1995), Sigma Theta Tau, Phi Kappa Phi. Methodist. Home: 5207 Doe Valley Ln Austin TX 78759-7103 Office: Austin C C 1020 Grove Blvd Austin TX 78759-3300

RICHARDSON, DEANNA RUTH, microbiologist; b. Columbus, Ohio, Jan. 7, 1956; d. Raymond and Anna Mary (Underwood) R. BS, Ohio State U., 1978. Lab tech. Ohio Dept. Agr., Reynoldsburg, Ohio, 1978-81, lab technologist, 1981-86, microbiologist, 1986—. Active East Columbus Christian Ch.; mem. Neighborhood Civic Assn., 1983-87. Mem. Ohio Valley Inst. Food Technologists, Vet. Microbiologists Assn., Ohio State U. Alumni Assn., Franklin County Alumni Club, Smithsonian Instn., Nat. Wildlife Fedn., Internat. Wildlife Fedn., World Wildlife Fund, African Wildlife Found., Columbus Zoo, Ohio State U. Century Club, Ohio State U. Friend of the Wexner Art Ctr. Home: 6267 Barberry Hollow Columbus OH 43213-3308 Office: Ohio Dept Agr Labs 8995 E Main St Reynoldsburg OH 43068-3398

RICHARDSON, DEBORAH KAYE, clinical nurse specialist, educator; b. Tyler, Tex., Mar. 31, 1953; d. Clarence Bruce and thelma Lee (McCarty) R. BS, Houston Bapt. U., 1975; BSN, Tex. Womans U., Houston, 1983, MSN, 1995. Hosp. aide M.D. Anderson Cancer Ctr., Houston, 1979-80, med. technologist, 1980-83, clinician, 1983-88, asst. nurse mgr., 1988-91, clin. instr., 1991-95, clinician IV, 1994-96, clin. nurse specialist, 1996—; coord. infusion therapy program Twelve Oak Hosp., Houston, 1990, outreach PICCS program, 1986—. Contbr. articles to profl. jours. Mem. Woodland Heights Assn., Houston, 1991—. Recipient Profl. Growth award Houston Bapt. U., 1974. Mem. Oncology Nurses Soc., Nat. Assn. Vascular Access Network, Phi Theta Kappa. Home: 1101 Highland St Houston TX 77009-6516 Office: University Texas MD Anderson Cancer Ctr 1515 Holcombe Houston TX 77030

RICHARDSON, DOT, softball player; b. Sept. 22, 1961. Student, Western Ill. U., UCLA. Ortho. surgeon. Recipient Gold medal Pan. Am. Games, 1979, 87, 95, ISF Women's World Championship, 1986, 94, South Pacific Classic, 1994, Superball Classic, 1995, Atlanta Olympics, 1996, Rev Linda award; named All-Am. Am. Softball Assn., MVP Am. Softball Assn. Major Fast Pitch Nat. Championship, Player of 1980s NCAA. Office: Amateur Softball Assn 2801 NE 50th St Oklahoma City OK 73111-7203*

RICHARDSON, ELSIE HELEN, retired elementary education educator; b. Vancouver, Wash., Feb. 1, 1918; d. Anthony William and Marie Julia (Dušek) Podhora-Clark; m. Clyde Stanley Richardson, Oct. 16, 1944 (dec. 1989). BA, Cen. Washington Coll. Edn., 1939. Cert. jr. high sch. prin.; cert. life elem. tchr., Calif., life spl. secondary to teach mentally retarded; cert. psychometrist, Calif. Tchr. 2d and 3d grades Randle (Wash.) Sch. Dist., 1939-40; remedial tchr. Randle, 1940-41; 2d grade tchr. Seattle Sch. Dist., 1941-44; remedial tchr., mental testing specialist Vancouver, Wash., 1944-45; tchr. 3rd grade Lancaster (Calif.) Sch. Dist., 1946-48; tchr. spl. edn. Bakersfield (Calif.) Sch. Dist., 1948-49; tchr. 2d grade Norco (Calif.) Sch. Dist., 1950-51; tchr. 4th grade Chino (Calif.) Sch. Dist., 1951-55, tchr. spl. edn., 1955-79, ret., 1979. Leader Girl Res., Camp Rimrock, Wash., summer 1939; leader Bluebird Club, 1939. Recipient Cert. of Appreciaiton, State Assembly of Calif., 1979. Mem. NEA, AAUW, Am. Assn. Ret. Persons, Calif. Tchrs. Assn. (rep.), Calif. Ret. Tchrs. Assn., Vancouver Edn. Assn., Chino Tchrs. Assn. (past v.p., sec.), Wash. State Tchrs. Assn. (rep.), PTA (life), Fun After Fifty Club, Delta Kappa Gamma.

RICHARDSON, GAIL MARGUERITE, community services agency executive; b. Brattleboro, Vt., Oct. 15, 1955; d. Guilford Elwin and Verna Marie (Buckey) Richardson; m. Eric Paul Johnson, Oct. 16, 1982. BS in Bus. Adminstrn., U. Vt., 1978. CPA, Vt. In-charge auditor P.F. Jurgs & Co., Burlington, Vt., 1978-81; assoc. R.F. Lavigne Co., Burlington, 1981-82; supr. fin. reporting C & S Wholesale Grocers, Inc., Brattleboro, Vt., 1982-86; audit supt., non-profit specialist Joseph Pieciak & Co., Brattleboro, 1986-89; comptroller, chief fin. officer Marlboro (Vt.) Coll., 1990-92; contr. Seventh Generation, Colchester, Vt., 1992-93; primary caregiver V. Buffum, Shelburne, Vt., 1993-94; personal support agt. Howard Cmty. Svcs., Burlington, Vt., 1994—; dir. Vt. Student Assistance Corp., Winooski, 1991—; prof. Cmty. Coll. Vt., Brattleboro, 1987-90; fin. cons. Assist, Inc., Wilder, Vt., 1982-86, 94—. Treas. Vt.-N.H. Belfast Kids, Inc., Brattleboro, 1987-91, Brattleboro Child Devel. Corp., 1989-90; active Big Bro. and Big Sister Program, Brattleboro, 1983-85; asst. basketball coach Vt. Spl. Olympics, Burlington. Office: Howard Cmty Svcs 109 S Winooski Ave Burlington VT 05401

RICHARDSON, GRACE ELIZABETH, consumer products company executive; b. Salem, Mass., Nov. 22, 1938; d. George and Julia (Sheridan) R.; m. Ralph B. Henderson, Mar. 3, 1979. B.S., Simmons Coll., 1960; M.S., Cornell U., 1962; M.B.A., NYU, 1981. Textile technologist Harris Research Lab., Washington, 1962-65; instr. Simmons Coll., Boston, 1965-66; dir. consumer edn. materials J.C. Penney, N.Y.C., 1966-73; dir. residential conservation Con Edison, N.Y.C., 1974-81; dir. consumer affairs Chesebrough-Ponds, Greenwich, Conn., 1981-85; v.p. global consumer affairs Colgate Palmolive, N.Y.C., 1985—. Bd. dirs. Cornell Club, N.Y.C., 1989—, chair Simmons Coll. Leadership Coun., 1993—; com. mem. Julliard Sch., 1996—; bd. dirs. City Vols. Corps, 1996—, SOCAP, 1996—. Named Nat. Bus. Home Economist of Yr., Home Economists in Bus., 1979. Mem. Cornell U. Coun. (chair pub. rels. com. 1988—), Nat. Coalition Consumer Edn. (bd. dirs. 1983—), Women's Forum. Home: 180 E 79th St New York NY 10021 Office: Colgate Palmolive Co 300 Park Ave New York NY 10022-7402

RICHARDSON, IRENE M., health facility administrator; b. Columbia, Tenn., Oct. 22, 1938; d. John Frank and Beatrice (Hill) Murphy; m. Joseph Richardson, Dec. 27, 1960; children: Pamela, Joseph, John, Karen. BS, Ramapo Coll., Mahwah, N.J., 1981; MBA, Farleigh Dickinson U., 1987; nursing diploma summa cum laude, St. Thomas Sch. of Nursing, Nashville, 1959. RN, N.J.; cert. sr. profl. in human resources. Clin. instr. St. Thomas Hosp., Nashville; coord. edn., staff nurse St. Clare's Hosp., Denville, N.J.; pres. Cygnus Assocs., Inc., Kinnelon, N.J., 1986-95; dir. edn. and tng. Northwest Covenant Med. Ctr. (formerly St. Clares Riverside), Denville, N.J., 1995—. Author: RN Job Satisfaction. Recipient U.S. Pub. Health Svc. scholarship. Mem. Am. Soc. for Health Care Edn. and Tng., Soc. for Health Care Edn. and Tng. N.J. (bd. dirs.), Women's Svc. Orgn. (pres. 1995-96). Home: 65 Fayson Lake Rd Kinnelon NJ 07405-3129

RICHARDSON, JANE, librarian; b. Sept. 16, 1946; d. Robert Clark and Evagene (Davis) Richardson; m. Frank Velasques Martinez Jr., May 28, 1966 (div. July 1970); 1 child, Robert Louis Martinez; m. William John Lorance, Feb. 14, 1983 (div. 1996). BA in History, U. Wyo., 1971; MLibr, U. Wash., 1972. Reference and fine arts libr. Clark County Libr., 1973; dept. head Clark County Libr. Dist., 1974-77; br. supr./adminstr. Newport Beach (Calif.) Pub. Libr., 1978-82; on-call libr. Santa Ana and Newport Beach Pub. Librs., Calif. State U., Fullerton, 1984; br. adminstr. Las Vegas-Clark County Libr. Dist., 1985—. Mem. Freedom to Read Found. Mem. ALA, Popular Culture Assn., Nev. Libr. Assn., Mountain Plains Libr. Assn., So. Calif. On-Line Users Group, Newport Beach Profl. and Tech. Employees Assn. Office: Las Vegas-Clark County Libr 833 Las Vegas Blvd N Las Vegas NV 89101-2030

RICHARDSON, KATHRYN V., financial services executive; b. Cedar Rapids, Iowa, May 12, 1955; d. George Ray and Loyola Margaret (Pauly) Keller; m. Jon Allan Richardson, Oct. 26, 1974; children: Ryan Thomas, Jaclyn Kay, Justin Lee. BS, Miss. U. Women, 1983. Sr. acct. Tesoro Petrolatum Corp., San Antonio, 1984-86; acct. Transportation Trendsetters, San Antonio, 1986-87, Mid-Continent Leasing, Inc., Rochester, Minn., 1987-89; playgroup lead parent U.S. Army Preschool, Berlin, 1990-91; fin. asst. Rochester (Minn.) C. of C., 1992-95; v.p. fin. Custom Iron, Inc., Zumbrota, Minn., 1995—. Pres. bd. Van Horn Libr., Pine Island, Minn., 1993—; vol. AA Jr. Olympics, Rochester, 1994; den leader Pack #69 Boy Scouts Am., Pine Island, 1994; mem. ACE SCORE, Rochester, Minn., 1995—. Named family of yr. Pine Island Jaycees, 1995; recipient Young Minnesotan award, 1996. Mem. Inst. Mgmt. Accts., Rochester Art Ctr., PTSA, Svc. Corps Ret. Execs. (cons. 1994—), Mu Rho Sigma. Office: Custom Iron Inc 201 E 1st St Zumbrota MN 55963

RICHARDSON, KAY CULVER, mathematics educator; b. Kansas City, Kans., July 23, 1950; d. Gordon Perry and Thelma Bernice (Pelikan) Culver; m. William Bert Richardson, Jr., Jan. 1, 1972; children: Amy, Todd, Scott. BA, Colo. State U., 1972; MA, U. Colo., 1986. Substitute tchr. Sch. Dist. #20, USAF Academy, Colo., 1976-78, tchr., 1978; tchr. math. Sch. Dist. #8, Fountain, Colo., 1980—, staff devel. cadre, 1991-93, math curriculum com. mem., 1994—; math. curriculum com. mem., 1994—, social studies curriculum mem., 1995—; site coord. Kids Vote; tutor for pvt. bus., Colorado Springs, Colo., 1974—. Mem. St. Stephen's Choir, Colorado Springs, 1989—. Mem. Colo. Coun. Tchrs. Math. Episcopalian.

RICHARDSON, LAUREL WALUM, sociology educator; b. Chgo., July 15, 1938; d. Tyrrell Alexander and Rose (Foreman) R.; m. Herb Walum, Dec. 27, 1959 (div. 1972); children: Benjamin, Joshua; m. Ernest Lockridge, Dec. 12, 1981. AB, U. Chgo., 1955, BA, 1956; PhD, U. Colo., 1963. Asst. prof. Calif. State U., Los Angeles, 1962-64; postdoctoral fellow Sch. Medicine Ohio State U., Columbus, 1964-65, asst. prof. sociology, 1970-75, assoc. prof., 1975-79, prof. sociology, 1979—; asst. prof. sociology Denison U., Granville, Ohio, 1965-69; mem. editorial bd. Jour. Contemporary Ethnography, Symbolic Interaction, Gender & Soc., Qualitative Sociology, Sociol. Quar. Author: Dynamics of Sex and Gender, 1977, 3d edit. 1988, The New Other Woman, 1985, Die Neve Andere, 1987, A Nova Outra Mulher, 1987, Writing Strategies: Reaching Diverse Audiences, 1990, Gender and University Teaching: A Negotiated Difference, 1995; editor: Feminist Frontiers, 1983, 4th edit., 1997; author more than 100 rsch. articles and papers. Ford Found. fellow, 1954-56; NSF dissertation fellow, 1960-62; post doctoral fellow Vocat. Rehab., Columbus, 1964; grantee Ohio Dept. Health, 1986-87, Nat. Inst. Edn., 1981-82, NIMH, 1972-74, NSF, 1963-64, NEH, 1992; recipient Disting. Affirmative Action award Ohio State U., 1983. Mem. Am. Sociol. Assn. (com. on coms. 1980-81, com. on pub. info. 1987—), North Ctrl. Sociol. Assn. (pres. 1986-87), Sociologists for Women in Soc. (coun. mem. 1978-80), Ctrl. Ohio Sociologists for Women in Soc. (past pres.), Women's Poetry Workshop, Soc. for Study of Symbolic Interaction (publs. com.). Democrat. Office: Ohio State Univ Dept of Sociology 190 N Oval Mall Columbus OH 43210-1321

RICHARDSON, LILY PENDARVIS, retired occupational health nurse; b. Columbia, N.C., Feb. 23, 1939; d. Theophilus Pendarvis and Comeller (Bowser) Johnson; m. Napoleon Richardson, Apr. 4, 1959; children: Donald Felton, Napoleon Jr. BS cum laude, N.C. A&T U., 1961. RN, D.C. Charge nurse L. Richardson Hosp., Greensboro, N.C., 1961-63; charge nurse medicine Georgetown U. Med. Ctr., Washington, 1963-64; charge nurse of nursery D.C. Gen. Hosp., Washington, 1964-67; occupational health nurse, occupational health adminstr. FBI, Washington, 1967-94; adminstr. nursing program FBI, 1994; part time instr. practical nurses Dudley High Sch., Greensboro, 1962; cons. Establishing Health Units, 1990-94, Med. Standard Task Force, Washington, 1993, Bloodborne Pathogen Task Force, 1993. Active cmty. svc. Rosemary Hills Sch., Silver Spring, Md., 1992-94, sch. bd., 1993; blood pressure screener, counselor at several cmty. chs. and cmty. health ctrs.; mail worker Health Reform Com., Washington, 1993-94. Mem. NAACP, Nat. Black Nurses Assn., Black Nurses Greater Washington D.C. ARea (rec. sec. 1985—), Met. Washington Assn. Occupational Health Nurses, Teloca Nursing Alumni (parliamentarian 1970—), A&T Alumni, Sigma Theta Tau (Mutau chpt. internat. charter, Gamma Beta chpt. 1 of 100 Extraordinary Nurses 1994). Home: 2212 Ross Rd Silver Spring MD 20910-2336

RICHARDSON, MARGARET MILNER, federal agency administrator, lawyer; b. Waco, Tex., May 14, 1943; d. James W. and Margaret Wiebusch Milner; m. John L. Richardson, July 22, 1967; 1 child, Margaret Lawrence. AB in Polit. Sci., Vassar Coll., 1965; JD with honors, George Washington U., 1968. Bar: Va. 1968, D.C. 1968, U.S. Dist. Ct. D.C. 1968, U.S. Ct. Appeals (4th, 5th, D.C. and Fed. cirs.) 1968, U.S. Claims Ct. 1969, U.S. Tax Ct. 1970, U.S. Supreme Ct. 1971. Clk. U.S. Ct. Claims, Washington; with Office Chief Counsel IRS, Washington, 1969-77; with Sutherland, Asbill and Brennan, Washington, 1977-80, ptnr., 1980-93; commr. IRS, Washington, 1993—; mem. commr.'s adv. group IRS, 1988-90, chair, 1990; mem. fed. tax adv. group Prentice Hall. Contbr. articles to profl. jours. Assisted Clinton 1992 gen. election campaign; served as team leader Justice Dept./Civil Rights Cluster during Presdl. Transition. Mem. ABA, D.C. Bar Assn. (tax sect.), Va. State Bar Assn., Fed. Bar Assn. (coun. taxation), Fin. Women's Assn. N.Y. Office: IRS 1111 Constitution Ave NW Washington DC 20224-0001

RICHARDSON, MARGO, middle school educator; b. Ottawa, Ill., Aug. 5, 1951; d. Francis Edward and Laurie Ann (Scherer) Sexton; m. Roy Neil Richardson, June 8, 1974; children: Brent (dec.), Dawn Marie, Dona Ann. BS, U. Ill., 1973, MS, 1977, cert. in advanced edn., 1981. Cert. tchr., Ill. Math. and algebra tchr., volleyball coach Sterling (Ill.) H.S., 1973-74; math. and algebra tchr. Urbana (Ill.) Mid. Sch., 1974—, synchronized swim club sponsor, 1975-79; pom pom sponsor Urbana Jr. H.S., 1975-76; facilitator for 8th grade team Urbana Mid. Sch., 1994—; conf. spkr. Ill. Coun. Tchrs. Math., Ea. Ill., 1995, Urbana Schs., 1995; Ctrl. Ill. Gifted Conf., 1995. Troop leader Girl Scouts USA, Urbana, 1990-94; room mother PTA, Urbana, 1987-95. Mem. NEA, Urbana Edn. Assn., Nat. Coun. Tchrs. Math., EC2TM, Delta Kappa Gamma (1st v.p. 1981—), Phi Delta Kappa. Office: Urbana Sch Dist 116 1201 S Vine St Urbana IL 61801-5016

RICHARDSON, MARTHA, nutrition analyst; b. Noble, La., Apr. 22, 1917; d. Alexander M. and Olive (Barlow) R.; A.B., U. Mo., 1938, Ph.D., 1953; M.S., Kans. State U., 1939. Dietitian, William Newton Meml. Hosp., Winfield, Kans., 1940-42, Molly Stark Sanatorium, Canton, Ohio, 1942-47; asst. dir. residence halls, instr. home econs. U. Mo., 1947-50, instr. home econs., 1951-53; head of foods and nutrition U. Utah, 1953-55; nutrition analyst Agrl. Research Service, Washington, 1955-80. Named Disting. Alumna, U. Mo., 1968. Fellow AAAS; mem. Am. Dietetic Assn., Am. Home Econs. Assn., Am. Med. Writers Assn., Am. Inst. Food Techologists, Am. Chem. Soc. Am. Assn. Cereal Chemists, Am. Forestry Assn., AAUW, N.Y. Acad. Scis., Sigma Xi, Gamma Sigma Delta, Phi Upsilon Omicron, Sigma Delta Epsilon. Contbr. articles to profl. jours. Home: 18700 Walkers Choice Rd Apt 302 Gaithersburg MD 20879-2552

RICHARDSON, MARY LOU, psychotherapist; b. Topeka, Oct. 4, 1953; d. Darrell and Beverly Nutter; m. Kenneth T Richardson Jr. children: Shad Martin, Cheralyn Pasbrig, Kenneth T Richardson III, Russ Richardson. Cert. addictions counselor, Ariz.; cert. Nat. Assn. of Alcolism and Drug Abuse Counselors. Counselor Compcare Alcoholism Ctr. The Meadows Treatment Ctr., Phoenix, 1986-88; co-dir. Phoenix Cons. & Counseling Assocs., Ariz., 1989—; founder and adminstr. The Orion Found., Ariz.; project mem. The Hutoomkhum Com. and Support Program, Hopi Reservation, Ariz.; cons. Baywood Hosp., 1988-89; faculty instr. The Recovery Source, 1989-90; chair Nat. Conv. Women, 1992. Author: Women's Acts of Power, 1991-93, Relationship Recover, 1992—, Women's Empowerment, 1992—, Body, Mind & Spirit, 1994—. Mem. Am. Mental Health Counselors, Am. Counseling Assn., Nat. Assn. Alcoholism & Drug Abuse Counselors, Nat. Reciprocity Consortium. Office: Phoenix Cons & Counseling Assocs 5333 N 7th St Ste A202 Phoenix AZ 85014

RICHARDSON, MARY WELD, training and organization specialist, company executive; b. Port Washington, N.Y., Dec. 8, 1946; d. Weld and Florence (McBeth) R. BA, Columbia U., 1970; MA in Psychology, Sonoma State U., Calif., 1992. Ops. dir. restaurant divsn. Newhall Land & Farming Co., Valencia, Calif., 1976-80; regional tng. specialist World Savs. and Loan Assn., Oakland, Calif., 1982-89; tng. specialist San Francisco Fed. Savs. and Loan, 1989-92; sr. ptnr. WorkLife Resources, Kenwood, Calif., 1990—; tng. and orgn. effectiveness specialist Sola Optical, Petaluma, Calif., 1995—; tng. cons. Redwood Conflict Resolution Svc., Santa Rosa, Calif., 1993—, SSU Cons. Group, Santa Rosa, 1990-93. Author: Client Centered Learning, 1993. Mediator RECOURSE, Santa Rosa, 1990—; family group facilitator Choices for Change, Santa Rosa, 1992-95; facilitator Am. Corps.-The Sonoma Project, 1993-95, Sonoma County AIDS Found., 1994—. Mem. Internat. Soc. Performance and Instruction (chpt. pres. 1993-94). Office: WorkLife Resources PO Box 886 842 Warm Springs Rd Kenwood CA 95452-0886

RICHARDSON, MIRANDA, actress; b. Lancashire, Eng., 1958. Studied, Drama Program Bristol. Stage performances London: Moving, All My Sons, Who's Afraid of Virginia Woolf, The Life of Einstein, A Lie of the Mind; others include The Changling, Mountain Language; TV appearances: The Hard World, Sorrel and Son, A Woman of Substance, Underworld, Death of the Heart, (series) Black Adder II, Sweet as You Are, (miniseries) Die Kinder; films: Dance with a Stranger, 1985, The Innocent, 1986, Empire of the Sun, 1987, Eat the Rich, 1987, Twisted Obsession, 1990, The Bachelor, 1991, Enchanted April, 1992, Damage, 1992 (B.A.F.T.A. award for Best Supporting Actress), The Crying Game, 1992 (Acad. award nominee for best supporting actress), Fatherland, HBO, 1994 (Golden Globe award), Tom & Viv, 1994 (Acad. award nominee for best actress 1995), La Nuit et Le Moment, 1994, Kansas City, 1996. *

RICHARDSON, NATASHA JANE, actress; b. May 11, 1963; d. Tony Richardson and Vanessa Redgrave; m. Liam Neeson, July 3, 1994; 1 son: Micheál Richard Antonio. Acting debut on stage at Leeds (England) Playhouse, 1983; appearences include (plays) A Midsummer's Night Dream, Hamlet, 1985, The Seagull, 1985, High Society, 1987, Anna Christie, 1993 (Tony award nominee 1993, Drama Desk award), (films) Every Picture Tells a Story, 1984, Gothic, 1987, A Month in the Country, 1987, Patty Hearst, 1988, Fat Man and Little Boy, 1989, The Handmaid's Tale, 1990, The Comfort of Strangers, 1991, The Favor, The Watch and the Very Big Fish, 1992, Past Midnight, Widows' Peak, 1994, Nell, 1994, (TV) In a Secret State, 1984, The Copper Beaches, 1984, Ghosts, 1986, Suddenly Last Summer, 1992, Hostages, 1993, Zelda, 1993. Recipient Most Promising Newcomer award Plays & Players, 1986; named Best Actress by London Theatre Critics, Plays & Players, 1990, Evening Standard Best Actress, 1990.

RICHARDSON, PATRICIA, actress; b. Bethesda, Md., Feb. 23, 1951; d. Laurence Baxter and Elizabeth (Howard) R.; m. Raymond Baker, June 20, 1982; children: Henry, Roxanne, Joseph. BFA, So. Meth. U., 1972. Appearences include (Broadway) Gypsy, Loose Ends, The Wake of Jamie Foster; (off-Broadway) The Collected Works of Billy the Kid, The Frequency, Vanities, The Coroner's Plot, Hooters, Company, Fables for Friends, The Miss Firecracker Contest, Cruise Control; (regional theatre) King Lear, The Killing of Sister George, Relatively Speaking, The Importance of Being Earnest, Of Mice and Men, The Philadelphia Story, Room Service, Fifth of July, About Face; (nat. tours) Gypsy, Vanities; (films) Gas, 1972, You Better Watch Out, Lost Angels, 1988, In Country, 1988; (TV) Double Trouble, 1984, Eisenhower & Lutz, 1988, FM, 1989-90, Home Improvement, 1991—

(Lead Actress in a Comedy Series Emmy award nominee, 1994, Golden Globe award nominee, 1993, 94). Office: William Morris Agy care Jonathon Howard 151 S El Camino Dr Beverly Hills CA 90212-2704*

RICHARDSON, RUTH GREENE, social worker; b. Washington, Mar. 30, 1926; d. Arthur Alonzo and Ruth Naomi (Conway) Greene; m. Frederick D. Richardson, June 7, 1968; 1 child, Arthur William Boler. BS, St. Louis U., 1948; MSW, Washington U., St. Louis, 1950. Exec. dir. Anna B. Heldman Cmty. Ctr., Pitts., 1962-64; assoc. dir. Hillhouse Assn., Pitts., 1964-67; assoc. dir. Dixwell House, also supr. group work services in community schs., New Haven, 1967-69; exec. dir. Three Rivers Youth Inc., Pitts., 1969-91; adv. bd. Sch. Social Work, U. Pitts., 1979-80; pres. Assn. Residential Youth Care Agys., 1973-77; artist, photographer, social work cons. Peoples Art Show Carnegie, 1991; pres., bd. dirs. Pa. Council Vol. Child Care Agys., 1973-78; asst. v.p. Allegheny Children and Youth Services Council, 1974-76, Ward Program Svcs. Participated in juried nat. art shows: Westmoreland County Mus., 1992, Three Rivers Art, 1992. Bd. dirs. Children's Council Western Pa.; adv. council Booth Home; bd. dirs. Nat. Assn. Homes for Children, Campfire Boys and Girls, 1988, South Arts, YWCA Greater Pitts. Recipient Social Assistance award Pitts. region Women's Am. ORT, 1975, Internat. Yr. of Child award region III, HEW, 1979; Jurors award, 1991, Images Show, 1991, Pitts., Black Artists William Pitt Union Gallery U. Pitts, 1986, Purchase prize Images III Waterworks, 1st prize in water color South Arts Sr. Citizen Show, Purchase prize C.C. Show, Ann. Svc. award Children's Coun. Western Pa., 1990, Best Of The Show award Carnegie Ethnic Art Show, 1993, Merit award South Hills Art League, 1993, Best Floral award Pitts. Garden Ctr., 1993, Real Pittsburgher award Pitts. Mag., 1993, First Place award Native Am. Heritage Com., 1993, Best Overall Artistic Achievement award Cranberry Area Coun. for the Arts, 1993, Community Svc. award Pitts. Club, Nat. Assn. Negro Bus. and Profl. Women's Club, Inc, 1993, Best of the Show award West Hills Art League, 1993, Outstanding Artistic Achievement award Cranberry Twp. Juried Art Exhibit, 3rd Prize award Pitts. Progressive Artist Annual Show, 1995, 3rd Prize award Native Am. Art Compition, 1995, 1st Place Westmoreland Heritage Nat., 1995, 1st Place Schoolhouse Art Ctr., 1995, Best of Show Bethel Park Art League Annual, 1995, 2nd Place Peoples Art Show, Carnegie, Eat and Park Gold Sable award West Hills Art League Annual, 1996, Vol. in Arts award, 1996—. Mem. Child Welfare League Am., Nat. Assn. Social Workers, Pitts. Watercolor Soc., Pa. Soc. Watercolor Painters, Pitts. Soc. Artist, Black Adminstrs. in Child Welfare, Creative Lens, Visions (v.p.), South Hills Art League (bd. dirs.). Presbyterian. Paintings exhibited in Pitts. region. Home and Office: 23 Stratford Ct Carnegie PA 15106-1575

RICHARDSON, SHARON YOUNG, writer; b. Washington, Mar. 13, 1961; d. James Thomas and Evelyn Pollard (Branche) Young; m. Claiborne Turner Richardson II, Nov. 5, 1988; 1 child, Lauren Evelyn. BS in Mass Comm., Va. Commonwealth U., 1983. Reporter Virginian-Pilot, Norfolk, Va., 1983-85; assoc. editor Times News Svc., Springfield, Va., 1985-87; state reporter Times-Dispatch, Richmond, Va., 1987-88; publs. dir. Nat. Assn. Black Journalists, Reston, Va., 1989-90; assoc. editor Assn. Governing Bds. Univ. and Colls., Washington, 1991-93; publs. writer George Mason U., Fairfax, Va., 1993-96; owner Richardson Comm., Woodbridge, Va., 1996—; writing cons. Dynamic Tech. Sys., Alexandria, Va., 1993—. Editor: Economic Prospects for American Higher Education, 1992, Alcohol and Drug Abuse: Policy Guidelines for Boards, 1992. Chairperson publicity com. St. Margaret's Episcopal, Woodbridge, 1994—. Mem. Nat. Assn. Black Journalists, Soc. Profl. Journalists (Sigma Delta Chi Mark of Excellence 1983), Washington Ind. Writers (sec. bd. dirs. 1996—), Washington Assn. Black Journalists. Episcopalian. Home: 11954 Cotton Mill Dr Woodbridge VA 22192-1508

RICHARDSON, SHIRLEY MAXINE, public relations director; b. Rising Sun, Ind., May 3, 1931; d. William Fenton and Mary (Phillips) Keith; m. Arthur Lee Richardson, Feb. 11, 1950; children—Mary Jane Hunt, JoDee Mayfield, Steven Lee Richardson. Personnel mgr. Mayhill Pubs., Knightstown, Ind., 1967-87, prodn. mgr., 1975-87, editor, 1967-87; info. staff, assoc. editor Ind. Farm Bur., Inc., 1987-89, dir. info. and pub. rels., 1989-94, ret., 1994; part time real estate agent Century 21, 1994-95; genealogy editor AntiqueWeek, 1996—. Mem. Newspaper Farm Editors of Am., Am. Agrl. Editors' Assn., Profl. Journalists of Am. Republican. Avocations: traveling, reading, boating, quilting. Home: 366 E Carey St Knightstown IN 46148-1208 Office: 27 N Jefferson St Knightstown IN 46148

RICHARDSON, SUE STOUGHTON, realtor, education advocate/policy maker; b. Shelbyville, Ind., July 16, 1948; d. Homer C. and Doris D. (Robison) Stoughton; m. Charles T. Richardson, Nov. 16, 1973; children: C. Todd, Lee Merritt. BS in Edn., Ind. U., 1970; MS in Edn., Butler U., 1972. Tchr. Indpls. Pub. Schs., 1970-75; realtor S. Richardson Homes, Indpls., 1973—; dir. Parent Power, Inc., Carmel, Ind., 1992—. Bd. visitors Butler U., Indpls., 1996—; adv. bd. Heartland Film Festival, Indpls., 1995—, Ind. Edn. Policy Ctr., Indpls., 1992—, Ind. Adolescent Adv. Bd., 1994—; mem. sch. bd. Carmel Clay Schs., 1986-94, State Bd. of Edn. of Ind., 1993—. Mem. Nat. Assn. State Bds. Edn. (chair, govt. affairs com. 1994—).

RICHARDSON-MELECH, JOYCE SUZANNE, secondary school educator, singer; b. Perth Amboy, N.J., Nov. 15, 1957; d. Herbert Nathaniel and Fannie Elaine (Franklin) Richardson; m. Gerald Melech, July 28, 1990. MusB, Westminster Choir Coll., 1979, MusM, 1981. Cert. music tchr., N.J. Musical play dir. Perth Amboy H.S., 1989-92, asst. band dir., 1984-94; music tchr. Perth Amboy Bd. Edn., 1981—, gifted and talented music tchr., 1992—; vocal soloist N.Y. Philharm. and Westminster Symphonic Choir, 1977, United Moravian Ch., N.Y.C., 1980-81, Ctrl. Jersey Concert Orch., Perth Amboy, 1994—. Participant Perth Amboy Adult Cmty. Theatre, 1983. Mem. Am. Fedn. Tchrs., Am. Fedn. Musicians (local 373), Music Educators Nat. Conf., Ctrl. Jersey Music Educators, Alpha Phi Omega. Democrat. Mem. African Meth. Episcopal Zion Ch. Home: 148 Carson Ct Somerset NJ 08873-4790 Office: Samuel Shull Sch 380 Hall Ave Perth Amboy NJ 08861-3402

RICHBART, CAROLYN MAE, mathematics educator; b. Catskill, N.Y., Aug. 12, 1945; d. George R. and Frances (Reynolds) Eden; m. Lynn A. Richbart, Aug. 15, 1987. BS, SUNY, Geneseo, 1967, MEd, 1982; PhD, U. Albany, 1992. Cert. math. tchr., elem. tchr., N.Y. Tchr. Wolcott St. Sch., Le Roy, N.Y., 1967-69; math. tchr. Le Roy Cen. High Sch., 1969-72, Attica (N.Y.) Mid. Sch., 1978-84; assoc. prof. Genesee C.C., Batavia, N.Y., 1984-87; grad. asst. U. Albany, 1987-90; asst. prof. Russell Sage Coll., Troy, N.Y., 1990-92, SUNY, New Paltz, 1992—; project dir. grades kindergarten through 6, N.Y. State Math Mentor Network. Contbr. articles to profl. jours. Mem. Nat. Coun. Tchrs. Math. (speaker), Assn. Math. Tchrs. N.Y. State (rec. sec. 1988-89, corr. sec. 1991-92, pres. 1995-96, chair workshop 1992, chair program 1989, chair Wyoming County sect. 1985-88), N.Y. State Assn. Two-Yr. Colls. (exec. bd. 1986-90, legis. chair 1986-89, curriculum chair 1989-90). Home: 25 Marthas Ct Saugerties NY 12477-4235 Office: SUNY at New Paltz Old Main New Paltz NY 12561-2499

RICHBURG, KATHRYN SCHALLER, nurse, educator; b. Picayune, Miss., Nov. 29, 1949; m. Edward Richburg Sr., June 24, 1972; children: William II, Kathryn. Diploma, Gilfoy Sch. Nursing, 1970; BSN, U. Miss. Med. Ctr., 1972. Cert. in nursing adminstrn., nursing continuing edn., infection control; cert. healthcare quality profl. Oper. rm. nurse, instr. ARC, 1970-82; infection control nurse U.S. Naval Hosp., Guam, 1982-83; nurse epidemiologist, utilization review coord. Nemours Children's Hosp., Jacksonville, Fla., 1983-86; utilization review coord. SunCare HMO, Jacksonville, Fla., 1986-87; program mgr. Trident Tech. Coll. Dept. Continuing Edn., Charleston, S.C., 1987-89; program mgr., acting dir. dept. continuing edn. Med. U. S.C., Charleston, 1989-90; edn. coord. quality mgmt. VA Med. Ctr., Charleston, 1990-93; quality assurance risk mgr. U.S. Naval Hosp., Yokosuka, Japan, 1993-95; health promotion dept. head U.S. Naval Hosp., Yokosuka, 1995—. Mem. S.C. Nurses Assn. (chmn. conv. com. 1992, mem. continuing edn. provider unit 1990-92), Trident Nurses Assn. (del. 1990-92, mem. planning com. Rsch. Day 1991, 92), Nat. Assn. Healthcare Quality.

RICHEIMER, MARY JANE, retired educator; b. Massillon, Ohio, Oct. 20, 1913; d. Thomas Carl and Nellie (Bea) R. AB, Lake Erie Coll., 1936; MA, Kent State U., 1951; postgrad., Northwestern U., 1960, U. London, 1968-69. Asst. libr. Lake Erie Coll., Painesville, Ohio, 1936-37; tchr. Edmund Jones Jr. High Sch., Massillon, 1937-45, Washington High Sch., Massillon, 1945-51; libr. New Trier High Sch., Winnetka, Ill., 1951-53; tchr., chmn. dept. English Evanston (Ill.) Twp. High Sch., 1953-74; mem. classified advt. staff Pioneer Press, Wilmette, Ill., 1975-82; now ret.; summer sch. instr. lit. for adolescents, Northwestern U., Evanston, 1960; mem. nat. bd. tchrs. of English, Scholastic mags., N.Y.C., 1960—; vol. libr. Evanston Hosp. Med. Libr., 1989—. Author: A Century of Education, 1947; co-author: Planning My Future, 1961; contbr. poetry, articles to various publs. Vol. tutor Walker Sch., Evanston, 1990—; editor The Chimes newsletter Presbyn. Homes, Evanston, 1990—; mem. vestry St. Augustine's Episcopal Ch., Wilmette. Mem. AAUW, Evanston Hosp. Women's Aux., Nat. Ret. Tchrs. Assn., North Shore Ret. Tchrs. Assn., Viewers for Quality Television. Republican. Episcopalian. Home: 601 Trinity Ct Evanston IL 60201-1909

RICHENS, MURIEL WHITTAKER, AIDS therapist, counselor and educator; b. Prineville, Oreg.; d. John Reginald and Victoria Cecilia (Pascale) Whittaker; children: Karen, John, Candice, Stephanie, Rebecca. BS, Oreg. State U.; MA, San Francisco State U., 1962; postgrad., U. Calif., Berkeley, 1967-69, U. Birmingham, Eng., 1973, U. Soria, Spain, 1981. Lic. sch. adminstr., tchr. 7-12, pupil personnel specialist, Calif., marriage, child and family counselor, Calif. Instr. Springfield (Oreg.) High Sch., San Francisco State U.; instr., counselor Coll. San Mateo, Calif., San Mateo High Sch. Dist., 1963-86; therapist AIDS Health Project U. Calif., San Francisco, 1988—; pvt. practice MFCC San Mateo; guest West German-European Acad. seminar, Berlin, 1975. Lifeguard, ARC. postgrad. student Ctr. for Human Communications, Los Gatos, Calif., 1974, U. P.R., 1977, U. Guadalajara (Mex.), 1978, U. Durango (Mex.), 1980, U. Guanajuato (Mex.) 1982. Mem. U. Calif. Berkeley Alumni Assn., Am. Contract Bridge League (Diamond Life Master, cert. instr., tournament dir.), Women in Comm., Computer-Using Educators, Commonwealth Club, Pi Lambda Theta, Delta Pi Epsilon. Republican. Roman Catholic. Home and Office: 847 N Humboldt St Apt 309 San Mateo CA 94401-1451

RICHMAN, GERTRUDE GROSS (MRS. BERNARD RICHMAN), civic worker; b. N.Y.C., May 16, 1908; d. Samuel and Sarah Yetta (Seltzer) Gross; B.S., Tchrs. Coll. Columbia U., 1948, M.A., 1949; m. Bernard Richman, Apr. 5, 1930; children—David, Susan. Vol. worker Hackensack Hosp., 1948-70; mem. bd. dirs. YM-YWHA, Bergen County, N.J., 1950-75, bd. mem. emeritus, 1975—; chmn. Leonia Friends of Bergen County Mental Health Consultation Center, 1959; founder, hon. pres. Bergen County Serv-A-Com., affiliated with women orgns. Div. Nat. Jewish Welfare Bd.; v.p. N.J. sect. Nat. Jewish Welfare Bd., 1964-71; hon. trustee women's div. Bergen County United Jewish Community; mem. adv. council Bergen County Office on Aging, 1968-83, reappointed, 1984—; mem. Hackensack Bd. Edn., 1946-51; mem. pub. relations com. Leonia Pub. Schs., 1957-58; N.J. del. White House Conf. on Aging, 1971; trustee Mary McLeod Bethune Scholarship Fund; v.p. Bergen County nat. women's com. Brandeis U., 1966-67. Recipient citation Nat. Council Jewish Women and YWCA in Bergen County, 1962; citation Nat. Jewish Welfare Bd., 1964, Harry S. Feller award N.J. Region, 1965; 14th Ann. Good Scout award Bergen council Boy Scouts Am., 1977; Woman Vol. of Distinction, Bergen County council Girl Scouts, 1979; Human Relations award Bergen County sect. Nat. Council Negro Women, 1982; recipient Gov.'s award, 1988, Cert. of Commendation County Exec. and the Bergen County Bd. of Chosen Freeholders, 1989; honored at testimonial United Jewish Community Bergen County, 1987; Senior Advocate award Divsn. on Aging, 1993. Mem. Kappa Delta Pi.

RICHMAN, JOAN F., television consultant; b. St. Louis, Apr. 10, 1939; d. Stanley M. and Barbara (Friedman) R. B.A., Wellesley (Mass.) Coll., 1961. Asst. producer Sta. WNDT, N.Y.C., 1964-65; researcher CBS News, N.Y.C., 1961-64, researcher spl. events unit, 1965-67; mgr. rsch. CBS News (Rep. and Dem. nat. convs.), N.Y.C., 1968; assoc. producer CBS News, N.Y.C., 1968, producer spl. events, 1969-72; sr. producer The Reasoner Report, ABC News, N.Y.C., 1972-75; exec. producer Sports Spectacular CBS, N.Y.C., 1975-76; exec. producer CBS Evening News weekend broadcasts CBS News, N.Y.C., 1976-81, v.p., dir. spl. events, 1982-87, v.p. news coverage, 1987-89; fellow Inst. Politics, John F. Kennedy Sch. Govt., Harvard U., 1990. Mem. nat. patrons com. Opera Theatre St. Louis. Recipient Emmy award for CBS News space coverage Nat. TV Acad. Arts and Scis., 1970-71; Alumnae Achievement award Wellesley Coll., 1973. Mem. Coun. on Fgn. Rels., Wellesley Coll. Alumnae Assn. (pres. class of 1961, 1966-70). Home: 14 Tinicum Creek Rd Erwinna PA 18920-9246

RICHMOND, ALICE ELENOR, lawyer; b. N.Y.C.; d. Louis A. and Estelle (Muraskin) R.; m. David L. Rosenbloom, July 26, 1981; 1 child, Elizabeth Lara. BA magna cum laude, Cornell U., 1968; JD, Harvard U., 1972; DLH (hon.), North Adams State U., 1987. Bar: Mass. 1973, U.S. Dist. Ct. Mass. 1975, U.S. Ct. Appeals (1st cir.) 1982, U.S. Supreme Ct. 1985. Law clk. to justices Superior Ct., Boston, 1972-73; asst. dist. atty. Office of Dist. Atty., Boston, 1973-76; spl. asst. atty. gen. Office of Atty. Gen., Boston, 1975-77; asst. prof. New Eng. Sch. of Law, Boston, 1976-78; assoc. Lappin, Rosen, Boston, 1978-81; ptnr. Hemenway & Barnes, Boston, 1982-92, Deutsch, Williams, Boston, 1993-95, Richmond, Pauly & Ault, Boston, 1996—; asst. team leader, faculty Trial Advocacy Course, Boston, 1978-82; examiner Mass. Bd. Bar Examiners, Boston, 1983—; trustee Mass. Continuing Legal Edn., Inc., Boston, 1985—. Author (2 chpts.) Rape Crisis Intervention Handbook, 1976; contbr. articles to profl. jours. Bd. of overseers Handel & Haydn Soc., Boston, 1985-94, mem. bd. govs. Handel & Haydn Soc., 1994—; mem. Pres. Adv. Com. on the Arts, 1995—. Named one of Outstanding Young Leaders Boston Jaycees, 1982; Sloan Found. Urban fellow, N.Y.C., 1969. Fellow Am. Coll. Trial Lawyers; mem. ABA (ho. of dels. 1980—, vice chmn. com. on rules and calendar 1986-88), Am. Law Inst., Mass. Bar Assn. (pres. 1986-87), Mass. Bar Found. (pres. 1988-91), Pres. Coun. of Cornell Women; (Trustee, legal def. and edn. fund 1995—), Harvard Club. Office: Richmond Pauly & Ault One Beacon St Boston MA 02108

RICHMOND, DEBORAH VANCE, civil engineer; b. Kansas City, Sept. 8, 1947; d. Gerald Griffith and Elizabeth Gosney (Moss) Riegel; m. Thomas Wayne Richmond, Apr. 4, 1987; children: Ray Gerald, Elizabeth Vance. BS in Civil Engring., U. Mo., 1970. Profl. engr. Mo. Engr. Maran-Ingram-Cooke, St. Charles, Mo., 1970-72, Crane & Fleming, Hannibal, Mo., 1972-75; from hwy. designer to dist. design engr. Mo. Hwy. & Trans. Dept., Hannibal, 1978—; geometric design com. Transp. Rsch. Bd., Washington, 1994—, friend of low volume roads, 1992—. Mem. Chi Epsilon, Tau Beta Pi. Republican. Episcopal. Office: Mo Hwy & Transp Dept PO Box 1067 Hannibal MO 63401

RICHMOND, JENNIFER LYNN, public relations specialist; b. Mount Clemens, Mich., June 11, 1964; d. Donald Earl Richmond and Joyce Ann-Yvonne (Lippard) Coles. AA, St. Petersburg Jr. Coll., 1987; BA, U. South Fla., 1990. Pub. rels. specialist ARC, Hyattsville, Md., 1990-95; cons. Silver Spring, Md., 1995—; pub. rels. cons., writer Housing Authority Balt. City, 1996—. Mem. Prince George's Jaycees, Hyattsville, Md., 1992-95, Prince George's Jaycees Found., Hyattsville, 1994-95, U. South Fla. Alumni Assn. Nat. Capital Chpt., 1994. Named Jaycee of the Yr., Prince George's Jaycees, 1991-92, 92-93; named for Individual Devel. Project of the Yr., 1993. Democrat. Home: 575 Thayer Ave #407 Silver Spring MD 20910

RICHMOND, LEE JOYCE, psychologist, educator; b. Balt., May 31, 1934; d. Alexander J. and Anne (Morganstern) Blank; m. Aug. 9, 1953 (div. 1983); children: Roth, Stephen, Sharon, Jessica. BS, Loyola Coll., 1961; MEd, Johns Hopkins U., 1968; PhD, U. Md., 1972. Licensed psychologist. Prof. psychology Dundalk Community Coll., Balt., 1971-75; prof. edn. Johns Hopkins U., Balt., 1975-86, Loyola Coll., Balt., 1986—; psychologist Counseling and Psychol. Svcs., Balt., 1975—; cons. in field; pres. Counseling & Psychol. Svcs., Balt., 1987—; speaker in field. Co-author: (monograph) Stress in Clergy, 1988; contbr. articles to profl. jours. Recipient Outstanding Contbn. to Psychology award Md. Psychol. Assn., 1986, Disting. Svc. award Nat. Vocat. Guidance Assn., 1984. Mem. ACA (gov.'s coun. 1988-90, pres. 1992, mem. ins. trust 1994—, Appreciation cert. 1990), Nat. Career Devel. Assn. (pres. 1988-89, Past Pres. award 1990). Home: 8907 Greylock Rd Baltimore MD 21208-1004 Office: Loyola Coll 105 Beatty Hall 4501 N Charles St Baltimore MD 21210-2601

RICHMOND, MARILYN SUSAN, lawyer; b. Bethesda, Md., Oct. 19, 1949; d. Carl Hutchins Jr. and Elizabeth Adeline (Saeger) R. BA with honors, U. Fla., 1971; JD, Georgetown U., 1974. Bar: Md. 1974, D.C. 1975. Atty. Office of Gen. Counsel, FTC, Washington, 1974-77, antitrust atty. Bur. of Competition, 1977-81; counsel, consumer subcom. of com. on commerce, sci. and transp. U.S. Senate, Washington, 1981-85; assoc. Heron, Burchette, Ruckert & Rothwell, Washington, 1985-87, ptnr., 1987-90; dep. asst. sec. for govtl. affairs U.S. Dept. Transp., Washington, 1990-91, acting asst. sec. for govtl. affairs, 1991-92; cons. Raffaelli, Spees, Springer & Smith, Washington, 1993-94; asst. exec. dir. govt. rels. APA Practice Directorate, 1995—; lectr. Brookings Instn. Ctr. for Pub. Policy Edn., Washington, 1985-88. Active Lawyers for Bush-Quayle, Washington, 1988. Mem. ABA (antitrust, adminstrv. law sect., vice chair transp. industry com. antitrust sect. 1992-95), Trade Assn. (vice chair com. antitrust sect. 1995). Republican. Methodist. Home: Apt 503 I 2725 Connecticut Ave NW Washington DC 20008-5305

RICHSTONE, BEVERLY JUNE, psychologist; b. N.Y.C., June 8, 1952; d. Max and Rosalyn Richstone. BA summa cum laude, Queens Coll., 1975; MEd, U. Miami, 1978; PsyD, Nova U., 1982. Lic. clin. psychologist. Clin. fellow Harvard Med. Sch., 1982-83; staff psychologist Met. State Hosp., Waltham, Mass., 1983-85; asst. attending psychologist McLean Hosp., Belmont, Mass., 1983-84; asst. psychologist Cambridge Hosp./N. Charles Mental Health Rsch./Tng. Found., Cambridge, Mass., 1984-85; assoc. dir. Coastal Geriatric Svcs., Hingham, Mass., 1985-86, Alpha Geriatric Svcs., Hingham, 1986-87; rsch. assoc. Harvard Sch. Pub. Health, Boston, 1992-94; instr. psychology Harvard Med. Sch., Boston, 1983-84; consulting psychologist Coastal Geriatric Svcs., Hingham, 1985. Contbg. author: The New Our Bodies, Ourselves, 1992. Cmty. advisor Mass. Office Disability, Boston, 1992—. Mem. APA, Phi Beta Kappa.

RICHTER, BARBARA DIANE MAEL, nursing administrator; b. Millis, Mass.; d. Edward Isaac and Esther (Sack) Mael; m. Joseph Eugene Richter; children: Stephen N., Elisa M. Zehnwirth, Attara J. Waxman. Diploma in nursing, Beth Israel Hosp., 1960; BSN, L.I. U., 1978; MA, NYU, 1988. RN, N.Y. Charge nurse Queen Hosp. Ctr., Hillcrest, N.Y., 1972-75; staff nurse City Hosp. Ctr., Elmhurst, N.Y., 1975-78; nursing supr. Booth Meml. Med. Ctr., Flushing, N.Y., 1978-80; pres., educator Dialysis Ednl. Svcs., Queens, N.Y., 1981—; adminstrv. supr. Einstein divsn. Montefiore Med. Ctr., Bronx, N.Y., 1983-94; clin. mgr. Mt. Sinai Hosp., N.Y.C., 1994. Author: (booklet) You're In Control of Your Hemodialysis, 1994; contbr. articles to profl. publs. Grantee Profl. Staff Congress-CUNY, 1987. Mem. N.Y. State Nurses Assn., Am. Nephrology Nurses Assn., N.Y. Orgn. Nurse Execs., Nat. Kidney Found. (grants com. 1993—, chmn. coun. nephrology nurses and technicians N.Y.-N.J. chpt. 1990—, vice chmn. 1991-93). Office: Mt Sinai Hosp 1 Gustave L Levy Pl New York NY 10029-6504

RICHTER, BERTINA, librarian; b. Scottsbluff, Nebr., Sept. 2, 1944; d. Herbert E. and Jean Roberta (Schaffer) R. AA, Monterey (Calif.) Jr. Coll., 1964; BA, Calif. State U., Sacramento, 1966; MLS, U. Calif., Berkeley, 1967; MA, Calif. State U., Fresno, 1980. Libr. Henry Madden Libr., Calif. State U., Fresno, 1967—. Author: Fort Miller, California, 1851-1865, 1988. Mem. ALA, Am. Hist. Assn., Archaeol. Inst. Am., Calif. Libr. Assn., Calif. Hist. Soc., Fresno Hist. Soc. Office: Henry Madden Libr Calif State Univ 5200 N Barton Fresno CA 93740-0034

RICHTER, CAROL DEAN, sales representative; b. Cummings, Ga., May 14, 1940; d. William Ralph and Mildred Mae (Heard) Bottoms; m. Cary James Simmons, July 5, 1959 (div.); children: Joel Perry, Carlton Wesley, Rebecca Lynn; m. Robert Warren Richter Sr., July, 1970 (div.); 1 child, Robert Warren Jr. Student, Unity Sch. of Christianity, Unity Village, Mo., 1974—; AS in Mental Sci., First Ch. of Religious Sci., 1979; degree in aesthesiology, Derma-Clinic, 1990. Cert. aromatherapist. Transcriptionist Med. Coll. Hosp., Charleston, S.C., 1960-64, St. Joseph's Infirmary, Atlanta, 1965-70, med. sec. Coal Mountain Clinic, Cummings, 1971-74; transcriptionist Northside Hosp., Atlanta, 1974-89, Gwinnett Med. Ctr., Lawrenceville, Ga., 1989-93; cert. image cons., 1986-90; esthetician Classy You Salon, Duluth, Ga., 1991-92, You-Nique Salon, Buford, Ga., 1990-92; distbr. Amway Distbrs. Assn., Ada, Mich., 1970—; owner, pres. Richter Rallies, Lawrenceville, 1970—. Mem. North Ga. Mountain Planning and Devel. Commn., Gainesville, 1970-74; bd. dirs. Breakthru House, Decatur, Ga., 1975-81. Mem. Internat. Platform Assn. Home and Office: 943 Terrace Ter Lawrenceville GA 30244-2717

RICHTER, JUDITH ANNE, pharmacology educator; b. Wilmington, Del., Mar. 4, 1942; d. Henry John and Dorothy Madelyn (Schroeder) R. BA, U. Colo., 1964; PhD, Stanford U., 1969. Postdoctoral fellow Cambridge (Eng.) U., 1969-70, U. London, 1970-71; asst. prof. pharmacology Sch. Medicine Ind. U., Indpls., 1971-78, assoc. prof. pharmacology and neurobiology, 1978-84, prof., 1984—; vis. assoc. prof. U. Ariz. Health Sci. Ctr., Tucson, 1983; mem. biomed. rsch. rev. com. Nat. Inst. on Drug Abuse, 1983-87. Mem. editorial bd. Jour. Neurochemistry, 1982-87; contbr. numerous articles to sci. jours. Scholar Boettcher Found., 1960-64; fellow Wellcome Trust, 1969-71. Mem. AAAS, Am. Soc. for Pharmacology and Exptl. Therapeutics (exec. com. neuropharmacology div. 1989-91), Am. Soc. for Neurochemistry, Internat. Soc. for Neurochemistry, Soc. for Neurosci., Women in Neurosci., Assn. Women in Sci., Phi Beta Kappa, Sigma Xi. Office: Ind U Sch Medicine 791 Union Dr Indianapolis IN 46202-4887

RICHTER, MARY KAYE, foundation director; b. Belleville, Ill., Apr. 20, 1945; d. Henry Charles and Lillian Frieda (Wittlich) Heberer; m. Norman George Richter, Nov. 21, 1964; children: Michael, Sharon, Charles. Student, U. Ill., 1962-63. Instr., florist Belleville Area Coll., 1970-81; exec. dir. Nat. Found. for Ectodermal Dysplasias, Mascoutah, Ill., 1981—. Dir. Nat. Orgn. Rare Disorders, New Fairfield, Conn., 1988—; mem. coun. Nat. Inst. Dental Rsch., Bethesda, Md., 1989—; chair Nat. Alliance Oral Health, Washington, 1989—; mem. Nat. Adv. Dental Rsch. Coun., Coalition Patient Advisers for Skin Disease Rsch.; commr. Horner Pk. Dist., Lebanon, Ill., 1976-80; bd. dirs. Lebanon Unit Sch. Dist. #9, U. Mo. Parents Assn., 1994-96; past leader 4-H; active United Ch. of Christ, past tchr. Sunday sch. Recipient Woman of Achievement award Nat. Synod United Ch. Christ, 1985, Belleville Zonta Orgn., 1989, Outstanding Achievement award St. Clair County YWCA, 1991, Exceptional Achievement award USPHS, 1993, Kimmel Svc. award, 1995, Humanitarian award ISMSA, 1995, Mascoutah Schs. Achievement award, 1996. Office: Nat Found for Ectodermal Dysplasias 219 E Main St # 114 Mascoutah IL 62258-2136

RICHTSMEIER, JANE, advertising executive. Sr. v.p., dir. group acct. Bayer Bess Vanderwarker, Inc., Chgo. Office: Bayer Bess Vanderwarker Inc 225 N Michigan Ave Ste 1900 Chicago IL 60601*

RICKARD, RUTH DAVID, retired history and political science educator; b. Fed. Republic Germany, Feb. 20, 1926; came to U.S., 1940; d. Carl and Alice (Koch) David; m. Robert M. Yaffe, Oct. 1949 (dec. 1959); children: David, Steven; m. Norman G. Rickard, June 1968 (dec. 1988); 1 stepson, Douglas. BS cum laude, Northwestern U., 1947, MA, 1948. Law editor Commerce Clearing House, Chgo., 1948; instr. history U. Ill., Chgo., 1949-51; instr. extension program U. Ill., Waukegan, 1960-67; instr. history Waukegan Schs., 1960-69; original faculty, prof. western civilization, polit. sci. Coll. of Lake County, Grayslake, Ill., 1969-92; mem. Inter-Univ. Seminar on Armed Forces and Soc.; mem. Hospitality Info. Svc. for Diplomatic Residents and Families affiliate Meridian Internat. Ctr. Author: History of College of Lake County, 1987 (honored by city of Waukegan 1987), (poem) I Lost My Wings, 1989, Au Revoir from Emeritusdom, 1993, Where are the Safety Zones, 1994; spkr. on various ind. radio and TV programs; contbr. articles to profl. jours. Mem. Econ. Devel. Com., Waukegan, 1992-93. Scholar Freedoms Found. Am. Legion, Valley Forge, Pa., 1967. Mem. AAUW (pres. Waukegan chpt. 1955-57, scholarship named for her 1985), LWV (charter, v.p. Waukegan chpt.), Nat. Press Club D.C. (co-writer/editor NPC History), Phi Beta Kappa.

RICKEL, ANNETTE URSO, psychology educator; b. Phila.; d. Ralph Francis and Marguerite (Calcaterra) Urso; m. Peter Rupert Fink, July 21, 1989; 1 child, John Ralph. BA, Mich. State U., 1963; MA, U. Mich., 1965, PhD, 1972. Lic. psychologist, Mich. Faculty early childhood edn. Merrill-Palmer Inst., Detroit, 1967-69; adj. faculty U. Mich., Ann Arbor, 1969-75;

asst. dir. N.E. Guidance Ctr., Detroit, 1972-75; asst. prof. psychology Wayne State U., Detroit, 1975-81; vis. assoc. prof. Columbia U., N.Y.C., 1982-83; assoc. prof. psychology Wayne State U., 1981-87, asst. provost, 1989-91, prof. psychology, 1987—; Am. Coun. on Edn. fellow Princeton and Rutgers Univs., 1990-91; dir. mental health and devel. Nat. Com. for Quality Assurance, Washington, 1995-96; clin. prof. dept. Psychiatry Georgetown U., Washington, 1995—; AAAS and APA Congl. Sci. fellow on Senate Fin. Subcom. on Health and Pres.'s Nat. Health Care Reform Task Force, 1992-93. Cons. editor Jour. of Cmty. Psychology, Jour. Primary Prevention; co-author: Social and Psychological Problems of Women, 1984, Preventing Maladjustment..., 1987; author: Teenage Pregnancy and Parenting, 1989; contbr. articles to profl. jours. Mem. Pres.'s Task Force on Nat. Health Care Reform, 1993; bd. dirs. Children's Ctr. of Wayne County, Mich., The Epilepsy Ctr. of Mich., Planned Parenthood League, Inc. Grantee NIMH, 1976-86, Eloise and Richard Webber Found., 1977-80, McGregor Fund, 1977-78, 82, David M. Whitney Fund, 1982, Katherine Tuck Fund, 1985-90; recipient Career Devel. Chair award, 1985-86; Congl. Sci. fellow AAAS, 1992-93. Fellow APA (div. pres. 1984-85); mem. Midwestern Psychol. Assn., Mich. Psychol. Assn., Soc. for Rsch. in Child Devel., Soc. for Rsch. in Child and Adolescent Psychopathology, Internat. Assn. of Applied Psychologists, Sigma Xi, Psi Chi. Roman Catholic.

RICKERSON, JEAN MARIE, video producer, journalist, photographer; b. Takoma Park, Md., Dec. 29, 1956; d. Charles Marvin and Rita Ann (Smith) Blackburn; m. Ronald Wayne Rickerson, Oct. 18, 1989; children: Drew Elliott, Ella Celine. BS, U. Md., 1978. Pres. Videofax Inc., Bethesda, Md., 1982-90; founder, dir. Found. for Acad. Excellence Inc., Bethesda, 1985-90; video prodr. Applied Measurement Systems Inc., Bremerton, Wash., 1990—; pres. Photo Graphics Inc., Bremerton, 1992—. Contbr. articles and photographs to profl. jours; writer, prodr., dir. videotape SEAFAC, 1992, USNS Hayes, 1993, High Gain Array Test Module, 1993, Advanced Mine Detection Sonar, 1995, BQH-9 Signal Data Recording Set, 1996, Submarine Acoustic Maintenance Program, 1996, Intermediate Scale Measurement System, 1996. Office: Applied Measurement Sys Inc 645 4th St Ste 202 Bremerton WA 98337-1402

RICKS, MARY F(RANCES), academic administrator, anthropologist; b. Portland, Oreg., July 6, 1939; d. Leo and Frances Helen (Corcoran) Samuel; m. Robert Stanley Ricks, Jan. 7, 1961; children: Michael Stanley, Allen Gilbert. BA, Whitman Coll., 1961; MA, Portland State U., 1977, MPA, 1981, PhD, 1995. Asst. to dir. auxiliary services Portland State U., 1975-79, instnl. researcher, 1979-85, dir. instnl. research and planning, 1985—, rsch. assoc. prof., 1994—. Contbr. articles and presentations to profl. socs. Vol. archeologist BLM-USDI, Lakeview, Oreg., 1983—. Fellow Soc. Applied Anthropology; mem. Soc. Am. Archaeology, Soc. Coll. and U. Planning, Pacific N.W. Assn. Instnl. Rsch. and Planning (pres. 1990-91), Assn. Oreg. Archaeologists (v.p. 1988-90), Assn. Instl. Rsch., City Club of Portland, Sigma Xi. Home: 5466 SW Dover Loop Portland OR 97225-1033 Office: Portland State U Office Instnl Rsch/Planning PO Box 751 Portland OR 97207-0751

RICO, PATRICIA, sports association administrator; b. N.Y.C., Sept. 25, 1933; m. Heliodoro Rico; one child. V.p. USA Track and Field; mem. U.S. Olympic Com.; co-dir. USA/Mobil Indoor Track and Field Championships. Co-founder Track Mirror. Mem. Internat. Amateur Athletic Fedn. (mem. women's com. 1976—, chair U.S. women's track and field com.). Office: USA Track and Field PO Box 120 Indianapolis IN 46206-0120

RIDDER, LINDA GAYLE, librarian; b. Chgo., Apr. 17, 1949; d. Gale Eugene and Yvonne Lucille (Marcotte) A.; m. George Larry Ridder, Mar. 29, 1970; 1 child, Michael Eric. BA English, St. Mary's U., 1971; MS Libr. Sci., Our Lady of the Lake U., 1977. Cert. media specialist; profl. libr.; provisional cert. secondary English and social studies, Tex. Tchr. fourth grade St. Thomas More Cath. Sch., San Antonio, Tex., 1971-72; tchr. English/dept. coord. Sam Rayburn Mid. Sch., San Antonio, 1972-77; libr. media specialist Gregorio Esparza Elem., San Antonio, 1977-85, H.B. Zachry Mid. Sch., San Antonio, 1985—; mem. Sch. Leadership Team, 1985—, Sch. Adv. Team, 1994—, recording sec.; mem. Northside Dist. Comm. Network Com., 1996—, Zachry Tech. Task Force Com., 1996—. Author Middle School Integrated Curriculum Guide of Library Skills, 1991; dir. accreditation reports, 1979, 84. Mem. St. Luke's Cath. Ch., San Antonio, 1975—. Mem. Nat. Reading Assn., Tex. Libr. Assn., Phi Delta Kappa. Home: 4607 Lightning Ln San Antonio TX 78238 Office: HB Zachry Mid Sch 9410 Timber Path San Antonio TX 78250

RIDDIFORD, LYNN MOORHEAD, zoologist, educator; b. Knoxville, Tenn., Oct. 18, 1936; d. James Eli and Virginia Amalia (Berry) Moorhead; m. Alan Wistar Riddiford, June 20, 1959 (div. 1966); m. James William Truman, July 28, 1970. AB magna cum laude, Radcliffe Coll., 1958; PhD, Cornell U., 1961. Rsch. fellow in biology Harvard U., Cambridge, Mass., 1961-63, 65-66, asst. prof. biology, 1966-71, assoc. prof., 1971-73; instr. biology Wellesley (Mass.) Coll., 1963-65; assoc. prof. zoology, U. Wash., Seattle, 1973-75, prof., 1975—; mem. study sect. tropical medicine and parasitology NIH, Bethesda, Md., 1974-78; mem. Competitive Grants panel USDA, Arlington, Va., 1979, 89, 95; mem. regulatory biology panel NSF, Washington, 1984-88; mem. governing coun. Internat. Ctr. for Insect Physiology and Ecology, 1985-91, chmn. program com., 1989-91; chmn. adv. com. SeriBiotech, Bangalore, India, 1989; mem. bio. adv. com. NSF, 1992-95. Contbr. articles to profl. jours. Mem. editorial bd. profl. jours. NSF fellow, 1958-60, 61-63; grantee NSF, 1964—, NIH, 1975—, Rockefeller Found., 1970-79, USDA, 1978-82, 89—; fellow John S. Guggenheim, 1979-80, NIH, 1986-87. Fellow AAAS, Am. Acad. Arts and Scis., Royal Entomol. Soc., Entomol. Soc. Am.; mem. Am. Soc. Zoologists (pres. 1991), Am. Soc. Biochem. and Molecular Biology, Entomol. Soc. Am., Am. Soc. Cell Biology, Soc. Devel. Biology. Methodist. Home: 16324 51st Ave SE Bothell WA 98012-6138 Office: U Wash Dept Zoology Box 351800 Seattle WA 98195-1800

RIDDLE, CAROL ANN, counselor; b. Houston, Jan. 29, 1936; d. Caddell Eugene and Alma (Abernathy) Scruggs; m. Arol Sumner Riddle, Aug. 15, 1958 (div. 1980); children: Prentiss A.S., Suzanne Elizabeth. MusB, Tex. Christian U., 1957; MS in Elem. Edn., Okla. State U., 1972, EdD in Counseling, 1978. Lic. prof. counselor, lic. chem. dependency counselor. Vis. asst. prof. U. Tex., Dallas, 1977; tng. dir. City of Ft. Worth, Tex., 1981-83, U. Tex., Arlington, 1983-85; pvt. practice Dallas, 1985-88; asst. prof. psychology Lamar U., Orange, Tex., 1988-89; counselor Pvt. Hosps., Webster, Tex., 1990-91, Pearland (Tex.) Ind. Sch. Dist., 1990-92; with Lewisville (Tex.) Ind. Sch. Dist., 1992—; cons. Dallas City Credit Union, Standard Meat Co. Author: (with Debra Julian) Students Helping Students, 1979. Mem. ACA (Nat. Disting. Svc. Registry 1990), Tex. Assn. Counseling and Devel., No. Metro Counseling Assn. (pres.), Phi Delta Kappa, Kappa Delta Pi. Unitarian. Home: 713 Mack Dr Denton TX 76201-6347

RIDDLE, JUDITH LEE, lawyer; b. Princeton, N.J., Nov. 27, 1950; d. Donald Husted and Leah Dunlap (Gallagher) R.; m. James Melvin Kohler, Aug. 20, 1976 (div. Dec. 1987). BS, West Chester U., 1973; MEd, Colo. State U., 1976; ABD, Temple U., 1982; JD cum laude, Villanova U. Sch. Law, 1986. Bar: Pa. 1986, U.S. Dist. Ct. (ea. dist.) Pa. 1988. Atty., assoc. Ballard Spahr Andrews & Ingersoll, Phila., 1986-87; law clk., hon. Robert S. Gawthrop III U.S. Dist. Ct. (ea. dist.) Pa., Phila., 1987-88; assoc. Dechert Price & Rhoads, Phila., 1988-91; asst. dist. atty. Dist. Atty. Office, Phila., 1992—; cons. in field. Assoc. editor: Villanova Law Review, 1985-86. Vol. atty. Support Ctr. Child Advs., Phila., 1988-92, Phila. Vol. Lawyers for Arts, 1986-90, Women's Law Project, Phila., 1991-92; bd. dirs. Young Women's Cmty. Ctr., 1978-79. Fulbright exchange tchr., 1978-79. Mem. Fed. Bar Assn. (chmn. young lawyers 1986-88, sec. 1988-90, 3d v.p. 1990-92, 2d v.p. 1992-93, 1st v.p. 1993—), Phila. Bar Assn., Order of Coif, Phi Delta Kappa. Democrat. Office: Dist Attys Office 1421 Arch St Philadelphia PA 19102-1507

RIDDLE, LAURA ELLEN, theatre educator; b. Flushing, N.Y., July 4, 1960; d. Phillip Granville and Renee Viola (Wood) R. BA in Theatre, Ind. State U., 1982; MFA in Acting, Goodman Sch. of Drama, Chgo., 1986; Cert. in Improvisation, Second City, Chgo., 1987. Assoc. prof. Ind. State U., Terre Haute, Ind., 1987-93; actor, dir. Ind. Summerstage, Terre Haute, Ind., 1988-93; assoc. prof., chair theatre U. Wis., Green Bay, 1993—; actor Peninsula Players, Fish Creek, Wis., 1994, Wis. Shakespeare Festival, Platteville, 1995; workshop presenter Am. Coll. Theatre Festival, 1988-95, regional festival host, 1994-95; play sect. Cmty. Theatre, Terre Haute, 1991-93; founding mem. improvisational theatre Milk Dogs, 1995-96. Appeared in stage play BAAL, 1992, 1 act play BERLIN, 1992 (Best of the Fest award), improvisational comedy in Comedy Sportz, 1993-96. Stand up comedy benefit mem. Lifelines, Terre Haute, 1990-91. Mem. NOW. Office: U Wis Green Bay 2420 Nicolet Dr Green Bay WI 54311

RIDDOCH, HILDA JOHNSON, accountant; b. Salt Lake City, July 25, 1923; d. John and Ivy Alma (Wallis) Johnson; m. Leland Asa Riddoch, Nov. 22, 1942; children: Ivy Lee, Leland Mark. Vocal student, Ben Henry Smith, Seattle; student, Art Instrn. Schs. Sales clk, marking room and dist. office Sears, Roebuck & Co., Seattle, 1940-42; with billing dept., receptionist C.M. Lovsted & Co., Inc., Seattle, 1942-51; acct., exec. sec. Viking Equipment Co., Inc., Seattle, 1951-54; acct., office mgr. Charles Waynor Collection Agy., Seattle, 1955-57; pvt. practice, 1957-96; acct., office mgr. Argus Mag., Seattle, 1962-67; acct. Law Offices Krutch, Lindell, Donnelly, Dempsey & Lageschulte, Seattle, 1967-72, Law Offices Sindell, Haley, Estep, et al, Seattle, 1972-77; co-founder, acct. Bus. Svc., Inc. and Diversified Design & Mktg., Fed. Way, Auburn & Orting, Wash., 1975-96; co-founder L & H Advt. and Distbg. Co., Wash., 1992—; sec.-treas., dir. Jim Evans Realty, Inc., Seattle, 1973-87; agt. Wise Island Water Co., P.U.D., Victoria, B.C., 1973-88, Estate Executrix, Seattle, 1987-95. Author: Ticking Time on a Metronome, 1989-90; writer, dir. hist. play Presidents of Relief Society Thru Ages; writer epic poetry; writer, dir. teenager activation video, 1984; pub., editor Extended Family Newsletter, 1983—. Dir. speech and drama LDS Ch., 1938-88, ward pres. young women's orgn., mem. ward and stake choirs, 1963-85, stake genealogy libr., Federal Way, 1983-85, ward and stake newsletter editors various areas, West Seattle, Seattle, Renton, Auburn, 1950-90, 1st counselor in presidency, tchr. various courses Ladies' Relief Soc. Orgn., 1965—; co-dir., organizer 1st Silver Saints Group, 1990-92; interviewer LDS Ch. Emplyment Svcs., 1992-93; founder WE CARE, 1993; co-resident mgr. Mountain View Estates, Orting. Recipient Letter of Recognition Howard W. Hunter, Pres. LDS Ch. Fellow Am. Biographical Assn. (life). Home: care 464 Lariat Cir Idaho Falls ID 83404

RIDE, SALLY KRISTEN, physics educator, scientist, former astronaut; b. L.A., May 26, 1951; d. Dale Burdell and Carol Joyce (Anderson) R.; m. Steven Alan Hawley, July 26, 1982 (div.). BA in English, Stanford U., 1973, BS in Physics, 1973, PhD in Physics, 1978. Teaching asst. Stanford U., Palo Alto, Calif.; researcher dept. physics Stanford U.; astronaut candidate, trainee NASA, 1978-79, astronaut, 1979-87; on-orbit capsule communicator STS-2 mission Johnson Space Ctr. NASA, Houston; on-orbit capsule communicator STS-3 mission NASA, mission specialist STS-7, 1983, mission specialist STS-41G, 1984; sci. fellow Stanford (Calif.) U., 1987-89; dir. Calif. Space Inst. of U. Calif. San Diego, La Jolla, 1989—; prof. Physics U. Calif. San Diego, La Jolla, 1989—; mem. Presdl. Commn. on Space Shuttle, 1986, Presdl. Com. of Advisors on Sci. and Tech., 1994—. Author: (with Susan Okie) To Space and Back, 1986, (with T.O'Shaughnessy) Voyager: An Adventure to the Edge of the Solar System, 1992, The Third Planet: Exploring the Earth From Space, 1994. Office: U Calif San Diego Calif Space Inst 0221 La Jolla CA 92093-0221

RIDEOUT, PHYLLIS MCCAIN, university director, medical educator; b. Macon, Ga., Sept. 15, 1938; d. Wayne Eugene and Lois Stone (Rollins) McC.; m. William Milford Rideout, Jr., Mar. 10, 1961; children: Christina Lynn, William Milford III, Julie Linda. AB in Modern European Lit., Stanford U., 1961; MA in English, Fla. State U., 1973, PhD in Humanities, 1981. Cert. community coll. life teaching credential, Calif. Teaching asst. Fla. State U., Tallahassee, 1974-75; program coord. humanities U. So. Calif., L.A., 1981-82, program adminstr. Norris Comprehensive Cancer Ctr., 1983-86, adminstrv. dir. Norris Comprehensive Cancer Ctr., 1986-89, assoc. dir. for adminstrn. and edn. Norris Comprehensive Cancer Ctr., 1989—, clin. instr. preventive medicine Sch. Medicine, Norris Comprehensive Cancer Ctr., 1989—. Leader, trainer Girl Scouts U.S.a., Tallahassee and Los Alamitos, Calif., 1975-81; bd. dirs. jr. and sr. high schs. PTA's, Los Alamitos, 1977-81; bd. dirs. Cancer Coalition Calif., 1986-91; bd. dirs., vice chair AIDS Healthcare Found., 1992—; treas. So. Calif. Cancer Pain Initiative, 1994—. Mem. Nat. Assn. Women in Edn., Cancer Ctr. Adminstrs. Forum (exec. com. 1987-91), Am. Assn. for Cancer Edn. (membership and bylaws coms.), U. So. Calif. Women in Mgmt. (bd. dirs. 1986-89, 90-96, pres. 1993-95), Stanford U. Alumni Assn. (life), Stanford Profl. Women (pres., bd. dirs. 1982-85), Stanford Club L.A. County (bd. dirs. 1985-88). Office: U So Calif Norris Comprehensive Cancer Ctr 1441 Eastlake Ave Los Angeles CA 90033-0800

RIDER, DIANE ELIZABETH, librarian; b. Kearny, N.J., June 25, 1951; d. Thomas Lindsay and Dorothy Jane (Sommer) R. MusB magna cum laude, Westminster Choir Coll., 1973; MLS, Fla. State U., 1993. Intern preservation dept. U. Fla., Gainesville, 1993; intern free-net libr. Tallahassee (Fla.) Free-Net, 1993; reference libr. Broward County Main Libr., Ft. Lauderdale, Fla., 1994-95; libr., instr. Art Inst. Ft. Lauderdale, 1995-96, dir. Learning Resource Ctr., 1996—; vice chair, assoc. mem. com. Southeast Fla. Libr. Info. Network, Ft. Lauderdale, 1995—; speaker in field. Soloist St. Paul's Chapel, Columbia U., N.Y.C., 1973, Ch. of St. Mary the Virgin, N.Y.C., 1974. Mem. Co-op Am., Washington, 1990—, Sierra Club, Broward & Leon Counties, Fla., 1988—. Fla. State U. fellow, 1993-94, Coll. Teaching fellow, 1992-93; Louis Shores scholar, 1992-93. Mem. ALA (intellectual freedom roundtable 1992—), Spl. Librs. Assn., Genealogical Soc. Southwestern Pa., NOW, Sierra Club, Phi Kappa Phi, Beta Phi Mu. Office: Art Inst Ft Lauderdale Learning Resource Ctr 1799 SE 17th St Fort Lauderdale FL 33316

RIDER, ELIZABETH ANN, elementary school educator; b. Oak Hill, Ohio, Sept. 10, 1968; d. Robert Dwight and Dorothy Florence (Wolfe) R. BS in Elem. Edn., U. Rio Grande, Ohio, 1990. Cert. elem. tchr., W. Va. Tchr. Walton (W. Va.) Elem. Sch., 1990—; co-author Sci. Curriculum, Roane County W. Va. Schs., 1991-92, Math. Curriculum, 1992-93. Tchr. Bible Sch., New Plymouth (Ohio) United Meth. Ch., July, 1994. Mem. Roane County Reading Coun., Faculty Senate.

RIDER, JANE LOUISE, artist, educator; b. Brownfield, Tex., Sept. 11, 1919; d. Oscar Thomas and Florence Myrtle (Bliss) Halley; m. Rolla Wilson Rider Jr., Mar. 26, 1944 (dec. July 1992); 1 child, Dorothy Jo Neil. BA, UCLA, Westwood, 1943, tchg. diploma in secondary art; postgrad., Chgo. Art Inst., 1945, Chouinards, L.A., U. Oreg., Scripps, Claremont, Calif. Art supr., elem. and jr. high art tchr. Tulare (Calif.) City Schs. Dist., 1943-44, 44-45; art tchr. Beverly Hills (Calif.) High Sch., 1946-47; art tchr. jr. high gen. art and ceramics Santa Barbara City Schs., Goleta, Calif., 1964-66; head art dept., tchr. Morro Bay (Calif.) Jr.-Sr. High Sch. Dist., 1967-70; pvt. practice studio potter Cambria, Calif., 1961-85; artist, Santa Rosa, Calif., 1985—; founder, dir., tech. La Canada (Calif.) Youth House Art Program, 1953-60; dir. Pinedorado Art Show, Allied Arts Assn., Cambria, 1970-80. Exhibited in group shows Wine Country Artist's Spring Show, 1991, 92, 93, 94, 95, Gualala Art in Redwoods, 1986, 87, 88, 96, Rodney Strong Vineyards Art Guild, 1994; revolving exhibits Berger Ctr. and Chalais-Oakmont, Santa Rosa, 1985-95, Oakmont Art Assn., Santa Rosa, 1985-96, Santa Rosa Art Guild, 1986-96; statewide art shows Spring Palettes Mumm Cuvee Winery, Napa, Calif., 1985-95, Women Creating, Luther Burbank Ctr., 1995, Summer House Gallery, Healdsberg, 1995, Armida Winery Show, 1995, Coddington Mall Show, 1995-96, Audubon-Bouverie Preserve Show, Glen Ellen, Calif., 1996, others. Mem. Nat. League Am. Pen Woman, Inc. (artist 1994, 94), Santa Rosa Art Guild (exhibits 1986-95, rec. sec. 1989), Ctrl. Coast Watercolor Soc. (charter 1977), Oakmont Art Assn. Republican. Home: 7019 Overlook Dr Santa Rosa CA 95409-6376

RIDGEWAY, LYNNE, insurance company executive. BA, New Sch. Social Rsch., 1983. Supr. Group Health Inc., N.Y.C., 1970-75, mgr., 1975-78, dir., 1978-90, asst. v.p., 1990—. Dir. Cmty. Edn. Resource Ctr., N.Y.C., 1992—. Mem. Westmoreland Assn., Inc. (dir. 1982—), Little Neck Cmty. Assn. (dir. 1990—). Office: Group Health Inc 88 West End Ave New York NY 10023

RIDGEWAY, TERESA MARIE, museum registrar; b. Kansas City, Mo., Jan. 10, 1961; d. Richard Thomas and Betty Marie (Holden) R. BA, Ind. U., 1986. Registration asst. Children's Mus. Indpls., 1985-90; registrar Bowers Mus., Santa Ana, Calif., 1990—; cons. registrar Nat. Art Mus. of Sport, Indpls., 1990. Mem. NOW, Am. Assn. Mus. (membership officer registrar's com. western region 1992-95, membership directory registrar's com. 1995, 96), Vegetarian Resource Group, Earthsave. Democrat. Office: Bowers Mus Cultural Art 2002 N Main St Santa Ana CA 92706

RIDGLEY, FRANCES AROC, principal; b. Manila, Jan. 29, 1936; came to U.S., 1966; d. Celestino Pascual and Urbana Oraliza (Velasco) Aroc; m. Ignacio Flores Rilloraza, Aug. 1, 1958 (div. July 1970); children: Ignacio Aroc Rilloraza II, Joel A. Rilloraza; m. Charles Delbert Ridgely, Jan. 29, 1983. BS, Philippine Normal Coll., 1964; MS in Edn., Ind. State U., 1967; EdD, U. Pacific, 1980. Tchr. Cuhao Elem. Sch., Quezon City, Philippines, 1955-61; exec. asst. GSIS, Manila, 1961-66; grad. asst. Ind. State U. Sch. Edn., Terre Haute, 1966-67; tchr. elem. sch. Vijo County Sch. Corp., Terre Haute, 1967-68; team leader, tchr. tng. supr. Tchr. Corps New Careers, Stockton, Calif., 1968-74; coord., sch. dist. cons. Stockton Unified Sch. Dist., 1974-80; tchr. intern supr., instr. U.O.P., Stockton, 1976-80; tchr. intern supr., instr., mem. basic edn. coun. Sch. Edn. U. Pacific, 1980-82; tchr. Alum Rock Union Elem. Sch. Dist., San Jose, 1982-85, coord., vice prin., 1985-93, prin., 1993—; guest lectr. U.O.P. Sch. Edn., 1974-80; cons. in field. Vol. ARC, San Jose, 1988; participant, mem. Poco Way Redevel. Project, San Jose, 1993—; mem. Filipino Affirmative Action, Oakland, Calif., 1995—. Recipient Disting. Educator award; Math. and Tech. grantee Santa Clara Office Edn., 1984, Global Edn. grantee Stanford U., 1978-80; Bilingual Edn. Doctoral fellow, 1976; I.D.E.A. fellow Kettering Found., 1981, 82; P.E.O. Internat. scholar, 1967. Mem. Filipino Am. Movement in Edn. (pres. 1986-88, LEadership award 1988), Filipino Am. Educators Assn. Calif. (v.p. 1987-89), Assn. Calif. Sch. Adminstrs. (pres. 1994-95), Calif. Sch. Leadership Acad., Phi Delta Kappa, Delta Kappa Gamma. Home: 755 Tramway Dr Milpitas CA 95035-3606 Office: Alum Rock Union Elem Sch 2930 Gay Ave San Jose CA 95127-2322

RIDGWAY, HELEN JANE, chemist, consultant; b. Ft. Worth, Aug. 10, 1937; d. Ralph Pope and Virginia Leah (Link) R. AS, Arlington (Tex.) State Coll., 1957; BA, North Tex. State Coll., Denton, 1959; MS, Baylor U., Waco, Tex., 1963, PhD, 1968. Rsch. asst. Wadley Rsch. Inst., Dallas, 1960-68; sr. investigator Wadley Insts. Molecular Medicine, Dallas, 1968-86, chmn. chemistry, 1986-92; R & D hemostasis mgr. Helena Labs., Beaumont, Tex., 1993—; cons. Helena Labs., Beaumont, 1986-92. Contbr. articles to sci. jours. AAUW scholar, 1955, 56. Fellow Internat. Soc. Hematology; mem. Am. Chem. Soc., Am. Heart Assn. (coun. on thrombosis).

RIDGWAY, MARCELLA DAVIES, veterinarian; b. Sewickley, Pa., Dec. 24, 1957; d. Willis Eugene and Martha Ann (Davies) R. BS, Pa. State U., 1979; VMD, U. Pa., 1983. Intern Univ. Ill., Urbana, 1983-84, resident in small animal internal medicine, 1984-87; small animal vet. Vet. Cons. Svcs., Savoy, Ill., 1987—. Contbr. articles to profl. jours. Mem. Am. Vet. Med. Assn., Am. Animal Hosp. Assn., Acad. Vet. Clinicians, Ednl. Resources in Environ. Sci. (bd. dirs.), Savoy Prairie Soc. (pres. 1989—), Grand Prairie Friends (bd. dirs. 1993-96). Home and Office: Vet Cons Svcs 194 Paddock Dr E Savoy IL 61874-9663

RIDGWAY, ROZANNE LEJEANNE, former diplomat, executive; b. St. Paul, Aug. 22, 1935; d. H. Clay and Ethel Rozanne (Cote) R.; m. Theodore E. Deming. BA, Hamline U., 1957, LLD (hon.), 1978; hon. degrees, U. Helsinki, George Washington U., Elizabethtown Coll.; hon. degree, Albright Coll., Coll. of William and Mary, Hood Coll. Career diplomat U.S. Fgn. Svc., 1957-89, amb. at large for oceans and fisheries, 1975-77; amb. to Finland, 1977-80; counselor of the Dept. State, Washington, 1980-81; spl. asst. to sec. state, 1981; amb. to German Dem. Republic, 1982-85; asst. sec. state Europe and Can., 1985-89; pres. The Atlantic Coun. U.S., Washington, 1989-92, co-chair, 1993—; chair Baltic-Am. Enterprise Fund, 1994—; bd. dirs. 3M Corp., RJR Nabisco, Union Carbide Corp., Bell Atlantic, Citicorp, Citibank, Emerson Electric Co., The Boeing Corp., Sara Lee Corp., Nat. Geog. Soc., Internat. Bd. Advisors, New Perspective Fund. Trustee Hamline U.; bd. dirs. Am. Acad. Diplomacy, Ptnrs. for Democratic Change, Catalyst, Aspen Inst., Brookings Instn. Recipient Profl. awards Dept. State, Presdl. Disting. Performance award, Joseph C. Wilson internat. rels. achievement award, 1982, Sharansky award Union Couns. Soviet Jewry, 1989, Grand Cross of the Order of the Lion, Finland, 1989; named Person of Yr., Nat. Fisheries Inst., 1977, Knight Comdr. of the Order of Merit, Fed. Republic Germany, 1989, U.S. Presdl. Citizens Achievement medal, 1989. Fellow Nat. Acad. Pub. Adminstrn.; mem. Met. Club, Army-Navy Country Club. Office: The Atlantic Coun of The US 910 17th St NW Ste 1000 Washington DC 20006-2601

RIDGWAY WHITE, LURENE JANE, neonatal nurse; b. Lindsay, Okla., Aug. 31, 1958; d. Jack Elijah and Geneva Clydene (Mariott) Matheson; m. Phillip H. Ridgway, May 11, 1996. AAS, Okla. State U., Oklahoma City, 1989; student, Cen. State U., Edmond, Okla., 1977-82. Cert. neonatal rescucication program instr.; cert. breastfeeding educator. Abstractor of land titles Co-Data, Inc., Oklahoma City, 1984-89; charge nurse Deaconess Hosp., Oklahoma City, 1993-94; resource nurse VHA Health Link, Oklahoma City. Mem. Phi Theta Kappa. Home: 11424 Walters Ave Oklahoma City OK 73162-1315 Office: Ste 675 4013 NW Expressway Oklahoma City OK 73116

RIDILL, WINIFRED MARIE MEYERS, English educator; b. Brownsville, Pa., July 11, 1949; d. George William and Sarah Winifred (Murray) Meyers; m. Jack Richard Ridill, Mar. 13, 1972. BA, Cleve. State U., 1971; MA, Old Dominion U., 1990. English tchr. Bay H.S., Bay Village, Ohio, 1972-81, Wando H.S., Mt. Pleasant, S.C., 1981-82, Bay H.S., 1982-83, First Colonial H.S., Virginia Beach, Va., 1983—. Vol. emergency rm. Va. Beach Gen. Hosp., 1986—; vol. reading tutor Lit. Coun. of Tidewater, Portsmouth, Va., 1994. Mem. Internat. Reading Assn., Nat. Coun. Tchrs. of English, Va. Assn. Tchrs. of English, Va. Beach Assn. Tchrs. English (sec. 1989-90, English Tchr. of Yr. 1992-93). Roman Catholic. Office: First Colonial HS 1272 Mill Dam Rd Virginia Beach VA 23454-2322

RIDINGS, DOROTHY SATTES, foundation admministrator; b. Charleston, W.Va., Sept. 26, 1939; d. Frederick L. and Katharine E. (Backus) Sattes; m. Donald Jerome Ridings, Sept. 8, 1962; children: Donald Jerome Jr., Matthew Lyle. Student, Randolph-Macon Woman's Coll., 1957-59; BSJ, Northwestern U., 1961; MA, U. N.C.-Chapel Hill, 1968; D.Pub. Svc. (hon.), U. Louisville, 1985; LHD (hon.), Spalding U., 1986. Reporter Charlotte Observer, N.C., 1961-66; instr. U. N.C. Sch. Journalism, 1966-68; freelance writer Louisville, 1968-77; news editor Ky. Bus. Ledger, Louisville, 1977-80, editor, 1980-83; communications cons., editor, 1983-86; mgmt. assoc. Knight-Ridder Inc., Charlotte, N.C., 1986-88; pres., pub. The Bradenton (Fla.) Herald, 1988-96; pres., CEO, Coun. on Founds., Washington, 1996—; adj. prof. U. Louisville, 1982-83; v.p. Nat. Mcpl. League, 1985-86; bd. dirs. com. on Constl. Sys., Nat. Com. Against Discrimination in Housing, 1982-87, Com. for Study of Am. Electorate, 1982—; bd. dirs. Ind. Sector, 1983-88, 92—; mem. exec. com. Leadership Conf. Civil Rights, 1982-86. Pres. LWV U.S., 1982-86, 1st v.p., 1980-82, human resources dir., 1976-80, chair edn. fund, 1982-86, 1st vice chair, 1980-82, trustee, 1976-80, pres. Louisville/Jefferson County, 1974-76, bd. dirs., 1969-76; trustee Louisville Presbyn. Theol. Sem., 1992—, Ford Found., 1989—, Manatee C.C., 1992-96; bd. dirs. Benton Found., Fla. Press Assn., 1994-96, Leadership Ky., 1984-87, Leadership Louisville, 1983-86, Louisville YWCA, 1978-80, Jr. League Louisville, 1972-74; mem. ABA Accreditation Com., 1987-93, Gov.'s Coun. Ednl. Reform, 1984-85; chair Prichard Com. Acad. Excellence, 1985-86; mem. Gov.'s Commn. Full Equality, 1982-83; mem. state adv. coun. U.S. Commn. Civil Rights, 1975-79; mem. steering com. Task Force for Peaceful Desegregation, 1974-75; elder 2d Presbyn. Ch., 1972-75, 78-81; mem. adv. coun. on ch. and soc. United Presbyn. Ch. in USA, 1978-84; mem. bd. visitors U. N.C., 1996. Recipient Disting. Alumna award U. N.C., 1995, Leadership award Nat. Assn. Cmty. Leadership Orgns., 1986, Alumnae Achievement award Randolph-Macon Woman's Coll., 1985, Disting. Citizen award Nat. Mcpl. League, 1983. Office: Council on Foundations 1828 L St NW Washington DC 20036

RIDINGS, SUSAN ELIZABETH, social worker; b. Bethlehem, Pa., July 6, 1949; d. Charles Frederick Schmidt and Eleanor Martin Jenico; m. Edward Haslam Ridings, Aug. 28, 1971; children: Alexis Katherine, Adam Edward. BSW, Pa. State U., 1971. Caseworker Pa. Dept. Welfare, Phila., 1973-78; bus. mgr. Vallemont Surg. Assocs., Lewistown, Pa., 1987—. Pres.

bd. dirs. Cmty. Counseling Ctr., Lewistown, 1986-88, Mifflin County Children and Youth Svcs., Lewistown, 1990—; bd. dirs. Mifflin-Juniata Assn. of the Blind, Lewistown, 1987-91, v.p., 1994—; pres.-elect Lewistown Hosp. Aux., 1989, pres., 1991-93, pres., 1996—; bd. dirs. Mifflin County 2000, 1995, chmn. Goal 8 Com.; mem. Mifflin County Sch. Dist. steering com.; rec. sec. P.A.H.A., 1994—; legis. chairperson State P.A.H.A., 1994—; trustee Mifflin County Libr. Assn., 1988-91, Lewistown Hosp., 1991—; co-founder Teen Parenting Program, Lewistown, 1985; mem. Lewistown Hosp. Found.; founding mem. Teen Pregnancy Coalition, 1995. Mem. AAUW (programming v.p. 1994-96, Outstanding Woman 1985), Pa. Assn. Hosp. Auxs. (chair ctrl. regional legis., record exec. ctrl. region, legis. chair state bd.), Alpha Omicron Pi. Home: 1 Pine Ln Lewistown PA 17044-2626 Office: Vallemont Surgical Assocs 100 Stine Dr Lewistown PA 17044-1339

RIDLEY, BETTY ANN, educator, church worker; b. St. Louis, Oct. 19, 1926; d. Rupert Alexis and Virginia Regina (Weikel) Steber; m. Fred A. Ridley, Jr., Sept. 8, 1948; children: Linda Drue Ridley Archer, Clay Kent. BA, Scripps Coll., Claremont, Calif., 1948. Christian sci. practitioner, Oklahoma City, 1973—; tchr. Christian sci., 1983—; mem. Christian Sci. Bd. Lectureship, 1980-85. Trustee Daystar Found.; mem. The First Ch. of Christ Scientist, Boston, Fifth Ch. of Christ Scientist, Oklahoma City. Mem. Jr. League Am. Home: 7908 Lakehurst Dr Oklahoma City OK 73120-4324 Office: Suite 100-G 3000 United Founders Blvd Oklahoma City OK 73112

RIEBER, RUTH B., artist; b. N.Y.C., Mar. 9, 1924; d. Joseph and Bessie (Fishman) B.; m. Martin Rieber; children: Jo-Anne F. Rieber Bakst, Suzanne B. Rieber Croes. BS, NYU, 1945; MA, Columbia U., 1948. Cert. tchr. K-12, N.J., art tchr., N.Y. Art tchr. N.Y. Bd. Edn., 1946-53; art tchr. Teaneck (N.J.) Sch. Sys., 1968-71, art therapist spl. svcs., 1970-75; artist in residence Project Impact, Midland Park, N.J., 1976-89; art inst. Tenafly (N.J.) Sr. Citizens Ctr., 1982-96; art instr. recreation dept. Teaneck, 1976-80; judge Bergen County Teenage Arts Festival, 1985—, Divsn. Cultural Affairs, Hackensack, N.J., 1990, 96. Collections include N.J. Treasury Dept., Trenton State Coll., Westinghouse Electric Corp., Jane Voorhees Zimmerle Art Mus., Nawa Collection. Recipient 1st prize Salmagundi Art Club, N.Y.C., 1985, award Nat. Acad. Design, N.Y.C., 1978. Mem. Nat. Assn. Women Artists (awards 1980, 82, 84, v.p. 1993-95), Audubon Artists, Printmaking Coun. N.J. Democrat. Home: 407 Warwick Ave Teaneck NJ 07666

RIEF, SANDRA FÁYE, special education educator; b. Chgo., Oct. 21, 1951; d. Jack H. and Edith Fisdel; m. Itzik Rief, Dec. 17, 1972. BA in Elem. Edn., U. Ill., Chgo., 1973; MEd, U. Ill., Urbana, 1976. Cert. tchr. elem. and spl. edn., Calif. Learning disabilities tchr. Peotone (Ill.) Sch. Dist., 1973, Beecher (Ill.) Sch. Dist., 1974; spl. edn. tchr., resource specialist San Diego Unified Sch. Dist., 1980—; cons. on tchr. tng.; lectr. in field; mentor tchr. San Diego Unified Schs., 1988-91, mentor tchr. emeritus, 1991—. Author: How to Reach and Teach ADD/ADHD Children, 1993, How to Reach and Teach All Children in the Inclusive Classroom, 1996, Systematic Phonics, 1986, Simply Phonics (curriculum), 1994; developer/presenter video: ADHD: Inclusive Instruction and Collaborative Practices, 1994, How to Help Your Child Succeed in School, 1996. Recipient EXCEL award Corp. for Excellence in Pub. Edn., San Diego County, 1993. Mem. Coun. for Exceptional Children, Children and Adults with Attention Deficit Disorder, Calif. Assn. for Resource Specialists (Calif. Resource Specialist of Yr. 1995), Learning Disabilities Assn., Phi Kappa Phi. Democrat. Address: PO Box 19207 San Diego CA 92159-0207

RIEGLE, ROSALIE GENEVIEVE, English educator; b. Flint, Mich., Feb. 19, 1937; d. John Louis and Eleanor Agnes (Hines) R.; m. Sept. 15, 1962 (div.); children: Kathryn Marie Troester, Maura Clare Troester, Ann Troester Lennon, Margaret Troester Murphy. BA, St. Mary's Coll., 1959; MA, Wayne State U., 1971; D of Arts, U. Mich., 1983. Prof. English Saginaw Valley State U., Univ. Ctr., Mich., 1990—; chair of hons. program Saginaw Valley State U., Univ. Ctr., 1986-93; oral historian Cath. Worker Movement; mem. Mustard Seed Cath. Worker Cmty., Saginaw, Mich. Editor: (books) Historic Women of Mich., 1987, Voices from the Catholic Worker, 1993. Office: Saginaw Valley State U Dept English University Center MI 48710

RIEHECKY, JANET ELLEN, writer; b. Waukegan, Ill., Mar. 5, 1953; d. Roland Wayne and Patricia Helen (Anderson) Polsgrove; m. John Jay Riehecky, Aug. 2, 1975; 1 child, Patrick William. BA summa cum laude, Ill. Wesleyan U., 1975; MA in Communication, Ill. State U., 1978; MA in English, Northwestern U., 1983. Tchr. English Blue Mound (Ill.) High Sch., 1977-80, West Chicago (Ill.) High Sch., 1984-86; editor The Child's World Pub. Co., Elgin, Ill., 1987-90; freelance writer Elgin, 1990—. Author: Dinosaur series, 24 vols., 1988, UFOs, 1989, Saving the Forests, 1990, The Mystery of the Missing Money, 1996, The Mystery of the UFO, 1996, Irish Americans, 1995, others. Recipient Summit award for best children's nonfiction Soc. Midland Authors, 1988. Mem. Soc. Am. Magicians, Children's Reading Round Table, Soc. Children's Book Writers and Illustrators, Mystery Writers of Am., Phi Kappa Phi. Democrat. Baptist.

RIEHL, JANE ELLEN, education educator; b. New Albany, Ind., Oct. 17, 1942; d. Henry Gabbart Jr. and Mary Elizabeth (McGraw) Willham; m. Richard Emil Riehl, June 15, 1968; 1 child, Mary Ellen. BA in Elem. Edn., U. Evansville, 1964; MS, Ind. U., Bloomington, 1966; postgrad., Spalding U., 1979, Ind. U. S.E., New Albany, 1991-93. Cert. 1-8 and kindergarten tchr., Ind.; lic. profl. kindergarten tchr., Ind. Elem. tchr. Clarksville (Ind.) Cmty. Sch., 1964-68, 70-75, 81-82, tchr. kindergarten, 1975-81; elem. tchr. Chapelwood Sch. Wayne Twp., Indpls., 1968-70; lectr. edn. Ind. U. S.E., 1988—, dir. tchg. and rsch. project, 1990-91, 92-93; cons. Riehl Assocs., Jeffersonville, Ind., 1995—. Co-author: An Integrated Language Arts Teacher Education Program, 1990, The Reading Professor, 1992, others; author procs. Parent vol. Girl Scouts U.S.A., Jeffersonville, 1988-95; mem. adminstrtv. bd. Wall Street United Meth. Ch., Jeffersonville, 1993-95; mem. women's health adv. coun. Clark Meml. Hosp., Jeffersonville, 1995—; team mem. People to People Citizen Amb. Program, 1993, 95, 96. Named Young Career Woman of Yr. Bus. and Profl. Women New Albany and Dist. 13 Ind., 1966; tchg. and rsch. grantee Ind. U. S.E., 1990, 94, 95. Mem. Nat. Coun. Tchrs. English, Profs. Reading Tchr. Edn., Altrusa Internat. Inc. (internat. bd. 1993-95, dist. gov.sovss 1993-95, svc. award 1995), Phi Delta Kappa (v.p. 1991-92, svc. award 1991), Kappa Kappa Kappa (pres. Jeffersonville 1975-76, 90-91, Outstanding Mem. award 1987). Home: 1610 Fox Run Trail Jeffersonville IN 47130 Office: Ind U SE 4201 Grant Line Rd New Albany IN 47150

RIEHM, SARAH LAWRENCE, writer, arts administrator; b. Iowa City, Sept. 8, 1952; d. Stuart Parker and Elizabeth Jane (Munson) Lawrence; m. Charles Curtis Riehm, May 18, 1974; children: Andrew, Amanda, Jennie Frances. BGS, U. Iowa, 1974; MA in Internat. Fin., U. Tex., 1981. Mgr., adminstr. IBM, Cedar Rapids, Iowa, 1974-75; program mgr. Rockwell Internat., Dallas, 1975-80; mgr. internat. tax Peat, Marwick, Mitchell, Hong Kong, 1981-82; writer, playwright, 1981—; exec. dir. Playwright's Project, Dallas, 1992-94, Tex. Composers Forum, Dallas, 1995-96; faculty mem. U. Tex., Dallas, 1996—; bd. dirs. Dallas Coalition Arts. Playwright: Liberty-A Drama in Two Acts, 1994 (So. Playwrights award 1994), The King & Me, 1994. Founder Playwrights Project; chair Dallas 10,000, 1995. Mem. NOW, Handgun Control. Democrat. Presbyterian. Office: Tex Composers Forum 7522 Campbell Rd Ste 113-181 Dallas TX 75248

RIEKE, ELIZABETH ANN, federal agency administrator; b. Buffalo, July 10, 1943; divorced; children: Frederick Martin, Eowyn Ann. BA in Polit. Sci. summa cum laude, Oberlin Coll., 1965; JD with highest distinction, U. Ariz., 1981. Rsch. asst. S.W. Environ. Svc., Tuscon, 1976-79; law clk. Snell & Wilmer (formerly Bilby, Shoenhari, Warnock & Dolph), Tuscon, 1979; law clk. Office of Solicitor Divsn. Conservation and Wildlife, Dept. Interior, Washington, 1980; law clk. to Hon. William C. Canby Jr. U.S. Ct. Appeals (9th cir.), 1981-82; dep. legal counsel Ariz. Dept. Water Resources, 1982-85, chief legal counsel, 1985-87, dir., 1991-93; assoc. Jennings, Strouss & Salmon, Phoenix, 1987-89, ptnr., 1989-91; asst. sec. for water and sci. Dept. Interior, Washington, 1993—; now dir. Natural Resouces Law Ctr Univ. Colorado, Boulder; adj. prof. Ariz. State U., Phoenix, 1989; speaker in field. Recipient Disting. Alumnus award U. Ariz., 1986. Office: Univ. Colorado Sch. Law Campus 401 Boulder CO 80309-0401*

RIEKE, GAIL, artist; b. Mt. Vernon, N.Y., Nov. 27, 1944; d. Bernard Cyril and Helen (Swartenberg) B.; m. Zachariah Rieke; children: Sialia, Daniel, Serena. BFA, U. Fla., Gainesville, 1966, MFA, 1968. Tchr. drawing and printmaking U. Fla., Gainesville, 1966-68; tchr. visual comm. U. Alta., Edmonton, Can., 1968-70; tchr. Lang. of Collage, Santa Fe (N.Mex.) C.C., 1990-92; tchr. pvt. classes and workshops in collage and creativity Santa Fe and L.A., 1992-95; tchr. founds. of design Coll.Santa Fe, 1990-95. Exhibited in group shows at Denver Art Mus., 1983, Am. Acad. and Inst. Arts and Letters, N.Y.C., 1986, L.A. Internat. Contemporary Art Exposition, 1987, 88, 89, Gail Rieke/Zachariah Rieke, Linda Durham Gallery, Santa Fe, 1984, 86, 88, 90, 91, 92, Chgo. Internat. Art Exposition, 1987, 88, 90, 91, 92, Santa Fe C.C., 1991, Allrich Gallery, San Francisco, 1991, Coll. Santa Fe, 1991, 94, 95, Owings Gallery, Santa Fe, 1991, 92, Seattle Art Exposition, 1992, Rieke Studio/Gallery, Sante Fe, 1993, 94, Cafe Gallery, Albuquerque, 1993, Charlotte Jackson Gallery, Santa Fe, 1994, Fuller Lodge Art Ctr., Los Alamos, N.Mex., 1995, Charlotte Jackson Gallery, Santa Fe, 1995, others; represented in permanent collections at Albuquerque Mus., Amoco Prodn., Denver, Fiberarts Mag., Asheville, N.C., Mountain Bell, Denver, Mus. Design Assocs., Coral Gables, Fla., N.Mex. Mus. Fine Arts, Santa Fe, Rocky Mountain Energy Corp., Denver, Roswell (N.Mex.) Mus. and Art Ctr., Security Pacific Nat. Bank, L.A., Sheldon Meml. Art Gallery, U. Nebr., Lincoln, U. Fla., Gainesville, Vesti Corp., Boston, also pvt. collections. Recipient 2nd awards Southwestern Crafts Biennial, Mus. Internat. Folk Art, Santa Fe, 1971, N.Mex. Crafts Biennial, Mus. Internat. Folk Art, Santa Fe, 1972, award of merit Mus. Albuquerque, 1974, award of merit Textiles N.Mex., 1976, Mus. Purchase award Southwestern Invitational Arts and Crafts Fair, Albuquerque, 1976, 2nd award Southwestern Crafts Biennial, Mus. Internat. Folk Art, Santa Fe, 1977, grant Western State Arts Found., 1977, Purchase award and award of merit Textiles N.Mex., Mus. Albuquerque, 1978, Purchase award and award of merit Fiberarts Mag., 1978. Home: 416 Alta Vista Santa Fe NM 87505

RIELY, CAROLINE ARMISTEAD, physician, medical educator; b. Washington, Feb. 1, 1944; d. John William and Jean Roy (Jones) Riely. AB, Mt. Holyoke Coll., 1966; MD, Columbia U., 1970. Diplomate Am. Bd. Internal Medicine. Med. intern Presbyn. Hosp., N.Y.C., 1970-71, resident in medicine, 1971-73; fellow in liver disease Yale U., New Haven, 1973-75, asst. prof., 1975-80, assoc. prof., 1980-88; prof. medicine U. Tenn., Memphis, 1988—. Fellow ACP, Am. Coll. Gastroenterology; mem. Am. Assn. Study Liver Disease, Internat. Assn. Study Liver, N.Am. Soc. for Pediatric Gastroenterology and Nutrition. Home: 1756 Central Ave Memphis TN 38104-5116 Office: U Tenn 951 Court Ave Rm 555D Memphis TN 38103-2813

RIENHOFF, JOANNE WINKENWERDER, artist; b. Balt., Nov. 2, 1938; d. Walter L. and Eleanor (Zouck) Winkenwerder; m. George Sloan Oldberg, July 7, 1962 (dec. Mar. 1966); m. MacCallum Rienhoff, Dec. 17, 1966 (dec. May 1994). AB, Radcliffe Coll., 1960; MA in Tchg., Johns Hopkins U., 1963; postgrad., U. Denver, 1984-85. Tchr. Garrison (Md.) Forest Sch., 1961-62, Latin Sch. Chgo., 1963-66, Graland Country Day Sch., Denver, 1972-80; artist, 1984—. Exhibited in group shows at U. Denver, Harvard U., Sigraph Soc., Denver, Mid. Pk. Bank, Granby, Colo., others. Bd. dirs., treas. Denver Sch. Vol. Program, 1969-71; leader Jr. Gt. Books program Denver sch. sys., 1967-69; mem. women's bd. Rush Presbyn. St. Luke's Hosp., Chgo., 1965-94. Mem. Rocky Mountain Harvard U. Club, Grand County Hist. Soc., Friends of Grand County Libr. Home: Ouray Ranch Granby CO 80446

RIENZI, BETH ANN MENEES, psychology educator; b. Grand Rapids, Mich., Jan. 31, 1944; d. Thomas Orville and Sylvia Anna (Graham) Menees; m. William David Sanders (dec. 1972); children: Michael Remington, Genevieve Demontremare, Jeannette Sanders, James William Sanders. AA, Porterville (Calif.) Coll., 1972; BA, Calif. State U., Bakersfield, 1974, MA, 1978; PhD, Calif. Sch. Profl. Psychology, Fresno, Calif., 1983. Lic. psychologist, Calif. Pvt. practice Visalia, Calif., 1975-80; clin. psychologist Kings View Mental health, Visalia, Calif., 1980-85, Tulare County Mental Health, Visalia, Calif., 1985-88; prof. pscyhology Calif. State U., Bakersfield, 1988—, coord. faculty mentor program; deafness specialist Kings View, 1980-85; sr. rsch. scientist Applied Rsch. Ctr., 1989—; cons. Head Start-Home Base, Tulare County, 1984-88. Contbr. articles to profl. jours. Recipient Alumnus of Yr. award Calif. State U., Bakersfield, 1996; Kern County Mental Health grantee, 1991-95. Mem. APA, Am. Psychology Soc. (charter), Western Psychology Assn., Assn. Women in Psychology, Coun. Tchrs. Udnergrad. Psychology, Alliance Against Family Violence (vol. sexual assault response team 1993—), Psi Chi (nat. coun., western v.p. 1995—, life). Office: Calif State U Dept Psychology Bakersfield CA 93311-1099

RIESZ, NANCY JEANNE, speaker, trainer, management consultant; b. Cin., Oct. 8, 1950; d. George Henry and Jeanne Elizabeth Cook; m. Jerome Martin Riesz, Sept. 8, 1973. BS, U. Cin., 1972; MBA, Xavier U., Cin., 1985; postgrad., The Union Inst., Cin., 1996—. Cert. clin. lab. scientist. Med. technologist Children's Hosp., Cin., 1972-73; lab. supr. Providence Hosp., Cin., 1973-82; regional mgr. Bio Mèrieux Vitek Inc., Hazelwood, Mo., 1982-93; pres. Attitudes for Success, North Bend, Ohio, 1993—; faculty, staff mem. Franciscan Wholistic Health Ctr., Cin., 1995—; mem. pres.'s adv. coun. McDonnell-Douglas Corp., St. Louis, 1980. Co-founder Ohio Coun. for Self-Esteem, Cin., 1994—; mem. com. adv. bd. West Park Retirement Com., Cin., 1994—; mem. Cin.-Kharkiv Sister Cities Project, 1994—; mem. United Way Amb.'s Group, 1995—, Team in Tng. Leukemia Soc., 1996—. Mem. ASTD, NAFE, Nat. Spkrs. Assn., Women Entrepreneurs Inc. (com. mem. 1993-95), Nat. Assn. Self-Esteem, Ky. Spkrs. Assn. (bd. dirs. 1996), Rotary Club Cin. Roman Catholic.

RIESZ, WANDA WALLACE, legislative specialist, educational consultant; b. Lafayette, Ind., July 13, 1942; d. George Murdock and Byrdena Maude (McDill) Wallace; m. William H. Riesz, July 28, 1963 (div. 1972); children: James W. (Jay) (dec.), Nicole Elies. Student, Purdue U., 1960-61, U. Md., Madrid, 1962; AB in Spanish, Ind. U., 1962, BS in Edn., 1963, MS in Edn., 1965, D in Cultural Studies, 1972; cert., U. Madrid, 1962; student, Berlitz Lang. Sch., Freiburg, Germany, 1966, Internat. U. Menendez Pelayo, Santander, Spain, 1967, Alliance Francaise, Paris, 1967. Lic. superintendent adminstr. K-12, tchr. Spanish K-9, elem. tchr., Ind.; lic. K-12 elem. sch., Spanish K-12, Va.; lic. real estate sales, broker, Ind. Tchr. elem. sch., French Fairfax (Va.) County Schs., 1963-65; dir. GED drop-out program U.S. Army, Kaiserslautern, Germany, 1965-66; assoc. prof. SUNY, Stony Brook, 1968-70; lectr. sch. edn. Ind. U., Purdue U., Columbus, Bloomington, Ind., 1970-78; founder, prin. Pub. Alternative H.S., Bloomington, 1970-80; legis. aide Ind. Ho. of Reps., Indpls., 1988—; cons. edn., legis., polit., drunk driving, vets.' affairs Hampton Inst., Little Rock, Lexington, Ky., L.A., Cleveland, Tenn., Grand Rapids, Mich., 1970—; grant writer Fed. Law Enforcement Agy., Ind., Washington, 1970—; spkr. in field. Contbr. articles to profl. jours.; co-developer: (video and board game) Peer Supervision, 1976. Rep. Ind. Baccalaureate Edn. Sys. Trust Ind. Ho. of Reps. Dem. Caucus; cons. Vietnam and Korean War Meml. Commn., 1990—, Goals 2000, 1990—, U.S. Sec. Edn., 1990—, Coalition Essential Schs., 1990—; bd. dirs. Luggage for Foster Kids, State of Ind., 1990—, Middle Way Shelter for Battered Women, Bloomington, 1984, State Juvenile Justice Task Force, 1982, Big Brothers/Big Sisters; bd. dirs., pres. Jay Riesz Found. to Prevent Drunk Driving, Women for Better Govt., Greater Indpls., 1994-96; legis. liaison State Mothers Against Drunk Driving; vol. Habitat for Humanity, Indpls., 1995; pres. Dem. Woman's Club, 1994—; founding mem. Ind. Victims of Violent Crimes, 1995—; elected del. Ind. Dem. State Conv., 1988, 92, 96; mem. youth adv. bd., New Directions Com. St. Paul's Episc. Ch., 1994—. Named Ky. Col., 1995; recipient State POW/MIA award DAV, Spl. Merit Recognition award State of Ind. Dept. Vets. Affairs, 1995, Spl. Legis. award Mothers Against Drunk Driving, State of Ind., 1990. Mem. Edn. Commn. of the States, NOW, Indpls. Athletic Club, Culver Mil. Acad. Club (Indpls.), Am. Legion Aux. (life), Metro. Indpls. Bd. Realtors, Studebaker Drivers Club, Mustang Owners Club, Maxinkuckee Yacht Club, Inpls. Ski Club, Phi Sigma Iota (treas. 1972), Pi Lambda Theta (sec. 1971), Psi Iota Xi. Home: 65 E Westfield Blvd Indianapolis IN 46220 Office: Ind Ho of Reps State House 4A6 Indianapolis IN 46204

RIFKIND, ARLEEN B., physician, researcher; b. N.Y.C., June 29, 1938; d. Michael C. and Regina (Gottlieb) Brenner; m. Robert S. Rifkind, Dec. 24, 1961; children: Amy, Nina. BA, Bryn Mawr Coll., 1960; MD, NYU, 1964. Intern Bellevue Hosp., N.Y.C., 1964-65, resident, 1965; clin. assoc. Endocrine br. Nat. Cancer Inst., 1965-68; research assoc., asst. resident physician Rockefeller U., 1968-71; asst. prof. medicine Cornell U. Med. Coll., N.Y.C., 1971-82, assoc. prof. medicine, 1983—, asst. prof. pharmacology, 1973-78, assoc. prof., 1978-82, prof., 1983—; chmn. Gen. Faculty Council Cornell U. Med. Coll., 1984-86; mem. Nat. Inst. Environ. Health Scis. Rev. Com., 1981-85, chmn., 1985-86; mem. toxicology study sect. Nat. Inst. Health, 1989-91, chmn. 1991-93; bd. sci. counselors USPHS Agy. for Toxic Substances and Disease Registry, 1991-95, adv. com. FDA Ranch Hand., Spl. Studies Relating to the Possible Long-Term Health Effects of Phenoxy Herbicides and Contaminents, 1995—. Mem. editorial bd. Drug Metabolism and Disposition, 1994—, Toxicology and Applied Pharmacology, 1996—, Biochem. Pharmacology, 1996—; contbr. articles to profl. jours. Chmn. Friends of the Library, Jewish Theol. Sem. Am., 1984-86; trustee Dalton Sch., 1986-92; mem. Environ. Health and Safety Coun. Am. Health Found., 1990—. Recipient Andrew W. Mellon Tchr.-Scientist award, 1976-78; USPHS spl. fellow, 1968-70, 71-72. Mem. Endocrine Soc., Am. Soc. Clin. Investigation, Am. Soc. Pharmacology and Exptl. Therapeutics, AAAS, Internat. Soc. Study Xenobiotics, Soc. Toxicology. Office: Cornell U Med Coll Dept Pharmacology 1300 York Ave New York NY 10021-4805

RIFMAN, EILEEN NISSENBAUM, music educator; b. Bklyn., June 10, 1944; d. Jack and Sarah (Bednarsh) Nissenbaum; m. Samuel Sholom Rifman, Aug. 12, 1972; children: Edward, Aimee. MusB, Manhattan Sch. Music, 1966, M Music Edn., 1967; MusM, Ind. U., 1970; cert., Fontainebleau, France, 1967. Music specialist N.Y.C. Pub. Sch. System, 1966-67; instr. Long Beach (Calif.) City Coll., 1970-72, Immaculate Heart Coll., Hollywood, Calif., 1971-74, U. Judaism, Hollywood, 1973-74; co-coord. Community Sch. Performing Arts, L.A., 1974-82, instr., 1973-83; pvt. piano tchr. Manhattan Beach, Calif., 1963—; tchr. gifted and talented edn. program GATE, Manhattan Beach, Calif., 1990-91; tchr. Etz Jacob Hebrew Acad., L.A., 1991-95, Ohr Eliyahu Acad., 1995-96. Performer Pratt Inst., Clinton Hill Symphony, N.Y.C., 1962, Sta. WNYC-FM, 1964. Chair Cultural Arts Com., Manhattan Beach, 1985-86; bd. dirs. Hermosa Beach (Calif.) Community Ctr., 1990-91. Mem. Nat. Fedn. Music Clubs (adjudicator 1970). Home: 1700 Lynngrove Dr Manhattan Beach CA 90266-4242

RIGER, STEPHANIE, psychology educator; b. Phila., Apr. 3, 1946; d. Martin and Anne (Cohen) R.; m. Dan A. Lewis, Jan. 3, 1986; children: Matthew, Jake. BA, U. Mich., 1967, PhD, 1973. Prof. Lake Forest (Ill.) Coll., 1973-90, U. Ill. Chgo., 1990—. Co-author: The Female Fear, 1990 (Choice award). Recipient disting. pub. award Assn. Women in Psychology. Office: U Ill at Chicago M/C 360 Womens Studies Program 1007 W Harrison St Chicago IL 60607-7137

RIGGS, JACKI PIERACCI, educational consultant; b. San Jose, May 13, 1954; d. Leo A. Pieracci and Laura B. Petersen LaRue; m. Joseph N. Riggs III, Aug. 27, 1978; children: Joseph N. IV, Amanda Marie, Austin Spenser. BS in Child Devel., Brigham Young U., 1981; MA in Spl. Edn., U. N.Mex., 1983, PhD, 1992. Treatment liaison ATASC Project, Albuquerque, 1976-79; dir. alcohol edn. program Juvenile Ct., Albuquerque, 1978-79; tchr. Children's Psychiat. Hosp., Albuquerque, 1985-88; div. dir. Juvenile Facilities, Santa Fe, N.Mex., 1988-89; cabinet sec. N.Mex. Youth Authority, Santa Fe, 1989-90; pvt. practice cons. Albuquerque, 1990—; dir. admissions Bosqee Prep. Sch., 1995—; mem. Gov. Johnson's Transitional Team Children, Youth and Families Dept., 1994. Commr. Youth Authority Commn., Santa Fe, 1988; mem. Gov.'s Substance Abuse Adv. Coun., 1989; mem. Community Corrections Panel, 1988; vol. Bosque Prep. U. N.Mex. fellow, 1986-87, 87-88, 91-92. Mem. NAFE, Coun. for Exceptional Children, Women Execs. in State Govt., Nat. Assn. Juvenile Correctional Adminstrs.

RIGGS, SONYA WOICINSKI, elementary school educator; b. Newhall, Calif., Oct. 9, 1935; d. Jack Lewis Woicinski and Mittie Mozelle (Bennett) Gillett; m. Eugene Garland Riggs, Dec. 21, 1956; children: Georgia Ann, Madeline Sue, Dana Eugene. BS in Elem. Edn., U. Tex., 1970; MEd in Reading Edn., S.W. Tex. State U., 1980. Cert. elem. tchr., Tex.; cert. reading specialist K-12. Sec. state govts., Nebr./Tex., 1955-57; piano instr. Elgin, Tex., 1961-66; tchr. 1st grade Elgin Elem. Sch., Elgin, 1967-69, tchr. Music 3rd/4th grades, 1971-72, tchr. 4th grade, 1972-73; pres. El Tesoro internacionale, 1973-74; sec. region office Planned Parenthood/World Population, Austin, 1975-76; tchr. 8th-12th grades Giddings (Tex.) State Sch., 1976-78; tchr. 4th/5th grades Thorndale (Tex.) Ind. Sch. Dist., 1979-80; tchr. remedial reading Brazosport Ind. Sch. Dist., Freeport, Tex., 1980-81; tchr. 6th grade reading and chpt. I Bastrop (Tex.) Mid. Sch., 1981-94, Bastrop Intermediate, 1994—; developer Enrichment Ctr., Bastrop Intermediate, 1995-96. Contbr. articles to Shih Tzu Reporter, 1993 French Bulldog Ann., French Bullytin, Boston Quar., Golden Retriever World; contbr. poetry to anthologies Garden of Life, 1996, Best Poems of 1996. Mem. Elgin Band Boosters, 1970-83, sec., 1976. Mem. Assn. Tex. Profl. Educators (campus rep. 1996-97), Austin Kennel Club (bd. dirs. 1990-91, 95—, sec. 1996-97), Am. Shih Tzu Club (edn. and rescue com. mem. south ctrl. regional hearing com.), French Bulldog Club Am. (rescue com.), Mission City Ring Stewards Assn., Internat. Soc. Poets, Austin Writers League.

RIGGS, SUZANNE MARIE, critical care nurse; b. Wheeling, W.Va., Feb. 13, 1963; d. William Edward and Mary Ann (Jacob) Simon; m. Donald Gregory Riggs, Nov. 14, 1987; children: Gregory Allen, Kassandra Elizabeth. Diploma, Ohio Valley Gen. Hosp. Sch. of Nursing, 1985; student, Ohio U., St. Clairsville, 1983. Nurse's aide Heartland-Lansing Care Ctr., Bridgeport, Ohio, 1983-84; staff nurse Fairfax Hosp., Falls Church, Va., 1985-87; staff nurse Ohio State U. Hosps., Columbus, 1987-92, renal med. transplant unit, 1987-90; cardiology telemetry unit, 1990-91, centralized scheduling dept., 1991-93; RN Ctrl. outpatient scheduling Ohio Valley Med. Ctr., Wheeling, W.Va., 1993—. Mem. Ohio Nurses Assn.

RIGGSBY, DUTCHIE SELLERS, education educator; b. Montgomery, Ala., Oct. 26, 1940; d. Cleveland Malcolm and Marcella (Bedsole) Sellers; m. Ernest Duward Riggsby, Aug. 25, 1962; 1 child, Lyn. BS, Troy (Ala.) State Coll., 1962, MS, 1965; postgrad., George Peabody Coll., 1963; EdD, Auburn U., 1972. Cert. tchr., Ala., Ga.; cert. libr., Ga. Tchr. Montgomery Pub. Sch.s, 1962-63, Troy City Schs., 1963-67; instr. Auburn (Ala.) U., 1968-69; asst. prof. Columbus (Ga.) Coll., 1972-77, assoc. prof., 1978-83, prof., 1983—; coord. Instrnl. Tech. Sch. Edn., 1996—; vis. prof. U. P.R., Rio Piedras, 1972, 73; cons. schs. Columbus and Ft. Benning, Ga., 1980; leader various workshops, 1989, 93—; software reviewer Nat. Sci. Tchrs. Assn. Contbr. more than 90 articles on state, regional, nat., and internat. programs to profl. jours., 1968—. Educator internal aerospace CAP, Maxwell AFB, 1980-90; dir. Air and Space Camp for Kids, 1990—. Recipient STAR Tchr. award Nat. Sci. Tchrs. Assn., Washington, 1968. Mem. Assn. for Ednl. Comms. and Tech. (non-periodical publs. com. 1994-96, awards com. 1994-96, chair awards com. 1996-97), Nat. Congress on Aviation and Space Edn. (dir. spl. promotions 1986-90), World Aerospace Edn. Orgn. (v.p. for the Americas 1996—), Ga. Assn. Instrnl. Tech. (bd. dirs. 1982-84), Phi Delta Kappa (pres. Chattahoochee Valley chpt. 1986-87, Svc. award 1989, Svc. Key award 1993). Baptist. Home: 1709 Ashwood Ct Columbus GA 31904-3009 Office: Columbus Coll Sch Edn 4225 University Ave Columbus GA 31907-5679

RIGONI, RENEE ANNE, accounting educator; b. Batavia, N.Y., Nov. 20, 1953; d. Roger Joseph and Cecilia Felicity (Falcon) Plossl; m. Gary Walter Rigoni, Jan. 6, 1973; children: Michael, Timothy, Emily, Megan, Amanda. AAS in Acctg., Rochester Inst. Tech., 1975, BS in Acctg., 1977, MBA in Fin., 1981. Fin. analyst, supr. Gleason Works, Rochester, N.Y., 1980-88; acctg. educator Monroe C.C., Rochester, 1988—. Co-author, editor: Accounting Demonstration Problems Workbook, Vol. 1, 1991, Vol. 2, 1993. Mem. Inst. Mgmt. Accts. (cert.). Republican. Roman Catholic.

RIGSBY, CAROLYN ERWIN, music educator; b. Franklinton, La., Apr. 11, 1936; d. Sheldon Aubrey and Edna Marie (Fussell) Erwin; m. Michael Hall Rigsby, May 30, 1959; 1 child, Laura Elaine Rigsby Boyd. B in Music Edn., Northwestern State U., La., 1958; MEd, Nicholls State U., 1970. Cert. vocal music tchr. k-12. Music tchr. Terrebonne Parish Sch., Houma, La., 1958-81, 81-83; music coord. Terrebonne Parish Sch., Houma, 1983-84; music tchr. Pasadena (Tex.) Ind. Sch. Dist., 1988—. Mem. Tex. Music Educators Assn., Packard Autombile Classics, Lone Star Packard Club,

Delta Kappa Gamma (pres. 1988-90). Republican. Methodist. Home: 16014 Mill Point Dr Houston TX 77059-5216

RIGSBY, JUDITH KAY, librarian; b. Pratt, Kans., Oct. 4, 1946; d. Lynn Logan and Vergie Lillian (Vansickle) Cannon; m. Albert Lee Rigsby, Sept. 4, 1971; 1 child, Jennifer Lynne. BA, Western State Coll., Gunnison, Colo., 1968; MLIS, U. Okla., 1994. Quality assurance specialist USAF, Okla. City, 1969-78; libr. acquisitions Oral Roberts U., Tulsa, 1983-89, circulation dir., 1990-92, libr. periodicals, 1992-93, acquisitions libr., 1994—. Dist. dir. CampFire Inc., Tulsa, 1989-90. Mem. ALA, Okla. Libr. Assn., Beta Phi Mu, Phi Theta Kappa. Office: Oral Roberts U Libr 7777 S Lewis Tulsa OK 74171

RIGSBY, LINDA FLORY, lawyer; b. Topeka, Kans., Dec. 16, 1946; d. Alden E. and Lolita M. Flory; m. Michael L. Rigsby, Aug. 14, 1963; children: Michael L. Jr., Elisabeth A. MusB, Va. Commonwealth U., 1969; JD, U. Richmond, 1981. Bar: Va. 1981, D.C. 1988. Assoc. McGuire, Woods, Battle & Boothe, Richmond, Va., 1981-85; dep. gen. counsel Crestar Fin. Corp., Richmond, 1985—. Recipient Disting. Svc. award U. Richmond, 1987; named Vol. of Yr. U. Richmond, 1986, Woman of Achievement, Met. Richmond Women's Bar, 1995. Mem. Va. Bar Assn. (exec. com. 1993-96), Richmond Bar Assn. (bd. dirs. 1992-95), Va. Bankers Assn. (chair legal affairs 1992-95), U. Richmond Estate Planning Coun. (chmn. 1990-92). Roman Catholic. Home: 10005 Ashbridge Pl Richmond VA 23233-5402 Office: Crestar Fin Corp 919 E Main St Richmond VA 23219-4625

RIKE, SUSAN, public relations executive; b. N.Y.C., Aug. 29, 1952; d. George Carson and Mildred Eleanor (Geehr) R. BA cum laude, Bklyn. Coll., 1975. Editl. asst. Artforum Mag., N.Y.C., 1975-77; co-owner Say Cheese, Bklyn., 1977-80; editl. asst. The Star, N.Y.C., 1980-82; acct. sec. Robert Marston and Assocs., N.Y.C., 1983-84; asst. acct. exec. Marketshare, N.Y.C., 1984; acct. exec. Doremus Pub. Rels. BBDO Internat., N.Y.C., 1984-86; pres. Susan Rike Pub. Rels., Bklyn., 1986—. Democrat. Office: Susan Rike Pub Rels 335 State St Ste 3C Brooklyn NY 11217-1719

RIKER, MARYANN JULIA, fine art consultant; b. Easton, Pa., Sept. 11, 1956; d. Charles R. and Mary T. (Kozari) R. BA, Moravian Coll., 1982; MA, Montclair State U., 1995; postgrad., Norwich U., 1996—. Designer Koh-I-Noor Rapidograph, Inc., Bloomsbury, N.J., 1974-82; graphics supr. Somerset County Coll., North Branch, N.J., 1982-83; account mgr. AT&T Visual Comms., Bedminster, N.J., 1984-90; advt./pub. rels. mgr. AT&T Comms., Basking Ridge, N.J., 1990-93; curatorial asst. AT&T Found., N.Y.C., 1993-95; owner, pers. InfoARTS, Phillipsburg, N.J., 1996—; fine artist Open Space Gallery, Allentown, Pa., 1990-93, City Without Walls, Newark, 1993—, Amos Enc Gallery, N.Y.C., 1994-96. Contbr. illustrations and articles to profl. jours. Polit. supporter Nat. Rep. Party, Phillipsburg, 1974-78. Recipient Excellence in Arts award Binney & Smith, Easton, Pa., 1993, Excellence in Arts award MCJ Techs., Inc., Tempe, Ariz. and Beijing, China, 1995. Mem. NAFE, Profl. Women's Bus. Owners Assn., Women's Caucus for the Arts. Roman Catholic. Home: 145 N Riverview Rd Phillipsburg NJ 08865

RILEY, ANN J., state legislator, technology specialist; b. Memphis, Oct. 27, 1940; m. Ray T. Riley, Apr. 28, 1962. BSBA, U. Albuquerque, 1985; MBA, Webster U., 1988; cert. in pub. policy, Harvard U., 1994. Loan officer Ravenswood Bank, Chgo., 1970-74; mgr. dist. sales Security Lockout, Chgo., 1974-77; owner AR Fasteners, Albuquerque, 1977-82; tech. transfer agt. Sandia Nat. Labs., Albuquerque, 1983—; mem. N.Mex. Senate, Santa Fe, 1993—; resolutions chair energy com. Nat. Order of Women Legis. Nat. Conf. State Legislators. Bd. dirs. All Faiths Receiving Home. Albuquerque, 1989-92, Law Enforcement Acad., Santa Fe, 1991-92; active Leadership Albuquerque, 1991, state federal task force U.S. Office Sci. & Tech., 1995. Flemming fellow Am. U. Ctr. for Policy Alternatives, 1996. Democrat. Home: 10301 Karen Ave NE Albuquerque NM 87111-3633

RILEY, CATHERINE IRENE, university official, cosultant, former state senator; b. Balt., Mar. 21, 1947; d. Francis Worth and Catherine (Cain) R. BA, Towson State U., 1969. Bacteriologist Balt. City Hosp., 1969-72; legis. aide Md. Ho. of Dels., Annapolis, 1973-74, mem., 1975-82; mem. Md. Senate, Annapolis, 1982-91; ret., 1991; asst. dir. Bur. Govtl. Rsch., U.Md. Sch. Pub. Affairs, College Park, 1992—; cons. Md. State Div. Alcoholism Control, 1973; mem. House Environ. Matters Com., 1975-82; mem. Spl. Joint Com. Energy, 1977-83, chmn., 1978-79, 1980-83; mem. So. Legis. Conf. Energy Com. 1978, Environ. Com., 1983—, vice chmn., 1985—, chair senate fin. com., 1987-91, joint budget & audit com., 1988-91; mem. So. Environ. Resource Coun., 1978, Power Plant Siting Adv. Com., 1977-91, State of Md. Energy Conservation Bd., 1978-83, mem. BiState Chesapeake Bay Commn., 1981-83, chmn. 1982; chmn. Forest Land Task Force, 1981-84, Budget and Taxation Senate Com., 1983-86, Subcom. Edn., Health, and Human Resources, 1983-86, Nat. Conf. State Legis. Energy Commn., 1983-91; senate chmn. adminstrv. exec. and legis. review com., 1983-86, various state govt. coms. and subcoms. Author: Maryland Profiles, Vol. 2, 1994; co-author: Maryland Policy Studies, vol. 4, 1991. Contbr. articles to profl. jours. Mem. adv. com. State Edn. Policy Seminars Adv. Com., 1983—, Protective Svcs. to Children and Families, 1983—; exec. bd. Balt. Area Coun. Boy Scouts Am., 1983-88; hon. chmn. Am. Cancer Soc., 1982-83; mem. Harford County Child Protection Coun., 1978-80, vice chmn. 1980; mem. Harford County Coun. Community Svcs., 1976—, Harford County legis. del., 1975-82 , chmn. 1976, 1980-82; mem. Md. Order Women Legislators, 1975—, sec. 1976-79; mem. adv. bd. Susquehanna State Park, 1975-91; mem. Joppatowne Womens Club, 1975—, No. Md. Assn. for Retarded Citizens, Inc., 1975—, Upper Cheasepeake Watershed Assn., Inc., 1975—. Recipient Disting. Svc. award Md. State Troopers, 1980, Community Svc. award, United Way, 1978, Disting. Svc. award Jaycees, 1976, Liberty award Harford Christian High Sch., 1975, Cert. of Appreciation Md. Mcpl. League, 1984, William P. Coliton Outstanding Community Svc. award Johns Hopkins U., 1985, Silver Chalice award Am. Coun. on Alsoholism, 1988, Outstanding Alumni award, Towson State U., 1989, Betty Tyler Pub. Affairs award Planned Parenthood of Md., 1989, Sarah T. Hughes Disting. Pub. Svc. award Goucher Coll., 1990; named Young Dem. of Yr. State of Md., 1975, Women of Yr. Soroptimist Club, 1980; Coun. Guide State Govt. Toll fellow, 1987, other state and civic awards. Mem. Am. Coun. on Alcoholism (bd. dirs.). Office: 20 Office St Bel Air MD 21014-3704

RILEY, DOROTHY COMSTOCK, judge; b. Detroit, Dec. 6, 1924; d. Charles Austin and Josephine (Grima) Comstock; m. Wallace Don Riley, Sept. 13, 1963; 1 child, Peter Comstock. BA with honors in Polit. Sci., Wayne State U., 1946, LLB, 1949; LLD (hon.), Alma Coll., 1988, U. Detroit, 1990. Bar: Mich. 1950, U.S. Dist. Ct. (ea. dist.) Mich. 1950, U.S. Supreme Ct. 1957. Atty. Wayne County Friend of Ct., Detroit, 1956-68; ptnr. Riley & Roumell, Detroit, 1968-72, 73-76; judge Wayne County Cir., Detroit, 1972, Mich. Ct. Appeals, Detroit, 1976-82; assoc. justice Mich. Supreme Ct., Detroit, 1982-83, 85—, chief justice, 1987-91; mem. U.S. Jud. Conf. Commn. on State-Fed. Ct. Rels.; chmn. tort reform com. Conf. of Chief Justices; bd. dirs. Nat. Ctr. for State Cts., Thomas J. Cooley Law Sch. Co-author manuals, articles in field. Mem. steering com. Mich. Children Skillman Found., 1992; mem. multistate profl. responsibility exam. com. Nat. Conf. Bar Examiners, 1992. Recipient Disting. Alumni award Wayne U., 1990; Headliner award Women of Wayne, 1977; Donnelly award, 1946; Law Enforcement Commendation medal Nat. Soc. Sons of Am. Revolution, 1991; inducted in Mich. Women's Hall of Fame, 1991. Mem. ABA (family law sect. 1965—, vice chmn. gen. practice sect. com. on juvenile justice 1975-80, mem. jud. adminstrn. sect. 1973—, standing com. on fed. ct. improvements, mem. judges adv. com. of standing com. on ethics and profl. responsibility 1992), Am. Judicature Soc., Fellows Am. Bar Found., Mich. State Bar Found., State Bar Mich. (civil liberties com. 1954-58), Detroit Bar Assn. (pub. rels. com. 1955-56, author Com. in Action column, Detroit Lawyers 1955, chmn. friend of ct. and family law com. 1974-75), Nat. Women Judges Assn., Nat. Women Lawyers Assn., Women Lawyers Assn. Mich. (pres. 1957-58), Mich. Sup. Ct. Hist. Soc., Karyatides, Pi Sigma Alpha. Republican. Roman Catholic. Office: Mich Supreme Ct 500 Woodward Ave Fl 20 Detroit MI 48226-3423*

RILEY, GEORGIANNE MARIE, lawyer; b. Chgo., Feb. 5, 1953. BA in Psychology, Drake U., 1974, JD, 1978. Bar: Ill., 1978. Chief counsel Ill. Indsl. Commn., Chgo., 1979-83; dep. chief counsel Ill. Dept. Transp., Chgo., 1983-89; counsel Chem. Waste Mgmt., Oakbrook, Ill., 1989-91, sr. counsel, 1991-92; gen. counsel, v.p., sec. Rust Indsl. Svcs., Westchester, Ill., 1993-96. Office: Waste Mgmt Inc 3003 Butterfield Rd Oak Brook IL 60521-1107

RILEY, HELENE MARIA KASTINGER, Germanist; b. Vienna, Austria, Mar. 11, 1939; came to U.S., 1959; d. Josef and Helene (Friedl) Kastinger; m. Edward R. Riley, Nov. 6, 1957 (div. May 1970); children: India Helene, John Edward, Jesse Dale, Michael Rutledge; m. Darius G. Ornston, May 11, 1983. Grad., bus. coll., Vienna, 1955; BA in Music, North Tex. State U., 1970; MA in Germanics, Rice U., 1973, PhD in Germanics, 1975. Teaching asst. Rice U., Houston, 1971-75; asst. prof. German Yale U., New Haven, Conn., 1975-78, head summer lang. inst., 1979-81, assoc. prof., 1979-85; chmn. Dept. Fgn. Langs. Wash. State U., Pullman, 1981-82; head Dept. Langs. Clemson (S.C.) U., 1985-86, prof., 1985-95, Alumni Disting. prof., 1996—; guest prof. Middlebury (Vt.) Coll., 1976; speaker in field. Author: Achim von Arnim, 1979, Virginia Woolf, 1983, Clemens Brentano, 1985, Die Weibliche Muse, 1986, Max Weber, 1991, others; contbr. numerous articles to profl. jours. Recipient German-Am. Friendship award Consul Gen. of the German Fed. Republic, 1989; grantee Griswold Found., 1975-76, 78, S.C. Dept. Edn., 1986, NEH, 1986, Provost's award Clemson U., 1989, Hilles Fund, 1976, 79, 82, S.C. Humanities Coun., 1996; NDEA fellow, 1972, 73, Rice fellow, 1971, 74, Morse fellow, 1977-78, Deutscher Akademischer Austausch-Dienst fellow, 1979, Yale U. sr. faculty fellow, 1981-82, Holland Fund fellow, 1982, Deutsche Forschungsgemeinschaft fellow, 1982, Mesda fellow, 1993. Fellow Davenport Coll., Yale U.; mem. AAUP (v.p. 1987-88, pres. 1988-89), MLA, Am. Assn. Tchrs. German, So. Comparative Lit. Assn., others. Democrat. Office: Clemson U Dept Langs 717 Strode Twr Clemson SC 29634-1515

RILEY, JOCELYN CAROL, writer, television producer; b. Mpls., Mar. 6, 1949; d. G.D. Riley and D.J. (Berg) Riley-Jacobson; m. Jeffrey Allen Steele, Sept. 4, 1971; children: Doran Riley, Brendan Riley. BA in English, Carleton Coll., 1971. Mng. editor Carleton Miscellany, Northfield, Minn., 1971; mktg. asst. Beacon Press, Boston, 1971-73; freelance writer, editor, producer, 1973—. Author: Only My Mouth Is Smiling, 1982 (one of Best Books of 1982, ALA, A. Tofte award 1982), Crazy Quilt, 1984; producer: (TV programs) Her Own Words, 1986 (Outstanding Achievement award Assn. for Multi-Image Internat. Festival 1987), Belle: The Life and Writings of Belle Case La Follette, 1987, Gold Medal Internat. Film and TV Festival, 1988, Zona Gale, 1874-1938, 1988, Patchwork, 1989, Prairie Quilts, 1990, Votes for Women?!, 1990, Mountain Wolf Woman, 1990, Prairie Cabin, 1991, Winnebago Women Songs & Stories, 1992, Ethel Kvalheim, Rosemaler, 1992, Her Mother Before Her, 1992, Women in Construction, 1993, America Fever, 1994, Women in Policing, 1994, Sisters & Friends, 1994, Big Sister, Little Sister, 1995, Audrey Handler, Glass Artist, 1995, Women in Dentistry, 1996, Sewing Together, 1996, Women in Nontraditional Careers, 1996, Women in Firefighting, 1996; contbr. articles to Christian Sci. Monitor, Pubs. Weekly, Writer, others; columnist Wis. State Jour., Madison, 1986-91. Active United Way of Dane County, 1984-90. Hon. fellow Women's Studies Research Ctr. U. Wis., Madison, 1986-91; Film in the Cities Regional Film/Video grantee; Bronze Apple award Nat. Ednl. Film & Video Festival, 1988; cert. of commendation Am. Assn. State and Local History, 1988, Gold medal Internat. Film & TV Festival, 1988, cert. of recognition Wis. Dept. Pub. Instrn. Am. Indian History & Culture Program, 1991, Write Women Back into History award Nat. Women's History Project, 1995, ALA award, 1996. Mem. Women in Communications (pres. Madison chpt. 1984-85, nat. del. 1983, Writers Cup 1985), Council for Wis. Writers (1st place for nonfiction article 1986), Authors Guild, Madison Assn. for Multi-Image (pres. 1986-87, nat. del. 1986), Downtown Madison Rotary Club. Address: PO Box 5264 Madison WI 53705-0264

RILEY, MATILDA WHITE (MRS. JOHN W. RILEY, JR.), sociology educator; b. Boston, Apr. 19, 1911; d. Percival and Mary (Cliff) White; m. John Winchell Riley, Jr., June 19, 1931; children: John Winchell III, Lucy Ellen Riley Sallick. BA, Radcliffe Coll., 1931, MA, 1937, DSc (hon.), 1994; DSc, Bowdoin Coll., 1972; LHD (hon.), Rutgers U., 1983. Rsch. asst. Harvard U., Cambridge, Mass., 1932; v.p. Market Rsch. Co. Am., 1938-49; chief cons. economist WPB, 1941; rsch. specialist Rutgers U., 1950, prof., 1951-73, dir. sociology lab., chmn. dept. sociology and anthropology, 1959-73, emeritus prof., 1973—; Daniel B. Fayerweather prof. polit. econ. and sociology Bowdoin Coll., 1974-78, prof. emeritus, 1978—; assoc. dir. Nat. Inst. on Aging, 1979-91, sr. social scientist, 1991—; mem. faculty Harvard U., summer 1955; staff assoc., dir. aging and society Russell Sage Found., 1964-73, staff sociologist, 1974-77; chmn. com. on life course Social Sci. Rsch. Coun., 1977-80; sr. rsch. assoc. Ctr. for Social Scis., Columbia U., 1978-80; adv. bd. Carnegie Aging Soc. Project, 1985-87; mem. Commn. on Coll. Retirement, 1982-86; vis. prof. NYU, 1954-61; cons. Nat. Coun. on Aging, Acad. Ednl. Devel.; mem. study group NIH, 1971-79, Social Sci. Rsch. Coun. Com. on Middle Years, 1973-77; chmn. NIH Task Force on Health and Behavior, 1986-91; cons. WHO, 1987—; Winkelman lectr. U. Mich., 1984, Selo lectr. U. No. Calif., 1987, Boettner lectr. Am. Coll., 1990, Claude Pepper lectr. Fla. State U., 1993, Disting. lectr. Southwestern Social Scis. Assn., 1990, Standing lectr. SUNY, 1992, Inaugural lectr. Cornell U., 1992; lectr. Internat. Inst. of Sociology, Plenary, 1993, Inter-Univ. Consortium Pol. and Social Rsch., U. Mich., 1993, Duke U., 1993. Author: (with P. White) Gliding and Soaring, (with Riley and Toby) Sociological Studies in Scale Analysis, 1954, Sociological Research, vols. I, II, 1964, (with others) Aging and Society, vol. I, 1968, vol. II, 1969, vol. III, 1972, (with Nelson) Sociological Observation, 1974, Aging from Birth to Death: Interdisciplinary Perspectives, 1979, (with Merton) Sociological Traditions from Generation to Generation, 1980, (with Abeles and Teitelbaum) Aging from Birth to Death: Sociotemporal Perspectives, 1982, (with Hess and Bond) Aging in Society, 1983; editor: (with M. Ory and D. Zablotsky) AIDS in an Aging Society: What We Need to Know, 1989; co-editor: Perspectives in Behavioral Medicine: The Aging Dimension, 1987, (with J. W. Riley) The Quality of Aging, 1989, The Annals, 1989; sr. editor: Structural Lag, 1994; editorial com.: Ann. Rev. Sociology, 1978-81, Social Change and the Life Course, vol. 1, Social Structures and Human Lives, (with B. Huber and B. Hess) Sociological Lives, vol. II, 1988, (with R. Kahn and Anne Foner) Structural Lag, 1994; contbr. chpts. to books, articles to profl. jours. Former trustee The Big Sisters Assn. Recipient Lindback Rsch. award Rutgers U., 1970, Social Sci. award Andrus Gerontology Ctr., U. So. Calif., 1972, Radcliffe Alumnae award, 1982, Commonwealth award 1984, Kesten Lecture award U. So. Calif., 1987, Sci. Achievement award Washington Acad. Scis., 1989, Disting. Sci. award, 1989, Disting. Creative award Gerontol. Soc. Am., 1990, Presdl. Meritorious award, 1990, Stuart Rice award Columbia Sociol. Soc., 1992, Kent award Gerontol. Soc. Am., 1992; fellow Advanced Study in Behaviorial Scis., 1978-79; Matilda White Riley award in rsch. and methodology established in her honor Rutgers U., 1977; Matilda White Riley prize established Bowdoin Coll., 1987; Matilda White Riley House dedicated Bowdoin Coll., 1996. Fellow AAAS (chmn. sect. on social and econ. scis. 1977-78); mem. NAS, Inst. Medicine of NAS (sr.), Acad. Behavioral Medicine Rsch., Am. Sociol. Assn. (exec. officer 1949-60, v.p. 1973-74, pres. 1986, 91, chmn. sect. on sociology of aging 1989, Disting. Scholar in Aging 1988, Career award 1992), Am. Assn. Public Opinion Rsch. (sec.-treas. 1949-51, Disting. Svc. award 1983), Eastern Sociol. Soc. (v.p. 1968-69, pres. 1977-78, Dis. Career award 1986), Soc. for Study Social Biology (bd. dirs. 1986-92), Am. Acad. Arts and Scis., D.C. Sociol. Soc. (co-pres. 1983-84), Sociol. Rsch. Assn., Internat. Orgn. Study Human Devel., Am. Philos. Soc. (membership lectr. 1987), Phi Beta Kappa, Phi Beta Kappa Assocs. Home: 4701 Willard Ave Apt 1607 Chevy Chase MD 20815-4630 Office: NIH Nat Inst on Aging 7201 Wisconsin Ave Bethesda MD 20814-4810

RILEY, MEG AMELIA, religion educator; b. Houston, Nov. 20, 1955; d. Charles Woodson and Martha (Moore) Wilson; m. Kendrick Wronski, Sept. 7, 1991. BA, Reed Coll., Portland, Oreg., 1977; MA, United Theol. Sem., New Brighton, Minn., 1987. Cons. religious edn. 1st Unitarian Soc., Mpls., 1983-85; dir. religious edn. 1st Universalist Ch., Mpls., 1985-89; youth program dir. Unitarian Universalist Assn., Boston, 1989—; dir. office for social justice Washington, 1995—. Editor: How to be a Con Artist, Conference Planning Handbook, 1991; creator, editor, team mgr. curriculum for adults: Ministry with Youth, 1991. Mem. Women Against Violence Against Women, Mpls., 1979-83; mem. Empowerment Group, Women Against Mil. Madness, Mpls., 1984-89; mem. Lesbian Feminist Organizing Com., Mpls., 1979-82. Recipient Ellie Morton award, Prairie Star Dist. Unitarian Universalist Assn., 1989. Mem. Soc. Larger Ministry, Unitarian Universalist Ministers Assn., Liberal Religious Educators Assn. Democrat. Office: Unitarian Universalist Assn 2026 P St NW Washington DC 20036

RILEY, NANCY MAE, retired vocational home economics educator; b. Grand Forks, N.D., May 1, 1939; d. Kenneth Wesley and Jeanne Margaret Olive (Hill) R. BS in Edn., Miami U., 1961; postgrad., Ohio U., 1964-69; MA, Marietta Coll., 1989. Cert. high sch. tchr. Tchr. home econs. Malta-McConnelsville (Ohio) High Sch., 1961-67; tchr. home econs. Waterford (Ohio) High Sch., 1968-92; advisor Malta-McConnelsville Future Homemakers, 1961-66, Waterford Future Homemakers Am., 1968-92; advisor to state officer Ohio Future Homemakers Am., McConnelsville, 1963, Waterford, 1976. Leader Girl Scouts Am., McConnelsville, 1962-66, camp counselor, 1962-76; fair judge Waterford Cmty. Fair, Waterford, 1970-85. Mem. NEA, Am. Vocat. Assn. (life), Ohio Edn. Assn. (life, del. 1979), Ohio Vocat. Assn. (life), DAR, Daus. Union Vets. (del. 1992—, tent pres. 1993-94, dist. pres. 1996), Daus. of War of 1812 (pres. 1991—, state sec. 1995—), Ohio Geneal. Soc., Order Ea. Star (worthy matron 1967-68, dep. grand matron 1978), White Shrine Jerusalem (worth high priestess 1979-81, 83). Republican. Baptist. Home: PO Box 137 Waterford OH 45786-0137

RILEY-DAVIS, SHIRLEY MERLE, advertising agency executive, marketing consultant, writer; b. Pitts., Feb. 4, 1935; d. William Riley and Beatrice Estelle (Whittaker) Byrd; m. Louis Davis; 1 child, Terri Judith. Student U. Pitts., 1952. Copywriter, Pitts. Mercantile Co., 1954-60; exec. sec. U. Mich., Ann Arbor, 1962-67; copy supr. N.W. Ayer, N.Y.C., 1968-76, assoc. creative dir., Chgo., 1977-81; copy supr. Leo Burnett, Chgo., 1981-86; freelance advt. and mktg. cons., 1986—; advt. and mktg. dir. Child and Family Svc., Ypsilanti, Mich., 1992—; vis. prof. Urban League Black Exec. Exch. Program; print, radio, and TV commercials; bd. dirs. Sr. Housing Bur., Ann Arbor; mem. adv. bd. Cmty. Diabetes, past bd. dirs. People's Hope for Housing, Ypsilanti, Mich. Recipient Grand and First prize N.Y. Film Festival, 1973, Gold and Silver medal Atlanta Film Festival, 1973, Gold medal V.I. Film Festival, 1974, 50 Best Creatives award Am. Inst. Graphic Arts, 1972, Clio award, 1973, 74, 75, Andy Award of Merit, 1981, Silver medal Internat. Film Festival, 1982, Corp. Mgmt. Assistance Program award, 1986, Good Sam award 1981, Svc. Advt. Creativity of Distinction cert., 1981; Senatorial scholar. Bd. dirs. Housing bur. for Srs. of the U. Mich. Med. Ctr., 1995—. Mem. Women in Film, Facets Multimedia Film Theatre Orgn. (bd. dirs.), Greater Chgo. Coun. for Prevention of Child Abuse, Internat. Platform Assn. Democrat. Roman Catholic. Avocations: dance, poetry, design, writing, volunteering. Office: 118 S Washington St Ypsilanti MI 48197-5427

RILEY-SCOTT, BARBARA POLK, retired librarian; b. Roselle, N.J., Nov. 21, 1928; d. Charles Carrington and Olive Bond P.; AB, Howard U., 1950; BS, N.J. Coll. Women, 1951; MS, Columbia U., 1955; m. George Emerson Riley, Feb. 23, 1957 (dec.); children: George E., Glenn C., Karen O.; m. William I. Scott, Oct. 6, 1990. Asst. librarian, Fla. A&M U., 1951-53; with Morgan State Coll., 1955; with Dept. Def., 1955-57, S.C. State Coll., 1957-59, U.Wis., 1958-59; asst. librarian Atlanta U., 1960-68; asst. dir. Union County Anti Poverty Council, 1968; librarian Union County Tech. Inst., Scotch Plains, N.J., 1968-82, Plainfield campus Union County Coll., 1982-95; ret., 1995. Mem. Roselle Bd. Edn., 1976-78; bd. dirs. Union County Anti Poverty Council, 1969-72; mem. Roselle Human Relations Commn., 1971-73, Plainfield Sci. Center, 1974-76, Union County Psychiat. Clinic, 1980-83, Pinewood Sr. Citizens Council, 1981-85; bd. dirs. Project, Women of N.J, 1985-93, Pinewood Sr. Citizen Housing, 1981-85, Black Women's History Conf., 1985-92, pres., 1989-91. Mem. N.J. Library Assn., Council Library Tech., ALA (Black caucas), N.J. Coalition of 100 Black Women, African Am. Women's Polit. Caucus, N.J. Black Librarians Network (bd. dirs.), Links, Inc. (North Jersey chpt.), Black Women's History Conf., Alpha Kappa Alpha. Mem. A.M.E. Ch. Club: Just-A-Mere Lit. Home: 114 E 7th Ave Roselle NJ 07203-2028

RIMA, INGRID HAHNE, economics educator; d. Max F. and Hertha G. (Grunsfeld) Hahne; m. Philip W. Rima; children: David, Eric. BA with honors, CUNY, 1945; MA, U. Pa., 1946, PhD, 1951. Prof. econs. Temple U., Phila., 1967—. Author: Development of Economic Analysis, 1967, 5th edit., 1996, Labor Markets Wages and Employment, 1981, The Joan Robinson Legacy, 1991, The Political Economy of Global Restructuring, Vol. I, Production and Organization, Vol. II, Trade and Finance, 1993, Measurement, Quantification and Economic Analysis, 1994, Labor Markets in a Global Economy, 1996. Fellow Ea. Econ. Assn.; mem. Am. Econ. Assn., History of Econs. Soc. (pres. 1993-4), Phi Beta Kappa. Office: Temple U Broad & Montgomery Ave Philadelphia PA 19122

RIMBACH, EVANGELINE LOIS, music educator; b. Portland, Oreg., June 28, 1932; d. Raymond Walter and Viola Clara (Gaebler) Rimbach. BA, Valparaiso (Ind.) U., 1954; MMus, Eastman Sch. Music, Rochester, N.Y., 1956; PhD, Eastman Sch. Music, 1967; student, Pacific Luth. U., Parkland, Wash., 1950-52. Vocal music instr. Goodwin Jr. High Sch., Redwood City, Calif., 1956-57; music instr. Calif. Concordia Coll., Oakland, Calif., 1957-62; prof. music Concordia U., River Forest, Ill., 1964—, chmn. dept., 1989—. Contbg. editor: Church Music, 1965-80; editor book: Johann Kuhnau: Magnificat, 1980; editor cantata: Johann Kuhnau: Lobe den Herrn, 1993; contbr. articles to profl. jours. Bd. dirs. Civic Symphony of Oak Park-River Forest, 1974-80, concert com. chmn., 1976-78, prog. annotator, 1976-80; mem. choir Grace Luth. Ch., River Forest, 1964—. AAUW postdoctoral fellow, 1969-70; DAAD grantee, Munich, 1980; recipient Rose of Honor award, Sigma Alpha Iota, 1987. Mem. Am. Musicol. Soc., Am. Recorder Soc., Luth. Edn. Assn., Sigma Alpha Iota. Republican. Lutheran. Home: 1115 Bonnie Brae Pl River Forest IL 60305-1515 Office: Concordia U 7400 Augusta St River Forest IL 60305-1402

RIMEL, REBECCA WEBSTER, foundation executive. BS, U. Va., 1973; MBA, James Madison U., 1983. RN, Va. Head nurse, emergency dept. U. Va. Hosp., Charlottesville, 1973-74, coord. med. out-patient dept., 1974-75, nurse practitioner dept. neurosurgery, 1975-77, instr. in neurosurgery, 1975-80, asst. prof., 1981-83; program mgr. health Pew Charitable Trusts, Phila., 1983-84; asst. v.p. Glenmede Trust Co., Pew Charitable Trusts, Phila., 1984-85; v.p. for programs Pew Charitable Trusts, Phila., 1985-88, exec. dir., 1988-94; pres., 1994—; mem. Coun. on Founds., Washington; prin. investigator dept. neurosurgery U. Va., 1981-85; adv. com. for U.S. Olympics on Boxing, 1983-86; adv. coun. Nat. Inst. of Neurol. Disorders & Strokes, 1988-91, also bd. dirs.; bd. dirs. Nat. Environ. Edn. and Tng. Found., Inc., Washington, Thomas Jefferson Meml. Found., Ind. Sector, Washington. Contbr. articles and abstracts to profl. jours., chpts. in books. Recipient Disting. Nursing Alumni award U. Va., 1988; Kellogg Nat. fellow, 1982. Mem. APHA, ANA, Va. State Nurses Assn. (membership and credentials com. 1982-86), Am. Acad. Nursing, Am. Assn. Neurosurg. Nurses, Emergency Dept. Nurses Assn.

RINEAMAN, LORNA M., psychotherapist, researcher; b. Cheverly, Md., June 18, 1967; d. Michael C. and Barbara E. (Marcus) Orndorff; m. Keith C. Rineaman, Sept. 15, 1990 (div. Sept. 1993). BA in Psychology, St. Mary's Coll. of Md., St. Mary's City, 1989; MA in Psychol. Svcs., Marymount U., Arlington, Va., 1992; MSW, Cath. U., Washington, 1996. Employee devel. asst. Dept Agr., USDA, Washington, 1990; sr. client svcs. coord. Employee Health Progams, Bethesda, Md., 1990; counseling intern Enhance, Employee Assistance Program, Fairfax, Va., 1992; ednl./vocational coord. George Washington U., U. Counseling Ctr., Washington, 1992-94; social work intern Cmty. Psychiat. Clinic, Bethesda, Md., 1994-95, social work cons., 1995; social work intern The Women's Ctr., Vienna, Va., 1995—; psychiat. social worker Ctr. for Posttraumatic and Dissociative Disorders Program, Washington, 1996—; grad. rsch. asst. Marymount U. Ctr. for Counseling and Career Svcs., Arlington, Va., 1991, U. Counseling Ctr., George Washington U., Washington, 1994-95, Sch. Social Svc., Cath. U. Am., Washington, 1995—; vol. data interpreter/videotape rater psychology dept. George Washington U., Washington, 1993; rsch. asst. psychology dept. George Mason U., Fairfax, Va., 1993-94. Vol. trainer No. Va. Hotline, Arlington, 1991-92, vol. listener, 1991-92; vol. intake worker AIDS Svcs., Whitman-Walker Clinic, Washington, 1993; vol. support group leader Whitman-Walker Clinic of No. Va., Arlington, 1993-94. Recipent award for leadership U.S. Achievement Acad., 1985. Mem. APA, ACA, NASW, N.Am. Assn. Masters in Psychology, Delta Epsilon Sigma. Democrat. Roman Catholic.

Home: 310 Ethan Allen Ave Takoma Park MD 20912 Office: PIW The Ctr 4th Fl 4228 Wisconsin Ave NW Washington DC 20016

RINER, ANGELA DAWN, elementary educator, adult education educator; b. Lynchburg, Va., May 12, 1969; d. Thomas William and Elizabeth Gayle (McGann) R. BS, Liberty U., 1991. 6th grade tchr. Halifax (Va.) County Pub. Schs., 1991-96, ABE/GED tchr., computer lab. mgr., 1993-96; kindergarten tchr. Amherst County Pub. Schs., Madison Heights, Va., 1996—; Coach Volens (Va.) Jump Rope Team. Baptist. Home: Rt 2 Box 248 Monroe VA 24574 Office: Elon Elem Sch Rt 1 Elon Rd Madison Heights VA 24572

RING, ALICE RUTH BISHOP, physician; b. Ft. Collins, Oct. 11, 1931; d. Ernest Otto and Mary Frances (Drohan) Bishop; m. Wallace Harold Ring, July 26, 1956 (div. 1969); children: Rebecca, Eric, Mark; m. Robert Charles Deifenbach, Sept. 10, 1977. BS, Colo. State U., 1953; MD, U. Colo., 1956; MPH, U. Calif., Berkeley, 1971. Physician cons. Utah State Div. HEalth, Salt Lake City, 1960-65; med. dir., project head start Salt Lake City Community Action Program, 1965-70; resident Utah State Div. Health, 1969-71; asst. assoc. reg. health dir. U.S. Pub. Health Svc., San Francisco, 1971-75; med. cons. U.S. Pub. Health Svc., Atlanta, 1975-77, dir. primary care, 1977-84; dir. div. diabetes control Ctrs. Disease Control, Atlanta, 1984-88; dir. WHO Collabor Ctr., Atlanta, 1986-91; dir. preventive medicine residency Ctrs. Disease Control, Atlanta, 1988-93; exec. dir. Am. Bd. Preventive Medicine, 1993—; trustee Am. Bd. Preventive Medicine, 1990-92 (diplomate); lectr. Emory U. Sch. Pub. Health, 1988-94. Co-author: Clinical Diabetes, 1991. Bd. dirs. Diabetes Assn. Atlanta, 1985-90, med. adv. com., 1990-94. Fellow Am. Coll. Preventive Medicine (bd. dirs. 1990-94); mem. APHA, AMA (grad. med. edn. adv. com. 1993—), Assn. Tchrs. Preventive Medicine, Am. Acad. Pediatrics, Sigma Xi. Office: Am Bd Preventive Medicine 9950 Lawrence Ave Schiller Park IL 60176-1310

RING, JENNIFER BETH, political science educator; b. L.A., Nov. 18, 1948; d. George Joseph and Frances (Kroll) R.; m. Norman Jacobson, Aug. 24, 1979; children: Johanna, Lillian. BA magna cum laude, UCLA, 1970; MA, U. Calif., Berkeley, 1973, PhD, 1979. Asst. prof. Columbia U., N.Y.C., 1979-80; lectr. U. Calif., Berkeley, 1981-89, Stanford (Calif.) U., 1983-89; assoc. prof. U. S.C., Columbia, 1989-95; assoc. prof. polit. sci., dir. women's studies U. Nev., Reno, 1996—; vis. assoc. prof. polit. sci. U. Calif., Berkeley, 1994-95; lectr. in field. Author: Modern Political Theory and Contemporary Feminism, 1991; contbr. articles to profl. jours. Mem. AAUW, Am. Polit. Sci. Assn., Nat. Womens Studies Assn., Phi Beta Kappa. Office: U Nev Womens Studies Program Dept Polit Sci Reno NV 89557

RING, NANCY GAIL, writer, artist; b. Irvington, N.J., Dec. 24, 1956; d. Frank and Dorothy (Kasoff) R.; m. Eric Mark Kaplan, Aug. 1, 1993. Student, Sch. of Mus. of Fine Arts, Boston, 1975-76; BFA, Syracuse U., 1978. Author, illustrator: Walking on Walnuts, 1996; art exhibited Women Figure, 1990. Recipient Drawing award Barbara Chase Burke, 1978; fellow Mid-Atlantic Arts Found., 1988, N.Y. Found. for Arts, 1987, Montalvo Ctr. for Arts, 1987.

RING, RENEE E., lawyer; b. Frankfurt, Germany, May 29, 1950; arrived in U.S., 1950; d. Vincent Martin and Etheline Bergetta (Schoolmeesters) R.; m. Paul J. Zofnass, June 24, 1982; Jessica Renee, Rebecca Anne. BA, Catholic U. Am., 1972; JD, U. Va., 1976. Bar: N.Y. 1977. Assoc. Whitman & Ransom, N.Y.C., 1976-83; assoc. Carro, Spanbock, Fass, Geller, Kaster & Cuiffo, N.Y.C., 1983-86, ptnr., 1986; ptnr. Finley Kumble Wagner et. al., N.Y.C., 1987; of counsel Kaye, Scholer, Fierman, Hays & Handler, N.Y.C., 1988; ptnr. Kaye Scholer Fierman Hays & Handler LLP, N.Y.C., 1989—. Mem. exec. com. Lawyers for Clinton, Washington, 1991-92; team capt. Clinton Transition Team, Washington, 1992-93; mem. Nat. Lawyers Coun. Dem. Nat. Com., 1993—. Mem. ABA, N.Y. Women's Bar Assn. Democrat. Roman Catholic. Office: Kaye Scholer Fierman Hays & Handler 425 Park Ave New York NY 10022-3506

RING, VICTORIA A., small business owner; b. Columbus, Ohio, July 5, 1958; d. James H. and Barbara C. (Wise) R. BA, East Tenn. State U., 1984; MA, Columbus Bus. U., 1986. Owner Tri-Angle Supreme Pizza, Sun, Va., 1981-86; typesetter, designer Battelle Meml. Inst., Columbus, Ohio, 1986-88; owner Graphico Pub., Columbus, Ohio, 1988—; instr. Ohio State U., Columbus, 1990-91; creator, designer GrapeVine News, 1992-94, The DynaWEB Link On-Line Newsletter, 1996—; spkr. at seminars and workshops in field. Author: Be "In The Know" With Adsheet Publishing, 1989, Word Perfect Just For Fun. 1991, Something From Nothing, 1993; contbr. articles to profl. publs.

RINGEL, ELEANOR, film critic; b. Atlanta, Nov. 3, 1950; d. Herbert Arthur and Sara (Finklestein) R.; m. John Gillespie, Nov. 18, 1989. BA magna cum laude, Brown U., 1972. With Alliance Theatre, 1974, S.C. Open Road Ensemble, 1974-75, N.Y. Shakespeare Festival, 1975-78, Children's TV Workshop, 1975-77; obituary writer Atlanta Jour., 1978; critic, editor Atlanta Jour.-Constitution Film, 1978—. Named Best Local Critic Atlanta Mag., 1990, Best of Cox Newspapers Critisims, 1987, Finalist Citations Critisims, 1984-85, Merit award, 1981. Mem. Nat. Soc. Film Critics (elected 1994). Home: 235 1/2 E Wesley Rd NE Atlanta GA 30305-3774 Office: Atlanta Journal Constitution Entertainment Desk 72 Marietta St NW Atlanta GA 30303-2804

RINGGOLD, FAITH, artist; b. N.Y.C., Oct. 8, 1930. B.S., CCNY, 1955; M.A., 1959; DFA (hon.), Moore Coll. Art, Phila., 1986, Coll. Wooster, Ohio, 1987, Mass. Coll. Art, Boston, 1991, CCNY of CUNY, 1991, DSc (hon.), Brockport (N.Y.) State U., 1992, Calif. Coll. Arts. and Crafts, Oakland, Calif., 1993, RISD, 1994. Art tchr. N.Y. Pub. Schs., 1955-73; lectr. Bank St. Coll. Grad. Sch., N.Y.C., 1970-80; prof. art U. Calif., San Diego, 1984—. Solo exhbns. include Spectrum Gallery, N.Y.C., 1967, 70, 10 year retrospective, Voorhees Gallery, Rutgers U., 1973, Summit Gallery, N.Y.C., 1979, 20 year Retrospective, Studio Mus. in Harlem, N.Y.C., 1984, Bernice Steinbaum Gallery, N.Y.C., 1987-88, Balt. Mus., Deland (Fla.) Mus., Faith Ruggold 25 Yr. Survey Fine Arts Museum L.I., Hempstead, 1990-93; exhibited in group shows at Meml. Exhibit for MLK, Mus. Modern Art, N.Y.C., 1968, Chase Manhattan Bank Collection, Martha Jackson Gallery, N.Y.C., 1970, Am. Women Artists, Gedok, Kunstalle, Hamburg, Ger., 1972, Jubilee, Boston Mus. Fine Arts, 1975, Major Contemporary Women Artists, Suzanne Gross Gallery, Phila., 1984, Committed to Print Mus. Modern Art, N.Y.C., 1988, The Art of Black Am. in Japan, Terada Warehouse, Tokyo, Made in the USA, Art in the 50s and 60s U. Calif. Berkeley Art Mus., Craft Today Poetry of the Physical, Am. Craft Mus., N.Y.C., Portraits and Homage to Mothers Hecksher Mus. Huntington, 1987; works in collections at Chase Manhattan Bank, N.Y.C., Philip Morris Collection, N.Y.C., Children's Mus., Bklyn., Newark Mus., The Women's House of Detention, Rikers Island, N.Y., The Studio Mus., N.Y.C., High Mus., Atlanta, Guggenheim Mus., Met. Mus. Art, Boston Mus. Fine Arts, MOMA. Author: Tar Beach, 1991, Aunt Harriet's Underground Railroad in the Sky, 1992; contbr. articles to profl. jours. Recipient AAUW travel award to Africa, 1976, Caldecott honor award, Coretta Scott King award best illustrated children's books Tar Beach, 1991; John Simon Guggenheim Meml. Found. Fellowship (painting), 1987, N.Y. Found. for Arts award (painting), 1988, Nat. Endowment Arts award (sculpture) 1978, (painting) 1989, La Napoule Found. award (painting in So. of France) 1990, Arts Internat. award (travel to Morocco) 1992. Office: Marie Brown Assocs 625 Broadway New York NY 10012-2611

RINGS, SALLY JO, English and reading educator; b. Kansas City, Mo., Dec. 21, 1941; d. Charles E. and Sarah E. (Baswell) R.; m. Alan L. Krueger, June 22, 1963 (div. Jan. 1977); children: David, Brian. AB, Baker U., 1963; MS, Emporia State U., 1979; PhD, Ariz. State U., 1986. Cert. C.C. tchr., Ariz. Tchr. Kansas City (Mo.) Pub. Schs., 1963-65, Shawnee Mission (Kans.) Unified Sch. Dist., 1965-67, 79-80, Cass R-1X Schs., Harrisonville, Mo., 1978-79; mem. faculty Maricopa C.C. Dist., Phoenix, 1981-87; faculty Paradise Valley C.C., Phoenix, 1987—; presenter in field. Named Innovator of the Yr., League for Innovation, 1989. Mem. Nat. Assn. for Devel. Edn., Coll. Reading and Learning Assn., Internat. Reading Assn., Nat. Coun. Tchrs. English. Presbyterian. Office: Paradise Valley Cmty Coll 18401 N 32nd St Phoenix AZ 85032-1210

RINGWALD, LYDIA ELAINE, artist, poet; b. L.A., Oct. 8, 1949; d. Siegfried Carl Ringwald and Eva M. (Macksoud) Mack; m. Hal von Hofe, July 31, 1972 (div. 1978). BA, Scripps Coll., 1970; student, Ruprecht-Karl Univ., Heidelberg, Germany, 1971; MA in Comparative Lit., U. Calif., Irvine, 1972; studied with William Bailey, Yale Art Sch., 1972-74; postgrad., U. Conn., 1976. Instr. English and German Cerritos (Calif.) Coll., 1975-83; instr. German Golden West Coll., Huntington Beach, Calif., 1976-83; instr. English Saddleback Coll., Mission Viejo, Calif., 1976-81, Long Beach (Calif.) City Coll., 1976-83; curator exhbns. Cultural Affairs Satellite Dept., L.A., 1994; cons., lectr. in field. Solo exhbns. include Great Western Bank, 1989, Atlantis Gallery, 1992, L.A. Pub. Libr., Sherman Oaks, Calif., 1993, Sumitomo Bank, 1993, Phoenix Gallery, 1994; group exhbns. include Long Beach (Calif.) Arts, 1988-89, Installations One, 1989, 90, Heidelberger Kunstverein, Heidelberg, Germany, 1990, Barbara Mendes Gallery, L.A., 1991, Folktree Gallery, 1991-92, Armand Hammer Mus., 1992, Jansen-Perez Gallery, L.A., 1993; author: Blessings in Disguise: Life is a Gift; Accept it with Both Hands, 1990, Blau: Kaleidescope einer Farbe, 1992. Mem. Internat. Friends Transformative Arts, Humanistic Arts Alliance, Nat. Mus. Women in Arts, L.A. Mcpl. Art Gallery, Mus. Contemporary Art, L.A. County Mus., U. Calif. Irvine Alumni Assn., Scripps Coll. Alumni Assn., Inst. Noetic Scis., Philosophical Rsch. Soc. Home and Office: Creative Realities 2801 Coldwater Canyon Dr Beverly Hills CA 90210-1305

RINSCH, MARYANN ELIZABETH, occupational therapist; b. L.A., Aug. 8, 1939; d. Harry William and Thora Analine (Langlie) Hitchcock; m. Charles Emil Rinsch, June 18, 1964; children: Christopher, Daniel, Carl. BS, U. Minn., 1961. Registered occupational therapist, Calif. Staff occupational therapist Hastings (Minn.) State Hosp., 1961-62, Neuropsychiat. Inst., L.A., 1962-64; staff and sr. occupational therapist Calif. Children's Svcs., L.A., 1964-66, head occupational therapist, 1966-68; researcher A. Jean Ayres, U. So. Calif., L.A., 1968-69; pvt. practice neurodevel. and sensory integraton Tarzana, Calif., 1969-74; pediat. occupational therapist neurodevel. & sensory integration St. Johns Hosp., Santa Monica, Calif., 1991-95; pvt. practice, cons. Santa Monica-Malibu Unified Sch. Dist., 1994—. Mem. alliance bd. Natural History Mus., L.A. County, 1983—; cub scouts den mother Boy Scouts Am., Sherman Oaks, Calif., 1986-88, advancement chair boy Scout Troop 474, 1989-92; mem. vol. League San Fernando Valley, Van Nuys, Calif., 1985-93; trustee Viewpoint Sch., Calabasas, Calif., 1987-90, Valley Women's Ctr., 1990-91. Mem. Am. Occupational Therapy Assn., Calif. Occupational Therapy Assn. Home: 19849 Greenbriar Dr Tarzana CA 91356-5428

RINTA, CHRISTINE EVELYN, nurse, air force officer; b. Geneva, Ohio, Oct. 4, 1952; d. Arvi Alexander and Catharina Maria (Steenbergen) R. BSN, Kent State U., 1974; MSN, Case Western Res. U., 1979. CNOR. Staff nurse in oper. rm. Euclid (Ohio) Gen. Hosp., 1974-76, oper. rm. charge nurse, 1977-79; commd. 1st lt. USAF, 1979, advanced through grades to lt. col.; staff nurse oper. rm. Air Force Regional Hosp., Sheppard AFB, Tex., 1979-82; staff nurse oper. rm., asst. oper. rm. supr. Regional Med. Ctr. Clark, Clark Air Base, Philippines, 1982-83; chief, nurse recruiting br. 3513th Air Force Recruiting Squadron, North Syracuse, N.Y., 1983-87; nurse supr. surg. svcs. 432d Med. Group, Misawa Air Base, Japan, 1987-89; course supr./instr. oper. rm. nursing courses 3793d Nursing Tng. Squadron, Keesler Med. Ctr., Keesler AFB, Miss., 1989-92; asst. dir., then dir. oper. rm. and ctrl. sterile supply Keesler Med. Ctr., Keesler AFB, Miss., 1992-93; comdr., enlisted clin. courses flight 383d Tng. Squadron, Sheppard AFB, Tex., 1993-94; comdr., officer clin. courses flight 383rd Tng. Squadron, Sheppard AFB, Tex., 1994-95; comdr. enlisted courses flight 383rd Tng. Squadron, Sheppard AFB, Tex., 1995—. Decorated Air Force Commendation medal, Air Force Achievement medal, Meritorious Svc. medal. Mem. ANA, Ohio Nurses Assn., Assn. Operating Rm. Nurses, Air Force Assn., Sigma Theta Tau. Home: 14 Pilot Point Dr Wichita Falls TX 76306-1000 Office: 383d Tng Squadron 939 Missile Rd Ste 3 Sheppard AFB TX 76311-2262

RIOS, ANGELYN MCLEOD, cell biologist, information analyst; b. Mpls., Aug. 20, 1946; d. Donald Robert and Frances Montana (Axtell) McLeod; children: Aisha, Alexander. BS in Exptl. Oncology, U. Minn., 1976. Rsch. assoc. U. Minn., Mpls., 1969-78; sr. rsch. asst. U. Calif., Irvine, 1978-80; rsch. fellow Mich. Cancer Found., Detroit, 1980-82; rsch. assoc. Mt. Carmel/Sinai Hosp., Detroit, 1982-87; evaluation specialist City of Detroit, 1987; grants writer SPARC, Gainesville, Fla., 1991; biol. scientist U. Fla., Gainesville, 1987-94; rsch. assoc. Georgians for Children, Atlanta, 1994—; cons. U. Pa., Phila., 1973, U. Kans., Kansas City, 1974, Nat. Cancer Inst., Bethesda, Md., 1976. Contbr. articles to Sci., N.Y. Acad. Scis., Cancer Immunology and Immunotherapy, Jour. Immunological Methods. Bd. dirs. YMCA, Gainesville, 1991. Mem. N.Y. Acad. Scis., Audubon Soc. Democrat.

RIOS, EVELYN DEERWESTER, columnist, musician, artist, writer; b. Payne, Ohio, June 25, 1916; d. Jay Russell and Flossie Edith (Fell) Deerwester; m. Edwin Tietjen Rios, Sept. 19, 1942 (dec. Feb. 1987); children: Jane Evelyn, Linda Sue Rios Stahlman. BA with honors, San Jose State U., 1964, MA, 1968. Cert. elem., secondary tchr., Calif. Lectr. in music San Jose State U., 1969-75; bilingual cons., then assoc. editor Ednl. Factors, Inc., San Jose, 1969-76, mgr. field research, 1977-78; writer, editor Calif. MediCorps Program, 1978-85; contbg. editor, illustrator The Community Family Mag., Wimberly, Tex., 1983-85; columnist The Springer, Dripping Springs, Tex., 1985-90; author, illustrator, health instr. textbooks elem. schs., 1980-82. Choir dir. Bethel Luth. Ch., Cupertino, Calif., 1965-66, Bethel Luth. Ch., 1968-83; dir. music St. Aban's Ch., Bogota Colombia; organist Holy Spirit Episcopal. Ch., Dripping Springs, Tex., 1987-94; music dir. Cambrian Park (Calif.) Meth. Ch., 1961-64; chmn. Dripping Springs Planning and Zoning Commn., 1991-93. Mem. AAUW, Am. Guild Organists (dean 1963-64), Phi Kappa Phi (pres. San Jose chpt. 1973-74). Episcopalian. Home and Office: 23400 FM 150 Dripping Springs TX 78620

RIOS, REBECCA ANGELA, social worker; b. Tucson, June 4, 1967; d. Peter Duarte and Gloria Ann (Mendoza) R.; m. Steve Leal; 1 child, Diego Esteban. AA, Ctrl. Ariz. Coll., 1987; BSW, Ariz. State U., 1989. Lic. by Behavioral Health Examiners, Ariz. Children's residential counselor Wayland Family Ctr., Phoenix, 1988-90; children's case mgr. Cmty. Care Network, Phoenix, 1990-92; case mgr. Pinal Gila Behavioral Health Assn., Apache Junction, Ariz., 1992—; state rep. Ariz. State Legis., Apache Junction, 1995—; adv. com. Ariz. Child Support Enforcement State of Ariz., Phoenix, 1996—; task force Ariz. Teen Pregnancy Task Force, State Legislature, Phoenix, 1996—. Mem. Dem. com. precinct person Ariz. Dem. Party, Dudleyville, Ariz., 1996—. Democrat. Roman Catholic. Home: 9620 N Malpais Box 517 Hayden AZ 85235

RIOUX, DONNA LOUISE, physical education educator; b. St. Foy, Que., Can., May 3, 1958; d. Donald and Nancy Anne (Burns) R. BS in Edn., Ohio State U., 1983; MS in Edn., U. Dayton, 1994. Tchr. adaptive phys. edn. Franklin County of MR/DD, Columbus, Ohio, 1988-89; tchr. phys. edn. Columbus Bd. Edn., 1989—; soccer coach Franklin Mid. Sch., Columbus, 1989—. Mem. Am. Alliance of Health, Phys. Edn., Recreation and Dance, Ohio Mid. Sch. Assn. Home: 294 Saint Thomas Dr Westerville OH 43081 Office: 1390 Bryden Rd Columbus OH 43205

RIPLEY, ALEXANDRA BRAID, author; b. Charleston, S.C., Jan. 8, 1934; m. Leonard Ripley, 1958 (div. 1963); m. John Graham, 1981; children Elizabeth, Merrill. BA in Russian, Vassar Coll., 1955. Former tour guide, travel agent, underwear buyer; former manuscript reader, publicity director N.Y.C. Author: Charleston, 1981, On Leaving Charleston, 1984, The Time Returns: A Novel of Friends and Mortal Enemies in Fifteenth Century Florence, 1985, New Orleans Legacy, 1987, Scarlett: The Sequel to Margaret Mitchell's Gone With the Wind, 1991, From Fields of Gold, 1994. Office: care Janklow-Nesbit Assoc 598 Madison Ave New York NY 10022-1614

RIPPENTROP, PATRICIA ANN, mental health services professional, family therapist; b. Sioux City, Iowa, Apr. 12, 1952; d. Robert Leo and Mary Terese (LaVelle) Cranny; m. John Patrick McSwiggan (div. Feb. 1984); children: Katy, Kelly, Michael Rippentrop. BA in Psychology, Augustana Coll., 1986; MA in Counseling, No. Am. Bapt. Sem., 1989. Cert. marriage and family therapist. Customer svc. rep. CitiBank, Sioux Falls, 1985-86; teaching asst. No. Am. Bapt. Sem., Sioux Falls, 1988-89; dir., co-founder, therapist Anchor Counseling, Sioux Falls, 1989—. Facilitator Mothers Without Custody Group, Sioux Falls, 1985-89. Mem. ACA (state and nat.). Roman Catholic. Office: Anchor Counseling Ctr 304 W 37th St Sioux Falls SD 57105

RIPPY, JODIE WRENN, artist; b. Concord, N.C., July 1, 1951; d. Charles Parnell Wrenn and Ruth (Marlin) Wrenn-Collins; m. Richard Allen Rippy, July 21, 1973; children: R. Allen Jr., Elizabeth Wrenn, Katherine Andersen. BS in Art Edn., U. N.C., 1973. Tchr. art & U.S. History Cape Fear Acad., Wilmington, N.C., 1973-77. One-woman shows include T. Williamson's Gallery, 1992, U. N.C., Wilmington, 1993, Davidson County Mus. Art, 1994, New Elements Gallery, 1996; exhibited in groups shows incuding Franklin Gallery, 1990-94 (Merit award 1990, Honorable Mention 1993, 2d place 1994), Wilmington Art Assn., 1991-93 (Honorable Mention 1993), Visual Arts Guild, 1993 (1st and 3d place for watercolor 1993), Bald Head Isl., 1993, N.C. Watercolor Soc., 1993, New Elements Gallery, 1993-94, The Women's Ctr., Chapel Hill, N.C., 1994-95 (Sothebys award for outstanding work 1995), Southport Art Assn., 1994, Wilmington Artists in France St. Johns Mus. Art, 1996, Dimentions, 1996; represented in permanent collections at Bald Head Isl. Corp., Pilot House Restaurants, Nat.'s Bank, Southport, N.C., Wilmington, New Elements Gallery, Wilmington, Comptons Art Gallery, Greensboro, N.C., City Art Works, New Bern, N.C., Creekside Art Gallery, Banner Elk, N.C., and pvt. collections. Moderator 1st Presbyn. Ch., Wilmington, Sunday sch. tchr., 1983-93, mem. personnel com., mem. edn. com., mem. search com., mem. ch. program rev. com., mem youth com., dir. bible sch., publicity chmn., chmn. chapel flower, cir. mem.; sch. vol. Cape Fear Acad., 1983-95; mem. Jr. League of Wilmington, 1976-83; bd. dirs., treas. YWCA. Mem. Nat. Mus. Women in the Arts, Nat. Oil Painters Assn., N.C. Mus. Art, N.C. Watercolor Soc., Friends of UNCW, St. John's Mus. Art (sec. bd. dirs. 1992-93, chair publicity com., mem. edn. com., organizer), Wilmington Art Assn. (co-chair hanging com. 1989—). Home: 2906 Park Ave Wilmington NC 28403

RISBY, BARBARA, special education educator; b. Balt., Apr. 12, 1952; d. Simon and Thelma (Peremel) Morrison; m. Terence Humphrey Risby, July 26, 1983; 1 child, Lauren Paige. BS, Towson State Coll., 1973; MS, Johns Hopkins U., 1983. Asst. tchr. Innovative Learning Ctr., Arnold, Md., 1983-84; primary spl. edn. tchr. Balt. City Schs., 1984-85, spl. edn. resource tchr., 1986—; mem. sch. improvement team Cross Country Elem. Sch., Balt., 1990-95, sch. support team, 1993—, chairperson spl. edn. team, 1988—. Mem. Coun. for Exceptional Children. Democrat. Jewish. Home: 6104 Greenspring Ave Baltimore MD 21209 Office: Cross Country Elem Sch 6100 Cross Country Blvd Baltimore MD 21215

RISDEN, NANCY DIKA, mathematics educator; b. Englewood, N.J., Sept. 14, 1948; d. John and Dorothy Louise (Eisberg) Macris; m. Dennis Richard Risden, Apr. 6, 1974; children: Jeannine, Steven, David. BS, Ursinus Coll., Collegeville, Pa., 1970; MA, Montclair State Coll., Upper Montclair, N.J., 1976. Cert. postgrad. prof. tchr. secondary math., Va., N.J. Tchr. math. West Essex Regional Mid. Sch., North Caldwell, N.J., 1970-71, South Jr. H.S., Bloomfield, N.J., 1971-79; substitute tchr. Oldham County Mid. Sch., Oldham County, Ky., 1981-82; instr. math. Watterson Coll., Louisville, 1984; tchr. math. Duke U. Hosp. Sch., Durham, N.C., 1988-90; substitute tchr. York County Pub. Schs., Yorktown, Va., 1991-93; tchr. math. Tabb Mid. Sch., Yorktown, 1993—. Treas. Mangum Primary Sch. PTA, Durham County, 1988-89; cookie chmn. Girl Scouts U.S., Durham County, 1989; den leader cub scouts Boy Scouts Am., Durham County, 1988-91, com. chairperson pack 104, Yorktown, Va., 1991-95. Mem. NEA, Va. Edn. Assn., York County Edn. Assn., Nat. Coun. Tchrs. Math., Va. Mid. Sch. Assn., Order Ea. Star N.J. (Worth Matron 1975-76, Grand Adah 1976-77). Presbyterian. Home: 113 Daphne Dr Yorktown VA 23692-3220 Office: Tabb Middle School 300 Yorktown Rd Yorktown VA 23693-3504

RISELEY, MARTHA SUZANNAH HEATER (MRS. CHARLES RISELEY), psychologist, educator; b. Middletown, Ohio, Apr. 25, 1916; d. Elsor and Mary (Henderson) Heater; BEd, U. Toledo, 1943, MA, 1958; PhD, Toledo Bible Coll., 1977; student Columbia U., summers 1943, 57; m. Lester Seiple, Aug. 27, 1944 (div. Feb. 1953); 1 child, L. Rolland, III; m. Charles Riseley, July 30, 1960. Tchr. kindergarten Maumee Valley Country Day Sch., Maumee, Ohio, 1942-44; dir. recreation Toledo Soc. for Crippled Children, 1950-51; tchr. trainable children Lott Day Sch., Toledo, 1951-57; psychologist, asst. dir. Sheltered Workshop Found., Lucas County, Ohio, 1957-62; psychologist Lucas County Child Welfare Bd., Toledo, 1956-62; tchr. educable retarded, head dept. spl. edn. Maumee City Schs., 1962-69; pvt. practice clin. psychology, 1956—; instr. spl. edn. Bowling Green State U., 1962-65; instr. Owens Tech. Coll., 1973-78; interim dir. rehab. services Toledo Goodwill Industries, summer 1967, clin. psychologist Rehab. Center, 1967—; staff psychologist Toledo Mental Health Center, 1979-84. Dir. camping activities for retarded girls and women Camp Libbey, Defiance, Ohio, summers 1951-62; group worker for retarded women Toledo YWCA, 1957-62; guest lectr. Ohio State U., 1957. Health care profl. mem. Nat. Osteoporosis Found., 1988—. Mem. Ohio Assn. Tchrs. Trainable Youth (pres. 1956-57), NW Ohio Rehab. Assn. (pres. 1961-62), Toledo Council for Exceptional Children (pres. 1965), Greater Toledo Assn. Mental Health, Nat. Assn. for Retarded Children, Ohio Assn. Tchrs. Slow Learners, Am. Assn. Mental Deficiency, Am. Soc. Psychologists in Marital and Family Counseling, Psychology and Law Soc. Am. (assoc.), Ohio, NW Ohio (sec.-treas. 1974-77, pres. 1978-79), Am. Theater Orgn. Soc., Ohio Psychol. Assn. (continuing edn. com. 1978—), NEA, AAUW, Am. Soc. Psychologists in Pvt. Practice (nat. dir. 1976—), State Assn. Psychologists and Psychol. Assts., Bus. and Profl. Women's Club, (pres. 1970-72), Ohio Fedn. Bus. and Profl. Women's Clubs (dist. sec. 1970-71, dist. legis. chmn. 1972-74), Toledo Art Mus., Women's Aux. Toledo Bar Assn., League Women Voters (pres. Toledo Lucas County 1991-93), Y Matrons (pres. 1993—), Toledo Area Theater Orgn. Soc. (sec. 1991—), Zonta Internat. (local pres. 1973-74, 78-79, area dir. 1976-78, Maumee River Valley Woman of Yr. for svc. to community and Zonta, 1992), Maumee Valley Hist. Soc., MBLS PEO (chpt. pres. 1950-51), Toledo Council on World Affairs, Internat. Platform Assn. Baptist. Home and Office: 2816 Wicklow Rd Toledo OH 43606-2833

RISHEILL, LILLIAN MARIE, microbiologist; b. Ft. Sill, Okla., Sept. 25, 1944; d. Clarence Elon and Edith Lillian (Reitnauer) R.; m. Charles Terence Guthrie, Aug. 21, 1966 (div. Dec. 1989); 1 child, Charles Terence Jr. BS in Microbiology, Colo. State U., 1966. Lab. asst. Letterman Army Inst., San Francisco, 1969; lab. tech. Larimer County Health Dept., Ft. Collins, Colo., 1970; substitute tchr. Poudre R-1 Schs., Ft. Collins, 1987-89, 89-90; microbiologist Colo. State U., Ft. Collins, 1989; tchr. English as a 2d lang. Poudre R-1 Schs., 1990-92; lab. coord. Colo. State U., 1992-95; lab. tech. Kodak Colo. Divsn., Windsor, 1995—. Active Cub Scouts, Boy Scouts Am., Tacoma, Wash., 1980-82. Independent. Methodist. Home: 3200 Azalea T-6 Fort Collins CO 80526 Office: Kodak Colo Divsn 9952 Eastman Park Dr Windsor CO 80551

RISHER, SARA, film company executive. With New Line Prodns./New Line Cinema Corp., L.A., 1974—; now chmn. prodn. New Line Prodns./ New Line Cinema Corp. Office: New Line Cinema 116 N Robertson Blvd 2nd Fl Los Angeles CA 90048-3103*

RISSMILLER, TAMMY LYNN, secondary school educator; b. Balt., Feb. 10, 1970; d. Paul Marion and Marie (Shirk) Hillebrand; m. Patrick Eugene Rissmiller, June 11, 1994. BA in Math., Lehigh U., 1992, MEd in Secondary Edn., 1994. Cert. math. tchr., Pa. Secondary math. tchr. Catasauqua (Pa.) Area Sch. Dist., 1993—; advisor, gifted and talented, sr. class, Catasauqua Area Sch. Dist., 1994—. Mem. Nat. Coun. Tchrs. of Math. Democrat.

RISSONE, DONNA, educator, financial executive; b. Stamford, Conn., July 13, 1943; d. Thomas and Carmela (Sabato) Galasso; m. Robert Rissone, Aug. 21, 1965; children: Robert, Jeannine. AB in Classics, Rosemont (Pa.) Coll., 1965; MSEd, Nazareth Coll., 1975. Cert. elem. secondary fgn. lang. tchr., N.Y. Tour escort various, Europe; fgn. lang. tchr. W. Irondequoit H.S., Rochester, N.Y., 1973—; treas. Door and Hardware Systems, Rochester, 1972—. Named Activity Advisor of Yr. N.Y. State Advisors/ Student Assn., 1993. Home: 134 Norcrest Dr Rochester NY 14617 Office: W Irondequoit High Sch 260 Cooper Rd Rochester NY 14617

RISTER, DIANA GAIL, rehabilitation nurse; b. Ashland, Ky., Apr. 9, 1965; d. Emmett Eugene and Mornie Mae (Wireman) R. AAS in Nursing, Ashland C.C., 1985. RN, Ky. Nurse Mercy Hosp., Portsmouth, Ohio, 1985-86, Kings Daughters Med. Ctr., Ashland, 1986—. Mem. Assn. Rehab. Nurses. Office: Kings Daughters Med Ctr 2201 Lexington Ave Ashland KY 41101

RISTOW, GAIL ROSS, art educator, paralegal, children's rights advocate; b. Carmel, Calif., Oct. 18, 1949; d. Kenneth E. and Lula Mae (Craft) Ross; m. Steven Craig Ristow, Sept. 15, 1971. BS in Biochemistry, Calif. Polytech State U., San Luis Obispo, 1972; MEd, Ariz. State U., 1980. Cert. tchr., Calif. Asst. instr. Calif. State Polytech U., Pomona, 1972; grad. asst. Calif. Polytech State U., Pomona, 1973-74; tchr. Mt. Carmel High Sch., L.A., 1974-76, Cartwright Sch. Dist., Phoenix, 1976-80; pres., owner Handmade With Love, Bay City, Tex., 1984-88; tchr. art Aiken, S.C., 1989-96; tchr. Community Edn., Bay City, 1986-88, Palacios, Tex., 1987. Sec. Chukker Creek Homeowners, Aiken, S.C., 1989-96; mem. S.C. Foster Care Rev. Bd., 1991-96; vol. tchr. elem. schs., Korea. Mem. AAUW, Am. Chem. Soc., Nat. Soc. Tole and Decorative Painters, Aiken Newcomer's Club (sec. 1989-91), Aiken Lioness Club (pres. 1991-94), Alpha Delta Kappa (v.p. 1986-87). Home: Kepco Apt 206/202, Bukmyon, Uljin-Gun, Kyongbuk 767-890, Korea

RITCH, KATHLEEN, diversified company executive; Harbor Beach, Mich., Jan. 23, 1943; d. Eunice (Spry) R.; B.A., Mich. State U., 1965: student Katharine Gibbs Sch., 1965-66. Exec. sec., adminstrv. asst. to pres. Katy Industries, Inc., N.Y.C., 1969-70; exec. sec., adminstrv. asst. to chmn. Kobrand Corp., N.Y.C., 1970-72; adminstrv. asst. to chmn. and pres. Ogden Corp., N.Y.C., 1972-74; asst. sec., adminstr. office services, asst. to chmn. Ogden Corp., N.Y.C., 1974-81, corporate sec., adminstr. office services, 1981-84, v.p., corporate sec., adminstr. office services, 1984-92, v.p. corp. sec., 1992—; part-owner Unell Mfg. Co., Port Hope, Mich., 1966-87. Bd. dir. Young Concert Artists, Inc., 1991—. Mem. Am. Soc. Corporate Secs. Home: 500 E 77th St New York NY 10162-0025 Office: Ogden Corp Two Pennsylvania Pla New York NY 10121

RITCHIE, CATHERINE D., correctional officer, deputy constable; b. Lynwood, Calif., Aug. 22, 1954; d. Harold Francis and Betty J. (Matlock) R.; m. Walter B. Ritchie Jr., July 21, 1977; children: Jeffrey, Bradley. Bookkeeper, sec. Severy Dental Labs., Orange, Calif., 1972-74, Shell Oil Co., Santa Ana, Calif., 1974-77; owner, ptnr. Vista (Calif.) Chevron Co., 1977-78; sec.-treas. Am. Battery Corp., Escondido, Calif., 1978-85; owner, operator Sophisticated 2ds, Vista, 1983-85, Bridal Elegance, Escondido, 1984-87; sr. correctional officer Humboldt County Sheriff's Dept., Eureka, Calif., 1988—; dep. marshal North Humboldt Jud. Dist., Arcata, Calif., 1991—; sgt. correction divsn. Humboldt County Sheriff's Dept., Arcata, 1991—, jail compliance sgt., vice chmn. jail population mgmt. team, 1995—; Co-pub. How to Avoid Auto Repair Rip-offs, 1981. Mem. Nat. Bridal Service (cert., cons.), Nat. Assn. Female Execs., Escondido C. of C., Calif. Farm Bur. Republican.

RITCHIE, KAREN, advertising agency executive. Former sr. v.p. Campbell-Ewald Co. (formerly Lintas: Campbell Ewald), Warren, Mich.; sr. v.p. McCann-Erickson/Detroit, Troy, Mich., 1989-94; exec. v.p., mng. dir. GM Mediaworks, GM Cyberworks, Warren, Mich., 1994—. Office: PO Box 6001 12200 Thirteen Mile Rd Warren MI 48090-6001

RITCHIN, BARBARA SUE, educational administrator, consultant; b. N.Y.C., Mar. 7, 1940; d. Harry and Miriam Rosalyn (Schoenberg) R. BS in Spl. Edn., SUNY, Buffalo, 1961; MS in Ednl. Guidance, CCNY, 1969; PhD in Urban Edn., Fordham U., 1990, postdoctoral student, 1991. Cert. tchr., spl. edn. tchr., counselor, adminstr., N.Y. Tchr. spl. edn. East Elem. Sch., Long Beach, N.Y., 1962-68; asst. prof. N.Y.C. Community Coll., Bklyn., 1970-76; ednl. cons. N.Y.C., 1976-92; dir. bus. programs N.Y.C. Tech. Coll., Bklyn., 1981-87; exec. dir. continuing edn. programs Queens Coll. CUNY, Flushing, N.Y., 1988—; bd. dirs. Foresight Sch., S.I., N.Y., 1986-92; cons. N.Y. Telephone Co., N.Y.C., 1988-92; chair subcom. on community outreach Queens Coll. Presdl. Com. on Multiculturalism. Co-author: Teachers Learn Metrics, 1981. Pres. bd. dirs. Greenwich Village Orchestra, 1991; admissions and rules com. mem. 401 E. 74 Corp., N.Y.C., 1990-92. Named Disting. Woman of Yr. Queens Women's Ctr., 1989. Mem. Continuing Edn. Assn. N.Y. (pres. 1995-96, regional chair 1990-91, membership chair 1988-90), UN Assn. N.Y. (bd. dirs.), Assn. Continuing Higher Edn. (sec.-treas. 1991-92), Phi Delta Kappa, Kappa Delta Pi. Office: Queens Coll CUNY 65-30 Kissena Blvd Flushing NY 11367-1575

RITSKO, NANCY LOUISE, counseling educator; b. Brownsville, Pa., Feb. 22, 1952; d. Edward W. and Helen P. (Costello) R. BS, Calif. U. Pa., Calif., Pa., 1974, MEd, 1976; EdD, Ind. U. Pa., Ind., Pa., 1985. Cert. elem. sch. counseling, secondary sch. guidance and counseling, pupil pers. specialist, nat. cert. counselor; lic. profl. counselor. Sch. counselor Intermediate Unit I, Calif., Pa., 1976-82, Punxsutawney Area Sch. Dist., Punxsutawney, Pa., 1985-93; assoc. prof. Clark Atlanta U., Atlanta, Ga., 1993—; coord. Dist. Guidance Svcs., Punxsutawney Area Sch. Dist., 1990-93; co-dir. Sch. Counseling Prog., Clark Atlanta U., 1994—. Vol. Habitat for Humanity, Am. Red Cross, Piedmont Pk. Conservancy, Zoo Atlanta, Chattooga Watershed Coalition, Atlanta, Ga., 1993—. Mem. ACA, Am. Sch. Counseling Assn., Assn. Counselor Edn. & Supervision, Assn. Multicultural Counselling & Devel., Ga. Sch. Counselor Assn., So. Assn. Counselor Educators & Suprs., Phi Delta Kappa. Home: 1101 Collier Rd NW Apt K5 Atlanta GA 30318-8209 Office: Clark Atlanta U Dept of Counseling Rec 301 Atlanta GA 30314

RITTER, ANN L., lawyer; b. N.Y.C., May 20, 1933; d. Joseph and Grace (Goodman) R. B.A., Hunter Coll., 1954; J.D., N.Y. Law Sch., 1970; postgrad. Law Sch., NYU, 1971-72. Bar: N.Y. 1971, U.S. Ct. Appeals (2d cir.) 1975, U.S. Supreme Ct. 1975. Writer, 1954-70; editor, 1955-66; tchr., 1966-70; atty. Am. Soc. Composers, Authors and Pubs., N.Y.C., 1971-72, Greater N.Y. Ins. Co., N.Y.C., 1973-74; sr. ptnr. Brenhouse & Ritter, N.Y.C., 1974-78; sole practice, N.Y.C., 1978—. Editor N.Y. Immigration News, 1975-76. Mem. ABA, Am. Immigration Lawyers Assn. (treas. 1983-84, sec. 1984-85, vice chair 1985-86, chair 1986-87, chair program com. 1989-90, chair speakers bur. 1989-90, chair media liaison 1989-90), N.Y. State Bar Assn., N.Y. County Lawyers Assn., Assn. Trial Lawyers Am., N.Y. State Trial Lawyers Assn., N.Y.C. Bar Assn., Watergate East Assn. (v.p., asst. treas. 1990—). Democrat. Jewish. Home: 47 E 87th St New York NY 10128-1005 Office: 420 Madison Ave New York NY 10017-1107

RITTER, DEBORAH ELIZABETH, anesthesiologist, educator; b. Phila., May 16, 1947; d. Charles William and Elizabeth Angeline (Coffman) R. BA, Susquehanna U., 1968; MS, U. Pa., 1969; MD, Med. Coll. Pa., 1973. Diplomate Am. Bd. Anesthesiology (assoc. examiner oral bds. 1990, 92). Intern Thomas Jefferson Univ. Hosp., Phila., 1973-74, resident in anesthesia, 1974-76, clin. fellow in anesthesiology, 1976-77; affiliate resident in anesthesia Children's Hosp. Pa., Phila., 1975; assoc. in anesthesiology Frankford Hosp., Phila., 1977-78; clin. instr. anesthesiology Med. Coll. Pa., Phila., 1977-78; clin. instr. anesthesiology Thomas Jefferson U., 1978-80, clin. asst. prof., 1980-86, clin. assoc. prof., 1986—, vice chmn. dept. anesthesiology, 1985—. Contbr. articles to profl. jours. Named Top Doc, Phila. Mag., 1994, 96. Mem. AMA, Am. Women's Med. Assn., Am. Soc. Anesthesiologists, Internat. Anesthesia Rsch. Soc., Soc. Edn. Anesthesia, Assn. Anesthesia Clin. Dirs. Lutheran. Office: Thomas Jefferson U Dept Anesthesiology 111 S 11th St Ste 6460G Philadelphia PA 19107-4824

RITTER, SALLIE, painter, sculptor; b. Las Cruces, N.Mex., May 9, 1947; d. John Barnes Ritter and Billie Ruth (Carter) Simpson; m. Kent Frederick Jacobs, Apr. 13, 1971. Student, U. Rome Coll. Art History, 1965, Edinburgh (Scotland) Coll. Art, 1967-68; BA, Colo. Coll., 1969. One-woman shows include Lubbock (Tex.) Art Ctr., 1970, N.Mex. Arts Commn., Santa Fe, 1974, Las Cruces Cmty. Ctr., 1975, Aldridge Fine Arts, Albuquerque, 1980, Woodrow Wilson Fine Arts, Santa Fe, 1989, Adobe Patio Gallery, Mesilla, N.Mex., 1991, 93, Contemporary Southwest Galleries, Santa Fe, 1996; exhibited in group shows at El Paso (Tex.) Mus. Art, 1988, Colorado Springs (Colo.) Fine Arts Ctr., 1995, Laguna Gloria Mus., Austin, Tex., 1979, Santa Fe Festival of the Arts, 1979, 83, The Governor's Gallery, Santa Fe, 1987, 94, Pioneer's Mus., Colo. Springs, 1985, 86, 88, N.Mex. State U., Las Cruces, 1988, 89, Dona Ana Arts Coun., Las Cruces, 1992, Tex. Commn. Arts, Austin, 1987, Tucson Mus. Art, 1995, Nat. Cowboy Hall of Fame, Oklahoma City, 1996, Autry Mus. Western Art, L.A., 1996, Albuquerque Mus. Art, 1996; represented in permanent collections U. Tex. Sch. of Law, Phelps Dodge Corp., Sunwest Bank, Albuquerque, N.Mex. State U., Mus. N.Mex., Santa Fe; featured in Contemporary Women Artists, 1984, Contemporary Western Artists, 1985. Bd. dirs. Women's Bd., Mus. N.Mex., Santa Fe, 1987—, Dona Ana Arts Coun., Las Cruces, 1990—. Mem. Nat. Mus. of Women in the Arts. Episcopalian. Home and Studio: 3610 Southwind Rd Las Cruces NM 88005-5556 also: 1114 Main Rd Ruidoso NM 88345

RITTER, SANDRA HELEN, psychotherapist, counselor; b. Kingston, Pa., Dec. 31, 1947; d. Earl Jean and Lois Mae (Hartley) R.; m. Billy Lee Ferguson, May 23, 1995; children: Christopher Andrew Hawkins, Alexander Cameron Hawkins (dec.); stepchildren: William Lee Ferguson, Ann Ferguson Bishop. BSME, Villanova U., 1969; MBA, Ctrl. Mich. U., 1981; MEd in Counseling, U. N.C., Greensboro, 1994; postgrad., U. N.C., 1995—. Nat. cert. counselor; lic. profl. counselor. Engr. Automation Industries, Silver Spring, Md., 1974-83; sr. engr. Naval Sea Sys. Command, Alexandria, Va., 1983-85; ptnr. Clemmons (N.C.) Primary Care, 1987-91; owner, proprietor Serendipity Resource Ctr., Clemmons, 1985-91; mental health asst. Charter Hosp., Greensboro, N.C., 1992-94; pvt. practice Greensboro, 1994—. Co-author: Assessment in Counseling and Therapy, 1995; sr. author: Leadership Development on a Shoestring, 1995. Vol. hospice, Winston-Salem, N.C., 1990-92; vol. counselor The Listening Post, Greensboro, 1993-94; mem. workshop com. Unitarian Universalist Fellowship, Greensboro, 1993-95, svc. leader coord., 1994-95. Mem. ACA, Internat. Assn. Addictions and Offenders Counselors (chair addictions com. 1993-96, mem. accreditation com. 1995-96, pres.-elect 1996—), Am. Mental Health Counselors Assn., Assn. for Counseling Edn. and Supervision (Outstanding Doctoral Student 1995), C.G. Jung Soc., N.C. Assn. for Adult Devel. and Aging (pres.-elect 1995-96, pres. 1996—), N.C. Assn. for Specialists in Group Work (pres.-elect 1995-96, pres. 1996—), N.C. Counseling Assn. (co-chair spl. task force 1995-96, treas. 1995-96), Chi Sigma Iota (fellow, mem. Upsilon Nu Chi chpt., treas. 1993-94, awards chair 1993-96, pres.-elect 1994-95, pres. 1995-96, Outstanding Master's Student 1994). Home: 2601 Woodview Dr Greensboro NC 27408 Office: 200 E Bessemer Ave Greensboro NC 27401

RITTER-CLOUGH, ELISE DAWN, consultant, former publishing company executive; b. Balt., Aug. 14, 1952; d. Nelson Fred and Marjorie Jean (Corke) Ritter; m. Philip Anthony Gibson, Apr. 7, 1979 (div. Feb. 1990); 1 child, Christopher Ritter Gibson; m. Victor Wayne Clough, Jr., Mar. 3, 1990; stepchildren: Wesley T., Lindsay, Sharon. Student, Austro-Am. Inst., Vienna, Austria, 1973; BS, U. Kans., 1974. Researcher, Impeachment Inquiry Staff U.S. Ho. of Reps., Washington, 1974; researcher APA, Washington, 1975; editor prodn. The New Republic Mag., Washington, 1976-77; copy editor Time-Life Books, Alexandria, Va., 1977-79, assoc. editor, 1979-83, series adminstr., 1983-87, asst. dir. editorial resources, 1988-90; dir. editorial resources Time Warner, Time-Life Books, Alexandria, 1990-94. Bd. dirs. Arlingtonians Ministering to Emergency Needs (AMEN), 1995—; chairperson outreach commn. Mt. Olivet Meth. Ch., Arlington, 1994—.

RITTERHOUSE, KATHY LEE, librarian; b. Hutchinson, Kans., May 24, 1952; d. Fayne Lee and Elizabeth Rose (Tener) R.; m. Michael Raymond Demmitt, July 8, 1972 (div. Apr. 1990). BA in English, Kans. State U., 1974; MLS, U. Okla., 1979. Circulation libr. Grand Prairie (Tex.) Meml. Libr., 1979-80, libr. dir., 1980—. Bd. dirs. Grand Prairie Arts Coun., 1980-95, pres., 1989. Named Pub. Svc. Employee of Yr. Grand Prairie C. of C., 1989. Mem. ALA, Tex. Libr. Assn. (Tex./SIRS Intellectual Freedom award 1993), Metro Rotary Club (bd. dirs. 1992-95), Beta Phi Mu. Office: Grand Prairie Meml Libr 901 Conover Dr Grand Prairie TX 75051-1521

RITTI, ALYCE RAE, artist; b. Moline, Ill., Jan. 18, 1934; d. Raymond Russell and Alice Linnea Matilda (Arvidson) Keagle; m. Raymond Richard Ritti, Jan. 26, 1957; children: Lesley, Jocelyn, Matthew, Susanna. BA with departmental honors, Grinnell Coll., 1956; MS, Purdue U., 1957; PhD, Columbia U., 1973; postrad., Pa. State U., 1985-90. Advanced cert. Am. Speech, Lang., and Hearing Assn. Speech therapist Rockford (Ill.) Coll. Summer Speech Ctr., summer 1956; instr. speech Cornell U., Ithaca, N.Y., 1957-59; exec. sec. Art Alliance of Cen. Pa., Lemont, 1978-80; test manual coord. NEA, Washington, 1980-82; rsch. assoc. E.P. Sys. Group, State College, Pa., 1980-82; visual artist Pt. Matilda, Pa., 1984—; com. mem., ad hoc projects Cen. Pa. Festival of Arts, State College, 1988—, artist in action, 1989-91, 93-94, instr. accessible arts collages, 1994-95; artist World's Women Online, 1995—. Artist collages and paintings in numerous solo shows, 1987—; exhibited in nat. and regional juried shows and galleries, 1990—, including So.Alleghenies Mus. Art Triennial VI. Bd. dirs., officer sch. dist. PTAs, PTOs, couns., Stamford, Conn., 1963-70, State College, 1971-87; mem. State College Cmty. Theatre, 1985—, Nittany Valley Symphony Guild, 1993—; mem., friend Palmer Mus. Art, 1984—, Pa. Dance Theatre, 1995. Office of Edn. fellow Columbia U. Tchrs. Coll., 1969, 70; Unified Art Event grantee (2) Cen. Pa. Arts Coun., 1984, 86. Mem. Nat. Mus. Women in the Arts, Art Alliance of Ctrl. Pa. (life, bd. dirs. 1981-86, v.p. 1982), Alliance of Women Artists, Phi Beta Kappa. Home: 170 Cherrywood Way Port Matilda PA 16870

RITTMER, ELAINE HENEKE, library media specialist; b. Maquoketa, Iowa, Feb. 4, 1931; d. Herman John and Clara (Luett) Heneke; m. Sheldon Lowell Rittmer, June 11, 1950; children: Kenneth, Lynnette, Robyn (dec.), infant son (dec.). BA, Marycrest Coll., 1973; MS, Western Ill. U., 1980. Permanent teaching cert. K-14, Iowa; cert. libr. media specialist K-14, Iowa. Sch. libr. Calamus-Wheatland (Iowa) Community Schs., 1970-74; high sch. libr. media specialist, libr. coord. Camanche (Iowa) Community Sch., 1974—; ind. tech. cons., 1988—. Mem. Iowa Edn. Media Assn., Iowa State Edn. Assn., Camanche Edn. Assn., Camanche Cmty. Schs. Tech. Com., Media Tech. Cons. Republican. Home: 3539 230th St De Witt IA 52742-9208 Office: Camanche High Sch PO Box 160 937 9th St Camanche IA 52730

RITZ, ESTHER LEAH, civic worker, volunteer, investor; b. Buhl, Minn., May 16, 1918; d. Matthew Abram and Jeanette Florence (Lewis) Medalie; m. Maurice Ritz, Apr. 8, 1945 (dec. 1977); children—David Lewis, Peter Bruce. B.A. summa cum laude, U. Minn, 1940, postgrad., 1940-41; postgrad., Duke U., 1941-42. Adminstrv. analyst, economist Office of Price Adminstrn., N.Y., Washington and Chgo., 1942-46. Pres., Nat. Jewish Welfare Bd., 1982-86; v.p. Council of Jewish Fedns., 1981-84; pres. World Conf. Jewish Community Ctrs., 1981-86; bd. dirs. Am. Jewish Joint Distbn. Com., 1977-93, bd. dirs. (hon. life mem.) Joint Distbn. Com., 1994; trustee United Jewish Appeal, 1982-87; vice-chmn. bd. dirs. Jerusalem Ctr. Pub. Affairs, 1984—; bd. dirs. Wurzweiler Sch. Social Work Yeshiva U., 1984-89, HIAS, 1983-86; mem. Jewish Agy. Com. on Jewish Edn., 1984-90, bd. govs., 1988-92; bd. dirs. Legal Aid Soc., Milw. County, 1983-85; mem. Community Issues Forum, Milw.; vice chmn. bd. United Way Greater Milw., 1977-81; pres. Florence G. Heller Jewish Welfare Bd. Research Ctr., 1979-83; pres. Mental Health Planning Council of Milw. County, 1976-79; vice chmn Large City Budgeting Conf., 1976-82; pres. Jewish Community Ctr. Milw., 1966-71; pres. Milw. Jewish Fedn., 1978-81; bd. dirs. Shalom Hartman Inst., 1989—; bd. dirs.; mem. exec. com., policy com. Nat. Jewish Dem. Coun., 1991—, vice-chmn. bd. dirs., 1994—; bd. dirs. Nat. Jewish Ctr. for Learning and Leadership, 1988-92, Ams. Peace Now, 1989—, vice-chmn. bd. dirs., 1995—, Coun. Initiatives Jewish Edn., 1990—, Friends of Labor Israel (steering com. 1988—, chair 1988-90); bd. vis. Ctr. for Jewish Studies U. Wis., Madison, 1994—. Named to Women's Hall of Fame YWCA, 1979; recipient Cmty. Svc. award Wis. Region NCCJ, 1977, William C. Frye award Milw. Found., 1984, Telesis award Alverno Coll., Milw., 1984, Hannah G. Solomon award. Nat. Coun. Jewish Women, ProUrbe award Mt. Mary Coll., Evan P. Helfer award Milw. chpt. Nat. Soc. of Fund Raising Execs., 1994, Margaret Miller award Planned Parenthood of Wis., 1994. Mem. LWV, NAACP, NOW, Hadassah, Na'amat, Common Cause, Nat. Women's Polit. Caucus, Nat. Coun. Jewish Women, Planned Parenthood. Democrat. Home: 626 E Kilbourn Ave Milwaukee WI 53202-3235

RITZ, JOSEPHINE MITCHELL, nursing resource development director; b. Bethlehem, Pa., Feb. 20, 1926; d. Adam Joseph and Mary Elizabeth (Smerk) Mitchell; m. George Ritz, Sept. 1, 1951 (dec.); 1 child, George Michael. Diploma in nursing, Allentown Hosp. Sch. Nursing, 1947; BSN, Cedar Crest Coll., 1961; MS in Edn., Temple U., 1974. Dir. Allentown (Pa.) Hosp. Sch. Nursing., curriculum coord., coord. fundamentals of nursing; coord. for nursing resource devel. program Health East Trust, Allentown; adv. bd. Kutztown U. Nursing Program; mem. bd. assocs. Lehigh Valley Hosp.; mem. devel. com. Cancer Soc.; mem. bd. dirs. Arthritis Soc., Allentown Hosp. Sch. Nursing Alumni Assn. Recipient Nursing Ethics award Allentown Hosp. Sch. Nursing. Mem. Nat. Assn. Fund Raising Execs., Nat. League for Nursing, Profl. Nursing Coun. Home: 1941 S Delaware St Allentown PA 18103-8523

RITZER, KAREN RAE, executive secretary, office administrator; b. Sioux City, Iowa, Nov. 26, 1946; d. Robert Leland and Wanda Lily (Kirby) Taylor; m. Thomas Arthur Ritzer, Nov. 23, 1963; children: Robert Arthur, Kristina Marie, Teresa Lynn Ritzer Jones, Carl Robert White. Grad., Arnolds Park (Iowa) High Sch., 1968. Office mgr., sec. Tom's Plumbing and Heating, Arnolds Park, 1964—; sec./treas., bd. dirs. Ritz Closet Seat Corp., Arnolds Park, 1985—. Sec./treas. Concerned Citizens Com., Arnolds Park, 1985, 86, 87; chairperson Centennial Bd. for Arnolds Park 100th Birthday Celebration. Mem. Nat. Trust for Hist. Preservation, The Smithsonian Assn., Am. Mus. Natural History (assoc.), United We Stand Am. (founding), Friends of Iowa Pub. TV, Ladies Aus. VFW. Address: PO Box 496 Arnolds Park IA 51331-0496

RIVE, SARELLE ROSELYN, manufacturing company executive; d. Max and Ruth Rae (Goldring) Raive; m. Norman E. Friedmann, June 22, 1952 (div. Nov. 1985); children: Marc David, Lance Alan, Keyla Ilene Friedmann Treitman; m. Robert A. Suhosky, July 4, 1986 (div. July 1994). BA with honors, Barat Coll., 1977. Owner, dir. Gallerie Sarelle, Highland Park, Ill., 1977-78, L.A., 1982-84, 86-90; owner, dir. A Neat Idea By Sarelle, L.A., 1992—; silver level exec. Quorum Internat., L.A., 1992—; pres. Internat. Export Concepts, L.A., 1994—; CFO Universal Diesel Products, Inc. USA subs., Vancouver, B.C., Can., 1995—. Den mother, pack leader cub scout troop Boy Scouts Am., 1959-63; day camp dir., leader Girl Scouts U.S., L.A., 1966-73; bd. dirs. YWCA, Highland Park, Ill., 1974-77; docent Mus. of Contemporary Art, L.A., 1985-88; assoc. Older People in a Caring Atmosphere (OPICA), L.A., 1981—; founding mem. Nat. Mus. Women in Arts, Washington, 1993—, Mus. Contemporary Art, L.A., 1985-93; mem. president's cir. L.A. County Mus. of Art, 1987—, mem. president's cir. of patrons. 1993-95. Mem. City of Hope (life), Kappa Gamma Pi, Delta Epsilon Sigma. Jewish. Home and Office: 401 N Carmelina Ave Los Angeles CA 90049-2703

RIVERA, BARBARA JEAN, healthcare administrator, nurse; b. St. Croix, Wis., Aug. 2, 1956; d. John Emmett and Erma Emily (Stimel) Broecker; m. Nick Anthony Rivera, Dec. 13, 1980; children: Nicole Renee, Natalie Marie. Lic. vocat. nurse, Hennipen Coll., 1976; cert. critical care nurse, Anoka Vocat., Mpls., 1977; cert. advanced coronary care nurse, Houston N.W. Med. Ctr., 1978; cert. compression therapist, Boston Sch., 1994. Crit. care case mgr. Houston N.W. Med. Ctr., 1977-84; clin. mgr. Cigna Health Plan, Houston, 1984-85; intensive care nurse Staff Relief, Houston, 1985-92; nurse mgr. neurology U. Tex., Houston, 1992-94; compression therapist S.W. Inst., Houston, 1994-96; regional sales mgr. Houston Theracare, 1994-96; dir. clin. affairs Lymphedema Rehab. Svcs., Houston, 1996—; regional spokeswoman Am. Dairy Assn., Mpls., 1976; prenatal/postnatal instr. Cigna Health Plan, 1985-86; clin. instr. neurology U. Tex., Houston, 1992-94, clinic coord. CQI, 1992-94. Adult leader Nat. 4-H Cmty. Assn., 1965-94. Mem. NAFE, Nat. Assn. Legal Nurse Cons., Nat. Lic. Vocat. Nurse Assn., Cmty. Health Care Com., N.W. Houston Chamber. Home: 25207 Tuckahoe Spring TX 77373 Office: Lymphedema Rehab Svcs Ste 588 11500 NW Fwy Houston TX 77092

RIVERA, CHITA (CONCHITA DEL RIVERO), actress, singer, dancer; b. Washington, Jan. 23, 1933; d. Pedro Julio Figuerva del Rivero; m. Anthony Mordente. Student, Am. Sch. Ballet, N.Y.C. Broadway debut: Call Me Madam, 1952; appeared on stage in: Guys and Dolls, Can-Can, Seventh Heaven, Mister Wonderful, West Side Story, Father's Day, Bye Bye Birdie, Three Penny Opera, Flower Drum Song, Zorba, Sweet Charity, Born Yesterday, Jacques Brel is Alive and Well and Living in Paris, Sondheim-A Musical Tribute, Kiss Me Kate, Ivanhoe, Chicago, Bring Back Birdie, Merlin, Jerry's Girls, 1985, The Rink, 1984 (Tony award 1984), Can-Can, 1988, Kiss of the Spider Woman (Tony award, Best Actress in a musical), 1993; performs in cabarets and nightclubs around world; starred in: film Sweet Charity, 1969; numerous TV appearances include Kojak and the Marcus Nelson Murders, 1973, The New Dick Van Dyke Show, 1973-74, Kennedy Ctr. Tonight-Broadway to Washington!, Pippin, 1982, The Mayflower Madam, 1987, Sammy Davis Jr.'s 60th Birthday Celebration, 1990. Mem. AFTRA, SAG, Actors Equity Assn. Office: William Morris Agy care Gayle Nachlis 1325 Ave Americas New York NY 10019•

RIVERA, JANE MARKEY, special education educator; b. Frederick, Md., Feb. 26, 1954; d. Willard Hanshew and Mary Leone (Palmer) Markey; m. Edric Rafael Rivera, Mar. 7, 1981; children: Edric Rafael Jr., Julian Rafael, Marisa Leona. BA, Wittenberg U., 1976; M in Spl. Edn., Antioch U., 1980. Remedial reading tchr. Cen. Bucks Sch. Dist., Doylestown, Pa., 1976-78; chpt. 1 reading tchr. Pennridge Sch. Dist., Perkasie, Pa., 1978-93, spl. edn. tchr., 1993—; student assistance team mem. Pennridge Sch. Dist., Perkasie, 1992—; youth aid panel Hilltown (Pa.) Police Dept., 1986—. Bd. mem. Deep Run. Valley Sports Assn., Hilltown, 1993—. Mem. St. Andrew's Ch. Handbell Choir. Home: 310 S Perkasie Rd Perkasie PA 18944-2454 Office: Pennridge Cen Jr High Sch 1500 N 5th St Perkasie PA 18944-2207

RIVERA, SOPHIE, photographer. Student, New Sch. for Social Rsch., N.Y.C. lectr. in field; photography resident, Syracuse, N.Y., 1987, SUNY, Buffalo, N.Y., 1987. Solo exhbns. include: Internat. Photo Optical Exhibit, N.Y.C., 1979, El Museo del Barrio, N.Y.C., 1987, En Foco Arts for Transit, N.Y.C., 1989, Windows on White, N.Y.C., 1990, Wilmer Jennings Gallery, N.Y.C., 1995; dual exhbns. include Cork Gallery, N.Y.C., 1980, Casa Aboy, P.R., 1981; group shows include: El Museo del Barrio, 1984, 87, El Museo Nat. del Bellas Artes, Havana, Cuba, 1984, Bronx Mus. Arts, N.Y.C., 1986, Salmagundi Club, N.Y.C., 1987, Camera Club N.Y., 1987, Goddard-Riverside Cmty. Ctr., N.Y.C., 1987, John Jay Coll. Criminal Justice, 1988, Intar Gallery, N.Y.C., 1988, Blum-Helman Warehouse Gallery, N.Y.C., 1989, Mus. Sci. and Industry, Chgo., 1989, Dia Art Found., N.Y.C., 1989, Flossie Martin Gallery, Radford, Va., 1990, Purdue Univ. Galleries, Lafayette, Ind., 1990, En Foco Gallery, 1990, Galleria El Bohio, N.Y.C., 1990, Kince Gallery, N.Y.C., 1990, Ctr. for Book Arts, N.Y.C., 1990, 80 Washington Sq. East Galleries, N.Y.C., 1991, 93, CCNY, 1991, Ctr. for Photography at Woodstock, N.Y., 1991, Scott Alan Gallery, N.Y.C., 1991, Rutgers U., N.J., 1991, Monasterio de Santa Clara, Spain, 1992, Tweed Gallery, N.Y.C., 1993, Mus. at Stony Brook, N.Y., 1993, Kenkeleba Gallery, N.Y.C., 1994, Foto Fest '94, Houston, Hostos Art Gallery, 1995. Recipient awards Pub. Art Fund, 1989, N.Y. Found. for the Arts (Photography), 1989. Home and Studio: 31 Tiemann Pl New York NY 10027-3309

RIVERA-URRUTIA, BEATRIZ DALILA, psychology and rehabilitation counseling educator; b. Bayamón, P.R., Jan. 16, 1951; d. José and Carmen B. (Urrutia) Rivera; m. Julio C. Ribera, July 1, 1978; 1 child, Alejandra B. BA, U. P.R., 1972, MA, 1975; PhD, Temple U., 1982. Staff psychologist Learning Plus, Inc., Phila., 1979-80; cons. Hispanic Mental Health Inst., Phila., 1981-82; staff psychologist J.F. Kennedy Community Mental Health Ctr., Phila., 1982-83; prof. U. P.R., Rio Piedras, 1983—; cons. Jewish Employment & Vocat. Svcs., Phila., 1980; staff psychologist San Juan VA Hosp., Rio Piedras, 1990—. Contbr. articles to profl. jours. Vol. Parroquia San Juan Apóstol y Evangelista, Caguas, P.R., 1988-90, ARC, San Juan, 1990. Faculty U. P.R. instnl. rsch. grantee, 1986-87. Mem. P.R. Psychol. Assn. (bd. editors jour. 1984-89, bd. dirs. 1989-91), P.R. Lic. Bd. Psychologists (pres. ethics com. 1991-92). Home: Roble D 23 Arbolada Caguas PR 00725 Office: PO Box 22724 San Juan PR 00931-2724

RIVERS, JOAN, entertainer; b. N.Y.C., June 8, 1937; d. Meyer C. Molinsky; m. Edgar Rosenberg (dec.), July 15, 1965; 1 child, Melissa. BA, Barnard Coll., 1958. Formerly fashion coordinator Bond Clothing Stores. Debut entertaining, 1960; mem. From Second City, 1961-62; TV debut Tonight Show, 1965; Las Vegas debut, 1969; nat. syndicated columnist Chgo. Tribune, 1973-76; creator: CBS TV series Husbands and Wives, 1976-

77; host: Emmy Awards, 1983; guest hostess: Tonight Show, 1983-86; hostess The Late Show Starring Joan Rivers, 1986-87, Hollywood Squares, 1987—, (morning talk show) Joan Rivers (Daytime Emmy award 1990), 1989—, Can We Shop? Home Shopping Netwrok, 1994—; originator, screenwriter TV movie The Girl Most Likely To, ABC, 1973; other TV movies include: How to Murder A Millionaire, 1990, Tears and Laughter: The Joan and Melissa Rivers Story, 1994; cable TV spl. Joan Rivers and Friends Salute Heidi Abromowitz, 1985; film appearances include The Swimmer, 1968, Uncle Sam, The Muppets Take Manhattan, 1984; co-author, dir.: (films) Rabbit Test, 1978 (also acted), Spaceballs, 1987; actress: theatre prodn. Broadway Bound, 1988, Sally Marr...and her escorts, 1994; recs. include: comedy album What Becomes a Semi-Legend Most, 1983; author: Having a Baby Can be a Scream, 1974, The Life and Hard Times of Heidi Abromowitz, 1984, (autobiography with Richard Meryman) Enter Talking, 1986, (with Richard Meryman) Still Talking, 1991; debuted on Broadway (play) Broadway Bound, 1988, creator Seminar You Deserve To Be happy, 1995. Nat. chmn. Cystic Fibrosis, 1982—, benefit performer for AIDS, 1984. Recipient Cleo awards for commls., 1976, 82, Jimmy award for best comedian, 1981; named Hadassah Woman of Yr., 1983, Harvard Hasty Pudding Soc. Woman of Yr., 1984. Mem. Phi Beta Kappa. *

RIVERS, LYNN N., congresswoman; b. Augres, Mich., Dec. 19, 1956; married; 2 children. BA, U. Mich., 1987; JD, Wayne State U., 1992. Mem. sch. bd. City of Ann Arbor, Mich., 1984-92; mem. Mich. House of Reps., 1992-94; mem. 104th Congress from 13th dist., 1994, mem. budget/science basic rsch., energy and environment, 1994. Office: US House Reps 1116 Longworth House Office Bldg Washington DC 20515-0513*

RIVERS, MARIE BIE, broadcasting executive; b. Tampa, Fla., July 12, 1928; d. Norman Albion and Rita Marie (Monrose) Bie; m. Eurith Dickinson Rivers, May 3, 1952; children—Eurith Dickinson, III, Rex B., M. Kells, Lucy L., Georgia. Student, George Washington U., 1946. Engaged in real estate bus., 1944-51, radio broadcasting, 1951—; pres., CEO, part owner Sta. WGUN, Atlanta, 1951—, Stas. KWAM and KJMS, Memphis, Sta. WEAS-AM-FM, Savannah, Ga., Stas. WGOV and WAAC, Valdosta, Ga., Sta. WSWN and Sta. WBGF, Belle Glade, Fla.; owner, chairperson, pres., CEO Sta. WCTH, Islamorado, Fla.; pres., CEO The Gram Corp., real estate com. Creative Christian Concepts Corp., 1985, pres., CEO Ocala, 1986; owner Suncoast Broadcasting Inc. Author: A Woman Alone, 1986; contbr. articles to profl. jours. Mem. Fla. Assn. Broadcasters (bd. dirs.), Ga. Assn. Broadcasters (bd. dirs., William J. Brooks award for exceptional svc. to radio broadcasting 1995), Coral Reef Yacht Club (Coconut Grove, Fla.), Palm Beach Polo and Country Club, Kappa Delta. Roman Catholic. Office: 11924 Forest Hill Blvd Ste 1 West Palm Beach FL 33414-6257

RIVERS, WILGA MARIE, foreign language educator; b. Melbourne, Australia, Apr. 13, 1919; came to U.S., 1970; d. Harry and Nina Diamond (Burston) R. Diploma in edn, U. Melbourne, 1940, BA with honors, 1939, MA, 1948; License es L., U. Montpellier, France, 1952; PhD, U. Ill., 1962; MA (hon.), Harvard U., 1974; D Langs. (hon.), Middlebury Coll., 1989. High sch. tchr. Victoria, Australia, 1940-48; asst. in English lang. France, 1949-52; tchr. prep. schs., 1953-58; asst. prof. French No. Ill. U., DeKalb, 1963-64; assoc. prof. Monash U., Australia, 1964-69; vis. prof. Columbia U., 1970-71; prof. French U. Ill., Urbana-Champaign, 1971-74; prof. Romance langs. and lit., coord. lang. instrn. Harvard U., 1974-89, prof. emerita, 1989—; cons. NEH, Ford Found., Rockefeller Found., others; lectr 41 countries and throughout U.S.; adv. coun. Modern Lang. Ctr., Ont. Inst. for Studies in Edn., Nat. Fgn. Lang. Ctr., Lang. Acquire Rsch. Ctr., San Diego. Author: The Psychologist and the Foreign-Language Teacher, 1964, Teaching Foreign-Language Skills, 1968, 2d edit., 1981, A Practical Guide to the Teaching of French, 1975, 2d edit., 1988; co-author: A Practical Guide to the Teaching of German, 1975, 2d edit., 1988, A Practical Guide to the Teaching of Spanish, 1976, 2d edit., 1988, A Practical Guide to the Teaching of English as a Second or Foreign Language, 1978, Speaking in Many Tongues, 1972, 3d edit., 1983, Communicating Naturally in a Second Language, 1983, Teaching Hebrew: A Practical Guide, 1989, Opportunities for Careers in Foreign Languages, 1993, others; editor, contbr. Interactive Language Teaching, 1978, Teaching Languages in College: Curriculum and Content, 1992; writing translated into 10 langs.; edtl. bd. Studies in Second Language Acquisition, Applied Linguistics, Language Learning, Mosaic, System; adv. com. Can. Modern Lang. Rev.; contbr. articles to profl. jours. Recipient Nat. Disting. Fgn. Lang. Leadership award N.Y. State Assn. Fgn. Lang. Tchrs., 1974. Decorated Chevalier des Palmes Académiques, 1995. Mem. MLA, Am. Assn. Applied Linguistics (charter pres.), Am. Coun. on Teaching Fgn. Langs. (Florence Steiner award 1977, Anthony Papalia award 1988), Mass. Fgn. Lang. Assn. (Disting. Svc. award 1983), Tchrs. of English to Speakers of other Langs., Am. Assn. Tchrs. French, Linguistic Soc. Am., Am. Assn. Univ. Suprs. and Coords. Fgn. Lang. Programs Northeast Conf. (Nelson Brooks award 1983), Internat. Assn. Applied Psycholinguistics (v.p. 1983-89), Japan Assn. Coll. English Tchrs. (hon.), Am. Assn. Tchrs. German (hon.), Internat. Assn. Lang. Labs. (hon.). Episcopalian. Home and Office: 84 Garfield St Watertown MA 02172-4916

RIVLIN, ALICE MITCHELL, economist; b. Phila., Mar. 4, 1931; d. Allan C. G. and Georgianna (Fales) Mitchell; m. Lewis Allen Rivlin, 1955 (div. 1977); children: Catherine Amy, Allan Mitchell, Douglas Gray; m. Sidney Graham Winter, 1989. B.A., Bryn Mawr Coll., 1952; Ph.D., Radcliffe Coll., 1958. Mem. staff Brookings Instn., Washington, 1957-66, 69-75, 83-93; dir. econ. studies Brookings Inst., 1983-87; dir. Congl. Budget Office, 1975-83; prof. pub. policy George Mason U., 1992; dep. dir. U.S. Office Mgmt. and Budget, 1993-94, dir., 1994—; dep. asst. sec. program coordination HEW, Washington, 1966-68, asst. sec. planning and evaluation, 1968-69; mem. Staff Adv. Commn. on Intergovtl. Rels., 1961-62. Author: The Role of the Federal Governemnt in Financing Higher Education, 1961, (with others) Microanalysis of Socioeconomic Systems, 1961, Systematic Thinking for Social Action, 1971, (with others) Economic Choices 1987, 1986, (with others The Swedish Economy, 1987, (with others) Caring for the Disabled Elderly: Who Will Pay?, 1988, Reviving the American Dream, 1992. MacArthur fellow, 1983-88. Mem. Am. Econ. Assn. (nat. pres. 1986). Office: U S Office Mgmt and Budget Office of the Director Old Exec Office Bldg Washington DC 20503*

RIVLIN, RACHEL, lawyer; b. Bangor, Maine, Sept. 1, 1945; d. Lawrence and A. Sara (Rich) Lait. BA, U. Maine, 1965; MA, U. Louisville, 1968; JD, Boston Coll., 1977. Bar: Mass. 1977, U.S. Dist. Ct. Mass. 1978, U.S. Ct. Appeals (1st cir.) 1983, U.S. Supreme Ct. 1985. Audiologist Boston City Hosp., 1969-72; dir. audiology Beth Israel Hosp., Boston, 1972-74; atty. Legal Systems Devel., Boston, 1977-78, Liberty Mutual Ins., Boston, 1978-82; counsel, sec. Lexington Ins. Co., Boston, 1982-85, v.p., assoc. gen. counsel, sec., 1985—. Mem. Civil Rights Com. Anti-Defamation League, Boston, 1982—; bd. dirs. DanceArt, Inc., Boston, 1985-92. Mem. ABA (com. on pub. regulation of ins. 1980—, vice chmn. 1980-81, vice chmn. pub. rels 1981-84, chmn. elect 1984-85, chmn. 1985-86, sr. vice chmn. 1989-90; excess surplus lines and reins. com. 1983—, vice chmn. 1986-87, chair-elect 1987-88, chmn. 1988-89; internat. ins. law com. 1983—; 1988 ann. meeting arrangements chmn. for TIPS; nat. inst. insurer involvency 1986, 89, nat. inst. reins. collections and involvency 1988), Boston Bar Assn. (council 1983-86; chmn. corp. counsel com., 1987, chmn. membership com. 1978-83, sub-com. on ABA model rules of profl. conduct 1980-81; chmn. ins. law com. 1987-90; chmn. profl. liability ins. com. 1990—; steering com. corp. bus. law and fin. sect. 1987-89; edn. com. 1987-89, 90-91; nominating com. 1988; dinner dance com. 1989, 94; ethics com. 1993—), Boston Coll. Law Sch. Alumni Assn. (ann. fund com. 1981-89, council 1983-87; chmn. telethon com. 1989-94; leadership gifts exec. com. 1994—; search com. for dean 1993; search com. for law sch. fund dir. 1993; nominating com. 1990; search com. for dir. of instl. advancement, 1995, Father James Malley award 1996). Home: 122 Lincoln St Newton MA 02161-1528 Office: Lexington Ins Co 200 State St Boston MA 02109-2694

RIZZI, DEBORAH L., public relations professional; b. Jersey City, N.J., Feb. 26, 1955; d. Edwin Joseph and Beulah Marie (Ardoin) R. BA, Rutgers U., 1977. Program dir. Am. Cancer Soc., Jersey City, 1977-79; internat. program asst. Stevens Inst. Tech., Hoboken, N.J., 1980; dir. pub. rels. United Hosps. Med. Ctr., Newark, 1981-90; dir. practice devel. Stryker Tams & Dill, Newark, 1990-92; comm. mgr. United Water, Harrington Park, N.J., 1992—; adv. bd. Nat. Boxing Safety Ctr., Newark, 1984-88; sr. producer Children's Miracle Network Telethon, N.J., 1985-90. Contbg. author: (book) Children With HIV Source Book, 1990, (booklet) Guide for Victims of Sexual Assault, 1985, Child With AIDS . . . Guide for the Family, 1986; co-producer: (video) Diagnosing Sexual Assault in Children, 1990. Recipient Mercury award Internat. Acad. Comm. Arts and Scis., 1993, 94, 95, Galaxy award, 1993, 94, 95, ARC award, 1994, 95, Jaspar award Jersey Shore Pub. Rels. and Advt. Assn., 1994, 95. Mem. Internat. Assn. Bus. Communicators (Ace award N.Y. chpt. 1993, 94, 95, EPIC award Phila. chpt. 1994, Silver Quill award U.S. Dist. I 1994, 95, Iris award N.J. chpt. 1994, 95), Am. Hosp. Assn. (Nat. Touch Stone award 1987), Pub. Rels. Soc. Am., Nat. Assn. Law Firm Marketers, N.J. Hosp. Assn. (Percy award 1986, 88, 90). Office: United Water 200 Old Hook Rd Harrington Park NJ 07640

RIZZO, JOANNE T., family nurse practitioner; b. Boston, Feb. 20, 1950; d. Anthony M. and Barbara A. Rizzo. BS, Northeastern U., 1972; MS, U. Colo., Denver, 1976. ACLS; cert. family nurse practitioner. RN pediatrics Mass. Gen. Hosp., Boston, 1972-75; family nurse practitioner Frontier Nursing Svc., Hyden, Ky., 1976-78; nurse practitioner migrant health program U. Colo., Alamosa, 1978-79; family nurse practitioner, clinic mgr. Plan de Salud del Valle, Ft. Lupton, Colo., 1979-82; family nurse practitioner Family Health Svc., Worcester, Mass., 1982-89; fgn. svc. nurse practitioner State Dept., Washington, 1989—; fgn. svc. nurse practitioner Am. Embassy, Bucharest, Romania, 1989-91, Lima, Peru, 1991—; nurse practitioner preceptor Robert Wood Johnson plan de salud del valle, Platteville, Colo., 1980-81, U. Lowell, Worcester, 1984-88, U. Wash., 1995. Recipient Cert. of Appreciation, Agy. Internat. Devel., Romania, 1990, Meritorious Honor award & Group Valor award, Romania, 1990, Dept. of State Health Practitioner of Yr. award, 1995. Mem. Sigma Theta Tau. Address: Dept State/ Kathmandu Washington DC 20521-6190

RIZZO, MARY ANN FRANCES, international trade executive, former educator; b. Bryn Mawr, Pa., Jan. 11, 1942; d. Joseph Franklyn and Armella Louise (Grubenhoff) R. BA magna cum laude (N.Y. State scholar), Marymount-Manhattan Coll., 1963; MA (fellow), Yale U., 1965, PhD (Lounsbury-Cross fellow), 1969; postgrad. Harvard U. Bus. Sch., 1979. Instr. Romance langs. and lit. Yale U., New Haven, 1966-70; asst. prof. Finch Coll., N.Y.C., 1971-73; v.p. Joseph F. Rizzo Co., Fla., 1969-87; owner, pres., 1987—; minister of the Word coordinator Our Lady of Perpetual Help Ch., Scottsdale, Ariz., 1986—, eucharistic min.; mem. bd. adv. Assn. Internat. des Etudiants en Sciences Economiques et Commerciales, Ariz. State U. Vice chmn., charter mem. bd. regents Cath. U. Am.; mem., coord. export counseling svc. Ariz. Dist. Export Coun.; 2d v.p. bd. advisors sch. bus. mgmt. Ariz. State U., Phoenix; bd. advisors bus. studies Paradise Valley (Ariz.) C.C. Mem. Il Circolo Italian Cultural Club (Palm Beach, Fla.), Fgn. Trade Coun. Palm Beach County (charter mem.), World Affairs Coun. of Ariz., Scottsdale C. of C. (internat. bus. devel. com.), World Trade Ctr., Alpha Chi. Republican. Roman Catholic (community coun. 1972-74). Clubs: Harvard Bus. Sch. Greater N.Y., Yale (N.Y.C. and Phoenix), Alliance Francaise (Phoenix), Ariz., Yale of Palm Beaches, Cercle Français de Palm Beach (Fla.), Ariz. Harvard Bus. Sch. Translator: From Time to Eternity, 1967; bibliographer: Italian Literature-Roots and Branches, 1976. Home: Villa Serein 2170 Ibis Isle Rd Palm Beach FL 33480-5350 Address: 5665 N 74th Pl Scottsdale AZ 85250-6416 Office: 7436 E Stetson Dr Ste 180 Scottsdale AZ 85251-3545

ROACH, ELEANOR MARIE, elementary education educator; b. Indpls., Nov. 30, 1932; d. Armand Dunnington and Ruth (Holman) R. BS in Art Edn., Ind. U., 1954; MS in Elem. Edn., Butler U., 1966. Cert. life K-12 art tchr., K-8 gen. elem. tchr., Ind. Tchr. art Wayne Twp. Pub. Schs., Indpls., 1954-57; freelance artist, 1957-60; artist, libr. designer Remington Rand, Indpls., 1960-61; elem. tchr. Indpls. Pub. Schs., 1962-70, tchr. academically talented, 1970-92, upper elem. tchr., 1992-94; content cons. Macmillan-McGraw Hill, N.Y.C., 1989-90, 1996; cons. Ind. State Mus., Indpls., 1988, 92. Photographer textbook Indiana, 1990. Former set designer Footlite Mus., Indpls.; stage mgr. Christian Theol. Sem. Repetory Theatre, Indpls., 1979-75. Recipient 1st place for ceramics Ind. State Fair, 1953, 2d place, 1954. Mem. NEA, Ind. Tchrs. Assn., Indpls. Edn. Assn., Ind. Coun. for Social Studies, Washington County Ind. Hist. Soc., Rush County Heritage, Inc., Nature Conservancy, Ind. Audubon Soc., Ind. Hist. Soc. Democrat. Roman Catholic. Home and Office: PO Box 635 Mooresville IN 46158-0635

ROACH, PATRICIA ROSANNE, elementary school educator; b. Brookline, Mass., June 17, 1957; d. Irma Valentine (Komisar) Gramer; m. John Ciccotelli, Aug. 22, 1976 (div. July 1980); 1 child, Nathaniel; 1 foster child, Andy Chee. BS in Edn., No. Ariz. U., 1985, MEd, 1991. 6th grade tchr. Flagstaff (Ariz.) Unified Sch. Dist., 1985—, also peer facilitator evaluator career ladder program; sec. Schs. for Today & Tomorrow, Flagstaff, 1994. Lic. foster parent for children with spl. needs Ariz. Dept. Econ. Security, Flagstaff, 1981—. Named Outstanding Young Woman of Am., Outstanding Young Women of Am., 1984, Foster Parent of Yr., City of Flagstaff Commn. on Disability Awareness, 1993. Mem. NEA (women's caucus 1992—, del. to rep. assembly 1994), Assn. Supervision and Curriculum Devel., AAUW, Nat. Coun. Tchrs. Math., Ariz. Sci. Tchrs. Assn., Ariz. Edn. Assn. (women's caucus 1992—, del. to del. assembly 1994, 95, 96), Flagstaff Edn. Assn. (exec. bd. 1993—). Democrat. Home: 1041 Tolani Trl Flagstaff AZ 86001-9614 Office: DeMiguel Elem Sch 3500 S Gillenwater Dr Flagstaff AZ 86001

ROADMAN, SHARON R., sales executive, communications coach; b. N.Y.C., Feb. 24, 1948; d. Max and Anita (Fried) Schwartz; m. Harry E. Roadman, Aug. 18, 1972 (div. Feb. 1991). BA in Mgmt., U. Redlands, 1983. Sr. assoc., v.p. Communispond, Inc., N.Y.C., 1984-95; dir. bus. devel. Koll Global Tng., Newport Beach, Calif., 1996—; prin., owner Recruiting Cons., Tustin, Calif., 1981-84. Mem. NAFE. Office: Koll Global Tng 4343 Von Karman Ave Newport Beach CA 92660

ROARK, BARBARA ANN, librarian; b. Evanston, Ill., July 24, 1958; d. Edward B. and Ann H. Rowe; m. Paul E. Roark, Sept. 18, 1982; children: Sarah, John. BA in History, U. Ky., 1981, MLS, 1982. Libr. dir. Hopkins County Madisonville (Ky.) Pub. Libr., 1983-85; ops. mgr. Wurzburg Inc., Nashville, 1985-91; libr. dir. Spies Pub. Libr., Menominee, Mich., 1991—; v.p. adv. coun. Mid-Peninsula Libr. Coop., Mich., 1993-95, sec. adv. coun., 1991-93. Grant writer Title II, 1994, Title I, 1995. Recipient Cert. of Excellence Libr. of Mich., 1995. Mem. ALA, Mich. Libr. Assn., Spies Pub. Libr. Found., PEO Chpt. BK, Order Ea. Star, U. Ky. Alumni Assn., Zeta Tau Alpha. Methodist. Office: Spies Public Library 940 1st St Menominee MI 49858

ROATH-ALGERA, KATHLEEN MARIE, massage therapist; b. Binghamton, N.Y., Feb. 7, 1952; d. Stephen James and Virginia Mary (Purdy) Roath; m. Parker Newcomb Wheeler Jr., Sept. 18, 1971 (div. June 1976); 1 child, Colleen Marie Wheeler; m. John M. Algera, Feb. 14, 1981. AS in Phys. Edn., Dean Jr. Coll., Franklin, Mass., 1971; BS in Edn., Boston U., 1977; postgrad., U. Ctrl. Fla., Orlando, 1981-82; grad., Reese Inst. Massage Therapy, Oviedo, Fla., 1988. Lic. massage therapist; master practitioner in myofascial release. Counselor Dept. Def., Orlando, 1979-84; tchr. Divine Mercy Cath. Sch., Merritt Island, Fla., 1984-85; courier Emery Worldwide, Orlando, 1985-89; massage therapist, dir., owner Massage Therapy Clinic of Titusville, Fla., 1989—; instr., supr. clin. internship Reese Inst., 1992-95; assoc. Todd Jaffe, M.D., 1995. Mem. Am. Massage Therapy Assn., Fla. State Massage Therapy Assn. (pres. Brevard County 1992—, Therapist of Yr. 1991-92), Nat. Cert. Bd. Therapeutic Massage and Bodywork (recert. chair 1994—). Home: 5538 River Oaks Dr Titusville FL 32780 Office: Massage Therapy Clinic Titusville 3410 S Park Ave Titusville FL 32780-5139

ROBAK, KIM M., state official; b. Columbus, Nebr., Oct. 4, 1955; m. William J. Mueller; children: Katherine, Claire. BA with distinction, U. Nebr., 1977, JD with high distinction, 1985. Tchr. Lincoln (Nebr.) Pub. Schs., 1978-82; clerk Cline Williams Wright Johnson & Oldfather, Lincoln, 1983; summer assoc. Cooley Godward Castro Huddleson & Tatum, San Francisco, 1984, Steptoe & Johnson, Washington, 1985; ptnr. Rembolt Ludtke Parker & Berger, Lincoln, 1985-91; legal counsel Gov. E. Benjamin Nelson/State of Nebr., Lincoln, 1991-92, chief of staff, 1992-93; lt. gov. State of Nebr., Lincoln, 1993—; chair Prairie Fire Internat. Symposium on Edn., 1986. Fellow Leadership Lincoln, 1986-87, program com., 1987-90; chair program com. Leadership Lincoln Alumni Assn., 1987, selection com., 1990; chair Landfill Alternatives and Ops. Task Force, 1986-87; chair Gladys Forsyth award subcom. YWCA Tribute! to Women, 1987, chair nominations, 1991; mem. adv. com. U.S. Constn. Bicentennial Competition, 1987; gen. Dem. counsel, Nebr., 1985-92; mem. bd. women's ministries First Plymouth Congl. Ch., 1988-91, trustee, 1991-94; mem. Toll Fellowship Program, 1995; chair Nat. Conf. Lt. Govs., 1996; hon. chair Daffodil Day campaign Am. Cancer Soc.; hon. chair Walktoberfest, Am. Diabetes Assn.; hon. chair Nebr.'s campaign Prevent Blindness; hon. mem. Red Ribbon campaign Mothers Against Drunk Driving, 1994-95. Mem. Nat. Conf. Lt. Govs. (fed. practice com. 1986-92), Nat. Inst. Trial Advocacy, Nebr. State Bar Assn. (ethics com. 1987-92, vice chair com. on pub. rels. 1988-92, chair com. on yellow pages advt. 1988, ho. of dels. 1988-95), Lincoln Bar Assn., U. Nebr. Coll. Alumni Assn. (bd. dirs. 1986-89), Updowntowners, Order of Coif.

ROBARDS, SHIRLEY JEAN NEEDS, education educator; b. Marietta, Ohio, Feb. 11, 1939; d. Lloyd Thomas and Wilma Imogene (Ballard) Needs; m. Frank Henry Robards, June 26, 1959; 1 child, Linda Renee Robards-Bull. BA, Ky. Wesleyan Coll., Owensboro, 1964; MA, Western. Ky. U., 1965; EdD, Ind. U., 1972. Cert. tchr., Ind., Ky., Okla. Tchr. Webster County Ky. Schs., Slaughters, Ky., 1959-64, Hopkins County Ky. Schs., Madisonville, Ky., 1964-66, Tell City (Ind.) Pub. Schs., 1966-68; assoc. instr. Ind. U., Bloomington, 1971-72; dept. chair, dir. field svcs. U. Tulsa, Tulsa, 1972—. Author (monograph) Webster's Baby Interpreting Research in Language Arts, 1971; contbr. articles to profl. jours. Recipient Integrating Math & Sci. award, 1992, Integrating Math, Sci. and Lang. Arts award, 1993, Integrating Core Disciplines with Aerospace award, 1994, Using Cmty. Resources to Integrate Sci. and Math. award, 1996. Mem. Assn. of Tchr. Educators (pres. 1989-92), Phi Delta Kappa (v.p. 1989-95, co-dir. edn. seminar Russia 1990), Kappa Delta Pi (counselor 1993-94). Methodist. Office: U Tulsa 600 S College Ave Tulsa OK 74104-3126

ROBB, CAROLE COLE, educational administrator, educator; b. Chariton, Iowa, Oct. 18, 1942; d. Harry A. and Mabel B. (Brown) Cole; m. Theodore E. Drish, Dec. 23, 1967 (div. Apr. 1981); children: Amy Allison; m. John Milton Robb, May 20, 1989. BS in Edn., Drake U., 1965, MS in Edn., 1978. Cert. tchr., Tex., Iowa. Tchr. West Des Moines (Iowa) Cmty. Sch., 1965-68, 76-85, Crystal City (Tex.) Ind. Sch. Dist., 1985-88, Tex. Youth Commn., Giddings, 1988—; tchr. alternative cert. program Region XIII Svc. Ctr., Austin, Tex., 1992—; cons. Tex. Assn. Bilingual Assn., Kingsville, 1992, Tex. Youth Commn., 1989-94. Author: Style Manual for Valley High School, 1982. Mission chair United Meth. Women, Giddings, 1995; mem. adv. bd. Mental Health Mental Retardation, Giddings, 1990-91. Connie Belin Ctr. for Gifted Edn. fellow, 1983, 92. Mem. NEA, Tex. State Edn. Assn., Texas Assn. Gifted and Talented, Internat. Reading Assn., Tex. State Reading Assn., Coalition Reading and Eng. Supr. Tex. (historian 1994—), S.W. Reading Assn. (pres.-treas. 1985-87). Office: Tex Youth Commn PO Box 600 Giddings TX 78942-0600

ROBBEN, MARY MARGARET, portrait artist; b. Bethesda, Md., Oct. 30, 1948; d. John Otto and Mary Margaret (McConnaughy) R. Student, Ohio U., 1967-71; B.Visual Art, Ga. State U., 1984. Visual merchandising staff Macy's Dept. Store, Union City, Ga., 1985-86; embroidery designer So. Promotions, Peachtree City, Ga., 1987-90; portrait artist Personal Touch Portraits, Peachtree City, Ga., 1991-95, Margy's Portraiture, Peachtree City, 1996—. Mortar Bd. scholar, 1984. Fellow Internat. Biographical Ctr. (life); mem. AAUW, Ga. State U. Alumni Assn., Golden Key, Am. Bus. Women's Assn., Nat. Mus. of Women in the Arts. Home and Office: 207 Battery Way Peachtree City GA 30269-2126

ROBBINS, ANNE FRANCIS See REAGAN, NANCY DAVIS

ROBBINS, ARLENE AGNES, elementary education educator; d. Raymond and Rose Goff; m. Carle B. Robbins Jr.; children: Carle III, Lauri. BS, So. Conn. State Coll; MEE, State of Pa., 1987. Tchr. instrl. support Palisades Sch. Dist., Kintnersville, Pa., tchr. elem. Trumbull (Conn.) Sch. Dist.; tchr. math. Palisades Mid. Sch., Kintnersville. Auditor Durham (Pa.) Township. Mem. Nat. Coun. Tchrs. Math., Pa. Edn. Assn., Pa. State Edn. Assn., Palisades Coun. Tchrs. Math., Buck County Coun. Tchrs. Math. Office: Palisades Mid Sch 425 Hilltop Rd Riegelsville PA 18077-9727

ROBBINS, BRENDA SUE, early childhood educator; b. Langdale, Ala., June 28, 1950; d. Richard Cecil and Audrey Millicent (Smallwood) R. Student, Mich. State U., 1968-72; BS in Edn., Auburn U., 1974, MS in Edn., 1977. Title 1 reading, math tchr. Muscogee Co. Sch. Dist., Columbus, Ga., 1977-78, fed. preschool tchr., 1978-80, tchr. grade 1, 1980-81, 1984-85, tchr. kindergarten, 1981-84, 1985—; staff devel. instr. Muscogee County Sch. Dist., Columbus, Ga., 1994; presenter in field. Mem. Georgia Assn. Educators, Nat. Edn. Assn. Office: Saint Marys Elem Sch 4408 Saint Marys Rd Columbus GA 31907

ROBBINS, ELIZABETH, stained glass artist, designer; b. N.Y.C., Dec. 17, 1941; d. Victor Ganales and Sylvia Sherrie (Woolf) R.; m. Jarvis Myers; children: Lorraine, Benjamin. BS in Art Edn., So. Conn. State Coll.; attended, Yale U., Cooper Union, N.Y.C., Silvermine (Conn.) Guild, Betzalel Art Sch., Jerusalem, Israel, Victoria & Albert Mus., London, Northeastern U., Boston, Wolverhampton (Eng.) Coll. Staff graphic layout and design Jarrett Press, N.Y.C., 1960-63; owner, operator Unique Boutique, Jerusalem, Israel, 1964-66; mem. staff, trainer Isratypeset, Jerusalem, 1967-72; costume designer MGM, Israel, 1967-72; graphic designer Time-Life Book Divsn., Amsterdam, Holland, 1973; originator, operator The Darkroom, Cambridge, Mass., 1976-82; owner, operatorr Elizabeth Robbins Studios, 1982-96. Gallery showings include Hartford (Conn.) Courant Art Competition, 1956-59 (Best in Show award (sculpture) 1957, 2d Place award (painting) 1958, (sculpture) 1959, 3d Place award (sculpture) 1956), So. Conn. State Coll., New Haven, 1965, Yale, New Haven Group Show, 1965, Betzalel, Israel Group Show, 1970, Amalgamated Gallery, N.Y.C., 1984, Art on the Green, Newton, Mass., 1982-86, Abrams Gallery, Cambridge, Mass., 1987, Corning (N.Y.) Show, 1988, Metro Show, Washington D.C., 1988 (Hon. Mention), Goldmine Gallery, Manchester, Vt., 1988, Catamount Gallery, St. Johnsbury, Vt., 1989, New England Art Glass Show, Derby Line, Vt., 1990-93, Pitts., The Orchid As Art, 1992, 94, Ventura, Calif. Group Show, 1992, 94, San Francisco Harvest Show, Calif. 1993, 95; represented in various pub. collections, including Amchad/Assn. for Hollocaust Survivors, Ramat Gan, Israel, Cobleigh Libr., Lyndonville, Vt., No. Vt. Regional Hosp., St. Johnsbury, Vt.; represented in numerous pvt. collections. Mem. Stained Glass Assn. Am., Vt. Coun. on the Arts, Vt. Handcrafters. Home: PO Box 1001 Lyndonville VT 05851 Office: Elizabeth Robbins Studio Vail Circle Lyndonville VT 05851

ROBBINS, HULDA DORNBLATT, artist, printmaker; b. Atlanta, Oct. 19, 1910; d. Adolph Benno and Lina (Rosenthal) Dornblatt. Student, Phila. Mus's. Sch. Indsl. Art, 1928-29, Prussian Acad., Berlin, 1929-31, Barnes Found., Merion, Pa., 1939. Poster designer and maker ITE Circuit Breaker Co. Inc., Phila., 1944; instr. serigraphy Nat. Serigraph Soc. Sch., N.Y.C., 1953-60; instr. creative painting Atlantic County Jewish Community Centers, Margate and Atlantic City, N.J., 1960-67; represented by WIlliam P. Carl, Fine Prints, Boston, The Picture Store, Boston. One-man shows, Lehigh U. Art Galleries, 1933, ACA Galleries, Phila., 1939, 8th St. Gallery, N.Y.C., 1941, Serigraph Gallery, N.Y.C., 1947, Atlantic City Art Center, 1961, 71, numerous group shows, 2d Nat. Print ann. Bklyn. Mus., Carnegie Inst., Library of Congress, LaNapoule Art Found., Am. Graphic Contemporary Art; represented in permanent collections, including, Met. Mus. Art, N.Y.C., Mus. Modern Art, N.Y.C., Bibliotheque Nationale, Smithsonian Instn., Art Mus. Ont., Can., Victoria and Albert Mus., London, U.S. embassies abroad, Lehigh U., Princeton (N.J.) Print Club. Recipient Purchase prize Prints for Children, Mus. Modern Art, N.Y.C., 1941; prize 2d Portrait of Am. Competition, 1945; 2d prize Paintings by Printmakers, 1948. Mem. Am. Color Print Soc., Print Club, Graphics Soc., Serigraph Soc. (mem. founding group, charter sec., Ninth Ann. prize 1948, 49). Home and Office: 16 S Buffalo Ave Ventnor City NJ 08406-2635

ROBBINS, JANE BORSCH, library science educator, information science educator; b. Chgo., Sept. 13, 1939; d. Reuben August and Pearl Irene (Houk) Borsch; married; 1 child, Molly Warren. B.A., Wells Coll., 1961; M.L.S., Western Mich. U., 1966; Ph.D., U. Md., 1972. Asst. prof. library and info.

sci. U. Pitts., 1972-73; asso. prof. Emory U., Atlanta, 1973-74; cons. to the bd. Wyo. State Library, 1974-77; asso. prof. La. State U., Baton Rouge, 1977-79; dean La. State U. (Sch. Library and Info. Sci.), 1979-81; prof., dir. Sch. Library and Info. Studies U. Wis., Madison, 1981-94; dean, prof. Sch. Libr. and Info. Studies Fla. State U., Tallahassee, 1994—. Author: Public Library Policy and Citizen Participation, 1975, Public Librarianship: A Reader, 1982, Are We There Yet?, 1988, Libraries: Partners in Adult Literacy, 1990, Keeping the Books: Public Library Financial Practices, 1992, Balancing the Books: Financing American Public Library Services, 1993, Evaluating Library Programs and Services: A Manual and Sourcebook, 1994; editor Libr. and Info. Sci. Rsch., 1982-92; contbr. articles to profl. jours. Mem. ALA (councilor 1976-80, 91-95), Am. Soc. Info. Sci., Assn. for Libr. and Info. Sci. Edn. (dir. 1979-81, pres. 1984), Wis. Libr. Assn. (pres. 1986), Fla. Libr. Assn. Democrat. Episcopalian. Office: Fla State U Sch Libr and Info Studies Louis Shores Bldg Tallahassee FL 32306

ROBBINS, MARJORIE JEAN GILMARTIN, elementary education educator; b. Newton, Mass., Sept. 19, 1940; d. John and Helen (Arbuckle) Gilmartin; m. Maurice Edward Robbins, Aug. 1, 1962; children: John Scott, Gregory Dale, Kris Eric. BS in Edn., Gordon Coll., 1962; postgrad., U. Maine, Augusta, 1976, U. Maine, Orono, 1986, U. Maine, Portland, 1987. Cert. tchr. Tchr. Ctr. St. Sch., Hampton, N.H., 1962-64, Claflin Sch., Newton, 1965-66, Israel Loring Sch., Sudbury, Mass., 1966-67, Cheney Sch., Orange, Mass., 1967-69, Palermo (Maine) Consolidated Sch., 1975—; founder, tchr. Primary Edn. Program, Palermo, 1990—; dir., author Child Sexual Abuse Program, Palmero, 1988—; mem. Title I Com., 1995—, Health Curriculum Com., 1995—. Mem. bd. Christian edn. Winter St. Bapt. Ch., Gardiner, Maine, 1993—, mem. bd. missions, 1993-94; bd. dirs. Hillside Christian Nursery Sch., 1994—; coord. student assistance team Maine Sch. Union #51, 1993—, bd. dirs. United Team, 1993—, mem. publicity com., 1991-92; coord. Nursing Home Ministry, Gardiner. Mem. NEA, Maine Tchrs. Assn., Palermo Tchrs. Assn. (pres. 1984-86), Maine Educators of the Gifted and Talented, Maine Sch. Union 51 (sec. certification steerin g com. 1988—, rep. gifted-talented com. 1976—), Palermo Sch. Club (exec. bd. 19 85-88. Home: 204 Dresden Ave Gardiner ME 04345-2618 Office: Palermo Consolidated Sch RR 3 Palermo ME 04354

ROBBINS, NANCY LOUISE See MANN, NANCY LOUISE

ROBBINS, RENE CORRINE, small business owner; b. St. Charles, Ill., July 5, 1960; d. Robert Clarence and Delores Lorraine Shuman; m. Gregory Keith Robbins. BA, William Penn Coll., 1981; postgrad., U. Tex., 1981-84. Lic. tchr. secondary edn. Iowa. Asst. mgr., disk jockey Sta. KIGC, Oskaloosa, Iowa, 1978-80; substitute tchr. Albia (Iowa) and Oskaloosa Pub. Schs., 1980-81; sales rep. Ginny's Printing Co., Austin, Tex., 1985-89; Macintosh coord. K-Graphics/Kinko's, Des Moines, 1989-91; owner, typesetter Rene's Resumes, Oskaloosa, 1991—; pvt. tutor; instr. resume workshops Ctrl. Coll., Pella, Iowa, 1996—. Active Peace and Social Concerns Com., Oskaloosa, 1992—. Mem. AAUW (bd. dirs., editor newsletter 1994—, Spl. Recognition for newsletter editing 1996), Nat. Women's Hall of Fame, Phi Alpha Theta, Alpha Chi. Mem. Soc. of Friends. Office: Renes Resumes & Typesetting 1110 4th Ave East Oskaloosa IA 52577

ROBBINS, SONIA JAFFE, editor, writer; b. Newport News, Va., June 4, 1942; d. Joseph and Lea (Leibowitz) Jaffe; m. Jack Robbins, Nov. 25, 1964; 1 child, Christie Megan. Student, Antioch Coll., 1960-62; BS, CCNY, 1969, MA in Women's Studies, 1990. Assoc. editor Bobbs-Merrill, N.Y.C., 1969-72; freelance editor, copyeditor N.Y.C., 1972-75; copyeditor Village Voice, N.Y.C., 1975-79, copy chief, dep. mng. editor, 1979-86; asst. prof. journalist NYU, N.Y.C., 1986-93; comm. coord. Network of East-West Women, N.Y.C., 1993—; panel organizer Socialist Scholars Conf., N.Y.C., 1992; seminar organizer N.Y. Inst. for the Humanities, N.Y.C., 1990-93; workshop co-organizer NYU Ctr. for European Studies, N.Y.C., 1992—; panelist Inst. for Study in Salzberg, Austria, 1994. Author of revs. for jours. Women's Rev. of Books, 1992-95, Columbia Journalism Review, 1988, Phila. Inquirer, 1987; author, editor, designer newsletter Network of East-West Women, 1992—; contbr. articles to Village Voice. Mem. No More Nice Girls, N.Y.C., 1977—; co-founder Network of East-West Women, N.Y.C., 1990—. Mem. Nat. Writers Union, Editl. Freelancers Assn. Democrat. Home: 395 Riverside Dr #2F New York NY 10025

ROBBINS-WILF, MARCIA, educational consultant; b. Newark, Mar. 22, 1949; d. Saul and Ruth (Fern) Robbins; 1 child, Orin. Student, Emerson Coll., 1967-69, Seton Hall U., 1969, Fairleigh Dickinson U., 1970; BA, George Washington U., 1971; MA, NYU, 1975; postgrad., St. Peter's Coll., Jersey City, 1979, Fordham U., 1980; MS, Yeshiva U., 1981, EdD, 1986; postgrad., Monmouth Coll., 1986. Cert. elem. tchr., N.Y., N.J., reading specialist, N.J., prin., supr., N.J., adminstr., supr., N.Y. Tchr. Sleepy Hollow Elem. Sch., Falls Church, Va., 1971-72, Yeshiva Konvitz, N.Y.C., 1972-73; intern Wee Folk Nursery Sch., Short Hills, N.J., 1978-81, dir. day camp, 1980-81, tchr., dir., owner, 1980-81; adj. prof. reading Seton Hall U., South Orange, N.J., 1987, Middlesex County Coll., Edison, N.J., 1987-88; asst. adj. prof. L.I. U., Bklyn., 1988, Pace U., N.Y.C., 1988—; ednl. cons. Cranford High Sch., 1988; presenter numerous workshops; founding bd. dirs. Stern Coll. Women Yeshiva U., N.Y.C., 1987; adj. vis. lectr. Rutgers U., New Brunswick, N.J., 1988. Chairperson Jewish Book Festival, YM-YWHA, West Orange, N.J., 1986-87, mem. early childhood com., 1986—, bd. dirs., 1986—; vice chairperson dinner com. Nat. Leadership Conf. Christians and Jews, 1986; mem. Hadassah, Valerie Children's Fund, Women's League Conservative Judaism, City of Hope; assoc. bd. bus. and women's profl. divsn. United Jewish Appeal, 1979; vol. reader Goddard Riverside Day Care Ctr., N.Y.C., 1973; friend N.Y.C. Pub. Libr., 1980—; life friend Millburn (N.J.) Pub. Libr.; pres. Seton-Essex Reading Coun., 1991-94. Co-recipient Am. Heritage award, Essex County, 1985; recipient Award Appreciation City of Hope, 1984, Profl. Improvement awards Seton-Essex Reading Council, 1984-86, Cert. Attendance award Seton-Essex Reading Counci, 1987. Mem. N.Y. Acad. Scis. (life), N.J. Council Tchrs. English, Nat. Council Tchrs. English, Am. Ednl. Research Assn., Coll. Reading Assn. (life), Assn. Supervision and Curriculun Devel., N.Y. State Reading Assn. (council Manhattan), N.J. Reading Assn. (council Seton-Essex), Internat. Reading Assn., Nat. Assn. for Edn. of Young Children (life N.J. chpt., Kenyon group), Nat. Council Jewish Women (vice chairperson membership com. evening br. N.Y. sect. 1974-75), George Washington U. Alumni Club, Emerson Coll. Alumni Club, NYU Alumni Club, Phi Delta Kappa (life), Kappa Gamma Chi (historian). Club: Greenbrook Country (Caldwell, N.J.); George Washington Univ. Home: 242 Hartshorn Dr Short Hills NJ 07078-1914 also: 820 Morris Tpke Short Hills NJ 07078-2619

ROBECK, MILDRED COEN, education educator; b. Walum, N.D., July 29, 1915; d. Archie Blane and Mary Henrietta (Hoffman) Coen; m. Martin Julius Robeck, Jr., June 2, 1936; children: Martin Jay Robeck, Donna Jayne Robeck Thompson, Bruce Wayne Robeck. BS, U. Wash., 1950, MEd, 1954, PhD, 1958. Ordnance foreman Sherman Williams, U.S. Navy, Bremerton, Wash., 1942-45; demonstration tchr. Seattle Pub. Schs., 1946-57; reading clinic dir. U. Calif., Santa Barbara, 1957-64; vis. prof. Victoria Coll., B.C., Can., summer 1958, Dalhousie U., Halifax, summer 1964; rsch. cons. State Dept. Edn., Sacramento, Calif., 1964-67; prof., head early childhood edn. U. Oreg., Eugene, Oreg., 1967-86; vis. scholar West Australia Inst. Tech., Perth, 1985; exec. faculty U. Santa Barbara, Calif., 1987-92, 92-95; trainer evaluator U.S. Office of Edn. Head Start, Follow Thru, 1967-72; cons., evaluator Native Am. Edn. Programs, Sioux, Navajo, 1967-81; cons. on gifted Oreg. Task Force on Talented and Gifted, Salem, 1974-76; evaluator Early Childhood Edn., Bi-Ling. program, Petroleum and Minerology, Dhahran, Saudi Arabia, 1985. Author: Materials KELP: Kgn. Evaluation Learning Pot, 1967, Infants and Children, 1978, Psychology of Reading, 1990; contbr. articles to profl. jours. Evaluation cons. Rosenburg Found. Project, Santa Barbara, 1966-67; faculty advisor Pi Lambda Theta, Eugene, Oreg, 1969-74; guest columnist Oreg. Assn. Gifted and Talented, Salem, Oreg., 1979-81; editorial review bd. ERQ, U.S. Calif., L.A., 1981-91. Recipient Nat. Dairy award 4-H Clubs, Wis., 1934, scholarships NYA and U. Wis., Madison, 1934-35, faculty rsch. grants U. Calif., Santa barbara, 1958-64, NDEA Fellowship Retraining U.S. Office Edn., U. Oreg., 1967-70. Mem. APA, Am. Ednl. Rsch. Assn., Internat. Reading Assn., Phi Beta Kappa, Pi Lambda Theta. Democrat. Home: 95999 Hwy 101 S Yachats OR 97498

ROBERGE, JILL QUIGLEY, editorial director; b. Englewood, N.J., Feb. 7, 1955; d. Charles Joseph and Constance (Osberg) Quigley; m. John Philip Roberge, Sept. 25, 1982; 1 child, Kelly Richard. BA, Franklin Pierce Coll., 1977. With Globetech Pub., Wilton, Conn., 1985—. Editl. dir. Med. Imaging Internat., Critical Care Internat., Chirurgia Internat., LabMedica Internat., 1989—. Mem. Internat. Fedn. Clin. Chemistry (editl. dir. Biotech. Lab. Internat.). Home: 182 Jockey Hollow Rd Monroe CT 06468-1235 Office: Globetech Pubs 30 Cannon Rd Wilton CT 06897-2625

ROBERGE, M. SHEILA, state legislator; b. Manchester, N.H.; m. A. Roland Roberge; 2 children. Ed. St. Anselm's Coll. Mem. N.H. Senate, 1985—; chmn. Manchester, N.H., Rep. com., 1979-80; del., Rep. Nat. Conv., 1980, 84; Rep. nat. committeewoman from N.H.; vice-chmn., Rep. Nat. Com., 1980-88. Roman Catholic. Office: Rep Nat Com 310 1st St SE Washington DC 20003-1801 also: Senate House 107 N Main St Rm 302 Concord NH 03301*

ROBERSON, CAREN, bank executive. Sr. v.p., dir. mktg. Calif. Fed. Bank, L.A. Office: Calif Fed Bank 5700 Wilshire Blvd Los Angeles CA 90036*

ROBERSON, CHERYL ANNE, lawyer; b. Phila., Mar. 7, 1963; d. Bruce Heerdt and Mary (Abrams) R. BA, Wofford Coll., 1984; JD, U. Fla., 1987. Bar: Fla. 1987, U.S. Dist. Ct. (mid. dist.) Fla. 1987. Assoc. Bledsoe, Schmidt & Lippes, Jacksonville, Fla., 1987—. Office: Ste 1818 1301 Riverplace Blvd Jacksonville FL 32207

ROBERSON, DEBORAH KAY, secondary school educator; b. Crane, Tex., Jan. 15, 1955; d. David B. and Virginia L. (King) Cole; m. Larry M. Roberson; children: Justin, Jenai, Julie. BS in Secondary Edn., Coll. S.W., 1981; MA in Sch. Adminstrn., Sul Ross State U., 1991. Cert. biology and history tchr., mid-mgmt. cert., supt. cert., Tex., biology and history tchr., Okla. Sci. and social studies tchr. Andrews (Tex.) Ind. Sch. Dist., 1987-95; forum tchr.- gifted social studies program, social studies dept. chair Ctrl. Mid. Sch. Broken Arrow (Okla.) Pub. Schs., 1995—; mem. 7th grade history curriculum com. Andrews Ind. Sch. Dist., 1988, mem. outdoor classroom com., 1989-90, chair sci. curriculum com., 1989-90, chair health curriculum com., 1990-91, mem. Tex. pub. schs. open house com., 1989-90, 92-93, mem. dist. textbook com., 1990-91; secondary edn. rep. Ptnrs. in Parliament, Berlin, 1993; site-based com. Broken Arrow Pub. Schs., 1995—, B.A.S.I.S. com., 1995—, nat. history day coord. Ctrl. Middle Sch., 1995, geography bee coord., 1995—, tech. com., 1996—, mem. discipline com., 1996, mem. remediation com., 1996—, Tools for Tomorrow Conf. com., 1996—, others. Livestock leader Andrews County 4-H Program, 1985-89; vol. Am. Heart Assn., Andrews, 1988; vol., team mother Little League, Andrews, 1990; vol., treas. Mustang Booster Club, Andrews, 1993-95. Recipient Appreciation awards Mustang Booster Club, 1993, 94, VFW Ladies Aux. Post 10887 award, Broken Arrow, 1996—. Mem. AAUW, Nat. Assn. Secondary Sch. Prins., Nat. Staff Devel. Coun., Assn. Tex. Profl. Educators (pres. local unit 1992-93, mem. resolutions com. 1994-95, appreciation award 1993, sec. region 1993-94, v.p. region 1994-95), ASCD, Tex. Assn. Supervision and Curriculum Devel., Tex. Network for Continuous Quality Improvement, Nat. Coun. Social Studies, Okla. Assn. Supervision and Curriculum Devel., Okla. Alliance Geographic Edn. Home: 708 N Sweet Gum Ave Broken Arrow OK 74012 Office: Broken Arrow Pub Schs Ctrl Mid Sch 210 N Main St Broken Arrow OK 74012

ROBERSON, LINDA, lawyer; b. Omaha, July 15, 1947; d. Harlan Oliver and Elizabeth Aileen (Good) R.; m. Gary M. Young, Aug. 20, 1970; children: Elizabeth, Katherine, Christopher. BA, Oberlin Coll., 1969; MS, U. Wis., 1970, JD, 1974. Bar: Wis. 1974, U.S. Dist. Ct. (we. dist.) Wis. 1974. Legis. atty. Wis. Legis. Reference Bur., Madison, 1974-76, sr. legis. atty., 1976-78; assoc. Rikkers, Koritzinsky & Rikkers, Madison, 1978-79; ptnr. Koritzinsky, Neider, Langer & Roberson, Madison, 1979-85, Stolper, Koritzinsky, Brewster & Neider, Madison, 1985-93, Balisle & Roberson, Madison, 1993—; lectr. U. Wis. Law Sch., Madison, 1978—. Co-author: Real Women, Real Lives, 1981, Wisconsin's Marital Property Reform Act, 1984, Understanding Wisconsin's Marital Property Law, 1985, A Guide to Property Classification Under Wisconsin's Marital Property Act, 1986, 2d edit. 1996, Workbook for Wisconsin Estate Planners, 2d edit., 1993, Look Before You Leap, 1996, Family Estate Planning in Wis., 1992, rev. edit. 1996. Fellow Am. Acad. Matrimonial Lawyers; mem. ABA, Wis. Bar Assn., Dane County Bar Assn., Legal Assn. Women, Nat. Assn. Elder Law Attys. Office: Balisle and Roberson 217 S Hamilton # 302 PO Box 870 Madison WI 53701-0870

ROBERSON, PATT FOSTER, mass communications educator; b. Middletown, N.Y., Dec. 3, 1934; d. Gilbert Charles and Mildred Elizabeth (O'Neal) Foster; m. Murray Ralph Roberson Jr., May 10, 1963 (dec. 1968). AA, Canal Zone Jr. Coll., 1954; BA in Journalism, La. State U., 1957, MA in Journalism, 1973; MA in Media, So. U., Baton Rouge, 1981; PhD in Mass Communication, U. So. Miss., 1985. Exec. sec. Lionel H. Abshire and Assocs., AIA, Architects, Baton Rouge, 1958-60, Murrell and Callari, AIA, Architects, Baton Rouge, 1960-63; bus. mgr. So. Rev. La. State U., Baton Rouge, 1963-69; free-lance researcher, ind. contractor Baton Rouge, 1969-74; rep. dept. info. State of La., Baton Rouge, 1974-75; asst. prof. mass. comm. So. U., 1976-86, assoc. prof. mass comm., 1986-93, prof. mass comm., 1993—; reviewer Random House Pubs., N.Y.C., 1981; profl. devel. intern Baton Rouge Morning Advocate, 1991, Baker Observer, 1991-92; cons. advt. Baton Rouge Little Theater, 1971—; reporter-photographer Canal Record, Seminole, Fla., 1967—; biographer of Edward Livermore Burlingame, John H. Johnson, Daniel Kimball Whitaker, (book) American mag. journalists series, Dictionary Literary Biography, Detroit, 1986-87; tutor Operation Upgrade, 1978-82; vol. reporter, photographer, proofreader The Platinum Record, Baton Rouge, 1996—. Co-editor: La. State U. cookbook Tiger Bait, 1976; biographer Frank E. Gannett in Biographical Dictionary of American Journalism, 1987; freelance writer/editl. cons.; editl. bd. Am. Journalism, 1986-87; reviewer Longman Publs. 1991-92; contbr. articles to profl. jours. Mem. poll commn. East Baton Rouge Parish Govt., 1978—; pres. Our Lady Lake Regional Med. Ctr., 1971-72; bd. dirs. Dist. Atty.'s Rape Crisis Commn., 1976-79, Plan Govt. Study Commn., 1973-76, Selective Svc. System Bd. 8, Baton Rouge, 1986—; docent Greater Baton Rouge Zoo, 1974-77; vol. ARC, 1989—; mem. East Baton Rouge Parish Commn. on Govtl. Ethics, 1992-93; mayoral appointee Baker Mobile Home Rev. Bd., 1990—; v.p. Baker Hist. and Cultural Found., 1990-93; mem. Baker Interclub Coun., 1990-91; organizer human-animal therapy svc. Baker Manor Nursing Home, 1994; mem. 1st class Citizens Basic Police Tng. Acad., Baton Rouge Police Dept., 1994; vol. reporter, photographer, proofreader The Platinum Record, Baton Rouge, 1996—. Mem. AAUP (sec.-treas. La. conf. 1988-89, sec. 1992-93, chmn. pub. rels. 1994-95), Assn. Edn. Journalism and Mass Comm., Am. Newspapers Pubs. Assn. (nat. coop. com. on edn. in journalism 1989-92), Women in Comm. (pres. Baton Rouge chpt. 1982, nat. judge Clarion awards 1987), Pub. Rels. Assn. La., La. State U. Journalism Alumni Assn. (pres. 1977), Soc. Profl. Journalists (pres. S.E. La. chpt. 1982), Am. Journalism Historians Assn., La. State U. Alumni Assn. (pres. East Baton Rouge Parish chpt. 1978-80), Popular Culture Assn., Investigative Reporters and Editors Assn., Baker C. of C., Toasmasters (adminstrv. v.p. Baton Rouge 1977), Pilot Club. Home: 2801 Allen Ct Baker LA 70714-2253

ROBERTS, ALIDA JAYNE, elementary school educator; b. Bristol, Conn., Aug. 11, 1967; d. James and Barbara Mae (Carlson) R. BA in Elem. Edn., Anna Maria Coll., Paxton, Mass., 1990; MS in Reading and Lang. Arts, Calif. State U., Fullerton, 1992. Cert. tchr., Conn., Mass., Calif. Elem. tchr. Rowland Unified Sch. Dist., Rowland Heights, Calif., 1990-94, Edgewood Elem. Sch., Bristol, Conn., 1994-95, Clara T. O'Connell Elem. Sch., Bristol, Conn., 1995—; tchr. Gifted and Talented Edn. After Sch. Program, West Covina, Calif., 1993-94, Chpt. 1 After Sch. Program, West Covina, 1993-94; intramural coach After Sch. Program Edgewood Elem. Sch., Bristol, Conn., 1994-95. Tchr. advisor PTA, La Puente, 1992-92, Clara T. O'Connell PTA, 1995-96. Scholar Bristol Fedn. Tchrs., 1986; grantee Anna Maria Coll., 1986-90. Mem. NEA, ASCD, Internat. Reading Assn., Calif. Reading Assn., Calif. Tchrs. Assn., Orange County Reading Assn., Bristol Fedn. Tchrs. Home: 291 Morris Ave Bristol CT 06010-4418

ROBERTS, ANITA MCEWEN, legislative aide, political organization worker; b. Bangor, Maine, June 11, 1962; d. Warren Martin and Mary Ellen (Keane) McEwen; m. Lawrence Roberts, May 29, 1993; 1 child, Thomas McEwen. BA in Psychology, U. Mass., 1987, BA in Comm., 1987. Publicist Lisa Ekus Pub. Rels., Hatfield, Mass., 1988-90; antique dealer Justine Mehlman Antiques, Washington, 1990-91; congrl. liaison/adminstrv. asst. Coastal States Orgn., Washington, 1991-93; nat. fundraiser Robb for U.S. Senate Com., McLean, Va., 1993-94; legis. asst. (to Del. Bob Hull) Va. Ho. of Dels., Richmond, 1995; legis. asst. (to Senator Janet Howell) Va. State Senate, Richmond, 1995—; commr. Arlington County, Va. Commn. on the Status of Women, 1994—; sec., asst. campaign mgr. Citizens for Janet Howell Campaign Com., Reston, Va., 1995; vice chair for fin., Arlington County Dem. Com., 1994-96; fundraiser Clinton-Gore Victory '92, 1992. Recipient Vol. Recognition award, The 52d Presdl. Inaugural Com., Washington, 1993. Mem. Nat. Women's Polit. Caucus, Nat. Women's Party, Nat. Abortion and Reproductive Rights Action League, Nat. Assn. Univ. Women, Dem. Party of Va., Arlington County Dem. Com. (Fundraiser of Yr. 1993). Democratic. Home: 2513 North Sycamore St Arlington VA 22207 Office: Office of Senator J Howell PO Box 2608 Reston VA 22090

ROBERTS, ANNA RUTH, financial consultant; b. Sweetwater, Tex., Apr. 10, 1942; d. Charles Heddington and Ethel Dorothy (Harris) Elliott; m. David Ira Roberts, Apr. 10, 1960; children: Craig Spencer, Edward Aaron. BA in Edn., Ariz. State U., 1976. CFP. Acct. Miller-Wagner & Co. Ltd., Phoenix, 1982-87; asst. v.p., sr. fin. cons. Merrill Lynch, Sun City, Ariz., 1987—; organizer, presenter seminars Pres.'s Club. Recipient Dist. Merit award Boy Scouts Am., Flagstaff, Ariz., 1975. Mem. Am. Bus. Women Assn., B'nai B'rith Women (Edith K. Baum chpt., Woman of Yr. 1976), Kiwanis (Disting. Svc. award 1991). Home: 6090 W Lone Cactus Dr Glendale AZ 85308-6280 Office: Merrill Lynch 9744 W Bell Rd Sun City AZ 85351-1343

ROBERTS, ANNE FINDLAY, humanities educator; b. San Diego, July 20, 1937; d. Francis McRae and Lois (Hopkins) Findlay; m. Warren Errol Roberts, June 22, 1957; children: Erin, James, Thomas, Peter. Degree in English Lit., U. Albany, 1966, degree in Libr. Sci., 1967, MA in Am. Lit., 1975, DA in Children's Lit., 1982. Cert. libr., N.Y. Libr. U. Albany, N.Y., 1967-89, lectr. reading dept., 1989—; adj. prof. Skidmore Coll., Saratoga, N.Y., 1995—. Author: Library Instruction for Librarians, 1982, Public Relations for Librarians, 1986, Experiencing Albany, 1986, Historic Albany's Churches and Synagogues, 1986. pres. PTA, Sch. 18, Albany, 1966-68; active Girl Scouts U.S. and Boy Scouts Am., Albany, 1968-70, ARC, Albany, 1970-80; elder First Presbyn. Ch., Albany, 1989—. Home: 13 Norwood St Albany NY 12203-3410

ROBERTS, BETTY JO, retired librarian, speech therapist; b. Ft. Worth, Tex., Nov. 11, 1927; d. Harry Pulliam and Mamie Josephine (Parker) Easton; m. Robert Lester Roberts, Jr.; children: Jo Lu, Lee Ann. Student, Tex. State Coll. Women, Denton, 1945-47, Tex. Wesleyan Coll.; BS, SW Tex. State U., 1952. Tchr. Milton H. Barry Sch. for Physical Rehab., Houston, United Cerebral Palsy Ctr., Ft. Worth, Tex., San Marcos Pub. Schs., Tex., 1952-53; supr. practice tchrs. S.W. Tex. State, 1952-53; tchr. Waco (Tex.) Ind. Schs., 1953-54; speech therapist Providence Crippled Children's Hosp., Waco; tchr. phonics, creative art Latin Am. Ctr., Waco, 1961-69; ch. librarian Trinity United Methodist Ch., Waco, 1979-88; ch. lib. Cen. United Methodist Ch., Waco, Tex., 1988-91. Compilor, Editor: Swedishes and More 1984. Democrat. Methodist. Home: 3248 Village Park Dr Waco TX 76708-1582

ROBERTS, CAROL STRUBE, educational consultant; b. Albany, N.Y., Mar. 28, 1939; d. Charles Edward and Ruth Jeanette (Barends) Strube; m. Rodman P. Roberts, Sept. 6, 1957; children: Karen Ruth Roberts Watson, Kenneth William, Rodman Scott. BS in Elem. Edn. and Sci., U. Md., 1972; AAS in Chem. Tech., Corning (N.Y.) C.C., 1981; MS in Environ. Sci., SUNY, Syracuse, 1985; MS in Instrnl. Design and Devel., Syracuse U., 1986. Cert. in ednl. adminstrn., N.Y. Dental asst. Schenectady, N.Y., 1957-58; underwriting dept. Mass. Mut. Ins. Co., Springfield, 1958-59; elem. tchr., sch. sci. coord. Frederick County Schs., Urbana/Frederick, Md., 1972-77; dir. in-sch. suspension program East H.S., Corning, 1978; math. tchr. spl. needs grades 7 and 8 Haverling Ctrl. Sch., Bath, N.Y., 1979-81; prin. Deposit (N.Y.) Ctrl. Sch. Dist., 1988-89; asst. to prin. Addison (N.Y.) Ctrl. Sch. Dist., 1988; owner edn./tng. cons. bus. Ed Tech Cons. Svc., Corning, 1990—; curriculum and program devel.-tng. Corning, Inc., 1990-93; steering com. Global Alliance for Transforming Edn., Grafton, Vt.; diversity trainer Corning-Painted Post Sch. Dist., 1994—. Contbr. articles to profl. jours.; photographer. Bd. dirs. Spencer Crest Nature Ctr., Corning, 1980-88; mem. steering com. YMCA Challenge Cup, 1989-91; vol. Meals on Wheels, Corning, 1992—; mem. Outreach com. First United Meth. Ch., Corning, 1991—; mem./supporter Adirondack Mus., Blue Mountain Lake, N.Y., 1991—, Watson Homestead, Corning, 1994—. Recipient grants and scholarships. Mem. ASCD, ASTD, Children and Adults with Attention Deficit Disorder, Support Group Celiac Disease. Home and Office: Box 43A Spencer Hill Rd Corning NY 14830

ROBERTS, CAROLE K., school system administrator; b. Plainfield, N.J., Jan. 28, 1947; d. Homer Clyde and Frances (Colquhoun) Korner; m. Thomas Edwards Roberts, May 26, 1972; children: Douglas Edwards, David Korner. BA in English, Cedar Crest Coll., 1968; MEd, Pa. State U., 1970; EdD with distinction, Temple U., 1993. Cert. elem. tchr., reading specialist, reading supr., elem. prin., Pa. 1st grade tchr. Wilson Sch. Dist., West Lawn, Pa., 1968-76, ESL tchr., 1984-88, reading specialist secondary, 1989-94; reading specialist Gov. Mifflin Sch. Dist., Shillington, Pa., 1988-89; dir. reading and lang. arts Antietam Sch. Dist., Reading, Pa., 1994—; exec. bd. Berks County project 2000 Berks County Intermediate Unit & County Bus. Coalition, Reading, 1995—; del. for lang. arts and literacy to China and Soviet Union, Citizen Amb. Program, 1993-95. Recipient Running Start award Chrysler Corp., 1995-96. Mem. Internat. Reading Assn., Tri County Reading Assn. (v.p. 1995-96, pres.-elect 1996—), Keystone State Reading Assn. (bd. dirs. 1996—), Phi Delta Kappa. Republican. Home: 7 Boardwalk Sinking Spring PA 19608 Office: Antietam Sch Dist 2310 Cumberland Ave Reading PA 19606

ROBERTS, CASSANDRA FENDLEY, investment company executive; b. Port St. Joe, Fla., Sept. 24, 1951; d. Pope and Sophie Virginia (McGee) Fendley; m. Charles Stanton Roberts, Aug. 7, 1971; 1 child, Davis McGee. BSBA, Edison State Coll., 1983. Sales assoc., v.p. Cooper Corp., Atlanta, 1979-85; sales assoc., broker WTM Investments, Atlanta, 1985-92, v.p., 1992—. Mem. Nat. Bd. Realtors, Ga. Bd. Realtors, Atlanta Bd. Realtors. Office: WTM Investments Inc PO Box 13256 Atlanta GA 30324-0256

ROBERTS, CELIA ANN, librarian; b. Bangor, Maine, Feb. 6, 1935; d. William Lewis and Ruey Pearl (Logan) R.; AA, U. Hartford, 1957, BA, 1961; postgrad. So. Conn. State Coll., 1963—. With catalog, acquistion and circulation depts. U. Hartford Library, 1956-65; librarian Simsbury (Conn.) Free Library, 1965; reference librarian Simsbury Public Library, 1969—. Tchr. ballet classes, 1965-66; ballet mistress Ballet Soc. Conn., Inc., 1968-70; with corps de ballet Conn. Opera Assn., 1963-64; active in prodns. Simsbury Light Opera Assn., 1964, 69; instr. in geneaology field. Contbr. articles to profl. jours. Vol. Family History Ctr., 1970—. Mem. ALA, Conn. Library Assn., Simsbury Hist. Soc., Ont. Geneal. Soc., New Eng. Historic and Geneal. Soc., AAUW (past pres. Greater Hartford br.), Pro Dance, DAR (Abigail Phelps chpt.), Conn. Soc. Genealogists (registrar Hartford 1983), Soc. Mayflower Descs. Conn., Dance Masters Am. Universalist. Office: 725 Hopmeadow St Simsbury CT 06070-2226

ROBERTS, CORINNE BOGGS (COKIE ROBERTS), correspondent, news analyst; b. New Orleans, Dec. 27, 1943; d. Thomas Hale and Corinne Morrison (Claiborne) Boggs; m. Steven V. Roberts, Sept. 10, 1966; children: Lee Harriss, Rebecca Boggs. BA in Polit. Sci., Wellesley Coll., 1964; hon. degrees, Amherst Coll., Columbia Coll., Loyola U. of the South, Manhattanville Coll., Gonzaga U., Boston Coll., Hood Coll., Chestnut Hill Coll. Assoc. prodr., host Altman Prodns., Washington, 1964-66; prodr. Altman Prodns., L.A., 1969-72; reporter, editor Cowles Communications, N.Y.C., 1967; prodr. Sta. WNEW-TV, N.Y.C., 1968, Sta. KNBC-TV, L.A., Greece, 1972-74; reporter CBS News, Athens, Greece, 1974-77; corr. Nat. Pub. Radio, Washington, 1977—, MacNeil/Lehrer Newshour, Washington, 1984-88; spl. Washington corr. ABC News, Washington, 1988—; interviewer, commentator This Week With David Brinkley, Washington, 1992—; lectr. in field. Co-host weekly pub. TV program on Congress, The Lawmakers, 1981-84; producer, host pub. affairs program Sta. WRC-TV, Washington; producer Sta. KNBC-TV Serendipity, L.A. (award for excellence in local programming, Emmy nomination for children's programming); contbr. articles to newspapers, mags. Bd. dirs. Dirksen Ctr., Pekin, Ill., 1988-95, Everett Dirksen awrd, 1987; bd. dirs. Fgn. Students Svc. Ctr., Washington, 1990—, Manhattanville Coll., Purchase, N.Y., 1991—, Children's Inn at NIH, Bethesda, Md., 1992—. Recipient Broadcast award Nat. Orgn. Working Women, 1984, Everett McKinley Dirksen disting. reporting of Congress, 1987, Weintal award Georgetown U., 1988, Corp. Pub. Broadcasting award, 1988, Edward R. Murrow award Corp. Pub. Broadcasting, 1990, Broadcast award Nat. Women's Polit. Caucus, 1990, David Brinkley Comm. award, 1992, Mother of Yr. award Nat. Mothers' Day Com., 1992, Emmy award news and documentary, 1992. Mem. Radio-TV Corrs. Assn. (pres. 1981-82, bd. dirs. 1980-94), U.S. Capitol Hist. Soc. Roman Catholic. Office: ABC News 1717 Desales St NW Washington DC 20036-4401 Office: Nat Pub Radio 635 Massachusetts Ave NW Washington DC 20001

ROBERTS, DORIS, actress; b. St. Louis, Nov. 4, 1930; d. Larry and Ann (Meltzer) R.; m. William Goyen, Nov. 10, 1963 (dec.); m. Michael E. Cannata, June 21, 1950; 1 child, Michael R. Student, NYU, 1950-51; studies with, Sanford Meisner, Neighborhood Playhouse, N.Y.C., 1952-53, Lee Strasberg, Actors' Studio, N.Y.C., 1956. Ind. stage, screen and TV actress, 1953—. Profl. stage debut, Ann Arbor, Mich., 1953; appeared in summer stock Chatham, Mass., 1955; Broadway debut in The Time of Your Life, 1955; other Broadway and off-Broadway appearances include The Desk Set, 1955, The American Dream, 1961, The Death of Bessie Smith, 1961, The Office, 1965, The Color of Darkness, 1963, Marathon 33, 1963, Secret Affair of Mildred Wilde, 1972, Last of the Red Hot Lovers, 1969-71, Bad Habits, 1973 (Outer Circle Critics award 1974), Cheaters, 1976, Fairie Tale Theatre, 1985, The Fig Tree, 1987, It's Only a Play, 1992; movie debut Something Wild, 1961, movies include Barefoot in the Park, 1968, No Way to Treat a Lady, 1973, A Lovely Way to Die, 1969, Honeymoon Killers, 1969, A New Leaf, 1970, Such Good Friends, 1971, Little Murders, 1971, Heartbreak Kid, 1972, Hester Street, 1975, The Taking of Pelham, One, Two, Three, 1974, The Rose, 1979, Good Luck, Miss Wyckoff, 1979, Rabbit Test, 1979, Ordinary Hero, 1986, #1 with a Bullet, 1987, For Better or for Worse-Street Law, 1988, National Lampoon's Xmas Vacation, 1989, Used People, 1992, The Night We Never Met, Momma Mia, 1994, Walking to Waldheim, 1995, The Grass Harp, 1995; TV debut on Studio One, 1958, Mary Hartman, Mary Hartman, 1975, Mary Tyler Moore Hour, 1976, Soap, 1978-79, Angie, 1979-80, Remington Steele, 1984-88, Lily Tomlin Comedy Hour, Barney Miller, Alice, Full House, Perfect Strangers, Sunday Dinner, A Family Man, The Fig Tree (Pub. Broadcasting System), 1987, (TV films) The Story Teller, 1979, Ruby and Oswald, 1978, It Happened One Christmas, 1978, Jennifer: A Woman's Story, 1979, The Diary of Anne Frank, 1982, A Letter to Three Wives, Blind Faith, 1989, The Sunset Gang, 1990, Crossroads, 1993, Dream On, 1993, The Boys, 1993, A Time To Heal, 1994, Murder She Wrote, Step By Step, Burk's Law Walker, Texas Ranger, 1994, Amazing Grace, 1995, High Society, 1996, Everybody Loves Raymond, 1996. Recipient Emmy award Nat. Acad. TV Arts and Scis., 1984, 85, Emmy nominations, 1986, 88, 91. Mem. Screen Actors Guild, AFTRA, Actors Equity Assn., Dirs. Guild Am.

ROBERTS, DORIS EMMA, epidemiologist, consultant; b. Toledo, Dec. 28, 1915; d. Frederic Constable and Emma Selina (Reader) R. Diploma, Peter Bent Brigham Sch. Nursing, Boston, 1938; BS, Geneva Coll., Beaver Falls, Pa., 1944; MPH, U. Minn., 1958; PhD, U. N.C., 1967. RN, Mass. Staff nurse Vis. Nurse Assn., New Haven, 1938-40; sr. nurse Neighborhood House, Millburn, N.J., 1942-45; supr. Tb Baltimore County Dept. Health, Towson, Md., 1945-46; Tb cons. Md. State Dept. Health, Balt., 1946-50; cons., chief nurse Tb program USPHS, Washington, 1950-57; cons. divsn. nursing USPHS, 1958-63; chief nursing practice br. Health Resources Adminstrn., HEW, Bethesda, Md., 1966-75; adj. prof. U. N.C. Sch. Pub. Health, 1975-92; cons. WHO, 1961-82. Contbr. articles to profl. jours. With USPHS, 1945-75. Recipient Disting. Alumna award Geneva Coll., 1971, Disting. Svc. award USPHS, 1971, Outstanding Achievement award U. Minn., 1983. Fellow APHA (v.p. 1978-79, Disting. Svc. award Pub. Health Nursing sect. 1975, Sedgwick Meml. medal 1979), Am. Acad. Nursing (hon. fellow); mem. Inst. Medicine of NAS, Common Cause, LWV, Delta Omega. Democrat. Episcopalian. Home: Apt 1112 9707 Old Georgetown Rd Bethesda MD 20814-1727

ROBERTS, ELLEN, social worker; b. Pitts., Jan. 19, 1947; d. Irving Roberts and Phyllis (Silver) Roberts Garnett; m. Theodore Hughes Wilson, Aug. 20, 1966 (dec. July 1989); 1 child, Amanda Michelle. AB with honors, U. Ill., Urbana, 1967, MSW, 1991; student, Catherine Spalding Coll., Louisville, 1968-70. Registered counselor, Wash.; lic. social worker, Ill. Asst. editor, reporter Jefferson Reporter, Louisville, 1967; tchr. Jefferson County Schs., Louisville, 1969-70; case mgr., social worker C-U Health Dist., Champaign, Ill., 1991-93; social worker S.W. Wash. Health Dist., Vancouver, 1993—. Soprano 1 sect. leader Aurora Chorus, Portland, Oreg., 1994, 95; vol. S.W. Wash. Fairness Coalition, Vancouver, 1993-95. Edmund J. James scholar, 1966-67. Mem. NASW, Women in Action, Alpha Deta Mu (cert. scholastic and profl. commitment 1990). Democrat. Jewish. Home: 2001 SE Blairmont Dr Vancouver WA 98683 Office: SW Washington Health Dist 2000 Fort Vancouver Way Vancouver WA 98663

ROBERTS, GERRY REA, elementary school educator, organist; b. Brady, Tex., Nov. 13, 1940; d. Willie Melvin and Mary Catherine (Brown) Howard; m. Leslie Wayne Templeton, July 28, 1961 (div. Feb. 1977); children: Todd Wayne, Gwen Marie; m. Harold James Roberts Jr., Sept. 24, 1977. Student, Sam Houston State U., 1959-60; MusB, U. Houston, 1962, postgrad., 1964-65; grad., North Tex. State U., 1966, Stephen F. Austin U., 1983; postgrad., East Tex. State U., 1984, Memphis State U., 1984-85, Las Vegas U., 1985. Cert. music tchr., 1-12, Tex., elem. tchr., 1-6, Tex., cert. music tchr., elem.-sec. (K-12), elem. edn. (K-8), Okla.; cert. Orff-Schulwerk levels I, II, III. Music tchr. Deer Park (Tex.) Ind. Sch. Dist., 1962-63, Dallas Ind. Sch. Dist., 1963, Richardson (Tex.) Ind. Sch. Dist., 1964-68; kindergarten tchr. Houston Ind. Sch. Dist., 1971, tchr. 1st grade, 1974-78; tchr. music Klein (Tex.) Ind. Sch. Dist., 1978-90; music tchr. grades 1-6 Choctaw (Okla.)-Nicoma Park Sch. Dist., Okla., 1993—. Pianist, mus. dir. 1960 Playhouse, 1979; pianist prodns. Klein Forest H.S., 1984-86, Klein H.S., 1987-90; singer Houston Symphony Chorale, 1960-62, Richardson Choral Club, 1963-64, Jeffrey Ross Chorale, 1988-89, Tomball (Tex.) Comty. Ch., 1988-90, Oklahoma City Met. Chorus, 1994—, Okla. Master Chorale, 1996—. Organist St. Paul's Ch., Houston, 1975-77, Lakewood United Methodist Ch., Tex., 1978-80, Windwood Presbyn. Ch., Cypress, Tex., 1981-90; Music dir. 1st United Meth. Ch., Choctaw, 1990-93; handbell dir., organist St. Matthews United Meth. Ch., 1994—. Recipient Tex. Pianist 2nd Pl. award Tex. Music Tchrs. Assn, 1959; Jesse Jones Foundation scholar, 1959, Houston 1st Pl. award-piano Houston Music Tchrs. Assn., 1959; Sam Houston State U. scholar, 1959, U. Houston scholar, 1960. Mem. NEA, Okla. Educators Assn., Music Educators Nat. Conf., Nat. Music Tchrs. Assn., Am. Guild Organists, Am. Guild of English Handbell Ringers, Inc., The Choristers Guild, Tex. Music Educators Assn., Tex. Tchrs. Assn., Klein Educators Assn., Okla. Music Tchrs. Assn., Okla. Kodály Educators, Kodály Educator Am., Am. choral Dirs.' Assn., Okla. Choral Dirs.' Assn., Okla. Orff-Schulwerk Assn., Am. Orff-Schulwerk Assn. (cert. levels I-III), Gulf Coast Orff-Schulwerk Assn., Sigma Alpha Iota (v.p. Houston alumni chpt. 1971-72, Sword of Honor 1972). Republican. Home and Office: RR 1 Box 799 Harrah OK 73045-7498

ROBERTS, GINNY BARKLEY, middle school language arts educator; b. Gainesville, Tex., Sept. 15, 1945; d. Edward Phillip and Myra Ruth (Durham) B.; m. Dennis LeRoy Roberts, Dec. 8, 1967 (div. May 1989); children: Danny Roberts, Ward Roberts, Seth Roberts. BA, U. North Tex., 1967, MEd, 1993. Cert. tchr., Tex.; cert. all level reading specialist. Traffic dir., newswriter Sta. KVET Radio, Austin, 1967-68; traffic/continuity dir. Sta. KOKE Radio, Austin, 1968-69, Sta. WINQ Radio, Tampa, 1969-71; title I reading aide Hedrick Middle Sch., Lewisville, Tex., 1986-89; radio-TV tchr. Griffin Middle Sch., The Colony, Tex., 1993-94, speech and drama tchr., 1993-94, 6th and 7th reading improvement tchr., 1993-94, 6th grade lang. arts tchr., 1989-94, 7th grade lang. arts tchr., 1994—; reading dept. chairperson Griffin Middle Sch., 1992—, mem. supt. adv. com., 1994—. Pres. Lewisville H.S. Cross Country/Track Booster Club, 1986-87, bd. dirs. 1986-90; charter mem. Lewisville H.S. Choir Booster Club, 1989-95; mem. Lewisville Football Booster Club, 1993-95. Mem. Internat. Reading Assn., Phi Kappa Phi. Baptist. Home: 5212 Gates Dr The Colony TX 75056 Office: Griffin Middle Sch 5105 N Colony Blvd The Colony TX 75056-1219

ROBERTS, JEANNE ADDISON, literature educator; b. Washington; d. John West and Sue Fisher (Nichols) Addison; m. Markley Roberts, Feb. 19, 1966; children: Addison Cary Steed Masengill, Ellen Carraway Masengill Coster. A.B., Agnes Scott Coll., 1946; M.A., U. Pa., 1947; Ph.D., U. Va., 1964. Instr. Mary Washington Coll., 1947-48; instr., chmn. English Fairfax Hall Jr. Coll., 1950-51; tchr. Am. U. Assn. Lang. Center, Bangkok, Thailand, 1952-56; instr. Beirut (Lebanon) Coll. for Women, 1956-57, asst. prof., 1957-60, chmn. English dept., 1957-60; instr. lit. Am. U., Washington, 1960-62; asst. prof. Am. U., 1962-65, asso. prof., 1965-68, prof., 1968-93; dean faculties Am. U., 1974; lectr. Howard U., 1971-72; seminar prof. Folger Shakespeare Libr. Inst. for Renaissance and 18th Century Studies, 1974; dir. NEH Summer Inst. for High Sch. Tchrs. on Teaching Shakespeare, Folger Shakespeare Libr., 1984, 85, 86; dir. NEH summer inst. Va. Commonwealth U. 1995, 96 Writings By and About Women in The English Renaissance. Author: Shakespeare's English Comedy: The Merry Wives of Windsor in Context, 1979, The Shakespearean Wild: Geography, Genus and Gender, 1991; editor: (with James G. McManaway) A Selective Bibliography of Shakespeare: Editions, Textual Studies, Commentary, 1975; (with Peggy O'Brien) Shakespeare Set Free, vol. 1, 1993, vol. 2, 1994, vol. 3, 1995; contbr. articles to scholarly jours. Danforth Tchr. grantee, 1962-63; Folger Sr. fellow, 1969-70, 88. Mem. MLA (chmn. Shakespeare div. 1981-82), Renaissance Soc. Am., Milton Soc., Shakespeare Assn. Am. (trustee 1978-81, 87-89, pres. 1986-87), AAUP (pres. Am. U. chpt. 1966-67), Southeastern Renaissance Conf. (pres. 1981-82), Phi Beta Kappa, Mortar Board, Phi Kappa Phi. Episcopalian. Home: 4931 Albemarle St NW Washington DC 20016-4359 Office: Am U Dept Lit Washington DC 20016

ROBERTS, JO ANN WOODEN, school system administrator; b. Chgo., June 24, 1948; d. Tilmon and Annie Mae (Wardlaw) Wooden; m. Edward Allen Roberts Sr. (div.); children: Edward Allen Jr., Hillary Ann. BS, Wayne State U., 1970, MS, 1971; PhD, Northwestern U., 1977. Speech, lang. pathologist Chgo. Bd. Edn., 1971-78, adminstr., 1978-88; dir. spl. svcs. Rock Island (Ill.) Pub. Schs., 1988-90; supt. Muskegon Hts. (Mich.) Pub. Schs., 1990-93; deputy supr. Chgo. Pub. Schs., 1993-96; supt. of schs. Hazel Crest (Ill.) Sch. Dist. #152 1/2, 1996—; instr. Chgo City Community Coll., 1976-77; project dir. Ednl. Testing Svc., Evanston, Ill., 1976-77; exec. dir. Nat. Speech, Lang. and Hearing Assn., Chgo., 1984-86; hon. guest lectr. Govs. State U., University Park, Ill., 1983-86; cons. in field. Author: Learning to Talk, 1974. Trustee Muskegon County Libr. Bd., 1990, Mercy Hosp. Bd., Muskegon, 1990, St. Mark's Sch. Bd. Dirs., Southborough, Mass., 1989, United Way Bd., Muskegon, 1990; mem. Mich. State Bd. Edn. Systematic Initiative in Math and Sci., 1991, Gov. John Engler Mich. 2000 Task Force, 1991, Chpt. II Adv. Commn., 1991. Recipient Leadership award Boy Scouts Am., 1990; named finalist Outstanding Young Working Women, Glamour Mag., 1984, Outstanding Educator, Blacks in Govt., 1990. Mem. Am. Assn. Sch. Adminstrs., Nat. Alliance Black Sch. Educators, Mich. Assn. Sch. Adminstrs., Assn. Supervision & Curriculum Devel., Phi Delta Kappa. Office: Hazel Crest Pub Schs Dist 15205 Hazel Crest IL 60429

ROBERTS, JOAN WARTHLING, English language educator; b. Buffalo, Mar. 4, 1930; d. Cyril Gerard and Edith Irene (Patterson) W.; m. Edward McCreery, May 8, 1954; children: Christopher, Elizabeth, Cecily, Julia, Margaret, Anne. AB, Nazareth Coll., 1951; MA, U. Cin., 1969, PhD, 1975. Instr. English U. Cin., 1969-73; dir. acad. remediation Mercy Coll., Dobbs Ferry, N.Y., 1974-76; adj. asst. prof. Manhattanville Coll., Purchase, N.Y., 1976-77; prof. English SUNY Coll. at Buffalo, 1978—. Author, editor: Sicily and Naples, 1984; author: (with others) Great Women Mystery Writers, 1994, Feminism in Women's Detective Fiction, 1995, Oxford Companion to Mystery/Detective Fiction, 1996. Recipient fellowship Danforth Found., 1967-75. Mem. MLA, Coll. English Assn. Home: 750 Mckinley Pky Buffalo NY 14220-1526 Office: SUNY Coll at Buffalo 1300 Elmwood Ave Buffalo NY 14222-1004

ROBERTS, JUDITH MARIE, librarian, educator; b. Bluefield, W.Va., Aug. 5, 1939; d. Charles Bowen Lowder and Frances Marie (Bourne) Lowder Alberts; m. Craig Currence Jackson, July 1, 1957 (div. 1962); 1 child, Craig, Jr.; m. Milton Rinehart Roberts, Aug. 13, 1966 (div. 1987). BS, Concord State Tchrs. Coll., 1965. Libr., Cape Henlopen Sch. Dist., Lewes, Del., 1965-91; with Lily's Gift Shop, St. Petersburg, Fla., 1991—. Pres. Friends of Lewes Pub. Libr., 1986-90; chmn. exhibits Govs. Conf. Librs. and Info. Svcs., Dover, Del., 1978; mem. Gov.'s State Library Adv. Coun., 1987-91. Mem. ALA, NEA, Del. State Edn. Assn., Sussex Help Orgn. for Resources Exchange (pres. 1984-85), Del. Library Assn. (pres. 1982-83), Del. Learning Resources Assn. (pres. 1976-77). Methodist.

ROBERTS, JUDITH VIRGINIA, social worker; b. Phoenix, Mar. 31, 1940; d. George Merle and Edith Virginia (Sevitz) Nycum; m. Kenneth Richard Dragoo, Dec. 28, 1958 (div. 1976); children: Kathryn Virginia Dragoo Lewis, Charles Allen, Kenson Michael; m. Ronald William Roberts, July 12, 1979; stepchildren: Shane Kugler, Noelle Brooke. AA, Mid Plains Community Coll., 1983; BSW, Kearney State Coll., 1986; MSW, U. N.D., Omaha, 1993. Cert. social worker, Nebr. Bookkeeping, payroll clk. Dragon Enterprise, North Platte, Nebr., 1972-76, City of North Platte, 1976-83; social worker Nebr. Dept. Social Svcs., North Platte, 1987-91, Ctrl. Plains Home Health & Hospice, Corad, Nebr., 1995—. Bassist, Omaha Symphony Orch., 1965-72, Lincoln (Nebr.) Symphony Orch., 1965-72; Lincoln County Republican del., North Platte, 1988. Mem. Nat. Assn. Social Workers, Nebr. Assn. Social Workers, Nebr. Cattlewomen (publicity chair 1980-88). Office: Ctrl Plains Home Health & Hospice 300 E 12th Cozad NE 69130

ROBERTS, JULIA FIONA, actress; b. Smyrna, Ga., Oct. 28, 1967; d. Betty and Walter Motes; m. Lyle Lovett, Jun. 27, 1993 (div. 1995). Film appearances include Blood Red, 1986, Satisfaction, 1987, Mystic Pizza, 1988, Steel Magnolias, 1989 (Acad. Award nominee, Golden Globe award), Pretty Woman,1990 (Acad. Award nominee, Golden Globe Award), Flatliners, 1990, Sleeping With the Enemy, 1991, Hook, 1991, Dying Young, 1991, The Player, 1992, The Pelican Brief, 1993, I Love Trouble, 1994, Ready to Wear (Prêt-à-Porter), 1994, Mary Reilly, 1996, Everybody Says I Love You, 1996; TV movies include Baja Oklahoma, 1988. Named Female Star of the Yr., Nat. Assn. Theatre Owners, 1991. *

ROBERTS, KATHLEEN ANNE, lawyer; b. L.A., Oct. 2, 1945. BA in English summa cum laude, U. Mass., Boston, 1971; PhD program in English Lit., Yale U., 1971-72, JD, 1977. Bar: N.Y. 1979, U.S. Dist. Ct. (so. and ea. dists.) N.Y. 1979, U.S. Ct. Appeals (2d cir.). Rsch. dir. Conn. Citizen Rsch. Group, 1972-73; investigator, monitor, evaluator grants, cons. Fund for City of N.Y., 1973-77; law clk. U.S. Dist. Ct. (so. dist.) N.Y., 1977-79; asst. U.S. atty. criminal div. So. Dist. N.Y., N.Y.C., 1979-83, asst. U.S. atty. civil div., 1983-85, U.S. magistrate, 1985-95; ADR neutral and dir. profl. svcs. JAMS/Endispute, N.Y.C., 1995—; law clk. San Francisco Neighborhood Legal Assistance Found., summer 1975, U.S. Attys. Office, So. Dist. N.Y., criminal div., summer 1976; adj. prof. law, trial advocacy inst. Bklyn. Law Sch., 1983—. Office: JAMS/Endispute 345 Park Ave New York NY 10154

ROBERTS, LAURA WILSON, secondary school educator; b. Mobile, Ala., Sept. 16, 1958; d. Douglas M.G. and Perilla A. Wilson; m. Mark H. Roberts; 1 child, Krisanna. BA, U. Dallas, 1980. Cert. art tchr. Drama dir. UMS-Wright Prep Sch., Mobile. Recipient Outstanding Educator award Mobile Area C. of C., 1988, Outstanding Drama Tchr. award Ala. Conf. Theatre & Speech, 1995. Mem. Nat. Art Edn. Assn., Edn. Theatre Assn. Office: UMS-Wright Prep Sch 65 N Mobile St Mobile AL 36607

ROBERTS, LAUREL LEE, lawyer; b. Lowell, Mass., Oct. 31, 1944; d. Angus Henry and Lorraine (Thompson) R. BA in History and Sociology, U. Calif., Santa Barbara, 1966, MA in Counseling, 1969, BA in Film Studies, 1973; PhD, U. So. Calif., 1976; JD, U. West L.A., 1982. Bar: Calif. 1984, U.S. Ct. Appeals 1985, U.S. Dist. Ct. (ctrl. dist.) Calif. 1985, U.S. Ct. Appeals (9th cir.) 1985; cert. secondary educator, Calif.; credential in pupil personnel svcs., Calif. Dormitory head resident U. Calif., Santa Barbara, 1964-69; counselor Foothill Elem. Sch., Goleta, Calif., 1968; univ. counselor U. Calif., Santa Barbara, 1969-73; adj. lectr. Grad. Sch. of Edn. U. So. Calif., L.A., 1975; asst. dean academic affairs Office of the Chancellor Calif. State U., Long Beach, 1976-86; atty. Law Office of Laurel Roberts, Hermosa Beach, Calif., 1984—; cons. U. So. Calif./Ind. U. Consortium on Instrnl. Devel., L.A., 1975, Nat. Commn. on Indsl. Innovation, Pasadena, Calif., 1986; lectr. Assn. for Devel. of Computer-based Instructional Systems, 1978. Author: (slide-tape presentation) CSU Educational Policy, 1980. Home legal svc. for elderly and infirmed, 1984—; participant Lt. Gov. Mike Curb's USA-Mexico Exch. Program, Fullerton, Calif., 1984; legal aid vol. U. West L.A., Culver City, 180-84; mem. Supt. of Pub. Instrn. Assessment Adv. Com., Sacramento, 1985. Recipient Am. Jurisprudence award Lawyers Coop. Pub. Co., 1982. Mem. Irish-Am. Bar Assn., Women Lawyers Assn. of L.A., L.A. County Bar Assn., Fed. Bar Assn. Republican. Roman Catholic. Office: 239 Pier Ave PO Box 594 Hermosa Beach CA 90254

ROBERTS, LYNNE JEANINE, physician; b. St. Louis, Apr. 19, 1952; d. H. Clarke and Dorothy June (Cockrum) R.; m. Richard Allen Beadle Jr., July 18, 1981; children: Richard Andrew, Erica Roberts. BA with distinction, Ind. U., 1974, MD, 1978. Diplomate Am. Bd. Dermatology, Am. Bd. Pediatrics, Am. Bd. Laser Surgery. Intern in pediats. Children's Med. Ctr., Dallas, 1978-79, resident in pediats., 1979-80; resident in dermatology U. Tex. Southwestern Med. Ctr., Dallas, 1980-83, chief resident in dermatology, 1982-83, asst. instr. dermatology and pediatrics, 1983-84, asst. prof., 1984-90, assoc. prof., 1990—; physician Cons. Dermatol. Specialists, Dallas, 1990-93; pres. Lynne J. Roberts, MD, PA, Dallas, 1993—; dir. dermatology Children's Med. Ctr., Dallas, 1986—; dermatology sect. chief Med. City Dallas Hosp., 1994-95, 95—. Contbr. articles to profl. jours., chpts. to books. Recipient Scholastic Achievement Citation Am. Med. Women's Assn., 1978. Fellow Am. Acad. Dermatology, Am. Acad. Pediatrics, Am. Soc. Laser Medicine and Surgery (bd. dirs. 1994—); mem. Soc. Pediatric Dermatology, Am. Soc. Dermatologic Surgery, Tex. Med. Assn., Dallas Zool. Soc., Dallas Arboretum, Kappa Alpha Theta, Alpha Omega Alpha. Office: 7777 Forest Ln Ste B314 Dallas TX 75230-2518

ROBERTS, MARGARET ANNE OTEY, lawyer; b. Cin., Apr. 5, 1961; d. Edward McCreery and Joan (Warthling) R. BA in History, Trinity Coll., Washington, 1983; cert. in Japanese lit. and lang., Sophia U., Tokyo, 1984; cert. in space studies, Internat. Space U., Kitakyushu, Japan, 1992; JD, Cath. U. Am., 1993. Bar: Va. 1993, D.C. 1995. Mem. faculty dept. English, Notre Dame Seishin U., Okayama, Japan, 1984-85; asst. to admissions dir. Beauvoir Elem. Sch., Washington, 1985-86; instr. English, field hand Maryknoll Vol. Program, Dzibalchen, Mex., 1986; dep. dir. legis. affairs Harris Group, Reston, Va., 1986-95; legal clk. Office Gen. Counsel, NASA Hdqs., Washington, 1993, atty.-advisor, 1995—; lectr. continuing edn. George Mason U., Centerville, Va., 1990, 91; bd. dirs. Internat. Small Satellite Orgn., Washington, 1993-94. Vol. Carter Reelection Com., Washington, 1979-80. Named One of 25 Stars of Space, Nat. Space Soc., 1994; scholar Trinity Coll.-Oxford U., 1980. Mem. Am. Astron. Soc. (edn. com. 1994-95), Internat. Inst. Space Law, Women in Aerospace (pres. 1989, bd. dirs. 1990-92, v.p. programs 1993), Nat. Space Club (rep. edn. com. 1989—, judge sci. fair 1990—, fellow 1992—). Home: 2501 N 20th Rd Apt 206 Arlington VA 22201 Office: NASA Hdqs Code GS 300 E St SW Washington DC 20546

ROBERTS, MARGARET HAROLD, editor, publisher; b. Aug. 18, 1928. A.B., U. Chattanooga, 1950. Editor, pub. series Award Winning Art, 1960-70, New Woman mag., Palm Beach, Fla., 1971-84; editor, pub. Going Bonkers mag., 1992—. Author: juvenile book series Daddy is a Doctor, 1965. Office: PO Box 189 Palm Beach FL 33480-0189

ROBERTS, MARGARET REYNOLDS, art educator; b. Nashville, Oct. 10, 1914; d. Elijah and Margaret (Sanders) Brugh; m. Morgan Boaz Reynolds, June 3, 1937 (dec. Mar. 1976); children: Margaret, Susanne, Morgan, Brugh, Liza, Elaine; m. William Clyde Roberts, Apr. 23, 1977. Student, Ward-Belmont Jr. Coll., Nashville, 1934; BA, Vanderbilt U., 1936; postgrad., William and Mary Coll., 1937-38, U. Wis. Tchr. decorating Watkins Inst., Nashville, 1965 70; tchr. Cheekwood, Nashville, 1973-74; tchr. period furniture Belle Meade Club, Nashville, 1994, 1994. One-woman exhibits include Vanderbilt U., 1986, 88, 94, Belmont U., 1989. Mem. Tenn. Art League, Le Petit Salon Literary Club (pres. 1979-80), Marsh Creek County Club, Centennial Club, Belle Meade Club, Kappa Alpha Theta. Roman Catholic. Home and Office: 5100 Boxcroft Pl Nashville TN 37205

ROBERTS, MARGOT MARKELS, business executive; b. Springfield, Mass., Jan. 20, 1945; d. Reuben and Marion (Markels) R.; children: Lauren B. Phillips, Debrah C. Herman. B.A., Boston U. Interior designer Louis Legum Furniture Co., Norfolk, Va., 1965-70; buyer, mgr. Danker Furniture, Rockville, Md., 1970-72; buyer W & J Sloane, Washington, 1972-74; pres. Bus. & Fin. Cons., Palm Beach, Fla., 1976-80, Margot M. Roberts & Assocs., Inc., Palm Beach, 1976—; dealer 20th century Am. art and wholesale antiques Margot M. Roberts, Inc., Palm Beach, 1989—; v.p., dir. So. Textile Svcs. Inc., Palm Beach. Pres. Brittany Condominium Assn., Palm Beach, 1983-87; v.p. South Palm Beach Civic Assn., 1983-88, South Palm Beach Pres.'s Assn., 1984-88; vice chmn. South Palm Beach Planning Bd., 1983-88, 90-91; elected town commr. Town South Palm Beach, Fla., 1991-92, elected vice mayor, 1992-93, elected mayor, 1993—; apptd. Commn. on Status of Women of Palm Beach County, 1992-95; voting mem. Palm Beach County Mcpl. League, 1992-95; vice chair Commn. Status of Women of Palm Beach County, 1994-95. Mem. Nat. Assn. Women in Bus., Palm Beach C. of C. Republican. Office: Town Hall South Palm Beach 3577 S Ocean Blvd Palm Beach FL 33480-5706

ROBERTS, MARIE DYER, computer systems specialist; b. Statesboro, Ga., Feb. 19, 1943; d. Byron and Martha (Evans) Dyer; BS, U. Ga., 1966; student Am. U., 1972; cert. systems profl., cert. in data processing; m. Hugh V. Roberts, Jr., Oct. 6, 1973. Mathematician, computer specialist U.S. Naval Oceanographic Office, Washington, 1966-73; systems analyst, programmer Sperry Microwave Electronics, Clearwater, Fla., 1973-75; data processing mgr., asst. bus. mgr. Trenam, Simmons, Kemker et al, Tampa, Fla., 1975-77; mathematician, computer specialist U.S. Army C.E., Savannah, Ga., 1977-81, 83-85, Frankfurt, W. Ger., 1981-83; ops. rsch. analyst U.S. Army Contrn. Rsch. Lab., Champaign, Ill., 1985-87; data base adminstr., computer systems programmer, chief info. integration and implementation div. U.S. Army Corps of Engrs., South Pacific div., San Francisco, 1987-93; computer specialist, IDEF repository coord., Functional Process Improvement Expertise, Defense Info. Systems Agy., Arlington, Va., 1993-95; computer specialist Ctr. Integration Def. Info. Systems Agy., MacDill AFB, Fla., 1995—. instr. computer scis. City Coll. of Chgo. in Franfurt, 1982-83. Recipient Sustained Superior Performance award Dept. Army, 1983, Nat. Performance Review Hammer award V.P. Gore, 1996. Mem. Am. Soc. Hist. Preservation, Data Processing Mgmt. Assn., Assn. of Inst. for Cert. Computer Profls., Assn. Women in Computing, Assn. Women in Sci., NAFE, Am. Film Inst., U. Ga. Alumni Assn., Sigma Kappa, Soc. Am. Mil. Engrs. Author: Harris Computer Users Manual, 1983.

ROBERTS, MARJORIE HELEN, editor; b. Port Chester, N.Y., Feb. 23, 1938; d. George and Blanche (Mulwitz) Goldowitz; m. Arthur W. Roberts, Aug. 23, 1959 (div. Aug. 1967); children: Scott Eric, Allison. BA in Journalism, U. Mich., 1959. Lic. real estate broker, N.Y. Reporter and editor Gannett Westchester Newspapers, Port Chester, N.Y., 1955-60; fin. adminstr. Investors Diversified Svcs., White Plains, N.Y., 1969-73; real estate adminstr. Schulman Realty Group, White Plains, 1973-78; exec. v.p. R.S. Silver & Co., Greenwich, Conn., 1978-89; freelance writer, editor. med. columnist Women's News, Westchester, N.Y., 1981-93; dir. mktg. pub. rels. Matthew J. Warshauer Architects, PC, Hawthorne, NY, 1989-90; editor Women's News, Westchester, N.Y., 1990-92; asst. dir. pub. rels. New York Med. Coll., Valhalla, N.Y., 1992—. Contbr. articles to mags. and newspapers. Mem. Harrison Archtl. Rev. Bd., N.Y., 1979-87, Harrison Com. Cable TV, 1977-79; bd. dirs. Home for Mentally Retarded, Harrison, 1982-87, Westchester Symphony, 1983-86. Home: 101 River W Greenwich CT 06831-4100

ROBERTS, MAURA M., secondary school educator; b. Washington, Mar. 2, 1944; d. John E. and Mary M. (McCann) Martin; m. Charles D. Roberts, Aug. 15, 1987; 1 child, Caragh M. McLaughlin. AB, U. Mass. at Lowell, 1965; MAT, Salem State Coll., 1973. Cert. tchr. English, Mass., S.C. Tchr. English Hilton Head (S.C.) Prep Sch.; with Concord (Mass.)-Carlisle Sch.

Dist.; tchr. English Concord-Carlisle Sch. Dist. Mem. edn. adv. bd. Orchard House Mus., Concord, 1994—. Mem. ASCD, Nat. Coun. Tchrs. of English, Concord Carlisle Tchrs. Assn., Mass. Tchrs. Assn.

ROBERTS, MICHELE ANN, nurse administrator; b. St. Louis, Apr. 6, 1961; d. William Joseph and Patricia Ann (Johnson) Zickel; m. Steven Mark Roberts, May 16, 1987; 1 child, Felicia. RN diploma, Mission Bapt., 1986; BSN, Maryville Coll., 1989; MS in Geriatric Nursing, St. Louis U., 1993; student, Jewish Sch. Nursing. Cert. geriatric nurse practitioner. Staff nurse St. John's Mercy, Creve Coeur, Mo., 1986-87; asst. DON Bridgeton (Mo.) Nursing Ctr., 1987-88; head nurse St. John's Hosp., Creve Coeur, 1988-93; asst. head nurse St. Luke's Survey Pl., Chesterfield, Mo., 1993; DON St. Luke's Survey Pl., 1996—; adminstr., profl. adv. mem. St. Andrew's Home Svcs., St. Andrew's Hosp., Chesterfield, 1993-96; cons. St. Andrew's Found., St. Louis, 1996. Mem. Geriatric Nursing Assn. Republican. Roman Catholic. Home: 156 Westridge Pk Ballwin MD 63021

ROBERTS, NANCY, computer educator; b. Boston, Jan. 25, 1938; d. Harold and Annette (Zion) Rosenthal; m. Edward B. Roberts, June 14, 1959; children: Valerie Friedman, Mitchell, Andrea. AB, Boston U., 1959, MEd, 1961, EdD, 1975. Elem. tchr. Sharon (Mass.) Pub. Schs., 1959-63; asst. prof. Lesley Coll., Cambridge, Mass., 1975-79, assoc. prof., 1980-83; prof., 1983—; dir. grad. programs in tech. in edn. Lesley Coll., Cambridge, Mass., 1980—, dir. Project Bridge,, 1987-92; dir. Ctr. for Math., Sci. and Tech. in Edn., Cambridge, Mass., 1990-91; rsch. assoc. MIT, Cambridge, 1976-79;mem. nat. steering com. Nat. Edn. Computing Conf., Eugene, Oreg., 1979—, co-chmn. nat. conf., 1989, vice chmn. steering com., 1991-95. Author: Dynamics of Human Service Delivery, 1976, Practical Guide to Computers in Education, 1982, Computers in Teaching Mathematics, 1983, Introduction to Computer Simulation, 1983 (J.W. Forrester award 1983), Integrating Computers into the Elementary and Middle School, 1987, Computers and the Social Studies, 1988, Integrating Telecommunications into Education, 1990; mem. editorial bd. Jour. Ednl. Computing, 1983—, Jour. Rsch. in Sci. Teaching; editor Computers in Edn. book series, 1984-89. Mem. Computer Policy Com., Boston, 1982-84, mem. adv. bd. Electronic Learning, 1989-91; bd. dirs. Computers for kids, Cambridge, 1983-85; mem. State Ednl. Tech. Adv. Coun., 1990-93. NSF grantee, 1985-96. Mem. System Dynamics Soc. (bd. dirs. policy com. 1987-89). Republican. Jewish. Home: 300 Boylston St Apt 1102 Boston MA 02116-3923 Office: Lesley Coll 29 Everett St Cambridge MA 02138-2702

ROBERTS, NANCY JEAN, secondary school educator; b. Evansville, Ind., Sept. 21, 1943; d. William E. and Vernell (Meeks) Morris; m. Harry F. Ransdell, June 19, 1965 (wid. Oct. 1967); m. Michael H. Roberts, Dec. 21, 1968; children: Stephanie Lyn, Jennifer Ann. BA, U. Evansville, 1965; MS, Ind. State U., 1971, Secondary Sch. Adminstr., 1990. Cert. tchr. Tchr. Central High Sch., Evansville, 1965-68, Evans Elem., Evansville, 1969-82; tchr. Reitz High Sch., Evansville, 1982—, social studies dept. chair, 1989—; adj. faculty U. of So. Ind., Evansville, 1984—. Mem. Ind. State Tchrs. Assn. (bd. dirs. 1978-88, exec. com. 1980-88), Evansville Tchrs. Assn. (bd. dirs. 1976-88), ASCD, Assn. of Tchr. Educators, Nat. Coun. Social Studies, Phi Delta Kappa, Delta Kappa Gamma. Home: 416 Red Bud Ln Evansville IN 47710 Office: Reitz HS Forest Hills Evansville IN 47712

ROBERTS, NICKOLENA GRECO (NICKY ROBERTS), small business owner; b. Syracuse, N.Y., Aug. 14, 1951; d. William James and Eileen (Knox) Greco; m. Robert B. Hegley, Dec. 27, 1974 (dec. 1983); m. Galen E. Roberts, Jan 2, 1987; children: Vera, David, Nicholas. Diploma, Gen. Motors Sch. Mdsing. and Mgmt., 1981, 82. Lead dancer Maori Polynesian Restaurant, W. Palm Beach, Fla., 1970-72; sales/mgmt. WJNO Radio, W. Palm Beach, 1970-76, WIRK & WNGS Radio, W. Palm Beach, 1976-80; truck/fleet mgr. Bob Hegley Inc., Clewiston, Fla., 1980-82; owner, pres. Nicky Hegley Chevrolet, Clewiston, Fla., 1983-87; v.p., co-owner, Roberts Auto Collection, Inc., Lake Wales, Fla., 1987—; account exec. Highlands Media Co., Inc., Sebring, Fla., 1990-92; advt. cons. Morris Comms. Corp. (dba Newschief Pub. Group), 1994—. Sec., Airport Authority, Clewiston, 1983-86; bd. dirs. Actor's Community Theater, 1983-86; mem. Bus. Improvement Council, 1984-85. Mem. Nat. Assn. Female Execs., Sales Mktg. Execs., C. of C. Jehovah's Witness. Avocations: polynesian dancing, flying, reading, crafts, snow skiing.

ROBERTS, NORA RUTH, English educator; b. L.A., Apr. 19, 1942; d. Daniel Robert Zhitlowsky and Frances Mary (James) Nicklas; m. (div. June 1975); children: Kit Adam Wainer, Robben Andrew Wainer. BA in English, CCNY, 1973, MA in Creative Writing, 1975; postgrad., Yale U., 1975-76; PhD in English, CUNY, 1995. Asst. fiction editor Good Housekeeping, N.Y.C., 1961-63; rsch. editor Voque Mag., N.Y.C., 1964-67; assoc. editor Daw Books, Inc., N.Y.C., 1976-85; English lectr. St. Peter's Coll., Jersey City, N.J., 1989-95, Medgar Evers Coll., Bklyn., 1993-95; lectr. Am. thought and lang. Mich. State U. Author: Three Radical Women Writers, 1996; Waterway Journey, 1968; published fiction and poetry, 1996; contbr. articles to profl. jours. Election chair Parents Assn., N.Y.C., 1970; mem. speakers bur. N.Y. Coun. Humanities, 1994—. Danforth fellow, 1973-75; grantee Theodore Goodman, 1971, Helena Rubinstein, 1992, Carolyn Heilbrun Dissertation award, 1995. Mem. MLA, Popular Culture Assn., Am. Studies Assn., Mich. Women's Hist. Assn., Jewish League for Edn. of women. Home: 705-104 Cherry Lane East Lansing MI 48823

ROBERTS, POLLY, writer, marketing consultant; b. Ware, Mass., Aug. 19, 1954; d. Edward Pierce and Alice (Jaques) Roberts; m. Rexford H. Swain, Apr. 23, 1988. BFA, R.I. Sch. Design, 1976. Asst. to editor, asst. fashion editor Vogue Patterns, N.Y.C., 1977, fashion editor, 1977-79; editor-in-chief Vogue Patters, N.Y.C., 1981-84; sr. editor McCall's Patterns, N.Y.C., 1979-80; editor-in-chief Vogue Patterns/Butterick, N.Y.C., 1981-84, Vogue Knitting mag., N.Y.C., 1981-84; writer, mktg. cons. N.Y.C. and Conn., 1985—. Trustee Gunn Meml. Libr. Mus., Washington, Conn., 1991—; alternate mem. Zoning Bd. Appeals, Washington, 1995—. Democrat. Home and Office: 8 South St Washington CT 06793

ROBERTS, POLLY JEANES, human resources consultant; b. Memphis, Mar. 18, 1948; d. Oliver and Martha Dabney Jeanes; m. Floyd Dodson Roberts Jr., Dec. 20, 1969; children: Dabney D., William D. BA, U. Memphis, 1994. Sr. v.p. Leader Svcs., Inc., Memphis, 1981-89; ptnr. Craddock and Roberts, Memphis, 1989-91; human resource cons. Internat. Paper, Memphis, 1994—. Sustaining mem. Jr. League Memphis, 1976—; chmn. ways and means Chickasaw Gardens Neighborhood Assn., Memphis, 1993—; lay minister Grace-St. Luke's Episcopal Ch., Memphis, 1990—. Mem. Pub. Rels. Soc. Am., Women in Communications (job link co-chmn. 1993—).

ROBERTS, PRISCILLA WARREN, artist; b. Montclair, N.J., June 13, 1916; d. Charles Asaph and Florence (Berry) R. Student, Art Students League, 1937-39, Nat. Acad., 1939-43. Represented in permanent collections Met. Mus., Cin. Art Mus., Canton Art Inst., Westmoreland County Mus. Art, Pa., IBM, Dallaas Mus., Walker Art Ctr., Mpls., Butler Inst., Youngstown, Ohio, Nat. Mus. Am. Art, Washington. Recipient Proctor prize, 1947, popular prize Corcoran Biennial, 1947, prize Westmoreland County Mus., 3d prize Carnegie Internat., Pitts., 1950, Nat. Mus. Women in Arts, Washington, Snite Mus., U. Notre Dame, Ind. Mem. NAD (Hallgarten prize 1945), Allied Artists Am. (Zabriskie prize 1944, 46), Catherine Lorillard Wolfe Assn. (hon.). Address: PO Box 716 Georgetown CT 06829-0716

ROBERTS, RITA LOUISE DOYLE, artist; b. McCook, Nebr., Oct. 15, 1964; d. Raymond Roy Doyle and Carla Marie (Cruver) Bales; m. Richard Joseph Roberts, Mar. 19, 1994. BFA, Kansas City (Mo.) Art Inst., 1987. Artist, art dir. Miner Container, Inc., Lenexa, Kans., 1986-91; freelance artist and designer Roberts Art & Design Studio, Weaverville, Calif., 1991—. Recipient First Place award and Hon. Mention award Snyder Highland Found., Weaverville, Calif., 1994, Best of Show award (for painting) Trinity County Arts Coun., Weaverville, 1994, Snyder Highland Found., Weaverville, 1995. Mem. Highland Art Ctr., North Valley Art League (Excellence award 1994), Mendocino Art Ctr. Home: PO Box 2262 Weaverville CA 96093 Office: Roberts Art & Design Studio 333 E Weaver Creek Rd Weaverville CA 96093

ROBERTS, ROBIN, sportcaster; b. Nov. 23, 1960. BA in Comms. cum laude, Southeastern La. U., 1983. Sports dir. WHMD/WFPR Radio, Hammond, La., 1980-83; spl. assignment sports reporter KSLU-FM, 1982; sports anchor, reporter WDAM-TV, Hattiesburg, Miss., 1983-84, WLOX-TV, Biloxi, Miss., 1984-86, WSMV-TV, Nashville, 1986-88, WAGA-TV, Atlanta, 1988-89; with WVEE-FM, Atlanta; host. Sunday SportsDay, contbr. NFL Prime Time, reporter, interviewer ESPN, Bristol, Conn., 1990-95, host, anchor SportsCenter, host In the SportsLight, 1995—; host Wide World of Sports ABC, 1995—. Apptd. adv. bd. Women's Sports Found., 1991; spkr. charity, civic functions. Recipient DAR T.V. Award of Merit, 1990, Women at Work Broadcast Journalism award, 1992, Excellence in Sports Journalism award Broadcast Media Northeastern U. Ctr. Study of Sport in Society and Sch. Journalism, 1993; inducted to Hall of Fame Women's Inst. Sport and Edn. Found., 1994. Office: ESPN Inc Comms Dept ESPN Plz Bristol CT 06010

ROBERTS, ROXANN MAE, educator; b. Dansville, N.Y., Oct. 28, 1941; d. James Vincent and Victoria Marie (Ashley) Argennia; m. James L. Roberts, Feb. 1, 1964; children: Donald James, Ronald Ashley, William Carl. BS in Edn., SUNY, Geneseo, 1969, MS in Edn., 1978. Cert. tchr., N.Y. Sub. tchr. Perry (N.Y.) Cen. Sch., 1965-71, reading aide, 1971-74, elem. tchr., 1974, 1975-86; tchr. remedial reading Keshequa Cen. Sch. Dist., Nunda, N.Y., 1975-86; prin. Wyoming (N.Y.) Cen. Sch. Dist., 1986-88; pupil personnel Pavilion (N.Y.) Cen., 1988-89; bridge coord. Genesee Community Coll., Batavia, N.Y., 1990-91; asst. dir. edn. Rochester (N.Y.) Mental Health Ctr., 1992; prin. St. Michael's, Warsaw, N.Y., 1993-94; vol. adminstr. liv. Wyo. Arc., Mt. Morris, N.Y., 1995—; adj. faculty State Univ. Coll. at Geneseo, Genesee Community Coll. in Batavia; charter mem. N.Y.State Staff Devel. Coun. Sec. Genesee-Wyoming Prins. Assn., N.Y., 1986-89. Mem. Sch. Adminstrs. Assn. N.Y. State, Internat. Reading Assn., Children's Book Coun., Assn. for Supervison and Curriculum Devel., NEA of N.Y., N.Y. State Tchrs. Retirement System, N.Y. Coll. Learning Skills Assn., Phi Delta Kappa. Home: 37 Watrous St Perry NY 14530-1538

ROBERTS, RUBY ALTIZER, poet, author; b. Floyd Co., Vt., Apr. 22, 1907; d. Waddy William and Dana Adeline (Cummings) Altizer; m. Laurence Luther Roberts, July 23, 1927; 1 child, Heidi. Grad., Christianburg (Va.) High Sch.; nursing course, Norfolk (Va.) Protestant Hosp.; DHL, Coll. William and Mary, 1961. Freelance writer, 1939—, newspaper corr.; rep. of Spirit of Va., 1993. Author: (with Rosa Altizer Bray) Emera Altizer and His Descendants, 1937, 2 vols. poetry, Forever is Too Long, Command the Stars, (biography) The Way It Was, 1979, The Way It Is, 1992, Look Down at the Stars, 1994; editor juvenile verse dept. Embers Mag., Batavia, N.Y., 1944—; owner, editor, pub. The Lyric Mag.; poetry columnist Va. newspaper; contbr. over 120 poems to anthologies, newspapes, mags., numerous articles to profl. jours. Recipient First Poetry prize Sanctuary Mag., Ballaman award Disting. Svc. to Poetry, 1956, citation Disting. Svc. Poetry Khalsa Coll.; named poet laureate Va. Gen. Assembly, 1950, poet laureate Va. emeritus Gen. Assembly Va., 1992. Home: 301 Roanoke St Christiansburg VA 24073-3150

ROBERTS, RUTH ANN, reading and English language educator; b. Fremont, Mich., Dec. 13, 1948; d. Melvin Curtis and Georgia Augusta (Hoyt) Davis; m. Steven Arthur Roberts, Aug. 30, 1980. AB in Sociology, Marion Coll., 1972; secondary cert., Tex. Woman's U., 1986; elem. cert., U. Tex., Tyler, 1992, MA in Edn., 1994. Cert. reading specialist. Head tchr. reading and math. Expressways to Learning, Waco, Tex., 1987-88; owner reading/math. clinic Expressways to Learning, Mt. Pleasant, Tex., 1988-93; tchr. reading recovery/1st grade Mt. Pleasant Ind. Sch. Dist., 1993-94; instr. reading and English Tex. State Tech. Coll., Marshall, 1994-95, lead instr. reading, 1995—; mem. adv. com. for reading/writing materials Tex. State Tech. Coll., Marshall, 1994—, adv. panel to devl. and implement improved testing measurements for incoming students, 1996—; mem. adv. bd. Expressways to Learning, Pearce, Ariz., 1988-93. Mem. Tex. Tchrs. Assn.

ROBERTS, SANDRA, editor; b. Humboldt, Tenn., July 22, 1951; d. Harold and Margaret (Headrick) R.; m. Parker W. Duncan Jr., Aug. 11, 1990. Student, Tex. Christian U., 1969-70; BS, U. Tenn., 1972; MLS, Peabody Coll. Libr. The Tennessean, Nashville, 1975-82, editorial writer, 1982-87, editorial editor, 1987—. Pres. Women's Polit. Caucus, Nashville, 1982. Recipient John Hancock award John Hancock Co., 1983, Freedom award Tenn. Trial Laywers Assn., 1988. Mem. Am. Soc. Newspaper Editors, Nat. Conf. Editorial Writers, Sigma Delta Chi (Nat. Headliner award 1982). Mem. Christian Ch. Office: The Tennessean 1100 Broadway Nashville TN 37203-3116

ROBERTS, SANDRA MILLER, middle school language arts educator; b. Owensboro, Ky., Apr. 30, 1947; d. Everett E. and Virginia Frances (Oldham) Miller; m. John Clayton Roberts, Nov. 20, 1941; children: Jason Eric, Ryan Alan, Gavin Clayton, Gretchen Elizabeth. BS in Spanish, French and English, Ky. Wesleyan U., 1969; postgrad., Western Ky. U., 1988, 92. 8th grade Spanish and French tchr. So. Jr. H.S., Owensboro, 1969-71; 8th grade lang. arts tchr. Daviess County Mid. Sch., Owensboro, 1988—, portfolio cluster leader, 1991-92, lang. arts curriculum coord., 1993-95; tchr. 6th grade lang. arts and French Coll. View Mid. Sch., Owensboro, 1995—. Mem. Christian Ch. (Disciples of Christ). Home: 4515 Loftwood Dr Owensboro KY 42303-2021

ROBERTS, SUSAN DIANNE GREEN, library media specialist; b. Natchez, Miss., Jan. 23, 1951; d. Vernie Newton and Susie Carolyn (Black) Green; m. Joel David Roberts, Dec. 15, 1990. BS, Miss. State Coll. Women, 1973; MA in Secondary Edn./History, U. Ala., Birmingham, 1976, MA in Sch. Libr. Media, 1982. Cert. secondary history tchr., sch. libr. media specialist. Tchr., libr. Bessemer (Ala.) Acad., 1973-80; libr. media specialist Abrams Elem. Sch., Bessemer, 1980-83, Davis Mid. Sch., Bessemer, 1984-87; head libr. media specialist Jess Lanier H.S., Bessemer, 1983-84, 87-94; libr. media specialist Mountain Brook H.S., Birmingham, 1994—; chmn. Bessemer City Schs. Librs., 1987-94; mem. Libr. Media Leadership Group ALa. Dept. Edn., 1993—. Mem. NEA, Ala. Edn. Assn., Ala. Instrnl. Media Assn., Ala. Libr. Assn., Ala. Cheerleader Coaches & Advisors Assn. (bd. dirs. 1988—). Methodist. Office: Mountain Brook HS 3650 Bethune Dr Birmingham AL 35223

ROBERTS, TERESA LOUISE, software consultant; b. Hammond, La., Aug. 5, 1955; d. Hulen O. and Nan (Robinson) Adams; m. Peter C. Crowe, Aug. 9, 1974; m. Randy M. Roberts, June 15, 1991. BS in Computer Sci., La. State U., 1983; postgrad., U. Tex., 1989-90. Software engr. Tex. Instruments, Dallas, 1983-91; object oriented advisor Object Internat., Austin, Tex., 1991-93; tech. trainer Berard Software Engring., Gaithersburg, Md., 1993; software analyst Maden Tech., Arlington, Va., 1993-94; sr. tech. rep. CenterLine, Cambridge, Mass., 1994-95; assoc. Tech. Resource Connection, Tampa, Fla., 1995; spkr. object-oriented software tech. confs., 1992-95. Contbr. tech. papers to profl. publs. and confs. Mem. IEEE Computer Soc. (voting mem.), NAFE, Assn. for Computing Machinery (voting mem.). Home: 107 Sherwood Blvd Los Alamos NM 87544

ROBERTS, THOMASENE BLOUNT, entrepreneur; b. Americus, Ga., Sept. 5, 1943; d. Thomas Watson and Mary Elizabeth (Smith) Blount; m. Henry Lee Roberts, Apr. 24, 1970 (div. 1991); 1 child, Asha Maia. Student, Fisk U., 1960-63; BA, Morris Brown Coll., 1965; MA, Atlanta U., 1970, postgrad., 1979-82; postgrad., Clark Atlanta U. Social worker Gate City Day Nursery Assn., Atlanta, 1965-66; ticket agt. Delta Air Lines, Inc., Atlanta, 1966-68; clk. accounts payable Kraft Foods, Inc., Decatur, Ga., 1968; cons. family svcs. Atlanta Housing Authority, 1970-72, supr. family svcs., 1972-73, mgr. family relocation, 1974-79; grad. rsch. asst. Sch. Edn. Atlanta U., 1979-82; city coun. asst. City of Atlanta, 1984-88, rsch. asst. Dept. Pub. Safety, 1988; dir. govtl. rels. Morris Brown Coll., Atlanta, 1988-93; owner TBR Ent., Atlanta, 1993—; adminstrv. analyst human svcs. City of Atlanta, 1995—; researcher/intern Project Focus Teen Mother Program, Atlanta, 1981-82; moderator Nat. Black Women's Health Project, Atlanta, 1985; workshop leader Assn. Human Resources Mgrs., Atlanta, 1989; pres.'s rep. U. Ctr. Devel. Corp., Inc., 1989-93; cons. entrepreneur devel. workshop Morris Brown Coll. Chairperson Ida Prather YWCA Cmty. Bd., Atlanta, 1985-90; bd. dirs. YWCA Met. Atlanta, 1986-90, Met. Atlanta Coalition 100 Black Women, 1988-90, 92—, sec., mem. bd. dirs., 1994—, Hammonds House Mus., 1995—; active fund dr. com. Jomandi Prodn., 1988-89; v.p. maj. gifts com. Camp Best Friends, City of Atlanta, 1989; mem. Multi-Cultural Leadership Group, Gov.'s Coun. on Developmental Disabilities. Mem. Atlanta-Trinidad/Tobago Exch. (sec., treas. 1983-89, Pt. of Spain cert. 1986), Nat. Polit. Congress Black Women (corr. sec. 1989-90), Nat. Assn. for Equal Opportunity Higher Edn. (coll. liaison 1988-93), Coun. for Advancement-Support of Edn., Info. Forum, Atlanta Urban League, Inc., Nat. Assn. for Equal Opportunity in Higher Edn. (Disting. Alumni award 1991), Nat. Soc. Fund-Raising Execs. (cert. 1992), Nat. Soc. Fund-Raising Execs. Leadership Inst., Friends of Morehouse Sch. Medicine, Delta Sigma Theta (pub. rels. asst. 1986-89). Home: 1817 King Charles Rd SW Atlanta GA 30331-4909 Office: TBR Enterprises Ste A-3165 2740 Greenbriar Pky SW Atlanta GA 30331-2614

ROBERTS, VICTORIA LYNN PARMER, antique expert; b. N.Y.C., Sept. 15, 1953; d. Edgar Alan Parmer and Nina Joyce (Ash) Gross; m. George E. Roberts, Dec. 1, 1978 (div. 1985); 1 child, Joshua Henry. Student, Yale U. Pres. High Gear Creative Svcs., Savannah, Ga., 1979-81; v.p. Rossignol Modeling Agy., N.Y.C., 1981-82; mgr., dir. Parc Monceau Antiques, Westport, Conn., 1982-85; pres., owner Victoria & Cie, Norwalk, Conn., 1985—; antiques tchr. Sacred Heart U., Fairfield, Conn., 1988, 89, Norwalk Community Coll., 1989; antique lectr. various hist. socs., Conn., 1989-90; speaker in antiques field; antique expert seminars to interior designers, Norwalk, 1989; creator, sole contbr. spls. on antiques CNBC TV, 1989, 90. Antiques editor Brooks Community Newspaper, Westport, 1989-91; contbr. Antiques Mag., 1991—. Mem. Appraisers Assn. Am. (sr.), Coll. Arts Assn., Alpha Sigma Lambda. Office: Victoria & Cie 3 Nelson Ave Norwalk CT 06851-3910

ROBERTS HARVEY, BONITA, secondary school educator; b. Detroit, June 24, 1947; d. Walter James and Mattie Louise (Pacely) Hall; stepfather, Dolphus Hall Sr.; m. Paul Randall Harvey, June 13, 1970 (div. Aug. 1980); 1 child, Paula Renee. BA, Grand Valley State U., 1974; Cert. in Continuing Edn., Western Mich. U. Art specialist Jenison (Mich.) Pub. Schs., 1974—; visual/performing artist Summer at Arts Place-Grand Rapids C.C., 1980-92; cons. art edn. Detroit Inst. Art, 1988. Bd. dirs., performing artist Robeson Players, Grand Rapids, Mich., 1973—, Cmty. Cir. Theatre, Grand Rapids, 1981-84, Coun. Performing Arts for Children, Grand Rapids, 1981-88; active First Cmty. African Meth. Episc. Ch., NAACP. Mem. ASCD, Nat. Art Edn. Assn., Mich. Art Edn. Assn., Mich. Edn. Assn. (tri-county pub. rels. 1994—), Mich. Alliance Arts Edn., Nat. Mus. Women in Arts, Jenison Edn. Assn. (pub. rels. 1993—), Delta Sigma Theta. Office: Jenison Pub Schs 8375 20th Jenison MI 49428

ROBERTSON, ALICE BOYKIN, secondary school educator; b. Fulton County, Ga., Oct. 4, 1939; d. Samuel Jefferson and Miriam (Stone) Boykin; m. Thomas Matthew Robertson, Dec. 22, 1962; children: Miriam Ann Robertson Threadgill, Samuel Thomas. BA, Agnes Scott Coll., 1961; MEd, West Ga. Coll., 1982, EdS in Math. Edn., 1989. Cert. in gifted edn., Ga. Secondary math. tchr. Avondale High Sch., Dekalb County Schs., Ga., 1961-63; secondary math. tchr., dept. head Dist. 88, Hinsdale Twp., Hinsdale, Ill., 1964-67, 68-70; mid. sch. and secondary math. tchr. Oak Mountain Acad., Carrollton, Ga., 1978-82; secondary math. and gifted edn. tchr. Ctrl. High Sch., Carroll County Schs., Carrollton, 1983—; editor, proofreader Ga. exit exam. in math.; developer Ga. GEMS math. program, 1993; evaluator, adminstr. tests for gifted program Ctrl. High Sch.; softball coach, 1983-84, golf coach, 1980-82; presenter in field. Mem. choir First United Meth. Ch., Carrollton, 1973—. Recipient Ga. High Tech. Month Outstanding Achievement in Edn. award Bus. and Tech. Alliance Ga., 1993; named STAR Tchr., 1992, 93, Tandy Outstanding Math./Sci./Computer Sci. Tchr., 1994; recipient grants in field. Mem. NEA, Nat. Coun. Tchrs. Math., Ga. Assn. Educators, Carroll County Assn. Educators, Carroll County and Ga. Supporters of the Gifted, Phi Delta Kappa, Kappa Delta Pi. Methodist. Home: 120 Fairlawn Dr Carrollton GA 30117-8867

ROBERTSON, CAREY JANE, musician, educator; b. Culver City, Calif., Apr. 18, 1955; d. Robert Bruce and Marjorie Ellen (Greenleaf) Coker;l m. Brian Collins Robertson, June 28, 1975 (div. July 1985); 1 child, Sean Kalen. BMus, Calif. State U., Northridge, 1977; MMus, U. So. Calif., L.A., 1979, PhD of Mus. Arts, 1987. Organist/choir dir. Village Meth. Ch., North Hollywood, Calif., 1972-75, St. Bede's Episcopal Ch., Mar Vista, Calif., 1975-79; organist interim St. Alban's Episcopal Ch., Westwood, Calif., 1985; organist Covenant Presbyn. Ch., Westchester, Calif., 1985-90; organist/choir dir. St. David's United Ch., West Vancouver, B.C., Can., 1990-91; prin. organist Claremont (Calif.) United Ch. of Christ, 1991—; prof. organ Claremont Grad. Sch., 1991—; concert organist Am. Guild of Organists, throughout U.S. and Can., 1974—; cons. Sch. Theology, U. B.C., 1990. Bd. dirs. Ruth and Clarence Mader Found., Pasadena, Calif., 1993—. Recipient Music Tchrs. Nat. Assn. Wurlitzer Collegiate Artist award, 1980; Irene Robertson scholar, 1977, 78. Mem. Am. Guild Organists (historian, sec. 1985-92, exec. com. 1983-85), Pi Kappa Lambda (Scholastic award 1987). Home: 7514 Pepper St Rancho Cucamonga CA 91730-2125

ROBERTSON, ELIZABETH ANN, office manager; b. Santa Clara, Calif., Mar. 27, 1968; d. Larry William and Anita Louise (Williams) R. Student, San Jose State U., 1986-91, Sonoma State U., 1993, Stanford U., 1994. Pub. rels. hostess Carl Karcher Enterprises, San Jose, Calif., 1984; sales mgr. The Book Mark, Milpitas, Calif., 1986-88; staff supr., account mgr. A Book Garden, Inc., Milpitas, 1988-95; office mgr. New Papyrus Tech., Saratoga, Calif., 1995—; owner, cons. The Geo List, Sunnyvale, Calif., 1995—. Editor newsletters A New Leaf, 1989-95, The SPPC News, 1994; features editor The Liberty newspaper, 1985-86. Admitting vol. Alexian Bros. Hosp., San Jose, 1985-86; booth mgr. Milpitas' Art and Wine Festival, 1994. Recipient Hon. Mention award Bulwer-Lytton Fiction Contest, 1988. Mem. Am. Booksellers Assn., No. Calif. Booksellers Assn., Nat. Geog. Soc. Democrat. Home: 1606 Peachwood Dr San Jose CA 95132-2128 Office: New Papyrus Tech 14585 Big Basin Way Saratoga CA 95070-6013

ROBERTSON, GAIL FIELDS, personnel director; b. Athens, Ga., Dec. 21, 1949; d. K.J. Jr. and Sedelia (Fagans) Fields; m. Emmett D. Robertson, Dec. 21, 1967. Personnel sec. Central Soya Athens Inc., 1970-73; personnel adminstr. 1st Nat. Bank Athens, 1973-80, personnel officer, 1981-83; asst. v.p., personnel dir. Trust Co. Bank NE Ga., Athens, 1983—; instr. personnel and law Am. Inst. Banking, Athens, 1985, 87. Chair Student Prep. Adv. Com., Athens, 1984-85; bd. dirs. Am. Cancer Soc., Athens, 1985-86; advisor Cedar Shoals High Sch., Athens, 1986-87. Mem. Athens Area Personnel Assn. (sec./treas. 1987, pres. 1989, bd. dirs.). Democrat. Baptist. Office: Sunstrust Bank NE Ga 101 N Lumpkin St Athens GA 30601

ROBERTSON, JANE RYDING, marketing executive; b. Dallas, Apr. 11, 1953; d. Ronald and Olive Stacey (Hodgkinson) Pearce; m. James Randall Robertson, May 25, 1974; children: James Andrew, Jessica Ryding. Assoc. degree, Tyler Jr. Coll., 1972; BS, Tex. Tech U., 1974. Store mgr. trainee Montgomery Ward, Dallas, Lubbock, Tex., 1974-75; dist. sales rep. Max Factor & Co., Dallas, 1975-78; sr. asst. buyer cosmetics Sanger Harris, Dallas, 1978-88, also cosmetic mktg.-divisional mktg. account exec., 1978-88; v.p. mktg. Dallas Market Ctr., 1988-90; dir. mktg.-pub. rels. Galleria/Hines Interests Dallas, 1990—. Bd. dirs. Ctr. for Profl. Selling, Baylor U., Waco, Tex., 1989—; mem. nat. bd. dirs. Susan G. Komen Found. for Breast Cancer, Dallas, 1990—. Mem. Internat. Coun. Shopping Ctrs., Fashion Group Internat., Univ. Club (bd. dirs. profl. women's com. 1990-92). Methodist. Office: Galleria Hines Interests Dallas 13355 Noel Rd Ste 250 Dallas TX 75240-6603

ROBERTSON, MARIAN ELLA (MARIAN ELLA HALL), small business owner, handwriting analyst; b. Edmonton, Alta., Can., Mar. 3, 1920; d. Orville Arthur and Lucy Hon (Osborn) Hall; m. Howard Chester Robertson, Feb. 7, 1942; children: Elaine, Richard. Student, Willamette U., 1937-39; BS, Western Oreg. State U., 1955. Cert. elem., jr. high. tchr., supt. (life) Oreg.; cert. graphoanalyst. Tchr. pub. schs. Mill City, Albany, Scio and Hillsboro, Oreg., 1940-72; cons. Zaner-Bloser Inc., Columbus, Ohio, 1972-85, assoc. cons., 1985-89; pres. Write-Keys, Scio, 1980-90; owner Lifelines, Jefferson, Oreg., 1991-94; tchr. Internat. Graphoanalysis Soc., Chgo., 1979; instr. Linn-Benton Community Coll., 1985-89. Sr. intern 5th Congl. Dist. Oreg., Washington, 1984, mem. sr. adv. coun.; precinct com. mem. Rep. Cen. Com., Linn County, 1986, alt. vice-chair, 1986, parliamentarian, 1988—; candidate Oreg. State Legis., Salem, 1986; del. Northwest Friends Yearly

Meeting, Newberg, Oreg., 1990, 91, 92; master gardener vol. Marion County, Oreg. State U. Extension Svc., 1992; floriculture judge Marion County Fair, 1992; master gardener clinic Oreg. State Fair, 1992; clerk Marion Friends Monthly Meeting, 1992-93. Mem. Altrusa Internat. (internat. chmn. 1985-86, chmn. pub. rels. 1989—, corr. sec. 1990-91), Internat. Platform Assn. Republican. Mem. Soc. of Friends. Home: 2757 Pheasant Ave SE Salem OR 97302-3170

ROBERTSON, MARTHA RAPPAPORT, state senator, consultant; b. Boston, Sept. 14, 1952; d. Jerome Lyle and Nancy (Vahey) Rappaport; m. T.L. Robertson, Nov. 22, 1980; 1 child, Colby. BA, Franklin & Marshall Coll., 1974; MBA, U. Pa., 1976. Mktg. and new bus. devel. exec. Gen. Mills, Inc., Mpls., 1976-91; state senator State of Minn., 1993—. Republican. Office: State of Minn 125 State Office Bldg Saint Paul MN 55155-1201

ROBERTSON, MARY LOUISE, archivist, historian; b. L.A., May 19, 1945; d. Snell and Dorothy (Tregoning) R. BA, UCLA, 1966, MA, 1968, PhD, 1975. Teaching asst. dept. history UCLA, 1967-70; acting instr. UCLA Extension, 1973-74; acting instr. dept. history Pepperdine U., L.A., 1970, Calif. State U., Northridge, 1972-73; asst. curator manuscripts Huntington Libr., San Marino, Calif., 1975, assoc. curator, 1977, chief curator, 1979—; adj. prof. English Claremont Grad. Sch., 1994. Author: Guide to British Historical Manuscripts in the Huntington Library, 1982; co-author, editor: Guide to American Historical Manuscripts in the Huntington Library, 1979; contbr. articles on Tudor history to profl. jours. Mabel Wilson Richards dissertation fellow, 1970-72. Mem. Am. Hist. Assn., Soc. Am. Archivists, Soc. Calif. Archivists, N.Am. Conf. on Brit. Studies, Pacific Coast Conf. on Brit. Studies (treas. 1986-88, pres. 1988-90), Phi Beta Kappa. Office: Huntington Libr 1151 Oxford Rd San Marino CA 91108-1218

ROBERTSON, MARY VIRGINIA, retired elementary education educator; b. Lincoln, Nebr., Oct. 1, 1925; d. Dean Leroy and Anna Charlotte (Boge) R. AB in Philosophy and Psychology, U. Nebr., Lincoln, 1949, BS in Elem. Edn., 1953; postgrad., U. Toronto, Ont., Can., 1949. Cert. elem. tchr., Nebr. Country sch. tchr. Lancaster County schs., Nebr., 1943-44, Otoe County schs., Palmyra, Nebr., 1944-45; 3d-5th grade tchr. Palmyra Schs., 1945-46; 3d grade tchr. Valley (Nebr.) Schs., 1953-57, Lincoln Pub. Schs., 1957-81; ret.; leader workshop in field; math. coord. Riley Elem. Sch., Lincoln, 1970-71. Author pamphlet A Letter for You, 1954. Mem. NEA, AAUW, Nebr. State Edn. Assn., Nat. Coun. Math. Tchrs., Am. Child Edn. Internat., Belmont PTA (life), Eastern Star, Lincoln Women's Club. Methodist.

ROBERTSON, MELVINA, construction company executive; b. Guilford, Mo., June 3, 1934; d. Charlie Gale and Christina Gertrude (Nelson) Turner; m. Ponnie Leonard Robertson, June 3, 1955; children: Raymond Edward, Richard Leonard. Student, Cen. Mo. State Coll., 1966. Mgr. Knowles Restaurant, Kansas City, Mo., 1954-55; v.p. P.L. Robertson Concrete Found. Co., Inc., Ozark, Mo., 1972-90; pres. P.L. Robertson Concrete Found. Co., Inc., 1990—. Mem. Rose Soc. of Ozark, Nat. Audubon Soc. Mem. Reorganized LDS Ch.

ROBERTSON, PATRICIA AILEEN, nursing consultant, educator; b. Washington, Dec. 15, 1950; d. John Thomas and Virginia Aileen (Parker) Dickmeyer; m. Lee Eiden Robertson; children: Jason Earle, Alyssa Michelle. BS, U. Mass., 1973; BSN with honors, George Mason U., 1982. Cert. intravenous therapy. Staff nurse, perdiem intravenous therapist St. Joseph's Hosp. and Tacoma Gen. Hosp., Tacoma; pediatric nurse, health educator Western Clinic, Tacoma; nurse cons., intravenous therapy educator Pharmacy Corp. Am., Seattle; developer, dir. Careline health adv. and case mgmt. program Weyerhaeuser, Tacoma; cons. Home IV Therapy Agys.; cons. UR Case Mgmt. Olympic Counseling Svcs., Tacoma; program developer Coord. Adolescent Assessment Ctr.; developer, AIDS edn. program for high sch. students and corp. employee, 1990; cons. alzheimer's dementia unit Weatherly Inn, 1992; speaker in field. Named Pierce County Nurse of Yr. nominee, 1986. Mem. ANA, Nat. League Nursing, Nat. Assn. Vascular Access Networks, Wash. State Nurses Assn., Intravenous Nurses Soc., South Sound AIDS Network, Healthcare Providers Coun. Wash., Sigma Theta Tau. Home and Office: 8621 Cherry Dr Fairfax VA 22031-2136

ROBERTSON, PAULINE DURRETT, publishing executive; b. Amarillo, Tex., Apr. 17, 1922; d. Walter Lucius and Mary Eddie (Jones) Durrett; m. Roy Lewis Robertson, Dec. 18, 1940; children: Kay Linda Robertson Savage, Kent Lewis, Robyn M. Robertson Turner Koock, Paula Jo Robertson Pierce, Roy Durrett, Laurel Annette Robertson FitzPatrick Gibson, Virginia Lee Robertson-Baker, Ellen Robertson Neal, Neil Thomas, Carrie Beth. AA, Amarillo Coll., 1969; BA in English Writing, St. Edward's U., Austin, Tex., 1992. Editor project history U.S. Reclamation Bur., Amarillo, 1942-43; editor post newsletter U.S. Army Air Force, Amarillo, 1943-44; freelance writer, 1944-73; writer books of history Staked Plains Press, Canyon, Tex., 1973-77; writer books of history and poetry Paramount Pub. Co., Amarillo, 1977—, pub. house pres., editor, 1977—; tchr. poetry writing, history Amarillo Coll., 1971-95; tchr. poetry writing Elderhostel, U. Tex., Austin, 1988-89; writer book revs. Amarillo Globe News, 1968—. Author: (with R.L. Robertson) Panhandle Pilgrimage: Illustrated Tales Tracing History in the Texas Panhandle, 1976, 77, 81, 85, 90, Tascosa: Historic Site in the Texas Panhandle, 1978, 2d edit., 1995, Mystery Woman of Old Tascosa: The Legend of Frenchy McCormick, 1979, 2d edit., 1995, Cowman's Country: Fifty Frontier Ranches in the Texas Panhandle 1876-1887, 1981, 95, (poetry books) Fringe Benefits: Light Verse From Living, 1985, Borrowed Moccasins: Poems From Other Viewpoints, 1986, Field Notes: Poems on Late Light, 1987; editor and designer: Austin Originals: Chats With Colorful Characters by Robyn Turner, 1982, Long Shadows: Indian Leaders Standing in the Path of Manifest Destiny 1600-1900, 1985; author, editor: (poetry) Bootsteps: Poems of the West-Then and Now, 1978, 83, Eve's Version: 150 Women of the Bible, 1983; featured in documentary on NBC-TV, 1960. Co-founder, sec. Cerebral Palsy Treatment Ctr., Amarillo, 1948-60, Opportunity House, Amarillo, 1970-87; founder, pres. Children's Cottage, Amarillo, 1964-84, Women's Coalition for Change: Focus on Poverty, Amarillo, 1989-95; founder, dir. for underprivileged children Camp Friendship, Ceta Glen, Tex., 1971-74; chair of elders First Christian Ch., 1979—; host family Internat. Christian Youth Exch., 1963-64, sending family, 1968, 78; mem. Potter County Hist. Commn., Tex., 1988—; pres.-elect Ch. Women United of Tex., 1996—. Named Amarillo's Family of the Yr., Amarillo Globe-News, 1957, Tex. Merit Mother, Am. Mothers Assn., Boston, 1991, 1995 Woman of the Yr. in Amarillo, Beta Sigma Phi, Amarillo, 1995; recipient Tex. Panhandle Disting. Svc. award West Tex. A&M U., Canyon, 1977, Lifetime Career Achievement award Amarillo Women's Network, 1996. Mem. LWV (v.p., Amarillo program chair), Western Writers Am., Acad. Am. Poets, Amarillo Photog. Soc. (publicity com., Salon award 1965-96), Panhandle Profl. Writers (pres., bd. mem.), Poetry Soc. Tex. (founder. area chpt. 1972, pres. area chpt. 1979-81, Tex. state councilor 1970—), Tex. Tchrs. of Creative Writing. Democrat. Home: 124 Wayside Dr Amarillo TX 79106 Office: Paramount Pub Co PO Box 3730 Amarillo TX 79116-3730

ROBERTSON, SARA STEWART, portfolio manager; b. N.Y.C., Feb. 4, 1940; d. John Elliott and Mary Terry (Schlamp) Stewart; m. James Young Robertson, Nov. 29, 1975 (dec. Mar. 1988). BA, Conn. Coll., 1961; MBA, Am. U., 1969. From trainee to officer First Nat. Bank/First Chgo. Corp., 1969-75, v.p., 1975-92; prin. Royall Enterprises, Chgo., 1992—; prin., dir. Zeppelin Press, Inc., Miami, Fla., 1995—; bd. dirs. Youth Guidance, Chgo., 1982-85, 92-95, chair individuals fundraising, mem. exec. com., 1993-95; bd. dirs. Harbor House Condominium Assn. Chgo., 1990-92; bd. trustees Sherwood Conservatory Music, 1993—, chair bd. devel., 1993-95; mem. allocations com. and family priority grants com. United Way-Chgo., 1992-95. Mem. Club 13 Palm Beach (pres. 1996—). Home and Office: 122 Peruvian Ave PH Palm Beach FL 33480-4477

ROBERTSON, SUZANNE MARIE, primary education educator; b. Canton, Ohio, Nov. 21, 1944; d. Jules Michael and Emma Louise (Olmar) Franzen; m. William K. Robertson, June 30, 1973 (dec. 1979). BS in Early Childhood Edn., Kent State U., 1966; M in Early Childhood Edn., Southern Conn. U., 1976; postgrad., Fairfield U. and U. Bridgeport, 1981-82. Kindergarten tchr. Ridgefield (Conn.) Bd. Edn., 1966—, Internat. Sch. Basel, Switzerland, 1993-94; children's gymnastics instr. Ridgefield (Conn.) YMCA, 1982-83, Sherman Parks and Recreation, Conn., 1983-85; mem. com., facilitator Young Writer's Conf., Ridgefield, Conn., 1996. Toy designer; mem. nat. adv. bd. Learning Mag. Campaign vol. Cancer Fund of Am., Sherman, 1980-81. Awarded Honorable Mention Learning Mag., 1989; recipient Profl. Best Teaching awards. Mem. NEA, Tchrs. Assn. Supporting Children (chmn. 1986-89, Fairfield County pub. rels. com. 1986-89), Conn. Edn. Assn., Internat. Platform Assn., Sherman Hist. Soc., Phi Delta Kappa (historian 1989-90, rsch. rep. 1990-91). Office: Farmingville Elem Sch 324 Farmingville Rd Ridgefield CT 06877-4241

ROBERTSON, WYNDHAM GAY, university official; b. Salisbury, N.C., Sept. 25, 1937; d. Julian Hart and Blanche Williamson (Spencer) R. AB in Econs., Hollins Coll., Roanoke, Va., 1958. Rsch. asst. Standard Oil Co., N.Y.C., 1958-61; rschr. Fortune Mag., N.Y.C., 1961-67, assoc. editor, 1968-74, bd. of editors, 1974-81, asst. mng. editor, 1981-86; bus. editor Time Mag., N.Y.C., 1982-83; v.p. comm. U. N.C., Chapel Hill, 1986-96; bd. dirs. Wachovia Corp., 1995—, Media Gen. Inc., 1996—. Contbr. numerous articles to Fortune Mag. Bd. dirs. N.C. Pub. TV Found., Mary Reynolds Babcock Found. Recipient Gerald M. Loeb Achievement award, U. of Conn., 1972. Mem. Phi Beta Kappa. Episcopalian.

ROBEY, KATHLEEN MORAN (MRS. RALPH WEST ROBEY), civic worker; b. Boston, Aug. 9, 1909; d. John Joseph and Katherine (Berrigan) Moran; B.A., Trinity Coll., Washington, 1933; m. Ralph West Robey, Jan. 28, 1941. Actress appearing in Pride and Prejudice, Broadway, 1935, Tomorrow is a Holiday, road co., 1935, Death Takes a Holiday, road co., 1936, Left Turn, Broadway, 1936, Come Home to Roost, Boston, 1936; pub. relations N.Y. Fashion Industry, N.Y.C., 1938-43. Mem. Florence Crittenton Home and Hosp., Women's Aux. Salvation Army, Gray Lady, ARC; mem. Seton Guild St. Ann's Infant Home. Mem. Christ Child Soc., Fedn. Republican Women of D.C. English-Speaking Union. Republican. Roman Catholic. Clubs: City Tavern, Cosmos (Washington), Nat. Woman's Republican. Home: 4000 Cathedral Ave NW Washington DC 20016-5249

ROBFOGEL, SUSAN SALITAN, lawyer; b. Rochester, N.Y., Apr. 4, 1943; d. Victor and Janet (Rosenthal) Salitan; m. Nathan Joshua Robfogel, July 12, 1965; children: Jacob Morris, Samuel Salitan. BA cum laude, Smith Coll., 1964; JD, Cornell U., 1967. Bar: N.Y.1967, U.S. Dist. Ct. (we. dist.) 1968, U.S. Ct. Appeals (2d cir.) 1971, U.S. Supreme Ct. 1971, U.S. Dist. Ct. (no. dist.) 1974, D.C. 1982. Asst. corp. counsel, then sr. asst. corp. counsel City of Rochester, N.Y., 1967-70; assoc. Harris, Beach & Wilcox, Rochester, 1970-75; ptnr. Harris, Beach, Wilcox, Rubin & Levey, Rochester, 1975-85; ptnr., chair health svcs. practice Nixon, Hargrave, Devans & Doyle, Rochester, 1985—; panel mem., Fed. Svc. Impasses Panel, Washington, 1983-94; mem., past chair Data Protection Rev. Bd., Albany, N.Y., 1984—. Mem. trustees vis. com. U. Rochester Med. Sch., 1990; mem. mgmt. adv. panel SUNY, 1990. Recipient Brockport Coll. Found. Community award, 1989. Fellow Am. Bar Found., N.Y. State Bar Found.; mem. ABA, N.Y. State Bar Assn., Washington D.C. Bar Assn., Monroe County Bar Assn. (Rodenbeck award 1988). Home: 1090 Park Ave Rochester NY 14610-1728 Office: Nixon Hargrave Devans & Doyle Clinton Sq PO Box 1051 Rochester NY 14603-1051 also: 437 Madison Ave New York NY 10022

ROBIN, CLARA NELL (CLAIRE ROBIN), English language educator; b. Harrisonburg, Va., Feb. 19, 1945; d. Robert Franklin and Marguerite Ausherman (Long) Wampler; m. Phil Camden Branner, June 10, 1967 (div. May 1984); m. John Charles Robin, Nov. 22, 1984 (div. Dec. 1990). BA in English, Mary Washington Coll., 1967; MA in English, James Madison U., 1974; postgrad., Jesus Coll., Cambridge, Eng., 1982, Princeton U., 1985-86; Auburn U., 1988, U. No. Tex., 1990-91. Cert. tchr. English, French, master cert., Tex. Tchr. 7th grade John C. Myers Intermediate Sch., Broadway, Va., 1967-68; tchr. 10th grade Waynesville (Mo.) H.S., 1968-70; tchr. 6th, 7th, 8th grades Mary Mount Jr. Sch., Santa Barbara, Calif., 1970-72; tchr. 9th grade Forest Meadow Jr. H.S. Richardson (Tex.) Ind. Sch. Dist., 1972-78, tchr. 10th grade Lake Highlands H.S., 1972-84; tchr. 11th, 12th grades Burleson (Tex.) H.S. Burleson Ind. Sch. Dist., 1986—, instr. composition Hill Coll., 1992-94. Contbg. author: (book revs.) English Journal, 1989-94, (lit. criticism) Eric, 1993. Vol. Dallas Theater Ctr., 1990—; mem. Kimbell Art Mus., Ft. Worth, 1990—, Modern Art Mus., Ft. Worth, 1992—, KERA Pub. TV, Dallas, 1990—. Fellow NEH, 1988, 89, 92, 95, Fulbright-Hays Summer Seminar, 1991; ind. study grantee Coun. Basic Edn., 1990; recipient Honorable Mention Tex. Outstanding Tchg. of the Humanities award, 1995. Mem. ASCD, NEA, Nat. Coun. Tchrs. English, Tex. State Tchrs. Assn., Epsilon Nu of Delta Kappa Gamma (1st v.p. 1988-94, v.p. 1992-94). Home: 4009 W 6th St Fort Worth TX 76107-1619 Office: Burleson High Sch 517 SW Johnson Ave Burleson TX 76028-5312

ROBINETTE, BETSYE HUNTER, school psychologist; b. Nashville, Sept. 30, 1960; d. Gerald Sylvan and Eleanor Louise (Felts) Hunter; m. Michael David Robinette, Aug. 13, 1988; 1 child, David. 030PhD, U. Tenn., 1993; MA cum laude, Wheaton (Ill.) Coll., 1984. Lic. psychol. examiner, cert. sch. psychologist, Tenn. Adolescent counselor Mercy Ctr., Aurora, Ill., 1983-84; mental health technician Glendale Heights (Ill.) Community Hosp., 1984; staff psychologist Cumberland River Comprehensive Care Ctr., Harlan, Ky., 1985-86; psychotherapist Family Svc. Ctr., Asheville, N.C., 1987; psychol. examiner Overlook Mental Health Ctr., Knoxville, Tenn., 1987-88; sch. psychology intern Cherokee Mental Health Ctr., Morristown, Tenn., 1989-90; sch. psychologist Knox County Schs., Knoxville, Tenn., 1990-94, Christian Acad. of Knoxville, 1994—; crisis intervention worker RAFT, Inc. Crisis Intervention, Blacksburg, Va., 1981-82; grad. asst. Wheaton Coll., 1984, U. Tenn., Knoxville, 1988-89; clinic coord. U. Tenn., 1989. Missionary Campus Crusade for Christ, Tokyo, 1982. Mem. Am. Psychol. Assn., Nat. Assn. Sch. Psychologists, Tenn. Assn. Sch. Psychologists, Christian Assn. Psychol. Studies, Phi Kappa Phi, Pi Lambda Theta, Psi Chi (v.p. 1981-82). Presbyterian. Home: 1624 Summerhill Dr Knoxville TN 37922-6257

ROBINS, BETTY DASHEW, antiques and arts dealer; b. N.Y.C., Feb. 14, 1923; d. Leon and Esther (Turits) Dashew; m. Arthur Joseph Robins, Sept. 26, 1948; children: Lisa Dale, Michael Lee. BA, NYU, 1952. Field staff Pearl Buck Open Door, N.Y.C., 1944-45; dir. MacArthur House, San Francisco, 1945-47, Georgetown House, Washington, 1948-50; asst. curator S. Asian Collection Mus. of Art and Archaeology, U. Mo., Columbia, 1967-68; owner BDR Assocs. Arts and Antiques, Columbia, 1976—; founding mem., 1st pres. Columbia Art League, 1959-61; gen. chmn. 1st Tenn. Artist Craftsman Fair, Nashville, 1971-72; bd. dirs. Mus. Assocs., Mus. Art and Archaeology, U. Mo., 1975-85, mem. S. Asian studies com., 1976-85; coord. Festival of India, 1985-86, Festival of China, 1986-87, Peace Through the Arts, 1987-88; mem. profl. visual arts adv. com. Mo. Arts Coun., 1980-82; cons. Denver Art Mus., 1991-92; organizer gallery exhibits. Co-author: Everyday Art of India, 1968; contbr. articles to profl. jours. Bd. dirs. PAST (hist. preservation of Mo.), 1978-79. Named Woman of the Yr., Women in Comms., 1977-78, Vol. of Yr., Vol. Action Coun., 1983; Columbia Art League Bldg. dedicated to Betty Dashew Robins, 1987. Home: 2316 Woodridge Rd Columbia MO 65203

ROBINS, LEE NELKEN, medical educator; b. New Orleans, Aug. 29, 1922; d. Abe and Leona (Reiman) Nelken; m. Eli Robins, Feb. 22, 1946 (dec. Dec. 1994); children: Paul, James, Thomas, Nicholas. Student, Newcomb Coll., 1938-40; BA, Radcliffe Coll., 1942, MA, 1943; PhD, Harvard U., 1951. Mem. faculty Washington U., St. Louis, 1954—, prof. sociology in psychiatry, 1968-91, prof. sociology, 1969-91, univ. prof. social sci., prof. social sci. in psychiatry, 1991—; past mem. Nat. Adv. Coun. on Drug Abuse; past mem. task panels Pres.'s Commn. on Mental Health; mem. expert adv. panel on mental health WHO; Salmon lectr. N.Y. Acad. Medicine, 1983. Author: Deviant Children Grown Up, 1966; editor 11 books; N.Am. Assoc. editor Internat. Jour. Methods in Psychiat. Rsch.; mem. editl. bd. Psychol. Medicine, Jour. Child Psychology and Psychiatry, Devel. and Psychopathology, Jour. Studies on Alcohol, Epidemiol. e Psychiat. Sociale, Criminal Behavior and Mental Health; contbr. articles to profl. jours. Recipient Rsch. Scientist award USPHS, 1970-90, Pacesetter Rsch. award Nat. Inst. Drug Abuse, 1978, Radcliffe Coll. Grad. Soc. medal, 1979, Sutherland award Soc. Criminology, 1991, Nathan B. Eddy award Com. on Problems of Drug Dependence, 1993; rsch. grantee NIMH, Nat. Inst. on Drug Abuse, Nat. Inst. on Alcohol Abuse and Alcoholism. Fellow Am. Coll. Epidemiology, Royal Coll. Psychiatrists (hon.); mem. APHA (Rema Lapouse award 1979, Lifetime Achievement award sect. on alcohol and drug abuse 1994), World Psychiat. Assn. (sect. com. on epidemiology and cmty. psychiatry, treas.), Soc. Life History Rsch. in Psychopathology, Am. Coll. Neuropsychopharmacology, Am. Sociol. Assn., Internat. Sociol. Assn., Inst. Medicine, Internat. Epidemiol. Assn., Am. Psychopath. Assn. (pres. 1987-88, Paul Hoch award 1978). Office: Washington U Dept Psychiatry Med Sch Saint Louis MO 63110

ROBINSON, ALICE JEAN MCDONNELL, drama and speech educator; b. St. Joseph, Mo., Nov. 17, 1922; d. John Francis and Della M. (Mavity) McDonnell; m. James Eugene Robinson, Apr. 21, 1956 (dec. 1983). BA, U. Kans., 1944, MA, 1947; PhD, Stanford U., 1965. Tchr. Garden City (Kans.) High Sch., 1944-46; asst. prof. Emporia (Kans.) State U., 1947-52; dir. live programs Sta. KTVH-TV, Hutchinson-Wichita, Kans., 1953-55; assoc. prof. drama and speech U. Md. Baltimore County, Balt., 1966—, rsch. theatre history. Author: The American Theatre: A History in Slides, 1992, Betty Comden and Adolph Green: A Bio-Bibliography, 1993; co-editor: Notable Women in the American Theatre, 1989; appeared in plays, including Landscape, 1983, Tartuffe, 1985, Rockaby, 1990. Mem. Am. Soc. Theatre Rsch., Assn. Theatre Higher Edn., East Central Theatre Conf., Phi Beta Kappa. Republican. Home: 606 Edgevale Rd Baltimore MD 21210-1904 Office: U Md Baltimore County Wilkens Ave Baltimore MD 21228

ROBINSON, AMY, film producer. Films include: Chilly Scenes of Winter, 1979, Baby It's You, 1983, After Hours, 1985, Running On Empty, 1987, White Palace, 1990, Once Around, 1991, With Honors, 1994. Office: Jersey Tomato Inc 1501 Broadway Ste 2600 New York NY 10036-5601

ROBINSON, ANNETTMARIE, entrepreneur; b. Fayetteville, Ark., Jan. 31, 1940; d. Christopher Jacy and Lorena (Johnson) Simmons; m. Roy Robinson, June 17, 1966; children: Steven, Sammy, Doug, Pamela, Olen. BA, Edison Tech. U., 1958; BA in Bus., Seattle Community Coll., 1959. Dir. perss. Country Kitchen Restaurants, Inc., Anchorage, 1966-71; investor Anchorage, 1971—; cons. Pioneer Investments, Anchorage, 1983—, M'RAL, Inc. Retail Dry Goods, Anchorage, 1985. Mem. Rep. Presdl. Task Force, Washington, 1984—, Reps. of Alaska, Anchorage, 1987; mem. chmn. round table YMCA, Anchorage, 1986—; active Sta. KWN2, KQLO, Reno, Nev.; active in child abuse issues and prosecution. Named Woman of Yr. Lions, Anchorage, 1989, marksman first class Nat. Rifle Assn., 1953. Mem. NAFE, Spenard Lion's Aux. (past pres.).

ROBINSON, BARBARA PAUL, lawyer; b. Oct. 19, 1941; d. Leo and Pauline G. Paul; m. Charles Raskob Robinson, June 11, 1965; children: Charles Paul, Torrance Webster. AB magna cum laude, Bryn Mawr Coll., 1962; LLB, Yale U., 1965. Bar: N.Y. 1966, U.S. Dist. Ct. (so. and ea. dists.) N.Y. 1975, U.S. Tax Ct. 1972, U.S. Ct. Appeals (2d cir.) 1974. Assoc. Debevoise & Plimpton (formerly Debevoise, Plimpton, Lyons & Gates), N.Y.C., 1966-75, ptnr., 1976—; mem. adv. bd., lectr. Practicing Law Inst.; arbitrator Am. Arbitration Assn., 1987—, bd. dirs. Contbr. articles to profl. jours. Mem. adv. coun., bd. visitors CUNY Law Sch., Queens, 1984-90; trustee Trinity Sch., 1982-86, pres., 1986-88; bd. dirs. Found. for Child Devel., 1989—, chmn., 1991—; mem. Coun. on Fgn. Rels.; bd. dirs. Catalyst, 1993—, Am. Judicature Soc., Fund Modern Cts., 1990—, Wave Hill, 1994—, Garden Conservancy, 1996—; trustee The William Nelson Cromwell Found., 1993—. Fellow Am. Coll. Trust and Estate Counsel, Am. Bar Found., N.Y. Bar Found.; mem. ABA, N.Y. State Bar Assn. (vice chmn. com. on trust adminstrn., trusts and estates law sect. 1977-81, ho. of dels. 1984-87, 90-92, mem. com. ann. award 1993-94), Assn. of Bar of City of N.Y. (chmn. com. on trusts, estates and surrogates cts. 1981-84, judiciary com. 1981-84, coun. on jud. adminstrn. 1982-84, chair nominating com. 1984-85, mem. exec. com. 1986-91, chair 1989-90, v.p. 1990-91, pres. 1994-96, chair com. on honors 1993-94, mem. com on long-range planning 1991-94), Assn. of Bar of City of N.Y. Fund Inc. (bd. dirs., pres.), Women's Forum, Yale Coun., Yale Law Sch. Assn. N.Y. (mem. devel. bd., exec. com. 1981-85, pres. 1988-93), Yale Club, Washington Club. Office: Debevoise & Plimpton 875 3rd Ave New York NY 10022-6225

ROBINSON, BARBARA S., cultural organization administrator; b. Cleve., Jan. 7, 1930; d. Alfred Cass and Rose (Markey) Shultz; m. Larry Robinson, May 29, 1953; children: Lisa, John, James. BA, Wellesley Coll., 1951; MBA, Harvard U./Radcliffe, 1952. Admin. asst. to mgr. Bonwit Teller, Cleve., 1952-53; artist in the classroom Cleve. Area Arts Coun., coord. Arts in Edn. project, seminar leader, project planner leadership devel. program, adv. arts mgr. internship program, 1969-73; asst. dir. pub. and pub. rels. Wellesley (Mass.) Coll., 1953-56; mkt. rsch. Harvard Bus. Sch., 1956-58; chmn., vice chmn. policy and planning com. Ohio Arts Coun., chair, 1987—; chair Nat. Assembly State Arts Agys., Washington, 1991—, Arts Midwest, 1996—; mem. piano faculty Cleve. Inst. Music., 1968-72, Ohio Arts and Sports Facilities Commn., 1992, Cleve. Found. Commn. Performing Arts, opera coun. Cleve. Opera, adv. com. Ohio Light Opera, program adv. com. Visual and Performing Arts Ctr. Jewish Com. Ctr., Cultural Initiative Task Force, Cleve.; v.p. Nat. Bd. Young Audience, Inc., N.Y.C., asst. treas., 1980—; pres. Cleve. Ballet, 1978-83, exec. com., bd. trustees; mem. exec. com. Cleve. Cultural Coalition, 1987—; dir., founding mem. Nat. Cultural Alliance, Washington, 1991—; mem. bd. Arts Midwest, Mpls., 1983—; trustee New Orgn. Visual Arts, Cleve., 1994 ; chmn. Cleve. Chamber Music Seminar, 1979-85, Mayor's Task Force Cultural Planning, adv. panel states and regions program NEA; chmn. founder Young Audiences Grtr. Cleve.; co-chair Ohio state com. Nat. Mus. Women in the Arts, Washington; mem. fine arts com. Shaker Heights (Ohio) Bd. Edn.; mem. bd. women's com. Cleve. Orch.; adv. com. Harvard Inst. Arts Mgmt., Cleve. Lyric Opera; adv. trustee Ohio Chamber Orch.; hon. chair Arts and Access Celebration and Awards, 1993. Columnist: Spotlight mag. Chmn., mem. univ. coun. Case Western Res. U., vice chmn. bd. overseers, mem. vis. com., mag. editl. adv. bd., pub. affairs adv. bd.; progrma advisor Arts Mgmt. Inst., Weatherhead Sch. Mgmt., 1982—; mem. exec. com., bd. trustees, mem. campaign cabinet U. Hosps. Cleve., 1985—, bd. trustees, 1986—; trustee Western Reserve AIDS Found.; mem. bd. Cleve. Conv. and Visitors Bur., Shaker Heights (Ohio) PTA Coun.; mem. leadership com. Capital Campaign Wellesley Coll., Boston, mem. pres.'s resources com.; trustee, chmn. capital projects com. Wooster Coll., 1983-90; mem. bicentennial adv. planning com. City of Cleve.; mem. adv. coun. U.S. Dept. Edn., Washington; mem. citizens adv. com. Cuyahoga C.C.; co-chmn. parent's com. parent's fund Wesleyan U.; hon. chmn. YWCA Corp. Campaign, 1987, Lake Erie coun. 75th anniversary Girl Scouts U.S., 1988, Svcs. for Ind. Living Week on Wheels Reality Rag Benefit, 1989; trustee Leadership Cleve., 1990—; bd. dirs. Nat. Found. for the Advancement of the Arts. Recipient Spl. Recognition award City of Cleve., 1977, Annual award in dance No. Ohio Live, 1982, Helen Homans Gilbert award for Disting. Vol. Svc. Radcliffe Coll., 1983, Mayor's Award for Volunteerism City of Cleve., 1986, Career Women of Achievement award in Cultural Arts YWCA, 1988, Gov.'s award Ohio Newspaper Assn., 1991, Vol. of Yr. award Leadership Cleve., 1991; named to Shaker Heights Hall fo Fame, 1990, Captain Cleveland, Cleve. Vis. and Convention Bur., 1991; honoree Benefit for Fairmount Theatre for the Deaf, 1994. Mem. Cleve. Soc. Contemporary Arts, Musical Arts Assn. Cleveland Orch., The Print Club Cleve., Wellesley Club, Radcliffe Club, The Social Study Club, Alzheimer's Assn. Gtr. Cleve., Clev. Mus. Art (hon., women's com.). Jewish. Office: Ohio Arts Coun 727 E Main St Columbus OH 42305

ROBINSON, BETH ANNE, acquired brain injury rehabilitation consultant; b. Barnstable, Mass., Sept. 27, 1963; d. Chester Arthur Jr. and Elizabeth (Estlin) R. AA, Cape Cod C.C., 1986; BS, Salem State Coll., 1989; MA, Johnson State Coll., 1995. Youth counselor Monomoy Youth and Family Svcs., Chatham, Mass., 1989-90; traumatic brain injury life skills aide Vocat. Rehab., Vt., 1991-92, Profl. Nurses Svc., Burlington, Vt., 1992-94; acquired brain injury cons., educator Whitefield, N.H., 1994-95; program dir. North Country Ind. Living, North Conway, N.H., 1995; presenter workshops and seminars on acquired brain injury, 1992—; co-chmn. Lifeskills Aide Support Group, Vocat. Rehab., Waterbury, 1993-94, co-chmn., organizer Head Injury Support Group, 1991-93; spkr. vocat. tng.-traumatic brain injury confs. and benefits, Vt., 1992-94; developer, trainer Traumatic Brain Injury Core Curriculum and Tngs., 1994-95; mem. traumatic brain injury re-entry team and adv. bd. Vocat. Rehab., 1993-95; mem. Head Injury and Stroke Independence Project, State NHIF chpt., 1992-95. Pub. video tng. core curriculum for tng. of traumatic brain injury svc. providers State of Vt., 1996. Vol. South Bay Rehab. Program, Hyannis, Mass., 1991. Margaret E. Small scholar Cape Cod C.C., 1986, Hyannis Rotary Club scholar, 1986. Mem.

Nat. Rehab. Assn., Nat. Head Injury Found. (Vt. chpt., N.H. chpt.). Home and Office: PO Box 2051 Brewster MA 02631

ROBINSON, CATHY, retail manager; b. Denison, Iowa, June 1, 1951; d. Teddy Junior and Ruth F. (Paulsen) Cornelius; m. Billy Don Turner, July 3, 1975 (div. Dec. 1979); 1 child, Michelle Suzanne; m. Gary L. Robinson, June 24, 1989; 1 child, Brittany Sue. BA, U. Iowa, 1973. Asst. store mgr. Casual Corner, Houston, 1975-77, store mgr., 1977-80, dist. mgr., Tampa, Fla., 1980-81, regional mgr., Tampa, 1981—; bd. dirs., sec. Galleria Mall, Houston, 1979-80. Mem. Nat. Assn. Female Execs., Gamma Phi Beta. Lutheran. Avocations: water skiing, skiing, snorkeling, softball. Office: Casual Corner 3302 W Buffalo Ave Ste 1022 Tampa FL 33607-6213

ROBINSON, CHARLOTTE HILL, artist; b. San Antonio, Nov. 28, 1924; d. Lucius Davis and Charlotte (Moore) Hill; m. Floyd I. Robinson, Mar. 1943; children: Floyd I. Jr., Lawrence H., Elizabeth H. Student, Incarnate Word Coll., 1943, 44, 45, NYU, 1947, 48, Corcoran Sch. Art, 1951-52. Painting instr. Art League No. Va., Alexandria, 1967-75; Condr. Art World Seminar Washington Women's Art Ctr., 1975-80, drawing workshop Smithsonian Instn. Resident Assocs. Program, Washington, 1977; program dir. Nat. Women's Caucus for Art, 1979; project coord., exhbn. curator The Artist and the Quilt, nat. mus. traveling exhbn., 1983-86; vis. artist S.W. Craft Ctr., San Antonio, 1983-85; lectr. WFUV 90 FM, Fordham U., N.Y.C., 1990, San Antonio Art Inst., 1991, Nat. Mus. for Women in Arts, Washington, 1991, Iowa State U., Ames, 1991. Editor: The Artist & The Quilt, 1983; one-person shows include Thames Sic. Ctr., New London, Conn., 1991, Brunner Gallery & Mus., Iowa State U., 1991, 92, San Antonio Art. Inst., 1991, de Andino Fine Arts, Washington, 1992, Masur Mus. Art, Monroe, La., 1993, 96, Lee Hansley Art Gallery, Raleigh, N.C., 1993, 96, Sol Del Rio, San Antonio, 1995, 1812 Artic Gallery, Virginia Beach, Va., 1995; exhibited in group shows at Franklin Square and Watkins Gallery, Washington, 1992, Rutgers U., New Brunswick, N.J., 1992, 96, Brody's Gallery, Washington, 1992, Lee Hansley Art Gallery, Raleigh, 1993, 96, Emerson Gallery, McLean, 1993, 95, No. Va. C.C., 1994, Harvard U., 1996. Trustee Bronx (N.Y.) Mus., 1977; bd. dirs. Washington Women's Art Ctr., 1977; nat. bd. dirs. Women's Caucus for Art, 1983-84; bd. dirs. New Art Examiner, 1985-86. Recipient Concourse award Corcoran Sch. Art, 1952, Scholarship award Telfair Acad. Art, Savannah, Ga., 1959; Nat. Endowment for Arts grantee, 1977, 78-81; fellow Va. Ctr. for Creative Arts, Sweet Briar, Va., 1985.

ROBINSON, DAWN, vocalist; b. New London, Conn.. Vocalist En Vogue, Atco/Eastwest Records, N.Y.C., 1988—. Albums include Born to Sing (Platinum 1990), Funky Divas, Remix to Sing, Runaway Love. Recipient Soul Train Music award, 1991; nominated Grammy award, 1990. Office: care En Vogue Atco/Eastwest Records 75 Rockefeller Plz New York NY 10019-6908*

ROBINSON, DOLORES MARGUERITE, legal secretary, retired; b. San Diego, July 6, 1930; d. Fernand and Roma Violet (Fingoe) Chevillard; m. Francis James Vingoe, Apr. 13, 1957 (div. Feb. 1966); 1 child, Sylvie Lamorna Vingoe; me. Milo Howard Robinson, May 9, 1969 (div. Mar. 1970). BA with high distinction, Colo. State U., 1969. Vol. Vols. In Svc. to Am., N.Y.C., 1972-74; legal sec. various cos., 1975-88; aide to Senator Bert Kobayashi Hawaii State Senate, Honolulu, 1983, Steefel, Levitt & Weiss, San Francisco, 1989-95; ret., 1995. One-woman shows (stand-up historian), San Francisco, 1992, 94, 95, Lee Glickstein, 1989-91; author, dir., prodr. (1 act play) The Treasures, 1969; consulting editor, editor Look Aloft newsletter, 1973; editor The Y at the Top of the Stairs newsletter, 1974; co-editor All Souls Unitarian Church newsletter, 1975. Bd. dirs. Uptown YMCA, N.Y.C., 1974; co-leader drama class Cmty. Ctr. for Creative Arts, Greeley, Colo., 1970; tutor Westside Cmty. Study Hall, Denver, 1969-70.

ROBINSON, DOROTHY K., lawyer; b. New Haven, Feb. 18, 1951; children: Julia Robinson Bouwsma, Alexandra Toby Bouwsma. BA in Econs. with honors, Swarthmore Coll., 1972; JD, U. Calif.-Berkeley, 1975, MA (hon.) Yale U., 1987. Bar: Conn. 1981, N.Y. 1976, Calif. 1975, U.S. Ct. Appeals (2d cir.) 1975, U.S. Dist. Ct. (so. dist.) N.Y. 1978, U.S. Dist. Ct. Conn. 1981, U.S. Tax Ct. 1981. Assoc. Hughes Hubbard & Reed, N.Y.C., 1975-78; asst. gen. counsel Yale U., New Haven, 1978-79, assoc. gen. counsel, 1979-84, dep. gen. counsel, 1984-86, gen. counsel, 1986-95, dir. fed. relations, 1986-88, acting sec., 1993, v.p., gen. counsel, 1995—. Trustee Hopkins Grammar Day Prospect Hill Sch., New Haven, 1983-88, sec., 1986-88; trustee Wenner-Gren Found. Anthrop. Rsch.,1991—; bd. dirs. Cold Spring Sch., New Haven, 1990-95; mem. adv. bd. Conn. Mental Health Ctr., New Haven, 1979-89; bd. dirs. Nat. Assn. Coll. and U. Attys., 1987-90, Nat. Assn. Indep. Coll. and U., 1994—. Editor articles and book revs. Calif. Law Rev. Fellow Ezra Stiles Coll. Yale U. Fellow Am. Bar Found.; mem. ABA, Nat. Assn. Coll. and Univ. Attys., Conn. Bar Assn., Calif. Bar Assn., Assn. of Bar of City of N.Y., New Eng. Assn. Schs. and Colls. Commn. on Instns. Higher Edn., Phi Beta Kappa. Office: Yale U Office of Gen Counsel PO Box 208255 Yale Sta New Haven CT 06520-8255

ROBINSON, ELAINE DIANE, electric power industry executive; b. N.Y.C., Feb. 13, 1940; d. William Emanuel and Sylvia (Eisenberg) R.; m. Leonard Adler, June 12, 1960 (div. Apr. 1979); children: Mona Jane, Sari Michele. BA, CUNY, 1960; MBA, Adelphi U., 1982. Sales svc. staff Crown Zellerbach, N.Y.C., 1960-61; tchr. N.Y.C. Schs., 1961-64; legis. Suffolk County Legis., Riverhead, N.Y., 1976-78; assoc. dir. pub. affairs L.I. Lighting Co., Hicksville, N.Y., 1978-87; mgr. nuclear info. Boston Edison Co., 1987-91, spl. asst. to pres. and mgr. transp. devel., 1991-93; v.p. pub. affairs Nashville Elec. Svc., 1993—. Active Consumer Protection Bd., Huntington, N.Y., 1970-72, Zoning Bd. Appeals, Huntington, 1972-76, Women's Polit. Caucus, Nashville, 1995—; econ. working group mem. Fed. Fleet Conv. Task Force, Washington, 1992-93. Mem. Phi Beta Kappa, Delta Mu Delta. Home: 113 Belle Glen Dr Nashville TN 37221 Office: Nashville Elec Svc 1214 Church St Nashville TN 37203

ROBINSON, ELIZABETH LEA, artist; b. Louisville, Miss., Oct. 19, 1954; d. Clarence Olyn and Doris Elaine (Ray) R. BA in Psychology, Miss. U. for Women, 1976, postgrad., 1977-78. V.p. Pearl River Glass Studio, Inc., Jackson, Miss., 1981-91; owner Mosquito Grill, Jackson, 1991-93; legal adminstr. Legal Resources, Inc., Jackson, 1994—; owner Oriental Express, Inc., Jackson, 1988-91, Gallery Restaurant, Jackson, 1990-91, Studio C, Jackson, 1991—. Hon. exhibit Yr. of Craft Miss. Mus. Art, Jackson, 1994. Mem. Craftsmen's Guild Miss. (sec.-treas. 1990-91, bd. dirs.), Miss. Forge Coun., Blacksmiths Am. Home: 1839 Linden Pl Jackson MS 39202 Office: Legal Resources Inc 206 W Pearl St Jackson MS 39201

ROBINSON, EMMA HAIRSTON, artist, educator; b. Lexington, N.C., Sept. 13, 1942; d. Cardell and Martha Ann (McCarter) Hairston; m. Daniel Louis Robinson, Dec. 26, 1963; 1 child, Gardell Lewis. BFA, Howard U., 1990, MFA, 1992. Sec. Dept. Navy, Washington, 1968-70, NSF, Washington, 1970-81; artist, tchr., lectr. Arts for Aging, Bethesda, Md., 1990—; office mgr., cons. Nat. Assn. Minority Contractors, Washington, 1993-94. Lucy E. Moten fellow, 1989; Spl. Talent scholar, 1988-92. Mem. Nat. Conf. Artists, New D.C. Collage Soc., Nat. Coun. Negro Women, Washington Area Lawyers for Arts, Golden Key Nat. Honor Soc., Zeta Phi Beta. Democrat. Home: 1523 Church St NW Washington DC 20005

ROBINSON, ESTHER MARTIN, secondary school educator; b. Buffalo, N.Y., Sept. 19, 1956; d. Douglas Charles and Esther (Hagen) Martin; m. Stephen Mark Robinson, May 6, 1978; children: Rachel Anne, Sarah Elizabeth. BA, Oral Roberts U., 1978; MA, U. Tulsa, 1983. Tchr. secondary sch. history Tulsa Pub. Schs., 1978-80; tchr. secondary sch. history Jenks (Okla.) High Sch., 1980-92, chair dept. social studies, 1990-92; tchr. world history, advanced placement U.S. history Langham Creek High Sch., Houston, 1992—; presenter in field. Mem. Nat. Coun. Social Studies, Tex. Coun. Social Studies, Cypress Fairbanks Coun. for Social Studies, Tex. Assn. Gifted and Talented. Home: 8022 Null Ct Spring TX 77379-6141 Office: Langham Creek High Sch 17610 FM 529 Houston TX 77095

ROBINSON, FLORINE SAMANTHA, marketing executive; b. Massies Mill, Va., Feb. 4, 1935; d. John Daniel and Fannie Belle (Smith) Jackson; m. Frederick Robinson (div. 1973); children: Katherine, Theresa, Freda. BS, Morgan State U., 1976; postgrad., U. Balt., 1977-81, Liberty U., 1987. Writer, reporter Phila. Independent News, 1961-63; freelance writer, editor Balt., 1963-71; asst. mng. editor Williams & Wilkins Pubs. Inc., Balt, 1971-76; mktg. rep., then mktg. mgr. NCR Corp., Balt., 1977-93; assoc. minister, trustee Christian Unity Temple, Balt., 1976—; pres. ABCOM, Inc., Balt., 1993—; bd. dirs. Armstrong & Bratcher, Inc., Balt. Editor: Stedman's Medical Dictionary, 1972; contbr. articles to profl. jours. Active PTA, Balt., 1963-65; bd. dirs. Howard Pk. Civic Assn., Balt., 1967—, pres. 1991—; leader, cons. Girl Scouts USA, 1970-73. Recipient Excellence in Rsch. award Psi Chi, 1976, Citizen citation Mayor of Balt. Mem. NAFE, Mid-Atlantic Food Dealers Assn., Am. Soc. Notaries, Internat. Platform Assn., Edelweiss Club, Order of Eastern Star. Democrat. Home: 3126 Howard Park Ave Baltimore MD 21207-6715

ROBINSON, GWENDOLYN POWELL, savings and loan executive, church executive. BS in Orgnl. Behavior and Pers., Northwestern U., 1979; MS in Cmty. Bank Mgmt., U. Tex., 1995. With Ill. Svc. Fed. Savs. and Loan Assn., Chgo., 1969—, asst. supr. mortgage loan scs., 1972-74, supr. teller ops., 1974-79, staff advisor and trainer, 1979-80, br. mgr., 1980-81, asst. v.p. adminstrv. svcs. and pers., br. coord., 1984-88, v.p., COO, pers. dir., 1988-91, sr. v.p., COO, 1991-92, exec. .p., COO, compliance officer, 1992—, also bd. dirs.; gen. sec. Ch. of Living God, Cin.; mem. Smith and Smith CPA Firm, Chgo., 1985—; mem. ad hoc com. Chgo. Mayor's Office Employment Tng., 1984. Mem. adv. coun. Jones Comml. H.S., Chgo. Bd. Edn.; deacon Chgo. United. Recipient Black and Hispanic achievers award, award Jr. Achievement, Leadership award, Cmty. and Bus. Leadership award. Mem. Ill. Svc. Fed. Savs. and Loan Assn. Chgo., Chgo. Urban League, Sigma Gamma Rho. Office: Ill Svc Fed Savs and Loan Assn 4619 S King Dr Chicago IL 60653 also: Ch of Living God Christian Workers Fellowship Workers Fellowship 430 Forest Ave Cincinnati OH 45229

ROBINSON, JENNIFER LYNN, nursing educator; b. Washington, Pa., Dec. 28, 1958; d. John and Jennie (Mucho) R. Diploma, Washington Hosp. Sch. Nursing, 1979; BSN, Wheeling Jesuit Coll., 1990; MSN in Cardiopulmonary Nursing, U. Pitts., 1995. RN, Pa.; CCRN. Med.-surg. staff nurse Washington Hosp., 1979-83, nurse trainer med. info. sys., 1983, staff nurse CCU, 1984-86, asst. nurse mgr. CCU, 1986-91, instr. critical care class, 1990—, nurse educator, 1991—; ACLS instr., Washington Hosp., Am. Heart Assn., 1989—. Mem. AACN, Respiratory Nursing Assn., Assn. Clin. Nurse Specialists, Nat. Honor Soc. Nurses, Washington Hosp. Sch. Nursing Assn., Sigma Theta Tau, Alpha Sigma Lambda, Alpha Sigma Nu. Office: Washington Hosp Sch Nursing 155 Wilson Ave Washington PA 15301

ROBINSON, JOAN LENORE, retired dietitian; b. Rochester, Minn., May 28, 1931; d. John Silas and Lenore Henrietta (Mittelstadt) Lundy; m. Donald N. Robinson, Sept. 17, 1960; children: Charles Lundy, Jonathan Paul. BS, U. Wash., 1953; MS, U. Minn., 1959. Dietetic intern Mass. Gen. Hosp., Boston, 1954; therapeutic dietitian Faulkner Hosp., Jamaica Plain and Boston, 1954-55; pediatric dietitian St. Mary's Hosp., Rochester, Minn., 1955-56; rsch. dietitian Lankenau Hosp., Phila., 1959-61; chief nutritionist U. Louisville Med. Sch., 1968-69; cons. dietitian Eagleville (Pa.) Hosp. and Rehab. Ctr., 1977-78; cons. dietitican North Penn Convalescent Residence, Eagleville, 1977-80, Ea. Mennonite Home, Souderton, Pa., 1980-81, River Crest, Mont Clare, Pa., 1973, 79-82, Arden Hall, Phila., 1983-84, Presbyn. Home for the Aged, Phila., 1978-95, Manatawny Manor, Pottstown, Pa., 1985-96. Pres. Trinity United Ch. of Christ, Collegeville, Pa., 1974-75; mem. Pa. State Extension Family Living Adv. Bd., Skippack, Pa., 1986-96. Mem. AAUW (life; Outstanding Women in Perkiomen Br. 1986), Am. Dietetic Assn., Pa. Dietetic Assn., Phila. Dietetic Assn., Mayo Found. Alumni, U. N.D. Alumni, Cons. Dieticians in Health Care Facilities (sec.-trea. 1982-83), Sigma Delta Epsilon. Home: 316 Colonial Ave Collegeville PA 19426-2538

ROBINSON, JOYCE MCPEAKE, administrator; b. Newark, July 28, 1941; d. Salvatore and Wilhelmina (Cervetto) Guinta; m. John David McPeake, June 15, 1963 (div. Aug. 1974); children: John Paul, David Samuel; m. Enders Anthony Robinson, Aug. 8, 1992. BA in English, Tufts U., 1962; MA in English, Boston U., 1965, EdD, 1979. Asst. to dean women & dept. adminstrn. Boston U., 1962-63, 65-67; reading specialist Hingham (Mass.) Pub. Schs., 1963-64; reading and learning specialist Manter Hall Sch., Cambridge, Mass., 1964-67; reporter Patriot Ledger, Quincy, Mass., 1967-69; dir. Christ Luth. Sch., Scituate, Mass., 1971-74; prin. and reading specialist Scituate Pub. Schs., 1974-80; chair English, dir. reading programs St. Andrew's Sch., Boca Raton, Fla., 1980-88; chair English, learning specialist Broadwater Acad., Exmore, Va., 1988-89; dir. learning resources, English Fountain Valley Sch., Colorado Springs, Colo., 1989-91; asst. prin. Islamic Saudi Acad., Alexandria, Va., 1991-93; chair English and lang. resources Masters Sch., Dobbs Ferry, N.Y., 1993-94; head QUEST program Dwight Sch., N.Y.C., 1994—, head of sch., 1996—; adj. prof. Nova U., Ft. Lauderdale, Fla., 1984-88, St. Thomas U., Miami, Fla., 1987-88; sch. evaluator Fla. Coun. Ind. Schs., 1985-88; cons. in field. Author: Teaching Study Skills, 1987, Wordworks, 1990; author of poems. Coord. Am. Inst. Fgn. Study, Boston, 1987; parent agt. Hamilton Coll. Parents Fund, Clinton, N.Y., 1986—; mem. town adv. com. Scituate Town Com., 1975-80. Mem. Nat. Coun. Tchrs. English, Am. Acad. Poets, Nat. Assn. Ind. Schs., Fla. Coun. Librs., Ea. Ednl. Rsch. Assn. (membership chair 1993—), Internat. Reading Assn., Coun. Exceptional Children, Modern Lang. Assn., Hemingway Soc. Home: 560 Riverside Dr Apt # 20J New York NY 10027 Office: Dwight Sch 291 Central Park W New York NY 10024

ROBINSON, JULIE CHRISTINE-LORD, elementary education educator; b. Peoria, Ill., Mar. 31, 1963; d. Farrell Stewart Lord and Patricia Lynn (Huisman) Hager; m. Thomas Lee Robinson, Aug. 6, 1988. AAS, Ill. Ctrl. Coll., 1984; BS in Edn., Ill. State U., 1986; MS in Math. Edn., Western Ill. U., 1992. Math. and sci. tchr. Lindbergh Middle Sch., Peoria, 1986-90; math. tchr. Blaine-Sumner Middle Sch., Peoria, 1992, Woodruff H.S., Peoria, 1992-94; math. dept. chair Von Steuben Mid. Sch., Peoria, 1994—, coach MATHCOUNTS, 1994—; supr. tchr. Ill. State U. and Bradley U., 1990—; spkr. in field. Math., Sci. and Tech. grantee Mid-Illini Ednl. Svc. Ctr., Creve Coeur, Ill., 1992, First Grant awardee 1995, Outstanding Tchr. award 1990, 95. Mem. Nat. Coun. Tchrs. Math., Ill. Coun. Tchrs. Math., West Ctrl. Coun. Tchrs. Math., Women in Math Edn., Phi Delta Kappa. Lutheran. Home: 8108 W Pfeiffer Rd Mapleton IL 61547-9753 Office: 801 E Forrest Hill Ave Peoria IL 61603-1341

ROBINSON, JUNE KERSWELL, dermatologist, educator; b. Phila., Jan. 26, 1950; d. George and Helen S. (Kerswell) R.; m. William T. Barker, Jan. 31, 1981. BA cum laude, U. Pa., 1970; MD, U. Md., 1974. Diplomate Am. Bd. Dermatology, Nat. Bd. Med. Examiners, Am. Bd. Mohs Micrographic Surgery and Cutaneous Oncology. Intern Greater Balt. Med. Ctr., Hanover, N.H., 1974; resident in medicine Greater Balt. Med. Ctr., 1974-75; resident in dermatology Dartmouth-Hitchcock Med. Ctr., Hanover, N.H., 1975-78, chief resident, clin. instr., 1977-78; instr. in dermatology Dartmouth-Hitchcock Med. Ctr., Hanover, 1978; fellow Mohs; chemosurgery and dermatologic surgery NYU Skin and Cancer Clinic, N.Y.C., 1978-79; instr. in dermatology NYU, N.Y.C., 1979; asst. prof. dermatology Northwestern U. Med. Sch., Chgo., 1979, asst. prof. surgery, 1980-85, assoc. prof. dermatology and surgery, 1985-91, prof. dermatology and surgery, 1991—; mem. consensus devel. conf. NIH, 1992; lectr. in field. Author: Fundamentals of Skin Biopsy, 1985, also audiovisual materials; editor: (textbooks) Atlas of Cutaneous Surgery, 1996, Cutaneous Medicine and Surgery: An Integrated Program in Dermatology, 1996; mem. editl. bd. Archives of Dermatology, 1988—; sect. editor The Cutting Edge: Challenges in Med. and Surg. Therapeutics, 1989—; contbg. editor Jour. Dermatol. Surgery and Oncology, 1985-88; mem. editl. com. 18th World Congress of Dermatology, 1982; contbr. numerous articles, abstracts to profl. publs., chpts. to books. Bd. dirs. Northwestern Med. Faculty Found., 1982-84, chmn. com. on benefits and leaves, 1984, nominating com. 1988. Grantee Nat. Cancer Inst., 1985-91, Am. Cancer Soc., 1986-89, Skin Cancer Found., 1984-85, Dermatology Found., 1981-83, Northwestern U. Biomed. Rsch., 1981, Syntex, 1984. Fellow Am. Coll. Chemosurgery (chmn. sci. program ann. meeting 1983, chmn. publs. com. 1986-87, chmn. task force on ednl. needs 1989-90, co-editor bull. 1984-87); mem. AMA, Am. Dermatol. Assn., Am. Acad. Dermatology (dist. sec. treas. 1985, Stephen Rothman Lectr. award 1992, Presdl. citation 1992), Dermatology Found. (trustee 1995—), Internat. Soc. Dermatol. Surgery, Am. Soc. Dermatol. Surgery (pres. 1994-95), Soc. Investigative Dermatology, Women's Dermatol. Soc. (pres. 1990-92), Chgo. Dermatol. Soc. Home: 132 E Delaware # 5806 Chicago IL 60611-1533

ROBINSON, LISA GALE LANGLEY, community health nurse; b. Carrollton, Ga., Apr. 27, 1959. AD, West Ga. Coll., 1985; BSN, U. Ala., Birmingham, 1988, MSN, 1990. RN, Ala., Ga. Charge, staff nurse Bowdon (Ga.) Area Hosp., 1979-86, 87-90, U. Ala. Hosps., Birmingham, 1986-90; family nurse practioner West Carroll Community Physicians, Bowdon, Ga., 1990; instr. practical nursing Carroll Tech. InstCarrollton, 1990-95; family nurse practitioner Cmty. Care Program, 1995—. Ala. Nursing scholar. Mem. ANA, Am. Heart Assn., Ala. State Nurses Assn., Sigma Theta Tau.

ROBINSON, LORNA JANE, marketing executive; b. N. Tonawanda, N.Y., Jan. 28, 1957; d. Lawrence Esdras and Irene Nancy (Sachuk) Cyr. AS in Bus. Methods, SUNY, Buffalo, 1983, BS in Bus. Adminstrn., 1987. Credit clk. Nat. Assn. Credit Mgmt., Buffalo, 1975-77; sec. to v.p. The Sample, Inc., Buffalo, 1977-78; credit rep. Liberty Nat. Bank and Trust, Buffalo, 1978-79, Spencer Kellogg Div. Textron, Buffalo, 1979-82; sr. customer svc. rep. Spencer Kellogg/NL Chems., Buffalo, 1982-86; account exec. WYRK-FM, Buffalo, 1986, Genigraphics Corp., Phila., 1986-90; mgr. advt. Trade Show Pubs., Morrisville, Pa., 1991—. Roman Catholic. Home: 5153 Judson Dr Bensalem PA 19020-3850 Office: Trade Show Pubs 20 N Pennsylvania Ave Morrisville PA 19067-1110

ROBINSON, LOUISE EVETTE, marriage family child counselor; b. San Francisco, May 8, 1952; d. Ellis Hart and Doris Sonia (Morris) R.; stepmother Anita Robinson. BA in Psychology, U. Calif., Berkeley, 1973; MA in Psychology, Sonoma State U., 1976. Lic. marriage, family and child counselor. Co-therapist John Champlin M.D., Berkeley, 1976, Jonothon Gross M.D., Napa, Calif., 1976; counselor Buckelew House, Kentfield, Calif., 1975-77, Petaluma (Calif.) Peoples Svcs. Ctr., 1977; intake counselor Youth Advocates C.C. Riders Clinic, Novato, Calif., 1978-80, clin. supr., 1980-82; psychotherapist Robert Cohen M.D., Santa Rosa, Calif., 1984-85; dir., founder Sonoma County Assocs. in Drug Edn., Rohnert Park, Calif., 1982-90; pvt. practice marriage, family and child counseling Kentfield, Rohnert Park and Petaluma, Calif.; speaker Marin Gen. Hosp. Pediatricians, 1981, Chope Hosp. Psychiatry Residents, San Mateo, Calif., 1984; guest speaker Marin County Grand Jury Edn. Com., 1981; instr. Sonoma State U., 1984. Contbr. articles to profl. jours. Mem. Internat. Platform Assn. Democrat. Office: 100 Avram Ave Ste 105 Rohnert Park CA 94928-3100

ROBINSON, MARY E. GOFF, retired historian, researcher; b. East Providence, R.I., Jan. 3, 1925; d. Newell Darius and Eva Agnes (Crane) Goff; m. Charles Albert Robinson, July 30, 1954; 1 child, Thomas Goff (dec.). BA, Wheaton Coll., Norton, Mass., 1947. Cataloger, fine arts Chester County Hist. Soc., Pa., 1973-80, trustee, 1974-80; cataloger artifacts Chadds Ford (Pa.) Hist. Soc., 1992—. Co-author: (monograph) Ada Clendenin Williamson, 1983, (history) The Ingalls and the Hoyts, The Crane Sawmill, The Ingalls-Crane House, 1995; author: (monograph) The Life of a Young Entrepreneur at the Turn of the Twentieth Century, 1992; editor: A Quiet Man from West Chester, 1974. Mem. Jr. League, Providence, 1957-62, Providence Athenaeum, 1955-63, Providence Preservation Soc., 1959-63, Brandywine Conservancy, Kennett Symphony Orch., Del. Symphony Orch., Winterthur Mus. Mem. AAUW, R.I. Hist. Soc. (trustee 1994—, founder Newell D. Goff Inst. for I & E Studies), Chester County Art Assn. (acting libr. 1994—), Danville (Vt.) Hist. Soc., Nat. Mus. of Women in the Arts, Hershey's Mill Country Club.

ROBINSON, MARY JO, pathologist; b. Spokane, Wash., May 26, 1954; d. Jerry Lee and Ann (Brodie) R. BS in Biology, Gonzaga U., 1976; DO, Coll. Osteo. Medicine and Surgery, U. Med. Health Scis., 1987. Diplomate Nat. Bd. Osteo. Med. Examiners, Am. Osteo. Bd. Pathology. Med. technologist Whitman Comty. Hosp., Colfax, Wash., 1977-81, Madigan Army Med. Ctr., Ft. Lewis, Wash., 1981-83; intern Des Moines Gen. Hosp., 1987-88; resident in pathology Kennedy Meml. Hosp., Stratford, N.J., 1988-92; asst. prof. pathology Sch. Medicine U. Medicine and Dentistry of N.J., Stratford, 1995—; staff pathologist Kennedy Meml. Hosp., Cherry Hill, N.J., 1995—; fellow in dermatopathology Jefferson Med. Coll., Phila., 1994. Fellow Coll. Am. Pathologists; mem. AMA, Am. Osteo. Coll. Pathologists (1st prize resident paper 1992), Am. Osteo. Assn., Am. Soc. Clin. Pathologists, N.J. Assn. Osteo. Physicians and Surgeons. Office: Kennedy Meml Hosp U Med Ctr 2201 Chapel Ave W Cherry Hill NJ 08002-2048

ROBINSON, MARY KATHERINE, school system administrator; b. Asheville, N.C., Sept. 11, 1943; d. William Robert Jr. and Iris Myrtle (Holden) Sherrill; m. Marcus William Sumner, Oct. 26, 1962 (div. June 1973); 1 child, Marcus Kevin; m. Frank Pearson Robinson, Jr., Oct. 26, 1974 (div. 1996). BS in Edn., Western Carolina U., Cullowhee, N.C., 1968, MA in Edn., 1983. Cert. tchr., N.C. Tchr. reading Jackson County Bd. Edn., Sylva, N.C., 1968-69, elem. tchr., 1970-76; instr. reading Western Carolina U., 1968, instr. remedial reading, 1972; Reading Program developer Haywood County Bd. Edn., Waynesville, N.C., 1976-82, Resource and Program developer, 1982—; cons. divsn. health, safety and phys. edn. N.C. Dept. Pub. Instrn., Raleigh, 1974-75; mem. adv. bd. Haywood Tech. Inst., Clyde, N.C., 1978-79; mem. N.C. Textbook Commn., Raleigh, 1989-93; mem. curriculum rev. com. in mktg. edn., bus. edn. N.C. Dept. Pub. Instrn., 1992, health edn., 1993. Compiler: Robert Lee Holden Family, 1993; contbr. to periodical; creator vocabulary game Jaw Breakers, 1977. Vol. Reading Is Fundamental project Haywood County Libr., 1978-79; treas. PTO, 1971-72; active Haywood County Found. Bd., 1995—. Recipient Gold Key award N.C. State Supt., 1991. Mem. NEA, ASCD, N.C. Assn. Educators (sec. 1977, v.p./pres. elect 1994-95, pres. 1995-96), Internat. Reading Assn. (v.p. 1978-79, pres. 1979-80), Bus. and Profl. Women's Orgn., Friends of Haywood County Libr., Delta Kappa Gamma (corr. sec. 1988-90, v.p. 1990-92, pres. 1992-94), Phi Delta Kappa, Kappa Delta Pi. Democrat. Home: PO Box 1017 Lake Junaluska NC 28745

ROBINSON, MARY LOU, federal judge; b. Dodge City, Kans., Aug. 25, 1926; d. Gerald J. and Frances Strueber; m. A.J. Robinson, Aug. 28, 1949; children: Rebecca Aynn Gruhlkey, Diana Ceil, Matthew Douglas. B.A., U. Tex., 1948, LL.B., 1950. Bar: Tex. 1949. Ptnr. Robinson & Robinson, Amarillo, 1950-55; judge County Ct. at Law, Potter County, Tex., 1955-59, (108th Dist. Ct.), Amarillo, 1961-73; assoc. justice Ct. of Civil Appeals for 7th Supreme Jud. Dist. of Tex., Amarillo, 1973-77; chief justice Ct. of Civil Appeals for 7th Supreme Jud. Dist. of Tex., 1977-79; U.S. dist. judge No. Dist. Tex., Amarillo, 1979—. Named Woman of Year Tex. Fedn. Bus. and Profl. Women, 1973. Mem. Nat. Assn. Women Lawyers, ABA, Tex. Bar Assn., Amarillo Bar Assn., Delta Kappa Gamma. Presbyterian. Office: US Dist Ct Rm 226 205 E 5th Ave # F13248 Amarillo TX 79101-1563

ROBINSON, MYRNA L(ORRAINE), cost analyst, financial/budget analyst; b. Fredericksburg, Va., Mar. 31, 1962; d. Charles Edward Sr. and Jeanette Carol R. BS, Morgan State U., 1984; postgrad., Averett Coll. Asst., clk. typist U.S. Army Pentagon, 1984-85; logistics technician E-Sys., Falls Church, Va., 1985-87; cost analyst Applied Rsch., Inc., Arlington, Va., 1987-89; sr. tech. support specialist Cost Based Sys., Inc., Fairfax, Va., 1989-91; program adminstr. EER Sys. Inc., Seabrook, Md., 1992-93; sr. cost analyst, LAN adminstr. Capstone Corp., Alexandria, Va., 1994-95; sr. project control specialist Nyma, Inc., 1995—; acct. Quality Catering, Acokeed, Md., 1995—; fin. asst. 2d Baptist Ch. S.W., Washington D.C. Contbg. author: (book) Cost Quality Management Assessment for the Richland Operation Office, 1994, Cost Quality Management Assessment for the Savannah River, 1995, Cost Quality Management Assessment for the Idaho Operations Office, 1995, Cost Quality Management Assessment for the Kansas City Plant, 1995. Mem. NAFE, Nat. Coun. of Negro Women, Inc., Am. Assn. Cost Engrs. Internat.

ROBINSON, NAN SENIOR, not-for-profit organization consultant; b. Salt Lake City, Jan. 11, 1932; d. Clair Marcil Senior and Lillian (Worlton) Senior Davis; m. David Zav Robinson; Sept. 6, 1954; children: Marc S. Robinson, Eric S. Robinson. BA with hons., Mills Coll., 1952; MA, Harvard U., 1953. Spl. asst. to undersec. Dept. Housing and Urban Devel., Washington, 1966-69; asst. to the pres. U. Mass. Statewide System, Boston, 1970-73, v.p. for planning, 1973-78; dep. commr. Conn. Bd. Higher Edn., Hartford, 1978-81; v.p. adminstrn. The Rockefeller Found., N.Y.C., 1981-90; mem. governing coun. Rockefeller Archive Ctr., Pocantico Hills, N.Y., 1986-89; com. mem.

Coun. on Founds. N.Y. Regional Assn. Grantmakers, 1985-89; mem. nat. advisory panel on governance Carnegie Found. for the Advancement of Teaching, Princeton, N.J., 1980-82. Trustee, chmn. fin. com. Inst. for Current World Affairs, Hanover, N.H., 1987-90; trustee Calif. Sch. Profl. Psychology, San Francisco, 1985-96. Recipient Centennial award Am. Assn. U. Women Hartford Br., 1981; named Woman of Yr. Hartford YWCA, 1980; named to Centennial Honor List of 100 Women Barnard Coll., 1989. Mem. Soc. for Coll. and U. Planning (com. chmn. 1985-86, nominating com. 1980-85, regional rep. 1975-77), Phi Beta Kappa. Home: 622 Greenwich St Apt 5B New York NY 10014-3305

ROBINSON, NANCY ELLEN, artist, writer; b. N.Y.C., Mar. 27, 1949; d. Edwin James Jr. and Marie Josette (Bentivoglio) R.; m. Ricky Michael Ponzio. BA in English cum laude, Lawrence U., 1971. Profl. fine artist Robinson Art Empire, Mpls., 1974—; vis. artist Mpls. Coll. of Arts and Design, 1983, guest lectr. U. Minn., 1983, painting instr. Lakewood C. C., St. Paul, Minn., 1993, mentor Women's Art Registry of Minn., St. Paul, 1991-94. Author: What We Eat, 1990; various paintings. Mem. Women's Art Registry of Minn., Women's Caucus for Art. Office: Robinson Art Empire PO Box 80503 Minneapolis MN 55408

ROBINSON, NELL BRYANT, nutrition educator; b. Kopperl, Tex., Oct. 15, 1925; d. Basil Howell and Lelia Abiah (Duke) Bryant; m. Frank Edward Robinson, July 14, 1945 (dec.); 1 child, John Howell Robinson. B.S., N. Tex. State U., 1945; M.S., Tex. Woman's U., 1958, Ph.D., 1967. Registered dietitian, Tex. Tchr. Comanche High Sch., Tex., 1945-46, Kopperl High Sch., Tex., 1946-48; county extension agt. Agrl. Extension Service, Tex., 1948-56; prof. nutrition Tex. Christian U., Fort Worth, 1957-92, chmn. dept. nutrition and dietetics, 1985-91, ret., 1992. Pres., bd. dirs. Sr. Citizens Svcs. of Greater Tarrant County, 1990-91. Contbr. chpt. to book. Named Top Prof., Tex. Christian U. Mortar Bd., 1978. Mem. Am. Dietetic Assn. (del. 1983-88, ethics com. 1985-88, coun. edn. 1988-90, chmn. coun. on edn. divsn. edn. accreditation/approval 1989-90, medallion award 1990), Am. Assn. Family and Consumer Scis., Tex. Dietetic Assn. (pres., 1972-73, Disting. Dietitian 1981), Tex. Assn. Family and Consumer Scis. (pres. 1978-80, Home Economist of Yr. 1975). Club: Fort Worth Women's. Lodge: Order Eastern Star. Home: 5729 Wimbleton Way Fort Worth TX 76133-3651

ROBINSON, PAMELA CHAMPION, school system administrator; b. Doylestown, Pa., Mar. 12, 1945; d. John Edward and Doris Estelle (Hammersley) Champion; children: William Champion, Sandra Lynn. BS in Edn., Miami U., Oxford, Ohio, 1967. 1st grade tchr. Middletown, Ohio, 1967-68; alumni coord. Fishburne Mil. Sch., Waynesboro, Va., 1986-94; alumni-devel. coord. Fishburne Mil. Sch., Waynesboro, 1994—. Bd. dirs. Mem. Hosp., Inc., Waynesboro, 1986-88, Big Brothers-Big Sisters, Waynesboro, 1994—; pres. Waynesboro Cmty. Hosp. Aux. Bd., 1985-87. Mem. Nat. Soc. Fund Raising Execs., Planned Giving Assn. Republican. Presbyterian. Office: Fishburne Mil Sch PO Box 988 Waynesboro VA 22980

ROBINSON, PATRICIA ANN, marketing educator; b. Tallulah, La., Sept. 30, 1952; d. Roosevelt Martin and Lorene Robinson. BA, Tarkio (Mo.) Coll., 1973; MBA, Prairie View (Tex.) A&M U., 1978; MS, Tex. So. U., 1980; PhD, Okla. State U., 1986. Cert. elem. tchr.; cert. home economist; lic. real estate broker. Catalogue inventory specialist Montgomery Ward & Co., Kansas City, Mo., 1974-77; fiscal affairs asst. Prairie View (Tex.) A&M U., 1977-78; adminstrv. asst., instr. Tex. So. U., 1978-82; grad. asst. Okla. State U., Stillwater, 1980-84; cons. Kate's McGehee (Ark.) Tng. Ctr., 1985-86; assoc. prof. mktg. U. Ark., Fayetteville, 1984-87; asst. prof. mktg. U. Akron, Ohio, 1987-88, Tenn. Tech. U., 1988-90; chancellor scholar Fayetteville State U., 1990-91, chmn. dept. acctg., mktg. and mgmt., assoc. prof. mktg., 1990-91, chmn. dept. mgmt. and mktg., 1991-92; cons. Kate's McGehee (Ark.) Tng. Ctr., 1975-76. Recipient Acad. Advising Svc. award U. Ark., 1986. Mem. Am. Collegiate Retailing Assn., Am. Home Econs. Assn., Am. Mktg. Assn., Consumer Rsch. Assn., So. Mktg. Assn., Internat. Assn. Black Bus. Educators, Acad. Internat. Bus., Midsouth Mktg. Assn., Midwest Mktg. Assn., Tenn. Home Econs. Assn., Southwestern Mktg. Assn., Pi Sigma Epsilon, Durcury Hon. Soc., Beta Gamma Sigma (first v.p.), Delta Mu Delta, Durcury Hon. Soc. Democrat. Baptist. Home: 1501 Londonderry Pl Fayetteville NC 28301-2886

ROBINSON, PATRICIA ELAINE, women's health nurse practitioner; b. St. Louis, June 30, 1955; d. Harold Winford and Robbie LaVeal (Ferguson) Hammett; m. Kenneth M. Robinson, Nov. 18, 1978 (div.); children: Barry Christopher, Emily Vanessa; m. C. gilbert, Nov. 20, 1990. ADN, St. Louis Community Coll., 1987; student, Webster U., 1990—; cert. in forensic pathology, St. Louis U., 1975; cert. in pharmacology, St. Louis Coll. Health, 1984; womens health nurse practioner, U. Mo., 1995. Per diem float nurse St. Louis U. Hosp.; coord. ob-gyn. unit Group Health Plan, St. Louis; staff nurse Barnes Hosp., St. Louis; staff nurse dept. ob-gyn. Washington U. Sch. Medicine, St. Louis, 1990-93; chief exec. study coord. women's health rsch. Obstetric & Gynecologic Diagnosis & Consultation, Florissant, Mo., 1992-96; nurse practitioner and exec. study coord. women's health rsch. Women's HealthPartners, 1996—; acting dir. Nurses for Reproductive Health Svcs., St. Louis, 1990-93. Mem. NAFE, Nurse Assn. Am. Coll. Obstetrics and Gynecologists, Med. Group Mgmt. Assn., Nat. Assn. Nurse Practitioners Reproductive Health, Phi Theta Kappa. Office: Ob-gyn Diagnosis & Consultation 1150 Graham Rd Ste 105 Florissant MO 63031-8013

ROBINSON, SALLY SHOEMAKER, canon, director church social ministries; b. N.Y.C., Dec. 31, 1931; d. Samuel M. and M. Shoemaker; m. James Courtland Robinson, Dec. 31, 1931; children: Samuel Shoemaker, W. Courtland, A. Alexander, Ellen Whitridge Robinson Mibalski. BA cum laude, Bryn Mawr Coll., 1953; postgrad. studies, Yonsei U. Lang. Inst., Korea, 1960-62, Children's Theatre Assn., 1964; MA, Towson State Coll., 1974. Ordained elder Brown Meml. Presbyn. Ch., 1985. Commd. missionary to Korea United Presbyn. Ch., 1959-71; dir. Brown Meml. Tutorial Program, 1974-84; exec. dir. Episcopal Social Ministries Diocese of Md., Balt., 1984—; canon for social ministry Episcopal Diocese of Md., Balt., 1985—; mem. Episcopal Housing Corp., Inc., bd. cons. East Balt. Hispanic Ministries Project; mem. Coalition for Homeless Children and Families, Balt., 1990—, steering com. 1990—, DaySpring Initiative Com., 1994—; Balt. Coalition Against Substance Abuse, day reporting ctr. Jericho Project, Emmanuel Ch., 1994—. Librettist: Jonah and the Great Fish (operetta), producer, dir. 1st performance, 1977; other libretti and anthems, 1978-85. Bd. edn. The Valley Sch., Balt., 1973-75; trustee and chmn. edn. com. Garrison Forest Sch., 1975-80; met. chmn. 10th Decade Campaign Bryn Mawr Coll., , 1974-76, nat. chmn. Centennial Campaign. 1980-85, trustee, 1985—; bd. trustees Am. Bible Soc., 1988—, v.p., 1993—; trustee United Bd. for Christian Higher Edn. in Asia, 1990—. Home: 2404 Burnside Farm Rd Stevenson MD 21153 Office: The Diocese of Maryland 4 East University Parkway Baltimore MD 21218

ROBINSON, SALLY WINSTON, artist; b. Detroit, Nov. 2, 1924; d. Harry Lewis and Lydia (Kahn) Winston; m. Eliot F. Robinson, June 28, 1949; children: Peter Eliot, Lydia Winston, Sarah Mitchell, Suzanne Finley. BA, Bennington Coll., 1947; postgrad. Cranbrook Acad. Art, 1949; grad. Sch. Social Work, Wayne U., 1948, MA, 1972; MFA, Wayne State U., 1973. Psychol. tester Detroit Bd. Edn., 1944; pyschol. counselor and tester YMCA, N.Y.C., 1946; social caseworker Family Service, Pontiac, Mich., 1947; instr. printmaking Wayne State U., Detroit, 1973—. One person shows U. Mich., 1973, Wayne State U., 1974, Klein-Vogol Gallery, 1974, Rina Gallery, 1976, Park McCullough House, Vt., 1976, Williams Coll., 1976, Arnold Klein Gallery, 1977; exhibited group shows Bennington Coll., Cranbrook Mus., Detroit Inst. Art, Detroit Artists Market, So. Women Painters, Soc. Arts and Crafts, Bloomfield Art Assn., Flint Left Bank Gallery, Balough Gallery, Detroit Soc. Women Painters, U. Mich., U. Ind., U. Wis., U. Pittsburg, Toledo Mus., Krannert Mus.; represented in permanent collections, Detroit, N.Y.C., Birmingham, Bloomfield Hills; tchr. children's art Detroit Inst. Art, 1949-50, now artistic advisor, bd. dirs. drawing and print orgn. Bd. dirs. Planned Parenthood, 1951—, mem. exec. bd., 1963—; bd. dirs. PTA, 1956-60, Roeper City and Country Sch., U. Mich. Mus. Art, 1978; trustee Putnam Hosp. Med. Research Inst., 1978; mem. Gov.'s Commn. Art in State Bldgs., 1978-79; mem. art and devel. coms. So. Vt. Art Ctr., 1987-88; mem. vol. com. Marie Selby Gardens. Mem. Detroit Artists Market (dir. 1956—), Bennington Coll. Alumnae Assn. (regional co-chmn. 1954), Detroit Soc. Women Painters, Birmingham Soc. Women Painters (pres. 1974-76), Bloomfield Art Assn. (program co-chmn. 1956), Founders Soc. Detroit Inst. Art., Village Women's Club (Birmingham, Mich.), Women's City Club (co-ordinator art shows Detroit 1950), Garden Club, Am. Club (Bennington, Vt., Sarasota, Fla.), Cosmopolitan (N.Y.C.). Unitarian. Home: 7 Monument Cir Bennington VT 05201-2134 also: 840 N Casey Key Rd Osprey FL 34229-9779 also: 200 E 69th St Apt 7B New York NY 10021

ROBINSON, SARA CURTIS, arts administrator; b. Amarillo, Tex., Jan. 6, 1967; d. Don Teel Curtis and Suzanne (Stokes) Brent; m. Benjamin Rowland Robinson, Oct. 5, 1991; children: Rowland Wyatt, Tristan Rodman. BA, Pine Manor Coll., 1989. Asst. dir. Sorota Fine Arts, Boston, 1989; asst. to curator Asiatic art Mus. Fine Arts, Boston, 1990-91; from devel. officer to dir. devel. Bank of Boston Celebrity Series, 1992—; mem. Women in Devel., Boston, 1993-96, Boston Arts Mktg. Group, 1992-94. Mem. Jr. League Boston, 1990-95, com. chair, 1993; mem. Mass. Advocates for the Arts, Boston, 1993-96, Cultural Diversity Com. for the Arts, Boston, 1993-96; com. Newbury St. League Auction, Boston, 1989. Mem. Internat. Soc. Performing Arts Adminstrs., Nat. Soc. Fundraising Execs. Episcopalian. Office: Bank of Boston Celeb Series 20 Park Plz Ste 1032 Boston MA 02116

ROBINSON, SARA LUCAS, business educator; b. Union, S.C., May 23, 1949; 1 child, Calvin Thomas Robinson. BS in Bus. Edn., Barber-Scotia Coll., 1970; MA in Ednl. Adminstrn., Kean Coll., N.J., 1996. Classification specialist Gen. Svcs. Adminstrn., Denver, 1971-73; social security adminstr. Alamosa, Colo., 1973-77; tchr. bus. edn. McManus Jr. H.S., Linden, N.J., 1977-78; exec. comms. specialist EPA, N.Y.C., 1978-85; tchr. bus. edn. Montclair (N.J.) H.S., 1985-87, Hillside (N.J.) H.S., 1987—; adv. Future Bus. Leaders Am., Hillside, N.J., 1987—. Mem. Nat. Edn. Assn., Nat. Bus. Edn. Assn., Barber-Scotia Alumni Assn., Alpha Kappa Alpha. Baptist. Office: Hillside HS 1085 Liberty Ave Hillside NJ 07205

ROBINSON, SARAH MARGARET, physical education educator; b. Portland, Oreg., Nov. 29, 1939; d. John Andrew and Margaret Elvira (Miller) R. BS in Phys. Edn., U. N.C., Greensboro, 1961; MS, Springfield Coll., 1964; PhD, U. Wis., 1974. Instr. U. Tex., Austin, 1961-63, 64-65; grad. asst. Springfield (Mass.) Coll., 1963-64; dir. camping and recreation Balt. (Md.) League for Handicapped Children & Adults, 1965-67; tchg./rsch. asst. U. Wis., Madison, 1967-70; asst. to assoc. prof. Northeastern U., Boston, 1970-76; assoc. prof. U. N.C., Greensboro, 1976—. Contbr. chpt. to book and articles to profl. jours. Mem. Am. Alliance for Health, Phys. Edn., Recreation, Sport and Dance (chair curriculum acad. 1975-77), Internat. Coun. for Health, Phys. Edn., Recreation, Sport and Dance, U.S. Fencing Assn. (cert. instr.), Delta Kappa Gamma Internat. (Beta Beta chpt. pres. 1988-90). Office: Univ NC Greensboro 237 HHP Bldg Greensboro NC 27412-5001

ROBINSON, SONDRA TILL, author; b. Santa Monica, Calif., Nov. 24, 1931; d. Charles G. and Gertrude L. (Till) Rhoads; m. David Starr Robinson, June 15, 1952; children: Kathleen T., Rebecca S. Robinson-Roberts. AA, UCLA, 1953. Author: Almansor, 1974, The Dark & Brilliant Places, 1977; co-author: Friends in High Places, 1979, "Dear John", 1981; author numerous short stories. Recipient Milton Glick award for Fiction, 1987. Mem. The Authors Guild. Home: 2396 Via Mariposa W Laguna Hills CA 92653 Office: Goodman/Andrew care Sasha Goodman 16 Fleet St #4 Marina Del Rey CA 90292

ROBINSON, SUE L(EWIS), federal judge; b. 1952. BA with highest honors, U. Del., 1974; JD, U. Pa., 1978. Assoc. Potter, Anderson & Corron, Wilmington, Del., 1978-83; asst. U.S. atty. U.S. Attys. Office, 1983-88; U.S. magistrate judge U.S. Dist. Ct. (Del. dist.), 1988-91, dist. judge, 1991—. Mem. Del. State Bar Assn. (sec. 1986-87). Office: US Dist Ct J Caleb Boggs Fed Bldg 844 N King St Lockbox 31 Wilmington DE 19801-3519*

ROBINSON, SUSAN MICHELLE, author, editor; b. N.Y.C., June 1, 1953; d. Arnold Friedman and Marion Perlstein; m. Frederick E. Robinson, May 27, 1983; 1 child, Marissa. Ba, Hofstra U., N.Y., 1975. Pub. rels. writer N.Y. Times Mag. Group, N.Y.C., 1980-86; editor newsletter Kid News, N.Y.C., 1986—; pub. rels. writer, cons. Virgin Records Group, N.Y.C., 1978-80; cons. Evins Comm., N.Y.C., 1984—; talk show host Sta. WGBB, N.Y.C. Appeared on Weekend Today, Today in N.Y., NY1 News, Good Morning Am., Fox Five News-Style, Queens, Eyewitness News; author: The Smart Shoppers Guide to The Best Buys for Kids, 1966; consumer writer Ladies Home Jour., 1992, 95; contbg. writer N.Y. Daily News, 1994—. Office: Kid News PO Box 797 Forest Hills NY 11375

ROBINSON, SUSAN MITTLEMAN, data processing executive; b. Bklyn., Nov. 18, 1941; d. Samuel and Ida (Priest) Mittleman; m. Sheldon N. Robinson, June 5, 1962; children: Edward Bruce, Nancy Michelle, Jonathan Scott, Karen Barbara, Judith Lynn. AAS in Computer Sci., BCC, Lincroft, N.J., 1981; BBA, CUNY, 1962; MS in Computer Sci., Fairleigh Dickinson U., 1983; postgrad., Seton Hall U., 1983-85. Engr. asst. United Technologies, East Hartford, Conn., 1962-64; programmer, systems analyst Litton Industries (Sweda), Pine Brook, N.J., 1981-83; asst. prof. data processing Mercer Coll., West Windsor, N.J., 1983-85; adj. instr. data processing Brookdale Community Coll., Lincroft, N.J., 1983—; coord. MIS N.J. Dept. Health and Sr. Svcs., Trenton, 1985—; Novell Lan adminstr. N.J. Dept. Health, Trenton, N.J., 1994—; world wide web webmaster N.J. Dept. Health, Trenton; med. data set liaison N.J. Dept. Health and HCFA, 1996—; outsource cons. Medicare/Medicaid, Trenton, 1989—; cons. Health Care Fin. Authority, Balt., 1995—. Author (reference material) Info-Henco, 1987, Automated Survey Processing Environment Users Training Manual, 1993; developer computerized sys. to help patients and their family select a nursing home. Exec. bd. Temple Beth Am, Parsippany, N.J., 1972-80. Mem. SAS Users Group, N.J. DOH Prime Users Group. Office: NJ Dept Health and Sr Svcs CN 367 Trenton NJ 08625

ROBINSON, VERNA COTTEN, retired librarian, property management owner; b. Enfield, N.C., Oct. 6, 1927; d. Ernest and Ida (Faulcon) Cotten; m. Elbert Crutcher Robinson, Aug. 14, 1953 (dec. Feb. 1992); children: Angela, Elbert Cotten. BS, N.C. Cen. U., 1948; MS in Libr. Sci., Carnegie Mellon U., 1950. Br. libr. Blyden br. Norfolk (Va.) Pub. Libr., 1950-51; serials libr. Howard U., Washington, 1951-52; sch. libr. Springarn H.S. D.C. Pub. Schs., Washington, 1952-53, sch. libr. Cardozo H.S., 1955-60, sch. libr. Roosevelt H.S., 1960-67; sch. libr. Roosevelt H.S. D.C. Pub. Schs., 1970-85; pres. Robinson Property Mgmt., Inc., Washington, 1993—; bd. dirs. New Birth Corp., Miami, Fla. V.p. D.C. Assn. Sch. Librs., Washington, 1972-74; mem. ALA, 1970-85. Recipient Pioneer's Achiever's award United Ch. Christ, 1995; Daisy Scarborough scholar N.C. Cen. U., 1946-47, 47-48, Carnegie Libr. Alumni scholar Carnegie Libr. Sch. Alumni Assn., 1948-50. Mem. African Am. Women's Assn. (mem. internat. com. 1992-95), Delta Sigma Theta (tuition scholar Grand chpt. 1948-50).

ROBINSON, VIANEI LOPEZ, lawyer; b. Houston, Mar. 6, 1969; d. David Tiburcio and Romelia Gloria (Guerra) Lopez; m. Noel Keith Robinson, Jr., Apr. 16, 1994. AB in Psychology cum laude, Princeton U., 1988; JD, U. Tex., 1991. Bar: Tex. 1991; mediator's cert. Assoc. Bracewell & Patterson LLP, Houston, 1991-94, Wagstaff Law Firm, Abilene, Tex., 1994—. Contbr. articles to profl. jours. Adv. bd. Sml. Bus. Devel. Ctr.; bd. dirs. Young Audiences of Abilene, 1995—, Ctr. for Contemporary Arts, Abilene, 1996—, Abilene Opera Assn., 1996—. Presdl. scholar, Nat. Merit scholar, Nat. Hispanic scholar, 1985, Vinson & Elkins scholar U. Tex. Sch. Law, Austin, 1988-91. Fellow Tex. Bar Found.; mem. ABA (labor and employment law planning bd. mem.), NSBA/TASB Coun. of Sch. Attys., State Bar Tex. (various coms.), Coll. of the State Bar of Tex., Tex. Young Lawyers Assn. (bd. dirs. 1994—), Abilene Bar Assn., Abilene Young Lawyers Assn. Home: 2410 Wyndham Ct Abilene TX 79606 Office: Wagstaff Law Firm 290 Cedar Abilene TX 79601

ROBINSON DEROSSI, FLAVIA, photographer, foundation executive; b. Torino, Italy; d. Daniele A. and Anna (Navissano) Derossi; m. Marshall A. Robinson, Oct. 12, 1974. MA, U. Torino, 1949, PhD, 1952. Asst. prof. IPSOA, Torino, 1952-58; dir. CRIS, Torino, 1961-74; fellow OECD Devel. Ctr., Paris, 1967-71; photographer, 1982—; pres. Daniele Agostino Found., N.Y.C., 1991—. Author: The Mexican Entrepreneur, 1971, The Technocratic Illusion, 1981; one-woman shows include: Soho Photo Gallery, N.Y.C., 1984, 86, 88, 90, Galleria Fotografis, Bologna, 1985, Galleria D'Alessandro, Torino, 1985, Galleria II Canale, Venezia, 1987, Fortezza Pisana, Elba, 1988, Bertha Urdang Gallery, N.Y.C., 1989, 92, Cathedral of St. John the Divine, N.Y.C., 1991, Dutot Mus., Pa., 1995, Piedmont Coll. Art Gallery, Ga., 1994; group shows include: Camera Club, N.Y.C., Met. Camera Coun., N.Y.C., Parsons Sch. Design, N.Y.C., Udinotti Galleries, Phoenix, Udinotti Galleries, San Francisco; permanent collections include: Bklyn. Mus., N.Y. Pub. Libr., Bibliotèque Nat. of Paris. Recipient Photography award Ariz. Bot. Soc., N.Y. Audubon Soc., Photographer's Forum. Mem. Cosmopolitan Club. Office: Daniele Agostino Found 870 UN Plz 35C New York NY 10017

ROBISON, BARBARA ANN, retired newspaper editor; b. Portland, Oreg., July 15, 1933; d. Louis Keith and Marjorie (Work) R.; 1 child, Nancy. Student, Coll. Idaho, 1951-54, U. Utah, 1968-70. Reporter Caldwell (Idaho) News Tribune, 1951-54; sports editor LaGrande (Oreg.) Evening-Observer, 1954-55; reporter Idaho Daily Statesman, Boise, 1955-57; asst. women's editor Tacoma (Wash.) News Tribune, 1958-59; lifestyle editor Salt Lake Tribune, 1967-93. Episcopalian. Home: 4210 Caroleen Way Salt Lake City UT 84124-2507

ROBISON, NANCY ANN, accountant; b. Ft. Smith, Ark., June 23, 1958; d. Frederick Joseph and Vera Marie (Shinert) Siebenmorgen; m. Gary Don Robison, Feb. 5, 1977; children: Travis, Joshua. BS magna cum laude, U. Ozarks, 1992. Office mgr. T.D. Jennings, D.D.S., P.A., Ft. Smith, 1979-93; accounts payable supr. Holt-Krock Clinic, Ft. Smith, 1993—. Tax return preparer Vol. Income Tax Assistance, Ft. Smith, 1993—. Mem. Inst. Managerial Accts. (sec. 1994), U. Ozarks Alumni Assn. (sec.-treas. Ft. Smith chpt. 1992—, alumni bd. dirs. 1993—). Roman Catholic. Home: 8800 Meadow Dr Fort Smith AR 72903 Office: Holt Krock Clinic 1500 Dodson Ave Fort Smith AR 72901-5193

ROBISON, PAULA JUDITH, flutist; b. Nashville, June 8, 1941; d. David Victor and Naomi Florence R.; m. Scott Nickrenz; Dec. 29, 1971; 1 child, Elizabeth Hadley Amadea Nickrenz. Student, U. So. Calif., 1958-60; B.S., Juilliard Sch. Music, 1963. Founding artist, player Chamber Music Soc., N.Y.C., 1970-90, NY ChôroBand, 1994; co-dir. chamber music Spoleto Festival, Charleston, S.C., 1978-88; Filene artist-in-residence Skidmore Coll., Saratoga Springs, N.Y., 1988-89; mem. faculty New Eng. Conservatory Music, 1991—; co-dir. (with Leon Kirchner) Gardner Chamber Orch., Boston, 1995—. Soloist with various major orchs., including N.Y. Philharm., London Symphony Orch.; player, presenter Concerti di Mezzogiorno, Spoleto (Italy) Festival, 1970—; commd. flute concertos by Leon Kirchner, Toru Takemitsu, Oliver Knussen, Robert Beaser, Kenneth Frazelle; author: The Paula Robison Flute Warmups Book, 1989, The Andersen Collection, 1994, Paula Robison Masterclass: Paul Hindemith, 1995; recos. on CBS Masterworks, Music Masters, Vanguard Classics, New World Records, Omega, Arabesque, Sony Classical, King Recs., Mode Recs. Recipient First prize Geneva Internat. Competition, 1966, Adelaide Ristori prize, 1987; named Musician of Month, Musical Am., 1979, House Musician for Isamu Noguchi Garden Mus., N.Y.C., 1988; Martha Baird Rockefeller grantee, 1966; Nat. Endowment for Arts grantee, 1978, 86; Fromm Found. grantee, 1980; Housewright Eminent scholar Fla. State U., 1990-91. Mem. Sigma Alpha Iota (hon.). Office: care Matthew Sprizzo 477 Durant Ave Staten Island NY 10308

ROBISON, SUSAN MILLER, psychologist, educator, consultant; b. Chgo., Nov. 15, 1945; d. William Louis and Constance Mary (Maloney) Miller; m. Philip Dean Robison, Dec. 27, 1969; 1 child, Christine Alyssa. BS, Loyola U., Chgo., 1967; MS, Ohio U., 1969, PhD, 1971. Lic. psychologist, Md. Asst. prof. psychology Ohio U., Lancaster, 1970-72; prof. psychology Coll. Notre Dame, Balt., 1972—; pvt. practice Ellicott City, Md., 1982—; leadership cons. Nat. Coun. Cath. Women, Washington, 1987—. Author: Sharing Our Gifts, 1987, 2d edit., 1992, Discovering Our Gifts, 1989, Thinking and Writing in College, 1991. Troop leader Girl Scouts U.S.A., Ellicott City, 1982-85, mem. adv. bd. Girl Scouts Central Md., 1987-88, mem. adv. bd. Archdiocese of Balt., 1986. Mem. Am. Psychol. Assn., Am. Assn. Sex Educators, Counselors and Therapists, Assn. for Advancement Behavior Therapy. Home: 3725 Font Hill Dr Ellicott City MD 21042-4932

ROBITAILLE, CLAUDIA LOUISE NICOLE (CLAUDIA LOUISE NICOLE BELLEAU), artistic director, writer, educator; b. Trois-Rivières, Québec, Can., July 31, 1953; d. Louis Joseph and M.C. Renée (LaRivière) R.; life ptnr. Thomas Alan Grace. BA in Eng., U. Dartmouth, 1978; MA in Eng., Creative Writing, Brown U., 1986. Co-editor Siren: A Women's Jour., N. Dartmouth, Mass., 1976-78; coord. residency project, artist in residence, poet Bristol Cmty. Coll., Fall River, Mass., 1980-81; writing tutor Brown U., Providence, R.I., 1984-86; comm. cons. PSI-TECH, New Bedford, Mass., 1986-93; artistic dir. A.C.C.E.S.S. Art Corp. Internat., New Bedford, 1994—; freelance journalist, 1979-86; pres. bd. dirs. A.C.C.E.S.S. Art Corp. Internat., New Bedford, 1994-96; tchr. Write for Life workshops, U. Mass., Dartmouth Coll., 1994—. Author: (plays) The Miracle of Why We're Here, 1986 (Rites & Reason Play-Rites Festival award), The Burgundy Letters, 1987, (theater multi-media) Earth Medicine, 1991, (Mass. Cultural Coun. award), (performance piece) Transformation Tales, 1992, (Mass. Cultural Coun. award). Chair bd. dirs. Gr. Fall River Family Planning Coun., 1980-81; battered women advocate Citizens for Citizens, Fall River, 1980-81; regional coord. cons. Am. Adoption Congress, Washington, 1995. Recipient A.C.C.E.S.S. Art award, 1994. Mem. NOW, New Eng. Artists Trust. Home and Office: ACCESS Art Corp Internat. 96 Mount Pleasant St New Bedford MA 02740-5609

ROBLE, CAROLE MARCIA, accountant; b. Bklyn., Aug. 22, 1938; d. Carl and Edith (Brown) Dusowitz; m. Richard F. Roble, Nov. 30, 1969. MBA with distinction, N.Y. Inst. Tech., 1984. CPA, Calif., N.Y. Compt. various orgns. various orgns., 1956-66; staff acct. ZTBG CPA'S, L.A., 1966-67; sr. acct. J.H. Cohn & Co., Newark, 1967-71; prin. Carole M. Roble, CPA, South Hempstead, N.Y., 1971-90; ptnr. Roble & Libman, CPAs, Baldwin, N.Y., 1990-93; prin. Carole M. Roble, CPA, Baldwin, N.Y., 1993—; speaker, moderator Found. for Acctg. Edn., N.Y., 1971—; lectr. acctg. various schs. including New Sch., Queens Coll., Empire State Coll., Touro Coll., N.Y. Inst. Tech., N.Y.C., Parsons Sch., 1971—. Guest various N.Y. radio and TV stas. Treas. Builders Devel. Corp. of L.I., Westbury, N.Y., 1985; dir. Women Econ. Devels. of L.I., 1985-87. Recipient Sisterhood citation Nat. Orgn. Women, 1984, 85, cert. of Appreciation Women Life Underwriters, 1988, Women in Sales, 1982, 84; named top Tax Practitioner Money Mag., 1987. Mem. AICPA, Am. Acct. Assn. (auditing sect.), Am. Soc. Women Accts. (pres. N.Y. chpt. 1980-81), Am. Woman's Soc. CPAs, Nat. Conf. CPA Practitioners (trustee L.I. chpt. 1981-82, sec. 1982-83, treas. 1983-84, v.p. 1984-85, 1st v.p. 1985-86, pres. 1986-87, nat. nominating com. 1983-84, 88-89, nat. continuing profl. edn. chmn. 1988-90, nat. treas. 1991-94, nat. v.p. 1994-96, exec. v.p. 1996—), Calif. Soc. CPAs, N.Y. State Soc. CPAs (bd. dirs. Nassau chpt. 1981-86, 91-93, bd. dirs. profl. devel., 1982-86, sec., mem. fin. acctg. standards com. 1990—), Kiwanis (program chmn. County Seat chpt. 1989-90, sec. 1990-91, pres. 1991-92), Baldwin C. of C. (treas. 1990-93). Home: 626 Willis St Hempstead NY 11550-8000

ROBOHM, PEGGY ADLER (PEGGY ADLER), private investigator, writer; b. N.Y.C., Feb. 10, 1942; d. Irving and Ruth (Relis) Adler; m. Jeremy Abbott Walsh, June 1, 1962 (div. Dec. 1968); children: Tenney Whedon, Avery Denison (Mrs. Adam Lapidus); m. Richard A. Robohm, Dec. 24, 1976 (div. May 1993). Student, Bennington Coll., 1959-60, Columbia U., 1962. Illustrator, author childrens books, 1958—; agt. Jan J. Agy., Inc., N.Y.C., 1981-82; freelance talent scout Cuzzins Mgmt., N.Y.C., 1982-83; personal mgmt. and pub. rels. cons. Madison, Conn., 1983-93; logistics ticket sales and mgmt. the world premiere "Butch Cassidy and the Sundance Kid," 1969; rsch. assoc. Steve Fredericksen, Pvt. Investigator, Conn. and N.Y., 1990-96; investigative rschr., writer, lit. cons., 1986—, pub. spkr., 1991—; asst. investigator Ho. of Reps. October Surprise Task Force, Washington, 1992; pvt. investigator Sterling Detective Agy., Milford, Conn., 1996—. Author, illustrator: The Adler Book of Puzzles and Riddles, 1962, The 2nd Adler Book of Puzzles, and Riddles, 1963, Metric Puzzles, 1977, Math Puzzles, 1978, Geography Puzzles, 1979; author: Hakim's Connection, 1988; co-author: Skull and Bones: The Skeleton in Bush's Closet?, 1988; illustrator numerous books including (Humane Soc. of U.S. pubs.), Pet Care, 1974, Caring for Your Cat, 1974, Hot and Cold, 1959, Numbers New and

Old, 1960, Do a Zoomdo, 1975, Reading Fundamentals for Teen-Agers, 1973; graphic designer various book covers, posters, co. logos; Promotional Work, Sweetie, Baby, Cookie, Honey (Freddie Gershon), 1986; rschr. Passion and Prejudice: A Family Memoir (Sallie Bingham), 1989, The Village Voice, 1991, 92, numerous others; cons. The President's Private Eye: The Journey of Detective Tony U. From N.Y.P.D. to the Nixon White House (Anthony Ulasewicz with Stuart McKeever), 1990; cons., rschr. Bush's Boys Club: Skull and Bones, 1990; cons. Spy Saga (Philip H. Melanson), 1990; contbr. Lies of Our Times; licensee/story cons. 60 Minutes, 1991; cons., rschr. London Sunday Times, 1991; rsch. asst. The Connecticut Cowboy, 1992; rsch. and document retrieval CNN, Kroll Assocs., 1992; contbr. the Independent, London, 1994, 95. Founder Shoreline Youth Theatre, Inc., 1979, bd. dirs., 1979-81; mem. adv. bd., 1981-86; bd. dirs. The Greens Condominium Assn. of Branford, Conn., 1975-78, Arts Coun. Greater New Haven, 1971-73, Planned Parenthood of Greater New Haven, 1972-73, Assassination Archives and Rsch. Ctr., Washington, 1990-96; v.p., bd. dirs. Pub. Info. Rsch., Washington, 1989; hon. mem. Forgotten Families; assoc. mem. Rep. Town Com., Clinton, rsch. and issues sub-com.; mem. study com. 10 Killingworth Turnpike bldg. Town of Clinton, chmn. majority subcom., study com. Mem. Shoreline Sailing Club (bd. dirs. 1994—, membership chmn. 1994-96, dir.-at-large 1996—), Assassination Archives and Rsch. Ctr. Washington (bd. dirs. 1990-96), Conn. Soc. Genealogists Inc., Assn. Former Intelligence Officers (assoc.), Assn. Former Intelligence Officers New Eng., Yale Club New Haven. Home and Office: 32 Founders Vlg Clinton CT 06413-1837

ROBOLD, ALICE ILENE, mathematician, educator; b. Delaware County, Ind., Feb. 7, 1928; d. Earl G. and Margaret Rebecca (Summers) Hensley; m. Virgil G. Robold, Aug. 21, 1955; 1 son, Edward Lynn. B.S., Ball State U., 1955, M.A., 1960, Ed.D., 1965. Substitute elem. tchr. Am. Elem. Sch., Augsburg, Germany, 1955-56; instr. Ball State U., Muncie, Ind., 1960-61; teaching fellow Ball State U., 1961-64, asst. prof. math. scis., 1964-69, assoc. prof., 1969-76, prof., 1976—. Mem. Nat. Coun. Tchrs. Math., Ind. Coun. Tchrs. Math., Sch. Sci. and Math. Assn., Pi Lambda Theta. Mem. Ch. of God. Office: Ball State U Dept Math Scis Muncie IN 47306

ROBY, CHRISTINA YEN, data processing specialist, educator; b. Shanghai, China; came to U.S., 1980; d. Hai Zhou and Yun Qui (Zhang) Yen; m: Ronald L. Roby; 1 child, Colin H. BS, Jiao-Tung U., Shanghai, 1957; MS, U. Balt., 1986. Lic. engr., Peoples Republic of China. Chief mech. engr. Shenyang Valve Rsch. Inst., China, 1958-1980; computer system operator U. Balt., 1984, rsch. asst., 1984-86; sales assoc. V. F. Assocs., Inc., Balt., 1986-88; system analyst Computer Data Systems, Inc., Rockville, Md., 1988-89; data processing specialist, sr. sys. analyst Dept. of Health and Mental Hygiene, Balt., 1989—; instr. Community Coll. of Balt., 1986, 88; cons. Nat. Ins. Agency, Balt., 1988. Author: Guide to Using MS-DOS, 1988; contbr. author Japanese-Chinese Electrical Mechanical Industry Dictionary, 1980; transl., editor Analysis of Gas, Impurities and Carbide in Steel, 1961; contbr. articles to profl. jours. Vol. tutor U. Balt., 1983; vol. tchr. Chinese Lang. Sch., Balt., 1985-86, 90—; lectr. Internat. Festival Exhbn., 1986. Recipient cert. of appreciation Chinese Lang. Sch., 1986. Mem. NAFE, Sci. and Tech. Assn., Beta Gamma Sigma, Delta Mu Delta.

ROBY, JENNIFER, accountant; b. Phila., Mar. 14, 1970; d. Albert Joseph Jr. and Margaret Jane (Daly) R. BS, LaSalle U., Phila., 1992. Jr. acct. Bruno C. Fiorenza, CPA, Phila., 1988-92; grant acct. Thomas Jefferson U., Phila., 1992-95; acct. with Thomas Havey LLP, Bala Cynwyd, Pa., 1995—. Vol. Spl. Olympics, Ft. Washington, Pa., 1990—. Mem. Inst. Mgmt. Accts. Republican. Roman Catholic. Home: 2115 S 21st St Philadelphia PA 19145 Office: Thomas Havey LLP Two Bala Plz Bala Cynwyd PA 19014

ROBY, PAMELA ANN, sociology educator; b. Milw., Nov. 17, 1942; d. Clark Dearborn and Marianna (Gilman) R.; m. James Peter Mulherin, July 15, 1977 (div. 1987). BA, U. Denver, 1963; MA, Syracuse U., 1966; PhD, NYU, 1971. Tchr. Jefferson County Schs., Denver, 1964; instrn. ednl. sociology NYU, 1966; asst. prof. George Washington U., Washington, 1970-71; asst. prof. sociology and social welfare Brandeis U., Waltham, Mass., 1971-73; chair cmty. studies bd. U. Calif., Santa Cruz, 1974-76, 79, assoc. prof., 1973-77, prof. sociology and women's studies, 1977—, dir. sociology grad. program, 1988-91; vis. scholar U. Wash., Seattle, 1991-92; mem. anthropology, linguistics and sociology panel NSF, Washington, 1993; mem. sociology doctoral program com. Northeastern U., Boston, 1990; assessor Social Scis. and Humanities Rsch. Coun. Can., Toronto, 1993; cons. James Irvine Found., San Francisco, 1986; vice chair Nat. Commn. on Working Women, Washington, 1977-80; mem. social sci. rsch. rev. com. NIMH, Washington, 1976-78. Author: Women in the Workplace, 1981; editor: The Poverty Establishment, 1974, Child Care: Who Cares? Foreign and Domestic Infant and Early Childhood Development Policies, 1973-75; co-author: The Future of Inequality, 1970; adv. editor: Sociol. Quar., 1990-93, Gender and Society, 1986-89. Andrew W. Mellon sr. scholar Wellesley Coll., 1978-79; vis. fellow Indian Coun. Social Sci. Rsch., 1979. Mem. Soc. for Study Social Problems (pres. 1996-97), Sociologists for Women in Soc. (pres. 1978-80), Am. Sociol. Assn. (chair sect. on sex and gender 1974-78), Internat. Sociol. Assn. (rsch. coun. mem.-at-large 1978-82), Pacific Sociol. Assn. (v.p. 1996-97), Ea. Sociol. Assn. (exec. coun. mem.-at-large 1973-74), Phi Beta Kappa, Alpha Kappa Delta. office: Merrill Coll U Calif 1156 High Sch Santa Cruz CA 95064

ROBYN, ELISA SOBELMAN, psychologist, consultant, author; b. L.A., Jan. 25, 1955; d. Lee and Dorothy Lee Sobelman; m. Rick Lee Murray, Oct. 3, 1987. BS, No. Ariz. U., 1976; MA, U. Calif., Santa Barbara, 1980; PhD, U. Colo., Boulder, 1991. Exploration geologist Phillips Petroleum, Denver, 1980-86; prof. Colo. Mountain Coll., Breckenridge, 1989—, Regis U., Denver, 1994-96; prin., owner E. Robyn Enterprises, Wheat Ridge, Colo., 1994—; cons. various industries, instns., govts., Denver, 1995—. Bd. dirs. Camp Fire Colo., Denver, 1995-96. Named Woman of the Month, Colo. Women Leaders, Denver, 1994. Office: E Robyn Enterprises 12215 W 42d Ave Wheat Ridge CO 80033

ROCCANOVA, JOHANNA D., lawyer; b. Rockville Center, N.Y., Aug. 28, 1945; d. Anthony and Marie (Marchese) DiBella; m. Rocky Roccanova, Sept. 25, 1965; children: Gina Marie, Anthony V. BA, Ramapo Coll., 1984; JD, Rutgers U., Newark, 1987. Bar: N.J. 1987, Pa. 1987, N.J. Dist. Ct. 1987. Law clk to Hon. Sylvia B. Pressler appellate divsn. Appellate divsn. N.J. Superior Ct., 1987-88; assoc. Margolis Chase, Verona, N.J., 1988-91, Dunn Pashman, Hackensack, N.J., 1991-92, D.A. Pressler & Assoc., Hackensack, 1992—. Participant Morris Pashman Inns of Ct., Bergen County, N.J., 1990-92. Mem. Women Lawyers in Bergen County (bd. dirs. 1987—, referral panel chmn. 1991—), Bergen County Bar Assn. Home: 126 Randolph Ave Emerson NJ 07630 Office: David A Pressler & Assocs 87 Essex St Hackensack NJ 07601

ROCCARO, ROSEANN JOANN, accountant; b. Bklyn., May 16, 1972; d. Giuseppe and Maria Giovanna (Lorenzo) R. BSBA, Pace U., 1994. CPA. Tax intern Shearson Lehman Bros., N.Y.C., 1992-93; from tax intern to staff acct. KPMG Peat Marwick LLP, N.Y.C., 1993—; mentor KPMG Peat Marwick, LLP, 1995—. Bd. dirs. Pace U. Recent Alumni Com., 1994—. Mem. Inst. Mgmt. Accts. Democrat. Roman Catholic. Home: 430 Ave Y Brooklyn NY 11223

ROCHE, JUNE BROWNELL, corporate fashion director; b. New Bedford, Mass., Jan. 18, 1938; d. Geroge Brownell and Freda Chongarlides. BS in Textile Design and Fashion, U. Mass., Dartmouth, 1960, DFA, 1977. Corp. fashion dir. Milliken & Co., N.Y.C., 1960—; bd. dirs. Napier Co., Meriden, Conn. Mem. Trends (program chairperson), Fashion Inner Circle (pres. 1994), Fashion Group Internat. (bd. mem., v.p. 1983). Home: 347 West 39th St Apt 9E New York NY 10018 Office: Milliken Co 1045 6th Ave New York NY 10018

ROCHELLE, LUGENIA, academic administrator; b. Maple Hill, N.C., July 14, 1943; d. John Edward and Ruby Lee (Holmes) R. BA, St. Augustine's Coll., 1965; MS, N.C. A & T State U., 1969; D of Pedagogy, Barbar-Scotia Coll., 1993. Cert. tchr., N.C. Tchr. French, English Butler High Sch., Barnwell, S.C., 1965-67; instr. English N.C. A & T State U., Greensboro, 1970-77; instr. English St. Augustine's Coll., Raleigh, N.C., 1977-86, dir. freshman studies program, 1986-91, dean lower coll., 1991-96, asst. to v.p. acad. affairs, 1991-92; dir. gen. studies, asst. prof. English Voorhees Coll., Denmark, S.C., 1996—; dir. Mellon program St. Augustine's Coll., Raleigh, 1980-83; adv. bd. cooperating Raleigh Colls., 1986—, Off to Coll., Montgomery, Ala., 1993—; mem. profl. practices commn. N.C. Dept. Pub. Instrn., 1994—. Author: English Manual of Writing, 1980. Judge oratorical contests, Optimist Club, Raleigh, 1985-93; chair pro tem Raleigh Bicentennial Hist. Com., Raleigh, 1991-92; initiated chartering of Phi Eta Sigma St. Augustine's Coll., 1995; bd. dirs. Garner Rd. YMCA, Raleigh, 1994—. Nat. teaching fellow N.C. A & T State U., Greensboro, 1968-70. NCTE. Fellow Nat. Coun. Tchrs. English; mem. ASCD (assoc.), Profl. Practices Commn. N.C. State Dept. Pub. Instrn. Home: Rt 2 Box 269-G Denmark SC 29042

ROCK, CAROL FAITH JOANN, journalist; b. Oakland, Calif., Apr. 7, 1954; d. Joseph charles and Anne (Kralovansky) Kochalka; m. Frank Everett Rock, Oct. 26, 1975; children: Sarah Tif, Kerry Joseph, Casey Jane. Student, San Jose State U., 1971-73, Calif. State U., L.A., 1978-80. Police cadet L.A. Police Dept., 1974-75, radio/telephone operation, 1976-77; office mgr. credit cards Home Savs. and Loan, L.A., 1978-81; data coord. NBC-TV, Burbank, Calif., 1981-88; owner MizRock Media, Santa Clarita, Calif., 1988-90; vol. program coord. City of Santa Clarita, 1990-92; auction coord. Santa Clarita Boys and Girls Club, 1992; life style editor The Signal, Santa Clarita, 1992—. Author col. on entertainment. Cons., liaison for earthquake recovery City of Santa Clarita, 1988—, for hist. resources, 1988—; chair, dir. Santa Clarita Film and Entertainment Bur., 1988-95; dir. Theatre Arts for Children; mem. Canyon Theatre Guild; pres., dir. Santa Clarita Valley Hist. Soc., 1986—; mem. Preservation Action, Washington, 1990—, Calif. Preservation Found., Oakland, 1987—, Nat. Trust for Hist. Preservation, Washington, 1990—; dir. Am. Heart Assn., Santa Clarita chpt., 1994-96. Recipient Cmty. Svc. award GE Co., 1988. Mem. Assn. of Sunday and Feature Editors, Nat. Soc. Newspaper Columnists, Am. Soc. Newspaper Editors, Santa Clarita Valley C. of C., Zonta. Office: The Signal 24000 Creekside Rd Santa Clarita CA 91355

ROCK, MILISSA A., pharmacist, diabetes educator; b. Troy, N.Y., Nov. 19, 1954; d. Kermit Allen and Ann Ange (Mennuti) R.; m. Donald Kevin Zettervall, Oct. 16, 1982; 1 child, Sara Lauren Zettervall. BS in Pharmacy, Albany Coll. Pharmacy, N.Y., 1978. Registered pharmacist Conn.; cert. diabetes educator Nat. Cert. Bd. for Diabetes Educators. Staff pharmacist Conn., 1979-86; pharmacist, store mgr. Drug City, Rocky Hill, Conn., 1986-89; staff pharmacist Old Lyme (Conn.) Pharmacy, 1990-93; co-owner, pharmacy cons. mktg. and merchandising Profits Unltd., Old Saybrook, Conn., 1984-92; co-owner, pharmacist, diabetes educator The Diabetes Edn. Ctr., Old Saybrook, Conn., 1992—; pharmacist CVS Pharmacy, Old Saybrook, Conn., 1994—. Mem. bd. edn. Old Saybrook Bd. Edn., 1994—. Mem. Am. Pharmacy Assn., Am. Assn. Diabetes Educators, Am. Diabetes Assn. (youth svcs. com. Conn. chpt. 1993), Conn. Pharmacy Assn. Office: The Diabetes Edn Ctr 134 Boston Post Rd Old Saybrook CT 06475

ROCK, SANDRA KAYE, retail executive; b. Lebanon, Pa., Feb. 4, 1952; d. John Edgar and Anna Elizabeth (Phillippy) Forney; m. Krall K. Hostetter, Jan. 1, 1972 (div. 1978); children: Todd Michael, Duane Eric; m. Darryl Lynn Rock, Oct. 5, 1985. Student, Lebanon Valley Coll., Annville, Pa., 1978-83, Lebanon Valley Coll., Annville, Pa., 1990. Clk., sewing instr. Singer Co., Lebanon, Pa., 1970-72; asst. mgr. Turkey Hill Minit Markets, Lancaster, Pa., 1977-78, store mgr., 1978-79, area mgr., 1979-84, gasoline mgr., store inventory mgr., 1985, tng. adminstr., 1986-87, dist. mgr., 1988-89, dir. store ops., 1989-92; dir. video ops. Turkey Hill Minit Markets, Lancaster, 1992-95, dir. store ops., 1995—; dir. video ops. Turkey Hill Minit Markets, Lancaster, Pa., 1992-95, dir. store ops., 1995—; dist. mgr. Avon Corp., York, Pa., 1987-88. Mem. NAFE. Mem. Brethren Ch. Home: 171 Ridings Way Lancaster PA 17601

ROCKBURNE, DOROTHEA GRACE, artist; b. Montreal, Que., Can, Oct. 18, 1934. Student, Black Mountain Coll. Milton and Sally Avery Disting. prof. Bard Coll., 1986; trustee Ind. Curators Inc., N.Y., Art in Gen.; artist in residence Am. Acad. in Rome, 1991; vis. artist Skowhegan Sch. Printing and Sculpture, 1984. One-person shows include Sonnabend Gallery, Paris, 1971, New Gallery, Cleve., 1972, Bykert Gallery, N.Y.C., 1970, 72, 73, Galleria Toselli, Milan, Italy, 1972, 73, 74, Galleria D'Arte, Bari, Italy, 1972, Lisson Gallery, London, 1973, Daniel Weinberg Gallery, San Francisco, 1973, Galerie Charles Kriwin, Brussels, 1975, Galleria Schema, Florence, Italy, 1973, 75, 92, John Weber Gallery, N.Y.C., 1976, 78, Galleria la Polena, Geona, Italy, 1977, Tex. Gallery, Houston, 1979, 80, 81, Xavier Fourcade Gallery, N.Y.C., 1980, 82, 83, 85, 86, David Bellman, Toronto, 1980, 81, Margo Leavin, Calif., 1982, Arts Club of Chgo., 1987, André Emmerich Gallery, N.Y.C., 1988, 89, 91, 92, 94, 95, 10 yr. retrospective Rose Art Mus., 1989, P. Fong & Spratt Galleries, San Jose, Calif., 1991, Sony Music Hdqs., N.Y.C., 1993, Frederick Spratt Gallery, San Jose, 1994; group shows include Whitney Mus. Am. Art, 1970, 73, 77, 79, 82, Mus. Modern Art; N.Y.C., 71, 73, 84, 86, 93, 94 ;Buenos Aires, 1971, Kolner Kunst Market, Cologne, Germany, 1971, Stedelijk Mus., Holland, 1971, Spoleto (Italy) Festival, 1972, Palazzo Taverna, Rome, 1973, Nat. Gallery Victoria, Melbourne, Australia, 1973, Art Gallery NSW, Sydney, 1973, Auckland (New Zealand) City Art Gallery, 1973, Inst. Contemporary Art, London, 1974, Mus. d'Arte de la Ville, Paris, 1975, Galerie Aronowitsch, Stockholm, 1975, Stadtiches Mus., Manchengladbach, Germany, 1975, Galleria D'Arte Moderna, Bologna, Italy, 1975, Art Gallery Ont., Toronto, Can., 1975, Mus. Fine Art, Houston, 1975, Contemporary Arts Ctr., Cin., 1973, 75, 81, Mus. Contemporary Art, Chgo., 1971, 77, 86, Corcoran Gallery of Art, Washington, 1975, 87, Städtisches Mus., Leverkusen, Germany, 1975, Cannaviella Studio d'Arte Rome, 1976, Phila. Coll. Art, 1976, 83, Balt. Mus. Art, 1976, New Mus., N.Y.C., 1977, 80, 84, 83, Renaissance Soc. of U. Chgo., 1976, Lowe Art Mus., U. Miami, Fla., 1976, Inst. Contemporary Art, Boston, 1976, Seibu Mus. Art, Tokyo, 1976, N.Y. State Mus., Albany, 1977, Drawing Ctr., 1977, Kansas City (Mo.) Art Inst., 1977, Smithsonian Inst., Washington, 1977, Kassel, Fed. Republic Germany, 1972, 77, Ackland Art Ctr., Chapel Hill, N.C., 1979, 84, Milw. Art Ctr., 1978, 81, Biblioteca Nacional, Madrid, 1980, Gulbenkian Mus., Lisbon, Portugal, 1980, Bklyn. Mus., 1981, 89, Guggenheim Mus., 1982, 88, 89, Albright Knox Art Gallery, Buffalo, 1979, 80, 88, 89, Kuustforeningen Mus., Copenhagen, 1980, Venice Biennale, 1980, Cranbrook (Mich.) Acad. Art, 1981, Mus. Fine Arts, Boston, 1983, Contemporary Arts Mus., Houston, 1983, Norman Mackenzie Art Gallery, U. Regina, Sask., Can., 1983, Gallerie, Sweden, 1983-84, Seattle Art Mus., 1979-84, Nat. Mus. Art., Osaka, Japan, 1984, Fogg Art Mus., Cambridge, Mass., 1984, Am. Acad. and Inst. Arts and Letters, N.Y.C., 1984, 87, L.A. County Mus. Art, 1984, 86, Wadsworth Atheneum, Hartford, Conn., 1981, 84, Evehart Mus., Pa., 1984, Grey Art Gallery, NYU, 1977, 84, 87, Avery Ctr. Arts, Bard Coll., N.Y., 1985, 87-88, Stamford (Conn.) Mus., 1985, Aldrich Mus., Conn., 1979, 82, Bronx Mus. Arts, N.Y.C., 1985, High Mus., Atlanta, 1975, 81, Phila. Mus. Art, 1986, Nat. Gallery Art, Washington, 1984, Mus. Art, Ft. Lauderdale, Fla., 1986, Nat. Mus. Women in Art, Washington, 1987, Xavier Fourcade Gallery, 1983, 87, L.A. County Mus. Modern Art, 1986-87, The Hague, The Netherlands, 1986, Carnegie-Mellon Art Gallery, Pitts., 1979, 87, Balt. Mus. Art, 1975, 76, 88, Ctr. for Fine Arts, Miami, 1989, Milw. Art Mus., 1989, Cin. Art Mus., 1989, New Orleans Mus., 1989, Denver Art Mus., 1989, Parrish Art Mus., South Hampton, N.Y., 1990, 91, Margo Leavin Gallery, L.A., 1991, Mus. of Modern Art, N.Y.C., 1991, Guild Hall Mus., East Hampton, N.Y., 1991, Am. Acad., Rome, 1991, Mus. Contemporary Art, L.A., 1991, Hunter Coll., N.Y., 1991, Centro Cultural/Arte Contemporanea, Mexico City, 1991, Hilton, San Jose, Calif., 1992, Hillwood Art Mus., L.I., N.Y., 1992, Am. Acad. and Inst. Arts and Letters, 1992, Neuberger Mus., 1992, Statue of Liberty Group, 1993, Foster Harmans Galliers of Am. Art, Sarasota, Fla., 1993, Kohn-Abrams Gallerie, L.A., 1993, The Gallery at Bristol Myers Squibb, N.J., 1993, Friends of Art and Preservation in Embassies, N.Y.C., 1993, Just Art, N.Y.C., 1993, Mus. Modern Art, N.Y.C., 1994, TZ Art and Co., N.Y.C., Andre Emmerich Gallery, N.Y.C., 1993, Nat. Gallery of Art, Washington, 1994, Fred Spratt Gallery, San José, Calif., 1994, RAAB Galarie, Berlin, 1994, Gallary at Bristol Myer Squibb, N.J., 1994, Moma, N.Y.C., 1994, N.Y. Studio Sch., N.Y.C., 1995, Aldrich Mus., Conn., 1995; represented in permanent collections Milw. Art Ctr., Mus. Modern Art N.Y.C., Fogg Mus., Cambridge, Mass., Phila. Mus. Art, High Mus. Art, Atlanta, Houston Mus. Fine Arts, Corcoran Gallery, Washington, Mpls. Art Inst., Mpls. Art Mus., Met. Mus. Art, N.Y.C., Guggenheim Mus., N.Y.C., Ludwig Mus., Aachen, Fed. Republic Germany, Holladay, Washington, Saatchi, London, Bard, Albright-Knox Art Gallery, Buffalo, Whitney Mus. Am. Art, N.Y.C., U. Mich., Ann Arbor, Ohio State U., Columbus, Gilman Paper Co., N.Y., Auckland (New Zealand) City Art Mus., Portland (Oreg.) Art Mus., Aaken Art Mus., Oberlin, Ohio, Highhold Internat., S. Africa, U. Ohio Art Gallery, Columbus, HHK Charitable Found., Milw., Art Gallery Ont., Toronto, Can., Nat. Mus. Women in Art, Washington, Chase Manhattan Bank, N.Y.C., Hilton Hotel, San Jose, Calif., Sony Music Hdqs. Mem. artists adv. bd. New Mus. of Contemporary Art, N.Y.C.; trustee Ind. Curators, N.Y.C. Recipient Witowsky prize 72d Am. Exhbn., Art Inst., Chgo., 1976, Creative Arts award Brandeis U., 1985, Bard Coll., 1986; Guggenheim fellow, 1972; Nat. Endowment Arts grantee, 1974, Am. Acad., Rome, 1991.

ROCKEFELLER, MARGARETTA FITLER MURPHY (HAPPY ROCKEFELLER), widow of former vice president of U.S.; m. Nelson Aldrich Rockefeller (dec.); children: James B. Murphy, Margaretta H. Bickford, Carol Murphy Lyden, Malinda Murphy Menotti, Nelson A. Rockefeller, Jr., Mark F. Rockefeller. Dir. Archer-Daniels-Midland Co., Decatur, Ill.; alt. rep. of U.S. to 46th Session of UN Gen. Assembly, 1991, 47th Session, 1992. *

ROCKETT-BOLDUC, AGNES MARY, nurse; b. Medford, Mass., Jan. 19, 1930; d. John Francis and Agnes Mary (Connor) R.; m. Richard Joseph Bolduc, Mar. 23, 1928. Diploma, Lawrence Meml. Hosp., 1951; BSN, Boston Coll., 1958; MEd, Tufts U., 1962. RN; cert. nurse oper. rm. Staff nurse Mass. Gen. Hosp., Boston, 1951-56; instr. nursing Lawrence Meml. Hosp., Medford, Mass., 1958-61; asst. dir. Boston Lying-In Hosp., 1962-67; asst. dean admissions Tufts Med. Sch., Boston, 1967-71; chmn. dept. oper. rm. nursing svcs. Mass. Gen. Hosp., 1971-86; nurse mgr. oper. rm. Portsmouth (N.H.) Regional Hosp., 1987-92; pres. Rover Sky Corp., Hampton, N.H., 1992—; part-time staff nurse Phillips Exeter (N.H.) Acad., 1992—. Author: The Roving Reporter, 1969; mem. editorial bd. Today's Oper. Rm. Nurse, 1978-86. Trustee St. Elizabeth's Hosp., Boston, 1969-72, St. Margaret's Hosp., Boston, 1972-74; bd. dirs. Lifewise, N.H., 1992—; vol. Spl. Olympics, N.H., 1991-92, Hampton C. of C., 1993; chmn. Seacoast Heart Assn., 1989-90; mem. State N.H. Health Ins. Adv. Com., 1981-88. Mem. Am. Assn. Oper. Rm. Nurses, Sigma Theta Tau. Roman Catholic. Home and Office: 15 Penniman Ln Hampton NH 03842-2714

ROCKLEN, KATHY HELLENBRAND, lawyer, banker; b. N.Y.C., June 30, 1951. BA, Barnard Coll., 1973; JD magna cum laude, New England Sch. Law, 1977. Bar: N.Y. 1978, U.S. Dist. Ct. (so. and ea. dists.) N.Y. 1982, U.S. Dist. Ct. (no. dist.) Calif. 1985. Interpretive counsel N.Y. Stock Exchange, N.Y.C.; 1st v.p. E.F. Hutton & Co. Inc., N.Y.C.; v.p., gen. counsel and sec. S.G Warburg (U.S.A.) Inc., N.Y.C.; counsel Rogers & Wells, N.Y.C; pvt. practice N.Y.C. Office mgr. Com. to elect Charles D. Breitel Chief Judge, N.Y. Named one of Outstanding Young Women in Am. Mem. N.Y. State Bar Assn., N.Y. Women's Bar Assn., Assn. Bar of City of N.Y. (sec. 2d century com., sex and law com., young lawyers'com., corp. law com., chair spl. com. drugs and law, chair fed. legis. com., securities law com.). Office: Law Office 515 Madison Ave New York NY 10022-5403

ROCKMAN, DEBORAH ANNE, art educator, artist, writer; b. Flint, Mich., Sept. 16, 1954; d. Richard Glenn and Ella Mae (Conrad) R.; m. Wendy Jo Carlton, Oct. 10, 1993. BS, We. Mich. U., 1977; MFA, U. Cin., 1981. Asst. prof. art Moorhead (Minn.) State U., 1981-83; prof. art Kendall Coll. Art and Design, Grand Rapids, Mich., 1983—, coord. life drawing program, 1983-92, coord. fine arts program, 1992—; panelist, presenter Aquinas Coll., Grand Rapids, Coll. Art Assn. Conf., San Antonio, 1995; spkr. Grand Valley State U., Grand Rapids, 1991-94; chairperson coll. senate Kendall Coll. Art and Design, Grand Rapids, 1990-92. One woman shows include U. Cin., 1992, Clack Art Ctr. Alma Coll., 1994, No. Ind. Arts Assn., 1994 South Bend (Ind.) Mus. Art. 1995. Mem. Coll. Art Assn. (gay and lesbian caucus 1994-96), Urban Inst. Contemporary Art (exec. com. bd. dirs. 1987-92). Office: Kendall Coll Art and Design 111 Division Ave N Grand Rapids MI 49503

ROCKOFF, SHEILA G., nursing and health facility administrator, educator, college administrator; b. Chgo., Mar. 15, 1945; d. Herbert Irwin and Marilyn (Victor) R.; divorced. ADN, Long Beach City Coll., 1966; BSN, San Francisco State U., 1970; MSN, Calif. State U.-L.A., 1976; EDD , South Ea. Nova U., 1993. RN, pub. health nurse, nursing instr., prof., health facility supr., Calif. Staff nurse Meml. Hosp., Long Beach, Calif., 1966-67, Mt. Zion Med. Ctr., San Francisco, 1967-69; instr. nursing Hollywood Presbyn. Med. Ctr., L.A., 1970-74; nursing supr. Orthopedic Hosp., L.A., 1974-76; instr. nursing Ariz. State U., Tempe, 1976-78; nurse supr. Hoag Meml. Hosp., Newport Beach, Calif., 1977-78; nurse educator U. Calif.-Irvine and Orange, Calif., 1978-80; nursing prof. Rancho Santiago Coll. (Calif.), 1980-89, dir. health svcs., 1989-95; dir., chair Health Occupations, 1995—; nursing prof. Rancho Santiago C.C., Santa Ana Campus; nurse cons. Home Health Care Agy., Irvine, 1983; educator, cons. Parenting Resources, Tustin, Calif., 1985-89. Contbr. articles to profl. jours. Mem. Nat. Assn. Student Personal Adminstrs., Am. Coll. Health Assn., Calif. Nurses Assn. (chmn. com. 1970-73), Assoc. of Calif. C.C. Administr., Calif C.C. Health Occpl. Educators, Assn. (bd. dirs.), Pacific Coast Coll. Health Assn., Phi Kappa Phi. Democrat. Jewish. Office: Rancho Santiago CC 1530 W 17th St Santa Ana CA 92706-3315

ROCKRISE, SALLY SCOTT, real estate broker; b. Mpls., Oct. 28, 1929; d. Harold Francis Scott and Mabel Vivien (Verdolyack) Alexander; m. George T. Rockrise, Dec. 18, 1959 (div. Jan. 1965); 1 child, Celia Rockrise Clarke. BS, Francis Shimer Coll., 1950. Pres./CEO Verdolyack Paper Specialties, 1952-57; mgr. ROMA, Inc., San Francisco, 1959-65; real estate agt. various cos., Palm Beach, Fla., 1965-82; mgr. Cutler Gardens, Inc., Miami, Fla., 1989-91; pres. S.E. Savs. Realty, Inc., West Palm Beach, 1982—; cons., paralegal to homeowner assns., 1991—. Mem. Community Assn. Inst., Million Dollar Club. Office: SE Savs Realty Inc 707 S Chillingworth Dr West Palm Beach FL 33409-4124

ROCKWELL, ELIZABETH DENNIS, retirement specialist, financial planner; b. Houston; d. Robert Richard and Nezzell Alderton (Christie) Dennis. Student Rice U., 1939-40, U. Houston, 1938-39, 40-42. Purchasing agt. Standard Oil Co., Houston, 1942-66; v.p. mktg. Heights Savs. Assn., Houston, 1967-82; sr. fin. planner Oppenheimer & Co., Inc., Houston, 1982—; 2d v.p. Desk and Derrick Club Am., 1960-61. Contbr. articles on retirement planning, tax planning and tax options, monthly article 50 Plus sect. for Houston Chronicle newspaper. Bd. dirs. ARC, 1985-91, Houston Heights Assn., 1973-77; named sr. v.p. Oppenheimer, 1986—; mem. Coll. Bus. U. found. bd. Houston, 1990, mem. million dollar roundtable, 1991—, mem. ct. of the table, 1991—, Top of Table, 1996—, mem. sys. planned giving coun., 1992—, mem. coll. bus. adv. bd., 1992—, mem. alumni bd., 1987-95; appointed trustee U. Houston Sys. Found., Inc., 1992; mem. adv. bd. Houston C.C., 1996. Named Disting. Alumnae Coll. Bus. Alumn. Assn. U. Houston, 1992; named YWCA Outstanding Woman of Yr., 1978, Disting. Alumna U. Houston Alumni Orgn., 1996. Mem. Am. Savs. and Loan League (state dir. 1973-76, chpt. pres. 1971-72; pres. S.W. regional conf. 1972-73; Leaders award 1972), Savs. Inst. Mktg. Soc. Am. (Key Person award 1974), Inst. Fin. Edn., Fin. Mgrs., Soc. Savs. Instns., U.S. Savs. and Loan League (com. on deposit acquisitions and adminstrn.), Houston Heights Assn. (charter, dir. 1973-77), Friends of Bayou Bend, Harris County Heritage Soc., U. Houston Alumni Orgn. (life), Rice U. Bus. and Profl. Women, River Oaks Bus. Womens Exchange Club, U. Houston Bus. Womens Assn. (pres. 1985), Greater Houston Women's Found. (charter). Office: Oppenheimer & Co Inc 1600 Smith St Ste 3100 Houston TX 77002-4103

ROCKWELL, ELIZABETH GOODE, dance company director, consultant, educator; b. Portland, Oreg., Sept. 10, 1920; d. Henry Walton and Elizabeth (Harmon) Goode; m. William Hearne Rockwell, Feb. 3, 1948; children: Enid, Karen, William. BA, Mills Coll., 1941; MA, NYU, 1946. Instr. dance Monticello Jr. Coll., Alton, Ill., 1941-42; dir. masters program in dance Smith Coll., Northampton, Mass., 1946-48; 1st dir. dance dept. High Sch. of Performing Arts, N.Y.C., 1948-51, 53-54; dir. Elizabeth Rockwell Sch. Dance, Bedford, N.Y., 1956-86, Rondo Dance Theater, Bedford, 1971-93; tchr. continuing dance classes CCAE, 1994—; mem. adv. ednl. com. Calif. Ctr. for Arts, Escondido, Calif., 1993-95, dir. dance workshops, 1994—. Choreographer (suite of dances) Jazz Suite, 1966, (50-minute dances) Catch the Wind, 1969, Genesis, 1972, (narrative modern ballet) The Executioner, 1974, Decathalon, 1982; dir. (subscription series) Dance-Art-Poetry-Jazz, 1978-79, (dance/music 1600-1900) Stages in Ages, 1981, (Am.

dance revivals) Masterpieces of American Dance, 1982-84, Dances of the Decades, 1985-90, (revival & new choreography) Dances of Our Times, 1991; dir. dance workshops for Calif. Ctr. Arts, 1994, 95, 96; creator, founder performing group of older dancers Golden Connections Dance Ensemble of Women, CCAE, 1996. Bd. dirs. Coun. for Arts in Westchester, White Plains, N.Y., 1978-79, affiliate, 1978—. Recipient Medal for Performance, Israeli Army, 1966, Award for Excellence in Arts Edn. Alumnae of High Sch. of Performing Arts, 1990, various grants N.Y. State Coun. on Arts, 1971-93, Coun. Arts in Westchester, 1973-92, dance touring program grant Nat. Endowment for Arts, 1975-79. Mem. Am. Dance Guild, Westchester Dance Coun. (program dir. 1965-69), Assn. Am. Dance Cos., San Diego Area Dance Alliance (bd. dirs. 1995—). Home: 205 Tampico Glen Escondido CA 92025-7359

ROCKWELL, KAY ANNE, elementary education educator; b. Brighton, Mich., Feb. 12, 1952; d. Philip Oscar and Patricia Irene (Bennett) Newton; m. Lawrence Edward Rockwell, Aug. 23, 1975. BA in Social Sci. & Elem. Edn. cum laude, Spring Arbor Coll., 1974; MA in Early Childhood Edn., Ea. Mich. U., 1981. Dir. child care St. Luke's Luth. Day Care Ctr., Ann Arbor, Mich., 1980-82; tchr. 3d grade Colo. Christian Sch., Denver, 1982-94; tchr. 1st grade Front Range Christian Sch., Littleton, Colo., 1994—; chmn. Nat. Children's Book Week Colo. Christian Sch., 1993-94, chmn. ACSI spelling bee, 1991-94, chmn. ACSI speech meet, 1985-86. Spring Arbor Coll. scholar, 1972-74. Office: Front Range Christian Sch 4001 S Wadsworth Blvd Littleton CO 80123-1358

ROCKWELL, VIRGINIA CONSIDINE, school counselor; b. Fall River, Mass., Dec. 27, 1940; d. John F. and Lucy (Graham) Considine; m. Ralph Edwin Rockwell Jr., Aug. 28, 1965; children: Richard, Katherine. BS in Edn., Bridgewater (Mass.) State U., 1962; MEd, U. Mass., 1965. English tchr. Arcturus Jr. High Sch., Ft. Richardson, Ala., 1962-64; sch. counselor Hopkins Acad., Hadley, Mass., 1964-65; sch. counselor, dept. chair High Point High Sch., Beltsville, Md., 1965-67; employment counselor State of Oreg., Eugene, 1967-69; libr. asst. UCLA, L.A., 1969-70; placement asst. Northwestern U., Evanston, Ill., 1970-71; counselor Swink (Colo.) Sch. Dist., 1982—. Mem. AACD, Am. Sch. Counselor Assn. (recipient Multi Level Sch. Counselor of Yr. Honorable Mention 1991), Colo. Assn. Counseling and Devel., Colo. Sch. Counselor Assn. (recipient Region I Counselor of Yr. Honorable Mention 1986, named Multi Level Sch. Counselor of Yr. 1990), Delta Kappa Gamma. Home: 30 Sierra Dr La Junta CO 81050-3335 Office: Swink Sch 610 Columbia Ave Swink CO 81077-9999

RODECAPE, PHYLLIS LORRAINE, bank officer; b. Fulton, Mo., Nov. 18, 1933; d. Frank Stephen and Bertha Pearl (Gentry) Gowin; m. Harry Rodecape, Apr. 5, 1953; children: Douglas, Stephanie Rodecape Davis. Grad. h.s., Fulton, Mo., 1951. Cashier J.C. Penney Co., Fulton, Mo., 1951-53; pvt. sec. Nolan B. Jones Ins. Agy., Rockford, Ill., 1953; sec. The Callaway Bank, Fulton, Mo., 1956-58, bookkeeper, 1958-70, teller, 1970-83, bank officer, 1983—. Sec., treas. ARC, Fulton, 1970-73; vol. Fulton C. of C., 1984—; bd. trustees Ct. St. United Meth. Ch., Fulton, 1984-90, 92-95. Recipient Respect for Law award Fulton Evening Optimist Club, 1984, Respect for Law award Optimist Internat., 1984. Mem. Am. Bus. Women's Assn. (corr. sec. 1988). Home: 1908 Dunham Dr Fulton MO 65251 Office: The Callaway Bank 5 E 5th St Fulton MO 65251

RODERICK, ANNE, critical care nurse; b. Akron, Ohio, Feb. 22, 1948; d. George Thomas and Frances Wells (Hutchinson) R. BS, Capital U., 1975; BSN, Hunter Coll., 1987. RN. Nurse aide, ward clk. Doctors Hosp., Columbus, Ohio, 1970-74; receptionist C.R.A.S.H., N.Y.C., 1976-77; dental asst. Dr. Bryks, N.Y.C., 1977-81; nurse psychiatry Downstate Infirmary, N.Y.C., 1982-83; nurse Cabrini Hospice, N.Y.C., 1983-84, Mens Shelter Cmty., N.Y.C., 1984-86, Bellevue AIDS Unit, N.Y.C., 1986, St. Clare's AIDS Unit, N.Y.C., 1986-88, Ridgewood Pl., Akron, Ohio, 1989-90, Lenox Hills AIDS Unit, N.Y.C., 1990-92, Village Care AIDS Unit, N.Y.C., 1992-94, Terminal Care Hospice, Akron, 1994-95, Rivington House Aids Unit, N.Y.C., 1996—. Fellow ANA (AIDS nursing, Hospice nursing). Democrat. Home: 5 Tudor City Pl # 739 New York NY 10017

RODERICK, DOROTHY PAETEL, retired secondary school educator; b. Portland, Oreg., Feb. 16, 1935; d. Henry William and Mildred (Wenzlaff) Paetel; m. William Rodney Roderick, Oct. 21, 1965. AB, Wheaton Coll., 1956. Libr.'s asst. Armour Rsch. Found., Chgo., 1956-59; chaplain's asst. Episcopal ch. Northwestern U., Evanston, Ill., 1959-63; trainer Stouffer Restaurants, Skokie, Ill., 1963-65; tchr. jr. high sch. English Kildeer Countryside Consol. Community Sch. Dist. 96, Buffalo Grove, Ill., 1967-94; ret., 1994. Dep. voter registrar Lake County, Waukegan, Ill., 1983—. Mem. AAUW (br. pres. 1985-87, Gift Honoree 1976), Ill. Edn. Assn. (local pres. 1983-85), Delta Kappa Gamma (mem. Lambda state com. on women and the arts 1989-92, chpt. pres. 1994-96). Home: 15193 W Redwood Ln Libertyville IL 60048-1447

RODGER, MARION MCGEE, medical and surgical nurse, nursing administrator; b. Waterville, Maine, Feb. 21, 1949; d. Audrey Renee (Kilgore) McGee. Diploma, Albany Med. Ctr., 1970; cert. in psychiat.-mental health nursing, U. Calif., San Diego, 1994. RN, Calif. Clin. nurse, med./surg. nurse Sharp Meml. Hosp., San Diego, 1970-78, mgr. vascular/trauma unit, 1978-84, div. mgr., orthopedics, 1985-91; br. dir. Nat. Staffing Agy., 1992; health facilities evaluator nurse State of Calif., 1994—. Mem. Nat. Orgn. Orthopedic Nurses.

RODGERS, AGGIE GUERARD, costume designer; m. Peter Laxton; children: James, Thomas. Grad., Fresno State Coll., 1967; MA in Theatre Arts, Calif. State U., Long Beach. Former wardrobe supr. Am. Conservatory Theatre, San Francisco. Costume designer: (films) American Graffiti, 1973, The Conversation, 1974, One Flew Over the Cuckoo's Nest, 1975, Corvette Summer, 1978, More American Graffiti, 1979, Return of the Jedi, 1983, The Adventures of Buckaroo Banzai: Across the 8th Dimension, 1983, Pee Wee's Big Adventure, 1985, Warning Sign, 1985, Cocoon, 1985, The Color Purple, 1985 (Acad. Award nomination best costume design 1985), Fatal Beauty, 1987, Leonard Part VI, 1987, The Witches of Eastwick, 1987, *batteries not included, 1987, My Stepmother is an Alien, 1988, Beetlejuice, 1988, I Love You to Death, 1989, In Country, 1989, Forever Young, 1992, Grand Canyon, 1992, Benny and Joon, 1993, The Fugitive, 1993. Office: care Lawrence Mirisch The Mirisch Agency 10100 Santa Monica Blvd Los Angeles CA 90067-4011*

RODGERS, DEBBIE JEAN, elementary school educator; b. Charleston, Ill., Mar. 29, 1956; d. Robert F. and Doris J. (Chism) Hawkins; m. Ron Rodgers, Nov. 19, 1983; children: Lauren and Lindsey (twins). BS, Ea. Ill. U. Cert. tchr. Tchr. grad. sch. Potomac, Ill.; tchr. Pinckneyville Jr. (Ill.) H.S., 1979—, mem. adv. coun., 1992-93, cheerleading sponsor, 1980-88; food judge Perry County 4-H, Pinckneyville, 1994-95; guest spkr. Potomac H.S., 1986. Mem. So. Ill. U. Recreation Ctr., 1994. Mem. Ill. Reading Coun. Office: Pinckneyville Jr HS 700 E Water St Pinckneyville IL 62274-1471

RODGERS, NANCY LUCILLE, corporate executive; b. Denver, Aug. 22, 1934; d. Francis Randolph and Irma Lucille (Budy) Baker; student public schs.; m. George J. Rodgers, Feb. 18, 1968; children by previous marriage: Kellie Rae, Joy Lynn, Timothy Francis, Thomas Francis. Mgr., Western Telearm, Inc., San Diego, 1973-93; pres. Rodgers Police Patrol, Inc., San Diego, 1973-80; br. mgr. Honeywell Inc., Protection Services div., San Diego, 1977-80; pres. Image, Inc., Image Travel Agy., Cairo, Egypt, 1981-83, Western Solar Specialties, 1979-80; founder, pres. Internat. Metaphysicians Associated for Growth through Edn., San Diego, 1979; founder, dir. Point Loma Sanctuary, 1983-86; co-founder, producer Zerciee Prodns. Unltd., 1986—, co-founder, producer, dir. mktg., 1986—; co-founder Philoe West, Breeder of Am. Bashkir Curleys. Bd. dirs. Cen. City Assn. Named Woman of Achievement Cen. City Assn., 1979. Mem. Nat. Assn. for Holistic Health, Am. Bus. Women's Assn. (Woman of Yr. 1980), Am. Union Metaphysicians, Inst. Noetic Scis., Am. Bashkir Curly Assn. Republican.

RODIN, JUDITH SEITZ, academic administrator, psychology educator; b. Phila., Sept. 9, 1944; d. Morris and Sally R. (Winson) Seitz. AB, U. Pa., 1966; PhD, U. Columbia, 1970. Asst. prof. psychology NYU, 1970-72; assoc. prof. Yale U., 1975-79, prof., dir. grad. studies, 1982-89, Philip R. Allen prof. psychology, medicine and psychiatry, 1984-94, chmn. dept. psychology, 1989-91, dean Grad. Sch., 1991-92, provost, 1992-94; pres. U. Pa., Phila., 1994—, prof. psychology, medicine and psychiatry, 1994—; chmn. John D. and Catherine T. MacArthur Found. Rsch. Network on Determinants and Consequences of Health-Promoting and Health-Damaging Behavior, 1983-93; vice chair coun. press. U. Rsch. Assn., 1994-95, chair, 1995-96; mem. Ind. Panel to Review Safety Procedures at The White House, 1994-95; chair adv. com. Robert Wood Johnson Found., 1994—; mem. Pres. Clinton's Com. Advisors Sci. and Tech., 1994—; bd. dirs. Aetna Life & Casualty Co., Air Products, Allentown, Pa. Author: (with S. Schachter) Obese Humans and Rats, 1978, Exploding the Weight Myths, 1982, Body Traps, 1992; chief editor Appetite Jour., 1979-92; contbr. articles to profl. jours. Mem. Pa. Task Force on Higher Edn. Funding, 1994; bd. dirs. Catalyst, N.Y.C., 1994—; trustee Brookings Inst., 1995—. Fellow Woodrow Wilson Found., 1966-67, John Simon Guggenheim Found., 1986-87; grantee NSF, 1973-82, NIH, 1981—. Fellow AAAS, Am. Acad. Arts and Scis., Am. Psychol. Assn. (bd. sci. affairs 1979-82), Soc. Behavioral Medicine; mem. Am. Philosophical Soc., Inst. Medicine of NAS, Acad. Behavioral Medicine Rsch., Ea. Psychol. Assn. (exec. bd. 1980-82, pres. divsn. 38 health psychology 1982-83, Outstanding Contbn. award 1980, Disting. Sci. award 1977), Phi Beta Kappa, Sigma Xi (pres. Yale chpt. 1986-87). Office: U Pa 121 College Hall Philadelphia PA 19104-6380

RODMAN, ANGELA FAYE, telecommunications research executive; b. Arlington, Va., Apr. 3, 1963; d. John Ivan and Wanda Faye (Smith) Slane; m. Edward Ford Rodman, Oct. 12, 1985; children: Andrew Ford, Sarah Catherine, Jessica Anne. AS in Info. Systems/Computer Sci. with high honors, Chattanooga State Tech. Community Coll., 1983; BS in Math., Computer Sci., Monmouth Coll., 1987, postgrad., 1987-88; MS in Computer Sci., Fairleigh Dickinson U., 1990, M, 1993. Tech. assoc. AT&T Bell Labs., Holmdel, N.J., 1983-84; staff technologist Bell Communications Rsch., Red Bank, N.J., 1984-87, sr. staff technologist, 1987-91, mem. tech. staff, 1991-96, sys. engr., 1996—. Music software developer (book) Animation, Games and Sound for the IBM PC, 1983. Mem. Monmouth County Rep. Exec. Com., 1989—; chmn. Future Pioneers Chpt. 99 So. coun., 1990-91; leader, tchr. H.S. Out of Hours Program, Summer Tech. Edn. Program. Named Future Pioneer of Yr., 1990-91; Photography scholar, 1981. Mem. Assn. Computing Machinery (sec. 1982-83), Data Processing Mgmt. Assn. (sec. 1982-83), Phi Theta Kappa. Republican. Methodist. Home: 501 Oxford Way Neptune NJ 07753-4347

RODMAN, SUE ARLENE, wholesale Indian crafts company executive, artist; b. Fort Collins, Colo., Oct. 1, 1951; d. Marvin F. Lawson and Barbara I. (Miller) Lawson Shue; m. Alpine C. Rodman, Dec. 13, 1970; 1 child, Connie Lynn. Student Colo. State U., 1970-73. Silversmith Pinel Silver Shop, Loveland, Colo., 1970-71; asst. mgr. Traveling Traders, Phoenix, 1974-75; co-owner, co-mgr. Deer Track Traders, Loveland, 1975-85, v.p. Deer Track Traders, Ltd., 1985—. Author: The Book of Contemporary Indian Arts and Crafts, 1985. Mem. U.S. Senatorial Club, 1982-87, Rep. Presdl. Task Force, 1984-90; mem. Civil Air Patrol, 1969-73, 87-90, pers. officer, 1988-90. Mem. Internat. Platform Assn., Indian Arts and Crafts Assn., Western and English Sales Assn., Crazy Horse Grass Roots Club. Mem. Am. Baptist Ch. Avocations: museums, piano, recreation research, fashion design, writing. Office: Deer Track Traders Ltd PO Box 448 Loveland CO 80539-0448

RODRIGUEZ, CARMEN VILA, artist, art educator, art historian; b. N.Y.C., July 16, 1927; d. Manuel and Julia (Lopez) Vila; m. Sabino Rodriquez Jr., Aug. 22, 1948; children: Sabino III, Manuel. BA in Art, Hunter Coll., 1948; studied with muralist Raul Anguiano, U. Mexico, 1966; student in advanced Ceramics and Jewelry, Calif. Coll. Arts and Crafts, 1966; student, U. Madrid, Spain, 1968; MA in Art and Art History, Columbia U., 1969, EdD in Art and Art Edn., 1977; postgrad., Fairfield U., 1982-93. Cert. in adminstrn. and supervision, Conn., art tchr., Conn., N.Y. Art tchr. Yorkville Vocat. H.S., N.Y.C., 1951-52; art history lectr. Instituto de Bellas Artes, Caracas, Venezuela, 1953-55; art tchr., dept. chmn. Eastchester (N.Y.) Sch. Dist. 1, 1958-92; cons., pres. VILA, Inc., Visual Instrnl. Libr. Art, Inc., 1981—; art edn. leader, lectr. art history Discovery Mus., Bridgeport, Conn., 1992—; co-chair ednl. programs Lockwood-Mathews Manor Mus., Norwalk, Conn., 1992-94; adj. faculty Daytona Beach C.C., 1993—, Norwalk (Conn.) Cmty. Tech. Coll., 1996—; art instr. Norwalk Sr. Citizen Ctr., 1992-95, New Canaan (Conn.) Sr. Ctr., 1993—, Girl Scouts USA, Norwalk, 1990-93. Author: Tracy Loves Picasso, 1993; one-woman shows include Picture This Gallery, Westport, Conn., 1995, 1st Fidelity Bank, Norwalk, 1995, Sun Trust Bank, Daytona Beach, Fla.; group shows include Rowayton (Conn.) Arts Ctr., 1994 (ribbon 1994), Bonnie Blair Country Club, Scarsdale, N.Y., 1962, N.Y. Gallery, 1970, Scarsdale Pub. Libr., 1975, Portland Gallery, Norwalk, Conn., 1996, Sun Trust Bank, 1996; editor J. Walter Thompson Advt., N.Y.C., 1970; editor, head stylist Trimble Studios, N.Y.C., 1949-53; contbr. articles to profl. jours. Art instr. Norwalk (N.Y.) Sr. Citizen Ctr., 1992—, Girl Scouts USA, Norwalk, Conn., 1990-93. Recipient Painting ward Eastchester Womens Club, 1964, Premio Major de Arte U. Mex., 1961. Mem. NEA, AAUW, NOW, Nat. Art Edn. Assn., Rowayton Art Assn., Art League Daytona Beach, Port Orange Art Assn. Home: Oceans Seven-1906 2947 S Atlantic Ave Daytona Beach Shores FL 32118 Office: VILA Inc PO Box 466 466 E Norwall South Norwalk CT 06856

RODRIGUEZ, ELENA GARCIA, retired pension fund administrator; b. Havana, Cuba, Mar. 21, 1944; came to U.S., 1959; d. Eliseo and Elena (Suarez) Garcia; divorced; children: Victor, Yvonne, Daniel. B in Profl. Studies, Barry U., 1983; MS in Mgmt., St. Thomas U., 1985; postgrad., U. Phila., 1989, UCLA, 1990. With City of Miami, Fla., 1969-95, pension adminstr., 1978—, ret., 1995. Author: General and Sanitation Pension Benefit Booklet, 1982, Fire and Police Pension Benefit Booklet, 1982, Retirement Planning Booklet, 1985; author numerous programs dealing with pension and acctg. for pension assets. Mem. Leadership Miami, 1985—. Mem. NASD (arbitrator), Internat. Found. Employee Benefit Plans, Internat. Pers. Mgmt. Assn., Inst. Fiduciary Edn., Fla. Assn. City Clks., New York Stock Exch. (arbitrator), Am. Stock Exch. (arbitrator), Am. Arbitration Assn., Better Bus. Bur. (arbitrator). Republican. Roman Catholic.

RODRIGUEZ, LINDA TAKAHASHI, secondary school educator; b. L.A., June 22, 1941; d. Edward S. and Mary Takahashi; divorced; children: Regina Marie, Marla Sari. AA, Trinidad (Colo.) Jr. Coll., 1961; BA, We. State Coll., Gunnison, Colo., 1963; MA, U. Colo., Denver, 1991. Cert. tchr., adminstr., Colo. Tchr. Stratton (Colo.) Jr./Sr. High Sch., 1964-65, Pikes Peak Elem. Sch., Colorado Springs, 1966-68, Prince Sch., Tucson, 1968-70, Ipava (Ill.) Grade Sch., 1970-72, Macomb (Ill.) Schs., 1972-74, Colchester (Ill.) Jr./Sr. High Schs., 1979-83, Hazel Park (Mich.) Alternative Sch., 1984-85; tchr. 8th grade lang. arts and social studies Denver Pub. Schs., 1986-95, chair lang. dept., 1987-95, tchr. reading resource, 1987-92; creator, dir. Reading Summer Sch., 1987-95; presenter insvcs. Denver Pub. Schs., 1987-94; mentor Alternative Tchr. Cert. Program; mem. bd. dirs. Asian Cultural Ctr. Advisor Asian Edn. Adv. Bd., Denver, 1989-95; bd. dirs. Colo. Youth-at-Risk, Denver, 1992-93. Mem. Landmark Edn. Forum, Highland Park Optimists, Delta Kappa Gamma. Home: 1617 Daphne St Broomfield CO 80020-1155

RODRIGUEZ, LORRAINE DITZLER, biologist, consultant; b. Ava, Ill., July 4, 1920; d. Peter Emil and Marie Antoinette (Mileur) D.; m. Juan G. Rodriguez, Apr. 17, 1948; children: Carmen, Teresa, Carla, Rosa, Andrea. BEd, So. Ill. U., 1943; MS, Ohio State U., 1944; PhD, U. Ky., 1973. Asst. nutritionist OARDC, Wooster, Ohio, 1944-49; postdoctoral fellow U. Ky., Lexington, 1973-74, pesticide edn. specialist, 1978-89; pvt. cons. Lexington, 1974-79, 89—. Author ext. publs. in field; co-author rsch. publs. and book chpts. in field. Leader 4-H, Lexington, 1962-68. Named Outstanding 4-H Alumni Woman, Ky., 1969. Mem. Vegetation Mgmt. Assn. Ky. (chmn. adv. bd. 1985-89), Am. Chem. Soc. Democrat. Roman Catholic. Home: 1550 Beacon Hill Rd Lexington KY 40504-2304

RODRIGUEZ, SUSAN MILLER, geriatrics nurse; b. New Orleans, Sept. 1, 1950; d. Albert John Miller and Patricia (Shields) Di George; m. Fred H. Rodriguez, Jr., Dec. 22, 1973; children: Alison, Fred III, Kathryn, David. BSN, La. State U. Med. Ctr., 1972. RN, La. Home health nurse Home Health Svcs. of La. Inc., New Orleans, 1972-73; assoc. faculty mem. La. State U. Sch. of Nursing, New Orleans, 1973-75; rsch. nurse Tulane U., New Orleans, 1994; personal health coord. Total Health 65, New Orleans, 1994—. Mem. New Orleans Dist. Nurses Assn. (nominating com.1972-74), Faculty Wives Club of La. State U. Med. Ctr. (pres. 1990-91), La. State U. Sch. Nursing Alumni (treas. 1972-73), Sigma Theta Tau. Republican. Roman Catholic. Home: 5105 Green Acres Ct Metairie LA 70003-1005 Office: Total Health 65 Ochsner Clinic 1514 Jefferson Hwy New Orleans LA 70121

RODRIGUEZ, TERESA IDA, elementary education educator, educational consultant; b. Levittown, N.Y., Oct. 10, 1951; d. George Arthur and Frieda (Diaz) R. BA in Secondary Edn., Hofstra U., 1973, MA in Bilingual Edn., 1978; profl. diploma in multicultural leadership, L.I. U., 1990. Cert. permanent nursery, kindergarten, elem. Spanish, bilingual K-6, ESL tchr., sch. dist. adminstr., sch. adminstr., supr., N.Y. Bilingual elem. tchr. Long Beach (N.Y.) Pub. Schs., 1973-76, Hempstead (N.Y.) Pub. Schs., 1976-79; account exec. Adelante Advt., N.Y.C., 1979-81; adminstrv. asst. Assocs. and Nadel, N.Y.C., 1981-84; freelance outside prop and set decorator for TV commls. N.Y.C., 1984-88; tchr. ESL Central Islip (N.Y.) Pub. Schs., 1988-92; ednl. cons. Houghton Mifflin Co., 1992-95; bilingual tchr. 5th grade Central Islip (N.Y.) Pub. Schs., Princeton, N.J., 1995—; cons. on tchr. tng. Staff Devel. Ctr. Islips, Central Islip, 1989—; cons. on staff devel. Nassau Bd. Coop. Ednl. Svcs., Westbury, N.Y., 1990—, edn. instrn. specialist IBM, 1991; presenter confs., workshops, seminars; cons. and grant writer, N.Y.C. and suburbs. Grantee N.Y. State Div. Bilingual Edn., 1988-90, Staff Devel. Ctr. Islips, 1988, Suffolk Bd. Coop. Ednl. Svcs., 1989; WLIW Pub. TV mini grantee; Pres.'s fellow L.I.U., 1989-90. Mem. ASCD, Nat. Assn. Bilingual Educators, State Assn. Bilingual Educators, Internat. Reading Assn. (presenter nat. conf. 1992, 93), N.Y. State ASCD, Suffolk Reading Coun., Smithtown Township Arts Coun. Home: 30 Wheelwright Ln Levittown NY 11756-5233 Office: 1 Broadway Central Islip NY 11722

RODWELL-BELL, REGINA, museum director; b. Casablanca, Morocco, Aug. 19, 1954; came to U.S., 1955; d. Richard Francis and Roxie Jean (Fletcher) Rodwell; m. Jack D. Bell, Apr. 4, 1981; children: Spencer Bell, Noel R. Bell. BS in Orgnl. Mgmt., Nyack Coll., 1993; cert. in fund raising, Marymount Coll., 1994. Lic. real estate broker, N.Y. Profl. dancer, actress N.Y.C., 1977-81; dance tchr., choreographer Coll. Ozarks, Point Lookout, Mo., 1981-82; real estate broker Baer & McIntosh Real Estate, Nyack, N.Y., 1986-93; founder, pres. Hudson Valley Children's Mus., Nyack, N.Y., 1993-95, exec. dir., 1995—. Author, editor Big Ideas, 1995. Bd. dirs. Rockland Coun. Young Children, 1994—; bd. trustees Hudson Valley Childen's Mus., 1993-95. Recipient Appreciation cert. Town Orangetown, 1996. Mem. Assn. Youth Mus. (assoc.), New Eng. Mus. Assn. (assoc.). Democrat. Presbyterian. Office: Hudson Valley Childrens Mus Nyack Seaport 21 Burd St Nyack NY 10960

ROE, ALLIE JONES, technical writer; b. Greenville, S.C., Dec. 3, 1950; d. James Richard and Allie McGreg (Singletary) Jones; m. Eugene Bartlett Roe, Aug. 29, 1970 (div. 1986); 1 child, David Michael. AB in English, Valdosta State Coll., 1972; MA in Journalism, Ohio State U., 1982. Instr. II State of Ga. Health Svcs., Valdosta, 1972-74; prodn. asst. Easton (Md.) Publ. Co., 1974-75; sec. office of radiation safety Emory U., Atlanta, 1977-79; asst. mgr. classified The Booster Newspaper, Columbus, Ohio, 1980-81; editorial aide Battelle Columbus Labs., 1983-84; publs. coord. specialist Battelle Project Mgmt. Div., Columbus, 1984-85, adminstv. coord., 1985-87; free-lance editor Am. Ceramic soc., Westerville, Ohio, 1988; tech. writer, editor Resource Internat., Westerville, 1988-89; tech. writer Cons. & Designers, Winter Park, Fla., 1989-91; advanced tech. writer Westinghouse, Orlando, Fla., 1991—. Vol. Am. Heart Assn., Columbus, 1984-88, Am. Cancer Soc., Columbus, 1986-88. Mem. Women in Comms. Inc. (v.p. projects 1986-87, chair job placement com. 1987-89), Nat. Mus. for Women in the Arts (charter 1988—), Altrusa Internat. (v.p. Orlando chpt. 1994), Jr. League Greater Orlando, Phi Kappa Phi. Methodist. Home: 3732 E Grant St Orlando FL 32812-8417

ROE, RADIE LYNN, secondary school educator; b. Stuart, Fla., Nov. 14, 1962; d. Albert R. III and Martha Katherine (Brooks) Krueger; 1 child, Travis; m. Dan C. Roe, May 24, 1990. AB, Ga. Wesleyan Coll., 1984; postgrad., U. Cen. Fla. Tchr. English Brevard County Sch. System, Melbourne, Fla., 1984-86; bank officer, tng. dir. First Nat. Bank and Trust, Stuart, 1987-90; dir. Christian edn. 1st Presbyn. Ch., Stuart, 1990-91; prof. English, Indian River Community Coll., Ft. Pierce, Fla., 1990-91; employment comm. cons. Curtis and Assocs., Grand Island, Nebr., 1992-93; exec. dir. Community HelpCenter, Grand Island, 1993, Martin County Literacy Coun., Stuart, Fla., 1993-94; mgr. ednl. svcs. The Palm Beach Post subs. Cox Enterprises, Inc., West Palm Beach, Fla., 1994-95; with audiotext advt./programming dept. The Stuart (Fla.) News, 1995—; lang. arts tchr. Southport Middle Sch., Port St. Lucie, Fla., 1996—; presch. tchr. Appletree Acad., Palm City, Fla. 1995—. Active Laubach Literacy in Action. Mem. NAFE, Toastmasters, Habitat for Humanity, Audubon Soc. Republican. Lutheran. Home: 4119 SE Jacaranda St Stuart FL 34997-2220

ROE, WANDA JERALDEAN, artist, retired educator, lecturer; b. Batesville, Ark., Nov. 9, 1920; d. William Melvin and Luna Eva (Cockrum) Finley; m. Roy A. Roe, Dec. 25, 1940; children: Ramona Jeraldean, Roy A. II. BS in Edn., U. Cen. Ark., Conway, 1954, MS in Edn., Ark. State U., 1965; diploma Exec. Devel. Ctr., U. Ill., 1984; postgrad., U. Ark., 1981. Cert. educator, Ark.; lic. profl. counselor, Ark. Counselor Fountain Lake High Sch., Hot Springs, Ark., 1965-68; instr. art and home econs. Foreman (Ark.) High Sch., 1968-72; profl. counselor Pea Ridge (Ark.) High Sch., 1972-83; instr. art No. Ark. Community Coll., Rogers, 1980-90; profl. artist Rogers (Ark.) Art Guild Gallery, 1983-95, Big Spring Gallery, Neosho, Mo., 1989-96, Ark. Artists Registry, Little Rock, 1983-96; instr. art Wishing Springs Gallery, Bella Vista, Ark.; dir. workshops State Dept. Edn., Little Rock, 1965-83; supr. for practice tchrs. and counselor interns. Ark. Colls. and Univs., 1968-83; art instr. War Eagle Seminar, 1996; presenter in field. Exhibited in one-person show at Walton Art Ctr., 1996; contbr. poetry to mags.; mem. editorial adv. bd. Cmty. Pubs. Inc., 1994—. Mem. State Adv. Coun. for Gifted/Talented Edn., Little Rock, 1989-96; mem. Ark. Leadership Acad., 1996, G/T Coalition, 1996—; juror for art contests; guide for County Constn. Day, Benton County, 1987; pres. United Meth. Women, Pea Ridge, 1973-75; cmty. vol.; sec. Dem. Ctrl. Com., 1996—; White House vol., 1996. Travel Study grantee Delta Kappa Gamma, 1987; named Art Educator of Yr., N.W. Art Educators Assn., 1983; recipient numerous art awards. Mem. AAUW (state exec. bd., state pres. 1985-87), Nat. Art Educators Assn., Ark. Art Educators Assn., Spiva Art Ctr., Ozark Pastel Soc. (Signature mem., pres. 1990-93), Rogers Art Guild (pres. 1991-92), Dem. Women's Club (v.p. 1996—), Delta Kappa Gamma (state exec. bd., state pres. 1983-85). Democrat. Methodist.

ROEDER, GLORIA JEAN, civil rights specialist, private investigator; b. Des Moines, Iowa, Dec. 4, 1945; d. Gerald Arthur and Dorothy Jean (Pardekooper) R. BA, Simpson Coll., 1970; postgrad., Iowa State U., 1991. Examiner disability determination divsn. Disability Determination Div. State of Iowa, Des Moines, 1970-75; owner, pres. Aaron Investigations, Des Moines, 1975—; pvt. investigator Des Moines; cons. All Area Detective Agy., Des Moines, 1965-78. Civil rights specialist Iowa Civil Rights Commn., Des Moines, 1978—, local liaision; mem. citl. com. Iowa Dem. Com. Polk, Des Moines, 1991—; vol. Luth. Social Svcs., 1988—; mem. Christ the King Cath. Ch., mem. social concerns com., 1995-96, chair mem., 1995-96, eucharistic min., 1996. Mem. Nat. Assn. Human Rights Workers, Nat. Assn. Prevention Child Abuse (bd. dirs. 1988-91), Iowa Assn. Pvt. Investigators (chair constn. com. 1994-95, sec. bd. dirs. 1996). Democrat. Office: Iowa Civil Rights Commn 211 Maple St Des Moines IA 50309-1858

ROEDER, REBECCA EMILY, software engineer; b. Findlay, Ohio, Nov. 2, 1959; d. Brian Eldon and Barbara Lee (Melton) R.; m. Stephen William Bigley, May 28, 1983. BS in Edn. and Computer Sci., Bowling Green State U., 1983, MS in Computer Sci., 1993. Systems analyst NCR Corp., Dayton, Ohio, 1983-84; sr. systems analyst Unisys (Burroughs) Corp., Detroit, 1984-88; asst. dir. St. Vincent Med. Ctr., Toledo, 1988-95; sr. cons. Advanced Programming Resources, Inc., Columbus, Ohio, 1996—. Active Sta. WGTE/WGLE Pub. Radio, Toledo, 1984-96, Sta. WOSU Pub. Radio, Columbus, 1996—, Sta. WCBE Pub. Radio, Columbus, 1996—, Toledo Mus. Art, 1988-96, Toledo Zoo, 1993-96; presenter Women in Sci. Career Day, Lourde's Coll., 1992. Marathon scholar Marathon Oil Co., Findlay,

1978, Hancock scholar Findlay Area C. of C., 1978. Mem. AAUW, Assn. for Computing Machinery, Columbus Computer Soc. Republican. Episcopalian. Home: 4964 Vicksburg Ln Hilliard OH 43026 Office: Advanced Programming Resources Inc 2929 Kenny Rd Columbus OH 43221

ROEDIGER, JANICE ANNE, artist, educator; b. Trenton, N.J.; d. John and Anne Balint; m. Paul Margerum Roediger; children: Pamela Anne, Matthew Paul, Joan Margaret. Student, Beaver Coll., 1975-78; grad. cert., Pa. Acad. Fine Arts, 1988. Instr. multi-media Jane Law Long Beach Island Gallery, Surf City, N.J., 1992-94, 94-96; instr. drawing Long Beach Island Found., Loveladies, N.J., 1994-96; docent Mus. Am. Art, Pa. Acad. Fine Arts, Phila., 1992-96. Exhibited in group shows at Rittenhouse Galleries, Phila., 1988-94, Phila. Mus. Art, ASR Gallery, 1992-96, Schaff Gallery, Cin., 1995-96. Mem. vestry, rector's warden St. Anne's Episcopal Ch., Abington, Pa., 1970-73; chair med. staff aux. Abington Meml. Hosp., 1973-7, chair scholarship com., 1974; coord. student com. Pa. Acad. Fine Arts, Phila., 1986-88; active Phila. Mus. Art, 1972—. Recipient Rohm & Haas Outstanding Achievement award Pa. Acad. Fine Arts, 1987, Pearl Van Sciver award Woodmere Mus., 1991, Blumenthal award Cheltenham Ctr. for Arts, 1991, Lance Lauffler award for visionary painting Pa. Acad. Fine Arts, 1988, Award of Merit Long Beach Island Found., 1994, 96. Mem. Nat. Mus. Women in Arts, Phila. Art Alliance, Artists Cultural Exch. (bd. dirs. 1989—). Episcopalian. Home: 1244 Rydal Rd Rydal PA 19046-1415 Studio: 1010 Arch St Philadelphia PA 19107-3003

ROEHL, KATHLEEN ANN, financial executive; b. Chgo., June 1, 1948; d. Walter Steven and Catherine (Puss) Kalchbrenner; m. Eric C. Roehl, June 28, 1969; children: Aaron C., Marc E. BA with honors, U. Ill., 1969. Registered investment advisor. Tchr. Ft. Huachuca (Ariz.) Accomodation Schs., 1969-70; interior designer Key Kitchens, Dearborn Heights, Mich., 1979-80; stockbroker, fin. cons. Merrill Lynch, Dearborn, Mich., 1980-81; v.p., registered investment advisor Merrill Lynch, Northbrook, Ill., 1982—; bd. dirs. ATA Info. Systems. Mem. Ill. Govt. Fin. Officers Assn., Internat. Assn. for Fin. Planning (bd. dirs. 1987-88), Northbrook C. of C. (bd. dirs. 1991-93), Northbrook Early Risers Rotary (charter mem.). Office: Merrill Lynch 400 Skokie Blvd Northbrook IL 60062-2816

ROEHL, LILLIAN LANE, visual arts administrator; b. Gate City, Va., Nov. 19, 1923; d. Roy Clayton and Elizabeth Jane (Pierson) Lane; m. William E. Roehl, June 19, 1948; 1 child, Jon William. Cert. Bus., Whitney Sch. Bus., Kingsport, Tenn., 1943; ind. study art history, U. Tenn., Knoxville, 1945-62. Sec. to regional dir. Congress Indsl. Orgns., Region VIII, Knoxville, Tenn., 1945-74; sec. dirs. office George Meany Ctr. for Labor Studies, Silver Spring, Md., 1974-85, coord. visual arts, sec., dir., dep. dir., 1985—; vol. organizer Congress Indls. Orgns., 1945; chmn. exhbn. Dulin Gallery of Art's Second Nat. Print & Drawing Exhbn., Knoxville, 1966, mem. women's com., 1970, sec., 1970-72, co-chmn. catalog and exhbn. com., 1971, chmn. sales and rental gallery, 1972, mem. women's com. ann. membership and fund drive, 1973. Sec. Knoxville Art Ctr., 1957-61; sec. arts adv. com. Dulin Gallery of Art, Knoxville, 1960-70; co-chmn. Arts Adv. Com. for Exhbns., 1970-72; mem. com. to organize First Knoxville Dogwood Arts Festival, 1962; co-chmn. Second Nat. Art Competition McClung Mus., U. Tenn., 1961; mem. Knoxville Bldg. Code Com., 1964; sec. Com. for First Nat. Print Exhbn., Dulin Gallery of Art, Knoxville, 1965; bd. dirs. Olney Theatre, 1990—; rec. sec. Friend of Olney Theatre Ctr. for Arts, 1986—. Mem. Internat. Union Office and Profl. Employees, Bus. Women's Sorority (sec. 1995), Nat. Secs. Assn. (sec. 1955-66), Bus. and Profl. Women's Assn. (sec. 1950-60), Strathmore Hall Found., Cultural Alliance of Washington, Art Coun. of Montgomery County, Md. Citizens for the Arts, Md. State Arts Coun., Montgomery Coun. Arts. Assn. Democrat. Unitarian. Home: 1610 Overlook Dr Silver Spring MD 20903 Office: George Meany Ctr Labor Studies 10000 New Hampshire Ave Silver Spring MD 20903

ROEHL, NANCY LEARY, marketing professional, educator; b. Natick, Mass., Mar. 25, 1952; d. Norman Leslie and Dorothy (Holmquist) Pidgeon; m. Patrick J. Leary, Sept. 17, 1977 (div. May 1984); m. Patrick F. Roehl, July 2, 1995. AA, Mass Bay Coll., Wellesley, Mass., 1979; BS, Lesley Coll., Cambridge, Mass., 1988; MA in Edn., U. South Fla., 1992. Cert. tchr., Fla. Sec. GTE Corp., Needham, Mass., 1973-78; coord. edn. Cullinet Software Inc., Westwood, Mass., 1983-84, adminstrv. asst., 1984-85, mgr. adminstrn., 1985-86; specialist product mktg. Cullinet Co., Westwood, Mass., 1986-88; v.p. mktg. and adminstrn. Jonathan's Landscaping, Bradenton Beach, Fla., 1988-89; tech. support staff A Plus Tax Product Group, Arthur Andersen, Inc., Sarasota, Fla., 1989-90; cons. Palmetto, Fla., 1990—; tchr. Manatee County, 1992—. Contbr. articles to profl. jours. Mem. Fla. Community Assn. Mgrs., NAFE, AAUW, Nat. Coun. for the Social Studies, Zonta, Phi Kappa Phi. Office: PO Box 181 Bradenton FL 34206-0181

ROELS, SHIRLEY JEAN, college program director, writer; b. Kalamazoo, Mich., July 22, 1950; d. Herbert John and Gertrude (Ditmar) Wolthuis; m. John Michael Roels, June 10, 1992; children: Daniel, Steven. MBA with honors, U. Mich., 1977; PhD Higher Edn. Adminstrn., Mich. State U., 1993. Career counselor U. Mich., Ann Arbor, 1973-75; asst. budget dir. U. Detroit, 1977-78, dir. cost and fin. analysis, 1978-79; prof. bus. Calvin Coll., Grand Rapids, Mich., 1979-89, chairperson dept. econs. and bus., 1991-95, coord. coll. strategic planning, 1993-95, dir. degree completion programs, 1994—. Co-author: Business Through the Eyes of Faith, 1990, On Moral Business, 1995. Woodrow Wilson Adminstrv. Intern Woodrow Wilson Found., 1977-79. Mem. Inst. Mgmt. Accts., Christian Bus. Faculty Assn. (chair steering com. 1984-88), Beta Gamma Sigma. Office: Calvin Coll 3201 Burton St SE Grand Rapids MI 49546

ROEMER, ELIZABETH, astronomer, educator; b. Oakland, Calif., Sept. 4, 1929; d. Richard Quirin and Elsie (Barlow) R. BA with honors, U. Calif., Berkeley, 1950, PhD (Lick Obs. fellow), 1955. Tchr. adult class Oakland pub. schs., 1950-52; lab technician U. Calif. at Mt. Hamilton, 1954-55; grad. research astronomer U. Calif. at Berkeley, 1955-56; research asso. Yerkes Obs. U. Chgo., 1956; astronomer U.S. Naval Obs., Flagstaff, Ariz., 1957-66; asso. prof. dept. astronomy, also in lunar and planetary lab. U. Ariz., Tucson, 1966-69; prof. U. Ariz., 1969—; astronomer Steward Obs., 1980—; Chmn. working group on orbits and ephemerides of comets commn. 20 Internat. Astron. Union, 1964-79, 85-88, v.p. comm. 20, 1979-82, pres., 1982-85, v.p. commn. 6, 1973-76, 85-88, pres., 1976-79, 88-91; mem. adv. panels Office Naval Research, Nat. Acad. Scis.-NRC, NASA; researcher and author numerous publs. on astrometry and astrophysics of comets and minor planets including 79 recoveries of returning periodic comets, visual and spectroscopic binary stars, computation of orbits of comets and minor planets. Recipient Dorothea Klumpke Roberts prize U. Calif. at Berkeley, 1950, Mademoiselle Merit award, 1959; asteroid (1657) named Roemera, 1965; Benjamin Apthorp Gould prize Nat. Acad. Scis., 1971; NASA Spl. award, 1986. Fellow AAAS (council 1966-69, 72-73), Royal Astron. Soc. (London); mem. Am. Astron. Soc. (program vis. profs. astronomy 1960-75, council 1967-70, chmn. div. dynamical astronomy 1974), Astron. Soc. Pacific (publs. com. 1962-73, Comet medal com. 1968-74, Donohoe lectr. 1962), Internat. Astron. Union, Am. Geophys. Union, Brit. Astron. Assn., Phi Beta Kappa, Sigma Xi. Office: U Ariz Lunar and Planetary Lab Tucson AZ 85721-0092

ROEPKE, NANCY JO, psychologist; b. Humboldt, Nebr., Apr. 15, 1959; d. Keith Bernhardt and Dolores Mae (Krafft) R.; 1 child, Jessica Marie. BA in Psychology with high distinction, U. Ariz., 1982, MA in Psychology, 1990, PhD in Clin. Psychology, 1993. Lic. psychologist, Ariz. Psychology intern Pima County Superior Cts., 1986-88; therapist Ariz. State Prison, 1989-90; eating disorder clinic coord. Ariz. Health Scis. Ctr., Tucson, 1986-90; therapist dept. psychology Denver Gen. Hosp., 1990-91; therapist Jewish Family and Children's Svc., Glendale, Ariz., 1993-94; pvt. practice Scottsdale, Ariz., 1993—; biofeedback cons. Exercise and Sports Scis. Dept., U. Ariz., Tucson, 1986, psychology intern, 1986-90; therapist Sports Medicine Clinic, Dept. Psychiatry, Ariz. Health Scis. Ctr., Tucson, 1987-90; counselor, houseparent T-Grove Corp., Tucson, 1978-81; counselor Ariz. Tng. Program, Tucson, 1977-78; rsch. asst. U. Ariz., Tucson, 1984-85, 86; stress mgmt. instr. Cottonwood Drug and Alcohol Rehab. Ctr., Tucson, 1985-86; lectr. in field. Contbr. articles to profl. jours. Mem. APA, Ariz. Psychol. Assn., Assn. for Advancement of Applied Sport Psychology. Office: 6991 E Camelback #B114 Scottsdale AZ 85251

ROERDEN, CHRIS (CLAIRE ROERDEN), editor, business owner, publishing consultant; b. N.Y.C., Aug. 28, 1935; d. Marion Smolin; m. Harold H. Roerden (div. 1985); children: Ken, Doug. BA in English summa cum laude, U. Maine, 1969, MA in English cum laude, 1971. Mem. pub. rels. staff Shell Oil Co., N.Y.C., 1952-55; asst. to pub. rels. dir. Interchem. Corp., N.Y.C., 1956-59; staff editor Newkirk Assocs., Albany, N.Y., 1960-62; instr. in English U. Maine, Portland, 1969-71; mentor Empire State Coll., SUNY, Rochester and Syracuse, N.Y., 1973-74; mng. editor CPA Digest, Brookfield, Wis., 1983; owner Edit It, Brookfield, 1984—; lectr. U. Wis., Milw., 1991—; speaker and trainer in field. Author: Collections from Cape Elizabeth, 1965, Oops 'n Options Game, 1982, Open Gate: Teaching in a Foreign Country, 1990; editor: Life Skills Parenting Series, Mrs. Wheeler Goes to Washington (Elizabeth Wheeler Colman), 1989, Give This Man a Hand (Earl Harrell), 1990, Genetic Connections: A Guide to Documenting Your Individual and Family Health History, 1995 (7 awards), The Safety Minute (R.L. Siciliano), 1995, Secret's Shadow (Alex Matthews), 1995, The Body in the Transept (Jeanne Dams), 1995 (Agatha award). Pres. Brookfield Civic Chorus, 1986-88; v.p. Brookfield Civic Music Assn., 1989-91. Recipient cert. of honor Korean Nat. Commn. for UNESCO, 1989, Kate Mooney Vol. Svc. award Counseling Ctr. Milw., 1991, Disting. Tech. Commn. awards (2) STC, 1995, award of achievement STC, 1995, Merit award, 1996, 1st pl. tech. editing award MAPA Book awards, 1995, 2d pl. interior design award MAPA Book awards, 1995. Mem. Mid-Am. Pubs. Assn. (pres. 1995—), Am. Soc. Indexers, Soc. for Tech. Comm. (bd. dirs. 1991-95), Women in Comm. (bd. dirs. 1988), Am. Soc. Quality Control, Wis. Bus. Women's Coalition (bd. dirs. 1988-94), Wis. Women's Network (founding), Feminist Bus. and Profl. Women's Forum (coord. 1990—), Wis. Regl. Writers Assn., Brookfield C. of C., Coun. Wis. Writers, NOW (Wis. pres. 1978-81, Positive Action award for leadership 1977), Mensa Internat., Phi Kappa Phi. Office: Edit It 3225 Hillcrest Dr Brookfield WI 53045-1529

ROESSER, JEAN WOLBERG, state legislator; b. Washington, May 8, 1930; d. Solomon Harry Wolberg and Mary Frances Brown; m. Eugene Francis Roesser, Aug. 3, 1957; children: Eugene Francis, Jr., Mary Roesser Calderon, Anne. BA, Trinity Coll., Washington, 1951; postgrad. in econs., Cath. U. of Am., 1951-53. Congl. relations asst. U.S. Info. Agy., Washington, 1954-58; news reporter for Montgomery County Council Suburban Record, 1983-86; del. Md. Gen. Assembly, Annapolis, 1986-94; mem. State Senate, Md. Gen. Assembly, Annapolis, 1994—, mem. fin. com., ethics com., 1994—. Former mem. Md. Gov.'s Task Force on Energy; former pres. Montgomery County Fedn. Rep. Women, Potomac Women's Rep. Club; former 3d v.p. Md. Fedn. Rep. Women; founding mem. Montgomery County Arts Coun.; alt. del. Rep. Nat. Conv., 1992, del., 1996. Recipient Cmty. Achievement awrd Washington Psychiat. Soc., 1994, Trinity Coll. Leadership award, 1994, Common Cause Md. award, 1993, Md. Underage Drinking Preventio Coalition award, 1994. Mem. Women Legislators Md., also area citizens assns. and chambers commerce. Republican. Roman Catholic. Home: 10830 Fox Hunt Ln Potomac MD 20854-1553 Office: James Senate Office Bldg 110 College Ave Annapolis MD 21401-1991

ROETS, LOIS FLORENCE, elementary and secondary education educator; b. Breda, Iowa, Mar. 4, 1937; d. Charles G. and Mary Ann (Goecke) Schelle; m. Philip George Roets, June 7, 1969; children: Jacqueline, Ron. BS, Viterbo Coll., 1964; MS, U. Wis., 1975; EdD, Internat. Inst. for Advanced Studies, St. Louis, Mo., 1984. Cert. tchr., grades 1-8, Iowa, Wis., specialist in gifted and talented edn., grades 1-12, Iowa. Coord. of gifted talented edn. North Mahaska Schs., New Sharon, Iowa, 1980-88, Des Moines Pub. Schs., Iowa, 1988-90; pres. founder Leadership Pubs., Des Moines, Iowa, 1982—; dir. of curriculum WLVA schs., Lake View, Iowa, 1995—; edn. cons., Des Moines, Iowa, 1984—; bd. mem. Iowa Div.: Odyssey of the Mind, 1986-90; com. mem. Sheridan Scholarships, New Sharon, Iowa, 1985-88; book reviewer, Am. Libr. Assn., 1991-92; presenter conferences for gifted edn., state, regional, nat., world, 1982—. Author: (ednl. books) 16 gifted edn., over 20 gen. edn., 1976—; editor: Sharing Time.. (Larson), KOI & Portfolio (Kingore), Forums, Fairs... (Silverman), Alligators... (Sanders), What Do You Think? (Achterberg); composer, singer: collection of ballads. Organizer, commr. Sanitary Dist. (secure sewer, water svcs. around lake residential dist.), Pardeeville, Wis.; vol. Iowa Pub. TV, Des Moines, Iowa, 1992-96, Nat. Pub. Radio, Ames, Iowa, 1993. Grantee Coun. for Exceptional Children, 1984. Mem. Nat. Assn. for Gifted Children, Am. Educators Rsch. Assn, Iowa Talented & Gifted, Nat. Crane Found., Wildflower Assn., Women in the Arts, Smithsonian, Des Moines Opera. Office: Leadership Pubs PO Box 8358 Des Moines IA 50301

ROFFÉ, MERCEDES, poet; b. Buenos Aires, June 23, 1954; arrived in U.S., 1985; d. Isaac and Simona (Botbol) de R. Prof. Modern Lit., U. Buenos Aires, 1978; PhD in Spanish Lit., NYU, 1993. Vis. asst. prof. Vassar Coll., Poughkeepsie, N.Y., 1991-95; editor Spanish program Curriculum Concepts, NYC, 1995—; vis. asst. prof. NYU, 1995-96; pre-screener postdoc. fellowships ACLS, N.Y., 1994—; reviewer rsch. found. CUNY, 1993—. Author: Poems 1973-75, 1978 (Torre Ardoz award), The Tapestry, 1983, Subchamber, 1987, Night & Words, 1996, Gender and Genre in Grisel y Mirabella by Juan de Flores, 1996; contbg. editor Tokonoma, 1994—, De Azur 1994—. Home and Office: 322 E 89th St # 4D New York NY 10128

ROFFE-STEINROTTER, DIANN, Olympic athlete. Silver medalist, Giant Slalom Albertville Olympic Games, 1992. Silver medalist Giant Slalom, Albertville Olympic Games, 1992, Gold medalist Super-G, Lillehammar Olympic Games, 1994. Address: PO Box 611 Potsdam NY 13676-0611 Office: US Skiing 1500 Kearns Blvd PO Box 100 Park City UT 84060*

ROFFMAN, ANN ESTES, elementary school principal; b. Athens, Ga., June 24, 1954; d. Thomas H. and Lonazelle (Holloway) Estes; m. Allan R. Roffman, Oct. 2, 1977. BS, Ga. Coll., 1975; MEd, U. Ga., 1977, EdS, 1987. Cert. sch. adminstr. and counselor, Ga. Sci. tchr. Morgan County Bd. edn., Madison, Ga., 1975-76, counselor, 1984-91, curriculum dir., 1991-96; employment counselor Ga. Dept. Labor, Athens, 1977-79; social worker Ga. Dept. Human Resources, Madison, 1979-84; asst. prin. Collins Ford Elem. Sch., Oconee County, Ga., 1996—. Mem. AAUW (v.p.), ASCD, Ga. Assn. Curriculum & Instr. Suprs., Delta Kappa Gamma. Office: Morgan County Bd Edn 1065 East Ave Madison GA 30650

ROGAN, ELEANOR GROENIGER, cancer researcher, educator; b. Cin., Nov. 25, 1942; d. Louis Martin and Esther (Levinson) G.; m. William John Robert Rogan, June 12, 1965 (div. 1970); 1 child, Elizabeth Rebecca. AB, Mt. Holyoke Coll., 1963; PhD, Johns Hopkins, 1968. Lectr. Goucher Coll., Towson, Md., 1968-69; rsch. assoc. U. Tenn., Knoxville, 1969-73; rsch. assoc. U. Nebr. Med. Ctr., Omaha, 1973-76, asst. prof., 1976-80, assoc. prof. Eppley Inst., dept. pharm. scis. and dept. biochemistry and molecular biology scis., U. Nebr., 1980-90, prof., 1990—. Contbr. articles to profl. jours. Predoctoral fellow USPHS, Johns Hopkins U., 1965-68. Mem. AAAS, AAUP, Am. Assn. Cancer Rsch., Am. Soc. Biochem. Molecular Biology. Democrat. Roman Catholic. Home: 8210 Bowie Dr Omaha NE 68114-1526 Office: U Nebr Med Ctr Eppley Inst 600 S 42nd St Omaha NE 68198-6805

ROGENESS, MARY SPEER, state legislator; b. Kansas City, Kans., May 18, 1941; d. Frederic A. and Jeannette (Hybskmann) Speer; m. Dean Rogeness, Aug. 31, 1964; children: Emily, James, Paul. BA, Carleton Coll., 1963. Computer analyst Dept. Def., Ft. Meade, Md., 1963-66; freelance writer, editor Longmeadow, Mass., 1982-91; mem. Mass. Ho. of Reps., Boston, 1991—. Editor: Reflections of Longmeadow, 1983. Mem. Longmeadow Rep. Town Com., 1983—; Mass. alt. del. Rep. Nat. Conv., Houston, 1992. Mem. Am. Legis. Exch. Coun., World Affairs Coun. of Western Mass. (bd. dirs. 1990—). Office: Mass House of Reps State House Boston MA 02133

ROGERS, ALICE LOUISE, retired bank executive, writer, researcher; b. McLoud, Okla., Feb. 18, 1929; d. John Edmond and Katy McNora (Williams) Stanka; m. Jesse Ray Rogers, Apr. 18, 1948; children: Jimmy Allen, Bonnie Kay Rogers Calhoun. Student, Am. Inst. Banking, 1967-69. Clk. typist loan dept. Security Pacific Nat. Bank, L.A., 1960-64; office mgr., adminstrv. asst. to v.p. loan adminstn. divsn. City Nat. Bank, Beverly Hills, 1964-75, credit mgr. Pershing Square branch, 1975-77. Author, editor: Dance Bands and Big Bands Reference Book and Price Guide, 1986, Dance Bands, Big Bands and Swing Reference Book and Price Guide, 1993; contbr. articles to DISCoveries mag. Mem. Internat. Assn. Jazz Record Collectors, Big Band Acad. Am., Libr. Congress Assocs. (founding nat. mem.), Nat. Mus. Am. Indians. Republican. Home: Rte 1 Box 146 A Deming NM 88030

ROGERS, ANDREA MARIA, medical administrator; b. Sao Paulo, Brazil, Oct. 7, 1953; came to U.S., 1956; d. Andreas and Erna Josefa (Bihler) Strasser; m. Jerome Edward Rogers, Jan. 10, 1976; 1 child, Shane Jerome. BSN, Loretto Hts. Coll., 1976; MS in Health Svc. Adminstrn., Coll. St. Francis, 1988. RN, Colo., Wash.; cert. rehab. nurse; cert. nursing home adminstr., Colo. Staff nurse ortho/med.-surg. Beth Israel Hosp., Denver, 1976-77; nurse, patient and staff educator rehab. Julia Temple North Rehab., Denver, 1977-79; staff developer Christopher House, Wheat Ridge, Colo., 1979-80; charge nurse, med.-surg. staff nurse Provenant St. Anthony No. Hosp., Denver, 1980-83, charge nurse, med.-surg./oncol. nurse, 1983-87; staff developer Provenant Sr. Life Ctr., Denver, 1987-89, program mgr. Subacute/Extended Care Facility, 1989-92; medicare nurse specialist Denver dist. Hillhaven Corp., Aurora, Colo., 1992-94; medicare compliance case mgr. corp. office Hillhaven Corp., Tacoma, Wash., 1994-96; clin. reimbursement specialist Unison Healthcare, Scottsdale, Ariz., 1996—; cons. Hillhaven Corp., Aurora, 1992-94. Mem. Assn. Rehab. Nurses, Colo. Trout Unltd., Puget Sound Flyfishers. Roman Catholic. Home: 3006 31st Ave SE Puyallup WA 98374 Office: Unison Healthcare 3006 31st Ave SE Puyallup WA 98374 also: 4140 Marshall St Wheat Ridge CO 80033

ROGERS, ANN, small business owner; b. Malakoff, Tex., Jan. 7, 1933; d. Alvin and Lillian (Looney) Workman; m. Clemon Wayne Rogers, Mar. 2, 1951 (dec. Aug. 24, 1978); children: Larry Wayne, David Keith. AS, Cedar Valley Coll., 1995. Farmer Malakoff, 1939-47; labeling maching operator Figaro Co., Dallas, 1948; advt. mgr. Sears, Roebuck & Co., Dallas, 1949-87; mgr. Hutchins, Tex., 1979-95; pres. Plastic Grinders, Inc., Hutchins, Tex., 1992-94. City Coun. Woman, City Hutchins, 1980-82, mem. zoning bd., 1983-85. Mem. Phi Theta Kappa, Alpha Zeta Omicron. Democrat. Baptist. Home: PO Box 92 Hutchins TX 75141

ROGERS, BETTY GRAVITT, research company executive; b. Valdosta, Ga., June 24, 1945; d. Jim Aldine and Ruby Romell (Mann) Gravitt; m. Ennis Odean Rogers, May 8, 1967; children: Catheryne, Charles, Elizabeth, Susanne. Student, Fla. Community Coll., Jacksonville, 1988. Chief exec. officer Info. Rsch. Ctr., Inc., Jacksonville, 1982-96; co-mgr. Sizes Unltd., The Ltd., Tampa, Fla., 1982-96; visual merchandiser, sales cons. The Entertainer, Jacksonville, Fla., 1996—. Mem. Plan and City Bus. and Profl. Women's Club, Phi Theta Kappa, Beta Phi Gamma. Democrat. Methodist. Home: 3549 Chestnut Hill Ct Jacksonville FL 32223

ROGERS, BILLIE D., occupational health nurse; b. Charlotte, N.C.; d. Marion T. and Clara B. (Lanford) Dobbs; m. Wyatt M. Rogers Jr., Aug. 11, 1956; children: Constance, John. BSN, U. N.C., 1956; cert. mgmt., U. Denver, 1984. RN, Colo.; cert. Am. Bd. for Occupl. Health Nurses; cert. CPR and first aid instr. Sr. pub. health nurse Wake County Health Dept., Raleigh, N.C., 1956-58; night charge nurse new born nursery Charlotte (N.C.) Meml. Hosp., 1959; relief nurse United Packing Co., Denver, 1977-78, Sunstrand, Arvada, Colo., 1978; nurse world hdqrs. Manville, Denver, 1978-88; pvt. practice occupl. health cons. Denver, 1988—; case mgr. Luth. Bus. Health Svcs., 1994-95. Mem. Am. Assn. Occupl. Health Nurses, Colo. State Assn. Occupl. Health Nurses (past dir., chmn. govtl. affairs com.), Denver Colo. Assn. Occupl. Health Nurses (pub. and govtl. affairs chmn., legis. affairs com.), Sigma Theta Tau. Democrat. Baptist. Home: 5452 W Geddes Pl Littleton CO 80123

ROGERS, BONNIE CARR, elementary education educator; b. Petersburg, W.Va., Dec. 26, 1954; d. Glenn Granville and Viola Mae (Combs) Carr; m. Gregory Alan Rogers, Jan. 2, 1978; 1 child, John Colton. BA in Elem. Edn., Shepherd Coll., 1977; M of Curriculum and Instrn., Frostburg State U., 1989. Permanent cert. profl. tchg., W.Va.; cert. elem. edn. 1-8, social studies 1-9. Head Start tchr. Hardy County, W.Va., 1982-85; tchr. Hardy County Bd. Edn., Mathias, W.Va., 1985-89, Moorefield, W.Va., 1989—; com. mem. Hardy County Attendance Policy Com., Moorefield, W.Va., 1986-87, 87-89, Moorefield Elem. Curriculum Com., 1990-91, 91-92, County Curriculum Rev. Com., Moorefield, 1995-96; chmn. Faculty Senate, Moorefield, 1992-93. Mem. AAUW. Democrat. Home: PO Box 23 Moorefield WV 26836 Office: Moorefield Elem 400 N Main St Moorefield WV 26836

ROGERS, BONNIE JEAN, college program director; b. Ft. Worth, Tex., Oct. 10, 1969; d. Ronald Woodrow and Constance Jean (Kellar) Jones; m. Christopher Dwayne Rogers, Dec. 20, 1991; 1 child, Celestial Joye. AA, S.W. Tex. Jr. Coll., 1989; BA in English, S.W. Tex. State U., 1992. Tutor, special programs asst. S.W. Tex. State U., San Marcos, 1990-92, upward bound coord., 1992-95; fin. aid dir. Austin (Tex.) Presbyn. Theol. Sem., 1995—; bd. dirs. Tex. Assn. Student Special Svcs. Programs, 1994-95. Mem. Nat. Assn. Student Fin. Aid Officers. Presbyterian. Office: Austin Presbyn Theol Sem 100 E 27th Austin TX 78705

ROGERS, BRENDA GAYLE, educational administrator, educator, consultant; b. Atlanta, July 27, 1949; d. Claude Thomas and Louise (Williams) Todd; m. Emanuel Julius Jones, Jr., Dec. 17, 1978; children: Lavelle, Brandon, Albre Jede, Briana Adanne. BA, Spelman Coll., 1970; MA, Atlanta U., 1971, EdS, 1972; PhD, Ohio State U., 1975; postgrad. Howard U., 1980, Emory U., 1986. Program devel. specialist HEW, Atlanta, 1972; rsch. assoc. Ohio State U., Columbus, 1973-75; asst. prof. spl. edn. Atlanta U., 1975-78, program adminstr., 1978—, CIT project dir., 1977-91, exec. dir. Impact project, 1992—; tech. cons. Dept. Edn., Washington, 1978-93, 96, cons. head start, 1990-91, cons. Gluction Teasting Svcs., 1996—; due process regional hearing officer Ga. State Dept Edn., Atlanta, 1978-84, adv. bd., 1980-84; regional cons. Access Project, 1995—; mem. parent adv. coun. APS, 1988—; cons. program devel. Ga. Respite Care, Inc., 1988-89; mem. exec. bd., pres. PTA Stone Mountain Elem. Sch., 1989-92; mem. test verification panel Edn. Testing Svcs., Princeton, N.J., 1995-96. Mem. Ga. Assessment Project com., Atlanta Pub. Schs. Adv. Council, 1986—; bd. dirs. Mountain Pines Civic Assn., 1988—; mem. Grady Meml. Hosp. Community Action Network, Atlanta, 1982-83; exec. bd. PTA Shadow Rock Elem. Sch., 1992-94. Recipient disting. service award Atlanta Bur. Pub. Safety, 1982, disting. svcs. award Mountain Sch. P.T.A., 1995, award Atlanta Pub. Sch. System, 1980, 82, 83, 89-90; fellow Ohio State U., 1972-74, Howard U., 1980; mem. Assn. for Retarded Citizens, Council for Exceptional Children, NAFE, Phi Delta Kappa, Phi Lambda Theta. Democrat. Roman Catholic. Avocation: gourmet cooking. Office: Clark Atlanta U James P Brawley Atlanta GA 30314-3913

ROGERS, CATHERINE GAMBRELL, art conservator; b. Bennettsville, S.C., Feb. 10, 1957; d. Virginius Cullum and Catherine Brown (McCall) R. Cert., Inst. per L'Arte e il Restauro, Florence, Italy, 1982; BA in Art History, Va. Commonwealth U., 1983; MA in Arts/cert. advanced study in Conservation, SUNY, Buffalo, 1989; cert. advanced study, Harvard U., 1992. Paintings conservator Perry Huston & Assocs., Fort Worth, 1989-90, Corcoran Gallery, Washington, 1990-91, Harvard U. Art Mus., Cambridge, Mass., 1992-93, The Walters Art Gallery, Balt., 1993-96; pvt. practice art conservator Charleston, S.C., 1996—. Mem. Am. Inst. Conservation (profl. assoc.), Internat. Inst. Conservation (assoc.), Washington Conservation Guild, Western Assn. Art Conservation. Democrat. Presbyterian. Home: 29 Savage St Charleston SC 29401

ROGERS, DESIREE GLAPION, state official; b. New Orleans, June 16, 1959; d. Roy and Joyce Glapion; m. John Rogers, Jr.; 1 child, Victoria. B in Polit. Sci., Wellesley Coll., 1981; MBA, Harvard U., 1985. Customer svc. mktg. mgr. AT&T, N.J., 1985-87; dir. devel. Levy Orgn., Chgo., 1987-89; founder, pres. Mus. Ops. Consulting Assocs., Chgo., 1989-91; dir. Ill. State Lottery, Chgo., 1991—. Pres. The Chgo. Children's Mus.; bd. dirs. Mus. Sci. and Industry, Frances Xavier Warde Sch., WTTW/Ch. 11; bd. trustees Harvard Bus. Sch. Club Chgo.; mem. women's bd. Mus. Contemporary Art; sec. Marwen Found. Mem. The Econ. Club, Harvard Bus. Sch. Club, Wellesley Club. Office: Ill State Lottery Ste 2040 676 N Saint Clair St Chicago IL 60611

ROGERS, ELIZABETH PARKER, chemistry educator; b. Plymouth, Mass., Aug. 27, 1919; d. Edward R. and Helen L. (Barnes) Belcher; m. Warren H. Yudkin, Dec. 23, 1951 (dec. June 1954); children: Michael, David; m. Robert W. Rogers, Nov. 23, 1956; children: Susan, Sarah, John. BA, Mount Holyoke Coll., 1940, MA, 1942; PhD, Northwestern U., 1951. Rsch. chemist Armstrong Cork Co., Lancaster, Pa., 1942-45, Evanston (Ill.) Health Dept., 1951-54; asst. prof. U. Ill., Urbana, 1963-87. Author: (lab book) Beginning Chemistry, 1973, 76, 81, 91, 94, (textbook) Fundamentals of Chemistry, 1987, (with W.H. Brown) General, Organic and Biochemistry, 1980, 83, 87. Staff asst. ARC, France, 1945-46; sec. LWV, Champaign, 1987-89; dir., sec. East Ctrl. Ill. Alzheimer's, Champaign, Ill., 1989-91, pres., 1991-95; dir. Friends of Univ. of Ill. Libr., Champaign, 1989-92. Recipient Achievement award Sid Granet Aging Network, Ill. Area Agys. on Aging, 1992, Cert. of Lifetime Achievement, Ill. Dept. on Aging, 1995. Mem. Am. Chem. Soc.

ROGERS, EVELYN MAE, speech and language pathologist; b. Binghamton, N.Y., Sept. 21, 1951; d. Llewellyn L. and Mildred E. (Hodge) R. AA, Cazenovia Coll., 1971; BS, SUNY, Fredonia, 1974; MS, SUNY, Albany, 1976. Cert. tchr., N.Y.; cert. clin. competence. Speech therapist Mary Imogene Bassett Hosp., Cooperstown, N.Y., 1974-76; speech pathologist. No. Catskills Bd. Cooperative Ednl. Svcs., Stamford, N.Y., 1977-90, Cooperstown (N.Y.) Ctrl. Sch., 1990—. Named Pres.'s coun. award Am. Speech, Lang., Hearing Assn., 1992. Mem. Delta Kappa Gamma, Order Ea. Star. Republican. Methodist. Home: RR 1 Box 1216 Maryland NY 12116-9725 Office: Cooperstown Ctrl Sch Linden Ave Cooperstown NY 13326

ROGERS, FRANCES NICHOLS, assistant principal; b. Fontana Dam, N.C., July 25, 1944; d. Fred Edward and Violet Bernice (Slagle) Nichols; m. Terry William Rogers, July 3, 1970. BA in English, Berea Coll., 1966; MA in Elem. Edn., U. Ky., 1968; postgrad., U. N.C., 1992. Tchr. intern Breathitt County Schs., Jackson, Ky., 1966-68; tchr. elem. sch. Haywood County Schs., Waynesville, N.C., 1968-72, resource program developer, 1972-75, 77-83, asst. prin., 1983-89, 92—, prin., 1989-92; pres. Haywood County Chpt. N.C. Edn. Assn., 1969-70. Author: Mount Zion United Methodist Church: A History 1850-1982, 1982; author of poems; contbr. articles to profl. jours. Mem. Friends of Libr., Waynesville, 1980—, Haywood Animal Welfare Assn., Waynesville, 1980—, Youth for Christ, Waynesville, 1980—. Named Outstanding Young Educator Waynesville Jaycees, 1968-69, Leader of Am. Elem. Edn., 1971. Mem. Tarheel Assn. Prins. and Adminstrs., Haywood County Prins. Assn., Internat. Reading Assn. (sec. local chpt. 1973-74). Methodist. Home: 120 Arrowood Acres Rd Clyde NC 28721-9751

ROGERS, GLENDA NELSON, missionary; b. Greenville, N.C., Mar. 6, 1962; d. Luther Sullivan and Thelma Olivia (Joyner) Nelson; m. Theodore Courtney Jr. Rogers, July 30, 1983. BA in Psychology cum laude, So. Meth. U., 1984. Loaned exec., campaign coord. United Way, Fort Worth, Tex., 1985; human resources dept. MCorp, Fort Worth, 1985; investment counselor S.W. Savs., Dallas, 1985-88; br. mgr. S.W. Fed. Savs. Assoc., Dallas, 1988-90; pres. The Daily Grind, Inc., Plano, Tex., 1990-95; missionary, dir. receipting Global Missions Fellowship, Dallas, 1995—; annuities cons. S.W. Savs., 1987-90; spkr. various fellowship groups. Active cmty. svc. East Dallas Asian Outreach, 1987-88. Mem. Kappa Delta Pi, Psi Chi. Evangelical. Office: Global Missions Fellowship Ste 200 11910 Greenville Ave Dallas TX 75243

ROGERS, IRENE, retired librarian; b. Yonkers, N.Y., Oct. 12, 1932; d. Franklin Harold and Mary Margaret (Nealy) R.; BS in Edn., New Paltz State Tchrs. Coll., 1954; MLS (N.Y. State Tng. grantee), Columbia U., 1959. Tchr., West Babylon (N.Y.) Sch. System, 1954-57, Yonkers Sch. System, 1957-58; reference librarian Yonkers Pub. Library, 1959-67, adult services coordinator, 1967-73, asst. library dir., 1973-92, ret., 1993. Mem. Mayor's Adv. Com. Consumer Edn., Yonkers, 1970—; active United Way of Yonkers; mem. curriculum adv. com., report card revision com. Office Supt. Schs., 1982; mem. Yonkers unit Am. Cancer Soc. West Library System grantee, 1966. Mem. ALA, Westchester, N.Y. library assns., Soroptimists (pres. 1978-79, 80-81, sec. dist. I North Atlantic region), Bus. and Profl. Women's Club (pres. Yonkers chpt. 1989-90). Home: 41 Amackassin Ter Yonkers NY 10703-2213

ROGERS, JANET TAXIS, psychotherapist; b. Livingston, N.J., Sept. 29, 1946; d. Fred Edwin and Ann Eleanor (Matheson) Taxis; m. Jimmie Jerome Rogers, Aug. 20, 1984. BA, U. N.C., Greensboro, 1981; MA, Wake Forest U., 1985. Lic. profl. counselor; nat. cert. counselor; cert. substance abuse counselor, N.C.; internat. cert. alcohol and drug abuse counselor. V.p., clin. dir. Step One, Winston-Salem, N.C., 1983-91; therapist Charter Hosp., Winston-Salem, 1992-93, Ashleybrook Clinic, Winston-Salem, 1993-95; therapist, pres. The Taxis Ctr., Winston-Salem, 1995—. Com. mem. chpt. svcs. Nat. Multiple Sclerosis, Winston-Salem, 1994—. Mem. ACA, ASCH, AMHCA. Office: The Taxis Ctr Inc 258 Forsyth Medical Park Winston Salem NC 27103

ROGERS, JEANNE VALERIE, art educator, artist; b. Islip, N.Y., Dec. 1, 1935; d. Joseph Oliver and Louise Valerie (Bayer) Fields; m. James Aubrey Rogers, Jan. 1, 1956; children: Bradley, Tyler, Lisa, Todd. BFA in Ceramics Design, Alfred U., 1957; MS in Art Edn., SUNY, New Paltz, 1962; postgrad., L.I. U., 1986-90, Parsons Sch. Design, 1988-90. Cert. art edn. tchr. K-12, elem. tchr., N.Y. Elem. art tchr. Sayville (N.Y.) Sch. Dist., 1957-61, high sch. art tchr., 1987-90; art tchr. Bayport (N.Y.)/Bluepoint Sch. Dist., 1980; art dir., art tchr. The Hewlett Sch., East Islip, N.Y., 1984-87; field supr. of student tchrs. Dowling Coll., Oakdale, N.Y., 1990—; high sch. art tchr. Torah Acad., Commack, N.Y., 1991—; instr. watercolor painting Staff Devel. Ctr. of The Islips, East Islip 45, N.Y.C., N.Y., 1996—; instr. oil painting adult edn. East Islip High Sch., 1961-62; dir. children's art Summer Outdoor Art Workshops, East Islip, 1967-78; adj. prof. Dowling Coll., 1991-92, art cons., 1990—; instr. watercolor painting for tchrs. Staff Devel. Ctr. of the Islips, East Islip H.S., N.Y., 1996—. Co-author/illustrator: Suffolk Scribes Calligraphic Poetry, 1980 (Libr. award East Islip, 1980); exhibited juried show at Babylon (N.Y.) Citizens Coun. Arts, 1994 (Best in Show award), Invitational Exhibit of Women Artists, Patchogue, N.Y., 1995; reader children's poetry Women in the Arts cable TV show, 1974; contbr. painting as cover design Suffolk Woman Watch Newspaper (premier issues), 1994. Instr. life saving and water safety ARC, Islip, 1955-61; tchr. Sunday sch. Presbyn. Ch., Islip, 1957-63; instr., dir. lifesaving and water safety Shoreham Beach Club, Sayville, 1965-70; instr. preschool, youth and adult swimming Bayshore YMCA, Lasalle Acad., Oakdale, 1971-88, instr., swim dir., 1983-88; art judge C. of C. Summerfest, Sayville, 1990. Recipient award of merit in painting, Nat. League Am. PEN Women, Vanderbilt Mus., Centerport, N.Y., 1993, 94, Chem. Bank award for painting Arts Coun., 1992, East Islip Pub. Libr., 1992, hon. mention Huntington Township Art League, Northport Spoke Gallery N.Y., 1991, HTAL winners show Hutchins Gallery, CW Post Campus/L.I. U., 1991, Honorable Mention Huntington Twp. Art League, Northport Spoke Gallery, N.Y., 1991, others. Mem. AAUW (implementation chair soc.'s reflection in arts study 1972-74, legis. chair Islip area br. 1972-74, cultural interests chair 1973-75), summer socials chmn. General and Ednl. grants Fundraising, 1995—, historian 1996—), Suffolk Scribes (charter mem., corr. sec. 1988-89), Nat. League Am. PEN Women (corr. sec. 1996-97), South Shore Watercolor Soc., South Bay Art Assn., N.Y. State Tchrs. Assn., L.I. Art Tchrs. Assn. Republican. Presbyterian. Home: 274 Marilynn Ct East Islip NY 11730-3315

ROGERS, JOAN DIANE, counselor; b. Meadville, Pa., July 7, 1933; d. Carlyle Claarence and Marie Gertrude (Hagen) Conn; m. Francis Howard Rogers, May 3, 1952; children: Diane Lynn, Yvonne Marie, Patricia Kathleen, Renee Ann. Francis Howard, Christopher Gerard, Elayne Jean. BS magna cum laude, Kent State U., 1986, MEd, 1989. Payroll clerk Mc Crosky Tool, Meadville, 1951-52; biofeedback clinician Kent, Ohio, 1973-94; coord. Counseling and Human Devel. Ctr., Kent, 1989-90; counselor Kent Psychol., 1989-94, Ctr. for Psychol. Health, Kent, 1994—; adj. instr. Kent State U., 1995—, steering com. Pub. Policy Inst., Kent, 1995—. Author: contbr. articles to profl. jours. Bd. dirs. Friendship House, Ravenna, Ohio, 1961-72, leader Girl Scout of Am., Kent, 1971-83; mem. Northeast Ohio Leadership Com., Kent, 1994—. Recipient Gwendolyn D. Scott Outstanding Sr. award, Kent State U., 1985, Judith A. DeTrude Profl. Recognition award, Kent State U., 1996, Judith A. DeLinde award Kappa Sigma Upsilon chpt. of Chi Sigma Iota Internat. Mem. ACA, Am. Assn. for Marriage and Family Therapists, Chestnut Soc., Golden Key Nat. Honor Soc., Kappa Delta Pi, Chi Sigma Iota. Home: 237 E Williams St Kent OH 44240 Office: Ctr For Psychol Health PO Box 279 812 S Water St Kent OH 44240

ROGERS, JUDITH W., federal circuit judge; b. 1939. AB cum laude, Radcliffe Coll., 1961; LLB, Harvard U., 1964; LLM, U. Va., 1988; LLD (hon.), D.C. Sch. Law, 1992. Bar: D.C. 1965. Law clk. Juvenile Ct. D.C., 1964-65; asst. U.S. atty. D.C., 1965-68; trial atty. San Francisco Neighborhood Legal Assistance Found., 1968-69; atty. assoc. atty. gen.'s office U.S. Dept. Justice, 1969-71, atty. criminal divsn., 1969-71; gen. counsel Congl. Commn. on Organization of D.C. Govt., 1971-72; coordinator legis. program Office of Dep. Mayor D.C., 1972-74, spl. asst. to mayor for legis., 1974-79, corp. counsel, 1979-83; assoc. judge D.C. Ct. Appeals, 1983-88, chief judge, 1988-94; cir. judge U.S. Ct. Appeals-D.C. Cir., 1994—; mem. D.C. Law Revision Commn., 1979-83; mem. grievance com. U.S. Dist. Ct. D.C., 1982-83; mem. exec. com. Conf. Chief Justices, 1993-94. Bd. dirs. Wider Opportunities for Women, 1972-74; mem. vis. com. Harvard U. Sch. Law, 1984-90; trustee Radcliffe Coll., 1982-88. Recipient citation for work on D.C. Self-Govt. Act, 1973, Disting. Pub. Svc. award D.C. Govt., 1983, award Nat. Bar Assn., 1989; named Woman Lawyer of Yr., Women's Bar Assn. D.C., 1990. Fellow ABA; mem. D.C. Bar, Nat. Assn. Women Judges, Conf. Chief Justices (bd. dirs. 1988-94), Am. Law Inst., Phi Beta Kappa. Office: US Ct Appeals 333 Constitution Ave NW Washington DC 20001-2802*

ROGERS, KATE ELLEN, interior design educator; b. Nashville, Dec. 13, 1920; d. Raymond Lewis and Louise (Gruver) R.; diploma Ward-Belmont Jr. Coll., 1940; BA in Fine Arts, George Peabody Coll., 1946, MA in Fine Arts, 1947; EdD in Fine Arts and Fine Arts Edn., Columbia U., 1956. Instr., Tex. Tech. Coll., Lubbock, 1947-53; co-owner, v.p. Design Today, Inc., Lubbock, 1951-54; student asst. Am. House, N.Y.C., 1953-54; asst. prof. housing and interior design U. Mo., Columbia, 1954-56, assoc. prof., 1956-66, prof., 1966-85, emeritus, 1985—, chmn. dept. housing and interior design, 1973-85; mem. accreditation com. Found. for Interior Design Edn. Rsch., 1975-76, chmn. stds. com., 1976-82, chmn. rsch., 1982-85. Mem. 1st Bapt. Ch., Columbia, Mo.; bd. dirs. Meals on Wheels, 1989-91. Nat. Endowment for Arts rsch. grantee, 1981-82. Fellow Interior Design Educators Coun. (pres. 1971-73, chmn. bd. 1974-76, chmn. rsch. com. 1977-78); mem. Am. Soc. Interior Designers, (hon., medal of honor 1975), Am. Home Econs. Assn., Columbia Art League (adv. bd. 1988-93), Pi Lambda Theta, Kappa Delta Pi, Phi Kappa Phi (hon.), Gamma Sigma Delta, Delta Delta Delta (Phi Eta chpt.), Phi Upsilon Omicron, Omicron Nu (hon.). Democrat. Author: The Modern House, USA, 1962; editor Jour. Interior Design Edn. and Research, 1975-78.

ROGERS, KATHERINE DIANE, political consultant, state legislator; b. Concord, N.H., Mar. 7, 1955; d. Albert A. and Alta (Whittier) R. BA, Clark U., Worcester, Mass., 1977. Mem. N.H. Ho. of Reps., Concord, 1992—; bd. dirs. N.H. Bus. Fin. Authority. Mem. City Coun., Concord, 1991—. Democrat. Lutheran. Home: 4 Jay Dr Concord NH 03301-7831

ROGERS, KATHRYN EILEEN, secondary school educator, farmer; b. L.A., Nov. 29, 1949; d. James and Doris Arlene (Smith) Threlfall; m. Richard McCallum Rogers, Nov. 27, 1970; children: Glen McCallum, Kevin James. BA, Calif. State U., L.A., 1977; postgrad., various schs. Tchr., cons. Pasadena (Calif.) Sch. Dist., 1977-78; substitute tchr. San Luis Obispo County Schs., 1978-80; tchr. San Miguel Joint Union Sch. Dist., San Miguel, Calif., 1980—; DATE Coord. San Luis Obispo County Schs., 1990—; evaluator Calif. Future Problem Solvers, Sacramento, 1990; Student Assistance Program facilitator and coord., 1993—. Editor: Help You Spell, 1993-94. Bd. dirs., sec. North County Farmers Market, San Louis Obisbo County, 1980—; donation collector San Luis Obispo County Food Bank, Paso Robles, 1992—. Named Tchr. of Yr., San Miguel Sch. Dist., 1986-87, Woman of Yr./Distinction in Edn., Cuesta Coll., 1994. Mem. Calif. Assn. Health, Phys. Edn., Recreation and Dance, Emblem Club, Nat. Colored Wool Growers Assn., Calif. Tchrs. Assn., San Miguel Tchrs. Assn. (v.p., co-pres.), Kappa Delta Pi. Home: 2935 Nacimiento Lake Dr Paso Robles CA 93446-9757 Office: San Miguel Joint Union Sch Dist PO Box 299 San Miguel CA 93451

ROGERS, LISA HENNING, training consultant; b. Jersey City, Aug. 22, 1959; d. George Frank and June Phyllis (Fegely) Henning; m. Leo Paul Rogers Jr., May 27, 1984; children: Amy, Leo. BA, Coll. of William and Mary, 1981; MSW in Adminstrn., Rutgers U., 1983; EdS in Higher Edn., William and Mary, 1981. Asst. coordinator Rutgers U., New Brunswick, N.J., 1981-83; ednl. rep. March of Dimes, Fairfield, N.J., 1983-84; dir. facilities Coll. William and Mary, Williamsburg, Va., 1984-86; tng. cons. Child Devel. Resources, Lightfoot, Va., 1986—. Vol. Colonial Prevention Coalition, 1988—, Big Sisters, Williamsburg, 1985—; coord. Interagy. Coun. for Young Children, 1990—; mem. Tidewater Regional Interagy. Coord. Coun., 1990—; bd. dirs. Jr. Women's Club, 1992—. Named Outstanding Young Woman of Yr., Jr. Women's Club, 1992; Garden State scholar State of N.J., 1977-81, George Anderson Meml. scholar Coll. William and Mary, 1977-78, Chubb Found. scholar Chubb & Son, Inc., 1977-81. Mem. Am. Coll. Pers. Assn. (bd. dirs. 1980-81), Assn. of Coll. Unions Internat., Coun. for Exceptional Children (divsn. early childhood 1990), Rural Network, Jr. Women's Club, Psi Chi, Kappa Delta Pi, Alpha Chi Omega. Home: 110 Links Of Leith Williamsburg VA 23188-7461 Office: Child Devel Resources PO Box 280 Norge VA 23127-0280

ROGERS, LORENE LANE, university president emeritus; b. Prosper, Tex., Apr. 3, 1914; d. Mort M. and Jessie L. (Luster) Lane; m. Burl Gordon Rogers, Aug. 23, 1935 (dec. June, 1941). B.A., N. Tex. State Coll., 1934; M.A. (Parke, Davis fellow), U. Tex., 1946, Ph.D., 1948; D.Sc. (hon.), Oakland U., 1972; LL.D. (hon.), Austin Coll., 1977. Prof. chemistry Sam Houston State Coll., Huntsville, Tex., 1947-49; research scientist Clayton Found. Biochem. Inst. U. Tex., Austin, 1950-64, asst. dir., 1957-64, prof. nutrition, 1962-80, assoc. dean Grad. Sch., 1964-71, v.p. univ., 1971-74, pres., 1974-79, mem. exec. com. African grad. fellowship program, 1966-71; research cons. Clayton Found. for Research, Houston, 1979-81; Vis. scientist, lectr., cons. NSF, 1959-62; cons. S.W. Research Inst., San Antonio, 1959-62; mem. Grad. Record Exams Bd., 1972-76, chmn., 1974-75; adv. com. ITT Internat. Fellowship, 1973-83; dir. Texaco, Inc., Gulf States Utilities, Republic Bank, Austin. Bd. dirs. Tex. Opera Theatre, Austin Lyric Opera; chmn. bd. trustees Texaco Philanthropic Found.; chmn. council of presidents Nat. Assn. State Univs. and Land-Grant Colls., 1976-77, mem. exec. com., 1976-79; mem. com. on identification of profl. women Am. Council on Edn., 1975-79, mem. com. on govt. relations, 1978-79; mem. target 2000 project com. Tex. A&M U. System; mem. ednl. adv. bd. John E. Gray Inst., Lamar U., Beaumont, Tex. Eli Lilly fellow, 1949-50; Recipient U. Tex. Students Assn. Teaching Excellence award, 1963; Disting. Alumnus award N. Tex. State U., 1972; Outstanding Woman of Austin award, 1950, 60, 71, 80; Disting. Alumnus award U. Tex., 1976; Honor Scroll award Tex. Inst. Chemists, 1980. Fellow Am. Inst. Chemists; mem. AAAS, Am. Chem. Soc. (sec. 1954-56), Am. Inst. Nutrition, Am. Soc. Human Genetics, Nat. Soc. Arts and Letters, Assn. Grad. Schs. (internat. edn. com. 1967-71), Sigma Xi, Phi Kappa Phi, Iota Sigma Pi, Omicron Delta Kappa. Home: 4 Nob Hill Cir Austin TX 78746-3650

ROGERS, MARTHA PAUL, contractor; b. Henderson, Tex., Oct. 22, 1933; d. Paul Emmett and Mary Lucy (Craig) R.; widowed, 1992; children: Paul, Mary Ellen. MusB, Baylor U., 1955, MusM, 1957. Cert. music, spl. edn. tchr. Pvt. teaching Fla., Va., Tex., 1955-85; tchr. children with learning disabilities Va., 1975-85; organist, choirmaster St. Matthew's Episcopal Ch., Henderson, Tex., 1980-90; owner Home Makeovers, Henderson, Tex., 1980-95; operator, owner financed homes Real Estate Co., Henderson, 1980-95; builder Passive Solar Garden Homes for Srs. and Handicapped, Henderson, 1985-95. Performed piano duos. Pres. AAUW, 1982-86, Varied Arts Club, Henderson, Tex., 1984-85, guild mem. Tex. Shakespeare Festival, Kilgore, 1994-95. Episcopalian. Home: 1100 Foley St Henderson TX 75652-4269

ROGERS, NEVA LEE, healthcare executive; b. Columbus, Ohio, Nov. 22, 1958; d. Thomas Franklin and Virginia Ilene (Norvell) R.; m. Mark R. Shuler, Nov. 2, 1985. BSN, U. S. Ala., 1980, MSN, 1987; postgrad., Fla. Tech., 1993—. RN; cert. BCLS instr. Coord. obstetric outreach program and high risk clinic U. S. Ala. Coll. Medicine, Mobile, 1983-87; coord. maternal and child health svcs. area 6 Dept. Health State of Ala., 1987-88; mgr. labor and delivery svcs. Huntsville (Ala.) Hosp. Sys., 1988-90, dir. orgnl. devel. and tng., 1990—; cons. work redesign Edn. Mgmt. Corp., Nashville, 1993-94; v.p. mktg. Advanced Med. Tech., Inc., Huntsville, 1994—; nurse labor and delivery unit U. S. Ala. Med. Ctr., Mobile, 1981-83; instr. aerobic class New Dimensions Fitness Ctr., Mobile, 1986-88; sales assoc. Parisian Dept. Store Madison Sq. Mall, Huntsville, 1992-93; instr. childbirth class Women's Ctr., Huntsville, 1988-93. Lectr. in field; contbr. articles to newspapers. With U.S. Army Res., 1990—. Mem. ASTD (pres.-elect Huntsville chpt. 1995, v.p. 1994, profl. devel. com. chair 1993), Assn. Women's Health, Obstetric, and Neonatal Nurses (program chmn. Mobile chpt. 1985, coord. 1986-87, legis. chair Ala. sect. 1988-93, treas. 1994-96, program chair Huntsville chpt. 1992, nat. com. on practice appointee 1990-91), Nat. Perinatal Assn. (exec. bd. Ala. assn. 1984-89, newsletter editor 1984-88, nat. coun. rep. 1986-88, treas. 1989-90, pres. 1991-93), Assn. Mil. Surgeons U.S., Soc. Human Resource Mgrs., Sigma Theta Tau (Zeta Gamma newsletter editor 1982-84). Office: Huntsville Hosp Sys 101 Sivley Rd Huntsville AL 35801

ROGERS, PIER CAMILLE, management educator; b. Chgo., July 24, 1953; d. Walter Eugene and Alpha (Spikner) R.; m. David Nathaniel Heywood, July 23, 1983; 1 child, Gabriel Alexander Heywood. BA, Wellesley Coll., 1975; MA, MS, Boston U., 1977; PhD, N.Y.U., 1991. Coll. advisor Pine Manor Coll., Chestnut Hill, Mass., 1976-78; legis. liaison Mass. Dept. Pub. Welfare, Boston, 1977-79; agy. rels. mgr. United Way Mass. Bay, Inc., Boston, 1979-83; rsch. assoc. N.Y.C. Bd. Edn., 1984-85; lectr. N.Y.U., 1991-92; asst. project dir. La Guardia C.C., Long Island City, N.Y., 1990-92; asst. prof. non-profit mgmt. The New Sch. for Social Rsch., N.Y.C., 1992—; evaluation cons. La Guardia C.C., 1992-93, United Way of N.Y.C., 1990, 94; mem. faculty South African Nonprofit Mgmt. Inst., New Sch. for Social Rsch., summer 1994, 95. Mem. family life com. Unity Bapt. Tabernacle, Mt. Vernon, N.Y., 1988—; ednl. adv. com. Bridges & Boundaries, N.Y.C., 1991; annual fund vol. Riverdale Country Sch., Bronx, N.Y., 1993—; mem. exec. com. Jack & Jill Am., Westchester chpt., 1992—. Mem. Am. Soc. Pub. Adminstrn., Assn. Rsch. Nonprofit Orgns. & Voluntary Action, Conf. Minority Pub. Adminstrns. Office: New Sch Social Rsch 80 Fifth Ave 4th Fl New York NY 10011-8802

ROGERS, RITA DORIS LUCK, family nurse; b. Lincoln County, Kans., Feb. 6, 1948; d. Ernest F. and Rea N. (Nelson) Luck; m. Eugene W. Rogers, Mar. 15, 1969; children: R. Michelle, Sara J (dec.), Brandon G. Diploma, Wesley Sch. Nursing, 1969; BSN cum laude, Ft. Hays State U., 1992, MSN, 1996. RN, Kans.; cert. family nurse practitioner ANCC. Float, relief charge nurse Wesley Med. Ctr., Wichita, 1969-71; charge nurse Mitchell County Hosp., Beloit, Kans., 1971-72; dir. PHN III Jewell County Health Dept., Mankato, Kans., 1973-74; office nurse Dr. A.T. Llana, Superior, Nebr., 1975-76; head nurse Jewell County Hosp., 1977—; allied health adj. faculty Cloud C.C., Concordia, Kans., 1988—' Perkins grant coord. North Ctrl. Kans. Area Vo-Tech., Beloit, 1988—; county chair Am. Cancer Soc., Mankato, 1972-74; sec. Jewell County Mental Health Assn., 1973-75; parliamentarian Dist. XII Kans. State Nurses Assn., Topeka, 1975-79. Columnist Rap with Rita, 1973-74. County and club leader 4-H, Jewell County, 1977-91' tchr. Sunday sch. Luth. Ch., Mankato, 1979-82. Scholar Kans. Health Found., 1993, Midwest Organ Bank, 1994, Ft. Hays State U., 1994, Dane G. Hansen Found., 1994, Kans. Nurses' Found., 1995. Mem. Great Plains Nurse Practitioner Soc., Ft. Hays Grad. Nurses Assn., Ft. Hays Alumni Assn., Sigma Theta Tau Internat., Inc. (Nu Zeta chpt.). Home: Rte 2 Box 252 309 N Columbus Jewell KS 66949 Office: Jewell County Hosp PO Box 327 100 Crestvue Mankato KS 66956

ROGERS, ROSEMARY, author; b. Panadura, Ceylon, Dec. 7, 1932; came to U.S., 1962; naturalized citizen.; d. Cyril Allan and Barbara (Jansze); m. Summa Navaratnam (div.); children: Rosanne, Sharon; m. Leroy Rogers (div.); children: Michael, Adam; m. Christopher Kadison (div.). B.A., U. Ceylon. Writer features and pub. affairs info. Associated Newspapers Ceylon, Colombo, 1959-62; sec. billeting office Travis AFB, Calif., 1964-69; sec. Solano County (Calif.) Parks Dept., Fairfield, 1969-74; part-time reporter Fairfield Daily Republic. Author: (novels) Sweet Savage Love, 1974, The Wildest Heart, 1974, Dark Fires, 1975, Wicked Loving Lies, 1976, The Crowd Pleasers, 1978, The Insiders, 1979, Lost Love, Last Love, 1980, Love Play, 1981, Surrender to Love, 1982, The Wanton, 1985, Bound by Desire, 1988, The Tea Planter's Bride, 1995. Mem. Authors Guild of Authors League Am., Writers Guild Am.

ROGERS, RUBY ELIZABETH, artist; b. New Kensington, Pa., June 24, 1952; d. Claude Ray and Dora Jean (Remaley) Downing; m. Kenneth Michael Rogers, June 26, 1970; children: Aaron Nathan, Jason Edward. Student, Fed. Tax and Bus. Sch., Chgo., 1990, NRI Sch. Computer Programming, Washington, 1990-93, ICS Sch. Med. Tng., Scranton, Pa., 1996—. Owner Kenneth M. Rogers Gen. Contractor, Claysville, Pa., 1975-90, Art by R. Rogers, Claysville, 1991—. Exhibited in group show at Calif. State Coll., 1969 (cert. of merit Washington County Fedn. Women's Clubs). Occupl. therapy vol. Washington (Pa.) Hosp., 1994-96, United Cerebral Palsy of Southwestern, Inc., Washington, 1994—; ptnr. Spl. Olympics, 1996; mem. The Shepherd's Guide, Christian Advertisers Orgn., 1995-96; mem. WQED Pitts. Pub. Broadcasting, 1990—. Mem. AAUW, Nat. Mus. Women in Arts. Republican. Lutheran. Home and Office: 1285 Templeton Run Rd Claysville PA 15323

ROGERS, RYNN MOBLEY, community health nurse; b. Georgetown, S.C., Aug. 2, 1950; d. Ralph Edward and Pearl (Hill) Mobley; m. C. Rogers Jr., July 3, 1971 (div. Mar. 1992); 1 child, Julie Pearl. Student, Georgetown County Sch. Nursing, 1970; AS, SUNY, Albany, 1982; AS in Criminal Justice, Georgetown Tech. Coll., 1992; postgrad., 1994. Cert. community nurse, med. asst. Mem. staff Georgetown Meml. Hosp., 1969-71; office nurse Dr. L. Benton Williams, Georgetown, 1971—; jail nurse Georgetown County Detention Ctr., 1991-92; staff devel. nurse Prince George Village, 1992—. Mem. ANA, Am. Assn. Office Nurses, Nat. Assn. Physicians Nurses, S.C. Nurses Assn., Order Ea. Star. Baptist. Home: 217 Beneventum Rd Georgetown SC 29440-9461 Office: 1743 N Fraser St Georgetown SC 29440 also: Prince George Village 901 Maple St Georgetown SC 29440

ROGERS, SHARON J., university administrator; b. Grantsburg, Wis., Sept. 24, 1941; d. Clifford M. and Dorothy L. (Beckman) Dickau; m. Evan D. Rogers, June 15, 1962 (div. Dec. 1980). BA summa cum laude, Bethel Coll., St. Paul, 1963; MA in Libr. Sci., U. Minn., 1967; PhD in Sociology, Wash. State U., Pullman, 1976. Lectr., instr. Alfred (N.Y.) U., 1972-76; assoc. prof. U. Toledo, 1977-80; assoc. dean Bowling Green (Ohio) State U. Librs., 1980-84; univ. libr. George Washington U., Washington, 1984-92, asst. v.p. acad. affairs, 1989-92, assoc. v.p. acad. affairs, 1992—, co-dir. Univ. Teaching Ctr., 1990—; mem. Online Computer Libr.Ctr. Users Coun., 1985-92, pres., 1989-90, mem. rsch. adv. com., 1990-92, trustee, 1992—. Contbr. articles to profl. jours. Bd. dirs. ACLU, Toledo, 1978-84, CapAccess, 1993—, treas., 1993-95. Jackson fellow U. Minn., 1964-65; NSF trainee Wash. State U., 1969-72. Mem. ALA (exec. coun. 1987-91, pub. com. 1989-93, chair 1990-93), Assn. Coll. and Rsch. Librs. (pres. 1984-85), Am. Sociol. Assn., Washington Rsch. Libr. Consortium (bd. dirs 1987-90), Universal Serials and Book Exch. (bd. dirs., treas. 1987). Office: George Washington Univ 2121 I St NW Washington DC 20037-2353

ROGERS, SUZANNE PROVOST, foreign language educator; b. Montreal, Que., Can., June 11, 1952; came to U.S., 1982; d. Jean and Madeleine (Poirier) Provost; m. Carl Connell Rogers, Feb. 25, 1982; 1 child, John Xavier. BA in Mass Comm., U. du Québec, Montreal, 1987; MA in Francophone Lit., U. Ariz., 1990, PhD in French Lit., 1995. Cert. C.C. tchr., Ariz. Grad. assoc. tchr. U. Ariz., 1988-95; assoc. tchr. Pima C.C., Tucson, 1990-91; tchr. Spanish and French Acad. Tucson, 1992-93; pres. Diplome Elementaire de Langue Francaise and Diplome Avance de Langue Francaise Ariz. U. Ariz., 1995—. Author: (radio novella) Le Retour à la ruelle, 1983. Mem. ACLU, AAUW, MLA, Conseil Internat. d'Etudes Francophones, Am. Assn. Tchrs. of French, Phi Delta Phi. Home: PO Box 4101 Tubac AZ 85646

ROGGE, PATIENCE, librarian; b. Bradford, Pa., Sept. 11, 1936; d. Albert Anthony and Constance Margaret (Ward) Griffin; m. David Michael Rogge, Aug. 31, 1957; children: Rachel Maria, Michelle Angela. Student, Pa. State U., 1954-57; BA, U. Calif., Berkeley, 1962, MLS, 1963. Libr. asst. U. Del., Newark, 1957-58; libr. asst. U. Calif., Berkeley, 1959-61, libr., 1963-66; libr. Armstrong Coll., Berkeley, 1968; gallery dir. Richmond (Calif.) Art Ctr., 1976-77; libr. ARAMCO Schs., Dhahran, Saudi Arabia, 1978-80, Livermore (Calif.) Pub. Libr., 1984-92; docent Coyote Point Mus., San Mateo, Calif., 1983-86, Sunol (Calif.) Regional Wilderness, 1986-91. Contbr. articles to profl. jours. and newsletters. trustee, sec., chair Jefferson County Rural Libr. Dist., Port Hadlock, Wash., 1994—; bd. dirs., pres. Friends of the Vineyards, Livermore, 1983-1992; active Jefferson County Higher Edn. Access, Port Townsend, Wash., 1995—. Recipient Vol. Svc. award Valley Col. Ctr., Pleasanton, Calif., 1989. Mem. Wash. Libr. Friends and Trustees Assn. (bd. dirs. 1995—), Wash. Libr. Assn., AAUW, Univ. Women's Found. (sec. 1995—), Am. Libr. Trustees Assn. Democrat. Home: 531 Pinecrest Dr Port Townsend WA 98368

ROGIN, RONNE ANN, government contract specialist; b. N.Y.C., Oct. 23, 1948; d. Maurice and Marjorie Doris (Markel) R. BS, George Washington U., 1970, MA, 1972. Head dept. athletics The Potomac Sch., McLean, Va., 1970-80; contract specialist U.S. Geol. Survey, Reston, Va., 1980-90; supervisory contract specialist Dept. Treasury, Washington, 1990-93; contract specialist State Dept., Washington, 1993—. Mem. NOW, Nat. Contract Mgmt. Assn. Democrat. Home: 13711 Springhaven Dr Chantilly VA 20151-3215

ROGO, KATHLEEN, safety engineer; b. Carrollton, Ohio, Sept. 28, 1952; d. Silvio and Mary (Siragusano) R. Grad. high sch., Carrollton; PhD in Med. Sci. (hon.), Ohio Valley Pathologists, Inc., 1992. Cert. histotechnologist, emergency med. technologist, safety engr. Rsch. pathology trainee Aultman Hosp., Canton, Ohio, 1970-75, supr. anatomic pathology, 1974-75; lab. mgr. W. Morgan Lab., Canton, 1973-74; supr. anatomic pathology Dr.'s Hosp., Massillon, Ohio, 1975-78; emergency med. technician Canton Fire Dept., 1976-81; safety engr. Ashland Oil Co., Canton, 1980-82; rsch. pathologist assoc., med. cons, v.p. Ohio Valley Pathologists, Inc., Wheeling, W.Va., 1990—. Mem. Am. Soc. Clin. Pathology (cert. histotechnician), Am. Soc. Safety Engrs. (cert.), Am. Soc. Emergency Med. Technicians (cert.), Ohio State Med. Soc., Internat. Platform Assn. Democrat. Roman Catholic.

ROGOSKI, PATRICIA DIANA, financial executive; b. Chgo., Dec. 29, 1939; d. Raymond Michael and Bernice Rose (Konkol) R. BS in Acctg. and Econs., Marquette U., 1961, postgrad., 1965-66; postgrad., NYU, 1966-68, St. John's U., N.Y.C., 1975-76; cert. mgmt. acct., 1979. Sr. fin. analyst Blackhawk Mfg. Co., Milw., 1961-66; mgr., sr. analyst Shell Oil Co., N.Y.C., 1966-71; mgr. data processing Bradford Nat./Penn Bradford, Pitts., 1971-75; asst. mgr. fin. controls ITT, N.Y.C., 1975-79; v.p., comptr. ITT Consumer Fin. Corp., Mpls., 1979-80; sr. v.p. fin. ITT Fin. Corp., St. Louis, 1980-84; v.p., exec. asst., group exec. ITT Coins, Secaucus, N.J., 1984-85; pres. Patron S., Ltd., Wilmington, Del., 1986—; CFO, sr. v.p. Guardsmark, Inc., Memphis, 1989-94; sr. v.p. Peoplemark, Inc., Memphis, 1989-94. Bd. dirs. St. Louis Repertory Theater, 1983-84. Named to Acad. Women Achievers, YWCA, N.Y.C., 1980. Mem. Fin. Execs. Inst., Inst. Mgmt. Acctg., Econ. Club. Office: Patron S Ltd NE Hercules Plz 1313 N Market St Ste 3410 Wilmington DE 19801-1151

ROHE, SUZANNE ELLEN, bond trader; b. Baldwin, N.Y., June 5, 1966; d. Victor Joseph and Grace (White) R.; m. John Gerald Fitzgibbon, June 24, 1995. BS, St. John's U., Jamaica, N.Y., 1988; postgrad. in bus., NYU, 1993—. Trading asst. Shearson Lehman, N.Y.C., 1988-90; bond trader Sanwa BGK Securities, N.Y.C., 1990-92; sr. bond trader Spear Leeds & Kellogg, N.Y.C., 1992—. Vol. N.Y. Cares, N.Y.C., 1993-94. Home: 230 E 79th St Apt 12A New York NY 10021

ROHNER, BONNIE-JEAN, small business owner, computer consultant; b. Waltham, Mass., Aug. 2, 1946; d. Gerrit John and Marjorie Lorraine (Hollis) R.; children: David Harrison Sackett, Amanda Marjorie Sackett. BFA in Fashion, Pratt Inst., Bklyn., 1967; BA in Biology, Adelphi U., Garden City, N.Y., 1983; MS, CIS, U. New Haven, Conn., 1993. Freelance fashion designer Garden City, 1971-76; owner, mgr. The Printing Workshop, Massapequa, N.Y., 1976-78; personnel mgr. Doron Ltd., Norwich, Conn., 1978-79; computer related trainer Gen. Dynamics, Groton, Conn., 1979-89; acad. computing coord. Three Rivers Com./Tech. Coll., Norwich, 1989-94; owner, mgr. bytestream, Norwichtown, Conn., 1993—; computer cons. U. New Haven, Groton, 1990-92; tech. advisor Countywide Network Com., 1989-90; sec. Connbug, Rocky Hill, Conn., 1992-93. Mem. NAFE, AAUW, AAUP, ACM, Women's Network of S.E. Conn.

ROHRBACH, HEIDI A., lawyer; b. Buffalo, N.Y., Jan. 25, 1953; d. William R. and A.T. R.; m. Leonard Lance, Aug. 9, 1996; 1 child, Peter R. Frank. BA, Northwestern U., Evanston, Ill., 1974; JD, Vanderbilt U., Nashville, 1977. Bar: N.Y., 1978. V.p., and asst. gen. counsel Chase Manhattan Bank, N.Y.C., 1985—. Office: Chase Manhattan Bank 270 Park Ave Fl 40 New York NY 10017-2014

ROHRBAUGH, LISA ANNE, librarian; b. Girard, Ohio, Sept. 17, 1956; d. John Michael and Josephine Antoinette (Oliva) Sultan; m. Paul Hugh Rohrbaugh Jr., July 28, 1979. BA, Youngstown State U., 1978; MLS, Kent State U., 1979. Libr.. readers assistance dept. Youngstown (Ohio) Pub. Libr., 1979-86; libr., researcher Ajax Magnethermic Corp., Warren, Ohio, 1986-90; asst. reference libr. Youngstown State U., 1990-93; dir. East Palestine (Ohio) Meml. Pub. Libr., 1993—; helped edit articles for Ency. Libr. Sci., 1978-79; translator articles dealing with electronics and induction heating/melting tech. from Spanish, German and French into English. Reviewer childrens books State Libr. of Ohio; reviewer for Libr. Jour. Recipient Quest '91 Creative Scholarship award Youngstown State U., 1991. Office: East Palestine Meml Pub Libr 309 N Market St East Palestine OH 44413-2153

ROHRBOUGH, ELSA CLAIRE HARTMAN, artist; b. Shreveport, La., Sept. 26, 1915; d. Adolph Emil and Camille Claire (Francis) Hartman; m. Leonard M. Rohrbough, June 19, 1937 (dec. Jan. 1977); children: Stephen, Frank, Leonard. Juried exhbns. (painting) Massur Mus. Art, Monroe, La., Mobile (Ala.) Art Gallery, Gulf Coast Juried Exhibit, Mobile, Juried Arts Nat., Tyler, Tex., Greater New Orleans Nat., La. Watercolor Soc. Nat., Ky. Watermedia Nat., So. Watercolor Ann., La. Women Artist, many others. One-woman shows include Le Petit Theatre du Vieux Carre, New Orleans World Trade Ctr.'s Internat. House, Singing River Art Assn., Pascagoula, Miss., La. Font Inn, Pascagoula, Mandeville (La.) City Hall, St. Tammany Art Assn., Covington, La., others; exhibited in groups shows at 1st Guaranty Bank, Hammond, La., St. Tammany Art Assn., Ft. Isabel Gallery, Covington, S.E. La. State U. Mem. Nat. League Am. Pen Women (v.p. S.E. La. br. 1986-87, pres. 1987-92, 94-98), St. Tammany Art Assn. (bd. dirs. 1985-86, 87, instr. 1977-78, classes chmn. 1986-88). Republican. Roman Catholic. Home: 2525 Lakeshore Dr Mandeville LA 70448-5627

ROHREN, BRENDA MARIE ANDERSON, therapist, educator; b. Kansas City, Mo., Apr. 18, 1959; d. Wilbur Dean and Katheryn Elizabeth (Albright) Anderson; m. Lathan Edward Rohren, May 10, 1985; 1 child, Amanda Jessica. BS in Psychology, Colo. State U., 1983; MA in Psychology, Cath. U. Am., 1986. Lic. mental health practitioner. Mental health therapist, sr. case mgr. Rappahannock Area Community Svcs. Bd., Fredericksburg, Va., 1986-88; mental health therapist, case mgmt. supr. Rappahannock Area Community Svcs. Bd., 1988; rsch. assoc. Inst. Medicine, NAS, Washington, 1988-89; supr. adult psychiat. program Lincoln (Nebr.) Gen. Hosp., 1989, program supr. mental health svcs., 1989-91; adj. instr. S.E. Community Coll., Lincoln, 1990—; assessment & referral specialist Rivendell Psychiat. Ctr., Seward, Nebr., 1993-95; therapist Lincoln Day Treatment Ctr., Lincoln, Nebr., 1993-95; adj. inst. Coll. of St. Mary, 1994—; therapist Rape/Spouse Abuse Crisis Ctr., Lincoln, 1996—; computer cons. Syscon Corp., Washington, 1983-84. Author: (report) Bottom Line Benefits: Building Economic Success Through Stronger Families; editor: (newsletter) Alliance for Mentally Ill, Lincoln. Active Lincoln Alliance for the Mentally Ill, Nebr. Domestic Violence/Sexual Assault Coalition. Mem. NOW, APA (assoc.), Nat. Alliance for Mentally Ill, Nebr. Psychol. Assn. (assoc.). Democrat. Roman Catholic. Home: 3821 S 33rd St Lincoln NE 68506-3806 Office: SE Community Coll 8800 O St Lincoln NE 68520-1227 also: Coll of St Mary 4600 Valley Rd Rm 403 Lincoln NE 68510

ROHRLICH, RUBY, anthropologist; b. Montreal, Can., June 7, 1913; d. Maurice and Elise (Haimovici) Rohrlich; m. Milton G. Leavitt, Aug. 31, 1935 (div. 1975); children: Michael, Matthew. BA cum laude, NYU, 1940, PhD in Anthropology, 1969; MS in Speech and Hearing Rehab., Adelphi U., 1962. Office mgr. Parkinson, Joncas, Montreal, 1930-35; propaganda analyst Office War Info., N.Y.C., 1940-42; tchr. Levittown (N.Y.) Sch. Dist., 1954-62, speech pathologist, 1962-67; anthropologist CUNY, New York, 1969-83, George Washington U., Washington, 1995—. Author: The Puerto Ricans: Culture Change and Language Deviance, 1974, Peaceable Primates and Gentle People, 1976; author, editor: Women Cross-Culturally: Change and Challenge, 1975, Women in Search of Utopia: Mavericks and Myth Makers, 1984; contbr. articles to profl. jours. NEH grantee, 1976; NEH fellow U. Calif., Santa Cruz, 1977-78. Fellow Am. Anthrop. Assn.; mem. Washington Assn. Profl. Anthropologists, Assn. for Anthropology and Gerontology, Internat. Interdisciplinary Congress for Women, Older Women's League, Nat. Coun. Sr. Citizens. Home and Office: Apt S-520 3003 Van Ness St NW Washington DC 20008

ROISMAN, HANNA MASLOVSKI, classics educator; b. Wroclaw, Poland; d. Leon and Eugenia (Shlager-Katz) Maslovski; m. Joseph Roisman, Aug. 5, 1971; children: Elad L., Shalev G. BA in Classics, MA in Classics, Tel Aviv U., Ramat Aviv, Israel, 1977; PhD in Classics, U. Wash., 1981. Lectr. classics Tel Aviv U., 1981-87, sr. lectr. classics, 1987-90; assoc. prof. classics Colby Coll., Waterville, Maine, 1990-94, prof., 1994—; jr. fellow Ctr. Hellenic Studies, Washington, 1985-86; vis. scholar U. Wash. Seattle, 1983, Cornell U., Ithaca, N.Y., 1989, 1995-96; sec. Israel Soc. for Promotion of Classical Studies, 1987-89; vis. assoc. prof. Cornell U., 1986-94, vis. prof., 1995—. Author: Loyalty in Early Greek Epic and Tragedy, 1984; co-author: The Odyssey Re Formed, 1996; contbr. articles to profl. jours. AAUW fellow, 1980-81. Office: Colby Coll Mayflower Hill Waterville ME 04901

ROITMAN, JUDITH, mathematician; b. N.Y.C., Nov. 12, 1945; d. Leo and Ethel (Gottesman) R.; m. Stanley Lombardo, Sept. 26, 1978; 1 child, Ben Lombardo. BA in English, Sarah Lawrence Coll., 1966; MA in Math., U. Calif., Berkeley, 1971, PhD in Math., 1974. Asst. prof. math. Wellesley (Mass.) Coll., 1974-77; from asst. prof. to prof. math. U. Kans., Lawrence, 1977—. Author: Introduction to Modern Set Theory, 1990; contbr. articles to profl. jours. Grantee NSF, 1975-87, 92-95. Mem. Math. Assn. Am., Assn. Symbolic Logic, Am. Math. Soc., Assn. Women in Math. (pres. 1979-81, Louise Hay award 1996), Kans. Assn. Tchrs. Math., Nat. Assn. Tchrs. Math.

ROLL, MARY KRISTIN, entrepreneur; b. Clinton, Md., Feb. 8, 1968; d. William Corneilius and Virginia Kay (Gissendaner) R. BA in Bus. Adminstrn., U. San Diego, 1990. Concierge Am./Intercontinental Concierge Corp., Washington, 1991-94; pres. Exec. Concierge Svcs., Inc., Washington, 1994—. Jr. friend/fundraiser Campagna Ctr. for Head Start Program, Alexandria, Va., 1995—; ch. sch. tchr. Christ Ch., Alexandria, 1993—, tutor for underpriveleged child, 1994-95. Mem. Property Mgmt. Assn. Democrat. Episcopalian. Home: #3-C 1201 N Pitt St Alexandria VA 22314 Office: Exec Concierge Svcs Inc Ste 501 1100 17th St NW Washington DC 20036

ROLLA, CHERYL KAY, retail executive; b. Carmi, Ill., May 8, 1961; d. Joel Nicholas and Beverly June (Sylvia) R. BA in Telecomm./Mktg., Ind. U., 1982. Mgr. expense analysis May Dept. Store Co., St. Louis, 1988-89, mgr. fin. analysis, 1989-90; dir. fin planning Kaufamann's divsn. May Dept. Store Co., Pitts., 1990-91; dir. merchandise planning Famous Barr divsn. May Dept. Store Co., St. Louis, 1991-93, asst. contr., 1993-95, dir. process planning, 1995—. Mem. NAFE. Republican. Office: Famous Barr 601 Olive St Saint Louis MO 63101

ROLLASON, MARY KATHERINE, artist, art educator; b. Balt., Jan. 18, 1908; d. Clarence Irving and Mary Agnes (Sadler) Drenner; m. Fred Rollason, Sept. 27, 1941 (dec. Mar. 1994). Student, Sch. Music Arts, Balt., 1928-33; student in fgn. lang., Costa Rican Consulate, Balt., 1936-40, Italian Consulate, Balt., YMCA, Balt.; pvt. student of Clyde Taylor,, Carnegie Mellon Inst., Pa., Md., 1941-45. Coloratura soprano Balt. Civic Opera Co., 1930; singer WBAL Radio, Balt., 1930-32; art tchr., owner Kay's Art Gallery, Crossville, Tenn., 1980—. Exhbn.: Salon des Nations à Paris, Internat. D'Art Contemporium, 1985; founder,mem. Black-Eyed Susans chpt. Sweet Adelines, Catonsville, Md., 1959-65. Aide-de-camp Hon. Shirley Duer, Tenn. Ho. Rep., 1981. Named Artist of the Month Cumberland Cmty. Bank, Crossville, 1981. Mem. Nat. Mus. Women in the Arts (charter), N.Y. Internat. Soc. Artists, Women of Moose (libr. chmn. Balt., 1945, conservation chmn. Balt., 1946, Acad. Friendship degree). Home and Office: Rt 11 Box 99 Crossville TN 38555-8920

ROLLBERG, JEANNE NORTON, educator; b. Jacksonville, Fla., Oct. 31, 1957; d. James Thomas and Joan Wade (Jennings) N.; m. Charles Anthony Rollberg, Aug. 4, 1956. BA, Wesleyan Coll., Macon, Ga., 1979; MA in Journalism, U. Mo., 1980. Stringer Dayton (Ohio) Daily News, 1981; asst. news dir. KAMU-TV/FM, Tex. A&M U., College Station, 1981-82, news dir., 1983; asst. prof. U. Ark., Little rock, 1983—; pub. affairs show producer KLRE-KUAR/FM, Little rock, 1987—; gen. asst. rep. part time KTHV-TV, Little Rock, 1984, 89—. Recipient 1st place pub. affairs award Ark. AP, 1989-93, award for talk show Am. Women in Radio and TV, Inc., 1989, 92. Mem. Assn. Edn. Journalism and Mass Communications, Soc. Profl. Journalists, Broadcast Edn. Assn., Ark. Press Women, Internat. Communication Assn. Office: U Ark 2801 S University Ave Little Rock AR 72204-1000

ROLLE, ESTHER, actress; b. Pompano Beach, Fla., Nov. 8; d. Jonathan Rolle. Student, Spellman Coll., Hunter Coll., New Sch. for Social Research. Dancer, Shogola Obola Dance Co., then mem., Negro Ensemble Co.; off-Broadway debut: The Blacks, 1962; London stage debut: God is a (Guess What?), 1969; numerous stage appearances include Macbeth, Amen Corner, Blues for Mister Charlie, Don't Play Us Cheap; toured Scandinavia in stage prdn. The Skin of Our Teeth; toured Australia, New Zealand in stage prdns. Black Nativity; other stage prdns. The Member of the Wedding, 1988, Nothing But a Man, 1964, Cleopatra Jones, 1973, Don't Play Us Cheap, 1973, P.K. and the Kid, 1982, Driving Miss Daisy, 1989, The Mighty Quinn, 1989, Color Adjustment, 1991, House of Cards, 1993, Nobody's Girls, 1994; TV series include Maude, 1972-74, One Life to Live, 1972-74, Good Times, 1974-77, 78-79, Singer and Sons, 1990; TV appearances include Summer of My German Soldier, 1979 (Emmy award 1979), I Know Why the Caged Bird Sings, 1979, Age Old Friends, 1989, The Kid Who Loved Christmas, 1990, Dinah's Place, N.Y.P.D., Like It Is, East Side, West Side, To Dance with a White Dog, 1993, Message From Nam, 1993, Scarlet, 1994. Hon. chmn. Pres.'s Com. on Employment of Handicapped.; Grand Marshall Cherry Blossom Festival, Washington, 1975. Named Woman of Yr. 3d World Sisterhood, 1976; recipient Image awards, NAACP, 1973, 74, 79, Leadership award, 1990, Hall of Fame, 1987; guest Bahamian gov. dedication Nat. Bank, 1993. Office: William Morris Agy 152 S El Camino Dr Beverly Hills CA 90212-2705*

ROLLÉ, JANET LYDIA, marketing executive; b. Mt. Vernon, N.Y., Dec. 25, 1961; d. William Arthur Sr. and Barbara Monica (Goldson) Rollé; m. Mark Damon Keye, Apr. 14, 1995. BFA in Dance, SUNY, Purchase, 1984; MBA in Mktg. and Film, Columbia U., 1991. Profl. dancer London, 1984-88; spl. asst. to chmn. Home Box Office, N.Y.C., 1991-92; mgr. multiplex mktg. Home Box Office, 1992-93; dir. mktg. HBO Home Video, 1993-96, dir. mktg. and sales promotion, 1996—. Mentor Harlem YMCA Mentoring Program, N.Y.C., 1993—; sponsor Black Filmmaker Found. Recipient Black Achievers in Industry award Harlem YMCA, 1993. Mem. Am. Film Inst. (3d decade coun.), N.Y. Women in Film and TV. Office: HBO Home Video 1100 6th Ave New York NY 10036

ROLLE, MYRA MOSS See MOSS, MYRA ELLEN

ROLLEFSON, MEGAN ELIZABETH, secondary school educator; b. Oconomowoc, Wis., Aug. 17, 1953; d. Irving G. and Mary E. (Griffith) R. BS in Edn., U. Wis., Whitewater, 1975, MS in Tchg., 1983. Life cert. 7-12 comprehensive bus. edn. tchr., Wis.; cert. in elem. keyboarding. Tchr. bus. edn. Mishicot (Wis.) H.S., 1975—; adult instr. Lakeshore Tech. Coll., Cleveland, Wis., 1979—. Mem. NEA, Wis. Edn. Assn., Wis. Bus. Edn. Assn. (life), Nat. Bus. Edn. Assn., Mishicot Edn. Assn. (sec. 1987—), Delta Pi Epsilon. Democrat. Lutheran. Office: Mishicot HS 660 Washington St Mishicot WI 54228

ROLLENCE, MICHELE LYNETTE, molecular biologist; b. Takoma Park, Md., Nov. 23, 1955; d. John Francis and Martha Jo (Jackson) R.; m. David H. Specht, June 3, 1978 (div. Sept. 1982). AA, Montgomery Coll., 1976; BS, U. Md., 1978; MS, Johns Hopkins U., 1995. Lab. technician Dairy and Food Labs., San Francisco, 1979-81; rsch. asst. Genex Corp., Gaithersburg, Md., 1981-82, rsch. assoc., 1982-86, sr. rsch. assoc., 1986-88, rsch. scientist, 1989-93; rsch. assoc. Genetic Therapy, Inc., Gaithersburg, Md., 1993—. Contbr. articles to profl. publs.; patentee in field. Pres. Explorer Post div. Boy Scouts Am., Gaithersburg, 1973; youth advisor Neelsville Presbyn. Ch., Germantown, Md., 1990. Recipient Nat. Exploration award TRW/Explorers Club, 1973. Mem. AAAS, Am. Soc. Microbiology, DAR, Pleasant Plains of Damascus. Republican. Presbyterian. Office: Genetic Therapy Inc 19 Firstfield Rd Gaithersburg MD 20878-1703

ROLLIN, BETTY, author, television journalist; b. N.Y.C., Jan. 3, 1936; d. Leon and Ida R.; m. Harold M. Edwards, Jan. 21, 1979. BA, Sarah Lawrence Coll., 1957. Assoc. features editor Vogue mag., 1964; sr. editor Look mag., 1965-71; network corr. NBC News, N.Y.C., 1971-80, contbg. corr., 1985—; network corr. ABC News Nightline, 1982-84; lectr. in field. Profl. actress on stage and television, 1958-64; Author: I Thee Wed, 1958, Mothers Are Funnier Than Children, 1964, The Non-Drinkers' Drink Book, 1966, First, You Cry, 1976, reissue, 1993, Am I Getting Paid for This?, 1982, Last Wish, 1985; columnist Hers, N.Y. Times; Contbr. articles to popular mags. Office: care NS Bienstock Inc 1740 Broadway New York NY 10019-4315

ROLLIN, MIRIAM ANN, child advocate; b. Jersey City, Oct. 7, 1960; d. Martin and Shirley (Korasek) Rosenberg; m. Michael David Rollin, May 27, 1990; 1 child, Samantha Elise. BA, Yale U., 1981; JD, Catholic U. Am., 1987. Bar: N.Y. 1988, D.C. 1988, Md. 1989. Nat. dir. Nat. Coalition Ind. Coll. & Univ. Students, Washington, 1981-83; govt. rels. specialist AACD, Washington, 1983-85, Nat. PTA, Washington, 1985-87; asst. dist. atty. King's County Dist. Atty.'s Office, Bklyn., 1987-88; staff atty. child advocacy unit Legal Aid Bur., Riverdale, Md., 1988-90; project atty. ctr. on child & the law ABA, Washington, 1990-92; v.p. policy and program Nat. Assn. Child Advocates, Washington, 1992—. Recipient Unsung Hero award Youth Law Ctr., San Francisco, 1994. Mem. Nat. Assn. Counsel for Children (pres., bd. dirs. 1995—). Jewish. Office: Nat Assn Child Advocates 1522 K St NW #600 Washington DC 20005

ROLLINGER, MARY ELIZABETH, secondary school educator; b. Jamestown, N.Y., May 12, 1950; d. Ernest Robert and June Armina (Carlson) Furlow. BS, Edinboro U., 1974; MEd, St. Bonaventure U., 1994. Cert. secondary edn. and elem. edn., N.Y., adv. cert. in counseling, 1996; advanced tng. in critical incident stress debriefing, 1996. English tchr. Bemus Point (N.Y.) Ctrl. Sch., 1974—; part-time clothing buyer Good Morning Farm, Stow, N.Y., 1976-84; part-time GED instr. Erie 2 BOCES, Fredonia, N.Y., 1979-84; creative writing tchr. Chautauqua County Sch. Bd., Fredonia, 1986—; adj. prof. SUNY, Fredonia, 1994—; turnkey trainer for N.Y. State syllabus N.Y. State Dept. Edn., Albany, 1985. Vol. Reg Lenna Civic Ctr., Jamestown, 1992; tchr. rep. Parent/Tchr./Student Assn., Bemus Point, 1980-94; bd. dirs. Amicae-Hotline for Rape/Battering/Abuse, Jamestown, 1986-88, Mutuus Mime Theater, Jamestown, 1982-86. Mem. Am. Counseling Assn., Am. Sch. Guidance Counselors Assn., Nat. Coun. Tchrs. English, Chautauqua County Counselors Assn., Internat. Reading Assn., Delta Kappa Gamma (publicity chair 1985-90). Home: PO Box 551 Bemus Point NY 14712 Office: Bemus Point Ctrl Sch Dutch Hollow Rd Bemus Point NY 14712

ROLLINS, LYNNE SATTERFIELD, family nurse practitioner, community health nurse; b. Canton, Ga., Oct. 24, 1952; d. Donald Eugene and Agnes Fay (Goss) Satterfield; m. Ray Daniel Abernathy, Sept. 28, 1974 (div. Dec. 1985); children: James Ray, Rana Lynne; m. Raymond Curtis Rollins, Oct. 21, 1989. ASN, Kennesaw Jr. Coll., Marietta, Ga., 1972; BSN magna cum laude, Kennesaw State Coll., 1994; postgrad., Emory U., 1983. RN, Ga.; cert. family nurse practitioner. Staff nurse R.T. Jones Hosp., Canton, Ga., 1972; office nurse William H. Nichols, M.D., Canton, 1972-73; staff nurse, relief supr. R.T. Jones Hosp., Canton, 1973-74; operating rm. supr. Cherokee Atomedic Hosp., Woodstock, Ga., 1974-77; sr. staff nurse Cherokee Health Dept., Canton, 1977-82, family nurse practitioner, 1983-93; nurse practitioner Planned Parenthood, Marietta, Ga., 1987-90; health dept. mgr. Pickens County Health Dept., Jasper, Ga., 1993-95; family nurse practitioner Promina N.W. Physicians Group, Marietta, Ga., 1995—. Bd. dirs. Cherokee Family Violence Ctr., Canton, 1981-82; profl. adv. bd. N.W. Ga. Home Health, Jasper, 1994-95; sex edn. adv. Pickens Sch. Sys., Jasper, 1993-94; emergency svcs. bd. Pickens Emergency Mgmt., Jasper, 1993-94; chmn. policy com. Headstart, Jasper, 1994. 1st lt. U.S. Army, 1990-91. Decorated Army Commendation medal (3); Ga. Cmty. Health Nurses scholar, 1994. Mem. ANA, Ga. Nurse Practitioner Coun., Ga. Nurses Assn., Am. Legion (historian Post 45, 1995, 96), Golden Key, Sigma Theta Tau (treas. 1995, 96), Beta Sigma Phi (v.p. 1994-95, pres. 1996, Woman of Yr. 1978, 88, 95). Baptist. Home: 6345 Reinhardt College Pky Waleska GA 30183-3257 Office: Towne Lake Primary Care 145 N Medical Pkwy Woodstock GA 30189

ROLLINS, SHERRIE SANDY, television executive; b. Roanoke, Va., June 11, 1958; d. William Gresham and Charlotte (Weeks) Sandy; m. Edward John Rollins, Jr., May 2, 1987. BA, U. Va., 1980. Sr. v.p. ABC TV Network, N.Y.C., 1994—; advt. dir. Georgetown mag., Alexandria, Va., 1980-81; exec. dir. Bus. and Profl. Assn. Georgetown, Washington, 1981-84; v.p. communications The Oliver Carr Co., Washington, 1985-89; asst. sec. for pub. affairs HUD, Washington, 1989-90; dir. news info. ABC News, N.Y.C., 1990-92; asst. to Pres. of U.S. for pub. liason and intergovtl. affairs The White House, Washington, 1992; sr. v.p. U.S. News and World Report, Washington, 1992-94; sr. v.p. Network Comms. ABC TV Network, N.Y.C., 1994-96, exec. v.p. network comm., 1996—; bd. dirs. Am. Coun. Young Pol. Leaders, Cities in Schs. Mem. U. Va. Alumni Assn. (bd. mgrs.). Home: 107 Dellwood Rd Bronxville NY 10708 Office: Capital Cities/ABC 77 W 66th St New York NY 10023-6201

ROLLMAN, CHARLOTTE, art educator; b. Harrisburg, Pa., Oct. 15, 1947; d. Joseph and Beulah (Overton) R.; m. Edward H. Shay, 1971 (div. 1982); m. William B. Holland, 1987; 1 child, Danielle Suzanne Holland. BFA, Murray State U., 1969; MFA, U. Ill., 1971. Instr. art Ball State U., Muncie, Ind., 1971-75; supr. hand-painted silk garments Nicole, Ltd., Chgo., 1980-84; textile designer, stylist Thybony Wallcovering, Chgo., 1983-88; prof. art No. Ill. U., DeKalb, 1987—. Exhibitions include New Harmony (Ind.) Gallery Art, Charlotte Brauer, Munster, Ind., Jan Cicero, Chgo., Roy Boyd, Chgo, Locus, St. Louis, Suzanne Brown, Scottsdale, Ariz, Nestle's Corp., DeKalb, Capitol State Bank, St. Louis, others; illustrator New Internat. Dictionary Music, 1991; AV coord. Women's Caucus Art, Beijing, 1995. Grad. Sch. Rsch. grantee No. Ill. U., 1993, Faculty Enhancement grantee, 1995, Undergrad. Improvement grantee No. Ill. U., 1996. Mem. AAUW, Women's Caucus Art, Nat. Mus. Women Arts, Chgo. Area Women's Studies, DeKalb Area Women's Ctr. Office: No Ill U Sch Art De Kalb IL 60115

ROLOF, MARCIA CHRISTINE, sales executive; b. Green Bay, Wis., Sept. 1, 1950; adopted d. William August Rolof and Marcella S. (Rantanen) R.; m. Gerald W. Mattson, July 5, 1969 (div. 1974); 1 child, Shannon M. Mattson; m. Louis Glenn Mitchell, Nov. 12, 1994. Mgr., sales rep. Cameo Photography, 1980-82; tchr., physically challenged resource coord. U. Wis., 1982-85; dist. mgr. Women's Specialty Retail Group, U.S. Shoe, 1985-90; regional sales dir. Decor/Claire Corp., 1990-93; corp. adminstr. FLC, Inc., Houston, 1993-94; dist. sales mgr. United Retail Group, Inc., Houston, 1994—; tutor, reading and lang. Pasadena Ind. Sch. Dist., Houston. Author: Tie the Moon to Your Car (My Cancer, My Way), 1994; author short stories; spokesperson childrens radio program. Network vol. U. Tex. M.D. Anderson Cancer Ctr., Houston, 1993—; vol. counselor R to R Cancer Soc., Houston, 1994. Mem. Houston C. of C., Pasadena C. of C.

ROMAIN, BELLA MARY, graphic designer; b. Oakland, Calif., June 16, 1949; d. John Thomas Kondrup and Anna (Rabinowitz) Friedman; m. Stewart Jay Romain, Mar. 19, 1972. Student, SUNY, Stony Brook, 1967-68, Sch. Visual Arts, 1973-75; BFA magna cum laude, West Ga. Coll., 1989. Asst. to editor Dell Pub. Co., N.Y.C., 1968-72; reporter, proofreader Local News, Long Island, N.Y., 1973-76; graphic designer, editor Yellow Book Corp., N.Y.C., 1976-78; freelance graphic designer, editor N.Y.C., 1978-82; owner, graphic designer, editor designplus, Carrollton, Ga., 1982—; publs. cons. West Ga. Coll., Carrollton, 1985—. Paintings exhibited in numerous juried shows, including Alexandria Mus. Art, 1992. Speaker to civic groups, Carrollton, 1993; vol. Amateur Radio Emergency Svcs., Carrollton, 1985—; vol. designer Carroll County Humane Soc., Carrollton, 1993—. Recipient Fine Arts Achievement award Binney & Smith, 1989. Mem. Nat. Mus. Women in Arts, Lions Internat., Am. Bus. Women's Assn., Toastmasters (chair membership local chpt. 1993), Carroll County C. of C., Phi Kappa Phi. Home and Office: 285 Timber Ridge Trl Carrollton GA 30117-8884

ROMAIN, CARLINE JOSEPH, physical and life sciences educator, consultant; b. N.Y.C., Sept. 5, 1962; d. Franck Arsace and Lucine (St. Fleur) R. AB, Cornell U., 1983; MS, Adelphi U., 1996; student, Polytech. U. Cert. tchr., N.Y. Resident advisor dept. Residence Life Cornell U., Ithaca, N.Y., 1981-82; translator, interpreter, writer, proofreader, editor Freelance Svcs., N.Y.C., 1984—; interpreter Univ. Lang. Svcs., N.Y.C., 1984—; pro-bono English lang. instr. Refugee Assistance Program Flatbush Devel. Corp., Bklyn., 1986; early childhood tchr. Day-Care Ctr./After-Sch. Program Practical Learning Ctr., Bklyn., 1986-87; pro-bono tchr., cons. St. Francis of Assisi/Holy Innocents Elem. Schs., Bklyn., 1988; computer cons., tutor, English-as-second-lang. instr. N.Y.C. Tech. Coll., Bklyn., 1986-90; editl. intern Intertec Pub. Corp., White Plains, N.Y., 1989; English-as-second-lang. tchr., sci. tchr. N.Y.C. Pub. Schs., Bklyn., 1986—; pres., founder Winsight Corp., Bklyn., 1992—; founder, chairwoman Winsight Ednl. Internat. Consulting., Inc., Bklyn., 1995—; workshop facilitator, writer, translator N.Y.C. Bd. Edn., also pvt. practice. Pro-bono ednl. referral svc. counselor Karico, Bklyn., 1983—; intake coord., counselor Eng. as a second lang., adult basic edn. N.Y.C. Tech. Coll. Nat. Laureate, Am. Assn. Tchrs. of French, 1977. Mem. AAAS, ACA, ASCD, IEEE (Profl. Comm. Soc.), Am. Coun. on Tchg. of Fgn. Langs., Nat. Coun. Tchrs. English, Nat. Coun. Tchrs. math., Nat. Sci. Tchrs. Assn., N.Y. Acad. Scis., Soc. Tech. Comm., Soc. Women Engrs., Tchr. English to Speakers of Other Langs. Office: Winsight Corp PO Box 260584 Brooklyn NY 11226-0011

ROMAN, CYNTHIA HUNTER, education educator, consultant; b. Richmond, Va., May 6, 1954; d. Jack Rogene and Marion (Balzer) Hunter; m. Christopher Scott Roman, July 18, 1981; 1 child, Katrina. BA, U. Va., 1976; MEd, U. Ga., 1977; EdD, Va. Tech. U., 1994. Asst. dir. U. Va. Richmond Ctr., 1977-78; admissions dir. Westminster-Canterbury, Lynchburg, Va., 1978-80; asst. adminstr. Hermitage of No. Va., Alexandria, Va., 1980-84; dir. mktg. Va. United Meth. Homes, Richmond, 1984-85; program mgr. Dynamic Systems, Inc., Alexandria, Va., 1985-90; pres. and cons. Roman and Assocs., Springfield, Va., 1990—; adj. prof. Nat.-Louis U., McLean, Va., 1990, Marymount U., Arlington, Va., 1993—, George Washington U., Washington, 1995—; cons. to over 50 orgns.; presenter AAHA Ann. Conf., New Orleans, 1990, ASTO Internat. Conf., Dallas, 1995, Orlando, 1996. Author: book chpt. The Invisible Academics, 1996. Mem. ASTD, Assn. for Psychol. Type, Am. Assn. Homes for Aging. Democrat.

ROMANANSKY, MARCIA CANZONERI, book company executive; b. Bklyn., Apr. 22, 1941; d. Nicholas C. and Ellen (Zukas) Canzoneri. BA in History, Coll. of Misericordia, Dallas, Pa., 1962; MLS, Pratt Inst., 1969; MA in Edn., Seton Hall U., 1973; postgrad. Fairleigh Dickinson U., 1980—. Acquisitions libr. St. Peter's Coll., Jersey City, 1963-68; sch. libr. Roselle (N.J.) High Sch., 1968-72; selection libr. Baker & Taylor, Somerville, N.J., 1972-74, chief libr., 1974-80, asst. mgr. program services, 1980-81, mgr. program svcs., 1981-87, dir. pub. libr. mktg., 1987-88; v.p. Yankee Book Peddler, Contoocook, N.H., 1988-89; dir. collection devel. svcs. Blackwell N.Am., Blackwood, N.J., 1989-90, v.p. purchasing and ops., 1990-96, sr. v.p. purchasing and ops., 1996—. Contbr. articles to profl. jours. Mem. publicity com. Showhouse, Aux. Muhlenberg Hosp., Plainfield, N.J., 1982, 84. Mem. ALA (tech. svcs. com. 1982-84), Beta Phi Mu. Home and Office: Blackwell NAm Inc 100 University Ct Blackwood NJ 08012-3214

ROMANELLO, MARGUERITE MARIE, librarian; b. San Francisco, Feb. 14, 1939; d. Antonio Joseph and Josephine Remilda (Magliano) R. BA cum laude, Lone Mountain Coll., 1960, MA, 1961. Cert. secondary tchr. and librarian, Calif. Instr. Portola Jr. High Sch., San Francisco, 1961-74, Abraham Lincoln High Sch., San Francisco, 1978-81; libr. Francisco Jr. High Sch., San Francisco, 1974-75, instr., 1975-78; libr., media specialist Raoul Wallenberg Traditional High Sch., San Francisco, 1981—; judge U.S. Acad. Decathalon, San Francisco, 1988, 89. Author: MOSAIC, 1975, (play) Scenes from Sense and Sensibility, 1986; editor San Francisco Guitar Soc. Newsletter, 1975-76; exhibitor Festival of Needlework, San Francisco, 1979. Founder, curator Raoul Wallenberg Mus., San Francisco, 1981—; active in Community Adv. Coun., San Francisco, 1968-70, KRON Community Adv. Com., San Francisco, 1985-94, Adopt-A-Sch. Program, San Francisco, 1988—, San Francisco Opera Guild; vol. Humanities West, 1993-96. Grantee Office of Supt., San Francisco, 1972, Calif. State Assembly, Sacramento, 1988; hist. Dickens Fellowship of San Francisco, 1992. Mem. Jane Austen Soc. North Am. (chmn. mem. 1986-89, mem. ann. grand meeting planning com. 1996—), Assoc. Alumni of Sacred Heart, Alpha Psi (treas. Alpha Delta Kappa chpt. 1978-80, corr. sec. 1976-78, 92-94, recording sec. 1994-96). Roman Catholic. Home: 15 Red Rock Way Apt 301N San Francisco CA 94131-1715 Office: Wallenberg High Sch 40 Vega St San Francisco CA 94115-3826

ROMANO, MENA N., artist, educator; b. Bronx, N.Y., Oct. 16, 1943; d. Gerardo and Paulina (Sciurba) DeSanctis; m. Nicholas Carmine Romano, Nov. 23, 1963; children: Dina Marie Girola, Nicholas Carmine Jr. AS in Fine Arts with distinction, Suffolk County C. C., Selden, N.Y., 1983; BFA summa cum laude, Long Is. U., 1986, MFA, 1988. Adj. asst. prof. art Suffolk County C. C., Selden, N.Y., 1988—, Dowling Coll., Oakdale, N.Y., 1992—, Lond Island Univ., Brookville, N.Y., 1994—, Nassau C. C., Garden City, N.Y., 1996—; vis. artist B.O.C.E.S. Art in Edn. program, 1992—; gallery exhibit cons. Smithtown Arts Coun., 1989-91; curator art, exhbns. Chess Collectors Internat., 1990; lectr. in field. Exhbns. include Islip Art Mus., 1990, S.W. Tex. State U. Gallery, 1994, Fine Art Mus. Long Island, 1996. juror Mentathlon, A Competition of the Mind Suffolk County C. C., Selden, N.Y., 1989, Earth Day competition Dowling Coll., Oakdale, N.Y., 1993, outdoor exhibit Smithtown (N.Y.) Arts Coun., 1994; vol. Connetquot Sch. Dist., Oakdale, Ronkokoma, Bohemia, N.Y., 1972-82. Grantee Artist Space, N.Y., 1990. Mem. Nat. Drawing Assn. (chair membership 1990-91), Long Island Craft Guild (pres. 1994-95), Phi Theta, Pi Alpha Sigma.

ROMANO, REBECCA KAY, counselor; b. Zanesville, Ohio, Mar. 26, 1958; Charles Ronald Fulkerson and Margaret Jane (Kiser) Williams; m. Richard Ralph Romano, May 24, 1986; children: Nicholas Robert, Kaitlin Kristine. BA, Walsh U., 1980; MEd, Bowling Green State U., 1981, 82. Lic. profl. counselor; nat. cert. counselor. Day program instr. Devel. Opportunities, Cañon City, Colo., 1983-85; clin. behavior specialist Pueblo Regional Ctr. Colo. Divsn. Devel. Disabilities, 1985-86; career devel. tchr. Colo. Dept. Corrections, Cañnon City, 1986-87, facility mental health therapist, 1987—, devel. disabilities coord., 1991—, facility mental health coord., 1995—; therapist sex offender treatment team Colo. Dept. Corrections, 1986—; presenter in field. Mem. ACA, Am. Assn. Mental Retardation (past state bd. dirs. 1987-91), Am. Correctional Assn., Nat. Assn. for Dually Diagnosed. Lutheran. Office: Colo Dept Corrections CTCF Mental Health PO Box 1010 Canon City CO 81215-1010

ROMANO, SUSAN VICTORIA KNIGHT, special education educator; b. Birmingham, Ala., Oct. 4, 1953; d. George Frederick Knight and Esther Faith (Bullard) Savela; m. Joseph James Romano, Aug. 1, 1987. B in elem. edn., U. Ala., 1975, M in elem. edn., 1980, M in behavioral & learning disorders, 1993. Cert. elem. tchr., learning disabilities, mental retardation. Elem. tchr. Birmingham Bd. Edn., 1975-88, Cath. Diocese of Birmingham, 1988-89; learning disabled/emotional conflict tchr. Etowah County Bd. Edn., Altoona, Ala., 1989-94; freelance reporter The Blount Countian Newspaper, 1989; textbook adoption com. Birmingham Bd. Edn., 1985, grant com., 1982, profl. orgn. rep. Birmingham Edn. Assn., 1983-86, ins. adoption com., 1983; reading rsch. participant U. Ala., 1982. Vol. Blount County Children's Ctr., Oneonta, Ala., 1992, Salvation Army, Birmingham, 1970-75, Oneonta, 1994, vol. cancasser John Katapodis Campaign for Mayor, Birmingham, 1981. Named Spl. Edn. Tchr. of West End. Elem. Sch., Altoona, 1993. Mem. Etowah County Edn. Assn., Ala. Edn. Assn., Coun. for Exceptional Children, Kappa Delta Pi. Roman Catholic. Home: 2542 Swann Bridge Rd Cleveland AL 35049-3566 Office: West End Elem Sch 6795 Highway 132 Altoona AL 35952

ROMANO-FOTHERGILL, NANCY LYNN, music director; b. Stamford, Conn., Dec. 14, 1959; d. James Edward and Dolores Anne Romano; m. James Herbert Fothergill, Aug. 8, 1994. BMus in Piano, Notre Dame Coll., 1986, postgrad., 1987, 89; postgrad., Lesley Coll., 1989, U. New Eng.; vocal tng., 1973—. Printed circuit solderer Raytheon Co., Manchester, N.H., 1978-79; sales clk. Lechmere, Manchester, 1980-86; music tchr. Windham (N.H.) Sch. Dist., 1986—; pvt. practice as piano tchr. Windham, N.H., 1986-90; lead singer, keyboards The Moonlighter's Band, Londonderry, 1990-94; coach summer theater camps. Dir. (musical play) Tribute to Beauty and The Beast, 1992, Tribute to Aladdin, 1993, Surfin' Santa, 1991, other holiday concerts. Sec. Music Club, N.H., 1984; mem. Ch. Choir, Hudson, N.H., 1981-86. Mem. MENC, MTNA, Alpha Sigma Lambda (Delta Epsilon chpt. 1984). Home: 5 Constance Dr Londonderry NH 03053-3283

ROMBERGER, JEAN LOUISE, retired educator; b. Camp Hill, Pa., Apr. 17, 1935; d. Austin Ira and Elizabeth Ann (Koons) R. BS in Edn., U. Pa., 1957; MS in Edn., Temple U., 1963. Cert. tchr., Pa. Tchr. Camp Hill Sch. Dist., 1957-65, 66-93, Shippensburg (Pa.) U., 1965-66; ret., 1993; mentor/tutor Harrisburg (Pa.) Sch. Dist., 1994—. Co-author curriculum in field. Mem. credit com. West Shore Tchrs. Fed. Credit Union, Camp Hill, 1993—; vol. Hospice of Ctrl. Pa., Enola, 1994—; mem. Susquehanna Consort, TLC Choir. Mem. NEA (life), Pa. Assn. Sch. Retirees (life), Pa. State Edn. Assn. (life), Capital Area Edn. Assn. (life), Camp Hill Civic Club, Delta Gamma (chpt. pres. 1956-57). Home: 300 S 24th St Camp Hill PA 17011

ROME, ILAYA ELIZABETH, academic exchange specialist; b. Aspen, Colo., May 11, 1968; d. Jeffrey Dozier and Sharon Elizabeth (O'Connell) R. BA in Internat. Rels. with distinction, U. Wis., 1990; postgrad., U. Florence, Italy, 1991; MA in Internat. Rels., Johns Hopkins U., 1993. V.p. adminstrn. Internat. Assn. Students in Econs. and Commerce, Madison, 1989-90; student advisor, lead worker Wis. Union Travel Ctr., Madison, 1990; profl. exch. programs intern Inst. Internat. Edn., Washington, 1992; with alumni affairs office SAIS, Washington, 1993—; presdl. mgmt. intern Bur. Edn. and Cultural Affairs USIA, Washington, 1993-95, acad. exch. specialist Office of Acad. Programs, 1996—. Mem. Career Devel. Group (com. head 1993), Johns Hopkins Alumni Assn. (SAIS alumni coun.), Golden Key.

ROME, PAULA DOZIER, language consultant; b. San Francisco, May 20, 1918; d. Thomas Bona and Viva Alexandra (Radovich) Dozier; m. Howard Phillips Rome, Mar. 15, 1941 (dec. 1992); children: John Dozier, Jeffrey Dozier, Alexandra Rome Mudd, Howard Phillips Jr., Paul Phillips. BA, U. Pa., 1942; postgrad., Inst. Pa. Hosp., 1942-44. Lang. cons., tutor Remedial Reading Ctr., Washington, 1944-46; founder, dir. Reading Ctr., Rochester, Minn., 1950-60, co-dir., 1960-90; ednl. cons. Bishop Whipple Schs., Faribault, Minn., 1969-73, Constance B. Wilson Ctr., Faribault, 1971-87, Pinewood Acad., Eagle River, Wis., 1974-80; adj. instr. Carleton Coll., Northfield, Minn., 1976-78, instr., 1978-90; ednl. program dir. Fed. Med. Ctr., Rochester, 1985-88; lectr. in field, 1960-91; co-dir. tchr. tng. workshops, 1968-91; mem. adv. bd. Assn. Children with Learning Disabilities, Minn., 1969-72. Contbr. articles to profl. jours.; co-editor: Dyslexia: Un Problema qui Afrontar, 1980; co-author manual and teaching materials. Founding bd. mem. Rochester Civic Theater, 1950's, Rochester Art Ctr., 1950's; bd. dirs. Minn. Mental Health Assn., Mpls., 1950's; pres. bd. Aldrich Meml. Nursery Sch., Rochester, 1950's. Recipient Disting. Svc. award Minn. soc. for Child and Adolescent Psychiatry, 1995, Outstanding Leadership award Assn. Children with Learning Disabilities, 1975. Mem. Dyslexia Inst. Minn. (bd. dirs. 1991—), C.B. Wilson Found. (bd. dirs. 1985—), Menninger Found. (trustee 1993—), Orton Dyslexia Soc. (mem. adv. bd. 1994—, nat. bd. mem., 3d, 2d, and 1st v.p. 1968-71, 76-92, pres. Upper Midwest br. 1968-72, Outstanding Leadership award 1975, Samuel T. Orton Ann. Award 1972, Outstanding Svc. and Dedication award 1992), Phi Beta Kappa. Unitarian. Home: 207 5th Ave SW # 1202 Rochester MN 55902

ROMES, MARILYN KYSER, surgical nurse; b. LaCross, Kans., Jan. 3, 1938; d. John Kyser and Katharine Harrett (Heidenrich) Arensmann; m. Ronald Andrew Romes, July 30, 1971; 1 child, Jennifer Katharine. AAS, diploma in nursing, Dallas County Jr. Coll., 1971. RN, Tex. Staff nurse Drs. Hosp., Dallas, 1969-72, Presbyn. Hosp., Dallas, 1972-76, Kaiser Permanent Hosp., San Francisco, 1976-77, Children's Hosp., Dallas, 1978-81; staff-charge nurse Dallas VA Med. Ctr., 1981—; mem. Dinster Cadré staff ARC, Dallas, 1969—. Mem. Casa Linda Homeowners Assn. (pres. 1990-91, treas. 1995—). Roman Catholic. Home: 1548 San Saba Dallas TX 75218

ROMINE, JOAN MARIE WINTERS, comptroller; b. Teaneck, N.J., July 13, 1951; d. Robert Grant and Joan Clare (Mooney) Winters; m. Mario Alejandro Romine, Oct. 31, 1972 (div. Dec. 1985); children: Jeremy Patrick, Kelly Marie, Christopher Grant. BS in Acctg., Kean Coll., 1988; postgrad. in Fine Arts, Coll. of New Rochelle, 1969-72. Staff acct. Shader & Co. CPA's, Westfield, N.J., 1988; CFO, sec. to bd. dirs., co. sec.-treas. Hanita Cutting Tools, Inc., Montainside, N.J., 1988-95; contr. Magic Cinemas, L.L.C., Livingston, N.J., 1995-96, Clearview Cinema Group, Inc., Madison, N.J., 1996—. Republican. Home: 925 Harding St Westfield NJ 07090-1216 Office: Clearview Cinema Group Inc 7 Waverly Pl Madison NJ 07940

ROMITI, SISTER STEPHANIE ANN, religious education educator; b. Sault Ste. Marie, Ont., Can., Mar. 30, 1961; came to U.S., 1980; d. Leo and Veronica Ann (Baic) R. BS in Elem. Edn. cum laude, Northern Mich. U., 1987; MS in Ednl. Adminstrn., Trinity Coll., 1996. Joined Sisters of St. Paul of Chartres, Roman Cath. Ch., 1980. Tchr. 4th grade Menominee (Mich.) Cath. Ctrl. Sch., 1988-92; tchr. 1st grade Nativity Cath. Sch., Washington, 1992-95; dir. religious edn. and youth ministry Nativity Cath. Ch. and Sch., 1995—; tchr. moderator-sch. choir Nativity Cath. Acad., 1994—, dir. sch. Christmas parade, 1992, 93; tchr. moderator-sch. newspaper Menominee Cath. Ctrl. Sch., 1991-92. Mem. ch. ministry Sisters of St. Paul Chartres, Marquette, Mich., 1980—; vol. ch. ministry Holy Spirit Resurrection and Holy Redeemer Chs., Menominee, 1987-92, Nativity Cath. Ch., Washington, 1992—. Mem. ASCD, NCEA, ACLA, NPCD. Home and Office: 6010 Georgia Ave NW Washington DC 20011

ROMM, JESSICA BETH, policy research/project implementation executive; b. San Francisco, Mar. 17, 1944; d. Arthur and Esther (Orloff) R. BA in Social Welfare, U. Calif., Berkeley, 1965; MA in Urban Planning, CUNY, 1970; PhD in Pub. Policy and Adminstrn., NYU, 1976. Vol. Peace Corps, San Cruz, Bolivia, 1965-67; rsch. asst. Hunter Coll. Urban Rsch. Ctr., N.Y.C., 1968-69; planning process cons. Office of Econ. Opportunity and Model Cities Program, N.Y.C., 1968-70; project dir. Environ. Resource Assocs., N.Y.C., 1970-72; cons., rsch. assoc. Office of Children's Svcs., N.Y. Family Ct., N.Y.C., 1972-74; asst. dir. edn. fund Dist. Coun. 37, AFSCME, N.Y.C., 1976-79; mng. of programs Planning Assistance, Inc, Costa Rica, 1979; sr. planner Bechtel Civil Corp., Caracas, Venezuela, 1980; labor rels. coord. stragegic planning and mktg. profl. Bechtel Civil Corp., San Francisco, 1980-91; pres. J.B. Romm Bechtel Corp., 1991—; cons. Baytrade Cons., 1994—, San Francisco Redevel. Agy., 1994—; cmty. econ. devel. cons. for base closure Hunters Point Shipyard, San Francisco, 1994—; jazz preservation dist. cons. San Francisco, 1994—; adj. prof. Golden Gate U., San Francisco, 1993—, UN Devel. Program, 1989, 93; presenter in field. Producer/dir.: ednl. TV programs, 1977. Vol. Am. Cancer Soc., Marin County, Calif., 1993—, Big Bros./Big Sisters, Marin County, 1992—, Christmas in April, San Francisco, 1991—; bd. dirs. Alumnae Resources, San Francisco, 1990-94, Soc. for Internat. Devel., 1994—, Am. Jewish Congress, 1994—. Recipient recognition from Gov. Bellon, Okla., 1986, Gov. Dukakis, Mass., 1986, ILO award, 1990; Fulbright fellow, Buenos Aires, 1974-75. Mem. ASPA, Soc. Internat. Devel. (bd. dirs. 1994), Women Constrn. Owners and Execs., Pan Am. Soc. (bd. dirs. 1981), Women in Internat. Trade, Indsl. Rels. Assn., U. Calif.-Berkeley Alumnae Assn., NYU Alumnae Assn. Home: 504 Seaver Dr Mill Valley CA 94941-2249

ROMOSZ, REBECCA ELLEN, psychiatric nurse; b. Benson, Minn., Apr. 14, 1952; d. Herbert Carlton and Inez Marie (Olson) Larson; m. Steven Edward Romosz, May 6, 1978 (div. May 1984); 1 child, Eric S. Nursing diploma, Fairview Hosp. Sch. Nursing, Mpls., 1973; BA in Psychology/Social Work, Luther Coll., Decorah, Iowa, 1977. Psychiat. cert. Minn. Bd. Nursing. Staff nurse Rice Hosp., Willmar, Minn., 1973-74, 77; clinic nurse Luther Coll. Health Svc., Decorah, Iowa, 1974-77; staff nurse Kandiyohi County Cmty. Health Svc., Willmar, 1977-88; psychiat. nurse Willmar Regional Treatment Ctr., 1988—; adj. faculty Willmar C.C., 1986—; pub. edn. chairperson Am. Cancer Soc., Willmar, 1980-88; Willmar Involved in Nutrition, Willmar Collaborative, 1984-86. Co-leader Cub Scouts, Willmar, 1993-94, awards chair, 1995-96; active Parent Tchrs. Student Assn., 1995-96. Recipient Pacesetter award Am. Cancer Soc., Willmar, 1983, 84, 86, 87. Mem. AAUW, Minn. Nurses Assn. Lutheran. Home: PO Box 374 Willmar MN 56201-0374 Office: Willmar Regional Treatment Ctr Hwy 71-N Willmar MN 56201

RONALD, PAULINE CAROL, school system administrator; b. York, Yorkshire, Eng., Feb. 28, 1945; came to U.S., 1966; d. Peter Vincent Leonard and Doris Annie (Clark) Hume-Shotton; m. James Douglas Ronald, July 16, 1966 (div. 1986); 1 child, Alexia Denise; m. James Donald Wadsworth, Feb. 15, 1991 (div. July 1994). Diploma, Harrogate Sch. Art, Yorkshire, 1965, U. New Castle, Upon Tyne, 1966; MA, Ball State U., 1977. Cert. art tchr., Ind. Art tchr. Knightstown (Ind.) Schs., 1966-67, Dunkirk (Ind.) Schs., 1967-68, Richmond (Ind.) High Sch., 1968—; part time tchr. Ind. U., Earlham Coll., Richmond 1974-84; set painter Richmond Civic Theatre. Exhibited in numerous group shows; illustrator History of Wayne County, History of Centerville, 1996. Coach State Acad. Fine Arts State Team Champions, 1988, 96, 2d Pl. for the state, 1989, 95; bd. dirs., mem. permanent collection com. Richmond Art Mus. Recipient Best Set Painting awards, also numerous awards for drawing and painting, Indpls. Art Mus. Mem. NEA, Ind. State Tchrs. Assn., Art Assn. Richmond, Indpls. Mus. Art. Home: 417 S 20th St Richmond IN 47374-5729

RONAYNE, JOAN BERNICE, business strategy consultant; b. Needham, Mass., Sept. 23, 1966; d. Joseph Stephen and Joan Bernice (Mack) Ronayne. AB magna cum laude, Harvard U., 1988, MBA, 1993. Rsch. assoc. Ctr. for Strategic and Internat. Studies, Washington, 1985; analyst Union Francais de Banques-Locabail, Paris, 1986; cons. Alternative Investment Corp., Boston, 1987; cons., mgr. rsch. assocs. Monitor Co., Cambridge, Mass., 1988-91; investment banking assoc. Goldman Sachs, 1992; real estate investment banking assoc. Merrill Lynch & Co., 1993-96; investment banking assoc. in tech. sect. Cowen & Co., Boston, 1996—; cons. in field; joint participant Washington Internat. Studies Ctr. Program and Harvard Summer in Washington Program, 1985. Bus. editor Harvard Crimson, Cambridge, Mass., 1984-88. Mem. Needham Town Meeting, 1989-94; religious edn. tchr. St. Joseph's Parish, Needham, 1989-90; mem. vis. fellows com. John F. Kennedy Sch. Govt., Cambridge, 1985-87; mem. exec. bd. Harvard Crimson Key Soc., 1985-88. John Harvard scholar, 1986, 87, Kosciuszko Found. scholar, 1991; recipient Cert. of Appreciation, Archdiocese of Boston, 1990, Elizabeth Cary Agassiz award Radcliffe Coll., 1986, 87, 88. Mem. NAFE, Radcliffe Club, Harvard Club, Rotary (Goodwill Ambassador to Soviet Union 1990), Phi Beta Kappa. Home: 15 Douglas Rd Needham MA 02192-4503 Office: Cowen & Co 2 International Pl Boston MA 02110

RONSTADT, LINDA MARIE, singer; b. Tucson, July 15, 1946; d. Gilbert and Ruthmary (Copeman) R. Rec. artist numerous albums including Evergreen 1967, Evergreen Vol. 2, 1967, Linda Ronstadt, The Stone Poneys and Friends, Vol. 3, 1968, Hand Sown, Home Grown, 1969, Silk Purse, 1970, Linda Ronstadt, 1972, Don't Cry Now, 1973, Heart Like a Wheel, 1974, Different Drum, 1974, Prisoner In Disguise, 1975, Hasten Down the Wind, 1976, Greatest Hits, 1976, Simple Dreams, Blue Bayou, 1977, Living in the U.S.A., 1978, Mad Love, Greatest Hits Vol. II, 1980, Get Closer, 1982, What's New, 1983, Lush Life, 1984, For Sentimental Reasons, 1986, Trio (with Dolly Parton, Emmylou Harris), 1986, 'Round Midnight, 1987, Canciones de Mi Padre, 1987, Cry Like a Rainstorm-Howl Like the Wind, 1989, Mas Canciones, 1991, Frenesi, 1992, Winter Light, 1993, Feels Like Home, 1995; starred in Broadway prodn. of Pirates of Penzance, 1981, also in film, 1983, off Broadway as Mimi in La Boheme, 1984. Recipient Am. Music awards, 1978, 79, Grammy awards, 1975, 76, 87 (with Emmylou Harris and Dolly Parton), 1988, 89 (with Aaron Neville), 1990 (with Aaron Neville, 1992 (2), Acad. Country Music award, 1987, 88. Office: care Peter Asher Mgmt Inc 644 N Doheny Dr West Hollywood CA 90069-5526

ROOK, JUDITH RAWIE, producer, writer; b. Long Beach, Calif., Jan. 25, 1942; d. Wilmer Ernest and Margaret Jane (Towle) Rawie; children: Daryn Kirsten, Dawn Malia; m. Timothy Daniel Rook. BBA, Loyola-Marymount Coll., 1964; BA in Visual Arts and Communications, U. Calif., San Diego, 1978. Producer/writer PBS series Achieving (Emmy award 1982, ACE nominee), assoc. dir. rsch. and video/producer IABC, San Francisco, 1982; dir. programming Group W Cable, Westinghouse Co., 1983-85; devel. Nelson/Embassy Home Entertainment, 1986-87; ptnr. Real Magic, 1988-89; ind. prodr.- screenwriter R2 Prodns., 1989—. Mem. adv. bd. U. Calif.-Irvine Screenwriting/Film Prodn., 1996—; active Found. U. Art Mus., 1996—; co-pres. Contemporary Coun., U. Art Mus., 1996—. Mem. Am. Film Inst., Women in Film, Ind. Features Assn., Found. Long Beach Mus. Art, Democrat. Episcopalian.

ROOME, KRISTINE ANN, college administrator; b. Pequannock, N.J., Sept. 3, 1967; d. Michael Wesley and Joan Ann (Dooley) Roome. BS, Montclair State U., 1990; postgrad. in anthropology, Columbia U., 1993—. Fin. acct. JP Morgan Co., N.Y.C., 1990-93; sr. acct. Tchr.'s Coll. Columbia U., N.Y.C., 1993, asst. dir. office of instnl. studies, 1993—; assoc. dir. Wright Gallery, N.Y.C., 1994—, curator several exhbns., 1995. Alumni scholar, Student Govt. Assn. scholar Montclair State U., 1989, 90, Columbia U. Tchr.'s Coll. scholar, 1995, travel grantee, 1995, Field Lang./Area Studies fellowship Inst. for African Studies Columbia U., N.Y.C., 1996—. Mem. NAFE, Assn. Inst. Rschrs. Office: Tchrs Coll Columbia U 525 W 120th St New York NY 10027

ROONEY, CAROL BRUNS, dietitian; b. Milw., Dec. 20, 1940; d. Edward G. and Elizabeth C. (Lemke) Bruns; m. George Eugene Rooney Jr., July 1, 1967; children: Steven, Sean. BS, U. Wis., 1962; MS, U. Iowa, 1965. Registered dietitian; cert. nutrition specialist; disting. health care food svc. adminstr.; cert. dietitian, Wis. Intern VA Med. Ctr., Hines, Ill., 1962-63; resident in nutrition and food svc. VA Med. Ctr., Iowa City, 1963-65; dietitian nutrition clinic VA Med. Ctr., Hines, 1965-67, 69-70, chief clin. dietetics, 1970-71, chief adminstrv. dietetics, 1971-73, clin. dietitian VA Med. Ctr., Memphis, 1967-68; asst. chief nutrition and food svc. Zablocki VA Med. Ctr., Milw., 1974-85, chief nutrition and food svc., 1985-96, divsn. mgr., cons. care, 1996—, cons. nutrition and food svc. mgmt., 1995—; adj. lectr. Loyola U. Coll. Dentistry, Maywood, Ill., 1969-72; investigator nutrition VA/Med. Coll. Wis., Milw., 1975—, co-dir. ann. clin. nutrition symposium, Milw., 1979—; chmn. task force on ration allowance VA, Washington, 1977-84, mem. nutrition and food svc. spl. interest users group Washington, 1983-85, chmn. tech. adv. group region IV, 1986; mem. Dept. Vets. Affairs Mktg. Ctr. Subsistence Task Force, 1991—, dietetic internship adv. bd. St. Luke's Hosp., Milw., 1983-87; mem. Dept. Vets. Affairs Nat. Cost Containment Ctr. Nutrition & Food Svc. Benchmarking Tech. Adv., 1995—; lectr. in field, 1965—; mem. Dept. Vets. Affairs, Nutrition and Food Svc. Policy Manual Rev. Task Force, 1992-96, Dept. Vets. Chiefs, Food and Nutrition Svc. Mentor Group, 1992—. Author: (videocassette) VA Ration Allowance as a Management Tool 1976; editor: Nutrition Principles and Dietary Guidelines for Patients Receiving Chemotherapy and Radiation Therapy, 1980; contbr. articles to profl. jours., 1978—. Mem. profl. edn. com. Milw. South unit Am. Cancer Soc., 1976-86, bd. dirs. Milw. South unit, 1984-86, Milw. div., 1986-87, Wis. div., 1987-91, media spokesperson, 1983-91, del. to Milw. div., 1984-85, mem. organizational and expansion com. Milw. div., 1986-87, profl. edn. com. Milw. div., 1986-87, Wis. div., 1987-91, mem. taking control Wis. div., 1987-91, chmn. nutrition Wis. div., 1989-91; mem. med. adv. com. YMCA Met. Milw., 1985—; mem. Marquette U. High Sch. Mothers Guild, 1990-94. Recipient Disting. Svc. award Am. Cancer

Soc. Milw. South unit, 1980, Women of Achievement award Girl Scouts USA Milw. area, 1987, Leadership award VA, 1989, Dept. Vets. Affairs Dietitian of Yr., 1994, Dept. Vets. Affairs Fed. Women's Program cert. merit for outstanding profl. leadership, 1994, Paralyzed Vets. Am. rsch. grantee, 1981-83. Fellow Am. Dietetic Assn. (registered, practice groups in mgmt. responsibilities in health care delivery, gerontology nutrition 1980—, dietetics in phys. medicine and rehab. 1983—, clin. nutrition mgmt. 1987—, amb. nat. media spokesperson 1983-89, Resource Amb. 1991—, Outstanding Svc. award 1983-89), FADA; mem. Am. Soc. Health Care Food Svc. Adminstrs. (dir.-at-large Wis. chpt. 1993-95, pres.-elect Wis. chpt. 1995-96, pres. 1996-97, Disting. Health Care Food Svc. Adminstr. 1995—), Wis. Dietetic Assn. (co-chmn. divsn. mgmt. practice 1976-77, chmn. 1977-78, bd. dirs. 1981-83, coord. cabinet 1984-91, pres. 1988-89, chmn. nominating com. 1989-90, chmn. long-range planning com. 1989-90, legis. com. 1988—, Wis. Medallion award 1986), Milw. Dietetic Assn. (cmty. nutrition and clin. dietetics and rsch. coms. 1975-76, chair ad hoc com. for nutrition and oncology patients 1976-79, clin. dietetics and rsch. study group 1981-90, chair 1983-85, pres. 1982-83, by-laws com. 1983-84, chair policies and procedures com. 1983-87, pub. rels. com. 1983-87, chair nominating com. 1984-85), Fed. Execs. Assn., Leadership Vets. Affairs Alumni Assn. (charter, life), Phi Upsilon Omicron, Kappa Delta. Home: 18230 Le Chateau Dr Brookfield WI 53045-4922 Office: Zablocki VA Med Ctr 5000 W National Ave Milwaukee WI 53295-0001

ROONEY, GAIL SCHIELDS, college administrator; b. St. Francis, Kans., Feb. 15, 1947; d. Fred Harlan and Darlene Mary (Saint) Schields; m. Thomas Michael Rooney, June 27, 1970; children: Shane Michael, Shauna Meghan. BA, U. Colo., 1969; MS, George Williams Coll., 1974; PhD, U. Ill., 1982. Asst. dir. Spl. Svcs. Program Cleve. State U., 1970-71; admissions counselor George Williams Coll., Downers Grove, Ill., 1972-73; coord. of career exploration ctr. Women's Programs Cuyahoga Community Coll., Cleve., 1973-76; vis. asst. prof. Sch. Clin. Medicine U. Ill., Champaign, 1981-82; counselor, instr. Cuyahoga Community Coll., Cleve., 1982-84, dir. counseling, career and psychol. svcs., 1984-85; dir. career, counseling and health svcs. Briar Cliff Coll., Sioux City, Iowa, 1985-88, v.p. for student devel., 1988-95, ednl. cons. and adj. faculty, 1996—; mem. faculty psychology Mesa (Ariz.) C.C., 1995; adj. instr. counselor edn. Wayne (Nebr.) State Coll., 1988, 96; adj. grad. faculty U. S.D., 1996; program presenter Myers Briggs Type Indicator, Sioux City, 1986—. Bd. dirs. Gordon Chem. Dependency Ctr., Sioux City, 1986-89, St. Luke's Gordon Recovery Ctr., Sioux City, 1991-95. Mem. ACA, Am. Coll. Pers. Assn., Nat. Assn. Student Pers. Adminstrs. Home: 52 Red Bridge Dr Sioux City IA 51104

ROONEY, MARIA DEWING, photographer; b. N.Y.C., July 25, 1949; d. Madeleine L'Engle (Camp) Franklin; m. John Bryon Rooney, Jan. 21, 1984; children: Bryson, Alexander. BFA, Phila. Coll. Art, 1971. Tchr. photography Bishop Bright Grammar Sch., Leamington Spa, Eng., Mid-Warwickshire Sch. of Further Edn., Leamington Spa, 1976-80; photographer, owner The Studios, Shipston-on-Stour, Eng., 1977-80; photographer Gary Studios & Comini Studios, Dallas, 1980-83; owner, photographer studio, Essex, Conn., 1990—. Exhbns. include Warwick (Eng.) Gallery, Derby (Eng.) Coll. Art Gallery, Bath (Eng.) Place Cmty. Ctr., Midland Group Gallery, Nottingham, Eng., Wimbledon Sch. Art, London, Warwich U. Arts Ctr., Birmingham, Eng., Essex Art Assn.; photographer (book) Anytime Prayers, 1994; photographs published in Co-Optic Publs., London, 1976-80. Mem. Child and Family Svcs. Mem. AAUW, Essex Art Assn. Home and Office: 48 N Main St PO Box 340 Essex CT 06426

ROONEY, MARIJO TEARE, psychologist; b. Wichita, Kans., Feb. 19, 1960; d. Max Eugene and H. Charlene (Smith) T.; m. H. Davis Rooney, Apr. 3, 1993. BS, U. Kans., 1982; MA, U. Louisville, 1988, PhD, 1991. Team leader child acute unit Western Mo. Mental Health Ctr., Kansas City, 1991-93; child psychology fellow dept. psychiatry U. Kans., Wichita, 1993-94; psychologist Area Mental Health Ctr., Dodge City, Kans., 1994-95; pvt. practice Shawnee Mission, Kans., 1995—. Home: 14050 W 114th Ter Lenexa KS 66215

ROOS, MARIANNE LOUISE, library director; b. Ft. Belvoir, Va., Nov. 27, 1955; d. William Fredrick and Miriam (Kelley) R.; m. David Wayne Bland, Aug. 23, 1980; children: Elizabeth, Gregory. BA, UCLA, 1976, MLS, 1978. Maunuscript librarian Library of Congress, Washington, 1978-83; v.p. Bland, Roos & Assocs., Inc., Winchester, Va., 1983-89; pres., owner Morgan's Choice Restaurant, Winchester, 1986-88; dir. Handley Regional Libr., Winchester, 1988—. Presbyterian. Office: Ramsey County Libr 4570 N Victoria St Shoreview MN 55126

ROOS, PAULA SPARROW, manufacturer's representative; b. Bklyn., Nov. 4, 1932; d. Alexander J. and Tillie A. (Shapiro) Sparrow; m. William J. Roos, Nov. 17, 1951; children: Liza, Sigmund, Joel. Profl. ski instr. Pa., 1962-92; ind. yarn rep. Honesdale, Pa., 1983—. Co-author: Hi Kids - Welcome to the World of Skiing, 1995. Sec., bd. dirs. Scranton (Pa.) Cmty. Concerts, 1960—, N.E. Pa. Easter Seal Soc., Scranton, 1971-82; bd. dirs. Pocono coun. Girl Scouts U.S., Scranton, 1955-70; bd. dirs. Maternal and Family Health Svc. N.E. Pa., 1974-95; mem. com. Dorflinger Glass Mus., Hawley, Pa., 1996, Wayne Hosp. Aux., Honesdale, 1952—. Recipient Brace for an Ace award Easter Seal Soc., 1980, Citizen of Yr. award B'nai B'rith, 1982, Last Bid award PBS-WVIA, 1996. Mem. Ladies Improvement Assn. (pres 1993—), Women's Club of Honesdale (bd. dirs. 1953—, Outstanding Women of Am. award 1965). Home: 7 Hillcrest Cir Honesdale PA 18431

ROOS, SYBIL FRIEDENTHAL, elementary school educator; b. L.A., Jan. 29, 1924; d. Charles G. and Besse (Weixel) Friedenthal; m. Henry Kahn Roos, May 8, 1949 (dec. Dec. 1989); children: Catherine Alane Cook, Elizabeth Anne Garlinger, Virginia Ann Bertrand. BA in Music, Centenary Coll., 1948; MEd, Northwestern State U., 1973. Cert. elem. edn. tchr., spl. edn. tchr. Tchr. Caddo Parish Schs., Shreveport, 1968-75, Spring Branch Ind. Schs., Houston, 1975-85; vol. Houston Grand Opera/Guild, 1979—, Houston Mus. of Fine Arts/Guild, 1990—. Author tchrs. guides. Pres. Nat. Coun. Jewish Women, Shreveport, 1958, Houston Grand Opera Guild, 1989-91; bd. dirs. Mus. Fine Arts; area coord. Spl. Olympics, Shreveport, 1974-75; mem. Houston Symphony League, Houston Ballet Guild. With USN, 1944-46. Mem. AAUW (pres. Spring Valley Houston chpt. 1985-87), Houston Grand Opera Guild, Houston Symphony League, Houston Ballet Guild, Mus. of Fine Arts Guild (bd. dirs.), Am. Needlepoint Guild, Delta Kappa Gamma (bd. dirs., treas. 1987-89), Phi Mu. Republican. Home: 10220 Memorial Dr Apt 78 Houston TX 77024-3227

ROOSEVELT, EDITH KERMIT, journalist; b. N.Y.C., Dec. 19, 1927; d. Archibald Bulloch and Grace Stackpole (Lockwood) R. Grad., Barnard Coll., 1948. Reporter UPI, San Francisco, L.A., 1951-53, Siskiyou Daily News, 1953, UPI, Washington, 1953-55; writer McCann Erickson Co., N.Y.C., 1956-57; assoc. editor Spadea Syndicate, N.Y.C., 1957-59; reporter, feature writer Newark Star Ledger, 1959-63; syndicated columnist numerous newspapers, 1963-80; Washington editor, corr. Nutrition & Health Review, 1980—; lectr. in field. Contbr. numerous articles to profl. jours. Recipient J.C. Meriam, Ervin S. Cobb & Rupert Hughes award of merit Am. Acad. Pub. Affairs. Address: 1661 Crescent Pl NW Washington DC 20009-4048

ROOT, DORIS SMILEY, portrait artist; b. Ann Arbor, Mich., June 28, 1924; d. George O. and Hazel (Smith) Smiley. Student, Art Inst. of Chgo., 1943-45, N.Y. Sch. Design, 1976-77, Calif. Art Inst., 1984-85. Creative dir. All May Co.'s, L.A., 1962-63; advt. sales pro. dir. Seibu, L.A., 1963-64; v.p. Walgers & Assoc., L.A., 1964-70; owner, designer At The Root of Things, L.A., 1970-73; adv. sales pro. dir. Hs. of Nine, L.A., 1973-74; asst. designer MGM Grand, Reno, Nev., 1974-76; designer, office mgr. Von Hausen Studio, L.A., 1976-82; ABC libr. ABC/Cap Cities, L.A., 1982-89; portrait artist (also known as Dorian), AKA Dorian, art studio, L.A., 1982—. One-man shows include Cookeville, Tenn., 1989, Beverly Hills, Calif., 1991; artist in residence, Cookeville, 1989-90. Republican. Presbyterian.

ROOT, M. BELINDA, chemist; b. Port Arthur, Tex., May 2, 1957; d. Robert A. and Charlene (Whitehead) Lee; m. Miles J. Root, Nov. 8, 1980; children: Jason Matthew, Ashley Erin. BS in Biology, Lamar U., 1979; MBA, U. Houston, 1994. Asst. chemist Merichem Co., Houston, 1979-81, project chemist, 1982-84, instrument chemist, 1984-85, quality assurance coord., 1986-89, product lab. supr., 1989-91; quality control supr. mfg. Welchem Inc. subs. Amoco, 1991—; mgr. Quality Control Petrolite Corp., 1993; mgr. quality control/quality assurance Akzo-Nobel Chems., Pasadena, Tex., 1994—. Editor (newsletter) Merichemer, 1989-91. Mem. MADD, 1989—, PTA, 1988—. Recipient Gulf Shore Regional award Cat Fanciers Assn., 1981, Disting. Merit award, 1990. Mem. NAFE, Am. Soc. Quality Control (cert. quality auditor, quality engr.), Am. Chem. Soc., United Silver Fancier (sec. 1980-82), Lamar U. Alumni Assn., Beta Beta Beta (sec. 1978-79), Beta Gamma Sigma. Office: Akzo-Nobel Chem Inc 13000 Bay Park Dr Pasadena TX 77507

ROOT, MARGARET GOHEEN, public relations executive; b. Quinwood, W.Va., Mar. 27, 1937; d. Martin Richard and Maysel Irene (Brown) Goheen; m. Arthur Ross Sleasman, Jr., Mar. 6, 1959; 1 child, Christopher Squire; m. Stephen Noble Root, Aug. 27, 1970. AA, Towson State U., 1957; BA, U. Md., 1959; MA, Ball State U., 1983. Accredited in pub. rels. Pub. health info. officer Balt. County Dept. Health, Towson, Md., 1969-71; pub. info. officer State Ill., Springfield, 1971-72; dir. pub. rels. Mount Saint Vincent U., Halifax, N.S., Can., 1973-77; mgr. comm. Blue Cross & Blue Shield Iowa, Des Moines, 1977-78; asst. v.p. pub. rels. Ind. Nat. Bank, Indpls., 1978-82; v.p. corp. comm. Conn. Nat. Bank, Hartford, 1982-91; v.p. pub. rels. St. Francis Hosp. & Med. Ctr., Hartford, 1991-93; exec. dir. corp. comm. Tenneco, Inc., Houston, 1993—. Women's exec. com. Greater Hartford C. of C., 1992-93, comm. com., 1990, 93; exec. com. Conn. Joint Coun. Econ. Edn., Storrs, 1986-90; bd. dirs. Alley Theatre, Houston, 1994-95. Recipient Ohio State award Ohio State U., 1977, Merit award Can. Pub. Rels. Soc., 1977. Mem. Pub. Rels. Soc. Am. (chmn., vice chmn., sec. Northeast dist. 1986-88, pres., v.p., treas. Hoosier chpt. 1979-82). Office: 1275 King St Greenwich CT 06831-2946

ROOT, NINA J., librarian; b. N.Y.C., Dec. 22; d. Jacob J. and Fannie (Slivinsky) Root; BA, Hunter Coll.; MSLS, Pratt Inst.; postgrad. U.S. Dept. Agr. Grad. Sch., 1964-65, City U. N.Y., 1970-75. Reference and serials libr. Albert Einstein Coll. Medicine Libr., Bronx, N.Y., 1958-59; asst. chief libr. Am. Cancer Soc., N.Y.C., 1959-62; chief libr. Am. Inst. Aeros. and Astronautics, N.Y.C., 1962-64; head ref. and libr. svcs. sci. and tech. div. Libr. Congress, Washington, 1964-66; mgmt. cons. Nelson Assocs., Inc., N.Y.C., 1966-70; dir. libr. svcs. Am. Mus. Natural History, N.Y.C., 1970—; freelance mgmt. cons. and libr. planning, 1970—. Trustee Barnard Found., 1984-91; mem. libr. adv. coun. N.Y. State Bd. Regents, 1984-89, trustee Metro, 1987-92; bd. dirs. Hampden/Booth Libr., Players, 1990—; trustee Mercantile Libr. N.Y., 1993-95. Recipient Meritorious Svc. award Libr. of Congress, 1965. Mem. ALA (preservation com. 1977-79, chmn. libr./binders com. 1978-80, chmn. preservation sect. 1980-81, mem. coun. 1983-86), Spl. Librs. Assn. (sec. documentation group N.Y. chpt. 1972-73, 2d v.p. N.Y. 1975-76, treas. sci. and tech. group N.Y. 1975-76, mus. arts and humanities div. program planning chairperson-conf. 1977), Archons of Colophon (convener 1978-79), Soc. Natural History (N.Am. rep. 1977-85), N.Y. Acad. Scis. (mem. publs. com. 1975-80, 89-91, archives com. 1976-78, search com. 1976). Home: 400 E 59th St New York NY 10022-2342

ROPER, BERYL CAIN, writer, publisher, retired library director; b. Long Beach, Calif., Mar. 1, 1931; d. Albert Verne and Ollie Fern (Collins) Cain; m. Max H. Young, Aug. 22, 1947 (div. 1958); children: Howard, Wade, Debra, Kevin, John R., Christopher; m. George Albert Roper, Mar. 24, 1962 (dec. July 1978); children: Ellen, Georgianne; m. Jack T. Hughes, Sept. 21, 1993. BA, West Tex. State U., 1986; MA, Tex. Womans U., 1989. Libr. clk. Cornette Libr., West Tex. State U., Canyon, 1981-87; dir. Clarendon (Tex.) Coll. Libr., 1988-96; lectr. in history and archaeology; co-owner Aquamarine Publs. Editor, pub.: In the Light of Past Experience, 1989, Transactions of the Southwest Federation of Archaeological Societies, 1993, Greenbelt Site, 1996; author, pub.: Trementina, 1990, Trementina Revisited, 1994; author articles on women and history. Mem. Clarendon Archaeol. Soc. (charter, v.p. 1990-91), Tex. Libr. Assn., Tex. Jr. Coll. Tchrs. Assn., Tex. Intertribal Indian Orgn. (charter), Pi Gamma Mu, Beta Phi Mu, Alpha Chi, Phi Alpha Theta. Republican. Mem. LDS Ch. Office: Aquamarine Publs 1903 3d Ave Canyon TX 79015

RORKE, LUCY BALIAN, neuropathologist; b. St. Paul, June 22, 1929; d. Aram Haji and Karzouhy (Ousdigian) Balian; m. Robert Radcliffe Rorke, June 4, 1960. A.B., U. Minn., 1951, M.A., 1952, B.S., 1955, M.D., 1957. Diplomate Am. Bd. Pathology. Intern Phila. Gen. Hosp., 1957-58, resident anat. pathology and neuropathology, 1958-62, asst. neuropathologist, 1963-67, chief pediat. pathologist, 1967-68, chief neuropathologist, 1968-69, chmn. dept. anat. pathology and chief neuropathologist, 1969-73, chmn. dept. pathology, 1973-77, pres. med. staff, 1973-75; practice medicine specializing in neuropathology Phila., 1962—; neuropathologist Children's Hosp., Phila., 1965—, pres. med. staff, 1986-88, acting pathologist-in-chief, 1995—; cons. neuropathologist Wyeth Rsch. Labs., Radnor, Pa., 1961-87, Wistar Inst. Anatomy and Biology, Phila., 1967-93; assoc. prof. pathology U. Pa. Sch. Medicine, Phila., 1970-73, prof., 1973—, clin. prof. neurology, 1979—; forensic neuropathologist Office of Med. Examiner, Phila., 1977—. Author: Myelinization of the Brain in the Newborn, 1969, Pathology of Perinatal Brain Injury, 1982; mem. editl. bd. Jours. Neuropathology Exptl. Neurology, 1980-85, 93—, Pediatric neurosurgery, 1984—, Child's Nervous System, 1984-88, Brain pathology, 1990-95; contbr. articles to profl. jours. NIH fellow in neuropathology, 1961-62; NIH grantee for study of neonatal brain, 1963-68. Fellow Coll. Am. Pathologists; mem. Phila. Gen. Hosp. Med. Staff (pres. 1973-75), Phila. Neurol. Soc. (v.p. 1971-72, editor Transactions 1973, pres. 1975-76), Am. Assn. Neuropathologists (exec. council 1976-85, v.p. 1979-80, pres. 1981-82), Am. Neurol. Assn., AMA, Burlington County Med. Soc., Phila. Coll. Physicians. Home: 120 Chestnut St Moorestown NJ 08057-2937 Office: Childrens Hosp of Philadelphia 324 S 34th St Philadelphia PA 19104-4301

ROSA, MARGARITA, agency chief executive, lawyer; b. Bklyn., Jan. 5, 1953; d. Jose and Julia (Mojica) R.; 1 child, Marisol Kimberly Rosa-Shapiro. BA in History cum laude, Princeton U., 1974; JD, Harvard U., 1977. Bar: N.Y. Assoc. Rosenman & Colin, N.Y.C., 1977-79, Rabinowitz & Boudin, N.Y.C., 1981-84; staff atty. Puerto Rican Legal Def. Edn. Fund, N.Y.C., 1979-81; teaching fellow Urban Legal Studies program CUNY, 1984-85; gen. counsel N.Y. State Div. Human Rights, N.Y.C., 1985-88, exec. dep. commr., 1988-90, commr., 1990-95; exec. dir. Grand St. Settlement, 1995—; vice chmn. N.Y. State Task force on ADA Implementation, 1991-95; mem. N.Y. Gov.'s Task Force on Sexual Harrassment, 1992; bd. dirs. Pub. Interest Law Found., NYU Law Sch., 1982-84; adj. prof. of law Fordham Law Sch., 1995; adj. prof. pub. policy Wagner Sch. NYU, 1995—; mem. bd. dirs. Martin Luther King Jr. Commn. N.Y. State, 1990-95, Feminist Press CUNY, 1990-95. Bd. dirs. N.Y. Civil Liberties Union, 1981-86, Lower East Side Family Union, N.Y.C., 1982-84. Recipient Hispanic Women Achievers award N.Y. State Gov.'s Office Hispanic Affairs, 1990, Woman of Excellence award CUNY, 1992, Oscar Garcia Rivera award P.R. Bar Assn., 1996; Lombard Assn. fellow Office of U.S. Atty., So. Dist. N.Y., 1975; Revson Teaching fellow Charles Revson Found., 1984-85. Office: Grand St Settlement 80 Pitt St New York NY 10002

ROSA, MELANIE ANN DOWNS, minister; b. Denver, Oct. 8, 1957; d. Harmon Jay Jr. and Maryann (Hambrick) D.; m. Fredric David Rosa, May 31, 1986; children: Mark, Katherine. BA summa cum laude, Met. State Coll., 1979; MDiv, Iliff Sch. Theology, 1984. Chaplain Hendrix Coll., Conway, Ark., 1982-83; assoc. min. Grace Meth. Ch., Denver, 1984-86; min. Eagle (Colo.)-Gypsum Meth. Ch., 1986-89; sr. min. Trinity Meth. Ch., Colorado Springs, Colo., 1989-95, Lakewood (Colo.) United Meth. Ch., 1995—. Mem. bd. ordained ministry United Meth. Ch. Named Outstanding Recent Grad., Iliff Sch. Theology, 1990. Mem. Acad. for Preaching, Joint Rev. Com., Garden of the Gods Rotary Club. Democrat. Office: Lakewood United Methodist Church 1390 Brentwood Lakewood CO 80215

ROSALES, SUZANNE MARIE, hospital coordinator; b. Merced, Calif., July 23, 1946; d. Walter Marshall and Ellen Marie (Earl) Potter; children: Anita Carol, Michelle Suzanne. AA, City Coll., San Francisco, 1966. Diplomate Am. Coll. Utilization Review Physicians. Utilization review coord. San Francisco Gen. Hosp., 1967-74; mgr. utilization review/discharge planning UCLA Hosp. and Clinics, 1974-79; nurse III Hawaii State Hosp., Kaneohe, 1979-80; review coord. Pacific Profl. Std. Review Orgn., Honolulu, 1980-81; coord. admission and utilization reviewq The Rehab. Hosp. of the Pacific, Honolulu, 1981-85; coord. Pacific Med. Referral Project, Honolulu, 1985-87; dir. profl. svcs. The Queen's Healthcare Plan, Honolulu, 1987-88; utilization mgmt. coord. Vista Psychiat. Physician Assocs., San Diego, 1989; admission coord. utilization review San Francisco Gen. Hosp., 1989-91, quality improvement coordinator, 1991—; cons. Am. Med. Records Assn. Contbr. articles to profl. jours. Mem. Nat. Assn. Utilization Review Profls. Home: 505 Hanover St Daly City CA 94014-1351 Office: San Francisco Gen Hosp 1001 Potrero Ave San Francisco CA 94110-3518

ROSALSKY, BARBARA ELLEN, artist, home health aide; b. N.Y.C., Nov. 16, 1948; d. Ellis M. Rosalsky and Claire (Schwartz) Rosalsky Shapiro; m. Dennis Robinson. BA, SUNY, Plattsburgh, 1970. Sales girl Cambridge (Mass.) Artist mag., 1970-71; artist Pillar of Fire mag., Zarephath, N.J., 1977; home health aide CMR, Bound Brook, N.J., 1978-95; designer New Brunswick (N.J.) Tomorrow, 1980-87; art therapist Middlesex Hosp., New Brunswick, 1981-83. Solo exhibitions include The Bird and Me, 1980; group exhibitions include Other Artists Other Art, 1983. Advisor Cultural Arts Commn., Piscataway, N.J., 1993-95. SUNY Plattsburgh scholar, 1970. Mem. Women's Caucus Art, Marriott Swim Club. Democrat. Home: 114 Woodland Rd Piscataway NJ 08854

ROSANOFF, NANCY, management consultant; b. San Gabriel, Calif., Dec. 24, 1949; d. William Ross Rosanoff and Margaret (Miller) Dorr; m. John A. Ragir, June 21, 1972 (div. June 1980); 1 child, Tamar Anga Ragir; m. John W. Krysko, Sept. 3, 1980; children: Jessie Anne Rosanoff Krysko. BA, U. Calif., Berkeley. Prin. Energy Strategies, Pleasantville, N.Y., 1981—, N. Rosanoff & Assoc., Inc., Pleasantville, N.Y., 1992—. Author: Intuition Workout, 1989. Vestry mem. St. Johns Episcopal Ch., Pleasantville, 1993—. Home: 109 Sunnyside Ave Pleasantville NY 10570

ROSAR, VIRGINIA WILEY, librarian; b. Cleve., Nov. 22, 1926; d. John Egbert and Kathryn Coe (Snyder) Wiley; m. Michael Thorpe Rosar, April 8, 1950 (div. Feb. 1968); children: Bruce Wiley, Keith Michael, James Wilfred. Attended, Oberlin Coll., 1944-46; BA, U. Puget Sound, 1948; MS, C.W. Post Coll., L.I.U., Greenvale, N.Y., 1971. Cert. elem. and music tchr., N.Y.; cert. sch. library media specialist, N.Y. Music programmer Station WFAS, White Plains, N.Y., 1948; prodn. asst. NBC-TV, N.Y.C., 1948-50; tchr. Portledge Sch., Locust Valley, N.Y., 1967-70; librarian Syosset (N.Y.) Schs., 1970-71, Smithtown (N.Y.) Schs., 1971-92; ret., 1992; pres. World of Realia, Woodbury, N.Y., 1969-86; founder Cygnus Pub., Woodbury, 1985-87. Active local chpt. ARC, 1960-63, Community Concert Assn., 1960-66, Leukemia Soc. Am., 1978—. Mem. AAAS, N.Y. Acad. Scis., L.I. Alumnae Club of Pi Beta Phi (pres. 1964-66). Republican. Presbyterian. Home: 10 Warrenton Ct Huntington NY 11743-3750

ROSAS, SUSAN JANE, designer, graphic artist, illustrator, art director; b. Oakland, Calif., June 30, 1937; d. Clarence Francis and Barbara Hischier Matthews; m. John Anthony Roach, July 28, 1958 (div. 1968); children: Jennifer, Adam; m. Gilbert Joseph Rosas, June28, 1975. BA, U. Calif., Santa Barbara, 1961; postgrad., Ventura Coll., 1993-94. With La Cumbre Animal Hosp., Santa Barbara, 1967-76; artist Rood Assocs., Santa Barbara, 1969-71. Designer, artist: (seasonal brochures) Ventura County Chamber Orchestra, 1994-95; designer: (nutcracker collectibles featured in Hammacher Schlemmer catalog and Collector's Mart Mag.) "Nutcracker Prince" for Adrian Taron & Sons and "Clara," 1994-95. Recipient Best of Show award Fine Arts Exhibit-Acrylics U. Calif., Santa Barbara, 1961, Fine Arts Exhibit-Oils, 1961. Mem. AAUW (sec. 1961-62), Nat. Mus. Women in the Arts, U. Calif. Santa Barbara Alumni Assn., Buenaventura Art Assn., Carmel Art Assn. Home: 1131 Windward Way Oxnard CA 93035 Office: Adrian Taron & Sons 801 Linden Ave Carpinteria CA 93013

ROSATO, LAURA MARIE, toxicologist, educator; b. Pitts., Jan. 13, 1958; d. William A. and Mary (Wachter) R. BS, U. Pitts., 1981, MS, 1985, PhD, 1990. Grad. student rschr. U. Pitts., 1983-85, rsch. asst. III, 1982-83, coord. & lectr., 1987-89, grad. student rschr., 1985-90; divsnl. toxicologist Procter & Gamble Co., Cin., 1990-92; prin. toxicologist Quantum Chemical Co., Cin., 1992-94, sr. prin. toxicologist, 1994—; adj. prof. U. Cin., 1995—; ind. cons. Pitts., 1985-90. Contbr. numerous articles to sci. jours. Recipient Student Leadership award U. Pitts., 1989. Mem. Ohio Valley Soc. Toxicology, Greater Cin. Women's Network (bd. dirs. 1996—, chair awards and recognition com.), Internat. Soc. Regulatory Toxicology and Pharmacology, Ohio Valley Soc. Environ. Toxicology and Chemistry, Soc. Toxicology, Vinyl Acetate Toxicology Group (v.p. and treas. 1994—), Toastmasters Internat. (sec.). Home: 7027 Waterview Way Apt # 13 Cincinnati OH 45241 Office: Quantum Chemical Co 11530 Northlake Dr Cincinnati OH 45249

ROSCHER, NINA MATHENY, chemistry educator; b. Uniontown, Pa., Dec. 8, 1938; d. Charles Kenneth and Wilma Pauline (Solomon) Matheny; m. David Roscher, Dec. 27, 1964. BS in Chemistry, U. Del., 1960; PhD in Chemistry, Purdue U., 1964. Phys. chemist Nat. Bur. of Standards, 1958-61; rsch. and teaching asst. Purdue U., West Lafayette, Ind., 1960-64, fellow in chemistry, instr. chemistry, 1964-65; instr. U. Tex., Austin, 1965-67; sr. staff chemist Coca-Cola Export Corp., 1967-68; asst. prof. Douglass Coll., Rutgers U., The State U., 1968-74, asst. dean, 1971-74; dir. acad. adminstrn. Am. U., Washington, 1974-76, assoc. prof. chemistry, 1974-79, prof., 1979—, assoc. dean grad. affairs Coll. Arts and Scis., 1976-79, vice-provost acad. svcs., 1979-82, vice provost for acad. affairs, 1982-85, dean faculty affairs, 1981-85, chair chemistry dept., 1991—; program dir. sci. edn., NSF, 1986—; lectr. in field. Contbr. articles to profl. jours. Recipient Disting. Alumna award Purdue Univ. Sch. Sci., 1996, Am. Chem. Soc. award for encouraging women into careers in the chem. scis. Camille and Henry Dreyfus Found., 1996; Standard Oil fellow, 1961-62, David Ross fellow, 1963-64, Rutgers U. Rsch. Fund, Biomed. Support grantee. Fellow AAAS, Am. Inst. Chemists (profl. opportunities for women com., pres. dist. inst. chemists 1978-79, sec. 1976-77, fin. com. 1983-87, exec. com., bd. dirs. 1986); mem. Am. Chem. Soc. (treas. Monmouth County sect. 1970-72, chmn. 1974, pres. Washington sect. 1995, profl. programs planning and coord. com. 1976-78, admissions com. 1981-89, 91—, GM scholar 1956-60, Virgil F. Payne award, numerous others), N.Y. Acad. Scis., AAUA, Assn. Women in Sci., Soc. Applied Spectroscopy, Sci. Manpower Commn. Profls. in Sci. Home: 10400 Hunter Ridge Dr Oakton VA 22124-1616 Office: Am Univ Dept Chemistry Washington DC 20016-8014

ROSE, ANITA CARROLL, retired educator; b. New Bedford, Mass., Oct. 14, 1922; d. Louis Arthur and Aline (Chicoine) Carroll; m. Anthony E. Rose, Sept. 24, 1955 (dec.); children: Anthony David, Stephen Arthur. BA, U. Mass., Dartmouth, 1971; MAT, R.I. Coll., 1975. Exec. sec. Berkshire-Hathaway, Inc., New Bedford, 1941-55, New Bedford Cancer Soc., 1956-59; tchr. French and English New Bedford Pub. Schs., 1971-88; ret., 1988; clk. Friends of Coastline Elderly Svcs., Inc., 1991-93; mem. bd. dirs. Our Lady's Haven, 1995—. Pres. New Bedford Jr. Women's Club, 1950-51; v.p. Cath. Women's Club, 1957-59, del. Coun. of Women's Orgns., 1989-91; pres. Fairhaven Mothers' Club, 1967-69, book chmn., 1989-91, sunshine chmn., 1991-93, nominating com. chmn., 1993—; mem. Fairhaven Town Mtg., Mass., 1965—; trustee Millicent Libr., Fairhaven, 1980—; rec. sec. Fairhaven Improvement Assn., 1982—; sec. Fairhaven Rep. Town Com., 1980—; bd. dirs. St. Anne Credit Union, New Bedford, 1988—, asst. treas., mem. investment com. 1991-93, pres., chmn. bd., 1993—; mem. adv. coun. Coastline Elderly Svc. Inc., 1988-92; del. Mass. Rep. Conv., 1974, 82, 86, 90, 94; mem. YWCA, Old Dartmouth Hist. Assn., Friends of the Zeiterion Theatre. Mem. AAUW (pres. Coll. Club New Bedford Inc. 1983-85, 1st v.p. 1989-91, del. nat. conv. 1981, 83, 85, 93, chmn. nominating com. Mass. divsn. 1988-90), Tri-County Music Assn. (pres. 1992-95, bd. dirs. 1988—), R.I. Coll. Alumni Assn., U. Mass.-Dartmouth Alumni Assn., Southeastern Mass. Assn. Social Studies, Mil. Order World Wars, Am. Ex-Prisoners of War, St. Joseph's Couples Club (pres. 1987-88), Fairhaven Colonial Club (2d v.p. 1988-89). Home: 49 Laurel St Fairhaven MA 02719-2817

ROSE, BEVERLY ANNE, pharmacist; b. Lewiston, Idaho, June 11, 1950; d. Burton Roswell and Nell Dora (Greenburg) Stein; m. Fred Joseph Rose, July 21, 1973 (div. Aug. 1980). BS in Pharmacy, Ohio No. U., 1973; MBA, Cleve. State U., 1987. Registered pharmacist, Ohio, N.Y. Staff pharmacist Lorain (Ohio) Community Hosp., 1973-79, dir. pharmacy, 1979-91; dir. dept. pharmacy svcs. The House of the Good Samaritan Health Care Complex, Watertown, N.Y., 1991-93; adj. faculty, clin. tng. specialist U. Toledo Coll. Pharmacy, 1980-91; computer cons. Hosp. Pharmacy Network; mem. State Bd. Legis. Rule Rev., Ohio State Bd. Pharmacy, 1987, 88; mem. pres. adv.

bd. Ohio No. U., Ada, 1990—. Mem. editl. bd. Aspen Publs., 1992—. Mem. Am. Soc. Health Sys. Pharmacists (apptd. coun. legal and pub. affairs 1988-89, 89-90, state del. ho. of dels. Ohio 1984, 85, 86, 87, 88, 89, mem. psychotherapeutics-spl. practice group 1990—), Adminstrs. Practice Mgmt. Group, Am. Pharm. Assn., Ohio Soc. Hosp. Pharmacists (pres. 1985-89, Squibb Leadership award 1988, Ciba-Geigy Svc. award 1988, Evlyn Gray Scott award 1987), N.Y. State Coun. Hosp. Pharmacists, Am. Soc. Parenteral and Enteral Nutrition, Fedn. Internat. Pharmaceutique, N.Y. Chpt. Am. Coll. Clin. Pharmacy, others. Home: 20 Cambridge Dr Apt 4 Georgetown OH 45121-9746

ROSE, BONNIE LOU, state official; b. Philipsburg, Pa., Feb. 24, 1951; d. Wasil and Ethel Louise (Crain) Harsomchuck; m. James Edward Rose, Aug. 31, 1975 (sept. 1981). Student, Harrisburg Area Community Coll, 1969-70; diploma, Harrisburg Hosp. Sch. Nursing, 1972; postgrad., Pa. State U., 1987. RN, Pa. Charge nurse Plasmapheresis Ctr., Harrisburg, Pa., 1973-75, Longterm Care Facility, Harrisburg, Pa., 1975; nurse Oral Surgery Practice, Harrisburg, Pa., 1975; nurse, utilization review Pa. Dept. Pub. Welfare, Harrisburg, 1975-79; chief planning, implementation Pa. Dept. Pub. Welfare, Office Med. Assistance, Harrisburg, 1979-83, dir. provider inquiry, 1983-87, dir. provider rels., 1987, dir. long term care provider svcs., 1989—; cons. in field; instr. Pa. Dept. Pub. Welfare, 1985—, coping with difficult behavior, 1985—, coping with difficult behavior, 1985—, stress mgmt., 1985—, burnout, 1986—, team bldg., facilitator-organizational devel., 1987—, team building, 1992—. Mem. Harrisburg Hosp. Alumni Assn. Home: 1704 Creek Vista Dr New Cumberland PA 17070-2212

ROSE, CAROL ANN, air transportation executive; b. Toledo, Jan. 4, 1942; d. Donald Lucien and Dorothy Josephine (Maus) Edmunds; m. Saul Rose, Feb. 3, 1971 (div. 1976). BA, Kent State U., 1963. Entertainer, restaurant supr. S.S. Aquarama Cruiseship, Cleve., 1961-63; airline reservation agt. United Airlines, Cleve., 1963-68; internat. passenger svc. rep. United Airlines, Miami, Fla., 1969-70; V.I.P. customer svc. receptionist-expediter United Airlines, Phila., 1971-79, account exec., 1980-84; spl. events mgr. United Airlines, Chgo., 1984-87, red carpet club coord., 1987-88, corp. meeting planner, 1988-90; comml. aircraft weight and balance planner United Airlines, Seattle, 1991-96, comms. coord., 1996—; speaker Am. Mktg. Assn., Chgo., 1989. Author: Red Carpet Club Procedure Manual-O'Hare, 1987, Corporate Meeting Planners Manual, 1989; editor: Sky Lines Seattle Station Newsletter, 1992. Recipient Oustanding Svc. award Airline Passengers Assn., Phila., 1981, Outstanding Contbn. award Muscular Dystrophy Assn.-Jerry Lewis Telethon, Las Vegas, 1985, 86, 89, Leadership award United Way Campaign, Chgo., 1988. Mem. Meeting Planners Assn., Mgmt. Club (v.p. 1983, pres. 1984), Women United (exec. bd. 1982-83), Delta Zeta. Home: 609 S 222nd St Apt 202 Des Moines WA 98198-6277 Office: United Airlines Seattle-Tacoma Airport Seattle WA 98158

ROSE, ELIZABETH, author, satirist, poet, publisher, environmental poisoning expert; b. N.Y.C., Sept. 18, 1941; children: Kimberly, Dana. Nurse, Lenox Hill Hosp. Sch. Nursing, 1962; BA summa cum laude, U. Redlands, 1976. Asst. head nurse emergency room N.Y.C., 1963-66; head nurse San Pedro (Calif.) Hosp., 1968-69; pub. Butterfly Pub. Co., Santa Monica, 1985; radio and TV personality L.A., 1985—; founder Candida Anonymous, Santa Monica, 1985; cons. health profls. Author: Lady of Gray: Healing Candida-The Nightmare Chemical Epidemic, 1985, 2d edit. 1987, 3d edit. 1989, Sainthood and Single Motherhood, 1990. Recipient Internat. World Leader award, Cambridge, Eng., 1989; N.Y. State Regents scholar, 1959. Mem. UCLA Alumni Assn. (life), Cousteau Soc., Tesla Soc., L.A. Blue Book Club.

ROSE, JOAN L., computer security specialist; b. N.Y.C., June 27, 1946; d. Vincent A. LaVertu and Joan (Mileti) Ellis; children: Robert, Lauren. BA, Bklyn. Coll./CUNY, Bklyn., 1967. Cert. info. sys. security profl. Internat. Info. Sys. Security Cert. Consortium. Programmer Met. Life Ins., N.Y.C., 1967-68; sys. analyst Western Electric, Oklahoma City, 1968-74, Pacific Intermountain Express, Oakland, Calif., 1974-78, Chevron, San Francisco, 1978—; project mgr. GUIDE (IBM Users Group), Chgo., 1983—. Participant Habitat for Humanity, 1995—. Mem. Info. Sys. Security Assn. (Bay Area chpt. treas. 1983—). Democrat. Home: 3299 Pine Valley Rd San Ramon CA 94583 Office: Chevron H2196 6001 Bollinger Canyon Rd San Ramon CA 94583

ROSE, JOANNE, lawyer, rating service executive. BA in Polit. Sci. magna cum laude, U. Rochester; JD, Columbia U. Assoc. White & Case, N.Y.C.; sr. mng. dir., gen. counsel Standard & Poor's Rating Svcs. divsn. McGraw Hill, N.Y.C., chair rating policy bd. Office: McGraw-Hill Inc 25 Broadway New York NY 10004-1064

ROSE, JODI, opera company founder and artistic director; b. Phila., Nov. 27, 1952; d. Hubert Michael and Rita Gervase (Schubert) Rosenberger; m. Edward A. Caycedo; children: Gervase-Teresa, Thomas Schubert, Tanya-Katrina, Edward-Michael. Student, Vienna (Austria) Hochshule, 1973; BS in Edn. and Music, Chestnut Hill Coll., Phila., 1974; postgrad. in performing arts, NYU, 1976-77. Vocalist various musicals and operas, various cities, 1974-88; founder, artistic dir. Opera on the Go, Ltd., Jamaica Estates, N.Y., 1988—. Commd., staged and choreographed many children's and adult operas, including Goldilocks, Little Red Riding Hood, The Tortoise and the Hare, The Pirate Captains, Telephone, Sweet Betsy from Pike, The Medium, and La Pizza Con Funghi. Exec. chair PTA cultural com., Jamaica Estates, 1990—; founder, dir. musical theater workshops for youths, Queens Theater, N.Y., 1993—;. Recipient numerous cmty. and corp. grants, as well as grants from N.Y. State Coun. on Arts; selected as guest performers at Lincoln Ctr., N.Y.C.; recipient 3-yr. grant N.Y.C. Dept. Youth Svcs. Republican. Roman Catholic. Home and Office: 184-61 Radnor Rd Jamaica Estates NY 11432

ROSE, JOY H., playwright, poet; b. Phila., May 24, 1927; d. Abraham Eliazer and Deborah (Feinberg) Hurshman; m. Bernard Rose, June 20, 1948; children: Joan Rose Easley, Linda Rose Hallowell. BA, Temple U., 1950, MFA, 1983. Co-owner, mgr. Roses' Newstand, Media, Pa., 1962-87; mng. dir. Rose and Swan Theater, Media, 1988-93. Author of 5 chap books of poetry; plays include This Is My Land, No Lovers To Scare, Sweet Vibella, Atlantis, In The Shadow of The Liberty Bell. Tchr. Russel Sch. Broomall, Pa., 1992, home-schoolers, Delaware County, 1994; tchr./storyteller, Media Fellowship House, Media, 1995. Recipient prize for short story, Woman's Clubs of Delaware County, 1962, Cmty. Svc. award Media, 1989, Emma Lazarus award Shalom Aleichem Club, Phila., 1954; winner Twin City Sister award Pew Found., 1996; tied 1st place Pa. State Med. Sch., Hershey, 1994. Mem. Theatre Assn. of Pa., Delco Poets Co-op. Jewish.

ROSE, KATHY LERNER, artist; b. N.Y.C., Nov. 20, 1949; d. Ben and Miriam (Burden) R. BFA, Phila. Coll. Art, 1971; MFA, Calif. Inst. of Arts, 1974. Vis. lectr. Harvard U., Cambridge, Mass., 1979-80; self-employed artist N.Y.C., 1976—. Dir., animator (animated films) 10, 1972-78; dir., performer 11 performance pieces (combining film with live performance); numerous articles about this pioneering work appeared in : Print, Dance Mags.; N.Y. Times, Boston Globe, Phila. Inquier, Washington Post and others. Grantee: NEA, 1981, 83, 84, 85, 86, 87, N.Y. Found. for Arts, 1984, 91; N.Y. State Coun. for the Arts, 1985, 86, Am. Filmmakers Inst., 1976.

ROSE, LEATRICE, artist, educator; b. N.Y.C., June 22, 1924; d. Louis Rose and Edna Ades; m. Sol Greenberg (div.); children: Damon, Ethan; m. Joseph Stefanelli, Oct. 10, 1975. Student, Cooper Union, 1941-45, Arts Students League, 1946, Hans Hoffman Sch., 1947. Solo exhbns. include Hansa Gallery, N.Y.C., 1954, Zabriskie Gallery, N.Y.C., 1965, Landmark Gallery, N.Y.C., 1974, Tibor de Nagy Gallery, N.Y.C., 1975, 78, 81, 82, Elaine Benson Gallery, Bridgehampton, N.Y., 1980, Armstrong Gallery, N.Y.C., 1985, Benton Gallery, Southampton, N.Y., 1987, Cyrus Gallery, N.Y.C., 1989; group exhbns. include Sam Kootz Gallery, N.Y.C., 1950, Peridot Gallery, N.Y.C., 1952, Poindexter Gallery, N.Y.C., 1959, Tanager Gallery, N.Y.C., 1960, 62, Riverside Mus., N.Y.C., 1964, Frumkin Gallery, N.Y.C., 1964, Pa. Acad. Fine Arts, Phila., 1966, N.Y. Cultural Ctr., 1973, The Queens (N.Y.) Mus., 1974, 83, Nat. Acad. Design, N.Y.C., 1974, 75, 76, 92, 93, Weatherspoon Art Gallery, Greensboro, N.C., 78, 81, Whitney Mus. Am. Art, N.Y.C., 1978, Albright-Knox Gallery, Buffalo, 1978, 81, Met. Mus. Art, 1979, Vanderwoude Tananbaum Gallery, N.Y.C., 1982, Benton Gallery, 1986, 87.; public collections include Albrect Gallery, St. Joseph, Mo., Guild Hall Mus., East Hampton, N.Y., Tibor de Nagy, Met. Mus. Art. Grantee N.Y. State Coun. Arts, 1974, The Ingram Merrill Found., 1974, AAUW, 1975, NEA, 1977, Esther and Aldolph Gottlieb Found., 1980, 88; recipient Altman prize NAD, 1974, Phillips prize NAD, 1992, award AAAL, 1992, Am. Inst. Art award. Mem. NAD. Office: Apt A924 463 West St New York NY 10014

ROSE, MARGARETE ERIKA, pathologist; b. Esslingen, Germany, Feb. 12, 1945; came to U.S., 1967; d. Wilhelm Ernst and Lina (Schurr) Pfisterer; m. Arthur Caughey Rose, Feb. 3, 1967; children: Victoria Anne, Alexandra Julia, Frederica Isabella. MD, U. So. Calif., L.A., 1972. Diplomate Am. Bd. Anatomic and Clin. Pathology. Pathologist St. Joseph Med. Ctr., Burbank, Calif., 1977-78, Glenview Pathology Med. Ctr., Culver City, Calif., 1979—; dir. anatomic pathology Glenview Meml. Pathology, Culver City, 1988—; dir. Life Chem. Lab., Woodland Hills, Calif.; co-dir., lab. Holy Cross Med. Ctr., Mission Hills, Calif., 1994-95. Mem. Because I Love You, L.A., 1994. Fellow Am. Soc. Pathology, Coll. Am. Pathology. Office: Brotman Med Ctr Dept Pathology 3828 Hughes Ave Culver City CA 90232-2716

ROSE, MARY ETTA, retired educator; b. Indpls., Oct. 3, 1917; d. Robert and Florence Etta (Brooking) T.; divorced, 1972. BS, Ball State U., 1937; MS, Butler u., 1947; DHL, Martin U., Indpls., 1995. Tchr. music Indpls. Pub. Schs., 1943-88. Choir dir., organist Bethel African Methodist Episcopal Ch., Indpls., 1942-64; organist, choir dir. Witherspoon Presbyn. Ch., Indpls., 1978—. Martin Luther King Human Rights award Indpls. Edn. Assn., 1987. Mem. NAACP (life), Internat. Soc. Music Educators, Nat. Assn. Black Sch. Educators, Ind. Retired Tchrs. Assn., Nat. Alliance of Black Sch. Educators, U.S. China Peoples Friendship Assn., Ctr. for Black Music Rsch./Columbia Coll., Phi Delta Kappa (sec. 1992-94). Home: 6431 Hoover Rd #D Indianapolis IN 46260-4635 Office: W-PAC 5136 N Michigan Rd Indianapolis IN 46208

ROSE, MARY PHILOMENA, business educator; b. Detroit, Sept. 27, 1943; d. Henry Joseph and Marie Frances (Wilt) Mueller; m. Robert Henry Rose, June 24, 1966; children: Christopher, Jennifer, Matthew. BS, U. Detroit, 1966; MA in Tchg., Oakland U., 1992. Cert. secondary tchr., Mich.; adminstrv. cert. Tour guide First Fed. Savings and Loan, Detroit, 1965-66; vocat. tchr. Detroit Public Schs., 1966-70; tchr. presch. Utica Cmty. Schs., Sterling Heights, Mich., 1980-82, tchr. computers, 1982-92, tchr. in charge, computers adult edn., 1987-92, acad. adv., 1987-92, coord. bus. partnership programs, 1992—; instr. Lotus macomb Intermediate Sch. Dist., Clinton Twp., Mich., 1988-90; adj. faculty Oakland Cmty. Coll., Auburn Hills, Mich., 1991; co-chairperson UCS adult edn. sch. improvement team, Sterling Heights, Mich., 1992—; chairperson Millage Switzer elections, Sterling Heights, Mich., 1981-84. Mem. Utica Cmty. Schs. Citizen's adv. com., Sterling Heights, Mich., 1975-85; pres. PTO, Shelby Twp., Mich., 1980-83; coord. Doug Carl election, Utica, Mich., 1985. Mem. Mich. Assn. Acad. Adv. Adult and Cmty. Edn. (pres. 1994-95), Grtr. Detroit Employment Opportunity Assn., Macomb County Assn. Placement Personnel, Mich. Assn. Cmty. and Adult Edn., Nat. Ctr. Cmty. Edn. Office: Utica Cmty Schs Adult Edn 11303 Greendale Sterling Heights MI 48312

ROSE, MELISSA EVA ANDERSON, small business owner; b. Grayson, Ky., Sept. 24, 1959; d. thomas Erwin and Betty Jane (Mauk) Hall; m. William David Rose, JUne 19, 1992. Student, Araphoe Bus. Coll., Denver, 1976-78; BA, Morehead State U., 1979-84. Sales clk. Cases Hardware and Antiques, Olive Hill, Ky., 1970-72; waitress Los Gringitos, Morehead, Ky., 1975; tele-mktg. operator Citi-Corp Fin. Svcs., Denver, 1977-78; model, spokeswoman Ford Agy. NY, N.Y.C., 1979-81; counselor Christian Social Svcs., 1979-81; activities coord. Dept. Corrections, Denver, 1979; pres. ops. Dimensions Unltd. Inc., Denver, 1981—; owner, pres. Dimensions Unltd. Inc., Huntington, W.Va., 1985—; cons. Home Interior Designs, Inc., Denver, 1985-86; sec. Denver County Real Estate Commn., 1987-88; bd. dirs. Found. for Human Concerns, Morehead, Ky., 1987-88, Excalibur Fin. Svc., Olive Hill, Ky., Melissa E. Rose Inc.; cons. Ky. C. of C., Glasgow, 1988—; founder, pres. Unified Fortress Group, Inc., 1989, Gold Link Publs., 1991-92; contr. Alpha Mktg. Corp., 1992-95; owner Mystic Limousine, 1992—. Author: Business Ethics 2nd Moral Values, 1987, Life After Death 2 Cultural Explorations, 1987, Business Marketing-Sales for the 90s, 1992. Spokesperson Nat. Rep. Group, Morehead, 1981; chairperson Tiffany's Gold Charity Soc., Denver 1986; sec. Bus. Devel. Soc., Las Vegas, 1987; charter sponsor NATO Culture Exch. in W.Va., NY, 1989. Named Dutchess Hutt River Province, Australia, 1996. Mem. NAFE, Dunn V. Bradstree, Inc., Nat. Assn. Mchts., Encore Gold Purchasing Club, League Human Rights, Nat. Assn. Euroeoan Bus. Cmtys., Met. Mus. Art, Smithsonian Instn., Citizens for a Better Govt. (chair), Olive Hill C. of C. Office: Dimensions Unltd Inc 3845 Bluestone Bratton Bridge Rd Morehead KY 40351-9788 also: Golden Link Publs PO Box 869 Olive Hill KY 41164-0869

ROSE, MERRILL, public relations counselor; b. Beaufort, N.C., Apr. 20, 1955; d. Robert Lloyd Rose and Betty Lou (Merrill) Ellis. Student, U. N.C., 1977. Reporter, editor Consumer News, Washington, 1978-79; v.p. Fraser/Assocs., Washington, 1979-82; sr. assoc. Porter/Novelli, Washington, 1982-83, v.p., 1983-87; sr. v.p., food practice leader Porter/Novelli, N.Y.C., 1989-91, exec. v.p., 1990—; gen. mgr. Chgo. Porter/Novelli, 1991-96. Bd. dirs. CARE, 1991—; bd. visitors U. N.C. Sch. Journalism, Chapel Hill, 1992—; bd. dirs. Friends of Prentice affiliate Northwestern Meml. Hosp., 1993—; mem. accrediting com. Accrediting Coun. for Edn. in Journalism and Comm., 1994—. Mem. Am. Inst. of Wine and Food, Pub. Rels. Soc. Am. Office: Porter/Novelli 303 E Wacker Dr Ste 12 Chicago IL 60601-5212

ROSE, PEGGY JANE, artist, art educator; b. Plainfield, N.J., Oct. 4, 1947; d. Kenneth Earl and Mary Elizabeth (Taylor) R.; m. Byram Soli Daruwala, July 30, 1988; 1 child, Mathew Byram Daruwala. BA magna cum laude, U. Tex., Austin, 1971; BFA with distinction, Acad. of Art Coll., San Francisco, 1980. Painting instr. Calif. Coll. Arts and Crafts, Oakland, 1985-86; painting and drawing instr. Walnut Creek (Calif.) Civic Arts, 1985-95, Acad. of Art Coll., 1983—; solo show Dragon Gallery, Mill Valley, Calif., 1987; Brenda Hall Gallery, San Francisco, 1993; featured artist Sausalito (Calif.) Art Festival, 1986; group shows U.S. Art, San Francisco, 1994; Marin open studios Marin Arts Coun., San Rafael, Calif., 1996—; curriculum devel. com. Calif. Coll. Arts and Crafts, Oakland, 1986; faculty exec. com. Acad. of Art Coll., 1986-88; art exhbn. juror, No. Calif., 1994—. Prin. works include Portrait and Landscape Commissions, 1984— (oil and pastel paintings); exhibited in group shows at City of Walnut Creek, Calif., 1984-93, Carmel Gallery, Danville, Calif., 1990, Marin Arts Coun., Larkspur, Calif., 1994-95, Marin County Fair, San Rafael, Calif., 1993. Recipient Lila Atcheson Wallace award N.Y. Soc. Illustrators, 1981-82, Best Illustration of Show and merit awards Acad. Art Coll., 1979-82, Best of Show, Grambacher Gold Medallion awards Alamo Danville Artists Soc., 1984-86, Handell award Pastels U.S.A., 1996. Mem. San Francisco Soc. Illustrators, Marin Soc. Artists, San Francisco Women Artists, Marin Arts Coun., Pastel Soc. of the West Coast. Home: 53 Sonora Way Corte Madera CA 94925

ROSE, PHYLLIS, English language professional, author; b. N.Y.C., Oct. 26, 1942; d. Eli and Minnie Davidoff; m. Mark Rose, (div. 1975); 1 son, Ted.; m. Laurent de Brunhoff, 1990. BA summa cum laude, Radcliffe Coll., 1964; M.A., Yale U., 1965; Ph.D., Harvard U., 1970. Teaching fellow Harvard U., Cambridge, Mass., 1966-67; acting instr. Yale U., New Haven, 1969; asst. prof. Wesleyan U., Middletown, Conn., 1969-76, assoc. prof., 1976-81, prof. English, 1981—; vis. prof. U. Calif., Berkeley, 1981-82; chmn. fiction jury Nat. Book Awards, 1993; bd. dirs. Wesleyan Writers Conf. Key West Literary Seminar. Author: Woman of Letters: A Life of Virginia Woolf, 1978, Parallel Lives: Five Victorian Marriages, 1983, Writing of Women, 1985, Jazz Cleopatra: Josephine Baker in Her Time, 1989, Never Say Goodbye: Essays, 1991; editor: The Norton Book of Women's Lives, 1993; book reviewer N.Y. Times Book Rev., The Atlantic; essayist; contbr. editor Civilization mag. Nat. Endowment for Humanities fellow, 1973-74; Rockefeller Found. fellow, 1984-85; Guggenheim fellow, 1985. Mem. PEN, Nat. Book Critics Circle, Authors Guild. Home: 122 E 82 2D New York NY 10028 Office: Wesleyan U Dept English Middletown CT 06457

ROSE, ROSLYN, artist; b. Irvington, N.J., May 28, 1929; d. Mark and Anne Sarah (Green) R.; m. Franklin Blou, Nov. 26, 1950; 1 child, Mark Gordon Blue (dec.). Student, Rutgers U., 1949-51, Pratt Ctr. for Contemporary, Printmaking, N.Y.C., 1967; BS, Skidmore Coll., 1976. Artist. One-person shows include Midday Gallery, Caldwell, N.J., 1972, Caldwell Coll., 1972, Kean Coll., Union, N.J., 1973, Art Corner Gallery, Millburn, N.J., 1974, Brandeis U., Mass., 1974, Newark (N.j.) Mus., 1974, George Frederick Gallery, Rochester, N.Y., 1981, Robbins Gallery, Washington, 1981, Signatures Gallery, Washington, 1981, Arnot Art Mus., Elmira, N.Y., 1982, Douglas Coll. Rutgers U., New Brunswick, 1987, Nathans Gallery, West Paterson, N.J., 1984, 86, 89, 96; exhibited in group shows at Seattle Art Mus., Portland (oreg.) Mus., NYU U. Small Works Show, Montclair Art Mus., N.J., Middlesex County Mus., Piscataway, N.J., and others; permanent collections include N.J. State Mus., Trenton, Citibank of N.Y., Russia, N.J. State Libr., Trenton, Roddenbery Meml. Libr., Cairo, Ga., Rosenberg Libr., Galveston, Tex., Newark Mus., Newark Pub. Libr., AT&T, BASF Wyandotte Corp., Canon Calculator Systems, N.Y.C., First Fed. Bank, Rochester, Gulf & Western Industries, Irving Trust Co., N.Y., Kidder, Peabody & Co., N.Y., McAllen Internat. Mus., Tex., Nabisco Brands Corp., East Hanover, N.J., N.J. Bell, Readers Digest Collection, Voorhees-Zimmerli Mus., Rutgers U., New Brunswick, N.J., others; creator UNCIF cards, 1979-80. Recipient graphic award Westechester (N.Y.) Art Soc., 1973, Best-in-Show award Livingston (N.J.) Art Assn., 1971, Best-in-Show award N.J. Ctr. for Visual Arts, Summit, 1969, Mixed Media Merit award Salmagundi Club, N.Y.C., 1995; numerous others. Mem. Nat. Assn. Women Artists (Innovative Painting award 1990), N.Y. Artists Equity, Pen and Brush Club (N.Y.C. Stauffer Mixed Media award 1996). Office: Atelier Rose PO Box 5095 Hoboken NJ 07030-5095

ROSE, SARA MARGARET, English as a second language educator; b. Johnstown, Pa., Sept. 22, 1950; d. William S. and Mary Margaret (Leberknight) R.; m. Akbar Ahamadian (common law, separated); 1 child, Meryem Rose. Student Sociology, Univ. Copenhagen, Denmark, 1971-73; MEd, Blagard Tchrs. Seminarium, Copenhagen, 1981. Cert. tchr., Denmark. Lang. tchr. and cons. Adult Edn., Hillerød, Denmark, 1981-90; cons. on immigrant and refugee issues Danish Dept. Welfare, Hillerød, 1983-88; ESL instr. Balt. City C.C., 1991-94, Catonsville C.C., Balt., 1992-96, Balt. Hebrew U., 1993-95; ESL instr. Balt. County Adult Edn., 1990-96, ESL facilitator, adminstr., 1994-96; dir. English Lang. Inst. Coll. Notre Dame of Md., Balt., 1996—; cmty. coord. Au Pair Care, Balt., 1991—. Lectr. on Immigrant and Refugee Issues, AOF Hillerød, 1983-90; founder, adminstr. Fgn. Women's Social Club, Hillerød, 1985-87; mem. People's Movement Against Racial Hatred and Discrimination, Denmark, 1983-90. Recipient Study Tour to Turkey, Danish Ministry of Edn., 1986. Mem. TESOL. Methodist. Home: 3905 Darleigh Rd Unit 2H Baltimore MD 21236 Office: English Lang Inst Coll Notre Dame of Md 4701 N Charles St Baltimore MD 21210

ROSE, SHARON MARIE, critical care nurse; b. Big Spring, Tex., Feb. 16, 1958; d. William Coleman Smith and Grace Marie (Arnett) Karns; m. Christopher Robin Rose, Jan. 21, 984; 1 child, Crystal Alyss. AAS, Odessa Coll., 1981; BS in Occupational Edn., Wayland Bapt., 1987. Critical care RN Univ. Med. Ctr., Lubbock, Tex., 1981-88; med-surg. instr. Lubbock (Tex.) Gen. Hosp., 1988-89; dialysis RN St. Mary of the Plains Hosp., 1989-91; asst. CCU mgr. St. Mary of the Plains Hosp., Lubbock, 1990-91; health occupations instr. Lubbock Ind. Sch. Dist., 1991-94; in-svc. coord. Dialysis Ctr. Lubbock, Tex., 1994—; tchr. summer session Asst. for Med. Terminology course, 1993; mem. Health Occupations Adv. Com., Lubbock, 1988. Mem. Nat. Kidney Found. Mem. Tex. Health Occupations Assn. (v.p. 1993-94), Health Occupation Students Am. (advisor 1991-94), Tex. Tech. Med. Alliance, Nat. Kidney Found. (coun. nephrology nurses and technicians). Baptist. Home: 4708 31st St Lubbock TX 79410 Office: Dialysis Ctr Lubbock 4110 22nd Pl Lubbock TX 79410

ROSE, SHARON MARIE, telecommunications professional; b. Mpls., July 21, 1962; d. Thomas Kevin and Jeanette Mary (Fasnacht) Lange; m. Mark Edward Tessier, July 3, 1981 (div. Dec. 1983); 1 child, Marie Elizabeth. Grad. H.S., Elk River, Minn. Installation and testing supr. N.Am. Satellite Transmission, Chgo., 1984-85; transmission tech. Sprint Comm. Long Distance Divsn., St. Paul, 1985-86, network ops. specialist III, 1986-91; sr. network ops. specialist Sprint Comm. Long Distance Divsn., Rancho Cordova, Calif., 1994-95; telecom. technician Hewlett-Packard, Roseville, Calif., 1996 . Home: PO Box 2771 Rancho Cordova CA 95741 Office. Hewlett-Packard Mailstop 5571 8000 Foothills Blvd Roseville CA 95747

ROSE, SUE ELLEN, elementary education educator; b. Alton, Ill., July 31, 1948; d. Paul F. and Agnes (Thompson) Day; children: Jennifer, Kelley. BA, U. South Fla., 1970, MA in Elem. Edn., 1975. Tchr. Shaw Elem. Sch., Tampa, 1972—; adj. instr. U. South Fla., Tampa, 1992; chair Shaw Sch. Improvement Team, 1993—; Early Literacy Insvc. Course facilitator Hillsborough County Schs., Tampa, 1994—. Dir. children's divsn. Sunday Sch. Bayshore Bapt. Ch., Tampa, 1994—. Faculty Study grant Hillsborough County Schs., 1994. Mem. Delta Kappa Gamma, Phi Kappa Phi. Office: Shaw Elem Sch 11311 N 15th St Tampa FL 33612-5935

ROSE, SUSAN PORTER, federal commissioner; b. Cin., Sept. 20, 1941; d. Elmer Johnson and Dorothy (Wurst) Porter; m. Jonathan Chapman Rose, Jan. 26, 1980; 1 child, Benjamin Chapman. BA, Earlham Coll., 1963; MS, Ind. State U., Terre Haute, 1970. Staff asst. Congressman Richard L. Roudebush, Washington, 1963-64; asst. dean George Sch., Bucks County, Pa., 1964-66; asst. dir. admissions Mt. Holyoke Coll., South Hadley, Mass., 1966-71; asst. dir. correspondence First Lady (Mrs. Nixon) The White House, 1971-72, appointments sec. to First Lady (Mrs. Nixon), 1972-74, to First Lady (Mrs. Ford), 1974-77; spl. asst. to asst. atty. gen. Office Improvements in Adminstrn. Justice, Washington, 1977-79, Justice Mgmt. div. U.S. Dept. Justice, 1979-81; chief of staff to Mrs. Bush, asst. to v.p. Office of V.P. of U.S. Washington, 1981-89; dep. asst. to Pres. of U.S., chief of staff to First Lady (Mrs. Bush) The White House, 1989-93; commr. U.S. Commn. Fine Arts, 1993—. Bd. dirs. Barbara Bush Found. for Family Literacy; bd. trustees Bush Presdl. Libr. and Ctr. Recipient Dist. Alumni award Earlham Coll., 1992, Ind. State U., 1991. Mem. Ind. Acad. Home: 501 Slaters Ln Apt 1001 Alexandria VA 22314-1118

ROSE, SUSAN (SIOUX), writer, columnist, counselor; b. Bklyn., Aug. 9, 1953; d. Abraham Rosenberg and Sybil Fichtelberg; children: Gabrielle Fernandez, Rachel Fernandez. Student, Empire Coll., 1974; BA signum laudis, SUNY, Albany, 1975. Cert. tchr. English, N.Y. Tchr. Robinson Sch., San Juan, P.R., 1976-81; writer Caribbean Bus. Newspaper, San Juan, P.R., 1977—; columnist Capitol Airlines mag., N.Y.C., 1980-84, Psychic Jour., Key West, Fla., 1987-88; writer Lear's mag., N.Y.C., 1989-94; tchr. Fla. Key C. C., Key West, Fla., 1993; lectr. Berlitz Sch. Langs., San Juan, P.R., 1978-79, Shape U Spa, Key West, Fla., 1994, Regency Health Spa, Hallandale, Fla., 1995—, Russell House Health Spa, Key West, Fla., 1987-93; t.v. host Channel 13, Fajardo, P.R., 1984-85, TCI, Fla. Keys, 1986-94; radio host Santurce, P.R., 1977-79. Author: La Guia Astrologica Hispana, 1986; co-author: Starmates, 1989. Mem. Unitarian Ch. Democrat. Home and Office: 8008 NW 31st Ave # 708 Gainesville FL 32606

ROSE, TERESA ANN, retail administrator; b. Queens, N.Y., Oct. 15, 1971; d. Michael Joseph and Joann Bella (Tubito) Ervolino; m. Stephen P. Rose, Apr. 1, 1995. AD in Mktg., Berkeley Coll., N.Y.C., 1991. Sales assoc. Steuben, N.Y.C., 1990-91, asst. to magr. sales, 1991-92, mgr. customer svc./warehouse, 1992—. Mem. NAFE. Office: Corning Inc/Steuben 717 Fifth Ave New York NY 10022

ROSE, VIRGINIA SHOTTENHAMER, secondary school educator; b. San Jose, Calif., Feb. 3, 1924; d. Leo E. and Mae E. (Slavich) Shottenhamer; m. Paul V. Rose, June 21, 1947; children: Paul V. Jr., David P., Alan P. AB, W. Calif., San Jose, 1945, MA, 1972. Tchr. grades 5-6 Evergreen Sch. Dist., San Jose, 1945-47; 6th grade tchr. Washington Sch., San Jose, 1947-57; elem. tchr. San Jose Unified Sch. Dist., 1967-82, reading specialist, 1982-93; ret., 1993; cons. in field; mem. project literacy San Jose Unified Schs., 1987-91; mem. instrnl. materials evaluation panel Calif. State Edpt. Edn., Sacramento, 1988; master tchr. U. Calif., San Jose, 1991. Co-author: Handbook for Teachers' Aides, 1967. Active Alexian Bros. Hosp. League, San Jose, 1965, bd. dirs., chair libr. cart, 1966-76. Mem. AAUW (com. chair 1978-81), Internat. Reading Assn., Calif. Reading Assn., Santa Clara County Reading Coun. (pres. 1986-87, Asilomar conf. chair 1991, IRA honor coun. pres. club

1987, bd. dirs.), Soroptimist Internat. (sec. 1993-94), Pi Epsilon Tau (pres. 1944-45), Kappa Delta Pi (pres. 1943-45), Pi Lambda Theta (pres. San Jose chpt. 1987-89, auditor 1980, sec. 1985-86, Biennium award 1987). Office: Willow Glen Ed Park S 2001 Cottle Ave San Jose CA 95125-3502

ROSE-ACKERMAN, SUSAN, law and political economy educator; b. Mineola, N.Y., Apr. 23, 1942; d. R. William and Rosalie (Gould) Rose; m. Bruce A. Ackerman, May 29, 1967; children: Sybil, John. B.A., Wellesley Coll, 1964; Ph.D., Yale U., 1970. Asst. prof. U. Pa., Phila, 1970-74; lectr. Yale U., New Haven, Conn., 1974-75, asst. prof., 1975-78, assoc. prof., 1978-82; prof. law and polit. economy Columbia U., N.Y.C., 1982-87, dir. Ctr. for Law and Econ. Studies, 1983-87; Ely prof. of law and polit. econ. Yale U., New Haven, 1987-92, Luce prof. jurisprudence (law and polit. sci.), 1992—; rev. panelist Program on Regulation and Policy Analysis, NSF, Washington, 1982-84, Am. studies program Am. Coun. Learned Socs., 1987-90; review panelist, faculty Fulbright Commn., 1993-96; vis. rsch. fellow World Bank, 1995-96. Author: (with Ackerman, Sawyer and Henderson) Uncertain Search for Environmental Quality, 1974 (Henderson prize 1982); Corruption: A Study in Political Economy, 1978; (with E. James) The Nonprofit Enterprise in Market Economies, 1986; editor: The Economics of Nonprofit Institutions, 1986; (with J. Coffee and L. Lowenstein) Knights, Raiders, and Targets: The Impact of the Hostile Takeover, 1988, Rethinking the Progressive Agenda: The Reform of the American Regulatory State, 1992, Controlling Environmental Policy: The Limits of Public Law in Germany and the United States, 1995; contbr. articles to profl. jours.; bd. editors: Jour. Law, Econs. and Orgn., 1984—, Internat. Rev. Law and Econs., 1986—, Jour. Policy Analysis and Mgmt., 1989—, Polit. Sci. Quar., 1988—. Guggenheim fellow 1991-92, Fulbright fellow, Free U. Berlin, 1991-92. Mem. Am. Law and Econs. Assn. (bd. dirs. 1993-96), Am. Econ. Assn. (mem. exec. com. 1990-93), Am. Polit. Sci. Assn., Assn. Am. Law Schs., Assn. Pub. Policy and Mgmt. (mem. policy coun. 1984-88). Democrat. Office: Yale U Law Sch PO Box 208215 New Haven CT 06520-8215

ROSEANNE, actress, comedienne, producer, writer; b. Salt Lake City, Nov. 3, 1952; d. Jerry and Helen Barr; m. Bill Pentland, 1974 (div. 1989); children: Jessica, Jennifer, Brandi, Buck, Jake; m. Tom Arnold, 1990 (div. 1994); m. Ben Thomas, 1994. Former window dresser, cocktail waitress; prin. Full Moon & High Tide Prodns., Inc. As comic, worked in bars, church coffeehouse, Denver; produced showcase for women performers Take Back the Mike, U. Boulder (Colo.); performer The Comedy Store, L.A.; showcased on TV special Funny, 1986, also The Tonight Show; featured in HBO-TV spl. On Location: The Roseanne Barr Show, 1987 (Am. comedy award Funniest female performer in TV spl., 1987, Ace award funniest female in comedy, 1987, Ace award Best Comedy Spl. 1987); star of TV series Roseanne ABC, 1988— (U.S. Mag. 2d Ann. Readers Poll Best Actress Comedy series, 1989, Golden Globe nomination Outstanding lead actress comedy series 1988, Emmy award Outstanding Lead Actress in a Comedy Series, 1993); actress: (motion picture) She-Devil, 1989, Look Who's Talking Too (voice), 1990, Freddy's Dead, 1991, Even Cowgirls Get the Blues, 1994, Blue in the Face, 1995; TV movies: Backfield in Motion, The Woman Who Loved Elvis, 1993; appeared in TV spl. Sinatra: 80 Years My Way, 1995; author: Roseanne: My Life as a Woman, 1989, My Lives, 1994. Active various child advocate orgns. Recipient Peabody award, People's Choice award (4), Golden Globe award (2), Am. Comedy award, Humanitas award. Office: Full Moon & High Tide Prodns 4024 Radford Ave # 916 917 Studio City CA 91604-2101

ROSEBROOKS, ANN COLBURN, artist; b. Gardner, Mass., Jan. 27, 1948; d. Warren Wallace and Ethel Elizabeth (Prigmore) Colburn; m. Nathan Bruce Rosebrooks, Mar. 22, 1969; children: Earl Warren, Sarah Ann. BFA in Painting, R.I. Sch. Design, 1970. represented by Artworks Gallery, Hartford, Conn. One woman shows include Steinway Gallery, Chapel Hill, N.C.; 2 person shows include Promenade Gallery, The Bushnell, Hartford, Conn.; also represented in pvt. collections. Mem. Conn. Acad. Fine Arts, Arts Worcester, Nat. Assn. Women Artists, Art XII. Home: 350 Ravenelle Rd North Grosvenordale CT 06255

ROSEBROUGH, CAROL BELVILLE, cable television company executive; b. Ironton, Ohio, June 5, 1940; d. Lindsey and Bessie (Reed) Belville; m. John R. Rosebrough, Mar. 4, 1960 (dec. Nov. 1974); children: G. Suzanne, John R., Rebecca J. Student, Columbia (Mo.) Coll., 1958-59; BSBA, Franklin U., 1985. Cons. CBR and Assocs., Columbus, 1978-82; dir. adminstrn. United Cerebral Palsy Columbus and Franklin County, 1972-82; bus. mgr. Times Mirror, Newark, Ohio, 1982-83; ops. mgr. Times Mirror, Newark, 1983-85; gen. mgr. Times Mirror, Logan/Waverly/Greenfield, Ohio, 1985-86, Times Mirror doing bus. as Dimension Cable Svcs., Marion, Ohio, 1986-88; gen. mgr. Cable TV div. Susquehanna Comms. (formerly Times Mirror and Cox Comms.), Williamsport, Pa., 1988—. Bd. dirs United Way, Marion County, 1987-88, Lycoming County, 1989—, Williamsport/Lycoming C. of C., 1995—. Mem. Ohio Cable TV Assn. (bd. dirs. 1986-88), Pa. Cable TV Assn. (bd. dirs. 1990-96), Pa. Edn. Communications Systems (bd. dirs. 1990—), Pa. Rural Devel. Coun. (exec. com., telecommunications task force 1992-95), Mid-Ohio Regional Planning Commn. (transp. com. 1980-82), Internat. Women's Writers Guild, Internat. Assn. Therapists and Counselors, Rotary. Office: Susquehanna Comms 330 Basin St Williamsport PA 17701-5216

ROSEIG, ESTHER MARIAN, veterinary researcher; b. Bklyn., July 23, 1917; d. Chone and Rebecca (Kaplan) Fogel; m. Seymour Roseig, Jan. 21, 1967. Cert., Med. Assts. Sch., N.Y.C., 1967; student, Orange County Community Coll., Middletown, N.Y., 1967-68. Cert. clin. lab. technician, N.Y. Gen. lab. technician Arden Hill Hosp., Goshen, N.Y., 1967-68; tech. rsch. asst. Lamont-Doherty Geol. Obs., 1968-70. Democrat.

ROSEL, CAROL ANN, artist; b. Dodge City, Kans., June 12, 1944; d. John Elbert and Mary Claire (Wetmore) Frazier; m. Herbert Carey Zortman, Aug. 21, 1960 (div. Jan. 1989); children: Elaine Marie, Anita Louise, Stanley Dale; m. George D. Rosel, Sept. 22, 1990 (dec. June 1995). Student, Ctrl. Coll., McPherson, Kans., 1961; BFA cum laude, Ft. Hays State U., 1994. Cert. machine embroidery instr. Dress designer Ms. Cosmo Ltd., Wichita, Kans., 1975-76; designer artistic embroidery garments, 1977-80; owner Carol Ann's Gallery, Liberal, Kans.; part-time art tchr. C.C.s, Baker Art Ctr., Seward County C.C., U.S. D 480, Liberal. One-woman show Ft. Hays Libr., 1993. Mem. Baker Art Ctr., Liberal, 1989—, Hays (Kans.) Arts Coun., 1993; tchr. Sunday sch.; counselor girls ch. camp; solo pianist ch. weddings and comty. functions. Recipient All Am. Scholar Collegiate award, 1994, Grand Champion award State Fair, 1989, 90, 95, Purple Champion award, 1990, others; named Woman of World, 1995-96. Mem. Mid. Am. Arts and Crafts Assn., Pinnacle Honor Soc., Art Club. Republican. Home and Office: 406 Harvard Ave Liberal KS 67901-3024

ROSEMAN, SUSAN CAROL, artist; b. Phila., June 20, 1950; d. Myer and Jeanette (Lewin) R.; m. James Robert Feehan, Feb. 21, 1985. Student, Art Inst. Pitts., 1967; 5-yr. cert., Pa. Acad. Fine Arts, 1973. Painter, printmaker, Pipersville, Pa., 1973—; sign painter Rose Moon Signs and Design, Pipersville, 1984—; curator Cafe Gallery, Rosemont, N.J., 1986—; pres. Riverbank Arts Inc., Stockton, N.J., 1994—; lectr. painting William Allen High Sch., Allentown, Pa., 1976; bd. dirs. Open Space Gallery, Allentown, 1980-81; mem. publicity and exhbn. com. Abington Art Ctr., Jenkintown, Pa., 1978-81; curator Gallery at Vineyards, New Hope, Pa., 1990; juror student show Pa. Acad. Fine Arts, Phila., 1990, Shad Festival, Lambertville, N.J., 1990, Plastic Club, Phila., 1994. One-woman shows include Moravian Coll., Bethlehem, Pa., 1980, Gallery 500, Elkins Park, Pa., 1981, 20th Century Gallery, Phila., 1983; exhibited in group shows at Women in the Arts, William Penn Mus., Harrisburg, Pa., 1981-82, Japan Internat. Artists Soc., Prefectural Mus. of Nara and Chiba, Japan, 1981-82, Trenton (n.J.) State Coll., 1986, Fellowship of Pa. Acad. Fine Arts, James A. Michener Art Mus., Doylestown, Pa., 1992, Woodmere Art Mus., 1994, Mus. Am. Art of Pa. Acad. Fine Arts, 1996, others; represented in permanent collections. Recipient 2nd pl. award Allentown Art Mus., 1979, Warga award Princeton Art Assn., 1979, Critics Choice award Lehigh Art Alliance, 1983; scholar Pa. Acad. Fine Arts, 1972; fellow Baum Sch. Art, 1980-81; LHP Found. grantee, 1994—. Mem. Woodmere Art Mus., Pa. Acad. Fine Arts Alumni Assn. (cochmn. exhbns. 1990-92, bd. dirs. 1991-92). Home and Office: 6588 Groveland Rd Pipersville PA 18947-1402

ROSEME, SHARON DAY, lawyer; b. Sacramento, Aug. 6, 1953; d. George Roseme and Alice Diane Day; m. Daniel George Glenn, June 26, 1982 (div. Nov. 1989); 1 child, Hilary. Student, San Francisco State U., 1971-72; BA, U. Calif., Santa Cruz, 1975; JD, Boalt Hall Sch. of Law, 1978. Jud. staff atty. Calif. State Ct. of Appeal, San Francisco, 1978-80; assoc. Feldman, Waldman & Kline, San Francisco, 1980-82, McDonough, Holland & Allen, Sacramento, 1982—; speaker to profl. and cmty. orgns. Contbr. articles to profl. jours. Mem. ABA, State Bar Calif., County Bar Sacramento, County Bar Placer, Am. Arbitration Assn. (arbitrator, Sacramento adv. com.), Sacramento Area Commerce and Trade Orgn. (devel. com. 1994-96, chmn. 1996-97), Comml. Real Estate Women Sacramento (chmn. cmty. svc. com. 1994-95, Mem. of Yr. award 1993), Order of Coif. Office: McDonough Holland & Allen 555 Capitol Mall Ste 950 Sacramento CA 95814-4601

ROSEN, ANA BEATRIZ, electronics executive; b. Guayaquil, Ecuador, May 16, 1950; came to U.S., 1962; d. Luis A. and Luz Aurora (Rodriguez) Moreira; m. Manuel Jose Farina, Dec. 15, 1979 (dec. Apr. 1990); children: Kevin, Mark; m. Michael G. Rosen, June 6, 1992. AA, Latin-Am. Inst., 1971. Adminstr. asst. M&T Chem. Inc., N.Y.C., 1971-75; mgr. sales Singer Products Co., N.Y.C., 1975-78; v.p. Argil Internat. Ltd., N.Y.C., 1978-83; pres. KMA Enterprises Inc., Bklyn., 1983-94, KMA Industries Inc., Palm Beach Gardens, Fla., 1994—; mem. U.S Trade Adv. Bd. Mem. NAFE, World Trade Coun. (Palm Beach County), Gold Coast Bus. and Profl. Women of the Palm Beaches. Roman Catholic.

ROSEN, ANN BETH, artist, photographer, educator; b. N.Y.C., Dec. 4, 1948; d. Sidney and Selma Ruth (Goldwater) R.; m. Owen Dean Long, Mar. 22, 1986; children: Maxwell A., Kyle I. BFA, SUNY, Buffalo, 1972, MFA, 1978. Cert. art tchr., N.Y. Art. tchr. clubhouse Hunter Coll. (campus schs.), N.Y.C., 1988-92; art tchr. Garfield Temple After Sch. Ctr., N.Y.C., 1992—; adj. prof. Parsons Sch. of Design, N.Y.C., 1990—, New Sch. for Social Rsch., N.Y.C., 1988—; founder Hard Press Printing/ABR Photographic, Buffalo, 1978—, N.Y.C., 1990—; ind. curator N.Y. State Coun. on Arts, 1980, 95-96; art tchr. Hunter Summer Program, N.Y.C., 1990-93; resident artist Va. Ctr. for Creative Arts, 1996. One-woman show, 1996. Democrat. Jewish. Home: 385 Douglass St # 1B Brooklyn NY 11217

ROSEN, BETH DEE, travel agency executive; b. N.Y.C., June 27, 1945. BA, Queens Coll., 1967, MA, 1970; cert. adminstrn. and supervision, CUNY, 1982. Master cruise counselor. Tchr. N.Y.C. Bd. Edn., 1967—; lectr. City U. N.Y., 1971-73; pres. Uniglobe Rainbow Travel Inc., Middletown, N.J., 1982-94; dir. Uniglobe Rainbow Travel Sch., 1983-87; travel counselor Excel Travel, Middletown, N.J., 1994—; mem. reader adv. panel Conde Nast Traveler, 1991, mem. travel agt. adv. panel, 1996—. Columnist "The Courier" newspaper, Middletown, N.J. Office: Excel Travel Ventura Plaza 1275 Highway 35 Middletown NJ 07748

ROSEN, CAROL MENDES, artist; b. N.Y.C., Jan. 15, 1933; d. Bram de Sola and Mildred (Bertuch) Mendes; m. Elliot A. Rosen, June 30, 1957. BA, Hunter Coll., 1954; MA, CUNY, 1962. Tchr. art West Orange (N.J.) Pub. Schs., 1959-85; co-curator exhibit Printmaking Coun. N.J., Somerville, 1981; exhibit curator 14 Sculptors Gallery, N.Y.C, 1988, Collection: Nat. Collection of Fine Arts, Smithsonian Instn., Newark Mus., N.J. State Mus., Bristol-Myers Squibb, AT&T, Noyes Mus. Contbr. articles to arts mags. Fellow N.J. State Coun. on Arts, 1980, 83; recipient Hudson River Mus. award, Yonkers, 1983. Jewish. Home: 10 Beavers Rd Califon NJ 07830-3433

ROSEN, CAROLE, cable television executive. BS, Russell Sage Coll., 1966; MS, SUNY, Bklyn., 1969. Tchr. N.Y.C. Pub. Schs.; v.p. family programming HBO, N.Y.C. Originator, exec. prodr.: (animated series) Happily Ever After: Fairy Tales for Every Child, Babar, Tintin, Cirque du Soleil (Emmy award), Lifestories: Families in Crisis (Emmy award, ACE award), Shakespeare: The Animated Tales (Emmy award), Going, Going, Gone: Animals in Danger (Emmy award Outstanding Children's Spl.). Office: HBO Time Warner Entertainment 1100 6th Ave New York NY 10036

ROSEN, JUDITH FAY FRIEDMAN, religious organization administrator, historian; b. Cin., Jan. 30, 1952; d. Gerald Manfred and Sue (Tyler-Theilheimer) Friedman; m. Stuart Morris Rosen, Feb. 16, 1975; children: David Ephraim, Daniel Michael, Jeremy Dale. BA, Stern Coll. Women, 1973; MA, Yeshiva U., 1975; PhD, NYU, 1992. Spl. projects coord. YIVO Inst. Jewish Studies, N.Y.C., 1973-75; rsch. cons. Displaycrafts for Mus. Diaspora, Tel Aviv, Israel, 1974-76, 76-78; program dir. United Synagogue, N.Y.C., 1985; interviewer Survivors of the Shoa Found., 1994—; spl. corr. L.I. Jewish World, Queens, N.Y., 1995—; pres. Ctrl. Queens Young Women's and Young Men's Hebrew Assn., 1989-96, chair bd., 1996—; mem. adv. bd. Mid-East Forum and Mid.-East Quarterly, N.Y.C., 1994—; mem. YIVO Inst. Advanced Jewish Studies, N.Y.C., 1975—; asst. prof. Bklyn. Coll./CUNY, 1996—. Bd. dirs. United Jewish Appeal Domestic Steering Com., 1991-94, Fedn. Domestic Assembly, 1988-94; mem. Jewish Agy. for Israel Com., 1994—, Queens Regional Planning Commn., 1990—; exec. bd. Queens Cmty. Bd. #6, 1993—; bd. dirs. Jewish Cmty. Rels. Coun., N.Y.C., 1995—, Queens Jewish Cmty. Coun., 1995—; exec. bd. Robert F. Kennedy Dem. Assn., Queens, 1992—; bd.dirs. Ctrl. Queens Hist. Soc., 1994—. Scholar-in-residence March of the Living, Poland and Israel, 1994, del. scholar Am. Zionist Movement, Ft. Lauderdale, Fla., 1995; rsch. fellow CUNY Grad. Sch., N.Y.C., 1994—; recipient Anne Frank award Jewish Cmty. Rels. Coun., 1989. Mem. Jewish Cmty. Ctr. Assn. (assoc.), Na'amat U.S.A. (bd. dirs. 1983—), Assn. Jewish Studies. Home: 43 Whitson St Forest Hills NY 11375

ROSEN, LORI, public relations executive; b. Phila., Dec. 9, 1955. BA in Comm., George Washington U., 1978. Acct. exec. John Adams Assocs., 1981-83; pres. Rosen Group, 1984—. Office: Rosen Group 200 Park Ave S # 1218 New York NY 10003

ROSEN, RHODA, obstetrician and gynecologist; b. Trenton, N.J., Jan. 17, 1933; d. Max and Gussie (Thierman) R.; m. Seymour Kanter, Aug. 19, 1956; children: Cynthia, Gregg, Larry, Brad. BA, U. Pa., 1954, MD, 1958. Diplomate Am. Bd. Obstetrics and Gynecology. Intern Albert Einstein Phila. Med. Ctr., 1958-59, resident, 1959-62; clin. prof. ob-gyn. Temple U. Med. Sch., Phila.; assoc. staff gyn. exec. com. Albert Einstein Med. Ctr., Phila.; attending physician Rolling Hill Hosp., Elkins Park, Pa.; pvt. practice obs/gyn Phila., 1962—; chmn. gynpathology com. Albert Einstein Med. Ctr., Phila. Bd. dirs. Joseph J. Peters Inst. Fellow ACOG, ACS; mem. AMA, Pa. Med. Soc., Phila. Colposcopy Soc. (past pres.), Ex-Residents Assn. (past pres. Albert Einstein Med. Ctr.), Philadelphia County Med. Soc. (com.), Phila. Bar Assn. (com.). Jewish. Home: 1011 Valley Rd Elkins Park PA 19027-3032

ROSEN, RITA BEATRICE, video producer, actress; b. Pitts., Jan. 14, 1926; d. Max and Anne (Ruben) Pochapin; m. Philip Rosen; children: Phyllis Rosen Raskin, Wendy Rosen Landes, Michael Edward. Student, Columbia U. creator Theater for a Cause, 1950s; tchr. acting class Temple Israel New Rochelle, 1957, creator, narrator dance drama, 1969; invited narrator Dance Coun. Westchester, 1959;. Prodr., creator: (video) The New Beginning, 1994 (3 Gold, Bronze, Crystal awards 1995); creator, narrator: (videos) The World Within, 1983, On the Threshold, 1986 (Gold award 1986), The Need, the Work & the Deed, 1988, Energy Is Life, 1989, The Greatest Contribution, The Gift of Healing, 1990, Born of Need, 1991, We Care, 1993. Bd. dirs. World Union for Progressive Judaism, 1996, Union of Am. Hebrew Congregations, 1993-96, mem. worship com. 1972; founder, hon. pres. women's divsn. Albert Einstein Coll. Medicine, 1981-84, v.p. N.Y. chpt., chmn. Spirit Achievement Luncheon, 1975. Recipient Creative Talent award Temple Israel New Rochelle, 1977, Spl. award, 1980, Or-Ami—Light Unto the People award, 1979, Harriet Jonas award Am. Jewish Com., Anti-Defamation League award, 1989, Spl. Cantorial citation Sacred Bridge award for outstanding contbn. to arts in Judaisim, Am. Conf. of Cantors, 1990, Family of Yr. award Family Svc. Westchester, 1991. Fellow Benjamin Cardozo Sch. of Law; mem. Prime Min.'s Club of United Jewish Appeal (So. bd. 1965-71, chair Save a Russian, Svc. award, Silver Jubilee Humanitarian award). Office: Image Comms Inc 550 Mamaroneck Ave Harrison NY 10528

ROSEN, RUTH CHIER, retired editor-in-chief; b. Mpls., June 13, 1925; d. Maurice Charles and Esther (Bentson) C.; m. Richard Rosen (dec.); children: Richard A., Roger C. BA, Smith Coll., 1947. V.p., editor-in-chief Rosen Press, N.Y.C., 1950-90, ret., 1990. Author 40 cookbooks. Home: 308 Eagle Dr Jupiter FL 33477

ROSENBACH, KATHRYN BETH KAYNE-SERIO, pianist, educator, choral director, organist, composer; b. Buffalo, Aug. 14, 1957; d. Daniel Walter and Carole Ann (Rosenbach) Kayne; m. Michael Thomas Serio, June 25, 1982 (div. May 30, 1991); 1 child, Anthony Michael. BFA magna cum laude, SUNY, Buffalo, 1979, MFA, 1981; postgrad., Eastman Sch. Music, 1982-86; artist diploma, Accademia Musicale di Chigiana, Siena, Italy, 1984. Choir dir., organist Stephen's-Bethlehem United Ch. Christ, Williamsville, N.Y., 1978-80, North Presbyn. Ch., North Tonawanda, N.Y., 1981-83, Leroy (N.Y.) Bapt. Ch., 1983-85; lectr. piano Genesee C.C., Batavia, N.Y., 1985-86; choir dir., organist 1st Congl. Ch., Stoughton, Mass., 1988-95; Park Ave. Congl. Ch., Arlington, Mass., 1994-95; lectr. piano Genesee C.C., Batavia, N.Y., 1985-86; organist Temple Beth Shalom, Peabody, Mass., 1995—; music dir. Islington (Mass.) Cmty. Ch., 1996—; instr. piano Eastman Sch. of Music, SUNY, Buffalo, 1978-80, Cmty. Music Sch., Buffalo, 1981-83; music dir. Cmty. Choir Sharon, Mass., 1988-90; mem. faculty Longy Sch. Music, Cambridge, Mass., 1989-91; adj. instr. Nazareth Coll., Rochester, N.Y., 1984; artistic coord. Composers in Red Sneakers, 1995—; mem. Janus Ensemble, 1995—, Baldwin-Rosenbach Duo, 1995—. Composer: (choral works) Gloria Alleluia, 1978, I Wonder What Child This Is, 1990, Christ the Lord Is Risen, 1991, Alleluia, Jesus Christ Is Coming, 1991, A Hymn of Celebration, 1993, Christmas Cameos, 1995; artistic coord.: Composers in Red Sneakers. Eastman Sch. Music grantee, Italy, 1984. Mem. Am. Guild of Organists, Coll. Music Soc.

ROSENBAUM, BELLE SARA, personal property appraiser, interior designer, educator, museum director; b. N.Y.C., Apr. 1, 1923; d. Harry and Hinda (Sits) Heimowitz; m. Jacob H. Rosenbaum, Mar. 12, 1939; children: Linda Zelinger, Simmi Brodie, Martin, Arlene Levene. Cert. N.Y. Sch. Interior Design, 1945. Sr. mem. Am. Soc. Appraisers, Washington, 1979—; tchr./Judaica, Yeshiva U., 1984—; dir. Mus. Contemporary Judaica; pres. Jarvis Designs, Inc., Union City, N.J., 1955-75, Design Assocs., BLS, Monsey, N.Y., 1970-78; v.p. Lord & Lady Inc., Union City, 1955-70, Cardio-Bionic Scanning, Inc., Spring Valley, N.Y., 1975-78; v.p., treas. Rapitech Sys., Inc., 1985; exec. bd. State of Israel Bonds Orgn., 1992—. Author of short stories, 1947-48, Chronicle of Jewish Traditions, 1992, Upon Thy Doorposts, 1996; contbr. articles on interior design to profl. jours. Bd. dirs. Migdal Ohr Schs., 1971—; chmn. bd. of artifacts Rockland Holocaust Ctr., 1991—; bd. trustees Rockland Ctr. Holocaust Studies, 1994. Named Woman of Valor State of Israel, 1960; ambulance driver North Hudson chpt. ARC during WWII. Mem. Internat. Soc. Artists (founding mem.), Yeshiva of North Jersey Women (hon. pres. 1955); bd. govs. Yeshiva U. mus.; mem. N.Y. State Coun. of Judaic Arts and Letters; mem. editl. bd. Light Found. Clubs: Amit Women (pres. 1955-57) (N.J.), AMI Women (treas. 1948-78), Cmty. Synogogue-Monsey (v.p. 1982—). Avocations: collector of art, antiques, Judaica, artist, gardening, communal and charity work.

ROSENBAUM, LISA LENCHNER, biochemist; b. Detroit, Dec. 31, 1955; d. Barbara Ellen (Krause) Lenchner; m. Richard Allen Rosenbaum, July 27, 1984; 1 child, Eric Marc. BS in Biochemistry, Mich. State U., 1978; MBA, U. Mich., 1992. Grad. asst. U. S.C., Columbia, 1978-79; rsch. assoc. Wayne State U., Detroit, 1979-80; project scientist biomed. sci. dept. GMC, Warren, Mich., 1980-93; decision risk analyst GMC Portfolio Planning, Warren, Mich., 1993—; chemistry tutor Berkley (Mich.) Pub. Schs., 1979-93. Coord. ARC, Warren, 1988—, United Way, Warren, 1990. Mem. Am. Chem. Soc., N.Y. Acad. Sci. Home: 4640 Pickering Bloomfield Village MI 48301 Office: GM Rsch & Devel 30500 Mound Rd Warren MI 48090-9055

ROSENBAUM, MARY HELÉNE POTTKER, writer, editor; b. Highland Park, Ill., Mar. 13, 1944; d. Ralph Eugene and Olga Norma (Somenzi) Pottker; m. Stanley Ned Rosenbaum, Sept. 2, 1963; children: Sarah Catherine, William David, Ephraim Samuel. Student, Bard Coll., 1962-63; BA magna cum laude, Dickinson Coll., 1975. Writing dir. Black Bear Prodns., Inc., Carlisle, Pa., Boston, Ky., 1989—; co-advisor Dickinson Coll. Hillel, Carlisle, 1991-92; exec. dir. Congregation Beth Tikvah, 1990-92; coord Interfaith Family Resources, 1995—. Co-author: Celebrating Our Differences: Living Two Faiths in One Marriage, 1994; columnist Interfaith Newsletter, 1995; mem. pubs. com. Cumberland County Hist. Soc.; editl. cons. Writers Cramp Inc., 1989—; assoc. editor Dovetail: A Jour. by and for Jewish Christian Families, 1996—; contbr. articles to profl. jours. Mem. Cable Commn., Carlisle, 1991-92. Recipient Jean Gray Allen Non-fiction award Harrisburg Manuscript Club, 1978, Founder's Fiction award, 1978. Mem. League Women Voters Carlisle Area (pubs. coord. 1990-92, pres. 1988-90). Democrat. Roman Catholic. Home: 431 S College St Carlisle PA 17013 Office: Black Bear Prodns Inc PO Box 1110 Carlisle PA 17013-6110

ROSENBERG, ALISON P., public policy official; b. Miami, Fla., Sept. 5, 1945; d. Mortimer I. and Gail (Sklar) Podell; m. Jeffrey Alan Rosenberg, May 4, 1969; 1 child, Robert Aaron. BS in Econs., Smith Coll., 1967. Mng. officer Citibank, N.Y.C., 1967-69; legis. aide Senator Charles Percy, Washington, 1969-80; profl. staff mem. Senate Fgn. Rels. Com., Washington, 1981-85; assoc. asst. adminstr. Agy. for Internat. Devel., Washington, 1985-87; dir. African affairs Nat. Security Coun., Washington, 1987-88; dep. asst. sec. for Africa State Dept., Washington, 1988-92; asst. admnstr. for Africa Agy. for Internat. Devel., Washington, 1992-93; regional co-financing advisor for Africa The World Bank, Washington, 1993—.

ROSENBERG, ELLEN Y., religious association administrator; married; 2 children. Student, Goucher Coll.; BS in Edn., Mills Coll.; postgrad., Columbia U. Assoc. dean for acad. affairs Marymount Manhattan Coll., N.Y.C.; assoc. dir. Nat. Fedn. Temple Sisterhoods; exec. dir. Women of Reform Judaism. V.p. Riverdale Temple, pres. Temple Sisterhood. Office: 838 Fifth Ave New York NY 10021

ROSENBERG, JILL, realtor, civic leader; b. Shreveport, La., Feb. 17, 1940; d. Morris H. and Sallye (Abramson) Schuster; m. Lewis Rosenberg, Dec. 23, 1962; children: Craig, Paige. BA in Philosophy, Tulane U., 1961, MSW, 1965; grad., Realtor Inst., 1994. Cert. residential specialist Residential Sales Coun.; grad. Realtor Inst. Social worker La. Dept. Pub. Welfare, 1961-62, 63-64; genetics counselor Sinai Hosp., Balt., 1967-69; ptnr. Parties Extraordinaire, cons., 1973-77; realtor assoc. Robert Weil Assocs., Long Beach, Calif., 1982—. Pres. western region Brandeis U. Nat. Women's Com., 1972-73; bd. dirs. Long Beach Symphony Assn., 1984-85; v.p. Jewish Cmty. Fedn. Long Beach and West Orange County, 1983-86, bd. dirs., 1982-86; pres. Long Beach Cancer League, 1987-88, exec. bd. dirs., 1984—; pres. Long Beach Jewish Cmty. Sr. Housing Corp., 1989-91; v.p. fundraising S.E. unit Long Beach Harbor chpt. Am. Cancer Soc., 1989-90; bd. dirs. Westerly Sch. Assoc., 1991—; bd. trustees St. Mary Med. Ctr. Found., 1991—; fund chair St. Mary Med. Ctr., 1992-94; pres. nat. conf. NCCJ, 1994-96; pres. Leadership Long Beach, 1994-95; Phoenix Long Beach Mus. Art, 1995—, Rotary Club of Long Beach, 1996—, numerous others. Recipient Young Leadership award Jewish Community Fedn. Long Beach and West Orange County, 1981, Jerusalem award State of Israel, 1989, Hannah G. Solomon award Nat. Coun. Jewish Women, 1992, Alumnus of Yr. award Leadership Long Beach, 1995; scholar La. Dept. Pub. Welfare, 1962, NIMH, 1964. Office: Robert Weil Assocs 5220 E Los Altos Plz Long Beach CA 90815-4251

ROSENBERG, JUDITH LYNNE, middle school educator; b. Bklyn., Nov. 1, 1944; d. Benjamin and Rose (Delbaum) Jackler; m. Joel Barry Rosenberg, Aug. 26, 1965; children: Jeffrey Alan, Marc David. BA in Edn., Queens Coll., Flushing, N.Y., 1966, MS in Edn., 1972. Lic. advanced profl. elem. and mid. sch. math., Md., elem. edn., N.Y. Elem. tchr. N.Y.C. and Cranston, R.I., 1966-68; tchr. math. Earl B. Wood Mid. Sch., Rockville, Md., 1981-82, Walt Whitman High Sch., Bethesda, Md., 1982-83, Robert Frost Mid. Sch., Rockville, Md., 1983-89; math. and interdiscipinary resource Julius West Mid. Sch., Rockville, 1989—. Mem. NEA, Nat. Coun. Tchrs. Math., Md. State Tchrs. Assn. Home: 16 Flameleaf Ct Gaithersburg MD 20878-5216 Office: Julius West Mid Sch Great Falls Rd Rockville MD 20850

ROSENBERG, JUDITH META, brokerage executive; b. N.Y.C., Sept. 17, 1964. BS in Fin., Lehigh U., 1986. With Morgan Stanley, N.Y.C., 1986;

broker Bear Stearns & Co., N.Y.C., 1987, v.p., 1988, assoc. dir., 1989; mng. dir., 1990. Bd. dirs. Henry Kaufmann Campgrounds. Mem. N.Y. Jr. League, Lehigh Alumni Assn., Women's Nat. Rep. Club. Republican. Office: 245 Park Ave Fl 9 New York NY 10167-0002

ROSENBERG, LESLIE KAREN, media director; b. Camden, N.J., Mar. 3, 1949; d. Lorimer and Doris Selma (Kohn) R. BS in Radio, TV, Film, U. Tex., 1971. Continuity dir. WEAT-TV/AM/FM, West Palm Beach, Fla., 1971-74; media buyer Wm. F. Haselmire Advt., West Palm Beach, 1974-75, media dir., 1982-85; program and pub. svc. dir. WTBS-TV, Atlanta, 1975-78; nat. traffic coord. WXIA-TV, Atlanta, 1978-80; sr. sales asst. CBS Radio Spot Sales, Atlanta, 1980-82; acct. exec. WRMF-FM, West Palm Beach, 1985; media dir., acct. exec. Merlin Masters & Nomes Advt., West Palm Beach, 1985-88; pres., media dir. Media Magic Plus, Inc., West Palm Beach, 1988—; advt. coord. Hearx, Inc., West Palm Beach, 1996—; communications adv. bd. Palm Beach Jr. Coll., Lake Worth, 1972-74; advtsg. coord. HEARX Ltd., 1996—. Talent, author various radio commercials (Addy award 1973, 74), talent various TV commercials (Addy award 1974). Bd. dirs. Lake Worth (Fla.) Playhouse, 1989-92, program co-chmn., 1989-91; producer Lake Worth Playhouse Internat. Cultural Exch. for 1994 trip to Eng., mem. com. for 97 trip to Eng., 1994-97. Mem. Advt. Club of the Palm Beaches (bd. dirs. 1983-85), NAFE, Nat. Acad. Arts & Sciences, Fireside Theatre, U.S. Racquetball Assn. (dir. tournament control 1976-80). Office: Media Magic Plus Inc PO Box 19962 West Palm Beach FL 33416-9962

ROSENBERG, MARILYN ROSENTHAL, artist, visual poet; b. Phila., Oct. 11, 1934; m. Robert Rosenberg, June 12, 1955; 2 children. B in Profl. Studies in Studio Arts, SUNY, Empire State Coll., 1978; MA in Liberal Studies, NYU, 1993. Author, pub., creator unique and edit. poetry/painting books; solo exhbns. include Irvine Gallery, State U. Calif., Irvine, 1981, The Sandor Tezsler Libr. Gallery, Spartanburg, S.C., 1983, U. Wis., River Falls, 1984, 361 Degrees Gallery, Greenfield, Mass., 1987; two-person exhbns. include SUNY Purchase Libr., 1982, The Hudson River Mus., Yonkers, N.Y., 1984, Women's Studio Workshop Inskirts Gallery, Rosendale, N.Y., 1986, Brownson Art Gallery, Purchase, N.Y., 1988, (with collaborator) Westchester County Gallery, White Plains, N.Y., 1989, Marymount Coll., Tarrytown, N.Y., 1993; group exhbns. include Long Beach (Calif.) Mus. Art, 1977, Kathryn Markel Fine Arts Gallery, N.Y.C., 1978, Pratt Graphic Ctr. Gallery, N.Y.C., 1978, Polytechnic State U. Gallery, San Luis Obispo, Calif., 1979, Phila. Art Alliance, Glassboro State Coll., Pa., 1979, Ridotte del Treatro Comunale, Italy, 1980, SUNY Purchase Gallery, 1982, Galerie Caroline Corre, Paris, 1983, Thorpe Intermedia Gallery, Sparkhill, N.J., 1983, U. Rochester Gallery, Rochester, N.Y., 1984, 14 Sculptors Gallery, N.Y.C., 1984, Georgetown U., Washington, 1984, Franklin Furnace, N.Y.C., 1986, Douglas & Cook Colleges, New Brunswick, N.J., 1985, City Without Walls, Newark, 1986, Galleri T.V., Malmo, Sweden, Post Machina Group and Am. Consulate, Bologna, Italy, 1986, Technical U. of Nova Scotia, Halifax, 1986, Museu Municipal, Figuira Da Foz, Portugal, 1987, King Stephen Mus., Szekesfehrvar, Hungary, 1987, Allen Meml. Art Mus., Oberlin, Ohio, 1987, Cultural Centre of San Paulo, Brazil, 1988, Centro Cultural de la Caja de Ahorros de Valencia, Spain, 1988, Cooper Union Art, N.Y.C., 1989, San Francisco Craft and Folk Art Mus., 1990, Alternatives Gallery, San Luis Obispo, Calif., 1990-91, San Antonio Art Inst., 1991, Sazama Gallery, Chgo., 1992, SUNY Oneonta, 1992, Ralston Fine Arts, Johnson City, Tenn., 1993, Va. Ctr. for Craft Arts, 1993, Libr. Can., 1993, Muée de la Post, Paris, 1993, Pratt Inst., N.Y.C., 1993, Musée de la Poste, Paris, 1993-94, Papertrail, Ottawa, Can., 1993-94, Nexus Found. for Arts, Phila., 1994, Va. Ctr. for Craft Arts, Richmond, 1994, Ormond Meml. Art Mus., Fla., 1994, Libr. Nat. Mus. Women, Washington, 1994-95, Spirit Sq. Ctr. Arts, Charlotte, N.C., 1995, Ellipse Arts Ctr., Arlington, Va., 1995, Monterserrat Coll. Art Gallery, Beverly, Mass., 1995, Yale U. Art Gallery Sculpture Hall, New Haven, Conn., 1995, Harper Collins, N.Y.C., 1995, Brookfield Craft Ctr., Conn., 1995, Muscatine Art Ctr., Iowa, 1995, Sangre de Cristo Art Ctr., Pueblo, Colo., 1995, Lake George (N.Y.) Art Project, 1995, Mus. Nebr. Arts, U. Nebr., Kearney, 1995, The Battery, Hastings-on-Hudson, N.Y., 1996, Ctr. for Book Arts, N.Y.C., 1996; public collections and archives include Art Gallery New South Wales, Sydney, Australia, Artpool Art Rsch. Ctr., Budapest, Hungary, Bibliotheque Nationale, Paris, Canadian Postal Mus. Archive, Ottawa, Electrografia Museo Internacional, La Mancha, Cuenca, Spain, Fogg Art Mus., Cambridge, Mass., Mus. of Modern Art Libr., N.Y.C., The Ruth and Marvin Sackner Archive, Miami Beach, Fla., Tate Gallery Libr., London, Yale U. Libr., New Haven, Ct., Canberra Sch. Art Gallery, Australia, Cleve. Inst. Art Libr., Harvard U. Fogg Mus. and Houghton Libr., Cambridge, Mass., Rochester (N.Y.) Inst. Tech., Sch. Art Inst. Chgo. Libr., Amherst (Mass.) Coll. Libr., Atlanta Coll. of Art Libr., Brown U. Libr., Cleve. Inst. of Art Libr., Dartmouth Coll., Sherman Art Libr., Georgetown U. Library, The N.Y. Pub. Libr., Rhode Island Sch. of Design, Stanford U. Libr., Temple U. Library, Phila., U. Calif. at Davis, Santa Barbara Librs., U. Chgo. Libr., U. Utah, Mariott Libr., U. Va. Libr., Va. Commonwealth U. Libr., Wellesley Coll. Libr., Libr. Mus. Fine Arts, Boston, Sch. Mus. of Fine Art Libr., Boston, Nat. Art Libr., Victoria and Albert Mus., London; works included in various pubs. and periodicals. Studio: 67 Lakeview Ave West Peekskill NY 10566-6415

ROSENBERG, SARAH ZACHER, institute arts administration executive, humanities administration consultant; b. Kelem, Lithuania, Jan. 10, 1931; came to U.S., 1938; d. David Meir Zacher and Rachel Korbman; m. Norman J. Rosenberg, Dec. 30, 1950; children: Daniel, Alyssa. BA in History, U. Nebr., 1970, MA in Am. History, 1973. Rsch. historian U. Mid-Am., Lincoln, Nebr., 1974-78, program developer dept. humanities, 1978-79, asst. dir. div. acad. planning, 1980-81, dir. program devel., 1981-82; exec. dir. Nebr. Humanities Coun., Lincoln, 1982-87, Nebr. Found. for Humanities, Lincoln, 1984-87; exec. dir. Am. Inst. for Conservation Hist. and Artistic Works, Washington, 1987—, exec. dir. found., 1991—; program officer, spl. cons. mus. div. NEH, Washington, 1987, external reviewer, 1981, 89; lay participant long-range planning conf. Nebr. Bar Assn., Hastings, 1986. Co-editor: The Great Plains Experience: Readings in the History of a Region, 1978; contbr. articles to profl. jours. Action mem. Haddasah, Lincoln, 1961-87, Tifereth Israel Synagogue, 1961-87, Beth El Congregation, Bethesda, Md., 1988—; bd. dirs. Sta. KUCV, affiliate Nat. Pub. Radio, Lincoln, 1986-87, Lincoln Community Playhouse, 1986-87. NEH grantee, 1981, 86, merit awards, 1983, 87; Humanities Resource Ctr. grantee, Peter Kiewit Found., 1984. Mem. Am. Hist. Assn., Western Hist. Assn., Alpha Theta. Democrat. Home: 8102 Appalachian Ter Potomac MD 20854-4050 Office: Am Inst for Conservation 1717 K St NW Ste 301 Washington DC 20006-1501

ROSENBERG, SHELI ZYSMAN, lawyer, financial management executive; b. N.Y.C., Feb. 2, 1942; d. Stephen B. and Charlotte (Laufer) Zysman; m. Burton X. Rosenberg, Aug. 30, 1964; children: Leonard, Marcy. BA, Tufts U., 1963; JD, Northwestern U., 1966. Bar: Ill. 1966. Ptnr. Schiff, Hardin & Waite, Chgo., 1973-80; exec. v.p., gen. counsel Equity Fin. Mgmt., Chgo., 1980-90; exec. v.p., gen. counsel Equity Group Investments, Inc., Chgo., 1988-94, pres., CEO, 1994—; pres., CEO Equity Fin. and Mgmt. Co., Chgo., 1994—; prin. Rosenberg & Liebentritt, P.C., Chgo., 1995—; bd. dirs. Gt. Am. Mgmt. & Investment, Chgo., 1984—, v.p., gen. counsel, 1985-90, sec., 1983-90; bd. dirs. CFI Industries, Inc., Am. Classic Voyages Co., Revco, D.S., Inc., Jacor Comm., Inc., Anixter Internat., Inc., Capsure Holdings Corp., Eagle Industries, Inc., Falcon Bldg. Products, Inc.; bd. trustees Equity Residential Properties Trust, Manufactured Home Cmtys., Inc. Bd. dirs., pres. Chgo. Network.

ROSENBERRY, CATHY LYNN, nursing administrator; b. Kewanee, Ill., Aug. 26, 1956; d. Irvin Eugene and Linda Lou (Lorenson) Flint; m. John Everett Rosenberry, Feb. 25, 1978; children: Rebecca Lynn, Elizabeth Marie. Diploma, Black Hawk Coll., 1975, ADN, 1978. RN, Ill. Staff nurse Kewanee (Ill.) Pub. Hosp., 1975-79; charge nurse, shift supr. Prairie View Home, Princeton, Ill., 1979-82, insvc. edn., 1982-83, asst. dir. nursing, 1983-88; rehab. supr. Toulon (Ill.) Health Care Ctr., 1988, dir. nursing svcs., 1988-90; coord. women, infants, children Henry County Health Dept., Kewanee, 1990—, coord. maternal child health, 1992—, clin. health svcs. supr., 1995—. Recipient Outstanding Nurse Recognition award March of Dimes, 1992. Mem. Local Interagy. Coun. (com. mem. 1993—), Ill. Pub. Health Nurse Adminstrn., Henry County Children's Coun., Ill. Maternal Child Health Coalition, Phi Theta Kappa. Methodist. Office: Henry County Health Dept 4424 US Highway 34 Kewanee IL 61443-8319

ROSENBLATT, JOAN RAUP, mathematical statistician; b. N.Y.C., Apr. 15, 1926; d. Robert Bruce and Clara (Eliot) Raup; m. David Rosenblatt, June 10, 1950. AB, Barnard Coll., 1946; PhD, U. N.C., 1956. Intern Nat. Inst. Pub. Affairs, Washington, 1946-47; statis. analyst U.S. Bur. of Budget, 1947-48; rsch. asst. U. N.C., 1953-54; mathematician Nat. Inst. Standards and Tech. (formerly Nat. Bur. Standards), Washington, 1955—, asst. chief statis. engring., 1963-68, chief statis. engring. lab., 1969-78, dep. dir. Ctr. for Applied Math., 1978-88; dep. dir. Computing and Applied Math. Lab., Gaithersburg, 1988-93, dir., 1993-95; mem. com. on indsl. rels. Dept. Stats. Ohio State U.; mem. adv. com. in math. and stats. USDA Grad. Sch., 1971—; mem. Com. Applied and Theoretical Stats., Nat. Rsch. Coun., 1985-88. Mem. editorial bd. Communications in Stats., 1971-79, Jour. Soc. for Indsl. and Applied Math., 1965-75, Nat. Inst. Stds. and Tech. Jour. Rsch., 1991-93; contbr. articles to profl. jours. Chmn. Com. on Women in Sci., Joint Bd. on Sci. Edn., 1963-64. Rice fellow, 1946, Gen. Edn. Bd. fellow, 1948-50; recipient Fed. Woman's award, 1971, Gold medal Dept. Commerce, 1976, Presdl. Meritorious Exec. Rank award, 1982. Fellow AAAS (chmn. stats. sect. 1982, sec. 1987-91), Inst. Math. Stats. (coun. 1975-77), Am. Statis. Assn. (v.p. 1981-83, dir. 1979-80, Founders award 1991), Washington Acad. Scis. (achievement award math. 1965); mem. AAUW, IEEE Reliability Soc., Am. Math. Soc., Royal Statis. Soc. London, Philos. Soc. Washington, Internat. Statis. Inst., Bernouilli Soc. Probability and Math. Stats., Caucus Women Stats. (pres. 1976), Assn. Women Math., Exec. Women Govt., Phi Beta Kappa, Sigma Xi (treas. Nat. Bur. Standards chpt. 1982-84). Home: 2939 Van Ness St NW Apt 702 Washington DC 20008-4628 Office: Nat Inst Stds and Tech Rm 353 NIST North Gaithersburg MD 20899-0001

ROSENBLATT, JULIE BISTRÉ, educator; b. Bagdad, Iraq, Apr. 24, 1927; came to U.S., 1959, naturalized, 1967; A.A., Am. Jr. Coll. Beirut, 1945; B.S. in Bus. Adminstrn., U. Richmond, 1966; M.B.A., U. Del., 1972; m. N. Walter Rosenblatt, Feb. 5, 1957; children—David J., Joel S. Instr., Bagdad, 1949; acct. H. Stern's, London, 1950-52; instr., Haifa, Israel, 1953; sr. acct. Am. Nat. Engring. Co., Haifa, 1954-57; instr. Del. Tech. and Community Coll., Wilmington, 1974-87, chairperson Bus. Adminstrn. Dept., 1987—. Mem. Nat. Assn. Accts. (dir. ednl. projects, v.p. adminstrn. and fin.). Home: 2703 Landon Dr Wilmington DE 19810-2211 Office: 333 N Shipley St Wilmington DE 19801-2412

ROSENBLOOM, KAREN S., psychologist; b. Rochester, N.Y., Nov. 2, 1959; d. Richard David and Beatrice (Melter) R.; m. Keith Raymond Wilson, Nov. 14, 1993; children: Amanda Wilson, Abigail Wilson, Nathaniel Wilson, Joel Wilson. BA, Skidmore Coll., 1980; MA, Alfred U., 1983; MS in Edn., U. Rochester, 1991, PhD, 1995. Cert. sch. psychologist, N.Y. Psychologist Brockport (N.Y.) Ctrl. Schs., 1983-88, Spencerport (N.Y.) Ctrl. Schs., 1984, West Frondequoit Schs., Rochester, 1990-91; rschr. U. Rochester, 1991-94; psychologist Penfield Ctrl. Schs., Rochester, 1993—; pvt. practice Rochester, 1994—; lectr. Nazareth Coll., Rochester, 1991—. Vol. crisis telephone hotline AIDS Rochester, 1987-89; vol. Big Bros./Big Sisters, Rochester, 1990—. Recipient Friends of Children award Rochester Area Childrens Collaborative, 1995. Mem. ACA, Am. Sch. Counselors Assn., N.Y. Assn. Sch. Psychologists. Home and Office: 46 Danforth Crescent Rochester NY 14618

ROSENBLUM, MINDY FLEISCHER, pediatrician; b. Bronxville, N.Y., June 5, 1951; d. Herman and Muriel (Gold) Fleischer; m. Jay S. Rosenblum, June 22, 1971; children: Meira, Tamar, Rafi, Rachel. BA, Yeshiva U., 1972; MD, Albert Einstein Coll., 1976. Diplomate Am. Bd. Pediatrics, Am. Bd. Pediatrics Endocrinology. Intern in pediatrics Bronx Mcpl. Hosp. Ctr., 1976-77, residency in pediatrics, 1977-79; fellow in pediatric endocrinology Children's Hosp. of Phila., 1981; asst. prof. U. Pa., Phila., 1981—; attending physician Bryn Mawr (Pa.) Hosp., 1981—, Lankenau Hosp., Wynnewood, Pa., 1983—. Fellow Am. Acad. Pediatrics; mem. Phila. Pediatrics Soc. (bd. dirs. 1988-92), Am. Diabetes Assn., Lawson Wilkins Pediatric Endocrine Soc.

ROSENBLUTH, LUCILLE MAXINE, health research facility administrator; b. N.Y.C., Sept. 18, 1931; d. David and Rhea (Farber) Moses; m. Sol Rosenbluth, June 8, 1952; children: Shelly Kratzer, Martin. BA in Polit. Sci., Bklyn. Coll., 1952; M in Pub. Adminstrn., NYU, 1953. Intern N.Y. State Adminstrn. Internship Program, 1953-54; rsch. aide N.Y. State Workmen's Compensation Bd., 1954-55; personnel asst. Dept. Personnel, N.Y.C., 1955-57; lectr. Bklyn. Coll., 1958, 59; rsch. asst. Temporary State Commn. on Operation N.Y.C. Govt., 1959-60; cons. Dept. Health, N.Y.C., 1960-61; rschr. study of profl., tech. and managerial manpower needs City of N.Y. Brookings Instn., 1961-63; cons. personnel utilization Dept. Health, N.Y.C., 1963-64; chief rschr. Med. and Health Rsch. Assn. N.Y.C., Inc., 1964-67, project coord., work com. chmn. systems study of sch. health records, 1967-70, project dir., policy com. chmn. N.Y.C. infant day care study, 1970-75, exec. v.p., 1975-86, pres., 1986—; cons. Commonwealth of Mass., 1982; mem. adj. faculty grad. sch. program in pub. health, dept. environ. and community medicine Rutger Med. Sch. U. Medicine and Dentistry N.J., 1984-86; mem. maternal and child health steering com. Sch. Pub. Health Columbia U., 1983—, lectr. pub. health, 1986—. Author: (with others) Caring Prescriptions: Comprehensive Health Care Strategies for Young Children in Poverty, 1993; contbr. articles to profl. jours. Fellow N.Y. Acad. Medicine (assoc., exec. com. on pub. health); mem. APHA (chair breastfeeding com. 1985, 86, 87), Family Planning Couns. Am. (chair grantee adv. com. Region II 1987, 88), N.Y. State Family Planning Advocates, N.Y. State Pub. Health Assn. (co-chmn. legis. com., bd. dirs. 1986—), Pub. Health Assn. N.Y.C., Soc. Rsch. Adminstrs., Health Care Execs. Forum (pres. 1988, 89), Hermann Biggs Soc., Women's City Club N.Y. (chair com. pub. health 1982-84). Office: Medical Health Rsch Assn of NYC 40 Worth St # 720 New York NY 10013-2904*

ROSENFELD, JUDITH LYNN, burn nurse; b. Poughkeepsie, N.Y., Aug. 4, 1964; d. Robert and Ida (Singer) R.; 1 child, Neil. AAS, Dutchess C.C., Poughkeepsie, N.Y., 1984; BSN, Western Conn. State U., Danbury, 1986; MSN, Mercy Coll., 1994. Cert. critical care nurse. Camp nurse Camp Poyntelle, Pa., 1985; staff nurse VA Med. Ctr., Castle Point, N.Y., 1986-87; emergency rm. nurse St. Francis Hosp., Poughkeepsie, N.Y., 1987-88; staff nurse Westchester County Med. Ctr., Valhalla, N.Y., 1988-89, burn nurse, 1989—; clin. instr. Westchester C.C., Valhalla, 1992; rsch. nurse N.Y. Med. Coll., Valhalla, 1993—; cardiac rehab. nurse Heart Health Cardiac Rehab., Poughkeepsie, 1994—; clin. instr. Dutchess C.C., Poughkeepsie, 1995—; human lyme disease vaccine study panel, Med. Coll., Valhalla; early lyme disease treatment study and CDC lyme disease diagnostic study panel NIH. Mem. AACN, ANA, N.Y. Nurses Assn., Sigma Theta Tau. Democrat. Jewish. Home: 19 Meadow Ln Poughkeepsie NY 12603-3253

ROSENFELD, NAOMI EVE, corporate communications specialist; b. Jerusalem, Oct. 14, 1944; d. Franz and Marianne Renate (Imberg) Winkler; m. Steven B. Rosenfeld, Aug. 21, 1965; children: Kathryn Anne, Elizabeth Jane. BA, Sarah Lawrence Coll., 1966. V.p. Drexel Burnham Lambert, N.Y., 1981-86, first v.p., 1986-90; ptnr. Morgen-Walke Assocs., N.Y., 1990—. Mem. Met. Opera Club. Office: Morgen Walke Assoc Inc 380 Lexington Ave New York NY 10168-0002*

ROSENFELD, SARENA MARGARET, artist; b. Elmira, N.Y., Oct. 17, 1940; d. Thomas Edward and Rosalie Ereny (Fedor) Rooney; m. Robert Steven Bach, June 1958 (div. 1963); children: Robert Steven, Daniel Thomas; m. Samson Rosenfeld III, June 5, 1976. Student, Otis/Parson Art Inst., L.A., 1994—, Idyllwild Sch. Music and Arts, 1994—. One-woman shows and group exhbns. include Robert Dana Gallery, San Francisco, Gordon Gallery, Santa Monica, Calif., Hespe Gallery, San Francisco, Gallery 444, San Francisco, Art Expressions, San Diego, Ergane Gallery, N.Y.C., Nat. Mus. of Women in the Arts, Washington, also in L.A., La Jolla, Calif., Aspen, Colo., New Orleans, Soho, N.Y.C., Santa Barbara, Calif., Tanglewood, Mass., Honolulu, Johannesburg, South Africa, La Sierra U., Riverside, Calif. Mem., vol., animal handler Wildlife Waysta., Angeles Nat. Forest, Calif. Recipient Best of Show award Glendale Regional Arts Coun., 1984-85, 1st pl. awards Santa Monica Art Festival, 1982, 83, 84, 85, 86, Sweepstakes award and 1st pl., 1986, Purchase prize awards L.A. West C. of C., 1986-87, Tapestry in Talent Invitational San Jose Arts Coun., 1986, 1st pl. awards Studio City and Century City Arts Couns., 1976-84. Mem. Nat. Mus. of Women in the Arts. Republican. Home: 6570 Kelvin Ave Canoga Park CA 91306-4021

ROSENHECK, BARA SUSAN, consulting company executive, consultant; b. N.Y.C., Nov. 27, 1940; d. Soloman and Fran (Bernstein) Ostrov; m. Arnold Herman Rosenheck, Aug. 11, 1962; children: Robert Steven, Spencer Scott. BA, C.W. Post Coll., L.I. U., N.Y., 1962; MA, Fairleigh Dickinson U., Rutherford, N.J., 1968. Cert. tchr. N.J., REACH (Respecting Ethnic & Cultural Heritage) trainer, trainer Anti Defemation League. Tchr. Wallington (N.J.) H.S., 1962-64; tng. dir. Consortium for Ednl. Equity, Rutgers U., New Brunswick, N.J., 1978-88; pers. cons. Craig Personnel, Saddle Brook, N.J., 1988-90; pres. Bara Rosenheck Cons., Skillman, N.J., 1990—; mem. steering and fundraising coms. Nat. Coalition for Sex Equity in Edn. (NCSEE), Clinton, N.J., 1994; mem. steering com. Women's Wellness Ctr., Robert Wood Johnson U. Hosp., New Brunswick, N.J., 1995—. Vol. fundraising/fin. com. Starfish Found. for Children With AIDS, Inc., Woodbridge, N.J., 1996; mem. N.J. gender equity adv. com. N.J. Dept. Edn.; mem. adv. coun. Internat. Women's Day. Mem. Northeast Coalition of Ednl. Leaders (NECEL), Middlesex County Reg. C. of C. Office: Bara Rosenheck Cons 11 Norfolk Way Skillman NJ 08558

ROSENHEIM, CHRISTINE LABODA, health management consultant; b. N.Y.C., June 22, 1952; d. Henry Oliver and Olga Caroline (Chupurdy) Laboda; m. Thomas Rosenheim, May 19, 1973; children: Brad Erik, Randy Thomas. AA in Nursing, Queensborough C.C., 1972; BS in Health Care Adminstrn., Stockton State Coll., 1976. RN, N.J., N.Y.; cert. med. case mgr., case mgr. Staff nurse N. Shore Med. Ctr., Manhassett, N.Y., 1972-73, W. Jersey Hosp., Voorhees, N.J., 1973-79; nurse Everett R. Curran Jr. M.D., Cherry Hill, N.J., 1979-83, Valley Rehab. Co., Hammonton, N.J., 1983-85; nurse auditor Consolidated Rehab. Co., Haddon Heights, N.J., 1986-87; pres. Medi Fax Cons., Atco, N.J., 1987—; presenter case mgmt. tng. Nursing Spectrum, 1994-95. Editor: Pediatric Press, 1982. Chairperson Cub Scouts Am., Atco 1986-87; v.p. Waterford Twp. Home and Sch. Assn., Atco 1985-87. Mem. NAFE, Emergency Dept. Nurses Assn., South Jersey Claims Assn., Profl. Rehab. Network (pres. 1994—, instr. nursing spectrum bus. network case mgmt. training), Nat. Assn. Rehab. Profls. Home: 2271 Linden Ave Atco NJ 08004-1210 Office: Medi-Fax Cons 639 Jackson Rd Atco NJ 08004-1108

ROSENHEIM, MARGARET KEENEY, social welfare policy educator; b. Grand Rapids, Mich., Sept. 5, 1926; d. Morton and Nancy (Billings) Keeney; m. Edward W. Rosenheim, June 20, 1947; children: Daniel, James, Andrew. Student, Wellesley Coll., 1943-45; J.D., U. Chgo., 1949. Bar: Ill. 1949. Mem. faculty Sch. Social Service Adminstrn., U. Chgo., 1950—, assoc. prof., 1961-66, prof., 1966—, Helen Ross prof. social welfare policy, 1975—, dean, 1978-83; lectr. in law U. Chgo., 1980—; vis. prof. U. Wsh., 1965, Duke U., 1984; acad. visitor London Sch. Econs., 1973; cons. Pres.'s Commn. Law Enforcement and Adminstrn. Justice, 1966-67, Nat. Advt. Commn. Criminal Justice Standards and Goals, 1972; mem. Juvenile Justice Standards Commn., 1973-76; trustee Carnegie Corp. N.Y., 1979-87, Children's Home and Aid Soc. of Ill., 1981—; dir. Nat. Inst. Dispute Resolution, 1981-89, Nuveen Bond Funds, 1982—; mem. Chgo. Network, 1983. Editor, contbr.: Justice for the Child, 1962, reprinted, 1977, Pursuing Justice for the Child, 1976, Early Parenthood and Coming of Age in the 1990s, 1992; contbr. articles and book revs. to profl. jours. Home: 5805 S Dorchester Ave Chicago IL 60637-1730 Office: 969 E 60th St Chicago IL 60637-2640

ROSENKRANTZ, LINDA, writer; b. N.Y.C., May 26, 1934; d. Samuel H. and Frances (Sillman) R.; m. Christopher Finch, Feb. 2, 1973; 1 child, Chloe. BA, U. Mich., 1955. Founding editor Auction Mag., N.Y.C., 1967-72; columnist Copley News Svc., San Diego, 1986-. Author: Talk, 1968; co-author: Gone Hollywood, 1979, SoHo, 1981, Beyond Jennifer and Jason, 1988, Beyond Charles and Diana, 1992, Beyond Shannon and Sean, 1992, Beyond Sarah and Sam, 1992, The Last Word on First Names, 1995.

ROSENSTEIN, BEVERLY BELLA, speech and language pathologist; b. N.Y.C., Aug. 8, 1921; d. George Solomon and Gretchen (Drucker) Gutterman; m. Solomon Nathan Rosenstein, Dec. 19, 1943; children: Roger, Dwight, Frederick, Elliott. BA, Hunter Coll., N.Y.C., 1943; postgrad., Cornell U., 1948, Montclair State U., 1966, 70, Patterson Coll., 1969. Lic. speech-lang. pathologist, N.J.; cert. tchr. English, speech arts and dramatics, N.J. On-call speech therapist Pascack Valley Hosp., Westwood, N.J., 1970-75; tchr. English, speech N.Y.C. Pub. Schs., 1947-49; tchr. speech Hunter Coll., N.Y.C., 1949; speech therapist in pvt. practice Hillsdale, N.J., 1956-66; speech pathologist No. Valley Parochial/Pub. Schs., N.J., 1966-68; speech-lang. pathologist River Dell Regional Sch. Dist., Oradell, N.J., 1968-93, Passaic County Career Ctr., Clifton, N.J., 1994-95; advisor lit. mag. River Dell Sr. H.S., Oradell, 1980-90, girls' varsity tennis coach, 1971-93. Dir. Pascack Players, Hillsdale, 1980-84; dir., actress Bergen County Players, Oradell, 1957—; town chmn. Girl Scouts U.S., Hillsdale, 1955-59; town chmn. Citizens for Eisenhower, Hillsdale, 1953; mem. debutante cotillion com. Project HOPE, N.Y.C., 1963, 64; pres. George G. White Sch. PTA, Hillsdale, 1966-67; mem., chmn. Columia Coll. Parents Coun., 1971—. 1st lt. WAC, U.S. Army, 1943-46. Recipient Svc. to Youth award YMCA of Greater Bergen County, 1992, Cert. of Commendation Bergen County Bd. of Chosen Freeholders, 1993; inducted to Hall of Fame N.J. Scholastic Coaches Assn., 1996. Mem. Am. Speech-Lang.-Hearing Assn. (cert. Clin. competence in Speech, Lang., Pathology, 1969), Bergen County Speech-Lang.-Hearing Assn. Home: 32 Saddlewood Dr Hillsdale NJ 07642-1336

ROSEN-SUPNICK, ELAINE RENEE, physical therapist; b. N.Y.C., May 7, 1951; d. Oscar Arthur and Sydell (Zimmerman) R.;m. Jed Supnick, Apr. 21, 1985. BS, CUNY-Hunter Coll., 1973; MS, L.I. U., Bklyn., 1977. Cert. orthop. specialist/Am. Bd. Specialists. Phys. therapy cons. Lenox Hill Hosp. Home Care, N.Y.C., 1977-83, Group Health Ins., Queens, N.Y., 1977-83, Vis. Nurse Assn., Bklyn., 1977-83; sr. phys. therapist Bird S. Coler Hosp., Roosevelt Island, N.Y., 1973-77; assoc. prof. Hunter Coll. CUNY-Hunter Coll., 1977—; ptnr. Queens Phys. Therapy Assocs., Forest Hills, N.Y., 1982—. Mem. Am. Phys. Therapy Assn. (cert. phys. therapist, dist. dir. greater N.Y. dist. 1984-88, dir. orthop. sect. 1994—, Merit award 1985, Outstanding Svc. award 1986, Disting. Svc. award 1988), Am. Acad. Orthop. Manual Therapists, Am. Assn. Orthop. Medicine, N.Y. State Assn. Coords. Clin. Edn. (treas. 1985-88). Democrat. Jewish. Office: Queens Phys Therapy Assocs 6940 108th St Flushing NY 11375-3851

ROSENTHAL, KATHY DONNA, social worker; b. Queens, N.Y., Sept. 16, 1959; d. Robert and Sheila Joyce (Golub) R. BA in Sociology, SUNY, Oneonta, 1982; MSW, SUNY, Stony Brook, 1997. Mktg. asst. Bantam Books, N.Y.C., 1983-86; mktg. mgr. St. Martin's Press, N.Y.C., 1986-87; mktg. dir. Bantam, Doubleday, Dell, N.Y.C., 1987-91; exec. mktg. dir. Random House, Inc., N.Y.C., 1991-94; mem. mktg. com. The Children's Book Coun., N.Y.C., 1988-89; co-host, prodn. asst. L.I. Rainbow Connection, pub. access cable TV show. Author: (poetry) The Green Fuse, 1978 (3d prize), Between the Raindrops, 1995; editor, author The LIGALY Jour., 1995. Vol. in Reading Is Recreation program Random House, Inc., N.Y.C., 1992-93; vol. coord., counselor, group facilitator, spkr. L.I. Gay and Lesbian Youth, Inc., Bay Shore, N.Y., 1995-96; mentor Children's House, Mineola, N.Y., 1995. Mem. NOW, NASW. Democrat. Jewish. Home: 99 Loop Dr Sayville NY 11782

ROSENTHAL, LEE H., federal judge; b. Nov. 30, 1952; m. Gary L. Rosenthal; children: Rebecca, Hannah, Jessica, Rachel. BA in Philosophy with honors, U. Chgo., 1974, JD with honors, 1977. Bar: Tex. 1979. Law clk. to Hon. John R. Brown U.S. Ct. Appeals (5th cir.), 1977-78; assoc. Baker & Botts, 1978-86, ptnr., 1986-92; judge U.S. Dist. Ct. (so. dist.) Tex., 1992—. Editor topics and comments Law Rev. U. Chgo., 1977-78. Active vis. com. Law Sch. U. Chgo., 1983-86, 94—; mem. devel. coun. Tex. Children's Hosp., 1988-92; pres. Epilepsy Assn. Houston/Gulf Coast, 1989-91; trustee Briarwood Sch. Endowment Found., 1991-92; bd. dirs. Epilepsy Found. Am., 1993—. Fellow Tex. Bar Found.; mem. ABA, Am. Law Inst., Texas Bar Assn., Houston Bar Assn. Office: US Dist Ct US Courthouse Rm 8631 515 Rusk St Houston TX 77002

ROSENTHAL, LISA BETH, editor; b. N.Y.C., Oct. 9, 1951; d. Jordan Alvin and Enid Harriet (Shapiro) Tartikoff; m. Mark Howard Rosenthal, Aug. 22, 1976; children: Emily, Lindsay. BA, Brandeis U., 1973; MA, San

Francisco State U., 1976. Dir. ESL program, assoc. prof. Coll. of Notre Dame, Belmont, Calif., 1976-84; editor, founder San Francisco Peninsula Parent, Burlingame, Calif., 1984—. Author: (books) Writing for a Specific Purpose, 1978, Academic Reading and Study Skills for International Students, 1984. Pres. Burlingame Comm. for Edn., 1991-92; trustee Burlingame Elem. Sch. Dist., Burlingame, 1993—. Recipient Yr. of the Child award San Mateo Cunty Bd. Suprs., 1995.

ROSENTHAL, NAN, curator, author; b. N.Y.C., Aug. 27, 1937; d. Alan Herman and Lenore (Fry) R.; m. Otto Piene (div.); m. Henry Benning Cortesi, Sept. 5, 1990. BA, Sarah Lawrence Coll., 1959; MA, Harvard U., 1970, PhD, 1976. Asst. prof. art history U. Calif., Santa Cruz, 1971-77, assoc. prof., 1977-84, prof., 1985-86, chair dept. art history, 1976-80; curator 20th-century art Nat. Gallery Art, Washington, 1985-92; cons. Dept. of 20th Century Art, Metro. Mus. of Art, N.Y.C., 1993—; Lila Acheson Wallace vis. prof. of Fine Arts Inst. of Fine Arts, NYU, 1996—; vis. prof. art history Fordham U., Lincoln Ctr., 1981, 85; vis. scholar N.Y. Inst. for Humanities, NYU, 1982-83; vis. lectr. visual arts Princeton U., 1985, 88, 92. Author: George Rickey, 1977; also exhbn. catalogues, catalogue essays and articles; art editor Show, 1963-64; assoc. editor, then editor at large and contbg. editor Art in Am., 1964-70. Radcliffe Inst. fellow, 1968-69, scholar, 1970-71; travelling fellow Harvard U., 1973-74, rsch. fellow U. Calif., 1978, Ailsa Mellon Bruce curatorial fellow Nat. Gallery of Art, 1988-89; rsch. and travel grantee U. Calif., Santa Cruz, 1974, 77-80, 82-85. Office: Met Mus of Art 20th Century Art 1000 Fifth Ave New York NY 10028-0113

ROSENTHAL, SUSAN LESLIE, psychologist; b. Washington, Sept. 27, 1956; d. Alan Sayre and Helen (Miller) R. BA, Wellesley Coll., 1978; PhD, U. N.C., 1986. Postdoctoral fellow Yale Child Study Ctr., New Haven, 1986-88; asst. prof. clin. pediatrics U. Cin., 1988-93, dir. psychology div. adolescent medicine, 1988—, assoc. prof. clin. pediatrics, 1993—; adj. faculty dept. psychology Miami U., Oxford, Ohio, 1992—. Contbr. articles to profl. jours. Grantee NIH, 1994—, Merck & Co., Inc., 1995, Wyeth-Ayerst Labs., 1995-96. Mem. APA (program chair divsn. 37 1992, sec. 1996—), Cin. Soc. Clin. Child Psychologists (treas. 1992-94, pres. 1994-96), Ohio Psychol. Assn., Soc. Behavioral Pediatrics, Soc. Rsch. on Adolescence, Cin. Acad. Profl. Psychology. Office: Children's Hosp Med Ctr Div Adolescent Medicine 3333 Burnet Ave Cincinnati OH 45229-3026

ROSENTHAL-ROSE, HOLLY ANNE, social services administrator; b. Cleve., Dec. 25, 1950; d. Steve and Mary Elizabeth (Appleby) Eschuk; m. Thomas Stephen Rosenthal, Apr. 16, 1971 (div. Sept. 1980); m. Thomas Michael Rose, Aug. 2, 1991. AA, Youngstown State U., 1971. Vol. coord. Cmty Crisis and Referral Ctr., Waldorf, Md., 1986-87; staffing supr. Norrell Health Care, Waldorf, 1987-88; night mgr. Tri-County Homeless Shelter, Hughesville, Md., 1988-90; social worker for homeless Lee County Social Svcs., Ft. Myers, Fla., 1990; libr. technician Lee County Libr. Sys., Ft. Myers, 1990-94; coord. hotline, case mgr. in battered women's shelter Abuse Counseling and Treatment, Ft. Myers, 1994—. Voter registrar LWV, St. Mary's County, Md., 1984, 85, 86, del. nat. conf., Indpls., 1982, New Orleans, 1985, Cin., 1987; co-founder Clothesline Project S.W. Fla., 1994—; bd. dirs. S.W. Fla. Gay and Lesbian Chorus, 1994—, for support of mems. Chorus Aid and Relief Endowment dir. Holly Rosenthal Appreciation Day named in her honor St. Mary's NOW, 1986. Mem. Ft. Myers NOW (chair pub. rels. 1993, pres. 1994-96), Planned Parenthood. Democrat. Home: 729 Sesame Ct Cape Coral FL 33904

ROSENZWEIG-LIPSON, SHARON JOY, pharmacologist; b. Queens, N.Y., July 8, 1966; d. Martin and Annette Nina (Epstein) Rosenzweig; m. Robert Steven Lipson, June 18, 1989; 1 child, Shelby Rachel. Student, Brandeis U., 1984-86; BA, U. Pa., 1988; MA, Harvard U., 1991, PhD, 1993. Grad. rsch. asst. Harvard Med. Sch., Southborough, Mass., 1989-92; postdoctoral rsch. scientist Am. Cyanamid Co., Pearl River, N.Y., 1992-94; sr. rsch. scientist Am. Home Products, Princeton, N.J., 1994—. Contbr. articles to profl. jours. William James Merit fellow Harvard U., 1988-90. Mem. Soc. for Neurosci., Soc. for the Stimulus Properties of Drugs, Behavioral Pharmacology Soc. Democrat. Jewish. Office: Wyeth-Ayerst Rsch Ridge Rd Princeton NJ 08543

ROSHONG, DEE ANN DANIELS, dean, educator; b. Kansas City, Mo., Nov. 22, 1936; d. Vernon Edmund and Doradell (Kellogg) Daniels; m. Richard Lee Roshong, Aug. 27, 1960 (div.). BMusEd., U. Kans., 1958; MA in Counseling and Guidance, Stanford U., 1960; postgrad. Fresno State U., U. Calif.; EdD, U. San Francisco, 1980. Counselor, psychometrist Fresno City Coll., 1961-65; counselor, instr. psychology Chabot Coll., Hayward, Calif., 1965-75; coord. counseling services Chabot Coll., Valley Campus, Livermore, Calif., 1975-81, asst. dir. student pers. svcs., 1981-89, Las Positas Coll., Livermore, Calif., 1989-91, assoc. dean student svcs., 1991-94, dean student svcs., 1994—; writer, coord. I, A Woman Symposium, 1974, Feeling Free to Be You and Me Symposium, 1975, All for the Family Symposium, 1976, I Celebrate Myself Symposium, 1977, Person to Person in Love and Work Symposium, 1978; The Healthy Person in Body, Mind and Spirit Symposium, 1979, Feelin' Good Symposium, 1980, Change Symposium, 1981, Sources of Strength Symposium, 1982, Love and Friendship Symposium, 1983, Self Esteem Symposium, 1984, Trust Symposium, 1985, Prime Time: Making the Most of This Time in Your Life Symposium, 1986, Symposium on Healing, 1987, How to Live in the World and Still Be Happy Symposium, 1988, Student Success is a Team Effort, Sound Mind, Sound Body Symposium, 1989, Creating Life's Best Symposium, 1990, Choices Symposium, 1991, Minding the Body, Mending the Mind Symposium, 1992, Healing through Love and Laughter Symposium, 1993, Healing Ourselves Changing the World Symposium, 1994, Finding Your Path Symposium, 1995, Build the Life You Want Symposium, 1996; mem. cast TV prodns. Eve and Co., Best of Our Times, Cowboy; chmn. Calif. C.C. Chancellor's Task Force on Counseling, Statewide Regional Counseling Facilitators, 1993-95, Statewide Conf. on Emotionally Disturbed Students in Calif. C.C.s, 1982—, Conf. on the Under Represented Student in California C.C.s, 1986, Conf. on High Risk Students, 1989. Choir dir. Tri-Valley Unity Ch., 1996, bd. dirs., 1996; title III activity dir. Las Positas Coll., 1995—. Mem. Assn. Humanistic Psychologists, Western Psychol. Assn., Nat. Assn. Women Deans and Counselors, Assn. for Counseling and Devel., Calif. Assn. Community Colls. (chmn. commn. on student services 1979-84), Calif. Community Colls. Counselors Assn. (Svc. award 1986, 87, award for Outstanding and Disting. Service, 1986, 87, Spl. Svc. award for outstanding svc Calif. advocated for re-entry edn., 1991), Alpha Phi. Author: Counseling Needs of Community Coll. Students, 1980. Home: 1856 Harvest Rd Pleasanton CA 94566-5456 Office: 3033 Collier Canyon Rd Livermore CA 94550-9797

ROSITA, ALMA See DAVIES, ALMA

ROS-LEHTINEN, ILEANA, congresswoman; b. Havana, Cuba, July 15, 1952; d. Enrique Emilio and Amanda (Adato) Ros; m. Dexter Lehtinen. AA, Miami (Fla.)-Dade C.C., 1972; BA, Fla. Internat. U., 1975, MS, 1987. Prin. Ea. Acad., from 1978; mem. Fla. Ho. of Reps., Tallahassee, 1982-86, Fla. Senate, 1986-89; mem. 101st-104th Congresses from 18th Fla. Dist., 1989—, mem. govt. reform and oversight com. nat. security, internat. affairs and criminal justice internat. rels. - Africa. Roman Catholic. Office: US Ho of Reps 2440 Rayburn Bldg Washington DC 20515-0918*

ROSMUS, ANNA ELISABETH, writer; b. Passau, Germany, Mar. 29, 1960; d. Georg Rudolf and Anna Johanna (Friedberger) R.; divorced; children: Dolores Nadine, Beatrice Salome Kassandra. M, U. Passau, 1994. speaker and organizer in field. Author: Resistance and Persecution, 1983 (Geschwister Scholl Preis 1984), Exodus In The Shadow of Mercy, 1988, Robert Klein A German Jew Looks Back, 1991, Wintergreen Suppressed Murders, 1993 (Concsience in Media award 1994), Pocking End and Renewal, 1995, What I Think, 1995; guest talk shows including Documentaries and Features in Germany, Austria, Great Britain, Denmark, Holland, France, Italy, Sweden, Poland, Can., U.S., South Am., Australia, 1983—. Fundraiser Anne Frank Found., Jewish Cmty. Ctrs., Holocaust Ctrs., others, 1992—. Named Best German Writer, European essay Competition, 1980; Oscar nomination for movie The Nasty Girl, 1991; Sarnat award Anti Defamation League, 1994; Anna Rosmus Day, City of Santa Cruz, 1994. Mem. PEN Internat., NAFE.

ROSNER, MARY WINWARD, lawyer; b. Salt Lake City, Dec. 18, 1947; d. Robert Wayne and Dorothy Cummock Winward; m. Alan Rosner, Oct. 25, 1986 (div. Dec. 1988). BS, U. N.Mex., 1975, JD, 1978. Bar: D.C. 1980, N.Mex. 1987; cert. in family law N.Mex. Bd. Specialization. Assoc. atty. fed. sector labor law Nat. Treasury Employees Union, Washington, 1980-84; assoc. Farrow, Shieldhouse, Wilson & Rains, Washington, 1984-87; pvt. practice Albuquerque, 1987-92, Las Cruces, N.Mex., 1992—; mentor N.Mex. Disciplinary Bd.; bd. dirs. Minimum Continuing Legal Edn., State of N.Mex., 1995—. Editor in family, author monthly column N.Mex. Trial Lawyers Assn., 1993-94. Mem. N.Mex. Mediation Assn. Office: PO Box 1239 Las Cruces NM 88004

ROSOF, PATRICIA J.F., secondary education educator; b. N.Y.C., May 19, 1949; d. Sylvan D. and Charlotte (Fischer) Freeman; m. Alan H. Rosof, Sept. 13, 1970; children: Jeremy, Simon, Ali. BA, NYU, 1970, MA, 1971, PhD, 1978. Cert. tchr. social studies, N.Y. Instr. history Iona Coll., New Rochelle, N.Y., 1978-81; tchr. social studies Profl. Children's Sch., N.Y.C., 1981-82, Hunter Coll. H.S., N.Y.C., 1984—; European history reader Advanced Placement Ednl. Testing Svcs. Co-editor Trends in History, 1978-84, Hunter Outreach, 1988-92; contbr. articles to profl. jours. Internat. Cultural Soc. Korea fellow, 1989; CUNY Women's Rsch. and Devel. Fund grantee, 1993-95. Mem. Am. Hist. Assn., Orgn. History Tchrs.

ROSOFF, JEANNIE I., foundation administrator; b. Clamart, France, Nov. 8, 1924; came to U.S., 1948; d. Georges Auguste Marie and Suzenne (Philomene) Martin; m. Morton Rosoff, Dec. 8, 1945 (div. 1958); 1 child, Ann Susan. BA in Law cum laude, U. Paris, 1946. Cmty. organizer East Harlem Project, N.Y.C., 1953-56; assoc. dir. N.Y. Com. for Dem. Voters, N.Y.C., 1960-64; spl. projects coord. Planned Parenthood Fedn. Am., N.Y.C., 1964-74, assoc. dir., 1968-74, assoc. dir. Ctr. for Family Planning Program Devel., 1968-74; v.p. govt. affairs Planned Parenthood Fedn. Am., Washington, 1974-77, dir. Washington office, 1976-81; sr. v.p. Alan Guttmacher Inst., Washington, 1974-78, pres., 1978—; participant in UN Population Conf., Bucharest, 1974, UN Conf. on Internat. Women's Yr., Mexico City, 1975; ofcl. U.S. del. UN Conf. on Population and Devel., Cairo, 1994; del.-at-large Internat. Women's Yr. Conf., Houston, 1977. Author: Teenage Pregnancy in Industrialized Countries, 1986, Health Care Reform: A Unique Opportunity, 1993, (govt. publs.) Family Planning: An Analysis of Laws, 1974, Family Planning: Contraception, 1979. Recipient merit award Nat. Family Planning and Repro. Health Assn., 1980, Ten for Ten award Ctr. for Population Options, 1990. Mem. APHA (pres., chair population sect. 1976, Carl S. Schultz award 1980; maternal and child health sec. 1973-76), Nat. Health Lawyers Assn., Population Assn. Am., Nat. Inst. Child Health and Human Devel., Pathfinder Internat. (bd. dirs. 1993—). Office: Alan Guttmacher Inst 120 Wall St Fl 21 New York NY 10005-4001

ROSS, ALLYNE R., federal judge; b. 1946. BA, Wellesley Coll., 1967; JD cum laude, Harvard Law Sch., 1970. Assoc. Paul, Weiss, Rifkind, Wharton & Garrison, 1971-76; asst. U.S. atty. U.S. Dist. Ct. (N.Y. ea. dist.), 2nd circuit, Brooklyn, 1976-83, chief, appeals div., 1983-86, magistrate judge, 1986-94, dist. judge, 1994—. Mem. Federal Bar Coun., New York City Bar Assn. Office: US District Court 225 Cadman Plz E Rm 252 Brooklyn NY 11201-1818*

ROSS, ANN DUNBAR, secondary school educator; b. Longview, Tex., Jan. 21, 1945; d. Louie and Myra Lee (Fanning) Dunbar; m. John Reuben Ross, Sept. 9, 1967; children: Jennifer Ann, John Byron. BA in Math., U. Tex., 1968; M in Liberal Arts, So. Meth. U., 1974; Endorsement in Gifted Edn., U. North Tex., 1992. Tchr. math. Dallas, 1968-72, Duncanville (Tex.) High Sch., 1979-89; tchr. math., dept. chairperson Duncanville Ninth Grade Sch., 1989—; vertical team mem. Math. Dept. Duncanville High Sch., 1993—; site based mgmt. mem. Duncanville Ninth Grade Sch., 1993; presenter in field at math. conf. Mem. Nat. Coun. Tchrs. Math., Tex. Coun. Tchrs. Math., Tex. Fedn. Tchrs., ASCD.

ROSS, BRENDA KAY, secondary school educator; b. Ft. Worth, Aug. 22, 1942; m. Martin P. Ross, July 22, 1961; children: Russ, DeeDee Betzel, Hunter. BA in Fine Arts, Sul Ross State U., Alpine, Tex., 1988. Cert. art tchr., Tex. Instr. art Alpine Ind. Sch. Dist., 1988—. Mem. Tex. Art Edn. Assn., Tex. State Tchrs. Assn., Alpine C. of C. Republican. Presbyterian. Address: PO Box 1419 Alpine TX 79831-1419

ROSS, CHARLOTTE PACK, suicidologist; b. Oklahoma City, Oct. 21, 1932; d. Joseph and Rose P. (Traibich) Pack; m. Roland S. Ross, May 6, 1951 (div. July 1964); children: Beverly Jo, Sandra Gail; m. Stanley Fisher, Mar. 17, 1991. Student U. Okla., 1949-52, New Sch. Social Rsch., 1953. Cert. tchr. Exec. dir. Suicide Prevention and Crisis Ctr. San Mateo County, Burlingame, Calif., 1966-88; pres., exec. dir. Youth Suicide Nat. Ctr., Washington, 1985-93; exec. dir. Death with Dignity Edn. Ctr., San Mateo, Calif., 1994—; pres. Calif. Senate Adv. Com. Youth Suicide Prevention, 1982-84; speaker Menninger Found., 1983, 84; instr. San Francisco State U., 1981-83; conf. coord. U. Calif., San Francisco, 1971—; cons. univs. and health svcs. throughout world. Contbg. author: Group Counseling for Suicidal Adolescents, 1984, Teaching Children the Facts of Life and Death, 1985; mem. editorial bd. Suicide and Life Threatening Behavior, 1976-89. Mem. regional selection panel Pres.'s Commn. on White House Fellows, 1975-78; mem. CIRCLON Svc. Club, 1979—, Com. on Child Abuse, 1981-85; founding mem. Women for Responsible Govt., co-chmn., 1974-79. Recipient Outstanding Exec. award San Mateo County Coordinating Com., 1971, Koshland award San Francisco Found., 1984. Fellow Wash. Acad. Scis.; mem. Internat. Assn. Suicide Prevention (v.p. 1985—), Am. Assn. Suicidology (sec. 1972-74, svc. award 1990), bd. govs. 1976-78, accreditation com. 1975—, chair region IX, 1975-82), Assn. United Way Agy. Execs. (pres. 1974), Assn. County Contract Agys. (pres. 1982), Peninsula Press Club.

ROSS, CONNIE LEE, special education educator; b. Jacksonville, Ill., Apr. 19, 1945; d. John Lee and Mary Priscilla (Walsh) Morath; m. Thomas Ferrell Ross, Dec. 21, 1969; 1 child, Melinda Jo. BS, Ill. State U., 1967. Cert. tchr., Ill. Tchr. talent preservation class Houston Ind. Sch. Dist., 1967-68; tchr. primary educable mentally handicapped Meredosia (Ill.)-Chambersburg Unit 11, 1968—. Author: Lookout, 1974, (poem) Harmony...I Long For Thee...a Joyful Noise, 1989. Recipient Ill. award for Excellence, Ill. Coun. on Econ. Edn., 1992. Mem. Reading Coun., Coun. for Exceptional Children, Precious Moments Collectors' Club. Democrat. Home: Box 326 W 2d St Versailles IL 62378 Office: Meredosia-Chambersburg Sch Main St Meredosia IL 62665

ROSS, DEBORAH ANN, customer relations professional, philatelist; b. Teaneck, N.J., Nov. 28, 1956; d. William George and Lillian Emily (Waraksaw) R. Grad. H.S., Old Tappan, N.J. Customer svc. staff Fleming H. Revell, Old Tappan, 1974-77; customer rels./export dept. staff Villazon & Co., Upper Saddle River, N.J., 1977—; photographer Villazon & Co., Upper Saddle River, 1988—. Mem. Smithsonian Assocs., Libr. Congress. Office: Villazon & Co 25 Park Way Upper Saddle River NJ 07458

ROSS, DEBORAH KOFF, lawyer; b. Phila., June 20, 1963; d. Marvin S. and Barbara A. (Klein) Koff; m. Stephen J. Wrinn, July 30, 1994. BA, Brown U., 1985; JD, U. N.C., 1990. Adminstrv./legis. coord. Citizens' Campaign, Washington, 1985-87; lawyer Hunton & Williams, Raleigh, N.C., 1990-94; exec./legal dir. ACLU of N.C., Raleigh, 1994—. Co-chair Betsy McCrodden for Judge, Raleigh, 1994; bd. dirs. Nat. Abortion Rights Action League-N.C. PAC Bd., Durham, N.C., 1992—, N.C. Vol. Lawyers for Arts, raleigh, 1991—; mem. Women's Polit. Caucus, Raleigh, 1993—. Friday Fellow for Human Rels., 1995. Mem. N.C. Bar Assn. (mem., sec. constnl. rights and responsibilities 1995—, childrens rights com. 1996—), Wake County Bar. Democrat. Home: 425 S Boylan Ave Raleigh NC 27603-1010

ROSS, DEBRA BENITA, marketing executive; b. Carbondale, Ill., May 1, 1956; d. Bernard Harris and Marian (Frager) R. BS, U. Ill., 1978; MS, U. Wis., 1979. Dir. mktg. Ambion Devel., Inc., Northbrook, Ill., 1983-89; dir. mktg. Fitness Horizons, Inc., Northbrook, 1989-91, v.p. mktg., 1991—; owner Benita Ross Designs, Northbrook, 1992—. Mem. Chgo. CitiWomen. Home: 1853 Mission Hills Ln Northbrook IL 60062-5760

ROSS, DIANA, singer, actress, entertainer, fashion designer; b. Detroit, Mar. 26, 1944; d. Fred and Ernestine R.; m. Robert Ellis Silberstein, Jan. 1971 (div. 1976); children: Rhonda, Tracee, Chudney; m. Arne Naess, Oct. 23, 1985; 1 son: Ross Arne. Grad. high sch. Pres. Diana Ross Enterprises, Inc., fashion and merchandising, Anaid Film Prodns., Inc., RTC Mgmt. Corp., artists mgmt., Chondee Inc., Rosstown, Rossville, music pub. Started in Detroit as mem. the Primettes; lead singer until 1969, Diana Ross and the Supremes; solo artist, 1969—; albums include Diana Ross, 1970, 76, Everything Is Everything, 1971, I'm Still Waiting, 1971, Lady Sings The Blues, 1972, Touch Me In The Morning, 1973, Original Soundtrack of Mahogany, 1975, Baby It's Me, 1977, The Wiz, 1978, Ross, 1978, 83, The Boss, 1979, Diana, 1981, To Love Again, 1981, Why Do Fools Fall In Love?, 1981, Silk Electric, 1982, Swept Away, 1984, Eaten Alive, 1985, Chain Reaction, 1986, Diana's Duets, 1987, Workin' Overtime, 1989, Red Hot Rhythm and Blues, 1987, Surrender, 1989, Ain't No Mountain High Enough, 1989, The Force Behind the Power, 1991, Stolen Moment: The Lady Sings... Jazz & Blues, 1993, Musical Memories Forever, 1993, The Remixes, 1994; films include Lady Sings the Blues, 1972, Mahogany, 1975, The Wiz, 1978; NBC-TV spl., An Evening With Diana Ross, 1977, Diana, 1981, numerous others; TV movie Out of Darkness, 1994; album Endless Love, 1982; author: Secrets of a Sparrow, 1993. Recipient citation Vice Pres. Humphrey for efforts on behalf Pres. Johnson's Youth Opportunity Program, citation Mrs. Martin Luther King and Rev. Abernathy for contbn. to SCLC cause, awards Billboard, Cash Box and Record World as worlds outstanding singer, Grammy award, 1970, Female Entertainer of Year NAACP, 1970, Cue award as Entertainer of year, 1972, Golden Apple award, 1972, Gold medal award Photoplay, 1972, Antoinette Perry award, 1977, nominee as best actress of year for Lady Sings the Blues Motion Picture Acad. Arts and Scis., 1972, Golden Globe award, 1972; named to Rock and Roll Hall of Fame, 1988. Office: ICM 8942 Wilshire Blvd Beverly Hills CA 90211 also: care Shelly Berger 6255 W Sunset Blvd Los Angeles CA 90028-7403*

ROSS, DONNA LEE, auditor; b. San Francisco, Dec. 1, 1956; d. Arthur J. and Myrtle Joan (Haynes) Lee; m. Eugene Ross Sr., Mar. 31, 1990. BS in Acctg., U. San Francisco, 1983. CPA, Calif. Sales supr. Macy's Calif., San Francisco, 1974-84; acctg. clk. 3/33 Ins. Co., San Francisco, 1979-80; advt. acct. San Francisco Newspaper Agy., 1980-83; supervising sr. auditor Arthur Young & Co., San Francisco, 1984-87; corp. auditor Hewlett-Packard Co., Palo Alto, Calif., 1987-90; ea. region audit mgr. Hewlett-Packard Co., Paramus, N.J., 1990-92, sr. internal auditor, 1992—. Author: (classroom tng. material) Understanding Basic Business Controls in a Changing Environment, 1992. Active Hist. Preservation Soc. Mem. Nat. Assn. Black Accts., State Soc. CPAs, Inst. Internal Auditors (mem. N.J. chpt.). Democrat. Roman Catholic.

ROSS, ELINOR, soprano; b. Tampa, Fla., Aug. 1, 1932; d. Joe D. and Lillian Rosenthal; m. Aaron M. Diamond; 1 son, Ross. Student, Syracuse U. Debuts include: Turandot, Met. Opera, N.Y.C., Il Trovatore, Cin. Opera, Cavalleria Rusticana, La Scala, Milan, Tosca, Bolshoi, Moscow; leading soprano roles with, Met. Opera, LaScala, Bolshoi, Chgo. Lyric Opera, San Francisco Opera, Tulsa Opera, Cin. Opera, Staatsoper, Vienna, LaFenice, Venice, Teatro Colon, Buenes Aires, Argentina, Arena de Verona, Massimo de Palermo; inaugurated Rossini Festival in Pesaro; televised concert tour in Peoples Republic of China, Taiwan; appeared in concerts, opera, symphony in Hong Kong, Japan, Thailand, Korea; appeared with symphony orchs. throughout world. Recipient medal of honor Novosibiresk, Siberia. Jewish.

ROSS, ELLEN, educator; b. Detroit, June 6, 1942; d. Jack Seymour Ross and Jeanette Charlotte Zide; m. W. Richard Glendon, Feb. 7, 1990; children: Zachary (dec.), Maude, Hope. BA, U. Chgo., 1964, PhD, 1975; MA, Columbia U., 1965. Instr., asst. prof. Conn. Coll., New London, 1971-76; asst. prof., prof. Ramapo Coll., Mahwah, N.J., 1976—, women's studies coord., 1976-86, 95—; coord. Ramapo women's studies Ramapo Coll., Mahwah, 1976-86, 95—. Author: Love & Toil: Motherhood in Outcast London, 1993; history editor Feminist Studies, College Park, Md., 1985—; contbr. articles to profl. jours. Mem. Parent's Assn. Manhattan Sch. Children, N.Y.C., 1995—. Woodrow Wilson fellow, 1964-65, Am. Coun. Learned Socs. fellow, 1982, Davis Ctr. fellow, 1986, NEH fellow, 1989-90. Mem. Am. Hist. Assn. (James Harvey Robinson Prize com. 1994-96), N.Am. Congress on British Studies, Nat. Women's Studies Assn., Phi Beta Kappa. Democrat. Jewish. Home: 890 West End Ave Apt 15D New York NY 10025 Office: Ramapo Coll Sch Social Sci & Human Svcs Mahwah NJ 07430

ROSS, EUNICE LATSHAW, judge; b. Bellevue, Pa., Oct. 13, 1923; d. Richard Kelly and Eunice (Weidner) Latshaw; m. John Anthony Ross, May 29, 1943 (dec. Jan. 1978); 1 child, Geraldine Ross Coleman. BS, U. Pitts., 1945, LLB, 1951. Bar: Pa. 1952. Atty., Pub. Health Law Research Project, Pitts., 1951-52; atty. jud. asst., law clk. Ct. Common Pleas, Pitts., 1952-70; adjunct law prof. U. Pitts., 1967-73; dir. family div. Ct. Common Pleas, Pitts., 1970-72; judge Ct. Common Pleas of Allegheny County, Pitts., 1972—; mem. Bd. Jud. Inquiry and Rev., Commonwealth of Pa., 1984-89, Gov's Justice Commn., 1972-78. Author: (with others) Survey of Pa. Public Health Laws, 1952. Author: Justice, 1995; co-author: Will Contests, 1992; contbr. articles to legal publs. Com. person for 14th ward, vice chmn. Democratic Com., Pitts., 1972; exec. com. bd. trustees U. Pitts., 1980-86, bd. visitors law sch., 1985—, bd. visitors sch. health, 1986—; adv. bd. Animal Friends, Pitts., 1973—; bd. mem. The Program, Pitts., 1983-87, Pitts. History and Landmarks FDTN., West Pa. Hist. Soc., West Pa. Conservancy. Recipient Disting. Amumna award U. Pitts., 1973, Medal of Recognition, 1987, Susan B. Anthony award Womens' Bar Assn. Western Pa., 1993, Probate and Trusts award, 1994; named Girl Scout Woman of Yr., Pitts. coun. Girl Scouts U.S., 1975; cert. of Achievement Pa. Fedn. Women's Clubs, 1975, 77. Mem. Scribes, Allegheny County Bar Assn. (vice chmn., exec. com. young lawyers sect. 1956-59), Pa. State Trial Judges Conf., Order of Coif. Home: 1204 Denniston Ave Pittsburgh PA 15217-1329 Office: Frick Bldg 3d Fl Pittsburgh PA 15219

ROSS, JEANETTE LYNN, art association administrator; b. Minot, S.D., Oct. 20, 1939; d. George John and Elmie Aurora (Erickson) Ross; m. George Graham Diskell, Oct. 15, 1966 (div. May 1980); children: Carol Driskell, Graham Driskell, Cary Driskell; m. Thomas Walthers von Alten. BA in English, Lewis-Clark State Coll., 1969; MA in English, U. Idaho, 1972, EdD, 1976. Journalist Lewiston (Idaho) Morning Tribune, 1968-72; dir. learning ctr. U. Idaho, Moscow, 1972-82; presenter arts performances and programs Moscow, Boise, Idaho, 1980—; coord. Wash. Prodns. First Night, Boise, 1995; reviewer Idaho Daily Statesman, Boise, 1984-89; critic Artweek & Reflex Mags., 1985—. Author: Telling Out Tales, 1995; playwright; editor regional Sierra Club newsletter, 1995. Past pres. bd. trustees Boise Unitarian Universalist Fellowship. Eugene O'Neill critic fellow, 1989. Mem. Am. Coll. Theatre Festival (regional chair critics sect. 1992—). Democrat. Home: 2824 Grandee St Boise ID 83704

ROSS, JENNIFER MARIE, paralegal; b. Hays, Kans., Nov. 26, 1960; d. Richard Raymond and Armella (Psannenstiel) R. BS in Sociology, Ft. Hays State U., 1989. Cert. paralegal. Case mgr. Golden West Skills Ctr., Goodland, Kans., 1989; telephone sales Olan Mills, Hays, 1991; tchr. asst. Northwest Kans. Day Care, Hays, 1990-93; telephone sales Intellisell, Victoria, Kans., 1992-93; paraprofl. Sch. Dist. # 489, Hays, 1990-93; with Hallmark, Kansas City, Mo., 1995—. Vol. Literacy Vol. of Am., Hays, 1990-93, Ct. Appt. Spl. Advocate, Hays, 1990-93, Cancer Council, Hays, 1990-91, HeadStart, Hays, 1993, Ellis County Dems. mem. AAUW (sec. 1989), NOW, Bus. and Profl. Women, Gen. Fedn. Women's Clubs, Feminist Coalition U. Kans. Roman Catholic. Home: 1001 Sherman #105 Denver CO 80203 Office: Hallmark 2450 Grand Ave Kansas City MO 64108

ROSS, JOYCE ADAMS, gerontological clinical specialist, nurse; b. Phila., June 29, 1944; d. Thomas Grandville and Dorothy (Anglea) Adams; m. Jerome Samuel Ross, June 8, 1963; children: Mary Teresa, Dorothy, Jerome Jr., Michael, Erin. ADN, Gwynedd Mercy Coll., 1987, BSN cum laude, 1988, MSN, 1992. RN Pa.; cert. gerontol. nurse., nurse practitioner/CRNP. Gerontol. nurse clinician Franklin Sq. Hosp. Ctr., Balt., 1988-89; instr. Fair Acres Geriatric Ctr., Lima, Pa., 1989; dir. staff devel., cert. gerontol. clin. specialist Dunwoody Village Continuing Care Retirement Cmty., Newtown Square, Pa., 1989—, mem. speakers bur., 1989—; with med. genetics dept. Hosp. of U. of Pa., Phila.; nursing home adminstr., mem. speakers bur.; long term care consortium Main Line, Inc.; evaluator continuing care accreditation Am. Assn. Homes for the Aged, 1993—, nursing home adminstr., 1994—. Nurst of Hope Am. Cancer Soc., Media, Pa., 1981, mem. edn. com., 1990-92. Mem. Delaware Valley Geriatric Soc., Sigma Theta Tau (Iota Kappa chpt.). Roman Catholic. Home: 347 Sussex Blvd Broomall PA 19008-4153 Office: Hosp U Pa Maloney Bldg Philadelphia PA 19104

ROSS, JUNE ROSA PITT, biologist; b. Taree, New South Wales, Australia, May 2, 1931; came to U.S., 1957; d. Bernard and Adeline Phillips; m. Charles Alexander, June 27, 1959. BS with honors, U. Sydney, New S. Wales, Australia, 1953, PhD, 1959, DSc, 1974. Research assoc. Yale U., New Haven, 1959-60, U. Ill., Urbana, 1960-65; research assoc. Western Wash. U., Bellingham, 1965-67, assoc. prof., 1967-70, prof. biology, 1970—, chair dept. biology, 1989-90; pres. Western Wash. U. Faculty Senate, Bellingham, 1984-85; conf. host Internat. Bryozoology Assn., 1986. Author: (with others) A Textbook of Entomology, 1982, Geology of Coal, 1984; editor (assoc.) Palaios, 1985-89; contbr. articles to profl. jours. NSF grantee; recipient Award of Excellence Sydney U. Grads. Union of N.Am., 1995. Mem. Australian Marine Scis. Assn., The Paleontol. Soc. (councillor 1984-86, treas. 1987-93), U.K. Marine Biol. Assn. (life), Microscopy Soc. of Am., Internat. Bryozoology Assn. (pres. 1992-95). Office: Western Wash U Dept Biology Bellingham WA 98225-9160

ROSS, KATHLEEN ANNE, college president; b. Palo Alto, Calif., July 1, 1941; d. William Andrew and Mary Alberta (Wilburn) R. BA, Ft. Wright Coll., 1964; MA, Georgetown U., 1971; PhD, Claremont Grad. Sch., 1979; LLD (hon.) Alverno Coll. Milw., 1990, Dartmouth Coll., 1991, Seattle U., 1992; LHD (hon.) Whitworth Coll., 1992, LLD (hon.) Pomona Coll., 1993. Cert. tchr., Wash. Secondary tchr. Holy Names Acad., Spokane, Wash., 1964-70; dir. rsch. and planning Province Holy Names, Wash. State, 1972-73; v.p. acads. Ft. Wright Coll., Spokane, 1973-81; rsch. asst. to dean Claremont Grad. Sch., Calif., 1977-78; assoc. faculty mem. Harvard U., Cambridge, Mass., 1981; pres. Heritage Coll., Toppenish, Wash., 1981—; cons. Wash. State Holy Names Schs., 1971-73; coll. accrediting assn. evaluator N.W. Assn. Schs. and Colls., Seattle, 1975—; dir. Holy Names Coll., Oakland, Calif., 1979—; cons. Yakama Indian Nation, Toppenish, 1975—; speaker, cons. in field. Author: (with others) Multicultural Pre-School Curriculum, 1977, A Crucial Agenda: Improving Minority Student Success, 1989; Cultural Factors in Success of American Indian Students in Higher Education, 1978. Chmn. Internat. 5-Yr. Convocation of Sisters of Holy Names, Montreal, Que., Can., 1981, 96; TV Talk show host Spokane Council of Chs., 1974-76. Recipient E.K. and Lillian F. Bishop Founds. Youth Leader of Yr. award, 1986, Disting. Citizenship Alumna award Claremont Grad. Sch., 1986, Golden Aztec award Washington Human Devel., 1989, Harold W. McGraw Edn. prize, 1989, John Carroll award Georgetown U., 1991, Holy Names medal Ft. Wright Coll., 1981, Pres. medal Eastern Washington U., 1994; named Yakima Herald Rep. Person of Yr. 1987, First Annual Leadership award Region VIII Coun. Advancement and Support Edn., 1993; Wash. State Medal of Merit, 1995; numerous grants for projects in multicultural higher edn., 1974—. Mem. Nat. Assn. Ind. Colls. and Univs., Am. Assn. Higher Edn., Soc. Intercultural Edn., Tng. and Rsch., Sisters of Holy Names of Jesus and Mary-SNJM. Roman Catholic. Office: Heritage Coll Office of Pres 3240 Fort Rd Toppenish WA 98948-9562

ROSS, LESA MOORE, quality assurance professional; b. New Orleans, Jan. 25, 1959; d. William Frank and Carolyn West Moore; m. Mark Neal Ross, Nov. 30, 1985; children: Sarah Ann, Jacquelyne Caroline. BS in Engring., U. N.C., Charlotte, 1981; MBA in Quality and Reliability Mgmt., U. North Tex., 1991. Seismic qualification engr. Duke Power Co., Charlotte, N.C., 1981-82; quality assurance engr. Tex. Instruments Inc., Lewisville, Tex., 1982-91; compliance mgr. Am. Med. Electronics, Inc., 1992-93; owner Ross Quality Cons., 1993-95; customer quality assurance sect. mgr. Hitachi Semiconductor (Am.) Inc., 1995-96; v.p. quality Ross Networking Cons. Inc., 1996—. Recipient Nat. Sci. Found. Rsch. Grant, U. N.C., Charlotte, 1980. Mem. Am. Soc. Quality Control (cert. quality engr., quality auditor, reliability engr., cert. quality technician, sec. Dallas sect. 1994-95, chair-elect Dallas sect. 1995-96, chair 1996-97), Zeta Tau Alpha (pres. 1984-85). Home: 4925 Wolf Creek Trl Flower Mound TX 75028-1955

ROSS, LUANA K., ethnic studies educator, researcher; b. Spokane, Wash., Mar. 21, 1949; d. V.L. (Sonny) Ross and Opal (Swaney) Cajune; 1 child, Shane. BA in Social Work, U. Mont., 1978; MSW, Portland State U., 1981; PhD in Sociology, U. Oreg., 1992. Instr. depts. sociology and Native Am. studies U. Mont., Missoula, 1981-82; instr. Salish Kootenai Coll., Pablo, Mont., 1982-83; grad. teaching fellow dept. sociology U. Oreg., Eugene, 1983-84, instr., grad. teaching fellow ethnic studies program, 1984-87; adj. asst. prof. Ctr. for Native Am. Studies Mont. State U., Bozeman, 1987-92; asst. prof. Native Am. studies dept. ethnic studies U. Calif., Berkeley, 1992-95; asst. prof. dept. Native Am. studies U. Calif., Davis, 1995—; advisor cultural diversity devel. divsn. ACT, 1995—; bd. dirs. Natives Voices Prodns., Bozeman; cons., rschr., lectr. in field. Jour. referee Jour. Am. Indian Edn., Am. Indian Culture and Rsch. Jour., Am. Indian Quar., Sociol. Quar.; assoc. editor Race, Gender, & Class; advisor (documentary film) Voices From Inside, 1994, Without Reservations: Notes on Racism in Montana, 1995; assoc. producer (video) White Shamans, Plastic Medicine Men, 1995; contbr. articles to profl. jours. Coord. Native Women's Support Group, Bozeman, 1988-92; mem. Women's Prison Site Selection Com., State of Mont., 1991; bd. dirs. Mont. State Bd. Pvt. Securities and Patrolmen, 1991-93, Mont. Indian Contemporary Artists, 1992—, Am. Indian Family Healing Ctr., Oakland, 1993-95. Rsch. grantee U. Calif., 1993-94, 94-95, Mentor grantee, 1993-94, Career Devel. grantee, 1994-95; Minority fellow Am. Soc. Assn., 1983-87, Dissertation fellow, 1989-90, fellow Newberry Libr., 1994, 95, Postdoctoral fellow Ford Found., 1994-95; K.W. Bergen scholar U. Mont., 1976-77, scholar NIMH, 1979-81. Mem. Am. Sociol. Assn. (sect. racial and ethnic minorities, sect. race, gender, and class), Am. Studies Assn., Mont. Hist. Soc., Sociologists for Women in Soc., Rural Sociol. Soc., Wanzi (conf. co-planner nat. Am. Indian women's conf. 1993), Native Am. Producers Assn. Office: U Calif Dept Native Am Studies Davis CA 95616

ROSS, MADELYN ANN, newspaper editor; b. Pitts., June 26, 1949; d. Mario Charles and Rose Marie (Mangieri) R. B.A., Indiana U. of Pa., 1971; M.A., SUNY-Albany, 1972. Reporter Pitts. Press, 1972-78, asst. city editor, 1978-82, spl. assignment editor, 1982-83, mng. editor, 1983-93; mng. editor Pitts. Post-Gazette, 1993—; bd. dirs. PG Pub. Co.; instr. Community Coll. Allegheny County, 1974-81; Pulitzer Prize juror, 1989, 90. Mem. Task Force Leadership Pitts., 1985-92; v.p. Old Newsboys Charity Fund; bd. dirs. Dapper Dan Charity. Mem. Am. Soc. Newspaper Editors, Women's Press Club. Democrat. Roman Catholic. Office: Pitts Post-Gazette 34 Blvd Of The Allies Pittsburgh PA 15222-1204

ROSS, MARIE HEISE, retired librarian; b. N.Y.C., June 19, 1930; d. Henry Albert and Sophie Elizabeth (Stoever) Heise; m. Leon T. Stark, Aug. 9, 1952 (div. 1977); children: Antony A. Stark, Kathy T. Stark, Leslie Stark Wolff; m. David H. Ross, May 2, 1982; 1 stepchild, Randolph E. BA, CUNY, 1952, MLS, 1969. Cert. libr., N.Y. Sr. libr. Queens Borough Pub. Libr., Jamaica, N.Y., 1969-82, 83-85; libr., indexer H.W. Wilson Co., Bronx, N.Y., 1986-92, ret., 1992. Home: 374 Los Ranchos Rd NW Albuquerque NM 87107-6530

ROSS, MARJORIE H., health care administrator; b. Boston, June 12, 1968; d. Richard B. and Rita A. (Ross) Gordon; m. Adam J. Decter, May 26, 1996. Cert., U. d'Aix-Marseille, France, 1989; BA in Biology and French, Lehigh U., Bethlehem, Pa., 1990; MHS in Health Policy and Mgmt., Johns Hopkins U., Balt., 1995. Cert. EMT. Pharm. sales specialist The Upjohn Co., Phila., 1990-93; rschr. Johns Hopkins U., Balt., 1993; policy analyst The White House Domestic Policy Coun., Washington, 1993-94; policy advisor HHS-Asst. Sec. Health, Washington, 1994-95; sr. policy analyst Principal Health Care, Rockville, Md., 1995—; cons. Nat. Health Policy Coun., Washington, 1994, 95; guest spkr. Johns Hopkins U., Balt., 1993-95. Contbr. chpt. to book. Recipient award for outstanding contbn. to nat. health care reform First Lady, The White House, Washington, 1994, award for role in nat. health reform Sec. HHS, Washington, 1995. Mem. APHA, Group Health Assn. Am. Home: 2300 18th St NW Apt 206 Washington DC 20009

ROSS, MARY RIEPMA COWELL (MRS. JOHN O. ROSS), retired lawyer; b. Oklahoma City, Okla., Oct. 1, 1910; d. Sears F. and Elizabeth (Van Zwaluwenburg) Riepma; AB, Vassar Coll., 1932; LLB, Memphis State U., 1938; LLD, U. Nebr., 1973; m. Richard N. Cowell, Mar. 1, 1946 (dec. Jan. 1953); m. 2d, John O. Ross, Mar. 31, 1962 (dec. June 1966). Bar: Tenn. 1938, D.C. 1944, N.Y. 1947. Atty. U.S. Govt., Washington, 1940-44; pvt. practice Cromelin & Townsend, Washington, 1944-46. Royall, Koegel & Rogers and predecessors, N.Y.C., 1946-61; individual practice law, 1961-88; dir. 39 E. 79th St. Corp., 1966-73; dir. 795 Fifth Ave. Corp., 1977-90; mem. adv. com. N.Y. Commn. on Estates, 1965-67. Bd. dirs. Silver Cross Day Nursery, N.Y.C., 1963-70, Cunningham Dance Found., 1969-72, Central Park Community Fund, 1977-81, Mary Riepma Ross Film Theatre, 1988—; trustee U. Nebr. Found., 1966—, bd. dirs., 1974-79; hon. trustee Nebr. Art Assn. Mem. Am. Bar Assn., N.Y. Women's Bar Assn. (pres. 1955-57, dir. 1957-63, 74-80, adv. coun. 1963—), Bar Assn. City N.Y. (surrogate cts. com. 1961-65, library com. 1965-78, com. on profl. responsibility 1972-75), Nat. Assn. Women Lawyers (assembly del. 1962-64, 73-74, UN observer 1965-67, v.p. 1967, chmn. 1971 ann. conv., distinguished service award 1973), Vassar Coll. Alumnae Assn., Phi Alpha Delta, Delta Gamma, Dinner Dances, Inc. (bd. govs. 1979-93). Address: 2 E 61st St Apt 2404 New York NY 10021-8402

ROSS, MOLLY OWINGS, gold and silversmith, jewelry designer, small business owner; b. Ft. Worth, Feb. 5, 1954; d. James Robertson and Lucy (Owings) R. BFA, Colo. State U., 1976; postgrad., U. Denver, 1978-79. Graphic designer Amber Sky Illustrators and Sta. KCNC TV-Channel 4, Denver, 1977-79; art dir. Mercy Med. Ctr., Denver, 1979-83, Molly Ross Design, Denver, 1983-84; co-owner Deltex Royalty Co., Inc., Colorado Springs, Colo., 1981—, LMA Royalties, Ltd., Colorado Springs, 1993—; art dir., account mgr. Schwing/Walsh Advt., Mktg. and Pub. Rels., Denver, 1984-87, prodn. mgr., 1987-88; jewelry designer Molly O. Ross, Gold and Silversmith, Denver, 1988—. Pres. Four Mile Hist. Park Vol. Bd., Denver, 1985-87; bd. dirs. Four Mile Hist. Park Assn., 1985-86, Hist. Denver, Inc., 1986-87, Denver Emergency Housing Coalition, 1989-90; coun. mem. feminization of poverty critical needs area coun. Jr. League Denver, 1989-90, chmn. children in crisis/edn. critical needs area, 1990-91, chmn. project devel., 1991-92, co-chmn. Done in a Day Comty. Project 75th Anniversary Celebration, 1991-93; mem. bd. dirs., 1993-94, v.p. comty. projects, 1993-94; co-chmn. Project IMPACT, 1994-95; exec. v.p. external affairs Jr. League of Denver, 1995-96; co-chmn. Comty. Coalitions Com., 1996-97; bd. dirs. Rocky Mountain PREP, 1994—; mem. steering com. Denver Urban Resources Partnership, 1995—. Named Vol. of Month (March), Jr. League Denver, 1990, Vol. of Yr., Four Mile Hist. Pk., 1988; recipient Gold Peak Mktg. award-team design Am. Mktg. Assn., 1986, Silver Peak Mktg. award-team design Am. Mktg. Assn., 1986, Gold Pick award-art dir. Pub. Rels. Soc. Am., 1980-81. Mem. Natural Resources Def. Coun., Physicians for Social Responsibility, Am. Farmland Trust, Nat. Trust for Hist. Preservation, Sierra Club, Environ. Def. Fund.

ROSS, PATTI JAYNE, obstetrics and gynecology educator; b. Nov. 17, 1946; d. James J. and Mary N. Ross; B.S., DePauw U., 1968; M.D., Tulane, U., 1972; m. Allan Robert Katz, May 23, 1976. Asst. prof. U. Tex. Med. Sch., Houston, 1976-82, assoc. prof., 1982—, dir. adolescent ob-gyn., 1976—, also dir. phys. diagnosis, dir. devel. dept. ob-gyn.; speaker in field. Bd. dirs. Am. Diabetes Assn., 1982—; mem. Rape Coun. Diplomate Am. Bd. Ob-Gyn, Children's Miracle Network Hermann's Children's Hosp; Olympic torch relay carrier, 1996; founder Women's Med. Rsch. Fund, U. Tex. Med. Sch., Houston. Mem. Tex. Med. Assn., Harris County Med. Soc., Houston Ob-Gyn. Soc., Assn. Profs. Ob-Gyn., Soc. Adolescent Medicine, AAAS, Am. Women's Med. Assn., Orgn. Women in Sci., Sigma Xi. Roman Catholic. Clubs: River Oak Breakfast, Profl. Women Execs. Contbr. articles to profl. jours. Office: 6431 Fannin St Houston TX 77030-1501

ROSS, RHODA, artist; b. Boston, Dec. 24, 1941. Student, Skowhegan Sch. Painting; BFA, RISD, 1964; MFA, Yale U., 1966. tchr. NYU, 1994—, Chautaqua (N.Y.) Sch. Art, 1991; participant Art in Embassies Program Dept of State, Havana, Cuba, 1991-93. One-woman shows include Frick Gallery, Belfast, Maine, Yale U., New Haven, Convent of the Sacred Heart, Mcpl. Art Soc., L.I. U., Emma Willard Sch. Dietal Gallery, Marymount Manhattan Coll., N.Y.C., N.Y.C. Landmarks Preservation Commn. 25th Silver Ann., numerous others; groups shows include The Crane Collection, Boston, Michael Ingbar Gallery, N.Y., N.Y. Studio Sch., N.Y.C., Am. U., Washington, Springfield (Mo.) Art Mus., numerous others; permanent collections include The White House, Gracie Mansion, N.Y.C., The Juilliard Sch., N.Y.C., Bankers Trust, Mus. City of N.Y., Chem. Bank Nat. Hqrs., Lehman Coll., Waldorf Astoria Hotel, N.Y.C., Russian Tea Rm., Rose Assocs., Bklyn. Union Gas, numerous other pvt. and pub. collections; artwork appears on New Sch. Social Rsch. catalog cover, Gifts and Decorative Accessories Mag. cover, UNICEF greeting card. Treas. R.I. Sch. Design Alumni Exec. com., 1986-90. Fellow Va. Ctr. for Creative Arts. Mem. RISD Alumni Assn. (treas. 1986, mem. alumni exec. com.), Phi Tau Gamma. Home and Studio: 473 W End Ave New York NY 10024-4934

ROSS, ROBINETTE DAVIS, publisher; b. London, May 16, 1952; d. Raymond Lawrence and Pearl A. (Robinette) Davis; m. William Bradford Ross, III, Mar. 16, 1979; children: Nellie Tayloe, William Bradford IV; 1 stepchild, Aviza Tayloe. Student, Am. U., 1977-78. Asst. to editor The Chronicle of Higher Edn., Washington, 1978, advt. mgr., 1978-82, advt. dir., 1983-88, assoc. pub., 1988-94; assoc. pub. The Chronicle of Philanthropy, 1988-94; publ. The Chronicle of Higher Edn., Washington, 1994—; pub. The Chronicle of Philanthropy, Washington, 1994—. Mem. Nat. Press Club, Am. News Women's Club, City Tavern Club. Episcopalian. Home: 3908 Virgilia St Chevy Chase MD 20815-5026 Office: The Chronicle of Higher Edn 1255 23rd St NW Washington DC 20037-1125

ROSS, SADYE LEE TATMAN, home health geriatrics nurse; b. Albuquerque, Dec. 5, 1937; d. Charles Robert Tatman and Cecilia Marie Zimmer; m. E. Ray Ross, Nov. 16, 1974. Diploma, Henry Ford Hosp., 1959. RN, Miss., Calif.; cert. gerontol. nurse. Head nurse Orange Meml. Hosp., Orlando, Fla., 1963-64; assoc. dir. Coll. of Calif. Med. Affiliates, San Francisco, 1964-65; ICU staff nurse So. Pacific Hosp., San Francisco, 1965-66; office mgr. Mortimer Weiss, M.D., San Francisco, 1966-70; staff nurse Kwajalein (Marshall Island) Missile Range Hosp., 1970-72, nursing supr., 1974-76; nursing svc. supr. St. Francis Hosp., San Francisco, 1972-74; staff nurse Lawrence County Nursing Ctr., Monticello, Miss., 1989-93, South Miss. Home Health, Prentiss, Miss., 1993—. Mem. Nat. Gerontol. Nurses Assn., Sorosis Club (pres. 1992-94). Home: RR 2 Box 372 Silver Creek MS 39663-9504 Office: South Miss Home Health PO Box 663 Prentiss MS 39474-0663

ROSS, SALLY PRICE, artist, mural painter; b. Cleve., Oct. 25, 1949; d. Philip E. and Mimi (Einhorn) Price; m. Howard D. Ross, Mar. 3, 1979; children: Sasha, Emily. BFA, Kent State U., 1971; MA, U. Iowa, 1974, MFA, 1975; student, Art Students League, N.Y.C., 1976-78. art cons. Art Options, Cleve., 1990-94; 1st and only woman artist to paint murals in the U.S. Capital/Ho. of Reps. corridors, 1978-79, Comm. to paint two Murals for Rainbow Babies and Children's Hosp., (Univ. Hosp.), Cleve. Art exhbns. include Cain Park Art Gallery, Cleve., 1967, Jewish Cmty. Ctr. Cleve., 1967, 86, Canton (Ohio) Art Inst., 1969, Studio Theatre, Iowa City, 1973; designed and executed murals Montefiore Nursing Home, Cleve., 2 murals Rainbow Babies and Children's Hosp. New Bldg., Cleve., 1996. Edwin Abbey scholar, 1975-77, Fresco scholar Skowhegan Sch. Painting and Sculpture, 1977. Home: 25 Millcreek Ln Chagrin Falls OH 44022-1265

ROSS, SHERILYN LOUISE, athletic director, educator; b. L.A., Sept. 3, 1949; d. Jack Edward and Ruth Louise (Kennedy) Danskin. BS, Calif. State U., Long Beach, 1971; MS, Azusa Pacific U., 1974, Adminstrv. Credential, 1974. Cert. athletic adminstr. Tchr. Mission Viego (Calif.) H.S., 1972-73; tchr., athletic dir. El Toro H.S., Lake Forest, Calif., 1973—; varsity swim coach, El Toro H.S., 1975—, tournament dir. state volleyball championships, Calif. Interscholastic Fedn., La Mirada, Calif., 1986—. Treas., pres. Sunset Place Homeowners Assn., Laguna Hills, Calif., 1990-92. Mem. Orange County Athletic Dirs. Assn. (pres. 1985-87), Calif. State Athletic Dirs. Assn. (pres. 1988-89, named Dir. of Yr. 1991), Calif. Interscholastic Fedn. (exec. com. so. sect. 1988-91, mem. state federated coun. 1983—), Nat. Fedn. H.S. Athletics (dirs. adv. com. 1990-93, citation 1990), Nat. Interscholastic Athletic Adminstrs. Assn. 9sect. VII rep.). Democrat. Roman Catholic. Office: El Toro HS 25255 Toledo Way Lake Forest CA 92630

ROSS, SUE, entrepreneur, author, fundraising executive; b. Chgo., Feb. 2, 1948; d. Irving and Rose (Stein) R. BA in Secondary Edn., Western Mich. U., 1971; postgrad., Northwestern U., Chgo. State U., U. Ill., 1971-75. Dir. youth employment Ill. Youth Svcs. Bur., Maywood, Ill., 1978-79; exec. dir. Edn. Resource Ctr., Chgo., 1979-82; asst. dir. devel. Art Inst. Chgo., 1982-83, mgr. govt. affairs, 1983-84, dir. govt. affairs, 1984-85; v.p. devel. Spertus Inst. of Judaica, Chgo., 1985-90; mgmt. and fundraising counsel Sue Ross Enterprises, Chgo. and San Francisco, 1990—; founder, pres. Kid Angels Internat., San Francisco, 1994—; lectr. Sch. Art Inst., Chgo., 1982-85, Episcopalian Archdiocese, Chgo., 1984, Nat. Soc. Fund Raising Execs. and Donor's Forum, Chgo., 1987; instr. DePaul U. Sch. for New Learning, 1987-88, Columbia Coll., Chgo., 1980-91. Resident counsel for devel. The Joffrey Ballet, 1990-91; adv. panelist Chgo. Office Fine Arts, 1981-82; v.p., bd. dirs. Lines Contemporary Ballet, 1995—; mem. adv. coun. Greater Chgo. Food Depository, 1984-85; exec. com. Chgo. Coalition Arts in Edn., 1981-82; mem. info. svcs. com. Donors' Forum Chgo., 1986-88, mem. internationally renowned Gospel Choir of Glide Meml., 1991-93, San Francisco City Chorus, 1994; mem. com. Congregation Sherith Israel, San Francisco Angel Club, 1994, Angel Collector's Club of Am., 1994—, Angels of World, 1994—; resident counsel for devel. The 1995 Children's World Peace Festival. Mem. Nat. Soc. Fund Raising Execs. (mem. svcs. com. Golden Gate chpt. 1993). Democrat. Jewish. Avocations: community service, singing. Home and Office: 1807 Octavia St San Francisco CA 94109-4328

ROSS, VONIA PEARL, insurance agent, small business owner; b. Taylorville, Ill., Dec. 4, 1942; d. Alvin Clyde and Lois Eva (Weller) Brown; m. Wyatt Gene Ross, Nov. 11, 1962 (Div. Nov. 1986); children: Craig Allen Ross, Cayle Allen Ross. Student, So. Ill. U., 1962-64, Palomar Coll., 1986-88, San Diego State U., 1988-90. Real estate agt. Joe Foster Agy., Collinsville, Ill., 1964-69; ofice mgr. real estate Bank of St. Louis, 1969-73; real estate agt. Palmer-Stelman, San Diego, 1986-89; office mgr. real estate McMillin Realty, San Diego, 1989-90; mgr., ins. agt. Calif. Plus Ins., San Diego, 1990-93; prin. Vonia Ross Ins. Agy., 1993—, Bernardo Flooring, 1993—; mem. Calif. Assn. Real Estate, Sacramento, 1986—, San Diego Bd. Realtors, 1986—, Health Underwriters, 1991—. Mem. adv. com. Rancho Bernardo Libr. Campaign, 1994—; active NOW, San Diego, 1988; mem. activist Barbara Boxer Campaign, San Diego, 1992, Susan Golding Campaign, San Diego, 1992, Barbara Warden Campaign for San Diego City Councilwoman. Scholar Ill. Assembly, 1962. Mem. Rancho Bernardo C. of C. (v.p., bd. dirs. 1993—, pres.-elect 1996—), Soroptimists (pres. Rancho Bernardo 1993-94, 95-96). Home: 18284 Fernando Way San Diego CA 92128-1213

ROSS, WENDY CLUCAS, newspaper editor, journalist; b. Balt., Apr. 15, 1942; d. Charles Max and Jean (Talbot) Clucas; m. David N. Ross, Sept. 5, 1964 (div. 1979). BA, Bradley U., 1964. Women's editor DeKalb (Ill.) Daily Chronicle, 1968-69; reporter Chgo. Tribune, 1969-70; copy editor, mag. editor Mpls. Tribune, 1970-72; copy editor Peoria (Ill.) Jour. Star, 1973-75, Miami (Fla.) Herald, 1975-77; asst. news editor Washington Post, 1977-83, dep. news editor, 1983-87, news editor, 1987-93; asst. mng. editor news desk, 1993—. Recipient award of excellence Soc. Newspaper Design, 1985, 87-91, Disting. Alumnae award Bradley U. Centurion Soc., 1994; Nieman fellow Harvard U., 1983-84. Office: The Washington Post 1150 15th St NW Washington DC 20071-0001

ROSSBACHER, LISA ANN, dean, geology educator, writer; b. Fredericksburg, Va., Oct. 10, 1952; d. Richard Irwin and Jean Mary (Dearing) R.; m. Dallas D. Rhodes, Aug. 4, 1978. BS, Dickinson Coll., 1975; MA, SUNY, Binghamton, 1978, Princeton U., 1979; PhD, Princeton U., 1983. Cons. Republic Geothermal, Santa Fe Springs, Calif., 1979-81; asst. prof. geology Whittier (Calif.) Coll., 1982-84; asst. prof. geology Calif. State Poly. U., Pomona, 1984-86, assoc. prof. geol. sci., 1986-91, assoc. v.p. acad. affairs, 1987-93, prof. geol. sci., 1991-93; v.p. acad. affairs, dean faculty Whittier (Calif.) Coll., 1993-95; dean of coll., prof. geology Dickinson Coll., Carlisle, Pa., 1995—; vis. researcher U. Uppsala, Sweden, 1984. Author: Career Opportunities in Geology and the Earth Sciences, 1983, Recent Revolutions in Geology, 1986; (with Rex Buchanan) Geomedia, 1988; columnist Geotimes, 1988—; contbr. articles to profl. jours. Recipient scholarship Ministry Edn. of Finland, Helsinki, 1984; grantee NASA, 1983-94. Mem. AAAS (geol. nominating com. 1984-87), Geol. Soc. Am., Sigma Xi (grantee 1976). Office: Dickinson Coll Dean of the Coll Carlisle PA 17013

ROSSELLINI, ISABELLA, actress, model; b. Rome, June 18, 1952; d. Roberto Rossellini and Ingrid Bergman; m. Martin Scorsese, Sept. 1979 (div. Nov. 1982); m. Jonathan Wiedemann (div.); 1 child, Elettra Ingrid. Student, Finch Coll., 1972, New Sch. for Social Research, N.Y.C. Became model for Lancôme, 1982. Appeared in films A Matter of Time, 1976, Il Pap'occhio, 1980, The Meadow, 1982, White Nights, 1985, Blue Velvet, 1986, Siesta, 1987, Red Riding Hood, 1987, Tough Guys Don't Dance, 1987, Zelly and Me, 1988, Cousins, 1989, Wild at Heart, 1990, Les Dames Galantes, 1990, Death Becomes Her, 1992, The Pickle, 1992, Fearless, 1993, Wyatt Earp, 1994, Immortal Beloved, 1994, The Innocent, 1995, The Funeral, Crime of the Century, 1996, Big Night, 1996; TV films: The Last Elephant, 1990, Lies of the Twins, 1991. Office: United Talent Agency 9560 Wilshire Blvd Fl 5 Beverly Hills CA 90212-2401*

ROSSER, ANNETTA HAMILTON, composer; b. Jasper, Fla., Aug. 28, 1913; d. Carlos Calvin and Jermai Reuben (Gilbert) Hamilton; m. John Barkley Rosser, Sept. 7, 1935 (dec. Sept. 1989); children: Edwenna Merryday, John Barkley Jr. BM, Fla. State U., 1932. Cert. tchr., Fla. Tchr. music Kirby-Smith Jr. High Sch., Jacksonville, Fla., 1932-35; 1st violinist Santa Monica (Calif.) Symphony, 1949-50; concertmaster Ithaca (N.Y.) Chamber Orch., 1948-56; concertmaster Cornell Univ. Orch., Ithaca, 1948-56, soloist, 1957; 1st violinist Princeton (N.J.) Symphony, 1959-61; concertmaster Madison (Wis.) Symphony Orch., 1963-66, 1st violinist, 1967-82. Composer of over 100 vocal and instrumental compositions including Meditations on Cross, song cycle for 2 voices, flute and piano, 1976, An Offering of Song, book of 48 songs, 1977, Songs of a Nomad Flute, song cycle for soprano, flute and piano, 1978, Six Songs of the T'ang Dynasty for soprano and violin, 1983, Nocturne for violin and piano, 1989, Trio for flute, violin and piano, 1991, Scherzo for flute ensemble, 1991. Bd. dirs. Madison Opera Guild, 1972-86, Madison Civic Music Assn., 1983-85; past pres. Madison Symphony Orch. League, Ithaca Federated Music Club, Ithaca Composers Club; trustee Madison Art Ctr., 1979-83, Madison Civics Club, 1976-79, Madison Woman of Distinction, 1980. Recipient Sr. Svc. award Rotary Club, 1994. Mem. AAUW, Univ. League, Univ. League Bird Study Group, Madison Club, Madison Federated Music Club, PEO, Phi Kappa Phi, Pi Kappa Lambda, Sigma Alpha Iota. Republican. Presbyterian. Home: 4209 Manitou Way Madison WI 53711-3703

ROSSER, RHONDA LANAE, psychotherapist; b. Champaign, Ill., Aug. 29, 1953; d. Neill Albert and Grace Lee (Byers) R.; (div. June 1, 1993); children: Anthony Neill Williams, Joseph Neill Jackson Hogan. BS in Psychology, Guilford Coll., 1975; MEd in Edn., U. N.C., Greensboro, 1979, PhD in Counseling, 1991. Joined 3rd Order of Secular Franciscans/Order of St. Francis. Instr. U. N.C., Greensboro, 1985-88; dir. Montagnard Program Luth. Family Svcs., Greensboro, 1985-88; psychotherapist pvt. practice, Greensboro, 1989—. Contbr. articles to profl. jours. Recipient Presdl. citation U.S. Govt., 1987. Mem. Am. Counseling Assn. (Outstanding Rsch. award 1991), Chi Sigma Iota. Democrat. Roman Catholic (3d order of Secular Franciscans/Order of St. Francis). Home and Office: 2318 W Cornwallis Dr Greensboro NC 27408-6802

ROSSET, LISA KRUG, editor; b. N.Y.C., Nov. 11, 1952; d. George William and Rita (Earle) Krug; m. Barney Rosset, Nov. 5, 1980 (div. Dec. 1990); 1 child, Chantal. B.A. magna cum laude, Smith Coll., 1974; M.A., Columbia U., 1976. Editor Latin Am. Series, N.Y.C., 1976-86; gen. editor Grove Press, N.Y.C., 1976-86; mng. editor Aperture, N.Y.C., 1987-90; pvt. practice N.Y.C., 1990—; cons. editor UNICEF, N.Y.C., 1995—. Author: James Baldwin, 1989, Thurgood Marshall, 1993, Outstanding Book For Teenagers, 1994. Mem. Phi Beta Kappa.

ROSSETTI, PAMELA A., advertising executive. Exec. v.p., chief fin. officer, chief adminstrv. officer Commonwealth USA (subsidiary WPP Group PLC), Parsippany, N.J. Office: Ferguson Comm Group 30 Lanidex Plz W Parsippany NJ 07054-2792*

ROSSI, COLUMBIA, foreign correspondent; b. Bklyn., Oct. 4, 1908; m. James Vincent Sileo, Sept. 20, 1928 (dec.); children: Gloria Sileo Smith, Joan V. Sileo Ziccardy, Felicia Sileo. Grad., Bay Ridge High Sch., Bklyn., 1926. Reporter, photographer Internat. News Svc., N.Y.C., 1939; speaker various orgns., experiences as a newswoman in Latin Am. and Europe. Author: Tiajuana Susie, 1951, On a Mission to Danger, Even the Sugarcane Weeps, Bertie: Life After Death of H. G. Wells, 1973. Mem. Overseas Press Club of N.Y. Roman Catholic. Home: 2 Hunter Ln Levittown NY 11756-5114

ROSSI, MARY ANN, research scholar; b. Torrington, Conn., Jan. 25, 1931; d. George James and Virginia Angelina (Negri) R.; m. John Bruce Brackenridge, June 19, 1954; children: Lynn, Sandy (dec.), Rob Brackenridge, Scot. BA in Classics, Conn. Coll. for Women, 1952; MA in Classics, Brown U., 1959; PhD in Classics, U. London, 1982. Asst. prof. English and classics Muskingum Coll., New Concord, Ohio, 1955-59; lectr. in classics and freshman studies Lawrence U., Appleton, Wis., 1959-71; lectr. in humanities U. Wis., Green Bay, 1973-76; lectr. in Greek and Latin City Lit. Inst., London, 1973-75, 80-81; asst. prof. classics Ball State U., Muncie, Ind., 1983-86; rsch. fellow Women's Studies Rsch. Ctr. U. Wis., Madison, 1989-95; ind. scholar London and Appleton, Wis., 1995—. Translator for articles in field. Pres. Fox Valley Human Rights Coun., Appleton, 1976-78; founder Appleton chpt. Archaeol. Inst. Am., 1978; treas. women's classical caucus Am. Classical Assn., 1980-85; mem. exec. bd. Nat. Assn. of Commn. for Women, Appleton, 1978-80; regional dir., reader Latin Exams for Advanced Placement, 1986-88; mem. exec. bd. Nat. Assn. Commns. for Women, Appleton, 1978-80. Fellow Princeton U., 1979, Am. Acad. in Rome, 1983, Stanford U., 1986; grantee NEH, U. Wis., 1991. Mem. NOW, ACLU, Amnesty Internat., So. Poverty Law Ctr. Democrat.

ROSSING, CATHERINE BARRETT SCHWAB, dental hygienist; b. San Francisco, Apr. 8, 1932; d. Richard James and Mary Ann (McAuliff) and Richard Thomas Barrett; m. Donald Theodore Schwab, Aug. 8, 1954 (div. 1965); 1 child, Carla Diane; m. Alan Robert Rossing, Mar. 31, 1989. AA, U. Calif., Berkeley, 1952, BS, 1954; MPA, Calif. State U., 1983. Registered dental hygienist, Calif. Preventive specialist Dr. Thomas Evans Office, Anaheim, Calif., 1968-72, 90; mem. T.E.A.M. program U. So. Calif., L.A., 1972-73; staff hygienist Dr. Joseph Berger Dental Office, Fountain Valley, Calif., 1974-88; pub. Rossing Enterprises, Pebble Beach, Calif., 1991—; co-founder Preventive Dental Care, L.A., 1985-90; co-owner Schwab/Flora Meeting Organizers, Anaheim, 1981-90. Mem. Calif. Dental Hygienists' Assn. (editor jour. 1974-76, 81-84, 89-95, Golden Pen award 1976), Am. Dental Hygienists' Assn. (trustee 1977-81, Recognition award 1981). Home: 1060 Old Dr Pebble Beach CA 93953-2509

ROSSMAN, JANET KAY, architectural interior designer; b. Lansing, Mich., Feb. 13, 1954; d. Elmer Chris and Jean Elizabeth (Schell) R.; m. Farzad Moazed; children: Alexander, Christina. BA with High Honors, Mich. State U., 1976. Designer Tilton & Lewis Assocs., Inc., Chgo., 1977-79, Swanke Hayden Connell & Ptnrs., N.Y.C., 1979-81, Bonsignore Brignati & Mazzotta Architects, N.Y.C., 1982-84; dir. design, assoc. SPGA Group, Inc., N.Y.C., 1984—; instr. Design Edn. Ctr., Lansing, 1975-76. Fellow Mus. Modern Art, N.Y.C., 1977—. Mem. Am. Soc. of Interior Designers (chair. 1973-76, editor Collage 1973-76), Inst. Bus. Designers, Nat. Assn. for Female Execs., Omicron Nu. Republican. Club: Atrium, Landmark. Home: 367 W Hill Rd Stamford CT 06902-1709

ROSSMAN, TOBY GALE, genetic toxicology educator, researcher; b. Weehawken, N.J., June 3, 1942; d. Norman N. and Sylvia Betty (May) Natowitz; m. Neil I. Rossman, Sept. 16, 1962 (div. Sept. 1980); m. Gordon Rauer, Aug. 19, 1990. AB, NYU, 1964, PhD, 1968; postgrad., Brandeis U., 1964-65. Instr. Polytech. Inst. of N.Y., N.Y.C., 1968-69; postdoctoral dept. pathology NYU, N.Y.C., 1969-71; from asst. to assoc. prof. Inst. for Environ Medicine NYU Med Ctr, N.Y.C., 1974-85; prof. Inst. for Environ. Medicine, 1985—; dir. molecular and genetic toxicology Nelson Inst. Environ. Medicine, NYU Med. Ctr., N.Y.C., 1995—. Mem. editorial bd. Molecular Toxicology, 1989-91, Teratogenesis, Carcinogenesis, Mutagenesis, 1990-91, Environmental and Molecular Mutagenesis, 1994—, Mutation Research, 1994—; contbr. numerous articles to profl. jours. EPA grantee, NIH grantee. Mem. AAAS, Assn. for Women in Sci., Am. Assn. for Cancer Rsch., Am. Soc. for Microbiology, Environ. Mutagen Soc. (councilor 1990-93). Office: NYU Inst Environ Medicine Long Meadow Rd Tuxedo Park NY 10987

ROSSO DE IRIZARRY, CARMEN (TUTTY ROSSO DE IRIZARRY), finance executive; b. Ponce, P.R., Feb. 9, 1947; d. Jorge Ignacio and Carmen Teresa (Descartes) Rosso Castain; m. Alfredo R. Irizarry Sile, Aug. 29, 1967. BBA, U. P.R., Rio Piedras. Vice pres. Alcay Inc., San Juan, P.R., 1972—, also bd. dirs.; v.p. J.I.C. Corp., M.I.C. Corp.; bd. dirs., now pres. bd. Construcciones Urbanas Inc., Internat. Fin. Corp. Troop leader Girl Scouts U.S.A., 1977-80; bd. dirs. PTA, San Juan, 1978-81, 86-88; activities coord. Colegio Puertorriqueño Niñas, San Juan, 1987-88; judge Miss P.R. Pageant, San Juan 1987-88, 94, Miss World P.R. Pageant, San Juan, 1987-88, Miss World of P.R., 1990; pres. fundacion dept. Oncologia Pediatrica Hosp. Universitario Dr. Antonio Ortiz, 1990; organizer Best of Saks Fifth Avenue Benefit, 1991, 92, 93, 94, 95, pres. 1992, 94, 96; com. mem. Make a Wish Found. Colleccion Alta Moda, 1994; mem. com. Muceo Ponce Gala, 1994; mem. com. Museo Ponce Coala, 1994; luminaria J.C. Penney, 1994; destellos de la Moda, 1994; pres. Best of Saks 5th Avenue Benefit, 1993, 94. Named to Ten Best Dressed List, San Juan Star, 1986-87, Hall of Fame of Ten Best Dressed, 1989; recipient luminaria J.C. Penney, 1994. Fellow Assn. Porcelanas; mem. Club de Leones (Garden Hills, P.R., Lady of Yr. award 1978), Caparra Country Club (pres. 1985-86), Club Civicos Damas (judge hat how 1989, in charge spl. events 1992), Mu Alpha Phi. Republican. Roman Catholic. Office: Internat Fin Corp PO Box 8486 Santurce San Juan PR 00910-0486

ROSSON, PEGGY, state legislator; b. Apr. 11, 1935. Mem. Tex. State Senate from 29th dist., 1991—. Democrat. Office: Tex State Senate State Capitol Austin TX 78711

ROSSOTTI, BARBARA JILL MARGULIES, lawyer; b. Englewood, N.J., Feb. 28, 1940; d. Albert and Loretta (Jill) Margulies; m. Charles Ossola Rossotti; children: Allegra Jill, Edward Charles. BA magna cum laude, Mount Holyoke Coll., 1961; LLB, Harvard U., 1964. Bar: D.C. 1966. Assoc. Nutter McClennen & Fish, Boston, 1964-65, Covington & Burling, Washington, 1965-72; assoc. Shaw, Pittman, Potts & Trowbridge, Washington, 1972-73, ptnr., 1973—. Trustee Mt. Holyoke Coll., South Hadley, Mass., 1984, vice chmn., 1989-94, chmn., 1994—; chmn. exec. com. Campaign for Mt. Holyoke Coll., 1986-91; trustee Legal Aid Soc., D.C., 1979-92, pres. 1985-89, mem. pres. coun., 1992—; trustee Choral Arts Soc., Washington, 1989-96, chair, 1993-95; bd. dirs. Washington Home, 1989—. Fellow Am. Bar Found.; mem. ABA, Am. Soc. Internat. Law, Internat. Law Assn., D.C. Bar. Office: Shaw Pittman Potts & Trowbridge 2300 N St NW Washington DC 20037-1122

ROSTEN, EMILY, phychologist; b. Ithaca, N.Y., Nov. 2, 1959; d. Arthur and Ellen Ida (Rich) R. BA in Spl. Edn., Mich. State U., 1981; MSW, U. Mich., 1983; PhD, SUNY, 1990. Coord. of counseling svcs. U. Utah Women's Resource Ctr., Salt Lake City, 1990-93; pvt. practice Salt Lake City, 1993—; cons. in field. Recipient Buras B. Crookston Doctural Rsch. award Am. Coll. Pers. Assn., 1990; grantee Sigma Xi in aid of rsch., 1989; Mary Switzer Merit fellow Nat. Inst. on Disability and Rehab. Rsch., 1989. Mem. APA (mem. program com. 1990-93), Am. Deafness and Rehab. Assn., Utah Psychol. Assn. Office: Suite L-5 1060 East 100 S Salt Lake City UT 84102

ROSTODHA, KAREN DEANNE, journalist, reporter; b. San Diego, Mar. 21, 1963; d. Phil L. and Shirley Ann (Quinn) R. BA in Journalism, San Diego State U., 1986. Rschr. San Diego, 1986-87, Sta. KGTV, San Diego, Calif., 1986-87; anchor, reporter Sta. KPRC, Redding, Calif., 1988-90; reporter Sta. KSEE, Fresno, Calif., 1990-93, Sta. KPRC-TV, Houston, 1993-95; freelance journalist Houston, 1995; reporter, anchor Sta. KSBW, Santa Cruz, Calif., 1996—; freelance journalist. Recipient Copley award Copley Newspapers, 1984. Mem. Nat. Assn. Black Journalists, Houston Press Club. Office: Sta KSBW-TV 555 Soquel #220 Santa Cruz CA 95062

ROSTOW, ELSPETH DAVIES, political science educator; b. N.Y.C.; d. Milton Judson and Harriet Elspeth (Vaughan) Davies; m. Walt Whitman Rostow, June 26, 1947; children: Peter Vaughan, Ann Larner. AB, Barnard Coll., 1938; AM, Radcliffe Coll., 1939; MA, Cambridge (Eng.) U., 1949; LHD (hon.), Lebanon Valley Coll.; LLD (hon.), Austin Coll., 1982, Southwestern U., 1988. Mem. faculty various instns. Barnard Coll., N.Y.C. and MIT, Boston, 1939-69; mem. faculty U. Tex., Austin, 1969—, dean div. gen. and comparative studies, 1975-77, prof. govt., 1976—, dean Lyndon B. Johnson Sch. Pub. Affairs, 1977-83, Stiles prof. Am. studies, 1985-88, Stiles prof. emerita, 1988—; mem. Pres.'s Adv. Com. for Trade Negotiations, 1978-82, Pres.'s Commn. for a Nat. Agenda for the Eighties, 1979-81; rsch. assoc. OSS, Washington, 1943-45; Geneva corr. London Economist, 1947-49; lectr. Air War Coll., 1963-81, Army War Coll., 1965, 68, 69, 78, 79, 81, Nat. War Coll., 1962, 68, 74, 75, Indsl. Coll. Armed Forces, 1961-65, Naval War Coll., 1971, Fgn. Svc. Inst., 1974-77, Dept. of State, Europe, 1973; bd. dirs. U.S. Inst. of Peace, vice chmn., 1991, chmn. 1991-92; co-founder The Austin Project, 1991; mem. Gov.'s Task Force on Revenue, Tex., 1991. Author: Europe's Economy After the War, 1948, (with others) American Now, 1968, The Coattailless Landslide, 1974; editor (with Barbara Jordan) The Great Society: A Twenty-Year Critique, 1986; columnist Austin Am. Statesman, 1985-92; contbr. articles to revs., poems to scholarly jours., newspapers, and mags. Trustee Sarah Lawrence Coll., 1952-59, Nat. Acad. Pub. Adminstrn., 1989-95, So. Ctr. for Internat. Studies, 1990—; bd. visitors and govs. St. John's Coll., 1986-89; bd. dirs. Barnard Coll., 1962-66, Lyndon Baines Johnson Found., 1977-83, Salzburg Seminar, 1981-89; vis. scholar Phi Beta Kappa, 1984-85; mem. bd. adv. to pres. Naval War Coll., Newport, R.I., 1995—. Recipient award Air U., ; Fulbright lectr., USIA participant, 1983-84, 90. Mem. Tex. Philos. Soc. (trustee 1989-95), Headliners Found. (vice-chmn. 1996—), Phi Beta Kappa, Phi Nu Epsilon (hon.), Mortar Bd. (hon.), Omicron Delta Kappa. Home: One Wild Wind Point Austin TX 78746 Office: U Tex Drawer Y Univ Station Austin TX 78713

ROTE, NELLE FAIRCHILD HEFTY, business consultant; b. Watsontown, Pa., May 23, 1930; d. Edwin Dunkel and Phebe Hill (Fisher) Fairchild; m. John Austin Hefty, Mar. 20, 1948 (div. June 1970); children: Harry E. Hefty, John B. Hefty, Susan E. Hefty DeBartolo; m. Keith Maynard Rote, Dec. 16, 1983 (dec. Aug. 1985). Student, Bucknell U., 1961, Williamsport Sch. of Commerce, 1968-69, Pa. State U., 1971-72, 83, Susquehanna U., 1986. Typesetter, page designer Colonial Printing House, Inc., Lewisburg, Pa., 1970-76; account exec. Sta. WTGC Radio, Lewisburg, 1976-78; co-owner Colonial Printing Co., Lewisburg, 1978-83; temp. HATS-Temps, Lewisburg, 1986-89; artist, editor Create-A-Book, Inc., Milton, Fla., 1980-92; census crew leader, spl. svc. Dept. Commerce, Washington, 1990; cons. Personalized Books, John B. Hefty Pub. Co., Inc., Gulf Breeze, Fla., 1991—. Artist: Children's Playmate Mag., 1942, Christmas Wish, Big Parade, 1989-90. Vol. proofreader Lewisburg Bicentennial Commn., 1976; editor-poet Holiday Newspaper Bus. Assn., Lewisburg, 1987; charter mem. Women's Art Mus., Washington; charter sponsor Women in Mil. Svc. Meml., Arlington, Va., 1991; chmn. Rooftop Garden Project Evang. Hosp., Pa., 1995—, Nelle Fairchild Rote Book Fund, Union County Libr. Recipient Humanitarian award Tri-County Fedn. Women's Clubs, Pa., 1965, Grand Prize in Cooking, Milton Std., 1966, Most Profl. Photo award, Lewisburg Festival of Arts, 1980, Hon. Mention award Women in Arts, Harrisburg, Pa., 1981, Photo Contest award Congressman Allen Ertel, Washington, 1981, Photo awards 2d and 3d place Union County Fair, Laurelton, Pa., 1981, Hon. Mention Photo award Susquehanna Art Soc., Pa., 1981, Silver award for poetry World of Poetry, 1990. Mem. DAR (nat. def. reporter Shikelimo chpt. 1989-95, sec. 1992-95, regent 1995—), Civic Club Lewisburg (v.p. 1994—), Orgn. United Environment, Nat. Wildlife Fedn. Assn. (cert.), Inst. Lifelong Learning Susquehanna U., Marine Corps League Aux. (life), Union County Hist. Soc. Republican. Home: 1015 Saint Paul St Lewisburg PA 17837-1213

ROTERT, DENISE ANNE, occupational therapist, army officer, educator; b. Sioux Falls, S.D., Nov. 18, 1949; d. Leonard Joseph and Irene Winnifred (Jennings) R. BS, U. Puget Sound, 1971; MA, U. No. Colo., 1975. Commd. 2d lt. Med. Specialist Corps, U.S. Army, 1970, advanced through grades to lt. col. , 1990; staff occupational therapist Tripler Army Med. Center, Honolulu, 1973-76, officer in charge occupational therapy sect. Ireland Army Hosp., Fort Knox, Ky., 1976-77; clin. supr. occupational therapy sect. Letterman Army Med. Center, Presidio of San Francisco, 1977-79; chief instr. occupational therapy asst. course Acad. Health Scis., Ft. Sam Houston, Tex., 1979-84; chief occupational therapy Tri-Service Alcohol Recovery Dept., Naval Hosp., Bethesda, Md., 1984-89, Womack Army Hosp., Ft. Bragg, N.C., 1989-90, ret., 1990; mem. faculty U. S.D., 1991—. Recipient Myra McDaniel Writer's award, 1989. Mem. Am. Occupational Therapy Assn., World Fedn. Occupational Therapists, S.D. Occupational Therapy Assn. Roman Catholic. Home: 2609 S Prairie Ave Sioux Falls SD 57105-4626 Office: USDSM OT Dept 414 E Clark St Vermillion SD 57069-2307

ROTH, ANN, costume designer. Student, Carnegie-Mellon U. costume designer Am. Conservatory Theatre, San Francisco, McCarter Theatre Co., Princeton, Am. Ballet Theatre, Am. Shakespeare Festival, Stratford, Kennedy Ctr. for Performing Arts, Minneapolis Opera, San Francisco Opera, Hartman Theatre Co., Stanford, Long Wharf Theatre, New Haven. Costume designer: (theatre) Maybe Tuesday, 1958, Make a Million, 1958, The Disenchanted, 1958, Edward II, 1958, A Desert Incident, 1959, The Cool World, 1960, Gay Divorcee, 1960, Ernest in Love, 1960, Face of a Hero, 1960, The Pleasure of His Company, 1960-61, A Far Country, 1961, Purlie Victorious, 1961, Look: We've Come Through, 1961, This Side of Paradise, 1962, Isle of Children, 1962, Venus at Large, 1962, A Portrait of the Artist as a Young Man, 1962, The Barroom Monks, 1962, We Comrades Three, 1962, Natural Affection, 1963, Hey You, Light Man!, 1963, Children from Their Games, 1963, A Case of Libel, 1963, The Last Analysis, 1964, Slow Dance on the Killing Ground, 1964, I Had a Ball, 1964, In the Summer House, 1964, The Odd Couple, 1965, 85, Mrs. Dally, 1965, The Impossible Years, 1965, Romeo and Juliet, 1965, The Wayward Stork, 1966, The Star-Spangled Girl, 1966, The Beard, 1967, Something Different, 1967, The Deer Park, 1967, Happiness Is Just a Little Thing Called a Rolls Royce, 1968, Play It Again, Sam, 1969, My Daughter, Your Son, 1969, Tiny Alice, 1969, The Three Sisters, 1969, Gantry, 1970, Purlie, 1970, What the Butler Saw, 1970, The Engagement Baby, 1970, Father's Day, 1971, Prettybelle, 1971, Fun City, 1972, Rosebloom, 1972, Twelfth Night, 1972, Children! Children!, 1972, 6 Rms Riv Vu, 1972, Enemies, 1972, The Merchant of Venice, 1973, Seesaw, 1973, The Women, 1973, The Royal Family, 1975, 85 (Tony award nomination best costume design 1985), The Heiress, 1976, The Importance of Being Earnest, 1977, Do You Turn Somersaults?, 1978, The Best Little Whorehouse in Texas, 1978, The Crucifer of Blood, 1978 (Tony award nomination best costume design 1979), First Monday in October, 1978, They're Playing Our Song, 1979, Strangers, 1979, Lunch Hour, 1980, Gardenia, 1982, Kaufman at Large, 1982, Present Laughter, 1982, The Misanthrope, 1983, Yankee Wives, 1983, Open Admissions, 1984, Hurlyburly, 1984, Design for Living, 1984, Biloxi Blues, 1984, 85, Arms and the Man, 1985, Juno's Swans, 1985, Singin' in the Rain, 1985, Social Security, 1986, The House of Blue Leaves, 1986-87 (Tony award nomination best costume design 1987), Light Up the Sky, 1986, Woman in Mind, 1988, O Pioneers!, 1989-90, Elliot Loves, 1990, Square One, 1990, Road to Nirvana, 1991, Any Given Day, 1993, (films) The World of Henry Orient, 1964, A Fine Madness, 1966, Up the Down Staircase, 1967, Pretty Poison, 1968, Sweet November, 1968, Midnight Cowboy, 1969, The Owl and the Pussycat, 1970, Jenny, 1970, The People Next Door, 1970, Klute, 1971, The Pursuit of Happiness, 1971, They Might Be Giants, 1971, The Valachi Papers, 1972, Law and Disorder, 1974, The Day of the Locust, 1975, The Happy Hooker, 1975, Mandingo, 1975, Murder by Death, 1976, Burnt Offerings, 1976, Independence, 1976, The Goodbye Girl, 1977, California Suite, 1978, Coming Home, 1978, Nunzio, 1979, Promises in the Dark, 1979, Hair, 1979, The Island, 1980, Dressed to Kill, 1980, Nine to Five, 1980, Honky Tonk Freeway, 1981, Only When I Laugh, 1981, Rollover, 1981, Blow Out, 1981, The World According to Garp, 1982, The Man Who Loved Women, 1983, Silkwood, 1983, The Survivors, 1983, Places in the Heart, 1984 (Academy Award nomination best costume design 1984), Sweet Dreams, 1985, The Slugger's Wife, 1985, Maxie, 1985, Jagged Edge, 1985, Heartburn, 1986, The Morning After, 1986, Biloxi Blues, 1988, Funny Farm, 1988, The Unbearable Lightness of Being, 1988, Stars and Bars, 1988, Working Girl, 1988, The January Man, 1989, Her Alibi, 1989, Family Business, 1989, Everybody Wins, 1990, Q & A, 1990, Pacific Heights, 1990, Postcards from the Edge, 1990, The Bonfire of the Vanities, 1990, Regarding Henry, 1991, Consenting Adults, 1992, The Mambo Kings, 1992, School Ties, 1992, A Stranger Among Us, 1992, Dennis the Menace, 1993, Dave, 1993, Guarding Tess, 1993, Wolf, 1994, (TV movies) The Silence, 1975, The Rivalry, 1975, Strangers: The Story of a Mother and Daughter, 1979, A Good Sport, 1984, (TV spls.) The House of Blue Leaves, PBS, 1987, O Pioneers!, PBS, 1991; costume design cons.: (TV spl.) Roanoak, 1986 (Emmy award nomination outstanding costume design 1986). Office: care United Scenic Artists 575 Fifth Ave New York NY 10018*

ROTH, CAROLYN LOUISE, art educator; b. Buffalo, June 17, 1944; d. Charles Mack and Elizabeth Mary (Hassel) R.; m. Charles Turner Barber, Aug. 4, 1991. Student, Art Student's League N.Y., 1965, Instituto Allende, San Miguel de Allende, Mex., 1966; BFA, Herron Sch. Art, 1967; MFA, Fla. State U., 1969. Asst. prof. art U. Tenn., Chattanooga, 1969-72; lectr. art So. Ill. U., Carbondale, 1973-75; asst. prof. art U. Evansville, Ind., 1975-80; lectr. art U. So. Ind., Evansville, 1984—; exhbn. coord., gallery dir. Krannert Gallery, U. Evansville, 1977-79; exhbn. coord., conf. advisor Ind. Women in Arts Conf., Ind. Arts Commn., Evansville, 1978. One woman shows include Wabash Valley Coll., Mt. Carmel, Ill., 1994, So. Ind. Ctr. for Arts, Seymour, Ind., 1996; exhibited in group shows Liberty Gallery, Louisville, 1992, Artlink Contemporary Art Gallery, Ft. Wayne, Ind., 1994, S.E. Mo. Coun. on Arts, Cape Girardeau, 1994, Lexington (Ky.) Art League, 1996, Mills Pond Horse Gallery, St. James, N.Y., 1996, SOHO Gallery, Pensacola, Fla., 1996; works appeared in Contemporary Batik and Tie-Dye, 1973, Kalliope: A Journal of Women's Art, vol. XIV, no. 1, 1992, Jour. Am. Vet. Med. Assn., vol. 203, no. 3, 1993. Mem. Nat. Mus. Women in Arts, Met. Mus. Art, J. B. Speed Mus., Evansville Mus. Arts and Sci., New Harmony Gallery of Contemporary Art. Democrat. Mem. Unity Ch. Home: 10801 S Woodside Dr Evansville IN 47712-8422 Office: U So Ind 8600 University Blvd Evansville IN 47712-3534

ROTH, JANE RICHARDS, federal judge; b. Philadelphia, Pa., June 16, 1935; d. Robert Henry Jr. and Harriett (Kellond) Richards; m. William V. Roth Jr., Oct. 9, 1965; children: William V. III, Katharine K. BA, Smith Coll., 1956; LLB, Harvard U., 1965; LLD (hon.), Widener U., 1986, U. Del., 1994. Bar: Del. 1965, U.S. Dist. Ct. Del. 1966, U.S. Ct. Appeals (3d cir.) 1974. Adminstrv. asst. various fgn. service posts U.S. State Dept., 1956-62; assoc. Richards, Layton & Finger, Wilmington, Del., 1965-73, ptnr., 1973-85; judge U.S. Dist. Ct. Del., Wilmington, 1985-91, U.S. Ct. Appeals (3d cir.), Wilmington, 1991—; adj. faculty Villanova U. Sch. Law. Hon. chmn. Del. chpt. Arthritis Found., Wilmington; bd. overseers Widener U. Sch. Law; bd. consultors Villanova U. Sch. Law; trustee Hist. Soc. Del. Recipient Nat. Vol. Service citiation Athritis Found., 1982. Fellow Am. Bar Found.; mem. ABA, Fed. Judges Assn., Del. State Bar Assn. Republican. Episcopalian. Office: US Ct House J Caleb Boggs Fed Bldg 844 N King St Rm 5100 Wilmington DE 19801-3519

ROTH, JUDITH SHULMAN, lawyer; b. N.Y.C., Apr. 25, 1952; d. Mark Alan and Margaret Ann (Podell) Shulman; m. William Hartley Roth, May 30, 1976; children: Andrew Henry, Caroline Shulman. AB, Cornell U., 1974; JD, Columbia U., 1977. Bar: N.Y. 1978, U.S. Dist. Ct. (ea. dist.) N.Y. 1978, U.S. Dist. Ct. (so. dist.) N.Y. 1978, U.S. Ct. Appeals (2d cir.) 1993. Assoc. Phillips Nizer Benjamin Krim & Ballon, N.Y.C., 1978-87, ptnr., 1988—; lectr. CLE Fordham Law Sch., N.Y.C., 1990. Mem. Cosmopolitan Club. Jewish. Office: Phillips Nizer Benjamin Krim & Ballon 666 Fifth Avenue New York NY 10103

ROTH, KATHRYN GAIE, government executive; b. Torrejon, Spain, Mar. 19, 1964; came to U.S., 1964; d. Edwin Isaac and Deborah (Weissman) R. BA, Bryn Mawr Coll., 1987; MPA, Princeton U., 1991. Founder, editor-in-chief Jour. for Pub. and Internat. Affairs, Princeton, N.J., 1989-91; asst. sec. to bd., dir. spl. projects Nathan Cummings Found., N.Y.C., 1991-92; assoc. dir. presdl. advance White House, Washington, 1993-95; v.p. Revlon Found. MacAndrews & Forbes Holding, Inc., N.Y.C., 1995-96; exec. dir. U.S. Dept. Def. Indsl. Affairs and Installations, 1996—; polit. cons. Mondale Campaign, Dukakis Campaign, Simon Campaign, Clinton for Pres. Campaign and Transition. Contbg. author: Public Opinion in U.S. Foreign Policy: The Controversy Over Contra Aid, 1994; contbr. articles to profl. publs. Mem. Dem. Bus. Coun. Women's Leadership Forum; bd. dirs. N.Y. Dem. Leadership Coun. Recipient Conf. Paper award Assn. Profl. Schs. of Internat. Affairs, 1991; Woodrow Wilson fellow, 1989-91. Mem. Women in Philanthropy, Coun. Fgn. Rels. (team member), Dem. Bus. Coun. N.Y., Dem. Leadership Coun. Democrat. Jewish. Home: 525 E 86th St Apt 10B New York NY 10028-7515 Office: DVSD CIA&I/A&T Rm 3E1074 3300 Defense Pentagon Washington DC 20301-3300

ROTH, MARTHA ALICE, writer, editor; b. Chgo., May 1, 1938; d. Joseph Russell and Sylvia (Weinstein) Silverman; m. Marty Roth, June 7, 1957; children: Molly, Jennifer, David. AB, U. Chgo., 1958. Author: (novel) Goodness, 1996; editor: Mother Journeys, 1994 (Minn. Book award 1995, Popular Culture Assn. award 1995), Transforming a Rape Culture, 1993. Fellow State Arts Bd., 1991. Mem. Nat. Writers Union (v.p. 1987-90), Nat. Writers United Svcs. Orgn. (pres. 1993—), The Loft (Loft-McKnight fellow 1992). Home: 2521 Irving Ave S Minneapolis MN 55405

ROTH, NANCY LOUISE, former nurse, veterinarian; b. Cin., June 24, 1955; d. Jack Leopold Jr. and Elsie Harriet (Shemin) R. BS in Agr., U. Mo., 1977, DVM, 1989; BSN, Avila Coll., 1980. Critical care RN. Staff nurse St. Louis Univ. Hosp., 1980-81, Barnes Hosp., St. Louis, 1981-85, U. Mo. Hosp. and Clinic, Columbia, 1985-89; assoc. veterinarian Ill. Equine Field Svc., North Aurora, 1989-95; proprietor Cedar Ln. Equine Clinic, New Haven, Mo., 1995—. Contbr. articles to profl. jours. Vol. instr. U.S. Pony Club, Wayne, Ill., 1991-95, 4-H Club, Wheaton, Ill., 1991-95; bd. dirs. Ill. Dressage and Combined Tng. Assn. Mem. AVMA, Am. Assn. Equine Practitioners (trails and events com.), Sigma Theta Tau, Phi Zeta. Home: 3134 Hwy E New Haven MO 63068 Office: Cedar Ln Equine Clinic PO Box 108 New Haven MO 63068-0108

ROTH, PAMELA JEANNE, marketing professional, web site developer; b. Huntington, N.Y., Sept. 9, 1955; d. Julius Leo and Constance Abby (Gettenberg) R. BA with honors, New Coll. Hofstra U., 1975; MS, Rensselaer Inst. Tech., 1977; JD, New England Sch. Law, 1983; postgrad., Sandler Sales Inst., 1996. Assoc. editor Functional Photography, Hempstead, N.Y., 1976; documentation specialist Allendale Ins., Johnston, R.I., 1977-78; systems analyst Comml. Union Ins., Boston, 1978-79; sr. software writer NEC Info. Systems, Lexington, Mass., 1979-82; pres. TEKDOC Tech. Communications, North Andover, Mass., 1978-86; sr. tech. writer Software Internat., Andover, Mass., 1983; pres., CEO SPIRAL Communications, Inc., SPIRAL Group, SPIRAL Books, Manchester, N.H., 1986—; developer Ofcl. Olympic Torch Relay event web site, Nashua, N.H., 1996; presenter in field. Author: The First Book of Adam, 1984, The Second Book of Adam, 1984, Using the PFS Family, 1985; editor: Data Warehousing and Decision Support-The State of the Art, 1995, Data Warehousing and Decision Support, vol. 2, 1996; contbr. articles to profl. jours. Gen. mgr. ImprovBoston, 1986. Mem. Women Owners Network. Office: SPIRAL Comms Inc Stark Mill Bldg Ste 401 500 Commercial St Manchester NH 03101-1151

ROTH, PAMELA SUSAN, lawyer; b. N.Y.C., Nov. 23, 1961; d. Edward Abraham and Susan Violet (Castro) R. BS in Biology, Adelphi U., 1982, MBA, 1986; JD, Pace U., 1990. Bar: N.Y. 1991, U.S. Dist. Ct. (ea. and so. dists.) N.Y. 1991, U.S. Ct. Appeals (10th cir.) 1993, Colo. 1995, U.S. Dist. Ct. Colo. 1995, U.S. Supreme Ct. 1995. Asst. gen. counsel N.Y.C. Dept. Probation, Bklyn., 1990-91; asst. dist. atty. Kings County Dist. Atty., Bklyn., 1992-93; assoc. Law Firm of Portales & Assocs., Denver, 1993-95; pvt. practice N.Y.C., 1995—; gen. counsel Hispano Crypto-Jewish Rsch. Ctr., Denver, 1994—. Mem. ABA, Am. Soc. Internat. Law, Hispanic Nat. Bar Assn., Bklyn. Bar Assn., Internat. Assn. Jewish Lawyers and Jurists, Kings County Criminal Bar Assn. Office: 26 Court St Ste 2003 Brooklyn NY 11242

ROTH, SHARON A., early childhood educational administrator; b. Watervliet, N.Y., Feb. 9, 1954; d. Patrick John Donlon Sr. and Elmina Helen (Wickware) McQuire; m. Richard L. Roth, June 16, 1973; children: Issac Jacob, SerahRose Gillett. AS, Norwalk C.C., 1984; BA, Goddard Coll., 1986, MA, 1988. Cert. tchr., Conn. Tchr., adminstr. Learning Comty., Westport, Conn., 1980-86; tchr. Mead Sch., Greenwich, Conn., 1988-90; adminstr. Inst. for Children's Lit., Redding, Conn., 1990-92, Saugatuck Child Care Svcs., Inc., Westport, 1992-96; validator Nat. Acad. for Edn. of Young Children, Washington, 1993—. Author: (student anthology) Goddard College Collection, 1987, 88. Mem. AAUW (bull. editor 1994-95), Nat. Assn. for Edn. of Young Children.

ROTH, SUSAN KING, design educator; b. Millville, N.J., Nov. 13, 1945; d. Frank N. and Ruth (Ludlam) King; m. Richard L. Roth, Sept. 17, 1973; 1 child, Justin King Roth. BFA, Cooper Union, 1968; MA, Ohio State U., 1988. With advt. prodn. Mayer/Martin, Inc., N.Y.C., 1968-70; dir. graphics N.Y.C. Parks, Recreation and Cultural Affairs Adminstrn., 1970-73; designer Whole Earth Epilog, Sausalito, Calif., 1974-75; asst. art dir. TV Guide mag., Radnor, Pa., 1975-77; design cons. various orgns., Chgo., 1978-80; instr., tchg. assoc. Ohio State U., Columbus, 1985-88, assoc. prof., 1988—, assoc. dean Coll. Arts, 1996; vis. designer Sch. Art Inst., Chgo., 1980-81, Ohio Wesleyan U., Delaware, 1982-84; co-founder, co-dir. Ctr. for Interdisciplinary Studies, Columbus, 1992—; vis. evaluator Nat. Assn. Schs. Art and Design, Reston, Va., 1994—; mem. faculty adv. com. to chancellor Ohio Bd. Regents, 1994—; cons. Elections Adminstrn., Franklin County Bd. Elections, Columbus, 1995—. Consulting editor Jour. Visual Literacy, 1992—; contbr. articles to profl. jours. Battelle grantee Battelle Endowment for Tech. & Human Affairs, 1993-94. Mem. Am. Ctr. Design, Assn. Computing Machinery, Graphic Design Edn. Assn., Internat. Visual Literacy Assn., Indsl. Designers Soc. Am. (mem. edn. bd. 1993-95). Home: 3158 Glenrich Pky Columbus OH 43221-2639 Office: Ohio State U 380 Hopkins Hall Columbus OH 43210

ROTH, SUZANNE ALLEN, financial services agent; b. Santa Monica, Calif., May 31, 1963; d. Raymond A. and Ethel Allen; m. Steve Milstein Roth, Dec. 27, 1992. BA, U. Calif., Santa Cruz, 1986; student, Calif. State U., L.A., 1987-93, Art Ctr. Sch. Design, Pasadena, Calif., 1994—. Cert. tchr., Calif.; lic. real estate agt., Calif. Interviewer L.A. Times Newspaper, 1986-88; educator L.A. Unified Sch. Dist., 1987-90; educator Burbank (Calif.) Unified Sch. Dist., 1990-94, vol., 1994—; ptnr. fin. svcs. Roth & Assocs./N.Y. Life, L.A., 1993—. Mem. NEA, Burbank Tchrs. Union.

ROTHACKER-PEYTON, SALLY STEPHANIE, clinical nurse specialist; b. Broadview Heights, Ohio, Oct. 13, 1954; d. Emil C. and Lillian Stephanie (Nebesar) Rothacker; m. Robert L. Peyton, June 25, 1983. AA, Cuyahoga Community Coll., 1974; BSN, Case Western Reserve U., 1977; MS in Nursing, U. Hawaii, 1983. RN; clin. nurse specialist in mental health, N.D. Clin. nurse U. Hosp. of Cleve., 1977-78; charge nurse Queen's Med. Ctr.-Kekela, Honolulu, 1978-83; instr. nursing U. Tex. at El Paso, 1984-89; clin. nurse specialist Fair Oaks Hosp., Delray Beach, Fla., 1989-90; coord. adult survivor program Fair Oaks, Delray Beach, 1990-91; mem. Nurse Healer's Profl. Assocs.; mem. N.D. critical incident stress debriefing team. Named Outstanding Young Women in Am., 1987. Mem. ANA, N.D. Nurses' Assn. (conv. spkr. 1996), So. Fla. Psychiat. Nursing Network (conf. spkr. 1990), Nurses Coalition for Action in Politics, NOW, Greenpeace, Sierra Club, Nat. Wildlife Fedn., Sigma Theta Tau. Office: Unimed Med Ctr South 600 17th Ave SE Minot ND 58701

ROTHENBERG, DEBRA L., photographer; b. Paterson, N.J., Feb. 18, 1962; d. Marvin Joseph and Janet Dorothy (Fives) R. BFA, Rochester (N.Y.) Inst. Tech., 1984. Staff photographer The Recorder, Amsterdam, N.Y., 1984-85, Public Opinion, Chambersburg, Pa., 1985-86; chief photographer Ocean County Reporter, Toms River, N.J., 1986-87; sr. photographer Monmouth County Park Sys., Lincroft, N.J., 1988—; photographer Names project AIDS Meml. Quilt, 1992—, March of the Living holocaust trip 1996. Solo exhbns. It's Only Rock-n-Roll: N.J. Musicians, 1990, Out of the Ashes: Poland to Israel, 1996; group exhbns. Women's Eye, 1995, Art Forms Gallery, Red Bank, N.J., 1996; editor/photographer (calendar) It's Only Rock-n-Roll: N.J. Musicians, 1990. Mem. Nat. Press Photographers Assn. (nat. 1st pl. award sports 1985), N.J. Press Assn., NOW. Democrat. Jewish. Home: Box 822 Matawan NJ 07747

ROTHENBERG, ELIZABETH JILL, editor; b. N.Y.C., Mar. 9, 1966; d. Jerry and Roslyn Diane (Rosenberg) R. BA, Colby Coll., 1989; M in Journalism, Northwestern U., Evanston, Ill., 1991; postgrad., U. Denver, 1992. Assoc. McKinzey-White Booksellers, Colorado Springs, Colo., 1989-90; reporter, Washington corr. Madison (Wis.) Capital Times, 1991; reporter Sonora (Calif.) Union Democrat, 1991-92; book editor in criminology, African Am. studies Westview Press/Harper Collins Pubs., Boulder, Colo., 1993—. Mem. Phi Beta Kappa. Office: Westview Press HarperCollins Pubs 5500 Central Ave Boulder CO 80301

ROTHERMEL, JOAN MARIE, occupational health nurse; b. Reading, Pa., Mar. 4, 1940; d. Andrew and Marie (Hilbert) Kuzan; m. James Carlton Rothermel, Dec. 15, 1965; 1 child, Wayne Lee. RN, Capitol City Sch. Nursing/, D.C. Gen. Hosp., 1960; BS, St. Joseph Coll., North Windham, Maine, 1983. Cert. occupational health nurse. Nurse Profl. Arts Ctr., Norwalk, Calif., 1962-64; pvt. duty nurse Reading (Pa.) Hosp. Med. Ctr., 1964-67; staff nurse/charge nurse Maple Farm Nursing Home, Akron, Pa., 1969-70; indsl. nurse Hamilton Tech., Lancaster, Pa., 1970-71; indsl. nurse/personnel sec. Rutt Custom Kitchens, Goodville, Pa., 1974-77; dir. nursing Ephrata (Pa.) Nursing Home, 1977-80; occupational health nurse C&D Batteries/Allied Corp., Leola, Pa., 1980-83, R.R. Donnelley & Sons, Lancaster, Pa., 1983-86; coord. occupational health svcs. Lancaster Gen. Hosp., 1986—. Profl. adv. com. March of Dimes, Lancaster, 1984-87; instr. CPR, standard first aid, ARC, Lancaster, 1983—. Mem. Ctrl. Pa. Assn. Occupl. Health Nurses (dir. 1985-88, 1st v.p. 1988-90), Pa. Assn. Occpl. Health Nurses (bd. dirs. 1988-90, chmn. 1991-94). Republican. Home: 126 W Metzler Rd PO Box 44 Brownstown PA 17508 Office: Lancaster Gen Hosp Corp Care Box 10547 1866 Colonial Village Ln Lancaster PA 17605

ROTHLEUTNER, PHYLLIS HARRIET, rancher; b. Neligh, Nebr., Apr. 24, 1928; d. Ralph Leslie and Marguerite L. Carnes; m. Wesley M. Rothleutner (dec. Aug. 1992); children: Elise M. Douglas, Todd W. BA, Nebr. Wesleyan U., 1950. Ptnr. Rothleutner Family Ranch, Todd County, S.D., Cherry County, Nebr.; mem. Cattlemen's Beef Bd., 1987-95, nominating com., dubget, rsch., adminstrn. and fgn. mktg. coms. Bd. trustees Cherry County Hosp., chmn.; charter mem. Cozy Fireside Ext. Club, Kilgore; state ext. sec., 1977-78; leader 4-H. Recipient Alumni Loyalty award Nebr. Wesleyan U., 1973. Mem. Am. Nat. Cattlewomen (exec. com. 1983-84, 88-93, membership chmn. 1987, 88, 2d v.p. 1988, 1st v.p. 1989, budget com. chmn. 1989, regional meetings chmn. 1990, pres. 1991, chmn. nominating com. 1992, chmn. outstanding cattlewomen com. 1992, nat. beef cookoff com. 1988-91, Outstanding Cattlewoman of Yr. award 1995, San Antonio, 1996), Nat. Cattlemen's Beef Assn., N.E. Cattlemen, Nebr. Cattlewomen (chmn. 1977, 78, sec.-treas. 1978-79, 2d v.p., chmn. Beef for Fathersday 1979-80, 1st v.p., membership chmn. 1980-81, pres. 1981-82, beeferendum chmn. 1981-82, Outstanding CattleWoman of Yr. award 1994), Agrl. Women's Leadership Network (treas., v.p., pres. 1995-96), Order of Ea. Star (Worthy Matron 1970, 93, 94, grand rep. Wash. state 1994, 95), Beta Sigma Phi (pres.). Home and office: PO Box 88 Kilgore NE 69216-0088

ROTHMAN, DEANNA, electroplating company executive; b. Bklyn., Sept. 20, 1938; d. Frank Philip and Elsie (Goldstein) Dukofsky; m. Edward Rothman, Dec. 8, 1956 (div. July 1984); children: Jeffrey Scott, Michele Dawn, Robert Jay; m. Ronald Friedman, Aug. 17, 1986. B.A., Bklyn. Coll., 1968. Exec. Bronzemaster Co., Bklyn., 1969-80, Perma Plating Co. Inc., Bklyn., 1980-84; pres. Duratron Finishing Corp., Bklyn., 1984—, Skillman Metal Corp., Bklyn., 1987—. Sec. Tenants Assn., S.I., 1973-77; v.p. Orgn. Rehab. and Tng., Woodmere, N.Y., 1978-80; sponsor Spl. Olympics; mem. East N.Y. Local Devel. Corp. Mem. Masters Electroplating Assn., Am. Metal Finishers, NAFE, NOW, SCORE. Republican. Avocations: painting, collecing art deco, dance, theatre. Office: Duratron Finishing Corp PO Box 789 East NY Sta Brooklyn NY 11207

ROTHMAN, ROSALIND WEISS, special education educator; b. N.Y.C., Aug. 12, 1930; d. Daniel and Sadye Tamor W.; children: Gwen Roginsky, Rachel Roginsky. BS Psychology, Columbia U., 1952; MA, Bank St. Coll. of Edn., 1954, MA/Tchr.'s Coll., 1967, EdD/Tchr.'s Coll., 1980. Spl. edn. tchr., cons. Mt. Vernon, Scarsdale and Eastchester Sch. Dists., 1976-82; asst. prof. spl. edn. Coll. New Rochelle, N.Y., 1971-79; assoc. prof. spl. edn. So. Conn. State U., New Haven, 1980-87; dir. Total Learning Ctr., Inc., Harrison, N.Y., 1983-91, Lang. and Learning Assocs., Harrison, 1991—; adj. instr. BOCES, Tchr. Ctr. of Ardsley, Greenburgh, Coll. New Rochelle, 1987—; lectr., adj. prof. L.I. U., Coll. of New Rochelle; presenter workshops and insvc. edn. N.Y., N.J., Conn., St. Thomas, V.I.; grant writer. Co-author: Fostering Young Learners: Activities for Parents and Teachers, 1990, Developing Your Baby's Potential, 1991; contbr. to publs. in field, profl. jours. Mem. Nat. Assn. Children with Learning Disabilities, Internat. Dyslexic Found., Orton Soc., Coun. Exceptional Children, Internat. and Westchester Reading Assn., Delta Kappa Gamma. Office: Lang and Learning Assn 550 Mamaroneck Ave Ste 103 Harrison NY 10528

ROTHMAN, SHARI LATZ, harpist, educator; b. Mpls., Feb. 16, 1970; d. Robert and Carolyn Mae (Spater) Latz; m. Michael J. Rothman, Aug. 1, 1993. MusB with highest distinction, U. Mich., 1992; postgrad., U. So. Calif., 1992—. Harpist various orchs., Mich., 1990-92; tchg. fellow harp U. So. Calif., L.A., 1992-95; instr. piano Calif. State U. Saturday Conservatory, L.A., 1995—; pvt. tchr. harp, L.A., 1995—, pvt. tchr. piano, 1996; tchr. art U.S. Art Ctr., L.A.; freelance harpist, L.A. Appeared with Long Beach (Calif.) Symphony Orch., Pasadena (Calif.) Symphony Orch., L.A. Master Chorale Sinfonia Orch., Music Acad. of West Festival Orch.; prin. harpist U. So. Calif. Symphony, Santa Monica (Calif.) Symphony, Young Musicians Found. Debut Orgn. Vol. White House Advance Staff, L.A., 1993-95, Mus. of Tolerance, L.A., 1996, My Jewish Discovery Place Children's Mus., L.A., 1996. Mem. Am. Harp Soc. (adjudicator music edn. workshops L.A. 1993-95), Am. String Tchrs. Assn., Pi Kappa Lambda. Democrat. Jewish. Home: 8722 Burton Way Apt 308 Los Angeles CA 90048

ROTHMAN, SHEILA MILLER, historian; b. Phila., Jan. 25, 1939; d. Harry and Rose (Newman) Miller; m. David J. Rothman, June 26, 1960; children: Matthew S., Micol S. BS, Simmons Coll., 1960, MSW, 1963; PhD, Columbia U., 1989. Rsch. assoc. Ctr. for Policy Rsch., N.Y.C., 1972-78, Columbia U., 1978-84; rsch. scholar Columbia Coll. Physicians and Surgeons, N.Y.C., 1984-95, sr. rsch. scholar, 1995—; bd. dirs. Asia Walch, N.Y.C., Profl. Med. Ctr., Albany, N.Y. Author: Living in the Shadow of Death, 1994, Woman's Proper Place, 1978; co-author: The Willowbrook Wars, 1984. Fellow NEH, 1987-90, NIH, 1979-81; rsch. grantee Field Found., 1976-78, Rudin Family Found., 1984-91. Office: Columbia Coll Phys/Surgeons 630 W 168th St New York NY 10032

ROTHMAN-BERNSTEIN, LISA J., operating room nurse; b. Toledo, Dec. 29, 1949; 1 child, Daniel Karvinen. Diploma, Mercy Hosp. Sch. Nursing, Toledo, 1974; B Individualized Studies magna cum laude, Lourdes Coll., Sylvania, Ohio, 1989; AS in Bus., U. Toledo, 1970; student, U. Florence, Italy, 1972. Buyer Lamson's of Toledo; owner/designer FUNKtional Art, Inc.; owner/baker Tres Bon Cheesecakes, Inc., Margate, Fla.; cruise ship nurse Costa Cruise Line, Miami, Fla.; home health nurse Upjohn, Ft. Lauderdale, Fla.; patient svcs. coord. Fla. Med. Ctr., Lauderdale Lakes, Fla.; vol. nurse in ob-gyn. Yoseftal Hosp., Eilat, Israel; staff nurse in ob-gyn. Mt. Sinai Med. Ctr., Miami Beach, Fla.; staff nurse on eye svc., oper. rm. St. Vincent Med. Ctr., Toledo; nursing and healthcare recruiter, customer svc. advocate emergency dept. Co-chmn. Lourdes Coll. Red Cross Blood Drive, 1988-89; publicity chairperson St. Vincent Med. Ctr. 1993 Nurses' Week. Mem. Assn. Operating Rm. Nurses, Nat. Assn. of Health Care Recruiters, Kappa Gamma Pi.

ROTHMAN-DENES, LUCIA BEATRIZ, biology educator; b. Buenos Aires, Feb. 17, 1943; came to U.S., 1967; d. Boris and Carmen (Couto) Rothman; m. Pablo Denes, May 24, 1968; children: Christian Andrew, Anne Elizabeth. Lic. in Chemistry, Sch. Scis., U. Buenos Aires, 1964, PhD in Biochemistry, 1967. Vis. fellow NIH, Bethesda, Md., 1967-70; postdoctoral fellow biophysics U. Chgo., 1970-73, rsch. assoc., 1973-74, asst. prof., 1974-79, assoc. prof., 1980-83, prof. molecular genetics and cell biology, 1983—; mem. microbial genetics study sect. NIH, 1980-83, 93-96, chair, 1994-96, genetic basis of disease study sect., 1985-89; mem. Damon Runyon and Walter Winchell Sci. Adv. Com., N.Y.C., 1989-93; mem. biochemistry panel NSF, 1990-92. Contbr. numerous articles to profl. publs. Fellow Am. Acad. Microbiology; mem. AAAS, Am. Soc. Microbiology (divsn. chair 1985, divsn. group II rep. 1990-92, vice chair GMPC 1995—), Am. Soc. Virology (councilor 1987-90), Am. Soc. Biochemistry and Molecular Biology. Office: Univ Chgo 920 E 58th St Chicago IL 60637-1432

ROTHROCK, JANE CLAIRE, nursing educator; b. Abington, Pa., Mar. 20, 1948; d. John Richard and Dorothea Ethel (Leser) Lynch; m. Joseph Rothrock, III, Apr. 17, 1977. BSN, U. Pa., 1974, MSN, 1978; DNSc, Widener U., 1987. Staff nurse Hosp. U. Pa., Phila., 1969-71, staff developer, 1971-74; dir. operating room Grad. Hosp., Phila., 1974-76; clin. instr. U. Pa., Phila., 1976-77; dir. operating room, Bryn Mawr Hosp., Pa., 1978-79; prof. Delaware County Community Coll., Media, Pa., 1979-87, prof., 1987—; pres. Quest RN Inc., Wallingford, Pa., 1983—; mem. adv. bd. Sch. of Nursing, U. Pa., 1990—. Bd. dirs. Community Mental Health Ctr., Chester, Pa., 1980-90. Author: Chesapeake Odysseys, 1984, Perioperative Care Planning, 1990, 96; editor: The RN First Assistant, 1986, 93, Core Curriculum for RN First Assistants, 1990, 94, Alexanders Care of the Patient in Surgery, 1991, 95; editor, pub. newsletter First Hand; contbr. articles to profl. jours. Assn. Operating Rm. Nurses scholar, 1974, 85-86, 86-87. Mem. ANA, Pa. Council Operating Rm. Nurses (pres. 1984-86), Assn. Operating Rm. Nurses (bd. dirs. 1987-91, treas 1991-93, pres. 1994-95, edit. bd. 1983-86, research com. 1986-87, pres.-elect 1993-94, pres. 1994-95), Soc. Research in Nursing Edn., Nursing Orgn. Liaison Forum (vice chair 1995—). Republican. Methodist. Clubs: Pine Ridge Garden, Jr. Womens. Avocations: sailing, skiing, needlework. Office: Del County CC 901 S Media Line Rd Media PA 19063

ROTHS, BEVERLY OWEN, organization executive; b. Kansas City, Kans., Aug. 25, 1935; d. Edward Charles and Josephine Mary (Vogel) Owen; m. Robert L. Roths, Sept. 4, 1954; children: Karen Kay, Daniel Owen, Nancy Jo. AA with honors, Antelope Valley Coll., 1975. Sec. McDonnell Aircraft Co., St. Louis, 1955-58; exec. dir. Florissant (Mo.) Valley C. of C., 1976-86; pres. Poppy Reserve/Mojave Desert Interpretive Assn., Lancaster, Calif., 1989—; pres. Soroptimist Internat., North St. Louis County, 1981-82; sec.-treas. St. Louis County League C. of C., Clayton, 1978. Prodr. Small Bus. Profiles, condr. interviews Storer Cable TV, Florissant, 1983-96. Mem. Florissant City Coun., 1968-72; bd. dirs. Mo. Mcpl. League First Woman, Florissant, 1970-71; co-chair Bicentennial, Florissant, 1985-86, Police Bldg. Bond Issue, Florissant, 1980. Recipient Woman of Achievement award Florissant Bus. and Profl. Women, 1979; Inst. Orgn. Mgmt. scholar C. of C., Jefferson City, Mo., 1980. Mem. Lancaster Woman's Club, Wildflower Preservation Found. (bd. dirs., treas. 1991—), League Calif. State Park Non-Profit Orgns. (bd. dirs., sec. 1994—). Roman Catholic. Office: PO Box 1408 Lancaster CA 93548

ROTHSCHILD, AMALIE RANDOLPH, filmmaker, producer, director, digital artist, photographer; b. Balt., June 3, 1945; d. Randolph Schamberg and Amalie Getta (Rosenfeld) R. BFA, R.I. Sch. Design, 1967; MFA in Motion Picture Production, NYU, 1969. Spl. effects staff in film and photography Joshua Light Show, Fillmore E. Theatre, NYC, 1969-71; still photographer TWA Airlines Pub. Relations Dept., Village Voice newspaper Rolling Stone magazine, Newsweek magazine, After Dark, N.Y. Daily News, numerous others, 1968-72; co-founder, partner New Day Films, distbn. coop., 1971—; owner, operator Anomaly Films Co., NYC, 1971—; mem., co-founder Assn. of Independent Video and Filmmakers, Inc., NYC, 1974, bd. dirs., 1974-78; instr. in film and TV, N.Y. U. Inst. of Film and TV, 1976-78; cons. in field to various organizations including Youthgrant Program of Nat. Endowment for Humanities, Washington, 1973-76; motion pictures include: Woo Who? May Wilson, 1969; It Happens to Us, 1972; Nana, Mom and Me, 1974; Radioimmunoassay of Renin, Radioimmunoassay of Aldosterone, 1977; Conversations with Willard Van Dyke, 1981; Richard Haas: Work in Progress, 1984; Painting the Town: The Illusionistic Murals of Richard Haas, 1990 (Emily award Am. Film and Video Festival 1990), A Meditation on the Olive, 1996; editor: Doing It Yourself, Handbook on Independent Film Distribution, 1977. Mem. Community Planning Bd. 1, Borough of Manhattan, N.Y.C., 1974-86. Recipient spl. achievement award Mademoiselle mag., 1972; independent filmmaker grant, Am. Film Inst., 1973; film grantee N.Y. State Coun. on the Arts, 1977, 85, 87, Nat. Endowment Arts, 1978, 85, 87, Md. Arts Coun., 1977, Ohio Arts and Humanities Couns., 1985. Mem. Assn. Ind. Video Filmmakers (bd. dirs. 1974-78) Univ. Film and Video Assn., N.Y. Women in Film, Ind. Documentary Assn., Laboratorio Immagine Donna. Democrat. Address: 135 Hudson St New York NY 10013-2102 also: Via delle Mantellate 19, Rome 00165, Italy

ROTHSCHILD, BARBARA, artist, educator; b. Chgo., Nov. 16, 1928; d. Nathan and Esther Mary (Fort) R.; m. Leon S. Katz, Aug. 25, 1951 (div. 1979); 1 child, Joseph Richard Katz; m. Harry Arnold Simon, June 23, 1985. AA, Am. Acad. Art, Chgo., 1949; BA, Coll. New Rochelle, 1974, MA in Art Edn., 1978. Registered art tchr., N.Y. Instr. Ctr. for Continuing Edn., Mamaroneck, N.Y., 1974-81, Boca Mus. Art, Boca Raton, Fla., 1995—; artist-in-residence New Rochelle, N.Y., 1974-85; adj. prof. Mercy Coll., Dobbs Ferry, N.Y., 1981-87; lectr. Pelham (N.Y.) Art Ctr., Coral Springs (Fla.) Art Guild, 1993, Women in Visual Arts, Boca Raton, 1994-96, Coconut Ctr. Art Guild, Fla., 1996; judge various orgns. Solo shows include Pelham Art Ctr., 1978, Mus. Gallery, White Plains, N.Y., 1979, MAG Gallery, Mamaroneck, N.Y., 1983, Lumen Winter Gallery, New Rochelle, 1987,Dover Gallery, Boca Raton, 1991, 93, Conservart Gallery, Boca Raton, 1993; group exhbns. include Bruce Mus., Greenwich, Conn., Hudson River Mus., Yonkers, N.Y., Nat. Arts Club, N.Y., Fla. Watercolor Soc., Broward Art Guild, Tallahassee Watercolor Soc. Ann., Mus. Fine Arts, St. Petersburg, Fla., Cornell Mus., Delray Beach, Fla., Profl. Artists Guild, Boca Raton, LeMoyne Art Found., Tallahassee; numerous pvt. and pub. collections. Recipient Artists Guild Norton Mus. award, 1990, Merit award, 1993, 2nd Pl. award Profl. Artists Guild, 1993-94, 96. Mem. Gold Coast Watercolor Soc., Profl. Artists Guild (pres. 1991-93), Fla. Watercolor Soc., Artists Guild Norton Gallery. Studio: 19577 Sedgefield Ter Boca Raton FL 33498

ROTHSCHILD, BERYL ELAINE, mayor; m. Edmund W. Rothschild; children: Margaret, Dan. BS in Journalism, Ohio U., 1951. Councilman City of University Heights, Ohio, 1968-78, mayor, 1979—; sec. Regional Coun. of Govts. Former mem. legis. policy com. Ohio Mcpl. League; past mem. exec. bd. N.E. Ohio Areawide Coord. Agy.; former trustee Citizens League Greater Cleve. and Citizens League Rsch. Inst., YWCA (Metro) Cleve., Meridia Suburban Hosp., 1987-90, chmn., Meridia Health System, 1987-90; bd. dirs. Cuyahoga County Nursing Home; mem. community adv. bd. Coop. Human Tissue Network, Case Western Res. U.; mem. adv. bd. Adult Basic and Literacy Edn.; charter mem., v.p. Ind. Living Experience Achievement Program; mem. adv. com. John Carroll U. Edn. Dept., 1988-90; past mem. com. on svcs. to the disabled Jewish Cmty. Fedn. of Cleve., special needs adv. com. Jewish Cmty. Ctr., advanced program employer adv. coun. Jewish Vocat. Svcs.; active mem. Learning Disabilities Assn. of Greater Cleve., Friends of the Cleveland Heights-Univ. Heights Libr. System, Hadassah, Pioneer Women, Coun. of Jewish Women, Heights Y, Univ. Heights Club 100, Fairmount Temple, Women's Com. of The Cleve. Orchestra, Cleve. Mus. Art. Recipient Career Woman of Achievement award Cleve. YWCA, 1986, Woman of Achievement Recognition award Greater Cleve. chpt. Hadassah, Recognition cert. Cleveland Heights-University Heights Bd. Edn., 1980-81, City of Peace award State of Israel Bonds, 1984, Kenneth R. Oldman Meml. award (with husband) Cleve. Assn. for Children and Adults with Learning Disabilities, 1988; named one of Outstanding Women of Yr. Greater Cleve. State of Israel Bonds, 1988. Mem. Nat. League of Cities and U.S. Conf. of Mayors, Cuyahoga County Mayors and Mgrs. Assn. (exec. bd., waste mgmt. com., legis. com., cable TV com.), Women in Comms., Inc., Alpha Sigma Nu (hon.). Office: City of University Heights 2300 Warrensville Center Rd University Heights OH 44118-3825

ROTHSTEIN, BARBARA JACOBS, federal judge; b. Bklyn., Feb. 3, 1939; d. Solomon and Pauline Jacobs; m. Ted L. Rothstein, Dec. 28, 1968; 1 child, Daniel. B.A., Cornell U., 1960; LL.B., Harvard U., 1966. Bar: Mass. 1966, Wash. 1969, U.S. Ct. Appeals (9th cir.) 1977, U.S. Dist. Ct. (we. dist.) Wash. 1971, U.S. Supreme Ct. 1975. Pvt. practice law Boston, 1966-68; asst. atty. gen. State of Wash., 1968-77; judge Superior Ct., Seattle, 1977-80; judge Fed. Dist. Ct. Western Wash., Seattle, 1980—, chief judge, 1987-94; faculty Law Sch. U. Wash., 1975-77, Hastings Inst. Trial Advocacy, 1977, N.W. Inst. Trial Advocacy, 1979—; mem. state-fed. com. U.S. Jud. Conf., chair subcom. on health reform. Recipient Matrix Table Women of Yr. award Women in Communication, Judge of the Yr. award Fed. Bar Assn., 1989; King County Wash. Women Lawyers Vanguard Honor, 1995. Mem. ABA (jud. sect.), Am. Judicature Soc., Nat. Assn. Women Judges, Fellows of the Am. Bar, Wash. State Bar Assn., U.S. Jud. Conf. (state-fed. com., health reform subcom.), Phi Beta Kappa, Phi Kappa Phi. Office: US Dist Ct 705 US Courthouse 1010 5th Ave Seattle WA 98104-1130

ROTHSTEIN, RUTH M., hospital administrator. Dir. Cook County Hosp., Chgo.; chief Cook County Bur. of Health Svcs. Office: Cook County Hosp 1835 W Harrison St Chicago IL 60612-3701*

ROTHSTEIN, SUSAN LYNN, fundraiser; b. Washington, Sept. 30, 1949; d. Robert J. and Sylvia (Werksman) R.; m. John A. Koeppel, Nov. 12, 1972; children: Adam Koeppel, Leah Koeppel. BS magna cum laude, Tufts U., 1971; MBA, Stanford U., 1978. Project mgr. Woodward-Clyde Conss., San Francisco, 1978-80, dir. corp. devel., 1980-83; sr. assoc. Strategic Decisions Group, Menlo Park, Calif., 1983-84, chief adminstrv. officer, 1984-85; dir. devel. Children Now, Oakland, Calif., 1989-91, v.p., 1991-94; also bd. dirs., 1995—; dir. devel. The San Francisco Sch., 1995—. Chair bd. mgrs. Stonestown YMCA, San Francisco, 1990-92; mktg. com. Asian Art Mus., San Francisco, 1987-89. Mem. Coun. for Advancement and Support of Edn., San Francisco C. of C. (bus. vol. for the arts 1987), Phi Beta Kappa. Office: The San Francisco Sch 300 Gaven St San Francisco CA 94134

ROTOLO, SUSAN, artist; b. N.Y.C., Nov. 20, 1943; d. Joachim Peter and Mary Theresa (Pezzati) R.; m. Enzo Bartoccioli, Dec. 23, 1967; 1 child, Luca. tchr. bookmaking. Designer textiles, compact disc cover art, scenery and props for theater; exhibited in shows at Visual Arts Ctr., N.Y.C., 1992, Galleria Todini, Perugia, Italy, 1992, Soc. for Contemporary Crafts, Pitts., 1993, AKA Artists Ctr., Saskatoon, Can., 1993, Ctr. for Book Arts, N.Y.C., 1994-96, ARC Gallery, Chgo., 1995, Appearances, N.Y.C., 1995, Spring Studio, N.Y.C., 1996, Nat. Mus. Women in Arts, Washington, 1996; artist one-of-a-kind sculptural books. Recipient Spl. Mention award for tech. expertise combined with creative risk, Appearances and West Village Coalition for Parks and Playgrounds, 1995. Mem. Ctr. for Book Arts, Am. Craft Coun., Book Arts Directory. Office: Suzart 682 Broadway New York NY 10012

ROTUNNO, PHYLLIS DI BUONO, accounting educator, researcher; b. Phila., Mar. 22, 1929; d. Salvatore and Rose (Pontolillo) di Buono; m. Rocco Michael Rotunno, Apr. 18, 1948; children: Roxane Rotunno Tise, Philip Anthony, Diane Rotunno Ellertsen. BS magna cum laude, N.Y. Inst. Tech., 1979; M in Acct., U. No. Fla., 1983. CPA, Fla. Mgr. acct. controls ITT Community Devel. Corp., Palm Coast, Fla., 1978-88; asst. prof. acct. Bethune-Cookman Coll., Daytona Beach, Fla., 1989-95, vis. prof., 1995—; dir. bd. Trustees ACT Corp., 1990-92; dir. student activities Inst. Mgmt. Accts., Daytona Beach, 1990-92; area coord. Acct. Bethune Cookman Coll., 1990-95. Study rschr. A Comparative Analysis of Test Scores in Principles of Acct. II, 1989; prin. rschr. Tchr. Effectiveness Evaluation; co-founder North Shore Sci. Mus., Manhasset, N.Y. Mem. AICPA, Fla. Inst. CPAs (mem. industry, govt. and edn. com. 1992-93). Office: Bethune-Cookman Coll 640 Mary McLeod Bethune Blvd Daytona Beach FL 32114-3099

ROUBIK, CHARLENE MARY, nursing administrator; b. Chgo., Mar. 12, 1956; d. Walter Francis and Florence Mary (Thomas) Nied; m. Robert Edward Roubik; children: Kristine, Robert, Jessica. BS in Nursing, No. Ill. U., 1978. Registered profl. nurse. Coord. women's health svcs. Des Plaines Valley Health Ctr., Summit, Ill., 1981-83; RN Mercy Hosp., Chgo., 1984-89; RN emergency rm. svcs. Olympia Fields Osteo. Med. Ctr., Chgo., 1989-93, Holy Cross Hosp., Chgo., 1990-92; RN Ingalls Hosp., Harvey, Ill., 1989-93; case mgr. Shay Health Care Svcs., Crestwood, Ill., 1992-96; dir. cmty. rels. Windsor Manor Nursing & Rehab. Ctr., Palos Hills, Ill., 1995—. Sec.

Conrady Jr. H.S. PTSA, 1994-95, publicity chair, 1995-96; publicity chair Oak Ridge PTA, 1992-95. Mem. AAUW, Palos Hills Baseball Assn. (sec. 1993-94, pres. 1994-95, past pres. 1995-96, sponsorship chair 1993-94, girls softball coach 1991-93). Roman Catholic.

ROUBINEK, SHARON MOEN, financial consultant; b. Lubbock, Tex., Feb. 8, 1951; d. Virgil Clayton and Wanona (Medlock) Moen; m. Jack Lewis Roubinek, Nov. 22, 1975 (div. Apr. 1992); children: Jeffrey, Justin. Student, Tex. Tech. U., 1975-76. Adminstr. Fin. Holding Co., 1973-75; ptnr. real estate firm, Lubbock, 1975-78; owner Designs in Mind, Beaumont, Tex., 1978-81; CEO Merit Fin. Group, Dallas, 1990-95; mgr. Ethan Allen Interiors, Dallas, 1995—. Mem. NAFE, Tex. Assn. Interior Designers, Profl. Photographers Assn, Gemological Alumni Assn. Republican. Office: Ethans Allen Interiors 6116 Luther Ln Dallas TX 75225

ROUDYBUSH, ALEXANDRA, novelist; b. Hyres, Cote d'Azur, France, Mar. 14, 1911; d. Constantine and Ethel (Wheeler) Brown; m. Franklin Roudybush, 1942. Student, St. Paul's Sch. for Girls, London, London Sch. Econs., 1930. Journalist London Eve. Standard, 1931, Time mag., 1933, French News Agy., 1935, CBS, 1936, MBS, 1940; White House corr. MBC Radio, 1940-48. Author: Before the Ball Was Over, 1965; Death of a Moral Person, 1967; Capital Crime, 1969; House of the Cat, 1970; A Sybaritic Death, 1972; Suddenly in Paris, 1975; The Female of the Species, 1977; Blood Ties, 1981. Mem. Crime Writers Am. and Brit., Am. Woman's Club (Paris), Miramar Golf Club (Porto, Portugal). Democrat. Episcopalian.

ROUKEMA, MARGARET SCAFATI, congresswoman; b. Newark, N.J., Sept. 19, 1929; d. Claude Thomas and Margaret (D'Alessio) Scafati; m. Richard W. Roukema, Aug. 23, 1951; children—Margaret, Todd (dec.), Gregory. B.A. with honors in History and Polit. Sci, Montclair State Coll., 1951, postgrad. in history and guidance, 1951-53; postgrad. program in city and regional planning, Rutgers U., 1975. Tchr. history, govt., public schs. Livingston and Ridgewood, N.J., 1951-55; mem. 97th-103rd Congresses from 5th N.J. dist., Washington, D.C., 1981—; mem. Banking, Fin. Urban Affairs com., subcom. Housing, Community devel., Internat. devel., Fin., Trade, Monetary Policy, Econ. Growth on; mem. Credit formation, Edn. Labor com., subcom. labor mgmt. rels., elementary, sec., vocat. edn., post-secondary edn. tng.; vice pres. Ridgewood Bd. Edn., 1970-73; bd. dirs., co-founder Ridgewood Sr. Citizens Housing Corp.; chairwoman Fin. Inst. and Consumer Credit Sub. Com. U.S. Congress; sponcer Family Med. Leave U.S. Congress. Trustee Spring House, Paramus, N.J.; trustee Leukemia Soc. No. N.J., Family Counseling Service for Ridgewood and Vicinity; mem. Bergen County (N.J.) Republican Com.; NW Bergen County campaign mgr. for gubernatorial candidate Tom Kean, 1977. Mem. Bus. and Profl. Women's Orgn. Clubs: Coll. of Ridgewood, Ridgewood Rep. Office: US Ho of Reps 2469 Rayburn Bldg Washington DC 20515-0005*

ROUMM, PHYLLIS EVELYN GENSBIGLER, English language educator, writer; b. New Alexandria, Pa., Jan. 1, 1927; d. Theodore Roosevelt and Daisy Isabelle (Patterson) Gensbigler; m. Milton Leonard Roumm, Nov. 23, 1946; children: David Lynn, Nikolyn, Dennis Eric, Janna Leigh. BS in English Edn., Indiana U. of Pa., 1945, MEd, 1963; postgrad., Ohio U., 1964, 65; PhD, Kent State U., 1977. Tchr. English Elders Ridge (Pa.) Joint High Sch., 1945-46, Apollo (Pa.) High Sch., 1946-47; tchr. English, speech Indiana Area Jr.-Sr. High Sch., 1959-67; teaching fellow Kent (Ohio) State U., 1970-71; prof. English Indiana U. of Pa., 1967-85, prof. emeritus, 1985—; freelance writer, 1985—. Bd. dirs. Hist. and Geneal. Soc. of Indiana County, 1984, Indiana Free Libr., 1988-91; mem. strategic planning steering com. Indiana (Pa.) Area Sch. Dist.; mem. health promotion com. Aging Svcs., Inc., Indiana. Mem. AAUW, Coll. English Assn. (life), Ligonier Valley Writers Assn., So. Humanities Conf., Pa. Ret. State Employees (v.p. Indico chpt. 1996—), Pa. Assn. Ret. Employees (v.p. 1996-97), Am. Assn. Ret. People, Assn. Pa. State Coll. and Univ. Ret. Faculty, Ind. (Pa.) Wordsmiths, Alpha Delta Kappa (pres. 1968-70, Silver Sister award 1991), Phi Delta Kappa. Home: 310 Poplar Ave Indiana PA 15701-3024

ROUND, ALICE FAYE BRUCE, school psychologist; b. Ironton, Ohio, July 19, 1934; d. Wade Hamilton and Martha Matilda (Toops) Bruce; children: Leonard Bruce, Christopher Frederick. BA, Asbury Coll., 1956; MS in Sch. Psychology, Miami U., Oxford, Ohio, 1975. Cert. tchr., sch. psychologist, supr., Ohio; cert. tchr., Calif. Tchr. Madison County (Ohio) Schs., 1956-58, Columbus (Ohio) Pub. Schs., 1958, San Diego Pub. Schs., 1958-60, Poway (Calif.) Unified Sch. Dist., 1960-64; substitute tchr. Princeton City Schs., Cin., 1969-75; sch. psychologist, intern Greenhills/Forest Park City Schs., Cin., 1975-76; sch. psychologist Fulton County Schs., Wauseon, Ohio, 1976-77, Sandusky (Ohio) pub. and Cath. schs., 1977-96; tchr. art cmty. group and pvt. lessons, Sandusky, 1962, Springdale, Ohio, 1962-69; mem. Youth Svcs. Bd., Sandusky, 1978-88; bd. dirs., cons. Sandusky Sch. Practical Nursing, 1983-91; presenter suicide prevention seminars for mental health orgns.; speaker at ch., civic and youth orgns., local radio and TV programs; cons. on teen pregnancy to various schs., health depts. Mem. Huron (Ohio) Boosters Club, 1978-92, Vols. in Action, Sandusky, 1987—. Mem. NAACP, NEA, Nat. Sch. Psychologist Assn., Ohio Sch. Psychologist Assn., Maumee Valley Sch. Psychologist Assn., Ohio Edn. Assn., Sandusky Edn. Assn., Phi Delta Kappa (historian 1984-88, Most Innovative Preservation of History award 1988). Home: 821 Seneca Ave Huron OH 44839-1842 Office: Sandusky Bd Edn 407 Decatur St Sandusky OH 44870-2442

ROUNDS, BARBARA LYNN, psychiatrist; b. L.A., Mar. 17, 1934; d. Ralph Arthur and Florene V. (Heyer) Behrend; divorced 1962; children: Steve, Mike, Pamela, Ronald, Thomas. BA, Stanford U., 1964, MD, 1966; postgrad., San Francisco Psychoanalytic, 1973-81. Diplomate Am. Bd. Psychiatry and Neurology; cert. psychoanalyst. Intern New Orleans Pub. Health Svc., 1966-67; resident psychiat. Mendocino State Hosp., 1967-69, U. Calif. Davis, 1969-70; staff psychiatrist U. Calif. Davis Med. Sch., Sacramento, 1970-77, clin. instr., 1970-76; psychiatrist pvt. practice, Sacramento, 1971—; asst. clin. prof. U. Calif. Davis, Sacramento, 1976-84, assoc. clin. prof., 1984—. Mem. Am. Psychiat. Assn., Am. Psychoanalytic Assn., AMA, Cen. Calif. Psychiat. Soc. (pres.-elect 1990-91, pres. 1991-92). Democrat. Home: 8910 Leatham Ave Fair Oaks CA 95628-6506 Office: 1317 H St Sacramento CA 95814-1906

ROUNDS-NICHOLS, LINDA L., school system administrator, consultant; b. San Diego, May 23, 1949; d. LaVerne W. and Ethyle N. (Erskine) Rounos; m. Harold L. Hovendick (widowed Jan. 15, 1988; children: Sean Hovendick, Michelle Hovendick;m. Philip B. Nichols, Dec. 18, 1994. BA in Edn., Wayne State Coll., 1973, MS in Edn., 1982; MA, We. N.Mex. U., 1986; student, Sophia Divinity Sch., 1995—, Newport U., 1995—. Cert. counselor. Tchr. Concordia (Kans.) H.S., 1973-74; tutor Scotland (S.D.) H.S., 1976-77, tchr., 1977-82; counselor JFK Middle Sch., Gallup, N.Mex., 1982-87; adminstr. assessment office Gallup (N.Mex.) McKinley County Schs., 1987—; instr. U. N.Mex. Gallup br., 1989—. Bd. dirs. Battered Families Svcs., Gallup, 1993-95, pres. 1995; cmty. coord. Red Ribbon Campaign, Gallup, 1988, 92; crisis counselor Crisis Life Line/Rape Crisis, Gallup, 1984-87, 90-91. Vol. award Crisis Life Line, 1987, 92. Mem. ASCD, ACA (western region br. assembly), N.Mex. Assn. Spiritual, Ethical, Religious Values in Counseling (pres. 1995—), N.Mex. Sch. Counseling Assn. (pres. 1984-88, bd. dirs. 1990—, editor Insights newsletter 1984-86, Counselor of Yr. 1985-86), N.Mex. Counseling Assn. (pres. 1986-84, bd. dirs. 1995—, editor Sunspots newsletter 1989-94, President's award for svc. 1987, 94), Internat. Reading Assn. Home: 427 Camino del Sol Gallup NM 87301 Office: Gallup McKinley County Schs P O Box 1318 Gallup NM 87305

ROUNTREE, PATRICIA ANN, youth organization administrator; b. Rochester, N.Y., Apr. 2, 1942; d. Robert James and Myrtle Margaret (Cuthbertson) R. AA, Cazenovia Coll., 1961; BA, Parsons Coll., 1965. Gen. clk. Eastman Kodak, Rochester, 1961-63; 6th grade tchr. Wayland (N.Y.) Ctrl. Sch., 1965-67; field dir. Seven Lakes Coun. Girl Scouts U.S.A., Phelps, N.Y., 1967-73; program dir. Palm Glades Coun. Girl Scouts U.S.A., Lake Worth, Fla., 1973-76; asst. exec. dir. Seven Lakes Coun. Girl Scouts U.S.A., 1976-86; exec. dir. Mich. Trails Coun. Girl Scouts U.S.A., Grand Rapids, 1986-89; exec. dir. Ctrl. N.Y. Coun. Girl Scouts U.S.A., Syracuse, 1989—. Pres., bd. dirs. Planned Parenthood of Fingerlakes, Geneva, N.Y., 1982-86. Mem. Zonta Internat. Rotary Syracuse. Presbyn. Home: 4 Robinson Dr Baldwinsville NY 13027 Office: Ctrl NY Girl Scout Coun 6724 Thompson Rd Box 482 Syracuse NY 13211

ROUP, BRENDA JACOBS, nurse, retired army officer; b. Petersburg, Va., July 8, 1948; d. Eugene Thurman and Sarah Ann (Williams) Jacobs; m. Clarence James Roup, May 8, 1976. BSN, Med. Coll. Va., Richmond, 1970; MSN, Cath. U. Am., 1977; PhD, U. Md., 1995. Commd. 2d lt. U.S. Army, 1970, advanced through grades to lt. col., 1986; infection control cons. 7th MEDCOM, Fed. Republic Germany, 1982-83; chief infection control Brooke Army MEDCEN, San Antonio, 1983-86; chief infection control Walter Reed MEDCEN, Washington, 1986-92, ret., 1992; Johnson & Johnson faculty scholar Johns Hopkins U. Sch. Nursing, Balt., 1995—; nurse cons. in infection control to U.S. Army Surgeon Gen., 1986-92. Contbr. articles to profl. jours. Mem. Assn. Profls. in Infection Control , Sigma Theta Tau. Avocations: reading, gardening, cooking. Office: Johns Hopkins U Sch Nursing Baltimore MD 21205

ROUPP, HEIDI SCHNEIDER, secondary school educator; b. Pampa, Tex., Oct. 8, 1940; d. Paul Alex Schneider and Christine Campaigne; m. David Kent Roupp, July 8, 1962. BA in Speech and Drama, U. Wyo., 1962, postgrad., 1963-78; postgrad., U. Colo., Colo. State U., 1980-84; MA, Columbia U., 1995. Cert. tchr., Colo. Tchr. English, social studies, speech Aurora (Colo.) South Jr. H.S., 1962-68; tchr. Am. history Aurora Ctrl. H.S.; tchr. English, social studies, reading, speech Aspen (Colo.) Pub. Schs., 1968-70, tchr. social studies, prodns., drama, outdoor edn., reading, 1970-78, tchr. multiple social, hist., polit. and English subjects, 1985—, chair history dept., 1992-94; conf. chmn. tchg. and curriculum workshop U. Chgo, 1991; mem. Colo. Gov's. com. Japanese Sister-State Dels. in Colo., 1986-88; founder Colo.-Yamaga Exch., Colo, 1988; mem. world history curriculum task force Nat. History Stds., writing com., 1993. Editor: World History Bull., 1992—, Treasures of the World: Literature and Source Readings for World History Teacher's Guide to Treasures of the World American Voices: A History of the United States, Source Readings The Aspen World History Handbook, Teaching World History, 1996, Barron's Study Guide to the World History Achievement Test, 1996; contbr. articles to profl. jours. Fulbright fellow, India, 1987, Japan Found., Japan, 1985, DeWitt Wallace fellow Woodrow Wilson Nat. Fellowship Found., 1990, Korean Soc., 1995-96. Mem. Aspen Edn. Assn. (pres. 1982-83) Aspen Hist. Assn. (trustee 1984-86), World History Assn. (sec. 1992-94, mem. nat. exec. coun. 1987-94, nominating com. 1985-87, v.p. 1996—), Rocky Mountain Reg. World History Assn. (steering com. 1984-91, vice chair 1990-95, chair 1995—), Am. Hist. Assn. (program com. 1993), Colo. Coun. for Studies (bd. dirs. 1989-91). Home: PO Box 816 Aspen CO 81612-0816

ROUSE, ELAINE BURDETT, retired secondary school educator; b. Point Pleasant, W.Va., Feb. 4, 1915; d. John Wallace and Edna Ada (Johnson) Burdett; m. Douglas Philip Rouse, Sept. 27, 1943 (dec. June 1971); 1 child, Julia Ann. BA, W.Va. U., 1938, MA in Econs., 1953; MA in Pub. Svc. (hon.), U. Rio Grande, 1990. Cert. secondary tchr., W.Va., Ohio. H.S. tchr. Mason County Schs., Point Pleasant, 1938-40, 46-53, 64-77; H.S. tchr. Pomeroy (Ohio) Schs., 1953-64; sec. field office FBI, Huntington, W.Va., 1940-43; part-time tchr. Rio Grande (Ohio) Coll., 1960-65, Point Pleasant br. Marshall U., 1978-83. Chmn. bd. dirs. Rio Grande C.C., 1993-95, Gallia County Bd. Elections, Gallipolis, Ohio, 1994—; mem. Gallia County Dem. Exec. Com., 1985—. Recipient 1st pl. econs. edn. in W.Va. award Pub. Utilities of the Virginias, 1971. Mem. NEA, Gen. Fedn. Women's Clubs (pres. Riverside Study Club 1990-92). Presbyterian.

ROUSE, LORRAINE JEAN, nursing administrator; b. Orlando, Fla., Nov. 8, 1959; d. Leon Jesse Rouse and Patricia Jean (Fisher) Gombash. BA, Fla. Tech. U., 1981; ASN, Valencia C.C., Orlando, Fla., 1991. Residential advisor Seminole Cmty. Mental Health Inc., Sanford, Fla. Home: 5930 Village Cir Orlando FL 32822

ROUSH, DOROTHY EVELYN, medical laboratory educator, consultant; b. Flatwoods, Ky., July 16, 1930; d. William Arch and Mary Jane (Frasure) Salyers; m. Gilbert Riley Dush, Aug. 26, 1951 (div. 1972); m. Virgil Bernard Roush, Nov. 18, 1972. Med. tech. degree, Clin. Lab., Mt. Vernon, Ohio, 1953; student, Ohio State U., 1967-72. Registered med. tech. Med. tech. Hosp. & Tb Hosp., Newark, Ohio, 1953-60; office nurse various physicians, Newark and Columbus, Ohio and Seattle, 1960-93; nursing home coord. Med. Lab., Seattle, 1980-89; sr. phlebotomist Roche BioMed. Lab., Burlington, N.C., 1990-95; nurse, phlebotomist ARC Blood Program, Columbus, Ohio, 1961-72; instr. in field; cons. in field. Contbr. articles to profl. jours. Vol. ARC, 1957-72, Boulder (Colo.) County Foster Parents, 1976, Cath. Shared Missions, Seattle, 1987. Recipient Appreciation award Gt. Brit. Red Cross Nursing Svc., 1969, Internat. Cancer Congress, 1982. Mem. Am. Assn. Med. Assts., Am. Med. Techs. (chairperson com., sci. chairperson Ariz. chpt., expert adhoc rev. com. 1994-95, Disting. Achievement award 1991), Wash. State Soc. Am. Tech. (sec., v.p., Tech. of Yr. 1989, 90), Am. Legion Aux. (pres.). Roman Catholic. Home and Office: 18002 N Hyacinth Dr Sun City West AZ 85375-5348

ROUSON, VIVIAN REISSLAND, alcohol and drug abuse services professional; b. New Orleans, July 18, 1929; d. Albert Isaac and Ophelia (Scott) Reissland; m. W. Ervin Rouson, June 22, 1953 (dec. May 1979); children: Lizette Hélène, Darryl Ervin, Brigette Maria, Janine Patrice, Damian William. BA, Xavier U., 1951; MS, Nova U., 1979; postgrad., U. Ky., 1965, U. South Fla., 1970. Tchr., cons. Gibbs Jr. Coll., St. Petersburg, Fla., 1958-60; tchr., cons. Pinellas County Schs., St. Petersburg,, Clearwater, Fla., 1960-78; freelance opinion editorial columnist U.S. newspaper, 1976-82; columnist Evening Independent, Pinellas County, Fla., 1976-78, Palm Beach (County, Fla.) Post, 1979-82; tchr., cons. Palm Beach County Sch., Lake Worth, W. Palm Beach, Fla., 1978-82; editorial writer St. Petersburg Times, 1979; program coord., interim dir. Women's Resource Ctr. Normandale C.C., Bloomington, Minn., 1986-89; interim dir. Women's Resource Ctr., Normandale Community Coll., Bloomington, Minn., 1989; vol., intern program coord. Inst. on Black Chem. Abuse, Mpls., 1989-90; assoc. editor Nat. Black Media Coalition, Washington, 1991—; V.I.P. coord. Inst. on Black Chem. Abuse, Mpls., 1989-90; writing and fgn. lang. cons. Pinellas County and Palm Beach County, fla., 1960-82; bd. dirs. Carroll Pub. Co. Author: The Hummingbird Within Us, 1980, Like a Mighty Banyan, 1982, Alcohol and Drug Abuse in Black America, 1988; editor conf. proceedings; editorial writer-columnist; editorial bd. St. Petersburg Times, 1979. Bd. dirs. St. Petersburg Cath. High Sch., 1976, Minn, divsn. Am. Cancer Soc., Mpls., 1983-90, Ind. Sch. Dist. 191, Burnsville, Eagan, Savage, Minn., 1984-87, Minn. Valley YMCA, Dakota County, Minn., 1987-90; pres. D.C. chpt. Hook-Up Plack Women, 1992—; sec., bd. dirs. Ionia Whipper Home, Inc., 1992—; mem. D.C. chpt. Nat. Urban League. Named Outstanding Journalist south Atlantic region Alpha Kappa Alpha, 1978, 79, 80; recipient Appreciation Pub. Svc. cert. Nat. Assn. Black Accts., 1992. Mem. AAUW, Twin Cities Black Journalists (co-chair 1985-86, v.p. 1989-90), Minn. Polit. Congress Black Women (charter), Nat. Urban League (subscribing life, Washington chpt.), Minn. Elected Women Ofcls., Dakota County Soc. Black Women (founder 1983, v.p. 1983-84), Pinellas County Fgn. Lang. Tchrs. (treas., pres.), The Links (sec. Capital City chpt.), Alpha Kappa Alpha (life). Roman Catholic. Home: 2311 N Capitol St NE Washington DC 20002-1105 Office: One Church-One Addict Ste 630 1101 14th St NW Ste 630 Washington DC 20005

ROUSSEL, LEE DENNISON, economist; b. N.Y.C., May 15, 1944; d. Ethan Allen and Frances Isabel (Ferry) Dennison; m. Andre Homo Roussel, Sept. 6, 1980; children: Cecilia Frances, Stephanie Anne. AB, Wellesley Coll., 1966; MA, Northeastern U., 1973. Mgmt. intern U.S. Dept. HEW, 1966-68; with Planning Office Commonwealth of Mass., 1968-70; exec. dir. Gov.'s Commn. Citizen Participation, Boston, 1973; with Boston Area Office U.S. Dept. HUD, 1970-78; fgn. svc. officer USAID, 1978—; with Housing and Urban Devel. Office USAID, Washington and Tunis, 1978-82; chief Housing and Urban Devel. Office for C.Am. USAID, Honduras, 1982-87; asst. dir. Office Housing and Urban Programs USAID, Washington, 1987-91; country rep. for Czech and Slovak Fed. Rep. USAID, 1991-92, country rep. for Czech Rep., 1993-94; min. counselor, U.S. rep. to Devel. Assistance Com. OECD, Paris, 1994—. Episcopalian. Office: USOECD, 19 rue de Franqueville, 75016 Paris France also: OECD/USAID PSC 116 APO AE 09777-9998

ROUTT, KAREN ELIZABETH, real estate consultant; b. Detroit, May 3, 1955; d. Robert Fletcher and Catherine (Weiss) R. Student, Denison U., 1973-75; BA, U. Mich., 1977; MBA, Stanford U., 1983. Cons. Arthur Andersen & Co., Detroit, 1977-79, sr. cons., 1979-81; project mgr. Bank One Columbus, N.Am., Ohio, 1983-84, project mgr., officer, 1984, mgr. on-line support, 1984-85, mgr. interest rate swap portfolio, 1985-86, mgr. check capture, 1986-87; sr. assoc. Index Group Inc., Cambridge, Mass., 1988-89; assoc. dir. Prism, 1989-92; chief of staff to the mayor Cambridge, Mass., 1992-93; pres., assisted living/health care cons. K. Routt & Assocs., Cambridge, 1993—. Active Big Sister, 1986-89; chmn. Commn. to Promote and Enhance Cen. Square Now!, 1992-93; bd. dirs. Shelter, Inc., 1992-96; chair Devel. Commn., 1995—, Property Mgmt. Com., 1994, S&H Investments, 1989-95, pres. 1990-91; charter mem. Coalition of 100 Black Women, Boston chpt., 1991—, chmn. nominating com., 1992-93; pres. Boston chpt. Stanford Bus. Sch. Alumni Club, 1995—. Mem. Zonta (bd. dirs. Columbus club 1987-88, chair girls group home 1986-88), Am. Soc. on Aging. Mem. United Ch. Christ.

ROUX, MILDRED ANNA, retired secondary school educator; b. New Castle, Pa., June 1, 1914; d. Louis Henri and Frances Amanda (Gillespie) R. BA, Westminster Coll., 1936, MS in Edn., 1951. Tchr. Farrell (Pa.) Sch. Dist., 1939-55; tchr. Latin, English New Castle (Pa.) Sch. Dist., 1956-76; ret., 1976; chmn. sr. high sch. fgn. lang. dept. New Castle Sch. Dist., 1968-76, faculty sponsor sch. fgn. lang. newspapers, 1960-76, 71-76, Jr. Classical League, 1958-76. Mem. Lawrence County Hist. Soc., Am. Classical League, 1958-76. Mem. AAUW (chmn. publicity, chmn. program com. Lawrence County chpt. 1992-96), Am. Assn. Ret. Persons, Nat. Ret. Tchrs. Assn., Pa. Assn. Sch. Retirees (chmn. cmty. participation com. Lawrence County br. 1976-81), Coll. Club New Castle (chmn. sunshine com. 1989-91, social com. 1991-92), Woman's Club New Castle (chmn. pub. affairs com. 1988-90, internat. affairs com. 1990-92, program com. 1990-92, telephone com. 1992-95). Republican. Roman Catholic. Home: 6 E Moody Ave New Castle PA 16101-2356

ROVANO, ROSANN, leasing consultant; b. Pitts., Apr. 26, 1948; d. Frank Anthony and Francis Marie (Zeleskey) R.; m. James Victor Zdanek, June 26, 1974 (div. 1983). BS in Edn., Duquesne U., 1970, BSBA, 1970; postgrad., U. Pitts., 1973. Tchr. Penn Trafford, Harrison City, Pa., 1972-84; account exec. Diskriter, Pitts., 1984-86; dist. mgr. U.S. Leasing, Pitts., 1986-91; area mgr. AT&T Credit, Pitts., 1991-95; dist. sales mgr. Assoc. Comml. Credit, Pitts., 1995—. Mem. People for Animal Welfare Soc., Pa. Ednl. Assn.

ROVELSTAD, MATHILDE VERNER, library science educator; b. Kempten, Germany, Aug. 12, 1920; came to U.S., 1951, naturalized, 1953; d. George and Therese (Hohl) Hotter; m. Howard Rovelstad, Nov. 23, 1970. Ph.D., U. Tubingen, 1953; M.S. in L.S, Catholic U. Am., 1960. Cataloger Mt. St. Mary's Coll., Los Angeles, 1953; sch. librarian Yoyogi Elem. Sch., Tokyo, 1954-56; mem. faculty Cath. U. Am., 1960-90, prof. library sci., 1975-90, prof. emeritus, 1990—; vis. prof. U. Montreal, 1969. Author: Bibliotheken in den Vereinigten Staaten, 1974; translator Bibliographia, an Inquiry into its Definition and Designations (R. Blum), 1980, Bibliotheken in den Vereinigten Staaten von Amerika und in Kanada, 1988; contbr. articles to profl. jours. Research grantee German Acad. Exch. Svc., 1969, Herzog August Bibliothek Wolfenbüttel, Germany, 1995. Mem. ALA (internat. relations com. 1977-80), Internat. Fedn. Library Assns. and Instns. (standing adv. com. on library schs. 1975-81), Assn. for Library and Info. Sci. Edn. Home: PO Box 111 Gibson Island MD 21056-0111 Office: Cath U Am Sch Libr & Info Sci Washington DC 20064

ROVER, ELENA RACHEL, magazine writer; b. N.Y.C., Sept. 12, 1966; d. Theodore Allen and Rita Norma (Gabler) Rover. BA, Barnard Coll., N.Y.C., 1988; MS, Columbia U., 1994. Copy clk. N.Y. Times, N.Y.C., 1987-88; prodn. chief Food Arts Mag., N.Y.C., 1988-89; editl. asst. Self Mag., N.Y.C., 1989-92, fitness editor, 1992-94; contbg. editor Walking Mag., Boston, 1994-95; freelance writer various mags. N.Y.C., 1994—; columnist Shape mag., Woodland Hills, Calif., 1994—; sr. editor Snow Country Mag., N.Y. Times Sports/Leisure Group, 1996—; founder Editl. Slaves Club, N.Y.C., 1990-92; mentor Columbia U. Sch. Journalism, N.Y.C., 1994—. Home: 140 Beachview Ave #274 Bridgeport CT 06605

ROVERE, ELIZABETH ANN, research associate; b. N.Y.C., Feb. 2, 1966; d. George Davitto and Patricia Ann (Severin) R. BA in Politics with honors, Wake Forest U., 1989; MA, Yale U., 1992; MST, Harvard Div. Sch., 1994; postgrad., Mass. Sch. Profl. Psychology, 1995—. Russian lang. tutor Wake Forest U., Winston-Salem, N.C., 1985-89; rsch. assoc. Inst. of Oriental Sudies of USSR Acad. of Sciences, Moscow, Russia, 1991; pastoral counselor intern McLean Hosp., Belmont, Mass., 1992-93; rsch. assoc., asst. to dir. Ctr. for Psychology and Social Change, Cambridge, Mass., 1993-95; rsch. asst. Harvard Program in Refugee Trauma, Cambridge, Mass., 1995—. Mem. writing staff Refugee Notes; contbr. newsletter Habiba Chaouch Found. Internat. Dept. scholar Wake Forest U., Moscow, 1987; USAID grantee Croatia and Bosnia. Mem. Soc. for the Psychol. Study of Social Issues, Psychologists for Social Responsibility, Network of East West Women, Appalachian Mountain Club, Pi Sigma Alpha. Democrat. Mem. Soc. of Friends. Home: 334 Harvard St Apt B-6 Cambridge MA 02139 Office: Harvard Program in Refugee Trauma 8 Storey St Cambridge MA 02138

ROVERUD, ELEANOR, pathologist, neuropathologist; b. Spring Grove, Minn., Oct. 24, 1912; d. Henry S. and Sigrid (Bakken) R.; m. Stuart Henry Nam (dec. Nov. 1986); adopted children: Sue, Kay, Becky, Howard, Signe, Sonia, Tom, Ted, Kurt. Diploma, Kahler Sch. Nursing, Rochester, Minn., 1934; BS in Nursing Edn., U. Minn., 1940; MD, Med. Coll. Pa., 1947. Intern Swedish Hosp., Mpls., 1947-48; resident in pathology, resident instr. Sch. of Tropical Medicine U. P.R., San Juan, 1949-52; fellow in Neuropathology Columbia U., Presbyn. Hosp., N.Y.C., 1952-54; neuropathologist Wayne County Gen. Hosp., Eloise, Mich., 1954-59; assoc. prof. Woman's Med. Coll./Med. Coll. Pa., Phila., 1959-61; pathologist Women's Hosp., Phila., 1961-62, St. Anthony Regional Hosp., Carroll, Iowa, 1962-77; cons. in pathology Carroll, Iowa, 1977-87, Spring Grove, 1987—; expert witness forensic cases Carroll County, Iowa, 1962-77. Chmn., v.p., sec. Carroll chpt. ARC, 1968-75. Mem. AMA, Am. Assn. Neuropathologists, Iowa Med. Soc. (life), Carroll County Med. Assn. (sec. 1968-74), Am. Med. Women's Assn., Zumbro Valley Med. Soc., Minn. Med. Assn. Democrat. Lutheran. Office: PO Box 706 Spring Grove MN 55974-0706

ROVNER, ILANA KARA DIAMOND, federal judge; b. Aug. 21, 1938; came to U.S., 1939; d. Stanley and Ronny (Medalje) Diamond; m. Richard Nyles Rovner, Mar. 9, 1963; 1 child, Maxwell Rabson. AB, Bryn Mawr Coll., 1960; postgrad., U. London King's Coll., 1961, Georgetown U., 1961-63; JD, Ill. Inst. Tech., 1966; LittD (hon.), Rosary Coll., 1989, Mundelein Coll., 1989; DHL (hon.), Spertus Coll. of Judaica, 1992. Bar: Ill. 1972, U.S. Dist. Ct. (no. dist.) Ill. 1972, U.S. Ct. Appeals (7th cir.) 1977, U.S. Supreme Ct. 1981, Fed. Trial Bar (no. dist.) Ill. 1982. Jud. clk. U.S. Dist. Ct. (no. dist.) Ill., Chgo., 1972-73; asst. U.S. atty. U.S. Atty.'s Office, Chgo., 1973-77; dep. chief of pub. protection, 1975-76, chief pub. protection, 1976-77; dep. gov., legal counsel Gov. James R. Thompson, Chgo., 1977-84; dist. judge U.S. Dist. Ct. (no. dist.) Ill., Chgo., 1984-92; cir. judge U.S. Ct. Appeals (7th cir.), Chgo., 1992—. Trustee Bryn Mawr Coll., Pa., 1983-89; mem. bd. overseers Ill. Inst. Tech./Kent Coll. Law, 1983—; trustee Ill. Inst. Tech., 1989—; mem. adv. coun. Rush Ctr. for Sports Medicine, Chgo., 1991-96; civil justice reform act adv. com. for the 7th cir., Chgo., 1991-95; bd. vis. No. Ill. U. Coll. Law, 1992-94; vis. com. Northwestern U. Sch. Law, 1993—, U. Chgo. Law Sch., 1993-96, 7th cir. race and gender fairness com., 1993—, U.S. Ct. Appeals (7th cir.) fairness com., 1996—, 7th cir. gender study task force, 1995—. Recipient Spl. Commendation award U.S. Dept. Justice, 1975, Spl. Achievement award 1976, Ann. Nat. Law and Social Justice Leadership award League to Improve the Cmty., 1975, Ann. Guardian Police award, 1977, Profl. Achievement award Ill. Inst. Tech., 1986, Louis Dembitz Brandeis medal for Disting. Legal Svc. Brandeis U., 1993, 1st Woman award, Valparaiso U. Sch. Law, 1993, ORT Women's Am. Cmty. Svc. award, 1987-88, svc. award Spertus Coll. of Judaica, 1987, Ann. award Chgo. Found. for Women, 1990; named Today's Chgo. Woman of Yr., 1985, Woman of Achievement Chgo. Women's Club, 1986, more. Mem. ABA, Fed. Bar Assn. (jud. selection com. Chgo. chpt. 1977-80, treas. Chgo. chpt. 1978-79, sec. Chgo. chpt. 1979-80, 2d v.p. Chgo. chpt. 1980-81, 1st v.p. Chgo. chpt.

1981-82, pres. Chgo. chpt. 1982-83, 2d v.p. 7th cir. 1983-84, v.p. 7th cir. 1984-85), Fed. Judges Assn., Nat. Assn. Women Judges, Ill. Bar Assn., Women's Bar Assn. Ill. (ann. award 1989, 1st Myra Bradwell Woman of Achievement award 1994), Chgo. Bar Assn. (commendation def. of prisoners com. 1987), Chgo. Coun. Lawyers, Decalogue Soc. (citation of honor 1991), Kappa Beta Pi, Phi Alpha Delta (hon.). Republican. Jewish. Office: 219 S Dearborn St Ste 2774 Chicago IL 60604-1803

ROWAN, MARY ELIZABETH, hydrogeologist, consultant; b. Athens, Tenn., June 26, 1957; d. George Wilburn and Dorothy Jean (Oliphant) Anderson; m. Charles D.V. Rowan, Jan. 3, 1981. BS, U. Tenn., Chattanooga, 1980; MS, U. Nebr., 1986. Cert. profl. geologist, Tenn., ground water profl. Hydrogeologist Nebr. Dept. Environ. Control, Lincoln, 1983-86, Wash. Dept. Ecology, Olympia, 1986-88, Dames & Moore, Seattle, 1988-89, Rust Environ. & Infrastructure, Greenville, S.C., 1989-93, RMT, Inc., Greenville, 1993—. Mem. Am. Geophys. Union, Nat. Ground Water Assn., Am. Fedn. Aviculture (S.C. coord. 1995, 96). Office: RMT Inc 100 Verdae Blvd Greenville SC 29606

ROWARK, MAUREEN, fine arts photographer; b. Edinburgh, Midlothian, Scotland, Feb. 28, 1933; came to U.S., 1960, naturalized, 1970; d. Alexander Pennycook and Margaret (Gorman) Prezdpelski; m. Robert Rowark, May 3, 1952 (div. July 1965). 1 child, Mark Steven. Student, Warmington Bus. Coll., Royal Leamington Spa, Eng., 1950-51, Royal Leamington Spa Art Sch.; diploma, Speedwriting Inst., N.Y.C., 1961; AS in Edn., St. Clair County Community Coll., Port Huron, Mich., 1977, AA, 1978. Supr. proof reading Nevin D. Hirst Advt., Ltd., Leeds, Eng., 1952-55; publicity asst. Alvis Aero Engines, Ltd., Coventry, Eng., 1955-57; adminstrv. asst. Port Huron Motor Inn, 1964-66; adminstrv. asst. pub. rels. dept. Geophysics and Computer Svcs., Inc., New Orleans, 1966-68; sales mgr. Holiday Inn, Port Huron, 1968-70; adminstrv. asst. Howard Corp., Port Huron, 1971-73; sales and systems coord. Am. Wood Products, Ann Arbor, Mich., 1973-74; systems coord. Daniels & Zermack Architects, Ann Arbor, 1974; systems coord., cataloger fine arts dept. St. Clair County Community Coll., Port Huron, 1976-79; freelance fine arts photographer Port Huron, 1978—; photographer Patterns mag. front cover, 1978, Erie Sq. Gazette, 1979, Bluewater Area Tourism Bur. brochure, 1989, Port Huron, Can. Legion, Wyo., Ont. Br., 1987, 88—, Grace Episcopal Ch. Mariner's Day, Port Huron, 1987, 92, 93, 94, 95, 96, Homes mag., 1989. One-woman shows at Grace Episcopal Ch., 1995, Port Huron Mus., 1995; Mich. Waterways Coun. Girl Scouts Exhibit, 1996; exhibited in internat. shows at Ann. Ea. Mich. Internat. Exhbn., 1982, 83, 84 (awards of excellence 1982, 83, Best Photography award 1995), St. Clair County C.C., 1983, 86 (award of excellence), Sarnia (Ont.) Gallery, 1983-92, 94 (honorable mention), Bluewater Bridge Exhibit, 1988, Kaskilaaksontie Exhibit, Finland, 1991 (Par Excellence award), Swann Gallery, 1996, others; contbr. short stories to mags. Cons., buyer interior decor Grace Episcopal Ch., 1994; active Port Huron Mus., 1985—. Recipient Hon. Mention award Sarnia Art Gallery, 1981; named Best Photographer, Sarnia Art Gallery, 1988; winner 2d and 3d Pl. awards Times Herald Newspaper, 1988. Mem. St. Clair County C.C. Alumni Assn., Phi Theta Kappa, Lambda Mu. Democrat. Episcopalian. Home and Office: 2005 Riverside Dr #15 Port Huron MI 48060-2677

ROWBO, SANDRA BROWN, artist, educator; b. Jamestown, N.Y., July 10, 1952; d. Forbes Harold and Elsie June (Van Vranken) Brown; m. Alexander John Rowbo, May 15, 1983. BS, SUNY, New Paltz, 1976. Elem. tchr. art Greater Amsterdam (N.Y.) Sch. Dist., 1977-78, secondary tchr. art, 1979-80; secondary tchr. art Shenendehowa Sch. Dist., Clifton Park, N.Y., 1978-79; artist, owner Studio Brown, Schenectady, from 1980, Amsterdam. One-woman show So. Vt. Art Ctr., Manchester, 1990, Schenectady Mus., 1991, Canajoharie (N.Y.) Libr. and Art Gallery, 1994, Walter Elwood Mus., Amsterdam, 1995; exhibited in group shows Adirondack Nat. Exhbn., Old Forge, N.Y., 1993, 95, Pa. Watercolor Soc., Erie, 1995, Nat. Watercolor Soc., Brea, Calif., 1995. Recipient 1st prize Montgomery County Ann., 1988, 3d prize for graphics Art Guild Old Forge, 1989, So. Vt. Art Ctr., 1991, Smith Packing Co. award Adirondack Nat. Exhbn. Am. Watercolors, 1993. Mem. Adirondack Aquanaut. Soc., N.Y. State Divers Assn. Methodist. Home and Studio: 28 DeWitt St Amsterdam NY 12010

ROWE, AUDREY, postal service administrator; b. Albuquerque, June 26, 1958; d. James Franklin Ringold and Geneva Doris (Jennings) Robinson. ASB in Acctg., ICS Ctr. for Degrees, Scranton, Pa., 1988, ASB in Fin., 1989; BSBA, Century U., 1991, MBA, 1995, grad. paralegal studies, 1996. Svc. rep. Mountain and Southwestern Bell Telephone Co., Albuquerque, Houston, 1978-83; clk., carrier U.S. Postal Svc. PS05, Bellaire, Sugar Land, Tex., 1983-86; supr. mails U.S. Postal Svc. EAS15, Sugar Land, 1986-87; officer-in-charge U.S. Postal Svc. EAS 18, Rosharon, Tex., 1987; from supr. mails EAS 15 to gen. supr. mails EAS 17 U.S. Postal Svc., Houston, 1987-89; relief tour supt. U.S. Postal Svc. EAS 21 (Detail Assignment), Houston, 1989; mgr. gen. mail facility U.S. Postal Svc. EAS22 (Detail Assignment), Capitol Heights, Md., 1989-90; mgr. mail processing U.S. Postal Svc. EAS21, Charlottesville, Va., 1990-91; MSC dir. city ops. U.S. Postal Svc. EAS23 (Detail Assignment), Roanoke, Va., 1991; mgr. gen. mail facility U.S. Postal Svc. EAS24, Washington, 1991—; plant mgr. U.S. Postal Svc. EAS25, Dulles, Va., 1992. Mem. NAFE, Am. Soc. Notaries. Home: PO Box 220411 Chantilly VA 22022-0411

ROWE, MARIELI DOROTHY, media literacy education consultant, organization executive; b. Bonn, Germany, Aug. 13; came to U.S., 1939; m. John Westel Rowe; children: Peter Willoughby, William Westel, Michael Delano. BA, Swarthmore Coll.; postgrad., U. Colo., 1990; MA, Edgewood Coll., 1990. Interim exec. dir. Friends of Sta. WHA-TV, Madison, Wis., 1976; exec. dir. Nat. Telemedia Coun., Madison, 1978—; project assoc. Loyola U., Chgo., 1989-92; bd. dirs. Sta. WYOU, Madison. Co-prodr., author TV documentary Kids Meet Across Space, 1983; editor Telemedium, Jour. of Media Literacy, 1980—. Co-founder, bd. dirs., pres. Friends of Pub. Stas. WHA-TV, radio, Madison, 1968-78; v.p. bd. Nat. Friends of Pub. Broadcasting, N.Y. and Washington, 1970-76; pres., v.p. bd. Wis. Coun. and Am. Coun. for Better Broadcasts, Madison, 1963-75; commr. Gov.'s Blue Ribbon Commn. on Cable Communications, Wis., 1971-73; bd. dirs. Broadband Telecommunications Regulatory Bd., Madison, 1978-81. Recipient Spl. Recognition award Am. Coun. Better Broadcasts, 1981, Spl. award Joint Congress and World Meeting on Media Literacy, Spain, 1995. Mem. Soc. Satellite Profls. Internat. (charter), Internat. Visual Literacy Assn., Zeta Phi Eta (1st v.p. 1992, pres. 1993, Marguerite Garden Jones award 1989). Unitarian. Home: 1001 Tumalo Trl Madison WI 53711-3024

ROWE, MARJORIE DOUGLAS, retired social services administrator; b. Bklyn., July 29, 1912; d. Herbert Lynn and Mary Manson (Hall) Douglas; m. Richard Daniel Rowe, July 29, 1937; 1 child, Richard Douglas. AB cum laude, Whitman Coll., 1933; MS in Social Adminstrn., Case Western Res. U., 1936. Caseworker Children's Svcs., Cleve., 1933-36, supr., 1937-39; dir. Adoption Svc. Bur., Cleve., 1940-41; social work supr., psychiat. social work cons. Ea. State Hosp., Medical Lake, Wash., 1962-67; dir. social svcs. Interlake Sch.for Developmentally Disabled, Medical Lake, 1967-74, supt., 1975-82. Pres. chpt. R.P.E.O., Spokane, Wash., 1949, Spokane Alumnae chpt. Delta Delta Delta, 1955-57; chpt. mem. ARC, Orofino, Idaho, 1941-45, Orofino chpt. chmn., 1945-46; sec. Idaho state chpt. AAUW, 1945-46. Mem. Am. Assn. for Mental Deficiency (region I chmn. 1976-77, social work chmn. 1971-73), NASW (gold card mem.), P.E.O. (pres. Spokane Reciprocity 1950), Acad. Cert. Social Workers, Spokane Women of Rotary (pres. 1960-61), Phi Beta Kappa, Delta Sigma Rho, Mortar Bd. Episcopalian. Home: 946 E Thurston Ave Spokane WA 99203-2948

ROWE, MELISSA A., biologist; b. Rome, N.Y., May 31, 1962; d. Frank Alan and Alicia Ann (Carrillo) R.; m. Jonathan Andrew Soll, Mar. 16, 1996. BA, U. Calif., Santa Cruz, 1985; M Forest Resources, U. Wash., 1992. Rsch. and maintenance asst. U. Calif. Arboretum, Santa Cruz, 1983-84; staff mem. Saturn and Blue Moon Cafes, Santa Cruz, 1982-85; carpenter asst. U. Calif. Natural Area Res., Big Creek, Calif., 1986; rsch. asst. environ. studies dept. U. Calif., Riverside, Calif., 1987; English tchr., tech. editor Gifu, Japan, 1988; vol. coord./protection adminstr. The Nature Conservancy, Seattle, 1989-91; wildlands ranger Wash. State Dept. Natural Resources, Cypress Island, Wash., 1991; environ. planner Wash. State Dept. Natural Resources, Sedro Woolley, Wash., 1992-95; wildlife habitat biologist and info. coord. Yakama Indian Nation, Toppenish, Wash., 1995—; advising biologist Timber, Fish and Wildlife Coop., Olympia, Wash., 1995-96, Yakima Resource Mgmt. Coop., Ellensburg, Wash., 1995-96. Author agy. guidelines: Natural Resources Conservation Area Planning Guide, 1992. Peer counsellor, Personal Counsellors, Seattle, 1990-96. Fellow Patricia Harris Roberts Fund, U. Wash., 1990-92. Mem. The Wildlife Soc., Soc. for Ecol. Restoration, Soc. for Conservation Biology. Office: Yakima Indian Nation DNR PO Box 151 Toppenish WA 98948

ROWE, SANDRA LEE, elementary school and adult education educator; b. Augusta, Maine, Mar. 22, 1962; d. Leland James and Theresa (Boldue) K.; m. Mark Ashley Rowe, July 24, 1982; children: Seth Gerald, Ashley Marie. BS in Elem. Edn., U. Maine, Farmington, 1991, BS in Adult Edn., 1993. Substitute tchr. Maine Pub. Schs., Chelsea, Gardiner, etc., 1991-93; math. instr. Adult Edn. Hall-Dale Sch., Hallowell, Maine, 1994—; instr. adult edn. all levels Kennebec Learning Ctr., Augusta, 1993—; cons. Maine Math. Motivators, Orono, 1993—. Mem. Nat. Coun. Tchrs. of Math. Home: RR1 Box 1263 Hallowell ME 04347 Office: Kennebec Learning Ctr 43 Melville St Augusta ME 04330

ROWE, SANDRA MIMS, newspaper editor; b. Charlotte, N.C., May 26, 1948; d. David Lathan and Shirley (Stovall) Mims; m. Gerard Paul Rowe, June 5, 1971; children—Mims Elizabeth, Sarah Stovall. BA, East Carolina U., Greenville, N.C., 1970; postgrad., Harvard U., 1991. Reporter to asst. mng. editor The Ledger-Star, Norfolk, Va., 1971-80, mng. editor, 1980-82; mng. editor The Virginian-Pilot and The Ledger Star, Norfolk, Va., 1982-84, exec. editor, 1984-86, v.p., exec. editor, 1986-93; editor The Oregonian, Portland, 1993—; mem. Pulitzer Prize Bd., 1994—. Bd. visitors James Madison U., Harrisonburg, VA., 1991-95. Named Woman of Yr. Outstanding Profl. Women of Hampton Rds., 1987. Mem. Am. Soc. Newspaper Editors (bd. dirs. 1992—, v.p. 1996), Va. Press Assn. (bd. dirs. 1985-93). Episcopalian. Office: The Oregonian 1320 SW Broadway Portland OR 97201-3469

ROWE, SHERYL ANN, librarian; b. Stephenville, Tex., Sept. 29, 1946; d. Horace Milton and Letha Faye (Hensley) Hughes; m. Darrell Vanoy Rowe, Nov. 27, 1969; children: Jason Burt, Shelley Jean. BA in English, Tarleton State U., Stephenville, 1967; MS in Libr. Sci., Tex. Women's U., Denton, 1986. Cert. tchr. secondary edn. Tchr. Lake Worth (Tex.) H.S., 1967-69; tchr. Aledo (Tex.) H.S., 1967-73, 78-84, libr., 1984—. Mem. Tex. Libr. Assn., Region XI Librs. Assn. (treas. 1984—). Office: Aledo High School 412 FM1187 S Aledo TX 76008

ROWE, SUSAN VICTORIA, artist; b. Skokie, Ill., Jan. 4, 1965; d. William John and Ellen (McCabe) R. Cert. of proficiency, Instituto Di Lingua E Cultura Michelangelo, Florence, Italy, 1986; BA, U. Calif., Berkeley, 1987; attended, Sch. Art Inst., Chgo., 1990-91. Asst., inpainter Baumgartner Fine Art Restoration, Chgo., 1992-95; inpainter Chgo. Conservation Ctr., 1996—. Artist: (cover art) Sonora Rev., 1993, 94, (artist's book) Collection of Newberry Libr., Chgo. Recipient Cmty. Arts Assistance Program Grant award Dept. Cultural Affairs, Chgo., 1992, 93. Mem. Womens Caucus For Art. Home and Studio: 2328 W Thomas St #2R Chicago IL 60622

ROWELL, BARBARA C., volunteer; b. New Orleans, Sept. 5, 1922; d. Carlos Fernando and Antoinette (Angelo) Caballero; m. J.C. Rowell, Dec. 17, 1941; children: Jerrie Carlene, Kerry Gene, Ricky Ray. AA in Bus. Adminstrn., Okaloosa Walton Jr. Coll., Niceville, Fla., 1973; BA in Social Scis., U. West Fla., 1987. Exec. sec. Bishop Enterprises, Ft. Walton Beach, 1961-64; office mgr./property mgr. Fred Cooke Real Estate, Ft. Walton Beach, Fla., 1964-71; adminstrv. sec. to v.p. Okaloosa Walton Jr. Coll., Niceville, 1971-74. Leader brownie scouts Girl Scouts U.S., 1954-56, cub scouts Boy Scouts Am., 1957-59; bd. dirs. U. West Fla., Sr. Ctr. for Life Long Learning, 1993-96, chair univ svc. com., 1993-94, pres. 1995; originator, implementor U. West Fal Tutor Program, 1993, Career Fair, 1994, started scholarship program, 1995, Proctor Program, 1995; presenter S.E. Conf. Insts. of Learning in Retirement, Charleston, S.C., 1995; gov.'s campaign vol., 1970; state legislature campaign vol., 1992. Mem. DAV Aux., Sr. Friends, Order Eastern Star (worthy matron, mem. bd. govs. melody assembly order of the rainbow for girls, 1963-65, Nieeville, chair, 1964). Democrat. Roman Catholic.

ROWEN, RUTH HALLE, musicologist, educator; b. N.Y.C., Apr. 5, 1918; d. Louis and Ethel (Fried) Halle; m. Seymour M. Rowen, Oct. 13, 1940; children: Mary Helen Rowen, Louis Halle Rowen. B.A., Barnard Coll., 1939; M.A., Columbia U., 1941, Ph.D., 1948. Mgmt. ednl. dept. Carl Fischer, Inc., N.Y.C., 1954-63; assoc. prof. musicology CUNY, 1967-72, prof., 1972—, mem. doctoral faculty in musicology, 1967—. Author: Early Chamber Music, 1948, reprinted, 1974; (with Adele T. Katz) Hearing-Gateway to Music, 1959, (with William Simon) Jolly Come Sing and Play, 1956, Music Through Sources and Documents, 1979, (with Mary Rowen) Instant Piano, 1979, 80, 83, Symphonic and Chamber Music Score and Parts Bank, 1996; contbr. articles to profl. jours. Mem. ASCAP, Am. Musicol. Soc., Music Library Assn., Coll. Music Soc., Nat. Fedn. Music Clubs (nat. musicianship chmn. 1962-74, nat. young artist auditions com. 1964-74, N.Y. state chmn. Young Artist Auditions 1981, dist. coord. 1983, nat. bd. dirs. 1989—, rep. UN 1991—), N.Y. Fedn. Music Clubs (pres.), Phi Beta Kappa. Home: 115 Central Park W New York NY 10023-4153

ROWINSKY, JANE GANTT, healthcare administrator; b. Andalusia, Ala., Jan. 13, 1944; d. Edward and Annie Lee (Foshee) Gantt; m. Edson Oberlin Scanlan, Dec. 7, 1962 (div. Nov. 24, 1972); children: Kelley Sue, Michael John, Benjamin Lee; m. Bruce Walton Rowinsky, Jan. 1, 1974. AS in Nursing, Troy State U., 1975, BSN, 1987, MSN, 1991. Cert. profl. in healthcare quality Healthcare Cert. Bd. Nursing asst. St. Margaret's Hosp., Montgomery, Ala., 1973-75; nursing supr. Valley Meml. Hosp., Langdale, Ala., 1975-77; home health nurse Omni-Care, Opp, Ala., 1977-79; nursing supr. Andalusia Hosp., 1979-89; office nurse R. R. Daniel, M.D., Andalusia, 1989-91; utilization rev. nurse Andalusia Hosp., 1991-93; utilization mgmt. dir. Pioneers Meml. Healthcare Dist., Brawley, Calif., 1993—; mem. Imperial Valley adv. bd. San Diego Rehab. Inst., El Centro, Calif., 1994—. Mem. Am. Assn. Utilization Mgmt. Nurses (chairperson profl. devel. 1995-96), Am. Assn. Healthcare Quality, Calif. Assn. Healthcare Quality (mem. nominating com. 1994-95), Troy State Alumni Assn., Grad. Nurses Assn. of Troy (past pres.), Sigma Theta Tau, Gamma Beta Phi. Home: 1585 Ross Ave El Centro CA 92243 Office: Pioneers Meml Healthcare Dt 207 W Legion Rd Brawley CA 92227

ROWLAND, ESTHER E(DELMAN), college dean, retired; b. N.Y.C., Apr. 12, 1926; d. Abraham Simon and Ida Sarah (Shifrin) Edelman; m. Lewis P. Rowland, Aug. 31, 1952; children: Andrew, Steven, Judith. B.A., U. Wis., 1946; M.A., Columbia U., 1948, M.Phil., 1984. Instr. in polit. sci. CCNY, 1947-51, Mt. Holyoke Coll., South Hadley, Mass., 1948-49; dir. health professions adv. bd. U. Pa., Phila., 1971-73; adviser to pre-profl. students Barnard Coll., N.Y.C., 1974-79, dean for pre-profl. students, 1980-93, assoc. dean studies, 1989-95; ret., 1995—. Mem. exec. com. Nat. Emergency Civil Liberties Com., N.Y.C., 1975-90; mem. exec. com. Women's Counseling Project, 1981-86. Mem. N.E. Assn. Health Professions Advisers (exec. com. 1973-74), N.E. Assn. Pre Law Advisors (exec. com. 1981-83, 85-86), Neurol. Inst. Aux. Home: 404 Riverside Dr New York NY 10025-1861

ROWLAND, SUSAN SCOTT, artist, writer; b. Boston, June 7, 1940; d. Robert Walter and Catherine (Buff) Scott; m. George B. Rowland, Jun. 1961 (div. 1968); children: Christopher F. Rowland, Alix B. Rowland; m. Charles P. Sifton, Jun. 1986. BA, Vassar Coll., 1962; student, Art Student's League, N.Y.C., 1972-74. Contbr. (author): articles on beauty and travel to N.Y. Times, 1987-96, Vogue, 1995—; shows include Albuquerque Mus., 1987, P.S. I, Queens, 1990; one-woman show Bklyn. Arts Coun., 1990; group shows include Tunisian Comm. Agy., Tunis, 1995, and numerous others; permanent collections include Albuquerque Mus., U.S. Office of the Contr. of the Currency, Roswell N.Mex. Art Mus., Warner Amex Cable, Tex. Arts Ctr. Active artist/homeless collabration Women's Armory, N.Y.C., 1992-94. NEA fellow, 1978.

ROWLES, ARLENE BEVERLY, geriatric social program administrator; b. Johnstown, Ohio, July 12, 1935; d. John Wesley and Ruth Margaret (Johnston) Thomas; m. Edward William Rowles, July 21, 1957; children: Kenneth Alan, Keith Thomas, Diane Elizabeth. BS in Home Econs., Ohio State U., 1957. Lic. dietitian. Tchr. home econs. Southwestern City Schs., Grove City, Ohio, 1958-59; dir. Meals on Wheels of Fairfield County, Inc., Lancaster, Ohio, 1975—; mem. state, area ext. adv. com. Ohio State Univ. Ext., 1980—, v.p., pres. state adv. com., 1993-96; mem., past officer Fairfield County Adv. Com., 1971—; adv. com. Vis. Nurses Fairfield County, Lancaster, 1983—, pres., 1993-96; mem., past officer Fairfield County Com. on Aging, Lancaster, 1975—; mem. Millersport United Meth. Ch. Fellow Nat. Assn. Meal Providers (presenter 1980), Nat. Assn. Nutrition and Svc. Providers, Ohio Assn. Nutrition and Svc. Providers. Republican. Office: Meals on Wheels Fairfield Cty Inc 253 Boving Rd SW Lancaster OH 43130-4240

ROWLEY, JANET DAVISON, physician; b. N.Y.C., Apr. 5, 1925; d. Hurford Henry and Ethel Mary (Ballantyne) Davison; m. Donald A. Rowley, Dec. 18, 1948; children: Donald, David, Robert, Roger. PhB, U. Chgo., 1944, BS, 1946, MD, 1948; DSc (hon.), U. Ariz., 1989, U. Pa., 1989, Knox Coll., 1991, U. So. Calif., 1992. Cert. Am. Bd. Med. Genetics. Rsch. asst. U. Chgo., 1949-50; intern Marine Hosp., USPHS, Chgo., 1950-51; attending physician Infant Welfare and Prenatal Clinics Dept. Pub. Health, Montgomery County, Md., 1953-54; rsch. fellow Levinson Found., Cook County Hosp., Chgo., 1955-61; clin. instr. neurology U. Ill., Chgo., 1957-61; USPHS spl. trainee Radiobiology Lab. The Churchill Hosp., Oxford, Eng., 1961-62; rsch. assoc. dept. medicine and Argonne Cancer Rsch. Hosp. U. Chgo., 1962-69, assoc. prof. dept. medicine and Argonne Cancer Rsch. Hosp., 1969-77, prof. dept. medicine and Franklin McLean Meml. Rsch. Inst., 1977-84; Blum-Riese Disting. Svc. prof., dept. medicine and dept. molecular genetics and cell biology, 1984—; mem. Nat. Cancer Adv. Bd., 1979-84; bd. sci. counsellors Nat. Ctr. for Human Genome Rsch., NIH, 1994—, chmn., 1994—; Bernard Cohen Meml. lectr. U. Pa., 1993, Katherine D. McCormick Disting. lectr. Stanford U., 1994; Donald D. Van Slyke lectr. Brookhaven Nat. Lab., 1994. Co-founder, co-editor Genes, Chromosomes and Cancer; mem. editl. bds. Oncology Rsch., Cancer Genetics and Cytogenetics, Internat. Jour. Hematology, Genomics, Internat. Jour. Cancer, Leukemia; past mem. editorial bd. Blood, Cancer Rsch., Hematol. Oncology, Leukemia Rsch.; contbr. chpts. to books., articles to profl. jours. Mem. Bd. Sci. Counsellors, Nat. Inst. Dental Rsch., NIH, 1972-76, chmn., 1974-76; mem. Nat. Cancer Adv. Bd. Nat. Cancer Inst., 1979-84; mem. adv. com. Frederick Cancer Rsch. Facility, 1983-85; mem. adv. bd. Leukemia Soc. Am., 1979-84; mem. MIT Corp. vis. com. Dept. Applied Biol. Scis., 1983-86; mem. selection com. scholar award in Biomed. Sci., Lucille P. Markey Charitable Trust, 1984-87; trustee Adler Planetarium, Chgo., 1978—; bd. dirs. am. Bd. Med. Genetics, 1982-83, Am. Bd. Human Genetics, 1985-88; bd. sci. cons. meml. Sloan-Kettering Cancer Ctr., 1988-90; nat. adv. com. McDonnell Found. Program for Molecular Medicine in Cancer Rsch., 1988—; adv. com. Ency. Britannica U. Chgo., 1988—; mem. adv. bd. Howard Hughes Med. Inst., 1989-94; adv. com. for career awards in biomed. scis. Burroughs Wellcome Fund, 1994—. Recipient First Kuwait Cancer prize, 1984, Esther Langer award Ann Langer Cancer Rsch. Found., 1983, A. Cressy Morrison award in natural scis. N.Y. Acad. Scis., 1985, Past State Pres.' award Tex. Fedn. Bus. and Profl. Women's Clubs, 1986, Karnofsky award and lecture Am. Soc. Clin. Oncology, 1987, prix Antoine Lacassagne Lique Nationale Francaise Contre le Cancer, 1987, King Faisal Internat. prize in medicine (co-recipient), 1988, Katherine Berkan Judd award Meml. Sloan-Kettering Cancer Ctr., 1989, (co-recipient) Charles Mott Prize GM Cancer Rsch. Found., 1989, Steven C. Beering award U. Ind. Med. Sch., 1992, Robert de Villiers award Leukemia Soc. Am., 1993, Kaplan Family prize for cancer rsch. excellence Oncology Soc. Dayton, 1995, Cotlove award and lecture Acad. Clin. Lab. Physicians and Scientists, 1995, Nilsson-Ehle lecture Mendelian Soc. and Royal Physiographic Soc., U. Lund, 1995, The Gardner Found. award, 1996. Mem. NAS (chmn. sect. 41 1995—), Am. Acad. Arts and Scis., Am. Philos. Soc., Am. Soc. Human Genetics (pres.-elect 1992, pres. 1993, Allen award and lectr. 1991), Genetical Soc. (Gt. Britain), Am. Soc. Hematology (Presdl. Symposium 1982, Dameshek prize 1982, Ham-Wasserman award 1995), Am. Assn. Cancer Rsch. (G.H.A. Clowes Meml. award 1989), Inst. Medicine (coun. 1988-90), Sigma Xi (William Proctor prize for sci. achievement 1989), Alpha Omega Alpha Alumnus. Episcopalian. Home: 5310 S University Ave Chicago IL 60615-5106 Office: U Chgo 5841 Maryland Ave MC 2115 Chicago IL 60637

ROWLEY, MARCIA LYNN, middle school educator; b. Terre Haute, Ind., May 6, 1952. BA in English Lit., U. Cin., 1974, BS in Secondary Edn., 1974; MEd in Curriculum Adminstrn., Xavier U., 1978. Tchr., coach, dean of girls Harrison (Ohio) Jr. Sch., 1975—. Named Ohio Mid. Sch. Lang. Arts Tchr. of Yr., 1993. Home: 6915 Rob Vern Dr Cincinnati OH 45239 Office: Harrison Jr Sch 9830 West Rd Harrison OH 45030

ROY, CATHERINE ELIZABETH, physical therapist; b. Tucson, Jan. 16, 1948; d. Francis Albert and Dorothy Orme (Thomas) R.; m. Richard M. Johnson, Aug. 31, 1968 (div. 1978); children: Kimberly Anne, Troy Michael. BA in Social Sci. magna cum laude, San Diego State U., 1980; MS in Phys. Therapy, U. So. Calif., 1984. Staff therapist Sharp Meml. Hosp., San Diego, 1984-89, chairperson patient and family edn. com., 1986-87, chairperson sex edn. and counselling com., 1987-89, chairperson adv. bd. for phys. therapy, asst. for edn. program, 1987-89; mgr. rehab. phys. therapy San Diego Rehab. Inst., Alvarado Hosp., 1989-91; dir. therapeutic svcs. VA Med. Ctr., San Diego, 1991—; lectr. patient edn., family edn., peer edn.; mem. curriculum rev. com. U. So. Calif. Phys. Therapy Dept., 1982; bd. dirs. Ctr. for Edn. in Health; writer, reviewer licensure examination items for phys. therapy Profl. Examination Services.. Tennis coach at clinics Rancho Penasquitos Swim and Tennis Club, San Diego, 1980-81; active Polit. Activities Network, 1985; counselor EEO, 1992-95. Mem. Am. Phys. Therapy Assn. (rsch. presenter nat. conf. 1985, del. nat. conf. 1986-94, rep. state conf. 1987-89, 92-94, Mary McMillan student award 1984, mem. exec. bd. San Diego dist. 1985-88, 92-94), AAUW, NAFE, Am. Congress Rehab. Medicine, Phi Beta Kappa, Phi Kappa Phi, Chi Omega. Home: 5067 Park West Ave San Diego CA 92117-1048 Office: San Diego VA Med Ctr Spinal Cord Injury Svc 3350 La Jolla Village Dr San Diego CA 92161-0002

ROY, ELSIJANE TRIMBLE, federal judge; b. Lonoke, Ark., Apr. 2, 1916; d. Thomas Clark and Elsie Jane (Walls) Trimble; m. James M. Roy, Nov. 23, 1943; 1 son, James Morrison. JD, U. Ark., Fayetteville, 1939; LLD (hon.), U. Ark., Little Rock, 1978. Bar: Ark. 1939. Atty. Rose, Loughborough, Dobyns & House, Little Rock, 1940-41, Ark. Revenue Dept., Little Rock, 1941-42; mem. firm Reid, Evrard & Roy, Blytheville, Ark., 1945-54, Roy & Roy, Blytheville, 1954-63; law clk. Ark. Supreme Ct., Little Rock, 1963-65; assoc. justice Ark. Supreme Ct., 1975-77; U.S. dist. judge then sr. judge Ea. and We. Dists. Ark., Little Rock, 1977—; judge Pulaski County (Ark.) Cir. Ct., Little Rock, 1966; asst. atty. gen. Ark., Little Rock, 1967; sr. law clk. U.S. Dist. Ct., Little Rock and Ft. Smith, 1967-75; Mem. med. adv. com. U. Ark. Med. Center, 1952-54; Committeewoman Democratic Party 16th Jud. Dist., 1940-42; vice chmn. Ark. Dem. State Com., 1946-48; mem. chmn. com. Ark. Constnl. Commn., 1967-68. Recipient disting. alumnae citation U. Ark., 1978, Gayle Pettus Pontz award, 1986, Brooks Hays Meml. Christian Citizenship award, 1994; named Ark. woman of yr., Bus. and Profl. Women's Club, 1969, 76, outstanding appellate judge, Ark. Trial Lawyers Assn., 1976-77, Delta Theta Phi mem. of yr. 1989; named among top 100 women in Ark. bus., 1995; Paul Harris fellow Rotary Club Little Rock, 1992. Recipient disting. alumnae citation U. Ark., 1978, Gayle Pettus Pontz award, 1986, Brooks Hays Meml. Christian Citizenship award, 1994; named Ark. Woman of Yr., Bus. and Profl. Women's Club, 1969, 76, Outstanding Appellate Judge, Ark. Trial Lawyers Assn., 1976-77, Mem. of Yr., Delta Theta Phi, 1989; named among top 100 women in Ark. bus., 1995, Ark. Bus. Top 100 Women in Ark., 1995; Paul Harris fellow Rotary Little Rock, 1992. Office: US Dist Ct 600 W Capitol Ave Rm 423 Little Rock AR 72201-3326

ROY, GAIL FLORINE, nursing administrator; b. Rumford, Maine, Sept. 2, 1947; d. Alanson W. Jr. and Florine E. (Bean) Bowden; m. Henry R. Roy Sr.; children: Henry Jr., Michael, Debra, Vaughn, Lauren, Ross. ADN, C.C. R.I., 1990; U. Md. RN, R.I.; cert. med. surg. nurse, gerongol. nurse; notary pub., R.I. Staff nurse, charge nurse Mt. St. Francis Health Ctr., Woonsocket, R.I., 1990, nursing supr., 1991-95; nursing supr. St. Antoine Residence, North Smithfield, R.I., 1995—. Relief mgr. Ronald McDonald House, Providence, 1993; vol. Vet. Ctr., Pautucket, R.I., 1983-87; chair R.I. Vietnam Vet. Honor Roll Com., 1984. Pell grantee State of R.I., 1987-90, R.I. Higher Edn. grantee, 1987-90; Woonsocket Landmark Med. Ctr. scholar, 1989. Mem. ANA, Gerontol. Nursing Assn., R.I. State Nurses Assn., Vietnam Vets. Am. (assoc.). Independent. Home: St Antoine Residence 42 Roy Ave Woonsocket RI 02895-5955 Office: St Antoine Residence 400 Mendon Rd North Smithfield RI 02896-6999

ROYAL, DOROTHY PATRICIA, retired library media specialist; b. Washington, Oct. 13, 1935; d. Frederick James and Willie Nora (Levister) Constantine; m. H.B. Royal, Feb. 16, 1957; children: Duane Alan, Brett Ashley, Craig Stephen. BA, U. Md., 1977, MLS, 1982. Cert. advanced profl. in ednl. media, Md. Libr. media specialist Charles Carroll Middle Sch., New Carrollton, Md., 1977-83, Crossland H.S., Temple Hills, Md., 1983-95. Editor film festivals, 1977-83; book reviewer Sch. Libr. Jour., 1985—, Kliatt Paperbacks, Wellesley, Mass., 1990—. Mem. adv. com. Friends of Sampson County Pub. Libr., 1996, exec. bd. Sampson County Arts Coun., 1996. Mem. AAUW, NOW, Md. State Tchrs. Assn., Md. Ednl. Media Orgn., Ednl. Media Assn. Prince Georges County (v.p. 1983-84), Smithsonian Assocs., Nat. Mus. Women in Arts, Clinton Women's Club. Home: 11500 Keener Rd Faison NC 28341

ROYBAL-ALLARD, LUCILLE, congresswoman; b. Boyle Heights, Calif., June 12, 1941; d. Edward Roybal; m. Edward T. Allard; 4 children. BA, Calif. State U., L.A. Former mem. Calif. State Assembly; mem. 103rd Congress from 33rd Calif. dist., 1993—; mem. Banking and Fin. Svcs., Budget Com. Office: Ho of Reps 324 Cannon Washington DC 20515*

ROYCE, MARY WELLER SA'ID, artist, poet; b. Tupper Lake, N.Y., July 9, 1933; d. Gerard Charles and Mary Weller (McCarthy) de Grandpré; m. Majed Farhan Sa'id, Nov. 19, 1960 (dec. 1966); children: Mary Weller Richardson, Emily Ann Bacon; m. William Ronald Royce, Sept. 2, 1974. AA with honors, Georgetown Visitation Jr. Coll., 1953; BS cum laude, Georgetown U., 1960; MA in Italian, Middlebury Coll., 1968. Writer, artist, 1954—; translator, adminstrv. asst. U.S. Army, Orleans, France, 1956-58; tchg. asst. dept. Italian Rutgers U., New Brunswick, N.J., 1968-70; translator N.J., Ariz., 1971-84; owner, designer The Stamp Act, Rockville, Md., 1990-93. Groups shows include Rockville (Md.) Arts Pl., 1992—, Rockville Art League, 1993—, Montpelier Cultural Arts Ctr., Laurel, Md., 1994—, Strathmore Hall Arts Ctr., North Bethesda, Md., 1994—; poetry collected in anthologies. Coord. Equal Rights Coalition, Utah, 1975; ACLU rep. So. Ariz. Coalition for ERA, Tucson, 1975-78; mem. steering com. Ariz. ERA, 1976-78; Md. state activist Caths. for a Free Choice, 1991-93; mem. The Alliance of Rockville Citizens, 1995—. Fulbright grantee, 1960. Mem. Acad. Am. Poets (assoc.), Nat. Mus. Women in Arts (charter), Washington Project for Arts, Rockville Art League, Strathmore Hall Arts Ctr., Rockville Arts Pl., Arlington Arts Ctr., Montpelier Cultural Arts Ctr. Avocations: photography, jazz, swimming.

ROYER, KATHLEEN ROSE, pilot; b. Pitts., Nov. 4, 1949; d. Victor Cedric and Lisetta Emma (Smith) Salway; m. Michael Lee Royer, June 6, 1971 (div. Aug. 1975). Student, Newbold Coll., 1968-69; BS, Columbia Union Coll., 1971; MEd, Shippensburg U., 1974; student, Lehigh U., 1974-75. Cert. tchr. Pa. Music tchr. Harrisburg (Pa.) Sch. Dist., 1971-77; flight instr. Penn-Air, Inc., Altoona, Pa., 1977; capt., asst. chief pilot Air Atlantic Airlines, Centre Hall, Pa., 1977-80; capt., chief pilot Lycoming Air Svc., Williamsport, Pa., 1980-81; govs. pilot Commonwealth of Pa., Harrisburg, 1981-87; flight engr. Pan-Am, N.Y.C., 1987-91; pilot, 1st officer B737 United Airlines, Chgo., 1992-96; 1st officer B767 United Airlines, N.Y.C., 1996—; first woman pilot/engr. crew mem. on 747, 1989-91, chief pilot, cons. Mem. Internat. Soc. Women Airline Pilots, Flight Engrs. Internat. Assn. (scheduling rep. 1989, scheduling dir. 1990, 1st vice chmn., mem. bd. adjustments 1989, v.p., dir. scheduling 1991-92), UAL-Airline Pilots Assn. (coord. critical incident stress program 1994—), 99's (local chair Ctrl. Pa. chpt. 1987-92), Whirley-Girls (Washington), Hershey Country Club. Republican. Office: United Airlines PO Box 66140 O'Hare Internat Airport Chicago IL 60666

ROYLE, LIA B., lawyer; b. Stuttgart, Germany, Jan. 17, 1956. BA, U. N.C., 1977; MA, Oxford U., 1981; JD, Columbia U., 1985. Ptnr. Anderson Kill Olick & Oshinsky, N.Y.C. Harlan Fiske Stone scholar. Mem. ABA, N.Y. State Bar Assn., Phi Beta Kappa. Office: Anderson Kill Olick & Oshinsky 1251 Ave of the Americas New York NY 10020-1182*

ROYSE, MARY KAY, judge; b. Hutchinson, Kans., Oct. 3, 1949; d. J.R. and Patricia Ann (Lamont) R. BS in Edn., Emporia State U., 1970, MA, 1972; JD, Kans. U., 1978. Instr. Miami U., Hamilton, Ohio, 1972-75; assoc. atty. Foulston & Siefkin, Wichita, 1978-82, Law Offices Bryson E. Mills, Wichita, 1982-86; judge Dist. Ct. (18th dist.) Kans., Wichita, 1986-93, Kans. Ct. Appeals, Topeka, 1993—; mem. Kans. Jud. Coun. Com. Pattern Instructions Kans., 1989—. Bd. dirs. Work Option Women, Wichita, 1980, Emporia State U. Alumni Assn., 1982-85, Kans. Dialysis Assn., Wichita, 1986-93. Named Woman Achievement, Women in Communications, Wichita, 1988, Disting. Alumni, Emporia State U., 1990. Mem. ABA, Kans. Bar Assn., Kans. Commn. Bicentenial U.S. Constitution, Kans. Bar Assn. Commn. Status of Women in Profession, Wichita Bar Assn.

ROZARTO, DENISE, nurse; b. Phila., Dec. 23, 1958; d. Francis John and Ercolina Marie (Madotto) R. BSN, Widener U., 1980. Cert. CNOR, ACLS. Staff nurse ICU/CCU stepdown unit Met. Hosp., Phila., 1981-83; ICU staff RN Phila. Coll. Osteopathic Medicine, Phila., 1983; staff RN parenteral therapy Methodist Hosp., Phila., 1983-88; staff RN oper. rm. Misericodia Hosp., Phila., 1988-90, Pa. Hosp., Phila., 1990—. Mem. Am. Found. for AIDS Rsch., 1989—. Widener U. grantee, 1976. Mem. AORN. Home: 515 A Country Club Pkwy Mount Laurel NJ 08054 Office: Pa Hosp Philadelphia PA 19107

ROZENBERG, MARY JACCOMA, environmental activist, aerosol researcher; b. Flint, Mich., Jan. 23, 1946; d. John August Green and Evelyn Ada Rockafellow; m. Albert Jaccoma, Nov. 7, 1967 (div. Jan. 1978); m. Donald Pryce Rozenberg, June 15, 1981. MusB, Manhattan Sch. of Music, N.Y.C., 1969; MusM, Manhattan Sch. of Music, 1970. Profl. cellist, N.Y.C., 1967-87. Contbr. articles to sci. profl. publs. Founder Burning Issues, Nat. USA, 1989, pres. Clean Air Revival, 1995; bd. dirs. Clean Air Revival, 1993; leader Self Help Course, Arthritis Found., Stanford U., 1993. Recipient New Activist award Sierra Club, 1993, Conservation award, 1994; grantee The Strong Found., 1995, Sierra Club Found., 1994. Mem. Am. Assn. for Aerosol Rsch., Sierra Club (air quality chair 1992-95). Green. Episcopalian. Home: 24800 Ten Mile Rd Point Arena CA 95468 Office: Burning Issues/ Clean Air Revival PO Box 1045 Point Arena CA 95468

RUANE, KAY, artist; b. Chgo., Apr. 21, 1956; d. Michael L. and Joan E. R.; m. Doug Bolin, June 27, 1981. Student, Sch. Art Inst. Chgo., 1975; BFA, U. Ill., 1978; postgrad., Ind. State U., 1981-82. One woman shows include MC Gallery, Mpls., 1985, 88, 91, U. Ill., Champaine-Urbana, Ill., 1978, WARM Gallery, Mpls., 1986, Gallery K, Washington, 1990; exhibited in group shows at Ind. State U., 1982, WARM Gallery, Mpls., 1983, 84, 85, 89, Lehigh U., Bethlehem, Pa., 1984, Art Ctr. of Minn., 1984, 85, N.D. State U., Fargo, 1985, St. Mary's Coll., Winnona, Minn., 1985, Duluth (Minn.) Art Inst. 1985, Tweed Mus., Duluth, Minn., 1985, U. Wis., 1986, ARC Gallery, Chgo., 1987, Katherine Nash Gallery, U. Minn., Mpls., 1987, Moyer Gallery, Green Bay, Wis., 1989, Gallery K, Washington, 1988, Concept Gallery, Pitts., 1990, Carnegie Mus., Pitts., 1989, 90, 91, Oglebay Steifel Fine Arts Ctr., Wheeling, W.Va., 1990, St. Paul(Minn.) Cos., 1990, Gallery K, Washington, 1990, 91, 92, MC Gallery, Mpls., 1984, 85, 86, 89, 90, 93, 94, 95, San Diego Art Inst., 1994; represented in permanent collections at Kreindler & Kreindler, N.Y.C., Am. Embassy, Reykjakik, Iceland, AT&T, Mpls., Fed. Res. Bank, Mpls., St. Paul Cos., Travelers, Express, St. Louis Park, Minn., also numerous pvt. collections; contbr. photographs, articles, cover art for various newspapers, mags., and calendar. Arts Midwest/NEA Regional Visual Artist fellowship, 1996; recipient Mildred K. Cohen award Carnegie Mus. AAP Exhibit; named emerging artist Am. Artist Mag., 1985. Mem. Associated Artist of Pitts., Woman's Caucus for Art. Home: 4325 Xerxes Ave S Minneapolis MN 55410 Studio: 700 Washington Ave N #323 Minneapolis MN 55401

RUBELL, BONNIE LEVINE, occupational therapist; b. Bklyn., Aug. 6, 1957; d. Seymour and Gladys Levine; m. Paul Rubell, June 3, 1990. BS in Occupational Therapy, NYU, 1979. Staff occupational therapist Main Campus Vocat. Workshop United Cerebral Palsy, Bklyn., 1980-83; sr. occupational therapist N.Y.C. Bd. Edn. Office Related and Contractual Svcs., 1983-86, supr. occupational therapy, 1986-87; sr. staff occupational therapist United Cerebral Palsy Treatment and Rehab. Ctr., Roosevelt, N.Y., 1987-89; master profl. occupational therapist The Sch. for Lang. and Communication Devel., North Bellmore, N.Y., 1987-92; staff occupational therapist Nassau Bd. Coop. Ednl. Svcs., The Lewis Ames Sch., 1992—; cons. On Your Mark program Staten Island Jewish Community Ctrs., 1984-85. Author: Big Strokes for Little Folks, 1995. Mem. Assn. Occupational Therapists Am., N.Y. Met. and L.I. Dists. Occupational Therapy Assn.

RUBEN, IDA GASS, state senator; b. Washington, Jan. 7, 1929; d. Sol and Sonia E. (Darman) Gass; m. L. Leonard Ruben, Aug. 29, 1948; children: Garry, Michael, Scott, Stephen. Del. Md. Ho. of Dels., Annapolis, 1974-86; mem. Md. Senate, Annapolis, 1986—, majority whip, 1995—; chair Montgomery County House Delegation, 1981-86, Montgomery County Senate Delegation, 1987—; mem. house econ. matters com., 1974-85, house ways and means com., 1985-86, legis. policy com., 1991—, senate budget and taxation com., joint budget and audit com., 1991—, exec. nominations com., 1991—, joint protocol com., 1991—, chair subcom. on pub. safety, transp., econ. devel. and natural resources, 1995—, mem. joint com. on spending affordability, 1995—, mem. capital budget subcom., 1995—; mem. Gov.'s Motor Carrier Task Force, 1989—; conv. chair Nat. Order Women Legislators, 1980. Chair Women Legislators Caucus Md., 1982-84; trustee Adventist Health Care Mid-Atlantic, Takoma Park, Md.; bd. dirs. Ctrs. for Handicapped, Silver Spring, Md.; former internat. v.p. B'nai Brith Women. Recipient Cert. of Appreciation Ctrs. for Handicapped, 1987, Meritorious Svc. award Safety and Survival, 1989, Cover Those Trucks award AAA Potomac, 1989, Leadership Laurel award Safety First Club Md., 1989, Woman of Valor award B'nai B'rith Women, 1991, Pub. Affairs award Planned Parenthood Md., 1992, ESOL support recognition Montgomery County Pub. Schs., 1992, Appreciation award Fraternal Order Police, 1992, John Dewey award Montgomery County Fedn. Tchrs., 1992, Appreciation award ARC of Md., 1992, Safety Leader award Advocates for Hwy. and Auto Safety, 1993, Disting. Svc. award Gov.'s Commn. Employment of People with Disabilities, 1993, award Faculty Guild U. Md. for support of faculty and univ., 1993, Sincere Appreciation award for commitment to Md.'s youth Md. Underage Drinking Prevention Coalition, 1994, Faithful Svc. to citizens of Montgomery County award Montgomery County Assn. of Realtors, 1994; named Most Effective Pub. Ofcl. by residents of Silver Spring, 1990, One of 100 Most Powerful Women in Washington Metro Area by Washingtonian Mag., 1994, Legislator of Yr. award Nat. Commn. Against Drunk Driving, 1995, Legislator of Yr. award Montgomery County Med. Soc., 1995, Carmen S. Turner Achievement in Cmty. Svc. award Montgomery County Dept. Transp., 1995; inducted into Washington, Md., Del., Pa. Svc. Sta. Assn. Hall of Fame, 1994. Mem. Coun. State Govts. (com. on suggested legislation), Hadassah. Democrat. Jewish. Home: 11 Schindler Ct Silver Spring MD 20903-1329 Office: Md State Senate 204 James Senate Off Bldg 110 College Ave Annapolis MD 21401-8012

RUBESCH, SANDRA M., credit manager consultant; b. Auburn, Wis., July 29, 1942; d. Merlin O. and Evelyn K. (Pitts) Schnoor; m. Leonard J. Rubesch, Jr., Feb. 20, 1965; children: David J., Stephanie A. Rubesch Wilcox. Rsch. contracts & grants U. Minn., Mpls., 1960-64; dep. registrar City-County Health Dept., Eau Claire, Wis., 1964-70; from adminstrv. asst. to exec. sec. Royal Credit Union, Eau Claire, 1979—. Chair women's group Sacred Heart Ch., Eau Claire, 1972-76. Mem. Am. Bus. Women's Assn. (membership com. 1996). Roman Catholic.

RUBIN, ANNA ITA, composer, educator; b. Akron, Ohio, Sept. 5, 1946; d. Leo and Sophie (Fitterman) R.; m. Howard Edward Herrnstadt, Dec. 10, 1989; 1 child, Eli Joseph Herrnstadt. BA cum laude, Pomona Coll., 1968; MFA in Composition, Calif. Inst. of the Arts, 1981; postgrad., Princeton U., 1994—. Freelance composer, pvt. tchr. piano and composition, 1988—. Culture editor Jour. of L.Am. Parents Adoption Assn., N.J., 1996—; composer De Nacht, 1983, Freedom, Sweet and Bitter, 1991, Crying the Laughing and Golden, 1992, Remembering, 1992. Fellow in composition N.Y. Found. for the Arts, N.Y.C., 1988, 94. mem. Am. Soc. Composers, Authors and Pubs. (Yearly awards 1989—), Soc. for Electron-Acoustic Music, U.S. (contbg. editor jour. 1992—), Internat. Computer Music Assn., Am. Music Forum. Jewish.

RUBIN, BARBARA HELENE, pastor; b. N.Y.C., Oct. 12, 1948; d. Milton Joseph and Miriam (Stermer) Cooperman; separated; 1 child, Jeremiah Micheal. Grad. h.s., N.Y.C.; hon. cert. divinity and ministry, United Christian Ch., 1995. Cert. degree of divinity and ministry United Christian Church, 1995. Pastor, founder The Ch. of Deliverance and Life, 1993—. Vol. nursing home. Address: Ch of Deliverance and Life 244 E 52d St New York NY 10022

RUBIN, CHANDA, professional tennis player; b. Lafayette, La., Feb. 18, 1976; d. Edward and Bernadette Rubin. Grad., Episcopal Sch. Acadiana, 1993. Mem. USTA Jr. Devel. Team, 1989, USTA Nat. Team, 1990; prof. tennis player, 1991—; player 20 tournaments and Fed. Cup with 43 wins, 19 losses, 1995, named to Olympic Team, Atlanta,1996,. Recipient 3 U.S. Jr. Titles, 12 Singles, 1988, 14 Singles, 1989, 16 Indoor Doublles, 1989; winner U.S. nat. title and Rolex Orange Bowl 12s crown, 1988, 14 Nat., 1989, 16 Indoor Doubles, 1989, U.S. Tennis Assn. Challenge of Midland Mich.

RUBIN, JANE LOCKHART GREGORY, lawyer, foundation executive; b. Richmond, Va., May 27, 1944; d. Phillip Henry and Jane Ball (Lockhart) Gregory; m. Reed Rubin, Jan. 22, 1966; children: Lara Ross, Maia Ayers, Peter Lyon. BA, Vassar Coll., 1965; JD, Columbia U., 1975; LLM in Taxation, NYU, 1984. Bar: N.Y, 1976. Assoc. Coudert Brothers, N.Y.C., 1977-84; of counsel Lankenau, Kouner & Kurtz, N.Y.C., 1985-95; dir. Interamericas, N.Y.C., 1992—; bd. dirs., treas. Reed Found., N.Y.C., 1985—; mem. adv. bd. Vt. Studio Ctr., 1985—; mem. Mcpl. Archives Reference and Rsch. Adv. Bd., 1991-94; mem. N.Y.C. Commn. for Cultural Affairs, 1992-94; mem. profl. adv. coun. Lincoln Ctr. for the Performing Arts, 1994—; mem. bd. visitors Columbia Law Sch., 1994—. Author: intro. and catalog for exhibit Temple of Justice: The Appellate Division Court House; (with others) The Art World and the Law, 1987. Bd. dirs., vice chair Vol. Lawyers for the Arts; mem. profl. advisors coun. Lincoln Ctr. for the Performing Arts, 1994—; bd. govs. The John Carter Brown Libr. Harlan Fiske Stone scholar Columbia U. Sch. Law. Mem. ABA (sect. real property and probate law, sect. internat. law and practice), N.Y. Bar Assn., Union Internationale des Avocats, Assn. Bar City of N.Y. (com. on non-profit orgns. 1984—), Copyright Soc. of U.S.A. Office: Inter Americas 162 East 78 St New York NY 10021 Home: 135 Central Park West New York NY 10023

RUBIN, JUDITH DIANE, medical educator; b. Pitts., 1944. MD, U. Pa., 1969. Diplomate Am. Bd. Pediatrics, Am. Bd. Preventive Medicine. Intern in pediats. Children's Hosp., Phila., 1969-70; resident in pediats. Pahlavi U., Shiraz, Iran, 1970-71; resident in pediats. U. Md. Hosp., Balt., 1975-76, resident preventive medicine, 1973-77; fellow in pub. health Johns Hopkins Sch. Pub. Health, Balt., 1974-75; assoc. prof. U. Md. Sch. Medicine. Contbr. numerous articles to profl. jours. Fellow Am. Acad. Pediatrics, Am. Coll. Preventive Medicine; mem. Am. Bd. Preventive Medicine (trustee). Office: U Md Sch Med Epid & Prev Medicine 132 E Howard Hall 660 W Redwood St Baltimore MD 21201-1596

RUBIN, KAREN BETH, publishing, marketing and representation executive; b. N.Y.C., Aug. 30, 1951; d. Samuel M. and Eleanor (Spiegel) Rubin; m. Neil Leiberman, Dec. 29, 1983; children: David, Eric. BA magna cum laude, SUNY, Binghamton, 1972. Sr. editor Travel Agt. mag., N.Y.C., 1973-86, Tour & Travel News, Manhasset, N.Y., 1986-89; pres. Workstyles, Inc., Great Neck, N.Y., 1989—; founder, pub., editor Making It!, Great Neck, 1981—, Family Travel Letter, Great Neck, 1995—; adj. prof. NYU, 1992—. Author: Flying High in Travel, 1986, 92; contbr. thousands of articles to newspapers and profl. jours. Recipient Neal Cert. of Merit, Am. Bus. Press, 1984. Office: Workstyles Inc 5 Rose Ave Great Neck NY 11021-1530

RUBIN, NANCY RUTH ZIMMAN, journalist, author; b. Boston, Nov. 25, 1944; d. Stuart Wendell and Ethel Charlotte (Rabinovitz) Zimman; children: Elisabeth, Jessica. BA, Tufts U., 1966; MA in Teaching, Brown U., 1967; PhD (hon.), Mt. Vernon Coll., 1995. English tchr. Rochester, N.Y., 1967-70; playwright, dir. Equity Library Theatre, Roundabout, Joseph Jefferson and St. Clement's theaters, N.Y.C., 1971-74; writer Westchester-Gannett newspapers and mags., 1975-77; free-lance reporter N.Y. Times, N.Y.C., 1977-96; faculty affiliate Bush Ctr. in Child Devel., Yale U., New Haven, 1981—; mem. Westchester County Women's Adv. Bd., chair, 1988; mem. faculty SUNY, Purchase, 1994—, Fordham U., N.Y.C., 1996—. Author: The New Suburban Women; Beyond Myth and Motherhood, 1982, The Mother Mirror: How a Generation of Women is Changing Motherhood in America, 1984, Isabella of Castile: The First Renaissance Queen, 1991, American Empress: The Life and Times of Marjorie Merriweather Post, 1995, (TV series) America's Castles, 1996—. contbg. editor Parents mag., 1987-91, McCalls, Savvy, Travel & Leisure, Ladies Home Journal, 1980-92; theater critic Stamford Advocate, 1994-96. Recipient Washington Irving award Westchester Libr. Assn., 1993; Time, Inc.-Bread Loaf Writers' Colony scholar, 1979. Fellow MacDowell Colony; mem. Author's Guild, Am. Soc. Journalists and Authors (Author of Yr. award 1992), PEN, NOW. Office: care Elaine Markson Agy 44 Greenwich Ave New York NY 10011-8347

RUBIN, SANDRA MENDELSOHN, artist; b. Santa Monica, Calif., Nov. 7, 1947; d. Murry and Freda (Atliss) Mendelsohn; m. Stephen Edward Rubin, Aug. 6, 1966. BA, UCLA, 1976, MFA, 1979. Instr. Art Ctr. Coll. Design, Pasadena, Calif., 1980, UCLA, 1981. One-woman exhbns. include L.A. County Mus. Art, 1985, Fischer Fine Arts, London, 1985, Claude Bernard Gallery, N.Y.C., 1987, L.A. Louver Gallery, L.A., 1992; group exhbns. include L.A. County Mus. Artm 1977, 82, 83, L.A. Mcpl. Art Gallery, 1977, 83, 93, L.A. Contemporary Exhbns., 1978, L.A. Inst. Contemporary Arts, 1978, Newport Harbor Art Mus., Newport Beach, Calif., 1981, Odyssia Gallery, N.Y.C., 1981, Nagoya (Japan) City Mus., 1982, Long Beach (Calif.) Mus. Art, 1982, Brooke Alexander Gallery, N.Y.C., 1982, Laguna Beach (Calif.) Mus. Art, 1982, Jan Baum Gallery, L.A., 1984, San Francisco Mus. Art, 1986, Claude Bernard Gallery, 1986, Struve Gallery, Chgo., 1987, Boise (Idaho) Mus., 1988, Judy Youen's Gallery, London, 1988, Tatistscheff Gallery, Inc., Santa Monica, Calif., 1989, Tortue Gallery, Santa Monica, 1990, Contemporary Arts Forum, Santa Barbara, Calif., 1990, San Diego Mus. Art, 1991, Fresno (Calif.) Met. Mus., 1992, Jack Rutberg Fine Arts, L.A., 1993. Recipient Young Talent Purchase award L.A. County Mus. Art, 1980; Artist's Fellowship grant NEA, 1981, 91.

RUBIN, VERA COOPER, research astronomer; b. Phila., July 23, 1928; d. Philip and Rose (Applebaum) Cooper; m. Robert J. Rubin, June 25, 1948; children: David M., Judith S. Young, Karl C., Allan M. BA, Vassar Coll., 1948; MA, Cornell U., 1951; PhD, Georgetown U., 1954; DSc (hon.), Creighton U., 1978, Harvard U., 1988, Yale U., 1990, Williams Coll., 1993. Research assoc. to asst. prof. Georgetown U., Washington, 1955-65; physicist U. Calif.-LaJolla, 1963-64; astronomer Carnegie Inst., Washington, 1965—; Chancellor's Disting. prof. U. Calif., Berkeley, 1981; vis. com. Harvard Coll. Obs., Cambridge, Mass., 1976-82, 92—, Space Telescope Sci. Inst., 1990-92; Beatrice Tinsley vis. prof. U. Tex., 1988; Commonwealth lectr. U. Mass., 1991, Yunker lectr. Oreg. State U., 1991, Bernhard vis. fellow Williams Coll., 1993, Oort vis. prof. U. Leiden, The Netherlands, 1995; lectr. in field, U.S., Chile, Russia, Armenia, India, Japan, China, Europe; trustee Associated Univs., Inc., 1993—. Assoc. editor: Astrophys. Jour. Letters, 1977-82; editorial bd.: Sci. Mag., 1979-87; contbr. numerous articles sci. jours.; assoc. editor: Astron. Jour., 1972-77. Pres.'s Disting. Visitor, Vassar Coll., 1987. Recipient Gold medal Royal Astron. Soc. London, 1996, Weizmann Women and Sci. award, 1996; President's disting. visitor Vassar Coll., 1987; mem. President's Commn. To Select U.S. Nat. Medal Sci. Awardees; named Henry Norris Russell lectr. Am. Astron. Soc., 1994. Mem. NAS (space sci. bd. 1974-77, chmn. sect. on astronomy 1992-95), Am. Astron. Soc. (coun. 1977-80, Russell prize lectr. 1994), Internat. Astron. Union (pres. Commn. on Galaxies 1982-85), Assn. Univ. Rsch. in Astronomy (trustee 1973-76, 94—), Am. Philos. Soc., AAAS, Commn. Nat. Med. Sci., Phi Beta Kappa (scholar 1982-83). Democrat. Jewish.

RUBINSTEIN, EVA (ANNA), photographer; b. Buenos Aires, Argentina, 1933; d. Arthur and Aniela (Mlynarska) R.; m. William Sloane Coffin Jr., 1956 (div. 1968); children: Amy, Alexander (dec.), David. Ballet tng., Paris, N.Y.C., Calif., 1938-53; student, Scripps Coll., 1950-51, UCLA, 1952-53; student in photography, Lisette Model, 1969, Jim Hughes, 1971, Ken Heyman, 1970, Diane Arbus, 1971. lectr. numerous workshops, seminars, confs.; instr. photo seminars Lodz Film Sch., Poland, 1986, 86-87. Dancer, actress: off-Broadway and Broadway, including original prodn. The Diary of Anne Frank, 1955-56; European dance tour, 1955; one-person shows of photographs include Underground Gallery, N.Y.C., 1972, Dayton Art Inst., Ohio, 1973, Arles Festival, France, 1975, Canon Photo Gallery, Amsterdam, 1975, Neikrug Gallery, N.Y.C., 1975, 79, 81, 82, 85, La Photogalerie, Paris, 1975, Friends of Photography, Carmel, Calif., 1975, Galerie 5.6, Ghent, Belgium, 1976, Gallery Trochenpresse, Berlin, 1977, Frumkin Gallery, Chgo., 1977, Galeria Sinisca, Rome, 1979, Hermitage Found. Mus., Norfolk, Va., 1982, Photographers Gallery, London, 1983, Galerie Forum Labo, Arles, France, 1983, Galerie Nicephore, Lyon, France, 1983, Image Gallery, Madrid, 1984, Muzeum Sztuki, Lodz, Poland, 1984, Il Diaframma/Canon Gallery, Milan, 1984, A.R.P.A. Gallery, Bordeaux, 1984, Chateau d'Eau, Toulouse, France, 1985, Galerie Demi-Teinte, Paris, 1985, Associated Artist Photographers galleries in Warsaw, Krakow, Lodz, Katowice and Gdansk, Poland, 1985-86, Foto/Medium/Art Gallery, Wroclaw, Poland, 1986, Visions Gallery, San Francisco, 1986, Canon Galerie, Paris, 1986, Salone Internat. SICOF, Milan, 1987, St. Krzysztof Gallery, Lodz, 1987, L'Image Fixe, Lyon, 1988, Artotheque, Grenoble, 1988, Neikrug Photographica, N.Y.C., 1989, Heuser Art Ctr. Gallery, Bradley U., Peoria, Ill., 1989, 3-os Encontros da Imagem, Braga, Portugal, 1989, Bibliotheque Nat. Galerie Colbert, Paris, 1989, Galerie Picto-Bastille, Paris, 1989-90, Portfolio Gallery, London, 1990, Vaison-La-Romaine, France, 1990, Hist. Mus. of City of Lodz, 1990, Galerie Artem, Quimper, France, 1993, Galerie F.N.A.C. Etoile, Paris, 1994, other F.N.A.C. galleries (France, Belgium, Spain), 1994—, Galerie Augustus, Berlin, 1995, L'Imagerie, Lannion, France, 1995, Zacheta Gallery, Warsaw, 1996; group shows include, Internat. Salon, Krakow, Poland, 1971, Delgado Mus., New Orleans, 1972, Neikrug Gallery, 1972, 73, 75, Salone Internationale, Milan, Italy, 1973, Photo-OVO, Montreal, Que., Can., 1974, Nat. Portrait Gallery, London, 1976, Hera Gallery, R.I., 1977, Musee National d'Art Moderne Georges Pompidou, Paris, 1977, Centre Culturel de l'ouest Aquitain, Bordeaux, France, 1978, Fotografiska Museet, Stockholm, 1978, Nat. Arts Club, N.Y.C., 1979, Chrysler Mus., Norfolk, 1979, Maine Photog. Gallery, 1981, Floating Found. Photography, N.Y.C., 1970, 71, 72, 73, 79, 82, Ffoto Gallery, Cardiff, Wales, 1983, Musée d'Art Moderne de la Ville de Paris, 1987-88, Boca Raton (Fla.) Mus., 1989, Galerie PICTO Bastille, Paris, 1989, Galerie Arena, Arles, 1989-90, Settimana della Fotografia, Palermo, 1990, Festival de l'Image, Le Mans, France, 1993, Quimper (France), 1995, Galerie Camera Obscura, Paris, 1996; represented: in permanent collections Library of Congress, Washington, Met. Mus. Art, N.Y.C., Bibliotheque Nationale, Paris, Musee Reattu, Arles, France, Kalamazoo Inst. Arts, Israel Mus., Jerusalem, Fotografiska Museet, Stockholm, Muzeum Sztuki, Lodz, Poland, Histo Mus. of City of Lodz, others; author 2 monographs, 2 ltd. edit. portfolios with introductions by John Vachon and André Kertész; contbr. photographs in various books, mags., profl. jours.

RUBIO, ETHEL GRIÑO, architect; b. Manila, Oct. 27, 1965; came to U.S., 1986; d. Armando Lina and Norma Libre (Griño) R. BArch, U. So. Calif., L.A., 1992. Designer Siegel Diamond Architects, L.A., 1992-93; asst. project mgr. HNTB, L.A., 1993-95; planner, designer, owner Ethel G. Rubio, Assoc. AIA, L.A., 1996—; mem. Woodbury U. Archtl. Consultancy Bd., 1996—. Vol. Craft and Folk Art Mus., L.A., 1986—, UNICEF, L.A. Chpt., 1990—, Exceptional Children's Found., L.A., 1992—; assoc. Riordan Vol. Leadership Devel. Program Class 10. mem. AIA (student affairs com. chair 1991-93, assoc. pres. 1994, Landworth Meml. scholarship chair 1994—, Intern Devel. Program chair 1995), Assn. for Women in Arch. (membership chair 1992, program chair 1993, pres. 1996). Democrat. Roman Catholic.

RUBIO, PATRICIA JEAN, secondary educator; b. Madison, Wis., Aug. 4, 1965; d. David Russell and Catherine (Tormey) Sommer; m. Abelardo Rubio Jr., July 6, 1992 (dec. Nov. 1993). BS in Math. Edn., U. Wis., 1987, postgrad.; postgrad., U. Wis., 1995—. Tchr. United Intermediate Sch., Laredo, Tex., 1988-90, United South H.S., Laredo, Tex., 1990-94, Edgewood H.S., Madison, Wis., 1994-95; mem. prin. adv. com. United South H.S., Laredo, 1992-94. Mem. Nat. Coun. Tchrs. Math., Pi Lambda Theta, Sigma Delta Pi. Home: 505 Blue Ridge Pky Madison WI 53705

RUBLEY, CAROLE A., state legislator; b. Bethel, Conn., Jan. 18, 1939; d. George B. and Evelyn M. (Maloney) Drumm; m. C. Ronald Rubley, Aug. 25, 1962; children: Lauren M. Rubley Simpson, Stephen R., Kristin A. BA in Biology, Albertus Magnus Coll., 1960; MS in Environ. Health, West Chester U., 1988. Tchr. biology Danbury (Conn.) High Sch., 1960-62, Waltham (Mass.) High Sch., 1962-63; real estate salesperson Henderson-Dewey, Wayne, Pa., 1976-81; solid waste coord. Chester County Health Dept., West Chester, Pa., 1981-88; environ. cons. Environ. Resources Mgmt., Exton, Pa., 1988-92; mem. Pa. Ho. Reps., Valley Forge, 1992—; mem. environ. resources, energy, consumer affairs, finance and urban affairs coms. House of Reps. Author: (with others) Leading Pennsylvania into 21st Century, 1990. Chmn. Ea. Chester County Regional Planning Commn., 1976-85; vice chmn. planning commn. Tredyffrin Twp., Berwyn, Pa., 1976-86, mem. bd. suprs., 1987-92; bd. dirs. Pa. Resources Coun., exec. v.p., 1988-92. Mem. LWV (pres. Upper Main Line chpt. 1976-78, Involved Voter of Yr. award 1993), Pa. Environ. Coun., Green Valleys Assn., Open Land Conservancy. Republican. Roman Catholic. Home: 621 Vassar Rd Wayne PA 19087-5312

RUCCI, DEBORAH DERRICK, special education educator; b. Maryville, Tenn., Mar. 18, 1956; d. Cecil Curtis and Betty Jo (White) Martin; m. Thomas Lee Rucci, Aug. 30, 1986. BS in English Edn., Tenn. Wesleyan Coll., 1978. Cert. English tchr., spl. edn. tchr., applied comm. tchr. Tchr. Turtletown (Tenn.) Elem. Sch., 1979-81; tchr. spl. edn. Sewanee (Tenn.) Pub. Sch., 1982-85, DeLaSalle Sch. for Behavior Disordered, Kansas City, Mo., 1985-86, Palmer Jr. H.S., Independence, Mo., 1986-88; tchr. spl. edn. English Sequatchie County H.S., Dunlap, Tenn., 1988—, tchr. spl. edn. math., 1995—; cheerleading coach Sequatchie County H.S., Dunlap, 1989-92, prom com. chair, 1988—. Coach Spl. Olympics, Franklin County and Sequatchie, 1982-85, 88-90. Mem. NEA (Nat. Edn. Week com. chmn. 1988—), Delta Kappa Gamma. Baptist. Home: RR 3 Box 290 Signal Mountain TN 37377-9721 Office: Sequatchie County H S Dunlap TN 37327

RUCH, MARCELLA JOYCE, educator, biographer; b. Brutus, Mich., Sept. 20, 1937; d. Virgil Murray and Grace Milbry (Collier) Wallace; m. Robert Kirkman McMain, Aug. 29, 1956 (div. Aug. 1970); children: Melodie Froom, Kirk McMain, Nancy Hedges, Elizabeth Curran; m. Peter Jerome Ruch, Dec. 22, 1973; children: David, Dan, Michael and Justin Moore Ruch. BS, Western Mich. U., 1964; MA, U. Colo., Colorado Springs, 1973; PhD, U. Colo., Boulder, 1980. Cert. tchr., prin., counselor, Colo. Tchr. Colorado Springs Pub. Schs., 1964-69; supr. child care El Paso County Social Svcs., Colorado Springs, 1970-73; exec. dir. Antlers Day Care Ctr., Colorado Springs, 1973-77, Green Shade Schs., Colorado Springs, 1977-81, Pueblo (Colo.) Toddler Ctr., 1981-83; tchr. Penrose (Colo.) Elem. Sch., 1983-86; adminstrv. intern Cottonwood Elem. Sch., Denver, 1986-87; elem. prin. Simla (Colo.) Pub. Schs., 1987-89; tchr. Colorado Springs Pub. Schs., 1989—; mem. adv. bd. for early childhood edn. Pikes Peak C.C., Colorado Springs, 1970-75; child care specialist Cmty. Agencies Working Together, Colorado Springs, 1970-75. Founder Green Shade Schs., 1977; campaign chair United Way, Canon City, Colo., 1983-84, pres., 1984-85; chair adult coun. St. Paul's United Meth. Ch., 1994—. Mem. Delta Kappa Gamma (v.p. membership 1994-96), Phi Delta Kappa. Methodist. Home: 2444 Virgo Dr Colorado Springs CO 80906 Office: Lincoln Elem Sch 2727 Cascade N Colorado Springs CO 80907

RUCHALA, LINDA VIRGINIA, accounting educator; b. Dearborn, Mich., July 10, 1954; d. Alexander L. and Virginia F. R.; m. F. Duncan Case Jr., 1978; children: Celeste, Marya. BS, Mich. State U., 1976; M in City & Regional Planning, Harvard U., 1978; PhD, Ind. U., 1991. Quality assurance coord. McNabb Mental Health Ctr., Knoxville, 1981-84; asst. instr. Ind. U., Bloomington, 1985-91; asst. prof. U. Nebr., Lincoln, 1991—. Mem. Am. Acctg. Assn., Inst. Mgmt. Accts., Soc. Judgement & Decision Making. Office: U Nebr Lincoln 380 CBA Lincoln NE 68588-0488

RUCKER, DELLA LEE (BOBBI RUCKER), broadcasting company executive; b. Servilla, Tenn., June 9, 1921; d. William L. and Donnie C. (Forrester) Lee; m. Arthur C. Rucker, Sept. 1, 1940 (dec. Dec. 1988); children: Rita Jean, James William. Student, Massey Bus. Coll., Atlanta, 1951. With Copper Basin Broadcasting, Copperhill, Tenn., 1964-82; sta. mgr. Mountain Broadcasting, Jasper, Ga., 1981-93; pres., owner Lee Broadcasting Co., Inc., Ellijay, Ga., 1985—; bd. dirs. Pinnacle Ins. Co., Carrollton, Ga. Talk show host, Let the Peeple Speak, Sta. WLJA AM/FM. Mem. LWV. Home: PO Box 613 Copperhill TN 37317-0613 Office: Lee Broadcasting Co Inc PO Box 545 Ellijay GA 30540-0545

RUCKER-HUGHES, WAUDIEUR ELIZABETH, educator; b. Washington, July 30, 1947; d. Jeter and Jeannette Belle (Toomer) Rucker; B.S., D.C. Tchrs. Coll., 1969; M.A. in Edn. Admin., U. Redlands, 1974; 1 child, Teliece E.M. Tchr. history J.W. North High Sch., Riverside, Calif., 1969-76, dean students, 1976-79; lectr. Afro-Am. history Riverside City Coll., 1972-74; exec. dir. Inland Area Opportunities Industrialization Center, Riverside, 1979-90; tchr., coord. steps of success program RUSD, 1990-92; asst. prin. J.W. North High Sch., 1992—; cons. in field. Commr. Community relations City of Riverside, 1972-76; sec. State Inter-Group Relations Educators, 1976-77; pres. Coalition of Urban Peoples, 1978-80; lay mem. Riverside County Jud. Selection Com., 1978-84; Calif. State Bar ct. referee, 1979-84. NSF fellow, 1970-71; Center for Leadership Edn. grantee, 1978. Mem. NAACP, Urban League, Riverside Women's Polit. Caucus, Nat. Women's Polit. Caucus, Exec. Dirs. Assn. (sec. 1983-84, nat. historian), Officers In Charge Am. (community devel. adv. com.), Nat. Council Negro Women, Delta Kappa Gamma, Hunter Pk. C. of C. (treas., pres.), Delta Kappa Gamma. Mem. C.M.E. Ch. Club: The Thurs. Group, Phi Delta Kappa. Author: Canine Capers, 1976; A Book to Match our Diversity, 1980. Home: 8907 Delano Dr Riverside CA 92503-2718 Office: 1550 3rd St Riverside CA 92507-3404

RUDACILLE, SHARON VICTORIA, medical technologist; b. Ranson, W. Va., Sept. 11, 1950; d. Albert William and Roberta Mae (Anderson) R.; BS cum laude, Shepherd Coll., 1972. Med. technologist VA Ctr., Martinsburg, W.Va., 1972—, instr. Sch. Med. Tech., 1972-76, assoc. coord. edn., 1976-77, edn. coord., 1977-78, quality assurance officer clin. chemistry, 1978-80, lab. svc. quality assurance and edn. officer, 1980-84, clin. chemistry sect. leader, 1984-86, staff med. technologist, 1986-94, supervisory med. technologist, 1994-95, sr. med. technologist, 1995—; adj. faculty mem. Shippensburg (Pa.) State Coll., 1977-78, Shepherd Coll., 1977-78. Mem. Am. Soc. Med. Tech., Am. Soc. Clin. Pathologists, W.Va. Soc. Med. Technologists, Shepherd Coll. Alumni Assn., Sigma Pi Epsilon. Baptist. Home: PO Box 14 Ranson WV 25438-0014

RUDDEN, MARIE GEORGINE, psychiatrist; b. Bklyn., Aug. 22, 1951; d. Francis Joseph and Georgette (Heinecke) R.; m. Howard B. Levy (div. 1984); 1 child, Daniel; m. Peter Michael Lazes; 1 child, Adrienne. BA, Yale Coll., 1973; MD, NYU Sch. Medicine, 1977; grad., N.Y. Psychoanalytic Inst., 1994. Diplomate Am. Bd. Psychiatry and Neurology, 1984. Intern Meml. Sloan Kettering Cancer Ctr. and N.Y. Hosp., 1977-78; resident Payne Whitney Clinic/Cornell Med. Sch., 1978-82; clin. instr. Cornell U. Sch. of Medicine, N.Y.C., 1982-92; clin. asst. prof. Cornell U. Sch. Medicine, N.Y.C., 1992—. Contbr. articles on delusional disorders to Am. Jour. Psychiatry, 1980-90. Recipient Rock Sleyster Meml. scholarship AMA, 1976. Mem. Am. Psychiat. Assn., Am. Psychoanalytic Assn., Internat. Psychoanalytic Assn. Home and Office: 25 Van Dam St New York NY 10013-1215

RUDDER, CATHERINE ESTELLE, political science association administrator; b. Atlanta, Dec. 16; d. James M. and Virginia Rudder. BA, Emory U., 1969; MA, Ohio State U., 1972, PhD, 1973. Asst. prof. U. Ga., Athens, 1973-77; chief staff to Rep. W. Fowler, Jr. U.S. House Reps., Washington, 1978-81, assoc. dir., 1983-87; exec. dir. Am. Polit. Sci. Assn., Washington, 1987—. Office: Am Polit Scis Assn 1527 New Hampshire Ave NW Washington DC 20036-1206

RUDE, MAUREEN JOY, state agency administrator; b. East Lansing, Mich., Apr. 26, 1962; d. William Raymond Lassey and Marion Hogarty (Lassey) Rosa; m. Mathew Charles Rude, Aug. 11, 1959. BSBA, U. Mont., 1985. CPA, Mont. Resident asst. U. Mont., Missoula, 1982-83; clk. UPS, Missoula, 1983-86; fin. compliance auditor Legis. Auditor, Helena, Mont., 1986-87, performance auditor, sr. performance auditor, 1987-92; multifamily program mgr. Bd. of Housing, Helena, 1992-95; adminstr. housing divsn., exec. dir. Bd. of Housing Dept. Commerce, Helena, 1995—. tutor, mentor Helena Pub. Schs./Hosts, 1992—; mem. Helena Jaycees, 1991-92; vol. Helena Jazz Festivals/Rocky Mountain Elk Found., Helena, 1990—. Named Outstanding New Jaycee of Quar., Helena Jaycees, 1991. Mem. Nat. Coun. State Housing Agys. Office: Mont Bd Housing Housing Divsn PO Box 200528 Helena MT 59620

RUDE, PHYLLIS AILEEN, secondary school educator; b. Jacksonville, Ill., Oct. 2, 1943; d. Chester Raymond and Thelma Grace (Pahlmann) Stewart; m. Gary Rude, Sept. 11, 1966; children: Richard Gary, Meredith Arlene. BA, Ill. State U., 1964; AM, U. Chgo., 1967. Cert. tchr. Alaska. Tchr. Farmington (Ill.) H.S., 1963-65, Wheeling (Ill.) H.S., 1965-67; tchr. Mears Jr. H.S., Anchorage, Alaska, 1967-74, lang. arts dept. chair, 1984—. Recipient scholarship Carnegie Found., 1966. Mem. Nat. Coun. Tchrs. English, Alaska Coun. Tchrs. English (Honor award 1987), Anchorage Coun. Tchrs. English. Lutheran. Home: 2567 Arlington Dr Anchorage AK 99517-1304 Office: Mears Jr HS 2700 W 100th Ave Anchorage AK 99515-2214

RUDIN, ANNE NOTO, former mayor, nurse; b. Passaic, N.J., Jan. 27, 1924; m. Edward Rudin, June 6, 1948; 4 children. BS in Edn., Temple U., 1945, RN, 1946; MPA, U. So. Calif., 1983; LLD (hon.), Golden Gate U., 1990. RN, Calif. Mem. faculty Temple U. Sch. Nursing, Phila., 1946-48; mem. nursing faculty Mt. Zion Hosp., San Francisco, 1948-49; mem. Sacramento City Council, 1971-83; mayor City of Sacramento, 1983-92; ind. pub. policy cons. Pres. LWV, Riverside, 1957, Sacramento, 1961, Calif., 1969-71, Calif. Elected Women's Assn., 1973—; bd. trustees Golden Gate U.; adv. bd. U. So. Calif., Army Depot Reuse Commn.; bd. dirs. Sacramento Theatre Co., Sacramento Symphony, Calif. Common Cause, Japan Soc. No. Calif., Sacramento Edn. Found.; v.p. Sacramento Traditional Jazz Soc. Found. Recipient Women in Govt. award U.S. Jaycee Women, 1984, Woman of Distinction award Sacramento Area Soroptimist Clubs, 1985, Civic Contbn. award LWV Sacramento, 1989, Woman of Courage award Sacramento History Ctr., 1989, Peacemaker of Yr. award Sacramento Mediation Ctr., 1992, Regional Pride award Sacramento Mag., 1993, Humanitarian award Japanese Am. Citizen's League, 1993, Outstanding Pub. Svc. award Am. Soc. Pub. Adminstrn., 1994; named Girl Scouts Am. Role model, 1989.

RUDISILL, CATHY MARIE, lawyer; b. Hickory, N.C., Mar. 20, 1958; d. Joe Harlin and Mary Jane Elizabeth (Reese) R.; m. Gary William Bigelow, Aug. 4, 1991; children: William Maxwell Bigelow, Mary Catherine Bigelow. AB, U. N.C., 1980, JD, 1984; MLT, Georgetown U., 1987. Bar: N.C. 1984, U.S. Tax Ct. 1985, D.C. 1986. Atty., advisor U.S. Tax Ct., Washington, 1984-86; assoc. Hunton & Williams, Washington, 1986-88; ptnr. Poyner & Spruill, L.L.P., Raleigh, N.C., 1989—. Contbr. articles to profl. jours. Mem. Phi Beta Kappa. Office: Poyner & Spruill 3600 Glenwood Ave Raleigh NC 27612

RUDMAN, JOAN ELEANOR, artist, educator; b. Owensburg, Ind., Oct. 7, 1927; d. William Hobart and Elizabeth Joaquin (Edington) Combs; m. William Rudman, June 9, 1951; children: Mary Beth, Pamela Ann. BA, Mich. State U., 1949, MA, 1951. tchr. Arlington Jr. and High Sch., Poughkeepsie, N.Y., Rippowam High Sch., Stamford, Conn., North Branch Club, West Dover, Vt., Greenwich (Conn.) Art Soc.; lectr., demonstrator Round Hill Community House, Greenwich; artist-in-residence So. Vt. Art Ctr., Manchester; arts reporter to 42 newspapers, N.Y., N.J. and Conn.; jurist of selection Hudson Valley Art Assn., 1971—; selection and awards jurist 2d Bergen County Mus. Open Mems. Juried Awards-Allied Artist, N.Y.; dir. Watercolor Workshops, Greenwich; liaison to Metro. Mus. Catharine Lorillard Wolfe Art Club; watercolor lectr. and demonstrator tri-state area. One-woman shows include Burning Tree Country Club, Greenwich, Town and Country Club, Hartford, Conn., U. Conn., Stamford, Conn. Valley Art Gallery, New Milford, So. Vt. Art Ctr., Manchester, The Nathaniel Witherall Gallery, Greenwich, Burke Rehab. Ctr., White Plains, N.Y.; exhibited in group shows at Wadsworth Antheneum, 1970, Mus. of Am. Art, New Britain, Conn., So. Vt. Art Ctr., Manchester, 1980-81, Nature Ctr., Westport, Conn., 1979-80, Mus. Fine Arts, Springfield, Mass., 1977, Wadsworth Antheneum, 1970, Mus. Am. Art, New Britain, Conn., Nat. Arts Club Open Show, 1969, 78, 79, 81, 82, Salmagundi Club, N.Y.C., 1978, 79, 80, 82, Am. Watercolor Soc., N.Y.C., 1974, 77, 82, Nat. Acad. Design, 1986, 94; represented in permanent collection Kresge Mus., East Lansing, Mich., numerous others; contbr. chpts. to books. Active North Stamford Congl. Ch. Recipient Nat. Art League awards, 1969, 71, 72, 73, Art Soc. Old Greenwich award, 1989, 94, Windsor Newton award, 1982, YWCA Greenwich Contemporary Women's Art Exhibit award, 1985, Best in Show award Art Soc. Old Greenwich, 1991, 1st Prize Graphics award Art Soc. Old Greenwich, 1994, 2nd Prize award Watercolor. Mem. Am. Watercolor Soc. (bd. dirs., asst. editor newsletter), Acad. Artists, Inc., Hoosier Salon (awards 1975, 76), Am. Artists Profl. League (50th Nat. Exhbn. award 1978), Hudson Valley Art Assn. (bd. dirs., publ. rels. editor, awards 1970, 80-90), Conn. Watercolor Soc. (award 1978), Conn. Artists 33, Whiskey Painters Am. (award 1978), Conn. Women Artists, Catharine Lorillard Wolfe Art Club (awards 1989, 90, chmn. 1989-90, co-chair 1994), Pen and Brush (award 1977-78), Nat. League Am. Pen Women (awards 1967, 69, 76-87), Nat. Press Club, Round Hill Community Guild (art dir.), New Canaan - Am. Assn. Univ. Women, Columbia U. Alumni Club (hon.), Nat. Soc. Daus. Am. Revolution (mem. Stamford chpt., historian), Mich. State Alumni Club, Delta Phi Delta (hon.), Phi Kappa Phi (hon.), Alpha Xi Delta. Republican. Home: 274 Quarry Rd Stamford CT 06903-5004

RUDNER, SARA, dancer, choreographer; b. Bklyn., Feb. 16, 1944; d. Henry Nathaniel and Jeannette (Smolensky) R.; 1 child, Eli Rudner Marschner. A.B. in Russian Studies, Barnard Coll., 1964. Dancer Sansardo Dance Co., N.Y.C., 1964-65, Am. Dance Co. at Lincoln Ctr., N.Y.C., 1965, Shakespeare Festival Touring Children's Show, N.Y.C., 1966; featured dancer Twyla Tharp Dance Found., N.Y.C., 1966-85; artistic dir., dancer 18th St. Dance Found., N.Y.C., 1977—; guest dancer Joffrey Ballet, N.Y.C., 1973, Pilobolus Dance Theatre, N.Y.C., 1975, Lar Lubovitch Dance Co., N.Y.C., 1975-76; guest lectr., choreographer grad. dance dept. UCLA, 1975; tchr. master workshop NYU Theater Program, 1988, 89, 90. Choreographer: Palm Trees and Flamingoes, 1980, Dancing for an Hour or So, 1981, Minute by Minute, 1982, Eight Solos, 1991, Heartbeats, Inside Out, 1993 (with Jennifer Tipton and Dana Reitz) Necessary Weather, 1994. Grantee Creative Artists Pub. Svc. Program, N.Y., 1975-76, N.Y. State Coun. on Arts, 1975-78, Nat. Endowment for Arts, 1979-81, 91-92, 94-97; Guggenheim fellow, 1981-82; recipient N.Y. Dance and Performance award, 1984.

RUDNICK, ELLEN AVA, health care executive; b. New Haven; d. Harold and C. Vivian (Soybel) R.; children from previous marriage: Sarah, Noah; m. Paul W. Earle. BA, Vassar Coll., 1972; MBA, U. Chgo., 1973. Sr. fin. analyst Quaker Oats, Chgo., 1973-75; various positions Baxter Internat., Deerfield, Ill., 1975-80, dir. planning, 1980-83, corp. v.p., 1985-1990; pres. Baxter Mgmt. Svcs., Deerfield, 1983-1990, HCIA, Balt., 1990-92, CEO Advs., Northbrook, Ill., 1992—; prin., chmn. Pacific Biometrics, Irvine, Calif., 1993—; bd. dirs. NCCI. Chief crusader Met. Chgo. United Way, 1982-85; pres. coun. Nat. Coll. Edn., Evanston, Ill., 1983—; cir. of friends Chgo. YMCA, 1985-89; bd. dirs. Highland Park Hosp., 1990—, NCCI. Mem. Chgo. Network, Econs. Club Chgo. (officer, bd. dirs.). Office: CEO Advs 255 Revere Dr Ste 111 Northbrook IL 60062-1595

RUDNICK, IRENE KRUGMAN, lawyer, former state legislator, educator; b. Columbia, S.C., Dec. 27, 1929; d. Jack and Jean (Getter) Krugman; AB cum laude, U. S.C., 1949, JD, 1952; m. Harold Rudnick, Nov. 7, 1954; children: Morris, Helen Gail. Admitted to S.C. bar, 1952; individual practice law, Aiken, S.C., 1952—, now ptnr. Rudnick & Rudnick; instr. bus. law, criminal law U. S.C., Aiken, 1962—; tchr. Warrenville Elem. Sch., 1965-70; supt. edn. Aiken County, 1970-72; mem. S.C. Ho. of Reps., 1972-78, 80-84, 86-94; pres. Adath Yeshurun Synagogue; active Aiken County Dem. Party, S.C. Dem. Party, Network Aiken; hon. mem. Aiken Able-Disabled. Recipient Citizen of Yr. award, 1976-77, Bus. and Profl. Women's Career Woman of Yr., 1978, 94, Aiken County Friend of Edn. award, 1985, 93, Outstanding Legis. award Disabled Vets., 1991, Citizen of the Yr. award Planned Parenthood, 1994, Sertoma Svc. to Mankind award, 1996. Mem. NEA, S.C. Tchrs. Assn., Aiken County Tchrs. Assn., Am. Bar Assn., Aiken County Bar Assn., Nat. Order Women Legislators, AAUW, Network Aiken, Aiken Able-Disabled (hon.), Alpha Delta Kappa. Jewish. Clubs: Order Eastern Star, Hadassah, Am. Legion Aux. Office: PO Box 544 135 Pendleton NW Aiken SC 29802

RUDNICK, REBECCA SOPHIE, lawyer, educator; b. Bakersfield, Calif., Nov. 26, 1952; d. Oscar and Sophie Mary (Loven) R.; m. Robert Anthoine, Dec. 2, 1990. BA, Willamette U., Salem, Oreg., 1974; JD, U. Tex., 1978; LLM, NYU, 1984. Bar: Tex. 1978, La. 1979, N.Y. 1980, Calif. 1980. Law clk. to Hon. Charles Schwartz, Jr. U.S. Dist. Ct., New Orleans, 1978-79; assoc. Winthrop, Stimson, Putnam & Roberts, N.Y.C., 1979-85; spl. counsel N.Y. Legis. Tax Study Commn., N.Y.C., 1983-84; asst. prof. law Ind. U., Bloomington, 1985-90; assoc. prof. of law Ind. U. Sch. of Law, Bloomington, 1990-94; assoc. prof. law London Law Consortium, Eng., 1994; vis. assoc. prof. law U. Conn., Hartford, 1984-85; vis. asst. prof. law U. Tex., Austin, 1988; vis. assoc. prof. law U. N.C., Chapel Hill, 1991, Boston U., 1994-95, U. Pa., Phila., 1995-96; prof.-in-residence, IRS, 1991-92; vis. scholar NSW, Australia, 1994, U. Sydney, Australia, 1994; vis. prof. law Seattle U., 1996—. Contbr. articles to various profl. jours. and publs. Dir., gen. counsel Project GreenHope: Svcs. for Women, N.Y.C., 1980-83; advisor, tech. asst. Internat. Monetary Fund, Washington, 1994. Mem. ABA (tax sect. 1982—, sec. tax sect. passthrough entities task force 1986-88, subcom. chairs for incorps. and CLE/important devel. tax sect., 1989—, corp. tax com. 1989—, tax sect. task force on integration 1990—), Am. Assn. Law Schs. (editor tax sect. newsletter 1987—), Assn. Bar of City of N.Y. (admiralty com. 1982-85), Internat. Fiscal Assn., Internat. Bar Assn. Office: Seattle U Sch Law 950 Broadway Plz Tacoma WA 98402

RUDOLPH, MARY KAY, college dean, psychologist; b. Peoria, Ill., June 17, 1957; d. Ward Walker and Mildred Pauline (Armbright) R.; m. Aug., 1983 (div. Mar. 1990); m. John William Kolhoven, Dec. 28, 1991; 1 child, Colin Blake. BA in Psychology and Sociology, Fla. State U., 1978; MA in Psychology and Clin. Edn., Calif. State U., Sacramento, 1987; EdD in Counseling Psychology, U. San Francisco, 1995. Cert. C.C. instr. social sci. (lifetime), counselor (lifetime), adminstr. (lifetime). Dep. probation officer Sacramento County, Calif., 1983-89; coord. pub. safety ctr. Sacramento (Calif.) City Coll., 1989-95, dean occupational tech., 1995—; instr. Los Rios C.C. Dist., Sacramento, 1989—, guest lectr. Vantaa (Finland) Polytech., 1993, Viterbo Coll., La Crosse, Wis., 1996; mem. program devel. com., Sacramento C.C., 1993-95, chair staff devel. com. 1993-94, affirmative action rep. Mem. subcom. on crime prevention Calif. Police Officers Assn., citizen's adv. com. for Calif. Youth Authority, adv. com. for child abuse, juvenile law, supervisory, etc. Police Officers Standards in Tng., Calif., tng. subcom. Sacramento Child Abuse Coun. Mem. APA, Assn. for Advancement Behavior Therapy, Assn. Calif. C.C. Adminstrs., Calif. Crime Prevention Officers Assn., Calif. Psychol. Assn., No. Calif. Am. Coun. on Edn.-Nat. Identification Program, Western and Pacific Assn. Criminal Justice Edn., Sacramento Area Tng. Mgrs. Assn., Phi Beta Kappa. Office: Sacramento City Coll Occupat Tech Dept 3835 Freeport Blvd Sacramento CA 95822

RUDOLPH, NANCY K., photographer, writer; b. N.Y.C., Dec. 26, 1923; d. Morris and Eva (Cohn) Kallman; m. Alan Goldsmith Rudolph, div. 1970. BA, Union Inst., 1989. Pub. rels. asst. Mus. Modern Art, N.Y.C., 1947-48; press attaché Econ. Cooperation Adminstrn., Rome, 1949-49; photography workshops Elizabeth Irwin H.S., 1969-70; pvt. instr.; tchr. New Sch. of Social Work, N.Y.C., 1978, guest lectr. Author: New Neighborhoods, New Lives, 1964, Workyards, Playgrounds Planned for Adventure, 1974; contbr. articles to profl. jours.; one-woman shows include Menemsha Gallery, Martha's Vineyard, Mass., 1962, Bank St. Coll. Edn., N.Y.C., 1962, Parents Mag. Gallery, N.Y.C., 1969, City Hall, Boston, 1970, Met. Mus. Art, N.Y.C., 1971, Dept. Interior, Washington, 1971, Jefferson Mkt. Br. of the N.Y. Pub. Libr., N.Y.C., 1975, 209 Photo Gallery, N.Y.C., 1976, Carver Cultural Cmty. Ctr., San Antonio, Tex., 1977, Photo Ctr. Gallery N.Y.U., 1981, Open Ctr. SOHO, N.Y.C., 1984, Seacliff Gallery, N.Y., 1989, Espacio Y Eventos, Valenzia, Venezuela, 1992; group shows include Neikrug Gallery, N.Y.C., 1975, Cooper Hewitt Mus., 1979, Foto Gallery, N.Y.C., 1981, Mus. of the City of N.Y., 1984, 88, Visual Arts Mus., N.Y.C., 1989, Nikon House, N.Y.C., 1991, U.N., N.Y.C., Copenhagen, Beijing, 1994-95, others; represented in permanent collections at Ministry of Health, Mex. City, Mex., The Schomburg Collection of the N.Y. Pub. Libr., Phila. Mus. Art, Mus. of the City of N.Y., Union Inst., Cin., Helen Keller Internat., N.Y.C., The Ctr. for Creative Photography, Tucson, Ariz. Mem. Citizen's Com. for Children of N.Y.C., 1970—, bd. dirs., 1972-81; mem. Citywide Headstart Com., 1974. Recipient Excellence in Photography award Comm. Arts, Excellence in Photography award Am. Inst. Graphic Arts, award Internat. Assn. Bus. Comm., 1996. Mem. Am. Soc. Media Photographers (dir. 1974-76, dir. N.Y. chpt. 1986-87), Dronmenon. Home: 35 W 11th St New York NY 10011

RUDY, RUTH CORMAN, state legislator; b. Millheim, Pa., Jan. 3, 1938; d. Orvis E. and Mabel Jan (Stover) Corman; m. C. Guy Rudy, Nov. 21, 1956; children: Douglas G., Donita Rudy Koval, Dianna F. Degree in x-ray tech. Carnegie Inst., 1956; student Pa. State U.,1968-71. Clk. of cts. County of Centre (Pa.), Bellefonte, 1976-82; rep. Pa. Gen.Assembly, Harrisburg, 1982—. Mem. Dem. Nat. Com., 1980—, chair women's caucus,1989-91; past pres. Pa. Fedn. Dem. Women, Harrisburg; pres. Nat. Fedn. Dem. Women, 1987-89; mem. exec. com. Dem. Nat. Com., 1987-89, chmn. women's caucus, 1989-91; candidate U.S. Congress, 5th Dist., 1995—. Named Woman of Yr., Pa. Fedn. Dem. Women, 1982. Methodist. Granted U.S. Patent on hair spray face shield 1995. Office: Pa Ho Reps PO Box 202020 Harrisburg PA 17120-2020 also: 141 E High St Bellefonte PA 16823

RUECKER, MARTHA ENGELS, retired special education educator; b. South Gate, Calif., Sept. 22, 1931; d. Eugene and Minna (Wilhelm) Engels; m. Geert Frank Ruecker, Aug. 10, 1959 (div. 1964); 1 child, Ann. MusB, U. So. Calif., 1954, Calif. tchr. credentiala, 1955. Tchr. educationally handicapped Downey (Calif.) Unified Schs., 1964-92. Recipient award for work with mentally gifted Johns Hopkins U., 1992; South Gate Kiwanis scholar U. So. Calif., 1949-54. Mem. NEA (life), Los Angeles County Art Mus. Republican. Methodist. Home: PO Box 630 Downey CA 90241

RUEHL, MERCEDES, actress; b. Queens, N.Y.. BA in English, Coll. of New Rochelle; studied acting with Uta Hagen, Tad Danielewski. Appearances include (theatre) Vanities, 1977-78, Billy Irish, 1980, Much Ado About Nothing, Misalliance, Androcles and the Lion, Tartuffe, Medea, 1980-82, Three Sisters, 1982-83, The Day They Shot John Lennon, 1982-83, Flirtation, 1983, June Moon, 1983-84, Monday After the Miracle, 1983-84, Coming of Age in Soho, 1985, The Marriage of Bette and Boo, 1985, I'm Not Rappaport, 1985 (Obie Award), American Notes, 1988, Other People's Money, 1989, Lost in Yonkers, 1991 (Tony award, 1991, Drama Desk award, 1991, Outer Critics Circle award 1991), The Shadow Box, 1994 (Tony nominee - Featured Actress in a Play, 1995), The Rose Tattoo, 1995, (film) The Warriors, 1979, Four Friends, 1981, Heartburn, 1986, 84 Charing Cross Road, 1987, Leader of the Band, 1987, The Secret of My Success, 1987, Radio Days, 1987, Big, 1988, Married to the Mob, 1988, Slaves of New York, 1989, Crazy People, 1990, Another You, 1991, The Fisher King, 1991 (Academy award Best Supporting Actress 1991), Lost in Yonkers, 1993, Last Action Hero, 1993, Roseanna's Grave, 1996, (TV movie) Indictment: The McMartin Trial, 1995, (TV series) Frazier, 1996. Recipient Nat. Film Critics Circle award, 1988, Clarence Derwent award, 1989. *

RUEHLE, DIANNE MARIE, retired elementary education educator; b. Detroit, Aug. 14, 1943; d. Richard Francis and Luella Mary (Kopp) R. BS, Ea. Mich. U., 1966, MA, 1971, adminstrv. cert., 1990, renewed adminstrv. cert., 1995. Cert. tchr., adminstr., Mich. Tchr. Cherry Hill Sch. Dist., Inkster, Mich., 1966-85; tchr. elem. sch. Wayne-Westland (Mich.) Community Schs., 1985-95; dist. com. Pub. Act 25 for State of Mich., Westland, 1990-93, chair bldg., 1991-95. Improvement Instrn. grantee Wayne Westland Found., 1992-94. Mem. ASCD, NEA, Mich. Edn. Assn. Home: 26117 La Salle Ct Roseville MI 48066-3285

RUEHLMANN, VIRGINIA JUERGENS, foundation administrator, writer; b. Cin., Dec. 31, 1924; d. Arthur Henry and Florence Johanna (Doogan) Juergens; m. Eugene Peter Ruehlmann, Aug. 30, 1947; children:

Virginia Wiltse, E. Peter, Margaret Straus, Andrea Cornett, Gregory, James, Mark, Rick. BS in Edn., U. Cin., 1946, M in Adminstrn., 1948. Swimming instr. Williams YMCA, Cin., 1942-43; recreation leader City of Cin., 1942-43; camp dir. U. Cin. Girls Summer Camp, 1943-45; instr. U. Cin., 1946-47, Wellesley Coll., Wellesley, Mass., 1947-48; homemaker Cin., 1948-84; adminstr., researcher, editor, writer Helen Steiner Rice Found., Cin., 1984—; contr. Revell Pub., Baker Book House, Grand Rapids, Mich., 1984—; cons. Gibson Greeting, Cin., 1989—. Editor, compiler devotional and inspirational books, author of prayers, researcher. Chair Spl. Olympics Greater Cin., Ohio, Ind., Ky., 1974; pres. Cin. chpt. Freedom Found. Valley Forge, 1974-76; pres. Cath. Social Svc. S.W. Ohio, 1984-86; trustee Glenmary Missions, 1989-91; mem. Western Hamilton County Econ. Coun., Nat. Fedn. Rep. Women, Rep. Women's Club Hamilton County; mem. nat. adv. bd. United Theol. Sem.; bd. dirs. Anthenaeum of Ohio. Named Woman of Yr. Cin. Enquirer, 1977, Lady Equestrian Order of Holy Sepulchre of Jerusalem, 1989; named to Ohio Women's Hall of Fame, 1991. Mem. Coun. on Founds., Cin. Woman's Club, Queen City Club, Argus Club, Donors Forum Ohio, Mortar Bd., Chi Omega, Kappa Delta Pi. Republican. Roman Catholic. Home: 1150 Gleneagles Ct Cincinnati OH 45233-4865 Office: Helen Steiner Rice Found Atrium 2 221 E 4th St # 2100 Cincinnati OH 45202

RUE-POTTER, JOYCE, nurse, actress, talk show host, columnist; b. Chgo., July 20, 1942; d. John West and Bertha L. (Delopez) Rue; m. Robert Irwin Potter, Mar. 31, 1990. BA in Advt., U. Wash., 1966; grad., Grant Hosp Sch. Nursing, Chgo., 1963. Nurse multiple hosps., 1964-77; social dir. R&B Enterprises, Inc., L.A., 1977-80; founder, dir. Abundantly Yours, Inc., San Diego, 1979—; ind. counselor, publicist, educator, speaker; founder Enthusyattituditiks Social Support Group, Fletcher, N.C. Author: Waist Size Isn't About Self worth, Enthusiologist Handbook, Making Lemonade Out of Prunes; columnist for 3 publs.; appeared in plays Our Town, 1986, Shadow Box, 1987, Sea Horse, 1988 (Best Actress award), Amadeus, 1988; appeared on TV shows Oprah, Donahue, Geraldo, Joan Rivers, Group; radio talk show host Sta. KMJC, 1988-89, Joyce Rue (Hyphen) Show, Stas. WISE-WTZQ; inventor The Rehabmobile, 1994. Mgr. Charitable Benefit Bingo for Unity Ctr. Mem. Performing Arts Theatre Handicapped (Svc. award 1985, bd. dirs. 1986-89), Actors Network San Diego County (pres., bd. dirs. 1985-89). Office: Enthusyattituditiks PO Box 907 Fletcher NC 28732-0907

RUESCH, JANET CAROL, federal magistrate judge; b. New Brunswick, N.J., May 9, 1943. AB in Polit. Sci., Gettysburg Coll., 1965; JD, Ind. U., 1970. Bar: Tex. 1971, U.S. Dist. Ct. (we. dist.) Tex. 1973, U.S. Ct. Appeals (5th cir.) 1975, U.S. Dist. Ct. (so. dist.) Tex. 1977, U.S. Supreme Ct. 1979. Law clk. Malcolm McGregor and Mark Howell, El Paso, Tex., 1970-71; ptnr. Malcolm McGregor, Inc., El Paso, 1971-78; substitute mcpl. ct. judge City of El Paso, 1977-78; asst. U.S atty. Western Dist. Tex., El Paso, 1978-79; U.S. magistrate judge El Paso divsn. U.S. Dist. Ct. (we. dist.) Tex., 1979—. Bd. dirs. El Paso County Gen. Assistance Agy., 1977-79; past mem. profl. adv. bd. El Paso Mental Health Assn.; v.p. El Paso Women's Pol. Caucus, 1977, program chair, 1976, pub. chair, 1975. Mem. Tex. Bar Assn., El Paso Bar Assn. (pres. 1984), El Paso Women's Bar Assn. (pres. 1975).

RUETER, MARY LOU, journalist; b. Davenport, Iowa, Mar. 12, 1945; d. D. Lant and Florine H. (Kneipp) Kimberly; m. Alan R. Rueter, Mar. 6, 1965 (dec. Feb. 1992); children: Kristi, David, Matthew, Kyle. Student, Iowa State U., 1963-65. Staff writer The Observer, DeWitt, Iowa, 1974-87; office mgr. Clinton (Iowa) Title Co., 1987-88; mng. editor The Observer, DeWitt, 1988-92, gen. mgr., 1992—; mem. journalism adv. bd. Mt. St. Clare Coll., Clinton, 1990—. Author numerous news and feature stories, and spl. articles. Mem. adv. bd. Samaritan Hospice, Clinton, 1993—; bd. dirs. Mississippi Bend Area Edn. Agy., Bettendorf, Iowa, 1989—. Named Woman of Yr., DeWitt Bus. and Profl. Women, 1988, others. Mem. Nat. Fedn. Press Women (Communicator of Achievement 1994), Iowa Press Women Inc. (v.p., bd. dirs. 1974—, Communicator of Achievement 1994), Iowa Newspaper Assn. (awards), DeWitt C. of C. (bd. dirs. 1994—). United Methodist. Office: The Observer PO Box 118 De Witt IA 52742

RUFFALO, MARIA THERESE, real estate developer; b. Seattle, Feb. 26, 1963; d. Patrick and Helen (Eckhardt) R.; m. Joseph Patrick Otterbine, May 5, 1987. BS in Mech. Engring., U. Rochester, 1985. Proj. engr. Polycast Tech. Corp., Hackensack, N.J., 1985-86, sr. project engr., 1986-87; cons. Polycast Tech. Corp., Hackensack, 1987; project engr. ink divsn. J.M. Huber Corp., Edison, N.J., 1987-89; sr. engr. Himont USA, Inc., East Brunswick, N.J., 1990-93; engring. team leader Anchor Glass Container, Cliffwood, N.J., 1993-95; real estate developer, 1995—. Mem. NOW. Home: 601 Pine St Lanoka Harbor NJ 08734

RUFFING, JANET KATHRYN, spirituality educator; b. Spokane, Wash., July 17, 1945; d. George Benjamin and Dorothy Edith (Folsom) R. BA, Russell Coll., 1968; M of Applied Spirituality, U. San Francisco, 1978; lic. in Sacred Theology, Jesuit Sch. Theology, 1984; PhD in Christian Spirituality, Grad. Theol. Union, 1986. Joined Sisters of Mercy Congregation, Roman Cath. Ch., 1963. Tchr. reading and English Mercy High Sch., Burlingame, Calif., 1968-72, 75-77, San Francisco, 1972-75; tchr., dept. head Marian High Sch., San Diego, 1978-80; faculty and originating team mem. Fully Alive, Burlingame, 1980-86; faculty, facilitator Permanent Diaconate Formation Program, Oakland, Calif., 1984-86; faculty Internship in Art of Spiritual Direction, Burlingame, 1984, 85, 87; assoc. prof. spirituality and spiritual direction Fordham U., Bronx, N.Y., 1986—; spkr. Villanova Theol. Inst., 1995, Roger Williams Symposium, Pullman, Wash., 1985; vis. faculty Australian Cath. U., Brisbane, summer 1994, San Francisco Theol. Sem., summer 1993, U. San Francisco, summer 1991, St. Michael's Coll., Vt., summer 1990. Author: Uncovering Stories of Faith, 1989; assoc. editor The Way; contbr. articles to profl. jours. Mem. Cath. Theol. Soc. Am. (seminar moderator 1987-90), Am. Acad. Religion (chairperson mysticism group 1994—), Mercy Assn. in Scripture and Theology (treas. 1987-96, mem. editorial bd. MAST jour.), Spiritual Dirs. Internat. (founding coord. com. mem. 1990-93, coord. of regions 1990-93), Women's Ordination Conf. Democrat. Office: Fordham U Grad Sch Religion and Religious Bronx NY 10458

RUFFOLO, MARILYN CLAIRE, primary education educator; b. Harvey, Ill., Aug. 2, 1952; d. Carmen Anthony and Helen Elaine (Welch) R. AA with high honors, Thornton C.C., 1972; BS in Edn. with high honors, Ill. State U., 1974; MEd, Nat.-Louis U., 1990. Cert. K-9, Ill. Tchr. kindergarten Primary Acad. Ctr., Markham, Ill., 1976-91, tchr. K-3, 1991—. Ill. State scholar, 1969. Mem. Ill. Edn. Assn. (assn. rep. 1976-88), Kappa Delta Pi, Phi Theta Kappa. Republican. Home: 2522 183rd St Homewood IL 60430-3037 Office: Prairie-Hills Prim Acad Ctr 3055 W 163rd St Markham IL 60426-5626

RUFFOLO, MARY, lawyer; b. Kenosha, Wis., Jan. 9, 1967; d. Louis Anthony and Dora Antonia Ruffolo; m. David Richard Rauch, Aug. 14, 1993. BA, Carthage Coll., Kenosha, 1989; JD, Valparaiso U., 1992. Bar: Ill. 1992, U.S. Dist. Ct. (no. dist.) Ill. 1992. Assoc. Jenner & Block, Lake Forest, Ill., 1992—. Mem. ABA, Women's Bar Assn. Ill., Ill. Bar Assn. Office: Jenner & Block 1 Westminister Pl Lake Forest IL 60045

RUGALA, KAREN FRANCIS, television producer, painter; b. Memphis, Apr. 27, 1950; d. Ben Porter Francis and Marguerite K. Higginbotham; children: Sarah Helfinstein, Ben Helfinstein. BA in Communication Arts, Rhodes Coll., 1971; MA, U. Mo., 1973. Cert. tchr., Tenn. Secondary sch. tchr. Memphis City Schs., 1971-72; speech tchr. U. Ga., Athens, 1973-75; dir. computer systems installations Planning Rsch. Corp., McLean, Va., 1976-78; dir. account mgmt. TDX Systems, Cable & Wireless, Vienna, Va., 1978-80; cons. telecommunications MCI, Washington, 1985-87; producer Fairfax Cable Access, Merrifield, Va., 1991—; owner Art Promotions, McLean, 1989—. Exhibited paintings in numerous group and one-woman shows including Clark & Co. Gallery, Washington, 1994, McLean Project for Arts, 1992, Hospice of No. Va. Auction Gala, 1992, Touchstone Gallery Benefit Auction, McLean, 1991, Great Falls Art Ctr., Va., 1990, many others; paintings represented in numerous pvt. collections. Active Family AIDS Housing Found., 1992, Hospice No. Va., 1991, 92, Friends of Vietnam Vets. Meml., 1992; founding bd. mem. Jobs for Homeless People, 1988-90. Office: Art Promotions PO Box 3104 Mc Lean VA 22103-3104

RUGGIERI, CATHERINE JOSEPHINE, management educator; b. Bklyn., Dec. 28, 1951; d. Joseph A. and Elvira E. (Brillante) R. BA, St. John's U., N.Y.C., 1973, MBA, 1979; postgrad., CUNY, 1993-94, Bklyn. Law Sch., 1994—. Asst. to dean St. Vincent's Coll. of St. John's U., N.Y.C., 1973-77, asst. dean acad. advisement, 1977-79, asst. dean, 1979-80, acting dean, 1980-81, dean, 1981-86, asst. v.p., dean, 1986-87, assoc. v.p., dean, 1987-93, univ. dir. study abroad, 1987-92, prof. mgmt., 1993—; chair St. John's Telecomm. Inst. for Non-Profit Video Prodns., N.Y.C., 1987-93. Recipient Hon. Citation Ministry of Edn. Hungary, Budapest, 1986. Mem. AAUW, ASCD, AAUP, Am. Assn. Higher Edn.; student mem. ABA, N.Y. State Bar Assn., N.Y. County Lawyers Assn. Roman Catholic. Office: St Johns U 8000 Utopia Pky Jamaica NY 11432-1335

RUHE, SHIRLEY LOUISE, government official, budget and legislative consultant; b. Des Moines, Mar. 20, 1943; d. Merritt Elton and Grace Alberta (Crabtree) Bailey; B.S., Iowa State U., 1965, M.S., 1969; m. Jonathan Mills Ruhe, Feb. 28, 1970; children—Alix-Nicole, Jonathan G. B. Wire editor, photographer Ames (Iowa) Daily Tribune, 1968-69; legis. asst. Congressman John Culver, 1969-72; staff asst. Congressman John Blatnik, 1973-75; dep. dir. budget process and ops. Ho. of Reps., Washington, 1978-82, assoc. dir., 1983-86, dir. budget policy, 1987-94; co-staff dir. Reconciliation Task Force, 1981—; adviser Spl. Rules Com. Task Force on Budget Process, 1982-83; chmn. bd. dirs. Le Neon French-Am. Theatre; mem. social action bd.Rock Spring Congl. Ch.; Resource Coun. Inst. Ednl. Policy. Ford Found. grantee, 1969. Mem. Delta Sigma Phi, Phi Kappa Phi. Democrat. Home: 3915 N Woodstock St Arlington VA 22207-2941 Office: Budget 203 O'Neill House Office Bldg Washington DC 20515

RUIZ, ARLENE M., foreign language educator; b. N.Y.C., July 24, 1970; d. Pedro and Aida (Figueroa) R. BA in Comms., Manhattan Coll., Bronx, 1993. Bookeeper Arista Stationery, N.Y., 1985-87; leader, asst. ctr. mgr. Weight Watchers, N.Y., 1987-94; computer programmer BT Summit, N.Y., 1993-94; tchr. Spanish N.Y.C. Bd. of Edn., Bronx, 1994—; intern-rschr. Inside Edition, N.Y., 1992; assoc. prodr., intern WABC-TV, N.Y., 1993. Advocate March of Dimes, 1984—; active Nat. Hispanic Coalition, 1993—; leader, pres. Aspira, 1986-87. Home: 3233 Corlear Ave Bronx NY 10469 Office: NYC Bd Edn 2545 Gunther Ave Bronx NY 10469

RUIZ, MARYBETH, clinical and health psychologist; b. Harbor City, Calif., May 6, 1964; d. Alfred Juan and Carol Loraine (Clark) Ruiz; m. Steven Gordon Walton, Aug. 18, 1993. BA, San Francisco State U., 1989; PhD, Calif. Sch. Profl. Psychology, Berkeley, 1993. Rsch. assoc. Alameda (Calif.) Minority Youth Project, 1991-93, Chicana/Latina Rsch. Ctr., Davis, Calif., 1993—; lectr. Chicano/a Studies program U. Calif., Davis, 1993—, postgrad. rschr. dept. psychology, 1994-96; presenter in field. Mem. APA, Am. Psychol. Soc., Mujeres Activas en Letra y Cambio Social. Office: U Calif Davis Chicana Latina Rsch Ctr 2102 Hart Hall Davis CA 95616

RUIZ, VANESSA, judge; b. San Jaun, P.R., Mar. 22, 1950; D. Fernando and Irma (Bosch) Ruiz-Suria; m. Eduardo Elejalde, Feb. 11, 1972 (div. Jan. 1982); children: Natalia, Alexia; m. David E. Birenbaum, Oct. 22, 1983; stepchildren: Tracy, Matthew. BA, Wellesley Coll., 1972; JD, Georgetown U., 1975. Bar: D.C. 1972, U.S. Supreme Ct. 1981. Assoc. Fried, Frank, Harris, Shrives & Kampelman, Washington, 1975-83; sr. mgr., counsel Sears World Trade Inc., Washington, 1983-94; assoc. judge D.C. Ct. of Appeals, 1994—; speaker in field. Mem. ABA, Inter-Am. Bar Assn. Office: 500 Indiana Ave NW Washington DC 20001 also: Pepper Hamilton & Scheetz 1300 19th St NW Washington DC 20036-1609*

RUIZ-VALERA, PHOEBE LUCILE, law librarian; b. Barranquilla, Colombia, Jan. 27, 1950; d. Ramon and Marion (Mehlman) Ruiz-Valera; m. Thomas Patrick Winkler, Mar. 27, 1981. BA cum laude, Westminster Coll., 1971; MLS, Rutgers U., 1974; MA, NYU, 1978. Libr. trainee Passaic (N.J.) Pub. Libr., 1973-74, reference libr., 1974; libr. assoc., cataloger NYU Law Libr., N.Y.C., 1974-79, asst. curator, cataloger, 1979-81; libr. III, cataloger Rutgers U. Library, New Brunswick, N.J., 1981-82; chief cataloger Assn. Bar City N.Y., 1982-85, head tech. svcs., 1985—. Mem. ALA, Am. Assn. Law Librs., Am. Translators Assn. (cert. translator English to Spanish), Law Libr. Assn. Greater N.Y., Reforma, Salalm. Democrat. Presbyterian. Office: Assn Bar City NY 42 W 44th St New York NY 10036-6604

RULE, WILMA LOUISE BANTA, political science educator; b. Basin, Wyo.; m. Irving Krauss. BA and MA in Polit. Sci., U. Calif., Berkeley; PhD, U. Hawaii, 1968. Adj. prof. polit. sci. U. Nev., Reno, 1991—. Co-editor: Russian Women in Politics and Society, 1996, Electoral Systems in Comparative Perspective, 1994, U.S. Electoral Systems, 1992; contbr. articles to profl. jours. Mem. exec. bd. dirs. Ctr. for Voting and Democracy, Washington, 1992—, Nat./Internat. Election Systems and Representation, 1993—, No. Calif. Citizens for Proportional Representation, Albany, 1994. Home: 14 Hawkside Ct Markleeville CA 96120 Office: U Nev Dept Polit Sci # 302 Reno NE 89557

RUMBAUGH, SHELIA ANN, educational technologist, consultant; b. Mexico, Mo., Feb. 25, 1957; d. William Arch and Gerald Jean (Bailey) Colley; m. Charles David Rumbaugh, Aug. 17, 1974 (div. Jan. 17, 1996); 1 child, Amanda Nicole. BS in Elem. Edn., U. Mo., 1982, MEd in Curriculum & Instrn. Elem., 1984, postgrad., 1989—. Cert. tchr. grade K-8, media specialist grades K-12. Computing instr. William Woods Coll., Fulton, Mo., 1985-90; rsch. asst. U. Mo., Columbia, 1989-91; edn. tech. Columbia (Mo.) Pub. Schs., 1992-95; cons.PC software installation and tng. Columbia, Mo., 1996—; cons. U. No. Iowa, Cedar Falls, 1993-94, Columbia (Mo.) Cath. Schs., 1994. 4-H project leader Hardin Huslers, Fulton, 1989—. Devel. grantee William Woods Coll., Fulton, 1988-89, Pvt.-Parent Group, Columbia Pub. Schs., 1994-95, Software grantee MicroMedia, U. Mo., 1991-92, NATO researcher workshop tech. grantee, 1994. Mem. Internat. Soc. for Tech. in Edn. (conf. com. 1993-95), Assn. for Ednl. Comm. and Tech. (com. mem. 1994—), Am. Ednl. Rsch. Assn. Home and Office: 7541 E Abc Ln Columbia MO 65202

RUMBERGER, REGINA, retired English language educator; b. Pitts., Aug. 6, 1921; d. Edward T. and Margaret (Berry) Flynn; m. Wilson A. Rumberger, July 31, 1943 (div. 1974); children: Edward, Wilson J., Susan A., Gerard, Paul, Nancy, Joe. BEd, Duquesne U., 1942; MEd, U. Pitts., 1950; grad., State Office Div. Blind Svcs., Ft. Myers, Fla., 1984. Professed Lay Carmelite, 1990. Primary tchr. Allegheny County Pub. Sch., Pa., 1942-43, Sharpsburg (Pa.) Schs., 1943-50; instr. English, Edison C.C., Ft. Myers, 1964-78; ret., 1978; media cons., Lee County and Ft. Myers, 1956; cons., evaluator State of Fla. and Lee County, 1987-88; cons., evaluator Lee County Dept. Transp., Ft. Myers, 1988-90. Chmn. water and safety ARC, Ft. Myers, 1960-65, first aid adminstr., 1965-68; pres. Lee County Med. Aux., 1965-66; consumer rep. Lee County Dept. Transp.; bd. dirs. Met. Planning Orgn., Ft. Myers, 1990—; v.p. S.W. Fla. Curia, 1988—; asst. tour guide to Fr. Stanislaw Pierog, tour dir. Andrew's Pilgrimages, Stockbridge, Mass., 1990—; cons. on accessibility for handicapped Mayor's Alliance, mem. Coun. Disabled, 1991-92; cons., citizen adv. Divsn. Blind Svcs., State of Fla., 1990-91; vol. Lee Mem. Hosp., 1992, Caloosa Retirement Ctr., 1988-96; mem. coun. Lee County Bd. Parks and Recreation, 1994—; mem. citizen's adv. com. Metro. Planning Orgn., 1996—; amb. of Mass. Trans., State of Fla.; spokesperson for disabled Lee County CAC. Recipient award Boy Scouts Am., Ft. Myers, 1967, State of Fla., 1984, Ft. Myers Care Ctr./Lee Convalescence, 1990, Vol. of Yr., State of Fla., 1994, award Caloosa Retirement Ctr., 1996. Mem. AAUW (pub. rels. com. Ft. Myers 1987-90). Roman Catholic. Home: 2140 Cottage St Apt 109 Fort Myers FL 33901-3666

RUMLER, DIANA GALE, geriatrics nurse; b. Manchester, Tenn., Feb. 23, 1943; d. Donald Yale and Thelma Irene (Beach) Miller; m. Herschel Hinkle, Aug. 1961 (div. Jan. 1978); children: David, John, Jody Hinkle West; m. Lester Rumler, Jr. (div. June 1984). AA in Nursing, Ind. U.-Purdue U., Indpls., 1974; BS in Pub. Health-Journalism-Psychology, Ball State U., Muncie, 1983. RN; cert. ACLS, BLS. Psychiat. nurse Meth. Hosp., Indpls., 1974-78; women's infant and children's coord. Cmty. & Family Svcs. Inc., Portland, Ind., 1978-81, Ball Meml. Hosp., Muncie, Ind., 1981-84; pub. health nurse Health & Rehab. Svcs., Ft. Lauderdale, Fla., 1984; med.-surg. nurse Holy Cross Hosp., Ft. Lauderdale, 1985; pre-op/post-op nurse VA Med. Ctr., Nashville, 1986-89; nurse vascular, orthopedics, intensive care, telemetry, tchg VA Med. Ctr., Tucson, 1990—; WIC advocate hearings/radio show, Ind., 1978-81; health vol. outreach clinic St. Mary's Hosp., Tucson, 1993-94; vol. Hospice Family Care, Tucson. Contbr. articles to profl. jours. Mem. Nurses of Vet. Affairs, Am. Fedn. Govt. Employees, Ladies' Hermitage Assn. Democrat. Roman Catholic. Home: PO Box 17764 Tucson AZ 85731-7764 Office: VA Med Ctr S 6th Ave Tucson AZ 85723

RUMORE, CHARLOTTE FOWLER, city official; b. Memphis, Oct. 5, 1937; d. Charles Calvin and Malinda (McDonald) Fowler; m. Marc Miller, Mar. 4, 1956 (div. Jan. 1980); children: Shai, Marc Jr., Chriss, Rachelle, Brett, Brandi; m. Anthony John Rumore, Oct. 16, 1982. Student, Sacred Heart Coll., 1968, 74, U. Ala., Huntsville, 1990, U. Ala., Tuscaloosa, 1991, 92. Dep. dir. Cullman (Ala.) County Civil Def., 1966-68; editor, co-owner The Cullman Tribune, 1968-77; reporter Cullman Times, 1978-82, Decatur (Ala.) Daily, 1983-84; sales rep., designer Monroe Bus. Equip., Huntsville, 1984-91; aide to mayor City of Madison, Ala., 1991—. Mem. Dem. Exec. Com., Cullman, 1972-76, City Coun., Cullman, 1976-80; mem. cmty. devel. com. Ala. League of Municipalities, Montgomery, 1977-80. Named Person of the Yr., Madison County Record, 1992, Outstanding Bus. Woman Bus. and Profl. women's Club, 1973. Mem. C. of C. (Leadership class 1993-94). Roman Catholic. Home: 12206 Greenleaf Cir Huntsville AL 35803 Office: 100 Hughes Rd Madison AL 35758-1110

RUNDIO, JOAN PETERS (JO RUNDIO), public administrator; b. Dearborn, Mich., Mar. 17, 1941; d. Joe and Donna (Sells) Peters; m. Florian (Pug) Frank Rundio Jr., Sept. 8., 1971; children: Jeffrey Daniel, David Eric. Diploma, Bronson Meth. Sch. Nursing, 1962; BA, U. Redlands, 1978; MPA, U. South Ala., 1987. RN Mich., 1962. Emergency nurse Bronson Meth. Hosp., Kalamazoo, 1962-63, The Queen's Med. Ctr., Honolulu, 1963-65; orthopaedic nurse The Honolulu Med. Group, 1965-72; sch. nurse Corpus Christi (Tex.) Sch. Dist., 1979-81; pub. health nurse Tri-County Health Dept., Traverse City, Mich., 1983-85; adminstrv. intern City of Troy (Mich.), 1987-88; acring econ. devel. dir. City of Traverse City, 1988-89; mgr. personal health svcs. Tri-County Health Dept., Traverse City, 1989; asst. city mgr. City of Traverse City, 1990—. V.p. Women's Econ. Devel. Orgn., Traverse City, 1993-95, mem., 1984—; mem. Traverse City Planning Commn., 1995—; rep. Traverse City Schs. Adv. Com., 1982-85, 88-89. Recipient James H. Boyd award U. South Ala., Mobile, 1987. Mem. Michigan City. Mgmt. Assn. (bd. dirs. 1996—), Internat. City Mgmt. Assn., Cherryland Humane Soc., Pi Sigma Alpha. Office: City of Traverse City 400 Boardman Ave Traverse City MI 49684

RUNFOLA, SHEILA KAY, nurse; b. Canton, Ohio, Feb. 8, 1944; d. Benjamin and M. Suzanne (deBord) Suarez; m. Steven Joseph Runfola, Aug. 17, 1968; children: Michael, Janine, Christine; stepchildren: Stephanie Bufalini, Darlene Teran. BS in Nursing, St. John Coll. Cleve., 1966; teaching credential jr. coll. nursing, UCLA Ext., San Diego, 1973. RN, Calif.; cert. occupational health nurse, cert. pub. health nurse. Staff nurse emergency rm. Leland Meml. Hosp., Riverdale, Md., 1966-67; staff nurse/team leader med./surg. Mercy Hosp., San Diego, 1967-68; staff nurse, charge nurse emergency dept., dept. radiology U. Calif.-San Diego Med.Ctr., 1968-76; staff devel./asst. dir. nurses TLC Nursing Home, El Cajon, Calif., 1978-80; staff nurse/charge nurse emergency dept. Kaiser Permanente Hosp., San Diego, 1980-89; staff nurse emergency dept. Kaiser Permanente Hosp., Sacramento, Calif., 1989-90; house supr. Kaiser Permanente Hosp., Sacramento, 1992-94, case mgr. occupational medicine, 1995—; health svcs. nurse U.S. Automobile Assn., Sacramento, 1990-95. Contbr. articles to profl. jours. Leader Girls Scouts Am., San Diego and Sacramento, 1982-91, treas., local svc. team, 1986-89, 90; parent rep. Elk Grove (Calif.) Sch. Bd. for Elk Grove H.s., 1994, co-chair Sober Grad. Night, 1993-95. Mem. Sacramento Valley Occupational Health Nurses (v.p. 1992-95), Newcomers Club. Democrat. Roman Catholic. Office: Kaiser Permanente Dept Occupl Med 6600 Bruceville Rd Sacramento CA 95823

RUNGE, BARBARA KAY, lawyer, arbitrator, mediator; b. Houston, July 15, 1949; d. William A. and Martha Ellen (Boynton) R.; m. W.R. Howard, May 26, 1979. BA in govt., Tex. Tech. U., Lubbock, 1971; JD, Tex. Tech. Sch. of Law, Lubbock, 1974. Bar: Tex. 1974, U.S. Supreme Ct. 1986. Owner, operator Law Offices of Barbara K. Runge, Houston, 1975—; pres., bd. trustees Tex. Tech. Sch. of Law, 1993—; treas. tax chpt. Am. Acad. of Matrimonial Lawyers, 1995— (fellow 1992). Contbr. articles to profl. jours. Life fellow Tex. Bar Found., Austin, Tex., 1981. Fellow Houston Bar Found. (past pres. Family Law Section); mem. ABA, Tex. Bar Assn., Assn. of Woman Attorneys (past pres.), Charter 100 of Houston (v.p. social 1996—). Presbyterian. Office: Law Ofcs of B K Runge 5615 Kirby Dr Ste 920 Houston TX 77005

RUNGE, KAY KRETSCHMAR, library director; b. Davenport, Iowa, Dec. 9, 1946; d. Alfred Edwin and Ina (Paul) Kretschmar; m. Peter S. Runge Sr., Aug. 17, 1968; children: Peter Jr., Katherine. BS in History Edn., Iowa State U., 1969; MLS, U. Iowa, 1970. Pub. service librarian Anoka County Library, Blaine, Minn., 1971-72; cataloger Augustana Coll., Rock Island, Ill., 1972-74; dir. Scott County Library System, Eldridge, Iowa, 1974-85, Davenport (Iowa) Pub. Libr., 1985—. Bd. dirs. River Ctr. for Performing Arts, Davenport, 1983—, Am. Inst. Commerce, 1989—, Quad-Cities Conv. and Visitors Bur., 1991—, Quad-Cities Grad. Study Ctr., 1992—, Downtown Davenport Devel. Corp., 1992—, Hall of Honor Bd. Davenport Ctrl. H.S., 1992-95, Brenton Bank, 1996—; mem. steering com. Quad-Cities Visions for the Future, 1987-91; bd. govs. Iowa State U. Found., 1991—. Recipient Svc. Key award Iowa State U. Alumni Assn., 1979. Mem. ALA (chmn. library adminstrs. and mgrs. div., fundraising section 1988), Iowa Library Assn. (pres. 1983), Pub. Library Assn. (bd. dirs. 1990-96), Iowa Edn. Media Assn. (Intellectual Freedom award 1984), Alpha Delta Pi (alumni state pres. 1978). Lutheran. Office: Davenport Pub Libr 321 N Main St Davenport IA 52801-1409

RUNYAN, ANNE SISSON, political science educator; b. Cin., Mar. 30, 1955; d. Richard Van Pelt and Margery Wing (Sisson) R.; m. Albert Adrian Kanters, Nov. 8, 1976. BA, U. Windsor, Ont., Can., 1976; MS, Am. U., 1979, PhD, 1988. From. asst. prof. to assoc. prof. politics dept. SUNY, Potsdam, 1988-96, chair politics dept., 1990-95, women's studies dir., 1992-96; assoc. prof. polit. sci. dept. Wright State U., Dayton, Ohio, 1996—, women's studies dir., 1996—; vis. scholar U. Amsterdam, The Netherlands, 1994-95; rsch. cons. Capital Counselors, Washington, 1978-80, Inst. Govt. Pub. Info. Rsch., 1980-81, Alta. Soc. Women Against Violence, Edmonton, 1983-84, Soc. Svcs. Dept. Niagara Regional Municipality, St. Catharines, Ont., 1985. Co-author: Gendered States, 1992, Global Gender Issues, 1993, Women, Gender and World Politics, 1994, Globalisation Theory & Practice, 1996; contbg. author: Gendered States, 1992; contbr. articles to profl. jours. bd. dirs. Alta. Status Women Action Com., Edmonton, 1982-83, Canadian Voice Women Peace, Toronto, Can., 1985-86; faculty advisor No. N.Y. Model UN Project, 1988-90; coord. Women's Caucus SUNY, Potsdam, 1992-96. Travel grantee Am. Coun. Learned Socs., 1994; rsch. fellow Rsch. Ctr. Socs. Internat. Polit. Economy, 1995. Mem. Am. Polit. Sci. Assn. (rsch. grantee 1994), Nat. Women's Studies Assn., Internat. Studies Assn. (sect. chair, bd. dirs. 1990-95). Democrat. Office: Wright State U Dept Polit Sci Dayton OH 45435

RUOFF, CYNTHIA OSOWIEC, foreign language educator; b. Chgo., Mar. 1, 1943; d. Stephen R. and Estelle (Wozniak) O.; m. Gary Edward Ruoff, June 5, 1965; children: Gary S., Laura A. AB, Loyola U., 1965; MA, Western Mich. U., 1973; PhD in French Lang. and Lit., Mich. State U., 1992. Tchr. Kalamazoo (Mic.) Pub. Schs., 1965-68; instr. Western Mich. U., Kalamazoo, 1980—; nat. and internat. spkr. in field. Contbr. articles to profl. jours. Mem. MLA, N.Am. Soc. Seventeenth-Century French Lit., Am. Assn. Tchrs. of French, Mich. Fgn. Lang. Assn., Internat. Soc. Phenomenology and Lit., L'Alliance Française, Soc. Interdisciplinary French Seventeenth-Century Studies, Phi Sigma Iota, Pi Delta Phi. Office: Dept Fgn Langs & Lit Western Mich Univ Kalamazoo MI 49008

RUPE, SUSAN YOCCA, editor; b. Windber, pa., Mar. 6, 1956; d. Nunzio Silvio and Flora Dorene (Santucci) Yocca; m. Joseph W. Rupe Jr., Oct. 3, 1981; 1 child, Christopher. BA in Comms., Shippensburg State Coll., 1978. Reporter Lewistown (Pa.) Sentinel, 1978-87; editor, gen. mgr. County Observer, Yeagertown, Pa., 1984—; owner Joseph Comms., Lewistown, 1987—.

Editor mag. Travel Host of the Keystone Mountains, 1987-91, PA Today, 1991. Mem. Soroptimist Internat. (rec. sec. Lewistown chpt. 1995—), Sigma Delta Chi (pres. Ctrl. Pa. chpt. 1984-86). Roman Catholic. Office: County Observer 310 S Main ST Yeagertown PA 17099

RUPINSKI, JANETTE MARIE, banker; b. Sheboygan, Wis., Jan. 7, 1946; d. Reuben Roy and Marie (Horn) Friedel; m. Albin Michael Hoffart, June 24, 1967 (div. Feb. 1993); children: Craig Michael, Curtis Marc.; m. Michael A. Rupinski, July 29, 1996. BS in Bus. Adminstrn., Cardinal Stritch Coll., Milw., 1992. Sec.-treas. Cmty. Fin. Svcs., Inc., Port Washington, Wis., 1979-84; teller Port Washington Savs. & Loan, 1977-79, asst. v.p., 1984-86; v.p., br. mgr. Port Washington Savs. & Loan, Saukville, Wis., 1986-88, Port Savs. Bank, S.A., Grafton, Wis., 1988-90; asst. v.p., mgr. St. Francis Bank, FSB, Thiensville, Wis., 1990-94; ops. mgr. Horizon Credit Union, Racine, Wis., 1994—; bd. dirs. Inst. Fin. Edn., Milw., 1984-90, membership chair, 1986-88, chpt. excellence chair, 1988-90. Vol. Port Washington Pub. Schs., 1976-79, Advocates for Victims of Abuse, Ozaukee County, Wis., 1992-94; bd. dirs. Ozaukee County Vol. Ctr., Port Washington, 1993-94; asst. cubmaster Boy Scouts Am., Port Washington, 1977-79. Mem. Wis. Credit Union League. Office: Horizon Credit Union 1931 Grove Ave Racine WI 53405

RUPPERT, MARY FRANCES, management consultant, school counselor; b. Flushing, N.Y., May 14; d. Raymond Edward and Mary Josephine (Reilly) R.; m. Donald Francis O'Brien (div.); children: Donald Francis O'Brien III, Kevin Raymond O'Brien; m. Patrick J. Falzone, July 31, 1993. BA in English, Loyola Coll.; MS in Psychology, Counseling, Queens Coll., 1965. Counselor Plainview (N.Y.)-Old Bethpage Schs., 1965—; trainer, cons. stress mgmt., time mgmt., comm., pres. Productivity Programs, Huntington, N.Y., 1975—. Contbr. articles in field; author audiotapes on stress mgmt., 1975—; appearances radio and TV. Mem. ASTD (pres. 1988, chmn. bd. dirs. 1989-95), AAUW, N.Y. State Counselors Assn., Nassau Counselors Assn., Huntington Camera Club (treas. 1996—). Office: 20 Richard Ln Huntington NY 11743-2354

RUPPRECHT, CAROL SCHREIER, comparative literature educator, dream researcher; b. Stafford Springs, Conn., June 30, 1939; d. William Joseph and Caroline Brown (Comstock) Schreier; divorced; children: Jody Francine, Whitney Glenn; m. Richard P. Suttmeier, May 8, 1987. BS, U. Va., 1962; MA, Yale U., 1963, M in Philosophy, 1973, PhD, 1977. Teaching fellow Yale U., 1973; asst. prof. Kirkland Coll., Clinton, N.Y., 1974-78; asst. prof. Hamilton, Coll., Clinton, 1978-81, assoc. dean, 1981-82, assoc. prof. comparative lit., 1982-89; prof., 1989—, chmn. dept., 1984-89; lectr. Switzerland, Israel, The Netherlands, Ireland, People's Republic China, Eng., Japan. Author, editor: The Dream and the Text: Essays on Literature and Language, 1993; co-editor and author: Feminist Archetypal Theory, 1985; sr. editor, cons. editor Dreaming; contbr. articles to profl. jours., chpts. to books. NEH fellow Dartmouth Dante Inst., 1986. Founding mem. Assn. for Study Dreams, 1983, Conn. Assn. Jungian Psychology, 1981. Merrill fellow Bunting Inst., 1970-72. Mem. MLA, Am. Comparative Lit. Assn., Shakespeare Soc., Assn. Study of Dreams (pres., v.p. bd. dirs., mem. editorial bd.), Conn. Assn. for Jungian Psychology (bd. dirs.). Avocations: sports; wilderness activities. Address: 198 College Hill Rd Clinton NY 13323-1218

RUPPRECHT, NANCY ELLEN, historian, educator; b. Coeur d'Alene, Idaho, Sept. 23, 1948; d. George John and Nancy Berneeda (Baird) R. BA with honors, U. Mo., 1967, MA, 1969; PhD, U. Mich., 1982. Acad. dir. pilot program U. Mich., Ann Arbor, 1971-73, lectr. in women studies, 1973-75; vis. lectr. history U. Mo., St. Louis, 1976-77; vis. instr. of history Wash. U., St. Louis, 1977-79, Grinnell (Iowa) Coll., 1979-81; asst. prof. Oakland U., Rochester, Mich., 1981-83; asst. prof. of history Mid. Tenn. State U., Murfreesboro, 1985-91, assoc. prof., 1991—; dir. women's studies program Middle Tenn. State U., 1988—, publicity dir. women's history month, 1989-92, mem. faculty senate, 1992-95. Contbr. articles to profl. jours. Mem. AAUP (chpt. v.p. 1988-89, pres. 1989-93), AAUW, NOW, Am. Hist. Assn., S.E. Women's Studies Assn., So. Hist. Assn., So. Humanities Assn., Holocaust Studies Assn., Mid. Tenn. Women's Studies Assn., German Studies Assn., Women in Higher Edn. in Tenn., Concerned Faculty and Adminstrv. Women (chpt. v.p. 1993-95, chpt. pres. 1995-96), Assn. of Faculty and Adminstrv. Women (chpt. pres. 1995—). Home: 1106 Jones Blvd Murfreesboro TN 37129-2310 Office: Middle Tenn State U 275 Peck Hall Murfreesboro TN 37132-0001

RUSCIO, NANCY STOKER, school system administrator; b. Cortland, N.Y., June 12, 1954; d. Max Alson and Shirley Margaret (Cook) Stoker; m. Joseph John Ruscio, Nov. 20, 1976; children: Stephanie Rae, Joey Corin, Kiley Christine, Justin Maxwell. BS, SUNY, Oswego, 1976; MS, SUNY, Cortland, 1982, Cert. of Advanced Study, 1985. Grade 2 tchr. Moravia (N.Y.) Ctrl. Sch., 1976-81, staff devel. trainer, 1981-84, asst. H.S. prin., 1984-85; elem. sch. prin. Manchester-Shortsville (N.Y.) Ctrl Sch., 1985-95; dir. instrn. Manchester-Shortsville Consol. Sch. Dist., 1995—; facilitator Wayne Finger Lakes, Stanley, N.Y., 1986—. Bd. dirs. Ontario County Youth Mus., Canandaigua, N.Y., 1989; chairperson of pastor's parish com., Farmington (N.Y.) United Ch., 1994—. Republican. Methodist. Home: 95 Bowerman Rd Farmington NY 14425 Office: Manchester-Shortsville 1506 Rt 21 Shortsville NY 14548

RUSHING, DOROTHY MARIE, historian, educator; b. Bonham, Tex., Aug. 28, 1925; d. Van Bain and Ada Belle (Price) Hawkins; m. J. E. Rushing, Aug. 6, 1960 (dec. 1985); children: Charles Maret, Bill Maret, Bob Maret, Charles Rushing, Martha Rushing Sosebee. BA, Tex. Woman's U., 1972; MA, East Tex. State U., 1974; PhD, U. North Tex., 1981. Cert. history, lang. arts. secondary tchr., Tex. Tchr. pub. schs., 1972-86; instr. East Tex. State U., Commerce, 1972-74, 80-81; teaching fellow U. North Tex., Denton, 1975-76; prof. Richland Coll., Dallas, 1975-95, ret., 1995; prof. Collin County Community Coll., McKinney, Tex., 1975-95; historian-archivist J.C. Penney, Inc., Dallas, 1988-95; lectr., Dallas, 1972—; vis. prof. Johns Hopkins U., 1985, U. Va., 1989; statis. analyst Dallas County C.C., 1982; lay rep. N.E. Tex. Libr. System, 1984-89. Editor, author: Texas: The Lone Star State, 1984; contbg. author: Beyond Sundown, 1975, Handbook of Texas, 1994. Decorated Honorary Cross of Lorraine (France); named Outstanding Instr., Richland Coll., 1987; postdoctoral fellow NEH, 1985, 89; grantee Dallas County C.C. Dist., 1984. Mem. Phi Kappa Phi, Sigma Tau Delta, Phi Alpha Theta. Home: 1214 Patricia Ln Garland TX 75042-8041

RUSHMER, ESTELLA VIRGINIA DIX (DIXIE RUSHMER), artist; b. Sullivan, Ind., Oct. 17, 1919; d. William Porter Jessop and Roxie Gertrude (Johnson) Dix; m. Robert Frazer Rushmer, Apr. 5, 1942; children: Donald Scott, Anne, Elizabeth. BS, Purdue U., 1940. cert. Am. Dietetic Assn. docent Wash. State Burke Mus., 1963-78. Author, artist: Whidbey Island Sketchbook, 1985; one-woman shows include Good Years Gallery, Edmonds, Wash., 1975, 75, 77, Stillwater Gallery, Seattle, 1979, Artists Gallery Northwest, 1979, 82, 83, Stonington Gallery, Seattle, 1985, Port Angeles (Wash.) Fine Arts Ctr., 1988; group shows include Bellevue (Wash.) Art Mus., 1979, 82, 84, 86-90, Peter Kirk Gallery, Kirkland, Wash., 1985-90, Frye Mus., Seattle, 1979, Frederick and Nelson Gallery, Seattle, 1980, 82, Fremont Fine Art Gallery, Seattle, 1987, Black Swan Gallery, Seattle, 1989, Portico Gallery, Kobe, Japan, 1987, Meguro Mus., Tokyo, Japan, 1987, Columbia Art Ctr., Vancouver, Wash., 1990, Nat. Watercolor Soc. Show, Muckenthaler Cultural Ctr., Fullerton, Calif., 1990; represented in permanent collections at Rainier Bank, Samotomo Bank, Alpac Corp., Honeywell, Seattle; represented in pvt. collections. Pres. U. Wash. Med. Sch. Aux., Seattle, 1948; leader Girl Scouts U.S.A., Lake Forest Park, Wash., 1958-63. Mem. Northwest Watercolor Soc., U. Wash. Auxiliary, U. Wash. Med. Auxiliary, U. Wash. Retiree Assn., Women Painters of Wash. Home: 10901 176 Circle NE # 3526 Redmond WA 98052

RUSIN ACKER, KATHLEEN ALICE, writer, editor, poet, spiritual counselor; b. Port Jefferson, N.Y., Sept. 4, 1945; d. Edward and Alice Catherine (Gniazdowski) Rusin.; m. David Henry Acker, Aug. 24, 1968 (div. 1979); children: Sherry Lynn Acker, Wendy Kay Acker. AAS, Suffolk County C.C., Selden, 1965. Legal sec. Block, Namm & Baranello, Port Jefferson, 1965-67; exec. sec. Hoffman Majesty, Inc., Port Jefferson, 1967; sr. steno Physics Dept. SUNY, Stony Brook, 1968-74, sr. steno Ecology & Evolution Dept., 1976-78; legal sec. Howard Bergson & Roy Dragotta, Port Jefferson, 1978-80, Neil Abelson, Port Jefferson, 1983-85; exec. asst. J.B. Kimberly & Assoc., Woodbury, N.Y., 1985-86; office svcs. mgr., personnel cons. Arrow Employment Agy., Melville, N.Y., 1986-90; author, editor, poet. Author: (book) Love Takes Time, 1996; editor, contbg. writer: (book) The Colors of God's Love, 1994; poet: (anthology) Dance on the Horizon, 1994; editor, contbg. writer, poet: (newsletter) Family Self Sufficiency Program, 1993-95. Sec., organizer "Blockettes" Group, Campaign to Elect Frederic Block, Esq. to State Assmbly, Port Jefferson, 1966; co-chmn. Post Office Customer Adv. Coun., Commack, N.Y., 1992—. Mem. Nat. Mus. Women in the Arts, Internat. Soc. Poets (Named Internat. Poet of Merit 1994, 96), Babylon Citizens Coun. on the Arts. Democrat. Roman Catholic. Home: 70-9 Fairfield Way Commack NY 11725

RUSKAI, MARY BETH, mathematics researcher, educator; b. Cleve., Feb. 26, 1944; d. Michael J. and Evelyn (Gortz) R. BS, Notre Dame Coll., Cleve., 1965; MA, PhD, U. Wis., 1969. Battelle fellow in theoretical physics U. Geneva, 1969-71; rsch. assoc. in math. MIT, Cambridge, Mass., 1971-72; rsch. assoc. in physics U. Alta., Edmonton, Can., 1972-73; asst. prof. math. U. Oreg., Eugene, 1973-76; asst. prof. U. Lowell, Mass., 1977-82, assoc. prof., 1982-86, prof. dept. math., 1986—, pres. faculty senate, 1990-91; sci. scholar Bunting Inst., Cambridge, Mass., 1983-85; vis. prof. Rockefeller U., N.Y.C., 1980-81, U. Vienna, Austria, 1981, Rome, 1988; faculty rsch. assoc. Naval Surface Warfare Ctr., Silver Springs, Md., 1986; vis. prof. math. U. Mich., Ann Arbor, 1991-92; vis. mem. Courant Inst. Math. Sci., NYU, 1988-89; cons. Bell Labs., Murray Hill, N.J., 1972, 83, 88-89; conf. dir. NSF/CBMS Conf. on Wavelets, 1990; Flora Stone Mather vis. prof. Case Western Res. U., Cleve., 1995. Editor-in-chief Wavelets and Their Applications, 1990-92; mem. editorial bd. Notices of Am. Math. Soc., 1994—; mem. editorial adv. bd. Internat. Jour. Quantum Chemistry, 1996—; contbr. articles to profl. jours. NSF predoctoral fellow, 1965-69; recipient NSF Career Advancement award, 1988-89. Fellow AAAS (symposium organizer 1991, 94, nominating com. math. sect. 1991-94); mem. Internat. Assn. Math. Physicists, Am. Math. Soc. (reviewer, session chmn., com. 1987—, com. chmn.), Math. Assn. Am. (com.), Am. Phys. Soc. (reviewer), Assn. Women in Math., Assn. Women in Sci. (pres. New Eng. chpt. 1986-87), Appalachian Mountain Club (Boston; winter leader 1979—), Sigma Xi. Office: U Lowell Dept Math 1 University Ave Lowell MA 01854-2881

RUSS, JOANNA, writer, English language educator; b. N.Y.C., Feb. 22, 1937; d. Evarett and Bertha (Zinner) R. B.A. in English with high honors, Cornell, U., 1957; M.F.A. in Playwriting and Dramatic Lit, Yale U., 1960. Lectr. in English Cornell U., 1967-70, asst. prof., 1970-72; asst. prof. English, Harpur Coll., State U. N.Y. at Binghamton, 1972-75, U. Colo., 1975-77; asso. prof. English, U. Wash., 1977-90, prof., 1984-90. Author: Picnic on Paradise, 1968, And Chaos Died, 1970, The Female Man, 1975, We Who Are About To, 1977, Kittatinny: A Tale of Magic, 1978, The Two of Them, 1978, On Strike Against God, 1980, The Adventures of Alyx, 1983, The Zanzibar Cat, 1983, How To Suppress Women's Writing, 1983, Extra (Ordinary) People, 1984, Magic Mommas, Trembling Sisters, Puritans and Perverts: Feminist Essays, 1985, The Hidden Side of the Moon, 1987; also numerous short stories. Mem. Sci. Fiction Writers Am. (Nebula award for best short story 1972, Hugo award for best novella 1983). Address: 8961 E Lester St Tucson AZ 85715-5568

RUSS, NIKKI L., SR., inventory management professional; b. Chgo., Jan. 21, 1947; d. Elmer and Mary (Patch) Geisler; m. Richard E. McNair, Aug. 13, 1966 (div. 1968); 1 child, Adam F. McNair; m. Steven A. Russ, Aug. 18, 1970 (div. 1989); children: Virginia Marie, Nikki L. Jr. Attended, U. Detroit, 1967-68; BSBA, Roosevelt U., 1983. Dist. mgr. Dodge/Scan Photronics, Chgo., 1968-71; asst. dir. meat merchandising Dominick's Finer Foods, Northlake, Ill., 1977-84; sr. buyer BWD Automotive, Northlake, 1984-90; dir. inventory mgmt. Cooper Aviation, Elk Grove Village, Ill., 1990—; treas. Pet Pride of Ill., Chgo., 1973-75; CEO NRL, Inc., Hanover Park, Ill., 1995—. Contbr. articles to profl. jours. Den leader Cub Scouts Am., Chgo., 1974-77; election judge City of Chgo., 1974-78. Recipient Boy Scouts Am. award, 1977. Lutheran. Office: Cooper Aviation Industries Inc 2149 East Pratt Blvd Elk Grove Village IL 60007

RUSSAVAGE, KATHY A., research director; b. Pittston, Pa., Oct. 18, 1955; d. Clement Joseph and Elinor Ruth (Ostrowski) R. BS in Music Edn., Mansfield U., 1977; MA in Conducting & MA in Composition, U. Denver, 1980, 81; D of Musical Arts in Composition Theory, U. Ill., 1988, postgrad., 1988-89. Instr. vocal, gen. music Pittston (Pa.) Area Sch. Dist., 1977-78; dir. music St. Vincent De Paul Ch., Denver, 1979-81; grad. teaching asst., asst. conductor U. Denver Lamont Sch. Music, 1978-81, mgr. concert Phipps concert series, 1979-81; grad. teaching asst. U. Ill. Sch. Music, Urbana, 1982-84; officer placement & alumni rels. U. Ull. Grad. Sch. libr. & Info. Sci., Urbana, 1987-89; adminstrv. assoc. Singing City, Phila., 1989-90; coord. institutional rsch. U. of Arts, Phila., 1990-93; dir. instnl. rsch. St. Peter's Coll., Jersey City, N.J., 1993—; com. mem. St. Peter's Coll., 1994—, U. of Arts, 1990-93. Contbr. articles to profl. jours.; composer music. U. Denver Grad. Student Assn. Study grantee, 1979. Mem. NAFE, North East Assn. Instnl. Rsch., Phila Area Computer Soc. (mem. adv. com. 1992—), Assn. Instnl. Rsch., Coll. Music Soc. (mem. northeast dist. program sel. com. 1990-93), Phi Kappa Phi. Office: St Peters Coll 2641 John F Kennedy Blvd Jersey City NJ 07306-5943

RUSSEK, JANET ANN, photographer; b. Bklyn., Oct. 3, 1947; d. Harry and Esther Laura (Weinstein) Goldberg; m. Michael Russek (div. 1978); children: Jonathan, Andra; m. David I. Scheinbaum, Mar. 22, 1982; 1 child, Zachary. BA, Hunter Coll., 1970; MA, Bklyn. Coll., 1973. Co-owner, dir. Scheinbaum & Russek Ltd. Gallery of Photography, Santa Fe, 1980—; apprentice Bklyn. Mus., 1979-80; ind. curator photography Santa Fe Festival of the Arts, 1982; designer, co-coord. Santa Fe Ctr. Photography, 1982, 83, bd. dirs., 1983-85; founder, dir. N.Mex. Coun. Photography, 1984-95, Santa Fe Children's Mus., 1986-88; mem. visual arts adv. coun. Coll. Santa Fe, 1995—; coord. spl. projects in field. Exhibited in group shows at Armory for the Arts, Santa Fe, 1981, 84, 85, Sea Breeze Gallery, Block Island, R.I., 1982, 83, 84, Sweeney Ctr., Santa Fe, 1982, Phoenix (Ariz.) Art Mus., 1982, Jewish Cmty. Coun. Albuquerque, 1983, N.Mex. State U., Las Cruces, 1983, Santa Fe Ctr. Photography, 1983, 87, 89, The Jean Cocteau, Santa Fe, 1984, 91, St. John's Coll., Santa Fe, 1984, Fogelson Gallery, Coll. Santa Fe, 1985, Fox and Fowle, N.Y.C., 1985, The Periscope, Santa Fe, 1986, Scheinbaum & Russek Gallery, Santa Fe, 1987, 90, 93, Susan Spiritus Gallery, Newport Beach, Calif., 1987, Photo Gallery Internat., Tokyo, 1988, Art Ctr. Corpus Christie, Tex., 1990, 91, Abiquiu (N.Mex.) Inn Gallery, 1990, Sangre de Cristo Arts Ctr., Pueblo, Colo., 1991, Guadalupe Ch., Santa Fe, 1992, 93, N.Mex. Repertory Theatre, Santa Fe, 1993, Mus. N.Mex. at Gov.'s Gallery, Santa Fe, 1993, Coll. Santa Fe, 1993, Ctr. Photography at Woodstock, N.Y., 1993; represented in permanent collections Biblioteque Nationale, Paris, Chase Manhattan Bank, N.Y.C., Farnsworth Mus., Rockland, Maine, U. Tex., Austin, High Mus. Art, Atlanta, Mus. Fine Arts, Santa Fe, Rockwell Mus., Corning, N.Y.; contbr. to various publs. Santa Fe Coun. Arts grantee, 1983. Mem. Assn. Internat. Photography Art Dealers. Democrat. Jewish. Office: Scheinbaum & Russek Ltd 369 Montezuma Box 345 Santa Fe NM 87501

RUSSELL, ATTIE YVONNE, academic administrator, dean, pediatrics educator; b. Washington, Aug. 10, 1923; d. George and Kathleen L. (Milliner) Werner; m. Rex Hillier, Apr. 19, 1954 (dec.); m. Henry J. Russell, 1960 (div. 1971); children: Richard Russell, Margaret Jane Russell-Harde; m. Harry F. Camper, Sept. 2, 1984. BS, Am. U., 1944; PhD, State U. Iowa, 1952; MD, U. Chgo., 1958. Intern Phila. Gen. Hosp., 1958-59; resident in pediatrics Bronx (N.Y.) Mcpl. Hosp., 1960-61, Del. Hosp., Wilmington, 1962-63; dir. maternal and child health, crippled children's svcs. Del. State Bd. Health, Dover, 1963-68; asst. dean community health affairs, assoc. prof. pediatrics U. Cin. Coll. Medicine, 1968-71; clin. assoc. prof. pediatrics Med. Coll. Pa., Phila., 1966-68, 71-74; dep. dir. div. pub. health State of Del., Dover, 1971-74; dir. Santa Clara Valley Med. Ctr., San Jose, Calif., 1974-79; assoc. dean, clin. prof. pediatrics, family medicine Stanford (Calif.) U. Sch. Medicine, 1974-79; dir. USPHS Hosp., Boston, 1979-81, Balt. City Hosps., 1981-82; asst. v.p. community affairs, prof. pediatrics U. Tex. Med. Br., Galveston, 1982-87, asst. v.p. student affairs, dean students, prof. pediatrics, 1987-92, clin. prof. pediatrics, 1992—; reviewer Coun. for Internat. Exchange of Scholars, Washington, 1987-94; dir. III Symposium on Health and Human Svcs. in the U.S.-Mex., Brownsville, 1988; mem. sci. coun. Am. Fedn. for Aging Rsch., Inc., 1983-86. Contbr. articles and abstracts to profl. jours. Mem. budget com. United Way, Galveston, 1982-84; mem. Mayor's Adv. Com. for Sr. Citizens and Handicapped Persons for the City of Galveston, 1983-85; bd. dirs. Galveston County Coordinated Community Clinics, 1983-87; bd. advisors Galveston Hist. Found., 1983-88; mem. Com. for Coop. Action Planning, 1983-88, Houston-Galveston Health Promotion Consortium, 1983-88, Injury Control Prevention (Houston), 1984-89, aging programs adv. com. Houston-Galveston Area Coun., 1985-92. Recipient Disting. Alumni award Am. U., 1984. Fellow Am. Acad. Pediatrics, Am. Pub. Health Assn.; mem. AMA, Am. Coll. Preventive Medicine, Soc. for Adolescent Medicine, Am. Physiol. Soc., Am. Fedn. for Aging Rsch., Am. Geriatrics Soc., Mass. State Med. Soc., Galveston Med. Soc., Tex. Med. Assn., Tex. Pediatric Soc., Galveston C. of C. (legis. com. 1983-88), Order of Eastern Star, Sigma Xi, Alpha Omega Alpha.

RUSSELL, CARMEN MARTIN, guidance counselor; b. Bogalusa, La., Nov. 13, 1941; d. Gilbert Thomas and Flora Ina (McQuaig) Martin; m. Duane L. Russell; June 4, 1966; children: Ethan Alan, David Duane. BA, Southeastern La. U., 1970; MEd, 1974; edn. specialist, Jackson (Miss.) State U., 1987. cert. guidance counselor, elementary edn. Elem. tchr. St. Tammany Schs., Slidell, La., 1964-68, 1968-72; tchr. Brookhaven (Miss.) Sch. Dist., 1972-79, guidance counselor, 1979—; presenter Internat. Reading Assn., Toronto, Can., 1994; trainer Too Good for Drugs, C.E. Mendez, 1990. Recipient Tchr. Appreciation grant Urban Found., Brookhaven, Miss., 1981, 87. Mem. Order of the Eastern Star, Mumbling Mums, Miss. Counseling Assn., Kappa Kappa Iota, Phi Delta Kappa, Delta Kappa Gamma. Baptist. Home: RR 1 Box 141A Monticello MS 39654-9717

RUSSELL, CAROL ANN, personnel service company executive; b. Detroit, Dec. 14, 1943; d. Billy and Iris Koud; m. Victor Rojas (div.). BA in English, CUNY-Hunter Coll., 1993. Registered employment cons. Various positions in temp. help cos. N.Y.C., 1964-74; v.p. Wollborg-Michelson, San Francisco, 1974-82; co-owner, pres. Russell Staffing Resources, Inc., San Francisco and Sonoma, 1983—; media guest, spkr., workshop and seminar leader in field; host/cmty. prodr. Job Net program for TCI Cable T.V. Pub. Checkpoint Newsletter; contbr. articles to profl. publs. Named to the Inc. 500, 1989, 90. Mem. Am. Women in Radio & TV, Soc. to Preserve and Encourage Radio Drama Variety and Comedy, No. Calif. Human Resources Coun., Soc. Human Resource Mgmt., Calif. Assn. Pers. Cons. (pres. Golden State chpt. 1984-85), Calif. Assn. Temp. Svcs., Bay Area Pers. Assn. (pres. 1983-84), Pers. Assn. Sonoma County, Profl. Resume Writers of Am. Office: Russell Staffing Resources Inc 351 California St 8th Fl San Francisco CA 94104-4303

RUSSELL, CHARLOTTE SANANES, biochemistry educator, researcher; b. N.Y.C., Jan. 4, 1927; d. Joseph and Marguerite (Saltiel) Sananes; m. Joseph Brooke Russell, Dec. 20, 1947; children: James Robert, Joshua Sananes. BA, Bklyn. Coll., 1946; MA, Columbia U., 1947, PhD, 1951. Asst. prof. biochemistry CCNY, N.Y.C., 1958-68, assoc. prof., 1968-72, prof., 1972—; peer reviewer NSF, NIH; ad hoc reviewer sci. jours. including Jour. Bacteriology, Biochemistry. Contbr. articles to profl. jours. Mem. AAAS, AAUP, AAUW (internat. fellowship panel 1986-89), Am. Soc. Biochemistry and Molecular Biology, Am. Chem. Soc., Amnesty Internat., Urgent Action Network, Sigma Xi. Office: CCNY Dept Chemistry 138th St & Convent Ave New York NY 10031

RUSSELL, CONNIE B., elementary education educator; b. Union City, Tenn., June 9, 1941; d. Verne Edward Bolen and Mayme M. (Chambers) Dillard; m. Mac F. Barton, 1968 (div. 1980); children: Mandy, Bethany Ann; m. William C. Russell Jr., Feb. 14, 1988. BS in Edn., U. Tenn., 1962; postgrad., U. Memphis, 1979. Tchr. 5th grade Irondale Elem., Birmingham, Ala., 1962-64; various to tchr. fifth grade Una Elem., Nashville, 1964-65; tchr. fourth and sixth grades Lee Elem., Paris, Tenn., 1965-67; tchr. Raineshaven Elem., Memphis, 1967-70, Springdale Elem., Memphis, 1970-72; staff tchr. MCS Reading Ctr., Memphis, 1972-73; remedial reading tchr. Ga. Ave. Elem., Memphis, 1979-80; tchr. Lara Kendall Elem., Ridgely, Tenn., 1980-81; tchr. ABE, GED, devel. coll. courses Lake County Regional Prison, Tiptonville, Tenn., 1982-83; remedial reading tchr./tchr. fifth grade Caldwell Elem., Memphis, 1983-91; tchr. fourth/fifth grade Keystone Elem., Memphis, 1991-96; career ladder evaluator Tenn. State Dept. Edn., 1996—; presenter workshops in field. Dir. vacat. Bible sch., Decatur Trinity Christian Ch., Memphis, 1993, edn. dept., 1992; fundraiser Am. Cancer So. Grantee Rotary, Memphis, 1989, 91. Mem. NEA, Tenn. Edn. Assn., Memphis Edn. Assn., Nat. Coun. Tchrs. Math., PTA. Home: 231 W Main St Hornbeak TN 38232 Office: Keystone Elem 4301 Old Allen Rd Memphis TN 38128-1729

RUSSELL, FRANCIA, ballet director, educator; b. Los Angeles, Jan. 10, 1938; d. W. Frank and Marion (Whitney) R.; m. Kent Stowell, Nov. 19, 1965; children: Christopher, Darren, Ethan. Studies with, George Balanchine, Vera Volkova, Felia Doubrouska, Antonina Tumkovsky, Benjamin Harkarvy; student, NYU, Columbia U. Dancer, soloist N.Y.C. Ballet, 1956-62, ballet mistress, 1965-70; dancer Ballets USA/Jerome Robbins, N.Y.C., 1962; tchr. ballet Sch. Am. Ballet, N.Y.C., 1963-64; co-dir. Frankfurt (Fed. Republic Germany) Opera Ballet, 1976-77; dir., co-artistic dir. Pacific N.W. Ballet, Seattle, 1977—; dir. Pacific N.W. Ballet Sch., Seattle; affiliate prof. of dance U. Wash. Dir. staging over 100 George Balanchine ballet prodns. throughout world, including the Soviet Union and People's Republic of China, 1964—. Named Woman of Achievement, Matrix Table, Women in Comm., Seattle, 1987, Gov.'s Arts award, 1989, Dance Mag. award, 1996. Mem. Internat. Women's Forum. Home: 2833 Broadway E Seattle WA 98102-3935 Office: Pacific NW Ballet 301 Mercer St Seattle WA 98109-4600

RUSSELL, HARRIET SHAW, social worker; b. Detroit, Apr. 12, 1952; d. Louis Thomas and Lureleen (Hughes) Shaw; m. Donald Edward Russell, June 25, 1980; children: Lachante Tyree, Krystal Lanae. BS, Mich. State U., 1974; AB, Detroit Bus. Inst., 1976; BA in Pub. Adminstrn., Mercy Coll. Detroit, 1988; MSW, Wayne State U., 1992. Factory employee Gen. Motors Corp., Lansing, Mich., 1973; student supr. tour guides State of Mich., Lansing, 1974; mgr. Ky. Fried Chicken, Detroit, 1974-75; unemployment claims examiner State of Mich. Dept. Labor, Detroit, 1975-77, asst. payment worker, 1977-84, social svcs. specialist, 1984-90; ind. contractor Detroit Compact pres. Victory Enterprises, 1991; sch. social worker Detroit Bd. of Edn., 1992—; moderator Michigan Opportunity Skills and Tng. Program, 1985-86. Vol. Mich. Cancer Soc., East Lansing, 1970-72, Big Sisters/Big Bros., Lansing, 1972-73; elected rep. Mich. Coun. Social Svcs. Workers; speaker Triumphant Bapt. Ch., Detroit, 1976-80; chief union steward Mich. Employees Assn., Lincoln Park, 1982-83; leader Girl Scouts U.S.; area capt. Life Worker Project Program. Recipient Outstanding Work Performance Merit award Mich. Dept. Social Services, 1979, Unsung Hero award Neighborhood Found., 1995; grad. profl. scholar, 1990-91, Dean's scholar, 1991-92; elected to Wayne State Sch. Social Work Bd., 1992—. Mem. NAFE, Am. Soc. Profl. and Exec. Women, Assn. Internat. Platform Speakers, Mich. Coun. Social Svcs. Workers, Nat. Fedn. Bus. and Profl. Women's Clubs, Inc. U.S.A. (elected del. to China), Nat. Assn. Black Social Workers, Wayne State U. Social Work Alumni Assn. (bd. dirs. 1992—), Delta Sigma Theta. Democrat. Baptist. Office: PO Box 361 Lincoln Park MI 48146-0361

RUSSELL, JOYCE ANNE ROGERS, librarian; b. Chgo., Nov. 6, 1920; d. Truman Allen and Mary Louise (Hoelzle) Rogers; m. John VanCleve Russell, Dec. 24, 1942; children: Malcolm David, John VanCleve. Student, Adelphi Coll., 1937; B.S. in Chemistry, U. Ky., 1942; M.L.S., Rosary Coll., 1967; postgrad., Rutgers U., 1970-71. Research chemist Sherwin Williams Paint Co., Chgo., 1942-45; reference librarian Chicago Heights (Ill.) Pub. Library, 1959-61; librarian Victor Chem. Works, Chicago Heights, 1961-62; lit. chemist Velsicol Chem. Corp., Chgo., 1964-67; chemistry librarian U. Fla., Gainesville, 1967-69; interim assoc. prof. U. Fla., 1967-69; librarian Thiokol Chem. Corp., Trenton, N.J., 1969-73; supr. library operations E.R. Squibb Co., Princeton, N.J., 1973-80, sr. research info scientist, 1980-91; mem. library adv. commn. Mercer Community Coll., 1979—; adv. asso. Rutgers U. Grad. Sch. Library and Info. Scis., 1978—. Editor: Bibliofile, 1967-69; contbg. articles to profl. jours. Mem. PTA, 1950-66; den mother Cub Scouts, 1952-59. Mem. Spl. Libraries Assn. (sec., dir., v.p., pres. Princeton-Trenton 1971, 75-80), Am. Chem. Soc. (bus. mgr., sec., dir. Trenton sect. 1969-78), AAUW, Mortar Board, Beta Phi Mu, Sigma Pi

Sigma, Chi Delta Phi, Pi Sigma Alpha. Home: 1189 Parkside Ave Trenton NJ 08618-2625

RUSSELL, JOYCE WEBER, principal; b. Detroit, Feb. 21, 1948; d. Ronald Robert and Eleanor Treva (Burns) Weber; m. James Edward Russell, Mar. 25, 1970; 1 child, Jennifer Eileen. AA, Palm Beach C.C., Lake Worth, Fla., 1968; BA, Fla. Atlantic U., 1970, MA, 1975. Cert. tchr., prin. Tchr. Palm Beach County Sch. Bd., West Palm Beach, Fla., 1970-79, staff devel. specialist, 1979-84; asst. prin. Allamanda Elem., 1984-88; prin. Addison Mizner Elem., Boca Raton, Fla., 1988-90, South Olive Elem., West Palm Beach, 1990-95; adminstr. Safe Schs. AFTER Sch. Programs, Sch. Police, 1995—. Chair Vision 2000 Good Shepherd Meth. Ch., West Palm Beach, 1990-95; mem. Leadership Palm Beach County, 1990-96. Mem. NAESP, ASCD, Fla. Assn. Sch. Administrs., Palm Beach County Adminstr. Assn., Phi Delta Kappa. Office: Sch Bd Palm County Dept Sch Police # 121B 3330 Forest Hill Blvd West Palm Beach FL 33405-4769

RUSSELL, JUDY ELAINE, family and consumer science educator; b. Ohio County, Ky., Apr. 14, 1950; d. Ralph and Ruby Jean (Nabours) R. BS, Western Ky. U., 1972, MA in Edn., 1974. Home econs. tchr. Ohio County Schs., Hartford, Ky., 1972-73, 74-75; child care svcs. instr. Meade County Vocat., Brandenburg, Ky., 1975-78, 85-88; home econs. curriculum specialist U. Ky., Lexington, 1978-79, Ky. Dept. of Edn., Frankfort, 1979-85; home econs. tchr. Franklin County Schs., Frankfort, 1988-91; head start tchr. Audubon Area Community Svc., Fordsville, Ky., 1992; life skills tchr. Ohio County Schs., Hartford, 1992—; freelance writer Nat. Instructional Media Co. Mem. Youth Svcs. Ctr. Adv. Coun., Hartford, 1992-95; babysitting instr. Ohio County ARC, Hartford, 1992—; rep. Edn. Found., 1995-96, v.p. leadership, 1996-97. Recipient Golden Apple award Ashland Oil Co., 1994. Mem. NEA, ASCD, Am. Vocat. Assn., Ky. Vocat. Assn., Nat. Vocat. Assn., Ohio County Edn. Assn., Ky. Edn. Assn., Alpha Delta Kappa (Pi chpt., v.p. 1994-96), Phi Delta Kappa. Democrat. Mem. LDS.

RUSSELL, LAURA WIMBERLY, artist; b. Rapid City, S.D., Aug. 17, 1949; d. Charles Leslie Wimberly and Peggy (Whitehead) Minier; m. Michael L. Russell, Aug. 21, 1971 (dec. Feb. 1986). BA in Creative Studies, U. Calif., Santa Barbara, 1970; MA, San Jose State U., 1974. art tchr., Cusco, Peru; developer, dir. The Mobile Art Studio, Cusco, Peru, 1991—. One-woman shows William Sawyer Gallery, San Francisco, 1976, Art Mus. South Tex., Corpus Christi, 1980, Watson de Nagy Gallery, Houston, 1988, Watson/Willour Gallery, Houston 1981, U. Redlands, Calif., 1982, Contemporary Arts Mus., Houston, 1983, Hadler/Rodriguez Gallery, Houston, 1983, 84, Canancuhua Gallery, Corpus Christi, 1985, Southwest Tex. U., 1985, Fuller Goldeen Gallery, Houston, 1987, 88, Berman Gallery, Palo Alto, Calif., 1988, Butler Gallery, 1989, 90, Kimpton Gallery, San Francisco, 1991, Lew Allen Gallery, Santa Fe, 1991, Brian Gross Fine, San Francisco, 1992, 93, 96, Inst. Cultural Peruano Nonteamericana, Lima, Peru, 1993, Ctr. de Estudios Andinos, Cusco, Peru, 1994, 95. Fellow NEA, 1981. Home: 110 De La Costa Ave Santa Cruz CA 95060-6321 Studio: 2537B Mission St Santa Cruz CA 95060-5727

RUSSELL, LILLIAN, medical, surgical nurse; b. N.Y.C., Feb. 21, 1942; d. Joserelle Russell; 1 child, Evan Gregory. AAS, N.Y.C. Community Coll., 1973; BS, St. Xavier Coll., Chgo., 1986; MS, Spertus Coll. of Judaica, Chgo., 1989. Staff/charge nurse Beth Israel Med. Ctr., N.Y.C., 1973-76; charge nurse Roosevelt Hosp., N.Y.C., 1977-78; staff/charge nurse U. Ill. Hosp., Chgo., 1979-90; asst. adminstrv. coord. Bethany Hosp., Chgo., 1990-91; adminstv. nurse I Mile Square Health Ctr. & U. Ill. Hosp., Chgo., 1991-95; asst. dir. nursing Mile Square Health Ctr., Chgo., 1995—; mem. instnl. rev. com. Bethany Hosp., 1987—; adj. asst. prof. Trinity Christian Coll., Palos Heights, Ill., 1996—. Mem. Great Cities Com., Chgo., 1994—. Mem. ANA, NAFE, AAUW, Ill. Nurses Assn., Res. Officers Assn. Home: 1342 N Oakley Blvd Chicago IL 60622-3048

RUSSELL, LINDA GAIL, accountant, consultant; b. Yakima, Wash., July 4, 1955; d. Bobby and Idella Mae (Rice) Crain; m. Thomas McCord, Apr. 1, 1972 (div. Mar. 1983); children: Michelle L., Heather Nicole. BS in Fin., Okla. State U., 1990. CPA. Staff acct. Melton Truck Lines, Inc., Tulsa; contr. Borg Compressed Steel, Tulsa; acct. Integral Mgmt. Svcs., Tulsa. Vol. Tulsa Rep. Com., 1992—; vol. ASTA Tulsa Opera, Tulsa, 1985, Kanchi Fund Raiser, Tulsa, 1985, Mayfest, Tulsa, 1983; class planner So. Hills Bapt. Ch., 1994. Mem. Inst. Mgmt. Accts., Am. Soc. Women Accts. (v.p. attendance 1993), Soc. Women Against Abuse of Kids, Golden Key, Tulsa C. of C. (bd. mem. Goals for Tomorrow), Phi Theta Kappa, Beta Gamma Sigma. Office: Integral Mgmt Svcs PO Box 29 Tulsa OK 74101-0029

RUSSELL, MARGARET JONES (PEG RUSSELL), secondary school educator; b. Durham, N.C., Apr. 25, 1938; d. Roderic O. and Margaret (Moore) Jones; m. Michael Morgan Russell; children: Lauren Skinner, Carol Martin, Seth Russell, Jay Russell. BA, Muskingum Coll., 1961. Ordained deacon Presbyn. Ch., 1970. Tchr. Sarasota (Fla.) County Sch. Bd., 1962—, Sarasota H.S., 1982—; sponsor literary mag. Quest, 1988—. Editor: (newsletter) The Mainsail, 1992-95; contbr. poems to profl. pubs. ARC vol. Sarasota Meml. Hosp., 1966-83, aux. vol., 1994—; reader Fla. Studio Theatre, Sarasota, 1980—. Sarasota Herald Tribune scholar, 1993; Fla. Writing Project fellow, 1990. Mem. Nat. Coun. Tchrs. English, Fla. Coun. Tchrs. English, Fla. Freelance Writers, Light Verse Workshop (co-chair 1995), Sarasota Fiction Writers, Meadows Country Club, Alpha Gamma Delta. Republican. Presbyterian. Home: 1150 Willis Ave Sarasota FL 34232-2148 Office: Sarasota HS 1000 S School Ave Sarasota FL 34237-8016

RUSSELL, MARJORIE ROSE, manufacturing company executive; b. Welcome, Minn., Sept. 3, 1925; d. Emil Frederick and Ella Magdalene (Sothman) Wohlenhaus; m. Kenneth Kollmann Russell, Sept. 15, 1947 (div. May 1973); children: Jennie Rose, Richard Lowell, Laura Eloise, James Wesley. Student, Northwestern Sch., Mpls., 1944-45, St. Paul Bible Inst., 1946-47. Cook U. Minn., Mpls., 1943-45; maintenance person U. Farm Campus/N.W. Schs., St. Paul, 1945-46; clk. Kresge Corp., Mpls., 1945; cook, waitress, mgr. Union City Mission Bible Camp, Mpls., 1944-47; caterer for v.p. Gt. No. R.R., St. Paul, 1947; custodian Old Soldiers Home, St. Paul, 1946; nurse Sister Elizabeth Kenney Polio Hosp., St. Paul, 1946; seamstress Hirsch, Weis, White Stag, Pendleton, Mayfair, Portland, Oreg., 1960-72; owner, operator, contract mgr., creative designer The Brass Needle, Portland, 1972—; contractor Forrester's Sanderson Safety, Scotsco, Nero & Assocs., Gara Gear, Portland, 1972—, Columbia Sportswear; tchr. Indo Chinese Cultural Ctr., Portland, 1982; mfr. of protective chaps and vests for the Pacific Northwest hogging industry. Designer, producer Kisn Bridal Fair, 1969; composer: He Liveth in Me, 1968; prodr. Safety Chaps for Loggers. Sec. Model Cities Com., Portland, 1969; com. mem. Neighborhood Black Christmas Parade, Portland, 1970; custume designer Local Miss Jr. Black Beauty Contest, Portland, 1973; nominating com. Nat. Contract Mgmt. Assn., Portland, 1978; mem. nominating com. Multi-Cultural Sr. Adv. Com., 1988-91. Mem. NAFE, Urban League, Urban League Guild (historian 1991-92), Am. Assn. Ret. Persons, Nat. Contract Mgmt. Assn. Democrat. Mem. United Ch. of Christ. Home and Office: The Brass Needle 2809 NE 12th Ave Portland OR 97212-3219

RUSSELL, MARY WENDELL VANDER POEL, non-profit organization executive, interior; b. N.Y.C., Feb. 6, 1919; d. William Halsted and Blanche Pauline (Billings) Vander Poel; m. George Montagu Miller, Apr. 5, 1940 (div. 1974); children: Wendell Miller Steavenson, Gretchen Miller Elkus; m. Sinclair Hatch, May 14, 1977 (dec. July 1989); m. William F. Russell, June 24, 1995 (dec. Apr. 1996). Pres. Miller Richard, Inc., Interior Decorators, Glen Head, N.Y., 1972—; bd. dirs. Eye Bank Sight Restoration, N.Y.C., 1975—, pres., 1980-88, hon. chair, 1988—; bd. dirs. Manhattan Eye Ear and Throat Hosp., N.Y.C., 1966-92, v.p., 1978-90; sec. Cold Spring Harbor Lab., N.Y., 1985-89, 92—, bd. dirs., 1985-90; chair DNA Learning Ctr., 1991—; bd. dirs. Cold Spring Harbor Lab, 1991—, sec., 1992—. V.p. North Country Garden Club, Nassau County, N.Y., 1979-81, 1983-85; dir. Planned Parenthood Nassau County, Mineola, N.Y., 1982-84, Hutton House C.W.Post Coll.,Greenvale, N.Y., 1982—; chair Hutton House, 1992-94. Recipient Disting. Trustee award United Hosp. Fund, 1992. Mem. Colony Club (N.Y.C.), Church Club (N.Y.C.), Piping Rock Club (Long Island), Order St. John Jerusalem (N.Y.C.). Republican. Episcopalian. Home: Mill River Rd # 330 Oyster Bay NY 11771-2733

RUSSELL, PAMELA REDFORD, writer, film documentarian; b. Long Beach, Calif., June 11, 1950; d. George Martin and Helen Glyn (Brewen) R.; m. Robert John Colleary, 1984 (div. 1993); children: Caitlin, Maggie, Tess. Student, UCLA, 1970-74. Field prodr. Santa Fe Comm., L.A., 1983-84; exec. prodr. Guiding Star Prodns., L.A., 1994—. Author: The Woman Who Loved John Wilkes Booth, 1978, Wild Flowers, 1982, (screenplay) Am American Woman, 1993; writer for Mary Tyler Moore Show, 1974, also 14 scripts for Sears and Mut. Radio Theater, 1980-81. Mem. Nat. Trust for Hist. Preservation, Civil War Trust., Pacific Grove Heritage Soc. Mem. Authors Guild, Writers Guild Am. West. Agency: Parradigm # 2500 10100 Santa Monica Blvd Los Angeles CA 90067-4003

RUSSELL, PATRICIA COOPER, foundation administrator; b. Houston, Feb. 5, 1944; d. Austin Eli and Sarah Lorraine (Rountree) Dawkins; children from previous marriage: Catherine Sloane, Sarah Riley, Patricia Daily; m. Robert B. Russell, Jr., Aug. 3, 1996. BA, Columbia Coll., 1965; grad. Williamsburg Devel. Inst., 1990. Appointments sec. to Congressman Tom Gettys, Washington, 1965; tchr. Lugoff (S.C.) Elem. Sch., 1967-68, Camden (S.C.) Elem. Sch., 1969-70; ombudsman State of S.C., 1970-73; asst. dir. Carolina Cup and Colonial Cup Internat. Steeplechase, Camden, 1973-87; adminstr. Camden Feed Co., 1973-87; office mgr. Camden Tng. Ctr., thoroughbreds, 1973-87; asst. sec. Mulberry Resources, Inc., 1980-82; sec.-treas. Equistar Products Co., 1980-87; mktg. dir. Holiday Inn of Lugoff-Camden, Holiday Inn of Sumter, S.C., 1987-88; dir. Devel. Bapt. Med. Ctr. Found., 1988-89; exec. v.p. S.C. State Mus. Found., Columbia, 1989—. Bd. dirs. Kershaw County Fine Arts Ctr., Columbia Devel. Corp.; sustaining mem. Camden Jr. Welfare League; mem. Inaugural Class, Leadership Kershaw County, 1986-87, participant Statewide Program, 1987-88; adv. com. Charleston Steeplechase; mem. Santee-Lynches Coun. Govts., 1987-88; bd. dirs. Kershaw County unit Am. Cancer Soc., 1980-90; chmn. bd. dirs. Kershaw unit Am. Heart Assn., 1984-86; bd. dirs. Palmetto Balloon Classic, 1983-86; mem. Bd. Appeals, City of Camden, 1985-87; vice chmn. Kershaw County Tourism Adv. Com., 1987-88; adminstrv. bd. Lyttleton St. United Meth. Ch., Camden, 1986-88; chmn. leadership com. Kershaw County, 1988-89; mem. Columbia Action Coun., 1988-90, Columbia Forum, 1988—; adv. com. S.C. Joint Legis. Com. on Cultural Affairs, 1989-96; active Assembly on the Future of S.C., 1989; trustee S.C. bd. Leukemia Soc. of Am., 1987-91; mem. strategic planning com. City of Columbia, 1995-96. Mem. Nat. Soc. Fundraising Execs. (mem. regional bd. 1993—), Am. Assn. Mus., Media Club of Columbia, Greater Kershaw County C. of C. (v.p. pub. affairs 1983-86, William F. Nettles award 1988), Thoroughbred Assn. S.C. (sec.-treas. 1986-88), Leadership S.C. Alumni (bd. dirs. 1988-93, pres. 1992-93), S.C. Exec. Inst., Future Group of Richland County (cultural resources chair 1994), Newcomen Soc. of the U.S., S.C. Bd. Dirs., Greater Columbia C. of C., Capital City Club, Sprindale Hall Club, Univ. Assocs. Club, Rotary (mem. bd. dirs. Columbia, 1993-96, Paul Harris fellow). Methodist. Home: 115 Shallow Brook Dr Columbia SC 29223 Office: SC State Mus Found PO Box 100107 Columbia SC 29202-3107

RUSSELL, PEGGY TAYLOR, soprano, educator; b. Newton, N.C., Apr. 5, 1927; d. William G. and Sue B. (Cordell) Taylor; Mus.B. in Voice, Salem Coll., 1948; Mus.M., Columbia U., 1950; postgrad. U. N.C., Greensboro, 1977; student Am. Inst. Mus. Studies, Austria, 1972, 78; student of Clifford Bair, Nell Starr, Salem Coll., Winston-Salem, N.C., Edgar Schofield, Chloe Owen, N.Y.C.; student opera-dramatics Boris Goldovsky, Southwestern Opera Inst., Ande Andersen, Max Lehner, Graz, Austria; m. John B. Russell, Feb. 23, 1952; children: John Spotswood, Susan Bryce. Mem. faculty dept. voice Guilford Coll., Greensboro, 1952-53, Greensboro Coll., 1971-72; pvt. tchr. voice, Greensboro, 1963—; co-founder, v.p. sales, mktg. Russell Textiles, Inc., 1988; vis. instr. in voice U. N.C., Chapel Hill, 1973-77; founding artistic dir., gen. mgr. Young Artists Opera Theatre, Greensboro, 1983; staged and produced 18 operatic prodns., 1983-91; guest lectr. opera workshop U. N.C., Greensboro, 1990-91; lectr. opera Friends of Weymouth, So. Pines, N.C., 1994; lectr. on music history and opera, High Point, N.C., Center for Creative Leadership, Greensboro, 1979-80, First Presbyn. Ch., 1982; debut in light opera as Gretchen in The Red Mill, Winston-Salem Opera Assn., 1947; debuts include: Rosalinda in Die Fledermaus, Piedmont Festival Opera Assn., 1949, Lola in Cavalleria Rusticana, Greensboro Opera Assn., 1951, Violetta in La Traviata, Greensboro Opera Assn., 1953, Fiordiligi in Cosi fan tutte, Piedmont Opera Co., 1956; appeared as Marguerite in Faust, Brevard Music Center Resident Opera Co., 1967, First Lady in The Magic Flute, Am. Inst. Mus. Studies, Graz, Austria, 1972; mem. Greensboro Oratorio Soc., 1955-59, soprano soloist in The Messiah, 1952, 58, The Creation, 1955, Solomon, 1958; soprano soloist Presbyterian Ch. of the Covenant, Greensboro, 1958-71; guest appearances Sta. WFMY-TV, Greensboro, 1958-62; soprano soloist with Greensboro Symphony Orch., 1964, 80, Eastern Music Festival Orch. 1965, Greensboro Civic Orch., 1980; soloist in numerous recitals including: Wesleyan Coll., 1964, Roanoke Symphony Guild, 1967, Am. Inst. Mus. Studies, Austria, 1972, 78, U. N.C., Chapel Hill, 1974, 75, 76, 77, N.C. Mus. of Art, 1978; recital, masterclass Mars Hill Coll., 1981. Bd. dirs. Music Theater Assocs., Greensboro Friends of Music, N.C. Lyric Opera; judge Charlotte Opera Guild Auditions, 1994. Mem. Friendship Force of Guilford County, Holland, 1985, No. Germany, 1987. scholarship grantee N.C. Arts Council and Nat. Endowment for the Arts, 1991. Mem. Nat. Opera Assn. (chmn. regional opera cos. com. 1985-91, judge vocal competition auditions 1991, 92, 94, chmn. trustees Cofield Endowment 1991), Central Opera Service, Nat. Assn. Tchrs. of Singing (state gov. 1976-82, coordinator Regional Artist Contest 1982-84), N.C. Fedn. Music Clubs (dir. 1956-58), Music Educators Nat. Conf., Greensboro Music Tchrs. Assn. (pres. 1966-67), Symphony Guild (dir. 1977-78), Broadway Theater League (chmn. 1961-63), Atlanta Opera Guild, Civic Music Assn. (chmn. 1963-64), English Speaking Union (bd. dirs. Greensboro chpt., chmn. Shakespeare competition 1995), N.C. Symphony Soc., Piedmont Triad Coun. Internat. Vis. (Appreciation award Nat. Coun. Internat. Visitors 1994), Greensboro Preservation Soc., Guilford County Planning/Devel. Office (Forecast 2015 Com.). Presbyterian. Clubs: Sherwood Swim and Racquet, The Greensboro City. Home: 3012 W Cornwallis Dr Greensboro NC 27408-6730

RUSSELL, ROSEMARIE M., artist, consultant; b. Albuqueque, May 21, 1953; d. Richard Anthony Michael and Edna Geraldine Helm Garrison; m. M. Reid Russell, Mar. 4, 1978. Bd. cert. dental ceramist; bd. cert. in crown and bridge. Technician Lifemark Dental Svcs., Albuquerque, 1972; dept. head Lifemark Dental Svcs., New Orleans, 1974; prodn. mgr. Lifemark Dental Svcs., Salt Lake City, 1976-80; owner Oral Arts Lab., Salt Lake City, 1980-91; sculptor, painter, goldsmith By Rosemarie, Salt Lake City, 1980—. Patentee process for finishing a bronze sculpture, process for finishing a painting. Bd. dirs., lobbyist Women State Legis. Coun., Salt Lake City, 1982-86; mem., com. chair, lobbyist Jr. League of Salt Lake City, 1983-88; mem., del. Salt Lake Coun. of Women, 1981-83. Mem. Internat. Sculpture Ctr., Nat. Sculpture Soc., Nat. Assn. Parliamentarians (parliamentarian, cons. 1983—), Utah Opera Guild, Salt Lake Ballet Guild, U. Utah Mus. Fine Arts. Home: 3986 Mt Olympus Way Salt Lake City UT 84124

RUSSELL, SALLY LYNN KOLITZ, clinical and neuropsychologist; b. Jersey City, Mar. 31, 1943; d. Norman and Sylvia (Goldstein) Ostrow; m. Elbert W. Russell, Apr. 2, 1989; 1 child, Brent Kolitz. BA, Vanderbilt U., 1965; MEd, U. Fla., 1967; PhD in Clin. Psychology, U. Miami (Fla.), 1986. Lic. psychologist, Fla.; diplomate Am. Bd. Profl. Disability Cons. Tchr. Bronson (Fla.) High Sch., 1965-66; dir. counseling Chamberlayne Jr. Coll., Boston, 1967-68; indsl. psychologist Gillette Co., Boston, 1968-69; dir. family life edn. Family Svc., Miami, 1971-75; researcher, grantee Am. Heart Assn., Miami, 1978-80; pvt. practice psychology Miami, 1986—. Author: Psychology of the Cardiac Patient, 1980, 88. Mem. APA, Nat. Acad. Neuropsychologists, Internat. Neuropsychology Soc., Sigma Xi. Office: 6262 Sunset Dr Ph 228 Miami FL 33143-4843

RUSSELL, STELLA PANDELL, artist, author, educator; b. N.Y.C., June 14, 1927; d. James C. and Dorothy (Ross) Pandell; m. George Russell, Aug. 10, 1951 (dec.); children: Janna, Jonathan, Loriann. BA, Hunter Coll., 1948; MA, Columbia U., 1950, PhD, 1972; M in Comml. Arts, N.Y. Inst. Tech., 1986. Animator, Loucks and Norling Co., 1948; dir. art Alexander's Dept. Stores, N.Y.C., 1948-51; tchr. art pub. schs., N.Y.C., 1951-53; co-dir. Russell-Pandell Art Studies, N.Y.C., 1953-61; lectr. art Hunter Coll., N.Y.C., 1961-65; pres., chmn. art Nassau Community Coll., N.Y., from 1965; one-woman shows include: Oyster Bay Library (N.Y.), 1962, 63, Huntington Library, 1970, Nassau Community Coll., 1971, South Nassau Library, 1973, 83, Firehouse Gallery, 1975, 84, Country Art Gallery, 1977; group shows include: N.Y. State U. traveling exhbn., 1969, St. John's U., 1975, Central Hall Gallery, 1976, C.W. Post Coll., 1977, Royal Acad., Stockholm, 1978, 82, Islip Mus., 1985, Fine Art Mus. of Lit., 1987; represented permanent collections Hunter Coll., Sallskapet, Sweden; host Art in World sta. WHPC, Garden City, 1972—. Author: Art in the World, 1975, 84, 89; contbr. articles to profl. jours. Winner Chancellor's award excellence in teaching, 1982. Mem. Profl. Artists Guild, N.Y. State Ann. Jr. Colls., N.Y. State African Studies Assn. Unitarian. Club: Mensa. Home: 29 Tiffany Rd Oyster Bay NY 11771-1907 also: 190 Lawton Rd Hilton Head SC 29928 Office: Stewart Ave Garden City NY 11530

RUSSELL, SUE ELLEN, lawyer; b. Centre, Pa., Aug. 17, 1959; d. Richard Basil and Patricia Ann (Garofolo) Glazer; m. David Tyler Russell, Oct. 6, 1990. BA, U. Va., 1981; JD, Am. U., Washington, 1987. Bar: Va. 1987, D.C. 1988. Staff asst. Rep. Stanley Lundine, Washington, 1981-84, Senator Gary Hart, Washington, 1984-85; law clk. Legal Aid Soc., Prince Georges County, Md., 1985; appellate clk. U.S. Atty's. Office, Appellate, Washington, 1986-87; jud. clk. to Chief Judge William C. Pryor, Washington, 1987-88; assoc. Brand & Lowell, Washington, 1988-94, ptnr., 1994-95; mng. ptnr. Russell & Russell, PC, Falls Church, Va., 1995—; del. Jud. Conf., Washington, 1988-90. Mem. ABA, Va. State Bar, D.C. Bar. Democrat. Office: Russell & Russell PC 211 Park Ave Falls Church VA 22046

RUSSELL, THERESA LYNN, actress; b. San Diego, Mar. 20, 1957; d. Jerry Russell Paup and Carole (Mall) Platt; m. Nicholas Jack Roeg, Feb. 12, 1986; children: Statten Jack, Maximilian Nicolas Sextus. Appeared in films including The Last Tycoon, 1976, Straight Time, 1977, Blind Ambition, 1978, Bad Timing, 1980, Eureka, 1981, Razor's Edge, 1983, Insignificance, 1984, Aria, 1984, Black Widow, 1985 (Nat. Assn. Theater Owners award 1985), Track 29, 1986 (Newcomer of Yr. award), Physical Evidence, 1987, Impulse, 1988, Cold Heaven, 1989 (Best Actress award Viareggio Film Festival 1991), Whore, 1990, Kafka, 1990, Thicker Than Water, 1992, Flight of the Dove, 1994, The Trade Off, 1994, (narrator) Being Human, 1994, Grotesque, 1995; TV movies Blind Ambition, 1979, Women's Guide to Adultery, 1993; BBC radio play Double Indemnity, 1993. *

RUSSO, D. CHRISTINE FIORELLA, English educator; b. N.Y.C., July 24, 1931; d. Anthony Joseph and Assunta Mary (Moroni) Fiorella; m. Victor Donald Russo, Jr., Apr. 30, 1960. BA, Marymount Manhattan Coll.; MS, Fordham U., 1959; diploma in reading, Hofstra U., 1978, PhD, 1987, postgrad., 1987—; cert. in litigation, Adelphi U. and Nat. Ctr. for Paralegal Tng., 1980. Cert. elem. and secondary English tchr., N.Y., reading specialist, N.Y. Tchr. St. Margaret's Sch., Bronx, N.Y., 1955-56, Sacred Heart, Manhattan, N.Y., 1956-57, Bd. Edn., N.Y.C., 1957-60, Harborfields Dist. 6, L.I., 1960—; 1st v.p. Marymount Manhattan Coll.; English instr. Marymount Manhattan Coll., N.Y., 1st v.p. Bd. dirs. Marymount Alumnae Adv. Coun., N.Y., 1985—, 1st v.p.; bd. dirs. Fordham U. Pres.'s Coun., Bronx, 1985-87, Fordham U. Recruitment Program, Bronx, 1983-87, Fordham U. Alumnae/i Adv. Bd. Coun., 1994—; campaign worker Dem. Party, N.Y.C., 1990, 92; Marymount rep. N.Y. State Bundy/Affairs Fund, 1982-83; L.I. rep. Marymount Recruitment Program, 1992; chmn. Ft. Salong Assn., L.I., 1979-83; campaign worker Dem. Party, N.Y.C., 1992, 94; vol. St. John's Hosp., L.I.; co-dir. Just Say No Thomas J. Lahey Sch. Recipient Tchr.-Student Participation award Suffolk Reading Coun., 1991-96, Tchr.-Student Participation award 3d, 4th, and 5th N.Y. Senate Earth Day Competition, 1994, 95. Mem. APA, Guilford Internat. Soc. Intelligence Edn. (v.p. 1991—, bd. dirs. 1990—), N.Y. Acad. Scis., N.Y. Orton Dyslexia Soc., Nat. Dyslexia Rsch. Found., Coun. for Exceptional Children, World Coun. for Gifted and Talented Children, Children and Adults with Attention Deficit Disorder, Am. Assn. Higher Edn., Marymount Manhattan Coll. (1st v.p. 1995—), Fordham U. Alumni Assn. (bd. dirs. adv. coun. Sch. Edn. 1995, 96). Roman Catholic. Home: 7 Bonnie Dr Northport NY 11768-1448

RUSSO, IRMA HAYDEE ALVAREZ DE, pathologist; b. San Rafael, Mendoza, Argentina, Feb. 28, 1942; came to U. S., 1972; d. Jose Maria and Maria Carmen (Martinez) de Alvarez; m. Jose Russo, Feb. 8, 1969; 1 child, Patricia Alexandra. BA, Escuela Normal MTSM de Balcarce, 1959; MD, U. Nat. of Cuyo, Mendoza, 1970. Diplomate Am. Bd. Pathology. Intern Sch. of Medicine Hosps., Argentina, 1969-70; resident in pathology Wayne State U. Sch. Medicine, Detroit, 1976-80; rsch. asst. and instr. Inst. of Histology and Embryology Sch. Medicine U. Nat. of Cuyo, 1963-71, assoc. prof. histology Faculty of Phys., Chem. and Math. Scis., 1970-72; rsch. assoc. Inst. for Molecular and Cellular Evolution, U. Miami, Fla., 1972-73; rsch. assoc. exptl. pathology lab. div. biol. scis., Mich. Cancer Found., Detroit, 1973-75, rsch. scientist, 1975-76, vis. rsch. scientist, 1976-82, asst. mem., pathologist, 1982-89, assoc. rsch. mem., 1989-91, co-dir. pathology reference lab., 1982-86, chief exptl. pathology lab., 1989-91; co-dir. Mich. Cancer Found. Lab. Svcs., 1986-91; mem. Dept. Pathology Fox Chase Cancer Ctr., 1991—, dir. anatomic pathology, 1991-92; dir. Lab. Svcs., 1992-94; chief molecular endocrinology sect. Breast Cancer Rsch. Lab. Fox Chase Cancer Ctr., 1994—; mem. dept. pathology Fox Chase Cancer Ctr., Phila., 1992—; chief resident physician dept. pathology Wayne State U. Sch. Medicine, 1978-80, asst. prof., 1980-82; mem. staff Harper-Grace Hosps., Detroit, 1980-82; adj. prof. Pathology and Cell Biology Jefferson Sch. of Medicine/Thomas Jefferson Univ., 1992—; mem. endocrinology panel peer rev. com. breast cancer rsch. program U.S. Army R&D Command, 1994, 95, 96; ad-hoc mem. biochem. endocrinology study sect. NIH, DHHS, 1994; mem. bd. scientific counselor, sec. of health & human svcs. Nat. Toxicology Program Bd., 1994—; mem. Internat. Life Scis. Inst.-Risk Sc. Inst. Mammary Working Group, 1992—; pres., founder League of Women Against Cancer, Rydal, Pa., 1994—. Rockefeller grantee, 1972-73; Nat. Cancer Inst. grantee, 1978-81, 84-87, 1994—; Am. Cancer Soc. grantee 1988-89, 91-94, U.S. Army Med. R&D Command grant, 1994—; Recipient Shannon award Nat. Cancer Inst./NHHSS, 1992-94. guest lectr. dept. obstetrics Sch. Medicine U. Nat. of Cuyo, 1965-71. Mem. AAAS, Nat. Cancer Inst. (breast cancer working group, breast cancer program 1984-88), Nat. Alliance Breast Cancer Orgns. (med. adv. bd. N.Y.C. chpt. 1986—), Eastern Coop. Oncology Group, 1992—, Coll. Am. Pathologists, Am. Soc. Clin. Pathologists, Am. Assn. for Cancer Research, Mich. Soc. Pathologists, Am. Assn. Clin. Chemistry, Electron Microscopy Soc. Am., The Endocrine Soc, Internat. Assn. Against Cancer, Mich. Electron Microscopy Forum, Sigma Xi. Roman Catholic. Contbr. numerous articles on pathology to profl. jours. Office: Fox Chase Cancer Ctr 7701 Burholme Ave Philadelphia PA 19111-2412

RUSSO, JOAN MILDRED, special education educator; b. New Haven, Aug. 23, 1933; d. Stanley Alfred and Mildred Mary (Burns) Marcotte; div.; children: David C., Thomas E., Mary Russo Herrmann, Elizabeth Russo Sant, Robert J., James E. Goeth. AA, Coll. DuPage, 1975; BS in Edn., No. Ill. U., 1977; MEd, Lewis U., Evanston, Ill., 1985. Cert. K-12 educable mentally handicapped, K-12 learning disabilities, K-12 Trainable mentally handicapped, K-9 elem tchg., Ill. Tchrs. aid Pioneer Sch., West Chgo., 1977-78; pvt. practice Wheaton, Ill., 1978—. Co-editor: Yes, You Can, 1994. Active Dem. political campaigns, Ill., 1960—; sec. Winfield Libr. Assn., 1963-68; bd. dirs. Orton Dyslexia Soc., Ill., 1980-81, sec., 1981-82. Mem. LWV (con-con com., 1972), Orton Dyslexia Soc. (bd. dirs. 1980-81, sec. 1981-82), Nat. Assn. Learning Disabilities, Nat. Ctr. Learning Disabilities. Home & Office: 26 W 270 Menomini Dr Wheaton IL 60187

RUSSO, PATRICIA JOAN, marketing professional; b. New Brunswick, N.J., Mar. 9, 1954; d. Thomas and Athena (Zikakis) R. BA, Trenton State Coll., 1976; cert., New Horizons Computer Sch., Orange County, Calif., 1992. Owner, pres. P.J. Graphics Inc., Irvine, 1980-92; advt. mgr. Orange Micro, Anaheim, Calif., 1981-83; sr. designer Martin Advt., Irvine, Calif., 1983-92; instr. advt. Platt Coll., Irvine, 1986-88; mgr. mktg. comm. James Hardie Irrigation, Laguna Niguel, Calif., 1993-95; mgr. advt./mktg. svcs. RYOBI Outdoor Products Inc., Chandler, Ariz., 1995—. Designer for various orgns. including Orange County Advertising Federation, 1981 (Award of Excellence 1981), Nat. Mature Media Award, 1993, Hospitality Design mag., 1993, Book of American Trade Marks, 1987. Exec. bd. dirs., advt. sponsor Tustin (Calif.) Tiller Days, 1992.

RUSSO, RENE, actress; b. Calif., 1955. Fashion model Eileen Ford Agy. Movie appearances include Major League, 1989, Mr. Destiny, One Good Cop, Freejack, Lethal Weapon 3, In the Line of Fire, Outbreak, Get Shorty;

TV appearances in clude (series) Sable. Office: Progressive Artists Agy 400 S Beverly Dr Ste 216 Beverly Hills CA 90212*

RUSSO, TARA MARIE, broadcast journalist; b. Teaneck, N.J., May 20, 1974; d. Thomas and Maria Russo. BS, Syracuse U., 1996. Contbg. sports writer Daily Orange Newspaper, Syracuse, N.Y., 1992-93; sports writer WAER Radio, Syracuse, 1993-94; disc jockey, sports announcer WJPZ Radio, Syracuse, 1993-96; intern WJLK FM Radio, Asbury Park, N.J., 1993; prodn. ass.t CBS Radio Sports Network, N.Y.C., 1994—; peer advisor Newhouse Sch. Pub. Comm., Syracuse, 1995-96; rep. Newhouse Rep. Com., Syracuse, 1994-95; freelance prodn. asst. NewsTalk TV, N.Y.C., 1996—; logger N.B.A. Entertainment, 1996—. Basketball team mgr. Syracuse U. Men's Basketball Team, 1992-96; tour guide, amb. Univ. 100, Syracuse, 1992-96. Mem. Women in Comm., Inc. Home: 1103 Boulevard New Milford NJ 07646

RUTENBERG-ROSENBERG, SHARON LESLIE, journalist; b. Chgo., May 23, 1951; d. Arthur and Bernice (Berman) Rutenberg; m. Michael J. Rosenberg, Feb. 3, 1980; children: David Kaifel and Jonathan Reuben (twins), Emily Mara. Student, Harvard U., 1972; B.A., Northwestern U., 1973, M.S.J., 1975; cert. student pilot. Reporter-photographer Lerner Home Newspapers, Chgo., 1973-74; corr. Medill News Service, Washington, 1975; reporter-newsperson, sci. writer UPI, Chgo., 1975-84. Interviewer: exclusives White House chief of staff, nation's only mother and son on death row; others. Vol. Chgo.-Read Mental Health Ctr. Recipient Peter Lisagor award for exemplary journalism in features category, 1980, 81; Golden Key Nat. Adv. Bd. of Children's Oncology Service Inc., 1981; Media awards for wire service feature stories, 1983, 84, wire service news stories, 1983, 84, all from Chgo. Hosp. Pub. Relations Soc. Mem. Profl. Assn. Diving Instrs., Nat. Assn. Underwater Instrs., Hon. Order Ky. Cols., Hadassah, Sigma Delta Chi, Sigma Delta Tau. Home: 745 Marion Ave Highland Park IL 60035-5123

RUTGERS, KATHARINE PHILLIPS (MRS. FREDERIK LODEWIJK RUTGERS), dancer; b. Butler, Pa., Sept. 2, 1910; d. Thomas Wharton and Alma (Sherman) Phillips; m. Frederik Lodewijk Rutgers, Feb. 2, 1942; children: Alma, Corinne Tolles. Diploma Briarcliff Coll., 1928; student L'Hermiage, Versailles, France, 1929-30; pupil ballet Vera Trefilova, Paris, Carl Raimund, Vienna, Varga Troyanoff, Budapest; pupil modern dance with Iris Barbura, Bucharest Ballet, Vincenzo Celli, N.Y.C., Igor Schwezoff, N.Y.C., Jean Yazvinsky, N.Y.C. Performed dance concerts Bucharest, 1937-40, U.S., 1941—; repertoire includes patriotic, dramatic, poetical dances, religious interpretations; dance therapist St. Barnabas Hosp., N.Y.C., 1965-70; author numerous pamphlets on dance, verses for choreographies. Chmn. ethnol. dance dept. Bruce Mus. Assocs., Greenwich, Conn., 1970—. Bd. dirs. Bruce Mus. Recipient citation for promoting culture with dance programs Nat. Fedn. Music Clubs, 1973. Mem. DAR, Conn. Fedn. Music Clubs (chmn. dance dept. 1965-66), Nat. League Am. Pen Women (local pres. 1973-78), Alliance Francaise, Mayflower Soc., Colonial Dames Am., Federated Music Club N.Y.C. (dir., dance chmn.), Met. Farm and Garden Club (dir.), Indian Harbor Club. Home: 9 Riversville Rd Greenwich CT 06831-3666

RUTH, BETTY MUSE, school system administrator; b. Florence, Ala., Oct. 24, 1943; d. Paul and Mary Lucille (Gresham) Muse; m. Thomas Gary Ruth, Dec. 17, 1965 (div. Sept. 1979); 1 child, Thomas Paul; m. Charles Larry Oliver, Jr., Mar. 10, 1990. BSBA, Athens State Coll., 1982; MBA, U. N.Ala., 1986. Sec., bookkeeper Anderson News Co., Florence, 1963-65; acct. receivable bookkeeper McConnell AFB, Wichita, Kans., 1967-68; legal sec. Reynolds Law Firm, Selmer, Tenn., 1973-74; subs. tchr. Athens (Ala.) City Schs., 1974-78, dir. RSVP, 1978—; del. White House Conf. on Aging, 1995; mem. Nat. Coun. on Aging, 1985—. Active United Way, Athens, 1990-94; sec. Gov.'s Commn. Nat. and Comty. Svc., Ala, 1994; vice chair Tenn. Valley Exhibit Commn., Ala., 1984—; past pres. Athens-Limstone County Beautification Bd., 1991-94; People-to-People internat. del. to People's Republic of China, 1994. Named outstanding project dir. Action, Atlanta, 1985, outstanding woman of Ala., 1989. Mem. NEA, Ala. Edn. Assn., Nat. Assn. RSVP Dirs. (v.p., treas., del. 1985—, svc. award 1993), Region IV Assn. RSVP dirs. (pres., v.p., treas. 1979—, svc. award 1989), Ala. Assn. RSVP Dirs. (v.p., sec., treas. 1978—, Citizens award 1991), Athens State Coll. Alumni Assn. (bd. dirs. 1993—). Mem. Ch. of Christ. Home: 15705 Kings Dr Athens AL 35611 Office: Athens State Coll PO Box 852 Athens AL 35612-0852

RUTH, CAROL A., public relations executive; b. N.Y.C., June 19, 1942; d. Edward McDonald and Dorothea (Beauman) Smith. BBA, CUNY, 1979. Sr. v.p. Hill and Knowlton, Inc., N.Y.C., 1968-86; pres., chief exec. officer Dewe Rogerson, Inc., N.Y.C., 1986—, also bd. dirs.; Dewe Rogerson Group, London; exec. dir. Dewe Rogerson Asia. Recipient Woman Achievers award YWCA of N.Y. 1985, bd. dirs. 1991—. Mem. Nat. Investors Rels. Inst. (bd. dirs. 1981-85, chmn. bd. 1984-85). Office: Dewe Rogerson Inc 850 3rd Ave New York NY 10022-6222

RUTH, LOIS-JEAN, social welfare company administrator, statistical analyst; b. Abbottstown, Pa., Aug. 24, 1931; d. Stewart Philip and Florence Kathryn (Mummert) Ruth. BA, Pa. State U., 1953. Engring. expeditor AMP Inc., Harrisburg, Pa., 1953-56, statis. analyst, 1956-59, head statis. analysis, 1959-73, systems procedures coord., 1957-73, mem. divisional cost improvement com., 1966-73, sales stats. tng. coord., 1963-73; v.p., asst. sec. Mobile Home Brokers Inc., Hanover, Pa., 1973-83; co-owner Suburban Developers, Gettysburg, Pa.; office mgr., loan processor Shelter Am. Corp, Aurora, Colo., 1984; v.p., treas. GTP Enterprises, Inc., Gettysburg; supr. caseworkers. Domestic Rels. Office Adams County, Pa., 1986-88; with Harry Ness & Co., 1988; v.p. fin. and adminstrn. Adams County United Way, 1988—. Chmn. legis. task force Pa. Mfg. Housing Assn., Harrisburg, Pa., 1979-80. Mem. Gov.'s Com. for Constl. Rev., State of Pa., 1963-66; chmn. Parks and Recreation Commn., 1966-72; sec. Zoning Hearing Bd., 1972-79; mem. Zoning Revision Com., Boro of New Cumberland, Pa., 1977-79; mem. exec. bd., chmn. personnel YWCA, Gettysburg, 1980-83; mem. Indoor Sports Complex Fund Commn., 1978-81; active Coll. Liberal Arts Endowment Fund; mem. alumni coun. Pa. State U., 1984—, bd. advisers, Mont Alto. Mem. AAUW (bd. dirs. 1954-56), Coll. of Liberal Arts Alumni Soc. (pres. 1982-88, career exploration task force 1995, 96, Alumni award 1988), Dwight Eisenhower Soc., Pa. Fedn. Women's Clubs (pres., chmn. legis. com. New Cumberland, Pa. chpt.), Lions, Phi Mu. Republican. Presbyterian. Home: 70 Hunters Trl Gettysburg PA 17325-8472

RUTH, TARA LYNN, artist; b. Phila., July 12, 1956; d. Thomas Arron and Barbara Jean (Miller) R. BA, Sarah Lawrence Coll., Bronxville, N.Y., 1995. Computer graphics operator Bankers Trust, N.Y.C., 1987—. Home: 62 Yale Rd Hartsdale NY 10530

RUTHCHILD, GERALDINE QUIETLAKE, training and development consultant, writer, poet; d. Nathan and Ruth (Feldman) Stein; m. Neil Wolinsky, Dec. 31, 1993; m. Nathaniel G. Wolinsky. BA summa cum laude, Queens Coll., 1977; MA in Am. Lit., Johns Hopkins U., 1980, PhD in Am. Lit., 1983. Asst. prof. Albion (Mich.) Coll., 1982-84; assoc. Investor Access Corp., N.Y.C., 1984-85; program dir. Exec. Enterprises, Inc., N.Y.C., 1985-86; pres. Ruthchild Assocs., N.Y.C., 1987-90, Exemplar, N.Y.C., 1991-95, Examplar, Ltd., N.Y.C., 1995—; cons. J.P. Morgan & Co., Inc., Bankers Trust Co., Chase Manhattan Bank N.A., Merill Lynch, NatWest Bank, U.S.A., Citibank N.A., Robert Morris Assocs., Goldman, Sachs & Co., Dean Witter Reynolds, Inc., also others, 1987—. Contbr. articles, poems to profl. and lit. jours. Vol. handicapped children N.Y. Foundling Hosp., N.Y.C., 1988-90, Fgn. Visitors Desk, Met. Mus. Art, N.Y.C., 1989—. Hopkins fellow Johns Hopkins U., 1979-80, Andrew Mellon Found. fellow, 1980-81, 81-82. Mem. ASTD, Assn. Bank Trainers and Cons., Internat. Soc. Philos. Enquiry, Phi Beta Kappa. Office: Exemplar 501 E 87th St Fl 12 New York NY 10128-7665

RUTHERFOORD, REBECCA HUDSON, computer science educator; b. Elkhart, Ind., Feb. 24, 1948; d. Charles Melvin Hudson and Eunice Klaire (Lund) Edmonds; m. James Kincanon Rutherfoord, Aug. 31, 1968; children: James Kincanon Jr., Charles Penn. BS, Ind. State U., 1971, MS, 1972, EdD, 1975; MS in Computer Sci., So. Poly State U., Marietta, Ga., 1995. Cert. data processor. Staff asst. Ind. State U., Terre Haute, 1969-71; vocal music tchr. S.W. Parke Schs., Rockville, Ind., 1971-73; fellowship asst. Ind. State U., Terre Haute, 1974-75; vocal music tchr. Slidell (La.) High Sch., 1977-78; programmer, analyst La. State U., Baton Rouge, 1978-79, dir. computer rehab. program, 1979-80; programmer, analyst Hanes Corp., Atlanta, 1980-81; asst. prof. Devry Inst., Atlanta, 1981-83; acting dept. chair So. Poly. State U., Marietta, Ga., 1989-92, prof. computer sci., 1983—, computer sci. grad. program coord., 1996—; cons. The Assocs. Group, Inc., Roswell, Ga., 1986-88, Crawford Communications, Atlanta, 1987; adj. prof. Cobb County Bd. Edn., Marietta, Ga., 1985-87, Joseph T. Walker Sch., Marietta, 1985-86; vis. prof. Leicester (U.K.) Polytechnic, 1990. Choir dir. St. Peter and Paul Episcopal Ch., Marietta, 1981-85, choir mem., 1992—; Christian edn. dir. St. Francis Episcopal Ch., Denham Springs, La., 1978-80; choir mem. St. David's Episcopal Ch., Roswell, 1985-92; bd. dirs., mem. Cherokee Comty. Habitat for Humanity, 1994—. Mem. Data Processing Mgmt. Assn., Assn. Computing Machinery, Sigma Alpha Iota. Republican. Office: So Poly State Univ 1100 S Marietta Pky Marietta GA 30060-2855

RUTHERFORD, JEAN, rancher; b. Gooding, Idaho, Sept. 25, 1933; d. Orval Liman and Willa Alice (Chapman) R.; m. Drew Williams Jensen, Jan. 25, 1967 (div. Mar. 1971); 1 child Bille Jensen. Vet. asst. Jerome (Idaho) Vet. Hosp., 1954-58; cattle owner Burnt River Ranch, Durkee, Oreg., 1958—; sales rep. Sports Apparel Mktg., 1982—; sec. Oreg. Cattle Women, 1964-65; cons. Western World Promotions, Denver, 1987—; queen judge Nat. H.S. Rodeo Assn., Denver, 1991, 93-94; rodeo judge, Miss., Oreg., Wash, Idaho, Ariz, 1985-92; news corres. Qtr. Horse Jour., 1959-63, Record Courier, 1963. Contbr. articles to mags. Organizer Blue Mountain Qtr. Horse Assn., Baker, Oreg., 1960, 4H Horse Club, Idaho, 1955. Named Best Dressed Westerner Gross Tailors, 1962, Best in Sales, Rodeo Am., 1992. Mem. Am. Angus Assn. (life, mfrs. rep. 1982—). Republican. Episcopalian. Home and Office: Rt 4 Box 4131 Hermiston OR 97838

RUTHERFORD, LINDA MARIE, hospital official; b. Chgo., Sept. 13, 1947; d. Allen A. and Marie (Romano) Gregory; children: Jason Alan Hunt, Lisa Marie Hunt; m. John H. Rutherford; stepchildren: Maury, Helena. BS, U. Phoenix, 1987. Adminstrv. asst. Old Tucson/Old Vegas, 1975-78; asst. mgr. W & W Mktg. Corp., Houston, 1978-83; adminstr. profl. rels. Tucson Gen. Hosp., 1983-84; mgr. Romero Road Med. Clinic, Tucson, 1984-89; mgr. physician svcs. El Dorado Hosp. and Med. Ctr., Tucson, 1989—; with N.W. Hosp., Tucson, 1994—. Bd. dirs. Flowing Wells Community Effort Coun., 1988; mem. Concerned Women for Am., 1986—. Mem. NAFE, Med. Group Mgmt. Assn. Baptist. Office: NW Hosp 6200 N La Cholla Blvd Tucson AZ 85741-3529

RUTHERFORD, VICKY LYNN, special education educator; b. Florence, S.C., Sept. 12, 1947. BS, Hampton U., 1969, MA, 1971; PhD, Mich. State U., 1991. Cert. tchr. French, spl. edn., reading specialist, Va., tchr. spl. edn., S.C. Social worker day care Hampton (Va.) Dept. Social Svc., 1970-72; reading therapist, asst. dir., dir. Bayberry Reading Clinic, Hampton, 1973-77; tchr. reading, English, counselor York County Schs., Yorktown, Va., 1977-85; staff advisor, asst. to course coord. Mich. State U., East Lansing, 1985-90; tchr. emotionally handicapped Florence (S.C.) Dist. 1 Sch. Sys., 1992-96, tchr. emotionally impaired, 1996—. Instrnl. designer: Addiction Severity Index #1, 1987, #2, 1988, Managing a Diverse Workforce, 1990; designer, trainer: Project Teach, 1991; designer, developer: (video) Camp Takona Summer Experience, 1992. Bass guitarist, Sun. sch. sec., youth worker, Sun. sch. supt. Progressive Ch. of Jesus, Florence, 1992—. Fellow Mich. Dept. Edn., 1987-89. Mem. Internat. Reading Assn. Office: Briggs Elem Sch 1012 Congaree Dr Florence SC 29501-5791

RUTHERFORD-CORREALE, LISA MARY, psychotherapist; b. Point Pleasant, N.J., Oct. 30, 1963; d. Melvyn Franklin and May Mary (Sommerrock) Rutherford; m. David Scott Correale, Sept. 30, 1989. BA in English, Rowan Coll., 1989; MSW, Rutgers U., 1992. Lic. social worker, Pa. Psychotherapist Osteo. Guidance Ctr., Bala cynwyd, Pa., 1992-94; pvt. practice Blue Bell, Pa., 1994 . Mem. NASW, NOW, Small Bus. Assn. of Delaware Valley. Home and Office: 711 Elmway Circle Blue Bell PA 19422

RUTHRUFF, KATHERYN A., educator, public school librarian; b. Greenville, Tex., Sept. 19, 1942; d. Winfred W. and Katie M. (Greenwade) Alfred; m. William E. Ruthruff, Apr. 12, 1971 (div. Aug. 1992); children: Paula Foster, Laura Eden. BA, East Tex. State U., 1964, MEd, 1966; MSLS, Our Lady of the Lake U., 1975. Cert. h.s. English tchr., Tex., h.s. Spanish tchr., Tex., all level libr., Tex. Tchr. Kimball H.S., Dallas, 1964-65, Browne Jr. H.S., Dallas, 1966-68; media dir. Region VIII Edn. Svc. Ctr., Mt. Pleasant, Tex., 1968-72; elem. libr. East Terrell Hills Elem., San Antonio, Tex., 1977-84; mid. sch. libr. John H. Wood Mid. Sch., San Antonio, Tex., 1984-92, Clara Driscoll Mid. Sch., San Antonio, Tex., 1992—. Vol. Habitat for Humanity, San Antonio, 1992-93; vol. usher Majestic Theatre, San Antonio, 1994—. Recipient Tex. PTA Life Membership award East Terrell Hills PTA, San Antonio, 1983, Terrific Tchr. award 5th Dist. Tex. Congress of PTA, 1984. Mem. NEA, Tex. Libr. Assn. (life), Tex. State Tchrs. Assn., North East Tchrs. Assn., Delta Kappa Gamma. Democrat. Episcopalian. Home: 8243 Capricorn Dr Universal City TX 78148 Office: Clara Driscoll Mid Sch 17150 Jones Maltsberger San Antonio TX 78247

RUTKOWSKI, JACQUELINE MARY, counseling administrator; b. Balt., Dec. 11, 1940; d. Frances Virginia (Janczewska) R. M, Loyola U., Balt., 1981; D, St. Mary's U., Balt., 1986. Cert. profl. counselor. Tchr. Md., Pa., N.J., Wash., 1962-85; dir. edn. St. Patrick's Cath. Ch., Balt., 1985-87; tchr.dept. epidemiology U. Md., Balt., 1987-90; dir. guidance Inst. Notre Dame, Balt., 1991—; pvt. practice counseling Balt., 1981—. Mem. ACA. Home: 938 Starbit Rd Baltimore MD 21286-2953

RUTLEDGE, MARIAN SUE, middle school language arts and social studies educator; b. New Albany, Ind., Feb. 21, 1946; d. Harold Berry Colvin and Wilma Louise (Kingsley) Abel; m. Mark Alan Rutledge, Nov. 30, 1974 (div. Sept. 1985); 1 child, Krista. BS in Elem. Edn., Ind. U., 1968, MS in Elem. Edn., 1971. Cert. tchr. elem. edn., mid. sch. lang. arts, social studies. Tchr. grades 4, 5, 6 Rogers Elem. Monroe County Comty. Sch. Corp., Bloomington, Ind., 1968-75; tchr. grades 3, 5 Ind. State U. Lab. Sch., Terre Haute, 1975-79; tchr. grades 3, 6 Union Elem. Sch. Eagle-Union Comty. Sch. Corp., Zionsville, Ind., 1979-88, tchr. lang. arts and social studies Zionsville Mid. Sch., 1988—; math. club sponsor, 1984-94; future problem solving coach, 1984—, cheerleading coach, 1991-95; mem. adv. bd. Ind. Future Problem Solving, Indpls., 1991—. Mem. NEA, Ind. State Tchrs. Assn., Ind. Gifted Edn., Eagle-Union Tchrs. Assn. (v.p., pres. 1979—), Kappa Kappa Kappa (v.p., pres. 1977—). Republican. Methodist. Home: 7326 Harbour Isle Indianapolis IN 46240-3471 Office: Zionsville Mid Sch 900 Mulberry St Zionsville IN 46077-1141

RUTTINGER, JACQUELYN, director of exhibitions; b. Great Falls, Mont., July 21, 1940; d. Robert Muir and Amy Rosalie (Kernaghan) R.; m. Lee Alan Boye, July 1961 (div. 1969); 1 child, Richard William. BFA, Sch. of Art Inst. Chgo., 1963; MA, No. Ill. U., 1976, MFA, 1977. Instr. art Kankakee (Ill.) C.C., 1977-79, Prairie State Coll., Chicago Heights, Ill., 1977-81; cmty. prof. Govs. State U., University Park, Ill., 1982; chair dept. art St. Mary-of-the-Woods (Ind.) Coll., 1983-85; dir. exhbns. Western Mich. U., Kalamazoo, 1986—. One woman shows include Freeport (Ill.) Art Mus., 1979, Jesse Besser Mus., Alpena, Mich., 1987, Saginaw (Mich.) Art Mus., 1988, Kalamazoo Inst. of Arts, 1990; exhibited in group shows at Mitchell Mus., Mt. Vernon, Ill., 1981, Millikin U., Decatur, Ill., 1982 (Purchase award), No. Ill. U., DeKalb (Purchase award State of Ill.), Ea. Ill. U., Charleston (Purchase award State of Ill.), Western Mich. U., Kalamazoo (2 Purchase awards State of Mich.); represented in permanent collections Ill. State Mus., Springfield, Freeport Art Mus., Sheldon Swope Art Mus., Terre Haute, Ind., Jesse Besser Mus. Project Completion grantee Ill. Arts Coun., 1981; Rsch. grantee Coll. Fine Arts, Western Mich. U., 1986, 87, 88-89, 90-91; recipient Best of Show award Jackson Area Juried Show, Ella Sharp Mus., Jackson, Mich., 1996; Creative Artists grantee Arts Found. of Mich and Mich. Coun. for Arts and Cultural Affairs, 1996-97. Mem. Assn. Coll. and Univ. Museums and Galleries, Mich. Mus. Assn., Arts Coun. Greater Kalamazoo (Mini grantee 1987-88), Detroit Inst. Arts. Home: 1110 Dwillard Dr Kalamazoo MI 49001 Office: Western Mich U Art Dept Kalamazoo MI 49008

RUTZEN, EVE TERESA, elementary school educator; b. Rochester, N.Y., Jan. 12, 1966; d. Frank Maarten Lefor and Rita Pollard Kent; m. Douglas Bruce Rutzen, July 2, 1994. BS, SUNY, Cortland, 1987; MS in Edn., U. Rochester, 1993. Cert. in elem. edn. Md. Substitute tchr. Rochester City Schs., 1987-88; adminstrv. asst. U. Rochester, 1988-90; tchr. 4th grade Balt. County Pub. Schs., Balt., 1990-94, Arlington County Pub. Schs., 1994—. Mem. NEA, Nat. Coun. Tchrs. Math., Va. Edn. Assn., Phi Delta Kappa. Office: Patrick Henry Elem Sch 701 S Highland St Arlington VA 22204-2449

RYALL, JO-ELLYN M., psychiatrist; b. Newark, May 25, 1949; d. Joseph P. and Tekla (Paraszczuk) R.; BA in Chemistry with gen. honors, Douglass Coll., Rutgers U., 1971; MD, Washington U., St. Louis, 1975. Diplomate Am. Bd. Psychiatry and Neurology. Resident in psychiatry Washington U., 1975-78, psychiatrist Student Health, 1980-84, clin. instr. psychiatry, 1978-83, clin. asst. prof. psychiatry, 1983—; inpatient supr. Malcolm Bliss Mental Health Ctr., St. Louis, 1978-80, psychiatrist outpatient clinic, 1980-82; pvt. practice medicine specializing in psychiatry, St. Louis, 1980—. Bd. dirs. Women's Self Help Ctr., St. Louis, 1980-83. Fellow APA, Soc. (pres. Ea. Mo. Dist. Br. 1983-85, sect. coun. AMA 1986—, dep. rep. to assembly 1994—); mem. AMA (alt. del. Mo. 1988-90, 93-94, del. 1995—), Am. Med. Women's Assn. (pres. St. Louis Dist. br. 1981-82, 92, regional gov. VIII 1986-89, spkr. house of dels., 1993—), St. Louis Met. Med. Soc. (del. to state conv. 1981-86, 93—, councilor 1985-87, v.p. 1989), Mo. State Med. Assn. (vice speaker ho. of dels. 1986-89, speaker 1989-92), Manic Depressive Assn. St. Louis (chmn. bd. dirs. 1985-89), Washington U. Faculty Club. Office: 9216 Clayton Rd Saint Louis MO 63124-1560

RYAN, BARBARA EILEEN, sociologist, educator; b. Granite City, Ill., Sept. 13, 1942; d. John Mahlon and Edith Eileen (Dougherty) R.; m. Robert Harris, July 21, 1962 (div. Oct. 1989); children: David Harris, Paul Harris, Jeanne Harris. BS in Edn., So. Ill. U., 1976, MS in Counseling, 1978, MA in Sociology, 1980; PhD in Sociology, Washington U., St. Louis, 1986. Asst. prof. sociology No. Ill. U., DeKalb, 1985-88; assoc. prof. sociology, coord. women's studies Widener U., Chester, Pa., 1988—; chair com. on acad. freedom and responsibility Midwest Sociol. Soc., 1991-94; pres. Midwest Sociologists for Women in Soc., 1990-91. Author: Feminism and the Women's Movement: Dynamics of Change in Social Movement Ideology and Activism, 1992, The Women's Movement: References and Resources, 1996; contbr. to profl. jours. Summer rsch. grantee NEH, 1995. Mem. NOW, Sociologists for Women in Soc. (elected mem. publs. com. 1996-99), Phi Kappa Phi, Kappa Delta Pi. Democrat. Home: # B 1709 Green Philadelphia PA 19130-3911 Office: Widener U Social Scis Divsn Chester PA 19013

RYAN, BARBARA TRESIDDER, musician, Celtic arts promotion company executive; b. Colombo, Sri Lanka, May 29, 1950; came to U.S., 1953; d. Argus John and Nancy (Palmer) Tresidder; m. David Bernard Ryan (div. 1986); children: Christopher David, Mark Edward. BA, George Washington U., 1971. Tchr. Vienna (Va.) Day Care Ctr., 1971-72; technician HUD, Washington, 1972-73, U.S. Treas. Libr., Washington, 1973-74; lead singer Iona (Celtic music group), Burke, Va., 1986—; festival and concert promoter, pres. Barnaby Prodns., Burke, Va., 1987—; voice tchr., Burke, 1993—. Albums include Nutmeg & Ginger, Holding Our Own, Back to Our Roots, Off The Beaten Track. Grantee Mid Atlantic Arts Found., 1994, Wrinkle in Time Found., 1995, 96. Mem. Washington Area Music Assn., Mid-Atlantic Coalition Folk Music Presenters. Democrat. Home: 9811 Pebble Weigh Ct Burke VA 22015 Office: Barnaby Prodns Inc PO Box 11160 Burke VA 22009-1160

RYAN, CATHLEEN COLLETTE, resource development manager; b. Bountiful, Utah, June 1, 1962; d. Philip John and Isabel Faye (McPhee) R. BA, Assumption Coll., 1984. Adminstrv. analyst and various entry adminstrv. positions IBM, Mt. Pleasant, N.Y., 1984-89; office systems adminstrv. mgr. IBM, Somers, N.Y., 1989-92, office systems and site ops. mgr., 1992-94, resource devel. mgr., 1994—. Mem. Young Reps., Wilton, Conn., 1976-80. Baptist. Home: 25 Muller St New Fairfield CT 06812 Office: IBM Rt 100 Somers NY 10589

RYAN, CHARLOTTE MURIEL, oncology nurse; b. Beedeville, Ark., Sept. 2, 1939; d. Eugene Sanford and Edith Elizabeth (Goforth) Breckenridge; children: Russell Kent, Cary Randall, Molly Renee. BSN cum laude, Calif. State U., Fresno, 1991, MSN, 1996. OCN cert. nurse. Psychiat. technician Porterville (Calif.) State Hosp., 1959-67; tchr. developmentally disabled Ariz. Tng. Ctr., Coolidge, 1967-71; Montessori tchr. Tucson, 1972-77; tchr. developmentally disabled Heartland Opportunity Ctr., Madera, Calif., 1977-79; med. office mgr. office of orthopedic surgeon, Madera, 1979-83, office mgr., x-ray technician, 1983-87; staff nurse in oncology St. Agnes Med. Ctr., Fresno, 1991—; instr. nursing dept. Calif. State U., Fresno, 1992, 93, 95. Treas. Hospice of Madera County, 1990-92, bd. dirs., 1992; peer counselor Calif. State U., Fresno, 1989-91; pres. bd. dirs. Easter Seals Soc., Madera, 1981. Mem. Oncology Nursing Soc., Nightingale Soc., Golden Key, Sigma Theta Tau (chair pub. com., editor MUNEWS newsletter 1994-95). Republican. Home: 4544 N Barton Fresno CA 93726 Office: St Agnes Med Ctr 1303 E Herndon Ave Fresno CA 93720-3309

RYAN, DEBBIE KAYE, financial planner; b. West Bend, Wis., Aug. 22, 1961; d. Allen August and Diann Marie (Yecke) Goldammer; m. Gregory Vincent Ryan, Aug. 12, 1991. Grad. H.S., Albuquerque. Cert. fin. paraplanner, Colo. Exec. sec. Mass Mutual Life Ins. Co., Albuquerque, 1979-82; adminstrv. asst. Mass Mutual Life Ins. Co., Phoenix, 1988-89; sec., receptionist Lyle Talbot Agy., Inc., Albuquerque, 1983-84; fin. paraplanner, adminstrv. asst. Charles Stephen & Co., Albuquerque, 1984-86; office mgr., fin. paraplanner Asset Planning Co., Inc., Albuquerque, 1986-87; brokerage rep. Monarch Life Ins. Co., Phoenix, 1988; from adminstrv. asst. to ins. agt., registered rep. Sun Life Can., Phoenix, 1990-94; mng. mem. GDR Benefits Group LLC, Phoenix, 1993—. Mem. Jr. League Phoenix (com. mem. 1994—), John C. Lincoln Guild (com. mem. 1995), Moon Valley Country Club (com. mem. 1991—). Republican. Lutheran. Home and Office: 2 West Country Gables Dr Phoenix AZ 85023-5236

RYAN, HOLLY ANNE, nurse, civic worker; b. Oak Park, Ill., Dec. 25, 1945; d. Bernard Lawrence and Ethel Eleanor (Kropf) Daleske; m. Patrick Michael Ryan, Aug. 31, 1968; children: Rebecca, Brendan, Abigail, Lucas. Student, Coll. St. Teresa, 1963-65; diploma in nursing, Oak Park Hosp., 1968. R.N., Wis. Staff nurse Misericordia Hosp., Milw., 1968-69, Dean Clinic, Madison, Wis., 1969-70, Marina View Manor, Milw., 1970-76. Co-chair gen. gifts United Performing Arts Fund, Milw., 1976-77; mem. panel United Way Ozaukee County, Milw., 1978-84; pres. Cedarburg (Wis.) Presch., 1980-81; chair Citizen Rev. Bd. Milw. County, 1981-84; bd. dirs. Cedarburg Youth Ctr., 1987-92, Cedarburg Athetic Booster Club, 1994—, Applaud Cedarburg, 1992—; mem., treas. Cedarburg Sch. Dist. Bd. Edn., 1988-94; active Ctr. for Integrated Living, 1989-93; mem. Ozaukee County NAACP, 1990—. Mem. Jr. League Milw. (chair 1981-84), Cedarburg Soccer Club (sec. 1987-89). Home: 363 Huntington Dr Cedarburg WI 53012-9507

RYAN, IONE JEAN ALOHILANI, retired educator, counselor; b. Honolulu, Oct. 18, 1926; d. William Alexander and Lilia (Nainoa) Rathburn; m. Edward Parsons Ryan, June 23, 1962 (dec.); children: Ralph M., Lilia K. BEd, U. Hawaii, 1948; MS in Pub. Health, U. Minn., 1950; EdD, Stanford U., 1960. Lic. marital and family therapist, N.C. Tchr. W.R. Farrington High Sch., Honolulu, 1948; instr. to asst. prof. U. Hawaii, Honolulu, 1950-66; assoc. prof. to prof. East Carolina U., Greenville, 1966-90; prof. emerita East Carolina U., Greenville, N.C., 1990—; adv. com. Eastern Regional Tng. Program, Greenville, N.C., 1975-80; cons. Title III Grant, Lenoir Community Coll., Kinston, N.C., 1981; adult svcs. adv. com. Pitt County Mental Health, Greenville, N.C., 1976-78. Contbr. articles to profl. publs. Recipient first scholarship Honolulu C. of C., 1948-50. Mem. APA.

RYAN, SISTER JANICE E., college administrator. BA in English, Trinity Coll., 1965; MEd in Spl. Edn., Boston U., 1967; postgrad., U. Minn., 1968, U. Lund, Sweden, 1971, Harvard U., 1974-76, 80. Joined Sisters of Mercy, Roman Cath. Ch., 1954. Dir. pub. relations Trinity Coll., Burlington, Vt., 1967-71, asst. prof. spl. edn., 1967-74; lobbyist Vt. Legis., 1974-79; chair spl. edn. div., pres. Trinity Coll., Burlington, Vt., 1979—; mem. Am. Council on Edn.'s Govtl. Relations Commn. on Nat. Challenges in Higher Edn.;

corporator, dir. Bank of Vt., trustee Vt. Law Sch.; task force on econ. devel. infrastructure, edn. and tng. NE-Midwest Leadership Council. Exec. com. Campus Compact, chair fed. initiatives task force; active Vt. Higher Edn. Coun.; lobbyist Vt. Legislature (chmn. spl. edn. div.), 1974-79. Mem. NACIU (bd. dirs. 1990), Am. Assn. Higher Edn. (participant Spring Hill Conf. 1987), Gov.'s Econ. Coun. Office: Trinity Coll Office of the President 208 Colchester Ave Burlington VT 05401-1470

RYAN, MARILYN CURRAN, special education educator; b. Omaha, Nebr., Dec. 12, 1931; d. James Michael and Alvena Elizabeth (Siepmann) Curran; m. Thomas Edward Ryan, June 26, 1954 (div. Aug. 1969); children: James, Kathryn, Michael, Margaret, John, Patrick. BA, Duchesne Coll., Omaha, 1953; MS, U. Nebr., 1971. Cert. spl. edn. tchr. and adminstr., Nebr. Tchr. 2d grade Omaha Pub. Schs., 1953-55, tchr. emotionally disturbed, 1969-74, supr. emotionally disturbed program, 1974—. Mem. adv. coun. Ea. Nebr. Cmty. Mental Health, Omaha, 1988-92; adv. bd. mem. Salvation Army, Omaha, 1992—; cons. Nebr. Dept. Edn., Lincoln, 1989-93; alumnae bd. em. Acad. Sacred Heart, Omaha, 1994—. Mem. NEA, Nebr. Edn. Assn., Omaha Edn. Assn., Omaha Coun. Exceptional Children (membership chair), Coun. Exceptional Children, Coun. Children with Behavioral Disorders (pres. local chpt. 1979-81). Democrat. Roman Catholic.

RYAN, MARLEIGH GRAYER, Japanese language educator; b. N.Y.C., May 1, 1930; d. Harry and Betty (Hurwick) Grayer; m. Edward Ryan, June 4, 1950; 1 child, David Patrick. B.A., NYU, 1951; M.A., Columbia U., 1956, Ph.D., 1965; Cert., East Asian Inst., 1956; postgrad., Kyoto U., 1958-59. Research assoc. Columbia U., N.Y.C., 1960-61, lectr. Japanese, 1961-65, asst. prof., 1965-70, assoc. prof., 1970-72; vis. asst. prof. Yale U ., New Haven, 1966-67; assoc. prof. U. Iowa, Iowa City, 1972-75, prof., 1975-81, chmn. dept., 1972-81; prof. Japanese SUNY, New Paltz, 1981—, dean liberal arts and scis., 1981-90; vice chmn. seminar on modern Japan, Columbia U., 1984-85, chmn., 1985-86; co-chmn. N.Y. State Conf. on Asian Studies, 1986, editor, 1993—, mem. exec. com., 1993-96, sec., 1993—. Co-author: (with Herschel Webb) Research in Japanese Sources, 1965; author: Japan's First Modern Novel, 1967, The Development of Realism in the Fiction of Tsubouchi Shoyo, 1975; assoc. editor: Jour. Assn. Tchrs. Japanese, 1962-71, editor, 1971-75. East Asian Inst. fellow Columbia U., 1955; Ford Found. fellow, 1958-60; Japan Found. fellow, 1973, Woodrow Wilson Ctr. Internat. Scholars fellow, 1988-89; recipient Van. Am. Disting. Book award Columbia, 1968. Mem. MLA (sec. com. on teaching Japanese Lang. 1962-68, mem. del. assembly 1979-87, mem. exec. com. div. Asian lit. 1981-86), Assn. Tchrs. Japanese (exec. com. 1969-72, 74-77), Assn. Asian Studies (bd. dirs. 1975-78, coun. of confs., 1993—), Midwest Conf. Asian Studies (pres. 1980-81). Office: SUNY Ft # 414 New Paltz NY 12561

RYAN, MARY A., diplomat; b. New York, N.Y., Oct. 1, 1940. B.A., St. John's Univ., 1963, M.A., 1965. With Foreign Service, Dept. of State, 1966—; consular and adminstrv. officer Naples, Italy, 1966-69; personnel officer Am. Embassy, Tegucigalpa, Honduras, 1970-71; consular officer Am. Consulate Gen., Monterrey, Mexico, 1971-73; adminstrv. officer Bur. of African Affairs, Dept. of State, Washington, 1973-75, post mgmt. officer, 1975-77; career devel. officer Bur. of Personnel, Dept. of State, 1977-80; adminstrv. counselor Abidjan, Ivory Coast, 1980-81, Khartoum, Sudan, 1981-82; inspector, Office of Insp. Gen. Dept. of State, Washington, 1982-83, exec. dir. Bur. of European and Can. Affairs, 1983-85, exec. asst. to Under Sec. of State for Mgmt., 1985-88; ambassador to Swaziland, 1988-90; dep. asst. sec. Bur. of Consular Affairs, Washington, 1990; dir. Kuwait task force, 1990-91, ops. dir. UN spl. commn. on elimination of Iraqi weapons, 1991; dep. asst. sec. Bur. European & Can. Affairs, Washington, 1991-93; asst. sec. Bur. of Consular Affairs, Washington, 1993—. Office: Dept State Bureau of Consular Affairs 2201 C St NW Washington DC 20520-0001*

RYAN, MARY CATHERINE, pediatrician; b. N.Y.C., Mar. 22, 1938; d. Thomas Michael and Catherine (Scullin) McLaughlin; m. Enda Kieran Ryan, Feb. 8, 1969; children: Denise Marie, Kathleen May. BS in Chemistry, St. John's U., Bklyn., 1959; MD, NYU, 1963; MPH, George Washington U., 1996. Diplomate Am. Bd. Pediatrics. Cons. Hampton health dept. Va. State Dept. Health, 1969-71; med. coord. N.Y.C. Bur. Handicapped, 1971-72; asst. prof. pediatrics L.I. Coll. Hosp., Bklyn., 1972-73; pub. health clinician Fairfax County Health Dept., Fairfax, Va., 1973—; pvt. contractor pediatrics PHP Healthcare Corp., Fairfax, 1987-93. Tchr. religious edn. St. Thomas à Becket Ch., Reston, Va., 1978-81. Maj. M.C., U.S. Army, 1969. Fellow Am. Acad. Pediatrics; mem. AMA, Med. Soc. Va., No. Va. Pediatric Soc., Fairfax County Med. Soc., Soc. Devel. Pediatrics. Home: 1423 Aldenham Ln Reston VA 22090-3903 Office: Fairfax County Health Dept 1850 Cameron Glen Dr Ste 100 Reston VA 22090-3310

RYAN, MARY NELL H., training consultant; b. Milw., Oct. 17, 1956; d. Robert Healey and Elizabeth Anne (Schulte) R.; 1 child, Katharine Scarlett. BA, Marquette U., 1979; MS, U. Wis., Milw., 1991. Tchr. St. Francis Borgia Sch., Cedarburg, Wis., 1979-81; dir. pub. rels. Aerobics West Club, N.Y.C., 1981; unit head, team leader Northwestern Mut. Life Ins. Co., Milw., 1982-84, asst. supr., 1984-86, tng. coord., 1986-87, mgr. tng., 1987-92; tng. cons. for ins. industry Workplace Learning, Inc., Milw., 1992—; cons. Aetna Life and Casualty Co., Hartford, Conn., 1988, Robertson-Ryan & Co., Milw., 1989, Blue Cross/Blue Shield United of Wis., Northwestern Mut. Life Ins. Co., CMI Group, Inc., Homes for Ind. Living, Inc., Aurora Health Care, Literacy Svcs. Wis., Executrain, Inc., Milw. First in Quality, Wis. Quality Network, United Wis. Svcs., Inc., Ameritech, Milw. Art Mus., Blood Ctr. Southeastern Wis., Meretz, Inc., Radiology Assocs. Wis., Deluxe Data, Inc., Portable Solution, Inc., Hewlett-Packard Users Group of Wis., Miller Brewing Co.; guest lectr. U. Wis., Milw., 1989, Milw. Area Tech. Coll., 1990, Marquette U., 1990; speaker confs., developer/trainer workshops. Mem. exec. com. Lakefront Festival Arts, Milw., 1985—, vol. com. chair, silent auction chair; exec. fundraiser United Performing Arts Fund, Milw., 1986; com. chmn. Jr. League Milw., 1983-87; fundraiser YMCA Ptnr. Youth, Milw. 1987-88; tutorHead Start Read with Me program, 1993—. Recipient gold medal Life Communicators Assn., 1987. Mem. ASTD (bd. dirs. Wis. chpt., membership com. 1989-90, chmn. Train Am.'s Workforce and comty. svcs. 1992-94), Milw. Mgmt. Support Orgn. (bd. dirs. 1988), Wis. Ins. Club (spkr.), InRoads (bd. dirs. Wis. chpt.), Phi Kappa Phi. Office: Workplace Learning Inc 1426 W Westport Cir Mequon WI 53092-5753

RYAN, MEG, actress; b. Fairfield, Conn., Nov. 19, 1961; m. Dennis Quaid, 1991; 1 child, Jack Henry. Student, NYU. Appearences include (TV) One of the Boys, 1982, As The World Turns, 1982-84, Wild Side, 1985, (films) Rich and Famous, 1981, Amityville 3-D, 1983, Top Gun, 1986, Armed and Dangerous, 1986, Innerspace, 1987, Promised Land, 1987, D.O.A., 1988, The Presidio, 1988, When Harry Met Sally, 1989, Joe Versus the Volcano, 1990, The Doors, 1991, Prelude to a Kiss, 1992, Sleepless in Seattle, 1993, Flesh and Bone, 1993, When a Man Loves a Woman, 1994, Restoration, 1994, I.Q., 1994, French Kiss, 1995, Two for the Road, 1996, Courage Under Fire, 1996, Addicted to Love, 1996; owner Prufrock Pictures movie prodn. co. Recipient Golden Apple award Hollywood Women's Press Club, 1989. Office: care ICM 8942 Wilshire Blvd Beverly Hills CA 90211*

RYAN, PAMELA JEANNE, guidance director; b. Evergreen Park, Ill., Jan. 16, 1955; d. Harold C. and Marilyn J. (Wales) Holck; m. Philip J. Ryan, July 15, 1983. BA, Coll. of St. Francis, Joliet, Ill., 1976; MA, Govs. State U., University Park, Ill., 1984. Tchr. Providence Cath. H.S., New Lenox, Ill., 1976-88, dir. guidance, 1988—, coord. student assistance program, 1993—; mem. critical incident stress debriefing team St. Joseph's Med. Ctr., Joliet, 1993—; conf. presenter in field. Mem. ACA, Am. Sch. Counseling Assn., Ill. Sch. Counseling Assn. Democrat. Roman Catholic. Office: Providence Cath HS 1800 W Lincoln Hwy New Lenox IL 60451

RYAN, PATRICIA ANN ADAMS, minister; b. Akron, Ohio, Aug. 30, 1943; d. Jim Floyd and Maggie Bell (Hargrove) Adams; m. James Richard Ryan, Feb. 10, 1962; children: Kent Richard, Connie Lynn Ryan Terrell. BA summa cum laude, Drake U., 1982; MDiv, St. Paul Sch. of Theology, 1985. Ordained to ministry, Disciples of Christ, 1985. Chaplain Ramsey Home, Des Moines, 1983-94, Hospice of Ctrl. Iowa, Des Moines, 1994—; min. Runnells (Iowa) Christian Ch., 1994—; exec. com. Commn. on the Order of Ministry, Des Moines, 1993—; pres. Inst. of Ministry, Des Moines, 1989-91; mem. program and arrangements com. Gen. Assembly of the Christian Ch., U.S. and Can., 1993-95; tchr., lectr. on aging issues Christian Chs., Iowa, 1985—; spkr. in field. Adv. bd. Ctrl. Coll., Pella, Iowa, 1985-92; adv. com. Govs. Conf. on Aging, Des Moines, 1986-88; keynote spkr. Iowa Assn. of Homes for the Aging, Des Moines, 1981. Mem. NOW, Grad. Assn. St. Paul Sch. of Theology, Phi Beta Kappa. Democrat. Office: Christian Ch 304 Maple Runnells IA 50237

RYAN, SARAH (SALLY RYAN), elementary education educator; b. Cornwall, N.Y., Apr. 8, 1938; d. Benjamin Marco and Sarah Loretta (McEvilly) Santoro; m. Leo Joseph Ryan, Aug. 12, 1961 (dec. July 1988); children: Sean, Ada, Sarah, Caithlin. BA in English, Coll. New Rochelle, 1959; MS in Edn. and Reading, SUNY, New Paltz, 1985; cert. reading recovery, NYU, 1991. Cert. elem. tchr., N.Y.; cert. English 7-12 grade. 3rd grade tchr. Willow Ave. Sch., Cornwall, 1959-64; jr. high English tchr. Cornwall H.S., 1964-70; from 6th-4th grade tchr. Temple Hill Sch., New Windsor, N.Y., 1970-80, title I reading tchr., 1990—; acad. specialist Temple Hill Acad., Newburgh, N.Y., 1992-95; reading tchr. Temple Hill Acad., New Windsor, N.Y., 1980-90, 1990-95; 3d grade tchr., reading recovery tchr. Temple Hill Acad., Newburgh, N.Y., 1990-95, tchr. third grade, 1995—; jr. league trainer Vol. Career Devel., 1978-82; cons. student leadership Cornwall H.S., 1985-86. Pres. Jr. League Orange County, 1972-73, sustainer rep., 1988-90; v.p. Hudson Valley Philharmonic, 1974-76; bd. dirs., v.p. Orange County YWCA, New Windsor, N.Y., 1988-94, vol., 1994—; vol. Mus. Hudson Highlands, Cornwall, 1994—. Mem. Newburgh Tchrs. Assn. (del. 1986-92), N.Y. State United Tchrs., Reading Recovery Inst. Democrat. Roman Catholic. Home: 49 Clinton St Cornwall NY 12518-1561 Office: Temple Hill Sch 525 Union Ave Newburgh NY 12553-6140

RYAN, SUSAN MAGNESS, librarian; b. Takoma Park, Md., May 27, 1958; d. Donald Eaton and Shirley Anne (Lusby) Magness; m. Edward Timothy Ryan, Sept. 1, 1984; 1 child, Shannon Kelsey. BS, Fla. State U., 1981, MS, 1982; MLS, UCLA, 1989. Intelligence analyst CIA, Washington, 1983-84; libr., assoc. prof. Stetson U., DeLand, Fla., 1989—; bd. mem. Coun. Advisers, Sch. Libr. and Info. Studies, Fla. State U., Tallahassee, 1995—. Author: Downloading Democracy: Government Information in an Electronic Age, 1996; contbg. author: Government CD-Roms: A Practical Guide to Searching Electronic Databases, 1994; editl. bd. Jour. Govt. Info., 1993-96; series and cons. editor Librs. Unltd., 1994—; column editor Jour. Govt. Info., 1994-96; contbr. articles to profl. jours. Mem. ALA (govt. documents round table 1989—, Catharine J.Reynolds award 1996), Fla. Libr. Assn. (chair govt. documents caucus 1992-93, chair elect 1991-92), Ctrl. Fla. Libr. Consortium (chair govt. documents interest group 1991-92). Office: duPont Ball Libr Stetson U Campus Box 8418 Deland FL 32720

RYAN, SUZANNE IRENE, nursing educator; b. Yonkers, N.Y., Mar. 13, 1939; d. Edward Vincent and Winifred E. (Goemann) R. BA in Biology, Mt. St. Agnes Coll., Balt., 1962; BSN, Columbia U., 1967, MA in Nursing Svc., 1973, MEd in Nursing Edn., 1975; MS in Oncology, San Jose (Calif.) State Coll. U., 1982. RN, N.Y.; cert. AIDS educator, N.Y. Prof. nursing Molloy Coll., Rockville Centre, N.Y., 1970—, co-dir. health svcs., dir. ednl. programs, 1987-94, dir. health svcs., 1994—, health educator, 1992—, co-dir. mobile health van, adminstr. health edn., 1992—; pres., CEO SIR Enterprises, Inc., 1982—; photographer Molloy Coll. Pubs., 1991—; photographic dir. Bali-Art, Inc., 1992—; mem. N.Y. State AIDS Coun., 1987—, L.I. Alcohol Consortium, 1987—; educator Nassau County Dept. Sr. Citizens Health, 1991—; photographer-in-residence Molloy Coll., 1992—; lectr. on landscape, wildlife and flower photography, L.I., N.H., Can., 1993—. Represented in permanent collections in photographic galleries in Carmel, Calif., Laconia, Wolfboro and Moultonboro, N.H., 1963—; one-woman shows include Mollay Coll., Rockville Ctr. Library; photographer 4 books on Monterey Peninulsa, New Eng. and N.H.; writer, editor Health News Letter Molloy Coll., 1990—. Health educator Nassau County Dept. of Sr. Citizens Outreach Program, Molloy Coll., AIDS educator, 1991—; adminstr., chief AIDS counselor Interaction AIDS Counseling, Babylon, N.Y., 1992—; lic. AIDS educator N.Y. Metro Area; chairperson of grants com. in higher edn. Nassau U. USPHS fellow, 1962, Nat. Cancer Inst. fellow, 1981-82. Mem. AAUP, AAUW, Nat. Congress Oncology Nurses, N.Y. State Fedn. Health Educators, Inc., Nurses Assn. Counties L.I. Dist. 14, N.Y. State Nurses Assn., World Wildlife Orgn., Audubon Soc., Internat. Ctr. Photography, Nature Conservancy, Sierra Club, Sigma Theta Tau (Epsilon Kappa chpt., rsch. grantee 1985, 87), Zeta Epsilon Gamma. Roman Catholic. Home: 16 Walker St Malverne NY 11565-1829

RYAN, SYLVIA FORGES, writer; b. N.Y.C., Apr. 6, 1937; d. Frank and Ottilie (Knöchlein) F.; m. Edward Robert Ryan, Nov. 7, 1964; children: Susanna, Eric. BA in English, Bucknell U., 1958, MA, 1963; postgrad., Wesleyan U. Editor: Frogpond, 1991-93; poetry pub. in anthologies and mags. Freedom writer Amnesty Internat., 1986-96. Recipient Phi Beta Kappa prize for fiction Bucknell U., 1958, Henderson award Haiku Soc. Am., 1993, Mainichi award, 1986. Unitarian. Home: 87 Bayard Ave North Haven CT 06473

RYAN, TERESA WEAVER, obstetrical nurse; b. Dallas, July 18, 1956; d. J.E. and Mary (Davis) Weaver; m. Patrick Hallaron Ryan, Apr. 7, 1991. BS, Troy State U., 1983; BSN, Tex. Christian U., 1987; MSN, U. South Ala., 1994; postgrad., La. State U. RN, Fla.; cert. maternal-newborn nurse ANCC. Intelligence analyst USN, Dallas, 1983-87; enlisted USAF, 1987, advanced through grades to capt. (obstetrical nurse), 1987—; childbirth educator USAF, 1988—. Mem. NOW, Assn. Women's Health, Obstetrical and Neonatal Nurses, Nat. Humane Soc. Educators, People for the Ethical Treatment of Animals, Sigma Theta Tau (sec. 1987—, rsch. grant 1987), Phi Kappa Phi. Roman Catholic. Home: 35 Imperial Woods Dr Harahan LA 70123

RYAN, THERESA ANN JULIA, accountant; b. N.Y.C., Mar. 1, 1962; d. John Patrick and Diane Elizabeth (Duggan) R. BA in Math. and Econs., Fordham U., 1984, MBA in Profl. Acctg., 1989. CPA, N.Y. With sales dept. Abraham & Straus, White Plains, N.Y., 1980-84; adminstrv. asst. Companion of N.Y., Rye, 1984-86, asst. fin. analyst, 1986-87; with tech. ctr. Fordham U., N.Y.C., 1987-88; staff acct. Konigsberg Wolf & Co., N.Y.C., 1989-91; sr. audit assoc. Coopers & Lybrand, L.L.P., N.Y.C., 1992-95; internal auditor N.Y. Power Auth., White Plains, 1996—. Mem. Beta Gamma Sigma. Republican. Roman Catholic. Home: 5 Clare Ter Yonkers NY 10707-3201 Office: NY Power Auth 123 Main St White Plains NY 10601

RYAN, VERONICA MAUDLYN, artist; b. Plymouth, Montserrat, Aug. 22, 1956; came to the U.S., 1990; d. Cyril and Elenor (Daily) R.; m. Paul Chevannes, Oct. 21, 1952; children: Zahra, Paloma. BFA with honors, Bath Acad. Art, 1978; MA, Slade Sch. Art U. Coll., London, 1980. vis. lectr. various colls., 1982-94. Exhibited sculpture in one-person shows including Camden Arts Ctr., London, 1995, Wood Street Gallery, Pitts., 1993, Kettle's Yard Gallery, Cambridge, England, 1988-89, Riverside Studios, London, 1988, Arnolfini Gallery, Bristol, Englanf, 1987, Wolverhampton (England) Art Gallery, 1987, others; exhibited sculpture in group shows including Six Sculptors L.I. U., 1995, Weltkunst Found. Irish Mus. Modern Art, Dublin, 1995, Body as Metaphor Bard Coll., N.Y., 1995, Trophies from the Civil Wars Meml. Arch Grand Army Plaza Bklyn. Natural Order Tate Gallery, Liverpool, England, 1993, Arts Coun. Touring Exhbn., England, 1993, many others; works represented in collections including Mellon Bank, Pitts., 1993, Tate Gallery, London, 1991, Contemporary Art Soc., London, 11990, Weltkunst Found., 1989, Salsbury Collection, England, 1988; many others. Recipient award Henry Moore Found., 1987, Prize Winner Cleveland Internat. Drawing Biennale, 1983, award Great London Arts Assn., 1983; Boise traveling scholar, 1980. Home: 362 6th Ave New York NY 11215

RYAVEC, ISABEL SEATON, librarian, media specialist; b. Cin., June 2, 1936; d. John Thomas and Isabella (Seaman) Seaton; m. Karl William Ryavec, Aug. 24, 1957; children: Karen Lenore Ryavec, Karl Ernest Ryavec. MSLS, Simmons Coll., 1971; BS in Edn., Miami U., 1957. Cert. sch. libr., Mass. Desk asst. Jones Libr., Amherst, Mass., 1968-70; sch. libr. Hinchcliff H.S., Wilbraham, Mass., 1971-73, Amherst Regional H.S., 1973-95; ret., 1995; mem. Media Coun., Amherst, 1973-95; co-chair, founder Joint Tech. Com., Amherst, 1992-95. Recipient Sonia Wexler award Multi-Cultural Edn. Com., 1986. Democrat.

RYCHLAK, BONNIE LEE, artist, museum curator; b. Culver City, Calif., July 7, 1951; d. Walter Arthur and Margaret (Miller) Rychlak; m. Brian Stewart Gayman, Dec. 23, 1973. BA, UCLA, 1973; MFA, U. Mass., 1976. Dir. collections, curator Isamu Noguchi Found., L.I. Solo exhbns. include St. Peter's Ch., N.Y.C., 1986, Rastovsky Gallery, N.Y.C., 1989, Shoshana Wayne Gallery, Santa Monica, Calif., 1991, The Sculpture Ctr., N.Y.C., 1993, Gallery Three Zero, N.Y.C., 1994; exhibited in group shows at Artists' Space, N.Y.C., 1986, White Columns, N.Y.C., 1986, Bess Cutler Gallery, N.Y.C., 1986, Mission Gallery, N.Y.C., 1987, A.I.R. Gallery, N.Y.C., 1988, Space III, Birmingham, Ala., 1988, Longwood Gallery, Bronx, 1987, Rastovsky Gallery, 1988, Shoshana Wayne Gallery, 1989, Stux Gallery, N.Y.C., 1990, Penine Hart Gallery, N.Y.C., 1990, Emily Sorkin Gallery, 1990, Sue Spaid Fine Art, L.A., 1990, Hallwalls Pleasure, N.Y.C., 1991, Internat. House, N.Y.C., 1992, 55 Ferris St., Bklyn., 1992, Wyn Kamarsky Inc., N.Y.C., 1993, T'zart Test Wall, N.Y.C., 1993, No. Ill. U., DeKalb, 1994, K & E Gallery, N.Y.C., 1994, Adam Baumgold Gallery, N.Y.C., 1994; works in pub. collection of Harvard U. NEA grantee, 1976; Bellagio residency Rockefeller Found., 1985. Mem. Orgn. Ind. Artists, Assn. Am. Mus. Democrat. Home: 248 Lafayette St New York NY 10012-4030 Office: The Isamu Noguchi Found 32-37 Vernon Blvd Long Island City NY 11106

RYDER, GEORGIA ATKINS, university dean, educator; b. Newport News, Va., Jan. 30, 1924; d. Benjamin Franklin and Mary Lou (Carter) Atkins; m. Noah Francis Ryder, Sept. 16, 1947; children: Olive Diana, Malcolm Eliot, Aleta Renee. B.S., Hampton (Va.) Inst., 1944; Mus.M., U. Mich., 1946; Ph.D., NYU, 1970. Resource music tchr., Alexandria, Va., 1945-48; faculty music dept. Norfolk State U., 1948—, prof., 1970—, head dept., 1969-79, dean Sch. Arts and Letters, 1979-86. Contbr. articles to profl. jours., contbr. chpts. to books. Trustee Va. Symphony, Va. Wesleyan Coll.; bd. dirs. Black Music Rsch. Ctr., Columbia Coll., Chgo., Nat. Assn. Negro Musicians, Southeastern Va. Arts Assn.; mem. advisory com. Norfolk chpt. Young Audiences, Va. Coalition for Mus. Edn., Gordon Inst. Music Learning, Temple U. Grantee So. Fellowship Fund, 1967-69, Consortium Rsch. Tng., 1973; recipient Norfolk Com. Improvement Edn. award, 1974, People's Acad. of Arts award, 1985, City of Norfolk award, 1989, Nat. Assn. Negro Musicians award, 1989, Nat. Conf. Christians and Jews award, 1990, Va. Laureate in Music award, 1992, Cultural Alliance award Greater Hampton Roads, 1992, Disting Alumni award Hampton U., 1993, Norfolk State U. Alumni. award, 1994, MECA Found. award, 1995. Mem. Music Educators Nat. Conf., Coll. Music Soc., Intercoll. Music Assn., Va. Music Educators Assn., Delta Sigma Theta.

RYDER, MICHELE CAIN, counselor, speech therapist; b. McKeesport, Pa., Aug. 12, 1946; d. Michael Patrick and Rose Elizabeth (Keddie) Cain; m. Dennis E. Ryder, May 26, 1973; children: Patrick Cain, Christian Cain. BS, Indiana U. Pa., 1968; MEd, Shippensburg U., 1972. Speech therapist Capital Area Intermediate Unit, Lemoyne, Pa., 1968-73; vol. in speech programs various pub. schs., Hawaii and, Germany, 1975-82; tchr. U. Md. European Divsn., Stuttgart, Germany, 1982; supr. child care ctr. Dept. Army, Moehringen, Germany, 1982-83; counselor Manassas Park (Va.) City Schs., 1987-89, Arlington (Va.) County Pub. Schs., 1989—. Sec. Kings Park West Civic Assn., Fairfax, Va., 1986, mem. cmty. affairs, 1988. Fellow Pa. State U., 1969, Gallaudet Coll., 1973. Mem. ACA, NEA, Va. Counseling Assn., Am. Sch. Counselor Assn., Va. Sch. Counselor Assn., No. Va. Sch. Counselor Assn. Home: 4910 Orkney Ct Fairfax VA 22032

RYDER, WINONA (WINONA LAURA HOROWITZ), actress; b. Winona, Minn., Oct. 29, 1971; d. Michael and Cynthia (Istas) Horowitz. Films include: Lucas, 1986, Square Dance, 1987, 1969, 1988, Beetlejuice, 1988, Great Balls of Fire, 1989, Heathers, 1989, Edward Scissorhands, 1990, Mermaids, 1990, Welcome Home, Roxy Carmichael, 1990, Night On Earth, 1992, Bram Stoker's Dracula, 1992, Age of Innocence, 1993 (Golden Globe for Best Supporting Actress, 1994, Academy award nominee, Best Supporting Actress, 1993), The House of the Spirits, 1994, Reality Bites, 1994, Little Women, 1994 (Acad. Awd. nom., Best Actress), Boys, 1995, How to Make An American Quilt, 1995, Looking for Richard, 1995, The Crucible, 1996, Boys, 1996. Office: care Carole Obie Arts Entertainment 9460 Wilshire Blvd 7th Fl Beverly Hills CA 90210*

RYLANT, CYNTHIA, author; b. Hopewell, Va., June 6, 1954; d. John Tune and Leatrel (Rylant) Smith; 1 child, Nathaniel. BA, Morris Harvey Coll., 1975; MA, Marshall U., 1976; MLS, Kent State U., 1982. English instr. Marshall U., Huntington, W.Va., 1979-80, U. Akron, Ohio, 1983-84; children's libr. Akron (Ohio) Pub. Libr., 1983; part-time lectr. Northeast Ohio Univs. Coll. Medicine, Rootstown, Ohio, 1991—. Author: (picture books) When I Was Young in the Mountains, 1982 (Caldecott Honor book 1983, English Speaking Union Book-Across-the-Sea Amb. of Honor award 1984, Am. Book award nomination 1983), Miss Maggie, 1983, This Year's Garden, 1984, The Relatives Came, 1985 (Horn Book Honor book 1985, Children's Book of Yr. Child Study Assn. Am. 1985, Caldecott Honor Book 1986), Night in the Country, 1986, Birthday Presents, 1987, All I See, 1988, Mr. Grigg's Work, 1989, An Angel for Solomon Singer, 1992, The Everyday Town, 1993, The Everyday School, 1993, The Everyday House, 1993, The Everyday Garden, 1993, The Everyday Children, 1993, The Everyday Pets, 1993, Mr. Putter and Tabby Pour the Tea, 1994, Mr. Putter and Tabby Walk the Dog, 1994, The Old Woman Who Named Things, 1994, The Blue Hill Meadows and the Much Loved Dog, 1994, Gooseberry Park, 1995; (Henry and Mudge series) Henry and Mudge: The First Book of Their Adventures, 1987, Henry and Mudge in Puddle Trouble, 1987, Henry and Mudge in the Green Time, 1987, Henry and Mudge Under the Yellow Moon, 1987, Henry and Mudge in the Sparkle Days, 1988, Henry and Mudge and the Forever Sea, 1989, Henry and Mudge Get the Cold Shivers, 1989, Henry and Mudge and the Happy Cat, 1990, Henry and Mudge and the Bedtime Thumps, 1991, Henry and Mudge Take the Big Test, 1991, Henry and Mudge and the Long Weekend, 1992, Henry and Mudge and the Wild Wind, 1993, Henry and Mudge and the Careful Cousin, 1994, Henry and Mudge and the Best Day Ever, 1995; (poetry) Waiting to Waltz ... a Childhood, 1984 (Nat. Coun. for Social Studies Best Book 1984), Soda Jerk, 1990, Something Permanent, 1994; (novels) A Blue-Eyed Daisy, 1985 (Children's Book of Yr. Child Study Assn. Am. 1985), A Fine White Dust, 1986 (Newbery Honor Book 1987), A Kindness, 1988; (stories) Every Living Thing, 1985, Children of Christmas: Stories for the Season, 1987, A Couple of Kooks: And Other Stories About Love, 1990; (autobiography) But I'll Be Back Again: An Album, 1989, Best Wishes, 1992; (other) Appalachia: The Voices of Sleeping Birds, 1991 (Boston Globe/Horn Book Honor book for nonfiction 1991), Missing May, 1992 (John Newbery medal 1992), I Have Seen Castles, 1993, The Dreamer, 1993. *

RYMAN, RUTH (STACIE) MARIE, primary education educator; b. Moline, Ill., July 22, 1952; d. Henry Joseph and Gladys Julia (Campbell) DeKeyzer; m. Phillip DeForrest Ryman, Aug. 14, 1976; children: Michelle, Daniel, Jennifer. BA, Augustana Coll., 1974; MA, U. Denver, 1988. Cert. tchr. Resource tchr. Notre Dame Sch., Denver, 1986-91, 2nd grade tchr., 1991—; cons. Notre Dame Sch., Denver, 1991—. mem. Nat. Cath. Edn. Assn., Nat. Coun. Tchrs. Math. Office: Notre Dame Sch 2165 S Zenobia St Denver CO 80219-5058

RYMER, PAMELA ANN, federal judge; b. Knoxville, Tenn., Jan. 6, 1941. AB, Vassar Coll., 1961; LLB, Stanford U., 1964; LLD (hon.), Pepperdine U., 1988. Bar: Calif. 1966, U.S. Ct. Appeals (9th cir.) 1966, U.S. Ct. Appeals (10th cir.), U.S. Supreme Ct. V.p. Rus Walton & Assoc., Los Altos, Calif., 1965-66; Assoc. Lillick McHose & Charles, L.A., 1966-72, ptnr., 1973-75; ptnr. Toy and Rymer, L.A., 1975-83; judge U.S. Dist. Ct. (cen. dist.) Calif., L.A., 1983-89, U.S. Ct. Appeals (9th cir.), L.A., 1989—; faculty The Nat. Jud. Coll., 1986-88; mem. com. summer ednl. programs Fed. Jud. Ctr., 1987-88; chair exec. com. 9th Cir. Jud. Conf., 1990; mem. com. criminal law Jud. Conf. U.S., 1988-93, Ad Hoc com. gender-based violence, 1991-94, fed.-state jurisdiction com., 1993—. Mem. editorial bd. The Judges' jour., 1989-91; contbr. articles to profl. jours. and newsletters. Mem. Calif. Postsecondary Edn. Commn., 1974-84, chmn., 1980-84; mem. L.A. Olympic Citizens Adv. Commn.; bd. visitors Stanford U. Law Sch., 1986—, chair, 1993-96, exec. com.; bd. visitors Pepperdine U. Law Sch., 1987—; mem. Edn. Commn. of States Task Force on State Policy and Ind. Higher Edn., 1987-89; bd. dirs. Constnl. Rights Found., 1985; Jud. Conf. U.S. Com. Fed.-State Jurisdiction, 1993, Com. Criminal Law, 1988-93, ad hoc com. gender based violence, 1991-94; chair exec. com. 9th cir. jud. conf., 1990-94. Recipient Outstanding Trial Jurist award L.A. County Bar Assn., 1988. Mem. ABA (task force on civil justice reform 1991—), State Bar Calif.

(antitrust and trade regulation sect., exec. com. 1990-92), L.A. County Bar Assn. (chmn. antitrust sect. 1981-82), Assn. of Bus. Trial Lawyers (bd. govs. 1990-92), Stanford Alumni Assn., Stanford Law Soc. Soc. Calif., Vassar Club So. Calif. (past pres.). Office: US Ct Appeals 9th Cir 304 US Court of Appeals Bldg 125 S Grand Ave Pasadena CA 91109-1510*

RYNEAR, NINA COX, retired registered nurse, author, artist; b. Cochranville, Pa., July 11, 1916; d. Fredrick Allen and Nina Natalie (Drane) Cox; m. Charles Spencer Rynear, Aug. 22, 1934 (dec. May 1941); children: Charles Joseph, Stanley Spencer. RN, Coatesville Hosp. Sch. Nursing, 1945; BS in Nursing Edn., U. Pa., 1954. Interviewer Nat. Opinion Rsch. Ctr., U. Denver, Colo., 1942-47; sch. nurse West Goshen Elem. Sch., West Chester, Pa., 1946-47; pub. health nurse Pa. Dept. Health Bur. Pub. Health Nursing, Harrisburg, 1947-51; staff nurse V.A. Hosp., Coatesville, Pa., 1951-54; staff nurse, asst. head nurse V.A. Hosp., Menlo Park, Calif., 1954-56; asst. chief nursing svc. Palo Alto and Menlo Park VA Hosps., Palo Alto, Menlo Park, Calif., 1956-76; self employed Reno, Nev., 1976—. Author: (poems, musical compositions) Old Glory and the U.S.A., 1989, Mister Snowman, 1988, Dawn Shadow of Lenape, 1988; (poem and song compilation) This Side of Forever, 1990; (musical compositions) Blessed Are Those Who Listen, What Can I Leave, The Hobo's Promise; (childrens' stories) Wilyum of Orange 1st, Lady Harley and Pepper, 1995; contbr. sonnets to Newsletter of N.Am. Acad. Esoteric Studies; paintings represented in numerous pvt. collections. Pres. Chester County Pub. Health Nurses Assn., 1950. Staff nurse Cadet Corps, 1944-45. Mem. VFW Aux. (patriotic instr. 1989-90, chmn. safety div. Silver State #3396 chpt. 1990-91), New Century Rebekah Lodge #244. Methodist. Home and Office: 3476 Harbor Beach Dr Lake Wales FL 33853-8082

RYNEARSON, PATRICIA HEAVISIDE, elementary school educator; b. Balt., Dec. 19, 1951; d. William and Evelyn (Davis) Heaviside; m. Leo E. Rynearson, Jr., Aug. 6, 1977; children: Courtney, Clipp. BS, U. Del., 1973; MA, U. N. Mex., 1979. Cert. tchr. multiple subjects and reading, Calif. Tchr. Lavaland Sch., Albuquerque, N. Mex., 1977-78, Santo Domingo Sch., Albuquerque, 1978-79, Chapparal Sch., Albuquerque, 1979-80, Liberty Sch., Buckeye, Ariz., 1980-86, Royal Palm Sch., Phoenix, 1986-87, Juniper Sch., Fontana, Calif., 1987-89, Almeria Middle Sch., Fontana, 1989-90, Redwood Sch., Fontana, 1990—; mem. planning com. Environ. EXPO Calif. State Univ., San Bernardino, Calif., 1995-96. Named Inland Empire Environ. Educator of Yr., Calif. State U., San Bernardino, 1996; recipient Eleanor Roosevelt Tchg. fellowship AAUW, 1996. Home: 2233 Drummond St Riverside CA 92506 Office: Redwood Elem Sch 8570 Redwood Ave Fontana CA 92335

RYPCZYK, CANDICE LEIGH, employee relations executive; b. Norman, Okla., Apr. 24, 1949; d. John Anthony and Lee (Brunswick) Wirth; m. Peter Charles Rypczyk, Nov. 27, 1976. BA, Kalamazoo Coll., 1971; cert. labor studies extension program, Cornell U., N.Y. Sch. Indsl., Labor Relations, Middletown, 1985. Personnel asst. PFW divsn. Hercules Inc., Middletown, N.Y., 1973-77, asst. personnel mgr., 1977-79, mgr. employee relations, 1979-92; mgr. human resources Huck Internat., Kingston, N.Y., 1992—. Mem. Am. Soc. for Pers. Adminstrn. (v.p. Mid-Hudson Valley chpt. 1985, pres. 1986, treas. N.Y. State coun. 1986, dist. bd. dirs. 1988-90, cert.), Orange County C. of C. (Vol. of the Yr. 1986, program com., treas., exec. com.). Office: Huck Internat 85 Grand St Kingston NY 12401-3907

RYSER, GAIL RENEE, education educator; b. Madison, Wis., June 2, 1954; d. Robert Lee and Marie Adele (DeWaide) R.; children: Renee Marie Young, Roderick Stuart Young. BS in Edn., Ill. State U., 1975; MA, U. Tex., 1985; PhD, 1990. Teaching asst. Fairchild Sch., Normal, 1976-78; elem. tchr. Houston Ind. Sch. Dist., 1979-81; math. tchr. Kirby Hall Sch., Austin, Tex., 1981-82, 84-85; tchr., planner, evaluator Inst. for Young Disadvantaged Gifted Children, Austin, 1988; tchr. of gifted and talented MasterSch., Manor, Tex., 1989-91, Judson Ind. Sch. Dist., Converse, Tex., 1989-90; lectr. U. Tex., Austin, 1990-92; asst. prof. Baylor U., Waco, Tex., 1992—; cons. Austin, Tex., 1989—, statistician Pro-Ed Publ. Co., Austin, 1989. Contbr. articles to profl. jours. Mem. ASCD, Tex. Assn. for Gifted and Talented, Nat. Assn. for Gifted Children, Am. Ednl. Rsch. Assn. Office: Baylor U PO Box 97314 Waco TX 76798

RYSER, PAMELA HORTON, small business owner; b. Grove Hill, Ala., June 13, 1952; d. Glover Wade and Gwendolyn (Finch) Horton; m. William Edward Ryser; children: William Joseph, Edward Wade. AA, Ala. So. Coll.; student, U. S. Ala. Cert. accomplishment H&R Block. Head teller Merchants Bank, Jackson, Ala., 1972-79; sec., bookkeeper McLain Constrn. Co., Jackson, 1978-80, Melton DuBose, P.A., Jackson, 1982-84; pres., owner McLain Hardware, Inc., Jackson, 1984—. Den leader Cub Scouts Am., Jackson, 1988-89; Sunday Sch. tchr. Goodsprings Bapt. Ch. Mem. NAFE, Jackson C. of C. (vice chair Christmas Parade 1993, chair 1994), Downtown Merchants Assn., Phi Theta Kappa. Home: RR 1 Box 52-f Jackson AL 36545-9801 Office: McLain Hardware Inc 108 Carroll St Jackson AL 36545-2710

RYU, KYOO-HAI LEE, physiologist; b. Seoul, Republic of Korea, Sept. 5, 1948; came to U.S., 1972; d. Hee Soon and Jung Ock Lee; m. David Tai Hyung Ryu, May 13, 1978; children: Eugenia, Christina, John. BS, Yonsei U., Seoul, 1971; PhD, U. Minn., 1981. Postdoctoral fellow U. Minn., Mpls., 1980-81, staff scientist, 1981-82; sr. rsch. assoc. Wright State U., Dayton, Ohio, 1985-91; adminstr. Ohio Ctr. of Cosmetic Surgery, Bellefontaine, Ohio, 1991—. Mem. Am. Physiol. Soc., Biophys. Soc., Soc. Gen. Physiologists. Home: 15 Bexley Ave Springfield OH 45503-1103

SAAB, DEANNE KELTUM, real estate appraiser, broker; b. Allentown, Pa., Jan. 27, 1945; d. James A. and Agnes G. (Hanzlik) S. BA, Cedar Crest Coll., 1966; MS, U. Calif., Santa Barbara, 1973; realtors cert., Pa. State U., 1978. Cert. appraiser, Pa.; state accredited affiliate Appraisal Inst.; cert. sales profl. Tchr. Ojai (Calif.) Unified Sch. Dist., 1966-74; pvt. practice Allentown, Pa., 1978—; pres./treas. DeAnne & Assoc., Inc., Allentown, Pa., 1987—; owner Heritage Gardens, Allentown, Pa., 1981—. Mem. AAUW (various offices), Nat. Assn. Realtors, Pa. Assn. Realtors, Allentown Lehigh County Bd. Realtors (various offices), Cedar Crest Coll. Alumnae Assn. (various offices), Lehigh Valley Guild Craftsmen (various offices). Home and Office: 1360 Dorney Ave Allentown PA 18103-9731

SAARI, JOY ANN, family nurse practitioner, geriatrics medical and surgical nurse; b. Chippewa Falls, Wis., July 14, 1953; d. Harry R. and Hilda R. (Christianson) Harwood; m. Allan A. Saari, Dec. 31, 1973 (dec.); children: Christopher, Erik. BSN summa cum laude, U. Wis., Eau Claire, 1978; postgrad., Blue Ridge Community Coll., Verona, Va., 1987; MSN, FNP, George Mason U., 1995; MSN. RN, Mich., Wis., Va.; FNP, Va.; cert. BLS instr., ACLS. Staff nurse Portage View Hosp., Hancock, Mich., 1979-80; evening supr., asst. dir. nursing Chippewa Manor, Chippewa Falls, 1980-86; staff nurse Bridgewater (Va.) Home, Inc., 1986-90; p.m. charge nurse Medicalodge Leavenworth, Kans., 1990-91; outdoor edn. nurse Montgomery County (Md.) Schs., 1991-93; FNP Leesburg/Sterling Family Practice, 1995—. Capt. USAR Nurse Corps. Mem. Am. Acad. Nurse Practitioners, Nat. League of Nursing, No. Va. Nurse Practitioner Assn., Res. Officer Assn., Am. Legion Aux., Phi Kappa Phi.

SAAS, DEBORAH ANNE, investment advisor, securities broker; b. Cleve., Mar. 17, 1955; d. Efrom Youngstein and Gerda Lillian (Klipper) Levine; m. Henry Ivan Saas, Jan. 8, 1977; children: Tyler Reed, Jonathan David, Jordan Peter. BS, Miami U., Oxford, Ohio, 1977. Cert. fin. mgr.; registered prin., registered rep. Asst. buyer May Co., Cleve., 1977-79; retail buyer Diamonds, Tempe, Ariz., 1979-84, Broadway Southwest, Mesa, Ariz., 1984-86; fin. cons. Merrill Lynch, Mesa, Ariz., 1986-91; br. mgr. Linsco/Pvt. Ledger, Tempe, Ariz., 1991—. Mem. Home Based Bus. Assn. Ariz. Office: Linsco Pvt Ledger 1835 E Citation Ln Tempe AZ 85284

SABA, BETTYE MILLER, librarian; b. Evansville, Ind., Oct. 3, 1917; d. James Monroe and Helene Wilhelmina (Thiele) Miller; m. Ralph Francis Saba, Jan. 17, 1976. AB, U. Evansville, 1939; BLS, Simmons Coll., 1947; MS in Edn., Ind. U., 1962. Cert. libr., Ind. Children's libr. Evansville (Ind.) Pub. Libr., 1939-44, order libr., 1946, east br. libr., 1947-69, adult program supr., 1969-72; head libr. Willard Libr., Evansville, 1972-75; ret. Adv. mem. Evansville Arts and Edn. Coun., 1969. Petty officer USN, 1944-46. Mem. ALA (life), AAUW (life), Ind. Libr. Assn. (life). Home: 19 Dreier Blvd Evansville IN 47712-5034

SABAROFF, ROSE EPSTEIN, retired education educator; b. Cleve., Sept. 4, 1918; d. Hyman Israel and Bertha (Glaser) Epstein; m. Bernard Joseph Sabaroff, Dec. 28, 1940; children: Ronald Asher, Katya Nina. B.A., U. Ariz., 1941; M.A., San Francisco State U., 1954; Ed.D., Stanford U., 1957. Tchr. Presidio Hill Elem. Sch., San Francisco, 1951-55; asst. prof. edn. Oreg. State U., Corvallis, 1958-61; asst. dir., then dir. elem. edn. Harvard Grad. Sch. Edn., Cambridge, Mass., 1961-66; prof. edn., head elem. edn., head reading program Va. Poly. Inst. and State U., Blacksburg, 1967-82; dir. Grad. Edn. Ctr. Calif. Luth. Coll., North Hollywood, 1982-84; reading specialist How to Learn, Inc., West Los Angeles, Calif., 1983-88. Author: (with Hanna, Davies, Farrar) Geography in the Teaching of Social Studies, 1966, (with Mary Ann Hanna) The Open Classroom, 1974, Teaching Reading with a Linguistic Approach, 1980, Developing Linguistic Awareness, 1981; contbr. articles to profl. jours. Recipient Disting. Research award Va. Edn. Research Assn., 1977; Phi Delta Kappa grantee, 1980. Mem. AAUP, Internat. Reading Assn., NEA, Va. Edn. Assn., Va. Coll. Reading Educators (pres. 1976-77), Va. Reading Assn., Phi Delta Kappa, Pi Lambda Theta, Gamma Theta Upsilon. Democrat. Jewish. Home: 23826 Villena Mission Viejo CA 92692-1818

SABATINI, ALICE CHANDLER, volunteer, artist; b. Lamar, Colo., Feb. 1, 1931; d. William Woods and Thelma Elisabeth (Gillespie) Chandler; m. Frank Carmine Sabatini, Dec. 28, 1954; children: Frank Marcus, Matthew Carmine, Michael William, Daniel Martin. BS, Kans. State U., 1952; MFA, U. Kans., 1955. Instr. fine arts U. Kans., Lawrence, 1954-55; instr. art Holy Name Sch., Topeka, 1963-66, St. Matthew Sch., Topeka, 1966-69; mem. adv. bd. Topeka Zoo, 1964-80; graphics artist Topeka Zool. Park, 1965—; mem. adv. bd. Fine Arts U. Kans., Lawrence, 1972-73; mem. sculpture com. M.K. Beach MOA, Manhattan, Kans., 1994-96. Designer posters Topeka Zool. Park, 1965—. Active Kans. Soc. Crippled Children, Topeka, 1965—; co-chair major gifts, archtl. com. adv. com. St. Lawrence Cath. Ctr., Lawrence, 1986-89, 94—; charter mem. Concerned Citizens of Topeka, 1996—. Recipient Wisdom award St. Lawrence Ctr., 1993, Appreciation award Mulvane Art Mus., 1994-96.

SABATINI, GABRIELA, tennis player; b. Buenos Aires, May 16, 1970; d. Osvaldo and Beatriz S. *

SABATINI, SANDRA, physician; b. N.Y.C., Dec. 1, 1940. BS in Chemistry, Millsaps Coll., 1962; MS in Pharmacology, Marquette U., 1966; PhD in Pharmacology, U. Miss., 1968; MD in Internal Medicine, Tex. Med. Sch., 1974. Lic. physician, Ill., Tex. Intern in medicine U. Ill. Hosp., Chgo., 1974-75; asst. prof. U. Tex. Med. Sch., San Antonio, 1968-70; assoc. dir. U. Ill. Hosp., Chgo., 1977-78; asst. prof. U. Ill. Coll. of Medicine, Chgo., 1977-83, assoc. prof. medicine and physiology, 1983-84; attending physician in nephrology VA, Chgo., 1977-84; med. dir. Dialysis Unit U. Ill., Chgo., 1978-84; prof. internal medicine and physiology Tex. Tech. U. Health Sci. Ctr., Lubbock, 1985—, chmn. dept. physiology, 1993—; attending physician in nephrology U. Med. Ctr., Lubbock, 1985—; lab. instr. Millsaps Coll., Jackson, Miss., 1961-62; instr. in pharmacology, Bapt. Hosp. Sch. Nursing, Jackson, 1966-68; merit rev. mem. NSF, 1987, 91, 92; rev. mem. several orgns. including Chgo. Heart Assn., 1984, NIH, 1982, 86, 89-93, Nat. Kidney Found., 1987, 89—, Am. Heart Assn., 1981-84, others. Editorial referee Am. Jour. Kidney Disease, Am. Jour. Physiology, Am. Jour. Nephrology, Annals of Internal Medicine, others; editorial bd. Am. Jour. Nephrology, 1989-93, Seminars in Nephrology, 1984—; ; author numerous publs. and abstracts in field; contbr. articles to profl. jours. Recipient predoctoral fellowship grant, Marquette U., 1963-66, pub. health predoctoral fellow U. Miss. Med. Sch., 1967-69, gen. medicine sci. rsch. grant U. Tex. Med. Sch., 1968-70, post-grad. fellowship award Karolinska Inst., Swedish Med. Coun., 1971, 73, NIH grants, 1979-82, 1984—, Chgo. Heart Assn. grant-in-aid, 1979-85, Nat. Eye Inst. grant, 1979-80, Banes Charitable Trust award U. Ill.,1984-85, U.S. Olympic Com. Rsch. Found. Clin. Study, 1986-87, numerous others awards in field. Fellow Am. Coll. Physicians; mem. AAAS, AAUP, AOA (hon.), Am. Fedn. Clin. Rsch., Am. Heart Assn., Am. Physiol. Soc., Am. Soc. Nephrology, Am. Soc. Pharmacology and Exptl. Therapeutics, Am. Soc. Renal Biochemistry and Metabolism (pres. elect 1994), Cen. Soc. Clin. Rsch., Ill. Kidney Found., Internat. Soc. Nephrology, Italian-Am. Nephrologists, Inc., Nat. Kidney Found. (numerous offices including chmn. several coms.), Nat. Kidney Found. of West Tex. (bd. dirs. 1993—, Outstanding Vol. 1995). Office: Tex Tech U Health Sci Ctr 3601 4th St Lubbock TX 79430-0001

SABBAGH, SHERAINE KAY, textile designer; b. Springfield, Ill., Mar. 2, 1959; d. Russ B. and Beverly Jane (McCarthy) Dhondy; m. John Peter Sabbagh, July 26, 1986; 1 child, Elliott Cyrus. BFA in Textile Design, Sophia Polytechnic, Bombay, India, 1981; AOS, Pratt Inst., N.Y.C., 1983. Cert. CPR and first aid, ARC. Trainee designer Laxmi-Vishnu Textile Mills, Ltd., Bombay, 1981; lectr. history of textiles Sophia Polytechnic, Bombay, 1981-82, assoc. of occupational studies in textile design, 1981-82; textile designer Piramal Spinning and Weaving Mills, Ltd., Bombay, 1981-82; colorist Quaker Fabric Corp., N.Y.C., 1984; spl. asst. designer Spectrum Fabrics Corp., N.Y.C., 1984-85; pres., owner, designer Sheraine Kay Designs, 1983—; computer aided stylist West Point Stevens, 1991—; cons. The Master Weavers India show, Smithsonian Instn., Washington, 1986; guest lectr., film prodr. Mus. Natural History, N.Y.C., 1988, 90, N.Y. Pub. Lib., N.Y.C., 1988, Great Neck (N.Y.) Libr., 1987. Producer, art dir. documentary film Journey to Arhikkal, 1988; set designer play The Elephant Man, Bombay, 1981; exhibited textile designs Sophia Poly., Bombay, 1979, 80, 81, Internat. House, N.Y.C., 1983, Pratt Inst., N.Y.C., 1983. Active Friends and Advs. the Mentally Ill, N.Y.C., 1989—; mem. W.P.P. Recycling Task Force, 1991—. Scholar Maharashtra State Directorate, 1979; recipient 1st prize woven divsn. 11th ann. competition Home Fashion Products Assn., 1983. Democrat. Office: 1185 Avenue Of The Americas New York NY 10036-2601

SABINI, BARBARA DOROTHY, art educator, artist; b. Bklyn., June 11, 1939; d. Joseph and Fannie (Ciazzia) Gugliucci; m. John Sabini Jr., June 22, 1957 (div. 1982); children: Michael, John, Gerald, Barbara-Jo. AAS in Psychology, Orange County C.C., Middletown, N.Y., 1979; BFA in Painting, SUNY, New Paltz, 1984, MFA in Painting, 1988. Cert. tchr. art edn. Tchg. asst. drawing and design SUNY, New Paltz, 1986; art tchr. Newburgh (N.Y.) Free Acad. H.S., 1987—; lectr. freshman drawing SUNY, Nw Paltz, 1990; painting instr. Orange County C.C., 1991; faculty supr. teen art projects Newburgh Free Acad. H.S., 1990-91; inst. Kosciuszko Found./ UNESCO, Poland, 1995, 96. One-woman shows include White Herron Lounge, Virginia Beach, Va., 1986, Ave. A Cafe, N.Y.C., 1987, Pumpkin Eater, N.Y.C., 1989, Painters Tavern, Cornwall-on-Hudson, N.Y., 1992; exhibited in group shows including Hammerquist Gallery, N.Y.C., 1984, Ariel Gallery, N.Y.C., 1985, James Callahan Gallery, Palm Springs, Calif., 1985, The Real Gallery, Cornwall, N.Y., 1986, Cork Gallery, Lincoln Ctr., N.Y.C., 1986, Mid Hudson Arts and Sci. Ctr., Poughkeepsie, N.Y., 1986, Ledo Gallery, N.Y.C., 1987, Outer Space Gallery, N.Y.C., 1989, 91, Wall Gallery, N.Y.C., 1989, 90, Women in the Arts Found. Gallery, N.Y.C., Ledger DeMain Gallery, N.Y.C., China Phoenix Gallery Store, Albuquerque, 1995. Recipient Appreciation cert. N.Y. State Art Tchrs. Assn. Mem. N.Y. State Tchrs. Assn., N.Y. State Art Tchrs. Assn. Home: 131 Willow Ave Apt 3P Cornwall NY 12518 Office: Newburgh Free Acad 201 Fulerton Ave Newburgh NY 12550

SABINO, CATHERINE ANN, magazine editor; b. N.Y.C., May 6, 1952; d. Joseph A. and Frances (Phelan) S. AB, Barnard Coll., 1973. Beauty editor, editor-at-large Harper's Bazaar, Italia, Men's Bazaar, 1976-79; beauty editor Seventeen mag. Triangle Comms., 1979-83; N.Y. editor Linea Italiana Mondadori, 1983-85; N.Y. editor Moda RAI, 1985-86; editor in chief Worldstyle The Aegis Venture Group, 1987-88; editor in chief In Fashion Murdoch Mags., 1988-89; editor mag. devel. European Home, 1989-91; cons. Hachette Mags., 1992; editor in chief Woman's Day Beauty Hachette Mags., 1993, N.Y. Times Custom Pub., 1993—. Author: Italian Style, 1985, Italian Country, 1988. Mem. Am. Soc. Mag. Editors, Barnard-Columbia Club N.Y. (dir. at large 1991-93), Yale Club. Office: NY Times Custom Pub 122 E 42nd St New York NY 10168-0002

SABLE, BARBARA KINSEY, former music educator; b. Astoria, L.I., N.Y., Oct. 6, 1927; d. Albert and Verna Rowe Kinsey; B.A., Coll. Wooster, 1949; M.A., Tchrs. Coll. Columbia U., N.Y.C., 1950; D.Mus., U. Ind., 1966; m. Arthur J. Sable, Nov. 3, 1973. Office mgr., music dir. sta. WCAX, Burlington, Vt., 1954; instr. Cottey Coll., 1959-60; asst. prof. N.E. Mo. State U., Kirksville, 1962-64; asst. prof. U. Calif., Santa Barbara, 1964-69; prof. music U. Colo., Boulder, 1969—, prof. emeritus, 1992—. Author: The Vocal Sound, 1982; contbr. poetry to literary jours. Mem. Nat. Assn. Tchrs. Singing (past state gov., asso. editor bull.), AAUP, Colo. State Music Tchrs. Assn. Democrat. Avocation: poetry. Home: 3430 Ash Ave Boulder CO 80303-3432 Office: U Colo Coll Music Campus Box 301 Boulder CO 80309

SABLOTNY-EISENHAUER, TRACY MICHELLE, elementary physical education educator; b. Springfield, Ill., May 15, 1968; d. Harvey Herbert and Marilyn Jane Sisson. BS, MacMurray Coll., Jacksonville, Ill., 1990. Cert. tchr., Ill. Phys. edn. tchr. Winchester (Ill.) Elem. Sch., 1990—, volleyball coach, 1992—; mem. Dist. Learning Leadership Team; co-chair Natural Helpers. Active Jacksonville Theatre Guild, 1994. Nominated Outstanding Young Educator, Jacksonville Jaycees. Home: 1610 S West St Jacksonville IL 62650 Office: Winchester Elem Sch 183 S Elm St Winchester IL 62694-1202

SABNIS, VASUMATI SUMAN, librarian; b. Bombay, India, Dec. 5, 1933; came to U.S., 1959; d. Vasant Murlidhar and Manorama Kulkarni; m. Suman Trimbak Sabnis, Aug. 13, 1960; children: Samir, Sushil, Kalpana. BA, Bombay U., 1956; MS, Drexel U., 1974. Libr. asst. Atomic Energy Commn., Bombay, 1957-59; libr. asst. tech. svcs. Drexel U., Phila., 1960-61, Somerset County Libr., Somerville, N.J., 1962-66; children's libr. Bethlehem (Pa.) Pub. Libr., 1963-66; reference libr. Am. Internat. Coll., Springfield, Mass., 1973-74; asst. dir. West Haven (Conn.) Pub. Libr., 1979—. Mem. AAUW. Democrat. Hindu. Home: 843 Garden Rd Orange CT 06477 Office: West Haven Pub Libr 300 Elm West Haven CT 06516

SABO, CORINNE MAE, property manager, advocate; b. San Antonio, Tex., Apr. 23, 1948; d. James Beard and Mary Rita (Veer) S. Contbr. articles to various jours. Mem. Tex. Freedom Network; mem. bd. dirs. Alamo Breast Cancer Coalition and Found., co-chair advocacy com.; co-founder Valley Info. of AIDS Svc. for Lower Rio Grande Valley; mem. Women's Inst. for Freedom of the Press; mem. nat. adv. coun. Pastors For Peace; mem. Poverty and Race Rsch. Action Coun.; del. Tex. State Dem. Party Convention, 1996; del. 26th Senatorial Convention Dem. Party; mem. 21st Century Democrats; mem. Metro Alliance; mem. Tex. Interfaith Network, Liberty Tree, Bexar County Women's Polit. Caucus. Democrat. Roman Catholic. Home: PO Box 12212 San Antonio TX 78212

SABO, MARY JANE, secondary school educator in English, reading; b. Perth Amboy, N.J., Apr. 16, 1953; d. John William and Mary (Toth) S. AA, Middlesex County Coll., Edison, N.J., 1973; BA, Kean Coll. of N.J., 1976, MA, 1982. Cert. tchr., adminstr., N.J. reading specialist, English. Tchr. English, reading Woodbridge (N.J.) H.S., 1977—; tchr.-in-charge 3 program sites after-care program Woodbridge Twp. Schs., 1995—; cons. Holistic Scoring, N.J., 1984—; participant Woodbridge-Rutgers project, 1988; mem. student rev. assessment com. Woodbridge Twp. Schs., 1994. Com. rels. dir. Mayor's Adv. Com., Woodbridge Twp., 1988-92, cons. to News Letter editor Blinded Vets. Assn., 1987-89. Mem. Woodbridge Twp. Edn. Assn. (bldg. rep.). Democrat. Roman Catholic. Home: 265 East Rd Belford NJ 07718 Office: Woodbridge HS Rt 35 Woodbridge NJ 07095

SABOSIK, PATRICIA ELIZABETH, publisher, editor; b. Newark, Aug. 25, 1949; d. George Aloysius and Elizabeth Ann (Simko) S.; m. Kenneth Donald Gursky, Apr. 21, 1972 (div. 1980). BA in English, Kean Coll. N.J., 1976; MBA in Mktg., Seton Hall U., 1984; cert. advanced study in fin., Fairfield U., 1989. Proofreader Baker & Taylor, Somerville, N.J., 1969-71, database coordinator, 1971-74, prodn. editor, 1974-77, publs. mgr., editor, 1977-82; dir. mktg. services H.W. Wilson Pub. Co., Bronx, N.Y., 1982-84; editor, pub. Choice mag. Am. Library Assn., Middletown, Conn., 1984-94; project dir. Books for Coll. Librs. Am. Library Assn., Middletown, 1985-88, project dir. Guide to Ref. Books, 1988-94; v.p. electronic text Booklink Technologies, Wilmington, Mass., 1994; v.p. Linked Media, Navi Soft Divsn. Am. Online, Inc., Needham, Mass., 1994-96; editor in chief Whole Internet Catalog, GNN an Am. Online, Inc. Co., 1996—; membership chmn. Serials Industry Systems Adv. Com., 1983-89, vice chmn., 1985-86, newsletter editor, 1986-87. Editor-in-chief Whole Internet Catalog, 1995—; contbr. articles to profl. jours. Party rep. Twp. Com. Cranford, N.J., 1977-79; hon. bd. advisors U. Conn. Women's Ctr., 1989-91; mem. Conn. Women's Edn. and Legal Fund; nat. bd. dirs. Literacy Vols. of Am., 1992-94, also chair pub. and mktg. com. Mem. ALA (coms., editorial bd. Choice), AAUW, Assn. Coll. and Rsch. Librs. (publs. com.), Soc. for Scholarly Pub. (membership com., editor newsletter 1988-91, budget and fin. com. 1990-92, sec.-treas. 1994—, bd. dirs. 1994—), Appalachian Mountain Club, Women's Outdoors Club (newsletter editor 1984-86, regional rep. 1986-87). Republican. Roman Catholic. Office: Am Online Inc 75 2d Ave Ste 710 Needham MA 02194

SACCA, HARRIET WANDS, music educator; b. Pittsfield, Mass; d. Harry J. and Anna F. (Mara) Wands; BS, Coll. St. Rose, 1939, MA, 1962; student SUNY, Albany, Oneonta. Tchr. pub. schs., Albany, N.Y., 1942-66; instr. Coll. St. Rose, 1962-63; dir. music edn. Albany (N.Y.) Bd. Edn., 1966—; bur. assoc. examiner personnel N.Y. State Dept. Edn. Past pres. Soroptimist Internat., 1969-70, City Club Albany, Inc., 1974-75; active Albany County Dem. Com., 1962—; jud. del. 3d Jud. Dist. N.Y. State, 1975-96; mem. Albany Local Devel. Corp.; bd. dirs. St. Joseph's Housing Corp., Albany Tulip Festival; mem. adv. bd. capital Region Ctr. Arts in Edn., 1983—, Albany County Alteratives to Incarceration, 1983-96, chair sub com., 1985—; bd. dirs. Coop. Extension Community Resources Devel., 7 County Youth Symphony Orch., 1970-84; project dir. N.Y. Council on Arts; chair festival N.Y. Sch. Music, 1988; mem. com. of 5 appointed select name for 16, 000 seat Civic Arena; trustee assoc. Coll. of St. Rose, 1996—; mem. exec. bd. N.Y.S. Coun. Music Adminstrs., 1996—; area 3 rep. N.Y. State Coun. Music Adminstrs., 1995—. Recipient Citizen of Yr. award Ford Motor Co., 1971; Women Helping Women award Soroptimist, 1975; Disting. Service award N.Y. State PTA, 1985. Fellow Harry Truman Library; mem. Nat. Coun. Music Adminstrs., Music Educators Nat. Conf., N.Y. State Sch. Music Assn., Capitol Hill Choral Soc. (dir.), N.Y. St. Council Arts Award Childrens Opera (dir. project), Albany Adminstrs. Assn., Albany Civic Auditorium (dir.), Delta Kappa Gamma, Delta Epsilon. Democrat. Roman Catholic. Clubs: Bus. and Profl. Women's, Soroptimist, Club of Albany, Cath. Women's Service League, Coll. St. Rose Alumni, Pres.'s Soc. Home: 226 Morris St Albany NY 12208-3525 Office: Albany Bd Edn Acad Park Albany NY 12207

SACHS, MARILYN STICKLE, author, lecturer, editor; b. N.Y.C., Dec. 18, 1927; d. Samuel and Anna (Smith) Stickle; m. Morris Sachs, Jan. 26, 1947; children: Anne, Paul. BA, Hunter Coll., 1949; MSLS, Columbia U., 1953. Children's libr. Bklyn. Pub. Libr., 1949-60, San Francisco Pub. Libr., 1961-67. Author: Amy Moves In, 1964, Laura's Luck, 1965, Amy and Laura, 1966, Veronica Ganz, 1968, Peter and Veronica, 1969, Marv, 1970, The Bears' House, 1971 (Austrian Children's Book prize 1977, Recognition of Merit award George C. Stone Ctr. for Children's Books 1989), The Truth About Mary Rose, 1973 (Silver Slate Pencil award 1974), A Pocket Full of Seeds, 1973 (Jane Addams Children's Book Honor award 1974), Matt's Mitt, 1975, Dorrie's Book, 1975 (Silver State Pencil award 1977, Garden State Children's Book award 1978), A December Tale, 1976, A Secret Friends, 1978, A Summer's Lease, 1979, Bus Ride, 1980, Class Pictures, 1980, Fleet Footed Florence, 1981, Hello...Wrong Number, 1981, Call Me Ruth, 1982 (Assn. Jewish Librs. award 1983), Beach Towels, 1982, Fourteen, 1983, The Fat Girl, 1984, Thunderbird, 1985, Underdog, 1985 (Christopher 1986), Baby Sister 1986, Almost Fifteen, 1987, Fran Ellen's House, 1987 (award Bay Area Book Reviewers Assn. 1988, Recognition of Merit award George C. Stone Ctr. for Children's Books 1989), Just Like A Friend, 1989, At the Sound of the Beep, 1990, Circles, 1991, What My Sister Remembered, 1992, Thirteen, 1993, Ghosts in the Family, 1995; co-editor: (with Ann Durell) Big Book for Peace, 1990 (Calif. Children's Book award 1991, Jane Addams Children's Book prize 1991); reviewer books N.Y. Times, San Francisco Chronicle, 1970—. Mem. PEN, ACLU, SANE-Freeze, Sierra Club,

Authors' Guild, Soc. Children's Bookwriters. Democrat. Jewish. Home: 733 31st Ave San Francisco CA 94121

SACHS, ROMAYNE LIEBER, education administrator; b. Scranton, Pa., Feb. 20, 1931; d. Samuel and Anna (Ouslander) Lieber; m. David Morton Sachs, July 15, 1958; children: Paul, Jean. BA, U. Pa., 1952. Exec. sec. Civil Svc. Commn., Phila., 1954-61; vol. resource group Lower Merion Sch. Dist., Ardmore, Pa., 1974-77; admissions dir. Oak Lane Day Sch., Bluebell, Pa., 1980-84; program coord. Phila. Futures, 1988—. Dem. committeewoman Lower Merion Dem. Party, Ardmore; mem. intersch. coun. Lower Merion Sch. Dist., Ardmore, 1970-80; mem. adv. bd. Moore Coll.-Levy Gallery, Phila., 1994—. Jewish. Office: Phila Futures 230 S Broad Philadelphia PA 19002

SACKETT, DIANNE MARIE, city treasurer, accountant; b. Oil City, Pa., Dec. 29, 1956; d. Clarence Benjamin and Donna Jean (Grosteffon) Knight; m. Mark Douglas Sackett, May 26, 1984; children: Jason Michael, Cory James. BBA, Ea. Mich. U., 1979, MBA, 1986. Cert. mcpl. fin. adminstr. Accounts payable supr. Sarns, Inc., Ann Arbor, Mich., 1979-81; cost acct. Simplex Products Divsn., Adrian, Mich., 1981-83, gen. acctg. supr., 1983-88; city treas. City of Tecumseh, Mich., 1991—. Mem. Mich. Mcpl. Treas.' Assn., Mich. Mcpl. Fin. Officers Assn., Mcpl. Treas.' Assn. of the U.S. and Can. Pentecostal. Office: 309 E Chicago Blvd Tecumseh MI 49286-1550

SACKETT, SUSAN DEANNA, film and television production associate, writer; b. N.Y.C., Dec. 18, 1943; adopted d. Maxwell and Gertrude Selma (Kugel) S. B.A. in Edn., U. Fla., 1964, M.Ed., 1965. Tchr. Dade County Schs., Miami, Fla., 1966-68, L.A. City Schs., 1968-69; asst. publicist, comml. coordinator NBC-TV, Burbank, Calif., 1970-73; asst. to creator of Star Trek Gene Roddenberry, 1974-91; prodn. assoc. Star Trek: The Next Generation TV Series, 1987-91; writer Star Trek: The Next Generation, 1990-92; lectr. and guest speaker STAR TREK convs. in U.S., Eng., Australia, 1974-93. Author and editor: Letters to Star Trek, 1977; co-author: Star Trek Speaks, 1979; The Making of Star Trek-The Motion Picture, 1979; You Can Be a Game Show Contestant and Win, 1982, Say Goodnight Gracie, 1986; author: The Hollywood Reporter Book of Box Office Hits, 1990, 2nd edit., 96, Prime Time Hits, 1993, Hollywood Sings, 1995. Mem. ACLU, Writers Guild Am., Am. Humanist Assn., Mensa, Sierra Club. Democrat. Address: PO Box 3372 Carefree AZ 85377

SACKLOW, HARRIETTE LYNN, advertising agency executive; b. Bklyn., Apr. 12, 1944; d. Sidney and Mildred (Myers) Cooperman; m. Stewart Irwin, July 2, 1967; 1 child, Ian Marc. BA, SUNY, Albany, 1965, postgrad., 1967-69; postgrad., Union Coll., 1969-70, Telmar Media Sch., N.Y.C., 1981. Tchr. math. Guilderland (N.Y.) Cen. Schs., 1967-76; v.p. Wolkcas Advt., Inc., Albany, N.Y., 1975—; supr. internship programs Coll. St. Rose, Albany, 1981; lectr. to area colls., Albany, 1981-83. V.p. Sisterhood Congregation Ohav Sholom, Albany, 1983-86; bd. dirs. Northeastern N.Y. chpt. Arthritis Found.; key market coord. Partnership for a Drug Free Am., 1994—; advisor Ronald McDonald House; bd. dirs. Takundewide Homeowners Assn. Mem. NAFE, Am. Women in Radio and TV (pres. 1982-84, chmn. task force for new mem. acquisition, v.p. N.E. area 1987-89, chmn. area conf. 1987, pres. 1982-84, speaker, dist. dir.), N.Am. Advt. Agy. Network (bd. dirs. 1992—), Advt. of the Capital Dist., Albany (N.Y.) Yacht Club. Office: Wolkcas Comms Group Ste 500 41 State St Albany NY 12209

SACKS, CLAUDIA LUPOLETTI, specialty leasing agent; b. Queens, N.Y., Nov. 11, 1961; d. Richard Mark and Joy E. (Betty) L. BA in English Lit., Gettysburg Coll., 1983. Cert. elem. tchr. Asst. buyer Harris Originals, Inc., Hauppauge, N.Y., 1983-85, TSS Seedmans/Finders Keepers, Bklyn., 1985-86; mktg. dir., account assoc. Sunrise Mall/Mitchell Manning Assocs., N.Y.C. and Massapequa, N.Y., 1986-88; mktg. dir. Kravco, Inc./Green Acres Mall, King of Prussia, Pa., Valley Stream, N.Y., 1988-90, Compass Retail/Green Acres Mall, Atlanta, Valley Stream, 1991; dir. specialty leasing Compass Retail, Inc./Green Acres Mall, Atlanta, Valley Stream, 1991-93, EQK Green Acres Trust/Green Acres Mall Corp. subs. of Arbor Property Trust, Valley Stream, N.Y., 1994-96; specialty leasing mgr. Faison & Assocs., Inc., Charlotte, N.C., 1996—. Mem. Pvt. Industry Coun., Hempstead, N.Y., 1989-91. Mem. Internat. Coun. Shopping Ctrs., NY/NJ Coun. Shopping Ctrs., Valley Stream C. of C. Home: Apt 1118 7710 Waterford Sq Dr Charlotte NC 28226 Office: Faison & Assocs 5471 Central Ave Charlotte NC 28212

SACKS, PATRICIA ANN, librarian, consultant; b. Allentown, Pa., Nov. 6, 1939; d. Lloyd Alva and Dorothy Estelle (Stoneback) Stahl; m. Kenneth LeRoy Sacks, June 27, 1959. A.B., Cedar Crest Coll., 1959; M.S. in L.S., Drexel U., 1965. News reporter Call-Chronicle, Allentown, 1956-59, 1961-63; reference librarian Cedar Crest Coll., Allentown, 1964-66, head librarian, 1966-73; dir. libraries Muhlenberg and Cedar Crest Colls., Allentown, 1973-94; dir. libr. svcs. Cedar Crest Coll., 1994; sr. fellow Lehigh Valley Assn. Ind. Colls., 1994—. del. On Line Computer Library Ctr. Users Council, Columbus, Ohio, 1977-84; cons. colls./health care orgns., libr. orgns. 1981—. Author: (with Whildin Sara Lou) Preparing for Accreditation: A Handbook for Academic Librarians, 1993; mem. editorial bd. Jour. Acad. Librarianship, 1982-84. Trustee Cedar Crest Coll., 1985-89. Mem. United Way Lehigh Valley Coms., 1993—; bd. dirs. John and Dorothy Morgan Cancer Ctr., 1994—. Named Outstanding Acad. Woman, Lehigh Valley Assn. for Acad. Women, 1984, Muhlenberg Coll. Outstanding Adminstr., 1987, Alumni Tricorn award Muhlenberg Coll., 1989, Alumnae Achievement award Cedar Crest Coll., 1994. Mem. ALA (chmn. copyright com. 1985-87), Assn. Coll. and Research Libraries (chmn. standards and accreditation com. 1976-78, 81-84), Lehigh Valley Assn. Ind. Colls. (chmn. librarians sect. 1967-81, 88-92), AAUW, LWV Lehigh Valley Conservancy, Appalachian Mountain Club, Phi Alpha Theta, Phi Kappa Phi, Beta Phi Mu. Democrat. Home: 2997 Fairfield Dr Allentown PA 18103-5413 Office: Lehigh Valley Assn Ind Colls 119 W Greenwich St Bethlehem PA 18018

SACKS, TEMI J., public relations executive; b. Phila.; d. Jule and Adeline (Levin) S. BA, Temple U. Pubs. editor Del. Valley Regional Planning Commn., Phila.; communications assoc. Fedn. Jewish Agys., Phila.; pres. T. J. Sacks Pub. Relations, Phila.; exec. v.p., mng. dir. healthcare div. Lobsenz-Stevens Inc., N.Y.C.; guest lectr. Temple U. Sch. Communications. Mem. Healthcare Businesswomen's Assn., Pharm. Advt. Coun., Women Execs. in Pub. Rels. Home: 142 W End Ave New York NY 10023-6103 Office: 460 Park Ave S New York NY 10016-7301

SADER, CAROL HOPE, former state legislator; b. Bklyn., July 19, 1935; d. Nathan and Mollie (Farkas) Shimkin; m. Harold M. Sader, June 9, 1957; children: Neil, Randi Sader Friedlander, Elisa. BA, Barnard Coll., Columbia U., 1957. Sch. tchr. Bd. Edn., Morris, Conn., 1957-58; legal editor W. H. Anderson Co., Cin., 1974-78; freelance legal editor Shawnee Mission, Kans., 1978-87; mem. Kans. Ho. of Reps., 1987-94; chair Ho. Pub. Health and Welfare Com., 1991-92; chair Joint Ho. and Senate Com. on Health Care Decisions for the 90's, 1992; vice chair Ho. Econ. Devel. Com., 1991-92; policy chair Ho. Dem. Caucus, 1993-94. Dem. candidate for Kans. Lt. Gov., 1994; chmn. bd. trustees Johns County C.C., Overland Park, Kans., 1984-86, trustee Johnson County Cmty. Coll., 1981-86; pres. League of Women Voters, Johnson County, 1983-85; State of Kans. League of Women Voters Bd, 1986-87; bd. dirs. United Cmty. Svcs. of Johnson County Shawnee Mission, 1984-92, Jewish Vocat. Svc. Bd., 1983-92; chmn. Kans. State Holocaust Commn., 1991-94; pres. Mainstream Coalition of Johnson County, 1995-96. Recipient Trustee award Assn. of Women in Jr. and C.C., 1985, awards Kans. Pub. Transit Assn., 1990, AARP, 1992, Assn. Kans. Theater, 1992, Nat. Coun. Jewish Women, 1992, Kans. Assn. Osteo. Medicine, 1992, Kans. Chiropractic Assn., 1992, United Com. Svcs. Johnson County, 1992, Disting. Pub. Svcs. award Johnson County, 1993, Hallpac Kans. Pub. Svc. award Hallmark Cards, Inc., 1993. Mem. Coun. Women Legislators, Phi Delta Kappa. Democrat. Home: 8612 Linden Dr Shawnee Mission KS 66207-1807

SADLER, PAMELA L., fundraising executive; b. Karachi, Pakistan, Nov. 8, 1965; came to U.S., 1966; d. T. Brooke and Patricia J. (McFadden) S. BS, So. Coll., Collegedale, Tenn., 1988. Cert. fund raising exec. Dir. devel. Battle Creek (Mich.) Acad., 1989-93; assoc. dir. Philanthropic Svcs. for Instns., Silver Spring, Md., 1993—. Trustee Silent Observer, Battle Creek, 1990-93; mgr. Milton Murray Found., Silver Spring, 1993-96. Mem. Nat. Soc. Fund Raising Execs., Coun. for Aid to Secondary Edn. Mem. Seventh-Day Adventist Ch. Office: Adventist World Headquarters 12501 Old Columbia Pike Silver Spring MD 20904-6600

SADLER, SALLIE INGLIS, psychotherapist; b. Phila., Nov. 16, 1941; d. H. Barton Off and Janet (Miller) Nelson; m. William A. Sadler, Jr., Apr. 23, 1977; children: Bill, Lisa, Nelson, Ashley, Kirsten. BA, Rollins Coll., Winter Park, Fla., 1964; MSW with high acad. achievement, Rutgers U., 1979; postgrad., Pa. State U., 1986-89. Cert. social worker. Caseworker II, dir. group work Family and Children's Svc. West Essex, Caldwell, N.J., 1979-81; dir. Single Parent Ctr. West Essex, Montclair, N.J., 1981-85; pvt. practice Upper Montclair, N.J., 1981-85; chief clin. svcs. Family Svc. Ctr., U.S. Naval Air Base, Alameda, Calif., 1990-95; sr. psychiat. social worker dept. psychiatry Kaiser Permanente Med. Ctr., San Francisco, 1995—; oral license examiner Calif. Bd. Behavioral Sci. Examiners; adj. instr. div. social scis. Bloomfield (N.J.) Coll., 1979-81, N.J. Inst. Tech., 1984-85; instr. psychology dept. Lock Haven (Pa.) U., 1985-90. Mem. NASW, APA, Assn. Women Faculty in Higher Edn.

SADLER, TAMMY KAY, junior high school educator; b. Anna, Ill., July 11, 1959; d. Freddie Edward and Mary Ruth (Lewis) Walker; m. Rodney Dale Sadler, Aug. 3, 1979; 1 child, Rodney Dale II. AS, Shawnee Jr. Coll., 1979; BS in Edn., Southeast Mo. State U., 1981. Cert. elem. tchr., English specialization, Mo. Elem. tchr. St. Vincent Elem. Sch., Perryville, Mo., 1981-90; tchr. St. Vincent Jr./Sr. High Sch., Perryville, Mo., 1991—; great books leader St Vincent Elem. Sch., Perryville, 1983-85; project star facilitator St. Vincent Jr./Sr. High Sch., Perryville, 1991—, pub. rels. coord., 1994-95. Jr. high volleyball coach St. Vincent Jr./Sr. High Sch., Perryville, 1982, 90—, cheerleading moderator, 1992—; jr. high basketball coach St. Vincent Elem., Perryville, 1981-82; speech and drama coach, judge Bellarmine Speech League, Archdiocese of St. Louis, 1984-91. Mem. Nat. Cath. Educators Assn., Southeast Mo. State U. Alumni Assn. Office: St Vincent Jr Sr High 210 S Waters Perryville MO 63775

SADOWSKI, CAROL JOHNSON, artist; b. Chgo., Mar. 20, 1929; d. Carl Valdamar Johnson and Elizabeth Hilma (Booth) Johnson-Chellberg; m. Edmund Sadowski, July 9, 1949; children: Lynn Carol Mahoney, Christie Sadowski Cortez. AAS, Wright-Ill. Coll., 1949. Tchr. art Malverne (N.Y.) H.S., 1968-69; artist Valley Stream, N.Y., 1968-76, Hollywood, Fla., 1976—; guest speaker Mus. Art Ft. Lauderdale, Fla., 1991, others; TV appearances on WCGB, Gainesville, WSVN, Miami, Storer and Hollywood Cable. One-woman shows include Mus. Fla. History, 1984-85, 87, Hist. Mus. South Fla., Miami, 1986, Thomas Ctr. Arts, Gainesville, Gla., 1985, 87, Hist. Mus. South Fla., Miami, 1986, Thomas Ctr. Arts, Gainesville, Gla., 1985, 87, Elliott Mus., Stuart, Fla., 1987, Hemingway Mus. & Home, Key West, Fla., 1986, Mus. Fla. History, Tallahassee, 1985, 87, Alliance Francaise de Miami, 1995; commd. painting St. Agustin Antigua Found., St. Augustine, Fla., 1985, Atlantic Bank, Ft. Lauderdale, Fla., Bonnet House Fla. Trust, Ft. Lauderdale, Tropical Art Gallery, Naples, Fla., 1981-83, Tequesta (Fla.) Art Gallery, 1985-89, Gingerbread Square Gallery, Key West, 1990—, Wally Findlay Galleries, Inc., Palm Beach, Key West Graphics, Tamarac. Recipient Hemingway medal Ernest Hemingway Mus., Cuba, 1990, appreciation award City of Hollywood. Mem. Internat. Platform Assn., Broward Art Guild, Fla. Hist. Assn., Ernest Hemingway Soc., Chopin Found., Am. Inst. for Polish Culture, Alliance Francaise de Miami, Internat. Platform Assn., Women in the Arts Nat. Mus. (charter mem.). Home and Studio: 1480 Sheridan St Apt B-17 Hollywood FL 33020-2295

SAEGESSER, MARGUERITE M., artist; b. Bern, Switzerland, May 27, 1922; came to U.S., 1974; d. Wilhelm and Fanny (Keupfer) Ruefenacht; m. Max Saegesser, May 27, 1952; 1 child, Francisca Marguerite; stepchildren: Anne-Marie Logan, Elisabeth, Barbara, Ursula L'Eplattenier. Solo exhbns. include De Saisset Mus., Santa Clara, Calif., 1995, Smith Andersen Gallery, Palo Alto, Calif., 1981, 85, 89, 91, 92, 95, Galerie Schindler, Bern, 1968, 90, Art Fair, Basel, Switzerland, 1990, many others; group exhbns. include Long Beach, Calif., 1971, Bienne Open Air Sculpture Show, Switzerland, 1958, 62, 66, Soc. Painters & Sculptors, Bern, 1945-46, 52, 56. Grantee Swiss Endowment Arts, 1995. Mem. South Bay Area Women's Caucus for Arts. Democrat. Home: 840 Mesa Ave Palo Alto CA 94306

SAFADI-PSYLLOS, GINA MONI, administrative assistant, business owner; b. Astoria, N.Y., Nov. 21, 1966; d. Juan Safadi and Lourdes Jannette (Navarette-Zavala) Achury; m. Peter John Psyllos, Nov. 15, 1992. BA, Marymount Manhattan Coll., 1988; Art Adminstrn. Cert., NYU, 1996; BS, U. of the State of N.Y., Albany, 1996. Computer lab. asst. Marymount Manhattan Coll., N.Y.C., 1986-88; adminstrv. aide NYU, N.Y.C., 1988-90; adminstrv. asst. BBDO, N.Y.C., 1990—; owner, art dealer SPace Art Corp., Auberndale, N.Y., 1996—; pub. chair dance dept. Marymount Manhattan Coll., 1987-88; artist, newsletter Streetlife Serenade, 1996. Chairperson St. Vincent Ferrer H.S. Class of '84 Reunion Com., N.Y.C., 1993-94; vol. Nassau County Mus. of Art, Roslyn, N.Y., 1996. Mem. Nat. Assn. of Fine Artists, Am. Assn. of Mus. Roman Catholic. Home: 40-26-171 St Flushing NY 11358

SAFARS, BERTA See FISZER-SZAFARZ, BERTA

SAFERITE, LINDA LEE, library director; b. Santa Barbara, Calif., Mar. 25, 1947; d. Elwyn C. and Polly (Frazer) S.; m. Andre Doyon, July 16, 1985. BA, Calif. State U., Chico, 1969; MS in Library Sci., U. So. Calif., 1970; cert. in Indsl. Relations, UCLA, 1976; MBA, Pepperdine U., 1979. Librarian-in-charge, reference librarian Los Angeles County Pub. Libr. System, 1970-73, regional reference librarian, 1973-75, sr. librarian-in-charge, 1975-78, regional adminstr., 1978-80; libr. dir. Scottsdale (Ariz.) Pub. Libr. System, 1980-93, Fort Collins (Colo.) Pub. Libr., 1993—; task force del. White House Conf. on Libr. and Info. Svcs., 1992—, rep. Region V, 1992-94. Bd. dirs. Scottsdale-Paradise Valley YMCA, 1981-86, Ariz. Libr. Friends, 1990-92; bd. dirs. AMIGOS, 1990, chmn., 1992-93; mem. Class 5, Scottsdale Leavership, 1991. Recipient Cert. Recognition for efforts in civil rights Ariz. Atty. Gen.'s Office, 1985, Libr. award Ariz. Libr. Friends, 1988, Women of Distinction award for Edn., 1989, State Project of Yr. award, 1995, Ariz. Disting. Svc. award, 1993; named State Libr. of Yr., 1990. Mem. ALA, Ariz. State Libr. Assn. (pres. 1987-88), Ariz. Women's Town Hall Alumni-Assn., Met. Bus. and Profl. Women (Scottsdale, pres. 1986-87), Soroptimist (pres. 1981-83). Republican. Office: Fort Collins Pub Libr 201 Peterson St Fort Collins CO 80524-2919

SAFFER, AMY BETH, foreign language educator; b. N.Y.C., Apr. 19, 1950; d. William and Evelyn (Yankowitz) S. BA, Fairleigh Dickinson U., 1972, MA, 1983; postgrad., Jersey City State Coll., 1983-84. Cert. tchr. Spanish K-12, N.J. Tchr. Madison (N.J.) High Sch., 1973, Livingston (N.J.) High Sch., 1973—; mem. faculty and dist. coms. Livingston Sch. Dist., 1975—; advisor to class of 1977, Livingston High Sch., 1975-77, chair mid. states subcom., 1990. Inducted Livingtion H.S. Alumni Hall of Fame, 1993. Mem. NEA, Am. Assn. Tchrs. of Spanish and Portuguese, N.J. Edn. Assn., Fgn. Lang. Educators of N.J., Livingston Edn. Assn. (negotiations rep. 1980—), Essex County Edn. Assn. Office: Livingston High Sch Livingston NJ 07039

SAFFIR, CYNTHIA RUTH, lawyer; b. N.Y.C., Oct. 13, 1954; d. Richard Benjamin and Leona (Rostov) S. BA with honors, U. Calif., Santa Cruz, 1976; JD, Loyola U., L.A., 1980. Bar: Calif. 1980, U.S. Dist. Ct. (ctrl. dist.) Calif. 1980. Assoc. Kahn, Stern, Blaney & Kittrell, L.A., 1981-82, Silver Kreisler Goldwasser and Shaeffer, Santa Monica, Calif., 1982-86; assoc. counsel Writers Guild of Am., West Inc., L.A., 1987-91, dir. legal svcs., 1991—. Activist, rschr., paralegal United Farmworkers Union, Salinas, Calif., 1974-75. Mem. L.A. County Bar Assn. (exec. com. labor and employment sect. 1993-95, mem. planning com. entertainment law and employment conf. 1990), Beverly Hills Bar Assn. Democrat. Office: Writers Guild of Am W Inc 7000 W 3d St Los Angeles CA 90048

SAFIAN, GAIL ROBYN, public relations executive; b. Bklyn., Dec. 12, 1947; d. Jack I. and Harriet S.; m. Jay Mark Eisenberg, Jan. 6, 1979; children: Julia, Eric. BA, SUNY, Albany, 1968; MBA, NYU, 1982. Reporter Albany (N.Y.)-Knickerbocker News/Times-Union, 1969, Athens (Ohio) Messenger, 1969-71; pub. relations asst. Mountainside Hosp., Montclair, N.J., 1971-74; dir. pub. relations Riverside Hosp., Boonton, N.J., 1974-78; consumer affairs coordinator Johnson & Johnson Personal Products Div., Milltown, N.J., 1978-79; v.p., group mgr. Harshe Rotman & Druck, N.Y.C., 1979-82; exec. v.p., dir. Health Care Div. Ruder Finn & Rotman, N.Y.C., 1982-84; v.p., mgr. client services Burson-Marsteller, N.Y.C., 1984-86; v.p., group mgr. health care Cohn & Wolfe, N.Y.C., 1986-90; exec. v.p., gen. mgr. MCS, Summit, N.J., 1990-94; pres. Safian Comm. Inc., Maplewood, N.J., 1994—. Mem. devel. com. Cancer Care, N.Y.C., 1985—. Recipient MacEachern award Am. Hosp. Assn., 1974, Communications Award Internat. Assn. Bus. Communicators, 1976, Creativity in Pub. Rels. award Inside PR, 1992, 93. Mem. N.Y. Acad. Scis., Drug Info. Assn., Women in Communications (Clarion award 1974), Healthcare Businesswomen's Assn. (mem. bd. dirs.). Jewish. Home: 31 Hickory Dr Maplewood NJ 07040-2107 Office: Safian Comm Inc 31 Hickory Dr Maplewood NJ 07040-2107

SAFIAN, SHELLEY CAROLE, advertising agency executive; b. Bklyn., May 29, 1954; d. Jack Israel and Harriet Sara (Cohen) S. BFA, Parsons Sch. Design/New Sch. for Social Rsch., 1975. Asst. art dir. Axelrod and Assocs., N.Y.C., 1975-77; art dir. Sta. WDBO-TV-AM/FM, Orlando, Fla., 1978-80; owner, pres. Safian Comm. Svcs., Inc., Winter Park, 1981—, Bonté Sportswear, Inc., Winter Park, 1993—; mem. adv. com. Career Edn., Orange County, Fla., 1981-88, chmn., 1982-83. Exec. producer/dir. March of Dimes Telethon, Orlando, 1984; bd. dirs. Boy Scouts Am., 1987-91; exec. dir. United Cerebral Palsy Telethon, Orlando, 1982-83; pub. rels. liaison United Cerebral Palsy, Orlando, 1983-84; founder Career Dir. for the Deaf, Orlando, 1985; trustee, pub. rels. chair Nat. Multiple Sclerosis Soc., 1991-92, bd. dirs., 1990, 91. Recipient 1st pl. Addy awards Orlando Advt. Fedn., 1981, 87, 88, 89, 1st pl. Addy award, 2d pl. awards, merit awards, 1982, 84, 85, 87, 88, Nat. Telly award Bronze Statue, 1988, Up and Coming award Price Waterhouse/Orlando Bus. Jour., 1988, Pro-Mark 1st pl. awards Fla. Coun. Shopping Ctrs., 1989, 90, merit award, 1990, Telly awrad Bronze finalist, 1989, 91. Mem. Broadcast Promotion and Mktg. Execs. Assn. (Silver Medallion 1983, nat. finalist 2 Silver Microphone awards 1986, 87), Broadcast Designer's Assn. (bd. dirs. 1980-82), Am. Women in Radio and TV (bd. dirs. 1980-81). Republican. Avocation: horseback riding. Office: Safian Communications Svcs PO Box 1016 Winter Park FL 32790-1016

SAFRAN-NAVEH, GILA OLIVIA, literature and Jewish studies educator; b. Balky, U.S.S.R., May 11, 1944; came to U.S., 1969; d. Isaac and Sara (Ghitelman) Safran; m. Michael M. Naveh, Nov. 8, 1965; 1 child, Dorian Naveh. PhD, U. Calif., San Diego, 1981. Lectr. San Diego State U., 1969-72; lectr., vis. prof. U. Calif., San Diego, 1972-86; assoc. prof. U. Cin., 1986—. Author: From Apples of Gold in Silver Settings to Imperial Messages: Parables from the Bible to Present, 1996, (book of poetry) Other Inquisitions; editor: The Formal Complexity of Natural Language, 1987. Mem. commn. on status of women U. Cin., 1991—, assn. women faculty, 1991-95, race rels. com., 1990—. Recipient A.B. Dolly Cohen Excellence in Univ. Teaching award, 1996; Skirball fellow Oxford (Eng.) Ctr. for Postgrad. Studies, 1995; NEH grantee, 1993-94. Mem. MLA, Nat. Women's Assn., Semiotic Studies Assn. (bd. dirs. 1986—). Office: U Cin 2006 Clifton Ave Cincinnati OH 45221

SAGAWA, SHIRLEY SACHI, lawyer; b. Rochester, N.Y., Aug. 25, 1961; d. Hidetaka H. and Patricia (Ford) S.; m. Gregory A. Baer; children: Jackson Ford Baer, Matthew Sagawa Baer. AB, Smith Coll., 1983; MSc, London Sch. Econs., 1984; JD, Harvard U., 1987. Bar: Md. 1988. Chief counsel youth policy, labor and human resources com. U.S. Senate, Washington, 1987-91; sr. counsel and dir. family and youth policy Nat. Women's Law Ctr., Washington, 1991-93; spl. asst. to Pres. Clinton for domestic policy, 1993; exec. dir., mng. dir., exec. v.p. Corp. for Nat. and Comty. Svc., Washington, 1993—. Mem. exec. bd. Orgn. for Pan-Asian Am. Women, Washington, 1987-89; mem. Women of Color Leadership Coun., 1991-92; vice chair, bd. dirs. Nat. Community Svc. Commn., 1991-93. Recipient Philip V. McGance award Coun. for Advancement of Citizenship, 1991, cert. of recognition Nat. Coun. Jewish Women, 1989, Alexandrine medal Coll. St. Catherine, St. Paul, 1995; Harry S. Truman scholar, 1981; Smith Coll. Alumnae Assn. fellow, 1983, AAUW fellow, 1986. Mem. Md. Bar Assn. Democrat. Episcopalian. Office: Corp for Nat and Community Svc 1201 New York Ave NW Washington DC 20005-3917

SAGER, SUSAN JOY, business educator; b. Schenectady, N.Y., Jan. 10, 1959; d. Robert Wendell and Clare June (Sussdorf) S.; m. Scott Edward Moody, Oct. 10, 1993. Diploma, Lake Placid Sch. of Art, 1979; BA, Hampshire Coll., 1981. Sr. staff asst. artisanry program Boston U., 1983-85; registrar Swain Sch. of Design, New Bedford, Mass., 1985-87; acting registrar Harvard U., Cambridge, Mass., 1987-88; acad. dir. Maine Photo Workshop, Rockport, 1988; student svcs. coord. Portland (Maine) Sch. of Art, 1989-90; asst. dir. Haystack Mt. Sch. of Crafts, Deer Isle, Maine, 1990-92; owner ArtBiz, Bangor, Maine, 1992—; exec. dir. Bangor Hist. Soc., 1995—; sec., exec. com., Watershed Ctr. for Ceramic Arts, Edgecomb, Maine, 1989-94' regional rep. Maine Crafts Assn., Deer Isle, 1993-95. Maine alumni admissions rep. Hampshire Coll., Amherst, Mass., 1989—. Mem. NOW, Maine Crafts Assn. Office: ArtBiz PO Box 2403 Bangor ME 04402

SAHATJIAN, MANIK, nurse, psychologist; b. Tabris, Iran, July 24, 1921; came to U.S., 1951; d. Dicran and Shushanig (Der-Galustian) Mnatzaganian; m. George Sahatjian, Jan. 21, 1954; children: Robert, Edwin. Nursing Cert., Am. Mission Hosps.-Boston U., 1954; BA in Psychology, San Jose State U., 1974, MA in Psychology, 1979. RN, Calif., Mass. Head nurse Am. Mission Hosp., Tabris, 1945-46; charge nurse Banke-Melli Hosp., Tehran, 1946-51; vis. nurse Vis. Nurse Assn., Oakland, Calif., 1956-57; research asst. Stanford U., 1979-81, Palo Alto (Calif.) Med. Research Found., 1981-84; documentation supr. Bethesda Convalescent Ctr., Los Gatos, Calif., 1985-86; sr. outreach worker City of Fremont (Calif.) Human Svcs., 1987-90, case mgr., 1990—; guest rsch. asst. NASA Ames Lab., Mountain View, Calif., summers 1978, 79. Author (with others) psychol. research reports. Fulbright scholar, 1951; Iran Found. scholar, 1953. Mem. AAUW, Western Psychol. Assn. Democrat. Mem. St. Andrew Armenian Church. Home: 339 Starlite Way Fremont CA 94539-7642

SAHS, MAJORIE JANE, art educator; b. Altadena, Calif., Aug. 27, 1926; d. Grayson Michael and Janie Belle (Aaron) McCarty; m. Eugene Otto Sahs, July 21, 1949; children: Victoria, Stephen, Jeffry. Student, Art Ctr. of L.A., 1943-45, Emerson Coll., Boston, 1945; BA, Sacramento State U., 1970; MA in Art Edn., Calif. State U., Sacramento, 1972, postgrad., 1973-79. Cert. secondary tchr., Calif. Tchr. art Sacramento County Schs., 1971-80; cons. Whole Brain Learning Modes, Sacramento, 1980-84; tng. specialist Art Media, Sacramento, Calif., 1983—; instr. Found. for Continuing Med. Edn., Calif., 1985; presenter Nat. Art Edn. Conf., Chgo., 1992, 93, Asian Pacific Conf. on Arts Edn., Franklin, Australia, Internat. Conf., Montreal, Can., 1993; cons., lectr. in field; judge U.S. Treas., 1994, 95, 96, Dept. of Calif. Student Art. Prodr., writer guide and video Gesture Painting Through T'ai Chi, 1992; editor, pub. Calif.'s state newspaper for art edn., 1987-90; editor: Crocker Mus. Docent Guide, 1990; mem. editl. bd. Jour. for Nat. Art Edn. Assn., 1990—; editor: (newsletter) U.S. Soc. for Edn. Through Art, 1994-96; designer of ltd. edits. scarves and cards for Nat. Breast Cancer Rsch. Fund, Exploration Inspiration '95. Del. Calif. Arts Leadership Symposium for Arts Edn., 1979, Legis. Coalition Through The Arts, Calif., 1989, 95; judge Calif. State Fair Art Show, 1989, 95, Fed. Treasury Poster Contest, 1994, 95, 96; organizer and host art show and fundraiser for women candidates, 1992. Recipient Patriotic Svc. award Fed. Treasury Dept., 1996, State award of Merit. Mem. Internat. Assn. Edn. through Art, U.S. Soc. Edn. through Art (editor newsletter 1994-96), Nat. Art Edn. Assn. (mem. editl. bd. jour. 1990—, Nat. Outstanding Newspaper Editor award 1988, 89), Calif. Art Edn. Assn. (mem. state coun., mem. area coun., editor state paper, State Award of Merit), Calif. Children's Homes Soc. (pres. Camellia chpt. 1990-91), Asian Pacific Arts Educators Assn., Art Ctr. L.A. Alumni. Home and Office: 1836 Walnut Ave Carmichael CA 95608-5417

SAIBLE, STEPHANIE, magazine editor; b. Mobile, Ala., Sept. 11, 1954; d. Lewis J. Slaff and Phoebe-Jane (Berse) Deats; m. Mark Saible, May 31, 1981 (div. 1983). Student, Va. Commonwealth U., 1972-75. Editorial asst. Woman's World Magazine, Englewood, N.J., 1980-81, service copywriter, 1981-83, assoc. articles editor, 1983-84, articles editor, 1984-85, sr. editor features dept., 1985-86, sr. editor services dept., 1986, now editor-in-chief. Contbr. articles to Woman's World, Modern Bride, New Body, Celebrity

Beauty, Trim & Fit. Named Wonder Woman of the Yr., Bus. Jour. N.J., 1986. Mem. Women in Communications. Office: Woman's World Mag 270 Sylvan Ave Englewood Cliffs NJ 07632*

SAID, PHYLLIS DIANNE, elementary school educator; b. Muncie, Ind., Aug. 21, 1942; d. Russel Philip and Edna Ann (Kiracofe) Donhauser; m. William Lee Said, Aug. 24, 1963; children: Denise Janine, Douglas James. BS, Ball State U., Muncie, Ind., 1970, MA in Edn., 1976. Kindergarten tchr. Delaware Cmty. Schs., Eaton, Ind., 1970-76, tchr. 1st grade, 1976—. Author/prodr.: (video prodn.) Prime Time - Indiana Dept. of Edn., 1986, 87, 89. Vol. Minnetrista Cultural Ctr., Muncie, Delaware County Coalition for Literacy, Muncie. Lilly Endowment Tchr. Creativity fellow, Indpls., 1992; Ind. Dept. Edn. Tchr. Tech. grantee, 1988, 90, Energy Edn. grantee, 1990, Bell grantee, 1995, Ctrl. Bur. Eng. Enhancement grant, 1996; recipient Fulbright Tchr. Exch. award, Eng., 1995—, Eisenhower Sci. and Math. award, 1995, Ind. Wildlife Fedn. Conservation Educator of Yr., 1995, Nila Purvis Animal Helper of Yr., 1994. Mem. Internat. Reading Assn., Ind. Wildlife Assn., Audubon Soc., Muncie Area Reading Coun., Hoosier Mgrs. (pres. 1993-94), Alpha Delta Kappa (treas. 1992-94). Republican. Methodist.

SAIKI, PATRICIA (MRS. STANLEY MITSUO SAIKI), former federal agency administrator, former congresswoman; b. Hilo, Hawaii, May 28, 1930; d. Kazuo and Shizue (Inoue) Fukuda; m. Stanley Mitsuo Saiki, June 19, 1954; children: Stanley Mitsuo, Sandra Saiki Williams, Margaret C., Stuart K., Laura H. BA, U. Hawaii, 1952. Tchr. U.S. history Punahou Sch., Kaimuki Intermediate Sch., Kalani High Sch., Honolulu, 1952-64; sec. Rep. Party Hawaii, Honolulu, 1964-66, vice chmn., 1966-68, 82-83, chmn., 1983-85; rsch. asst. Hawaii State Senate, 1966-68; mem. Hawaii Ho. of Reps., 1968-74, Hawaii State Senate, 1974-82, 100th-101st Congresses from 1st Hawaii dist., Washington, 1987-91; adminstr. SBA, Washington, 1991-93; mem. Pres.'s Adv. Coun. on Status of Women, 1969-76; mem. Nat. Commn. Internat. Women's Yr., 1969-70; commr. We. Interstate Commn. on Higher Edn.; fellow Eagleton Inst., Rutgers U., 1970; fellow Inst. of Politics, Kennedy Sch. Govt., Harvard U., 1993; bd. dirs. Bank of Am.-Hawaii, Landmark Systems Corp., Internat. Asset Recovery Corp. Mem. Kapiolano Hosp. Aux.; sec. Hawaii Rep. Com., 1964-66, vice chmn., 1966-68, chmn., 1983-85; del. Hawaii Constl. Conv., 1968; alt. del. Rep. Nat. Conv., 1968, del., 1984, Rep. nominee for lt. gov. Hawaii, 1982, for U.S. Senate, 1990, for. gov. Hawaii, 1990; mem. Fedn. Rep. Women; trustee Hawaii Pacific Coll.; st bd. govs. Boys and Girls Clubs Hawaii; mem. adv. coun. ARC; bd. dirs. Nat. Fund for Improvement of Post-Secondary Edn., 1982-85; past bd. dirs. Straub Med. Rsch. Found., Honolulu, Hawaii's Visitors Bur., Honolulu, Edn. Commn. of States, Honolulu, Hawaii Visitors Bur., 1983-85; trustee U. Hawaii Found., 1984-86, Hawaii Pacific Coll., Honolulu. Episcopalian. Home: 784 Elepaio St Honolulu HI 96816-4710

SAILORS, EMMA LOU, pediatrician; b. Lincolnville, Ind., Aug. 21, 1923; d. Lee J. and Ethel Lavonne (Wingard) S.; m. Thomas E. Louis (dec.), Mar. 16, 1957; children: Susan, Julie, Tracy, Hilarie. BA, Manchester Coll., North Manchester, 1944; MD, Ind. U., Indpls., 1949. Diplomate Am. Bd. Pediat. Intern U. Ill., Chgo., 1949-50; resident in pediat. N.E. Med. Ctr.-Tufts, Boston, 1950-51; resident, then fellowship La. State U., New Orleans, 1951-54; instr. Tulane U. Sch. Med. dept. pediat., New Orleans, 1954-57; asst. prof. Tulane U. Sch. Med. dept. pediat., 1957-61, assoc. clin. prof., 1961-67; sch. physician Yonkers (N.Y.) Pub. Schs., 1971-77, chief sch. physician, 1977—; clinician Westchester County (N.Y.) Dept. Health, 1971-95; mem. task forces (adolescent pregnancy, immunization), Yonkers. Contbr. articles to prof. jours. Bd. mem. 1st Unitarian Ch., New Orleans, 1955-67, Cmty. Unitarian Ch., White Plains, N.Y., 1967—, Youth Svcs. Coun. former chair, Dobbs Ferry, N.Y., 1975—, sch. bd. nominating com., Dobbs Ferry, 1970's, 1980's, Sheltering the Homeless is Our Responsibility, White Plains, 1993—; ch. sch. tchr. Unitarian Chs., New Orleans, 9 yrs. Mem. Med. Soc. N.Y. State, Am. Sch. Health Assn., LWV. Democrat. Home: 125 Bellair Dr Dobbs Ferry NY 10522 Office: Yonkers Pub Schs Health Svc care Burroughs Sch 150 Rockland Ave Yonkers NY 10705

SAINE, BETTY BOSTON, elementary school educator; b. Newton, N.C., Dec. 1, 1932; d. Glenn and Carrie Queen Boston; m. Thomas Paul Saine, Aug. 3, 1968; 1 child, Carrie Ann. BA, Lenoir Rhyne Coll., 1956. Tchr. grade 4 High Point (N.C.) City Schs., 1956-59, Charlotte City Schs./Charlotte-Mecklenburg Schs., 1959-66; art tchr. grades 1-8 Newton-Conover City Schs., 1966-67; tchr. grade 4 Charlotte-Mecklenburg Schs., 1967-68; tchr. grade 6 Lincolnton (N.C.) City Schs., 1968-70; tchr. grades 5 and 6 Lincolnton City Schs./Lincoln County Schs., 1972-90; ret. Historian, publicity chair beautification com. Sunflower Garden Club, Lincolnton, 1976-87. Mem. Alpha Delta Kappa (various offices and coms.). Methodist. Home: 2492 Pickwick Pl Lincolnton NC 28092-7748

SAINT, EVA MARIE, actress; b. Newark, July 4, 1924; d. John Merle and Eva Marie (Rice) S.; m. Jeffrey Hayden, Oct. 28, 1951; children: Darrell, Laurette. BA, DFA, Bowling Green State U., 1946; student, Actors Studio, after 1950. Appeared in various radio and TV dramatic shows, N.Y.C., 1947—; theater roles include The Trip to Bountiful, 1953 (Outer Circle Critics award, N.Y. Drama Critics award, 1953), The Rainmaker, 1953, Winesburg, Ohio, 1970, The Lincoln Mask, 1972, Summer and Smoke, 1973, Desire Under the Elms, 1974, The Fatal Weakness, 1976, Candida, 1977, Mr. Roberts, First Monday in October, 1979, Duet for One, 1982-83, The Country Girl, 1986 (L.A. Dramalogue award 1986), Death of a Salesman, 1994, Love Letters, 1994; appeared in films On the Waterfront, 1954 (Acad. Award for best supporting actress, 1955), Raintree County, 1957, That Certain Feeling, 1956, A Hatful of Rain, 1957, North by Northwest, 1959, Exodus, 1961, All Fall Down, 1962, 36 Hours, 1963, The Sandpiper, 1964, The Russians Are Coming, The Russians Are Coming!, 1965, Grand Prix, 1966, The Stalking Moon, 1969, Loving, 1970, Cancel My Reservation, 1972, Nothing in Common, 1986; TV dramas The Macahans, 1976 (Emmy nom.), The Fatal Weakness, 1976, Taxi!!, 1978 (Emmy nom.), A Christmas to Remember, 1978, When Hell Was in Session, 1980, The Curse of King Tut's Tomb, The Best Little Girl in the World, 1981, Splendor in the Grass, 1981, Love Leads the Way, 1983, Jane Doe, 1983, Fatal Vision, 1984, The Last Days of Patton, 1986, A Year in the Life, 1986, Breaking Home Ties, 1987, I'll Be Home for Christmas, 1988, Voyage of Terror: The Achille Lauro Affair, 1990, People Like Us, 1990 (Emmy award, 1990), Palomino, 1991, Kiss of the Killer, ABC, 1992, documentary Primary Colors: The Story of Corita, 1991, My Antonia, 1994; also appeared in TV series Moonlighting, 1986-89.

ST. AUBIN, SUSAN, writer; b. Detroit, Feb. 10, 1944; d. Ernest Burton and Katherine (Crittenden) St. A.; m. Keith James Anderson, July 10, 1984. BA, San Jose State U., 1974; MA, San Francisco State U., 1980. Author of short stories in Herotica, Vols. 1-5, 1988-96, Yellow Silk: Erotic Arts and Letters, 1990, Fever, 1994, Best American Erotica, 1995. Home: 5 Pastori Ave San Anselmo CA 94960-1815

ST. CLAIR, GLORIANA STRANGE, librarian, dean; b. Tonkawa, Okla., Dec. 13, 1939; d. Glen Leroy and Doris Mildred (Furber) Strange. BA in English, U. Okla., 1962, PhD in Literature, 1970; MLS, U. Calif., Berkeley, 1963; MBA in Mgmt., U. Tex., San Antonio, 1980. Rsch. asst. U. Calif., Berkeley, 1962-63, asst. libr., 1963-65; cataloguer U. Okla., Norman, 1965-68; supervising libr. San Antonio Pub. Libr., 1980-84; head acquisitions divsn. Tex. A&M U. Librs., College Station, 1984-87, humanities bibliographer, 1985, head pers. ops., 1986; asst. dir. tech. automation and adminstrv. svc. Kerr Libr., Oreg. State U., Corvallis, 1987-90; assoc. dean, head info. access svcs. Pa. State U. Librs., University Park, 1990—. Editor Coll. & Rsch. Librs., 1990-96, Jour. Academic Librarianship, 1996—. Bd. dirs. Towers Condo. Bd., State College, 1993-94; mem. vestry, mem. book discussion group St. Andrew's Episcopal Ch., State College, 1991—; examiner Pa. Quality Leadership, 1994. Sr. fellow UCLA, 1991. Mem. Assn. Coll. and Rsch. Librs. (chair editl. adv. bd. 1990-96). Home: 403 S Allen St Apt 602 State College PA 16801-5254 Office: Pa State U Librs E506 Pattee Libr University Park PA 16802

ST. CLAIR, JANE ELIZABETH, management executive; b. Concord, Mass., Aug. 15, 1944; d. James F. and Mary E. (Clyne) Connell. BA, Salem State Coll., 1969; MPH, Columbia U., N.Y.C., 1990. Field rep., safety program Am. Red Cross of Greater N.Y., 1971-72; program dir. Bronx Community Coll., N.Y., 1973-75; dir. edn. Council N.Y.C., Inc., 1975-77, asst. exec. dir., 1978; exec. dir. Regional Emergency Med. Services, N.Y., 1979-91; dir. Peace Corps, Kenya, 1991-94, Gulfcoast South Area Health Edn. Ctr., Sarasota, Fla., 1995—; adjunt asst. prof., Hunter Coll. N.Y., 1973-91. Contbr. articles to profl. jours. Mem. Emergency Cardic Care Com. N.Y., Heart Assn., Am. Soc. Safety Engrs., Profl. Edn. Com., Am. Red Cross, First Aid Com. Address: 1749 S Highland Ave Apt 12A Clearwater FL 34616-1869

ST. GEORGE, JUDITH ALEXANDER, author; b. Westfield, N.J., Feb. 26, 1931; d. John Heald and Edna (Perkins) Alexander; m. David St. George, June 5, 1954; children: Peter, James, Philip, Sarah Anne. BA, Smith Coll., 1952. Author: Turncoat Winter, Rebel Spring, 1970, The Girl with Spunk, 1975, By George, Bloomers!, 1976, The Chinese Puzzle of Shag Island, 1976, The Shad Are Running, 1977, The Shadow of the Shaman, 1977, The Halo Wind, 1978, The Halloween Pumpkin Smasher, 1978, Mystery at St. Martin's, 1979, The Amazing Voyage of the New Orleans, 1980, Haunted, 1980, Call Me Margo, 1981, The Mysterious Girl in the Garden, 1981, The Brooklyn Bridge: They Said It Couldn't Be Built, 1982 (Am. Book award), Do You See What I See?, 1982, In The Shadow of the Bear, 1983, What's Happening to My Junior Year?, 1983, Who's Scared? Not Me!, 1984, The Mount Rushmore, 1985 (Christopher award), Panama Canal: Gateway to the World, 1989 (Golden Kite award), The White House, 1990, Mason and Dixon's Line of Fire, 1991, Dear Dr. Bell...Your Friend Helen Keller, 1992, Crazy Horse, 1994; (from filmscript) A View to a Kill, 1985; (from screenscript) Tales of the Gold Monkey, 1983. Mem. adv. coun. on children's lit. Rutgers U., 1977—; chmn. ednl. com. Bklyn. Bridge Centennial Commn., 1981-83. Mem. Soc. Children's Book Writers, Author's Guild. Episcopalian. Home: 8 Binney Rd Old Lyme CT 06371-1445

ST. GERMAIN, JEAN MARY, medical physicist; b. N.Y.C.; d. Herbert and Mary J. (Newman) S.; BS, Marymount Manhattan Coll., 1966; MS, Rutgers U., 1967. Diplomate Am. Bd. Med. Physics, Am. Bd. Health Physics. Fellow radiol. health USPHS, Rutgers U., New Brunswick, N.J., 1967; fellow dept. med. physics Meml. Hosp., N.Y.C., Cornell U. Med. Coll., 1967-68, asst. physicist, 1968-71, instr. radiology (physics), 1971-78, clin. asst. prof., 1979-94, assoc. prof. clin. radiology, 1995—; assoc. attending physicist Meml. Sloan-Kettering Cancer Ctr., 1993—; cons. in field. Fellow Am. Assn. Physicists in Medicine (sec., bd. dirs.); mem. Am. Inst. Physics (gov. bd.), Am. Acad. Health Physics (treas. 1996—), Am. Bd. Health Physics, Health Physics Soc. (pres. N.Y. chpt., pres. med. health physics sect.), Am. Acad. of Health Physics (treas.), Radiol. & Med. Physics Soc. N.Y. (past pres.), Nat. Soc. Arts and Letters (regional dir., pres. N.Y. chpt., nat. music chair). Iota Sigma Pi (treas., pres. V chpt.). Author: The Nurse and Radiotherapy, 1978; contbr. articles, chpts. to med. jours., texts. Office: 1275 York Ave New York NY 10021-6007

ST. JAMES, LYN, business owner, professional race car driver; b. Willoughby, Ohio, Mar. 13, 1947; d. Alfred W. and Maxine W. (Rawson) Cornwall; m. John Raymond Carusso, Dec. 7, 1970 (div. 1979); m. Roger Lessman, Feb. 27, 1993; 1 stepchild, Lindsay. Cert. in piano, St. Louis Inst. Music, 1967. Sec. Cleve. dist. sales office U.S. Steel Corp., 1967-69, Mike Roth Sales Corp., Euclid, Ohio, 1969-70; co-owner, v.p. Dynasales Fla., Hollywood, 1970-79; owner, pres. Autodyne, Ft. Lauderdale, Fla., 1974-91, Creative Images, Inc., 1979—; professional race car driver, 1979—; ranked 11th Indpls. 500, 1992; race car driver Ford Motor Co., Dearborn, Mich., 1981—, spokesperson, cons., 1981—; media spokesperson JC Penney, 1992—. Author: Lyn St. James Car Owner's Manual, 1989; contbg. editor automotive articles Seventeen mag., 1987—, Cosmopolitan mag., 1989-90. Bd. trustees Women's Sports Found., N.Y.C., 1988—. Recipient Rookie of the Year, AutoWeek Magazine, 1984, Woman of Yr. award McCalls mag., 1986, Leadership award Girl Scouts U.S., 1988, Rookie of Yr. at the Indy 500, 1992, Touchstone award Girls Inc. Indpls., 1995; first woman since Janet Guthrie to qualify for the Indpls. 500. Mem. Internat. Motorsports Assn., Sports Car Club of Am. Republican. Office: Creative Images Ste F 2570 International Speedway Blvd Daytona Beach FL 32114

SAINT JAMES, SYNTHIA, artist, writer; b. L.A., Feb. 11, 1949. Author: Can I Touch You, Girlfriends; author, illustrator: (children's picture books) The Gifts of Kwanzaa, Sunday; illustrator: Tukama Tootles the Flute, Snow on Snow on Snow, How Mr. Monkey Saw the Whole World, Neeny Coming...Neeny Going; commns. include House of Seagram, Mark Taper Forum, Nat. Bar Assn., Cultural Affairs Dept., ALA, UNICEF, Dance Africa Am., Girl Scouts USA, Cornerstone Creative Apparel, Nat. Urban League, Mus. African Am. Art; works featured on more than 40 book covers, also numerous greeting cards, gift bags, T-shirts, magnets, boxes, deck cards, puzzles, mugs, calendars, clocks, and watches.

ST. JOHN, JULIE, mortgage company executive. BA in English, U. Mich.; MBA, Fla. State U. CPA, Fla. Prin. Arthur Young & Co.; v.p. info. sys. Residence Inn divsn. Marriott; sr. v.p. transaction processing and mgmt. sys. Fed. Nat. Mortgage Assn., Washington, 1990—. Office: Fed Nat Mortgage Assn 3900 Wisconsin Ave NW Washington DC 20016

ST. JOHN, MARIA ANN, nurse anesthetist; b. Rochester, Pa., Dec. 15, 1953; d. James Edward and Evelyn Marie (Sayers) St. J.; m. Paul David Dworsky, Aug. 19, 1978 (div. Dec. 13, 1991); children: Lauren Marie Dworsky, Michael David Dworsky. BSN, U. Pitts., 1975; cert. reg. nurse anesthetist, U. Health Ctr. Pitts. Sch. Anesthesia for Nurses, 1984. RN Pa.; adv. reg. nurse practitioner Fla.; cert. reg. nurse anesthetist. Nurse Presbyn. U. Hosp., Pitts., 1975-77, VA Hosp., Pitts., 1977-82; nurse anesthetist Anesthesia Assocs. of Hollywood, Fla., 1984-87, North Hills Anesthesia Assocs., Pitts., 1987—. Vol. tchr. art history, fundraiser St. Alexis Sch., Wexford, Pa., 1991—, recording sec. PT6 Bd., 1996—. Recipient scholarship March of Dimes, Beaver County, Pa., 1971. Mem. Am. Assn. Nurse Anesthetists, Pa. Assn. Nurse Anesthetists. Republican. Roman Catholic. Home: 436 Anna Marie Dr Cranberry Township PA 16066

ST. JOHN, PATRICIA ANNE, academic administrator, art therapist; b. Johnson City, N.Y., Dec. 6, 1943; d. Michael and Helen (Gordan) Wovkulich; m. Mark Gregory St. John, Aug. 28, 1966 (div. Nov. 1970); m. Jack Tager, Dec. 4, 1987. BS, SUNY, Buffalo, 1964; MA, Ohio U., 1968; EdD, Columbia U., 1978; MA, NYU, 1986. Registered art therapist (A.T.R.), bd. cert. art therapist. Art tchr. Bd. Coop. Ednl. Svcs., Potsdam, N.Y., 1964-65, Gouverneur (N.Y.) Pub. Schs., 1965-66; therapeutic art specialist Wellesley (Mass.) Pub. Schs., 1969-73; pvt. practice Amherst, 1984—; art edn. instr. Kean Coll., Union, N.J., 1974-79; asst. prof. art U. Mass., Amherst, 1979-86; dir. grad. art programs Coll. New Rochelle, N.Y., 1986-94, div. head grad. art, comm. arts, 1994—; cons. editor Davis Publs., Inc. Worcester, Mass., 1989-90, Magnolia Pubs., Inc. Chgo., 1995—. Assoc. editor: Art Therapy, 1991-95; contbr. articles to profl. jours. N.J. state rep. Nat. Com. Arts for the Handicapped (ea. divsn.), Washington, 1976; co-dir. Western Mass. Scholastic Art awards, Amherst, 1982, 83; exhibit coord. Western Mass. Youth Art Month Exhibit, Chicopee, 1984, 85. Recipient 2d prize exptl. weaving, Midwest Weavers Conf., 1967; rsch. grantee Kean Coll. N.J., 1978. Fellow Am. Soc. Psychopathology Expression; mem. Nat. Art Edn. Assn. (rev. panelist, 1990—), Am. Art Therapy Assn., New Eng. Assn. Art Therapists (hon. life mem., pres. 1984-86), Mass. Art Edn. Assn. (v.p. 1985). Office: Coll New Rochelle 29 Castle Pl New Rochelle NY 10805-1902

ST.MARIE, SATENIG, writer; b. Brockton, Mass., June 2, 1927; d. Harry and Mary K. Sahjian; m. Gerald L. St. Marie, Dec. 26, 1959. B.S., Simmons Coll., Boston, 1949; M.A., Columbia U., 1959; LL.D. (hon.), N.D. State U., 1976. Extension home economist U. Mass. Extension Service, 1949-52, U. Conn. Extension Service, 1953-56; with J.C. Penney Co., Inc., 1959-87, mgr. endl. and consumer relations, 1967-73, dir. consumer affairs, 1973-87, div. v.p., 1974-87; dir. Nat. Reins. Co.; mem. U.S. Metric Bd. Author: Homes Are For People, 1973, Romantic Victorian Weddings: Then and Now, 1992; pub. J.C. Penney Consumer Edn. Services, 1981-87; lifestyles editor: Victorian Homes Mag., 1987—. Mem. Am. Home Econs. Assn. (past pres.), Antiques Dealers Assn. Am. (exec. dir. 1987—). Office: PO Box 335 Greens Farms CT 06436-0335

ST. MARK, CAROLE F., business executive. Formerly v.p. corp. planning and devel. Pitney Bowes, Inc., pres. bus. supplies and svcs. unit, 1988—, pres. logistics systems and bus. svcs. unit, pres., CEO bus. svcs. unit, 1994—. Office: Pitney Bowes Inc 1 Elmcroft Rd Stamford CT 06926-0700*

ST. ONGE, BARBARA S., media services coordinator, educator; b. Hartford, Conn., Dec. 3, 1949; d. Bruno P. and Marguerite C. (Wunsch) Skaroupski; m. Robert J. St. Onge; children: Bethany, Bryan. BS in Elem. Edn., Cen. Conn. State U., New Britain, 1971; M in ELem. Edn., Cen. Conn. State Coll., New Britain, 1977, postgrad., 1990; cert. libr. media specialist K-12, U. Conn., Storrs, 1992. Cert. intermediate adminstr. and supr. Tchr. 2d grade Bristol (Conn.) Bd. Edn., 1971-73, chpt. I instr., 1977-81, tchr. 3d grade, 1981-82, tchr. reading and lang. arts, 1982-85, instr. chpt I, 1985-90, coord. media svcs., 1990—; mem. bd. dirs. Bristol Pub. Library, 1991-92, Conn. Edn. Media Assn., 1993-94, Conn. Educators Computer Assn., 1995—; mem. adv. bd. TCI Cable TV, 1995—. Contbr. articles to profl. jours. Chair craft show Bristol Mum Festival, 1990; pres. Women's Coll. Club, 1990-91; assoc. bd. mem. New England Carousel Mus., Bristol, 1993. Recipient PLUS (Providing Leadership and Unselfish Svc.) award for outstanding woman honoree 1990; Danforth Found. scholar U. Conn., 1993. Mem. ASCD, Internat. Reading Assn., Am. Assn. Sch. Librs., Conn. Assn. for Supervision and Curriculum Devel., Conn. Reading Assn., Info. Literacy Network, Pi Lambda Theta. Home: 592 East Rd Bristol CT 06010

ST. PIERRE, CHERYL ANN, art educator; b. Buffalo, Apr. 26, 1945; d. Guy Thomas and Madeline (Duncan) St. P. BS in Art Edn., SUNY, Buffalo, 1967, MS in Art Edn., 1970; MA in Italian, Middlebury Coll., 1976; PhD in Humanities, NYU, 1992. K-12 art tchr. Kenmore-Town of Tonawanda (N.Y.) Union Free Sch. Dist., 1967—; cooperating tchr. for art student tchrs. SUNY, Buffalo, 1972—; advisor on original multi-media prodn. N.Y. State Coun. for Arts, Tonawanda, 1990—; coord., tchr. Parents As Reading Ptnrs. Artwork, Tonawanda, 1990—; grad. asst. NYU, N.Y.C., 1987-88. Illustrator jour. Italian Americana, 1971-81; designer greeting cards for State of N.Y. and Maine, Am. Lung Assn., 1978-79. Earthwatch vol. Identity through Native Costume, Macedonia, 1995. Mem. N.Y. State United Tchrs., Nat. Art Edn. Assn., N.Y. State Tchrs. Assn., Am. Fedn. Tchrs., Kenmore Tchrs.' Assn. Home: 3881 Bailey Ave Buffalo NY 14226-3202

SAITO-FURUKAWA, JANET CHIYO, primary school educator; b. L.A., June 29, 1951; d. Shin and Nobuko Ann (Seki) Saito; m. Neil Yasuhiko Furukawa, June 30, 1990. BS, U. So. Calif., 1973; MA, Mt. St. Mary's Coll., L.A., 1990. Cert. elem. tchr. K-8, adminstrn. 1st tier, lang. devel. specialist, Calif. Tchr. grades four through six Rosemont Elem. Sch., L.A., 1973-80, psychomotor specialist, 1979-80; tchr. mid. sch. lang. arts Virgil, Parkman Mid. Schs., L.A./Woodland Hills, Calif., 1980-87, 87-90, dept. chairperson, 1974-77, 80-84, 1989-90; drama tchr. Virgil Mid. Sch., L.A., 1980-81, dance tchr., 1984-87; mid. sch. advisor L.A. Unified Sch. Dist., Encino, Calif., 1990-91; practitioner facilitator L.A. Unified Sch. Dist., Encino, 1991—; young authors chairperson Parkman Mid. Sch., Woodland Hills, 1988-90; multicultural performance educator, Great Leap, L.A., 1988-93; mentor tchr. L.A. Unified Sch. dist., 1980-90; presenter/cons. in field. Tchr./leader Psychomotor Grant, 1979; writer Level II Teamin' and Theme-in, 1994. Recipient Nancy McHugh English award English Coun. L.A., Woodland Hills, 1987, 88, 91, Outstanding Reading and Lang. Tchr. award L.A. Reading Assn., Woodland Hills, 1991, Apple award L.A. Mayor's Office, 1990, Tchr. of the Month award Phi Delta Kappa, San Fernando, Calif., 1989. Mem. ASCD, Nat. Mid. Schs. Assn. (presenter), Nat. Coun. Tchrs. Math., Calif. Sci. Tchrs. Assn., Nat. Coun. Tchrs. English, The Learning Collaborative. Lutheran. Office: Practitioner Ctr LA Unified Sch Dist 3010 Estara Ave Los Angeles CA 90065-2205

SAIZAN, PAULA THERESA, oil company executive; b. New Orleans, Sept. 12, 1947; d. Paul Morine and Hattie Mae (Hayes) Saizan; m. George H. Smith, May 26, 1973 (div. July 1976). BS in Acctg. summa cum laude, Xavier U., 1969. CPA, Tex.; notary pub. Systems engr. IBM, New Orleans, 1969-71; acct., then sr. acct. Shell Oil Co., Houston, Tex., 1971-76, sr. fin. analyst, 1976-77, fin. rep., 1977-79, corp. auditor, 1979-81, treasury rep., 1981-82, sr. treasury rep., 1982-86; asst. treas. Shell Credit Inc., Shell Leasing Co., Shell Fin. Co. 1986-88, sr. pub. affairs rep., 1988-89, sr. staff pub. affairs rep., 1990-91, program mgr., 1991-96, sr. program mgr., 1996—. Bd. dirs. Houston Downtown Mgmt. Dist., Greater Houston Conv. and Visitors Bur. (exec. com.), St. Joseph Hosp. Found., United Negro Coll. Fund, Associated Cath. Charities, Houston, Galveston; mem. adv. coun. U.S. SBA region VI, Houston; acctg. dept. adv. bd. Tex. So. U.; del. White House Conf. on small bus., 1995. Mem. AICPA, NAACP, Tex. Soc. CPAs, Leadership Houston, Greater Inwood Partnership, LWV of Houston, Xavier U. Alumni Assn., Nat. Assn. Black Accts., Nat. Coun. Negro Women, Inc., Nat. Political Congress Black Women, Alpha Kappa Alpha, Phi Gamma Nu, Kappa Gamma Pi. Roman Catholic. Home: 5426 Long Creek Ln Houston TX 77088-4407 Office: Shell Oil Co PO Box 2463 Houston TX 77252-2463

SAKAI, HIROKO, trading company executive; b. Nishiharu, Aichi-ken, Japan, Jan. 9, 1939; came to U.S., 1956; d. Kichiya and Saki (Shiraishi) S. BA, Wellesley Coll., 1963; MA, Columbia U., 1967, PhD, 1972. Journalist Asahi Evening News, Tokyo, 1963-65; escort interpreter Dept. State, Washington, 1967-68; econ. analyst Port Authority N.Y. and N.J., N.Y.C., 1968-69; sr. cons. Harbridge House, Inc., Boston, 1970-84, Quantum Sci. Corp., White Plains, N.Y., 1984-87; corp. planner ITOCHU Internat. Inc., N.Y.C., N.Y., 1988-92; dir. bus. devel. ITOCHU Internat. Inc., N.Y.C., 1993-94, dir. venture and investment, 1995—. Interpreter Govt. Mass., Boston, 1974. Wellesley Coll. fellow, 1960-63, Columbia U. fellow, 1965-68; Columbia U. grantee, 1969. Mem. Regional Sci. Assn., Assn. Am. Geographers. Buddist. Home: 235 E 51st St Apt 5C New York NY 10022-6523 Office: ITOCHU Internat Inc 335 Madison Ave New York NY 10017-4605

SAKAMOTO, NANCY MASTERSON, cultural studies educator; b. L.A., Nov. 26, 1931; d. Manoah H. and Alice May (Lunn) Masterson; m. Satoru Sakamoto, Nov. 28, 1960; children: Gen Paul, Shiyo Philip. BA in English with honors, UCLA, 1952. Cert. prof. Japanese Nat. U., Japanese Ministry Edn. Tchr. English Am. Cultural Ctr., Osaka, Japan, 1968-82, Osaka Edn. U., 1969-72, YMCA English Sch., Osaka, 1972-82, Osaka Prefectural Edn. Inst., 1976-82; prof. Hawaii br. Shitennoji Gakuen U., Honolulu, 1982—; vis. prof. U. Osaka, 1981-82; lectr. Japanese civic and profl. orgns., Osaka, Kobe, Wakayama, and Shizuoka, Japan, 1972-82. Author: Polite Fictions: Why Japanese and Americans Seem Rude to Each Other, 1982; co-author: Mutual Understanding of Different Cultures, 1981; contbr. articles to Japanese English-tchg. publs. Bd. dirs. Orgn. Women Leaders, Honolulu, 1989-93. Mem. AAUW, Japan-Am. Soc. Hawaii (com. chair 1993-94), Phi Beta Kappa (UCLA chpt.). Home: 1936 Citron St Honolulu HI 96826

SAKAS, CATHY JO, naturalist, consultant, documentary filmmaker; b. Portsmouth, Va., Feb. 4, 1951; d. Joseph and Katherine (West) S.; m. John Anthony Crawford, May 12, 1976 (div. June 1989). BS in Biology, Armstrong State Coll., 1976, MEd in Sci., 1989. Food mgr. and naturalist field leader Wilderness Southeast, Inc., St. Simons Island, Ga., 1976-79; program dir. and naturalist field leader Wilderness Southeast, Inc., 1982-84, head resource naturalist and field leader, 1989—; guest mgr. and interpretive naturalist Little St. Simons Island (Ga.), Inc., 1979-82; environ. educator and animal caretaker Outland Island Edn. Ctr., Savannah, 1984-88; owner and pres. Coastal Naturalist, Inc., Tybee Island, Ga., 1989—; v.p. and chief interpretive naturalist Spartina Trails, Inc., Savannah, 1992-94; curator of natural history Mus. of Hilton Head Island, S.C., 1993-96; survey coord. New England Aquarium, Savannah, 1993-94, Atlanta Com. for Olympic Games, 1996; cons. Coastwise Consulting, 1996—; supervisor Loggerhead Sea Turtle Hatchery, Little Cumberland Island-Jekyll Island, Ga., 1990; adj. prof. Ga. So. U., 1986, 87. Originator, writer, host natural history documentary series The Coastal Naturalist, 1990, 1994 (Emmy award 1995), children's video Acorns, Oaks and Trees that Talk, 1984; author h.s. curriculum Environ. Sci., 1986. Bd. dirs. Wilderness Southeast, Inc., 1987—, pres. bd. dirs. 1984-89, 93-95; active Coastal Citizens for Clean Environment, Savannah, 1984-89. Recipient Special Conservation Achievement award Ga. Wildlife Federation, 1995. Mem. Union Concerned Scientists, Sierra Club, Audobon Soc., The Nature Conservancy, The Ga. Conservancy, Mus. of Hilton Head Island. Home: PO Box 2028 Tybee Island GA 31328

SAKELLARIOS, GERTRUDE EDITH, retired office nurse; b. Lowell, Mass., Mar. 14, 1929; d. William V. and Eileen E. (Hale) Yoachimciuk; m. Angelos D. Sakellarios, Dec. 30, 1966. Diploma, Lowell Gen. Hosp., 1949; student, Boston U., 1949-53, Boston Coll./St. Josephs Hosp., Lowell, 1951. Gen. duty med.-surg. nurse Lowell Gen. Hosp., 1949-50, operating room nurse, 1950-52; office nurse gen. practitioner's office, Lowell, 1952-83. Home: 124 Cashin St Lowell MA 01851-2004

SAKRY, MARY ELIZABETH, software engineer, process improvement consultant; b. Mpls., Apr. 28, 1954; d. Edward S. and June M. (Hackett) S.; m. David R. Dodge, Aug. 9, 1980 (div. Aug., 1990). BS in Computer Sci., U. Minn., 1976; MBA, St. Edwards U., 1980. Software engr. Tex. Instruments, Austin, 1976-78, software project leder, 1978-89; software process engr. Tex. Instruments, Dallas, 1989-90; software process cons. The Process Group, Dallas, 1990—. Contbr. articles to profl. jours. Mem. Assn. for Software Engring. Excellence, Toastmasters. Home: 801 Legacy Dr # 1628 Plano TX 75023 Office: The Process Group 2121 W Springcreek Pkwy Ste 206 Plano TX 75023

SAKS, JANE, management consultant, psychologist; b. N.Y.C., May 18, 1947; d. Milton Edelstein and Dorothy (Moskowitz) Litt; m. Michael Saks, June 1973 (div. 1979); 1 child, Brianna. Psychologist Needham (Mass.) Pub. Schs., 1974-76, Human Resources, Inc., Boston, 1976-78, DARE, Inc., Boston, 1978-80; human resources/mktg. specialist Computek, Inc., Burlington, Mass., 1981-82, Matra Datavision, Inc., Burlington, 1982-83; orgnl. cons. Computervision Corp., Burlington, 1983-85; gen. mgr. Info./Edn., Waltham, Mass., 1986-89; mgmt. cons. Saks Assocs., Watertown, Mass., 1982-90; orgnl. cons. Unisys Corp., Cambridge, Mass., 1990—; cons. to various govt. orgns., Washington, 1990—; spkr. in field. Mem. Orgnl. Devel. Network, Single Mothers by Choice, Single Parents Adopting Children Everywhere. Office: Unisys Corp 4 Cambridge Ctr Cambridge MA 02172

SAKS, JUDITH-ANN, artist; b. Anniston, Ala., Dec. 20, 1943; d. Julien David and Lucy-Jane (Watson) S.; student Tex. Acad. Art, 1957-58, Mus. Fine Arts, Houston, 1962, Rice U., 1962; BFA, Tulane U., 1966; postgrad. U. Houston, 1967; m. Haskell Irvin Rosenthal, Dec. 22, 1974; 1 child, Brian Julien. One-man shows include: Alley Gallery, Houston, 1969, 2131 Gallery, Houston, 1969; group shows include: Birmingham (Ala.) Mus., 1967, Meinhard Galleries, Houston, 1977; Galerie Barbizon, Houston, 1980, Park Crest Gallery, Austin, 1981; represented in permanent collections including: L.B. Johnson Manned Space Mus., Clear Lake City, Tex., Harris County Heritage Mus., Windsor Castle, London, Smithsonian Instn., Washington: commns. include: Pin Oak Charity Horse Show Assn., Roberts S.S. Agy., New Orleans, Cruiser Houston Meml. Rm., U. Houston; curator student art collection U. Houston, 1968-72; artist Am. Revolution Bicentennial project Port of Houston Authority, 1975-76. Recipient art awards including: 1st prize for water color Art League Houston, 1969, 1st prize for graphics, 1969, 1st prize for sculpture, 1968, 1st place award for original print, DAR, Am. Heritage Com., 1987. Mem. Art League Houston, Houston Mus. Fine Arts, DAR (curator 1983-85, 93-95, contbr. Tex. sesquicentennial drawing for DAR mag.), Daus. Republic Tex. Home: 2215 Briar Br Houston TX 77042-2959

SAKSON, SHARON R(OSE), journalist, writer, educator; b. Trenton, N.J., June 6, 1952; d. John Andrew and Helen Hope (Haggerty) S. BA, Georgetown U., 1974. Desk asst. ABC News, Washington, 1972-73, prodn. asst., 1973-74; TV news field prodr. ABC-TV News, London and Miami, Fla., 1979-85; news producer Sta. WBAL-TV, Balt., 1974-75; news prodr. Stas. ABC-TV/CBS-TV, Chgo., 1976-77; exec. producer Sta. KPIX-TV (Westinghouse), San Francisco, 1977-79; freelance writer Lawrenceville, N.J., 1985—; tchr. Oxbridge Acads., Paris, 1990-94; exec. dir. Oxbridge Academics, 1994—. Author: (short stories) 2d Gazette Fiction Collection, 1987, Streetsongs, 1990, (book) Miami, 1990, Florida, 1991. Recipient Katherine Ann Porter prize for fiction, 1989, Nimrod Lit. prize, 1989; grantee Commonwealth of Pa., 1989. Mem. Am. Whippet Club (Top Breeder of Whippet Champions 1994), Dog Writers Assn. Am., Trenton Kennel Club. Roman Catholic. Home: #273 3375 Brunswick Pike Lawrenceville NJ 08648

SALAGI, DORIS, educational administrator; b. Perth Amboy, N.J., July 30, 1947; d. Joseph William and Anna Salagi. BA, Trenton State Coll., 1969, MA, 1973. Cert. elem. sch. tchr., supr., tchr. of the handicapped. 3d grade tchr. Willingboro (N.J.) Bd. Edn., 1969-79, basic skills math. tchr., 1979-83, resource rm. tchr., 1983-87, tchr. of the handicapped, 1987-92, individualized ednl. plan facilitator, 1992—; curriculum writer Willingboro Bd. Edn., 1973, 77, 79-83. Co-author: (composition curriculum) The Care and Handling of Compositions, 1973. Vol. Rancocas Hosp., Willingboro, 1978—. Named for Outstanding Achievement in Edn., Trenton State Coll. Alumni Assn., 1991. Mem. Willingboro Edn. Assn. (rep. 1974-76), Twin Hills PTA, Rancocas Hosp. Aux. (pres. 1987-89, rec. sec. 1983-87, bazaar chair 1981-85, scholarship chair 1978-81), Delta Kappa Gamma (rec. sec. Alpha Zeta state 1995—, Eta chpt., treas. 1992—, pres. 1990-92, 1st v.p. 1988-90, fundraising 1985-88). Office: Willingboro Bd Edn Levitt Bldg 50 Salem Rd Rm A8 Willingboro NJ 08046-2847

SALAMAN, MAUREEN KENNEDY, nutritionist; b. Glendale, Calif., Apr. 4, 1936; d. Ted and Elena (Peters) Kennedy; 1 child, Sean. West Coast Report, Sta. WMCA-AM, N.Y.C., 1980—; hostess Maximize Your Life with Maureen Kennedy Salaman, KFCB, Concord, Calif.; pres. Nat. Health Fedn., Monrovia, Calif., 1982—; cons., lectr., rschr. on cancer rsch. and metabolic medicine, nutrition; freedom of choice lobbyist. Author: Foods That Heal, Nutrition: The Cancer Answer, 1983, The Diet Bible, The Light at the End of the Refrigerator, Health Freedom News, 1982-85, Nutrition: The Cancer Answer II, 1995. Contbr. articles to profl. jours.; hostess TV show Maureen Salaman's Maximize Your Life. Developer nutrition programs for radio and TV. Office: Nat Health Fedn PO Box 688 Monrovia CA 91017-0688 also: Maureen Kennedy Salaman Inc 1259 El Camino Real Ste 1500 Menlo Park CA 94025-4227

SALAMON, LINDA BRADLEY, university administrator, English literature educator; b. Elmira, N.Y., Nov. 20, 1941; d. Grant Ellsworth and Evelyn E. (Ward) Bradley; divorced; children: Michael Lawrence, Timothy Martin. B.A., Radcliffe Coll., 1963; M.A., Bryn Mawr Coll., 1964, Ph.D., 1971; Advanced Mgmt. Cert., Harvard U. Bus. Sch., 1978; D.H.L., St. Louis Coll. Pharmacy, 1993. Lectr., adj. asst. prof. Eng. Dartmouth Coll., Hanover, N.H., 1967-72; mem. faculty lit. Bennington Coll., Vt., 1974-75; dean students Wells Coll., Aurora, N.Y., 1975-77; exec. asst. to pres. U. Pa., Phila., 1977-79; assoc. prof. English Washington U., St. Louis, 1979-88, prof., 1988-92, dean Coll. Arts and Scis., 1979-92; prof. English, dean Columbia Sch. Arts and Scis. George Washington U., Washington, 1992-95, interim v.p. for acad. affairs, 1995—; mem. faculty Bryn Mawr Summer Inst. for Women, 1979—. Author, co-editor: Nicholas Hilliard's Art of Limning, 1983; co-author: Integrity in the College Curriculum, 1985; contbr. numerous articles to literary and ednl. jours. Bd. dirs. Assn. Am. Colls., vice chmn., 1985, chmn., 1986; bd. dirs. Greater St. Louis council Girl Scouts U.S.A.; trustee Coll. Bd., St. Louis Coll. Pharmacy. Fellow Radcliffe Coll. Bunting Inst., 1973-74; Am. Philos. Soc. Penrose grantee, 1974; fellow Folger Shakespeare Library, 1986, NEH Montaigne Inst., 1988. Mem. MLA, Cosmos Club, Phi Beta Kappa. Office: George Washington U Off VP Acad Affairs Washington DC 20052

SALAMON, RENAY, real estate broker; b. N.Y.C., May 13, 1948; d. Solomon and Mollie (Friedman) Langman; m. Maier Salamon, Aug. 10, 1968; children: Mollie, Jean, Leah, Sharon, Eugene. BA, Hunter Coll., 1969. Licensed real estate borker, N.J. Mgr. office Customode Designs Inc., N.Y.C., 1966-68; co-owner Salamon Dairy Farms, Three Bridges, N.J., 1968-86; assoc. realtor Max. D. Shuman Realty Inc., Flemington, N.J., 1983-85; pres., chief exec. officer Liberty Hill Realty Inc., Flemington, N.J., 1985—; cons. Illva Saronna Inc. (Illva Group), Edison, N.J. 1985—; real estate devel. joint venture with M.R.F.S. Realty Inc. (Illva Group), 1986—. Mem. Readington twp. Environ. Commn., Whitehouse Sta., N.J., 1978-87, N.J. Assn. Environ. Commrs., Trenton, 1978—; fundraiser Rutgers Prep. Sch., Somerset, N.J., 1984—; bd. dirs. Hunterdon County YMCA, 1987-95. Named N.J. Broker Record, Forbes Inc., N.Y.C. 1987. Mem. Nat. Assn. Realtors, N.J. Assn. Realtors, Hunterdon County Bd. Realtors (mem. chair 1986), Realtor's Land Inst. Republican. Jewish. Office: Liberty Hill Realty Inc 415 US Highway 202 Flemington NJ 08822-6021

SALAMONE-KOCHOWICZ, JEAN GLORIA, banker; b. White Deer, Pa., Dec. 28, 1929; d. Dewey and Pearl Viola (Bastian) Smith; m. Daniel W. Salamone, Nov. 2, 1946 (div. 1977); children: Daryl Joseph, John Daniel; m. John T. Kochowicz, Feb. 10, 1990 (dec. 1993). Student, Bloomsburg State Coll., 1946, Am. Inst. Banking, 1974-85. Sec. Chef Boy-ar-Dee Foods, Milton, Pa., 1946-48, Arthur Andersen & Co., Washington, 1948-58; exec. sec. Citizens Bank and Trust Co., Riverdale, Md., 1970-74, asst. treas., 1974-77, asst. v.p., 1977-84; v.p. Citizens Bank and Trust Co. (name now Citizens Bank Md.), Riverdale, Laurel, Md., 1984—; also corp. sec. Citizens Bancorp (holding co. for Citizens Bank Md.), Laurel. Trustee Prince George's Arts Coun., Riverdale, 1983—, treas., 1983-89, pres. 1990-91. Mem. Fin. Women Internat. (pres. met. Md. group 1977-78). Roman Catholic.

SALAND, LINDA CAROL, anatomy educator, researcher; b. N.Y.C., Oct. 24, 1942; d. Charles and Esther (Weingarten) Gewirtz; m. Joel S. Saland, Aug. 16, 1964; children—Kenneth, Jeffrey. B.S., CCNY, 1963, Ph.D. in Biology, 1968; M.A. in Zoology, Columbia U., 1965. Research assoc. dept. anatomy Columbia U. Coll. Physicians and Surgeons, N.Y.C., 1968-69; sr. research assoc. dept. anatomy Sch. Medicine, U. N.Mex., Albuquerque, 1971-78, asst. prof., 1978-83, assoc. prof., 1983-89, prof., 1989—. Ad hoc reviewer NIH study sect., 1994, 95, site visit team. Mem. editorial bd. Anat. Record, 1980—; contbr. articles to profl. jours. Predoctoral fellow NDEA, 1966-68; research grantee Nat. Inst. on Drug Abuse, 1979-83, NIH Minority Biomed. Research Support Program, 1980—; NIH research grantee, 1986-95. Mem. AAAS, Am. Assn. Anatomists, Soc. for Neurosci., Women in Neuroscience (chair steering comm. 1991-93), Am. Soc. Cell Biology, Sigma Xi. Office: U NMex Sch Medicine Dept Anatomy Basic Med Sci Bldg Albuquerque NM 87131

SALAT, CRISTINA, writer; b. N.Y.C.. Student, Long Island Univ. author, editor, manuscript cons., workshop facilitator, 1985—. Author: Living in Secret, 1993, Alias Diamond Jones, 1993, Defending the Dreamcatchers, 1995, Once Upon A Time, 1996; contbr. to anthologies including Sister/Stranger, 1993, Am I Blue, 1994; contbr. to popular publ.; freelance editor, 1987—. Home: PO Box 1519 Forestville CA 95436*

SALAVERRIA, HELENA CLARA, educator; b. San Francisco, May 19, 1923; d. Blas Saturnino and Eugenia Irene (Loyarte) S. AB, U. Calif., Berkeley, 1945, secondary teaching cert., 1946; MA, Stanford U., 1962. High sch. tchr., 1946-57; asst. prof. Luther Coll., Decorah, Iowa, 1959-60; prof. Spanish, Bakersfield (Calif.) Coll., 1961-84, chmn. dept., 1973-80. Vol., Hearst Castle; mem. srs. adv. group edn. Cuesta Coll. Community Svcs. Mem. AAUW (edn. com.), NEA, Calif. Fgn. Lang. Tchrs. Assn. (dir. 1976-77), Kern County Fgn. Lang. Tchrs. Assn. (pres. 1975-77), Union Concerned Scientists, Natural Resources Def. Coun., Calif. Tchrs. Assn. (chpt. sec. 1951-52), Yolo County Coun. Retarded, Soc. Basque Studies in Am., RSVP, Amnesty Internat., Common Cause, Sierra Club, Prytanean Alumnae, U. Women of Cambria, U. Calif. Alumni Assn., Stanford U. Alumni Assn. Democrat. Presbyterian. Address: PO Box 63 Cambria CA 93428-0063

SALAY, CINDY ROLSTON, technical specialist, nurse; b. Roanoke, Va., July 18, 1955; d. Gilbert Wilson and Elinor Patterson (Sandridge) Rolston; m. John Matthew, July 7, 1988; 1 child, David. AAS, Va. Western Community Coll., 1976; AS, J. Sargeant Reynolds Community Coll., 1982; BS, Va. Commonwealth U., 1984. RN. Operating room RN Henrico Doctors Hosp., Richmond, Va., 1979-80; nursing supr. Johnston Willis Hosp., Richmond, 1980-87; systems analyst, coord. Health Corp Va., Richmond, 1983-87, sr. project leader, 1987-88; sr. systems analyst Hosp. Corp. Am., Nashville, 1987; sr. systems cons. IBAX Healthcare Systems, Reston, Va., 1988-94; sys. analyst MCV Hosps. Info. Sys., Richmond, Va., 1994-95; specialist HBO & Co., Atlanta, Ga., 1995—. Presbyterian. Home: 12800 Sunrise Bluff Rd Midlothian VA 23112-2512 Office: HBO & Company 301 Perimeter Center N Atlanta GA 30346

SALAZAR, LAURA ALICE GARDNER, theater educator; b. Gilbert, Minn., Feb. 22, 1935; d. Lloyd William and Isabel Mary (Aldrich) Gardner; m. Hugo Salazar, June 12, 1962; children: Anthony, Catherine. BS, U. Wis., River Falls, 1957; MA, Kent State U., 1960; PhD, U. Mich., 1984. H.s. tchr. various pub. schs., Wis., 1957-59, Mich., 1960-64; instr. Mich. State U., East Lansing, 1964-65; prof. Grand Valley State U., Allendale, Mich., 1966—; cons., writer, Mich. 4H, East Lansing, 1995—; cons. Goals 2000, U. S. Dept. Edn. and MENC, Reston, Va., 1992-95; pres. Am. Alliance for Theater and Edn., Tempe, Ariz., 1993-95; pres. Internat. Am. Theatre/USA, Detroit, 1990-94. Author: Teaching Dramatically: Learning Thematically, 1995 (Ann. Disting. Book award Am. Alliance for Theatre and Edn. 1996); co-author (with S. Harbin): International Theatre Events, 1991; writer, creator performance art pieces performed in Europe, the Caribbean, Australia, and the U.S., 1992-96; dir. over 60 stage plays, mostly at Grand Valley State U., 1966—; contbr. over 30 articles to profl. jours. Leader Theatre for At-Risk Youth, Grand Rapids/Trinidad, Mich., 1985—; pres. Coun. of Performing Arts, Children, Grand Rapids, 1976-77; cons. Leadership Grand Rapids, 1993, 95; team mem. Kent County Jail Ministry, Grand Rapids, 1995—; bd. mem. Grand Rapids Ballet, 1994—. Recipient Fulbright rsch. grant, 1992, Australia-Am. Edn. Found. grant, 1995. Mem. Internat. Amateur Theatre Assn. N.Am. (mem. bd. 1990—), Internat. Theatre for Youth (six internat. offices), Internat. Amateur Theatre Assn. (editor, info. officer, 1991—), Am. Alliance for Theatre and Edn. (past pres. 1995, mem. bd. 1987—, Presdl. award 1989), Internat. Drama in Edn. Assn. (U.S. rep. 1993-95), Music Educators Nat. Conf. Democrat. Methodist. Office: Grand Valley State Univ 1 Campus Dr Allendale MI 49401

SALAZAR, PAMELA SUE, secondary education educator; b. Pensacola, Fla., Aug. 24, 1951; d. Raymond Earl and Mary JoAnn (Lister) Cummins; m. George Watson (div. Sept. 1975); 1 child, Jason Watson; m. Thomas Joseph Salazar, Mar. 26, 1980; children: cortney Diann, Cresen Denise. BS, U. Nev., Las Vegas, 1975; MS in Physics and Edn., 1980. Tchr. sci. and math. Woodbury Jr. H.S., Las Vegas, 1975-78; tchr. physics Basic H.S., Henderson, Nev., 1978-90, Green Valley H.S., Henderson, 1990—; assoc.dir. Nev. Inst. for Gifted and Talented, U. Nev., Las Vegas, 1991—; project dir. Dept. Energy MST Grant, 1994—. Author: (lab. experiments) Mesur-NASA, 1992. Asst. coord. pub. events So. Nev. Muscular Dystrophy, Las Vegas, 1990-93; race dir. sporting events Multiple Sclerosis Soc., Las Vegas, 1986-92. Named Tandy Tech. Techr., 1992. Mem. Am. Assn. Physics Tchrs., Nat. Sci. Tchrs. Assn. (Presdl. award in sci. 1993), So. Nev. Computer Using Educators, So. Nev. Sci. Tchrs. Assn., So. Nev. Math. Tchrs. Assn. Democrat. Roman Catholic. Home: 7145 W Le Baron Ave Las Vegas NV 89124 Office: Green Valley HS 460 Arroyo Grande Blvd Henderson NV 89014-3900

SALEH, FARIDA YOUSRY, chemistry educator; b. Cairo, Egypt, June 17, 1939; came to U.S., 1968; d. Michael Yousry and Fakiha Yousef (Badawy) Wassif; m. Hosny Gabra Saleh, Oct. 8, 1959; children: Magda, Nagwa. BS, Ain Shams U., 1959; MS, Alexandrial U., Egypt, 1967; PhD, U. Tex., 1976. Postdoctoral rsch. assoc. Tex. A&M U., College Station, 1977-78; rsch. scientist II U. North Tex., Denton, 1978-83, asst. prof. chemistry, 1980-83, assoc. prof., 1985-94, prof., 1994—; cons. Stanford Rsch. Inst., Menlo Park, Calif., 1983-84, Allied Chems. Co., Hackettstown, N.J., 1985-86, Am. Chrome Chems., Corpus Christi, Tex., 1988-89, USEPA Rev. Panel, Washington, 1986—. Contbg. author book chpts. in field; contbr. more than 60 articles to profl. jours. Recipient Svc. award U.S. EPA, Washington, 1993; recipient numerous grants in field. Mem. Am. Chem. Soc., Internat. Union of Pure and Applied Chemistry, Internat. Humic Substances Soc., Assn. Women in Sci. Home: 1314 Valley Pkwy Lewisville TX 75067 Office: Univ North Tex Corner Mulberry & Ave B Denton TX 76203

SALEMBIER, VALERIE BIRNBAUM, publishing executive; b. Teaneck, N.J., July 2, 1945; d. Jack and Sara (Gordon) Birnbaum; m. David J. Salembier, June 23, 1968 (div. 1980); m. Paul J. Block, Dec. 9, 1990. B.A., Coll. of New Rochelle, 1973. Merchandising mgr. Life Internat., Time, Inc., N.Y.C., 1964-69; merchandising copywriter Newsweek, Inc., N.Y.C., 1970; promotion prodn. mgr. Newsweek, Inc., 1971, adv. sales rep., 1972-76; advt. dir. Ms. Mag., N.Y.C., 1976-79, assoc. pub., 1979-81; pub. Inside Sports Mag., N.Y.C., 1982; v.p., pub. 13-30 Corp., N.Y.C., 1983; sr. v.p. advt. USA Today, 1983-88; pub. TV Guide, Radnor, PA, 1988-89; pres. N.Y. Post, N.Y.C., 1989-90; pub. Family Circle Mag., N.Y.C., 1991-93; v.p. advt. The N.Y. Times, 1993-94; pres. Quest Mag., 1995-96; v.p. mag. devel. Meigher Comms., 1995-96; pub. Esquire Mag., 1996—; lectr. in field. Trustee Coll. New Rochelle; trustee, exec. com. N.Y.C. Police Found.; mem. exec. com. Women of Distinction, United Jewish Appeal; pres., bd. dirs. Nat. Alliance Breast Cancer Orgns., BOX (Beneficial Orgn. to Aid Ex-Fighters). Mem. C200, Women in Comm., Womens Forum, Nat. Coun. Jewish Women (bd. dirs.). Home: 1075 Park Ave New York NY 10128-1003 Office: Esquire 250 West 55th St New York NY 10019

SALEMME, (AUTORINO) LUCIA, artist, writer; b. N.Y.C., Sept. 23, 1919; d. Salvatore and Teresa (Iovino) Autorino; m. Attilio Salemme, Sept. 26, 1943 (dec. 1955); children: Vincent, Lawrence. Student, Art Students League, N.Y.C. Instr. art Peoples Art Ctr., 1957-69, Mus. Modern Art, N.Y.C., 1957-69, Art Students League, N.Y.C., 1970-90; adj. asst. prof. NYU, 1959-72. Exhibited in group shows at N.Y.C. galleries and museums including 19 solo shows; author: Color Exercises for the Painter, 1970, Compositional Exercises for the Painter, 1974, The Complete Book of Painting Techniques, 1983; represented in permanent collections including Guggenheim Mus., Whitney Mus. Am. Art, N.Y.C., Nat. Gallery Art, Washington, Bates Coll. Mus. Art, Lewiston, Maine, Mus. City of N.Y., Met. Mus. N.Y. Grantee Solomon R. Guggenheim Found., 1942; resident at McDowell Colony, 1963. Mem. Pen and Brush Club (chmn. painting sect. 1989—). Democrat. Roman Catholic. Home: 55 Bethune St Apt B641 New York NY 10014-1703 Office: Assoc Am Artists Gallery 20 W 57th St New York NY 10019

SALERNO, CHERIE ANN (C. S. MAU), artist; b. Chgo., Nov. 21, 1948; d. Henry Jasper and Helen (Polyak) Mau; m. Kenneth Daniel Salerno; children: Nick Anthony, Brittney Ann. AAS in Advertising, Triton Coll., 1985; student, Art Inst. Chgo., 1996. Freelance comml. artist Chgo., 1986-90; artist Chgo. Fine Arts Exch., 1994-95; artist, owner C.S. Mau Studio, River Grove, Ill., 1992—; Designer Centennial Quilt, River Grove Libr., 1988; logo designer, River Grove Sch., 1984. Vol. tchr. art Bethlehem Luth. Sch., River Grove,Ill., 1996—; vol. ElderCare, 1990-94. Fellow Chgo. Artist Coalition, Glenview Art League (Excellence award 1996), North Shore Art League, West Suburban Art League (excellences honor 1991-93); mem. Oak Park Art League (bd. dirs. 1989—, sch. bd. 1993-94, excellences merit 1990-94, arts and stds. judge 1991-93, active fundraising 1994). Lutheran.

SALERNO, HEIDI TERESA, lawyer; b. Fontana, Calif., Nov. 14, 1966; d. Robert Francis Salerno and Bobbette Aikin Marschik. BA, UCLA, 1988; JD, Hastings Coll. of Law, San Francisco, 1991. Bar: Calif. 1991, U.S. Dist. Ct. (no., ea. and so. dists.) Calif. 1993, U.S. Ct. Appeals (9th cir.) 1993. Grad. legal asst. Legal Svcs. Corp. Ala., Montgomery, 1991-92; pvt. practice L.A., 1992-93; dep. atty. gen. Dept. Justice, Oakland, Calif., 1993—. Co-editor Hastings Women's Law Jour., 1990-91; pub. editor Hastings Internat. & Comparative Law Rev., 1990-91. Campaign vol. Calif. Dem. Party, San Francisco, 1994, nat. Dem. Party, 1992; clinic vol. NOW, L.A., San Francisco, 1988—. Mem. Nat. Women's Polit. Caucus (governing mem. 1994—). Office: Dept of Justice 12th Fl 2101 Webster St Oakland CA 94612

SALERNO-SONNENBERG, NADJA, violinist; b. Rome, Jan. 10, 1961; came to U.S., 1969; d. Josephine Salerno-Sonnenberg. Grad., Curtis Inst. Music, 1975, Juilliard Sch., 1982. Profl. debut with Phila. Orch., 1971; appearances include Am. Symphony Orch., Balt., Chgo., Cin., Detroit, Houston, Indpls., Milw., Montreal, N.J., Pitts. symphonys, Cleve., L.A. Chamber, Phila., Minn. orchs., New Orleans, N.Y., L.A. philharms.; guest appearance include Mostly Mozart Festival, Ravinia, Blossom, Meadow Brook, Gt. Woods, Caramoor, Aspen, Hollywood Bowl; internat. appearances include Vienna, Munich, Stuttgart, Frankfurt, Geneva, Rotterdam, Lisbon, Tokyo; featured on 60 Minutes, CBS, CBS Sunday Morning, NBC Nat. News, PBS Live from Lindoln Ctr., Charlies Rose Show; numerous appearances on The Tonight Show with Johnny Carson; rec. artist Angel, 1987, Nonesuch, 1996. Recipient 1st prize Naumburg Violin Competition, N.Y.C., 1981; Avery Fisher Career grantee, N.Y.C., 1983. Mem. AFTRA, Screen Actors Guild. Office: care M L Falcone Pub Rels 155 W 68th St New York NY 10023-5808

SALESMAN, JANET FAY, speech language pathologist; b. Sullivan, Ind., Nov. 29, 1951; d. Howard N. and Margaret F. (Aaron) Lee; m. Jerry L. Salesman, June 1, 1975; 1 child, Elizabeth A. BS, Ind. State U., 1975, MS, 1977. Speech, lang. pathologist Bloomfield (Ind.) Sch. Dist., 1974-85, Met. Sch. Dist. of Shakamak, Jasonville, Ind., 1985—; mem. tech. com. Met. Sch. Dist. of Shakamak, Jasonville, 1993-94. Pres. Shakamak Jr. Sr. High Choir Boosters, Jasonville, Ind., 1994-95. Mem. VFW Aux., Delta Kappa Gamma. Home: PO Box 127 Coalmont IN 47845-0127

SALHANICK, BRENDA CRANE, lawyer; b. Keene, N.H., Aug. 2, 1951; d. Clayton Howard and Anita (Barry) Crane; BA cum laude, St. Anselm Coll., 1974; CLU Northeastern U. 1978; JD cum laude Suffolk U. Law Sch. 1987; m. Joel A. Salhanick, Sept. 16, 1978; children: Marc Allan, Scott Joseph. With Jules Meyers Assocs., Chestnut Hill, Mass. 1975-83, dir. pension dept. 1977-83, v.p. Employee Benefit Plan Services 1979-83; assoc. Jenkens & Gilchrist, P.C., Dallas, 1987-92, Settle and Pou P.C., Dallas, 1992—. Instr. first aid ARC 1972-81; bd. dir. Our Friends Place, 1993-96; cub scout den leader, 1993—; adj. prof. U. Dallas.

SALICRUP, MADELINE, nurse; b. Bronx, N.Y., Jan. 16, 1968; d. Natanael and Mirriam (Echevarria) S. BS cum laude, Coll. Mt. St. Vincent, 1990. Specialized clin. asst. Albert Einstein Coll. Medicine, Bronx, 1988-90; RN Mt. Sinai Hosp., Bronx, 1990-91, Bronx (N.Y.) Lebanon Hosp., 1991—; del., 1993—. Recipient Woman of Yr. award, 1996. Mem. ANA, N.Y. State Nurses Assn., Sigma Theta Tau, Delta Epsilon Sigma. Democrat. Home: 80 Mcclellan St Apt 5L Bronx NY 10452-8614

SALIERS, AMY RAY, singer; b. Atlanta, 1964. Student, Vanderbilt U., Emory U. Mem. folk rock duo "Indigo Girls", 1983—; represented by Epic Records, 1988—. Albums include Back on the Bus Y'All, 1991 (Grammy award nom. best contemporary fold album), Indigo Girls, 1989 (Grammy award as best contemporary folk recording), Nomads Indians Saints, 1990, Rites of Passage, 1992 (Gold on Billboard's Top Pop Albums), Strange Fire, 1989, Swamp Ophelia, 1994; appeared on Tonight Show, 1991, Late Night with David Letterman, 1991; appeared in movie Boys on the Side. Grammy award nom. for best new artist, 1990; Grammy award nom. for single "Hammer and A Nail" as best contemporary folk recording, 1991. Office: care Epic Records 550 Madison Ave New York NY 10022-3297*

SALINAS, ANITA TERESA, computer specialist; b. Grand Rapids, Mich., Mar. 27, 1959; d. Horacio and Martenia (LaBlanc) S. BS in Computer Sci., U. Tenn., 1988. Programmer IBM, Kingston, N.Y., 1988-90; mktg. support rep. IBM, Dallas, 1990-93; tech. cons. Hewlett-Packard, Dallas, 1993-94; lead tech. architect Citicorp, Dallas, 1994-95; sr. tech. mktg. cons. Novell, Dallas, 1995-96; sr. tech. advisor BEA Systems, Dallas, 1996—. Vol. Big Bros./Big Sisters, Dallas/Ft. Worth, 1990-96, Multiple Sclerosis, Dallas/Ft. Worth, 1993, 94, 95. Home and Office: 2185 Randol Mill Ave Southlake TX 76092

SALISBURY, ALICIA LAING, state senator; b. N.Y.C., Sept. 20, 1939; d. Herbert Farnsworth and Augusta Belle (Marshall) Laing; m. John Eagan Salisbury, June 23, 1962; children: John Eagan Jr., Margaret Salisbury La Rue. Student Sweet Briar Coll., 1957-60; BA, Kans. U., 1961. Mem. Kans. Senate, 1985—, v.p., chmn. commerce com., telecomm. strategic planning com.; vice chmn. ways and means com., mem. legis. post audit com., mem. joint com. on econ. devel.(mem. orgn. and calendar rules comm.). Elected mem. State Bd. Edn., Topeka, 1981-85, Kans.,; past pres. Jr. League of Topeka; trustee Leadership Kans., 1982-89; bd. dirs. Topeka Community Found., 1983—, Topeka Pub. Sch. Found., 1985-89, Capitol Area Pla. Authority, 1989—, Mid-Am. Mfg. Tech. Ctr., mem. workers' compensation fund oversight com., mem. Kids Count steering com., mem. Stormont-Vail Hosp. Aux.; mem. adv. comm. Juvenile Offenders Program, Kans., 1985—; mem. adv. bd. Topeka State Hosp., Kans. Action for Children, 1982—, Kans. Ins. Edn. Found., 1984—, Youth Center at Topeka, 1987-95; steering com. One Stop Career Ctr., Interstate Cooperation Com. Coun. State Govts.;

mem. Nat. Fedn. Rep. Women; past bd. mem. United Way Greater Topeka, ARC, Family Service and Guidance, Topeka, Shawnee County Mental Health Assn., Florence Crittenton Services, Topeka, Topeka City Commn. Govtl. Adv. Com. Mem. Nat. Conf. State Legislators (exec. com.), Nat. Rep. Legislators' Assn. (Nat. Rep. Legislator of Yr. 1993, Bus. Guardian award 1990, Outstanding Individual Legis. Achievement award 1989), Nat. Fedn. Ind. Bus., Shawnee County Rep. Women, Kappa Kappa Gamma. Episcopalian. Avocations: tennis; downhill skiing; water sports; horseback riding; gardening. Office: Kans State Senate State Capital Topeka KS 66612

SALISBURY, MARGARET MARY, retired educator; b. LaGrange, Tex., Oct. 23, 1932; d. Charles Frederick and Hedwig Mary (Fajkus) Meyer; m. Harrison Bryan Salisbury, Jan. 8, 1955; children: Elaine, Kathleen, David, Stephen, Mark, Margaret II. BA, Our Lady of the Lake, San Antonio, 1954; MA, U. Tex., San Antonio, 1975. Lic. elem., secondary edn., English and sch. adminstrn. High sch. tchr. St. Joseph's Sch. for Girls, El Paso, Tex., 1954-55; tchr. 1st grade St. Patricks Cathedral Sch., El Paso, 1955; tchr. 2d grade S.W. Ind. Sch. Dist., San Antonio, 1971-74, tchr. 6th grade, 1974-75, supr. testing, reading, 1975-81, 82-86, jr. high sch. prin., 1981-82, dir. alternative sch., 1986-87, tchr. 3d grade, 1987-96; pres. Cooperating Tchr./Student Tchr. U. at Tex., San Antonio, 1986-87. Mem. AAUW (chairperson pub. policy com. 1995—), Internat. Reading Assn., Tex. State Reading Assn., Alamo Reading Coun., Reading Improvement, Pres. Club, San Antonio Ret. Tchrs. Assn. Republican. Roman Catholic. Home: 126 Meadow Trail Dr San Antonio TX 78227-1639

SALISBURY, TAMARA PAULA, foundation executive; b. N.Y.C., Dec. 14, 1927; d. Paul Terrance and Nadine (Korolkova) Voloshin; m. Franklin Cary Salisbury, Jan. 22, 1955; children: Franklin Jr., John, Elizabeth, Elaine, Claire. BA, Coll. Notre Dame, 1948; postgrad., Am. U., George Washington U. Chemist depts. pathology and chemotherapy NIH Cancer Inst., Bethesda, Md., 1946-52; asst. to chief of Chemistry Br. Office of Naval Rsch., Bethesda, 1953-55; v.p., COO Nat. Found. Cancer Rsch., Bethesda, 1973—. Mem. Assn. Internat. Cancer Rsch., 1995. Decorated d'Officier De L'Ordre De Leopold II; outstanding contbns. award Internat. Soc. Quantum Biology, 1983, award of appreciation Beth Israel Hosp., Harvard Med. Sch., Brigham & Women's Hosp., 1993. Mem. AAAS, Am. Chem. Soc., N.Y. Acad. Scis., Inst. Phys. and Chem. Biology (fgn.), Krebforschung Internat., Nat. Liberal Club. Home: 10811 Alloway Dr Potomac MD 20854-1504 Office: Nat Found Cancer Rsch 7315 Wisconsin Ave Ste 500W Bethesda MD 20814

SALJINSKA-MARKOVIC, OLIVERA T., oncology researcher; b. Skopje, Macedonia, Oct. 27, 1938; d. Trajko and Radmila Saljinska; m. Nenad Markovic, July 9, 1961; children: Svetomir, Mila. MD, Med. Faculty, Skopje, 1962; PhD, Med. Faculty, Belgrade, 1977; Specialist Med. Biochemistry, U. Kiril and Metodij, Skopje, 1969. Asst. prof. Med. Faculty, Skopje, 1964-79, assoc. prof., 1979-84; dir. clin. lab. U. Children's Hosp., Skopje, 1974-84; sr. rsch. assoc. Pa. State U., State College, 1984-85; sr. fellow U. Pa., Phila., 1985-88; prof. U. Belgrade, 1988-93; adj. prof. Med. Coll. of Pa., 1993-95; vis. scientist MIAMDH, NIH, Bethesda, 1976-77; vis. scientist ATCC, Rockville, Md., 1995-96; dir. BioSciCon, Md., 1996—; primarius Univ. Children's Hosp., Skopje, 1983-86; head lab. for rsch. and devel., Clin. Ctr., Belgrade, 1990-93; mem. exam. com., State of Macedonia, 1980-90. Author: Quantitative Cytoch of Enzymes, 1986; contbr. articles to profl. jours., publs. Postdoctoral intern rsch. fellowship Fogarty Internat. Ctr., NIH, Bethesda, 1971-73; recipient several rsch. grants NIH, Pharm. Co., 1984-95. Mem. Histochem. Soc., Am. Assn. Clin. Chem., N.Y. Acad. Scis., Am. Assn. Cell Biology. Home: Apt 602 259 Congressional Ln Rockville MD 20852 Office: BioSciCon Inc Rockville MD 20852

SALLMEN SMITH, LAURA JANE, economist; b. Warren, Ohio, Sept. 19, 1964; d. John W. and Sylvia J. (Lewis) Sallmen; m. Anning Hiram Smith Jr., Aug. 30, 1986. BA in Econs., Hiram (Ohio) Coll., 1986; MA in Tech. & Human Affairs, Washington U., St. Louis, 1989. Economist U.S. EPA, Washington, 1989—; pres., CEO Shenandoah Brewing Co., Falls Church, Va., 1994—; vis. scholar Inst. Alternative Agr., Beltsville, Md., 1992. Mem. nat. steering com. Luth. Vol. Corps, Washington, 1995; vol. Luther Pl. Womens Shelter, Washington, 1990—. Recipient Presdl. Point of Light award U.S. EPA, 1992, Bronze medal, 1993, Silver medal, 1996. Mem. NOW, Arlington Met. Chorus, Springfield Cmty. Theatre (Best Mus. 1995). Democrat. Lutheran. Home: 6704 Farragut Ave Falls Church VA 22042

SALMERON, ANGELINA, social worker; b. Las Vegas, Nev., Jan. 13, 1945; d. Silverio and Victoria (Archuleta) H.; m. Santiago Bustamente, May 29, 1965 (div. Dec., 1982); children: Anna Jean, Cynthia Marie, Delfido Jimmie, Rexann Vicky; m. Frank Salmeron, June 12, 1993. BA, N. Mex. Highlands U., 1980, M in Social Work, 1981. Lic. social worker, N. Mex. Dep. assessor San Miguel County Assessor's Office, Las Vegas, N. Mex., 1964-65; various positions in educational and social work field N. Mex. Highlands U. and cooperating instns., Las Vegas, N. Mex., 1977-81; from comty. support counselor to day activity coord. Sangre de Cristo Comty. Mental Health, N. Mex., 1981-85; from social worker III to social worker clinician State of N. Mex., Las Vegas Med. Ctr., 1982-90; social worker clinician State of N. Mex., Social Svcs. Divsn., 1990-93, Profl. Ednl. Assocs. Psycho. Ancillary Svcs., Las Vegas, 1993-94; med. social worker Frances' Home Health Care, Las Vegas, N. Mex., 1994—; mem. San Miguel/Mora Comty. mental health adv. bd., 1990-94, Greater Las Vegas Coun. on Alcoholism; presenter, speaker to numerous local civic groups on drug and alcohol prevention, rape, sexual abuse and suicide prevention; radio presenter on play therapy; trained home care providers for the mentally ill; assisted in initiating support groups for eating disorders, and alcoholism-endangered families. Bd. dirs. DayCare-Headstart Program, pers. com., budget com., Las Vegas, N. Mex.; Channel One Youth Program, pers. com.; mem. Cursillo groups In Roman Cath. Chs. Our Lady of Sorrows, Las Vegas, N. Mex., Immaculate Conception, Las Vegas, advisor to Encuentro Groups at both chs. lay tchr. in catechism religion classes to elem. sch. children of Roman Cath. faith. Mem. Nat. Assn. Social Workers, Image de Nuevo Mex., Las Vegas (chpt. pres. 1990-92). Home: 2425 Jesse Lee Ln Las Vegas NM 87701

SALMON, KATHLEEN A., insurance company executive; b. 1945. With Commonwealth of Penn., Harrisburg, 1967-79, Penn. Blue Shield, Camp Hill, Penn., 1979-83; sr. v.p.-adminstrn. Capital Blue Cross, Harrisburg, Penn., 1983—. Office: Capital Blue Cross 2500 Elmerton Ave Harrisburg PA 17110-9763*

SALMON, LAURA BETH, public relations director; b. Oskaloosa, Iowa, Oct. 10, 1938; d. John Bertrand Pooley and Anna Laura Brasher; m. Nathan O. Folland, Dec. 28, 1960 (div. 1976); children: Elizabeth G. Folland, Meredith J. Folland, Jonathan L. Folland; m. Fredrec Eugene Salmon, Aug. 22, 1986; 1 stepchild, Elizabeth Grace Sweet. BS, Iowa State U., 1960; MS, Kans. State U., 1976. Copywriter Nat. Rsch. Bur., Burlington, Iowa, 1960; editor, grad. asst. Kans. State U., Manhattan, 1975-76; real estate agt. Sullivan & Assocs., Manhattan, 1976-79; health educator Kans. Dept. Health & Environ., Topeka, 1979-82; pub. info. officer No. Okla. Coll., Tonkawa, 1982-86; head libr. Attalla (Ala.)-Etowah County Libr., 1987; exec. dir. Found. Women's Health in Ala., Birmingham, 1987-90; pub. rels. dir. Gadsden (Ala.) State Community Coll., 1990—; interviewer PARTNERS, Ala., 1989-90. Co-editor: Education for a Lifetime booklet, 1991; health columnist Birmingham Bus. Jour., 1987-88; editor curriculum materials Kans. Foster Parent Project, 1975-76, Found. News, 1988-90; contbr. articles to profl. jours. Mem. Literacy Coun., Gadsden, 1991-95, chmn., 1994, chair comm. com., 1992, chair vol. recruitment and tng. com., 1993; mem. Infant Mortality Task Force, Kans., 1982, Gadsden Community Chorus, 1988-92; publicist Nat. Issues Forums, Tonkawa, Okla., 1985-86; actress Manhattan Civic Theater, 1970-75. Mem. Found. for Womens Health in Ala. (forum moderator, program com. 1991, sec. 1990-93, co-chmn. internat. conf. 1990), Ala. Edn. Assn., Ala. Coll. System Pub. Rels. Assn. (exec. com., exhbn. steering com. sec. 1994, pres.-elect 1996, Communicator of Yr. award 1995), Gadsden State C.C. Alumni Assn. (life), Gadsden-Etowah LWV (1st v.p. 1992), Kappa Omicron Nu. Methodist. Home: 3166 Rocky Hollow Rd Attalla AL 35954-5757 Office: Gadsden State Community Col Wallace Dr Gadsden AL 35903

SALMON, PHYLLIS WARD, early education educator; b. Dallas, Aug. 10, 1948; d. Clinton David and Reba (Gilbert) Ward; m. James Y. Barbo, Dec. 12, 1970 (div. Jan. 1975); m. William Wellington Salmon, Jan. 21, 1977; 1 child, Megan Alyssa. A. in Acctg., Richland Coll., 1977; B.S. in Edn., Stephen F. Austin U., 1971. Cert. tchr. secondary edn., Tex. Cost acct. Jackson-Shaw, Dallas, 1975-79, Dal-Mac Devel., Dallas, 1979-81; store mgr. Shepard & Vick, Dallas, 1983-84; mktg. coordinator Tex. Instruments, Dallas, 1984-85; pres. Computer Expertise, Richardson, Tex., 1985-91; pres. TI's Only, 1986-91, pres. TechnaServe, 1987-91; early edn. tchr. The da Vinci Sch., Dallas, 1992-94; mgr. Kids Town, 1994—. Mem. NAFE, Tex. Computer Dealers Assn. (organizing mem.), Dallas Needlework and Textile Guild. Republican. Episcopalian. Club: St. Clare's Guild (bd. dirs. 1980-81, Dallas). Avocations: needlepoint, photography, travel. Office: Kids Town 7151 S Central Expy Richardson TX 75080-7410

SALTER, AVRIL, technologist; b. Windsor, Eng.; arrived in U.S., 1992; d. Edmund J. and Gabriel E. (Fookes) Benke; m. Antony P. Salter. BS in Math., U. London, 1978; PhD in Engring., U. Reading, Eng., 1982. Sys. engr. IBM Australia, Ltd., Melbourne, 1982-85; mgr. Helix Cons., Ltd., London, 1988; mgr. sys. stragety Motorola, Ltd., Basingstoke, Eng., 1991; mgr. Motorola, Ltd., Swindon, Eng., 1992; dir. mktg. Motorola, Inc., Arlington Heights, Ill., 1994, dir. strategy, 1996—; orgnl. dir. In Forum, Tex. Contbr. papers to profl. jours. Office: Motorola Inc 1501 W Shure Dr Arlington Heights IL 60004

SALTER, LANORA JEANETTE, corporate financial officer; b. Omaha, Nebr., June 7, 1964; d. Phillip Ray Sr. and Charlene (Sanford) Hinton; m. Howard Douglas Salter, Mar. 26, 1964; children: Ryan Douglas, Erin Jeanette, Evan Tainter. AS, Chattohochee Valley C.C., 1988; diploma, Am. Inst. Banking, 1988; BS, Spring Hill Coll., 1995. Office mgr. Zales, Mobile, Ala., 1983-85; customer svc. rep. Columbus (Ga.) Bank & Trust, 1985-88; adminstrv. asst. First Atlanta Bank, Augusta, Ga., 1988-90; customer svc. specialist Am. South Bank, Mobile, 1990-92; v.p. finance adminstrn. Performance Rehab. Assocs., Inc., Fairhope, Ala., 1992—; treas. bd. dirs. AIB, 1989-90. tutor Am. Literacy Coun., 1994. Republican. Episcopalian. Office: Performance Rehab Assoc Inc PO Box 1100 Point Clear AL 36564

SALTER, LINDA LEE, security officer; b. Garden City, Mich., Oct. 10, 1953; d. Bertram Edward Salter and Gertrude Theresa (Barnes) Ashby; children: Korina Reshell Irene Miller, Terry Wayne Tomlin II. Student, Henry Ford C.C., 1990. Security supr. Guardsmark, Memphis, 1979-86; security officer Detroit Newspapers, 1986—; emergency first aid specialist ARC, Dearborn, Mich., 1993—. Pres. Downriver/Monroe County Women Involved in Wings, South Rockwood, Mich., 1991—; mem. Mich. Lupus Found., 1995—, Monroe County Humane Soc., 1993—, Ladies Aux., 9363, 1971—; reunion class tchr. Carlson H.S., Gibraltar, Mich., 1971; ch. treas. South Rockwood United Meth. Ch.; mem. United Meth. Women. Mem. NOW, Woman's Bowling Assn. Methodist. Home: 19544 S Glen Blvd Trenton MI 48183 Office: Detroit Newspapers 615 W Lafayette Detroit MI 48226

SALTZMAN, ELLEN S., mediator; b. Bklyn., Apr. 6, 1946; d. Joseph and Hilda (Lazar) Estrin; m. Stuart Saltzman, June 25, 1966; children: Todd, Michael. BA in Sociology, L.I. U., 1967; JD, CUNY, 1993. Bar: Pa. 1993, N.J. 1994. Fin. cons. Cigna Fin. Svcs., Syosset, N.Y., 1983-84; pension cons. Pension Svcs. Corp., Port Washington, N.Y., 1984-86, Consulting Actuaries Internat., Inc., N.Y.C., 1986-89; mktg. mgr. New Eng. Life Ins. Co., N.Y.C., 1986-89; atty. Vaccaro & Prisco, Hauppauge, N.Y., 1993-95; mediator pvt. practice, 1996—. Mem. task force Women on the Job, Port Washington, N.Y., 1989—, bd. dirs., 1994—; bd. dirs., chair pub. affairs com. L.I. region March of Dimes, 1994—; mem. N.Y. State legis. com. March of Dimes. Recipient Women of Distinction award March of Dimes, 1994, Spl. Congl. cert., 1994, Nassau County Exec. citation, 1994, Suffolk County Exec. citation, 1994; named to Town of North Hempstead's Women's Roll of Honor, 1995. Mem. Am. Acad. Family Mediators, Nat. Women's Polit. Caucus, L.I. Ctr. for Bus. and Profl. Women (pres. 1992-94). Home: 28 Driftwood Dr Port Washington NY 11050-1717

SALUSSO, CAROL JOY, apparel design educator, consultant; b. Butte, Mont., Dec. 25, 1950; d. George B. and Ruth M. (Richards) S.; (div.); children: Ryan R. and Daron A. Deonier. BS, Mont. State U., 1975; MS, U. Minn., St. Paul, 1977, PhD, 1983. Grad. asst. U. Minn., St. Paul, 1975-81; asst. prof. Iowa State U., Ames, 1981-86; assoc. prof. Mont. State U., Bozeman, 1986-94, Wash. State U., Pullman, 1994—; cons. product devel., Bozeman, Mont., 1986-94. Author: (handbook) Users Guide to Fabrics, 1993. Challenge grantee USDA, Faculty grantee Sunbury Textiles. Mem. Internat. Textiles and Apparel Assn., (chair spl. events 1986-88, chair electronic comm. 1993-95, book rev. editor 1995—, co-author World Wide Web ITAA server 1995—). Home: 345 W Main St Pullman WA 99163-2829 Office: Wash State U Dept Apparel Merch Int Design White Hall 209 Pullman WA 99164-2020

SALVESEN, B(ONNIE) FORBES, artist; b. Elgin, Ill., Nov. 6, 1944; d. Donald Behan and Helen Elaine (Krajacik) Forbes; m. Bruce Michael Salvesen, Sept. 3, 1966. Studied with Elvira Spivey, Barrington, Ill., 1972-74; studied with Peter Schoelch, Cary, Ill., 1975-82; student, Am. Acad. Art, 1976, Sch. Art Inst. Chgo., 1980-82, Kulick-Startk Byzantine Jewelry Sch., 1983. Asst. to purchasing agt. Harnischfeger, Crystal Lake, Ill., 1962-64; rec. sec. Electric Mfrs. Credit Bur., Cary, Ill., 1964-66; student and practicing artist, 1968—. Illustrator: (book) There were Reasons, 1983. Recipient Award of Excellence, Ill.-Arlington Heights Fine Arts Festival, 1995, Best of Show award 20th Ann. Cambridge Art Fair, 1995, 19th Ann. Fine Arts Festival, Downers Grove, Ill., 1995. Democratic. Roman Catholic. Home and Office: 1312 Whippoorwill Dr Crystal Lake IL 60014-2614

SALZILLO, MARJORIE H., artist, educator; b. Trenton, N.J., Oct. 6, 1949; d. Edward and Jean (Lavine) Hellman; 1 child, Ben. BFA, R.I. Sch. Design, 1971; MFA, Syracuse U., 1978. Prof. art Munson-Williams-Proctor Inst., Utica, N.Y., 1978—. Exhibited in groups shows at Anita Shapolsky Gallery, N.Y.C., 1991, Roberson Mus., Binghamton, N.Y., 1992, Rutger's Nat. Stedman Art Gallery, Camden, N.J., 1994, Links and Layers, St. Mark's in the Bowery, N.Y.C., 1995. Va. Ctr. for Creative Arts fellow, 1996, Byrdcliffe Arts Colony fellow, 1996. Mem. Coll. Art Assn., Women's Caucus for Art. Office: Munson Williams Proctor 310 Genesee St Utica NY 13502

SALZMAN, DEBRA GAYLE, clinical psychologist; b. Manhasset, N.Y., Dec. 16, 1965; d. Stanley Philip and Leona (Schames) S.; m. David Lee Blumberg, May 29, 1994. BA, Emory Univ., 1987; PhD, SUNY, Albany, 1992. Lic. psychologist. Clinical psychologist Behavior Therapy Assocs., Somerset, N.J., 1992—. Contbr. articles to profl. jours. Mem. Am. Psychological Assn., Assn. Advancement of Behavior Therapy, N.J. Psychological Assn. Office: Behavior Therapy Assocs Profl Ctr At Somerset 11 Clyde Rd Ste 103 Somerset NJ 08873

SAMA, VICTORIA E., television broadcast executive; b. Bellville, N.J., Nov. 19, 1962; d. Frank Lincoln and Jennie (Bonoccorso) S. BA in Journalism, Montclair (N.J.) State Coll., 1984. Prodn. asst. ABC Wide World of Sports, N.Y.C., 1982-84, Cable News Network, N.Y.C., 1984-85; writer CNN Headline News, Atlanta, 1985-88; producer CNN Spanish News, Atlanta, 1988-92, CNN Internat., Atlanta, 1992—; N.E. regional coord. Alpha Epsilon Rho, N.Y.C., 1984-85; qualifier 1996 Olympic Trials Women's Cycling. Alumni Award scholar Montclair State Alumni Com., 1983; Spanish Lang. fellow Nat. Press Found., Washington, 1990. Mem. Handgun Control, Nature Conservancy. Office: Cable News Network 1 Cnn Ctr NW Atlanta GA 30303-2705

SAMBI, MARGARET ANN, curator; b. Uniontown, Pa., Apr. 28, 1945; d. Thomas Joseph and Helen Adrienne (Reagan) Meehan; m. Walter John Sambi, Dec. 15, 1973; children: Elizabeth A., Tiffany R. BA in Art History, U. Cin., 1971, MA in Art History, 1973. Cert. in non-profit orgn. mgmt. and volunteer adminstrn. Archtl. historian Miami Purchase Assn., Cin., 1974-76; lectr. fine arts U. Cin., 1975-87; dir. Summerfair, Inc., Cin., 1987-89; asst. curator mus. edn. Cin. Art Mus., 1989-91; curator mus. edn. Contemporary Arts Ctr., Cin., 1991—; mem. nat. adv. com. Save Our Sculpture, Smithsonian Inst., Nat. Mus. Am. Art, 1991-95, edn. adv. com. Cin. Arts Assn., 1994-95; chair off-site mus. visits Ohio Art Edn. Assn., 1994-95; provider adv. com. Assn. Advancement of Arts Edn., 1994-95. Author: Joyce J. Scott: Dream Weaver, 1994. Trustee, bd. dirs. A Day in Eden, Inc., Cin., 1991; mem. nominating com. Greater Cin. Beautiful, Inc., 1991-93. Mem. Am. Assn. Muss., Nat. Art Edn. Assn., Mid-West Assn. Muss., Mus. Edn. Roundtable. Home: 3945 Clifton Ave Cincinnati OH 45220 Office: Contemporary Arts Ctr 115 E 5th St Cincinnati OH 45202

SAMIMI, SANDRA, lawyer; b. Wooster, Ohio, Sept. 20, 1959; d. Kenneth Earl and June Eileen (Miller) Weaver; children: Daniel Abraham, Elizabeth Mariam. BA, Miami U., 1980; JD, U. Mich., 1983. Bar: N.Y. 1984. Ct. atty. State of N.Y. Supreme Ct., N.Y.C., 1984-92; pvt. practice Spring Valley, N.Y., 1992-94; ptnr. Samimi & Murphy, New City, N.Y., 1995—; surrogate decision making com. N.Y. State Commn. on Quality of Care for the Mentally Disabled, 1993-96. Author: (with others) Criminal Defense Techniques, 1991. Bd. dirs. Rockland Parent-Child Ctr., N.Y.C., Nyack, 1994-96, Hudson Valley Children's Mus., Nyack, 1993-96, Chestnut Rotary, Chestnut Ridge, N.Y., 1993-96; mem. New City United Meth. Ch., 1990-96. Mem. Rockland County Bar Assn., Rockland County Women's Bar Assn., N.Y. State Bar Assn., Tappan Zee Bus. and Profl. Women. Office: Samimi & Murphy 616 S Main St New City NY 10956

SAMMET, JEAN E., computer scientist; b. N.Y.C.; d. Harry and Ruth S. B.A., Mt. Holyoke Coll., Sc.D. (hon.), 1978; M.A., U. Ill. Group leader programming Sperry Gyroscope, Great Neck, N.Y., 1955-58; sect. head, staff cons. programming Sylvania Electric Products, Needham, Mass., 1958-61; with IBM, 1961-88; adv. program mgr. Boston, 1961-65; program lang. tech. mgr. IBM, 1965-68; programming tech. planning mgr. Fed. Systems div., 1968-74, programming lang. tech. mgr., 1974-79, software tech. mgr., 1979-81, div. software tech. mgr., 1981-82, programming lang. tech. mgr., 1983-88; programming lang. cons. Bethesda, Md., 1989—; chmn. history of computing com. Am. Fedn. Info. Processing Socs., 1977-79; mem. exec. com. Software Patent Inst., 1991—, edn. com., 1992—, chair edn. com., 1992-93; bd. dirs. Computer Mus., 1983-93. Author: Programming Languages: History and Fundamentals, 1969; editor-in-chief: Assn. Computing Machinery Computing Revs, 1979-87; contbr. articles to profl. jours. Fellow Assn. for Computing Machinery, 1994, (charter, pres. 1974-76, Disting. Svc. award 1985); mem. NAE, Upsilon Pi Epsilon. Office: PO Box 30038 Bethesda MD 20824-0038

SAMPAS, DOROTHY M., government official; b. Washington, Aug. 24, 1933; d. Lawrence and Anna Cornelia (Henkel) Myers; m. James George Sampas, Dec. 8, 1962; children: George, Lawrence James. AB, U. Mich., 1955; postgrad., U. Paris, 1955-56; PhD, Georgetown U., 1970; cert., Nat. War Coll., Washington, 1987, Naval Post Grad. Sch., 1993. With Bur. Pub. Affairs Dept. State, Washington, 1958-60, analyst Bur. of Adminstrn., 1973-75, div. chief, dep. chief Office of Position and Pay Mgmt., 1979-83, div. chief Office of Mgmt., 1983-84, dir. Office of Mgmt., 1984-86; vice consul Am. Consulate Gen., Hamburg, Fed. Republic Germany, 1960-62; cons. Trans Century Corp., Washington, 1972; gen. svcs. officer Am. Embassy, Brussels, 1975-79; embassy minister-counselor Am. Embassy, Beijing, 1987-90; minister-counselor U.S. Mission to UN, N.Y.C., 1991-94; Am. ambassador to Islamic Republic of Mauritania, 1994—. Presbyterian. Home: 4715 Trent Ct Chevy Chase MD 20815-5516 Office: Am Embassy Nouakchott Dept State Washington DC 20521-2430 also: Am Embassy, Boite Postale 222, Nouakchott Mauritania

SAMPERE, ROBERTA LYNN, English language educator, consultant; b. South Amboy, N.J., June 12, 1954; d. Wilbur and Betty Ruth (Wyckoff) Farley; m. Charles Rogers Curran II, Jan. 16, 1971 (div. Feb. 1978); 1 child, Jason Samuel Curran; m. Michael Sampere, Aug. 3, 1991. BS in English, Emporia State U., 1988, MA in English, 1991. Homemaker, 1971-75, 79-86; adminstrv. specialist US Army, 1975-79; grad. asst. Emporia (Kans.) State U., 1988-91; adminstrv. asst. The Farm, Inc., Emporia, Kans., 1990-91; adj. faculty Brevard C. C., Melbourne, Fla., 1991—. Contbr. article to The Body Politic mag.; contbg. editor Space Coast Review; guest editor Florida Today newspaper. Co-dir. Clinic Def. Project, Melbourne, Fla., 1993—; exec. dir. Brevard County Voters' Alliance, Melbourne, 1995-96; coord. Mainstream Voters' Alliance, Melbourne, 1996—. Mem. NOW, Nat. Audubon Soc., Nature Conservancy. Home: 1864 Glenwood Dr Melbourne FL 32935 Office: Brevard C C 1534 Clearlake Rd Cocoa FL 33333

SAMPSON, DAPHNE RAE, library director; b. Milw., Aug. 11, 1943; d. Gerald Joseph and Helene Virginia Babbitt; m. Charles Sargent Sampson, Oct. 23, 1971. BA, U. Wis., 1965, MLS, 1966. Reference libr. Def. Intelligence Agy., Washington, 1966-68; sr. reference libr. U.S. Dept. of State, Washington, 1968-78, Exec. Office of the Pres., Washington, 1978-80; chief readers' svcs. Fed. Trade Commn., Washington, 1980-81; chief readers' svcs. U.S. Dept. of Justice, Washington, 1981-84, asst. dir. libr. staff, 1984-86, dep. dir. libr. staff, 1986, acting dir. libr. staff, 1986-87, dir. libr. staff, 1987—, sr. exec. svc., 1995—. Active Berkshire Civic Assn., Alexandria, Va., 1976—. Mem. Am. Assn. Law Librs., Law Librs. Soc. of Washington, Fed. Libr. and Info. Ctr. Com. (bd. mem. 1992). Home: 5838 Wyomissing Ct Alexandria VA 22303-1634 Office: US Dept of Justice Libr Rm 5317 10th & Pennsylvania Ave NW Washington DC 20530

SAMPSON, EARLDINE ROBISON, education educator; b. Russell, Iowa, June 18, 1923; d. Lawrence Earl and Mildred Mona (Judy) Robison; m. Wesley Claude Sampson, Nov. 25, 1953; children: Ann Elizabeth, Lisa Ellen. Diploma, Iowa State Tchrs. Coll., 1943, BA, 1950; MS in Edn., Drake U., 1954; postgrad., No. Ill. U., Iowa State U., 1965-66, 74. Cert. tchr., guidance counselor, Iowa. Tchr. elem. sch. various pub. sch. sys., 1943-48; cons. speech and hearing Iowa Dept. Pub. Instrn., Des Moines, 1950-52; speech therapist Des Moines Pub. Schs., 1952-54, 55; lectr. spl. edn. No. Ill. U., DeKalb, 1964-65; tchr. of homebound Cedar Falls (Iowa) Pub. Schs., 1967-68; asst. prof. edn. U. No. Iowa, Cedar Falls, 1968; asst. prof., counselor Wartburg Coll., Waverly, Iowa, 1968-70; instr. elem. edn., then head of advising elem. edn. Iowa State U., Ames, 1972-82; field supr. elem. edn. U. Toledo, 1988, 89; ind. cons. Sylvania, Ohio, 1989—; cons. Des Moines Speech and Hearing Ctr., 1958-59, bd. dirs., 1962, 63; cons. Sartori Hosp., Cedar Falls, 1967-69; bd. dirs. Story County Mental Health Ctr., Ames, 1972-74. NDEA fellow, 1965. Mem. AAUW, Univ. Women's Club, Zeta Phi Eta. Methodist. Home: 4047 Newcastle Dr Sylvania OH 43560-3450

SAMPSON, SUSAN J., corporate communications consultant, writer; b. St. Louis, Sept. 22, 1939; d. Robert Mantheny Sampson and Lee Quinn Fischbach; m. William Craig Borneman, May 20, 1960 (div. Apr. 1972); children: Katherine Lee Borneman, William Craig Borneman. BA in English Lit., U. Cin., 1969. Writer/photographer WKRC-TV, Cin., 1972-73, art dir., 1973-74; mgr. sta. advt. and promotion WDAF-TV, Kansas City, Mo., 1974-78; creative svcs. dir. WBZ-TV, Boston, 1978-79; supr. comml. prodn. Procter & Gamble Co., Cin., 1979-83, supervising producer Search for Tomorrow, 1983-85, project mgr. corp. comms., 1985-91, exec. producer corp. comms., 1991-95; pres. Insight Comms., Covington, Ky., 1995—. Exec. producer video news mag. P&G This Quarter , 1991-95; author numerous mag. articles. Recipient numerous advt. awards. Mem. Women in Comms. Home: 312 Garrard St Covington KY 41011

SAMPSON, THYRA ANN, mediator; b. Oakland, Calif., Apr. 22, 1948; d. Harold Joseph and Velma Louise (Robinson) S.; 1 child, Leon Broussard III. BA, U. Calif., 1970; JD, Hastings Coll of Law, 1978. Project dir. Univ. Calif. Medical Sch., L.A., 1980-81; legislative staff Calif. State Assembly, Sacramento, 1981-85; adminstr. support for dir. Toward Utility Rate Normalization, San Francisco, 1985-86; program devel. rep. Network Solutions Inc., Sacramento, 1988-89; mediator Sacramento Mediation Ctr., 1990—; founder Realistic Solutions, Inc., Sacramento, 1991; staff cons. Calif. Legislative Black Caucus, Sacramento, 1982, Angel City Dental Soc., L.A., 1978-79. Campaign cons., precinct leader Jessie Jackson for Pres., 1988.

SAMS, TERRI ANN, telecommunications executive; b. Gary, Ind., Jan. 1, 1963; d. Richard Milton and JoAnn (Preston) S. AB in Econs., U. Mich., 1985; cert. telecomm., DePaul U., 1994. Comml. accounts rep. MCI Telecomm. Corp., Chgo., 1987-89, account coord., corp. accounts, 1989-93, account rep., tech. svcs., 1993-94, support cons., strategic nat. accounts,

1994-95, client specialist, strategic nat. accts., 1995—. Mem. scholarship com. Galilee Bapt. Ch., Gary, Ind. Mem. Nat. Black MBA Assn., U. Mich. Alumni Assn. Democrat. Baptist. Home: Apt J-106 5802 Kennedy Terr Gary IN 46403 Office: MCI Telecomm Corp Ste 1100 8750 W Bryn Mawr Ave Chicago IL 60631

SAMSEL, MAEBELL SCROGGINS (MIDGE SAMSEL), paralegal; b. Yazoo City, Miss., Aug. 15, 1940; d. Robert and Lela Estelle (Hammons) Scroggins; m. John Sanders Swain, Dec. 30, 1960 (div. Oct. 1968); 1 child, Stacy Melissa Swain Ramsey; m. Howard Swinehart Samsel, Oct. 8, 1981. BA, Miss. Coll., 1963. Sec. Standard Life Ins. Co., Jackson, Miss., 1963-64; legal sec. Gray & Montague Law Firm, Hattiesburg, Miss., 1964-65; personnel sec. Adj. Gen.'s Office, State of Miss., Jackson, 1965-70; paralegal State of Miss., Atty. Gen.'s Office, Jackson, 1970-79, 84-86; sales agt. Prudential Ins. Co. Am., Jackson, 1979-84. Chmn. acquisitions Miss. Mus. Art, Jackson, 1983, acquisitions vol., 1982, 89, chmn. Vols. at the Palette Restaurant, 1990-95, music chair Miss. Mus. Art Palette Restaurant, 1996, pres. aux., 1991-92, trustee, 1991-92; mem. Jackson Symphony League, 1988—, Miss. Opera Guild, Jackson, 1991—; bd. dirs. Friends of the Ballet, Internat. Ballet Competition. Named Vol. of the Week, Miss. Mus. Art Palette Restaurant, 1989, Vol. of Yr., Miss. Mus. of Art, 1991-92. Mem. AAUW, Jackson Assn. Legal Secs. (pres. 1975-76, 77-78, del. to nat. convs. 1975-77, Outstanding Legal Sec. of Yr. 1975-76), Miss. Assn. Legal Secs., Nat. Assn. Legal Secs. (chmn. nat. spring bd. mtg. 1980), Miss. Coll. Alumni Assn., Petroleum Aux. (v.p. 1986-87, pres. 1988-89, treas. 1989-90, pres. 1994-96), Revelers Dance Club, Serendipity Bridge Club (treas. 1989-93, v.p. 1991-92, pres. 1992-93), Met. Supper Club. Republican. Baptist. Home: 1206 Bay Vis Brandon MS 39042-8650

SAMSON, WANDA KAY, secondary school educator, consultant; b. Shenandoah, Iowa, July 1, 1950; d. Carl Frederick and Margaret Ann (Vette) Sickman. BA, Midland Luth Coll., Fremont, Nebr., 1972; MA in Bus. Edn., U. Nebr., 1983. Cert. tchr., Nebr. Tchr. bus. edn. Fremont (Nebr.) H.S., 1972—; cons. Cortez Peters Keyboarding, 1991—. Bd. dirs., coord. bloodmobile ARC of Dodge County, Fremont, 1990—. Recipient Belong Excel Study Travel award Nebr. Dept. Edn., 1991-96. Mem. NEA, Am. Vocat. Assn., Nat. Assn. Classroom Educators Bus. Edn., Nebr. Edn. Assn., Fremont Edn. Assn., Nat. Bus. Edn. Assn., Mountain-Plains Bus. Edn. Assn., Nebr. Bus. Edn. Assn. (met. rep. 1990-91, pres.-elect 1993-94, pres. 1994-95, past pres. 1995-96), Delta Pi Epsilon (rec. sec., newsletter editor). Lutheran. Office: Fremont HS 1750 N Lincoln Ave Fremont NE 68025-3206

SAMS SCHREIBER, CAROL MARIE HOUSER, artist, graphic designer; b. Knoxville, Tenn., Sept. 28, 1952; d. Harrison Barton Houser and Doris Marie McFarland; m. Richard Vernon Sams (div. 1980); m. Robert William Schreiber, 1990. BFA, U. Tenn., 1973. Prodn. artist Cope Studios, Memphis, 1973-75, Brunner Printing Co., Memphis, 1975-76; graphic designer Smith & Nephew Richards, Memphis, 1976-78, art mgr., designer, 1978-87, creative svcs. coord., 1987-89; owner, electronic designer, illustrator, free-lancer Square One Studio, St. Louis, 1989—. Solo exhbns. include The Bell Gallery, Memphis, 1993-95, numerous others; group exhbn. Nat. Watercolor Soc. Annual, 1980, Tenn. Watercolor Soc., 1974-82, The Bell Gallery, 1993, 94, 95, William Shearburn Gallery, St. Louis, 1996, numerous others. Mem. Memphis Soc. of Visual Communicators, Memphis Watercolor Group, Tenn., So. Ga., Ky., Watercolor Soc. Office: Square One Studio 208 Wolfner Dr Fenton MO 63026

SAMUEL, GWENDOLYN B., director external publications university, writer; b. Detroit, Aug. 25, 1936; d. George Nayf and Josephine Viola Bashara; children: Carol Ann Thomas, Stephanie Elaine Samuel. BA in English, History, U. Mich., 1957; MEd in Sociology, Wayne State U., 1967. Cert. secondary sch. tchr., Mich. Ins. underwriter Firemans Fund Ins. Co., Detroit, 1958-61; tchr. Detroit Pub. Schs., 1961-63, West Covina (Calif.) Unified Sch. Dist., 1963-65, Inglewood (Calif.) Sch. Dist., 1966-68; owner, mgr. Grosse Pointe (Mich.) Book Village, 1974-89; dir. external pubs. Detroit Coll. Law at Mich. State U., 1989—. Playwright: Daddy's Girls, 1986; author: (book) The First Hundred Years Are the Hardest, 1993. Recorder Recording for the Blind, L.A., 1963-68; worthy matron Order of Eastern Star, 1957-62. Recipient Best Overall Design award in New Ednl. Mag., Mag. Design and Prodn., 1990. Mem. Grosse Pointe Theatre (child selection com., sec., treas., ticket chair, workshop chair). Office: Detroit Coll Law at Mich State U 130 E Elizabeth St Detroit MI 48230

SAMUEL, JANET ELLEN, artist, designer; b. N.Y.C., Jan. 7, 1953; d. Ray and Beverly (Burke) S. Student, Franconia Coll., 1971-73; cert., Pa. Acad. Fine Arts, 1983, MFA, 1995. Ptnr., designer Davies & Samuel, Phila., 1988—; faculty mem. Chester Springs (Pa.) Studio, 1994-95; juror Conshocken (Pa.) Arts League, 1995. One-woman exhibits include Zone One Gallery, Phila., 1991-92, Nexus Found. Today's Art, Phila., 1994; group exhibits include Pa. Acad. Fine Arts, 1983, NYU, 1985, Rutgers U., Camden, N.J., 1986, Cheltenham (Pa.) Art Ctr., 1989, 95, Suzanne Gross Gallery, Phila., 1989, Momenta Art Alts., Phila., 1989, Cmty. Edn. Ctr., Phila., 1990, Zone One Gallery, 1991, Villanova U., 1991, Del. Art Mus., Wilmington, 1991, John Post Lee Gallery, N.Y., 1992, Kirkbride Gallery, Phila., 1992, Gallery Continental Bank, Phila., 1992, Nexus Found. Today's Art, 1993, 95, Sande Webster Gallery, Phila., 1993, U. Pa., Phila., 1993, Hallwalls Contemporary ARts Ctr., Buffalo, 1993, Alt. Mus., N.Y., 1993-94, Viridian Gallery, 1994, Maitland (Fla.) Arts Ctr., 1995; represented in pvt. collections; artwork appeared in film Renaissance, 1994. Recipient First prize Muhlenberg Coll. Ctr. Arts, 1992; J. Henry Schiedt Meml. Traveling scholar Pa. Acad. Fine Arts, 1983. Mem. Nexus Found. Today's Art (sec. 1994—), Fellowship Pa. Acad. Fine Arts (bd. dirs. 1995). Home: 1166 E Passyunk Ave Philadelphia PA 19147

SAMUEL, KATHERINE ALICE, artist, painter; b. Paris, Sept. 2, 1948; arrived in U.S., 1970; d. George Albert Samuel and Claude (Keller) Kamin. One-woman shows include 700 S. Clinton Ave., Rochester, 1995, Vassar Coll., Poughkeepsie, N.Y., 1994, Womens Caucus of U. of Rochester, 1992; exhibited in group shows Shoestring Gallery, Rochester, 1995, Snite Mus., U. Notre Dame, 1993; created CD cover: American Women Composers, 1995. Home and Studio: 39 Sumner Park Rochester NY 14607

SAMUELS, ANGELLA V., academic administrator; b. Jamaica, Jan. 14, 1961; came to U.S., 1980; d. Solomon and Victoria (Godfrey) S.; m. Everald Mendis, Aug. 28, 1986; children: Dirk Smith, Glenese Smith. BA, Marymount Manhattan, 1987; MSc, Coll. New Rochelle, 1990; AA, Borough Manhattan C.C., 1996. Sec. United Jewish Appeal, N.Y.C., 1982-84; adminstrv. asst. Travelers Ins., N.Y.C., 1985-87; asst. to editor-in-chief Am. Inst. Physics, N.Y.C., 1987-90; exec. asst. SUNY, N.Y.C., 1990-93, asst. dir. pub. rels., 1993—; mem. employee adv. Am. Inst., N.Y.C., 1989; sch. vol. tchr. N.Y.C. Sch. Vol. Program; mem. strategic planning com. Women in Comm., Va., 1993-94. Mem. N.Y. State Assn. Coll. Admission, N.Y. Women in Comm. Mem. Ch. of God. Home: 724 E 231st St Bronx NY 10466

SAMUELS, CYNTHIA KALISH, communications executive; b. Pitts., May 21, 1946; d. Emerson and Jeanne (Kalish) S.; m. Richard Norman Atkins, Sept. 12, 1971; children: Joshua Whitney Samuels Atkins, Daniel Jonathan Samuels Atkins. BA, Smith Coll., 1968. Press aide McCarthy for Pres. Campaign, Washington, 1968; assoc. producer Newsroom program Sta. KQED, San Francisco, 1972-73; with CBS News, 1973-80, researcher, Washington, 1969-71, documentary researcher, N.Y.C., 1973-74, asst. fgn. editor, 1974-76, asst. N.Y. bur. chief, 1976-80; writer, field producer Today program NBC News, N.Y.C., 1980-84, polit. producer Today program, 1984-89; planning producer, 1988-89; sr. producer Main Street program NBC News, N.Y.C., 1987; founding exec. producer Channel One Program, 1989-92; exec. v.p. Whittle Communications, N.Y.C., 1989-94; now interactive TV and multi-media cons., 1994—. Author: It's A Free Country!: A Young Person's Guide to Politics and Elections, 1988; contbr. book revs. to N.Y. Times Book Rev., Washington Post Book World. Recipient Emmy award No. Calif. Acad. TV Arts and Scis., 1974, Columbia DuPont citation, 1975, Media Access award Calif. Office of Handicapped, 1991, Silver award Nat. Mental Health Assn., 2 Bronze awards Nat. Assn. Edn. in Film and TV, 1993.

SAMUELS, HANNA, artist; b. Buffalo, Apr. 26, 1908; d. Emil and Rachel (Span) S. Student, Art Inst. Buffalo, 1937-54. sr. clk. in charge of catalog SUNY, Buffalo, 1966-73, vol. cons. on art. Represented in permanent collections at Erie County Hist. Mus., Vincent Price Collection, Judaic Mus., Temple Beth Zion, Buffalo, sculpture at Burchfield-Penny Art Ctr., Buffalo. Vol. USO, Buffalo, 1942-45. Mem. Patteran Artists (rec. sec.). Democrat.

SAMUELSON, ANN ELIZABETH, archaeologist; b. Nassau, N.Y., Nov. 11, 1954; d. Dale Silas and Lillian Elizabeth (Thompson) S. BA, New Coll., 1975; MA, SUNY, Albany, 1981; postgrad., U. Calif., Berkeley, 1989-91. Cert. Soc. Profl. Archaeologists. Vol. archaeology projects Harvard, Cambridge, SUNY-Albany, various locations, 1977, 78; crew chief Midwest Archaeol. Ctr., U.S. Pk. Svc., Yellowstone Nat. Park, 1978, 80; forest archaeologist Gallatin Nat. Forest, Bozeman, Mont., 1982-84; pvt. practice English tchr. Shingu, Japan, 1984-85; computer cons., R&D historian, libr. Advanced Cardiovascular Sys., Santa Clara, Calif., 1987-92; computer programmer Summation Legal Techs., San Francisco, 1991; field tech. monitor various contract archaeology firms, 1992-93; supervising archaeologist William Self Assocs., Orinda, Calif., 1993-96; pres. Cultural Resource Cons., 1996—. Bd. mem. Bozeman (Mont.) Alliance for a Nuclear-Free Future, 1982-84, Peninsula Peace Ctr., Palo Alto, Calif., 1987-89, Agape Fund for Non-Violent Social Change, San Francisco, 1990-91; vol. Internat. Com. of Lawyers for Tibet, Berkeley, Calif., 1996. Mem. Soc. for Am. Archaeology, Soc. Calif. Archaeology. Home: 1705 Lexington Ave El Cerrito CA 94530

SAMUELSON, BILLIE MARGARET, artist; b. Long Beach, Calif., Apr. 11, 1927; d. William Christian and Gladys Margaret (Caffrey) Newendorp; m. Fritz Eric Samuelson, Aug. 12, 1950 (div. 1985); children: Craig Eric, Clark Alan, Dana Scott. Student, Long Beach City Coll., 1945-46. Pvt. art tchr. Wycokoff/Allendale, N.J., 1985—; workshop instr. Jane Law Studio, Long Beach Island, N.J., 1990—. Exhibited in solo show at Ridgewood (N.J.) Art Inst., 1985, West Wing Gallery, 1991; group shows include Craig Gallery, Ridgewood, 1979, Charisma Gallery, Englewood, N.J., 1981-83, Custom Gallery, Waldwick, N.J., 1985, Wyckoff (N.J.) Gallery, 1987-90, West Wing Gallery, Ringwood State Park, N.J., 1991, Union Camp Corp., 1992. Recipient 1st in State N.J. Womens Clubs, 1978-80, Watercolor award N.J. Painters and Sculptors, 1981. Mem. DAR, Community Arts Assn. (pres. 1978-79), Am. Artists Profl. League (bd. dirs. 1985-87, watercolor prize 1992), Ringwood Manor Arts Assn. (sr. profl.), Catherine Lorillard Wolfe Art Club (cash award 1993), Salute to Women in the Arts, Art Ctr. Watercolor Affiliates, Nat. Mus. of Women in the Arts. Home: 1-3 Chestnut Pl Waldwick NJ 07463-1125

SAMUELSON, ELLEN BANMAN, state legislator; b. Mathiston, Miss., Dec. 11, 1930; d. Alvin Kornelius and Florence Ellen (True) Banman; m. Armin Otto Samuelson, June 22, 1952; children: Alida Jayne, Ronald Ramin, Eric Carl, Mark Alan. BS, Kans. State U., 1952, MS, 1974. Tchr. elem. sch. Newton (Kans.) Pub. Schs., 1952-53, tchr. home econs., 1957-58; tchr. home econs. Hesston (Kans.) Unified Sch. Dist. 460, 1965-79; prof. home econs. Bethel/Hesston Coll., North Newton, Hesston, Kans., 1979-82, Bethel Coll., North Newton, 1982-87; cons., 1987-88; legislator ho. of reps. State of Kans., Topeka, 1989—; chmn. Joint Com. Children and Families, 1992-94. Precinct committeewoman Rep. Ctrl. Com., Harvey County, Kans., 1956-68, 88—; mem., sec. Harvey County Extension Coun., 1960-64; mem. Family Life Adv. Coun. for Community Mental Health, Kans., 1967-71, Ct. Appointed Spl. Advocate Adv. Bd., Harvey County, 1991—; mem. Hertzler Rsch. Found. Bd., 1993—. Mem. Am. Home Econs. Assn. (speaker ann. meeting student sect. 1989), Am. Vocat. Home Econs. Assn., Kans. Home Econs. Assn. (past sec., past pres., bd. dirs.), Kans. Vocat. Home Econs. Assn. (past pres. bd. dirs.), Kans. State U. Alumni Assn., Kans. State U. Coll. Human Ecology Alumni (bd. dirs. 1991-94), Harvey County Rural Life, Soroptomists, Delta Kappa Gamma (pres. 1984-86), Kappa Omicron Phi. Methodist. Office: House Reps State House Topeka KS 66612

SAMUELSON, NORMA GRACIELA, architectural illustrator, artist; b. Mar del Plata, Argentina, May 29, 1957; came to U.S., 1979; d. Jose and Elsa Florinda (Camaras) Nunez; m. Jeffrey Thomas Samuelson, Oct. 9, 1982; 1 child, Taylor Sebastian. Student, Conservatory Mendelssohn, Mar del Plata, 1970-76; MFA, Superior Sch. Visual Arts, Mar del Plata, 1976. Tchr. art Domingo F. Sarmiento, Mar del Plata, 1976; graphic artist Atelier Marzoratti Munoz, Mar del Plata, 1976-79; archtl. illustrator Szabo Inc., Irvine, Calif., 1981-84; owner, archtl. illustrator Norma Samuelson Illustrations, Mission Viejo, Calif., 1985—. Illustrator: Centennial of Immigration Law, 1975 (2d nat. award), Historical Buildings in Los Angeles, 1995 (ltd. edits.); art work published in Best of Colored Pencil III. Mem. Color Pencil Soc. Am., Mus. Contempoary Art L.A. Home: 24392 Chrisanta Dr Mission Viejo CA 92691 Office: 27001 La Paz Rd Ste 406-B Mission Viejo CA 92691

SAMUELSON, RITA MICHELLE, speech language pathologist; b. Chgo., July 15, 1954; d. Mike Dabetic and Rita Lorraine (Stasny) Dabertin; m. K. Alan Samuelson, May 7, 1977; children: Amber Michelle, April Claire. BS, Ind. U., 1976, MA in Teaching, 1977. Speech lang. therapist East Maine Dist. 63, Des Plaines, Ill., 1977-80, Cmty. Cons. Dist. 59, Elk Grove, Ill., 1980-83, Fenton High Sch. Dist. 100, Bensenville, Ill., 1988-93, Addison (Ill.) Dist. 4, 1993-94, Elgin (Ill.) Dist. U-46, 1994—. Author: Sound Strategist, 1989, The Birthday Party Adventure, 1991, The Lizard Princess Adventure, 1991; contbr. chpt.: Yuletide Reverie, 1993. Mem. Am. Speech Lang. Hearing Assn., DuPage County Speech Hearing Lang. Assn. (v.p. bd. dirs. 1995—), Ill. Speech Lang. Hearing Assn., Villagers Club Bloomingdale, Writer's Workshop of Bloomingdale. Roman Catholic. Home: 156 Longridge Dr Bloomingdale IL 60108-1416 Office: Oakhill Elementary Sch 502 S Oltendorf Rd Streamwood IL 60107

SANABRIA, DIANE MARIA, music education specialist; b. Bklyn., Jan. 14, 1954; d. Pascual and Margarita (De Grazia) S. Student, Friends World Coll., Mineola, N.Y., 1975, SUNY, Stony Brook, 1973-75; BA in Music Edn. cum laude, U. Mass., 1987. Cert. gen. and vocal music educator, Mass. Tchr. substitute, intern gen. and vocal music Fort River Elem. Sch., Amherst, Mass., 1986, Mark's Meadow Elem. Sch., Amherst, Mass., 1987; instr. gen. and vocal music Bernardston and Warwick Elem. Schs., Amherst, Mass., 1986-88; arts cons. Very Special Arts Massachusetts, 1988-91; music instr. gen. and vocal South Hadley (Mass.) Middle Sch., 1988-89; music cons. Theatre Dept. Mount Holyoke Coll., South Hadley, 1991; music instr. gen. and vocal Mosier Elem. Sch., South Hadley, 1987-90, 92—, Glenbrook Middle Sch., Longmeadow, Mass., 1990-91, Plains Elem. Sch., South Hadley, 1992-95. Recordings include: Varela, Sunlost Records, 1970, Valley Partners, Old Homestead, 1980, Pioneer Valley Jamboree I, 1980, Pioneer Valley Jamboree II, 1981; performed in bands including Diane and Roger, 1977-80, Guiding Star Contradance Ensemble, 1980—, Debbie Fish and Diane Sanabria, 1981-88, Briar Hill Ramblers, 1983-87, Lyn Hardy and Diane Sanabria, 1987—, Rude Girls, 1988—, Lyn Hardy and the New Nohemians, 1993—; solo performer in field, 1970—; musician, performer: Sidewalk Theater Co., 1981-84; folk traditions artist: Pioneer Valley Folklore Soc., 1980-94. Recipient First Place award Newfane Vt. Banjo Contest, 1979, recipient first place Banjo and Fiddle 17th Annual Banjo and Fiddle Contest, Lowell Nat. Historical Park, 1996, Christa McAuliffe Tchr. Incentive grant, 1986-87. Mem. Pioneer Valley Folklore Soc. (bd. dirs. 1981-89), Kappa Delta Pi. Office: Mosier Elem Sch Mosier St South Hadley MA 01075

SANBORN, ANNA LUCILLE, pension and insurance consultant; b. Bklyn., Mar. 29, 1924; d. Peter Francis and Matilda M. (Stumpp) Galligen; B.A., Bklyn. Coll., 1945; 1 son, Dean Sanborn. Head dept. benefit and estate planning Union Central Life Ins. Co., N.Y.C., 1949-51; adminstr. employee benefits Seaboard Oil Co., N.Y.C., 1952-56; with Frank J. Walters Assocs., Inc., N.Y.C., 1957—, pres., 1970—. Bd. dirs. Archdiocesan Service Corp. Mem. Am. Acad. Actuaries, Republican. Roman Catholic. Home: 58-11 Seabury St Elmhurst NY 11373-4825 Office: Frank J Walters Assocs 58-13 Seabury St Flushing NY 11373-4825

SANBORN, NANCY L., lawyer; b. Hartford, Conn., Sept. 4, 1958; d. John Bradford and Doris Virginia (Rogers) S. BA, Bowdoin Coll., 1980; JD, Columbia U., 1991. Bar: N.Y. 1992. From staff to v.p. Morgan Guaranty Trust Co. N.Y., N.Y.C., 1980-88; assoc. Davis Polk & Wardwell, N.Y.C., 1991—. Editor Columbia Law Rev., 1990-91. Mem. ABA, Assn. of the Bar of the City of N.Y., Am. Bankruptcy Inst. Home: 92 Remsen St Apt 4B Brooklyn NY 11201 Office: Davis Polk & Wardwell 450 Lexington Ave New York NY 10017

SANCETTA, CONSTANCE ANTONINA, oceanographer; b. Richmond, Va., Apr. 17, 1949; d. Anthony Louis and Joyce Louise (Kellogg) S. BA, Brown U., 1971, MSc, 1973; PhD, Oreg. State U., 1976. Rsch. assoc. Stanford (Calif.) U., 1977-78; assoc. rsch. scientist Columbia U., N.Y.C., 1979-84, rsch. scientist, 1985-87, sr. rsch. scientist, 1988-94; assoc. program mgr. divsn. ocean sci. NSF, Washington, 1992—; mem. adv. com. divsn. ocean sci. NSF, 1981-86, 89-92. Editl. bd. Marine Micropaleontology, Oceanography, 1983—; contbr. articles to profl. jours. Fellow AAAS, Geol. Soc. Am.; mem. Am. Quaternary Soc. (councilor 1988-90), Am. Geophys. Union (sec. ocean sci. sect. 1988-90), Oceanography Soc. (councilor 1989-93), Paleontol. Rsch. Instn. (trustee 1991-92). Home: 1637 Irvin St Vienna VA 22182-2119 Office: NSF Assoc Prog Mgr Divsn Ocean Sci 4201 Wilson Blvd Rm 725 Arlington VA 22230

SANCHEZ, JANICE PATTERSON, psychotherapist, educator; b. Indpls., Nov. 5, 1948; d. Jack Downey and Elizabeth (Evard) Patterson; m. Adel Sanchez, Sept. 20, 1972; children: Christina, Alison. BS in Edn., Ind. U., 1970; MSW, Cath. U. Am., 1983; grad. adv. psychotherapy tng. prog., Washington Sch. Psychiatry, 1988-91, grad. nat. group psychotherapy tng., 1994-96. Lic. clin. social worker, Va., Washington. Tchr. Fairfax County Pub. Schs., McLean, Va., 1970-76; psychotherapist D.C. Inst. Mental Hygiene, Washington, 1984-89; pvt. practice Arlington, Va., 1989—. Vol. tchr. Jr. Gt. Books, Taylor Elem. Sch., Arlington, Va., 1987-89; active Columbia Bapt. Ch. Mem. Am. Group Psychotherapy Assn., Inst. Contemporary Psychotherapy, Greater Washington Soc. for Clin. Social Workers, Jr. League No. Va. Office: Ste 14 3801 Fairfax Dr Arlington VA 22203-1762

SANCHEZ, MARLA RENA, finance director; b. Espanola, N.Mex., Mar. 3, 1956; d. Tomas Guillermo and Rose (Trujillo) S.; m. Bradley D. Gaiser, Mar. 5, 1979. BS, Stanford U., 1979, MS, 1979; MBA, Santa Clara U., 1983. Rsch. biologist Syntex, Palo Alto, Calif., 1980-81; fin. analyst Advanced Micro Devices, Sunnyvale, Calif., 1983-85; fin. mgr. ultrasound divsn. Diasonics, Inc., Milpitas, Calif., 1985-86, contr. therapeutic products divsn., 1989-93, contr. internat. divsn., 1992-93; contr. Ridge Computers, Santa Clara, Calif., 1986-88; dir. fin. VLSI Tech., Inc., San Jose, Calif., 1993—. Home: 1234 Russell Ave Los Altos CA 94024-5541

SAND, PHYLLIS SUE NEWNAM (PHYLLIS SUE NEWNAM), retired special education educator; b. Epworth, N.D., Feb. 12, 1931; d. Zelnoe Jackson and Susie Ella (Lindley) Newnam; m. Shirley Sylvester Sand, Aug. 24, 1952; children: Thomas Richard, James Waldow, Catherine Roberta, Constance Renae. AA, Minot State Tchrs. Coll., 1952; BS in Edn., U. N.D., 1970, MEd, 1971. Cert. profl. educator, N.D., tchr., Minn. Tchr. various rural schs. Ward/Cavalier Counties, N.D., 1950-53; cons., tchr. Griggs, Steele, & Trail Spl. Edn. Unit, N.D., 1976-78; diagnostician, tchr. learning disabled Larimore (N.D.) Elem., 1978-92. Mem. NEA (life), N.D. Edn. Assn. (life), Coun. for Exceptional Children, N.D. Ret. Tchrs. Assn., Greater Grand Forks Sr. Citizens Assn., DAV Aux., North Star Quilters Guild (charter), Minnkota Geneal. Soc., Delta Kappa Gamma (pres. 1990-92, program chmn.). United Methodist. Home: 418 Conklin Ave Grand Forks ND 58203-1669

SANDA, KRIS(TA LINNEA), state commissioner; b. Detroit Lakes, Minn., Dec. 26, 1937; d. K.I. and Luella E. (Meyer) Gandrud; m. Donald J. Sanda, Dec. 28, 1957 (div. 1990); children: John, Karin Luebke, Steven, Timothy, Paul, David; m. Richard O. Johnson, June 15, 1991; children: Lisa Johnson Wahlberg, Scott Johnson. Student, St. Cloud State U., 1955-57; cert., Humphrey Inst. of Pub. Affairs, U. Minn., 1983. Substitute tchr. Staples (Minn.) Pub. Schs., 1957-67; with customer svc. dept. Benson Optical Co., Staples, 1968-79; reporter, columnist Staples World, 1962-68; officer Rep. Party of Minn. State, 1968-79; nat. conv. del., 1972, 76; consumer advocate State of Minn., St. Paul, 1979-83; commr. dept. pub. svc. State of Minn., 1991—; with sales dept. Rural Ventures Inc. (Control Data Corp.), Mpls., 1983-87; pres. Rural Tech. Partnership, St. Paul, 1987-91; bd. dirs. St. Paul Combined Charities State of Minn. Employees. Contbr. editorials and columns to local newspapers; polit. analyst Pub. TV Almanac, KTCA-TV, St. Paul. Bd. dirs. St. Paul Downtown Coun., 1991-93, Rasmussen Bus. Colls. Minn., St. Paul Area United Way, Boy Scouts Am. Indianhead Coun., St. Paul Conv. Bur., also officer; bd. dirs. Gloria Dei Luth. Ch., St. Paul; mem. Minnehaha Park restoration com.; nat. conv. del. Reps., 1972, 76; Todd County chair woman 7th congl. dist., state vice chair, 1964-79; mem. Minn. Hist. Soc. Mem. Nuc. Waste Strategy Coalition (exec. com.), Nat. Assn. Regulated Utility Commrs., Nuc. Regulatory Commn. (Minn. state liaison), State of Minn. Environ. Quality Bd., Rotary (treas. 1987-88, Youth Leadership award St. Paul chpt. 1990), St. Paul C. of C. (bd. dirs. 1987-91), Sons of Norway. Republican. Office: Minn Dept Pub Svc 200 Metro Sq Saint Paul MN 55101

SANDAHL, BONNIE BEARDSLEY, pediatric nurse practitioner, clinical nurse specialist, nurse manager; b. Washington, Jan. 17, 1939; d. Erwin Leonard and Carol Myrtle (Collis) B.; m. Glen Emil Sandahl, Aug 17, 1963; children: Cara Lynne, Cory Glen. BSN, U. Wash., 1962, MN, 1974, cert. pediatric nurse practitioner, 1972. Dir. Wash. State Joint Practice Commn., Seattle, 1974-76; instr. pediatric nurse practitioner program U. Wash., Seattle, 1976, course coordinator quality assurance, 1977-78; pediatric nurse practitioner/health coordinator Snohomish County Head Start, Everett, Wash., 1975-77; clin. nurse educator (specialist), nurse manager Harborview Med. Ctr., Seattle, 1978—, dir. child abuse prevention project, 1986—; speaker legis. focus on children, 1987; clin. assoc. Dept. of Pediatrics, U. Wash. Sch. medicine, 1987—, clin. faculty Sch. Nursing. Mem. Task Force on Pharmacotherapeutic Courses, Wash. State Bd. Nursing, 1985-86; Puget Sound Health Systems Agy., 1975-88, pres., 1980-82; mem. child devel. project adv. bd. Mukilteo Sch. Dist., 1984-85; mem. parenting adv. com. Edmonds Sch. Dist., 1985—; chmn. hospice-home health task force Snohomish County Hospice Program, Everett, 1984-85, bd. dirs. hospice, 1985-87, adv. com. 1986-88; mem. Wash. State Health Coordinating, Council, 1977-82, chmn. nursing home bed projection methodology task force, 1986-87; mem., interim chair Nat. Council Health Planning and Devel., HHS, 1980-87; mem. adv. com. on uncompensated care Wash. State Legislature, 1983-84; mem. Joint Select Com., Tech. Adv. Com. on Managed Health Care Systems, 1984-85. Pres., Alderwood Manor Community Council, 1983-85; treas. Wash. St. Women's Polit. Caucus, 1983-84; mem. com. to examine changes in Wash. State Criminal Sex Law, 1987; appointee county needs assessment com. Snohomish County Govt. United Way, 1989; chair human svcs. adv. coun. Snohomish County Human Svcs. Dept., chair adv. com., 1992-96. Recipient Golden Acorn award Seattle-King County PTA, 1973, Katherine Rickey Vol. Participation award, 1987. Mem. Am. Nurses Assn. (chmn. pediatric nurse practitioner subcom. Com. Examiners Maternal-Child Nursing Practice, 1986-92, chair Com. Examiners Maternal-Child Nursing Practice 1988-90), Wash. State Nurses Assn. (hon. leadership award 1981, chair healthcare reform task force 1992—), King County Nurses Assn. (Nurse of Yr. 1985, 1st v.p. 1992—, pres. 1996—), Wash. State Soc. Pediatrics, Sigma Theta Tau. Democrat. Methodist. Home: 1814 201st Pl SW Lynnwood WA 98036-7060 Office: Harborview Med Ctr 325 9th Ave # Za-53 Seattle WA 98104-2420

SANDARG, PENELOPE J., accountant; b. Hartford, Conn., Sept. 11, 1945; d. Frederick Van Horn and Gloria Benidict (Mitchell) Judd; m. Robert Morrison Sandarg, Aug. 1967 (div. Oct. 1968); 1 child, Mitchelle E. BBS in Acctg., U. No. Fla., 1982, MBA, 1987. CPA, Fla. V.p. fin. Aeroacoustic Corp., Jacksonville, Fla. and Copiague, N.Y., 1968-90; cons. Fla. Products, Jacksonville, 1990-91; acctg. mgr. World Cars, Jacksonville, 1991-92, West Group, Jacksonville, 1992—. Fund raiser Hubbard House, Jacksonville, 1988. Mem. AICPA, Nat. Assn. Purchasing Mgrs. (cert., treas.), Fla. Inst. CPAs, Inst. Mgmt. Acctg. (pres. 1994-95). Office: West-Wayne 401 E Jackson St Ste 3600 Jacksonville FL 32602

SANDERS, ALMA, broadcast executive. Sr. v.p. fin. and adminstrn. CNN, Atlanta. Office: CNN 100 Internat Blvd PO Box 105366 Atlanta GA 30348-5366*

SANDERS, JACQUELYN SEEVAK, psychologist, educator; b. Boston, Apr. 26, 1931; d. Edward Ezral and Dora (Zoken) Seevak; 1 son, Seth. BA, Radcliffe Coll., 1952; MA, U. Chgo., 1964; PhD, UCLA, 1972. Counselor, asst. prin. Orthogenic Sch., Chgo., 1952-65; research assoc. UCLA, 1965-68; cons. Osawatomie State Hosp. (Kans.), 1965-68; asst. prof. Ctr. for Early Edn., L.A., 1969-72; assoc. dir. Sonia Shankman Orthogenic Sch., U. Chgo., 1972-73, dir., 1973-93, dir. emeritus, 1993—; curriculum cons. day care ctrs. L.A. Dept. Social Welfare, 1970-72; instr. Calif. State Coll., L.A., 1972; lectr. dept. edn. U. Chgo., 1972-80, sr. lectr., 1980-93, clin. assoc. prof. dept. psychiatry, 1990-93, emeritus, 1993—; instr. edn. program Inst. Psychoanalysis, Chgo., 1979-82; reading cons. Foreman High Sch., Chgo. Author: Greenhouse for the Mind, 1989; editor: (with Barry L. Childress) Psychoanalytic Approaches to the Very Troubled Child: Therapeutic Practice Innovations in Residential & Educational Settings, 1989, Severly Disturbed Children and the Parental Alliance, 1992, (with Jerome M. Goldsmith) Milieu Therapy: Significant Issues and Innovative Applications, 1993; contbr. articles to profl. jours. Mem. vis. com. univ. sch. rels. U. Chgo. UCLA Univ. fellow, 1966-68; Radcliffe Coll. Scholar, 1948-52; recipient Alumna award Girls' Latin Sch., Boston. Mem. Assn. Children's Residential Ctrs. (past pres.). Clubs: Quadrangle, Radcliffe of Chgo. (sec/treas. 1986-87, pres. 1987-89); Harvard of Chgo. (bd. dirs. 1986—). Home: 5842 S Stony Island Ave Apt 2G Chicago IL 60637-2023

SANDERS, KAREN ELEY, academic director; b. Newport News, Va., Sept. 8, 1962; d. Alvin Earl and Margaret (Edwards) Eley; m. Reliford Theopolis Sanders Jr., July 6, 1991; children: Reliford III, Micaela Karynne. BS, Va. State U., 1986, MS, 1992. Instr. dept. psychology Va. State U., Petersburg, 1990-91; program analyst Security Assistance Tng. Field Activity, Hampton, Va., 1991; acad. counselor student support svcs. dept. U. Ark., Fayetteville, 1992, dir. Boyer Ctr. for Student Svcs., Coll. Edn., 1992—. Grad. fellow Va. State U., 1986-88. Mem. ACA, Am. Coll. Counseling Assn., Nat. Acad. Advising Assn., Mental Health Assn. N.W. Ark., Fayetteville Women's Bowling Assn., Ark. Acad. Advising Network (v.p. comms.). Democrat. Baptist. Home: 4309 Chaparral Ln Fayetteville AR 72704 Office: U Ark Coll Edn 8 Peabody Hall Fayetteville AR 72701

SANDERS, MARION YVONNE, geriatrics nurse; b. St. Petersburg, Fla., Dec. 4, 1936; d. Ira Laurey and Maude Mae Cherry Sanders; children: Dwayne Irwin Parker, Princess Charrie Ferrette, Henry, Pelote. BS, Fla. A&M U., 1959; MS, Nova U., Ft. Lauderdale, Fla., 1992. RN, Fla. Staff nurse Lantana (Fla.) TB Hosp., 1960-61, Mercy Hosp., St. Petersburg, 1961; gen. duty nurse VA, Tuskegee, Ala., 1961-62; staff nurse John Andrews Hosp., Tuskegee, 1962-63; gen. duty staff nurse Brewster Meth. Hosp., Jacksonville, Fla., 1963-65, Duval Med. Ctr., Jacksonville, 1965-66; pvt. duty nurse Dist. 2 Registry, Jacksonville, 1966-70; supr. Eartha White Nursing Home, Jacksonville, 1970; staff nurse Bapt. Hosp., Jacksonville, 1971-73, City-County Methadone Clinic, Jacksonville, 1976-78; pvt. duty nurse Home Nursing, Jacksonville, 1982-86; pvt. duty geriatric nursing and gerontology specialist Home Nursing, 1995—. Active St. Stephen African Meth. Episcopal Ch., Jacksonville; advocate for poor, homeless and prisoners; vol. shelter mgr. ARC, Miami, Fla., 1992-94; vol. cmty. activist, Miami, 1994; vol. Jacksonville Cmty. Rels. Bd., 1996. Recipient Cert. of Recognition, Rep. Party, Fla. and Wash., 1990, Rep. Congl. Orgn., 1988, 90, 91. Mem. ANA (mem. polit. action coms.), Fla. Nurses Assn. Republican. Methodist. Home: 4832 N Main St Apt 14 Jacksonville FL 32206

SANDERS, MARLENE, anchor; b. Cleve., Jan. 10, 1931; d. Mac and Evelyn (Menitoff) Sanders; m. Jerome Toobin, May 27, 1958 (dec. Jan. 1984); children: Jeff, Mark. Student, Ohio State U., 1948-49. Writer, prodr. Sta. WNEW-TV, N.Y.C., 1955-60, P.M. program Westinghouse Broadcasting Co., N.Y.C., 1961-62; asst. dir. news and public affairs Sta. WNEW, N.Y.C., 1962-64; anchor, news program ABC News, N.Y.C., 1964-68, corr., 1968-72, documentary prodr., writer, anchor, 1972-76, v.p., dir. TV documentaries, 1976-78; corr. CBS News, N.Y.C., 1978-87; host Currents Sta. WNET-TV, N.Y.C., 1987-88; host Met. Week in Review, 1988-90; host Thirteen Live Sta. WNET-TV, 1990-91; prof. dept. journalism NYU, 1991-93; adj. prof. journalism, adminstr. Columbia U. Grad. Sch. Journalism, N.Y.C., 1994-95; tv anchor Prime Life Network, N.Y., 1996—. Co-author: Waiting for Prime Time: The Women of Television News, 1988. Recipient award N.Y. State Broadcasters Assn., 1976, award Nat. Press Club, 1976, Emmy awards, 1980, 81, others. Mem. Am. Women in Radio and TV (Woman of Yr. award 1975, Silver Satellite award 1977), Women in Comm. (past pres.), Soc. Profl. Journalists.

SANDERS, SUMMER, Olympic athlete; b. 1972; d. Bob and Barbara S. Gold medalist, 200m Butterfly Barcelona Olympic Games, 1992, Silver medalist, 200m Individual Medley, 1992, Bronze medalist, 400m Individual Medley, 1992. Address: US Swimming Inc One Olympic Plaza Colorado Springs CO 80909-5724*

SANDERSON, CATHY ANN, histotechnician, researcher; b. Key West, Fla., Apr. 12, 1954; d. Robert Gary and Cheri Dae (Colin) S.; 1 child, Nichole Renee. Grad. h.s., Phoenix, Ariz., 1972. Histology trainee St. Luke's Medical Ctr., Phoenix, 1972-73, histotechnician, 1973-83; histotechnician/rsch. Harrington Arthritis Rsch. Ctr., Phoenix, 1983-87, Emory U., Atlanta, 1987-88, VA Medical Ctr, Salt Lake City, 1988—; founder, chair hard tissue com. Nat. Soc. Histotech., Bowie, Md., 1989 , editor, 1992—, vet. indsl. rsch. com., 1989—, health and safety com., 1988—, mem. ednl. com., 1989-91; owner Wasatch Histo Cons., 1988—. Mem. editl. bd. Jour. Histotechnology, 1993—; contbr. articles to numerous profl. jours. Organizer Neighborhood Watch, West Valley City, Utah, 1993—. Named Histotechnologist of Yr., Nat. Soc. Histotechnology, 1992; recipient Hacker Instruments; Membership Incentive award, 1991-92, Superior Performance award, 1989-92, 95-96, William J. Hacker award, 1988, Rsch. Technician of Yr. award, 1989. Mem. European Soc. Histotechnology, Nat. Wildlife Fedn., Ga. Soc. Histotechnology, Utah Soc. Histotechnology, Am. Assn. Lab Animal Sci. (bd. dirs. 1989-91), The Cousteau Soc., Inc., Nat. Soc. Histotechnology. Office: VA Medical Ctr 500 Foothill Blvd 151F Salt Lake City UT 84148

SANDERSON, HOLLADAY WORTH, domestic violence advocate; b. Raleigh, May 17, 1950; d. Hal Venable Jr. and Mary Simmons (Andrews) W.; M. Glen Wessel Potter, Apr. 15, 1978 (div. Sept. 1980); m. Stanley McNaughton Sanderson, July 2, 1984. Cert. advanced acctg./data processing, Kinman Bus. U., 1985. Orch. tchr. New Hanover County Schs., Wilmington, N.C., 1972-74, 75-78, Fairfax (Va.) County Schs., 1978-80, 86-89, Missoula (Mont.) Elem. Sch. Dist., 1983-84; musician, music tchr. Coeur d'Alene, Idaho, 1980-83, 84-86, 1989-91; adj. music faculty, violin, viola, chamber music North Idaho Coll., Coeur d'Alene, 1980-83, 84-86; organist, choir dir. St. Luke's Episcopal ch., Coeur d'Alene, 1980-83, 84-86, St. Luke's Episcopal Ch., Coeur d'Alene, 1989-95; gen. mgr., artistic dir. Coeur d'Alene Summer Theatre, Coeur d'Alene, 1991-92; bookkeeper, adminstrv. asst. Women's Ctr., Coeur d'Alene, 1993-95, exec. dir., 1995—. Sec. Idaho Coalition Against Sexual and Domestic Violence, 1995—; sec.-treas. North Idaho Coalition on Domestic Violence, 1995—; paliamentarian Vestry of St. Luke's Episcopal Ch., 1996—, audit com. chair, 1992-95, lay reader, chalice bearer, 1992—; orch. dir. Pend Oreille Chamber Orch., Sandpoint, Idaho, 1994-95, North Idaho Symphony, 1991, Coeur d'Alene Summer Theatre, 1982-85; cert. QPR suicide prevention gatekeeper instr. Greentree Behavioral Ctr., Spokane, 1996—; mem. Nat. Coalition Against Domestic Violence, Washington State Coalition Against Domestic Violence. Mem. Coeur d'Alene Sunrise Rotary. Democrat. Home: 504 N 15th St Coeur D Alene ID 83814 Office: Womens Ctr 2201 N Government Way Ste E Coeur d'Alene ID 83814

SANDERSON, MARY LOUISE, medical association administrator; b. Fairmont, W. Va., Oct. 29, 1942; d. Lawrence Oliver and Frances Evelyn (Shuttleworth) Shingleton; m. William W. Olmstead III, Dec. 1966 (div. June 1974); children: William W. IV, Happy; m. Lester F. Davis, III, Oct. 1979 (div. Dec. 1986); m. David S. Sanderson, Sept. 1992. Student, Vassar Coll., 1960-62, Carnegie Mellon, 1962-63. Real estate broker, N.C. Exec. sec. Creative Dining, Raleigh, N.C., 1980-83, Sea Pines Plantation Co., Hilton Head, S.C., 1973-79; adminstr. Am. Bd. Neurological Surgery, Houston, 1983—. Vol. Interact, Raleigh, 1984-86, M.D. Anderson Cancer Ctr./Camp Star Trails, 1994—; docent Mordicai House Hist. Preservation, Raleigh, 1981-83; mem. Reach to Recovery, 1995—. Recipient Vol. award N.C. State Gov., 1986. Mem. Am. Soc. Assn. Execs. Democrat. Episcopalian. Office: Am Bd Neurol Surgery 6550 Fannin St Ste 2139 Houston TX 77030-2722

SANDFORD, JUANITA DADISMAN, sociologist, educator, writer; b. Wichita, Kans., June 20, 1926; d. Carol Orville and Mabel Bernice (Stearman) Dadisman; m. Herman Prestridge Sandford, Dec. 22, 1946; children: Susan Jane, Linda Ann, Mary Kaye. BA, Baylor U., 1947, MA, 1948; LLD (hon.), Hendrix Coll., 1991. Instr. sociology Wayland Bapt. Coll., Plainview, Tex., 1948-49, Ft. Smith (Ark.) Jr. coll., 1959; instr. sociology Ouachita Bapt. U., Arkadelphia, Ark., 1960-68, adj. prof., 1996—; asst. prof. sociology Henderson State U., Arkadelphia, Ark., 1968-89, coord. women's studies, 1975-89; ret., 1989; adj. tchr. Ouachita Bapt. U., 1996—; chmn. bd. Coll. Cmty. Action, Inc., 1974-78; cons. human rels. Ark. Tech. Assistance & Consultative Ctr., 1964-78; mem. Gov. Ark. Commn. on Status of Women, 1975-80, Atty. Gen. Consumer Adv. Bd., 1977-79. Author: I Didn't Get a Lot Done Today, 1974, Poverty in the Land of Opportunity, 1978, Sunbonnet Sue: The Crone, 1996; contbg. author Women & Religion: Images of Women in the Bible, 1977, Arkansas: State in Transition, 1981, Arkadelphia: 2000 AD, 1982. Bd. dirs. Ctrl. Ark. Devel. Coun., 1975-80, Ark. Hunger Project, 1983-86, Ark. Advs. for Children and Families, 1986-89. Recipient Ark. Woman of Achievement award Ark. Womens Polit. Caucus, 1975. Mem. NOW, Ark. Sociolog. & Anthropolog. Assn. (pres. 1991-92), Inst. Noetic Sci. Home: 959 N 8th St Arkadelphia AR 71923-3201

SANDIDGE, KANITA DURICE, communications company executive; b. Cleve., Dec. 2, 1947; d. John Robert Jr. and Virginia Louise (Caldwell) S. AB, Cornell U., 1970; MBA, Case Western Res. U., 1979. Supr. assignments service ctrs. and installation AT&T, Cleve., 1970-78, chief dept. data processing and acctg., 1979-80; adminstrn. mgr. exec. v.p. staff AT&T, N.Y.C., 1980-83; sales forecasting and analysis mgr. resources planning AT&T, Newark, 1983-86; planning and devel. mgr. material planning and mgmt. AT&T Network Systems, Morristown, N.J., 1986-87; dir. adminstrv. services AT&T Network Systems, Lisle, Ill., 1987-89; dir. divsn. staff customer support and ops. AT&T Network Systems, Morristown, 1990-94; dir. global procurement minority and women bus. enterprises AT&T, Basking Ridge, N.J., 1994—. Mem black exchange program Nat. Urban League, N.Y.C., 1986—. Named Black Achiever in Industry, Harlem YMCA, 1981; recipient Tribute to Women and Industry Achievement award YWCA, 1985. Mem. Nat. Black MBA's, Alliance Black AT&T Mgrs., Am. Mgmt. Assn., Nat. Assn. for Female Execs., NAACP, Beta Alpha Psi. Mem. African Meth. Episcopal Ch. Home: 10 Trade Winds Dr Randolph NJ 07869-1238 Office: AT&T 295 N Maple Ave Basking Ridge NJ 07920-1002

SANDIDGE, PEGGY G., therapist, counselor; b. Cleveland, Tenn., Oct. 11, 1944; d. Donald C. and Florence M. Pierce; m. Sterling C. Sandidge, Nov. 21, 1967. AS, Cleveland State Cmty. Coll., 1991; BA, Lee Coll., 1993; MEd, U. Tenn., 1995. Correction officer Juvenile Court, Cleveland, 1993-94; drug edn. coord. Polk County Sch. Sys., Chattanooga, 1993-95; family counselor New Life Homes for Boys, Inc., Chattanooga, 1995—. Mem. Am. Counseling Assn., Chi Sigma Iota, Delta Kappa Phi. Democrat. Baptist. Home: 3298 Sugar Creek Rd Crandall GA 30711 Office: New Life Home for Boys Inc PO Box 15676 Chattanooga TN 37415

SAND LEE, INGER, artist; b. Sauda, Norway, Apr. 8, 1938; came to U.S., 1960; d. Inge Sigvald and Johanne Elise (Hamre) Sand; m. Charles Allen Lee, Aug. 28, 1981. Cert. in decorative art, N.Y. Sch. Interior Design, 1968; BFA, Marymount Manhattan Coll./N.Y. Sch. Interior Design, 1980; cert. completion, Art Students League, 1993; postgrad., Nat. Acad. Design, 1993-94. One-woman shows include Art 54, N.Y.C., 1988, Pyramid Gallery, N.Y.C., 1990, Exhbn. Space, N.Y.C., 1991, Denise Bibro Fine Art, N.Y.C., 1993, 95; selected exhbns. include Lincoln Ctr., N.Y.C., 1988, Avery Fisher Hall, N.Y.C., 1988, Mus. Atheism and Realism, Lviv, USSR, 1990, Lever House, N.Y.C., 1991, Nat. Acad. Mus., N.Y.C., 1994; group exhbns. include Pyramid Gallery, N.Y.C., 1989, 90, 91, Ariel Gallery, N.Y.C., 1991, Broome Street Gallery, N.Y.C., 1992, 93, Ward-Nasse Gallery, N.Y.C., 1992, Hudson Guild Art Gallery, N.Y.C., 1992, Denise Bibro Fine Art, N.Y.C., 1992, 94, 95, Frank Bustamante Gallery, N.Y.C., 1993, Southern Alleghenies Mus. Art, Loretto, Pa., 1994, Edward William Gallery, 1996, Knoxville (Tenn.) Opera Guild, 1996, Fairleigh Dickinson U., 1996; represented in numerous permanent pvt. and pub. collections. Recipient Alumni award N.Y. Sch. Interior Design, 1979; merit scholar Art Student's League, 1991. Mem. Archtl. League N.Y.

SANDLER, BERNICE RESNICK, women's rights specialist; b. N.Y.C., Mar. 3, 1928; d. Abraham Hyman and Ivy (Ernst) Resnick; children: Deborah Jo, Emily Maud. BA cum laude, Bklyn. Coll., 1948; MA, CCNY, 1950; EdD, U. Md., 1969; LLD (hon.), Bloomfield Coll., 1973, Hood Coll., 1974, R.I. Coll., 1980, Colby-Sawyer Coll., 1984; LHD (hon.), Grand Valley State Coll., 1974; Dr. Pub. Service (hon.), North Adams State Coll., 1985; LLD (hon.), Goucher Coll., 1991; LHD (hon.), Plymouth State Coll., 1992, Wittenberg U., 1993. Research asst., nursery sch. tchr., employment counselor, adult edn. instr., sec.; psychologist HEW, 1970; tchr. psychology Mt. Vernon Coll., 1970; head Action Com. for Fed. Contract Compliance, Women's Equity Action League, 1970-71; edn. specialist U.S. Ho. Reps., Washington, 1970; dep. dir. Womens Action program, HEW, Washington, 1971; dir. project on status and edn. of women Assn. Am. Colls., Washington, 1971-91; sr. assoc. Ctr. for Women Policy Studies, 1991-94; sr. scholar in residence Nat. Assn. Women in Edn., Washington, 1994—; cons., 1991—; expert witness, 1990—; writer, 1971—; vis. lectr. U. Md., 1968-69; adv. bd. Women's Equity Action League Ednl. and Legal Def. Fund, 1980—, trustee, 1974-80, Women's Equity Action League, 1971-78; adv. com. Math./Sci. Network, 1979, Wider Opportunities for Women, 1978-85, Women's Legal Def. Fund, 1978-84; adv. bd. N.J. project Inst. for Rsch. on Women Rutgers U., New Brunswick, 1987—, Nat. Coun. for Alternative Work Patterns Inc., 1978-85, Women's Hdqs. State Nat. Bank for Women's Appointments, 1977-78, and others. Mem. adv. bd. Jour. Reprints Documents Affecting Women, 1976-78, Women's Rights Law Reporter, 1970-80; editor: (newsletters) On Campus With Women, 1971-91, About Women on Campus, 1991—; contbr. articles to profl. jours. Mem. bd. overseers Wellesley Coll. Ctr. for Rsch. on Women, 1975-87; bd. dirs. Ctr. for Women's Policy Studies, 1972-75; mem. exec. com. Inst. for Ednl. Leadership, 1982-87, mem. program adv. com., 1987—, chair bd. dirs., 1981, chair adv. com., 1975-81; mem. affirmative action com., task force on family, nat. affairs commn. Am. Jewish Com., 1978, bd. dirs. D.C. chpt.; tech. adv. com. Nat. Jewish Family Ctr., 1980-89; adv. coun. Ednl. Devel. Ctr., 1980-85; adv. bd. Urban Inst., 1981-85, Women Employed Inst., 1981-84, Ex-New Yorkers for N.Y., 1978-79; mem. adv. com. Arthur and Elizabeth Schlesinger Libr. History of Women in Am., 1981-85; nat. adv. com. Shelter Rsch. Inst., Calif., 1980-82; chair adv. panel project on self-evaluation Am. Insts. for Rsch., 1980-82; bd. dirs. Equality Ctr., 1983, Evaluation and Tng. Inst., Calif., 1980, Inst. for Studies in Equality, 1975-77. Recipient Athena award Intercollegiate Assn. Women Students, 1974, Elizabeth Boyer award Women's Equity Action League, 1976, Rockefeller Pub. Svc. award Princeton U., 1976, Women Educators award for activism, 1987, Anna Roe award Harvard U., 1988, Readers Choice honors Washington Woman Mag., 1987, Woman of Distinction award Nat. Assn. Women in Edn., 1991, Georgina Smith award AAUP, 1992, Woman of Achievement Turner Broadcasting System, 1994; named one of 100 Most Powerful Women Washingtonian Mag., 1982, one of the nation's 100 Most Important Women, Ladies Home Jour., 1988. Mem. Assn. for Women in Sci. Found. (bd. dirs. 1977—), Am. Soc. Profl. and Exec. Women (adv. bd. 1980). Office: Nat Assn Women in Edn 1350 Connecticut Ave NW Ste 850 Washington DC 20036-1701

SANDLER, JENNY, dancer; b. N.Y.C.. Scholarship student, The Joffrey Ballet Sch. Dancer Joffrey II Dancers, N.Y.C., 1988-90, The Joffrey Ballet, N.Y.C., 1990—. Featured in mag. Mirabella, Aug., 1994. Office: 25 E 9th St #7A New York NY 10003

SANDLER, LUCY FREEMAN, art history educator; b. N.Y.C., June 7, 1930; d. Otto and Frances (Glass) Freeman; m. Irving Sandler, Sept. 4, 1958; 1 child, Catherine Harriet. B.A., Queens Coll., 1951; M.A., Columbia U., 1957; Ph.D., NYU, 1964. Asst. prof. NYU, 1964-70, assoc. prof., 1970-75, prof. fine arts, 1975-86, Helen Gould Sheppard prof. art history, 1986—, chmn. dept., 1975-89; editorial cons. Viator, UCLA, 1983—. Author: The Peterborough Psalter in Brussels, 1974, The Psalter of Robert De Lisle in the British Library, 1983, Gothic Manuscripts 1285-1385, 1986, 'Omne Bonum': A Fourteenth-Century Encyclopedia of Universal Knowledge, 1996; editor: Essays in Memory of Karl Lehmann, 1964, Art the Ape of Nature: Studies in Honor of H.W. Janson, 1981, Monograph Series, 1970-75, 86-89, Gesta, 1991-94; asst. editor Art Bull., 1964-67, mem. editl. bd., 1994; mem. editl. bd. Jour. Jewish Art, 1978, Speculum, 1994. Trustee Godwin-Ternbach Mus., Queens Coll., 1982-94. NEH fellow, 1967-68, 77; fellow Pierpont Morgan Library; Guggenheim fellow, 1988-89. Fellow Soc. Antiquaries (London); mem. AAUP, Coll. Art Assn. (pres. 1981-84), Medieval Acad. Am., Internat. Ctr. Medieval Art (adv. bd., bd. dirs. 1976-80, 84-87, 89-92, 95—). Home: 100 Bleecker St Apt 30A New York NY 10012-2207 Office: NYU Dept Fine Arts New York NY 10003

SANDLER, MARION OSHER, savings and loan association executive; b. Biddeford, Maine, Oct. 17, 1930; d. Samuel and Leah (Lowe) Osher; m. Herbert M. Sandler, Mar. 26, 1961. BA, Wellesley Coll., 1952; postgrad., Harvard U.-Radcliffe Coll., 1953; MBA, NYU, 1958; LLD (hon.), Golden Gate U., 1987. Asst. buyer Bloomingdale's (dept. store), N.Y.C., 1953-55; security analyst Dominick & Dominick, N.Y.C., 1955-61; sr. fin. analyst Oppenheimer & Co., N.Y.C., 1961-63; sr. v.p., dir. Golden West Fin. Corp. and World Savs. & Loan Assn., Oakland, Calif., 1963-75, vice chmn. bd. dirs., CEO, mem. exec. com., dir., 1975-80, pres., co- chief exec. officer, dir., mem. exec. com., 1980-93, chmn. bd. dirs., CEO, mem. exec. com., 1993—; pres., chmn. bd. dirs., CEO Atlas Assets, Inc., Oakland, 1987—, Atlas Advisers, Inc., Oakland, 1987—, Atlas Securities, Inc., Oakland, 1987—; mem. adv. com. Fed. Nat. Mortgage Assn., 1983-84. Mem. Pres.'s Mgmt. Improvement Coun., 1980, Thrift Insts. Adv. Coun. to Fed. Res. Bd., 1989-91, v.p., 1990, pres., 1991; mem. policy adv. bd. Ctr. for Real Estate and Urban Econs. U. Calif., Berkeley, 1981—, mem. exec. com. policy adv. bd., 1985—; mem. ad hoc com. to rev. Schs. Bus. Adminstrn. U. Calif., 1984-85; vice chmn. industry adv. com. Fed. Savs. and Loan Ins. Corp., 1987-88, Ins. Corp., 1987-88; bd. overseers NYU Schs. Bus., 1987-89; mem. Glass Ceiling Commn., 1992-93. Mem. Phi Beta Kappa, Beta Gamma Sigma. Office: Golden W Fin Corp 1901 Harrison St Oakland CA 94612-3574

SANDLER, MICHELLE GAIL, librarian; b. Long Beach, Calif., Oct. 22, 1956; d. Arthur Nelson and Annabelle (Marks) S. AA in History, Cypress C.C., 1977; BA in History, U. Ariz., 1979; cert. in cartography, Calif. State U., Long Beach, 1983; MLS, San Jose State U., 1993. Cartographer Teledyne Geotronics, Long Beach, 1983-84; tech. illustrator Oldershaw Engring., Anaheim, Calif., 1984-85, Cons. and Designers, Anaheim, 1985-86; sales clk. Aaron Bros. Art Marts, Garden Grove, Calif., 1987-90; libr. asst. County of Orange Environ. Mgmt. Agy., Santa Ana, Calif., 1990-93, County of Orange-Orange County Pub. Libr., Santa Ana, 1993; libr. Jewish Cmty. Ctr., Costa Mesa, Calif., 1992-94, Morasha Day Sch., Aliso Viejo, Calif., 1993—, Temple Bat Yahm, Newport Beach, Calif., 1994—; profl. genealogist, Calif., 1986-90. Environ. educator Sierra Club, Tucson, 1977-79. Mem. Assn. Jewish Librs., Jewish Genealogy Soc. (pres. 1987-94). Democrat. Home: 5773 Centerstone Ct Westminster CA 92683 Office: Temple Bat Yahm 1011 Camelback St Newport Beach CA 92660

SANDLIN, ANN MARIE, real estate broker; b. Ft. Worth, Sept. 17, 1940; d. Joseph Gustave Rountree and Jessie Margaret (Piatt) Ford; m. James Gordon Anderson, Apr. 28, 1961 (div. May 1981); children: James Gordon Jr., Edward Joseph; m. George Wilson Sandlin, Nov. 11, 1984. Mail clk. State Comptroller's Dept., Austin, Tex., 1960-62; Realtor, relocation dir., office mgr. Sandlin & Co. Real Estate, Austin, 1976—. Mem. Women's Coun. Realtors (past pres.), Tex. Assn. Realtors (bd. dirs. 1988—, chmn. pub. rels. 1991), Austin Bd. Realtors (bd. dirs. 1990—, pres. 1996), Daus. Republic of Tex. Office: Sandlin & Co PO Box 202738 Austin TX 78720-2738

SANDOWSKI, NORMA JEWELL, safety engineer; b. Tulsa, Dec. 30, 1940; d. Norman Jesse Sandusky and Gulia Ida (Poynor) Foster; divorced; children: Sheila Jewell Lester, Sheryl Lee Sanders, Michael Lance Sandowski. AS in Welding Tech., Tulsa Jr. Coll., 1970; BS in Indsl. Safety, Cen. State U., 1983; MS in Environ. Sci., Nova U., 1987; cert. in hazardous materials mgmt., U. Calif., Davis, 1988. Cert. assoc. risk mgmt.; cert. assoc. loss control mgmt. Safety and personnel dir. Utility Contractors, Tulsa, 1976-77; safety officer City of Tulsa Water and Sewer Dept., 1977-78; risk control rep. Comml. Union Ins., Dallas, Oklahoma City, 1978-81; cons. Parallel Resources, Oklahoma City,, San Francisco, 1981-86; mgr. environ. and occupational health Linde div. Union Carbide, Santa Rosa, Calif., 1987; mgr. tech. svcs., asst. v.p. risk engring. dept. Zurich-Am. Ins., Schaumburg, Ill., 1987—; mgr. safety & indsl. hygiene JLM Chems. Inc., Blue Island, Ill. Author: Right to Know in Educational Institutions, 1986, Environmental Auditing and Recordkeeping, 1987, Chemical Industry and its Accidents, 1991, Future of Ammonia, 1992. Mem. Adult Literacy Coun., Make Today Count-Am. Cancer Soc.; vol. Take-A-Hike. Pres.' scholar Tulsa Jr. Coll., 1969, Flint Steel scholar, Tulsa, 1970; recipient Danforth award Cities Svc. Oil, Bartlesville, Okla., 1958, Silver Trefoil Woman of Achievement award Ill. Crossroads coun. Girl Scouts U.S.A., 1994. Mem. Am. Soc. Safety Engrs. (profl.). Jewish. Office: 3350 W 131st St Blue Island IL 60406-3354

SANDROCK, DONNA, gallery director; b. Coon Rapids, Iowa, July 27, 1948; d. Forrest Orrie and Eleanor Caroline (Sieg) S. BA, Calif. State U., 1980-87, cert. mus. studies, 1987. Curatorial asst. Art Mus. Calif. State U., Long Beach, 1985-86; asst. curator Long Beach (Calif.) Art Mus., 1986-90; asst. to registrar Laguna Art Mus., Laguna Beach, Calif., 1990-92; dir./curator Golden West Coll., Huntington Beach, Calif., 1992—. Address: Fine Art Gallery PO Box 2748 Huntington Beach CA 92647-0748

SANDRY, KARLA KAY FOREMAN, industrial engineering educator; b. Davenport, Iowa, Apr. 2, 1961; d. Donald Glen and Greta Geniveve (VanderMaten) Foreman; m. William James Sandry, Oct. 12, 1985; children: Zachary Quinn, Skyler David. BS in Indsl. Engring., Iowa State U., 1983; MBA, U. Iowa, 1992. Quality control supr., indsl. engr. Baxter Travenol Labs, Hays, Kans., 1983-84; indsl. engr. HQ Amccom, Rock Island, Ill., 1984-86; mgmt. engr. St. Lukes Hosp., Davenport, 1986-90; adj. instr. engring. St. Ambrose U., Davenport, 1990—; chair space allocations St. Luke's Hosp., Davenport, 1987-90; pres. employee rels. coun. HQ Amccom, Rock Island, 1986, chair savings bonds, 1985; speaker in field. Vol., past counselor Fellowship Christian Athletes Ctrl. H.S., Davenport, 1984-87, vol., adult chpt., 1988—; counselor Explorer Scout Troop, Davenport, 1984-85; leader, counselor ch. youth group, 1985-89; v.p. Crisis Pregnancy Ctr., 1996—, co-chmn. walkathon, 1996, pres. ch. choir, 1992, 95-96, orch. ch., 1994—, fin. com. 1995, dream team, 1996—, security com. 1996—. Mem. Inst. Indsl. Engrs. (sr. mem.), Healthcare Info. & Mgmt. Systems Soc. (recognition & comms. com. 1988), Soc. for Health Systems (founding mem.), Found. for Christian Living, Iowa State U. Alumni Assn., U. Iowa Alumni Assn.; Positive Thinkers Club. Office: St Ambrose U 518 W Locust St Davenport IA 52803-2829

SANDS, CORI EILEEN, artist; b. Balt., Nov. 15, 1959; d. Reginald and Phyllis Emily (Johnson) S. Exhbns. include American Dream Festival, L.A., 1987, Currents, Balt., 1989, 4th Annual Am. Artist With Disabilities Lincoln Ctr., N.Y.C., 1990, City Hall Galleries, Balt., 1990, African Am. Artist With Disabilities, N.Y., 1992, Towson Town Art Festival, 1992, 94, Artscape, Balt., 1993, 95, 96, Out of Order Md. Art Place, Balt., 1995. Served in U.S. Army, 1979-83. Democrat. Roman Catholic. Home: 912 Lenton Ave Baltimore MD 21212

SANDS, ROBERTA ALYSE, real estate investor; b. N.Y.C., Oct. 7, 1937; d. Harry and Irene (Mytelka) S. BEd, U. Miami, 1960; postgrad., U. Oslo, 1960. Cert. secondary educator biology, Mass. Phys. edn. instr. Key Biscayne and Ludlam Elem. Sch., Miami, 1961-63; sci. tchr. Plantation (Fla.) Mid. Sch., 1969-71, Rickards Middle Sch., Ft. Lauderdale, Fla., 1972-76; founder U. Miami Diabetes Rsch. Inst., 1989. Author: Biology on the Secondary Level, 1970. Vol. Douglas Garden Retirement Home, Miami, 1988-92, Mus. of Art, Ft. Lauderdale, 1988-92, Imperial Point Hosp., Ft. Lauderdale, 1981-83. Mem. AAUW (rec. sec. 1988-92, cultural chair 1993-94, legis. chair Ft. Lauderdale br. 1994-95, women's issue chair Ft. Lauderdale 1994—, edn. chair Pompano Beach br. 1994-96, Recognition of Significant Svc. award 1983). Home: 4250 Galt Ocean Dr Fort Lauderdale FL 33308-6138

SANDS, ROBERTA G., social work educator; b. Bklyn., Oct. 28, 1941; d. Alan Nathan and Alice Louise Goldsamt; m. Morris M. Wilhelm, Mar. 13, 1966 (div. Nov. 1972); children: Philip Wilhelm, Bonnie Wilhelm Moskoff; m. Samuel Z. Klausner, Nov. 26, 1992. BA, Bryn Mawr Coll., 1963; MSW, Hunter Coll., 1965; PhD, U. Louisville, 1979. Psychiat. social worker River Region Mental Health, Louisville, 1972-75; psychiat. social worker/rschr. U. Louisville, 1975-78; instr. Spalding Coll., Louisville, 1978-80; lectr. Cornell U., Ithaca, N.Y., 1979-80; psychiat. social worker Willard (N.Y.) Psychiat. Ctr., 1980-81; asst. prof. Ohio State U., Columbus, 1981-87; assoc. prof. Ohio State U., 1987-90, U. Pa., Phila., 1990—. Author: Clinical Social Work Practice in Community Mental Health, 1991; contbr. articles to Social Work, Families in Soc. Rsch. grantee AARP Andrus Found., Washington, 1995-96. Mem. NASW (bd. dirs. Ohio chpt. 1985-87), Coun. on Social Work Edn. Jewish. Office: U Pa Sch Social Work 3701 Locust Walk Philadelphia PA 19104

SANDS, SHARON LOUISE, graphic design executive, art publisher, artist; b. Jacksonville, Fla., July 4, 1944; d. Clifford Harding Sands and Ruby May (Ray) MacDonald; m. Jonathan Michael Langford, Feb. 14, 1988. BFA, Cen. Washington U., 1968; postgrad, UCLA, 1968. Art dir. East West Network, Inc., L.A., 1973-78, Daisy Pub., L.A., 1978; prodn. dir. L.A. mag., 1979-80; owner, creative dir. Carmel Graphic Design, Carmel Valley, Calif., 1981-85; creative dir., v.p. The Video Sch. House, Monterey, Calif., 1985-88; graphic designer ConAgra, ConAgra, Nebr., 1988; owner, creative dir. Esprit de Fleurs, Ltd., Carmel, Calif., 1988—; lectr. Pub. Expo, L.A., 1979, panelist Women in Mgmt., L.A., 1979; redesign of local newspaper, Carmel, Calif., 1982. Contbr. articles to profl. mags. Designer corp. ID for Carmel Valley C. of C., 1981, 90, redesign local newspaper, Carmel, Calif., 1982. Recipient 7 design awards Soc. Pub. Designers, 1977, 78, Maggie award, L.A., 1977, 5 design awards The Ad Club of Monterey Peninsula, 1983, 85, 87, Design awards Print Mag. N.Y., 1986, Desi awards, N.Y., 1986, 88. Mem. NAFE, Soc. for Prevention of Cruelty to Animals, Greenpeace. Democrat. Home and Office: 15489 Via La Gitana Carmel Valley CA 93924-9669

SANDSTROM, ALICE WILHELMINA, accountant; b. Seattle, Jan. 6, 1914; d. Andrew William and Agatha Mathilda (Sundius) S. BA, U. Wash., 1934. CPA, Wash. Mgr. office Star Machinery Co., Seattle, 1935-43, Howe & Co., Seattle, 1943-46; pvt. practice acctg., Seattle, 1945-85; controller Children's Orthopedic Hosp. and Med. Ctr., Seattle, 1948-75, assoc. adminstr. fin., 1975-81; lectr. U. Wash., Seattle, 1957-72. Mem. Wash. State Title XIX Adv. Com., 1975-82, Wash. State Vendors Rate Adv. Com., 1980-87, Mayor's Task Force for Small Bus., 1981-83; bd. dirs. Seattle YWCA, 1981—, pres., 1986-88; bd. dirs. Sr. Svcs. Seattle King Co., 1989-95, bd. dirs. Sr. Services Seattle/King County, 1985, treas., 1986, pres. 1988-90; bd. dirs. Children's Orthopedic Hosp. Found., 1982-90. Fellow Hosp. Fin. Mgmt. Assn. (charter, state pres. 1956-57, nat. treas. 1963-65, Robert H. Reeves Merit award 1970, Frederick T. Muncie award 1985), Wash. State Hosp. Assn. (treas. 1956-70), Am. Soc. Women Accts. (pres. Seattle chpt. 1946-48), Am. Soc. Women CPAs, Wash. Soc. CPAs, Women's Univ. Club (Seattle), City Club (Seattle, charter mem.). Home and Office: 5725 NE 77th St Seattle WA 98115-6345

SANDSTROM, DEBORAH SNAPP, sales executive; b. Bethesda, Md., June 24, 1946; d. Roy Baker and Dorothy (Loftis) Snapp; m. Roy Sandstrom, Oct. 1, 1983. BA, Wake Forest U., 1968; MA, Tulane U., 1970. Educator Old Lyme (Conn.) Pub. Schs., 1974-80; fed. account mgr. NBI, Arlington, Va., 1981-88; nat. account mgr. Apple Computer, Reston, Va., 1988—. Mem. Columbia Country Club (Washington), Mortar Board. Presbyterian. Home: 9724 Brimfield Ct Potomac MD 20854-4338 Office: Apple Computer 1892 Preston White Dr Reston VA 22091-4325

SANDWEISS, MARTHA A., museum director, author, American studies educator; b. St. Louis, Mar. 29, 1954; d. Jerome Wesley and Marilyn Joy (Glik) S. BA magna cum laude, Radcliffe Coll., 1975; MA in History, Yale U., 1977, MPhil in History, 1981, PhD, 1985. Smithsonian-Nat. Endowment Humanities fellow, Nat. Portrait Gallery, Washington, 1975-76; curator photographs Amon Carter Mus., Ft. Worth, 1979-86, adj. curator photographs, 1987-89; dir. Mead Art Mus. Amherst Coll., 1989—, adj. assoc. prof. of fine arts and Am. studies, 1989-94, assoc. prof. Am. studies, 1994—. Author: Carlotta Corpron: Designer with Light, 1980, Masterworks of American Photography, 1982, Laura Gilpin: An Enduring Grace, 1986, (catalogue) Pictures from an Expedition: Early Views of the American West, 1979; co-author: Eyewitness to War: Prints and Daguerreotypes of th Mexican War, 1989; editor: Historic Texas: A Photographic Portrait, 1986, Contemporary Texas: A Photographic Portrait, 1986, Denizens of the Desert, 1988, Photography in Nineteenth Century America, 1991; co-editor: Oxford History of the American West, 1994. Fellow Ctr. for Am. Art and Material Culture, Yale U., 1977-79, NEH, 1988, Am. Coun. Learned Socs., 1996—. Office: Amherst Coll Mead Art Mus Amherst MA 01002

SANFORD, DIANNE H., lawyer; b. Pittston, Pa., July 29, 1948. BA, Cornell U., 1970, MA, 1973; JD cum laude, Harvard U., 1976. Asst. U.S. atty. D.C., 1971-81; atty. Office of the Solicitor U.S. Dept. Interior, 1981-82; trial atty. wildlife and marine resources U.S. Dept. Justice, 1982-86, asst. chief environmental enforcement sect., 1987-91; ptnr. Akin, Gump, Strauss, Hauer & Feld, LLP, Washington. Author: Assault with a Deadly Weapon: The Autobiography of a Street Criminal, 1977. Mem. D.C. Bar. Office: Akin Gump Strauss Hauer & Feld 1333 New Hampshire Ave NW Washington DC 20036*

SANFORD, GLENDA LEVONNE, educational administrator; b. Mpls., Apr. 3, 1935; d. Robert Emmanuel and Stella Glendora (Larson) Carlson; m. Reed Ellis Sanford, June 17, 1955 (div. June 1979); children: Kenneth, Paul, Sheryl Sanford Vanscoy; m. Vernon Edward Almlie, Aug. 12, 1995; stepchildren: Jurgan, William, Ann Almlie Iglehart. AA, U. Minn., 1955; BA, Moorhead (Minn.) State U., 1979; MS, N.D. State U., 1986. Bus. office mgr. U. Minn. Health Svc., Mpls., 1955-58; office mgr. Reed E. Sanford Inc., Fargo, 1958-77; exec. dir. YWCA of Fargo-Moorhead, 1979-85; owner, mgr. farm and rental properties, Fargo, 1981-89; pres. Sanford Money Mgmt. Inc., Fargo, 1987—; program coord. Early Childhood Tracking Sys. State of N.D., Bismarck, 1989—; spl. pub. adminstr. Cass County, Fargo, 1988-89; spkr. Women in Leadership N.D. State U. and KFME, Fargo, 1975-76; advisor N.D. Office Vol. Svcs., Bismarck, 1984-86. Mem. bds. YWCA, LWV, AAUW, Fargo, 1989-92; pres., treas. Jr. League Fargo-Moorhead, 1971-75; pres., bd. mem. Hot Line, Inc., Fargo, 1970-76, United Way of Cass County, Fargo, 1983, N.D. Dental Aux., Fargo, 1975-77; del. White House Conf. on Family, L.A., 1981. Recipient Women Helping Women award Soroptomist Internat., Moorhead, 1984. Mem. AAUW, LWV (treas. 1990-92), Women's Polit. Caucus (fundraising chair 1989-94), N.D. Mental Health Assn. Republican. Lutheran. Home: 2101 S 10th St Fargo ND 58103 Office: ND Early Childhood Tracking Sys Box 5065 State U Sta Fargo ND 58105-5065

SANFORD, JOANNE KAY, counselor, psychology educator; b. San Angelo, Tex., Dec. 31, 1956; d. Lawrence M. and Jessie S. (McDaniel) S.; children: Stacy, Rebecca, Robert, Deborah. AA, Odessa Coll., 1991; BA magna cum laude, U. Tex. of the Permian Basin, Odessa, 1992, MA, 1994. Lic. profl. counselor intern, Tex. Spl. projects coord. Odessa (Tex.) Coll., 1990, counselor, 1991-95, dir. student activities/leadership devel., 1995-96, dir. admissions, 1996—; mem. adv. bd. Allied Health Programs, Odessa (Tex.) Coll., 1991-95; advisor Eta Tau chpt. Phi Theta Kappa, Odessa, 1992; grad. liaison U. Counselors Assn., Odessa, 1995. Mem. Tex. C.C. Tchrs. Assn., Tex. Counseling Assn., Orgn. Chpt. Advisors-Phi Theta Kappa, Permian Basin Counselors Assn. Home: 1613 W 20th Odessa TX 79763

SANFORD, KATHERINE KOONTZ, cancer researcher; b. Chgo., July 19, 1915; d. William James and Alta Rachel (Koontz) S.; m. Charles Fleming Richards Mifflin, Dec. 11, 1971. BA, Wellesley Coll., 1937; MA, Brown U., 1939, PhD, 1942; DSc (hon.), Med. Coll. Pa., 1974, Cath. U. Am., 1988. Teaching asst. Brown U., Providence, 1937-39, rsch. asst., 1939-41; instr. biology Western coll., Oxford, Ohio, 1941-42, Allegheny Coll., Meadville, Pa., 1942-43; asst. dir. Johns Hopkins Nursing Sch., Balt., 1943-47; rsch. biologist Nat. Cancer Inst. NIH, Bethesda, Md., 1947-74; head cell physiology and oncogenesis sect. Lab. Biochemistry, Bethesda, 1974-77; chief in vitro carcinogenesis sect. Nat. Cancer Inst. NIH, Bethesda, 1979—. Contbr. 150 articles to profl. jours. Ross Harrison fellow, 1954. Mem. Phi Beta Kappa, Sigma Xi. Home: 101 Stuart Dr Dover DE 19901-5817 Office: Nat Cancer Inst In Vitro Carcinogenesis Bethesda MD 20892

SANGER, EILEEN, gallery owner, artist; b. Far Rockaway, N.Y., Mar. 24, 1952; d. Edward Herbert and Gladys Minerva Sanger; m. Freddy Profit, May 28, 1989; 1 child, Kristen. Attended, Roslyn (N.Y.) Sch. Painting, 1975-77. Accounts receivable supr. Kwik Kopy Printers, Inc., N.Y.C., 1978-82; acctg. supr. Insul-lite Window Mfg., Inc., Garden City, N.Y., 1984-89; ptnr., owner Sweet'ms, Rocky Point, N.Y., 1991-93, Bellport (N.Y.) Lane Art Gallery, 1994—; represented by Robley Gallery, Roslyn, John Christopher Gallery, Stony Brook, N.Y., Chrysalis Gallery, Southampton, N.Y., Robley Gallery, Roslyn, N.Y. Group shows include: Mills Pond House Gallery, St. James, N.Y., 1993, 94, Guild Hall, East Hampton, N.Y., 1993, 94, 95, Gallery North, Setauket, N.Y., 1993, 94, 95, Vanderbilt Mus., Northport, N.Y., 1993, 94, B.J. Spoke Gallery, Huntington, N.Y., 1994; represent in permanent collections at Neo-Futurarium Hall of Pres., Chgo., 1994. Recipient N.Y. Found. for Arts spl. opportunity stipend, 1994, 96, Stu-Art Oils award Suburban Art League, 1993, Grumbacher Oils award Wet Paint Studio Group, 1994, 1st Pl. award South Bay Arts Assn., 1995. Mem. Nat. League Am. PEN Women, Smithtown Twp. Arts Coun., Huntington Twp. Arts Coun., Southbay Arts Assn. (1st place 1995, 2d place 1996), East Ends Arts Coun., Brookhaven Arts Coun. Home: 49 Rolling Rd Miller Place NY 11764-2223

SANGIULIANO, BARBARA ANN, tax specialist; b. Bronx, N.Y., Dec. 28, 1959; d. Patrick John and Mildred (Soell) Gallo; m. John Warren Sangiuliano, Aug. 28, 1982. BA, Muhlenberg Coll., 1982; MST, Seton Hall U., 1989. CPA, N.J.; CMA. Sr. tax mgr. KPMG Peat Marwick, Short Hills, N.J., 1988-92; sr. tax analyst Allied Signal, Morristown, N.J., 1992-93; tax mgr. AT&T, Morristown, 1993-96, Lucent Techs., Morristown, 1996—. Mem. N.J. Soc. CPAs (dir. Union County chpt.), AICPA, Inst. Mgmt. Accts., Mensa, Omicron Delta Epsilon, Phi Sigma Iota. Republican. Roman Catholic. Home: 340 William St Scotch Plains NJ 07076-1430 Office: Lucent Techs Inc 412 Mount Kemble Ave Morristown NJ 07962

SAN MIGUEL, SANDRA BONILLA, social worker; b. Santurce, P.R., May 23, 1944; d. Isidoro and Flora (Carrero) Bonilla; m. Manuel San Miguel, July 12, 1969. BA, St. Joseph's Coll., 1966; MS in Social Work, Columbia U., 1970. Case worker Dept. Labor, Migration Div., N.Y.C., 1966-68; clin. social worker N.Y.C. Housing Authority, N.Y.C., 1968-69, Children's Aid Soc., N.Y.C., 1969-71; sr. social worker Traveler's Aid Soc., San Juan, P.R., 1971-74; coord., supr. Dept. Addiction Control Svcs., San Juan, P.R., 1974-77; substance abuse div. dir. Seminole County Mental Health Ctr., Altamonte Springs, Fla., 1978-81; cons. pvt. practice Hispanic Cons. Svcs., Winter Springs, Fla., 1982—; adj. prof. Seminole Community Coll., Lake Mary, Fla., 1986-90; sch. social worker I Seminole County Pub. Schs., Sanford, Fla., 1986-91, lead sch. social worker, 1991—; mem. pres.'s minority adv. coun. U. Ctrl. Fla., 1982—, vice chair, 1982-86, chair, 1986-90; mem. bd. regents EEO adv. com. State Univ. System Fla., 1985-89; bd. dirs. Seminole Cmty. Mental Health Ctr., 1986-94, 95—, v.p., 1988-90, pres., 1990-91; adv. bd. Nat. Devereux Found. Ctrl. Fla., 1993—, women's adv. bd. South Seminole Hosp., Fla., 1994—; v.p.; mem. Fla. Consortium on Tchr. Edn. for Am. Minorities, 1990—; mem. local com. Hispanic Info. and Telecomms. Network, 1990; mem. Seminole County (Fla.) Juvenile Justice Coun., 1993—; mem. statewide student svcs. adv. com. Dept. Edn., Fla., 1993-96; student svcs. adv. pool, 1996—. Mem. NASW, Fla. Assn. Sch. Social Workers (co-founder minority caucus 1988, columnist quar. newsletter Minority Corner 1988-92, bd. dirs. 1989—, sec. 1990-92, v.p. 1992-93, pres. 1993-94), Sch. Social Work Assn. of Am., Fla. Assn. Student Svcs. Adminstrs., Collegiate Social Workers P.R., Columbia U. Alumni Assn., St. Joseph's Coll. Alumni Assn. Home: 1214 Howell Creek Dr Winter Springs FL 32708-4516 Office: Seminole County Pub Schs 1401 S Magnolia Ave Sanford FL 32771-3400

SANNS, ANNA MARIA, clinical social worker; b. Pinar Del Rio, Cuba, May 16, 1957; d. Narciso Manuel and Josefina (Medio) Sanchez. AA, Miami Dade Coll., 1980; BSW, Fla. Internat. U., Miami, 1982; MSW, Barry U., Miami, 1983. Lic. clin. social worker; cert. case mgr. Social worker Dodge Hosp., Miami, 1983-84; clin. social worker Miami Jewish Home and Hosp., 1984; social work dir. Hebrew Home, Miami Beach, Fla., 1984-85; activities dir., social work cons. Four Freedoms, Miami Beach, 1985-86; social work dir. Pan Am. Hosp., Miami, 1986-89, West Gables Rehab. Hosp., Miami, 1989; social work supr. Jackson Meml. Hosp., Miami, 1989—. Mem. NOW, Individual Case Mgmt. Assn. Office: Jackson Meml Hosp 1611 NW 12th Ave Miami FL 33136

SANQUIST, NANCY JOHNSON, international facility management professional; b. Muncie, Ind., Aug. 31, 1947; d. Charles Elof and Pauline Lydia (Murphy) S.; m. James M. Johnson, Dec. 1988. BA, UCLA, 1970; MA, Bryn Mawr Coll., 1973; MS, Columbia U., 1978. Instr. Lafayette Coll., Easton, Pa., 1973-74, Muhlenberg Coll., Bethlehem, Pa., 1974-75, Northampton Area Community Coll., Bethlehem, 1974-75; dir. Preservation Office City of Easton, 1977-78; cons. El Pueblo de Los Angeles State Historic Park, 1978-79; dir. restoration Bixby Ranch Co., Long Beach, Calif., 1979-82; mgr. computer applications Cannel-Heumann & Assoc., Los Angeles, 1982-84; dir. Computer-Aided Design Group, Marina del Rey, Calif., 1984-93; v.p. PAE Facility Mgmt. Svcs., L.A., 1993—; adj. instr. UCLA, 1979-86, Grad Sch. Calif. State U., Dominguez Hills, 1981. Author numerous tech. articles and manuals. Bd. dirs. Historic Easton, Inc., 1977-78, Simon Rodia's Towers in Watts, Los Angeles, 1979-81, Los Angeles Conservancy, 1982-86, Friends of Schindler House, West Hollywood, Calif., 1978—, pres., 1982-85. Recipient Outstanding Contbn. award Nat. Computer Graphics Assn., 1987. Mem. Internat. Facility Mgmt. Assn. (seminar leader, lectr. N.Am., Asia, Australia, Europe and Mid. East 1987—).

SANSONE, SUSAN MARY, health facility administrator; b. Cin., Aug. 15, 1957; d. Paul Lucian and Florence Margaret (Kaiser) Back; m. Joseph A. Sansone, May 23, 1981; 1 child, Joseph Anthony. Diploma, Deaconess Hosp. Sch. Nursing, 1978; BS magna cum laude in Nursing Mgmt., Coll. Mt. St. Joseph, 1991. Cert. ACLS, BLS, PALS; cert. post anesthesia nurse. Nursing asst. Deaconess Hosp., Cin., 1976-78, staff nurse med./surg., 1978-79, staff nurse ICU/critical care unit, 1979-82, staff nurse recovery rm., 1982-86, post anesthesia care unit asst. mgr., 1986-87, post anesthesia care unit mgr., 1987-93; mgr. post anesthesia care, same day surgery, pre-admissions testing St. Elizabeth Med. Ctr., Edgewood and Covington, Ky., 1993—; mem. rsch. adv. bd. Hill-Rom, Batesville, Ind., 1991—. Mem. Am. Soc. Post Anesthesia Nurses, Ohio Post Anesthesia Nurses Assn., Cin. Post Anesthesia Nurses Assn., Kappa Gamma Pi Honor Soc. Home: 3390 Cherryridge Dr North Bend OH 45052-9522 Office: 1 Medical Village Dr Edgewood KY 41017

SANSONETTE-SICÉ, GENEVIÈVE-ANTOINETTE, nurse midwife; b. Kouba, Algeria, Sept. 26, 1952; came to U.S., 1971; d. Félix and Antoinette Sansonetti; m. Pierre Henri Sicé, June 3, 1971; children: Chantal Marie, Christel Marie. ADN, A in Psychology, Rancho Santiago Coll., 1985; BSN, Calif. State. U., 1987; nurse midwifery cert., U. S.C., 1990. Cert. nurse midwife Am. Coll. Nurse Midwives, pub. health nurse; RN, Calif. RN Riverside (Calif.) Gen. Hosp., 1986-87; RN, charge nurse Anaheim (Calif.) Gen. Hosp., 1989—. Mem. NOW, AAUW, ACNM. Roman Catholic. Office: Kaiser Permanente 9400 E Rosecrans Ave Bellflower CA 90706

SAN SOUCIE, PATRICIA MOLM, artist, educator; b. Mpls., Nov. 4, 1931; d. Ralph Frederick and Evangeline Mary (Nusbaum) Molm; m. Robert Louis San Soucie, Sept. 5, 1953; children: Richard Peter, Marc David, Mary Frances. BS in Applied Arts, U. Wis., 1953. Chmn. juror selection St. Louis Artists Guild, 1968-70; exhibition chmn. Summit (N.J.) Art Ctr., 1973-76, instr. watercolor, 1981—; pres. N.J. Watercolor Soc., 1988-90; freelance watercolor painter, 1970—. Publs. include Watermedia Techniques for Releasing the Creative Spirit, 1992, Color Section/Master Class in Watercolor, 1975, How to Discover Your Personal Painting Style, 1995; works in permanent collections at Jane Voorhees Zimmerli Mus. Art, New Brunswick, N.J., Cultural Exch./Zheijang Art Mus., Hangzhow, China; presenter workshop Watercolor U.S.A. Honor Soc. Conf., 1995. Recipient Watercolor Purchase award Springfield (Mo.) Art Mus. Travel Exhbn., 1974, Taiwan Mus. Fine Arts, 1986, Chateau de Tours, France, 1987, Butler Inst. Fine Arts, 1985, Ariz. Aqueous awards of excellence, 1991, 93; Walser Greathouse medals and awards Am. Watercolor Soc., 1991, 93, Millard Sheets Meml. medal and award, 1995, Ida Wells Stroud Meml. award, 1996; Dolphin fellow. Mem. Am. Watercolor Soc., Nat. Assn. Women Artists, Nat. Watercolor Soc., Watercolor U.S.A. Honor Soc., N.J. Watercolor Soc. Roman Catholic. Home: 68 Dortmunder Dr Manalapan NJ 07726-3800

SANTAELLA, IRMA VIDAL, state supreme court justice; b. N.Y.C., Oct. 4, 1924; d. Rafael and Sixta (Thillet) Vidal; children: Anthony, Ivette. Acctg. degree, Modern Bus. Coll., 1942; BA, Hunter Coll., 1959; LLB, Bklyn. Law Sch., 1961, JD, 1967; LLD, Sacred Heart U., Conn., 1990. Bar: N.Y. 1961. Sole practice N.Y.C., 1961-63, with ptnr., 1966-68; dep. commr. N.Y.C. Dept Correction, 1963-66; mem. N.Y. State Human Rights Appeal Bd., N.Y.C., 1968-83, chmn., 1975-83; justice N.Y. State Supreme Ct., N.Y.C., 1983-94; mem. N.Y.C. Adv. Council on Minority Affairs, 1982—, N.Y.C. Commn. on Status of Women, 1975-77. Founder, chmn. Legion of Voters, 1962-68; nat. del. Presdl. Democratic Convs., 1968, 72, 76, 80; vice chmn. N.Y. State del. 1976 Conv.; founder Nat. Assn. for Puerto Rican Civil Rights, 1962, Hispanic Community Chest Am., 1972; chmn. bd. dirs. Puerto Rican Parade, 1962-67; bd. dirs. Catholic Interracial Council, 1968-81; nat. co-chmn. Coalition Hispanic People, 1970; fund raiser Boy Scouts Am., 1962-63; chmn. Children's Camp, South Bronx (N.Y.) 41st Police Precinct, 1967; active City-Wide Steering Com. for Quality Edn., 1962-64, Community Service Soc., 1972-74, Talbott Perkins Children's Services, 1973-75, Planned Parenthood Assn., 1968-69, Puerto Rican Crippled Children's Fund, 1965-69; founder N.Y. chpt. Clinica Grillasca, P.R. Cancer Assn., 1974—. Recipient citations for civic work Gov. Rockefeller, 1972, Gov. Carey, 1982, First Puerto Rican woman to be elected to the N.Y. State Supreme Ct., County of Bronx, 1983; recipient Recognition award Gov. Mario M. Cuomo, 1990, Nat. Puerto Rican Coalition Life Achievement award, 1990, Life Achievement award Pres. of Dominican Republic, 1991, Life Achievement award Nat. Coun. Hispanic Women, 1991, others. Mem. Am. Judicature Soc. Roman Catholic. Home: 853 7th Ave New York NY 10019-5215 Office: Supreme Ct State NY 60 Centre St New York NY 10007-1402

SANTANGELO, BETTY J., lawyer; b. N.Y.C., Sept. 5, 1950; d. Alfred E. and Betty L. Santangelo; m. Thomas Egan, Oct. 11, 1981. BA, Trinity Coll., 1971; JD, Fordham U., 1974. Bar: N.Y. 1975, Fla. 1975, U.S. Dist. Ct. (so. and ea. dists.) N.Y. 1975, U.S. Ct. Appeals (2d cir.) 1975. Assoc. Martin, Obermaier & Morvillo, N.Y.C., 1974-76; law clk. to justice U.S. Dist. Ct. (so. dist.) N.Y., N.Y.C., 1976-77; asst. U.S. atty. So. Dist. N.Y., N.Y.C., 1977-83; 1st v.p., asst. gen. counsel Merrill Lynch, Pierce, Fenner & Smith, N.Y.C., 1983—; adj. prof. law Fordham U., N.Y.C., 1982-84. Mem. ABA (divsn. dir. litigation com. 1991-92), Assn. of Bar of City of N.Y. Office: Merrill Lynch 250 Vesey St 12th Fl New York NY 10281-1312

SANTAVICCA, PAMELA FERGUSON, social welfare administrator; b. Plainfield, N.J., Apr. 15, 1949; d. Russell L. and Laura Esther (Telander) Ferguson; children: Daniel, Elizabeth. BA, Douglass Coll., 1971; MEd, Rutgers U., 1972. Cert. elem. tchr., N.J. Tchr. Orchard Road Sch., Montgomery Twp., N.J., 1972-84; county coord. Congrl. Campaign, Centre County, Pa., 1986; dir. Christian edn. St. Andrews Ch., State College, Pa., 1987-88; exec. dir. Food Bank State Coll., 1992—; del. Coun. Human Svcs., Centre County, 1992—, Interfaith Mission, State College, 1992—; rep. County Food Banks, Bellefonte, Pa., 1992—; com. mem. Supercupboard Program, Centre County, 1995—. Committeewoman State Coll. Bd. Dems., 1986—; vestry mem. St. Andrews Episc. Ch., 1988-95, reader, chalice bearer, 1992—. Named Citizen of Yr., Elks Club of State College, 1996. Mem. NOW, Hunger Project, Leadersip Ctr. County, Rotary Internat. (group study exch. 1996—), Episc. Peace and Justice Network. Home: 520 W Fairmount Ave State College PA 16801 Office: Food Bank State College 208 W Foster Ave State College PA 16801

SANTIAGO, NELLIE, state legislator; m. Ben Fernandez. BA, Hunter Coll., 1970; MA, Columbia U., 1972; PhD, U. Mass., 1977. Dir. chronic mental health svcs. Jefferson County Health Dept., Birmingham, Ala., 1978-84; adminstr. Bklyn. Manor Home for Adults, 1987-92; asst. bur. dir. N.Y. State Health, Albany, 1984-87; mem. N.Y. State Senate, Albany, 1992—; health care adminstrn. cons.; mem. adj. faculty U. Ala., Birmingham, 1978-84; mem. White House Conf. on Families, 1980. Recipient Pub. Health award Kings County Dist. Atty., 1992, also awards from Johns Hopkins U. Sch. Hygiene and Pub. Health, SUNY Ctr. for Women in Govt.. Office: NY State Senate Legis Office Bldg Rm 513 Albany NY 12247

SANTIAGO, ROXANA VIOLETA, auditor; b. Guatemala, Guatemala, Nov. 14, 1968; came to U.S., 1976; d. Augusto Celestino and Aura Violeta (Morales) Oliva; m. John Anthony Santiago, July 19, 1995; 1 child, Fabiana Oliva. BS in Acctg., No. Ill. U., Dekalb, 1992. CPA, Ill. Fin. assoc. Baxter, Deerfield, Ill., 1992-94; internal auditor Baxter Internat., Deerfield, Ill., 1994—; spkr. in field.

SANTILLI, LAURA ANNE, market researcher; b. Bridgeport, Conn., Apr. 11, 1958; d. Edward and Yolanda Mary (Benedetto) S. MBA, Stern Grad. Sch., N.Y.C., 1985; BA cum laude, Fordham U., 1980. Credit analyst, sr. fin. analyst Credit Lyonnais, N.Y.C., 1985-89, comml. lending officer, 1989-94; rsch. specialist Sumitomo Trust & Banking Co., N.Y.C., 1994-96; mgr. market rsch. and analysis Andersen Cons., N.Y.C., 1996—. Mem. Mayer-Avedon Women's Support Group, N.Y.C., 1991-95. Mem. Fin. Women's Assn. N.Y., YMCA. Home: 589 Lincoln Ave Bridgeport CT 06606 Office: Andersen Cons 1345 Ave of the Americas New York NY 10105

SANTILLI, LAURA ELIZABETH, psychologist; b. Columbus, Ohio, May 7, 1963; d. Robert Leo and Rosalyn Ann (Crawford) Fisher; m. William Francis Morrow, Jr., Jul. 16, 1993. AB, Washington Univ., 1985; MA, Univ. Ala., 1989, PhD, 1991. Lic. psychologist. Psychology fellow Alfred I DuPont Inst., Wilmington, Del., 1991-92; pediatric psychologist Eastern Maine Medical Ctr., Bangor, Maine, 1992—; clinical faculty mem. Tufts Univ. Sch. of Medicine, Boston, 1992—; clinical staff Univ. Maine, 1993—. Contbr. articles to profl. jours. Bd. dirs. United Cerebal Palsy Ctr., Bangor, 1993—. Recipient Grad. Council fellowship Univ. Ala., 1985-86. Mem. Am. Psychological Assn., Soc. Pediatric Psychology, Maine Assn. Infant Mental Health, Bangor Area Psychologists Assn., Phi Beta Kappa. Office: EMMC BDP 417 State St Ste 310 Bangor ME 04401

SANTIN, JEAN, cosmetic company executive, consultant; b. Trenton, N.J., May 31, 1938; d. Joseph and Angeline (Parziale) Inverso; m. Louis Santin, Apr. 12, 1958; children: Renee, Scott. Grad. high sch., Trenton. Self employed jewelry bus. Hamilton Square, N.J., 1967-71; credit mgr. Lenape Products, Inc., Pennington, N.J., 1971-80; sales dir. Mary Kay Cosmetics, Ringoes, N.J., 1979—; fashion, beauty and color analysis cons. Mary Kay Cosmetics, Ringoes, 1980-91. Beauty cons. for drug and alcohol rehab. area hosps., 1980-91; organizer of Christmas gifts for the underpriviledged, Hunterdon County, 1989, 90. Mem. Hunterdon County C. of C. Home and Office: Mary Kay Cosmetics 23 Runyon Mill Rd Ringoes NJ 08551-1514

SANTISTEVAN, LORETTA CREDO, government official; b. New Orleans, Dec. 6, 1956; d. Henry Paul and Margaret Elizabeth (Sandy) Credo; m. Alfredo Carlos Santistevan, Oct. 30, 1975 (div. Feb. 1994); children: Tara Nicole and Trinia Leigh (twins). A Gen. Studies, Delgado C.C., New Orleans, 1994. Owner, operator Childcare Referrals, Casper, Wyo., 1978-83; consumer mktg. mgr. West Bldg. Materials, New Orleans, 1984-87; letter carrier U.S. Postal Svc., New Orleans, 1987—. Mem. A Child's Wish, New Orleans, 1994-95. Mem. Nat. Assn. Letter Carriers, Nat. Assn. Investors Corp., La. Stock Marketeers, Alpha Lambda Delta, Phi Theta Kappa. Democrat. Presbyterian. Home: 8913 Camille Dr River Ridge LA 70123

SANTO, LORRAINE A. RAITERI, property manager; b. Detroit, Jan. 19, 1943; d. Charles Pierre and Gina Domenica (Passerini) Raiteri; m. John A. Santo, Aug. 1, 1964; children: Suzanne Santo Peresich, Toni-Michelle Santo Coons, Danielle. Grad. high sch., Detroit; grad., Am. Real Estate Inst., Birmingham, 1976. Cert. residential specialist; realtors/CRS, LTG. With Mark IV Realty, 1976-81, C-21 Bayou Riley, 1981-82, C-21 "K" Realty, 1982-84, Janis Pittman Realty, 1984-93, Intown Properties, Inc., 1993-94; realtor, assoc. Gulfport, Miss., 1976-90; realtor, 1990—; realtor, owner Lorraine Santo, Realtor, Gulfport, 1993—; project mgr. Hammett & Assocs., Inc., Gulfport, 1994—. Mem. Women's Coun. Realtors (sec./treas. state chpt. 1995, Mem. of Yr. Gulf Coast chpt. 1990-95, local and state chpts. 1995), Realtors Coun. Miss. (Mem. of Yr. 1995), West Gulf Coast Assn. Realtors (life mem. round table 1985—), Gulf Coast C. of C. (chair mil. affairs 1990-95), Irem Chpt. # 80 Miss., Resdl. Coun. of Miss. Democrat. Roman Catholic. Home: 902 W Birch Dr Gulfport MS 39503-5808 Office: 902 W Birch Dr Gulfport MS 39503-5808

SANTONA, GLORIA, lawyer; b. Gary, Ind., June 10, 1950; d. Ray and Elvira (Cambeses) S.; m. Douglas Lee Frazier, Apr. 12, 1980. BS in Biochemistry, Mich. State U., 1971; JD, U. Mich., 1977. Bar: Ill. 1977. Atty. McDonald's Corp., Oak Brook, Ill., 1977-82, dir., 1982-86, assoc. gen. counsel, 1986-92, asst. v.p., 1989—, v.p., sec., 1996—. Mem. ABA, Chgo. Assn., Am. Corp. Counsel Assn., Am. Soc. Corp. Secs. (corp. practices law com.). Office: McDonalds Corp 1 McDonalds Plz Oak Brook IL 60521

SANTORE, CARRIE-BETH, computer management professional; b. Torrington, Conn., July 28, 1953; d. Michael and Dolores Leonard S. BA History and Am. Studies cum laude, Conn. Coll., 1975; MA History, U. Conn., 1977; MBA Mktg., Va. Polytechnic Inst., 1988. Analyst CIA, Washington, 1980-90; prin. tng. specialist Quality Sys., Inc., Fairfax, Va., 1990-93, dep. dir. ops. programs, 1993-95; mgr. Proposal Ctr. Quality Systems, Inc., Fairfax, Va., 1995-96; tech. publs. mgr. Sci. & Tech. Analysis Corp., Fairfax, Va., 1996—; Lotus cert. cons., 1994. Bd. dirs., sec. Seminary Walk Condo Assn., Alexandria, Va., 1987-88, editor newsletter, 1986-87; vol. Alexandria Waterfront ARC, 1989-90; mem. com. to devel. internat. studies program Conn. Coll., New London, 1988-89. Mem. SALT, Balt. Washington Info. Systems, AAUW, Women's Nat. Book Assn., Assn. Proposal Mgmt. Profls., Phi Alpha Theta. Office: Sci & Tech Analysis Corp Ste 300 11250 Waples Mill Rd Fairfax VA 22030

SANTORE, MARCIA LUCINDA GREEN, artist, college administrator; b. Hartford, Conn., Nov. 25, 1960; d. Douglass Marshall Green and Marquita Yvonne Dubach; m. Jonathan Conrad Santore, May 30, 1987. BFA, U. Tex., 1982. Devel. asst. Mount St. Mary's Coll., L.A., 1987-91; alumni coord. physics dept. UCLA, 1991-93; gen. mgr. Minnetonka (Minn.) Orchestral Assn., 1994; advancement coord. Coll. Lifelong Learning, Concord, N.H., 1995—; tchr. Batchelder Artist Studios, Plymouth, N.H., 1995—. Exhbns. include UCLA Kerckhoff Art Gallery, San Francisco Mus. Modern Art Rental Gallery, Mpls. Coll. Art and Design, U. Oreg., Tex. Mus. Natural History, Austin, Mus. Art and History, Ontario, Calif., L.A. Mcpl. Art Gallery, One Congress Plz., Austin, Dougherty Arts Ctr., Austin, Arts Warehouse, Austin, U. Tex. Huntington Art Gallery, Austin. Coun. Advancement and Support Edn. Newcomer scholar, 1991. Mem. AAUW, NSFRE, Coun. Advancement & Support Edn. Democrat. Episcopalian. Office: Coll Lifelong Learning 125 N State St Concord NH 03301

SANTOS, ADELE NAUDE, architect, educator; b. Cape Town, South Africa, Oct. 14, 1938; came to U.S., 1973; d. David Francois Hugo and Aletta Adèle Naudé. Student, U. Cape Town, South Africa, 1956-58; Diploma, Archtl. Assn., 1961; MArch in Urban Design, Harvard U., 1963; M in City Planning, U. Pa., 1968, MArch, 1968. Pvt. practice architecture with Antonio de Souza Santos, 1966-73; ptnr. Interstudio, Houston, 1973-79; assoc. prof. architecture Rice U., Houston, 1973-78, prof., 1979; prof. architecture and urban design, dept. architecture U. Pa., Phila., 1981-90; founding dean Sch. Architecture U. Calif., San Diego, 1990-94; pvt. practice architecture and urban design Adele Naude Santos, Architect, Phila., 1979-90, Adele Naude Santos and Assocs., San Diego and Phila., 1991—; prof. architecture Coll. Environ. Design U. Calif., Berkeley, 1994—; founding dean Sch. of Architecture, U. Calif., San Diego, 1990—. Project dir., co-filmmaker for 5 part series, 1979-80. Wheelwright Travelling fellow, Harvard U., 1968; NEA grantee, 1976, Tex. Com. for Humanities grantee, 1979; recipient (with Hugo Naudé) Bronze medal for House Naudé Capt. Inst. South African Architects, 1967, award for public TV program So. Ednl. Communications Assn., 1980, 3d place award Inner city Infill Competition, 1986; winner Internat. Design Competition, Hawaii Loa Coll., hon. mention Cin. Hillside Housing Competition and City Visions, Phila., 1986; winner competition for Franklin/La Brea Affordable Housing Project Mus. Contemporary Art and Community Redevel. Agy. City L.A., 1988, Pa. Soc. Architects design award for Franklin/La Brea Multi-Family Housing, 1988; winning entry collaborative competition for amphitheater, restaurant and natural history mus., Arts Pk., La., 1989; winner competition for 24-unit residential devel., City of Camden, N.J., 1989, for New Civic Ctr., City of Perris, Calif., 1991. Office: 2527 South St Philadelphia PA 19146-1037 also: 629 J St Ste 102 San Diego CA 92101

SANTOS, EILEEN, management consultant; b. Morristown, N.J., Feb. 27, 1965; d. Angel Jesus and Arsenia (Quiles) S. BS in Engring., Rutgers U., Piscataway, N.J., 1987; MBA, Columbia U., 1992. Assoc. engr. Westinghouse Elec. Corp., Balt., 1987-89; asst. mgr. N.J. Bell, Newark, 1989-90; ops. specialist Philip Morris Mgmt. Corp., N.Y.C., 1992-94; sr. bus. cons. Am. Mgmt. Systems, Inc., Roseland, N.J., 1994—. chairperson profl. com., Soc. Hispanic Profl. Engrs., Washington, 1988, client svc. team Vols. for Med. Engring, 1988; chairperson pub. rels. com., mem. exec. bd. Coun. of Action for Minority Profls., Newark, 1989; v.p. Hispanic Bus. Assn., 1991. Recipient Cora and Rose Morgan fellowship Columbia U., 1991. Mem. NAFE, Nat. Soc. Hispanic MBAs. Democrat. Roman Catholic. Home: 8 Sand Spring Rd Morristown NJ 07960 Office: Am Mgmt Systems Inc 75 Livingston Ave Roseland NJ 07068

SANTOS, LISA WELLS, critical care nurse; b. Richardson, Tex., Oct. 25, 1963; d. Malcolm R.N. and Maitland Anne (MacIntyre) Wells; m. Ignacio Santos, Jr., Dec. 17, 1988. Cert. med. asst., x-ray-lab. technician, Tex. Coll. Osteopathy, 1983; ASN, El Centro Coll., 1988; postgrad., U. North Tex.; BS in Bus. Mgmt., Le Tourneau U., 1993; postgrad., U. Phoenix, 1995—. RN, Tex.; cert. in CPR; cert. case mgr., cert. profl. in health care quality; advanced competency certification in continuity of care; assoc. cert. mgr. Med. technologist Family Med. Ctr., Dallas, 1984-85, Beltline Med. Clinic, Dallas, 1985-86; nurse, lab. technician Primacare, Dallas, Plano, Richardson, Tex., 1986-88; charge nurse telemetry unit NME Hosp.-RHD Meml. Hosp., Denton, Tex., 1988-89; nurse ICU Denton (Tex.) Regional Med. Ctr.; nurse Angel Touch, Dallas, 1989; nurse cons. Travelers Ins., Richardson, Tex., 1990-91; med. rev. specialist Nat. Group Life, Las Colinas, Tex., 1991-94; mgr. coordinated care Nat. Group Life, 1994-95; pres. San Cal Health Care Options, Lewisville, Tex., 1994-95; clin. dir. PRN Associated Care/ Am. Care Source, Dallas, 1995—. Contbr. articles to profl. jour. Mem. AACN, NAFE, Nat. Assn. Health Care Quality, Nat. Assn. Quality Assurance Profls., Assn. Nurses in AIDS Care, Case Mgmt. Soc. Am., Am. Assn. Law Ethics and Medicine, Am. Assn. Continuity of Care, Alpha Epsilon Delta, Alpha Beta Kappa, Gamma Beta Phi.

SANTOS-ZOUGHY, MARIA VICTORIA, portfolio management professional; b. Jersey City, N.J., Oct. 29, 1965; d. Teodoro Manuel and Flor Maria (Rosa) S.; m. A. Zoughy, Oct. 21, 1989. Student, Rutgers U., 1984-85; AAS, NYU, 1996. Supr. Am. Savs. Bank, N.Y.C., 1985-86; SUPV Dean Witter Reynolds, N.Y.C., 1986-90; asst. v.p. Fiduciary Trust Co. Internat., N.Y.C., 1990—. Author poems. Vol. homeless food pantry Let's Celebrate!, Jersey City, N.J., 1988, Big Sister, Bronx, N.Y., 1995, Literacy Plus, N.J., 1995. Republican. Roman Catholic. Home: 228 Broadway Union Beach NJ 07735

SANZ, KATHLEEN MARIE, management consultant; b. L.A., Sept. 29, 1955; d. Jess Quevedo and Rosemary Helen (Debley) S. Student, Chabot Coll., 1975-76, City of Costa Mesa (Calif.), 1985. Lic. tax preparer, Calif. Admistrv. positions, 1973-80; office mgr. The Printery, Laguna Hills, Calif., 1980-83, Astro Vista, Inc., Irvine, Calif., 1983-85; adminstrv. dir. Orange County Pacific Symphony, Santa Ana, Calif., 1985-86, Image Printing, Irvine, 1986-88; adminstr. Conant Constrn. Corp., Corona Del Mar, Calif., 1988-90; owner, cons. KMS & Assocs., Mission Viejo, Calif., 1990—; nat. coord. PED Inc., Reno, 1985-86; cons. Forms Mgmt. Co., Reno, 1987-89; spkr. Human Resources Saddleback Coll. Continuing Edn.; developer seminar series Now What. Author: (collection of poetry) In the Twighlight of Life, 1978; author acctg. system; contbr. poetry to anthologies and articles to profl. jours.; developer Keeping Mgmt. Simple sys. Mem. Santa Ana City Renovation Com., 1985, Environ. Def. Fund, Washington, 1989—; team capt. San Clemente (Calif.) Triathlon, 1988; vol. Orange County Rep. Orgn., Santa Ana, 1989-90; mem. coun. South County Region, 1990-95, officer, sec., 1991-93, logistics coord. Cmty. Expo, 1993; vol. south region Orange County United Way, logistics chmn. corp. campaign kick-off, 1994, cmty. rels. chmn., liaison to corp. mktg. dept., 1994; mem. Saddleback Valley Cmty. Task Force. Named Outstanding Vol., Lake Forest Showboaters, 1988, South Orange County region United Way, 1993, Shining Star award United Way. Mem. NAFE, Lake Forest Showboaters (bd. govs. 1987-88), World Wildlife Found., Greenpeace, Soc. Poets. Presbyterian. Home and Office: KMS & Assocs 26196B Sanz Mission Viejo CA 92691-6822

SANZONE, DONNA S., publishing executive; b. Bklyn., Apr. 4, 1949; d. Joseph J. Seitz and Faye (Brooks) Rossman; m. Charles F. Sanzone, Jan. 2, 1972; children: Danielle, Gregory. BA magna cum laude, Boston U., 1970; MA, Northeastern U., 1979. Grad. placement specialist Inst. Internat. Edn., N.Y.C., 1970-72; adminstr. AFS Internat. Scholarships, Brussels, 1972-74; editor Internat. Ency. Higher Edn., Boston, 1974-76; editor G.K. Hall & Co., Pubs., Boston, 1977-81, exec. editor, 1981-91, editor-in-chief, 1991-96; v.p. Oryx Press, Boston, 1996—. Contbg. author: Access to Power, 1981. Mem. ALA, Assn. Am. Pubs., Assn. Coll. and Rsch. Librs., Libr. and Info. Tech. Assn. Office: Oryx Press 18 Pine St Weston MA 02193-1116

SAPADIN, LINDA ALICE, psychologist, writer; b. N.Y.C., Mar. 20, 1940; d. Samuel Miles and Helen Leah (Bogen) Fink; m. Seymour Sapadin, Nov. 10, 1962 (div. 1980); children: Brian, Glenn, Daniel; m. Ronald J. Goodrich, May 15, 1983. BA, Bklyn. Coll., 1960; MA, Temple U., 1961, CUNY, 1986; PhD, CUNY, 1986. Lic. psychologist, N.Y. Sch. psychologist N.Y.C. Bd. Edn., 1962-66, rsch. cons., 1985-87; tchr. Hewlett-Woodmere (N.Y.) Adult Edn., 1975-84; devel. dir. Ctr. for Women and Achievement, Island Park, N.Y., 1984-89; dir. Biofeedback and Stress Reduction Ctr., Valley Stream, N.Y., 1990—; pvt. practice Valley Stream, 1987—; forum leader, adj. prof. Hofstra U., N.Y. Inst. Tech., Five Towns Coll., Nassau Community Coll., L.I., 1974-90; cons. Nassau County Town of Hempstead, N.Y., 1986; adj. prof. continuing edn. Hofstra U., Uniondale, N.Y., 1985—; talk show host Sta. WGBB Radio, Merrick, N.Y., 1987. Author: It's About Time! The 6 Styles of Procrastination and How to Overcome Them, 1996; columnist Chanry Communications, 1987-90, Richner Publs., 1992; contbr. articles to profl. jours. Chmn. psychology com. Nassau County NOW, Uniondale, 1983; spkr. Smithsonian Assocs., Learning Annex, L.I. Assn. Planned Parenthood, Econ. Opportunities Coun., L.I. Libr. Sys., B'nai Brith, Women's Forum, Nat. Coun. Jewish Women, 1984—. Recipient Outstanding Community Svc. award State Senator Carol Berman, 1984. Mem. APA (media div., psychology of women div.), Nassau County Psychol. Assn. (women's studies com.). Home and Office: Biofeedback and Stress 19 Cloverfield Rd Valley Stream NY 11581-2421

SAPHIRE, NAOMI CARROL, account executive; b. Cleve., Mar. 22, 1938; d. Ben F. and Marian (Lackritz) S.; m. Sanford M. Goldstein (div. 1979); children: Jodi Hayes, Jonathan Goldstein, Daniel Goldstein. BS, CSU, Fullerton, 1980; postgrad. cert., U. Calif., Irvine, 1991-93. Tax svc. coord. ADP, LaPalma, Calif., 1980-87; conversion analyst Bank of Am., Anaheim, Calif., 1987-91; account exec. Systems Tax Svc., Fountain Valley, Calif., 1992—; bookkeeper constrn. notebook Dickinson Printers, Las Vegas, Nev., 1994. Home: 910 N Harbor #115 La Habra CA 90631 Office: Systems Tax Svc 17390 Brookhurst St #300 Fountain Valley CA 92728

SAPINSLEY, LILA MANFIELD, state official; b. Chgo., Sept. 9, 1922; d. Jacob and Doris (Silverman) Manfield; BA, Wellesley Coll., 1944; D. Pub. Service, U. R.I., 1971; D. Pedagogy, R.I. Coll., 1973, LHD, Brown U., 1993; m. John M. Sapinsley, Dec. 23, 1942; children—Jill Sapinsley Mooney, Carol Sapinsley Rubenstein, Joan Sapinsley Lewis, Patricia Sapinsley Levy. Mem. R.I. Senate, 1972-84, minority leader, 1974-84; dir. R.I. Dept. Community Affairs, 1985; bd. dirs. Lifespan Corp.; chmn. R.I. Housing and Mortgage Fin. Corp., 1985-87; Commr. R.I. Pub. Utilities Commn., 1987-93. Mem. R.I. Gov.'s Commn. on Women; commr. Edn. Commn. of States; pres. bd. trustees Butler Hosp., 1978-84; trustee R.I. State Colls., 1965-70, chmn., 1967-70; trustee U. R.I., R.I. Coll. Found.; bd. dirs. Hamilton House, Trinity Repertory Co., Lincoln Sch., Wellesley Center for Research on Women, 1980, Providence Pub. Libr. Recipient Alumnae Achievement award Wellesley Coll., 1974; Outstanding Legislator of Yr. award Republican Nat. Legislators Assn., 1984. Republican. Jewish. Home: 25 Cooke St Providence RI 02906-2022

SAPIRO, VIRGINIA, political science educator; b. East Orange, N.J., Feb. 28, 1951. AB, Clark U., 1972; MA in Polit. Sci., U. Mich., 1976, PhD in Polit. Sci., 1976. Asst. prof. polit. sci. and women's studies program U. Wis., Madison, 1976-81, assoc. prof., 1981-86, prof., 1986—, Sophonisba P. Breckinridge prof., 1995—; vis. lectr. dept. govt. U. Essex, 1979-80, lectr., 1981, 82-83, vis. prof., 1989. Author: Women in American Society: An Introduction to Women's Studies, 1986, 3d edit., 1994, Women, Biology and Public Policy, 1985, The Political Integration of Women: Roles, Socialization and Politics, 1983, A Vindication of Political Virtue: The Political Theory of Mary Wollstonecraft, 1992; contbr. articles to profl. jours. Rsch. grantee U. Wis., 1977, 79, 83, 87, 96. Mem. Am. Polit. Sci. Assn. (nominations com. chair 1993-94, chair nomination com. 1993, chair Woodrow Wilson Book award com. 1995-96), Midwest Polit. Sci. Assn. (nominations com. 1992-94), Internat. Soc. Polit. Psychology (nominations com. 1990-91, governing coun. 1988-90), Phi Beta Kappa. Office: U Wis Dept Polit Sci 1050 Bascom Mall Madison WI 53706

SAPP, MARY ELLEN, state official, educator; b. Bethesda, Md., Aug. 6, 1945; d. Richard Friend and Anne Carr (Garges) S. BA in Math., Incarnate Word Coll., 1968; MS in Health Care Adminstrn., Trinity U., 1972; M in Theol. Studies, Oblate Sch. Theology, San Antonio, 1984. Tchr. Archdiocese of San Antonio, 1965-71; adminstrv. resident Spohn Hosp., Corpus Christi, 1971, Morningside Manor, San Antonio, 1972; exec. dir. St. Benedict Health Care Ctr., San Antonio, 1972-85, Benedictine Health Resource Ctr., Austin/ San Antonio, 1985-89, Tex. Dept. Aging, Austin, 1992—; town meeting specialist Alamo Area Coun. of Govts., San Antonio, 1990-91; pres. Tex. Conf. Cath. Health Facilities, Austin, 1980-81; cmty. advisor San Antonio Light Newspaper, 1989-91; mem. adj. faculty Inst. on Aging Incarnate Word Coll., San Antonio, 1991-93; mem. Tex. Indigent Health Care Task Force, Austin, 1983-84. Recipient Headliners award for pub. endeavors Women in Comm., 1990; named Regional Citizen, Alamo Area Coun. Govts., 1987. Office: Tex Dept Aging 4900 N Lamar Blvd Austin TX 78751

SAPP, NANCY L., assistant principal; b. Joplin, Mo., July 22, 1951; d. Jim L. and Leah (Smith) Hayes; children: Michael A., Julie D. B in Music Edn., Pittsburg (Kans.) State U., 1973; MEd in Psychology, Wichita State U.; cert. in elem./secondary sch. adminstrn., Emporia State U., 1994. Cert. elem./ secondary vocal/instrumental music tchr., learning disabled tchr., behavior disorder tchr., adminstr. Vocal and instrumental music instr. Cherokee, Kans., 1973-75, Holy Cross Grade Sch., Hutchinson, Kans., 1980-85, Trinity H.S., Hutchinson, 1980-82; learning disabilities tchr. Unified Sch. Dist. # 308, Hutchinson, 1987-89, behavior disorder tchr., 1989-95, behavior cons., 1990-95, asst. sch. prin., 1995—. Prin. second violin Hutchinson Symphony, 1991—; pres. exec. bd. Hutchinson Regional Youth Symphony, 1994-95; bd. dirs. Reno Choral Soc., Kans. Youth Soc. Grantee Southwestern Bell Tel., Hutchinson, 1992. Mem. Internat. Reading Assn., NEA, Kans. NEA, Kans. Reading Assn., Hutchinson NEA (bldg. rep. 1992-94), Ark Valley Reading Assn. (pres. 1994-95). Republican. Presbyterian. Home: 11 Truman Dr South Hutchinson KS 67505

SAPPINGTON, SHARON ANNE, librarian; b. West Palm Beach, Fla., Sept. 15, 1944; d. A. D. and Laura G. (Jackson) Chambless; m. Andrew Arnold Sappington III, June 11, 1966; children: Andrew Arnold IV, Kevin Sean. Student, Fla. So. coll., 1962-64; BA in Edn., U. Fla., 1966; media specialist, U. Ala., 1980. 5th grade tchr. Tates Creek Elem., Lexington, Ky., 1966-68; 4th grade tchr. Sadieville (Ky.) Elem., 1968-69; libr. media specialist A.H. Watwood Elem., Childersburg, Ala., 1980—; guest storyteller Young Author's Conf., Winterboro, Lincoln, Sylacauga, and Fayetteville, Ala., 1982-94; vis. com. mem. Southeastern Accreditation Assn.; program presenter Internat. Reading Assn., Birmingham, Ala., 1983; guest speaker rare children's books "By the Way" TV talk show, 1983. Creator, presenter: (slide presentation) Tellers of Tales and Sketchers of Dreams, 1983, (multimedia programs) Dinosaurs, Teddy Bears, and Wild Things, 1990, Shanghaied in the Beijing Airport, 1994. Circle chmn., Sunday tchr. Grace United Meth. Ch., Birmingham, 1973, 92-95; delivery mem. Meals on Wheels, Birmingham, 1975-76; radio reader for the blind WBHM Pub. Broadcasting, Birmingham, 1980; guest speaker, program presenter Jaycees, Kiwanis, and C. of C., Childersburg, 1993-94. Title I grantee, 1991, Stutz Bearcat grantee, 1992. Mem. AAUW, ALA, Am. Assn. Sch. Librs., Ala. Libr. Assn. (children's and sch. divsn. publicity chmn. 1991-93, chmn. Nat. Libr. Week 1993-94, Outstanding Youth Svcs. award 1989), People to People Internat. (libr. del. to China 1993), Kappa Delta Pi. Democrat. Methodist. Home: 5278 Cornell Dr Birmingham AL 35210 Office: A H Watwood Elem Sch Limbaugh Blvd Childersburg AL 35044

SARACELLI, KRISTINE DORTHIE, systems engineer, consultant; b. N.Y.C., May 24, 1954; d. George R. and Dorothy L. (Weidmann) Stegmann; m. Paul R. Saracelli, June 5, 1982. BS, Ramapo (N.J.) Coll., 1982. Computer ops. staff Marlyn Steel Co., Tampa, Fla., 1977-78; computer ops. supr. IBM, Sterling Forest, N.Y., 1979-83; info. ctr. support staff IBM, Franklin Lakes, N.J., 1983-84; data processing mgr. IBM, Sterling Forest, 1984-86; competitive analysis staff IBM, Montvale, N.J., 1987-88; decision support ctr. facilitator IBM, Southbury, Conn., 1988-89; decision support tech. mgr. IBM, Southbury, 1989-90, methodology devel. staff, 1990-93; cons. IBM Consulting Group, Raleigh, N.C., 1993-94; sr. bus. area mgr. ISSC/IBM, Raleigh, N.C., 1995—; instr. skill dynamics, Thornwood, N.Y., 1992-93; IBM project rep. G.U.I.D.E. Internat., 1993-94 (invited speaker Lisbon, Portugal, 1993). Contbr. articles to profl. jours. Mem. IEEE, Assn. for Computing Machinery, N.C. Quality Assurance Discussion Group (invited speaker Raleigh 1993). Democrat. Methodist. Home: 14200 Wyndfield Cir Raleigh NC 27615-1317 Office: IBM Integrated Sys Solutions Corp 1001 Winstead Dr Cary NC 27513

SARAH, EDITH, writer; b. Boston, Jan. 16, 1921; d. Samuel and Sarah (Rubin) Duboff; m. Eugene Abber, Aug. 30, 1940 (dec. Aug. 1956); children: Joan Sokoloff, Marlene Faust; m. Lou Stein, Sept. 20, 1963. BS, Northeastern U., Boston, 1970; master's degree, Boston U., 1975. Dir. foster grandparent program Action for Boston Cmty. Devel., 1972-87. Author: A Time for Every Purpose, 1994. Recipient Disting. Alumni award Boston U., 1995; Vis. scholar Northeastern U., 1995-96. Home: 615 Washington St Brookline MA 02146

SARANDON, SUSAN ABIGAIL, actress; b. N.Y.C., Oct. 4, 1946; d. Phillip Leslie and Lenora Marie (Criscione) Tomalin; m. Chris Sarandon, Sept. 16, 1967 (div. 1979); children: Eva Maria Livia Amurri, Jack Henry Robbins, Miles Guthrie Robbins. B.A. in Drama and English, Cath. U. Am., 1968. Actress: (plays) include An Evening with Richard Nixon, 1972, A Coupla White Chicks Sittin' Around Talkin', 1980-81, A Stroll in the Air, Albert's Bridge, Private Ear, Public Eye, Extremities, 1982, (films) Joe, 1970, Lady Liberty, 1972, The Rocky Horror Picture Show, 1975, Lovin' Molly, 1974, The Front Page, 1974, The Great Waldo Pepper, 1975, Dragon Fly, 1976, Crash, 1976, The Other Side of Midnight, 1977, The Last of the Cowboys, 1978, Checkered Flag or Crash, 1978, Pretty Baby, 1978, King of the Gypsies, 1978, Something Short of Paradise, 1979, Loving Couples, 1980, Atlantic City, 1980 (Prix Genie Best Fgn. Actress award 1981, Acad. award nominee 1981), Tempest, 1982 (Best Actress award Venice Film Festival 1982), The Hunger, 1983, Buddy System, 1984, Compromising Positions, 1985, The Witches of Eastwick, 1987, Bull Durham, 1988, Sweet Hearts Dance, 1988, A Dry White Season, 1989, The January Man, 1989, White Palace, 1990, Thelma and Louise, 1991 (Acad. award nominee for best actress 1992, Golden Globe award nominee 1992), The Player, 1992, Light Sleeper, 1992, Bob Roberts, 1992, Lorenzo's Oil, 1992 (Acad. award nominee 1993), The Client, 1994 (Acad. award nominee for best actress), Little Women, 1994, Safe Passage, 1994, Dead Man Walking, 1995 (Golden Globe award nominee for best actress 1996, Acad. award for best actress 1996); TV appearances The Haunting of Rosalind, 1973, F. Scott Fitzgerald and The Last of the Belles, 1974, Who Am I This Time, 1982, A.D., 1985. Mussolini: The Deline and Fall of Il Duce, 1985, (TV series) A World Apart, 1970-71, Search for Tomorrow, 1972-73. Mem. AFTRA, Screen Actors Guild, Actors Equity, Acad. Motion Picture Arts and Scis., NOW, MADRE, Amnesty Internat., ACLU. Office: Internat Creative Mgmt Martha Luttrell 8942 Wilshire Blvd Beverly Hills CA 90211

SARATH, CAROL ANN, library/media specialist; b. Ossining, N.Y., Apr. 2, 1952; d. Edward Noah and Florence Louise (Cafarelli) S.; m. Karl Burton Lohmann, July 9, 1986; children: Maria Estella, Patrick Noah. BS in Early Childhood Edn., So. Conn. State U., 1974; MLS, U. Ariz., 1980. Tchr. Gallup (N.Mex.) McKinley County Schs., 1975-79, libr./media specialist, 1982—; rschr. Fenn Galleries, Santa Fe, N.Mex., 1980-82; vice-chair libr. br. Octavia Fellin Pub. Libr., Gallup, 1990—; libr. adv. coun. State of N.Mex., Santa Fe, 1992—. Contbr.: Exploring the Southwest Through Childrens Literature, 1994. Bd. mem. Red Rock Balloon Rally Assocs., Gallup, 1983—. Mem. ALA, AECT, N.Mex. Libr. Assn. Office: Gallup McKinley County Schs 1000 E Aztec Ave Gallup NM 87301-5509

SARAVANJA-FABRIS, NEDA, mechanical engineering educator; b. Sarajevo, Yugoslavia, Aug. 2, 1942; came to U.S., 1970; d. Zarko and Olga Maria (Majstorovic) Saravanja; m. Gracio Fabris, Nov. 4, 1967; children: Drazen Fabris, Nicole. Diploma in mech. engring., U. Sarajevo, 1965; MSME, Ill. Inst. Tech., 1972, PhD in Mech. Engring., 1976. Lectr. in mech. engring. U. Sarajevo, 1965-70; teaching asst. Ill. Inst. Tech., Chgo., 1970-76; lectr. U. Ill., Chgo., 1974-75; mem. tech. staff Bell Telephone Lab., Naperville, Ill., 1976-79; prof. mech. engring. Calif. State U., L.A., 1979—, chair mech. engring. dept., 1989-92; assoc. researcher Lab. for Machine Tools, Aachen, Fed. Republic Germany, 1966-67; cons. Northrop Corp., L.A., 1984; COO FAS Engring. Inc., Burbank, Calif., 1993—. Contbr. articles to profl. pubs. Grantee NSF, 1986, Brown & Sharpe Co., 1989; German Acad. Exch. fellow DAAD, 1966-67, Amelia Earhart fellow Zonta Internat., 1973-74, 75-76; recipient Engring. Merit award San Fernando Valley Engring. Coun., 1990, Disting. Chair award sch. of engring. and tech. Calif. State U., L.A., 1993. Mem. AAUW, Soc. for Engring. Edn., Soc. Women Engrs. (sr.), Soc. Mfg. Engrs. (sr., chpt. v.p. 1984-88). Home: 2039 Dublin Dr Glendale CA 91206-1006 Office: Calif State U 5151 State University Dr Los Angeles CA 90032

SARDESON, LYNDA SCHULTZ, nursing, diabetes educator; b. LaPorte, Ind., Nov. 5, 1946; d. Wilbur W. and Helen (Winkfein) Schultz; children: Brian Michael, Eric Matthew. BS, Purdue U., Westville, Ind., 1976. Cert. diabetes educator. Emergency room nurse LaPorte Hosp., inpatient ctr. rep., sr. clin. instr. diabetes edn. program coord.; parish nurse Bethany Luth. Ch., LaPorte; guest presenter 1st Ann. Med. Congress, Izheusk, Russia, 1996. Active N.Am. Cultural Exch. League; past pres. People to People Internat., Vietnam Women's Meml.; mem. bd. elders, chmn. svc. divsn. Bethany Luth. Ch. With AUS, 1967-70. Mem. ANA, ADA, Am. Assn. Diabetes Educators, No. Ind. Assn. Diabetes Educators (sec., bd. dirs.), Am. Legion.

SARFATY, SUZANNE, internist and educator; b. Irvington, N.Y., Apr. 11, 1962; d. Sam and Pat (Petrovich) S. BS, Boston U., 1984, MD, 1988, MPH, 1994. Diplomate Am. Bd. Internal Medicine. Intern and resident Boston City Hosp., 1988-91; attending/clin. instr. Boston U., 1991-93, asst. prof. medicine and pub. health, 1995—, asst. dean of student affairs, 1995—. Mem. prof. com. Am. Cancer Soc., Boston, 1991—; mentor Boston Ptnrs. for Edn., 1991—. Recipient Cmty. Svc. award CIBA Geigy, 1986; Dana Farber cancer prevention fellow, 1993-94. Fellow ACP. Home: 11 Verndale St Brookline MA 02146-2423

SARGENT, LIZ ELAINE (ELIZABETH SARGENT), safety consulting executive; b. Meadville, Pa., Apr. 17, 1942; d. Melvin Ellsworth and Roberta Jean (Beach) Taylor; m. Lawrence Sargent, Sept. 6, 1969; 1 child, Kathy-Dawn. Student, Allegheny Coll., 1964; AA cum laude, Cuyahoga C.C., Cleve., 1987, Assoc. in Transp. cum laude, 1989; BA, Ithaca Coll., 1993. Car distbr. Norfolk and Western R.R., Cleve., 1963-69; account mgr. Ill. Cen. R.R., Cleve., 1970-73; traffic coord. Carlon Pipe, Mantua, Ohio, 1973-75; chief dispatcher X.L. Trucking, Coshocton, Ohio, 1975-77; corp. log auditor Anchor Motor Freight, Beachwood, Ohio, 1977-78; cons. Saf-T, Parma, Ohio, 1978-84; v.p. safety Saf-T, Shaker Heights, Ohio, 1987-91; dir. safety Sherwin Williams, Cleve., 1984-87; pres. Safety Advisors for Transp., Inc., Beachwood, Ohio, 1991—; founder Love Keepers, 1996; speaker Coshocton (Ohio) Traffic Club, 1984, Am. Indsl. Hygiene, Cleve., 1985. Author: Hall Chemical-Safety Procedures, 1983-84, Progressive Insurance, 1987, RL Lipton Co. manual, 1995; contbr. articles to profl. jours.

Chairperson intergenerational com. Ch. in Aurora, Ohio, 1984-86, Valley View Village Ch. libr. chairperson, mem. choir; bd. dirs. Shaker Heights Teen Recreational Com., 1984-87. Delta Nu Alpha scholar, 1977. Mem. Ohio Trucking Assn. (nat. safety coun.), Cleve. Bd. Realtors, Motor Fleet Safety Suprs. (nat. com.), Fleet Maintenance Coun., Phi Theta Kappa. Republican. Office: Saf-T 14716 Rockside Rd Maple Heights OH 44137-4016

SARGENT, PAMELA, writer; b. Ithaca, N.Y., Mar. 20, 1948. BA, SUNY, Binghamton, N.Y., 1968, MA, 1970. Mng. editor, Binghamton, N.Y., 1970-73, asst. editor, 1973-75; Am. editor Bull. Sci. Fiction Writers Am., Johnson City, N.Y., 1983-91. Author: Cloned Lives, 1976, Starshadows, 1977, The Sudden Star, 1979, Watchstar, 1980, The Golden Space, 1982, The Alien Upstairs, 1983, Earthseed, 1983, Eye of the Comet, 1984, Homesmind, 1984, Venus of Dreams, 1986, The Shore of Women, 1986, The Best of Pamela Sargent, 1987, Alien Child, 1988, Venus of Shadows, 1988, Ruler of the Sky, 1993 (Nebula best novelette award 1992, Locus best novelette award 1993, Electric Sci. Fiction award 1993); edit: (anthology) Women of Wonder, 1975, Bio-Futures, 1976, More Women of Wonder, 1976, The New Women of Wonder, 1978, (with Ian Watson) Afterlives, 1986, Women of Wonder, The Classic Years, 1996, Women of Wonder, The Contemporary Years, 1995, Nebula Awards 29, 1995, Nebula Awards 30, 1996. Office: care Richard Curtis Assocs Inc 171 E 74th St New York NY 10021-3221

SARGENT, SANDRA KAY, accountant; b. Springfield, Ill., Mar. 18, 1969; d. John E. and Connie E. Stevens; m. Brian Keith Sargent, Sept. 12, 1992. BS, Millikin U., 1991. CPA, Ill. Supr. III acctg. State Farm Ins. Co., Bloomington, Ill., 1991-95; acct. III State Farm Ins. Co., Salem, Oreg., 1995—; newsletter editor Inst. of Mgmt. Accts., Bloomington and Salem, 1991-96. Cons. Jr. Achievement, Salem, 1996; vol. Spl. Olympics, Bloomington, 1989-96. Scholarship Am. Bus. Women, 1987, DAR, 1987. Mem. Toastmasters Internat. (sec., sgt. at arms), Pi Beta Phi. Office: State Farm Ins Co 4600 25th St Salem OR 97313

SARICKS, JOYCE GOERING, librarian; b. Nov. 8, 1948; d. Joe W. and Lovella Goering; m. Christopher L. Saricks, Aug. 21, 1971; children: Brendan James, Margaret Katherine. BA with highest distinction in Eng.& Ger, U. Kans., 1970; MA in Comparative Lit., U. Wis., 1971; MA/MAT in Library Sci., U. Chgo., 1977. Reference librarian Downers Grove (Ill.) Pub. Library, 1977-80, head tech. svcs., 1980-83, coord. lit. and audio svcs., 1983—; presenter workshops in field. Author: (with Nancy Brown) Readers' Advisory Service in the Public Library, 1989. Mem. Read Ill. adv. com., 1990-91. Woodrow Wilson fellow, 1970; recipient Allie Beth Martin award Pub. Library Assn., 1989, No. Ill. Lib. of Yr. award Windy City Romance Writers, 1995. Mem. ALA, Ill. Library Assn., Adult Reading Round Table (founder), Phi Beta Kappa, Delta Phi Alpha, Pi Lambda Theta, Beta Phi Mu. Home: 1116 61st St Downers Grove IL 60516-1819 Office: Downers Grove Pub Library 1050 Curtiss St Downers Grove IL 60515-4606

SARIS, PATTI B., federal judge; b. 1951. BA magna cum laude, Radcliffe Coll., 1973; JD cum laude, Harvard U., 1976. Law clerk to Hon. Robert Braucher Mass. Supreme Judicial Ct., 1976-77; atty. Foley Hoag & Eliot, Boston, 1977-79; staff counsel U.S. Senate Judiciary Com., 1979-81; atty. Berman Dittmar & Engel, Boston, 1981-82; chief civil divsn. U.S. Atty.'s Office, 1984-86; U.S. magistrate judge U.S. Dist. Ct. Mass., 1986-89; assoc. justice Mass. Superior Ct., 1989-94; dist. judge U.S. Dist. Ct. Mass., 1994—; mem. com. on civil rules Supreme Judicial Ct. Comments editor civil rights Civil Liberties Law Rev. Bd. trustees Beth Israel Hosp.; active Wexner Heritage Found. Nat. Merit scholar, 1969; recipient award Mothers of Murdered Children, 1993. Mem. Nat. Assn. Women Judges, Am. Jewish Com., Women's Bar Assn. (bd. dirs. 1982-86), Mass. Bar Assn., Mass. Assn. Women Judges, Boston Bar Assn., Boston Inns Ct., Phi Beta Kappa. Office: John W McCormack Courthouse 90 Devonshire St Rm 707 Boston MA 02109-4501

SARKISIAN, PAMELA OUTLAW, artist; b. Spokane, Sept. 26, 1941; d. Willard Clinton and Frances (Montieth) Outlaw; m. Ronald Edward Sarkisian, Nov. 11, 1960; children: Ronald Abraham, Michelle Suzanne. Grad. high sch., Stockton, Calif. Art student Oceanside, Calif., 1972-80; founder Palette 'N Easel Studio, Oceanside, Calif., 1980—, operator, mgr., 1980-85; art tchr. in residence Palette 'N Easel Studio, Oceanside, 1985-96; publisher greeting cards Polytint, Ltd., England, 1995, 96. Designer floral collector plate series Danbury Mint/MBI, Inc.; represented by Casay Gallery, Kailau, Kona, Hawaii, 1991, Galeria Jean Lammelin, Paris, 1991, 2d St. Gallery, Encinitas, Calif., 1991, Blondes Gallery, San Diego, 1992, Valentine-Owens Gallery, Santa Monica, Calif., 1992, Sodarco Gallery, Montreal, 1993, Surtex, 1993, Jacob G. Javity Conv. Ctr., N.Y.C., 1993, Laura Larkin Gallery, Del Mar, Calif., 1993-94, Charles Hecht Galleries, Tarzana and Palm Desert, Calif., 1993-94, 95-96, Lou Martin Gallery, Laguna Beach, Calif., 1994, Charles Hecht Gallery, La Jolla, Calif., 1995-96, Calif. Art Gallery, Laguna Beach, 1996, Hunter Gallery, Tucson, 1996, Cottage Gallery at Carmel, Calif., 1996. Pres. Zonta Internat., Oceanside, 1980-81; mem. Emblem Club #177, Oceanside, 1971-96; princess Daughters of the Nile, San Diego, 1974; bd. dirs. Oceanside Girls Club, 1980. Recipient 1st Pl. award San Dieguito Art Guild, 1978, 85, 2nd Pl. award, 1983, 89, 3rd Pl. award, 1983, 1990; winner People's Choice award Internat. Show of Women Artists of the West, Las Vegas, 1992. Mem. North County Art Assn. (founder), Carlsbad Oceanside Art League, 1978, San Dieguito Art Guild, Fallbrook Art Assn., San Diego Art Inst., Assn. pour Promotion Artiste Français, ARTISPHERE. Office: Palette 'N Easel Studio 1021 S Coast Hwy Oceanside CA 92054-5004

SARLAT, GLADYS, public relations consultant; b. Elizabeth, N.J., July 22, 1923; d. Max and Dora (Levin) S. BS, U. Wash., 1946. Asst., Kay Sullivan Assocs. N.Y.C., 1949-50; fashion dir. Warsaw & Co., N.Y.C., 1950-54; asst. fashion coordinator Emporium Dept. Store, San Francisco, 1955-56; asst. prodn. mgr. Cunningham & Walsh Advt., San Francisco, 1958-59; v.p., pub. rels. dir. Harwood Advt. Inc., Tucson and Phoenix, 1959-68; v.p., dir. Waller & Sarlat Advt. Inc., Tucson, 1968-69; pres. Godwin & Sarlat Pub. Rels., Inc., Tucson, 1970-87; counsel, Godwin Sarlat Pub. Rels., 1987-88, cons., 1988—; of counsel Liess Peck & Godwin, Tuscon, 1993—; cons. in field. Mem. adv. com. Downtown Devel. Corp., 1979-85, Festival in the Sun; bd. dirs. Tuscon Conv. and Visitors Bur., 1993-95. Named Woman of Yr. for Bus., Ariz. Daily Star, 1963; recipient Lulu award L.A. Woman in Advt., 1962. Mem. Pub. Rels. Soc. Am. (past bd. mem., counselors acad.), Fashion Group, Tucson Met. C. of C. (v.p., dir. 1976-85, chmn bd. 1986-87), Tucson Trade Bur. (dir. 1977-80). Republican. Jewish. Home: 5530 N Camino Arenosa Tucson AZ 85718-5417 Office: 177 N Church Ave Ste 301 Tucson AZ 85701-1118

SARMIENTO, SHIRLEY JEAN, counselor, court advocate; b. Buffalo, Nov. 28, 1946; d. John Clyde and Claudia Mary (Hall) Laughlin; 1 child, Tolley C.; m. William Sarmiento, May 6, 1981. BS in Liberal Studies and Social Sci., Medaille Coll., 1980; M Arts and Scis., SUNY, Buffalo, 1996. Cmty. health worker Jesse Nash Health Ctr., Buffalo, 1979-83; educator Western N.Y. Peace Ctr., Buffalo, 1984-89; substitute tchr. Buffalo Bd. Edn., 1990-91; counselor, ct. advocate LHI, Buffalo, 1990—. Narrator fundraising video, 1993; editor: Drum Beats, 1996. Mem. Art Space, 1995—; founder Urban Arts, Buffalo, 1994—; vol. Burchfield/Penny Art Gallery, Buffalo, 1994—; bd. dirs. Jubilee Fund, Buffalo, 1989-91; vol. MLK Com., 1993, Movin On Residential House, 1995-96. Home: 205 Marine Dr # 4D Buffalo NY 14202

SARNAK, NANCY JEAN, elementary education educator; b. Elizabeth, N.J., Aug. 14, 1952; d. Norman John Olsen Jr. and Patricia June (Peterson) Schmidt; m. Paul Robert Sarnak, June 18, 1977. BS in Elem. Edn., Athens Coll., 1974. Pharm. technician Thrift Drugs, Spotswood, N.J., 1969—; tchr. Immaculate Conception Sch., Spotswood, 1974—; mem. com. to reevaluate standardized tests Diocese of Metuchen, N.J., 1992; co-chmn. steering com. mid. states assn. colls. and schs. Immaculate Conception, Spotswood. Vol. St. Peter's Ch. Fellowship Dinners, Spotswood, 1993—. Mem. Nat. Cath. Edn. Assn. Episcopalian. Office: Immaculate Conception Sch 23 Manalapan Rd Spotswood NJ 08884-1658

SARNOFF, LILI-CHARLOTTE DREYFUS (LOLO SARNOFF), artist, business executive; b. Frankfurt, Germany (Swiss citizen), Jan. 9, 1916; came to U.S., 1940, naturalized, 1943; d. Willy and Martha (Koch von Hirsch) Dreyfus; m. Stanley Jay Saronff, Sept. 11, 1948; children: Daniela Martha Bargezi, Robert L. Grad. Reimann Art Sch. (Germany), 1936, U. Berlin, 1936-38; student U. Florence (Italy), 1948-54. Rsch. asst. Harvard Sch. Pub. Health, 1955-69; rsch. assoc. cardiac physiology Nat. Heart Inst., Bethesda, Md., 1954-59; pres. Rodana Rsch. Corp., Bethesda, 1959; v.p. Catrix Corp., Bethesda, 1958-61; inventor FloLite light sculptures under name Lolo Sarnoff, 1968; one-woman shows include Agra Gallery, Washington, 1969, Corning Glass Ctr. Mus., Corning, N.Y., 1970, Gallery Two, Woodstock, Vt., 1970, Gallery Marc, Washington, 1971, 72, Franz Bader Gallery, Washington, 1976, Gallery K, Washington, 1978, 81, Alwin Gallery, London, 1981, Galerie von Bartha, Basel, Switzerland, 1982, Gallery K, Washington, 1982, 83, 84, 85, 87, 88, 89, 90, 91, La Galerie L'Hotel de Ville, Geneva, Switzerland, 1982, Pfalzgalerie, Kaiserlautern, Fed. Republic of Germany, 1985, Gallery K, Washington, 1987-91, Galerie Les Hirondelles, Geneva, 1988, Rockville (Md.) Civic Ctr., 1988, Washington Square Sculpture Group, 1989, Internat. Sculpture Congress, Washington, 1990, Retrospective show Gallery K, Washington, 1995; represented in collections: Fed. Nat. Mortgage Assn., Washington, Brookings Inst., Washington, Corning Glass Ctr. Mus., Nat. Air and Space Museum, Washington, Kennedy Ctr., Washington, Nat. Acad. Sci., Chase Manhattan Bank, N.Y.C., Israel Mus., Jerusalem, Nat. Mus. Women in the Arts, Washington, others. Past trustee Nat. Ballet, Mt. Vernon Coll.; founder, pres. Arts for the Aging, Inc., Bethesda, Md., 1988—; active Washington Opera Soc., Washington Ballet Soc.; bd. overseers Corcoran Gallery Art, 1991. Recipient Gold medal Accademia Italia delle Arti e del Lavoro, 1980, Golda Meir award, 1995. Mem. City Tavern Club (Washington), Cosmos Club. Democrat. Co-inventor electrophrenic respirator; inventor flowmeter. Home: 7507 Hampden Ln Bethesda MD 20814-1331

SARPANEVA, PIA MARIAANA, architect, educator; b. Helsinki, Finland, Feb. 2, 1956; arrived in U.S., 1994; d. Pentti Akseli Sarpaneva and Kirsti Anneli Qveflander. MArch, Helsinki U. Tech., 1986. Registered arch., Finland. Staff arch. Heliövaara and Uksila Archs., Helsinki, 1977-81; project arch. Kahri Ky Archs., Helsinki, 1981-85; project leader Helin and Siitonen Archs., Helsinki, 1986-94; asst. prof. Coll. Arch. and Urban Design Va. Poly. Inst. and State U., Blacksburg, 1994—; vis. design instr. faculty of arch. Helsinki U. of Tech., 1989-94; artist-in-residence Visual Arts Found. in U.S., N.Y.C., 1993. Mem. editl. bd. Finnish Archtl. Rev., 1996—. Recipient Helsinki City Cert. of Honor for Arch., 1986. Mem. Finnish Assn. Archs. Home: 408 Clay St SW Blacksburg VA 24060 Office: Va Tech 202 Cowgill Hall Blacksburg VA 24061-0205

SARRY, CHRISTINE, ballerina; b. Long Beach, Calif., May 25, 1946; d. John and Beatrice (Thomas) S.; m. Jim Varriale, Sept. 12, 1984; 1 child, Maximilian Sarry Varriale. With Joffrey Ballet, 1963-64; With Am. Ballet Theatre, 1964-68, prin. dancer, 1971-74; leading dancer Am. Ballet Co., 1969-71; ballerina Eliot Feld Ballet, 1974-81; mem. faculty New Ballet Sch., also freelance guest tchr. Performed ballets for Agnes DeMille, Antony Tudor, Jerome Robbins, Eliot Feld; appeared at White House, 1963, 67; U.S. Dept. State tours include, Russia, 1963, 66, S.Am., 1964, 76, various tours of N.Am., Orient, Europe, various appearances U.S. nat. TV; partnered by Mikhail Baryshnikov.

SARTORI, BRIDGET ANN, home health care nurse; b. Plattsburg, N.Y., July 17, 1957; d. Francis McCarthy and Phyllis (Harvey) McCarthy/Haegler; m. Robert S. Sartori, May 20, 1978; children: Robert F., Ryan R. BSN, Mt. St. Mary's Coll., Newburgh, N.Y., 1990. RN, N.Y. Staff nurse CCU White Plains (N.Y.) Hosp., 1990-91; nurse in home care divsn. Putnam Hosp. Ctr., Carmel, N.Y., 1991—, acting LTHHCP coord. home care divsn., 1995—; intravenous therapy nurse Anytime Home Care, Poughkeepsie, N.Y., 1992—; substitute tchr., substitute sch. nurse Dover Union Free Sch. Dist., 1994—; children's adv. Astor Head Start, Dover Plains, N.Y., 1989-92. Mem. rescue squad J.H. Ketcham Hose Co., Dover Plains, 1978—, mem. ladies aus., 1978—, fire prevention officer, 1994-95, corp. sec., 1996; 1st v.p. J.H. Ketcham Hose Co. Fire Police, 1994—; coach Dover Little League, 1994, 95. Recipient Army Nurse Perseverance award U.S. Army, 1990. Republican. Roman Catholic. Office: Putnam Hosp Ctr Home Care Divsn Stoneleigh Ave Carmel NY 10512

SARTORIS, GEORGIA PORTER, artist; b. Denver, Sept. 8, 1943; d. Glen Porter and Marguerite C. (Downey) Arnold; m. James J. Sartoris, Apr. 30, 1966; 1 child, Aspen Claire. BA, Colo. State U., 1965. One-woman shows include Volcano Art Ctr., Hawaii, 1994, Emmanuel Gallery U. Colo. Auraria Ctr., Denver, 1989, Robischon Gallery, Denver, 1984, 86, 87, Cohen Gallery, Denver, 1982, Colo. Mountain Coll., Breckenridge, 1981, Ohio State U., Newark, 1979; exhibited in group shows at Hawaii Craftsmen Ann. Exbhn., Honolulu, 1994, Denver Art Mus., 1983, 84, 86, San Angelo (Tex.) Mus. Fine Arts, 1989, Craft Nat., Buffalo, 1985, Colo. Springs (Colo.) Fine Arts Ctr., 1985, 8th Ann. Biennial of Ceramic Art, Vaullaris, France, 1982, Marietta (Ohio) Coll. Craft Nat., 1981, Aspen (Colo.) Found. for Arts, 1978, Tweed Mus., Duluth, Minn., 1975, 77; represented in permanent collections at Colo. U., Boulder, Colo. Springs Fine Arts Ctr., Forum Hotel, Chgo., Paine Weber, Tucson, Mountain Bell, Denver, Pa. Bell, Phila., Kimball Internat. Design, L.A., Hughes Aircraft PNL, L.A. Bd. dirs. Hamakua Incubator Kitchen and Craft, Inc., Honokaa, Hawaii, 1993-96. Recipient Best of Show award Foothills Art Ctr., Golden, Colo., 1975, Excellence in Ceramics award Colo. Artist Craftsman, Denver, 1979, 80, 81, Cash award Craft Design Ctr., 1988. Mem. Hawaii Artist/Craftsmen.

SARWAR, BARBARA DUCE, school system administrator; b. Mpls., Aug. 9, 1938; d. Harold Taylor and Barbara (Thayer) Duce; m. Mohammad Sarwar, Dec. 28, 1972; 1 child, Barbara Sara Depies. BS, U. Colo., 1972; M Spl. Edn., Ea. N.Mex. U., 1975, Edn. Specialist, 1979. Cert. tchr., adminstr., N.Mex. Tchr. 2d grade, English as 2d lang. Lake Arthur (N.Mex.) Mcpl. Schs., 1972-74; tchr. spl. edn. Artesia (N.Mex.) Pub. Schs., 1974-79, ednl. diagnostician, 1979-88, dir. spl. edn., 1988—. Contbr. to profl. publs. Pres. Altrusa Club Artesia, 1981-82, 86-87, The Arc of Artesia, 1990-92. Named Employee of Yr. Arc of N.Mex., 1994. Mem. Artesia Edn. Assn. (pres. 1978-79), Internat. Reading Assn. (pres. Pecos Valley chpt. 1975-76, sec. N.Mex. unit 1977-78), Nat. Assn. Sch. Psychologists, N.Mex. Sch. Adminstrs. Assn., Assoc. Sch. Curriculm Divsn., Phi Kappa Phi, Phi Delta Kappa. Home: PO Box 1493 Artesia NM 88211-1493 Office: Artesia Pub Schs 1106 W Quay Ave Artesia NM 88210

SASEK, GLORIA BURNS, English language and literature educator; b. Springfield, Mass., Jan. 20, 1926; d. Frederick Charles and Minnie Delia (White) Burns; BA, Mary Washington Coll. of U. Va., 1947; EdM, Springfield Coll., 1955; postgrad. Sorbonne, summer 1953; MA, Radcliffe Coll., 1954; postgrad. Universita per Stranieri, Perugia, Italy, summer 1955; m. Lawrence Anton Sasek, Sept. 5, 1960. Tchr., head dept. jr. and sr. h.s. English, Somers, Conn., 1947-51, 52-59; tchr. English, Winchester (Mass.) pub. schs., 1959-60; faculty La. State U., Baton Rouge, 1961—, asst. prof. English, 1971—, chmn. freshman English, 1969-70; mem. South Ctrl. Conf. on Christianity and Literature. Recipient George H. Deer Disting. Tchr. award La. State U., 1977, Gumbo Favorite Prof., 1978, Disting. Undergrad. Teaching award Amoco Found., 1994. Mem. MLA, AAUP (chpt. v.p. 1981-84), South Ctrl. Modern Lang. Assn., South Ctrl. Renaissance Soc., South Ctrl. Conf. on Christianity and Lit., South Ctrl. Soc. for 18th Century Studies. Address: 1458 Kenilworth Pky Baton Rouge LA 70808-5737

SASMAN, SUZETTE MARY, insurance company executive; b. Clintonville, Wis., Oct. 31, 1981; d. Joseph Arthur and Marcille Georgia (Diemel) Stilen; m. Kevin Raymand Sasman, Oct. 31, 1981. Assoc. Supervisory Mgmt., Northcentral Tech. Coll., 1994; postgrad., Cardinal Stritch Coll., 1994—. Gen. mgr. Marriott Corp., Wausau, 1982-86; mgr., dir. Wausau Ins. Co., 1986—. Vol. bus. cons. Jr. Achievement, Wausau, 1986, bd. dirs., com. chair, 1995—; alumni Leadership Wausau Program, 1993; chair com. Wausau Visitors Coun., 1987-94; chair Vol. Corp., Wausau, 1993—. Mem. Wausai Area Innkeepers Assn., Internat. Assn. Conf. Ctrs., Wis. Soc. Assn. Execs., Wine N Roses Dance Club (past pres.). Office: Wausau Ins PO Box 4834 Syracuse NY 13221-4834

SASMOR, JEANNETTE LOUISE, educational consulting company executive; b. N.Y.C., May 17, 1943; d. Sol and Willmyra J. (Reilly) Fuchs; m. James C. Sasmor, May 30, 1965. BS, Columbia U., 1966, MEd, 1968, EdD, 1974; adult primary care nurse practitioner, U. Md., Balt., 1982; MBA, U. South Fla., 1990. Cert. adult primary care nurse practitioner; cert. women's health nurse practitioner; cert. risk mgr. Coord. ANA Div. Maternal Child Health, N.Y.C., 1972-73; maternal child health cons. test constrn. div. Nat. League for Nursing, N.Y.C., 1973; prof., dir. continuing nursing edn. U. South Fla., Tampa, 1973-89; v.p. and dir. edn. Continuing Edn. Cons. Inc., Tampa, Fla., 1976-89, Sedona, Ariz., 1989—; coord. maternal child health and 2d yr. nursing curriculum Yavapai Coll., Prescott, Ariz., 1994—; dir. internat. study tours USSR, 1986, New Zealand/Australia, 1990, Scandinavia, 1992, China, 1996; mem. scope practice com. Ariz. Bd. Nursing, 1994—. Author: What Every Husband Should Know About Having a Baby, 1972, Father's Labor Coaching Log and Review Book, 1972, 82, Childbirth Education: A Nursing Perspective, 1979. Del. White House Conf. on Children and Youth, 1970, White House Conf. on Families, 1980; bd. dirs. Ariz. divsn. Am. Cancer Soc., 1992—, sec., 1995-96. Am. Acad. Nursing fellow, 1977, Robert Wood Johnson Nurse faculty fellow in primary care, 1981-82; recipient NEAA Nursing Practice award Tchrs.'s Coll. Columbia U., 1992, Vol. of Yr. award Sedona-Oak Creek unit Am. Cancer. Soc., 1992. Mem. Am. Soc. Childbirth Educators (pres. 1972-78), Fla. Nurses Assn. (pres. dist. 4 1976-77), Ariz. Nurses Assn. (continuing edn. review com. 1990—), Ariz. Bd. Nursing (scope of practice com. 1994—), Lions (treas. Sedona-Oak Creek Canyon Club 1990—, Melvin Jones fellow 1996), One Good Turn Inc. (pres. 1992-95), Phi Theta Kappa (founding pres. Lambda Nu chpt. 1962, faculty advisor Beta Gamma Pi chpt. 1996—), Pi Lambda Theta, Sigma Theta Tau (chpt. treas. 1992-96, newsletter editor 1991-94, Outstanding Cmty. Leader award Lambda Omicron chpt. 1994), Kappa Delta Pi. Office: Yavapai Coll 1100 E Sheldon St Prescott AZ 86301-3220

SASS, ANNE MICHELE, pediatric nurse practitioner, clinical nurse specialist; b. N.Y.C., Apr. 17, 1965; d. William Kenneth and Panthie (Hopper) S. BSN, SUNY, Buffalo, 1989; MSN, Emory U., 1995. RN, Tex., Ga. Staff nurse orthopedics Buffalo Gen. Hosp., 1989; charge nurse gen. surgery Millard Fillmore Hosp., Buffalo, 1990; staff nurse newborn nursery, postpartum unit USAF Wilford Hall Med. Ctr., Lackland AFB, Tex., 1990-94; childbirth educator Wilford Hall, 1993-94. 1st lt. USAF, 1990-94. Mem. Nat. Assn. Pediat. Nurse Assocs. & Practitioners, Am. Heart Assn., Internat. Nursing Honor Soc., Sigma Theta Tau (Alpha Epsilon chpt.). Baptist.

SASSEN, GEORGIA, psychologist, educator; b. N.Y.C., July 27, 1949; d. Bernard Nicholas Sassen and Rose Ellen Benjamin; m. L.S. Laing, Aug. 27, 1983; 1 child. BA, Wesleyan U., 1971; EdM, Harvard U., 1977; MS, U. Mass., 1981, PhD, 1985. Lic. psychologist, Mass. Program assoc. Am. Friends Svc. Com., Cambridge, Mass., 1971-76; field faculty Goddard-Cambridge Grad. Program, 1974-76; dir. field study Hampshire Coll., Amherst, Mass., 1977-80; asst. prof. U. Mass. Med. Sch., Worcester, 1985-88, asst. clin. prof., 1988-91, assoc. in psychiatry, 1991-94; affiliate asst. prof. psychology Clark U., Worcester, 1989—; pvt. practice Shrewsbury, Mass., 1988—; active staff Med. Ctr. Ctrl. Mass., Worcester, 1993—; summer faculty Smith Coll. Sch. Social Work, Northampton, Mass., 1985-90; cons. Mass. Sch. Profl. Psychology, Dedham, 1991, Syndicate Nat. des Psychologues, Paris, 1985, Mass. Dept. Elder Affairs and Other Mental Health Agys., 1981—; dir. Women's Relational Devel. Group, Boston, 1990-93. Co-author: Corporations and Child Care, 1974, The Abortion Business, 1975; contbr. articles to profl. jours. Vice pres. Women's Rsch. Action Project, Boston/Cambridge, 1975—. U. Mass. fellow in gerontology, 1986-87; Joseph P. Healey Found. grantee, 1986, AARP/Andrus Found. grantee, 1985, Sigma Xi grantee, 1985; NIMH and Harvard U. traineeship. Mem. APA, Assn. for Women in Psychology. Office: 48 Maple Ave Shrewsbury MA 01545-2922

SASSOON, JANET, ballerina, educator; b. Sorabaya, Indonesia, Sept. 2, 1936; came to U.S., 1937; d. Edward and Flora (Bar) S.; m. John Roland Upton Jr., Aug. 7, 1983. Began training with Christensen brothers, Ruby Asquith, and Gisella Caccialanza, San Francisco; Studied with Leo Staats, Lubov Egorova, Olga Preobrajenska, Mathilde Kshessinskaya, Paris, 1951. Dancer Grand Ballet du Marquis de Cuevas, Paris, 1952-55, Chgo., Utah and San Francisco Ballets, 1955; prima ballerina Berlin Ballet, 1956; assoc. dir. Acad. of Ballet, San Francisco, 1974—; condr. master classes in ballet, movement therapy for numerous profl. dancers including Natalia Makarova. Office: 2121 Market St San Francisco CA 94114-1321

SATIN, KAREN W., university publications director; b. Chgo., Apr. 12, 1938; d. Harry E. and Gertrude (Plotkin) Weiss; m. Lawrence Z. Satin, Sept. 11, 1960 (div. 1980); children: Wendy, Scott, Kimberly. BA in English and Sociology, U. Conn., 1958; MA in Journalism, U. Md., 1984. Prodn. editor Encyclopedia Britannica, Chgo., 1960-64; freelance editor Washington, 1977-81; program editor Nat. Sci. Tchrs. Assn., Washington, 1981-83; sr. tech. writer Computer Scis. Corp., Arlington, Va., 1983-84; publs. mgr. Sci. Applications Rsch., Lanham, Md., 1984-89; dir. publs., adj. faculty comm. studies U. Md. Univ. Coll., College Park, 1989—. Mem. Capitol Assn. for Women in Edn. Office: U Md Univ Coll University Blvd at Adelphi Rd College Park MD 20742-1671

SATO-VIACRUCIS, KIYO, inventor, nurse, entrepreneur, consultant; b. Sacramento, May 8, 1923; d. John Shinji and Mary Tomomi (Watanabe) Sato; m. Gene Viacrucis, Aug. 9, 1958 (div. May 1976); adopted children: Cia, Jon, Paul, Tanya. BS, Hillsdale Coll., 1944; MSN in Grad. Studies/Pub. Health Nursing, Western Res. U., 1951. Cert. health and devel. specialist, Calif., pub. health nurse, Calif., audiologist. Nursery sch. attendant Poston (Ariz.) II Concentration Camp, 1942; staff nurse U. Hosps., Cleve., 1948; pub. health nurse Sacramento County Health Dept., 1948-50, 52-53; sch. nurse U. Oslo, 1953, Sacramento County Schs., 1954-58; presch. nurse Sacramento City Unified Sch. Dist., 1973-85; pvt. practice cons. Blackbird Vision Screening System, Sacramento, 1985—; cons., speaker Blackbird Vision Screening System, 1973—; cons. state task force Vision Screening Guidelines, 1981. Inventor Blackbird presch. vision screening method; cons. vision screening; contbr. articles to profl. jours. Served to capt. USAF, 1951-52. Recipient Excellence in Nursing award RN Mag. Found., 1983. Mem. Nat. Sch. Nurses Assn., Calif. Sch. Nurses Orgn., Japanese Am. Citizens League (pres. 1950), Am. Assn. Ret. Persons, VFW (pub. rels., post surgeon 1985—, cmty. activities 1986—, speaker's bur. Internment of Am. of Japanese Descent and the U.S. Constn.). Democrat. Home: 9436 Americana Way Sacramento CA 95826-4621 Office: Blackbird Vision Screening PO Box 277424 Sacramento CA 95827-7424

SATTERFIELD-HARRIS, RITA, workers compensation representative; b. Bklyn., Oct. 14, 1949; d. Wilton Anthony and Hattie Eva (Tunstall) Satterfield; m. Sidney Harris, Jan. 5, 1973; 1 child, Marcial A.H. BA in Psychology, Bernard Baruch Coll., N.Y.C., 1983; student, CCNY, 1971-74; Cert. in Paralegal Studies, L.I. U., Bklyn., 1982; cert. unemployment ins. benefits law, Cornell U., 1984. Lic. claimant's workers compensation rep. N.Y.; registered agt. N.Y. State Unemployment Ins. Dir. social svcs. Lincoln Sq. Neighborhood Ctr., N.Y.C., 1979-88; pvt. practice N.Y.C., 1988—; writer proposals funded by N.Y.C. Dept. for Aging Inc., 1980-82, and N.Y.C. Cmty. Devel. Agy., 1984-88. Recipient Cert. of Appreciation for participation in vol. income tax assistance program Dept. Treasury, IRS, 1985, 86, Ptnrs. in Change award Nat. Displaced Homemakers Network, 1991. Mem. Workers' Def. League, Nat. Orgn. Social Security Claimant's Reps. Office: 141 Livingston St Brooklyn NY 11201-5133

SATTLER, NANCY JOAN, curriculum chair; b. Toledo, July 14, 1950; d. Thomas Joseph and Margaret Mary (Linenkugel) Ainsworth; m. Rudolph Henry Sattler, June 17, 1972; children: Cortland, Clinton, Corinne. BS, U. Toledo, 1972, MEd, 1988. Office worker/bookkeeper Gilbert Mail Svc., 1967-71; computer typesetter Quality Composition, Toledo, 1971-89; instr. Terra Tech. Coll. (now Terra C.C.), Fremont, Ohio, 1988-89; dept. head Terra Tech. Coll., Fremont, Ohio, 1989-95, curriculum chair bus., social scis., math. and arts, 1995—; adj. instr. Terra Tech. Coll., Fremont, 1982-88, U. Toledo, 1988, Lucas County Bd. Edn. Gifted Program, Toledo, 1988-92; computer coord. St. Joseph Elem. Sch., Fremont, 1987-94, coord. quiz bowl, 1993; extern in quality control Atlas Crankshaft, Fostoria, Ohio, 1990; instr. devel. math. A.O. Smith, Bellevue, Ohio, 1991, 93, 94; adult edn. computer instr. St. Joseph Ctrl. Cath. Sch., Fremont, 1990-92, sec. sch. bd., 1989-94, pres., 1991-94; instr. devel. math. and sci. Whirlpool Corp., Findlay, Ohio,

1992; presenter Am. Math. Assn. Two-Yr. Colls., 1991-95, Nat. Coun. Tchrs. Math. Conf., 1993, 95; co-presenter Continuous Improvements Through Faculty Externship, League for Innovation, 1992; co-chmn. Ohio Gt. Tchrs. Seminar, 1993-96; chmn. Kids Coll., Fremont, 1993-95; facilitator Mo. Gt. Tchrs. Seminar, 1993, Ohio Gt. Tchrs. Retreat, 1994, 95, 96, N.Y. Gt. Tchrs. Seminar, 1994, Inventing Our Future, 1995—; co-chmn., presenter Ohiomatyc Winter Inst., 1994, 95, 96; TOM trainer Terra C.C., 1994-96. Author: The Implication of Math Placement Testing in the Two Year College, 1988, Applied Math for Industrial Technology, 1989; co-author: Math and Science Made Easy, 1992, The Metric System, Preparing for the Future, 1992, Workplace Literacy, 1994, The Basics of Using the TI-85 Graphing Calculator, 1995. Sec. St. Joseph Ctrl. Cath. Sch. Bd., 1989-94, pres., 1991-94; Sunday sch. dir. St. Joseph Ch., Fremont, 1977-87; pres. Plant 'N Bloom Garden Club, Fremont, 1977-79; clk. Sandusky County Fair, 1977—; rep. for deanery Early Childhood Devel., 1982-84; parliamentarian Welcome Wagon, 1980; Eucharistic min., 1991—; chair communications Inventing Our Future, 1996. Mem. Ohio Math. Assn. Two-Yr. Colls. (pres. 1992-95, NSF grant com. 1992), Am. Math. Assn. Two-Yr. Colls. (assessment com. 1990—, chmn. 1993—, program com. 1993), Nat. Coun. Tchrs. Math., Ohio Coun. Tchrs. Math., Ohio Assn. Garden Clubs, Alumni and Friends (bd. mem. 1995-96, bd. viss. 1995—), Ohio Math. and Sci. Coalition (co-chmn. collaboration com. 1996—). Democrat. Roman Catholic. Home: 712 Hayes Ave Fremont OH 43420-2914 Office: Terra C C 2830 Napoleon Rd Fremont OH 43420-9670

SATTY, ANDREA N., lawyer; b. Queens, N.Y., Oct. 6, 1958. BA, CUNY, 1981; JD, Fordham U., 1985. Bar: N.Y. 1985. Ptnr. Chadbourne & Parke LLP. Office: Chadbourne & Parke LLP 30 Rockefeller Plz New York NY 10112*

SATUR, NANCY MARLENE, dermatologist; b. Philipsburg, Pa., Apr. 12, 1953; d. Nicholas and Mary (Kutzer) S.; m. John David Lortscher, Oct. 20, 1979; children: David Nicholas, Glenn William, Stephen John. BS magna cum laude, Pa. State U., 1974; MD, Thomas Jefferson U., 1976. Diplomate Am. Bd. Dermatology. Intern Allentown (Pa.) Gen. Hosp., 1976-77; resident in pathology U. Ill. Hosp., Chgo., 1978-79; resident in dermatology Case Western Res. U. Hosp., Cleve., 1979-82; dermatologist Encinitas, Calif., 1985—; sr. instr. dermatology Case Western Res. U. Hosp., 1982-83, sr. clin. instr. dermatology, 1983-84. Fellow Am. Acad. Dermatology; mem. Am. Soc. Dermatologic Surgery, Am. Soc. Laser Medicine and Surgery, N.Am. Soc. Phlebology, San Diego Dermatologic Soc., Pacific Dermatologic Assn. Office: Ste C308 477 N El Camino Real #C308 Encinitas CA 92024-1331

SATURNELLI, ANNETTE MIELE, school system administrator; b. Newburgh, N.Y., Dec. 1, 1937; d. William Vito and Anna (Marso) M.; m. Carlo F. Saturnelli, Oct. 15, 1960; children: Anne, Karen, Carla. BA, Vassar Coll., 1959; MS, SUNY, New Paltz, 1978; EdD, NYU, N.Y.C., 1993. Rsch. chemist Lederle Labs/Am. Cyanamid, Pearl River, N.Y., 1959-64; sci. coord. Marlboro (N.Y.) Cen. Sch. Dist., 1974-84; state sci. supr. N.Y. State Dept. Edn., Albany, 1984-86; dir. sci. edn. Newburgh (N.Y.) City Sch. Dist., 1986—; project dir., proposal reviewer NSF, Washington, 1984—; state coord. N.Y. State Sci. Olympiad, 1985-86; mem. Gov. Cuomo's Task Force on Improving Sci. Edn., Albany, N.Y., 1989—; mem. adv. bd. N.Y. State Systemic Initiative, 1993—, N.Y. State Tech. Edn. Network, 1993—. Author: Focus on Physical Science, 1981, 87; editor: Transforming Testing in New York State--A Collection of Past, Present and Future Assessment Practices, 1994. Recipient Presdl. award Excellence in Sci. Tchg., Washington, 1983; NSF 3-yr. summer sci. camp grantee, 1995, 96, 97, N.Y. State Edn. Dept. Workforce Preparation grantee, 1993-94, N.Y. State Edn. Dept. Sch.-to-Work grantee, 1995-96. Mem. ASCD, Nat. Sci. Tchrs. Assn. (exemplary sci. tchrs. award 1982), N.Y. State Sci. Suprs. (bd. dirs., pres. 1991), Sci. Tchrs. Assn. N.Y. State (outstanding sci. tchrs. award 1983, fellows award 1990, pres. 1993), Phi Delta Kappa. Home: 3 Taft Pl Cornwall On Hudson NY 12520-1713 Office: Newburgh Free Acad 201 Fullerton Ave Newburgh NY 12550-3718

SAUBEL, KATHERINE SIVA, Indian culture consultant, educator; b. Los Coyotes Indian Reservation, Calif., Mar. 7, 1920; d. Juan C. and Melana Sewaill; m. Mariano Saubel, Oct. 2, 1940 (dec.); 1 child, Allen. Grad. high sch., Palm Springs, Calif. Tchr.'s asst. dept. anthropology UCLA, 1959-60; cons. to Dr. Hansjakob Seiler, U. Cologne, Banning, Calif., Germany, 1964-74; on Cahuilla Indian culture throughout U.S., 1960—; pres., editor press Malki Mus., Banning, 1964—; lectr. U. Cologne, 1971; vis. lectr. U. Calif., Riverside, 1990; lectr. to sch. classes, Indian gatherings, 1958—. Author: Kunvachmal: A Cahuilla Tale, 1969; co-author: Temelpakh: Cahuilla Knowledge and Use of Plants, 1972, Chem'villu' (Lets Speak Cahuilla), 1981. Mem. Native Am. Heritage Commn., Calif.; speaker to various orgns. fighting nuclear and hazardous waste dumps in areas significant to Native Ams.; keynote spkr. Symposium on Am. Indian Religious Freedom, UCLA, 1992. Named County Historian of Yr., Riverside County Hist. Soc., 1986; named to Nat. Women's Hall of Fame, 1993. Home: PO Box 373 Banning CA 92220 Office: Malki Mus Morongo Indian Reservation PO Box 578 Banning CA 92220

SAUDEK, MARTHA FOLSOM, artist, educator; b. Palo Alto, Calif., Nov. 27, 1923; d. David Morrill and Clinton Erwin (Stone) Folsom; m. William Morrison Kingsley, Dec. 3, 1943 (div. 1971); 1 child, Lucy Clinton Kingsley; m. Victor Mead Saudek, Aug. 18, 1973. BA, Pomona Coll., 1947. Tchr. Concord (Calif.) Sch. Dist., 1949-51; tchr. Hermosa Beach (Calif.) City Schs., 1966-76, adminstrv. asst. to supt., 1977-81. Contbg. artist: (books) Painting With Passion, 1994, How to Paint Trees, Flowers, and Foliage, 1995, How to Paint Water, 1996. Sch. bd. dirs. Manhattan Beach (Calif.) Sch. Dist., 1964-72, pres., 1965. Named to Top 100, Arts for the Parks, 1994, 96, One of Nat. Gold Winners, Grumbacher Hall of Fame, 1995. Mem. Calif. Art Club, Salmagundi Club (assoc.), Allied Artists Am. (assoc.). Democrat. Home: 7216 Kentwood Ave Los Angeles CA 90045-1222

SAUER, ANNE KATHERINE, glass blower, artist, educator; b. Madison, Wis., Sept. 2, 1958; d. Collin Harold and Margaret (Isabell (Roberts) S. BS, U. Wis., 1982; MFA, Mass. Coll. Art, Boston, 1987. Owner, mgr. Brick House Glass, Madison, 1989; lectr., demonstrator Madison Art Ctr., 1992, Madison East H.S., 1992, Univ. League, 1993. Exhibited in group shows Valperine Gallery, Madison, 1992, City-County Arts, Madison, 1993, Newell Gallery, Waunakee, Wis., 1993, 94, Blue Bird Gallery, Prairie du Sac, Wis., 1994; work represented in various mags. Home: 3860 N River Hills Dr Tucson AZ 85720 Office: Brick House Glass 6777 E River Rd Tucson AZ 85715-2045

SAUER, CLAIRE, state legislator; b. Valley Stream, N.Y., Mar. 12, 1929; d. Harry Charles and Florence Gertrude (Tews) Essig; m. Frederick Sauer, Oct. 7, 1953 (dec. May 1989); children: Frederick, David. BS in Indsl. and Labor Rels., Cornell U., 1951. Asst. to pres. Glover Assocs., mgmt. cons., 1951-53; rschr., writer L.I. Assn. Commerce and Industry, 1972-74; asst. to dir. program for urban and policy scis. SUNY, Stony Brook, N.Y., 1974-76; legislator Suffolk County, Riverhead, N.Y., 1976-78; realtor S.M. Strong, Inc., Old Lyme, Conn., 1980-90; mem. Conn. Gen. Assembly, Hartford, 1995—. Former chmn. Suffolk County Charter Revision Commn.; former mem. Suffolk County Youth Bd., Huntington Youth Bd.; former mem. Huntington Town Dem. Com.; former mem. bd. dirs. Literacy Vols., Lyme (Conn.) Land Conservation Trust, Lymes Youth Svc. Bur.; former mem. Lyme Bd. Fin.; former registrar of voters Town of Lyme; chmn. Lyme Affordable Housting Com.; sec.-treas. Joshuatown Assn.; v.p. Taxpayers Alliance To Serve Conn.; former selectwoman Town of Lyme. Mem. ACLU, AAUW, LWV (past bd. dirs. N.Y. State, past pres. Suffolk County coun., former govt. dir. and fiscal affairs specialist Conn. bd. dirs., pres. Lower Conn. Valley 1982-88, mem. state bd. dirs. 1989-94), NOW, Lyme-Old Lyme C. of C. (pres. 1982), Audubon Soc., Ams. United for Separation Ch. and State, Child and Family Assn. Southeastern Conn., Coalition To Stop Gun Violence, Common Cause, Concord Coalition, Conn. Nat. Abortion Rights League, Connecticut River Mus., Florence Griswold Mus., Goodspeed Opera House Found., Handgun Control, Literacy Vols., Lyme Pub. Hall Assn., Lyme Art Assn., Am. Assn. Ret. Persons, Mental Health Assn. Conn., Nature Conservancy, Nat. Women's Polit. Caucus, Old Saybrook C. of C., People for Am. Way, Planned Parenthood. Congregationalist. Home: 47 Mitchell Hill Rd Lyme CT 06371 Office: Conn Legislature Legis Office Bldg Hartford CT 06106

SAUER, MELANIE SUZANNE, college dean; b. Mesa, Ariz., Feb. 1, 1963; d. Cliff and Jacqueline F. (Wisherd) S. BA in Acctg. and Bus. Mgmt., Whitworth Coll., 1985; MA in Edn., Azusa Pacific U., 1988. Cons. mktg. Spokane (Wash.) Symphony, 1985-86; residence hall dir. Azusa (Calif.) Pacific U., 1986-88; career counseling intern, residence hall dir. San Diego State U., 1988-89; instr. Sch. Edn., area dir. U. So. Calif., L.A., 1989-93; activities coord. Marymount, Rancho Palos Verdes, Calif., 1994; asst. dean students Scripps Coll., Claremont, Calif., 1994—; orgnl. cons. ednl. opportunity programs Cerritos (Calif.) Coll., 1993; women's issues office adv. U. So. Calif., 1989-94. Campaign asst. Bill Clinton for U.S. Pres., Pasadena, Calif., 1992. Mem. Nat. Assn. Student Pers. Adminstrs. (chairperson new profls. network region VI 1994-95), Assn. Coll. Pers. Adminstrs., Western Assn. Chief Housing Officers (chairperson so. rap 1991-92, exec. com. 1995-96). Democrat. Episcopalian. Office: Scripps Coll Dean Students 1030 Columbia Claremont CA 91711

SAUERBREY, ELLEN ELAINE RICHMOND, radio talk show host; b. Balt., Sept. 9, 1937; d. Edgar Arthur and Ethel Frederika (Landgraf) Richmond; m. Wilmer John Emil Sauerbrey, June 27, 1959. AB summa cum laude in Biology and English, Western Md. Coll., 1959. Biology instr., chmn. sci. dept. Baltimore County Sch. System, 1959-64; dist. mgr. Baltimore County U.S. Census, 1970; Md. Ho. of Dels., Annapolis, 1978-95, minority leader, 1986-95; radio talk show host Sta. WBAL; Rep. candidate for Gov., 1994. Rep. Nat. Committee Woman, Md., 1996—; del. Rep. Nat. Convs., 1968, 76, 84, 88, 92, 96, mem. credentials com., 1984, platform com., chmn. subcom. on economy, 1977; vice chmn. Rep. State Ctrl. Com. of Balt. County, 1966-71; trustee Md. Coun. Econ. Edn., Franklin Sq. Hosp.; founder United Citizens for Md.'s Future; mem. govt. activities com. United Cerebral Palsey Ctrl. Md.; nat. chmn. Am. Legis. exec. Coun., 1990-91. Recipient Pvt. Property award Greater Balt. Bd. Realtors, 1984; named Legislator of Yr., Md. Assn. Builders and Contractors, 1982, Am. Legis. Exec. Coun., 1986, Western Md. Coll. Alum of Yr., 1988, Outstanding Legis. Leader, Am. Legis. Exec. Coun., 1992, Rep. Woman of Yr., Md. Rep. Party, 1995. Mem. DAR, Nat. Fedn. rep. Women (Margaret Chase Smith award 1995), Md. Fedn. Rep. Women, Am. Legis. exch. Coun. (chmn. emeritus), Md. Farm Bur., Md. Conservative Union, Beta Beta, Beta, Phi Beta Kappa. Presbyterian.

SAUERBRUN, SUSAN JO, artist; b. Warren, Ohio, Mar. 9, 1949; d. Jack Edward and Mary Colette (Lins) S. AA, Stephens Coll., Columbia, Mo., 1969, BFA, 1971; student, Sir John Cass Sch. Art, London, 1973-75, Johnson Atelier, Princeton, N.J., 1980; MFA Mason Gross Sch. of Art, Rutgers U., 1979. lectr. painting Havering Coll., Hornchurch, Eng., 1976-77; vis. artist Queens Coll., CUNY, N.Y.C., 1983; exch. scholar Am. Field Svc. Austria, 1966; artist in residence Henry St. Settlement, N.Y.C., 1981-82, Bronx (N.Y.) Coun. on Arts, 1984-90; one on one program Air Gallery, N.Y.C., 1982, 84. One-person shows include Amp Gallery, London, 1973, Maynard Gallery, Herts, Eng., 1975, Brownson Art Gallery, Manhattanville Coll., Purchase, N.Y., 1991; exhibited in group shows at White Chapel Art Gallery, London, 1977, Westbeth Gallery, N.Y.C., 1982, Morivioi Gallery, N.Y.C., 1983, Inter Art Gallery, N.Y.C., 1985, Longwood Art Gallery, Bronx, N.Y., 1986, 87, The City Gallery, N.Y.C., 1981, 89, Bronx Mus. Art, 1991, The Times Sq. Hotel, N.Y.C., 1993, The Water Book Show, Albuquerque, 1996. Recipient Artist's Grant Artist's Space, N.Y.C., 1991. Mem. Coll. Art Assn., Long River T'ai Chi Circle.

SAUL, ANN, public relations executive; b. Columbia, Miss.; d. Otto and Ruth (Stamps) Saul. BS in Edn., Miss. Coll., 1961; postgrad., U. Louisville. Staff writer, circulation mgr. Louisville Mag. and Louisville Area C. of C., 1971-77; employee communications staff Brown & Williamson Tobacco Corp., 1977-79; media rels. staff NKC Hosps., 1979-80; pub. rels. and sales promotion staff Am. Temp. Svcs., 1980-82; sr. account supr. Daniel J. Edelman Pub. Rels., Chgo., 1982-87; dr. communication svcs. Nat. Easter Seal Soc., Chgo., 1987-89; v.p. Sam Huff & Assocs., Pub. Rels., Chgo., 1989-91; founder Ann Saul Pub. Rels., 1991—. Mem. Pub. Rels. Soc. Am., Publicity Club of Chgo. (Silver Trumpet 1985, 95, bd. dir.).

SAUL, BARBARA ANN, English studies educator; b. Vincennes, Ind., Feb. 20, 1940; d. Charles Dudley and Essie Faye (York) Green; children: Beth Suzanne, Becca Lynn, Brian William. BA with honors, So. Ill. U., Carbondale, 1961; MS, So. Ill. U., Edwardsville, 1988. Cert. secondary English tchr., spl. reading K-12 tchr., Mo.; cert. lang. arts specialist, K-12, English 6-12, Ill. English tchr. James Island High Sch., Charleston, S.C., 1961-63, Waterloo (Ill.) High Sch., 1963-65; instr. rhetoric and composition Belleville Area Coll., 1966-67; homebound tchr. Belleville Twp. High Sch., 1966-73; Title I reading tchr. Freeburg (Ill.) Community High Sch., 1973-80; grad. asst. So. Ill. U., Edwardsville, 1986-87; reading specialist Hazelwood Schs., St. Louis, 1987-92; tchr. English East Richland H.S., Olney, Ill., 1995-96; instr. Lion's Quest, 1988-91; team mem. Write-On project Highland (Ill.) Cmty. Schs., 1980-83; clinician Edwardsville Adult Literacy Prescription Project, 1986-88; presenter Mo/IRA State Conv., 1991; coordinating tchr. Intergenerational Oral History Gateway Writing Project, 1991-92; securities rep. Equitable Assurance Co. Bd. dirs. presch. 1st Presbyn. Ch., Belleville, 1969-73; mem. coun., conf. del. Evang. United Ch. of Christ, Highland, 1979-85, mem. choir, 1985-87; mem. Jr. High Reading Curriculum Revision Com. Mem. Sigma Kappa, Phi Kappa Phi, Kappa Delta Pi, Beta Sigma Phi. Home and Office: 1209 N Morgan St Olney IL 62450-1941

SAUL, STEPHANIE, journalist; b. St. Louis, Jan. 28, 1954; d. Elmer William and Nancy (Cromer) S.; m. Walt Bogdanich, Jan. 2, 1982; children: Nicholas Walter, Peter Eric. BA, U. Miss., 1975. Reporter New Albany (Miss.) Gazette, 1974, Clarion-Ledger, Jackson, Miss., 1975-80, The Plain Dealer, Cleve., 1980-84; nat. corr. Newsday, Melville, N.Y., 1984—. Recipient Silver Gavel award ABA, 1980, George Polk award for regional reporting, 1981, Nat. Press Club award, 1990, IRE award Investigative Reporters and Editors, 1995, Headliner award Atlantic City Press Club, 1995, Roy Howard award Scripps Howard Found., 1995, Pulitzer prize for investigative reporting, 1995. Office: Newsday 235 Pinelawn Rd Melville NY 11747-4250

SAULMON, SHARON ANN, librarian; b. Blackwell, Okla., June 13, 1947; d. Ellis Gordon and Willa Mae Overman; 1 child, John Henry. AA, No. Okla. Coll., 1967; BA, Ctrl. State U., 1969, MBA, 1987; MLS, U. Okla., 1974; postgrad., Okla. State U., 1982. Children's libr. Met. Libr. Sys., Oklahoma City, 1969-74, coord. pub. svcs., 1974-77, asst. chief ext. svcs., 1977-80; reference/special projects libr. Rose State Coll., Midwest City, Okla., 1980-91, head libr., 1991—; adj. faculty Rose State Coll., 1983—; program chair Global Okla. Multi-Cultural Festival, 1993; mem. nat. adv. panel for assessment of sch. and pub. librs. in support of nat. edn. goals, 1995—; spkr. various civic and profl. orgns. Contbr. articles to profl. jours. Bd. dirs. Areawide Aging Agy., 1974-77; chair Met. Libr. Commn., 1990—, disbursing agt., chair fin. com., 1986-88, long-range planning com., 1985-87; chair bd. dirs. Met. Librs. Network Ctrl. Okla., 1989-90, chair alternative funding com., 1990—, newsletter editor, 1987-89, chair electronic media com., 1987-89. Recipient Outstanding Contbn. award Met. Libr. Sys., Friends of the Libr., 1990, Disting. Svc. award Okla. Libr. Assn., 1995. Mem. AAUW, Am. Libr. Trustee Assn. (pres. 1994-95, 1st v.p., pres. elect 1993-94, newsletter editor 1989-93, chair publs. com. 1987-92, regional v.p. 1985-88, chair speakers bur. com. 1991-92), Assn. Coll. and Rsch. Librs. (Cmty. and Jr. Coll. sect.), Pub. Libr. Assn., Am. Mktg. Assn., Okla. Libr. Assn. (conf. preview editor 1990-91, chair trustees divsn. 1989-90, mem. coms., disting. svc. award 1995). Democrat. Methodist. Office: Rose State Coll Libr 6420 SE 15th St Midwest City OK 73110-2704

SAULS, ALLISON HOUSTON, art educator; b. Columbus, Ohio, Aug. 4, 1949; d. Loren Charles and Beulah Mae (Veal) Miller; m. James Mack Sauls, Aug. 31, 1979; children: Zachary Houston, Christopher Bennett. BA, Huntingdon Coll., 1971; MA, U. Ga., 1981; PhD, Emory U., 1993. Instr. U. Ga., Athens, 1982-85; asst. prof. U. Tenn., Chattanooga, 1985; libr. cons. Nat. Park Svc. Regional, Atlanta, 1987-89; asst. prof. Mo. Western State Coll., St. Joseph, 1993—. Co-author: Historic Places in Central Alabama: A Preliminary Inventory, 1973; rsch. asst. (book) Frederic Guitheim at 80-A Festschrift, 1988, (film) The Making of Atlanta, 1989-90, Emmy nomination, 1990; editl. asst. About Atlanta: A Research Guide, 1988. Commr. Landmarks Commn., St. Joseph, 1995—. Grantee Nat. Endowment Arts, 1985, Dept. Interior, 1972-73; Mary Wallace Kirk scholar Agnes Scott Coll., Decatur, Ga., 1987-89. Mem. Coll. Art Assn., Soc. for Cinema Studies. Democrat. Episcopalian. Home: 1308 N 11th St Saint Joseph MO 64501 Office: Mo Western State Coll 4525 Downs Dr Saint Joseph MO 64507

SAULS, BETTY JANE, educator; b. Lake City, Fla., July 25, 1952; d. William Robert and Martha Jean (Jenkins) Terry; m. Perry Robert Sauls, May 7, 1977; children: Heather Lorraine, Jerrad Kyle. AA, Lake City C.C., 1972; B of Elem. Edn., U. West Fla., 1974; M of Elem. Edn., Fla. A&M U., 1991. Tchr. elem. sch. Dixie County Sch. Dist., Cross City, Fla., 1974-79; tchr. elem. sch. Columbia County Sch. Dist., Lake City, Fla., 1979-92, tchr. mid. sch., 1992—; chair Ft. White (Fla.) Sch. Adv. Coun., 1994-96, co-chair, 1992-94, 96—. Pianist United Meth. Ch., Branford, Fla., 1995—; booster mem. Columbia Youth Soccer Assn., Lake City, 1986—, Columbia High Soccer Boosters, Lake City, 1994—. Mem. AAUW, Columbia Tchrs. Assn. (sec. 1991-92, pres. 1994—), Columbia Pub. Schs. Found. (bd. dirs. 1994—). Democrat. Home: Rt 2 Box 506 Lake City FL 32024 Office: Ft White Pub Sch Rt 4 Box 1000 Fort White FL 32038

SAUM, ELIZABETH PAPE, community volunteer; b. Evanston, Ill., Aug. 7, 1930; d. Karl James and Catherine (Schwall) Pape; m. William Joseph Saum, Dec. 31, 1960; children: JeanMarie, Katherine Anne, Mary Elizabeth. BA in English cum laude, Fontbonne Coll., 1952; MA in English, Northwestern U., 1958. Cert. tchr., Ill. Tchr. Our Lady of Perpetual Help, Glenview, Ill., 1952-55, Wilmette (Ill.) Jr. High Sch., 1955-61; dir. religion edn. St. Paul's Ch., Valparaiso, Ind., 1972-76; activities dir. Heritage Manor Nursing Home, Plano, Tex., 1982-84; exec. dir. Jessamine County Assn. Exceptional Citizens, Nicholasville, Ky., 1985-89; ret., 1989. Pres. bd. dirs. Women's Neighborly Orgn., Lexington, 1977-81; mem. Bluegrass Long-Term Care Ombudsman, Lexington, 1984-89, pres., 1986-88; bd. dirs. Women's History Coalition Ky., Midway, 1985-90; bd. dirs. Sr. Citizens East, Louisville, 1991-93, treas., 1992-93; creator, pres. Ky. Women's Heritage Mus., Lexington, 1986-90; adminstrn. coord. Transfiguration Ch., Goshen, Ky., 1991-93. Mem. AAUW (bd. dirs. Ky. br. 1977-81, 85—, named gift honoree 1988, v.p. Ednl. Found. 1988-94, 95-96, co-pres. Ky. chpt. 1994-96, named gift honoree Lexington br. 1987, pres. 1984-86, 88-90, Louisville br. editor newsletter 1990-93, treas. 1991-93, v.p. Ednl. Found. 1991-93), Lexington Newcomers (editor newsletter 1976-78), Trigg County Quilter's Guild (pres. 1995—). Democrat. Roman Catholic. Home: PO Box 1510 Cadiz KY 42211-1510

SAUNDERS, ADAH WILSON, physical education educator; b. Balt.; d. William Llewellyn and Irene Bertha (Dorkins) Wilson; 1 child, Leigh Robert. BS, Hampton U., 1967; MS, Columbia U. Teacher's Coll., 1971. Instr. phys. edn. Hunter Coll CUNY, N.Y.C., 1967-68, Bronx C.C., N.Y.C., 1968-69; phys. edn. tchr. N.Y.C. Bd. Edn., 1971—, dean students, 1993—; coach N.Y. Jr. Tennis League; dir. summer camps N.Y.C. Dept. of Human Resources, 1969-72. Inventor: (bd. game) The Presidency; patentee: Rollice Shoe, 1991. Grantee N.Y.C. Bd. Edn., The Early Morning Health Club, 1985. Mem. United Fedn. Tchrs., Am. Fedn. Tchrs., Queens C. of C. Home: 41-10 Bowne St Apt 7V Flushing NY 11355-5612 Office: Leonardo Da Vinci Sch 98-50 50th Ave Corona NY 11368-2757

SAUNDERS, ARLENE, opera singer; b. Cleve., Oct. 5, 1935. MusB, Baldwin-Wallace Coll., 1957. Tchr. voice Rutgers U., New Brunswick, N.J., 1987-88; tchr. classical vocal repertoire Abraham Goodman Sch., N.Y.C., 1987-88; advisor, tchr. vocal dept. NYU, 1990—, tchr. master classes, head opera dept., 1990-96; tchr. master classes Baldwin Wallace Coll., Santa Fe Opera Co., etc.; founder, dir. Opera Mobilé, Inc., N.Y.C., 1991—; adjudicator Met. Opera Regional Auditions, Liederkranz Voice Auditions, etc. Debut Milan Opera, 1961; Met. Opera debut in Die Meistersinger, 1976; specializes in Strauss and Wagner; performer with Phila. Opera, Lyric Opera, Houston Opera, Covent Garden, London, Teatro Colon, Buenos Aires, San Francisco Opera, Vienna Staatsoper, Paris Opera, Australian Opera, Sydney, Berlin Deutsche Opera, Munich Staatsoper, Hamburg State Opera, 1963-86, Rome Opera, Brussels Opera, Maggio Musicale, Florence, Italy, Geneva (Switzerland) Opera, Berlin Festival, Lisbon Opera, Glyndebourne Festival Opera, Eng., English Opera North, Boston Opera, N.Y.C. Opera; performed world premieres of Beatrix Cenci, 1971, Jakobowsky und der Oberst, 1965, Help, Help, The Globolinks, 1968, Ein Stern Geht Auf Aus Jaakob, 1970 (Gold medal Vercelli (Italy) voice competition); appeared in opera films including Arabella (title role), Meistersaenger (Eva), Marriage of Figaro (Countess), Help, Help the Globolinks (Mme. Euterpova), Der Freischuetz (Agathe), Gasparone (Carlotta); recs. for Philips and Victor. N.Y.C. Mayor's award, 1962; Kammersängerin Hamburg, 1967. Mem. Pi Kappa Lambda (Epsilon Phi chpt.). Address: 535 E 86th St New York NY 10028-7533

SAUNDERS, BETTY MARIE, musician, educator; b. Jamesport, Mo., June 17, 1940; d. Walter Charles Stoller and Enna Mabel Purdy; m. William Saunders, Oct. 4, 1986. B Music, Eastman Sch. Music, 1961, M Music, 1963. Owner Walker Music Sch., Rochester, N.Y., 1966-87, Peak Performance Tng., Rochester, N.Y., 1988-96; contract trainer Eagle Internat., Rochester, N.Y., 1993-96; aerobics instr. Pat Drum Aerobics, Rochester, N.Y., 1980-86; adj. voice prof. Monroe C.C., Rochester, 1978-96; pres. Accordion Tchrs. Guild, 1964-65; program dir. Rochester Profl. Sales Assn., 1992-93. Author: You Are the Music: Discovering God's Plan for Your Life, 1995; composer: Choose Your Own Flight, 1980, Start Living Today, 1995, You Are the Music, 1996. Cons. Jasco Scholarship Program East H.S., Rochester, 1992-96; mem. exec. com. Christian Women's Club, Rochester, 1983-91. Mem. Toastmasters (v.p. 1989, pres. 1990-91, Toastmaster of Yr. 1990), Success Communicators Coalition. Republican. Home: 18 Sibley Pl Rochester NY 14607

SAUNDERS, DANIELLE MICHELLE, physician, educator; b. Smithtown, N.Y., Nov. 14, 1970; d. Richard Gilbert and Maureen Eileen (Pardee) S. BA, Columbia (S.C.) Coll., 1991; MD, U. South Fla., 1995. Tchr. Bapt. Hosp., Columbia, S.C., 1989-91; clin. fellow Harvard U., Boston, 1995—; resident in gen. surgery Mass. Gen. Hosp., Boston, 1995—. Chair cmty. svc. project Downtown Boston Young Adults, 1996. Recipient Leader of Leaders award Key Club Internat., 1988; Downtown Tampa Bus. and Profl. Women's Assn. scholar, 1995. Mem. AMA, Assn. Women Surgeons, Alpha Omega Alpha, Omicron Delta Kappa. Home: 10 Emerson Pl # 24H Boston MA 02114 Office: Mass Gen Hosp Dept Surgery 32 Fruit St Boston MA 02114

SAUNDERS, DORIS EVANS, editor, educator, business executive; b. Chgo., Aug. 8, 1921; d. Alvesta Stewart and Thelma (Rice) Evans; m. Vincent E. Saunders Jr., Oct. 28, 1950 (div. 1963); children: Ann Camille, Vincent E. III. B.A., Roosevelt U., 1951; M.S., M.A., Boston U., 1977; postgrad., Vanderbilt U., 1984. Sr. library asst. Chgo. Pub. Library, 1942-46, prin. reference librarian, 1946-49; librarian Johnson Pub. Co., 1949-66, dir. book div., 1961-66, 73-77; prof., coord. print journalism Jackson (Miss.) State U., 1977—, acting chair dept. mass communication, 1990—, chair, 1991—; Disting. minority lectr. U. Miss., Oxford, 1986-96; ret., 1996; pres. Ancestor Hunting, Inc., Chgo., 1982—; dir. community rels. Chgo. State Coll., 1968-70; acting dir. instnl. devel. and community rels Chgo. State Coll., 1969-70; columnist Chgo. Daily Defender, 1966-70, Chgo. Courier, 1970-73; staff assoc. Office of Chancellor, U. Ill. at Chgo. Circle, 1970-73. Host: radio program The Think Tank, 1971-72; writer, producer: (TV) Our People, 1968-70; producer, host: Faculty Review Forum, Sta. WJSU, 1987-93; author: Black Society, 1976; assoc. editor: Negro Digest mag, 1962-66; editor: The Day They Marched, 1963, The Kennedy Years and the Negro, 1964, DuBois: A Pictorial Biography, 1979, Wouldn't Take Nothin' for My Journey (L. Berry), 1981; compiler, editor: The Negro Handbook, 1966, The Ebony Handbook, 1974; pub. Kith and Kin; contbr. to profl. jours., mags. Bd. dirs. Arts Alliance, Jackson-Hinds County, Miss., 1993; mem. com. on racial recognition Diocese of Miss. Mem. NAACP. Democrat. Episcopalian. Address: PO Box 2413 Chicago IL 60690-2413

SAUNDERS, DOROTHY ANN, insurance company executive, sales management; b. Roxbury, N.C., Nov. 29, 1932; d. James William and Anna Bell (Wesley) Rice; m. Bernard L. Lewis, June 10, 1950 (dec. Jan. 1957); m. J.R. Saunders, Nov. 26, 1976 (dec. May 1981). Student, Md. U., 1950-53. Bookeeper, office mgr. TTN Cosmetics, Bethesda, Md., 1958; owner, mgr. Donnel's Hall of Gifts, Washington, 1959-63, Gifts, Inc., Washington, 1959-63; with U.S. Govt. Health, Edn., Welfare, Bethesda, 1965-73; owner, mgmt.

in sales Dorothy Saunders Ins. Agy., Forest, Va., 1973—; vis. spkr. Bus. & Profl. Woman's Assn., Brookneal, Va., 1986-87; mem. bd. rsch. advisor ABI. Mem. Nat. Trust for Historic Preservation. Fellow Am. Biog. Inst.; mem. Internat. Platform Assn., Am. Lyceum Assn. Democrat. Baptist. Home and Office: RR 1 Box 166D Huddleston VA 24104-9765

SAUNDERS, HELEN MARIE, realtor, real estate company executive; b. Garnett, Kans., Aug. 18, 1924; d. David George and Julia Teresa (Prochaskova) Brecheisen; m. Robert Leroy Saunders, Aug. 24, 1946; children: Robert L. Jr., J. Michael, Gregory Wayne. Teaching cert., Kans. State Tchrs. Coll., 1942. Rchr. Washington Rural Sch., Garnett, Kans., 1942-43; cost acctg. clk. Beech Aircraft, Wichita, Kans., 1943-44; sec. Farm & Home Adminstrn., Kansas City, Mo., 1944-46, War Dept., Wiesbaden, Germany, 1946-49, USAF, various locations, 1949-65; owner Sec. Svcs., Universal City, Tex., 1965-66; realtor Aero, Tucker, Schoolcraft, Universal City, Tex., 1966-88; owner Kirk & Saunders Realty, Universal City, Tex., 1988—. Dir. Metrocom C. of C., Randolph AFB, 1979-82. Mem. Beta Sigma Phi (pres. 1964—). Republican. Methodist.

SAUNDERS, KATHRYN A., retired data processing administrator; b. Elgin, Minn., Apr. 12, 1920; d. William P. and Mathilda M. (Mielke) Hagner; m. James L. Saunders, June 14, 1952; children: Gary, Wade, Brian. BA, U. Calif., Berkeley, 1941; cert., Coll. of Marin, Kentfield, Calif., 1948. Mem. gen. staff Fed. Res. Bank, San Francisco; with civilian pers./payroll dept. USAF, Hamilton AFB, Calif.; coord. data processing Sir Francis Drake High Sch., San Anselmo, Calif. Sec. program resource United Meth. Women, 1988—, treas., 1994—. Mem. AAUW, Calif. Sch. Employees Assn., Calif. Scholarship Fedn. (life), Nat. Assn. Ret. Fed. Employees, Coll. of Environ. Design Alumni Assn. of U. Calif. Berkeley, Order of Golden Rose of Delta Zeta. Address: 118 Tamal Vista Dr San Rafael CA 94901-1646

SAUNDERS, LAURA S., education educator; b. Augusta, Ga., Aug. 22, 1953; d. John C. and Mary G. (Fields) S.; children: Danielle Sheehan, Mary Truesdale, Willie Truesdale. BA, U. S.C., 1975, MEd, 1990, PhD, 1993. Cert. tchr., S.C. Dir. Rebekah Christian Sch., Corpus Christi, Tex., 1982-83; tchr. North Ctrl. H.S., Kershan, S.C., 1987-93; asst. prof. edn. U. S.C., Aiken, 1993—; cons. S.C. Dept. Edn., Columbia, 1995—. Contbr. articles to profl. publs. S.C. Dept. Edn. classroom grantee, 1990, 91. Mem. Aiken County Reading Assn. (v.p. 1995—), Nat. Coun. Tchrs. English, Internat. Reading Assn. Home: 615 Douglas Dr Aiken SC 29803 Office: U SC-Aiken 171 University Pkwy Aiken SC 29801

SAUNDERS, PATRICIA GENE, textbook editor; b. Tulsa, Okla., Nov. 29, 1946; d. Eugene Merritt and Patricia May (Hough) Knight; m. Joseph Eugene Saunders, June 24, 1989. BA, Baylor U., 1969. Nat. advt. sec. KTVT-TV, Ft. Worth, 1969-71; tchr. Arlington (Tex.) Ind. Sch. Dist., 1971-77, Garland (Tex.) Ind. Sch. Dist., 1977-79; spl. projects assoc. Electronic Data Systems, Dallas, 1979-81; adminstrv. asst. Diversified Innovators, Dallas, 1981-82; system ops. mgr. Span Instruments, Plano, Tex., 1982-86; data processing mgr. Claire Mfg., Addison, Ill., 1986-87, Everpure, Inc., Westmont, Ill., 1987-88; software cons. Software Alternatives, Inc., Downers Grove, Ill., 1988-89; data processing asst., cons. J&J Maintenance, Inc., Austin, Tex., 1989-90; pres., computer cons. Cardinal Software Solutions, Inc., Austin, 1990-93; editor Holt, Rinehart & Winston, Inc., Austin, 1993—. Contbr. articles to Tex. Hwy. Patrol Assn. Mag., Hill Country Sun, South Austin News, Police Vet. Mem. Smithsonian Instn., N.Y. Met. Mus. Fine Art, Soc. of Children's Book Writers and Illustrators, Austin Writers' League, Baylor Alumni Assn., Nat. Wildflower Ctr. Republican. Baptist. Home: 410 Teal Ln Kyle TX 78640-8888 Office: Holt Rinehart & Winston 1120 Capital Of Tex Hwy S Austin TX 78746

SAUNDERS, SANDRA GRANT, secondary school educator; b. Houston, Sept. 26, 1947; d. James Mingaye and Jane Ethel (Singleton) Grant; m. Douglas Jay Saunders, Aug. 10, 1968; children: Ian Grant, Julie Elizabeth. BA, Alfred (N.Y.) U., 1968; ADN, Broome C.C., Binghamton, N.Y., 1976; postgrad., Elmira Coll., 1987. Nurse various hosps., 1976-85; tchr. Whitney Point (N.Y.) Ctrl. Sch., 1985-88, Newark Valley (N.Y.) Ctrl. Sch., 1988—. Mem. Tioga County Dem. Com., Owego, N.Y.; sec. ch. coun. St. John's Ch., Newark Valley; sec. Project Neighbor, Newark Valley; tchr. Literary Vols. of Am., Endwell, N.Y. Mem. N.Y. State Assn. Fgn. Lang. Tchrs., N.Y. State United Tchrs., Newark Valley United Tchrs. (former sec.).

SAUNDERS, SUSAN PRESLEY, real estate executive; b. South Bend, Ind., Feb. 27, 1956; d. William Presley Jr. and Anne Summers (Winburn) S. Student, Converse Coll., 1974-77, Sandhills Community Coll., Southern Pines, N.C., 1978-86. Lic. real estate broker, N.C.; ins. lic., N.C.; notary pub.; accredited Relo coord. With Gouger, O'Neal & Saunders, Southern Pines, 1973-74, 75, Ceralon Mfg., Aberdeen, N.C., 1976; bank teller The Carolina Bank, Aberdeen, 1977-78; from clk. to v.p. fin. G.O.S., Inc., Southern Pines, 1978—. Mem. NAFE, Am. Soc. Profl. and Exec. Women, Am. Inst. Profl. Bookkeepers, Sandhills Area C. of C. (membership com. So. Pines chpt. 1989-94), Moore County Leadership Inst. Democrat. Presbyterian. Home: 130 Pebble Bch Southern Pines NC 28387-2345 Office: GOS Inc 177 W Pennsylvania Ave Southern Pines NC 28387-5428

SAUNDERS, TERRY ROSE, lawyer; b. Phila., July 13, 1942; d. Morton M. and Esther (Hauptman) Rose; m. George Lawton Saunders Jr., Sept. 21, 1975. BA, Barnard Coll., 1964; JD, NYU, 1973. Bar: D.C. 1973, Ill. 1976, U.S. Dist. Ct. (no. dist.) Ill. 1976, U.S. Ct. Appeals (7th cir.) 1976, U.S. Supreme Ct. 1983. Assoc. Williams & Connolly, Washington, 1973-75; assoc. Jenner & Block, Chgo., 1975-80, ptnr., 1981-86; ptnr. Susman, Saunders & Buehler, Chgo., 1987-94; pvt. practice Law Offices of Terry Rose Saunders, Chgo., 1995—. Author: (with others) Securities Fraud: Litigating Under Rule 10b-5, 1989. Recipient Robert B. McKay award NYU Sch. Law. Mem. ABA (co-chair class actions and derivative suits com. sect. litigation 1992-95, task force on merit selection of judges), Ill. State Bar Assn., Chgo. Bar Assn., NYU Alumni Assn. (bd. dirs. 1985—), Order of Coif, Union League Club. Office: 30 N La Salle St Chicago IL 60602-2508

SAUNDERS-SMITH, GAIL ANN, educational administrator, consultant; b. Pitts., Nov. 23, 1952; d. John E. and Ruth L. Saunders; m. Charles D. Smith, June 21, 1975. BS in Early Childhood Edn., Kent State U., 1974, MA in Early Childhood Edn., 1977; MS in Adminstrn. and Supervision, Youngstown State U., 1981; PhD in Elem. Edn., U. Akron, 1994. Classroom tchr. Youngstown Diocese, Warren, Ohio, 1974-76; cooperating tchr. Kent (Ohio) State U. Lab. Sch., 1976-77; classroom tchr. Maplewood Bd. Edn., Cortland, Ohio, 1977-85; reading/lang. arts supr. Summit County Bd. Edn., Akron, Ohio, 1985-90; reading recovery tchr. leader Summit County Bd. Edn., Akron, 1986-89, coord. state and fed. programs, 1990-94; mgr. cons. svcs. Rigby, Chgo., 1994-96, mgr. content devel. for profl. devel. dept., 1996—; part-time faculty Kent (Ohio) State U., 1986-89; bd. mem. Stark, Summit, U. of Akron (Ohio) Tchrs. Applying Whole Lang. Group, 1987-96, Ohio Coun. Tchrs. English Lang. Arts, Columbus, Ohio, 1989-92; bd. mem. edn. com. Akron Symphony Orch., 1993-94. Author: (children's books) Giant's Breakfast, 1993, Half for You, Half for Me, 1993, Worms, 1993, How Dogs and Man Became Friends, 1993, Laughing Giraffes, 1991. Mem. Internat. Reading Assn., AAUW, Nat. Staff Devel. Coun., Phi Delta Kappa, Kappa Delta Pi, Pi Lambda Theta.

SAUNTRY, SUSAN SCHAEFER, lawyer; b. Bangor, Maine, May 7, 1943; d. William Joseph and Emily Joan (Guenter) Schaefer; m. John Philip Sauntry, Jr., Aug. 18, 1968; 1 child, Mary Katherine. BS in Foreign Service, Georgetown U., 1965, JD, 1975. Bar: D.C. 1975, U.S. Dist. Ct. D.C. 1975, U.S. Ct. Appeals (D.C. cir.) 1975, (4th cir.) 1977, (6th cir.) 1978, (10th cir.) 1983, U.S. Supreme Ct. 1983. Congl. relations asst. OEO, Washington, 1966-68; program analyst EEO Com., Washington, 1968-70, U.S. Dept. Army, Okinawa, 1970-72; assoc. Morgan, Lewis & Bockius, Washington, 1975-83, ptnr., 1983-94; of counsel Howe, Anderson & Steyer, PC, Washington, 1994—. Co-author: Employee Dismissal Law: Forms and Procedures, 1986; contbr. articles to profl. jours. Mem. ABA, D.C. Bar Assn., D.C. Women's Bar Assn., Am. Assn. Univ. Women, USA, Phi Beta Kappa, Pi Sigma Alpha. Democrat. Office: Ste 1050 1747 Pennsylvania Ave NW Washington DC 20006-4604

SAURWEIN, VIRGINIA FAY, international affairs specialist; b. Madrid, Feb. 24, 1928; d. George Nelson and Ruth Augusta (Zimmerman) S. BA, Carleton Coll., Northfield, Minn., 1950; MA, U. Denver, 1952. Adminstrv. sec. Collegiate Coun. for UN, Am. Assn. UN, N.Y.C., 1952-55; dir. edn. dept. Am. Assn. UN, N.Y.C., 1955-57; dir. publs. ctr. and program U.S. Com. for UN, UN Assn. U.S., N.Y.C., 1957-63, 63-65; program dir., editor Intercom Ctr. for War/Peace Studies, N.Y.C., 1965-70; non-govtl. orgns. officer UN Devel. Programme, N.Y.C., 1970-75; chief non-govtl. orgns. office Dept. Econ. and Social Affairs, UN, N.Y.C. and Geneva, 1975-88, 89-90; non-govtl. orgn. liaision officer UN Office, Geneva, 1988-89; liaison officer Vienna UN, N.Y.C., 1990; non-govtl. orgn. officer UN Crime Congress, Havana, Cuba, 1990, UN World Conf. on Women, Beijing, China, 1995; sec. com. on non-govtl. orgns. UN, N.Y.C., 1976-87; non-govtl. orgn. officer 19 major confs., 1975-88. Editor: Hommage to a Friend, 1964; updated: A Visual History of the United Nations, 1962; author, editor Intercom, 1968-70, Commitment, 1972-75. Founder, convenor, bd. mem.Women's World Banking, N.Y.C., 1975-85; mem. adv. com. YWCA, N.Y.C., 1960's; mem. bd. Sustainable End of Hunger Found., Accra, Ghana, 1991—. Mem. Soc. Internat. Devel., Fedn. Former Internat. Civil Servants (UN rep., chair non-govtl. affairs com. 1995—), Airedale Terrier Club Am. (rep. Am. Kennel Club 1990—), Airedale Terrier Club New Eng. (pres. 1976-77), Airedale Terrier Club Met. N.Y. (pres. 1989-90, 94-96). Democrat. Lutheran. Home: 32 Glen Dr South Salem NY 10590

SAUSMAN, KAREN, zoological park administrator; b. Chgo., Nov. 26, 1945; d. William and Annabell (Lofaso) S. BS, Loyola U., 1966; student, Redlands U., 1968. Keeper Lincoln Park Zoo, Chgo., 1964-66; tchr. Palm Springs (Calif.) Unified Sch., 1968-70; ranger Nat. Park Svc., Joshua Tree, Calif., 1968-70; zoo dir. The Living Desert, Palm Desert, Calif., 1970—; natural history study tour leader internat., 1974—; part-time instr. Coll. Desert Natural History Calif. Desert, 1975-78; field reviewer conservation grants Inst. Mus. Svcs., 1987—, MAP cons., 1987—, panelist, 1992—; internat. studbook keeper for Sand Cats, 1988—, for Cuvier's Gazelle, Mhorr Gazelle, 1990—; co-chair Arabian Oryx species survival plan propogation group, 1986-95; spkr. in field. Author Survival Captive Bighorn Sheep, 1982, Small Facilities- Opportunities and Obligations, 1983; wildlife illustrator books, mags, 1970—; editor Fox Paws newsletter Living Desert, 1970—, ann. reports, 1976—; natural sci. editor Desert Mag., 1979-82; compiler Conservation and Management Plan for Antelope, 1992; contbr. articles to profl. jours. Past bd. dirs., sec. Desert Protective Coun.; adv. coun. Desert Bighorn Rsch. Inst., 1981-85; bd. dirs. Palm Springs Desert Resorts Convention and Visitors Bur., 1988-94; bd. dirs., treas. Coachella Valley Mountain Trust, 1989-92. Named Woman Making a Difference Soroptomist Internat., 1989, 93. Fellow Am. Assn. Zool. Parks and Aquariums (bd. dirs., accredation field reviewer, desert antelope taxon adv. group, caprid taxon adv. group, felid taxon adv. group, small population mgmt. adv. group, wildlife conservation and mgmt. com., chmn. ethics com. 1987, mem. com., internat. rels. com., ethics task force, pres'. award 1972-77, outstanding svc. award 1983, 88, editor newsletter, Zool. Parks and Aquarium Fundamentals 1982); mem. Internat. Species Inventory System (mgmt. com., policy adv. group 1980-96), Calif. Assn. Mus. (v.p. 1992-96), Calif. Assn. Zoos and Aquariums, Internat. Union Dirs. Zool. Gardens, Western Interpretive Assn. (so. Calif. chpt.), Am. Assn. Mus., Arboreta and Botanical Gardens So. Calif. (coun. dirs.), Soc. Conservation Biology, Nat. Audubon. Soc., Jersey Wildlife Preservation Trust Internat., Nature Conservancy, East African Wildlife Soc., African Wildlife Found., Kennel Club Palm Springs (past bd. dirs., treas. 1978-80), Scottish Deerhound Club Am. (editor Scottish Deerhounds in N.A., 1983, life mem. U.K. chpt.), Internat. Bengal Cat Soc. (pres. 1994-96). Office: The Living Desert 47 900 Portola Ave Palm Desert CA 92260

SAUTER, MARSHA JEANNE, elementary school educator; b. Ft. Wayne, Ind., Apr. 13, 1951; d. Donald Paul and Juanita Mae (Foltz) Harsch; m. Michael Charles Sauter, Dec. 11, 1971; 1 child, Paul Michael. Student, Ball State U., 1969-71; BS in Edn. summa cum laude, U. Cin., 1974. Cert. tchr., Ohio, Okla. 6th grade tchr. Norwood (Ohio) Schs., 1974-75, 1st grade tchr., 1975-77; kindergarten tchr. Mason (Ohio) Schs., 1979-81; 1st grade tchr. Oak Park Elem. Sch. Bartlesville (Okla.) Schs., 1988—, primary curriculum coord., 1992-95, 96—, mem. edn. com., 1991—, mem. English/math. textbook selection com., 1992, 93. Jr. H.S. youth advisor Good Shepherd Presbyn. Ch. Bartlesville, 1982-85, Sr. H.S. youth advisor, 1991-92, elder on session, 1985-88, 96—; mem. sunshine squad-crisis line Women Children in Crisis, Bartlesville, 1993—; sec. Bartlesville Cmty. Singers. Grantee Bartlesville Sch. Found., 1992, 94, 95. Mem. NEA, Nat. Coun. Tchrs. Math., Tchrs. Assn. of Whole Lang., Nat. Reading Assn., Okla. Reading Assn., Soc. for Prevention of Cruelty to Animals, Okla. Edn. Assn., Toastmasters (Competent Toastmaster award 1993, sec.-treas. 1994-95, v.p. membership 1995-96), Elks. Home: 365 Turkey Creek Rd Bartlesville OK 74006-8116 Office: Bartlesville Pub Schs Oak Park Elem 200 Forest Park Rd Bartlesville OK 74003-1503

SAUVÉ, JUDITH DIANE, healthcare services director; b. Winchester, Ontario, Can., Sept. 24, 1950; d. John Dwight and Myrtle Irene (Simmons) Dawley; m. Jean-Louis Sauvé, Sept. 9, 1972; children: Shawn Christopher, Danielle Andreé. Diploma in Nursing, Cornwall Regional Sch. Nursing, Can., 1971; BS, Upsala Coll., 1991; postgrad., East Stroudsburg U., 1995—. RN, N.J.; cert. BLS, sch. nurse. Staff nurse The Grace Hosp., Ottawa, Ontario, Can., 1971-72; staff and charge nurse Hotel Dieu Hosp., Cornwall, Ontario, Can., 1972-81; relief supr., staff nurse Andover (N.J.) Care Ctr., 1983-85; ind. pvt. duty nurse Andover, Hackettstown, N.J., 1985-87; staff nurse Blair Acad., Blairstown, N.J., 1987-88, dir. health svcs., 1988—; dept. head for health Blair Acad., Blairstown, 1989—. Mem. APHA, Nat. Assn. Sch. Nurses, Ind. and Sch. Health Assn., Warren County Sch. Nurses Assn., N.J. State Sch. Nurses Assn. Office: Blair Acad PO Box 600 Park St Blairstown NJ 07825

SAVAGE, DOROTHY, religious organization administrator; b. Cleve., Sept. 3, 1936; d. Thomas James and Nora Martha (Johnson) S. BA, St. Francis Coll., 1961; MA, Fordham U., 1974. Elem. sch. tchr. Bklyn. Roman Cath. Diocese, 1956-66; tchr. sci. St. Pascha Baylon Jr. High Sch., Queens, N.Y., 1966-68; assoc. youth ministries Nat. Coun. Chs., N.Y.C., 1968-73, dir. edn., 1976—; tchr. religion high Sch., Tampa., 1974-76. Mem. Religious Edn. Assn. (exec. dir. 1977-79, bd. dirs. 1990-96). Democrat. Office: Nat Coun Churches 475 Riverside Dr Rm 848 New York NY 10115

SAVAGE, M. SUSAN, mayor. Student, U. Aix-Marseilles, Aix-en-Provence, France, 1969, City of London Poly., Eng., 1972; BA in Sociology with honors, Beaver Coll., 1974. Pre-trial rep. Phila. Ct. Common Pleas, 1974-75; criminal justice planner Montgomery County Criminal Justice Unit, 1975-77; exec. dir. Met. Tulsa Citizens Crime Com., 1977-87; vol. coord. Vote Yes For Tulsa, 1987; chief of staff to mayor City of Tulsa, 1988-92, mayor, 1992—. Active Lee Elementary Sch. PTA; bd. dirs., treas. Okla. Crime Prevention Assn.; bd. dirs. Youth Svcs. of Tulsa County, 1984-88, pres., 1986-87; co-chair Safe Streets/Enhanced 911 Steering Com., 1987; mem. C. of C. Task Force/Community Edn. Network, 1983. Office: Office of Mayor City Hall Rm 1115 200 Civic Ctr Tulsa OK 74103-3827*

SAVAGE, RUTH HUDSON, poet, writer, speaker; b. Childress, Tex., Apr. 29, 1932; d. John Floyd and Eula Jemima (Cornelius) Hudson; m. Robert Berkes, Nov. 6, 1950 (div. June 1963); children: Donna, Mike, Kelly, Rex; m. Martin Thomas Savage, Sept. 18, 1965. Pres. Poets of Tarrant County, 1995-96. Author: (book of poetry) Voices in the Wind, 1982, (play) Tumbleweed Christmas, 1989; author of numerous poems; author, performer Audio Poetry Cassette: Simply Savage, 1992; contbg. writer to newspapers; newsletter editor Arlington Women's Shelter, 1988-91; mem. newsletter publicity LWV, Arlington, 1991-92. Dir. Arlington Friends of the Libr., 1987-90; judge Tex. Student Poetry, Storyteller for Students, Retirement Ctrs., 1987—. Mem. Am. Lit. Scholars and Critics, Acad. Am. Poets. Home: 1700 Ocho Rios Ct Arlington TX 76012

SAVAGE-NEUMAN, MARY SUSAN, art dealer; b. Deerfield, Mass., Dec. 15, 1944; d. John George and Mary Margaret (Sabolinski) Savage; m. Robert Sterling Neuman, June 3, 1979; 1 child, Christina Mary Savage Neuman. Student, U. de Mediterranee, Nice, France, 1965; BA, Lake Erie Coll., 1966; postgrad., Western New Eng. Law Coll., 1967-68. Asst. to adminstr. Mayor's Office of Pub. Svc., Boston, 1968-70; dir. art rental gallery Inst. Contemporary Art, Boston, 1970-71; art cons. Cir. Art Gallery, Boston, 1971-75; dir., owner Sunne Savage Gallery, Boston, 1975-83; pvt. art dealer Sunne Savage Gallery, Winchester, Mass., 1983—; curator of Herbert W. Plimpton Collection, 1976-80, Wingspread Gallery, Northeast Harbor, Maine, 1990—; conceptual advisor to Monumenta Exhibit, Newport, R.I., 1976; initiated various art shows including Rose Art Mus., Waltham, Mass., Oakland Mus. Art, Calif.; represents various early 20th century Am. artists. Conservation chair Winchester (Mass.) Home & Garden, 1994-96; active Fogg Mus., Harvard U., 1985—, Mus. Fine Arts Boston, 1985—, Gore Place, Waltham, Mass., 1990—. Mem. Archives of Am. Art (co-chair state street benefit 1989, vice chair art fair 1990, co-chair arslibr 1992), William Farnsworth Libr. and Art Mus. (Rockland, Maine), Mus. Modern Art (N.Y.C.). Republican. Roman Catholic. Home: 135 Cambridge St Winchester MA 01890

SAVARD, CHRISTINE ELIZABETH, music educator; b. Boston, Apr. 25, 1940; d. Albert Eugene and Catherine Marie (Lusk) Lloyd; m. Emile Joseph Savard, June 27, 1964; children: Peter Joseph, Paul Eugene, Elizabeth Jane. BS, New Eng. Conservatory of Music, 1964. Music tchr. Glen Cove (Maine) Christian Academy, 1962-63, The Pub. Schs., Malden, Mass., 1964-65, Vestal (N.Y.) Cen. Schs., 1965-68, Johnson City (N.Y.) Cen. Sch. Dist., 1969, Cen. Baptist Christian Acad., Binghamton, N.Y., 1975-78, Ross Corners Christian Academy, Vestal, 1978-82, Tamworth (N.H.) Sch. Dist., 1987-90, Rogers City (Mich.) Area Schs., 1991—; music tchr. Freedom & Madison (N.H.) Sch. Dists., 1988-89. Competition judge N.Y. State Talents for Christ, 1977-85; choir dir. First Baptist Ch., N. Conway, N.H., 1970-74; organist Mich. Home Health Care Hospice, Indian River, Mich., 1993. Mem. No. Mich. Gen. Assn. Regular Baptist Chs. (pres., spkr. ladies group 1991—). Home: 190 W Huron Ave Rogers City MI 49779-1336

SAVELLO, CHERYL ADAMSON, art educator; b. Twin Falls, Idaho, Aug. 17, 1946; d. Robert Calvin and Lois LaVern (Timm) Adamson; m. Paul Alexander Savello, June 29, 1974; children: Denise, Robert Alexander, Catherine Jane Allison. BFA, U. Utah, 1970, MEd, 1975. Tchr. art Granite Sch. Dist., Salt Lake City, 1972-75, Jordan Sch. Dist., Sandy, Utah, 1977-80, Cache County Sch. Dist., North Logan, Utah, 1989-90, Marsh Valley Sch. Dist., Arimo, Idaho, 1990-91, West Side Sch. Dist. #202, Dayton, Idaho, 1992—. Tchr. Peace Corps, Saipan, Mariana Islands, 1970-72. Mem. NEA, Idaho Art Edn. Assn., Utah Art Edn. Assn., Nat. Art Edn. Assn., Logan Golf and Country Club. Mem. Ch. LDS. Home: 85 N 400 E PO Box 613 Hyde Park UT 84318-0613 Office: West Side High Sch 775 N West Side Hwy Dayton ID 83232

SAVIDGE, SARAH ELIZABETH, artist; b. Seattle, Jan. 18, 1962; d. Samuel Leigh and Joan Virginia (Harris) S.; m. Matthew Edward Owens, Oct. 1, 1995. Student, Middlesex Polytechnic, London, 1982-83, Cornell U., 1984, Skowhegan (Maine) Sch. of Painting, 1986; BFA, Empire State Coll., 1988. Artist asst. Elyn Zimmerman, Sculptor, N.Y.C., 1985-86, Mary Miss, Pub. Artist, N.Y.C., 1985-86; gallery asst. Sarah Rentschler Gallery, N.Y.C., 1986, Landfall Press, N.Y.C., 1987; mng./dir. A.I.R. Gallery, N.Y.C., 1988-92; asst. Susan Rothenberg, Artist, Galisted, N.Mex., 1993-95; mem. Bklyn. Waterfront Artists Coalition, 1990-93; bd. dirs. Assn. Artist Run Galleries, N.Y.C., 1989-92. One woman shows include Grover/Thurston Gallery, Seattle, 1992, Vevey, Switzerland, 1994; exhibited in group shows at Jan Weiss Gallery, N.Y.C., 1995, Casa Grande Art Mus., Ariz., 1995. Empire State Coll. grantee, 1988; Palenville Interarts Colony fellow, 1990, Yaddo fellow, 1994; Assistance grantee Contemporary Artists Ctr., 1995. Home and Office: PO Box 19397 Seattle WA 98109

SAVIGNAC, AMY LYNN NORRIS, special education educator; b. Richmond, Va., Sept. 10, 1969; d. Bruce Charles Norris and Trude Newman Young; m. Kevin R. Savignac, Oct. 1, 1994. BS, Longwood U., 1991, MS, 1992. Cert. spl. edn. tchr. for emotionally disturbed, mentally retarded, learning disabled, Va. Learning disabled resource tchr. Stonewall Jackson Middle Sch., Hanover, Va., 1992-93; learning disabled self contained, resource tchr. Richard C. Haydon Elem. Sch., Manassas, Va., 1993-94, tchr. educable retarded, self contained, 1994—. Mem. NEA, Coun. for Exceptional Children. Home: 4146 Rectortown Rd Marshall VA 20115

SAVITRIPRIYA, SWAMI, religious leader, author; b. Apr. 1, 1930; divorced; three children. Ordained Hindu nun, Holy Order of Sannyas, 1975. Psychotherapist, 1970-75; founder, spiritual dir. Shiva-Shakti Kashmir Shaivite Hindu Ch., Ashram, Marin County, Calif., 1975-77, Shiva-Shakti Ashram, Oakland, Calif., 1978, Convent of the Divine Mother, Kona, Hawaii, 1979-80, Holy Mountain Monastery and Retreat Ctr., Groveland, Calif., 1984-92, Holy Mountain U., Groveland, Calif., 1985-92; founder, spiritual dir. Inst. for New Life, Groveland, Calif., 1990-92, Santa Cruz, Calif., 1993-95; founder, spiritual dir. Shiva-Shakti Ashram, Lake Chapala-Ajijic, Jalisco, Mexico, 1995—. Author (books) Kundalini-Shakti: From Awakening to Enlightenment, 1980, The Psychology of Mystical Awakening: The Yoga Sutras, 1991, The Cloud of the Universe, 1986, The Worlds of the Chakras, 1987, Arising Woman, 1988, Arising Man, 1988, Tantras of Personal and Spiritual Unfoldment, 1989, New World Hinduism, 1990, others; translator: Bhagavad Gita, 1974, Narada Bhakti Sutras, 1976, Upanishads, 1981, Shiva Sutras, 1984, Pratyabhijnahridayam, 1987, Vijnana Bhairava, 1989, others. Office: Shiva-Shakti Ananda Ashram 9297 Siempre Viva Rd # 71-270 San Diego CA 92173

SAVITZ, MAXINE LAZARUS, aerospace company executive; b. Balt., Feb. 13, 1937; d. Samuel and Harriette (Miller) Lazarus; m. Sumner Alan Savitz, Jan. 1, 1961; children: Adam Jonathan, Alison Carrie. BA in Chemistry magna cum laude, Bryn Mawr Coll., 1958; PhD in Organic Chemistry, MIT, 1961. Instr. chemistry Hunter Coll., N.Y.C., 1962-63; sr. electrochemist Mobility Equipment Rsch. and Devel. Ctr., Ft. Belvoir, Va., 1963-68; prof. chemistry Federal City Coll., Washington, 1968-72; program mgr. NSF, Washington, 1972-74; dir. FEA Office Bldgs. Policy Rshc. U.S. Dept. Energy, Washington, 1974-75, dir. div. indsl. conservation, 1975-76, from dir. div. bldgs. and community systems to dep asst sec., 1975-83; pres. Lighting Rsch. Inst., 1983-85; asst. to v.p. engring. Ceramic Components div. The Garrett Corp., 1985-87; gen. mgr. ceramic components divsn. AlliedSignal Inc., Torrance, Calif., 1987—; lectr. in field; bd. dirs. Am. Coun. for Energy Efficient Economy, 1984—, Internat. Inst. Energy Conservation, 1984-94, Energy Found., 1991—; cons. State Mich. Dept. Commerce, 1983, N.C. Alternative Energy Corp., 1983, Garrett Corp., 1983, Energy Engring. Bd., Nat. Rsch. Bd., 1986-93, Office Tech. Assessment, U.S. Congress Energy Demand Panel, 1987-91, nat. materials adv. bd. NRC, 1989-94; bd. dirs. U.S. Advanced Ceramic Assn., 1989—, chmn., 1992; adv. com. div. ceramics/materials ORNL, 1989-92, adv. com. dir., 1992—; adv. bd. Sec. Energy, 1992—; mem. Def. Sci. Bd., 1993-96; vis. com. adv. tech. Nat. Inst. Standards and Tech., 1993—. Editor Energy and Bldgs.; contbr. articles to profl. jours. Policy com. mem. NAE, 1994—. NSF postdoctoral fellow, 1961, 62, NIH predoctoral fellow, 1960, 61. Mem. Nat. Acad. Engring. Office: AlliedSignal Ceramic Components Divsn 2525 W 190th St Torrance CA 90504-6002

SAVOCCHIO, JOYCE A., mayor; b. Erie, Pa.; d. Daniel and Esther S. BA in History, Mercyhurst Coll., 1965; MEd, U. Pitts., 1969; cert. secondary sch. adminstrn., Edinboro U., 1975; LLD (hon.), Gannon U., 1990. Tchr. social studies Erie Sch. Dist., 1965-85, asst. prin. Strong Vincent High Sch., 1985-89, tchr. coord. high sch. task force, 1971-75; pres. Erie Edn. Assn., 1975-76; mem. coun. City of Erie, 1981-90, pres. coun., 1983, mayor, 1990—; pres. Pa. League League of Cities and Municipalities, Northwestern Pa. Mayors' Roundtable; mem. subcoms. on transp. and comms. U.S. Conf. of Mayors; bd. dirs. State Job Tng. Partnership Bd.; mem., sec. Electoral Coll. for Commonwealth of Pa. Past pres. Erie Hist. Mus.; past mem. editl. bd. Erie Hist. Soc.; mem. Pa. Gov.'s Flagship Commn., Cmty. Task Force on Drug and Alcohol Abuse. Named Woman of Yr., Dem. Women Erie, 1981, Italian Am. Women's Assn., 1987, Outstanding Citizen of Yr., MECA, 1991; recipient Disting. Alumna award Mercyhurst Coll., 1990, Community Svc. award Roosevelt Mid. Sch., 1990, Disting. Citizen award French Creek coun. Boy Scouts Am., 1991. Roman Catholic. Office: Office of Mayor Mcpl Bldg 626 State St Erie PA 16501-1128

SAVOY, SUZANNE MARIE, critical care nurse; b. N.Y.C., Oct. 18, 1946; d. William Joseph and Mary Patricia (Moclair) S. BS, Columbia U., 1970; M in Nursing, UCLA, 1978. RN, CCRN, cert. CCRN, CS. Staff nurse

MICU, transplant Jackson Meml. Hosp., Miami, 1970-72; staff nurse MICU Boston U. Hosp. (Mass.), 1972-74; staff nurse MICU VA Hosp., Long Beach, Calif., 1974-75; staff nurse MIRU Cedars-Sinai Med. Ctr., L.A., 1975-77; critical care clin. nursing specialist Anaheim (Calif.) Meml. Hosp., 1978-81; practitioner, instr. Rush-Presbyn.-St. Luke's Med. Ctr. Coll. Nursing, Chgo., 1982-88; rsch. assoc. dept. neurosurgery, Rush U., 1984-88; clin. rsch. assoc. Medtronic, Inc. Drug Adminstrn. Systems, Mpls., 1988-91; staff nurse critical care Harper Hosp., Detroit, 1992-93; clin. nurse specialist, surg./trauma critical care, Detroit Recieving Hosp., 1993-95; critical care clin. nurse specialist Saginaw (Mich.) Gen. Hosp., 1996—; clin. instr. Wayne State U. Coll. of Nursing, Detroit, 1991-96, adj. faculty, 1996—; program coord. Critical Care ACNP-CC MSN, Wayne State U., 1993-96; neurosci. clinician acute stroke unit Harper Hosp., Detroit, 1989; edn. cons. Critical Care Svcs., Inc., Orange, Calif., 1979-81. Co-author articles for profl. jours. Mem. Am. Assn. Neurosci. Nurses (treas. Ill. chpt. 1983-85, pres. 1986-87, SE Mich. chpt. 1992—, bd. dirs., treas., program chair), Am. Assn. Critical Care Nurses (bd. dirs. Long Beach chpt. 1981-82), Am. Assn. Sci. Nursing (mem. rsch. com. 1993-95), Lambda Gamma Phi (bd. dirs. 1994-96), Sigma Theta Tau. Roman Catholic. Office: Saginaw Gen Hosp 1447 N Harrison Saginaw MI 48602

SAWI, ELIZABETH GIBSON, brokerage house executive. Exec. v.p. electronic brokerage The Charles Schwab Corp., San Francisco, 1995—. Office: Schwab & Co 101 Montgomery St San Francisco CA 94104-4122*

SAWIN, LISA JEAN, school social worker; b. Rockford, Ill., Apr. 4, 1969; d. Eugene George and Elaine Cecilia (Happ) S. BA, Coll. St. Francis, 1991; MSW, Aurora U., 1993. Social worker Aunt Martha's Youth Ctr., Joliet, Ill., 1990-92; intern social worker Hinsdale (Ill.) Ctrl. H.S., 1992-93; sch. social worker Wilmington (Ill.) Sch. Dist. 208-U, 1993—; Operation Genesis Adv. Bd. Dist. 209-U Spl. Edn., 1995—, sponsor Operation Snowball, Operation Snowflake, 1993—, founder, adv. S.O.A.P. Club, 1995—, sponsor Snowclub, 1994—. Vol. TLC for Children's Sake, Wilmington, 1993—, Ill. Teenage Inst., Bloomington, Ill., 1994—, Ctr. for Adult Basic Edn. and Literacy, Joliet, 1994-95. Mem. Am. Fedn. Tchrs., Nat. Assn. Social Workers, Ill. Assn. Student Assistance Profls., Ill. Assn. Sch. Social Workers. Home: 1123 Elizabeth Ct #4 Crest Hill IL 60435 Office: Wilmington Sch Dist 209-U 715 S Joliet Wilmington IL 60481

SAWIN, NANCY CHURCHMAN, educator, artist, historian; b. Wilmington, Del., June 21, 1917; d. Sanford W. and Ellen (Quigley) S. BA, Principia Coll., 1938; MA, U. Del., 1940; EdD, U. Pa., 1962; PhD (hon.), Golden Beacom Coll., 1987. With Sanford Sch., Hockessin, Del., 1938-74; dean girls Sanford Sch., 1945-62, head sch., 1962-74; coordinator student services U. Del. Div. Continuing Edn., Newark, 1974-77; ednl. cons. DuPont Co., ICI Ams., 1976-80; chmn. Del. State Sci. Fair com., 1962; mem. com. Jr. Sci. and Humanities Symposium, 1962-76; mem. English, lang. arts adv. com. State Del., 1965-68; sec., dir. Recreation, Promotion and Service, Inc., 1963-74; mem. All-Am. Hockey Team, 1948-59. One-person shows include Ctr. for Creative Arts, 1993—, others; editor: The Eagle, 1961-62; co-pub., illustrator: Between the Bays, 1977, Delaware Sketchbook, 1976, Backroading Throuth Cecil County, 1977, Brick and Ballast, 1985; author, illustrator: Man-O-War My Island Home, 1978, Up the Spine and Down the Creek, 1982, Locks Traps and Corners, 1984, China Sketchbook, 1985, A Hockessin Diary, 1987, Privy to the Council, 1987, The Oulde King's Roade, 1989, North from Wilmington by Oulde Roads and Turnpikes, 1992, Once Upon a Time in the Country, 1994. Trustee Goldey Beacom Coll., pres., 1974-81, mem. safety coun., 1964-74; pres. Del. Sports Hall of Fame, 1982—; pres. bd. dirs. Del. Soc. for Preservation of Antiquities, 1986-88, chair, 1990—; chair fundraising com. Hockessin County Libr., 1989-94; bd. dirs. Preservation Del., 1996—. 2d lt. CAP, 1942-45. Recipient Medal of Merit, U. Del., 1989, DAR History medal, 1990, Hist. Preservation award New Castle County, 1996, gold medals Sr. Olympic Swimming, 1994, 95; named to Del. Sports Hall of Fame, 1977; charter mem. U.S. Field Hockey Hall of Fame, 1988; named to Hall of Fame of Del. Women, 1991, Wall of Fame, U. Del., 1991. Mem. Headmistress Assn. East, Del. Art Mus., Rehoboth Art League, Middle Atlantic States Assn. Colls. and Secondary Schs. (past pres.), Commn. on Secondary Schs., Red Clay Creek Assn., Internat. Fedn. Women's Hockey Assns. (past pres.), U.S. Field Hockey Assn. (past pres., named to Sports Hall of Fame 1987), Del. Field Hockey Assn. (past pres.), Nat. League Am. Pen Women, DAR (History medal), Daus. of Founders and Patriots, Nat. Soc. New Eng. Women, Daus. Colonial Wars, Del. Greenbank Questars (pres. 1993-94), Delta Kappa Gamma (past pres.), Pi Lambda Theta. Republican. Presbyterian (elder). Club: Quota (pres. Wilmington 1971-73, gov. 10th Dist. 1979-80). Address: North Light Studio 147 Sawin Ln Hockessin DE 19707-9713

SAWYER, ANA MARIA RAMIREZ, clinical psychologist; b. Tegucigalpa, Honduras, Mar. 21, 1954; came to U.S., 1965; d. Jaime Antonio Ramirez Quesada and Ofelia Ochoa de Ramirez; m. Richard S. Sawyer, Dec. 21, 1984 (div. June 1990); children: Briant Boru, Rory Conor, Brendan Patrick. Cert. stenographer, Soulé Bus. Coll., 1976; BS, U. South Ala., 1980, MS, 1982. Counselor Cuban Haitian concerns Mobile (Ala.) Mental Health Ctr., 1982; sec. I U.S. Agy. Internat. Devel. Procurement and Contracting, Tegucigalpa and Honduras, 1982; visa examiner Am. Consulate, Am. Embassy, Tegucigalpa and Honduras, 1982; habilitation supr. Albert P. Brewer Devel. Ctr., Mobile, 1983-85; temp. sec. Kelly Svcs. Inc., Mobile, 1985-86; contract therapist Cath. Soc. Svcs. Counseling Program, Mobile, 1985-88; coord. students with spl. needs U. South Ala., Mobile, 1986-88; coord. day treatment program Searcy Hosp., Mt. Vernon, Ala., 1988-91; behavior mgmt. specialist Albert P. Brewer Devel. Ctr., Mobile, Ala., 1991—; bd. mem. Ala. Orgn. Mental Health Technologists and Human Svc. Workers, 1988-89; designer/developer behavioral mgmt. programs. Presentor/trainer Cath. Soc. Svcs., Mobile, 1987-88, Cath. Youth Ministries, 1988. Mem. APA (assoc.), Ala. Orgn. for Mental Health Technologists and Human Svc. Workers (bd. mem. 1988-89), Ala. Coun. on Learning Disabilities (Mobile County chpt. edn. chmn. 1987), Alpha Lambda Delta, Omicron Delta Kappa. Democrat. Roman Catholic. Home: 2528 Woodland Rd Mobile AL 36693

SAWYER, ANITA DAWN, special education educator; b. Harrison, Ark., July 8, 1963; d. Donnie Frank and Myrtle Darline (Curbow) Coxsey; m. Timothy Clarence Sawyer, Mar. 26, 1988; children: Benjamin Aram, Lukas Ryan, Lauren Nicole. AS, North Ark. Cmty. Tech. Coll., Harrison, 1984; BS in Edn., U. Ctrl. Ark., 1986. Cert. spl. edn.-mildy handicapped grades K-12. Jr. and sr. H.S. spl. educator Omaha (Ark.) Pub. Schs., 1986-91; extended yr. svcs. coord. Boone County Spl. Svcs., Harrison, summer 1987; tchr.-leader summer youth program Job Tng. Partnership Act, Harrison, summer 1991; jr. and sr. H.S. spl. educator Alpena (Ark.) Pub. Schs., 1991; indirect svcs. coord. Omaha (Ark.) H.S., 1986-91, Alpena (Ark.) H.S., 1991—, dist. spl. olympics coord., Omaha Pub. Schs., 1987-91, Alpena Pub. Schs., 1991—; adv. bd. mem. Omaha H.S. Future Bus. Leaders Am., 1990-91; coord. transitional svcs. Omaha, 1986-91, Alpena, 1991—; pres. pers. policies committee, Alpena, 1995-96. Vol. internat. cert. Omaha (Ark.) and Ark. Spl. Olympics, 1986-91; fundraising and cmty. contact rep. United Way-Omaha (Ark.) H.S., 1989; spl. olympics coach in bowling, basketball, floor hockey and athletics Alpena (Ark.) and Ark. Spl. Olympics, 1991—. Mem. NEA, Ark. Edn. Assn. (bldg. rep., gen. assembly 1986-90), Omaha Edn. Assn. (v.p. 1986-87, pres. 1987-90, rep.), Coun. Exceptional Children, Omaha Booster Club (v.p. 1988-89), Omaha PTO, Alpena PTO. Baptist. Home: RR 4 Box 391C Harrison AR 72601-9155 Office: Alpena Pub Schs PO Box 270 300 S Denver Alpena AR 72611

SAWYER, CHERYL LYNNE, foundation administrator, educator, consultant; b. Balt., Mar. 8, 1954; d. Carolyn (Brooks) Bulcken; m. Gary W. Sawyer, July 16, 1976; children: Jesse, Stacy. BA in English, Sam Houston State U., 1976; MA in Behavioral Scis., U. Houston, 1984, EdD in Adminstrn. and Supervision, 1993. Lic. psychol. assoc., Tex.; cert. English, history, psychology, learning disabilities tchr., Tex.; cert. diagnostician, counselor, spl. edn. counselor, assoc. sch. psychologist, Tex. Tchr. Alvin (Tex.) Ind. Sch. Dist., 1976-84, LaMarque (Tex.) Ind. Sch. Dist., 1985-90; ednl. cons. Dickinson, Tex., 1992—; from vis. asst. prof. to adj. prof. U. Houston, 1990—; dir. acute children's programs Devereux Found., League City, Tex., 1994—; mem. adv. bd. spl. edn. Santa Fe Sch. Dist., 1993, 94, 95; mem. adv. bd. drug and alcohol prevention LaMarque Sch. Dist., 1989, 90, 91, 92; presenter in field. Contbr. articles to profl. jours. Spkr. child-related psychol. issues Devereux Found., 1993, 94, 95, 96. Mem. Nat. Assn. for Gifted, Coun. for Exceptional Children, Nat. Assn. for Bilingual Edn., Beta Sigma Phi, Phi Delta Kappa. Home: 12308 Marion Ln Dickinson TX 77539

SAWYER, (L.) DIANE, television journalist; b. Glasgow, Ky., Dec. 22, 1945; d. E.P. and Jean W. (Dunagan) S.; m. Mike Nichols, Apr. 29, 1988. BA, Wellesley Coll., 1967. Reporter Sta. WLKY-TV, Louisville, 1967-70; adminstr. press office White House, 1970-74; rschr. Richard Nixon's memoirs, 1974-78; gen. assignment reporter, then Dept. State corr. CBS News, 1978-81; co-anchor Morning News CBS, from 1981, co-anchor Early Morning News, 1982-84; corr., co-editor 60 Minutes CBS-TV, 1984-89; co-anchor Prime Time Live ABC News, 1989—; co-anchor Day One, 1995—, Turning Point. Recipient 2 Peabody awards for Pub. Svc., 1988, Robert F. Kennedy award 9 Emmy awrds, Spl. Dupont award, IRTS Lifetime Achievement award. Mem. Coun. Fgn. Rels. Office: PrimeTime Live 147 Columbus Ave Fl 3 New York NY 10023-5900

SAWYER, LINDA, advertising executive. Exec. v.p., group acct. dir. Deutsch, Inc., N.Y.C. Office: Deutsch Dworin 215 Park Ave S New York NY 10003-1603*

SAWYER, MARIAN A., law librarian; b. San Francisco, Aug. 28, 1950; d. James Edward and Virginia (Mannina) S.; 1 child, Mark Edward. BA, Calif. State U., Sacramento, 1976; M Libr. and Info. Sci., U. Calif., Berkeley, 1980. Acquisitions libr. McGeorge Sch. of Law, U. of Pacific, Sacramento, 1976-81, tech. svcs. libr., 1981-84; law libr. Calif. Dept. Justice, Office of Atty. Gen., Sacramento, 1984—. Mem. Am. Assn. Law Librs., State Ct. and County Law Librs., No. Calif. Assn. Law Librs. Office: Calif Dept Justice Office of Atty Gen 1300 I St Sacramento CA 95814

SAWYER, MARY CATHERINE, hospital administrator; b. Borger, Tex., Dec. 8, 1931; d. Andrew Rodgers and Mary Elizabeth (Slater) Hill; m. Edmond Eugene Sawyer, Aug. 26, 1963; children: Slater Shane, Anthony Barrett, Maronda Rae. BBA, Tex. Tech U., 1956; cert. in med. records, U. Tex. Med. Br., Galveston, 1957. Registered med. adminstr.; cert. coding specialist. Med. record adminstr. Taylor Hosp., Inc., Lubbock, Tex., 1957-63; pvt. practice cons. Paris, Tex., 1963-79; med. record adminstr., coding specialist St. Joseph's Hosp., Paris, 1979—. Mem. DAR (corr. sec. 1989-91, treas. 1991-93, 1st vice regent 1994-96, def. chmn. 1990-96), Gordon Country Club, Phi Gamma Nu. Methodist. Home: PO Box 128 Deport TX 75435-0128 Office: St Joseph's Hosp PO Box 9070 Paris TX 75461-9070

SAWYERS, CLAIRE ELYCE, arboretum administrator; b. Maryville, Mo., May 30, 1957; d. Scott Kirkir and Betty Jane (Alexander) S. BS with distinction, Purdue U., 1978, MAg., 1981; MS, U. Del., 1984. Adminstrv. asst. Mt. Cuba Ctr. Study of Piedmont Flora, Greenville, Del., 1983-90; dir. Scott Arboretum of Swarthmore (Pa.) Coll., Swarthmore, Pa., 1990—. Office: Scott Arboretum 500 College Ave Swarthmore PA 19081-1306

SAWYERS, ELIZABETH JOAN, librarian, administrator; b. San Diego, Dec. 2, 1936; d. William Henry and Elizabeth Georgiana (Price) S. A.A., Glendale Jr. Coll., 1957; B.A. in Bacteriology, UCLA, 1959, M.L.S., 1961. Asst. head acquisition sect. Nat. Library Medicine, Bethesda, Md., 1962-63, head acquisition sect., 1963-66, spl. asst. to chief tech. services div., 1966-69, spl. asst. to assoc. dir. for library ops., 1969-73; asst. dir. libraries for tech. services SUNY-Stony Brook, 1973-75; dir. Health Scis. Library Ohio State U., Columbus, 1975-90, spl. asst. to dir. Univ. librs., 1990—. Mem. Assn. Acad. Health Scis. Library Dirs. (sec./treas. 1981-83, pres. 1983-84), Med. Library Assn., Am. Soc. for Info. Sci., Spl. Libraries Assn., ALA. Office: Ohio State Univ Librs 1858 Neil Ave Columbus OH 43210-1225

SAX, MARY RANDOLPH, speech pathologist; b. Pontiac, Mich., July 13, 1925; d. Bernard Angus and Ada Lucile (Thurman) TePoorten; m. William Martin Sax, Feb. 7, 1948. BA magna cum laude, Mich. State U., 1947; MA, U. Mich., 1949; cert. clin. competence in speech and language pathology. Supr. speech correction dept. Waterford Twp. Schs., Pontiac, 1949-69; lectr. Marygrove Coll., Detroit, 1971-72; pvt. practice in speech and lang. pathology, Wayne and Oakland Counties, Mich., 1973—; co-investigator Support Personnel Profl. Practice of Speech-Lang. Pathology; counselor to divsn. stroke liaisons Am. Heart Assn. Mich.; liaison, staff Scientific Coun. Stroke AHA Mich. and Dallas, 1996—; adj. speech pathologist Southfield, Mich.; lectr. on stroke Mich. Speakers Bur., Am. Heart Assn., 1990—; pub. speaking coach, 1989—; adj. faculty SS. Cyril and Methodius Sem., Orchard Lake, Mich., 1989-90, St. Mary's Preparatory Sch., Orchard Lake, Mich., 1990—; founder, mem. Stroke Project Task Force for Detroit, 1993—; com. mem. Charrette, study Architecture and Design for physical restructuring Franklin, Mich., 1993. Mem. sci. coun. stroke Am. Heart Assn. Grantee Inst. Articulation and Learning, 1969, others, project choices and funding Meadow Lake Cmty. Coun., Birmingham, Mich., 1989—; christian svc. commn. St. Owen, Birmingham co-chmn. blood drive Red Cross, Franklin, Mich., 1991—. Mem. Am. Speech-Lang.-Hearing Assn. (clin. competence cert.), Mich. Speech-Lang.-Hearing Assn. (com. cmty. and hosp. svcs., pvt. practitioner liaison 1991—), Am. Heart Assn. of Mich. (mem. stroke awareness seminar, planning and operation ednl., liaison sci. coun. stroke 1996—, counselor divsn. stroke liaisons), Stroke Com. of Am., Internat. Assn. Logopedics and Phoniatrics (Switzerland), Franklin Found. (mem. natural resources adv. coun. 1991—, bd. dirs. 1994—), Founders Soc. of Detroit Inst. Arts, Mich. Humane Soc., Theta Alpha Phi, Phi Kappa Phi, Kappa Delta Pi, Gamma Phi Beta Internat. Contbr. articles to profl. jours. including Language and Language Behavior Abstracts, Language Speech & Hearing Services, Speech Language Hearing Jour. Achievements include research in language and speech acquisition in children in reference to the development of and prediction of biological speech change; research interests developmental phonatory voice disorders in adult acquisition of language and speech relative to central and autonomic nervous systems. Home and Office: 31320 Woodside Dr Franklin MI 48025-2027

SAXE, THELMA RICHARDS, secondary school educator, consultant; b. Ogdensburg, N.J., Apr. 21, 1941; d. George Francis and Evelyn May (Howell) Richards; m. Kenneth Elwood Meeker, Jr., June 22, 1957 (div. 1965); children: Sylvia Lorraine Meeker Hill, Michelle Louise Meeker Aromando, David Sean (dec.); m. Frederick Ely Saxe, Feb. 18, 1983; stepchildren: Jonathan Kent, Holly Harding Schenker. BA, William Paterson Coll., Wayne, N.J., 1972, MEd, 1975, postgrad., 1983-84; Dyslexia cert., Fairleigh Dickinson U., 1994. Cert. paralegal, dyslexia specialist Fairleigh Dickonson U. Tchr. handicapped Sussex (N.J.)-Wantage Regional Sch. Dist., 1972-75; resource rm. tchr. Sussex County Vo-Tech Sch., Sparta, N.J., 1975-77; learning cons. Sussex County Vo-Tech Sch., 1977-83; learning specialist Bennington-Rutland Supervisory Union, Manchester, Vt., 1986-87; learning cons. Stillwater (N.J.) Twp. Sch., 1987-88, Independence Twp. Cen. Sch., Great Meadows, N.J., 1989; learning cons., tutor in pvt. practice specializing dyslexia Sparta, 1986—; asst. prin. Harmony Twp. Sch., Harmony, N.J., 1989-92; learning cons. Montague (N.J.) Elem. Sch., 1996—; coord. gifted/talented Sussex Vo-Tech, 1980-83; coord. child study team Stillwater Twp. Sch., 1987-88, Montague Twp. Sch., 1996—. Mem. Coun. Exceptional Children, Learning Disabilities Assn., Orton Dyslexia Soc., N.J. Assn. Learning Cos., Kappa Delta Pi. Republican. Presbyterian. Home: 17 Park Rd Sparta NJ 07871-2002 Office: Accent on Comm 350A Sparta Ave Sparta NJ 07871

SAXL, JANE WILHELM, state legislator; b. N.Y.C., Aug. 26, 1939; d. Seymour F. and Doris (Fuld) Wilhelm; m. Joseph Saxl, Nov. 17, 1957; children: Susan S., Ruth L., Mary-Anne, Michael V. BA, Sangamon State U., 1973, MA, 1974. City councilor City of Bangor, Maine, 1987-93; mem. Maine Ho. Reps., Augusta, 1992—. sec./treas. Penobscot Valley Coun. Govts., 1988-91. Active Bangor Sch. Bd., 1984-87, Family Planning Maine, Natural Resources Coun., Penobscot Dem. Com.; bd. dirs. Bangor Beautiful, Bangor Conv. and Visitors Bur.; past chmn. Bangor Recycling. Mem. LWV (pres. Maine chpt. 1987-93), Nat. League State Legislators, Nat. Women's Polit. Caucus, Maine Women's Lobby, Friends of Bangor Pub. Libr., Spruce Run Assocs., Maine Audubon Soc., Tuesday Forum, Women's Legis. Lobby, N.Y. Pub. Libr. Democrat. Jewish. Home: 37 Pond St Bangor ME 04401-4641 Office: Maine Legislature State House Sta # 3 Augusta ME 04330

SAXTON, CAROLYN VIRGINIA, fund raising executive; b. Charleston, W.Va., June 24, 1948; d. Robert Everett and Jo Ann (Rader) S.; children: Jon Hamilton Rickey Jr., Leigh Ann Rickey; m. Harlow William Gregory Jr., May 27, 1989. BA, W.Va. Wesleyan Coll., 1971; postgrad., Loma Linda U., 1989-91. Cert. Fund Raising Exec. Counselor Open Door, Annapolis, Md., 1971-73; social worker Salvation Army, Charleston, 1977-79; patient educator Womens Health Ctr., Charleston, 1979-83; community edn. specialist Shawnee Hills Mental Health, Charleston, 1983; exec. dir. W.Va. Nat. Abortion Rights Action League, Charleston, 1983-86; lobbyist Charleston, 1986; exec. dir. Community Hospice, Ashland, Ky., 1986-89; dir. home hospice Home Hospice VNA North, Evanston, Ill., 1989-90; exec. dir. Community Chest Oak Park/River Forest, Ill., 1990—, Oak Park/River Forest Cmty. Found., 1993—. Mem. Ky. Cancer Program Network, Ashland, 1986-89, Ky. Religious Coalition for Abortion Rights, Frankfort, 1987-88; mem. Citizens Coun. Oak Park/River Forest H.S., 1991-93; mem. W.Va. Task Force on Adolescent Residential Treatment Ctr./Drug Abuse, 1983; mem. Nat. Abortion Rights Task Force on Minor's Access, 1986-87; mem. com. on minor's access W.Va. Dept. Health, 1986-87; mem. Jr. League Charleston, 1982-86; chmn., usher com. Paramount Women's Assn., Ashland, 1988-89; mem. choir 1st Presbyn. Ch., Ashland, 1986-89, Sunday sch. tchr., 1988-89; choir mem. Fair Oaks Presbyn. Ch., 1990-92, bd. deacons; mem. First United Meth. Ch.; mem. task force linkage cmty. svcs. for high risk adolescents, 1995. Mem. NAFE, Nat. Soc. Fundraising Execs. (programming com. 1991-93, internat. conf. com. 1994-95, scholarship com. 1994-95, bd. dirs. 1995—, spl. interest group com. chair 1995—), Nat. Hospice Orgn. (award of excellence 1988), Ky. Assn. Hospice (bd. dirs., mem.-at-large 1989, chmn. nominating com. 1988-89), Coun. for Non-Profits (vol. action com. 1988-89, co-chmn. cmty. support com. 1989), Zonta (status of women com., program com.), Women in Mgmt. (treas. 1993-95), Rotary (program co-chair, bd. dirs. 1993-95, co-chair spl. events 1994-95, sec. 1996—). Democrat. Home: 851 Fair Oaks Ave Oak Park IL 60302-1546 Office: Community Chest Oak Park River Forest 1042 Pleasant St Oak Park IL 60302-3002

SAXTON, CATHERINE PATRICIA, public relations executive; b. Sheffield, Eng., July 5, 1944; d. Clifford and Kate Ann (Ruane) S. B.A. cum laude, Fordham U., 1978. Mgr. corp. comms. Westinghouse Broadcasting & Cable Co., N.Y.C., 1981-82; prin., pres. Saxton & Assocs., N.Y.C., 1983—; CEO Potter/Saxton Assocs., Inc., 1985-90; CEO The Saxton Group Ltd., 1990—; prof. pub. speaking Katharine Gibbs Coll., N.Y.C., 1977—. Mem. exec. com. Mayor's Commn. for a Vietnam Vet's Meml., 1982-90. Roman Catholic. Home: 325 E 90th St New York NY 10128-5260

SAXTON, MARY JANE, management educator; b. Syracuse, N.Y., Mar. 3, 1953; d. John Cook and Florence (Cooper) S.; m. Paul Hood. BA, SUNY, Cortland, 1975; MBA, U. Pitts., 1979, PhD, 1987. Counselor Methadone Mgmt. Svcs., Inc., N.Y.C., 1975-76; resident mgr. Crossroads Svcs., Inc., Jackson, Miss., 1976; outreach worker Jackson Mental Health Ctr., 1977-78; cons. Organizational Design Cons., Inc., Pitts., 1982-83, mktg. dir., 1984-86; asst. prof. mgmt. U. Houston, 1988-93; lectr. mgmt. U. Colo., Denver, 1994—, U. Denver, 1994-96, Colo. Christian U., Denver, 1996—; instr. mgmt. Met. State Coll., Denver, 1996—, lectr. human resource mgmt., 1996—; part-time lectr. Sch. Indsl. Adminstrn., Carnegie Mellon U., Pitts., 1986, U. Pitts., 1983-87; cons. Wessex, Ctr. for Creative Comm., Children's Hosp., Pullman Swindell, Westinghouse Elec. Corp. Co-editor: Gaining Control of the Corporate Culture, 1985; co-author: The Kilmann-Saxton Culture-Gap Survery, 1983, contbr. articles to profl. jours. Mem. Greater Houston Women's Found., 1991-93. U.S.-Soviet Joint Ventures grantee U. Houston, 1990. Mem. ASTD, Acad. of Mgmt., Colo.-Wyo. Assn. Indsl./Orgnl. Psychologists, Inst., Ops. Rsch. and Mgmt. Svcs.

SAXTON, RUTH OLSEN, educator, dean; b. Spokane, Wash., Apr. 18, 1941; d. O. Martin and Edith M. (Halsey) Olsen; m. Paul Malcom, Mar. 16, 1963; children: Kirsten Teresa, David Malcom, Katherine Blair. BA, Wheaton Coll., 1963; MA, Mills Coll., 1972; PhD, U. Calif., Berkeley, 1986. Calif. C.C. credential. Tchr. English Hyde Park H.S., Chgo., 1963-64; instr. English Coll. of Alameda, Calif., 1972-76, Mills Coll., Oakland, Calif., 1974-85; asst. prof. English Mills Coll., Oakland, 1985-90, assoc. prof. English, 1990—, dean of letters, 1993—; bd. mem. Calif. Writing Project Adv. Bd. Editor: Woolf & Lessing: Breaking the Mold, 1994; assoc. editor Woolf Studies Annual. Recipient Outstanding Tchr. award Sears Found., 1990. Mem. MLA, Va. Woolf Soc., Doris Lessing Soc. (newsletter editor 1991—). Democrat. Home: 800 Portal Ave Oakland CA 94610 Office: Mills College 5000 Macarthur Blvd Oakland CA 94613

SAYERS, MARY ANNA GLADDEN, county official; b. Nassawadox, Va., Sept. 10, 1947; d. William Haywood and Lou Emma (Burroughs) Gladden; m. Edward James Sayers, Sr., June 2, 1966 (div. Aug. 1984); children: Edward James Jr., Michael Charles, William Guy. Grad. high sch., Eastville, Va. Admissions clk. NAM Hosp., Nassawadox, 1969-78; dep. commr. of the revenue Northampton County, Eastville, Va., 1978-90, commr. of the revenue, 1990—. Mem. Cape Charles Rotary Club, Internat. Assn. of Assessing Officers, Va. Assn. of Assessing Officers. Baptist. Office: Commr of the Revenue 16404 Courthouse Rd Eastville VA 23347

SAYRE, LINDA DAMARIS, human resources professional; b. Washington, Nov. 26, 1945; d. Wallace Stanley and Kathryn Louise (McKnight) S. BA in English, Wells Coll., 1967; MA in Sociology, U. Sussex, Brighton, Eng., 1969; postgrad., Rutgers U., 1993—. Human resources specialist N.Y.C. Human Resources Adminstrn., 1967-68; rsch. assoc. Presdl. Campaign Gov. Nelson Rockefeller, N.Y.C., 1968; ednl. coord. Isabella Geriat. Ctr., N.Y.C., 1970-72; rsch. assoc. N.Y.C. Mayor's Commn. on City Fins., 1973-75; project mgr. The Urban Acad. for Mgmt., N.Y.C., 1976-80; intern and external tng. cons. Boston and N.Y.C., 1980-83; tng. cons. N.Y.C. Bd. of Edn., N.Y.C., 1983-84; tng. and edn. dir. Gen. Hosp. Ctr., Passaic, N.J., 1984-87; dir. human rels. Bronx (N.Y.) Lebanon Hosp., 1987-90; external cons. Atlanta, N.Y.C., 1990-95; tng. & devel. mgr. BOC Gases, Murray Hill, N.J., 1995—. Mem. steering com. Broadway Dems., N.Y.C., 1974-80, 1993-96, pres., 1975, 77; coord. Carter Presdl. Campaign, N.Y. 20th Congl. Dist., 1976; bd. Westside Cares Food Voucher, N.Y.C., 1993-95. Mem. ASTD (v.p. programs No. N.J. 1985-86, chmn. nat. affairs Atlanta 1991), N.Y. ASTD (v.p. prof. edn. 1993, pres. 1994, past pres. 1995, co-chair adv. coun. 1996, nat. leadership design com. 1995—). Democrat. Home: 448 Riverside Dr New York NY 10027

SAYSETTE, JANICE ELAINE, vertebrate paleontologist, zoo archaeologist; b. San Francisco, Feb. 27, 1949; d. James Monroe and Isabel Christine (Saysette) Heffern; m. Thomas Arthur Haygood, Aug. 6, 1978 (div. June 1991); children: Grant Thomas, Ian James. AA in Nursing, Ohlone Coll., 1974; BSN, Metro State, 1981; MS in Nursing, U. Colo., 1982; MA in Anthropology, Colo. State U., 1990, postgrad., 1991—. Staff nurse Palo Alto (Calif.) VA Hosp., 1974-75, San Jose (Calif.) Hosp., 1975-78, O'Connor Hosp., San Jose, 1978-80; clin. nursing instr. U. No. Colo., Greeley, 1982-87; nursing supr. Poudre Valley Hosp., Ft. Collins, Colo., 1988-89; grad. teaching asst. Colo. State U., Ft. Collins, 1988-90, ind. contractor-zooarchaeology, 1990—; crew mem. U. Wyo. Lookingbill Archaeological Site, 1991; crew chief Denver Mus. Natural History Porqupine Cave Paleontological Site, 1993; lectr., presenter in field. Mem. Am. Soc. Mammalogists, Internat. Coun. Archaeozoology, Soc. Am. Archaeology, Soc. Vertebrate Paleontology. Democrat. Office: Colo State U Dept of Biology Fort Collins CO 80523

SAZAMA, KATHLEEN, pathologist, lawyer; b. Sutherland, Nebr., May 8, 1941; d. Roger William and Esther Mary (Reitz) Paulman; m. Franklin Jed Sazama, Aug. 26, 1962; children: Clare Ann, Jill Patrice. BS, U. Nebr., 1962; MS, Am. U., 1969; MD, Georgetown U., 1976; JD, Cath. U. Am., 1990. Diplomate Am. Bd. Pathology; lic. pathologist Mich., Va., Md., D.C., Calif., Pa.; bar: Md. Intern and resident Georgetown U. Med. Ctr., Washington, 1976-78; resident NIH, Bethesda, Md., 1978-79; clin. asst. prof. pathology Uniformed Svcs. U. Health Scis., Bethesda, 1981-89; clin. affiliate Ferris State Coll., Big Rapids, 1985-86; chief lab. of blood bank practices FDA Ctr. for Biologics Evaluation and Rsch., Bethesda, 1986-89; cons. Ober, Kaler, Grimes & Shriver, Balt., 1989-90; assoc. med. dir. Sacramento (Calif.) Med. Found. Blood Ctr., 1990-92; asst. clin. prof. pathology U. Calif., Davis, 1990-92, assoc. prof., dir. clin. pathology, 1992-93; prof. pathology and lab. medicine Allegheny U. of the Health Scis., Phila., 1994—;

v.p. Bd. Met. Washington Blood Banks, Inc., 1981-84; speaker in field. Author: (with others) Stat: The Laboratory's Role, 1986; contbr. numerous articles to profl. jours. Comdr. USPHS, 1986-89. Fellow Coll. Am. Pathologists, Am. Soc. Clin. Pathologists; mem. AMA, ABA, Pa. Med. Soc., Am. Assn. Blood Banks (bd. dirs.), Pa. Blood Bank Assn., Nat. Health Lawyers Assn., Phi Kappa Phi, Beta Beta Beta. Office: Allegheny U Health Scis Broad and Vine Sts MS 435 Philadelphia PA 19102

SBUTTONI, KAREN RYAN, reading specialist; b. Albany, N.Y., Sept. 9, 1953; d. Patrick Frederick and Virginia Mary (Moore) Ryan; m. Michael James Sbuttoni, Aug. 9, 1975; children: Michael Louis, Ashley Ryan. BS in Bus. Edn., Buffalo State Coll., 1979; MS in Bus. Edn., SUNY, Albany, 1983, MS in Reading, 1991, CAS in reading, 1994. Cert. reading specialist K-12 and bus. edn. 7-12, N.Y. Tchr. Williamsville East H.S., Buffalo, N.Y., spring 1979, East Irondequoit H.S., Rochester, N.Y., 1979-81; tchr., mem. admissions com. and outcomes com. The Albany Acad., 1992—; tchg. asst. SUNY, Albany, 1992. Religious edn. tchr. St. Pius X Ch., Loudonville, N.Y., 1982-84. Mem. Internat. Reading Assn., Nat. Coun. Tchrs. English. Office: The Albany Acad Academy Rd Albany NY 12208

SCACCHI, GRETA, actress; b. Milan, Feb. 18, 1960. Films include Das Zweite Gesicht, 1982, Heat and Dust, 1982, Defence of the Realm, 1985, The Coca-Cola Kid, 1985, White Mischief, 1987, Un Homme Amoureux, 1987, Good Morning, Babylon, 1987, Paura e Amore, 1988, La Donna della Luna, 1988, Presumed Innocent, 1990, Turtle Beach, 1991, Fires Within, 1991, The Player, 1992, Desire, 1993, Country Life, 1994, The Browning Version, 1994, Jefferson in Paris, 1995, Emma, 1996, Bravo Randy, 1996; TV movies include The Ebony Tower, 1984, Camille, 1984, Dr. Fischer of Geneva, 1985, Rasputin, 1996 (Emmy award). Office: c/o Susan Smith & Assocs 121 San Vicente Blvd Beverly Hills CA 90211*

SCAFFIDI, JUDITH ANN, school volunteer program administrator; b. Bklyn., Aug. 2, 1950; d. Anthony William and Rose Virginia (Nocera) S. BA, SUNY, Plattsburg, 1972, MS, 1973; postgrad. Kennedy Learning Ctr., Einstein Coll. Medicine, 1983; PhD (hon.), Internat. U. Bombay, 1993; HHD (hon.), London Inst. Applied Rsch., 1993. Cert. secondary edn. English. VISTA mem. ACTION, N.Y.C., 1976-77; coord. cultural resources N.Y.C. Sch. Vol. Program, N.Y.C., 1977-80; dist. coord. in Bklyn. N.Y.C. Sch. Vol. Program, 1980—; field supr., adj. faculty Coll. for Human Svcs., N.Y.C., 1984-86; adv. coun. chairperson Ret. Sr. Vol. Program in Bklyn., 1983-86; adv. bd. Ret. Sr. Vol. Program in N.Y.C., 1983-86. Mem. Am. Friends Svc. Com., 1994—. Recipient award for svcs. in promotion literacy Internat. Reading Assn. and Bklyn. Reading Coun., 1986, award for outstanding leadership Ret. Sr. Vol. Program, 1986, cert. of appreciation Mayor City of N.Y., 1991,. Mem. NAFE, Cath. Tchrs. Assn. Bklyn. (del. sch. dist. 18, 1982-91), Internat. Platform Assn., World Found. Successful Women, Am. Biog. Inst. (rsch. bd. advisors 1992-93), Am. Biog. Inst. Rsch. Assn. (bd. govs. 1992—), Internat. Parliament for Safety and Peace (dep. mem. and diplomatic passport), Maisson Internat. de Intellectuels (Acad. MIDI), Cath. Alumni Club N.Y., Amnesty Internat. Roman Catholic. Home: 2330 Ocean Ave Apt 3H Brooklyn NY 11229-3036 Office: NYC Sch Vol Program 352 Park Ave S 13th fl New York NY 10010

SCAGLIOLA, GERALDINE, accountant; b. Bklyn., Nov. 2, 1961; d. Jack P. and Christine (Lasala) Surdi; m. Graziano Scagliola, Nov. 16, 1991; 1 child, Nicole Elizabeth. MBA in Quantitative Analysis, St. John's U., 1990; BS in Acctg., L.I. U., 1993. Staff dir. NYNEX Corp., N.Y.C., 1983—. Mem. Inst. Mgmt. Accts., Nat. Assn. Purchasing Mgrs. Office: NYNEX Corp 3 Stephen Ln Hicksville NY 11801-6516

SCALA, MARILYN CAMPBELL, special education educator, writer, consultant; b. Lansing, Mich., June 25, 1942; d. Coral Edward and Eloise (Doolittle) Campbell; children: Nicholas, Anne. BS Edn., U. Mich., 1964; MA Spl. Edn., Columbia U., 1967. Cert. elem. edn., spl. edn. tchr., N.Y. Tchr. physically handicapped Multi-Age, Port Chester, N.Y., 1964-66; tchr. spl. edn. PS 199, N.Y.C., 1966-69, Manhattan Sch. for Seriously Disturbed, N.Y.C., 1969-70; tchr. regular and spl. edn. Munsey Park Sch., Manhasset, N.Y., 1970—. Co-author: Three Voices: An Invitation to Poetry Across the Curriculum; contbr. articles to profl. jours. Recipient Disting. Svc. award Bd. Edn., Manhasset, 1989-90. Mem. Manhasset Edn. Assn. (corr. sec. 1992-95), Tchr. Resource Ctr. Bd., Dist. Shared Decision Making Team, Delta Kappa Gamma. Office: Munsey Park Sch Hunt Lane Manhasset NY 11030

SCALETTA, HELEN MARGUERITE, volunteer; b. Sioux City, Iowa, Apr. 13, 1927; d. Ralph J. and Ruth Cora (Coyle) Beedle; m. Phillip Jasper Scaletta, May 21, 1946; children: Phillip Ralph, Cheryl Diane Kesler. AA in Bus., Edwards Coll. Bus., Sioux City, 1946. Acct. Towners Dept. Store, Iowa City, 1947-48; legal sec. Phillip Scaletta, Sioux City, 1950-74; service chmn. Easter Seal Soc., Lafayette, Ind., 1970-88; recording sec. Home Hosp. Aux., Lafayette, 1989; danced in Civic Theatre Follies, 1962. Orch. mem. June's All-Girl Ensemble, 1943-50. Pres. Newcomers club YWCA, Lafayette, 1967-68, mem. chmn., bd. dirs., 1979; leader Girl Scouts Am., Ft. Wayne, Ind., 1960-63; chmn. Mental Health Inc., Ft. Wayne, 1960-61, Cancer Crusade, West Lafayette, 1973-74; precinct worker Rep. Cen. Com., West Lafayette, 1974-76; Nat. Missions sec. 1st Presbyn. Ch., 1957. Recipient Citation Easter Seal Soc., 1981. Mem. Purdue U. Women's Club (pres. 1973-74), Lafayette Country Club (golf chmn. 1971, 90, bowling pres. 1992-93, golf co-chair Battleground 9-hole group 1996), Purdue Women's Bowling League (treas. 1978-79), Cosmopolitan Club, Sigma Kappa (corp. bd., sec., treas. 1971—), Kappa Kappa Sigma (pres. 1972), Sigma Kappa Lafayette Alumnae (pres. 1970, 1988-93). Home: One Via Verde Lafayette IN 47906

SCALETTA-CARONE, STACIA ANN, social worker; b. Johnstown, Pa., July 6, 1967; d. Samuel August and Claire Joanne (Foreman) Scaletta; m. Patrick Patteson Carone, June 3, 1995. BA, Chatham Coll., 1989; MA, Ind. U. Pa., 1991; EdD, U. Va., 1995. Cert. counselor, nat. Clin. therapy coord. Appalachian Youth Svc., Ebensburg, Pa., 1991-92; instr. U. Va., Charlottesville, 1992-94; social worker Med. Coll. Va., Richmond, 1995—; treatment specialist St. Joseph's Villa, Richmond, 1995—; pres. Counselor Edn. Student Assn., Indiana, Pa., 1990-91; grant coord. Ind. U. Pa., 1991. Mem. Internat. Assn. Addiction and Offender Counselors, Am. Counseling Assn., Richmond Area Counselor's Assn.

SCALFANO, JENNIE LOU, real estate executive; b. Beaumont, Tex., Nov. 4, 1956; d. Willie Slaton and Pauline (Leight) Spears; m. Dennis Allen Knapp, Dec. 23, 1973 (div. 1984); 1 child, Myron Allen; m. Thomas Charles Scalfano, Nov. 1, 1986; children: Rachael Michelle, Thomas Charles Jr. Student, Lamar U., Beaumont, 1981-85. Bookkeeper Heufelder Masonry & Sons, Beaumont, 1976-78; accounts payable staff M&I Ind., Beaumont, 1979-80, acctg. clk. supr., 1980-81, credit/collections supr., staff acct., 1981-82; acctg. supr., staff acct. Jefferson Ind. Inc., Port Arthur, Tex., 1982, corp. controller, 1982-84; v.p., sec., treas., gen. mgr. B.M. Odom Estate, R.E. Odom, Odom Bldg., Inc., Duphil, Inc., Orange, Tex., 1984—; dir. Ta-Lo Co., Orange, Odom Bldg. Co., Orange, Duphil, Inc., Orange. Roman Catholic. Home: 3326 Pheasant St Orange TX 77630-2042 Office: Estate of BM Odom PO Box 458 Orange TX 77631-0458

SCANLON, DERALEE ROSE, registered dietitian, educator, author; b. Santa Monica, Calif., Aug. 16, 1950; d. Stanley Ralph and Demba (Runkle) S.; m. Alex Spataru, July 20, 1970 (div. 1974). AA, Santa Monica Coll., 1968; accred. med. record tech., East L.A. Coll., 1980; BS, U. Calif., L.A., 1984. Registered dietitian. V.p. corp. sales, nutrition dir. LIfeTrends Corp., Carlsbad, Calif., 1984-86; dir. media, nutrition Irvine Ranch Farmers Markets, L.A., 1987-88; spokesperson for media Calif. Milk Adv. Bd., San Diego, 1986; nutrition reporter Med-NIWS, L.A., 1990-91; dietitian Sta. ABC-TV The Home Show, L.A., 1991-92, Sta. NBC-TV David Horowitz Fight Back, L.A., 1991-92; dietitian, nutrition reporter Sta. KTTV-TV Good Day L.A., 1994-95; nutritionist Sta. KABC-TV Kids View, 1994—; co-host talk radio show Light and Lively, KABC, 1994—; mgr. Nutrition Svcs. Vitex Foods, Inc., 1995-96; spokesperson Sandoz Nutrition, 1995-96; host nat. cable TV health show To Your Health, 1996—; media spokesperson Lifetime Food Co., Seaside, Calif., 1992—, Interior Design Nutritionals, Provo, Utah, 1993—, Weight Watchers, 1993-94; contbr. writer L.A. Parent Mag., Burbank, Calif., 1991—; syndicated nutrition reporter Live N'Well TV Series, Utah, 1992-93; nutrition educator Emeritus Coll. Sr. Health, Santa Monica, 1990-92; nutrition lectr. Princess Cruises, L.A., 1987; nutrition video host AMA Campaign Against Cholesterol, 1989; lectr. on nutrition and health to various orgns., 1993—; leader seminar series on I.B.S. UCLA Med. Ctr., 1994-95, others. Author: The Wellness Book of IBS, 1989, Diets That Work, 1991, rev. edit., 1992, 93; newspaper columnist: Ask the Dietitian, 1990-94; columnist Natural Way Mag.; Ask the Dietitian column in The Natural Way Mag., 1995; contbr. articles to profl. jours. Mem. AFTRA, Dietitians in Bus./Comms. (regional rep. 1990-92, So. Calif. chairperson 1991-92, editor nat. newsletter 1994-96), Am. Dietetic Assn. (pub. rels. chair 1985-87), Calif. Dietetic Assn. (Dietitian of Yr. in Pvt. Practice, Bus. and Comm. 1993), Soc. for Nutrition Edn., Nat. Speakers Assn. Home and Office: 10613 Eastborne Ave Los Angeles CA 90024-5920

SCANLON, DOROTHY THERESE, history educator; b. Bridgeport, Conn., Oct. 7, 1928; d. George F. and Mazie (Reardon) S.; AB, U. Pa., 1948, MA, 1949; MA, Boston Coll., 1953; PhD, Boston U., 1956; postdoctoral scholar Harvard U., 1962-64, 72. Tchr. history and Latin Marycliff Acad., Winchester, Mass., 1950-52; tchr. history Girls Latin Sch., Boston, 1952-57; prof. Boston State Coll., 1957-82, Mass. Coll. Art, 1982-95, prof. emerita, 1995—. Recipient Disting. Svc. award Boston State Coll., 1979, Faculty Award of Excellence, Mass. Coll. Art, 1985, Faculty Disting. Service award, Mass. Coll. Art, 1987. Mem. Pan-Am. Soc., Latin Am. Studies Assn., Am. Hist. Assn., Orgn. Am. Historians, Am. Studies Assn., Am. Assn. History of Medicine, History of Sci. Soc., AAUP, AAUW, Phi Alpha Theta, Delta Kappa Gamma. Author: Instructor's Manual to Accompany Lewis Hanke, Latin America: A Historical Reader, 1974; contbr. Biographical Dictionary of Social Welfare, 1986. Home: 23 Mooring Ln Dennis MA 02638 Office: Mass Coll Art Dept History 621 Huntington Ave Boston MA 02115-5801

SCANLON, GAIL GRETCHEN, librarian, nurse; b. Holyoke, Mass., Aug. 2, 1955; d. Rudy John and Josephine Sophia (Burek) Wojnarowski; m. Michael John Scanlon, June 5, 1976; children: Jonathan Spencer Scanlon, Douglas Todd, Abigail Jillian. Diploma in Nursing, Framingham (Mass.) Union Hosp. Sch. of Nursing, 1976; BA, Mount Holyoke Coll., South Hadley, Mass., 1995. RN; lic. real estate agent. Nurse Seaside Nursing Home, Portland, 1979-80, Upjohn Health Care, Torrance, Calif., 1983-85, Meadowood Nursing Home, South Hadley, Mass., 1988-91; owner The Elegant Basket, South Hadley, 1988-91; real estate sales agent Chestnut Hill Real Estate, South Hadley, 1987—; library circulation asst. Mount Holyoke Coll., South Hadley, 1993—; asst. dir. access svcs. Mt. Holyoke Coll. Libr., South Hadley, 1996—. Creator: (mus. exhibit) Past, Present and Future: Women Making a Difference in South Hadley, 1995. Mem. bd. dirs. South Hadley (Mass.) Swim Club, 1988-94; library trustee South Hadley Pub. Library, 1989—; mem. town mtg. Town of South Hadley, 1990—; dir. South Hadley Youth Ctr., 1994—. Mem. ALA, Mass. Library Trustees Assn., Mass. Friends of Libraries Assn., Know Your Town. Home: 3 Chestnut Hill Rd South Hadley MA 01075 Office: Mount Holyoke Library South Hadley MA 01075

SCANLON, JENNIFER ROSE, women's studies educator; b. N.Y.C., Dec. 23, 1958; d. William Edward and Mary Catherine (Barry) S. BS in English/Secondary Edn., SUNY, Oneonta, 1980; MA in English, U. Del., 1982; MA in Women's History, Binghamton U., 1986, PhD in History, 1989. Asst. prof. women's studies SUNY, Plattsburgh, 1989-95; assoc. prof., dir. women's studies, 1995—; chair SUNY women's studies coun., 1994—, pres.'s adv. com. on personal safety, 1994-96; lectr. in field. Author: Inarticulate Longings; The Ladies' Home Journal, Gender and the Promises of Consumer Culture, 1995; co-author: American Women Historians, 1770s-1990s: A Biographical Dictionary, 1996; manuscript reader NWSA Jour., 1994—, Transformations, 1993-94; contbr. articles to profl. jours. Bd. dirs. No. Adirondack Planned Parenthood, 1992—, exec. com., 1995—, v.p. 1996, pres., 1996—; facilitator Celebration of Cultural Diversity, 1989-93. Recipient N.Y. State/UUP New Faculty Devel. award for rsch., 1991, Phi Eta Sigma disting. faculty award for excellence in teaching, 1992, Chancellor's award for excellence in tchg. SUNY, 1996. Mem. N.Y. Women's Studies Assn. (conf. and steering com. 1993-94), Nat. Women's Studies Assn. (continuing edn. com. 1993-94, N.Y. to state del. to conf. 1992-95), United Univ. Profls. (exec. bd. 1990-93, 94—), Am. Journalism Historians Assn. (pub. com. 1991-92), Am. Hist. Assn., Orgn. Am. Historians, Conf. Group on Women's History, Am. Studies Assn., Berkshire Conf. on Women's History. Office: SUNY Women's Studies Program Hawkins 106 Plattsburgh NY 12901

SCANLON, JERILYN AILEEN, advertising executive; b. Bronx, N.Y., May 30, 1949; d. Sam and Shirley (Schubert) Winkler; m. Thomas Anthony Scanlon, Mar. 23, 1974; children: Michelle Reneé, Jeffrey Andrew. BS in Elem. Edn., U. Bridgeport. Owner Winklers for Parties, Trumbull, Conn., 1972-83; from sales rep. to dir. sales Getting to Know You Internat., Westbury, N.Y., 1983-89, v.p. West Coast ops., 1990—. Home: 21652 High Country Dr Trabuco Highlands CA 92679

SCARBROUGH-LUTHER, PATSY WURTH, geographic information systems specialist; b. Paducah, Ky., Dec. 5, 1947; d. James Edward and Olean Barbara (Sietz) Wurth; m. Jerry Leon Scarbrough, Aug. 7, 1965 (div. 1985); children: Tracy Ann, Ashli Michele, Scott Jeremy; m. Robert W. Luther, Feb. 25, 1995. BS magna cum laude, Murray (Ky.) State U., 1988, MS, 1991. Cert. emergency med. technician. Instr. Ky. Cabinet for Human Resources, Frankfort, 1983-93, Vocat. Edn. Region I, Paducah, Ky., 1983-91, Murray State U., 1983-91, Calloway County Red Cross, Murray, 1985-89; exec. dir. Marshall County Red Cross, Benton, Ky., 1985-88; first aid attendant Ohio River Steel, Calvert City, Ky., 1985-86; profl. intern Johnson Controls, Cadiz, Ky., 1986; grad. asst. Murray State U., 1988-91; fellow U.S. Dept. Energy/Oak Ridge (Tenn.) Nat. Lab., 1989-90; postgrad. rsch. fellow U.S. Army Corps Engrs. Constrn. Engring. Rsch. Lab., Champaign, Ill., 1991-92, acting team leader spatial techs. support team, 1992-93; GIS facility mgr. environ. scis. divsn. Oak Ridge (Tenn.) Nat. Lab., 1993-95; mgr. GIS svcs. Solutions to Environ. Problems, Inc., Oak Ridge, 1995-96, AEgis Svcs. Corp., Clinton, Tenn., 1996—; adj. prof. Roane State C.C., Hariman, Tenn., 1996—. Troop leader Kentuckiana Girl Scouts, Benton, 1973-84, fund drive chmn., 1973-84. Mem. LWV, Am. Soc. Safety Engrs., Ky. EMT Instrs. Assn. (instr.), Western Ky. EMT Assn., Am. Soc. Photogrametry and Remote Sensing (Western Great Lake region sec., treas. 1992), Nat. Safety Coun. (cmty. health and emergency svcs. com.), Assn. Women in Sci., Tenn. Geog. Info. Coun., S.E. Regional ARC/INFO Users Group (chair 1995), Nat. Assn. Environ. Profls., Oak Ridge Area ARC/INFO Users Group (chairperson 1996), Epsilon Pi Tau, Alpha Chi. Democrat. Roman Catholic. Home: 330 Melton Hill Dr Clinton TN 37716 Office: Aegis Svcs Corp PO Box 160 Clinton TN 37717

SCARF, MARGARET (MAGGIE SCARF), author; b. Phila., May 13, 1932; d. Benjamin and Helen (Rotbin) Klein; m. Herbert Eli Scarf, June, 1953; children: Martha Samuelson, Elizabeth Stone, Susan Merrell. BA, South Conn. State U., 1989. Writer in residence Jonathan Edwards Coll., Yale U.; contbg. editor New Republic, Washington, DC, 1978—, Self Mag., N.Y.C., 1991—; writer-in-residence Jonathan Edwards Coll., 1995—; assoc. fellow Jonathan Edwards Coll. Yale U., New Haven, 1979, 81, 83; sr. fellow Bush Ctr. in Child Devel. and Social Policy, Yale U., 1991—; mem. adv. bd. Am. Psychiat. Press, Poynter Fellowship Journalism Yale U., 1995-96. Author: Meet Benjamin Franklin, 1968, Antarctica: Exploring the Frozen Continent, 1970, Body, Mind, Behavior, 1976 (Nat. Media award Am. Psychological Assn. 1977), Unfinished Business: Pressure Points in the Lives of Women, 1981, Intimate Partners: Patterns in Love and Marriage, 1987, Intimate Worlds: Life Inside the Family, 1996; contbr. numerous articles to jours. including N.Y. Times mag. and book rev., Psychology Today. Recipient Nat. Media award Am. Psychol. Found., 1971, 74, Conn. UN award Outstanding Conn. Women, 1987; grantee Smith Richardson Found., 1991-94; Ford Found. fellow, 1973-74, Neiman fellow Harvard U., 1975-76, Ctr. Advanced Study in Behavioral Scis. fellow, 1977-78, 85-86, Alicia Patterson Found. fellow, 1978-79. Mem. Conn. Soc. Psychoanalytic Psychologists, Am. Psychiat. Press (mem. adv. bd. 1992), Lawn Club, Elizabethans.

SCARPITTI, ELLEN CANFIELD, elementary school counselor; b. Tulsa, Feb. 4, 1938; d. Glenn Owen and Ellen Elizabeth (Hartwell) Canfield; m. Frank R. Scarpitti, Sept. 5, 1959; children: Susan Denise, Jeffrey Alan. BA, Antioch Coll., Yellow Springs, Ohio, 1960; MEd in Spl. Edn., Antioch U., Phila., 1978, postgrad., U. Del., 1986-89. Cert. counselor, Del. Spl. edn. tchr. Columbus (Ohio) Schs., 1960-61, Louisville Schs., 1961-63, Sommerset Schs., New Brunswick, N.J., 1963-66; ednl. diagnostician New Castle County Schs., Wilmington, Del., 1978-80; tchr. spl. edn. autistic pre-sch. Christina Sch. Dist., Newark, Del., 1981-82, spl. edn. kindergarten tchr., 1982-88, elem. sch. counselor, 1989—; instr. grad. program U. Del., Newark, 1991—. Bd. dirs. Mental Health Assn., 1993—, West Ctr. City Day Care, Wilmington, 1975-92, First Days Record, Newark, 1991—, Newark Unitarian Ch., 1970-74, Martin Luther King Co-op, Newark, 1970-73. Mem. NEA, ACA, Am. Sch. Counseling Assn., Del. Edn. Assn., Del. Sch. Counselor Assn. (bd. dirs. 1990-94). Home: 104 Radcliffe Dr Newark DE 19711-3147

SCARROW, PAMELA KAY, health care manager; b. Washington, Nov. 4, 1949; d. Edward Charles and Elsie Lorine (Kay) Scarrow; m. Antonio Joseph Franz, Sept. 4, 1979; 1 child, Vanessa Motil Franz. AA, Navarro Coll., Tex., 1981; BS, Golden Gate U., 1983. Cert. med. staff coordinator, 1986, cert. profl. healthcare quality, 1996. Adminstrv. asst. Trust Ter. of the Pacific Islands, Saipan, Mariana Islands, 1976-79; adminstrv. asst. Navarro Coll., Corsicana, Tex., 1979-81; staff asst. San Francisco Symphony, 1981-82; med. staff liaison Calif. Med. Assn., San Francisco, 1982-87; provider, practitioner cons. Calif. Med. Rev., Inc., San Francisco, 1987-90; med. rev. specialist Am. Med. Peer Rev. Assn., Washington, 1990-93; adminstr. quality assessment Am. Coll. Ob-gyn., 1993—. Democrat. Roman Catholic. Office: Am Coll Ob-gyn 409 12th St SW Washington DC 20024-2125

SCARSE, OLIVIA MARIE, cardiologist, consultant; b. Chgo., Nov. 10, 1950; d. Oliver Marcus and Marjorie Ardis (Olsen) S. BS, North Park Coll., 1970; MD, Loyola U., Maywood, Ill., 1973. Diplomate Am. Bd. Internal Medicine, Am. Bd. Cardiovascular Diseases. Surg. intern Resurrection Hosp., Chgo., 1974; resident in internal medicine Northwestern U., Chgo., 1974-77; cardiovascular disease fellow U. Ill., Chgo., 1977-80; dir. cardiac catherization lab. Cook County Hosp., Chgo., 1981; dir. heart sta. MacNeal Hosp., Berwyn, Ill., 1983; dir. electrophysiology Hines VA Hosp., Maywood, Ill., 1984-85; dir. progressive care Columbus Hosp., Chgo., 1985-88, pvt. practice, 1984—; pvt. practice Ill. Masonic Hosp., Chgo., 1989—; founder Physician Cons. for Evaluation of Clin. Pathways, Practice Parameters and Patient Care Outcomes, 1991—. Dir. continuous quality improvement Improvement Columbus, 1990-95. Pillsbury fellow Pillsbury Fund, 1980. Fellow Am. Coll. Cardiology; mem. AMA, ACP, Chgo. Med. Assn., Ill. State Med. Assn., Am. Heart Assn., Crescent Countries Found. for Med. Care, Physicians Health Network, Cen. Ill. Med. Review Orgn. Home and Office: 2650 N Lakeview Ave Apt 4109 Chicago IL 60614-1833

SCATENA, LORRAINE BORBA, rancher, women's rights advocate; b. San Rafael, Calif., Feb. 18, 1924; d. Joseph and Eugenia (Simas) de Borba; m. Louis G. Scatena, Feb. 14, 1960; children: Louis Vincent, Eugenia Gayle. BA, Dominican Coll., San Rafael, 1945; postgrad., Calif. Sch. Fine Arts, 1948, U. Calif., Berkeley, 1956-57. Cert. elem. tchr., Calif. Tchr. Dominican Coll., 1946; tchr. of mentally handicapped San Anselmo (Calif.) Sch. Dist., 1946; tchr. Fairfax (Calif.) Pub. Elem. Sch., 1946-53; asst. to mayor Fairfax City Recreation, 1948-53; tchr., libr. U.S. Dependent Schs., Mainz am Rhine, Fed. Republic Germany, 1953-56; translator Portugal Travel Tours, Lisbon, 1954; bonding sec. Am. Fore Ins. Group, San Francisco, 1956-60; rancher, farmer Yerington, Nev., 1960—; hostess com. Caldecott and Newbury Authors' Awards, San Francisco, 1959; mem. Nev. State Legis. Commn., 1975; coord. Nevadans for Equal Rights Amendment, 1975-78, rural areas rep., 1976-78; testifier Nev. State Senate and Assembly, 1975, 77; mem. adv. com. Fleischmann Coll. Agr. U. Nev., 1977-80, 81-84; speaker Grants and Rsch. Projects, Bishop, Calif., 1977, Choices for Tomorrow's Women, Fallon, Nev., 1989. Trustee Wassuk Coll., Hawthorne, Nev., 1984-87; mem. Lyon County Friends of Libr., Yerington, 1971—, Lyon County Mus. Soc., 1978; sec., pub. info. chmn. Lyon County Rep. Women, 1968-73, v.p. programs, 1973-75; mem. Lyon County Rep. Ctrl. Com., 1973-74; mem. Marin County Soc. Artists, San Anselmo, Calif., 1948-53; charter mem. Eleanor Roosevelt Fund Women and Girls, 1990, sustaining mem., 1992—; Nev. rep. 1st White House Conf. Rural Am. Women, Washington, 1980; participant internat. reception, Washington, 1980; mem. pub. panel individual presentation Shakespeare's Treatment of Women Characters, Nev. Theatre for the Arts, Ashland, Oreg. Shakespearean Actors local performance, 1977; mem. Nev. Women's History Project, U. Nev., 1996—. Recipient Outstanding Conservation Farmer award Mason Valley Conservation Dist., 1992, Soroptimist Internat. Women Helping women award 1983, invitation to first all-women delegation to U.S.A. from People's Republic china, U.S. House Reps., 1979; Public Forum Travel grantee Edn. Title IX, Oakland, Calif., 1977; fellow World Lit. Acad., 1993. Mem. Lyon County Ret. Tchrs. Assn. (unit pres. 1979-80, 84-86, v.p. 1986-88, Nev. div. Outstanding Svc. award 1981, state conv. gen. chmn. 1985), Rural Am. Women Inc., AAUW (br. pres. 1972-74, 74-76, chair edn. found. programs, 1983—, state convention gen. chmn. 1976, 87, state div. sec. 1970-72, state div. legis. program chmn. 1976-77, state div. chmn. internat. rels. 1979-81, state div. pres. 1981-83, br. travelship, discovering women in U.S. history Radcliffe Coll. Div. Humanities award 1975, Future Fund Nat. award 1983), Mason Valley Country Club, Italian Cath. Fedn. Club (pres. 1986-88), Uniao Portuguesa Estado da Calif. Roman Catholic. Home: 521 Hwy 339 Yerington NV 89447-0247

SCATIZZI, PATRICIA LYNN, media specialist, consultant; b. Rapid City, S.D., Apr. 27, 1964; d. Roger Nelson and Carolyn Ann (Sheffield) Manville; m. Michael Richard Scatizzi, Oct. 26, 1985; children: Andrew Roger, Mary Caroline. B of Journalism, U. Mo., 1985; MA in Edn., U. Ctrl. Fla., 1993. Media specialist Cambridge Elem. Sch., Cocoa, Fla., 1993—; presenter Fla. Assn. for Media Edn., 1993-94. Recipient Tech. Incentive award Fla. Dept. Edn., 1993-95. Office: Cambridge Elem Sch 2000 Cambridge Dr Cocoa FL 32922

SCAVETTI, LINDA VERONICA, librarian; b. Queens, N.Y., Dec. 14, 1947; d. Joseph and Vera S.; m. Wayne Clauss, Nov. 9, 1977. BA, NYU, 1969; MLS, St. John's U., 1971. Cert. pub. libr., N.Y. Libr. trainee Queensborough Pub. Libr., Jamaica, N.Y., 1969-71; libr. Queensborough Pub. Libr., Jamaica, 1971-80, sr. libr., 1980-85, 91—, asst. divsn. head, 1985-91, acting divsn. head, 1989-91, reference libr., 1991-96. Mem. NAFE, Disabled Am. Vets. Aux., N.Y. Libr. Club. Roman Catholic. Office: Queens Libr 89-11 Merrick Blvd Jamaica NY 11432

SCEARSE, PATRICIA DOTSON, nurse educator, college dean; b. Wabash, Ind., Sept. 4, 1931; d. Claude Richard and Lilly Etta (Colvill) D.; m. Vernon Quinton Scearse, June 26, 1955 (dec. Mar. 1990); 1 child, Victoria Lynn Lenderman. BS, Earlham Coll., 1955; MS, U. Colo., 1968; D in Nursing Sci., U. Calif., San Francisco, 1974. RN. Staff nurse Reid Meml. Hosp., Richmond, Ind., 1954-55; head nurse, instr. Hillcrest Bapt. Hosp., Waco, Tex., 1955-56; instr. Sch. Nursing Candler Hosp., Savannah, Ga., 1956-60; adminstrv. asst., edn. cons. Wyo. State Bd. Nursing, Cheyenne, 1964-68; asst. prof. San Diego State U., 1969, Ball State U., Muncie, Ind., 1969-71; assoc. prof., area chairperson U. Mich., Ann Arbor, 1974-80; prof., dean Coll. Nursing Tex. Christian U., Ft. Worth, 1980-95, emeritus dean, prof., 1995—. Pub. policy editor Jour. Profl. Nursing, Phila., 1986-89; editorial cons. Jour. Pub. Health Nursing, New Haven, 1984-89; contbr. articles to profl. jours. Recipient Outstanding Nurse award Sigma Theat Tau, Beta Alpha, Ft. Worth, 1986; Kennedy Inst. Ethics postdoctoral fellow, Georgetown U., 1978. Mem. ANA, APHA (bd. govs. 1976), Am. Assn. Colls. of Nursing (bd. dirs. 1982-84, 85-87), Nat. League for Nursing, Coun. Baccalaureate and Higher Degree Programs (bd. rev.), Assn. Community Health Nurse Educators (named Great 100 Nurses 1992). Home: 5108 Ledgestone Dr Fort Worth TX 76132-2019

SCEERY, BEVERLY DAVIS, genealogist, writer, educator; b. Hartford, Conn.; d. Howard Coe and Gladys (Cotton) Davis; m. Walter Raymond Sceery; children: Nancy Bazar, Edward Sceery, Walter Sceery Jr., Martha Creed, Mary Heaton. BS magna cum laude, U. Md., 1975, MS, 1977, postgrad., 1977-82. Fin. counselor U. Md., College Park, 1975-77, lectr., 1977-82; realtor Jack Lawlor Realty, Washington, 1982-95; genealogist DAR, Washington, 1992—; dir. handicapped program U. Md., College Park, 1975-77. Editor Capital Gardener mag., 1980-84; contbr. articles to profl. jours. Leader Girl Scouts Am., Potomac, Md., 1963-73, chmn., 1970-73, dir., Bethesda, Md., 1973. Mem. AAUW (chmn. nomination com. 1991), DAR (state registrar 1994—, chmn. Am. History, 1991-94, nat. vice chmn. vol.

genealogists, mus. docent, mem. speakers staff, organizing regent Potomac Hundred chpt. 1992—, hon. regent Great Falls chpt.), Nat. Capital Area Fedn. Garden Clubs (chmn. 1992—, flower show sch., 1989-91, master judge flower shows, landscape design 1972—), Phi Kappa Phi, Alpha Lambda Delta, Omicron Nu. Home: 10307 Riverwood Dr Potomac MD 20854-1539

SCHAAF, MARTHA ECKERT, author, poet, library director, musician, composer, educator, lecturer; b. Madison, Ind., Sept. 21, 1911; d. Frederick William and Julia (Richert) Eckert; m. Clarence William Schaaf, Dec. 27, 1941 (dec. 1987); 1 child, Susan Elizabeth Lee. AB with distinction, Ind. U., 1933; MLS, Columbia U., 1945; postgrad., Butler U., Ind. U. Lic. tchr. English, French, Spanish, music. Libr. dir. Twp. System, Crothersville, Ind., 1936-38; libr. music instr. Angola, Ind., 1938-39, Howe High Sch., Indpls., 1939-42; libr. dir. Reitz High Sch., Evansville, Ind., 1942; county libr. organizer County Brs. Libr., Columbus, Ga., 1943; hosp. libr. dir. Camp Van Dorn, Woodville, Miss., 1943-44; organized libr. Bulova Sch. for Disabled Vets., L.I., N.Y., 1944-45; organized bus. rsch. libr. Eli Lilly & Co., Indpls., 1946-50; rsch. libr. Wallace Collection Ind. Hist. Soc. Libr., 1958-61; dir. Pub. Libr., Pompano Beach, Fla., 1967-72; pres. Ind. Spl. Libr. Assn., 1948. Author: Lew Wallace: Boy Writer, 1961, Duke Ellington: Music Master, 1975; contbg. author: War Paint and Wagon Wheels, 1968, Reading Incentive Series, 1969, The Nat. Library of Poetry; contbr. articles to profl. jours. Named Valedictorian, Madison (Ind.) H.S., 1929; recipient History award DAR, 1930, C. of C. award Pompano Beach, Fla., 1970, Editor's Choice award Nat. Libr. Poetry award, 1995, Disting. Alumni award Ind. U., 1983. Mem. Nat. League Am. Pen Women (Svc. award Boca Raton br. 1995), Internat. Soc. Poets, Acad. Am. Poets, Pen Women, Mortar Board, Ind. U. Alumni Assn., Columbia U. Alumni Assn., Boca Raton Music Guild, Phi Beta Kappa, Pi Lambda Theta, Chi Omega (Found. award Theta Beta chpt.).

SCHAAFSMA, CAROL ANN, librarian; b. Ft. Wayne, Ind., Jan. 9, 1937; d. Ralph E. Armey and Georgia E. Roush Armey Swisher; m. Henry M. Schaafsma Jr., June 21, 1958 (div. 1977); 1 child, Julie Keiko. BS in Edn., Ind. U., 1958; MLS, U. Hawaii, 1968, MBA, 1977. Libr. U. Hawaii Libr., Honolulu, 1968-74, head acquisition dept., 1974-79, head serials dept., 1987-94, head collection svcs. divsn., 1995—. Treas. Friends of Libr. Hawaii, Honolulu, 1992-94, pres., 1995—; mem. Hawaii State Libr. Reengring. Adv. Com., 1995. Mem. ALA, Hawaii Libr. Assn. Office: U Hawaii Libr 2550 The Mall Honolulu HI 96822

SCHAAL-MAEDEL, ALLYSON BROOKE, psychotherapist, researcher; b. Mt. Holly, N.J., Dec. 13, 1965; d. Walter Richard and Alice Mae (Robbins) S. BS, Chestnut Hill (Pa.) Coll., 1988; MA, Rider Coll., 1991. Psychotherapist intern Family Svc. Burlington County, Moorestown, N.J., 1990; rsch. asst. Ctr. for Children's Support U. Medicine and Dentistry N.J., Stratford, 1990-91, coord. rsch., 1991—; counselor, 1992—. Office: U Medicine & Dentistry NJ Sch Osteopathic Medicine 42 E Laurel Rd Ste 3400 Stratford NJ 08084-1504

SCHAAR, SUSAN CLARKE, state legislative staff member; b. Lawrenceville, Va., Dec. 21, 1949; d. Garland Lewis and Frances Virginia (Matthews) Clarke; m. William Berkley Schaar Jr., Nov. 24, 1990. BA, U. Richmond, 1972. Engrossing clk. Senate Va., Richmond, 1974, legis. rsch. analyst, 1974-77; asst. to the clk. Senate of Va., Richmond, 1977-83; asst. clk. Senate Va., Richmond, 1983-90, clk. of the Senate, 1990—. mem. YMCA Model Gen. Assembly Adv. com., Richmond, 1990—; trustee U. Richmond, 1990-94; pres. Richmond Club of Westhampton, 1988-90; mem. Spider Club Athletic Bd., Richmond, 1988-90; co-chair Arts Around the Lake, Richmond, 1990-91. Mem. Am. Soc. Legis. Clks. and Secs. (mem. exec. com. 1995—, sec.-treas. 1996), Omicron Delta Kappa, Pi Sigma Alpha. Baptist. Office: Senate of Va PO Box 396 Richmond VA 23218-0396

SCHABNER, DAWN FREEBLE, artist, educator; b. Mercer, Pa., Jan. 30, 1933; d. Benjamin Frederick and Mary Emma (McElheny) Freeble; m. Donald Russell Schabner, Jan. 5, 1954; children: Donald Russell Jr., Dean Aaron. Student, Phila. Mus. Sch. Art, 1950-52; BA in Fine Arts magna cum laude, Hofstra U., 1971; student, Cleve. Inst Art., Stony Brook, 1976. Designer Am. Greetings, Cleve., 1953; art educator Islip (N.Y.) Pub. Schs., 1967-95, Dowling Coll., Oakdale, N.Y., 1991—. One-woman shows include East Islip (N.Y.) Pub. Libr., 1977, 88; group shows include Hofstra U., 1970, Patchogue-Medford Pub. Libr., 1983, East End Arts & Humanities Coun., Riverhead, N.Y., 1984, Islip Art Mus. Juried Exhibit, 1985, 87, 88, Suffolk County Legis. Bldg., Hauppage, N.Y., 1988, Bennington Coll., 1989, Goat Alley Gallery, Sag Harbor, N.Y., 1989, Canio's Books, Sag Harbor, 1990, South Country Libr., Bellport, N.Y., 1991; featured artist East End Arts and Humanities Coun., Riverhead, N.Y., 1986; featured at Clayton Liberatore Art Gallery, Bridgehampton, N.Y., 1994, 95. Mem. Met. Mus. Art, East End Arts Coun., Smithtown Twp. Arts Coun., Guild Hall.

SCHACHT, ARLENE MILLER, school system administrator; b. N.Y.C., Dec. 2, 1932; d. David and Esther (Nissman) Miller; m. Kenneth Schacht, July 24, 1952 (div. Sept. 1975); children: Scott, Glenn. BS, NYU, 1954; MA, Newark State Coll., 1969. Cert. counselor, sch. counselor. Tchr. N.Y.C. Sch. Sys., 1955-60; social studies tchr. Neptune (N.J.) Twp. Sch. Sys., 1967-70, sch. counselor, 1970-86, sch. counseling supr., chair dept., 1986-95; cons., sch. to work curriculum coord. New Brunswick (N.J.) Sch. Sys., 1995—; co-chair N.J. core curriculum content stds. in career edn. N.J. Dept. Edn., Trenton, 1995. Developer career curriculum, N.J. Recipient Planning for Life award U.S. Army, 1994, Counselor of County award Monmouth County Sch. Counselors Assn., 1995. Mem. Am. Sch. Counselor Assn., N.J. Sch. Counselor Assn. (advocacy chair 1995—).$Dat. Assn. Counseling. Office: Horizon Cons Svcs 7 Eisele Ave Ocean NJ 07712

SCHACHT, LINDA LOUISE, secondary school educator; b. Watertown, S.D., Feb. 5, 1964; d. Lester Eugene and Lois Maxine (Wolcott) S. BS in Edn., U. N.D., 1986; MA in Theatre Arts, U. S.D., 1988. Instr. secondary sch. lang. arts Alpena (S.D.) Sch. Dist., 1989—. Mem. Nat. Coun. Tchrs. English. Roman Catholic.

SCHACHTEL, BARBARA HARRIET LEVIN, epidemiologist, educator; b. Rochester, N.Y., May 27, 1921; d. Lester and Ethel (Neiman) Levin; m. Hyman Judah Schachtel, Oct. 15, 1941; children: Bernard, Ann.Mollie. Student Wellesley Coll., 1939-41; BS, U. Houston, 1951, MA in Psychology, 1967; PhD, U. Tex.-Houston, 1979. Psychol. examiner Meyer Ctr. for Devel. Pediatrics, Tex. Children's Hosp., Houston, 1967-81; instr. dept. pediatrics Baylor Coll. Medicine, Houston, 1967-81, asst. prof. dept. medicine, 1982—; asst. dir. biometry and epidemiology Sid W. Richardson Inst. for Preventive Medicine, Meth. Hosp., Houston, 1981-88, dir. quality assurance, 1988-93; retired 1993; mem. instl. rev. bd. for human rsch. Baylor Coll. Medicine, Houston, 1981-87; mem. devel. bd. U. Tex. Health Sci. Ctr., Houston, 1987—; mem. dean's adv. bd. Sch. Architecture U. Houston, 1987; bd. dirs. Tex. Medical Ctr, 1990-93. Contbr. articles to profl. jours. Vice pres., bd. dirs. Houston-Harris County Mental Health Assn., 1966-67; vice-chmn. bd. mgrs. Harris County Hosp. Dist., Houston, 1974-90, chmn. 1990-92, bd. dirs., 1970-93; trustee Inst. Religion in Tex. Med. Ctr., 1990— bd. mem. Planned Parenthood of Houston, Inc., 1994—, Houston Ind. Sch. Dist. Found., 1993—; sec. Bo Harris County Hosp. Dist. Found. Bd., 1993—. Named Great Texan of Yr., Nat. Found. for Ilietis and Colitis, Houston, 1982, Outstanding Citizen, Houston-Harris County Mental Health Assn., 1985; recipient Good Heart award B'nai Brith Women, 1984, Women of Prominence award Am. Jewish Com., 1991, Mayor's award for outstanding vol. svc., 1994. Mem. APA, APHA, Wellesley Club of Houston (pres. 1968-70). Avocations: golf, tennis, books. Home: 2527 Glen Haven Blvd Houston TX 77030-3511

SCHACK, EDNA ANN O'BRIEN, education educator; b. St. Louis, July 4, 1957; d. S. Vincent and Claire Elizabeth (McCarthy) O'Brien; m. Markham B. Schack, Dec. 27, 1979; children: Brian, Kevin, Claire, Rachel. AA Paralegal Studies, St. Louis C.C., 1977; BA, Northwestern State U., 1980, MS Child Devel., 1982; EdD Curriculum & Instr., Ill. State U., 1987. Lead presch. classroom tchr., Lab Sch. Northwestern State U., Natchitoches, La., 1981-82; grad. asst. Grad. Coord.'s Office Ill. State U., Normal, 1983-85, asst. prof. ednl. computing, 1985, grad. asst. Ctr. for High Edn., 1985-87; instr. computer sci. Lincoln Coll., Normal, 1985; grad. asst. Gifted Area Svc. Ctr. Ill. Region III, Normal, 1985-86; assoc. prof. Morehead (Ky.) State U., 1987—; ann. judge Northeast Ky. Regl. Sci. Fair, 1988—; reviewer Nat. Coun. Tchrs. Maths. Jour., 1988—; textbook reviewer Merrill/MacMillan and West Ednl. and Longman Group; cons. pub. schs. in ea. Ky.; presenter in field. Editor: (newsletter) Make Today County Support Group, Morehead, 1990-95; contbg. editor: Media & Methods, 1988-91; contbr. articles to profl. jours. Recipient Ora Bretall Dissertation scholarship Ill. State U., 1986. Mem. Nat. Coun. Tchrs. Math., Nat. Assn. Edn. Young Children, Mid-South Ednl. Rsch. Assn., Ky. Coun. Tchrs. Math., Kappa Delta Pi (assoc. coun. Epsilon Theta chpt. 1994—), Kappa Delta Pi (scholarship 1986). Roman Catholic. Home: 550 Crestview Ln Morehead KY 40351 Office: Morehead State U 304 Ginger Hall Morehead KY 40351

SCHADE, CHARLENE JOANNE, adult and early childhood education educator; b. San Bernardino, Calif., June 26, 1935; d. Clarence George Linde and Helen Anita (Sunny) Hardesty; m. William Joseph Jr., Apr. 12, 1958 (div., 1978); children: Sabrina, Eric, Camela, Cynthia; m. Thomas Byron Killens, Sept. 25, 1983. BS, UCLA, 1959. Tchr. dance & pe L.A. Unified Secondary Schs., Calif., 1959-63; dir., instr. (Kindergym) La Jolla YMCA, Calif., 1972-76; instr. older adult San Diego Community Colls., 1977—; artist in residence Wolf Trap/Headstart, 1984-85; workshop leader S.W. Dance, Movement and Acro-Sports Workshop, prime-time adult activities coord., 1988—, Am. Heart Assn., Arthritis Found., Am. Lung Assn., AAHPERD, S.W. Dist. AHPERD, Calif. Assn. Health, Phys. Edn., Recreation and Dance, Head Start, San Diego Assn. Young Children, Calif. Assn. Edn. Young Child, Calif. Kindergarten Assn., Assn. Childhood Edn. Internat., IDEA Internat. Assn. Fitness Profls., San Diego C.C., Am. Soc. on Aging, 1977—; cons. to Calif. Gov.'s Coun. on Phys. Fitness, 1993; feature guest Sta. KFMB and KPBS TV shows, San Diego, 1980-88. Author: Move With Me From A to Z, 1982, Move With Me, One, Two, Three, 1988; co-author: Prime Time Aerobics, 1982, Muevete Conmigo, uno, dos, tres, 1990; co-writer: Guide for Physical Fitness Instructors of Older Adults, Grant Project, 1990, The Empowering Teacher, 1990, Handbook for Instructors of Older Adults, 1994. Dir. We Care Found., San Diego, 1977-79, Meet the Author programs San Diego County Schs., 1988—; founder SOLO, San Diego, 1981-83; adminstr., v.p. ODEM chpt. Toastmasters, San Diego, 1982; chmn. People with Arthritis Can Exercise com. San Diego chpt. Arthritis Found., 1994-95; trainer PACE instrs. Nat. Arthritis Found., 1995—. Grantee Video Showcase of Exercises for Older Adults, 1992-93. Mem. AAPHERD (workshop leader), Calif. Assn. Health, Phys. Edn., Recreation and Dance (workshop leader). Office: Exer Fun/Prime Time Aerobic 3089C Clairemont Dr Ste 130 San Diego CA 92117-6802

SCHAEFER, BEVERLY JEAN, elementary education educator; b. Havre, Mont., May 29, 1953; d. Leo J. Schaefer and Agnes May (Peters) S.; m. Gene R. DiRe, June 26, 1981; children: Patrick DiRe, Lauren DiRe. BA, Gonzaga U., 1974, MA, 1990. Cert. K-12 tchr., Wash. Clerical worker dept. psychology Gonzaga U., Spokane, Wash., 1972-74; 1st grade tchr. East Valley Sch. Dist., Spokane, Wash., 1975-80, 4th grade tchr., 1980-93, 5th grade tchr., 1993—; mem. reading com. East Valley Sch. Dist., 1985-94, tech. com., 1984-92, restructuring com., 1993-95. Mem. neighborhood accountability bd. Spokane County, 1981; leader March of Dimes neighborhood Spokane City, 1988. Mem. Wash. Edn. Assn. (rep. 1977, S.T.A.R. cadre 1992-94), East Valley Edn. Assn. (bldg. rep. 1976-77, exec. com. 1984-85, treas. 1985-86, sec. 1995). Home: N 8211 Lucia Ct Spokane WA 99208

SCHAEFER, MARILYN LOUISE, artist, writer, educator; b. Cedar Rapids, Iowa, Apr. 22, 1933; d. Henry Richard and Maria Augusta (Dickel) S. AA, Monticello Coll. for Women, 1953; BFA, Cranbrook Acad. Art, 1956, MFA, 1960; MA cum laude, U. Chgo., 1958; MA, St. John's Coll., Santa Fe, 1979. Rsch. asst. editor Encyclopaedia Britannica, Chgo., 1960-63; humanities editor Encyclopedia Americana, N.Y., 1964-68; acquisitions editor Litton Ednl. Pub., N.Y., 1968-70; from instr. to prof. art and advt. design dept. N.Y.C. Tech. Coll. CUNY, 1970—; contbg. editor Encyclopedia Americana, 1979—, Coll. Teaching Jour., 1979. Contbr. articles to profl. publs. including Art and Auction mag., Art and Antiques mag., Am. Artist mag., Encyclopedia Americana, 1970—. Luce Found. postgrad. study fellow St. John's Coll., 1976-79; Ingram Merrill Found. grantee, 1983-84. Mem. AAUW, CUNY Acad. Arts and Scis. Home: 306 W 76th St New York NY 10023-8065 Office: NYC Tech Coll CUNY 300 Jay St Brooklyn NY 11201-2902

SCHAEFER, MARY ANN, health facility administrator, consultant; b. Chgo., May 18, 1942; d. Joseph and Mary A. (Kozyra) Strosnik; m. Robert Earl Schaefer, May 18, 1963; children: Debra Ann, Robert Joseph. Diploma in nursing, St. Francis Hosp. Sch. Nursing, Evanston, Ill., 1962; BA, Nat. Coll. Edn., Evanston, 1980; MBA in Health Svc. Mgmt., Webster U., 1990; MJ in Health Law, Loyola U., Chgo., 1993. Med. and surg. nurse Resurrection Med. Ctr., Chgo., 1962-79, charge nurse labor and delivery, 1978-79; coord. maternal child care Humana, Hoffman Estates, Ill., 1979-81; nurse mgr. labor and delivery Resurrection Med. Ctr., Chgo., 1981-91; mgr. Family Birthplace Resurrection Med. Ctr., Chgo., 1991—; cons., prin. M/B Assocs.-Consultants Perinatal Healthcare and Edn., Barrington, 1994—; seminar leader on childbirth edn., legal issues in nursing. Contbr. to Motor Facilitation Handbook; editorial bd. Essentials publ., Resurrection Med. Ctr. Mem. NAFE, NAACOG (cert. in inpatient obstetric nursing), Ill. Pub. Health Assn., Nat. Perinatal Assn., Perinatal Assn. Ill. (mem. exec. bd.), Am. Orgn. Nurse Execs. Home: 23370 N Juniper Ln Barrington IL 60010-2936

SCHAEFER, NANCY TURNER, artist, educator; b. Hamilton, Ohio, July 4, 1940; d. Edward and Leota (Taylor) Turner; m. Richard Burton Price, June 16, 1967 (div. July 1970); m. Donald Raymond Schaefer, July 6, 1970 (dec. Nov. 1990). BA in English and Art, Ea. Ky. U., 1965; postgrad., Cin. Art Acad., 1995—. Cert. tchr., Ky., Ohio, Va. Tchr. Boone County Bd. Edn., Florence, Ky., 1965-67, Rockingham County Bd. Edn., Harrisonburg, Va., 1967-69, Hamilton County Bd. Edn., Cin. and Greenhills, Ohio, 1969-86; pvt. tchr. art, instr. cmty. colls., Sarasota and Bradenton, Fla., 1986—; demonstrator Palm Aire Artists Orgn., Sarasota, 1995; bd. dirs. Art League Manatee County. Works exhibited in two woman show Longboat Key (Fla.) Edn. Ctr., 1996, four woman show Art League of Manatee County, 1995 (Equal Merit award 1995), group shows Hilton Leech Studio, Sarasota, Fla., 1995 (1st honorable mention for mixed media 1995); represented in permanent collections Art League of Manatee County and many pvt. collections. Recipient numerous awards for paintings. Mem. Fla. Suncoast Watercolor Soc., Art League Manatee County (demonstrator 1995), Nat. Mus. Women in Arts (assoc.).

SCHAEFFER, ANNE A., trade association executive; b. Hackensack, N.J., July 6, 1953; d. Llewellyn Walter and Rosalind (Sweet) Bley; m. Peter M. Schaeffer, June 22, 1975; children: Matthew Stephen, Lee Jonathan. BA in Eng. and Secondary Edn., SUNY, Oswego, 1975; MBA in Mktg. Mgmt., Baruch Coll., 1984. Dir. edn. Direct Mktg. Assn., N.Y.C., 1982-85; dir. membership Direct Mktg. Assn., 1985-88, v.p. confs., 1988-91, v.p. profl. devel., tng. and ops., 1991—. Vol. Temple Beth Abraham, Tarrytown, N.Y., 1995—. Democrat. Jewish. Office: Direct Mktg Assn 1120 6th Ave New York NY 10036

SCHAEFFER, BARBARA HAMILTON, retired rental leasing company executive; b. Newton, Mass., Apr. 26, 1926; d. Peter Davidson Gunn and Harriet Bennett (Thompson) Hamilton; m. John Schaeffer, Sept. 7, 1946; children—Laurie, John, Peter. Student, Skidmore Coll., 1943-46; AB in English, Bucknell U., 1948; postgrad. Montclair State U., 1950-51, Bank St. Coll. Edn., 1959-61, Yeshiva U., 1961-62; student Daytona Beach Coll., 1984. Cert. primary, secondary tchr., N.J. Dir. Pompton Plains Sch., N.J., 1959-62; adviser Episcopal Sch., Towaco, N.J., 1968-70; v.p. Deltona-De Land Trolley, Orange City, Fla., 1980-81; pres. Monroe Heavy Equipment Rentals, Inc., Orange City, 1981—, also Magic Carpet Travel, 1985-88 cons., founder, pres. TLC Travel Club, Orange City, 1981-88; lectr. on children's art, 1959-70. Contbr. articles to profl. publs. Mem. LWV, AAUW, Internat. Platform Assn., Small Bus. Devel. Regional Ctr. (Stetson U. chpt.), Nat. Trust Historic Preservation. Episcopalian. Avocations: restoring old homes, oil painting, piano, writing. Home: 400 Foothill Farms Rd Orange City FL 32763-5502 Address: PO Box 688 Debary FL 32713-0688

SCHAEFFER-ROWE, HARRIET BEA, retired speech and language pathologist; b. North Platte, Nebr., July 23, 1934; d. Harry Alfred and Phoebe Cary (Spence) Potter; m. Harry Earl Schaeffer, Sept. 25, 1955 (div. Apr. 1979); children: Clinton Earl, Jeffrey Wade; m. James Robert Rowe, Sept. 4, 1994. BS in Edn., U. Nebr., 1969, MA, 1970. Tchr. Rural Sch. Dist. 82, Hebron, Nebr., 1952-53; sec. Fairbury (Nebr.) Light and Power Co., 1954-55; receptionist Olin-Mathieson Chem. Corp., St. Louis, 1955; sec. Atty. Johnson, Lexington, Nebr., 1956, Sate of Nebr., Lincoln, 1957-59; speech/lang. pathologist Lincoln (Nebr.) Pub. Schs., 1970-95; ret., 1995. Author of poetry. Den mother Boy Scouts, Lincoln, 1967; coord. social involvement Dist. United Meth. Women, Lincoln and Cortland, 1983, 84, 96; legis. rep. Nebr. Assn. Tchr. Educators, 1985-86; pres., sec.-treas. Cortland United Ch., 1988-94, del., 1995-96. Mem. NEA (life, rep. 1991), Nebr. State Edn. Assn. (life, del. del. assembly 1987, 91, 93, 94, 95), Lincoln Edn. Assn. (life, liaison 1986, 87, 91, 93, 95)), Nebr. Speech Hearing Assn. (life, chairperson schs. com. 1993-94, Recognition of Svc. Cert. 1995), Am. Legion Aux. Democrat. Home: PO Box 286 Cortland NE 68331

SCHAFER, ALICE TURNER, mathematics educator; b. Richmond, Va., June 18, 1915; d. John H. and Cleon (Dermott) Turner; m. Richard Donald Schafer, Sept. 8, 1942; children: John Dickerson, Richard Stone. AB, U. Richmond, 1936, DSc, 1964; MS, U. Chgo., 1940, PhD (fellow), 1942. Tchr. Glen Allen (Va.) High Sch., 1936-39; instr. math. Conn. Coll., New London, 1942-44; asst. prof. Conn. Coll., 1954-57, asso. prof., 1957-61, prof., 1961-62; prof. math. Wellesley Coll., 1962-80, Helen Day Gould prof. math., 1969-80, Helen Day Gould prof. math. emerita, 1980—, affirmative action officer, 1980-82; prof. math. Marymount U., Arlington, Va., 1989-96; instr. U. Mich., Ann Arbor, 1945-46; lectr. Douglass Coll., New Brunswick, N.J., 1946-48; asst. prof. Swarthmore (Pa.) Coll., 1948-51, Drexel Inst. Tech., Phila., 1951-53; mathematician Johns Hopkins Applied Physics Lab., Silver Spring, Md., 1945; lectr. Simmons Coll., Boston, 1980-88, Radcliffe Coll. Seminars, Cambridge, Mass., 1980-85. Contbr. articles on women in math. and other articles to math. jours. Recipient Disting. Alumna award Westhampton Coll., U. Richmond, 1977; NSF sci. faculty fellow Inst. for Advanced Study, Princeton, N.J., 1958-59. Fellow AAAS (math. sect. A nominating com. 1979-83, mem.-at-large 1983-86, chair-elect sect. A 1991, chair 1992, retiring chair 1993, Assn. for Women in Math. rep. 1993—), AAUP (chmn. nat. com. W 1980-83, mem. nat. coun. 1984-87), Am. Math. Soc. (chmn. postdoctoral fellowship com. 1973-76, affirmative action procedures com. 1980-82, chair com. on Human Rights of Mathematicians 1988-94), Soc. Indsl. and Applied Math., Am. Statis. Assn., Inst. Math. Stats., Nat. Coun. Tchrs. of Math. (chair com. on women 1976-81), Math Assn. Am. (adv. com. for Women and Math. program 1987-89, dir. fund raising 1989-92, lectr. 1982—, chair devel. com. 1988-92), Internat. Congress Mathematicians (mem. fund raising com. 1986), Assn. for Women in Math. (pres. 1973-75, Alice T. Schafer Prize established 1989, chair fund raising com. 1992-94, leader math. del. women mathematicians to China 1990, U.S. chair postsecondary math. edn., U.S./China Joint Conf. on Edn. 1992, co-chair Citizen Amb. program People to People U.S. and China Joint Conf. on Women's Issues 1995, session women in sic. and math., rept. to sect. A, Disting. Svc. award 1996), Cosmos Club, Phi Beta Kappa, Sigma Xi, Sigma Delta Epsilon. Home: 2725 N Pollard St Arlington VA 22207-5038 Office: Marymount U Dept Math 2807 N Glebe Rd Arlington VA 22207-4299

SCHAFER, MARIANNE MARKS, television production company executive, actress; b. Jakarta, Indonesia; m. Stanley M. Marks; m. Jerry S. Schafer, Oct. 1, 1979; children: Mark, Morgan, Martin, Erik, Aaron. Actress more than 20 roles various internat. TV prodn. cos. and Hollywood studios, 1975—; actress, ops. dir. Sanford Internat. Entertainment, Inc., Malibu, Calif., Las Vegas, Nev., 1979-88; actress, ops. dir. Internat. Video Comm., Inc., Las Vegas, 1988—; TV spokesperson and program prodr. Nev. Hwy. Patrol, 1990—, Nev. Dept. Motor Vehicles and Pub. Safety, 1991—, MADD, Las Vegas, 1990-93, Stop D.U.I., Las Vegas, 1993—. Host, narrator over 50 TV programs; co-prodr. over 75 TV programs; TV host, co-prodr. documentaries, ednl. programs, game and talk shows; co-prodr., narrator, host pub. svc. documentary Get M.A.D.D., 1992 (MADD appreciation award 1992); co-prodr., narrator, host documentary Inside the Nevada Highway Patrol, 1992; co-star movies Wrong Is Right, Wild Times, Adventure: The Billion Dollar Threat; lead Fists of Steel, 1988. Recipient Gov.'s Appreciation award State of Nev., 1993, Racers Against Impaired Drivers award Nev. Hwy. Patrol, 1993; named Hon. Constable No. Las Vegas Constables Office, 1985—. Mem. SAG, AFTRA, Nev. Constables Assn. (sec.-treas. 1996). Office: Internat Video Comm Inc PO Box 15101 Las Vegas NV 89114-5101

SCHAFER, RUTH ERMA, artist, educator; b. Thompson, Mo., Nov. 23, 1923; d. Lewis Maxwell and Maude Ethel (Keller) Johnson; m. Paul Linzy Starlin (dec. Jan. 1987); children: Barbara Ann White, Larry David, Stephen Paul, Paula Lynn Norris, Randal Lee; m. Justin Schafer. Student, Art Sch. of Ft. Wayne, Ind. Bus. mgr. Chevrolet Dealership, Portland, Ind.; tchr. Portland Art Sch., 1964-88. Artist oil paintings, portraits, sea scapes, landscapes, still life; exhibited in shows in Atlanta, Chgo., N.Y.C., Indpls., Ft. Wayne, Brown County Art Guild. Leader Girl Scouts U.S., Boy ScoutsAm., 4-H Club; head art booths Jay County Fairs; tchr. Sunday sch. Ch. of Christ; selected by Gov. Bowen of Ind. to serve as Ind. Arts Commn. cultural rep., 1967. Named Mother of the Yr., C. of C. of Portland, 1957; honored by Sen. Birch Bayh as one of the Ind. Artists, Washington, 1965. Mem. Ind. Fedn. Art Clubs (pres. 1975-77, treas. 1971-75), Nat. Endowment for the Arts (charter), The Hoosier Salon.

SCHAFER, SHARON MARIE, anesthesiologist; b. Detroit, Mar. 23, 1948; d. Charles Anthony and Dorothy Emma (Schweitzer) Pokriefka; m. Timothy John Schafer, Nov. 12, 1977; children: Patrick Christopher, Steven Michael. BS in Biology, Wayne State U., 1971, MD, 1975. Diplomate Am. Bd. Anesthesiology. Intern, resident Sinai Hosp. Detroit, 1975-78; pvt. practice anesthesiology Troy, Mich., 1988—. Mem. AMA, Am. Soc. Anesthesiologists. Roman Catholic. Home and Office: 5741 Folkstone Dr Troy MI 48098-3154

SCHAFF, BARBARA WALLEY, artist; b. Plainfield, N.J., May 6, 1941; d. Miron M. and Silvia S. (Solott) Walley; m. John A. Schaff, Apr. 10, 1963 (div. 1992); children: Elizabeth A., Joshua L. BA, Syracuse U., 1963; cert., Pa. Acad. Fine Arts, 1994; grad., China Nat. Acad. Fine Art, Hangzhou, 1994. Clay artist Stockton, N.J., 1968-88; advisor to faculty BFA program Kean Coll., Union, N.J., 1987—; painter Phila., 1989—; mem. adv. bd. Hunterdon Art Ctr., Clinton, N.J., 1988, 89; workshop leader, U.S. and Can. One person shows include N.J. State Mus., Trenton, 1985, Lee Sclar Gallery, Morristown, N.J., 1986, Howe Gallery, Kean Coll., Union, 1989, ITT Boston Sheraton, 1995, Thos. Moser Cabinetmakers, Phila., 1995; exhibited in group shows Newark Mus., 1973, 77, Morris Mus., Morristown, N.J., 1973, 77, Carnegie Ctr., Princeton, N.J., 1984, Newman Galleries, Phila., 1986, Ednl. Testing Svc., Princeton, 1987, Monarch Title Nat., San Angelo (Tex.) Mus. Art, 1989, U.S. Artists, Phila., 1992, 93, China Nat. Acad. Fine Art, 1994, Am. Drawing Biennial V, Muscarelle Mus. Art, Williamsburg, Va., 1996, others; represented in permanent collections N.J. State Mus., Trenton, Fuller Mus. Art, Brockton, Mass., also corp. collections; commns. include N.J. Natural Gas, Wall, 1983, Bell Comms. Rsch., Red Bank, N.J., 1985, Kenneth Endick, Boca Raton, Fla., 1987; works featured in N.J. Mag., Star Ledger, N.Y. Times, Am. Artists, An Illustrated Survey of Leading Contemporaries. Recipient Medal of Excellence for promotion and design Art Dirs. Club N.J., 1986; fellow N.J. State Coun. on Arts, 1984-85, resident fellow Va. Ctr. Creative Arts, 1996. Mem. Fellowship of Pa. Acad. of Fine Arts (com. mem., exhibitor 1994—, Mable Wilson Woodrow Meml. award 1994), Artist Equity. Home: 528 Queen St Philadelphia PA 19147 Office: Barbara Schaff Studio 314 Brown St Philadelphia PA 19123

SCHAFFNER, CYNTHIA VAN ALLEN, writer, researcher; b. Washington, Jan. 28, 1947; d. James Alfred and Abigail Fifthian (Halsey) Van Allen; m. Robert Todd Schaffner, June 11, 1972; 1 child, Hilary Van Allen. BA, Western Coll., 1969; MAT, Simmons Coll., 1971; postgrad., Cooper-Hewitt, N.Y.C., 1994—. Editor Mademoiselle mag., N.Y.C., 1972-79; dir. devel. Am. Acad. in Rome, N.Y.C., 1987-89. Author: Discovering American Folk Art, 1991; co-author: Folk Hearts, 1984, Nineteenth Century American Painted Furniture, 1977; also mag. articles. Co-chairperson Fall Antiques Show, N.Y.C., 1979-93; trustee Mus. Am. Folk Art, N.Y.C., 1980-

95. Mem. Coll. Art Assn., Decorative Arts Soc., Cosmopolitan Club, Colonial Soc. (trustee 1996—). Home: 850 Park Ave New York NY 10021

SCHAFFNER, ROBERTA IRENE, medical, surgical nurse; b. Vero Beach, Fla., Oct. 5, 1926; d. Robert Wesley and Harriett Louise (Davis) Routh; m. David Leonard Schaffner, Apr. 25, 1947 (div. July 1975); children: Penny Routh S., David Leonard II. Mem. cadet nurse corps, Charity Hosp., New Orleans, La., 1944-45; ADA, Montgomery County C.C., Blue Bell, Pa., 1978; BSN, Gwynedd (Pa.) Mercy Coll., 1982, MSN, 1984. RN Pa. Med.-surg. nurse Chestnut Hill Hosp., Phila., 1978—; mem. delegation to study health care delivery sys., Moscow, Tbillisi, Azerbeijan, Kiev, 1981, Shanghai, Beijing, Nanjing, Hong Kong, 1984, Milan, Pisa, Bologna, Florence, Rome, Sorento, Naples, 1985. Cadet U.S. Nurse Corps, 1945. Mem. Oncology Nursing Soc., Sigma Theta Tau. Republican. Home: 1600 Church Rd # A 214 Wyncote PA 19095-1926 Office: Chestnut Hill Hosp 8835 Germantown Ave Philadelphia PA 19118-2718

SCHALLER, JOANNE FRANCES, nursing consultant; b. Columbus, Ga., July 15, 1943; d. John Frank and Ethel Beatrice (Spring) Lanzendorfer; m. Robert Thomas Schaller, Jan. 22, 1977; 1 child, Amy. BS, Pacific Luth. U., 1969; M in Nursing, U. Wash., 1971. House supr. UCLA Hosp., 1971-72; outpatient supr. Harborview Hosp., Seattle, 1973-75; outpatient clinic and emergency room supr. U. Wash. Hosp., Seattle, 1975-77; co-author, researcher with Robert Schaller MD Seattle, 1977-87; prin. Nursing Expert-Standards of Care, Seattle, 1987—; cons. Wash. State Trial Lawyers, Wash. Assn. Criminal Def. Lawyers, 1989—; founder, CEO Present Perfect, Seattle, 1991—; appt. Breast Cancer cons. UWMC, 1995—. Contbr., editor articles to profl. jours. Bd. dirs. Pacific Arts Ctr., 1992—; vol. guardian ad litem King County Juvenile Ct., 1978—; vol. Make a Wish Found. U.S. Bank, 1984—, Multiple Sclerosis Assn., 1986—, Am. Heart Assn., 1986—, Internat. Children's Festival, 1987—, Seattle Children's Festival, 1987—, Seattle Dept. Parks and Recreation Open Space Com., 1990—, Pacific N.W. Athletic Congress, 1991—, Wash. Fed. Garden Clubs Jr. Advisor, 1992—, Fred Hutchison Cancer Rsch. Ctr., 1993—; mem. parent coun. Seattle Country Day Sch., 1986—; mem. Photo Coun. Seattle Art Mus., 1986—, Native Am. Coun., 1989—; mem. N.W. Coun. Seattle Art Mus., 1992—, mem. NAOO Coun. Seattle Art Mus., 1989—, Plestcheeff Inst. Decorative Arts, 1992—; mem. fundraiser Children's Hosp. Med. Ctr., 1977—, Breast Cancer Fund, 1994—, Susan G. Komen Breast Cancer Found., 1994—. Named 1st Migrant Health Care Nurse, State of Wash., 1969, 1st Am. nurse visiting China, 1974. Mem. AAUW, ANA, Wash. State Nurses Assn., U. Wash. Alumni Assn. Home and Office: 914 Randolph Ave Seattle WA 98122-5267

SCHANFIELD, FANNIE SCHWARTZ, community volunteer; b. Mpls., Dec. 25, 1916; d. Simon Zouberman and Mary (Schmilovitz) Schwartz; m. Melvin M. Stock, Oct. 27, 1943 (dec. Apr. 1944); 1 child, Moses Samuel Schanfield; m. Abraham Schanfield, Aug. 28, 1947; children: David Colman, Miriam Schanfield Kieffer. Student, U. Minn., 1962-75. Author: My Thoughts, 1996. Bd. dirs. Jewish Cmty. Ctr., Mpls., 1975-96, chairperson older adult needs, 1982-88; past pres. Bnai Emet Women's League, Mpls., 1988-90; rschr., advocate Hunger Hennepin County, Mpls., 1969-75; sec. Joint Religious Legis. Coalition; v.p., bd. dirs. Cmty. Housing Svc., Mpls., 1971-85. Recipient Citation of Honor, Hennepin County Commn., 1989, Lifetime Achievement award Jewish Cmty. Ctr. Greater Mpls., 1995. Mem. NOW, Lupus Found. Minn., Internat. Soc. Poets, Hadassah (prs. 1967-69, Citation 1969). Jewish. Home: 3630 Phillips Pky Minneapolis MN 55426-3792

SCHANSTRA, CARLA ROSS, technical writer; b. Berwyn, Ill., Sept. 4, 1954; d. Caroles Schanstra and Heather Millar (Thomson) Alonso. BA, Western Ill. U., 1976; postgrad., U. Ill. Circle, Chgo., 1980-81. Assoc. editor Hitchcock Pub., Wheaton, Ill., 1976-80; assoc. product mgr. Advanced Systems, Inc., Elk Grove Village, Ill., 1980-81; tech. writer Profl. Computer Resources, Oak Brook, Ill., 1982; sr. tech. writer AT&T Bell Labs., Naperville, Ill., 1982—; freelance writer, 1980-85. Author: (stage plays) A Little Bit of Both, The Reversible Play, Survivors, Snakes and Apple Pie, It Should Be Obvious, Pastiche, The Model Home; contbr. articles to profl. jours. Violist DuPage Symphony, Glen Ellyn, Ill., 1984-87, 90-93, Elgin (Ill.) Symphonette, 1985-87. Mem. So. Tech. Comm. Assn. (award of excellence 1985), Dramatists Guild, Feminist Writers Western Suburbs (founder), Feminist Writers Guild Chgo. (adv. panel), Internat. Soc. Dramatists, Ill. Theatre Assn., Writers Workshop (co-founder). Office: AT&T Bell Labs IH 2A-173 2000 N Naperville Rd Naperville IL 60563-1443

SCHAPIRO, MARY, federal agency administrator, lawyer; b. N.Y.C., June 19, 1955; d. Robert D. and Susan (Hall) S.; m. Charles A. Cadwell, Dec. 13, 1980. BA, Franklin and Marshall Coll., 1977; JD, George Washington U., 1980. Bar: D.C. 1980. Trial atty., 1980-81; counsel to chmn. Commodity Futures Trading Commn., 1981-84; gen. counsel Futures Industry Assn., 1984-88; commr. SEC, Washington, 1988-94; chmn. Commodity Futures Trading Commn. (CFTC), Washington, 1994-96; pres. NASDR, Washington, 1996—. Office: NASDR 1735 K St NW Washington DC 20006

SCHAPIRO, MIRIAM, artist; b. Toronto, Ont., Can., Nov. 15, 1923; d. Theodore and Fannie (Cohen) S. BA, State U. Iowa, 1945, MA, 1946, MFA, 1949; hon. doctorate, Wooster Coll., 1983, Calif. Coll. Arts and Crafts, 1989, Mpls. Coll. Art and Design, 1994, Miami U., 1995, Moore Coll. Art, Phila., 1995. co-originator Womanhouse, Los Angeles, 1972, Heresies mag., N.Y.C., 1975; co-originator feminist art program Calif. Inst. Arts, Valencia, 1971; founding mem. Feminist Art Inst., N.Y.C.; mem. adv. bd. Women's Caucus for Art; assoc. mem. Heresies Collective; lectr. dept. art history U. Mich., 1987. Works in numerous books and catalogues; numerous one-woman shows including, Galerie Liatowitsch, Basel, Switzerland, 1979, Lerner Heller Gallery, N.Y.C., 1979, Barbara Gladstone Gallery, N.Y.C., 1980, Spencer Mus. Art, Lawrence, Kans., 1981, Everson Mus., Syracuse, N.Y., 1981, Galerie Rudolf Zwirner, Cologne, Fed. Republic Germany, 1981, Staatagalerie, Stuttgart, Fed. Republic Germany, 1983, Dart Gallery, Chgo, 1984, Bernice Steinbaum Gallery/Steinbaum Krauss Gallery, N.Y.C., 1986, 88, 90, 91, 94, Brevard Art Ctr. and Mus., Melbourne, Fla., 1991, Guild Hall Mus., East Hampton, N.Y., 1992, ARC Gallery, Chgo., 1993, James Madison U., Harrisburg, Va., 1994. others; retrospective exhbn., Wooster (Ohio) Coll. Art Mus., 1980; exhibited in numerous group shows, including, Palais de Beaux Arts, Brussels, 1979, Inst. Contemporary Art, Phila., 1979, Delahunty Gallery, Dallas, 1980, Indpls. Mus., 1980, Va. Mus., Richmond, 1980, Laguna Gloria Mus., Austin, Tex., 1980, R.O.S.C., Dublin, Ireland, 1980, Biennale of Sydney, Australia, 1982, Zurich, Switzerland, 1983, Sidney Janis Gallery, N.Y.C., 1984, Am. Acad. Arts and Letters, N.Y.C., 1985, Mus. Modern Art, N.Y.C., 1988, Whyte Mus. Can. Rockies, Banff, Alta., 1991, Nat. Mus. Women in Arts., Wash., 1993, Jane Voorhees Zimmerli art mus. Rutger's U., New Brunswick, N.J., 1994, Mus. of F.A. Boston, 1994, Santa Barbara Mus. of Art, 1994, Hudson River Mus. of Westchester, Yonkers, N.Y., 1995, Mus. Los Angeles, Calif. Bronx Mus. of the Arts, N.Y., 1995; represented in permanent collections, Hirshhorn Mus., Washington, Bklyn. Mus., Met. Mus. Art, N.Y.C., Mus. Contemporary Art, San Diego, Mpls. Inst. Art, Mulvane Art Center, Topeka, Nat. Gallery Art, Washington, N.Y.U., Peter Ludwig Collection, Aachen, Germany, Stanford U., Palo Alto, Calif., Univ. Art Mus., Berkeley, Calif., Whitney Mus., N.Y.C., Worcester (Mass.) Art Mus., Santa Barbara (Calif.) Mus. Art, also others; author: (books) Women and the Creative Process, 1974, Rondo: An Artists Book, 1988; sculpture Anna and David, Rosslyn, Va., 1987. Guggenheim fellow, 1987, Nat. Endowment for Arts fellow; grantee Ford Found.; recipient numerous other grants and fellowships. Mem. Coll. Art Assn. (past dir.). Office: Steinbaum Krauss Gallery 132 Greene St New York NY 10012

SCHAPPELL, ABIGAIL SUSAN, speech, language and hearing therapist; b. York, Pa., May 25, 1952; d. Felix and Ann (Getty) DeMoise; m. Gery Mylan Schappell, Oct. 20, 1979; 1 child, Jonathan Michael. BS with Master's equivalency, U. Va., 1974; postgrad., Bloomsburg U., 1975-77. Lic. speech-lang. pathologist, Pa. Speech-lang.-hearing specialist dept. pub. welfare Hamburg (Pa.) Ctr., 1975; judge deaf posters and essays Virginville (Pa.) Grange, 1990—, tchr. emergency pers. on communicating with deaf and hard of hearing, 1991, 92; leader demonstrations and workshops on sign lang. and dysphagia, non-verbal comms., active listening to various orgns., 1978—. Pub: (Boy Scouts Coun. manual), Scouting for the Handicapped, Hawk Mountain, 1981-82. Sign/del. to conf. Bible Sch. dir., mem. Zion's United Ch. of Christ, Windsor Castle, Pa., 1985—. Named Virginville Grange Comty. Citizen of Yr., 1994-95, Outstanding Young Woman of Am., 1984. Mem. AAUW, Am. Assn. Mental Retardation (presenter at state conf. 1994, regional conf. 1995, mem. Region 9 core com. for speech 1976), Pa. Speech and Hearing Assn., Berks Deaf and Hard of Hearing Svcs., Schuykill Bus. and Profl. Women (pres 1983-84, involvement on dist. and state level, Young Careerist local, dist. and state honors 1980-81), Yorktown chpt. DAR, Smithsonian Assocs., Order Ea. Star (mem., chaplain Blue Mountain chpt. 1981, 82), Hamburg Area Soccer Assn. (sec. 1989-94), Young Careerist Alumni Assn. (life). Republican. Home: 531 S 4th St Hamburg PA 19526 Office: Hamburg Ctr Old RR 22 Hamburg PA 19526

SCHARFF, LAUREN FRUH VANSICKLE, psychology educator, researcher; b. Austin, Tex., May 31, 1966; adopted d. Donald R. VanSickle; d. E. Gus Fruh and Gwen (Fruh) VanSickle. BA with honors, U. Tex., 1987, MA in Psychology, 1989, PhD in Psychology, 1992. Asst. prof. of psychology Stephen F. Austin State U., Nacogdoches, Tex., 1993—. Contbr. articles to profl. jours. Advisor, Psychology Club, Nacogdoches, Tex., 1993—. Mem. AAUW, Assn. for Rsch. in Vision and Ophthalmology, Optical Soc. of Am., Psychonomic Soc., Sigma Xi. Office: Stephen F. Austen State U. Psychology Dept Box 13046 SFA Station Nacogdoches TX 75962

SCHAROLD, MARY LOUISE, psychoanalyst, educator; b. Wichita Falls, Tex., Mar. 3, 1943; d. Walter John and Louise Helen (Hartman) Baumgartner; m. William Ballew McCollum, Aug. 23, 1964 (div. 1981); m. Harry Karl Scharold, June 19, 1982; children: Margaret Louise, Walter Ballew. BA with highest distinction, U. Kans., 1964; MD, Baylor Coll. Med., 1968; postgrad. Topeka Inst. for Psychoanalysis, 1981. Diplomate Am. Bd. Psychiatry and Neurology. Intern Meml. Baptist. Hosp., Houston, 1968-69; resident in psychiatry Baylor Coll. Med., Houston, 1969-72, chief resident, 1971-72; practice of medicine specializing in psychoanalysis, Houston, 1972—; asst. prof. Baylor Coll. Med., Houston, 1973-76, asst. clin. prof., 1981-84, assoc. clin. prof., 1984—; dir. Baylor Psychiat. Clinic, Houston, 1973-76; co-dir. Rice U. Psychiat. Service, Houston, 1981-82; asst. clin. prof. U. Kans. Sch. Medicine, Kansas City, 1977-81; teaching assoc. Topeka Inst. Psychoanalysis, 1980-81; instr. Houston-Galveston Psychoanalytic Inst., 1984-86, teaching analyst, 1986-90, tng. and supervising analyst, 1990—, v.p., 1994—; Adv. bd. Leavenworth Mental Health Assn., Kans., 1977-81. Watkins scholar U. Kans., 1961-64. Fellow Am. Psychiatric Assn. (chmn. Tex. peer review 1984-88); mem. Am. Psychoanalytic Assn. (cert. 1982, peer rev. com. 1985-90, prof. ins. commn. 1986-93, bd. profl. stds., 1994—, CME com., 1994—, mem. exec. coun. 1994-96, cert. com. 1994—), Am. Group Psychotherapy Assn., Houston Psychiatric Soc. (v.p. 1984-85, pres. elect 1985-86, pres. 1986-87), Houston-Galveston Psychoanalytic Soc. (sec.-treas. 1984-86, pres.-elect 1986-88, pres. 1988-90, alter councillor 1994-96), Psychiat. Assn. (quality assurance com. 1986-87), Houston Group Psychotherapy Soc. (adv. bd. 1984-85), Mortar Bd., Phi Beta Kappa, Delta Phi Alpha, Alpha Omega Alpha, Hilltopper, Pi Beta Phi Alumni Assn. Republican. Lutheran. Office: 3400 Bissonnet St Ste 170 Houston TX 77005-2153

SCHARPER, C. DIANE, poet, educator; b. Balt., Oct. 23, 1942; d. Franklin Willard and Constance (Karpers) Waesche; m. Philip H. Scharper, June 16, 1962; children: Philip H., Jr., Mia Diane, Julie Anne. BA in English, Coll. Notre Dame, Balt., 1964; MA in Writing, Johns Hopkins U., 1972. adj. prof. Towson State U., Md., 1987-96; lectr. in field. Author: (books of poetry) The Laughing Ladies, A Collection of Poems, 1993, Radiant, 1996; author of numerous poems; contbg. editor: Maryland Poetry Review, 1995—. Recipient Poetry award 3rd place Artscape, 1988. Mem. AAUW, Acad. Am. Poets, Assn. for Gen. and Liberal Studies, Coll. English Assn. (Middle Atlantic group), Delta Epsilon Sigma. Democrat. Roman Catholic. Office: Towson State U English Dept Towson MD 21204

SCHARUDA, VICTORIA, lawyer; b. Vineland, N.J., Aug. 3, 1967; d. Victor Scharuda and Elizabeth (Repin) Bennett. BA in History, Ursinus Coll., 1989; JD, Temple U., 1992. Bar: Ga. 1993. Corp. counsel Wells Fargo Armored Svc. Corp., Atlanta, 1993—. Active 1000 Lawyers for Justice, Atlanta, 1993. Recipient James D. Mandarino award Phila. Trial Lawyers Assn., 1992. Mem. NAFE. Office: Wells Fargo Armored Svc Corp 6165 Barfield Rd NE Ste 200 Atlanta GA 30328-4309

SCHATKEN, NANCY LEAH, medical editor; b. N.Y.C., Jan. 7, 1938; d. Robert V. and Lillian Belle (Neff) S. BS, U. N.C., 1959; cert. med. tech., Albany Sch. Med. Tech., 1960. Med. tech., instr. various orgns., 1960-66; acting mng. editor Harper & Row, N.Y.C., 1966-69; assoc. editor Med. World News-McGraw-Hill, N.Y.C., 1969-70; owner, founder Mostly Med., N.Y.C., 1970-78, Mullins St. Peter, Barbados, 1978—. Home and Office: North Beacon, Mullins St Peter, Barbados

SCHATZ, LILLIAN LEE, playwright, molecular biologist, educator; b. N.Y.C., Apr. 8, 1944; d. Joseph Louis and Rose (Zakalik) S. BA in Biology, SUNY, Buffalo, 1965, MA in Biology, 1970. Cert. h.s. tchr. biology, chemistry, gen. sci., N.Y., 1968. Rsch. asst. dept. biology SUNY at Buffalo, 1965-68, rsch. asst. dept. pharmacology Sch. Medicine, 1969; rsch. assoc. dept. biology SUNY, Buffalo, 1971-74; cancer rsch. scientist dept. viral oncology Roswell Park Meml. Inst., Buffalo, 1969-70; tchr. biology Kenmore East Sr. H.S., Buffalo, 1970-71; playwright Buffalo, 1976—; presenter workshop Rosa Coplon Jewish Home and Infirmary, Buffalo, N.Y., 1982, N.Y. State Community Theater Assn., 1982. Plays include Solomon's Court, 1979, Neshomah, 1983, Bernie, 1985, The Jonah Men, 1991; contbr. rsch. articles to sci. jours. Charter mem. B'not Israel Group Buffalo chpt. Hadassah, life mem. Recipient N.Y. State Regents Coll. Scholarship, 1961-65; semi-finalist Sergel Drama prize Ct. Theatre, U. Chgo., 1985, Nat. Play Award Competition Nat. Repertory Theatre Found., 1981; Playwriting fellow, N.Y. State Creative Artists Pub. Svc. fellow, 1980-81, Roswell Park Meml. Inst. fellow, 1962, Summer Sci. fellow. Democrat. Jewish. Home and Office: 31 Twyla Pl Buffalo NY 14223-1526

SCHAUB, MARILYN MCNAMARA, religion educator; b. Chgo., Mar. 24, 1928; d. Bernard Francis and Helen Katherine (Skehan) McNamara; m. R. Thomas Schaub, Oct. 25, 1969; 1 dau., Helen Ann. B.A., Rosary Coll., 1953; Ph.D., U. Fribourg, Switzerland, 1957; diploma, Ecole Biblique, Jerusalem, 1967. Asst. prof. classics and Bibl. studies Rosary Coll., River Forest, Ill., 1957-69; prof. Bibl. studies Duquesne U., Pitts., 1969-70, 73—; participant 8 archeol. excavations, Middle East; adminstrv. dir. expedition to the Southeast Dead Sea Plains, Jordan, 1989—; hon. assoc. Am. Schs. Oriental Rsch., 1966-67, trustee, 1986-89; Danforth assoc., 1972-80. Author: Friends and Friendship for St. Augustine, 1964; translator: (with H. Richter) Agape in the New Testament, 3 vols, 1963-65. Mem. Soc. Bibl. Lit., Catholic Bibl. Assn., Am. Acad. Religion. Democrat. Home: 25 Mckelvey Ave Pittsburgh PA 15218-1452 Office: Duquesne U Theology Dept Pittsburgh PA 15282

SCHAUB, THERESA MARIE, early childhood educator; b. Milw., Oct. 12, 1951; d. Joseph and Mary (Huberty) S. BS in Early Childhood, U. Wis., 1975. Cert. exceptional-edn.-early childhood, Wis. Kindergarten tchr. Sacred Heart, Milw., 1981-82, Ebenezer Child Care, Milw., 1982-83; presch.-head tchr. Ragamuffin Child Care, Milw., 1984-85, 86-87; asst. dir., head tchr. Country Kare, Albuquerque, 1985-86; kindergarten tchr. Holy Angels Sch., Milw., 1987-90, St. Rose Sch., Milw., 1990-94; head start tchr. Children's Outing Assn., Milw., 1994-96, Parkman Sch., Milw., 1996—; supportive cons. St. Rose Sch., Milw., 1990-94, peer mediation supr., 1991-94, AV coord., 1990-94; parent vol. com. Children's Outing Assn., 1995-96. Author: ABC's of Peace, 1990. Pres. Young Dems.; vol. Homeless Shelter Casa Maria Hospitality, Milw., 1975-80; vol. tchr. Peacemakers Camp, Milw., 1992; bd. dirs. Clear Horizons Food Coop., Milw., 1978. Mem. Milw. Peace Ctr., NAEYC, Sierra Club, NOW, Nat. Audubon Soc., Wis. Edn. for Social Responsibility, Habitat for Humanity. Office: Parkman Sch 3620 N 18th St Milwaukee WI 53206

SCHAUBER, NANCY ELLEN, educator; b. White Plains, N.Y., Mar. 25, 1960; d. Edgar and Lois (Gold) S,; m. A. John Simmons, May 30, 1987. AB, St. John's Coll., 1981; MA, U. Va., 1987; PhD, Yale U., 1993. Prof. U. Richmond (Va.), 1993—. Home: 275 Lego Dr Charlottesville VA 22901-8604 Office: U Richmond Dept Philosophy Richmond VA 23173

SCHAUENBERG, SUSAN KAY, educational counselor, educator; b. Taylor Ridge, Ill., Oct. 23, 1945; d. Albert George and Elizabeth (Stedman) Grill; m. Robert Dale Schauenberg Jr.; 1 child, Trevor Alan. BA, Marycrest Coll., 1967; MA, U. Iowa, 1968. From assoc. prof. to prof. Black Hawk Coll., Moline, Ill., 1971—; bus. cons., Rock Island, 1984—; v.p. faculty senate Black Hawk Coll., 1980-82. Planning com. United Way Orgn., Quad-Cities, Ill., 1981-84, agy. rels. com., 1981-82, allocations com., 1980-82; den mother Rock Island chpt. Boy Scouts Am., 1978-79; sponsor Christmas fundraiser for 100 children, yearly. Named one of Most Admired Women of the Quad-Cities, 1975; won L.I.V.E. Volunteerism honor for peer counselor-aide program, 1991. Mem. Assn. of Psychol. Type, Friends of Jung, Am. Fedn. Tchrs., Ill. Guidance and Personnel Assn. (Black Hawk chpt.), U. Iowa Alumni Assn., Phi Gamma Delta (mem. Parents Assn.). Home: 8428 104th Ave W Taylor Ridge IL 61284-9210 Office: Black Hawk Coll 6600 34th Ave Moline IL 61265-5870

SCHAUER, CATHARINE GUBERMAN, public affairs specialist; b. Woodbury, N.J., Sept. 24, 1945; d. Jack and Anna Ruth (Felipe) Guberman; m. Irwin Jay Schauer, July 4, 1968; children: Cheryl Anne, Marc Cawin. AB, Miami-Dade Jr. Coll., 1965; BEd, U. Miami, 1967; postgrad. Mercer U., 1968, MPA, Troy State U., 1995. Writer, Miami (Fla.) News, 1962-63; tchr. Dade County Schs., Miami, Fla., 1967-68; coord. pub. info. Macon Jr. Coll. (Ga.), 1968-69; writer Atlanta Jour., 1969-72; editor Ridgerunner newspaper, Woodbridge, Va., 1973-75; pub. info. specialist Dept. Interior, Washington, 1980-82; writer Dept. Army, Ft. Belvoir, Va., 1982-84, chief prodn., design and editl., publs. div., 1984-85; head writer-editor SE region U.S. Naval Audit Svc., Virginia Beach, Va., 1986; pub. affairs specialist, tech. rep. for vis. ctr. ops., NASA Langley, 1986-90, project mgr., chmn. 75th anniversary yr., 1991-92; NASA Langley Rsch. Ctr., Hampton, Va., 1987-89, acting head Office Pub. Svcs., 1989, pub. affairs officer for space NASA Langley, 1993—; columnist, writer Potomac News, Woodbridge, 1972-85. Contbr. articles to profl. jours. Historian, publicity chmn. PTO, Woodbridge, 1974; publicity chmn. Boy Scouts Am., Woodbridge, 1974-83, Girl Scouts U.S., Woodbridge, 1974-79; bd. dirs. Congregation Ner Tamid, Woodbridge, 1984-85. Recipient Outstanding Tng. Devel. Support award U.S. Army, 1983; 1st place news writing award and 1st place for advt. design Fla. Jr. Coll. Press Assn., 1964, 1st place feature writing award, 1964, 1st place news writing award Sigma Delta Chi, 1965, 70th anniversary team NASA, 1988, Long Duration Exposure Facility Team award NASA. Mem. Va. Press Women (1st Pl. Govt. Mags. 1991, 3d Pl. Govt. Brochures 1991, 1st Pl. Govt. Brochures 1993, 1st Pl. Govt. Media Campaign 1993, award 1996), Women in Comms., Nat. Fedn. Press Women (life, 1st Pl. Govt. Mags. 1991, 1st Pl. Govt. Media Campaign 1993). Democrat. Home: 120 Tide's Run Yorktown VA 23692-4333 Office: NASA Langley Rsch Ctr Mail Code 154 Hampton VA 23681-0001

SCHAUER, JOANN LUISE, social worker; b. Denver, Oct. 21, 1967. BA, U. Colo., 1989; MSW, U. Denver, 1991; MBA, U. Colo., 1996. Social worker emergency psychiatric svcs. Mental Health Ctr., Boulder, Colo., 1991-94; clin. social worker Denver Health Med. Ctr., 1992-94; sr. clin. social worker Denver Gen. Hosp., 1994—. V.p. Rotaract, Denver, 1994, 95, pres., 1996. Jacob van Eck scholar, 1989, Rotary Group Study Exch. scholar, 1993. Mem. AAUW, Mortar Bd. Alumni Assn. Home: 34 Albion St Denver CO 80220

SCHAUF, VICTORIA, pediatrician, educator, infectious diseases consultant; b. N.Y.C., Feb. 17, 1943; d. Maurice J. and Ruth H. (Baker) Bisson; m. Michael Delaney; 2 children. BS with honors in Microbiology, U. Chgo., 1965, MD with honors, 1969. Intern pediatrics U. Chgo. Hosp., 1969-70; resident pediatrics Sinai Hosp. of Balt., 1970-71; chief resident pediatrics Children's Hosp. Nat. Med. Ctr., Washington, 1971-72; rsch. trainee NIH, Bethesda, Md., 1972; asst. prof. microbiology Rush Med. Coll., Chgo., 1972-74; prof. pediatrics, head pediatric infectious diseases U. Ill., Chgo., 1974-84; med. officer FDA, Rockville, Md., 1984-86; chmn. dept. pediatrics Nassau County Med. Ctr., East Meadow, N.Y., 1986-90; prof. pediatrics SUNY, Stony Brook, 1987-94; vis. prof. Rockefeller U., 1990-92; mem. vis. faculty Chiang Mai (Thailand) U., 1978; mem. ad hoc com. study sects. NIH, Bethesda, 1981-82; bd. dirs. Pearl Stetler Rsch. Fond., Chgo., 1982-84; cons. FDA, 1987-88, 93-95, Can. Bur. Human Prescription Drugs, Ottawa, 1990—, biotech. investors, 1993—; course dir. pediatric infectious diseases rev. course Cornell U. Med. Coll., N.Y.C., 1994, faculty, 1995. Co-author: Pediatric Infectious Diseases: A Comprehensive Guide to the Subspecialty, 1996; prodr. TV programs in field; contbr. articles to profl. jours., chpts. to books. Vol. physician Cook County Hosp., Chgo., 1974-84; mem. adv. com. Nat. Hansen's Disease Ctr., La., 1986, Nassau County Day Care Coun., N.Y., 1988-90; mem. adv. bd. Surg. Aid to Children of World, N.Y., 1986-90. Am. Lung Assn. grantee U. Ill., 1977; recipient contract NIH, U. Ill., 1978-81, grantee, 1979-84. Fellow Infectious Diseases Soc. Am.; mem. Pediatric Infectious Diseases Soc. (exec. bd.), Soc. Pediatric Rsch., Am. Pediatric Soc., AAAS, Am. Soc. Microbiology, Am. Acad. Pediatrics, NOW, Phi Beta Kappa, Alpha Omega Alpha.

SCHAUPP, JOAN POMPROWITZ, trucking company executive, writer; b. Green Bay, Wis., Sept. 29, 1932; d. Joseph and Helen Elizabeth (Vander-Linden) Pomprowitz; m. Robert James Schaupp, Sept. 4, 1956; children: Margaret Schaupp Siebert, Frederick, John Robert, Elizabeth Schaupp Sidles. BS cum laude, U. Wis., 1954; cert. in theology, St. Norbert Coll., 1979; MA, U. Wis., Green Bay, 1982; DMin, Grad. Theol. Found., 1996. Rsch. asst. Calif. Inst. Tech., Pasadena, 1954-55; woman's editor Green Bay Press-Gazette, 1955-56; freelance writer Green Bay, 1957-75; sec.-treas., dir. L.C.L. Transit Co., Green Bay, 1962-70; dir. P & S Investment Co., Green Bay, 1982—, mgmt. cons., 1984-89, dir. strategic planning, 1992, vice chmn., 1994—; pres. The Manna Co., Green Bay, 1992. Author: Jesus Was a Teenager, 1972, Woman Image of Holy Spirit, 1975 (Thomas Moore Book award), Elohim: A Search for a Symbol for Human Fulfillment, 1995. Master gardener De Pere (Wis.) Beautification Com., 1991-92; lector, lay min. St. Francis Xavier Cathedral, Green Bay, 1991-92. Mem. Am. Acad. Religion, Nat. Fedn. Press Women, Nat. Press Club, Soc. Bibl. Lit., Equestrian Order of the Holy Sepulchre Jerusalem (lady, grand cross with star), Secular Franciscan Order (vice min. Assumption Province 1991-92), Franciscans Internat. Home: PO Box 358 De Pere WI 54115-0358

SCHECHTER, GERALDINE POPPA, hematologist; b. N.Y.C., Jan. 16, 1938; d. Josif and Victoria (Nosi) P.; m. Alan Neil Schechter, Feb. 6, 1965; children: Daniele Malka, Andrew M.R. AB, Vassar Coll., Poughkeepsie, N.Y., 1959; MD, Columbia U., 1963. Diplomate Am. Bd. Internal Medicine, Am. Bd. Hematology. Intern, resident Presbyn. Hosp., N.Y.C., 1963-65; resident, fellow, rsch. assoc. VA Med. Ctr., Washington, 1965-70, staff physician, 1970-74, chief hematology, 1974—; asst., assoc. prof. medicine George Washington U., Washington, 1971-81, prof. medicine, 1981—; mem. hematology com. Am. Bd. Internal Medicine, Phila., 1985-91, bd. dirs., 1990-95, residency review com. internal medicine, 1996—. Mem. editl. bd. Blood, 1985-89; contbr. articles to hematologic jours. Office: VA Med Ctr Hematology Sect 50 Irving St NW Washington DC 20422-0001

SCHECK, BARBARA ANN JEANNE, artist; b. Englewood, N.J., Dec. 26, 1943. Assoc., Southwestern U., Chula Vista, Calif., 1976. lectr. Munson-Williams-Proctor Inst., Utica, N.Y., 1986, Hartwick Coll., Oneonta, N.Y., 1990. One-person shows include Cocharan Studio, N.Y.C., 1980, Honey Sharp Gallery, Lenox, Mass., 1983, Mt. Utsayantha Gallery, Stamford, N.Y., 1984, Aurora Gallery, Annapolis, Md., 1986, Schoharie County Arts, Cobleskill, N.Y., 1987, ArtTrek, Flagstaff, Ariz., 1993; exhibited in group shows at Wenniger Gallery, Boston, 1982, Gallery Beni, Kyoto, Japan, 1983, Md. Art Ctr., Balt., 1984, Pyramid Paper, Balt., 1985, Mini-Micronesian Paper Conf., Guam, 1985, Leopold-Hoesch Mus., Duran, Germany, 1986, First Internat. Biennial of Paper Art JurriedExhbn., 1986, Leonarda De Mauro Gallery, N.Y.C., 1987, Grosvenor Gallery, Cobleskill, N.Y., 1988, Ruth Volid Gallery, Chgo., 1989, Lee-Lanning Gallery, Sedona, Ariz., 1989, Gallery 53, Cooperstown, N.Y., 1990, Bremer Farm, Otego, N.Y., 1991, Kubiak Gallery, Oneonta, N.Y., 1992, Alize, Scottsdale, Ariz., 1994, Aurora Gallery, Annapolis, Md., 1995; represented in permanent collections at Eno (Japan) Paper Mus., Dard Hunter Paper Mus., Appleton, Wis., Pitts. Ctr. for Arts, Kubiak Gallery, Oneonta, Gallery 53, Cooperstown; also pvt. collections. Mem. Internat. Assn. Hand Papermakers and Paper Artists, N.Y. State Arts in Edn. Program. Home and Office: PO Box 66 Treadwell NY 13846

SCHECKTER, STELLA JOSEPHINE, retired librarian; b. Phila., Nov. 30, 1926; d. Isaar Jerome and Rose (Levin) S. AB, Temple U., 1948; MLS, Drexel U., 1952. Continuations asst. acquisitions dept. Temple U. Libr., Phila., 1949-52; jr. asst. ref. libr. Hartford (Conn.) Pub. Libr., 1952-53, asst. br. libr., 1953-54; asst. lit. and lang. dept. Enoch Pratt Free Libr., Balt., 1954-56, asst. bus. and econs. dept., 1956-58; dir. ref. and loan bur. N.H. State Libr., Concord, 1958-90, ret., 1990. Vol. Concord Cmty. Concert Assn., 1975—, bd. dirs. 1977-90; selected participant Concord's Civic Profile, The City of Concord, 1991. Recipient Best Set Design award New England Theatre Conf., 1968; nominated Charles McCarthy award for outstanding svc. to state govt. Coun. of State Govts., 1989. Mem. Am. Libr. Assn. (state membership com. chair 1964-69), N.H. Libr. Assn. (life, pub. rels. com. 1971-74), New England Libr. Assn. (chmn. bibliography com. 1971-72), N.H. Hist. Soc. (libr. vol. 1992—), State Employees Assn. (councillor 1991—), Freedom to Read Found., Cmty. Players Concord (bd. dirs. 1965-67), Music Club Concord (bd. dirs. 1967-69), Hadassah (life, bd. dirs. 1989-91, 96—). Home: 27 Church St Concord NH 03301-6417

SCHECTER, ELLEN L., writer, producer, developer children's and family entertainment, educational consultant; b. Phila., Mar. 6, 1944; d. George and Pearl (Grossman) S.; m. James M. Altman, Sept. 27, 1980; children: Alexander, Anna. BA in English and Philosophy, Beaver Coll., 1966; MA in English and Comparative Lit., Hunter Coll., 1969. Head writer, assoc. prodr. Reading Rainbow PBS/Lancit Media, N.Y.C., 1979-86; co-writer, co-prodr. Miracle at Moreaux PBS/WQED, Washington, Pitts., 1983-85; writer, ednl. cons. TV series The Magic Schoolbus Scholastic/PBS, N.Y.C., 1989-90; ednl. cons., scriptwriter TV series Allegra's Window Topstone Prodn. & Nickelodeon, N.Y.C., 1992-96; exec. prodr. video Voices of Lupus Hosp. For Spl. Surgery, N.Y.C., 1991-93; dir. Publs. and Media Group Bank Street Coll. of Edn., N.Y.C., 1990—; tchr. Upward Bound, U. Mass., Boston, 1968-70; cons., writer CD-Rom Virgin Sound & Vision, L.A., 1995—; cons. I Can Read CD-Roms HarperCollins Interactive, N.Y., 1994-95. Author: (books) Career Connections, 1976, Work or Play?, 1976, Who? What? When?, 1976, Television Critikit, 1980, Voyage of the MIMI, 1985, Hide and Seek, 1986, Starting Free, 1987, The Warrior Maiden: A Hopi Legend, 1992, I Love to Sneeze, 1992, Sim Chung and the River Dragon, 1993, The Town Mouse and the Country Mouse, 1994, Sleep Tight, Pete, 1994, (with Doris Orgel and Emily Coplon) She'll Be Coming Round the Mountain, 1994, Diamonds and Toads, 1994, The Boy Who Cried Wolf, 1994, (with Orgel) The Flower of Sheba, 1994, (as Suzanne Altman with Orgel) Worst Days Diary, 1995, Real-Live Monsters!, 1995, The Big Idea, 1996, The Pet-Sitters, 1996; contbr. numerous articles to profl. jours. Mem. patient adv. bd. Hosp. for Spl. Surgery, N.Y.C.; dir. Bank Street Writers' Lab., N.Y.C., 1990—. Mem. ASCAP, Writer's Guild of Am., N.Y. Women in Film, Soc. of Children's Book Writers/Illustrators. Democrat. Jewish. Office: Bank Street Coll Edn 610 W 12th St New York NY 10025

SCHEER-DOERFERT, JILL ANNE, state official; b. Milw., June 10, 1958; d. James F. and Joyce M. Scheer; m. David L. Doerfert, May 18, 1991; 1 child, Michael. AA, U. Wis., West Bend, 1978; BSW, U. Wis., Oshkosh, 1980; M Cmty. Human Svcs., U. Wis., Green Bay, 1991. Program dir. Daybreak, Inc., Horicon, Wis., 1980-85; cmty. svcs. specialist Calumet County Dept. Human Svcs., Chilton, Wis., 1985-88; juvenile ct. disposition worker Brown County Dept. Social Svcs., Green Bay, 1988-90, family therapist, 1990-91; state juvenile justice specialist State of Wis. Office Justice Assistance, Madison, 1991-93; state youth diversion coord. Dept. Health and Social Svcs., Madison, 1993; rehab. treatment svcs. supr. Iowa State U., Ames, 1993-96; Violence Against Women program specialist State of Wis. Office Justice Assistance, Madison, 1996—; trainer Phantom Lake YMCA Camp, Mukwonago, Wis., 1986—; nat. trainer Nat. Inst. for Alternative Care Profls., 1995, Foster Family Based Treatment Assn., 1995. Recipient Achievement award Wis. Social Svc. Assn., 1990, Exemplary Performance award State of Wis., 1992. Home: 436 Bowlavard Belleville WI 53508 Office: State of Wis Office Justice Assistance 222 State St Madison WI 53702-0001

SCHEETER, STEPHANIE ANN, special education and elementary school educator; b. Cape Girardeau, Mo., Aug. 5, 1967; d. Gerald Elmer and Bernadette Mary (DeBrock) Schlitt; m. Dennis James Scheeter, Aug. 13, 1988; children: Chelsey Nicole, Caitlin Marie, Courtney Ann. BS in Elem. Edn., S.E. Mo. State U., 1992. Cert. tchr., Mo. Spl. edn. tchr. Scott County R-II Schs., Chaffee, Mo., 1992—. Mem. Coun. for Exceptional Children, Mo. Tchrs. Assn. Home: RR 1 Box 585 Chaffee MO 63740-9729

SCHEETZ, SISTER MARY JOELLEN, English language educator; b. Lafayette, Ind., May 20, 1926; d. Joseph Albert and Ellen Isabelle (Fitzgerald) S. A.B., St. Francis Coll., 1956; M.A., U. Notre Dame, 1964; Ph.D., U. Mich., 1970. Tchr. English, Bishop Luers High Sch., Fort Wayne, Ind., 1965-67; acad. dean St. Francis Coll., Fort Wayne, 1967-68; pres. St. Francis Coll., Ft. Wayne, Ind., 1970-93; pres. emeritus; English lang. prof. St. Francis Coll., Ft. Wayne, Ind., 1993—. Mem. Nat. Coun. Tchrs. English, Delta Epsilon Sigma. Office: St Francis Coll 2701 Spring St Fort Wayne IN 46808-3939

SCHEID, ANN FRANCES, preservation planner, consultant; b. Rochester, Minn., Jan. 30, 1940; d. Joseph Frank and Clara Josephine (Larson) Underleak; m. John Allen Scheid, Dec. 24, 1977. AB in German, Vassar Coll., 1962; MA in Germanic Langs., U. Chgo., 1963, postgrad., 1964-68; M in Design, Harvard U., 1993. Fgn. svc. officer USIA, Stockholm, 1963-65; sr. planner City of Pasadena, Calif., 1977-91; assoc. planner City of Redlands, Calif., 1991-92; archtl. historian Calif. Dept. Transp., L.A., 1992-95; prin. Ann Scheid, Pasadena, 1995—; tchg. assoc. UCLA, 1975-76; adj. prof. Pasadena (Calif.) City Coll., 1978; lectr. in field. Author: Pasadena: Crown of the Valley, 1986, The Valley Hunt Club: 100 Years, 1988; contbr. chpts. to books and articles to profl. jours. NDEA fellow, 1966-68, Fulbright-Hays fellow, 1968-69. Mem. Am. Planning Assn., Nat. Trust Hist. Preservation, Soc. Archtl. Historians (bd. dirs. So. Calif. chpt. 1988-93), Soc. Am. City and Regional Planning History, Calif. Preservation Found., Calif. Coun. Promotion History, Hist. Soc. So. Calif. Home and Office: 500 S Arroyo Blvd Pasadena CA 91105

SCHEIMAN, KATHLEEN ANNE, insurance operations analyst; b. Cleve., Mar. 8, 1957; d. Walter Edward and Bernice Agnes (Nemeth) S. AS in Acctg., Lakeland C.C., Kirtland, Ohio, 1993; student in Psychology, Ursuline Coll. Analyst Progressive Ins., Mayfield Village, Ohio, 1976—. Mem. Inst. Internal Auditors, Phi Theta Kappa. Home: 5219 Franklyn Blvd # B Willoughby OH 44094-3372

SCHEIN, SALLY JOY, special services and learning disabilities consultant, marriage and family therapist; b. Chgo., July 6, 1930; d. Rudolph James and Lillian (Cohen) Good; m. Michael Schein, Apr. 9, 1955; children: Jack Edward, David Lee. BA, U. Chgo., 1950, Columbia U., 1952; MS, CCNY, 1953; EdS, Seton Hall U., 1982, also doctoral coursework; EdD. Nova U., 1986. Occupational therapist Monmouth Meml. Hosp., Longbranch, N.J., 1953-54; tchr. nursery kindergarten N.Y. Dept. Welfare, N.Y.C., 1954-55; tchr. kindergarten Yonkers Pub. Sch., N.Y., 1955, Dumont Pub. Sch., N.J., 1955-56; learning disabilities teaching cons. Haworth, N.J., 1968-72, Caldwell, N.J., 1972-79, Cranford Pub. Sch., N.J., 1979-90; psychologist extern North Caldwell, Closter, N.J., 1976-77; counselor Community Mental Health Ctr., Dumont, 1981-82. Author: Welcome to Danish International Studies, 1979; (with E. Riley et al) Sparking Divergent Ability, 1985, Reducing Children's Vulnerability After Divorce, 1987. Founding mem. clin. bd. Community Mental Health Ctr., Dumont, 1958-60. Mem. Am. Assn. Marriage and Family Therapists, Nat. Assn. Sch. Psychologists, Assn. Learning Cons., Council Exceptional Children, Orton Soc. Avocations: Sculpting; art; jogging; travel. Home: 4 Harding Ave Dumont NJ 07628-1211

SCHEIN, VIRGINIA ELLEN, psychologist; b. Rahway, N.J., June 23, 1943; d. Jacob Charles and Anne S.; m. Rupert F. Chisholm. BA cum laude, Cornell U., 1965; PhD, N.Y.U., 1969. Lic. psychologist, Pa. 1 child, Alexander Nikos. Sr. research assoc. Am. Mgmt. Assn., N.Y.C., 1969-70; mgr. personnel research Life Office Mgmt. Assn., N.Y.C., 1970-72; dir. personnel research Met. Life Ins. Co. N.Y.C., 1972-75; asso. prof. Sch. Mgmt. Case Western Res. U., Cleve., 1975-76; vis. asso. prof. Sch. Orgn. and Mgmt., Yale U., New Haven, 1976-77; assoc. prof. mgmt. Wharton Sch. U. Pa., Phila., 1977-80; mgmt. cons. Virginia E. Schein, PhD, P.C., 1975—; assoc. prof. psychology Bernard M. Baruch Coll., City U. N.Y., 1982-85; prof. mgmt. Gettysburg Coll., Pa., 1986—, chair mgmt. dept., 1993-95. Co-author: Power and Organization Development, 1988; Author: Working from the Margins, 1995; mem. editorial rev. bds. Women Mgmt. Rev., Acad. Mgmt. Execs.; contbr. articles to profl. jours. Bd. dirs. Keystone Rsch. Ctr., Family Planning Ctr., Survivors, Inc., past pres. bd.; bd. dirs. Pvt. Industry Coun. Mem. Am. Psychol. Assn. (council reps. 1978-80, com. on women 1980-83), Met. Assn. Applied Psychology (pres. 1973-74), Acad. Mgmt., (rep. orgn. devel. div. 1979-81, mem. exec. com. women mgmt. divsn.), Internat. Assn. Applied Psychology, Am. Psychol. Soc., Psi Chi. Office: Gettysburg Coll Dept Mgmt Gettysburg PA 17325

SCHEINDLIN, SHIRA A., federal judge; b. Washington, Aug. 16, 1946; d. Boris and Miriam (Shapiro) Joffe; m. Stanley Friedman, May 22, 1982; 2 children. BA cum laude, U. Mich., 1967; MA in Far Ea. Studies, Columbia U., 1969; JD cum laude, Cornell U., 1975. Bar: N.Y. 1976. With Stroock, Stroock & Lavan, 1975-76; law clerk to Hon. Charles L. Brieant, Jr. U.S. Dist. Ct. (so. dist.) N.Y., 1976-77; asst. U.S. atty. Ea. Dist. N.Y., 1977-81; gen. counsel N.Y.C. Dept. of Investigation, 1981-82; U.S. magistrate U.S. Dist. Ct. (ea. dist.) N.Y., 1982-86; with Budd, Larner, Gross, Rosenbaum, Greenberg & Sade, Short Hills, N.J., 1986-90, ptnr., 1990; ptnr. Herzfeld & Rubin, N.Y.C., 1990-94; endispute mem. Judicial Panel, 1992-94; judge U.S. Dist. Ct. (so. dist.) N.Y., 1994—; adj. prof. law Bklyn. Law Sch., 1983—; mem. 2d Cir. Conf. Planning Com., So. Dist. Adv. Com., 1991-94. Recipient Spl. Achievement award Dept. of Justice, 1980. Mem. Fedn. Bar Coun. (trustee 1986-88, 90—, v.p. 1988-90), N.Y. State Bar Assn. (chair comml. and fed. litigation sect. 1991-92), N.Y. County Lawyers Assn. (bd. dirs. 1992-95, chair tort sect. 1992-94), Assn. of Bar of City of N.Y. Office: US Courthouse 500 Pearl St Rm 1050 New York NY 10007

SCHELAR, VIRGINIA MAE, chemistry consultant; b. Kenosha, Wis., Nov. 26, 1924; d. William and Blanche M. (Williams) S. BS, U. Wis., 1947, MS, 1953; MEd, Harvard U., 1962; PhD, U. Wis., 1969. Instr. U. Wis., Milw., 1947-51; info. specialist Abbott Labs., North Chgo., Ill., 1953-56; instr. Wright Jr. Coll., Chgo., 1957-58; asst. prof. No. Ill. U., DeKalb, 1958-63; prof. St. Petersburg (Fla.) Jr. Coll., 1965-67; asst. prof. Chgo. State Coll., 1967-68; prof. Grossmont Coll., El Cajon, Calif., 1968-80; cons. Calif., 1981—. Author: Kekule Centennial, 1965; contbr. articles to profl. jours. Active citizens adv. coun. DeKalb Consol. Sch. Bd.; voters svc. chair League Women Voters, del. to state and nat. convs., judicial chair, election laws chair. Standard Oil fellow, NSF grantee; recipient Lewis prize U. Wis. Fellow Am. Inst. Chemists; mem. Am. Chem. Soc. (membership affairs com., chmn. western councilor's caucus, exec. com., councilor, legis. counselor, chmn. edn. com., editor state and local bulletins).

SCHELL, JOAN BRUNING, information specialist, business science librarian; b. N.Y.C., June 9, 1932; d. Walter Henry and Gertrude Emily (Goossen) Bruning; m. Harold Benton Schell, Aug. 27, 1955 (div. 1978); children: Jeffrey Mark, Sue Lynne. AB, Wittenberg U., 1954; postgrad., Syracuse U., 1963, U. Md., 1965-66; MLS, U. Pitts., 1968. Actuarial, claims asst. Nationwide Ins., Columbus, Ohio, 1954-57; tech. report typist Cornell U., Ithaca, N.Y., 1957; bus. libr. asst. U. Pitts., 1969; bus. reference libr. Dallas Pub. Libr., 1971-73, Pub. Libr. Cin. and Hamilton County, Cin., 1973-79; book selection coord. Pub. Libr. Cin. & Hamilton County, Cin., 1979-83, asst. to main libr., 1983-85; literacy tutor Cin. LEARN, 1985-89; recorder feminist lit. Womyn's Braille Press, Mpls., 1985-89; wellness program asst. Times Pub. Co., St. Petersburg, Fla., 1989-96, Taoist Tai Chi Soc., 1995—; dir. Wittenberg U., Springfield, Ohio, 1988—; bd. dirs. Crazy Ladies Ctr. Inc., Cin., 1989-93; coord. Fla. west coast Old Lesbians Organizing for Change, 1993-95; sec., trustee Clio Found., Inc., 1995—; docent Fla. Internat. Mus., 1994—. Compiler: (reference source) Greater Cincinnati Business Index, 1975-79; editor: New Reference Materials, 1983, 84. Mem. Tampa Bay YWCA Women's Guild, St. Petersburg, 1991-95; vol. NOW Elect Women Campaign, St. Petersburg, 1990-92, Senator Helen G. Davis Reelection, St. Petersburg, 1992. Mem. ALA, Spl. Librs. Assn. (treas., archivist 1974-83), Am. Assn. Individual Investors, Laubach Literary Action, Taoist Tai Chi Soc., Beta Phi Mu Libr. Sci. Hon., Phi Delta Gamma Grad. Women Hon. Address: PO Box 7472 Saint Petersburg FL 33734-7472

SCHELL, VICKI J., mathematics educator; b. Terre Haute, Ind., Oct. 10, 1948; d. Earl Jackson and Roberta Jean (Brown) S. BS, Davis & Elkins Coll., 1970; MA, N.E. Mo. State U., 1980; PhD, No. Ill. U., 1991. Math tchr. Campbell County Schs., Rustburg, Va., 1970-73; devel. engr. space shuttle Honeywell Avionics, St. Petersburg, Fla., 1973-79; math tchr. Darüssafaka Lisesi, Istanbul, Turkey, 1976-77; tchr. math. and computers Salzburg (Austria) Internat. Sch., 1977-79; cons. math. Mo. Dept. Edn., Jefferson City, 1980-81; assoc. prof. math. and computers Pensacola (Fla.) Jr. Coll., 1981-90; asst. prof. math. U. West Fla., Pensacola, 1990-93; assoc. prof. math., dept. chmn. Lenoir-Rhyne Coll, Hickory, N.C., 1993—; cons. Escambia County Schs., Pensacola, 1981-93. Contbr. articles to profl. jours. Mem. Nat. Coun. Suprs. Math., Nat. Coun. Tchrs. Math., N.C. Coun. Tchrs. Math., Assn. Women in Math., Sch. Sci. and Math. Assn., Math. Assn. Am., Rsch. Coun. for Diagnostic and Prospective Math. Office: Lenoir-Rhyne Coll PO Box 7281 Hickory NC 28603-7281

SCHELLING, JOYCE ELAINE, account executive; b. Fort Wayne, Ind., Oct. 14, 1937; d. George Martin and Lucille Alice (Schuckel) Schmeling. BA, St. Francis Coll., 1962; MA, Catholic U., 1968; PhD, NYU, 1987. Lic. tchr., Ind., N.J. Dir. drama St. Francis Coll., Ft. Wayne, 1966-70; instr. South Plainfield (N.J.) High Sch., 1970-80, NYU, N.Y.C., 1980-82; account exec. On-Line Software, Fort Lee, N.J., 1982-86, SDI, Hackensack, N.J., 1986-88, Microbank Software, Inc., N.Y.C., 1988-91, Performance Mgmt., Inc., N.Y.C., 1991-95, BBN Planet, Inc., 1995—. Mem. NAFE, NOW, N.J. Network Bus. and Profl. Women, N.J. Assn. Women Bus. Owners. Democrat. Home: 2100 Linwood Ave Apt 15R Fort Lee NJ 07024-3159 Office: BBN Planet 485 Madison Ave 11th Fl New York NY 10020

SCHENK, SUSAN KIRKPATRICK, geriatric psychiatry nurse; b. New Richmond, Ind., Nov. 29, 1938; d. William Marcius and Frances (Kirkpatrick) Gaither; m. Richard Dee Brown, Aug. 13, 1960 (div. Feb. 1972); children: Christopher, David, Lisa; m. John Francis Schenk, July 24, 1975 (widowed Apr. 1995). BSN, Ind. U., 1962; postgrad., U. Del., 1973-75. RN, PHN, BCLS; cert. community coll. tchr., Calif. Staff nurse, then asst. dir. nursing Bloomington (Ind.) Hosp., 1962-66; charge nurse Newark (Del.) Manor, 1967-69; charge nurse GU Union Hosp., Terre Haute, Ind., 1971-72; clin. instr. nursing Ind. State U., Terre Haute, 1972-73; clin. instr. psychiatric nursing U. Del., Newark, 1974-75; psychiatric nursing care coord. VA Med. Ctr., Perry Point, Md., 1975-78; nurse educator Grossmont Hosp., La Mesa, Calif., 1978-90, cmty. rels. coord., 1990-91; dir. psychiat. svcs. Scripps Hosp. East County, El Cajon, Calif., 1991—; tech. advisor San Diego County Bd. Supervisors, 1987; tech. cons. Remedy Home and Health Care, San Diego, 1988; expert panelist Srs. Speak Out, KPBS-TV, San Diego, 1988; guest lectr. San Diego State U., 1987. Editor: Teaching Basic Caregiver Skills, 1988; author, performer tng. videotape Basic Caregiver Skills, 1988. Mem. patient svcs. com. Nat. Multiple Sclerosis Soc., San Diego, 1986-89; bd. dirs. Assn. for Quality and Participation, 1989. Adminstrn. on Aging/DHHS grantee, 1988. Mem. Am. Psychiat. Nurses Assn., Ind. U. Alumni Assn. (life), Mensa, Sigma Theta Tau. Home: 9435 Carlton Oaks Dr # D Santee CA 92071-2588 Office: Scripps Hosp East County 1688 E Main St El Cajon CA 92021-5204

SCHENKEL, SUZANNE CHANCE, natural resource specialist; b. Phila., Mar. 12, 1940; d. Henry Martyn Chance II and Suzanne (Sharpless) Jameson; m. John Lackland Hardinge Schenkel, June 15, 1963; children: John Jr., Andrew Chance. BS in Edn., Tufts U., 1962. Tchr. Roland Pk. Country Sch., Balt., 1962-65; exec. dir. Mass. Citizens' Com. for Dental Health, Springfield, 1981-83; pub., editor Women's Investment Newsletter, Longmeadow, Mass., 1985-89; pub. affairs officer USDA's Soil Conservation Svc., Amherst, Mass., 1990-93; resource conservationist divsn. conservation & ecosys. assistance USDA's Natural Resources Conservation Svc., Washington, 1993—; staff Merchant Marine and Fisheries com. U.S. Ho. of Reps., Washington, 1993. Author Wetlands Protection and Management Act. Chmn. Longmeadow (Mass.) Conservation Commn., 1984-90; supr. Hampden County (Mass.) Conservation Dist., 1985-90; bd. dirs., v.p. League of Women Voters of Mass., Boston, 1974-85; exec. com. Water Supply Citizens' Adv. Com.; adv. bd. Water Resources Authority, Mass., 1979-90. Mem. Soil and Water Conservation Soc., Nat. Assn. Conservation Dists. Episcopalian. Home: 1052 Carriage Hill Pky Annapolis MD 21401-6505 Office: USDA Natural Resources Conservation Svc/Ecosystem Asst Divsn/PO Box 2890 Washington DC 20013

SCHENSTED, ELIZABETH MALONEY, editor; b. Yakima, Wash., June 30, 1929; d. Thomas Gleason and Eunice Elizabeth (Montague) Maloney; m. Warren Curtis Schensted, Sept. 25, 1954; children: David Patrick, Robert Michael. BA, Wash. State U., 1951. Editor Mercer Island (Wash.) Reporter, 1972-79; chief regional editor Soundings Nat. Boating News Mag., Seattle, 1979-81; editor-in-chief Argus Publs., Seattle, 1981-84; chief copy editor Soundings Publs., Essex, Conn., 1985-87; west coast editor Soundings Publs., Newport Beach, Calif., 1987-91; Northwest editor Waterfront Mag., Seattle, 1992-94, Dockside Mag., Seattle, 1995—. Bd. dirs. Cystic Fibrosis Found., 1977, Mercer Island C. of C., 1977-79. Lt. (j.g.) USN, 1951-54. Mem. AAUW, Wash. Press Assn. (bd. dirs. 1995, dir. judges 1995), Soc. Profl. Journalists (bd. dirs. 1992-94). Democrat. Roman Catholic. Home: 10045 NE 1st St # 326 Bellevue WA 98004 Office: Dockside Magazine 754 Garfield St Seattle WA 98109

SCHEPPNER, KATHLEEN, metal products executive; b. Erie, Pa., Feb. 7, 1949; d. Albin C. and Dorothy (Carlson) S. Student, Denison U. Pres., CEO Carlson-Erie Corp., Erie, 1970-94, v.p., sec., 1995—; pres. Am. Tinning & Galvanizing Co., Erie, Pa., 1984—; co-owner Cup.A.Ccino's Coffie House, Erie, 1990—. Bd. corporators St. Vincent Health Ctr.; bd. trustees St. Vincent Health Sys., Boys' and Girls' Club of Erie; mem. Pa. Environ. Coun., Gannon U. Ambs., Enterprise Zone Loan Rev. Commn.; mem. Erie-Enterprise Zone Econ. Devel. Coun.; charter mem. Women Leaders' Summit, Washington. Mem. Am. Electroplaters and Surface Finishers Soc. (pres. Erie br. 1988-92, v.p. 1995-96), Am. Galvanizers Assn., Nat. Assn. Metal Finishers, Pvt. Industry Coun., Mfrs. Assn. (environ. roundtable), Erie Conf. Cmty. Devel., Aluminum Anodizers Coun. Address: 552 W 12th St Erie PA 16501-1507

SCHEPPS, VICTORIA HAYWARD, lawyer; b. Brockton, Mass., June 11, 1956; d. William George and Lucy Victoria (Mitcheroney) Hayward; m. Frank Schepps, Sept. 18, 1982; children: Frank IV, Lucia. BA, Suffolk U., 1977; JD, U. San Diego, 1981. Instr., Northeastern U., Boston, 1981-83; assoc. Hoffman & Hoffman, Boston, 1983-85, Mark J. Gladstone, P.C., 1985-87; Doktor, Hirschberg & Schepps, 1987-88, Schepps & Reilly, 1988-90; pvt. practice Law Office of Victoria Hayward Schepps, Stoughton, Mass., 1990— . Mem. Mass. Bar Assn., Mass. Conveyancing Assn., Mass. Assn. Bank Counsel, Inc. Democrat. Roman Catholic. Office: 6 Cabot Pl Ste 9 Stoughton MA 02072-4625

SCHERER, KARLA, foundation executive, venture capitalist; b. Detroit, Jan. 13, 1937; d. Robert Pauli and Margaret (Lindsey) S.; m. Peter R. Fink, Sept. 14, 1957 (div. July 1989); children: Christina Lammert, Hadley McKenzie Tolliver, Allison Augusta Scherer; m. Theodore Souris, Sept. 5, 1992. Student, Wellesley Coll., 1954-55; BA, U. Mich., 1957. Chmn. Karla Scherer Found., Detroit, 1989—; advisor on shareholders' rights; speaker on corp. governance to various univs. and profl. assns.; condr. workshops in field; leader only successful proxy contest of maj. U.S. publicly held corp., 1988. Trustee Eton Acad., Birmingham, Mich., 1989—; mem. vis. com. Fordham U. Grad. Sch. Bus. Adminstrn.; former mem. bd. dirs. Cottage Hosp., Univ. Liggett Sch., Music Hall, Detroit League for Handicapped; former mem. adv. bd. Wellesley Coll; former mem. Rep. Dennis M. Hertel's Candidate Selection Com. for Armed Svcs. Acads.; mem. U. Mich. Ctr. for the Edn. of Women Leadership Coun. Named Outstanding Woman Leader of Yr. Oakland U., 1990, one of Metro Detroit's Dynamic Women Women's Econ. Club, 1992, Entrepreneur of Yr. Finalist, 1993. Mem. Am. Mgmt. Assn. (gen. mgmt. coun. for growing orgns.), Women's Forum Mich., Econ. Club Detroit (bd. dirs. 1991—), Women's Econ. Club Detroit, Detroit Club, Detroit Athletic Club, Country Club Detroit, Grosse Pointe Club, Renaissance Club (bd. dirs. 1995—). Office: 100 Renaissance Ctr Ste 1680 Detroit MI 48243-1009

SCHERER, SUZANNE MARIE, artist, educator; b. Buffalo, Sept. 12, 1964; d. Robert Henry Scherer and Judith Louise Le Bar; m. Pavel Victorovich Ouporov, Oct. 25, 1991. AA, Broward C.C., 1984; BFA magna cum laude, Fla. State U., 1986; MFA summa cum laude, Bklyn. Coll., 1989; postgrad., Surikov State Art Acad., Moscow, 1989-91. Educator Bklyn. Mus., 1987-89; profl. artist N.Y.C., 1989—; guest lectr. Bklyn. Coll., 1992, Pa. Sch. Art and Design, Lancaster, 1996; artist-in-residence Lancaster Mus. and Pa. Sch. Art and Design, 1996; lectr. Lancaster Mus. Artist: (books) The Basics of Buying Art, 1996, Monumental Propaganda, 1994, Genesis: A Living Conversation, 1996, (jour.) The Scis., 1995-96; (TV) Genesis: A Living Conversation, 1996, (radio) Radio Free Europe: Interview with Raya Vail, 1995, WBAI FM: Interview with Charles Finch, 1994. Mem. Internat. Women's Orgn., Moscow, 1989-91. Grantee Internat. Rsch. and Exchs. Bd., 1989; Visual Arts Residency grantee Mid-Atlantic Arts Found., 1996. Democrat. Home and Office: Scherer and Ouporov 2d Fl 56 First Pl Brooklyn NY 11231

SCHERMER, JUDITH KAHN, lawyer; b. N.Y.C., Feb. 28, 1949; d. Robert and Barbara Kahn; m. Daniel Woodrough Schermer; 1 child, Sarah Nicole. BA, U. Chgo., 1971; JD, William Mitchell Coll. Law, 1987. Bar: Minn. 1987, U.S. Dist. Ct. Minn. 1987. Advt. and promotion specialist U. Chgo. Press, 1971-75; systems analyst Allstate Ins. Co., Northbrook, Ill., 1975-78, Lutheran Brotherhood, Mpls., 1980-83; polit. aide Mpls. City Coun., 1986-87; ptnr. Schermer & Schermer, Mpls., 1987—. Pres., feminist caucus, assoc. chair 5th dist., state exec. com. Dem. Farm Labor Party; bd. dirs. Women Candidates Devel. coalition. Mem. ATLA, Minn. Trial Lawyers Assn. (bd. govs., chair employment law sect.), Minn. State Bar Assn., Minn. Women Lawyers, Nat. Employment Law Assn. Home: 4624 Washburn Ave S Minneapolis MN 55410-1846 Office: Schermer and Schermer Lumber Exch Bldg 10 S 5th St Ste 700 Minneapolis MN 55402-1033

SCHETLIN, ELEANOR M., retired university official; b. N.Y.C., July 15, 1920; d. Henry Frank and Elsie (Chew) Schetlin; B.A., Hunter Coll., 1940; M.A., Tchrs. Coll., Columbia U., 1942, Ed.D., 1967. Playground dir. Dept. of Parks, N.Y.C., 1940-42; librarian Met. Hosp. Sch. Nursing, N.Y.C., 1943-44, dir. recreation, 1944-48, dir. recreation and guidance, 1948-59; coordinator student activities SUNY, Plattsburgh, 1959-63, asst. dean students, 1963-64; asst. prof., coordinator student personnel services CUNY, Hunter Coll., 1967-68; asst. dir. student personnel Columbia U., Coll. Pharm. Scis., N.Y.C., 1968-69, dir. student personnel, 1969-71; assoc. dean for students Health Scis. Center, SUNY, Stony Brook, 1971-73, asst. v.p. for student services, 1973-74, assoc. dean of students, dir. student services, 1974-85; mem. Sea Cliff unit 300 Nassau County Auxiliary Police. Recipient Lifetime Achievement award Nassau NOW, 1992. Mem. Nat. Assn. Women in Edn., Nat. Women's Studies Assn. Contbr. articles to profl. jours. Home: 20 Barberry Ln Sea Cliff NY 11579-2052

SCHEU, JEAN W. MORRISON, retired school library media specialist; b. St. Paul, Jan. 30, 1927; d. Roy Chesterfield and Laura Ida (Zempel) Morrison; m. James William Scheu; children: Steven James, Susan Kathryn, Sara Anne, Stuart Morrison. BA, U. Minn., 1949, MA in Libr. Sci., 1966, postgrad. Lic. sch. libr. and media specialist. Sch. libr. media specialist Pilgrim Ln. Elem. Sch., Plymouth, Minn., 1966-93; sec. Dist. 281 Continuing Edn. Com., New Hope, Minn., 1971-75, chair, 1975-91; mem. edn. policies com. Minn. Fedn. Tchrs., 1975-92. Vol. Plymouth Pub. Libr., 1995; active Citizens League, 1993-95, NOW, 1985-95, Planned Parenthood, 1980-95. Recipient 25 Yr. Svc. pin Dist. 281 Robbinsdale, 1991; named Chess Coach of Yr., Minn. Sch. Chess Assn., 1988. Mem. AAUW, Am. Fedn. Tchrs., Robbinsdale Fedn. Tchrs. Democrat. Episcopal. Home: 1170 N Evergreen Ln Plymouth MN 55441-4834

SCHEUFFELE, TRACY LYNNE, accountant; b. Battle Creek, Mich., Feb. 7, 1968; d. Kent Allan Schwartz and Marie Elaine (Decker) Dowd; m. Scott Dwight Scheuffele, Sept. 21, 1990 (div.). BA, Western Mich. U., 1990; postgrad., Ind. U. Acctg. assoc. James River Corp., Kalamazoo, Mich., 1990-91, cost acct., 1991-92; contr. James River Corp., Kendallville, Ind., 1992-96, contr. Sys. Implementation Project, 1995—. Mem. Inst. Mgmt. Accts. (sec. 1990-91, treas. 1991-92, v.p. membership 1992-93, v.p. fin. and adminstrn. 1993-94), Internat. Mgmt. Coun. Republican. Roman Catholic. Home: 57 F Adams Cir Fairfield OH 45014 Office: James River Corp One Better Way Rd Milford OH 45150-3266

SCHEURER, CHERYL ANN, accountant; b. Redwood City, Calif., Nov. 10, 1954; d. Jack L. and Thelma M. (Jaton) S. Student, Peterson Sch. Bus., 1971-72, Golden Gate U., 1980-83. Acctg. clk. Seattle First Nat. Bank, 1973-74, Simpson Timber Co., Kirkland, Wash., 1974-76; controller, office mgr. Maida Constrn. Co., Walnut Creek, Calif., 1978-80; acct. Castle, CPA, Oakland, Calif., 1981-82; pvt. practice acctg., tax planning Alameda, Calif., 1980—; guest speaker ESL Adult Sch., Alameda, 1988. Creator, writer, artist (first story and art) Power Angels (TM), 1996. Active Big Bros./Big Sisters Am., Oakland, 1986-87; bd. mem., treas. Marin Ch. of Religious Sci., 1992-93; chairperson Madison Sch. Cite Coun., 1995-96.

SCHEVILL, MARGOT BLUM, anthropologist; b. Stockton, Calif., Aug. 15, 1931; d. Gay Frederick Helmuth and Ruth Carolyn (Zuckerman) Hartmann; m. Robert C. Blum, Sept. 9, 1951 (div. June 1965); children: Sherifa Zuhur, Paul Helmuth; m. James Erwin Schevill, Aug. 2, 1966. BA, Brown U., 1972, MA, 1981. Rsch. assoc. Haffenreffer Mus. Anthropology, Brown U., Bristol, R.I., 1982-97; rsch. assoc. P. Hearst Mus. Anthropology, U. Calif., 1995-97, guest curator, 1996—; asst. curator Haffenreffer Mus. Anthropology, Brown U., Bristol, R.I., 1987-91; sr. mus. scientist P. Hearst Mus., U. Calif., Berkeley, 1988-93; guest curator M.H. de Young Meml. Mus., San Francisco, 1995-96, P. Hearst Mus., U. Calif., 1996—; cons. in field. Author: Evolution in Textile Design, 1985, Costume as Communication, 1986, Maya Textiles of Guatemala, 1993; editor: Textile Traditions of Mesoamerica and the Andes, 1996; editor, contbr. The Maya Textile Tradition, 1997. Bd. dirs. Composers, Inc., San Francisco, 1993-96, Music in Schs. Today, San Francisco, 1991-93; pres. New Music Ensemble, Providence, 1968-84. Grantee NEA, 1984, 88, 90, 95-96, NEH, 1991-93. Mem. Am. Anthropol. Assn., Native Am. Art Studies Assn., The Textile Soc. (arts coun. 1991—), Coun. Mus. Anthropology (v.p. 1981—, sec. 1986-89). Home: 1309 Oxford St Berkeley CA 94709 Office: P Hearst Mus Anthropology U Calif Berkeley CA 94720

SCHEWEL, ROSEL HOFFBERGER, education educator; b. Balt., Mar. 1, 1928; d. Samuel Herman and Gertrude (Miller) Hoffberger; m. Elliot Sidney Schewel, June 12, 1949; children: Stephen, Michael, Susan. AB, Hood Coll., 1949; MEd, Lynchburg Coll., 1974; EdS, 1982. Reading resource tchr. Lynchburg Pub. Schs., Va., 1967-75; adj. prof. edn. Lynchburg Coll., 1973-79; cons., seminar leader Woman's Resource Ctr., Lynchburg, 1980-92; assoc. prof. edn. Lynchburg Coll., 1980-92. Trustee, vice chair bd. trustees Lynchburg Coll., Va., 1992—; bd. dirs. Va. Found. for Humanities and Pub. Policy, 1985-90, New Vistas Sch., Lynchburg Human Rights Commn., 1992—, Lynchburg Youth Svcs., 1993—; bd. dirs. Venture Enterprising Women, Planned Parenthood of the Blue Ridge; trustee Va. Mus. of Fine Arts, 1985-90; apptd. Commn. on Edn. for All Virginians, 1990; bd. dirs. Action Alliance for Virginia's Children and Youth, 1995—; bd. trustees Amazement Sq. Children's Mus., 1996—. Recipient Disting. Svc. award NCCJ, 1973, Outstanding Woman in Edn. award YWCA, 1988, Disting. Alumni award Lynchburg Coll., 1993. Democrat. Jewish. Address: 4316 Gorman Dr Lynchburg VA 24503-1948

SCHEXNAYDER, CHARLOTTE TILLAR, state legislator; b. Tillar, Ark., Dec. 25, 1923; d. Jewell Stephen and Bertha (Terry) Tillar; m. Melvin John Schexnayder Sr., Aug. 18, 1946; children: M. John Jr., Sarah Holden, Stephen. BA, La. State U., 1944, postgrad., 1947-48. Asst. editor La. Agrl. Extension, Baton Rouge, 1944; editor The McGehee (Ark.) Times, 1945-46, 48-53; editor, co-publisher The Dumas (Ark.) Clarion, 1954-85, publisher, 1985—; mem. Ark. Ho. of Reps., Little Rock, 1985—, asst. speaker pro tem, 1995—; pres. Ark. Assn. Women, 1955, Nat. Newspaper Assn., Washington, 1991-92, Ark. Press. Assn., Little Rock, 1982, Nat. Fedn. Press Women, Blue Springs, Mo., 1977-78, Litte Rock chpt. Soc. Profl. Journalists, 1973; mem. pres.'s coun. Winrock Internat., 1990—. Editor: Images of the Past, 1991. 1st woman mem. Ark. Bd. Pardons and Parole, 1975-80; mem. Ark. Legis. Coun., 1985-92; v.p. Desha County Mus., 1989—; dir. Dumas Indsl. Found., 1986—; mem. exec. com. Ark. Ctrl. Radiation Therapy Inst., 1991-92; mem. adv. bd. Ark. Profl. Women Achievement, 1992—; vice chair Ark. Rural Devel. Commn., 1991-96; mem. Winrock Internat. Adv. Coun., 1991—. Named Disting. Alumnus Ark. A&M Coll., 1971, Woman of Achievement Nat. Fedn. Press Women, 1970, Outstanding Arkansan C. of C., 1986; recipient Ark. Profl. Women of Distinction award No. Bank, Little Rock, 1990, Emma McKinnery award Nation's Top Cmty. Newspaper Woman, 1980, Journalist award Nat. Conf. of Christians and Jews, 1989, Lifetime Achievement award Nat. Fedn. Press Women, 1992, Outstanding Svc. award Ark. Assn. Elem. Prins., Disting. Svc. award Ark. Press Assn., 1993; named to La. State U. Alumni Hall of Distinction, 1994; named one Top 100 Ark. Women, Ark. Bus., 1995, 96. Mem. Pi Beta Phi (Crest award 1992), Ark. Delta Coun. (chmn. of bd. dirs. 1989—). Democrat. Roman Catholic. Home: 322 Court St Dumas AR 71639-2718 Office: Clarion Publishing Co Inc 136 E Waterman St Dumas AR 71639-2227

SCHIAVO, A. MARY FACKLER, aviation consultant, lawyer; b. Pioneer, Ohio, Sept. 4, 1955. AB cum laude, Harvard U., 1976; MA, Ohio State U., 1977; JD, NYU, 1980. Bar: Mo. 1980, U.S. Dist. Ct. (we. dist.) Mo. 1980, U.S. Ct. Appeals (8th cir.) 1983, U.S. Ct. Appeals (10th cir.) 1985, U.S. Supreme Ct. 1990, D.C. 1993, Md. 1994. Assoc. law firm, Kansas City, Mo., 1980-82; asst. U.S. atty. we. dist. Mo. U.S. Dept. Justice, Kansas City, 1982-85, fed. prosecutor organized crime and racketeering strike force, 1985-86; White House fellow, spl. asst. to U.S. Atty. Gen. U.S. Dept. Justice, Washington, 1987-88; exec. dir. Bush/Quayle '88 Campaign, State of Mo., 1988; atty. law firm, Kansas City, 1989; asst. sec. labor-mgmt. standards U.S. Dept. Labor, Washington, 1989-90; insp. gen. U.S. Dept. Transp., Washington, 1990-96; aviation consultant ABC News, 1996—; instr. U.S. Atty. Gen.'s Adv. Inst., Washington, 1986, 88, FBI Acad., Quantico, Va., 1988; guest lectr. NYU Sch. Law, 1986, 88, 91; bd. dirs. Dept. Labor Acad., 1989-90; bd. dirs. White House Fellows Assn. and Found., 1992-96, 2d v.p., 1992-93, chair ann. meeting, 1993, 1st v.p., 1993-94, pres. 1994-95; mem. Pres.'s Coun. on Integrity and Efficiency, 1990-96, Pres.'s Commn. on White House Fellowships, 1994-95. Bd. dirs. Root-Tilden Scholarship program NYU, 1982-89. Recipient Thompson award Ohio State U. Alumni, 1988, Aviation Laurel citation Aviation Week and Space Tech. mag., 1992, Aviation Laurel award Aviation Week and Space Tech. mag., 1995; named one of Top Ten Coll. Women in U.S., 1975, one of ten Outstanding Young Working Women in Am., 1987, Kansas City Career Woman of Yr., 1988; Ohio State U. fellow, 1976-77; U.S.-Japan Leadership fellow, 1995; Root-Tilden legal scholar NYU, 1977-79. Mem. ABA (ho. of dels. 1986-89, assembly del. 1986-89, litigation sect. complex crimes com.), Mo. Bar Assn. (bd. govs. 1986-89, chmn. pro bono task force 1984-86, young lawyers coun. 1983-86, Outstanding Svc. award 1986), Women Fgn. Policy Group. Office: US Dept Transp Office of Insp Gen 1401 N Taft #1421 Arlington VA 20590-0001

SCHIAVO, ANTOINETTE MARIE, administrator; b. Phila.. AA, Peirce Coll.; MS, Cath. U. Am., MD; EdD, Temple U. Instr. Immaculata (Pa.) Coll., registrar, dir. admissions; dir. acad. svcs. Temple U., Phila.; exec. asst. Coax Comm., Jay, N.Y.; dean grad. studies and acad. support Holy Family Coll., Phila. Mem. AERA, NACADA, AAHE, Nat. Coun. Tchrs. Math., ACAFAD, KGP. Office: Holy Family Coll Grant & Frankford Aves Philadelphia PA 19114

SCHIAVO, GERALDINE ELIZABETH (GERI SCHIAVO), poet, screenwriter; b. Phila., Apr. 2; d. Francis Anthony and Helen Nancy (Capaldo) S. BA, Rugers U.; student, Performing Arts of N.J., The Actor's Lab., Phila., Weist-Barron Sch. TV. Cons. Ultima II Cosmetics, N.Y.C., 1981-85; realtor Old Colony, Moorestown, N.J., 1985-88; account exec. Success Pub., Hillside, N.J., 1986-88, Fragrances Du Monde, N.Y.C., 1987-88, Max Factor, L.A., 1989-90; freelance poet, screenwriter, 1990—. Contbr. poetry to Life Poems, An Anthology, 1996; author screenplays When Hearts Entwine, 1991, My Life in Boxes, 1993, Solitary Man, 1995, Obsession, 1995, others. Vol. Am. Cancer Soc. South Jersey, 1995. State scholar State of N.J. Fellow Am. Film Inst. Democrat.

SCHICK, KATHY DIANE, archaeologist, anthropology educator; b. Akron, Ohio, June 6, 1949; d. Vernon Richard Schick and Dorothy Elizabeth (Stimpfel) Kleppel; m. Nicholas Patrick Toth, June 18, 1977. BA in Anthropology, Kent State U., 1974; MA in Anthropology, U. Calif., Berkeley, 1980, PhD in Anthropology, 1984. Vis. asst. prof., rschr. in anthropology U. Calif., Berkeley, 1985-86; vis. asst. prof. Ind. U., Bloomington, 1986-89, asst. prof. anthropology, 1989-94, assoc. prof. anthropology, 1994—, co-dir. CRAFT Rsch. Ctr., 1988—; co-dir. Nihewan Archaeology Project, Hebei Province, China, 1996—. Author: Stone Age Sites in the Making, 1986; co-author: Making Silent Stones Speak, 1993; contbr.: Encyclopedia of Human Evolution, 1988; mem. editl. bd. African Archaeol. Rev., 1994—; contbr. articles to profl. jours. Rsch. grantee NSF, China, 1995. Mem. Soc. Africanist Archaeologists (pres. 1992-94), Soc. for Am. Archaeology, Am. Anthropol. Assn., Paleoanthropology Soc. Office: Craft Human Origins Rsch Ctr 419 N Indiana Bloomington IN 47405

SCHIER, MARY JANE, science writer; b. Houston, Mar. 10, 1939; d. James F. and Jerry Mae (Crisp) McDonald; B.S. in Journalism, Tex. Woman's U., 1961; m. John Christian Schier, Aug. 26, 1961; children—John Christian, II, Mark Edward. Reporter, San Antonio Express and News, 1962-64; med. writer Daily Oklahoman, also Oklahoma City Times, 1965-66; reporter, med. writer Houston Post, 1966-84; sci. writer, univ. editor U. Tex. M.D. Anderson Cancer Ctr., 1984—. Recipient award Tex. Headliners Club, 1969, Tex. Med. Assn., 1972-74, 76, 78, 79, 80, 82 Tex. Hosp. Assn., 1974, 82, Tex. Public Health Assn., 1976, 77, 78, others. Mem. Houston Press Club Ednl. Found. (pres 1992—). Lutheran. Home: 9742 Tappenbeck Dr Houston TX 77055-4102 Office: 1515 Holcombe Blvd Houston TX 77030-4009

SCHIER, MARY LAHR, public relations consultant; b. St. Paul, Minn., Apr. 30, 1956; d. Thomas N. and Jeanette D. (Buysse) Lahr; m. Steven E. Schier, July 10, 1987; children: Anna, Teresa. BA, U. Minn., 1977. Reporter, city editor St. Cloud (Minn.) Daily Times, 1978-84; media rels. specialist Land O'Lakes, Inc., St. Paul, 1984; press sec. U.S. Sen. Rudy Boschwitz, Washington, 1985-87; prin. Mary Schier Pub. Rels., Northfield, Minn., 1988—. Steering com. Citizens for Ctrl. Park, Northfield, 1992-95. Mem. Women in Comms., Inc., The Loft: A Ctr. for Writing. Republican. Roman Catholic. Office: 403 Division St Northfield MN 55057

SCHIEROW, LINDA-JO, environmental policy analyst; b. Milw., Aug. 17, 1947; d. Joseph August Schierow and Ruth Eleanore (Beyersdorff) Heuer. BS in Edn. with honors, U. Wis., 1969, MS in Land Resources, 1980, PhD in Land Resources, 1983. Cert. tchr., Wis. Tchr. elem. Cedarburg (Wis.) Pub. Schs., 1972-78; project assoc. Water Resources Ctr. U. Wis., Madison, 1985; asst. prof. U. Okla., Oklahoma City, 1985-88; rsch. fellow U. Okla., Norman, 1988; rsch. assoc. MIT, Cambridge, 1989-90; ind. cons., 1990-91; policy analyst Environ. and Natural Resources Policy div. U.S. Congress Congl. Rsch. Svc., Libr. of Congress, Washington, 1991-95, policy specialist Environ. and Natural Resources Policy div., 1995—; cons. U.S.-Can. Internat. Joint Commn., Windsor, Ont., Can., 1985; mem. editorial bd. RISK: Health, Safety & Environ., 1990—. Mem. Okla. State Groundwater Protection Strategy Com., Oklahoma City, 1985-88; bd. dirs. Ctr. for Community Tech., Madison, 1983-84. Mem. AAAS, Soc. for Risk Analysis, Risk Assessment and Policy Assn. Democrat. Office: Congl Rsch Svc Libr of Congress Washington DC 20540-7450

SCHIESS, BETTY BONE, priest; b. Cin., Apr. 2, 1923; d. Evan Paul and Leah (Mitchell) Bone; m. William A. Schiess, Aug. 28, 1947; children: William A. (dec.), Richard Corwine, Sarah. BA, U. Cin., 1945; MA, Syracuse U., 1947; MDiv, Rochester Ctr. for Theol. Studies, 1972. Ordained priest Episcopal Ch., 1974; priest assoc. Grace Episc. Ch., Syracuse, N.Y., 1975; mem. N.Y. Task Force on Life and Law (apptd. by gov.) 1985—; chaplain Syracuse U., 1976-78, Cornell U., Ithaca, N.Y., 1978-79; rector Grace Episc. Ch., Mexico, N.Y., 1984-89; cons. Women's Issues Network Episc. Ch. in U.S., 1987—; writer, lectr., cons. religion and feminism, 1979—. Author: Take Back the Church, Indeed The Witness, 1982, Creativity and Procreativity: Some Thoughts on Eve and the Opposition and How Episcopalians Make Ethical Decisions, Plumline, 1988, Send in the Clowns, Chrysalis, Journal of the Swedenborg Foundation, 1994; contbr. forward to book. Bd. dirs. People for Pub. TV in N.Y., 1978, Religious Coalition for Abortion Rights; trustee Elizabeth Cady Stanton Found., 1979; mem. policy com. Coun. Adolescent Pregnancy; mem. N.Y. State Task Force Life and the Law, 1983—. Recipient Gov.'s award Women of Merit in Religion, 1984, Ralph E. Kharas award ACLU Cen. N.Y., 1986 Goodall disting. alumna award & Hills Sch., 1988, Human Rightes award Human Rights Commn. of Syracuse and Onondaga County, N.Y., 1989; inducted into Nat. Women's Hall of Fame, 1994. Mem. NOW (Syracuse), Internat. Assn. Women Ministers (dir. 1978, pres. 1984-87), Na'amat U.S. (hon. life), Mortar Bd., Theta Chi Beta. Democrat. Home and Office: 107 Bradford Ln Syracuse NY 13224-1901 Office: Grace Episcopal Ch Main St Mexico NY 13114

SCHIFF, JAYNE NEMEROW, underwriter; b. N.Y.C., Aug. 8, 1945; d. Milton E. Nemerow and Shirley (Kaplan) Wachtel; m. Albert John Schiff, Mar. 7, 1971; children: Matthew Evan, Kara Anne. BS in Bus., Marymount Coll., 1981; M of Profl. Studies in Elem. and Spl. Edn., Manhattanville Coll., 1995. Corporate sec., treas. Albert J. Schiff Assocs., Inc., N.Y.C., 1970-78; field underwriter Mut. N.Y. Fin. Svcs., Greenwich, Conn., 1973—; freelance employee benefit cons. Greenwich, 1979—; regional dir. mktg., MONY Fin. Services, N.Y.C., 1978-79. Bd. dirs. N.Y. League Bus. and Profl. Women, 1976-78, Temple Sinai, Stamford, Conn., 1979-84, N.Y. Ctr. Fin. Studies; leader Webelos Cub Scouts, 1977-78; treas. Ann. Mothers Bd. Benefit Greenwich Acad., 1988, upper sch. acquisitions chmn., 1989, chmn. spl. acquisitions Greenwich Acad. Benefit, 1990-91, chmn. advt., 1992; ESL tutor Lit. Vols. Am., ESL tutor, trainer, 1993. Named Conn.'s Outstanding Young Woman, 1979. Mem. LWV, Am. Soc. Chartered Life Underwriters, N.Y. Ctr. Fin. Studies (bd. dirs.), N.Y.C. Life Underwriters Assn. (bd. dirs. 1977-78). Jewish. Office: 30 Stanwich Rd Greenwich CT 06830-4860

SCHIFF, LAURIE, lawyer; b. Newark, Apr. 24, 1960; d. Norman Nathan and Claire Jane (Schott) S.; m. Ralph Conrad Shelton II, 1992. BS in Law, We. State U., Fullerton, Calif., 1987, JD, 1988. Bar: Calif. 1989. Ptnr. Schiff Mgmt., Newport Beach, Calif., 1983-89; pvt. practice Schiff & Assocs., Irvine, Calif., 1989-91; ptnr. Schiff & Shelton, 1991—; probation monitor State Bar Ct. Calif., 1991—. Producer: (record album) Boys Just Want to Have Sex, 1984. Bd. dirs. Jewish Family Svcs. of Orange County, 1994—. Mem. Orange County Bar Assn. (arbitrator 1995—), Am. Mensa, Am. Polocrosse Assn., Saddlebrook Polocrosse (treas. 1991), Am. Quarterhorse Assn., Internat. Cat Assn. (chair legis. com. 1995—), Tonks West (v.p. 1994-96, pres. 1996—), Tonkinese Breed Assn., Online Feline Fanciers (v.p. 1995—), IPICa.C. (v.p. 1996—). Democrat. Jewish. Office: Schiff & Shelton Ste 620 3 Hutton Centre Dr Santa Ana CA 92707-5736

SCHIFFMAN, SUSAN STOLTE, medical psychologist, educator; b. Chgo., Aug. 24, 1940; d. Paul R. and Mildred (Glicksman) Stolte; m. Harold Schiffman (div.); 1 child, Amy Lise; m. H. Troy Nagle, July 22, 1989. BA, Syracuse U., 1965; PhD, Duke U., 1970. Lic. psychologist, N.C. Postdoctoral fellow Duke U., Durham, N.C., 1970-72, asst. prof., 1972-77, assoc. prof., 1978-83, full prof., 1983—; cons., mem. adv. bd. Nutrasweet, Chgo., 1978—, Nestle, Vevey, Switzerland, 1990, Fragrance Rsch. Fund, N.Y.C., 1986—, and others. Author: Introduction to Multidimensional Scaling: Theory, Methods and Applications, 1981, Flavor Set-Point Weight Loss Cookbook, 1990. Nat. Inst. Aging grantee, 1972—. Mem. Assn. Chemoreception Scis., European Chemoreception Rsch. Orgn., Soc. for Neurosci. Office: Duke U Med Sch Dept Psychiatry Box 3259 Durham NC 27708-0086

SCHILKE, SARAH, editor; b. Oregon City, Oreg., Aug. 12, 1970; d. John Frederick and Susan (Saubert) S. Student, U. Hamburg, Germany, 1990; BA, U. Oreg., 1995. Cert. motorcycle safely instr. Office asst. U. Oreg., Eugene, 1994-95; instr. Team Oreg. motorcycle safety program Oreg. State U., Corvallis, 1994—, office coord. Team Oreg. motorcycle safety program, 1994-96; assoc. editor, seminar leader Women's Motorcycle Market Jou. Jessie Cahill & Assocs. Inc., Portland, 1996—, developer curriculum She's Got the Ticket to Ride Seminar, 1995. Vol. Cultural Ctr. Performing Arts, Eugene, Oreg., 1993—, Project Saferide, Eugene, 1993-94. Mem. NOW, Women on Wheels, Chrome Plated Hearts, Honda Rider's Club. Am., Delta Phi Alpha, Delta Gamma. Home: 12612 SW 9th St Beaverton OR 97005

SCHILLER, SOPHIE, artist, graphic designer; b. Moscow, Feb. 10, 1940; came to U.S., 1974; d. Samuel and Rebecca (Lagovier) Elinson; m. Mikhail Schiller, Apr. 29, 1960; 1 child, Maria. Student, Moscow State Art Sch., 1954-58; MA, Moscow Inst., 1964; cert. in graphic and book design, Mass. Coll. Art, 1977. Graphic artist Progress Pub. House, Moscow, 1964-70, Popular Sci. mag., Moscow, 1970-74; artist, graphic designer Boston, 1974—; freelance graphic designer Harvard Press, Boston, M.E. Sharpe Pub., N.Y., Ginn Press, Simon & Schuster, Boston, Tech. Rev., MIT, Cambridge, Mass. One person shows include Galleria del Corso, Rome, 1974, Wennigar Gallery, Weningar Gallery Boston, 1977; exhibited in group shows Taganka Exhibit, Moscow, 1962, Moscow Artists Union, 1962, Am. Painters in Paris Exhbn., 1975, Unofficial Art from Soviet Union, Washington, 1977, Mariland Gallery, St. Mary's City, 1977, Bard Coll., N.Y., 1991, Rose Art Mus., Brandeis U., Boston, 1992, Toffias Gallery, Boston, 1994, Zimmerly Art Mus., Rutgers U., N.J., 1995. Mem. Nat. Mus. Women in the Arts. Home and Studio: 63 University Rd Brookline MA 02146

SCHILLING, EMILY BORN, editor, association executive; b. Lawton, Okla., Oct. 2, 1959; d. George Arthur and Sumiko (Nagamine) Born; m. Mark David Schilling, June 26, 1995. BS, Ball State U., 1981. Cert. rural electric communicator Nat. Rural Electric Coop. Assn. Feature writer The News-Sentinel, Fort Wayne, Ind., 1981-83; wire editor The Noblesville (Ind.) Daily Ledger, 1983; staff writer Ind. Statewide Assn. Rural Electric Coops., Indpls., 1983-84, mng. editor, 1984-85, editor, 1985—. Author: Power to the People, 1985. Mem. Coop. Communicators Assn. (Michael Graznak award 1990), Internat. Assn. Bus. Communicators (award of excellence dist. 7 1985), Elec. Women's Round Table Inc. (Power award 1994), Electric Inst. Ind., Nat. Electric Cooperatives Statewide Editors Assn. Office: Ind Statewide Assn RECs 720 N High School Rd Indianapolis IN 46214-3756

SCHILLING, EYDIE ANNE, science educator, consultant; b. Columbus, Ohio, June 17, 1965; d. Phyllis Anne (Helsel) Radugge. BS in Bilog. Scis., Ohio State U., 1989, MA in Sci. Edn., 1994. Cert. tchr., Ohio; comprehensive sci., biology sci. gen. sci. Tchr. integrated 7th and 8th grade sci. Wynford Middle Sch., Bucyrus, Ohio, 1989-93; tchr. tech. biology and integrated 8th grade sci. Ridgedale Jr./Sr. H.S., Marion, Oho, 1993-94; tech. chemistry and integrated 8th grade sci. Ridgedale Jr./Sr. H.S., Marion, 1994-95; tchr. biology, chemistry, tech. biology Teays Valley H.S., Asheville, Ohio, 1995-96; cons. Tech.-Prep. Consortium, Marion, 1993-95, Marion County Schs., 1993-95, Buckeye Assessment Teams in Sci., Columbus, 1995—; mem. math-sci. adv. subcom. Ctrl. Ohio Regional Profl. Devel. Ctr., Columbus, 1995—; instr. Project Discovery, Columbus, 1995—; tchr. biology, chemistry Tech. Prep II Teays Valley H.S., Ashville, Ohio, 1995—; coach high sch. girls track, high sch. cross country Teays Valley Schs., Ashville, 1995—. Grantee Project Discovery, Columbus, 1991; intern Young Exptl. Scientist C.O.S.I., Columbus, 1991, 92. Mem. Nat. Sci. Tchrs. Assn., Sci. Elem. Coun. Ohio (presenter conf. 1995-96), Ohio State Univ. Alumni, Phi Delta Kappa. Republican. Lutheran. Home: 1039 Vernon Bexley OH 43209 Office: Teays Valley Schs SR 752 Ashville OH 43103

SCHILLING-NORDAL, GERALDINE ANN, secondary school educator; b. Springfield, Mass., Feb. 4, 1935; d. Robert Milton and Helen Veronica (Ewald) Schilling; m. Reidar Johannes Nordal. BS, Boston U., 1956, MEd, 1957; postgrad., Springfield Coll. Tchr. art Agawam (Mass.) Jr. H.S., 1957-58; tchr. art Agawam H.S., 1958—, K-12 art acad. coord., 1995-96, head art dept., 1970-95; instr. oil painting univ. ext. course Agawam Night Sch., 1957-58; instr. creative arts Agawam Evening Sch., 1973-80. Active Agawam Town Report Com., 1967-77, Agawam Hist. Commn., 1979-87, Agawam Arts and Humanities Com., 1979-85, Agawam Minerva Davis Libr. Study Com., 1987—, Agawam Cultural Coun., 1994—; sec. Agawam Town Beautification Com., 1974-87; mem. town tchrs. rep. Agawam Bicentennial Com., 1975-77; chmn. 40th anniversary St. John the Evangelist Ch., Agawam, 1986, co-chmn. 50th anniversary com., 1996, mem. renovation com., 1983; decoration chmn. town-wide Halloween parties, Agawam, 1971-93; recruiter Miss Agawam Pageant. Mem. NEA, ASCD, Agawam Edn. Assn. (sec. 1970-74, 76-77), Hampden County Tchrs. Assn., Mass. Tchrs. Assn., Mass. Art Edn. Assn., Nat. Art Edn. Assn., New Eng. Art Edn. Assn., Mass. Alliance for Art Edn., Am. Assn. Ret. Persons, Mass. Cath. Order Foresters, West Springfield Neighborhood House Alumni Assn. (pres. 1966, advisor 1968), West Springfield H.S. Alumni Assn. (3d v.p. 1968-70, 1st v.p. 1970-71, pres. 1972-74), Boston U. Alumni Club Springfield Area (organizer area giving campaigns 1957-62, class agt. 1985—, mem. area scholarship com. 1995—), Am. Legion (life), Zeta Chi Delta (pres. 1955-56), Delta Kappa Gamma (Alpha chpt., art chairperson, reservation chmn. art work and hist. archives). Office: Agawam Sr High Sch 760 Cooper St Agawam MA 01001-2177

SCHILPLIN, YVONNE WINTER, educational administrator; b. Mahnomen, Minn., May 26, 1946; d. Milo Joseph and Lucille Margaret (Schoenborn) Winter; m. Frederick Colegrove Schilplin III, Dec. 30, 1975; children: Frederick IV, Chad. Student, St. Cloud State U., 1964. Retail fashion buyer Fandel's Dept. Store, St. Cloud, Minn., 1968-75; mem. graduation standards exec. com. Minn. Dept. Edn., Mpls., 1988—; mem. Annandale (Minn.) Sch. Bd. Dist. 876, 1988-94, chmn., 1991-94; co-owner, cons. Am. Rsch. Grant Writing & Tng., Inc., 1993—. Edn. chmn. Minn. PTA, Mpls., 1989-91; mem. legis. com. St Cloud Reading Rm., 1991-92, v.p., 1996—; liaison for sch. bd. Annandale PTA, 1989-94; co-chmn. Living Wax Mus., Minn. Pioneer Park, 1991-92; mem. facilities planning com. Sch. Dist. 876, mid. sch. steering com. Recipient Minn. Sch. Bd. Mem. of Yr., 1994. Mem. Stearns County Hist. Soc., Minn. Sci. Mus., St. Cloud Country Club. Home: RR 3 Annandale MN 55302-9803

SCHIMBERG, BARBARA HODES, organizational development consultant; b. Chgo., Nov. 30, 1941; d. David and Tybe Zisook; children from previous marriage: Brian, Valery; m. A. Bruce Schimberg, Dec. 29, 1984. BS, Northwestern U., 1962. Ptnr. Just Causes, cons. not-for-profit orgns., Chgo., 1978-86; cons. in philanthropy, community involvement, and organizational devel., 1987—; Chgo. cons. Population Resource Ctr., 1978-82. Woman's bd. dirs. Mus. Contemporary Art; bd. dirs., vice chmn. Med. Rsch. Inst. Coun., Michael Reese Med. Ctr.; bd. dirs., chmn. Midwest Women's Ctr.; trustee Francis W. Parker Sch.; bd. dirs. Women's Issues Network, 1991—, pres., 1993-94; mem. honorary bd. Med. Rsch. Inst. Coun., Children's Meml. Hosp. Mem. ACLU (adv. com.). Office: 132 E Delaware Pl Apt 5002 Chicago IL 60611-1442

SCHIMEK, DIANNA RUTH REBMAN, state legislator; b. Holdrege, Nebr., Mar. 21, 1940; d. Ralph William and Elizabeth Julia (Wilmot) Rebman; m. Herbert Henry Schimek, 1963; children: Samuel Wolfgang, Saul William. AA, Colo. Women's Coll., 1960; student, U. Nebr., Lincoln, 1960-61; BA magna cum laude, U. Nebr., Kearney, 1963. Former tchr. and realtor; mem. Nebr. Legislature, Lincoln, 1989—, chmn. govt., mil. and vets. affairs com., 1993-94, vice chair urban affairs com., 1995—. Chmn. Nebr. Dem. Com., 1984-88, mem. exec. com., 1987-88; past pres., sec. bd. dirs. Downtown Sr. Ctr. Found.; mem. exec. bd. Midwest Conf. of State Govts., co-chair health and human svcs. com. Mem. Nat. Conf. State Legislators Women's Network (bd. dirs.), P.E.O., Soroptomists. Democrat. Unitarian. Home: 2321 Camelot Ct Lincoln NE 68512-1457 Office: Dist # 27 State Capital Lincoln NE 68509

SCHIMMEL, CLEO RITZ, volunteer; b. Canton, Ohio, Jan. 28, 1940; d. John Vail and Jesse (Roderick) Ritz; m. Paul R. Schimmel, Dec. 30, 1962; children: Kirsten Leah, Katherine Diane. AB, Ohio Wesleyan U., 1958-62. Cert. tchr. Ohio, Mass. Tchr. 2d grade Quincy (Mass.) Pub. Sch., 1962-63; adminstrn. assist counseling Counseling Ctr., Lexington, Mass., 1978-79; assist dir. coop. edn. program Middlesex Coll., Bedford, Mass., 1979-80; instr. adult edn. Middlesex Coll., Lexington, Mass., 1984-88; adminstrn. assist MIT, Cambridge, Mass., 1980-83, office of the pres.; substitute tchr., Cambridge Pub. Sch., 1964-66, Quincy Pub. Sch., 1964-66, Lexington Pub. Sch., 1977-79, interior design cons., 1985-88, program chair MIT Womens League, Cambridge, 1995—. Bd. Trustee Lexington Christian Acad., 1977-79, ch-chair Ohio Wesleyan Alumae Sesquifest Celebration, Delaware, 1992, bd. gov. and overseers New England Med. Ctr., Boston, 1992—. Home: 75 Cambridge Pkwy W-900 Cambridge MA 02142 Office: MIT Womens League 77 Mass Ave Cambridge MA 02139

SCHINDEHETTE, JACQUELYN LEE, artist; b. Miami, Fla., June 5, 1946; d. Clarence Judson and Damie Eloise (Brown) Modesitt; m. Harry Martin Schindehette Jr., June 24, 1967; children: Chad Aaron, David Scott. AA, Indian River C.C., Ft. Pierce, Fla., 1992. painting instr. Ft. Pierce, Fla. and Provo, Utah, 1990-96; studio/gallery owner Brush Strokes Gallery, Ft. Pierce, 1992-94; mentor, art St. Lucie County Pub. Schs., Ft. Pierce, 1993. One-woman show Fla. State Capitol Bldg., Tallahassee; group exhibits include Art Encounter, Naples, Fla., Miami Mus. Sci., Coconut Grove, Fla., Palma Ceia Country Club, Tampa, Fla., Riviera Country Club, Coral Gables, Fla., Rod and Reel Country Club, Hibiscus Island, Fla., A.E. Beanie Backus Art Gallery, Ft. Pierce, St. Lucie West Country Club, Port St. Lucie, Fla., Lighthouse Gallery, Tequesta, Fla., Loxahatchee Hist. Soc. Mus., Jupiter, Fla., Hist. Utah County Courthouse, Provo; represented in permanent collections The State of Fla., Fla. Power and Light Co., Miami, Bernard Egan and Co., Ft. Pierce, Riverside Nat. Bank, St. Lucie, Harbor Fed. Savs. and Loan Assn., Port St. Lucie, MBNA Am. Bank, N.A., Newark, Integon Ins. Corp., Winston-Salem, N.C., Hav-A Tampa (Fla.) Tobacco Co., numerous pvt. collections. Recipient First Place/Landscape, Backus Arts Festival, Ft. Pierce, 1990, First Place/Landscape, On The Green Arts Festival, St. Lucie County, Fla., 1992, 5 Purchase awards Treasure Coast Art Festival, St. Pierce, 1993. Mem. Nat. Assn. Women in the Arts, Art Students League, Utah Valley Art Assn., Vero Beach (Fla.) Ctr. for the Arts, A.E. Backus Gallery (dir.), Artists of Fla. Home: 1800 Friday Rd Cocoa FL 32926

SCHINDLER, JUDITH KAY), public relations executive, marketing consultant; b. Chgo., Nov. 23, 1941; d. Gilbert G. and Rosalie (Karlin) Cone; m. Jack Joel Schindler, Nov. 1, 1964; 1 child, Adam Jason. BS in Journalism, U. Ill., 1964. Assoc. editor Irving Cloud Publs., Lincolnwood, Ill., 1963-64; asst. dir. publicity Israel Bond Campaign, Chgo., 1965-69; v.p. pub. relations Realty Co. of Am., Chgo., 1969-70; dir. pub. relations Pvt. Telecommunications, Chgo., 1970-78; pres. Schindler Communications, Chgo., 1978—; del. White House Conf. on Small Bus., Washington, 1980, 86; mem. adv. bd. Entrepreneurship Inst., Chgo., 1988-92. Bd. dirs. Family Matters Comty. Ctr.; mem. Chgo. bd. Roosevelt U.; leader luncheon coun. YWCA, Chgo., 1987, 89-90, 92; appointee small bus. com. Ill. Devel. Bd., 1988-89. Named Nat. Women in Bus. Adv. SBA, 1986, Chgo. Woman Bus. Owner of Yr., Continential Bank and Nat. Assn. Women Bus. Owners, 1989, Ill. Finalist Entrepreneur of Yr. award, 1991, 92. Mem. Nat. Assn. Women Bus. Owners (pres. Chgo. chpt. 1980-81, nat. v.p. membership 1988-89), Small Bus. United of Ill., Ill. Coun. Growing Cos. (vice chair 1993-94), Publicity Club Chgo., Alpha Epsilon Phi. Office: Schindler Comm 500 N Clark St Chicago IL 60610-4202

SCHINE, CATHLEEN, writer; b. Westport, Conn., 1953; m. David Denby, 1981; children: Max, Thomas. Student, Sarah Lawrence Coll., Barnard U., U. Chgo. Author: Alice in Bed, 1983, To the Birdhouse, 1990, Rameau's Niece, 1993 (one of best books of 1993 N.Y. Times, Voice Literary Supplement, finalist Book prize L.A. Times 1992-93), The Love Letter, 1995; contbr. articles, reviews, columns to popular publs. including N.Y. Times Mag., N.Y. Times Book Review, Village Voice, Vogue. Office: care Candida Donadio Donadio & Ashworth Inc 121 West 27TH St Ste 704 New York NY 10001*

SCHINE, WENDY WACHTELL, foundation administrator; b. White Plains, N.Y., May 5, 1961; d. Thomas and Esther Carole (Pickard) Wachtell; m. Jonathan Mark Schine, Sept. 2, 1990; children: Jameson Myer, Bradley Thomas. BA, Wellesley Coll., 1983; MA in Journalism, U. So. Calif., L.A., 1987. Legis. asst. U.S. House Reps., Washington, 1983-85; varied positions KCBS-TV, L.A., 1986-88; v.p. Joseph Drown Found., L.A., 1988—; bd. dirs. L.A. Urban Funders, L.A. Cities in Schs.; advisor Psychol. Trauma Ctr., L.A., 1988—, Ctr. for Talented Youth, Glendale, Calif., 1989—. Mem. oversight com. Pathways Project, Big Sisters, L.A. Office: Joseph Drown Found Ste 1930 1999 Avenue Of The Stars Los Angeles CA 90067-6051

SCHIPPER, REBECCA ANDRA, executive assistant; b. Phoenix, Nov. 25, 1966; d. Don Leo and Wanda June (Phillips) Daggett; m. Eliot Lewis Schipper, Aug. 28, 1970. BS, No. Ariz. U., 1993. Comml. real estate loan processor 1st Interstate Bank, Phoenix, 1985-88; fin. svc. rep. Selco Credit Union, Eugene, Oreg., 1993-95; exec. asst. Grand Canyon Trust, Flagstaff, Ariz., 1995—. Active Flagstaff Leadership Program, 1996—; founder Earth Save No. Ariz., Flagstaff, 1995; treas., bd. dirs. Big Bros./Big Sisters, Springfield, Oreg., 1993-95; pres. Kayettes, Flagstaff, 1991-93. Office: Grand Canyon Trust 3100 N Ft Valley Rd # 8 Flagstaff AZ 86001

SCHIRBER, ANNAMARIE RIDDERING, speech and language pathologist, educator; b. Somerset County, N.J., Dec. 18, 1941; d. Pieter C. and Marie Louise (Kerk) Riddering; m. Eric R. Schirber, Aug. 25, 1960; children: Stefan Rene, Ashley Brooke. BA in Speech and Hearing Therapy, Rutgers U., 1964; MA in Edn. of Deaf and Hard of Hearing, Smith Coll., 1968; postgrad., Rutgers U., 1987-93. Cert. tchr. of deaf, hard of hearing, spl. edn., speech correctionist, speech-lang pathologist, N.J. Speech therapist Manatee County Bd. Edn., Bradenton, Fla., 1968-69; speech-lang. specialist Lawrence Twp. Pub. Schs., Lawrenceville, N.J., 1969—; adj. instr. comm. dept. Trenton (N.J.) State Coll., 1983-87; vis. lectr. Rutgers U., New Brunswick, 1993. Author: Teaching Auditory Processing Skills to Children, 1994; co-author: (with Erica Winebrenner) Speech Activities for Children, 1994, Language Activities to Teach Children at Home, 1994. Mem. exec. com. Women's Coll. Symposium, Princeton, N.J., 1982-84; mem. nat. alumnae admissions com. Smith Coll., Northampton, Mass., 1984-86. Grantee Lawrence Twpw. Bd. Edn., 1973, 89, 90. Mem. N.J. Speech-Lang. and Hearing Assn. (legis. com. 1996), Ctrl. Jersey Speech-Lang. and Hearing Assn. (exec. com. 1984, v.p. 1985, pres. 1986-87). Office: Lawrence Twp Pub Schs Princeton Pike Trenton NJ 08648

SCHIRMER-SMITH, SARA JANE (SALLY SCHIRMER-SMITH), director student activities; b. Saginaw, Mich., June 5, 1963; d. Charles Albert and Jeanne Marie (Ashbaugh) Schirmer; m. Steven John Smith, June 20, 1992. BS, Ctrl. Mich. U., 1985; MEd, Springfield Coll., 1989. Dir. student activities Bay Path Coll., Longmeadow, Mass., 1989—. Mem. AAUW, NAFE, Zonta Internat. (co-chair program com. 1995-96). Home: 588 Longmeadow St Longmeadow MA 01106 Office: Bay Path Coll 588 Longmeadow St Longmeadow MA 01106

SCHIRO, STEPHANIE, performing company executive. Exec. dir. San Jose Ballet, Cleve. Ballet. Office: 40 N 1st St San Jose CA 95133 also: One Playhouse Sq 1375 Euclid Ave Cleveland OH 44115*

SCHIRO-GEIST, CHRISANN, rehabilitation counselor; b. Chgo., Dec. 31, 1946; d. Joseph Frank and Ethel (Fortunato) Schiro; m. John J. Conway Sr., Oct. 26, 1985; children: Jennifer, Daniel; stepchildren: Patricia, Nicole, John Jr., Denise, Christine. BS, Loyola U., Chgo., 1967, MEd, 1970; PhD, Northwestern U., 1974. Registered psychologist, Ill.; cert. sex edn. cons. Tchr. sci. Northbrook (Ill.) Jr. High Sch., 1967-70; dir. career counseling and placement Mundelein Coll., Chgo., 1972-74; counselor human devel. Regional Service Agy., Skokie, Ill., 1975-87; assoc. prof. psychology, rehab. counselor Ill. Inst. Tech., Chgo., 1975-87; full prof. rehab. U. Ill., Champagne-Urbana, 1987—. Co-author: Placement Handbook for Counseling Disabled Persons, 1982; author, editor: Vocational Counseling with Special Populations, 1990. Rsch. grantee Northwestern U., 1974; Region V Short-Term Tng. grantee Rehab. Svcs. Adminstrn., 1978-79, Long-Term Tng. grantee, 1983—; Mary E. Switzer fellow NIDRR, 1989-90, VA, 1991-92, World Rehab. Fund fellow, 1993. Mem. APA, ACA, Nat. Rehab. Assn., Nat. Coun. Rehab. Edn. (named Educator of Yr. 1987), Ill. Rehab. Counseling Assn. (pres. 1979-80), Coun. on Rehab. Edn. (pres. 1982-85, editor jour. 1986-92), Ill. Rehab. Assn. (pres.-elect), Kappa Beta Gamma Alumni Assn. (nat. officer). Office: U Ill Divsn Rehab Edn 1207 S Oak St Champaign IL 61820-6901

SCHISLER, KAY ELLEN, human services administrator; b. N.Y.C., Oct. 17, 1948; d. Harold Jack and Rhea (Gardner) Schoenfeld; children: Matthew David, Jenny Serina. BS, SUNY, Albany, 1985; postgrad., Fla. State U., 1995—. Exec. dir. Dutchess County Child Devel. Coun., Poughkeepsie, N.Y., 1985-89, Fla. Children's Forum, Tallahassee, 1989-93, Brehon Inst. Human Svcs., Tallahassee, 1993—. Author: (industry manuals) School Age Child Care - Start Up and Operation, 1987, CCR&R Standard Levels of Service, 1993. Bd. dirs. Blueprint 2000, Poughkeepsie, 1988-89, Nat. Leadership Childcare Resource and Referral, Boston, 1990, United Way of Big Bend, Tallahassee, 1995-96. Mem. Am. Assn. Pub. Adminstrs. Democrat. Jewish. Home: 4126 Arklow Dr Tallahassee FL 32308 Office: Brehon Inst Human Svcs 1260 Paul Russell Rd Tallahassee FL 32301

SCHLACHTER, DEBORAH BRISTOW, special education educator, consultant; b. Ajo, Ariz., Dec. 21, 1957; d. John Edward Jr. and Anne Elizabeth (Butler) Bristow; m. James Martin Schlachter Jr., July 25, 1981; children: James Martin, Katie Elizabeth, Joshua Timothy, Jacob Leslie, Jean Nicole. BE, Stephen F. Austin, 1981; MEd, U. N. Tex., 1991. Cert. tchr., Tex. Pvt. practice spl. needs tutor Dallas/Ft. Worth, 1981-91; pvt. practice family in home child care Lancaster, Tex., 1982-89; instr., coord. Cedar Valley Coll., Lancaster, 1989—; tchr. DeSoto (Tex.) Ind. Sch. Dist., 1990-91; kindergarten tchr. Dallas Ind. Sch. Dist., 1991-92, ESL tchr. 1st grade, 1992-93; 4-6th grade Montessori tchr. Dallas Pub. Sch., 1993-95; co-leader strategic planning Lancaster Ind. Sch. Dist., 1992-93. Co-editor: Resource Handbook for Educators on American Indians, 1993-94. Vol. tutor Women's Halfway House, Nacogdoches, Tex., 1980-81; trainer in spl. needs children PTA, Dallas-Ft. Worth, 1990—, active Dallas-Lancaster, 1984—; voting mem. Dallas Native Am. Parent Adv. Com., 1992-94; vol. Harry Stone Montessori Acad. PTA, v.p., 1995-96, 96-97. Mem. ASCD, AAUW, Nat. Assn. Edn. Young Children, Nat. Indian Edn. Assn., Nat. Mus. Am. Indian, Am. Montessori Soc., So. Assn. Children Under Six, Dallas Assn. Edn. Young Children, Native Am. Rights Funds, Am. Indian Resource and Edn. Coalition. Episcopalian. Home: 532 Laurel St Lancaster TX 75134-3220

SCHLAFLY, PHYLLIS STEWART, author; b. St. Louis, Aug. 15, 1924; d. John Bruce and Odile (Dodge) Stewart; m. Fred Schlafly, Oct. 20, 1949; children: John F., Bruce S., Roger S., Phyllis Liza Forshaw, Andrew L., Anne V. BA, Washington U., St. Louis, 1944, JD, 1978; MA, Harvard U., 1945; LLD, Niagara U., 1976. Bar: Ill. 1979, D.C. 1984, Mo. 1985, U.S. Supreme Ct. 1987. Syndicated columnist Copley News Svc., 1976—; pres. Eagle Forum, 1975—; broadcaster Spectrum, CBS Radio Network, 1973-78; commentator Cable TV News Network, 1980-83, Matters of Opinion sta. WBBM-AM, Chgo., 1973-75. Author, pub.: Phyllis Schlafly Report, 1967—; author: A Choice Not an Echo, 1964, The Gravediggers, 1964, Strike From Space, 1965, Safe Not Sorry, 1967, The Betrayers, 1968, Mindszenty The Man, 1972, Kissinger on the Couch, 1975, Ambush at Vladivostok, 1976, The Power of the Positive Woman, 1977, First Reader, 1994; editor: Child Abuse in the Classroom, 1984, Pornography's Victims, 1987, Equal Pay for Unequal Work, 1984, Who Will Rock the Cradle, 1989, Stronger Families or Bigger Government, 1990, Meddlesome Mandate: Rethinking Family Leave, 1991. Del. Rep. Nat. Conv., 1956, 64, 68, 84, 88, 92, 96, alt., 1960, 80; pres. Ill. Fedn. Rep. Women, 1960-64; 1st v.p. Nat. Fedn. Rep. Women, 1964-67; mem. Ill. Commn. on Status of Women, 1975-85; nat. chmn. Stop ERA, 1972—; mem. Ronald Reagan's Def. Policy Adv. Group, 1980; mem. Commn. on Bicentennial of U.S. Constn., 1985-91; mem. Adminstrv. Conf. U.S., 1983-86. Recipient 10 Honor awards Freedoms Found., Brotherhood award NCCJ, 1975; named Woman of Achievement in Pub. Affairs St. Louis Globe-Democrat, 1963, one of 10 most admired women in world Good Housekeeping poll, 1977-90. Mem. ABA, DAR (nat. chmn. Am. history 1965-68, nat. chmn. bicentennial com. 1967-70, nat. chmn. nat. def. 1977-80, 83-95), Ill. Bar Assn., Phi Beta Kappa, Pi Sigma Alpha. Office: Eagle Forum 7800 Bonhomme Ave Saint Louis MO 63105-1906

SCHLAGER, KRISTINE MARIE, middle school educator; b. Elgin, Ill., June 11, 1963; d. Kenneth Calvin and Florence Therese (Majewski) Bork; m. John Benedict Schlager, July 25, 1992; 1 child, Dylan Bennett Schlager. Student, Northwestern U., 1985, U. Wis., 1987-89; BA, Lawrence U., 1985; MA, U. Colo., 1991. Cert. tchr., Colo. Rsch. specialist in physiology U. Wis., Madison, 1986-87, rsch. specialist in nutrition/soil sci., summer 1988; rschr. Colo. Dept. Edn., Denver, 1991, 92, 94; tchr. Mandalay Mid. Sch. Jefferson County Sch. Dist. R-1, Westminster, Colo., 1992—; mem. adv. panel State Accountability Bd., Denver, 1992-93. Contbr. articles to profl. publs. Recipient First Yr. Tchr. award Sallie Mae, 1993, Jefferson County Pub. Schs. Grant award for pilot project on creating time as a variable in learning, Classroom Connection Disseminator Grant award for interdisciplinary math activity. Mem. NSTA, ASCD, Am. Assn. Educators in Pvt. Practice, Nat. Coun. Tchrs. Math., Colo. Assn. Sci. Tchrs., Phi Beta Kappa, Phi Sigma. Home: 1223 S Elmoro Ct Superior CO 80027-8067 Office: Mandalay Mid Sch 9651 Pierce St Broomfield CO 80021-6437

SCHLAIN, BARBARA ELLEN, lawyer; b. N.Y.C., May 28, 1948; d. William and Evelyn (Youdelman) S.; B.A., Wellesley Coll., 1969; M.A., Columbia U., 1970; J.D., Yale U., 1973. Bar: N.Y. 1974, U.S. Dist. Ct. (so. dist.) N.Y. 1974, U.S. Ct. Appeals (2d cir.) 1975, U.S. Dist. Ct. (ea. dist.) N.Y. 1977. Assoc. firm Donovan Leisure Newton & Irvine, N.Y.C., 1973-76, Graubard Moskovitz McGoldrick Dannett & Horowitz, N.Y.C., 1976-79; atty. McGraw-Hill, Inc., N.Y.C., 1979-80, asst. gen. counsel, 1980-86, v.p., assoc. gen. counsel, asst. sec., 1986—. sec. proprietary rights com. Info. Industry Assn., 1982-83. Author outlines Practicing Law Inst., 1983, 84, 85, 86, 88; contbr. numerous articles to profl. jours. Bd. dirs., v.p., sec. Dance Research Found., N.Y.C., 1983-86, chmn. 1986—. Phi Beta Kappa scholar, Durant scholar Wellesley Coll., 1967-69. Mem. ABA, Assn. Am. Pubs. (lawyers com. 1979—), Assn. Bar City N.Y. (communications law com. 1985-88). Office: The McGraw-Hill Companies 1221 Ave Of The Americas New York NY 10020-1001

SCHLEGEL, NANCY BROWNING, small business owner; b. Camden, N.J., May 4, 1929; d. Stanley Holland and Sara N. (Finley) Browning; m. Arthur J. Schlegel, Nov. 10, 1962; children: Janice, Richard, Arthur, Joy, John, Eraka. Student, Pa. Bus. Coll., 1945, N.Mex. Pub. Sch., 1970. Bookkeeper Louis Shoe Salons, Tucson, Ariz., 1961-63; speech and hearing aide N.Mex. Pub. Schs., Moriarty, 1970-71, substitute tchr., 1971-78; field supr. Office of the Aging, Wilkes Barre, Pa., 1979-86; owner Nancy's Vinyl Repair & Restore, White Haven, Pa., 1986—. Inventor Nancy's Spaghetti Sauce. Mem. Internat. Traders, Am. Assn. Retired Persons. Republican. Episcopalian. Office: Nan Art Enterprises PO Box 242 White Haven PA 18661-0242

SCHLEICHER, NORA ELIZABETH, banker, treasurer, accountant; b. Balt., Aug. 10, 1952; d. Irvin William and Eleanor Edna S.; m. Ray Leonard Settle Jr., July 27, 1985. AA cum laude, Anne Arundel Community Coll., 1972; BS summa cum laude, U. Balt., 1975. CPA, Md. Staff auditor Md. Nat. Bank, Balt., 1975-76, sr. staff auditor, 1976-77, supr. auditing dept., 1977-78; full charge acct. Wooden & Benson, CPA's, Balt., 1978-81; asst. to treas. First Fed. Savs. & Loan Assn., Annapolis, Md., 1981, asst. treas., 1982-83, v.p., 1984; v.p., treas. First Fed. Savs. & Loan Assn. (now First Annapolis Bank), 1984—. Bd. dirs., treas. Coll. Manor Community Assn. Mem. AICPA, Md. Assn CPA's, Fin. Mgrs. Soc., Coll. Manor Community Assn. (bd. dirs., treas.). Methodist. Office: First Annapolis Savs Bank 1832 George Ave Annapolis MD 21401-4103

SCHLEIN, MIRIAM, author; children: Elizabeth Weiss, John Weiss. B.A. in Psychology, Bklyn. Coll., 1947. Author over 85 books for children, natural sci. books, concept books, story books, picture books, including: A Day at the Playground, 1951, The Four Little Foxes, 1952 (Jr. Lit. Guild selection), Shapes, 1952, Go with the Sun, 1952, Tony's Pony, 1952, Fast is Not a Ladybug, 1953 (Boys' Club Am. Jr. Book award 1953), When Will the World Be Mine?, 1953 (Caldecott Honor Book), The Sun Looks Down, 1954, How Do You Travel?, 1954, Heavy is a Hippopotamus, 1954, Elephant Herd, 1954 (Jr. Lit. Guild selection, Herald Tribune Honor Book award 1954), Oomi, the New Hunter, 1955, Little Red Nose, 1955, It's About Time, 1955, City Boy, Country Boy, 1955 (Jr. Lit. Guild selection), Puppy's House. 1955, Big Talk, 1955, Lazy Day, 1955, Henry's Ride, 1956, Something for Now, 1956, Deer in the Snow, 1956, The Big Cheese, 1957 (Jr. Lit. Guild selection), Little Rabbit, The High Jumper, 1957, Amazing Mr. Pelgew, 1957, A Bunny, A Bird, A Funny Cat, 1957, Here Comes Night, 1957, The Bumblebee's Secret, 1958, Home: The Tale of a Mouse, 1958, Herman McGregor's World, 1958, The Raggle Taggle Fellow, 1959, Little Dog Little, 1959, The Fisherman's Day, 1959, Kittens, Cubs and Babies, 1959, My Family, 1960, The Sun, the Wind, the Sea and the Rain, 1960, Laurie's New Brother, 1961, Amuny, Boy of Old Egypt, 1961, The Pile of Junk, 1962 (Jr. Lit. Guild selection), Snow Time, 1962, The Snake in the Carpool, 1963, Who?, 1963, The Big Green Thing, 1963, The Way Mothers Are, 1963, Big Lion, Little Lion, 1964, Billy, the Littlest One, 1966, The Best Place, 1968, My House, 1971, Moon-months and Sun-days, 1972, The Rabbit's World, 1973, Juju Sheep and the Python's Moonstone, 1973, What's Wrong with Being a Skunk?, 1974, Metric: The Modern Way to Measure, 1975, The Girl Who Would Rather Climb Trees, 1975, Giraffe: The Silent Giant, 1976 (Children' Book of Yr. Child Study Assn. 1976), Bobo, the Troublemaker, 1976, Antarctica: The Great White Continent, 1978, I Hate It, 1978, On the Track of the Mystery Animal, 1978, I, Tut: The Boy Who Became Pharaoh, 1979, Snake Fights, Rabbit Fights and More: A Book About Animal Fighting, 1979 (Outstanding Sci. Trade Book for Children Nat. Sci. Tchrs. Assn./Children's Book Council Joint Com. 1979), Lucky Porcupine!, 1980 (Outstanding Sci. Trade Book for Children Nat. Sci. Tchrs. Assn./Children's Book Council Joint Com. 1980), Billions of Bats, 1982 (Outstanding Sci. Trade Book for Children Nat. Sci. Tchrs. Assn./Children's Book Council Joint Com. 1982), Our Holidays, 1983, Project Panda Watch, 1984 (Children's Sci. Book award N.Y. Acad. Scis. 1985), What the Elephant Was, 1986, The Dangerous Life of the Sea Horse, 1986 (Outstanding Sci. Trade Book for Children Nat. Sci. Tchrs. Assn./Children's Book Council Joint Com. 1986), Pigeons, 1989, Big Talk, 1990, The Year of the Panda, 1990 (Outstanding Sci. Trade Book for Children Nat. Sci. Tchrs. Assn./Children's Book Council Joint Com. 1990), That's Not Goldie, 1990, Jane Goodall's Animal World: Elephants, 1990, I Sailed With Columbus, 1991, Discovering Dinosaur Babies, 1991 (Outstanding Sci. Trade Book for Children Nat. Sci. Tchrs. Assn./Children's Book Council Joint Com. 1991), Let's Go Dinosaur Tracking, 1991, Squirrel Watching, 1992, Secret Land of the Past, 1993, Just Like Me, 1993, Before the Dinosaurs, 1996, The Puzzle of the Dinosaurs-Bird: The Story of Archaeopteyx, 1996, More than One, 1996; contributor: (as Miriam Weiss) Redbook, McCall's, Ladies Home Jour., Good Housekeeping, Univ. Rev., Creative Living, Colorado Quar.; included in anthologies; transl. into Danish, Swedish, Italian, French, Dutch, Norwegian, German, Braille. Mem. Authors Guild, PEN Am. Center (children's book com.), Nat. Writers Union. Author filmstrip materials Guidance Assocs.; textbook editor Harcourt Brace Jovanovich, 1980; editor Scribner Ednl. Pubs., 1985. Home and Office: 19 E 95th St New York NY 10128

SCHLESINGER, CAROLE LYNN, elementary education educator; b. Detroit, May 13, 1961; d. Robert Schlesinger and Regenia Compere. Student, Kalamazoo Coll., 1981-84; BA, U. Mich., 1986; teaching cert., Eastern Mich. U., 1992. Cert. elem. tchr., Mich. Bank teller U. Mich. Credit Union, Ann Arbor, 1987; rsch. asst. dept. postgrad. medicine U. Mich., Ann Arbor, 1987; fin. planner IDS Fin. Svcs., Ann Arbor, 1988-89; telemarketer U. Mich. Telefund, Ann Arbor, 1989-90; enumerator U.S. Bur. Census, Ann Arbor, 1990; reading and math. tutor Reading and Learning Skills Ctr., Ann Arbor, 1991-92; interpreter Living Sci. Found., Wixom, Mich., 1992-94; intern planning and mgmt. info. div. Peace Corps., Washington, 1985; intern Com. for Econ. Devel., Washington, 1985. Elder 1st Presbyn. Ch., Ann Arbor, 1992-94; canvasser, vol. Pub. Interest Rsch. group in Mich., Ann Arbor, 1986-87; trainee Groundwater Edn., Easter Mich. U., Ypsilanti, 1991, mem. dean's adv. com., 1992; mem., group leader Ann Arbor Dems., 1984-87. Mem. ASCD, Mich. Reading Assn., Washtenaw Reading Coun., Mich. Coun. Tchrs. Math., Nat. Coun. Tchrs. Math., Mich. Sci. Tchrs. Assn., Kappa Delta Pi.

SCHLESINGER, RUTH HIRSCHLAND, art curator, consultant; b. Essen, Germany, Mar. 11, 1920; came to U.S., 1936; d. Kurt M. and Henriette (Simons) Hirschland; m. Rudolf B. Schlesinger, Sept. 4, 1942; children: Steven, June, Fay. BA cum laude, Wheaton Coll., Norton, Mass., 1942; intern, Met. Mus. of Art, N.Y.C., 1941. Dir. Upstairs Gallery, Ithaca, N.Y., 1960-67; curatorial asst. Andrew D. White Mus. Cornell U., Ithaca, N.Y., 1967-70; curator of prints Herbert F. Johnson Mus. Cornell U., 1970-75; art curator Hastings Coll. of the Law U. Calif., San Francisco, 1978—. Author: (mus. catalog) 15th and 16th Century Prints of No. Europe from the Nat. Gallery of Art-Rosenwald Collection, 1973, other catalogs. Mem. UN World Centre founding com., 1979-84; mem. art adv. com. N.Y. State Fair, Syracuse, 1973; cons. Gallery Assn., State of N.Y., 1972-74. Recipient History of Art prizes Wheaton Coll., 1941, 42. Home: 1333 Jones St Apt 810 San Francisco CA 94109-4112 Office: U Calif Hastings Coll of Law 200 McAllister San Francisco CA 94102

SCHLESINGER, VIOLET MURRAY, biomedical consultant; b. Denver, June 14, 1929; d. Robert Robertson Ferguson and Virginia Lee (Murray) Corbin; m. Robert Alexander Schlesinger, June 14, 1953; children: Roberta Diane, William Alexander. BA, U. Colo., 1952; MA, Goddard Coll., 1967; mins. license, Bethesda Sch. Ministry, 1990; PhD, Columbia Pacific, 1993. Prof. Ecole Normale, Tours, France, 1952-53; tchr. Denver and L.A. Pub. Schs., 1953-56; exec. dir. Wilde Woode Children's Ctr., Palm Springs, Calif., 1980-87; trustee Anderson Children's Found., Palm Springs, 1987-90; pastor Candle Cross Chapel, Palm Springs, 1990-95; exec. dir. Prevention Pays, Palm Springs, 1990-95. Author: Spiritual, Mental and Physical, 1967, A Wholistic Approach to Wellness A Needed Answer to American Healthcare Crises, 1993. Pastor Candle Cross Chapel, 1990-94. Republican. Home: 380 Pablo Dr Palm Springs CA 92262

SCHLICHTING, NANCY MARGARET, hospital administrator; b. N.Y.C., Nov. 21, 1954. B, Duke U., 1976; M, Cornell U., 1979. Adminstrv. resident Meml. Hosp. Cancer, N.Y.C., 1978; fellow Blue Cross-Blue Shield Assn., Chgo., 1979-80; asst. dirs. ops. Akron (Ohio) City Hosp., 1980-81, assoc. dir. planning, 1981-83, exec. v.p., 1983-88; exec. v.p. Riverside Meth. Hosps., Columbus, Ohio, 1988-92, pres., COO, 1992-93; pres., CEO, 1993-95; pres. Catholic Health Initiatives, eastern region, 1995—. Home: 887 Neil Ave Columbus OH 43215-1334 Office: Catholic Health Initiatives 1 McIntire Dr Chester PA 19014-1196*

SCHLISSEL, LILLIAN, English educator, writer; b. N.Y.C., Feb. 22, 1930; d. Abraham and Mae (Isaacson) Fischer; children: Rebecca Claire, Daniel. BA, Bklyn. Coll., 1951; PhD, Yale U., 1957. From asst. prof. to prof. English Bklyn. Coll. and Grad. Ctr., CUNY, 1957—; dir. Am. studies program Bklyn. Coll., CUNY, 1974—; guest lectr. Am. studies U. N.Mex., Albuquerque, 1981, 83, 89; guest lectr. English U. Santa Clara, Calif., 1971. Editor: Conscience in America, 1968, World of Randolph Bourne, 1970, Journals of Washington Irving, Vol. II, 1981, Women's Diaries of the Westward Journey, 1982, Black Frontiers, 1995; co-editor: Western Women: Their Land, Their Lives, 1988, Far From Home, Families of Westward Journey, 1989; author: Introduction to Covered Wagon Women, 1996, Black Frontiers, 1995. Mem. Am. Studies Assn., Orgn. Am. Historians, Western Hist. Assn. Office: Bklyn Coll Dept Am Studies Brooklyn NY 11210

SCHLITT, JEAN WANAMAKER, secondary school educator; b. Gary, Ind., July 27, 1944; d. John Edward and Louise Margarette (Bach) Wanamaker; m. Raymond John Schlitt, June 29, 1968; children: Theresa M., Carol A., Rachel L. Student, Eckerd Coll., 1962-64; BA, U. Fla., 1966, MEd, 1967. Cert. tchr., Fla. Tchr. St. John's Sch. Bd., St. Augustine, Fla., 1967-68, Alachua Sch. Bd., Gainesville, Fla., 1968-69, Okaloosa Sch. Bd., Niceville, Fla., 1985—. Councilwoman Town of Mary Esther, 1982-86. Mem. APA, Nat. Coun. Tchrs. Social Studies, Okaloosa County Edn. Assn., Delta Kappa Gamma. Home: 61 Mary Esther Dr Mary Esther FL 32569-1831 Office: Niceville HS 800 John Sims Pky E Niceville FL 32578-1210

SCHLOESSER, PATRICIA TURK, pediatrician, consultant; b. Okmulgee, Okla., Apr. 10, 1924; d. Alonzo Benjamin and Ruth (Powe) Turk; m. Harvey Leopold Schloesser, Dec. 31, 1945; children: Lysa Lynn, Nina Ruth, Peter Ernst, Anne Carol, David Turk. Student, Okla. State U., 1941-44, BS, 1965; BA, U. Wis., 1945; MD, U. Okla., Oklahoma City, 1949. Diplomate Am. Bd. Pediatrics; lic. healing arts. Internship Univ. Hosp., Oklahoma City, 1949-50; pediat. residency Crippled Children's Hosp., Oklahoma City, 1950-52; pediatric cons. Kans. Bd. Health, Topeka, 1952-58, dir. divsn. maternal and child health, 1958-71; chief of party maternal and child health US Agy. for Internat. Devel. and U. Calif. Berkeley, Kampala, Uganda, 1971-73; med. officer Mental Retardation Svcs. Western Australia, Perth, 1973; dir. bur. maternal and child health Kans. Dept. Health & Environment, Topeka, 1974-83, med. dir. maternal and child health programs, 1984-87, dir. divsn. health, 1987-88, dep. dir. fed. and state rels., 1988-89; pvt. practice as maternal and child health cons. Topeka, 1989—; rsch. assoc. coping project Menninger Found., Topeka, 1955-62; clin. asst. prof. dept. pediatrics med.

sch. U. Kans., Kansas City, 1977-94. Author: (with others) Widening World of Childhood, 1962; author, editor: Health of Children in Day Care, 1986; contbr. chpt. to Encyc. Britannica Med. & Health Ann., 1994; contbr. articles to profl. jours. Mem. adv. com. Kans. Action Children, Topeka, 1980-96; cons. Kans. Children's Svc. League, Topeka, 1980-85; mem. nat. adv. com. Nat. Resource Ctr. for Health and Safety in Child Care, 1996—. Recipient Samuel J. Crumbine award Kans. Pub. Health Assn., 1983, Kans. Action Children award, 1985. Fellow Am. Acad. Pediatrics (mem. coms. child care 1969-74, emeritus fellow); mem. APHA (chair MCH sect. 1985-86, cons. child care 1987-94, mem. action bd. 1991—, Martha May Eliot award 1992), Kans. Med. Soc. (mem. maternal health com.), Assn. Maternal & Child Health Programs (bd. dirs. 1981-87, mem. various coms.). Republican. Presbyterian. Home and Office: 1914 SW Warner Ct Topeka KS 66604-3267

SCHLOSSER, ANNE GRIFFIN, librarian; b. N.Y.C., Dec. 28, 1939; d. C. Russell and Gertrude (Taylor) Griffin; m. Gary J. Schlosser, Dec. 28, 1965. BA in History, Wheaton Coll., Norton, Mass., 1962; MLS, Simmons Coll., 1964; cert. archives adminstrn. Nat. Archives and Records Service, Am. U., 1970. Head UCLA Theater Arts Library, 1964-69; dir. Louis B. Mayer Libr., Am. Film Inst., L.A., 1969-88, dir. film/TV documentation workshop, 1977-87; head Cinema-TV Libr. and Archives of the Performing Arts, U. So. Calif., L.A., 1988-91; dir. Entertainment Resources Seminar, 1990; dir. rsch. libr. Warner Bros., 1991—. Project dir.: Motion Pictures, Television, Radio: A Union Catalogue of Manuscript and Special Collections in the Western U.S., 1977. Active Hollywood Dog Obedience Club, Calif. Numerous grants for script indexing, manuscript cataloging, library automation. Mem. Soc. Am. Archivists, Soc. Calif. Archivists (pres. 1982-83), Theater Library Assn. (exec. bd. 1983-86), Women in Film, Spl. Librs. Assn.. Democrat. Episcopalian. Avocations: running, swimming, reading, dog obedience training. Office: Warner Bros Rsch Libr 5200 Lankershim Blvd Ste 100 North Hollywood CA 91601-3100

SCHLOSSER, THEA SUSSANNE, advocate, association executive; b. Hasenfeld, Germany, June 1, 1937; d. Theodor and Anna (Poppe) Hermesmeyer; divorced; children: Ingrid, Evelyn. Ed. in home econs., Austria; attended, N.Y. Inst. Photography, Modern Sch. Photography; postgrad., Am. Coll. Nutrition. Prin. World Wide Slides, Santa Barbara; founder Chronic Fatigue and Immune Dysfunction Media Awareness Assn., Santa Barbara; assoc. TV show Growing Younger; promotional dir. Kuhnan MD Xenotransplant Ctr.; advt. and bus. cons.; speaker, lectr. on chronic fatigue immune dysfunction of TV, radio, others. Author, publisher: Beyond the Dark Cloud, Road to Recovery from Chronic Fatigue and Immune Dysfunction after 25 Years, 1996; founder-pres., publisher-editor CFID Health Update Internat. Newsletter; inventor game show Challenge Your IQ. Recipient numerous gold medals in photography; swimming champion Austria, 1950. Mem. AMa, Internat. Platform Assn. Office: Chronic Fatigue Media Awareness Assn PO Box 41028 Santa Barbara CA 93140

SCHLOTFELDT, ROZELLA MAY, nursing educator; b. DeWitt, Iowa, June 29, 1914; d. John W. and Clara C. (Doering) S. BS, State U. Iowa, 1935; MS, U. Chgo., 1947, PhD, 1956; DSc (hon.), Georgetown U., 1972, Adelphi U., 1979, Wayne State U., 1983, U. Ill., Chgo., 1985, Kent State U., 1987, U. Cin., 1989, Case Western Res. U., 1996; LHD (hon.), Med. U. S.C., 1976. Staff nurse State U. Iowa, VA Hosp., 1935-39; instr., supr. maternity nursing (State U. Iowa), 1939-44; asst. prof. U. Colo. Sch. Nursing, 1947-48; asst., then asso. prof. Wayne State U. Coll. Nursing, 1948-55; prof., asso. dean Wayne State U. Coll. Nursing (Coll. Nursing), 1957-60; dean Frances Payne Bolton Sch. Nursing, Case Western Res. U., 1960-72, prof., 1960-82, prof., dean emeritus, 1982-95; vis. prof. Rutgers U., 1984-89, 90—, U. Pa., 1985-86; spl. cons. Surgeon Gen.'s Adv. Group on Nursing, 1961-63; mem. nursing research study sect. USPHS, 1962-66; mem. Nat. League for Nursing-USPHS Com. on Nursing Edn. Facilities, 1962-64; mem. com. on health goals Cleve. Health Council, 1961-66; mem. Cleve. Health Planning and Devel. Commn., 1969-72; adv. com. div. nursing W.K. Kellog Found., 1959-67; v.p. Ohio Bd. Nursing Edn. and Nurse Registration, 1970-71, pres., 1971-72; mem. Nat. Health Services Research Tng. Com., 1970-71; mem. supply and edn. panel Health Manpower Com., 1966-67; rev. com. Nurse Tng. Act, 1967-68; bd. visitors Duke U. Med. Center, 1968-70; mem. council, exec. com. Inst. Medicine of Nat. Acad. Scis., 1971-75; mem. nat. adv. health services council Health Services and Mental Health Adminstrn., 1971-75; mem. def. adv. com. on women in services Dept. Def., 1972-75; bd. mem., treas. Nursing Home Adv. and Research Council, 1975—; mem. adv. panel Health Services Research Commn. on Human Resources, Nat. Acad. Sci., 1977-85; cons. Walter Reed Army Inst.; adv. council on nursing, U.S. VA, 1965-69, chmn., 1966-69; mem. Yale U.; Council Com. on Med. Affairs, 1981-86; mem. adv. bd. Scholarly Inquiry for Nursing Practice, 1987—. Mem. editorial bd.: Advances in Nursing Sci, Inquiry, 1982-85, Jour. Nursing Edn., 1982-91; contbr. numerous articles to profl. jours. Bd. vis. Syracuse U., 1990—. Served to 1st lt. Army Nurse Corps, 1944-46. Recipient Disting. Svc. award U. Iowa, 1973, Case Western Res. U., 1991, N. Watts Lifetime Achievement award, 1995; named Living Legend, Am. Acad. Nursing, 1995. Fellow Am. Acad. Nursing (v.p. 1975-77, Living Legend award 1995), Nat. League Nursing; mem. ANA (chmn. commn. on nurse edn. 1967-70, mem. com. for studying credentialling 1976-79, adv. com. W.K. Kellogg Nat. Fellowship program 1981-85), Pi Lambda Theta, Sigma Theta Tau (nat. v.p. 1948-50, selection com., disting. lectr. program 1986-87, Founders award for creativity 1985). Home: 1111 Carver Rd Cleveland OH 44112-3635 Office: 2121 Abington Rd Cleveland OH 44106-2333

SCHLOTZHAUER, VIRGINIA HUGHES, parliamentarian; b. Washington, July 24, 1913; d. William and Secy Alice (Royston) Hughes; m. Elbert O. Schlotzhauer, May 16, 1936; children: Carol Schlotzhauer Hinds, Jean Schlotzhauer Sumner, Jude Schlotzhauer Wilson. AB in LS, George Washington U., 1934. Mem. libr. staff George Washington U., Washington, 1934; various clerical positions U.S. Govt., ARC, Washington, Phoenix, mid-1930s; cons. parliamentarian Washington, 1967—; cons. Nat. Parliamentarian Edn. Project for Colls. and Univs. sponsored by Am. Inst. Parliamentarians funded by William Randolph Hearst Found., 1993-95; presenter seminars. Author: A Parliamentarian's Book of Limericks, 1984; (with others) Parliamentary Opinions, 1982, Parliamentary Opinions II, 1992; primary contbr./cons. column Parliamentary Jour.; contbr. articles to profl. publs. Mem. steering and bylaws coms., sec. Nominating Conv. for Endorsement of Candidates for Bd. Edn., Montgomery County, Md., 1966; election reporter ABC-LWV, Prince George's County, Md., 1970s; v.p., bylaws com. Planned Parenthood Am., Prince George's County, late 1960s and 70s; group leader, bd. dirs., sec., trustee Potomac Area coun. Camp Fire Girls, Md. and D.C. area, 1940s and 50s; participant nonpartisan and Dem. polit. campaigns; judge various contests Future Bus. Leaders Am., Washington, 1970s. Mem. AAUW (life, named gift Bethesda-Chevy Chase br. 1962, named gift Md. divsn. 1972), Am. Inst. Parliamentarians (cert. profl. parliamentarian, mem. adv. coun. or bd. dirs. 1966—, pres. D.C. chpt. 1966-68, opinions com. 1974—, chmn. 1974-78, cons., named changed to Virginia Schlotzhauer D.C. chpt. 1984), Nat. Assn. Parliamentarians (profl. registered parliamentarian, mem. coms.), D.C. Assn. Parliamentarians (founding pres., 1st hon. pres., Achievement award 1976), Westerners. Home and Office: 9819 Indian Queen Point Rd Fort Washington MD 20744-6904

SCHLUETER, ERIKA MANRIQUEZ, civil engineer research scientist; b. Santiago, Chile; came to U.S., 1980; d. Javier Bustos Manriquez and Constantina Vilos Anso; m. Ross Donald Schlueter, May, 1981; children: Dietrich, Kurt. B of Civil Constrn., Cath. U., Santiago, 1980; postgrad., MIT, 1980-81, San Jose State U., 1983; MS in Civil Engring., U. Wash., 1986; PhD in Engring. Sci., U. Calif., Berkeley, 1995. Instr. continuing edn. Cath. U., Santiago, 1975-77, tchg. asst., 1976-77; hydrogeologist Celzac Co., Santiago, 1978; med. asst. Stanford (Calif.) U. Med. Ctr., 1981, fin. aids analyst, 1981-82; homemaker Pleasanton, 1986-88; rsch. asst. Lawrence Berkeley Nat. Lab. U. Calif., Berkeley, 1988-95; rsch. scientist Lawrence Berkeley Nat. Lab. U. Calif., Berkeley, 1995—. Contbr. numerous articles to profl. jours. Fulbright fellow, 1980-81, James Lewis fellow, 1990-91. Mem. ASCE, Soc. Petroleum Engrs., Am. Geophys. Union, Soc. Exploration Geophysicists (Award of Merit 1994-95). Republican. Roman Catholic. Home: 780 Cragmont Ave Berkeley CA 94708 Office: Lawrence Berkeley Nat Lab MS 90-1116 1 Cyclotron Rd Berkeley CA 94720

SCHLUETER, MARGARET COX, principal; b. Van Nuys, Calif., June 3, 1940; d. Percy Atlas and Martha Eleln (Luening) Cox; m. Ralph Schlueter, Dec. 26, 1958; children: Tammara, Scott, Matthew. B in Edn., Incarnate Ward Coll., 1969; MA, St. Mary's U., 1993. Cert. tchr. elem., music, English, Tex. Tchr. Adams Elem. Sch., San Antonio, Tex., 1966-81; music coord. Hariandale ISD, San Antonio, 1979-81; music cons. YMCA, San Antonio, 1982-85; religion coord. Holy Spirit Sch., San Antonio, 1986-93; vice prin. St. Joseph Cath. Sch., San Antonio, 1993-94, prin., 1994—; Project 30 evaluator St. Mary's U., San Antonio, 1988; PTC fedn. Sch. San Antonio, 1992-93; workshop tchr. Sch. San Antonio Archdiocese, 1991-94, chair cath. high sch. exposition, 1992-93. Religious edn. bd. mem. Holy Spirit Parish, San Antonio, 1987-93; chair Alamo dist Music Tchrs. Assn., San Antonio, 1978. Chaminade scholarship recipient St. Mary's U., San Antonio, 1989. Mem. Nat. Cath. Edn. Assn., Tex. Middle Sch. Assn., Tex. Music Edn. Assn. Republican. Roman Catholic. Home: 13322 Langtry St San Antonio TX 78248-1232 Office: St Joseph Cath Sch 535 New Laredo Hwy San Antonio TX 78211-1927

SCHMEER, ARLINE CATHERINE, cancer research development chemotherapy scientist; b. Rochester, N.Y., Nov. 14, 1929; d. Edward Jacob and Madeline Margaret (Haines) S. BA, Coll. St. Mary of the Springs, Columbus, Ohio, 1951; MS in Biology, Notre Dame U., 1961; PhD in Biomedicine, U. Colo., 1969; DSc (hon.), Albertus Magnus Coll., New Haven, Conn., 1974, SUNY, Potsdam, 1990. Chmn. sci. dept. Watterson High Sch./Diocese of Columbus, 1954-59, St. Vincent Ferrer High Sch./Archdiocese of N.Y., N.Y.C., 1959-62; chmn. dept. biology Ohio Dominican Coll., Columbus, 1963-72; chmn. dept. anti-cancer agents of marine origin Am. Cancer Rsch. Ctr., Denver, 1972-82; dir. Mercenene Cancer Rsch. Inst., New Haven, 1982-93; dir. Mercenene Cancer Rsch. Inst. U. Cin. Med. Sch., 1996—; sr. prin. investigator Marine Biol. Lab., Woods Hole, Mass., 1962-72, corp. mem., mem. libr. com., 1964—; rsch. prof. Med. Sch., U. Würzburg, Germany, 1969-70; pres., chief exec. officer Med. Rsch. Found., 1972—; participant, contbr. Internat. Cancer Congress, 1966—. Contbr. articles to biol. publs. Grantee Am. Cancer Soc., 1965; NSF fellow, 1957-62, NIH fellow, 1966-69; recipient numerous teaching awards, Ohi Acad. Scis. and others. Fellow Royal Microscopical Soc. Eng. (life); mem. N.Y. Acad. Sci. (life), Am. Soc. Cell Biology, Internat. Cancer Congresses. Roman Catholic. Office: Mercenene Cancer Rsch Inst U Cin Med Sch 3130 Highland Ave Cincinnati OH 45202

SCHMELZ, BRENDA LEA, legal assistant; b. Washington, Mo., June 13, 1958; d. Edward G. and Wilma D. (Hektor) R.; m. Jan M. Schmelz, Oct. 7, 1978; children: Edward L., Brent T. Secretarial sci. cert. with honors, East Ctrl. Coll., Union, Mo., 1977. Sec., paralegal Mittendorf & Mittendorf, Union, 1976-83, Eckelkamp, Eckelkamp, Wood & Kuenzel, Washington, 1983—; mem. legal secretarial adv. bd. East Ctrl. Coll., 1978, chmn., 1987; mem. legal secretarial adv. bd. State Fair C.C., 1995. Mem. Nat. Assn. Legal Assts. (cert.), Nat. Assn. Legal Secs. (cert.), Mo. Assn. Legal Secs. (v.p. 1986, 91, pres. 1989-92, 94-96, sec. 1984-86, 89-90, dir. pub. rels. 1987-89, Legal Sec. of Yr. 1987), Franklin County Legal Secs. (pres. 1989-92, Legal Sec. of Yr. 1986, 95), Union of Women Today, Phi Beta Kappa. Republican. Roman Catholic. Home: 142 Highland Dr Union MO 63084-2014 Office: Eckelkamp Eckelkamp Wood & Kuenzel Bank of Washington Bldg Main & Oak Washington MO 63084

SCHMERLER, MARCI P., lawyer; b. Phila., Sept. 1, 1959. BS cum laude, U. Pa., 1981; JD cum laude, Temple U., 1986. Bar: Ga. 1986, U.S. Dist. Ct. (no. dist.) Ga. 1986, U.S. Ct. Appeals (11th cir.) 1986. Ptnr. Alston & Bird, Atlanta. Recipient Am. Jurisprudence award in Constitutional Law. Mem. ABA, State Bar of Ga. (real property sect.), Atlanta Bar Assn. (sects. on real estate, bus. and finance law), Nat. Assn. Bond Lawyers. Office: Alston & Bird 1 Atlantic Ctr 1201 W Peachtree St Atlanta GA 30309-3424*

SCHMERTZ, MILDRED FLOYD, editor, writer; b. Pitts., Mar. 29, 1925; d. Robert Watson and Mildred Patricia (Floyd) S. B.Arch., Carnegie Mellon U., 1947; M.F.A., Yale U., 1957. Archtl. designer John Schurko, Architect, Pitts., 1947-55; assoc. editor Archtl. Record, N.Y.C., 1957-65; sr. editor Archtl. Record, 1965-80, exec. editor, 1980-85, editor-in-chief, 1985-90; vis. lectr. Yale Sch. Architecture, 1979—. Editor, contbr.: New Life for Old Buildings; other books on architecture and planning. Bd. mgrs. Jr. League, City of N.Y., 1964-65; commr. N.Y. Landmarks Preservation Commn., 1988-91. Fellow AIA; mem. Archtl. League N.Y., Mcpl. Art Soc. N.Y., Century Assn. (N.Y.C.). Home and Office: 310 E 46th St New York NY 10017-3002

SCHMID, LYNETTE SUE, child and adolescent psychiatrist; b. Tecumseh, Nebr., May 28, 1958; d. Mel Vern John and Janice Wilda (Bohling) S.; m. Vijendra Sundar, June 13, 1987; children: Jesse Christopher Mikaéle, Eric Lynn Kalani, Christina Elizabeth Ululani. BS, U. Nebr., 1979; MD, U. Nebr., Omaha, 1984; postgrad., U. Mo., 1984-89. Diplomate Am. Bd. Med. Examiners, Am. Bd. Psychiatry and Neurology. Child and adolescent psychiatrist Fulton (Mo.) State Hosp., 1990-91, Mid-Mo. Mental Health Ctr., Columbia, Mo., 1991—; clin. asst. prof. psychiatry U. Mo., Columbia, 1990—. Contbr. articles to profl. jours. Mem. Am. Psychiat. Assn., Am. Acad. Child and Adolescent Psychiatry, Ctrl. Mo. Psychiat. Assn. (sec.-treas. 1992-93, pres.- elect 1993-94, pres. 1994-95), U. Nebr. Alumni Assn., Phi Beta Kappa, Alpha Omega Alpha. Republican. Baptist.

SCHMIDT, ANN MARIE, foundation administration; b. Mankato, Minn., Feb. 13, 1963; d. Michael John and Mary Katherine (Showers) S. BA in Psychology, BA in Sociology, U. Kans., 1986; postgrad., Antioch Coll., 1996—. Counselor Caremark, L.A., 1987-89; program mgr. Sunrise Cmty. Counselling Ctr., L.A., 1989-92; exec. dir. Courage To Care Found., L.A., 1992—; cons. AIDS Care, L.A. 1989-91; human rights task force monitor Med. Aid for El Salvador, 1989-90. Vol. Shanti, L.A., 1987-90, AIDS Project L.A., 1990—; coord. spkr. fellowship YMCA, Santa Monica, Calif., 1993-95; mem. peace and justice com. St. Monica's Cath. Ch., Santa Monica, 1994-96; mem. alumnae adv. coun., chpt. adviser Calif. State U., Northridge, 1993—. Recipient outstanding vol. award Johnson County Assn. Against Battered Women, 1987, commendation County of Los Angeles, 1990; Outstanding Greek Adviser award Order of Omega, Calif. State U., Northridge, 1995, 96, Outstanding Alumnae Adv. Coun. award, 1995. Mem. NAFE, Alpha Omicron Pi (pres. West L.A. alumnae chpt. 1993-96, sec. So. Calif. coun.). Democrat. Office: Courage To Care Found 1015 Gayley Ste 434 Los Angeles CA 90024

SCHMIDT, B. JUNE, education educator; b. Alleghany County, Pa., Dec. 26, 1932; d. Ralph F. and Elizabeth M. (Gottschall) Hoffman; m. Richard E. Schmidt, Sept. 3, 1956; children: Amy Elizabeth, Stephen F. BBA, U. Pitts., 1956; MS, Va. Poly. Inst., 1959, EdD, 1974. Tchr. Montgomery County (Va.) Schs., 1959-62; free-lance writer Blacksburg, Va., 1963-68, 69-71; instr. Radford U., Redford, Va., 1968-69; grad. rsch. asst. Va. Poly. Inst. and State U., Blacksburg, 1971-74, from asst. to prof., 1979—; supr. bus. edn. Va. Dept. Edn., Radford, 1974-79; vis. scholar Inst. Edn. Rsch., Jyvaskyla, Finland, 1992; rschr. NAt. Ctr. Rsch. in Vocat. Edn., U. Calif., Berkeley, 1988—. Named Collegiate Tchr. of Yr., Nat. Bus. Edn. Assn., 1991, Tchr. Educator of Yr., So. Bus. Edn. Assn.; recipient John Robert Gregg award McGraw Hill Pub., 1992; U. Coun. for Vocat. Edn. vis. scholar, 1994-95. Mem. Am. Vocat. Edn. Rsch. Assn. (pres. 1991, chair editl. bd. jour. 1989), Delta Pi Epsilon (pres. 1996—, editor jour. 1988-89). Office: Va Poly Inst & State U Coll of Edn Blacksburg VA 24061-0254

SCHMIDT, CAROL DOROTHY, mathematics educator; b. Chgo., Dec. 18, 1939; d. Herbert H. and Irma D. (Lietz) Gross; m. Alvin J. Schmidt, Aug. 15, 1964; children: Timothy J., Mark A. BA cum laude, Augustana Coll., 1961; MS, Ill. State U., 1962. Cert. tchr., Ind. Instr. in math., asst. registrar Concordia Coll., Seward, Nebr., 1962-67; instr., math. Ind. U.-Purdue U., Fort Wayne, 1977-89; instr. math. Concordia Luth. H.S., Fort Wayne, 1984-88; instr. in math Lincoln Land C.C., Springfield, Ill., 1990—. Chair Holy Cross Luth. Sch. Bd., Fort Wayne, 1979-84; mem., sec. Coll. Hill Literary Soc., Jacksonville, Ill., 1992—. Mem. Ill. Math. Assn. of C.C. (bd. dirs.), Am. Math. Assn. of Two-Yr. Colls. (edn. com. 1994—), Math. Assn. of Am., Nat. Coun. of Tchrs. of Math., Ill. Coun. of Tchrs. of Math. Office: Lincoln Land Community Coll Shepherd Rd Springfield IL 62794

SCHMIDT, CHARLOTTE ANN, fund raiser, public relations, marketing officer; b. Birnamwood, Wis., Apr. 25, 1943; d. Roland Lewis and Myrtle Agnes (Nelson) Rothman; m. Jack Gerald Schmidt, Aug. 27, 1966 (div. Feb. 1995); children: Charné Lee, Darcey Dejon. BS, U. Wis., 1965. Cert. fund raising exec. Y-Teen dir. YWCA, Janesville, Wis., 1965-66; dir. spl. events and fund raising Black Hawk coun. Girl Scouts U.S., Madison, Wis., 1966-71; cmty. devel. mgr. Mile Hi coun. Girl Scouts U.S., Denver, 1980-87; dir. ann. fund Colo. Christian Home, Denver, 1987-92; chief devel. officer Rocky Mountain Multiple Sclerosis Ctr., Englewood, Colo., 1992—. Mem. Gov.'s Coun. on Employing People with Disabilities, Colo., 1994—; co-chair Rocky Mountain Philanthropy Inst., Colo., 1990; participant Leadership Denver, 1989—; mem., newsletter editor Denver Sister Cities, 1981-85. Mem. Nat. Soc. Fund Raising Execs. (bd. dirs. Colo. chpt. 1981—, pres. 1991, mem. long-range planning com. 1993-94, participant Exec. Leadership Inst. 1996), Zonta Club of Denver, Alpha Gamma Delta. Christian. Office: Rocky Mountain MS Ctr 701 E Hampden Ste 430 Englewood CO 80110

SCHMIDT, ELLEN R., public health administrator, occupational therapist; b. White Plains, N.Y., May 28, 1949; d. Leslie and Gladys S. BS, Boston U., 1971; MS, Johns Hopkins U., 1979. Registered occupl. therapist; cert. tchr. Md. Dir. occupl. therapy dept. Children's Hosp., Balt., 1974-77, Md. Gen. Hosp., Balt., 1977-81, Calif. Hosp. Med. Ctr., L.A., 1981-84; occupl. therapy cons. Md. Dept. Health, Balt., 1984-88, chief divsn. injury and disability prevention, 1988-95; mgmt. and program analyst U.S. Consumer Product Safety Commn., Bethesda, Md., 1995—; mem. CDC Prevention Adv. Com. for Nat. Ctr. for Injury Prevention and Control, Atlanta, 1993-95; lectr./presenter in field; mem. grant rev. panel DHHS, Bur. Maternal and Child Health, 1992; invited lectr. on injury prevention U. Md. Sch. Nursing, 1993. Mem. APHA, State and Territorial Injury Prevention Dirs. Assn. (founding mem., pres. 1992-95). Office: US Consumer Prod Safety Com 4330 East-West Hwy Bethesda MD 20814

SCHMIDT, GLORIA JEAN, elementary educator; b. Phila., June 23, 1943; d. Adolph J. and Elizabeth M. (Sokolowski) R.; m. Arthur F. Schmidt, Oct. 11, 1969 (dec. 1992); 1 child, Christopher. BA, Immaculate Coll., 1964; MEd, Temple U., 1967. Tchr. grade 4 Springfield (Pa.) Schs., 1964—. Republican. Roman Catholic. Home: 36 Darlington Rd Glen Mills PA 19342

SCHMIDT, GRETCHEN R., foundation administrator; b. St. Louis, Sept. 27, 1964; d. Christopher and Sandra Jane (Sabin) Rhodes; m. Michael Gerard, Apr. 29, 1995. BS, Southwest Mo. State U., Springfield, 1986; M in Public Policy Adminstrn., U. Mo., St. Louis, 1992. Acctg. para-profl. Mortland & Co. P.C., St. Louis, 1988-91; adminstrv. asst. St. Louis Cmty. Fund, 1991-95, asst. dir., 1995-96; exec. dir. Circus Arts Found./Circus Flora, 1996—. Democrat. Roman Catholic.

SCHMIDT, JANICE LAVONNE, bank executive; b. Larimore, N.D., May 29, 1941; d. Erwin Hugo William and Gertrude Lydia Maria (Wolfgram) Schmidt. Student, Mayville State Coll., 1959, U. N.D. Sch. Banking, Grand Forks, 1988, 1994. Bookkeeper Citizens State Bank, Petersburg, N.D., 1966-82, asst. cashier, 1982-94, br. mgr., 1994-95, v.p., bd. dirs., 1995—. Sec., treas. Petersburg City Job Devel., 1990—; pres., treas. Petersburg Civic Club, 1990—; bd. dirs. Nelson County Hist. Soc., Lakota, N.D., 1994—; bd. dirs. Lakota (Mich.) Unity Dollars for Scholars (pres. 1994, v.p. 1989—, treas. 1989—); organist St. Andrew Lutheran Ch., 1957—, Sunday Sch. tchr., 1966—. Mem. Aid Assn. for Lutherans (sec., treas. 1989—). Office: Citizens State Bank 202 S 5th St Petersburg ND 58272

SCHMIDT, JANIS ILENE, elementary education educator; b. Wyandot County, Ohio., Feb. 4, 1930; d. Floyd Dale and Edith June (Clark) Herbert; m. William Frederick Schmidt, Aug. 27, 1950; children: Lon William, Randy Floyd. BS, Findlay Coll., 1968; MEd, Ashland Coll., 1986. Cert. elem. tchr., Ohio. Elem. tchr. Wharton (Ohio) Elem., 1950-52, Upper Sandusky (Ohio) Schs., 1967—. Author: Improvement of Retention, 1986. Officer Beta Usando Literary Club, Upper Sandusky, 1993; mem. Wyandot Meml. Hosp. Guild, 1980-95, North Salem Luth. Ch. Tchr., officer, 1950—, Tri-G Mothers League, 1953-80. Jennings scholar The Martha Holden Jennings Found., Ohio, 1969-73. Mem. Internat. Reading Assn. (com. chmn. 1990). Republican. Lutheran. Home: 569 N Warpole St Upper Sandusky OH 43351-9332 Office: East Sch 401 3rd St Upper Sandusky OH 43351-1105

SCHMIDT, JEAN MARIE, microbiology educator; b. Waterloo, Iowa, June 5, 1938; d. John Frederick and Opal Marie (Lowe) S. BA, U. Iowa, 1959, MS, 1961; PhD, U. Calif., Berkeley, 1965. NIH postdoctoral fellow U. Edinburgh, Scotland, 1965-66; asst. prof. Ariz. State U., Tempe, 1966-71, assoc. prof., 1971-79, prof. microbiology, 1979—, assoc. dir. for biology Cancer Rsch. Inst., 1982—, acting chair dept. microbiology, 1988-89. Author: (with others) Bergey's Manual of Systematic Bacteriology, 1989; contbr. articles to jours. NSF grantee, 1981. Fellow AAAS; mem. Am. Soc. Microbiology (divsn. chmn. 1979-80), Phi Beta Kappa, Sigma Xi. Democrat. Methodist.

SCHMIDT, KAREN ANNE, travel company executive, state legislator; b. L.A., Nov. 27, 1945; d. Ernest Potter and Anne Ruth (Cieslar) Jacobi; m. Gary Manning Schmidt, Jan. 30, 1970 (div. Jan. 1984); children: Geoffrey, Gavin; m. Simeon Robert Wilson III, Mar. 20, 1993. Student, Ariz. State U., 1963-66. Stewardess TWA, Kansas City, Mo., 1966-67, Western Airlines, L.A., 1967-68; sales rep. Delta Airlines, Atlanta, 1968-70; owner Go Travel Svc., Bainbridge Island, Wash., 1971—; mem. Wash. Legislature, 1980—, chmn. transp. com. and organized crime com. Named Legislator of Yr. Hwy. Users Fedn., 1992, 95, Legislator of Yr. Wash. State Patrol, 1995. Mem. Bainbridge Island C. of C. (dir. 1971-81, pres. 1976), Rotary (named Woman of the Yr. 1979). Office: Go Travel Svc 155 Madrone Ln N Bainbridge Is WA 98110-1862 also: Wash Ho of Reps 328 Jlob Olympia WA 98504

SCHMIDT, KATHLEEN MARIE, lawyer; b. Des Moines, June 17, 1953; d. Raymond Driscoll and Hazel Isabelle (Rogers) Poage; m. Dean Everett Johnson, Dec. 21, 1974 (div. Nov. 1983); children: Aaron Dean, Gina Marie; m. Ronald Robert Schmidt, Feb. 7, 1987. BS in Home Econs., U. Nebr., 1974; JD, Creighton U., 1987. Bar: Nebr. 1987, U.S. Dist. Ct. Nebr. 1987, U.S. Ct. Appeals (8th cir.) 1989, U.S. Supreme Ct. 1991. Apprentice printer, journeyman Rochester (Minn.) Post Bull., 1978-82; dir. customer info. Cornhusker Pub. Power Dist., Columbus, Nebr., 1982-83; artist Pamida, Omaha, 1983; offset artist Cornhusker Motor Club, Omaha, 1983-84; assoc. Lindahl O. Johnson Law Office, Omaha, 1987-88; pvt. practice Omaha, 1988-90; ptnr. Emery, Penke, Blazek & Schmidt, Omaha, 1990-91; pvt. practice, Omaha, 1992—; atty. in condemnation procs. Douglas County Bd. Appraisers, Omaha, 1988—. Mem. Millard Sch. Bd., Omaha, 1989-96, treas. 1991, 92; mem. strategic planning com. Millard Sch. Dist., 1990; mem. Omaha Mayor's Master Plan Com., 1991-94. Named hon. mem. Anderson Mid. Sch., Omaha, 1991. Mem. Nebr. Bar Assn., Omaha Bar Assn. (spkrs. bur. 1992—), Nat. Sch. Bd. Assn. (del. federal rels. network 1991-96, cert. recognition 1991), Nebr. Sch. Bd. Assn. (presenter 1991, 92, award of achievement 1991, 94). Republican. Lutheran. Home: 15936 Cuming St Omaha NE 68118-2241 Office: 399 N 117th St Ste 305 Omaha NE 68154-2507

SCHMIDT, KATHY MARGARET, special education educator; b. Butte, Mont., Nov. 16, 1949; d. Fred Joseph and Sara Katherine (McLaughlin) Godbout; m. Todd D. Schmidt, Apr. 23, 1976; children: Lance, Trista, Lane. BE, Ea. Mont. Coll., 1972, MEd, 1976. Tchr. spl. edn. Lewistown (Mont.) Sch. Dist., 1972-74; resource tchr. Philipsburg (Mont.) Sch. Dist., 1974; resource tchr. Anaconda (Mont.) Pub. Schs., 1975-88, pre-sch. specialist, 1989—. Head coach Mont. Spl. Olympics, Anaconda, 1989—. Mem. Coun. Exceptional Children (Mont. pres. 1988, 93, gov. Mont. divsn. 1985-88, 94—, Tchr. of Yr. 1989), Ancient Order Hibernians (v.p., social action chairperson 1986—), Anaconda Fedn. Tchrs. (exec. com.). Democrat. Roman Catholic. Home: 709 Main St Anaconda MT 59711-2938 Office: Anaconda Sch Dist PO Box 1281 Anaconda MT 59711-1281

SCHMIDT, LAURA LEE, elementary and middle school gifted and talented educator, special education educator; b. South Bend, Ind., Sept. 6, 1960; d. Max A. and Sandra Lee (Engmark) Tudor; m. William Michael

Schmidt, Aug. 7, 1982; children: Sandra Lorena, Charlotte Lee. BA, U. Ky., 1982; postgrad., Augustana Coll., Sioux Falls, S.D., U. S.D.; MEd, S.D. State U., 1991. Cert. elem. K-8, spl. edn. K-12, mid./jr. h.s., gifted edn. K-12, S.D. Spl. edn. tchr. Owen County Sch. Dist., Owenton, Ky.; elem. sch. tchr. White River (S.D.) Sch. Dist.; elem. and music tchr. St. Liborius Sch., Orient, S.D.; spl. edn. and chpt. I tchr. Cresbard (S.D.) Sch.; gifted edn. tchr. Douglas Mid. Sch., Douglas Sch. Dist., Box Elder, S.D. Easter seals camp counselor; vol. Spl. Olympics; accompianist high sch. choir. Mem. Dir. Spl. Edn., Mortar Board, Lambda Sigma. Home: 614 Bluebird Dr Box Elder SD 57719-9509

SCHMIDT, LAURA LEE, secondary school educator; b. Roswell, N.Mex., June 5, 1951; d. Gilbert Glenn Ford and Janis Jo Neill Ford Smothermon; m. Gerald Wayne Schmidt, May 27, 1972; children: Stacey Darlene, Bradley Neill. BS, East Tex. State U., Commerce, 1973; MA, U. Tex., Tyler, 1978. Secondary tchr. math. Brownsboro (Tex.) Ind. Sch. Dist., 1973—; cons. Region VII Ednl. Svc. Ctr., Kilgore, Tex., 1985-92. Recipient Tex. Excellence award for Outstanding Tchr., U. Tex. Alumni, 1987; GTE Gifts for Tchrs. grantee, 1987. Mem. Nat. Coun. Tchrs. Math., Tex. Coun. Tchrs. Math., East Tex. Coun. Tchrs. Math. (membership chmn., sec.-treas., v.p.), Tex. Computer Educators Assn. Democrat. Baptist. Home: PO Box 264 419 4th St Chandler TX 75758 Office: Brownsboro Ind Sch Dist Hwy 31 Brownsboro TX 75756

SCHMIDT, MARTHA MARIE, educator, counselor; b. Cadott, Wis., Sept. 28, 1912; d. Karl Christian and Lydia Sarah (Keller) Bubeck; m. Eugene Milton Schmidt, Sept. 11, 1943; children: Eugene Karl, Fredric John. BS, U. Wis., Stout, 1934; MPhil, U. Wis., Madison, 1947, M in Psychology and Behavioral Studies, 1959. Tchr. home econs. Barron (Wis.) High Sch., 1934-37; supr. student teaching U. Wis., Stout, 1937-38; state supr. home econs. edn. Wis. State Bd. Vocat. Edn., Madison, 1938-48; instr. adult evening sch. Madison Area Tech. Coll., 1949-69; guidance counselor Madison Met. Schs., 1959-79; coord. AARP and Wis. Ret. Tchrs. Assn., Madison, 1986-90; state chmn. health/long term care action group AARP, Wis., 1990-91; coord. health advocacy svcs. AARP, 1991—; founder Future Homemakers of Am., 1943, past advisor; condr. fgn. study programs, Europe, Asia, Australia, 1971-88. Bd. dirs. Madison Oakwood Retirement Ctr., 1983-89; com. mem. Wis. Legis. Study Elderly Abuse, 1985-88. Mem. AARP, Wis. Ret. Tchrs. Assn. (recording sec. 1983-89), AAUW, Nat. Honor Soc. Home Econs., Luth. Women Missionary League, Valparaiso U. Guild (state pres. 1981-85), Madison Civics Club. Lutheran. Home: 3709 Zwerg Dr Madison WI 53705-5229

SCHMIDT, MARY ELIZABETH, mathematics educator; b. Hamilton, Ohio, Nov. 28, 1963; d. W. Frederick and Dorothy Elizabeth (Brandhoff) Schmidt. B in secondary math. edn., Miami U., 1986. Math. tchr. Lakota H.S., West Chester, Ohio, 1986—. Mem. Nat. Coun. Tchrs. Math., Ohio Coun. Tchrs. Math. Home: 4118 Privet Ct Hamilton OH 45011 Office: Lakota HS 5050 Tylersville Rd West Chester OH 45069

SCHMIDT, MERRY SUE, elementary school educator; b. St. Louis, Dec. 25, 1946; d. William Fred and Elizabeth Mae (Clay) S. BS in Early Childhood Edn., U. Mo., 1970; MA in Edn., Lindenwood Coll., 1984. Elem. tchr. Wentzville (Mo.) R-IV Sch., 1970—. Mem. Internat. Reading Assn., Alpha Delta Kappa. Office: Wentzville R-IV Sch Dist One Campus Dr Wentzville MO 63385

SCHMIDT, PATRICIA FAIN, nurse educator; b. Chgo., June 17, 1941; d. Lawrence D. and Catherine B. (Schira) Fain; m. Donald W. Schmidt, July 16, 1966; children: Kathryn, Kristine, Michael. BSN, Coll. of St. Teresa, 1963; MSN, Marquette U., 1965; EdD, U.S. Internat. U., 1981. Instr. Coll. of St. Teresa, Winona, Minn.; asst. prof. San Diego State U.; interim dean for mathematics and natural and health scis. Palomar Coll., San Marcos, Calif. Mem. Sigma Theta Tau. Home: 12573 Utopia Way San Diego CA 92128-2229

SCHMIDT, RUTH ANN, college president emerita; b. Mountain Lake, Minn., Sept. 16, 1930; d. Jacob A. and Anna A. (Ewert) S. B.A., Augsburg Coll., Mpls., 1952; M.A., U. Mo., 1955; Ph.D., U. Ill., 1962; LLD, Gordon Coll., 1987. Asst. prof. Spanish Mary Baldwin Coll., Staunton, Va., 1955-58; asst. prof. Spanish SUNY-Albany, 1962-67, assoc. prof., 1967-78, dean of humanities, 1971-76; prof. and provost Wheaton Coll., Norton, Mass., 1978-82; pres. Agnes Scott Coll., Decatur, Ga., 1982-94; pres. emerita Agnes Scott Coll.,, Decatur, Ga., 1994—; chair Women's Coll. Coalition, 1986-88. Author: Ortega Munilla y sus novelas, 1973, Cartas entre dos amigos del teatro, 1969. Trustee Gordon Coll., Wenham, Mass., 1980-86, Lyon Coll., 1993—; bd. dirs. DeKalb C. of C., 1982-85, Atlanta Coll. Art, 1984-94; mem. exec. com. Women's Coll. Coalition, 1983-88; v.p. So. Univ. Conf., 1993. Named Disting. Alumna Augsburg Coll., 1973. Mem. Assn. Am. Colls. (dir. 1979-82, treas. 1982-83), Soc. Values in Higher Edn., Am. Coun. Edn. (commn. on women in higher edn. 1985-88), AAUW, Assn. Pvt. Colls. and Univs. Ga. (pres. 1987-89), Internat. Women's Forum, Young Women's Christian Assn. Acad. Women Achievers. Democrat. Presbyterian.

SCHMIDT, RUTH A(NNA) M(ARIE), geologist; b. Bklyn., Apr. 22, 1916; d. Edward and Anna M. (Range) S. AB, NYU, 1936; MA, Columbia U., 1939, PhD, 1948. Cert. profl. geologist. Geologist U.S. Geol. Survey, Washington, 1943-56; dist. geologist U.S. Geol. Survey, Anchorage, 1956-63; prof., chmn. geology dept. U. Alaska, Anchorage, 1959-84; cons. geologist Anchorage, 1964—; lectr. Elder Hostels, Alaska Pacific U., Anchorage, 1988-89, U. Alaska, Anchorage, 1994; coord. Engring. Geol. Evaluating Group, Alaskan 1964 Earthquake, Anchorage, 1964; environ. cons. Trans Alaska Pipeline, Office of Gov., Anchorage, 1975-76. Editor: Alaska geology field trip guide books, 1984, 89; contbr. articles to profl. jours. Trustee, pres. Brooks Range Libr., Anchorage, 1979-91; bd. dirs., com. chmn. Anchorage Audubon Soc., 1989—; mem. exec. bd., chmn. various coms. Alaska Ctr. Environment, Anchorage. Fellow AAAS, Arctic Inst. N.Am. (bd. govs. 1983-94), Geol. Soc. Am.; mem. Am. Inst. Profl. Geologists (charter), Am. Assn. Petroleum Geologists, Internat. Geol. Congress (del.), Alaska Geol. Soc. (hon. life mem., bd. dirs. 1993-95), Sigma Xi.

SCHMIDT, SANDRA JEAN, financial analyst; b. Limestone, Maine, Mar. 21, 1955; d. Dale Laban and Marie Audrey (Bailey) Winters; m. Lee Lloyd Schmidt, Oct. 20, 1973; children: Colby Lee, Katrina Leesa. AA summa cum laude, Anne Arundel Community Coll., 1987; BS summa cum laude, U. Balt., 1990. CPA, Md. Enlisted U.S. Army, 1973, traffic analyst, 1973-85, resigned, 1985; auditor Md. State Office of Legislative Audits, Balt., 1990-93; fin. analyst Md. Ins. Adminstrn., Balt., 1993—. Tutor Anne Arundel County Literacy Coun., Pasadena, Md., 1990—; mentor U. Balt., 1991; host family Am. Intercultural Student Exchange, 1992—. Mem. AICPA, Am. Soc. Women Accts., Md. Assn. CPAs, Soc. Fin. Examiners, U. Balt. Alumni Assn., Alpha Chi, Beta Gamma Sigma, Phi Theta Kappa. Republican. Baptist. Home: 7716 Pinyon Rd Hanover MD 21076-1585

SCHMIDT, SUSAN MARY, school counselor, education consultant to industry; b. L.I., N.Y., Feb. 5; d. Joseph and Emma (Brunner) Bebon; m. Frederick Karl Schmidt, Feb. 5, 1966; children: Diane, Derek. BS, U. Fla., 1963; MEd, N.C. State U., 1983, EdD, 1991. Cert. counselor, N.C.; nat. cert. counselor. Tchr. sci. Pub. Schs. in Fla., Va., N.C., 1963-82; guidance supr. Wake County Pub. Schs., Raleigh, N.C., 1988; guidance counselor Wake County Pub. Schs., Raleigh, 1989-91; edn. cons. Burroughs Welcome Co., Research Triangle Park, N.C., summers 1988-89. Mem. N.C. and Nat. Women's Polit. Caucus, Raleigh, 1987-91. Am. Soc. Biol. Chemists fellow, 1986. Mem. ASTD, ASCD, Am. Mental Health Counselors Assn., Am. Sch. Counselor Assn., Assn. Women in Sci., Career Devel. Counselors Assn., Employment Counselors Assn., Nat. Bd. Cert. Counselors, N.C. Bd. Registered Practicing Counselors,N.C. Sch. Counselors Asns., N.C. Assn. Educators. Roman Catholic. Home: 219 Queensferry Rd Cary NC 27511-6313

SCHMIT, SHARYN KEARNEY, secondary school educator; b. New Orleans, Sept. 10, 1945; d. William Frank and Mercedese Marie (Marks) Kearney; m. Kenneth Arthur Schmit, Dec. 29, 1973; children: Kenneth Kearney, Allison Katherine. BS, Southeastern La. U., 1967; MA, Ga. State U., 1971, Southeastern La. U., 1974. Tchr. Andrew Jackson High Sch., Chalmette, La., 1967-68, Floyd Jr. High Sch., Mableton, Ga., 1968-71, Lockett Elem. Sch., New Orleans, 1972-75, Jos. S. Clark Sr. High Sch., New Orleans, 1975-80; curriculum area specialist New Orleans Pub. Schs., 1980; tchr. Livingston Mid. Sch., New Orleans, 1980-81, Sixth Ward Jr. High Sch., Pearl River, La., 1981-82; tchr., dept. chair Northshore High Sch., Slidell, La., 1982—; cognitive coach tng. St. Tammany Parish, Covington, La., 1991—, prospective adminstr., math. articulation com. mem., 1992—; model career options La. State Dept. Edn., Baton Rouge, 1991-93; master tchr. assessor for intern tchrs., 1994—. Tchr. Sunday sch. 1st United Meth. Ch., Slidell, La., ch. edn. com.; active Girl Scouts Am., Slidell. Mem. Nat. Coun. Tchrs. Math., St. Tammany Fedn. Tchrs. Home: 97 Live Oak Dr Slidell LA 70461-1305 Office: Northshore High Sch 100 Panther Dr Slidell LA 70461-2326

SCHMITT, MARGARET SCHOMBURG, librarian; b. LaCrosse, Wis., Apr. 25, 1927; d. Frederick and Ida (Nuttleman) Schomburg; m. Elroy Henry Schmitt, Sept. 24, 1949; children: Katherine Anne, Lawrence Elroy. BA, U. Wis., 1948; MLS, Rosary Coll., River Forest, Ill., 1970. Ref. librarian, asst. libr. dir. LaGrange (Ill.) Pub. Libr., 1971-74; libr. dir. Alsip-Merrionette Park (Ill.) Pub. Libr., 1974-92; ret., 1992; mem. Ill. Authors Com., 1986-88; sec. Joint Advancement of Ill. Librs., 1987-89. Mem. ALA, Ill. Libr. Assn., South Suburban Libr. Assn. (pres. 1980-81), Phi Beta Kappa, Phi Kappa Phi, Beta Phi Mu. Lutheran. Home: 1409 W 53rd Pl La Grange IL 60525-6509

SCHMITT, MARILYN LOW, foundation program manager, art historian; b. Chgo., May 24, 1939; d. Abraham A. and Mae (Willett) Low. BA, Lawrence U., 1960; MA, U. Calif., Berkeley, 1962; PhD, Yale U., 1972. Instr. Dickinson Coll., Carlisle, Pa., 1964-66; acting instr. Yale Univ., New Haven, 1969-70; asst. prof. So. Conn. State U., New Haven, 1970-75; assoc. prof. U. Miami, Coral Gables, Fla., 1976-82; program officer J. Paul Getty Trust, L.A., 1983-85; program mgr. Getty Info. Inst., Santa Monica, Calif., 1985—; ex-officio bd. dirs. Recovery, Inc., Chgo., 1971—; 1st v.p. Abraham A. Low Inst., Chgo., 1989—. Author: Random Reliefs and Primitive Friezes: Re-used Sources of Romanesque Sculpture?, 1981, The Siren Song of Cybermedia, 1993; co-author: Object, Image, Inquiry: The Art Historian at Work, 1988; co-editor: Report on Data Processing Projects in Art, 1988. Recipient Woodrow Wilson fellowship, 1960-61, AAUW fellowship, 1968-69, NEH fellowship for ind. rsch., 1981-82. Mem. Coll. Art Assn. Am., Art Librs. Soc. N.Am., Phi Beta Kappa. Home: 1440 Veteran Ave Apt 362 Los Angeles CA 90024-4832 Office: Getty Art History Info Program 401 Wilshire Blvd Ste 1100 Santa Monica CA 90401-1430

SCHMITT, MARLENE LOUISE, healthcare executive; b. Wheeling, W.Va., July 7, 1933; d. D. Joseph and Ruth (Bryer) Greschner; m. Raymond J. Schmitt, July 3, 1954; children: Louise Ann, Raymond D. Student, U. Calif., Santa Cruz, 1992. Cert. master practioner in neuro-linguistic program Soc. Neuro-Linguistic Programming. Pres. Watkins & Trott, Inc., Wheeling, 1972—; founder TERRAP Program (now Anxiety and Panic Disorders Ctr. W.Va.), 1984—; presenter workshops in field; founder, developer Mindfulness-Based Stress Reduction Program, Wheeling, 1995. Named Leading Bus. Woman, Wheeling, 1986. Office: Anxiety and Panic Disorders Ctr PO Box 383 Wheeling WV 26003

SCHMITT, NANCY CAIN, public and corporate relations executive, writer; b. Fayetteville, N.C., June 12, 1942; d. Carlton White and Cleo Margaret (Parnell) Cain; m. Louis Dennis Schmitt, July 13, 1974 (div.). BA, Wake Forest U., 1960-64. Intern Winston-Salem (N.C.) Jour.-Sentinel, 1963-64; reporter Gastonia (N.C.) Gazette, 1964-66; copy editor, reporter Twin City Sentinel, Winston-Salem, 1966-67; entertainment editor Fayetteville Observer, 1967-78; lifestyle editor Anchorage Times, 1978-83; pub. rels. specialist Multivisions Cable TV Co., Anchorage, 1983-84; editor Alaska Jour. of Commerce, Anchorage, 1984-85; sr. comms. specialist U.S. Postal Svc., 1985—. Author: How to Care for Your Car: A Women's Guide to Car Care in Alaska, 1978 (award 1979); mem. editorial bd. Episc. Diocean of Alaska, Fairbanks, 1983-86; contbr. articles to profl. jours. and nat. publs. Recipient Asst. Postmaster Gen.'s award for excellence, USPS Legis. Affairs Corp. Rel. Sr. VP Opportunity award, Op-Ed Writing award. Mem. Nat. Fedn. Press Women (bd. mem. 1990-91), Pub. Rels. Soc. Am., Alaska Press Women (pres. treas., sec., communicator of achievement, recipient numerous awards), Alaska Press Club (recipient 3 awards), Rotary Internat. (bd. dirs. 1991-92). Home: 6716 E 16th Ave Apt A Anchorage AK 99504-2513 Office: U S Postal Svc Corp Rels 3720 Barrow St Anchorage AK 99599-0041

SCHMITZ, DOLORES JEAN, primary education educator; b. River Falls, Wis., Dec. 27, 1931; d. Otto and Helen Olive (Webster) Kreuziger; m. Karl Matthias Schmitz Jr., Aug. 18, 1956; children: Victoria Jane, Karl III. BS, U. Wis., River Falls, 1953; MS, Nat. Coll. Edn., 1982; postgrad., U. Minn., Mankato, 1969, U. Melbourne, Australia, 1989, U. Wis., Milw., 1989, Carroll Coll., 1990, Cardinal Stritch, 1990. Cert. tchr., Wis. Tchr. Manitowoc (Wis.) Pub. Schs., 1953-56, West Allis (Wis.) Pub. Schs., 1956-59, Lowell Sch., Milw., 1960-63, Victory Sch., Milw., 1964; tchr. Palmer Sch., Milw., 1966-84, 86-94, unit leader, 1984-86; ret., 1994; co-organizer Headstart Tchg. Staff Assn., Milw., 1968; insvc. organizer Headstart and Early Childhood, Milw., 1969-92; pilot tchr. for Whole Lang., Hi-Scope and Math. Their Way, 1988-93; bd. dirs. Cuurriculum Devel. Ctr. of Milw. Edn. Ctr., 1993-94. Author: (curriculum) Writing to Read, 1987, Cooperation and Young Children (ERIC award 1982), Kindergarten Curriculum, 1953. Former supporter Milw. Art Mus., Milw. Pub. Mus., Milw. County Zoo, Whitefish Bay Pub. Libr., Earthwatch Riveredge Nature Ctr.; vol. fgn. visitor program Milw. Internat. Inst., 1966-94, holiday folk fair, 1976-94, Earthwatch, 1989; lobbyist Milw. Pub. Sch. Bd. and State of Wis., 1986-93; coord. comty. vols., 1990-94. Grantee Greater Milw. Ednl. Trust, 1989. Mem. NEA (life), ASCD, Milw. Kindergarten Assn. (rec. sec. 1986-93), Nat. Assn. for Edn. of Young Children, Tchrs. Applying Whole Lang., Wis. Early Childhood Assn., Milw. Tchrs. Ednl. Assn. (co-chmn. com. early childhood 1984-86), Assn. for Childhood Edn. Internat. (charter pres. Manitowoc chpt. 1955-56), Milw. Educating Computer Assn., Alpha Psi Omega. Roman Catholic. Home: 312 8th Ave Apt 1 Tierra Verde FL 33715-1800

SCHMITZ, MARIANN, infection control specialist; b. Sept. 8, 1956; d. Paul E. and Mary J. (Macchi) S.; m. Charles J. Thompson, July 24, 1993. BS in Med. Tech., U. Ala., Tuscaloosa, 1978; MPH, U. Ala., Birmingham, 1985. Cert. in infection control Certification Bd. of Infection Control. Med. technologist U. Ala. Birmingham Hosps., 1978-85; epidemiology specialist Cooper Green Hosp., Birmingham, 1985—; infection control cons. South Haven Nursing Home, Birmingham, 1995—. Citizen's adv. Jefferson County Assn. for Retarded Citizens, 1979-81; bd. dirs. AIDS Task Force Ala., 1988. Mem. Assn. Profls. in Infection Control and Epidemiology (pres. Ala. State chpt. 1991), Alpha Eta. Office: Cooper Green Hosp 1515 6th Ave S Birmingham AL 35233

SCHMITZ, MARY MARGARET, educational development director, consultant; b. Sauk Centre, Minn., July 30, 1954; d. Arthur Frank and Eileen Barbara (Johnston) S.; m. Roger Ray Mehling, Sept. 10, 1983; stepchildren: Chad Mehling, Jason Mehling. BS, U. Minn., 1976, postgrad., 1981. Lic. tchr., Minn. Child care counselor Bethany Children's Home, Duluth, 1976-78; tchr. Duluth Pub. Schs., 1978-80, U. Minn., Duluth, 1980-81; therapeutic recreation specialist Courage Ctr., Duluth, 1981-85; mktg. and devel. dir. Polinsky Med. Rehab. Ctr., Duluth, 1985-89; devel. dir. Holy Rosary Sch., Duluth, 1989-94, Cathedral Sch., Superior, Wis., 1994—; cons. Mary M. Schmitz Consulting, Duluth, 1989—; Nat. Conf. Children's Program dir. Spina Bifida Assn. Am., Washington, 1989-94; endowment dir. Cathedral of Our Lady of the Rosary, Duluth, 1992—. Bd. dirs., pres. YMCA, Duluth, 1987-93, 90-92. Named Coach of Yr., Nat. Women's Sports Found., 1983. Mem. Nat. Soc. Fund Raising Execs., Lake Superior Fund Raising Execs. (co-chair 1992-94). Roman Catholic. Home: 4146 Charles Rd Duluth MN 55803

SCHMITZ, SHIRLEY GERTRUDE, marketing and sales executive; b. Brackenridge, Pa., Dec. 19, 1927; d. Wienand Gerard and Florence Marie (Grimm) S. BA, Ariz. State U., 1949. Tchr., guidance counselor Mesa High Sch., Ariz., 1949-51; area mgr. Field Enterprises Ednl. Corp., Phoenix, 1951-52, dist. mgr., 1952, regional mgr., 1953-55, br. mgr., Montreal, Que., Can., 1955-61, nat. supr., Chgo., 1961-63, asst. sales mgr., 1963-65, nat. sales mgr., 1965-70; v.p., gen. sales mgr. F.E. Compton Co. div. Ency. Brit., Chgo., 1970-71, exec. v.p., dir. sales, 1971-73; pres. CHB Port-A-Book Store, Inc., 1973-76; gen. mgr. Bobbs-Merrill Co., Inc., Indpls., 1976-82; v.p. sales U.S. Telephone Communications of Midwest, Inc., Chgo., 1982-83; exec. v.p. sales and market devel. Entertainment Publs., Corp., Birmingham, Mich., 1983-89, sr. v.p. mktg. and sales, Troy, Mich., 1989-92; prin. S.G. Schmitz and Assocs., Chgo., 1992—; bd. dirs. Ariz. Tech. Incubator; bd. advisors Ctr. Advancement of Small Bus., Ariz. State U. Sch. Bus; bd. dirs. Spectral, Inc., Colourtech, Inc. Recipient Twin award Nat. Bd. YWCA, 1987. Recipient Honors award Beta Gamma Sigma, 1995, Disting. Achievement award Sch. Bus. Ariz. State U., 1995; Angel award Nat. Assn. Women Bus. Owners, 1996. Mem. USGA (assoc.), Internat. Platform Assn., Am. Mgmt. Assn., Nat. Bus. Incubation Assn., Nat. Geographic Soc., Nat. Space Soc., World Future Soc., Ariz. State U. Alumni Assn. Republican. Roman Catholic. Home: 93 Miller Rd Lake Zurich IL 60047-1395

SCHMOLDER, EULALIA LEFFERS, food and nutrition educator; b. Omaha, July 4, 1919; d. Fred John and Ida Martha (Meyer) Leffers; m. Carl James Schmolder, Sept. 15, 1950. BS, Ohio State U., 1943; MS, Tex. Woman's U., 1967, PhD, 1969. Registered and lic. dietitian, Tex. Dietitian dormitory food svc. Ohio State U., Columbus, 1944-49; dir. food svc. Deshler Walleck Hotel, Columbus, 1949-50; dietitian Dallas Ind. Sch. Dist., 1951-58, 59-60, 1965-66; grad. asst. food preparation labs. Tex. Woman's U., Denton, 1967-68, from asst. to assoc. prof., 1969-70, 78; dir. dietetics Baylor U. Med. Ctr., Dallas, 1970-73; asst. prof. home econs. Sam Houston State U., Huntsville, Tex., 1975-81; ret., 1981, presenter in field food and nutrition, , 1981—; with food svc. mgmt. dept. Parkland Meml. Hosp., Dallas, part-time 1950, 51-53. Author: Organization and Management of a Hospital Department of Dietetics, 1985. Vol. Sr. Citizens Cmty. Ctr., Ferris, Tex., 1992, Ellis county and nat. polit. candidates, 1992—, Nursing Home, Ferris, 1992-93; tchr. Bible studies, 1992; sec. United Meth. Women, 1992—. Faculty grantee Sam Houston State U. Mem. Am. Dietetic Assn., Am. Home Econ. Assn., Tex. Dietetic Assn., Tex. Nutrition Coun., Dallas Dietetic Assn., Dallas Dietetic Assn. Cons. Interest Group, Soc. Nutrition Edn., Nutrition Today Soc., Ea. Star (officer 1992-93), 3 Garden Club (v.p. 1992-93), Book Rev. Club (pres. 1993—). Methodist. Home and Office: 1200 S Interstate Highway 45 Ferris TX 75125-8106

SCHMOLDT, PEGGY SUE, cosmetology educator; b. International Falls, Minn., Apr. 11, 1959; d. John Herbert and Elizabeth Ann (Powers) Hauptli; m. Stephen Michael Schmoldt, Jan. 5, 1980 (div. Feb. 1996); children: Jillian Marie, Megan Elizabeth. Student, U. Iowa, 1977-78; diploma, Capri Cosmetology Coll., 1979; student, Regis U., 1993—. Lic. cosmetologist, Colo., Fla.; cert. pvt. cosmetology tchr., vo-tech. tchr., Colo. Hair designer Fashion Ave., Dubuque, Iowa, 1979-81, LaVonne's, Denver, 1981-83, A Unique Boutique, Destrehan, La., 1984-85, V.I.P. Salon, Boca Raton, Fla., 1987-89; sch. mgr., instr. LaVonne's Acad. of Beauty, Denver, 1981-83; nat. platform educator Anion Labs., Inc., Harvey, La., 1984-85; salon mgr., designer, publ. rels. specialist, educator Lord & Taylor Salons, Boynton Beach/Boca Raton, Fla., 1985-87; dir. edn. Cantwell/Creative Sch. Beauty, Pompano Beach, Fla., 1988-91; dir. cosmetology edn. Boca Raton Inst., 1991-92; freelance cosmetologist, educator Profl. Salon Svcs., Westminster, Colo., 1993—; mem., educator La. Hair Fashion Com., New Orleans, 1985; tchr. Le Team Styles Group, Ft. Lauderdale, Fla., 1986-87; mem. Colo. Edn. Com., Denver, 1993; educator Inter Mountain Beauty Supply, Denver, 1995; cosmetology educator Inst. Hair Design, Arvada, Colo., 1996—; mem. Nexxus Design Team, 1994, Nat. Hair Am., 1994. Pres. New Orleans Cosmetology Assn., 1984; treas., membership chair Palm Beach Cosmetology Assn., 1986-88; vol. Look Good-Feel Better program Am. Cancer Soc., Palm Beach/Broward County, Fla., 1989, Denver, 1993; mem. nat. planning com. trainer's panel LGFB, 1995; sec., mem. legislation/edn. com. Broward County Cosmetology Assn., 1990-92; mem. spkrs. bur. Planned Parenthood of Rocky Mountains, Denver, 1993. Mem. Denver Cosmetology Assn. (pres. 1993, 94), Colo. Cosmetology Assn. (3d v.p. 1993, 1st v.p. 1994, mem. legislation/by-laws com., pres. 1995=96). Roman Catholic.

SCHNABEL, DANA CAROL, elementary education educator; b. Albertville, Ala., Apr. 16, 1965; d. Danny Bruce and Carolyn Joan (Childers) Snow; m. Jeffrey Allen Schnabel, Oct. 11, 1986; 1 child, Berend Vaughn. BS, Bob Jones U., 1986; BA, Met. State Coll. Denver, 1991; MA in Curriculum and Instrn., U. Colo., 1996. Head tchr. Children's World Daycare, Aurora, Colo., 1987-88; kindergarten tchr. Country Presch., Littleton, Colo., 1988-90; tutor, advisor Met. State Coll. Denver, 1990-91; substitute tchr. Adams and Jefferson Counties, 1991; classroom tchr. Jefferson County Schs., Lakewood, Colo., 1991—; presenter in field. Election judge Rep. Party, Denver. Mem. Nat. Coun. Tchrs. Math., Profl. Alternative Consortium for Tchrs., Kappa Delta Pi. Republican. Home: 2726 S Linley Ct Denver CO 80236

SCHNACK, GAYLE HEMINGWAY JEPSON (MRS. HAROLD CLIFFORD SCHNACK), corporate executive; b. Mpls., Aug. 14, 1926; d. Jasper Jay and Ursula (Hemingway) Jepson; student U. Hawaii, 1946; m. Harold Clifford Schnack, Mar. 22, 1947; children: Jerrald Jay, Georgina, Roberta, Michael Clifford. Skater, Shipstad & Johnson Ice Follies, 1944-46; v.p. Harcliff Corp., Honolulu, 1964—, Schnack Indsl. Corp., Honolulu, 1969—, Nutmeg Corp., Cedar Corp.; ltd. ptnr. Koa Corp. Mem. Internat. Platform Assn., Beta Sigma Phi (chpt. pres. 1955-56, pres. city council 1956-57). Established Ursula Hemingway Jepson art award, Carlton Coll., Ernest Hemingway creative writing award, U. Hawaii. Office: PO Box 3077 Honolulu HI 96802-3077 also: 1200 Riverside Dr Reno NV 89503

SCHNALL, BELLA, lawyer; b. Phila., June 23, 1951; d. Charles and Flora (Snyder) S.; m. Eric L. Frank, Nov. 10, 1985; children: Rachel Schnall Frank, Deborah Schnall Frank. BA, U. Pa., 1972, JD, 1976. Bar: Pa. 1976, Mass. 1979. Staff atty. U. Mass. Legal Svcs., Springfield, 1976-82; clin. prof., lectr. Law Sch. U. Pa., Phila., 1982-86; atty. Phila., 1986—. Mem., bd. dirs. Family Planning Coun.-S.E.P.A., Phila., 1982—; vol. atty. Phila. Vols. Indigent, 1988—. Mem. Phila. Bar Assn. Jewish. Home: 722 W Sedgwick St Philadelphia PA 19119 Office: 1420 Walnut St Ste 1500 Philadelphia PA 19102

SCHNALL, EDITH LEA (MRS. HERBERT SCHNALL), microbiologist, educator; b. N.Y.C., Apr. 11, 1922; d. Irving and Sadie (Raab) Spitzer; AB, Hunter Coll., 1942; AM, Columbia U., 1947, PhD, 1967; m. Herbert Schnall, Aug. 21, 1949; children: Neil David, Carolyn Beth. Clin. pathologist Roosevelt Hosp., N.Y.C., 1942-44; instr. Adelphi Coll., Garden City, N.Y., 1944-46; asst. med. mycologist Columbia Coll. Physicians and Surgeons, N.Y.C., 1946-47, 49-50; instr. Bklyn. Coll., 1947; mem. faculty Sarah Lawrence Coll., Bronxville, N.Y., 1947-48; lectr. Hunter Coll., N.Y.C., 1947-67; adj. assoc. prof. Lehman Coll., City U. N.Y., 1968; asst. prof. Queensborough Community Coll., City U. N.Y., 1967, assoc. prof. microbiology, 1968-75, prof., 1975—, adminstr. Med. Lab. Tech. Program, 1985—; vis. prof. Coll. Physicians and Surgeons, Columbia U., N.Y.C., 1974; advanced biology examiner U. London, 1970—. Mem. Alley Restoration Com., N.Y.C., 1971—; mem. legis. adv. com. Assembly of the State of N.Y., 1972. Mem. Community Bd. 11, Queens, N.Y., 1974—, 3d vice-chmn., 1987-92, 2nd vice chmn., 1992—; public dir. of bd. dirs. Inst. Continuing Dental Edn. Queens County, Dental Soc. N.Y. State and ADA, 1973—. Rsch. fellow NIH, 1948-49; faculty rsch. fellow, grantee-in-aid Rsch. Found. of SUNY, 1968-70; faculty rsch. grant Rsch. Found. City U. N.Y., 1971-74. Mem. Internat. Soc. Human and Animal Mycology, AAAS, Am. Soc. Microbiology (coun., N.Y.C. br. 1981—, co-chairperson ann. meeting com. 1981-82, chair program com. 1982-83, v.p. 1984-86, pres. 1986-88), Med. Mycology Soc. N.Y. (sec.-treas. 1967-68, v.p. 1968-69, 78-79, archivist 1974—, fin. advisor 1983—, pres. 1969-70, 79-80, 81-82), Bot. Soc. Am., Med. Mycology Soc. Americas, Mycology Soc. Am., N.Y. Acad. Scis., Sigma Xi, Phi Sigma. Clubs: Torrey Botanical (N.Y. State); Queensborough Community Coll. Women's (pres. 1971-73) (N.Y.C.). Editor: Newsletter of Med. Mycology Soc. N.Y., 1969-85; founder, editor Female Perspective newsletter of Queensborough Community Coll. Women's Club, 1971-73. Home: 21406 29th Ave Flushing NY 11360-2622

SCHNEIDER, ADELE SANDRA, clinical geneticist; b. Johannesburg, South Africa, Mar. 21, 1949; came to U.S., 1976, naturalized, 1981; d. Michael and Annette (Sive) S.; m. Gordon Mark Cohen, July 2, 1978; children: Jeffrey, Brian, Adrienne. MB, BChir, Witwatersrand U., Johannesburg, South Africa, 1973. Intern in internal medicine Baragwanath Hosp., Johannesburg, 1974, intern in gen. surgery, 1974; sr. house officer in pediatrics Coronation Hosp., Johannesburg, 1975; sr. house officer in radiation therapy Johannesburg Gen. Hosp., 1975-76; resident in pediatrics Wilmington (Del.) Med. Ctr., 1976-78; fellow in clin. genetics and metabolic diseases Children's Hosp. of Phila., 1978-81, staff physician Cystic Fibrosis Clinic, 1987-88; staff pediatrician Children's Rehab. Hosp., Phila., 1981-82, dir. pediatrics, 1982-87, acting med. dir., 1984-85; clin. instr. dept. pediatrics Jefferson Med. Coll., Phila., 1982-84, clin. asst. prof. dept. pediatrics, 1984—; clin. geneticist Hahnemann Univ. Hosp., Phila., 1987-90, asst. clin. prof. dept. pediatrics and neoplastic diseases, 1987-90; clin. geneticist Albert Einstein Med. Ctr., Phila., 1990-92, acting dir. med. genetics, 1992-93, dir. clin. genetics program, 1993—; mem. courtesy faculty Sch. Medicine Temple U., Phila., 1987; clin. geneticist St. Christopher's Hosp. for Children, Phila., 1987; genetics cons. dept. pediatrics Bryn Mawr (Pa.) Hosp.; presenter, lectr. in field. Contbr. articles to profl. jours. Bd. dirs. Phila. Parenting Associates, 1986-93. Fellow Am. Coll. Med. Genetics; mem. Am. Soc. Human Genetics, Am. Chem. Soc. Office: Albert Einstein Med Ctr Dept Pediatrics 5501 Old York Rd Philadelphia PA 19141-3001

SCHNEIDER, CARMEN MARIE, elementary school educator; b. Plymouth, Wis., Oct. 10, 1970; d. Allen Roy and Patricia Margaret (Olsson) S. BS in Edn., Alverno Coll., Milw., 1993. Cert. tchr., Wis. Field student U.S. Grant Elem. Sch., Sheboygan, Wis., 1989; swim instr. Sheboygan Falls (Wis.) YMCA, 1990-91, Sports Core Health Club, Kohler, Wis., 1991; field student Mitchell Elem. Sch., Milw., 1991, St. Alphonsus Elem. Sch., Glendale, Wis., 1991, Greenfield (Wis.) Middle Sch., 1992; student tchr. Fairview Elem. Sch., Milw., 1992, St. Mary's Parish Sch., Hales Corners, Wis., 1992-93; case mgr. Rehab. Ctr. of Sheboygan, Inc., 1993—; writing asst. Alverno Coll. Writing Ctr., Milw., 1992—. Recipient Alverno Presdl. Merit award, 1992. Mem. NEA, Wis. Edn. Assn. Republican. Lutheran. Home: 835 Mead Ave Sheboygan WI 53081 Office: Rehab Ctr of Sheboygan Inc 1305 St Clair Ave Sheboygan WI 53082

SCHNEIDER, CHRISTINE LYNN, customs inspector; b. Staten Island, N.Y., Feb. 3, 1960; d. Howard Thomas and Ina Elise (Beyer) S. BS, SUNY Maritime Coll., Bronx, 1984. Lic. 3d mate, U.S. Mcht. Marine; cert. U.S. customs firearms instr. Sr. inspector U.S. Customs Svc., San Diego, 1989—. Served to lt. comdr. USNR, 1984-87, 91—. Democrat. Lutheran. Home: 2940 Alta View Dr Apt F202 San Diego CA 92139-3365 Office: US Customs Svc 720 E San Ysidro Blvd San Ysidro CA 92173-3115

SCHNEIDER, ELAINE FOGEL, special education educator, consultant; b. Bklyn., Mar. 6, 1947; d. Maurice Seymour and Lillian (Marowitz) F.; m. Jack Schneider, June 12, 1977; 1 child, Karli. BA, Hunter Coll., 1967; MA, Queens Coll., 1969, NYU, 1977; PhD, Calif. Coast U., 1985. Cert. tchr.; registered dance/movement therapist. Speech-lang. pathologist N.Y. Dept. Edn., 1969-72; dir. Dance Theatre, Coconut Grove, Fla., 1972-75; chairperson Lancaster (Calif.) Sch. Dist., 1978-81; exec. dir. Antelope Valley Lang. Movement Therapy, Lancaster, 1981—, Antelope Valley Infant Devel., Lancaster, 1983—. Author: Pictures Please! Adult Language Supplement, 1990, The Power of Touch: Infant Message, 1995, In Infants and Young Children, 1996; contbr. articles to profl. jours.. Bd. dirs. Families for Families Resource Ctr., Lancaster, 1993—, United Way, Lancaster, 1988—; mem. adv. bd. L.A. County Child Care, 1991—; mem. L.A. County teen pregnancy program State of Calif. Interagy. Coord. Coun., 1988—, state coun. appointee, 1988—; mem. Assistance League of Antelope Valley, 1992-94. Recipient L.A. County award Bd. Suprs., 1993, People Who Make a Difference award Antelope Valley Press, 1994; grantee March of Dimes, 1993. Mem. Am. Speech-Lang.-Hearing Assn.cert. infant massage instr., dir.-elect dist. 7), Am. Dancer therapy assn., Am. Speech-Lang. Pathologists in Pvt. Practice, Infant Devel. Assn., Nat. Assn. for Edn. Young Children, So. Calif. Assn. Edn. of Young Children, Rotary. Office: Antelope Valley Infant Dev 1051 W Avenue M Ste 205 Lancaster CA 93534-8156

SCHNEIDER, ELEONORA FREY, physician; b. Basel, Switzerland, Jan. 17, 1921; came to U.S., 1952; d. Friedrich Ernst and Clara Melanie (Heiz) Frey; m. Jurg Adolf Schneider, Aug. 22, 1946; children: Andreas George, Daphne Eleanor, Diana Veronica, Claudia Elizabeth. MD, U. Basel, 1945. Lic. MD. Pharmacologist Sandoz Pharms., Basel, 1946-47; resident in anesthesiology U. Hosp., Basel, 1950-51; resident Pediatric Dept. Del. Div., Wilmington, 1971-73; physician Wilmington Pub Schs., 1973-79, Pub. Health, Wilmington, 1975-80; staff physician student health svc. U. Del., Newark, 1979—; v.p. Pharmacon, Inc., Wilmington, 1985—. Contbr. articles to profl. jours. V.p. del. Citizens for Clean Air, 1969-71; mem. com. Gov.'s Adv. Coun. for Exceptional Children, Dover, Del.; mem. adv. panel YWCA; vol. Girl Scouts U.S.A., ARC. Mem. AAUW (study group leader 1966-67, area chmn. community problems 1967-69, edn. com. 1968-69, new mems. advisor 1969-70, bd. dirs. 1967-70), AMA, Am. Acad. Pediatrics, Med. Soc. Del., New Castle County Med. Soc. Republican.

SCHNEIDER, GAIL ALPERN, bank executive. Sr. v.p. Chase Manhatten Bank, N.Y.C., 1991—. Office: Chase Manhattan Corp 350 Park Ave 7th Fl New York NY 10022-1000*

SCHNEIDER, GRETA SARA, economist, financial consultant; b. Bklyn., May 26, 1954; d. Irving Victor and Anne Joyce (Goldberg) S. BA, MA, CUNY, 1975, MA, 1976, PhD, 1977. Writer, cons. Pitts., 1972-73; cons. Flushing, N.Y., 1973-85; sr. writer, cons. Buck Cons. Inc., N.Y.C., 1985-86; chmn., CEO Schneider Cons. Inc., N.Y.C., 1986-90; pvt. cons. Greta Schneider Cons., N.Y.C., 1991—; CEO Schneider Cons. Group, 1996—; lectr. The Learning Annex, 1995-96, others. Author: Exploding the Bankruptcy Mystique, 1993. Mem. Little Theatre Group, Marathon Cmty. Ctr., Little Neck, N.Y., 1980-83; founder, pres. Bankruptcy Anonymous, 1996; hon. mem. bd. dirs. Am. Biographical Inst. Nat. Adv. Bd., 1996. Cambridge Biographical Inst. fellow, 1993. Mem. AFTRA, Nat. Assn. Women Bus. Owners, Nat. Assn. Bus. Communicators, Internat. Platform Assn., Employee Assistance Profls. Assn., Soc. Human Resource Mgmt., U.S. C. of C., Writers Guild Am., Rotary. Home: 252-37 60th Ave Little Neck NY 11362-2423 Office: 130 W 30th St 5th Fl New York NY 10001-4004

SCHNEIDER, JANE HARRIS, sculptor; b. Trenton, N.J., Jan. 2, 1932; d. Leon Harris and Dorothy (Perlman) Rosenthal; m. Alfred R. Schneider, July 25, 1953; children: Lee, Jeffry, Elizabeth. BA, Wellesley Coll. Exhibited work in numerous group and one-person shows including June Kelly Gallery, 1988, 90, 93, 95, Nassau County Mus. Fine Art, Roslyn, N.Y., 1988, Alternative Mus., N.Y.C., 1985, Phila. Art Alliance, 1984, Atrium Gallery, St. Louis, 1993, 96, Bill Bace Gallery, 1992, Triplex Gallery, N.Y.C., 1991, Rockland Ctr. for Arts, West Nyack, N.Y., 1990, Hudson River Mus., Yonkers, N.Y., 1989, Sculpture Ctr., N.Y.C., 1988, many others; sculpture represented in numerous pub. and pvt. collections. Office and Studio: 75 Grand St New York NY 10013-2219

SCHNEIDER, JANET M., arts administrator, curator, painter; b. N.Y.C., June 6, 1950. d. August Arthur and Joan (Battaglia) S.; m. Michael Francis Sperendi, Sept. 21, 1985. BA summa cum laude, Queens Coll., CUNY, 1972; spl. study fine arts Boston U. Tanglewood Inst., 1971. With Queens Mus., Flushing, N.Y.C., 1973-89, curator, 1973-75, program dir., 1975-77, exec. dir., 1977-89. Collections arranged include: Sons and others, Women Artists See Men (author catalog), 1975, Urban Aesthetics (author catalog), 1976, Masters of the Brush, Chinese Painting and Calligraphy from the Sixteenth to the Nineteenth Century (co-author catalog), 1977, Symcho Moszkowicz: Portrait of the Artist in Postwar Europe (author catalog), 1978, Shipwrecked 1622, The Lost Treasure of Philip IV (author catalog), 1981, Michaelangelo: A Sculptor's World (author catalog), 1983, Joseph Cornell: Revisited (author catalog), 1992, Blueprint for Change: The Life and Times of Lewis H. Latimer (co-author catalog), 1995. Chmn. Cultural Instns. Group, N.Y.C., 1986-87; mem. N.Y.C. Commn. for Cultural Affairs, 1991-93; bd. dirs. N.Y.C. Partnership, 1987-88, Gallery Assn. N.Y. State 1979-81. Mem. Artists Choice Mus. (trustee 1979-82), Am. Assn. Mus., Phi Beta Kappa.

SCHNEIDER, JO ANNE, anthropologist, educator; b. Seattle, Jan. 11, 1959. BA, Lewis and Clark Coll., 1979; student, Montgomery Coll., 1980-81, George Washington Univ., 1980-81; MA, PhD, Temple Univ., 1988. Programmer, rschr. Westat, Inc., Rockville, Md., 1979-81; sr. rsch. assoc. Child Guidance Clinic, Phila., 1983; ethnohistorian Cultural Heritage Rsch. Svcs., Inc., Brookhaven, Pa., 1983-84; rsch. coord. Ctr. Rsch. on Acts of Man, Phila., 1985; rsch. asst. Phila. Geriatric Ctr., 1985-87; project coord., adj. asst. prof. anthrop. Temple Univ., Phila., 1988-91; program dir. Inst. for Sutdy of Civic Values, Phila., 1992-94, asst. dir., 1992—; adj. asst. prof. Holy Family Coll., 1993—; workshop leader. Co-author: (with Judith Goode) Reshaping Ethnic and Racial Relations in Philadelphia: Immigrants in a Racially Divided City, 1994; contbr. to books including Strructuring Diversity, 1992; contbr. to profl. jours., newspapers. Exec. dir. Bridges, Ctrl. Phila. Monthly Meeting of Friends, 1992—; bd. dirs. Friends Neighborhood Guild, 1992—; job developer, employment counselor, tchr. ESL, U.S. Cath. Conf. Penn-SERVE Cmty. Based Svc. Learning fellow, 1994-95. Mem. Soc. Anthrop. N.Am., Am. Anthrop. Assn. (Congl. fellow 1989-90), Soc. Applied Anthrop., Urban Anthrop. Assn. *

SCHNEIDER, KAREN LEE, psychotherapist; b. Houston, July 16, 1965; d. Robert Louis and Gloria Jean (Craft) S. B Religious Edn., Bayridge Christian Coll., 1991; MA, Houston Grad. Sch. Theology, 1991. Asst. dir., tchr. Tchrs. Listening to Children, Houston, 1987-91; asst. dir., psychotherapist TLC Counseling & Tng. Ctr., Houston, 1991—, co-developer esteem enhancing discipline, 1987, co-developer self-esteem measure for young children-TLC esteem scale, rschr., co-developer anti-violence/anti-gang program, 1991—; v.p., co-founder Luminé, Inc., Houston, 1989—; lectr. on esteem enhancing dipscipline, 1987—. Author: TLC Theory and Technique, 1991, (booklets) TLC Philosophy, 1993; contbr. articles to profl. jours.; appeared in TV news programs, 1991—. Psychotherapist Houston Pub. Schs., 1994-95; vol. psychotherapist Mayor's Anti-Gang Office, 1995, mem. summit meetings, 1994; vol. Houston Police Dept. Cmty. Outreach Dept., 1995-96. Recipient benefit concert Musicians Band Together to UnPlug Violence, Houston, 1995; grantee Amoco, 1995, Houston Endowment, 1995, Mayor's Anti-Gang Office, Houston, 1996. Mem. ACA, Assn. for Humanistic Edn. and Devel., Am. Mental Health Counselors Assn. Methodist. Office: TLC Counseling & Tng Ctr 50 Briar Hollow Ln Ste 303E Houston TX 77027

SCHNEIDER, KATHLEEN ANN, secondary school educator; b. Wisconsin Rapids, Wis., Jan. 5, 1949; d. Walter Edward and Darlene Emma (Schwoch) Reynolds; m. Gregory Russell Schneider, June 17, 1972; children: Gregory John. BA, Luther Coll., 1971; MED, Nat. Louis U., 1988. Cert. speech educator. Tchr. Sts. Mary and Joseph, Fond du Lac, Wis., 1973-75, St. Mary Sch., Pewaukee, Wis., 1975-78, Sch. Dist. Kettle Moraine, Wales, Wis., 1979—; writing coord. Sch. Dist. Kettle Moraine, Wales, 1988-93. Mem. WCTE, Nat. Coun. Tchrs. English (newsletter editor 1981, dir. 1994-97), Wis. Edn. Assn. Coun., Phi Delta Kappa. Roman Catholic. Home: 183 Willow Dr Hartland WI 53029-1313 Office: Kettle Moraine High Sch PO Box 902 Wales WI 53183-0902

SCHNEIDER, MARY LEA, college administrator. Student, Cardinal Stritch Coll., 1960-63; BA in Theology and Philosophy, Marquette U., 1966, MA in Theology, 1969, PhD in Religious Studies, 1971. Asst. prof. dept. religious studies Mich. State U., 1971-79, assoc. prof., 1979-84, prof., 1984-90, acting chair dept. religious studies, 1988-90; pres. Cardinal Stritch Coll., Milw., 1990—; vis. instr. theology dept. U. San Francisco, summer 1969, Creighton U., summers 1974-77; spkr., presenter papers, mem. seminars in field; cons. Lilly Endowment, 1988; various TV and radio interviews, 1985—. Contbr. articles, revs. to profl. publs. Trustee Pub. Policy Forum; mem. program Peter Favre Forum; mem. Greater Milw. Com. NEH travel grantee, 1986-87, 1990, rsch. grantee Coll. Arts and Letters Mich. State U., 1987-88. Mem. Am. Acad. Religion (chair Thomas Merton consultation 1979-81), Coll. Theology Soc. (chair Detroit-Cleve. region 1975-77, mem. com. on membership and objectives 1977-79, program dir., chair ann. conv. 1981-84, 88, convenor ecclesiology sect. ann. conv. 1984-87, pres. 1988-90, bd. dirs. 1990-92), Cath. Theol. Soc. Am., Am. Cath. Hist. Soc., History of Women in Religious Network, Tempo, Wis. Assn. Ind. Colls. and Univs. (exec. com. 1995—). Home: 225 W Bradley Rd Milwaukee WI 53217 Office: Cardinal Stritch Coll 6801 N Yates Rd Milwaukee WI 53217

SCHNEIDER, PHYLLIS LEAH, writer, editor; b. Seattle, Apr. 19, 1947; d. Edward Lee Booth and Harriet Phyllis (Ebbinghaus) Russell; m. Clifford Donald Schneider, June 14, 1969; 1 child, Pearl Brooke. B.A., Pacific Luth. U., 1969; M.A., U. Wash., 1972. Fiction, features editor Seventeen Mag., N.Y.C., 1975-80; mng. editor Weight Watchers Mag., N.Y.C., 1980-81; editor YM mag., N.Y.C., 1981-86. Author: Parents Book of Infant Colic, 1990, Kids Who Make a Difference, 1993, Straight Talk on Women's Health: How to Get the Health Care You Deserve, 1993, Hot Health Care Careers, 1993, What Kids Like To Do, 1993. Recipient Centennial Recognition award Pacific Luth. U., 1990. Democrat. Episcopalian.

SCHNEIDER, SYLVIA ISAACSON, retired psychological counselor; b. N.Y.C., Dec. 12, 1915; d. Harry and Rebecca Isaacson; m. Aaron David Schneider, Dec. 29, 1934 (dec. Jan. 1973); children: Judith Schneider Wertheimer, Deborah Schneider Poleshuck. BA in English, NYU, 1936; MS in Edn., CUNY, 1963. Rehab. counselor Divsn. Vocat. Rehab.-N.J. State, 1963-83, mgr. Union County, 1977-81, mgr. Passaic County, 1981-83; past pres. No. N.J. Nat. Rehab. Assn., 1979-83. Vol. bereavement counselor with widowed people We Care of Century Village, Deerfield Beach, Fla., 1984; vol. counselor Ctr. for Group Counseling, Boca Raton, Fla., 1985—. Recipient Cert. Appreciation, N.E. Focal Point Sr. Ctr., Deerfield Beach, 1984, We Care, Deerfield Beach, 1990, Ctr. for Group Counseling, Boca Raton, 1995; Cert. Achievement, Ctr. for Group Counseling, Boca Raton, 1985. Democrat. Jewish. Home: 1039 Lyndhurst J Deerfield Beach FL 33442

SCHNEIDER, VALERIE LOIS, speech educator; b. Chgo., Feb. 12, 1941; d. Ralph Joseph and Gertrude Blanche (Gaffron) S. BA, Carroll Coll., 1963; MA, U. Wis., 1966; PhD, U. Fla., 1969; cert. advanced study Appalachian State U., 1981. Tchr. English and history Montello High Sch. (Wis.), 1963-64; dir. forensics and drama Montello High Sch., 1963-64; instr. speech U. Fla., Gainesville, 1966-68, asst. prof. speech, 1969-70; asst. prof. speech Edinboro (Pa.) State Coll., 1970-71; assoc. prof. speech East Tenn. State U., Johnson City, 1971-76, prof. speech, 1976—; instr. newspaper course Johnson City Press Chronicle, 1979, Elizabethton Star, Erwin Record, Mountain City Tomahawk, Jonesboro Herald and Tribune, 1980; mem. investor panel USA Today, 1991-92. Editor East Tenn. State U. evening and off-campus newsletter, 1984-91; assoc. editor: Homiletic, 1974-76; columnist Video Visions, Kingsport Times-News (Tenn.), 1984-86; book reviewer Pulpit Digest, 1986-90; contbr. articles on speech to profl. jours. Chmn. AAUW Mass Media Study Group Com., Johnson City, 1973-74. Recipient Creative Writing award Va. Highlands Arts Festival, 1973; award Kingsport (Tenn.) Times News, 1984, 85, Tri-Cities Met. Advt. Fedn., 1983, 84; Danforth assoc., 1977; finalist Money mag. contest 'Best Personal Fin. Mgrs.', 1994. Mem. Speech Communication Assn. (Tenn. rep. to states adv. council 1974-75), So., Tenn. (exec. bd. 1974-77, publs. bd. 1974-78, pres. 1977-78), Religious Speech Communication Assn. (Best article award 1976), Tenn. Basic Skills Council (exec. bd. 1979-80, v.p. 1980-81, pres. 1981-82), AAUW (v.p. chpt. 1974-75, pres. 1975-76, corp. rep. for East Tenn. State U. 1974-76), Am. Assn. Continuing Higher Edn., Bus. and Profl. Women's Club (chpt. exec. bd. 1972-73, v.p. 1976-77), Mensa, Delta Sigma Rho-Tau Kappa Alpha, Phi Delta Kappa, Delta Kappa Gamma, Pi Gamma Mu. Presbyterian. Home: 3201 Buckingham Rd Johnson City TN 37604-2715 Office: East Tenn State U PO Box 23098 Johnson City TN 37614-0124

SCHNEIDER, WILLYS HOPE, lawyer; b. N.Y.C., Sept. 27, 1952; d. Leon and Lillian (Friedman) S.; m. Stephen Andrew Kals, Jan. 21, 1979; children: Peter, Josefine. AB, Princeton U., 1974; JD, Columbia U., 1977. Bar: N.Y. 1978, U.S. Dist. Ct. (ea. and so. dists.) N.Y. 1978, U.S. Tax Ct. 1979. Law clk. to hon. Jack B. Weinstein U.S. Dist. Ct. (ea. dist.) N.Y., Bklyn., 1977-78; assoc. Paul, Weiss, Rifkind, Wharton & Garrison, N.Y.C., 1978-83; ptnr. Kaye, Scholer, Fierman, Hays & Handler, N.Y.C., 1983—. Contbr. articles to profl. jours. Mem. ABA, N.Y. State Bar Assn., Assn. of Bar of City of N.Y. Home: 320 W End Ave New York NY 10023-8110 Office: Kaye Scholer Fierman Hays & Handler 425 Park Ave New York NY 10022-3506

SCHNEIDER-CRIEZIS, SUSAN MARIE, architect; b. St. Louis, Aug. 1, 1953; d. William Alfred and Rosemary Elizabeth (Fischer) Schneider; m. Demetrios Anthony Criezis, Nov. 24, 1978; children: Anthony, John and Andrew. BArch, U. Notre Dame, 1976; MArch, MIT, 1978. Registered architect, Wis. Project designer Eichstaedt Architects, Roselle, Ill., 1978-80, Solomon, Cordwell, Buenz & Assocs., Chgo., 1980-82; project architect Gelick, Foran Assocs., Chgo., 1982-83; asst. prof. Sch. Architecture U. Ill., Chgo., 1980-86; exec. v.p. Criezis Architects, Inc., Evanston, Ill., 1986—. Graham Found. grantee MIT, 1977, MIT scholar, 1976-78; Prestressed Concrete Inst. rsch. grantee, 1981. Mem. AIA, Chgo. Archtl. Club, Chgo. Women in Architecture, Am. Solar Energy Soc., NAFE, Jr. League Evanston, Evanston C. of C. Roman Catholic. Office: 1007 Church St Ste 101 Evanston IL 60201-5910

SCHNEIDMAN, BARBARA SUE, psychiatrist; b. Mpls., Jan. 18, 1944; d. Norman Reuben and MIldred (Roberts) S.; m. William McAllister. BA, U. Minn., Mpls., 1966, MD, 1970; MPH, U. Wash., 1974. Diplomate Am. Bd. Psychiatry and Neurology. Resident ob-gyn. U. Wash., Seattle, 1972-74, dir. gynecology, 1974-78, resident in psychiatry, 1978-81, cons. primary care, 1981-88; pvt. practice Seattle, 1981-93; cons. Sexual Assault Ctr., Seattle, 1981-93, Cen. Area Mental Health, Seattle, 1990-92; assoc. v.p. Am. Bd. Med. Specialties, Evanston, Ill., 1993—; mem., chair Wash. State Bd. Med. Examiners, 1982-93; pres. Fedn. State Med. Bds., 1991-92. Mem. AMA, Am. Psychiat. Assn., Ill. State Med. Assn., Ill. Psychiat. Soc., Chgo. Med. Soc. Office: ABMS 1007 Church St Ste 404 Evanston IL 60201-5913

SCHNELLER, ESTHER LYNN, emergency trauma nurse; b. Tawas City, Mich., June 13, 1966; d. Garrie Lee and Naomi Ruth (Atwood) S. BS in Christian Secondary Edn., Ozark Bible Inst. & Coll., Neosho, Mo., 1988; BSN, Ind. Wesleyan U., Marion, 1991; MS in Cmty. Health Nursing, U. Colo. Health Scis. Ctr., Denver, 1995. RN, Colo.; CEN; cert. ACLS, pediatric advanced life support, trauma nurse core course; cert. type E cert. Colo. Dept. Edn. Staff nurse emergency dept. Marion Gen. Hosp., 1991-92, Penrose-St. Francis Healthcare Sys., Colorado Springs, Colo., 1992-95; staff nurse registry QS Nurses Corp., Colorado Springs, 1992—; staff devel. nurse 302d ASTS-USAFR, Peterson AFB, Colo., 1994—; mentor various healthcare instrnl. facilities, 1991—; vol. tchr. health classes Knowledge is Power, Red Cross Shelter, Colorado Springs, 1995—. Mem. orch. Living Springs Worship Centre, 1993—. Mem. Emergency Nurses Assn., Res. Officers Assn., Sigma Theta Tau.

SCHNIPPER, SYDRA, mathematics educator; b. N.Y.C., Oct. 31, 1944; d. Leo and Deborah Ruth (Deane) S.; children: Merritt, Deborah, Claudia. BA, Queens Coll., 1965; MEd, Cambridge Coll., 1989. Cert. secondary edn., Mass. Tchr. Canarsie H.S., Bklyn., 1965-68, West Haven (Conn.) H.S., 1968-70, Brookline (Mass.) H.S., 1974—; sch. com. City of Newton, Mass., 1985-93. Alderman City of Newton, 1994—; ward comm. Newton Dem. City Commn., 1985—. Grantee NSF, 1966-68. Jewish. Home: 273 Ward St Newton MA 02159 Office: Brookline HS 115 Greenough St Brookline MA 02146

SCHNITZER, IRIS TAYMORE, financial management executive; b. Cambridge, Mass., Aug. 3, 1943; d. Joseph David and Edith (Cooper) Taymore; m. Stephen Mark Schnitzer, Sept. 10, 1966. BA in Econs., Boston U., 1967; JD, Mass. Sch. Law, 1996. Lic. real estate broker, life ins. advisor, life ins. and health ins. broker; registered rep. NASD; CFP; CLU; cert. in fin. counseling, advanced pension planning. Real estate broker Woods Real Estate, Braintree, Mass., 1968; real estate broker, property mgr. Village Gate Realty, Brockton, Mass., 1969; agt. Prudential Ins., Boston, 1970-73; supr. edn. and advanced underwriting, agt. Northwestern Mutual Life, Boston, 1973-78; fin. planning cons. Iris Taymore Schnitzer Assocs., Boston, Mass., 1973-79; trainer fin. planners Gerstenblatt Co., Newton, Mass., 1978-79; founder, pres. The Fin. Forum, Inc., Boston, 1979-91, TFF, Inc. at the Chase Exchange, N.Y.C., 1980-83; pres. I&S Assocs., Boston, 1991-93; v.p. Fleet Investment Svcs., Boston, 1993—; bd. dirs., clk. Mister Tire, Inc., Abington, Mass.; arbitrator Nat. Assn. Securities Dealers, 1992—. Contbr. articles to profl. jours. Chmn. credit com., bd. dirs. Mass. Feminist Fed. Credit Union, Boston, 1975-77; bd. dirs. Ledgewood, Brookline, Mass., 1967-70, LWV, Brockton, Mass., 1968-70, NOW, Boston, 1972-73; bd. govs. Women's City Club, Boston, 1976-80; pres. Mass. divsn. Women's Equity Action League, 1977-79; life mem. Navy League U.S, Boston, 1985—; treas., bd. dirs. Festival of Light and Song, 1989-92; bd. dirs. Achievement Rewards for Coll. Scientists, Boston, 1991-93, 94-95; mem. steering com. Fleet Bank of Mass. United Way, 1994—. Named One of the Best Fin. Planners in the U.S., Money Mag., 1987, to Mutual Funds Panel, Sylvia Porter's Personal Fin. Mag., 1988, 89. Mem. Am. Assn. Individual Investors (pres. Boston chpt. 1987-89, bd. dirs. 1985-95), Boston Estate Planning Coun., Boston Club. Republican. Jewish. Office: Fleet Investment Svcs MABOFO5A 75 State St Boston MA 02109-1807

SCHNITZLER, BEVERLY JEANNE, designer, art educator, writer; b. Berkeley, Calif.; children: Erich Gregory. BS, Ariz. State U., 1954; MA, Calif. State U., L.A., 1959; postgrad., Claremont Grad. Sch., 1956-59, Chouinard Art Inst., L.A., 1960-63. Spl. art tchr. and cons. Alhambra (Calif.) City Sch. Dist., 1958-60; prof. art Calif. State U., L.A., 1960—; cons. in art and creative fabric art Calif. State U., L.A., 1960—; lectr. in field; Calif. State U. del. for internat. acad. exch. guidelines to Yunnan Art Inst., Kunming, China, 1993. Author: New Dimensions in Needlework, 1978; project dir. and head designer heraldic banners Calif. State U., L.A., 1986-87; exhibiting artist in fiber art. Participant student/prof. exch. program Kunming, 1993. Calif. State U. L.A. instl. grantee, 1978, 79; AAUW Found. grantee, 1988; recipient Award for Outstanding Artistic Merit, Calif. State U. L.A. Assoc. Students, 1987; scholar conf. Spain and Portugal of the Navagators: The Age of Discovery to the Enlightenment, Georgetown U., 1990, scholar conf. participant Portugal and Spain of the Navigators: The Age of Exploration, George Washington U., 1992; recipient Emily Gates Nat. Alumna Achievement award Sigma Sigma Sigma, 1995. Mem. Nat. Surface Design Assn., Costume and Textile Coun. of L.A. County Mus., Internat. Designers Assn., Internat. World Conf. of Educators, AAUW, Am. Craftsman's Coun., Fine Art Club of Pasadena. Office: Calif State U Art Dept 5151 State University Dr Los Angeles CA 90032

SCHNOLIS, KATHY BUSH, university program director; b. Chgo., Jan. 15, 1969; d. Raymond and Lou Vernia (Campbell) Bush; m. Marc J. Schnolis, July 3, 1993. BA, U. Iowa, 1991; MS, Western Ill. U., 1993. Cert. counselor, nat. Asst. dir. counseling Albion (Mich.) Coll., 1993-95; coord. student affairs U. Fla., Gainesville, 1995—. mem. Am Counseling Assn., Am. Coll. Counseling Assn., Am. Coll. Pers. Assn. Democrat. Home: PO Box 12837 Gainesville FL 32604 Office: Univ Fla 1001 Stadium Dr Gainesville FL 32611

SCHNURSTEIN, ANGELA ANN, secondary school educator; b. Ames, Iowa, Apr. 1, 1971; d. Roger Kent and Virginia Sue (Martin) Swenson; m. Mark James Schnurstein, June 4, 1993. BA in Elem. Edn., U. No. Iowa, 1993. Chpt. 1 math. tchr. Kansas City (Mo.) Sch. Dist., 1993—. Recipient Enhancing the Tchr.'s Role in Assessment award U. Mo.-Kansas City, 1994-95. Mem. Mo. Edn. Assn., Kappa Delta Pi, Omicron Delta Kappa, Tau Beta Sigma (sec., historian, regional chpt. del.).

SCHOCK, JACQUI VIRGINIA, counselor, data operations specialist; b. Atlanta, Nov. 24, 1938; d. Herman Lee and Martha Jane (Hunsecker) Turner; m. Raymond J. Torres, Oct. 20, 1990. AA in Human Svcs., Bucks County Community Coll., 1986; BA in Human Svcs., Antioch U., 1987; MS in Addictions, Chestnut Hill Coll., 1988; MA in Applied Psychology, U. Santa Monica, Calif., 1990. Counselor Bucks County Rehab. Ctr., Doylestown, Pa., 1983-88; addictions counselor Clearbrook Friendship Ctr., Phila., 1988-89; in-patient counselor Penn Found., Sellersville, Pa., 1988-89; pvt. practice Willow Grove, Pa., 1989—; outpatient therapist Westmeade Med. Ctr., 1992—; instr. self-esteem Upper Moreland Adult Eveing Sch., 1991—; founder, dir. Crossroads Counseling Svc., Willow Grove, 1990—; data entry operator SPS Techs., Jenkintown, Pa., 1963-65, data engry supr., 1965-70, data mgr., 1970-94; pvt. instr. in computer concepts, 1991—. Mem. exec. bd. Counseling Assn. Greater Phila., 1988—, pres., 1994-95; exec. bd. West Phila. Fund for Human Devel., 1989-92. Mem. NAFE, APA, Am. Counseling Assn., Pa. Counselors Assn., Data Entry Mgrs. Assn., Nat. Coun. on Self-Esteem, Fraternal Order of Police, Phi Theta Kappa Alumni Assn. Office: Cross Roads Counseling Svc 7600 Stenton Ave 1-G Philadelphia PA 19118

SCHOCKAERT, BARBARA ANN, operations executive; b. Queens, N.Y., Dec. 13, 1938; d. Lawrence Henry and Eleanor Veronica (Tollner) Grob; children: Donna Ann, Don. Student, Ocean County Coll., Toms River, N.J., 1987, 94—. Cert. notary pub. V.p. ops. Am. Vitamin Products, Inc.,

Freehold, N.J., 1977-89, v.p. ops. Foods Plus div., 1990-94, sales coord., 1994—; assoc. Ocean County Realty, Toms River, N.J., 1987-90, Crossroads Realty, Toms River, 1990—. Contbg. author: Greatest Poems of the Western World, 1989 (Golden Poet award). Past pres. mayor's adv. coun., past pres. of help line Town of Jackson, N.J.; past bd. dirs. Big Bros. of Ocean County; speaker community svc. orgns. Named Woman of Yr., Jaycees, 1974; recipient Capitol award Nat. Leadership Coun., 1991, Silver Bowl award for 1st pl. poetry contest, 1996. Mem. N.J. Realtors Assn., Internat. Platform Assn., Alpha Beta Gamma. Home: 977 Fairview Dr Toms River NJ 08753-3064 Office: 500 Halls Mill Rd Freehold NJ 07728-8811

SCHOEBERL, BETH JO, zoologist; b. Chgo., Mar. 13, 1951; d. William Claude and Diane Marie (Jarmer) Skelnik; m. Bernard William Schoeberl, Sept. 1972 (div. Oct. 1986); children: Jason William, Amy Jo. BS, U. Minn., St. Paul, 1973. Zookeeper Minn. Zool. Garden, Apple Valley, 1984-89, zoologist, 1989—. Mem. Am. Zoo and Aquarium Assn., Am. Assn. Zookeepers (profl. mem.). Home: 3820 36th Ave S Minneapolis MN 55406 Office: Minn Zool Garden 13000 Zoo Blvd Apple Valley MN 55124

SCHOEN, CAROL BRONSTON, retired English language educator; b. Plainfield, N.J., May 14, 1926; d. Harry E. and Yetta (Cohen) Bronston; m. Andrew J. Schoen, June 26, 1949 (div.); children: Douglas, Sarah. BA, Radcliffe, 1948; MA, Columbia U., 1963, PhD, 1968. Lectr. Lehman Coll. CUNY, N.Y.C., 1968-75, asst. prof., 1975-85, assoc. prof., 1986-91; ret., 1991. Author: The Writing Experience, 1978, Anzia Yezierska, 1982, Sara Teasdale, 1986, Thinking & Writing in College, 1986. Democrat. Jewish.

SCHOEN, REGINA NEIMAN, psychotherapist; b. Bronx, N.Y., Feb. 21, 1949; d. Louis and Bertha (Hoffman) Neiman; m. Dennis Leo Schoen, Dec. 2, 1979; 1 child, Leah F. B, Hunter Coll., N.Y.C., 1969; M, Columbia U., N.Y.C., 1971; M (social work), Hunter Coll., N.Y.C., 1977. Cert. Psychoanalytic Psychotherapist, Wash. Square Inst. N.Y.C., 1983, Family Therapist, Postgrad. Ctr. for Mental Health N.Y.C., 1986. Tchr., advisor Brandeis High Sch., N.Y.C., 1972-75; family service counselor N.Y. Assn. for New Am., N.Y.C., 1978-82; psychiatric social worker Lutheran Med. Ctr., Bklyn., 1982-84; mental health practitioner Montefiore Med. Ctr., Riker's Island, N.Y., 1984-86; moderator, spkr. Nat. Assn. Social Workers Alcoholism Inst. N.Y.C., 1989, 91; presenter YWCA, N.Y.C., 1987—; spkr. Greater N.Y. Hosp. Assn., 1983; commentator WNYC Radio Women and Rape N.Y.C., 1982; mem. faculty Postgrad. Ctr. Mental Health, 1990—; spkr. Empire Blue Cross/Blue Shield, N.Y., 1990-95, Fashion Inst. Employee Assistance Program, 1994—. Mem. Nat. Assn. Social Workers. Office: Regina Schoen CSW 488 7th Ave Apt 9A New York NY 10018-6808

SCHOENBERG, APRIL MINDY, nursing administrator; b. Nassau, N.Y., June 2, 1955; d. Robert and Eleanor (Marks) Christian; m. Gerald Duggan, 1979 (div.); children: Lance, Craig, Danielle; m. Bruce Schoenberg; 1 child, Michael. BSN, Long Island U., 1978. Intravenous cert., 1994, cen. line intravenous cert., 1995; cert. Nassau Fire Commn. Head nurse Sunrise Manor Nursing Home, Bayshore, N.Y., 1982-87; unit coord. East Neck Nursing Ctr., Babylon, N.Y., 1987-89; dir. nursing svcs., asst. dir. nursing svcs. Oceanside (N.Y.) Care Ctr., 1988-91; PRI nurse, medicare nurse, rehab. coord., MDST coord. Ctrl. Island Health Care, Plainview, N.Y., 1993-95; reviewer, monitor restraints and psychoactive medications Quality of Care Mgmt., N.Y.C., 1995—; RN discharge planner Northshore Hosp. Plainview (N.Y.), 1995—; Asst. info. Tumor Registry Northshore Hosp., Manhasset, N.Y., 1975. Assoc. mem. Am. Mus. Natural History; sponsor Child Reach, 1984—. Mem. N.Y. State Nurses Assn., Multiple Sclerosis Soc., Nat. Trust Hist. Preservation (elected).

SCHOENBERG, BETTY REBECCA, artist; b. N.Y.C., June 13, 1916; d. Abraham and Sonja (Weisband) Cohen; m. Albert Schoenberg, Dec. 26, 1952; children: Steven Mark, Lisa Hillary. Dental hygienist, U. So. Calif., 1948; BA in Art History, Calif. State U., Carson, 1978. Registered dental hygienist, Calif., 1949. Dental hygienist Dr. Mark Shulman, L.A., 1948-88; artist L.A., 1973—. Exhibited at Westwood Ctr. for the Arts, 1980 (1st prize). With U.S. Army, 1943-46. Grantee Women's Bldg. L.A., 1985. Mem. Women's Caucus for Art (bd. dirs., Achievement award 1995), Neighbors United (del. 1991-95), World's Women On-Line, Internet Installation, UN Fourth World Conf. on Women (participant 1995-96). Democrat. Jewish.

SCHOENBERG-SWARTCHILD, COCO, sculptor; b. Paris, May 3, 1939; came to U.S., 1941; d. Heinz Ernst and Kathe (Gassman) Oppenheimer; m. Bernard Schoenberg, Aug. 11, 1963 (dec. Apr. 1979); children: Nara, Jonathan Alexander, Amanda; m. William G. Swartchild III, June 5, 1988. BS in Lit., Sci., Arts, U. Mich., 1961; MA in Art, Columbia U., 1964. Tchr. handicapped children Steven Sch., N.Y.C., 1962-63; assoc. in pottery for occupational therapy Columbia Tchrs. Coll., N.Y.C., 1963; studio potter, tchr., lectr. various cities, N.Y., 1965—; chmn. N.J. Designer Craftsman, New Brunswick, 1983-85; coord. Ctr. Crafts Fair-Old Ch., Demarest, N.J., 1983-84, ACC Craft Fair, Balt., 1985-94, West Springfield, 1985-94; juror Lincoln Ct. Craft Fair, N.Y.C., 1985, Art Rider Craft Fairs, N.Y.C., 1986, Sta. WBAI Craft Fair, N.Y.C., 1989; commd. by Gulick Group, 1988, Harrison, Star Weiner and Beitler Advt., N.Y.C., 1989; juror Am. Craft Exposition, 1992. Two-person shows include Latitude, Greenwich, Conn., Handworks Gallery, Manchester, Vt.; exhibited in group shows at Montclair (N.J.) Mus., Bergen Mus., Paramus, N.J., Morris Mus., Morristown, N.J., Noyes Mus., Oceanville, N.J., Mus. Am. Jewish History, Phila., High Mus., Atlanta, Craft and Folk Mus., L.A., Brockton (Mass.) Mus., Summit (N.J.) Art Ctr., Campbell Mus., and various other galleries, craft fairs and stores. N.J. State Coun. on the Arts grantee 1983-84; recipient Innovative Sculpture award Texaco, 1982, purchase award Noyes Mus., 1986, highest award for crafts Craft Concepts, 1986, Juror's award Summit Art Ctr., 1985, Mamoroneck Artist Guild award, 1984, Charlotte Simons Glicksman Meml. award, 1983, merit award in ceramics N.Y.C. Artist/Craftsmen of N.Y., 1987, Most Innovative Use of Medium award Toshiko Tokaezu, 1994. Home: 119 Erledon Rd Tenafly NJ 07670-2503

SCHOENE, KATHLEEN SNYDER, lawyer; b. Glen Ridge, N.J., July 24, 1953; d. John Kent and Margaret Ann (Bronder) Snyder. BA, Grinnell Coll., 1974; MS, So. Conn. State Coll., 1976; JD, Washington U., St. Louis, 1982. Bar: Mo. 1982, U.S. Dist. Ct. (we. and ea. dists.) Mo. 1982, Ill. 1983. Head libr. Mo. Hist. Soc., St. Louis, 1976-79; assoc. Peper, Martin, Jensen, Maichel & Hetlage, St. Louis, 1982-88, ptnr., 1989—; bd. dirs. Legal Svcs. of Eastern Mo. Author: (with others) Missouri Corporation Law and Practice, 1985; contbr. articles to profl. jours. Trustee Grinnell (Iowa) Coll., ex officio voting mem., 1991-93; bd. dirs. Jr. League St. Louis, 1995-96, Leadership Ctr. Greater St. Louis, 1995-96, FORUM St. Louis, 1996—. Mem. ABA, Nat. Health Lawyers Assn., Nat. Assn. Bond Lawyers, The Mo. Bar, Ill. State Bar Assn., Bar Assn. Met. St. Louis (treas. 1991-92, sec. 1992-93, v.p. 1993-94, pres.-elect 1994-95, pres. 1995-96, chairperson small bus. com. 1987-88, mem. exec. com. 1988-96, chairperson bus. law sect. 1988-89, mem. exec. com. young lawyers sect. 1988-90), St. Louis Bar Found. (bd. dirs. 1994—, v.p. 1995-96, pres. 1996—). Home: 7824 Cornell Ave Saint Louis MO 63130-3701 Office: Peper Martin Jensen Maichel & Hetlage 720 Olive St Fl 24 Saint Louis MO 63101-2338

SCHOENFELD, ALISSA DIANE, art gallery director; b. Porterville, Calif., Mar. 2, 1966; d. Edward Louis and Mary Ruth (Yeasting) S. BA, San Francisco State U., 1990; MA, SUNY, Stony Brook, 1994. Dir., curator Canessa Gallery Artists Resource, San Francisco, 1991-92; dir. A.I.R. Gallery, N.Y.C., 1994—; mng. editor Critical Rev. Mem. Nat. Assn. Artists Orgns., Coll. Art Assn., N.Y. Women's Agenda. Office: AIR Gallery 40 Wooster St Fl 2 New York NY 10013

SCHOENL, LYNNE M., accountant; b. Buffalo, Feb. 2, 1968; d. Robert R. and Sharon M. (Noll) S.; m. W. Morgan Adams Jr., Jan. 2, 1988 (div. 1995). Student, Auburn U., 1986-87; BS in Acctg., U. Md., 1990. CPA. Staff acct. Keller Bruner & Co. LLC, Bethesda, Md., 1990-92, sr. acct., 1992-93, advanced sr. acct., 1993-95, supr. auditing dept., 1995—, recruiting dir., 1993—. Mem. Am. Inst. CPAs, Md. Assn. CPAs, Inst. Mgmt. Accts. (dir. 1994), Prince George's C. of C., Phi Chi Theta (pres. 1993, Alumni Leadership award 1990). Roman Catholic. Home: 13600 Colgate Way #632 Silver Spring MD 20904 Office: Keller Bruner & Co LLC 6701 Democracy Blvd Ste 600 Bethesda MD 20817

SCHOENRICH, EDYTH HULL, academic administrator, physician; b. Cleve., Sept. 9, 1919; d. Edwin John and Maud Mabel (Kelly) Hull; m. Carlos Schoenrich, Aug. 9, 1942; children: Lola, Olaf. AB, Duke U., 1941; MD, U. Chgo., 1947; MPH, John Hopkins U., 1971. Diplomate Am. Bd. Internal Medicine, Am. Bd. Preventive Medicine. Intern John Hopkins Hosp., Balt., 1948-49, asst. resident medicine, 1949-50, postdoctoral fellow medicine, 1950-51, chief resident, pvt. wards, 1951-52; asst. chief, acting chief dept. chronic and cmty. medicine Balt. City Hosp., Balt., 1963-66; dir. svc. to chronically ill and aging Md. State Dept. Health, Balt., 1966-74; dir. divsn. pub. health adminstrn. Sch. Pub. Health, John Hopkins U., Balt., 1974-77, assoc. dean academic affairs, 1977-86, dir. part time profl. programs and dep. dir. MPH program, 1986—, prof. dept. health policy and mgmt., 1974—, joint appointment medicine, 1978—. Contbd. articles to profl. jours. Bd. trustees Friends Life Care Cmty., 1984—; Kennedy-Krieger Inst., Balt., 1985—, Vis. Nurses Assn., 1990—. Recipient Stebbins medal John Hopkins U., 1989. Fellow Am. Col. Physicians, Am. Coll. Preventive Medicine; mem. Assn. Tchrs. Preventive Medicine, Am. Pub. Health Assn., Med. Chirurg. Soc. Md., Balt. City Med. Soc., Phi Beta Kappa, Alpha Omega Alpha, Delta Omega. Home: 1402 Boyce Ave Baltimore MD 21204-6512 Office: Johns Hopkins Univ Sch Pub Health 615 N Wolfe St Baltimore MD 21205-2103

SCHOETTLER, GAIL SINTON, state official; b. Los Angeles, Oct. 21, 1943; d. James and Norma (McLellan) Sinton; children: Lee, Thomas, James; m. Donald L. Stevens, June 23, 1990. BA in Econs., Stanford U., 1965; MA in History, U. Calif., Santa Barbara, 1969, PhD in History, 1975. Businesswoman Denver, 1975-83; exec. dir. Colo. Dept. of Personnel, Denver, 1983-86; treas. State of Colo., Denver, 1987-94, lt. govern., 1995—; bd. dirs. Nat. Jewish Hosp., Nat. Taxpayers' Union, Douglas County Edn. Found.; past bd. dirs. Pub. Employees Retirement Assn., Mi Casa Resource Ctr., Women's Bank, Denver, Equitable Bankshares of Colo., Equitable Bank, Littleton; chair Colo. Commn. Indian Affairs, Aerospace States Assn.; mem. adv. com. on external regulation of nuclear safety U.S. Dept. Energy, 1995—; mem. bd. trustees U. No. Colo., 1981-87. Mem. Douglas County Bd. Edn., Colo., 1979-87, pres., 1983-87; trustee U. No. Colo., Greeley, 1981-87; pres. Denver Children's Mus., 1975-85. Recipient Disting. Alumna award U. Calif. at Santa Barbara, 1987. Mem. Nat. Women's Forum (bd. dirs. 1981-89, pres 1983-85), Internat. Women's Forum (mem. bd. dirs. 1981-89, pres. 83-85), Women Execs. in State Govt. (bd. dirs. 1981-87, chmn. 1988), Leadership Denver Assn. (bd. dirs. 1987, named Outstanding Alumna 1985), Nat. Assn. State Treas., Stanford Alumni Assn., Denver Rotary. Democrat.

SCHOFFMANN, CAROL LOUISE NAJI, art gallery director, artist; b. Summit, N.J., Mar. 23, 1957; d. Edwin and Jeanette (Levine) S.; m. Loren Naji, June 25, 1995. BFA, Cleve. Inst. Art, 1980; MA in Art Edn., Case Western Reserve U., 1987. Gallery mgr. Scheele Galleries, Cleveland Heights, Ohio, 1989-90; dir., owner Badawang Art Gallery, Cleve., 1991—. Represented in permanent collections at Great No. Corp. Ctr., Traub Container Corp., Steichen Vending, Sherwin-Williams Co. Recipient First award Kansas City Plz. Art Fair, 1983, Ohio Sculpture & Craft Show Butler Inst. Am. Art, 1983, Purchase award Cleve. Artists Assn. at Cleve. Mus. Art, 1984, Best Mixed Media Painting Trumbull Art Guild, 1985. Mem. Murray Hill Area Arts Assn. (pres. 1991-95). Office: Badawang Art 2026 Murray Hill Rd Cleveland OH 44106

SCHOLER, SUE WYANT, state legislator; b. Topeka, Oct. 20, 1936; d. Zint Elwin and Virginia Louise (Achenbach) Wyant; m. Charles Frey Scholer, Jan. 27, 1957; children: Elizabeth Scholer Truelove, Charles W., Virginia M. Scholer McCal. Student, Kans. State U., 1954-56. Draftsman The Farm Clinic, West Lafayette, Ind., 1978-79; assessor Wabash Twp., West Lafayette, 1979-84; commr. Tippecanoe County, Lafayette, Ind., 1984-90; state rep. Dist. 26 Ind. Statehouse, Indpls., 1990—; asst. minority whip, 1992-94, majority whip, 1994—; mem. Tippecanoe County Area Plan Commn., 1984-90. Bd. dirs. Crisis Ctr., Lafayette, 1984-89, Tippecanoe Arts Fedn., 1990—, United Way, Lafayette, 1990-93; mem. Lafayette Conv. and Visitors Bur., 1988-90. Recipient Salute to Women Govt. and Politics award, 1986, United Sr. Action award, Outstanding Legislator award, 1993, Small Bus. Champion award, 1995, Ind. Libr. Fedn. Legislator award, 1995. Mem. Ind. Assn. County Commrs. (treas. 1990), Assn. Ind. Counties (legis. com. 1988-90), Greater Lafayette C. of C. (ex-officio bd. 1984-90), Sagamore Bus. and Profl. Women, LWV, P.E.O., Purdue Women's Club (past treas.), Kappa Kappa Kappa (past pres. Epsilon chpt.), Delta Delta Delta (past pres. alumnae, house corp. treas.). Republican. Presbyterian. Home: 807 Essex St West Lafayette IN 47906-1534 Office: Indiana Statehouse Rm 3A-4 Indianapolis IN 46204

SCHOLIN, MARGO S., lawyer; b. Sioux Center, Iowa, Nov. 16, 1950. BSN with highest distinction, U. Iowa, 1973; MSN, Tex. Woman's U., 1980; JD summa cum laude, U. Houston, 1983. Bar: Tex. 1983; RN, Tex. Ptnr. Baker & Botts, LLP, Houston. Assoc. editor Houston Law Rev., 1982-83. Recipient U. Houston Law Found. Acad. Excellence award, 1983. Fellow Houston Bar Found.; mem. ABA, State Bar of Tex., Houston Bar Assn., Order of the Coif, Order of the Barons, Sigma Theta Tau. Office: Baker & Botts 1 Shell Plz Houston TX 77002*

SCHOLTES, TINA FISHER, elementary education educator; b. Okolona, Miss., May 16, 1959; d. Harvey Dale and Celia (Coleman) Fisher; m. Robert Beck Scholtes, July 31, 1982; children: Sara Elizabeth, Beck Fisher. Elem. edn. chpt. 1 tchr. Kosciusko (Miss.) Pub. Schs., 1982; elem. edn. chpt. 1 tchr. Starkville (Miss.) Sch. Sys., 1984, elem. edn. classroom tchr., 1985—; staff devel. presenter Starkville (Miss.) Sch. Sys., 1993-95; presenter Miss. State U., Starkville, 1994-96; summer helper Math Their Way, 1995, follow-up instr., 1995-96. Math. Manipulative Classrm. grantee Starkville (Miss.) Found. for Pub. Edn., 1995, Cross Age Enrichment grantee Starkville (Miss.) Found. for Pub. Edn., 1996. Mem. Nat. Coun. Tchrs. Math., Kappa Kappa Iota (pres. 1994-95), Delta Kappa Gamma, Phi Delta Kappa. Presbyterian. Home: 1095 E Lee Blvd Starkville MS 39759 Office: Overstreet Elem S Jackson Starkville MS 39759

SCHOMER, CAROLYN DICKSON, social services administrator; b. Indpls., May 4, 1939; d. Willard E. and Sarah Grace (Huggins) Dickson; m. David Lawrence Schomer, July 24, 1964; children: Scott David, Douglas Lee. BS, Ind. U., 1961; MEd, Tex. Christian U., 1963; MSW, U. Ga., 1988. Assoc. dir. Ind. Univ. YWCA, Bloomington, 1962-63; exec. dir. U. Cin. YWCA, 1963-64; teen program dir. Bethlehem Cmty. Ctr., Ft. Worth, 1964-65; adult edn. instr. Houston County Bd. Edn., Warner Robbins, Ga., 1968-70; supervisor child welfare Houston County Dept. Children & Family Svcs., Warner Robbins, Ga., 1971-89; cons., trainer Ga. Dept. Family & Children Svcs., Macon, 1989—. Pres. Cmty. Concert Assn., Warner Robbins, 1995—; mem. Jamaica mission team, 1993—. Mem. AAUW, NASW, Phi Kappa Phi. Home: 604 Arrowhead Tr Warner Robins GA 31088

SCHOMMER, TRUDY MARIE, pastoral minister, religion education; b. Wayzata, Minn., May 18, 1937; d. Edward and Gertrude (Mergen) S. BA, Coll. St. Catherine, St. Paul, 1966; MA, Manhattanville Coll., 1971. Joined Order of Franciscan Sisters of Little Falls, Minn., 1955. Dir. religious edn. St. Pius X, White Bear Lake, Minn., 1971-77; campus min., theology tchr. St. Cloud (Minn.) State Univ., 1977-81; pastoral min. St. Galls, St. Elizabeth, Milw., 1981-85; dir. religious edn. St. Alexander's, Morrisonville, N.Y., 1985-90; pastoral min. of religious edn. St. Mary's, Bryantown, Md., 1990-91; diocesan dir. religious edn. Diocese of New Ulm, Minn., 1991—; exec. bd. mem. Nat. Assembly Religious Women, Chgo., 1974-78. Author: Easiest Gospel Stories Ever, 1993; book reviewer Sister's Today, 1988-91. Mem. Network, Washington, 1978—. Mem. Nat. Cath. Edn. Assn., Nat. Parish Coords. and Dirs. Democrat. Roman Catholic. Home and Office: 1725 Oxford St Apt 201 Berkeley CA 94709-1701

SCHONAUER, ANNE MILLER, music educator; b. Houston, July 29, 1965; d. George Louquet and Marilyn Ann (Rhoades) Miller; m. Paul Richard Schonauer, July 2, 1988; 1 child, Paul David. BA in Music, BMusEd, Southwestern Okla. State U., 1987; MA, 1991. Cert. music tchr., Okla., Tex., Ala., Ga. Tchr. band 5-6 Dallas Ind. Schs., 1988-89; tchr. gen. music, K-5 Norman (Okla.) Pub. Schs., 1991—. Mem. NEA, Orgn. of Am. Kodaly Educators, Music Edn. Nat. Conf. Office: Monroe Elem Sch 1601 S McGee Norman OK 73072

SCHÖNBERG, BESSIE, dance educator; b. Hanover, Germany, Dec. 27, 1906; m. Dimitry Varley Jan. 6, 1934. Student, U. Oreg., 2 yrs.; studied with Martha Hill, Martha Graham; BA, Bennington Coll., 1936. Dancer Martha Graham Dance Co., N.Y.C., 1931; asst. to Martha Hill Bennington Coll. and/or Bennington Sch. of the Dance, 1933-35, 34-41; dance instr. Sarah Lawrence Coll., Bronxville, N.Y., 1936-41, head dance dept., 1941-75, 1941, prof. emerita, 1975—; tchr. dance dept. Juilliard, N.Y.C., 1993—; guest tchr. Ohio State U., Wesleyan U., U. N.H., George Mason U., The Art of Movement Ctr., London, Contemporary Dance Ctr., London, Dance Theatre Workshop, N.Y.C., Dance Theatre Harlem, N.Y.C.; dance cons. Hunter Coll., N.Y.C., Oberlin (Ohio) Coll., Dennison U., Wesleyan U.; mem. appeals bd. N.Y. State Coun. on Arts; mem. adv. panel NEA Dance Program; chmn., bd. dirs. Dance Theatre Workshop. Appeared in Martha Graham's dances including Primitive Mysteries, Ceremonials, Heretic, Project in Movement for a Divine Comedy. Mentor fellow NEA, 1994; recipient citation Assn. Am. Dance Cos., 1975, Lifetime Achievement in Dance Bessie award, 1987-88, Gov. Arts award N.Y. State, 1989, Ernie award Dance/USA, 1994; The N.Y. Dance and Performance Awards are named in her honor as The BESSIES. Office: Sarah Lawrence Coll Dept Dance 1 Meadway Bronxville NY 10708-5931

SCHONEMAN, PATRICIA JANE, elementary school educator; b. Wadena, Minn., Mar. 13, 1950; d. Sylvester Joseph and Marian Jean (Schloeder) Schmith; m. Michael Joseph Schoneman, May 15, 1971; children: Kristine, Lisa. AA in Art, N.D. State U., 1971; BS in Edn., St. Cloud (Minn.) State U., 1986. Cert. tchr. elem./kindergarten edn., Minn. Kindergarten tchr. New London-Spicer (Minn.) Schs., 1987—. Clk., Irving Twp., Hawick, Minn., 1978-82; mem. edn. adv. com. Rep. Tom Van Engen, Dist. 15A Legis., 1994—. Ag in the Classroom Agr. Edn. grantee, 1994, 95. Mem. Nat. Coun. Tchrs. Math., New London-Spicer Edn. Assn. (meet and confer com.), Minn. Reading Assn., Minn. Kindergarten Assn. (region 3 rep. 1991—), Kappa Delta Pi. Home: 16067 195th Ave NE Hawick MN 56246-9789 Office: New London Spicer Schs New London MN 56273

SCHONHOLTZ, JOAN SONDRA HIRSCH, banker, civic worker; b. N.Y.C., Sept. 8, 1933; d. Joseph G. and Mildred (Klebanoff) Hirsch; m. George J. Schonholtz, Aug. 21, 1951; children: Margot Beth, Steven Robert, Barbara Ellen. Student, Vassar Coll., 1950-52; B.A., Barnard Coll., 1954; postgrad., Am. U., 1963. Chmn. bd. dirs., founding mem. Ist Women's Bank of Md., Rockville, 1976—; chmn. FWB Bancorp., Rockville, 1982—. Pres. Ft. Benning Med. Wives, Ga., 1962-63; sec. Montgomery County Women's Med. Aux., Md., 1968; bd. dirs. Svc. Guild of Washington, 1968-77, sec., 1969-70, pres., 1975-77; bd. dirs. Pilot Sch. for Blind Multiple Handicapped Children, Washington, 1968-77; bd. dirs. Strathmore Hall Arts Ctr., N. Bethesda, Md., 1992—; spl. gifts chmn. Cancer Soc. Montgomery County, 1968, 69; mem. Washington Adv. Coun. on Deaf-Blind Children, 1972-74; chmn. Friends of Wash. Adventist Hosp., Takoma Park, Md., 1993-94. Recipient Outstanding Service award Service Guild of Washington, 1969. Republican. Jewish. Clubs: Vassar, Barnard. Home: 10839 Lockland Rd Potomac MD 20854-1855

SCHOOLAR, LAUREL ANN, artist, educator; b. Phoenix, Jan. 17, 1950; d. Robert Day and Mary Ellen (Smith) Skelton; m. James Robert Schoolar; children: Tom, Ellen. BFA, Old Dominion U., 1973. Profl. artist, 1973—; drawing and painting instr. enrichent program Millsaps Coll., Jackson, Miss., 1990—; painting instr. cmty. edn. program Rankin County Sch. Dist., Brandon, Miss., 1989-94. Designer cover artwork for enrichment program Millsaps Coll., 1991-96. Vol. New State Theatre, CONTACT Crisis Line, Miss. Symphony, Jackson, 1990—. Mem. Nat. Mus. Women in Arts (assoc.), Miss. Mus. Art (assoc.), Mcpl. Art Gallery (exhibiting mem.), Miss. Watercolor Soc. (charter mem., signature artist, 2d pl. award Grand Nat. Watercolor Exhbn. 1995), Profl. Artists League of Miss. (rec. sec. 1995—). Home and Studio: 175 Summit Ridge Dr Brandon MS 39042

SCHOONOVER, JEAN WAY, public relations consultant; b. Richfield Springs, N.Y.. AB, Cornell U., 1941. With D-A-Y Pub. Rels., Ogilvy & Mather Co., N.Y.C., 1949-91, D-A-Y Pub. Rels. Inc. and predecessor, N.Y.C., 1949—; owner, pres. Dudley-Anderson-Yutzy Pub. Rels. Inc. and predecessor, N.Y.C., 1970—; chmn. Dudley-Anderson-Yutzy Pub. Relations Inc. and predecessor, 1984-88; merger with Ogilvy & Mather, 1983; sr. v.p. Ogilvy & Mather U.S., 1984-91; vice chmn. Ogilvy Pub. Relations Group, 1986-91; ind. cons., 1992—; pres. YWCA of the City of N.Y., 1994—; mem., historian, Pub. Relations Seminar; mem. U.S. Dept. Agriculture Agribusiness Promotion Council, 1985—. Trustee Cornell U., 1975-80; mem. Def. Adv. Com. on Women in Svcs., 1987-89. Named Advt. Woman of Yr. Am. Advt. Fedn., 1972, one of Outstanding Women in Bus. & Labor, Women's Equity Action League, 1985; recipient Matrix award, 1976, Nat. Headliner award, 1984, N.Y. Women in Comm., 1976, Leadership award Internat. Orgn. Women Bus. Owners, 1980, Entrepreneurial Woman award Women Bus. Owners N.Y., 1981, Women of Distinction award Soroptimists Internat. N.Y., 1995. Mem. Women Execs. in Pub. Rels. N.Y.C. (pres. 1979-80), Pub. Rels. Soc. Am., Pub. Rels. Soc. N.Y. (pres. 1979), Womens Forum, Women's City Club. Home: 25 Stuyvesant St New York NY 10003-7505

SCHOONOVER, MARGARET See LEFRANC, MARGARET

SCHOR, MIRA, artist; b. N.Y.C., June 1, 1950; d. Ilya and Resia (Ainstein) S. BA, NYU, 1970; MFA, CalArts, 1973. Co-editor M/E/A/N/I/N/G, N.Y.C., 1986-96; faculty Parsons Sch. Design, N.Y.C., 1989—; faculty Sarah Lawrence Coll., Bronxville, N.Y., 1991-94, Skowhegan (Maine) Sch., 1995, SUNY, Purchase, 1983-86; asst. prof. Nova Scotia Coll. Art & Design, Halifax, Nova Scotia, Can., 1974-78; visual arts com. Fine Arts Work Ctr., Provincetown, Mass., 1994—; adv. bd. Provincetown Arts Press, Inc., 1993—. One-person exhbns. Horodner Romley Gallery, N.Y.C., 1993, 95. Guggenheim fellow, 1992, NEA fellow, 1985. Mem. Coll. Art Assn.

SCHOR, SUZI, lawyer; b. Chgo., Feb. 1, 1947; d. Samuel S. and Dorothy Helen (Hineline); 1 child, Kate. BABA, Ind. U., 1964; MBA Mktg., Northwestern U., 1967, JD, 1970; PhD in Fine Arts (hon.), U. Nev., PhD in Clin. Psychology, 1989. Bar: Ill., 1971. Pvt. practice L.A., 1971-80; v.p. legal affairs Little Gypzy Mgmt., Inc., Beverly Hills, Calif., 1980—; mem. Pres.'s Coun. on Alcoholism. Author: 13th Step to Death; contbg. author Wine and Dine Mag.; contbr. articles to profl. jours. Bd. dirs. Nat. Ctr. for Hyperactive Children, L.A., 1989-91, sec. Rainbow Guild Cancer Charity, L.A., 1985-89, ind. cons. Jewish Legal Aid, L.A., 1988—; campaign coord. advisor Dem. Nat. Campaign, L.A., 1990, 94. Recipient Poet of Yr. award, 1995. Mem. ABA (criminal justice com. 1994), AAUW, NAADAC, CAADAC, L.A. Breakfast Club (chmn. entertainment 1988-90), Rotary. Jewish.

SCHORR, LISBETH BAMBERGER, child and family policy analyst, author, educator; b. Munich, Jan. 20, 1931; d. Fred S. and Lotte (Krafft) Bamberger; m. Daniel L. Schorr, Jan. 8, 1967; children—Jonathan, Lisa. BA with highest honors, U. Calif., Berkeley, 1952; LHD (hon.), Wilkes U., 1991, U. Md., 1994. Med. care cons. U.A.W. and Community Health Assn., Detroit, 1956-58; asst. dir. Dept. Social Security AFL-CIO, Washington, 1958-65; acting chief CAP Health Svcs., OEO, 1965-66; chief program planning Office for Health Affairs, OEO, Washington, 1967; cons. Children's Def. Fund, Washington, 1973-79; scholar-in-residence Inst. of Medicine, 1979-80; chmn. Select Panel on Promotion Child Health, 1979-80; adj. prof. maternal and child health U. N.C., Chapel Hill, 1981-85; lectr. social medicine Harvard U. Med. Sch., 1984—; dir. project on effective interventions Harvard U., 1988—; nat. coun. Alan Gutmacher Inst., 1974-79, 82-85; pub. mem. Am. Bd. Pediatrics, 1978-84; vice chmn. Found. for Child Devel., 1978-84, bd. dirs., 1976-84, 86-94; mem. coun. Nat. Ctr. for Children in Poverty, 1987-96; mem. children's program adv. com. Edna McConnell Clark Found., 1987—; bd. dirs. Pub. Edn. Fund Network, 1991-93; co-chair Roundtable on Comprehensive Cmty. Inititatives Aspen Inst., 1992—, chair roundtable steering com. on evaluation, 1994—; mem. bd. on children and families NAS, 1993-95; mem. nat. Commn. State and Local Pub. Svcs., 1992-94; mem. task force on young children Carnegie Corp., 19-94; mem. sec.'s adv. com. Head Start quality and expansion, 1993-94; trustee City Yr., 1994—; mem. exec. com. Harvard Project on Schooling and Children. Author: Within Our Reach: Breaking the Cycle of Disadvantage, 1988. Recipient Dale Richmond Meml. award Am. Acad. Pediatrics, 1977, 9th Ann. Robert F. Kennedy Book award, 1989, Nelson Cruikshank award nat.

Coun. Sr. Citizens, 1990, Porter prize, 1993. Mem. Inst. Medicine, NAS, Nat. Acad. on Social Ins., Phi Beta Kappa. Home: 3113 Woodley Rd NW Washington DC 20008-3449

SCHORR-RIBERA, HILDA KEREN, psychologist; b. N.Y.C., May 2, 1942; d. Leon and Rosa Schorr-Ribera; m. Ira Eli Wessler, Aug. 6, 1971; children: Mike, Daniel. BA, Hunter Coll., 1963; MEd, U. No. Fla., 1982; PhD, U. Pitts., 1988. Lic. psychologist, Pa. Psychotherapist South Hills Interfaith Ministries, Bethel Park, Pa., 1989-92, Profl. Psychol. Assn. of Greater Pitts., 1992; pvt. practice psychologist Pitts., 1993; group facilitator Burger King Cancer Caring Ctr., Pitts., 1989—, Allegheny Hospice, Pitts., 1994—; child therapist Forbes Hospice, Pitts., 1993; psychol. evaluator Washington (Pa.) County Ct., 1993—, Allegheny County Ct., Pitts., 1995—. Author: (with others) Educating the Child With Cancer, 1993. Keynote speaker on illness and bereavement to hosps., schs., and agys., Pitts., 1989—. Fellow Am. Bd. Med. Psychotherapists and Psychodiagnosticians (diplomate); mem. APA, Am. Counseling Assn., Am. Coll. Forensic Examiners, Am. Bd. Forensic Examiners, Greater Pitts. Psychol. Assn. Office: 117 Ridgeway Ct Pittsburgh PA 15228

SCHOTT, LINDA KAY, historian, educator; b. Hondo, Tex., June 7, 1957; d. Rudolph Robert and Elsie Emma (Boehle) S.; m. Horace Jeffrey Hodges, Dec. 22, 1979 (div. Aug. 1985); m. Ralph Joseph Noonan III, May 16, 1987; 1 child, Decker Joseph Schott-Noonan. BA, Baylor U., 1979; MA, Stanford U., 1982, PhD, 1986. Seminar instr. Stanford U., 1984-85; asst. prof. history S.W. Tex. State U., San Marcos, 1985-86, Tex. Luth. Coll., Seguin, 1986-89; asst. prof. history U. Tex., San Antonio, 1989-95, assoc. prof., 1995—, dir. Ctr. for Study of Women and Gender, 1994—; mem. governing bd. Conf. of Women Historians in Tex., 1992-95. Author: Reconstructing Women's Thoughts, 1997, also articles. Mem. Am. Hist. Assn., Orgn. Am. Historians, Berkshire Conf. Women Historians, So. Assn. Women Historians. Democrat. Office: U Tex at San Antonio 6900 N Loop 1604 W San Antonio TX 78249

SCHOU, GAYLE EVELYN, academic administrator; b. Morrison, Ill., Oct. 6, 1941; d. Francis Kneale and Dorothy Pearl (Hockman) Nelson; m. Thomas Gordon Mode, Oct. 5, 1961 (dec. Oct. 1972); 1 child, Laurel; m. Wayne Albert Schou, May 29, 1976. BS, No. Ill. U., 1970, MS, 1977, EdD, 1980. Tchr. Thomson (Ill.) Pub. Schs., 1963-76; dir. spl. programs St. Mary's U., San Antonio, 1980-82; asst. prof. S.W. Tex. State U., San Marcos, 1982, U. Tex., San Antonio, 1983; assoc. dean Coll. of St. Mary, Omaha, 1983-86; assoc. dean continuing edn. George Washington U., Washington, 1986-89; assoc. dean Rio North Rio Salado C.C., Phoenix, 1989-92; dean gen. edn. and spl. programs Clarkson Coll., Omaha, 1992-94; exec. dir. St. Louis Ctr. Nat. Louis U., 1994-95; exec. dir. Corp. Ednl. Svcs., Clarke Coll., 1995—. Democrat. Office: Clarke Coll 1550 Clarke Dr Dubuque IA 52001

SCHOUTEN, ROSE-MARY, adult education educator; b. Hilversum, The Netherlands, May 10, 1944; arrived in U.S., 1968; d. Marinus Hendrikus and Lebertha (van den Nulft) S.; children: Kadrian Schouten Talley, Julian Schouten Talley. MA in French, Sorbonne, Paris, 1964; BA in Anthropology, Tarkio (Mo.) Coll., 1972; MA in Anthropology, So. Meth. U., 1976. Hotel mgr. Hotel Spaans, Haarlem, The Netherlands, 1966-67; law clk. Freeman, Freeman, Chgo., 1968-69; freelance translator/interpreter Dallas, 1979-85; ESL instr. English Lang. Specialists, Houston, 1985-94, Houston Cmty. Coll., 1995—; part-time tchr. U. Houston, 1996; part-time tutor Russian Lang. Svcs., Houston, 1995-96. Recipient grants NSF, 1975-76, Social Sci. Found., 1975, Houston Cmty. Coll., 1995. Mem. TESOL, Tex. TESOL (bd. mem. 1995—), Houston Grand Opera, Houston Art Mus., YMCA. Office: Houston Community Coll 5407 Gulfton Houston TX 77081

SCHOWALTER, ELLEN LEFFERTS, financial planner; b. Milw., Apr. 23, 1937; d. William George and Alice (Virgin) Lefferts; m. John Erwin Schowalter, June 11, 1960; children: Jay, Bethany. BS, U. Wis., 1958, MS, 1959; MA, Yale U., 1982. Cert. fin. planner. Tchr. English West Allis (Wis.) Bd. Edn., 1959-60, New Haven (Conn.) Bd. Edn., 1960-61, Cin. Bd. Edn., 1961-63; dir. Bethesda Nursery Sch., New Haven, 1971-80; registered rep. First Investors Corp., Hamden, Conn., 1982-85; sr. rep. Jonathan Alan and Co., Inc. (name changed to Schowalter & Seymour Assocs.), White Plains, N.Y., 1985-90; cert. fin. planner Schowalter Assocs., New Haven, 1990—; seminar leader, tchr., Successful MOney MgmtSeminars, Fairfield Continuing Edn. Program, Fairfield, Conn., 1987-92; seminar leader Pace U. Exec. Nurses,1988-92, K Mart Employees, Morrisville, Pa, North Bergen, N.J., 1994—. ,. Mem. Internat. Assn. Fin. Planners, Coll. Fin. Planning, Mortar Bd. Democrat. Lutheran. Home: 606 Ellsworth Ave New Haven CT 06511-1636 Office: Schowalter Assocs 68 Putnam Ave New Haven CT 06517-2825

SCHRADER, DEBORAH LYNN, social insurance representative; b. Ludington, Mich., Sept. 8, 1953; d. Obe Jackson and Lois Amelia (Tower) S. AA, West Shore C.C., Scottville, Mich., 1973; BA, Western Mich. U., Kalamazoo, 1975; cert. in Humanities, U. f.ENGL. SPR. u. LIT, Salzburg, Austria, 1973; cert. in Computers, No. Mich. Coll., Traverse City, 1985. Social ins. specialist Social Security Adminstrn., L.A., 1976-81; Traverse City, Mich., 1983-86; field specialist Ludington, Mich., 1987—; author pvt. practice, 1982—; cons. Washtenaw Assn. Retarded Citizens Ann Arbor, Mich., 1984-87, Mason County Human Svcs. Coun., Ludington, Mich., 1986—. Author: A Gentleman's Agreement, 1984; author, pub.: Company Policy, 1991, Balance Due, 1992; editor, contbr.: (newsletter) News: From Olmos Productions, 1989—; contbr.: (newspapers) Lake County Star, 1986-93, Mason County Press, 1986-90, Ludington Daily News, 1986-93; soloist: J. Rutter's "Requiem," 1993, 96. Bus. mgr. Lakeshore Chorale, Ludington, Mich., 1992—; assoc. mem. Gang Intervention Task Force, Ludington, Mich., 1994—. Recipient Spl. Act or Svc. award Social Security Adminstrn., 1984, 85, 87, 88, 90. Mem. Edward James Olmos Fan Club (pres.), Mason County Human Svc. Coun., Gang Intervention Task Force, West Mich. Rock and Mineral Club.

SCHRADER, DIANA LEE, secondary education educator; b. N.Y.C., Oct. 9, 1946; d. Edward Schrader and Virginia (Felleman) Buck. Assocs. degree, Concordia Coll., 1966, BA, 1968. Cert. tchr., N.Y. Tchr. grade 1 Emanuel Luth., Patchogue, N.Y., 1968-70; tchr. grades 3-4, 1-2 Grace Luth., Bronx, N.Y., 1970-74; tchr. grades 3-4, 5 Queens Sch., Kew Gardens, N.Y., 1974-77; writer, home tutor N.Y.C., 1977-79; tchr. grade 8 St. Matthew Luth. Sch., N.Y.C., 1979—; co-dir. upper sch. program grades 5-8, 1991—. Author: Television in Classroom, 1978, Take My Hands, 1980; contbr. articles to ednl. jours. and mags. Pres. congregation St. Matthew Ch., N.Y.C., 1991-96, choir dir., 1990—. Mem. ASCD, Luth. Schs. Assn. (Tchr. of Yr. 1990). Lutheran. Office: St Matthew Luth Sch 200 Sherman Ave New York NY 10034-3301

SCHRADER, HELEN MAYE, retired municipal worker; b. Akron, Ohio, June 8, 1920; d. Simon P. and Helen Cecelia (Fennessy) Eberz; widowed; children: Alfred E., Kathleen Therese Schrader Wein. Notary pub., Ohio. Insp., clk. Fed. Govt. agys., 1940; stenographer Chem. Warfare divsn. USAF, Akron, 1954; clk., stenographer VA; elected clk./treas. of twp. Springfield (Ohio) Twp., 1956-92. Sec. Springfield Dem. Club, Akron, 1957—; sec., treas. Springfield Twp. Civic Club, 1980—. Mem. Summit County Assn. of Trustees and Clks. (sec. 1959-78, 83-92, Svc. plaque 1979, 92). Roman Catholic. Home: 693 Neal Rd Akron OH 44312-3709

SCHRAGE, ROSE, educational administrator; b. Montelimar, France, Apr. 15, 1942; came to U.S., 1947; d. Abraham and Celia (Silbiger) Levine; m. Samuel Schrage, Dec. 12, 1935 (dec. 1976); children: Abraham, Leon. BRE, Beth Rivkah Tchrs. Sem., Bklyn., 1968; Paralegal, Manpower Career Devel. Agy., Bklyn., 1973; MS, L.I. U., 1975; Advanced Cert. Ednl. Adminstrn., Bklyn. Coll., 1983. Cert. sch. dist. adminstr., guidance counselor, tchr., asst. prin. Sec. N.Y.C., 1964-68; police adminstrv. aide N.Y.C. Police Dept., 1974-75; coordinator state reading aid program Sch. Dist. 14, Bklyn., 1977-78, project dir. Title VII, 1978-81, asst. dir. reimbursable fed. and state programs, 1981-85, dist. bus. mgr., 1985-94, asst. prin., 1994—; chmn. N.Y.C. Bd. Edn. IMPACT Com., Bklyn., 1986—. Author (poem): Never Again, 1983; contbg. editor Chai Today; contbr. articles on current affairs and concerns to profl. jours. Del. Republican. Jud. Conf., 1968; founder, pres Concerned Parents, Bklyn., 1977; radio co-host Israeli War Heroes Fund-Radiothon, Bklyn.; family counselor local social agys., Bklyn. Recipient Cert. of Appreciation as vol. regional coord. N.Y. State Mentoring Program N.Y. Gov. Cuomo, 1991. Mem. Am. Assn. Sch. Adminstrs., Assn. Orthodox Jewish Tchrs. (v.p. exec. bd.), N.Y. State Assn. Sch. Bus. Ofcls., N.Y.C. Assn. Sch. Bus. Ofcls., Coun. Suprs. and Adminstrs.

SCHRALL, ROBERTA LEE, elementary school educator; b. New Kensington, Pa., Nov. 1, 1952; d. Robert Lee and Rose Marie (Lentz) Adams; m. Donald George Schrall, June 23, 1973; children: Julie Ann, Laurie Anne. BS in Elem. Edn., Edinboro U. Pa., 1973, MEd, 1975. Cert. tchr., Pa. Kindergarten, 1st grade tchr. Greenville (Pa.) Sch. Dist., 1973-76; substitute tchr. Conneaut Sch. Dist., Linesville, Pa., 1977-87, kindergarten tchr., chpt. 1 math. tchr., 1987-88, chpt. 1 math. tchr., 1988—; 5th grade math. adv. bd. Pa. Dept. Edn., Harrisburg, 1994—. Pres. PTO, Linesville, Pa., 1980-81; religious edn. instr. St. Phillips Ch., Linesville, Pa., 1981-83. Mem. NEA, Pa. State Edn. Assn., Conneaut Edn. Assn. (pres.-elect 1995—), Nat. Coun. Tchrs. Math. Home: 15721 Kings Dr Meadville PA 16335 Office: Conneaut Lake Elem Sch Box AB-630 Line St Conneaut Lake PA 16316

SCHRAM, GERALDINE MOORE, security consultant; b. Kinde, Mich., Jan. 1, 1935; d. Charles Harold and Stella Mary (Horetski) Moore; children: Robert Charles, Kelly Jo. Cert. Bus., Cleary Coll., Ypsilanti, 1954; BAA in Bus., Delta Coll., University Center, Mich., 1983; BS in Mgmt./Mktg., Northwood Inst., Midland, Mich., 1988. Registered med. sec. Hubbard Meml. Hosp., U. Mich., Ann Arbor, 1955-58; account mgr. Bloom Assocs., Detroit, 1960-62; pub. rels. staff Dow Chem. Co., Midland, Mich., 1980-96; govt. security adminstr. Dow Corning Corp., Midland, 1980-96; cons./lectr. Janus Assocs., Midland, 1977—; lectr. in field; facilitator World Assn. Document Examiners, Chgo., 1989—. Author: Personalities at Risk, 1993; contbr. articles to profl. jours. Mem. Am. Def. Preparedness Assn., World Assn. Document Examiners, Internat. Graphoanalysis Soc. (instr. 1976—), C. of C., Am. Soc. Indsl. Security. Republican. Roman Catholic. Home and Office: 302 Hollybrook Dr Midland MI 48642-3350

SCHRAMM, BRENDA GOFF, psychology and medical/health educator, counselor; b. Ithaca, N.Y., Dec. 31, 1963; d. Charles William and Mary Bertha Goff; m. Daniel Brian Schramm; 1 child, Dakota Brendan. AS in Liberal Arts with honors, Tomkins Cortland C.C., Dryden, N.Y., 1986; BS in Health Psychology with hons., Andrews U., 1989; MA in Counseling, Liberty U., 1994. Lang. instr. U. de Montemorelos, Nueva Leon, Mex., 1988; workforce rep. Iowa City Workforce Ctr., Iowa City, 1994; counselor William Underwood PhD, Cedar Rapids, Iowa, 1994; advocacy asst. N.W. Aging Assn., Spencer, Iowa, 1994; family therapist N.W. Iowa Mental Health Ctr., Spencer, 1994-95; adj. prof. Spencer Coll., 1994—, Third Age Coll., 1996—, Iowa Lakes C.C., 1996—; student counselor, 1995—. Vol. flood clean-up, Iowa City, 1993; guest spkr. Single Ministries, 1995—, Iowa Kiwanis Clubs, 1995—. Acad. scholar Andrews U., 1987-88. Mem. ACA. Office: Iowa Lakes CC Gateway North Mall Spencer IA 51301

SCHREIBER, EILEEN SHER, artist; b. Denver; d. Michael Herschel and Sarah Deborah (Tannenbaum) Sher; student U. Utah, 1942-45, N.Y.U. extension, 1966-68, Montclair (N.J.) State Coll., 1975-79; also pvt. art study; m. Jonas Schreiber, Mar. 27, 1945; children—Jeffrey, Barbara, Michael. Exhibited Morris Mus. Arts and Scis., Morristown, N.J., 1965-73, N.J. State Mus., 1969, Lever House, N.Y.C., 1971, Paramus (N.J.) Mus., 1973, Newark Mus., 1978, Am. Water Color Soc., Audubon Artists, N.A.D. Gallery, N.Y.C., Pallazzo Vecchio Florence (Italy), Art Expo 1987, 1988, Newark Mus., 1991-92; represented in permanent collections Tex. A&M U., Sunbelt Computers, Phoenix, Ariz., State of N.J., Morris Mus., Seton Hall U., Bloomfield (N.J.) Coll., Barclay Bank of Eng., N.J., Somerset Coll., NYU, Morris County State Coll., Broad Nat. Bank, Newark, IBM, Am. Telephone Co., RCA, Johnson & Johnson, Champion Internat. Paper Co., SONY, Mitsubishi, Celanese Co., Squibb Corp., Nabisco, Nat. Bank Phila., NYU, Data Control, Sperry Univac, Ga. Pacific Co., Pub. Svc. Co. N.J., Forms Galleries, Delray Beach, Fla., Robin Hutchins Galleries, Maplewood, N.J., others; also pvt. collections. Recipient awards N.J. Watercolor Soc., 1969, 72, Marian E. Halpern Memorial award Nat. Assn. Women Artists, 1970; 1st award in watercolor Hunterdon Art Center, 1972, Best in Show award Short Hills State Show, 1976, Tri-State Purchase award Somerset Coll., 1977, Art Expo, N.Y.C. 1987, 88, ; numerous others. Mem. Nat. Assn. Women Artists (chmn. watercolor jury; Collage award 1983, Marian Halpren meml. award 1995), Nat., N.J. Artists Equity, Printmaker Coun. Visual Artists (1st award in printmaking 1996). Home: 22 Powell Dr West Orange NJ 07052-1337

SCHRENKER, VIRGINIA MCCRARY, math and Latin educator; b. Nashville, Jan. 20, 1949; d. James Watts and Georgia Ruth (Kesterson) McC.; m. Carl James Schrenker, Jr., Aug. 17, 1974; children: Michael James, David Alexander. BA, Memphis State U., 1970; MA, Fla. State U., 1973. Cert. tchr., Fla. Tchr. Dade County Pub. Schs., Coral Gables, Fla., 1973-84, 1973—; advanced placement faculty cons. Coll. Entrance Examination Bd., Princeton, N.J., 1993—; adv. com. for Nat. Latin Exam. Am. Classical League, Oxford, Ohio, 1990-93; ednl. cons. Fla. Dept. Edn., Tallahassee, 1987-88; textbook evaluation com. for fgn. langs. Dade County Pub. Schs., Miami, 1983. Asst. editor Archaeological News, 1971-73; editor (newsletter) Bromeliadvisory, 1988-94. Mem. Nat. Coun. Tchrs. Math., Fla. Coun. Tchrs. Math., Classical Assn. Fla. (exec. sec. 1986-93), Am. Philol. Assn., Am. Classical League, Classical Assn. Midwest and South, Dade County Coun. Tchrs. Math., Cryptanthus Soc. (pres. 1996—), Bromeliad Soc. (student judge), Eta Sigma Phi, Pi Mu Epsilon.

SCHREYER, NANCY KRAFT, medical science researcher; b. Chelsea, Mass., Apr. 18, 1952; d. Meyer Louis and Eileen Marguerite (McCauley) Kraft; m. Raymond Scott Schreyer, Aug. 22, 1976; children: Kraftin Ellice, Evan Kraft. BS, Simmons Coll., 1974; PhD, Hahnemann Med. Coll., 1979. Instr. Hahnemann Med. Coll., Coll. Allied Health Professions, Phila., 1977-79, sr. instr., 1979-80; asst. instr. Hahnemann Med. Coll., Phila., 1977-79, instr., 1979-80, sr. instr., 1980-81; asst. prof. Hahnemann U., Sch. Allied Health Professions, Phila., 1980-88, Hahnemann U. Sch. Medicine, Phila., 1981-88, Hahnemann U. Grad. Sch., Phila., 1983—; non-affiliated mem. animal care and use com. Bristol Myers-Squibb Co. N.J., 1988—. Contbr. articles to profl. jours. Rsch. grantee Hahnemann U., 1983, Am. Heart Assn., 1986. Mem. Am. Soc. Hypertension, N.Y. Acad. Scis., Am. Soc. Primatologists, Physiol. Soc. Phila., Am. Assn. Lab. Animal Sci., Am. Physiol. Soc.

SCHRICKER, ETHEL KILLINGSWORTH, business management, public relations, and marketing consultant, public speaker; b. Hagerstown, Md., July 22, 1937; d. Lloyd Granville and Ethel Mull; children: Jeanne, Lori, Jerri. BA in Mgmt., Hood Coll., 1994; postgrad. in Psychology, Hood Coll, 1994—. Vol. Literacy Coun., Frederick, 1976-84, Dept. Social Svcs., Frederick, 1984; bd. ruling elders Frederick Presbyn. Ch., 1989-92; active Frederick County Commn. for Women, 1996—. Named Bus. Woman of Yr. Frederick Bus. and Profl. Women, 1992. Mem. Assn. Sch. Bus. Ofcls. (chairperson seminar devel. com. 1990-94), Frederick County Assn. Adminstrv. and Supervisory Pers., Frederick County C. of C., Frederick County Advt. Fedn., Carroll Creek Rotary Club, Toastmasters Internat. (area gov. 1991-92, pub. rels. 1991-93, v.p. pub. rels. 1995—). Home: PO Box 15 Frederick MO 21705-0015

SCHRODER, MARILYN A., mathematics educator; b. Troy, N.Y., May 17, 1969; d. David T. and Mary E. S. BS Mgmt., SUNY, Binghamton, 1991; Cert. Edn., Russell Sage Coll., 1992. Math. reasoning instr. Johns Hopkins Ctr. for Talented Youth, Towson, Md., 1993, New London, Conn., 1994; math. tchr. North Warren Cen. High Sch., Chestertown, N.Y., 1993——; math. reasoning instr. Johns Hopkins Ctr. for Talented Youth, Stanford, Calif., 1996; tutor gifted edn., North Warren Cen., 1994—. Mem. Bus. and Profl. Women's Assn. Office: North Warren Central Main St Chestertown NY 12866

SCHROEDER, JOYCE KATHERINE, research analyst; b. Moline, Ill., Apr. 1, 1951; d. Reinhold J. and Miriam-May Schroeder. BS in Math., U. Ill., 1973, MA in Ops. Rsch., 1978. Underwriter, programmer Springfield, Ill., 1973-76; ops. rsch. analyst Ill. Dept. Transp., Springfield, 1976-78, data analyst, 1978-80, team leader, fatal accident reporting sys., 1980-83, mgr. safety project evaluation, 1983-92, mgr. accident studies and investigation, 1992—; sys. engrng. del. to China China Assn. for Sci. and Tech., 1986; mem. staff Driving While Intoxicated Adv. Coun. and Task Force, State of Ill., 1983-86, 89-92, Gov. Task Force on Occupant Protection, 1988-90; active Ill. Traffic Safety Info. Sys. Coun., 1993—. Vol. Animal Protective League, Springfield; leaderbd. co-chairperson LPGA Rail Classic, Springfield, 1983-87; amb. of goodwill Lions of Ill. Found., 1993, trustee, 1995—. Lions Clubs Internat. Melvin Jones fellow, 1993, Lions of Ill. Found. fellow, 1995. Mem. Lions of Ill. Found. (amb. of goodwill 1993, trustee 1995—), Springfield Lincoln Land Lions Club (charter pres. 1988-90, treas. 1993-95, news editor 1995—), Lions Club (dist. gov. Ill. 1992-93, state membership coord. 1994—, Melvin Jones fellow 1993), Past. Dist. Gov. Assn. (sec.-treas. 1993—), Phi Kappa Phi, Kappa Delta Pi. Office: Ill Dept Transp 3215 Executive Park Dr Springfield IL 62703-4509

SCHROEDER, MARSHA ANN, therapist, counselor; d. Francis and Marcella Cardinal; m. Tim Edwin Schroeder; children: Tim E. II, Steven M. BA in Psychology, Saginaw Valley State U., 1985; M Counseling, Ctrl. Mich. U., 1992, lic. profl. counselor, 1993. Adj. faculty mem. Delta Coll., University Center, Mich., 1990—; therapist Cath. Family Svc., Saginaw, Mich., 1992—; sch. counselor St. Peter and Paul Cath. Sch., Saginaw, 1994—. Mem. ACA. Roman Catholic.

SCHROEDER, MARY MURPHY, federal judge; b. Boulder, Colo., Dec. 4, 1940; d. Richard and Theresa (Kahn) Murphy; m. Milton R. Schroeder, Oct. 15, 1965; children: Caroline Theresa, Katherine Emily. B.A., Swarthmore Coll., 1962; J.D., U. Chgo., 1965. Bar: Ill. 1966, D.C. 1966, Ariz. 1970. Trial atty. Dept. Justice, Washington, 1965-69; law clk. Hon. Jesse Udall, Ariz. Supreme Ct., 1970; mem. firm Lewis and Roca, Phoenix, 1971-75; judge Ariz. Ct. Appeals, Phoenix, 1975-79, U.S. Ct. Appeals (9th cir.), Phoenix, 1979—; vis. instr. Ariz. State U. Coll. Law, 1976, 77, 78. Contbr. articles to profl. jours. Mem. ABA, Ariz. Bar Assn., Fed. Bar Assn., Am. Law Inst. (coun. mem.), Am. Judicature Soc., Soroptimists. Democrat. Office: US Ct Appeals 9th Cir 6421 Courthouse & Fed Bldg 230 N 1st Ave Phoenix AZ 85025-0230

SCHROEDER, PATRICIA SCOTT (MRS. JAMES WHITE SCHROEDER), congresswoman; b. Portland, Oreg., July 30, 1940; d. Lee Combs and Bernice (Lemoin) Scott; m. James White Schroeder, Aug. 18, 1962; children: Scott William, Jamie Christine. B.A. magna cum laude, U. Minn., 1961; J.D., Harvard U., 1964. Bar: Colo. 1964. Field atty. NLRB, Denver, 1964-66; practiced in Denver, 1966-72; hearing officer Colo. Dept. Personnel, 1971-72; mem. faculty U. Colo., 1969-72, Community Coll., Denver, 1969-70, Regis Coll., Denver, 1970-72; mem. 93d-104th Congresses from 1st Colo. dist., 1973-96; co-chmn. Congl. Caucus for Women's Issues, 1976-96; mem. Ho. of Reps., ranking minority mem. judiciary subcom. on the Constitution, mem. Nat. Security Com. Inducted, National Women's Hall of Fame, 1995. Congregationalist. Office: US Ho of Reps 2307 Rayburn House Office Washington DC 20515

SCHROEDER, RITA MOLTHEN, retired chiropractor; b. Savanna, Ill., Oct. 25, 1922; d. Frank J. and Ruth J. (McKenzie) Molthen; m. Richard H. Schroeder, Apr. 23, 1948 (div.); children—Richard, Andrew, Barbara, Thomas, Paul, Madeline. Student, Chem. Engring., Immaculate Heart Coll., 1940-41, UCLA, 1941, Palmer Sch. of Chiropractic, 1947-49; D. Chiropractic, Cleve. Coll. of Chiropractic, 1961. Engring.-tooling design data coordinator Douglas Aircraft Co., El Segundo, Santa Monica and Long Beach, Calif., 1941-47; pres. Schroeder Chiropractic, Inc., 1982-93; dir. Pacific States Chiropractic Coll., 1978-80, pres. 1980-81. Recipient Palmer Coll. Ambassador award, 1973. Parker Chiropractic Research Found. Ambassador award, 1976, Coll. Ambassador award Life West Chiropractic Coll. Mem. Internat. Chiropractic Assn., Calif. Chiropractic Assn., Internat. Chiropractic Assn. Calif., Assn. Am. Chiropractic Coll. Presidents, Council Chiropractic Edn. (Pacific State Coll. rep.), Am. Pub. Health Assn., Royal Chiropractic Knights of the Round Table. Home: 8701 N State Highway 41 Spc 18 Fresno CA 93720-1010 Office: Schroeder Chiropractic Inc 2535 N Fresno St Fresno CA 93703-1831

SCHROER, JANE HASTINGS, nurse practitioner; b. Pender, Nebr., Aug. 24, 1947; d. John Dean and Florence (Meier) Hastings; m. Ronald L. Schroer, May 13, 1967; 1 child, Patricia Schroer Kennedy. LPN, Antonian Sch. Prac. Nursing, Carroll, Iowa, 1966; Diploma, St. Joseph Sch. Nursing, Sioux City, Iowa, 1980; B.Applied Sci., Teikyo Westmar U., LeMars, Iowa, 1985; Women's Health Care Nurse Practitioner, S.W. Med. Ctr./U. Tex., Dallas, 1990. Cert. nurse practitioner Tex., Iowa, Ariz., Nebr., Fla.; RN. Nurse cardiac catheterization lab. Marian Health Ctr., Sioux City, 1980-85; ob-gyn. nurse practitioner Drs. Goodman and Partridge, Chandler, Ariz., 1991-93; nurse practitioner STD Clinic, Austin, Tex., 1994-95; women's health nurse practitioner Round Rock (Tex.) Rural Health Clinic, 1995—. Mem. ACOG (edn. affiliate), Austin Area Nurse Practitioner Assn., Tex. Nurse Practitioner Assn., Tex. Nurses Assn. Republican. Roman Catholic. Home: 2008 Rosemary Ln Round Rock TX 78664 Office: Round Rock Health Clinic 2000 N Mays Ste 109 Round Rock TX 78664

SCHROER, MARY, state legislator; b. St. Marys, Ohio, Feb. 11, 1947; m. J. Michael Schroer; children: Jennifer, Amy, Rebecca. Student, Washtenaw C.C., Ea. Mich. U. Legis. asst. to State Sen. Lana Pollack Inst. Study of Mental Retardation and Related Disabilities, 1983-92; state rep. 52d dist. State of Mich., 1992—. Mem. Washtenaw County (Mich.) Dem. Party, Washtenaw County Area Auto Plant Coaltion, Ann Arbor, Pittsfield Twp. Econ. Deve. Corp. Bd.; past pres. Carpenter Sch. PTO, Ann Arbor; former bd. dirs. Ann Arbor (Mich.) Cmty. Ctr. Roman Catholic. Office: 907 Olds Plz Bldg Lansing MI 48913

SCHROM, ELIZABETH ANN, educator; b. Princeton, Minn., June 7, 1941; d. Raymond Alois and Grace Eleanor (Hayes) S. Student, U. Minn., 1960; BA, St. Scholastica Coll., Duluth, Minn., 1963; postgrad., Princeton U., 1965; MEd, Temple U., 1972; MLS, Drexel U., 1974; postgrad., NYU, 1981, Russian Temple U., 1983. Tchr. Strandquist (Minn.) H.S., 1963-64, Hutchinson (Minn.) H.S., 1964-65, Peace Corps, Ankara, Turkey, 1965-67, Phila. Sch. Dist., 1968-80; children's libr. Laurel (Del.) Pub. Libr., 1983. Mem. Jewish Com. on Middle East, Washington, 1988-90, 93, Nat. Coun. Returned Peace Corps. Vols., Washington, 1989-96, Nat. Taxpayers Union, Washington, 1988-92; mem. bd. policy Liberty Lobby, Washington, 1989-96; mem. Emergency Com. to Stop Immigration, Marietta, Ga., 1989-91. Populist. Roman Catholic. Home: RR 2 Box 206 Ortonville MN 56278-9784

SCHUBERT, HELEN CELIA, public relations executive; b. Washington City, Wis.; d. Paul H. and Edna (Schmidt) S. BS, U. Wis., Madison. Dir. pub. rels. United Cerebral Palsy, Chgo., 1961; adminstrv. dir. Nat. Design Ctr., Chgo., 1962-67; owner Schubert Pub. Rels., Chgo., 1967—; bd. dirs. Fashion Group, Chgo., 1988-95. Mem. women's bd. Am. Cancer Soc., Chgo., 1988-96, Art Resources in Tchg., Chgo., 1988-92. Recipient Comm. award Am. Soc. Interior Designers, Chgo., 1979, 83, 88, 94; named to Chgo. Women's Hall of Fame City of Chgo., 1990. Fellow Nat. Home Fashion League; mem. Women's Ad Club Chgo. (pres. 1981-83, Woman of Yr. award 1987), Women in Comm. (pres. 1969-70, Matrix award Lifetime Achievement 1996), Am. Advt. Fedn. (lt. gov. 1983-85). Lutheran. Home: 1400 N Lake Shore Dr Chicago IL 60610-1674

SCHUCK, MARJORIE MASSEY, publisher, editor, authors' consultant; b. Winchester, Va., Oct. 9, 1921; d. Carl Frederick and Margaret Harriet (Parmele) Massey; student U. Minn., 1941-43, New Sch., N.Y.C., 1948, N.Y.U., 1952, 54-55; m. Ernest George Metcalfe, Dec. 2, 1943 (div. Oct. 1949); m. 2d, Franz Schuck, Nov. 11, 1953 (dec. Jan. 1958). Mem. editorial bd. St. Petersburg Poetry Assn., 1967-68; co-editor, pub. poetry Venture Mag., St. Petersburg, Fla., 1968-69, editor, pub., 1969-79; co-editor, pub. Poetry Venture Quar. Essays, Vol. I, 1968-69, Vol. 2, 1970-71; pub., editor poetry anthologies, 1972—; founder, owner, pres. Valkyrie Press, Inc. (name changed to Valkyrie Pub. House 1980), 1972—; cons. designs and formats, trade publs. and ann. reports, lit. books and pamphlets, 1973—; founder Valkyrie Press Roundtable Workshop and Forum for Writers, 1975-79; established Valkyrie Press Reference Libr., 1976-80; pub., editor The Valkyrie Internat. Newsletter, 1986—; exec. dir. Inter-Cultural Forum Villanor Ctr., Tampa, Fla., 1987-94; dir. edn. The Villanor Mus. Fine and Decorative Arts, Tampa, 1994, St. Petersburg, 1994—; pres. Found. for Human Potentials, Inc., Tampa, 1988-94; representative distbr. Marg Art Publs. of India

(Bombay), 1992—; mem. pres. coun. U. South Fla., 1993-95; lectr. in field. Judge poetry and speech contests Gulf Beach Women's Club, 1970, Fine Arts Festival dist. 14. Am. Fedn. Women's Clubs, 1970, South and West, Inc., 1972, The Sunstone Rev., 1973, Internat. Toastmistress Clubs, 1974, 78, Beaux Arts Poetry Festival, 1983, 89, 92-96; judge poetry contest Fla. State conf. Nat. League Am. Pen Women, 1989, Tampa Bay Poetry Coun., 1994-96; judge Fla. Gov.'s Screenwriters Competition, 1984—; judge poetry contest Tampa Bay Poetry Coun., 1996. Corr.-rec. sec. Women's Aux. Hosp. for Spl. Surgery, N.Y.C., 1947-59; active St. Petersburg Mus. Fine Arts (charter), St. Petersburg Sister City Com., St. Petersburg Arts Ctr. Assn.; mem. Orange Belt express com. 1988 Centennial Celebration for St. Petersburg; mem. Com. of 100 of Pinellas County, Inc., exec. bd., 1975-77, membership chmn., 1975-77; pub. rels. chmn. Soc. for prevention Cruelty to Animals, 1968-71, bd. dirs., 1968-71, 75-77; founder, mem. Pinellas County Arts Coun., 1976-79, chmn., 1977-78; mem. grant rev. panel for lit. Fine Arts Coun. of Fla., 1979; mem. pres.'s coun. U. South Fla., 1994-95; mem., bd. dirs. Tampa Bay Poetry Found., Inc., 1995—. Named One of 76 Fla. Patriots, Fla. Bicentennial Commn., 1976; a recipient 1st ann. People of Dedication award Salvation Army, Tampa, 1984; named to Poetica Hall of Fame, Tampa Bay Poetry Coun., 1994. Mem. Am. Assn. Museums, Acad. Am. Poets, Fla. Suncoast Writers' Confs. (founder, co-dir., lectr. 1973-83, adv. bd. 1984—), Coordinating Council Lit. Mags., Friends of Libr. of St. Petersburg, Suncoast Mgmt. Inst. (exec. bd.; chmn. Women in Mgmt. 1977-78), Pi Beta Phi. Republican. Episcopalian. Author: Speeches and Writings for Cause of Freedom, 1973. Contbr. poetry to profl. jours. Home and Office: 8245 26th Ave N Saint Petersburg FL 33710-2857

SCHUELER, BETTY JANE, writer; b. Washington, Feb. 21, 1944; d. Grover Cleveland and Mary (Bruce) Sherlin; m. Gerald Joseph Schueler, Aug. 17, 1963; children: Diane Sue, Joseph Carroll, Andrew Tyson, Crystal Ann. AA, Harford C.C., Bel Air, Md., 1975; BS, SUNY, Albany, 1992; MS in Adminstrn., Ctrl. Mich. U., 1993; PhD in Interdisciplinary studies, The Grad. Sch. Am., 1996. Owner Copy Cats, Aberdeen, Md., 1975-88; instr. Harford C.C., Bel Air, Md., 1978-84; owner Compucats Computer Store, Aberdeen, 1982—, Harford Writers Group, Aberdeen, 1988—, Creative Sales and Svc., Aberdeen, 1988—; computer cons., Aberdeen, 1982—, tutor, Aberdeen, 1989—. Co-author: Coming Into the Light, 1989, Enochian Yoga, 1990, Enochian Workbook, 1993. Bd. dirs. Friends of the Harford County Librs., Riverside, Md., 1991—; treatment foster parent FACETS, Belcamp, Md., 1992—. Adult scholar Harford County C. of C., Bel Air, 1992. Mem. Am. Counseling Assn., Internat. Assn. Marriage and Family Counselors, Assn. Multicultural Counseling and Devel. Democrat. Methodist. Office: Harford Writers Group 680 W Bel Air Ave Aberdeen MD 21001

SCHUELER, JAN FRANCES MENIER, early childhood special education administrator; b. Port Clinton, Ohio, July 3, 1955; d. Vito Joseph and Isabelle Mae (Robron) Menier; m. Jerold Douglas Schueler, Mar. 18, 1977; children: Ryan, Blair, Chase. BEd in Spl. Edn., Bowling Green State U., 1977; MEd in Early Childhood, U. Toledo, Ohio, 1991. Cert. spl. edn. tchr., elem. prin., supr., pre-sch. and K-8 tchr., Ohio. Kindergarten tchr. Sandusky County (Ohio) Ednl. Svc. Ctr., 1977-80; kindergarten tchr. Huron (Ohio) City Schs., 1986-89, pre-sch. tchr., 1989-90, pre-sch. spl. edn. tchr., 1989-90; early childhood svcs. coord. No. Ohio Spl. Edn. Regional Resource Ctr., Oberlin, Ohio, 1991-94; early childhood spl. edn. dir. Sandusky County Office of Ednl. Svcs., Fremont, Ohio, 1994—; developer Huron City Schs. Pre-sch. Program, 1989-91; cons. No. Ohio SERRC, Oberlin, 1991-94, Early Childhood divsn. Ohio Dept. Edn., Columbus, 1991-94; mem. adv. bd. Berlin-Milan (Ohio) Schs. Pre-sch., 1992-94, Lorain County Office of Edn. Pre-schs., Elyria, Ohio, 1992-94. Supr. Middleground Family Reunification Program, Norwalk, Ohio, 1993-95; mem. com. Huron Athletic Boosters, Inc., 1992—, sec. 1995—; concession co-chair Huron Baseball Program, Inc., 1993-95. Mem. ASCD, Nat. Assn. for Edn. of Young Children, Coun. for Exceptional Children, Assn. for Early Childhood Edn. Internat., Children and Adults with Attention Deficit Disorder (chpt. coord. 1993-95), Phi Delta Kappa (v.p. membership Firelands chpt. 1996—), Pi Lambda Theta. Home: 307 Wexford Dr Huron OH 44839-1459 Office: Sandusky County Ednl Svc Ctr 602 W State St Fremont OH 43420-2534

SCHUELKE, CONSTANCE PATRICIA, mortgage company executive; b. Cedar Rapids, Iowa, Feb. 9, 1953; d. Emmo August and Ruth Otilia (Firnhaber) S.; m. Kevin Dennis Curran, May 21, 1983 (div. Dec. 1986); 1 child, Emma Kate Schuelke-Curran. BA, U. Nebr., 1973. Asst. mgr. Jaeger Internat., Atlanta, 1973-75; pres., owner Domani of Florence (Italy), Inc., 1975-82; assoc. broker Downtown Properties, Inc., Atlanta, 1982-85; v.p. Dunwoody Mortgage, Inc., Atlanta, 1985-90; owner, exec. v.p. FSM, Inc. dba First So. Mortgage, Atlanta, 1990-91; v.p. Dunwoody Mortgage, Inc., Atlanta, 1991-95, Regency Mortgage, Atlanta, 1995-96; Vanguard Mortgage Corp., Atlanta, 1996—. Neighborhood adv. Inman Park Civic Assn., Atlanta, 1973—, Castelberry Hill Neighborhood, Atlanta, 1988—; fund raiser Design Industry Found. for AIDS, Atlanta, 1989. Mem. Mortgage Bankers Ga., Ga. Assn. Mortgage Brokers (individual sr.), Midtown Bus. Assn., Atlanta Bd. Realtors, Ravinia Club, Pi Beta Phi, Phi Upsilon Omicron (Hon.), Nat. Honor Soc. Democrat. Home: 35 Ivy Gates Atlanta GA 30342 Office: Vanguard Mortgage Corp Ste 125 4840 Roswell Rd Bldg B Atlanta GA 30342

SCHUESSLER, ANNEMARIE, pianist, educator; b. Wheaton, Ill., Apr. 20, 1951; d. Joseph John and Maureen Eileen (Harrington) S. MusB, Manhattanville Coll., 1973; MusM, Northwestern U., 1980, MusD, 1987; artists diploma with honors, Hochschule für Musik, Wurzburg, Germany, 1982. Music dir. Am. Mil. Community of Kitzingen, Germany, 1976-78; tchr. Music Arts Sch., Highland Park, Ill., 1978-82, Jack Benny Fine Arts Ctr., Waukegan, Ill., 1982-88; lectr. DePaul U. Sch. Music, Chgo., 1984-88; asst. prof. La. State U. Sch. Music, Baton Rouge, 1988-89, Ithaca (N.Y.) Coll. Sch. Music, 1989-92; asst. prof., piano Ball State U. Sch. Music, Muncie, Ind., 1992—; adj. prof. Suzuki program Wheaton (Ill.) Coll., 1982-88, Triton Coll., River Grove, Ill., 1980-82; adjudicator nat. competitions; vis. asst. prof. Eastman Sch. Music, Rochester, N.Y., 1990-91; adj. instr. Northwestern U., Evanston, Ill., 1980-81; lectr. Kang Reung, South Korea, 1990, Teagu, Korea, 1993; lectr., performer European Piano Tchrs. Assn., Eng., 1991; performer Maly Hall, St. Petersburg, Russia, 1993—. Contbr. articles to profl. jours. Eckstein scholar Northwestern U., 1978—. Mem. ISSTIP, EPTA, Nat. Conf. on Piano Pedagogy, Coll. Music Soc. (Sec. N.E. chpt. 1992-94), Ind. Music Tchrs. Assn. (bd. dirs.), Music Tchrs. Nat. Assn., Pi Kappa Lambda. Office: Ball State U Sch Music Muncie IN 47305

SCHUESSLER FIORENZA, ELISABETH, theology educator; b. Tschanad, Romania, Apr. 17, 1938; parents German citizens; d. Peter and Magdalena Schuessler; m. Francis Fiorenza, Dec. 17, 1967; 1 child, Chris. MDiv, U. Wuerzburg, Federal Republic of Germany, 1962; Dr of Theology, U. Muenster, Federal Republic of Germany, 1970; Lic. Theol, U. Wuerzburg, 1963. Asst. prof. theology U. Notre Dame, South Bend, Ind., 1970-75, assoc. prof., 1975-80, prof., 1980-84; instr. U. Muenster, 1966-67; Talbot prof. New Testament Episcopal Div. Sch., Cambridge, Mass., 1984-88; Krister Stendahl prof. div. in scripture and interpretation Harvard U., Cambridge, Mass., 1988—; Harry Emerson Fosdick vis. prof. Union Theol. Sem., N.Y.C., 1974-75; guest prof. U. Tuebingen, Federal Republic of Germany, 1987, Cath. Theol. faculty Luzern, Switzerland, 1990. Author: Der Vergessene Partner, 1964, Priester für Gott, 1972, The Apocalypse, 1976, Invitation to the Book of Revelation, 1981, In Memory of Her, 1983, Bread not Stone, 1984, Judgement or Justice, 1985, Revelation: Vision of a Just World, 1991, But She Said - Feminist Practices of Biblical Interpretation, 1992, Discipleship of Equals: A Critical Feminist Ekklesialogy of Liberation, 1993, Jesus: Miriam's Child and Sophia's Prophet, Critical Issues in Feminist Christology, 1994; editor: Searching the Scriptures, 2 vols, 1993, 94; founding co-editor Jour. Feminist Studies in Religion; also editor other works. Mem. Am. Acad. Religion, Soc. Bibl. Lit. (past pres.). Office: Harvard Div Sch 45 Francis Ave Cambridge MA 02138-1911

SCHUK, LINDA LEE, legal assistant, business educator; b. Scott Field, Ill., July 19, 1946; d. Frank A. Schuk and Jessie (Bumpass) Stearns; divorced; 1 child, Earl Wade. BBA, U. Tex., El Paso, 1968. Lic. life and health ins. agt., Tex. Acct., traffic mgr. Farah Mfg. Co., El Paso, 1970-71; adminstrv. asst. Horizon Corp., El Paso, 1971-76; adminstrv. asst. in charge office ops. Foster-Scwartz Devel. Corp., El Paso, 1976-78; legal sec. Howell and Fields, El Paso, 1978-80; supr. Southland Corp., San Antonio, Waco, El Paso, 1980-83; sales mgr. Southland Corp., San Antonio, 1983-84, dist. mgr., 1984-87; dist. supr. E-Z Mart Convenience Stores, San Antonio, 1987-89; legal asst. Brock & Brock, San Antonio, 1989—; instr. San Antonio C.C., 1989—. Mem. NAFE. Democrat. Baptist. Home: 11903 Parliment Apt 323 San Antonio TX 78216 Office: Brock & Brock 803 E Mistletoe Ave San Antonio TX 78212-3524

SCHULER, CYNTHIA LEIGH, art educator, artist; b. Casablanca, Morocco, Aug. 13, 1954; d. E. J. and Shirley M. (Baker) Teachout; m. Warren H. Schuler, Aug. 19, 1973; children: Vanessa, Kirk. BA, Briar Cliff Coll., 1987. Cert. tchr. Art tchr. Sioux City (Iowa) Art Ctr., 1985-86, Red Oak (Iowa) Cmty. Schs., 1987—. Exhibits include Adam Whitney Gallery, Omaha, 1994-96, Jct. Days Art Exhibit, 1995. Bd. dirs. Red Oak Cmty. Theatre, 1987-89; bd. dirs., sec. Red Oak Tennis Assn., 1991-96. Mem. NEA, Iowa State Edn. Assn., Iowa Alliance Arts Edn. Republican. Lutheran.

SCHULER, DEBRA L., accounting executive; b. Milw., Dec. 23, 1964; d. Dan F. and Carol J. (Schofield-Drew) Lang; m. Randall J. Schuler, Aug. 4, 1984; children: Jessica J., Randall Jr. Student, MATC, 1991—. Acctg. supr. MLG, Brookfield, Wis., 1984—; treas. MVFC, Muskego, Wis., 1985-87. Treas. St. Pauls, K. Com., Muskego, 1995—, treas D. com., 1995—, funding com. 1996. Mem. S.E. Wis. Comml. Realtors Assn. Republican. Lutheran. Office: Mlg Mooney LeSage Group Ste 500 16620 W Bluemound Rd Brookfield WI 53005-5958

SCHULLER, EILEEN MARIE, religious studies educator; b. Edmonton, Alta., Can., 1946; d. Norbert Schuller and Elizabeth Deutsch. BA with honors, U. Alta., 1970; MA, U. Toronto, Can., 1973; PhD, Harvard U., 1983. Asst. prof. Newmann Theol. Sch., Edmonton, 1973-77; assoc. prof. Atlantic Sch. Theology, Halifax, 1982-89; prof. dept. religious studies McMaster U., Hamilton, Ont., Can., 1990—. Author: Non-Canonical Psalms from Queran, 1986, Post-Exilic Prophets, 1988; contbr. articles to profl. jours. Doctoral fellow Can. Coun., 1977-81, rsch. fellow Annenberg Inst., 1993; grantee Social Scis. & Humanities Rsch. Coun., 1992-96. Mem. Can. Soc. Biblical Studies (pres. 1993-94), Soc. Biblical Lit. (co-chair Qumen sect. 1992—), Cath. Biblical Soc. (editl. bd. 1992—). Roman Catholic.

SCHULMAN, GRACE, poet, English language educator; b. N.Y.C.; d. Bernard and Marcella (Freiberger) Waldman, m. Jerome L. Schulman, Sept. 6, 1959. Student, Bard Coll., Johns Hopkins U.; BS, Am. U., 1955; MA, NYU, 1960, PhD, 1971. Prof. Baruch Coll., N.Y.C., 1971—; poetry editor The Nation, N.Y.C., 1971—. Author: (poetry) Burn Down the Icons, 1976, Hemispheres, 1984, For That Day Only, 1994, (critical study) Marianne Moore: The Poetry of Engagement; translator (postry) At the Stone of Losses, Carmi/Present Tense Award. Fellow Yaddo, 1973, 75, 77, 79, 81, 93, MacDowell Colony, 1973, 75, 77, Rockefeller Inst., 1986, fellow in poetry N.Y. Found. for Arts, 1995; recipient Delmore Schwartz Meml. award for poetry, 1996. Mem. PEN (past v.p.), Poetry Soc. Am., Nat. Book Critics Cir., Authors Guild. Home: 1 University Pl Apt 14F New York NY 10003-4519

SCHULTE, JILL MARIE, elementary education educator; b. Platte, S.D., Apr. 12, 1968; d. Donavon Ray and Arlene Dorothy (Pedersen) Mason; m. Dale Mark Schulte, June 16, 1990; 1 child, Kyle Mason. BS in Edn., U. S.D., 1990; MA in Edn., U. No. Iowa, 1994. Cert. elem. tchr. Tchr. elem. Hansen Elem. Sch., Cedar Falls, Iowa, 1991—. Republican. Lutheran. Office: Helen A Hansen Elem Sch 616 Holmes Dr Cedar Falls IA 50613-2043

SCHULTE, SISTER LORETTA, social services consultant, educator; b. Cleve., Sept. 22, 1927; d. Frank and Mary (Berendsen) S. BS in Edn., St. John Coll., Cleve., 1958, MS in Edn., 1968. Joined Congregation of St. Joseph, Roman Cath. Ch. Elem. sch. tchr. Cath. Sch. System, Akron, Lorain, Ohio, 1950-59; elem. sch. prin. Cath. Sch. System, Akron, Lorain, 1959-75; missionary Cath. Diocese of Cleve., El Salvador, 1975-78; founder, exec. dir. West Side Cath. Ctr. Shelter, Cleve., 1979-83, Transitional Housing Inc., Cleve., 1983-90; ret., 1990; part-time mem. office staff Congregation of St. Joseph Cmty., Cleve., 1990—; cons. Transitional Housing Inc., Cons. Svcs. Inc., 1987-90; initiator First Nat. Conf. on Transitional Housing, Cleve., 1990. Author: Inn-Between: A Manual on Transitional Housing, 1989, (with others) Vision Statement for a United States Housing Policy, 1989. Mem. Ohio Coalition for the Homeless, Columbus, 1984-87; participant Housing Activist Conf., Washington, 1989. Recipient Congl. Merit-Achievement award for Peace and Justice, U.S. Congress, Washington, 1988, Peace, Jusitce and Human Dignity award Commn. on Cath. Community Action, Cleve., 1988, Berkman-Lowry Community Achievement award Legal Aid Soc. Cleve., 1989, Peace, Justice, Merit award Cuyahoga County COmmrs., Cleve., 1988. Democrat. Home: 3430 Rocky River Dr Cleveland OH 44111-2937

SCHULTZ, BARBARA MARIE, insurance company executive; b. Chgo., Sept. 9, 1943; d. Edwin and Bernice (Barstis) Legner; m. Ronald J. Schultz Sr., May 1, 1965; 1 child, Ronald J. Grad. high sch., Chgo. Account rep. Met. Ins. Co., Aurora, Ill., 1981—; qualifier Met. Life Leaders Conf., 1990. Fellow Nat. Assn. Life Underwriters (edn. chmn. 1988-91, nat. quality award Robert L. Rose award 1990), Life Underwriters Tng. Coun. (chmn. 1986-88, citation 1987), South Cook County Assn. Life Underwriters (edn. chmn. 1988-91). Roman Catholic. Office: Met Ins Co 15255 94th Ave Orland Park IL 60462-3800

SCHULTZ, CARMEN HELEN, copywriter, translator; b. Caracas, Venezuela, Jan. 22, 1962; came to U.S., 1975; d. Arthur Henry and Alicia M. (Mercedes) S. BA in Fgn. Langs. cum laude, So. Meth. U., 1984; postgrad. studies, U. Tex., Dallas, 1987-94, Monterey Inst. Internat. Studies, 1985-86; Bus. Cert., U. Tex., 1995, U. Tex., Austin, 1995. Tech. translator Mobil Oil Exploration & Producing Svcs., Dallas, 1984-85; freelance translator/interpreter Dallas, 1985-87; abstractor/rsch. asst. Rand Corp., Santa Monica, Calif., 1987; Hispanic comm. coord. Mary Kay Cosmetics, Inc., Dallas, 1987-93; bilingual copywriter Rapp Collins Worldwide, Irving, Tex., 1993-94; translator/copy editor Ornelas & Assocs., Dallas, 1994-95; translator, writer Assocs. Corp. of N.Am., Irving, 1995—. Editor/translator: Belleza Total, 1992 (Internat. Mercury award); founder, editor (newsletter) Entérate, 1988 (Hispanic 100 1990, 91); contbg. writer Applause, 1992 (Award of Merit IPBC). So. Meth. U. scholar, 1980-84. Mem. Am. Translators Assn., Am. Lit. Translators Assn., Metroplex Interpreters and Translators Assn., Dallas Hispanic C. of C., Pi Delta Phi, Sigma Delta Pi. Roman Catholic. Home: 7008 Town Bluff Dr Dallas TX 75248-5524 Office: Assocs Corp of North America 250 Carpenter Freeway Irving TX 75062

SCHULTZ, CAROLE LAMB, community volunteer; b. Corning, N.Y., May 14, 1946; d. Arthur Martin and Jane Ursula (Oehler) Lamb; m. John Charles Schultz, July 13, 1968; children: David Michael, Geoffrey Brian. BS in Math. magna cum laude, St. Lawrence U., Canton, N.Y., 1968. Systems engr. IBM, Williamsport, Pa., 1968-71; invited attendee Gov.'s Cong. of Bus./Edn. Partnerships, Harrisburg, Pa., 1991. Helped establish Children's Hands-on Mus., Children's Discovery Workshop, 1979-88. Treas. Jr. League Williamsport, Inc., 1980-82, cmty. v.p., 1985-86, pres.-elect, 1986-87, pres., 1987-88; area II coun. mem. Assn. Jr. Leagues Internat., Inc., 1988-90, chair nominating com., 1989-90; NE regional coun. United Way Am., 1993—; pers. chair Faxon-Kenmar United Meth. Ch., Williamsport, 1991-92; trustee St. Lawrence U., 1988—, chair honors com., 1994—; ednl. tech. adv. com. Williamsport Area Sch. Dist., 1994—; 2d v.p., sec., divsn. chair, planning mem. Lycoming United Way, Williamsport, 1991—, vice-chair campaign 1992, chair campaign 1993; candidate Williamsport Area Sch. Bd., 1989; panelist Leadership Lycoming, 1987, mentor, 1990—; chair steering com. Lycoming County Sch.-to-Work Partnership, 1995—; cmty. adv. bd. Williamsport-Lycoming Found., 1995—; bd. govs. Cmty. Arts Ctr. Recipient Lycoming County Brotherhood award, 1996. Mem. AAUW (program v.p. 1973-75, pres. 1975-77, treas. Pa. conv. 1973, 85, Woman of Yr. 1981), Williamsport-Lycoming C. of C. (chair edn. subcom. on partnerships 1991-92), Lycoming Bus.-Edn. Coalition (exec. com., steering com., co-chair task force on skills/curriculum), Phi Beta Kappa. Methodist. Home: 300 Upland Rd Williamsport PA 17701-1852

SCHULTZ, CAROLYN JOYCE, nurse practitioner, educator; b. Johnstown, Pa., Aug. 26, 1949; d. Robert Charles and Marion Elizabeth (Beatty) Miller; children: Melissa Lynn, Allison Marie. ADN, Mt. Aloysius Coll., 1972; BSN, Indiana U. Pa., 1979; MSN, W.Va. U., 1984, postgrad., 1996—. RN, Pa. Staff nurse Conemaugh Valley Meml. Hosp., Johnstown, 1975-84, faculty Sch. of Nursing, 1984-92; clin. rsch. nurse Laurel Highlands Cancer Program, Johnstown, 1992-94; mem. faculty St. Francis Coll., Loretta, Pa., 1983-84; chair svc. and rehab. com., bd. dirs. Johnstown unit Am. Cancer Soc., 1985-94, Cambria dist. dir., Johnstown, 1992-94. Recipient Vol. of Yr. award Am. Cancer Soc., 1990. Fellow Oncology Nursing Soc. (cert.). Home: 330 Phillips St Johnstown PA 15904-1226

SCHULTZ, EILEEN HEDY, graphic designer; b. Yonkers, N.Y.; d. Harry Arthur and Hedy Evelyn (Morchel) S. B.F.A., Sch. Visual Arts, 1955. Staff artist C.A. Parshall Studios, N.Y.C., 1955-57; editorial art dir. Paradise of the Pacific, Honolulu, 1957-58; graphic designer Adler Advt. Agy., N.Y.C., 1958-59; art dir. Good Housekeeping Mag., N.Y.C., 1959-82; creative dir. advt. and sales promotion Good Housekeeping Mag., 1982-86; creative dir. Hearst Promo, 1986-87; pres. Design Internat., N.Y.C., 1987—; creative dir. The Depository Trust Co., 1987—. Art dir., editor, designer, 50th Art Directors Club Annual, 1973; columnist: Art Direction, 1969—. Dir. Sch. Visual Arts, N.Y.C., 1978—; trustee Sch. Art League, 1978—; advisor Fashion Inst. Tech., 1979—; mem. adv. commn. N.Y.C. Community Colls., 1979—. Named Yonkers Ambassador of Good Will to Netherlands, 1955; recipient Outstanding Achievement Sch. Visual Arts Alumni Soc., 1976, Sch. Art League Youth award, 1976. Mem. Art Dirs. Club (pres. 1975-77), Soc. Illustrators (pres. 1991-93), Joint Ethics Com. (chmn. 1978-80), Am. Inst. Graphic Arts, Soc. Publ. Designers, Type Dirs. Club.

SCHULTZ, JANET W., intelligence research analyst; b. Balt., Nov. 25, 1957; d. Richard W. and Minna M. (Glaser) S.; m. Jacob L. Williams Jr., Feb. 1, 1992. BA cum laude, U. Md., 1979, BS, 1986; MA, George Washington U., 1982. Crew leader U.S. Bur. of Census, Baltimore County, Md., 1980; mgmt. analyst NASA Hdqrs., Washington, 1981; tech. writer Dynatech Data Sys., Springfield, Va., 1982-85, Catalyst Rsch., Owings Mills, Md., 1985-86; intelligence rsch. analyst Nat. Security Agy., Ft. Meade, Md., 1986—; intern U.S. Dept. of State, Washington, 1978. Coach, umpire Arbutus Girls' Athletic Assn., Balt., 1969-80; Sunday sch. tchr. Emmanuel Luth. Ch., Balt., 1972-80; basketball coach Luth. Ch. of St. Andrews, Wheaton, Md., 1984-85; branch v.p. Aid Assn. for Lutherans Holy Nativity Lutheran Ch., Balt., 1996—. Recipient Merit Scholastic award State of Md., 1975; Wolcott Found. fellow High Twelve Internat., 1980-82. Mem. Phi Beta Kappa, Phi Kappa Phi, Pi Sigma Alpha, Phi Alpha Theta, Alpha Lambda Delta. Democrat.

SCHULTZ, JOANN THOMAS, clinical nurse specialist; b. Cleve., Jan. 2, 1954; d. Frank John and Coletta Florence (Smith) Thomas; m. Stephen Joseph Schultz, June 30, 1984; children: Brittany L., Brian S. ADN, Cuyahoga C.C., Parma, Ohio, 1974; BSN, Cleve. State U., 1985; MSN, U. Akron, 1992. RN, Ohio; cert. critical care nurse; cert. BLS instr., ACLS instr. Staff nurse Lakewood (Ohio) Hosp., 1974-81, charge nurse med. unit, 1976-77, preceptor coronary care, 1981-89, asst. clin. nurse mgr., 1989-90, nurse clinician, 1990-92, clin. nurse specialist, 1992—; tchr. continuing nursing edn. Cleve. State U., Lorain (Ohio) C.C., 1993-95. Mem. AACN, Soc. Critical Care Medicine, Am. Heart Edn. (nursing edn. com. 1993—), Sigma Theta Tau (pres. chpt. 1995—, Lillian DeYoung Rsch. award 1992, Rsch. grantee 1992). Republican. Roman Catholic. Home: 4371 Jennings Rd Cleveland OH 44109-3632 Office: Lakewood Hosp 14519 Detroit Ave Lakewood OH 44107-4316

SCHULTZ, JOANNE MARIE, artist; b. Cleve., Jan. 5, 1954; d. Joseph and Martha Ann (Ducas) S. BA, Goddard Coll., Plainfield, Vt., 1975. Touring co. performer Bread & Puppet Theater, Glover, Vt., 1978-82; cmty.-based artist Elders Share the Arts, N.Y.C., 1984—; artistic dir. Ninth St. Theater, N.Y.C., 1986—; panelist N.Y. Found. for the Arts, N.Y.C., 1995. Dir.: The Ideal: The Life and Times of Rosa Luxemburg, 1988, Accident: A Day's News, 1991; contbg. author: Generating Community, 1994; performer: Medeamaterial (theater), 1992. Grantee for projects with 9th St. Theatre N.Y. State Coun. on the Arts, 1991, 92, 95, 96, N.Y.C. Dept. Cultural Affairs, 1995, Puffin Found., 1995. Home: 309 E 9th St New York NY 10003

SCHULTZ, KAREN ROSE, clinical social worker, author, publisher, speaker; b. Huntington, N.Y., June 16, 1958; d. Eugene Alfred and Laura Rose (Palazzolo) Squeri; m. Richard S. Schultz, Apr. 8, 1989. BA with honors, SUNY, Binghamton, 1980; MA, U. Chgo., 1982. Lic. clin. social worker, Ill. Unit dir., adminstr. Camp Algonquin, Ill., 1981; clin. social worker United Charities Chgo., 1982-86; social worker Hartgrove Hosp., Chgo., 1986-87; pvt. practice, Oak Brook, Ill., 1987—; trainer, speaker various groups, schs. and orgns., DuPage County, Ill., 1988-89; group leader Optifast Program, Oak Park and Aurora, Ill., 1989-90; instr. social work Morraine Valley C.C., Palos Hills, Ill., 1989-90; instr. eating disorders Coll. of Dupage, Glen Ellyn, Ill., 1990-92, mem. eating disorder com., 1989—, tchr. intuition and counseling, 1995—. Editor, contbg. author The River Within newsletter, 1989—. Com. mem. DuPage Consortium, 1987-89. Mem. NASW (registerd, diplomate), acad. Cert. Social Workers, Nat. Speakers Assn., Profl. Speakers Ill., Toastmasters Interant., Women Entrepreneurs DuPage. Office: 900 Jorie Blvd Ste 234 Oak Brook IL 60521-2230

SCHULTZ, MARIAN CLARE, business science educator; b. Blue Water Bay, Fla., Nov. 4, 1953; d. Bernard Joseph and Margaret Theresa Stine; m. James Thomas Schultz, Oct. 15, 1977; children: Jeremy, Joshua. AA, BA, U. Detroit, 1977; MA, Pepperdine U., 1978; D of Edn., U. So. Calif., 1983. Rsch. asst. Mercy Coll., Detroit, 1977-79; instr. U. Hawaii, Hilo, 1979-80, Hawaii Pacific U., Honolulu, 1980-83, Chaminade U., Honolulu, 1983, U. Tex., San Antonio, 1983-84, Our Lady of the Lake U., San Antonio, 1984; asst., assoc. prof. bus. sci. St. Mary's U., San Antonio, 1984-89; assoc. prof. bus. sci. U. West Fla., Pensacola, 1989—; cons. Pace Foods, San Antonio, 1985-86, Tex. Air N.G., San Antonio, 1985-86. Contbr. articles to profl. jours. Mem. Southwestern Soc. Economists, Ft. Walton Beach C. of C. Home: 230 Windward Way Niceville FL 32578 Office: U West Fla 11060 University Pkwy Eglin AFB FL 32542

SCHULTZ, MELANIE MARGARET, artist, educator; b. Huntsville, Ala., Oct. 17, 1960; d. David Norman and Mary Suzanne (Tissier) S. Student, U. Perugia, Italy, 1989; BA, U. South Fla., 1990; MFA, Fla. State U., 1993. Asst. coord. for policy issue Bankers Fidelity Life Ins., Atlanta, 1986-87; gallery asst. Fla. State U. Gallery and Mus., Tallhassee, 1991-92; instr. painting Fla. State U., Tallhassee, 1991-93, LeMoyne Art Found., Tallhassee, 1993, Tallahassee Sr. Ctr. for the Arts, 1993; with Bus. Express Airlines, 1994—. Exhibited works in shows at Fla. State U. Pres.'s Gallery, 1992, Arts Night, Tallahassee NOW, 1992, Fla. State U. Mus. and Gallery, 1993, RRios Photography, Tallahassee, 1993, Silent Shade Gallery, St. Petersburg, Fla., 1993, others. Fla. State U. Art Dept. grad. stipend awardee, 1991-93. Mem. Coll. Art Assn., Fla. Sate U. Gallery and Mus., DAR.

SCHULTZ, PHYLLIS MAY, financial property manager; b. Knox County, Ill., Dec. 17, 1933; d. Clarence Cleo and Mildred Ruth (Hultberg) Cooper; m. Wayne Willard Mohr, Apr. 23, 1955 (div. Sept. 1965); Jeffery Lee Mohr, Kelly Marie Mohr (dec.); m. Robert William Schultz, Sept. 14, 1968. Student, L.A. Valley Coll., 1979-82. Fire and casualty ins. lic., Calif. Keypunch operator Gale Products Outboard Marine Corp., Galesburg, Ill., 1952-55; office mgr. movie and video distbn. Rainbow Distbrs., Inc., 1965-89; fin. property mgr. and acctg. John Lamb, L.A., 1989—; co-owner Real Estate Investments, Ill., Calif., 1980-89. Mem. Lutheran Social Svcs., L.A., 1989. Republican. Home: 6309 Morella Ave North Hollywood CA 91606-3413

SCHULTZ, RUTH ANNE, home economics educator, parenting educator, consultant; b. Oneida, N.Y., Jan. 27, 1953; d. Herman Lyon and Anna Marie (Jarvis) S. BS, Cornell U., 1975; MS, Syracuse U., 1982; postgrad., Plattsburgh State U., 1986, 89, L.I. U., 1990—. Cert. tchr., N.Y.; cert. in family and consumer scis. Tchr. home econs. Phelps-Clifton Springs (N.Y.) Cen. Schs., 1975-77, adult educator, 1976-77, 93; home econs. tchr. Fabius (N.Y.)-

SCHULZ 962 WHO'S WHO OF AMERICAN WOMEN

Pompey Cen. Schs., 1977-82; tchr. home econs. Chittenango (N.Y.) Ctrl. Schs., 1982—, adviser Future Homemakers Am. club, 1986—, mem. bldg. planning team, 1994—; parenting educator Cornell Coop. Extension, Madison County, Morrisville, N.Y., 1985—; cons. N.Y. Dept. Edn., 1988-96. Primary author curriculum materials. Community rep. Madison County Head Start Policy Coun., Morrisville, 1985-88; chmn. program com. Cornell Coop. Extension, Madison County, 1990-92, Long Range Planning Com.; bd. dirs. Community Action Program of Madison County. Recipient N.Y. State Edn. Dept. Region 7 Disting. Occupational Educator ward, 1990. Mem. ASCD, N.Y. State Future Homemakers Am. (trustee, vice chmn.), Home Econs. Edn. Assn. (v.p. 1988-90, pres.-elect 1990-91, pres. 1991-93, past pres. 1993-94), N.Y. State Home Econs. Tchrs. Assn. (pres. 1986-88, state conv. chmn. 1989-90, 96, legis. co-chmn. 1989-90), N.Y. State Home Econs. Assn. (elem., secondary and adult chmn. 1989-93, New Achiever award 1988, Tchr. of Yr. award 1989), Am. Home Econs. Assn. (nat. leadership com. 1989-91), Ctrl. N.Y. Home Econs. Tchrs. Assn. (Tchr. of Yr. award 1985), N.Y. State Occupl. Edn. Assn. (affiliate v.p. 1986-88, state conv. chmn. 1988-89, 93, 95, regional rep. 1994—, Disting. Svc. award 1990), Nat. Assn. Vocat. Home Econs. Tchrs. (spl. award of merit 1991), Am. Vocat. Assn. (Region I Vocat. Tchr. of Yr. award 1994). Democrat. Roman Catholic. Home: RR 3 Cazenovia NY 13035-9803 Office: Chittenango Mid Sch RR 2 1732 Fyler Rd Chittenango NY 13037-9802

SCHULZ, CELIA HOPE, occupational therapist; b. N.Y.C., Mar. 4, 1959; d. Richard Frederick Schulz and Constance Gorman. BA, Cornell U., 1982; MA, Tufts U., 1993. Lic. occupl. therapist, Mass., Oreg. Staff occupl. therapist VA Med. Ctr., Brockton, Mass., 1993-94, Oreg. State Hosp., Salem, Oreg., 1994—. Mem. Am. Occupl. Therapy Assn., World Fedn. Occupl. Therapists, Occupl. Therapy Assn. Oreg., Cornell Club of Oreg. Democrat. Episcopalian. Office: Oreg State Hosp 2600 Center St NE Salem OR 97310

SCHULZ, KAREN A., medical and vocational case manager; b. Detroit, Aug. 18, 1952; d. Donald E. and Ethel B. (Johnston) Wallinger; m. Kirk C. Hamlin (dec. Sept. 1987); m. Paul R. Schulz, Feb. 19, 1993; children: Jennifer, Carolyn. BA, Concordia U., 1974; MA, Wayne State U., 1991. Case mgr. IntraCorp., Southfield, Mich., 1990-92, S. Yangouyian Assocs., Southfield, 1992-93, Comprehensive Case Mgmt. Svcs., Dearborn, Mich., 1993—; mem. faculty Detroit Coll. Bus., Dearborn, 1993—; sch. dir. Ross Career Schs., Oak Park, Mich., 1980-90; Cert. rehab. counselor, addictions counselor, Am. Bd. Disability Analysts; lic. profl. counselor. Mem. NAFE, Am. Counseling Assn., Mich. Self Insurers Orgn. Office: Comprehensive Case Mgmt Svcs PO Box 7455 Dearborn MI 48121-7455

SCHULZ, MARIANNE, accountant; b. East Orange, N.J.; d. Clifford W. Schulz; m. James A. Willits, Dec. 29, 1991; 1 child, Lukas James. BA in Bus., U. Wash., 1979. Cert. mgmt. acct. Contr. Farwest Spl. Products, Bellevue, Wash., 1974-88; acct. Lakeside Industries, Bellevue, Wash., 1988—. Mem. Inst. Mgmt. Accts. (bd. dirs. 1990-92, v.p. 1992-93).

SCHULZ, MARY ELIZABETH, lawyer; b. New Ulm, Minn., Oct. 6, 1950; d. Paul F. and Elizabeth B. (Wichtel) S. BA cum laude, Mankato State U., 1972; JD, So. Meth. U., 1976. Bar: Tex., 1976, Ky., 1992, Ohio, 1993. Atty. Kagay, Turner, Eyres & Robertson, Dallas, 1976-78; asst. regional counsel U.S. EPA, Dallas, 1978-86; atty. Gardere & Wynne, Dallas, 1986-89, Valvoline, Inc., Lexington, Ky., 1989-90; counsel Olin Corp., E. Alton, Ill., 1990-92; sr. environ. counsel B.F. Goodrich Co., Akron, Ohio, 1992—. Mem. ABA. Office: B F Goodrich Co 3925 Embassy Pky Akron OH 44333-1763

SCHULZ, RENATE ADELE, German studies and second language acquisition educator; b. Lohr am Main, Germany, Feb. 24, 1940; came to U.S., 1958; 1 child, Sigrid Diane. BS, Mankato State Coll., 1962; MA, U. Colo., 1967; PhD, Ohio State U., 1974. Edn. officer U.S. Peace Corps, Ife Ezinihitte, Nigeria, 1963-65; asst. prof. Otterbein Coll., Westerville, Ohio, 1974-76, State U. Coll. N.Y., Buffalo, 1976-77; from asst. to assoc. prof. U. Ark., Fayetteville, 1977-81; from assoc. to prof. U. Ariz., Tucson, 1981—, chair PhD program in second lang. acquisition and teaching, 1994—; disting. vis. prof. USAF Acad., Colorado Springs, Colo., 1990-91. Author: Options for Undergraduate Foreign Language Programs, 1979, Lesen, Lachen, Lernen, 1983, Aktuelle Themen, 1987, Im Kontext: Lesebuch zur Landeskunde, 1990; mem. editorial bd. Modern Lang. Jour., 1985—. Recipient Creative Tchg. award U. Ariz. Found., Tucson, 1984, Stephen A. Freeman award N.W. Conf. Tchg. Fgn. Langs., 1984, Bundesverdienstkreuz, Fed. Govt. Germany, 1990. Mem. Am. Coun. Tchg. Fgn. Langs. (exec. coun. 1979-81, Florence Steiner award 1993), Am. Assn. Tchrs. German (v.p. 1988-90, pres. 1990-91, editor Die Unterrichtspraxis 1980-85), MLA (del. 1989-91), Tchrs. of ESL, Am. Assn. Applied Linguistics, Am. Assn. Tchrs. French. Office: Univ of Ariz Dept German Studies Tucson AZ 85721

SCHULZ, SUZON LOUISE, fine artist; b. Chgo., Sept. 2, 1946; d. Carl George and Ruth Ada (Eberhardt) S. BFA, R.I. Sch. Design, 1968. Studio ptnr. Michael Eaton Smith, El Valle, N.Mex., 1976-79; artist-in-residence Idaho Com. on the Arts, 1980—, Wash. State Arts Com., 1980-82, Mississippi County C.C. Libr., Blytheville, Ark., 1984-85, various art couns., Oreg., 1983—; tchr. elem. art seminar Ea. Oreg. Coll. Bend Br., Bend, 1996; owner Flying Shoes Studio, Bend, 1982—; cartoonist, writer, illustrator NOW News, Bend, 1991-94. Painter: (series) In the Home, 1982—, The World Beyond, 1984—, Living With a Man, 1986—, Tipi Now, 1988—. Mem. Nat. Mus. Women in Arts, Cen. Oreg. Arts Assn. Home and Studio: 16881 Varco Rd Bend OR 97701

SCHULZE, ANTOINETTE MALUSKA, research laboratory analyst, accountant; b. Chgo., Jan. 26, 1918; d. Joseph and Anna Maluska m. Oliver Gordon Craker, Sept. 15, 1943 (div. 1955); children: Barbara, Andrea, Annette Helen, Dennis Albert; m. Ervin Walter Schulze, Apr. 18, 1959 (dec. 1985). Student, Costa Mesa Coll., 1973-75; student Acctg., Sawyer Bus. Sch., 1975. Rsch. lab. analyst Hughes Aircraft, Culver City, Calif., 1952-60; elec. assembler Lockheed, Sunny Vale, Calif., 1960-62; assembly work Hughes Tool Co., Culver City, Calif., 1962-64; acct., tax cons. The Mid.-Class Person's Tax Svc., Roy, Utah, 1980-95. Author: Lithuania's Seed, 1995. Home: 3800 S 1900 W 181 Roy UT 84067

SCHUMACHER, CYNTHIA JO, secondary education educator, retired; b. Sebring, Fla., Sept. 24, 1928; d. Floyd Melvin and Espage Love (Rogers) S. BA, Fla. State U., 1950, MA, 1951; MS, Nova U., 1978; postgrad., Fla. State U., 1968-69. English tchr. Grady County Sch. System, Cairo, Ga., 1951-53; elem. tchr. Brevard County Sch. System, Melbourne, Fla., 1953-55; elem. tchr., curriculum generalist, secondary tchr. Lake County Schs., Tavares, Fla. area, 1955-85; retired, 1985; mem. Edn. Standards Commn., Fla., 1980-85, Quality Instrn. Incentives Coun., Fla., 1983-84. Author: (poetry) Seeds from Wild Grasses, 1988, Creekstone Crossings, 1993; (poetry and stories) Butterfly Excursions, 1996. Pres. League of Women Voters of Lake County, 1989-91; mem. Lake Conservation Coun., The Nature Conservancy, Habitat for Humanity of Lake County. named Fla. Tchr. of Yr., Fla. Fedn. Women's Clubs, 1966, Lake County Tchr. of Yr., Lake County Sch. Systems, 1985, East Cen. Fla. Tchr. of Yr., finalist State of Fla., 1986; recipient Good Egg award Leesburg Area C. of C., 1991. Mem. Lake County Edn. Assn. (pres. 1971-72, cons. 1985—). Democrat. Roman Catholic. Office: Lake County Edn Assn PO Box 490816 Leesburg FL 34749-0816

SCHUMACHER, ELIZABETH SWISHER, garden ornaments shop owner; b. Webster City, Iowa, Apr. 1, 1940; d. Andrew Dale and Harriet Elizabeth (Hudson) Swisher; m. H. Ralph Schumacher Jr., July 13, 1963; children: Heidi Ruth, Kaethe Beth. BS, U. Colo., 1961; student, Barnes Found. Sch Horticulture, 1978. Owner Garden Accents, West Conshohocken, Pa., 1979—; lectr. on garden ornaments, hillside gradening, water in the garden, 1979—; exhibitor designer show house Vassar Coll., Phila. area sites, 1984—, Phila. Flower Show, 1996—. Contbr. articles to Fine Gardening, Green Scene, Gardens and Landscapes. Recipient Outstanding Landscaping award Pa. Nurserymen's Assn., 1972, Residential Beautification award Upper Merion Twp., 1974, 76, 86, Exhibit of Distinction award Phila. Flower Show, 1989, 1st prize Comml. Exhibit, 1996, Best of Philly, Phila. Mag., 1996. Mem. Pa. Hort. Soc. (hotline vol. 1987—). Office: Garden Accents 4 Union Hill Rd W Conshohocken PA 19428-2719

SCHUMACHER, LOIS MERYL, counselor; b. Englewood, N.J., Aug. 26, 1949; d. Isadore and Sally (Darlow) Diamond; m. Marc Schumacher, June 6, 1971; children: Erin Leigh, Kevin Chip. BS, Boston U., 1972; MS, Nova U., 1990; postgrad., St. Thomas U., Miami, Fla., 1992; PhD, The Union Inst., Cin., 1996. Tchr. Pinewood Acres Day Sch., Miami, 1977-80; jazz instr. Dade County Pks. and Recreation, Miami, 1982-85; food broker, owner Diamond Food Sales, Miami, 1985-88; tchr. Dade County Pub. Schs., Miami, 1988-92, guidance counselor, 1992—. Mem. APA, ACA, United Tchrs. of Dade, Dade County Counseling Assn. Democrat. Jewish. Office: Dade County Pub Schs 7955 SW 152d St Miami FL 33157

SCHUMACHER, MARY LOU, secondary education educator; b. Cando, N.D., Mar. 1, 1946; d. Harold J. and Ella (Baerwald) Campbell; m. Herbert Don Schumacher, Apr. 3, 1969; 1 child, Marissa Dawn. BS, Mayville State U., 1967; MS, U. Ariz., 1974. Tchr. San Manuel (Ariz.) High Sch., 1967-69; tchr. Flowing Wells High Sch., Tucson, 1969—, chmn. math. dept., 1988—. Mem. NEA, Ariz. Tchr. Math., Nat. Coun. Tchrs. Math., Con Sortium for Math. Home: 6338 N Carapan Pl Tucson AZ 85741-3401

SCHUMACHER, SUZANNE LYNNE, artist, art educator; b. San Francisco, Apr. 20, 1951; d. Martin John and Evelyn Lucinda (Andrews) S.; m. Timothy Van Ert, June 24, 1983 (div. Aug. 1988). BA, St. Marys Coll., 1972; MFA, San Francisco Art Inst., 1983. Instr. art Coll. Marin (Calif.), 1984-90; tchr. Montera Jr. High Sch., Oakland, Calif., 1989-92; prof. art St. Marys Coll., Moraga, Calif., 1990—; developer, dir. Myrtle Street Art Studios, Oakland, 1978—. Home: 3037 Myrtle St Oakland CA 94608 Office: St Mary's Coll Dept Art St Mary's Rd Moraga CA 94575

SCHUMACHER, THERESA ROSE, singer, musician; b. Muskegon, Mich.; d. Boles and Marguerite (Lassard) Pietkiewicz; m. Glenn O. Schumacher, 1968 (div. 1988); children: Pamela Harrington Boller, Daniel Mark Harrington. BS in Sociology, Fairmont State Coll., 1975. Active W.Va. U. Symphony Choir, 1988—, 93 Fairmont State Coll. Choir; musician with spl. knowledge of music from 1735-1850, Nat. Park Svcs., 1989—. Mem. AAUW, W.Va. Poetry Soc., Morgantown, W.Va. Poetry Soc. Home: PO Box 162 Mannington WV 26582-0162

SCHUMACK, MAXINE LYNNE, community college counselor; b. N.Y.C., Jan. 6, 1951; d. Selig-David and Ruth-Helen (Weinstock) S. AA, L.A. Valley Coll., Van Nuys, Calif., 1974; BA, Calif. State U., Northridge, 1976; MA, Pepperdine U., Malibu, Calif., 1983. Cert. mental health counselor; lifetime counselor credential Calif. C.C. Case aide, social work assoc. United Way Agy., Van Nuys, 1976-78; pers. asst. L.A. Unified Sch. Dist., West Los Angeles, 1979-80; psychol. asst. Vera Wayman, MD, Glendale, Calif., 1980-84; entrepreneur Seminars for Industry, Sherman Oaks, Calif., 1984-89; resources specialist Ind. Living Ctrs. So. Calif., Van Nuys, 1989-92; cultural diversity specialist ARC, Van Nuys, 1991-92; litigation specialist, advocate Protection and Advocacy, Glendale, 1992-93; counselor Calif. Cmty. Colls., Sacramento, 1993—. Recipient Vol. award MADD of L.A., 1992, Cert. of Appreciation, ARC, 1991. Mem. AAUW, Calif. State Psychol. Assn., Calif. Assn. Marriage and Family Counselors, Psi Chi. Home: 13621 Addison St Sherman Oaks CA 91423

SCHUMAN, PATRICIA GLASS, publishing company executive, educator; b. N.Y.C., Mar. 15, 1943; d. Milton and Shirley Rhoda (Goodman) Glass; m. Alan Bruce Schuman, Aug. 30, 1964 (div. 1973). AB, U. Cin., 1963; MS, Columbia U., 1966. Libr. trainee Bklyn. Pub. Libr., 1963-65; tchr. libr. Brandeis High Sch., N.Y.C., 1966; asst. prof. libr. N.Y. Tech. Coll., Bklyn., 1966-71; assoc. editor Sch. Libr. Jour., N.Y.C., 1970-73; sr. editor R.R. Bowker Co., N.Y.C., 1973-76; pres. Neal-Schuman Pubs., N.Y.C., 1976—; vis. prof. St. John's U., Queens, N.Y., 1977-79, Columbia U., N.Y.C., 1981-90, Pratt Inst., 1993—; cons. N.Y. State Coun. on Arts, 1987, Office Tech. Assessment, U.S. Congress, 1982, 84, Coord. Coun. Lit. Mags., N.Y.C., 1987, NEH, 1980, Temple U., 1978-80; bd. visitors Sch. Libr. and Computer Studies Pratt Inst., 1987—; juror Best of Libr. Lit., 1980-88; mem. adv. bd. Sch. Libr. and Info. Studies, Queens Coll., 1989-91. Author: Materials for Occupational Education, 1973, 2d edit., 1983 (Best Edn. Book award 1973), Library Users and Personnel Needs, 1980, Your Right to Know: The Call for Action, 1993; editor: Social Responsibilities and Libraries, 1976; mem. editorial bd. Urban Acad. Libr., 1987-89, Multicultural Review, 1991—; contbr. articles to profl. jours. Bd. dirs. Women's Studies Abstracts, Albany, N.Y., 1970-74; mem. Com. To Elect Major Owens to U.S. Congress, 1983, N.Y.C. Mayor's Com. for N.Y. Pub. Ctr., 1984-85. Recipient Fannie Simon award Spl. Librs. Assn., 1984, Disting. Alumni award Columbia U., 1992; U.S. Office Edn. fellow, 1969. Mem. ALA (councillor 1971-79, 84-88, exec. bd. 1984-88, 90—, treas. 1984-88, chmn. legis. com. 1989-90, 94—, v.p., pres.-elect 1990-91, pres. 1991-92, Disting. Coun. Svc. award 1979, 88, Equality award 1993), ALA, N.Y. Libr. Assn., Assn. for Libr. and Info. Sci. Edn., Spl. Librs. Assn. Office: Neal-Schuman Pubs Inc 100 Varick St New York NY 10013-1506

SCHUMANN, ALICE MELCHER, medical technologist, educator, sheep farmer; b. Cleve., Sept. 1, 1931; d. John Henry and Marian Louise (Clark) M.; m. Stuart McKee Struever, Aug. 21, 1956 (div. June 1983); children: Nathan Chester, Hanna Russell; m. John Otto Schumann, July 3, 1985. BS, Colby Coll., New London, N.H., 1953. Cert. tchr.; cert. med. technologist. Rschr. Lakeside Hosp., Cleve., 1953-54, Bambridge (Ohio) Schs., 1954-55, Shalersville (Ohio) Schs., 1955-56, Richtnior Sch., Overland, Mo., 1956-57; sci. tchr. Tonica (Ill.) High Sch., 1956-58, Morton Grove (Ill.) High Sch., 1958-60, Univ. Chgo. Lab Sch., 1960-65; co-founder Ctr. for Am. Archeology, dir. flotation rsch. U. Chgo. Campus, Kampsville, Ill., 1957-71, head of supplies distbn., dir. food svcs. dept.; head mailing dept. Found. for Ill. Archeology, Evanston and Kampsville, Ill., 1971-83; sheep farmer, wool processor Gravel Hill Farm, Kampsville, 1983—. Vol. Mt. Sinai Hosp., Cleve., 1948-49; tchr. Title I Dist. 40, Kampsville, 1970-71. Recipient Beverly Booth award Colby Coll., 1953, 1st prize for hand spun yarn DeKalb County Fair, Sandwich, Ill., 1987, 88. Mem. Precious Fibers Found., Natural Colored Wool Growers Assn., Farm Bur. of Calhoun County. Home and Office: Gravel Hill Farm RR 1 Box 121A Kampsville IL 62053-9720

SCHUNKE, HILDEGARD HEIDEL, accountant; b. Indpls., Nov. 24, 1948; d. Edwin Carl and Hildegard Adelheid (Baumbach) S. BA, Ball State U., Muncie, Ind., 1971, MA in German/English, 1973, MA in Acctg., 1975. CPA, Ind., Calif. Exch. teaching grad. asst. Padagogische Hochschule, Germany, 1971-72; teaching grad. asst. German/acctg. Ball State U., Muncie, 1972, 74-75, asst. prof. acctg., 1975-78; investing rschr. Family Partnership, Muncie, 1977-83; staff acct. Am. Lawn Mower Co., Muncie, 1984-88, G&J Seiberlich, CPAs, St. Helena, Calif., 1988-89, R.A. Gullotta, MBA, CPA, Sonoma, Calif., 1989-90; plant acct. Napa Pipe Corp., Napa, Calif., 1990—; continuing edn. instr. Calif. Soc. CPAs, Redwood City, 1990. ESOL instr. Napa County Project Upgrade, 1988-92; ticketing and refreshments com. North Ba Philharmonic Orch., Napa, 1988—, North Bay Wind Ensemble, Napa, 1988—. Mem. AICPAs, Calif. Soc. CPAs, Ind. Soc. CPAs, Inst. Internal Auditors, Environ. Auditing Roundtable, Am. Soc. Quality Control. Home: 1117 Devonshire Ct Suisun City CA 94585-3343 Office: Napa Pipe Corp 1025 Kaiser Rd Napa CA 94558-6257

SCHUR, SUSAN DORFMAN, public affairs consultant; b. Newark, Feb. 27, 1940; d. Norman and Jeanette (Handelman) Dorfman; children: Diana Elisabeth, Erica Marlene. BA, Goucher Coll., 1961. Adminstr. fed. housing, fgn. aid, anti-poverty programs, 1961-67; mem. Mass. Housing Appeals Com., 1977-86; mem., v.p. Bd. of Alderman, Newton, Mass., 1974-81; mem. Mass. Ho. of Reps., 1981-94; pvt. pub. affairs cons., Newton, Mass., 1995—. Mem. Newton Dem. City Com., 1970—.

SCHURTER, BETTE JO, realtor; b. Salem, Oreg., July 7, 1932; d. Walter Robert and Dixie Wayne (Gayman) Haverson; m. John J. Schurter, Oct. 2, 1954; children: John Thomas, Steven Robert, Brian Douglas. BS, Portland State U., 1980. Mgr. Ball, Ball & Brosamer, Danville, Calif., 1982-87; realtor Stan Wiley, Inc. Realtors, Wilsonville, Oreg., 1988—. Mem. Draft Bd., Aurora, Oreg., 1980—. Mem. AAUW, Clackamas County Bd. Realtors, Clackamas County Million Dollar Club, Wilsonville C. of C., Aurora Colony Hist. Soc. Home: 10616 E Navajo Pl Sun Lakes AZ 85248 Office: Stan Wiley Inc 8750 SW Citizens Dr Wilsonville OR 97070-6404

SCHUSTER, CARLOTTA LIEF, psychiatrist; b. N.Y.C., Sept. 16, 1936; d. Victor Filler and Nina Lincoln (Rayevsky) Lief; m. David Israel Schuster, Sept. 2, 1962; 1 child, Amanda. BA, Barnard Coll., 1957; MD, NYU, 1964. Cert. Am. Bd. Psychiatry and Neurology; cert. addiction psychiatry. Intern Lenox Hill Hosp., N.Y.C., 1964-65; resident St. Luke's Hosp., N.Y.C., 1965-68; fellow Inst. Sex Edn., U. Pa., Phila., 1968-69; instr. N.Y. Med. Coll., N.Y.C., 1969-72; asst. attending Met. Hosp., N.Y.C., 1969-72; assoc. attending St. Luke's-Roosevelt Hosp. Ctr., N.Y.C., 1972—; staff psychiatrist Silver Hill Found., New Canaan, Conn., 1972-95; clin. assoc. instr. Columbia U., N.Y.C., 1990—; chief substance abuse svc. Silver Hill Found., New Canaan, 1976-95; clin. faculty dept. psychiatry Sch. Medicine NYU, 1995—; dir. recovery clinic Bellevue Hosp., N.Y.C., 1995—. Author: Alcohol and Sexuality, 1988; co-author: Chapter in Advances in Alcohol and Substance Abuse, 1987; contbr. chpt. Mental Health in the Workplace, 1993. Mem. Am. Psychiat. Assn., Am. Med. Soc. on Addictions, Am. Acad. Psychiatrists in Alcohol and Addictions. Democrat. Jewish. Office: 207 E 30th St New York NY 10016

SCHUSTER, CHERYL DENISE JAHN, speech, language pathologist; b. Aurora, Ill., Sept. 8, 1957; d. Harold Arthur and Marilyn Louise (Brennemann) Jahn; m. Terence Kenneth Schuster, Mar. 13, 1978; children: Jessica Leigh, Logan Kenneth. BA in Edn., No. Ill. U., 1981, MA, 1985. With Tri-County Cooperative, Freeport, Ill., 1981-82; with Belvidere (Ill.) Schs., 1982-83, speech-lang. pathologist, 1983-86; speech-lang. pathologist Freeport Schs., 1986-90, Rockford (Ill.) Schs., 1990—; mem. adv. bd. StarNet, Macomb, Ill., 1991—. Dir. Logos Bethlehem Luth. Ch., Rockford, 1993-96, mem. youth com., 1996. Grantee Project APPLES, 1991, 95. Mem. NOW. Office: Early Childhood Ctr 512 S Fairview Ave Rockford IL 61108

SCHUSTER, INGEBORG IDA, chemistry educator; b. Frankfurt, W. Ger., Oct. 30, 1937; came to U.S. 1947; d. Ludwig Karl and Mariluise (Kautetzky) S. BA, U. Pa., 1960; MS, Carnegie Inst. Tech., Pitts., 1963; PhD, Carnegie Inst. Tech., 1965. Postdoctoral fellow Bryn Mawr (Pa.) Coll., 1965-67; asst. prof. chemistry Pa. State U., Abington, 1967-73; assoc. prof. chemistry Pa. State U., 1973-83, prof. chemistry, 1983—. Contbr. articles to profl. jours. Huff fellow, 1966; E. Gerry fellow, 1982. Mem. Am. Chem. Soc. Republican. Roman Catholic. Office: Pa State Univ 1600 Woodland Rd Abington PA 19001-3918

SCHUSTER, SARAH C., art educator, painter, artist; b. Boston, Mass., Oct. 15, 1957; d. Melvin M. and Arian C. (Fowler) S.; m. Gregory Allen Little, Dec. 17, 1983. BFA in Painting, Boston U., 1979; MFA in Painting, Yale U., 1982. Summer instr. summer program Yale U., New Haven, Conn., 1986-88; lectr. Brandeis U., Waltham, Mass., 1988; assoc. prof. art Oberlin Coll., Ohio, 1988—; vis. prof. summer workshop Cleve. Inst. Art, 1991; adj. instr. Paier Coll. Art U. New Haven, U. Bridgeport, Conn.; presenter in field. One woman shows include Ceres Gallery, N.Y.C., 1992, 95; two women shows include The Coll. Wooster Art Mus., Ohio; group shows include Michael Kohler Arts Ctr., 1995, Woods-Gerry Gallery, R.I. Sch. Design, Providence, Women's Caucus for Arts, New Haven, Sister Coty Exch., New Haven, Leon, Mus. Ams., Leon, Nicaragua, Housatonic Mus. Art, Housatonic C.C., Bridgeport, Cummings Art Ctr., Conn. Coll., New London, 1986, Munson Gallery, New Haven. Mem. Women's Caucus for the Arts, N.Y., Ohio, 1989-95, Spaces. Recipient R&D grant Oberlin Coll., 1989, 94, Powers Travel grant Oberlin Coll., 1990. Mem. Ceres Art Gallery (assoc.), The Coll. Art Assn. Home: 249 Oak St Oberlin OH 44074 Office: Oberlin Coll Dept Art N Main St Oberlin OH 44074

SCHUTH, MARY MCDOUGLE, interior designer, educator; b. Kansas City, Mo., Jan. 19, 1942; d. William Darnall and Marie DeArmond (Meiser) McDougle; m. Howard Wayne Schuth, Sept. 4, 1965; 1 child, Andrew Wayne. BS in Interior Design, Communications, Northwestern U., 1964; Cert. Basic Mgmt., U. Mo., 1966. Lic. interior designer, La. Interior designer Cottington's Interiors, Glen Ellyn, Ill., 1964-65, Robnett-Putman Interiors, Columbia, Mo., 1966-67, Nu-Idea Furniture Co., New Orleans, 1973, Maison Blanche, New Orleans, 1974-75, Mary M. Schuth Interior Design, Metairie, La., 1977—; instr. interior design U. New Orleans div. Continuing Edn., 1973—; judge model homes U.S. Homes, Mandeville, La., 1978, 80; bd. dirs. Interior Design Adv. Com. Delgado Coll., New Orleans, 1981—; mem. Alpha Chi Omega Frat. housing rev. com., 1991-96; guest lectr. Delta Queen Steamboat Co., 1995-96; spkr. in field. Co-author: cookbook From the Privateers' Galley, 1980; design work featured in profl. jours.; contbr. to Metairie Mag., 1993-94. Recipient 3rd place Batik Design Juried Art Show Columbia (Mo.) Art League, 1969. Mem. AIA (profl. affiliate), Am. Soc. Interior Designers (profl.), La. Landmarks, Alpha Chi Omega, Alumnae Club (New Orleans).

SCHUTT, CHERYL ANN, auditor; b. Houston, Feb. 13, 1967; d. Oscar Earl and Billie Jean (Warren) S. BBA in Acctg., U. Tex., Arlington, 1989. CPA, Tex. Staff acct. Finkelstein, Allgeier & Co., Addison, Tex., 1989; sr. auditor Tex. Credit Union League, Farmers Branch, 1990—. Mem. AICPA, Tex. Soc. CPA's, Am. Women's Soc. CPA's, Amnesty Internat., Greenpeace, Sierra Club, Dallas Zool. Soc. Democrat. Office: Tex Credit Union League 4455 LBJ Freeway #904 Farmers Branch TX 75244

SCHUTZA, JUDY L., forester; b. Ft. Worth, July 1, 1950; d. Henry J. and Nan S. (Eggner) S. BS, Stephen F. Austin State U., 1971; MS, U. Mont., 1975. Forestry tech. Nezperce Nat. Forest USDA Forest Svc., Red River, Idaho, 1973; forester Montana Pacific Internat., Missoula, 1974; forestry tech. Clearwater Nat. Forest USDA Forest Svc., Kamiah, Idaho, 1975; forester Lassen Nat. Forest USDA Forest Svc., Susanville, Calif., 1975-78; reforestation forester Kootena Nat. Forest USDA Forest Svc., Troy, Mont., 1978-81; silviculturist Bitterroot Nat. Forest USDA Forest Svc., Darby, Mont., 1981-89; resource asst. Bridger-Teton Nat. Forest USDA Forest Svc., Big Piney, Wyo., 1989-91; timber mgmt. officer to Sequoia Nat. Forest Hot Springs (Calif.) Ranger Dist., USDA Forest Svc., 1991-94, dist. ranger, 1994—. Mem. Soc. Am. Foresters. Home: 1923 W Forest Ave Porterville CA 93257 Office: USDA Forest Svc Rt 4 Box 548 Hot Springs CA 93207

SCHUTZLER, KATHRYN GRACE, information systems specialist; b. Silver Spring, Md., Feb. 24, 1966; d. James E. and Suellen (Jones) Durkin; m. Peter H. Schutzler, May 22, 1992; 1 child, Magdalena G. BS in BA, U. Dayton, Ohio, 1988; MBA, Lehigh U., 1992. Office info. cons. Society Bank N.A., Dayton, 1987-90; video conf. technician Fuller Co., Bethlehem, Pa., 1990-91, info. ctr. programmer, 1991-92, project mgr. info. tech., 1992-95, mgr. adminstrn., info. svcs., 1995—. Mem. Soc. for Info. Mgmt. Republican. Roman Catholic. Home: 720 N 12th St Allentown PA 18102 Office: Fuller Co 2040 Ave C Bethlehem PA 18017-2118

SCHUUR, DIANE JOAN, vocalist; b. Tacoma, Dec. 10, 1953; d. David Schuur. Ed. high sch., Vancouver, Wash. Albums include Pilot of My Destiny, 1983, Deedles, Schuur Thing, 1986, Timeless (Grammy award for female jazz vocal 1986), Diane Schuur and the Count Basie Orchestra (Grammy award for female jazz vocal 1987), Talkin' 'Bout You, 1988, Pure Schuur, 1991 (reached #1 on Billboard contemporary jazz chart, nominated for Grammy award 1991), In Tribute, 1992, Love Songs, 1993 (Grammy nomination, Best Traditional Vocal), 1993 (Grammy nomination, The Christmas Song), (with B.B. King) Heart to Heart, 1994 (entered at #1 on Billboard contemporary jazz chart), Love Walked In, 1996; performed at the White House, Monterey Jazz Festival, Hollywood Bowl; toured Japan, Far East, South Am., Europe.

SCHUYLER, JANE, fine arts educator; b. Flushing, N.Y., Nov. 2, 1943; d. Frank James and Helen (Oberhofer) S. BA, Queens Coll., 1965; MA, Hunter Coll., 1967; PhD, Columbia U., 1972. Asst. prof. art history Montclair State Coll., Upper Montclair, N.J., 1970; assoc. prof. C.W. Post Coll., L.I. Univ., Greenvale, N.Y., 1971-73, adj. assoc. profl, 1977-78; coord. fine arts, asst. prof. York Coll., CUNY, Jamaica, 1973-77, 78-87, assoc. prof., 1988-92, prof. 1993-96, prof. emerita 1996—. Author: Florentine Busts: Sculpted Portraiture in the Fifteenth Century, 1976; contbr. articles to profl. jours. Mem. fine arts com. Internat. Women's Arts Festival, 1974-76; pres. United Cmty. Dems. of Jackson Heights, 1987-89. N.Y. Columbia U. summer travel and rsch. grantee, 1969; recipient PSC-CUNY Rsch. award, 1990-91. Mem. Coll. Art Assn., Nat. Trust for Hist. Preservation, Renaissance Soc. Am. Roman Catholic. Home: 35-37 78th St Jackson Heights NY 11372

SCHWAB, BARBARA, advertising executive; b. Bklyn., Feb. 21, 1942; d. Samuel Al and Heidi (Weisskirch) Schnitzer; m. Jeffrey Alan Schwab, July 6, 1963; children: Debra Brandt, Michael. BA, Adelphi U., 1963; MS in Edn., Queens Coll., 1965. Tchr. Roosevelt (N.Y.) Jr. Sr. High Sch., 1963-65, Dix Hills, N.Y., 1977-79, Norwalk (Conn.) High Sch., 1980, Weston (Conn.) High Sch., 1980-82; pres. Barbara Schwab & Assoc., Inc., Norwalk, 1982—. Named Top Sales Distributor, Benchmark Products Ohio, 1992-93. Mem. Specialty Advt. Assn. Greater N.Y., Advt. Specialty Inst.

SCHWAB, EILEEN CAULFIELD, lawyer, educator; b. N.Y.C., Feb. 11, 1944; d. James Francis and Mary Alice (Fay) Caulfield; m. Terrance W. Schwab, Jan. 4, 1969; children: Matthew Caulfield, Catherine Grimley, Claire Gillespie. BA, Hunter Coll., 1965; JD, Columbia U., 1971; BA magna cum laude. Bar: N.Y. 1972, U.S. Dist. Ct. (so. and ea. dists.) N.Y. 1975, U.S. Ct. Appeals (2d cir.) 1975, U.S. Tax Ct. 1980, U.S. Ct. Appeals (10th cir.) 1993. Assoc. Poletti Friedin, N.Y.C., 1971-72, Hughes Hubbard & Reed, N.Y.C., 1972-75, Davis Polk & Wardwell, N.Y.C., 1975-81; dep. bur. chief Charities Bu., Atty. Gen. of N.Y., 1981-82; counsel Brown & Wood, N.Y.C., 1983—, ptnr., 1984; adj. prof. N.Y. Law Sch.; mediator atty. disciplinary com. first dept., N.Y. Co-chmn. gift planning adv. com. Archdiocese of N.Y.C.; dir. Cath. Found. for the Future, Cath. Communal Fund. Fellow Am. Coll. Trust and Estate Counsel; mem. N.Y. State Bar Assn. (exec. com. trust and estate sect.), Assn. Bar City N.Y., Phi Beta Kappa. Democrat. Roman Catholic.

SCHWAB, KATHERINE ANNE, art history educator; b. Pomona, Calif., May 15, 1954; d. Paul Edward and Shirley (Barnes) S.; m. Ronald M. Davidson, June 27, 1993; 1 child, Stephanie L. Davidson. BA, Scripps Coll., 1976; MA, Southern Meth. U., 1979; PhD, NYU, 1988. Vis. prof. UNC, Chapel Hill, 1986-88; asst. prof. fine arts Fairfield (Conn.) U., 1988-95, assoc. prof. visual and performing arts, 1995—. Recipient Andrew W. Mellon Sr. fellow Met. Mus. of Art, N.Y.C., 1995. Mem. Archaeol. Inst. Am., Coll. Art Assn., Am. Sch. Classical Studies at Athens. Office: Dept Visual Performing Arts Fairfield Univ Fairfield CT 06430-5195

SCHWAB, SUSAN CAROL, university dean. BA in Polit. Economy, Williams Coll., 1976; MA in Applied Econs., Stanford U., 1977; PhD in Pub. Adminstrn., George Washington U., 1993. U.S. trade negotiator Office of Pres.'s Spl. Trade Rep., Washington, 1977-79; trade policy officer U.S. Embassy, Tokyo, 1980-81; chief economist, legis. asst. for internat. trade for Senator John C. Danforth, 1981-86, legis. dir., until 1989; asst. sec. commerce, dir. gen. U.S. and Fgn. Comml. Svc. Dept. Commerce, 1989-93; with corp. strategy office Motorola, Inc., Schaumburg, Ill., 1993-95; dean U. Md. Sch. Pub. Affairs, College Park, 1995—. Office: U Md Sch Pub Affairs College Park MD 20742

SCHWALB, CLAUDIA EMILYN, artist; b. N.Y.C., Aug. 25, 1952; d. Lloyd Daniel Schwalb and Audrey (Rogow) Hall; 1 child, Heather. BFA, Pratt Inst., 1974. Legal sec. to Andrew M. Manshel, Esq., N.Y.C., 1990-91, Melito & Adolfsen, N.Y.C., 1991—. Solo exhbns. include The Clocktower Gallery, N.Y.C., 1977, El Bohio Cmty. & Cultural Ctr., N.Y.C., 1986, Horse Nostrils Gallery, N.Y.C., 1988, The Knitting Factory, 1990, Visionary Gallery, 1992, The Cedar Tavern, 1993, Momotaro, 1993; group exhbns. include Magoo's Bar, 1976, Gallery of July & August, Woodstock, N.Y., 1977, New Mus. Contemporary Art, N.Y.C., 1978, Blondies Contemporary Art, N.Y.C., 1992-94, Smithsonian Instn. Archives of Am. Art, 1996. Office: Melito & Adolfsen 233 Broadway 28th Fl New York NY 10279-0118

SCHWANZ, DEBORAH ANN, psychiatric nurse; b. South Bend, Ind., Jan. 1, 1952; d. Ned Christian and Rita Jane (Witucki) S. Diploma in nursing, Meml. Hosp. Sch. Nursing, South Bend, 1973; BS in Health Arts, Coll. of St. Francis, Joliet, Ill., 1991. RN, Fla.; cert. psychiat. and mental health nurse ANCC. House float nurse Meml. Hosp., 1973; psychiat. team leader St. Anthony's Hosp., St. Petersburg, Fla., 1974-81, asst. head nurse, 1981-84, clin. mgr. psychiatry, instr. aggression control techniques, 1984-89; weekend nursing supr. Boley, Inc., St. Petersburg, 1989-92; nurse therapist various nursing homes, St. Petersburg, 1992-93, Physicians' Cmty. Hosp., St. Petersburg, 1993-94; contract psychiat. nurse St. Anthony's Home Health Care, St. Petersburg, 1986-94; psychiat. home health nurse Shands Home Care, Largo, Fla., 1995—; presenter on psychiat. nursing at seminars and workshops, St. Petersburg and Clearwater, Fla., 1984-88. Mem. St. Petersburg Dem. Club. Mem. NOW (past sec. Pinellas chpt.), Mental Health Assn., Meml. Hosp. Sch. Nursing Alumni Assn. Office: 7249 Bryan Dairy Rd Largo FL 33777

SCHWARTZ, ADELE, education educator; b. N.Y.C., Apr. 15, 1944; d. Bernard and Minna (Snetkoff) S. BSEd in Elem. and Spl. Edn., CCNY, 1964, MEd in Diagnostic and Remedial Reading, 1968, postgrad., 1974-76; EdD in Spl. Edn., Columbia U., 1993. Cert. nursery-6th grade tchr., spl. edn. tchr., sch. dist. adminstr., sch. adminstr. and supr., N.Y. Spl. edn. tchr. N.Y.C. Pub. Schs., 1964-71, 83-86, coord. outreach program in spl. edn., 1971-76, coord. N.Y.C. Child Find Project, 1976-79; project dir. dean's grant Hunter Coll., CUNY, N.Y.C., 1979-83, dir. ednl. svcs. divsn. programs in edn., 1986-94, dir. spl. svcs. Sch. Social Work, 1994-96; assoc. prof. tchr. edn. Marymount Manhattan Coll., N.Y.C., 1996—; ednl. cons. Life Skills Sch. and Early Intervention Program, N.Y.c., 1979-82, Medgar Evers Coll., CUNY, N.Y.C., 1981-83, The Lorge Sch., N.Y.C., 1995-96. Editor Coalition of Voluntary Mental Health Agys., N.Y.C., 1995; contbr. articles to profl. publs., chpt. to book. Bd. dir. Coalition to End Ableism, N.Y.C., 1993-95; mem. subcom. on edn. Manhattan Borough Pres.'s Adv. Coun. on People with Disabilities, 1992-93; active Nat. Abortion Rights Activist League, Anti Defamation League of B'nai B'rith. Gail Coates scholar Nat. Coun. Jewish Women, 1988-89; dean's grantee Columbia U., 1993, grantee N.Y. State Consortium on Disability Studies, 1993-96. Mem. NOW, Assn. for Help of Retarded Children, Coun. for Exceptional Children, Soc. for Disability Studies, Kappa Delta Pi. Democrat. Jewish. Office: Marymouth Manhattan Coll 221 E 71st St New York NY 10021

SCHWARTZ, ALLYSON Y., state senator; b. N.Y.C., Oct. 3, 1948; d. Everett and Renee Perl Young; m. David Schwartz, 1970; children: Daniel, Jordan. BA, Simmons Coll., 1970; MSS, Bryn Mawr Coll., 1972. Founder, exec. dir. Elizabeth Blackwell Health Ctr. for Women, 1975-88; acting commr., 1st dep. commr. Dept. Human Svcs., 1988-90; mem. Pa. State Senate 4th dist., 1990—; minority chmn. Edn. Com., 1994—; mem. Aging and Youth Com., Pub. Health and Welfare Com., Comty. and Econ. Devel. Com. Policy. Mem. State Bd. Edn., 1995—; mem. Pa. Coun. on Higher Edn., Pa. 2000, 1990—, Pa. Hist. and Mus. Commn.; vice chair assembly on fed. issues Nat. Coun. State Legislators, 1994; v.p. Women's Network; bd. dirs. Ctr. for Policy Alternatives, 1992—. Named Social Worker of Yr. Nat. Assn. Social Workers, 1990. Mem. Child Welfare League. Office: Senate State Capital Harrisburg PA 17101

SCHWARTZ, ANNA JACOBSON, economic historian; b. N.Y.C., Nov. 11, 1915; married; four children. BA, Barnard Coll., 1934; MA, Columbia U., 1935, PhD, 1964; LittD (hon.), U. Fla., 1987; ArtsD (hon.), Stonehill Coll., 1989; LLD (hon.), Iona Coll., 1992. Researcher USDA, 1936, Columbia U. Social Sci. Research Council, 1936-41; mem. sr. research staff Nat. Bur. Econ. Research Inc., N.Y.C., 1941—; instr. Bklyn. Coll., 1952, Baruch Coll., 1959-60; adj. prof. econs. grad. CCNY, 1967-69, grad. sch. CUNY, 1986—, NYU Grad. Sch. Arts and Sci., 1969-70; hon. vis. prof. City U. Bus. Sch., London, 1984—. Mem. editorial bd. Am. Econ. Rev., 1972-78, Jour. Money, Credit and Banking, 1974-75, 84—, Jour. Monetary Econs., 1975—, Jour. Fin. Svcs. Rsch., 1993—; contbr. numerous articles to profl. jours. Disting. fellow Am. Econ. Assn., 1993. Mem. Western Econ. Assn. (pres. 1987-88). Office: Nat Bur Econ Research 50 East 42nd St 17th Fl New York NY 10017-5405

SCHWARTZ, BARI-LYNNE, social services specialist, social worker; b. Cambridge, Mass., Jan. 27, 1943; d. William and Pearl (Levin) Hurwitz; children: Alec, Alison. BA, U. Mass., 1964; MSW, Rutgers U., 1988. Lic. social worker, N.J.; cert. secondary edn. tchr., N.J., Mass. Coord. of monitoring Morris County Dept. Human Svcs., Morristown, N.J.; contract adminstr., intern Bergen County Dept. Human Svcs., Hackensack, N.J.; tchr. Livingston (N.J.) Bd. of Edn.; tchr. English Haddon Twp. Bd. of Edn., Westmont, N.J. Mem. NASW. Home: 181 Long Hill Rd Apt 5M Little Falls NJ 07424-2050 Office: Commission Status Women Adminstrn Bldg Ct Plz South 21 Main St Rm 115W Hackensack NJ 07601-7023

SCHWARTZ, BRENDA KEEN, lawyer; b. Ft. Smith, Ark., Dec. 5, 1949; d. James Pritchard and Era Erline (Jones) Denniston; m. Dean Edward Keen, June 23, 1973 (dec. June 1990); 1 child, Duncan Denniston Keen; m. Sylvan Schwartz, Jr., Apr. 26, 1992. BA, U. Houston, 1972, JD magna cum laude, 1975. Bar: Tex. 1975, U.S. Dist. Ct. (so. dist.) Tex. 1975. Assoc. Haynes & Fullenweider, P.L.C., Houston, 1975-79, v.p., ptnr., 1979-87; ptnr., officer Wallis & Keen, P.C., Houston, 1988-92; prin. Brenda Keen Schwartz P.C., Houston, 1992—. Contbr. articles to legal publs. Fellow Am. Acad. Matrimonial Lawyers (pres. Tex. chpt. 1996—), Tex. Bar Found., Houston Bar Found.; mem. State Bar Tex. (family law coun. 1989-93). Roman Catholic. Office: Brenda Keen Schwartz P C 5718 Westheimer Rd Ste 1320 Houston TX 77057-5732

SCHWARTZ, BRENDA SUE, psychotherapist, artist; b. N.Y.C., Feb. 16, 1939; d. Abraham and Edythe Enya (Bennis) S.; m. Ben Rosenfeld, June 22, 1962 (div. 1964); 1 child, Paula Rosenfeld; m. Don Friedman, Jan. 15, 1972 (div. 1981); 1 child, Lynn Friedman. BFA magna cum laude, CUNY, 1978; MSW, Fordham U., 1994. Cert. social worker, N.Y. Artist N.Y.C., Calif., 1950—; pvt. practice Bronx, 1994—; psychotherapist Our Lady of Mercy Mental Health Clinic, Bronx, 1993—. Mem. NASW.

SCHWARTZ, CAROL LEVITT, former government official; b. Greenville, Miss., Jan. 20, 1944; d. Stanley and Hilda (Simmons) Levitt; m. David H. Schwartz (dec.); children: Stephanie, Hilary, Douglas. BS in Spl. and Elem. Edn., U. Tex., 1965. Mem. transiton team Office of Pres. Elect, 1980-81; con. office presdl. personnel The White House, Washington, 1981; cons. U.S. Dept. Edn., Washington, 1982; pres. sec. U.S. Ho. Reps., Washington, 1982-83; mem. at large Coun. of D.C., Washington, 1985-89; candidate for mayor, Washington, 1986, 94; vice chmn. Nat. Edn. Commn. on Time and Leaarning, 1992-94, Nat. Adv. Coun. on Disadvantaged Children, 1974-79; lectr. in field; radio commentator, 1990-91. Regional columnist Washington Jewish Week, 1995—. Mem. D.C. Bd. Edn., 1974-82, v.p., 1977-80; bd. dirs. Met. Police Boys and Girls Club, 1st v.p., 1989-93, pres., 1994—, chmn. membership com., 1984-93; mem. adv. com. Am. Coun. Young Polit. Leaders, 1982-90; mem. Nat. Coun. Friends Kennedy Ctr., 1984-91; bd. dirs. Whitman-Walker Clinic, 1988—, v.p., 1995—; bd. dirs. St. John's Child Devel. Ctr., 1989-91; trustee Kennedy Ctr. Cmty. and Friends Bd., 1991—, chmn. ednl. task force, 1993—; trustee Jewish Coun. on Aging, 1991-93; v.p. adv. bd. Am. Automobile Assn., 1988—; bd. dirs. Washington Hebrew Congregation, 1995—. Mem. Cosmos Club. Republican. Jewish.

SCHWARTZ, CHERIE ANNE KARO, storyteller; b. Miami, Fla., Feb. 24, 1951; d. William Howard and Dorothy (Olesh) Karo; m. Lawrence Schwartz, Aug. 12, 1979. BA in Lit., The Colo. Coll., 1973; MA in Devel. Theater, U. Colo., 1977. Tchr. English, drame, mime, creative writing, speech coach South High Sch., Pueblo, Colo., 1973-76; tchr. drama St. Mary's Acad., Denver, 1979-81; tchr. English and drama Rocky Mountain Hebrew Acad., Denver, 1981-83; full-time profl. storyteller throughout N.Am., 1982—; storyteller, docent, tchr. tng., mus. outreach Denver Mus. Natural History, 1982—; trainer, cons., performer, lectr, keynote speaker various orgns., synagogues, instns., agys., confs. throughout the country, 1982—; co-founder, chairperson Omanim b'Yachad: Artists Together, Nat. Conf. Celebrating Storytelling, Drama, Music and Dance in Jewish Edn., Denver, 1993. Storyteller: (audio casette tapes) Cherie Karo Schwartz Tells Stories of Hanukkah from Kar-Ben Books, 1986, Cherie Karo Schwartz Tells Stories of Passover From Kar-Ben Books, 1986, Miriam's Trambourine, 1988, Worldwide Jewish Stories of Wishes and Wisdom, 1988; storyteller, actor: (video tape) The Wonderful World of Recycle, 1989; author: (book) My Lucky Dreidel: Hanukkah Stories, Songs, Crafts, Recipes and Fun for Kids, 1994; author numerous stories in anthologies of Jewish literature. Title III grantee State of Colo. Edn., Pueblo, 1975-76. Mem. Coalition for Advancement of Jewish Edn. (coord. Jewish Storytelling Conf. 1989—, coord. Nat. Jewish Storytelling Network), Nat. Assn for Preservation and Perpetuation of Storytelling, Nat. Storytelling Assn. (Colo. state rep. and liaison), Rocky Mountain Storytelling Guild. Democrat. Jewish. Home: 996 S Florence St Denver CO 80231-1952

SCHWARTZ, DORIS RUHBEL, nursing educator, consultant; b. Bklyn., May 30, 1915; d. Henry and Florence Marie (Shuttleworth) S. BS, NYU, 1953, MS, 1958. RN, N.Y. Staff nurse Meth. Hosp., Bklyn., 1942-43; pub. health nurse Vis. Nurse Assn., Bklyn., 1947-51; pub. health nurse Cornell U. Med. Coll., Cornell-N.Y. Hosp. Sch. Nursing, N.Y.C., 1951-61, tchr. pub. health nursing, geriatric nursing, 1961-80; ret., 1990; sr. fellow U. Pa. Sch. Nursing, Phila., 1981-90; mem. bd. dirs. Elders With Adult Dependants. Author: Give Us to Go Blithely, 1990 (Book of Yr. award Am. Jour. Nursing 1991); sr. author: The Elderly Chronically Ill Patient: Nursing and Psychosocial Needs, 1963; co-author: Geriatrics and Geriatric Nursing, 1983 (Book of Yr. award Am. Jour. Nursing 1984); contbr. articles to profl. jours. Mem. adv. com. nursing WHO, Geneva, 1971-79; adv. com. Robert Wood Johnson Found., Teaching Nursing Home Project, Princeton, N.J., U. Pa. Wharton Sch. Study of Continuing Care Retirement Communities, 1981-83; vol. Foulkeways Continuing Care Retirement Cmty., Gwynedd, Pa. Served to capt. N.C., U.S. Army, 1943-47, PTO. Rockefeller fellow U. Toronto, 1950-51, Mary Roberts fellow Am. Jour. Nursing, 1955, Fogarty fellow NIH, 1975-76; recipient Diamond Jubilee Nursing award N.Y. County RNs Assn., 1979. Fellow Inst. Medicine of NAS, APHA (Disting. Career award nursing sect. 1979), Am. Acad. Nursing (charter, coun. 1973-74); mem. ANA (Pearl McIver award 1979), Soroptimist (v.p. N.Y.C. club 1974-75), Sigma Theta Tau (Founders award 1979, Mentor award Alpha Upsilon chpt. 1992). Democrat. Mem. Soc. of Friends.

SCHWARTZ, ELAINE CAROLE (LAINEY SCHWARTZ), lawyer; b. Irvington, N.J., Mar. 3, 1964; d. Edward and Harriet M. (Cohen) S. BA, Boston U., 1987; MS, No. Ill. U., 1991; JD, Vt. Law Sch., 1993. Bar: N.J. 1993, N.Y. 1994. Clk. N.H. Pub. Defender, Keene, 1992, South Royalton (Vt.) Legal Clinic, 1993; law clk. Ocean County Courthouse, Toms River, N.J., 1993-94; assoc. DeNoia and Tambasco, Toms River, 1994—. Vol. ARC, Ocean County, 1993—; vol., supporter Pearl S. Buck Found., Planned Parenthood. Mem. NOW, N.J. Bar Assn., N.Y. Bar Assn., Ocean County Bar Assn. Home: 52 North Ave Seaside Park NJ 08752 Office: DeNoia & Tambasco PO Box 1266 202 Rt 37W Toms River NJ 08754

SCHWARTZ, ELEANOR BRANTLEY, academic administrator; b. Kite, Ga., Jan. 1, 1937; d. Jesse Melvin and Hazel (Hill) Brantley; children: John, Cynthia. Student Mercer U., Ga., 1954-55; student U. Va., 1955, Ga. Southern Coll., 1956-57, BBA, Ga. State U., 1962, MBA, 1963, DBA, 1969. Adminstrv. asst. Fin. Agy., 1954, Fed. Govt., Va., Pa., Ga., 1956-59; asst. dean admissions Ga. State U., Atlanta, 1961-66, asst. prof., 1966-70; assoc. prof. Cleve. State U., 1970-75, prof. and assoc. dean, 1975-80; dean, Harzfeld prof. U. Mo., Kansas City, 1980-87, vice chancellor acad. affairs, 1987-91, interim chancellor, 1991-92, chancellor, 1992—; disting. vis. prof. Berry Coll., Rome, Ga., N.Y. State U. Coll., Fredonia, Mons U., Belgium; cons. pvt. industry, U.S., Europe, Can.; bd. dirs. ANUHCO, Rsch. Med. Ctr., United Group of Mutual Funds, Waddell & Reed Funds, Inc., Torchmark/ United Funds, Toy and Miniature Mus., Menorah Med. Ctr. Found., NCCJ, Econ. Devel. Corp. of Kansas City, Midwest Grain Products, Silicon Prairie Tech. Assn., Mo. Planning Coun. for Devel. Disabilities, 1995—, Am. Coun. Edn. Commn. on Minorities in Higher Edn., 1995—, Assn. Gov. Bds. Univs. and Colls., 1995—. Author: Sex Barriers in Business, 1971, Contemporary Readings in Marketing, 1974; (with Muczyk and Smith) Principles of Supervision, 1984. Chmn., Mayor's Task Force in Govt. Efficiency, Kansas City, Mo., 1984; mem. community planning and research council United Way Kansas City, 1983-85; bd. dirs. Jr. Achievement, 1982-86; Mo. Planning Coun. Devel. Disabilities, 1995—. Recipient Disting. Faculty award Cleve. State U., 1974, Cleve., 60 Women of Achievement Girls Scouts Council Mid Continent, 1983; named Career Woman of Yr. Kansas City, Mo., 1989; recipient disting. svc. award Kansas State U., 1992. Mem. Am. Mktg. Assn., Acad. Internat. Bus., Am. Mgmt. Assn., Am. Case Research Assn., Internat. Soc. Study Behavioral Devel., Greater Kansas City C. of C. (ex. officio, bd. dirs.), Phi Kappa Phi, Golden Key, Alpha Iota Delta.

SCHWARTZ, ELISABETH H., physical education educator; b. Holyoke, Mass., May 29, 1967; d. Wayne E. and Dorothy G. (Green) Leininger; m. Anthony A. Schwartz, Oct. 20, 1990. BS in Phys. Edn., Wheaton (Ill.) Coll., 1989; MA in Counseling edn., No. Ill. U., 1995. Cert. phys. edn. tchr., sch. counselor, Ill. Youth ministry intern Willow Creek Cmty. Ch., Barrington, Ill., 1989-90; tchr. phys. edn. Fox River Grove (Ill.) Sch. Dist. # 3, 1991-94, Barrington Sch. Dist. # 220, 1994—. Mem. ACA, Am. Sch. Counseling Assn., Ki Sigma Iota. Republican. Home: 336 Carl Sands Dr Cary IL 60013 Office: Barrington Mid Sch Prairie Campus 40 E Dundee Rd Barrington IL 60010

SCHWARTZ, ESTAR ALMA, lawyer; b. Bklyn., June 29, 1950; d. Henry Israel and Elaine Florence (Scheiner) Sutel; m. Lawrence Gerald Schwartz, June 28, 1976 (div. Dec. 1977); 1 child, Joshua (dec.). JD, N.Y.U., 1980. owner Estaris Paralegal Svc., Flushing, N.Y., 1992—. Mgr., ptnr. Scheiner, Scheiner, DeVito & Wytte, N.Y.C., 1966-81; fed. govt., social security fraud specialist DHHS, OI, OIG, SSFIS, N.Y.C., 1982-83; pensions Todtman, Epstein, et al, N.Y.C., 1983-85; office mgr., sec. Sills, Beck, Cummis, N.Y.C., 1985-86; office mgr., bookkeeper Philip, Birnbaum & Assocs., N.Y.C., 1986-87; office mgr., sec. Stanley Posses, Esq., Queens, N.Y., 1989-90. Democrat. Jewish. Home and Office: 67-20 Parsons Blvd Apt 2A Flushing NY 11365-2960

SCHWARTZ, HILDA G., retired judge; b. N.Y.C.; d. Solomon and Anna Leah (Rubin) Ginsburg; m. Herman N. Schwartz, Feb. 21, 1930; 1 child, John Michael. BS, Washington Sq. Coll. of NYU; LLB, NYU, 1929. Bar: N.Y. 1930. Pvt. practice, 1930-46; sec., bur. head, trial commr. Bd. Estimate, N.Y.C., 1946-51; city magistrate City of N.Y., 1951-58, city treas., head dept. finance, 1958-62, dir. finance, 1962-64, judge civil ct., 1965-71; justice state supreme ct. State of N.Y., 1972-83; ret., 1983; counsel to law firm, 1984; chmn. law com. Bd. Magistrates, 1953-58; chmn. home term panel judges, 1954-56; judge adolescent ct., 1953-58. Mem. welfare adv. bd. N.Y. Jr. League, 1953-56; bd. mgrs. Greenwich House, 1946-48; v.p. Young Dem. club 1935-37; trustee Village Temple, 1956-61, chair dedication com., 1957; chair exec. bd. Coun. Org. Am. Jewish Congress, 1958; hon. chair, bd. dirs. Women's League for Histadrut, 1959; vice-chair Greenwich Village Fresh Air Fund, 1962; co-chair community breakfast State of Israel Bonds, 1956; bd. dirs. Washington Sq. Outdoor Art Exhibit, 1950-58, Washington Sq. Coll. Alumni Assn., 1967. Recipient Citation by Women for Achievement, 1951, Award of Merit Women Lawyers Assn. State of N.Y., 1957, Scroll of Key award Key Women, 1959, Honor award Am. Jewish Congress Coun. of Orgns., 1959, Honor award Greenwich Village Community for State of Israel Bonds, 1960, Mother of Yr. award Justice Lodge Masons, 1960, First Egalitarian award Aegis Soc., Fed. Negro Civil Svc. Orgns., 1961, Honor award B'nai B'rith, 1963, Interfaith award, 1963, Alumni Achievement award NYU Washington Sq. Coll. Alumni Assn., 1968; named Woman of Achievement Fedn. Jewish Women Orgns., 1959, Patron ann. bridge, Cath. Ctr. NYU, 1960. Mem. ABA, Assn. of Bar of City of N.Y. (mem. lectr., legal aid, matrimonial law, profl. and jud. ethics coms.), N.Y. State Assn. Women Judges (hon. mem., bd. dirs., Outstanding Jud. Achievement award 1983), Supreme Ct. Justices Assn. of City of N.Y. (bd. dirs. 1976-89), Ins. Arbitrator Forums (arbitrator), N.Y. County Lawyers Assn. (profl. ethics com.), N.Y. State Bar Assn. (jud. sabbaticals com.), N.Y. Women's Bar Assn. (past pres., founder, mem. adv. bd., scroll of honor 1958, Disting. Svc. award 1977, Lifetime Contbn. to Justice award 1984), Nat. Assn. Women Judges, Assn. Supreme Ct. Justices State of N.Y. (community rels., retirement and pensions, jud. sabbaticals coms.), Hadassah (hon. mem. N.Y. chpt. 1961), United HIAS Women's Div. (life), Emerald Soc. (hon. mem. 1961), Histadrut (hon. mem. 1960), Iota Tau Tau (hon.). Office: 43 5th Ave New York NY 10003-4368

SCHWARTZ, ILENE, psychotherapist, educator; b. Phila., June 19, 1942; d. Israel Gerson and Susan (Soloway) Schiffman. BS, Temple U., 1970; MEd, Antioch U., 1990. Counselor pvt. practice, Phila., 1978—; cons., crisis counselor in the field; instr. psychology and education, 1974-79. Mem. AAUW, Am. Counseling Assn., Freud Friends.

SCHWARTZ, ILSA ROSLOW, neuroscientist; b. Bklyn., Aug. 20, 1941; d. David and Lottie (Warshall) Roslow; m. Alan Gordon Schwartz, July 19, 1964; children: Leah Ellen, Seth Roslow. AB magna cum laude, Vassar Coll., 1962; MS, Yale U., 1964, PhD, 1968. Postdoctoral fellow Albert Einstein Coll. Medicine, Bronx, N.Y., 1968-69; rsch. assoc. ctr. for neural scis. Ind. U., Bloomington, 1970-73, asst. prof. anatomy and physiology, 1973-75; asst. prof. med. scis. Ind. U. Sch. Medicine, Bloomington, 1976-77; vis. rsch. anatomist UCLA Sch. Medicine, 1976-77, asst. prof. in- residence head and neck surgery, 1977-81, assoc. prof., 1981-87; assoc. prof. Yale U. Sch. Medicine, New Haven, 1987-89, prof. surgery (otolaryngology) and neurobiology, 1989—; mem. communicative disorders rev. com. Nat. Inst. Neurol. Communicative Disorders and Stroke, Bethesda, 1981-83, chair, 1983-85; sci. adv. coun. House Ear Inst., L.A., 1989, chair, 1991-94. Recipient Jacob Javits Neurosci. Investigator award Nat. Inst. Neurol. Communicative Disorders and Stroke, 1988-95; grantee NIH, 1973—; fellow Vassar Coll., 1962-63, NIH, 1962-68, 68-69. Mem. Assn. for Rsch. in Otolaryngology (coun. mem. 1986-89, pres. elect 1989-90, pres. 1990-91, past pres. 1991-92), Nat. Inst. on Deafness and Other Communication Disorders (adv. coun. 1989-93), Soc. for Neurosci. (chair Bloomington, Ind. chpt. 1975-76), Am. Assn. Anatomists, Women in Neurosci., AAAS, Friends of NIDCD, Inc. (bd. dirs.). Jewish. Office: Yale U Sch Medicine 333 Cedar St New Haven CT 06510-3206

SCHWARTZ, JANE LINKER, social worker, nurse; b. Tampa, Fla., Sept. 4, 1925; d. Sydney Linker and Sadie Friedman; m. Lawrence Schwartz (div. 1976); children: Karen, Joel, David. BS, Russell Sage Coll., 1948; MSW, U. Wash., 1967; M in Nursing, 1973; PhD, Union Inst., 1982. Diplomate Am. Bd. Examiners Clin. Social Work; lic. clin. social worker Acad. Cert. Social Workers, Fla. Clin. social worker Navy Regional Med. Ctr., Guam, U.S.A., 1983-84; pvt. practice Honolulu, 1985-89; clin. social worker, psychotherapist VA Med. Ctr., Tampa and Miami, Fla., 1989-90; pvt. practice Miami, 1990-94; clin. social worker Eglin (Fla.) AFB, 1994-95; clin. social worker, psychotherapist Emerald Coast Psychol. Care, Ft. Walton, Fla., 1995—. Author: The Psychodynamics of Patient Care, 1972, Vulnerable Infants-A Psychosocial Dilemma, 1977. 2nd lt. U.S. Army Nurse Corp, 1948-49. Mem. ANA (registered profl. nurse, cert. psychiat. and mental health nurse), NASW, Sigma Theta Tau. Democrat. Jewish. Home: 4471 D Luke Ave Destin FL 32541 Office: Emerald Coast Psychiat Care Fort Walton Beach FL 32548

SCHWARTZ, KATHRYN COX, journalist; b. Ogallala, Nebr., Dec. 21, 1942; d. Howell Winfred and Beverly Jean (Hennings) C.; m. Guenther Leopold Schwartz, Mar. 4, 1962; children: Elizabeth Shanti, Christopher Paul. Urban 4-H aide UNL Extension Svc., Blair, Iowa, 1974-76; reporter, editor Enterprise Publ., Blair, 1976-84; editor, advt. mgr. Contemporary Women, Des Moines, Lincoln, Nebr., 1986-87; asst. editor, mng. editor, pubs. coord. Enterprise Pub., Blair, 1989—; reporter Contemporary Women, Des Moines, 1986-87, Midlands Bus. Jour., Omaha, Nebr., 1984-86. Pub. info. officer Civil Def. Emergency Preparedness Staff, Blair, 1990—; amb. Blair Area C. of C., 1992—; bd. dirs. John G. Neihardt Found., 1996—. Mem. Nebr. State Hist. Soc., Washington County Hist. Soc. (2d v.p. 1996), Children's Mus. Kansas City, Josyln Art Mus., Order of Eastern Star, Nebr. Press Assn., Northeast Nebr. Dist. Press Assn. (sec. 1996—). Office: Enterprise Publ Co 138 N 16th PO Box 328 Blair NE 68008

SCHWARTZ, KATHY LOU, nursing administrator; b. Camp Atterbury, Ind., Mar. 26, 1953; d. Marvin H. and Vernita Rippe; m. Allen C. Schwartz, Aug. 23, 1975; children: Sarah Anne, Kyle Lynn. Diploma, Stormont-Vail Sch. of Nursing, 1974. RN; cert. BLS, ACLS. Staff nurse Hanover (Kans.) Hosp., 1974-75; house supr. Meml. Hosp., Manhattan, Kans., 1975-78, 80—, oper. rm. nurse, 1978-79, pediatric nurse, 1979-80. Home: 2213 Snowbird Dr Manhattan KS 66502-1943 Office: Memorial Hospital 1105 Sunset Ave Manhattan KS 66502-3575

SCHWARTZ, LILLIAN FELDMAN, artist, filmaker, art analyst, author, nurse; b. Cin., July 13, 1927; d. Jacob and Katie (Green) Feldman; m. Jack James Schwartz, Dec. 22, 1946; children: Jeffrey Hugh, Laurens Robert. RN, U. Cin., 1947; Dr. honoris causa, Kean Coll., 1988. Nurse Cin. Gen. Hosp., 1947; head supr. premature nursery St. Louis Maternity Hosp., 1947-48; cons. AT&T Bell Labs., Murray Hill, N.J., 1968—; pres. Computer Creations Corp., Watchung, N.J., 1989—; cons. Bell Communications Research, Morristown, N.J., 1984-92; artist-in-residence Sta. WNET, N.Y.C., 1972-74; cons. T.J. Watson Rsch. Lab. IBM Corp., Yorktown, N.Y., 1975, 82-84; vis. mem. computer sci. dept. U.. Md., College Park, 1974-80; adj. prof. fine arts Kean Coll., Union, N.J., 1980-82, Rutgers U., New Brunswick, N.J., 1982-83; adj. prof. dept. psychology NYU, N.Y.C., 1985-86, assoc. prof. computer sci.; guest lectr. Princeton U., Columbia U., Yale U., Rockefeller U.; mem. grad. faculty Sch. Visual Arts, N.Y.C., 1990—. Co-author: The Computer Artist's Handbook; contbd. articles to profl. jours including Scientific Am., 1995; contbr. chpts. to books, also Trans. Am. Philos. Soc., vol. 75, Part 6, 1985; one-woman shows of sculpture and paintings include Columbia U., 1967, 68, Rabin and Krueger Gallery, Newark, 1968; films shown at Met. Mus., N.Y.C., Franklin Inst., Phila., 1972, U. Toronto, 1972, am. Embassy, London, 1972, L.A. County Mus., Corcoran Gallery, Washington, 1972, Whitney Mus., N.Y.C., 1973, Grand Palais, Paris, Musee Nat. d'Art Moderne, Paris, IBM, and others. Recipient numerous art and film awards, Emmy award Mus. Modern Art, 1984, Computer Graphics World Smithsonian awards for virtual reality, art analysis, inventing computer medium for art and animation, 1993; named Outstanding Alumnus, U. Cin., 1987; grantee Nat. Endowment for Arts, 1977, 81, Corp. Pub. Broadcasting, 1979, Nat. Endowment Composers and Librettists, 1981. Fellow World Acad. of Art and Sci.; mem. NATAS, Am. Film Inst., Info. Film Prodrs. Am., Soc. Motion Picture and TV Engrs., Internat. Sculptors Assn., Centro Studi Pierfrancescani (Sansepolcro, Italy, founding mem.).

SCHWARTZ, LITA LINZER, psychologist, educator; b. N.Y.C., Jan. 14, 1930; d. Aaron Jerome and Dorothy Claire (Linzer) Linzer; m. Melvin Jay Schwartz, June 18, 1950 (div. 1983); children: Arthur Lee, Joshua David, Frederic Seth. AB, Vassar Coll., 1950; EdM, Temple U., 1956; PhD, Bryn Mawr Coll., 1964. Diplomate Am. Bd. Forensic Psychology, Am. Bd. Profl. Psychology; lic. psychologist, Pa. Part-time instr., counselor Pa. State U., Ogontz, Campus, Abington, 1961-66, asst. prof. ednl. psychology, 1966-71, assoc. prof., 1971-76, prof., 1976-93, disting. prof., 1993-95, prof. women's studies, 1993-95, disting. prof. emerita, 1995—; pvt. practice, 1964—; cons. in field. Recipient Humanitarian Award N.Y. Philanthropic League, 1973, Christian R. and Mary F. Lindback award, 1982, Outstanding Tchr. award Pa. State U. Coll. Edn. Alumni, 1982. Fellow APA, Am. Orthopsychiatric Assn.; mem. Am. Bd. Forensic Psychology, Soc. Reproductive Medicine, Internat. Council of Psychologists (bd. dirs. 1995—), Assn. Tchr. Educators (Tchr. Laureate 1993-94), Coun. for Exceptional Children, Assn. Family and Conciliation Cts., Nat. Assn. for Gifted Children, Pa. Assn. Gifted Children, Soc. for Advancement of Field Theory (exec. bd. 1991-93), Acad. Family Mediators (Pa. and Del. Valley chpts., evaluation com. child custody mediation project Del. Valley), Ethnic Studies Assn. Del. Valley (co-chair program com. 1986-88), Psi Chi. Author: American Education, 1969, 74, 78; Educational Psychology, 1972, 77; The Exceptional Child: A Primer, 1975, 79; Exceptional Students in the Mainstream, 1984; (with Natalie Isser) The American School and The Melting Pot, 1985, 89, (with Florence W. Kaslow) The Dynamics of Divorce, 1987; (with Natalie Isser) The History of Conversion and Contemporary Cults, 1988; Alternatives to Infertility: Is Surrogacy the Answer?, 1991, Why Give Gifts to the Gifted?: Investing in a National Resource, 1994; editor: Mid-Life Divorce Counseling, 1994; contbr. over 60 articles to profl. jours., numerous chapters to books. Office: Pa State U Ogontz Campus Abington PA 19001

SCHWARTZ, MARTI ANN, management consultant; b. San Rafael, Calif., Aug. 16, 1955; d. Sidney and Sylvia Schwartz; m. Kenneth Steven; 1 child, Erin Ashley. BFA, UCLA, 1977. Talent coord. L.A., 1979-85; promotions coord. Salem, Oreg., 1986-90; author, spkr. The Consummate Consumer, Beaverton, Oreg., 1991—. Author: Listen to Me, Doctor, 1995. Mem. Portland C. of C. Office: The Consummate Consumer PO Box 1397 Beaverton OR 97075

SCHWARTZ, MELISSA LEE, fashion designer; b. Honolulu, Aug. 22, 1968; d. Kenneth Edward and Carole Lee (Tanda) S. A in Fashion Design, SUNY, 1991. Asst. designer Deborah Marquit, N.Y.C., 1992; pattern maker Jacques Moret, N.Y.C., 1992-94; freelance designer various industry clients, N.Y.C., 1992-94; designer The Finals/Ankhka Swimwear, N.Y.C., 1994—; decorator ballroom for Pre-Bening Women's Conf. Party, Ngo Women's Forum Ball, N.Y.C., 1995. Designer, editor: (catalogues) Finals 1997, Ankhka, 1997, Finals 1996, Ankhka 1996; graphic designer Ankhaka co. logo name, 1995; costume designer outfits for Architect's Ball, Wigstock, 1992-96. Asst. Rainbow Coalition, Eugene, Oreg., 1984. Recipient Christian Francis Roth Critic award F.I.T. Design Adminstrn., N.Y.C., 1991, Saks Fifth Ave. scholarship, 1990, 91. Liberal. Wiccan. Avocations: dancing, mountain climbing, cliff diving, gymnastics.

SCHWARTZ, MINA A., counselor; b. Brklyn., Jan. 13, 1945; d. Harry and Lillian (Sachs) Alexander; m. Morton D. Schwartz; children: Lowell, Sara. BA, U. Mich., Ann Arbor, 1962-66; MA, U. Md., College Park, 1975-78. Cert. profl. counselor, cert. rehab. counselor, cert. ins. rehab. specialist, Md. Rehab. counselor C.R.C., Bethesda, Md., 1978-82; rehab. mgr. Vocational Counseling Assoc., Bethesda, 1982—; bd. dirs. Head Injury Referral Svcs., Rockville, Md., 1991—. Pres., bd. mem. Kehilah Chadasho, Bethesda, 1988-90. Mem. Nat. Assn. Rehab. Practitioners in the Pvt. Sector (organized nat. conv. 1990-91), Chesapeake Assn. Rehab. Profls. in the Pvt. Sector (pres. 1990).

SCHWARTZ, NEENA BETTY, endocrinologist, educator; b. Balt., Dec. 10, 1926; d. Paul Howard and Pauline (Shulman) S. A.B., Goucher Coll., 1948, D.Sc. (hon.), 1982; M.S., Northwestern U., 1950, Ph.D., 1953. From instr. to prof. U. Ill. Coll. Medicine, Chgo., 1953-72; asst. dean for faculty U. Ill. Coll. Medicine, 1968-70; prof. physiology Northwestern U. Med. Sch., Chgo., 1973-74; Deering prof. Northwestern U., Evanston, Ill., 1974—, chmn. dept. biol. scis., 1974-78, acting dean, Coll. Arts and Scis., 1996—. Contbr. chpts. to books, articles to profl. jours. NIH research grantee, 1955—. Fellow AAAS; mem. Am. Acad. Arts Scis., Endocrine Soc. (v.p. 1970-71, mem. coun. 1979-83, pres. 1982-83, Williams award 1985), Soc. for Study of Reprodn. (dir. 1975-77, exec. v.p. 1976-77, pres. 1977-78, Carl Hartman award 1992), Am. Physio. Soc., Soc. for Neurosci., Phi Beta Kappa. Home: 1511 Lincoln St Evanston IL 60201-2338

SCHWARTZ, RUTH LEAH, poet; b. Geneva, N.Y., Feb. 22, 1962; d. George Robert Schwartz and Loretta Jean (Rosenberg) Schwartz Nobel. BA in Writing/Women's Studies, Wesleyan U., 1983; MFA in Writing, U. Mich., 1985. Author: (poems) Accordion Breathing and Dancing, 1996. Recipient Nimrod Poetry award, 1991, New Letters Poetry award, 1991, N.C. Writers Network award, 1993; Emerging Writers grantee Astraea Found., 1992; Individual Writers grantee NEA, 1993. Home: 6035 Majestic Ave Oakland CA 94605-1862

SCHWARTZ, RUTH WAINER, physician; b. New London, Wis.; d. Louis M. and Kathryn Ann (Schwall) W.; m. Seymour I. Schwartz, June 18, 1949; children: Richard, Kenneth, David. BS, U. Wis., 1947, MD, 1950. Diplomate Am. Bd. Ob-Gyn. Intern Genesee Hosp., Rochester, N.Y., 1950; resident Strong Meml. Hosp., Rochester, N.Y., 1951-54; pvt. practice ob-gyn. Rochester, 1954—; examiner Am. Bd. Ob-Gyn., 1976-95, bd. dirs., 1981-89; dir. colposcopy, dysplasia and DES Clinic, colposcopy and laser tutor Genesee Hosp.; prof. ob-gyn. U. Rochester Sch. Medicine and Dentistry, dir. Menopause Ctr.; pres. med. staff Genesee Hosp., 1972-74; bd. dirs. Genesee Health Svc., 1972-75, ARC, med. adv. com.; trustee Rochester Acad. Medicine, 1975-78; vis. prof. U. Kuwait Med. Sch., 1984, U. Toledo Sch. Medicine, 1985, U. N.Mex. Sch. Medicine, 1989. Contbr. numerous articles to med. jours. and chpts. to med. textbooks; cons. editor and contbr. to The Merck Manual, 15th edit., 1983, 16th edit., 1987, 17th edit., 1991. Mem. med. adv. bd. N.Y. State Task Force on Child Abuse. Named one of Best Women Doctors in Am., Harper's Bazaar mag., Nov., 1985. Mem. AMA (accreditation coun. on continuing med. edn. 1988-93), ACS, ACOG (health care commn., Women in Ob-Gyn task force, patient edn. com. 1979-83, asst. sec. 1994-95, task force on hysterectomy 1987-89, vice chmn. fin. com. 1996-99, adv. bd. dist. II 1993-96, sec. 1993-96), Am. Soc. Colposcopy and Colpomicroscopy, Gynecologic Laser Soc. (bd. dirs.), Am. Fertility Soc., N.Y. State Med. Assn., Monroe County Med. Soc. (maternal mortality com., pub. health com.). Home: 18 Lake Lacoma Dr Pittsford NY 14534-3956

SCHWARTZ, SHIRLEY E., chemist; b. Detroit, Aug. 26, 1935; d. Emil Victor and Jessie Grace (Galbraith) Eckwall; m. Ronald Elmer Schwartz, Aug. 25, 1957; children: Steven Dennis, Bradley Allen, George Byron. BS, U. Mich., 1957, Detroit Inst. Tech., 1978; MS, Wayne State U., 1962, PhD, 1970. Asst. prof. Detroit Inst. Tech., 1973-78, head divsn. math. sci., 1976-78; mem. rsch. staff BASF Wyandotte (Mich.) Corp., 1978-81, head sect. functional fluids, 1981; sr. staff rsch. scientist GM, Warren, Mich., 1981—. Contbr. articles to profl. jours.; patentee in field. Recipient Gold award Engring. Soc. Detroit, 1989, lifetime achievement award Mich. Women's Hall of Fame, 1996. Fellow Soc. Tribologists and Lubrication Engrs. (treas. Detroit sect. 1981, vice chmn. 1982, chmn. 1982-83, chmn. wear tech. com. 1987-88, bd. dirs. 1985-91, assoc. editor 1989-90, contbg. editor 1989—, Wilbur Deutsch award 1987, P.M. Ku award 1994); mem. Am. Chem. Soc., Soc. In Vitro Biology, Soc. Automotive Engrs. (Excellence in Oral Presentation award 1986, 91, 94, Arch T. Colwell Merit award 1991, Lloyd L. Withrow Disting. Spkr. award 1995), Mensa, Classic Guitar Soc. Mich., U.S. Power Squadrons, Detroit Navigators, Sigma Xi. Lutheran. Office: GM Rsch & Devel Ctr 30500 Mound Rd Warren MI 48090-9055

SCHWARTZ, SUSAN LYNN HILL, principal; b. Portland, Ind., Aug. 15, 1951; d. Leland Alfred and Marjorie (Halberstadt) Hill; m. William Samuel Schwartz, July 6, 1974; children: Angelica Martinique, Allysia Dominica. BA, DePauw U., 1973; MA, Ball State U., 1976; postgrad., Tri-Coll. U., Fargo, N.D., 1986, Ind. U., 1993—. Cert. tchr. and aminstr., Ind., N.D. 2d and 3d grade tchr. Jay Sch. Corp., Portland, 1973-76; 1st to 3d grade tchr. Minot (N.D.) Pub. Schs., 1976-80; prin. elem. sch. Ward County Schs., Minot, 1980-82, LaPorte (Ind.) Schs., 1988-89; prin. 3d to 4th grade and spl. edn. Western Wayne Schs., Cambridge City, Ind., 1989—; mem. State Sch. Evaluation Team, Bismarck, N.D., 1980-81. Bd. dirs. Am. Cancer Soc., Muncie, Ind., 1985-88, Richmond, Ind., 1992—, Suzuki Music Assn., Muncie, 1986-87; mem./leader Work Area on Edn.-Meth., Muncie, 1985-87; philanthropic chair Delaware County Welcome Wagon, Muncie, 1982-88; treas./fin. sec. Christian Women's Club, Muncie, 1983-86; pres. N.D. State U. Sch. Adminstrs. Assn., Fargo, 1980-81; mem. Wayne County Step Ahead Edn. Com., 1991—. Named Outstanding Young Educator, Jaycees, 1980, Outstanding Young Career Woman, Bus. and Profl. Women, 1981. Mem. Phi Delta Kappa, Pi Lambda Theta, Delta Kappa Gamma, Psi Iota Xi. Methodist. Home: 12522 W Us Highway 40 Trlr 30 Cambridge City IN 47327-9481 Office: Milton Elem Sch PO Box 308 Milton IN 47357-0308

SCHWARTZKOPF, DENISE LESLIE, nurse; b. Denver, July 9, 1963; d. Walter Lee and Kathleen Angela (Hyland) S. BSN, U. Colo. Health Sci. Ctr., 1992. RN, Colo. Program dir. Am. Diabetes Assn., Denver, 1986-92; staff nurse Rose Med. Ctr., Denver, 1992-96; admissions dir. Mediplex Rehab. Hosp., Thornton, Colo., 1996—; pres. Rose Med. Ctr. Nursing Congress, 1995-96. Newsletter editor Washington Park Cmty. Ctr., Denver, 1994-96. Mem. Colo. Nurses Assn. (co-pres. dist. 19 1994—), Am. Assn. Diabetes Educators, NAFE, Friends of Nursing. Democrat. Home: 830 Leyden St Denver CO 80220

SCHWARTZMAN, ROBIN BERMAN, lawyer; b. Mobile, Ala., Aug. 22, 1941; d. Hyman E. and Lillian (Cooperman) B.; m. Edward Schwartzman, May 21, 1971 (div. 1994); 1 child, Daniel Berman. BA, Bryn Mawr Coll., 1961; MA, Harvard U., 1963; JD, NYU, 1975. Bar: N.Y. 1976, D.C. 1982. Rsch. analyst, Slavic reference libr. and area specialist for Yugoslavia, U.S. Library of Congress, 1965-67; reference libr. and archivist Council Fgn. Relations, N.Y.C., 1967-70; program officer Internat. Rsch. and Exchange Bd., N.Y.C., 1970-72; assoc. Morgan, Lewis & Bockius, N.Y.C., 1975-77; assoc. Fried, Frank, Harris, Shriver & Jacobson, N.Y.C., 1977-79; deputy dir. Bur. Trade Regulation U.S. Dept. Commerce, Washington, 1979-81; sr. atty. Burlington Industries, Greensboro, N.C., 1984-87, asst. gen. counsel, 1987-88; of counsel Heron, Burchette, Ruckert & Rothwell, Washington, 1988-90; sr. atty. Weadon & Assocs, Washington, 1991-92; assoc. atty. Dickstein, Shapiro & Morin, Washington, 1992-93; sr. legal & regulatory officer USAgy. Internat. Devel. Bereau of Europe and New Independent States, Washington, 1993-96. Contbr. articles to profl. jours. Carnegie Scholarship for Study in Soviet Union, Bryn Mawr Coll., 1960, Woodrow Wilson fellow, Harvard U., 1961-62, Nat. Defense Fgn. Language fellow, Harvard U., 1962-64, Jr. fellow Ctr. for Internat. Studies NYU Sch. Law, 1974-75. Mem. ABA (sect. internat. law, com. NIS law, coord. Ukraine, com. Ctrl. European law), Women in Internat. Trade, Exec. Women in Govt. (vice chmn. 1981), Fed. Bar Assn. (steering com. democracy devel. initiative 1991-93). Democrat. Jewish. Home and Office: 5510 Surrey St Chevy Chase MD 20815-5524

SCHWARZ, BARBARA RUTH BALLOU, elementary school educator; b. East Orange, N.J., Aug. 8, 1930; d. Robert Ingram Ballou and Ruth Edna Sweeney; m. Eugene A. Schwarz, Jr., Dec. 24, 1954 (div. 1977); children: Ruth Ellen, Eugene A. III. BS, Trenton State Coll., 1952. Tchr. West Orange N.J. Schs., 1952-54, Franklin Sch., Ft. Wayne, Ind., 1955-56, Parliament Place Sch., North Babylon, N.Y., 1965-91; trustee welfare trust fund North Babylon Tchrs. Orgn., N.Y., 1988-91. Vol. Safe Home, L.I. Women's Coalition, Bayshore, N.Y., 1979—; sec. Victims Info. Bur., Suffolk, 1987-88, v.p., 1989-90, pres. bd. dirs., 1990-94, rep. to Women's Equal Rights Coalition, Suffolk County Human Rights Commn., 1989-94; mem. adv. bd. Suffolk County Women's Svcs., 1990—, vice-chmn., 1991-93; bd. dirs. Suffolk Abortion Rights Coun., 1992—; mem. Suffolk-Nassau Abortion Def., 1991-94; mem. pub. affairs com. Planned Parenthood Suffolk County; mem. adminstrv. bd. Babylon Meth. Ch.; mem. Long Islanders for Fairness and Equality 94. Women's History Month Community Svc. honoree Town of Babylon. Mem. AAUW (mem. v.p. Islip area br. 1982-84, pres. 1984-88, legis. chmn. 1988-93, mem. com. promoting individual liberties Nassau-Suffolk dist. VI 1989-91, pro-choice coord. N.Y. state 1990-92, rep. to women on job task force 1986—, chmn. dist. VI inter-br. 1991-92, chair N.Y. state pub. policy 1992-96, rep. on L.I. and N.Y. State Pro-Choice Coalitions), N.Y. State Ret. Tchrs. Assn., Western Suffolk Ret. Tchrs. Assn., Coalition Ret. Tchrs. L.I., North Babylon Tchrs. Orgn. (retirees chpt.). Republican. Home: 23 Wyandanch Ave Babylon NY 11702-1920

SCHWARZ, GRETCHEN CAROLYN, retired government administrator; b. Mar. 16, 1944; d. George Anthony and Grace Katherine (Mahoney) S. BS in Bus. Adminstrn. and Acctg., Kansas State U., 1966; M in Pub. Adminstrn., George Washington, 1979. Auditor, audit mgr. U.S. GAO, Washington, 1966-79; spl. asst. to the dir. bur. accounts ICC, Washington, 1979-80; spl. asst. to the insp. gen. and assoc. insp. gen. U.S. Dept. Edn., Washington, 1980-95; ret., 1995. Mem. Assn. Govt. Accts. (Disting. Leadership award No. Va. chpt. 1975, pres. No. Va. chpt. 1973, nat. fin. bd. 1981-84), Inst. Internal Auditors (v.p. Wash. 1984-86, internat. membership com. 1984-88, co-chair Ea. Regional Conf., 1988, Disting. Service award 1986, mem. standards bd. 1993-95), Phi Alpha Alpha. Roman Catholic.

SCHWARZKOPF, GLORIA A., education educator, psychotherapist; b. Chgo., Apr. 20, 1926; m. Alfred E. Grossenbacher. BE, Chgo. State U., 1949, MEd in Libr. Sci., 1956. Cert. nat. recovery specialist, reality therapist; libr. sci. endorsement; cert. hypnotherapist; nat. forensic counselor. Tchr. Chgo. Bd. Edn., 1949-91, inservice trainer in substance abuse, 1990, 91; co-therapist ATC outpatient unit Ingalls Meml. Hosp., Chgo., 1981-86; recovery specialist Interaction Inst., Evergreen Park, Ill., 1993-95; instr. Govs. State U., University Park, Ill., 1987, 91, South Suburban Coll., South Holland, Ill., 1991, Prairie State Coll., Chicago Heights, Ill., 1993, 96. columnist Peoples Choice Weekly, 1991-93. Citizens Amb. Program del. to Russia and Czechoslovakia, 1996. Recipient Sci. Tchr. of Yr. award, 1976, Svc. Recognition award, 1985, IMSA Recognition award, 1988; grantee Chgo. Pub. Sch., 1981. Mem. NEA, Nat. Assn. Forensic Counselors, Sci. Tchrs. Assn., Ill. Alcoholism Counselors Alliance, Nat. Alcoholism Coun., Am. Assn. Hypnotherapists, Am. Assn. Behavioral Therapists, Soc. of Am. for Recovery (nat. cert. recovery specialist). Home: 2216 W 91st St Chicago IL 60620-6238

SCHWARZROCK, SHIRLEY PRATT, author, lecturer, educator; b. Mpls., Feb. 27, 1914; d. Theodore Ray and Myrtle Pearl (Westphal) Pratt; m. Loren H. Schwarzrock, Oct. 19, 1945 (dec. 1966); children: Kay Linda, Ted Kenneth, Lorraine V. BS, U. Minn., 1935, MA, 1942, PhD, 1974. Sec. to chmn. speech dept., U. Minn., Mpls., 1935, instr. in speech, 1946, team tchr. in creative arts workshops for tchrs., 1955-56, guest lectr. Dental Sch., 1967-72, asst. prof. (part-time) of practice adminstrn. Sch. Dentistry, 1972-80; tchr. speech, drama and English, Preston (Minn.) H.S., 1935-37; tchr. speech, drama and English, Owatonna (Minn.) H.S., 1937-39, also dir. dramatics, 1937-39; tchr. creative dramatics and English, tchr.-counselor Webster Groves (Mo.) Jr. H.S., 1939-40; dir. dramatics and tchr.-counselor Webster Groves Sr. H.S., 1940-43; exec. sec. bus. and profl. dept. YWCA, Mpls., 1943-45; tchr. speech and drama Covent of the Visitation, St. Paul, 1958; editor pro-tem Am. Acad. Dental Practice Adminstrn., 1966-68; guest tchr. Coll. St. Catherine, St. Paul, 1969; vol. mgr. Gift Shop, Eitel Hosp., Mpls., 1981-83, Edina Cmty. Resource Pool, 1992-95; cmty. citizen mem. planning, evaluating, reporting com. Edina Pub. Sch. System, 1993-96; tutor for reading, writing, and speaking, 1993-96; cons. for dental med. programs Normandale C.C., Bloomington, Minn., 1968; cons. on pub. rels. to dentists, 1954-96; guest lectr. to various dental groups, 1966-95; lectr. Internat. Congress on Arts and Communication, 1980, Am. Inst. Banking, 1981; condr. tutorials in speaking and profl. office mgmt., 1985-96; owner Shirley Schwarzrock's Exec. Support Svc., 1989—; cons. to mktg. communications mgr. Ergodyne Corp., St. Paul, 1991-92; freelance editor med. support bus., 1992. Author books (series): Coping with Personal Identity, Coping with Human Relationships, Coping with Facts and Fantasies, Coping with Teenage Problems, 1984; individual book titles include: Do I Know the "Me" Others See?, My Life-What Shall I Do With It?, Living with Loneliness, Learning to Make Better Decisions, Grades, What's So Important About Them, Anyway?, Facts and Fantasies About Alcohol, Facts and Fantasies About Drugs, Facts and Fantasies About Smoking, Food as a Crutch, Facts and Fantasies About the Roles of Men and Women, You Always Communicate Something, Appreciating People-Their Likenesses and Differences, Fitting In, To Like and Be Liked, Can You Talk With Someone Else? Coping with Emotional Pain, Some Common Crutches, Parents Can Be a Problem, Coping with Cliques, Crises Youth Face Today, Effective Dental Assisting, (with L.H. Schwarzrock) 1954, 59, 67, (with J.R. Jensen) 1973, 78, 82, (with J.R. Jensen, Kay Schwarzrock, Lorraine Schwarzrock) 1990, Workbook for Effective Dental Assisting, 1960, 68, 73, (with Lorraine Schwarzrock), 1978, 82, 90, Manual for Effective Dental Assisting, 1968, 73, 78, 82, 90; (with Donovan F. Ward), Effective Medical Assisting, 1969, 76; Workbook for Effective Medical Assisting, 1969, 76, Manual for Effective Medical Assisting, 1969, 76; (with C.G. Wrenn) The Coping with Series of Books for High School Students, 1970, 73; The Coping With Manual, 1973, Contemporary Concerns, of Youth, 1980. Pres. University Elem. Sch. PTA, 1955-56. Fellow Internat. Biog. Assn.; mem. Minn. Acad. Dental Practice Adminstrn. (hon.), Minn. Historical Soc., 1992—, Minn. Geneaolgical Soc., 1992—, Zeta Phi Eta (pres. 1948-49), Eta Sigma Upsilon. Home: 7448 W Shore Dr Edina MN 55435-4022

SCHWEBEL, RENATA MANASSE, sculptor; b. Zwickau, Germany, Mar. 6, 1930; d. George and Anne Marie (Simon) Manasse; came to U.S., 1940, naturalized, 1946; m. Jack P. Schwebel, May 10, 1955; children: Judith, Barbara, Diane. BA, Antioch Coll., 1953; MFA, Columbia U., 1961; student Art Students League, 1967-69. Cartographer, Ecostate, Inc., Ridgewood, N.J., 1949; display artist Silvestri, Inc., Chgo., 1950-51; asst. Mazzolini Art Found., Yellow Springs, Ohio, 1952; one-person show Columbia U., 1961, Greenwich Art Barn, Conn., 1975, Sculpture Ctr., N.Y.C., 1979, Pelham Art Ctr., N.Y., 1981, New Rochelle Libr. Gallery, N.Y., 1980, outdoor installation Alfresco, Katonah Gallery, 1989, Berman/Daferner Gallery, N.Y.C., 1992-93; exhibited in group shows Stamford Mus., Conn., 1967, 96, Hudson River Mus., Yonkers, N.Y., 1972, 74, Wadsworth Atheneum, Hartford, 1975, Silvermine New Eng. Anns., 1972, 76, 80, 95, Silvermine Gallery, 1991, New Britain Mus. Am. Art, Conn., 1974, Sculptors Guild Anns., 1974—, Imprimatur Gallery, St. Paul, 1985, Bergen County Mus., N.J., 1983, Sculpture Ctr., N.Y.C., 1978-88, Katonah Gallery, N.Y., 1986-90, Cast Iron Gallery, N.Y.C., 1991, 93, Kyoto (Japan) Gallery, 1993; traveling show exhibited in Am. cultural ctrs. in Egypt and Israel, 1981, FFS Gallery, N.Y.C., 1994, 95; represented in permanent collection S.W. Bell, Columbia U., Colt Industries, Am. Airlines, ComCraft Industries, Nairobi, Grüber Haus, Berlin, Mus. Fgn. Art, Sofia, Bulgaria. Bd. dirs. Fine Arts Fedn., N.Y., 1985-87; trustee Sculpture Ctr., 1980-88, chmn. exhbn. com., 1986-88; mem. adv. bd. Pehlham Art Ctr., 1982. Mem. Sculptors Guild (bd. dirs., pres. 1980-83), Antioch Coll. Assn. (bd. dirs. 1971-77), Ams. for Peace Now (bd. dirs. 1991—), Nat. Assn. Women Artists (Willis Meml. prize 1974, Medal of Honor 1981, Paley Meml. award 1979), Audubon Artists (Chaim Gross award 1980, medal of honor 1982, Rennick award 1986, 90, 92, 95), Conn. Acad. Fine Arts, N.Y. Soc. Women Artists, Artists Equity N.Y., Katonah Gallery (artist mem. 1986-90). Home: 10 Dogwood Hills Pound Ridge NY 10576-1508

SCHWEGMAN, MONICA JOAN, artist; b. Hamilton, Ohio, Apr. 19, 1958; d. David Michael and LaVerne Henrietta (Mergy) Kiley; m. Craig Alfred Schwegman, Oct. 6, 1978; children: Craig, Sarah. Student, U. Cin., 1976-78; AAS, Brookdale C.C., 1978; postgrad., Kansas City Art Inst., 1990. Mgmt. trainee coll. coop. Marshall Fields, Chgo., 1977-78; decorator, cons. Sears, Toms River, N.J., 1985-88; artist, owner studio and gallery Lampasas, Tex., 1990-94; chmn. Keystone Art Alliance, Lampasas, 1991-94; art dir. Theatre for Lampasas, 1993-94. Exhibited in group shows at Gallery One, Marble Falls, Tex., Found Art, Lampasas, KBVO TV Set Design, Austin, Tex., Breckenrdge Fine Arts Ctr., Pasillo De Artes Gallery, Austin, Contemporary Art Exhibit, Lampasas, Gannon U., Erie, Pa., Glass Growers Gallery, Erie, Barnes & Noble, Erie, Springhill, Erie. Instr. art City of Lampasas/Sparts, 1993. Mem. Lampasas C. of C. (mem. tourism com. 1993). Republican. Roman Catholic.

SCHWEGMANN, MELINDA, supermarket executive, former state official; b. Austin, Tex., Oct. 25, 1946; m. John F. Schwegmann; 3 children. Student, La. State U.; grad. in Edn., U. New Orleans, 1968. Former pub. sch. tchr.; past pres. La. Soc. for Prevention of Cruelty to Animals; lt. gov. La., 1991-95; now dir. Schwegmann's Giant Supermarkets. Mem. bd. Schwegmann Giant Super Markets; chmn. bd. Goodwill Industries; bd. dirs. Met. Area Com. New Orleans; sec. bd. dir.s Jr. Achievement; former mem. Jefferson Beautification Com. Office: PO Box 26099 New Orleans LA 70186*

SCHWEIG, MARGARET BERRIS, meeting and special events consultant; b. Detroit, Mar. 23, 1928; d. Jacob Meyer and Anne Lucille (Schiller) Berris; m. Eugene Schweig Jr., Nov. 24, 1951 (dec.); children: Eugene III, John A., Suzanne. Student, U. Mich., 1945-47. Founder, pres. St. Louis Scene, Inc., 1975-94. Mem. St. Louis Conv. and Visitors Commn., St. Louis Forum. Mem. Meeting Planners Internat., Am. Soc. Assn. Execs., Profl. Conv. Mgmt. Assn., Nat. Assn. Exposition Mgrs., Internat. Spl. Events Soc., Hotel Sales Mgmt. Assn. (bd. dirs. 1977-80), Regional Commerce and Growth Assn., The Network (pres. 1980-81).

SCHWEIKER-MARRA, KARYN ELIZABETH, educator; b. Englewood, N.H., Aug. 8, 1948; d. Robert E. and Kathleen E. (Hand) Pollard; m. William F. Schweiker, Nov. 19, 1977 (div. July 1994); children: Alyosha, Kyra, J.T., Davin, MaryBeth, Heather, Sabrina; m. William T. Marra, Aug. 6, 1994. BS cum laude, W.Va. U., 1971, MA, 1979, EdD, 1994. Instr. early childhood Alice's Wonderland, Morgantown, W.Va., 1971-72, Nat. Elem. Sch., Morgantown, W.Va., 1973-75, Daybrook-Wadestown, Morgantown, W.Va., 1975-78; tchr. various schs., Morgantown, W.Va., 1978-82; tchr. elem. sch. Oak Grove Sch., Morgantown, W.Va., 1982-83, Sabraton Sch., Morgantown, W.Va., 1983-90, 92-93; supr. tchr. interns Frostburg (Md.) State U., 1991-92; tchr. mid. sch. Sabraton Sch., 1993-94, Brookhaven Sch., Morgantown, 1993-94; computer lab. supervisor Cheat Lake Mid. Sch., 1994—; instr. ednl. found. California U. Pa., 1995—; vis. instr. W.Va. U., Morgantown, 1992; researcher in field. Author: Suggestions for Involving Parents in Primary Grade Activities, 1979, School Cultural Norms Relationship to Teacher Change, 1994; contbr. articles to profl. jours. W.Va. Staet Mini grantee, 1989-90, 90-91, W.Va. Humanities grantee, 1993-94. Mem. Nat. Coun. Tchrs. English, Nat. Reading Conf., Ea. Ednl. Rsch. Assn. Alliance Calif. U. and We. Pa. English Tchrs., Inmternat. Reading Assn., Monongalia Reading Coun., Phi Kappa Delta.

SCHWEITZER, LINDA TAYLOR, artist, nurse; b. Fairmont, W.Va., Apr. 1, 1943; d. Frederic Thompson and Louise Elizabeth (Taylor) S.; m. Robert William LoPresti, June 22, 1965 (div. Aug. 1984); children: Eric Robert, Shanna Louise. BA in Sociology, W.Va. U., 1965, MS in Rehabilitation Counseling, 1967; BSN, W.Va. Wesleyan, 1988. RN, W.Va. Social worker W.Va. Dept. Welfare, Kingwood, 1965-66; group leader LaLeche League

Internat., 1971-79; staff nurse St. Joseph's Hosp., Buckhannon, W.Va., 1988-92; freelance artist, 1991—; clin. RN W.Va. U. Hosps., Morgantown, 1992—. Group exhibits include Cultural Ctr., Charleston, W.Va., 1994-95, Crosscurrents, Stiffel Fine Arts Ctr., Wheeling, W.Va., 1994, Aqueous '94 juried show, W.Va. Watercolor Soc. at Parkersburg (W.Va.) Art Ctr., 1994, Westmoreland Art Nat., Youngwood, Pa., 1994 (Merit award), Women and Creativity Conf. W.Va. U. Creative Arts Ctr., Morgantown, 1994, Exhibit '60, Monongalia Arts Ctr., Morgantown, 1996 (Best of Show), Realism '96, Parkersburg Art Ctr., 1996 (Purchase award), Mid-Atlantic Regional Watercolor Exhibit, Johns Hopkins U., Balt., 1996 (Merit award). Mem. W.Va. Watercolor Soc. (chmn. membership 1989-92).

SCHWEITZER, MARSHA L., musician, consultant; b. Canton, Ohio, Aug. 26, 1949; d. Paul and Florence Schweitzer; m. Kenji Otani, Mar. 10, 1979 (dec. May 1986). BM, Oberlin Coll., 1971. Assoc. prin. bassoon Honolulu Symphony, 1971—, asst. pers. mgr., 1975-81; bassoon Spring Wind Quintet, Honolulu, 1974—; exec. dir. Chamber Music Hawaii, Honolulu, 1982-87; mgr. Music Projects Honolulu, 1985-94; tchr. Mid Pacific Inst., Honolulu, 1993-94; 2d bassoon Ohio Chamber Orch., Cleve., 1994—; mgr. Spring Wind Quintet, 1974—; vice chair, treas. Honolulu Symphony Orch. Com., 1987-94; v.p. Hawaii Assn. Music Socs., Hilo, 1988-94; founder Hawaii Symphony, Honolulu, 1994. Editor: Senza Sordino news letters, contbr. articles to profl. jours.; music arranger, 1977—. Dir. ex officio Honolulu Symphony Honolulu Symphony Soc., 1987-89; mem. exec. bd. Hawaii Alliance Art Edn., Honolulu, 1980; lobbyist Hawaii State Legis., Honolulu, 1975-76; mem. grants review panelist Hawaii State Found. Culture & Arts, Honolulu, 1982, 84, Internat. Conf. of Symphony and Opera Musicians, 1996—. Mem. ASCAP, Am. Soc. Music Copyists, Am. Fedn. Musicians, Internat. Double Reed Soc. Home: 905 Spencer St #404 Honolulu HI 96822

SCHWEITZER, NANCY N., retired science educator, writer; b. La Place, La., Dec. 2, 1937; d. Gustave Joseph and Georgie Marie (Talbot) Naquin; m. James P. Schweitzer (dec.), June 8, 1975; children: Merlin James, Ricky John. BS, Dominican Coll., 1963; MEd, La. State U., 1978. Sci. tchr. Orleans Parish, New Orleans, 1963-70, Jefferson Parish Pub. Sch. Sys., Harvey, La., 1970-75, E. Baton Rouge Parish, 1975-92; sci. tchr. Sch. Nursing So. U., Baton Rouge, 1991, 92; ret., 1992; coord. marine sci. E. Baton Rouge Sch. Sys., 1981-82, phys. sci., 1991-92; chair sci. dept. Baton Rouge Magnet H.S., 1986-88, Scottondville Magnet H.S., Baton Rouge, 1989-92. Contbr. articles to profl. jours. Named La. State Outstanding Biology Tchr. Nat. Assn. Biology Tchrs., 1974, Disting. Sci. Tchr. La. Acad. Sci., 1987. Mem. AAUW, Delta Kappa Gamma. Roman Catholic. Home: 4272 Lancaster Dr Niceville FL 32578

SCHWEITZER, PAMELA BIFANO, psychiatric and mental health nurse; b. Detroit, Apr. 18, 1958; d. Daniel Frank and Roberta Rosemary (Hudson) Bifano; m. Jeffrey William Schweitzer, June 10, 1989; children: Elizabeth Gabrielle, Katherine Eleanore. ADN, Henry Ford C.C., Dearborn, Mich., 1980; BSN, Madonna U., 1986; MS, U. Mich., 1991. RN, Mich.; cert. nurse practitioner, Mich.; cert. clin. specialist adult psychiat. and mental health nursing, ANCC. RN, charge nurse, preceptor Sinai Hosp. Detroit, 1980-83, Henry Ford Hosp., Detroit, 1983-86; mental health nurse, case mgr. Washtenaw County Cmty. Mental Health Ctr., Ann Arbor, Mich., 1986-87; rsch. nurse, clin. care coord. U. Mich. Psychiat. Hosps., Ann Arbor, 1987-91, clin. nurse specialist, 1991—; pvt. practice as cognitive and behavioral therapist, Ann Arbor, 1993—; panic disorder trainer NIMH and Soc. Fdn. & Rsch. Psychiat. Nursing, Midwestern region, 1993-95; state clusters convener Kellogg and Coalition Psychiat. Nursing Orgns., Mich., 1994. Editor: (with others) Nursing Diagnosis Handbook: A Guide to Planning Care, 2d edit., 1994. Parent rep. to bd. dirs. U. Mich. Child Care Ctr., Ann Arbor, 1993—. Mem. ANA, Anxiety Disorders Assn. Am. (profl. mem.), Mich. Nurses Assn., Soc. Edn. & Rsch. Psychiat. Nursing (midwestern region), Sigma Theta Tau (Rho chpt.). Home: 2130 Steeplechase Dr Ann Arbor MI 48103-6033 Office: U Mich Anxiety Disorders Program 1500 E Medical Center Dr Ann Arbor MI 48109-0999

SCHWEIZER, VALÉRIE, otolaryngologist, phoniatrician; b. La Chaux-de-Fonds, Switzerland, Feb. 10, 1961; d. Eric René Schweizer and Madeleine Ruth Mosimann. BS, Gymnase of Lausanne, Switzerland, 1979; diploma in phoniatrics, U. Besançon, France, 1995. Resident in gen. surgery Ctr. Hospitalier Universitaire Vaudois, Lausanne, 1986, Cantonal Hosp. of Monthey, Monthey, Switzerland, 1987-88; resident in pediatric surgery Ctr. Hospitalier Universitaire Vaudois, Lausanne, 1986-87, resident in otolaryngology, head and neck surgery, 1988; resident in otolaryngology, head and neck surgery Cantonal Hosp. of Fribourg, Switzerland, 1990-91; resident in maxillo-facial surgery Ctr. Hospitalier Universitaire Vaudois, Lausanne, 1988-89, resident in oncol. otolaryngology, 1989-90, fellow, 1991-93; fellow Cantonal Hosp. of Lucern, Switzerland, 1993-94; vis. doctor in neurolaryngology, HNO-Universität Klinik, Innsbruck, Austria, 1994, in laryngology, Univ. Hosp. of Iowa City, Iowa, 1995; rsch. physician in laryngology U. Tenn. Med. Ctr., Memphis, 1995—; lectr. in field. Contbr. articles to profl. publs. Grantee U. Lausanne, 1994, Assn. Vaud-Genève, Santé Publique & Hôpitaux Universitaires, 1995. Mem. Soc. Française de Phoniatrie, Internat. Assn. Logopedics and Phoniatrics. Office: Coll Medicine Dept Otolaryngology 956 Court Ave Ste A 220 Memphis TN 38163

SCHWEMLER, DEBORAH A., psychotherapist, educator; b. Fresno, Calif., Nov. 18, 1958; d. Edward R. and Ardith G. (Henderson) S. BS in Bus., Calif. State U., Fresno, 1980, MS, 1991; postgrad., Calif. Sch. of Profl. Psychology, Fresno, 1992—. Legal advocate Calif. Assn. of Physically Handicapped, Fresno, 1982-83; instrnl. computing cons. Calif. State U., Fresno, 1985-95; therapist Cedar Vista Psychiatric Hosp., Fresno, 1989-94, Charter Behavioral Health Systems of Cen. Calif., Visalia, 1994-95, Tulare County Mental Health, Visalia, 1995—; adj. prof. Nat. U., Fresno, 1995—; therapist Family Comms. Ctr., Fresno, 1995—. Mem. ACA, APA, Calif. Assn. of Marriage and Family Therapists. Republican. Lutheran. Home: 1507 E Andrews Fresno CA 93704 Office: Family Comms Ctr 1039 U St Fresno CA 93721

SCHWIER, PRISCILLA LAMB GUYTON, television broadcasting company executive; b. Toledo, Ohio, May 8, 1939; d. Edward Oliver and Prudence (Hutchinson) L.; m. Robert T. Guyton, June 21, 1963 (dec. Sept. 1976); children—Melissa, Margaret, Robert; m. Frederick W. Schwier, May 11, 1984. B.A., Smith Coll., 1961; M.A., U. Toledo, 1972. Pres. Gt. Lakes Communications, Inc., 1982—; vice chmn. Seilon, Inc., Toledo, 1981-83, also dir. Contbr. articles to profl. jours. Trustee Wilberforce U., Ohio, 1983—, Planned Parenthood, Toledo, 1979-83, Maumee Valley Country Day Sch., Toledo; bd. dirs. N.W. Ohio Hospice, 1991—. Episcopal Ch., Maumee, Ohio, 1983—; bd. trustees Toledo Hosp., Maumee Country Day Sch., 1986-92; pres. Edward Lamb Found., 1987—. Democrat. Episcopalian. Home: 345 E Front St Perrysburg OH 43551-2131 Office: 129 W Wayne St Ste 100 Maumee OH 43537-2150

SCHWINGE, JOAN HILLS, retired preschool education educator; b. Portland, Oreg., Mar. 11, 1929; d. Gentry M. and Freda (Miller) Hills; m. Norman W. Schwinge; children: Robert, Craig, Mark, Scott. BA, Lewis & Clark Coll., 1951, postgrad., 1952-60. Cert. specialist in early childhood edn. Tchr. Portland (Oreg.) Pub. Schs., 1951-52; tchr. Cmty. United Meth. Ch. Presch., Pacific Palisades, Calif., 1957-65, dir., 1966-79; hotel owner, mgr. Friday Harbor, Wash., 1979-90; substitute tchr. Friday Harbor Pub. Schs., 1981-85; founding bd. dirs.. Presbyb. Presch., Friday Harbor, 1990—. Author: (children's book) Sunny Sunflower, 1990. Bd. dirs. San Juan Island Sch. Dist., Friday Harbor, 1986-94; active Animal Protection Soc., Friday Harbor, 1982—, Wash. Lit., Friday Harbor, 1984-90. Mem. AAUW (v.p. 1984-86, treas. 1986-87, grantee 1984). Republican. Home: 4865 Victoria Dr Friday Harbor WA 98250

SCHWINN-JORDAN, BARBARA (BARBARA SCHWINN), painter; b. Glen Ridge, N.J.; d. Carl Wilhelm Ludwig and Helen Louise (Jordan) Schwinn; m. Frank Bertram Jordan, Jr.; children: Janine Jordan, Frank Bertram III. Grad. N.Y. Sch. Fine and Applied Art (Parsons), N.Y. and Paris; student Grand Cen. Art Sch., Art Students League, Grand Chaumiere, Academie Julien-Paris, Columbia U., NAD. Illustrator mags. including Vogue, 1930's, Ladies Home Jour., Saturday Evening Post, Colliers, Good Housekeeping, Cosmopolitan, McCall's, American, Town and Country, 1940's-60's. Women's Jour., Eng., Hors Zu, Fed. Republic Germany, Marie Claire, France, other fgn. publs., 1950's-60's. Portrait painter, including Queen Sirikit, Princess Margaret, Princess Grace; freelance painter, 1970—; one-man shows include Soc. of Illustrators, 1940, 50, Barry Stephens Gallery, 1950, Bodley Gallery, N.Y.C., 1971, 80, C.C., West Mifflin, Pa., 1973, Duquesne U., 1973, Mus. Am. Illustration, N.Y.C., 1991, Illustration House, N.Y.C., 1991, Giraffics Gallery, East Hampton, N.Y., 1991-95 (also rep.); exhibited in group shows including NAD, 1955, Royal Acad., London, Guild Hall, N.Y., 1981, Summit N.J. Art Ctr., 1981, Meredith Long Gallery, Houston, 1983, Mus. Soc. Illustrators, N.Y., 1985, The Marcus Gallery, Sante Fe, 1985, 86, The Gerald Peters Gallery, Santa Fe, 1985, 86, Brandywine Mus., Pa., 1986, New Britain (Conn.) Mus. Am. Art, 1986, Armory Show, N.Y.C., 1992-94, The Women's Ctr., Chapel Hill, N.C., 1993-94, Greenville County Mus. Art, S.C., 1995, The Soc. of the Four Arts, Palm Beach, Fla., 1995, The Hyde Collection, Glens Falls, N.Y., 1995, Ga. Mus. Art, 1995, Heckscher Mus., L.I., N.Y., 1995; works represented Holbrook Collection, Ga. Mus. Art, Eureka Coll., Ill., New Britain Mus. Am. Art, Mus. of Soc. of Illustrators, N.Y.C., Brandywine Mus., Pa., Sanford Low Meml. Collection, Del. Art Mus., Wilmington, Mus. Am. Illustration, N.Y.C., Glenbow Mus., Calgary, Alberta, Can.; represented in traveling show Del. Art Mus. 1994-95; various pvt. and gallery collections; work featured in America's Great Women Illustrators 1850-1950, 1985; lectr., instr. illustration Parsons Sch., 1952-54; founder adv. coun. Art Instrn. Sch., 1956-70. Chmn. art com. UNICEF greeting cards, 1950-61 mem. com. Spence Chapin Sch., Philharm. Soc., 1950's-60's. Winner prizes Art Dirs. Club, 1950, Guild Hall, 1969. Assoc. mem. Guggenheim Mus. Mem. Cosmopolitan Club N.Y. Author: Technique of Barbara Schwinn, 1956; World of Fashion Art, 1968. Home and Studio: 579 Fearrington Post Pittsboro NC 27312

SCILLIA, DIANE GRAYBOWSKI, art historian, researcher; b. Queens, N.Y., Aug. 20, 1945; d. Joseph Francis and Grace Virginia (McNeil) G.; m. Charles Edward Scillia, June 9, 1968 (div. Apr., 1993); 1 child, Matthew Thomas. BA, SUNY, Stony Brook, 1967; PhD, Case Western Reserve U., 1975. Rsch. asst. Cleve. Mus. of Art, 1967-72; vis. lectr. Case Western Reserve U., Cleve, 1971-72, Franklin and Marshall Coll., Lancaster, Pa., 1974; adj. curator, asst. to dir. Chrysler Mus. of Art, Norfolk, Va., 1979-80; adj. asst. prof. Va. Wesleyan Coll., Norfolk, VA., 1980-84, Old Dominion U., Norfolk, 1982-84; asst. prof. art history Kent (Ohio) State U., 1985-91, assoc. prof. art history, 1992—; juror travel awards NEH, Washington, 1991, juror grants, 1992. Contbr. articles to profl. jours. and to the Encyclopedia Dutch Art. Mem. Coll. Art Assn., Scholars of Early Modern Europe, Historians of Netherlandish Art (sec.-treas. 1989-91), Mid-West Art Hist. Soc. (bd. dirs. 1992-95). Home: 2941 Somerton Rd Cleveland Heights OH 44118-2044 Office: Kent State U Sch of Art Kent OH 44242-0001

SCIRGHI, ROSE MARIE, sister, artist; b. Bklyn., Nov. 17, 1922; d. Joseph and Livia (Bargoni) S. Diploma, Internat. Corr. Sch., Scranton, Pa., 1987. Cert. tchr. religion; joined Sisters for Christian Cmty., 1970. Sec. to v.p. fin. Ins. Svcs. Office, Inc., 1975-83; sister Parish Visitors of Mary Immaculate, 1946-68, Sisters for Christian Cmty., 1970—. Artist oil paintings, mixed media, black and white. Mem. Nat. Mus. Women in Arts (assoc.), Artist League Bklyn., Humane Soc. U.S. Roman Catholic.

SCLAR, JENNIFER, lawyer; b. Boston, Sept. 26, 1969. BA magna cum laude, Barnard Coll., 1991; JD, Columbia U., 1995. Ptnr. Anderson, Kill, Olick, Oshinsky, P.C., N.Y.C., 1995—. Stone scholar, Columbia U. Office: Anderson Kill Olick Oshinsky PC 1251 Avenue of the Americas New York NY 10020-1182*

SCOBEL, JENNY, artist; b. Orrville, Ohio, Feb. 1, 1955; d. Donald Nathaniel and Carol (Schmid) S. Student, Cleve. Inst. Art, 1973-75; BFA, Colo. State U., 1979; postgrad., Pratt Inst., 1982-84. One-woman shows Bologna (Italy) Ctr., 1983, Salena Gallery, L.I. U., Bklyn., 1991, One Square Mile Gallery, Seacliff, N.Y., 1992, Cynthia McCallister Gallery, N.Y.C., 1994; exhibited in group shows Zenith Gallery, Washington, 1984, Rubelle and Norman Schafler Gallery, Bklyn., 1989, Pratt Manhattan Gallery, N.Y.C., 1989, Cork Gallery and The Clocktower, N.Y.C., 1990, Mus. Modern Art, N.Y.C., 1991, Trenkman Gallery, N.Y.C., 1991, The Atrium Gallery, Schenectady, 1991, White Columns, N.Y.C., 1992, Bard Coll., Annandale-on-Hudson, N.Y., 1992, Muranushi Lederman, N.Y.C., 1992, Cynthia McCallister Gallery, 1993, 450 Gallery, N.Y.C., 1993, Chgo. Art Fair, Muranushi Lederman, 1993, Gallery 30, N.Y.C., 1993, Orgn. Ind. Artists, N.Y.C., 1993, The Drawing Ctr., N.Y.C., 1993, Muranushi/Lederman, L.A., 1993, Front Street Gallery, Housatonic, Mass., 1994, Mt. San Antonio Coll., Walnut, La., 1994, Geoffrey Young Gallery, Gt. Barrington, Mass., 1994, Rotunda Gallery, Bklyn., 1994, Miami (Fla.)-Dade C.C., 1995, Thread Waxing Space, N.Y.C., 1995, K&E Gallery, N.Y.C., 1995, also others. Active Women's Action Coalition, N.Y.C., 1991-92. Artist's grantee Artists Space, N.Y.C., 1991, grantee E.D. Found., 1995. Democrat. Home and Studio: 135 Plymouth St Brooklyn NY 11201

SCOBEY, JOAN MOISSEIFF, writer, editor; b. N.Y.C.; d. Siegfried and Frieda (Loewe) Moisseiff; children: David, Richard. BA, Smith Coll. Author: Stained Glass, 1979, Short Rations, 1980, I'm A Stranger Here Myself, 1984, Fannie Farmer Junior Cookbook, 1993, numerous others; editor: Cooking with Michael Field, 1978; contbr. numerous articles to mags. Mem. PEN, Authors Guild, Am. Soc. Authors and Journalists, Soc. Am. Travel Writers.

SCOBIE, ILKA TERI, poet, educator; b. Bklyn., Aug. 15, 1950; d. Philip and Mildred (Machenberg) Verowitz; (div. June 1979); 1 child, Risa Scobie; m. Luigi Cazzaniga. Student, Sch. of Visual Arts, N.Y.C., 1968; hon. degree in ESL Methodology, New Sch. for Social Rsch., N.Y.C., 1993. Poet in residence Poets in Pub. Svc., N.Y.C., 1979-95; dep. editor Cover mag., N.Y.C., 1989—; instr. AAA program Parsons Sch. Design, N.Y.C., 1989—; poet in residence Tchrs. and Writers Collaborative, N.Y.C., 1995—. Author: (poetry) There for the Taking, 1979, Any Island, 1993, Exquisite Corpse, 1991. Mem. Women's Action Coalition, N.Y.C., 1990. Mem. Tchrs. and Writers Collaborative, Poets and Writers. Democrat. Jewish. Home: 39 Great Jones St New York NY 10012-1136

SCOGNO, STACIE JOY, financial services company executive; b. Camden, N.J., Dec. 5, 1957; d. Albert Joseph Scogno and Josephine Geovanni Fiorello. AAS, Bay State Coll., Boston, 1978; BS in mgmt., Boston Coll., 1986; cert. of mgmt. and spl. scis., Harvard Ext. Sch., 1994. Software sys. cons., owner North Shore Svcs., Boston, 1984-88; tech. cons. Lotus Devel. Corp., Boston, 1988-90; mgr. MIS Blackwell Sci. Publs., Boston, 1990-93; product design analyst Thomson Fin. Corp., Boston, 1993-95; sr. cons. The Hunters Group, Boston, 1995-96; N.E. regional mgr. nat. fin. systems Coopers & Lybrand, Boston, 1996—; notary pub. Commonwealth of Mass., 1980—. Trustee Action Dance Theater, treas., 1980-91. Office: 144 Middlesex Trnpke Burlington MA 02129

SCOLLARD, DIANE LOUISE, retired elementary school educator; b. Seattle, Mar. 12, 1945; d. James Martin and Viola Gladys (Williams) S. BA in Edn., Wash. State U., 1967; 5th yr. cert. in edn., U. Wash., 1970; cert. edn., Oakland U., 1977. Tchr. Battle Ground (Wash.) Sch. Dist., 1967-70, Lapeer (Mich.) Cmty. Schs., 1970-95; ret. Mem. AAUW, NEA, NAFE, Nat. Assn. Career Women, Am. Bus. Women's Assn., Mich. Edn. Assn., Lapeer Edn. Assn. (bldg. rep. 1985, 89), Beta Sigma Phi. Democrat. Episcopalian.

SCOTT, ADRIENNE, social worker, psychotherapist; b. N.Y.C.; d. William and Anne Scott; m. Ross F. Grumet, Nov. 10, 1957 (div. Aug. 1969). BA, Finch Coll., 1957; postgrad., NYU, 1958-62, MA in English, 1958; MSW, Adelphi U., 1988. Mem. English faculty Fordham U., N.Y.C., 1966-68; editor Blueboy Mag., Miami, Fla., 1974, "M" Mag., N.Y.C., 1976; freelance writer N.Y.C., 1958—; mem. English faculty NYU, 1958-65; pres. Googolplex Video, N.Y.C., 1981-86; clin. social worker Mt. Sinai Hosp., N.Y.C., 1988-93, Stuyvesant Polyclinic, N.Y.C., 1993—; presenter Nat. Methadone Conf., 1992. Author: Film as Film, 1970; contbg. editor Menstyle Mag., 1995; contbr. articles to numerous mags., including Vogue, Interview, N.Y. mag.; pioneer in fashion video; videographer documentaries; performance artist in Robert Wilson's King of Spain, 1973. Mem. exec. com. Adopt-An-AIDS Rschr. Program Rockefeller U.; nat. co-chairperson Gay Rights Nat. Lobby, 1976. Mem. NASW (cert.), AAUW, Assn. for Psychoanalytic Self Psychology. Home: 165 E 66th St New York NY 10021-6132 Office: 7 Patchin Pl New York NY 10011-8341

SCOTT, ALICE H., librarian; b. Jefferson, Ga.; d. Frank D. and Annie D. (Colbert) Holly; m. Alphonso Scott, Mar. 1, 1959; children—Christopher, Alison. A.B., Spelman Coll., Atlanta, 1957; M.L.S., Atlanta U., 1958; Ph.D., U. Chgo., 1983. Librarian Bklyn. Pub. Library, 1958-59; br. librarian Chgo. Pub. Library, 1959-72, dir. Woodson Regional Library, 1974-77, dir. community relations, 1977-82, dep. commr., 1982-87, asst. commr., 1987—. Doctoral fellow, 1973. Mem. ALA (councilor 1982-85), Ill. Library Assn., Chgo. Spelman Club, DuSable Mus., Chgo. Urban League. Democrat. Baptist. Office: Chgo Pub Library 400 S State St Chicago IL 60605-1203

SCOTT, AMY ANNETTE HOLLOWAY, nursing educator; b. St. Albans, W.Va., Apr. 10, 1916; d. Oliver and Mary (Lee) Holloway; m. William M. Jefferson, June 22, 1932, (div. Oct. 1933); 1 child, William M. Jefferson, m. Vann Hyland Scott, Mar. 15, 1952, (dec. Dec. 1972). BS in Nursing Edn., Cath. U., Washington, 1948; cert. in psychiat. nursing, U. Paris, Paris, 1959. Indsl. nurse Curtiss Wright Air Plane Co., Lambert Field, St. Louis, 1941-44; faculty St. Thomas U., Manila, Philippines Island, 1948-50; pub. health nurse St. Louis Health Dept., 1951-56; capt. USAF Nursing Corps, Paris, 1956-60; resigned as maj. USAF (Nurse Corps), 1960, 1960; faculty St. Louis State Hosp., 1960-67; dept. head St. Vincents Hosp., St. Louis, 1967-68; faculty RN, creator psychiat. program Sch. of Nursing Jewish Hosp., 1968-72; adminstrv. nurse St. Louis State Hosp., 1972-84; initiated first psychiatric program sch. nursing, Jewish Hosp. Author: (short story) Two Letters, 1962, (novel) Storms, 1987, Life's Journey, 1993. Past bd. dirs. county bd. Mo. U., 1984-88; hon. citizen Colonial Williamsburg, Va.; mem. Rep. Presdl. Task Force; mem. Women in the Arts '94. Recipient Key to Colonial Williamsburg, Va., Medal of Merit, Rep. Presdl. Task Force, 1992; named to Rep. Presdl. Task Force Honor Roll, 1993, Nat. Women's Hall of Fame, 1995, Women's Hall of Fame, 1996. Mem. AAUW, NAFE, Internat. Fedn. Univ. Women, Internat. Soc. Quality Assurance in Health Care, N.Y. Acad. Scis., Am. Biog. Inst. (life, governing bd.), Women in the Arts, Cambridge Centre Engring., Internat. Platform Assn. Roman Catholic.

SCOTT, ANDREA LYNNÉ, entrepreneur; b. Rochester, N.Y., Oct. 21, 1962; d. Eleanore Jeanne (Vinci) S. BA, U. Rochester, 1985; Student, NYU, 1985-87. Sr. acct. rep. Siemens Info. Systems, N.Y.C., 1986-89; prin., pres. The Hudson Agy., Speakers Bur., Washington, 1991—. Home: 23 Native Dancer Ct North Potomac MD 20878 Office: The Hudson Agency 4401A Connecticut Ave NW Washington DC 20008-2302

SCOTT, ANNE BYRD FIROR, history educator; b. Montezuma, Ga., Apr. 24, 1921; d. John William and Mary Valentine (Moss) Firor; m. Andrew Mackay Scott, June 2, 1947; children: Rebecca, David MacKay, Donald MacKay. AB, U. Ga., 1941; MA, Northwestern U., 1944; PhD, Radcliffe Coll., 1958; LHD (hon.), Lindenwood Coll., 1968, Queens Coll., 1985, Northwestern U., 1989, Radcliffe Coll., 1990, U. of the South, 1990, Cornell Coll., 1991. Congressional rep., editor LWV of U.S., 1944-53; lectr. history Haverford Coll., 1957-58, U. N.C., Chapel Hill, 1959-60; asst. prof. history Duke U., Durham, N.C., 1961-67; assoc. prof. Duke U., 1968-70, prof., 1971-80, W.K. Boyd prof., 1980-91, W.K. Boyd prof. emerita, 1992—, chmn. dept., 1981-85; Gastprofessor Universität, Bonn, Germany, 1992-93; vis. prof. Johns Hopkins U., 1972-73, Stanford U., 1974, Harvard U., 1984, Cornell U., 1993, Williams Coll., 1994; Times-Mirror scholar Huntington Libr., 1995; vice chmn. Nat. Humanities Ctr., 1991—; mem. adv. com. Schlesinger Libr.; Fulbright lectr., 1984, 92-93. Author: The Southern Lady, 1970, 25th anniversary edit., 1995, (with Andrew MacKay Scott) One Half the People, 1974, Making the Invisible Woman Visible, 1984, Natural Allies, 1991; editor: Jane Addams, Democracy and Social Ethics, 1964, The American woman, 1970, Women in American Life, 1970, Women and Men in American Life, 1976, Unheard Voices, 1993; mem. editl. bd. Revs. in Am. History, 1976-81, Am. Quar., 1974-78, Jour. So. History, 1978-84; contbr. articles to profl. jours. Chmn. Gov.'s Commn. on Status of Women, 1963-64; mem. Citizens Adv. Council on Status of Women U.S., 1964-68. AAUW fellow, 1956-57; grantee NEH, 1967-68, 76-77, Nat. Humanities Ctr., 1980-81; grad. medal Radcliffe Coll., 1986, Duke U. medal, 1991, John Caldwell medal N.C. Humanities Coun., 1994; fellow Ctrl. Advanced Study in Behavioral Sci., 1986-87, Fulbright scholar, 1984, 92-93. Mem. Am. Antiquarian Soc., Orgn. Am. Historians (exec. bd. 1973-76, pres. 1983), So. Hist. Assn. (exec. bd. 1976-79, pres. 1989), Soc. Am. Historians, Phi Beta Kappa. Democrat. Office: Duke U Dept History Durham NC 27708

SCOTT, CAROL LEE, child care educator; b. Monte Vista, Colo., Jan. 10, 1944; d. Robert A. and Thelma G. (Allen) Jay; m. Bates E. Shaw, June 4, 1966 (dec. Feb. 1976); children: Crystal A., Sharon L.; m. James W. Scott, July 23, 1977. BA in Home Econs., Friends U., 1965; MS, Okla. State U., 1973. Cert. in family and consumer scis., child and parenting specialist; lic. profl. counselor. Receptionist Cen. Assembly of God Ch., Wichita, Kans., summer 1965; office worker Henry's Inc., Wichita, 1965-66; tchr. home econs. Wichita High Sch. South, 1966, Cir. High Sch., Towanda, Kans., 1966-68, Fairfax (Okla.) High Sch., 1968-74; tchr. vocat. home econs. Derby (Kans.) High Sch., 1974-75; child devel. specialist Bi-State Mental Health Found., Ponca City, Okla., 1975-87; instr. child care Pioneer Tech. Ctr., Ponca City, 1987—, dir., 1987-89, 93—; cons. Phil Fitzgerald Assocs. Archs., Ponca City, 1980, Head Start Okla., 1981-86; trainer, paraprofl. Child Care Careers, 1980—; validator Nat. Assn. Edn. Young Children 1992—. Contbg. author Child Abuse Prevention Mini Curriculum. Mem. sch. bd. Ponca City Schs., 1982-85, title IV-A parent com., 1985-89; area chmn. Heart Fund, 1985; chmn. edn. com. Dist. XVII Child Abuse Prevention Task Force, Okla., 1985—, treas., 1989—; mem. cultural affairs com. Ponca City Adv. Bd., 1986-89; co-chair Week of the Young Child Com. for Kay County, 1991—. Mem. NEA, Am. Vocat. Assn., Am. Assn. Family and Consumer Scis., Okla. Vocat. Assn., Okla. Assn. Vocat. Home Econs. Tchrs., Okla. Edn. Assn., Okla. Assn. for Edn. Young Children, Okla. Early Childhood Assn., So. Early Childhood Assn. (chmn. 1992-93, past chmn. 1993-94, exec. coun. at-large 1994-96), Nat. Assn. Vocat. Home Econs. Tchrs., Nat. Assn. for Edn. Young Children (validator for early childhood programs seeking accreditation by divsn. Nat. Acad. Early Childhood Programs 1992—), Friends of Day Care. Republican. Methodist. Home: 414 Virginia Ave Ponca City OK 74601-3436

SCOTT, CATHERINE DOROTHY, librarian, information consultant; b. Washington, June 21, 1927; d. Leroy Stearns Scott and Agnes Frances (Meade) Scott Schellenberg. AB in English, Cath. U. Am., 1950, MS in Library Sci., 1955. Asst. Librarian Export-Import Bank U.S.A., Washington, 1951-55; asst. librarian Nat. Assn. Home Builders, 1955-62, reference librarian, 1956-62; founder, chief tech. librarian, Bellcomm, Inc., subs. AT&T, Washington, 1962-72; chief librarian Nat. Air and Space Mus., Smithsonian Instn., Washington, 1972-82, chief librarian Mus. Reference Ctr., 1982-88, sr. reference librarian, 1989-95; info. cons., 1995—; bd. visitors Cath. U. Am. Library Sci. Sch. and Libraries, 1984-93; apptd. by Pres., mem. Nat. Commn. Libraries and Info. Sci., 1971-76. Editor International Handbook of Aerospace Awards and Trophies, 1980, 81; guest editor Aeronautics and Space Flight Collections, 1985, in Spl. Collections, 1984. Vice-chmn. D.C. Rep. Com., 1960-68; mem. platform com. Rep. Nat. Com., 1964, sec., 1968; del. Rep. Nat. Conv., San Francisco, 1964, Miami, Fla., 1968. Recipient Sec.'s Disting. Service award Smithsonian Instn., 1976, Alumni Achievement award Cath. U. Am., 1977, Disting. Fed. Svc. Nat. Commn. Libr. and Info. Sci. medal, 1985. Mem. Spl. Librs. Assn. (pres. Washington chpt. 1973-74, cons. 1976-89, chmn. cons. com. 1994—, chmn. aerospace div. 1980-81, aerospace divsn. 30th anniversary com. 1995, Disting. Svc. award 1982, nat. dir. 1986-89, bd. dirs. 1986-89, 91-94, Washington chpt. awards com. 1990-91, assn. pres.-elect 1991-92, pres. 1992-93, immediate past pres. 1993-94, chair assn. awards and honors 1994-95), Am. Soc. Assn. Execs. (internat. roundtable), Am. Soc. Info. Scis. (com. chmn.), Internat. Fedn. Library Assns. (del. 1976, 83, 85, 88, 89), Friends of Cath. U. Libraries (founder, pres. 1984-88, exec. coun. 1984—), Nat. Fedn. Rep. Women, Rep. Women's Fed. Forum, League Rep. Women D.C. (dir. mem. 1995—, mem. nominating com. 1996—), Capital Yacht Club (Washington). Roman Catholic.

SCOTT, CATHERINE LEDFORD, therapist; b. Greenville, S.C., Aug. 28, 1953; d. Field Holtzclaw and Mary Elizabeth (Traynaham) Ledford; m. Randolph L. Scott, July 29, 1972; 1 child, John Kevin Scott. BA in Econs.,

Converse Coll., 1986; M in Counseling, Clemson U., 1991. Lic. profl. counselor, S.C. Social worker Chestnut Hills, Travelers Rest, S.C., 1990-92; therapist Foothills Counseling Ctr., Easley, S.C., 1991-94; exec. dir., therapist Mountain Meadows Group Home, Pickens, S.C., 1993—; cons. Abbeville (S.C.) Sch. Dist., 1992-93, Laurens (S.C.) Sch. Dist., 1992-93, McCormick (S.C.) Sch. Dist., 1992-93. Bd. dirs. Pickens County Coun. for Prevention of Child Abuse, 1990-91, Greenville Rape Crisis Coun., 1990-93, Dept. Mental Health, 1991—. Mem. Easley Bus. & Profl Womens Club (bd. dirs. 1993—, Career Woman of Yr. 1994), Easley C. of C. (amb. 1993—). Presbyterian. Home: 647 Old Bethlehem Sch Rd Pickens SC 29671

SCOTT, CLAIRE NELLE, psychotherapist; b. Tampa, Fla., May 13, 1946; d. Clarence Sylvester and Nelle Juanita (Palmer) S.; m. Vester Cleveland Lokey III, Dec. 18, 1975 (dec. July 1990). BA, U. N.C. Charlotte, 1982, MHDL, 1986; postgrad., Fla. State U., 1991-95. Nat. certified counselor; registered practicing counselor, N.C., 1988; lic. profl. counselor, Ga., 1995. Counselor Queens Coll., Charlotte, N.C., 1986-88; pvt. practice clinician, psychotherapist Charlotte, 1986-91; clinician, psychotherapist Family Counseling Svc., Athens, Ga., 1995—; psychology intern Counseling and Testing Ctr. U. Ga., Athens, 1994-95. Mem. ACA, APA. Episcopalian. Office: Family Counseling Svc 468 N Milledge Ave Ste 202 Athens GA 30601

SCOTT, DEBORAH EMONT, curator; b. Passaic, N.J.; d. Rhoda (Baumgarten) Emont; m. George Andrew Scott, June 4, 1983; children: Meredith Suzanne, Diana Faith. BA, Rutgers U., 1973; MA, Oberlin Coll., 1979. Asst. curator Allen Meml. Art Mus., Oberlin, Ohio, 1977-79; curator collections Memphis Brooks Mus. Art, 1979-83; curator The Nelson-Atkins Mus. Art, Kansas City, 1983—; project dir. Henry Moore Sculpture Garden, 1986—. Author: (catalogue) Alan Shields, 1983, (essay) Jonathan Borofsky, 1988, (essay) Judith Shea, 1989, (interview) John Ahearn, 1990, (essay) Gerhard Richter, 1990, (essay) Kathy Muehlemann, 1991, (essay) Nate Fors, 1991, (essay) Julian Schnabel, 1991, (essay) Louise Bourgeois, 1994, (essay) Joel Shapiro, 1995, (essay) Lewis deSoto, 1996. Office: Nelson-Atkins Mus Art 4525 Oak St Kansas City MO 64111-1818

SCOTT, ELIZABETH, social service administrator; b. Aberdeen, Md., Sept. 28, 1954; d. Thomas and Mary Alberta (Adams) S.; 1 child, Cha Rae L'Nise. Student, Md. Inst. Coll. Art, Balt., 1972-75, U. Balt., 1977-79. Employment counselor City of Balt., 1976-78; supr. U.S. Postal Svc., Balt., 1978-83; work study counselor Westside Skill Ctr., Balt., 1984-85; gen. mgr. 32d St. Pla., Balt., 1985-87; office mgr. Md. Citizen Action Coalition, Balt., 1988-89; exec. dir. Coalition of Peninsula Orgns., Balt., 1989-93, Heart, Body and Soul, Inc., Balt., 1993; legis. coord. Planned Parenthood of Md., Balt., 1993-94; exec. dir. Balt. Housing Roundtable, 1994—; faculty assoc. Johns Hopkins U., Balt., 1993—, cons. Sch. Pub. Health, 1991—; mem. exec. com. Inner City Cmty. Devel. Corp., 1990-92. Bd. dirs. Light St. Housing Corp., Balt., Balt. Cable Access Corp., Md. Citizen Action Coalition, Md. Low Income Housing Info. Svc., 1989-91, Jobs with Peace, 1989-91, Women's Housing Coalition; bd. dirs. South Balt. Youth Ctr., pres., 1992-93; mem. gubernatorial transition subcom. on neighborhood revitalization and cmty. devel. Md. Forward, 1994; media rep. Save Our Cities March on Washington, 1991-92; mem. jazz com. Md. Mus. African Art, Columbia, 1994—; mem. Walters Art Gallery, Washington; mem. Gov.'s Task Force on Home Ownership; adv. coun. Empower Balt. Mgmt. Corp. Adv. Coun., 1996—; mem. women's caucus U.S. Network for Habitat II, 1995—; rep. UN preparatory com. Habitat II, N.Y.C., 1996; rep. UN mega conf. on human settlements Habitat II, Istanbul, Turkey, 1996. Recipient Contbn. award Balt. Commonwealth, 1992, Balt. City Pub. Schs., 1990, Community Svc. award State of md., 1990, 91, 92, Svc. award United Way of Cen. Md., 1991, Svc. award U.S. Postal Svc., 1983. Mem. Smithsonian Instns., Md. Assn. Housing Redevel. (bd. dirs. 1995—). Home: 3609 Kimble Rd Baltimore MD 21218-2027

SCOTT, ELIZABETH JANE, chemical engineer; b. Culpeper, Va., July 12, 1970; d. James Herbert Jr. and Roberta Jane (Lucas) S. BSChemE, Va. Poly. Inst. and State U., 1992; MBA, U. Houston, 1995. Process engr. Chevron Chem., Baytown, Tex., 1992-96; quality improvement advisor, 1995—, product devel. engr., 1996—. Tchr. Jr. Achievement, Tex., 1994-95; counselor, panel dir. Hugh O'Brien Youth Found., Tex., 1995. Mem. Cedar Bayou Employees Club (founder, pres. 1992-95, treas. 1995-96), Toastmasters (treas. 1995-96). Home: 4400 Memorial Dr Apt 1214 Houston TX 77007 Office: Chevron Chem Co 9500 I-10 East Baytown TX 77521

SCOTT, ELOISE HALE, state legislator; b. Benton County, Miss., Jan. 24, 1932; m. Lex B. Scott; children: Kenny, Kimble. BS, Miss. U. for Women; MA, U. Miss. Mem. Miss. Ho. of Reps.; vice chmn. edn. com., mem. appropriations, banks and banking, and ethics coms. Active Lee County Ext. Svc. Mem. LWV, Dem. Women. Methodist. Democrat. Home: 1218 W Main St 237RD53 Tupelo MS 38801-9439 Office: Miss State House State Capitol Jackson MS 39201

SCOTT, GINI GRAHAM, writer, speaker, consultant. PhD in Sociology, U. Calif., Berkeley, 1976, postdoctoral studies in Anthropology, 1979-82; JD, U. San Francisco, 1990. Founder, dir. Creative Comm. and Rsch., Oakland, Calif., Changemakers, Oakland, 1968—. Author: Cult and Countercult, 1980, The Magicians, 1983, rev. edit. 1986, Erotic Power, 1985, French and German edits., Strike it Rich in Personal Selling, 1985, Effective Selling and Sales Management, 1987, Debt Collection, 1987, It's Your Money, 1987, Mind Power: Picture Your Way to Success, 1987, Audio Version, 1989, (Russian edit.), The Creative Traveler, 1989, Shaman Warrior, 1989, Shamanism for Everyone, 1989, Get Rich Through Multi-Level Selling, 1989, Italian edits., Resolving Conflict, 1990, (Russian edit.), The Open Door--Traveling in the USSR, 1990, Building a Winning Sales Team, 1991, (Italian, Spanish, Malaysian edits.), Shamanism and Personal Mastery, 1991, Success in Multi-Level Marketing, 1991, Collect Your Court Judgment, 1993, The Empowered Mind, 1993 (Bk. of the Month Club Selection 1994), Secrets of the Shaman, 1993, Collection Techniques for Small Business, 1994, The Truth About Lying, 1994, The Power of Fantasy, 1994, The Small Business Credit and Collection Guide, 1995, Mind Your Own Business: The Battle for Personal Privacy, 1995, Can We Talk?: The Power and Influence of Talk Shows, 1996; author: (with others) Brain Boosters, 1993, You the Jury: Recovered Memories, 1996, also children's books; designer Glasnost: The Game of Soviet-American Peace and Diplomacy, 1988; songwriter: The Truth About Lying, What I Told You on the Pillow. Mem. Am. Soc. Journalists and Authors, Authors Guild, Nat. Fedn. Presswomen, Calif. Press Women, Am. Booksellers Assn., Soc. of Children's Book Writers, Women's Nat. Book Assn., No. Calif. Songwriters Assn., Tenn. Songwriters Assn., Broadcast Music, Inc., No. Calif. Book Publicists, Media Alliance, Nat. Assn. Radio and Talk Show Hosts, Bay Area Organizational Devel. Network, Privacy Internat., Bay Area Assn. for Psychol. Type, Calif. Assn. Lic. Investigators (affiliate), Commonwealth Club San Francisco, San Francisco Mus. Modern Art, YLEM: Artists Using Sci. and Tech. Office: Changemakers 6114 La Salle Ste 358 Oakland CA 94611

SCOTT, GLORIA, publishing marketing consultant; b. N.Y.C., May 22, 1927; d. Matthew and Ethel Lindenberg; m. Sidney Steinberg, Mar. 2, 1947 (dec. 1969); children: Marcy Lea Chessler, Cindy Ann Sachs; m. John Lenard Scott, Dec. 1, 1974 (div. May 1991). BBA, CCNY, 1947; MEd, Temple U., 1963. Adminstr. Rahmani Trading Corp., N.Y.C., 1947-50; acct. Pola Stout Corp., Phila., 1950-54; adminstr. Bristol Twp. Police Dept., Pa., 1954-58; acct. Odora Corp., N.Y.C., 1958-59, Middletown Twp., Neshaminy, Pa., 1959-60; tchr., chmn. social studies dept. Pennsbury Schs., Falls Twp., Pa., 1960-70; mktg. dir., dir. profit ctr. Bantam Books, N.Y.C., 1970-77; exec. officer Infocom Broadcast Svc., Hawley, Pa., 1977-89; ind. mktg. cons. Bantam, Doubleday, Dell Publishing Group, Random House, Assn. Am. Pubs., World Book Inc., N.Y.C., 1989—; ptnr. Scott/Satz Group, Walnut Creek, Calif., 1991—, LetterLink, Walnut Creek, Calif., 1992—; mem. negotiating team Pa. Tchrs. Assn., 1963-67. Contbr. articles to profl. jours. Active Pa. Bd. Edn. Mem. AAUW, LWV (treas.), Nat. Women's Polit. Caucus, Great Books Club (sec. 1986—), Walnut Creek C. of C., Rotary Internat. Avocations: running, aerobics, reading. Home and Office: 539 Monarch Ridge Dr Walnut Creek CA 94596-2955

SCOTT, IRENE FEAGIN, federal judge; b. Union Springs, Ala., Oct. 6, 1912; d. Arthur H. and Irene (Peach) Feagin; m. Thomas Jefferson Scott, Dec. 27, 1939 (dec.); children: Thomas Jefferson, Irene Scott Carroll. A.B., U. Ala., 1932, LL.B., 1936, LL.D., 1978; LL.M., Catholic U. Am., 1939. Bar: Ala. 1936. Law libr. U. Ala. Law Sch., 1932-34; atty. Office Chief Counsel IRS, 1937-50, mem. excess profits tax coun., 1950-52, spl. asst. to head appeals div., 1952-59, staff asst. to chief counsel, 1959-60; judge U.S. Tax Ct., 1960-82, sr. judge serving on recall, 1982—. Contbr. articles to Women Lawyers Jour. Bd. dirs. Mt. Olivet Found., Arlington. Mem. ABA (taxation sect.), Ala. Bar Assn., Fed. Bar Assn., D.C. Bar Assn. (hon.), Nat. Assn. Women Lawyers, Nat. Assn. Women Judges, Kappa Delta, Kappa Beta Pi. Office: US Tax Ct 400 2nd St NW Washington DC 20217-0001

SCOTT, JACQUELINE DELMAR PARKER, educational association administrator, business administrator, consultant, fundraiser; b. L.A., May 18, 1947; d. Thomas Aubrey and Daisy Beatrice (Singleton) Parker (div.); children: Tres Mali, Olympia Ranee, Stephen Thomas. AA in Theatre Arts, L.A. City Coll., 1970; BA in Econs., Calif. State U., Dominquez Hills, Carson, 1973; MBA, Golden Gate U., 1979. Cert. parenting instr. 1994. Sales clk. Newberry's Dept. Store, L.A., 1963-65; long distance operator Pacific Telephone Co., L.A., 1965-66; PBX operator Sears, Roebuck & Co., L.A., 1966-68; retail clk. Otey's Grocery Store, Nashville, 1968-69; collector N.Am. Credit, L.A., 1970-71; office mgr. Dr. S. Edward Tucker, L.A., 1972-74; staff coord. sch. edn. dept. Calif. State U., 1973-74; bank auditor Security Pacific Bank, L.A., 1974-76, corp. loan asst., 1976-77; dist. credit analyst Crocker Nat. Bank, L.A., 1977-78, asst. v.p., 1978-80; capital planning adminstr. TRW, Inc., Redondo Beach, Calif., 1980-82, ops. bus. adminstr., 1982-84, lab. sr. bus. adminstr., 1984-86, project bus. mgr., 1986-87, div. sr. bus. adminstr., 1987-92; ptnr., co-author, co-facilitator, cons. Diversified Event Planners, Inc., L.A., 1990-93; asst. area devel. dir. United Negro Coll. Fund, L.A., 1993—. Co-founder career growth awareness com. TRW Employees Bootstrap, Redondo Beach, Calif., 1980, pres., 1983-84; role model Inglewood High Sch., TRW Youth Motivation Task Force, Redondo Beach, 1981-83, Crozier Jr. High Sch., 1981-83, Monroe Jr. High Sch., Redondo Beach, 1981-83, Frank D. Parent Career Day, TRW Affirmative Action Com., Redondo Beach, 1987, St. Bernard's Career Day, 1991; chairperson community involvement com., 1981, chairperson disaster com., 1989-90; chairperson gen. and local welfare com. TRW Employees Charitable Orgn., 1989-90, disaster com. chair, 1988-89, bd. dirs. 1987-89; pres. Mgmt. Effectiveness Program Alumnae, L.A., 1982-83, TRW Employees Bootstrap Program Alumnae, 1983-84; group leader Jack & Jill of Am., Inc., South L.A., 1980-81, parliamentarian, 1986-87, v.p., 1981-82, chpt. pres., 1984-86, regional dir., 1987-89, nat. program dir., 1992—, liaison to Young Black Scholars Program, 1986—; bd. dirs. Adolescent Pregnancy Child Watch, 1993—; nat. program dir., founder Jack & Jill Am. Found., 1992—; L.A. mem. Nat. Black Child Devel. Inst., 1994—; vol. ARC, 1994—; parenting instr. Am. Red Cross, 1994—; founder Jack & Jill of Am. Leadership Devel. Program, 1993. Recipient commendation NAACP, 1985, United Negro Coll. Fund, 1986, United Way, 1988, Austistic Children's Telephon, 1980, Inglewood Sch. Dist., 1981, Pres. award Harbor Area Chpt. Links, Inc., 1985, Women of Achievement award City of L.A., Black Pers. Assn., 1994. Mem. Black Women's Forum (sponsor), Delta Sigma Theta.

SCOTT, JANE WOOSTER, artist; b. Phila.; d. Martin J. Wurster and Irella Jacobs; m. Vernon Scott (div. 1990); children: Vernon IV, Ashley. BA, Harcum Jr. Coll. One person shows include Ankrum Gallery, Beverly Hills, Calif., 1972-75, De Ville Gallery, Beverly Hills, 1976-78, Grand Cen. Gallery, N.Y.C., 1977-79, Petersen Gallery, Beverly Hills, 1980-86, Wentworth Gallery, 1990-95; works featured in (book) An America Jubilee: The Art of Jane Wooster Scott. Recipient Disting. Alumnae award Friends Cen., Pa., 1987; named Best Artist in Idaho, City of Boise, 1995. Office: Scott Art Graphics Ste H 19205 Parthenia St Northridge CA 91324

SCOTT, JUDITH MYERS, elementary education educator; b. Loredo, Mo., Dec. 29, 1940; d. Wilbur Charles and Dora Emma (Frazier) Myers; m. David Ronald Scott, Dec. 18, 1965; children: Russell Myers, Geoffrey Douglas. BA in Edn., Ariz. State U., 1962, MA in edn., 1970. Cert. tchr., Ariz. Tchr. 2d grade Scottsdale (Ariz.) Elem. Dist., 1962-64; tchr. 1st grade Cahuilla Sch., Palm Springs, Calif., 1965, Palm Crest Sch., La Canada, Calif., 1968-69; tchr. Ak Chin Community Sch., Maricopa, Ariz., 1969-70; grad. asst. Ariz. State U., Tempe, 1970-71; pvt. tutor Tempe, 1970-77; tchr. Dayspring Presch., Tempe, 1978-83; tchr. 3d grade Waggoner Elem. Sch., Kyrene, Ariz., 1984-86; reading specialst Tempe Elem. Sch. Dist., 1986-90, tchr., trainer collaborative literacy intervention program, 1990—; exec. dir. Beauty for All Seasons, Tempe, 1982-86; presenter in field. Coord. New Zealand Tchr. Exch., Tempe Sister Cities, 1992—. Mem. NEA, ASCD, IRA, ARA, Ariz. Sch. Admisntrs., Ariz. Edn. Assn. Methodist. Home: 1940 E Calle De Caballos Tempe AZ 85284-2507 Office: Tempe Elem Sch Dist 3205 S Rural Rd Tempe AZ 85282-3853

SCOTT, LINDA GAE, charitable organization executive; b. Fullerton, Calif., June 15, 1947; d. Arthur Lendel and Genevieve (Waddell) Brookshire; m. Daniel N. Scott, Dec. 30, 1965; children: Trisha, Kenneth, Kara, Melissa. BS with honors, Calif. State U., Fullerton, 1995. Parent support coord. Children's Hosp. of Orange County, 1985-95; tng. and referral coord. Family Support Network, Orange, 1987-94; coord. immunization coalitioin United Way Orange County, Irvine, 1996—; cons. in field. Named Spl. Judge award Hosp. Parent Support Group, 1987, Cmty. Svcs. award Hos. Parent Support Group, 1988. Mem. Parent Care Inc. (Outstanding Parent Support Group 1989), So. Calif. Mediation Assn. Office: United Way Orange County 18012 Mitchell Ave S Irvine CA 92614

SCOTT, LOTTIE BELL, retired civil rights administrator; b. Ridgeway, S.C., Nov. 5, 1936; d. Joe and Estelle (Stone) Bell; m. Charles Wright, 1961 (div. 1965); 1 child, Clyburn. AS, Mohegan Community Coll., Norwich, Conn., 1982; B of Gen. Studies, U. Conn., Storrs, Conn., 1986. Clk.-typist Conn. Dept. of Mental Health, Norwich, 1962-70; neighborhood resource worker Conn. Commn. on Human Rights & Opportunities, Norwich, 1970-73, investigator, 1973-79, regional mgr., 1979—; owner LBS Human Resource Cons., Norwich, 1992—. Dir. Thames Valley Coun. for Cmty., Jewett City, Conn., 1965-68; br. sec. NAACP, Norwich, 1967-74, br. pres., 1974-80; asst. sec. Conn. State Conf. of the NAACP, 1971-73, v.p., 1973-79; bd. dirs. Conn. Civil Liberties, Hartford, 1972-76; vice chmn. Norwich Redevelopment Agy., 1974; vice moderator, Unitarian Universalist Ch., 1977-81; bd. dirs. United Cmty. Svc., 1977-80, 85-88; com. chmn., bd. dirs. William W. Backus Hosp. Long Range Planning, 1981-88, chmn. bd. dirs., 1988-90; bd. dirs. Conn. Hosp. Assn., Wallingford, Conn., 1990-92, YMCA, Norwich, 1991—. Mem. Rotary. Democrat. Home: 85 Church St Norwich CT 06360-5001 Office: LBS Human Resource Cons 85 Church St Norwich CT 06360-9999

SCOTT, MARGARET SIMON, mortgage broker; b. Boston, May 12, 1934; d. Frank A. and Margaret Alice (Gotham) Simon; m. Walter Neil Scott, Nov. 21, 1959; 1 child, Walter David Kimbley. BA in Physics, Wellesley Coll., 1956; MA in Polit. Sci., Boston U., 1965; MS in Human Resources Mgmt., U. Utah, 1974. Registered mortgage broker, N.Y. Rsch. asst. Bell Tel. Labs., Whippany, N.J., 1956-58; rsch. asst. med. sch. U. Louisville, 1959-60, Harvard U., Boston, 1960-64; instr. polit. sci. Trinity U., San Antonio, 1966-67; cons. info. systems U.S. Dept. Labor, Washington, 1968; dir. manpower planning N.Y.C. Human Resources Adminstrn., 1968-71; asst. v.p. First Nat. City Bank, N.Y.C., 1972-77; v.p. Citibank, N.A., N.Y.C., 1978-86, AMEV Asset Mgmt., Inc., N.Y.C., 1986-88; pres. Mortgage Adv. Svcs., Inc., N.Y.C., 1988—. Vol. Jr. League, Louisville, 1957—; bd. mgr. N.Y. Jr. League, N.Y.C., 1970-74; sec. 1095 Park Ave Corp., N.Y.C., 1977-86; bd. dirs. YWCA, N.Y.C., 1980-85; trustee First Presbyn. Ch. in the City N.Y., N.Y. City Presbytery; bd. mgrs. McBurney YMCA, N.Y.C. Mem. Nat. Assn. Mortgage Brokers (cert. mortgage cons.), N.Y. Assn. Mortgage Brokers, Met. N.Y. Mortgage Brokers Assn. (founding pres. 1990-91), Am. Assn. Residential Mortgage Regulators, Nat. Assn. Women Bus. Owners, Assn. Real Estate Women, Fin. Women's Assn., Women's Econ. Roundtable, Spinsters' Cotillion Club, Wellesley Club. Democrat. Home: 441 W 24th St New York NY 10011-1253

SCOTT, MARIANNE FLORENCE, librarian, educator; b. Toronto, Dec. 4, 1928; d. Merle Redvers and Florence Ethel (Hutton) S. BA, McGill U., Montreal, Que., Can., 1949, BLS, 1952; LLD (hon.), York U., 1985, Dalhousie U., 1989; DLitt (hon.), Laurentian U., 1990. Asst. librarian Bank of Montreal, 1952-55; law librarian McGill U., 1955-73, law area librarian, 1973-75, dir. libraries, 1975-84, lectr. legal bibliography faculty of law, 1964-75; nat. librarian Nat. Library of Can., Ottawa, Ont., 1984—. Co-founder, editor: Index to Can. Legal Periodical Lit, 1963—; contbr. articles to profl. jours. Decorated Officer of the Order of Can., 1995. Mem. Internat. Assn. Law Libraries (dir. 1974-77), Am. Assn. Law Libraries, Can. Assn. Law Libraries (pres. 1963-69, exec. bd. 1973-75, honored mem. 1980—), Can. Library Assn. (council and dir. 1980-82, 1st v.p. 1980-81, pres. 1981-82), Corp. Profl. Librarians of Que. (v.p. 1975-76), Can. Assn. Research Libraries (pres. 1978-79, past pres. 1979-80, exec. com. 1980-81, sec.-treas. 1983-84), Ctr. for Research Libraries (dir. 1980-83), Internat. Fedn. Library Assns. (honor com. for 1982 conf. 1979-82), Conf. of Dirs. of Nat. Libraries (chmn. 1988-92). Home: 119 Dorothea Dr, Ottawa, ON Canada K1V 7C6 Office: Nat Libr Can, 395 Wellington St, Ottawa, ON Canada K1A 0N4

SCOTT, MARY RODDY, business educator; b. Houma, La., Feb. 13, 1954; d. Gordon Joseph and Lillian Eve (Brunet) Roddy; m. Richard Wayne Chauvin, Nov. 11, 1972 (div. Mar. 1984); children: Amy Beth Chauvin, Timothy John Chauvin; m. Douglas Alan Scott, May 18, 1985; 1 child, Rachel Rebecca. BS, Nicholls State U., 1979, MBA, 1988; DBA, La. Tech. U., 1996. CPA, La.; CMA. Staff acct. E. J. Porche, Acct., Houma, 1974-77, Main, Hurdman and Cranston, New Orleans, 1977-78; acct. Mathews and Broussard, CPAs, Houma, 1978-80, Mary R. Scott, CPA, Houma, 1980-88; tchg. asst. La. Tech. U., Ruston, 1988-89; asst. prof. Grambling (La.) State U., 1989-96, N.W. Mo. State U., Maryville, Mo., 1996—. Recipient 1st Alumni Employee award Pvt. Industry Coun. for Work Connection, 1990, Disting. Paper award S.W. Bus. Symposium, 1993. Mem. AICPA, Inst. Mgmt. Accts. (CMA), Am. Acctg. Assn., Acad. Acctg. Historians, La. Soc. CPAs, Beta Gamma Sigma. Republican. Home: PO Box 104 Maryville MO 64468-0104 Office: N W Mo State U Dept Acctg 800 University Dr Maryville MO 64468

SCOTT, MELLOUISE JACQUELINE, educational media specialist, master storyteller; b. Sanford, Fla., Mar. 1, 1943; d. Herbert and Mattye (Williams) Cherry; m. Robert Edward Scott, Jr., July 1, 1972; 1 child, Nolan Edward. B.A., Talladega Coll., 1965; M.L.S., Rutgers U., 1974, Ed.M., 1976, Ed.S., 1982. Media specialist Seminole County Bd. Edn., Sanford, 1965-72, Edison Bd. Edn. (N.J.), 1972—. Mem. ALA, N.J. Edn. Assn., NEA, Ednl. Media Assn. N.J. Baptist. Home: PO Box 8 Fords NJ 08863-0008 Office: Edison Bd Edn Mcpl Complex Edison NJ 08817

SCOTT, MIMI KOBLENZ, psychotherapist, actress, publicist, journalist; b. Albany, N.Y., Dec. 15, 1940; d. Edmund Akiba and Tillie (Paul) Koblenz; m. Barry Stuart Scott, Aug. 13, 1961 (dec. Nov. 1991); children: Karen Scott Zantay, Jeffrey B. BA in Speech, English Edn., Russell Sage Coll., 1962; MA in Speech Edn., SUNY, Albany, 1968; M in Social Welfare, SUNY, 1985; PhD in Psychology, Pacific Western U., Encino, Calif., 1985. Cert. tchr., social worker. Tchr. English, speech Albany Pub. Schs., 1961-63; hostess, producer talkshow Sta. WAST-TV 13, Albany, 1973-75; freelance actress N.Y.C., 1975-77; producer, actress Four Seasons Dinner Theater, Albany, 1978-82; instr. of theatre Albany Jr. Coll., 1981-83; pvt. practice psychotherapy Albany, N.Y., 1985-92; exec. producer City of Albany Park Playhouse, 1989-92; actor self-employed N.Y.C., 1992—; actor Off Broadway show Grandma Sylvia's Funeral, 1996; guest psychotherapist Sally Jessy Raphael Show, 1992, 93, Jane Whitney Show, 1994, A Current Affair, 1995, News Talk TV, 1995. Scriptwriter, dir., actress TV movie, 1995; feature writer Backstage, 1995-96; (off-Broadway) Grandma Sylvia's Funeral. Event organizer AmFar, 1985; co-chmn. March of Dimes Telethon, 1985-86; fundraiser Leukemia Found., 1987, Aids Benefit, N. Miami Beach, Fla., 1988; elected to SUNY Albany U. Found., 1990. Recipient FDR Nat. Achievement award March of Dimes, 1985, Recognition Cert. Capital Dist. Psychiat. Ctr., 1983, 84, 85; named Woman of Yr. YWCA, 1986, Commr. Albany Tricentennial Celebration, 1986; Mimi Scott Day proclaimed by Mayor of Albany, 1989. Mem. AEA, SAG, AFTRA, NASW. Jewish. Home and Office: 211 West 71st # 6C New York NY 10023

SCOTT, PAMELA MOYERS, physician assistant; b. Clarksburg, W.Va., Jan. 5, 1961; d. James Edward and Norma Lee (Holbert) Moyers; m. Troy Allen Scott, July 19, 1986. BS summa cum laude, Alderson-Broaddus Coll., 1983. Cert. physician asst. Physician asst. Weston (W.Va.) State Hosp., 1983-84, Rainelle (W.Va.) Med. Ctr., 1984—; support faculty physician asst. program Coll. W.Va., 1994—, mem. physician asst. adv. coun. 1993—, physician asst. program admission selection com., 1994—; keynote spkr. Alderson-Broadous Coll. Ann. Physician Assn. Banquet, 1992; presenter civa. Task Force on Adolescent Pregnancy and Parenting State Meeting, Charleston, 1992, W.Va. Primary Care Assn. Ann. Conf., Beckley, W.Va., 1994, W.Va. State Rural Health Conf., Morgantown, 1992, Chinese Med. Soc., Beijing, 1992; guest Lifetime TV med. program Physician Jour. Update, 1993; adv. coun. W.Va. Rural Health Networking, 1994—, W.Va. Rural Networking Managed Care Policy Group, 1996. Mem. edtl. bd. Jour. Am. Acad. Physician Assts., dept. editor Procedures in Family Practice Dept., 1996; contbr. articles to profl. jours. Mem. W.Va. State Task Force on Adolescent Pregnancy and Parenting, 1992—; W.Va. Rural Networking Managed Care Study Group, 1995, W.Va. Rural Networking Managed Care Policy Group, 1996. Named Young Career Woman of Yr. Rainelle chpt. and Dist. V of W. Va., Citation of Honor at State Level of Competition, Bus. and Profl. Women's Club, 1986, Nominee for W. Va. Women's Commn. Celebrate Women award, 1996. Fellow Am. Acad. Physician Assts. (del. to People's Republic China 1992, W.Va. chief del. Ho. of Dels. Nat. Conv. 1992, 94, 95, 96, W.Va. del. 1993, mem. rural health caucus 1991—, chair pub. edn. com. 1996—, presenter ann. CME conf. San Antonio 1994, Las Vegas 1995), W.Va. Assn. Physician Assts. (chair membership com. 1989-91, nominations and elections com. 1990-91, pres. 1991-94, immediate past pres. 1994-95, presenter Continued Med. Edn. Conf. 1993). Republican. Baptist. Home: PO Box 43 Williamsburg WV 24991-0043 Office: Rainelle Med Ctr 645 Kanawha Ave Rainelle WV 25962-1013

SCOTT, PEGGY S., academic administrator; b. Beaumont, Tex., Apr. 27, 1958; d. Fred S. and Cora Elizabeth (McDermott) Dow; m. Steve Eric Scott, Mar. 7, 1980; 1 child, Jennifer Noel. BS, Lamar U., 1979; MS, East Tex. State U., 1981, EdD, 1985. Lic. profl. counselor. Asst. to exec. dir. student affairs East Tex. State U., Commerce, 1982-83, writer, 1983-84, instr., 1985; dir. promotion & cmty. rels. Sta. KETR-FM, Commerce, 1984-85; asst. dean student devel. Stephen F. Austin State U., Nacogdoches, Tex., 1986—; coach pom pon squad Stephen F. Austin State U., Nacogdoches, 1986—, dir. student wellness ctr., 1988—; presenter, rschr. in field of women's leadership, 1988—; program dir. wellness retreats, 1993—; wellness model, spokesperson, 1993—. Pres. Am. Heart Assn., Nacogdoches, 1991, state vol. svcs. com., Austin, Tex., 1992-95; cons. East Tex. AIDS Project, Nacogdoches, 1993; mem. transit com. City of Nacogdoches, 1995—. Recipient Disting. Svc. award Am. Heart Assn., 1991. Mem. Am. Counseling Assn., Am. Coll. Pers. Assn., Nat. Wellness Assn. Republican. Mem. Christian Ch. (Disciples of Christ). Office: Stephen F Austin State U 1936 North St Box 13020 SFA Nacogdoches TX 75962

SCOTT, PHYLLIS JEAN, mathematics educator; b. Oneida, Ky., July 9, 1950; d. Herbert and Zona (Bowling) Gibson; m. Victor Errol Arnett, Jan. 2, 1970 (div. June 1982); 1 child, Errol Scott; m. Jasper Scott, July 31, 1983. BS Sigma Cum Lauda, Cumberland Coll., 1976; MA, Ea. Ky. U., 1980; Rank I/Supervision, Union Coll., 1982. Elem. educator Clay County Bd. Edn., Oneida, Ky., 1976-83, Laurel County Bd. Edn., London, 1983—; trainer Tchr. Expectations of Student Achievement, London, Ky., 1987, Ky. Internship Program, London, 1985—, Effective Schs., London, 1988, Implementing Ky. Edn. Reform Act, London, 1994; presenter Nat. Middle Sch. Conf., New Orleans, Nov. 1995.

SCOTT, ROSA MAE, artist, educator; b. East Hampton, N.Y., Apr. 12, 1937; d. James Alexander and Victoria (Square) Nicholson; m. Frank Albert Hanna, Apr. 1, 1957 (div. Mar. 1985); 1 child, Frank Albert Hanna III; m. Warner Bruce Scott, Aug. 3, 1985; children: Bernadine, John, Patricia, Charlene, Lawrence. AA, Dabney Lancaster, 1989; BA, Mary Baldwin, 1992. Cosmetologist Rosa's Beauty Shop, East Hampton, 1962-68; sec. Frank Hanna's Cleaning Co., East Hampton, 1962-77; cashier, clk. Brook's Pharmacy, East Hampton, 1992; lead tchr. East Hampton Day Care, 1992-94; substitute tchr. Lexington (Va.) Schs., 1994—; sec. Lylburn Downing Cmty. Ctr., Inc., Lexington, 1985-92. Acrylic painter. Pres. Rockbridge Garden Club, Lexington, 1996; co-organizer Va. Co-op. Ex. Garden Clubs,

Lexington, 1995; bd. dirs. Rockbridge Area Pres. Homes, 1996, Fine Arts of Rockbridge, 1985-92, Friends of Lime Kiln, Lexington, 1985-92. Mem. Rockbridge Arts Guild. Home: PO Box 1061 Lexington VA 24450

SCOTT, SHARON ROSENFELD, artist; b. N.Y.C., Apr. 8, 1954; d. Andrew F. and Leonor R. (Cassel) Romney; m. Kenneth Wayne Scott, Nov. 6, 1988; children: Andrew James, Lewis Gardner. BFA, Pratt Inst., 1977; MA, NYU, 1983. Artist-in-residence Millay Colony for Arts, Austerlitz, N.Y., 1985. One-woman shows 80 Washington Square East Gallery, N.Y.c., 1983, Century Galleries, Henley on Thames, Eng., 1992, Gallery Galimberti, Vaduz, Liechtenstein, 1992, Righetti Knie Fine Arts Trading, Muri-Bern, Switzerland, 1992, Alumni Exhbn.-Pres. Office, Pratt Inst., N.Y., 1992, Art Addiction, Stockholm, 1993. Recipient spl. mention In Search of Am. Experience, 1989. Home and Studio: 16 E 96th St Apt 4B New York NY 10128

SCOTT, SUSAN, lawyer; b. Orange, N.J., July 25, 1943; d. Bailey Bartlett and Regina Margaret (Butler) S.; m. Robert John Gillispie, Aug. 20. 1966 (div. 1979); children: Robert John Jr., Megan Anne. BA in Math, Catholic U. Am., 1965; JD, Rutgers U., 1975. Bar: N.J. 1975, U.S. Dist. Ct. N.J. 1975, U.S. Ct. Appeals (3d cir.) 1988, U.S. Supreme Ct. 1993. Applied math. CIA, Washington, 1965-68; assoc. Pitney, Hardin, Kipp & Szuch, Morristown, N.J., 1975-76; assoc. Riker, Danzig, Scherer, Hyland & Perretti, Morristown, 1979-85, ptnr., 1986—; corp. counsel Allied-Signal, Inc., Morristown, 1977-78; mem. Child Placement Rev. Bd., Morristown,1992—; commr. Morris County Bd. Condemnation, Morristown, 1989—. Mem. ABA, N.J. State Bar Assn., Morris County Bar Assn. Democrat. Roman Catholic. Home: 20 Vinton Rd Madison NJ 07940-2506 Office: Riker Danzig Scherer Hyland & Perretti Headquarters Plz 1 Speedwell Ave Morristown NJ 07960-6845

SCOTT, SUSAN C., art history educator, editor; b. Drexel Hill, Pa., July 13, 1942; d. William Edwin and Clar-Monna (Darby) S. BS in Art Edn./English, Pa. State U., 1964, MA in Art History, 1978, PhD in Art History, 1995. Art/English tchr. Phoenixville (Pa.) Area H.S., 1964-65; art tchr. K-6 Newark (Del.) Spl. Sch. Dist., 1965-70; art/English 7-9 Emmaus (Pa.) Jr. H.S., 1970-71; instr. art history Pa. State U., University Park, 1980—, editor, papers in art history, 1983—, asst. prof. art history, 1995—. Editor, author: Projects and Monuments..., 1984; editor: Light on the Eternal City, 1987, The Age of Rembrandt, 1988, Paris, Center of Artistic Enlight, 1988 and subsequent vols. in 1989-90, 92-93, 95-96; editor articles . Mem. Soc. of Architectural Historians, Coll. Art Assn., Alpha Delta Kappa. Home: 465 Galen Dr State College PA 16803 Office: Dept Art History PSU 229 Arts Bldg University Park PA 16802-2901

SCOTT-FINAN, NANCY ISABELLA, government administrator; b. Canton, Ohio, June 13, 1949; d. Milton Kenneth and Gertrude (Baker) Scott; m. Robert James Finan II, Aug. 23, 1986. Student, Malone Coll., 1970-73; BA magna cum laude, U. Akron, 1976, postgrad., 1976; postgrad., Kent State U., 1977; MA in Internat. Transactions, George Mason U., 1995. Legal sec. Krugliak, Wilkins, Griffiths & Dougherty, Canton, 1969, Amerman, Burt & Jones, Canton, 1970-77; legal sec., paralegal Black, McCuskey, Souers & Arbaugh, Canton, Ohio, 1977-81; adminstrv. staff mem. com. on judiciary U.S. Senate, Washington, 1981-86; adminstrv. asst. to counsel to Pres., The White House, Washington, 1986-89; adminstrv. asst. to former counsel to pres. O'Melveny & Myers, Washington, 1989; asst. dir. congl. rels. Office Legis. Affairs U.S. Dept. Justice, Washington, 1989-91; spl. asst. to asst. atty. gen. U.S. Dept. of Justice, Washington, 1991—; substitute tchr. North Canton City Sch. System, 1979-80; residential tutor Canton City Sch. System, 1980-81, Fairfax (Va.) County Sch. System, 1983;instr. dance and exercise Siffrin Home for Developmentally Disabled, Canton, 1980. East coast regional v.p. for spl. projects Childhelp U.S.A., Washington, 1988-90; mem. Rep. Women of Capitol Hill, Washington, 1984-95; bd. mem. Have a Heart Homes for Abused Children, Washington, 1990-91. Mem. AAUW, Women of Washington. Presbyterian. Office: US Dept Justice 10th and Constitution Washington DC 20530

SCOTTI, RITA ANGELICA, novelist; b. Providence, Dec. 25, 1946; d. Ciro Ottorino and Rita Ward (Dwyer) S.; children: Francesca, Ciro. Student, U. Rome, 1963-64, Loyola U., 1964-65. Author: The Devil's Own, 1965, Kiss of Judas, 1984, Cradle Song, 1987, The Hammer's Eye, 1987, For Love of Sarah, 1995. Roman Catholic. Home: 224 E 18th St Apt 3A New York NY 10003-3632

SCOTTO, MARY LEE, columnist; b. Hartford, Conn., July 27, 1946; d. Leno J. Rinaldi and Mary Louise (Morgan) Hewitt; m. Frank J. Scotto, Oct. 30, 1975; children: John, Frank Jr. Student pub. schs., Hartford, Conn. Editor IHMSA News, Burlington, Iowa, 1989—; columnist FMG Publications, San Diego, 1993—; dir. industry IHMSA, Inc., 1990—. Contbr. articles on guns to profl. jours; author numerous poems. Mem. Rep. Nominating Com., Washington, 1996. 1st woman dir. of silhouette com., 1986, outstanding sportsman of yr., 1985, Conn. State Rifle & Pistol Assn., Wallingford; 1st woman dir. of industry rels. Ctrl. Conn. Handgun Silhouette Assn., Wallingford, 1985. Mem. Internat. Handgun Metallic Silhouette Assn. (outstanding support 1986, 87, 88, 89; outstanding family 1988; dir. of internat. championship 1986-89; dir. of industry, editor 1990—; outstanding mem. 1992, 1st woman dir. of industry, 1990). Republican. Roman Catholic. Office: IHMSA Inc PO Box 5038 Meriden CT 06451

SCOTTO, RENATA, soprano; b. Savona, Italy, Feb. 24, 1935; m. Lorenzo Anselmi. Studied under, Ghirardini, Merlino and Mercedes Llopart, Accademia Musicale Savonese, Conservatory Giuseppe Verdi, Milan. Debut in La Traviata, Teatro Nuevo, Milan, 1954; then joined La Scala Opera Co.; appeared with Met. Opera, N.Y.C., 1965, Convent Garden, Hamburg (Fed. Republic of Germany) State Opera, Vienna (Austria) State Opera, Nat. Theatre Munich, San Francisco Opera, Chgo. Lyric Opera, 1988; roles include: Ballo in Maschera, La Sonnambula, I Puritani, L'Elisir d'amore, Lucia di Lammermoor, La Boheme, Turandot, Otello (Verdi), Trovatore, Le Prophete, Madama Butterfly, Adriana Lecouvreur, Norma, Tosca, Manon Lescaut, Rosenkavalier (Marschallin), La Voix Humaine, Pirata, Italy; dir. Madama Butterfly, N.Y. Met. Opera, 1986; recordings include Christmas at St. Patrick's Cathedral, French Arias with Charles Rosekrans, Live in Paris with Ivan Davis, Great Operatic Scenes with Jose Carreras, various recitals and concerts. Office: care Robert Lombardo Assocs One Harkness Plaza 61 W 62d St Ste 6F New York NY 10023 also: care Il Teatro la Scala, via Filodrammatici 2, Milan Italy*

SCOTT-WILLIAMS, WENDY LEE, publishing company executive; b. Buffalo, Jan. 22, 1953; d. Arthur Raymond and June Amelia (Dittmann) Schutt; m. Nigel Simon Scott-Williams, Feb. 29, 1980. BA cum laude, SUNY, Buffalo, 1975; MA with honors, Cambridge U., 1979; MLIS with honors, CUNY-Queens Coll., 1987. Applications rep. Barrister, N.Y.C., 1982-83; coord. computer systems Stroock & Stroock & Lavan, N.Y.C., 1983-87; tech. svcs. mgr. Batten, Barton, Durstein & Osborn (BBDO) Worldwide, N.Y.C., 1987-92; adminstr., mgr. info. resources Fairchild Publs., N.Y.C., 1992—. Active N.Y. Zool. Soc. Mem. Am. Soc. Info. Sci., Cambridge Union Soc., Oxford-Cambridge Soc., Nature Conservancy, Greenpeace. Presbyterian. Office: Fairchild Publs 7 W 34th St C Level New York NY 10001-8100

SCOTT-WILSON, SUSAN RICE, educator; b. Brownsville, Tenn., Aug. 11, 1942; d. Moreau Estes and E. Estelle (Walker) Rice; m. Charles E. Scott, Feb. 28, 1969 (div. July 1985); children: Tamera W., David W.; m. Lloyd Curlin Wilson, Apr. 7, 1994. BS, U. Tenn., Martin, 1964; EdM, Memphis State U., 1979, EdD, 1989. Cert. master tchr., Tenn. Elem. tchr. Lauderdale County Bd. Edn., Ripley, Tenn., 1964-65; exchange tchr. USIA, Washington, Netherlands, 1986-87; chmn. English dept. Am. Sch. of The Hague, Netherlands, 1987-88; secondary tchr. Haywood County Bd. Edn., Brownsville, Tenn., 1974-86, tchr. vocat. English, 1989-90, dir. adult basic edn., 1990-96; vice prin. Haywood H.S., Brownsville, Tenn., 1995—; mem. curriculum task force Tenn. Dept. Edn., Nashville, 1985-86, mem. collaborative task force, 1989-92. Local elector Tenn. Pres.'s Trust, Knoxville, 1989—; mem. Sister Cities Commn., Brownsville, 1990; com. mem. Ptnrs. in Edn., Brownsville, 1992-93; mem. West Star Leadership, 1993, Tenn. Reorgnl. Improvement Mgmt. Sys., 1994-95; mem. steering com. Fayette County-Haywood County Cmty. Enterprise, Brownsville, 1994—; bd. dirs. YMCA, Brownsville, 1996—. Named Outstanding Tchr. by students U. Chgo., 1989. Mem. NEA, Nat. Coun. Tchrs. English (regional composition judge 1984-86), Am. Assn. Adult and Continuing Edn., Tenn. Edn. Assn., Tenn. Assn. Adult and Continuing Edn., Tenn. Tchrs. Study Coun. (state steering com. 1984-86), Sigma Tau Delta, Phi Delta Kappa. Methodist. Home: 321 N Washington St Brownsville TN 38012-2063 Office: Haywood HS 1175 E College St Brownsville TN 38012-2647

SCOVEL, MARY ALICE, music therapy educator; b. Grand Rapids, Mich., Jan. 28, 1936; d. Carl Edward and Alice Bertha (Bieri) Sennema; m. Ward Norman Scovel, July 7, 1956; children: Marcia, Katherine. MusB, Western Mich. U., 1969; MusM, Mich. State U., 1975. Registered music therapist; bd. cert. Asst. prof. music Grand Valley State U., Allendale, Mich., 1969-75; instr. U. Dayton (Ohio), 1975-78, Muskegon (Mich.) Community Coll., 1978-80; intern dir. Battle Creek (Mich.) Adventist Hosp., 1980-84; prof. music therapy Western Mich. U., Kalamazoo, 1984-95; cons. Pre-sch. Physically Handicapped, Wyo., Mich., 1974, Doris Klausen Devel. Ctr., Battle Creek, 1985-86, Sancta Sophia Sem., Tahlequah, Okla., music therapist, sound practitioner and trainer at Wellness Ctr.; chmn. Multi-clinic, Kalamazoo, 1988-89. Author: Music Therapy in Treatment of Adults, 1990; co-editor Music Therapy Perspectives; contbr. articles to profl. jours. Lay del. United Meth. Ch., Albion, Mich., 1991. Mem. Nat. Assn. Music Therapy (del.), Nat. Assn. Mental Illness, Great Lakes Region Music Therapy (past pres.), Mich. Music Therapists, AAUW, Pi Delta Alpha, Pi Kappa Lambda. Home: 502 Summit Ridge Dr Tahlequah OK 74464

SCOVILL, DEBRA ANSELMO, elementary education educator; b. Price, Utah, Oct. 13, 1952; d. John and Juanita (Pilling) Anselmo; m. Kent O. Scovill, Mar. 1975 (dec. Dec. 1990); children: Lance K., Kimberly Ann. AS, Coll. Eastern Utah, 1972; BS, Utah State U., 1975, MEd, 1994. Libr. Utah State U., Logan, 1973-75; acctg. Coll. Eastern Utah, Price, 1975-76; elementary educator Carbon County Schs., Price, 1978—. Mem. Delta Kappa Gamma, Phi Kappa Phi. Democrat. Home: 96 N 1230 W Price UT 84501-4215 Office: Wellington Elem Sch 250 W 200 N Wellington UT 84542

SCRIMENTI, BELINDA JAYNE, lawyer; b. Dayton, Ohio, Jan. 30, 1956. BS in Journalism, Ohio U., 1978; JD, Ohio State U., 1981. Bar: Ohio 1981, U.S. Dist. Ct. (no. dist.) Ohio 1981, U.S. Dist. Ct. (ea. dist.) Mich. 1983, U.S. Ct. Appeals (3d and 6th cirs.) 1984, U.S. Dist. Ct. Md. 1988, D.C. 1989, U.S. Dist. Ct. D.C. 1989, U.S. Ct. Appeals (2d cir.), 1995. Assoc. Baker & Hostetler, Cleve., 1981-88; assoc. Baker & Hostetler, Washington, 1988-90, ptnr., 1991—. Contbr. articles to profl. jours. Sec. Chagrin Condominiums Homeowners' Assn., Chagrin Falls, Ohio, 1985-87. Mem. ABA (sect. on litigation, patent, trademarks and copyritghts, entertainment and sports law), D.C. Bar Assn. (sects. on copyright, trademarks, patent and entertainment and sport law), Internat. Trademark Assn. (firm rep., coms. 1990—), Internat. Anti-Counterfeiting Coaliton (firm rep.), Womens Bar Assn. D.C. Office: Baker & Hostetler 1050 Connecticut Ave NW Washington DC 20036-5303

SCULLION, ANNETTE MURPHY, lawyer, educator; b. Chgo., Apr. 6, 1926; d. Edmund Patrick and Anna (Nugent) Murphy; 1 son, Kevin. B.Ed., Chgo. Tchrs. Coll., 1960; J.D., DePaul U., 1964, M.Ed., 1966; M.Ed., Loyola U., Chgo., 1970; Ed.D., No. Ill. U., 1974. Bar: Ill. 1964, U.S. Dist. Ct. (no. dist.) Ill. 1965, U.S. Ct. Appeals (D.C. cir.) 1978. Lectr. Chgo. Community Coll., 1964-68; pvt. practice law, Chgo., 1964—; asst. prof. bus. edn. Chgo. State U., 1966-69, assoc. prof., 1970-73, prof., 1974—. Club founder, adviser Bus. Edn. Students Assn., Chgo. State U., 1976—; sch. law workshop coordinator Ill. Div. Vocat. and Tech. Edn., 1981. Mem. Nat. Bus. Edn. Assn., Women's Bar Assn. Ill., ABA, Am. Tchr. Edn., Beta Gamma Sigma Home: 386 Muskegon Ave Calumet City IL 60409-2347 Office: Chgo State U 95 And King Dr # 203 Chicago IL 60601

SCULLION, TSUGIKO YAMAGAMI, non-profit organization executive; b. China, June 30, 1946; d. Hajime and Akemi (Murazumi) Yamagami; m. William James Scullion, Nov. 26, 1971; 1 child, James. BA, Baldwin-Wallace Coll., 1970; MA, Sch. Internat. Tng., 1971. Area cons. Conn. AFS Internat./Intercultural Programs, N.Y.C., 1972-73, regional mgr. for Asia and Pacific, 1973-78, dir. internat. ops., 1978-81, v.p. Europe, Africa, Middle East, 1981-83, v.p. program svcs., 1083-85, exec. v.p., 1985-87; exec. v.p. U.S. Com. UNICEF, N.Y.C., 1988-95; mgmt. cons. strategic planning, mktg. and fundraising, 1995-96; chief oper. officer Synergos Inst., 1996—. Bd. dirs. Oberlin Shansi Meml. Assn. Home: 7 Chasmar Rd Old Greenwich CT 06870-1404

SCULLY, MARTHA SEEBACH, speech and language pathologist; b. S.I., Nov. 1, 1951; d. Henry F. and Rose Anne (Callahan) Seebach; m. Roger Tehan Scully, Dec. 29, 1979; 1 child, Roger Tehan. BA, Trinity Coll., 1972; MS, George Washington U., 1974; postgrad., Syracuse (N.Y.) U., 1976-79. Lic. speech-lang. pathologist, Md. Clin. supr. Syracuse U., 1976-79; speech-lang. pathologist Fairfax (Va.) County Pub. Schs., 1979—. Bd. dirs. Trinity Coll., Washington, Nat. Children's Choir, 1987-91; trustee Davis Meml. Goodwill Industries, 1994-96, bd. dirs. Goodwill Guild, 1990—, chair ball; docent Folger Shakespearean Libr.; chmn. Nat. Challenge Com. of Disabled, 1985; mem. Ear Ball, 1988, 89; mem. Salvation Army garden party, 1992, mem. internat. children's festival, 1990, 91; co-chmn. Jr. League of Washington Capital Collection, 1990. Recipient First Order Affiliation Order of Franciscans mirror, 1985; named Outstanding Woman in Am., 1987, 88. Mem. Am. Biog. Inst., Am. Speech-Lang.-Hearing Assn., Coun. for Exceptional Children, Montgomery County Assn. for Hearing Impaired Children. Home: 10923 Wickshire Way Rockville MD 20852-3220

SCULLY, PAULA CONSTANCE, journalist; b. Carlisle, Pa., Nov. 7, 1948; d. Alfred Albert and Concetta (Rosati) Sanelli. BA in Anthropology, U. Wis., 1970. Pub. rels. writer Valley Forge Mil. Acad., Wayne, Pa., 1977-79; reporter Main Line Times, Ardmore, Pa., 1979-81; mng. editor Kane Communications, Phila., 1981-82; publicist Running Press Book Publishers, Phila., 1982-84; sr. writer Paolin & Sweeney Advt., Cherry Hill, N.J., 1984-87; free-lance pub. rels., 1987; reporter Beach Haven Times, Manahawkin, N.J., 1989—. Mem. Beach Haven WWII Commemorative Com., 1992-95. Mem. Mystery Writers Am., Romance Writers Am. Home: 331 Mcmull Dr Wayne PA 19087-2025 Office: Beach Haven Times 345 E Bay Ave Manahawkin NJ 08050-3314

SCURLOCK, JUDY B., early childhood educator; b. Florence, S.C., May 19, 1950; d. Charles James Jr. and Catherine (Finklea) Brockington; m. Gregory Blair Scurlock, June 10, 1972; children: Blair, Brian. BA, Columbia Coll., 1972; MEd, U. S.C., 1989. Tchr. Aiken (S.C.) County Schs., 1972-74, Richland County Schs., Columbia, S.C., 1974-76, Episcopal. Day Sch., Augusta, Ga., 1978-89; instr., dept. chair Aiken Tech. Coll., 1989—. Mem. Visions for Youth, Aiken, 1992-94; validator early childhood programs Nat. Acad. Early Childhood Programs. Recipient Gov. Disting. Prof. award, 1994. Mem. S.C. Assn. Edn. Young Children (pres. 1994-95, pub. rels. chair 1990-93, conf. chair 1993, pub. policy/advocacy chair 1996), S.C. Early Childhood Assn., Nat. Coalition Campus Child Care (conf. com. 1993), Nat. Assn. Edn. Young Children (affiliate pres. 1994-95), Sandhills Assn. Edn. Young Children (pres. 1993-94), Phi Delta Kappa. Presbyterian. Home: 821 Heard Ave Augusta GA 30904 Office: Aiken Tech Coll PO Drawer 696 Aiken SC 29802-0696

SCURRY, BRIANA COLLETTE, amateur soccer player; b. Mpls., Sept. 7, 1971. BS in Polit. Sci., U. Mass., 1995. Named Nat. Goalkeeper of Yr. Mo. Athletic Club Sports Found., 1993, 2d Team All-Am., 1993, Gold medal Atlanta Olympics, 1996. Office: US Soccer Fedn US Soccer House 1801-1811 S Prairie Ave Chicago IL 60616*

SEAGREN, ALICE, state legislator; b. 1947; m. Fred Seagren; 2 children. BS, SE Mo. State U. Mem. Minn. Ho. of Reps., 1993—. Active Bloomington (Minn.) Sch. Bd., 1989-92. Mem. Bloomington C. of C. (bd. dirs. 1990-92), Phi Gamma Nu, Alpha Chi Omega. Republican. Home: 9730 Palmer Cir Bloomington MN 55437-2017 Office: Minn Ho of Reps State Capital Building Saint Paul MN 55155-1606

SEAMAN, ARLENE ANNA, musician, educator; b. Pontiac, Mich., Jan. 21, 1918; d. Roy Russell and Mabel Louise (Heffron) S. BS, life cert., Ea. Mich. U., 1939; MMus, Wayne State U., 1951; postgrad., Colo. Coll., 1951-52, Acad. Music, Zermatt Switzerland, 1954, 58, U. Mich. guest conductor Shepherds and Angels, Symphonie Concertante, 1951; asst. conductor Detroit Women's Symphony, 1960-68; adjudicator Mich. State Band and Orch. Festivals, Solo and Ensemble Festivals, 1950-70, Detroit Fiddler's Band Auditions, 1948-52, Mich. Fedn. Music Clubs, 1948-55; tchr. Ea. Mich. U., 1939-42, Hartland Sch. Music, 1939-42, Pontiac (Mich.) Pub. Schs., 1942-45, Detroit Pub. Schs., 1945-73, pvt. studio, 1973-90. Performer cello South Oakland Symphony, 1958-65, Detroit Women's Symphony, 1951-68, Riviera Theatre Orch., 1959, 60, Masonic Auditorium Opera, Ballet Seasons, 1959-65, Toledo Ohio Symphony, 1963-70, others; performer trumpet Detroit Brass Quartet, 1974-78; piano accompanist various auditions, recitals, solo and ensemble festivals; composer: Let There Be Music, 1949, Fantasy for French Horn and Symphonic Band, 1951. Mem. Quota Internat., Delta Omicron. Home: 14650 N Alamo Canyon Dr Tucson AZ 85737-8812

SEAMAN, EMMA LUCY, artist, poet; b. West Freedom, Pa., Dec. 5, 1932; d. Roger Leslie and Lillian Emeline (Phillips) Eddinger; m. Roger John Seaman, Sept. 14, 1958; 1 child, Roger Kent. Grad. H.S., Seneca, Pa. Sec. to supt. Cranberry H.S., Seneca, 1951-56; flight attendant, hostess Trans World Airlines, Newark, 1956-57; copy writer Radio St. WFRA, Franklin, Pa., 1957-58. Works have been exhibited at Art League of Marco Island, Fla., 1985-93, Sussex County Arts and Heritage Coun. Fine Arts Exhbns., Newton, 1990-94, N.J. Herald Art Show, Newton, 1990, Annual Sparta (N.J.) Day Event, 1990, St. Mary's Art Festival, Sparta, 1991-94, Hilltop Art Exhibit, Sparta, 1991-94, Edison Festival of Light, Ft. Myers, Fla., 1992; represented in permanent collection of Fame Mus. Teterboro (N.J.) Airport; one woman show: Sparta Libr., N.J., 1994; contbr. numerous poems to publs. Sunday sch. tchr., Sparta, 1965-74; organizer, operator Paper Drives, Sparta, 1965-74. Recipient First Pl. Beginners Oils award Creative Canvas Art Assn., Newton, 1982, Purchase award St. Mary's Art Festival, Sparta, N.J., 1991, honorable mention, 1993. Mem. ASPCA, AARP, People for the Ethical Treatment Animals, Art League Marco Island, Sussex County Arts and Heritage Coun., Sussex County Arts Assn., Studio A Art Assn., Edison Festival of Light, Nat. Humane Edn. Soc., Human Soc. U.S., Doris Day Animal League, Animal Legal Def. Fund, Women's Mus. Art, Smithsonial Assn., Antique Airplane Assn., Newton (N.J.) Meml. Hosp. Aux., Sparta (N.J.) Woman's Club, Lake Mohawk Country Club. Home: 54 Alpine Trl Sparta NJ 07871-1509

SEAMAN, JUDITH D., adult education educator; b. Merrill, Oreg., Oct. 14, 1940; d. Donald Dungan and Annabelle J. (Stockton) Dod; m. David William Seaman, June 10, 1962 (div. Oct. 1986); children: Amanda Catherine, Natasha Thérèse. BA, Coll. Wooster, 1962; MA, Stanford U., 1967; MS, Marshall U., 1996. Case worker, translator Planned Parenthood, Waukegan, Ill., 1971-72; lectr. in humanities Davis & Elkins Coll., Elkins, W.Va., 1972-75; ESL tchr. Internat. Lang. Inst., Elkins, W.Va., 1975-78; Adult Basic Edn. tchr. Randolph County Schs., Elkins, W.Va., 1980—; tutor trainer Literacy Vols. Am.-W.Va. Tygart Affiliate, Elkins, 1985—, pres., 1991-95; peer trainer W.Va. Adult Basic Edn., Elkins, 1990—. Bd. dirs. Women's Aid in Crisis, Elkins, 1991—, pres., 1993-95. Mem. W.Va. Adult Edn. Assn. (pres. 1991-92), W.Va. Edn. Assn. (W.Va. adult tchr. of yr. award 1990), W.Va. NOW (pres. 1986-88). Mem. Soc. of Friends. Home: 1316 S Davis Ave Elkins WV 26241 Office: Randolph County Vo-Tech Ctr 200 Kennedy Dr Elkins WV 26241

SEAPKER, JANET KAY, museum director; b. Pitts., Nov. 2, 1947; d. Charles Henry and Kathryn Elizabeth (Dany) S.; m. Edward F. Turberg, May 24, 1975. BA, U. Pitts., 1969; MA, SUNY, Cooperstown, 1975. Park ranger Nat. Park Svc., summers 1967-69; archtl. historian N.C. Archives and History, Raleigh, 1971-76, hist. preservation adminstr., 1976-77, grant-in-aid adminstr., 1977-78; dir. Cape Fear Mus. (formerly New Hanover County Mus.), Wilmington, N.C., 1978—; bd. dirs. Bellamy Mansion Found., Wilmington, 1986-89, 91—, Lower Cape Fear Hist. Soc., Wilmington, 1985-88; N.C. rep. S.E. Mus. Conf., 1986-90; field reviewer Inst. Mus. Svcs., 1982—. Contbr. articles to profl. jours. Bd. dirs. Downtown Area Revitalization Effort, Wilmington, 1979-81, Thalian Hall Ctr. for Performing Arts, 1996—; bd. dirs. Hist. Wilmington Found., 1979-84, pres., 1980-81; mem. Cmty. Appearance Commn., Wilmington, 1984-88, 250th Anniversary Commn., Wilmington, 1986-90. Grad. program fellow SUNY, Cooperstown, 1969-70; recipient Profl. Svc. award N.C. Mus. Coun., 1982, Woman of Achievement award YWCA, 1994. Mem. Am. Assn. Mus. (accreditation vis. com. 1983—, reviewer mus. assessment program 1982—), Nat. Trust Hist. Preservation, Southeastern Mus. Conf. (N.C. state rep. 1986-90), N.C. Mus. Coun. (sec.-treas. 1978-84, pres. 1984-86), Hist. Preservation Found N.C. (sec. 1976-78). Democrat. Presbyterian. Home: 307 N 15th St Wilmington NC 28401-3813 Office: Cape Fear Mus 814 Market St Wilmington NC 28401-4731

SEARIGHT, CAROL CHIPMAN, mortgage banker; b. Ashland, Ohio, July 21, 1942; d. Kenneth Gordon Chipman and Ruth Collins Canzonari; m. Nicholas Reis Snyder, Sept. 15, 1962 (div. 1971); children: Nicholas Scott Snyder, Kenneth Matthew Snyder; m. Scott Charles Searight, July 11, 1993. AS in Fine Arts, Penn Hall, Chambersburg, Pa., 1962. Lic. real estate broker, Calif. V.p. Anaheim (Calif.) Savs., 1976-84; sr. v.p. Meritor Mortgage Corp., Phila., 1984-89, M-West Mortgage Corp., Orange, Calif., 1989-93; exec. v.p. MCS Fin., Dallas, 1993—. Bd. dirs. Santa Ana Community Housing Authority, 1985. Gold medalist in Art, 1962. Mem. Western Assn. Affiliated Agys., Calif. Mortgage Bankers Assn. (ins. com. 1991-93), Am. Assn. Residential Mortgage Regulators, Am. Soc. Quality Control. Home: 2 Monticello Irvine CA 92720-2728 Office: MCS Financial 5485 Belt Line Rd Ste 225 Dallas TX 75240-7656

SEARING, JANIS LYNN (DEE SEARING), early childhood education educator; b. N.Y., Apr. 27, 1946; d. John Stuart and Shirle (Caterson) Colety; m. John Thomas Searing, July 30, 1966; children: Jodilyn, Jennifer, John. BA, Towson (Md.) State U., 1977, MEd, 1987. Cert. tchr., reading specialist, Md. Early childhood specialist Harford County Pub. Schs., Bel Air, Md., 1977—; sr. lectr. Towson State U., 1990—; presenter in field. Author articles. Recipient Curriculum award Harford County Pub. Schs., 1990, 93, Most Disting. Early Childhood Educator award Towson State U., 1992, Cmty. Svc. award Md. Cystic Fibrosis Found., 1977. Mem. ASCD, NEA, Assn. for Childhood Edn. Internat. (nat. publs. com., br. sec., chair Internat. Study Conf. Program 1995), Internat. Reading Assn. (chair Md. Parents and Reading Com., coord. programs), Nat. Assn. for Edn. of Young Children (validator Acad. Early Childhood Programs), Active Parenting Inc. (cert. group leader, parent trainer), Md. Com. for Children, Phi Delta Kappa, Kappa Delta Pi.

SEARING, MARJORY ELLEN, government official, economist; b. N.Y.C., Mar. 29, 1945; d. William Edgar Searing and Jean Frances (Smith) Searing Fusaro; m. Warren Eugene Lane, Mar. 3, 1977; children—Gary Francis, Jennifer Rebecca, Stephanie Anne. B.A. in Econs., SUNY-Binghamton, 1966; M.A. in Econs., Georgetown U., 1969, Ph.D. in Econs., 1972. Economist Bur. Econs. Analysis U.S. Dept. Commerce, Washington, 1967-73, internat. economist Bur. East-West Trade, 1973-74, dir. Office Internat. Sector Policy, 1980-84, dir. Office Industry Assessment, 1984-86, acting dep. asst. sec. sci. and electronics, 1984-85, dir. Office Multilateral Affairs, 1986-90; dep. asst. sec. for Japan U.S. Dept. Commerce, 1991—; sr. internat. economist Office Trade Policy U.S. Dept. Treasury, Washington, 1974-76, dir. Office East-West Econ. Policy, 1976-79. Contbr. numerous articles to profl. publs. N.Y. State Regents scholar, 1962-65; Georgetown U. fellow, 1966-71. Office: US Dept Commerce 14th Pl SE Rm 2320 Washington DC 20230

SEARLE, ELEANOR MILLARD, history educator; b. Chgo., Oct. 29, 1926; married. BA, Harvard U., 1948; Licentiate Medieval Studies, Pontifical Inst. Medieval History, 1961, D Medieval Studies, 1972; D honoris causa, Pontifical Inst., 1994. Lectr. history Calif. Inst. Tech., Pasadena, 1962-63, prof. history, 1979-87, Edie and Lou Wasserman prof. history, 1987—; rsch. fellow Rsch. Sch. Social Sci., Australian Nat. U., 1963-65, fellow, 1965-68; assoc. prof. UCLA, 1969-72, prof., 1972-79; vis. fellow Cambridge U., 1976, 81; sr. rsch. fellow Hungtington Libr., 1986—; cons. Huntington Libr., 1980-82. Author: Lordship and Community: Battle Abbey and Its Banlieu, 1066-1538, 1974; editor: The Chronicle of Battle Abbey, 1980; co-editor: Accounts of the Cellarers of Battle Abbey, 1967,

Predatory Kinship and the Creation of Norman Power, 840-1066, 1988; contbr. articles to profl. jours. Fellow Royal Hist. Soc., Royal Soc. Antiquaries of London; mem. Am. Hist. Soc., Medieval Acad. Am. (pres. 1985-86), Econ. History Soc., Am. Soc. Legal History, Haskins Soc. (bd. dirs. 1982—, pres. 1990-96). Office: Calif Inst Tech Dept History Pasadena CA 91125

SEARLES, ANNA MAE HOWARD, educator, civic worker; b. Osage Nation Indian Terr., Okla., Nov. 22, 1906; d. Frank David and Clara (Bowman) Howard; A.A., Odessa (Tex.) Coll., 1961; BA, U. Ark., 1964; M.Ed., 1970; postgrad. (Herman L. Donovan fellow), U. Ky., 1972—; m. Isaac Adams Searles, May 26, 1933; 1 dau., Mary Ann Rogers (Mrs. Herman Lloyd Hoppe). Compiler news, broadcaster sta. KJBC, 1950-60; corr. Tulsa Daily World, 1961-64; tchr. Rogers (Ark.) H.S., 1964-72; tchr. adult class rapid reading, 1965, 80; tchr. adult edn. Learning Center Benton County (Ark.), Bentonville, 1973-77, supr. adult edn., 1977-79; tchr. North Ark. C.C., Rogers, 1979-90, CETA, Bentonville, 1979-82; tchr. Joint Tng. Partnership Act, 1984-85; coordinator adult edn. Rogers C. of C. and Rogers Sch. System, 1984—. Sec. Tulsa Safety Council, 1935-37; leader, bd. dirs. Girl Scouts U.S.A., Kilgore, Tex., 1941-44, leader, Midland, Tex., 1944-52, counselor, 1950-61; exec. sec. Midland Community Chest, 1955-60; gray lady Midland A.R.C., 1958-59; organizer Midland YMCA, Salvation Army; dir. women's div. Savings Bond Program, Midland; mem. citizens com. Rogers Hough Meml. Library, women's aux. Rogers Meml. Hosp.; vol. tutor Laubach literacy orgn., 1973—; sec. Beaver Lake Literacy Council, Rogers, 1973-83, Little Flock Planning Commn., 1975-77, Benton County Hist. Soc., 1981—; pub. relations chmn. South Central region Nat. Affiliation for Literacy Advance, 1977-79; bd. dirs. Globe Theatre, Odessa, Tex., Midland Community Theatre, Tri-County Foster Home, Guadalupe, Midland youth centers, DeZavala Day Nursery, PTA, Adult Devel. Center, Rogers CETA, 1979-81; vol. recorder Ark. Hist. Preservation Program, 1984—; docent Rogers Hist. Mus., 1988—. Recipient Nice People award Rogers C. of C., 1987, Thanks badge Midland Girl Scout Assn., 1948, Appreciation Plaque award Ark. Natural Heritage Commn., 1988; Cert. of recognition, Rogers Pub. Schs., 1986, Cert. of Recognition, Beaver Lake Literacy Coun., 1993; Instr. of Yr. award North Ark. Community Coll. West Campus, Conservation award Woodmen of the World Life Ins. Soc., 1991, Vol. of Yr. award Rogers Hist. Mus., 1993. Mem. NEA (del. conv. 1965), Ark. Assn. Public Continuing and Adult Edn. (pres. 1979-80), South Central Assn. for Lifelong Learning (sec. 1980-84), PTA (life), Future Homemakers Am. (life; sec. 1980—), Delta Kappa Gamma (Disting. Acheivement award Beta Pi chpt. 1992). Episcopalian. Clubs: Altrusa (pres. 1979—), Apple Spur Community (Rogers), Garden Club Rogers (publicity chmn. 1994-95, garden therapy 1994-96). Home: 2808 N Dixieland PO Box 03319400 Rogers AR 72756

SEARLS, EILEEN HAUGHEY, lawyer, librarian, educator; b. Madison, Wis., Apr. 27, 1925; d. Edward M. and Anna Mary (Haughey) S.; BA, U. Wis., 1948, JD, 1950, MS in Libr. Sci., 1951. Bar: Wis. 1950. Cataloger Yale U., 1951-52; instr. law St. Louis U., 1952-53, asst. prof., 1953-56, asso. prof., 1956-64, prof., 1964—, law librarian, 1952—; chair Coun. Law Libr. Consortia, 1984-90; sec. Bd. of Conciliaton and Arbitration, Archdiocese of St. Louis, 1986—. Named Woman of Yr., Women's Commn., St. Louis U., 1986—. Mem. ABA, Am. Lib. Assn., Wis. Bar Assn., Bar Assn. Met. St. Louis, Am. Assn. Law Librs., Mid-Am. Assn. Law Librs. (pres. 1984-86), MALSLC (chair 1980-84), Southwestern Assn. Law Librs., Altrusa Club. Office: 3700 Lindell Blvd Saint Louis MO 63108-3412

SEARS, DONNA MAE, technical writer and illustrator; b. St. Paul, Oct. 23, 1951; d. Raymond and Shirley Marie (Dupre) Waldoch; m. Mark D. Sears, Sept. 4, 1993. BA in Art and Edn., Cardinal Stritch Coll., Milw., 1969-73; postgrad., Rock Valley Coll., Rockford, Ill., 1985, 87, 89-90, So. Ill. U., 1983; cert. of tng., Computervision Tech. Ctr., Itasca, Ill., 1986, 88. Electronic assembler Warner Electric Co., Marengo, Ill., 1973-75, machine hand, 1976-78, quality assurance lead insp., 1978-80, draftswoman, 1980-86, CAD-sr. draftswoman, 1986-87; tchr. art Stephen Mack Sch. Dist., Rockford, 1975, Harrison Sch. Dist., Wonder Lake, Ill., 1975-76; CAD specialist Greenlee Textron Inc., Rockford, 1988-89, resigned, 1989; asst. buyer Ingersoll Milling, Rockford, 1989-90; asst. office mgr. and sign maker Shake-A-Leg Signs, Rockford, 1990-92; tech. writer and illustrator Mathews Co., Crystal Lake, Ill., 1992; tech. writer and CAD support Clinton Electronics, Loves Park, Ill., 1993—. Author: (with others) Treasured Poems of America, 1990, Poetic Voices of America, spring 1992, Anthology of American Poetry, fall 1991 (awards of Poetic Excellence 1992), Distinguished Poets of America, spring 1993, The Sound of Poetry, spring 1993. Vol. Boone County Conservation Dist.; mem. choir St. James Ch., Belvidere, Ill., 1985-93; assoc. mem. Spl. Olympics. Recipient Leadership award YWCA, Rockford, 1988. Mem. Internat. Soc. Poets, Exptl. Aircraft Assn., Nat. Right to Life Assn., Macktown Restoration Found. Roman Catholic.

SEARS, LEAH J., state judge; d. Thomas E. and Onnye J. Sears; married; children: Addison, Brennan. BA, Cornell U.; JD, Emory U.; M in Apellate Jud. Process, U. Va.; JD (hon.), Morehouse Coll., 1993. Judge City Ct. Atlanta; atty. Alston & Bird, Atlanta; trial judge Superior Ct. Fulton County; justice Supreme Ct. Ga., Atlanta. Contbr. articles to profl. jours. Bd. dirs. Sadie G. Mays Nursing Home, Ga. chpt. Nat. Coun. Christians & Jews; mem. adv. bd. United Way Drug Abuse Action Ctr., Outdoor Activity Nature Ctr.; mem. Cornell U. Women's Coun.; mem. steering com. Ga. Women's History Month, Children's Def. Fund Black Cmty. Crusade Children; founder Battered Women's Project, Columbus, Ga. Recipient Outstanding Young Alumna award Emory U., One of 100 Most Influential Georgians Ga. Trend mag., Excellence in Pub. Svc. award Ga. Coalition Black Women, 1992, Outstanding Woman of Achievement YWCA Greater Atlanta, One of Under Forty & On the Fast Track, 1993. Mem. ABA (chair bd. elections), Nat. Assn. Women Judges, Ga. Bar Assn., Women's Forum Ga., Gate City Bar Assn., Atlanta Bar Assn. (past chair jud. sect.), Ga. Assn. Black Women Attys. (founder, pres.), Fourth Tuesday Group, Jack & Jill Am. (Atlanta chpt.), Links Inc. (Atlanta chpt.), Alpha Kappa Alpha. Office: Ga Supreme Ct 244 Washington St SW Atlanta GA 30334*

SEARS, SANDRA LEE, computer consultant; b. Rochester, N.Y., Apr. 25, 1952. AB with distinction, Cornell U., 1974; MA, U. Conn., 1976, postgrad., 1976-81. Cert. in data processing, 1983. Tng. cons. Ins. Crime Prevention Inst., Westport, Conn., 1977-78; systems analyst Data Directions, Bloomfield, Conn., 1978-79; prin. S. S. Prindle Consulting, Manchester, Conn., 1979-81; dir. info. svcs. Conn. Attys. Title Ins., Rocky Hill, Conn., 1981-85; mgr., systems, programming Community Health Care Plan, Inc., Wallingford, Conn., 1985-87; assoc. dir. Mass. Mutual Life Ins., Springfield, Mass., 1987-91; cons. mgr. Coopers & Lybrand Cons., East Hartford, Conn., 1991—; dir. info. architecture and data warehousing CIGNA Healthcare, Bloomfield, Conn., 1996—; adj. faculty U. New Haven, West Haven, Conn., 1976-77, Eastern Conn. State U., Willimantic, 1986—, Manchester Community Coll., 1989—; participant Tex. Instruments' Case Satellite Seminar, 1989. Mentor Career Beginnings, Hartford, 1991—. Presdl. scholar Nat. Merit Program, 1970, William Stout scholar Cornell U., 1973, AAUW fellow U. Conn., 1981. Mem. Cornell Club of Greater Hartford (mem. admissons vol. programs alumni adv. com., exec. bd., book award chair 1987—), Cornell Alumni Admissions Amb. Network (chair 1983-86), Mortar Board, Phi Kappa Phi, Pi Mu Epsilon. Office: Coopers & Lybrand LLP 333 E River Dr East Hartford CT 06108-4201

SEASHORE, MARGRETTA REED, physician; b. Red Bank, N.J., June 20, 1939; d. Robert Clark Reed and Lillie Ann (Heaviland) R.; m. John Seashore, Dec. 26, 1964; children: Robert H., Carl J., Carolyn L. BA, Swarthmore Coll., 1961; MD, Yale U., 1965. Diplomate Am. Bd. Pediatrics, Am. Bd. Med. Genetics, Nat. Bd. Med. Examiners. Intern in pediatrics Yale U. Sch. Medicine, Haven, Conn., 1965-66, asst. resident in pediatrics, 1966-68; postdoctoral fellow in genetics and metabolism, depts. of pediatrics and medicine Yale U. Sch. Medicine, 1968-70; clin. asst. prof. pediatrics U. Fla. Coll. Medicine, Gainesville, 1970-71; attending physician Hope Haven Children's Hosp., Jacksonville, Fla., 1970-73; asst. prof. pediatrics Duval Med. Ctr., Jacksonville, Fla., 1970-71; attending physician Duvall Med. Ctr. U. Hosp. Jacksonville, 1970-73; asst. prof. pediatrics U. Fla. Coll. Medicine, 1971-73; attending physician Shands Teaching Hosp., Gainesville, Fla., 1971-73; asst. clin. prof. human genetics and pediatrics Yale U. Sch. Medicine, 1974-78; attending physician Yale-New Haven Hosp., 1974—; cons. physician Bridgeport (Conn.) Hosp., 1974—; attending physician Danbury (Conn.) Hosp., 1977—; dir. Genetic Consultation Svc. Yale-New Haven Hosp., 1977-86; from asst. prof. to assoc. prof. human genetics and pediatrics Yale U. Sch. Medicine, 1978-90; cons. physician Lawrence and Meml. Hosp., New London, Conn., 1979—, Norwalk (Conn.) Hosp., 1981—; dir. Genetic Consultation Svc. Yale-New Haven Hosp., 1989—; prof. genetics and pediatrics Yale U. Sch. Medicine, 1990—. Contbr. chpts. to books. Fellow Am. Acad. Pediatrics (chair com. on genetics 1990-94, mem. screening com. Conn. chpt. 1977—, mem. genetics com. 1989—), Am. Coll. Med. Genetics (founder, mem. screeing subcom. 1993—); mem. AMA, AAAS, Am. Soc. Human Genetics (mem. genetic svcs. com. 1986-91), Soc. Inherited Metabolic Disorders (bd. dirs. 1989—, sec. 1991-96, pres.-elect 1996), Soc. for Study of Inborn Errors of Metabolism, New Eng. Genetics Group (co-dir. 1992-95, chmn. outreach com. 1979-89, chmn. screening com. 1989-93, mem. steering com. 1979—). Office: Yale U Sch Med Dept Genetics 333 Cedar St New Haven CT 06510-3206

SEASTRAND, ANDREA H., congresswoman; b. Chgo., Aug. 5, 1941; m. Eric Seastrand (dec.); children: Kurt, Heidi. BA in Edn., DePaul U., 1963. Prof. religion U. Santa Barbara; mem. Calif. Assembly, 1990-94, U.S. Ho. of Reps., 1995—; asst. Rep. leader; mem. Rep. caucus; mem. edn. com., agr. com., consumer protection com., new tech. com., govtl. efficiency com., and ways and means com.; mem. rural caucus and select com. on marine resources. Mem. Calif. Fedn. Rep. Women (past pres.). Office: US Ho of Reps 1216 Longworth HOB Washington DC 20515-0522*

SEATON, ALBERTA JONES, biologist, consultant; b. Houston, Dec. 31, 1924; d. Charles Alexander and Elizabeth (Polk) Jones; m. Earle Edward Seaton, Dec. 24, 1947 (dec. Aug. 1992); children: Elizabeth Wamboi, Dudley Charles. BS in Zoology and Chemistry, Howard U., 1946, MS in Zoology, 1947; DSc in Zoology, U. Brussels, 1949. Asst. prof. Spelman Coll., Atlanta, 1953-54; assoc. prof. biology Tex. So. U., Houston, 1954-60, prof. biology, 1960-72, 91-95; adminstr. Ministry Edn., Bermuda, 1973-76; lectr. biology Bermuda Coll., Devonshire, 1976-78; prof. anatomy Sch. Allied Health U. Tex. Health Ctr., Houston, 1979-80; cons. sci. sect. Nat. Inst. Pedagogy Ministry of Edn. Sci., Victoria, Seychelles, 1980-89; head dept. biology Wiley Coll., Marshall, Tex., 1950-51; dir. NSF Summer Sci. Inst. Tex. So. U., 1957-59, gen. studies program, 1970-72, undergrad. and grad. rsch. in biology, 1954-72; mem. Univ. Honors Program Com., Tex. So. U., 1960-70; chair self-study com., Tex. So. U., 1969-71, ednl. policies com., 1968-72; lectr. biology U. Md., USN Air Sta., Bermuda, 1972-78; supr. adminstrn. and budget Office of the Minister Ministry Edn., Bermuda, 1973-76; lectr. in field. Author, editor: Conserving the Environment, Part 1, 1984; editor: Reprints of Agrinews, 1982; co-author, co-editor: Conserving the Environment, Part 2, The Seychelles, 1986, Conserving the Environment, Part 3, Focus on Aldabva, 1991; contbr. articles to profl. jours. Evaluator grant proposals NSF, 1957-72; active regional meetings Com. on Undergrad. Edn. in Biol. Sci., 1967-72, AAC-AAUP confs. on curriculum improvement, 1970-72; chair nurses licensing bd., Hamilton, Bermuda, 1973-75; mem. Endangered Species Com., Hamilton, 1974-77. Postdoctoral fellow Calif. Inst. Tech., Pasadena, 1959-60, NSF postdoctoral fellow Roscoe B. Jackson Lab., Bar Harbor, Maine, 1959, U. Brussels, 1965-66. Mem. AAAS, AAUP (apptd. to ad hoc coms. 1968-71, sec.-treas. Tex. State Conf. 1968-70), AAUW, Am. Assn. Zoologists, Assn. des Anatomistes, Assn. Women in Sci., Tex. Acad. Sci., Beta Kappa Chi, Beta Beta Beta. Episcopalian. Home and Office: 3821 Gertin St Houston TX 77004

SEATON, SANDRA JEANNE, women's health nurse; b. St. Louis, Apr. 29, 1945; d. Lloyd Otto Hampe and Yvonne Jacqueline (Wagenbach) Reiner; m. Francis Bruce Seaton, Jan. 30, 1971; children: Theresa, Kyle. BA, Webster U., 1968; MA, St. Louis U., 1972; ADN, SUNY, Albany, 1980; BSN, Barry U., 1993. RN, Fla., cert. inpatient obstet. nurse, profl. healthcare quality, instr. neonatal resuscitation providers, cardiopulmonary resuscitation and emergency cardiac care instr. Staff nurse Baptist Hosp. of Miami, 1979-91, nurse clinician, 1991—, care coord., clinician Mother/Baby Unit, 1994—; expert witness Cohen, Berke, Bernstein, Brodie, Kondell & Laslo, P.A., Miami, 1993. Deacon Pinecrest Presbyn. Ch., Miami, 1990-93; mem. Bapt. Hosp. Environ. Task Force, Miami, 1990-94. Mem. AWHONN, Nat. Assn. Healthcare Quality, Dade Assn. for Healthcare Quality, South Fla. Perinatal Network, Macrobiotic Found. of Fla., Sigma Theta Tau Internat. Office: Bapt Hosp of Miami 8900 N Kendall Dr Miami FL 33176-2118

SEATS, PEGGY CHISOLM, marketing executive; b. Lisman, Ala., Oct. 12, 1951; d. William H. and Bernice (Berry) Chisolm; m. Melvin Seats (div.). BA in Communications cum laude, Lewis U., 1974; grad. cert. in event mgmt., George Washington U., 1995; postgrad., Am. U., 1996—. Account exec. Globe Broadcasting, Chgo., 1976-78, Merrill Lynch, Chgo., 1978-79, Transp. Displays, Inc., Chgo., 1979-81; with Reverie, Inc., 1981—; nat. accounts mgr. Soft Sheen Products Co., Chgo., 1981-83; mktg. cons. Reverie, Inc., Chgo., 1983-85; pres., mktg. cons. Reverie, Inc., Washington, 1987—; pub. rels., mktg. mgr. Proctor & Gardner Advt., Chgo., 1985-86; dir. pub. rels., mktg. Morris Brown Coll., Atlanta, 1986-87; mgr. mktg. Howard U. Press, Washington, 1989-90; cons. White House Initiative on Historically Black Colls., Univs., 1990-92; founder Black Pub. Rels. Soc., Atlanta, 1987. Contbr. numerous articles to newspapers and mags. Bd. dirs Lewis U. Alumni, Ill., 1979; state advisor U.S. Congl. Adv. Bd., Ill. 1982. Recipient Kizzie award Black Women Hall of Fame, Chgo., 1981, Svc. award Nat. Assn. Women in Media, Chgo., 1982; inductee Outstanding Women of Am., 1975, 87. Mem. Internat. Platform Assn., Internat. Assn. Bus. Communicators, Internat. Spl. Events Soc., Pub. Rels. Soc. Am., Black Pub. Rels. Soc. (Atlanta chpt. pres. emeritus), Nat. Assn. Market Developers, World Affairs Coun. Democrat. Baptist. Home: 2020 Pennsylvania Ave NW Washington DC 20006-1846 Office: 1825 Eye St NW #400 Washington DC 20006

SEAVEY, ARLINE JOYCE, educator; b. Old Town, Maine, Nov. 25, 1941; d. Richard Brown and Bernice Irene (Littlefield) Cousins; m. Richard E. Snowden, July 24, 1965 (div.); m. Wayne L. Seavey, July 8, 1979; children: Barbara, Mark, Kathryn, Douglas. Student, Maine Med. Sch. Nursing, 1960-61; BS in Edn., U. Maine, 1965; postgrad., U. N.H., 1971-72, Antioch Coll., 1991-94. Tchr. 4th grade Wentworth Dennett Sch., Kittery, Maine, 1965-67, tchr. 2d grade, 1967-68; beauty cons. Mary Kay, Austin, Tex., 1970-71; tchr. day care Cmty. Day Care Ctr., Portsmouth, N.H., 1972-73, dir. Latch Key Ctr., 1973-74; tchr. jr. high sch. English Greenland Ctrl. Sch., N.H., 1974-91, tchr. 3d grade, 1991—; coach Odysey of the Mind, Greenland, 1982-92, judge state competitions, 1992-96; mem. staff devel. com., Greenland, 1974-81, pres. 1980. Treas. Assn. Coastal Tchrs., 1976-86. Mem. ASCD, NEA (grievance chair), Greenland Tchrs. Asns. (v.p. 1987-90), ADK Hon. Tchrs. Sorority (Theta Theta pres. 1980-81, 96—). Office: Greenland Ctrl Sch 70 Post Rd Greenland NH 03840-2312

SEAVY, MARY ETHEL INGLE, art educator; b. Alpena, S.D., Mar. 23, 1910; d. James Albert and Mollie (Ceny) Ingle; m. Donald Lee Seavy, Mar. 19, 1940; 1 child, Judith Ann. BS, No. State Tchrs. Coll., Aberdeen, S.D., 1934; MA in Art, U. Iowa, 1937, postgrad., 1949-53; postgrad., Columbia U., 1940. Cert. permanent profl. tchr., Iowa. Art coord. pub. schs., Decorah, Iowa, 1937-38, Waterloo, Iowa, 1938-40, Whiting, Ind., 1940-41; instr. art Luther Coll., Decorah, 1942-43, U. Iowa, Iowa City, 1945-47; tchr. Solon (Iowa) Elem. Sch., 1949-53; art coord. Mil. Sch., Aschaffenburg, Fed. Republic Germany, 1962-64; tchr. Iowa City Pub. Schs., 1965-75; artist, tchr. Stauffenburg Studio, Marengo, Iowa, 1987-90. One-woman show Hawkeye State Bank, Coralville, Iowa, 1987; exhibited in group shows State Fair, Des Moines, 1989, Cmty. Theatre, 1990, Heart Ctr. for Arts, Cedar Falls, 1992, Fern Hill Gallery, 1992, Dubuque (Iowa) Art Show, 1993, Iowa City Art Ctr., 1994, Hawkeye State Bank, 1994, art show, Iowa City, 1994, Cedar Rapids Art Show, 1994. Recipient award for short story State Federated Women's Club, 1987, 90, award for essay, 1987, 90, 1st place award for short story, 1996; 1st place print award, 2d place oil award State Regional Art Show, Dubuque, 1994, 2d place award, Cedar Rapids, 1994; Mil. Edn. Achievement award, 1994; 1st and 2d oil and watercolor awards Iowa Artists State Regional Ar t Show, 1995; 2d place watercolor award Federated Woman's Art Club Show, Des Moines, 1995, 96; named to Internat. Profl. and Bus. Women's Hall of Fame, 1994. Mem. AAUW, DAR (past regent Iowa City), Iowa Watercolor Soc., Iowa City Women's Club, Order Ea. Star, Order White Shrine of Jerusalem (past worth high priestess), Order of Amaranth, Delta Kappa Gamma, Zeta Tau Alpha (v.p. Alpha Omicron chpt. 1970-71). Christian Scientist. Home and Studio: 534 Clark St Iowa City IA 52240-5616

SEAWRIGHT, GAYE LYNN, education consultant; b. San Angelo, Tex., Dec. 20, 1958; d. Denson Woodrow and Eddie Carolyn (Dusek) Henry; m. Jimmy Don Seawright, Aug. 17, 1980; children: John Weston, Emily Kaye. BS in Poultry Sci., Tex. A&M U., 1981; MEd in Edn. Adminstrn., East Tex. State U., 1995. Cert. tchr. secondary biology, English. With Security State Bank, Pecos, Tex., 1976-77; bookkeeper Lowake (Tex.) Gin, 1978; cashier, pharmacy asst. K-Mart, College Station, Tex., 1980-81; sec./land title rsch. asst. Bosque Title Co., Meridian, Tex., 1981-82; cake decorator/instr. Lagniappe Bakery, M.J. Designs, DeSoto, Duncanville, Tex., 1987-88; tchr. sci. Red Oak (Tex.) Ind. Sch. Dist., 1988-93; poultry sci. instr. Cedar Valley Coll., Lancaster, Tex., 1989; outside sci. cons. Region 10 Edn. Svc. Ctr., Richardson, Tex., 1990-93, edn. cons., 1993—. Commr. Tex. Animal Health Commn., Austin, 1988-95; mem. Ellis County 4-H youth adv. bd. Ellis County Ext. Svc., Waxahachie, Tex., 1990-94; dir. youth poultry show Ctrl. Tex. Youth Fair, Clifton, 1981-83; adv. bd. Garland (Tex.) Ind. Sch. Dist. Single Parent Program, 1993-96; adv. bd., coord. 21st Century Work Study Program, Celina, Tex., 1993-96; Johnson County campaign chmn. Gov. Bill Clements Campaign, Cleburne, Tex., 1985-86; DeSoto campaign chmn. George Bush campaign, 1988; del. Rep. Senatorial Dist. Meeting, Duncanville, 1988; del., nominee for state officer Rep. State Conv., Houston, 1988. Recipient Cert. of Appreciation, Operation We Care, Mayor Bruce Todd, Austin, 1995, 96; Tex. Edn. Agy. grantee, 1994, 95. Mem. AAUW, ASCD, NAFE, Sigma Tau Delta. Republican. Presbyterian. Home: Rte 1 Box AA 161 Stephenville TX 76401 Office: Region 10 Edn Svc Ctr 400 E Spring Valley Rd Richardson TX 75083

SEBA, KATE PROCTOR GRANT, legal assistant, paralegal; b. Portland, Maine, Nov. 23, 1965; d. Edward Donald Jr. and Lydia (Smith) Grant; m. David Andrew Seba, Jan. 18, 1992; children: Emily Lee Dutton, Sophie Maria Grant. Student, La. State U., 1983-88. Legal asst., paralegal Byron Magbee, Baton Rouge, 1984-89; office mgr., legal asst., paralegal Brook, Pizza & Van Loon, L.L.P., Baton Rouge, 1989—. Republican. Episcopalian. Home: 16803 Ft Pulaski Ave Baton Rouge LA 70817

SEBANZ, VICTORIA JEAN, dance educator, artist; b. Milw., Dec. 24, 1957; d. Robert Joseph and Elaine Iris (Ignera) Sebanz; m. Mark David Sturwold, June 30, 1979 (div. Aug. 1986); 1 child, Jenifer Leigh Sturwold. BA in Art and Theater Arts, Calif. State U., L.A., 1992, MA in Interdisciplinary Arts Edn., 1996. Asst. dance tchr. Calif. State U., L.A., 1990-91; art specialist Alhambra Sch. Dist., Calif., 1990-93, East L.A. Coll., 1991-95; fin. aid cons. Talent Search, L.A., 1993; dance/arts educator 32d St Magnet Visual, Performing Arts, L.A., 1994—; fitness cons. Orange County, 1986-91. Activist Native Am. issues, 1977—. Mem. NOW, Calif. Dance Educator's Assn., Sierra Club. Home: 3334 N Campus Ave Claremont CA 91711

SEBASTIAN, DEBORAH KAY, secondary school educator; b. Mt. Pleasant, Mich., Jan. 30, 1950; d. Wesley J. and Joan K. (Bowne) Smith; m. David A. Sebastian, July 8, 1972; children: Rebecca, Matthew. BS in Edn., Ctrl. Mich. U., 1971; MS in Edn., Fresno Pacific Coll., 1989. Cert. tchr., journalism educator, Calif. Market rschr. Brown Shoe Co., St. Louis, 1972-73; math. tchr. Edgewood Ind. Sch. Dist., San Antonio, 1973-74; sec. St. Louis Art Mus., 1974-75; freelance photographer, writer Chowchilla (Calif.) News, 1978-83; coop. presch. dir. Trinity Luth. Ch., Chowchilla, 1979-83; reporter, photographer Sierra Star, Oakhurst, Calif., 1984-85; math. and journalism tchr. Madera (Calif.) H.S., 1985-91, mentor tchr., 1990-91; math. and journalism tchr. Yosemite H.S., Oakhurst, 1991—; project participiant San Joaquin Valley Math. Project, 1993; presenter Calif. Math. Coun., Fresno, 1994. Presch. tchr. Oakhurst Luth. Ch., 1984—. Mem. Western Assn. Schs. and Colls. (visitation com. 1990—), Nat. Coun. Tchrs. Math., Calif. Math. Coun. (no. sect.), Journalism Edn. Assn. (5-Yr. award 1991), Journalism Edn. Assn. No. Calif. Home: 51617 Coyote Ridge Rd Oakhurst CA 93644-9624 Office: Yosemite HS 50200 Road 427 Oakhurst CA 93644-9506

SEBASTIAN, SANDRA MARY THOMPSON, mental health counselor, social worker; b. Moncton, Can., June 14, 1943; came to U.S., 1965; d. Alan G. E. Thompson and Jean Glenn Hyde Thompson Hart; m. John Francis Sebastian, Jr., Aug. 12, 1967; children: Byron David, Colin Alan. Diploma, Queen Elizabeth's Coll., Surrey, Eng., 1962, Morley Coll, London, 1965; BA in Sociology, Miami U., 1986; MS in Mental Health Counseling, Wright State U., 1995. Rsch. sec. St. Thomas' Hosp. Med. Sch., London, 1962-65; prodn. editor Ency. Britannica, Chgo., 1966-67; sec. Miami U., Oxford, Ohio, 1980-86; social worker Butler CY.CSB, Hamilton, Ohio, 1987-95, Family Preservation, 1992-95; mental health counselor, child/adolescent therapist Hamilton Counseling Ctr., 1995—; Spkr. in field. Apptd. commr. on volunteerism State Ohio, 1986-87; mem. Conflict Resolution Svcs., 1991—, Oxford Citizens for Peace & Justice, 1988—, Butler County AIDS Task Force, 1990; v.p. McGuffey Sch. PTA, Oxford, 1978. Mem. ACA, Am. Mental Health Counselors Assn., Internat. Assn. Play Therapy, NAACP (Oxford chpt.), UN Assn. USA, Miami U. Women's Club (v.p. 1980), Sigma Chi Iota. Democrat. Unitarian. Home: 220 McKee Ave Oxford OH 45056 Office: Hamilton Counseling Ctr 111 Buckeye St Hamilton OH 45011

SEBELA, VICKI D., association executive, freelance writer; b. Des Plaines, Ill., Mar. 7, 1964; d. James Edward and Mary Nell (Davis) S.; m. Julius Michael Colangelo, Oct. 8, 1988. AA, AS, Harper Coll., 1984; BS, Roosevelt U., 1986; student, Inst. Orgnl. Mgmt., Boulder, Colo., 1991-93. Adminstrv. asst. McDonald's Corp., Rolling Meadows, Ill., 1979-83; info. specialist William Rainey Harper Coll., Palatine, Ill., 1983-84; teller Arlington Fed. Savs. and Loan, Arlington Heights, Ill., 1984-85; asst. to the pres. Ill. Women's Agenda, Chgo., 1984-85; student outreach coord. William Rainey Harper Coll., Palatine, 1985-86; adminstrv. asst. women's affairs Office of the Gov., Chgo., 1986-88; exec. adminstr. Social Engring. Assocs., Inc., Chgo., 1988-89; exec. dir. Greater Wheaton (Ill.) C. of C., 1989-94; internat. conf. dir. Environ. Planning Group, Barrington, Ill., 1994-95; pres. SEBCO Enterprises, Wheaton, Ill., 1995—; freelance writer, 1996—; founder Wheaton Womens Bus. Coun., Greater Wheaton Cycle Classic; freelance writer, Wheaton, Ill., 1996—. Columnist Daily Herald, 1992—; corr. Wheaton Leader, Warrenville Post, Winfield Estate, 1996—; contbr. articles to Ency. Brit. Cert. paraprofl. Talk Line/Kids Line Crisis Hot Line, Elk Grove Village, Ill., 1983; plan commr. City of Wheaton, 1994—, vice chair plan commn., 1995, chair, 1996—; mem. Wheaton History Ctr., chair Silver and Gold Ball Auction, 1995, publicity coord. Heritage Tour, 1996. Harper Coll. scholar, 1982, Roosevelt U. scholar, 1984. Mem. APA, Chgo. Women in Govt. Rels. (membership chair, bd. dirs. 1988-89), Women's Opportunity Internat., Greater Wheaton C. of C. (hon. life, chair clubs and orgn. autumnfest 1995), South Wheaton Bus. Assn., Phi Theta Kappa. Republican.

SEBELIUS, KATHLEEN GILLIGAN, state representitive; b. Cin., May 15, 1948; d. John J. and Mary K. (Dixon) Gilligan; m. Keith Gary Sebelius, 1974; children: Edward Keith, John McCall. BA, Trinity Coll., 1970; MA, U. Kans., 1977. Dir. planning Ctr. for Cmty. Justice, Washington, 1971-74; spl. asst. Kans. Dept. Corrections, Topeka, 1975-78; mem. Kans. Ho. of Reps., 1987-95. Founder Women's Polit. Caucus; mem. Friends of Cedar Crest, Florence Crittendon Svcs.; precinct committeewoman, 1980-86; mayor-elect, Potwin, 1985-87; exec. com. NAIC, Kans. Health Care Commn. Mem. Common Cause (state bd., nat. gov. bd. 1975-81), Kans. Trial Lawyers Assn. (dir. 1978-86). Democrat. Roman Catholic. Home: 224 SW Greenwood Ave Topeka KS 66606-1228

SEBRING, MARJORIE MARIE ALLISON, former home furnishings company executive; Burnsville, N.C., Oct. 8, 1926; d. James William and Mary Will (Ramsey) Allison Shockey; student Mars Hill Coll., 1943, Home Decorators Sch. Design, N.Y.C., 1948, Wayne State U., 1953; cert. home furnishings rep. U. Va., 1982; 1 child, Patricia Louise Banner Krohn. Dir. decorating div. Robinson Furniture, Detroit, 1949-57; head buyer Tyner Hi-Way House, Ypsilanti, Mich., 1957-63; head buyer Town and Country, Dearborn, Mich., 1963-66; instr. Nat. Carpet Inst., 1963-71; owner Adams House, Inc., Plymouth, Mich., 1966-72; exec. v.p. mktg. and sales, regional sales and mktg. mgr. Triangle Industries, L.A., 1972-89; co-owner Markham-

Sebring, Inc., St. Petersburg, Fla., 1983-89; dir. contract div. Kane Furniture, 1984-85; co-owner Accessories, Etc., 1985-89; chmn. bd. Heritage Lakes, U.S. Home. Vol. coord. Pasco County Clerk Ct., Suncoast Theatre; mem adv. bd. Webster Coll; charter mem. Presdl. Task Force; pres. Presbyn. Ch. Seven Springs; bd. dirs. Fla. Health and Human Svc.; chmn. bd. dirs. Two Westminster Condominium Assn., Inc. Recipient nat. sales awards, recognition for work with youth and aged; named to Fla. Finest list by Fla. Gov., 1994. Mem. Internat. Home Furnishings Assn., Fla. Home Furnishings Rep. Assn. (officer), Am. Security Coun. (coun.), Williamsburg Found., USCG Aux., Nat. Audubon Soc., Internat. Platform Assn. Republican. Contbr. creative display to Better Homes and Gardens, 1957-64. Home: 4902 Cathedral Ct New Port Richey FL 34655-1486

SEBRING, PATRICIA LOUISE, scientist, administrator; b. N.Y., Oct. 3, 1956; d. Ray McCarty and Louise Arlene (Bender) S. BA, Wilkes Coll., 1978; MS, East Stroudsburg State U., 1981. Environ. compliance coord. Bechtel Power Corp., Berwick, Pa., 1981-84; safety engr. Dynamac Corp., Rockville, Md., 1984; exec. dir. Susquehanna-Wyoming Counties Solid Waste Authority, Tunkhannock, Pa., 1985-88; bus. devel. rep. Bechtel Civil, Inc., Vienna, Va., 1988-89; supr. pubs. Bechtel Power Corp., Gaithersburg, Md., 1989-94; bus. devel. rep. Bechtel Power Corp., 1994—; strategic planning coord. Grace United Meth. Ch., Gaithersburg, Md., 1995-96. Adult ministries coord., 1994-96, strategic planning chairperson, 1996—, Grace United Meth. Ch., Gaithersburg, Md., 1994-95. Mem. Nat. Mgmt. Assn. (chmn. bd. dirs. 1993-95). Methodist. Office: Bechtel Power Corp 9801 Washingtonian Blvd Gaithersburg MD 20878-5355

SECOR, ELIZABETH KAPLAN, public information specialist; b. N.Y.C., Apr. 24, 1936; d. Theodore and Alma (Denenholz) Kaplan; m. Robert Miller Secor, June 3, 1956 (div.); children: Anne Deborah, Richard Alan; m. James Bayly Woy, Aug. 7, 1987; stepchildren: Patricia Ruth Woy West, Susan Woy Moore, Jeffrey Bayly Woy. BA, Bryn Mawr (Pa.) Coll. Pub. rels. dir. Greater Wilmington Devel. Coun., 1971-82; dir. spl. assignment Media Ctr. for Sch Desegregation, Wilmington, 1978; pub. rels. mgr. Kent Gen. Hosp., Dover, Del., 1982-85; dir. state commn. gov.'s commn. on health care costs State of Del., 1985-88, dir. publ. info. dept. of health and social svcs., 1988; assoc. dir of pub. rels. Mercy Cath. Med. Ctr., Darby, Pa., 1988; assoc. dir. pub. rels. Moss Rehab. Hosp., Phila., 1989; info./devel. officer Monell Chem. Senses Ctr., Phila., 1990—. Editl bd. Bryn Mawr Coll. Alumni Bull., 1996. Bd. dirs. LWV, Greater Wilmington, 1961-88. Recipient Silver Anvil Pub. Rels. Soc. Am., 1979. Mem. Nat. Soc. of Fund Raising Execs. (various coms.). Home: 1420 Locust St 13-K Academy House Philadelphia PA 19102 Office: Monell Chem Senses Ctr 3500 Market St Philadelphia PA 19104

SEDDON, JOHANNA MARGARET, ophthalmologist, epidemiologist; b. Pitts.; m. Ralph Hingson, 1974. BS, U. Pitts., 1970, MD, 1974; MS in Epidemiology, Harvard U., 1976. Intern Framingham (Mass.) Union Hosp., 1974-75; resident Tufts New Eng. Med. Ctr., Boston, 1976-80; fellow ophthalmic pathology Mass. Eye and Ear Infirmary, Boston, 1980-81, clin. fellow vitreoretinal Retina Svc., 1981-82; instr. clin. ophthalmology Harvard Med. Sch., Boston, 1982-84, asst. prof., asst. surgeon ophthalmolgy, 1984, assoc. prof., 1989—; assoc. surgeon, dir. ultrasound svc. Mass. Eye and Ear Infirmary, Boston, 1989—, orgn. epidemiology rsch. unit, 1984-85, dir. epidemiology unit, 1985—, surgeon in ophthalmology, 1992—; assoc. prof. faculty dept. epidemiology Harvard Sch. Pub. Health, Boston, 1992—; mem. com. vision Commn Behavioral and Social Scis. and Edn., NRC, NAS, Washington, 1984; mem. divsn. rsch. grants NIH, 1987-89, 94—; mem. sci. adv. bd. Found. for Fighting Blindness, 1985—, Mecular Internat., 1994—. Author books and articles in field; mem. editl. staff ophthalmic jours. Recipient NIH Nat. Svc. Rsch. awards, 1975, 80-81, Lewis R. Wasserman merit award from rsch. to prevent blindness for contbns. to ophthalmic rsch., 1996; grantee, prin. investigator Nat. Eye Inst., 1984-96, Nat. Cancer Inst., 1986; med. sch. scholar, 1970-74, Henry H. Clark Med. Edn. Found. scholar, 1973. Mem. AMA, APHA, Am. Acad. Ophthalmology (Honor award 1990), Am. Med. Women's Assn., Assn. Rsch. in Vision and Ophthalmology (elected, chair epidemiology sect. 1990, trustee clin. vision epidemiology sect. 1992—), Soc. Epidemiologic Rsch., New Eng. Ophthal. Soc., Am. Coll. Epidemiology, Retina Soc., Macula Soc. Home: 4 Louisburg Sq Boston MA 02108-1203

SEDGWICK, KYRA, actress; b. N.Y.C., Aug. 19, 1965; m. Kevin Bacon; 1 child, Travis. Appeared in off-Broadway prodns. Time Was, 1981, Dakota's Belly Wyoming, 1989; stage appearances in Ah Wilderness!, 1988 (Theatre World award), Maids of Honor, 1990, Oleanna, 1994; TV appearances include (miniseries) Family Pictures, 1983, (spls.) ABC Afternoon Spls., 1985, Am. Playhouse, 1987, 88, (TV movies) The Man Who Broke 1,000 Chains, 1987, Women & Men II, 1991, Hallmark Hall of Fame, 1992 (Golden Globe award nomination 1993), (series) Another World, 1981; film appearances include War and Love, 1985, Tai-Pan, 1986, Kansas, 1988, Born on the Fourth of July, 1989, Mr. and Mrs. Bridge, 1990, Pyrates, 1991, Singles, 1992, Heart and Souls, 1993. Office: care InH Creative Mgmt 8942 Wilshire Blvd Beverly Hills CA 90211*

SEDGWICK, SALLY STOWELL, philosophy educator; b. L.A., Sept. 14, 1956; d. Robert Post Sedgwick and Catherine Park (Stowell) Sedgwick Peppard; m. George Stephen Boolos, Jan. 23, 1996. BA in Philosophy, U. Calif., Santa Cruz, 1978; PhD, U. Chgo., 1985. Asst. prof. philosophy Dartmouth Coll., Hanover, N.H., 1985-91, assoc. prof., 1991—; vis. assoc. prof. U. Pa., Phila., 1992, Harvard U., Cambridge, Mass., 1996-97; rev. panelist Applications for Univ. Teaching Fellowships NEH, Washington, 1996. Contbr. articles to profl. jours.; mem. adv. bd. Jour. Hegel Soc. N.Am., 1994—. Rsch. fellow Alexander von Humboldt Stiftung, 1990, 97; conf. grantee NEH, 1996, summer rsch. grantee DAAD, 1987. Mem. AAUW, Am. Philos. Assn., Hegel Soc. N.Am., N.Am. Kant Soc., Kant Gesellschaft a.v. Bonn. Office: Dartmouth Coll Dept Philosophy 6035 Thorton Hall Hanover NH 03755

SEDLACEK, EVELYN ANN, library developer; b. Mpls., Sept. 18, 1919; d. Guy Galen and Eleanor Rose (Stein) Harper; m. James Arthur Sedlacek, June 6, 1945; children: Judith, Joan, Karen. BS, U. Nebr., Omaha, 1973, MS, 1981. Rsch. libr. Joslyn Art Mus., Omaha, 1974-75; law libr. Smith, Peterson Law Firm, Council Bluffs, Iowa, 1977-84; libr. developer Papio Natural Resources Devel., Omaha, 1977-81; pres. BHS and Assocs., Omaha, 1982—. Bd. dirs. Etc. Camp Fire Girls, Omaha, 1955-76; mem. Omaha Opera, 1959—; mem. coms. Omaha Symphony Guild, 1946-49; sewing com. Omaha Home for Girls, 1958-66; sorting com. KVNO Radio Sta., U. Nebr., St. Robert's Elem. Sch.; vol. archival/photography dept. Western Heritage Mus. Omaha History Mus., Joslyn Art Mus.; sorting com. Friends of Omaha Pub. Libr., bd. dirs., 1995—. Recipient Vol. of Yr. award Friends of the Omaha Pub. Libr., 1994. Mem. AAUW, Omaha History Mus., Nebr. Libr. Assn., Mountain Plains Libr. Assn., Civil War Round Table of Omaha, Daus. of Union Vets. of Civil War 1861-1865, Phi Alpha Theta (history hon.), Kappa Delta Pi (edn. hon.), Phi Delta Gamma. Home: 8628 Broadmoor Dr Omaha NE 68114-4243

SEDLAK, VALERIE FRANCES, English language educator, university administrator; b. Balt., Mar. 11, 1934; d. Julian Joseph and Eleanor Eva (Pilot) Sedlak; 1 child, Barry. AB in English, Coll. Notre Dame, Balt., 1955; MA, U. Hawaii, 1962; PhD, U. Pa., 1992. Grad. teaching fellow East-West Cultural Ctr. U. Hawaii, 1959-60; adminstrv. asst. Korean Consul Gen., 1959-60; tchr. Boyertown (Pa.) Sr. High Sch., 1961-63; asst. prof. English U. Balt., 1963-69; assoc. prof. Morgan State U., Balt., 1970—, asst. dean Coll. Arts and Scis., 1995—, sec. to faculty, 1981-83, faculty research scholar, 1982-83, 92-93, communications officer, 1989-90, dir. writing for TV program, 1990—; cons. scholar Md. Humanities Coun., 1992—. Author poetry and lit. criticism; asst. editor Middle Atlantic Writer's Assn. Rev., 1989—; assoc. editor Md. English Jour., 1994—, Morgan Jour. Undergrad. Rsch., 1995—. Coord. Young Reps., Berks County, Pa., 1962-63; chmn. Md. Young Reps., 1964; election judge Baltimore County, Md., 1964-66; regional capt. Am. Cancer Soc., 1978-79; mem. adv. bd. Md. Our Md. Anniversary, 1984, The Living Constitution: Bicentennial of the Fed. Constitution, 1987. Fellow Morgan-Penn Faculty, 1977-79, Nat. Endowment Humanities, 1984; named Outstanding Teaching Prof., U. Balt. Coll. Liberal Arts, 1965, Outstanding Teaching Prof. English, Morgan State U., 1987. Mem. MLA, South Atlantic MLA, Coll. Lang. Assn., Coll. English Assn. (v.p. Mid-Atlantic Group 1987-90, pres. 1990-92, exec. bd. 1992—), Women's Caucus for Modern Langs., Md. Coun. Tchrs. English, Md. Poetry and Lit. Soc., Md. Assn. Depts. English (bd. dirs. 1992—), Mid. Atlantic Writers' Assn. (founding mem. 1981, asst. editor Mid. Atlantic Writers' Assn. Rev. 1989—), Delta Sigma Epsilon (v.p. 1992-94, pres. 1994-96). Roman Catholic. Home: 102 Gorsuch Rd Lutherville Timonium MD 21093-4318 Office: Morgan State U Coll Arts & Scis Dean Baltimore MD 21239

SEE, SAW-TEEN, structural engineer; b. Georgetown, Penang, Malaysia, Mar. 23, 1954; came to U.S., 1974; d. Hock-Eng and Ewe-See (Lim) S.; m. Leslie Earl Robertson, Aug. 11, 1982; 1 child, Karla Mei. BSc in Civil Engring., Cornell U., 1977, M in Civil Engring., 1978. Registered profl. engr., N.Y., Calif., Conn., Fla., Md., N.J., Ohio, Pa., Wash. Design engr. Leslie E. Robertson Assocs., N.Y.C., 1978-81, assoc., 1981-85, ptnr., 1986—, mng. ptnr., 1990—; profl. cons. M of Engring. class Cornell U., 1994-95; project dir., project mgr. Shinji Shumeikai Mus., Kyoto, Japan, West Side H.S., N.Y.C., Jr. H.S. 234, Bklyn., Jewelry Trade Ctr., Bangkok, Bilbao (Spain) Emblematic bldgs., Internat. Trade Ctr., Barcelona, Spain, Seattle Art Mus., San Jose (Calif.) Convention Ctr., San Jose Arena; project dir. Balt. Conv. Ctr., Rock 'N Roll Hall of Fame and Mus., Cleve., Pontiac Marina Hotel and Retail, Singapore, acad. bldgs. and greenhouse, SUNY, Binghamton, N.Y.; project mgr. Coll. of Law bldg. U. Iowa, Iowa City, Neiman-Marcus store, San Francisco, AT&T Exhbn. bldg., N.Y.C., Bank of China Tower, Hong Kong, PPG Hdqs., Pitts., AT&T Corp. Hdqs., N.Y.C. Contbr. articles to profl. jours. Named to Those Who Made Marks in the Constrn. Industry in 1988, Engring. News Record, N.Y.C., 1989. Mem. ASCE, Archtl. League, Coun. on Tall Bldgs. and Urban Habitat (past chairperson com. on gravity loads and temperature effects 1982-85), Architects, Designers, Planners for Social Responsiblity, N.Y. Assn. Cons. Engrs. (dir. 1989-93, structural codes com. 1991—). Home: 45 E 89th St Apt 25C New York NY 10128-1230 Office: Leslie E Robertson Assocs 211 E 46th St New York NY 10017-2935

SEEBACH, LYDIA MARIE, physician; b. Red Wing, Minn., Nov. 9, 1920; d. John Henry and Marie (Gleusen) S.; m. Keith Edward Wentz, Oct. 16, 1959; children: Brooke Marie, Scott. BS, U. Minn., 1942, MB, 1943, MD, 1944, MS in Medicine, 1951. Diplomate Am. Bd. Internal Medicine. Intern Kings County Hosp., Bklyn., 1944; fellow Mayo Found., Rochester, Minn., 1945-51; pvt. practice Oakland, Calif., 1952-60, San Francisco, 1961—; asst. clin. prof. U. Calif., San Francisco, 1981—; mem., vice chmn. Arthritis Clinic, Presbyn. Hosp., San Francisco, 1961-88, pharmacy com., 1963-78; chief St. Mary's Hosp. Arthritis Clinic, San Francisco, 1968-72; exec. bd. Pacific Med. Ctr., San Francisco, 1974-76. Contbr. articles to med. jours. Fellow ACP; mem. AMA, Am. Med. Womens Assn. (pres. Calif. chpt. 1968-70), Am. Rheumatism Assn., Am. Soc. Internal Medicine, Pan Am. Med. Womens Assn. (treas.), Calif. Acad. Medicine, Calif. Soc. Internal Medicine, Calif. Med. Assn., San Francisco Med. Soc., San Francisco Med. Assn., San Francisco Soc. Internal Medicine, No. Calif. Rheumatism Assn., Internat. Med. Women's Assn., Mayo Alumni (bd. dirs. 1983-89), Iota Sigma Pi. Republican. Lutheran. Office: 490 Post St Ste 939 San Francisco CA 94102-1410

SEEBERT, KATHLEEN ANNE, international sales and marketing director; b. Chgo.; d. Harold Earl and Marie Anne (Lowery) S. BS, U. Dayton, 1971, MA, U. Notre Dame, 1976; MM, Northwestern U., 1983. Registered commodity rep. Publs. editor ContiCommodity Services, Inc., Chgo., 1977-79, supr. mktg., 1979-82; dir. mktg. MidAm. Commodity Exchange, 1982-85; internat. trade cons. to Govt. of Ont., Can., 1985-90; dir. mktg. and program devel. Internat. Orientation Resources. 1990-94; v.p. Am. Internat. Group, 1995—. guest lectr. U. Dayton, U. Notre Dame, Northwestern U., Kellogg Alumni Chgo., French-Am. C. of C., Internat. Employee Relocation Coun., Soc. Intercultural Educators, Trainers and Researchers, Am. Soc. Tng. and Devel., Ill. CPA Soc., SBA, KPMG Peat Marwick, Price Waterhouse, Arthur Andersen, Coopers & Lybrand, Nat. Fgn. Trade Coun., William M. Mercer, Inc., Minn. Employee Relocation Coun., MRA, CRC, Chgo. Relocation Coun., Ky. Relocation Coun., Mpls. Employee Relocation Coun., Chgo.-Midwest Credit Mgmt. Assn. Mem. Futures Industry Assn. Am. (treas.), Greater Cin. C. of C., Notre Dame Club Chgo., Kellogg Mgmt. Club Chgo. Republican. Roman Catholic. Office: 500 W Madison St Ste 1000 Chicago IL 60611

SEEBRUCK, NANCY JEAN, reading and mathematics educator; b. Mauston, Wis., Sept. 30, 1965; d. Marvin Martin and Ruth Mildred (Gantner) Jensen; m. Michael Charles Seebruck, May 2, 1987; children: Michael Marvin, Samantha Jean. Assoc. in Med. Asst., Western Wis. Tech. Coll., 1985; BS, U. Wis., Stevens Point, 1990, Cert. Reading, 1995. Cert. med. asst. Tchr. EKW Sch. Dist., Elroy, Wis., 1993—; 7th grade boys basketball coach EKW Schs., 1993—. Mem. Wis. Edn. Assn. Coun. Home: W6403 23d St West Necedah WI 54646 Office: EKW Schs PO Box A Elroy WI 53929

SEEFELDT, GENEVIEVE MARIE, elementary education educator, music educator; b. La Crosse, Wis., Sept. 25, 1947; d. Walter and Anne (Staron) Bania; m. David C. Seefeldt, Aug. 22, 1970. BA in Vocal Performance, St. Norbert Coll., 1970; BA in Elem. and Secondary Vocal Edn., Lakeland Coll., 1974; BA in Spl. Edn., Cardinal Stritch Coll., 1993; MAT, Aurora U., 1996. Cert. educator K-12 vocal music, spl. edn. vocal music K-12, Wis. Music educator Christ Child Acad., Sheboygan, Wis., 1970-92, Holy Name of Jesus Sch., Sheboygan, Wis., 1970-92, St. Dominic Sch., Sheboygan, Wis., 1970-92, Sheboygan (Wis.) Area Sch. Dist., 1992—; tchr. pvt piano lessons, Plymouth, Wis., 1970—, pvt. voice lessons, Plymouth, 1993—. Named Outstanding Educator, Milw. Archdiocese, 1990. Home: W4872 CTR U Plymouth WI 53073 Office: Sheboygan Area Sch Dist 830 Virginia Ave Sheboygan WI 53081

SEEFER, CAROLYN MARIE, business educator, curriculum developer; b. Rochester, N.Y., Apr. 9, 1962; d. Francis Michael and Joan Louise (Haitz) Brault; m. Christopher Paul Seefer, July 4, 1991; 1 stepchild, Christopher Jacob. BBA in Indsl. Rels., U. Ga., 1984, Cert. in Bus. Edn., 1987, MEd in Bus. Edn., 1990; MBA in Fin. Mgmt., John F. Kennedy U., 1996. Cert. secondary edn. tchr., bus. edn. tchr., adult edn. tchr. Personnel adminstr. U. Ga., Athens, 1985-86; substitute tchr. Clarke County Sch. Dist., Athens, 1987-90; edn. dir. Interactive Learning Systems, Athens, 1987-90; corp. trainer Martinez (Calif.) Unified Sch. Dist., 1990-91; tchr. Ctr. for Employment Tng., San Francisco, 1991; tchr., curriculum developer Heald Bus. Coll., Concord, Calif., 1991-96; instr. Diablo Valley Coll., Pleasant Hill, Calif., 1996—; cons. Holton & Assocs., Ltd., Walnut Creek, Calif., 1992-95, SRD Assocs., Walnut Creek, 1993-95, Fitzpatrick and Assocs., Walnut Creek, 1993-95; curriculum advisor Heald Bus. Coll., Concord, 1993-96. Vol. Ga. Spl. Olympics, Athens, 1987. Mem. NEA, ASCD, ASTD, NAFE, Nat. Bus. Edn. Assn., Alpha Omicron Pi (historian 1980-84, pledge advisor 1984-85, fin. advisor 1985-87), Commonwealth Club Calif., Kappa Delta Pi, Delta Pi Epsilon (sec. 1989-90). Republican. Roman Catholic. Home: 574 Cesar Ct Walnut Creek CA 94598-2229 Office: Diablo Valley Coll Bus Divsn 321 Golf Club Rd Pleasant Hill CA 94523

SEEGER, LEINAALA ROBINSON, law librarian, educator; b. Wailuku, Hawaii, July 2, 1944; d. John Adam and Anna Hiilani (Leong) Robinson; 1 child, Maile Lea. BA, U. Wash., 1966; JD, U. Puget Sound, 1977; M in Law Librarianship, U. Wash., 1979. Bar: Wash. 1977. Reference librarian U. Puget Sound Sch. Law., Tacoma, 1977-79, assoc. law librarian, 1981-86; asst. librarian McGeorge Sch. Law, U. of Pacific, Sacramento, 1979-81; assoc. librarian pub. svc. Harvard Law Sch., Cambridge, Mass., 1986-89; dir. law library, assoc. prof. law U. Idaho Coll. Law, Moscow, 1989—; bd. dirs. Inlan, Spokane, Wash., 1989—. Mem. Palouse Asian-Ams. Assn., Moscow, 1989—. Mem. Wash. STate Bar Assn., Am. Assn. Law Librs. (chmn. minority com. 1990-91, v.p., pres.-elect Western Pacific chpt. 1985-86, 90-91, pres. 1991-92, vice chmn. edn. com. 1991-92, chmn. 1992-93), Idaho Coun. Acad. Librs. Office: U Idaho Coll Laws Moscow ID 83844-2324

SEEGER, PEGGY, musician, singer, songwriter; b. N.Y.C., June 17, 1935; d. Charles Louis and Ruth Porter (Crawford) S.; m. Ewan MacColl, Jan. 25, 1977 (dec. Oct. 1989); children: Neill, Calum, Kitty. Attended, Radcliffe Coll., 1953-55. Dir. Ewan MacColl, Ltd., London, 1959—. Co-author: Travellers Songs of England and Scotland, 1977, Till Doomsday in the Afternoon, 1986; 17 solo albums, 120 shared albums. Office: 520 S Clinton Oak Park IL 60304

SEEGER, SONDRA JOAN, artist; b. L.A., May 27, 1942; d. Reinhold Josheph and Bertha Catherine (Monese) S.; m. Richard John Pahl, Aug. 18, 1961 (div. 1974); children: Catherine Marie, Douglas Richard, Angela Gay, Susan Joan; m. David Ernest Matteson, Apr. 25, 1990. Student, Marylhurst Coll., 1960. Pvt. practice musician various locations, 1973-81; security guard MGM Hotel, Las Vegas, 1981-82; real estate salesperson Century 21, Kent, Wash., 1983-85; mgr. Viera Land & Cattle, Inc., La Grande, Oreg., 1984-92; freelance artist, Casper, Wyo., 1991—; ptnr. Old West Saddle Shop, Casper, 1989-93, Casper, Wyo., 1993—; com. mem. Oreg. State Forest Practices Com., N.E. Region, 1990-91. Named Union Co. Tree Farmer of Yr., Am. Tree Farm System, 1987. Mem. NRA, Nat. Soc. Artists, Women Artists of the West, Allied Artists, Cider Painters of Am., Australian Soc. of Miniature Art, Small Woodlands Assn., Knickerbocker Artists (assoc.), United Pastelists of Am. (signature), Nat. Soc. Artists (signature), Women Artists of the West, Pacific Art League, The Art League of Alexandria, Va., Miniature Art Soc. Fla., Oil Painters Am., Wyo. Artists Assn., Cody Country Art Guild, Am. Soc. Classical Realism, Gen. Artist Mem., Internat. Platform Assn., Oreg. Forest Resources Inst., Am. Artists' Profl. League. Republican. Home and Office: Old West Saddle Shop PO Box 4300 Casper WY 82604-0300

SEEGERS, LORI C., lawyer; b. Miami Beach, Fla., June 17, 1955. BA cum laude, U. Pa., 1977; JD, Fordham U., 1982. Bar: N.Y. 1983, U.S. Dist. Ct. (so. dist.) N.Y. 1983. Ptnr. Anderson, Kill, Olick & Oshinsky, P.C., N.Y.C. Contbr. articles to profl. jours. Mem. ABA, N.Y. State Bar Assn. (sect. banking, corp. and bus. law), Assn. of Bar of City of N.Y. Office: Anderson Kill Olick & Oshinsky PC 1251 Avenue of the Americas New York NY 10020-1182*

SEEKINS, SHARON EILEEN, city official; b. Phoenix, Nov. 19, 1953; d. Donald Frederick and Virginia Lee (Greenwood) Witt; m. David Lester Seekins, Jan. 15, 1972; 1 child, Brian William. BA in Mgmt., U. Phoenix, 1996. Cert. profl. pub. purchasing officer Univ. Pub. Purchasing Cert. Coun. Underwriting clk. Gt. S.W. Fire Ins. Co., Mesa, Ariz., 1973-74; purchasing clk. City of Mesa, 1974-76, purchasing asst., 1976-79, purchasing supr., 1979-82, purchasing adminstr., 1982—; mem. purchasing rev. bd. State of Ariz., Phoenix, 1978-80; mem. buy recycled taask force U.S. Conf. Mayors, Washington, 1990-92. Mem. Nat. Inst. Govt. Purchasing (bd. dirs. 1990—, pres. 1996, Pub. Purchasing Mgr. of Yr. award 1989), Nat. Assn. Purchasing Mgmt. (cert. purchasing mgr.), Optimists (treas., v.p. Mesa 1990-93). Republican. Methodist. Office: City of Mesa PO Box 1466 Mesa AZ 85211

SEELBACH, ANNE ELIZABETH, artist; b. Detroit, July 27, 1944; d. William Otto and Elizabeth (Simonds) S. BA, NYU, 1967; MFA, CUNY, 1985. Curator Monhegan (Maine) Mus., 1992—; art instr. The Victor d'Amico Inst. of Art, Napeague, N.Y., 1994—, Arts Pro Tem, Hancock, N.H., 1991—. One-woman shows include Tower Gallery, Southampton, N.Y., 1981, Newark (N.J.) Mus., 1984, Tower Gallery, N.Y.C., 1985, The Conn. Gallery, Marlborough, 1989, Bunting Inst. of Radcliffe Coll., Cambridge, Mass., 1990, Frick Gallery, Belfast, Maine, Simmons Coll., Boston, 1991, The Painting Ctr., N.Y.C., 1994, Kouros Gallery, N.Y.C., 1996; group shows include Kommunale Galerie, Berlin, 1987, Frauenmuseum, Bonn, Germany, 1988, Northeastern U., Boston, 1990, Fed. Res. Bank, Boston, 1995, Kouros Gallery, 1995—, Met. Mus. and Art Ctr., Coral Gables, Fla., others; represented in permanent collections at Newark Mus., Frauenmuseum, Bonn, Centrum Frans Masereel, Kasterlee, Belgium, Bunting Inst. of Radcliffe Coll., Simmon Coll., Prudential Ins. Co., Newark, Continental Grain Corp., N.Y.C., Phoenix Mut. Life Ins. Co., Hartford, Conn., The Hillier Group, Princeton, N.J. Recipient painting fellowship Bunting Inst., Radcliffe Coll., 1989-90, artist fellowship Triangle Artists' Workshop, Pine Plains, N.Y., 1988, MacDowell Colony, Peterborough, N.H., 1987. Mem. Coll. Art Assn., Soc. of Bunting Fellows.

SEELER, RUTH ANDREA, pediatrician, educator; b. N.Y.C., June 13, 1936; d. Thomas and Olivia (Patten) S. BA, U. Vt., 1959, MD, 1962. Diplomate Am. Bd. Pediatrics, Am. Bd. Pediatric Hematology/Oncology. Intern Bronx (N.Y.) Mcpl. Hosp., 1962-65; pediats. hematology/oncology fellow U. Ill., 1965-67; dir. pediatric hematology/oncology Cook County Hosp., 1967-84; prof. pediatrics, dir. pediatric edn. coll. medicine U. Ill., Chgo., 1984—; assoc. chief pediatrics Michael Reese Hosp., Chgo., 1990—; course coord. pediatrics Nat. Coll. Advanced Med. Edn., Chgo., 1987—; mem. subboard Pediatric Hematology/Oncology, Chapel Hill, 1990-95. Mem. editl. bd. Am. Jour. Pediatric Hematology/Oncology, 1985-95. Jr. and sr. warden, treas. Ch. Our Saviour, Chgo., 1970-92; founder camp for hemophiliacs Hemophilia Found., Ill., 1973—, current med. dir.; pres. Hemophilia Found. Ill., 1981-85. Mem. Gamma Phi Beta Found. (trustee 1994—), Phi Beta Kappa. Office: Michael Reese Hosp Dept Pediat 2929 S Ellis Ave Chicago IL 60616-3302

SEELHAMMER, CYNTHIA MAE, town manager; b. Fargo, N.D., Oct. 29, 1957; d. John Robert and Betty Jane (Brausen) S.; m. Barry Minett Robinson, May 31, 1980 (div. 1983); m. Douglas Lynn Myrland, Oct. 19, 1984 (div. 1994). Student Kerevan Yhteskoulu, Kerava, Finland, 1975-76; BA in English, St. Cloud State U., 1976-80; MPub. Adminstrn. Golden Gate U., 1987; postgrad. Hamline U., 1989—, Mich. State U., 1992. Editor Sherburne County Hist. Soc., Becker, Minn., 1978-80; assoc. editor SCS Chronicle, St. Cloud, Minn., 1979-80; reporter Chandler Arizonan, Ariz, 1980-81; coord. pub. rels. Bashas' Markets, Inc., Chandler, 1981-84; owner, mgr. Seelhammer Pub. Rels., 1984—; pub. info. specialist City Mesa, Ariz., 1984-88; asst. to Library dir. for fiscal and personnel mgmt., City of Mesa, 1988-89; asst. to mayor City of St. Paul, 1989; mgmt. analyst City Mgr.'s Office, La Mesa, Calif., 1991-94; town mgr. Town of Queen Creek, Ariz., 1994—. Author feature stories for papers, mags., 1980—. Editor: The Growth of Sherburne County, 1980, The St. Paul Experiment: Initiatives of the Latimer Adminstrn., 1989; editor short story in fiction mag., 1996 . Chmn. Chandler Neighborhood Coun., 1981-82; exec. bd. dirs. Chandler Boys and Girls Club of the East Valley, 1985; judge for Ariz. Tchr. Yr. awards, 1984, 85. Recipient Best Editorial award Minn. Newspaper Assn., 1980; MECCA fellow U. Denver, 1980. Mem. LVW, Internat. Assn. Bus. Communicators, Soc. Profl. Journalists (Best Editorial award Region 6 1980), Ariz. Press Women (v.p. pub. rels. 1981-82, Best Feature award 1980), Internat. City Mgrs. Assn. (scholarship to Montreal conf.1987), Internat. Visitors Coun. San Diego, Ariz. Fed. Credit Union (mem. supr. com. 1987-89), Minn. Assn. Urban Mgmt. Assts. (chair bylaws com. 1990), Internat. Assn. City Mgmt., Toastmasters (CTM 1989), Soroptimists (officer Mesa chpt. 1985, 86, 87, pres. 1988), Minn. Internat. Ctr. Avocations: gourmet cooking, gardening, travel, horseback riding. Office: Town of Queen Creek 22350 S Ellsworth Rd Queen Creek AZ 85242

SEELIN, JUDITH LEE, rehabilitation specialist; b. Bklyn., Feb. 22, 1941; d. Sidney and Helene Agnes (Minkowitz) S.; m. Mel Schwartz, Sept. 30, 1965 (div. 1983); children: Jeffrey, Robin; m. Arnold Seelin, Oct. 16, 1983. AAS, SUNY, Farmingdale, 1972; BSN, SUNY, Stony Brook, 1973. CRRN, CIRS, CCM. Staff nurse surg. unit L.I. Jewish Med. Ctr., New Hyde Park, N.Y., 1962-67; DON Home Health Aids, Inc., Hempstead, N.Y., 1973-78, Able Home Health Care, Wantagh, N.Y., 1978-84; nursing adminstr. Aides at Home, Inc., Hicksville, N.Y., 1984-86; asst. ADON Savana Cay Manor, Port Saint Lucie, Fla., 1986; Fla. state supr. CCM, Hollywood, Fla., 1987-93; med. team leader Resource Opportunities, Fort Lauderdale, Fla., 1993-95; ind. med. case mgr., 1993-95; W.C. resource nurse Humana Health Care Plan, Mirama, Fla., 1995—; spkr. Am. Inst. Med. Law; adv. bd. mem. Whithal, Boca Raton. Mem. AARN, CMSA. Home: 14090 Fair Isle Dr Delray Beach FL 33446-3395

SEELY, ELLEN WELLS, endocrinologist; b. N.Y.C., Sept. 25, 1955; d. Robert Daniel and Marcia (Wells) S.; m. Jonathan David Strongin, June 11, 1983; children: Jessica, Matthew. BA magna cum laude, Brown U., 1977; MD, Columbia U., 1981. Diplomate Am. Bd. Internal Medicine, Endocrinology and Metabolism. Residency internal medicine Brigham & Women Hosp., Boston, 1981-84, fellow in endocrinology, 1984-87; rsch. fellow medicine Harvard U., Boston, 1984-87; dir. clin. rsch. endocrine hypertension divsn. Brigham & Women's Hosp., Boston, 1987—, dir. and assoc. program dir. ambulatory clin. rsch. ctr., 1995—; instr. medicine Harvard

Medical Sch., Boston, 1987-91; asst. prof. medicine Harvard Med. Sch., Boston, 1991-95; assoc. physician Brigham & Women's Hosp., 1987-95, physician, 1996—; assoc. physician Beth Israel Hosp., Boston, 1988—; med. internship selection com. Brigham and Women's Hosp., 1983-94, co-dir. endocrinology fellowship tng. program, 1993-95, dir. Pregnancy-Related Endocrine and Hypertensive Disorders Clinic, 1988—; coord. Diabetes and Pregnancy Clinic, 1988—, coord. osteoporosis program Harvard Pilgrim Health Plan, Boston, 1995—. Contbr. articles to profl. jours. Capps scholar in diabetes Harvard Med. Sch., 1994-96. Mem. ADA, Endocrine Soc., Am. Fedn. Clin. Rsch., Internat. Soc. Study of Hypertension in Pregnancy, Coun. for High Blood Pressure Rsch., Am. Heart Assn., Sigma Si. Office: Brigham & Women's Hosp 221 Longwood Ave Boston MA 02115-5817

SEFCHEK, KATHY ANN, government official; b. N.Y.C., Dec. 3, 1948; d. Henry Francis and Emily Madeleine (Finck) Meier; children: Brett Alexander, Miles Garrett. BA, Queens Coll., 1979. Supr. claims dept. Travelers Ins. Co., Mineola, N.Y., 1968-72; exec. sec. to pres. Nassau County P.B.A., Mineola, 1972-85; exec. sec. to county exec. Nassau County Dept. Labor, Mineola, 1985-94, asst. to dir., 1994—. Vol. Com. to Re-Elect, Merrick, N.Y., 1986—. Mem. Women's Sports Found. (hon.), United Way Found. (dept. rep. 1994—). Republican. Roman Catholic. Office: 1 West St Mineola NY 11501-4813

SEFER, JOYCE WILLIAMS, speech pathologist; b. Mpls., Feb. 8, 1924; d. Joseph Grant and Inez (Warren) Williams; m. Norman Roy Sefer, Aug. 26, 1950; children: Susan Ann Sefer Liebert, Laurel Mary Sefer Anderson. BS, U. Minn., 1948, MA, 1965. Clin. speech pathologist Aphasia Clinic Mpls. VA Hosp., 1962-70, acting dir., 1970; assoc. ctr. for rsch. in learning U. Minn., Mpls., 1981-83; chief speech pathologist St. Mary's Hosp. and Extended Care Ctr., Mpls., 1973-74; cons. Right to Read Acad. Byers Libr., Denver, 1974-75; mem. faculty U. No. Colo., Denver, 1975-76; acting dir. Alaska Crippled Children and Adults, Fairbanks, 1977-78; aphasiologist Home Health Care Assn., San Antonio, 1979-86; vol., chmn. bd., ednl. cons. Project Learn to Read, San Antonio, 1988—; cons. in aphasia Fairbanks Psychiat. and Psychol. Clinic, 1977; cons., lectr. various ednl. and literacy groups, San Antonio, 1990—; mem. adv. bd. Project Learn to Read, 1995—; guest lectr. Laubach Conf., Ark., 1995. Contbr. articles to profl. jours. and chpts. to books. Active in local lobbying for literacy; del. People to People Amb. Program, Moscow, St. Petersburg, Latvia, 1993. With USCGR, 1945-46. Recipient Vol. award J.C. Penney & Co., 1992. Mem. Laubach Literacy Action, Orton Dyslexia Soc., NOW, Am. Lit. Coun. Home: 6223 Forest Bend San Antonio TX 78240 Office: Project Learn to Read Bazan Libr 1800 W Commerce San Antonio TX 78204

SEGA, DENISE ANNE, language professional educator English; b. Pitts., Dec. 21, 1970; d. Robert A. and Suzanne A. (Kaminski) S. BS in Edn., Slippery Rock (Pa.) U., 1993; postgrad., Northeastern U. cert. instr., Pa. English tchr. New Brighton (Pa.) Area Sch. Dist., 1993—. Recipient Nat. Collegiate Edn. award USAA, 1993, U.S. Achievement Acad. All Am. Scholar, 1993. Mem. NEA, Nat. Coun. of Tchrs. of English, Internat. Reading Assn., Pa. State Edn. Assn. Home: 846 Thorn St Apt 70 Sewickley PA 15143

SEGAL, BARBARA JEANNE, sculptor, educator; b. Bronxville, N.Y., Jan. 27, 1953; d. Jacques Segal and Suzanne (Friedman) Shepard; m. Steve Mack, Oct. 2, 1983; 1 child, David. Student, Pratt Inst., Bklyn., 1970-72, 96, L'Ecole Nat. Superieure des Beaux-Arts, 1972-74. Tchr., prof. Sch. Visual Arts, N.Y.C., 1990—, Westchester Art Workshop, White Plains, N.Y., 1993—, Nat. Acad. Design, N.Y.C., 1994-95; exec. dir. Art on Main St./Yonkers (N.Y.) Inc., 1995—. Exhibitions include Soho Gallery, N.Y.C., 1985-96, Contemporary Crafts Mus., Portland, Oreg., 1992, Mus. at Fashion Inst., N.Y.C., 1994, Westchester County Ctr., White Plains, N.Y., 1994, Art on Main St./Yonkers Inc., 1995; dir., participating artist (documentary) The Stone Symposium, 1996. Home: 88 Alta Ave Yonkers NY 10705

SEGAL, DIANE SUSAN, art educator, artist; b. Albany, N.Y., Apr. 16, 1955; d. Emanual Joseph and Bertha (Burrick) Kotlow; m. David D'Anthony, June 6; m. Donald Paul, June 24, 1979; children: Todd Alan, Jenna Lauren. BS in Art Edn., SUNY, Buffalo, 1977; MS, Coll. of St. Rose, Albany, 1988. Cert. tchr. K-12, N.Y. Art tchr. St. Anne Inst., Albany, 1979-86, Vander & Heyden Hall, Troy, N.Y., 1978-79, Bethlehem Cen. H.S., Delmar, N.Y., 1986—; freelance artist, designer, cons., Albany, 1978—. Exhibited in group shows Rensselaer County Coun. for Arts, Troy, N.Y., 1982, Harmanus Bleecker Ctr., Albany, 1985-86, Schnecteday Mus., 1985-86, Ginger Man Restaurant, Albany, 1986-87, Wolfert's Roost Country Club, Albany, 1986-87, Gala Gallery Art Exhbn., Albany, 1986-87, Ann Grey Gallery, Congress Park, Saratoga Springs, N.Y., 1988, Ulster County C.C., Stone Ridge, N.Y., 1990, Style Works Gallery, St. Louis, 1991, New Eng. Quilt Mus. 1st Ann. Quilt Festival, Lowell, Mass., 1992, Thompson Art Prodns., Sacramento, 1993, Internat. Traveling Wearable Art Fashion Show, 1994, Fairfield Processing Corp., 1995, Internat. Quilt Market, Holland, 1995, Rice Gallery, Albany, 1995, Ctr. Galleries, Albany, 1995; works featured in Am. Quilter's Soc. Mag., 1990; artist (book) Creative Silk Painting, 1995. Vol., design chairperson Temple Israel, Albany, 1978—; ADL trainer World of Difference, Albany. S.O.S. Spl. Opportunity stipendee N.Y. Found. for Arts, 1991. Mem. NEA, Am. Quilters Soc. (author), N.Y. State Art Tchrs. Assn., Design Com. (chairperson), Art/Quilt Design and Critique Group (co-chair), Visual Critique Alliance, Designer Crafts Coun. of Schenectady Mus., Am. Crafts Coun., Network for Wearable Arts, Eastcoast Quilters Assn., Internat. Quilt Art Assn. Jewish. Home: 1738 New Scotland Rd Slingerlands NY 12159 Office: Bethlehem Cen H S 600 Delaware Delmar NY 12154

SEGAL, GERALDINE ROSENBAUM, sociologist; b. Phila., Aug. 26, 1908; d. Harry and Mena (Hamburg) Rosenbaum; m. Bernard Gerard Segal, Oct. 22, 1933; children: Loretta Joan Cohen, Richard Murry. BS in Edn., U. Pa., 1930, MA in Human Rels., 1963, PhD in Sociology, 1978; MS in Libr. Sci., Drexel U., 1968; Dr. Letters (Hon.), Franklin & Marshall Coll., 1990. Social worker County Relief Bd., Phila., 1931-35; sociologist, Phila., 1935—; cons. and lectr. in field. Author: In Any Fight Some Fall, 1975; Blacks in the Law, 1983. Bd. dirs. NCCJ, 1937-47, 82—, sec., 1983-91; bd. overseers U. Pa. Sch. Social Work, 1983—; bd. dirs., Juvenile Law Ctr., 1984—; chair Phila. Tutorial Project, 1966-68; 1st v.p. U. Pa. Alumnae Assn., 1967-70. Co-recipient Nat. Neighbors Disting. Leadership in Civil Rights award, 1988; recipient Drum Major award for Human Rights, Phila. Martin Luther King, Jr. Assn. for Nonviolence, 1990, Brotherhood Sisterhood award NCCJ, 1994. Democrat. Jewish. Home: 2401 Pennsylvania Ave Apt 19-C-44 Philadelphia PA 19130-3001

SEGAL, HELENE R., editor; b. L.A., Jan. 31, 1955; d. Alan and Lila E. Segal; m. David Scott Wright, May 6, 1979. Student, Calif. State U., Fullerton, 1973-75; BA in English, U. Calif., Santa Barbara, 1978. Library asst. ABC-CLIO, Santa Barbara, 1979-80, editorial asst., 1980-81, asst. editor, 1981-83; mng. editor ABC POL SCI, ABC-CLIO, Santa Barbara, 1983—. Mem. Am. Polit. Sci. Assn., Current World Leaders (adv. bd. 1989—). Home: 142 La Vista Grande Santa Barbara CA 93103-2817 Office: ABC-CLIO 130 Cremona Dr Santa Barbara CA 93117-3075

SEGAL, JOAN SMYTH, library consultant, business owner; b. Bklyn., Sept. 14, 1930; d. John Patrick and Anna Catherine (Green) Smyth; m. William Segal, June 25, 1955; children: Harold M., Nora A. BA, Douglass Coll., Rutgers U., 1951; MS in LS, Columbia U., 1955; PhD, U. Colo., 1978. Cert. assn. exec., 1988. Librarian, Math Inst., NYU, 1955-58, Western Interstate Commn. for Higher Edn., Boulder, Colo., 1970-76; libr. cons., Boulder, 1976-78; resource sharing program mgr. Bibliog. Ctr. for Rsch., Denver, 1978-80, exec. dir., 1980-84; exec. dir. Assn. of Coll. and Rsch. Librs., ALA, Chgo., 1984-90; assoc. exec. dir. programs ALA, 1990-93; owner Vintage Ventures, 1993—; trainer library automation, group devel., resource sharing; cons. in field. Contbr. articles to profl. publs. Named Colo. Librarian of Yr., Colo. Library Assn., 1984; named to Douglass Soc. Mem. ALA, Spl. Libraries Assn. (chmn. edn. div. 1981-82, pres. Rocky Mountain chpt. 1981-82, 1994—, bd. dirs. 1983-86), OCLC Network Dirs. (chmn. 1983), Mountain Plains Library Assn., Am. Soc. Assn. Execs. Colo. Soc. Assn. Execs.

SEGAL, LINDA GALE, insurance executive; b. Panama City, Fla., Dec. 14, 1947; d. Homer Ford Jr. and Mary Virginia (Phillmon) F. m. Howard Arthur Segal, Dec. 29, 1970; 1 child, David Samuel. Student, Orlando (Fla.) Jr. Coll., 1966-69, Rollins Coll., 1972. Sales asst. Sta. WESH-TV, Orlando, Fla., 1973-76; mktg. coordinator Sta. WFBC-TV, Grenneville, S.C., 1976-77; traffic mgr. STa. WRDW-TV, Augusta, Ga., 1978-80; field underwriter Liberty Life Ins. Co., Greenville, 1980-81; agt. benefits dept. J. Rolfe Davis Ins. Agy., Orlando, 1981-84; sr. market sales rep. Humana, Inc., Orlando, 1984-86; dir. mktg. Nat. Med. Mgmt., Orlando, 1986-87; sr. account exec. Physicians Health Plan Fla., Inc., Tampa, 1987-88, N.E. Fin. Services, Orlando, 1988-89; mktg. mgr. Ins. Mgmt. Svcs., Inc., Greenville, S.C., 1989-90; regional mktg. dir. Horizons Internat. Inc., St. Augustine, Fla., 1991-92; dir. bus. devel. ResCare Home Health, Inc., Jacksonville, Fla., 1992—; pvt. practice ins. cons., Tampa and Orlando, Fla., 1986-89. Mem. Am. Bus. Women's Assn., Nat. Assn. Profl. Saleswomen, Nat. Assn. Health Underwriters, Assn. Life Underwriters, Women Life Underwriters Confedn., Nat. Assn. Securities Dealers (registered rep.). Republican. Club: University (Jacksonville). Office: 4329 Falling Leaf Ct Jacksonville FL 32258

SEGAL, PHYLLIS NICHAMOFF, lawyer, federal agency administrator; b. Bklyn., Apr. 18, 1945; d. Sidney and Theresa Helen (Uroff) Nichamoff; m. Eli J. Segal, June 13, 1965; children—Jonathan, Mora. Student, Brandeis U., 1962-65; B.A., U. Mich., 1966; J.D., Georgetown U., 1973. Bar: N.Y. 1974, U.S. Dist. Ct. (so. and ea dists.) N.Y. 1975, Mass. 1983, U.S. Supreme Ct. 1979. Assoc. Weil, Gotshal and Manges, N.Y.C., 1973-77; legal dir. NOW Legal Def. and Edn. Fund, N.Y.C., 1977-82; gen. counsel, 1986—; now chmn. Fed. Labor Rels. Auth., Washington; gen. counsel Exec. office Transp. and Constrn., Commonwealth of Mass., 1984-86; past dep. Atty. Gen. State of Mass., Boston; adj. asst. prof. law NYU, 1980-82; fellow Bunting Inst. Radcliffe Coll., 1982-83; cons. U.S. Commn. Civil Rights. Mem. Commn. on Party Reform Nat. Democratic Party, 1972-73, mem. Compliance Rev. Commn., 1974-76; mem. adv. bd. Mass. Commn. Against Discrimination, 1983—. Mem. ABA, Fedn. Women Lawyers Jud. Screening Panel, Mass. Bar Assn. Contbr. articles to profl. jours. Home: 314 Dartmouth St Ph Boston MA 02116-1809 Office: Fed Labor Rels Auth 607 14th St NW Washington DC 20424-0001*

SEGAL, RENA BETH, artist; b. New Brunswick, N.J., May 27, 1953; d. George and Helen (Steinberg) S. BFA, Montclair State Coll., 1975; MFA, Rutgers U., 1977. One person shows include Ocean County Coll., Toms River, N.J., 1978, Piscataway (N.J.) Mcpl. Bldg., 1983, Johnson and Johnson, New Brunswick, N.J., 1985, N.J. State Mus., Trenton, 1989, Mystic Knight Gallery, New Brunswick, 1990, Advocate Bldg., Stamford, Conn., 1991; exhibited in group shows Dumont Landis Gallery, New Brunswick, 1981, Sidney Janis Gallery, N.Y.C., 1984, Laforet Mus. Harajunku, Tokyo, 1986, Morris Mus., Morristown, N.J., 1987, Tobia-Krass Gallery, Upper Montclair, N.J., 1988, 89, Hunterdon Art Ctr., Clinton, N.J., 1990, Phoenix Group, Metuchen, N.J., 1993, Sound Shore Gallery, Stamford, Conn., 1994, Williams Gallery, Princeton, N.J., 1995, others; represented in permanent collections Pub. Svc. and Electric, Newark, Pepsico, Purchase, N.Y., Bristol-Meyers Squibb, Lawrenceville, N.J., others. N.J. State Coun. on Arts fellow, 1985.

SEGAL, SABRA LEE, artist, graphic designer, illustrator, educator; b. Boston. Student, Elmira Coll., 1955-57; BFA, Boston U., 1963; MA in Art Edn., U. Wis., 1968, MFA, 1969. Author: (book of poems) All Things Alive, 1968; author of poems; works exhibited in one-woman shows Watermark/Cargo Gallery, Kingston, N.Y., 1991, Woodstock (N.Y.) Artists Assn., Inc., 1992, Cultural Ctr., Stoneridge, N.Y., 1994, Hasbrouck House, Stonebridge, 1994-95; group exhibits include Froebel Gallery, Albany, N.Y., 1994, Donskoj & Co., Kingston, 1994, Watermark/Cargo Gallery, Kingston, 1994, Taliesin Gallery, Red Hook, N.Y., 1995, Park West Gallery, Kingston, 1995, The Group Delamater Conf. Ctr. of the Beekman Arms, Rhinebeck, N.Y., 1995. Lady exercisor, vis. guest Perfo Prodns. N.C., 1993. Home and Studio: PO Box 821 Woodstock NY 12498

SEGEL, KAREN LYNN JOSEPH, lawyer; b. Youngstown, Ohio, Jan. 15, 1947; d. Samuel Dennis and Helen Anita Joseph; m. Alvin Gerald Segel, June 9, 1968 (div. Sept. 1976); 1 child, Adam James. BA in Soviet and East European Studies, Boston U., 1968; JD, Southwestern U., 1975. Bar: U.S. Tax Ct., U.S. Dist. Ct. (cen. dist.) Calif., U.S. Supreme Ct., Calif. Adminstrv. asst. Olds Brunel & Co., N.Y.C., 1968-69, U.S. Banknote Corp., N.Y.C., 1969-70; tax acct. S.N. Chilkov & Co. CPA's, Beverly Hills, Calif., 1971-74; intern Calif. Corps. Commr., 1975; tax. sr. Oppenheim Appel & Dixon CPA's, L.A., 1978, Fox, Westheimer & Co. CPA's, L.A., 1978, Zebrak, Levine & Mepos CPA's, L.A., 1979; ind. cons. acctg., taxation specialist Beverly Hills, 1980—; bd. dirs. World Wide Motion Pictures Corp., L.A. Editorial adv. bd. Am. Biog. Inst. High sch. amb. to Europe People-to-People Orgn., 1963. Named 1991, 93 Woman of Yr., Am. Biog. Inst. Mem. Nat. Assn. Tax Profls., Nat. Assn. Tax Practitioners, Nat. Soc. Tax Profls., Nat. Trust for Hist. Preservation, Am. Mus. Natural History, Calif. State Bar, Winterthur Guild, Women's Inner Circle of Achievement, Consumer Lawyers of L.A., Calif. Young Lawyers Assn., Beverly Hills Bar Assn., Santa Monica Bar Assn., Complex Litigation Inns of Ct.

SEGER, LINDA SUE, script consultant, writer; b. Peshtigo, Wisc., Aug. 27, 1945; d. Linus Vauld and Agnes Katherine Seger; m. Theodore Newton Youngblood, Jr., Aug. 28, 1968 (div. Jan. 1970); m. Peter Hazen LeVAr, April 12, 1987. BA in English, Colo. Coll., Colorado Springs, 1967; MA in theatre arts, Northwestern U., Evanston, 1968; MA in religion and arts, Pacific Sch. of Religion, Berkeley, 1973; ThD in drama and theology, Graduate Theological U., Berkeley, 1976; postgrad., Immaculate Heart Coll. Ctr., L.A., 1996—. Instr. drama Grand Canyon Coll., Phoenix, 1969-71; instr. drama and theology McPherson (Kans.) Coll., 1976-77; instr. drama and humanities LaVerne (Calif.) U., 1977-79; asst. Provisional Theatre, L.A., 1979-80, Tandem/TAT, L.A., 1980-81; story analyst EMI Films, L.A., 1982-83; pvt. practice script cons. L.A., 1981—, pvt. practice lectr., author, 1984—. Author: Making a Good Script Great, 1988, Creating Unforgettable Characters, 1990, The Art of Adaptation, 1992, When Women Call the Shots, 1996; co-author: From Script to Screen, 1994. Mem. NOW, Women in Film, Acad. of TV Arts and Scis., Ind. Feature Project-West. Democrat. Mem. Soc. of Friends. Home and Office: 2038 Louella Ave Venice CA 90291

SEGGEL, HEATHER LYNN, writer, bookseller; b. Santa Monica, Calif., Sept. 22, 1969; d. Albert Charles and Gail Marie (Conway) S. AA in Gen. Studies, Santa Rosa Jr. Coll., 1990; BA in English, Sonoma State U., 1992. Office temporary Remedy-Temp Agy., Santa Rosa, Calif., 1992-94, Manpower Agy., Santa Rosa, Calif., 1992-94; bookseller Copperfield's Books, Sebastopol, Calif., 1994—. Editor, pub. Slumber, 1993-96. Coord., solicitor Teach-In, 1991. Democrat. Home: 3585 Cazadero Hwy Cazadero CA 95421

SEGIL, LARRAINE DIANE, materials company executive; b. Johannesburg, South Africa, July 15, 1948; came to U.S., 1974; d. Jack and Norma Estelle (Cohen) Wolfowitz; m. Clive Melwyn Segil, Mar. 9, 1969; 1 child, James Harris. BA, U. Witwatersrand, South Africa, 1967, BA with honours, 1969; JD, Southwestern U., L.A., 1979; MBA, Pepperdine U., 1985. Bar: Calif. 1979, U.S. Supreme Ct. 1982. Cons. in internat. transactions, L.A., 1976-79; atty. Long & Levit, L.A., 1979-81; chmn., pres. Marina Credit Corp., L.A., 1981-85; pres., chief exec. officer Electronic Space Products Internat., L.A., 1985-87; mng. ptnr. The Lared Group, L.A., 1987—. Bd. govs. Cedars Sinai Med. Ctr., L.A., 1984—; bd. dirs. So. Calif. Tech. Execs. Network, 1984-86. Mem. ABA (chmn. internat. law com. young lawyers div. 1980-84), Internat. Assn. Young Lawyers (exec. coun. 1979-81, coun. internat. law and practice 1983-84), World Tech. Execs. Network (chmn.), Regency Club (house com. 1986). Avocations: piano, horseriding. Office: The Lared Group 1901 Avenue Of The Stars Los Angeles CA 90067-6004

SEGRÈ, NINA, lawyer; b. New Haven, Apr. 4, 1940; d. Victor M. and Naomi (Berlin) Gordon; m. Gino Segrè, Dec. 31, 1962 (div. 1983); children: Katia, Julie, Michele; m. Frank F. Furstenberg, Jr., Feb. 2, 1985; stepchildren: Sarah Furstenberg, Ben Furstenberg. BA, Radcliffe Coll., 1961; MAT, Harvard U., 1963; JD, U. Pa., 1974. Bar: Pa. 1974, U.S. Dist. Ct. (ea. dist.) Pa. 1974. Law clk. U.S. Ct. Appeals (3d cir.), Phila., 1974-75; assoc. Dechert Price & Rhoads, Phila., 1976-83, ptnr., 1983-93; ptnr. Segrè & Senser, P.C., Phila., 1993—; bd. dirs., course preparer, panelist Phila. (Pa.) Bar Edn. Ctr., 1994—. Trustee Radcliffe Coll., Cambridge, Mass., 1991-95, chair fund com., chair program com.; mem. fin. com. Lynn Yeakel for U.S. Senate, Phila., 1992, Lynn Yeakel for Gov. Pa., 1994. Mem. Phila. Bar Assn. (mem. real property sec., mem. exec. bd.), The Harvard-Radcliffe Club (v.p., mem. exec. bd.), College Works (founder). Home: 2316 Delancey Pl Philadelphia PA 19103-6407 Office: Segrè & Senser PC 2 Penn Center Plz Ste 414 Philadelphia PA 19102-1704

SEHRING, HOPE HUTCHISON, library science educator; b. Akron, Ohio; d. Wesley Harold and Jane (Brown) H.; m. Frederick Albert Sehring, July 15, 1978. BS, Slippery Rock U., 1968; MEd, U. Pitts., 1973, MLS, 1984. Cert. instructional media specialist. Reference libr.-intern Carnegie Mellon U., Pitts., 1981; libr. media specialist Gateway Sch. Dist., Monroeville, Pa., 1968—. Contbr. articles to profl. jours. Active Pa. Citizens for Better Libraries. Recipient Gift of Time Tribute Am. Family Inst., 1996; Henry Clay Frick Found. U. of London scholar, 1969, 73. Mem. NEA, ALA, Pa. Sch. Librs. Assn. (treas. 1982-84), Pa. State Edn. Assn., Gateway Edn. Assn., Alpha Xi Delta. Home: RD #2 Box 467 New Alexandria PA 15670 Office: Gateway Sch Dist Mosside Blvd Monroeville PA 15146

SEIBERT, MARGARET ARMBRUST, art historian, educator; b. Cin., Oct. 12, 1945; d. John Jost and Gertrude C. (Pohl) A.; m. Jack Seibert. BS in Advtg. Design, U. Cin., 1967; MA in Art History, Ohio State U., Columbus, 1971, PhD in Art History, 1986. Prof. Columbus (Ohio) Coll. of Art & Design, 1971-95. Contbr. chpt. to book, articles to profl. jours. Office: Columbus Coll Art & Design 107 N 9th St Columbus OH 43215

SEIBERT, MARY LEE, college official; b. Evansville, Ind., Jan. 30, 1942; d. Ernest Hensley and Lillian (Schmadel) S.;. BS, Ind. U., 1963, MS, 1973, EdD, 1979. Cert. med. technologist, med. asst. Lab. supr. Wishard Meml. Hosp., Indpls., 1964-67; chmn. life scis. div. Ind. Vocat. Tech. Coll., Indpls., 1967-73; assoc. prof., program dir. Ind. U. Sch. Medicine, Indpls., 1973-79; assoc. project coordinator Am. Assn. State Colls. and Univs., Washington, 1979-81; dean coll. allied health professions Temple U., Phila., 1981-90; assoc. provost, dean grad. studies Ithaca (N.Y.) Coll., 1990—; vis. prof. U. Tex. Med. Br., Galveston, 1985. Assoc. editor Jour. Med. Tech., 1985-86. Fellow Am. Soc. Allied Health Profls. (hon., chmn. forum on allied health data, rsch. com. 1983-89, bd. dirs. 1990-92, Outstanding Mem. award 1986); mem. Am. Soc. Med. Technologists (profl. affairs com. 1986-89), Am. Assn. Med. Assts. (hon.), Nat. Coun. on Health Professions Edn., Nat. Acad. Scis. (bd. health care svcs. inst. of medicine 1993—), Phi Delta Kappa, Pi Lambda Theta. Republican. Home: 16 Bean Hill Ln Ithaca NY 14850-9750

SEIDEL, DIANNE MARIE, finance executive; b. Reading, Pa., Feb. 1, 1959; d. Frederick Jacob and Claire Marie (Paskey) S. ASBA, Pa. State U., 1986; BA, Alvernia Coll., Reading, Pa., 1988. Office asst. Berks-Lehigh Valley Farm Credit Service, Fogelsville, Pa., 1977-80, sr. office asst., 1980, office supr., 1980-83, office mgr., 1983-86; chief fin. officer, 1986-88; exec. v.p. Keystone Farm Credit ACA, Lancaster, 1989-92, sr. v.p. fin. svcs., CFO, 1992—. Home: 218 Candalwood Ln Exton PA 19341-3023

SEIDEL, JOAN BROUDE, stockbroker, investment advisor; b. Chgo., Aug. 16, 1933; d. Ned and Betty (Treiger) Broude; m. Arnold Seidel, Aug. 18, 1957; children: David, Craig. BA, UCLA, 1954; postgrad., N.Y. Inst. Fin. Registered prin., investment advisor Morton Seidel & Co. Inc., L.A., 1970-74, v.p., 1974-93; pres., 1993—; also bd. dirs. Morton Seidel & Co. Inc., L.A.; instr. UCLA Extension, 1979-84. Treas. City of Beverly Hills, Calif., 1990—, chmn. rent adjustment bd., 1989-90, mem., 1983-89; mem. investment com. YWCA, L.A., 1987—, chmn. bd. dirs., 1989—, treas. Greater L.A., 1992-95; bd. dirs. Discovery Fund for Eye Rsch., L.A., 1987-95. Named Citizen of Yr. Beverly Hills C. of C., 1993. Fellow Assn. for Investment Mgmt. and Rsch.; mem. Nat. Assn. Security Dealers (dist. bus. conduct com. 25 1993-95), L.A. Soc. Fin. Analysts, Orgn. Women Execs., Women in Bus., City Club, Bond Club, Phi Sigma Alpha. Home: 809 N Bedford Dr Beverly Hills CA 90210-3023 Office: Morton Seidel & Co Inc 350 S Figueroa St Ste 499 Los Angeles CA 90071-1203

SEIDELMAN, SUSAN, film director; b. Pa., Dec. 11, 1952. Student, Drexel U., NYU. Dir. films, including: Smithereens, 1982, Desperately Seeking Susan, 1985, Making Mr. Right, 1987, Cookie, 1989, She-Devil, 1990, The Dutch Master (nominee Acad. award in dramatic short category), 1994, The Barefoot Executive, 1995; directorial debut with short film: You Act Like One, Too (Student Film award AMPAS). Office: care Michael Shedler 225 W 34th St Ste 1012 New York NY 10122-0049 also: William Morris Agy 151 El Camino Los Angeles CA 90048

SEIDENBERG, RITA NAGLER, education educator; b. N.Y.C., Mar. 24, 1928; d. Jack and Anna (Weiss) Nagler; m. Irving Seidenberg, Apr. 10, 1949; children: Jack, Melissa Kolodkin. BA, Hunter Coll., 1948; MS, CCNY, 1968; PhD, Fordham U., 1985. Cert. reading tchr., specialist, N.Y. Reading tchr. East Ramapo (N.Y.) Sch. Dist., 1967-68, clinician reading ctr., 1968-83, reading diagnostician, 1983-85, student support specialist, 1985-94; instr. N.Y. State Dept. Edn., 1978; presenter Northeastern Rsch. Assn., 1978, 85, N.Y. State Reading Assn., 1986-94, N.Y. State Reading Assn., 1996; adj. asst. prof. Fordham U. Grad. Sch. Edn., 1986-89, adj. assoc. prof., 1989—. Mem. Internat. Reading Assn., N.Y. State Reading Assn., Phi Delta Kappa, Kappa Delta Pi. Office: Fordham U Grad Sch Edn 113 W 60th St New York NY 10023

SEIDL, JANE PATRICIA, lawyer; b. Stamford, Conn., June 9, 1958; d. Francis Xavier and Frances (Nizolek) S. BA magna cum laude, Boston Coll., 1980; JD, U. Conn., 1985. Bar: Conn. 1985, U.S. Dist. Ct. Conn. 1985. Fin. editor Fin. Acctg. Standards Bd., Stamford, 1980-82; assoc. Schatz & Schatz, Ribicoff & Kotkin, Hartford, Conn., 1985-92; sr. counsel Northeast Utilities, Hartford, Conn., 1992—. Mem. ABA, Conn. Bar Assn., Hartford County Bar Assn., Hartford Assn. Women Attys. (pres. dir 1992—). Office: Northeast Utlities PO Box 270 Hartford CT 06141-0270

SEIDMAN, ELLEN SHAPIRO, lawyer, government official; b. N.Y.C., Mar. 12, 1948; d. Benjamin Harry Shapiro and Edna (Eysen) Stern; m. Walter Becker Slocombe, June 14, 1981; 1 child, Benjamin William. AB, Radcliffe Coll., 1969; JD, Georgetown U., 1974; MBA, George Washington U., 1988. Bar: D.C., 1975. Law clk. U.S. Ct. of Claims, Washington, 1974-75; assoc. Caplin & Drysdale, Washington, 1975-78; atty., advisor U.S. Dept. of Transportation, Washington, 1978-79, dep. asst. gen. counsel, 1979-81; assoc. gen. counsel Chrysler Corp Loan Guaranty Bd., Washington, 1981-84; atty., advisor U.S. Dept. of Treasury, Washington, 1981-86, spl. asst. to the Under Sec. Fin., 1986-87; dir. strategic planning Fed. Nat. Mortgage Assn., Washington, 1987-88, v.p., asst. to chmn., 1988-91, sr. v.p. regulation rsch. and econs., 1991-93; spl. asst. to the pres. for econ. policy The White House, Washington, 1993—. Office: Federal Nat'l Mortgage Assoc 3900 Wisconsin Ave Washington DC 20016

SEIDMAN, MARIAN TAYLOR, adult education educator; b. Montclair, N.J., Oct. 25, 1954; d. John Albert and Virginia Anne (Cooney) Taylor; m. Stephen Michael Seidman, Aug. 17, 1979; 1 child, Julie Anne. BS in Elem. Edn., U. Hartford, West Hartford, Conn., 1976; MEd, West Chester (Pa.) U., 1990. Cert. reading specialist, elem. edn. tchr. Tchr. Our Lady of Mt. Carmel Sch., Boonton, N.J., 1977-79, Catawba County Schs., Hickory, N.C., 1980-82, St. Joseph Sch., Big Bend, Wis., 1982-87; tchr., evaluator, asst. coord. Del. County Lit. Coun., Chester, Pa., 1991—. Mem. Internat. Reading Assn., Del. Valley Reading Assn., Keystone State Reading Assn., Laubach Lit. Action, Kappa Delta Pi. Office: Del County Lit Coun Chester PA 19013

SEIFER, JUDITH HUFFMAN, sex therapist, educator; b. Springfield, Ill., Jan. 18, 1945; d. Clark Lewis and Catherine Mary (Fisher) Huffman; married; children: Christopher, Patrick, Andrea. RN, St. John's Hosp./Quincy Coll., 1965; MHS, Inst. Advanced Study Human Sexuality, 1981, PhD, 1986. RN, Ohio; Diplomate Am. Bd. Sexology. Charge nurse Grandview Hosp., Dayton, Ohio, 1967-70; v.p. Sego, Inc., Dayton, 1970-84, pres., 1984—; marital and sex therapist Grandview Ob-Gyn., Inc., Dayton, 1975-87; asst. clin. prof. psychiatry and ob-gyn Wright State U. Sch. Medicine, Dayton,

1985-93; edn. cons., screenwriter The Learning Corp., Ft. Lauderdale, Fla., 1990—; COO Am. Sex Inst., Hillsborough Beach, Fla., 1995—; CEO In Good Co., Inc., Lewisburg, W.Va., 1995—; adj. prof. psychology U. dayton, 185-90; profl. spkr. The Upjohn Co., Kalamazoo, 1986—, CIBA-GEIGY Co., 1987-90; chmn. tech. adv. com. Mercari Comm., Inc., Englewood, Colo., 1988-89; cons. dept. psychology VA Hosp., Dayotn, 1990-93. Author, screenwriter film script: Mercari Communications, 1988; editor: Jour. Sexuality and Relationships, 1995—; author, screenwriter film script: In Good Co., Inc., 1994—; guest editor: The D.O., 1985; contbr. articles to profl. jours. Pres. Dayton Osteopathic Aux., 1974-75, Aux. Ohio Osteopathic Assn., Columbus, 1981-82, Sister City Assn., Oakwood, Ohio, 1985-86; bd. dirs. Grace House Sexual Abuse Resource Ctr., Dayton, 1987-89, Planned Parenthood Miami Valley, Ohio, 1985-86, Social Health Assn., Dayton, 1976-87. Grantee Dayton Found., 1980-82; fellow Masters and Johnson Inst., 1984. Fellow Internat. Coun. Sex Educators, Am. Acad. Clin. Sexologists; mem. Am. Assn. Sex Educators, Counselors and Therapists (cert., rec. sec. 1986-91, pres. 1994—), Am. Coll. Sexologists. Roman Catholic. Office: Sego Corp 2 Deerfield Rd PO Box 426 Lewisburg WV 24901-0426

SEIFERT, CAROL JOY, goverment administrator; b. Paducah, Tex., July 21, 1953; d. Charles Gene Bragg and Anita Joy (Bates) Hurta; m. Stephen Charles Seifert. BA in Psychology, U. Tex., 1974. Contract specialist NASA, Houston, 1974-77; collections supr. U.S. Dept Edn., Dallas, 1977-80, lender examiner, 1980-84; chief, fin. mgmt. sect. U.S. Dept Edn., Washington, 1984-86, chief, guaranteed student loan policy br., 1986-87, chief, guaranteed student loan ops. br., 1987-92; dir. div. Guaranteed Student Loan Systems U.S. Dept. Edn., Washington, 1992-95, acting dir. program sys. svc., 1995—. Baptist.

SEIFERT, SHELLEY JANE, human resources specialist; b. Aug. 12, 1954. BS in Consumer Econs. and Journalism, U. Mo., 1976; MBA in Fin. with honors, U. Louisville, 1980. Fin. analyst Nat. City Bank, Ky., 1979-81; compensation analyst Nat. City Bank, 1981-85, mgr. compensation, 1985-86, mgr. compensation, recruiting and tng., 1986-91; mgr. compensation and devel. Nat. City Corp., Cleve., 1988-91, human resource dir., 1991-94, sr. v.p., corp. human resource dir., 1994—; spkr. in field. Recipient Woman of Distinction award YMCA. Mem. Urban League (bd. dirs., chair employment com., Ohio labor adv. com.). Office: Nat City Corp Nat City Ctr 1900 E 9th St Cleveland OH 44114-3484*

SEIFERT, TERESA DISTEFANO, physical education educator; b. Alexandria, Va., Aug. 9, 1957; d. S. John and Evelyn M. (Bender) diS.; m. Paul Joseph Seifert, Nov. 14, 1992; 1 child, Steven Robert. BS, U. Md., 1979; MEd, Bowie State U., 1983. Dept. chair Acad. of the Holy Name, Silver Spring, Md., 1981-83; grad. asst. U. Md., College Park, 1984-85; assoc. prof. Prince George's C.C., Largo, Md., 1983—; asst. women's basketball coach Prince Georges C.C., Largo, Md., 1985-88, head women's basketball coach, 1988-94, prof. Mem. 23d legis. dist. Prince George's Rep. Cen. Com., 1988-94; 1st vice chmn. 5th dist. Congl. Rep. Com., Md., 1992—; chmn. Md. Fedn. Young Reps., 1990-95; mem. Calvert County Rep. Ctrl. Com., 1994—. Named Young Rep. Woman of Yr., Young Rep. Nat. Fedn., 1993. Mem. AAHPERD, Nat. Jr. Coll. Athletic Assn. Basketball Coaches Assn., Nat. Assn. for Sport and Phys. Edn., Assn. for Rsch., Adminstrn., Profl. Couns. and Socs., Md. Assn. for Health, Phys. Edn., Recreation and Dance. Roman Catholic.

SEIGFRIED, CHARLENE HADDOCK, humanities educator; b. San Diego, Jan. 26, 1943; d. Charles Richard and Allene Theresa (McLeod) Haddock; m. Hans Haddock Seigfried, Aug. 15, 1970; 1 child, Karl Erik Haddock. BA, St. Joseph Coll., Orange, Calif., 1965; MA, Loyola U., Chgo., 1970, PhD, 1973. Instr. Oakton C.C., Morton Grove, Ill., 1976-78; asst. prof. Purdue U., West Lafayette, Ind., 1979-83; assoc. prof. Purdue U., 1983-91, prof., 1991—; cons., spkr. NEH Masterwork Seminar, Lab. Sch. U. Chgo., 1993; seminar leader Summer Idea Seminar, St. Mary's Coll., Notre Dame, Ind., 1992, sesquicentennial lectr., 1994; Irving Thalberg lectr. U. Ill., Chgo., 1996. Author: Chaos and Context, 1978, William James's Radical Reconstruction of Philosophy, 1990, Pragmatism and Feminism, 1996; editor: Hypatia (spl. issue), 1993; mem. editl. bd.: Jour. Speculative Philosophy, Vanderbilt U. Press. Postdoctoral fellow Northwestern U., Evanston, Ill., 1978-79, Kellogg Nat. fellow Kellogg Found., Battle Creek, Mich., 1980-83. Mem. Am. Philos. Assn., Soc. for Advancement of Am. Philosophy (pres. 1996—), Soc. for Women in Philosophy, Soc. for Study of Women Philosophers (bd. dirs. 1994—), Soc. for Phenomenology and Existential Philosophy, Soc. for Philosophy and Tech. Office: Purdue U Dept Philosophy 1360 LAEB West Lafayette IN 47907

SEIGLER, RUTH QUEEN, college nursing administrator, educator, consultant, nurse; b. Conway, S.C., July 31, 1942; d. Charles Isaac and Berneta Mae (Weaks) Queen; m. Rallie Marshall Seigler, Sept. 1, 1963; children: Rallie Marshall Jr., Scot Monroe. ADN, Lander Coll., 1962; BSN, U. S.C., 1964, MSN, 1980. Pub. health nurse Richland County Health Dept., Columbia, S.C., 1964-66; dir. nurses Columbia Area Mental Health Ctr., 1966-69; program nurse specialist Midlands Health Dist., 1969-72; discharge planner Richland Meml. Hosp., 1972-73, clin. dir., 1973-75; exec. dir. S.C. State Bd. Nursing, 1976-83, v.p. nursing dept. Self Meml. Hosp., Greenwood, S.C., 1983-86; exec. dir. S.C. Commn. on Aging, Columbia, 1986-95; asst. dean Coll. Nursing U. S.C., Columbia, 1995-96, assoc. clin. prof., 1996—; bd. dirs. Queen Gas Co., Barnwell, S.C.; nurse cons. Creative Nursing Mgmt., Mpls., 1984—. Advisor: The Role of County Mental Health Nurse, 1971. Recipient Disting. Alumni award Lander Coll., 1978, career Woman recognition award Columbia YWCA, 1980, William S. Hall award S.C. Assn. Residential Care Homes, 1988, U. S.C. Coll. Nursing Disting. Alumni award, 1993, award for excellence S.C. League for Nursing, 1995, Svc. Recognition award S.C. AARP, 1995; named one of Ten Women of Achievement, S.C. March of Dimes, 1987. Mem. ANA, APHA, S.C. Nurses Assn. (sec. 1965-68, bd. dirs. 1986-88, Excellence award 1984, Recognition award 1984), S.C. Hosp. Assn., S.C. Gerontol. Soc., S.C. Nurses Found., S.C. Healthy People 2000 (vice chair), Partnership for Older South Carolinians (founder, chair bd. dirs.), Columbia Luncheon Club, S.C. Fedn. Older Ams., Evening Mission Action Group, Bd. Nursing Home Examiners, Pilot Club, Inc. (pres. 1988-89), Rotary Internat., Sigma Theta Tau. Presbyterian. Home: 2220 Bermuda Hills Rd Columbia SC 29223-6710 Office: U SC Coll Nursing Dept Adminstrv and Clin Nursing Columbia SC 29208

SEILER, KAREN PEAKE, psychologist; b. Seattle, Jan. 31, 1952; d. Louis Joseph and Donna Mae (Waters) Tomaso; m. Arthur J. Seiler; children from previous marriage: Jeremy S. Peake, Anthony K. Peake. BA/BSW magna cum laude, Carroll Coll., 1987; postgrad., MIT, 1994. Cert. strategic planning Pacific Inst.; cert. orgnl. cons. Covey Learning Ctr., 1993. Admissions counselor Shodair Children's Hosp., Helena, Mont., 1984-86; asst. dir., counselor Career Tng. Inst., Helena, 1986-90, pres. Corp. Cons., Helena, 1990—; apptd. amb. Mont. Ambs., 1990—; active Gov.'s Task Force on Econ. Devel., 1991-94; chairperson Mont. Dist. Export Coun./U.S. Dept. Commerce, 1992—; exec. com. mem. Mont. World Trade Ctr., Missoula, 1995—;. Mem. YWCA, 1986-90, pres., 1989; mem. Bus. and Profl. Women's Orgn., 1987-93, sec., 1990; pres. Helena Area Econ. Devel. Coun., 1989-92; exec. com. Leadership Helena, 1990-91; monitoring chair Concentrated Employment Program Pvt. Industry Coun., Mont., 1990—; bd. dirs., exec. com. Mont. Women's Capital Fund, 1990-95; exec. com. Mont. Race for the Cure, 1994—. Mem. NAFE, Partnership for Employment and Tng., Delta Epsilon Sigma (Outstanding Citizen award). Roman Catholic. Home and Office: 315 N Park Ave Helena MT 59601

SEIPP, RITA MARY, principal; b. Passaic, N.J., Aug. 16, 1950; d. William Joseph and Agnes (Dennison) Galop; m. Charles Richard Seipp; children: Richard, Charles. BA in Elem. Edn., Fairleigh Dickinson U., Madison, N.J., 1973; MA in Secondary Edn./Adminstrn., East Stroudsburg (Pa.) U., 1987. Cert. chief sch. adminstr. K-12, supr. K-12, prin. K-12, tchr. K-8. Tchr. grades 2, 3, 5 and 6 Parsippany (N.J.) Bd. Edn., 1973-83; tchr. grade 5 Mansfield Twp. (N.J.) Bd. Edn., 1985-88; asst. prin. K-6 Knowlton Twp. (N.J.) Bd. Edn., 1988-89; prin. K-5 Denville Twp. (N.J.) Bd. Edn., 1989-92, Jefferson Twp. (N.J.) Bd. Edn., 1992—. Geraldine Dodge Found. fellow, 1993. Mem. NEA, ASCD, PSA. Office: Ellen T Briggs Sch One Jefferson Dr Lake Hopatcong NJ 07849

SEISER, VIRGINIA, librarian; b. Anchorage, Aug. 9, 1948; d. Virgil Owen and Marjorie (Betts) S. BS in Psychology, U. Oreg., 1971; MA in Libr. Sci., U. Chgo., 1974; MS in Psychology, Portland State U., 1982. Libr. I Multhnoman County Libr., Portland, Oreg., 1973-74; ednl. psychology libr. Portland State U., 1974-82; readers svcs. dept head, 1982-85; ref. libr. U. N.Mex., Albuquerque, 1985; assoc. to dean of Libr. Scis., 1986—. Coauthor: Mountaineering and Mountain Club Serials, 1990; column editor: Serials Review (periodical), 1978-80; contbr. articles to profl. jours. Libr. com. Mazamas Portland, 1981-84 vol. worker Cave Rsch. Found., Carlsbad, N.Mex., 1990—; rescue team mem. Albuquerque Mountain Rescue, 1987—. Recipient Sixteen Peaks award Mazamas, Portland, 1987; Watson/Chadwick Meml. Fund grant Am. Alpine Club, Golden, Colo., 1983. Mem. AAUP, Am. Alpine Club, N.Mex. Libr. Assn., Assn. Coll. Rsch. Librs. Office: General Library University of New Mexico Albuquerque NM 87131

SEITZ, MARY LEE, mathematics educator. BS in Edn. summa cum laude, SUNY, Buffalo, 1977, MS in Edn., 1982. Cert. secondary tchr., N.Y. Prof. math. Erie C.C.-City Campus, Buffalo, 1982—; Reviewer profl. jours. and coll. textbooks. Reviewer profl. jours. Mem. Nat. Coun. Tchrs. Maths., N.Y. Maths. Assn. Two Yr. Colls., Assn. Maths. Tchrs. N.Y., N.Y. Assn. Two Yr. Colls., Inc., Pi Mu Epsilon. Office: Erie C C-City Campus 121 Ellicott St Buffalo NY 14203-2601

SEITZ, NANA TUCEK, food service manager, realtor; b. Saint Louis, Sept. 13, 1948; d. Albert John and Lillian Mae (Hisle) Tucek; m. James Gardner, Oct. 9, 1964 (dec.); m. Joe C. Quick, Oct. 31, 1968 (div. 1976); m. Paul Kenneth Seitz, Jr., Mar. 8, 1980; 1 child, Stacy Lynn. Student, Broward C.C., Fort Lauderdale, 1976. Cert. realtor. Cashier Grand Union, Fort Lauderdale, 1965-67; officer mgr. Vance Baldwin, Fort Lauderdale, 1967-68; pvt. sec. Burnside-Aviation, Fort Lauderdale, 1968-69; planetarium sec. Broward C.C., Fort Lauderdale, 1969-71; with Harry M. Stevens Cat., Pompano Race Track, 1969-70; catering mgr. Volume Svcs., Pompano Race Track, 1970-76; mgr., dist. mgr. Jones Beach Catering, N.Y.C., 1976-80; restaurant mgr. Stones Bowling Lns., Cin., 1980; real estate sales cons. Century 21, Virginia Beach, Va., 1980—; owner, gen. mgr. Pungo Pl. Lighthouse Restaurant, Virginia Beach, Va., 1986-95; with Beechwood Ave. Entertainment Catering, Starlake Amphitheatre, Burgettstown, Pa., 1996. Food svc. coord. Pungo Strawberry Festival, Virginia Beach, 1986-95. Broward County Restaurant Assn. scholar, 1975. Republican. Roman Catholic.

SEITZINGER, SHEILA MARIE, elementary education educator; b. Atlanta, July 8, 1948; d. Kenneth Earl and Mildred (Booth) Davis; m. Philip Cary Seitzinger, Feb. 14, 1970; children: Lori Beth, Amy Marie. BS, So. Ill. U., 1970. Second grade tchr. Alton (Ill.) Sch. Dist. # 11, 1970-73; presch. tchr. Evangelical Sch. for the Young Years, Godfrey, Ill., 1980-83; first grade tchr. Evangelical Elem. Sch., Godfrey, 1983—. Adult sponsor Encounter-Sr. Youth, sec., 1993—, treas. 1996—. Republican. Methodist. Home: 1509 Colonial Dr Godfrey IL 62035 Office: Evangelical Elem Sch 1212 Homer Adams Pkwy Godfrey IL 62035

SEKELY, MARY ANN, editorial, marketing and systems associate; b. Pitts., Sept. 25, 1950. BS, Pa. State U., 1973; MLS, U. Pitts., 1980. Info. specialist Info. and Vol. Svcs., Pitts., 1980-81; adminstrv. asst. The Bank Ctr., Pitts., 1982-84; indexer H.W. Wilson Co., Bronx, N.Y., 1984-87; asst. editor Pub. Affairs Info. Svc., N.Y.C., 1987-95, editl., mktg. and systems assoc.,, 1995—. Asst. editor (index) Pub. Affairs Info. Svc. Internat. Interviewer Mayor's Vol. Action Ctr., N.Y.C., 1992-95. Mem. ALA, Spl. Libr. Assn., Am. Soc. Indexers (pres. N.Y. chpt. 1988-89). Office: Pub Affairs Info Svc 521 W 43d St New York NY 10036-4396

SEKHON, KATHLEEN, state legislator; b. 1948; m. David Sekhon; 3 children. BS, U. Minn. Mem. Minn. Ho. of Reps., St. Paul, 1992—, mem. environ. and natural resources com., labor and mgmt. rels. com.; tchr. Home: 6619 189th Ln NW Anoka MN 55303-9519*

SEKINE, DEBORAH KEIKO, systems analyst, programmer; b. Honolulu, Dec. 1, 1952; d. Yoshiteru and Yaeko (Matsuda) Isa; m. Andrew K. Sekine, May 8, 1993. BA in Math. with distinction, U. Hawaii, 1974, BEd with distinction, 1974, MS in Computer Sci., 1976, MBA, 1987. Data analyst, engr. in-charge Kentron, Honolulu, 1977-81; sys. analyst Am. Savs., Honolulu, 1981-82; analyst, programmer City and County of Honolulu, 1982—; cons. Am. Savs., Honolulu, 1982. Contbr. articles to profl. jours. Vol. Hawaii Dem. Conv., Honolulu, 1984, Mayoral campaign, 1988, 92; com. co-chair Hui Makaala, Honolulu, 1989—; caregiver Makiki Christian Ch., Honolulu, 1991—. Mem. IEEE, Assn. for Computing Machinery, Am. Fedn. State County Mcpl. Employees, U. Hawaii MBA Alumni Assn., Phi Kappa Phi. Mem. United Ch. of Christ. Home: 3322 George St Honolulu HI 96815-4319

SEKOWSKI, CYNTHIA JEAN, corporate executive, contact lens specialist; b. Chgo., Feb. 14, 1953; d. John L. and Celia L. (Matusiak) S. PhD in Health Svcs. Adminstrn., Columbia Pacific U., 1984, PhD in Health Scis., 1984. Chief contact lens dept. Lieberman & Kraff, Chgo., 1974-87; pres., CEO Seko Eye Care, Inc., Chgo., 1988—; realtor-assoc. Country Club Realty Group, Naples, Fla., 1995—; researcher, technologist U. Ill., Chgo., 1976-78. Mem. Chgo. Zool. Soc., 1984—, Little City Inner Circle, 1991—; sponsor Save the Children Orgn., 1983—; asst. to campaign mgr. Rep. state senatorial candidate, Chgo., 1972; pres. Compass Point Condo Assn., Naples, Fla., 1996—; mem. budget com. Windstar Masters Assn., Naples. Fellow Contact Lens Soc. Am.; mem. Ill. Soc. Opticianry, Opticians Assn. Am., Better Vision Inst., Nat. Contact Lens Examiners, Fla. Assn. Realtors, Nat. Assn. Realtors, Naples Area Bd. of Realtors, Women's Coun. of Realtors, Nat. Geographic Soc., Columbia Pacific U. Alumnae Assn., Nat. Wildlife Fedn. Roman Catholic. Office: Country Club Realty Ste 105 2640 Golden Gate Pkwy Naples FL 34105

SELBY, BARBARA KENAGA, bank executive; b. San Francisco, July 14, 1942; d. George W. and Margaret (Spencer) Kenaga; m. Robert I. Selby, June 19, 1965; 1 child, Michael S. BBA, Ill. Wesleyan U., 1964. Corp. activities analyst Harris Bank, Chgo., 1969-77; asst. to gen. mgr. Harriscorp Fin., Inc., Chgo., 1978-80; with Bank Ill., Champaign, 1984-86; pers. officer BankIll., Champaign, 1986-87, asst. v.p. human resources, 1988-95, v.p. human resources, 1995—. Mem. Champaign-Urbana Pers. Assn. (treas. 1987-88), Women's Bus. Coun. (treas. 1991, bylaws chairperson 1996). Home: 909 W Union St Champaign IL 61821-3323 Office: Bank Ill 100 W University Champaign IL 61820

SELBY, CECILY CANNAN, dean, educator, scientist; b. London, Feb. 4, 1927; d. Keith and Catherine Anne Cannan; m. Henry M. Selby, Aug. 11, 1951 (div. 1979); children: Norman, William, Russell; m. James Stacy Coles, Feb. 21, 1981. A.B. cum laude, Radcliffe Coll., 1946; Ph.D. in Phys. Biology, MIT, 1950. Teaching asst. in biology MIT, 1948-49; adminstrv. head virus study sect. Sloan-Kettering Inst., N.Y.C., 1949-50; asst. mem. inst. Sloan-Kettering Inst., 1950-55; research assoc. Sloan-Kettering div. Cornell U. Med. Coll., N.Y.C., 1953-55; instr. microscopic anatomy Cornell U. Med. Coll., 1955-57; tchr. sci. Lenox Sch., N.Y.C., 1957-58; headmistress Lenox Sch., 1959-72; nat. exec. dir. Girl Scouts U.S.A., N.Y.C., 1972-75; adv. com. Simmons Coll. Grad. Mgmt. Program, 1977-78; mem. Com. Corp. Support of Pvt. Univs., 1977-83; spl. asst. acad. planning N.C. Sch. Sci. and Math., 1979-80, dean acad. affairs, 1980-81, chmn. bd. advisors, 1981-84; cons. U.S. Dept. Commerce, 1976-77; dir. Avon Products Inc., RCA, NBC, Loehmanns Inc., Nat. Edn. Corp. pres. Am. Energy Ind., 1976; co-chmn. commn. precoll. math. and sci. Nat. Sci. Bd., 1982-83; adj. prof. NYU, 1984-86, prof. sci. edn., 1986—; mem. policy steering com. Gov. Cuomo's Conf. on Sci. and Engring., 1989-90. Contbr. articles to profl. jours., chpt. to book. Founder, chmn. N.Y. Ind. Schs. Opportunity Project, 1968-72; mem. invitational workshops Aspen Inst., 1973, 75, 77, 79; trustee MIT, Bklyn. Law Sch., Radcliffe Coll., Woods Hole Oceanographic Instn., Women's Forum N.Y., Skin Disease Found., N.Y. Hall of Sci., 1982—, vice chmn., 1989—, trustee Girls Inc., 1992—, Nat. Coun. Women in Medicine, 1990-94; mem. Yale U. Peabody Mus. Adv. Coun., 1981-89. Recipient Woman Scientist of Yr. award N.Y. chpt. Am. Women in Sci., 1992. Mem. Headmistresses of East (hon., pres. 1970-72), Sigma Xi, Phi Delta Kappa. Clubs: Cosmopolitan (N.Y.C.). Home and Office: 1 E 66th St New York NY 10021 also: 100 Ransom Rd Falmouth MA 02540-1652

SELBY, MYRA CONSETTA, state supreme court justice; b. Bay City, Mich., July 1, 1955; d. Ralph Irving and Archie Mae (Franklin) S.; m. Bruce Curry; 1 child, Lauren. BA with honors, Kalamazoo (Mich.) Coll., 1977; JD, U. Mich., 1980. Bar: D.C. 1980, Ind. 1983, U.S. Dist. Ct. (so. dist.) 1983, Ct. Appeals (D.C. cir.) 1984, U.S. Ct. Appeals (8th cir.) 1985. Assoc. Seyfarth, Shaw, Fairweather & Geraldson, Washington, 1980-83; ptnr. Ice, Miller, Donadio & Ryan, Indpls., 1983-93; dir. Ind. Healthcare Policy, 1993-94; assoc. justice Ind. Supreme Ct., 1995—. Bd. dirs. Alpha Nursing Home, Flanner House, Inpls. Ballet Theatre. Office: Ind Supreme Ct 200 W Washington St Rm 324 Indianapolis IN 46204-2732*

SELDES, MARIAN, actress; b. N.Y.C.; d. Gilbert and Alice (Hall) S.; m. Julian Claman, Nov. 3, 1953 (div.); 1 child, Katharine; m. Garson Kanin, June 19, 1990. Grad., Neighborhood Playhouse, N.Y.C., 1947; D.H.L., Emerson Coll., 1979. Mem. faculty drama and dance div. Juilliard Sch. Lincoln Center, N.Y.C., 1969-91. Appeared with Cambridge (Mass.) Summer Theatre, 1945, Boston Summer Theatre, 1946, St. Michael's Playhouse, Winooski, Vt., 1947-48, Bermudiana Theatre, Hamilton, Bermuda, 1951, Elitch Gardens Theatre, Denver, 1953; Broadway appearances include Medea, 1947, Crime and Punishment, 1948, That Lady, 1949, Tower Beyond Tragedy, 1950, The High Ground, 1951, Come of Age, 1952, Ondine, 1954, The Chalk Garden, 1955, The Wall, 1960, A Gift of Time, 1962, The Milk Train Doesn't Stop Here Any More, 1964, Tiny Alice, 1965, A Delicate Balance, 1967 (Tony award for best supporting actress), Before You Go, 1968, Father's Day, 1971 (Drama Desk award), Mendicants of Evening (Martha Graham Co.), 1973, Equus, 1974-77, The Merchant, 1977, Deathtrap, 1978; off-Broadway appearances include Diff'rent, 1961, The Ginger Man, 1963 (Obie award), All Women Are One, 1964, Juana LaLoca, 1965, Three Sisters, 1969, Am. Shakespeare Festival, Stratford, Conn., Mercy Street at Am. Place Theater, N.Y.C., 1969, Isadora Duncan, 1976 (Obie award), Painting Churches, 1983, 84 (Outer Critics Circle award 1984), Other People, Berkshire Theatre Festival, 1969, The Celebration, Hedgerow Theater, Pa., 1971, Richard III, N.Y. Shakespeare Festival, 1983, Remember Me, Lakewood Theatre, Skowhegan, Maine, Gertrude Stein and a Companion, White Barn Theatre, Westport, Conn., 1985, Lucile Lortel Theatre, N.Y.C., 1986, Richard II, N.Y. Shakespeare Festival, 1987, The Milk Train Doesn't Stop Here Anymore, WPA Theatre, N.Y.C., 1987, Happy Ending, Bristol (Pa.) Riverside Theatre, 1988, Annie 2 John F. Kennedy Ctr., Washington, 1989-90, Goodspeed Opera House, Chester, Conn., 1990, A Bright Room Called Day, N.Y. Shakespeare Festival, 1991, Three Tall Women, River Arts, Woodstock, N.Y., 1992, Another Time, Am. Jewish Theatre, 1993, Breaking the Code, Berkshire Theatre Festival, 1993, Three Tall Women, Vineyard Theatre, N.Y.C., 1994, Promenade Theatre, 1994-95; engaged in nat. tour Medea, 1947; U.S. entry Berlin Festival, 1951, nat. tour Three Tall Women, 1995-96; motion picture appearances include The Greatest Story Ever Told, Gertrude Stein and a Companion, 1988, In a Pig's Eye, 1988, The Gun in Betty Lou's Handbag, 1992, Tom and Huck, 1995; (ABC series) Good and Evil, 1991, Murphy Brown, 1992, Truman, 1995; also appeared on CBS Radio Mystery Theater, 1976-81, as well as numerous dramatic shows; author: The Bright Lights, 1978, Time Together, 1981. Bd. dirs. Neighborhood Playhouse, The Acting Co., nat. repertory theatre. Inducted into Theater Hall of Fame, 1996. Mem. Players Club, Century Assn. Home: Apt 19 D 210 Central Park West New York NY 10019

SELDNER, BETTY JANE, environmental engineer, consultant, aerospace company executive; b. Balt., Dec. 11, 1923; d. David D. and Miriam M. (Mendes) Miller; m. Warren E. Gray, June 20, 1945 (div. 1965); children: Patricia, Deborah; m. Alvin Seldner, Nov. 15, 1965; children: Jack, Barbara. BA in Journalism, Calif. State U., Northridge, 1975, MA in Communications, 1977. Dir. pub. info. United Way, Van Nuys, Calif., 1958-63; dir. edn. United Way, Los Angeles, 1963-68; dir. pub. relations, fin. San Fernando Valley Girl Scout Council, Reseda, Calif., 1968-73; asst. dir. pub. info. Calif. State U., Northridge, 1973-75; dir. environ. mgmt. HR Textron Corp., Valencia, Calif., 1975-87; environ. engr. Northrop Aircraft, Hawthorne, Calif., 1987-88, EMCON Assocs., Burbank, Calif., 1988-92, Atkins Environ., 1992-93, Seldner Environ., Valencia, Calif., 1993—; prin. Seldner Environ. Svcs., 1993—. Author non-fiction. Mem. Santa Clarita Valley Environ. Mgrs. Soc. (chmn. bd. dirs. 1984), San Fernando Valley Round Table (pres. 1971-72), Hazardous Materials Mgrs.' Assn., Zonta Internat. Republican. Jewish.

SELES, MONICA, tennis player; b. Novi Sad, Yugoslavia, Dec. 2, 1973; came to U.S., 1986; d. Karol and Esther Seles. Profl. tennis player. Winner Houston, 1989, 91, 92, Oakland, 1990, 92, L.A., 1990, 91, Tampa, 1990, 91, U.S. Hardcourts, 1990, Lipton, 1990, 91, Roland Garros, 1990, 91, 92, Italian Open, 1990, German Open, 1990, French Open, 1990, 91, 92, Va. Slims, 1990, 91, 92, Phila., 1991, Milan, 1991, Tokyo Nichirie, 1991, 92, U.S. Open, 1991, 92, Australian Open, 1991, 92, 93, 96, Italian Open Doubles (with Kelesi) 1990, (with Capriati) 1991, (with Sukova), 1992, Essen, 1992, Indian Wells, 1992, Barcelona, 1992, Chgo., 1993, Can. Open, 1995, 96; finalist Dallas, 1989, Brighton, 1989, Palm Springs, 1991, U.S. Hardcourts, 1991, Hamburg, 1991, Italian Open, 1991, San Diego, 1991, Oakland, 1991, Wimbledon, 1992, Italian Open, 1992, L.A., 1992, Can. Open, 1992, Paris indoors, 1993, U.S. Open, 1995; singles semifinalist , New Orleans, 1988, Roland Garros, Washington, 1989, European indoors, 1989, Washington, 1990; doubles semifinalist (with A. Smith) Australian Open, 1991, (with Nagelsen), Chgo., 1993; named Yugoslavia's sportswoman of yr., 1985, World #1 ranked player, 1991, 92, #3 players in terms of career titles as a teenager, 1993; recipient 1990 Rado Topspin award, Ted Tinling Diamond award Va. Slims, 1990, Grand Slam Title, 1996; named Tennis Mag./Rolex Watch Female Rookie of Yr., 1989, World Champion, 1991, 92, Comeback Player of Yr. Tennis mag., 1995, Profl. Female Athlete by Yr., 1995. Office: care Internat Mgmt Group 1 Erieview Plz Cleveland OH 44114-1715*

SELF, CHRIS LUMBLEY, insurance company executive; b. Houma, La., Dec. 21, 1954; d. Joseph Powell, Sr. and Lucille (Tyner) Lumbley; m. Monte Darryl Self, Feb. 27, 1988. BA in Sociology, U. Tex., Arlington, 1979. Lic. ins. agent (life and health, property and casualty); lic. securities agent. Sales mgr. Allstate Ins., Dallas, 1979-92; ins. agent various cos., Dallas, 1993-96; owner Wise Fin. Group, Inc., Dallas, 1996—. Vol. Am. Cancer Soc. fundraisers, Senior Women's Coun. Mem. AAUW, NAFE, Dallas Assn. Life Underwriters. Republican. Methodist. Home: 915 Greenway Cir Duncanville TX 75137

SELIG, PHYLLIS SIMS, architect; b. Topeka, Nov. 16, 1931; d. Willis Nolan and Victoria Clarinda (Oakley) Sims; m. James Richard Selig, Mar. 31, 1957; children: Lin Ann, Susan Nan, Sarah Jo. BS in Architecture, U. Kans., 1956. Realtor Assoc. Realty, Lawrence, Kans., 1965-70; v.p. finance and housing Alpha Phi Internat. Fraternity, Inc., Evanston, Ill., 1968-74, chief exec. officer, internat. pres., 1974-78, trustee, 1978-80; sr. engr. tech. Nebr. Pub. Power, Columbus, 1980-86, staff architect, 1986-89, archtl. supr., 1989—. Republican. Lutheran. Office: Nebr Pub Power 1414 15th St Columbus NE 68601-5226

SELIGMAN, ROXY PACE, artist, educator; b. Sweetwater, Tex., July 27, 1948; d. Otho Reese Pace and Lillian Jeanne Gebhardt; m. Robert Harold Seligman, Aug. 12, 1985; children: Shay, Suzannah, Julianna. BA, U. Tex., Arlington, 1970; MS, North Tex. State U., 1976. Cert. tchr., Tex. Vocat. evaluator Goodwill Industries, Waco, Tex., 1970-71; tchr. Waco Ind. Sch. Dist., 1972-74, Plano (Tex.) Ind. Sch. Dist., 1974-75; regional edn. cons. Region 10 Tex. Edn. Agy., Richardson, 1975-80; edn. cons. Braniff Edn. Systems, Dallas, 1980-81; owner Roomate Agy., Dallas, 1981; art cons. Roxy S. & Assocs., Dallas, 1980-83; gallery owner, coord. Gallery Cascade, Burlingame, Wash., 1994-95; artist Seligman Studios, Sedro Woolley, Wash., 1989—; cons. and spkr. in field. Author: The Effect of Career & Economic Education Upon High School Seniors, 1976, Utilizing Community Resources, 1978, The Classroom That Manages Itself, 1979, Roommates Make Sense, 1980. Pres. Relief Soc., Anacortes, Wash., 1992, Young Women's Orgn., Sedro Woolley, 1994. Grantee Econ. Edn., 1972; Tex. Youth Coun. scholar, 1968. Mem. Nat. Art Assn., Women in Arts, Allied Arts, Whatcom Art Guild, Skagit Art Assn. (program chair 1994-95), Madronna. Republican. Mem. LDS Ch. Home: 1155 Zarahemla Sedro Woolley WA 98284

SELK, ELEANOR HUTTON, artist; b. Duboise, Nebr., Oct. 21, 1918; d. Anderson Henry and Florence (Young) Hutton; R.N., St. Elizabeth Hosp., Lincoln, Nebr., 1938; m. Harold Frederick Selk, Aug. 3, 1940; children: Honey Lou, Katherine Florence. Nurse, Lincoln, 1938-40, Denver, 1940-50; with Colo. Bd. Realtors, 1956-66; owner, mgr. The Pen Point, graphic art studio, Colorado Springs, 1974-94; instr. history and oil painting, 1994—; one-woman shows: Colo. Coll., 1970, 72, Nazarene Bible Coll., 1973, 1st Meth. Ch., 1971 (all Colorado Springs); exhibited in group shows: U. So. Colo., 1969, 70, 71, 72, Colorado Springs Art Guild, 1969-72, Pike's Peak Artists Assn., 1969-73, Mozart Art Festival, Pueblo, Colo., 1969-74, numerous others; represented in permanent collection U.S. Postal Service, Pen-Arts Bldg., Washington, Medic Alert Found. Internat. Hdqrs., Turlock, Calif., Colorado Springs Music Co. Piano Gallery. Rec. sec. Colo. chpt. Medic Alert Found. Internat., 1980-90, chairperson El Paso County and Colorado Springs chpt., 1980-90, Colo. bd. dirs., 1980-89, rec. sec., 1980-89. Recipient 3d pl. award Nat. Tb and Respiratory Disease and Christmas Seal Art Competition, 1969, finalist award Benedictine Art competition Hanover Trust Bank, N.Y.C., 1970, numerous awards and certs. for pub. service and art, award Music of the Baroque, 1991, Editors Choice award Nat. Libr. Poetry, 1993. Mem. Nat. League Am. Pen Women (rec. sec. 1972-74, traveling art slide collection 1974—, designer jewelry, awards for book cover art, numerous Gold Bangle awards). Contbr. med. articles, short stories, poetry to newspapers. Home and Studio: 518 Warren Ave Colorado Springs CO 80906-2343

SELKOWITZ, LUCY ANN, security officer; b. Pitts., Oct. 15, 1956; d. Thomas Francis and Matilda Margaret (Carlini) Donato; m. Jeremiah Anthony Barry, Jan. 10, 1976 (div. July 1979); 1 child, Jeremiah; m. Stanley Irwin Selkowitz, Aug. 19, 1987; children: Lori, Lee, Mattie. Grad., William Boyd, 1974. Cert. EMT, Pa. Owner, buyer Tillie's Antiques, Pitts., 1972-86; legal aide Selkowitz & Assoc., Pitts., 1986-94; armed security officer Wackenhut Corp., Pitts., 1992—. Dance performer Shade Sisters, 1992—. Counselor troubled youths, Clairton, Pa., 1986—; active PTA, chair 1995—. Mrs. Am. Finalist, 1990-91. Home: 100 Farm Ln Jefferson Boro PA 15025 Office: Wackenhut Inc Rt 88 Castle Shannon PA 15234

SELL, JOAN ISOBEL, mobile home company owner; b. Johnson City, Tenn., May 5, 1936; d. Earl Walter and Jeanne Mason (Lyle) S.; m. Dale L. Moss, Jan. 15, 1956 (div. Nov. 1977); children: Carol Anne, John D. BS, East Tenn. State U., Johnson City, 1961. Cert. tchr., Tenn., Ga. Tchr. Asbury Sch., Johnson City, 1961-62, Richard Arnold High Sch., Savannah, Ga., 1964-66, Windsor Forest High Sch., Savannah, 1966-67, Boones Creek High Sch., Jonesborough, Tenn., 1967-77; co-owner Moss-Sell Mobile Homes, Johnson City, 1978-88; co-owner Biddix Budget Homes, Inc. (formerly Budget Mobile Homes), Johnson City, 1978-87, v.p., sec., 1987—; pres., treas. Budget Homes, Inc. (formerly Biddix Budget Homes), Johnson City, 1988-92; owner McKinley Park, Johnson City, 1970—; sec. Piedmont Fin. Svcs. Inc., 1995—. Mem. Tenn. Manufactured Housing Assn. (state bd. dirs. 1993-95), N.E. Tenn. Manufactured Housing Assn. (pres.), DAR, UDC, Order Ea. Star. Mem. Brethren Ch. Home: 3 Caitlin Ct Johnson City TN 37604-1147 Office: McKinley Park PO Box 5189 Johnson City TN 37603-5189

SELLERS, ANNETTE CABANISS, secondary education educator; b. Tuscaloosa, Ala., Mar. 3, 1947; d. Jack A. and Ruth (Gilliland) Cabaniss; m. Ronald A. Sellers, Aug. 24, 1968; children; Melanie, Brian. BS in Maths., U. Ala., Tuscaloosa, 1968, MA in Secondary Edn., 1971. Cert. secondary tchr., Miss. Tchr. math. and English Gordo (Ala.) High Sch., 1968-69; tchr. maths. Killeen (Tex.) High Sch., 1971-72, Tuscaloosa Acad., 1973-74; tchr. chpt. I math. Guin (Ala.) Elem. Sch., 1974-75; tchr. maths. and English Hamilton (Ala.) High sch., 1975-81; tchr. maths. Winfield (Ala.) High Sch., 1981-87; tchr. aid Shrine Sch. for Exceptional Children, Jasper, Ala., 1987-89; tchr. maths. Caledonia (Miss.) High Sch., 1989—; tchr. asst. math. camp Miss. State U., Starkville, 1993; presenter workshops and sessions. Mem. com. Troop 9 Boy Scouts Am., Caledonia, 1991—; tchr. Sunday sch. 1st United Meth. Ch., Columbus, Miss., 1992—. Named Tchr. of Yr., Lowndes County Sch. Dist., 1992, Educator of Yr., Columbus-Lowndes C. of C., 1994; D.D. Eisenhower grantee, 1991, 93. Mem. Nat. Coun. Tchr. Maths., Miss. Coun. Tchrs. Maths., Kappa Delta Pi.

SELLERS, BARBARA JACKSON, federal judge; b. Richmond, Va., Oct. 3, 1940; m. Richard F. Sellers; children: Elizabeth M., Anne W., Catherine A. Attended, Baldwin-Wallace Coll., 1958-60; BA cum laude, Ohio State U., 1962; JD magna cum laude, Capital U. Law Sch., Columbus, Ohio, 1979. Bar: Ohio 1979, U.S. Dist. Ct. (so. dist.) Ohio 1981, U.S. Ct. Appeals (6th cir.), 1986. Jud. law clk. Hon. Robert J. Sidman, U.S. Bankruptcy Judge, Columbus, Ohio, 1979-81; assoc. Lasky & Semons, Columbus, 1981-82; jud. law clk. to Hon. Thomas M. Herbert, U.S. Bankrupcty Ct., Columbus, 1982-84; assoc. Baker & Hostetler, Columbus, 1984-86; U.S. bankruptcy judge So. Dist. Ohio, Columbus, 1986—; lectr. on bankruptcy univs., insts., assns. Recipient Am. Jurisprudence prize contracts and criminal law, 1975-76, evidence and property, 1976-77, Corpus Juris Secundum awards, 1975-76, 76-77. Mem. ABA (corp., litigation sect. 1986—, banking and bus. law sect. 1981-94, jud. adminstrv. sect. 1983-84), Columbus Bar Assn., Comml. Law Leage of Am., Am. Bankruptcy Inst., Nat. Conf. Bankruptcy Judges, Order of Curia, Phi Beta Kappa. Office: US Bankruptcy Ct 170 N High St Columbus OH 43215

SELLERS, JILL SUZANNE, lawyer; b. Baton Rouge, Oct. 24, 1967; d. Tommy Davis Sellers and Rhonda Lynn (Zimmerman) Ross. BA, La. State U., 1988; vis. student cum laude, Suffolk U. Sch. Law, 1991-92; JD, Franklin Pierce Law Ctr., 1992. Bar: Mass. 1993, U.S. Dist. Ct. 1993, U.S. Ct. Appeals (1st cir.) 1993. Summer assoc. Law Office of Robert Hernandez, Malden, Mass., 1990; vol. intern Disability Rights Ctr., Concord, N.H., 1990, N.H. Pub. Defender, Manchester, N.H., 1991, N.H. Appellate Defender, Concord, 1991; summer assoc. Law Office of David Bownes, Laconia, N.H., 1991; vol. legal asst. Com. for Pub. Counsel Svcs., Dedham, Mass., 1992; atty. Jill S. Sellers, Atty. at Law, Concord, 1994-95; atty., bar adv./pub. defender Middlesex Def. Attys., Inc., Concord, 1993-95; atty. Law Office of Robert S. Potters P.C., Boston, 1992-95; notary pub., Mass., 1994; pub. defender divsn. Com. for Pub. Counsel Svcs., 1995—. Vol./chair vols. Habitat for Humanity, Roxbury, Mass., 1994. Mem. ATLA (state gov. young lawyers sect. 1993-94, 94-95-96, liaison 1993-95-96, sec./treas. criminal law sect. 1993-94, 1st vice-chair criminal law sect. 1995—, Pub. Svc. award 1994), Mass. Acad. Trial Attys. (exec. com. young lawyers sect. 1994-95), Boston Bar Assn., Cen. Middlesex Bar Assn. Democrat. Home: 72 Marion Rd Ext Marblehead MA 01945 Office: Ste 408 One Salem Green Salem MA 01970

SELLERS, SUSAN TAYLOR, assistant principal; b. Melrose, Mass., Jan. 8, 1948; d. Walter Edmund and Lucille (Clark) Taylor; m. Burton Chance Sellers, Oct. 6, 1989; children: Heather, Heidi. BA in English, Syracuse U., 1970; MA in Ednl. Leadership, Immaculata (Pa.) Coll., 1993. Cert. early childhood, elem., elem. prin. Dir. Head Start The Neighborhood Ctr., Utica, N.Y., 1970; tchr. Mt. Markham Sch. Dist., Bridgewater, N.Y., 1970-72; dir. Little People Day Sch., Malvern, Pa., 1987-88; tchr. Friendship Elem. Sch., Coatesville, Pa., 1988-93; asst. prin. Rainbow Elem. Sch., Coatesville, 1993—; grad. adv. bd. Immaculata Coll., 1993—. Recipient Artist in Edn. award Pa. Coun. Arts, 1990, 91, 92, Presdl. award for excellence in elem. math. Pa. Dept. Edn., 1991. Mem. ASCD, Nat. Assn. Edn. Young Children, Nat. Coun. Tchrs. Math., Pa. Coalition Arts in Edn., Pa. Lit. Coun., Local Children's Team. Home: 10 Oak Hill Cir Malvern PA 19355-2017 Office: Coatesville Area Sch Dist Rainbow Elem Sch 50 Country Club Rd Coatesville PA 19320

SELMAN, CAROL, secondary school teacher; b. N.Y.C., Oct. 28, 1946; d. Edward and Gertrude (Feldman) S.; m. Andrew W. Barchas, June 19, 1966 (div. 1983); m. Jules L. Schneider, May 24, 1986; stepchildren: Karen Schneider Dellaripa, Nancy Schneider. BA with distinction, Cornell, 1969; MA, SUNY, 1981, postgrad., 1982-83. Cert. secondary sch. social studies tchr., N.J. Tchg. fellow SUNY, Stony Brook, 1982-83; tchr. history Millburn (N.J.) Sr. H.S., 1969—. Pub. mem. N.J. Hist. Commn., 1992—; adv. organizer Millburn H.S. chpt. Amnesty Internat., 1985—; mem. Sing-Out Found.; alumni amb. Cornell U., 1992—. Fellow Nat. Endowment for the Humanities, 1986. Mem. Millburn (N.J.) Edn. Assn. (chmn. legis. action team 1983-86), Orgn. Am. Historians, Cornell Club (no. N.J.), Phi Beta Kappa. Office: Millburn Sr H S 462 Millburn Ave Millburn NJ 07041

SELMAN, MINNIE CORENE PHELPS, elementary school educator; b. Freedom, Okla., Mar. 25, 1947; d. Maxwell Jack and Mary Elizabeth (Mountain) Phelps; m. Thomas O. Selman, Aug. 8, 1966; children: T. Justin, Jeffrey L. BS in Elem. Edn., Northwestern Okla. State U., 1969; diploma in aerospace sci. and tech. edn., Okla. City U./Internat. Space, 1996. Cert. elem. tchr., early childhood edn. tchr., elem. sci. tchr., Okla.; cert. early experiences insci., Okla. Tchr. Woodward (Okla.) Pub. Sch., 1969-72; pre-sch. tchr. Free Spirit Pre-sch., Woodward, 1974-75; tchr. Montessori Discovery World Pre-sch., Woodward, 1975-78; tchr. kindergarten Woodward Pub. Sch., Woodward, 1978—; host Leaderhip Okla. in the Classroom, 1991; tng. tchr. Okla. State U., Stillwater, 1987, 90. Benefit vol. Western Plains Shelter Orgn., Woodward, 1990, 91; life mem. Plains Indians and Pioneers Hist. Found., Woodward. Woodward Pub. Schs. Ednl. Found. grantee, 1990, 91, 92, NASA/NSTA grantee, 1995. Mem. NEA, Okla. Edn. Assn., Woodward Edn. Assn. (pub. rels. com. 1990—), Nat. Sci. Tchr. Assn. (cert. in elem. sci.), Okla. Sci. Tchrs. Assn. Democrat. Home: 318 Spruce Park Dr Woodward OK 73801-5945

SELTZER, LINDA WEISBAUM, school principal; b. Springfield, Ill., May 15, 1950; d. M. Byron and Marilyn Joyce (Rossiter) Weisbaum; m. William Seltzer; stepchildren: Karen, David, Daniel. BA, Ill. State U., 1973; MA in Human Devel. Counseling, Sangamon State U., 1976, MA in Psychology, 1979; PhD in Ednl. Adminstrn., So. Ill. U., 1992. Coord. West Ctrl. Diagnostic Ctr., Springfield, Ill., 1973-83; supr. alternative programs, prin. Webster Springfield Pub. Schs., 1983-94; prin. Webster Acad., Springfield, 1994—; pvt. practice counselor, Springfield, 1976-86; pres. bd. dirs. Family Svc. Ctr. Young Parents Support Svcs., Springfield, 1993-95; chair Sangamon County Juveinle Probation and Ct. Svcs. Adv. Bd., Springfield, 1993—; mem. Sangamon County Interagy. Coun., Springfield, 1984-96; pres. Sangamon County Truants Alternative Bd. of Control, 1994—; mem. Ill. Truants Alternative and Optional edn. Ad hoc com., 1994—. Mem. Human Rels. Coun., Springfield, 1996—. Recipient scholarship award Ill. Assn. Sch. Bds., 1990. Mem. ASCD, Assn. Ill. H.S., Ill. Alternative Edn. Assn., Kiwanis (pres. 1993-95). Office: Webster Acad 2530 E Ash St Springfield IL 62703-5600

SELTZER, VICKI LYNN, obstetrician-gynecologist; b. N.Y.C., June 2, 1949; d. Herbert Melvin and Marian Elaine (Willinger) S.; m. Richard Stephen Brach, Sept. 2, 1973; children: Jessica Lillian, Eric Robert. BS, Rensselaer Poly. Inst., 1969; MD, NYU, 1973. Diplomate Am. Bd. Ob-Gyn. Intern Bellevue Hosp., N.Y.C., 1973-74, resident in ob-gyn, 1974-77; fellow gynecol. cancer Am. Cancer Soc., N.Y.C., 1977-78, Meml. Sloan Kettering Cancer Ctr., N.Y.C., 1978-79; assoc. dir. gynecol. cancer Albert Einstein Coll. Medicine, N.Y.C., 1979-83; assoc. prof. ob-gyn., SUNY, Stony Brook, N.Y.C., 1983-89; prof. ob-gyn. Albert Einstein Coll. Medicine, 1989—; chmn. ob-gyn. L.I. Jewish Med. Ctr., 1993—; dir. ob-gyn., Queens Hosp. Ctr., Jamaica, N.Y., 1983-93, pres. med. bd., 1986-89. Author: Every Woman's Guide to Breast Cancer, 1987; editor-in-chief: Primary Care Update for the Ob-Gyn, 1993—; editor: Women's Primary Health Care, 1995; mem. editorial bd. Women's Life mag., 1980-82, Jour. of the Jacobs Inst. Women's Health, 1990—; contbr. over 75 articles to profl. jours.; host Weekly Ob-Gyn. TV Program, Lifetime Med. TV. Chmn. health com. Nat. Coun. Women, N.Y.C., 1979-84; mem. Mayor Beame's Task Force on Rape, N.Y.C., 1974-76; bd. govs. Regional Coun. Women in Medicine, 1985—; chmn. Coun. on Resident Edn. in Ob-Gyn., 1987-93. Galloway Fund fellow 1975; recipient citation Am. Med. Women's Assn., 1973, Nat. Safety Coun., 1978, Achiever award Nat. coun. Women, 1985, Achiever award L.I. Ctr. Bus. and Profl. Women, 1987. Fellow N.Y. Obstet. Soc., Am. Coll. Ob-Gyn (v.p. 1993-94, pres.-elect 1996—, gynecol. practice com. 1981, examener Am. Bd. Obstetrics and Gynecology 1988—); mem. Women's Med. Assn. (v.p. N.Y. 1974-79, editorial bd. jour. 1985—, resident review com. for obstetrics and gynecology 1993—), Am. Med. Women's Assn. (com. chmn. 1975-77, 78-79, editorial bd. jour. 1986—), N.Y. Cancer Soc., NYU Sch. Med. Alumni Assn. (bd. govs. 1979—, v.p. 1987-91, pres. 1992-93), Alpha Omega Alpha. Office: LI Jewish Med Ctr New Hyde Park NY 11040

SELTZER, VIVIAN CENTER, psychology educator; b. Mpls., May 27, 1931; d. Aaron M. and Hannah (Chazanow) Center; m. William Seltzer; children: Jonathan, Francesca S. Rothseid, Aeryn S. Fenton. BA summa cum laude, U. Minn., 1951; MSW, U. Pa., 1953; PhD, Bryn Mawr Coll., 1976. Lic. psychologist; cert. sch. psychologist; lic. social worker, Pa.; cert. marriage and family therapist. Family counselor Phila. and Miami, Fla., 1953-60; pvt. practice psychology cons. Phila., 1965—; prof. human devel. and behavior U. Pa., Phila., 1976—; exch. prof. U. Edinburgh, 1979-80; vis. prof. Hebrew U., Jerusalem, 1984-85; chair internat. com. U. Pa., various other cosm., chair faculty senate. Author: Adolescent Social Development: Dynamic Functional Interaction, 1982, The Psychosocial Worlds of the Adolescent, 1989; contbr. articles to profl. jours. Mem. bd. overseers Gratz Coll., Phila., 1965—, v.p., 1989—, chair acad. affairs com., 1980—. Mem. APA, Pa. Psychol. Assn., Phila. Soc. Clin. Psychologists (bd. dirs. 1975-86, program chair 1980-86), Phi Beta Kappa. Office: U Pa 3701 Locust Walk Philadelphia PA 19104-6214

SELVY, BARBARA, dance instructor; b. Little Rock, Jan. 20, 1938; d. James Oliver and Irene Balmat Banks; m. Franklin Delano Selvy, Apr. 15, 1959; children: Lisa Selvy Yeargin, Valerie Selvy Miros, Lauren, Franklin Michael. Student, U. Ctrl. Ark., 1955-57. Founder, dir. Carolina Ballet Theater, Greenville, S.C., 1973—; pres. Dance Arts Inc. and Incentives, Inc.; Advisory bd. dirs. Met. Arts Council and S.C. Governors Sch. Appeared in numerous TV commls., on Goodson-Toddman game show Play Your Hunch, 1958-59; toured Far East with TV show Hit Parade, 1958; named Miss Ark., 1956, Mrs. S.C., 1981; dir. and staged Mrs. Va., Mrs. N.C., Mrs. S.C. pageants; choreographed Little Theater prodns., Furman U. Opera. Mem. So. Assn. Dance Masters (ballet adviser, regional dir.), Dance Educators Am., Dance Masters of Am., Profl. Dance Tchrs. Home: 206 Honey Horn Dr Simpsonville SC 29681-5814 Office: Carolina Ballet Theatre 872 Woodruff Rd Greenville SC 29607-3538

SEMAN, JILL DIANA, engineering manager; b. Salt Lake City, Mar. 30, 1967; d. Edward Michael Seman and Barbara Louise Abbott. BSEE, Boston U., 1989. Assoc. engr. Digital Equipment Corp., Shrewsbury, Mass., 1988-89; tech. mktg. engr. Chips & Techs., San Jose, Calif., 1991-93, tech. mktg. mgr., 1993-94; sys. mgr. Cirrus Logic, Fremont, Calif., 1994-95; applications mgr. S3 Inc., Santa Clara, Calif., 1995—; presenter in field. Contbr. chpt. to book. Tutor Santa Clara County Office Edn., Calif., 1993-95; student mentor Santa Clara Valley Youth Found., Calif., 1995—.

SEMBER, JUNE ELIZABETH, retired elementary education educator; b. Apr. 3, 1932; d. Charles Benjamin and Cora Emma (Miller) Shoemaker; m. Eugene Sember, Oct. 18, 1975. BS with honors, Ea. Mennonite, 1957; post-grad., Columbia U., 1958, U. W.Va., 1960. Tchr. grades 1-6 Cross Roads Pvt. Sch., Salisbury, Pa., 1953-55; tchr. grade 5 Connellsville (Pa.) Area Schs., 1957-58, tchr. grade 2, 1958-66, tchr. grade 1, 1967-92, classroom vol., 1992—; supervising tchr. California (Pa.) U., 1970-90. Mem. Delta Kappa Gamma (pres. 1978-80). Presbyterian. Home: 1125 Pittsburgh St Scottdale PA 15683-1630 Office: Connellsville Area Schs 7th Ave Connellsville PA 15425

SEMLER STRONG, MARGOT, association administrator; b. N.Y.C., June 26, 1933; d. Philip Grandin and Margot Violet (Berglind) Strong; m. Ralph Semler, Feb. 19, 1955; children: Ralph Parker, Christopher Strong, Michael. Student, Nat. Cathedral Sch., Bryn Mawr Coll., 1954. Exec. dir. Nat. Cathedral Assn., Washington Nat. Cathedral, 1974-95, canon, exec. dir. for nat. outreach, 1995—; comdr. sister Order of St. John of Jerusalem, 1983—. Mem. Alumnae Assn. Nat. Cathedral Sch. (pres., trustee 1994-96). Episcopalian. Office: Massachusetts & Wisconsin Aves NW Washington DC 20016

SEMORE, MARY MARGIE, abstractor; b. Cowlington, Okla., Feb. 11, 1920; d. William Leonard and Bessie Mae (Bellah) Barnett; m. Jack Sanford Semore, Mar. 3, 1940 (dec. Jan. 1985). Grad. high sch., Wagoner, Okla., 1938. Legal sec. W.O. Rittenhouse, Wagoner, Okla., 1938-40; abstractor Wagoner County Abstract Co., 1941—. Mem. Title Industry Polit. Action Com., Washington, 1986, Am. Legion Women's Aux., Wagoner Hist. Soc. Mem. Okla. Land Title Assn., Am. Land Title Assn., Wagoner C. of C., DAR, Daus. Am. Colonists. Democrat. Methodist. Home: 902 S White Ave Wagoner OK 74467-7239 Office: Wagoner County Abstract Co 219 E Cherokee PO Box 188 Wagoner OK 74477

SENECHAL, ALICE R., judge, lawyer; b. Rugby, N.D., June 25, 1955; d. Marvin William and Dora Emma (Erdman) S. BS, N.D. State U., 1977; JD, U. Minn., 1984. Bar: Minn. 1984, U.S. Dist. Ct. Minn. 1984, N.D. 1986, U.S. Ct. Appeals (8th cir.) 1987. Law clk. U.S. Dist. Judge Bruce M. Van Sickle, Bismarck, N.D., 1984-86; assoc. Robert Vogel Law Office, Grand Forks, N.D., 1986—; U.S. magistrate judge, 1990—. Office: Robert Vogel Law Office 106 N 3rd St Ste M102 Grand Forks ND 58203-3798

SENERCHIA, DOROTHY SYLVIA, urban planner, author; b. Warwick, R.I., Apr. 20, 1933; d. Vincenzo Ralph and Theresa Felicia (Petrarca) S. BA, Pembroke Coll., Brown U., 1955; Cert., U. Florence, Italy, 1956. Cert. urban planner, N.Y.C. Tchr. Berlitz Sch. Langs., Florence, 1955-56; adminstrv. asst. Sheraton Corp. Am., N.Y.C., 1956-57, Inter-Am. Coun., N.Y.C., 1958-59, Roger Stevens Devel. Corp., N.Y.C., 1960-61; urban planner N.Y.C. Dept. City Planning, 1962-96. Author: Silent Menace, 1990; co-producer, co-star film The Funeral, 1980; solo concert violinist, 1945-62; co-founder singing group The Chattertocks of Brown U., 1952. One of the pioneers in cmty organization in the Urban Planning Process, N.Y.C., 1962-68; one of the early pioneers in women's movement, N.Y.C., 1969; mem. planning com. 1970 Women's March, N.Y.C., 1970; counselor Big Sisters Orgn., N.Y.C., 1969-82. Mem. Vet. Feminists Am. (co-founder, mem. founding bd.), The French Round Table (founder), Life-Affirming Group (founder). Democrat.

SENG, ANN FRANCES, civic organization executive; b. Chgo., Jan. 5, 1936; d. William John and Helen Christine (Steger) S. BA, Alverno Coll., Milw., 1957; MA, Loyola U., Chgo., 1970. Tchr. Alvernia High Sch., Chgo., 1958-65; exec. dir. Community House Cath. Charities, Chgo., 1965-67; adminstr. Sch. Sisters St. Francis, Chgo., 1967-69; dir. uptown advocacy program Chgo. Cath. Interracial Coun., 1970-71; community devel. dir. Uptown Ctr. Hull House, Chgo., 1971-81; dir. rsch. and pub. policy Hull House Assn., Chgo., 1981-88; pres., chief exec. officer Chgo. Coun. Urban Affairs, 1988—; bd. dirs. Jane Addams Conf., Chgo., 1987—, Chgo. Capital Fund, 1988-95, Women Employed Inst., Chgo., 1988-91. Mem. Pvt. Industry Coun., Chgo., 1988-95; vice-chair Chgo. Com. Urban Opportunity, 1988-92. Mem. LWV, NOW, Ill. Women's Agenda (chair 1983-84),. Office: Chgo Coun Urban Affairs 6 N Michigan Ave Ste 1308 Chicago IL 60602-4808

SENGSTACKE, ASTRID SANDRA, poet; b. Chgo., Sept. 4, 1938; d. Whittier A. and Mattie Astrid (Pryor) S.; children: Taasha Kaundart, Sylkija Creamer, Seratiel Jones, LaTheena Jones. BA, Goddard Coll., 1995. Circulation mgr. Memphis Tri-State, 1960-62; asst. gen. mgr., journalist Defender, Memphis, 1960-70. Lobbyist Wash. Assoc. Churches, Olympia, 1987-96.

SENKEVICH, LISA KAY, telecommunications software company executive; b. Denville, N.J., June 27, 1957; d. William Lawrence and Patricia Ruth (Anderson) Watson; m. Joseph Martin Phillips, Feb. 19, 1977 (div. Aug. 1985); m. Arthur SenKevich, Sept. 28, 1985; children: Timothy Lawrence, Stephen Andrew. Sec. City of Liberty, Mo., 1976-77; computer ops. Std. Steel Specialty, Beaver Falls, Pa., 1978-87; v.p. The FreeSoft Co., Beaver Falls, 1987—. Republican. Lutheran. Home: 147 Hickory Dr Beaver Falls PA 15010 Office: The FreeSoft Co 105 McKinley Rd Beaver Falls PA 15010

SENKO, MARY GAEL, advertising executive. Sr. v.p., group mgmt. supr. W.B. Doner & Co., Southfield, Mich. Office: WB Doner & Co 25900 Northwestern Hwy Southfield MI 48075*

SENSABAUGH, MARY ELIZABETH, financial consultant; b. Eastland, Tex., Aug. 15, 1939; d. Johnnie and L.G. (Tucker) Roberts; m. Dwight Lee Sensabaugh, Dec. 22, 1956; children: Robert Lee, Mark Jay. Student, Odessa Jr. Coll., 1959-63, U. North Tex., 1963-67. Sr. acct. Braniff Internat. Airlines, Dallas, 1967-68; acct. Computer Bus. Services, Dallas, 1968-72; sec.-treas. Robert D. Carpenter, Inc., Dallas, 1972-76; controller Broadway Warehouses, Dallas, 1976-78; asst. controller S.W. Offset, Dallas, 1978-79; sec.-treas., cons. Carpenter, Carruth & Hover, Inc., Dallas, 1979-92; sec.-treas. Roberts, Taylor and Sensabaugh, Inc., Hurst, Tex., 1992—. Mem. Nat. Assn. Women in Constrn. (bd. dirs. Dallas chpt. 1983-84), Internat. Platform Assn., Beta Sigma (pres. Irving, Tex. chpt. 1973-74), NAFE. Home: 702 Hughes Dr Irving TX 75062-5601 Office: 204 W Bedford Euless Rd Ste E Hurst TX 76053-4042

SENSENICH, ILA JEANNE, magistrate judge; b. Pitts., Mar. 6, 1939; d. Louis E. and Evelyn Margaret (Harbourt) S. BA, Westminster Coll., 1961; JD, Dickinson Sch. Law, 1964, JD (hon.), 1994. Bar: Pa. 1964. Assoc. Stewart, Belden, Sensenich and Herrington, Greensburg, Pa., 1964-70; asst. pub. defender Westmoreland (Pa.) County, 1970-71; U.S. magistrate judge for We. Dist. Pa., Pitts., 1971—; adj. prof. law Duquesne U., 1982-87, vis. fellow Daniel & Florence Guggenheim program in criminal justice Yale Law Sch., 1976-77. Trustee emeritus Dickinson Sch. Law. Mem. ABA, Fed. Magistrate Judges Assn. (sec. 1979-81, sec. 1988-89, treas. 1989-90, 2d v.p. 1990-91, pres.-elect 1992-93, pres. 1993-94), Pa. Bar Assn., Allegheny County Bar Assn. (fed. ct. sect.), Nat. Assn. Women Judges, Westmoreland County Bar Assn., Allegheny Bar Assn. (civil litigation sect., com. women in law), Womens Bar Assn. of We. Pa., Am. Judicature Soc. Democrat. Presbyterian. Avocations: skiing, sailing, bicycling, classical music, cooking. Author: Compendium of the Law of Prisoner's Rights, 1979; contbr. articles to profl. jours. Office: 518B US PO And Courthouse Pittsburgh PA 15219

SENTENNE, JUSTINE, corporate ombudsman; b. Montreal, Que., Can.; d. Paul Emile and Irene Genevieve (Laliberte) S. MBA, U. Que., Montreal, 1993, postgrad. McGill U., Ecole Nat. d'Adminstrn. Publique, 1989-91. Fin. analyst, assoc. mgr. portfolio Bush Assocs., Montreal, 1970-82; city councillor, mem. exec. com. City of Montreal and Montreal Urban Com., 1978-82; adminstrv. asst. Montreal Conv. Ctr., 1983; dir. sponsorship Cen. Com. for Montreal Papal Visit, 1984; dir. pub. rels. Coopers & Lybrand, Montreal, 1985-87; exec. dir. Que. Heart Found., 1987-89; corp. ombudsman Hydro-Que., Montreal, 1991—; tchr. DSA program Concordia U.; v.p., bd. dirs. Armand Frappier Found., Can., Chateau Dufresne Mus. Decorative Arts, Montreal, 1985-90; chmn. bd. Wilfrid Pelletier Found., Montreal, 1986-91; bd. dirs. St. Joseph's Oratory, 1979-92, Caisse Populaire Desjardins Notre Dame de Grace, Montreal, 1980-96; mem. jury John Labatt Ltd., London, Ont., 1982-86. Notre Dame de Grace v.p. riding assoc. Liberal Party of Can., chairperson Women's Commn.; mem. bd. govs. Youth and Music Can., Montreal, 1981-86; chmn. bd. The Women's Ctr., Montreal, 1986-88, Vol. Bur. Montreal, 1986-87; bd. dirs. Palais des Congres de Montreal, 1981-89, Port of Montreal, 1983-84, Can. Ctr. for Ecumenism, Montreal, 1968-85, Villa Notre-Dame de Grace, Montreal, 1979-87, Montreal Diet Dispensary, 1989— (chairperson 1996), Pathways to Faith, 1990—, The Ombudsman Assn., 1996—; bd. mgmt. Saidye Bronfman Ctr. for Arts, 1994—. Named Career Woman of Yr., Sullivan Bus. Coll., 1979; recipient Silver medal Ville de Paris, 1981, Women's Kansas City Assn. for Internat. Rels. and Trade medal, 1982. Fellow Fin. Analysts Fedn. N.Y., Inst. Fin. Analysts, Montreal Soc. Investment Analysts; mem. Cercle Fin. et Placement, The Ombudsman Assn. Roman Catholic.

SENTER, GAIL W., educator; b. Bethesda, Md., Sept. 21, 1947; d. Leonard C. and Ida Mae (Low) Wolff; m. Al D. Senter, Dec. 19, 1970 (dec. 1974); 1 child, Hollie Lyn. BA in Speech/Drama, Colo. State U., 1969, MA in English, 1979; EdD, U. So. Calif., 1989. Cert. K-12 English, Calif., C.C. lang. arts and lit., Calif., secondary speech/drama/English, Colo. Lectr. Calif. State U., San Marcos, 1990-91, 92—, San Diego State U., 1989-90, 1991; lectr. Calif. State U., San Bernardino, 1991-93; adj. instr. Chapman U., San Diego, 1987—; part-time cohort coord. Calif. State U., San Marcos, 1993—; interim edn. program coord. Chapman U., San Diego North Acad. Ctr., San Diego, 1990; program developer Ft. Collins Docents, 1977-78; publs. com. So. Calif. Assn./Tchr. Educators, San Bernardino, 1992—. Co-author: Elementary Classroom Management, 2d edit., 1995, (with author) Building Classroom Discipline, 4th edit., 1992, 5th edit., 1995. Trainer, field mgr. Youth for Understanding, San Diego, 1991—; ad hoc adv. com. Internat. Exch., Los Altos, Calif., 1994; vol. devel. com. mem. Youth for Understanding, Washington, 1994. Mem. ASCD, Calif. ASCD, Nat. Coun. of Tchrs. of English, Calif. Assn. of Tchrs. of English, So. Calif. Assn. of Tchr. Educators.

SENTER, MERILYN P(ATRICIA), former state legislator and freelance reporter; b. Haverhill, Mass., Mar. 17, 1935; d. Paul Barton and Mary Etta (Herrin) Staples; m. Donald Neil Senter, Apr. 23, 1960; children: Karen Anne Hussey, Brian Neil. Grad., McIntosh Bus. Coll., 1955. Sec. F.S. Hamlin Ins. Agy., Haverhill, Mass., 1955-60; free lance reporter Plaistow-Hampstead News, Rockingham county newspapers, Exeter and Stratham, N.H., 1970-89; mem. N.H. Gen. Ct., Rockingham Dist. 9, 1988-96. Sec. Hwy. Safety Com., Plaistow, N.H., 1976—; sec., bd. dirs. Region 10 Commn. Support Svcs. Inc., Atkinson, N.H., 1982-88; chmn. Plaistow Area Transit Adv. Com., 1990-93; active Devel. Disabilities Coun., 1993—; mem. Plaistow Bd. Selectmen, 1996-99. Named Woman of Yr., N.H. Bus. and Profl. Women, 1983, Nat. Grange Citizen of Yr., 1992. Republican. Home and Office: 11 Maple Ave Plaistow NH 03865-2221

SENTURIA, YVONNE DREYFUS, pediatrician, epidemiologist; b. Houston, Jan. 16, 1951. BA in Biology and Sociology, Rice U., 1973; MD, U. Tex., San Antonio, 1977; MSc in Epidemiology, London Sch. Hygiene and Tropical Medicine, 1985. Diplomate Am. Bd. Pedias. Pediat. resident Shands Tchg. Hosp., Gainesville, Fla., 1977-79, Tex. Children's Hosp., Houston, 1979-80; instr., asst. prof. Coll. Medicine, Baylor U., Houston, 1980-82; sr. clin. med. officer Hammersmith and Fulham Health Authority, London, 1982-83; cons. pediatrician Kingston (Eng.) Hosp., 1983, Northwick Park Hosp., London, 1983; rsch. pediatrician Charing Cross Hosp. Med. Sch., London, 1984-85; clin. lectr. Inst. Child Health, London, 1985-88; attending pediatrician and epidemiologist Children's Meml. Hosp., Chgo., 1989—. Fellow Am. Acad. Pediats.; mem. Ambulatory Pediat. Assn., Midwest Soc. Pediat. Rsch. Address: 17 Blue Ribbon Dr Westport CT 06880-2219

SEPAHPUR, HAYEDEH C(HRISTINE), investment executive; b. Lincoln, Nebr., Dec. 8, 1958; d. Bahman and Marylin Lou (Duffy) S.; m. Bahman Robert Kosrovani, May 2, 1992; 1 child, Cyrus Thomas Simonson Kosrovani. BS, Lehigh U., 1983. V.p. Drexel Burnham Lambert Inc., N.Y.C., 1982-90, Donaldson, Lufkin & Jenrette, New York City, 1990-92, Lehman Bros., Inc., N.Y.C., 1992—. Sponsor Jr. Statesmen of Am. Found., Washington, 1976—; charter mem. Nat. Mus. Women in the Arts, Washington, 1985—; bd. dirs. Coll. Express Project, Bronx, N.Y., 1987—; mem. Inst. Asian Studies, St. Thomas Episc. Ch. Mem. Nat. Trust Hist. Preservation, The Asia Soc., Women's Campaign Fund, N.Y. Soc. Libr., French Inst., WISH List, Parents League, N.Y. Women's Found., Fin. Women's Assn. (N.Y. chpt.), Persian Heritage Found., Mensa, Gamma Phi Beta. Club: Downtown Athletic (N.Y.C.). Home: 220 E 67th St Apt 12-d New York NY 10021-6255 Office: Lehman Bros Inc 3 World Fin Ctr 200 Vesey St Fl 6 New York NY 10285-0600

SEPKO, KAREN LUCIA, chemical engineer, consultant; b. Moses Lake, Wash., Apr. 9, 1962. BS in Chem. Engring., U. Ariz., 1987. Project engr. Manville Sales Corp., Corona, Calif., 1987-90; plant engr. NCR Corp., Brea, Calif., 1990-91; process engr. Martin Marietta Magnesia Specialties, Woodville, Ohio, 1994—; environ. cons., Fontana, Calif., 1991. Author: (book) Paint Tng. Manual, 1985. Home and Office: 8945 Rolling Hill Dr Holland OH 43528

SEPPALA, KATHERINE SEAMAN (MRS. LESLIE W. SEPPALA), retail company executive, clubwoman; b. Detroit, Aug. 22, 1919; d. Willard D. and Elizabeth (Miller) Seaman; B.A., Wayne State U., 1941; m. Leslie W. Seppala, Aug. 15, 1941; children: Sandra Kay, William Leslie. Mgr. women's bldg. and student activities adviser Wayne State U., 1941-43; pres. Harper Sports Shops, Inc., 1947-85, chmn. bd., treas., sec., v.p. 1985—; ptnr. Seppala Bldg. Co., 1971—. Mich. service chmn. women grads. Wayne State U., 1962—, 1st v.p., fund bd., Girl and Cub Scouts; mem. Citizen's adv. com. on sch. needs Detroit Bd. Edn., 1957—, mem. high sch. study com., 1966—; chmn., mem. loan fund bd. Denby High Sch. Parents Scholarship; bd. dirs., v.p. Wayne State U. Fund; precinct del. Rep. Party, 14th dist., 1956—, del. convs.; mem. com. Myasthenia Gravis Support Assn. Recipient Ann. Women's Service award Wayne State U., 1963. Recipient Disting. Alumni award Wayne State U., 1971. Mem. Intercollegiate Assn. Women Students (regional rep. 1941-45), Women Wayne State U. Alumni (past pres.), Wayne State U. Alumni Assn. (dir., past v.p.), AAUW (dir. past officer), Council Women as Public Policy Makers (editor High lights) Denby Community Ednl. Orgn. (sec.), Met. Detroit Program Planning Inst. (pres.), Internat. Platform Assn., Detroit Met. Book and Author Soc. (treas.), Mortar Bd. (past pres.), Karyatides (past pres.), Anthony Wayne Soc., Alpha Chi Alpha, Alpha Kappa Delta, Delta Gamma Chi, Kappa Delta (chmn. chpt. alumnae adv. bd.). Baptist. Clubs: Zonta (v.p., dir.); Les Cheneaux. Home: 22771 Worthington Ct Saint Clair Shores MI 48081-2603 Office: Harper Sport Shop Inc 23208 Greater Mack Ave Saint Clair Shores MI 48080-3422

SEPRODI, JUDITH CATHERINE, accounting administrator; b. Terre Haute, Ind., June 16, 1955; d. Ferris Lee and Mary Ann (Tully) Roberson; m. Donald Matthew Seprodi, Aug. 1, 1972 (div. Oct. 1994); children: Antoinette, Autumn, Jacob, Brooklyn. AA, Ivy Tech., 1990; grad., Dale Carnegie Course. Lic. property/casualty ins. agt.; notary public. Sec. Equifax, Oklahoma City, 1975-76; ins. clk. Northside Family Medicine, Del City, Okla., 1976; office mgr. Dick Clark Ins., Terre Haute, 1981, Simrell's, Terre Haute, 1981-85; ADC acctg. clk./typist V Vigo County Welfare, Terre Haute, 1985-86, head ADC acctg., clk./typist IV, 1986-87; purchasing agt. Bruce Fox, Inc., New Albany, Ind., 1987-88; acctg. mgr. Terre Haute Coke and Carbon, 1988-96, acting sec. bd. dirs., 1989; ptnr., owner Thistlehare; office mgr. Terre Haute (Ind.) Truck Ctr., 1996; ptnr., owner Thistlehare; bookkeeper Seprodi Constrn., Terre Haute, 1989—; grad. asst. Dale Carnegie Inst.; owner Take-A-Letter. Author employee manuals. Coach, Terre Haute Youth Soccer Assn., 1979-82, bd. dirs., 1979-82; player North Tex. Women's Soccer Assn., Plano, 1977-78. Recipient Dale Carnegie highest award for achievment. Mem. NAFE, AIPB, Am. Notary Assn., Profl. Bookkeepers Assn., Vigo County Taxpayers Assn. Democrat. Roman Catholic. Home: PO Box 323 Sandborn IN 47578

SEPTER, ELIZABETH BYRNSIDE, secondary education educator; b. Harrodsburg, Ky., May 29, 1939; d. Minor Colonel and Esther Katherine (Christman) Byrnside; divorced; children: Gregory, Michael. Student, Ea. Ky. U., 1957-60; BS, Austin Peay U., 1962; social studies cert., Holy Family Coll., Phila., 1966; MEd, spl. edn. cert., Antioch Coll., Phila., 1989. Tchr. English Lumpkin County Schs., Dahlorega, Ga., 1963-65, 68-89, Washington County Schs., Springfield, Ky., 1967-68, Pennsbury Schs., Fairless Hills, Pa., 1970-80, Hightstown (N.J.) H.S., East Windsor Schs., 1980—. Mem. Delta Kappa Gamma. Home: 17 New School Ln Levittown PA 19054-3405 Office: Hightstown H S 25 Leshin Ln Hightstown NJ 08520-4001

SERAFINE, MARY LOUISE, psychologist, educator, lawyer; b. Rochester, N.Y., July 2, 1948. B.A. with honors in music, Rutgers U., 1970; Ph.D., U. Fla., 1975; JD, Yale U., 1991. Bar: Calif., D.C.; U.S. Tax Ct. Teaching and research fellow U. Fla., Gainesville, 1970-76; vis. asst. prof. U. Tex.-San Antonio, 1976-77; asst. prof. U. Tex.-Austin, 1977-79; postdoctoral fellow dept psychology Yale U., New Haven, 1979-83, lectr., 1981-83; asst. prof. dept. psychology Vassar Coll. Poughkeepsie, N.Y., 1983-88; with O'Melveny & Myers, L.A., 1988-96, Chadbourne & Parke, L.A. Author: Music as Cognition: The Development of Thought in Sound, 1988. Contbr. articles to profl. jours. Editorial reviewer Child Devel., Devel. Psychology, Am. Scientist, Jour. Experimental Child Psychology, Jour. Applied Developmental Psychology, Yale Law Jour. Grantee State of Fla., 1974-75, U. Tex.-Austin, 1977, Spencer Found., 1979-85. Office: Chadbourne & Parke Ste 1600 601 South Figueroa St Los Angeles CA 90017

SERBUS, PEARL SARAH DIECK, former freelance writer, former editor; b. Riverdale, Ill.; d. Emil Edwin and Pearl (Kaiser) Dieck; m. Gerald Serbus, Jan. 26, 1946 (dec. Aug. 1969); children—Allan Lester, Bruce Alan, Curt Lyle. Mem. home econs. staff, writer Chgo. Herald Examiner, 1934-39; operator test kitchen Household Sci. Inst., Mdse. Mart, Chgo., 1940-45; freelance writer grocery chains, Chgo., 1945-49; Riv.-Dolton corr. Calumet Index, Chgo., 1953-58, editorial asst., 1958-60, asst. editor, 1960-68, editor, 1968-72; with Suburban Index, Chgo., 1959-72, editor, 1960-72; mng. editor Index Publs., 1972-74; free lance writer, 1974-94, ret., 1994. Public relations vol. New Hope Sch., 1959-67; bd. dirs. United Fund of Riverdale, Roseland Mental Health Assn., Thornton chpt. Am. Field Service; cmty. rels. vol. Ctrl. Ark. Therapy Inst. Recipient Disting. Service Meml. scroll PTA, 1959, Sch. Bell award Ill. Edn. Assn., 1965, Outstanding Citizen award Chgo. South C. of C., 1972. Named Outstanding Civic Leader Am.; recipient Vol. citation Ctrl. Ark. Radiation Therapy Inst., 1994. Mem. Ill. Woman's Press Assn. (past pres. Woman of Distinction 1968, recipient 46 state awards, 3 nat. awards), Ark. Press Women (Communicator of Achievement award 1991, honored 50 Yr. member 1994), Nat. Fedn. Press Women (past pres. parley past presidents 1981, past dir. protocol, Honors 50 Yrs. Membership 1994), Riverdale (v.p. 1966-68), Chgo. South (v.p., dir.) chambers commerce. Home: 1421 N University Ave Apt 215N Little Rock AR 72207-5241

SERFOZO, MARY, writer; b. Seattle, Feb. 21, 1925; d. Patrick and Olive Cannon; m. John Serfozo, Aug. 8, 1953; children: Stephan, David. BA, U. Wash. freelance author, copywriter; past asst. editor Mademoiselle; past publicity Elizabeth Arden, N.Y.C., Pan Am. Airways, Hawaiian sugar industry, Honolulu. Author: Welcome, Roberto!/Bienvenido, Roberto!, 1969, Who Said Red?, 1988 (Pick of List, Am. Booksellers, Cert. of Excellence, Children's Choice), Who Wants One?, 1989 (Reading Magic award Parenting), Rain Talk, 1990, Dirty Kurt, 1992, Benjamin Bigfoot, 1993, Joe Joe, 1993, There's a Square, 1996, What's Waht, 1996. *

SERGE, ANITA LOUISE, elementary education educator; b. Quakertown, Pa., May 24, 1962; d. Santo Anthony and Althea Fern (Wieand) S. BS, Pa. State U., 1984; M in Secondary Edn., Kutztown U., 1991; postgrad., Lehigh U., 1992—. Cert. elem. edn. Tchr. Quakertown (Pa.) Cmty. Sch. Dist., 1985—; asst. basketball coach H.S., Quakertown (Pa.) Sch. Dist., 1988-90, mem. parent/tchr. task force, 1989, asst. softball coach H.S., 1990-91, head girls' basketball coach, 1995—, mem. tesing com., 1992, mem. long range planning com., 1992. Mem. NEA, Quakertown Cmty. Edn. Assn. (v.p. 1988-91, negotiations com. 1994-95), Pa. State Edn. Assn. Home: 6832 Ridge Rd Zionsville PA 18092

SERGI, ROSE ANNE, journalism educator; b. Somerville, Mass., Feb. 28, 1946; d. Guy John and Adeline (Ministeri) S.; children:Guy Doyon, Matthew Doyon. BA, Northeastern U., 1968, MA, 1970. Asst. prof. Bryant-McIntosh Jr. Coll., Lawrence, Mass., 1970-72; instr. Daniel Webster Jr. Coll., Nashua, N.H., 1971-74; tchr. Billerica (Mass.) Meml. High Sch., 1972-75; instr. U. Lowell, Mass., 1975-77; gen. assignment reporter, then investigative reporter Lowell Sun, 1985-87; instr. Regis Coll., Weston, Mass., 1987-88; sr. lectr. Northeastern U., Boston, 1971—; assoc. prof. journalism Middlesex C.C., Bedford, Mass., 1988-95, prof., 1995—. Appointee Svc. Acad. Rev. Bd., Boston, 1983. Mem. NEA, Mass. Tchrs. Assn., Northeastern U. Journalism Alumni Assn. (pres. 1990—). Roman Catholic. Office: Middlesex Community Coll Springs Rd Bedford MA 01730

SEROTA, BARBARA JO BEANE, librarian; b. Edinburg, Tex., July 13, 1946; d. William Edward and Katie Frances (Woodruff) Beane; m. Thomas Dean Serota, June 4, 1967; children: Scott Thomas, Susan Renee. BA, Pan Am. Coll., 1969; MLS, U. Tex. at Austin, 1973. Tchr. Kingsville (Tex.) Ind. Sch. Dist., 1969-71, Marion County Sch. Bd., Ocala, Fla., 1971-72; adminstrv. asst. Grad. Sch. Libr. Sci. U. Tex., Austin, 1974-75; cataloger, acquistions libr., assoc. libr. State Law Libr., Austin, 1975-84; sch. libr. Corpus Christi (Tex.) Ind. Sch. Dist., 1985-89, Flour Bluff Ind. Sch. dist., 1989—. Mem. Tex. Libr. Assn. Methodist. Office: Flour Bluff High Sch 2505 Waldron Rd Corpus Christi TX 78418

SEROTA, SUSAN PERLSTADT, lawyer; b. Chgo., Sept. 10, 1945; d. Sidney Morris and Mildred (Penn) Perlstadt; m. James Ian Serota, May 7, 1972; children: Daniel Louis, Jonathan Mark. AB, U. Mich., 1967; JD, NYU, 1971. Bar: Ill. 1971, D.C. 1972, N.Y. 1981, U.S. Dist. Ct. (no. dist.) Ill. 1971, U.S. Dist. Ct. (so. dist.) N.Y. 1981, U.S. Dist. Ct. (ea. dist.) N.Y. 1985, U.S. Ct. Claims 1972, U.S. Tax Ct. 1972, U.S. Ct. Appeals (D.C. cir.) 1972. Assoc. Gottlieb & Schwartz, Chgo., 1971-72, Silverstein & Mullens, Washington, 1972-75, Cahill Gordon & Reindel, N.Y.C., 1975-82; assoc. Winthrop, Stimson, Putnam & Roberts, N.Y.C., 1982, ptnr., 1983—; adj. prof. Sch. Law, Georgetown U., Washington, 1974-75; mem. faculty Practicins Law Inst., N.Y.C., 1983—. Editor: ERISA Fiduciary Law, 1995; assoc. editor Exec. Compensation Jour., 1973-75; dep. editor Tax Mgmt., Estate and Gift Taxation and Exec. Compensation, 1973-75; mem. editl. adv. bd. Benefits Law Jour., 1988—, Tax Mgmt. Compensation Jour., 1993—; mem. bd. editor ERISA and Benefits Law Jour., 1992—; contbr. articles to profl. jours. Fellow Am. Coll. Tax Counsel; mem. ABA (chmn. joint com. employee benefits taxation sect. 1991-92, coun. mem. taxation sect. 1994—), Internat. Pension and Employee Benefits Lawyers Assn. (co-chair 1993-95), N.Y. State Bar Assn. (exec. com. tax sect. 1988-92), Am. Bar Retirement Assn. (dir. 1994—). Democrat. Office: Winthrop Stimson Putnam & Roberts One Battery Park Pla New York NY 10004-1490

SERRAINO, JOANNE FRANCES, art director; b. Passaic, N.J., Aug. 27, 1942; d. Charles and Ann Rose (Molica) S. BA, Rutgers U., Newark, 1964; MA, Jersey City State Coll., 1976; MFA, Pratt Inst., 1983. Cert. art tchr. grades K-12, N.J. 5th grade tchr. St. Peter the Apostle Sch., River Edge, N.J., 1965; art tchr. grades K-8 Little Ferry (N.J.) Pub. Sch. Sys., 1967-79; vet. asst. Hasbrouk Heights (N.J.) Vet. Clinic, 1979-85; N.J. dept. labor, chief fine arts Divsn Vocat. Rehab. Svcs., Hackensack, N.J., 1985—; adj. art prof. Jersey City State Coll., 1975; adj. prof. Bergen C.C., Paramus, N.J., 1979-81; exec. bd. mem. Very Spl. Arts/N.J., New Brunswick, 1987-93; mem. Art Pride, Trenton, 1995. Exhibited drawing and sculpture in one-person show Jersey City State Coll., 1976; sculptures exhibited St. John's 9th Annual Exhbn. of Contemporary Religious Art, 1984, Nat. Show of Contemporary Religious Art, 1985. Mem. Nat. Rehab. Assn. North East, N.J. Art Edn. Assn. (Profl. award for work as art dir. 1990). Home: 204 Harrison Ave Hasbrouck Heights NJ 07604 Office: NJ Dept Labor NJ Divsn Vocat Rehab Svcs 60 State St Hackensack NJ 07601

SERRILL, PATRICIA WHITFIELD, media and management consultant; b. Walhalla, S.C., Feb. 26, 1941; d. C. and O. Glayds (McCurry) Whitfield; m. Theodore A. Serrill, Feb. 21, 1987; children: Marc Schaffer, Eric Schaffer, Jill D. Schaffer Smith. AA, Wingate (N.C.) Coll., 1975; student, Cen. Fla. Tech. Coll., Valencia Community Coll., Orlando, Fla. Lic. real estate sales, Fla. Mem. circulation staff Orlando (Fla.) Sentinel; real estate agt. Park Place Assocs., Winter Park, Fla.; bus. mgr. Pinllas Review Inc., Pubs., Clearwater, Fla.; pvt. cons. Clearwater, Fla., 1994—. Asst. editor: Counterpoint, Wingate Coll. 1974-75. Treas. Clearwater Rep. Club, 1987-88; v.p., bd. dirs. Imperial Park Owners Assn.; bd. dirs. So. Pinellas Cmty. Coun., 1995—, recording sec., 1995—; treas. Canterbury Chase HOA, 1995-96, pres., 1996—. Mem. ABWA, FALs, NALs, NAFE, Clearwater Bar Assn. (aux.-hon.), Clearwater Legal Secs. Assn.

SERSTOCK, DORIS SHAY, retired microbiologist, educator, civic worker; b. Mitchell, S.D., June 13, 1926; d. Elmer Howard and Hattie (Christopher) Shay; BA, Augustana Coll., 1947; postgrad. U. Minn., 1966-67, Duke U., summer 1969, Communicable Disease Center, Atlanta, 1972; m. Ellsworth I. Serstock, Aug. 30, 1952; children: Barbara Anne, Robert Ellsworth, Mark Douglas. Bacteriologist, Civil Service, S.D., Colo., Mo., 1947-52; research bacteriologist U. Minn., 1952-53; clin. bacteriologist Dr. Lufkin's Lab., 1954-55; chief technologist St. Paul Blood Bank of ARC, 1959-65; microbiologist in charge mycology lab. VA Hosp., Mpls., 1968-93; instr. Coll. Med. Scis., U. Minn., 1970-79, asst. prof. Coll. Lab. Medicine and Pathology, 1979-93. Mem. Richfield Planning Commn., 1965-71, sec., 1968-71. Contbr. articles to profl. jours. Extended ministries commn. Wood Lake Luth. Ch., Richfield, Minn., 1993-94; rep. religious coun. Mall Am., Bloomington, Minn., 1993-94, chief nursery caregiver Christ the King Lutheran Ch., Bloomington, Minn. 1994—. Fellow Augusta Coll.; named to Exec. and Profl. Hall of Fame; recipient Alumni Achievement award Augustana Coll., 1977; Superior Performance award VA Hosp., 1978, 82, Cert. of Recognition, 1988; Golden Spore awards Mycology Observer, 1985, 87. Mem. Minn. Planning Assn. Republican. Clubs: Richfield Women's Garden (pres. 1959), Wild Flower Garden (chmn. 1961). Home: 7201 Portland Ave Minneapolis MN 55423-3218

SERVERIAN, HEIDI SUE WHITAKER, accountant, systems developer; b. Framingham, Mass., Sept. 21, 1964; d. Charles Harvey and Judith R. (Reich) Whitaker; m. Raymond Serverian, Oct. 8, 1988; 1 child, William Michael. BS in Acctg., BS in Mgmt. Info. Sys., U. Ariz., 1987. Acctg. clk. Inventory Auditors, Inc., Denver, 1984; leasing and adminstrv. asst. James Presley Co., Tucson, 1985-86; office mgr. Sid's Appliance and TV, Tucson, 1986; assoc. acct., acct. GTE Calif., Thousand Oaks, Calif., 1987-89; auditor I and II GTE Svc. Corp., Westlake Village, Calif., 1989-91, sr. auditor, 1991-94; staff acct., staff adminstr. regulatory acctg. GTE Telephone Ops., Irving, Tex., 1994-96; bus. process specialist sys. GTE Long Distance, Irving, 1996—; mem. Project Mgmt. Inst., 1996. Mem. Inst. Mgmt. Accts. (CMA), Inst. Internal Auditors, Lions Club Internat. (Lionette 1990-95). Office: GTE Long Distance PO Box 152211 Irving TX 75015-2211

SERVINSKI, SARAH JANE (JEROUE), language arts educator; b. Detroit, Sept. 13, 1944; d. Edward Lawrence and Frances Elizabeth (Henne) Jeroue; m. Leonard Charles Servinski, July 31, 1965; children: Charles, Mary, Michael, Katherine, Andrew. BA, Mich. State U., 1965, MA, 1978; EdS, Cen. Mich. U., 1990. Cert. tchr., adminstr., Mich. Tchr. elem. and secondary schs. Mich., 1965-80; assoc. prof. lang. arts Northwood U., Midland, Mich., 1980-90; field placement coord. Saginaw Valley State Univ./Coll. of Edn., University Center, Mich., 1991-95; owner Maple Hill Farm, Midland, Mich., 1990—; communications cons.; co-founder Maple Hill Nursery and Flowers, Midland, 1977, Maple Hill Equip. Sales and Svc., Midland, 1987; founder Maple Hill Children's Shop, Midland, 1983; adj. prof. lang. arts Delta Coll., University Center, Mich., 1990—. mem. Dow Corning Citizens Community Adv. Panel, Midland, Mich, 1991-92. Republican. Roman Catholic. Home: 2674 N Eastman Rd Midland MI 48640-8833

SERVISS, ALICIA J., secondary school educator; b. N.Y.C., May 28, 1968; d. Roy Irwin and Diane (Kulberg) Pasternack; m. Kenneth L. Serviss, Aug. 27, 1995. BA, SUNY, Albany, 1990; MA in Tchg., Fairleigh Dickinson U., 1993. Cert. secondary math. tchr., N.J. Hebrew sch. tchr. Ctrl. Synagogue, Rockville Center, N.Y., 1990-91; computer and math. tchr. The Harding (N.J.) Sch., 1991-94; math. tchr. Woodbridge (N.J.) Twp. Bd. Edn., 1994—; math. tutor, N.J., 1993—; yearbook advisor Colonia Mid. Sch., 1994-95; newspaper advisor Harding Twp. Sch., 1993-94. Jewish. Home: 11 Deborah Way Fanwood NJ 07023 Office: Woodbridge Twp Schs Colonia Mid Sch Delaward Ave Colonia NJ 07067

SESSIONS, JUDITH ANN, librarian, university library dean; b. Lubbock, Tex., Dec. 16, 1947; d. Earl Alva and Anna (Mayer) S. BA cum laude, Cen. Fla. U., 1970; MLS, Fla. State U., 1971; postgrad., Am. U., 1980, George Washington U., 1983. Head libr. U. S.C., Salkehatchie, 1974-77; dir. Libr. and Learing Resources Ctr. Mt. Vernon Coll., Washington, 1977-82; planning and systems libr. George Washington U., Washington, 1981-82, asst. univ. libr. for adminstrn. svcs., acting head tech. svcs., 1982-84; univ. libr. Calif. State U., Chico, 1984-88; univ. libr., dean of libr. Miami U., Oxford, Ohio, 1988—; cons. Space Planning, S.C., 1976, DataPhase Implementation, Bowling Green U., 1982, TV News Study Ctr., George Washington U., 1981; asst. prof. Dept. Child Devel., Mt. Vernon Coll., 1978-81; mem., lectr. U.S.-China Libr. Exch. Del., 1986, 91; lectr., presenter in field; mem. coord. com. OhioLink Adv. Coun., 1995—, v.p., 1996. Contbr. articles, book revs. to profl. jours. Trustee Christ Hosp., Cin., 1990-94, Deaconness Gamble Rsch. Ctr., Cin., 1990-94; bd. dirs. Hamilton (Ohio) YMCA, 1994-97, pres., 1995-96, v.p., 1996-97; v.p. Ohio Link Co-ordinating Coun., 1995-98, v.p., 1995, pres., 1996. Recipient award for outstanding contbn. D.C. Libr. Assn., 1979; rsch. grantee Mt. Vernon Coll., 1980; recipient Fulbright-Hayes Summer Travel fellowship to Czechoslovakia, 1991. Mem. ALA (Olofson award 1978, councillor-at-large policy making group 1981-94, coun. com. on coms. 1983-84, intellectual freedom com. 1984-88, directions and program rev. com. 1989-91, fin. and audit subcom. 1989-90, mem. exec. bd. 1989-94), Assn. Coll. and Rsch. Librs. (editorial bd. Coll. and Rsch. Librs. jour. 1979-84, nominations and appointments com. 1983-85, faculty status com. 1984-86), Libr. and Info. Tech. Assn. (chair legis. and regulation com. 1980-81), Libr. Adminstrn. and Mgmt. Assn. (bd. dirs. libr. orgn. and mgmt. sect. 1985-87), Calif. Inst. Librs. (v.p., pres. elect 1987-88), Mid-Atlantic Regional Libr. Fedn. (mem. exec. bd. 1982-84), Jr. Mems. Round Table (pres. 1981-82), Intellectual Freedom Round Table (sec. 1984-85), Freedom to Read Found. (trustee 1984-88, v.p. 1985-86, treas. 1986-87, pres. 1987-88), Rotary, Beta Phi Mu. Home: 45 Waters Way Hamilton OH 45013-6324 Office: Miami U Edgar W King Oxford OH 45056

SESTANOVICH, MOLLY BROWN, writer; b. Denver, Nov. 30, 1921; d. Ben Miller and Mary (McCord) Brown; m. Stephen Nicholas Sestanovich, July 9, 1949; children: Stephen, Mary, Robert Benjamin. Student, Fairmont Jr. Coll., 1939-41. Radio comml. writer Young & Rubicam Advt., N.Y.C. and Hollywood, Calif., 1941-47; radio scriptwriter Korean Broadcasting Co., Seoul, 1947-48; substitute tchr. County Sch. Bd., Montgomery County, Md., 1956-58; syndicated polit. columnist Lesher Newspapers, various locations, 1971-91; freelance polit. writer Moraga, Calif., 1991—; active internat. women's orgns., Italy, Thailand, Singapore, Finland, Venezuela, 1949-70. Writer, spokesperson LWV, Diablo Valley, Calif., 1970. Recipient prize for contbn. to cause of peace and justice Mt. Diablo Peace Ctr., 1989. Mem. Am. Fgn. Svc. Assn., Lamorinda Dem. Club (program chmn. 1985). Unitarian. Home: 15 Idlewood Ct Moraga CA 94556

SETLOW, CAROLYN EVE, marketing professional; b. New Haven, Conn., June 18, 1946; d. Herbert David and Claire (Rappaport) S.; m. Philippe Lazard Felix Sommer, Jan. 8, 1983; children: Alexander, Daniel. BA, Smith Coll., Northampton, Mass., 1968; MA, The Fletcher Sch. Law and Diplomacy, Medford, Mass., 1970; postgrad., Harvard Bus. Sch., 1982. Exec. v.p. Louis Harris & Assocs., N.Y.C., 1970-77; v.p., corp. planning Newsweek, Inc., N.Y.C., 1978-82; pres. Setlowear, Inc., Orange, Conn., 1982-88, Harris Scholastic Rsch., N.Y.C., 1989-91; mktg. and opinion rsch. profl., group sr. v.p. Roper Starch Worldwide, N.Y.C., 1991—; mem. exec. com. Roper Starch Worldwide, N.Y.C., 1994—. Bd. dirs. Northside Ctr. for Child Devel., N.Y.C., 1980—, chmn., 1988-90; bd. dirs. Fedn. of Protestant Welfare Agys., N.Y.C., 1981-91; bd. dirs. Nat. Coun. of Aging, Washington, 1975-83; chmn. The Dalton Coun./The Dalton Sch., N.Y.C., 1993-95. Recipient The Buddy award NOW Legal Def. and Edn. Fund, N.Y. chpt., 1986. Jewish. Avocation: skiing. Office: Roper Starch Worldwide 205 E 42nd St New York NY 10017

SETLOW, NEVA DELIHAS, artist, research biologist; b. New Haven, Dec. 29, 1940; d. Nevins Donald and Eve Mary (Kokojan) Cummings; m. Nicholas Delihas, Aug. 21, 1961 (div. 1986); m. Richard Burton Setlow, Mar. 3, 1989; children: Nicholas Delihas, Marcia Hermus, Cynthia DiGiacomo. BA, Empire State Coll., 1975. Rschr. Brookhaven Nat. Lab., Upton, N.Y., 1976—. Group exhibits include Goodman Gallery, Southampton, N.Y., 1993, Ward Nasse Gallery, N.Y.C., 1993, 94, 95, Islip Art Mus., 1993, 96, East Hampton Visual Art Festival, 1995. Recipient Purchase prize Berkshire Art Assn., Pittsfield, Mass., 1972, 25th Anniversary award Silvermine Art Guild, New Canaan, Conn., 1972, Sculpture award Huntington Twp. Art League, 1974, 76. Mem. Internat. Sculpture Coun., Southampton Artists. Home: 4 Beachland Ave East Quogue NY 11942

SETSER, CAROLE SUE, food science educator; b. Warrenton, Mo., Aug. 26, 1940; d. Wesley August and Mary Elizabeth (Meine) Schulze; m. Donald Wayne Setser, June 2, 1969; children: Bradley Wayne, Kirk Wesley, Brett Donald. BS, U. Mo., 1962; MS, Cornell U., 1964; PhD, Kans. State U., 1971. Grad. asst. Cornell U., Ithaca, N.Y., 1962-64; instr. Kans. State U., Manhattan, 1964-72, asst. prof., 1974-81, assoc. prof., 1981-86, prof., 1986—. Recipient Rsch. Excellence award Coll. of Human Ecology, Manhattan, 1990. Mem. Am. Assn.Cereal Chemists (assoc. editor 1989-93), Inst. Food Techs. (chmn. sensory evaluation divsn. edn. com. 1989-92, continuing edn. com. 1992—, other offices), Kappa Omicron Nu (Excellence for Rsch. award 1987), Sigma Xi, Phi Upsilon Omicron, Gamma Sigma Delta, Phi Tau Sigma. Office: Kansas State U Justin Hall Dept Foods Nutrition Manhattan KS 66506

SETTEMBRO, JANET MARY, secondary education educator; b. Springfield, Mass., Nov. 20, 1953; d. Michael J. Settembro. BA in Maths., Coll. of Our Lady of the Elms, Chicopee, Mass., 1975; MBA, Western New Eng. Coll., 1982. Cert. secondary tchr., Mass. Tchr. maths. Cathedral High

Sch., Springfield, 1975-77, Van Sickle Jr. High Sch., Springfield, 1977-86, Springfield Ctrl. High Sch., 1986—; tchr. math. Digital Equipment Corp., Springfield, summers 1982-84, Am. Internat. Coll. Springfield, 1985-87; mentor for students Western New Eng. Coll., Springfield, 1988—. Mem. Nat. Coun. Tchrs. Math. (chairperson com. regional and nat. confs. 1982, 88, 95), Adriatic Club, Alpha Delta Kappa. Home: 85 Woodmont St Springfield MA 01104-1205 Office: Springfield Ctrl High Sch 1840 Roosevelt Ave Springfield MA 01109-2437

SEVALSTAD, SUZANNE ADA, accounting educator; b. Butte, Mont., Mar. 26, 1948; d. John Cornelius and Ivy Jeanette (Cloke) Pilling; m. Nels Sevalstad, Jr., Mar. 11, 1975. BS in Bus. with high distinction, Mont. State U., 1970, MS in Bus., 1972. CPA, Mont. Internal auditor Anaconda Co., Butte, 1970-71; mgr. Wise River (Mont.) Club, 1976-79; instr. acctg. Bozeman (Mont.) Vocat./Tech. Ctr., 1970-72, Ea. Mont. Coll., Billings, 1972-73, Mont. State U., Bozeman, 1973-76, U. Nev., Las Vegas, 1979—. Recipient Women of Month award Freshman Class Women, 1976, Disting. Tchr. Coll. Bus. U. Nev., 1983, 86, 89, 93, Prof. of Yr. award Student Acctg. Assn. U. Nev., 1984, 87, 88, 90, 91, Outstanding Acctg. Prof. award Acctg. Students of U. Nev., 1987, 88, 89, Spanos Disting. Teaching award, 1989, 94. Mem. AICPA, Am. Acctg. Assn., Nat. Inst. Mgmt. Acctg. (campus coord. 1988—), Inst. Mgmt. Accts., Assn. for Female Execs., Golden Key Soc. (hon.). Office: U Nev Dept Acctg 4505 S Maryland Pky Las Vegas NV 89154-9900

SEVERIN, CHARLOTTE WOOD, nurse, health consultant, artist; b. Evanston, Ill., Oct. 25, 1936; d. Emerson and Lydia (Weber) Wood; m. Gerald Lang Severin, June 14, 1958; children: John Gerald, Kimberly Sue, Juliana Leigh. BS with honors, Stanford U., 1959. RN, Calif.; lic. pub. health nurse; lifetime school health credential. Staff nurse Stanford U. Hosp., San Francisco, 1959; vis. pub. health nurse Mpls., 1959-60; clinic coordinating nurse Stanford U. Hosp. Neurology Clinic, Palo Alto, Calif., 1965-66; sch. health cons. Livermore (Calif.) Sch. Dist., 1967-69, Pleasanton (Calif.) Unified Sch. Dist., 1969-94; artist in residence, watercolor instr. Pleasanton and Livermore Sch. Dists., 1969—; art tchr. City of Pleasanton Pks. and Community Svcs., 1992—. Over 25 one-woman shows, including Wente, Concannon and Stoneyridge vineyards, various galleries; represented in pvt. and corp. collections in U.S., Japan, Guatemala, France, Germany, Africa, Ireland, Mex., also fgn. consultates and embassies in San Francisco. Chmn. 75th birthday hist. mural City of Pleasanton, 1970, chmn. refurbishing it for 100th birthday of city City of Pleasanton, 1995, chmn. bicentennial festivals com., 1976; founder Pleasanton Cultural Arts Coun., pres., bd. dirs., 1973-94; vol., coord. BSE instrn. Am. Cancer Soc., 1976—; chmn. renovation Amador Theater, 1981-89; founding chmn. bd. Pub. Access TV Channel, 1983—; founder Arts in Schs. Program, Tri-Valley, Calif., 1984-94. Recipient Gen.'s commendation 3d inf. divsn. arty. 7th Army Germany, 1962, commendation City of Pleasanton, 1976, 89, Edn. award Bay Area Sch. Adminstrs. and Phi Delta Kappa, 1983, 86, award Am. Cancer Soc., 1983, 85; named Woman of Yr., City of Pleasanton, 1976, Woman of Distinction, Pleasanton Soroptomists, 1986. Mem. AAUW (life, press. 1972-74, state officer 1973-74, chmn. major fundraiser for ednl. fellowships Livermore, Pleasanton, Dublin br. 1995, 96, keynote spkr. 1996, fellow 1974, 89), Calif. Watercolor Soc. (Signature award 1992), Pleasanton Art League (charter), Stanford U. Nurse Alumnae Assn. Presbyterian.

SEVERNS, PENNY L., state legislator; b. Decatur, Ill., Jan. 21, 1952. BS in Polit. Sci. and Internat. Relations, So. Ill. U., 1974. Spl. asst. to adminstr. AID, Washington, 1977-79; city councilwoman Decatur, from 1983; mem. 51st dist. Ill. State Senate, 1987—, chief budget negotiator for Senate Dems., 1993—, minority spokesperson appropriations com., 1994—. Office: Ill State Senate State Capitol Springfield IL 62706

SEVERSON, LOIS I, secondary education educator, chairperson; b. Madison, Wis., Sept. 25, 1941; d. Jacob J. and Laura Theresa (Brunner) Z.; m. Robert T. Severson, June 3, 1972; children: Jeanne M., Patricia A. BA in Physics, Alverno Coll., 1965; MS, U. Wis., Mllw., 1972. Cert. tchr. math. and sci grades 7, 8, 9, Wis. Math. and sci. tchr. St. Mary's Sch., Hales Corners, Wis., 1963-67; math. tchr. Madison Pub. Schs., 1967-69; math. tchr., chairperson Elmbrook Middle Sch., Elm Grove, Wis., 1969—. Religious edn. tchr. Roman Cath. Chs., Cross Plains, Wis., Hales Corners, 1964-68, Men. Falls, Wis., Pewaukee, Wis., 1981—. Grantee (summers) in math. NSF, St. Cloud, Minn. 1967, in sci. Madison, Wis., 1968. Mem. Nat. Coun. Tchrs. of Math., Wis. Math. Coun., Wis. Middle Level Educators. Office: Elmbrook Middle Sch 1500 Pilgrim Pkwy Elm Grove WI 53122

SEWARD, GRACE EVANGELINE, retired librarian; b. L.A., Feb. 2, 1914; d. William Henry and Maud Leuty (Elphingstone) S. BA, Calif. State, L.A., 1959; MLS, U. So. Calif., L.A., 1961. Cert. tchr., Calif. Page L.A. County Pub. Library, San Gabriel, Calif., 1927-37, asst. branch librarian, 1938-40; various clerical positions Zoss Const./Consolidated, San Diego, 1941-42; time keeper Cal Ship Constrn., Wilmington, Calif., 1942-45; turkey ranch mgr. Bagnard Turkey Ranch, Baldwin Park, Calif., 1945-47; filing clerk Union Hardware, L.A., 1947-49; library asst. Rosemead (Calif.) H.S., 1949-60; librarian Anaheim (Calif.) Union H.S., 1960-61; catalog head librarian Pasadena (Calif.) City Coll., 1961-79; library classifier Pasadena City Coll., 1979-81. Author: (bibliographies) Man and Environment, 1970, Black America, 1978, (index) American Rose Mag., 1989-91; editor: Bulletin Rose Soc. Rose Parade, 1974-87. Mem. Am. Rose Soc. (life, life judge, cons. 1978—, elected dist. dir. Pacific S.W. 1985-88, Pacific Southwest Dist. Silver Honor medal 1991, Outstanding Dist. Judge award 1995), Royal Nat. Rose Soc. (life), Calif. Garden Clubs (pres. Ranche De Duarte 1991-96), Calif. Library Assn., Beta Phi Mu (hon.). Home: 2397 N Morslay Rd Altadena CA 91001

SEWELL, BEVERLY JEAN, financial executive; b. Oklahoma City, July 10, 1942; d. Benjamin B. Bainbridge and Faith Marie (Mosier) Allision; m. Ralph Byron Sewell, Jan. 23, 1962; children: M. Timothy, Pamela J. Student, U. Okla., 1960-61, Jackson C.C., 1973-77; BA in Bus., Mesa Coll., 1982; cert., Coll. Fin. Planning, 1984, MS in Fin. Planning, 1994. Sole practice fin. planning Grand Junction, Colo., 1985-87; fin. planner, broker Interpacific Investors Services, Grand Junction, 1987-88; investment broker A.G. Edwards & Sons, Inc., Grand Junction, 1988-92, v.p., 1992—. Mem. ctrl. com. Grand Junction Rep. Orgn., 1988; mem. Grand Junction Planning Commn., 1987-89; bd. dirs. Grand Junction Symphony, 1991-94, Downtown Devel. Authority, St. Mary's Hosp. Mem. Inst. Cert. Fin. Planners, Internat. Assn. Fin. Planning. Home: 717 Wedge Dr Grand Junction CO 81506-1866 Office: A G Edwards & Sons Inc 501 Main St Grand Junction CO 81501-2607

SEWELL, PHYLLIS SHAPIRO, retail chain executive; b. Cin., Dec. 26, 1930; d. Louis and Mollye (Mark) Shapiro; m. Martin Sewell, Apr. 5, 1959; 1 child, Charles Steven. B.S. in Econs. with honors, Wellesley Coll., 1952. With Federated Dept. Stores, Inc., Cin., 1952-88, research dir. store ops., 1961-65, sr. research dir., 1965-70, operating v.p., research, 1970-75, corp. v.p., 1975-79, sr. v.p., research and planning, 1979-88; bd. dirs. Lee Enterprises, Inc., Davenport, Iowa, Pitney Bowes, Inc., SYSCO Corp. Bd. dirs. Nat. Cystic Fibrosis Found., Cin., 1963—; chmn. divsn. United Appeals, Cin., 1982; mem. bus. adv. coun. Sch. Bus. Adminstrn., Miami U., Oxford, Ohio, 1982-84; trustee Cin. Cmty. Chest, 1984-94, Jewish Fedn., 1990-92, Jewish Hosp., 1990—; mem. bus. leadership coun. Wellesley Coll., 1990—, Fordham U. Grad. Sch. Bus., 1988-89. Recipient Alumnae Achievement award Wellesley Coll., 1979, Disting. Cin. Bus. and Profl. Woman award, 1981, Directors' Choice award Nat. Women's Econ. Alliance, 1995; named one of 100 Top Corp. Women Bus. Week mag., 1976, Career Woman of Achievement YWCA, 1983, to Ohio Women's Hall of Fame, 1982.

SEWER, DORIS E., critical care nurse, educator; b. Charlotte, St. Thomas, V.I., Oct. 23, 1934; d. Richard and Rachel (Callwood) Donovan; m. Edmundo Valerius Sewer, Mar. 19, 1959; children: Milagros Holden, Melinda Muganzo Mignel Sewer, Maria Vantine. Diploma, Bella Vista Sch. Nursing, Mayaguez, P.R., 1969; BSN, Andrews U., 1975; MA in Edn., Counseling, Calif. State U., San Bernardino, 1979; cert. in clin. pastoral edn., Loma Linda U., 1989; PhD, Walden U., 1996. Staff nurse ICU Lincoln (Nebr.) Gen. Hosp., 1969-72; charge nurse ICU Loma Linda (Calif.) Community Hosp., 1974-75; staff nurse ICU Loma Linda U. Med. Ctr., 1975-77; dir. nursing Mountain View Child Care Ctr., Loma Linda, 1977-79; asst. prof. nursing Chaffey Coll., Ont., Calif., 1979-82; nursing instr., missionary nurse Antillian Coll., Mayaguez, P.R., 1982—; counselor, lectr. Suicide and Crisis Intervention, San Bernardino, Calif., 1977-80; part-time clin. instr. psychiat. nursing Riverside (Calif.) City Coll., 1976-78; instr. ICU course Bella Vista Hosp., Mayaguez, 1984, 86, 88, 89; participating instr. Intensive Care Course Antillian Coll., Mayaguez, 1989; mem. San Bernardino Adv. Com. Drug Abuse, 1979-82; vis. prof. nursing U. V.I., St. Thomas, 1991; pres. Tutorial Nursing and Edn. Unlimited. Mem. Nat. League Nursing.

SEWITCH, DEBORAH E., health science association administrator, educator, sleep researcher; b. Perth Amboy, N.J., Nov. 21, 1954; d. Myron David and Barbara A. (Werner) S. BA, Duke U., 1976; MA, CCNY, 1980; MA and PhD in Psychology, CUNY, 1982. Diplomate Am. Bd. Sleep Medicine. Assoc. dir. Sleep Disorders Ctr. Columbia-Presbyn. Med. Ctr., N.Y.C., 1980-81; sr. clinician Sleep Evaluation Ctr. Western Psychiat. Inst. & Clinic, Pitts., 1982-84; assoc. dir. Sleep Evaluation Ctr. U. Pitts., 1985, instr. in psychiatry Sch. of Medicine, 1984-85; dir. Sleep Disorders Ctr. The Griffin Hosp., Derby, Conn., 1985-89; asst. clin. prof. psychiatry Sch. of Medicine Yale U., New Haven, 1987-89; rsch. dir. unit for exptl. thermoregulation Inst. of Pa. Hosp., Phila., 1989-91; clin. asst. prof. psychology U. Pa., Phila., 1990-91; dir. Sleep Disorders Ctr. Hampstead (N.H.) Hosp., 1991—; chair PhD part II exam. subcom. for bd. certification in clin. sleep disorders Am. Bd. Sleep Medicine, Rochester, Minn., 1989-92; cons. reviewer Jour. Sleep, Jour. Psychophysiology, Jour. Biol. Psychiatry; cons. in clin. sleep disorders and rsch. dept. psychiatry U. Pa., 1990-91. Mem. APA, Am. Sleep Disorders Assn., Internat. Brain Rsch. Orgn., Soc. for Neurosci., Sleep Rsch. Soc. Jewish. Office: Hampstead Hosp Sleep-Wake Disorders Ctr 218 East Rd Hampstead NH 03841

SEXTER, DEBORAH RAE, lawyer; b. Bklyn., May 28, 1939; d. Benjamin and Minnie (Popkewitz) Rochkin; m. Jay Sexter, Apr. 14, 1957; children: David, Michael. BBA, CCNY, 1961; AAS, Bergen C.C., 1975; MS, Fordham U., 1978, JD, 1987; profl. diploma, United Hosps. Sch. Nurse Anesthesia, 1980. Bar: N.J. 1987, U.S. Dist. Ct. N.J. 1987, N.Y. 1988; RN, N.J., N.Y.; cert. RN anesthetist, Am. Assn. Nurse Anesthetists; cert. fraud examiner, Assn. Cert. Fraud Examiners. Community organizer N.Y.C., 1965-70; staff nurse community hosps., Bergen County, N.J., 1975-78; staff anesthetist Columbia-Presbyn. Med. Ctr., N.Y.C., 1980-83, Manhattan Eye, Ear, Throat Hosp., N.Y.C., 1983-84; chief nurse anesthetist Anesthesia Assocs., Nyack, N.Y., 1984-87; pvt. practice law Grand View-on-Hudson, N.Y., 1987-90; sr. asst. gen. counsel, inspector gen. Met. Transp. Authority, N.Y.C., 1990-94; pvt. practice Irvington, N.Y., 1994—. Village justice Village of Grand View-on-Hudson, 1986-92; vice chmn. ethics com. Village of Irvington, N.Y., 1992—; mem. ethics com. Cmty. Hosp., Dobbs Ferry, N.Y., 1995—. Mem. Nat. Assn. Scholars, Fedn. Am. Immigration Reform, N.Y. State Magistrates Assn. Home and Office: 2 Hudson Rd E Irvington NY 10533-2612

SEXTON, BRENDA ATWELL, nursing educator; b. Abingdon, Va., Oct. 20, 1962; d. Carl Edward Jr. and Barbara Jean (Testerman) Atwell; 1 child, Joshua Casey. ADN, Wytheville (Va.) C.C., 1984; BSN cum laude, East Tenn. State U., 1985; postgrad., U. Tenn., 1985—. RN, Va.; Registered Nurse Cert., ANCC, Va.; cert. cmty. 1st aid instr., Va.; cert. ACLS, Va., BLS instr., ARC, Va.; cert. instr. Breast Self-Exam, Testicular Self-Exam and smoking cessation classes, ARC, Va. Staff, charge nurse Bristol (Tenn.) Meml. Hosp., 1985-87; staff nurse Meml. Mission Hosp., Asheville, N.C., 1987-88; staff, relief charge nurse oncology Humana Hosp. Bayside, Virginia Beach, Va., 1988-89; staff nurse orthopedic unit Chesapeake (Va.) Gen. Hosp., 1989-92, clin. nurse educator, 1992—; clin. instr. Tidewater C.C., Portsmouth, Va., 1991. Mem. Am. Soc. Health Edn. and Tng. (Va. chpt.), Educators Awareness Group Hampton Rds., Sigma Theta Tau (Epsilon chpt.). Baptist. Home: 1332 Fallmouth Ct Virginia Beach VA 23464-6320 Office: Chesapeake Gen Hosp 736 Battlefield Blvd N Chesapeake VA 23320-4941

SEXTON, CAROL BURKE, financial institution executive; b. Chgo., Apr. 20, 1939; d. William Patrick and Katharine Marie (Nolan) Burke; m. Thomas W. Sexton Jr., June 30, 1962 (div. June 1976); children: Thomas W., J. Patrick, M. Elizabeth. BA, Barat Coll., 1961; cert. legal, Mallinckrodt Coll., 1974. Tchr. Roosevelt High Sch., Chgo., 1961-63, St. Joseph's Sch., Wilmette, Ill., 1975-80; dir. Jane Byrne Polit. Com., Chgo., 1980-81; mgr. Chgo. Merc. Exch., 1981-84, sr. dir. govt. and civic affairs, 1984-87, v.p. pub. affairs, 1987-94, exec. v.p. corp. rels., 1994—; mem. internat. trade an investment subcom. Chgo. Econ. Devel. Commn., 1989, 90. Bd. dirs. Chgo. Sister Cities, 1992—; chmn. Chgo.-Toronto Sister Cities Com., 1992—; bd. dirs. Ill. Ambs., 1991—, pres., 1994; bd. dirs., sec. Internat. Press Ctr., 1992—, chmn. bd., 1994. Mem. Exec.'s Club of Chgo. (bd. dirs.), Chgo. Conv. and Tourism Bur. (sec. 1989—, exec. com. 1987—, chmn.-elect 1990, chmn. 1991-92), Econ. Club of Chgo. Roman Catholic. Office: Chgo Merc Exch 30 S Wacker Dr Chicago IL 60606-7402

SEXTON, CHARLENE ANN, education consultant; b. Mobile, Ala., Sept. 13, 1946; d. J.D. and Melvina Grace (Kisner) S.; m. Joseph Michael Hesse, May 26, 1978; 1 child, Caroline Aimee Sexton Hesse. BA, St. Mary Coll., 1968; MA, U. Mich., 1969-70; postgrad., U. Wis., 1977-85. Clin. social worker Topeka State Hosp., 1970-72; ESL tchr. Peace Corps, U.S., Korea, Japan, 1974-76; instr. Troy State U., Berlin, 1985-87; asst. prof. edn. Kans. State U., Manhattan, 1988-89, U. Nebr., Lincoln, 1989-90; assoc. dir. The Internat. Ctr. St. Norbert Coll., DePere, Wis., 1990-95; edn. cons. Global Awareness Pub. Co., Madison, Wis., 1995—; adv. bd. Global Studies Resource Ctr. for K-12 Tchrs., DePere, 1992—. Contbg. editor Adult Edn. Quarterly, 1993—; cons. editor Global Awareness Publ. Co., Madison, Wis. 1992—. Bd. dirs. Oneida (Wis.) Workplace Literacy Program, 1993-94. Fellow Womens Rsch. Ctr. U. Wis. Madison; mem. LWV, Am. Assn. Adult & Continuing Edn., Assn. Internat. Edn. Adminstrs., Am. Edn. Rsch. Assn. (womens ednl. rsch. group), Nat. Coun. History Edn., Nat. Acad. Advisors Assn. (book reviewer 1991), Bay Creek Neighborhood Assn., Green Bay C. of C. (adv. com. on internat. trade 1991-93). Home: 1102 Hickory St Madison WI 53715-1726

SEXTON, JEAN ELIZABETH, librarian; b. Boone, N.C., June 24, 1959; d. Warren G. and Carol Jean (Smith) S. AA, Chowan Coll., Murfreesboro, N.C., 1979; AB, U. N.C., 1981, MS in Libr. Sci., 1983. Cataloging libr. Pembroke (N.C.) State U., 1983-89, coord. tech. svcs., 1989-92, asst. dir., coord. tech. svcs., 1992—; cons. Whitaker Libr. Chowan Coll., 1989—. Editor Libr. Lines, 1992; contbr. articles to profl. jours. Order of Silver Feather. Mem. N.C. Libr. Assn., Southeastern Libr. Assn. Democrat. Baptist. Home: 118 Charles St Apt 3 Lumberton NC 28358 Office: U NC Pembroke Livermore Libr Pembroke NC 28372

SEXTON, VIRGINIA STAUDT, retired psychology educator; b. N.Y.C., Aug. 30, 1916; d. Philip Henry and Kathryn Philippa (Burkard) Staudt; m. Richard J. Sexton, Jan. 21, 1961. B.A., Hunter Coll., 1936; MA, Fordham U., 1941, PhD, 1946; LHD, Cedar Crest Coll., 1980. Elem. tchr. St. Peter and St. Paul's Sch., Bronx, N.Y., 1936-39; clk. N.Y.C. Dept. Welfare, 1939-44; lectr., asst. prof., assoc. prof. psychology Notre Dame Coll. of S.I., 1944-52; instr. Hunter Coll. of CUNY, 1953-56, asst. prof., 1957-60, assoc. prof., 1961-66, prof., 1967-68; prof. psychology Herbert H. Lehman Coll., 1968-79, prof. emeritus, 1979—; disting. prof. St. John's U., Jamaica, N.Y., 1979-92; mem. profl. conduct rev. bd. N.Y. State Bd. for Psychology, 1971-78; mem. adv. bd. Archives of History Am. Psychology, 1966—. Author: (with H. Misiak) Catholics in Psychology; A Historical Survey, 1954, History of Psychology: An Overview, 1966, Historical Perspectives in Psychology: Readings, 1971, Phenomenological, Existential and Humanistic Psychologies: A Historical Survey, 1973, Psychology Around the World, 1976. Editor: (with J. Dauben) History and Philosophy of Science: Selected Papers, 1983, (with R. Evans, T. Cadwallader) 100 Years: The American Psychology Assn., 1992, (with J. Hogan) International Psychology: Views From Around The World, 1992; mem. editorial bd. Jour. Phenomenological Psychology, 1977—, Jour. Mind and Behavior, 1979—, Interamerican Jour. Psychology, 1982—, The Humanistic Psychologist, 1984—, Professional Psychology: Research and Practice, 1984-89, Clinician's Research Digest, 1984-92. Contbr. articles to profl. jours. Recipient Margaret Floy Washburn award N.Y. State Psychol. Assn., 1995. Fellow Am. Psychol. Assn., AAAS, N.Y. Acad. Scis., Charles Darwin Assocs.; mem. Am. Hist. Assn., AAUP, AAUW, Am. Assn. for Advancement Humanities, Internat. Assn. Applied Psychology, Internat. Council Psychologists (pres. 1981-82), Interam. Soc. Psychology, Internat. Soc. History of Behavioral and Soc. Scis., Eastern Psychol. Assn., N.Y. Soc. Clin. Psychologists, N.Y. Psychol. Assn., N.Y. Assn. Applied Psychologists, Assn. for Women in Psychology, N.Y. Acad. Scis. (Charles Darwin Assocs. award 1995), Psychologists Social Responsibility, Phi Beta Kappa, Psi Chi (v.p. eastern region 1982-86; pres. 1986-87). Roman Catholic. Avocation: stamp collecting. Home: 188 Ascan Ave Flushing NY 11375-5947

SEYBERT, JOANNA, federal judge; b. Bklyn., Sept. 18, 1946; married; 1 child. BA, U. Cin., 1967; JD, St. John's U., 1971. Bar: N.Y. 1972, U.S. Dist. Ct. (ea. and so. dists.) N.Y. 1973, U.S. Ct. Appeals (2d cir.) 1973. Trial staff atty. Legal Aid Soc., N.Y.C., 1971-73; sr. staff atty. Legal Aid Soc., Mineola, N.Y., 1976-80; sr. trial atty. Fed. Defender Svc., Bklyn., 1973-75; bur. chief Nassau County Atty's Office, Mineola, 1980-87; judge Nassau County Dist. Ct., Hempstead, N.Y., 1987-92, Nassau County Ct., Mineola, 1992-94, U.S. Dist. Ct. (ea. dist.) N.Y., Bklyn., 1994—. Past mem. environ. bd. Town of Oyster Bay; mem. Rep. com. Nassau County, 1979-87. Recipient Norman F. Lent award Criminal Cts. Bar Assn., 1991. Mem. ABA, N.Y. State Bar Assn., Bar Assn. Nassau County, Nassau County Women's Bar Assn., Theodore Roosevelt Am. Inns of Ct., Fed. Judges Assn., Nassau Lawyer's Assn. (past pres.), Nat. Assn. Women Judges. Office: 2 Uniondale Ave Uniondale NY 11553-1259

SEYFFARTH, LINDA JEAN WILCOX, corporate executive; b. Montour Falls, N.Y., May 10, 1948; d. Maurice Roscoe and Theodora (Van Tassell) Wilcox; m. P. Tomlin Agnew, June 29, 1991; 1 child by previous marriage, Kristin. BA magna cum laude, Syracuse (N.Y.) U., 1970; MBA with honors, NYU, 1977. Programmer Prudential Ins. Co., Newark, 1970-73; with Hoffmann-La Roche Inc., Nutley, N.J., 1973—, corp. controller, 1985-88, v.p., contr., 1989-95; v.p. fin. Roche Labs., 1995—. Bd. dirs. St. Barnabas Burn Found., West Orange, N.J., Glen Ridge (N.J.) Ednl. Found., Ind. Coll. Fund, Summit, N.J. Mem. Nat. Assn. Accts., Fin. Execs. Inst., Leadership N.J., Phi Beta Kappa, Beta Gamma Sigma. Office: Hoffmann-LaRoche Inc 340 Kingsland St Nutley NJ 07110-1150

SEYKORA, MARGARET S., psychotherapist; b. N.Y.C., June 18, 1947; d. Stanley Sneider and Janet Pick (Sneider) Smith; m. Sern A. Seykora, Jan. 19, 1968 (div. 1984); m. H. Lester Mower, Jr., Nov. 19, 1993. BS in Journalism, U. Fla., 1970; MA in Edn. and Human Devel. Counseling, Rollins Coll., 1991. Lic. mental health counselor, Fla.; lic. mortgage broker, Fla., lic. real estate broker, Fla. Advt. profl. Gainesville (Fla.) Sun, 1968-75, TV mag. editor, 1968-75, Sunday/lesiure/book editor, 1970; stoneware potter, owner Old Town (Fla.) Pottery, 1975-82; real estate salesperson Jack McCormick Realty, Chiefland, Fla., 1982-85, Coldwell Banker, Orlando, Fla., 1985-90; real estate broker The Hood Group, Inc., Orlando, 1990-92; psychotherapist, facilitator, pres. Personal Dynamics Inst., Altamonte Springs, Fla., 1989—; career instr. The Knowledge Shop, Winter Park, Fla., 1992—; outpatient clin. svcs. supr. Lakeside Alternatives, Winter Park, Fla., 1992—; adj. instr. Seminole C.C., Sanford, Fla., 1992—, Valencia C.C., Winter Park, 1992—. Author/facilitator workshops in field. Mem. Nat. Bd. Counselors, Am. Counseling Assn., Assn. for Specialists in Group Work, Nat. Bd. Realtors. Mem. Ch. of Religious Sci. Office: Personal Dynamics Inst 421 Montgomery Rd Ste 105 Altamonte Springs FL 32714-3140

SEYLER, MONIQUE GEORGINA, artist; b. Jersey City, Dec. 3, 1956; d. John Joseph and Claude Marie (Jordan) S.; m. Chet Zoltak, May 25, 1985; children: Danielle, Matthew. Student, Art Students League, N.Y.C., 1976, 80-83; cert. of honors, U. Sorbonne, Paris, 1976, Fu Jen U., Hsinchu, Taiwan, 1978; BA in Asian Studies cum laude, Seton Hall U., 1979; postgrad., Sch. Visual Arts, N.Y.C., 1983-85. Freelance China Hand (lang. and culture) China Inst., N.Y.C., 1980-85; ind. curator Maxwell's, Hoboken, N.J., 1991, Westchester Land trust, Bedford Hills, N.Y., 1993, 94, Working Artists, Hastings-on-Hudson, N.Y., 1994. One-woman shows include Westchester C.C., 1993, Westchester Arts Coun., 1995; exhibited in group shows including Pace U., 1995, Nat. Assn. Women Artists, 1995, Nardin Gallery, 1995, Elaine Benson Gallery, Bridgehampton, N.Y., 1996. Chmn. Concerned Somers (N.Y.) Residents, 1990-96; assoc. Westchester Land trust, Bedford Hills, 1992-94; bd. dirs. Valley Pond assn., Somers, 1994-95, pres., 1996—. Recipient hon. mention Putnam Arts Coun., 1993; painting scholar N.J. Ctr. for Visual Arts, 1988. Mem. Nat. Assn. Women Artists (Miriam E. Halpern award 1993), Katonah Mus. Art Artists Assn. (program chmn. 1993—). Home and Studio: 15 Colonial Dr Katonah NY 10536

SEYMOUR, CAROLYN CATHERINE, housing agency administrator; b. Rochester, N.Y., May 11, 1939; d. George Stetson and Catherine Augusta (Buckelew) Gifford; m. James Elwood Zull, July 22, 1961 (div. May 1968); m. C. Bruce Melville, Jan. 1, 1970 (div. Mar. 1972); m. Douglas Frank Seymour, Sept. 1, 1972 (div. May 1995); 1 child, Richard James. BA magna cum laude, Houghton Coll., 1961; PhD, U. Wis., 1966. Rsch. assoc., asst. prof. linguistics Case We. Res. U., Cleve., 1966-70; founder, publ., editor East Cleve. Citizen, 1969-72; rsch. asst. Chautauqua County, Mayville, N.Y., 1972-73; asst. to mayor City of Jamestown, N.Y., 1974-77; coord. housing and econ. devel. So. Tier West Regional Planning Bd., Salamanca, N.Y., 1977-79; family editor Post-Jour., Jamestown, 1985-88; owner, operator The Bookshop, Jamestown, 1976-94; mayor City of Jamestown, 1992-93; exec. dir. Chautauqua Home Rehab. and Improvement Corp., Mayville, 1994—. Fellow NSF, 1965. Mem. N.Y. State Rural Housing Coalition (dir.), Chautauqua County Women's Polit. Caucus (founder), Jamestown Housing Partnership, Jamestown Fortnightly Club, Jamestown C. of C. (dir. 1989-95). Democrat. Office: Chautauqua Home Rehab and Improvement Corp Hall Clothier Bldg Mayville NY 14757

SEYMOUR, JANE, actress; b. Hillingdon, Middlesex, Eng., Feb. 15, 1951; came to U.S., 1976; d. John Benjamin and Mieke Frankenberg; m. David Flynn, July 18, 1981 (div. 1991); 2 children; m. James Keach, May 15, 1993. Student, Arts Ednl. Sch., London. Appeared in films Oh What A Lovely War, 1968, The Only Way, 1968, Young Winston, 1969, Live and Let Die, 1971, Sinbad and the Eye of the Tiger, 1973, Somewhere in Time, 1979, Oh Heavenly Dog, 1979, Lassiter, 1984, Head Office, Scarlet Pimpernel, Haunting Passion, Dark Mirror, Obsessed with a Married Woman, Killer on Board, The Tunnel, 1988, The French Revolution; TV films include Frankenstein, The True Story, 1972, Captains and The Kings, 1976 (Emmy nomination), 7th Avenue, 1976, The Awakening Land, 1977, The Four Feathers, 1977, Battlestar Galactica, Dallas Cowboy Cheerleaders, 1979, Our Mutual Friend, PBS, Eng., 1975, Jamaica Inn, 1982, Sun Also Rises, 1984, Crossings, 1986, Keys to Freedom, Angel of Death, 1990, Praying Mantis, 1993; A Passion for Justice: The Hazel Brannon Smith Story, 1994; Broadway appearances include Amadeus, 1980-81, I Remember You, 1992, Matters of the Heart, 1991, Sunstroke, 1992, Praying Mantis, 1993, Heidi, 1993; TV mini-series include East of Eden, 1980, The Richest Man in the World, 1988 (Emmy award), The Woman He Loved, 1988, Jack the Ripper, 1988, War and Remembrance, 1988, 89; host PBS documentary, Japan, 1988; TV series: Dr. Quinn: Medicine Woman, 1993— (Emmy nomination, Lead Actress - Drama, 1994); author: Jane Seymour's Guide to Romantic Living, 1986. Named Hon. Citizen of Ill., Gov. Thompson, 1977. Mem. Screen Actors Guild, AFTRA, Actors Equity, Brit. Equity. Office: Metropolitan Talent Agency 4526 Wilshire Blvd Los Angeles CA 90010-3801*

SEYMOUR, JANET MARTHA, psychologist; b. Mineola, N.Y., June 13, 1957; d. John Andrews and Eileen (Brudie) S.; children: Heide Lynn Adams, Hartley Ann Adams, John Kyle Bergerson; m. John Douglas Bergerson, Mar. 26, 1995. BA in Psychology and Music, Wheaton Coll., 1979; MA in Clin. Psychology, Rosemead Sch. Psychology, La Mirada, Calif., 1981, PsyD in Clin. Psychology, 1988. Lic. psychologist, Calif. Psychology intern Colmery Oneil VA Med. Ctr., Topeka, 1985-86; psychotherapist Concord (N.H.) Psychol. Assocs., 1987-88; psychologist Jolliffe & Assocs., Long Beach, Calif., 1989—. Sunday sch. tchr. 1st Evang. Free Ch. Fullerton, Calif., 1990-91, orch. flutist, 1980—; mem. Flutes Fantastiques Trio, 1993—; instr. flute tones course Whittier Cmty. Ctr., 1994—. Mem. Calif. Assn. Marriage and Family Therapists, Christian Assn. for Psychol. Studies. Republican. Office: Jolliffe & Assocs 3740 Atlantic Ave Ste 200 Long Beach CA 90807-3440

SEYMOUR, JOYCE ANN, elementary school educator; b. Lafayette, Ind., Nov. 24, 1947; d. Richard Max and Helen Lois (North) Taylor; m. Timothy

Joe Seymour, Dec. 27, 1969; children: Christy Nicole, Chad Richard. BS, Purdue U., 1970; MS, Wright State U., 1974. Cert. tchr. elem. edn.; cert. counselor. Tchr. grade 5 Fairborn (Ohio) City Schs., 1970-84, elem. guidance counselor, 1984-94, tchr. grade 6, 1994-95, elem. guidance counselor, 1995—; adv. com. Sch. Counseling, Wright State U., Dayton, 1986—. Mem. Phi Delta Kappa. Lutheran. Home: 1100 Medway-Carlisle Rd Medway OH 45341

SEYMOUR, STEPHANIE KULP, federal judge; b. Battle Creek, Mich., Oct. 16, 1940; d. Francis Bruce and Frances Cecelia (Bria) Kulp; m. R. Thomas Seymour, June 10, 1972; children: Bart, Bria, Sara, Anna. BA magna cum laude, Smith Coll., 1962; JD, Harvard U., 1965. Bar: Okla. 1965. Practice Boston, 1965-66, Tulsa, 1966-67, Houston, 1968-69; assoc. Doerner, Stuart, Saunders, Daniel & Anderson, Tulsa, 1971-75, ptnr., 1975-79; judge U.S. Ct. Appeals (10th cir.) Okla., Tulsa, 1979—, now chief justice; assoc. bar examiner Okla. Bar Assn., 1973-79; trustee Tulsa County Law Library, 1977-78; mem. U.S. Jud. Conf. Com. Defender Svcs., 1985-91, chmn., 1987-91. Mem. various task forces Tulsa Human Rights Commn., 1972-76, legal adv. panel Tulsa Task Force Battered Women, 1971-77. Mem. Am. Bar Assn., Okla. Bar Assn., Tulsa County Bar Assn., Phi Beta Kappa. Office: US Courthouse 333 W 4th St Rm 4-562 Tulsa OK 74103-3819*

SGARLAT, MARY ANNE E. A., marketing professional; b. Boston, Apr. 5, 1958; d. Francis Abbott and Elizabeth Maria (Paragallo) S. Diploma, Milton Acad., 1974; student, Roedean Sch., Brighton, Eng., 1975; BA, Bennington Coll., 1979. Adminstr. Harvard U., Cambridge, Mass., 1979-86; pub. rels. dir. Graham Gund Architects, Cambridge, 1986-89; mktg. and comms. mgr. Elkus/Manfredi Architects, Boston, 1989-90; comms. mgr. Turan Corp., Boston, 1990-92; mktg. mgr. The Design Partnership of Cambridge, 1992—. Mem. LWV, Bennington Coll. Alumni Assn. (regional dir. 1993—, exec. com. 1986-93). Home: 1214 Brook Rd Milton MA 02186-4136

SGOUTAS-EMCH, SANDRA APHRODITE, psychology educator, researcher; b. Urbana, Ill., Sept. 20, 1964; d. Demetrios and Maria (Plytaria) Sgoutas; m. Todd Emch, May 2, 1992. AA, Oxford (Ga.) Coll., 1984; BA, Emory U., 1986; MS, U. Ga., 1989, PhD, 1991. Grad. asst. U. Ga., Athens, 1987-91; postdoctoral fellow Ohio State U., Columbus, 1991-93; asst. prof. psychology U. San Diego, 1993—; mem. Nat. Women's Health Resource Commn., 1991—; vice-chair Com. Comty. Svc. Learning, 1995—. Author: (book chpt.) Nociception and the Neuro-Immune Connection, 1996; contbr. articles to profl. jours. Vol. Sierra Club, Columbus and San Diego, 1991—, UNICEF, Columbus and San Diego, AIDS Walk, San Diego, 1993—. Hebert Zimmer scholar of psychology U. Ga., 1991. Mem. AAUW, APA, Am. Psychol. Soc., Soc. Behavioral Medicine, Psi Chi, Sigma Xi. Office: U San Diego Dept Psychology 5998 Alcala Park San Diego CA 92110

SHABAZZ, AIYSHA MUSLIMAH, social work administrator; b. Columbia, S.C., Aug. 9, 1942; d. Jerry James Gadson and Edna Louise (Bellinger) Gadson Smalls; m. Abdullah Muslim Shabazz, July 28; children: Ain, Wali. BA, Fed. City Coll., Washington, 1973; MSW with honors, U. S.C., 1994, postgrad., 1994-95. Cert. child protective svcs. investigator, S.C., adoption investigator, S.C.; lic. social worker and ACBSW; cert. AIDS instr. ARC; lic. notary pub., S.C. Social work asst. Family Service Ctr., Washington, 1966-68; admission counselor Washington Tech. Inst., Washington, 1968-70; program dir. Park Motor Community Ctr., Washington, 1970-75; adminstrv. asst. Neighborhood Planning Council, Washington, 1974-75; substitue tchr. D.C. Pub. Sch. System, Washington, 1974-75; substitute tchr. Dist. I Pub. Schs., Columbia, 1977; home sch. program dir. Community Care, Inc., Columbia, 1977-81; monitor summer program U. S.C., Columbia, 1982; program dir. Dept. Social Services, Columbia, 1984—, case auditor, 1987-88, social worker supr., 1988—, project adminstr. for a alcohol and drug abuse program, 1994—; writer Acad. of Bacholu-Social Workers Exam, 1991; cons. substance abuse resch. program evaln., 1994—. substance abspeaker in field. Bd. dirs. Frederick Douglas Inst., Washington, 1968-69; pres. Park Motor Resident Coun., Washington, 1972-75; expert witness Family Ct.; bd. dirs. Coun. on Child Abuse and Neglect; adv. com., v.p. Benedict Coll. Sch. Social Work, S.C. Protection and Advocacy Handicapped Children; vol. AIDS instr. ARC, 1994; chairperson coordinating com. Voice of the Customer, 1995—. Mem. NASW (bd. dirs. 1993-95), S.C. Child Abuse and Neglect Task Force, AIDS Task Force (chmn. 1987-89). Democrat. Office: Dept Social Services 3220 Two Notch Rd Columbia SC 29204-2826

SHADE, LINDA BUNNELL, university chancellor; m. William Shade. BA in English and Comm., Baylor U., 1964; MA in English Lang. and Lit., U. Colo., 1967, PhD in English Lit., 1970. Asst. prof. English, acting assoc. dean Coll. Humanities U. Calif., Riverside, 1970-77; dean acad. affairs for acad. programs and policy studies Calif. State U., Riverside, 1977-87; vice chancellor acad. affairs Minn. State Univs., Mpls., 1987-93; chancellor U. Colo., Colorado Springs, 1993—; active Minn. Women's Econ. Round Table, 1989; mem. exec. com. Nat. Coun. for Accreditation Tchr. Edn., 1996-99. Bd. dirs. St. Paul chpt. ARC; active St. Paul Chamber Orch., Baylor U. Coun. Sesquicentennial Coun. of 150, 1990, Grace Episcopal Ch., Colorado Springs. Recipient Disting. Alumni award Baylor U., 1995; Woodrow Wilson dissertation fellow U. Colo. Office: U Colo 1420 Austin Bluffs Pkwy Colorado Springs CO 80933-7150

SHADER, KAREN KATHLEEN, education coordinator and system designer; b. Birmingham, Ala., Aug. 17, 1958; d. Stephen Joseph and Mary Catherine (Scribner) S.; m. David B. Heiman, Jan. 13, 1993; 1 child, Katherine Shader Heiman. BA in Sociology, Loyola U., New Orleans, 1980; MS in Instructional Systems Design, Fla. State U., 1983, PhD in Instructional Systems Design, 1990. Asst. producer, news gatherer Stas. WEAR-TV, WJHG-TV, Pensacola, Panama City, Fla., 1980-81; mktg. rep. Fin. Mktg. Concepts, Tallahassee, Fla., 1982-83; instructional systems designer Digital Video Group, Tallahassee, 1983, Arthur Andersen & Co, Chgo., 1983-86; rsch. asst. Ctr. for Needs Assessment and Planning Fla. State U., Tallahassee, 1986-89; adminstrv. rsch. asst. Los Alamos (New Mex.) Nat. Lab., 1989-91; quality assurance and instructional designer Continental Systems Tech., Atlanta, 1991; edn. project mgr. VA Southeastern Regional Med. Edn. Ctr., Birmingham, Ala., 1991-92; education coord. Univ. Ala. Birmingham Hosp., 1992—; cons. on design and devl. of edn. systems Univ. Ala. Hosp., Birmingham, 1992—. Contbr. articles to profl. jours., presentations to profl. orgns. Mem. ASTD, Nat. Soc. for Performance and Instruction, Am. Ednl. Rsch. Assn., Ala. Soc. for Healthcare Edn. and Tng. of the Ala. Hosp. Assn. Office: Univ Ala Hosp 1917 5th Ave S Rm 230 B Birmingham AL 35233-2015

SHADEROWFSKY, EVA MARIA, photographer, writer; b. Prague, Czechoslovakia, May 20, 1938; came to U.S., 1940; d. Felix Resek and Gertrude (Telatko) Frank; children: Tom, Paul. Student, Oberlin Coll., 1955-56; BA, Barnard Coll., 1960. Women's channel coord., moderator America Online: Evenings with Eva. Exhibited in one-person shows at The Left Bank Gallery, Wellfleet, Mass., 1974, Art Ctr. No. N.J., Tenafly, 1975, Soho Photo, N.Y., 1974, 80, Esta Robinson Gallery, 1982, Fairleigh Dickinson U., 1983, Donnell Libr., N.Y.C., 1985, Piermont (N.Y.) Libr., 1987, The Turning Point, Piermont, N.Y., 1988, Hopper House, Nyack, N.Y., 1989, Puchong Gallery, N.Y., 1991, Rockland Ctr. for Arts, 1992; group shows include Soho Photo Gallery, N.Y., 1974, Fashion Inst. Tech., N.Y.C., 1975, Portland (Maine) Mus. Art, 1977, Maine Photog. Workshop, Rockport, 1978, Marcuse Pfeifer, N.Y., 1977, 78, Chrysler Mus., Norfol,, Va., 1978, Exposure Gallery Wellfleet, 1978, 79, The Art Ctr. No. N.J., Tenafly, 1980, Neuberger Mus., Purchase, N.Y., 1982, Hudson River Mus., 1982, Foto, N.Y., 1982, Barnard Coll., N.Y.C., 1983, Rockland Ctr. for Arts, 1978, 87, 89, 96, Print Club, Phila., 1988; represented in collections at Bklyn. Mus., Portland (Maine) Mus. Art, Met. Mus. Art, N.Y.C.; author and photographer (book) Suburban Portraits, 1977; photographer Women in Transition, 1975, (book) Earth Tones, 1993, The Womansource Catalog and Review: Tools for Connecting the Community of Women, 1996; poetry critic/essayist Contact II, 1980-93; contbr. story to anthology, 1980-93, Touching Fire, 1989, Sexual Harassment: Women Speak Out, 1992, Lovers, 1992, The Time of Our Lives, 1993; contbr. photography to Camera 35 mag., Shots mag., Shutterbug. Recipient Photography award Rockland Ctr. for Arts, 1978, Gt. Am. Photo Contest, 1981, Demarais Press, 1982, Harrison Art Coun., SUNY-Purchase, 1982, The Cape Codder, 1976, 79-82. Home and Office: 265 Maple Rd Valley Cottage NY 10989-1426

SHADRACH, (MARTHA) JEAN HAWKINS, artist; b. La Junta, Colo., Nov. 7, 1926; d. Lloyd Marion Hawkins and Martha May (Hawkins) Sudan; widowed, 1987; children: John M., Karolyn Sue Shadrach Green. BA, U. Colo., 1948. Owner Artique, Ltd. Gallery, Anchorage, Alaska, 1971-87; instr. Foothills Art Ctr., Golden, 1988-89, Prince William Sound C.C., Homer, Alaska, 1993, Kachemak Bay C.C., Homer, 1994; facilitator mktg. art seminars; guest lectr. Cunard Cruise Lines, 1988-90, 95. Bd. dirs. Bird Treatment and Learning Ctr., Anchorage, 1994, Anchorage Art Selection Com., 1984. Recipient gov.'s award for excellence in art, Anchorage, 1970, drawing award All Alaska Juried Show, 1970, 1st prize Fairbanks Watercolor Soc., 1987, Paul Schwartz Meml. award Sumi-e Soc. Am., 1993. Mem. Alaska Watercolor Soc. (v.p. 1994—, award 1988). Home and Studio: 3530 Fordham Dr Anchorage AK 99508-4558

SHAEFFER, THELMA JEAN, primary school educator; b. Ft. Collins, Colo., Feb. 1, 1949; d. Harold H. and Gladys June (Ruff) Pfeif; m. Charles F. Shaeffer, June 12, 1971; 1 child, Shannon Emily. BA, U. No. Colo., 1970, MA, 1972. Cert. profl. tchr., type B, Colo. Primary tchr. Adams County Dist #12 Five Star Schs., Northglenn, Colo., 1970-84; chpt. I (lang. arts) tchr. Adams County Dist #12 Five Star Schs., Northglenn, 1984-92, chpt. I, read succed tchr., 1992—; mem. policy coun. Adams County Dist. # 12 Five Star Schs., Northglenn, 1975-79, dist. sch. improvement team, 1987-89; presenter Nat. Coun. Tchrs. of English, 1990. Vol. 1992 election, Denver, alumni advisor for Career Connections U. No. Colo., 1993—. Mem. Colo. Tchrs. Assn. (del. 1992), Dist. Tchrs. Edn. Assn. (exec. bd. mem. 1991-93), Internat. Reading Assn. (pres. Colo. coun. 1988), Internat. Order of Job's Daughters (coun. mem.), Order of Eastern Star, Delta Omicron. Episcopalian. Home: 6502 Perry St Arvada CO 80003-6400 Office: Hulstrom Elem Sch 10604 Grant Dr Northglenn CO 80233-4117

SHAFER, ANNE WHALEN, volunteer civic worker; b. Memphis, Tenn., Aug. 22, 1923; m. Robert W. Shafer, June 5, 1948. BLS in Cmty. Devel., Memphis State U. (U. Memphis), 1982. Pres., cons. Colonial Neighborhood Assn., Memphis Ctr. for Neighborhoods, Memphis, 1980—; sec., past pres., founder, Colonial Acres Neighborhood Assn., Neighborhood Watch, Memphis, 1980—. Mem., officer, Ch. Women United, 1960—, Mid South Peace and Justice Ctr., 1970, W. Tenn. Hist. Soc., 1980. Recipient Race Rels. award Mid South Peace and Justice Ctr., Memphis, 1996; named one of Women Who Made a Difference, Mattie Sengstacke Civil Rights Mus., Memphis, 1994; grantee: Thanks Be to Grandmother Winifred Fedn., Wainscott, N.Y., 1995-96. Mem. LWV (past pres. local chpt. many coms., other offices), Chickasaw Bluffs Conservancy Memphis, Pub. Issues Forum Memphis. Democrat. Home: 4963 Essexshire Memphis TN 38117

SHAFER, DIANNE DEAVOURS, educational administrator; b. Knoxville, Feb. 5, 1948; d. George S. and Reba M. (Johnson) Deavours; m. John W. Shafer, Dec. 13, 1969; 1 child, J. Michael. BS in English Edn., Auburn U., 1969, MEd in English Edn., 1977; EdS in Adminstrn., U. Ga., 1994. Tchr. English, dept. chair Ctrl. High Sch., Phenix City, Ala., 1972-79; tchr. English & journalism Auburn (Ala.) High Sch., 1979-80; tchr. English & history Lee Scott Acad., Auburn, 1980-81, Franklin Road Acad., Nashville, 1981-82; tchr. English Hilsman Mid. Sch., Athens, Ga., 1982-88; tchr. English, instructional team leader, adminstrv. asst. Clarke Ctrl. High Sch., Athens, Ga., 1988-94; project dir. Action Heat Start Transition Demonstration Project, Athens, Ga., 1994—; mem. coms. Clarke County Schs., 1992-94. Chair craft show and registration Am. Cancer Soc. Aux., Athens, 1982-94; mem. Athens Regional Med. Ctr. Annual Giving Com. Found. of Excellence grantee, Athens, 1994; recipient D. Shafer Leadership award, 1994. Mem. ASCD, Ga. Assn. Adminstrs., Ga. Assn. Supervision and Curriculum Devel., Phi Delta Kappa, Phi Kappa Phi. Office: Action Head Start Transition Demo Project PO Box 1072 574 Oconee St Athens GA 30603

SHAFER, ELIZABETH JANE, writer; b. Colorado Springs, Colo., Jan. 18, 1924; d. Ira Elmer and Grace Leota (Groves) S. Student, Colo. Coll., 1942-45. Mem. advt. staff Colorado Springs News, 1944; continuity writer KVOR, Colorado Springs, 1944-46; editor Western Advt., L.A., 1958-59; CS reporter Fairchild Publs., N.Y.C., 1959-70; reporter Religious News Svc., N.Y.C., 1961-73, USIA, Washington, 1969—; asst. editor Earth Sci. Mag., Colorado Springs, 1973-80. Co-author: 7 Keys to the Rocky Mountains, 1968; author: The Ellen T. Brinley Guild, 1992; editor, ghostwriter numerous regional books, 1980—; contbr. numerous articles, fiction and poems to profl. publs. Mem. Nat. League Am. Pen Women (pres. 1958-60, cert. appreciation 1984), Colo. Aauthors League (Top Hand awards 1968-88), Poetry Soc. Colo. (Colorado Springs workshop dir. 1966—), Colorado SPrings Poetry Fellowship (pres. 1960-62, life mem.). Democrat. Home and Office: 215 N Custer Ave Colorado Springs CO 80903

SHAFER, RITA MAE, educator; b. Elmhurst, Ill., Nov. 5, 1955; d. Albert Anton and Gertrude Ruth (Hagerman) Westphal; m. Richard Anthony Shafer, Nov. 6, 1976; children: Theresa, Jack. AA, Coll. of DuPage, Glen Ellyn, Ill., 1974; BA, Nat.-Louis U., Wheaton, Ill., 1990; MA, Nat.-Louis U., 1995. Elem. tchr. William Hammerschmidt Sch., Lombard, Ill., 1990—; presenter Ill. Reading Coun., Springfield, 1994. Grantee Partnership in Ednl. Progress, 1994. Mem. ASCD, Internat. Reading Assn., Ill. Reading Assn. Home: 106 N Ahrens Ave Lombard IL 60148-2080 Office: 617 Hammerschmidt Lombard IL 60148

SHAFER, SUSAN WRIGHT, retired elementary school educator; b. Ft. Wayne, Dec. 6, 1941; d. George Wesley and Bernece (Spray) Wright; 1 child, Michael R. BS, St. Francis Coll., Ft. Wayne, 1967, MS in Edn., 1969. Tchr. Ft. Wayne Community Schs., 1967-69, Amphitheater Pub. Schs., Tucson, 1970-96; ret., 1996; Odyssey of the Mind coord. Prince Elem. Sch., Tucson, 1989-91, Future Problem Solving, 1991-95. Tchr. Green Valley (Ariz.) Cmty. Ch., Vacation Bible Sch., 1987-89, dir. vacation bible sch., 1989-93. Mem. AAUW, NEA (life), Delta Kappa Gamma (pres. Alpha Rho chpt.), Alpha Delta Kappa (historian Epsilon chpt. 1990—), Phi Delta Kappa (life, Tucson chpt.). Republican. Methodist. Home: 603 W Placita Nueva Green Valley AZ 85614-2827

SHAFFER, BECKY MARIE, secondary mathematics educator; b. Cleve., June 14, 1969; d. Robert Earle and Bonnie Barbara (Hantl) S. BS in Edn. magna cum laude, Bob Jones U., 1991; MA in Math., Ohio State U., 1992. Substitute tchr., math. tutor Mentor (Ohio) Bd. Edn., 1992-94, tchr. math., 1994—; asst. track coach Ridge Jr. H.S., Mentor, 1995—. Mem. Nat. Coun. Tchrs. Math., Gtr. Clev. Coun. Tchrs. Math., Ohio Coun. Tchrs. Math. Office: Ridge Jr HS 7860 Johnnycake Ridge Rd Mentor OH 44060

SHAFFER, CYNTHIA JANE, management executive; b. Grove City, Pa., Sept. 11, 1957; d. Oliver Eugene and Carol Ann (Winger) W.; m. Stephen Walter Shaffer, Mar. 15, 1980; children: Matthew Eugene, Cody Aaron, Kayla Janelle. BS, Fla. So. Coll., 1979. Various positions Interstate Chem. Co., West Middlesex, Pa., 1980-89; dir. customer/rsch. svc. DeVilbiss HC, Somerset, Pa., 1993-95; v.p. customer svc. Sunmed Svcs., Somerset, 1995—. Mem. NAFE, Phi Chi Theta. Home: 1404 Ridgeview Dr Somerset PA 15501

SHAFFER, DEBORAH, nurse; b. Tampa, Fla., Jan. 20, 1954; d. Frank Solomon and Mary Louise (Swann) Shaffer; children: Danny, Dionne. LPN, Suwanee-Hamilton Nursing Sch., Live Oak, Fla., 1984; student, Hillsborough CC, 1992—. LPN, Fla. Nursing experience various hosps. and nursing homes, 10 yrs. Author poems, songs and short stories. Active Neighborhood Crime Watch, Parents Without Ptnrs., The Spring, Literacy Vols. Am.; ESL tutor First Bapt. Ch.; activities instr. A.D.C. Osborne Ctr.

SHAFFER, DOROTHY BROWNE, retired mathematician, educator; b. Vienna, Austria, Feb. 12, 1923; d. Hermann and Steffy (Hermann) Browne; arrived U.S., 1940; m. Lloyd Hamilton Shaffer, July 25, 1943 (dec. 1978); children: Deborah Lee, Diana Louise, Dorothy Leslie. AB, Bryn Mawr Coll., 1943; MA, Harvard U., 1945, PhD, 1962. Mathematician, MIT, Cambridge, 1945-47; tchg. fellow, research asso., Harvard U., Cambridge, 1947-48; asso. mathematician Cornell Aeronautical Lab, Buffalo, N.Y., 1952-56; mathematician Dunlap & Assoc., Stamford, Conn., 1958-60; lectr. grad. engrng. U. of Conn. at Stamford, 1962; prof. math Fairfield (Conn.) U., 1963-92, prof. emeritus, 1992—; vis. prof. Imperial Coll. Sci. and Tech., London, fall 1978, U. Md., College Park, spring 1981; vis. prof. U. Calif.-San Diego, summer 1981; vis. scholar, 1986; NSF faculty fellow IBM-T.J. Watson Research Center, Yorktown Heights, N.Y., 1979. Contbr. numerous papers in math. analysis. Mem. Am. Math. Soc., Math. Assn. of Am., Assn. for Women in Math., London Math. Soc. Achievement include patent in Viscosity Stabilized Solar Pond. Home: 156 Intervale Rd Stamford CT 06905-1311 Office: Fairfield U Dept Math & Computer Sci Fairfield CT 06430

SHAFFER, JENNIFER LYNN, elementary education educator; b. Plymouth, Wis., Mar. 19, 1971; d. Wayne Lee and Jean Levern (Miske) S. BA in Elem. Edn. minor, computer sci., Concordia U., Mequon, Wis., 1993. Tchr. 3d and 4th grades Redeemer Luth. Sch., Warsaw, Ind., 1993—. Mem. Tippkee Coun. Lutheran. Office: Redeemer Luth Sch 1720 E Center St Warsaw IN 46580

SHAFFER, JILL, clinical psychologist; b. Columbus, Ohio, May 18, 1958; d. Melvin Warren and Emily (White) S.; m. Robert K. Yost, Jan. 9, 1991; children: Melanie Jill Yost, Robison Kimber Yost. BS in Psychology with honors, Wright State U., 1984, PsyD, 1988. Lic. psychologist, Ohio. Psychology talk show producer/participant Sta. WHIO-AM, Dayton, Ohio, 1981-83; psychology asst. and organizer Terrap S.W. Ohio, Dayton, 1981-83; psychology trainee Oakwood Forensic Ctr., Lima, Ohio, 1984-85, Wright State U., Dayton, 1984-87; predoctoral resident South Community Mental Health Ctr., Dayton, 1987-88; postdoctoral trainee Fulero and Assoc., Dayton, 1988-89; pvt. practice Dayton, 1989—; supervising psychologist GERI-Tech of Dayton, 1990-92; cons. psychologist disability evaluations for worker's compensation and social security disability, 1989-94; state examiner Indsl. Commn. of Ohio, 1989—; owner, mgr. rental properties, 1988—. Author: (article) Strategic Intervention with Transvestism, 1989. Recipient scholarship Sch. of Profl. Psychology, 1985. Mem. APA, NOW, Ohio Psychol. Assn., Dayton Area Psychol. Assn. Office: 2705 Far Hills Ave Ste 4 Dayton OH 45419-1606

SHAFFER, MARGARET MINOR, retired library director; b. New Orleans, Sept. 20, 1940; d. Milhado Lee and Margaret Minor (Krumbhaar) S. BS, Nicholls State U., Thibodaux, La., 1962; MLS, La. State U., 1965. Asst. dir. Terrebonne Parish Pub. Libr., Houma, La., 1965-72, dir., 1973-95; ret., 1995. Named Woman of Yr., Houma Bus. and Profl. Women's Club, 1981. Mem. ALA, La. Libr. Assn. (chmn. pub. libr. com. 1986-87), Southeastern Libr. Assn. Democrat. Episcopalian. Home: 1726 Highway 311 Schriever LA 70395-3240

SHAFFER, SHEILA WEEKES, mathematics educator; b. Syracuse, N.Y., Oct. 20, 1957; d. Carroll Watson and Reina Lou (Yonkers) Judd; m. Jason Craig Shaffer, June 4, 1983 (div. Sept. 1994). BA, SUNY, Albany, 1979, MS, 1983. Cert. tchr. English/Math., N.Y.; cert. advanced profl. cert. in English and Math, Md. English tchr. Cortland (N.Y.) HS, 1979-81; English tchr. Prince George's County, Upper Marlboro, Md., 1984-86, math. tchr., 1986-87; math. tchr./coord. Prince George's County, 1990-95; math./English tchr. Camden HS, St. Mary's, Ga., 1988-90; math tchr. Frederick County, Va., 1995-96, Prince George's County, Upper Marlboro, Md., 1996—; mem. SAT Com., The Coll. Bd., N.Y.C., 1993-96. Mem. Nat. Coun. Tchrs. Math. Office: Potomac High Sch 5211 Boydell Ave Oxon Hill MD 20745

SHAFFER, TERI R., marketing educator; b. Castro Valley, Calif., Jan. 9, 1958; d. John and Jeannie (Hamilton) Root; m. Gary Paul Shaffer, Aug. 4, 1984. BA in Sociology, U. Calif., Santa Barbara, 1981; PhD in Mktg., La. State U., 1991. Instr. La. State U., Baton Rouge, 1989-90; prof. mktg. Southeastern La. U., Hammond, 1990—. Contbr. articles to profl. jours. Bd. dirs. Hammond (La.) Housing Authority, Friends of the Shelter, Hammond; mem. com. Habitat for Humanity, Hammond. Mem. Am. Mktg. Assn. (Doctoral Consortium fellow 1988), So. Mktg. Assn., Southwestern Mktg. Assn. Office: Southeastern La Univ Box 302 Hammond LA 70402

SHAGHOIAN, CYNTHIA LYNNE, accountant; b. Niagara Falls, N.Y., Apr. 23, 1962; d. Ralph and Joanne Lynne (Ishman) S. AAS in Acctg. with merit, Niagara County C.C., Sanborn, N.Y., 1982; BBA in Acctg. magna cum laude, Niagara U., 1984. CPA, N.Y. Staff acct. Salada Wynne Kling and Co. CPAs, Niagara Falls, 1985-88; fin. analyst Lockport (N.Y.) Meml. Hosp., 1988-90; acctg. mgr. Brown & Co. CPAS, Niagara Falls, 1990—; mem. fundraising com. Lockport Meml. Hosp., 1990. Vol. United Way of Niagara, 1991, Arthritis Found., Tonawanda, N.Y., 1992—; mem. membership subcom. Niagara Falls Area C. of C., 1994—; mem. Campaign Com. to Elect Greg Danoian to Niagara Falls City Coun., 1994. Mem. AICPA, N.Y. State Soc. CPAs, Inst. Mgmt. Accts. Democrat. Home: 504 22nd St Niagara Falls NY 14301

SHAH, MOKLESA DEWAN, artist; b. Panchbibi, Bogra, Bangladesh, Aug. 17, 1947; came to U.S., 1970; d. Manjer Ali and Azimunnessa (Begum) Dewan; m. Dhiraj M. Shah, May 29, 1969; children: Rajanya, Anuny, Melissa. AAS, Jr. Coll., Albany, N.Y., 1985; BA in Art, SUNY, Albany, 1990, MA in Art, 1995. Ward sister, staff nurse Dacca (Bangladesh) P.G. Hosp., 1965-69, supr. nursing, 1970. Exhibited work in shows at Inst. of History of Art, Albany, 1990, Albany Med. Ctr., 1991, Guilderland Pub. Libr., 1993, Albany Airport, 1994, Schenectady Mus. Planetarium, 1995, Chapel and Cultural Ctr., Troy, N.Y., Mus. SUNY at Albany, 1995, others. Mem. Upstate 88, Albany Artists Guild, Albany Inst. History and Art. Home: 4262 SR 66 Malden Bridge NY 12115-9701

SHAHEEN, C. JEANNE, state legislator; b. St. Charles, Mo., Jan. 28, 1947; m. William H. Shaheen; 3 children. BA, Shippensburg U., 1969; M of Social Sci. in Polit. Sci., U. Miss., 1973. Mem. N.H. Senate, 1991—. Democrat. Protestant. Office: NH Senate State Capital Concord NH 03301

SHAHIDI, PARISIMA, school psychologist; b. Tehran, Iran, June 14, 1951; came to U.S., 1966; d. Emil and Victoria (Dadras) Shahidi; m. Abbas Behbehani, Aug. 24, 1979; 1 child, Sara. BS, Queens Coll./CUNY, 1973, MS, 1976, MFA, 1978; EdD, U. So. Calif., L.A., 1996. Cert. sch. psychologist, pupil pers. credential, resource specialist, learning handicapped credential, severely handicapped credential, art edn. credential, all Calif. Art instr. Met. Mus. Art, N.Y.C., 1976-79; spl. edn. tchr. Dorothy Brown Sch., L.A., 1980-82; resource specialist Alhambra (Calif.) Sch. Dist., 1982-84; resource specialist Long Beach (Calif.) Unified Sch. Dist., 1984-87, sch. counselor, 1987-92, sch. psychologist, 1992—. Mem. Assn. Long Beach Ednl. Mgrs., Calif. Assn. Sch. Psychologists, Long Beach Pupil Pers. Assn., Phi Delta Kappa. Office: Long Beach Unified Sch Dist Fremont Sch 4000 E 4th St Long Beach CA 90814

SHAINESS, NATALIE, psychiatrist, educator; b. N.Y.C., Dec. 2, 1915; d. Jack and Clara (Levy-Hart) S.; div.; children: David Spiegel, Ann Spiegel. BA in Chemistry, NYU, 1936; MD, Va. Commonwealth U., 1939. Diplomate in psychiatry; cert. in psychoanalysis. Pvt. practice N.Y.C., 1955—; faculty William Alanson White Inst. Psychiatry, Psychoanalysis, N.Y.C., 1961-81; asst. clin. prof. psychiatry N.Y. Sch. Psychiatry, N.Y.C., 1964-67; faculty med. edn. div. N.Y. Acad. Medicine, 1966-67; lectr. psychiatry Columbia U. Coll. Physicians and Surgeons, N.Y.C., 1966-80; faculty, supervising analyst L.I. Inst. Psychoanalysis, N.Y., 1980—; invited participant 1st and 2nd Internat. Conf. on Abortion, 1967, 68; research project on menstruation. Editorial bd. Jour. of the Am. Women's Med. Assn., 1985—; author: Sweet Suffering: Woman as Victim, 1984; contbr. over 100 articles to profl. jours. and over 90 profl. book revs. Mem. Physicians for Social Responsibility, Nuclear Freeze, several other anti-nuclear orgns. Fellow Am. Acad. Psychoanalysis (past trustee, organizer several panels), Am. Psychiat. Assn. (life mem., organizer several panels), N.Y. Acad. Medicine (hon.), Soc. Med. Psychoanalyst (councillor, honored for keen erudition, lively imagination and professionalism 1993); mem. Assn. for Advancement Psychotherapy, Women's Med. Assn. N.Y.C. (fin. assistance com., 1st President's award 1990). Home and Office: 140 E 83rd St New York NY 10028-1931

SHAINSWIT, CAROL, marketing professional; b. N.Y.C.; d. George and Lisa Shainswit. BBA, Baruch Coll., 1973. Product forecast analyst, mgr., mktg. mgr. Revlon, Inc., N.Y.C., 1970-78; dir. mktg. Helena Rubinstein, Inc., N.Y.C., 1978-80, Am. Cyanamid Co., N.Y.C. and Wayne, N.J., 1980-82, Warner Cosmetics, Inc., N.Y.C., 1982-84; dir. sales promotion Swatch Watch, N.Y.C., 1984-86; adv. dir. Citizen Watch Co., Lyndhurst, N.J., 1986-89; mktg. dir. TAG Heuer Sports Watches, Springfield, N.J., 1990—. Mem. Fashion Group, Women's Jewelry Assn.

SHALACK, JOAN HELEN, psychiatrist; b. Jersery City, Mar. 6, 1932; d. Edward William and Adele Helen S.; m. Jerome Abraham Sheill (dec. June 1996). Student, Farleigh Dickinson U., 1950-51; BA cum laude, NYU, 1954; MD, Women's Med. Coll. Pa., 1958. Intern Akron (Ohio) Gen. Hosp., 1958-59; resident in psychiatry Camarillo (Calif.) State Hosp., 1959-62; resident in physchiatry UCLA Neuropsychiat. Inst., 1962, U. So. Calif., L.A., 1963; pvt. practice Beverly Hills, Calif., 1963-83, Century City L.A., Calif., 1983-86, Pasadena, Calif., 1986—; pres., chair bd. dirs. Totizo Inc., Beverly Hills, 1969-71; mem. staff Westwood Hosp., 1970-75. Mem. AMA, Calif. Med. Assn., L.A. County Med. Assn., Physicians for Social Responsibility, Union of Concerned Scientists, Phi Beta Kappa, Mu Chi Sigma. Home and Office: 1405 Afton St Pasadena CA 91103-2702

SHALALA, DONNA EDNA, federal official, political scientist, educator, university chancellor; b. Cleve., Feb. 14, 1941; d. James Abraham and Edna (Smith) S. AB, Western Coll., 1962; MSSC, Syracuse U., 1968, PhD, 1970; 16 hon degrees, 1981-91. Vol. Peace Corps, Iran, 1962-64; asst. to dir. met. studies program Syracuse U., 1965-69; instr. asst. to dean Syracuse U. (Maxwell Grad. Sch.), 1969-70; asst. prof. polit. sci. CUNY, 1970-72; assoc. prof. politics and edn. Tchrs. Coll. Columbia U., 1972-79; asst. sec. for policy devel. and research HUD, Washington, 1977-80; prof. polit. sci., pres. Hunter Coll., CUNY, 1980-88; prof. polit. sci., chancellor U. Wis., Madison, 1988-93; sec. Dept. HHS, Washington, 1993—. Author: Neighborhood Governance, 1971, The City and the Constitution, 1972, The Property Tax and the Voters, 1973, The Decentralization Approach, 1974. Bd. govs. Am. Stock Exch., 1981-87; trustee TIAA, 1985-89, Com. Econ. Devel., 1981-93; bd. dirs. Inst. Internat. Econs., 1981-93, Children's Def. Fund, 1980-93, Am. Ditchley Found., 1981-93, Spencer Found., 1988-93, M&I Bank of Madison, 1991-93, NCAA Found., 1991; mem. Trilateral Commn., 1988-93, Knight Commn. on Intercollegiate Sports, 1990-93; trustee Brookings Inst., 1989-93. Ohio Newspaper Women's scholar, 1958, Western Coll. Trustee scholar, 1958-62; Carnegie fellow, 1966-68; Nat. Acad. Edn. Spencer fellow, 1972-73; Guggenheim fellow, 1975-76; recipient Disting. Svc. medal Columbia U. Tchrs. Coll., 1989. Mem. ASPA, Am. Polit. Sci. Assn., Nat. Acad. Arts & Scis., Nat. Acad. Pub. Adminstrn., Coun. Fgn. Rels., Nat. Acad. Edn., Nat. Acad. Arts and Scis. Office: Dept Health and Human Svcs Office of Sec 200 Independence Ave SW Rm 615F Washington DC 20201-0004

SHAMBAUGH, JOAN DIBBLE, writer, educator; b. Hillsdale, Mich., Mar. 14, 1928; d. Edwin Andrew and Helen Melissa (Crum) Dibble; m. Benjamin Shambaugh, Dec. 26, 1950 (div. Apr. 1964); children: Benjamin Dibble, Jeannette Melissa, Nathaniel Capps. AB, Duke U., 1949; MEd, Lesley Coll., 1980. Cert. elem. and secondary tchr., Mich. Fourth grade tchr. Grand Traverse Pub. Schs., Traverse City, Mich., 1949-50; asst. prof. Harvard Extension, Cambridge, Mass., 1966-74; moderator, tchr. creative writing workshop Lincoln Sudbury (Mass.) Adult Edn., 1972-79; tchr. creative writing workshop Concord Carlyle Continuing Edn., 1978-89; tchr. writing workshops Out & About, Morrisville, Vt., 1995; tchr. jour. keeping Trapp Family Lodge, Stowe, Vt., 1995; Invitedpapers to Duke U. Libr.Manuscript Dept. Will Perkins Library, 1982; Directory of American Poets and Fiction Writers, 1980-81. Author: The New Road to China, 1995, sequel China, 1996; editor, pub. Acorn Press, Lincoln, Mass., 1975-95; poet. Home: Box 106 Rte 1 Craftsbury VT 05826

SHANAFELT, NANCY SUE, organizational development specialist, career counselor; b. Northampton, Mass., Nov. 21, 1947; m. John D. Shanafelt; children: Amy, Nicholas. BS, U. Mass., 1969; MA in Human Resources/Orgnl. Devel., U. San Francisco, 1991. Tchr. Southwick (Mass.) Pub. Schs., 1969-70; acctg. asst. Maricopa County Schs., Phoenix, Ariz., 1973-74; tax auditor to br. chief IRS, San Jose, 1974-89; enrolled agt., 1984-85; OD specialist IRS, San Jose, 1991-93; creator IRS Women's Network, San Francisco, 1981—. Leader Girl Scouts U.S., Santa Clara, 1980-96, Golden Valley, 1996—, cons., 1981-82, svc. mgr., 1982-84, trainer, 1982-84; leader Boy Scouts Am., 1992-96; facilitator Unwed Parents Anonymous, 1992—; master catechist Diocese of San Jose, 1992-96. Recipient Disting. Performance award IRS, 1993. Mem. AAUW, NAFE, ASTD, Calif. Assn. for Counseling and Devel., Federally Employed Women, Commonwealth Club Am., Italian Cath. Fedn. (sec. 1991—), Bay Area Orgnl. Devel. Network, Medugorje PGL. Office: Mail Stop FR4300 821 M St Fresno CA 93721

SHANAHAN, EILEEN FRANCES, secondary education educator; b. Bethlehem, Pa., Sept. 10, 1949; d. Edward Vincent and Geraldine Mary (Gilligan) S. BA, Moravian Coll., 1971. Cert. secondary tchr. in Spanish, English, N.J. Tchr. Kingsway Regional High Sch. Dist., Swedesboro, N.J., 1971—. Mem. NEA, N.J. Edn. Assn., Gloucester County Edn. Assn., Fgn. Lang. Educators N.J., Kingsway Edn. Assn. (sec. membership), Hellertown Hist. Soc. Democrat. Roman Catholic.

SHANAHAN, ELIZABETH ANNE, art educator; b. High Point, N.C., Apr. 5, 1950; d. Joe Thomas and Nancy Elizabeth (Moran) Gibson; m. Robert James Shanahan, Aug. 31, 1969 (div. Mar. 1987); children: Kimberly Marie Shanahan Conlon, Brigette Susanne. Student, Forsyth Tech. Coll., 1974-83, Tri-County Tech. Coll., 1989, Inst. of Children's Lit., 1989. Owner cleaning bus. Winston-Salem, N.C., 1985-86, 87; instr. Anderson (S.C.) Arts Coun., 1987—, Tri-County Tech. Coll., Pendleton, S.C., 1987—. Artist Wild Geese, 1985 (Best in Show). Active Libr. of Congress, 1994. Mem. Anderson Art Assn. (con. 1987—), Met. Arts Coun. (Upstate Visual Arts divsn.), Triad Art Assn. (pres. Kernersville, N.C. chpt. 1984-85), Nat. Mus. Women in Arts (charter), Libr. of Congress (charter). Home: 7 Woodbridge Ct Anderson SC 29621-2260 Office: Tri County Tech Coll PO Box 587 Pendleton SC 29670-0587

SHANAS, ETHEL, sociology educator; b. Chgo., Sept. 6, 1914; d. Alex and Rebecca (Rich) S.; m. Lester J. Perlman, May 17, 1940; 1 child, Michael Stephen. AB, U. Chgo., 1935, AM, 1937, PhD, 1949; LHD (hon.), Hunter Coll., N.Y.C., 1985. Instr. human devel. U. Chgo., 1947-52, rsch. assoc. prof., 1961-65; sr. rsch. analyst City of Chgo., 1952-53; sr. study dir. Nat. Opinion Rsch. Ctr., Chgo., 1956-61; prof. sociology U. Ill., Chgo., 1965-82, prof. emerita, 1982—; vice chmn. expert com. on aging UN, 1974; mem. com. on aging NRC, Washington, 1978-82, panel on statistics for an aging population, 1984-86; mem. U.S. Com. on Vital and Health Stats., Washington, 1976-79. Author: The Health of Older People, 1962; (with others) Old People in Three Industrial Societies, 1968; editor: (with others) Handbook of Aging and the Social Sciences, 1976, 2d edit., 1985. Bd. govs. Chgo. Heart Assn., 1972-80; mem. adv. council on aging City of Chgo., 1972-78. Keston lectr. U. So. Calif., 1975; recipient Burgess award Nat. Council on Family Relations, 1978; Disting. Chgo. Gerontologist award Assn. for Gerontology in Higher Edn., 1988. Fellow Gerontol. Soc. Am. (pres. 1974-75, Kleemeier award 1977, Brookdale award 1981), Am. Sociol. Assn. (chmn. sect. on aging 1985-86 Disting. Scholar award, 1987); mem. Midwest Sociol. Soc. (pres. 1980-81), Inst. Medicine of Nat. Acad. Scis. (sr. mem.). Home: 222 Main St Evanston IL 60202-2467

SHAND, KAREN LOUISE HANES, art educator; b. Peru, Ind., Jan. 1, 1949; d. Elmer Eugene and Opal Catherine (Wray) Hanes; m. Stanley Lee Shand, June 7, 1970; children: Shelby Lynnette, Tiffanie Dawn, Kimberly Krestin. BA, Ball State U., 1970; MA, St. Francis Coll., 1973. Art tchr. Wiley H.S., Terre Haute, Ind., 1971, Clay City (Ind.) H.S., 1971-72, Ctrl. Noble H.S., Albion, Ind., 1972-76, Northwestern H.S., Kokomo, Ind., 1978; owner Batik Boutique, Flora, Ind., 1978—; art tchr. Carroll H.S., Flora, Ind., 1979—. Exhibited in group shows at Ball State U., 1970, Ft. Wayne Mus. Art, 1971, Hoosier Salon Art Gallery, 1981-96 (Merit award), Indpls. Mus. Art, 1985-90, Lafayette Art Mus., 1989-92, Logansport Art Gallery, 1989-95 (Best of Show award 1990). Bd. dirs. Am. Cancer Soc., Albion, Ind., 1974; art judge Logansport (Ind.) Art League, 1988, Kokomo Artist Assn., 1992, 94; vol. house restorations in Ind., 1992—. Ind. Artist in Residency grantee, 1995. Mem. Indpls. Art Leauge, Logansport Art Assn., Mich. Guild Artists and Artisans, Am. Watercolor Soc. Home and Office: Batik Boutique 11806 W 400 N Flora IN 46929

SHANE, RITA, opera singer; b. N.Y.C.; d. Julius J. and Rebekah (Milner) S.; m. Daniel F. Tritter, June 22, 1958; 1 child, Michael Shane. BA, Barnard Coll., 1958; postgrad., Santa Fe Opera Apprentice Program, 1962-63, Hunter Opera Assn., 1962-64; pvt. study with, Beverly Peck Johnson, Elizabeth Schwartzkopf, Bliss Hebert. Adj. prof. voice Manhattan Sch. of Music, 1993-95; prof. voice Eastman Sch. Music Rochester U., 1989—; pvt. teachng, N.Y.C., 1978—. Performer with numerous opera cos., including profl. debut, Chattanooga Opera, 1964, Met. Opera, San Francisco Opera, N.Y.C. Opera, Chgo. Lyric Opera, San Diego Opera, Santa Fe Opera, Teatro alla Scala, Milan, Italy, Bavarian State Opera, Netherlands Nat. Opera, Geneva Opera, Vienna State Opera, Phila., New Orleans, Balt. Opera, Opera du Rhin, Strasbourg, Scottish Opera, Teatro Reggio, Turin, Opera Metropolitana, Caracas, Portland Opera, Minn. Opera, also others; world premiere Miss Havisham's Fire, Argento; Am. premieres include Reimann-Lear, Schat-Houdini, Henze-Elegy for Young Lovers; participant festivals, including Mozart Festival, Lincoln Center, N.Y.C., Munich Festival, Aspen Festival, Handel Soc., Vienna Festival, Salzburg Festival, Munich Festival, Perugia Festival, Festival Canada, Glyndebourne Festival, performed with orchs. including Santa Cecilia, Rome, Austrian Radio, London Philharmn., Louisville, Cin., Cleve., Phila., RAI, Naples, Denver, Milw., Israel Philharm., rec. artist, RCA, Columbia, Louisville, Turnabout labels, also radio and TV. Recipient Martha Baird Rockefeller award, William Matheus Sullivan award. Mem. Am. Guild Mus. Artists, Screen Actors Guild. Office: care Daniel F Tritter 330 West 42nd St New York NY 10036

SHANE, SANDRA KULI, postal service administrator; b. Akron, Ohio, Dec. 12, 1939; d. Amiel M. and Margaret E. (Brady) Kuli; m. Fred Shane, May 30, 1962 (div. 1972); 1 child, Mark Richard; m. Byrl William Campbell, Apr. 26, 1981 (dec. 1984). BA, U. Akron, 1987, postgrad., 1988-90. Scheduler motor vehicle bur. Akron Police Dept., 1959-62; flight and ops. control staff Escort Air, Inc., Akron and Cleve., 1972-78; asst. traffic mgr. Keen Transport, Inc., Hudson, Ohio, 1978-83; mem. ops. and mktg. staff Shawnee Airways and Essco, Akron, 1983-86; in distbn. U.S. Postal Svc., Akron, 1986—; rec. sec. Affirmative Action Coun., Akron, 1988-90. Asst. art tchr. Akron Art Mus., 1979; counselor Support, Inc., Akron, 1983-84; com. chmn. Explorer post Boy Scouts Am., Akron, 1984-85. Mem. Bus. and Profl. Women's Assn. (pres.), Delta Nu Alpha. Democrat. Roman Catholic. Home: 455 E Bath Rd Cuyahoga Falls OH 44223-2511

SHANER, LESLIE ANN, lawyer; b. Lynchburg, Va., Oct. 1, 1948; d. George Leslie and Ruby Ann (Ward) S.; 1 child, Jennifer Ann; m. Harris Sol Levy, Mar. 15, 1992. BA, Randolph-Macon Women's Coll., 1989; JD, Washington & Lee U., 1992. Bar: U.S. Dist. Ct. (we. dist.) Va. 1993, U.S. Ct. Appeals (4th cir.) 1993. Assoc. Singleton & Deeds, Warm Springs, Va., 1992-94, O'Keefe & Spies, Lynchburg, Va., 1994—. Chmn. Ctrl. Shenandoah Disabilities Svcs. Bd., 1993-94; bd. dirs. Highland Med. Ctr., Inc., 1992-93, Valley Cmty. Svcs. Bd., 1993—. Recipient Nat. Collegiate Humanities award, Am. Jurisprudence award, Future Interests. Mem. ABA, Va. State Bar Assn., Va. Bar Assn., Va. Trial Lawyers Assn., Allegheny-Bath-Highland Bar Assn. (sec.-treas. 1993-94, chmn. social com. 1993-94), Lynchburg Bar Assn., The Federalists Soc. (sec.), Phi Delta Phi, Phi Beta Kappa, Omicron Delta Kappa (pres.), Eta Sigma Phi, Phi Alpha Phi. Office: O'Keefe & Spies 828 Main St Ste 1803 Lynchburg VA 24504

SHANK, CLARE BROWN WILLIAMS, political leader; b. Syracuse, N.Y., Sept. 19, 1909; d. Curtiss Crofoot and Clara Irene (Shoudy) Brown; m. Frank E. Williams, Feb. 18, 1940 (dec. Feb. 1957); m. Seth Carl Shank, Dec. 28, 1963 (dec. Jan. 1977). B in Oral English, Syracuse U., 1931. Tchr., 1931-33, merchandising exec., 1933-42; Pinellas County mem. Rep. State Com., 1954-58; life mem. Pinellas County Rep. Exec. Com.; exec. com. Fla. Rep. Com., 1954-64; Fla. committeewoman Rep. Nat. Com., 1956-64, mem. exec. com., 1956-64, asst. chmn. and dir. women's activities, 1958-64; alt., mem. exec. arrangements com., major speaker Rep. Nat. Conv., Chgo., 1960; alt., program and arrangement coms. Rep. Nat. Conv., 1964. Pres. St. Petersburg Women's Rep. Club, 1955-57; Mem. Def. Adv. Com. on Women in Services, 1959-65; trustee St. Petersburg Housing Authority, 1976-81. Recipient George Arents medal Syracuse U., 1959; citation for patriotic civilian service 5th U.S. Army and Dept. Def.; 1st woman to preside over any part of nat. polit. conv., Rep. Nat. Conv., Chgo., 1960. Mem. AAUW, DAR, Gen. Fedn. Women's Clubs, Colonial Dames 17th Century, Fla. Fedn. Women's Clubs (dist. pres. 1976-78), Women's Club (St. Petersburg, pres. 1974-76, Yacht Club, Lakewood Country Club (St. Petersburg). Methodist.

SHANKLE, MONIQUE VAN VOOREN, law clerk; b. Crockett, Tex., Dec. 11, 1963; d. Carl Wesley Shankle and Barbara Jean Leopold Rachal Williams. BA, Rice U., 1986; MEd, Tex. So. U., 1990; JD, U. Houston, 1993. Vol. People's Workshop for the Visual and Performing Arts, Houston, 1985—. Mem. Houston Young Lawyers Assn., Rice Univ. Bus. and Profl. Women. Home: PO Box 20453 Houston TX 77225

SHANKLIN, ELIZABETH E., secondary education educator; b. Nashville, July 23, 1934; d. J. Gordon and Emily (Shacklett) S. BS, Columbia U., 1956; MA, Sarah Lawrence Coll., 1990. Tchr. N.Y.C. Bd. of Edn., 1968—. Mem. AAUW, AFT, Am. Hist. Assn., Orgn. Am. Historians, The Feminists. Home: 2600 Netherland Ave Bronx NY 10463

SHANKS, ANN ZANE, filmmaker, producer/director, photographer, writer; b. N.Y.C.; d. Louis and Sadye (Rosenthal) Kushner; m. Ira Zane (dec.); children—Jennifer, Anthony; m. Robert Horton Shanks, Sept. 25, 1959; 1 child, John. Student, Carnegie-Mellon U., Columbia U., 1949. tchr., moderator spl. symposiums Mus. Modern Art, N.Y.C.; tchr. New Sch. for Social Research. Photographer, writer for numerous mags. and newspapers; producer, dir.: (movie shorts) Central Park, 1969 (U.S. entry Edinburgh Film Festival, Cine Golden Eagle award, Cambodia Film Festival award), Denmark... A Loving Embrace (Cine Golden Eagle award 1973), Tivoli, 1972-79 (San Francisco Film Festival award, Am. Film Festival award), (TV series) American Life Style (Silver award, 5 Gold medal awards Internat. TV and Film Festival N.Y., 2 Cine Golden Eagle awards), He's Fired, She's Hired; producer CBS TV Drop-Out Mother; producer, dir., writer (TV short) Mousie Baby; dir. (TV movie) Friendships, Secrets and Lies, NBC; producer: (TV movie) Drop-out Father, CBS, (video spl.) The Avant-Garde in Russia 1910-1930, Arts and Entertainment channel, ABC Morning Show, Good Afternoon Detroit; producer, dir. (TV spl.) A Day in the Country, PBS, (Emmy award nomination); producer, dir. play S.J. Perelman in Person; producer Broadway play, Lillian; exec. producer Gore Vidal's Am. Pres. series Channel Four, London, Discovery channel, U.S.; exhibited photographs Mus. Modern Art, Mus. City N.Y., Transit Mus., Brooklyn Heights, N.Y., Met. Mus. Art, Jewish Mus.; author: (photographs and text) The Name's the Game, New Jewish Ency; author, photographer, writer Old Is What You Get, Busted Lives...Dialogues with Kids in Jail, 1983; writer, photographer Garbage and Stuff. Recipient awards from internat. competitions. Mem. Am. Soc. Mag. Photographers (bd. govs.), Overseas Press Club Am., Women in Film (v.p.), Dirs. Guild Am.

SHANKS, JUDITH WEIL, editor; b. Montgomery, Ala., Nov. 2, 1941; d. Roman Lee and Charlotte (Alexander) Weil; m. Hershel Shanks, Feb. 20, 1966; children: Elizabeth Jeannette, Julia Emily. BA in Econs., Wellesley Coll., 1963; MBA, Trinity Coll., 1980. Econs. asst. Export-Import Bank, Washington, 1963-68; cons. econs. and social sci., 1968-76; researcher Time-Life Books, Alexandria, Va., 1976-80, prin. researcher, 1980-83, illustrations editor, 1983, adminstrv. editor, 1984-95, dir. editl. adminstrn., 1996. Vol. dinner program for homeless women, Mentors, Inc., vol. mentor with Mentors, Inc.; bd. dirs. Anne Frank House, for formerly homeless women. Mem. Garden Writers Am., Internat. Alliance, Washington Alliance Bus. Women, Leadership Greater Washington, Washington Wellesley Club (career caucus). Democrat. Jewish. Home: 5208 38th St NW Washington DC 20015-1812

SHANKS, KATHRYN MARY, health care administrator; b. Glens Falls, N.Y., Aug. 4, 1950; d. John Anthony and Lenita (Combs) S. BS summa cum laude, Spring Hill Coll., 1972; MPA, Auburn U., 1976. Program evaluator Mobile Mental Health, Ala., 1972-73; dir. spl. projects Ala. Dept. Mental Health, Montgomery, 1973-76; dir. adminstrn. S.W. Ala. Mental Health/Mental Retardation, Andulusia, Ala., 1976-78; adminstr. Mobile County Health Dept., 1978-82; exec. dir. Coastal Family Health Ctr., Biloxi, Miss., 1982-95; cons. med. group practice, 1995—; ptnr. Shanks & Allen, Mobile, 1979—; healthcare consulting pvt. practice, 1995—; cons. S.W. Health Agy., Tylertown, Miss., 1984-86; preceptor Sch. Nursing, U. So. Miss., Hattiesburg, 1983, 84; advisor Headstart Program, Gulfport, Miss., 1984-95; LPN Program, Gulf Coast C.C., 1984-95; lectr. Auburn U., Montgomery, 1977-78. Bd. dirs. Mobile Cmty. Action Agy., 1979-81, Moore Cmty. House; mem. S.W. Ala. Regional Goals Forum, Mobile, 1971-72, Cardiac Rehab. Study Com., Biloxi, Miss., 1983-84, Mothers and Babies Coalition, Jackson, Miss., 1983-95, Gulf Coast Coalition Human Svcs., Biloxi, Miss., 1983-95; exec. dir. Year for Miss., 1993-94. Spring Hill Coll. Pres.'s scholar, 1972. Mem. Miss. Primary Health Care Assn. (pres.), Med. Group Mgmt. Assn., Biloxi C. of C., ACLU, Soc. for Advancement of Ambulatory Care, Spring Hills Alumni Assn. Avocations: tennis, home restoration, golf.

SHANNON, CYNTHIA JEAN, biology educator; b. Phila., Feb. 19, 1961; d. Foster Lloyd and Nancy Ellen (Chapman) S.; ptnr. Gerald Thomas Braden. AA, Fullerton (Calif.) Coll., 1981; BA in Psychology, Calif. State U., Fullerton, 1986; BS in Zoology, Calif. Poly. State U., 1985, MS in Biology, 1991. Biology instr. Calif. State Poly. U., Pomona, Calif., 1986-91, Mt. San Antonio Coll., Walnut, Calif., 1986—. Mem. AAAS, Ornithological Soc. N.Am., So. Assn. Naturalists, Golden Key, Phi Kappa Phi. Democrat. Office: Mt San Antonio Coll 1100 N Grand Ave Walnut CA 91789

SHANNON, MARY LOU, adult health nursing educator; b. Memphis, Apr. 4, 1938; d. Sidney Richmond Shannon and Lucille (Gwaltney) Cloud. BSN, U. Tenn., 1959; MA, Columbia U., 1963, MEd, 1964, EdD, 1972. Staff nurse City of Memphis Hosps., 1959-60, instr. Sch. Nursing, 1960-62; asst. prof. U. Tenn., Memphis, 1964-70, assoc. prof., 1970-73, prof., 1973-89; prof., chair adult health dept. Sch. Nursing U. Tex., Galveston, 1989—; bd. dirs. Nat. Pressure Ulcer Adv. Panel, Buffalo, 1987-96; vis. prof. U. Alta., Edmonton, Can., 1982; mem. project adv. bd. RAND, Santa Monica, Calif., 1994. Contbr. chpts. to books in field and to periodicals; mem. editl. bd. Advances in Wound Care, 1987—. Trustee Nurses Edn. Funds, N.Y.C., 1972-86. Mem. ANA, Nat. League Nursing (bd. of rev. 1983-86), Orthopedic Nurses Assn., So. Nursing Rsch. Soc., Am. Assn. for History of Nursing. Office: U Tex Sch Nursing 301 University Blvd Galveston TX 77550-2708

SHAPERO, ESTHER BAILEY GELLER, artist; b. Boston, Oct. 26, 1921; d. Harry Gregor and Fannie (Geller) Geller; m. Harold Samuel Shapero, Sept. 21, 1945; 1 child, Hannah. Diploma, Sch. Boston Mus. Fine Arts, 1943. Tchr. Boston Mus. Fine Arts, Natick Art Assn., 1945-70. One woman shows include Mus. of Fine Arts Boston, Boris Mirski Art Mus., De Cordova Mus., Am. Acad. Rome, Worcester Art Mus., Decenter Gallery, Denmark, Danforth Mus. Art; exhibited in group shows at Chgo. Art Inst., San Francisco Mus., Smith Coll. Mus. Cabot fellow Am. Acad. Rome, 1949, 49-50, 70-71; named Boston's Honored Artists, 1995. Office: Firehouse Studios 5 Summer St Natick MA 01760

SHAPIRO, ANNA, microbiologist, researcher; b. N.Y.C., Jan. 11, 1910; d. Samuel and Esther (Cohen) Lewis; m. Joseph Shapiro, Feb. 7, 1933 (dec. 1985); children: Joan Elisabeth Brandston (dec.), Joel Elias. BS in Biology and Chemistry, NYU, 1931, MS in Bacteriology, 1934, PhD in Microbiology, 1971. Lab. asst. Bellevue Med. Sch., NYU, 1931-33, instr., 1933-36; lectr. Hofstra U., L.I., 1963, Queensborough U., CUNY, Queens, 1964; rsch. asst. Haskins Lab. of Pace Univ., N.Y.C., 1971-80, rsch. assoc., 1980-83. Author: Methods of Enzymology, 1980, The In Vitro Cultivation of Pathogens of Tropical Diseases, 1980; contbr. articles to profl. jours. Mem. AAAS, N.Y. Acad. Sci. (Disting. Svc. award 1992), Sigma Xi. Home: 2 Fifth Ave Apt 9J New York NY 10011

SHAPIRO, DEBORAH ANNE, corporate training specialist, software support executive; b. Bristol, Pa., Feb. 27, 1959; d. Seymour and Frances (Kaplan) S.; life ptnr. Beth Spivak. BA, SUNY, Purchase, N.Y., 1980; MBA, Widener U., Chester, Pa., 1988. Instr. Pennco Tech., Bristol, Pa., 1982-89, Computer Learning Ctr., Phila., 1989-95; training support staff Compudata, Inc., Phila., 1995—. Active various political marches, Phila., Washington, N.Y. Mem. Congregation Beth Ahavah (pres. 1986-87, chair ritual affairs 1981-86). Democrat. Jewish. Office: CompuData Inc 10501 Drummond Rd Philadelphia PA 19154

SHAPIRO, EILEEN, education professional; b. Kew Gardens, N.Y., Dec. 25, 1944; d. Emanuel E. and Beatrice (Miller) Lichtenberg; m. Howard Shapiro, June 25, 1966; children: David, Rachel. BS in Edn., U. Cin., 1966; MS in Reading, Nova U., 1987. Mem. instrl. support team Sch. Dist. Palm Beach County, West Palm Beach, Fla. Recipient Outstanding Cmty. Involvements Joining Bus. and Edn. Together award No. Palm Beach C. of C., 1988; Louie Camp Creative Tchg. grantee Fla. Coun. on Elme. Edn., 1987. Mem. Internat. Reading Assn., Fla. Reading Assn., Palm Beach Reading Coun. (Outstanding Sch. Reading Project award 1988), Phi Delta Kappa, Delta Kappa Gamma. Home: 371 Kelsey Park Dr Palm Beach Gardens FL 33410 Office: Sch Dist Palm Beach County 3505 Shiloh Dr West Palm Beach FL 33407

SHAPIRO, FLORENCE, state legislator, advertising, public relations executive; b. N.Y.C., May 2, 1948; d. Martin Nmi and Ann (Spiesman) D.; m. Howard Nmi Shapiro, Dec. 28, 1969; children: Lisa, Todd, Staci. BS, U. Tex., 1970. Tchr. Richardson High Sch., Tex., 1970-72; advt., pub. rels. Shapiro, Small and Assocs., Plano, Tex., 1982—; formerly mayor and mem. city coun. City of Plano, Tex.; now mem. Tex. Senate, 1992—; vice chair Senate Criminal Justice Com. Bd. dirs. Plano C. of C., Presbyn. and Children's Healthcare Ctr., Plano Econ. Devel. Bd., U. Tex. at Dallas Adv. Coun., The North Tex. Commn., The Dallas Regional Mobility Coalition; mem. nat. bd. dirs. Susan B. Komen Breast Cancer Found.; mem. adv. bd. Children's Edn. Fund Dallas. Recipient Plano Vol. of Yr. award, 1983, Plano Citizen of Yr. award, 1985, Athena award Plano C. of C. for Businesswoman of Yr., 1990, Child Advocate award Dallas Children's Advocacy Ctr., 1995, Legislator of Yr. award Tex. Mcpl. League, 1995, Outstanding Legislator of Yr. award Tex. Police Chiefs Assn., 1995. Mem. Alpha Epsilon Phi (v.p., soc. chmn. 1968-69), Plano Rotary Club (Paul Harris fellow award 1990). Republican. Jewish. Home: 2005 Crown Knls Plano TX 75093-4103 Office: Tex Senate PO Box 12068 Austin TX 78711

SHAPIRO, JOAN ISABELLE, laboratory administrator, nurse; b. Fulton, Ill., Aug. 26, 1943; d. Macy James and Frieda Lockhart; m. Ivan Lee Shapiro, Dec. 28, 1968; children: Audrey, Michael. RN, Peoria Methodist Sch. Nursing, Ill., 1964. Nurse, Grant Hosp., Columbus, Ohio, 1975-76; nurse Cardiac Thoracic and Vascular Surgeons Ltd., Geneva, Ill., 1977—, mgr. non-invasive lab., 1979—; owner, operator Shapiro's Mastiff's 1976-82; sec.-treas. Sounds Svcs., 1976—, Mainstream Sounds Inc., 1980-84; cofounder Cardio-Phone Inc., 1982—, Edgewater Vascular Inst., 1987-89, Associated Profls., 1989-92; v.p., bd. dir. Computer Specialists Inc., 1986-89; founder, pres. Vein Ctr., Edema Ctr. Ltd. Mem. Soc. Non-invasive Technologists, Soc. Peripheral Vascular Nursing (community awareness com. 1984—), Oncology Nursing Soc., Internat. Soc. Lymphology, Kane County Med. Soc. Aux. (pres. 1983-84, adviser, 1984-85). Lutheran. Office: Cardiac Thoracic and Vascular Surgeons Ltd PO Box 564 Geneva IL 60134-0564

SHAPIRO, JUDITH R., anthropology educator, university official; b. N.Y.C., Jan. 24, 1942. Student Ecole des Haute Etudes Institut d'Etudes Politiques, Paris, 1961-62; BA, Brandeis U., 1963; PhD, Columbia U., 1972. Asst. prof. U. Chgo., 1970-75; postdoctoral fellow U. Calif.-Berkeley, 1974-75; Rosalyn R. Schwartz lectr., asst. prof. anthropology Bryn Mawr Coll., Pa., 1975-78, assoc. prof., 1978-85, prof., 1985—, chmn. dept., 1982-85, acting dean undergrad coll., 1985-86, provost, 1986-94; pres. Barnard Coll., N.Y., 1994—; contbr. articles to profl. jours., chpts. to books. Fellow Woodrow Wilson Found., 1963-64, Columbia U., 1964-65, NEH Younger Humanist, 1974-75, Am. Coun. Learned Socs., 1981-82, Ctr. for Advanced Study in the Behavioral Scis., 1989; grantee NSF summer field tng., 1965, Ford Found. 1966, NIMH, 1974-75, Social Sci. Rsch. Coun., 1974-75. Mem. Phila. Anthrop. Soc. (pres. 1983), Am. Ethnol. Soc. (nominations com. 1983-84, pres. elect 1984-85, pres. 1985-86), Am. Anthrop. Assn. (ethics com. 1976-79, bd. dirs. 1984-86, exec. com. 1985-86), Social Sci. Rsch. Coun.

(com. social sci personnel 1977-80), mem. bd. dirs. consortium on financing higher edn.; dir. Fund for the City of N.Y.; mem. exec. com. Women's Coll. Coalition; mem. nat. adv. com. Woodrow Wilson Nat. Fellowship Found., Women's Forum, Phi Beta Kappa, Sigma Xi. Office: Barnard Coll Office of the Pres 3009 Broadway New York NY 10027-6598

SHAPIRO, LUCILLE, molecular biology educator; b. N.Y.C., July 16, 1940; d. Philip and Yetta (Stein) Cohen; m. Roy Shapiro, Jan. 23, 1960 (div. 1977); 1 child, Peter; m. Harley H. McAdams, July 28, 1978; stepchildren: Paul, Heather. BA, Bklyn. Coll., 1961; PhD, Albert Einstein Coll. Medicine, 1966. Asst. prof. Albert Einstein Coll. Medicine, N.Y.C., 1967-72, assoc. prof., 1972-77, Kramer prof., chmn. dept. molecular biology, 1977-86, dir. biol. scis. div., 1981-86; Eugene Higgins prof., chmn. dept. microbiology, Coll. Physicians and Surgeons Columbia U., N.Y.C., 1986-89; Joseph D. Grant prof., chmn. dept. devel. biology Sch. Medicine, Stanford U., 1989—; bd. dirs. Silicon Graphics; bd. sci. counselors NIH, Washington, 1980-84, DeWitt Stetten disting. lectr., 1989; bd. sci. advisors G.D. Searle Co., Skokie, Ill., 1984-86; sci. adv. bd. Mass. Gen. Hosp., 1990-93, SmithKline Beecham, 1993—, PathoGenesis, 1995—; bd. trustees Scientists Inst. for Pub. Info., 1990-94; lectr. Harvey Soc., 1993; commencement address U. Calif., Berkeley, 1994. Editor: Microbiol. Devel., 1984; mem. editorial bd. Jour. Bacteriology, 1978-86, Trends in Genetics, 1987—, Genes and Development, 1987-91, Cell Regulation, 1990-92, Molecular Biology of the Cell, 1992—, Molecular Microbiology, 1991—, Current Opinion on Genetics and Devel., 1991—; contbr. articles to profl. jours. Mem. sci. bd. Helen Hay Witney Found., N.Y.C., 1986-94; co-chmn. adv. bd. NSF Biology Directorate, 1988-89; vis. com., bd. overseers Harvard U., Cambridge, Mass., 1987-90; mem. sci. bd. Whitehead Inst., MIT, Boston, 1988-93; mem. sci. rev. bd. Howard Hughes Med. Inst., 1990-94, Cancer Ctr. of Mass. Gen. Hosp., Boston, 1994; mem. Presidio Coun. City of San Francisco, 1991-94; mem. Pres. Coun. U. Calif., 1991—. Recipient Hirschl Career Scientist award, 1976, Spirit of Achievement award, 1978, Alumna award of honor Bklyn. Coll., 1983, Excellence in Sci. award Fedn. Am. Soc. Exptl. Biology, 1994; Jane Coffin Child fellow, 1966. Fellow AAAS, Am. Acad. Arts and Scis., Am. Acad. Microbiology; mem. NAS, Inst. Medicine of NAS, Am. Soc. Biochemistry and Molecular Biology (nominating com. 1982, 87, coun. 1990-93), Am. Heart Assn. (sci. adv. bd. 1984-87). Office: Stanford U Sch Medicine Beckman Ctr Dept Devel Biology Stanford CA 94305

SHAPIRO, MARIAN KAPLUN, psychologist; b. N.Y., July 13, 1939; d. David and Bertha Rebecca (Pearlman) Kaplun; m. Irwin Ira Shapiro, Dec. 20, 1959; children: Steven, Nancy. BA, Queens Coll., 1959; MA in Teaching, Harvard U., 1961, EdD, 1978. Cert. psychologist. Tchr. North Quincy High Sch., Quincy, Mass., 1962-64; instr. Carnegie Inst., Boston, 1968-74; staff psychologist South Shore Counselling Assn., Hanover, Mass., 1978-80; pvt. practice psychologist Lexington, Mass., 1980—; adj. instr. Mass. Sch. Profl. Psychology, Dedham, 1985—. Author: 2nd Childhood: Hypnoplay Therapy with Age--Regressed Adults, 1989; contbr. articles on teaching reading, hypnotherapy, multiple personality and other clin. issues to profl. jours. Fellow Am. Orthopsychiat. Assn.; mem. APA, Mass. Psychol. Assn., N.E. Soc. Group Psychotherapy, Am. Soc. Group Psychotherapy (clin.), Am. Soc. Clin. Hypnosis (cert. cons.), New Eng. Soc. for the Study of Multiple Personality Disorders, Internat. Soc. for the Study of Multiple Personality Disorders, New Eng. Soc. Clin. Hypnosis, Sigma Alpha, Pi Lambda Theta. Jewish. Home and Office: 17 Lantern Ln Lexington MA 02173-6029

SHAPIRO, MARY J., writer, researcher, speech writer; b. Buffalo, Oct. 30, 1945; d. Peter J. and Margaret (McMahon) Crotty; m. Barry H. Shapiro, Apr. 22, 1972; children: Michael, Eben. BA, Manhattanville Coll., 1967; MFA, NYU, 1970. Editor Francis Thompson, Inc., N.Y.C., 1973-76; exhbn. coord., writer, researcher Chermayeff & Geismar, Inc., N.Y.C., 1987-92; writer, researcher Edwin Schlossberg Inc., N.Y.C., 1991-92, Ralph Appelbaum Assocs. Inc., N.Y.C., 1994—; exhbn. coord. Mus. Jewish Heritage, N.Y.C., 1987-88, Carnegie Hall Mus., N.Y.C., 1990; writer Ellis Island Immigration Mus., N.Y.C., 1988-90, Johnston (Pa.) Flood Mus., 1989, Chickamauga (Ga.) Battlefield Visitor Ctr., 1991, Oklahoma City Zoo Great Apes Habitat, 1992, Sony Wonder Tech. Mus., N.Y.C., 1993; writer, rschr. Women's Rights Nat. Hist. Park, Seneca Falls, N.Y., 1988-91, Old South Mtg. House, Boston, 1994-96. Author: Picture History of the Brooklyn Bridge, 1983, How They Built The Statue of Liberty, 1985, Gateway to Liberty, 1986, Ellis Island: An Illustrated History of the Immigrant Experience, 1991. Recipient Outstanding Science Trade Book citation Children's Book Coun., 1985, Garden State Children's Book award N.J.. Libr. Assn., 1986. Home: 370 1st Ave Apt 4B New York NY 10010-4928

SHAPIRO, MYRA STEIN, poet; b. Bronx, N.Y., May 21, 1932; d. David M. and Ida Betty (Leader) Stein; m. Harold M. Shapiro, Feb. 15, 1953; children: Karen S., Judith M. BA, U. Tenn., 1968; MA in English, Middlebury Coll., 1973; MFA, Vt. Coll., 1993. reader, Internat. Women's Day, Jefferson Market Libr., N.Y.C., 1989; reading performance Midday Muse Series, Folger Shakespeare Libr., Washington, 1983, NEA Hunter Mus., Chattanooga, 1985, Bower's Mus., Santa Ana, Calif., 1986, 88. Author: (poetry) The Ohio Review, 1989, Education for Peace, 1988, Kalliope, 1988, Ploughshares, 1990-91, The Harvard Review, 1994. Recipient Dylan Thomas Poetry award, The New Sch., N.Y.C., 1981, The MacDowell Colony Fellowship, The MacDowell Colony, Peterborough, N.H., 1985, 87. Mem. Poetry Soc. Am., Poets House (bd. dirs.). Office: 111 4th Ave Apt 12I New York NY 10003-5240

SHAPIRO, NELLA IRENE, surgeon; b. N.Y.C., Nov. 13, 1947; d. Eugene and Ethel (Pearl) S.; m. Jack Schwartz, Oct. 16, 1977; children: Max, Molly. BA, Barnard Coll., 1968; MD, Albert Einstein Coll., 1972. Resident in gen. surgery Montefiore Hosp., N.Y.C., 1972-76; mem. staff North Cen. Hosp., Bronx, N.Y., 1976-77, Bronx Mcpl. Hosp., 1977-87; chief gen. surgery Bronx Mcpl. Hosp. Ctr., 1983-87; mem. staff in gen. surgery Albert Einstein Coll. Hosp., Bronx, 1977-93, chief gen. surgery, 1991-93; atty. Lear Surg. Assocs., 1993-94; pvt. solo practice Bronx, 1994—; asst. prof. surgery Albert Einstein Coll., Bronx, 1980—; assoc. dir. gen. surgery Weller Hosp., Bronx, 1991-93; co-founder Whaecom Breast Ctr., Bronx, 1991—. Fellow Am. Coll. Surgeons. Office: 1695 Eastchester Rd Ste 304 Bronx NY 10461-2335

SHAPIRO, ROBYN SUE, lawyer, educator; b. Mpls., July 19, 1952; d. Walter David and Judith Rae (Sweet) S.; m. Charles Howard Barr, June 27, 1976; children: Tania Shapiro-Barr, Jeremy Shapiro-Barr, Michael Shapiro-Barr. BA summa cum laude, U. Mich., 1974; JD, Harvard U., 1977. Bar: D.C., 1977, Wis., 1979, U.S. Supreme Ct., 1990. Assoc. Foley & Lardner, Washington, 1977-79; ptnr. Barr & Shapiro, Menomonee Falls, Wis., 1980-87; assoc. Quarles & Brady, Milw., 1987-92; ptnr. Michael Best & Friedrich, Milw., 1992—; adj. asst. prof. law Marquette U., Milw., 1979-83; assoc. dir. bioethics ctr. Med. Coll. Wis., Milw., 1982-85, dir., 1985—; asst. prof. bioethics Med. Coll. Wis., 1984-89, assoc. prof. bioethics, 1989—; dir. Wis. Ethics Com. Network, 1987—; bd. mem. Wis. Health Decisions, 1990-93. Editorial bd. mem: Cambridge Quarterly, 1991—, HEC Forum, 1988-91; contbr. articles to profl. jours. Mem. ethics com. St. Luke's Hosp., Milw., 1983—, Elmbrook Meml. Hosp., Milw., 1983-86, Cmty. Meml. Hosp., Menomonee Falls, 1984—, Sinai Samaritan Hosp., Milw., 1986—, Milw. County Med. Complex, 1984—, Froedtert Meml. Luth. Hosp., 1985—; mem. subcom. organ transplantation Wis. Health Policy Coun., Madison, 1984, bioethics com., 1986-89; mem. com. study on bioethics Wis. Legis. Coun., Madison, 1984-85; bd. dirs. Jewish Home and Care Ctr., 1994—, chair ethics com., 1994—; chair Bayside Ethics Bd., 1994—; bd. dirs. Milw. area chpt. Girl Scouts U.S., Am. Bioethics Assn., 1995—. James B. Angell scholar, 1971-72. Mem. ABA (forum com. health law, individual rights and responsibilities sec., health rights com. chair 1994—, mem. coordinating com. on bioethics and law, chair 1995—), Nat. Health Lawyers Assn., Am. Soc. Law & Medicine, Am. Hosp. Assn. (bioethics tech. panel 1991-94, spl. com. HIV & practitioners 1991-93), Wis. Bar Assn. (coun. Wis. health law sect. 1988-89, individual rights sect. coun. 1987-90), Assn. Women Lawyers, ACLU, Wis. Found. (Atty. of Yr. 1988), Milw. Acad. Medicine (coun. 1992—, chair bioethics com. 1992—), Milw. AIDS Coalition (steering com. 1988-91), Internat. Bioethics Assn. (chair task force on ethics coms.), Profl. Dimensions (Golden Compass award 1994), Phi Beta Kappa, others. Home: 9474 N Broadmoor Rd Milwaukee WI 53217-1309 Office: Med Coll Wis Bioethics Ctr 8701 W Watertown Plank Rd Milwaukee WI 53226-3548

SHAPIRO, SANDRA, lawyer; b. Providence, Oct. 17, 1944; d. Emil and Sarah (Cohen) S. AB magna cum laude, Bryn Mawr Coll., Pa., 1966; LLB magna cum laude, U. Pa., 1969. Bar: Mass. 1970, U.S. Dist. Ct. Mass. 1971, U.S. Ct. Appeals (1st cir.) 1972, U.S. Supreme Ct. 1980. Law clk. U.S. Ct. Appeals (1st cir.), Boston, 1969-70; assoc. Foley, Hoag & Eliot, Boston, 1970-75, ptnr., 1976—; bd. dirs. Mass. Govt. Land Bank; mem. Bd. Bar Overseers Mass. Supreme Judicial Ct., 1988-92, Gender Bias Study Com., 1986-89. Contbr. articles to profl. jours. Bd. dirs. Patriots' Trail coun. Girl Scouts U.S., 1994—; mem. bd. overseers Boston Lyric Opera, 1993—, New England Conservatory of Music, 1995—. Woodrow Wilson fellow, 1966. Mem. ABA (ethics, professionalism and pub. edn. com. 1994—), Women's Bar Assn. of Mass. (prs. 1985-86), New Eng. Women in Real Estate, Nat. Women's Law Ctr. Network, Mass. Bar Assn. (chmn. real property sect. coun., com. on profl. ethics), Boston Bar Assn. (mem. coun.), U. Pa. Law Sch. Alumni Assn. (bd. mgrs. 1990—), Order of Coif, Boston Club. Office: Foley Hoag & Eliot 1 Post Office Sq Boston MA 02109-2170

SHAPIRO, SHARON LYNN, journalist; b. Tulsa, Okla.; d. Joseph Hubert and Bess Bailey. B of Journalism, U. Mo., 1989. Screenwriter L.A., 1985-86; editor, columnist The Tampa (Fla.) Tribune, 1989-95; writer Tampa, 1995—. Contbr. articles to profl. publs. Mem. AAUW. Office: PO Box 10245 Tampa FL 33679

SHAPIRO, SUSAN HILLARY, director, producer, lawyer; b. Nyack, N.Y., Nov. 3, 1957; d. Milton B. S. and Sonya Libby Fienne. BA, U. Pa., 1979; BFA, NYU, 1990; JD, Cardoza Sch. Law, 1993. Bar: N.Y. 1994. Prodr. Skouras Pictures, L.A., 1990, Fries Entertainment and Locus Solus, L.A., 1991; prodr., dir. Flying Wolf Prodns., N.Y.C., 1992-93, 7th Level, Glendale, Calif., 1994; prodr. Jonathan Krane Group, Palm Beach, Fla., 1994; line prodr. Dream Entertainment, L.A., 1994-95; head prodn., dir. Rocket Pictures, Beverly Hills, Calif., 1995; prodr. Cineville Pictures, 1996. Contbr. chpt. to book; exhibitions include Around the Clock Gallery, N.Y.C., 1986, Santa Monica (Calif.) Place Gallery, 1993, Directors Guild of Am., L.A., 1994, Alliance for the Wild Rockies, Missolua, Mont., 1994. Mem. Women in Film, Heal the Bay, Women in the Arts, Greenpeace. Office: 237 Amalfi Dr Santa Monica CA 90402

SHAPO, HELENE S., law educator; b. N.Y.C., June 5, 1938; d. Benjamin Martin and Gertrude (Kahaner) Seidner; m. Marshall S. Shapo, June 21, 1959; children: Benjamin Mitchell, Nathaniel Saul. BA, Smith Coll., 1959; MA in Teaching, Harvard U., 1960; JD, U. Va., 1976. Bar: Va. 1976, U.S. Dist. Ct. (we. dist.) Va. 1977, Ill. 1993. Tchr. Dade County, Miami, Fla., 1960-64; assoc. Robert Musselman & Assocs., Charlottesville, Va., 1976-77; law clk. to presiding justice U.S. Dist. Ct. Va., Charlottesville, 1977-78; asst. prof. law Northwestern U., Chgo., 1978-81, assoc. prof. law, 1981-83, prof. law, 1983—; instr. Sweet Briar Coll., Va., 1976-77, U. Va., Charlottesville, 1976-78; mem. com. law sch. admissions council/testing and devel., 1983—; cons. in field. Mem. ABA, Va. Bar Assn., Assn. of Am. Law Schs. (sect. chairperson 1985—), Women's Bar Assn. Chgo. Office: Northwestern U Sch Law 357 E Chicago Ave Chicago IL 60611-3008*

SHARBEL, JEAN M., editor; b. Lansford, Pa.; d. Joseph and Star (Nemr) Sharbel. BA in Journalism, Hunter Coll., N.Y.C. Editorial dir., v.p. Dauntless Books, N.Y.C., 1962-75; editor romance mags., True Confessions Mag., Macfadden Holdings, Inc., N.Y.C., 1976-92; freelance editor fiction and nonfiction books, 1989—. Home: 165 E 66th St New York NY 10021-6132

SHARBONEAU, LORNA ROSINA, artist, educator, author, poet, illustrator; b. Spokane, Wash., Apr. 5, 1935; d. Stephen Charles Martin and Midgie Montana (Hartzel) Barton; m. Thomas Edward Sharboneau, Jan. 22, 1970; children: Curtis, Carmen, Chet, Cra, Joseph. AA in Arts, Delta Coll., 1986; studies with Steve Lesnick, Las Vegas, Nev.; studies with Bette Myers/Zimmerman, Phoenix and Bonners Ferry, Idaho. Prin. Sharboneau's Art Gallery, Spokane, 1977-80; tchr. art Michell's Art Gallery, Spokane, 1978-79; art therapist Vellencino Sch. Dist., Calif., 1981-83, ind. artist Lind, Wash., 1948—; dir., producer, stage designer Ch. of Jesus Christ of LDS, San Jose, Sonora, Modesto, Calif., 1978 (1st. place road show San Jose); dir. Sharboneau's Art Show, Spokane, 1979, Hands On-Yr. of the Child; platform spkr., poet, fundraiser, libr., 1984-87; asst., apprentice to Prof. Rowland Cheney, Delta Coll., Stockton, Calif., 1985, 86, 87; demonstrated drip oil technique, Bonners Ferry, Idaho, Spokane, Wash., Stockton, Calif., Delta Coll. Author, illustrator: Through the Eyes of the Turtle Tree, The One-Armed Christmas Tree, The Price of Freedom, William Will, Bill Can, Song of the Turtle Tree, Chet's Ottle-Bottle: The Unbreakable Bottle, One Drop of Water and a Grain of Sand; poet; prolific artist completed over 4000 paintings and drawings, displayed works in galleries through western states; featured in Magnolia News, Seattle, Delta Coll. Impact, Stockton, Calif., Stockton Record, Union Democrat, Sonora, Calif., Lincoln Center Chronicle, Stockton, Calif., Spokesman Rev., Spokane, Wash., Modesto (Calif) Bee, Angels Camp, Calif., Union Democrat, Sonora, Calif., New-Letter, Ch. of Jesus Christ of L.D.S 1st ward, Sonora; artist mixed media, oil, drip oil works, sculptures, pastel, watercolor; illustrations pen and ink, acrylic; sculptor bronze, lost wax method, ceramic art, soap stone, egg-tempra, original techniques, collage, variation on a theme. Dir., programmer, fundraiser Shelter Their Sorrows, Sonora, Calif., 1989-92, vol. Community Action Agency and Homeless Shelter. Recipient Golden Rule award J.C. penny, 1991, Recognition award Pres. George Bush, cert. Spl. Congl. Recognition Congressman Richard H. Lehman, 3rd Pl. Best Show East Valley ARtists/Pala Show, 1973, 74, 75, 3d Pl. Artist of Yr., 1974, Valley Fair, Santa Clara, Calif., 1974, 1st and 2d Pl. Spokane County Fair, 1978, 3 honorable mentions, 4 premiums, 1979, 3 1st Pl., 3 2d Pl., 2 3rd Pl., honorable mention Calaveras County Fair/Angels Camp, Calif., 1983, 1st and 3rd Pl. Unitarian Art Festival, Stockton, Calif., 1984, 2d Pl., 1985, 3d Pl., 1986, 1st Pl. Lodi Art Ann., 1985, 3rd Pl., 1986, 1st Pl. 1987, 1st Pl., 1988, honorable mental SJCAC Junque Art Show, Stockton, 1985, 1st Pl Ctrl. Calif. Art League, Modesto, 1986, 88, 2d Pl. 1995; 3d Pl. Camilla Art Show, San Jose, Calif., 1974, and numerous others; 1st, 2d, and 3d Pl., Spokane County Fair, 1978; 4 honorable mentions, Sonora, Calif., 1993, 2nd Pl. Ctrl. Calif. Art Show, 1996. Mem. Ctrl. Sierra Arts Coun., Mother Lode Artists Assn., Sacramento Fine Arts Ctr., Inc., Internat. Platform Assn. (Judges Choice conv. arts competition 1993), The Planetary Soc., The Nat. Mus. of Women of Arts. Mem. Ch. of Jesus Christ of LDS. Office: Internat Platform Assn PO Box 250 Winnetka IL 60093-0250

SHARKEY, COLLEEN MARY, law firm administrator, business consultant; b. Jersey City, Sept. 26, 1950; d. Martin and Helen (Sirangelo) Powers; 1 child, Jessica; stepchildren: Matthew, Debra, Janet. BA, U. Ctrl. Fla., Orlando, 1986; MBA, Crummer Grad. Sch. Bus., Winter Park, Fla., 1995. Keypunch supr. Alpha Metals Inc., Jersey City, 1969-71, computer operator, 1971-73, computer programmer, 1973-75; computer lab. trainer Seminole C.C., Sanford, Fla., 1982-86; litigation support paralegal Rumberger, Kirk, Caldwell, Cabaniss, Burke & Wechsler, PA, Orlando, 1986-91; adminstr. Cabaniss & Burke, PA, Orlando, 1991—. Author seminar Keeping the Good Ones, 1995. Recipient Nat. Collegiate award U.S. Achievement Acad., 1986. Mem. NAFE, AAUW, Assn. Legal Adminstrs. Republican. Roman Catholic. Office: Cabaniss & Burke PA 800 N Magnolia Ave Orlando FL 32803

SHARKEY, KATHLEEN, accountant; b. Phila., Jan. 25, 1951; d. Joseph Philip and Florence Veronica (Noykoff) Sharkey; m. Joel David Delpha, Sept. 24, 1977; children: Daniel Joseph, Madeleine Day. BA, John Carroll U., 1973. Tchr. St. Michael's Sch., St. Louis, 1976-79; acct. Citicorp Acceptance, St. Louis, 1986-89; fin. dir., adminstr. Women's Self Help Ctr., St. Louis, 1989—. Bd. dirs. Mo. Religious Coalition for Reproductive Choice, St. Louis, 1992—; co-chair St. Louis Caths. for a Free Choice, 1992—; treas. Shaw Neighborhood Improvement Assn., 1994—, Mo. Coalition Against Domestic Violence, 1995—. Democrat. Roman Catholic. Home: 4047 Magnolia Pl Saint Louis MO 63110-3914 Office: Women's Self Help Ctr Inc 2838 Olive St Saint Louis MO 63103-1428

SHARMA, RASHMI, toxicologist, researcher; b. Mathura, India, Aug. 10, 1960; came to U.S., 1989; d. Ghanshiam Nath and Gomati (Ramnathji) S. BSc, U. Allahabad, India, 1979, MSc, 1981, PhD, 1989. Rsch. assoc. U. Miss., Jackson, 1989-91; postdoctoral fellow U. Tex. Med. Br., Galveston, 1991—; attendee workshops and meetings Congress Zoology, Gwalior (India) U., 1983, Meerut (India) U., 1985, Indian Sci. Congress Assn., Lucknow (India), 1984, Delhi U., 1985, Bangalore (Karnataka) India, 1986, USA Internat. Conf., Stanford (Calif.) U., 1987, Young Scientist Workshop on Environ. Nematology, U. Allahabad, India, 1987, South Ctrl. Soc. Toxicology, Oxford (Miss.) U., 1989, Nat. Ctr. for Toxicol. Rsch., Jefferson, Ark., 1990, Miss. Acad. Sci., Biloxi, 1990, Jackson, Miss., 1991, Soc. Toxicology, Dallas, 1991, New Orleans, 1993, Am. Assn. Cancer Rsch., San Diego, 1992, Orlando, Fla., 1993, San Francisco, 1994, Toronto, Can., 1995. Contbr. articles to profl. jours. Fellow Coun. Sci. and Indsl. Rsch., Govt. of India, 1984-87; grantee NIH, 1989-91. Mem. AAAS, Am. Assn. for Cancer Rsch. Home: 515 1st St Apt 335 Galveston TX 77550-5743 Office: U Tex Med Br 7 138 MRB Rt J-67 Galveston TX 77555-1067

SHARMA, SALLY A., bank executive. Sr. v.p. corp. planning Calif. Fed. Bank, L.A. Office: Calif Fed Bank 5700 Wilshire Blvd Ste 328A Los Angeles CA 90036*

SHARMA, SANTOSH DEVRAJ, obstetrician, gynecologist, educator; b. Kenya, Feb. 24, 1934; came to U.S., Jan. 1972; d. Devraj Chananram and Lakshmi (Devi) S. BS, MB, B.J. Medical Sch., Pune, India, 1960. House surgeon Sasson Hosp., Poona, India, 1960-61; resident in ob-gyn. various hospitals, England, 1961-67; house officer Maelor Gen. Hosp., Wrexham, U.K., 1961-62; asst. prof. ob-gyn. Howard U. Med. Sch., Washington, 1972-74; assoc. prof. John A. Burns Sch. Med., Honolulu, 1974-78, prof., 1978 --. Fellow Royal Coll. Ob-Gyn., Am. Coll. Ob-Gyn. Office: 1319 Punahou St Rm 824 Honolulu HI 96826-1032

SHARMAN, DIANE LEE, secondary school educator; b. Harvey, Ill., May 12, 1948; d. Eric Melvin and Josephine A. (Kut) Van Patten; m. Sharman Richard Lee, Nov. 13, 1973; children: Doria Lee, Deedra Lee. BS, Purdue U., 1970; MBA, U. Chgo., 1973. Cert. secondary sch. math. tchr., Tex. Computers sales rep. GE, Chgo., 1970-73; mgr. sold equipment Xerox Corp., Rochester, N.Y., 1973-81; mgr. fin. ops. analysis worldwide Xerox Corp., Stamford, N.Y., 1981-84; math. tchr. Conroe (Tex.) Ind. Sch. Dist., 1993—. Mem. DAR, Nat. Coun. Tchrs. of Math., Assn., Tex. Profl. Educators, Purdue Alumni Assn. (life), Episcopal Womens Assn. Trinity Ch., Woodlands, Tex., Lions Club. Home: 26 Fernglen Dr Woodlands TX 77380 Office: York Jr HS 27310 Oak Ridge Sch Rd Conroe TX 77385

SHARMAN, JOELLE COOPERMAN, lawyer; b. Phila., Dec. 10, 1969. BS, U. Miami, 1991; JD, Duke U., 1994. Assoc. Schwartz, Gold, Cohen, Zakarin & Kotler, Boca Raton, Fla., 1995—. Active South Palm Beach County Fedn., 1995—. Mem. ABA, Acad. of Fla. Trial Lawyers, Ft. Lauderdale. Office: Schwartz Gold Cohen Zakarin & Kotler 54 SW Boca Raton Blvd Boca Raton FL 33432

SHARP, ANNE CATHERINE, artist, educator; b. Red Bank, N.J., Nov. 1, 1943; d. Elmer Eugene and Ethel Violet (Hunter) S. BFA, Pratt Inst., 1965; MFA (teaching fellow 1972), Bklyn. Coll., 1973. tchr. art Sch. Visual Arts, 1978-89, NYU, 1978, SUNY, Purchase, 1983, Pratt Manhattan Ctr., N.Y.C., 1982-84, Parsons Sch. Design, N.Y.C., 1984-90, Visual Arts Ctr. of Alaska, Anchorage, 1991, Anchorage Mus. Hist. and Art, 1991, 93, 94, 95, U. Alaska, Anchorage, 1994—; lectr. AAAS, The 46th Arctic Divsn. Sci. Conf., U. Alaska, Fairbanks, 1995. One-person shows Pace Editions, N.Y.C., Ten/Downtown, N.Y.C., Katonah (N.Y.) Gallery, 1974, Contemporary Gallery, Dallas, 1975, Art in a Public Space, N.Y.C., 1979, Eatontown Hist. Mus., N.J., 1980, N.Y. Pub. Library Epiphany Br., 1988, Books and Co., N.Y., 1989, The Kendall Gallery, N.Y.C., 1990, Alaska Pacific U., Carr-Gottstein Gallery, Anchorage, 1993, Internat. Gallery Contemporary Art, Anchorage, 1993, Art Think Tank Gallery, N.Y.C., 1994, U.S. Geol. Survey, Reston, Va., 1994, Stonington Gallery, Anchorage, 1994; group shows include Arnot Art Mus., Elmira, N.Y., 1975, Bronx Mus., 1975, Mus. Modern Art, N.Y.C., 1975-76, Nat. Arts Club, N.Y.C., 1979, Calif. Mus. Photography, Riverside, 1983-92, Jack Tilton Gallery, N.Y.C., 1983, Lincoln Ctr., N.Y.C., 1983, Cabo Frio Print Biennale, Brazil, 1983, Pratt Graphic Ctr., N.Y.C., 1984, State Mus. N.Y., Albany, 1984, Kenkeleba Gallery, N.Y.C., 1985, Hempstead Harbor Art Assn., Glen Cove, N.Y., 1985, Mus. Mod. Art, Weddel, Fed. Republic of Germany, 1985, Kenkeleba Gallery, N.Y.C., 1985, Paper Art Exhbn. Internat. Mus. Contemporary Art, Bahia, Brazil, 1986, Mus. Salon-de-Provence, France, 1987, Mus. Contemporary Art, Sao Paulo, Brazil, 1985-86, Salon de Provence, France, 1987, Adirondack Lakes Ctr. for Arts, Blue Mountain Lake, N.Y., 1987, Kendall Gallery, N.Y.C., 1988, Exhibition Ctr. Parsons Sch. Design, N.Y.C., 1989, F.M.K. Gallery, Budapest, Hungary, 1989, Galerie des Kulturbundes Schwarzenberg, German Dem. Republic, Q Sen Do Gallery, Kobe, Japan, 1989, Anchorage Mus. History and Art, 1990-91, 94, U. Alaska, Anchorage, 1990, 91, Coos Art Mus., Coos Bay, Oreg., 1990, Spaceship Earth, Mus. Internat. de Neu Art, Vancouver, Can., 1990, Councourse Gallery, Emily Carr Coll. Art and Design, 1990, Nat. Mus. Women in the Arts, Washington, 1991, Visual Arts Ctr. Alaska, 1991, 92, Nomad Mus., Lisbon, Portugal, 1991, Mus. Ostdeutsche Gallery, Regensberg, Germany, 1991, Mcpl. Mus. Cesley Krumlov (So. Bohemia) CSFK, Czechoslovakia, 1991, Böltmiche Dörter Exhbn. Hochstrass 8, Munich, 1992, BBC-TV, Great Britain, U.K., Sta. WXXI-TV, Rochester, N.Y., 1992-93, Site 250 Gallery Contemporary Art., Fairbanks, 1993, Santa Barbara (Calif.) Mus. Art, 1993, The Rochester (N.Y.) Mus. and Sci. Ctr., 1990-94, Space Arc: The Archives of Mankind, Time Capsule in Earth Orbit, Hughes Comm., Divec TV Satellite Launch, 1994, Stonington Gallery, Anchorage, 1994, 95, UAA Art Galley U. Alaska, 1995, Arctic Trading Post, Nome, Alaska, 1995, Lawrenceville (N.J.) Sch., 1996; represented in permanent collections Smithsonian Instn., Nat. Air and Space Mus., Washington, Albright Knox Gallery, Buffalo, St. Vincent's Hosp, N.Y.C., N.Y. Pub. Libr., N.Y.C., U.S. Geol. Survey, Reston, Va., White House (Reagan, Bush adminstrns.), Site 250 Gallery Contemporary Art, Anchorage Mus. History and Art, others; Moon Shot series to commemorate moon landing, 1970-76, Cloud Structures of the Universe Painting series, 1980-86, Am. Landscape series, 1987-89, Thoughtlines, fall 1986, Swimming in the Mainstream with Her, U. Va., Charlottesville; author: Artist's Book - Travel Dreams U.S.A., 1989, Artworld-Welt Der Kunst, Synchronicity, 1989—, Art Think Tank: Projects in Art and Ecology, 1990—, The Alaska Series, 1990—, Potraits in the Wilderness, 1990—; columnist: Anchorage Press, 1995—. Sponsor IDITOROD Trail Com., Libby Riddles. Artist-in-residence grantee Va. Center for Creative Arts, 1974, Artpark, Lewiston, N.Y., 1980, Vt. Studio Colony, 1989; recipient Pippin award Our Town, N.Y.C., 1984, certificate of Appreciation Art in Embassy program U.S. Dept. State, 1996. Mem. Nat. Space Soc., Nat. Mus. Women in Arts, Alaska Photography Ctr., Pratt Inst. Alumni Assn., The Planetary Soc., Internat. Assn. Near-Death Studies, Art and Sci. Collaborations, The Internat. Gallery of Contemporary Art. Address: PO Box 100480 Anchorage AK 99510-0480 Gallery: 621 W 6th Ave Anchorage AK 99501 also: 250 Custaman St Ste 2A Fairbanks AK 99701

SHARP, JANE ASNTON, art historian, educator; b. Seattle, Aug. 4, 1956; d. Benjamin Thomas and Jane (Shriver) S.; m. James Page Hersey, Aug. 16, 1986; 1 child, Samuel Ashton. BA, UCLA, 1979; MA, Yale U., 1983, PhD, 1992. Assoc. curator Solomon R. Guggenheim Mus., N.Y.C., 1989-92; vis. asst. prof. Vassar Coll., Poughkeepsie, N.Y., 1992-93; asst. prof. U. Md., College Park, 1993—; Mem. adv. bd. Md. Art Pl., 1996. Contbr. articles to profl. jours. Fellow Internat. Rsch. Exch., 1985-87, Fulbright-Hayes Found., 1985-87, Social Sci. Rsch. Coun., 1993-96. Mem. Am. Assn. Advancement Slavic Studies, Coll. Art Assn. Democrat. Office: U Md Dept Art History/Archeology College Park MD 20742-1335

SHARP, SHARON LEE, gerontology nurse; b. Beatrice, Nebr., Jan. 14, 1939; d. Clarence Alfred and Edna Clara (Grosshuesch) Wolters; m. Philip Butler, June 27, 1959 (div. 1964); m. Ted C. Sharp, Sept. 21, 1966 (div. 1988); children: Sheryl Butler, Philip Butler. Diploma, Lincoln Gen. Hosp., 1959. RN Nebr. Charge nurse Mary Lanning Meml. Hosp., Hastings, Nebr., 1960-61; asst. head nurse Ingleside State Hosp., Hastings, Nebr., 1961-62; charge nurse Rio Hondo Meml. Hosp., Downey, Calif., 1969-71, Santa Barbara (Calif.) Cottage Hosp., 1974-78; supr. Marlora Manor Convalescent Hosp., Long Beach, Calif., 1979-80; supr. Marlinda Nursing Home, Lynwood, Calif., 1982-84, dir. nursing, 1984-89; dir. nursing Ramona Care Ctr., El Monte, Calif., 1989-90, Oakview Convalescent Hosp., Tujunga, Calif., 1990-91, North Valley Nursing Ctr., Tujunga, Calif., 1992—; asst. dir. nursing Skyline Health Care Ctr. (Gran Care), L.A., 1993-94; resident assessment coord. Country Villa Rehab. Ctr., L.A., 1994-95; case mgr. Vitas Innovative Hospice Care, West Covina, Calif., 1996—; mem. adv. bd. Regional Occupational Program, Downey, 1985-86. Home: 2875 E Del Mar Blvd Pasadena CA 91107-4314

SHARP, SUSAN S., artist, art educator; b. N.J., Jan. 4, 1942; d. William Herman and Myrtle Hadassah (Walter) Silverstein; m. Ronald Case Sharp, June 17, 1962; children: Nancy, Greg. Student, Syracuse U., 1961-62; BS cum laude, U. Hartford, 1964. Tchr. Wethersfield Pub. Schs., Conn., 1963-64, Westport Pub. Schs., Conn., 1964-66, Spl. Edn. Program, Fairfield, Conn., 1975-77; tchr. painting Silvermine Sch. Arts, New Canaan, Conn., 1994—. One-woman shows include Stamford Mus., 1983, Palace Theater Art Gallery, Stamford, Conn., Kohn Pederson Fox Gallery, N.Y.C., 1995, Soho 20, N.Y.C., Silvermine Guild, also others; exhibited in group shows at Artspace, New Haven, Conn., 1994, Kouros Gallery, N.Y.C., 1995, Reece Gallery, N.Y.C., 1995, Butters Gallery, Portland, Oreg., also others; represented in numerous pub. and pvt. collections including General Electric, Chase Manhattan, Kidder/Peabody. Trustee Silvermine Artists Guild, New Canaan, Conn., 1993-96, bd. govs. 1992—; co-founder Inst. for Visual Arts-Programming, New Canaan, pres. 1989-91. Recipient Conn. Painters award Stamford Mus., 1982.

SHARPE, KATHRYN MOYE, psychologist; b. Barnesville, Ga., Nov. 27, 1922; d. Herbert Johnston and Henri Lucile (Winter) Moye; m. William Herschel Sharpe, Mar. 2, 1946; children: William Herschel Jr., Mark Stephens. AB, Piedmont Coll., Demorest, Ga., 1942; MA, U. N.C., 1947; PhD, U. S.C., 1975. Tchr., guidance counselor Charleston (S.C.) Pub. Schs., 1947-66; prof. sociology, chmn. dept. Bapt. Coll. at Charleston, 1966-88, prof. emeritus, 1988—; pvt. practice psychology, Charleston, 1975—. Kathryn Moye Sharpe scholarship given in her honor Bapt. Coll. at Charleston, 1988. Fellow Am. Assn. for Marriage and Family Therapy (approved supr., pres. S.C. div. 1975-77). Congregationalist. Home and Office: 6 Cavalier Ave Charleston SC 29407-7702

SHARPE, ROCHELLE PHYLLIS, journalist; b. Gary, Ind., Apr. 27, 1956; d. Norman Nathaniel and Shirley (Kaplan) S. BA, Yale U., 1978. Reporter Concord (N.H.) Monitor, 1979-81; statehouse rep. Wilmington News Jour., Dover, Del., 1981-85; statehouse corr. Gannett News Svc., Albany, N.Y., 1985; nat. reporter Gannett News Svc., Washington, 1986-93; staff reporter social issues The Wall St. Jour., Washington, 1993—. Contbr. articles to profl. jours. Recipient Pulitzer prize for series in child abuse, Columbia U., 1991. Home: 2500 Q St NW Apt 315 Washington DC 20007-4360 Office: Wall St Jour Washington Bur 1025 Connecticut Ave NW Ste 800 Washington DC 20036-5405

SHARROW, MARILYN JANE, library administrator; bd. Oakland, Calif.; d. Charles L. and H. Evelyn S.; m. Lawrence J. Davis. BS in Design, U. Mich., 1967, MALS, 1969. Librarian Detroit Pub. Libr., 1968-70; head fine arts dept. Syracuse (N.Y.) U. Librs., 1970-73; dir. libr. Roseville (Mich.) Pub. Libr., 1973-75; asst. dir. librs. U. Wash., 1975-77, assoc. dir. librs., 1978-79; dir. libraries U. Man., Winnipeg, Can., 1979-82; chief libr. U. Toronto, Can., 1982-85; univ. libr. U. Calif., Davis, 1985—. Recipient Woman of Yr. in Mgmt. award Winnipeg YWCA, 1982; named Woman of Distinction, U. Calif. Faculty Women's Rsch. Group, 1985. Mem. ALA, Assn. Rsch. Librs. (bd. dirs., v.p., pres-elect 1989-90, pres. 1990-91, chair sci. tech. work group 1994—, rsch. collections com. 1993-95), Online Computer Libr. Ctr.-Rsch. Librs. Adv. Com. (vice chmn. 1992-93, chair 1993-94), Calif. State Network Resources Lib. Com. Office: U Calif Shields Lib Davis CA 95616

SHATLES, DIANE ARLENE, school system administrator, educator; b. N.Y.C., Jan. 28, 1945; d. Samuel S. and Minerva (Berkowitz) Krulik; m. Arthur Mark Shatles, Nov. 20, 1966; 1 child, Rebeca. BA, Bklyn. Coll., 1966, MA, 1972; cert. advanced study, N.Y. U., 1982. Cert. reading tchr., asst. prin., English tchr., ednl. adminstrn., curriculum devel. and staff. devel. Elem. educator Pub. Sch. Dist. 184, Bklyn., 1966-72; reading tchr. ECIA Non.-Pub. Sch. Program, Bklyn., 1973-83, Pub. Sch. Dist. 230, Bklyn., 1983-92; sch. based mgmt. facilitator N.Y.C. Bd. Edn., 1992-94; supr. rsch. and evaluation N.Y.C. Cmty. Sch. Dist. 18, 1995—; adj. lectr. Bklyn. Coll., 1972-78, Bklyn. Coll. Grad. Divs., 1991—. Curriculum author Learning Magazien, 1989, Profl. Best award. Mem. Women's League for Peace and Freedom, Rockaway, N.Y., 1966—. Impact II grantee, N.Y.C., 1988, 90. Mem. ASCD, Internat. Reading Assn., Nat. Coun. Tchrs. of English, Educators Social Responsibility, Bklyn. Reading Coun., Phi Delta Kappa. Home: 338 Beach 145th St Neponsit NY 11694-1148

SHATTER, SUSAN, artist, art educator; b. N.Y.C., Jan. 17, 1943; d. Aubrey and Florence (Breines) S.; married (div. June 1975); children: Paul Brown, Scott Brown. Student, Skowhegan Sch. Sculpture, Maine, 1964; BFA, Pratt Inst., 1965; MFA, Boston U., 1972. Artist in residence Skowhegan (Maine) Sch Painting and Sculpture, 1977, 79; art instr. Sch. Visual Arts, N.Y.C., 1980-84, Tyler Sch. of Art, Phila., 1985, San Francisco Art Inst., 1989, Vt. Studio Ctr., Johnson, 1989, Bklyn. Coll., 1991-95; vis. critic, U. Pa., 1974-85, acting co-chair, 1983-84; bd. govs. Skowhegan Sch. Painting and Sculpture, 1979—, chair, 1988-91. One-woman exhbns. include Fischbach Gallery, N.Y.C., 1973-95, Harcus Gallery, Boston, 1975-87, Mattingly Baker Gallery, Dallas, 1981, John Berggruen Gallery, San Francisco, 1986, Heath Gallery, Atlanta, 1987; works reproduced in America '76: A Bicentennial Exhibition, 1976, Boston Watercolor Today, 1976, Realist Drawings and Watercolors: Contemporary Works on Paper, 1980, Contemporary Realism Since 1960, 1981, Perspectives on Contemporary American Realism: Works of Art on Paper from the Collection of Jalane and Richard Davidson, 1983, New Vistas: Contemporary American Landscapes, 1984, American Realism: Twentieth Century Drawings and Watercolors from the Glenn C. Janss Collection, 1984, A Graphic Muse: Prints by American Women, 1987, Spirit of Place: Contemporary Landscape Painting & the American Tradition, 1989, Twentieth Century Watercolors, 1990, American Realism and Figurative Art: 1952-1991, 1991; represented in permanent collections Art Inst. Chgo., Mus. Fine Arts, Boston, MIT, Cambridge, Currier Gallery of Art, Manchester, N.H., Hood Art Mus., Dartmouth Coll., Hanover, N.H., Phila. Mus. Art, Utah Mus. Fine Art, Salt Lake City, Farnesworth Mus., Maine. Recipient grants Mass. Creative Artists Humanities, Radcliff Inst., Ingram-Merrill Found., NEA, N.Y. State Found. for the Arts, Yadoo Corp. Mem.-elect Nat. Acad. Design. Home and Studio: 26 W 20th St New York NY 10011

SHATTO, GLORIA MCDERMITH, academic administrator; b. Houston, Oct. 11, 1931; d. Ken E. and Gertrude (Osborne) McDermith; m. Robert J. Shatto, Mar. 19, 1953; children: David Paul, Donald Patrick. BA with honors in Econs., Rice U., 1954, PhD (fellow), 1966. Mkt. rsch. Humble Oil & Refining Co., Houston, 1954-55; tchr. pub. sch. C.Z., 1955-56; tchr. Houston Ind. Sch. Dist., 1956-60; asst. prof. econs. U. Houston, 1965-69, assoc. prof., 1969-72; prof. econs., assoc. dean Coll. Indsl. Mgmt., Ga. Inst. Tech., Atlanta, 1973-77; George R. Brown prof. bus. Trinity U., San Antonio, 1977-79; pres. Berry Coll., Mt. Berry, Ga., 1980—; sml. bus. adv. com. U.S. Treasury, 1977-81; trustee Joint Coun. Econ. Edn., 1985-88; dir. Ga. Power Co., So. Co., Becton Dickinson and Co., Tex. Instruments, Inc. Contbr. articles to profl. jours.; Editor: Employment of the Middle-Aged, 1972; mem. editorial bd.: Ednl. Record, 1980-82. Mem. Tex. Gov.'s Commn. on Status of Women, 1970-72, Gov.'s Commn. on Economy and Efficiency in State Govt., 1991; trustee Ga. Tech. Rsch. Inst., 1975-77, Berry Coll., Ga., 1975-79, Ga. Forestry Commn., 1987-95; mem. Ga. Gov.'s Commn. on Status of Women, 1975; mem. commn. on women in higher edn. Am. Coun. on Edn., 1980-82, chmn., 1982; mem. Ga. Study Com. on Pub. Higher Edn. Fin., 1981-82; v.p. Ga. Found. Ind. Colls., 1981, pres. 1982, 94; mem. adv. bd. to Sch. Bus. Adminstrn., Temple U., Phila., 1981-83; mem. Study Com. on Ednl. Processes, Soc. Assn. Colls. and Schs., 1981-82, Ga. United Meth. Commn. on Higher Edn. and Campus Ministry, 1981-82; trustee Redmond Park Hosp., Rome, Ga., 1981-87, 1st United Meth. Ch., 1986-89. Recipient Disting. Alumni award Rice U., 1987; OAS fellow, summer 1968. Mem. Royal Econ. Assn., Am. Econ. Assn., So. Econ. Assn., Southwestern Econ. Assn. (pres. 1976-77), Am. Fin. Assn. (nominating com. 1976), Southwestern Social Scis. Assn., Fin. Execs. Inst. (chmn. Atlanta edn. com. 1976-77, mem. com. on profl. devel. 1981), AAUW (area rep. 1967-68, Tex. chmn. legis. program 1970-71, mem. internat. fellowships-awards com. 1970-76, chmn. 1974-76), Ga. Newcomen Soc. (chmn. 1991—), Newcomen Soc. U.S. (trustee), Phi Beta Kappa, Phi Kappa Phi, Omicron Delta Epsilon. Office: Berry Coll Office of the President 39 Mount Berry Sta Mount Berry GA 30149-0159

SHATTUCK, CATHIE ANN, lawyer, former government official; b. Salt Lake City, July 18, 1945; d. Robert Ashley S. and Lillian Culp (Shattuck). B.A., U. Nebr., 1967, J.D., 1970. Bar: Nebr. 1970, U.S. Dist. Ct. Nebr. 1970, Colo. 1971, U.S. Dist. Ct. Colo. 1971, U.S. Supreme Ct. 1974, U.S. Ct. Appeals (10th cir.) 1977, U.S. Dist. Ct. D.C. 1984, U.S. Ct. Appeals (D.C. cir.) 1984. V.p., gen. mgr. Shattuck Farms, Hastings, Nebr., 1967-70; asst. project dir. atty. Colo. Civil Rights Commn., Denver, 1970-72; trial atty. Equal Employment Opportunity Commn., Denver, 1973-77; vice chmn. Equal Employment Opportunity Commn., Washington, 1982-84; pvt. practice law Denver, 1977-81; mem. Fgn. Svc. Bd., Washington, 1982-84, Presdl. Personnel Task Force, Washington, 1982-84; ptnr. Epstein, Becker & Green, L.A. and Washington, 1984—; lectr. Colo. Continuing Legal Edn. Author: Employer's Guide to Controlling Sexual Harrassment, 1992; mem. editorial bd. The Practical Litigator, 1988—. Bd. dirs. KGNU Pub. Radio, Boulder, Colo., 1979, Denver Exchange, 1980-81, YWCA Met. Denver, 1979-81. Recipient Nebr. Young Career Woman Bus. and Profl. Women, 1967; recipient Outstanding Nebraskan Daily Nebraskan, Lincoln, 1967. Mem. ABA (mgmt. chair labor and employment law sect. com. on immigration law 1988-90, mgmt. chair com. on legis. devels. 1990-93), Nebr. Bar Assn., Colo. Bar Assn., Colo. Women's Bar Assn., D.C. Bar Assn., Nat. Women's Coalition, Delta Sigma Rho, Tau Kappa Alpha, Pi Sigma Alpha, Alpha Xi Delta, Denver Club.

SHATZ, JAYNE EILEEN, artist, educator; b. Bklyn., Mar. 24, 1950; d. George Benton and Ann Ruth (Winick) Shatz; m. Mark Brayden Goor, May 16, 1971 (div. May 1976); m. Ronald Michael Allen, June 26, 1994. BA, SUNY, Albany, 1972; MA, Goddard Coll., Plainfield, Vt., 1979; PhD, Union Inst., Cin., 1992. Cert. tchr. in art, N.Y. Tchr. art Niskayuna (N.Y.) Ctrl. Sch., 1971-72; artist potter Kilnhaus Potters, Slingerlands, N.Y., 1972-76; dir. ceramics Coll. Continuing Studies SUNY, Albany, 1979-82; tchr. art Richmondville (N.Y.) Ctrl. Sch., 1984-87; dir. ceramics Hudson Valley C.C./Rensselaer County Coun. for the Arts, Troy, N.Y., 1982-94; tchr. art Shenandehowa Ctrl. Sch., Clifton Park, N.Y., 1987—; artist potter Jayne Shatz Pottery, Schenectady, N.Y., 1976—; founder, gallery dir. Albany Ceramic Inst., 1982; founder, bd. v.p. Hudson River Clay Factory Coop, Troy, 1990-94; tutor/evaluator Empire State Coll., Albany, 1985-86; artist-in-residence N.Y. Found. for the Arts, 1985-87. Contbr. articles to profl. jours.; ceramic exhbns. include Arts Ctr., Old Forge, N.Y., 1980, Lynn Kottler's Gallery, N.Y.C., 1980, Peter's Valley Craft Gallery, N.J., 1983, Farmington Valley Arts Ctr., Conn., 1984, Albany Inst. History and Art, 1985, Brookfield (Conn.) Craft Ctr., 1985, Home Gallery, 1976-95, Ctr. Galleries, Albany, 1995, SUNY-Albany, 1996. Vol. artist N.E. Assn. for Blind, Albany, 1983, VA Hosp. Day Ctr., Albany, 1979; fundraising vol. art auction WHMT-Pub. TV, Capital Dist., N.Y., 1985; tchr. U.S. Holocaust Mus., 1994. Recipient Nat. Award Excellence in Ceramic Edn. Studio Potter Found., N.H., 1989; grantee N.Y. State Coun. on the Arts, 1984, N.Y. State Dept. Edn., 1995. Mem. N.Y. State Union for Tchrs., SUNY-Albany Alumni Assn. Democrat. Jewish. Home: 724 Bedford Rd Schenectady NY 12308

SHAUGHNESSY, ELIZABETH ANN, surgeon, researcher; b. Evanston, Ill., Jan. 4, 1959; d. Terrence Joseph and Mary Ann (Nugent) S.; m. James Dennis Stapleton, Oct. 3, 1987. BS in Biology, U. Ill., 1981; MD in Medicine, U. Ill., Chgo., 1985, PhD in Cell Biology, 1990. Cert. Am. Bd. Surgery. Resident in gen. surgery U. Ill. and affiliated hosps. dept. surgery, Chgo., 1985-87, 90-93; fellow in surg. oncology City of Hope Nat. Med. Ctr., Duarte, Calif., 1993—. Contbr. articles to profl. jours. Mem. bd. dirs. L.A. County chpt. Susan G. Komen Breast Cancer Found., L.A., 1996—, mem. exec. com. Race for the Cure, 1995, chair spkrs. bur., 1995. Fellow ACS (assoc.), Am. Soc. Clin. Oncology (Young Investigator award 1995), Soc. for Surg. Oncology (candidate mem.), Am. Med. Women's Assn., Am. Assn. for Cancer Rsch., Physicians for Social Responsibility, Sierra Club, Glendale chpt. Zeta Tau Alpha (fedn. rep. 1993—). Roman Catholic. Office: City of Hope Nat Med Ctr 1500 E Duarte Rd Duarte CA 91010-3000

SHAUGHNESSY, MARIE KANEKO, artist, business executive; b. Detroit, Sept. 14, 1924; d. Eishiro and Kiyo (Yoshida) Kaneko; m. John Thomas Shaughnessy, Sept. 23, 1959. Assocs. in Liberal Arts, Keisen Women's Coll., Tokyo, 1944. Ops. mgr. Webco Alaska, Inc., Anchorage, 1970-88; ptnr. Webco Partnership, Anchorage, 1983—, also bd. dirs. Paintings include Lilacs, 1984, Blooms, 1985, The Fence, 1986 (Purchase award 1986). Bd. dirs. Alaska Artists Guild, 1971-87; commr. Mcpl. Anchorage Fine Arts Commn., 1983-87; organizing com. Japanese Soc. Alaska, 1987. Recipient arts affiliates award Anchorage C. of C., 1975, 78, 84, Univ. Artists award Alaska Pacific U., 1986, Am. Juror's Choice award Sumi-E Soc. Am., 1994, Ikebana Internat. award, 1994, Dorothy Klein Meml. award, 1995. Mem. Potomac Valley Watercolorists (bd. dirs., awards 1989, 91, Spl. award 1995), Va. Watercolor Soc. (pres.), Sumi-E Soc. Am. (past pres., bd. dirs., Nat. Capital Area chpt. award 1990, 91, 92, 94, Purchase award 1993), Vienna Art Soc. (bd. dirs. 1995-96), Alaska Watercolor Soc. (charter and life, Grumbacher Silver medal 1989), McLean Arts Club (1st pl. award 1991), Nat. League Am. Penwomen (Grumbacher gold medal award excellence 1993), Potomac Valley Watercolorists (bd. dirs. 1995-95). Republican. Episcopalian.

SHAVER, CONSTANCE ANNE, social worker; b. Lawrence, Kans., Nov. 2, 1946; d. Odell and Wave Lucille (Boyer) S.; m. Merwin S. Hall II, Oct. 3, 1982; 1 child, Meredith Hall. BA, U. Kans., 1968, MA in Tchg., 1970; MSW, U. Wis., Milw., 1974. Cert. alcohol and drug counselor, Wis. Pub. assistance worker Jackson County Welfare Dept., Kansas City, Mo., 1970-72; therapist/intern Racine (Wis.) Family Svcs., 1972-73, Milw. Psychiat. Hosp., 1973-74; social worker Luth. Social Svcs., Milw., 1974-76; asst. dir. Horizons, Inc., Milw., 1977-80, program co-dir., 1981-87, exec. dir., 1987—; pvt. practice therapist New Prospects Counsling and Consultation, Milw., 1981-85. Bd. dirs. Cambridge House, Milw., 1981-82. Mem. Internat. Cmty. Corrections Assn. (Wis. pres. 1996), Wis. Coun. on Cmty. Corrections (pres. 1993-96). Home: 2648 N Farwell Milwaukee WI 53211 Office: Horizons Inc 2511 W Vine St Milwaukee WI 53205

SHAW, ANN, social worker, educator; b. Columbus, Ohio, Nov. 21, 1921; d. Pearl Daniel and Sarah Frank (Roberts) White; m. Leslie Nelson Shaw (dec.); children: Valerie Lynne, Leslie Jr., Rebecca. AB, U. Redlands, 1943; MA, Ohio State U., 1944; MSW, U. So. Calif., L.A., 1968; DHL (hon.), U. Redlands, 1971. Cert. tchr. with specialization in secondary edn. and jr. coll., Calif. Instr. Va. Union U., Richmond, 1944-46; asst. prof. Cen. State Coll., Wilberforce, Ohio, 1946-48; adminstrv. asst. Job Corps Ctr. for Women, L.A., 1963-65; instr. UCLA ext., 1968-70; guest faculty U. So. Calif., UCLA, 1970-75; with L.A. Neighborhood Initiative. Chmn. bd. founders Savs. & Loan Assn., L.A., 1986-87; bd. dirs. Lloyds Bank Calif., L.A., 1978-86; mem. Calif. Commn. Jud. Performance, 1976-80, Calif. Comty. Found., L.A., 1986-95, Citizens Rev. Panel Selection of Chiefs of Police, 1992, Cathedral Ctr. Corp. of Episcopal Diocese of L.A., 1986—, L.A. Neighborhood Initiative Bd., 1994—, Calif. Legis. Joint State Task Force on Family, 1988-91; pres., mem. nat. bd. YWCA L.A., 1963; corp. bd. dirs., met. bd. United Way, 1983-92; v.p., bd. dirs. L.A. Urban League, 1980-86; bd. counselors U. So. Calif. Sch. Social Work, 1987—; mem. Black Women of Achievement, NAACP Legal Def. and Ednl. Fund, 1986-90; mem. Mayor's Task Force on Econ. Devel. for South Cen. L.A., 1989-92. Recipient Vol. of Yr. award NASW, 1975, Woman of Yr. award Greater L.A. chpt. Calif. State Legis., 1987, Mayor's Cert. of Appreciation, 1987. Episcopalian.

SHAW, CAROLE, editor, publisher; b. Bklyn., Jan. 22, 1936; d. Sam and Betty (Neckin) Bergenthal; m. Ray Shaw, Dec. 27, 1957; children: Lori Eve Cohen, Victoria Shaw Locknar. BA, Hunter Coll., 1962. Singer Capitol Records, Hilton Records, Rama Records, Verve Records, 1952-65; TV appearances Ed Sullivan, Steve Allen, Jack Paar, George Gobel Show, 1957; owner The People's Choice, L.A., 1975-79; founder, editor-in-chief Big Beautiful Woman mag., Beverly Hills, Calif., 1979—; creator Carole Shaw and BBW label clothing line for large-size women. Author: Come Out, Come Out Wherever You Are, 1982. Office: BBW Mag PO Box K-298 Tarzana CA 91356

SHAW, DORIS BEAUMAR, film and video producer, executive recruiter; b. Pitts., July 13, 1934; d. Emerson C. and Doris Llorene (Rees) Beaumar; m. Robert Newton Shaw, July 6, 1957. BA summa cum laude, Lindenwood Coll., St. Charles, Mo., 1955. Writer, asst. to pres. Baker Prodns., Benton Harbor, Mich., 1955; asst. prodn. mgr. Condor Films, Inc., St. Louis, 1955-57; chief editor, asst. to v.p. Frederick F. Watson Inc., N.Y.C., 1957-58; v.p. Gen. Pictures Corp., Cleve., 1958-71; dir., editor, unit mgr. Cinecraft Inc., Cleve., 1971-72; mgr. audio-visual dept. Am. Greetings Corp., Cleve., 1972-73; proprietor Script to Screen Svcs., Chagrin Falls, Ohio, 1973-76; pres. D & B Shaw, Inc., Chardon, Ohio, 1976-87, Hudson, Ohio, 1987—; pres. Execusearch, Inc., Hudson, 1987—, Infosearch Inc., Hudson, 1994—, Cybersearch, Inc., Hudson, 1995—; film festival judge, tchr. Martha Holden Jennings Found./Hawken Sch., Gates Mills, Ohio, 1970-85; advisor teenage film contests, seminars Cleve. Bd. Edn., 1970-88; contest judge/film and video WVIZ-TV, Channel 25, Parma, Ohio, 1971—; guest lectr. Lindenwood Coll., 1973-80; adj. prof. U. Akron, 1990—; cons. to bus. and industry regarding sales, mktg., bus. mgmt., info. and rsch. svcs. Writer, dir., editor, prodr. of film, video, multi-image, multi-media, audio/visual prodn., radio, TV commls. and programs; contbr. articles to profl. jours. Bd. trustees Ohio Boys Town, Cleve., 1957-68; mem. alumnae coun. Lindenwood Coll., 1973-77; publicity chmn. Geauga County Preservation Soc., 1984-91; active various charitable orgns. Named Outstanding Young Woman of Am., Fedn. of Women's Clubs, 1965, Alumna of Yr. Merit award Lindenwood Coll., 1971; recipient numerous awards and grants for film, video projects including Gold Camera Best Documentary award, 1979. Mem. Soc. Motion Picture and TV Engrs., Info. Film Prodrs. Am., Assn. for Multi Image (charter), Detroit Prodrs. Assn., Internat. TV and Video Assn. (charter), Internat. Comm. Industries Assn., Alpha Epsilon Rho. Republican. Office: D & B Shaw Inc 118 W Streetsboro Rd Hudson OH 44236-2029

SHAW, GINA LOUISE, wallpaper designer; b. Ephrata, Pa., Sept. 26, 1960; d. Brenda L. (Enck) Roach; m. Jonathan Wayne Shaw, Sept. 28, 1985; children: Cameron, Stephanie Louise. BFA, Moore Coll. of Art, 1982. V.p. design Eisenhart Wallcoverings Co., Hanover, Pa., 1982—. Named 1 of 12 Achievers of Yr., Wallcoverings Windows & Interior Fashion mag., 1994. Mem. Color Mktg. Group. Home: 2 Timber Ln Hanover PA 17331-9381 Office: Eisenhart Wallcoverings Co PO Box 464 Hanover PA 17331-0464

SHAW, GLORIA DORIS, art educator; b. Huntington, W.Va., Nov. 10, 1928; d. Charles Bert and Theodosia Doris (Shimer) Haley; m. Arthur Shaw, July 13, 1954 (dec. Aug. 1985); children: Deirdra E. Franz, Stewart N. Student, SUNY, 1969-70, Art Students League, N.Y.C., 1969-70, 74; BA, SUNY, N.Y.C., 1980; postgrad., U. Tenn., 1982, Nat Kaz, Pietrasanta, Italy, 1992. Sculptor replicator Am. Mus. Natural History, N.Y.C., 1976-77; adj. prof. sculpture Fla. Keys C.C., Key West, 1983—; prof. TV art history Fla. Keys C.C., 1989—; host moderator Channel 5 TV, Fla. Keys, 1982—; presenter Humanities Studies and Art History Channel 19 TV, 1995—. Sculptor (portrait) Jimmy Carter, Carter Meml. Libr., 1976, Tennessee Williams, Tennessee Williams Fine Arts Ctr., 1982, UNICEF, 1978-79, (series) Fla. Panther and Audubon Wall Relief, 1985, (bust) AIDS Meml., 1990; one woman shows include Bank Street Coll., 1979, Hollywood Mus. of Art, 1985, Islander Gallery, 1983, Martello Mus., 1984, Greenpeace, 1987; exhibited in group shows at Montoya, West Palm Beach, Fla., 1989, N.Y.C. Bd. of Edn. Tour of Schs., 1979, Earthworks East, N.Y., 1987, Man and Sci., 1978, Cuban Club, Key West, Fla., 1991, Leda Bruce Gallery, Big Pine, 1992, Kaz, Pietrasanta, Italy, 1992, Fla. Keys C.C. Gallery, 1993, Tennessee Williams Fine Arts Ctr., Key West, 1993, Internat. Woman's Show, Fla. Keys, 1994, Joy Gallery, 1994, 95, 96, Baron Gallery, Girls of Mauritania to UNICEF; designer Windows at Greenpeace Bldg., Key West, 1985-88. Recipient Children and Other Endangered Species award Thomas Cultural Ctr., 1980, Purchase award Cuban C. of C., 1982, Sierra Club, 1983, Blue Ribbon, Martello Towers Art and Hist. Soc., 1985, Red Ribbon, South Fla. Sculptors, 1986, Endangered Species award Greenpeace, 1986. Mem. Nat. Sculpture Soc. of N.Y.C., Internat. Sculpture Ctr., Art Students League of N.Y.C. (life), Art and Hist. Soc. Democrat.

SHAW, GRACE GOODFRIEND (MRS. HERBERT FRANKLIN SHAW), publisher, editor; b. N.Y.C.; d. Henry Bernheim and Jane Elizabeth (Stone) Goodfriend; m. Herbert Franklin Shaw (dec. 1992); 1 son, Brandon Hibbs. Student, Bennington Coll.; BA magna cum laude, Fordham U., 1976, MS, 1991. Reporter Port Chester (N.Y.) Daily Item; editorial coordinator World Scope Ency., N.Y.C.; assoc. editor Clarence L. Barnhart, Inc., Bronxville, N.Y.; freelance-writer for reference books; editing supr. World Pub. Co., mng. editor, sr. editor; mng. editor Peter H. Wyden Co., N.Y.C., 1969-70; assoc. editor Dial Press, N.Y.C., 1971-72; sr. editor Dial Press, 1972, David McKay Co., N.Y.C., 1972-75, Grosset & Dunlap, 1975-79; chief editor Today Press (Grosset), 1977-79; sr. editor, coll. dept. Bobbs-Merrill, N.Y.C., mng. editor, exec. editor trade div., 1979-80; pub. Bobbs-Merrill, 1980-84; mng. editor Rawson Assocs. div. Macmillan Pub., 1985-91; pres. Grace Shaw Assocs., Scarsdale, N.Y., 1991—. Home and Office: 85 Lee Rd Scarsdale NY 10583-5212

SHAW, HELEN LESTER ANDERSON, university dean; b. Lexington, Ky., Oct. 18, 1936; d. Walter Southall and Elizabeth (Guyn) Anderson; m. Charles Van Shaw, Mar. 14, 1988. BS, U. Ky., 1958; MS, U. Wis., 1965, PhD, 1969. Registered dietitian. Dietitian Roanoke (Va.) Meml. Hosp., 1959-60, Santa Barbara (Calif.) Cottage Hosp., 1960-61; dietitian, unit mgr. U. Calif., Santa Barbara, 1961-63; rsch. asst., NIH fellow U. Wis., Madison, 1963-68; from asst. prof. to prof. U. Mo., Columbia, 1969-88, assoc. dean, prof., 1977-84; prof., chair dept. food and nutrition U. N.C., Greensboro, 1989-94, dean Sch. Human Environ. Scis., 1994—; cluster leader Food for 21st Century rsch. program U. Mo., 1985-88. Contbr. articles to rsch. publs. Elder 1st Presbyn. Ch., Columbia, 1974-89, Greensboro, 1992—. Recipient Teaching award Home Econ. Alumni Assn., 1981, Gamma Sigma Delta, 1984; rsch. grantee Nutrition Found., 1971-73, NIH, 1972-75, NSF, 1980-83. Mem. Am. Inst. Nutrition, Am. Bd. Nutrition, Am. Soc. for Clin. Nutrition, Am. Dietetic Assn., Am. Family and Consumer Sci. Assn., Soc. for Nutrition Edn., Sigma Xi, Phi Upsilon Omicron, Kappa Omicron Nu. Democrat.

SHAW, HELEN LOUISE HAITH, educational administrator; b. Glen Raven, N.C., Oct. 6, 1931; d. Samuel and Robie (Summers) Haith; m. Benjamin Franklin Shaw, Apr. 9, 1954 (div. Dec. 1991); children: Ronald Elliott, Roland Eric. BS cum laude, N.C. Agrl. and Tech. State U., Greensboro, 1953; postgrad., D.C. Tchrs. Coll., 1962-64, Monterey Peninsula Coll., 1966, 86. 91, LaVerne Coll., 1975-77, Gavilan Coll., 1985-87. Cert. child devel. tchr., Calif. Elem. tchr. Lynchburg (Va.) City Schs., 1953-54, D.C. Pub. Schs., Washington, 1960-65; receptionist, dental asst. Dr. Benjamin Franklin Shaw, Seaside, Calif., 1970-85; from office pers. to adminstrv. asst. Infant Care Ctr., Inc., Seaside, 1984-92. Vol. Reach to Recovery; past stewardess, steward, sec. ch. conf., sec. ofcl. bd., sec. quar. conf., past pres. Women's Missionary Soc., now v.p.; ch. treas., mem. choir, sec.; mem. Lay Coun., adminstrv. asst. to pastor Hays Christian Meth. Episcopal Ch. Named Woman of Yr., Hays Christian Meth. Episcopal Ch., 1982, 91, 1st pl. award state rally, 1991, 92, 93, 96, 2d pl. award 1994, 95, stewardess award, 1992; honoree for outstanding cmty. svc. Sun St. Ctrs., Inc.-Sea Rina Cmty. Recovery Ctr., 1994. Mem. NAACP (Golden Heritage), AARP, Am. Legion Aux. (pres. 1993-95), Seaside Bus. and Profl. Women, Nat. Coun. Negro Women, Citizen's League for Progress (life), Order Ea. Star (past matron Golden State Grand chpt., Honoree for Contbns. to Cmty., 1994, past matron Carmelita chpt. 1994), Heroines of Jericho (most ancient matron and grand dep. Cypress Ct.), Alpha Kappa Alpha (past basileus and currently corr. sec. Kappa Gamma Omega chpt.), Sigma Rho Sigma. Democrat. Address: PO Box 331 Seaside CA 93955-0331

SHAW, JENNIFER DRU, elementary education educator; b. Davenport, Iowa, Sept. 26, 1967; d. Gary Allen and Rickie R. (Wildberger) Howard; m. Jeffrey Clifford Clark Shaw, June 4, 1994. BA in Elem. Edn., U. No. Iowa, 1990; MEd, Sam Houston State U., 1995. Cert. in elem. edn., reading edn., Tex. Tchr. 3d grade Glenloch Elem. Sch., Conroe Ind. Sch. Dist., The Woodlands, Tex., 1990—, tutorial dir., 1990-91, 93-94, 95-96, chair reading com., 1995—. Co-author lang. arts curriculum. Tchr. Edn. scholar U. No. Iowa, 1986-90. Mem. NEA, ASCD, Internat. Reading Assn., Tex. State Tchrs. Assn. Home: 2800 Hirschfield Rd Apt 86 Spring TX 77373-7475

Office: Glenloch Elem Sch 27505 Glen Loch Dr The Woodlands TX 77381-2913

SHAW, LAURIE JO, grant project director; b. Morris, Minn., Feb. 23, 1956; d. Edgar Allen and Dorothy Ruth (Harms) S.; m. Grant William Carlson, July 23, 1983 (div. Feb. 1986). Tchr. aide degree, Hutchinson Area Vocat. Tech., Minn., 1975; audio visual prodn., Hutchinson (Minn.) AVTI, 1976; BA in Psychology, S.W. State U., 1982; MA in Counseling, N.Mex. State U., 1987. Libr. tech. S.W. State U., Marshall, Minn., 1976-84; student svcs. coord. Mohave C.C., Bullhead City, Ariz., 1987-91; counselor, instr. Prestonsburg C.C., Pikeville, Ky., 1992-93; project dir. So. W.Va. C.C., Williamson, 1993—. Mem. AAUW (v.p. 1990-92), Nat. Assn. Student Pers. Adminstrs., Ky. Assn. Student Fin. Aid Adminstrs., Bus. and Profl. Women (pres. 1990-91, Young Career Woman award 1989), W.Va. Assn. Edn. Opportunity Program Pers., Mid.-East Assn. Edn. Opportunity Program Pers. Democrat. Methodist. Office: So WV Community Coll Armory Dr Williamson WV 25661

SHAW, LILLIE MARIE KING, vocalist; b. Indpls., Nov. 27, 1915; d. Earl William and Bertha Louise (Groth) King; m. Philip Harlow Shaw, June 26, 1940. Student, Jordan Conservatory Music, Indpls., 1940-43; BA, Ariz. State U., 1959; MA, Denver U., 1962; pvt. vocal study, 1944-70. Educator, libr. Glendale (Ariz.) Schs., 1959-67; lectr. libr. sci. Ariz. State U., Tempe, 1962-68. Concertizing, oratorio, symphonic soloist, light opera, 1965-82; soloist First Ch. of Christ Scientist, Sun City West, Ariz., 1980—. Monthly lectr. Christian Women's Fellowship, Phoenix, 1989-96; World Conf. del. Soc. of Friends, 1967. Mem. Nat. Soc. Arts and Letters (sec. 1990-94, nat. del. 1992), Am. Philatelic Assn. (life), Am. Topical Assn., Phoenix Philatelic Soc., Auditions Guild Ariz. (sec. 1989-92), Phoenix Opera League, Phoenix Symphony Guild, Sigma Alpha Iota Alumnae (Phoenix chpt., life, treas. 1988-96, Sword of Honor 1972, Rose of Honor 1982, Rose of Dedication 1995). Republican. Home: 6802 N 37th Ave Phoenix AZ 85019-1103

SHAW, LOIS BANFILL, economist; b. Billings, Mont., July 23, 1924; d. William Hail and Lessie Edna (Dutton) Banfill; m. Richard Franklin Shaw, June 17, 1944; children: Rachel A., Alan F., Sarah Shaw Tatuonova, Wayne B. AB, U. Calif., Berkeley, 1946; MA, U. Mich., 1965, PhD, 1973. Lectr., asst. prof. St. Mary's U., Halifax, N.S., Can., 1968-72; economst Ind. U. N.W., Gary, 1973-75; rsch. assoc. U. Ill., Chgo., 1975-77; sr. rsch. assoc. Ctr. Human Resource Rsch., Ohio State U., Columbus, 1977-85; sr. economist U.S. Gen. Acctg. Office, Washington, 1986-91; sr. rsch. assoc., cons. Inst. Women's Policy Rsch., Washington, 1992—. Author: British and American Women at Work, 1986; editor: Unplanned Careers, 1983, Midlife Women at Work, 1986; contbr. articles to profl. jours. Grantee Social Security Adminstrn., Washington, 1995. Mem. Internat. Assn. Feminist Econs., Am. Econ. Assn., Population Assn. Am., Midwest Econ. Assn. (2nd v.p. 1985-86). Office: Inst Womens Policy Rsch 1400 20th St NW Ste 104 Washington DC 20036

SHAW, MARILYN MARGARET, artist, photographer; b. San Diego, Dec. 19, 1933; d. George Louis and Helen Frances (Wright) Mitchell; m. Robert Dale Shaw, Feb. 19, 1952; children: Austin Allen, Kenneth Duane, Frank Lloyd. BA in Fine Arts and Photography, Juniata Coll., 1989. Photographer The Daily News, Huntingdon, Pa., 1988-92; owner, tchr. Marilyn Shaw Studios, Tyrone, Pa., 1989—; photographer The Jamesyouth, St. James. Luth. Ch., Huntingdon, 1987-92; photojournalist Easter Seals Telethon, 1991-92; art dir. Allegheny Riding Camp-The GrierSch., Tyrone, Pa., 1992. One-woman shows include Shoemaker Gallery, Huntingdon, 1989; group shows include Standing Stone Art League, Huntingdon, 1978-92, Washington St. Art Gallery, Huntingdon, 1991, 94; author, illustrator The Prize, 1989. Vol. The Huntingdon House, 1992—, Presbyn. Ch., Huntingdon, 1992-95, Tyrone Presbyn. Ch., 1995—. Recipient numerous ribbons Huntingdon County Fair, 1978, 90, 91, Sinking Valley Farm Show, 1992, 94, 95, Huntingdon County Arts Coun., 1989, 90, 91, Merit cert. Photographers Forum, 1989, Vila Gardner Metzger art award, 1989, others. Mem. Standing Stone Art League, Huntingdon County Arts Coun., Women's League Juniata Coll., Nat. Mus. of Women in the Arts (charter mem.). Home and Office: 104 W 12th St Tyrone PA 16686-1634

SHAW, NANCY RIVARD, museum curator, art historian, educator; b. Saginaw, Mich.; d. Joseph H. and Jean M. (O'Boyle) Marcotte; m. Danny W. Shaw, Feb. 29, 1980; 1 stepchild, Christina Marie. BA magna cum laude, Oakland U., 1969; MA, Wayne State U., 1973. Asst. curator Am. art Detroit Inst. Arts, 1972-75, curator, 1975—; adj. prof. art and art history Wayne State U., Detroit, 1991—. Contbg. author: American Art in the Detroit Institute of Arts, 1991; contbr. articles to exhbn. catalogues and profl. jours. Mem. Wayne State U. Alumni Assn. Roman Catholic. Office: Detroit Inst Arts 5200 Woodward Ave Detroit MI 48202-4008

SHAW, ROSLYN LEE, elementary education educator; b. Bklyn., Oct. 1, 1942; d. Benjamin Biltmore and Bessie (Banilower) Deretchin; m. Stephen Allan Shaw, Feb. 1, 1964; children: Laurence, Victoria, Michael. BA, Bklyn. Coll., 1964; MS, SUNY, New Paltz, 1977, cert. advanced study, 1987; cert. gifted edn., Coll. New Rochelle, 1986. Cert. sch. adminstr., supr., sch. dist. adminstr., reading tchr., tchr. N-6. Tchr. Hillel Hebrew Acad., Beverly Hills, Calif., 1965-66, P.S. 177, 77, Bklyn., 1964-65, 66-67; tchr. Middletown (N.Y.) Sch. Dist., 1974-77, reading specialist, 1977—, compensatory edn. reading tchr., 1977-95, tchr. gifted children, 1984-87, asst. project coord. pre-K, 1988-89, instrnl. leader, 1989-93. Pres. Middletown H.S. Parents' Club, 1983-86; bd. dirs. Mental Health Assn., Goshen, N.Y., 1980-81; mem. Middletown Interfaith Coun., 1983-85. Mem. ASCD, Amy Bull Crist Reading Coun. (pres. 1989-91, 93-95), N.Y. State Reading Assn. (Coun. Svc. award 1990, regional dir. 1991-94, bd. dirs. 1991—, chair reading tchrs. spl. interest group 1993-94, newsletter editor The Empire State Reading Scene), Internat. Reading Assn., Univ. Women's Club, Delta Kappa Gamma. Home: 133 Highland Ave Middletown NY 10940-4712 Office: Liberty St Sch 6 Liberty St Middletown NY 10940-5508

SHAW, SONDRA CHASE, university administrator; b. Flint, Mich., July 6, 1936; d. Montelle Irwin and Nedra Beatrice (Walcutt) Chase; children: Heather Shaw Cauchy, Laurie Shaw Smith, Campbell Chase. BA, Mich. State U., 1958, JD, 1985. Ptnr. Cooper-Shaw Pub. Rels., Traverse City, Mich., 1973-75; sales and mktg. Coll. Am. Pathologists, Traverse City, 1978-81; exec. dir., senatorial aide Senate Republican Caucus, Lansing, Mich., 1981-85; polit. fundraiser Rep. Nat. Senatorial and Congl. Cmtys., Washington, 1985-86; fundraising cons. Madison, Wis., 1986-87; devel. dir. Madison Festival of the Lakes, 1987-88; asst. dir. State Hist. Soc. Wis., Madison, 1988-94; asst. v.p. external affairs Western Mich. U., Kalamazoo, 1994—; co-dir. Nat. Network of Women as Philanthropists, U. Wis., Madison, 1991—; presenter in field. Co-author: Reinventing Fundraising: Realizing the Potential of Women's Philanthropy, 1996 (Grenzebach award 1995, McAdam Book award 1995). County commr. Grand Traverse County Bd. Commrs., 1970-76; mem. Traverse City Planning Commn., 1979-81. Named one of 10 Outstanding County Commrs., Mich. Assn. Counties, 1975. Mem. Kalamazoo Rotary Club, Mich. Women's Found. (devel. com.). Home: 2200 Parkview Ave E1 Kalamazoo MI 49008

SHAW, SUSAN HOLLY, federal agency administrator; b. Phila., Dec. 23, 1950; d. Earl Ward and Dorothy Mae (Archer) Foote; m. David Franklin Shaw, Dec. 24, 1971 (div. Oct. 1993); 1 child, Holly Christine. BS in Math., U. Del., 1972, MS in Math., 1975. Ops. rsch. analyst FEA, Washington, 1973-77; ops. rsch. analyst Energy Info. Adminstr., U.S. Dept. Energy, Washington, 1977-90, ops. rsch. analyst Nat. Energy Modeling Sys. Project Office, 1990-91, tech. asst. to adminstr., 1991-92, chief natural energy modeling sys. br., 1992—. Joint editor: Advanced Techniques of Operations Research, 1981; contbr. articles to profl. jours. Faculty fellow for grad. work math. dept. U. Del. Mem. Inst. for Ops. Rsch. and Mgmt. Scis. Democrat. Lutheran.

SHAW, TAMMY SHEALY, speech and language pathologist; b. Greenwood, S.C., Oct. 5, 1959; d. Harvey Edward and Jerolene Berry Shealy; m. Robert Wayne Shaw, Aug. 16, 1980; children: Rebeccca Lynn, Andrew Wayne. BA, Columbia Coll., 1980; MEd, U. S.C., 1989. Cert. tchr. speech correction and elem. edn., S.C. Speech clin. Saluda (S.C.) Dist. # 1, 1980—; mem. Sch. Restructuring Com., Saluda, 1993—, Sch. Improvement Coun., 1994—; presenter S.C. CEC Conv., 1993-94. Mem. Saluda Garden Club. Tchr. incentive grantee S.C. Dept. Edn., Columbia, 1991-92. Mem. S.C. Speech and Hearing Assn., Coun. Exceptional Children. Baptist. Home: RR 5 Box 208 Saluda SC 29138-8902

SHAW, VIRGINIA RUTH, clinical psychologist; b. Salina, Kans., Dec. 10, 1952; d. Lawrence Eugene and Gladys (Wilbur) S.; m. Joseph Eugene Scuro Jr., July 14, 1990. BA magna cum laude, Kans. Wesleyan U., 1973; MA, Wichita State U., 1975; PhD, U. Southern Miss., 1984. Diplomate Am. Bd. Med. Psychotherapists (fellow). Rsch. fellow Wichita (Kans.) State U., 1973-75; rsch. fellow, teaching fellow U. So. Miss., 1978-79, 80-81; staff psychologist Big Spring (Tex.) State Hosp., 1976-78; predoctoral clin. psychology intern U. Okla. Health Scis. Ctr., Oklahoma City, 1981-82; postdoctoral fellow in neuropsychology Neuropsychiat. Inst., UCLA, 1982-83; rsch. psychologist, neuropsychologist L.A. VA Med. Ctr. Wadsworth Div., 1983-84; clin. neuropsychologist Patton (Calif.) State Hosp., 1984-85; clin. neuropsychologist Brentwood div. LA VA Med. Ctr., 1985; clinical, neuropsychologist Timberlawn Psychiatric Hosp., Dallas, 1985-87, Dallas Rehab. Inst., 1987-93; cons. clin. neuropsychology Dallas area hosps., Willowbrook Hosp., Waxahachie, Tex., Cedars Hosp., Waxahachie, 1988-96; clin. psychologist Maui child and adolescent mental health team State of Hawaii Dept. Health, 1996—; presenter profl. meetings, 1975—. Contbr. articles to profl. jours. Mem. Dallas Mayor's Com. for Employment of the Disabled (cert. appreciation), 1987, 500 Inc., Dallas, 1988-96. Remiatte Meml. scholar Kans. Wesleyan U., 1970-73; recipient Nat. Disting. Svc. Registry award in rehab., 1989, Early Career Contbns. to Clin. Neuropsychology award candidate Nat. Acad. Neuropsychology, 1993, 94. Mem. APA Divsn. 35/ Psychology of Women (student rsch. prize com. 1996), Internat. Neuropsychol. Soc., Nat. Head Injury Found., Assn. for Women in Psychology, Tex. Head Injury Found., Dallas Head Injury Found. (Vol. award, cert. appreciation 1991), Am. Congress Rehab. Medicine, Nat. Rehab. Assn., Nat. Acad. Neuropsychology (membership com. 1991-94, rsch. consortium 1991—, co-chair poster program com. 1994, 95). Office: 444 Hana Hwy # 202 Kahului HI 96732

SHAW-COHEN, LORI EVE, magazine editor; b. Manhattan, N.Y., Apr. 22, 1959; d. Ray and Carole (Bergenthal) Shaw; m. Robert Mark Cohen, Sept. 20, 1981; children: Joshua Samuel, Drew Taylor, Logan Shaw. BA in Journalism, U. So. Calif., 1981. Editorial asst., writer BBW: Big Beautiful Woman Mag., Los Angeles, 1979-80; editorial asst., writer Intro Mag., Los Angeles, 1980-81; mng. editor 'Teen Mag., Los Angeles, 1981-86; writer, interviewer Stan Rosenfeld & Assocs. Pub. Relations, Los Angeles, 1980-81; cons. BBW: Big Beautiful Woman Mag., Los Angeles, 1981—, Media Research Group, Los Angeles, 1984; condr. seminars Women in Communication, Los Angeles, 1983, Pacific N.W. Writers Conf., Seattle, 1984. Patentee children's toy, 1971; lyricist for songs, 1977—; contbr. articles and poems to profl. jours. and mags. Office: BBW: Big Beautiful Woman Mag 19528 Ventura Blvd # 298 Tarzana CA 91356-2917

SHAWL, S. NICOLE, hypnobehavioral scientist; b. South Amboy, N.J., July 26, 1940; d. Michael Joseph and Kathleen Shawl; life ptnr. Donna J. Talcott. BA, Georgian Court Coll., 1971; MA, Kean Coll. of N.J., Union, 1975; PhD, Calif. Coast U., Santa Ana, 1992; postgrad., Saybrook Inst., San Francisco; postgrad. studies in hypno-behavioral psychology, The Union Inst., Cin. Joined Sisters of Mercy, 1958, left, 1966; cert. student pers. svcs. adminstr., prin., supr., dir. student pers. svcs., substance awareness coord. Georgian Ct. Coll., substance awareness coord. State of N.J.; cert. hypnobehavioral therapist. Tchr. pub. and parochial schs., Monmouth & Ocean Counties, N.J., 1960-79; interviewer, pub. rels. mgr. ARC, Toms River, N.J., 1980; editor, writer Prentice-Hall, Englewood Cliffs, N.J., 1980; counselor, asst. dir. coll. program Georgian Court Coll., Lakewood, N.J., 1980—; adj. instr. UCLA, 1975-76; owner, pres. Auntie Nuke Enterprises. Active NOW. Mem. AAUW, ACLU, ACA, NOW, So. Poverty Law Ctr., Mercy Higher Edn. Colloquium Assn., Nat. Guild Hypnotists, Am. Soc. Clin. Hypnosis, Nat. Psychology Adv. Assn., Nat. Bd. for Cert. Clin. Hypnotherapists, Ednl. Opportunity Assn. (nat. coun.), Assn., Union Inst. Ctr. for Women, Internat. Platform Assn., Am. Biog. Inst. (rsch. fellow). Democrat. Office: Georgian Court Coll 900 Lakewood Ave Lakewood NJ 08701-2600

SHEA, ANNE JOAN, fashion editor; b. Beacon, N.Y., Dec. 29, 1907; d. Patrick Henry and Mary Loretta (Walsh) S. AB in Liberal Arts, Syracuse (N.Y.) U., 1929. Fashion editor The Bride's Mag., N.Y.C., 1952-63; dir. fashion promotion Angelo Bridals, N.Y.C., 1964-65; asst. to N.Y. mgr. Nat. Home Fashions League, 1965; freelance sec. to mgr. Union League Club of N.Y., 1963, 65; fashion cons. to pub. rels. dir. French Lace Inst., Paris, 1965-67; freelance fashion cons., stylist, 1966-70. Bd. dirs. Dag Hammerskjold Fund; mem. mobile blood bank unit ARC; vol. Svcs. for Children, Bide-A-Wee Home, Fairchild Tropical Gardens, Miami Heart Inst. Aux., Am. Mus. Natural History. Mem. Women in Communications, Fashion Group (bd. dirs. Fashion Critics award), Syracuse U. Alumni Assn., AAUW, Am. Assn. Ret. Persons, English Speaking Union, Internat. Platform Assn., Lucy Stone League, Smithsonian Assocs., Theta Phi Alpha. Home: 4735 NW 7th Ct Lantana FL 33462

SHEA, KAREN BIUS, financial consultant; b. Memphis, Oct. 6, 1945; d. Ferdinand Lafayette Bius and Carolina Hope (Sudlow) Richards; divorced; children: Kelly Turns, Patrick Turns. Student, Drury Coll., 1963-64; BS in Secondary Edn. cum laude, U. Memphis, 1971, postgrad., 1993-94. Lic. broker series 7 and 63 Nat. Assn. Securities Brokers. Various mcpl. bond positions, 1968-76; broker Hibbard, O'Conner & Weeks, Houston, 1976-79, Cowen & Co., Houston, 1982-83, Shearson/Am. Express, Houston, 1983-84, Arnspiger, Cox & Iverson, Houston, 1984, Morgan Keegan & Co., Memphis, 1984-85, Vining-Sparks IBG, Memphis, 1991-95; broker, mgr. securities clearance Refco Mortgage Securities, Memphis, 1985-87; instnl. fixed income securities broker 1st Tenn. Bank, Memphis, 1987-91; fin. cons. Ameristar Investments & Trust, Memphis, 1995—. Prin. vol. Kathy Whitmire for Mayor, Houston, 1981; pres. Houston Area Women's Polit. Caucus, 1982, Memphis Women's Polit. Caucus, 1989-90; chmn. bd. M.K. Gandhi Inst. for Non Violence, Memphis, 1994-95; mem. Tenn. Commemorative Woman Suffrage Commn., 1995—; Stephen min. Calvary Episcopal Ch., Memphis, 1988-90. Recipient Cmty. Svc. award Memphis chpt. NCCJ, 1991, award for racial justice YWCA, Memphis, 1995. Mem. Nat. Assn. Securities Profls. Republican. Home: 322 Angelus St Memphis TN 38112 Office: Ameristar Investments/Trust Ste 113 6000 Poplar Memphis TN 38119

SHEA, MARY FRANCES, elementary school educator; b. Spring Valley, Ill., Nov. 23, 1949; d. Joseph Charles and Jean Violet (Stevenson) Mertel; m. Patrick Dennis Shea, Dec. 15, 1973; children: Megan, Patrick. AA, Ill. Valley C.C., Oglesby, 1969; BS in Edn. magna cum laude, No. Ill. U., 1971. Cert. elem. sch. educator K-9. Second grade educator Ladd (Ill.) Cmty. Consolidated Sch., 1971-77, chpt. 1 educator, 1978-80, chpt. 1 educator, gifted educator, 1980-85, kindergarten educator, chpt. 1 educator, gifted educator, 1985-93, kindergarten educator, computer educator, 1993-96, tech. cons., 1992—. Mem. Phi Theta Kappa. Roman Catholic. Home: 3105 E 5th Rd Tomahawk Bluff La Salle IL 61301 Office: Ladd Cmty Consolidated Sch 232 E Cleveland St Ladd IL 61329

SHEA, ROSANNE MARY, artist, art educator; b. Waterbury, Conn., Oct. 29, 1957; d. John Patrick and Helen Gertude (Goodridge) S.; 1 child, Matthew Shea. BFA, U. Conn., 1980; MFA, Vermont Coll., 1996. Freelance artist Waterbury, Conn., 1980-90; art tchr. Creative Summer program Mead Sch., Greenwich, Conn., 1991, 92, 93, 94; art tchr. We. Conn. State U., Danbury, 1994, Sacred Heart/St. Peter's Sch., New Haven, Conn., 1995—; arts and crafts program dir. Futures Initiative Program, Bridgeport, Conn., 1989; adj. art tchr. Naugatuck Valley Cmty. Tech. Coll., Waterbury, Conn., 1991—; v.p. Bank Street Artists, Waterbury, Conn., 1993-94. Appeared as lead character in play Tropical Blues, 1996; one-woman exhbns. include Mattatuck C.C., Waterbury, Conn., 1992, A Frame Come True Gallery, Torrington, Conn., 1992; group exhbns. include Waterbury Arts Resource Coun., 1992 (mem.), Bank St. Artists Gallery, Waterbury, 1994 (mem.), Northampton Coll., Bethlehem, Pa., 1995, Talk of the Town Coffee House, Torrington, 1996, Sacred Ground Coffee House, Watertown, Conn., 1996, Wood Gallery, Montpelier, Vt., 1996, Women Only, Waterbury, 1996. Leader Boy Scouts Am., Waterbury, Conn., 1990-94; state visitation mgr. Conn. chpt. Nat. Holiday Project, 1986-87; course vol., mem. bd. Bridgeport (Conn.) Youth at Risk, 1986-88, ropes course leader, vol. enrollment mgr., 1987-99. Scholar AAUW, 1993, Philanthropic Ednl. Orgn., 1993.

SHEA, VIRGINIA GALWAY, writer, editor; b. N.Y.C., Aug. 23, 1961; d. George Edward Shea and Charlotte Aiken (King) Rowlands; m. Andrew James Mendelsohn, Apr. 10, 1994. BA, Princeton U., 1982. Comms. cons. Electric Power Rsch. Inst., Palo Alto, Calif., 1988-93. Author: Netiquette, 1994; contbr. articles to profl. jours. Mem. AAUW, Nat. Writers Union.

SHEAD, DIANA M., elementary school educator; b. St. Louis, Sept. 23, 1943; d. Shellie McClure and Bessie Will (Hairston) Tatum (div.); 1 child, Melanie Dyan. BA, Harris Stowe Tchrs. Coll., 1969; MA, Webster U., 1979. Substitute tchr. St. Louis Pub. Schs., 1969-71, first grade tchr., 1972-74, reading specialist, 1974-76, data processing coord., 1976-80, first grade tchr., 1981-82, instructional coord., 1982-85; entrepreneur Lady D. Inc., St. Louis, 1984-87; 1st, 2d and 3d grade tchr. Atlanta Pub. Schs., 1987—. Author: (Novel) Teach at Your Own Risk, 1995. Mem. Am. Fedn. Tchrs. Home: 5490 Northcut Dr College Park GA 30349

SHEAR, IONE MYLONAS, archaeologist; b. St. Louis, Feb. 19, 1936; d. George Emmanuel and Lella (Papazouglou) Mylonas; BA, Wellesley Coll., 1958; MA, Bryn Mawr Coll., 1960, PhD, 1968; m. Theodore Leslie Shear, June 24, 1959; children: Julia Louise, Alexandra. Research asst. Inst. for Advanced Study, Princeton, N.J., 1963-65; mem. Agora Excavation, Athens, 1967, 72-94; lectr. art and archaeology Princeton U., 1983-84; lectr. Am. Sch. Classical Studies, Athens, summers 1989—; also excavator various other sites in Greece and Italy. Mem. Archaeol. Inst. Am., Greek Archaeol. Soc. (hon.). Author: The Panagia Houses at Mycenae, 1987; contbr. articles to profl. jours. Address: 87 Library Pl Princeton NJ 08540-3015 also: Demokratous 30, Athens 106-76, Greece

SHEAR, NATALIE PICKUS, public relations executive; b. N.Y.C., Oct. 18, 1940; d. Sam and Mildred (Shulman) Pickus; m. Daniel H. Shear, Dec. 14, 1968 (dec. Apr. 1989); children: Adam Brian, Tamara Beth. BA in Journalism, Fairleigh Dickinson U., 1962. Editorial asst. Show Bus. Newspaper, N.Y.C., 1962-64, The Jewish News, Newark, 1964-66; dir. Manhattan women's div., program asst. Am. Jewish Congress, N.Y.C., 1966-68; mng. editor The Jewish Week, Washington, 1968-71; dir. pub. rels. United Jewish Appeal, Washington, 1973-74; pub. affairs dir. Leadership Conf. on Civil Rights, Washington, 1977-83; pres. Natalie P. Shear Assocs., Inc., Washington, 1983—. Editor (newspaper) Books Alive, 1973-74; editor, pub. (newsletter) Trends, Inc., 1989-94. Vol. Nat. Jewish Dem. Coun., Washington, 1992—, D.C. Jewish Cmty. Ctr.; chairperson women's task force Am. Jewish Congress, Washington, 1984-86, mem. nat. women's task force, 1989—; v.p. Nat. Child Rsch. Ctr., Washington, 1974-76; pres. Ohr Kodesh Sisterhood, Chevy Chase, Md., 1980-82. Mem. Am. Jewish Pub. Rels. Soc., Jewish Cmty. Ctr. Home: 4701 Willard Ave Chevy Chase MD 20815-4635 Office: 1629 K St NW Ste 802 Washington DC 20006

SHEARER, LOUISE A., lawyer; b. Urbana, Ill., Sept. 18, 1958. BA summa cum laude, U. Ill., 1978; postgrad., U. Chgo., 1978-79; JD summa cum laude, U. Houston, 1982. Bar: Tex. 1982. Law clk. Hon. Carolyn Dineen King, U.S. Ct. Appeals, 5th cir., 1982-83; assoc. Baker & Botts, LLP, Houston, 1983-89, ptnr., 1990—. Casenote and comment editor Houston Law Rev., 1981-82. Recipient U. Houston Law Found. Acad. Excellence award, 1982. Mem. State Bar of Tex., Houston Bar Assn., Order of the Barons, Bronze Tablet, Phi Beta Kappa, Phi Kappa Phi. Office: Baker & Botts LLP 910 Louisiana St Houston TX 77002*

SHEARER, RHONDA ROLAND, artist; b. Aurora, Ill., June 12, 1954; d. Clarence N. and Mary (McKinley) Roland; m. Joseph Allen, May 18, 1983 (div. 1994); children: Jade Shearer Allen, London Shearer Allen; m. Stephen Jay Gould, Jan. 1, 1996. Student, Boston U., SUNY, 1973-74. lectr. Ctr. for Complex Sys. & Visualization, Curacao, 1995, Brown U., Providence, R.I., 1993, Harvard U., Cambridge, Mass., 1993. Solo exhbns. include Wildenstein Gallery, London, 1987, N.Y.C., 1989, 90, Pub. Art Fund, Inc., N.Y.C., 1993, Cheekwood Mus. Art, Nashville, 1993, James A. Mirchener Mus. Art, Doylestown, Pa., 1993, Jacksonville (Fla.) Art Mus., 1994, Gibbes Mus. Art, Charleston, S.C., 1994, Knoxville Mus. Art, 1994; contbr. articles to profl. jours. Founder, trustee Housing Works, N.Y.C., 1990—; trustee N.Y. Soc. for Prevention of Cruelty to Children, 1985—, Nat. Mus. Racing Hall of Fame, Saratoga Springs, N.Y., 1985-89. Mem. AAAS, Internat. Soc. Ecol. Psychology, Internat. Soc. Arts, Scis. and Tech., Coll. Art Assn., Nat. Coun. Tchrs. of Math. Office: 285 Spring St New York NY 10013

SHEARIN, BETTY SPURLOCK, retired educational administrator; b. Salem, Va., Nov. 7, 1931; d. Thomas Shirley and Willie Ann (Borden) Spurlock; m. Alexander Moore Shearin Jr. (dec.), June 1 1957; 1 child, Victoria Louise. BS, Va. State U., 1954. Mem. staff Benedict Coll., Columbia, S.C., 1957-94; acting pres. Benedict Coll., 1984-85, v.p. adminstrn., 1986-87, coord. archives, telecommunications, 1987-88, spl. asst. to v.p. bus. affairs, 1988-90; cons., 1990-94; vol. coord. Richland County Pub. Libr., Columbia, 1991-95. Bd. dirs. Benedict Coll. Fed. Credit Union, 1974-79, 84-91; asst. sec. bd. trustees Benedict Coll., 1976-85, sec., 1985-86; sec. Colonial Park Cmty. Home Assn., Columbia, 1988—; vol. Friends Richland County Pub. Libr., 1991—; mem. S.C. State Mus. Mem. NAFE, Assn. Records Mgrs. and Adminstrs. (sec. bd. dirs. 1983-85), Assn. Vol. Adminstrs. S.C. Assn. Vol. Adminstrs. (historian), Alpha Kappa Alpha. Democrat. Episcopalian. Home: 4116 Grand St Columbia SC 29203-6656

SHEARING, MIRIAM, justice; b. Waverly, N.Y., Feb. 24, 1935. BA, Cornell U., 1956; JD, Boston Coll., 1964. Bar: Calif. 1965, Nev. 1969. Justice of peace Las Vegas Justice Ct., 1977-81; judge Nev. Dist. Ct., 1983-92, chief judge, 1986; justice Nevada Supreme Ct., Carson City, 1993—. Mem. ABA, Am. Judicature Soc., Nev. Judges Assn. (sec. 1978), Nev. Dist. Ct. Judges Assn. (sec. 1984-85, pres. 1986-87), State Bar Nev., State Bar Calif., Clark County Bar Assn. Democrat.

SHEA-STONUM, MARILYN, judge; b. Anaconda, Mont., June 6, 1947. AB, U. Calif., Santa Cruz, 1969; JD, Case Western Res. U., 1975. Bar: Ohio 1975, Calif. 1976. Law clk. to Hon. Battisti U.S. Dist. Ct. (no. dist.), Ohio, 1975-76; ptnr. Jones, Day, Reavis & Pogue, Cleve., 1984-94; bankruptcy judge ea. divsn. U.S. Bankruptcy Ct. Ohio (no. dist.), Akron, 1984-94; bankruptcy judge U.S. Bankruptcy Ct. (no. dist.) Ohio, Akron, 1994—. Office: US Bankruptcy Ct No Dist Ohio Ea Divsn 2 S Main St Rm 240 Akron OH 44308*

SHEBESTA, LYNN MARIE, school administrator; b. Manitowoc, Wis., Dec. 16, 1955; d. Joseph J. Shebesta and Shirley Ann (Pietras) Kent. BS, U. Wis., La Crosse, 1978; MS, Mankato State U., 1986; postgrad. study Admissions, Harvard Grad. Sch. Edn., 1992. Admissions counselor Silver Lake Coll., Manitowoc, Wis., 1980-83; asst. dir. admissions Mankato (Minn.) State U., 1983-88; dir. admissions Lakeland Coll., Sheboygan, Wis., 1988-90; dean of admissions and fin. aid Wayland Acad., Beaver Dam, Wis., 1990-95; econ. devel. profl. Northeast Wis. Tech. Coll., Green Bay, Wis., 1995—; cons. to admissions Northwestern Military/Naval Acad., Lake Geneva, Wis., 1992; presenter Nat. Assn. Luth. Coll. Admission Officers, Concordia U. Wis., Mequon, Wis., 1993. Editor, designer, publisher (ednl. insts. brochures, viewbooks), 1986-93. Bd. dirs., founder Civitan, Mankato, 1986-88; bd. dirs. Big Brothers/Big Sisters, Manitowoc, Wis., 1989, Girl Scouts, Green Bay, Wis., 1996. Mem. Wis. Assn. Secondary Sch. and Coll. Admissions Counselors, Secondary Sch. Admission Test Bd., Midwest Boarding Schs. (bd. dirs.), Nat. Assn. Student Affairs Profls., Rotary Internat. (bd. dirs. DePere, Wis.), Green Bay Area C. of C. (advance econ. devel. com., advance retention com.). Home: 448 North Good Hope Rd De Pere WI 54115 Office: Northeast Wis Tech Coll PO Box 19042 2740 W Mason St Green Bay WI 54307-9042

SHEDDEN, EDYTHE MARIAN, artist; b. Dumont, N.J., Dec. 17, 1921; d. Milton and Vera Gladys (Meister) Bauer; m. Peter J. Shedden, Apr. 26, 1944 (div. June 1987); children: Darryl E., Peter Scott; m. William Parker Cowgill, Aug. 25, 1987. BA, Rutgers U., 1943; studied with, Adja Yunkers, Stuart Davis, Meyer Shapiro. Artist apprentice Abraham & Strause, Bklyn., 1943-44; artist/model Apfel Studios, N.Y.C., 1944-45, 46; tchr. art Allofus Workshop, Rochester, N.Y., 1970-75, Meml. Art Gallery, Rochester, 1970-80,

Monroe County Penitentary, Rochester, 1965-75; owner/dir. Oxford Gallery, Rochester, 1971-85. Exhibits include Meml. Art Gallery, Rochester, Albright-Knox, Buffalo, Everson, Syracuse, Alfred U., Nazareth Coll., Rochester; pvt. collections include SUNY, Oswego, Alfred U., Rochester Telephone Corp., Gannett Corp., Young & Rubicam, Rochester, Amalgamated Clothing Workers, Rochester, Charles Rand Penney Collection, others. Mem. coun. Meml. Art Gallery, Rochester, 1967—; bd. dirs. Broadway Theatre League, Rochester, 1962-70, Monroe County Arts Resources Ctr., 1970-75; committeeperson Dem. Party, Rochester, 1968, 75. Unitarian. Home: 5 Elmwood Hill Ln Rochester NY 14610

SHEEHAN, CAROLINE GRIFFIN (CARRIE SHEEHAN), medical researcher, writer; b. La Grande, Oreg., Dec. 13, 1928; d. John Henry and Lillian Louise (O'Connell) Griffin; m. Tom Edward Sheehan, Sept. 10, 1949 (wid.); children: Christie, Thomas, Patrick, Molly (dec.), Timothy, Mary, Michael, Caroline. BA in Public Affairs and Political Science, Seattle U., 1974. Rsch. coord. S.W. SIDS Rsch. Inst., Lake Jackson, Tex., 1992—; interviewer, chpt./Flash program U. Wash., Seattle, 1995-96; trustee Nat. SIDS Found., 1980, Jubilee Women's Ctr., Seattle, 1990—; charter mem. Citizens for Rational Handgun Control, Seattle. Contbr. articles to jours., chpts. to books. Planning commr. City of Seattle, 1970-78, mem. landmarks bd., 1975-78; mem. police and cmty. task force Ch. Coun. of Seattle, 1975-85; candidate Seattle City Coun., 1979. Mem. Holy Names Acad. Alumnae Assn. (trustee, bd. dirs. 1991—, Disting. Alumna award 1996). Democrat. Roman Catholic. Home: 915-16 East Seattle WA 98112

SHEEHAN, DEBORAH ANN, radio station and theater executive; b. Paterson, N.J., Mar. 29, 1953; d. John J. and Ruth (Badertschier) S.; m. Emidio S. Quattrocchi, Mar. 15, 1985; 1 child, Deirdre Emily Sheehan. B.A., William Paterson Coll., 1975. With radio Sta. WWDJ, Hackensack, N.J., 1980-83, Shadow Traffic, N.Y.C., 1981-83; dir. news, community affairs WPAT-AM/FM, N.Y.C., 1979—. Actress-tchr. Paterson Arts Ctr., 1975-79; host radio show Bus. Jour. N.J., 1984; host, producer radio show Debbie Sheehan mag., 1983; host FDU Focus, Cable Network N.J.; writer plays. Exec. dir., actress Learning Theater Co., Paterson, 1975—; sec. bd. dirs. YMCA Passaic Valley, Paterson, 1983-89; mem. N.J. Legal Bd., Montclair, N.J., 1984-86; mem. Paterson Edn. Found., 1984-89; bd. dirs. United Way Passaic Valley, Conn., 1985, chair allocations com., 1985-92. Recipient Edward R. Murrow Gold medal B'nai B'rith, 1983, finalist 1984-85; Gold medal Internat. Radio Festival, 1983; Best Reporter award Sigma Delta Chi, 1985-87, Personality Profile award local chpt., 1987, Best Pub. Service award, 1987; Best Feature award AP, 1985, 87; Angel Excellence award, Los Angeles, 1985, 87; Internat. Press Assn. fellow, Japan, 1985, New Zealand, 1988. Club: Zonta. Avocations: weaving; travel; acting. Office: WPAT-AM-FM 1396 Broad St Clifton NJ 07013-4222

SHEEHAN, PATTY, professional golfer. 4th ranked woman LPGA Tour, 1992; winner U.S. Women's Open, 1992, 94, LPGA Championship, 1983-84, 93. Inductee LPGA Hall of Fame, 1993, Sports Illustrated Sportsman of the Yr., 1987. Office: LPGA Ste B 2570 W Internat Speedway Blvd Daytona Beach FL 32114-1118*

SHEEHAN, SUSAN, writer; b. Vienna, Austria, Aug. 24, 1937; came to U.S., 1941, naturalized, 1946; d. Charles and Kitty C. (Herrmann) Sachsel; m. Neil Sheehan, Mar. 30, 1965; children—Maria Gregory, Catherine Fair. BA (Durant scholar), Wellesley Coll., 1958; DHL (hon.), U. Lowell, 1991. Editorial researcher Esquire-Coronet, N.Y.C., 1959-60; free-lance writer N.Y.C., 1960-61; staff writer New Yorker mag., N.Y.C., 1961—. Author: Ten Vietnamese, 1967, A Welfare Mother, 1976, A Prison and a Prisoner, 1978, Is There No Place on Earth for Me?, 1982, Kate Quinton's Days, 1984, A Missing Plane, 1986, Life For Me Ain't Been No Crystal Stair, 1993; contbr. articles to various mags., including N.Y. Times Sunday Mag., Washington Post Sunday Mag., Harper's, Atlantic, New Republic, McCall's, Holiday, Boston Globe Sunday Mag., Life. Judge Robert F. Kennedy Journalism awards, 1980, 84; mem. lit. panel D.C. Commn. on Arts and Humanities, 1979-84; mem. pub. info. and edn. com. Nat. Mental Health Assn., 1982-83; mem. adv. com. on employment and crime Vera Inst. Justice, 1978-86; chair Pulitzer Prize nominating jury in gen. non-fiction for 1988, 1994, mem., 1991. Recipient Sidney Hillman Found. award, 1976, Gavel award ABA, 1978, Individual Reporting award Nat. Mental Health Assn., 1981, Pulitzer prize for gen. non-fiction, 1983, Feature Writing award N.Y. Press Club, 1984, Alumnae Assn. Achievement award Wellesley Coll., 1984, Carroll Kowal Journalism award NASW, 1993, Disting. Grad. award Hunter Coll. H.S., 1995, Pub. Awareness award Nat. Alliance for Mentally Ill, 1995; fellow Guggenheim Found., 1975-76, Woodrow wilson Internat. Ctr. for Scholars, 1981. Mem. Soc. Am. Historians, Phi Beta Kappa, Authors Guild. Home: 4505 Klingle St NW Washington DC 20016-3580 Office: New Yorker Mag 20 W 43rd St New York NY 10036-7400

SHEEHAN, TRACI ANN, organization administrator; b. N.Y.C., Aug. 5, 1965; d. Phillip Tracy and Joan Catherine (Waldron) Sheehan. BA, Douglass Coll., Rutgers U., 1991. Field dir. N.J. PIRG Citizen Lobby, New Brunswick, 1990-95, Taxpayers for Common $ense, Washington, 1996—. Office: Taxpayers for Common $ense 651 Pennsylvania Ave SE Washington DC 20003

SHEEHY, LOUISE FRANKLIN, entertainment company executive; b. Boston, Feb. 18, 1939; d. David Saul and Hilda (Trachtenberg) Witkind; m. Frank Thomas Sheehy, Oct. 19, 1985; children: Jonathan, Anne. BA in Humanities cum laude, Rollins Coll., 1980. Asst. dir. Epicenter, Orlando, Fla., 1975-79; dir. Holocaust Project, Orlando, 1980-82; owner, operator Barnie's Coffee & Tea Co., Orlando, 1982-85; exec. dir. Mohawc Project, Orlando, 1985-88; program dir. Canterbury Retreat Ctr., Oviedo, Fla., 1988-93, Walt Disney Co., Orlando, 1993—; cons. to women's bus., Orlando, 1983-85, Found. for Mideast Comm., Orlando, 1983-88. Mem. adv. bd. Jr. League of Orlando, 1980-82, Fla. Hosp. Ctr. for Women's Medicine, Orlando, 1985—; mem. Downtown Devel. Com., Orlando, 1982-84. Recipient Leadership award Jewish Fedn. Orlando, 1977; named Downtown Woman of Yr., Women's Exec. Coun., 1981, 84. Democrat. Jewish. Home: 341 Alpine Dr Maitland FL 32751 Office: Disney Inst 210 Celebration Pl Celebration FL 34747

SHEEHY, PATRICIA ANN, environmental services manager; b. Rockaway Park, N.Y., July 6, 1960; d. James Patrick and Margaret Patricia (Maloney) Boyle; m. Neil Edward Sheehy, May 24, 1991; children: Patrick Joseph and Megan Eileen (twins). BS in Biology and Biochemistry, SUNY, Stony Brook, 1983; MS in Environ. Studies, L.I. U., 1985. Sec. Met. N.Y. Assn. Environ. Profls., Greenvale, 1984-85; intern Suffolk County Dept. Health Svcs., Hauppauge, N.Y., 1984-85; regulatory specialist Prentiss Drug & Chem. Co., Inc., Floral Park, N.Y., 1986-89; mgr. regulatory affairs Roussel Bio Corp., Lincoln Park, N.J., 1989-90; mgr. internat. regulatory affairs Merck & Co., Inc., Three Bridges, N.J., 1990-93, mgr. regulatory coord. and planning, 1993-96, assoc. dir. coordination and planning, 1996—; spokesperson endangered species task force Prentiss Drug & Chem. Co., Inc., Washington, 1986-89. Freelance designer. Mem. Nat. Agrl. Chems. Assn., Met. N.Y. Assn. Environ. Profls. (sec.), Chem. Spltys. and Mfr.'s Assn. (steering com. Washington chpt. 1989-90), Chem. Producers and Distbrs. Assn. (minor use com. Washington chpt. 1988), Codex Com. of Pesticide Residues. Office: Merck & Co Inc PO Box 450 Hillsborough Rd Three Bridges NJ 08887-0450

SHEELEY, VIRGINIA RUTH, civic volunteer; b. Walker, Mo., Jan. 6, 1936; d. Glenn Monroe and Edna Estella (Thomas) Stevens; m. Charles B. Sheeley, Aug. 3, 1955; children: Steven M., Craig B., Jeffrey A. BS in Edn., S.W. Mo. State U., 1958; postgrad., Drury Coll., Springfield, Mo., 1970. Tchr. Springfield (Mo.) R-12 Schs., 1958-59. Columnist Woodcarving Mag., 1978-85; woodcarver. Mem. dist. com. Boy Scouts Am., Springfield, 1980—; com. mem. S.W. Com. for UNICEF, Springfield, 1980—; regional v.p. Nat. Carvers Mus., 1970-85. Named Outstanding Young Women, Jr. Jaycee Wives, 1970, Silver Beaver award Boy Scouts Am., 1976. Mem. AAUW (hist./program chair), Ozarks Whittlers and Woodcarvers (organizer, pres.). Democrat.

SHEELY, CINDY JEAN, elementary education educator; b. Renton, Wash., July 21, 1956; d. Leonard Ivan and Adeline Elaine (Waddington) Backman; m. Kevin Dee Sheely, July 17, 1982. BA, Seattle Pacific U., 1978. Cert. tchr. K-9, Wash. Tchr. second/third grade Rainier Valley Christian, Seattle, 1978-80; tchr. first/second grade Seattle Christian Sch., 1980—. Mem. Skyway Ch. of God. Home: 12632 SE 211th Ct Kent WA 98031-2209 Office: Seattle Christian Sch 19639 28th Ave S Seattle WA 98188-5128

SHEERAN, SUSAN, television executive; b. Teaneck, N.J., Oct. 4, 1963; d. Philip A. and Geraldine (Hunter) S. BA in Speech Comm., Trenton State Coll., 1985. Duplication coord. Home Box Office, N.Y.C., 1986-88; ops. coord. Reiss Media Enterprises, Northvale, N.J., 1988-90; traffic ops. mgr. Mizlou Sports News Network, Arlington, Va., 1990-91; ops. mgr. Court TV, N.Y.C., 1991-93, dir. ops., 1993-95, v.p. ops., 1995—. Home: 57 Tallmadge Ave Chatham NJ 07928 Office: Court TV 600 Third Ave New York NY 10016

SHEETS, MARTHA LOUISE, civic activist; b. Toledo, Mar. 25, 1923; d. Ira Elmo and Nellie Gertrude Merrill; m. Ted Charles Sheets, Dec. 21, 1946; children: Thomas Merrill, Susan Ruth, Laura Louise, Charles Ira. B in Edn., U. Toledo, 1945. speaker in field. Charter mem., trustee, sec.-treas., v.p., pres. Citizens for Metroparks, Inc.; commr. Met. Park Dist. Bd., 1976; mem. Gov.'s Commn. Restoration of State Capitol Bldg., Nashville, 1986; historian designer show houses Chattanooga Symphony and Opera Guild, 1981-93; appointee City Commn. to Greenway Adv. Bd., 1989, re-appointed, 1992-93; active numerous civic orgns. including garden clubs and ch. groups; active Save Outdoor Sculpture project Tenn. State Mus. and Smithsonian Inst., 1992-93; mem. com. Hamilton County (Tenn.) Bicentennial, 1996. Mem. AAUW (chmn. 75th birthday luncheon 1982, grantee Ednl. Found prog.), ASME (chmn., pres. Northwest Ohio sect. women's aux.), Jr. Coterie Club (founding pres.), Zonta Internat. Svc. Club, Little Theatre Assocs. (past pres.), Murray Hills Garden Club (pres. 1991-92, 92-93), Tenn. Fedn. Garden Clubs (dist. hist. preservation chmn. 1981-85, state hist. preservation chmn. 1987-89, dist. III hist. preservation chmn. 1992-94), Chattanooga Coun. Garden Clubs (awards chmn., hist. preservation chmn. 1992-94), PEO.

SHEETZ-LISTER, DAWN MICHELLE, social studies educator; b. Washington, Sept. 16, 1971; d. Miles Lucas and Patricia Lynn (Smallwood) Sheetz; m. Paul Richard Lister, Feb. 18, 1995. BA in History/Edn., Salisbury State U., 1992. Tchr. social studies Calvert County Pub. Schs., Prince Frederick, Md., 1993—. Mem. Phi Alpha Theta, Pi Gamma Mu, Kappa Delta Pi.

SHEFFIELD, BENITA CARROLL, bank officer; b. Lexington, Mo., June 5, 1950; d. Bruce Byron and Willie Otella (Lorren) Carroll; m. James Wilbur Sheffield, Jr., May 8, 1982. Student, Jacksonville (Fla.) U., 1968-69; AA, Fla. Jr. Coll., 1980; BBA cum laude, U. North Fla., 1987; MBA summa cum laude, U. of North Fla., 1991. Cert. fraud examiner. Authorization and control clk. First Union Nat. Bank Fla., Jacksonville, 1970-74, supr. ops. and control, 1974-78; bankcard acctg. mgr. First Union Nat. Bank of Fla., Jacksonville, 1978-80; loss prevention officer First Union Nat. Bank Fla., Jacksonville, 1980-87, asst. v.p., 1987—, v.p., 1994—. Presdl. scholar Jacksonville U., 1968-69. Mem. Bank Security Assn. of N.E. Fla. (pres. Jacksonville chpt. 1986-87), Phi Kappa Phi, Beta Gamma Sigma, Golden Key Nat. Honor Soc. Home: 2331 Herschel St Jacksonville FL 32204-4313 Office: 1st Union Nat Bank Fla 214 N Hogan St Jacksonville FL 32202-4240

SHEI, JULIANA CHIANG, technology transfer manager; b. Tokyo, Aug. 27, 1948; d. Wellington J. and Yoshiko (Araki) Chiang; m. Shen-Ann Shei; children: Irene, Ryan. BS, Nat. Cheng Kung U., Taiwan, 1971; MS, U. Mass., 1975; MBA, Rensselaer Poly. Inst., 1987. Tech. interpreter Shionogi Pharm. Co., Taiwan, 1971-73; gen. mgr. Enterpreneurial Pub. Co., Los Alamitos, Calif., 1975-77; asst. chemist Ames Lab. Iowa State U., 1977-81; rsch. scientist Tech. Ctr. U.S. Steel Corp., Monroeville, Pa., 1982-85; group coord. Sterling Drug Inc., Rensselaer, N.Y., 1986-91; internat. tech. mgr. GE Corp. R & D, Schenectady, N.Y., 1991—. Contbr. to tech. publs. Mem. NAFE, Assn. Women in Sci., Am. Chem. Soc. (sec.-treas. Pitts sect. 1983-84), Am. Mgmt. Assn., Profl. Women's Network (pres. Capital dist. N.Y. 1986—).

SHEIL, WILMA ROHLOFF, psychiatry, mental health nurse; b. N.Y.C., Oct. 10, 1937; d. William G.H. and Marjorie (Marshall) Rohloff; m. John James Sheil, July 6, 1958; children: Shawn William (dec.), Marjorie Katherine. LPN diploma, Wilson Tech., 1975; ASN, SUNY, Albany, 1985. Staff nurse Hoch Psychiatric Ctr., Brentwood, N.Y., 1976-77; staff nurse Huntington (N.Y.) Hosp., 1977-85, 85-87, asst. nurse mgr., 1988—. Mem. MADD, 1994—, Planned Parenthood, 1994—, U.S.O., 1994—. Mem. AARP, NRA, Nat. Wildlife Fedn., Humane Soc. U.S., Ctr. Marine Conservation, Internat. Soc. of Poets. Roman Catholic. Office: Huntington Hosp 270 Park Ave Huntington NY 11743

SHELBY, NINA CLAIRE, special education educator; b. Weatherford, Tex., Oct. 23, 1949; d. Bill Hudson and Roselle (Price) S.; m. Richard Dean Powell, May 29, 1971 (div. 1975); 1 child, Stoney Hudson. BA in English, Sul Ross State U., 1974, MEd, 1984; MA in English, U. Tex., 1995. Jr. high lang. arts educator Liberty Hill, Tex., 1974-75; H.S. resource educator Georgetown (Tex.) I. S. D., 1976-77; intermediate resource educator Raymondille (Tex.) I. S. D., 1977-81; educator of severe profound Napper Elem. Pharr (Tex.) San Juan Alamo Ind. Sch. Dist., 1981-90; H. S. life skills educator Pharr (Tex.) San Juan Alamo ISD North H.S., 1990-93; intermediate inclusion educator Carman Elem. Pharr (Tex.) San Juan Alamo Ind. Sch. Dist., 1993—; coach asst. Tex. Spl. Olympics, Pharr, 1981—, sponsor vocat. adj. club, 1990-93, adaptive asst. device team, Edinburg, Tex., 1993-95. Asst. den leader Cub Scouts of Am., 1994-95, parent vol. Boy's and Girl's Club of McAllen, 1992—. Mem. DAR, Assn. of Tex. Profl. Educators, Alpha Delta Kappa. Democrat. Mem. Ch. of Christ. Home: 2501 Falcon Ave McAllen TX 78504-4315 Office: Pharr San Juan Alamo ISD Carman Elem 100 Ridge Rd San Juan TX 78589

SHELDON, BROOKE EARLE, librarian, educator; b. Lawrence, Mass., Aug. 29, 1931; d. Leonard Hadley and Elsie Ann (Southerl) Earle; m. George Duffield Sheldon, Mar. 28, 1955 (dec.); children: L. Scott, G. Stephen. B.A., Acadia U., 1952, D.C.L. (hon.), 1985; M.L.S., Simmons Coll., 1954; Ph.D., U. Pitts., 1977. Base librarian Ent AFB, Colorado Springs, Colo., 1955-57, U.S. Army, Germany, 1956-57; br. librarian Albuquerque Public Library, 1959-61; coordinator adult services Santa Fe Public Library, 1965-67; head library devel. N.Mex. State Library, Santa Fe, 1967-72; asst. dir. leadership tng. inst. U.S. Office Edn., Washington, 1971-73; head tech. svcs. and tng. Alaska State Library, Juneau, 1973-75; dean Sch. Library Info. Studies Tex. Woman's U., Denton, 1977-90; acting provost Library Info. Studies, Tex. Woman's U., Denton, 1979-80; dean Grad. Sch. Libr. Info. Sci. U. Tex., Austin, 1991—. Author: Leaders in Libraries: Styles and Strategies for Success, 1991; editor: Library and Information Science Education in the United States, 1996; contbr. articles to profl. jours. Bd. dirs. Am. Libr. in Paris, 1992—. Recipient Alumni Achievement award Simmons Coll., 1983; Disting. Alumni award Sch. Library Info. Sci., U. Pitts., 1986. Mem. ALA (pres. 1983-84, chmn. com. on accreditation 1995-96), Tex. Libr. Assn., Rotary Internat., Beta Phi Mu. Democrat. Episcopalian.

SHELDON, DEENA LYNN, television camera operator; b. Groveland, Mass., Mar. 10, 1962; d. Frederic J. and Penny Margolis. BS, Boston U., 1984. Youth counselor. Camera operator Sta. WSBK-TV, Boston, 1985; robotic camera operator Met. Life and Fuji Blimps, Crofton, Md., 1989—; camera operator ESPN, Bristol, Conn., 1986—, Sportschannel, Woodbury, N.Y., 1987-92, Sta. WWOR-TV, Shea Stadium, Flushing, N.Y., 1987-92, NBC, N.Y.C., 1986—; robotic camera operator NFL NFC Wild Card, Playoff, and Championship Games, 1994—; camera operator CBS, N.Y.C., 1987—, ABC, incl. Monday Night Football, The Triple Crown and the Indy 500, N.Y.C., 1992, Fox Sports, N.Y.C., 1994—, ABC, N.Y.C., 1992—. Camera operator on these shows: Late Night with David Letterman, 1986—, Major League Baseball, 1990 (Sports Emmy award),Dem. and Rep. Convs., 1992, Inaugaration, 1993, Daytona 500, 1993, (Sports Emmy award), Monday Night Football (ABC), The Indy 500 (ABC), NFL and NFC Wild Card Playoff and Championship Games, 1994 and others. Co. mem. Body Lang. Dancers, 1986; mem. Michael Macchio's Jazz Co., Boston, 1980-85, Danny Sloan's Repertory, Boston, 1980-82, N.Y. and Nat. Ballroom Championship Team, 1978, Celtics Green Gang, 1980-82. Recipient Sports Emmy award for postseason maj. league baseball NATAS, 1990, Sports Emmy award for Daytona 500, 1993, ESPN's Extreme Games, 1995, N.Y. Sports Emmy award for N.Y. Mets coverage, 1986-87, Sports Emmy nominee for 1995 Am.'s Cup, 1996. Mem. Nat. Assn. Broadcast Employees and Technicians (local 53), Internat. Brotherhood Elec. Workers (local 45). Home: 385 W I St Encinitas CA 92024

SHELDON, ELEANOR HARRIET BERNERT, sociologist; b. Hartford, Conn., Mar. 19, 1920; d. M.G. and Fannie (Myers) Bernert; m. James Sheldon, Mar. 19, 1950 (div. 1960); children: James, John Anthony. AA, Colby Jr. Coll., 1940; AB, U. N.C., 1942; PhD, U. Chgo., 1949. Asst. demographer Office Population Rsch., Washington, 1942-43; social scientist USDA, Washington, 1943-45; assoc. dir. Chgo. Community Inventory, U. Chgo., 1947-50; social scientist Social Sci. Rsch. Coun., N.Y.C., 1950-51, rsch. grantee, 1953-55, pres., 1972-79; rsch. assoc. Bur. Applied Social Rsch. Columbia U., 1950-51, lectr. sociology, 1951-52, vis. prof., 1969-71; social scientist UN, N.Y.C., 1951-52; rsch. assoc., lectr. sociology UCLA, 1955-61; assoc. rsch. sociologist, lectr. Sch. Nursing U. Calif., 1957-61; sociologist, exec. assoc. Russell Sage Found., N.Y.C., 1961-72; vis. prof. U. Calif., Santa Barbara, 1971; dir. Equitable Life Assurance Soc., Mobil Corp., H.J. Heinz Co. Author: (with L. Wirth) Chicago Community Fact Book, 1949, America's Children, 1958, (with R.A. Glazier) Pupils and Schools in N.Y.C., 1965; editor: (with W.E. Moore) Indicators of Social Change, Concepts and Measurements, 1968, Family Economic Behavior, 1973; contbr. (with W.E. Moore) articles to profl. jours. Bd. dirs. Colby-Sawyer Coll., 1979-85, UN Rsch. Inst. for Social Devel., 1973-79; trustee Rockefeller Found., 1978-85, Nat. Opinion Rsch. Ctr., 1980-87, Inst. East-West Security Studies, 1984-88, Am. assembly, 1976-95. William Rainey Harper fellow U. Chgo., 1945-47. Fellow Am. Acad. Arts and Scis., Am. Sociol. Assn., Am. Statis. Assn.; mem. AAAS, U. Chgo. Alumni Assn. (Profl. Achievement award), Sociol. Rsch. Assn. (pres. 1971-72), Coun. on Fgn. Rels., Am. Assn. Pub. Opinion Rsch., Ea. Sociol. Soc., Internat. Sociol. Assn., Internat. Union Sci. Study of Population, Population Assn. Am. (2d v.p. 1970-71), Inst. of Medicine (chmn. program com. 1976-77), Cosmopolitan Club. Home and Office: 630 Park Ave New York NY 10021-6544

SHELDON, INGRID KRISTINA, mayor; b. Ann Arbor, Mich., Jan. 30, 1945; d. Henry Ragnvald and Virginia Schmidt (Clark) Blom; m. Clifford George Sheldon, June 18, 1966; children: Amy Elizabeth, William David. BS, Eastern Mich. U., 1966; MA, U. Mich., 1970. Cert. tchr., Mich. Tchr. Livonia (Mich.) Pub. Schs., 1966-67, Ann Arbor Pub. Schs., 1967-68; bookkeeper Huron Valley Tennis Club, Ann Arbor, 1978—; acct. F.A. Black Co., Ann Arbor, 1984-88; coun. mem. Ward II City of Ann Arbor, 1988-92, mayor, 1993—; chair Housing Bd. Appeals, Ann Arbor, 1988-91; chair fin. and budget com. S.E. Mich. Coun. Govts. Mem. Huron Valley Child Guidance Clinic, Ann Arbor, 1984—, Ann Arbor Hist. Found., 1985—, Parks Adv. Commn., 1987-92, Ann Arbor Planning Commn., 1988-89; excellence com. Ann Arbor Pub. Schs. reorgn., 1985; treas. SOS Cmty. Crisis Ctr., Ypsilanti, Mich., 1987-93; precinct ward city vice-chair Ann Arbor Rep. City Com., 1978—. Recipient Community Svc. award Ann Arbor Jaycees, 1980; AAUW fellowship, 1982. Mem. Mich. Mcpl. League (del. 1989—), Ann Arbor Women's City Club (chair endowment com. 1989-90, fin. com. 1987-90, treas.), Rotary (dir. Ann Arbor chpt.), Kappa Delta Pi, Alpha Omnicron Pi. Republican. Methodist. Home: 1416 Folkstone Ct Ann Arbor MI 48105-2848

SHELET, DAWN ARDELLE, financial analyst; b. Lac La Biche, Alberta, Can., Feb. 23, 1954; d. Laura Myrtle (Gould) Thacher; m. Paul Buettiker, Aug. 30, 1983. Student, McMaster U., Hamilton, Ontario, Can., 1976-78, B of Commerce (with honours), 1986; MBA, U. Miami, 1988. Mktg. rsch. asst. U. Miami Mktg. Dept., Coral Gables, Fla., 1986-87; fin. mgmt. intern Am. Express TRS Inc., Latin Am. Hdqrs., Coral Gables, Fla., 1987; internat. law rsch. asst. U. Miami Bus. Law Dept., Coral Gables, 1987-88; fin. analyst mktg. Eastern Air Lines Hdqrs., Miami, 1988-89; fin. planning systems analyst Am. Airlines Hdqrs., Dallas, 1989-90, fin. analyst internat., 1990-93, sr. bus. analyst, 1993—. Fund raising coord. United Way, Dallas-Ft. Worth Airport, 1989, 90, 91, 93, 94. Recipient U. Miami Grad. scholarship, 1986, 87, 88, Fees scholarship McMaster U., 1977; named to Dean's Honours list McMaster U., 1976, 77, 84, 85, 86. Mem. AMR Mgmt. Club (sec. 1991, treas. 1990-91, dir. 1992-93, v.p. 1994-95), Internat. Bus. Assn. (treas. 1986-87), Beta Gamma Sigma.

SHELEY, JEAN H., elementary school educator; b. Sycamore, Ill., Jan. 2, 1941; d. Ivan N. and Betty M. (Schaub) S. BS in Edn., No. Ill. U., 1963; postgrad., U. Colo., summer 1965, U. Wash., summers 1970,76, Elmhurst (Ill.) Coll., summer 1993. Cert. elem. tchr., Ill. Elem. tchr. Sterling (Ill.) Pub. Schs., 1963-71, Bamboo River Acad., Borneo, Indonesia, 1971-73, Wheaton (Ill.) Christian Grammar Sch., 1973—. Mem. Assn. Christian Schs. Internat. Baptist.

SHELLEY, CAROLE AUGUSTA, actress; b. London, Aug. 16, 1939; came to U.S., 1964; d. Curtis and Deborah (Bloomstein) S.; m. Albert G. Woods, July 26, 1967 (dec.). Student, Arts Ednl. Sch., 1943-56, Prepatory Acad. Royal Acad. Dramatic Art, 1956-57; studies with Iris Warren. Studied with Iris Warren and Eileen Thorndike; Trustee Am. Shakespeare Theatre., 1974-82. Appeared in revues, films, West End comedies, including Mary Mary at the Globe Theatre; first appeared as Gwendolyn Pigeon in stage, film and TV versions of The Odd Couple, Absurd Person Singular; The Norman Conquests (L.A. Drama Critics Circle award 1975); appeared as Rosalind in As You Like It, as Regan in King Lear, as Neville in She Stoops to Conquer, Stratford, Ont., Can., 1972, as Mrs. Margery Pinchwife in The Country Wife, Am. Shakespeare Festival, Stratford, Conn., 1973, as Nora in A Doll's House, Goodman Theatre, Chgo., as Ann in Man and Superman, as Lena in Misalliance, Zita in Grand Hunt; appeared at Shaw Festival, 1977, 80, Stepping Out, 1986 (Tony nomination 1986), Broadway Bound, 1987-88; appeared in: The Play's the Thing, Bklyn. Acad. Music, 1978; played Eleanore in stage prodn. Lion in Winter, 1987; other stage appearances include Nat. Co. of The Royal Family (L.A. Drama Citics Circle award 1977), The Elephant Man (Outer Critics Circle award 1978-79 season, Tony award for best actress 1978-79 season), What the Butler Saw, 1989; appeared inaugural season, Robin Phillips Grand Theatre Co., London, Ont., Can., 1983-84, Broadway and Nat. Co. of Noises Off, 1985, Waltz of the Toreadors, 1986, Oh Coward, 1986-87 ; appeared as Kate in Broadway Bound by Neil Simon The Nat. Co. and L.A. Premiere, 1987-88; played Lettice in Lettice and Lovage Globe Theatre, London, 1989-90, Frosine in The Miser, 1990, Cabaret Verboten, 1991, The Destiny of Me, 1992-93, Later Life, 1993 (Outer Critics nominee), Richard II, 1994, London Suite (Neil Simon) 1995, N.Y. Shakespeare Festival, Show Boat, 1995; films include: The Boston Strangler, The Odd Couple, The Super, 1990, Devlin, 1991, Quiz Show, 1993, The Road to Wellville, 1993; created: voice characters in Walt Disney films Robin Hood, The Aristocats. Recipient Obie Award for Twelve Dreams N.Y. Shakespeare Festival, 1982. Jewish. Office: care Duva-Flack Assocs Inc 200 W 57th St New York NY 10019-3211

SHELLHORN, RUTH PATRICIA, landscape architect; b. L.A., Sept. 21, 1909; d. Arthur Lemon and Lodema (Gould) S.; m. Harry Alexander Kueser, Nov. 21, 1940. Student dept. landscape architecture, Oreg. State Coll., 1927-30; grad. landscape architecture program, Cornell U. Coll. Architecture, 1933. Pvt. practice landscape architecture, various cities Calif., 1933—; exec. cons. landscape architect Bullocks Stores, Calif., 1945-78, Fashion Sqs. Shopping Ctrs., Calif., 1958-78, Marlborough Sch., L.A., 1968—, El Camino Coll., Torrance, Calif., 1970-78, Harvard Sch., North Hollywood, Calif., 1974-90; cons. landscape architect, site planner Disneyland, Anaheim, Calif., 1955, U. Calif., Riverside Campus, 1956-64, numerous others, also numerous gardens and estates; landscape architect Torrance (Calif.) City Goals Com., 1969-70; cons. landscape architect City of Rolling Hills (Calif.) Community Assn., 1973-93. Contbr. articles to garden and profl. publs.; subject of Oct. 1967 issue Landscape Design & Constrn. mag. Named Woman of Year, Los Angeles Times, 1955, Woman of Year, South Pasadena-San Marino (Calif.) Bus. Profl. Women, 1955; recipient Charles Goodwin Sands medal, 1930-33, Landscape Architecture award of merit Calif. State Garden Clubs, 1984, 86, Horticulturist of the Yr. award So. Calif. Hort. Inst., numerous nat., state, local awards for excellence. Fellow Am. Soc. Landscape Architects (past pres. So. Calif. chpt.), Phi Kappa Phi, Kappa Kappa Gamma (Alumni Achievement award 1960). Home and Office: 362 Camino De Las Colinas Redondo Beach CA 90277-6435

SHELLY, CHRISTINE DEBORAH, foreign service officer; b. Pontiac, Mich., May 1, 1951; d. Chester Price and Margaret Alice (Neafie) S. BA cum laude, Vanderbilt U., 1973; MA, Tufts U., 1974, MA in Diplomacy, 1975. Fgn. affairs analyst Intelligence and Rsch. Bur. Dept. State, Washington, 1975-77, desk officer Near Eastern Affairs, 1977-79; fin. attache Am. Embassy Dept. State, Cairo, 1979-81; asst. v.p. BankAmerica Internat., N.Y.C., 1981-82; spl. asst. Near Eastern Affairs Dept. State, Washington, 1982-83; econ., polit. officer Am. Embassy Dept. State, Lisbon, Portugal, 1983-87; dep. econ. advisor U.S. Mission to NATO, Brussels, 1987-90, dep. cabinet dir. Sec. Gen., 1990-93; dep. spokesman, dep. asst. sec. pub. affairs Dept. State, Washington, 1993-95; mem. Sr. Exec. Seminar U.S. State Dept., 1995-96; min. counselor polit. affairs Am. Embassy, Ottawa, Ont., Can., 1996—. Office: US Embassy Ottawa (POL) PO Box 5000 Ogdensburg NY 13669-0430

SHELTON, BARBARA PAYNE, college department chairman; b. Arlington, Va., July 10, 1949; d. Conley Dallas and Juanita Ethel (Long) Payne; m. Gordon Burton Shelton, Aug. 22, 1970; children: Dianne, Wade, Drew. BA, Western Md. Coll., 1970; MSW, U. Pa., 1972; MEd, Towson State U., 1982; EdD, Nova U., 1993. Cert. advanced profl. tchr. Social worker Chgo. Comprehensive Care Ctrs., 1972-73, Carroll County Youth Svc. Bur., Westminster, Md., 1975; social work cons. Archdiocese of Balt., 1975-78; tchr. Brown Meml. Weekday Sch., Balt., 1979-84, Good Shepherd Sch., Ruxton, Md., 1984-89; divsn. chair edn. Villa Julie Coll., Stevenson, Md., 1986—. Mem. ASCD, Assn. Childhood Edn. Internat., Nat. Assn. Edn. Young Children, Assn. Assoc. Degree Early Childhood Educators (sec. 1994—), Assn. Tchr. Educators, Phi Delta Kappa. Office: Villa Julie Coll Greenspring Valley Rd Stevenson MD 21153-9999

SHELTON, BESSIE ELIZABETH, school system administrator; b. Lynchburg, Va.; d. Robert and Bessie Ann (Plenty) Shelton; B.A. (scholar), W.Va. State Coll., 1958; student Northwestern U., 1953-55, Ind. U., 1956; M.S., SUNY, 1960; diploma Profl. Career Devel. Inst., 1993. Young adult libr. Bklyn. Pub. Libr., 1960-62; asst. head cen. ref. div. Queens Borough Pub. Libr., Jamaica, N.Y., 1962-65; instructional media specialist Lynchburg (Va.) Bd. Edn., 1966-74; ednl. research specialist, 1974-77; ednl. media assoc. Allegany County Bd. Edn., Cumberland, Md., 1977—. Guest singer Sta. WLVA, 1966—, WLVA-TV Christmas concerts, 1966—;cons. music and market rsch. Mem. YWCA, Lynchburg, 1966—, Fine Arts Ctr., Lynchburg, 1966—; ednl. adv. bd., nat. research bd. Am. Biog. Inst.; mem. U.S. Congl. Adv. Bd., USN Nat. Adv. Coun.; amb. goodwill Lynchburg, Va., 1986. Named to Nat. Women's Hall of Fame. Mem. AAUW, NEA, NAFE, Md. Tchrs. Assn., Allegany County Tchrs. Assn., Va. Edn. Assn., State Dept. Sch. Librarians, Internat. Entertainers Guild, Music City Songwriters Assn., Vocal Artists Am., Internat. Clover Poetry Assn., Internat. Platform Assn., Nat. Assn. Women Deans, Adminstrs. and Counselors, Intercontinental Biog. Assn., World Mail Dealers Assn., N.Am. Mailers Exch., Am. Assn. Creative Artists, Am. Biog. Inst. Research Assn., Tri-State Community Concert Assn. Pi Delta Phi, Sigma Delta Pi. Contbr. poems to various publs. Democrat. Baptist. Clubs: National Travel, Gulf Travel. Home: PO Box 187 Cumberland MD 21501-0187

SHELTON, DOROTHY DIEHL REES, lawyer; b. Manila, Sept. 16, 1935; came to U.S., 1945; d. William Walter John and Hedwig (Glienecke) Diehl; m. Charles W. Rees, Jr., June 15, 1957 (div. 1971); children: Jane Rees Stebbins, John B., Anne Rees Slack, Esq., David C., Esq.; m. Thomas C. Shelton, Mar. 4, 1977 (dec.). BA in Music, Stanford Univ., 1957; JD, Western State Univ. Coll. Law, 1976. Bar: Calif. 1977, U.S. Dist. Ct. (so. dist.) Calif. 1977. Pvt. practice, San Diego, 1977—. Mem. ABA, Calif. State Bar, Calif. Attys. for Criminal Justice, San Diego County Bar Assn., Consumer Attys. San Diego, Stanford U. Alumni Assn., Jr. League San Diego, Gt. Pyrenees Club Am., Dachshund Club Am., Nu Beta Epsilon. Roman Catholic. Office: 110 W C St Ste 812 San Diego CA 92101-3906

SHELTON, ELIZABETH COLLEY, social worker; b. Atlanta, Ga., Mar. 26, 1920; d. John Edmonds and Bess (Hollowell) Colley; m. Charles Bascom Shelton Jr., Oct. 22, 1940 (dec. Febr. 1990); children: Charles III, Elizabeth Colley Case, Rosser Edmonds. Attended, Sweet Briar (Va.) Coll., 1937-40; BA in Sociology, U. Tenn., Chattanooga, 1963; postgrad., U. of the South, Sewanee, Tenn., 1990-96. Caseworker Hamilton County Family Svcs., Chattanooga, 1970-72; caseworker prin. Fulton County Dept. of Family and Children Svcs., Atlanta, Ga., 1973—; mem. bd. dirs. Midtown Assist. Ctr., Atlanta, 1988—. Sustainer Jr. League of Atlanta, 1946—. Mem. Ga. Conf. on Social Welfare (bd. dirs. 1993-96), Ga. County Welfare Assn., Daus. of the King, Svc. and Prayer Group, Soc. Companions of Holy Cross, Symphony and Alliance Theater. Republican. Episcopalian. Home: 643 Grove Pky Marietta GA 30067 Office: Fulton County Dept Family & Children Svcs 84 Walton St Atlanta GA 30303

SHELTON, LESLIE HABECKER, adult literacy program director; b. Lancaster, Pa., Feb. 15, 1948; d. William Powell and Mary Louise (Habecker) S. BS in Health and Phys. Edn., West Chester U., 1970; MA in Student Pers. Work, U. Iowa, 1972; cert. in graphic design, U. Calif., Santa Cruz, 1980; postgrad., Union Inst., 1996—. Cert. cmty. coll. instr., Calif., tchr., counselor, Iowa, tchr., Pa. Student devel. specialist U. Maine, Farmington, 1972-74; rsch. asst. career counseling U. Colo., Boulder, 1974-75; coord. student activities Iowa Lakes C.C., Estherville, 1975-76, coord. counseling svcs., 1976-78; career counselor, apt. mgr. Loyola Marymount U., L.A., 1978-79; exec. dir. Am. Cancer Soc. Monterey, Calif., 1979-82; patient svcs. coord. Am. Cancer Soc. San Mateo County, Calif., 1982-85; dir. Project READ South San Francisco Pub. Libr., 1985—. Author: Honoring Diversity: A Multidimensional Learning Model for Adults, 1991, The Dinner Buffet Approach to Learner Support, 1994; illustrator: The Tree Deva. Facilitator, moderator Nat. Issues Forums, South San Francisco, 1987-94; cons., co-creator Easy Reader Voter Guide New Reader Coun. San Francisco Bay Area, 1994; founding bd. dirs. Salinas Valley (Calif.) Hosp. Assn., 1979-81; c.c. rep. Iowa Alliance for Arts in Edn., 1977-78. Grant honoree AAUW, 1989; named one of Outstanding Young Women Am., 1979; Literacy Leader fellow Nat. Inst. Literacy, 1995-96. Mem. Calif. Libr. Assn. (coun. rep. 1991-95, chair literacy chpt. 1988-92), Bay Area Libr. Literacy Program (chair 1987, 88, 92), New Reader Coun. Bay Area (staff coord. 1989-96), AAUW (chair edn. San Bruno br. 1988), North County Literacy Coun. (chair 1986-94, coord. Calif. statewide adult learner conf. 1996). Office: Project Read South San Francisco Libr 840 W Orange Ave South San Francisco CA 94080

SHELTON, MURIEL MOORE, religious education administrator; b. Freeport, N.Y., May 29, 1921; d. Samuel Talbott and Agnes Jerolean (Trigg) Payne; m. Ernest William Moore, May 29, 1944 (dec. Apr. 2, 1978); children: Diana Moore Williams, David E. Moore, Cathi Moore Mount, Douglas L. Moore; m. Malcolm Wendell Shelton, Aug. 9, 1987. AB, Eastern Nazarene Coll., 1942; MusM, U. Tex., 1966. Cert. educator gen. and choral music, English, Tex., Tenn., Ark., Kans. Music dir. Coll. Ave. United Meth. Ch., Manhattan, Kans., 1969-71, Cen. United Meth. Ch., Lawrence, Kans., 1971-75, First United Meth. Ch., Horton, Kans., 1975-78; dir. Christian edn. St. Mark's United Meth. Ch., Bethany, Okla., 1980—; chmn. bd. dirs. Northwest Food Pantry, Oklahoma City, 1987-88; rep. St. mark's United Meth. Ch. Labor Link Ctr., 1989—; lectr. in field. Contbr. articles to quar. mags.; author: Song of Joy, 1985, Promises of Good, 1989, Healing in His Wings, 1992. Mem. Christian Educators' Fellowship. Home: 6404 NW 35th St Bethany OK 73008-4136 Office: St Mark's United Meth Ch 8140 NW 36th St Bethany OK 73008-3526

SHELTON, SLOANE, actress; b. Hahira, Ga., Mar. 14, 1934; d. Clarence Duffie and Ruth Evangeline (Davis) S. Student, Berea Coll., 1955; honors diploma, Royal Acad. Dramatic Art, London, 1959. Mem. O'Neill Found., Waterford, Conn., 1981-83, 85, 89, 91, 94; mem. theater panel N.Y. State Coun. on the Arts, 1979-81. Producer: (with Kevin Brownlow and Norma Millay Ellis) (documentary film) Millay at Steepletop, 1976; appearances in Broadway plays include: I Never Sang for My Father, Sticks & Bones, The Runner Stumbles, The Shadow Box, Orpheus Descending, Passione, Open Admissions; films include: All That Jazz, All the President's Men, Tiger Warsaw, Running on Empty, Jacknife, Lean on Me. Pres. Berrillz Kerr Found., N.Y.C., 1993-96. Mem. SAG, AFTRA, Actors Equity Assn., Actors Fund Am. Democrat.

SHELTON, STEPHANI, broadcast journalist, consultant; b. Boston; d. Phil and Babette (Belloff) Saltman; m. Frank Herold. BS, Boston U. Reporter, news broadcaster Sta. WPAT, Paterson, N.J., 1972-73; corr. CBS News, N.Y.C., 1973-84; news corr. WWOR-TV, N.Y.C., 1984-88; corr., anchor Fin. News Network, N.Y.C., 1989-91; ind. broadcast journalist, producer, cons., 1991—; freelance reporter Sta. WPIX-TV, 1991-95, Sta. WNBC-TV, 1993—; freelance radio documentary writer Westinghouse Group W Broadcasting, N.Y.C., 1970-73. Recipient Peabody award, 1972, N.J. Best Spot News award AP, 1987, 88, N.J. Working Press award, 1992, 93, 94; Emmy nominee, 1994-95. Mem. Radio and TV Working Press Assn. (v.p. 1985—), Soc. Profl. Journalists, Radio and TV News Dirs. Assn., N.Y.C. Press Club.

SHELTON-MOORE, ALICIA, marketing assistant; b. Chgo., Jan. 11, 1957; d. Wilbert Olesta (Dillon) Shelton; m. Gary Vernon Moore, June 16, 1984. BA in Comms., Trinity Coll., Deerfield, Ill., 1990. Supr. State of Ill., Chgo., 1980-84; office mgr. T.E.D.S., Deerfield, Ill., 1984-90; systems adminstr. Hyatt Deerfield, 1991-93; mktg. asst. Hyatt Hotel Corp., Chgo., 1993-95, Lakehurst Mall, Waukegan, Ill., 1995—. Democrat. Baptist. Office: Lakehurst Mall 199 Lakehurst Rd Waukegan IL 60085

SHEMORRY, CORINNE JOYNES, marketing executive; b. Rolla, N.D., Jan. 24, 1920; d. William H. and Edna Ruth (Conn) Joynes; children: Gay, Jan. Publisher, Williston (N.D.) Plains Reporter, 1953-78; mktg. dir. Western Credit Union, 1979-91; journalist, lectr., cons., author, reporter. Recipient numerous awards in journalism on state and nat. level, including Outstanding Woman in Journalism in N.D., 1987, 1st Place Golden Mirror award Credit Union Nat. Assn., Rough Rider Gov.'s Individual Community Pride Leadership award N.D. Gov. George A. Sinner, 1988. Chmn. Rough Rider Internat. Art Show & Auction, 1985—. Mem. N.D. Press Assn., N.D. Press Women (past pres.), Nat. Press Women, Williston C. of C., NAFE, Fin. Mktg. Assn. (charter). Club: Bus. and Profl. Women's (past pres.). Home: 210 E 14th St PO Box 1030 Williston ND 58801

SHEN, RONGER, artist, educator; b. Shanghai, China, Nov. 11, 1942; came to U.S., 1984; d. Jianping and Huijun (Peng) S.; m. Yi Wu, Dec. 31, 1965; 1 child, Yan Wu. BA, Nat. Nanjing Acad. Arts, 1965. Dir. arts and crafts dept. Jiangsu Light Industry Bur., Nanjing, 1965-79; dir. Jiangsu Acad. Arts and Crafts, 1982—; profl. painter Jiangsu Acad. Traditional Chinese Painting, 1979—; pres. Qigong Ctr., Inc., N.Y., 1989—; Qigong cons. to dept. orthopedics Mt. Sinai Sch. Medicine, N.Y.C., 1991—, N.J. Med. Ctr. Pain Mgmt. Ctr., Newark, 1991; NIH approved rsch. project on Life Info. Pictures, Life Info. Rhythm and Qigong, 1993; dir. Assn. Modern Chinese Arts Inc., 1994—. Mem. Artists Assn. China (Jiangsu br.), Acad. Arts and Crafts China, Eastern Am. Qigong U.S. (chmn. 1991—). Home and Studio: 32-05 146th St Flushing NY 11354-3151

SHENOSKY, BLANCHE ANN, nursing administrator; b. Hazleton, Pa., Oct. 22, 1946; d. Joseph Anthony and Blanche Mame (Farace) Leotilo; m. Joseph Thomas Shenosky, Aug. 3, 1968; children: Joseph Thomas, Thomas Joseph. Nurse diploma, Hazleton State Hosp., 1967; BS, St. Joseph's Coll., 1986; MS in Human Resource Devel., Villanova U., 1991. RN, Pa., Md. Registered staff nurse pediatric unit Robert Packer Hosp., Sayre, Pa., 1969-75, registered staff nurse float pool, 1975-77, registered staff nurse psychiatric unit, 1977-79, asst. head nurse psychiatric unit, 1979-81; supervisor Colonial Manor Nursing and Rehab. Home, York, Pa., 1981-82; charge nurse Margaret E. Moul Cerebral Palsy Home, York, 1982-83; oncology nurse York Hosp., 1983-88; registered staff nurse medical and oncology unit The Good Samaritan Hosp., Balt., 1988-90; registered staff nurse nephrology unit Polyclinic Med. Ctr., Harrisburg, Pa., 1990-91; resident care coord. Jewish Convalescent and Nursing Home, Balt., 1992-93, dir. nursing, 1994-95; dir. nursing Balt. City Detention Ctr., 1993-94, Gundry Glass Hosp., Balt., 1995-96, Cmty. Based Alternatives and Initiatives, Balt., 1996—; home health nurse cons. Cmty. Based Alternatives & Initiatives, Balt. Co-author: Standardized Care Plans, 1993. Mem. Oncology Nursing Soc. Republican. Roman Catholic. Home: 8009E Greenspring Way Owings Mills MD 21117-5435 Office: Cmty Based Alts and Initiatives 7222 Ambassador Rd Baltimore MD 21244-9999

SHENTON, MARTHA ELIZABETH, research psychologist; b. Concord, N.H., Nov. 11, 1952; d. Enoch and Loretta Marie (Halle) S., m. George Santiccioli; 1 child, Jessica. AB, Wellesley Coll., 1973; MS, Tufts U., Medford, Mass., 1976; MA, Harvard U., 1981, PhD, 1984. Research fellow Mclean Hosp. Mailman Research Ctr., Belmont, Mass., 1979-84; lecturer Brandis U., Walton, Mass., 1984-85; post doctoral research fellow Harvard Med. Sch., Mass. Mental Health Ctr., Boston, 1984-86; instr. Harvard Med. Sch., VA Med. Ctr., Boston, 1986-88, 1986-88; asst. prof. psychology, dept. psychiatry Med. Sch. Harvard U., 1988-93, now assoc. prof psychology. Contbr. articles to profl. jours. Mem. Am. Psychol. Assn., Mass. Psychol. Assn., Phi Beta Kappa. Office: VA Med Ctr Dept Psychiatry 116A 940 Belmont St Cambridge MA 02140-1704

SHEPARD, ELAINE ELIZABETH, writer, lecturer; b. Olney, Ill.; d. Thomas J. and Bernice E. (Shadle) S.; m. Terry D. Hunt, Apr. 16, 1938; m. George F. Hartman, Oct. 1, 1943 (div. June 1958). Covered nat. polit. convs. for Stas. WTTG-TV and WINS, Chgo., 1952, 1956, polit. reporter for NANA and WINS, Chgo. and Los Angeles, 1960; reporter Congo rebellion for N.Am. Newspaper Alliance and N.Y. Mirror, 1960-61; corr. covering Pres. Eisenhower's Middle East, Far East and S. Am. tour, 1959-60; Vietnam corr. MBS, 1965-66; granted interviews with Khrushchev, Castro, Tito, Chou En-lai, Nasser, Shah of Iran, King Hussein, King Faisel, Duvalier, Lumumba, Chiang-Kai-Shek, Nehru, Menzies, John F. Kennedy, Richard M. Nixon, others; mem. White House Press Corps accompanying Pres. Nixon to, Austria, Iran, Poland, Moscow, 1972. Film and theater actress, Hollywood, N.Y.C., Europe, 1939-50, cover girl, John Robert Powers, 1939-43, under contract to, RKO and Metro-Goldwyn-Mayer, 1940-45, guest commentator for, Voice of Am.; contbr.: feature articles to various mags., including N.Y. News Sunday Mag, 1953—; columnist, contbg. editor: feature articles to various mags., including Nat. Cath. Press, 1969-74; author: Forgive Us Our Press Passes, 1962, The Doom Pussy, 1967, The Doom Pussy II, 1991. Recipient 2 citations for participating in armed helicopter assaults with 145th Aviation Bn. Vietnam. Mem. Screen Actors Guild, AFTRA, Actors Equity. Club: Overseas Press (N.Y.C.). Home: 12 E 62nd St New York NY 10021-7218

SHEPARD, JANIE RAY (J. R. SHEPARD), software development executive; b. Montebello, Calif., Feb. 23, 1954; d. George Allen and Ada Janette (Barrow) Ray; 1 child, April Lynn. Grad. high sch., Albany, Ga., 1972. Adminstrv. asst. to pres. FRC Office Products, Jacksonville, Fla., 1979-82; adminstrv. asst. to v.p. comml. lending Stockton Savs., Dallas, 1983-84; exec. sec. to v.p. ops. Metromedia Long Distance, Ft. Lauderdale, Fla., 1985-87; owner, pres. RaceCom, Inc., Ormond Beach, Fla., 1986—, ALAdvt., Ormond Beach, 1986— . Developer computer text file editing system and computer artificial intelligence; developer optical character recognition neural network software. Active Jacksonville and Dallas areas Girl Scouts U.S., 1980-96, Citrus Coun., 1996—; vol. co-chair Jazz Matazz, 1992-94, adv. coord., 1995, 96; chair Home for the Holidays Parade, City of Ormond Beach, 1995, 96. Mem. Ormond Beach C. of C. Democrat. Methodist. Home: 10 Cypress View Trl Ormond Beach FL 32174-8295 Office: RaceCom Inc PO Box 730955 Ormond Beach FL 32173

SHEPARD, KATHRYN IRENE, public relations executive; b. Tooele, Utah, Jan. 6, 1956; d. James Lewis and Glenda Verleen (Slaughter) Clark; m. Mark L. Shepard, June 5, 1976. BA in History, Boise State U., 1980. On-air writer Sta. KTTV, Channel 11, L.A., 1982-85; publicity dir. Hollywood (Calif.) C. of C., 1985-87; pres. Kathy Shepard Pub. Rels., Burbank and Portland, 1987-93; dir. public relations Las Vegas Hilton, 1993-94; dir. comms. Hilton Gaming, 1994-96; dir. corp. comms. Hilton Hotels Corp., 1996—; instr. pub. rels. ext. program UCLA, 1991-92. Contbr. articles to profl. publs. Mem. Publicity Club L.A. (pres. 1991-92, bd. dirs. 1987-91), Pub. Rels. Assn. Am., Women in Comms. Office: Hilton Hotels Corp PR Dept 9336 Civic Center Dr Beverly Hills CA 90210

SHEPARD, MIKKI MAUREEN ALLISON, personal care company executive; b. Queens, N.Y., May 12, 1951; d. George William and June Rita (Ferrary) S.; m. Tom C. Blankenheim, July 2, 1983; 1 child, Jeffrey Thomas. BA, U. Colo., 1982. Cert. real estate brokerage mgr. Employment counselor Centennial Personnel, Colorado Springs, Colo., 1977-78; ins. auditor Associated Ins. Utah, Colorado Springs, 1978-79; broker, co-owner TCB Realty and Investment Co., Inc., Colorado Springs, 1979-90; exec. NuSkin, Castles of Am., Inc., Colorado Springs, Colo., 1989—; speaker Nat. Assn. Realtors, Chgo., 1985—. Contbr. articles to Real Estate Today, Colo. Realtor News Communiqué, Gazette Telegraph. Pres. Christmas Unlimited, Colorado Springs, 1988, 89; campaign worker El Paso County Reps., Colorado Springs, 1977-78; mem. Realtors Polit. Action Com., Chgo., 1979—; mem. Profl. Women's Rep. Club, Colorado Springs, 1987. Served with USAF, 1970-74. Mem. Colo. Assn. Realtors (dir. 1988—), Colorado Springs Bd. Realtors (bd. dirs. 1981, 84, treas. 1985-86, sec. 1987-88, pres. 1989-90), Realtors Nat. Mktg. Inst., Women's Coun. Realtors (Colo. chpt. pres. 1989—, gov. 1990, Pikes Peak chpt. treas. 1984-85, pres. 1986-87, Woman of Yr. Pikes Peak chpt. 1986, Woman of the Yr. Colo. State chpt. 1990), Nat. Women's Coun. Realtors (leadership tng. grad. 1987, edn. chmn. 1987-88). Methodist. Office: Castles of Am Inc 3960 Weather Vane Dr Colorado Springs CO 80920

SHEPARD, SUE ANNETTE, director fund raising; b. Bridgewater, Iowa, Mar. 5, 1943; d. Gerald L. and Sarah Shirley (Sullivan) Campbell; m. Joe Willwerth Shepard, June 10, 1962 (div. May 1984); children: Jonathan Willwerth, Christopher Campbell. BME, Ind. U., 1965; cert. arts adminstrn., U. Wis., 1978; MA in Philanthropic Studies, Ind. U., Indpls., 1995. Cert. fund raising exec. Tchr. St. Dominics Sch., Northfield, Minn., 1970-73; adminstr. Northfield Arts Guild, 1976-85; co-founder Northfield Musical Theater, dir. devel. Waterloo (Iowa) Cmty. Playhouse, 1986-88; officer spl. svcs. devel. U. Minn. Found., Mpls., 1988-89; dir. devel. Inst. Agr., Forestry, Home Econ. U. Minn., St. Paul, 1989-95, dir. devel. Coll. Agr., Food, and Environ. Sci., 1995—. Soprano Dale Warland Singers, 8 recordings; major roles, 2 recordings Opera and Broadway comedy. Mem. Nat. Soc. Fund Raising Execs., Coun. for Advancement and Support of Edn., Nat. Planned Giving Coun., Minn. Planned Giving Coun. Office: Univ Minn 277 Cofy Hall 1420 Eckles Ave Saint Paul MN 55108

SHEPARD, SUZANNE V., English language educator; b. Montour Falls, N.Y., Mar. 4, 1958; d. William Henry III and A. Louisa (Stenberg) S.; m. Tredwell Burch Jr., May 29, 1982. BA in Music and Lit., Eisenhower Coll., Seneca Falls, N.Y., 1980; MA in English, Binghamton U., 1983, PhD in English, 1995. Tchg. asst. Binghamton U., N.Y., 1981-87, adj. prof., 1987; adj. prof. Broome Cmty. Coll., Binghamton, 1991-95, asst. prof., 1996—. Elder Presbyn. Ch., Binghamton, 1988—, lay preacher, 1993—; mem. Multicultural Reading Group, Binghamton, 1995—. Mem. Nat. Coun. Tchrs. English, Phi Kappa Phi. Presbyterian.

SHEPHERD, CYBILL, actress, singer; b. Memphis, Feb. 18, 1950; d. William Jennings and Patty Shobe (Micci) S.; m. David Ford, Nov. 19, 1978 (div.); 1 child, Clementine; m. Bruce Oppenheim, March 1, 1987; children: Molly Ariel and Cyrus Zachariah (twins). Student, Hunter Coll., 1969, Coll. of New Rochelle, 1970, Washington Sq. Coll., NYU, 1971, U. So. Calif., 1972, NYU, 1973. Appeared in motion pictures Last Picture Show, 1971, The Heartbreak Kid, 1973, Daisy Miller, 1974, At Long Last Love, 1975, Taxi Driver, 1976, Special Delivery, 1976, Silver Bears, 1977, The Lady Vanishes, 1978, Earthright, 1980, The Return, 1986, Chances Are, 1988, Texasville, 1990, Alice, 1990, Once Upon a Crime, 1992, Married to It, 1993; star TV series The Yellow Rose, 1983-84, Moonlighting, 1985-89, Cybill, 1994—; TV films include A Guide for the Married Woman, 1978, Secrets of a Married Man, 1984, Seduced, 1985, The Long Hot Summer, 1985, Which Way Home, 1991, Memphis, 1992 (also co-writer, co-exec. prodr.), Stormy Weathers, 1992, Telling Secrets, 1993, There Was a Little Boy, 1993; record albums include Cybill Does It To Cole Porter, 1974, Cybill and Stan Getz, 1977, Vanilla with Phineas Newborn, Jr, 1978; appeared in stage plays A Shot in the Dark, 1977, Picnic, 1980, Vanities, 1981. •

SHEPHERD, GILLIAN MARY, physician; b. Belfast, U.K., Mar. 12, 1948; came to U.S., 1957; d. John Thompson and Helen (Johnston) S.; m. Eduardo Goar Mestre, Aug. 4, 1973; children: Laura Elena, Cristina Alicia., Eduardo Goar. BA, Wheaton Coll., Norton, Mass., 1970, postgrad. Tufts U., 1970-73; MD, N.Y. Med. Coll., 1976. Diplomate Am. Bd. Internal Medicine, Am. Bd. Allergy and Immunology. Intern, resident Lenox Hill Hosp., N.Y.C., 1976-79; fellow in allergy and immunology N.Y. Hosp./Cornell Med. Sch., N.Y.C., 1979-81; assoc. prof. medicine Cornell U. Med. Coll., N.Y.C., 1988—, clin. assoc. prof. medicine, 1995—; assoc. attending physician N.Y. Hosp., N.Y.C.; cons. allergy and immunology dept. medicine Meml. Sloan-Kettering Cancer Ctr., N.Y.C., 1982—. Contbr. articles in field to profl. jours. Fellow ACP, Am. Acad. Asthma, Allergy and Immunology; mem. AAAS, Am. Fedn. for Clin. Research, Joint Coun. Allergy and Immunology, N.Y. Allergy Soc. (exec. com. 1982-94, pres. 1991-92), N.Y. County Med. Soc. Office: 235 E 67th St Ste 203 New York NY 10021

SHEPHERD, PAMELA JEAN, real estate agent, marketing professional; b. Salt Lake City, Apr. 24, 1953; d. Lloyd Edgard and Kathelyne (Fonnesbeck) Metcalf; m. Kevin Patrick Shepherd, June 11, 1977 (div. June 1992); children: Patrick David, Peter Michael. BS in Mass Comm., U. Utah, 1974. Lic. salesperson Va. Real Estate Bd. Asst. promotion mgr. Deseret News, Salt Lake City, 1974-75, staff writer, youth editor, 1975-78; assoc. editor Metro Mag., Norfolk, Va., 1978; feature writer Daily Press, Newport News, Va., 1978-81; freelance writer, photographer Yorktown, Va., 1983-91; pub. rels. coord. Va. Living Mus., Newport News, 1990-93; owner P.J. Comm., Yorktown, 1993-94; real estate agt. Long & Foster, Newport News, 1994—; mktg. coord. Philanthropic Rsch., Inc., Williamsburg, Va., 1994—. Cotnbr. articles to profl. publs. Social coord. Millside Homeowners Assn., Yorktown, 1986-90; Dare PTA historian Dare Elem., Yorktown, 1987-88; jr. EYC youth leader Episcopal Ch., Yorktown, 1993-94; social coord. Brandywine Homeowners Assn., Yorktown, 1995. Mem. NAFE, Va. Real Estate Bd. Lutheran. Office: Philanthropic Rsch Ste 200 1318 Jamestown Rd Williamsburg VA 23185

SHEPPARD, ALICE G., psychology educator, writer; b. San Jose, Calif., Feb. 11, 1945; d. Robert Doumens and Doris Edith (Mount) Groch; m. Robert John Klak, Dec. 19, 1982 (dec. July 1993); m. Gary McGregor Boone, May 19, 1995. BA, Mills Coll., 1966; MA, Clark U., 1968, PhD, 1971. Instr., asst. prof. Vassar Coll., Poughkeepsie, N.Y., 1970-73; asst. prof. Kalamazoo (Mich.) Coll., 1973-76; lectr. Calif. State U., Fresno, 1976-78; assoc. prof. Ea. Oreg. State Coll., La Grande, 1979-87; asst. prof. Bloomsburg (Pa.) U., 1987-90; asst. prof. SUNY, Geneseo, spring 1991, Fredonia, 1991-94; asst. prof. U. Maine, Presque Isle, 1995—. Author: Cartooning for Suffrage, 1994. Fellow NEH, 1988. Mem. Am. Psychol. Soc., Nat. Women's Studies Assn. Office: U Main 181 Main St Presque Isle ME 04769

SHEPPARD, AUDREY DIANE, government official, public affairs consultant; b. Newton, Mass., July 31, 1948; d. Jack N. and Annabelle (Tofias) S.; m. Charles E. Zeitlin, Oct. 7, 1990; children: Katherine Z. Duckers, Elizabeth Zeitlin. BA, Syracuse U., 1970. Legis. & press asst. to Pete Stark, Washington, 1973-75; polit. and public affairs cons. Rothstein/Buckley, Washington, 1975-77; polit. cons. Washington, 1977-81; polit. dir. Dem. Senatorial Campaign Com., Washington, 1981-87; cons., exec. dir. Internat. Inst. Women's Polit. Leadership, Washington, 1988-89; polit. & pub. affairs cons. Washington, 1990-93; asst. to sec. def. Pentagon, Washington, 1993; spl. asst. presdl. pers. White House, Washington, 1994; dep. dir. Office Women's Health FDA, Rockville, Md., 1994-95, acting dir., 1996—. Mem. nat. adv. bd. Ctr. Nat. Policy, Washington, 1991-93; bd. dirs. Personal PAC, Chgo., 1991-93; mem. Women's Issues Network, Chgo., 1991-93, Clinton/Gore Women's Steering Com., Washington, 1992, Ferraro for Senate Nat. Fin. Com., N.Y., 1992; creator Clinton/Gore Older Women's Program, 1992; mem. adv. bd. Nat. Osteoporosis & Related Bone Diseases Nat. Resource Ctr., 1995—. Office: FDA Office Women's Health 5600 Fishers Ln Rockville MD 20857

SHEPPARD, HELEN BLAIR, retired educator; b. West Somerville, Mass., Mar. 16, 1927; d. Donald and Margaret (Burrett) Gunn; m. David Winston Sheppard, June 21, 1952;; children: Cheryl, Cynthia Sandy. Assoc. in Comml. Sci., Boston U., 1954; AB, Defiance Coll., 1966; MAT, W.Va. Wesleyan Coll., 1984. Cert. Mass Dental Assts. Cert. Bd. Tchr. Grove City Schs., Columbus, Ohio, Reynolds Dist. Schs., Greenville, Pa., Upshur Bd.

Edn., Buckhannon, W.Va.; mem. staff Learning Ctr., W.Va. Wesleyan Coll., Buckhannon; part-time instr. edn. W.Va. Wesleyan Coll., Buckhannon, spring, 1993. Mem. AAUW, W.Va. Profl. Educators, Delta Kappa Gamma. Address: 41 Boggess St Buckhannon WV 26201-2144

SHEPPERD, JONI L., elementary school educator; b. N.Y.C., Nov. 12, 1946; d. Frank L. and Ethel M. (Pellacani) Marfe; m. Robert A. Shepperd, Oct. 26, 1985. BA in Elem. Edn., King's Coll., 1993. 6th grade tchr. Sacred Heart Elem. Sch., Wilkes-Barre, Pa., 1993—; owner, pres. Manhattan Assistance Rsch. Svcs., N.Y.C. Mem. Internat. Reading Assn., Keystone State Reading Assn., Luzerne County Reading Coun., Kappa Delta Pi. Democrat. Roman Catholic. Home: 188 Market St Pittston PA 18640

SHEPPERD, SUSAN ABBOTT, special education educator; b. Pekin, Ill., May 12, 1942; d. Robert Fred and Martha Mae (Abbott) Belville; m. Thomas Eugene Shepperd, Oct. 7, 1960; children: Scott Thomas, Allison Marie Shepperd-Henry, Michele Lea. BA, Maryville Coll., 1990; MEd, U. Mo., 1994. Cert. elem. edn. tchr. grades 1-8, spl. reading tchr. grades K-12. Resource tchr. reading grades K-8 St. Joseph Sch., Ardiocese of St. Louis, Cottleville, Mo., 1990—. Mem. Pi Lambda Theta (pres. 1992-94), Assn. in Edn. (Gamma Zeta chpt.), Phi Kappa Phi, Delta Epsilon Sigma. Episcopalian. Home: 15977 Chamfers Farm Rd Chesterfield MO 63005-4717 Office: St Joseph Sch Motherhead Rd Cottleville MO 63304

SHER, LINDA ROSENBERG, lawyer; b. Chgo., May 16, 1938; d. Sidney and Rebecca Rosenberg; B.A., U. Chgo., 1959; LL.B., Yale U., 1962; m. Stanley O. Sher, Aug. 11, 1963; children—Jeremy Jay, Hellyn Sue. Admitted to D.C. bar, 1962; counsel constl. rights subcom. Senate Judiciary Com., 1962-64; atty. NLRB, 1964-77, asst. gen. counsel supreme ct. br., 1977-93, acting assoc. gen. counsel, 1994-95, assoc. gen. counsel, 1995—. Office: NLRB 1099 14th St NW Washington DC 20005-3419

SHER, PATRICIA RUTH, state legislator; b. Washington, June 19, 1931; d. Harry Eugene Hesse and Beatrice Ruth (Whitcomb) Cooper; m. William Sher, Feb. 13, 1955; children: Mark Stephen, Hunter Neal, Valerie Lynn, Tod David. Student, Montgomery Coll.; BS in Human Ecology and Applied Design, U. Md., 1983. Mem. House of Dels., Annapolis, Md., 1979-90, dep. majority whip, 1987-89, dep. majority leader, 1989-90, vice-chair task force to study deaths resulting from bldg. fires, 1985-88, mem. interdept. com. mandated health ins. benefits, spl. com. drug and alcohol abuse, chair nat. legis. task force fire gas toxicity, 1983-85; mem. Md. State Senate, 1991—; mem. finance com., state employees' health ins. adv. coun., spl. joint com. legis. data sys., 1991-94. Founder Friends of RAP-Regional Addiction Prevention, 1971; mem. Com. to Repeal Blue Laws, 1976; mem. adv. coun. Drug Abuse, 1972-78; Dem. precinct chair, 1966-78. Recipient Ann London Scott Meml. award, Md. NOW, 1989, Pres. Recognition award Md. Soc./AIA, 1991, Md. Senate Legis. Law Enforcement Friend of Yr. award Fraternal Order of Police, 1991, Child Advocacy award Md. chpt. Am. Acad. Pediat., 1992, Betty Tyler Pub. Affairs award Planned Parenthood Md., 1992. Democrat. Office: 2905 Barker St Silver Spring MD 20910-1004

SHER, PHYLLIS KAMMERMAN, pediatric neurology educator; b. N.Y.C., Aug. 13, 1944; d. Seymour K. and Shirley (Parmit) Kammerman; m. Kenneth Swaiman, Oct. 6, 1985. BA, Brandeis U., 1966; MD, U. Miami, 1970. Diplomate Am. Bd. Psychiatry and Neurology. Pediatric intern Montefiore Hosp., Bronx, N.Y., 1970-71; resident in neurology U. Miami (Fla.) Med. Sch., 1971-73, fellow in pediatric neurology, 1973-75, asst. prof. neurology, 1975-80; rsch. assoc. NIH, Bethesda, Md., 1980-83; asst. prof. neurology and pediatrics U. Minn. Med. Sch., Mpls., 1983-86, assoc. prof., 1986—; dir. Ripple program United Cerebral Palsy Found., Miami, 1972-75; chmn. med. svcs. com. 5-yr. action plan State of Fla., 1975; cons. Minn. Epilepsy Program for Children, 1983-85; vis. prof. Japanese Soc. Child Neurology, 1985, Chinese Child Neurology Ctr., 1989, Hong Kong Soc. Child Neurology & Devel. Pediat., 1995. Mem. editl. bd. Pediatric Neurology, 1991—, Brain and Devel., 1994—; contbr. articles and abstracts to med. jours., chpts. to books. Comdr. USPHS, 1980-83. Fellow United Cerebral Palsy Found., 1972-73; rsch. grantee Gillette Children's Hosp., U. Minn. Grad. Sch., Viking Children's Fund, Minn. Med. Found. Fellow Am. Neurol. Assn., Am. Acad. Neurology; mem. Child Neurology Soc. (exec. com., councillor 1993-95), Upper Midwest Child Neurology Soc., So. Clin. Neurology Soc. Office: U Minn Med Sch Divsn Pediat Neurology 1821 University Ave Ste W 188 Saint Paul MN 55104

SHERARD, BARBARA TROUSDALE, medical laboratory technologist; b. San Francisco, Apr. 4, 1924; d. Mallows Edward and Edna (Herbert) Trousdale; m. James Raymond Sherard, Oct. 6, 1950; children: Lynn Sherard Stuhr, Nan Rutledge, Mary Sherard, Paul Sherard, Alice Sherard. BA in Biochemistry, U. Calif., Berkeley, 1946; tchg. cert. secondary gen. sci., biology & chemistry, Adelphi U., 1972. Lic. med. technologist, Calif.; lic. tchr., N.Y. Rsch. technician Mt. Zion Hosp., San Francisco, Calif., 1946-47; med. technologist Seguoia Hosp., Redwood City, Calif., 1948-52; substitute tchr. sci. Sachem, Sayville, Bayport Sch., Suffolk County, N.Y., 1972-87. Mental health adv. bd. Suffolk County, N.Y., 1968-74; mem. Health Systems Agy. Suffolk Coun., 1975-80; bd. dirs. Planned Parenthood of Suffolk County, 1983—, pres. 1985-89; pres. Suffolk Abortion Rights Coun., Suffolk County, 1994-96; com. S.C. Dem. com., 1980—. Congregationalist. Home: 8 Ivy Hill Rd Oakdale NY 11769

SHERBELL, RHODA, artist, sculptor; b. Bklyn.; d. Alexander and Syd (Steinberg) S.; m. Mervin Honig, Apr. 28, 1956; 1 child, Susan. Student, Art Students League, 1950-53, Bklyn. Mus. Art Sch., 1959-61; also; pvt. study art, Italy, France, Eng., 1956. cons., coun. mem. Emily Lowe Gallery, Hofstra U., Hempstead, N.Y., 1978, pres., 1989-81, instr., 1991—, life mem. bd. friends, pres. bd. trustees; tchr. instr. Mus. Modern Art, N.Y.C., 1959, NAD Art Sch., N.Y.C., 1985—, Art Students League, N.Y.C., 1980—. Exhibited one-woman shows Country Art Gallery, Locust Valley, N.Y., Bklyn. Mus. Art Sch., 1961, Adelphi Coll., A.C.A. Galleries, N.Y.C., 1967, Capricorn Galleries, Rehn Gallery, Washington, 1968, Huntington Hartford Mus., N.Y.C., 1969, Morris (N.J.) Mus. Arts and Scis., 1980, Bergen Mus. Arts and Scis., N.J., 1984, William Benton Mus., Conn., 1985, Palace Theatre of the Arts, Stamford, Conn., Bronx Mus. Arts, 1986, Hofstra Mus. Art, L.I., N.Y., 1989, 90, County Art Gallery, N.Y.C., 1990; one-woman retrospective at N.Y. Cultural Ctr., 1970, Nat. Arts Collection, Washington, 1970, Montclair Mus. of Art, 1976, Nat. Art Mus. of Sport, 1977, Jewish Mus. of N.Y.C., 1980, Black History Mus., 1981, Queens Mus., 1981, 82, Nat. Portrait Gallery, Washington, 1981, 82, Bronx Mus., N.Y., Bklyn. Mus., Mus. Modern Art, N.Y.C., Country Art Gallery, 1990, Port Washington Library, Nat. Mus. Am. Art, The Smithsonian Instn., 1982, Nat. Acad. Design, N.Y.C., 1984, 89, Castle Gallery Mus., N.Y.C., 1987, Emily Lowe Mus., N.Y.C., 1987, Heckshire Mus., N.Y.C., 1989, Islip Art Mus., N.Y.C., 1989, Gallery Emanuel, N.Y.C., 1993, Sundance Gallery, Bridgehampton, N.Y., CASTIRON Gallery SoHo Show, 1995, Nat. Acad. Design Exhibition, 1995, Sundance Gallery, Bridgehampton, N.Y., 1995; exhibited group shows Heckscher Mus., 1989, Islip Mus., 1989, Nassau Dept. Recreation and Parks, 1989, Downtown Gallery, N.Y.C., Maynard Walker Gallery, N.Y.C., F.A.R. Gallery, N.Y.C., Provincetown Art Assn., Detroit Inst. Art, Pa. Acad. Fine Arts, Bklyn. and L.I. Artists Show, Old Westbury Gardens Small Sculpture Show, Audubon Artists, NAD, Allied Artists, Heckscher Mus., Nat. Art Mus. Sports, Mus. Arts and Scis., L.A., Am. Mus. Natural History, Post of History Mus., 1987, 88, Caslte Gallery Mus., N.Y.C., 1987, Emiloy Lowe Gallery Mus., N.Y., 1987, Bronx Mus. Arts, 1987, Chgo. Hist. Soc., Mus. of Modern Art, N.Y.C., 1988, Sands Point Mus., L.I., NAD, Hofstra Mus., 1990, Nat. Mus. Sports Art, 1991, Indpls. Art Mus., Phoenix Mus. Art, Corcoran Mus. Art, Washington, IBM, N.Y.C., Fire House Gallery Mus. Nassau Cmty. Coll., L.I., 1992, Nat. Arts Club Ann. Exhbn., 1992, Sports in Art From Am. Mus. at IBM, N.Y.C., 1992, Nat. Sculpture Soc. and The Regina A Quick Ctr. for The Arts Fairfield U.Centennial Anniversary Exbn., 1993, Mus. Modern Art, N.Y.C., Nat. Sculpture Soc. 100 Anniversary Exhbn., 1993, Italy, 1994, Provincetown Assn. and Art Mus., 1993, Kyoto (Japan) Mus. Sculpture Guild, 1993, Nat. Sculpture Soc. Exhbn. in Italy, Lucca, 1994, Sculptures Guild, N.Y.C., 1994-95, Cline Gallery, Santa Fe, 1995; represented permanent collections, Stony Brook Hall of Fame, William Benton Mus. Art, Colby Coll. Mus., Oklahoma City Mus., Montclair (N.J.) Mus., Schonberg Library Black Studies, N.Y.C., Albany State Mus., Hofstra U., Bklyn. Mus., Colby Coll. Mus., Nat. Arts Collection, Nat. Portrait Gallery, Smithsonian Instn., Baseball Hall of Fame Cooperstown, N.Y., Nassau Community Coll., Hofstra U. Emily Lowe Gallery, Art Students League, Jewish Mus., Queens Mus., Black History Mus., Nassau County Mus., Stamford Mus. Art and Nature Ctr., Jericho Pub. Library, N.Y., African-Am. Mus., Hempstead, N.Y., 1988, Stamford (Conn.) Mus. Art and Scis., Silvermine Artists North East exhibition, 1989, Nassau Community Coll. Fire House Gallery Exbn., 1992, Nat. Portrait Gallery Smithsonian Instn.; also pvt. collections, TV shows, ABC, 1968, 81; ednl. TV spl. Rhoda Sherbell-Woman in Bronze, 1977; important works include Sod Ballerina, portraits of Aaron Copland (Bruce Stevenson Meml. Best Portrait award Nat. Arts Club 1989), Eleanor Roosevelt, Variations on a Theme (36 works of collaged sculpture), 1982-86; appeared several TV shows; guest various radio programs; contbr. articles to newspapers, popular mags. and art jours. Council mem. Nassau County Mus., 1978, trustee, 1st v.p. council; asso. trustee Nat. Art Mus. of Sports, Inc., 1975—; cons., community liaison WNET Channel 13, cultural coordinator, 1975-83; host radio show Not for Artists Only, 1978-79; trustee Women's Boxing Fedn., 1978; mem. The Art Comm of The City of New York, 1993. Recipient Gold medal Allied Artists of Am., 1989, Alfred G. B. Steel Meml. award Pa. Acad. Fine Arts, 1963-64; Helen F. Barnett prize NAD, 1965, Jersey City Mus. prize for sculpture, 1961, 1st prize sculpture Locust Valley Art Show, 1966, 67, Ann. Sculpture prize Jersey City Mus., Bank for Savs. 1st prize in sculpture, 1950, Ford Found. purchase award, 1964, 2 top sculpture awards Mainstreams 77, Cert. of Merit Salmagundi Club, 1978, prize for sculpture, 1980, 81, award for sculpture Knickerbocker Artists, 1980, 81, top prize for sculpture Hudson Valley Art Assn., 1981, Sawyer award NAD, 1985, Gold medal of honor Audubon Artists, 1985, 39th Ann. Silvermine Exhbn. award, Gold medal Allied Artists Am., 1990, Pres' award Nat arts Club N.Y.C.; MacDowell Colony fellow, 1976 Am. Acad. Arts and Letters and Nat. Arts and Letters grantee, 1960, Louis Comfort Tiffany Found. grantee, 1962, Ford Found. grantee, 1964, 67, also award; named one of top 5 finalist World Wide Competition to do Monument of Queen Catherine of England, 1991. Fellow Nat. Sculpture Soc.; mem. Sculpture Guild (dir.), Nat. Assn. Women Artists (Jeffery Childs Willis Meml. prize 1978), Allied Artists Soc. (dir., Gold medal 1990), Audubon Artists (Greta Kempton Walker prize 1965, Chaim Gross award, award for disting. contbr. to orgn. 1979, 80, Louis Weskeem award, dir.), Woman's Caucus for Art, Coll. Art Assn., Am. Inst. Conservation Historic and Artistic Works, N.Y. Soc. Women Artists, Artists Equity Assn. N.Y., Nat. Sculpture Soc. (E.N. Richard Meml. prize 1989), Internat. Platform Assn., Profl. Artists Guild L.I., Painters and Sculptors Soc. N.J. (Bertrum R. Hulmes Meml. award), Am. Watercolor Soc. (award for disting. contbn. to orgn.), Catharine Lorillard Wolfe Club (hon. mention 1968), Nat. Arts Club (N.Y.C., Stevenson Meml. award 1989, Pres. award 1992), NAD Design (Leila Gordon Sawyer prize 1989; The Dessle Green Prize 1993). Home: 64 Jane Ct Westbury NY 11590-1410

SHERBY, KATHLEEN REILLY, lawyer; b. St. Louis, Apr. 5, 1947; d. John Victor and Florian Sylvia (Frederick) Reilly; m. James Wilson Sherby, May 17, 1975; children: Michael R.R., William J.R., David J.R. AB magna cum laude, St. Louis U., 1969, JD magna cum laude, 1976. Bar: Mo. 1976. Assoc. Bryan Cave, St. Louis, 1976-85; ptnr. Bryan Cave LLP, St. Louis, 1985—. Contbr. articles to profl. jours. Bd. dirs Jr. League, St. Louis, 1989-90, St. Louis Forum, 1992—, pres., 1995—); vice chmn. Bequest and Gift Coun. of St. Louis U., 1995—. Fellow Am. Coll. Trust and Estate Coun., Estate Planning Coun. of St. Louis (pres. 1986-87), Bar Assn. Met. St. Louis (chmn. probate sect. 1986-87), Mo. Bar Assn. (chmn. probate and trust com. 1996—, chmn. probate law revision subcom. 1988-96). Episcopalian. Home: 47 Crestwood Dr Saint Louis MO 63105-3032 Office: Bryan Cave LLP 1 Metropolitan Sq Ste 3600 Saint Louis MO 63102-2733

SHEREDOS, CAROL ANN, rehabilitation services director; b. N.Y.C., Jan. 29, 1944; d. Robert J. and Margaret M. (Adams) Ross; m. Saleem J. Sheredos, July 14, 1973; children: Emily Joy, Douglas Joseph. BS, Ithaca Coll., 1967; MA in Adulthood and Aging, Coll. of Notre Dame, Balt., 1994. Lic. phys. therapist, N.Y., Md., Fla., N.J. Staff phys. therapist Glen Cove (N.Y.) Community Hosp., 1967-68, Nassau County Health Dept., Mineola, N.Y., 1968-70; rsch. phys. therapist VA, N.Y.C., 1970-71, prosthetics rsch. and edn. specialist, 1971-73; chief phys. therapist Medicus, Wappingers Falls, N.Y., 1983-88; dir. Meridian Rehab. Svcs., Towson, Md., 1989-92; rehab. svcs. dir. Mariner Rehab. Svcs., Balt., 1992-95; dist. mgr. Mariner Rehab. Svcs., 1995—; pvt. practice phys. therapy, N.Y., 1967-83; cons. in disability and aging Alliance, Inc., Balt., 1990-93; co-instr. course The Challenge of Geriatric Rehab., 1994—. Contbr. articles to profl. jours. Host minister St. Joseph's Ch., Tex., Md., 1990—; mem. Gov's. Adv. Coun. Individuals with Disabilities, 1996—. Named One of Ten Most Outstanding Handicapped Americans, Pres.' Com. on Employment of Handicapped, 1971. Mem. Am. Phys. Therapy Assn., Md. Coalition for Assistive Tech., Assn. Christian Therapists, Am. Soc. Aging, Resna. Republican. Roman Catholic. Office: Mariner Rehab Svcs 2700 N Charles St Baltimore MD 21218-4318

SHERIDAN, ANGELIA JUNE, lawyer; b. Anderson, S.C., Dec. 20, 1952; d. Harold Ford and June Rose (Derrick) S.; 1 child, Yolanda Ashly. AA, L.A. City Coll., 1977; BA, Rollins Coll., 1982; JD, Whittier Law Sch., 1989. Bar: Calif. 1990, Fla. 1996, U.S. Ct. Appeals (9th cir.) 1991, U.S. Ct. Appeals (fed. cir.) 1995, U.S. Dist. Ct. (cen. dist.) Calif. 1990. Atty. Law Office of William L. Manuel, San Pedro, Calif., 1989—. Democrat.

SHERIDAN, DIANE FRANCES, public policy facilitator; b. Wilmington, Del., Mar. 12, 1945; d. Robert Kooch and Eileen Elizabeth (Forrest) Bupp; m. Mark MacDonald Sheridan III, Dec. 7, 1968; 1 child, Elizabeth Anne. BA in English, U. Del., 1967. Tchr. English Newark (Del.) Sch. Dist., 1967-68, Lumberton (Tex.) Ind. Sch. Dist., 1969-71, Crown Point (Ind.) Sch. Dist., 1972-75; sr. assoc. The Keystone (Colo.) Ctr., 1986—; environ. policy facilitator Taylor Lake Village, Tex., 1986—; chair Keystone Siting Process Local Rev. Com. 1st v.p. LWV, Washington, 1992-94, sec. treas. voters edn. fund, sec. treas. Nat. LWV, 1994-96, bd. dirs. 1996-98; pres. LWV of Tex., 1987-91, chair edn. fund, 1987-91, bd. dirs., 1983-87; pres. LWV of the Bay Area, 1981-83; mem. adv. com. Ctr. for Global Studies of Houston Advanced Rsch. Ctr., The Woodlands, Tex., 1991—, Ctr. for Conflict Analysis and Mgmt., bd. advisors Environ. Inst.; mem. U. Houston-Clear Lake Devel. Adv. Coun., 1989-95; mem. Bay Area Cmty. Awareness and Emergency Response Local Emergency Planning Com., 1988-92; active Tex. House-Senate Select Com. on Urban Affairs Regional Flooding Task Force, 1979-80, Congressman Mike Andrews Environ. Task Force, 1983-85, Gov.'s Task Force on Hazardous Waste Mgmt., 1984-85; dir. local PTAs, 1981-91; coord. Tex. Roundtable on Hazardous Waste, 1982-87; sec., v.p. Tex. Environ. Coalition, 1983-85; co-chair Tex. Risk Commn. Project, 1986-89; mem. Leadership Tex., Class of 1988. Mem. LWV (bd. dirs. Washington chpt. 1996—, trustee nat. fund), Soc. for Profls. in Dispute Resolution, Internat. Assn. for Pub. Participation Practitioners, Mortarboard, Pi Sigma Alpha, Kappa Delta Pi.

SHERIDAN, SUSAN M., mental health counselor; b. Sheffield, Ala., Jan. 31, 1961; d. Richard C. and Carol (Moore) S. BA, Carson-Newman Coll., 1983; MS in Counseling Psychology, U. So. Miss., 1985. Lic. profl. counselor, Va., lic. psychol. examiner; cert. substance abuse counselor, Tenn., nat. cert. addiction counselor, cert. employee assistance profl. Program dir., substance abuse counselor, psychol. examiner Holston Mental Health Ctr., Kingsport, Tenn., 1985-88; regional dir. quality improvement MCC Behavioral Care, Richmond, Va., 1988—, dir. quality improvement for the east region; orals examiner Licensure Bd. Profl. Counselors, Richmond, 1990-91; bd. dirs. Tenn. Assn. Alcohol and Drug Abuse Counselors, 1988; presenter on managed behavioral healthcare at state and nat. convs. Mem. ACA, AAUW, Am. Mental Health Counselors Assn., Va. Assn. Clin. Counselors, Richmond Assn. Clin. Counselors (v.p. 1994-95, pres. 1995-96). Home: 9006 Locksley Lane Richmond VA 23236 Office: MCC Behavioral Care 7501 Boulders View Dr, Ste 400 Richmond VA 23225

SHERMAN, BETTY HELEN, dental hygienist; b. San Diego, May 19, 1932; d. David Herman and Mildred Versie (Jones) Harris; m. Marvin Leon Sherman, July 29, 1950 (div. 1964); children: Susan Ann, Judy Lynn, Steven David. Cert. dental asst., Edison Tech., 1963; AA, dental hygienist, Lane C.C., 1970; BA, Ctrl. Wash. U. Dental asst., 1950-70, dental hygienist, 1970—; cons. in field; facilitator, spkr. in field. City councilwoman, Richland, Wash.; active Wash. State Housing Authority, Wash.; mem. Planning Commn., Richland; chair platform com. Benton County Rep. Cen. com., 1985-89; negotiator Richland City Coun. Mem. Am. Dental Hygienists Assn. (2d v.p., bd. dirs., trustee 1984-88), Greater Seattle Dental Hygienists Soc. (pres.-elect), Wash. State Dental Hygienists Assn. (pres. 1980), Nat. Air Racing Group (treas. 1994—). Home: 5508 7th Ave NW Seattle WA 98107

SHERMAN, ELAINE C., gourmet foods company executive, educator; b. Chgo., Aug. 1, 1938; d. Arthur E. and Sylvia (Miller) Friedman; m. Arthur J. Spiegel, Jan. 1989; children: Steven J., David P., Jaime A. Student, Northwestern U., 1956-58; diploma in cake decorating, Wilton Sch. Profl. Cake Decorating, 1973; diploma, Dumas Pere, L'école de la Cuisine Française. Tchr. cooking and adult edn. Maine, Oakton, Niles Adult and Continuing Edn. Program, Park Ridge, Ill., 1972-82; corp. officer The Complete Cook, Glenview, Ill., 1976-82, Madame Chocolate, Glenview, 1983-87; food columnist Chgo. Sun Times, 1985-87; dir. mktg. Sue Ling Gin, Chgo., 1987-88; co-owner Critical Eye, Chgo., 1988—; v.p., dir. merchandising, gen. mgr. Foodstuffs, Inc., Evanston, Ill., 1990-91, food cons. mgmt. and mktg., 1991—. Author: Madame Chocolate's Book of Divine Indulgences, 1984 (nominated Tastemaker award 1984). Bd. dirs. Chgo. Fund on Aging and Disability, 1989—; co-chmn. Meals on Wheels, 1989-90, 91. Mem. Les Dames D'Escoffier (founding pres.), Women's Foodservice Network (pres.), Confrerie de la Chaine Des Rotisseurs (vice conselliere gastronomique), Am. Inst. Wine and Food (bd. dirs.). Home and Office: 1728 Wildberry Dr # D Glenview IL 60025-1748

SHERMAN, FRIEDA FRANCES, writer; b. N.Y.C., Oct. 21, 1929; d. Benjamin and Anna (Brown) Jeffe; m. Alan Morton Sherman, Feb. 21, 1952; children: Steven, Daniel, Elizabeth, Richard. BA, Hunter Coll., 1951. Market researcher Am. Broadcasting Co., N.Y.C., 1953-55, Am. Inst. Mgmt., N.Y.C., 1955-56; tchr. dance Palo Alto (Calif.), 1960-70; co-founder Workshop Unltd., Palo Alto, 1970-74; dir. client support Prognostics, Palo Alto, 1982-85; dance therapist pvt. practice, Palo Alto, 1975-90; cons. Market Intelligence Rsch., Palo Alto, 1985. Author of poems and short stories. Coord. cmty. outreach Lively Arts Stanford (Calif.) U., 1990-92; bd. dirs. SPCA, Santa Cruz, Calif., 1994; judge Nat. Poetry Contest, Santa Cruz, 1994. Mem. Nat. Writers Union, Phi Beta Kappa. Home: 900 Glen Canyon Rd Santa Cruz CA 95060-1619

SHERMAN, JUDY, medical researcher; b. Darby, Pa., Apr. 7, 1942; d. Reynolds H. and Helen E. (Young) Wyatt; children from previous marriage: Alan, Pegi, Jason; m. Charles R. Sherman, Apr. 17, 1993. BSN, U. Tex., Houston, 1986, MS in Nursing, 1990. RN, Ga. Cardiology nurse specialist Cardiology Assn. Houston; network mgr. critical care Meml. City Med. Ctr., Houston; clin. instr. Sch. Nursing U. Tex. H.S.C., Houston; critical care clin. coord. Floyd Med. Ctr., Rome, Ga.; rsch. coord. Southeastern Cardiovascular Inst., Rome. Contbr. articles to profl. publs. Capt. U.S. Army, 1962-66. Mem. ANA, Ga. State Nurses Assn. (mem. pub. rels. com. 1990-92, mem. com. 1990-92, program rev. com. 1990-96, dist. bd. dirs. 1990-92), AACN (chpt. past pres., sec., treas., mem. and chair various coms., Nurse of Yr. Houston-Gulf Coast chpt. 1989). Home: 15 Rosalynn Dr SW Rome GA 30165-8589

SHERMAN, JULIA ANN, psychologist; b. Akron, Mar. 25, 1934; d. Roy V. and Edna Helen (Schultz) S.; m. Stanley George Payne, June 16, 1961 (div. Nov. 1995); 1 child, Michael George Sherman. BA, Case Western Res. U., 1954; PhD, U. Iowa, 1957. Diplomate Am. Bd. Psychology. Postdoctoral fellow U. Iowa, Iowa City, 1957-58; with VA Hosp., Mpls., 1958-60, Clinic of Psychiatry and Neurology, Madison, 1960-62; dir. Women Rsch. Inst. Wis., Madison, 1974-79; assoc. clin. cons. psychology dept. U. Wis., 1980-90; psychologist Madison Psychiatric Assn., 1980-87, Mental Health Assn., Madison, 1987-90; part-time tchr. U. Minn., 1959; various part-time clin., writing, rsch. and teaching positions U. Wis., 1962-79; clin. work at Luth. Social Svcs. and Cen. State Hosp. Author: Psychology of Women, 1971, Sex Related Cognitive Differences, 1978; editor: Prism of Sex, 1979, Psychology of Women, 1978; also articles. Rockefeller grantee NSF, NIE, 1972-79. Fellow Am. Psychol. Assn. (chmn. fellowship commn. div. 35 1979-81, pres. sect. IV clin. div. 1986); mem. Wis. Psychol. Assn., Wis. Women in Psychology (pres. 1984). Home: 6302 Mineral Point Rd # 303 Madison WI 53705

SHERMAN, KATHRYN ANN, communication professional; b. Phila., Mar. 12, 1964; d. Edward and Ann Elizabeth (Shields) S. AA, Bucks County C.C., Newtown, Pa., 1988; BBA, Temple U., 1993. Waitress Posh Nosh, Newtown, Pa., 1985-89, Blue Fountain Diner, Langhorne, Pa., 1989-93; comm. assoc. The Vanguard Group, Valley Forge, Pa., 1993—. Mem. Inst. Mgmt. Accts. (bd. dirs., dir. membership acquisition), Beta Alpha Psi, Phi Theta Kappa, Golden Key. Republican. Lutheran.

SHERMAN, MARY ANGUS, public library administrator; b. Lawton, Okla., Jan. 3, 1937; d. Donald Adelbert and Mabel (Felkner) Angus; m. Donald Neil Sherman, Feb. 8, 1958; children: Elizabeth Sherman Cunningham, Donald Neil II. BS in Home Econs., U. Okla., 1958, MLS, 1969. Br. head Pioneer Libr. System, Purcell, Okla., 1966-76; regional libr. Pioneer Libr. System, Norman, Okla., 1976-78, asst. dir., 1978-80, dir., 1987—. Named one of Distinguished Alumni Sch. Home Econs., U. Okla., 1980. Mem. ALA (councilor 1988-96, planning and budget assembly 1990-91, internat. rels. com. 1992-96), Pub. Libr. Assn. (divsn. of ALA, pres. pub. policy for pub. librs. sect. 1995-96), AAUW (pres. Okla. chpt. 1975-77, nat. bd. dirs. 1983-87, S.W. ctrl. region dir. 1983-85, v.p. nat. membership 1985-87, Woman of the Yr. Purcell chpt. 1982), Okla. Libr. Assn. (pres. 1982-83, interlibrary cooperation com. 1993-95, chair 1994-95, Disting. Svc. award 1986), Norman C. of C. (bd. dirs. 1988-96, pres. 1994-95), Rotary (program chair 1991-92, bd. dirs. 1993—, pres. 1995-96. Paul Harris fellow), Norman Assistance League Club (cmty. assoc.), Norman, Okla. Sister City Com. 1994—, Delta Gamma Mothers (pres. 1978-79), Kappa Alpha Theta (pres. Alpha Omicron House Corp. 1984-87, nat. dir. house corps. 1987-88), Beta Phi Mu, Phi Beta Kappa. Democrat. Methodist. Office: Pioneer Libr System 225 N Webster Ave Norman OK 73069-7133

SHERMAN, MONA DIANE, school system administrator; b. N.Y.C., Aug. 28, 1941; d. Hyman and Lillian (Baker) Ginsberg; m. Richard H. Sherman, May 9, 1964; children: Holly Baker, Andrew Hunter. BS, Hunter Coll., CUNY, 1962; MS, CUNY, 1965. Cert. elem. tchr., K-12 reading endorsement specialist, ESL tchr., elem. adminstrn. and supervision, instrnl. supervision, spl. edn. learning disabilities and neurologically impaired edn., Ind. Elem. tchr. N.Y.C. Pub. Schs., 1962-77; team leader Tchr. Corps Potsdam (N.Y.) State Coll., SUNY, 1977-79; dir. Tchr. Ctr., Sch. City of Hammond, Ind., 1979-87; lab. coord. PALS, Gary (Ind.) Sch. Corp., 1987-93, mentor, 1988—, facilitator of staff devel., 1993—; instr. Tex. Instrument Computer Co., Lubbock, 1983-84, Performance Learning Sys., Emerson, N.J., 1984—; cons. in classroom discipline and computer instrn. Gary Staff Devel. Ctr., 1987—; mentor Urban Tchr. Edn. program Ind. U. N.W., Gary, 1991—; chair sch. improvement team, tchr. of yr. com., 1993-94; mem., grantswriter Gary Tech. Com., Gary Distance Learning Com. Mem. Lake Area United Way Lit. Coalition NW Ind., 1990, Gary Reading Textbook Adoption Com.; sec. Martin Luther King Jr. Acad. PTSA, mem. sch. improvement team. Recipient Recognition NW Ind. Forum, 1988, Tchr. of Yr. award Merrillville (Ind.) Lions Club, 1988, Outstanding Tchr. of Yr. award Inland Ryerson, East Chicago, Ind., 1989. Mem. Ind. Reading Assn., Gary Reading Assn., Phi Delta Kappa, Delta Kappa Gamma. Home: 1112 Fran Lin Pky Munster IN 46321-3607

SHERMAN, NANCY, philosophy educator; b. Passaic, N.J., June 20, 1951; d. Seymour and Beatrice (Hoffman) S.; m. Marshall Presser, June 22, 1980; children: Kala, Jonathan. AB in Philosophy magna cum laude, Bryn Mawr Coll., 1973; postgrad., Boston U., 1973; MLitt in Philosophy, U. Edinburgh, Scotland, 1976; PhD, Harvard U., 1982. Tchg. asst. in philosophy Harvard U., Cambridge, Mass., 1980-81; asst. prof. Yale U., New Haven, 1982-88, assoc. prof., 1988-89; assoc. prof. Georgetown U., Washington, 1989-94, prof., 1994—; vis. rsch. scholar King's Coll., Cambridge (Eng.) U., spring 1978; vis. prof. Johns Hopkins U., Balt., spring 1995, U. Md., College Park, spring 1995, 96; cons. on ethics to undersec. Dept. Navy, 1994; dist. lectr. ethical theory and character devel. U.S. Naval Acad., Annapolis, Md., 1994, cons. on moral edn. and moral remediation, 1994; participant numerous confs., symposia, colloquia; lectr., spkr. in field. Author: The Fabric of Character: Aristotle's Theory of Virtue, 1989, paperback edit., 1991, Making a Necessity of Virtue: Aristotle and Kant on Virtue, 1996; contbr. articles and revs. to profl. jours. Vans Dunlop scholar U. Edinburgh, 1974-76;

Teschemacher fellow Harvard U., 1976-81, Newcombe fellow, 1981-82, fellow NEH, 1984-85, 96, Am. Coun. Learned Socs., 1987, Mellon fellow Yale U., 1988, Whitney Humanities fellow Yale U., 1987-88, fellow Kennedy Inst. Ethics, 1991-96, Mellon summer fellow, 1992, Georgetown U. summer fellow, 1990, 91, 94, 95. Mem. APA (program com. ea. divsn. 1995-97), Soc. for Ancient Greek Philosophy, N.Am. Kant Soc., Am. Philos. Assn., Washington Psychoanalytic Found. Office: Georgetown U Dept Philosophy 224 New North St NW Washington DC 20057

SHERMAN, RUTH TODD, government advisor, counselor, consultant; b. Memphis, July 3, 1924; d. Robbie M. and Lillie M. (Shreve) Todd. BS, Memphis State U., 1972, MEd, 1975; MA, Western Mich. U., 1986. Cert. tchr., counselor. Youth leader Assembly of God Ch., Memphis, 1962-64, youth dir., 1964-66; counselor Teen Challenge, Memphis, 1973-74; marriage and family therapist Memphis, 1976-77; govt. tng. advisor Def. Logistics Agy., Battle Creek, Mich., 1982-87; advisor Def. Logistics Agy., Alexandria, Va., 1987-94, ret., 1994; Agy. to Mil. Svc. cons. Def. Logistics Agy., Oklahoma City, 1990-94. Author: Federal Catalog Training Books/Videos, 1987 (Sustained Superior Performance award 1987). Mem. Internat. Assn. Marriage and Family Counselors, Nat. Employment Counseling Assn., Am. Mental Health Counseling Assn. Home: 3165 N Maranatha Ln # 22 Springfield MO 65803

SHERMAN, SIGNE LIDFELDT, portfolio manager, former research chemist; b. Rochester, N.Y., Nov. 11, 1913; d. Carl Leonard Broström and Herta Elvira Maria (Thern) Lidfeldt; m. Joseph V. Sherman, Nov. 18, 1944 (dec. Oct. 1984). BA, U. Rochester, 1935, MS, 1937. Chief chemist Lab. Indsl. Medicine and Toxicology Eastman Kodak Co., Rochester, 1937-43; chief rsch. chemist Chesebrough-Pond's Inc., Clinton, Conn., 1943-44; ptnr. Joseph V. Sherman Cons., N.Y.C., 1944-84; portfolio strategist Sherman Holdings, Troy, Mont., 1984—. Author: The New Fibers, 1946. Fellow Am. Inst. Chemists; mem. AAAS, AAUW (life), Am. Chem. Soc., Am. Econ. Assn., Am. Assn. Ind. Investors (life), Fedn. Am. Scientists (life), Union Concerned Scientists (life), Western Econ. Assn. Internat., Earthquake Engring. Rsch. Inst., Nat. Ctr. for Earthquake Engring. Rsch., N.Y. Acad. Scis. (life), Internat. Platform Assn., Cabinet View Country Club. Office: Sherman Holdings Angel Island 648 Halo Dr Troy MT 59935-9415

SHERMAN, SUSAN JEAN, English language educator; b. N.Y.C., Oct. 30, 1939; d. Monroe and Gertrude Jean (Horn) S. BA, Sarah Lawrence Coll., 1969, MA in Lit., 1971. Tchr. English Riverdale Country Sch., N.Y., 1972—. Author: Give Me Myself, 1961; editor: May Sarton: Among the Usual Days, 1993 (Huntington Hartford fellow 1961, Amy Loveman award 1960), (rec.) Promises to Be Kept, 1962, May Sarton: Selected Letters, 1995. Office: Riverdale Country Sch 5250 Fieldston Rd Bronx NY 10471

SHERMAN JUSTICE, DARCY LOU, nurse; b. Mitchell, S.D., May 27, 1953; d. Clarence Robert and Joanne Elaine (Dodge) Gosmire; m. Kenneth Frank Sherman, Aug. 9, 1975 (div. Oct. 1983); 1 child, Brian Barton; m. Jerry Jay Justice, Sept. 19, 1987; 1 child, Brandon James. ADN, Presentation Coll., 1973; BSN, S.D. State U., 1987; MS in Health Svcs. Adminstrn., U. S.D., 1995. Cert. nursing continuing edn. and staff devel. Dir. nursing Rivercrest Manor, Pierre, S.D., 1973-75; nurse, asst. head nurse Dakota Hosp., Vermillion, S.D., 1975-78; surg. staff devel. coord., nurse, enterostomal therapist Rapid City (S.D.) Regional Hosp., 1979-85, coord. nursing edn., 1985-90; specialist staff devel. McKennan Hosp., Sioux Falls, S.D., 1990-95; mgr. edn., tng. and devel. McKennan Hosp., 1995—. Contbr. articles to profl. jours. Mem. ANA, Nat. Nursing Staff Devel. Orgn., Am. Soc. for Health Care Eng. and Tng. (S.D. chpt. pres. 1995-96, Educator of Yr. 1991), S.D. Nurses Assn. (bd. dirs., Search for Excellence award 1993, Dist. 9 Nurse of Yr. 1994), Dist. 9 Nurses Assn. (bd. dirs.), Sioux Empire Nurses Com. (sec. 1993-94, pres. 1994-96), Sigma Theta Tau (pres. chpt. 1994-95). Democrat. Lutheran. Office: McKennan Hosp 800 E 21st St Sioux Falls SD 57105-1016

SHERR, LYNN BETH, television news correspondent; b. Phila., Mar. 4, 1942; d. Louis and Shirley (Rosenfeld) S.; m. Lawrence B. Hilford, Jan. 11, 1980. B.A., Wellesley Coll., 1963. Writer, editor Conde Nast Publications, N.Y.C., 1963-65; writer, reporter AP, N.Y.C., 1965-72; corre. Sta. WCBS-TV News, N.Y.C., 1972-74; anchor, corre. Pub. Broadcasting System, N.Y.C., 1975-77; nat. corre. ABC News, N.Y.C., 1977—. Co-author: (with Jurate Kazickas) The Liberated Woman's Appointment Calendar, 1971-82, The American Woman's Gazetteer, 1976, Susan B. Anthony Slept Here, 1994; author: Failure is Impossible: Susan B. Anthony in Her Own Words, 1995. Recipient Ohio State award Ohio State U., 1976; recipient spl. commendation Am. Women in Radio & TV, 1979, Emmy for Post Election Spl., 1980, Peabody, 1994; numerous others. Office: 20/20 147 Columbus Ave New York NY 10023-5900

SHERRED, CLAIRE LOUISE, sports program manager; b. Croydon, London, Eng., Nov. 5, 1956; d. Peter and Elizabeth (Penn) S.; m. Donald Jay Delnegro, June 23, 1990. BS in Comms., Ithaca Coll., 1978. Asst. dept. dir. Lake Placid (N.Y.) Olympic Organizing Com., 1978-80; programs asst. WCFE-TV Sta., Plattsburgh, N.Y., 1980-82; support svcs. L.A. Olympic Organizing Com., 1984, exec. dir. Lake Placid Horse Show Assn., 1985-88, also bd. dirs.; internat. program dir. U.S. Luge Assn., Lake Placid, 1988—; Olympic athlete luge Brit. Olympic Team Winter Olympics, Sarajevo, 1984. Adv. bd. mem. Women's Sports Found., N.Y.C., 1994—; sports commn. mem. Fedn. Internat. Luge, Berchtesgaden, Germany, 1994—. Home: 1200 Salem St Cedar Pond # 189 Lynnfield MA 01940 Office: US Luge Assn 35 Church St Lake Placid NY 12946

SHERRED, DAWN LARONDA, accountant; b. Greenville, S.C., Feb. 3, 1969; d. Gloria G. Sherred. BSBA, Univ. S.C. State, 1991. Cost acct. Vermont America, Fountain Inn, S.C., 1992—. Mem. Inst. Mgmt. Accts. Home: 325A Shemwood Ln Greenville SC 29605 Office: Vermont Am 800 Woodside Ave Fountain Inn SC 29644

SHERREN, ANNE TERRY, chemistry educator; b. Atlanta, July 1, 1936; d. Edward Allison and Annie Ayres (Lewis) Terry; m. William Samuel Sherren, Aug. 13, 1966. BA, Agnes Scott Coll., 1957; PhD, U. Fla.-Gainesville, 1961. Grad. teaching asst. U. Fla., Gainesville, 1957-61; instr. Tex. Woman's U., Denton, 1961-63, asst. prof., 1963-66; rsch. participant Argonne Nat. Lab., 1973-80, 93, 94; assoc. prof. chemistry N. Cen. Coll., Naperville, Ill., 1966-76, prof., 1976—. Ruling elder Knox Presbyn. Ch., 1971—, clk. of session, 1976-94. Mem. AAAS, AAUP, Am. Chem. Soc., Am. Inst. Chemists, Ill. Acad. Sci., Sigma Xi, Delta Kappa Gamma, Iota Sigma Pi (nat. pres. 1978-81, nat. dir. 1972-78, nat. historian 1989—). Presbyterian. Contbr. articles in field to profl. jours. Office: North Ctrl Coll Dept Chemistry Naperville IL 60566

SHERVE-OSE, ANNE, music educator; b. Minot, N.D., Feb. 11, 1953; d. Albin Gustav and Alvhild Margaret (Slen) Sherve; m. Alan Kent Ose, Jan. 19, 1980; children: Samuel Sherve Ose, Rachel Sherve Ose. BA in Phys. Edn. and Health, St. Olaf Coll., 1975; MusB in Music Composition, Iowa State U., 1982. Cert. tchr., Iowa. Asst. instr. Minn. Outward Bound Sch., Ely, 1977; tchr. phys. edn. and music Am. Girls Sch., Izmir, Turkey, 1978-79; tchr. elem. music N.E. Hamilton Schs., Blairsburg, Iowa, 1985-88, St. Thomas Aquinas Sch., Webster City, Iowa, 1992—; tchr. Blairsburg Community Presch., 1982-85, Iowa. Church organist Blairsburg United Ch. of Christ, 1980—; cmty. chorus dir. Williams (Iowa) Cmty. Chorus, 1988—; bd. dirs. William Pub. Libr., 1990—; asst. scout leader Brownie Scout Troop 150, Webster City, 1992—. Home: 2230 Wilson Ave Williams IA 50271-7571 Office: Saint Thomas Aquinas Sch 624 Dubuque St Webster City IA 50595-2245

SHER-WALTON, AUDREY HELENE, mental health therapist; b. N.Y.C., Oct. 1, 1957; d. Milton H. and Betty Sher; m. W. Dennis Walton, Sept. 15, 1984; children: Alexander, Shayna. BA in Psychology, U. Ariz., 1979. Residential therapist Fineson House, N.Y.C., 1979, Quadrante House, Tucson, 1980-81; owner, tchr. Mrs. Audrey's Playgroups, Tucson, 1982-89; therapist, vol. coord. Las Familias Counseling Agy., Tucson, 1987-93; owner, therapist SherWin Therapeutic Recreation, Tucson, 1993—; cons., trainer Shalom House, Tucson, 1993-95, Parent Edn. Com. Jewish Cmty. Ctr., Tucson, 1995, A.A.S.K., 1993; mem. adv. bd. Family to Family Initiative, Tucson, 1991-93 . Del., bd. dirs. Nat. Coun. Jewish Women, 1986-92; vol. Tucson Poetry Festival, 1977-90; fundraiser early childhood com. Jewish Cmty. Ctr., 1994-95; vol. Ariz. Theatre Co., Tucson, 1984-90; bd. dirs., events coord. Mothers on the Move, 1993-95. Mem. Assn. Vol. Coords. Office: SherWin Therapeutic Recreation PO Box 12794 Tucson AZ 85732-2794

SHERWOOD, CATHRINE (MITZI SHERWOOD), science educator; b. Chgo., Nov. 14, 1957; d. John Instone III and Nancy Elizabeth (Griffey) Crockett; m. William Stith Bynum, Mar. 12, 1978 (div. Dec. 1980); m. Travis Aaron Sherwood, May 28, 1983; children: Phillip Quinn, Travis Grant. BS, Tex. A&M U., 1979; MS, East Tex. State U., 1995. Sec. CORE Lab., Tyler, Tex., 1979-80; ops. mgr. Crockett Sales Co., Dallas, 1980-81; soil scientist, conservationist Soil Conservation Svc., Bonham, Tex., 1981-84, 87-89; tchr. Paris (Tex.) H.S., 1989—.

SHERWOOD, JOAN KAROLYN SARGENT, career counselor; b. Wichita, Kans., July 11, 1934; d. James Wirth and Ann K. (Freeburg) Sargent; m. Howard Kenneth Sherwood, Jan. 26, 1956 (div. 1966); children: Diane Elizabeth, Karolyn Sherwood Krause, David Matthew. BS, Kans. State U., 1956; MA, Wichita State U., 1964; PhD, U. Kans., 1978. Asst. dir. U. Kans., Lawrence, 1973-78, asst. vice chancellor/student affairs, 1978-81; asst. vice chancellor/student affairs U. Mo., Kansas City, 1981-84; v.p. student affairs Western Wash. U., Bellingham, 1984-87; cons. Corp. Tng. Assurance, Kansas City, 1987-95; career coord. Park Coll., Parville, Mo., 1995—; program chair Phi Delta Kappa, Lawrence, 1983-84; initiation chair Phi Kappa Phi, Kansas City, 1983-84; organizer Singles Connection, Kansas City, 1983-84; creator SummerStart, Bellingham, 1988-89. Contbr.: Theatre Companies of the World, 1986; female voice: (film) Junction City, 1973. Long range planning coord. Ch. Redeemer, Kansas City, 1994; workshop facilitator South Side Jr. C. of C., Kansas City, 1991; presenter Centurians, Kansas City, 1982; spkr. Pi Lambda Theta, 1983. NDEA fellow, 1969. Mem. ASTD, Phi Kappa Phi. Democrat. Episcopal. Home: 4901 NW Gateway #22 Kansas City MO 64151 Office: Park Coll 8700 NW River Park Dr Kansas City MO 64152

SHERWOOD, LILLIAN ANNA, librarian, retired; b. South Bend, Ind., Dec. 22, 1928; d. Julius Andrew and Mary (Kerekes) Takacs; m. Neil Walter Sherwood, May 31, 1953; children: Susan Kay Huff, Nancy Ellen Coney, James Walter. AB in Home Econs., Ind. U., 1951, postgrad., 1978-83. Cert. libr. IV, Ind., 1984. Lab. tech. Lobund Inst., Notre Dame (Ind.) U., 1951-53; substitute tchr. Plymouth (Ind.) Community Schs., 1969-73; bookkeeper, processing clk. Plymouth (Ind.) Pub. Libr., 1973-76, audio-visual coord., 1976-79, reference and genealogical libr., 1980-93; retired, 1994; project dir. Ind. Heritage rsch. grant, Ind. Humanities Coun. and Ind. Hist. Soc., 1992-93; orgn. and verification com. Geneal. Socs., Pioneer Soc., Marshall County, Ind., Plymouth, 1988—. Mem. bd. dirs. Child Day Care Ctr. of Plymouth, 1971-75, pres., 1974. Mem. AAUW (v.p. 1966-68, pres. 1971-73, 85-87, 91-93), Marshall County Geneal. Soc. (v.p. 1986-87), Omicron Nu. Methodist. Home: 808 Thayer St Plymouth IN 46563-2859

SHERWOOD, PATRICIA WARING, artist, educator; b. Columbia, S.C., Dec. 19, 1933; d. Clark du Val and Florence (Yarbrough) Waring; divorced; children: Cheryl Sherwood Kraft, Jana Sherwood Kern, Marikay Sherwood Taitt. BFA magna cum laude, Calif. State U., Hayward, 1970; MFA, Mills Coll., Oakland, Calif., 1974; postgrad., San Jose State U., 1980-86. Cert. tchr., Calif. Tchr. De Anza Jr. Coll., Cupertino, Calif., 1970-78, Foothill Jr. Coll., Los Altos, Calif., 1972-78, West Valley Jr. Coll., Saratoga, Calif., 1978—; artist-in-residence Centrum Frans Masereel, Kasterlee, Belgium, 1989. One-woman shows include Triton Mus., Santa Clara, Calif., 1968, RayChem Corp., Sunnyville, Calif., 1969, Palo Alto (Calif.) Cultural Ctr., 1977, Los Gatos (Calif.) Mus., 1992, Stanford U. faculty club, Palo Alto, 1993, d. P. Fong Gallery, San Jose, Calif., 1995, Heritage Bank, San Jose, Calif.; exhibited in group shows at Tresidder Union Stanford U., 1969, Oakland (Calif.) Mus. Kaiser Ctr., 1969, Sonoma (Calif.) State Coll., 1969, Bank Am., San Francisco, 1969, San Francisco Art Festival, 1969, 70, U. Santa Clara, 1967, Charles and Emma Frye Mus., Seattle, 1968, Eufrat Gallery DeAnza Coll., Cupertino, 1975, San Jose (Calif.) Mus. Art, 1976, Lytton Ctr., Palo Alto, 1968 (1st award), Zellerbach Ctr., San Francisco, 1970, Works Gallery, San Jose, 1994; represented in permanent collections Mills Coll., Bank Am., San Francisco. Art judge studnet show Stanford U., Palo Alto, 1977; mem. d.p. Fong Gallery, San Jose, Calif., 1994. Nat. Endowment for Arts/We. States Art Fedn. fellow, 1994. Mem. Calif. Print Soc., Womens Caucus for Arts, Internat. Platform Assn. Home: 1500 Arriba Ct Los Altos CA 94024-5941 Office: West Valley Jr Coll Art Dept 14000 Fruitvale Ave Saratoga CA 95070-5640

SHEVINS, BONNIE K., foundation administrator; b. N.Y.C., Aug. 12, 1955; d. Isadore and Barbara (Brodie) Klebanow; m. Jay Stanley Shevins; children: Russell, Jessica, Elizabeth. BA, SUNY, Buffalo, 1976; MA, U. Chgo., 1978. From asst. dir. to dir. info. sys. Greater N.Y. Fund United Way, N.Y.C., 1979-89; from exec. asst. to COO to group v.p. strategic mgmt. United Jewish Assn. Fedn. N.Y., N.Y.C., 1989—; asst. sec., dir. FEDVentures, Inc., N.Y.C., 1994—; ins. profl. adv. com. FOJP Svc. Corp., N.Y.C., 1992—; aging svc. network adv. com. N.Y. State Office of Aging, 1995—; human svc. info. tech. task force United Way, N.Y.C., 1995—; human svc. action group on tech. Human Svcs. Coun., N.Y.C., 1995—. Non-tax revenue com. Tenafly (N.J.) Bd. Edn., 1995—. Office: UJA Fedn New York 130 E 59th St New York NY 10022

SHEY, JANE ELIZABETH, agriculture and trade specialist; b. Algona, Iowa, Dec. 2, 1956; d. Daniel Jeremiah and Jean Lois (Balgeman) S. BA, Briar Cliff Coll., 1979. Caseworker Congressman Berkley Bedell, Sioux City, 1979-81; pastoral minister St. Cecelia's Ch., Algona, 1981-84; chaplain Washington Hosp. Ctr., 1984-86; congl. candidate 6th Congl. Dist. of Iowa, Algona, 1986; legis. asst. congressman Berkley Bedell, Washington, 1986; legis. asst. congressman Tim Penny, Washington, 1986-88, 92, staff dir. subcom. fgn. agriculture and hunger, 1993-94; dir. govt. affairs Corn Refiners Assn., Washington, 1988-92; agriculture policy and trade specialist Hessian, McKasy and Soderberg, Washington, 1994—. Mem. Women in Govt. Rels. (co-chair agrl. task force Washington chpt. 1988-89, 90-91), Women in Internat. Trade. Democrat. Roman Catholic. Office: Ste 420 499 S Capitol St SW Washington DC 20003-1827

SHIBATA, SETSUE, humanities educator; b. Nagoya, Aichi, Japan, July 2, 1952; came to U.S., 1978; d. Masuo and Sumako (Hasegawa) Hayashi; m. Tomoo Shibata; children: Lina, Kayu. BA, Keio U., 1975; MSW, U. S.C., 1982, PhD, 1985. Ednl. researcher Ednl. Rsch. Ctr., Irvine, Calif., 1986-89; statistician, researcher Rsch. Inst. Alcoholism, Buffalo, N.Y., 1989-91; sr. lectr. SUNY, Buffalo, 1991-95; asst. prof. Calif. State U., Fullerton, 1995—; dir. program coord. Buffalo Japanese Weekend Sch., 1989—. Mem. Am. Ednl. Rsch. Assn., Asian Studies Assn., Southern Calif. Japanese Tchrs. Assn. Home: 10456 Santa Marta Cypress CA 90630 Office: Calif State U Dept Fgn Lang & Literature Fullerton CA 92634

SHICKLE, LOUISE MARIE, mathematics educator; b. Lancaster, Pa., Feb. 5, 1949; d. George Edward and Marion (Borry) Grube; m. Wayne Lloyd Sittler, Oct. 17, 1969 (div. Oct. 1979); 1 child, Lisa Mae; m. Richard Charles Shickle Sr., June 14, 1980; children: Denise Jamais, Richard Charles Jr., Martha Frances. BA in Math., Dana Coll., 1969; MA Tchg. Math., U. Nebr., 1975. Cert. math. tchr., Va. Tchr. Army Edn. Ctr., Heilbronn, Fed. Republic Germany, 1970-73; math. tchr. Waynesboro (Pa.) Area H.S., 1976-80, James Wood H.S., Frederick County Schs., Winchester, Va., 1982-93, Sherando H.S., Frederick County Schs., Winchester, 1993—. Pres. James Wood H.S. Concert Choir Boosters, 1990-91, Apple Pie Ridge Elem. Sch. PTO, Winchester, 1991-92. Mem. Nat. Coun. Tchrs. Math., Va. Coun. Tchrs. Math., Valley of Va. Coun. Tchrs. Math., Math. Assn. Am. Methodist. Home: 292 Green Spring Rd Winchester VA 22603-2740 Office: Sherando HS 185 S Warrior Dr Stephens City VA 22655

SHIELDS, BROOKE CHRISTA CAMILLE, actress, model; b. N.Y.C., May 31, 1965; d. Francis A. and Teri (Schmon) S. BA, Princeton U., 1987. Model for Ivory Soap commls. starting in 1966, later for Calvin Klein jeans and Colgate toothpaste commls.; actress: (films) Alice, Sweet Alice, 1975, Pretty Baby, 1977, King of the Gypsies, 1978, Wanda Nevada, 1978, Just You and Me Kid, 1978, Blue Lagoon, 1979, Endless Love, 1980, Sahara, 1983, Backstreet Strays, 1989, Brenda Starr, 1992, Seventh Floor, 1993, Running Wild, 1993, Freaked, 1993, Freeway, 1996; (TV movies) The Prince of Central Park, 1977, After the Fall, Wet Gold, I Can Make You Love Me: The Stalking of Laura Black, 1993, Nothing Lasts Forever, 1995, (TV shows) The Tonight Show, Bob Hope spls., The Diamond Trap, 1988, Friends, 1996, Suddenly Susan, 1996; appeared on Broadway in Grease, 1994-95. Office: Christa Inc Ste 630 2300 West Sahara Box 18 Las Vegas NV 89102*

SHIELDS, CAROL ANN, writer, educator; b. Oak Park, Ill., June 2, 1935; came to Can., 1957, naturalized, 1974; d. Robert Elmer and Inez Adelle (Sellgren) Warner; m. Donald Hugh Shields, July 20, 1957; children: John, Anne, Catherine, Margaret, Sara. B.A., Hanover Coll., 1957; MA, U. Ottawa, Ont., Can., 1975. Editl. asst. Can. Slavonic Papers, Ottawa, 1972-74; lectr. U. Ottawa, 1976-77, U. B.C., Vancouver, Can., 1978-80; prof. U. Man., Winnipeg, Can., 1980—; chancellor U. Winnipeg, 1996—; mem. Can. Coun., 1994—. Author: (poems) Others, 1972, Intersect, 1974, Coming to Canada, 1991; (novels) Small Ceremonies, 1976, The Box Garden, 1977, Happenstance, 1980, A Fairly Conventional Women, 1982; Various Miracles, 1985, Swann: A Mystery, 1987, The Orange Fish, 1989, The Republic of Love, 1992, The Stone Diaries, 1993 (Nat. Book Critics Circle award for fiction 1994, Pulitzer Prize for fiction 1995); (play) Women Waiting, 1983, Departures and Arrivals, 1984, Thirteen Hands, 1993, (with Catherine Shields) Fashion Power Guilt. Grantee Can. Council, 1973, 76, 78, 86, Man. Arts Council, 1984, 85; recipient prize CBC, 1983, 84, Nat. Mag. award, 1985, Arthur Ellis award, 1987, Can. Book Sellers'award 1994, Manitoba Book of the Yr., 1994, Marian Engel award Writers' Devel. Trust, 1990, Gov. Gen.'s award Can. Coun., 1993. Mem. PEN, Writers Union Can., Writers Guild Man., Jane Austen Soc., N.Am. Can. Coun. Bd. Quaker. Home: 701 237 Wellington Crescent, Winnipeg, MB Canada R3M 0A1 Office: care Bella Pomer Agency Inc, 22 Shallmar Blvd Penthouse 2, Toronto, ON Canada M5N 2Z8

SHIELDS, CYNTHIA ROSE, college administrator; b. Monterey, Calif., June 1, 1954; d. William Lawrence and Rose Virdell (Turner) Jackson; m. Franklin Shields, Sept. 19, 1981; 1 child, Brett. AA, San Francisco City Coll., 1980; BS, U. San Francisco, 1986; MPA, Golden Gate U., 1988; MS, Nat. U., 1994; postgrad., U. Calif., Davis, 1994—. Cert. community coll. instr., supr., Calif. Acct. exec. KFSN-TV, Fresno, Calif., 1982-85; instr. Merced County (Calif.) Schs., 1985-89; gen. mgr., owner Ad Line Advt., Merced, 1986—; instr. Merced Coll., 1989-90; youth outreach specialist, 1990-91, re-entry coord., 1991—; sr. assoc. Sch. Leadership Ctr., Calif. Sch. Leadership Acad., 1989-92. Author curriculum materials. Bd. dirs. Merced Cmty. Med. Ctr. Found., 1991, MUHSD Found., 1992-94; mem. citizens adv. bd. Merced City Sch. Dist., 1985-87; chmn. Merced Conv. and Vis. Bur., 1991; coord. Merced Cmty. Housing Resource Bd., 1988-90; mem. Leaders program Nat. Inst. for Leadership Devel., 1996. Mem. AAUW, Merced City C. of C. (bd. dirs. 1991-93, v.p. fin. and ops. 1993-94), Phi Delta Kappa. Democrat. Office: Ad Line Advt Jackson Shields Assocs PO Box 3346 Merced CA 95344-1346

SHIELDS, MARLENE SUE, elementary school educator; b. Denver, Apr. 7, 1939; d. Morris and Rose (Sniderman) Goldberg; m. Charles H. Cohen, Dec. 22, 1957 (dec.); children: Lee, Richard, Monica; m. Harlan Shields. BA magna cum laude, Met. State Coll., 1980; MA, U. No. Colo., 1986. Preschool tchr. Temple Emanuel, Denver, 1970-75; tchr. Kindergarten Temple Sinai, Denver, 1975-80; tchr. pre-Kindergarten St. Mary's Acad., Englewood, Colo., 1980-83; tchr. Beach Court Elem., Denver, 1983-86, Valverde Sch., Denver, 1984-85; tchr. third grade Brown Elem., Denver, 1985-86; tchr. learning disabilities Cowell Elem. Sch., Denver, 1986-87, Sabin Elem. Sch., Denver, 1987-88; tchr. second grade Sabin Elem., Denver, 1988 ; mem. curriculum com. Denver Pub. Sch., 1989—, pers. subcom., 1991—; citizen amb. Spain joint tchr. conf., 1995. Mem. Colo. Copun. Internat. Reading Assn., Nat. Assn. for Young Children, Nat. Tchrs. Colo. Math., Internat. Reading Assn., Carousel of Intervention, Delta Kappa Gamma (sec., v.p., grade level chair), PRIDE (lang. curriculum com., math. curriculum com., impact com., CDM rep. 1994-95). Home: 5800 Big Canon Dr Englewood CO 80111-3516

SHIELDS, MEREDITH ANN, elementary school educator; b. Columbus, Ohio, Dec. 14, 1967; d. Ford David and Janice Ann (Besom) Smucker; m. James Douglas Shields, Aug. 14, 1993. BS in Edn., Ohio State U., 1991; MS in Edn., U. Dayton, 1994. Cert. tchr. grades 1-8 with grades kindergarten-12 reading concentration, Ohio. Tchr. Chpt. 1 reading Springfield (Ohio) City Schs., 1991—; mem. Right to Read com. Springfield City Schs., 1991-93; mem. Child Assistance Team, Springfield, 1993—. Vol. mentor Franklin County Children's Svcs., Grove City, Ohio, 1991-95. Recipient award for 3 yrs. svc. Franklin County Children's Svcs., 1994. Office: Simon Kenton Elem Sch 1221 E Home Rd Springfield OH 45503

SHIELDS, RANA COLLEEN, special education educator; b. Midland, Tex., Oct. 2, 1951; d. Robert Campbell and Edith Sue (Alexander) S.; m. Micheal Leggett; children: Daniel Robert Tilly, Casey Michelle Leggett; 1 stepchild, Laurie Ayn Leggett. B of Journalism, U. Tex., 1974; JD magna cum laude, South Tex. Coll. Law, 1984; MEd in Spl. Edn., S.W. Tex. State U., 1993. Bar: Tex., 1985; cert. generic spl. edn., reading, Tex. City editor Huntsville (Tex.) Item, 1976-78; asst. county atty. Travis County Atty.'s Office, Austin, Tex., 1986-87; tchr. spl. edn. Liberty Hill (Tex.) H.S., 1990-91, Tex. Sch. for the Blind, Austin, 1991-93; grad. rsch. asst. in spl. edn. U. Tex., Austin, spring 1994, tchg. asst. spl. edn., 1995-96. Asst. casenotes editor: South Tex. Law Jour., 1983. Recipient 1st Pl. Spot News Photography award AP Mng. Editors, 1978, Am. Jurisprudence awards, 1979, 82, 83; named Outstanding Sophomore Journalist, Women in Comm., 1971; Univ. fellow, 1996-97. Mem. Assn. Tex. Profl. Educators, Kappa Delta Pi, Phi Kappa Phi.

SHIENTAG, FLORENCE PERLOW, lawyer; b. N.Y.C.; d. David and Ester (Germane) Perlow; m. Bernard L. Shientag, June 8, 1938. BS, NYU, 1940, LLB, 1933, JD, 1940. Bar: Fla. 1976, N.Y. Law aide Thomas E. Dewey, 1937; law sec. Mayor La Guardia, 1939-42; justice Domestic Relations Ct., 1941-42; mem. Tchrs. Retirement Bd., N.Y.C., 1942-46; asst. U.S. atty. So. dist. N.Y., 1943-53; cir. ct. mediator Fla. Supreme Ct., 1992; pvt. practice N.Y.C., 1960—, Palm Beach, Fla., 1976—; lectr. on internat. divorce; mem. Nat. Commn. on Wiretapping and Electronic Surveillance, 1973—, Task Force on Women in Cts., 1985-86; circuit ct. mediator Fla. Supreme Ct., 1992. Contbr. articles to profl. jours. Candidate N.Y. State Senate, 1954; bd. dirs. UN Devel. Corp., 1972-95, Franklin and Eleanor Roosevelt Inst., 1985—; bd. dirs., assoc. treas. YM and YWHA; hon. commr. commerce, N.Y.C. Mem. ABA, Fed. Bar Assn. (exec. com.), Internat. Bar Assn., N.Y. Women's Bar Assn. (pres., Life Time Achievement award 1994), N.Y. State Bar Assn., N.Y.C. Bar Assn. (chmn. law and art sect.), N.Y. County Lawyers Assn. (dir.), Nat. Assn. Women LAwyers (sec.). Home: 737 Park Ave New York NY 10021-4256

SHIER, GLORIA BULAN, mathematics educator; b. The Philippines, Apr. 20, 1935; came to U.S., 1966.; d. Melecio Cauilan and Florentina (Cumagun) Bulan; m. Wayne Thomas Shier, May 31, 1969; children: John Thomas, Marie Teresita, Anna Christina. BS, U. Santo Tomas, Manila, Philippines, 1956; MA, U. Ill., 1968; PhD, U. Minn., 1986. Tchr. Cagayan (Philippines) Valley Coll., 1956-58, St. Paul Coll., Manila, 1959-62, Manila Div. City Schs., 1958-64; asst. prof. U. of East, Manila, 1961-66; rsch. asst. U. Ill., Urbana, 1968-69; instr. Miramar Community Coll., San Diego, 1974-75, Mesa Community Coll., San Diego, 1975-80, Lakewood Community Coll., St. Paul, 1984, U. Minn., Mpls., 1986-87, North Hennepin Community Coll., Brooklyn Park, Minn., 1987—; cons. PWS Kent Pub. Co., Boston, 1989—. Chairperson Filipino Am. Edn. Assn., San Diego, 1978-79. Fulbright scholar U.S. State Dept., U. Ill., 1966-70; fellow Nat. Sci. Found., Oberlin Coll., 1967; recipient Excellence in Teaching award UN Ednl. Scientific Cultural Organ., U. Philippines, 1960-62, Cert. Commendation award The Gov. of Minn., 1990, Outstanding Filipino in the Midwest Edn. Cat. award 1992, Cavite Assn. Mem. Am. Math. Soc., Math. Assn. Am., Phi Kappa Phi, Sigma Xi Rsch. Honor Soc., Nat. Coun. Tchrs. Math., Am. Math. Assn. for Two Yr. Colleges, Internat. Group for Psychology of Math. Edn., Minn. Coun. of Tchrs. Math., Minn. Math. Assn. of Two Yr. Colleges, Fil-Minnesotan Assn (bd.dirs. 1991—), Am. Statistical Assn. Roman Catholic. Home: 210 Wexford Heights Dr New Brighton MN 55112

SHIER, SHELLEY M., production company executive; b. Toronto, Mar. 15, 1957; d. Harry Shier and Rosaline (Cutler) Sonshine; m. Hank O'Neal,

May 14, 1985. Student, H.B. Studio, N.Y.C., 1975-76, Stella Adler Conservatory, N.Y.C., 1976-80. Company mem., actor Soho Artists Theater, N.Y.C., 1976-81; casting dir. Lawrence Price Prodns., N.Y.C., 1981-82; pres. Hoss, Inc., N.Y.C., 1983—; v.p. Chiaroscuro Records, N.Y.C., 1987—; cons. Peter Martin Assocs., N.Y.C., 1983, Kloster Cruise Ltd., Miami, Fla., 1983—, Floating Jazz Festival, Big Bands At Sea, Rhythm & Blues Cruise, Dixieland At Sea, Oslo (Norway) Jazz Festival, 1986—, New Sch. for Social Rsch., N.Y.C., 1989—, Beacons In Jazz Awards Ceremony, A Tribute to the Music of Bob Wills and The Texas Playboys, Mardi Gras at Sea. Talent acquisition agt. Save the Children, N.Y.C., 1986, Tomorrow's Children, N.Y.C., 1990, Royal Caribbean Cruise Ltd., Miami, 1994—, Ultimate Caribbean Jazz Spectacular, Country Music Festival in the Caribbean, CUNARD N.Y.C., 1994—, Barcelona Olympics, NBC, 1992, others. Office: HOSS Inc 830 Broadway New York NY 10003-4827

SHIFFMAN, LESLIE BROWN, management executive; b. Fresno, Calif., Dec. 9, 1936; d. Albert Brown and Marion Jean (Riese) Brown-Propp; married, Jan. 20, 1957 (div. 1972); m. Sydney Shiffman, July 4, 1993; children: Susan, Steven, David, Thomas. BS, U. So. Calif., 1958. Office mgr. pvt. practice physician, Long Beach, Calif., 1971-73; cost acct. Panavision, Inc., Tarzana, Calif., 1974-76; exec. sec. Hartman Galleries, Beverly Hills, Calif., 1976-78; adminstrv. asst. Galanos Originals, L.A., 1978—. Named L.A. Alumnae Panhellenic Assn. Women of Yr., 1977. Mem. Alpha Epsilon Phi (nat. pres. 1985-89, trustee, sec. Alpha Epsilon Phi Found. Inc. 1990-91, pres. 1991-95, Woman of Distinction award 1993), Order of Omega Honorary. Republican. Jewish. Home: 1745 S Bentley Ave # 1 Los Angeles CA 90025-4323 Office: Galanos Originals 2254 S Sepulveda Blvd Los Angeles CA 90064-1812

SHIFRIN, SUSAN, historian, small business owner; b. Oakland, Calif., Mar. 4, 1961; d. Seymour Jack and Miriam (Levine) S.; m. F. Michael Angelo, Nov. 11, 1988. Attended, Yale U., 1979-80; BA, Brandeis U., 1984; MA, Bryn Mawr Coll., 1991, postgrad. Intern Dept. Textiles and Costumes Mus. Fine Arts, Boston, summer 1985, sec., dept. asst., 1986-87; intern Dept. Drawings Pierpont Morgan Libr., summer 1988; dept. asst. Dept. Conservation The Bklyn. Mus., 1988-89; grad. asst. coll. archives Bryn Mawr Coll., 1989-90; curatorial asst. art collection Rosenbach Mus. & Libr., Phila., 1990-91; curator textiles, costumes Phila. Coll. Textiles and Sci., 1992-93; ind. historian, cons. Phoenixville, Pa., 1991—; owner Custom Vittles Vending, Phoenixville, 1995—. Contbg. author: Chronology of Women Worldwide: People, Places and Events That Shaped World History, 1996; contbr. articles to profl. jours. Dissertation travel fellow Bryn Mawr Coll., 1995-96, Theodore N. Ely Travel fellow, summers 1992, 94, grad. fellow, 1990-91, scholar, 1989-90, 92-96; Stella blum rsch. grantee The Costume Soc. Am., 1993-94, Coll. Art Assn. History Travel grantee, winter 1993, Sachar Post-Grad. Rsch. grantee Brandeis U., summer 1984, undergrad. rsch. grantee, 1983-84; Smithsonian Instn. Grad. Student fellow, summer 1993, resident rsch. fellow Francis C. Wood Inst. for History of Medicine Coll. Physicians Phila., spring 1993, M. Louise Carpenter Gloeckner, M.D. summer rsch. fellow Archives and Spl. Collections on Women in Medicine Med. Coll. Phila., summer 1991, others. Mem. AAUW, Assn. Am. Mus., Coll. Art Assn., Soc. Historians Brit. Art, Nat. Conf. Brit. Studies, Mid. Atlantic Conf. on Brit. Studies, Group for Early Modern Cultural Studies (conf. organizer 1996, session chair 1996). Democrat. Jewish.

SHIGEMOTO, APRIL FUMIE, English educator secondary school; b. Lihue, Hawaii, Apr. 22, 1948; d. Warren Itaru and Edith Yuriko (Yoshimura) Tanaka; m. Tom Hideo Shigemoto, July 21, 1973; children: Taylor, Tyron, Tryson, Thomas-Jay. BA in English, U. Hawaii Manoa, 1970, profl. diploma secondary, 1971. English tchr. Kapaa (Hawaii) H.S. and Intermediate Sch., 1971-81, Kauai H.S. and Intermediate Sch., Lihue, Hawaii, 1981-90; core curriculum coord. Kauai H.S. and Intermediate Sch., 1990—. Leader Boy Scouts of Am., Lihue, Hawaii, 1982—. Recipient one of seven Status of Women awards, Kauai, Lihue, Hawaii, 1988, Den Leader of the Yr. award Boy Scouts of Am., 1988, Milken Educator's award, Milken Found., L.A., 1992; named Outstanding Working Mother, Garden Island Newspaper, Lihue, Hawaii, 1989, Kauai Dist. Tchr. of Yr., State Dept. Edn., Hawaii, 1990, State Tchr. of Yr., Scottish Rite Order of Free Masons, Honolulu, 1991, one of Kauai's Outstanding Families, Garden Island Newspaper, Hawaii, 1992. Mem. Phi Delta Kappa, Delta Kappa Gamma. Democrat. Office: Kauai HS & Intermediate Sch 3577 Lala Rd Lihue HI 96766-9520

SHIH, J. CHUNG-WEN, Chinese language educator; b. Nanking, China; came to U.S., 1948, naturalized, 1960; d. Cho-kiang and Chia-pu (Fang) S. B.A., St. John's U., Shanghai, 1945; M.A., Duke U., 1949, Ph.D., 1955. Asst. prof. English Kings Coll. N.Y., 1955-56; asst. prof. U. Bridgeport, Conn., 1956-60; postdoctoral fellow East Asian Studies Harvard, 1960-61; asst. prof. Chinese Stanford, 1961-64; asso. prof. Chinese Pomona Coll., 1965-66; asso. prof. George Washington U., Washington, 1966-71, prof., chmn. dept. East Asian langs. and lit., 1971-93, prof. emeritus, 1993—, rsch. prof., 1994—. Author: Injustice to Tou O, 1972, the Golden Age of Chinese Drama: Yuan Tsa-chu, 1976, Return from Silence: China's Writers of the May Fourth Tradition, 1983. Bd. dirs. Sino-Am. Cultural Soc., Washington, 1971-80, 95—. AAUW fellow, 1964-65; Social Sci. Rsch. Coun. fellow, 1976-77; grantee NEH, 1979-80, 89-91, 96-97, Annenberg/CPB Project, 1989-92; sr. scholars exchange program NAS, China, Spring 1980. Mem. Assn. Asian Studies, Am. Council Fgn. Lang. Tchrs., Chinese Lang. Tchrs. Assn. (chmn. exec. bd. 1976-78). Home: 2500 Virginia Ave NW Washington DC 20037-1901 Office: George Washington U Dept East Asian Langs E Washington DC 20052

SHIH, MARIE, metaphysical healer; b. Florence, Ariz., Jan. 24, 1959; d. John Cecil and Josephine Marie (Carter) Lewis; m. Ravi Sundervardan Candadai, Aug. 13, 1982 (div. Aug. 1984); m. Tony Hu-Tung Shih, July 11, 1987 (div. Sept. 1991); m. Jack Hunter Caldwell, Jan. 2, 1995; 1 child, John Lewis Caldwell; step-children: Trevor Hunter, Levi Robert. BA, U. Ariz., 1982, postgrad., 1982-84. Musician, writer, illustrator, Tucson and Seattle, 1978-94; front desk clk. Ghost Ranch Lodge, Tucson, 1982-83; adminstrv. sec. Starnet Corp., Seattle, 1985-86; vol. U.S. Peace Corps, Mbalmayo, Cameroun, Africa, 1986; practitioner Christian Science Ch., 1994—, ch. vocalist, 1994; ind. team mgr. Noevir Natural Herbal Cosmetics, Seattle, 1987-92, author, editor mo. newsletter, 1989-92, attended nat. convs., 1989-92; lectr. So. Seattle Cmty. Coll., 1990-92. Author press releases, bus. forms local orgns., Tucson, Seattle, 1978-94; editor letters, speeches local orgns., Seattle; author, editor, designer mo. newsletter Fairmount News and Views, 1993-94; contbr. articles to jours. Bd. dirs., com. chmn. S.W. Seattle Liberacy Coalition, 1989-90; active ArtsWest, United Way, West Seattle Totem Theatre, 1990-94; bus. sponsor West Seattle Hi-Yu, 1991; active 6th Ch. of Christ, Scientist, Seattle, 1987-96, 1st reader, 1991-94; active 1st Ch. of Christ, Scientist, Boston, 1990—, Christian Sci. Soc. of Casa Grande, 1996—; mem. steering com. Constellation Park and Marine Res. at Ritchey Viewpoint, 1993-94; founding mem. Fairmount Ravine Preservation Group, 1993-94; substitute ch. soloist, Chehalis, 1994. Mem. NAFE, West Seattle C. of C. (area dir. 1990-91, com. mem. 1990-93, com. chair 1992-93), Neighborhood Promotion Com., Coolidge C. of C. Republican. Address: PO Box 1964 Coolidge AZ 85228

SHIH-CARDUCCI, JOAN CHIA-MO, cooking educator, biochemist, medical technologist; b. Rukuan, Chunghua, Republic of China, Dec. 21, 1933; came to U.S., 1955; d. Luke Chiang-hsi and Lien-chin (Chang) Shih; m. Kenneth M. Carducci, Sept. 30, 1960 (dec. July 1988); children: Suzanne R., Elizabeth M. BS in Chemistry, St. Mary Coll., Xavier, Kans., 1959; intern in med. tech., St. Mary's Hosp., Rochester, N.Y., 1960. Med. researcher Strong Meml. Hosp. (U. Rochester), 1960-61; pharm. chemist quality control Strasenburgh Labs., Rochester, 1961-62; cooking tchr. adult edn. Montgomery County Pub. Schs., Rockville, Md., 1973-79; cooking tchr. The Chinese Cookery Inc., Rockville, 1975-86; cooking tchr. The Chinese Cookery Inc., Silver Spring, Md., 1986—, pres., bd. dirs., 1975—; chemist NIH, Bethesda, 1987—; analytical chemist NIH/WRAIR, Rockville, Md., 1994-96. Author: The Chinese Cookery, 1981, Hunan Cuisine, 1984. Mem. Am. Chem. Soc., Internat. Assn. Cooking Profls. (Woman of the Yr. 1994, 95). Republican. Roman Catholic. Home and Office: The Chinese Cookery Inc 14209 Sturtevant Rd Silver Spring MD 20905-4448

SHILLINGSBURG, MIRIAM JONES, English educator, academic administrator; b. Balt., Oct. 5, 1943; d. W. Elvin and Miriam (Reeves) Jones; BA, Mars Hill Coll., 1964; MA, U. S.C., 1966, PhD, 1969; m. Peter L. Shillingsburg, Nov. 21, 1967; children: Robert, George, John, Alice, Anne Carol. Asst. prof. Limestone Coll., Gaffney, S.C., 1969; asst. prof. Mississippi State (Miss.) U., 1970-75, assoc. prof., 1975-80, prof. English, 1980-96, assoc. v.p. for acad. affairs, 1988-96, dir. summer sch., 1991-96; dean arts and scis. Lamar U., Tex., 1996—; vis. fellow Australian Def. Force Acad., 1989; Fulbright lectr. U. New South Wales, Duntroon, Australia, 1984-85. Nat. Endowment Humanities fellow in residence, Columbia U., 1976-77. Mem. Soc. Study So. Lit., Nat. Acad. Advising Assn., S. Ctrl. Modern Lang. Assn., Australia-New Zealand Am. Studies Assn., Phi Kappa Phi, Simms Soc. (pres.). Author: Mark Twain in Australasia, 1988; editor: Conquest of Granada, 1988; mem. editorial bd. Works of W.M. Thackeray; assoc. editor Miss. Quarterly; contbr. articles to profl. jours. and mags.

SHIMMIN, MARGARET ANN, women's health nurse; b. Forbes, N.D., Oct. 26, 1941; d. George Robert and Reba Aleda (Strain) S. Diploma in Nursing, St. Luke's Hosp. Sch. Nursing, Fargo, N.D., 1962; BSW, U. West Fla., 1978; cert. ob-gyn nurse practitioner, U. Ala., Birmingham, 1983, MPH, 1986. Lic. nurse, Fla., N.D., Ala. Head nurse, emergency room St. Luke's Hosps., Fargo, 1962-67; charge nurse, labor and delivery, perinatal nurse educator Sacred Heart Hosp., Pensacola, Fla., 1970-82; ARNP Escambia County Pub. Health Unit, Pensacola, 1983-89; cmty. health nursing cons. Dist. 1 Health and Rehab. Svcs., Pensacola, 1989—. Capt. nurse corps U.S. Army, 1967-70, Japan. Mem. NAACOG (cert. maternal-gynecol.-neonatal nursing 1978, ob-gyn nurse practitioner 1983), Fla. Nurses' Assn., ANA, N.W. Fla. ARNP (past sec./treas.), Fla. Perinatal Assn., Nat. Perinatal Assn., Healthy Mothers/Healthy Babies Coalition, Fla. Pub. Health Assn., U. West Fla. Alumni Assn., U. Ala. at Birmingham Sch. of Public Health Alumni Assn., Phi Alpha. Republican. Presbyterian. Home: 8570 Olympia Rd Pensacola FL 32514-8029 Office: Dist 1 HRS 160 Governmental Ctr Pensacola FL 32501

SHIMP, KAREN ANN, accountant, municipal financial executive; b. Atlantic, Iowa, July 17, 1959; d. Emerson Arnold and Verna Louise (Schmeling) Fett; m. Philip Kenneth Shimp, Jan. 30, 1988 (div.); 1 child, Keith Emerson. BSBA, Drake U., 1981. Acct. Midwest Mut. Ins. Co., West Des Moines, Iowa, 1981-84; staff acct. Deborah J. Kent, CPA, Palm Desert, Calif., 1985; fin. analyst Massey Sand & Rock Co., Indio, Calif., 1986-88; supr. interline Greyhound Lines, Inc., West Des Moines, 1989-93; fin. dir. City of Pella, Iowa, 1993—; coord. Drake U. Bus. Aid Soc., 1980; mem. Inland Soc. Tax Consultants, 1987-91. Treas. Luth. Women's Missionary League, Indio, 1986-88, sec., 1988-89; v.p. Aid Assn. for Lutherans, Indio, 1988-89. State of Iowa scholar, 1977. Mem. NAFE, Inst. Mgmt. Accts. (bd. dirs.), Kiwanis Internat. Democrat. Home: 808 W 1st St Pella IA 50219-1708 Office: City of Pella 717 Main St Pella IA 50219-1620

SHIN, JEAN KYOUNG, artist; b. Seoul, Korea, Aug. 25, 1971; came to U.S., 1978; d. Eui Sheen and Sung Hee (Chung) Shin. BFA, Pratt Inst. Art & Design, 1994, MS, 1996. Editor-in-chief Prattler, Bklyn., 1991-94; curatorial intern Bklyn. Mus., 1994; asst. to dir. Artists Talk on Art, N.Y.C., 1994-95; curatorial asst. The Whitney Mus. of Am. Art, N.Y.C., 1996—. U.S. Presdl. Scholar in the Arts, Washington, 1990.

SHINA, LISA ANNE, clinical social worker, psychotherapist; b. Cornwall, N.Y., Jan. 2, 1959; d. Joseph Edward and Lucille Barbara (Nazzaro) S. AAS, Orange County C.C., 1979; BA in Criminal Justice, L.I. U., 1981; MSW, Adelphi U., 1988. CSW-R; cert. alcoholism counselor, N.Y.; cert. addictions counselor, N.Y.; cert. social worker, N.Y. Youth counselor Town of Woodbury, Highland Mills, N.Y., 1981-83; youth counselor, coord. Town of Chester Police, Chester, N.Y., 1984-85; dir. of counseling svcs. Warwick Cmty. Bandwagon, Warwick, N.Y., 1985-89; employee assistance coord. Orange County Govt., Goshen, N.Y., 1986-88; adolescent addiction counselor Horton Hosp., Middletown, N.Y., 1989; clinician So. Orange Counseling Ctr., Warwick, 1991-93; peer mediation dir., sch. coord., student assistance counselor, student svcs. coord. Monroe-Woodbury Ctrl. Sch., Central Valley, N.Y., 1989—; clin. supr. Counseling Resource Ctr., Pine Island, N.Y., 1993—. Adv. bd. mem. PINS steering com., Goshen, 1992—; mem., cons. Orange County Student Assistance Orgn., Goshen, 1990—; v.p. Orange County Youth adv. bd., 1994—; membership com. Orange County AIDS Task Force, Goshen, 1994—. Mem. NASW, Nat. Coalition Bldg. Inst. Roman Catholic. Home: 15 Oak Dr Highland Mills NY 10930

SHINDER, MARCELLA MARIE, marketing professional; b. Indpls., Jan. 4, 1967; d. Anthony S. and Bernice (Duffy) Lazar,: m. Richard Shinder, June 29, 1991. BEd, Gonzaga U., 1989; MA, Villanova U., 1992. Mgr. Am. Express, N.Y.C., 1993—. Polit. analyst N.Y. for Guiliani, 1993. Republican. Roman Catholic. Home: 225 Rector Pl 20A New York NY 10280

SHINEVAR, KAREN KAY, lawyer; b. Marshall, Mich., Mar. 16, 1956; d. Wayne Alden and Elizabeth Marilyn (Albrecht) Coats; m. Peter O'Neil Shinevar, Aug. 25, 1979; children: Thomas Scott, William Joseph. BA in History and Econs., Albion Coll., 1978; JD, U. Mich., 1981. Bar: D.C. 1981, Md. 1982, N.Y. 1994. Assoc. Seifman, Semo & Slevin, Washington, 1981-82; atty. MCI Airsignal, Inc., Washington, 1983-86; v.p. McCaw Cellular Comm., Washington, 1986-91; v.p. ops., gen. counsel Cellular Telephone Co. dba AT&T Wireless Svcs., Paramus, N.J., 1992—. Mem. Md. Bar Assn., D.C. Bar Assn., N.Y. Women in Utilities, N.J. Corp. Counsel Assn., Phi Beta Kappa. Office: Cellular Telephone Co 15 E Midland Ave Paramus NJ 07652-2926

SHIPE, KATHLEEN MARIE, graphic designer; b. Chgo., Feb. 26, 1947; d. Philip Joseph and Margaret Elizabeth (Himmes) Browner; m. James Orrin Shipe, Oct. 11, 1986. BA in Edn., Ariz. State U., Tempe, 1969, MA, 1971; MPhil, Rutgers U., 1988. Adminstr. Rutgers U., New Brunswick, 1975-81; v.p. Bold Impressions, Inc., Scottsdale, Ariz., 1981-88, pres., 1988—; bd. dirs. Delta Dental, Phoenix. Editor newsletter CF, 1991-95; contbr. articles to profl. jours. Pres. ctrl. Ariz. chpt. Muscular Dystrophy Assn., Tempe, 1989-95; bd. dirs. Contemporary Forum, Phoenix, 1991-95, Phoenix Art Mus., 1994—; chmn. small bus. awards com. Scottsdale (Ariz.) C. of C., 1993-95. Named Small Bus. of Yr., Scottsdale C. of C., 1991; Russell Sage Found. grantee, 1973. Mem. Phoenix Direct Mkgt. Club (1st pl. Otto award 1994, 95, 96). Democrat. Roman Catholic. Office: Bold Impressions Inc 6990 E Main St Ste 205 Scottsdale AZ 85251

SHIPEK, KIM LINES, visual arts educator; b. Kodiak, Alaska, July 1, 1955; d. Joseph Elmer and Donna Mary (Smoot) Lines; m. David Connolly Shipek, June 11, 1977; 1 child, David Catlow. BS, No. Ariz. U., 1977; MS, Bank St. Coll. of Edn., 1990. Cert. visual art specialist K-12, Ariz. Tchr. h.s. art Sierra Vista (Ariz.) Pub. Schs., 1984—; instr. Cochise C.C., Sierra Vista, 1985, 87; chair fine arts dept. Buena H.S., Sierra Vista, 1986—; instr. U. Ariz., Sierra Vista, 1996; Sierra Vista pub. sch. rep. Sierra Vista Arts & Humanities Commn., 1987—. Mem. Nat. Art Edn. Assn. (educator 1991), Ariz. Art Edn. Assn. (exec. coun. mem., pres. 1986—), Toastmasters # 3198, Phi Delta Kappa. Christian Scientist. Office: Buena H S 3555 E Fry Blvd Sierra Vista AZ 85635-2972

SHIPHERD, SUSAN VAN HORN, sales representative; b. Irvington, N.J., Jan. 5, 1943; d. John Alfred and Dorothy (Blake) Van Horn; m. John Bennett Shipherd, Nov. 13, 1965 (div. Feb. 1991); children: Jon Peter, Jillian; m. James Peter Ferris, Mar. 7, 1992. BS, SUNY, Albany, 1964. Med. libr. Winthrop Labs., N.Y.C., 1964-65; lab. technician Cornell U., Ithaca, N.Y., 1965, 66, 69; fish and wildlife technician N.Y. State Dept. of Environ. Conservation, Delmar, 1972-73; lab. technician N.Y. State Dept. Health, Albany, 1974-75; rsch. asst. SUNY, Albany, 1977-78, Albany Med. Coll., 1979-82; sales rep. Krackeler Sci. Inc., Albany, 1982—. Pres., bd. dirs. Alumni Assn. U. Albany, 1986-94, co-chair capitol dist. chpt., 1994—. Democrat. Roman Catholic. Home: 10 Saddle Hill Rd Wynantskill NY 12198 Office: PO Box 1849 Albany NY 12201

SHIPLEY, LUCIA HELENE, retired chemical company executive; b. Boston, Oct. 26, 1920; d. Harry Jacob and Helen Merrill (Dillingham) Farrington; m. Charles Raymond Shipley, Oct. 11, 1941; children: Helen Merrill, Richard Charles. Student, Smith Coll., 1938-41. Chief exec. officer, treas. Shipley Co. Inc., Newton, Mass., 1957-92, also bd. dirs. Patentee for immersion tin, electroless copper. Recipient Winthrop Sears award Chem. Industry Assn., 1985, Semi award Semicon West, 1990. Mem. Garden Club (pres. 1954-56). Republican. Congregationalist.

SHIPPEE, PATRICIA MOREL, fine art dealer; b. Bklyn., Oct. 7, 1940; d. William Emil and Marian Agnes (Swager) Morel; m. Nathan Mathewson Shippee. BA, Fordham U., 1981. Corp. v.p., sec. Am. Stock Exch. Co., N.Y.C., 1964-80; owner, mgr. Old Lyme (Conn.) Art Works, 1983-89, Shippee Gallery, N.Y.C., 1980-89; fine arts dealer, cons. and curator various pvt. and corp. collections; trustee Griffis Art Ctr., New London, Conn./artist-in-residence program, 1990—; co-chair exhbn. com. Lyman Allyn Art Mus., New London, 1994—; co-editor, sponsor 1995-96 Directory of Fine Art and Artists of Southeastern Conn., 1995; curator exhbn. "New England Landscapes - Impressionist Paintings by Roger W. Dennis", Akus Gallery, Ea. Conn. State U., Willimantic, 1994; mem. auction com. Lyme Acad. of Fine Arts, 1994; co-curator exhbn. "On The Pond", Bradbury Mill, 1993, others; mem. art vis. com. Wheaton Coll., Norton, mass., 1970-76; TV program interviewer Art Talk, 1994-95. Home and Office: 209 Mile Creek Rd Old Lyme CT 06371

SHIPPEY, LYN, reading center director; b. Childress, Tex., Mar. 6, 1927; d. Robert Coke and Alta (Timmons) Elliott; m. James George Shippey, Mar. 29, 1947; children: James Robert, Deborah Shippey Meyer, Marilyn Shippey Buron. BS, U. Corpus Christi, 1963; MA in Edn., San Diego State U., 1977; EdD, U. San Diego, 1993. Cert. tchr., reading specialist, tchr. of learning handicapped, Calif. Substitute tchr. Dept. Edn., Guam, 1958-61; tchr. counselor Robstown Ind. Sch. Dist., Tex., 1964-65; elem. tchr. Cupertino Union Sch. Dist., Calif., 1965-68, tchr., secondary, 1968-71; dir. PIRK Reading Center, Poway, Calif., 1973—; cons., workshop presenter PIRK Reading Programs, Calif., Tex., 1974—. Author: Perceptual Integration Reading Kits, 1971, PIRK Reading Program, 1977, rev. 1987. Mem. Coun. for Exceptional Children, Alcala Soc. U. San Diego (scholar), Orton Dyslexia Soc., Learning Disabilities Assn., Coun. for Learning Disabilities. Office: PIRK Reading Center 16957 Cloudcroft Dr Poway CA 92064-1306

SHIPPEY, SANDRA LEE, lawyer; b. Casper, Wyo., June 24, 1957; d. Virgil Carr and Doris Louise (Conklin) McC.; m. Ojars Herberts Ozols, Sept. 2, 1978 (div.); children: Michael Ojars, Sara Ann, Brian Christopher; m. James Robert Shippey, Jan. 13, 1991. BA with distinction, U. Colo., 1978; JD magna cum laude, Boston U., 1982. Bar: Colo. 1982, U.S. Dist. Ct. Colo. 1985. Assoc. Cohen, Brame & Smith, Denver, 1983-84, Parcel, Meyer, Schwartz, Ruttum & Mauro, Denver, 1984-85, Mayer, Brown & Platt, Denver, 1985-87; counsel western ops. GE Capital Corp., San Diego, 1987-94; assoc. Page, Polin, Busch & Boatwright, San Diego, 1994-95; v.p., gen. counsel First Comml. Corp., San Diego, 1995—. Active Pop Warner football and cheerleading. Mem. Phi Beta Kappa, Phi Delta Phi. Republican. Mem. Ch. of Christ. Home: 11878 Glenhope Rd San Diego CA 92128-5002 Office: First Comml Corp 550 West C St Ste 1000 San Diego CA 92101

SHIRKEY, LINDA SUE, interior designer, film company executive, set designer; b. Denver, June 29, 1948; d. Roger L. and Virginia Ruth (Lee) Williams; m. Larry Wayne, May 2, 1972 (div. Aug. 1982); children Troy Lee, Ian Christopher. BFA, U. Colo., Denver and Boulder, 1970; AAS, Arapahoe C.C., Littleton, 1985. Figure skating coach Denver, 1972-84; interior design Possibilities For Design, Denver, 1983-85; interior designer For Men Only, Inc., Denver, 1985-95; film prodn. mgr., set styling & interior design Desciose Prodns., Denver, 1991—. Prodn. mgr.: (public svc. announcement) Going Home-Colo. Christian Home, 1992 (Emmy nom. 1992). mem. bd. dirs. Front Range Ctr. for Spiritual Growth, Denver, 1993-95, pres. 1995; treas. Spiritual Solutions, Denver, 1996. Mem. Internat. Interior Design Assn., Denver Mile High Rotary (chair cmty. svc. 1993-94, fellowship chair 1996-97). Office: Prodn & Design By Linda PO Box 100865 Denver CO 80250

SHIRLEY, COURTNEY DYMALLY, nurse; b. Trinidad, July 17, 1937; came to U.S., 1960; d. Andrew Hamid Dymally; m. Adolph Shirley, Apr. 8, 1960; children: Ingrid, Robyne, Andrea, Kirk, Sandra. Cert. mgmt./adminstrn. health facilities, UCLA, 1978; BBA, Calif. Coast U., 1980, MBA, 1983. Cert. critical care nurse, advanced critical care nurse, nursing home adminstr. Head nurse med. unit Prince of Wales Gen. Hosp., London, 1959-60; asst. head nurse, CCU staff nurse Cedars-Sinai Hosp., L.A., 1962-73; asst. dir. nursing, dir. in-svc. edn., staff nurse Beverly Glen Hosp., 1973-75; supr. ICU/CCU/house Imperial Hosp., 1975-76; house supr. Med. Ctr. of North Hollywood, 1976-77; dir. nursing Crenshaw Ctr. Hosp., 1977-78, Mid-Wilshire Convalescent, 1978-79; supr. ICU/CCU, coord. utilization rev. Temple U., 1979-80; house supr. East L.A. Doctors' Hosp., 1980-81; pvt. nurse various hosps. and homes, 1981-86; utilization rev. coord. Managed Care Resources, L.A., 1986-88; prof. rev. sys. utilization rev. coord., case mgr. Nat. Med. Enterprises, Santa Monica, Calif., 1988—, cert. case mgr., 1993—. Mem. AACN, Internat. Case Mgmt. Assn., Sci. of Mind, Toastmasters (sgt. at arms 1990). Office: Nat Med Enterprises 2700 Colorado Ave Santa Monica CA 90404-3521

SHIRLEY, NORMA, librarian, bibliographer; b. Chatham, N.Y., Mar. 22, 1935; d. George and Bertha (Shattuck) Shirley. B.A., Russell Sage Coll., 1962; M.L.S., SUNY-Albany, 1963, M.S. in Ednl. Adminstrn., 1980. Asst. reference librarian Jr. Coll. Albany, 1963-65; librarian Hudson Area Library (N.Y.), 1966-67; reference librarian Russell Sage Coll., Troy, N.Y., 1967-69; librarian Poughkeepsie High Sch. (N.Y.), 1970-71; library media specialist Spl. Edn. Ctr., Dutchess County BOCES, Poughkeepsie, 1971-92. Co-author: Checklist of Serials in Psychology and Allied Fields, 1969; Serials in Psychology and Allied Fields, 1976. Bd. dirs. Friends of Locust Grove, Deyo Family Assn., Huguenot Hist. Soc. Home: PO Box 2401 Poughkeepsie NY 12603-8401

SHIRLEY, VIRGINIA LEE, advertising executive; b. Kankakee, Ill., Mar. 24, 1936; d. Glenn Lee and Virginia Helen (Ritter) S. Student, Northwestern U., 1960-61. With prodn. control dept. Armour Pharm., Kankakee, 1954-58; exec. sec. Adolph Richman, Chgo., 1958-61; mgr. media dept. Don Kemper Co., Chgo., 1961-63, 65-69; exec. sec. Playboy mag., Chgo., 1964-65; exec. v.p. SMY Media inc., Chgo., 1969-96, CEO, chmn. bd., 1996—. Mem. Pla. Club. Home: 1502-J S Prairie Ave Chicago IL 60605-2856 Office: SMY Media Inc 333 N Michigan Ave Chicago IL 60601-3901

SHIRTCLIFF, CHRISTINE FAY, healthcare facility executive; b. Greenfield, Mass.; d. Francis E. and Doris E. (Olsen) S.; 1 child, Danielle Elizabeth. BS in Pub. Health, U. Mass., 1973, MBA, 1987; MEd, Antioch U., 1978. Lic. nursing home adminstr., social worker. Health program rep. Fulton County Health Dept., Atlanta, 1973-74; home health aide supv. County Health Care, Greenfield, Mass., 1974-77; adminstrv. asst. Mary Lane Hosp. (now Mary Lane Hosp./Baystate Health Sys.), Ware, Mass., 1977-79; asst. exec. dir. Mary Lane Hosp., Ware, Mass., 1979-85, exec. v.p., 1985—; founder, mem. steering com. We. Mass. Healthcare Mgrs. Group, 1983-86; active Mass. Rural Devel. Social Svcs. Subcom., 1986, Mass. Coun. Homemaker/Home Health Aide Svcs., 1976-85, bd. dirs., 1976-77, We. Mass. Health Planning Coun., 1974-78. Trustee Congl. Ch. in Belchertown, Mass., 1993-95; mem. Belchertown Collaboration for Excellence in Edn., 1993; mem. blue ribbon com. on excellence in edn.; corporator Country Bank, 1996. Fellow Am. Coll. Healthcare Execs. Office: Mary Lane Hosp 85 South St Ware MA 01082-1649

SHISLER, ROBIN ELLEN, occupational therapist; b. Phila., Feb. 3, 1961; d. Robert Helm and Ellen (Gindhart) H. Long; m. Dale Edward Shisler, Sept. 25, 1988; children: Kyle James, Keely Ann. BS in Occupational Therapy, Temple U., 1984. Occupational therapist Craig Hosp., Englewood, Colo., 1985-93, 95—, Home Health Profls., Englewood, Colo., 1988-89, Med. Resource Co., Ind., 1993-94, Vis. Nurses Assn., Denver, 1994-95, Holy Redemer Vis Nurses Assn., Erma, N.J., 1995; presenter in field. Home: 957 Yellowpine Bailey CO 80421 Office: Craig Hosp 3425 S Clarkson Rd Englewood CO 80110

SHIVELY, BETH ANN, elementary education educator; b. Plymouth, Ind., Dec. 5, 1947; d. Robert Floyd and Esther Louise (Grossman) Shaffer; m. Charles Daniel Shively, July 31, 1971 (div. Sept. 1987); 1 child, Michael

C. BS in Edn., Ball State U., 1970, MA in Edn., 1971. Elem. tchr. grades 4 & 5 Jefferson Sch., Plymouth, 1971-89, 90—; primary tchr. grade 5 Tongala (Victoria, Australia) Primary Sch., 1989; spkr. in field. Mem. Maxinkuckee Players Civic Theater, Culver, Ind., 1980-83, 85—, musical dir., 1988—; dir. Maxinkuckee Singers Singing Group, Culver, 1992—. Internat. Tchg. fellow tchr. exchange Internat. Tchg. Fellowship Australia, Victoria, 1989. Mem. NEA, Ind. State Tchrs. Assn., Plymouth Edn. Assn., Marshall County Reading Coun. (bldg. rep. 1986-94). Methodist. Home: 14380 Lawrence Lake Dr Plymouth IN 46563-8574

SHIVELY, JUDITH CAROLYN (JUDY SHIVELY), office assistant, contract administrator; b. Wilkinsburg, Pa., Jan. 30, 1962; d. John Allen and Edith (Crowell) S. BA in English, U. Nev., Las Vegas, 1984. Circulation aide Charleston Heights Libr., Las Vegas, 1979-86; asst. food editor Las Vegas Sun Newspaper, 1985-88, asst. horse racing editor, 1985-90, features writer, page editor, 1988-89, editor youth activities sect., 1989-90; racebook ticket writer, cashier Palace Sta. Hotel Racebook, Las Vegas, 1989-92; contract adminstr., gen. office asst. Loomis Armored, Inc., Las Vegas, 1992—; propr. Creative Computing, Las Vegas, 1996—; horse racing historian, rschr., Las Vegas, 1985—; vol. rsch. asst. Dictionary of Gambling and Gaming, 1982-84; part-time clk. Hometown News, Las Vegas, 1994-96. Staff writer horse race handicaps, columns, articles, feature stories Las Vegas Sun Newspaper, 1985-90; freelance writer for monthly horse racing publ. Inside Track, 1992-94. Mem. Phi Beta Kappa. Republican. Home: PO Box 26426 Las Vegas NV 89126-0426

SHIVERS, JANE, corporate communications executive, director; b. Georgetown, Tex., June 29, 1943; d. Marvin Bishop and Jewell (Petrey) Edwards; m. Harold E. Shivers; children: Clay Houston, Will Davis; m. Don Evans Hutcheson. BA, U. Md., 1965. Reseacher Amex Broadcasting Co., San Francisco, 1965-67; pub. info. officer Semester at Sea, Orange, Calif., 1967-69; dir. pub. rels. Atlanta Arts Alliance, 1974-78, RSVT, Atlanta, 1978-82; pres. Shivers Communications, Atlanta, 1982-84; exec. v.p., dir. Ketchum Pub. Rels., Atlanta, 1985—; pres. Midtown Bus. Assocs., Atlanta, 1987-91; bd. dirs. Crown Cryts, Inc. Trustee Alliance Theatre Co., Atlanta, 1980-93, Care, Internat., Atlanta, 1988-89; bd. dirs. Piedmont Park Conservancy, Emory Sch. Pub. Health. Recipient Mgmt. Woman Achievement award Women in Communication, Atlanta, 1984. Mem. Pub. Rels. Soc. Am. (bd. dirs.), Cen. Atlanta Progress Club, Commerce Club, Peachtree Club, Crown Crafts, Inc. (bd. dirs.). Episcopalian. Home: 238 15th St NE Atlanta GA 30309-3594 Office: Ketchum Pub Rels 999 Peachtree St NE Atlanta GA 30309-3964

SHOBE, NANCY, fundraising consultant; b. Detroit, Oct. 3, 1961; d. Richard William and Barbara Ann (Williams) S.; 1 child, Allison Elizabeth Stelyn; m. William Wright Watling, Aug. 23, 1996. BA, Mich. State U., 1983. Copywriter Wickes Lumber Hdqr., Vernon Hills, Ill., 1983-85; asst. to prodr. Music Ctr. of L.A., 1985, mercado coord., 1985-86; dir. comms. Candlelight Pavilion, Claremont, Calif., 1987-88, corp. dir. mktg., 1988; asst. dir. devel. The Webb Schs., Claremont, Calif., 1988-90; dir. devel. Crane Sch., Santa Barbara, Calif., 1991-96. Contbr. chpts. to books. Mem. Coun. Advancement and Support of Edn. (heavy hitter spkr. 1993, cir. of excellence award for ednl. fund raising 1995). Democrat. Episcopalian. Home and Office: 1705 Franceschi Rd Santa Barbara CA 93103

SHOCKED, MICHELLE, vocalist, songwriter; b. 1963; d. Bill Johnston. Student, U. Tex. Albums include The Texas Campfire Tapes, 1987, Short Sharp Shocked, 1988, Captain Swing, 1989, Arkansas Traveler, 1992, Kind Hearted Woman, 1995. Office: care Mercury/Polygram Records Worldwide Plaza 825 8th Ave New York NY 10019*

SHOCKEY, GEORGANNE MICHELLE, sales manager; b. St. Marys, Ohio, July 1, 1958; d. George Michael and Clover B. (Werner) Apelian; m. Gregory L. Shockey, June 22, 1985. BS in Home Econs., Ohio State U., 1980. Asst. dir. food svc. Meml. Hosp. Marriott Corp., Houston, 1981-84; assoc. dir. food svc. Cedars Med. Ctr. Marriott Corp., Miami, Fla., 1984-85; dir. food and nutrition svc. Children's Hosp. Stanford Sodexho USA, Calif., 1985-89; dir. food and nutrition Torrance (Calif.) Meml. Med. Ctr. Sodexho USA, 1989-92; regional sales mgr. Sodexho USA, Inc., Alameda, Calif., 1992—. Participant Shell Oil/L.A. Marathon Wheelchair Race, 1993-96, Children's Miracle Network, L.A. area, 1994, 95, Real Women Cook to Fight Breast Cancer, L.A., 1995. Recipient award Real Women Cook to Fight Breast Cancer, 1995, Salesperson of Yr. Sodexho USA, 1993, 95. Mem. NAFE, Am. Soc. Hosp. Food Svc. Assocs., Roundtable for Women in Food Svc., Phi Mu (past officer, nat. adv. dir. 1981-84, area coord.). Office: Sodexho USA Inc # 400 1001 Marina Village Pkwy Alameda CA 94501

SHOCKLEY, CAROL FRANCES, psychologist, psychotherapist; b. Atlanta, Nov. 24, 1948; d. Robert Thomas and Frances Lavada (Scrivner) S. BA, Ga. State U., 1974, MEd, 1976; PhD, U. Ga., 1990. Cert. in gerontology; Diplomate Am. Bd. Forensic Examiners. Counselor Rape Crisis Ctr., Atlanta, 1979-80; emergency mental health clinician Gwinnett Med. Ctr., Lawrenceville, Ga., 1980-86; psychotherapist Fla. Mental Health Inst., Tampa, 1987-89, Tampa Bay Acad., Riverview, Fla., 1990-91; sr. psychologist State of Fla. Dept. of Corrections, Bushnell, 1991-92; ind. practice psychology Brunswick, Ga., 1992—; mem. Adv. Bd. for Mental Health/Mental Retardation, 1992-94. Author: (with others) Relapse Prevention with Sex Offenders, 1989. Vol. Ga. Mental Health Inst., Atlanta, 1972; leader Alzheimer's Disease Support Group, Athens, Ga., 1984; vol. therapist Reminiscence Group for Elderly, Athens, 1984-85. Recipient Meritorious Svc. award Beta Gamma Sigma, 1975. Mem. Am. Psychol. Assn., Ga. Psychol. Assn., Sigma Phi Omega, Psi Chi. Office: 14 Saint Andrews Ct Brunswick GA 31520-6764

SHOCKLEY, SARAH ANNE, publishing company executive; b. Greenwich, Conn., Oct. 30, 1954; d. Robert Bartlett and Cora Merritt (Keith) S. BA in German, U. Vt., 1976; MBA in Internat. Mktg., Monterey Inst. Internat. Studies, 1982. Mgr. Caribbean, Ams. and Far East Computerland Corp., Hayward, Calif., 1984-85, mgr. internat. product mktg., 1985-86; contracts and grants adminstr. Lawrence Berkeley (Calif.) Lab., 1990-92; co-owner Dancing Video, El Cerrito, Calif., 1994—; owner Any Road Press, El Cerrito, 1994—; mem. faculty U. Phoenix, 1994—. Author: Traveling Incognito, 1994, The Critics' Choice Award, 1995; dir. video documentary Dancing From the Inside Out, 1994. Recipient Chris award Colombus Internat. Film and Video Festival, 1994, Golden plaque Intercom Chgo. Internal Film Festival, 1994. Office: Any Road Press 190 El Cerrito Plz Ste 204 El Cerrito CA 94530-4002

SHOE, MARGARET ELLEN, accountant; b. Phila., Feb. 10, 1944; d. Francis James and Margaret Edna (Hathaway) Wiedenmann; m. Richard Alan Shoe, Feb. 14, 1964 (div. Aug. 1975). Associates, Burlington County Coll., 1978; BS, Trenton State Coll., 1982. Lic. pub. acct.; lic. real estate salesperson. Acct., office mgr. Philmar Constrn. Co., Somerdale, N.J., 1967-72; acct. Microcircuit Engring., Medford, N.J., 1972-73, R.L. Fitzwater and Son, Inc., Merchantville, N.J., 1973-75; asst. contr. Bancroft Sch. and Instrn., Haddonfield, N.J., 1976-79; corp. contr. Paparone Constrn. Co. Inc., Mt. Laurel, N.J., 1979; asst. contr. Reutter Engring. Inc., Camden, N.J., 1979-80; corp. contr. CSI Electronics, Inc., Cinnaminson, N.J., 1980, Wagner Holm and Inglis, Inc., Mt. Holly, N.J., 1980-81; pub. acct. Shoe Acctg. and Consulting Svc., Mt. Laurel, N.J., 1981—; acctg. clk. Robert C. Perina, CPA, Camden, 1968-69; bookkeeper, acctg. clk. Lantern Lane Interiors, Cherry Hill, N.J., 1967; bookkeeper, cost acctg. clk. Drew Constrn. Co., Inc., Cherry Hill, 1964-66; bookkeeper, time study clk. Mailing Svcs., Inc., Pennsauken, N.J., 1963-64. Recipient Woman of Achievement award Burlington County Freeholders, 1990. Mem. N.J. Assn. Pub. Accts. (pres. 1992-93, bd. dirs. 1988—, Camden pres., v.p. 1988-91), N. J. Bd. Accountancy, N.J. Assn. Women Bus. Owners (bd. dirs. 1981—, del. White House conf. small bus. 1984), Inst. Managerial Accts. (assoc.), Cherry Hill C. of C., Rotary. Lutheran. Home and Office: Shoe Acctg and Consulting 623 Union Mill Rd Mount Laurel NJ 08054-9515

SHOEMAKER, CLARA BRINK, retired chemistry educator; b. Rolde, Drenthe, The Netherlands, June 20, 1921; came to U.S., 1953; d. Hendrik Gerard and Hendrikje (Smilde) Brink; m. David Powell Shoemaker, Aug. 5. 1955; 1 child, Robert Brink. PhD, Leiden U., The Netherlands, 1950. Instr. in inorganic chemistry Leiden U., 1946-50, 51-53; postdoctoral fellow Oxford (Eng.) U., 1950-51; rsch. assoc. dept. chemistry MIT, Cambridge, 1953-55, 58-70; rsch. assoc. biochemistry Harvard Med. Sch., Boston, 1955-56; project supr. Boston U., 1963-64; rsch. assoc. dept. chemistry Oreg. State U, Corvallis, 1970-75, rsch. assoc. prof. dept. chemistry, 1975-82, sr. rsch. prof. dept. chemistry, 1982-84, prof. emerita, 1984—. Sect. editor: Structure Reports of International Union of Crystallography, 1967, 68, 69; co-author chpts. in books; author numerous sci. papers. Bd. dirs. LWV, Corvallis, 1980-82, bd. dirs., sec., Oreg., 1985-87. Fellow Internat. Fedn. Univ. Women, Oxford U., 1950-51. Mem. Metall. Soc. (com. on alloy phases 1969-79), Internat. Union of Crystallography (commn. on structure reports 1970-90), Am. Crystallographic Assn. (crystallographic data com. 1975-78, Fankuchen award com. 1976), Sigma Xi, Iota Sigma Pi (faculty adv. Oreg. State U. chpt. 1975-84), Phi Lambda Upsilon. Office: Dept Chemistry Oreg State U Corvallis OR 97331

SHOEMAKER, ELEANOR BOGGS, television production company executive; b. Gulfport, Miss., Jan. 20, 1935; d. William Robertson and Bessie Eleanor (Ware) Boggs; m. D. Shoemaker, April 9, 1955 (div. 1987); children: Daniel W., William Boggs. Student in protocol, Southeastern U., 1952-53; student, George Washington U., Washington, 1953-56; BA in Communications and Polit. Sci. with honrs, Goucher Coll., 1981; postgrad., Villanova U. Feature writer Washington Times Herald, 1951-54; dir. Patricia Stevens Modeling Agy., Washington, 1955-56; free-lance model Julius Garfinkel, Woodward & Lothrop, Washington, 1951-56; research analyst Balt. County Council, Towson, Md., 1980-81; feature news reporter Sta. WGCB-TV, Red Lion, Pa., 1980—; pub. speaker, protocol The Reliable Corp., Columbia, Md., 1982-86; media cons. The Enterprise Found., Columbia, Md., 1985-86; faculty, TV prodn. and communication St. Francis Prep Sch., Spring Grove, Pa., 1985-88; owner Windswept Prodns. Co., Felton, Pa., 1984—; mktg. svcs. coord. Yorktowne, Inc., Red Lion, Pa., 1993-95; mem. conservation bd. Pa. Parks and Recreation Soc., 1984—; prodr. The Pa. County TV Prodn., 1981; prodr., host Westar 4 Channel 9 half hour weekly news program Keystone Report. Prodr. The Pa. County TV Prodn., 1981, The Pa. County TV Prodn., 1981, documentary Human Rights: A Special Report, Sta. WGCB-TV, 1989; prodr., host Westar 4 Channel 9 half hour weekly news program Keystone Report, 1990. Bd. dirs. York (Pa.) County Parks and Recreation, 1972-87, YWCA, York, 1957-82, Hist. York, 1990—; mem. exec. com. York County Reps., 1972-82; accreditation adv. com. York Coll. of Pa.; instr. YWCA Women in Politics; founder, mem. Child Abuse Task Force, York, 1983—; mem. select com. Pa. Agrl. Zoning, 1988; mem. steering com. York Forum, 1989—; co-chmn. Cross Mill Restoration, 1987—; mem. Displaced Homemaker's Bd., 1989—, pres., 1993—; bd. dirs. Hist. York, 1990—; founder, host Old Rose Tree Pony Club, 1967—; chair Spring Valley County Pk. Task Force, 1972; master of fox hounds Mrs. Shoemaker's Hounds, 1969—; master of beagles Mrs. Shoemaker's Weybright Beagles, 1988—. Recipient pro bono child legal representation grant Pa. Bar Assn., 1983, Pa. Tree Farmer of Yr. award, 1987, Outstanding Achievement in Broadcasting award Am. Women in Radio and TV, 1992, Lay Person of Yr. award Pa. Recreation and Parks Assn. and Gov. Thornburg, 1982, Jefferson award, 1992, Matrix award Ctrl. Pa. Women in Comm., 1993, First pl. corp. video prodn. Ctrl. Pa. Women in Comm., 1993; selected journalist for Novosti Press USSR-U.S. Press Exch. program, 1989. Mem. Am. Polled Hereford Assn., York Area C. of C., York County C. of C. (publicity com. 1985—, agri. bus. com.), Masters of Foxhounds Assn. Episcopalian. Home and Office: PO Box 167 Felton PA 17322-0167

SHOEN, MICHELLE SUZANNE, special education educator; b. Syracuse, N.Y., May 21, 1969; d. George William and Patricia Ann (Almasy) Miller; m. Duane Robert Shoen, June 13, 1992. BS in Elem. Edn. and Psychology, SUNY, Potsdam, 1991, MS in Elem. Edn., 1992, postgrad., 1992—. Cert. N-3 elem. tchr., N.Y., spl. edn. N-12. Home-based visitor Head Start, Canton, N.Y., 1992-95; spl. edn. tchr. Candor, N.Y., 1995—. Mem. Coun. for Exceptional Children. Home: 534A Valley Rd Brooktondale NY 14817

SHOFFNER, DONNA LOUISE, elementary education educator; b. Crystal River, Fla., Jan. 1, 1953; d. Donald Philip and Alexandra Isobel (Henry) Gerrits; m. Richard Louis Marta, Dec. 31, 1972 (div. Dec. 1, 1989); children: Cynthia Marie Marta, Cole Johnlouis Donald Marta; m. Thomas Jay Shoffner, Dec. 2, 1989; 1 child, Caleb Gerrits. BA, York U., 1974. Owner Crossed Sabres Ranch, Cody, Wyo., 1974-81, Scotty's Skate Odyssey, Green River, Wyo., 1981-83, The Wildflower Co., Billings, Mont., 1983-85; from substitute tchr. to primary grades tchr. Lancaster (Calif.) Sch. Dist., 1985—. Treas. Valley View PTA, Quartz Hill, Calif., 1988; registrar Antelope Coun. Girl Scouts U.S., Quartz Hill, 1987; vol. Com. to Elect Bill Clinton, 1992, 96. Mem. Tchrs. Assn. Lancaster (pres. 1996—). Democrat. Home: 42822 Tumblewood Way Lancaster CA 93536 Office: Tchrs Assn Lancaster 1027 W Lancaster Blvd Lancaster CA 93534

SHOHEN, SAUNDRA ANNE, health care communications and public relations executive; b. Washington, Aug. 22, 1934; d. Aaron Kohn and Malvina (Kleiman) Kohn Blinder; children: Susan, Brian. BS, Columbia Pacific U., 1979, MS in Health Svcs. Adminstrn., 1981. Adminstr. social work dept. Roosevelt Hosp., N.Y.C., 1978-79; adminstr. emergency dept. St. Luke's-Roosevelt Hosp. Ctr., N.Y.C., 1979-83, assoc. dir. pub. rels., 1983-87; pres. Saundra Shohen Assocs., Ltd., N.Y.C., 1987-1992; v.p. Prism Internat., N.Y.C., 1988-91, bd. dirs. Tureck Bach Inst., N.Y.C., 1985—; panelist ann. Emmy awards NATAS, N.Y.C., 1983, 84; tchr. healthcare mktg. Baruch Coll., N.Y.C., 1994. Author: EMERGENCY!, 1989, (health scripts for radio) Voice of America, 1983 (Presdl. Recognition award 1984), (with others) AIDS: A Health Care Management Response, 1987. Mem. NATAS, Internat. Hosp. Fedn., Am. Soc. Hosp. Mktg. and Pub. Rels., Vols. in Tech. Assistance. Democrat. Jewish. Home: 240 Central Park S New York NY 10019-1413

SHOJI, JUNE MIDORI, import and export trading executive; b. Long Beach, Calif., June 21, 1957; d. Sam Masatsugu and Tomiyo (Kinoshita) S. BA in Psychology and Econs., UCLA, 1975-79; cert. Japanese, Waseda U., Tokyo, 1980-82; Grad. Gemologist, Gemol. Inst., Santa Monica, Calif., 1984. Mktg. rep. IBM Corp., L.A., 1982-84, Xerox Corp., El Monte, Calif., 1984-86; adminstrv. drilling analyst Arco Internat. Oil & Gas, L.A., 1986-89; buyer OEM components & machinery Honda Trading Am., Torrance, Calif., 1989-94, asst. mgr. OEM components machinery and non-ferrous metals, 1994—. Home: 1865 W 166th St Gardena CA 90247-4664

SHOMO, SALLY WEAVER, middle school educator; b. Harrisonburg, Va., Dec. 9, 1960; d. Charles Franklin and Mary Katherine (Lineweaver) Weaver; m. Scott H. Shomo, 1996. BS, VPI and SU, 1982. Agrl. edn. instr. Augusta County Sch. System, Fishersville, Va., 1982—; FFA advisor Beverley Manor Mid. Sch., Staunton, Va., 1982—; young farmer advisor Augusta County Young Farmer Women, Staunton, 1988—; no. area young farmer advisor No. Area of Va., Staunton, 1990—; mem. adv. coun. Young Farmers of Va., Richmond, 1990-93, state young farmer advisor 1991— (Va. Outstanding Advisor 1990); chmn. Va. FFA Mid. Sch. Contest Com., Blacksburg, 1991—; chmn. Va. FFA Mid. Sch. Quiz Bowl Com., Blacksburg, 1991—; mem. Va. Mid. Sch. Agrisci. Curriculum Com., Blacksburg. Author: Country Cacklin' Cookbook, 1991, Grandmother's Cookbook, 1992, Weaver Family Cookbook, 1993. Instr. Va. Hunter Edn., Staunton, 1985—; mem. Valley Conservation Coun., Staunton, 1992—; com. chmn. Shenandoah Valley Rocky Mountain Elk Found., Staunton, 1994-95. Named Nat. Outstanding Advisor, Nat. Young Farmer Ednl. Assn., 1994. Mem. NEA, Nat. Vocat. Agrl. Tchrs. Assn., Nat. Young Farmer Ednl. Assn. (life), Va. Vocat. Agrl. Tchrs. Assn., Va. Edn. Assn., Augusta County Edn. Assn., Augusta County Agrl. Tchrs. Assn. Office: Beverley Manor Mid Sch Rte 8 Box 2 Staunton VA 24401

SHONTELL, JAYNE J., mortgage company executive. BS in Econs., Georgetown U., MS in Econs.; postgrad. studies in Econs., U. London, Eng., Sch. Planning and Stats., Warsaw, Poland. Chief economist Fed. Home Loan Mortgage Corp.; economist Fed. Nat. Mortgage Assn., Washington, 1982-85, v.p. mortgage backed securities, 1985-89, dir. corp. and bus. devel., 1989-92, sr. v.p. fin. and info. svcs., 1992-96, sr. v.p. investor rels., 1996—. Office: Fed Nat Mortgage Assn 3900 Wisconsin Ave NW Washington DC 20016-2806

SHOOK, ANN JONES, lawyer; b. Canton, Ohio, Apr. 18, 1925; d. William M. and Lura (Pontius) Jones; m. Gene E. Shook Sr., Nov. 30, 1956; children: Scott, William, Gene Edwin Jr. AB, Wittenberg U., 1947; LLB, William McKinley Law Sch., 1955. Bar: Ohio 1956, U.S. Dist. Ct. (no. dist.) Ohio 1961, U.S. Ct. Appeals (6th cir.) 1981. Cost acct. Hoover Co., North Canton, Ohio, 1947-51; asst. sec. Stark County Prosecutor's Office, Canton, Ohio, 1951-53; ins. adjuster Traveler's Ins. Co., Canton, 1953-56; ptnr. Shook & Shook Law Firm, Toledo, 1958-62, North Olmsted, Ohio, 1962—. Mem. at large coun. Olmsted Community Ch., Olmsted Falls, Ohio, 1987-90; chmn. ways and means com. North Olmsted PTA, 1968; area chmn. United Way Appeal, North Olmsted, 1963; v.p. LWV, Toledo, 1960-62. Mem. Cleve. Bar Assn.

SHOOK, ELIZABETH JANE, gallery owner, artist; b. Cin., Apr. 25, 1957; d. Elmer Arthur Jr. and Edith Jane (Hankins) Jahnke Maloney; 1 child, Elizabeth Anitre. AA, Clark State C.C., 1992. Co-owner The Looking Glass Gallery, Springfield, Ohio, 1993—; logo designer DAI Distributing, Springfield, 1993, Journey: A Ctr. for Healing, Springfield, 1993; card designer Springview Devel. Ctr., Springfield, 1994; centerpiece designer Project Woman, Springfield, 1995. Contbg. artist: Shades of Gray, 1991, 92, 93, 94, 95, 96, Treasured Poems of America, 1993, The Ohio Celebration of Art, 1993, Women's Dreams, Now Reality, 1995, Holistic Women, 1996. Poster designer Springfield Altrusa Lit. Club, 1990, 91, Northminster Presbyn. Ch., Springfield, 1993, 94, 95, Habitat for Humanity, 1996, Heartland of Urbana Springfield Jaycees, 1991; artist Clothesline Project, Washington, 1995; mem. Springfield Mus. Art, 1993—; assoc. mem. Nat. Mus. Women in Arts, 1994—; charter mem. Nat. Mus. Am. Indian, 1996. Recipient 1st pl. painting award, 1st pl. airbrush award, 2d pl. color illustration award, Judge's Best of Show award Clark State C.C. Juried Exhibit, 1992, 2d pl. 3-D award, 3d pl. collage award, 1991, 2d pl. award Clark State C.C. Ann. Writing Competition, 1992, 2d pl. award Springfield Art Mus., 1996. Democrat. Office: The Looking Glass Gallery 670 N Limestone St Springfield OH 45503

SHORENSTEIN, ROSALIND GREENBERG, physician; b. N.Y.C., Jan. 14, 1947; d. Albert Samuel and Natalie Miriam (Sherman) Greenberg; m. Michael Lewis Shorenstein, June 18, 1967; children: Anna Irene, Claire Beth. BA in Chemistry, Wellesley Coll., 1968; MA in Biochemistry and Molecular Biology, Harvard U., 1970, PhD in Biochemistry and Molecular Biology, 1973; MD, Stanford U., 1976. Diplomate Am. Bd. Internal Medicine. Resident in internal medicine UCLA Med. Ctr., 1976-79; pvt. practice internal medicine Santa Cruz, Calif., 1979—; mem. dept. internal medicine Dominican Hosp., Santa Cruz, 1979—; co-dir. med. svcs. Health Enhancement & Lifestyle Planning Systems, Santa Cruz, 1983—. Contbr. articles to profl. journals. Dir. Santa Cruz Chamber Players, 1993-94, pres., bd. dirs., 1994—. Recipient Charlie Parkhurst award Santa Cruz Women's Commn., 1989; NSF fellow, 1968-72, Sarah Perry Wood Med. fellow Wellesley Coll., 1972-76. Mem. Am. Soc. Internal Medicine (del. 1994, 95), Calif. Soc. Internal Medicine (trustee 1994—), Am. Med. Women's Assn. (Outstanding Svc. award 1987, br. #59 pres. 1986—), Calif. Med. Assn. (com. on women 1987-93), Santa Cruz County Med. Soc. (mem. bd. govs. 1993—), Phi Beta Kappa, Sigma Xi. Jewish. Office: 700 Frederick St Ste 103 Santa Cruz CA 95062-2239

SHORES, JANIE LEDLOW, state supreme court justice; b. Georgiana, Ala., Apr. 30, 1932; d. John Wesley and Willie (Scott) Ledlow; m. James L. Shores, Jr., May 12, 1962; 1 child, Laura Scott. J.D., U. Ala., Tuscaloosa, 1959; LLM, U. Va., 1992. Bar: Ala. 1959. Pvt. practice Selma, 1959; mem. legal dept. Liberty Nat. Life Ins. Co., Birmingham, Ala., 1962-66; assoc. prof. law Cumberland Sch. Law, Samford U., Birmingham, 1966-74; assoc. justice Supreme Ct. Ala., 1975—; legal adviser Ala. Constn. Revision Commn., 1973; mem. Nat. Adv. Coun. State Ct. Planning, 1976—. Contbr. articles to legal jours. Mem. bd. dirs. State Justice Inst., 1995—. Mem. Am. Bar Assn., Am. Judicature Soc., Farrah Order Jurisprudence. Democrat. Episcopalian. Office: Ala Supreme Ct 300 Dexter Ave Montgomery AL 36104-3741

SHORNEY, MARGO KAY, art gallery owner; b. Great Falls, Mont., July 5, 1930; d. Angus Vaughn McIver and Loneta Eileen Kuhn; m. James Thomas Shorney, Apr. 17, 1954; 1 child, Blair Angus. Student, Coll. Edn., Great Falls, Mont., 1948-50, U. Denver, 1950-53. Owner, dir. Shorney Gallery Fine Art, Oklahoma City, 1976—; pres. Mont. Inst. Arts, Great Falls, 1953-54, Okla. Art Gallery Owners Assn., Oklahoma City, 1981-83; lectr. Norman (Okla.) Art League, 1987-91; judge fine arts Ponca City (Okla.) 12th Ann. Fine Arts, 1986, Edmond (Okla.) Art Assn. Expo 1995, Fine Arts Festival 22nd Ann., 1996; appraiser Globe Life, Oklahoma City, Ponca City Juried Art Assn. 22nd Ann. Fine Arts. Works exhibited in group shows, various orgns., 1953-90. Mentor South Oklahoma City Coll., 1990; active Okla. Mus. Art, 1973-78. Mem. Nat. Assn. Women Bus. Owners, Okla. Sculpture Soc. (charter), Okla. Art Guild (bd. dirs. 1979-82, lectr. 1981, 82, 83, 92). Republican. Episcopalian. Office: Shorney Gallery Fine Arts 6616 N Olie Ave Oklahoma City OK 73116-7318

SHORT, BETSY ANN, elementary education educator; b. Macon, Ga., Mar. 18, 1958; d. Garland Brooks Jr. and Mary Eleanor (Jordan) Turner; m. Lynn Robin Short, July 21, 1984. BS in Early Childhood Edn., Ga. Coll., Milledgeville, 1981, M in Early Childhood Edn., 1993, EdS, 1995. Cert. elem. tchr. and tchr. support specialist, Ga. Tchr. 3d grade Stockbridge (Ga.) Elem. Sch., 1983-84, tchr. kindergarten, 1984-93; tchr. augmented spl. instructional assistance Locust Grove (Ga.) Elem. Sch., 1993—. Author: Spinning Yarns, 1995; mem. editl. adv. bd. Ga. Jour. Reading; contbr. articles to profl. jours.; artist oil painting/pen and ink drawing. Mem. Profl. Assn. of Ga. Educators, Ga. Coun. Tchrs. Maths., Ga. Coun. Internat. Reading Assn., Ga. Coun. Social Studies, Ga. Sci. Tchrs. Assn., Henry Heritage Reading Coun. Baptist. Office: Locust Grove Elem 1727 Griffin Rd Locust Grove GA 30248

SHORT, ELIZABETH M., physician, educator, federal agency administrator; b. Boston, June 2, 1942; d. James Edward and Arlene Elizabeth (Mitchell) Meehan; m. Herbert M. Short, Sept. 2, 1963 (div. 1969); 1 child, Timothy Owen; m. Michael Allen Friedman, June 21, 1976; children: Lia Gabrielle, Hannah Ariel, Eleanor Elana. BA Philosophy magna cum laude, Mt. Holyoke Coll., 1963; MD cum laude, Yale U., 1968. Diplomate Am. Bd. Internal Medicine, Am. Bd. Med. Genetics. Intern, jr. resident internal medicine Yale New Haven Hosp., 1968-70; postdoctoral fellow in human genetics Yale Med. Sch., 1970-72; postdoctoral fellow in renal metabolism U. Calif., San Francisco, 1972-73; sr. resident in internal medicine Stanford (Calif.) Med. Sch., 1973-74, chief resident in internal medicine, 1974-75; staff physician Palo Alto Veterans Med. Ctr., Stanford, Calif., 1975-80; asst. prof. of medicine Stanford Med. Sch., 1975-83, asst. dean Student Affairs, 1978-80, assoc. dean Students Affairs/Medical Education, 1980-83; dir. biomed. rsch. and faculty devel. Assn. Am. Med. Colls., Washington, 1983-87, dep. dir. dept. acad. affairs, 1983-87, dep. dir. biomedical rsch., 1987-88; dep. assoc. chief med. dir. for acad. affairs VA, Washington, 1988-92, assoc. chief medical dir. for acad. affairs, 1992—; vis. prof. Human Biology, Stanford U., 1983-86; resource allocation com. Veteran's Health Adminstrn., 1989-91; budget planning and policy review coun. 1991—; planning review com. Veterans Health Adminstrn., 1991—; chair resident work limit task force 1991—; managed care task force, 1993-94; co-chair com. status women Am. Fedn. Clin. Rsch., 1975-77; mem. numerous adminstrv. coms., Yale Med. Sch., Stanford U.; accreditation coun. grad. med. edn., 1988—; mem. public policy com. Am. Soc. Human Genetics, 1984—, chair, 1986-94; mem. White House Task Force on Health Care Reform, 1993-94. assoc. editor Clin. Rsch. Jour., 1976-79, editor elect, 1979-80, editor 1980-84; contbr. articles to profl. jours. Mem. nat. child health adv. coun. NIH, 1991—; mem. com. edn. and training Office Sci. and Tech. Policy, 1991—. Recipient Maclean Zoology award Mt. Holyoke Coll.; Munger scholar, Markle scholar, Sara Williston scholar Mt. Holyoke Coll., 1959-63, Yale Men in Medicine scholar, 1964-68; Bardwell Meml. Med. fellow, 1963. Mem. AAAS, Am. Soc. Human Genetics, Am. Fedn. Clin. Rsch. (bd. dirs. 1973-83, editor 1978-83, nat. coun., exec. com., pub. policy com. 1977-87), Am. Assn. Women in Scis., Western Soc. Clin. Investigation, Calif. Acad. Medicine, Phi Beta Kappa, Alpha Omega Alpha. Home: 6807 Bradley Blvd Bethesda MD 20817-3004 Office: Health Adminstrn Acad Affairs Dept Veterans 810 Vermont Ave VHA 14 Washington DC 20420

SHORT, LINDA HUFFSTETLER, state senator; b. Gastonia, N.C., July 9, 1947; d. Everett Rhyne and Violet Lucille (Kuykendall) Huffstetler; m. Paul

E. Short, Jr., June 14, 1968; children: Lindy Lee, Melanie Lynne. BA in Psychology, Winthrop U., 1984. Mem. S.C. Senate, Columbia, 1993—, asst. majority whip, 1993—. Mem. Chester County Sch. Bd., 1982-92, chmn., 1990-92; bd. dirs. Downtown Devel. Assn., 1989-93, Palmetto Leadership, 1990-91; bd. visitors Presbyn. Coll., 1990-93; mem. Chester County's Fall Affair, 1988-90; former coord. 6th Cir. Guardian Ad Litem Program; former jr. and sr. H.S. Sunday sch. tchr. Purity Presbyn. Ch., former pres. Presbyn. Women; former v.p. Providence Presbytery Presbyn. Women; mem. Children's Case Resolutions Sys. Panel, Joint Legis. com. Children and Families, 1992-95. Recipient S.C. Dept. Health and Environ. Control Bur. of Maternal and Child Health Legis.award 1995, Chester County's Econ. Devel. Efforts award 1995, Girl Scouts Women of Achievement award 1996, Ernestine C. Player Friend of Social Work award 1996. Mem. Bench Bar Com., Phi Kappa Phi, Delta Kappa Gamma. Democrat. Home: 120 W End St Chester SC 29706-1819

SHORT, LINDA MATTHEWS, reading educator; b. Winston-Salem, N.C., Mar. 25, 1949; d. Edwin Kohl and Nannie Mae (Bowen) Matthews; m. James Coy Short, June 18, 1972. BS, Appalachian State U., 1971, MA, 1981. Cert. elem. edn. tchr. Tchr. Mount Airy City Schs., Mount Airy, N.C., 1971-72, 88—, Surry County Schs., Dobson, N.C., 1972-88; mem. Mt. Airy City Schs. Adv. Bd., 1994-95. Pres.-elect Foothills Reading Coun., 1992-93; active Mt. Airy Women's Club, 1970s, Mt. Airy Jaycettes, 1970s. Mem. Foothills Reading Coun. (pres. 1993-96), N.C. Reading Assn. (area dir. 1995-96), N.C. Assn. Educators (treas. 1992-94), Internat. Reading Assn., Mt. Airy N.C. Assn. Educators (treas. 1992-94). Democrat. Baptist. Home: 107 Brentwood Dr Mount Airy NC 27030 Office: BH Tharrington Elem Sch 315 Culbert St Mount Airy NC 27030

SHORT, MARION PRISCILLA, neurology educator; b. Milford, Del., June 12, 1951; d. Raymond Calistus and Barbara Anne (Ferguson) S.; m. Michael Peter Klein; 1 child, Asher Calistus Klein. BA, Bryn Mawr Coll., 1973; diploma, U. Edinburgh (Scotland), 1975; MD, Med. Coll. Pa., 1978. Diplomate Am. Bd. Psychiatry and Neurology, Am. Bd. Internal Medicine. Intern in internal medicine Hahnemann Med. Coll. Hosp., Phila., 1978-79; med. resident in internal medicine St. Lukes-Roosevelt Hosp., N.Y.C., 1979-81; neurology resident U. Pitts. Health Ctr., 1981-84; fellow in med. genetics Mt. Sinai Med. Ctr., N.Y.C., 1984-86; fellow in neurology Mass. Gen. Hosp., Boston, 1986-90, asst. neurologist, 1990-95; asst. prof. dept. neurology Harvard Med. Sch., Boston, 1990-95; asst. prof. dept. neurology, pediat. and pathology U. Chgo., 1995—; cons. Spaulding Rehab. Hosp., Boston. Recipient Clin. Investigator Devel. award NIH, 1988-93. Mem. Am. Acad. Neurology, Am. Soc. for Human Genetics. Office: U Chgo Med Ctr WCHC 376 MC3055 5841 S Maryland Ave Chicago IL 60637

SHORT-MAYFIELD, PATRICIA AHLENE, business owner; b. Fort Benning, Ga., Oct. 12, 1955; d. William Pressley and Ilse Marie (Hofmann) Short; m. Thomas Hicks Fort, June 2, 1973 (div. Jan. 1981); m. Michael Patrick Mayfield, Aug. 11, 1984; 1 child, William Zachary. Grad. high sch., Butler, Ga., 1973. Notary pub., Ga. Staff mem. Fairyland Day Care, Canton, Ga., 1973-74, Small World Child Care, Thomaston, Ga., 1974-77; nurses aide Kenneston Hosp., Marietta, Ga., 1978-80; staff worker Mental Health Ctr., Smyrna, Ga., 1980-81; dir. Kiddie Kollege, Marietta, 1981-85; bus. owner, mgr. Spiffy Clean by Mayfield, Marietta, 1985-95, Petsmart, Kennesaw, Ga., 1994—. Choir staff Eastside Bapt. Ch., Marietta, 1988-89; vol. East Valley Elem. Sch., 1989-95, chorus vol., 1994-95; vol. East Cobb Middle Sch., 1995—; active Nat. Congress Parents and Tchrs., Cobb County Humane Soc., 1991—. Mem. NAFE, Cobb County C. of C., Atlanta High Mus. Art, Dog Lovers Am. Republican. Baptist. Office: Spiffy Clean By Mayfield 2791 Georgian Ter Marietta GA 30068-3625

SHOSS, CYNTHIA RENÉE, lawyer; b. Cape Girardeau, Mo., Nov. 29, 1950; d. Milton and Carroll Jane (Duncan) S.; m. David Goodwin Watson, Apr. 13, 1986; 1 child, Lucy J. Watson. BA cum laude, Newcomb Coll., 1971; JD, Tulane U., 1974; LLM in Taxation, NYU, 1980. Bar: La. 1974, Mo. 1977, Ill. 1978, N.Y. 1990. Law clk. to assoc. and chief justices La. Supreme Ct., New Orleans, 1974-76; assoc. Stone, Pigman et al, New Orleans, 1976-77, Lewis & Rice, St. Louis, 1977-79, Curtis, Mallet-Prevost, et al, N.Y.C., 1980-82; ptnr. LeBoeuf, Lamb, Greene & MacRae, L.L.P., N.Y.C., 1982—; mng. ptnr. London office LeBoeuf, Lamb, Leiby & MacRae, 1987-89; assoc. editor Tulane Law Rev., 1972-74; frequent speaker before profl. orgns. and assns. Contbr. articles to profl. jours. Mem. ABA, Am. Mgmt. Assn. (ins. and risk mgmt. coun.), Corp. Bar Westchester and Fairfield, Lawyers Alliance N.Y. (chair, bd. dirs.). Office: LeBoeuf Lamb Greene Et Al 125 W 55th St New York NY 10019-5369

SHOTWELL, CHERRIE LEIGH, speech and language pathologist; b. Munich, Nov. 15, 1950; parents Am. citizens; d. William Bedford and Pauline Leona (Bainbridge) S. BA with distinction, U. Redlands, 1973, MS, 1975. Cert. lang., speech and hearing tchr., Calif. Speech and lang. therapist Hawaii Dept. Edn., Wahiawa, 1976-86; lang. and speech specialist L.A. County Dept. Edn., Downey, Calif., 1986-87; day treatment instr. Assn. Retarded Citizens, Honolulu, 1987-88; speech and lang. pathologist Honolulu Cmty. Action Program, 1988-89, Hawaii Speech Pathology, Honolulu, 1989-90, Med. Pers. Pool, Honolulu, 1990-94, Hawaii Dept. Edn., Waipahu, 1994—. Mem. Hawaii Speech Lang. Hearing Assn. (com. chairperson Licensure and Ethics 1978-79). Democrat. Home: 1015 Laakea Pl Honolulu HI 96818

SHOTZ, ALYSON HARA, artist; b. Glendale, Ariz., Dec. 13, 1964; d. Fredric G. Shotz and Lois B. (Paul) Weinberg. BFA, RISD, 1987; MFA, U. Wash., 1991. Sr. cataloguer Mus. Modern Art, N.Y.C., 1992-95; curatorial asst. Werner H. Kramasky, N.Y.C., 1995—. Solo exhbns. at Ag 47 Gallery, Seattle, 1991, Susan Inglett Gallery, N.Y.C., 1996; group exhbns. include Mus. for Contemporary Arts, Balt., 1990, Ctr. on Contemporary Art, Seattle, 1991 (N.w. Ann. award), Fla. Mus. Contemporary Art, 1992, A/C Project Rm., N.Y.C., 1994, Domestic Setting, L.A., 1995; artist, curator group exhbn., 1994. Recipient award S.W. Tex. State U., 1992; Art Matters Found. fellow, 1996. Office: 560 Broadway #608 New York NY 10012

SHOUSHA, ANNETTE GENTRY, critical care nurse; b. Nashville, May 25, 1936; d. Thurman and Laura (Pugh) Gentry; m. Alfred Shousha, May 29, 1959; children: Mark André, Anne, Mary, Melanie. Diploma, St. Thomas Hosp., Nashville, 1957; student, Belmont Coll., Nashville, 1958, No. State U., Aberdeen, S.D., 1973; BSN, S.D. State U., 1985. Cert. coronary care. Instr. med. nursing Nashville Gen. Hosp., 1958-59, ob-gyn. nurse, 1959-60; insvc. educator Tri County Hosp., Ft. Oglethorpe, Ga., 1960-61; clin. mgr., office nurse Britton, S.D., 1962-90; med. nursing Nashville VA Hosp., 1990-92, gastrointestinal nurse, 1992-94, critical care nurse ICU, 1994-95. Contbr. essays to S.D. Jour. Medicine. Del., S.D. Dem. Conv. Recipient Gov.'s Recognition award for outstanding vol. svc. Mem. ANA, AMA Aux. (state pres.), Nat. Hospice Assn., Nurses Orgn. VA, Donelson/Hermitage C. of C. Home: 2809 Lealto Ct Nashville TN 37214-1813

SHOVER, JOAN, secondary school educator; b. St. Joseph, Mo., Apr. 7, 1948; d. Jay S. and Clara Lillian (Burkett) Marquis; m. Rolland Craig Shover, May 31, 1975; children: Terra Jayne, Thomas Jay. BS in Edn., Ctrl. Mo. State U., 1971, MS in Edn., 1976, postgrad., 1989—. Cert. tchr., Mo. Phys. edn. tchr. Worth County H.S., Grant City, Mo., 1971-73, Blue Springs (Mo.) H.S., 1973—; mem. rev. com. Mo. Dept. Elem. and Secondary Edn., Jefferson City, 1993—. Named Am. Cancer Soc. Educator of Yr., 1989, Top 36 Am. Tchrs. award, Disney Corp., 1992. Mem. AAHPERD, NEA, Am. Coun. on Exercise, Internat. Dance Exercise Assn., Mo. Assn. Phys. Edn., Health, Recreation and Dance (Kansas City Dist. Phys. Educator asard 1989, Prewsl. award, Kansas City rep. 1988—), Mo. State Tchrs. Assn., Pilot Club. Home: 1418 NW A St Blue Springs MO 64015-3605

SHOWALTER, DENISE M., communications marketing administrator; b. Bridgeport, Conn., June 26, 1946; d. Paul J. and Magdalena D. (Feske) Amato; m. George W. Showalter, Aug. 26, 1967; children: Anthony (dec.), Kristen. BS in Bus. Adminstrn., U. Redlands, 1985; MS in Sys. Mgmt., U. Denver, 1991. Cert. sys. profl. Mktg. rep. Pacific Telephone Co., L.A., 1967-69; real estate sales Whitehead Realtors, Rockford, Ill., 1972-77; mktg. mgmt. Pacific Bell, Orange/San Ramon, Calif., 1977—; bd. dirs. Switched Digital Svcs. Applications Forum, 1996—. Office: Pacific Bell 2600 Camino Ramon 3S000 San Ramon CA 94583

SHOWALTER, ELAINE, humanities educator; b. Cambridge, Mass., Jan. 21, 1941; married; 2 children. BA, Bryn Mawr Coll., 1962; MA, Brandeis U., 1964; PhD in English, U. Calif., Davis, 1970. Teaching asst. English U. Calif., 1964-66, from instr. to assoc. prof., 1967-78; prof. English Rutgers U., from 1978; prof. English, Avalon Found. prof. humanities, Princeton (N.J.) U., 1984—; Avalon Found. prof. humanities Princeton (N.J.) U., 1987—; vis. prof. English and women's studies U. Del., 1976-77; vis. prof. Sch. Criticism and Theory, Dartmouth Coll., 1986; prof. Salzburg (Austria) Seminars, 1988; Clarendon lectr. Oxford (Eng.) U., 1989; vis. scholar Phi Beta Kappa, 1993-94; numerous radio and TV appearances. Author: A Literature of Their Own, 1977, The Female Malady, 1985, Sexual Anarchy, 1990, Sister's Choice, 1991; co-author: Hysteria Beyond Freud, 1993; editor: These Modern Women, 1978, The New Feminist Criticism, 1985, Alternative Alcott, 1987, Speaking of Gender, 1989, Modern American Women Writers, 1991, Daughters of Decadence, 1993; also articles and revs. Recipient Howard Behrman humanities award Princeton U., 1989; faculty rsch. coun. fellow Ruthers U., 1972-73, Guggenheim fellow, 1977-78, Rockefeller humanities fellow, 1981-82, fellow NEH, 1988-89. Mem. MLA. Office: Princeton U Dept of English Princeton NJ 08544

SHOWALTER, KAREN JOAN, human resources executive; b. Roanoke, Va., 1933. Grad., Coll. William & Mary, 1955, Columbia U., 1963. Sr. v.p. human resources CBS, Inc., N.Y.C. Mem. Am. Mgmt. Assn., Human Resource Coun. Office: CBS Inc 51 W 52nd St New York NY 10019-6119*

SHOWALTER-KEEFE, JEAN, data processing executive; b. Louisville, Mar. 11, 1938; d. William Joseph and Phyllis Rose (Reis) Showalter; m. James Washburn Keefe, Dec. 6, 1980. BA, Spalding U., 1963, MS in Edn. Adminstrn., 1969. Cert. tchr., Ky. Tchr., asst. prin. Louisville Cath. Schs., 1958-71; cons. and various editorial positions Harcourt Brace Jovanovich Co., Chgo. and N.Y.C., 1972-82; dir. editorial Ednl. Challenges, Alexandria, Va., 1982-83; mgr. project to cons. Xerox Corp., Leesburg, Va., 1983-88, mgr. systems edn., 1988-89; curriculum devel. mgr. corp. edn. and tng. Xerox Corp. Hdqrs., Stamford, Conn., 1989-94; mem. bd. Belcastle Cluster Assocs., Reston, Va., 1994—, pres. bd., 1995—, 1995—, mgmt. and sys. cons., 1995—; mem. adv. bd. Have a Heart Homes for Abused Children, 1991-93; instr. Sales Exec. Club N.Y., 1974-79; cons., Houston, 1980-83. Moderator Jr. Achievement, Louisville, 1968-70; cons. Future Bus. Leaders Am., Dade County, Fla. 1983. Named Outstanding Young Educator Louisville Jaycees, 1968. Mem. Nat. Assn. Female Execs., Am. Soc. Tng. and Devel., Am. Mgmt. Assn. Home and Office: 1419 Belcastle Ct Reston VA 22094-1245

SHOWS, WINNIE M., professional speaker; b. L.A., Apr. 2, 1947; d. William Marion Arvin and Joan Catherine (Sperry) Wilson; m. George Albert Shows, Mar. 18, 1967 (div. May 1980); 1 child, Sallie; m. Michael P. Florio, Jan. 1, 1990. BA in English, UCLA, 1969; MEd, Calif. State U., Long Beach, 1976. Tchr. St. Joseph High Sch., Lakewood, Calif., 1969-71; tchr. high sch. Irvine (Calif) Unified Sch. Dist., 1972-79; freelance writer, 1979-80; mgr. pub. rels. Forth, Inc., Hermosa Beach, Calif., 1980-81; account mgr., account supr., dir. mktg. Franson & Assoc., San Jose, Calif., 1981-84; v.p., pres. Smith & Shows, Menlo Park, Calif., 1984-96. Author (newsletter) Smith & Shows Letter, 1989-94. Vol. Unity Palo Alto (Calif.) Cmty. Ch., 1989-94, Newcomers, Menlo Park, 1990-93, Kara, Palo Alto, 1991-94, Menlo Park Sch. Dist., 1993—. Named Woman of Vision, Career Action Ctr., 1994. Mem. Nat. Spkrs. Assn., Bus. Mktg. Assn. (program dir. 1985-87). Office: Smith & Shows 28 Holbrook Ln Atherton CA 94027

SHRAGE, LAURETTE, special education educator; b. Montreal, Jan. 15, 1951; d. Ivan and Adela (Zupnik) Benda; m. William Lee Shrage, Oct. 30, 1977; children: Robert, Jaclyn. BS in Elem. Edn., Adelphi U., 1972; MS in Reading, Coll. New Rochelle, 1994. Cert. elem. edn., spl. edn., reading, bilingual edn., N.Y. Mgr. Century Operating Corp., N.Y.C., 1973-82; substitute tchr. New Rochelle (N.Y.) Sch. Dist., 1992-93, bilingual spl. edn. tchr., 1993—; substitute tchr. Keller Sch., Yonkers, N.Y., 1992-93; parent rep. New Rochelle Com. Presch. Spl. Edn., 1990-91, New Rochelle Com. Spl. Edn., 1991-92; mem. adv. coun. Jefferson Sch., New Rochelle, 1993—, mem. Magnet Think Tank com., 1994—; mem. Ptnrs. in Policy Making N.Y. State, 1992. Pres. PTA Augustus St. Gardens Sch., N.Y.C., 1987-90; advt. mgr. Mitchell Lama Apt., N.Y.C., 1983-86; telethon vol. Channel 13, N.Y.C., 1977; sponsor Sagamore Children's Sch., Suffolk, N.Y., 1974. Recipient Parent Leadership award Coun. Suprs. and Adminstrs. City of N.Y., 1990. Home: 29 Reyna Ln New Rochelle NY 10804-1104 Office: Jefferson Sch 131 Weyman Ave New Rochelle NY 10805-1428

SHRAUNER, BARBARA WAYNE ABRAHAM, electrical engineering educator; b. Morristown, N.J., June 21, 1934; d. Leonard Gladstone and Ruth Elizabeth (Thrasher) Abraham; m. James Ely Shrauner, 1965; children: Elizabeth Ann, Jay Arthur. BA cum laude, U. Colo., 1956; AM, Harvard U., 1957, PhD, 1962. Postdoctoral researcher U. Libre de Bruxelles, Brussels, 1962-64; postdoctoral researcher NASA-Ames Rsch. Ctr., Moffett Field, Calif., 1964-65; asst. prof. Washington U., St. Louis, 1966-69, assoc. prof., 1969-77, prof., 1977—; sabbatical Los Alamos (N.Mex.) Sci. Lab., 1975-76, Lawrence Berkeley Lab., Berkeley, Calif., 1985-86; cons. Los Alamos Nat. Lab., 1979, 84, NASA, Washington, 1980, Naval Surface Weapons Lab., Silver Spring, Md., 1984. Contbr. articles on transport in semiconductors, hidden symmetries of differential equations, plasma physics to profl. jours. Mem. IEEE (exec. com. of standing tech. com. on plasma sci. applications), AAUP (local sec.-treas. 1980-82), Am. Phys. Soc. (divsn. plasma physics, exec. com. 1980-82, 96—), Am. Geophys. Union, Univ. Fusion Assn., Phi Beta Kappa, Sigma Xi, Eta Kappa Nu, Sigma Pi Sigma. Home: 7452 Stratford Ave Saint Louis MO 63130-4044 Office: Washington U Dept Elec Engring 1 Brookings Dr Saint Louis MO 63130-4862

SHREEVE, JEAN'NE MARIE, chemist, educator; b. Deer Lodge, Mont., July 2, 1933; d. Charles William and Maryfrances (Briggeman) S. BA, U. Mont., 1953, DSc (hon.), 1982; MS, U. Minn., 1956; PhD, U. Wash., 1961; NSF postdoctoral fellow, U. Cambridge, Eng., 1967-68. Asst. prof. chemistry U. Idaho, Moscow, 1961-65; assoc. prof. U. Idaho, 1965-67, prof., 1967-73, acting chmn. dept. chemistry, 1969-70, 1973, head dept., and prof., 1973-87, vice provost rsch. and grad. studies, prof. chemistry, 1987—, v.p. rsch. and grad. studies, prof. chemistry, 1995—; Lucy W. Pickett lectr. Mt. Holyoke Coll., 1976, George H. Cady lectr. U. Wash., 1993; mem. Nat. Com. Standards in Higher Edn., 1965-67, 69-73. Mem. editl. bd. Jour. Fluorine Chemistry, 1970—, Jour. Heteroatom Chemistry, 1988—, Accounts Chem. Rsch., 1973-75, Inorganic Synthesis, 1976—; contbr. articles to sci. jours. Mem. bd. govs. Argonne (Ill.) Nat. Lab., 1992—. Recipient Disting. Alumni award U. Mont., 1970; named Hon. Alumnus, U. Idaho, 1972; recipient Outstanding Achievement award U. Minn., 1975, Sr. U.S. Scientist award Alexander Von Humboldt Found., 1978, Excellence in Teaching award Chem. Mfrs. Assn., 1980; U.S. hon. Ramsay fellow, 1967-68, Alfred P. Sloan fellow, 1970-72. Mem. AAAS (bd. dirs. 1991-95), AAUW (officer Moscow chpt. 1962-69), Am. Chem. Soc. (bd. dirs. 1985-93, chmn. fluorine divsn. 1979-81, Petroleum Rsch. Fund adv. bd. 1975-77, women chemists com. 1972-77, Fluorine award 1978, Garvan medal 1972, Harry and Carol Mosher award Santa Clara Valley sect. 1992), Göttingen (Germany) Acad. Scis., Phi Beta Kappa. Office: U Idaho Rsch Office 111 Morrill Hall Moscow ID 83843

SHREEVE, SUSANNA SEELYE, educational planning facilitator. BA in Dance, Arts and Humanities, Mills Coll.; MA in Confluent Edn., U. Calif., Santa Barbara, 1989; postgrad., U. Calif., 1990, San Diego State U., 1992. Cert. elem. tchr., C.C. adminstr., tchr., Calif. Comm. instr. Brooks Inst., 1982; initiator Santa Barbara County Arts and Aging Forum, 1982; co-plannter PARTners "How Kids Learn" Conf., 1985; dir. Los Ninos Bilingual Head Start Program, 1986-87; writing counselor Am. and internat. students S.B. City Coll., 1988, U. Calif., Santa Barbara, 1989-90; writing counselor Upward Bound, 1989-90; edn. coord. Santa Barbara County Urban Indian Project, Santa Barbara, 1990; instr. Santa Barbara Youth Cultural Arts, Santa Barbara, 1993; planner/staff Tri-County Regional Team Youth Summit, 1993-94; planner SIG confluent edn. AERA, 1994—; DQ-U. math/sci. resources for tchrs. Indian Edn., 1992—; multi-cultural cmty. Regional Alliance Info. Network Internet Youth Programs, Santa Barbara, 1991—; Pro-Youth Coalition planner, NetDay 96, NAPF's Indigenous People's Issues Liaison to WWWebsite, City of Santa Barbara. Office: 527 Laguna St Santa Barbara CA 93101-1607

SHREM, EILEEN MERRY, insurance planner; b. Bklyn., Oct. 17, 1946; d. Joseph Isodor and Beverly Irene (Cohen) Pollak; 1 child, Andrea Joy. MS, Bklyn. Coll. Profl. actress N.Y.C., 1950-58; tchr. N.Y.C. Sch. Sys., Bklyn., 1968-70; recreation supr. East Brunswick (N.J.) Twp., 1973-80; ins. planner Bradley Beach, N.J., 1980—; bd. dirs. N.J. Individual Health Coverage Program, chair mktg. com.; instr. Life Underwriter Tng. Coun., N.J., 1993, 94. Sec., chair adv. com. N.J. Com. on Rec for Disabled, Trenton, 1979—. Named Woman of Achievement Mon. Couty Adv. Com. on Status of Women, 1992. Mem. N.J. Assn. of Women Bus. Owners (pres., v.p. 1989-93, state and chpt. bds. 1981-87, Woman of Yr. 1987). Home and Office: 215 McCabe Ave C1 Bradley Beach NJ 07720

SHREVE, ALLISON ANNE, former air traffic control specialist; b. Sturgeon Bay, Wis., Aug. 29, 1961; d. Kendil McLaren and Barbara Gail (Kellner) S. Student, U. Wis., Oshkosh, 1979-82, 95—, Madison Area Tch. Coll., 1993. Cert. control tower operator. Air traffic asst. FAA, Green Bay, Wis., 1985-87, air traffic control specialist, 1987-96. Active Earth Share Fund, Humane Assn., ASPCA; animal care vol. Wildlife Sanctuary, Green Bay, Wis. Mem. Wis. Wildlife Rehabilitator's Assn. Home: 411 S Francis St Brillion WI 54110-1338

SHREVE, PEG, state legislator, retired elementary educator; b. Spencer, Va., July 23, 1927; d. Hubert Smith and Pearl (Looney) Adams; m. Don Franklin Shreve, June 17, 1950 (dec. Sept. 1970); children: Donna, Jennifer, John, Don. BA, Glenville State U., 1948. Cert. elem. tchr., Va., Wyo. Reading tchr. Wood County Bd., Parkersburg, W.Va., 1948-50; elem. tchr. Mt. Solon, Va., 1950-52, Bridgewater, Va., 1952-53, Cody, Wyo., 1970-86; mem. Wyo. Ho. of Reps., 1983—, chmn.. com. travel, recreation and wildlife, 1983-91, majority whip, 1992-94, speaker pro tem, 1995—. Mem. coun. Girl Scouts U.S.A., White Sulpher Springs, W.Va., 1962-65; co-chmn. Legis. Exec. Conf., Wyo., 1987; mem. Nat. Com. State Legislatures, 1982—. Named Legislator of Yr., Wyo. Outfitters Assn., 1989, Ofcl. of Yr., Wyo. Wildlife Assn., 1990, Alumna of Yr., Glenville State Coll., 1994. Mem. AAUW (exec. bd.), Nat. Women Legislators, Soroptimists (Women Helping Women award 1985), Beta Sigma Phi (Lady of Yr. award 1986). Republican. Presbyterian. Home: PO Box 2257 Cody WY 82414-2257

SHREVE, SUE ANN GARDNER, retired health products company administrator; b. Bklyn., Jan. 26, 1932; d. Homer Frank and Grace Emily (Kohlhagen) Gardner; m. Eugene Sheldon Shreve II, Nov. 20, 1954; children: Pamela Ann, Cynthia Ann Shreve Richard. BBA, Hofstra U., 1955. Co. rep. N.Y. Tel. Co., Bay Shore, 1954-55; engr. Republic Aviation, Farmingdale, N.Y., 1955-58; substitute tchr. East Islip (N.Y.) Sch. Dist., 1966-71; mgr. Patchogue Surg. and Athletic Supplies, Sayville, N.Y., 1971-81, ret., 1981; invited guest writer Nat. Geneal. Soc. newsletter, 1996. Author, editor: The Kohlhagen Family Genealogy, 1994; compiler, editor newsletter Gardner/Gardiner Rschrs., 1993—; issue reviewer Geneal. Helper Mag., 1995. life mem. N.Y. State Congress of Parents and Tchrs., 1963—, past pres.; mem. Penataquit Aux. Southside Hosp., 1985—; mem., fund raiser Hospice of South Shore, 1983—. Recipient Ofcl. proclamation Village of Frankfort, Ill., 1996; named one of Outstanding Young Women of Am., 1967. Mem. AAUW (charter, past pres., past treas. Islip area br., rsch. and project grantee 1989), Daus. of Union Vets. of Civil War, 1st Families of Ohio, Bay Shore Garden Club (past pres., treas.). Republican. Methodist. Home: 5 Anderson Ct West Bay Shore NY 11706

SHREVE, SUSAN RICHARDS, author, English literature educator; b. Toledo, May 2, 1939; d. Robert Kenneth and Helen (Greene) Richards; children—Porter, Elizabeth, Caleb, Kate. U. Pa., 1961; MA, U. Va., 1969. Prof. English lit. George Mason U., Fairfax, Va., 1976—; vis. prof. Columbia U., N.Y.C., 1982—, Princeton U., 1991, 92, 93. Author: (novels) A Fortunate Madness, 1974, A Woman Like That, 1977, Children of Power, 1979, Miracle Play, 1981, Dreaming of Heroes, 1984, Queen of Hearts, 1986, A Country of Strangers, 1989, Daughters of the New World, 1992, The Train Home, 1993, Skin Deep: Women & Race, 1995, The Visiting Physician, 1995; (children's books) The Nightmares of Geranium Street, 1977, Family Secrets, 1979, Loveletters, 1979, The Masquerade, 1980, The Bad Dreams of a Good Girl, 1981, The Revolution of Mary Leary, 1982, The Flunking of Joshua T. Bates, 1984, How I Saved the World on Purpose, 1985, Lucy Forever and Miss Rosetree, Shrinks, Inc., 1985, Joshua T. Bates In Charge, 1992, The Gift of the Girl Who Couldn't Hear, 1991, Wait for Me, 1992, Amy Dunn Quits School, 1993, Lucy Forever & the Stolen Baby, 1994, The Formerly Great Alexander Family, 1995, Zoe and Columbo, 1995, Warts, 1996; co-editor: Narratives on Justice, 1996, The Goalie, 1996. Recipient Jenny Moore award George Washington U., 1978; John Simon Guggenheim award in fiction, 1980; Nat. Endowment Arts fiction award, 1982. Mem. PEN/Faulkner Found. (pres.), Phi Beta Kappa.

SHRIER, DIANE KESLER, psychiatrist; b. N.Y.C., Mar. 23, 1941; d. Benjamin Arthur and Mollie (Wortman) Kesler; BS magna cum laude in Chemistry and Biology (Regents scholar 1957-61), Queen's Coll., CUNY, 1961; student Washington U. Sch. Medicine, St. Louis, 1960-61; M.D., Yale U., 1964; m. Adam Louis Shrier, June 10, 1961; children: Jonathan Laurence, Lydia Anne, Catherine Jane, David Leopold. Pediatric intern Bellevue Hosp., N.Y.C., 1964-65; psychiat. resident Albert Einstein Coll. Medicine-Bronx (N.Y.) Mcpl. Municipal Hosp. Center, 1966-68, child psychiatry fellow, 1968-70; staff cons. Family Service and Child Guidance Center of the Oranges, Maplewood, Milburn-Orange, N.J., 1970-73, cons., 1973-79; pvt. practice, Montclair, N.J., 1970-92, Washington, 1994—; cons. Community Day Nursery, E. Orange, 1970-79, Montclair State Coll., 1976-78; psychiat. cons. Bloomfield (N.J.) public schs., 1974-75; clin. instr. Albert Einstein Coll. Medicine, 1970-73; clin. asst. prof. psychiatry U. Medicine and Dentistry N.J., 1978-82, clin. assoc. prof., 1982-89, prof. clin. psychiatry, 1989-92; vice chmn., dir. clin. psychiat. svcs. Dept. Psychiatry Children's Nat. Med. Ctr., 1992-94, attending staff, 1994—; prof. psychiatry and pediatrics George Washington U. Med. Ctr., 1992-94, clin. prof. psychiatry and pediatrics, 1994—. cons. Walter Reed Med. Ctr., 1994—. Trustee, Montessori Learning Center, Montclair, 1973-75. Diplomate Am. Bd. Psychiatry and Neurology. Fellow Am. Psychiat. Assn., Acad. Child Psychiatry; mem. Tri-County Psychiat. Assn. (exec. com., rec. sec. 1977-78, 2d v.p. 1978-79, 1st v.p. 1979-80, pres. 1977-81), N.J. Psychiat. Assn. (councillor 1981-84), Am. Acad. Child and Adolescent Psychiatry (councillor at large 1992-95), Phi Beta Kappa. Contbr. articles to med. jours. Home: Apt 317B 4000 Cathedral Ave NW Washington DC 20016-5249 Office: 1616 18th St NW Ste 104 Washington DC 20009-2530

SHRIVER, EUNICE MARY KENNEDY (MRS. ROBERT SARGENT SHRIVER, JR.), civic worker; b. Brookline, Mass.; m. Robert Sargent Shriver, Jr., May 23, 1953; children: Robert Sargent III, Maria Owings, Timothy Perry, Mark Kennedy, Anthony Paul Kennedy. BS in Sociology, Stanford U., 1943; student, Manhattanville Coll. of Sacred Heart, LHD (hon.), 1963; LHD (hon.), D'Youville Coll., 1962, Regis Coll., 1963, Newton Coll., 1973, Brescia Coll., 1974, Holy Cross Coll., 1979, Princeton U., 1979, Boston Coll., 1990; LittD (hon.), U. Santa Clara, 1962; also hon. degrees, U. Vt., Albertus Magnus Coll., St. Mary's Coll. With spl. war problems div. State Dept. Washington, 1943-45; sec. Nat. Conf. on Prevention and Control juvenile Delinquency, Dept. of Justice, Washington, 1947-48; social worker Fed. Penitentiary for Women, Alderson, W.Va., 1950; exec. v.p. Joseph P. Kennedy, Jr. Found., 1956—; founder Spl. Olympics Internat.; social worker House of Good Shepherd, Chgo., also Juvenile Ct., Chgo., 1951-54; regional chmn. women's div. Community Fund-Red Cross Joint Appeal, Chgo., 1958; mem. Chgo. Commn. on Youth Welfare, 1959-62; cons. to Pres. John F. Kennedy's Panel on Mental Retardation, 1961; founder Community & Caring, Inc., 1986. Editor: A Community of Caring, 1982, 85, Growing Up Caring, 1990. Co-chmn. women's com. Dem. Nat. Conv., Chgo., 1956. Decorated Legion of Honor; recipient Lasker award, Humanitarian award A.A.M.D., 1973, Nat. Vol. Service award, 1973, Phila. Civic Ballet award, 1973, Prix de la Couronne Française, 1974, Presdl. Medal of Freedom, 1984, others.

SHRIVER, MARIA OWINGS, news correspondent; b. Chgo., Nov. 6, 1955; d. Robert Sargent and Eunice Mary (Kennedy) S.; m. Arnold Schwarzenegger, Apr. 26, 1986; children: Katherine Eunice, Christina Aurelia, Patrick. BA, Georgetown U. Coll. Am. Studies, Washington, 1977. News producer Sta. KYW-TV, 1977-78; producer Sta. WJZ-TV, 1978-80; nat. reporter PM Mag., 1981-83; news reporter CBS News, Los Angeles,

1983-85; news correspondent, co-anchor CBS Morning News, N.Y.C., 1985-86; co-host Sunday Today, NBC, 1987-90; anchor Main Street, NBC, 1987; co-anchor Yesterday, Today, and Tomorrow, NBC, 1989; anchor NBC Nightly News Weekend Edition, 1989-90, Cutting Edge with Maria Shriver, NBC, 1990, First Person with Maria Shriver, NBC, 1991—; co-anchor summer olympics, Seoul, Korea, 1988; substitute anchor NBC News at Sunrise, Today, NBC Nightly News with Tom Brokaw. Recipient Christopher award for "Fatal Addictions", 1990, Exceptional Merit Media award Nat. Women's Political Caucus. Democrat. Roman Catholic. Office: NBC News First Person with Maria Shriver 30 Rockefeller Plz New York NY 10112*

SHRIVER, PAMELA HOWARD, professional tennis player; b. Balt., July 4, 1962. Profl. tennis player, 1979—; winner 21 career singles, 92 career doubles titles, 7 Australian Opens (with Martina Navratilova), 4 French Opens (with Navratilova), 5 Wimbledons (with Navratilova), 6 U.S. Opens, French Open mixed doubles (with Emilio Sanchez); mem. U.S. Fedn. Cup Team, 1986-87, 89, 92, U.S. Wightman Cup Team, 1978-81, 83, 85, 87. V.P. Internat. Tennis Hall of Fame; pres. of Women's Tennis Association, 1991, 92, 93. Recipient Gold medal 1988 Olympic Games in doubles (with Zina Garrison). Mem. Women's Tennis Assn. Tour Players Assn. Address: care PHS Ltd Ste 902 401 Washington Ave Baltimore MD 21204

SHRIVER, PEGGY ANN LEU, lay administrator; b. Muscatine, Iowa, July 23, 1931; d. George Chester and Zelda Marguerita (Wunder) Leu; m. Donald Woods Shriver, Aug. 9, 1953; children: Gregory, Margaret Ann, Timothy. BA, Central Coll., 1953, HHD (hon.), 1979. Staff exec. office rev. and evaluation Gen. Assembly Presbyn. Ch. U.S.A., Atlanta, 1973-75; asst. gen. sec. office rsch. evaluation and planning Nat. Coun. Chs. of Christ, U.S.A., N.Y.C., 1976-89, staff assoc. profl. ch. leadership, 1989—; nat. sec. United Christian Youth Movement, 1951-53; bd. dirs. Christianity and Crisis, 1977-90, Ctr. for Theology and Pub. Policy, Washington, 1978—; del. to World Coun. Chs. Faith, Sci. and Future Consultation, 1979; mem. interreligious delegation to Romania, Appeal to Conscience Found., 1980. Author: The Bible Vote: Religion and the New Right, 1981, Having Gifts That Differ, 1989, Pinches of Salt (poetry book), 1990; contbr. articles to profl. jours. Protestant cons. Girl Scouts Am., 1984—; cons. World Assn. Girl Guides and Girl Scouts, London, 1994—; mem. staff, ex-com. Resources for Civic Conversation, Nat. Coun. Chs. of Christ USA. Recipient Union medal Union Theol. Sem., 1991. Mem. Religious Rsch. Assn. (pres. 1993-94), John Milton Soc. (bd. dirs. 1989—). Democrat. Home: 440 Riverside Dr Apt 58 New York NY 10027-6830 Office: Nat Coun Chs of Christ USA 475 Riverside Dr New York NY 10115-0122

SHUBART, DOROTHY LOUISE TEPFER, artist, educator; b. Ft. Collins, Colo., Mar. 1, 1923; d. Adam Christian and Rose Virginia (Ayers) Tepfer; m. Robert Franz Shubart, Apr. 22, 1950; children: Richard, Lorenne. Grad., Cleve. Inst. Art, 1944-46; AA, Colo. Women's Coll., 1944; grad., Cleve. Inst. Art, 1946; student, Western Res. U., 1947-48; BA, St. Thomas Aquinas Coll., 1974; MA, Coll. New Rochelle, 1978. Art tchr. Denver Mus., 1942-44, Cleve. Recreation Dept., 1944-50; ind. artist, portrait painter, ceramist-potter Colo., Cleve., N.Y., and N.Mex., 1944—; adult edn. art tchr. Nanuet (N.Y.) Pub. Schs., 1950-65, Pearl River (N.Y.) Adult Edn., 1950-51; rec. sec. Van Houten Fields Assn., West Nyack, N.Y., 1969-74. Exhbns. include Hopper House, Rockland Ctr. for Arts, CWC, Cleve. Inst. Art, Coll. New Rochelle, Rockland County Ann. Art Fair, 1970-89. Leader 4-H Club, Nanuet, 1960-80, Girls Scouts U.S., Nanuet, 1961-68; mem. scholarship com., gen. com. PTA, Nanuet, 1964-68; rec. sec. Van Houten Fields assn., West Nyack, N.Y., 1969-74; com. mem. Eldorado (Santa Fe) Cmty. Improvement Assn.-Arterial Rd. Planning Com., 1992-94, Ams. for Dem. Action (coun. for a livable world), Environ. Def. Fund, Union of Concerned Scientists, Nat. Com. to Preserve Social Security and Medicare; capt. Neighborhood Watch; local organizer Eldorado chpt. Eldorado History Project Com.; worked for Jim Baca Gov.'s campaign, 1994; mem. Eldorado Hist. Com., 1995-96; mem. El Dorado Arterial Road Planning Com., Habitat for Humanity. Gund scholar Cleve. Inst. Art, 1946. Mem. AAUW, NOW, Audubon Soc., Ams. for Dem. Action, Environ. Def. Fund, Union Concerned Scientists, Nat. Com. To Preserve Social Security and Medicare, Action on Smoking and Health, Wilderness Club, Delta Tau Kappa, Phi Delta Kappa. Democrat. Home: 8 Hidalgo Ct Santa Fe NM 87505-8898

SHUCART, EVELYN ANN, sales and marketing professional; b. Covington, Ky., May 29, 1942; d. Frederick Holroyd and Evelyn Ann (Thomson) Eastabrooks; m. Rexford Lee Hill III, Sept. 12, 1964 (div. 1983); children: Eric Douglas, Rexford Alan, Gerald Alexander, Andrew David; m. James Wood Shucart, Sept. 21, 1991. BS in Design, U. Cin., 1965. Freelance artist St. Louis, 1960—; office mgr. United Ch. of Christ, St. Louis, 1983-84; program coord. Acme Premium Supply, St. Louis, 1984-86, mgr., 1986-93; v.p. I.B.A. Inc., St. Louis, 1993—. Illustrator: Life Through Time, 1975. Coord./advisor Guardian Angels N.Y., St. Louis, 1981-82; advisor Pres.'s Commn. on Continuing Edn., Eden Sem., St. Louis, 1982-83; advisor Ecumenical Task Force on Hunger, 1982; cons. Women's Task Force on Employment, 1975-76; cons. Nat. Bd. Homeland Ministries, United Ch. of Christ, 1982, mem. St. Louis Assn. United Ch. of Christ, pres., 1981-82. Best of Show award Siegfried Reinhardt County Artists, 1976. Mem. NAFE, LWV, Direct Mktg. Assn., Am. Mgmt. Assn., Amnesty Internat., Sierra Club. Home and Office: 2039 Brookcreek Ln Saint Louis MO 63122-2254

SHUE, ELISABETH, actress; b. Wilmington, Del., Oct. 6, 1963; m. Davis Guggenheim. Grad., Wellesley Coll., Harvard U.; studied with Sylvie Leigh. Appeared in Broadway plays including Some Americans Abroad, Birth and After Birth; appeared in films including The Karate Kid, 1984, Link, 1986, Adventures in Babysitting, 1987, Cocktail, 1988, Body Wars, 1989, Back to the Future Part II, 1989, Back to the Future Part III, 1990, Soapdish, 1991, The Marrying Man, 1991, Twenty Bucks, 1993, Heart and Souls, 1993, Radio Inside, 1994, Blind Justice, 1994, The Underneath, 1995, Leaving Las Vegas, 1995 (Oscar nominee for Best Actress), The Trigger Effect, 1996, The Saint, 1996; appeared in TV movies including Charles and Diana, Double Switch, 1987, Hale the Hero, 1992, Blind Justice; appeared in TV series Call to Glory, 1984. Office: Creative Arts Agy 9830 Wilkshire Blvd Beverly Hills CA 90212*

SHUEY, JUDITH LEWIS, counselor; b. Atlanta, Oct. 2, 1946; d. Oliver McCutchen and Hazel Kyle (Jones) Lewis; m. Theodore G. Jr. Shuey, June 21, 1969 (div. 1986); children: Ellen Lewis, Theodore G. III. BA in Econ., Bridgewater Coll., 1968; student, U. Va., 1969-71; MEd, James Madison U., 1990. Cert. fin. planner. Tchr. Augusta County Schs., Staunton, Va., 1968-70; sec.-treas. Cabinet Craft Va., Inc., Richmond, 1977-80; choir master Christ Luth. Ch., Staunton, 1982-88; career counselor Staunton City Schs., 1987-90; trainer student assistance programs Va. Dept. Edn., Broadway, 1991—; cons. on PULSAR to gov. of Va., 1990—; cons. interagy. comm. City of Petersburg; creater Student Assistance Program (winner state and local awards); speaker ann. conf. W.Va. Edn. Assn., 1992. Bd. dirs. Christ Luth. Ch., Staunton, 19185-88, 90—, Staunton CADRE, 1988—; bd. irs. Staunton Youth Commn. Recipient Citation for substance abuse prevention, Va. Atty. Gen. Mary Sue Terry, Richmond, 1990. Mem. NEA, Va. Edn. Assn. (presenter state instrn. conf. 1990), Va. Career Devel. Assn. (bd. dirs.), Staunton Mental Health Assn. (bd. dirs. 1989—), Va. Counselors Assn. Democrat. Home: 504 Rainbow Dr Staunton VA 24401-2141

SHUFFELTON, JANE WEISS, secondary education educator; b. Pitts., Dec. 3, 1940; d. Mark and Marion (Ballou) Weiss; m. Frank C. Shuffelton, Apr. 20, 1963; children: Amy, George. BA, Radcliffe Coll., 1962; MA in Tchg., Harvard U., 1963. Cert. secondary French, Russian, Spanish, and English tchr., Mass., N.Y. Tchr. Acton (Mass.)-Boxborough H.S., 1963-66, 68-69; tchr. fng. langs. Brighton H.S., Rochester, N.Y., 1972—. Contbr. articles to profl. publs. Elder 3d Presbyn. Ch., Rochester, 1987—; bd. dirs. Linkages of Rochester, 1988—. Grantee Ford Found., 1990, NEH, summer 1992. Mem. Am. Coun. Tchrs. Russian (bd. dirs. 1988—, exch. tchr. Leningrad 1986, sec.), Am. Assn. Tchrs. Slavic and East European Langs., Am. Assn. Tchrs. French, N.Y. State Assn. Fgn. Lang. Tchrs. (Ruth Wasley Disting. Tchr. award 1992), Women's Edn. Network, Assn. Learning Labs., Alliance Française. Office: Brighton HS 1150 Winton Rd S Rochester NY 14618-2244

SHUFFLER, SARA ANTONIA, social worker, researcher; b. Cali, Colombia, Nov. 4, 1968; d. Cecil Allen and Paulette Lucille (DiYanni) S. BA, U. Calif., 1990; MA, San Diego State U., 1994; M in Social Work, U. Mich., 1995. Info. svcs. coord. Harcourt Brace Jovanovich Pubs., San Diego, 1990-91; tchg. asst. San Diego Unified Sch. Dist., 1991-93, instructional aide, 1993-94; grad. asst. San Diego State U., 1993, rsch. asst., 1992-93, tchg. assoc., 1993-94; intern Mich. Dept. Social Svcs., Lansing, 1994-95, policy analyst, 1995—. Vol. White House Conf. on Aging, 1995. Mem. U. Mich. Alumni Soc. (rep.), Toastmasters (Humorous speech contest award 1995), Alpha Kappa Delta. Democrat. Roman Catholic. Home: 1746 Warrington St San Diego CA 92107

SHUGART, ANITA CAROL, research and development cosmetologist; b. Memphis, July 2, 1943; d. Thomas Edwin and Lula P. (Shults) Brumbelow; m. Cecil Glen Shugart, Dec. 14, 1985; m. Robert E. Henry (div. Jan. 1985); children: Robert Eugene Henry Jr., Lisa Carol Henry Brown. BA, Memphis State U., 1989, postgrad., 1990-91. Cert. cosmetologist, aesthetician. Cosmetologist Memphis, 1981-86; aesthetician mgr. Adian Arpel Cosmetics, 1991-92; cosmetologist Maybelline R & D, Memphis, 1992—. Mem. NAFE, Soc. Cosmetic Chemists, Adult Student Assn. (pres. 1987-89), Sigma Tau Delta (sec. 1987-89), Omicron Delta Kappa. Home: 475 N Highland St 3M Memphis TN 38122-4533 Office: Maybelline Corp 3030 Jackson Ave Memphis TN 38112

SHUHLER, PHYLLIS MARIE, physician; b. Sellersville, Pa., Sept. 25, 1947; d. Raymond Harold and Catherine Cecilia (Virus) S.; m. John Howard Schwarz, Sept. 17, 1983; 1 child, Luke Alexander. BS in Chemistry, Chestnut Hill Coll., 1971; MD, Mich. State U., 1976; diploma of Tropical Medicine and Hygiene, U. London, 1980. Diplomate Am. Bd. Family Medicine. With Soc. Cath. Med. Missionaries, Phila., 1966-82; ward clk., nursing asst. Holy Family Hosp., Atlanta, 1971-72; resident in family practice Somerset Family Med. Residency Program, Somerville, N.J., 1976-79; physician East Coast Migrant Health Project, Newton Grove, N.C., 1980; physician, missionary SCMM, Diocese of Sunyani, Berekum, Ghana, West Africa, 1980-81; emergency rm. physician Northeast Emergency Med. Assn., Quakertown, Pa., 1981-82; founder, physician Family Health Care Ctr., Inc., Pennsburg, Pa., 1982-90; physician Lifequest Med. Group, Pennsburg, 1990-93; pvt. practice Pennsburg, 1993—. Fellow Royal Soc. Tropical Medicine and Hygiene; mem. Am. Acad. Family Practice, Am. Bd. Family Practice, Am. Med. Women Assn. Pa. Acad. Family Practice, Lehigh Valley Women Med. Assn. Roman Catholic. Office: 101 W 7th St Ste 2C Pennsburg PA 18073

SHUKET-BARASHY, BARBARA SHARI, elementary school educator; b. N.Y.C., Sept. 20, 1960; d. Joseph and Muriel (Katzelnick) Shuket; m. Joseph Haim Barashy, June 30, 1985; children: Ezra Samuel, Mitchell Harris. BA, Queens Coll., 1984, MA, 1987. Elem sch. tchr. N.Y. State. Tchr. N.Y.C. Bd. Edn., 1984—, trip coord. asst. programmer, 1991—; tchr. Louis Armstrong Middle Sch. Home: 224-59 77th Ave Flushing NY 11364-3018

SHULDES, L(ILLIAN) JUNE, educator; b. Chgo.; d. Clarence Andrew Sr. and Lillian (Evans) Baldwin; m. Robert William Shuldes, June 19, 1954; children: Eugene Robert, Judith Yvonne Shuldes Turley. BS in Edn., Northwestern U., 1951, MA in Edn., 1956. Tchr. elem. sch. Chgo. Bd. Edn., 1951-87; lcctr. Chgo. Workshop, 1982; speaker in field. Vice chair 13th Congl. Dist. Rep. Women Orgn., Evanston, Ill., 1958-62; chmn. Am. history essay contest Signal Hill chpt. NSDAR, Barrington, Ill., 1988-92, chaplain, 1994-96; hon. condr. Elgin (Ill.) Symphony Orch., 1988. Recipient George Washington Honor medal Freedoms Foun., Valley Forge, Pa., 1971,72, Valley Forge Tchrs. medal, 1972, Pageant Honor cert., 1973. Mem. AAUW, Barrington Hist. Soc., Delta Kappa Gamma. Baptist. Home: 1 W Penny Rd Barrington IL 60010

SHULER, ARLENE, arts administrator; b. Cleve., Oct. 18, 1947; d. Myron and Rosalind (Albert) S.; m. Nigel Redden, June 21, 1986; children: William Austin Redden, Julia Austin Redden. BA magna cum laude, Columbia U., 1976, JD, 1978. Bar: N.Y. 1979. Dancer The Joffrey Ballet, N.Y.C., 1965-69; program adminstr. NEA, Washington, 1977-78; cons. Fed. Coun. on Arts and Humanities, Washington, 1978-79, legis. asst. Congressman Ted Weiss, Washington, 1979-81; exec. dir. Vol. Lawyers for Arts, N.Y.C., 1981-85; dep. dir. Wallace Funds, N.Y.C., 1985-88; pres. Gen. Atlantic Ptnrs. Found., N.Y.C., 1988-89; v.p. Atlantic Philanthropic Svc. Co., N.Y.C., 1989-90; v.p. planning and devel. Lincoln Ctr., Inc., N.Y.C., 1990—; bd. dirs. Second Stage Theater, N.Y.c.; chmn. bd. dirs. David Gordon/Pick up Performance, N.Y.C., 1982-95; panelist overview policy panel NEA, Washington, 1994, co-chmn. inter arts panel, 1986-88; chmn. dance panel Mass. Coun. on Arts and Humanities, Boston, 1987. Harlan Fiske scholar Columbia U., 1976-77. Mem. Phi Beta Kappa. Office: Lincoln Ctr Performing Arts 9th Fl 70 Lincoln Center Plz New York NY 10023

SHULER, SALLY ANN SMITH, telecommunications, computer services and software company executive; b. Mt. Olive, N.C., June 11, 1934; d. Leon Joseph and Ludia Irene (Montague) Simmons; m. Henry Ralph Smith Jr., Mar. 1, 1957 (div. Jan. 1976); children: Molly Montague, Barbara Ellen, Sara Ann, Mary Kathryn; m. Harold Robert Shuler, Aug. 2, 1987. BA in Math., Duke U., 1956; spl. studies, U. Liège, Belgium, 1956-57; postgrad. in bus. econs., Claremont Grad Sch., 1970-72. Mgr. fed. systems GE Info. Svcs. Co., Washington, 1976-78; mgr. mktg. support GE Info. Svcs. Co., Rockville, Md., 1978-81; dir. bus. devel. info. tech. group Electronic Data Systems, Bethesda, Md., 1981-82; v.p. mktg. optimum systems div. Electronic Data Systems, Rockville, 1982-83; v.p. planning and communications Electronic Data Systems, Dallas, 1983-84; exec. dir. comml. devel. U.S. West Inc., Englewood, Colo., 1984-90; v.p. mktg. devel. Cin. Bell Info. Systems Inc., 1990-92; mgmt. cons. in mergers and acquisitions Denver, 1992-93; v.p. major accounts U.S. Computer Svcs., Denver, 1993-95; mgmt. cons. in mergers and acquisitions Mktg., Telecom., Denver, 1995—. Recipient GE Centennial award, Rockville, 1978. Mem. Women in Telecommunications, Rotary (fellow Internat. Found.), Phi Beta Kappa, Tau Psi Omega, Pi Mu Epsilon. Democrat. Presbyterian. Office: 1626 S Syracuse St Denver CO 80231-2691

SHULER DONNER, LAUREN, film producer; b. Cleveland, OH. BS in Film and Broadcasting, Boston U. TV films include: Amateur Night at the Dixie Bar and Grill, 1979; fmils include: Thank God It's Friday, 1978 (assoc. prodr.), Mr. Mon, 1983, Ladyhawke, 1985, St. Elmo's Fire, 1985, Pretty in Pink, 1986, Three Fugitives, 1989, Radio Flyer, 1992, Dave, 1993, Free Willy, 1993, The Favor, 1994; (exec. producer) Free Willy 2: The Adventure Home, 1995, Assassins, 1995, Free Willy 3, 1996. Office: Donner/Shuler-Donner Prodns Warner Bros 4000 Warner Blvd Burbank CA 91522-0001

SHULGASSER, BARBARA, writer; b. Manhasset, N.Y., Apr. 10, 1954; d. Lew and Luba (Golante) S. Student, Sarah Lawrence Coll., 1973-74; BA magna cum laude, CUNY, 1977; MS, Columbia U., 1978. Feature writer Waterbury (Conn.) Rep., 1978-81; reporter, feature writer Chgo. Sun Times, 1981-84; film critic San Francisco Examiner, 1984—; freelance book critic N.Y. Times Book Rev., N.Y.C., 1983—. Co-author: (screenplay, with Robert Altman) Ready to Wear, 1994; freelance video columnist N.Y. Times Sunday Arts & Leisure, 1989, features for Vanity Fair, Glamour and Mirabella mags. Office: San Francisco Examiner 110 5th St San Francisco CA 94103-2918

SHULL, CLAIRE, documentary film producer, casting director; b. N.Y.C., Oct. 26, 1925; d. Barnet Joseph and Fannie (Florea) Klar; m. Leo Shull, Aug. 8, 1948; children: Lee Shull Pearlstein, David. Student, Am. Acad. Dramatic Arts, N.Y.C., 1943-44, NYU, 1973-74. Editor, assoc. pub. Show Bus. Publs., N.Y.C., 1957-85; owner, founder Claire/Casting, N.Y.C. and Miami, Fla., 1972—, Claire/Casting Film Prodns., N.Y.C. and Miami, 1978—; cons. dir., prodr., dir. film and TV, The Bass Mus., Miami Beach, Fla., 1992—. Actress in The Front Page, USO European tour, 1945-46, (on Broadway) Tenting Tonight, 1947; prodr., dir. HBO TV series How To Break into Show Business, 1980-81, Cable-TV seriesJoin Us at the Bass, 1993-95. Recipient gold award and distinctive merit TV award Advt. Club. Hartford, Conn., 1984, Clio award, 1989. Mem. Ind. Casting Dirs. Assn. N.Y., Actors Equity Assn., Drama Desk.

SHULMAN, ALIX KATES, writer; b. Cleve., Aug. 17, 1932; d. Samuel Simon and Dorothy (Davis) Kates; m. Martin Shulman, June 1959 (div. 1985); children: Ted, Polly; m. Scott York, Apr. 1989. BA, Case Western Res. U., 1953; MA, NYU, 1978. Instr. New Sch. for Social Rsch., N.Y.C., 1972-74, NYU Sch. of Continuing Edn., 1976-79, Yale U., New Haven, Conn., 1979-81, NYU, 1981-84; writer-in-residence U. Colo., Boulder, 1984-86; vis. writer-in-residence Ohio State U., Columbus, 1987; citizen's chair of lit. U. Hawaii at Manoa, Honolulu, 1991-92; vis. writer-in-residence U. Ariz., Tucson, 1994. Author: (memoir) Drinking the Rain, 1995; (novels) In Every Woman's Life..., 1987, On the Stroll, 1981, Burning Questions, 1978, Memoirs of an Ex-Prom Queen, 1972, Finders Keeper, 1971, Awake or Asleep, 1971, Bosley on the Number Line, 1970, To the Barricades: The Anarchist Life of Emma Goldman, 1971. Feminist activist Redstockings, N.Y., 1969-71, Carasa, N.Y.C., 1971-82, No More Nice Girls, N.Y.C. and Honolulu, 1986-92, Women's Action Coalition, N.Y.C., 1992-94. Fellowship in fiction Nat. Endowment for the Arts, 1983, DeWitt Wallace/Reader's Digest Fulton, 1979, MacDowell Colony for the Arts, 1975-77, 79, 81, Body Mind Spirit award of Excellence, 1996. Mem. Poets Essayists Novelists (exec. bd. 1974-91, v.p. 1982-83), Nat. Writers Union, Author's Guild and Author's League, Columbia U. Seminar on Women and Soc. (exec. bd. 1980-82).

SHULMAN, MYRA ANN, English language educator; b. Madison, Wis., Feb. 27, 1941; d. Herbert and Deana (Krantman) S.; m. Edward M. Mezvinsky, Aug. 27, 1961 (div. Nov. 1974); children: Margot Mezvinsky Sarch, Vera Mezvinsky Ovadia, Elsa Mezvinsky Smithgall, Eve Mezvinsky; m. K.W. Gooch, Aug. 16, 1981; 1 stepchild, Thomas Keith Gooch. Student, Smith Coll., 1959-61; BA, U. Calif., Berkeley, 1963; MA in Eng., The Am. U., 1976. Cert. tchr. ESL. Lang. specialist, adj. prof. The Am. U., Washington, 1976—. Author: Selected Readings in Business, 1991, Journeys Through Literature, 1995. Mem. Tchrs. English to Spkrs. of Other Langs., Washington Area Tchrs. English to Spkrs. of Other Langs., English Lang. Inst. Faculty Assn. (negotiator), Phi Beta Kappa. Home: 6683 McLean Dr McLean VA 22101 Office: The Am U Mass & Nebr Ave NW Washington DC 20016

SHULTS-DAVIS, LOIS BUNTON, lawyer; b. Elkton, Md., Sept. 29, 1957; d. Asa Grant Bunton and Carolyn Elizabeth Bunton Pate; m. David Reed Shults (Dec. 8, 1979 (div. Sept. 1990); children: Kenneth Grant, Joseph David, Lawrence Scott; m. Michael Howard Davis, June 14, 1992. BS, East Tenn. State U., 1977; JD, U. Tenn., 1980. Bar: Tenn. 1980, U.S. Dist. Ct. (ea. dist.) Tenn. 1985. Assoc. Jenkins & Jenkins, Knoxville, Tenn., 1980-82, R.O. Smith Law Offices, Erwin, Tenn., 1982-85; ptnr. Shults & Shults, Erwin, 1985—; gen. counsel Erwin Nat. Bank, 1985—. Bd. dirs. Unicoi County Heritage Mus., Erwin, 1986-87, Unicoi County Ambulance Authority, Erwin, 1990-91, YMCA, Erwin, 1991—; pres. Unicoi Elem. PTO, 1994; mock trial coach Mock Trial Competition Young Lawyers, 1993, 95-96. Recipient Contbn. to Edn. award Unicoi County Edn. Assn., 1994. Mem. Female Attys. of Mountain Empire, DAR (regent 1990-92). Republican. Methodist. Home: Rt 1 Box 258-B Unicoi TN 37692 Office: Shults & Shults Law Offices 111 Gay St Erwin TN 38650

SHULTZ, LEILA MCREYNOLDS, botanist, educator; b. Bartlesville, Okla., Apr. 20, 1946; 1 child, Kirsten. BS, U. Tulsa, 1969; MA, U. Colo., 1975; PhD, Claremont Grad. Sch., 1983. Curator Intermountain Herbarium Utah State U., 1973-92; rschr. Harvard U., Cambridge, Mass., 1994—. Co-author: Atlas of the Vascular Plants of Utah, 1988; taxon editor: Flora of North America (3 vols.), 1987. Mem. Am. Bot. Soc. (systematics rep. 1988-90), Am. Soc. Plant Taxonomists (coun. 1990-92). Office: Harvard U Herbaria 22 Divinity Ave Cambridge MA 02138-2020

SHULTZ, LINDA JOYCE, library director; b. South Bend, Ind., Aug. 25, 1931; d. Justin Russell and Gladys Ernstine (Miller) Nash; m. Dale Jay Shultz, Apr. 20, 1952; children: Donald Jay, Sally Janine, William Justin, Alan Joel, Kent Jon. AA, Stephens Coll., 1951; BS in Edn., Ind. U., Ft. Wayne, 1971, Cert. I in Libr. Edn., 1975. Sec. John R. Worthman, Inc., Ft. Wayne, 1951-54; farm wife, mother Noble County, Ind., 1954-68; libr. Noble County Pub. Libr., Albion, Ind., 1968—; mem. exec. bd. Tri-Alsa Libr. Svc. Authority, Ft. Wayne, 1988-90. Editor: Albion Memories, 1977. Mem. Albion Local Devel. Corp., 1989 92; sec. Cen. Noble Jr. Achievement, 1988-92. Named Albion Citizen of the Yr. Albion Rotary Club, 1977. Mem. DAR, Ind. Libr. Assn., Ind. Hist. Soc., Albion C. of C., Order Ea. Star, Rotary (pres. Albion club 1993-94), Toastmasters (pres. U.S. Six Shooters chpt. 1988-89), Gene Stratton Porter Meml. Soc., Ind. Soc. Mayflower Descendants. Republican. Methodist. Office: Noble County Pub Libr 813 E Main St Albion IN 46701-1038

SHUMARD, SALLY LEE, art educator; b. Tulsa, Okla., Nov. 26, 1957; d. Samuel Berry and Alice Elaine (Benzinger) S.; m. John C. Gibbs, Dec. 21, 1985; 1 child, Samuel Taylor Gibbs. BS in Fine Arts, Miami U., 1979; MA in Fine Arts, Ohio U., 1992. Cert. art tchr., Ohio. Art tchr. Wellston (Ohio) City Schs., 1979-92; tchg. assoc., supr. student tchrs., photography instr. Ohio State U., Columbus, 1992-95; asst. prof. dept. art edn. Va. Commonwealth U., Richmond, 1995—. Recipient grant State of Ohio, Dept. Edn., 1990, Arts in Edn. grant Ohio Arts Coun., 1991, grant Columbus Found., 1992. Mem. Nat. Art Edn. Assn., Am. Edn. Rsch. Assn., U.S. Soc. for Edn. in Arts, Internat. Soc. Edn. in Arts, Am. Edn. Rschrs. Assn., Ohio State U. Assn. for Grad. Students in Art Edn. (pres. 1992—), Wellston Tchrs. Assn. (bldg. rep. 1985-91, pres. 1988-90), Phi Delta Kappa, Delta Kappa Gamma. Democrat. Home: 4304 Cary Street Rd Richmond VA 23221 Office: Va Commonwealth Univ Sch of Arts Dept Art Edn Richmond VA 23284-2519

SHUMATE, CLARA ELAINE, realtor; b. Lorain, Ohio, Dec. 8, 1942; d. Elvin R. and Frances G. (McDonald) Culp; m. Arthur E. Shumate Jr., Sept. 14, 1963; children: Arthur III, John. Lic. realtor. Realtor Findeiss, Zanesville, Ohio, 1987-92, Lepi, 1993—. Mem. Ohio Hist. Soc., Nat. Trust Hist. Preservation, Pioneer and Hist. Soc. Muskingum County. Named Hon. Citizen Colonial Williamsburg, 1995. Mem. NAFE, Nat. Bd. Realtors, Ohio Assn. Realtors (pres. sales club 1993-95, alt. trustee 1995), Muskingum County Homebuilders Assn., Zanesville Bd. Realtors (sec.-treas. 1995, pres.-elect 1996, edn. chmn. 1994, trustee 1996), Mideast Ohio Womens Entrepreneurs (steering com. 1993—), Lepi and Assocs. Multi-Million Dollar Sales Club (charter), Zanesville C. of C., Pilot Club Zanesville, Inc. Roman Catholic. Home: 3430 Boggs Rd Zanesville OH 43701

SHUMATE, GLORIA JONES, retired educational administrator; b. Meridian, Miss., Jan. 8, 1927; d. Thomas Marvin and Flora E. (Suggs) Jones; m. Jack B. Shumate, Nov. 19, 1946; children: Jack B. Jr., Thomas Edward. BS, Miss. State U., 1960; MA, U. South Fla., 1969, postgrad. in vocat. edn., 1970-72. Cert. guidance counselor, psychology and social studies specialist, Fla. High sch. tchr. Lauderdale County Schs., Meridian, 1952-56; tchr. vocat. edn. Manpower Devel. and Tng., St. Petersburg, Fla., 1964-69; counselor City Ctr. for Learning St. Petersburg Vocat.-Tech. Inst., 1969-70, registrar, 1970-72, asst. dir., 1972-80, exec. dir., 1980-85; dir. vocat.-tech., adult edn. ops. Pinellas County Schs., Largo, Fla., 1985-89; chmn. Fla. Equity Council, 1980-81; mem. Fla. Adv. Council on Vocat. Edn., 1980-85, Fla. Job Tng. Coordinating Council, 1983-84. Named Outstanding Educator Pinellas Suncoast C. of C., 1980. Mem. Nat. Council Local Adminstrs., Am. Vocat. Assn., Fla. Vocat. Assn., So. Assn. Colls. and Schs. (standards com. 1975-81), Phi Delta Kappa, Kappa Delta Pi. Democrat. Baptist. Home: 900 63rd St S Saint Petersburg FL 33707-3016

SHUMICK, DIANA LYNN, computer executive; b. Canton, Ohio, Feb. 10, 1951; d. Frank A. and Mary J. (Mari) S.; 1 child, Tina Elyse. Student, Walsh Coll., 1969-70, Ohio U., 1970-71, Kent State U., 1971-77. Data entry clk. Ohio Power Co., Canton, 1969-70; clk. City of Canton Police Dept., 1971-73; system engr. IBM, Canton, 1973-81; adv. market support rep. IBM, Dallas, 1981-89; system engr. mgr. IBM, Madison, Wis., 1989-93; mktg. customer satisfaction mgr. IBM, Research Triangle Park, N.C., 1993; HelpCenter mgr. desktop and consumer sys. supporter IBM Personal Computer Co., Research Triangle Park, 1993—. Author: Technical Coordinator Guidelines, 1984. Pres., bd. dirs. Big Bros. and Sisters of Denton (Tex.) County, 1989, v.p., 1988, sec., 1987; mem. St. Philip Parish Coun., Lewisville, Tex., 1988-89, Western Stark County Red Cross, Canton, 1980; v.p. Parents Without Ptnrs., Madison, 1991; founding bd. mem. Single Parents

Network, 1991; vol. ARC, 1985—; mem. bd. dirs. Rape Crisis Ctr. Dane County, sec., 1990-91; vol. Paint-A-Thon, Dane County, 1990, Badger State Games Challenge, 1992, Cystic Fibrosis Found. Gt. Strides, 1992, 93, 94, 95, 96, Cystic Fibrosis Found. Mother's Day Tea, 1991, 92, 93, 94, 95, 96, Cystic Fibrosis Found. Golf Classic, 1995.

SHURBUTT, SYLVIA BAILEY, English language educator, department chairperson; b. Chamblee, Ga., Nov. 15, 1944. AB in English, West Ga. Coll., Carrollton, 1965; MA in English, Ga. So. U., Statesboro, 1974; PhD in English, U. Ga., Athens, 1982. Tchr. Jefferson (Ga.) High, 1965-67; tchr., English dept. chair S.E. Bulloch High, Brooklet, Ga., 1975-78; assoc. prof. Ga. So. U., Statesboro, 1979-87; prof., English dept. chair Shepherd Coll., Shepherdstown, W.Va., 1987—. Co-author: (textbook) Reading/Writing Relationships, 1986; contbr. chpts. to books, articles to profl. jours. Editor, historian (newsletter) N.O.W., W.Va. Eastern Panhandle, 1993—. Recipient STAR Tchg. award Ga. C. of C., 1975. Mem. Nat. Coun. Tchrs. of English, Phi Kappa Phi. Democrat. Methodist. Home: PO Box 599 Shepherdstown WV 25443 Office: Dept English/Modern Langs Shepherd Coll Shepherdstown WV 25443

SHURE, MYRNA BETH, psychologist, educator; b. Chgo., Sept. 11, 1937; d. Sidney Natkin and Frances (Laufman) S.; student U. Colo., 1955; BS, U. Ill., 1959; MS, Cornell U., 1961, PhD, 1966. Asst. prof. U. R.I., head tchr. Nursery Sch., Kingston, 1961-62; asst. prof. Temple U., Phila., 1966-67, assoc. prof., 1967-68; instr. Hahneman Med. Coll., Phila., 1968-69, sr. instr. psychology, 1969-70, asst. prof., 1970-73, assoc. prof., 1973-80, prof., 1980—. NIMH research grantee, 1971-75, 77-79, 82-85, 87, 88-93. Recipient Lela Rowland Prevention award Nat. Mental Health Assn., 1982; . lic. psychologist, Pa. Fellow Am. Psychol. Assn. (Disting. Contbn. award div. community psychology 1984), Am. Psychol. Assn. (divsn. clin. psychology, child sect. 1994, Task Force on Prevention award 1987, Task Force on Model Programs award 1994, award U. Utah and Juvenile Justice Dept. of Delinquency Prevention, 1996); mem. Nat. Assn. Sch. Psychologists, Nat. Assn. Edn. Young Children, Soc. Research in Child Devel., Phila. Soc. Clin. Psychologists. Author: (with George Spivack) Social Adjustment of Young Children, 1974; (with George Spivack and Jerome Platt) The Problem Solving Approach to Adjustment, 1976; (with George Spivack) Problem Solving Techniques in Childrearing, 1978, (child curricula manual) I Can Problem Solve, 1992, (trade book) Raising a Thinking Child, 1994, (audiotape, workbook), 1996; mem. editl. bd. Jour. Applied Developmental Psychology; spl. cons. to The Puzzle Place PBS Children's TV Show.

SHURTLEFF, AKIKO AOYAGI, artist, consultant; b. Tokyo, Jan. 24, 1950; d. Kinjiro and Fumiyo (Sugata) Aoyagi; m. William Roy Shurtleff, Mar. 10, 1977 (div. 1995); 1 child, Joseph Aoyagi. Grad., Women's Coll. Art, Tokyo, 1971; student, Acad. Art, San Francisco, 1991-92. Fashion designer, illustrator Marimura Co. and Hayakawa Shoji, Inc., Tokyo, 1970-72; co-founder, art dir. Soyfoods Ctr. consulting svcs., Lafayette, Calif., 1976-94; freelance illustrator, graphic designer; lectr. U.S. Internat. Christian U., Tokyo, 1977, Japanese Tofu Mfrs. Conv., Osaka, 1978; presenter cooking demonstrations, tchr. cooking classes. Co-author, illustrator: The Book of Tofu, 1975, The Book of Miso, 1975, The Book of Kudzu, 1977, Tofu and Soymilk Production, 1979, The Book of Tempeh, 1979, Miso Production, 1979, Tempeh Production, 1980; illustrator: Spirulina (by L. Switzer), 1982, The Book of Shiatsu-The Healing Art of Finger Pressure (by S. Goodman), 1990, Staying Healthy with Nutrition (by E. Haas), 1992, Culinary Treasures of Japan (by John and Jan Belleme), 1992, Yookoso, An Invitation to Contemporary Japanese, Vols. 1 & 2 (by Hasu-Hiko Tohsaku), 1994-95, Blue Collar & Beyond (by Yana Parker), 1995, Damn Good Ready to Go Resumes, 1995, Homework (by Peter Jeswald), 1995, Vegetarian's A to Z Guide to Fruits and Vegetables (by Kathleen Robinson with Pete Luckett), 1996, Hubert Keller's Cuisine, 1996, Doctor Generic Will See You Now (by Oscar London), 1996. Office: Akiko Aoyagi Shurtleff PO Box 443 Lafayette CA 94549-0443

SHURTLIFF, V. NORMA, property manager, sculptor, writer; b. Salt Lake City, Nov. 13, 1928; d. Francis Fielding and Jane (Boulton) Crompton; m. Lyman Folkman Shurtliff, Dec. 26, 1949; children: Marque, Carlie, Jen. BS in Biol. Sci., U. Utah, 1966. Cert. secondary tchr., Utah; note, avocations are limited to 5, per style. Switchboard operator Mountain Bell, Salt Lake City, 1948-58; pvt. instr. ballet, Ely and McGill, Nev., 1959-62; property mgr., builder, Tempe, Ariz., 1966-68; receptionist, acct. Lyman Shurtliff, M.D., Bountiful, Utah, 1969-90; property mgr., builder, Salt Lake City, 1980—; sculptor Le Motif, Bountiful, 1990—. Author: (novel) Alone in Timber Creek, 1980 (hon. mention Utah Arts Coun. 1981), (autobiography) Epiphany, 1986 (hon. mentin 1987), also 4 other novels, 1975-93. Candidate for White Pine County (Nev.) Sch. Bd., 1960; Nev. sec. Aux. to AMA, 1961; Davis County rep. Utah Women's Legis. Coun., 1970; precinct capt. Utah Dem. Com., 1972-80. Mem. AAUW (critics' circle), Daria Lit. Club (pres.), Salt Lake Swimming and Tennis Club (bd. dirs., v.p. 1985). Home and Office: 987 Canyon Crest Dr Bountiful UT 84010

SHUSS, JANE MARGARET, artist; b. Ost, Kans., Feb. 15, 1936; d. Leo and Mary Catharine (Thimesch) Nett; m. Robert Hamilton Shuss, Feb. 19, 1954; children: Patrick, Andrea, Matt, Lisa, Robert, Eric. Grad. high sch. sec. Found. for Plein Air Painting, Avalon, Calif., 1995—. One woman shows include Challis Galleries, Laguna Beach, Calif., 1981, 82, 83, Esther Wells Gallery, 1984, 85, 86, 87, 94; exhibited in group shows at Plein Air Painters of Am., 1985, 86, 87, 88, 89, 90, 91, 92, 93, 94, 95, 96, Western Acad. Women Artists, 1996, O'Brien's Gallery, Scottsdale, Ariz., 1996. Mem. Western Acad. Women Artists, Soc. Am. Impressionists, Plein Air Painters Am. (treas. 1996-97), Calif. Art Club. Republican. Office: Shuss Design 15222 1/2 Pipeline Ln Huntington Beach CA 92649

SHUSTER, DIANNA, musical theatre company executive, choreographer. Artistic dir. Am. Musical Theatre of San Jose, Calif. Office: Am Muscial Theatre 1717 Technology Dr San Jose CA 95110-1305

SHUTLER, MARY ELIZABETH, academic administrator; b. Oakland, Calif., Nov. 14, 1929; d. Hal Wilfred and Elizabeth Frances (Gimbel) Hall; m. Richard Shutler Jr., Sept. 8, 1951 (div. 1975); children: Kathryn Allice, John Hall, Richard Burnett. BA, U. Calif., Berkeley, 1951; MA, U. Ariz., 1958, PhD, 1967. Asst., assoc., full prof. anthropology, chmn. dept. San Diego State U., 1967-75; prof. anthropology, dept. chmn. Wash. State U., Pullman, 1975-80; dean Coll. Arts and Scis., prof. anthropology U. Alaska, Fairbanks, 1980-84; vice chancellor, dean of faculty, prof. anthropology U. Wis. Parkside, Kenosha, 1984-88; provost, v.p. for acad. affairs, prof. anthropology Calif. State U., L.A., 1988-94; provost West Coast U., L.A., 1994—; mem. core staff Lahav Rsch. Project, Miss. State U., 1975—. Co-author: Ocean Prehistory, 1975, Deer Creek Cave, 1964, Archaeological Survey of Southern Nevada, 1963, Stuart Rockshelter, 1962; contbr. articles to jours. in field. Mem. coun. Gamble House. Fellow Am. Anthropol. Assn.; mem. Soc. for Am. Archaeology, Am. Schs. for Oriental Rsch., Am. Coun. Edn., Am. Assn. for Higher Edn., Am. Assn. State Colls. and Univs., Delta Zeta. Republican. Roman Catholic. Office: West Coast U 440 Shatto Pl Los Angeles CA 90020-1704

SHUTRUMP, MARY JILL, writer, editor, photographer, educator; b. Youngstown, Ohio, Sept. 24, 1964; d. Albin George and Joanne Donna (Torello) S. BA in Journalism, Ohio State U., 1986; MFA in Creative Writing, Clayton U., 1990, PhD in Communications/English, 1991. Mgr. Riverwatch Tower, Columbus, Ohio, 1987-88; editor, writer UPS, Columbus, 1988-95; freelance writer Columbus, 1990-95, Folly Beach, S.C., 1995—; v.p. publicity Arc Entertainment, Columbus, 1992-94, copywriter, acct. mgmt. advt., 1993, asst. producer videos, 1994; publicist Pet Helpers Orgn., Folly Beach, S.C., 1995; writer The Connection Newspaper, Kiawah Island, S.C., 1995—; cons. Comms. and Advt., 1993-94; tech. writing cons. Mauswerks, Inc., Columbus, 1991; proofreader, Columbus, 1990-95; cons., commn./pub. rels. dir. FAN Engring. (U.S.A.) Inc., 1993-95; owner, freelance cons. Profl. and Acad. Svcs., 1991; instr. dept. English Columbus State C. C., 1991-93; owner Au Natural internat. health and beauty products brokers, 1995—; owner, publicist Moondog Cafè and Graphics Internat., 1995; comm. and speech instr. Trident Tech. Coll., Charleston, 1996—. Publicist and pub. rels. (rock band) Euragression, 1991—; prodr. MD Entertainment, 1994, 96; model and actress in music field, Europe, 1992—; music editor/writer Atlantic Surfer mag., 1994; asst., publicist Innovative Resources LLC, 1995—; asst. publicist Coyote Enterprises, 1995—. Active Greenpeace, Washington, 1987—, Environ. Def. Fund, Washington, 1988—, World Wildlife Fund, PETA, 1987—. Mem. Humane Soc. of the U.S. Home: PO Box 1356 Folly Beach SC 29439-1356 Office: PO Box 1396 Folly Beach SC 29439 also: 2426 Sawmill Village Ct Columbus OH 43235

SHUTT, BUFFY, marketing executive; d. Charles Byron and Jean Allison (Draegert) S. BA in Communication, Purdue U., 1983. With Paramount, N.Y.C., 1973-75, sec. to pub. staff, 1975-78, nat. mag. contact, 1978, dir. pub., 1978-80, exec. dir. pub., v.p. pub. and promotions, sr. v.p., asst. to pres. Motion Picture Group, 1981-84, exec. f.p. mktg., 1985, pres. mktg., 1986; v.p. East coast prodn. Time-Life Films, 1980-81; ptnr. Shutt-Jones Comm., 1987-89; mktg. pres. Columbia Pictures & Tri-Star Pictures, 1989-91, TriStar, 1991; pres. mktg. Universal Pictures, Universal City, Calif. Tutor Project Literacy U.S., Menlo Park, Calif., 1987-88; active in Combined Fed. Campaign, Washington, 1984, 86, U.S. savs. bond drive, Washington, 1985. Republican. Presbyterian. *

SHUTTLEWORTH, ANNE MARGARET, psychiatrist; b. Detroit, Jan. 17, 1931; d. Cornelius Joseph and Alice Catherine (Rice) S.; A.B., Cornell U., 1953, M.D., 1956; m. Joel R. Siegel, Apr. 19, 1959; children: Erika, Peter. Intern, Lenox Hill Hosp., N.Y.C., 1956-57; resident Payne Whitney Clinic-N.Y. Hosp., 1957-60; practice medicine, specializing in psychiatry, Maplewood, N.J., 1960—; cons. Maplewood Sch. System, 1960-62; instr. psychiatry Cornell U. Med. Sch., 1960; mem. Com. to Organize New Sch. Psychology, 1970. Mem. AMA (Physicians Recognition award 1975, 78, 81, 84, 87, 90, 93, 96), Am. Psychiat. Assn., Am. Med. Women's Assn., N.Y. Acad. Scis., Acad. Medicine N.J., Phi Beta Kappa, Phi Kappa Phi. Home: 46 Farbrook Dr Short Hills NJ 07078-3007 Office: 2066 Millburn Ave Maplewood NJ 07040-3715

SHUTTLEWORTH, REBECCA SCOTT, English language educator; b. Eupora, Miss., Aug. 18, 1919; d. Thaddeus William and Frances Lucinda (Willingham) Scott; m. Wallace Shuttleworth, June 12, 1943 (dec. Aug. 1961); children: Sally, Rebecca. BA, Miss. U. for Women, 1941, MEd, 1962. Tchr. Okolona (Miss.) High Sch., 1941-42, Indianola (Miss.) High Sch., 1942-43, 45-70; tchr. Miss. Delta Community Coll., Moorhead, 1970-89, chmn. lang. arts, 1978-89, tchr. extended learning, 1989-96; asst. organizer Miss. Community Coll. Creative Writing Assn., 1978. Past pres. Twentieth Century Club, Indianola, 1947-94. Mem. AAUW (Woman of Achievement 1992, Scholarship award 1989), DAR (Am. history chmn. 1990-92, vice-regent 1994-96, regent 1996—). Republican. Methodist. Home and Office: 401 Lee St Indianola MS 38751-2739

SHUTTS, SHARON E., psychologist; b. Macon, Mo., July 11, 1940; d. Clarence Miller and Margaret Jane (Burke) Cox; m. William Allen Bowlin, June 12, 1960 (div. 1973); children: Lori Christine, William Alan; m. Ellis Lynn Shutts, Sept. 3, 1976 (dec. 1978). BS Psychology, Mo. W. State Coll., 1975; MA Psychology, U. Mo., 1977, EdS in Counseling, 1989. Lic. profl. counselor. Mental health coord. Greater St. Joseph Area Head Start, St. Joseph, Mo., 1973-79; profl. counselor Child & Family Counseling, St. Joseph, Mo., 1991—; psychologist I Woodson Children's Psychiatric Hosp., St. Joseph, Mo., 1979—. Mem. ACA, Task Force on Sexual Assault and Interpersonal Violence, St. Joseph, Mo., Head Start Adv. Coun., Am. Psychol. Assn., Assn. Applied Psychophysiology and Biofeedback. Office: Woodson Children's Psychiatric Hosp 3400 Frederick Saint Joseph MO 64506 also: Child & Family Counseling 1018 W St Maartens Dr Saint Joseph MO 64506

SHWAYDER, ELIZABETH YANISH, sculptor; b. St. Louis; d. Sam and Fannie May (Weil) Yaffe; m. Nathan Yanish, July 5, 1944 (dec.); children: Ronald, Marilyn Ginsburg, Mindy; m. M.C. Shawayder, 1988. Student, Washington U., 1941, Denver U., 1960; pvt. studies. One-woman shows include Woodstock Gallery, London, 1973, Internat. House, Denver, 1963, Colo. Women's Coll., Denver, 1975, Contemporaries Gallery, Santa Fe, 1963, So. Colo. State Coll. Pueblo, 1967, others; exhibited in group shows: Salt Lake City Mus., 1964, 71, Denver Art Mus., 1961-75, Oklahoma City Mus., 1969, Joslyn Mus., Omaha, 1964-68, Lucca (Italy) Invitational, 1971, others; represented in permanent collections include Colo. State Bank, Bmh Synagogue, Denver, Colo. Women's Coll., Har Ha Shem Congregation, Boulder, Colo., Faith Bible Chapel, Denver, others. Chmn. visual arts Colo. Centennial-Bicentennial, 1974-75; pres. Denver Council Arts and Humanities, 1973-75; mem. Mayor's Com. on Child Abuse, 1974-75; co-chmn. visual arts spree Denver Pub. Schs., 1975; trustee Denver Center for the Performing Arts, 1973-75; chmn. Concerned Citizens for Arts, 1976; pres. Beth Israel Hosp. Aux., 1985-87; organizer Coat Drive for the Needy, Denver and N.Y.C., 1982-87, Common Cents penny dirve for homeless, 1991-93; bd. dirs. Mizel Mus., Srs., Inc.; active Mayor's Com. on Cultural Affairs, Nat. Mus., Women in the Arts Mus., Freedom Found. at Valley Force, Hospice of Metro Denver. Humanities scholar Auraria Librs.-U. Colo.; recipient McCormick award Ball State U., Muncie, Ind., 1964, Purchase award Color Women's Coll., Denver, 1963, Tyler (Tex.) Mus., 1963, 1st prize in sculpture 1st Nat. Space Art Show, 1971, Humanitarian award Milehi Denver Sertoma, 1994, The Gleitsman Found., 1994, Svc. to Mankind awards Freedom Found. at Valley Forge, Mile Hi Sertoma Club, Minoruyasui Found., Gleitsman Found. Mem. Artists Equity Assn., Rocky Mountain Liturgical Arts, Allied Sculptors Colo., Allied Arts Inc. Hist. Denver, Symphony Guild, Parks People, Beth Israel Aux. Home: 131 Fairfax St Denver CO 80220-6331

SIATRA, ELENI, English educator; b. Kozani, Greece, Oct. 22, 1961; came to U.S., 1985; d. Athanasios and Alexandra (Lanaras) S.; m. Todd Alan Reda, May 30, 1991. B of English, Aristotle U., 1983; MA in English, Miami U., 1990, PhD in English, 1996; MLS, Kent State U., 1986. Tchr. English as a 2d lang. Fgn. Langs. Inst., Kozani, Greece, 1983-85; asst. to dir. of ethnic studies ctr. Kent (Ohio) State U., 1986, student reference asst., 1985-86, instr., libr. adminstr., 1987; libr. readers' svcs. Bloomsburg (Pa.) U., 1987-88; grad. rsch. asst. Miami U., Oxford, Ohio, 1988-90, King Libr., Miami U., Oxford, Ohio, 1990-91; coord., portfolio rater Miami U., Oxford, Ohio, 1994-96, teaching assoc., 1991-94; vis. instr. Miami U., 1994-96; mem. Coll. of Arts and Scis. Comparative Lit. Com., Miami U., 1995-96. Sinclair Meml. scholar, 1995-96. Fulbright scholar, 1985-86; recipient Gordon Wilson award, 1994. Fellow Phi Kappa Phi; mem. ALA, Am. Soc. 18th Century Studies, Nat. Coun. Tchrs. English, Modern Lang. Assn., Internat. Soc. Study of European Ideas (workshop chair, 1996. Greek Orthodox. Home: PO Box 416 West College Corner IN 47003 Office: Miami U Dept English Oxford OH 45056

SIBBERSON, STEPHENIE LYNN REX, process engineer; b. Toledo, Mar. 31, 1970; d. Daryle Warren and Jill Suzanne (Rex) Damschroder; m. Jeffrey Gregg Sibberson, June 26, 1993. BSChE, U. Cin., 1993. Process engr. Sun Co., Inc., Toledo, 1993—. Mem. AIChE, Nat. Mgmt. Assn., Sigma Delta Tau. Office: Sunoco Mid-Am Mktg & Refining Co Inc P O Box 920 Toledo OH 43697

SIBLEY, DAWN BUNNELL, advertising executive; b. Jersey City, Nov. 14, 1939; d. Milton Joseph and Dorothy (Nicoll) Bunnell; m. John Winthrop Sibley, Mar. 5, 1962 (div. 1975). BA, Wellesley Coll., 1960. Planner to sr. v.p., media dir. Ted Bates & Co., N.Y.C., 1967-76; sr. v.p., media dir. Compton Advt., N.Y.C., 1977-82; exec. v.p., media dir. Ally & Gargano, N.Y.C., 1982—; chmn. Leading Ind. Agy. Network. Media dir. Gerald Ford Election Campaign, Washington, 1976. Named one of Women Achievers of Yr., YWCA, 1983. Mem. 4A's Media (policy com.). Home: 29 Craw Ave Norwalk CT 06853-1608 Office: Ally & Gargano Inc 805 3rd Ave New York NY 10022-7513

SIBLEY, PATRICIA, actress; b. Hollywood, Calif., Oct. 15, 1951; d. James Joseph and Catherine (Mallory) S. BS in Child Devel., Calif. Poly. State U., San Luis Obispo, 1973, postgrad., 1984-85. Cert. tchr., Calif. Actress, 1978—. Appeared in plays Cinderella at Pacific Conservatory of the Performing Arts, Santa Maria, Calif., Blithe Spirit at Spokane (Wash.) Interplayers Ensemble and Village Theatre, Issaquah, Wash., Lost in Yonkers at Idaho Repertory Theatre, Moscow and Spokane Civic Theatre. Democrat. Mem. Ch. of Religious Sci. Home: 118 SW 116th St D-24 Seattle WA 98146-2369

SIBOLSKI, ELIZABETH HAWLEY, academic administrator; b. Gt. Barrington, Mass., Aug. 18, 1950; d. William Snyder and Frances Harrington (Smith) Gallup; m. John Alfred Sibolski Jr., Aug. 15, 1970. BA, The Am. U., 1973, MPA, 1975, PhD, 1984. Acting dir. acad. adminstrn. The Am. U., Washington, 1974, planning analyst, 1974-79, asst. dir. budget and planning, 1980-83, dir. instl. rsch., 1984-85, dir. univ. planning and rsch., 1985—; trustee Mortar Bd. Nat. Found., 1989-95. Recipient Comencement award Am. U. Women's Club, 1973. Mem. ASPA, Assn. Instl. Rsch., Soc. Coll. and Univ. Planning (bd. dirs. 1995—), Am. Assn. for Higher Edn., Mortar Bd. (sect. coord. 1975-82), Pi Alpha Alpha, Phi Kappa Phi (chpt. officer 1986-92), Pi Sigma Alpha, Omicron Delta Kappa. Home: 565 Wayward Dr Annapolis MD 21401-6747 Office: The Am Univ Office of Planning 4400 Massachusetts Ave NW Washington DC 20016-8059

SICHERMAN, ROBBIN MERYL, library media specialist; b. N.Y.C., Sept. 13, 1949; d. Lester and Helen (Schnei) S. BA, Bklyn. Coll., 1970; MS in Libr. Sci., Palmer Sch. of Libr. & Info. Sci., 1972; MS in Reading, Adelphi U., 1981. Gen. asst. Queens (N.Y.) Borough Pub. Libr., 1972-73, asst. children's libr., 1973, children's libr., 1973-81, asst. br. mgr./children's libr., 1981-88; libr. media specialist # 4 Sch., Lawrence, N.Y., 1988—. Mem. Am. Libr. Assn., N.Y. Libr. Assn., Nat. Coun. Tchrs. of English, Internat. Reading Assn., Nat. Assn. for Edn. of Young Children, Med. Libr. Assn. Home: 2371 E 26th St Brooklyn NY 11229-4920

SICKEL, JOAN SOTTILARE, foundation administrator; b. Jersey City, Dec. 29, 1941; d. Peter S. and Rose M. (Maresca) Sottilare; m. Walter F. Sickel Jr., Jan. 4, 1964 (div. July 1979); children: Walter F. III (dec.), Linda Hilaire. AB, Georgian Ct. Coll., 1963. Dir. ann. giving Tucson Med. Ctr. Found., 1980-87; dir. devel. and pub. rels. Ariz. Children's Home, Tucson, 1987-93; exec. dir. Ariz. Children's Home Found., Tucson, 1993-94; curator edn. program devel. Ariz. Aerospace Found., Tucson, 1995—. Mem. women's studies adv. coun. U. Ariz. Mem. Nat. Soc. Fund Raising Execs., Nat. Assn. for Hosp. Devel., Pub. Rels. Soc. Am., Planned Giving Round Table of So. Ariz., AAUW, Ariz. Assn. for Hosp. Devel. (treas. 1986-88), U. Ariz. Presidents Club, U. Ariz. Wildcat Club, Soroptimists Internat. (chair fin. com. 1985). Home: 4151 N Camino Ferreo Tucson AZ 85750-6358 Office: 6000 E Valencia Tucson AZ 85706

SICKLER, JOAN LOUISE, retail store owner; b. Mpls., June 21, 1949; d. George Howard and Evelyn Amelia (Erickson) S.; m. Robert Lee Stableski, June 19, 1971 (div.); 1 child, Nicholas Richard; m. Michael P. Rosow, Oct. 15, 1989. BA cum laude, U. Minn., 1971. Editl. asst. UN Indsl. Devel. Orgn., Vienna, Austria, 1973-74; dir. undergrad. tchg. program Coun. on Learning, New Rochelle, N.Y., 1976-78; freelance writer, editor Putney, Vt., 1978-82, White Plains, N.Y., 1982-85; editor World of Work Report Work in Am. Inst., Scarsdale, N.Y., 1985-86, dir. The Productivity Forum, 1986-89, v.p., 1989-92; owner Purple Sage, Santa Fe, N.Mex., 1994—. Editor: (book) The State of Academic Science, 1978, (newsletter) Ednl. Marketer, 1984-85, also reports in field; contbr. articles to newspapers, chpts. to books. Democrat. Office: Purple Sage 110 Don Gaspar Santa Fe NM 87501

SICULAR, EVE, producer; b. N.Y.C., Oct. 12, 1961; d. Arthur and Lilian Marietta (Weinberger) S. Ba magna cum laude, Harvard-Radcliffe Coll., 1983. Prodr., dir., animator Food for Thought Prodns., Portland, Oreg., 1983-85; exec. prodr. Popcorn Sister Prodns., Seattle, 1988-90; curatorial asst. film series Mus. Modern Art, N.Y.C., 1991-92; curator film and photo archives YIVO Inst. Jewish Rsch., N.Y.C., 1992-94; exec. prodr. Rhythm Media, N.Y.C., 1995—; indep. film historian, 1984-96; drummer, mgr. Gr. Met. Klezmer Band, N.Y.C., 1993—; cons. Seattle Internat. Festival Women's Film, 1987-88, Internat. Conf. Gay and Lesbian Jews, 1995; writer, rschr., lectr. in field. Contbr. articles to popular and rsch. publs. Mem. FILMA Women's Eyeview Festival, Portland, 1983-86; bd. dirs. N.W. Lesbian-Gay Svc. Ctr., Seattle, 1989-90; founding mem., percussionist Lesbian Avengers Marching Band, N.Y.C., 1992. Recipient award Oreg. Com. Humanities, 1985, Pride Found., Seattle, 1989.

SIDAMON-ERISTOFF, ANNE PHIPPS, museum official; b. N.Y.C., Sept. 12, 1932; d. Howard and Harriet Dyer (Price) Phipps; m. Constantine Sidamon-Eristoff, June 29, 1957; children—Simon, Elizabeth, Andrew. B.A., Bryn Mawr Coll., 1954. Chmn., bd. dirs. Am. Mus. Natural History, N.Y.C.; dir.-at-large Black Rock Forest Consortium; trustee God Bless Am. Fund. Bd. dirs. Greenacre Found., Highland Falls (N.Y.) Pub. Libr., N.Y. Cmty. Trust, Storm King Art Ctr., Mountainville, N.Y., World Wildlife Fund.; former bd. dirs.Scenic Hudson, St. Bernard's Sch., N.Y.C., Mus. Modern Art, N.Y.C., Mus. Hudson Highlands. Home: 120 East End Ave New York NY 10028-7552

SIDAMON-ERISTOFF, CATHERINE BAXTER, securities broker; b. N.Y.C., Jan. 2, 1964; d. Comer Cash and Betty Nan (Carpenter) Baxter; m. Andrew Sidamon-Eristoff, Mar. 30, 1996. BA, Duke U., 1986, MBA, 1987. V.p. Morgan Stanley & Co., Inc., N.Y.C., 1987—; former alumni coun. mem. Fuqua Sch. Bus., Durham, N.C.; mem. alumnae bd. Hockaday Sch., Dallas. Chmn. bd.-elect Burden Ctr. for Aging, N.Y.C., 1991—; active Jr. League, N.Y.C., 1982—; mem. jr. coun. Am. Mus. Natural History. Mem. NAFE, Am. Women's Econ. Devel. Assn. Republican. Presbyterian. Office: Morgan Stanley & Co Inc 1251 Avenue Of The Americas New York NY 10020-1104

SIDDAYAO, CORAZÓN MORALES, economist, educator, energy consultant; b. Manila, July 26, 1932; came to U.S., 1968; d. Crispulo S. and Catalina T. (Morales) S. Cert. in elem. teaching, Philippine Normal Coll., 1951; BBA, U. East, Manila, 1962; MA in Econs., George Washington U., 1971, MPhil and PhD, 1975. Cert. Inst. de Francais, 1989. Tchr. pub. schs. Manila, 1951-53; exec. asst. multinational oil corps., 1953-68; asst. pensions officer IMF, Washington, 1968-71; cons. economist Washington, 1971-75; rsch. assoc. Policy Studies in Sci. and Tech. George Washington U., Washington, 1971-72, teaching fellow dept. econs., 1972-75; natural gas specialist U.S. Fed. Energy Adminstrn., Washington, 1974-75; sr. rsch. economist, assoc. prof. Inst. S.E.A. Studies, Singapore, 1975-78; sr. rsch. fellow energy/economist East-West Ctr., 1978-81, project dir. energy and industrialization, 1981-86; vis. fellow London Sch. Econ., 1984-85; sr. energy economist in charge energy program Econ. Devel. Inst., World Bank, Washington, 1986-94, ret., 1994; affiliate prof. econs. U. Hawaii, 1979—; vis. prof. econs. U. Philippines, intermittently, 1989—; co-dir. UPecon Inst. of Resource Studies, 1995—; vis. prof. U. Montpelier, France, 1992, 1995-96; cons. internat. orgns. and govts., 1995—; spkr. at confs. and symposia. Author or co-author: Increasing the Supply of Medical Personnel, 1973, The Offshore Petroleum Resources of Southeast Asia: Some Potential Conflicts and Related Economic Factors, 1978, Round Table Discussion on Asian and Multinational Corporations, 1978, The Supply of Petroleum Resources in Southeast Asia: Economic Implications of Evolving Property Rights Arrangements, 1980, Critical Energy Issues in Asia and the Pacific: The Next Twenty Years, 1982, Criteria for Energy Pricing Policy, 1985, Energy Demand and Economic Growth, 1986; editor: Energy Policy and Planning series, 1990-92, Energy Investments and the Environment, 1993; co-editor: Investissements Energetiques et Environnement, 1993; co-editor: (series) Energy Projecy Analysis for the CIS Countries (Russian), 1993, Politique d'Efficacité de l'Énergie et Environnement, Expérience pratiques, 1994, Matérial Pedagogique sur la Politique d'Efficacité de l'Energie et Environnement, 1994; contbr. chpts. to books, articles to profl. jours. Grantee in field. Mem. Am. Econ. Assn., Internat. Assn. Energy Economists (charter), Alliance Francaise, Omicron Delta Epsilon. Roman Catholic.

SIDDERS, EMMA ELIZABETH, principal; b. Waynoka, Okla., Aug. 7, 1950; d. Alan V. and Emma Louise (Curtis) Nutter; m. Jerry Glen Sheppard, Sept. 25, 1971 (div. 1973); m. Samuel C. Sidders Jr., Mar. 28, 1974; children: Samuel Vincent, Martin Alan. BS in Edn., Southwestern Okla. State U., 1972; MEd in Reading, Northwestern Okla. State U., 1991. Cert. tchr. elem., learning disabilities, reading, elem. prin. Dir. spl. edn. Gage (Okla.) Pub. Schs., 1988-89, 91-95, tchr. elem., 1989-91, prin. elem., 1992-96; prin. elem. Sharon-Mutual Pub. Schs., Okla., 1996—; adminstrv. asst. Ellis County Spl. Edn. Coop., Gage, 1992-95; grant reader Okla. State Dept. Edn., Oklahoma City, 1994; mem. Nat. Acad. Prins., Oklahoma City, 1994-95. Mem. ASCD, Okla. Elem. Prins., Ellis County Tchrs. Assn. (pres. 1988-95), Beta Sigma Phi (pres., sec. 1979-92). Republican. Home: RT 1 Box 72A Gage OK 73843

SIDDIQUI, KATHRYN L., school principal, social worker; b. Evergreen Park, Ill., Nov. 26, 1957; d. George P. and Marie M. Meyer; m. Farrukh R. Siddiqui, Oct. 7, 1989. BS, No. Ill. U., 1980; MSW, Loyola U., 1988; MA in Ednl. Adminstrn., Govs. State U., 1995. Cert. in sch. svc. pers., in gen. adminstrn. Caseworker Berwyn-Cicero (Ill.) Coun. on Aging, 1983-87; sch. social worker intern South Met. Assn.- Independence High Sch., Flossmoor, Ill., 1987-88; sch. social worker Echo Joint Agreement-Pace High Sch., Blue Island, Ill., 1988-95, Echo Joint Agreement-Pace Elem. Jr. High Sch., Phoenix, Ill., 1993; sch. prin., sch. social worker East DuPage Spl. Edn. Dist.- Villa Grove Sch., Villa Park, Ill., 1995—. Mem. ASCD, Sch. Social Worker Assn. Am., Ill. Assn. Sch. Social Workers.

SIDDONS, SARAH MAE, chemist; b. Conway, S.C., July 20, 1939; d. Willie C. and Lelia (Parker) Crawford; m. John Lathan, June 26, 1958 (div.); m. Ronald Gladstone Siddons, June 26, 1965; 1 child, Ronald George. BA, Coll. New Rochelle, 1980; postgrad., Cornell U., 1975. Lab. technologist DC37-Local 144, Bronx, 1961-65, 65-82; jr. chemist DC37-Local 375, Bronx, 1982-85, assoc. chemist, 1985-90, assoc. chemist, supr., 1990—; del. DC37-Lcoal 144, 1962-84, DC37-Local 375, 1984—. Mem. Am. Assn. Clin. Chemistry, Dynamic Five Social Club (pres. 1988—, v.p. 1980-88). Home: 3924 Carpenter Ave Bronx NY 10466 Office: Lincoln Med Ctr 234 E 149th St Rm 432 Bronx NY 10451

SIDEMAN, EVA STERN, marketing executive; b. Bucharest, Romania; d. Ernest and Rose Stern; m. Daniel Sideman, Oct. 27, 1974; children: Dawn Stern, Stephanie Anne. BA cum laude, U. Minn., 1968; MA, Ind. U., 1970, PhD, 1973; M. Mgmt., Northwestern U., 1982. Instr. English dept. U. Cin., 1970-71; instr. Ind. U., 1972-73; sr. rsch. analyst Amoco Corp., Chgo., 1973-77; communications and rsch. cons. Chgo., 1977-87; tech. writer Walgreen Co., Deerfield, Ill., 1987-90; tng. devel. specialist Covia Corp., Rosemont, Ill., 1990-93; mgr. documentation and tng. William M. Mercer, Deerfield, Ill., 1994—; lectr. Northwestern U., 1975-79. Trustee Northbrook (Ill.) Pub. Libr., 1986-91. Mem. ASTD, Nat. Soc. for Performance & Instrn., Soc. for Tech. Communications. Office: William M. Mercer Mercer Adminstrv Ctr 1417 Lake Cook Rd Deerfield IL 60015

SIDNEY, CORINNE ENTRATTER, journalist, actress; b. L.A., Apr. 13, 1937; d. Carl Smith and Alice (Polk) Kegley; m. Jack Entratter (dec. 1971); m. Robert Heffron, 1973 (div. 1980); 1 child, Benjamin Jack; m. George Sidney, Oct. 12, 1991. Student, U. Calif., Berkeley; Grad., U. Judaism, L.A., 1971; postgrad., UCLA, 1983. Feature editor Univ. Man fashion mag., 1972-86; columnist Beverly Hills, 1986-89; writer syndicated entertainment column Real to Real Capital News Svc., 1988-91; stringer USA Today, People weekly, Beverly Hills (Calif.) Post, 1990-91; pub. rels. cons., 1972-86. Film appearances include Murderers' Row, North to Alaska, Speed Limit 65, That Funny Feeling, The Big Mouth, The Journey, (with Peter Sellers) The Party, Road House, (George Sidney's film) The Swinger, Who's Minding the Mint?; TV appearances include Steve Allen, Caine's 100, Cannon, Bob Hope, Hazel, Home Show, Ironside, Monkees, Ozzie and Harriet, Bachelor Father, Tennessee Ernie Ford, General Hospital, FBI, Larry King, Bob Newhart, Shower of Stars, Johnny Carson Players, This is Alice; stage appearances include Born Yesterday, Seven Year Itch, Ninety Day Mistress, Tender Trap, Who Was That Lady I Saw You With?, Getting It; toured with Las Vegas lounge act The New Yorkers, also toured 1990-TV cir. with playmates of each decade; hostess TV talk show Westcoasting... with Corinne, 1991; co-host Real to Reel. Active civic orgns.; candidate Beverly Hills City Coun., 1980; mem. El Rodeo Sch. PTA, El Rodeo YMCA. 1st runner-up Miss U.S.A. Contest; named Playboy Ctr. Fold of 50's Decade, 1958; named Pin-up Girl of Atomic Nuclear Submarine Nautilus, 1958, one of 7 Top Playmates Fox-TV Am. Chronicles., 1990. Mem. AFTRA (women's com.), SAG, LWV, Women in Film, Am. Film Inst., C. of C. and Civic Assn., Hollywood Women's Press Club, Bus. and Profl. Women (conv. del., Olympic com., program chmn., founder West Side chpt. 1985), Hadassah (v.p., membership chmn., co-chmn. dinner-dance honoring Barbara Sinatra, founder & pres. Haifa chpt.), Israel Tennis Ctrs., UCLA Theatre Arts Alumni Assn.

SIDON, CLAUDIA MARIE, psychiatry and mental health nursing educator; b. Bellaire, Ohio, Feb. 6, 1946; d. Paul and Nell (Bernas) DePaulis; m. Michael Sidon; children: Michael II, Babe. Diploma, Wheeling (W.Va.) Hosp. Sch., 1966; BS in Nursing summa cum laude, Ohio U., Athens, 1979; MS in Nursing, W.Va. U., Morgantown, 1982. Cert. social worker. Various staff positions Bellaire City Hosp., 1966-67, 72-77; adj. nursing faculty W.Va. No. Community Coll., Wheeling, 1977-82; nurse clinician, psychotherapist Valley Psychol. and Psychiat. Svcs., Moundsville, W.Va., 1984; psychotherapist, nurse clinician, case mgr. No. Panhandle Behavioral Health Ctr., Wheeling, 1984-88; assoc. prof. ADN program Belmont Tech. Coll., St. Clairsville, Ohio, 1988—; presenter in field. Mem. Tri-State Psychiat. Nursing Assn. (pres., v.p., program chmn.), Nat. League for Nursing (presenter), Phi Kappa Phi, Sigma Theta Tau. Home: 52295 Sidon Rd Dillonvale OH 43917-9538 Office: Belmont Tech Coll 120 Fox Shannon Pl Saint Clairsville OH 43950-8751

SIDRAN, MIRIAM, retired physics educator, researcher; b. Washington, May 25, 1920; d. Morris Samson and Theresa Rena (Gottlieb) S. BA, Bklyn. Coll., 1942; MA, Columbia U., N.Y.C., 1949; PhD, NYU, 1956. Rsch. assoc. dept. physics NYU, N.Y.C., 1950-55, postdoctoral fellow, 1955-57; asst. prof. Staten Island Community Coll., Richmond, N.Y., 1957-59; rsch. scientist Grumman Aerospace Corp., Bethpage, N.Y., 1959-67; prof. N.Y. Inst. Tech., N.Y.C., 1967-72; NSF rsch. fellow Nat. Marine Fisheries Svc., Miami, Fla., 1971-72; assoc. prof. then prof. physics Baruch Coll., N.Y.C., 1972-89, chmn. dept. natural scis., 1983-89, prof. emerita, 1990—; v.p. Baruch chpt. Profl. Staff Congress, 1983-89. Contbr. numerous articles to profl. and govtl. publs., chpts. to books. N.Y. State Regents scholar, 1937-41; NSF summer fellow, Miami, 1970. Mem. N.Y. Acad. Scis., Am. Assn. Physics Tchrs. Home: 210 West 19 St Apt 5G New York NY 10011

SIDUN, NANCY MARIE, clinical psychologist, art therapist; b. Newark, July 9, 1955; d. Albert and Mae (Clement) S. BA, Colo. Womens Coll., 1976; MS, Emporia State U., 1978; PsyD, Ill. Sch. Profl. Psychology, 1986. Art therapy intern The Menninger Found., Topeka, 1978-79; art psychotherapist Childrens Med. Ctr., Tulsa, 1979-82; clin. psychologist, pvt. practice Chgo., 1983—; chief psychologist, adminstr. Ill. State Psych. Inst., Chgo., 1987-91; dir. practicum tng. Chgo. Sch. Profl. Psychology, 1991-95, dir. clin. tng., 1995—; adj. asst. prof. U. Ill., Chgo., 1982-84, 91-93; adj. asst. prof. Sch. Art Inst. Chgo., 1985-96, adj. assoc. prof., 1996—; clin. dir. Young Expressions, Chgo., 1985-87; psychologist Henry Horner Children's Ctr., Chgo., 1986-87; cons. Weight Mgmt. Svcs., Chgo., 1988-89, Touchstone Group, Chgo., 1987, Creative Devel. Ctr., Chgo., 1985-88. Contbr. articles to profl. jours. Mem. APA, Am. Art Therapy Assn., Ill. Psychol. Assn., Ill. Art Therapy Assn., Nat. Coalition Art Therapies Assn. Office: 3170 N Sheridan Rd Apt 210 Chicago IL 60657-4825

SIEBENMAN, JEANNE BOURBON, academic administrator; b. St. Louis, Sept. 15; d. William and Amelia (Noonan) McElwaine; m. David Robert Siebenman, May 23, 1953; children: Jeanmarie, Mary Ann, Joann. BS, Ariz. State U., 1968, MA, 1973, EdD, 1984. Tchr. Phoenix Union, 1972-73, St. Vincent DePaul Sch., 1965-71; tchr.-tutor trainer Phoenix Union H.S., 1973-79; asst. prof. edn. Grand Canyon U., Phoenix, 1982-84, assoc. prof., 1984-87, prof., 1987—, asst. dean, 1988-92, assoc. dean, 1993—; cons., vis. prof. Fgn. Lang. U., Almaty Kazakhstan, Commonwealth of Ind. States, 1991, Kashgar Tchrs. Coll., Xinjang, China, summer, 1988, August 1st Agrl. Coll., Urumqi, China, summer 1987. Habitat for Humanity. Named Outstanding Exemplary Advisor and Mentor Nat. Acad. Advisor Assn., 1988, Outstanding Undergrad. Prof. Sears Found., 1989; recipient Outstanding Contbn. to Republic of Kazakhstan award Ministry Edn., 1991. Mem. ASCD, Nat. Mid. Sch. Assn., Internat. Reading Assn., Ariz. Sch. Adminstrs. Assn., Ariz. Town Hall, Phi Delta Kappa. Democrat. Roman Catholic. Home: 145 Brady Rd Prescott AZ 86301-7362 Office: Grand Canyon U 3300 W Camelback Rd Phoenix AZ 85017-3030

SIEBER, RUTH E., music educator; b. Houston, Aug. 22, 1952; d. Glen P. and Martha N. (Grumbles) Armstrong; m. Richard E. Sieber, Mar. 21, 1982; children: Andrea, Jami, Kurt, Liesle, Jenny, Beth. MusB, U. Ark., 1983. Voice instr. at pvt. studio Little Rock, 1975-88; soprano Ark. Opera Theater, Little Rock, 1977-88; mus. theatre dir. U. N.C., Asheville, 1989—; music dir. Jubilee! Cmty. Ch., Asheville, 1989—; nat. exec. sec. Sigma Alpha Iota Internat. Music Fraternity, Asheville, 1992—; premiered opera songs by the composer Robert Boury, U. Ark., Litte Rock, 1989; concert soloist and recitalist/soprano. Pres. PTA Booker Magnet Sch., Little Rock, 1986-88. Singing fellow Stonybrook Bach Aria Festival, 1985. Mem. NAFE, Nat. Assn. Tchrs. Singing (nat. finalist Young Artist Awards 1987), Am. Guild Organists, Ptnrs. of the Americas (arts com. 1986—), Sigma Alpha Iota (state pres. 1984-88, nat. bd., Sword of Honor, Rose of Honor). Home: 83 Furman Ave Asheville NC 28801 Office: Sigma Alpha Iota 34 Wall St Ste 515 Asheville NC 28801

SIEBERT, DIANE DOLORES, author, poet; b. Chgo., Mar. 18, 1948; m. Robert William Siebert, Sept. 21, 1969. RN. Author: Truck Song, 1984 (Notable Childrens Book award ALA 1984, Sch. Libr. Jour. one of Best Books 1984, Outstanding Childrens Book award N.Y. Times Book Rev. 1984, Reading Rainbow Selection book 1991), Mojave, 1988 (Childrens Editors Choice 1988, Internat. Reading Assn. Tchrs. Choice award 1989, others), Heartland, 1989 (award Nat. Coun. for Social Studies/Childrens Book Coun. 1989, on John Burroughs List Nature Book for Young Readers 1989, Ohio Farm Bur. Women award 1991), Train Song, 1990 (Notable Childrens Book award ALA, 1990, Redbook Mag. one of Top Ten Picture Books 1990, one of Best Books award Sch. Libr. Jour. 1990, others), Sierra, 1991 (Outstanding Sci. Trade Book for Children award NSTA 1991, Notable Childrens Trade Book in Field Social Studies award Nat. Coun. Social Studies 1991, Beatty award Calif. Libr. Assn. 1992), Plane Song, 1993 (Outstanding Sci. Trade Book for Children 1994, Platinum award Oppenheim Toy Portfolio, Tchrs. Choice award Internat. Reading Assn. 1994). Home: 9676 SW Jordan Rd Culver OR 97734

SIEBERT, MURIEL, business executive, former state banking official; b. Cleve.; d. Irwin J. and Margaret Eunice (Roseman) Siebert; student Western Res. U., 1949-52; DCS (hon.), St. John's U., St. Bonaventure U., Molloy Coll., Adelphi U., St. Francis Coll., Mercy Coll., Coll. New Rochelle, St. Lawrence U., Manhattan Coll. Security analyst Bache & Co., 1954-57; analyst Utilities & Industries Mgmt. Corp., 1958, Shields & Co., 1959-60; partner Stearns & Co., 1961, Finkle & Co., 1962-65, Brimberg & Co., N.Y.C., 1965-67; individual mem. (first woman mem.) N.Y. Stock Exchange, 1967; chmn., pres. Muriel Siebert & Co., Inc., 1969-77; trustee Manhattan Savs. Bank, 1975-77; supt. banks, dept. banking State of N.Y., 1977-82; dir. Urban Devel. Corp., N.Y.C., 1977-82, Job Devel. Authority, N.Y.C., 1977-82, State of N.Y. Mortgage Agy., 1977-82; chmn., pres. Muriel Siebert & Co., Inc., 1983—; assoc. in mgmt. Simmons Coll.; mem. adv. com. Fin. Acctg. Standards Bd., 1981-84; guest lectr. numerous colls. Former mem. women's adv. com. Econ. Devel. Adminstrn., N.Y.C.; former trustee Manhattan Coll.; v.p., former mem. exec. com. Greater N.Y. Area council Boy Scouts Am.; mem. N.Y. State Econ. Devel. Bd., N.Y. Coun. Economy; bd. overseers NYU Sch. Bus., 1984-88; former bd. dirs. United Way of N.Y.C.; trustee Citizens Budget Commn., L.I. U.; mem. bus. com. Met. Mus., bus. com. of N.Y. State Bus. Coun.; active Women's Campaign Fund; bd. dirs. N.Y. Women's Agenda. Recipient Spirit of Achievement award Albert Einstein Coll. Medicine, 1977; Women's Equity Action League award, 1978; Outstanding Contbns. to Equal Opportunity for Women award Bus. Council of UN Decade for Women, 1979; Silver Beaver award Boy Scouts Am., 1981; Elizabeth Cutter Morrow award YWCA, 1983; Emily Roebling award Nat. Women's Hall of Fame, 1984; Entrepreneural Excellence award White House Conf. on Small Bus., 1986; NOW Legal Def. and Edn. Fund award, 1981, Brotherhood award Nat. Conf. of Christians and Jews, 1989, Women on the Move award Anti-Defamation League, 1990., award Borough of Manhattan, 1991, Benjamin Botwinick prize Columbia Bus. Sch.'s, 1992, Women in Bus. Making History award Women's Bus. Coun. N.Y. C. of C., 1993, Disting. Woman of the Yr. award Greater N.Y. Boy Scouts of Am., 1993, Woman of the Yr. award Fin. Women's Assn. N.Y., 1994, Medal of Honor award Ellis Island, 1994, Bus. Philanthropist of the Yr. award So. Calif. Conf. for Women Bus. Owner's,, 1990, Corning Excellence award N.Y.S. Bus. Coun., 1993, Star award N.Y. Women's Agenda, Established Siebert Entrepreneurial Philanthropic Plan, N.Y. Urban Coalition's Achievement award, 1994, Women of Distinction award Crohn's and Colitis Found., Entrepreneurial Leadership award Nat. Found. Teaching Entrepreneurship, 1994; inductee Nat. Woman's Hall of Fame, Seneca Falls, N.Y., 1994, Internat. Women's Forum Hall of Fame, 1994. Mem. Women's Forum (founding mem., pres.), Com. 200, Fin. Women's Assn. (Community Svc. award 1993), River Club, Doubles Club, Westchester Country Club, West Palm Beach Polo and Country Club, Nat. Assn. Women Bus. Owners (Veuve Clicquot Bus. Women of Yr. award 1992, Lifetime Achievement award 1993), Econ. Club. Home: 435 E 52nd St New York NY 10022-6445 Office: Muriel Siebert & Co Inc 885 3rd Ave New York NY 10022-4834

SIEBERT, STEPHANIE RAY, video production company executive; b. Phoenix, Sept. 17, 1949; d. Richard and Jacquelyn (Schmunk) S. AA, Yavapai Community Coll., 1967; BS, U. Minn., 1970. Acctg. mgr. Ski Mart of Newport Beach, Calif.; contr. Brown Jay Prodns., L.A.; gen. mgr. Video Tape Libr., Ltd., L.A.; pres. Film & Video Stock Shots Inc., L.A.; pres., chmn. Unfettered Mind, non-profit Calif. corp. Bd. dirs., officer Buddhist orgn. Mem. NAFE, NOW (past pres. Laguna Beach), Women's Bus. Enterprises, Assn. Women Entrepreneurial Developers, Am. Film Inst., Am. Mgmt. Assn., Am. Assn. Female Execs., Nat. Assn. Women Bus. Owners, Women in Film, Hollywood C. of C., Bus. and Profl. Women's Assn., Women in Show Bus. Office: Film & Video Stock Shots 10442 Burbank Blvd North Hollywood CA 91601-2217

SIEDENBURG, CARRIE, program manager; b. Chgo.; d. Reinhard and Carol Marie (Cheevers) S.; m. Michael R. Henn, Oct., 1991; 1 child, Charlotte Marie Henn. BS in Biochemistry with honors, Calif. Poly. Inst. Registered lead auditor. Space/brain rsch. asst. NASA/Ames, Mountain View, Calif., 1981-82; libr. rschr. Boston Consulting Group., Menlo Park, Calif., 1982-83; biotech. intern Atlantic Richfield Co. Plant Cell Rsch. Inst., Dublin, Calif., 1985; software quality assurance engr. Intelligenetics, Mountain View, 1986-87, mgr. quality assurance dept., 1987-88, project mgr., 1988-89; software designer Tandem Computers, Cupertino, Calif., 1989-92; lead auditor Nat. Stds. Authority of Ireland, 1993-96; program mgr. Borealis, Incline Village, Nev., 1996—; cons. Summit Quality Assocs., Tahoe City, Calif., 1992-93. Dir. Profl. Lifestyles Day, Cupertino, 1990-92. Mem. AAUW, Am. Soc. Quality Control (conf. chair 3d internat. conf. on software quality, software divsn.), Santa Clara Valley Software Quality Assn. (bd. dirs., local task force 1991, newsletter editor 1992-94, chair internat. conf. SW divsn. 1992-93), Women in Technology Internat., Phi Kappa Phi. Home: PO Box 7548 Tahoe City CA 96145-7548 Mailing Address: 2755 N Lake Blvd # 420 Tahoe City CA 96145

SIEDLECKI, NANCY THERESE, lawyer, funeral director; b. Chgo., May 30, 1954; d. LeRoy John and Dorothy Josephine (Wilczynski) Schielka; m. Jonathan Francis Siedlecki, June 18, 1977; children: Samantha Ann, Abigail Marie. Student Triton Jr. Coll., 1971-73; grad. funeral dir., Worsham Coll., 1974; student Loyola U., Chgo., 1974-76., U. Ill.-Chgo., 1976-77; JD with honors, Chgo.-Kent Coll. Law, 1980. Bar: Ill. 1980. Paralegal in real estate Rosenberg, Savner & Unikel, Chgo., 1974-77; pvt. practice law, Burr Ridge, Ill., 1980—; cons. probate and various small bus. corps., Chgo., 1980—. Mem. ABA, Ill. State Bar Assn., Chgo. Bar Assn. Roman Catholic. Office: 5300 Main St Downers Grove IL 60515

SIEFERT-KAZANJIAN, DONNA, corporate librarian; b. N.Y.C.; d. Merrill Emil and Esther (Levins) S.; m. George John Kazanjian, June 15, 1974; 1 child, Merrill George. BA, NYU, 1969; MSLS, Columbia U., 1973; MBA, Fordham U., 1977. Asst. librarian Dun & Bradstreet, N.Y.C., 1969-73; research assoc. William E. Hill & Co., N.Y.C., 1973-76; sr. info. analyst Info. for Bus., N.Y.C., 1976-77; librarian Handy Assocs., N.Y.C., 1979-90; mgr. Infoserve Fuchs Cuthrell & Co., Inc., N.Y.C., 1991-94; libr. Heidrick & Struggles, Inc., N.Y.C., 1994—. Mem. Spl. Librs. Assn., Rsch. Roundtable, Am. Mensa Ltd. Roman Catholic. Office: Heidrick & Struggles Inc 245 Park Ave New York NY 10167-0002

SIEG, SANDRA NISHKIAN, entrepreneur, dental hygienist; b. Long Beach, Calif., Oct. 16, 1938; d. Martin ARis and Rose (Boyd) Nishkian; m. Thomas Lyon Hall, Nov. 13, 1960 (div. 1965); 1 child, Gina; m. James Wallace Sieg Jr., Dec. 28, 1967; children: christine, Stephanie, Gina, Summer. BA in Dental Hygiene, U. So. Calif., 1960; postgrad., Loma Linda U., 1983; M in Liberal Studies, NYU, 1996. Dental hygienist David Brandon, DDS, Dana Point, Calif., 1985-95; artistic dir. Cosimo & Co., Laguna Beach, Calif., 1990-95; pres. Harbour Trading Children's Arts Games, Laguna Beach, 1989—. Vol. fund raiser Laguna Beach Volleyball Assn., 1989—, Laguna Beach Fire Victims, 1994—. Home: 453 Palmer Pl Laguna Beach CA 92651

SIEGAL, RITA GORAN, engineering company executive; b. Chgo., July 16, 1934; d. Leonard and Anabelle (Soloway) Goran; m. Burton L. Siegal, Apr. 11, 1954; children: Norman, Laurence Scott. Student, U. Ill., 1951-53; BA, DePaul U., 1956. Cert. elem. tchr., Ill. Tchr. Chgo. Public Schs., 1956-58; founder, chief exec. officer Budd Engring. Corp., Skokie, Ill., 1959—; founder, pres. Easy Living Products Co., Skokie, 1960—; pvt. practice in interior design, Chgo., 1968-73; dist. sales mgr. Super Girls, Skokie, 1976; lectr. Northwestern U., 1983; guest speaker nat. radio and TV, 1979—. Contbr. to profl. jours. Mem. adv. bd. Skokie High Schs., 1975-79; advisor Cub Scouts Skokie coun. Boy Scouts Am., 1975; bus. mgr. Nutrition for Optimal Health Assn., Winnetka, Ill., 1980-82, pres., 1982-84, v.p. med./profl., 1985-93; leader Great Books Found., 1972; founder Profit Plus Investment, 1970; bd. dirs. Noha, Internat. Recipient Cub Scout awards Boy Scouts Am., 1971-72, Nat. Charlotte Danstrom award Nat. Women of Achievement, 1988, Corp. Achievement award, 1988. Mem. North Shore Women in Mgmt. (pres. 1987-88), Presidents Assn. Ill. (bd. dirs. 1990-94, membership chairperson 1991-93), No. Ill. Indsl. Assn., Ill. Mfrs. Assn., Inventors Coun. Office: Budd Engring Corp 8707 Skokie Blvd Skokie IL 60077-2269

SIEGEL, ANNE JULIA, human resources consultant, clinical social worker; b. Norwalk, Conn., Feb. 7, 1965; d. Robert I. and Suzanne Dorothy (Kreisman) S.; m. Jerry Lynn Watson, Feb. 11, 1995. BA, Johns Hopkins U., 1987; MSW, Hunter Coll., 1992. Cert. social worker, N.Y.; cert. clin. social worker, N.C.; nat. cert. employee assistance profl. Account exec. Ruder Finn Pub. Rels., N.Y.C., 1987-89; assoc., prodr. ABC-TV Good Morning Am., N.Y.C., 1989; counselor Rheedlen Found., N.Y.C., 1990-91, Employee Devel. Ctr., Cornell Med. Coll., N.Y.C., 1991-92; employee assistance specialist City of N.Y. Dept. Health, 1992-94; client svcs. coord. Frank Horton Assn., Raleigh, N.C., 1994—; human resources cons. Wake Med. Ctr., Raleigh, 1994—; presenter in field. Co-chairperson Com. on Domestic Violence, 1993-94. Mem. NASW. Democrat. Home: 4101 Five Oaks Dr #18 Durham NC 27707 Office: Frank Horton Assocs 229 Goodhill Rd Weston CT 06883

SIEGEL, BETTY LENTZ, college president; b. Cumberland, Ky., Jan. 24, 1931; d. Carl N. and Vera (Hogg) Lentz; m. Joel H. Siegel, June 6; children: David Jonathan, Michael Jeremy. B.A., Wake Forest Coll., 1952; M.Ed., U. N.C., 1953; Ph.D., Fla. State U., 1961; postgrad., Ind. U., 1964-66; hon. doctorate, Miami U., 1985, Cumberland Coll., 1985, Ea. Ky. U., 1992. Asst. prof. Lenoir Rhyne Coll., Hickory, N.C., 1956-59; assoc. prof., 1961-64; asst. prof. U. Fla., Gainesville, 1967-70; assoc. prof. U. Fla., 1970-72, prof., 1973-76, dean acad. affairs for continuing edn., 1972-76; dean Sch. Edn. and Psychology Western Carolina U., Cullowhee, N.C., 1976-81; pres. Kennesaw State Coll., Marietta, Ga., 1981—; bd. dirs. Atlanta Gas Light Co., Equifax Inc., Nat. Services Industries, Acordia Benefits of the South Inc.; cons. numerous sch. systems. Author: Problem Situations in Teaching, 1971; contbr. articles to profl. jours. Bd. dirs. United Way Atlanta, Ga. Acad. Children and Youth Profls., Ga. Partnership for Excellence in Edn., Ga. Coun. Econ. Edn., Northside Hosp. Found., Atlanta Ballet. Recipient Outstanding Tchr. award U. Fla., 1969; Mortar Bd. Woman of Yr. award U. Fla., 1973, Mortar Bd. Educator of Yr., Ga. State U., 1983, CASE award, 1986, Alumna of Yr. award Wake Forest U., 1987, "Grad Made Good" award Fla. State U. Alumni Assn, Omicron Delta Kappa, 1991, Spirit of Life award City of Hope, 1992, Woman of Achievement award Cobb Chamber YWCA, 1992; named One of 100 Most Influential People in State of Ga., Ga. Trend Mag., Outstanding Alumni, Fla. State U. Coll. Edn. Alumni Assn., 1992. Mem. ASCD, Am. Psychol. Assn., Am. Assn. State Colls. and Univs. (bd. dirs., chmn. 1990), Am. Coun. Edn. (bd. dirs., bd. advisors), Am. Inst. Mng. Diversity (bd. dis.), Soc. Internat. Bus. Fellows, Internat. Alliance for Invitational Edn. (co-founder, co-dir.), Bus./Higher Edn. Forum 9mem. exec. com.), Assn. Tchrs. Educators' Commn. on Leadership in Interprofl. Edn. (task force on techr. edn.), Cobb C. of C. (chair 1996), Kiwanis (Atlanta chpt.), Phi Alpha Theta, Pi Kappa Delta, Alpha Psi Omega, Kappa Delta Pi, Pi Lambda Theta, Phi Delta Kappa, Delta Kappa Gamma. Baptist. Office: Kennesaw State Coll Office of the President PO Box 444 Marietta GA 30061-0444

SIEGEL, BONNIE RUTH, healthcare automation consultant; b. Chgo., Jan. 29, 1948; d. William Russell and Alma Shilling; m. Gary Michael Siegel; children: Scott, Michael. BS, U. Ill., 1990. Health care tech. assoc. Sheldon I Dorenfest & Assoc., Northbrook, Ill., 1979-84, mgr. market rsch., 1984-87, mgr. product devel., 1987-88; dir. corp. svcs. Sheldon I Dorenfest & Assoc., Chgo., 1988-90, v.p. corp. svcs., 1990-92, v.p. market rsch., 1992—.

SIEGEL, CAROLE ETHEL, mathematician; b. N.Y., Sept. 29, 1936; d. David and Helen (Mayer) Schore, m. Bertram Siegel, Aug. 18, 1957; children: Sharon, David. BA in Math., NYU, 1957, MS in Math., 1959, PhD in Math., 1963. With computer dept. Atomic Energy Commn., 1957-59; rsch. asst. Courant Inst. of Math. Sci., 1959-63; rsch. scientist dept. of engring. NYU, N.Y.C., 1963-64; rsch. math. Info. Scis. Div. Rockland Rsch. Inst., Orangeburg, N.Y., 1965-74; head Epidemiology and Health Svcs. Rsch. Lab Stat. Scis., Epidemiology Divsn./Nathan S. Kline Inst. Rsch., Orangeburg, N.Y., 1974—; rsch. prof. dept. psychiatry NYU, 1987—; dep. dir. WHO Collaborating Ctr., Nathan S. Kline Inst., 1987—; grant reviewer NIHM, 1988—; co-prin. investigator Ctr. for Study of Issues in Public Mental Health, NIMH, 1993-95, prin. investigator, dir., 1995—. Editor: (with S. Fischer) Psychiatric Records in Mental Health Care, 1981; contbr. articles to profl. jours. Recipient grants NIMH, 1993—, 88-91, Nat. Ctr. for Health Svcs. Rsch., 1979-82, Nat. Inst. Alcohol Abuse, 1978-82. Mem. Assn. for Health Svcs. Rsch., Am. Soc. Clin. Pharmacology and Therapeutics, Assn. Women in Math., Am. Statis. Assn. Office: Nathan S Kline Inst Orangeburg NY 10962

SIEGEL, CAROLYN AUGUSTA, state employee; b. Buffalo, Dec. 29, 1943; d. Joseph Frederick and Louise Augusta (Knecht) S.; m. Roger John Fenlon, Feb. 15, 1969 (div. Nov. 1, 1989); children: Kristin M. Fenlon, Jocelyn N. Fenlon. BA, St. Bonaventure U., 1965; MS, SUNY, Buffalo, 1973, postgrad., 1994—. Cert. elem. and exceptional tchr. Indsl. investigator N.Y. Dept. Labor, Buffalo, 1966-67; tchr. St. Bonaventure Grammar Sch., Buffalo, 1967; adminstrv. analyst N.Y. State Dept. Law, Albany, 1967-68; caseworker N.Y. State Dept. Social Svcs., Buffalo, 1968-72; resource agent N.Y. State Dept. Mental Hygiene, Buffalo, 1972-73; resource & reimbursement agent N.Y. State Office Mental Retardation and Developmental Disabilities, Buffalo, 1982—. Contbr. articles to profl. jours. Pres. Bd. Edn. Springville (N.Y.)-Griffith Inst. Ctrl. Sch. Dist., 1980-95; bd. visitors Buffalo Psychiat. Ctr., 1994—; bd. dirs. Erie County Mental Health Assn., Buffalo; 4H Group Leader Erie County Cooperative Extension, East Aurora, N.Y., 1974-92; town chmn. Am. Cancer Soc., Buffalo. Mem. AAUW, Delta Epsilon Sigma. Home: 7615 Irish Rd West Falls NY 14170 Office: NYS OMRDD Dept 70 1200 East and West Rd West Seneca NY 14224

SIEGEL, FRANCES, artist, educator; b. N.Y.C., Apr. 12, 1941; d. Meyer and Victoria (Stein) S.; m. Gerald Mancus; 1 child, Jedediah Rosenzweig. BS, Pratt Inst., 1962. Art tchr., lectr. Art Students League of N.Y., Bank St. Coll., Parsons Sch. of Design (grad. painting program), Women's Caucus for Art, N.Y. Univ., Wagner Coll., Am. Mus. of Natural History, Sch. of Visual Arts, Hofstra U. One-woman shows include Prince St. Gallery, N.Y.C., 1978, 81, 83, 85, 89, 93, Westbeth Galleries, N.Y., 1972, Sutton Gallery, N.Y., 1982, Queens Coll., N.Y., 1983, N.Y.C. Tech. Coll., 1985, Moravian Coll., Bethelhem, Pa., 1993; exhibited in group shows at Inaugural Exhibition, Westbeth Galleries, N.Y., 1968, Drawings USA '75 (travelling show circulated by the Minn. Museum of Art), Minn. Mus. of Art, St. Paul, Carleton Coll., Northfield, Minn., Civic Fine Arts Ctr., Sioux Falls, S.D., Albrecht Mus. of Fine Art, St. Joseph, Mo., Memphis Acad. of Arts, Flint Inst. of Arts, Mich., Arkansas Art Ctr., Little Rock, 1975-76, Hassam Fund Purchase Exhbn., Am. Acad. and Inst. of Arts and Letters,

N.Y., 1977, Black and White on Paper, Nat. Arts Club, N.Y., 1982, Rockford Internat. Biennale '83, Rockford Coll., Ill., 1983, Sense and Sensibility, Leonardo Di Mauro Gallery, N.Y., 1983, Costumes, Masks and Disguises, The Clocktower, N.Y. 1986, 165th and 161st annual exhibit Nat. Acad. of Design, N.Y. 1986, 90, Nat. Works on Paper Exhbn., Firehouse Gallery, Nassau C.C., N.Y., 1991, Am. Drawing Biennial III., Muscarelle Mus. of Art, The Coll. of William and Mary, Williamsburg, Va., 1992, Stockton (Calif.) Nat., Haggin Mus., 1988, 90, 94, Selections from the Scott Collection of Work by Women Artists, Bryn Mawr Coll., Pa., 1994. Home and Studio: 155 Bank St New York NY 10014

SIEGEL, JOY HAYES, banker, writer, educator, entrepreneur; b. Portland, Maine; d. Erwin Roland and Doris (Hazelton) Hayes; m. Frederick W. Siegel; 1 child, Christopher Erik. BA magna cum laude, U. Louisville, MBA; postgrad., East Tenn. State U., U. Fla.; student, Am. Acad. Dramatic Arts, N.Y.C., Acad. Radio-TV Broadcasting, Cleve. Inst. Tech. With Mid-Am. Bancorp and Bank of Louisville, Nat. City Bank, Ky., Ohio, S.E. Bank, Fla., Hamilton Bank, Tenn., Key Bank, Maine, Bankers Trust, N.Y.C.; sr. v.p. corp. credit Bank of Louisville; instr. fin., econs. and mgmt. U. Louisville; founder Joy's Creations, Hayes Boarding Stables, The Believings Power Press, YouCanDoIt! Western Apparel. Author textbooks on credit analysis, motivational books for children; creator, editor The Brilliant Banker. Active Focus Louisville, Boy Scouts Am. With U.S. Army, Vietnam. Mem. Robert Morris Assocs. (bd. dirs.), Bus. and Profl. Women (River City mem. state fin. com., state bd. dirs.), U. Louisville Women (bd. dirs.), Ky. Soc. Mayflower Descs. (bd. dirs.), Belle of Louisville (hon. capt.), Hon. Order Ky.Cols., Filson Club, Jefferson Club, Doe Valley Country Club, We.-English Retailers Assn., Oxford Hills C. of C., Nat. Assn. Women Bus. Owners, N. Am. Horsemen's Assn. Office: Bank of Louisville 322 Kenwood Hill Rd Louisville KY 40214

SIEGEL, KARINA, lawyer; b. Fulda, Germany, Aug. 14, 1959. BA, U. Calif., Irvine, 1981; JD, UCLA, 1985. Ptnr. Chadbourne & Parke LLP. Mem. ABA, State Bar of Calif. Office: Chadbourne & Parke LLP 30 Rockefeller Plz New York NY 10112*

SIEGEL, LUCY BOSWELL, public relations executive; b. N.Y.C., July 5, 1950; d. Werner Leiser and Carol (Fleischer) Boswell; m. Henry Winter Siegel, Nov. 11, 1979 (div.); children: David Alan Siegel, Joshua Adam Siegel. BA, Conn. Coll., 1972. Assoc. editor Conn. Western, Litchfield, Conn., 1972-73; assoc. editor, editor United Bus. Publ., N.Y.C., 1974-78; mgr. external communications Equitable Life Assurance Soc., N.Y.C., 1978-86; mgr. internat. affairs Cosmo Pub. Relations Corp., Tokyo, Japan, 1986-87; dir. internat. affairs Cosmo Pub. Relations Corp., Tokyo, 1987-88; pres. Cosmo Pub. Rels. Corp., N.Y.C., 1988-90, Siegel Assocs. Internat., N.Y.C., 1990—; bd. dirs. Cosmo Pub. Rels. Corp., Tokyo, N.Y.C., 1987-91. Contbr. articles to jours. and mags. Bd. dirs., sec. Am. Jewish Com. (N.Y.C. chpt.) 1993—. Mem. Pub. Rels. Soc. Am., Women Execs. in Pub. Rels., Japan Soc. Democrat. Jewish. Home: 41 W 96th St Apt 12B New York NY 10025-6519 Office: Siegel Assocs Internat Ltd 38 E 29th St Fl 7 New York NY 10016-7911

SIEGEL, NANCY ROSEN, educator; b. Albany, Oct. 28, 1938; d. Ralph and Bess D. (Hartman) Rosen; divorced; children: Andrew David, Todd Matthew, Robert Adam. BS in Edn., SUNY, Buffalo, 1960; MA, Columbia U., 1966. Tchr. 5th Ave Sch., Bay Shore, N.Y., 1960-65, Mark County Day Sch., Wantagh, N.Y., 1965-66, Case & North Jr. High Schs., Watertown, N.Y., 1966-67, Butterfield Sch., Waterton, N.Y., 1967-69, SUNY, Canton, N.Y., 1975-76; home sch. tutr Ogdensburg (N.Y.) Pub. Schs., 1974-76, elem. tchr., 1976—. Judge Odyssey of the Mind, 1990—. Mem. Ogdensburg Commd. Performance (v.p. mktg. 1994—), Delta Kappa Gamma, Gamma Epsilon (chpt. v.p. 1993-96, pres. 1996—). Democrat. Jewish. Home: 810 Linden St Ogdensburg NY 13669 Office: Sherman Sch 615 Franklin St Ogdensburg NY 13669

SIEGEL, PATRICIA ANN, management consultant; b. Louisville, Mar. 29, 1955; d. Roy John and Theresa (Preate) S. BS in Human Svcs., U. Scranton, 1977; M Psychosocial Sci., Pa. State U., 1982, cert. cmty. psychologist, 1982. Field rep. Am. Cancer Soc., Bethlehem, Pa., 1978-80; teen dir. YWCA, Harrisburg, Pa., 1980-82; mgr. membership devel. AAUW, Washington, 1982-85; mgr. membership Boat Owners Assn. U.S. (BOAT/US), Alexandria, Va., 1985-88; asst. v.p. leadership and membership devel. Nat. Assn. Home Builders, Washington, 1988-95; prin. Siegel & Assocs. Internat., Woodbridge, Va., 1995—; cons. to membership-based assns., 1991-95. Contbg. author: The National-Chapter Partnership, 1993; contbr. articles to profl. publs. Mem. Am. Soc. Assn. Execs. (cert., trainer, presenter confs. and meetings 1990-95, bd. dirs. 1993-95, edn. com. 1995, charter chmn. chpt. rels. sect. 1993-95, award of membership excellence in membership 1992, cert. assn. exec. 1990). Home and Office: 236 W Portal Ave # 136 San Francisco CA 94127

SIEGEL, RUTH K., customs official; b. Balt., Oct. 3, 1917; . Sigmund and Minnie (Hurwitz) Kleinman; m. Seymour Siegel (dec.), Nov. 20, 1940; children: Martin, Laurence Francis, Bruce. Student, Balt. Law Sch., Strayers Bus. Coll. Export, import control supr. U.S. Customs, 1964-79; realtor, 1975—; coord. Miami region fed. women's program U.S. Customs, 1974-76, hon. adv., 1976. Founder Federally Employed Women, Miami, Fla., 1975-85; pres. Women's Com. of 100, Miami; active Nat. Dem. Party, Miami; mem. Internat. Women's Yr. Com., Miami, Women's Leadership Forum, Miami. Recipient Outstanding Svc. Miami Bd. of Realtors, 1975, Cert. of Appreciation, Federally Employed Women, 1976, Outstanding Performance Rating, U.S. Dept. Treasury, 1978, Recognition of Disting. Svc., 1979. Democrat. Jewish. Home: 950 SW 138 Ave #B-113 Pembroke Pines FL 33027-3538

SIEGEL, SARAH ANN, lawyer; b. Providence, Aug. 29, 1956. BA in History cum laude, Brandeis U., 1978; JD, Washington U., St. Louis, 1981. Bar: Mo. 1982, U.S. Dist. Ct. (ea. dist.) Mo. 1983. Assoc. atty. St. Louis, 1982-83; staff atty. Land Clearance for Redevel. Authority, St. Louis, 1983-85, gen. counsel, 1985-88; gen. counsel Econ. Devel. Corp., St. Louis, 1988-90, St. Louis Devel. Corp., 1990-91; spl. counsel for devel. City of St. Louis, 1991-92; assoc. Suelthaus & Walsh, P.C., St. Louis, 1992-95, prin., 1995—. Pres. Central Reform Congregation, St. Louis, 1991-93, v.p., 1989-91, bd. dirs. 1987-89. Mem. ABA, Mo. Bar Assn. (vice chair com. on eminent domain 1990-91, steering com. 1987-89), Women Lawyer's Assn. (bd. dirs. 1985-90, v.p. 1989-90). Office: Suelthaus & Walsh PC 7733 Forsyth Blvd 12th Fl Saint Louis MO 63105

SIEGERT, BARBARA (MARIE), health care administrator; b. Boston, May 22, 1935; d. Salvatore Mario and Mary Kathleen (Wagner) Tartaglia; m. Herbert C. Siegert (dec. Apr. 1974); children: Carolyn Marie, Herbert Christian Jr. Diploma, Newton-Wellesley (Mass.) Hosp. Sch. Nursing, 1956; MEd, Antioch U., 1980. Diplomate Am. Bd. Med. Psychotherapists. Supr. nursing Hogan Regional Ctr., Hathorne, Mass., 1974-78; community mental health nursing advisor Cape Ann area office Dept. Mental Health, Beverly, Mass., 1978-79; dir. case mgmt. Dept. Mental Health, Beverly, 1979-87, dir. case mgmt. north shore area office, 1988-91; dir. case mgmt. Dept. Mental Health-north shore area-Lynn (Mass.) site, Lynn, Mass., 1991-92; mem. interdisciplinary faculty, profl. cons. com., lecture staff clin. pastoral counseling program Danvers State Hosp./Hogan/Berry Regional Ctrs., Hathorne, Mass., 1982-86; nursing edn. adv. com. North Shore Community Coll., Beverly, 1983-91; tng. staff Balter Inst., Ipswich, Mass., 1987-88. Mem. Internat. Cultural Diploma Honor, 1989—. Recipient Spl. Recognition award Lexington (Mass.) Pub. Schs., 1973, Peter Torci award Lexington Friends of Children in Spl. Edn., 1974; named Internat. Biog. Roll. of Honor, 1989—. Fellow Am. Biog. Inst. (life, Woman of Yr. 1990); mem. World Inst. Achievement. Home: 63 Willow Rd # B Boxford MA 01921-1218

SIEGLER, AVA LEE, psychologist; b. Lakewood, N.J., Dec. 17, 1939; d. Philip Jerome and Charlotte Francis (Gunsberg) Heyman; m. Robert Siegler, July 5, 1959; children: Dan Adam, Jess Gabriel. BA, Bennington Coll., 1959; MA, Columbia U., 1960; PhD, NYU, 1972. Lic. psychologist, N.Y., 1973. Liaison supr. Bellevue Hosp. Pediatric Project, 1971-75; dir. N.Y.C. Day Care, Prescott Early Intervention Project, 1972-87; assoc. clin. prof. NYU, 1976-88; dir. suicide prevention team Stuyvesant High Sch./LaGuardia High Sch., 1982-84; sr. supr. Postgrad. Ctr. Mental Health, 1985-90, dir. child adolescent and family clinic, 1981-88, dean tng., v.p. profl. acad. affairs, 1988-90; clin. psychologist, 1973—; dir. Inst. Child Adolescent and Family Studies, 1991—; cons. Childrens Aid Soc., 1971-73; cons. family project Bethlehem Day Care Ctr., 1971-75, Spence-Chapin Agy., 1973-76; lectr. NYU Med. Sch., 1983-88; forensic cons. N.Y. State Supreme Ct., 1987—; speaker in field. Author: What Should I Tell the Kids A Parent's Guide to Real Problems in the Real World, 1993; contbr. editor, columnist Child mag.; contbr. articles to profl. jours. Mem. APA, N.Y. State Psychol. Assn., NYU Postdoctoral Soc., N.Y. Freudian Soc., Internat. Psychoanalytic Assn. Office: 15 Charles St Apt 7E New York NY 10014-3024

SIEGMAN, MARION JOYCE, physiology educator; b. Bklyn., Sept. 7, 1933; d. C. Joseph and Helen (Wasserman) S. BA, Tulane U., 1954; PhD, SUNY, Bklyn., 1966. Instr. physiology Med. Coll. Thomas Jefferson U., Phila., 1967-68, asst. prof., 1968-71, assoc. prof., 1971-77, prof., 1977—; mem. physiology study sect. NIH. Editor: Regulation and Contraction of Smooth Muscle, 1987. Recipient award for excellence in rsch. and teaching Burlington No. Found., 1986, award for excellence in teaching Lindback Found., 1987, Outstanding Alumna award, Newcomb Coll./Tulane U., 1990; grantee NIH, 1967—. Mem. Am. Physiol. Soc., Biophys. Soc., Soc. Gen. Physiologists, Physiol. Soc. Phila. (pres. 1972-73). Office: Jefferson Med Coll 1020 Locust St Philadelphia PA 19107-6731

SIEGMUND, MELINDA GAYLE, marketing executive; b. Ft. Worth, Apr. 14, 1962; d. Grant and Betty Jean (Beil) Johnson; m. Martin Scott Siegmund, Nov. 9, 1985; children: Rachel Elizabeth, Colton Grant. BA in Advt. and Pub. Rels., Tex. Tech U., 1983; MA in Communications, U. Fla., 1984. Account exec. Phillip Poole and Assocs., Ft. Worth, 1984-85; account supr. Graphic Concepts, Ft. Worth, 1985-86; from mktg. mgr. physician svcs. to mktg. analyst satellite network Vol. Hosps. of Am., Irving, Tex., 1986-89; asst. mktg. dir. Bedford Meadows Hosp., Bedford, Tex., 1989-90; pvt. practice mktg. svcs. Bedford, Tex., 1991—. Exec. dir. Miss Hurst-Euless-Bedford Scholarship Found., 1987-92; vice chmn. Cen. Bus. Dist. Planning Com., Bedford, 1990-91; active Hurst-Euless-Bedford Econ. Devel. Com., 1988-90. Mem. Profl. Models Am. (charter adv., historian 1990-91), Hurst-Euless-Bedford C. of C., State Assn. Local Miss Tex. Scholarship Pageants (pres. 1992—). Baptist. Office: Siegmund Mktg Svcs 4208 Tanbark Trl Fort Worth TX 76109-3407

SIEGMUND-ROACH, SHERILYN LEIGH, educator; b. N.Y.C., Feb. 2, 1965; d. David Oliver and Sandra Sue (Melchert) S.; m. Jeffery Allen Roach, Aug. 16, 1986; children: Amber, J. Daniel, Victoria. BA cum laude, Vassar Coll., 1985; postgrad., U. Alaska, 1985-88, Curtin U. Tech., 1995—. Tchr. math., sci. Eagle (Alaska) Sch., 1988-92, Tok (Alaska) Sch., 1992-96; tchr. leader Concepts for All Project in Sci., Anchorage, 1992-95, Project on Leading Alaska Reform in Sci., Anchorage, 1995—. Pres. Tok-a-Tan Homemakers (homemaker of the yr. 1996), 1995-96. Teaching fellow Northfield (Mass.) - Mt. Herman, 1985. Mem. AAUW, ASCD, Nat. Sci. Tchrs. Assn. (life), Nat. Coun. Tchrs. Math. (life), Nat. Assn. Biology Tchrs. (life), Alaska Sci. Tchrs. Assn. (life, regional rep. 1988—), Tri Beta. Home: PO Box 876 Tok AK 99780

SIEHR, PAMELA ANNE, textile designer, fashion designer; b. Superior, Wis., Sept. 11, 1970; d. Steven O. and Barb A. (Becker) S. AAS, Fashion Inst. Tech., 1992; BAS, U. Wis., 1992. Textile artist Guilford Mills, N.Y.C., 1993-94; stylist Missbrenner Inc., N.Y.C., 1994—; designer, owner accessory bus., N.Y.C., 1990—. Mem. NAFE, Fashion Group, U. Wis. Alumni Assn., Fashion Inst. Tech. Alumni Assn. Office: Missbrenner Inc 1359 Broadway New York NY 10018

SIEMER, DEANNE CLEMENCE, lawyer; b. Buffalo, Dec. 25, 1940; d. Edward D. and Dorothy J. (Helsdon) S.; m. Howard P. Willens; 1 child, Jason L. BA, George Washington U., 1962; LLB, Harvard U., 1968. Bar: N.Y. 1968, D.C. 1969, Md. 1972, Trust Ter. 1976. Economist Office of Mgmt. and Budget, Washington, 1964-67; assoc., then ptnr. Wilmer, Cutler & Pickering, Washington, 1968-90; ptnr. Pillsbury, Madison & Sutro, Washington, 1990-95; mng. dir. Wilsie Co., Saipan, M.P., 1995—; gen. counsel U.S. Dept. of Def., Washington, 1977-79; spl. asst. to sec. U.S. Dept. of Energy, Washington, 1979-80. Author: Tangible Evidence, 1984, 3d edit., 1996, Understanding Modern Ethical Standards, 1985, Manual on Litigation Support Databases, 1986, supplement, 1992. Mem. Lawyers Com. for Civil Rights, Washington, 1973—; mediator D.C. Superior Ct., Washington, 1986—, U.S. Ct. Appeals, Washington, 1988—; chair Nat. Inst. Trial Advocacy, Am. Law Inst., 1995—. Recipient Citation Air Force Assn., 1977, Dist. Pub. Service medal Sec. of Def., 1979, Commendation Pres. of U.S. 1981. Mem. ABA, ATLA, Am. Law Inst., D.C. Bar Assn., No. Marianas Bar Assn., Womens Bar Assn. Episcopalian. Office: Wilsie Co Macaranas Bldg 1st Fl PO Box 909 Saipan MP 96950

SIETSEMA, KATHY ELAINE, internal medicine educator, researcher; b. Glen Ridge, N.J., Nov. 17, 1953; d. Raymond Jay and Dorathy (Luce) S.; m. Eric Paul Brass, Sept. 3, 1994; 1 child, Alexander Jay. BS, Seattle Pacific Coll., 1975; MD, Northwestern U., Chgo., 1979. Diplomate Am. Bd. Internal Medicine, Am. Bd. Pulmonary Medicine, Am. Bd. Critical Care Medicine. Intern in internal medicine U. Calif.-Davis, Sacramento, 1979-80; resident in internal medicine U. Wash., Seattle, 1080-82; fellow in pulmonary medicine Harbor-UCLA Med. Ctr., Torrance, 1982-85, organizer practicum in exercising testing, 1993—; asst. prof. medicine UCLA Sch. Medicine, Torrance, 1985-93, assoc. prof., 1993—; sci. reviewer various med. jours.; mem. spl. emphasis panel NIH, Bethesda, Md., 1994—. Contbr. articles on exercise physiology especially as related to cardiopulmonary diseases to med. and sci. jours. Recipient clin. investigator award NIH, 1987-92, rsch. grantee, 1993-96. Mem. Am. Thoracic Soc. (ad hoc com. 1994—), Am. Physiol. Soc., Am. Heart Assn. (cardiopulmonary coun.). Office: Harbor UCLA Med Ctr 1000 W Carson St Torrance CA 90509

SIEVERS, ANN ELISABETH FURIEL, clinical nurse specialist in otolaryngology; b. Utica, N.Y., Mar. 26, 1950; d. Ralph Edward and Mary Paula (Delahunt) Furiel; m. Mark Scott Sievers, Apr. 29, 1979; children: Elisabeth Ann, Katherine Tanner. BSN, Russell Sage Coll., 1972; MA in Human Resource Devel., George Washington U., 1979. Cert. in otorhinolaryngology nursing; RN, Calif., D.C., N.Y. Staff/charge nurse Rome (N.Y.) Murphy Meml. Hosp., 1972-73; staff/charge nurse ICU George Washington U. Hosp., 1973-74, respiratory clin. specialist, 1974-79; otolaryngology clin. nurse specialist U. Calif. Davis Med. Ctr., Sacramento, 1979—, staff Skull Base Surgery Ctr.; adj. clin. prof. U. Calif., San Francisco; lectr., presenter in field; mem. nursing rsch. com. U. Calif., Davis, 1982-89, mem. nursing ethics and practice com., 1983-92, mem. instnl. rev. bd., 1984-90, chmn. hospice adv. bd., 1984-87, mem. skull base surgery programmatic subcom., 1990-93. Contbr. articles to profl. jours. Bd. dirs., vol. D.C. Lung Assn., 1974-79; vol. Am. Cancer Soc. of Immigrant Trails, Sacramento, 1980—; fundraiser Calif. hospice North Bay Med. Ctr., 1987—. Recipient S.O.H.N. Nat. Clin. Excellence award, 1995. Mem. AACN, Soc. Otorhinolaryngology Head and Neck Nurses (coord. nat. rsch. project 1990—, nat. bd. dirs. 1989-92, nat. v.p. 1992-94, chmn. rsch. com. 1980-90, edn. com. 1990, 92-94, Nat. Honor award 1991, 94), Sigma Theta Tau (Clin. Excellence award Zeta Eta chpt. 1982).

SIEWERT, CONNIE RAE, marketing professional, accountant; b. Grand Forks, N.D., May 24, 1957; d. Reed Milton and Edith Eleanor (Sand) S.; m. Viatcheslav Anokhine, Oct. 26, 1990. BS in Acctg., U. N.D., 1979. CPA, N.D. Auditor Touche Ross & Co., Mpls., 1979-83; sr. opers. analyst No. Telecom, Nashville, 1983-85; regional controller No. Telecom, Atlanta, 1990-92; sr. fin. analyst Bell No. Rsch., Mountainview, Calif., 1985-86; mgr. US corp. reporting Bell No. Rsch., Ottawa, Can., 1986-87; regional controller Bell No. Rsch., Atlanta, 1987-90; dir. mktg. opers. Atlanta Centennial Olympic Properties, 1992—. Home: 3565 Mt Vernon Ct Lawrenceville GA 30244 Office: Atlanta Centennial Olympic Properties 250 Williams St Atlanta GA 30303

SIFF, MARLENE IDA, artist; b. N.Y.C., Sept. 20, 1936; d. Irving Louis and Dorothy Gertrude (Lahn) Marmer; m. Elliott Justin Siff, July 11, 1959; children: Bradford Evan, Brian Douglas. BA, Hunter Coll., 1957. Cert. elem. tchr., N.Y., N.J. Tchr. Stewart Manor (N.Y.) Sch. System, 1957-59, Teaneck (N.J.) Sch. System, 1959-60; free-lance interior designer Westport, Conn., 1966-70; designer indsl. plant Varo Inertial Products, Trumbull, Conn., 1970; corp. sec., treas. Belmar Corp., Westport, 1972—, also bd. dirs.; chmn. bd. Marlene Designs Inc., Westport, 1973-77; owner Marlene Siff Design Studio, Westport, 1978—; designer Signature Collections, J.P. Stevens & Co., Inc., 1974-78, J.C. Penney Co., N.Y.C., 1978, C.R. Gibson Co., Norwalk, Conn., 1980; aesthetic cons. ALCIDE Corp., Norwalk, 1980-88. One-woman shows include David Segal Gallery, N.Y.C., 1987, Conn. Pub. TV Gallery 24, Hartford, 1987, Paul Mellon Art Ctr. at Choate Rosemary Hall, Wallingford, Conn., 1989, Conn. Nat. Bank Hdqrs., Horwalk, 1990, The Michael Stone Collection, Washington, 1992, Bergdorf Goodman, N.Y.C., 1993, Joel Kessler Fine Art, Miami Beach, Fla., 1994, Park Pl., Stamford, Conn., 1995, Westport (Conn.) Arts Ctr., 1995. Decorator ann. charity ball Easter Seal Home Svc., 1976; bd. dirs. United Jewish Appeal, Westport, 1982-86; mem. com. Levitt Pavillion Performing Arts, Westport, 1982-89. Recipient award Lower Conn. Mfrs. Assn., 1970. Mem. Kappa Pi. Home: 15 Broadview Rd Westport CT 06880-2303

SIFTON, ELISABETH, book publisher; b. N.Y.C., Jan. 13, 1939; d. Reinhold and Ursula (Keppel-Compton) Niebuhr; m. Charles P. Sifton, 1962 (div. 1984); children: Peter Samuel, Charles Tobias, John Paul Gustav; m. Fritz R. Stern, 1996. B.A. magna cum laude, Radcliffe Coll., Cambridge, Mass., 1960; postgrad., U. Paris, 1960-61. Asst. to dep. asst. sec. of state U.S. Dept. of State, Washington, 1961-62; editorial asst., assoc. editor, editor, sr. editor Frederick A. Praeger Pubs., N.Y.C., 1962-68; editor, sr. editor, editor-in-chief The Viking Press, N.Y.C., 1969-83; v.p., pub. Elisabeth Sifton Books, Viking Penguin, N.Y.C., 1984-87; exec. v.p. Alfred A. Knopf, Inc., N.Y.C., 1987-92; sr. v.p. Farrar, Straus & Giroux, 1993—; pub. Hill & Wang, 1993—. Fulbright fellow, 1960-61. Democrat. Episcopalian. Home: 15 Claremont Ave New York NY 10027-6814 Office: Farrar Straus & Giroux 19 Union Sq W New York NY 10003-3307

SIGAFUS, EVELYN, secondary school educator; b. Phila., Apr. 1, 1945; d. Herman and Claire (Frank) Weiss; m. Martin Lewis Sigafus, Aug. 20, 1967; children: Michelle, Brent. BA in Edn., U. Ariz., 1967. Cert. tchr., Ariz. Math. tchr. Marana (Ariz.) H.S., 1967-70, Sabino H.S., Tucson, 1982, 84-91, Tucson H.S., 1983-84, Santa Rita H.S., 1991—; mem. math. core curriculum com. Tucson Unified Sch. Dist., 1988-92, mem. math. assessment com., 1992-93, mem. computer lab. com., 1993-95, mem. textbook selection com., 1993-94. Mem. com. advancement chair, sec. Troop 739, Boy Scouts Am., Tucson, 1986-93; pres. Wrightstown Neighborhood Assn., Tucson, 1988—; pres. Sahuaro High Drama Parents, Tucson, 1991-93; mem. 5-yr. planning com. Cong. Anshei Israel, Tucson, 1994—; mem. bd. trustees Cong. Anshei Israel, 1996—. Grantee NSF, 1990. Mem. NEA, Ariz. Edn. Assn., Tucson Edn. Assn., Nat. Coun. Thcrs. MAth. Home: 9424 E Calle Bolivar Tucson AZ 85715-5840 Office: Santa Rita HS 3951 S Pantano Rd Tucson AZ 85730-4014

SIGHOLTZ, SARA O'MEARA, nonprofit organization executive; b. Knoxville, Tenn.; m. Robert Sigholtz; children: John; stepchildren: Taryn, Whitney. Attended, Briarcliff Jr. Coll.; BA, The Sorbonne, Paris; D (hon.), Endicott Coll. Co-founder, chmn. bd., CEO CHILDHELP USA/Internat. (formerly Children's Village USA), Scottsdale, Ariz., 1974—. Bd. dirs. Internat. Soc. Prevention Child Abuse and Neglect, Children to Children, Inc.; hon. com. mem. Learning Disabilities Found., Inc.; mem. Mayor's adv. bd., Defense for Children Internat., Nat. Soc. Prevention Cruelty to Children, World Affairs Coun.; adv. bd. mem. Ednl. Film Co.; bd. dirs. Internat. Alliance on Child Abuse and Neglect; sustaining mem. Spastic Children's League, past pres.; mem., past recording sec. Assistance League So. Calif. Recipient Cross of Merit, Knightly Order of St. Brigitte, 1967, Victor M. Carter Diamond award Japan-Am. Soc., 1970, Dame Cross of Merit of Order of St. John of Denmark, 1980, Official Seal of 34th Gov. Calif., 1981, Woman of Achievement award Career Guild, 1982, Women Making History award Nat. Fedn. Bus. Profl. Women's Clubs, 1983, Disting. Am. award for svc., 1984, Humanitarian award Nat. Frat. Eagles, 1984, Nat. Recognition award outstanding leadership Am. Heritage Found., 1986, Notable Am. award svc. to Calif., 1986, Dove of Peace award Pacific Southwest and Ctrl. Pacific Regions B'nai B'rith, 1987, Paul Harris fellow award Rotary Found., 1989, Love and Help the Children award, 1990, Presdl. award, 1990, Hubert Humphrey award Touchdown Club Washington, 1994, numerous others. Mem. SAG, AFTRA, Victory Awards (exec. com.), Am. Biographical Inst. (nat. bd. advisors), Alpha Delta Kappa (hon.). Office: Childhelp USA 15757 N 78th St Scottsdale AZ 85260

SIGLAIN, HELEN See DE LUCA, ANDREA

SIGMAR, LUCIA ANNE STRETCHER, English educator, administrator; b. Waynesville, N.C., Oct. 24, 1959; d. Robert Hatfield and Amelia Joyce (Simpson) S.; m. Axel Michael Sigmar, Aug. 17, 1991. BA in French and English, Delta State U., 1981; MA in English, U. So. Miss., 1986; PhD in English, U. Tenn., 1995. Cert. tchr., Miss. English instr. Roane State C.C., Harriman, Tenn., 1987-89, dir. writing ctr., 1989-91; cons. corp. comm. and tech. writing, 1996—. Recipient Star Tchr. award, Miss. Econ. Coun., 1983-84. Mem. S. Atlantic Modern Lang. Assn., Nat. Coun. Tchrs. of English, Lambda Iota Tau. Office: PO Box 1892 Stafford TX 77497

SIGMON, JOYCE ELIZABETH, professional society administrator; b. Stanley, N.C., Oct. 4, 1935; d. Rome Alfred and Pearl Elizabeth (Beal) S. BS, U. N.C., 1971; MA, Loyola U., 1980. Cert. dental asst., assn. exec. Dental asst. Dr. Paul A. Stroup, Jr., Charlotte, N.C., 1953-63; instr. Wayne Tech. Inst., Goldsboro, N.C., 1963-65, Ctrl. Piedmont Community Coll., Charlotte, 1965-69; dir. Dental Assisting Edn. ADA, Chgo., 1971-85, asst. sec. Coun. Prosthetics Svcs., 1985-87, mgr. Office Quality Assurance, 1987-80, exec. dir. Aux., 1990-92; dir. adminstrv. activities Am. Acad. of Implant Dentistry, Chgo., 1993—; exec. sec. Am. Bd. of Oral Implantology/Implant Dentistry, 1993—. Deacon 4th Presbyn. Ch., 1973-75, elder 1975-77, 88-91, trustee, 1991-94; moderator Presbyn. Women in 4th Ch., 1987-91. Mem. Am. Soc. Assn. Execs., Chgo. Soc. Assn. Execs. (chair CAE com. 1991-92), Am. Dental Assts. Assn., N.C. Dental Assn. (pres. 1968-69), Charlotte Dental Assts. Soc. Presbyterian. Home: 260 E Chestnut St Chicago IL 60611-2423 Office: Am Acad Implant Dentistry 211 E Chicago Ave Chicago IL 60611-2616

SIGMUND, DIANE WEISS, judge; b. N.Y.C., Mar. 1, 1943. BS, Pa. State U., 1963; JD magna cum laude, Temple U., 1977. Bar: Pa. 1977. Lawyer Blank, Rome, Cominsky & McCauley, Phila.; judge U.S. Bankruptcy Ct. (Pa. ea. dist.), Phila., 1993—; course planner Pa. Bar Inst., 1991; mem. steering com. Ea. Dist. Pa. Bankruptcy conf., 1995—, 3d cir. task force equal treatment in cts., gender commn., 1995—. Office: US Courthouse Rm 3722 601 Market St Philadelphia PA 19106-1510

SIKES, CYNTHIA LEE, actress, singer; b. Coffeyville, Kans., Jan. 2, 1954; d. Neil and Pat (Scott) S.; m. Alan Bud Yorkin, June 24, 1989. Student, Am. Conservatory Theater, San Francisco, 1977-79. Appeared in TV series St. Elsewhere, 1981-83, L.A. Law, 1989; TV movies include His Mistress, 1990; films include Man Who Loved Women, That's Life, Arthur On The Rocks, Love Hurts, 1988; producer, actress Sins of Silence, 1996; also Broadway show Into The Woods, 1988-89. Active Hollywood Women's Polit. Com. Recipient Gov.'s Medal of Merit, Kans., 1986. Democrat.

SIKORA, SALLY MARIE, nursing administrator; b. Atlantic City, Aug. 9, 1949; d. R. Joseph and Julia G. (Myers) Wimberg; m. Paul A. Sikora, Aug. 15, 1970; children: Andrew Joseph, Paul A. II. ASN, Atlantic C.C., Mays Landing, N.J., 1971; BSN, Stockton State Coll., Pomona, N.J., 1990; MSN, LaSalle U., Phila., 1995. CCRN; cert. instr. ACLS, pediat. ACLS, neonatal ACLS, EMT, BLS trainer. Charge nurse surg. unit Atlantic City Med. Ctr., 1971; head nurse Senator Nursing Home, Atlantic City, 1972; ICU/Critical Care Unit staff and head nurse William Kessler Meml. Hosp., Hammonton, N.J., 1972-80, adminstrv. supr., 1980-82; adminstrv. supr. Atlantic City Med. Ctr., Atlantic Pomona, N.J., 1982-85; critical care mgr. Atlantic City Med. Ctr., Pomona, 1985-90, dir. edn., 1990-91; adminstrv. dir. nursing Shore Meml. Hosp., Somers Point, N.J., 1991—; adj. prof. nursing Atlantic County C.C., 1995—, Cumberland County C.C., 1996; bd. mem. So. N.J. Perinatal Coop., Camden, 1993; lectr., cons. cmty. orgns. and hosps.; establisher Coastal Critical Care Consortium N.J., first free-standing cardiac catheterization lab. without surg. back-up in State N.J.; sch. lectr. elem. and H.S., Pleasantville, N.J.; opened 1st hosp. based detoxifaction unit for outpatient svcs., 1995; adj. prof. nursing Atlantic C.C., Cumberland Coll. Vol. ARC, Pleasantville, N.J., 1980's. Recipient Citation of Merit United Way, Atlantic County, N.J., 1993-94, Pres.'s award for excellence, Atlanticare award. Mem. ANA, Am. Heart Assn. (mgr. tng. ctr. 1990-91), N.J. State Nurses Assn., Assn. Med./Surg. Nurses, So. N.J. Perinatal Cooperative (bd. dirs. 1993—). Republican. Roman Catholic. Home: 4 Maple Branch Ct Port Republic NJ 08241-9784 Office: Shore Meml Hosp New York Ave Somers Point NJ 08224

SIKORSKI-TUERPE, LAURA MARY, telecommunications and management consultant; b. Mineola, N.Y., Oct. 10, 1950; d. Adelbert Leonard and Eleonore Laura (Zuba) Sikorski; m. Donald Werner Tuerpe, July 19, 1975. BA in Liberal Arts, Fordham U., 1972. Dir. telecom. and facilities planning Hilton Svc. Corp., N.Y.C., 1971-86; mng. ptnr. Sikorski-Tuerpe & Assocs., Centerport, N.Y., 1986—. Contbr. articles to profl. jours. Founder Call Ctr. Networking Group; mem. Polish Gift of Life, Roslyn, 1988-90, Ladies Guild, St. Francis Hosp., Roslyn, N.Y., 1990—. Mem. Soc. Telecom. Cons. (pres. 1993-95). Roman Catholic. Office: Sikorski-Tuerpe & Assocs 20 Mill Pond Ln Centerport NY 11721-1644

SILAGI, BARBARA WEIBLER, corporate administrator; b. Chgo., June 26, 1930; d. Carleton Thomas and Catherine Josephine (Wolph) Weibler; m. Joseph Edward Sturgulewski (Sturgus), Feb. 12, 1953 (div. Aug. 1954); 1 child, Mariann Catherine; m. John Louis Silagi, Jr., July 2, 1960 (div. July 1968). BM in Edn., Northwestern U., 1958; MS in Edn., No. Ill. U., 1965. Cert. K-14 supervisory teaching, spl. edn. tchr., airline transport pilot, FAA dispatcher. Elem. sch. tchr. St. Mary's Sch., Chgo., 1947-49, Kingman, Ariz., 1949-52; legal sec. Judge Edward J. Mahoney, Quincy, Ill., 1954-55; elem. sch. tchr. C.M. Bardwell Sch., Aurora, Ill., 1955-76; flight instr. flight schs. Chgo., Aurora and Frankfort, Ill., Clinton, Iowa, 1960-77; aircraft dispatcher Transcontinental Airlines, Zantop Internat. Airlines, Ypsilanti, Mich., 1977-81; airline pilot Mannion Air Charter, Ypsilanti, 1977-80; head night auditor Howard Johnson, Quality Inn, Travelodge, BestWestern, others, Ocala, Fla., Silver Springs, Fla., 1983-87; sec.-treas. Diamond Design Svcs., Inc., Ocklawaha, Fla., 1985—; pub. Forest Shopper, Springs Shopper, Belle Shopper. Author: Dispatch Training, 1989; editor tng. manuals, 1977-85. Violist Chgo. Suburban Symphony, Naperville, Ill., 1956-60; contralto Palestrina A capella Choir, Aurora, Ill., 1956-60; life mem. Ill. PTA, Aurora, 1974—; apptd. vice chmn. adv. bd. Dunnellon Airport and Indsl. Park, 1992. Recipient 1st place Suburban Aviation Assn., Chgo., 1975, 5th place Illi-Nines Air Derby, Chgo., Moline, Ill., 1973, 2d place Leg prize Powder Puff Derby, McLean to Lincoln, Nebr., 1971; Eckstein scholar Northwestern U., 1952. Mem. AAUW (life), NEA (life), Ill. Edn. Assn., Ninety Nines Internat. (life), Illi-Nines Air Derby (handicap chmn. 1972-76, air marking chmn. 99's Chgo. chpt. 1972-76, corr. sec. Chgo. chpt. 1976-77, 1st pl. achievement awards 1972-78), Ocala Orchid Soc. (sec.), Lake Wier Garden Club, Pi Lambda Theta (charter, life, rsch. chmn. Beta Delta chpt. 1962-63). Roman Catholic. Home: RR 2 Box 1837-A Ocklawaha FL 32179-8757 also: 6385 SE 158th Ct Ocklawaha FL 32179 Office: Diamond Design Svcs Inc PO Box 186 Ocklawaha FL 32183

SILAK, CATHY R., judge; b. Astoria, N.Y., May 25, 1950; d. Michael John and Rose Marie (Janor) S.; m. Nicholas G. Miller, Aug. 9, 1980; 3 children. BA, NYU, 1971; M in City Planning, Harvard U., 1973; JD, U. Calif., 1976. Bar: Calif. 1977, U.S. Dist. Ct. (no. dist.) Calif. 1977, D.C. 1979, U.S. Ct. Appeals (D.C. cir.) 1979, U.S. Dist. Ct. (so. dist.) N.Y. 1980, Idaho 1983, U.S. Dist. Ct. Idaho 1983, U.S. Ct. Appeals (2nd cir.) 1983, U.S. Ct. Appeals (9th cir.) 1985. Law clk. to Hon. William W. Schwarzer U.S. Dist. Ct. (no dist.), Calif., 1976-77; pvt. practice San Francisco, 1977-79, Washington, 1979-80; asst. U.S. atty. So. Dist. of N.Y., 1980-83; spl. asst. U.S. atty. Dist. of Idaho, 1983-84; pvt. practice Boise, Idaho, 1984-90; judge Idaho Ct. Appeals, 1990-93; justice Idaho Supreme Ct., Boise, 1993—; assoc. gen. counsel Morrison Knudsen Corp., 1989-90; mem. fairness com. Idaho Supreme Ct. and Gov.'s Task Force on Alternative Dispute Resolution; instr. and lectr. in field. Assoc. note and comment editor Calif. Law Rev., 1975-76. Land use planner Mass. Dept. Natural Resources, 1973; founder Idaho Coalition for Adult Literacy; bd. dirs. Literacy Lab., Inc. Recipient Jouce Stein award Boise YWCA, 1992, Women Helping Women award Soroptimist, Boise, 1993. Fellow Idaho Law Found (ann., lectr.); mem. ABA (nat. conf. state trial judges jud. adminstrn. divsn.), Nat. Assn. Women Judges, Idaho State Bar (corp./securities sect., instr.). Office: PO Box 83720 Boise ID 83720-0002

SILBER, JOAN KAREN, writer, educator; b. Newark, June 14, 1945; d. Samuel Sanford and Dorothy (Arlein) S. BA, Sarah Lawrence Coll., 1967; MA, NYU, 1979. Mem. writing faculty 92d St. Y, N.Y.C., Sarah Lawrence Coll., Bronxville, N.Y., 1985, Warren Wilson Coll., Asheville, N.C., 1986—. Author: Household Words, 1980 (Hemingway award), In the City, 1987; also stories. Grantee N.Y. Found. Arts, 1986; Guggenheim fellow, 1984-85, NEA fellow, 1986. Home: 43 Bond St New York NY 10012 Office: Sarah Lawrence Coll 1 Mead Way Bronxville NY 10708

SILBER, JUDY G., dermatologist; b. Newark, July 26, 1953. MD, SUNY, Bklyn., 1978. Intern Brookdale Med. Ctr., Bklyn., 1978-79; resident in dermatology Kings County Hosp., Bklyn., 1979-82; pvt. practice dermatology; affiliated with Meadowlands Med. Ctr., Secaucus, N.J. Fellow Am. Acad. Dermatology; mem. AMA, N.J. Med. Soc. Office: 992 Clifton Ave Clifton NJ 07013-3502

SILBERBERG, INGA, dermatologist; b. Kassel, Germany, Sept. 16, 1934; came to U.S., 1938; d. Willi and Erna (Rosenbaum) S.; m. Herbert M. Sinakin, Feb. 16, 1969; 1 child, William Elias. BA, Hunter Coll., 1955; MD, SUNY, 1959; MS in Dermatology, NYU, 1965. Diplomate Am. Bd. Dermatologists, 1964. Instr., clin. dermatology NYU Med. Ctr., N.Y.C., 1963-65, clin. asst. prof., 1965-66, asst. prof. dermatology, 1966-71, clin. assoc. prof. dermatology, 1971-76; cons., dermatology Newcomb Hosp., Vineland, N.J., 1975—. Jonas Salk scholar, City of N.Y., 1955-59, Henry Silver award, Dermatologic Soc. Greater N.Y., 1962, 65, Dermatology Found. Discovery award, 1993. Fellow Am. Acad. Dermatology; mem. AMA.

SILBERMAN, ROSALIE GAULL, government official; b. Jackson, Miss., Mar. 31, 1937; d. Samuel and Alice (Berkowitz) Gaull; m. Laurence H. Silberman, Apr. 28, 1957; children: Katherine, Anne, Robert. BA, Smith Coll., 1958. Tchr., 1967-72; bd. dirs. Natl. Adv. Coun. on Edn. of Disadvantaged Children, 1973-75, Widening Horizons, 1973-75; dir. comm., press sec. Sen. Robert Packwood, 1977-79; exec. dir., sec., treas. New Coalition for Econ. and Social Change, 1981-83; dir. pub. rels. San Francisco Conservatory of Music, 1982-83; spl. asst. Commr. Mimi Weyforth Dawson FCC, 1983-84; commr. EEOC, 1984-86, vice chmn., 1986-94, commr., 1994-95; exec. dir. Office of Compliance, U.S. Congress, Washington, 1995—. Office: Office Compliance Rm LA 200 Washington DC 20540-1999

SILBERSTEIN, DIANE, publishing executive. Publisher The New Yorker, 1995—. Office: Advance Publ Inc 20 W 43rd St New York NY 10036*

SILBERT, LAYLE, photographer, writer; b. Chgo.; d. Morris and Rose (Davidson) S.; m. Abraham Aidenoff, May 9, 1945 (dec. Jan. 1976). BPh, U. Chgo., MA. Photographer, N.Y.C., 1971—. Author: (poems) Making A Baby in Union Park Chicago, 1982, (short stories) Imaginary People & Other Strangers, 1985, Burkah & Other Stories, 1992, New York, New York, 1996; one-woman photog. shows include Spertus Mus., Chgo., Am. Jewish Mus., Phila.,Hebrew Union Coll., Cin., Donnell Libr., N.Y.C.; exhibited in group shows at Columbia U., others; photographs in Libr. of Congress, London Mus. Mem. PEN Am. Ctr., Poetry Soc. Am. Home and Studio: 505 La Guardia Pl Apt 16C New York NY 10012

SILBEY, ROBYN ROSEN, elementary education educator; b. Phila., Dec. 6, 1952; d. Burton and Harriette (Kimmelsman) Rosen; m. Sam Silbey, Dec. 16, 1973; children: Marc Adam, Carrie Lynn. BS with honors, U. Md., 1974. Advanced profl. cert., 1984. Classroom tchr. Montgomery County Pub. Sch., Rockville, Md., 1974-87; tchr. of the disadvantaged Montgomery County Pub. Sch., Rockville, 1987-90, math specialist, 1990—; pvt. tutor, Gaithersburg, 1974—; cons. Marymount U., Reston, Va., 1993—; mem. evaluation and selection com. Montgomery County Pub. Sch., Rockville, 1989—, elem. math. adv. com., 1994—, author geometry for elem. tchrs., 1994; presenter and spkr. in effective instrnl. practices. Writer: Formal Assessment Houghton-Mifflin, Middle School Mathematics, 1993, Addison Wesley Mathematics, 1991, 93, McGraw-Hill Math, 1987, MacMillan Alternative Math Program, 1992, Holt Mathematics, 1983, Mathematics Plus/ Harcourt Brace, 1992, Houghton Mifflin Mathematics, 1994, Scholastic Math Place, 1994, McGraw Hill Reading, 1986, HRW Reading, 1989, World of Reading, 1991, World of Reading, 1993. Mem. ASCD, Nat. Coun. Tchrs. Math., Md. Coun. Tchrs. Math., Montgomery County Math. Tchrs. Assn. (elem. rep. 1994), Phi Delta Kappa. Home: 5 Tuckahoe Ct Gaithersburg MD 20878-4229 Office: Rosement Elem Sch 16400 Alden Ave Gaithersburg MD 20877-1508

SILBY, CAROLINE JANE, sport psychologist, educator; b. Cleve., June 21, 1965; d. Howard and Barbara (O'Loughlin) S. BA, Syracuse U., 1988; MEd, U. Va., 1991, PhD, 1994. Pvt. practice sport psychology cons. Washington, 1992—; counselor Kirov Acad. Ballet, Washington, 1994-95; prof. U. Del., Newark, 1995—, U. Va., Falls Church, 1995—; mem. sports medicine com. U.S. Figure Skating, Colorado Springs, Colo., 1989—; mem. collegiate sports coun. U.S. Olympic Com., Colorado Springs, 1992—, athletes adv. com., 1992—, athlete rep. World UN Games, 1995. Editor Skating, 1993; contbr. articles to profl. jours. Vol. D.C. Cares, Washington, 1995. Office: Ste 1005 701 Pennsylvania Ave NW Washington DC 20004

SILCOX, FRANCES ELEANOR, museum and exhibits planning consultant; b. Orange, Calif., Sept. 26, 1956; d. William Henry and M. Eleanor (Saulpaugh) S.; m. David William Smith, June 21, 1986; children: Lena Celeste, Reid Whitney. BA in English, U. San Francisco, 1979; MA in Mus. Studies, George Washington U., 1984. Intern divsn. performing arts Smithsonian Instn., Washington, 1978; adminstrv. asst. exhibits dept. Calif. Acad. Scis., San Francisco, 1979-81; gallery coord. The George Washington U., Washington, 1981-83; intern art dept. aide Smithsonian Instn., Washington, 1983-84; asst. dir. Torpedo Factory Arts Ctr., Alexandria, Va., 1983-84; accreditation coord. Am. Assn. Mus., Washington, 1984-86; interpretive planner Design and Prodn. Inc., Lorton, Va., 1986-88; mus. planner West Office Exhbn. Design, San Francisco, 1988-91; ind. mus. and exhibits planner, owner Dallas, 1991—. Bd. mem. St. Gerard Circle, St. Rita Cath. Cmty., Dallas, 1995-97; contbr. numerous natural and cultural resources orgns. Scholar Nat. Endowment for the Arts-Am. Law Inst.-ABA, Washington, 1982. Mem. Am. Assn. for State and Local History, Am. Assn. Mus., Archaeol. Inst. Am., Internat. Coun. Mus., Nat. Assn. for Mus. Exhibition, Tex. Assn. Mus. Democrat. Home and Office: 5816 Lindenshire Dallas TX 75230

SILER, NANCY MARGARET POWERS, dietitian, nutritionist; b. Houston, Oct. 20, 1950; d. Wallace Lewis and Margaret Van Elswyk Powers; m. Larry Wayne Siler, Mar. 31, 1973; children: Stacy Elizabeth, Steven Austin. Cert., Inst. Nutrit. Cen. Am./Panama, 1969; BS, U. Houston, 1971; dietetic intern, St. Paul Ramsey Med. Ctr., 1972; MS, S.W. Tex. State U., 1976. Lic. dietitian, Ill.; cert. Am. Assn. Family and Consumer Scis., foodsvc. mgr. Chgo. Dept. Health, applied foodsvc. sanitation Edni. Found. Nat. Restaurant Assn., foodsvc. sanitation tng. instr. Ill. Dept. Pub. Health Office Health Protection. Clin. dietitian Scott and White Med. Ctr., Temple, Tex., 1972-73, St. David's Comty. Hosp., Austin, Tex., 1973-74; cons. dietitian Health Care Facilities, Austin, 1974-88; specialist in dietetics U. Tex., Austin, 1980-88; asst. prof. Chgo. State U., 1989-92; clin. asst. prof., coordinated program dir. U. Ill., Chgo., 1992-95; dir. nutrition Hill and Knowlton, Inc., Chgo., 1995—; lectr. S.W. Tex. State U., San Marcis, summer 1986, 87. Author: Texas Dietetic Association Food Faddism, 1991, Dietetics Recruitment Manual, 1992, Quantity Food Production Manual, Model Clinical Preceptor Orientation Manual for HND 421 Clinical Practice II, 1992; co-author: The American Heart Association Nutrition Education Resource Guide, 1994; contbr. book chpts., revs., and articles to profl. publs. Named Young Dietitian of Yr., Tex. Dietetic Assn. and Am. Dietetic Assn., 1979, Outstanding Dietetic Educator, Chgo. Dietetic Assn., Ill. Dietetic Assn. and Am. Dietetic Assn., 1995; recipient numerous grants. Mem. NAFE, Am. Dietetic Assn. (registerd dietitian, appeals com. chmn. 1991-92, abstract rev. team 1994-96, state adv. com. chmn. ann. meeting 1994-95, Outstanding Svc. award 1988), Ill. Dietetic Assn. (bd. dirs., fin. com. 1994-96, pres.-elect 1994-95, pres. 1995-96, Outstanding Dietitian 1996), West Suburban Dietetic Assn. (legis. com. 1992-93, fundraising com. 1992-93), Dietitians in Bus. and Comms., Dietetic Educators Practitioners, Sports, Cardiovasc., and Wellness Nutritionists, Soc. for Nutrition Edn., Chgo. Nutrition Assn. (bd. dirs. 1993-95, pub. rels. chair 1992-93, nominating com. 1995-96). Home: 838 Franklin St Westmont IL 60559-1211 Office: Hill and Knowlton Inc Ste 2100 900 N Michigan Ave Chicago IL 60611

SILLANPÄÄ, MIA CHRISTINE, publishing company executive, educator; b. Seattle, Mar. 21, 1966; d. Kauko Johannes and Tuula Marita (Passi) S. BSW, U. Wash., 1988; MS, Seattle Pacific U., 1992. Registered counselor, Wash. Clarinetist, Tacoma and Seattle, 1984—; pub., cons. MCS Pub., Tacoma, 1993—; instr. Pacific Luth. U., Tacoma, 1993—, Renton Tech. Coll., 1993—; tchr. Tacoma City Schs., 1993—. Contbg. author: Beyond Bad Times, 1994; author: Poetic Truths, 1995; editor Poetry By the Kids, 1995. Mem. exec. team staff City of Redmond, 1994. With U.S. Army, 1995-96. Recipient local awards for ceramics. Mem. NAFE (pres. Wash. State chpt. 1994-96), Nat. Assn. Tax Practitioners, Nat. Assn. Tchrs. Singing. Lutheran. Home and Office: 937 NW 56th St Seattle WA 98107

SILLMAN, CATHERINE ANN, information specialist; b. Meriden, Conn., Jan. 16, 1960; m. William Lee Lynch, Aug. 12, 1994. BA, U. Conn., 1981; MLS, San Jose State U., 1994. Chef, owner Country Fare, Palo Alto, Calif., 1986-95; reference libr. Stanford (Calif.) Grad. Sch. Bus., 1994-95; info. specialist Frost & Sullivan, Mountain View, Calif., 1995, Heidrick & Struggles, Menlo Park, Calif., 1996—. Author: Country Fare for City Folk, 1993. Mem. ALA, NAFE, Soc. Competitive Intelligence Profls., Spl. Librs. Assn., Assn. for Ind. Info. Profls. Office: Heidrick & Struggles 2740 Sand Hill Rd Menlo Park CA 94025

SILLS, BEVERLY (MRS. PETER B. GREENOUGH), performing arts organization executive, coloratura soprano; b. Bklyn., May 25, 1929; d. Morris and Sonia (Bahn) Silverman; m. Peter B. Greenough, 1956; children: Meredith, Peter B.; stepchildren: Lindley, Nancy, Diana. Grad. pub. schs.; student voice, Estelle Leibling; student piano, Paolo Gallico; student stagecraft, Desire Defrere; hon. doctorates, Harvard U., NYU, New Eng. Conservatory, Temple U. Gen. dir. N.Y.C. Opera, 1979-1989; pres. N.Y.C. Opera Bd., 1989-90; mng. dir. Met. Opera, N.Y.C., 1991-94; chairwoman Lincoln Ctr. for Performing Arts, Inc., N.Y.C., 1994—; Bd. dirs. Am. Express, Macy's, Time/Warner Comm., Met. Opera; cons. Nat. Coun. on Arts. Radio debut as Bubbles Silverman on Uncle Bob's Rainbow House, 1932; appeared on Major Bowes Capitol Family Hour, 1934-41, on Our Gal Sunday; toured with Shubert Tours, Charles Wagner Opera Co., 1950, 51; operatic debut Phila. Civic Opera, 1947; debut, N.Y.C. Opera Co. as Rosalinda in Die Fledermaus, 1955; debut San Francisco Opera, 1953; debut La Scala, Milan as Pamira in Siege of Corinth, 1969, Royal Opera, Covent Garden in Lucia di Lammermoor, London, 1971, Met. Opera, N.Y.C., 1975, Vienna State Opera, 1967, Teatro Fenice in La Traviata, Venice; appeared Teatro Colon, Buenos Aires; recital debut Paris, 1971, London Symphony Orch., 1971; appeared throughout U.S., Europe, S. Am. including Boston Symphony, Tanglewood Festival, 1968, 69, Robin Hood Dell, Phila., 1969; title roles in: Don Pasquale, Norma, Ballad of Baby Doe, Thais, La Traviata, Anna Bolena, Maria Stuarda, Lucia de Lammermoor, Barber of Seville, Manon, Louise, Tales of Hoffmann, Daughter of the Regiment, The Magic Flute, Elizabeth in Roberto Devereaux, I Puritana, Julius Caesar, Suor Angelica, Il Tabarro, Gianni Schicchi, Faust, La Loca, Merry Widow, Turk in Italy, Rigoletto, I Capuleti e I Montecchi, Lucrezia Borgia, Ariodante, Le Coq D'Or, others; recordings include The Art of Beverly Sills, Welcome to Vienna, Great Scores (with Placido Domingo); ret. from opera and concert stage, 1980; numerous TV spls; author: Bubbles-A Self-Portrait, 1976, autobiography Beverly, 1987. Chmn. bd. March of Dimes, nat. chmn. Mothers' March on Birth Defects. Recipient Handel medallion, 1973, Pearl S. Buck Women's award, 1979, Emmy award for Profiles in Music, 1976, Emmy award for Lifestyles with Beverly Sills, 1978, Medal of Freedom, 1980, Kennedy Ctr. Honors award. Office: care Edgar Vincent 157 W 57th St Ste 502 New York NY 10019*

SILVA, DENISE MULLEN, management accountant; b. Everett, Mass., June 25, 1952; d. Joseph F. and Rita I. (Savage) Mullen; m. Mark D. Schneider, Aug. 16, 1975 (div. July 1986); children: Derek D., Scott A.; m. John H. Silva, Aug. 31, 1991. AS in Bus. Adminstrn. and Mgmt., Mitchell Coll., 1988; BS in Fin. Acctg., U. New Haven, 1992. Office mgr. Embry & Neusner Attys. at Law, Groton, Conn., 1986-89; bookkeeper Mashantucket Pequot Indian Nation, Ledyard, Conn., 1989-92, staff acct., 1992-95, supr. fin. acctg. and auditing, 1995—; vol. host Prodigy Online Svc., N.Y., 1995. Mem. Inst. Mgmt. Accts. (cert.), Conn. Soc. CPAs (Merit award). Home: 170 Seneca Dr Noank CT 06340

SILVA, OMEGA LOGAN, physician; b. Washington, Dec. 14, 1936; d. Louis Jasper and Ruth (Dickerson) Logan; m. C. Francis A. Silva, Oct. 25, 1958 (div. 1981); 1 child, Frances Cecile; m. Harold Bryant Webb, Nov. 28, 1982. Grad., Howard U., Washington, 1958, MD, 1967. Bio-chemist NIH, Bethesda, Md., 1958-63; asst. chief endocrinology Vets. Affairs Med. Ctr., Washington, 1967-96; physician Mitchell-Trotman Med. Group, P.C., 1996—; assoc. prof. George Washington U., Washington, 1975-91, prof. 1991—; prof. Howard U., Washington, 1977—. Author: (with others) Endocrinology, 1990; contbr. articles to profl. jours. Charter mem. Nat. Mus. of Women in the Arts, Washington, 1986; health cons. River Pk. Mutual Homes, Inc., Washington, 1987; vol. Career Day Chillum Elem. Sch., Career Week, George Washington U., Washington, 1988; trustee Howard U., 1991—. Fellow ACP (Best Sci. Presentation award 1974); mem. Am. Chem. Soc., Am. Med. Women's Assn. (br. I v.p. 1986-87, pres. 1987-88, anti-smoking task force 1989—, chair govtl. affairs nominations com. 1992), Howard U. Med. Alumni (pres. 1983-88), Alpha Omega Alpha.

SILVA, STEPHANIE, special education educator; b. Pensacola, Fla., Sept. 2, 1954; d. Ralph James and Sarah Geraldyn (Goodnight) S. BA in Spl. Edn., U. West Fla., 1975, MA in Clin. Tchg., 1980. Tchr. Walton County Schs., DeFuniak Springs, Fla., 1984-88, Escambia County Schs., Pensacola, Fla., 1988—. Recipient Above and Beyond award SEDNET (Network for Severely Emotionally Disturbed), 1986. Mem. ASCD, NEA/Escambia Uniserv (collective bargaining team mem. 1988-91, membership chair 1991), Coun. for Exceptional Children, Kappa Delta Pi, Phi Delta Kappa (historian 1993—). Home: 2656 Stallion Rd Cantonment FL 32533-7549

SILVA, SYLVIA ANNE, higher education administrator; b. Las Vegas, Nev., Dec. 11, 1937; d. Enrique A. Silva and Faustina Flores; m. Peter Paul Lopez, 1954 (div. 1976); children: Peter John, Marie Anne, Henry Matthew, Vincent Martin, Renee Marie. BA in Social Welfare cum laude, Calif. State U., Chico, 1973, BA in Spanish, 1973, MA in Edn., 1981; EdD, U. San Francisco, 1991. Migrant edn. community aide, 1968-70; case aide counselor Mental Retardation Service, Chico, Calif., 1970-72, elem. sch. tchr., 1973-75; instr., lectr. Calif. State U., Chico, 1975-91, adminstrv. fellow, 1982-83; coordinator Upward Bound project, Chico, 1976-80, dir. student affirmative action, 1980-86; dir. edml. equity svcs. programs, 1986-89, dir. univ. outreach programs, univ. ednl. equity officer, 1991-95; assoc. vice provost for student affairs, dean of students Ariz. State U., West Phoenix, 1995—; lectr. cross-cultural awareness for counseling program Laverne U., 1984-90; past mem. adv. bd. Western Assn. Ednl. Opportunity Programs; keynote spkr., workshop presenter in field; cons. workshop for county sch. tchrs. and adminstrs., 1990-91; past mem. adv. bd. Ednl. Equity Svcs.; cons. on early childhood edn. Orcut Sch. Dist., Santa Monica, Calif., 1976; instr. Calif. C.C., 1988—; participant Nat. Assn. Student Svc. Profls. Symposium for Women Preparing to Become Sr. Student Affairs Officers. Chmn. student affirmative action adv. bd. Calif. Acad. Partnership Program; co-founder Hispanic Profl. Group; past mem. community adv. bd. Upward Bound; cons. Mendocino Nat. Forest, 1991. Recipient Steve Holman award Western Assn. Ednl. Opportunity, 1988, Outstanding Latina Alumni recognition award Calif. State U., 1992. Mem. Am. Assn. for Higher Edn. (Hispanic caucus), Nat. Assn. Student Affairs Pers., Nat. Assn. for Women in Edn., Hispanic Assn. for Comty. and Edn. (bd. dirs., past pres.), S.E. Asian Student Assn., Ariz. Hispanic C. of C., Phi Delta Kappa, Lambda Theta Nu (founding advisor). Democrat. Roman Catholic. Home: # 26 2516 W Eugie Ave Phoenix AZ 85029-1407

SILVANO, JUDI, vocalist, composer; b. Phila., May 8, 1951; d. Arthur and Miriam (Schwartz) Silverman; m. Joseph S. Lovano, Sept. 30, 1984. BS in Edn., Temple U., 1973. mem. internat. tours Universal Lang. and Symbiosis bands, 1969—; mem. St. Bartholomew's Choir, N.Y.C., 1992—; mem., guest composer Jazz Composer's Collective, N.Y.C., 1993—; vocalist Joe Lovano's Rush Hour (Grammy nomination, Album of Yr., Downbeat Mag. 1996); condr. Choir of Jewish Comty. Ctr., Paramus, N.J., 1990—; assoc., singer Robert Shaw Conducting Workshop, Carnegie Hall, N.Y.C., 1993-96; cmposer, guest Muhlenberg Coll. Dance Dept., Allentown, Pa., 1992—; dir. Silvano Music Pub., 1993. Composer 35 original mus. compositions and lyrics for chamber music and jazz, (CDs) Dancing Voices, 1992, Judi Silvano, 1996. Featured composer Greenwich House Mostly New Music Series, 1995. Mem. NARAS (voting mem.), BMI, Internat. Assn. Women Composers, N.Y. Women Composers. Home and Office: Silvano Music # 2 206 W 23d St New York NY 10011

SILVER, BARBARA OAKS, lawyer; b. Phila., Sept. 17, 1934; d. Samuel and Sara R. Berger; m. Martin Oaks (div. 1967); 1 child, Robert; m. Edward W. Silver, May 28, 1967. BA, U. Pa., 1956; JD, Temple U., 1969. Bar: Pa. 1969. Assoc. Mason & Ringe, Phila., 1969-71, Ewing & Cochen, Phila., 1971-72; ptnr. Silver & Silver, Phila., 1972-91, Astor Weiss Kaplan & Rosenblum, Phila., 1991—; prof. corp. law Paralegal Inst., Phila., 1973-85; lectr., seminar leader Inst. Awareness, Phila., 1975-85; frequent lectr. on family law and estate planning throughout ea. U.S. Mem. Pa. Bar Assn., Phila. Bar Assn., Phi Beta Kappa. Office: Astor Weiss Kaplan Et Al The Bellevue Ste 600 Philadelphia PA 19103

SILVER, BEVERLEY ANN, museum educator; b. N.Y.C., Oct. 30, 1950; d. Malcolm and Johanna (Stern) Moss; m. Michael Silver, May 16, 1971; children: Sabina, Joseph. BFA, Washington U., St. Louis, 1972, MA, 1976. Cert. tchr., Mo., Wash. Art tchr. Pkwy. North Sr. H.S., St. Louis, 1972-77, Midwest Coun. on Aging, St. Louis, 1978; art reviewer, feature writer Citizen Newspapers, St. Louis, 1980-81; visual arts writer St. Louis Weekly, 1983; art tchr. Solomon Schechter Day Sch., St. Louis, 1985-86; curatorial asst. to chief curator Bellevue (Wash.) Art Mus., 1987-89, coord. children's edn., 1989-92, coord. children/docent edn., 1992—; art methods instr. Maryville Coll., St. Louis, 1976; visual arts writer St. Louis Weekly, 1983; creator edn. program Designing for the Future, 1989-90; project mgr. computer program Jacob Lawrence & Gwendolyn Knight, 1993-94, Roger Shimomurai: An Artist's Japanese American Experience, 1996. Exec. producer: (video) Two Voices in Contemporary Sculpture, 1992-93, Patti Warashina: Inside the Studio of a Ceramic Sculptor, 1991. Com. mem. SMART (Support More Art) Bellevue Pub. Schs., 1991—; com. mem. Chinese Outreach program Seattle Art Mus., 1990; co-chmn. cultural arts and recreation com. City of Bellevue, 1989-90. Mem. Nat. Art Edn. Assn., Wash. Art Edn. Assn. (Mus. Art Educator of Yr. 1990-91), Washington Alliance for Arts Edn., Mus. Educators Puget Sound. Office: Bellevue Art Mus 301 Bellevue Sq Bellevue WA 98004-5000

SILVER, JOAN MICKLIN, film director, screenwriter; b. Omaha, May 24, 1935; d. Maurice David and Doris (Shoshone) Micklin; m. Raphael D. Silver, June 28, 1956; children: Dina, Marisa, Claudia. BA, Sarah Lawrence Coll., 1956. Writer, dir. (movies) Hester Street, 1975 (Writers Guild best screenplay nomination), Chilly Scenes of Winter, 1981, (TV film PBS) Bernice Bobs Her Hair starring Shelly Du Vall, 1975; dir. (TV films HBO) Finnegan, Begin Again with Robert Preston and Mary Tyler Moore, Parole Board, A Private Matter with Sissy Spacek and Aidan Quinn, (TV film Showtime) In The Presence of Mine Enemies, 1996, (films) Between the Lines, 1976, Crossing Delancey with Amy Irving, 1988, Loverboy, 1989, Stepkids, 1991; dir. stage plays and musicals including Album, Maybe I'm Doing It Wrong, Off-Broaday prodn. A...My Name is Alice; prod. On The Yard, (radio) Great Jewish Stories from Eastern Europe and Beyond, 1995. Office: Silverfilm Prodns Inc 510 Park Ave New York NY 10022-1105

SILVER, MARY WILCOX, oceanography educator; b. San Francisco, July 13, 1941; d. Philip E. and Mary C. (Kartes) Wilcox; children: Monica, Joel. BA in Zoology, U. Calif., Berkeley, 1963; PhD in Oceanography, U. Calif., La Jolla, 1971. Asst. prof. biology San Francisco State U., 1971-72;

prof. marine sci. U. Calif., Santa Cruz, 1972—, chmn. dept., 1992-95. Contbr. numerous articles on biol. oceanography to profl. jours. Grantee NSF, 1979—; recipient Bigelow medal, 1992. Mem. AAAS, Am. Soc. Limnology and Oceanography, Am. Phycological Soc. Office: U Calif Dept Marine Sci Santa Cruz CA 95064

SILVER, SANDRA, school system administrator; b. Boston, Jan. 27, 1953; d. Aaron Alexander Silver and Marcia (Rosenbaum) Parker. BS, Boston U., 1974; MEd, Fitchburg (Mass.) State Coll., 1975; CAGS, Northeastern U., Boston, 1979; PhD, U. Calif., Berkeley, 1986. Tchr. spl. needs resources Methuen (Mass.) Pub. Schs., 1974-77; specialist learning disabilities, reading Pembroke Acad., Suncook, N.H., 1977-78; tchr. moderate spl. needs Chelsea (Mass.) Pub. Schs., 1978-79; coord. child study SW & WC ECSU, Windom, Minn., 1979-81; instr. Peralta C.C., Oakland, Calif., 1983-85; asst. prof. Bemidji (Minn.) State U., 1985-88; prin. Bemidji Area Schs., 1988-94; dir. curriculum, instrn., evaluation Windham Pub. Schs., Willimantic, Conn., 1994—. Dist. chair United Way, Bemidji, 1989-90. Mem. ASCD (assoc.), Am. Assn. Sch. Administrs., Coun. for Exceptional Children, Minn. Assn. Elem. Prins. (exec. bd.), Phi Delta Kappa (exec. bd.), Pi Lambda Theta, Kappa Delta Pi. Office: Windham Pub Schs 355 High St Willimantic CT 06226

SILVERANDER, CAROL WEINSTOCK, manufacturing executive; b. San Francisco, July 19, 1946; d. Vernon A. and Kathleen (Taylor) Davison; m. D. Michael Romano, Apr. 4, 1971 (div. Mar. 1979); children: Michael G. Romano, Kimberly A. Romano; m. Ronald D. Weinstock, Jan. 12, 1984 (div.); m. Michael David Silverander, Dec. 28, 1995. BA in Edn., U. Ariz., 1964-70, grad. work, 1977-82; MS in Photography, Brooks Inst. Photography, 1982-84. Exhibits Shalom-Salaam Liese Communal Svcs. Bldg., Tucson, 1980; photographer Jews of Ethiopia, 1982, Nat. Jewish Community Rels. Adv. Coun., 1983, Jews of Ireland, 1985-87, Bet Hatefutsot Mus. of Diaspora, Tel Aviv, Israel, 1987-88, Westside Jewish Community Ctr., L.A., 1989, Irish Jewish Mus., Dublin, Ireland, 1992—; pres., owner EthnoGraphics Greeting Cards, 1987—. exec. bd., adv. com. Jewish Fedn. So. Ariz., 1979-82 chmn. Run for Soviet Jewry, 1983-84. Recipient Internat. Greeting Card awards, 1988, 91, 92, 93, 94, 95, Cmty. Svc. award Jewish Fedn. So. Ariz., 1981, Simon Rockower award for excellence in Jewish journalism, Excellence in Photography mag. category, 1992. Mem. Am. Soc. Media Photographers, Greeting Card Assn. (bd. dirs. 1994—). Office: 417 Santa Barbara St # B 7 Santa Barbara CA 93101-2348

SILVERMAN, CATHERINE SCLATER PARKER, history educator; b. Portland, Maine, Apr. 9, 1921; d. Elliott MacDonald and Laura Virginia (Montague) Parker; m. Joseph Silverman, June 26, 1953 (dec. 1988); children: Jane Hoskins, Fay Elizabeth. BA, Sweet Briar Coll., 1943; MA, CCNY, 1964; PhD, CUNY, 1972. Edit. asst. U.S. Office War Info., N.Y.C., 1944-46; edit. asst., asst. editor Transport Workers Union, N.Y.C., 1946-64; lectr. CCNY, 1964-66, CUNY, 1969-70; vis. prof. SUNY, Stony Brook, 1972-73; sr. field rep., dir. regulatory affairs, dir. federal contra N.Y. State Div. Human Rights, N.Y.C., 1972-87; adj. assoc. prof. CCNY, 1987-88, Mercer County C.C., Lawrenceville, N.Y., 1989—. Fellow Ctr. for Study of Human Rights, Columbia U., N.Y.C., 1985-86; NDEA fellow, 1966-68, AAUW fellow, 1967-68. Mem. Am. Hist. Assn., So. Hist. Assn., Orgn. Am. Historians. Democrat. Home: 276C Milford Ln Jamesburg NJ 08831

SILVERMAN, ELLEN-MARIE, speech and language pathologist; b. Milw., Oct. 12, 1942; d. Roy and Bettie (Schlaeger) Loebel; m. Feb. 5, 1967 (div.); 1 child, Catherine Bette. BS, U. Wis., Milw., 1964; MA, U. Iowa, 1967, PhD, 1970. Rsch. assoc. U. Ill., Urbana, 1969-71; asst. prof. speech pathology Marquette U., Milw., 1973-79; assoc. prof. speech pathology Marquette U., 1979-85; pvt. practice speech and lang. pathology, Milw., 1985—; owner, pres. The Speech Source, Inc. Contbr. articles to profl. jours., chpts. to books. Marquette U. grantee, 1982. Fellow Am. Speech, Hearing, Lang. Assn.; mem. Wis. Speech, Hearing, Lang. Assn., Sigma Xi.

SILVERMAN, FRANCINE TERRY, writer; b. N.Y.C., Apr. 24, 1943; d. Michael and Jeanne (Friedman) Scherr; m. Ronald Silverman, May 26, 1968; 1 child, Amy. BA, Coll. Mt. St. Vincent, 1980. Freelance writer, 1980—; with Gannett Newspapers, Yonkers, N.Y., 1985-90; staff reporter News Communications, Bronx, 1993—. Mem. N.Y. Press Club, Deadline Club, Women's Nat. Book Assn. (bd. dirs., newsletter editor 1995-96). Home and Office: 4455 Douglas Ave Riverdale NY 10471

SILVERMAN, MARCIA, public relations executive; b. Lexington, Ky., Dec. 4, 1943; d. Harry and Rebecca (Green) S.; m. Stephen Regenstreif, Mar. 13, 1977; 1 child, Jacob Anthony. AB in Polit. Sci., U. Pa., 1965, MA in Econs., 1966. Reporter Nat. Jour., Washington, 1969-72; pub. rels. exec. J. Walter Thompson, N.Y.C., 1979-80; pub. rels. exec. Ogilvy, Adams & Rinehart, Washington, 1981-95, pres., 1992-95. Bd. dirs. Washington Internat Sch., 1994-95, Mex. Am. Legal Def. & Edn. Fund, L.A., 1994-95, Women's Campaign Fund, Washington, 1993-94. Office: Ogilvy Adams & Rinehart 1901 L St NW Ste 300 Washington DC 20036

SILVER REGHEB, CORINNE ALLYN, artist; b. Glace Bay, N.S., Can., Oct. 21, 1940; d. Robert Douglas and Euphemia Nell (MacKinnon) Silver; m. Samir Mikhail Ragheb; children: Nawal Ellen, Jennifer Fiona, Christopher Samir, Paul Ian. RN, Montreal (Can.) Gen. Hosp., 1961; BAF, Ctr. for Creative Studies, Detroit, 1984; MFA, Wayne State U., 1992. Nurse newborn intensive care Montreal Children's Hosp., 1961; adj. instr. art Southfield (Mich.) Pub. Schs., 1985-86, Birmingham (Mich.) Cmty. House, 1986-87, Schoolcraft C.C., Livonia, Mich., 1988-93; adj. instr. printmaking workshop Macomb C.C., Mt. Clemens, Mich., fall 1993; mem. alumni bd. Ctr. for Creative Studies, Coll. of Art and Design, Detroit, 1993—. One-woman shows include Civic Ctr. Gallery, Southfield, 1987, Art Loft Gallery, Birmingham, 1990, Macomb C.C., 1993, Port Huron (Mich.) Mus., 1996; group shows include North Miami (Fla.) Mus. and Art Ctr., 1984, Tokyo Met. Mus., 1985, Il Ritorno Studio Art Ctrs. Internat., Florence, Italy, 1995, Studio Art Ctrs. Internat., Bowling Green, Ohio, 1995. Recipient 1st place printmaking finalist sculpture Steelcase Scholarship Competition, 1984, Hon. Mention Purdue U. Small Print Nat., 1984, Best of Show, Ann Arbor Art Assn., 1986, Outstanding Award of Merit, 33d Mid-Mich. Exhbn., 1991. Mem. Detroit Inst. Arts (graphic arts coun. 1972), Coll. Art Assn., Wayne State U. (alumni). Home: 1130 Oxford Rd Bloomfield Hills MI 48304 Studio: St Fredericks Studio 120 E Wide Track Pontiac MI 48342

SILVERS, ANITA, philosophy educator, strategic planner; b. N.Y.C., Nov. 1, 1940; d. Seymour Harry and Sarah (R.) S. BA, Sarah Lawrence Coll., N.Y.C., 1962; PhD, The Johns Hopkins U., Balt., 1967. Prof. Philosophy San Francisco State U., 1967—, strategic planner, 1995—; mem. Nat. Coun. For the Humanities, Washington D.C., 1980-87; mem. Calif. Coun. for the Humanities, San Francisco, 1979-83; exec. sec. Coun. for Philosophical Studies, College Park, Md., 1978-82. Author: (book) Puzzles About Art; contbr. articles to profl. jours. Recipient Calif. Disting. Humanist award Calif. Coun. for the Humanities, 1978, Equal Rights award Calif. Faculty Assn., 1989. Mem. Am. Philosophical Assn. (bd. dirs. 1982—), Am. Soc. for Aesthetics (trustee 1976-79, 87-90), Calif. Faculty Assn. (bd. dirs. 1993-95). Home: 15 Otsego San Francisco CA 94112 Office: San Francisco State U Dept Philosophy 1600 Holloway Ave San Francisco CA 94132-1722

SILVERS, SALLY, choreographer, performing company executive; b. Greeneville, Tenn., June 19, 1952; d. Herbert Ralston and Sara Elizabeth (Buchanan) S.; life ptnr. Bruce Erroll Andrews. BA in Dance and Polit. Sci., Antioch Coll., 1975. Artistic dir. Sally Silvers & Dancers, N.Y.C., 1980—; mem. faculty Leicester Poly., 1986, 87, 89, summer choreography project Bennington Coll., 1988-92, Chisenhale Dance Space, London, 1989, 91, Am. Dance Festival, Durham, N.C., 1990, 92; guest tchr. European Dance Devel. Ctr., Arnhem, The Netherlands, 1992—. Choreographer: Politics of the Body Microscope of Conduct, 1980, Social Movement, 1981, Connective Tissue, 1981, Less Time You Know Praxis, 1981, Don't No Do And This, 1981, Lack of Entrepreneurial Thrift, 1982, Celluloid Sally and Mr. E, 1982, Mutate, 1982, Being Red Enough, 1982, Disgusting, 1982, Bedtime at the Reformatory, 1982, Eat the Rich, 1982, They Can't Get It in the Shopping Cart, 1982, Blazing Forceps, 1982, And Find Out Why, 1983, Tips for Totalizers, 1983, Choose Your Weapons, 1984, And Find Out Why, 1984, Extend the Wish for Entire, 1985, No Best Better Way, 1985, Every All Which is Not Us, 1986, Swaps Ego Say So, 1986, Be Careful Now, You Know Sugar Melts in Water, 1987, Fact Confected, 1987, Both, Both, 1987, Tizzy Boost, 1988, Moebius, 1988, Whatever Ever, 1989, Get Tough, Sports and Divertissement, 1989, Flap, 1989, Swan's Crayon, 1989, Fanfare Tripwire, 1990, Harry Meets Sally, 1990, Along the Skid Mark of Recorded History, 1990, Matinee Double-You, 1991, Grand Guignol, 1991, Dash Dash Slang Plural Plus, 1992, The Bubble Cut, 1992, Vigilant Corsage, 1992, Oops Fact, 1992, Small Room, 1993, Exwhyzee, 1993, Elegy, 1993, Now That It Is Now, 1994, Give Em Enough Rope, 1994, Swoon Noir, 1994, Radio Rouge, 1995, Braceletizing, 1995, Hush Comet, 1995, Bite the Pillow, 1995 and others; filmmaker: Little Lieutenant, 1993 (Silver award), N.Y. Dance on Camera Festival; co-author: Resurgant New Writings By Women, 1992; contbr. articles to profl. jours. Grantee Nat. Endowment Arts, 1987, 89, 90, 91, Jerome Found., 1993, Meet the Composer N.Y. Found. for the Arts, 1995; Guggenheim Found. fellow, 1988. Mem. Segue Found. (bd. dirs. Segue Performance Space 1992—). Home: 303 E 8th St Apt 4F New York NY 10009-5212

SILVERSTEIN, BARBARA ANN, conductor, artistic director; b. Phila., July 24, 1947; d. Charles and Selma (Brenner) S.; m. Bernard J. Taylor II, Aug. 19, 1978. Student Bennington Coll., 1965-67; B.Mus., Phila. Coll. Performing Arts, 1970. Assoc. music dir. Suburban Opera Co., Chester, Pa., 1967-75; asst. condr. Toledo Opera Assn., 1975-76; asst. condr., coach Curtis Inst. Music, Phila., 1973-77; asst. condr. Phila. Lyric Opera, 1971-74, Des Moines Opera Festival, Indianola, Iowa, 1974-78; music dir., condr. Savoy Co., Phila., 1977-80, Miss. Opera, Jackson, 1979-82; artistic dir., condr. Pa. Opera Theater, Phila., 1976-93; guest condr. Anchorage Opera, 1982, Opera Del., Wilmington, 1981, 83, Utah Festival Opera Co., 1993—, Lyric Opera of Kansas City, 1995—. Recipient Alumni award U. of Arts, 1989, Wash. H.S., 1991, Greater Phila. Mem. Am. Fedn. Musicians, Music Fund Soc., Pa. Council on the Arts (adv. panel 1987-90) OPERA Am. (bd. dirs. 1987-93, exec. com. 1988-93) . Jewish. Avocations: scuba diving; reading. Office: 1217 Samson St 6th Fl Philadelphia PA 19107*

SILVERSTEIN, KARIN, broadcast executive. V.p. talent and creative devel. VH1, N.Y.C. Office: VH1 1515 Broadway 20th Fl New York NY 10036*

SILVERSTEIN, LINDA LEE, secondary school educator; b. Riverside, Calif., July 1, 1953; d. John Conrad and Libbie Lola (Slovak) Woodard; m. Jerry Silverstein, Mar. 24, 1983. BS in Secondary Sci. Edn., Ohio State U., 1976, BS in Zoology, 1976, MA in Ednl. Adminstrn., 1992. Cert. tchr., Ohio; cert. prin., adminstr., Ohio. Tchr. Hilliard (Ohio) City Schs., 1978—; lectr. Dimensions of Learning, Hilliard, 1993-95; edn. vol. Ohio Wildlife Ctr., Dublin, 1985—. Co-author: Human Growth: Guide to a Healthier Your, 1992. Grantee Ohio Dept. Edn., 1994-95; named Martha Holden Jennings scholar Ohio State U., 1983, Tchr. Leader Ctrl. Ohio Regional Profl. Devel. Ctr., 1992-93. Mem. ASCD, Nature Conservancy, Phi Delta Kappa. Republican. Presbyterian. Home: 93 Garden Rd Columbus OH 43214-2131

SILVERSTONE, ALICIA, actress; b. Calif., 1977. Stage debut in Carol's Eve at Met Theater, L.A.; starred in three Aerosmith videos, including Cryin'; appeared in feature films: The Crush, The Babysitter, True Crime, Le Nouveau Monde, Hideaway, Clueless; appeared in TV programs including Torch Song, Shattered Dreams, The Cool and the Crazy, The Wonder Years. Office: care Premiere Artists Agy 8899 Beverly Blvd Ste 102 Los Angeles CA 90048*

SILVESTRI, ANTOINETTE GRACE, secondary education educator; b. N.Y.C.; d. Onofrio and Grace (Colucci) De Dominicis; m. Gino Silvestri; children: Dawn Michelle, Erica Jean, Cynthia Ann. BBA, CCNY, 1966; MS in Edn., CUNY, 1970; sch. dist. adminstrn. profl. diploma, L.I. U., 1995. Lic. bus. edn. tchr., N.Y., N.Y.C. Tchr. bus. edn. William Cullen Bryant H.S., Long Island City, N.Y., 1968, Glen Cove (N.Y.) City Schs., 1982—. Ednl. liaison Glen Cove Beautification Com., 1986-90; mem. Mayor's Steering Com. City of Glen Cove, 1990-92, dist. dir. One to One Teens in Bus., 1994—. Mem. Distributive Edn. Clubs Am. (advisor Glen Cove chpt. 1988—), N.Y. State Distributive Edn. Clubs Am. (hon. life), Lions. Roman Catholic. Office: Glen Cove HS 150 Dosoris Ln Glen Cove NY 11542

SILVEY, ANITA LYNNE, editor; b. Bridgeport, Conn., Sept. 3, 1947; d. John Oscar and Juanita Lucille (McKitrick) S.; m. Bill Clark, 1988. BS in Edn., Ind. U., 1965-69; MA in Comm. Arts, U. Wis., 1970. Editorial asst. children's book dept. Little Brown and Co., Boston, 1970-71; asst. editor Horn Book Mag., Boston, 1971-75; mng. editor, founder New Boston Rev., 1975-76; mktg. mgr. children's books, libr. svcs. mgr. trade divsn. Houghton Mifflin, Boston, 1976-84; editor-in-chief Horn Book Mag., Boston, 1985-95; v.p., pub. Children's Books Houghton Mifflin Co., Boston, 1995—. Editor: Children's Books and Their Creators, 1995; contbr. articles to profl. jours. Named one of 70 Women Who Have Made a Difference, Women's Nat. Book Assn., 1987. Mem. ALA (chmn. children's librs., Laura Ingalls Wilder award 1987-89), Internat. Reading Assn. (mem. IRA Book award com. 1985-87), Assn. Am. Pubs. (libr. com.), New England Round Table (chmn. 1978-79). Office: Horn Book Mag 11 Beacon St Boston MA 02108-3002

SIMARD, PATRICIA GANNON, economic development finance specialist; b. Methuen, Mass., June 25, 1965; d. Richard Edward and Barbara Lee (Selden) Gannon; m. Thomas Joseph Simard, Sept. 1, 1990. BA, Coll. Holy Cross, 1987; MPA, Suffolk U., 1997. Mng. dir. adminstrn., dir. non-profit fin. Mass. Indsl. Fin. Agy., Boston, 1989-95, exec. dir., 1995; mng. dir. non-profit fin. Mass. Devel. Fin. Agy., Boston, 1996—. Mem. Nat. Mus. Women in the Arts. Office: Mass Devel Fin Agy 75 Federal St Boston MA 02110

SIMECKA, BETTY JEAN, convention and visitors bureau executive; b. Topeka, Apr. 15, 1935; d. William Bryan and Regina Marie (Rezac) S.; m. Alex Pappas, Jan. 15, 1956 (div. Apr. 1983); 1 child, Alex William. Student, Butler County Community Coll., 1983-85. Freelance writer and photographer L.A., also St. Marys, Kans., 1969-77; co-owner Creative Enterprises, El Dorado, Kans., 1977-83; coord. excursions into history Butler County Community Coll., El Dorado, 1983-84; dir. Hutchinson (Kans.) Conv. & Visitors Bur., 1984-85; dir. mktg. div. Exec. Mgmt., Inc., Wichita, 1985-87; exec. dir. Topeka Conv. and Visitors Bur., 1987-91, pres., CEO, 1991-96; pres. Internat. Connections, Inc., 1996—; dir. promotion El Dorado Thunderboat Races, 1977-78. Contbr. articles to jours. and mags.; columnist St. Marys Star, 1973-79. Pres. El Dorado Art Assn., 1984; chmn. Santa Fe Trail Bike Assn., Kans., 1988-90; co-dir. St. Marys Summer Track Festival, 1973-81; chmn. spl. events Mulvane Art Mus., 1990, sec., 1991-92; membership chmn., 1993-94, bd. dirs., 1995-96; bd. dirs. Topeka Civic Theater, 1991-96, co-chmn. spl. events, 1992; Kans. chmn. Russian Festival Com., 1992-93; vice-chmn. Kans. Film Commn., 1993-94, chmn., 1994; bd. dirs. Kans. Expoctr. Adv. Bd., 1990-96; pres. Kans. Internat. Mus., 1994-96. Recipient Kans. Gov.'s Tourism award Kans. Broadcaster's Assn., 1993, Disting. Svc. award City of Topeka, 1995, Hist. Ward Meade Disting. award Topeka Parks & Recreation Dept., 1995; named Kansan of Yr., Topeka Capitol-Jour., 1995, Sales and Mktg. Exec. of Yr., Internat. Soroptimists, Topeka chpt., 1995, Woman of Distinction, 1996. Mem. Nat. Tour Assn., Sales and Mktg. execs. (bd. dirs. 1991-92), Internat. Assn. Conv. and Visitors Burs. (co-chmn. rural tourism com. 1994), Am. Soc. Assn. Execs., Travel Industry Assn. Kans. (membership chmn. 1988-89, sec. 1990, pres. 1991-92, Outstanding Merit award 1994), St. Marys C. of C. (pres. 1975), I-70 Assn. (v.p. 1989, pres. 1990), Optimists (social sec. Topeka chpt. 1988-89). Republican. Methodist.

SIMKINS, SANDRA LEE, middle school educator; b. N.Y.C.; d. Charles and Ray (Abramowitz) Fox; m. Alan Bruce Simkins, May 28, 1967; 1 child, Andrea. BA, Queens Coll., 1965; MA in Human Svcs., Wilmington Grad. Sch., 1987. Cert. elem. educator, middle sch. educator, Del. Elem. tchr. Valley Stream (N.Y.) Sch. Dist., 1965-66, Abington (Pa.) Sch. Dist., 1966-68; tchr. math. Mt. Pleasant Sch. Dist., Wilmington, Del., 1968-74; tchr. computers Brandywine Sch. Dist., Wilmington, Del., 1976—; treas. Assn. for Computers in Edn., Newark, Del., 1987-89; coach Del. Math. League, Dover, 1990-92; proctor, sponsor Del. Computer Faire, Dover, 1990-92; workshop leader Brandywine Tech. Seminar, Wilmington, 1993; internet homepage Webmaster Talley Mid. Sch.; coord. NetDay 96, Del. Pres. Greenview Civic Assn., Wilmington, 1980; v.p. Citizens Action Com., Wilmington, 1990-91, Booster Club, Wilmington, 1991-92; chairperson Concord Prom Com., Wilmington, 1992. Named Del. State Tchr. of Yr., Chpt. I Parents Com., 1988; nominee Presdl. award for Tchrs. of Math., Dept. Pub. Instrn., 1992. Mem. NEA, Del. Edn. Assn., Brandywine Edn. Assn., Brandywine Dist. Tech. Com. Home: 3316 Cross Country Dr Wilmington DE 19810-3311 Office: Talley Middle Sch 1110 Cypress Rd Wilmington DE 19810-1908

SIMKO, HELEN MARY, school library media specialist; b. Trenton, N.J., Feb. 25, 1950; d. Matthew John and Helen Catherine Harbach; m. Thomas F. Simko, Oct. 13, 1973; children: Jesse Matthew, Ian Christopher. BS in Home Econs. Edn., Immaculata Coll., 1972; postgrad. Home Econs. Design, Drexl U., 1972; MLS, So. Conn. State U., 1993, 6th Yr. Degree in Ednl. Founds., 1996. Cert. tchr. Conn. libr. media specialist (provl.) Conn. Substitute tchr. Pub. Schs. of Litchfield, Sch. Dist. #6, Litchfield, Conn., 1988-89; spl. edn. asst. Ctr. Elem. Sch., Litchfield, 1989-93, Litchfield Intermediate Sch., 1993; sch. libr. media specialist Burr Elem. Sch., Hartford, Conn., 1993-94, Swift Jr. H.S., Oakville, Conn., 1994—; mem. student handbook revision com. Ctr. Sch., Litchfield, 1992-93, mission statement revision com., 1992-93, faculty adv. com., 1992-93; mem. Litchfield adv. com. on Quality Edn. and Diversity, 1994; mem. libr. media selection policy revision com. Watertown Bd. Edn., 1994; mem. tech. planning com. Watertown Pub. Schs., 1995—. Active mem. Civic Family Svcs., Litchfield, 1983-89, LWV, Litchfield, 1986-89. Mem. ALA, ASCD, Conn. Edn. Media Assn. (bd. dirs., mem. co-chair), Am. Assn. Sch. Librs., Kappa Omicron Phi, Beta Phi Mu. Roman Catholic. Home: 45 Baldwin Hill Rd Litchfield CT 06759-3305

SIMMONDS, RAE NICHOLS, musician, composer, educator; b. Lynn, Mass., Feb. 25, 1919; d. Raymond Edward and Abbie Iola (Spinney) Nichols; m. Carter Fillebrown, Jr., June 27, 1941 (div. May 15, 1971); children: Douglas C. (dec.), Richard A., Mary L., Donald E.; m. Ronald John Simmonds, Oct. 9, 1971 (dec. Nov. 1995). AA, Westbrook Coll., Portland, Maine, 1981; B in Music Performance summa cum laude, U. Maine, 1984; MS in Edn., U. So. Maine, 1989; PhD, Walden U., 1994. Founder, dir. Studio of Music/Children's Studio of Drama, Portsmouth, N.H., 1964-71, Studio of Music, Bromley, Eng., 1971-73, Bromley Children's Theatre, 1971-73, Oughterard Children's Theatre, County Galway, Ireland, 1973-74, Studio of Music, Portland, Maine, 1977—; resident playwright Children's Theatre of Maine, Portland, 1979-81; organist/choir dir. Stevens Ave. Congl. Ch., Portland, 1987-95; field faculty advisor Norwich U., Montpelier, Vt., 1995; field advisor grad. program Vt. Coll., Norwich U., 1995; cons./educator mus. tng. for disabled vets. VA, Portsmouth, N.H., 1966-69; show pianist and organist, mainland U.S.A., 1939-59, Hawaii, 1959-62, Rae Nichols Trio, 1962—. Author/composer children's musical: Shamrock Road, 1980 (Blue Stocking award 1980), Glooscap, 1980; author/composer original scripts and music: Cinderella, If I Were a Princess, Beauty and the Beast, Baba Yaga - A Russian Folk Tale, The Journey - Musical Bible Story, The Perfect Gift - A Christmas Legend; original stories set to music include: Heidi, A Little Princess, Tom Sawyer, Jungle Book, Treasure Island; compositions include: London Jazz Suite, Bitter Suite, Jazz Suite for Trio, Sea Dream, Easter (chorale), others. Recipient Am. Theatre Wing Svc. award, 1944, Pease AFB Svc. Club award, 1967, Bumpus award Westbrook Coll., 1980; Nat. Endowment for Arts grantee, 1969-70; Women's Lit. scholar, 1980, Westbrook scholar, 1980-81, Nason scholar, 1983; Kelaniya U. (Colombo, Sri Lanka) rsch. fellow, 1985-86. Mem. ASCAP, Musicians Assn. of Hawaii, Internat. League Women Composers, Music Tchrs. of Maine, Am. Guild of Organists, Music Tchrs. Nat. Assn., Internat. Alliance for Women in Music, Doctorate Assn. N.Y. Educators, Inc., Delta Omicron, Phi Kappa Phi. Democrat. Episcopalian. Home: Back Bay Tower 401 Cumberland Ave Apt 1004 Portland ME 04101-2875

SIMMONS, ADELE SMITH, foundation executive, former educator; b. Lake Forest, Ill., June 21, 1941; d. Hermon Dunlap and Ellen T. (Thorne) Smith; m. John L. Simmons; children—Ian, Erica, Kevin. BA in Social Studies with honors, Radcliffe Coll., 1963; PhD, Oxford U., Eng., 1969; LHD (hon.), Lake Forest Coll., 1976, Amherst Coll., 1977, Franklin Pierce Coll., 1978, U. Mass., 1978, Alverno Coll., 1982, Marlboro Coll., 1987, Smith Coll., 1988, Mt. Holyoke Coll., 1989, Am. U., 1992, Tufts U., 1994. Asst. prof. Tufts U., Boston, 1969-72; dean Jackson Coll., Medford, Mass., 1970-72; asst. prof. history, dean student affairs Princeton U., N.J., 1972-77; pres. Hampshire Coll., Amherst, Mass., 1977-89, John D. and Catherine T. MacArthur Found., Chgo., 1989—; bd. dirs. Marsh & McLennan, N.Y.C., 1st Chgo. Corp./NBD, Synergos, Union of Concerned Scientists; cons. Ford. Found., Stockholm Internat. Peace Rsch. Inst., Radcliffe Coll.; former corr. in Mauritius and Tunisia for N.Y. Times, The Economist; high level adv. bd. UN, 1993—. Co-author: (with Freeman, Dunkle, Blau) Exploitation from 9 to 5: Twentieth Century Fund Task Force Report on Working Women, 1975; author: Modern Mauritius, 1982; contbr. articles on edn. and pub. policy in The N.Y. Times, Christian Sci. Monitor, The Bulletin of Atomic Scientist, Harper's, The Atlantic Monthly and others. Commr. Pres.'s Commn. on World Hunger, Washington, 1978-80, Pres.'s Commn. on Environ. Quality, 1991-92; mem. Commn. Global Governance; trustee Carnegie Found. for Advancement Teaching, 1978-86; chair Mayor Richard Daily's Youth Devel. Task Force, 1993-95. Fellow Am. Acad. Arts and Scis.; mem. Phi Beta Kappa. Office: MacArthur Found 140 S Dearborn St Ste 1100 Chicago IL 60603-5202

SIMMONS, ANNE L., federal official; b. Spencer, Iowa, Jan. 4, 1964; d. Donald Lewis and Lois Amber (Blass) S. B in Spl. Studies, Cornell Coll., 1986. Intern for Congressman Berkley Bedell Washington, 1986; field staff Iowans for Clayton Hodgson, Sioux City, Iowa, 1986; exec. sec. Atomic Indsl. Forum, Bethesda, Md., 1986-87; staff asst. House Armed Svcs. Com., Washington, 1987; legis. asst. to Congressman Tim Johnson Washington, 1988-93; staff dir. gen. farms commodities subcom. House Agriculture Com., Washington, 1993, staff dir. environ., credit and rural devel. subcom., 1994, minority resource conservation rsch. and forestry subcom., 1995—. Music scholar Cornell Coll., 1982-86. Mem. Delta Phi Alpha. Democrat. Office: House Agriculture Com 1301 Longworth House Office Bldg Washington DC 20515

SIMMONS, ANTOINETTE ELIZABETH, auditor; b. Chgo., Jan. 9; d. Sterling and Dorethea (Bryan) S. BA, U. Calif., Santa Barbara, 1976; MA, Calif. State U., L.A., 1982. Tax auditor Calif. State Bd. Equalization, Culver City, 1982-92; assoc. tax auditor Calif. State Bd. Equalization, Sacramento, 1992-96, staff tax auditor, investigator, 1996—, employee adv. com. Mem. Delta Sigma Theta. Home: 6785 Alamar Way Elk Grove CA 95758

SIMMONS, BETTY JO, materiel manager; b. Caddo, Okla., Dec. 13, 1936; d. Robert Lee and Beatrice (Alexander) S.; m. Donald Sherrill Stauffer, Jan. 3, 1959 (div. 1963); m. Daniel Oliver Amos, Oct. 20, 1972 (div. 1975). BA, City Coll.; student, U. Calif. Drafting clk. PacBell, 1956-59, jr. civil engr. draftsperson, 1959-61, sr. civil engr. draftsperson, 1961-62, civil engr. draftsperson, 1962-82, EEO counselor, 1973-77, supr., civil engr. draftsperson, 1982-83, liaison cons. civil rights, 1983-87; project adminstr. pre-apprenticeship tng. program Caltrans, Compton, Calif., 1987-89; coord. govtl. affairs Caltran, L.A., 1989, chief facilities ops., 1989-93, dist. claims officer, 1993-94, dist. materiel mgr., 1994—; facilitator Govs. Commn. on the Status of Women, Fresno, Calif., 1980. Producer: Building a Future, 1988 (bronze Cindy award Assn. Visual Communicators). Bd. dirs. Morgan Canyon Inst. of Higher Learning, Fresno, 1978-82; fund raiser Hunger Project, L.A., Fresno, 1980—, Youth at Risk, L.A., 1986—. Recipient Excellence in Transp. Facilities award, 1993. Office: Caltrans 120 S Spring St Los Angeles CA 90012-3606

SIMMONS, CAROLINE THOMPSON, civic worker; b. Denver, Aug. 22, 1910; d. Huston and Caroline Margaret (Cordes) Thompson; m. John Farr Simmons, Nov. 11, 1936; children: John Farr (dec.), Huston T., Malcolm M. (dec.). AB, Bryn Mawr Coll., 1931; MA (hon.), Amherst Coll. Chmn. women's com. Corcoran Gallery Art, 1965-66; vice chmn. women's com. Smithsonian Assos., 1969-71; pres. Decatur House Council, 1963-71; mem. bd. Nat. Theatre, 1979-80; trustee Washington Opera, 1955-65; bd. dirs. Fgn. Student Svc. Coun., 1956-79; mem. Washington Home Bd., 1955-60; bd. dirs. Smithsonian Friends of Music, 1977-79; commr. Nat. Mus. Am. Art, 1979-89; mem. Folger com. Folger Shakespeare Libr., 1979-86, trustee emeritus, 1986—; mem. Washington bd. Am. Mus. in Britain, 1970-93; bd. dirs. Found. Preservation of Historic Georgetown, 1975-89; trustee Marpat Found., 1987—, Amherst Coll., 1979-81, Dacor-Bacon House Found., Phillips Collection, 1990—, Georgetown Presbyn. Ch., 1989-91; v.p. internat. coun. Mus. Modern Art, N.Y.C., 1964-90, emeritus trustee; bd. dirs. Alliance Francaise. Recipient award for eminent svc. Folger Shakespeare Libr., 1986. Mem. Soc. Women Geographers, Sulgrave Club, Chevy Chase Club. Address: 1508 Dumbarton Rock Ct NW Washington DC 20007-3048

SIMMONS, CORINNE, hotel executive; b. Washington, Sept. 19, 1940; d. John Malloy Shaw and Ruby Louise (Jordan) Mau; m. James E. Hammock, Apr. 30, 1962 (div. 1981); children: Michele Marie, James E. Jr.; m. Michael Simmons, Nov. 21, 1981. BS, SW Tex. State U., 1971. Supr. purchasing N.E. Sch. Dist., San Antonio, 1976-78; dir. purchasing LaQuinta Motor Inns, San Antonio, 1978-82; v.p. Econo Lodges Am., Inc., Norfolk, Va., 1982-84; sr. v.p. Econo Lodges Am., Inc., Charlotte, N.C., 1986—; v.p. Mariner Corp., Houston, 1984-85; pres. Hotel Furnishings, Santa Ana, Calif., 1985-86; cons. Va. Beach Sales Assn., 1986. Mem. Ad Hoc Mayoral Com., San Antonio; instr. Women's Self Help Group, San Antonio, 1980. Recipient Citizen Achiever award Jefferson Circle, 1987. Mem. Bus. and Profl. Women's Club, Sales and Mktg. Execs., Nat. Purchasing Execs., NAFE, Motel and Hotel Assn., NRA. Republican. Baptist. Office: Crown Group 143 Eric Dr Kirbyville MO 65679

SIMMONS, DEIDRE WARNER, performing company executive; b. Easton, Pa., May 11, 1955; d. Francis Joseph and Irene Carol (Burd) Mooney; m. Robert D. Jacobson, June 27, 1981 (div. Mar. 1989); m. William Richard Simmons, Aug. 18, 1990; children: Caitlin Dawn, Abigail Patricia, Samantha Irene. BA in Music, Montclair State Coll., 1978. Music tchr. Warren Hills Regional Sch., Washington, N.J., 1978-80; devel. dir. N.J. Shakespeare Festival, Madison, 1981-83; dir. contbns. Parent Found., Lancaster, Pa., 1983-86; exec. dir. Fulton Opera House, Lancaster, 1986—, capital campaign counsel, 1990-95; mem. adv. bd. Mellon Bank. Vice chmn. bd. dirs. Ind. Eye, Lancaster, 1986-89; mem. adv. com. Lancaster Cultural Coun., 1988—. Mem. Theatre Communications Group, League Hist. Theatres. Office: Fulton Opera House 12 N Prince St PO Box 1865 Lancaster PA 17603

SIMMONS, GLENDA GRACE, librarian, media specialist, secondary educator; b. LaGrange, Ga., May 23, 1939; d. Alvin Carnie and Dillie Irene (Boggs) Bridges; m. Robert Webb Simmons, Oct. 30, 1961 (div. May, 1993); children: Robert Patterson, Cynthia Joy, Anna Elizabeth. AB in English Lit., U. Ga., 1961; MEd, Media, W. Ga. Coll., 1992. Cert. tchr. Ga. in English edn. and media specialist. Media specialist Whitfield County Schs., Dalton, Ga., 1983-88, Murray County Schs., Chatsworth, Ga., 1990—. Mem. Profl. Assn. Ga. Educators (divsn. dir.), Lesche Literary Club, (publicity com. 1976), Phi Beta Kappa, Phi Kappa Phi, Delta Kappa Gamma. Presbyterian. Office: Murray County Schs Green Rd Chatsworth GA 30705

SIMMONS, JEAN, actress; b. London, Jan. 31, 1929; d. Charles and Winifred Ada (Lovel) S.; m. Stewart Granger, Dec. 20, 1950 (div. June 1960); 1 dau., Tracy; m. Richard Brooks, Nov. 1, 1960; 1 dau., Kate. Ed., Orange Hill Sch., Burnt Oak, London. Motion picture actress, appearing in English and Am. films including Great Expectations, 1946, Black Narcissus, 1947, Hamlet, 1948 (Acad. award nomination), Adam and Evelyn, 1949, The Actress, 1953, Young Bess, 1953, Guys and Dolls, 1956, The Big Country, 1958, Home Before Dark, 1958, Spartacus, 1960, Elmer Gantry, 1960, The Grass Is Greener, 1960, All the Way Home, 1963, Rough Night in Jericho, 1967, Divorce American Style, 1967, The Happy Ending, 1969 (Acad. award nomination), The Dawning, 1989; also theatre appearance A Little Night Music, Phila. and on tour, 1974; appeared in: TV mini-series The Dain Curse, 1978, A Small Killing, 1981, Valley of the Dolls, 1981, The Thornbirds, 1983 (Emmy award), North and South, 1985, North and South Book II, 1986; TV film: December Flower, 1987, The Legend of Lost Loves, 1988, Great Expectations, 1989; guest TV series Murder She Wrote, 1989, In the Heat of the Night, 1993; TV series Dark Shadows, 1991. Office: care Geoffrey Barr 9400 Readcrest Dr Beverly Hills CA 90210-2552 Office: Susan Smith & Assocs 121 N San Vicente Blvd Beverly Hills CA 90211-2303*

SIMMONS, JEAN ELIZABETH MARGARET (MRS. GLEN R. SIMMONS), chemistry educator; b. Cleve., Jan. 20, 1914; d. Frank Charles and Sarah Anne (Johnston) Saurwein; m. Glen R. Simmons, Nov. 14, 1935; children: Sally Anne, (Frank) Charles, James Fraser. B.A., Western Reserve U., 1933; Ph.D. (Stieglitz fellow 1935-37), U. Chgo., 1938. Faculty Barat Coll., Lake Forest, Ill., 1938-58; prof., chmn. dept. chemistry Barat Coll., 1948-58; faculty Upsala Coll., East Orange, N.J., 1959—; prof. Upsala Coll., 1963-84, prof. emeritus, 1984—, chmn. dept. chemistry, 1965-71, 74, 76-81, chmn. sci. curriculum study, Luth. Ch. Am. grantee, 1965-68, chmn. div. natural scis. and maths., 1965-69, asst. to pres., 1968-73, 78-86; Coordinator basic scis. Evang. Hosp. Sch. Nursing, Chgo., 1943-46; lectr. sci. topics; participant various White House Confs. Contbr. articles to pubis. in field. Troop leader Girl Scouts U.S.A., Wheaton, Ill., 1952-58, neighborhood chmn., 1956-57, dist. chmn., DuPage County, 1958; chmn. U. Chgo. Alumni Fund Dr., Wheaton, 1957, 58, Princeton, N.J., 1964, 65; mem. nursing adv. com. East Orange (N.J.) Gen. Hosp., 1963-73; pres. Virginia Gildersleeve Internat. Fund, 1975-81, bd. dirs., 1969-83, chmn. nominating com., 1985-87, oral history com., 1981, hon. mem., 1996. Recipient Lindback Found. award for disting. teaching, 1964; vis. fellow Princeton U., 1977. Fellow Am. Inst. Chemists, AAAS (council 1969-71); mem. Am. Chem. Soc., AAUW (br. treas. 1960-62, chmn. sci. topic 1963-65, state v.p. program 1964, nat. sci. topic implementation chmn. 1965, 66, state dir. 1967-68, 71-72, state pres. 1968-70, 50 Yr. Cert. 1989), Fedn. Orgns. Profl. Women (nat. pres. 1974-75), Internat. Fedn. Univ. Women (alt. del. for U.S. at conf. 1968, 77, 83, del. conf. 1974, ofcl. observer UN Conf. Vienna 1979, Nairobi 1981, convenor membership com. 1980-84, adv. bd. 1980—, oral history com. 1990), AAUP (charter, past chpt. pres.), Phi Beta Kappa (pres. North Jersey alumni assn. 1973-74), Sigma Xi, Sigma Delta Epsilon (nat. pres. 1970-71, dir. 1972-78, edn. liaison 1978-87, chmn. nom. 1986-87, hon., award sci. edn. 1989). Episcopalian. Home: 40 Balsam Ln Princeton NJ 08540-5327

SIMMONS, JOY LOUISE, activist; b. Torrington, Wyo., Sept. 9, 1946; d. Jack Mervin and Betty Case Thompson; foster parents William R. and Ruth Martin; m. Richard L. Simmons, Sept. 9, 1971; children: Cheleen L. Simmons-Morgan, Michael L. Grad. H.S., Cheyenne, Wyo. Cocktail waitress Las Vegas, Nev., 1967-78; casino dealer Laughlin, Nev., 1979-85; owner Trifles of Arizona, 1985-92. Author: This of Joy, Celestial Arts, 1975. Activist Civil Rights, Wyo, Colo., Nev., 1962—, Feminist Movement ERA, Comty. Action Against Rape, Nev., 1969—, Worker's Rights, Nev., 1985-87, Silicone, 1991-92, Anti-Nuke; spearheaded class action suit against Dow Chem. for liquid injections of silicone. Mem. ACLU, Common Cause, Halt, Pub. Citizen. Democrat. Home: 3129 Palo Verde Laughlin NV 89029

SIMMONS, LYNDA MERRILL MILLS, educational administrator; b. Salt Lake City, Aug. 31, 1940; d. Alanson Soper and Madeline Helene (Merrill) Mills; m. Mark Carl Simmons, Nov. 17, 1962; children: Lisa Lynn Simmons Morley, William Mark, Jennifer Louise, Robert Thomas. BS, U. Utah, 1961, MS, 1983. Cert. sch. adminstr., Utah. Tchr. Wasatch Jr. H.S./Granite Dist., Salt Lake City, 1961-64, Altamont (Utah) H.S./Duchesne Dist., 1964-66; tchr. spl. edn. Park City (Utah) H.S., 1971-73; resource tchr. Eisenhower Jr. H.S., Salt Lake City, 1979-88; tchr. specialist Granite Sch. Dist., Salt Lake City, 1985-90; asst. prin. Bennion Jr. H.S., Salt Lake City, 1990-93; prin. Hartvigsen Sch., Salt Lake City, 1993—; adj. prof. spl. edn. U. Utah, Salt Lake City, 1987—, Utah Prin. Acad., 1994-95, co-chair Utah Spl. Educators for Computer Tech., Salt Lake City, 1988-90; mem. adv. com. on handicapped Utah State Office Edn., 1990-93; presenter at confs. Author: Setting Up Effective Secondary Resource Program, 1985; contbr. articles to profl. publs. Dist. chmn. Heart Fund, Cancer Dr., Summit Park, Utah, 1970-82; cub pack leader Park City area Boy Scouts Am., 1976-80; bd. dirs. Jr. League Salt Lake City, 1977-80; cookie chmn. Park City area Girl Scouts U.S., 1981; dist. chmn. March of Dimes, 1982—. Recipient Amb. award Salt Lake Conv. and Vis. Bur., 1993. Mem. Nat. Assn. Secondary Sch. Prins., Park City Young Women's Mut. (pres. 1989-93, family history cons. 1993—), Women's Athanaeum (v.p. 1990-93, pres. 1994—), Coun. for Exceptional Children (pres. Salt Lake chpt. 1989-90, pres. Utah Fedn. 1991-93, Spl. Educator of Yr.), Granite Assn. Sch. Adminstrs. (sec.-treas. 1992-94). Mem. LDS Ch. Office: Hartrigsen Sch 350 E 3605 S Salt Lake City UT 84115

SIMMONS, MARGUERITE SAFFOLD, pharmaceutical sales professional; b. Montgomery, Ala., Oct. 21, 1954; d. Arthur Edward and Gwendolyn Jane (Saffold) S. BS in Communications, U. Tenn., 1976. Press sec. Met. Mayor's Office, Nashville, 1976-77; advt. copywriter United Meth. Pub. House, Nashville, 1977-78; sales rep. No Nonsense Pantyhose, Houston, 1978-81, Breon Labs., Houston, 1981-82; profl. sales rep. Janssen Pharmaceutica, Inc., Houston, 1982-88, sr. sales rep., 1988—. Vol. Dem. Nat. Conv., Atlanta, 1988. Named to Outstanding Young Women in Am., 1981, 87. Mem. NAFE, U. Tenn. Alumni Assn. (bd. dirs. Atlanta chpt. 1989-90), U. Tenn. Black Alumni Assn. (bd. dirs. Atlanta chpt. 1989—, pres.- elect bd. dirs. 1995), Ga. Trust Hist. Soc., Ala. Geneal. Soc., Ga. Geneal. Soc., Nat. Trust Hist. Preservation, Delta Sigma Theta. Baptist. Office: PO Box 16934 Atlanta GA 30321-0934

SIMMONS, MIRIAM QUINN, state legislator; b. Jackson, Miss., Mar. 28, 1928; d. Charles Buford and Viola (Hamill) Quinn; m. Willie Wronal Simmons, July 10, 1952; children: Dick, Sue, Wronal. BS, Miss. U. for Women, 1949. Tchr. Columbia (Miss.) City Schs., 1949-51, 53-54, literacy coord., 1986-87; home demonstration agt. Coop. Extension Svc., Bay Springs, Miss., 1951-52; tchr. Marion County Schs., Columbia, 1952-53, 54-55, Columbia Tng. Sch., 1961-63, Columbia Acad., 1970-73; rep. Miss. Ho. of Reps., Jackson, 1988—; adv. bd. Magnolia Fed. Bank for Savs; trustee State Inst. Higher Learning, Jackson, 1972-84; dir. Miss. Authority for Ednl. TV, Jackson, 1976-88. Named Marion County Outstanding Citizen Columbia Jr. Aux., 1981. Mem. Miss. Fedn. Women's Clubs, Bus. and Profl. Women's Club, Hilltop Garden Club, Delta Kappa Gamma. Democrat. Methodist. Home: 45 Old Highway 98 E Columbia MS 39429-8172

SIMMONS, ROBERTA JOHNSON, public relations firm executive; b. St. Louis, June 28, 1947; d. Robert Andrew and Thelma Josephine (Bunch) J.; m. Clifford Michael Simmons, Aug. 10, 1968; children: Andrew Park, Matthew Clay, Jordan Michael. BA, Ind. U., South Bend, 1972. Lic. real estate broker, Ind.; accredited pub. rels. practitioner; mem. Inst. Residential Mktg. Account exec., supr. Juhl Advt., Inc., Mishawaka, Ind., 1971-74, pub. rels. dir., 1974-79, v.p., 1979; v.p., pub. rels. dir. Juhl Advt., Inc., Mishawaka and Indpls., 1984-89; v.p. E.L. Yoder & Assocs., Inc., Granger, Ind., 1979-80; pres. Simmons Communications, Inc., Mishawaka, 1981-82; v.p., gen. mgr. Juhl Bldg. Communications, Inc., South Bend, 1983-84; sr. v.p. Wyse Advt., Inc., Indpls., 1989-90; v.p., pub. rels. dir. Caldwell VanRiper, Inc., Indpls., 1990—. Contbr. articles to profl. publs. Mem. pub. rels. com. Ind. Adult Literacy Coalition, Indpls., 1989; chairperson pub. rels. com. Crossroads of Am. coun. Boy Scouts Am., Indpls., 1990-91; dep. community info. com. Indpls. C. of C. Infrastructure Study, 1990-91. Mem. PRSA (accredited, mem. counsellors acad., Hoosier chpt. job bank com. 1993—), Nat. Sales Mktg. Coun. (trustee 1991-92), Inst. Residential Mktg. Mem. Christian Ch. (Disciples of Christ). Office: Caldwell VanRiper Inc 1314 N Meridian St Indianapolis IN 46202-2303

SIMMONS, RUTH J., academic administrator; b. Grapeland, Tex., 1945; 2 children. Student, Universidad Internacional, Saltillo, Mex., 1965, Wellesley Coll., 1965-66; BA, Dillard U., 1967; postgrad., Universite de Lyon, 1967-68, George Washington U., 1968-69; AM, Harvard U., 1970, PhD in Romance Langs., 1973; LLD (hon.), Amherst Coll., 1995; LHD (hon.), Howard U., 1996, Dillard U., 1996; LLD (hon.), Princeton U., 1996. Interpreter lang. svcs. divsn. U.S. Dept. State, Washington, 1968-69; instr. French George Washington U., 1968-69; admissions officer Radcliffe Coll., 1970-72; asst. prof. French U. New Orleans, 1973-75, asst. dean coll. liberal arts, asst. prof. French, 1975-76; adminstrv. coord. NEH liberal studies project Calif. State U., Northridge, 1977-78, acting dir. internat. programs, vis. assoc. prof. Pan-African studies, 1978-79; asst. dean grad. sch. U. So. Calif., 1979-82, assoc. dean grad. sch., 1982-83; dir. studies Butler Coll. Princeton (N.J.) U., 1983-85, acting. dir. Afro-Am. studies, 1985-87, asst. dean faculty, 1986-87, assoc. dean faculty, 1986-90, vice provost, 1992-95; provost Spelman Coll., 1990-91; pres. Smith Coll., Northampton, Mass., 1995—; peer reviewer higher edn. divsn. NEH, 1980-83, bd. cons., 1981; mem. grad. adv. bd. Calif. Student Aid Commn., 1981-83; chair com. to visit dept. African-Am. studies Harvard U., 1991 ; mem. strategic planning task force N.J. Dept. Higher Edn., 1992-93; mem. nat. adv. commn. EQUITY 2000, Coll. Bd., 1992-95; mem. adv. bd. ctrl. N.J. NAACP Legal Def. Fund, 1992-95; mem. Mid. States Assn. Accreditation Team, Johns Hopkins U., 1993; chair rev. panel for model instns. planning grants NSF, 1993. Mem. editl. bd. World Edn. series Am. Assc. Collegiate Registrars and Admissions Officers, 1984-86; contbr. articles to profl. jours.; presenter, speaker and panelist in field. Mem. adv. bd. N.J. Master Faculty program Woodrow Wilson Nat. Fellowship Found., m 1987-90, bd. trustees, 1991—. KYOK scholar, 1963; Worthing Found. scholar, 1963-67; Danforth fellow, 1967-73; Fulbright scholar U. de Lyon, 1967-68; Sr. Fulbright fellow, 1981; Rsch. grantee AACRAO, 1987-88; recipient Disting. Svc. award Assn. Black Princeton Alumni, 1989, Dillard U., 1992, Pres.'s Recognition award Bloomfield Coll., 1993, TWIN award Princeton Area YWCA, 1993, Women's Orgn. Tribute award Princeton U., 1994, Leadership award Third World Ctr. Princeton U., 1995, Tex. Excellence award Leap Program, 1995, Benjamin E. Mays award A Better Chance, 1995. Office: Smith College Office of the President Northampton MA 01063

SIMMONS, SHARON DIANNE, elementary education educator; b. Woodruff, S.C., Apr. 5, 1961; d. James Madison and Lucy Nell (Carlton) Crow; m. Wayne Roy Simmons, Mar. 29, 1986; children: Zachary, Luke. BA in Elem. Edn., U. S.C., 1983, M of Elem. Edn., 1987. Tchr. 3d grade M.S. Bailey Elem. Sch., Clinton, S.C., 1984-85, tchr. 4th grade, 1985-86; tchr. 5th grade Eastside Elem. Sch., Clinton, S.C., 1986-88, tchr. 4th & 5th grades, 1988-90, 91-92, tchr. 5th grade, 1990-91, tchr. 4th grade, 1993-95, tchr. 3rd grade, 1995—; pilot tchr. authentic assessment Eastside Elem. Sch., 1992—, mem. sch. libr. com., 1993—, tchr. chair 4th grade, 1993-94, tchr. grad. course authentic assessment, 1996. Pres. libr. coun. Spartanburg-Woodruff (S.C.) Br. Libr., 1993-95, v.p., 1995—. Recipient Ambassador award The Edn. Ctr., 1993-94. Mem. S.C. Math. Tchrs. Assn., Sch. Improvement Coun. Baptist. Home: 651 Parsons Rd Woodruff SC 29388-8700 Office: Eastside Elem Sch 103 Old Colony Rd Clinton SC 29325-5917

SIMMONS, SHARON RITCHEY, counselor; b. Aurora, Ill., Aug. 9, 1949; d. Harold Eugene and Margaret Marion (Eby) Ritchey; childrens: Shane C., Scott M. BA in Edn., Concordia U., 1972; MS in Counseling and Human Devel., Troy State U., 1996. Cert. elem. tchr., Fla.; cert. occupational specialist. Tchr. Grace Luth. Sch., Winter Haven, Fla., 1972-75; customer svc. rep. Commonwealth Corp., Tallahassee, 1975-76; tchr. Hartsfield Elem. Sch., Tallahassee, 1976-89; clin. supv. Rose Speech and Acad. Ctr., Tallahassee, 1989-91; alternative edn. tchr. Hartsfield Sch., Tallahassee, 1991-92; occupational specialist Adult and Cmty. Edn., Tallahassee, 1992—, counselor, 1994—; chair-elect, mem. Tchr. Edn. Ctr., Tallahassee, 1993—; coord. Adult Edn. Mentor Program, 1992—; mem. Ltd. English Proficiency Com., 1995—. Editl. columnist I Declare, 1995. Mem. St. Stephen Luth. Ch., 1985—. Named Vol. of Yr. Rickards H.S., 1986. Mem. ACA, Leon Classroom Tchrs. Assn., Occpl. Specialist Guidance Assn. Office: Leon County Schs Adult and Cmty Edn 283 Trojan Trail Tallahassee FL 32311

SIMMONS, SYLVIA (SYLVIA SIMMONS NEUMANN), advertising agency executive, author; b. N.Y.C.; BA, Bklyn. Coll.; MA in English Lit., Columbia U.; m. Hans H. Neumann, 1962. Dir. sales promotion and direct mail div. McCann Erickson, Inc., N.Y.C., 1958-62; v.p., asst. to pres. Young & Rubicam, Inc., N.Y.C., 1962-73; sr. v.p., dir. spl. projects Kenyon & Eckhardt, Inc., N.Y.C., 1975-86; sr. v.p., dir. corp. communications Bozell, Jacobs, Kenyon & Eckhardt, 1985-86, cons., 1986-88; free-lance speech writer and coach advt. cons., 1987—. Recipient Medal of Freedom, 1946, award for best radio comml. N.Y. Radio Broadcasters Assn., 1976-77, award for contbns. in direct mail promotions Sales Promotion Execs. Assn. Mem. Authors Guild, Propylaea, Sigma Tau Delta. Clubs: Advt. Women of N.Y. Author: New Speakers Handbook, 1972; The Great Garage Sale Book, 1982; (with Hans H. Neumann) The Straight Story on VD, 1974; Dr. Neumann's Guide to the New Sexually Transmitted Diseases, 1983; co-author (with Thomas D. Rees) More Than Just a Pretty Face, 1987, How To Be The Life Of The Podium, 1991; also articles.

SIMMONS, SYLVIA JEANNE QUARLES (MRS. HERBERT G. SIMMONS, JR.), university administrator, educator; b. Boston, May 8, 1935; d. Lorenzo Christopher and Margaret Mary (Thomas) Quarles; B.A., Manhattanville Coll., 1957; M.Ed., Boston Coll., 1962, PhD, 1990, DHL (hon.) St. Joseph's Coll., 1994; m. Herbert G. Simmons, Jr., Oct. 26, 1957; children: Stephen, Alison, Lisa. Montessori tchr. Charles River Park Nursery Sch., Boston, 1970-76; registrar Boston Coll. Sch. Mgmt., Chestnut Hill, Mass., 1966-70; dir. fin. aid Radcliffe Coll., Cambridge, Mass., 1970-75, assoc. dean admissions and fin. aid, 1972-75, assoc. dean admissions, fin. aid and women's edn., 1975; assoc. dean admissions and fin. aid Harvard and Radcliffe, from 1975; assoc. v.p. for acad. affairs, central adminstrn. U. Mass., Boston, 1976-79, spl. asst. to chancellor, 1979; v.p. field services Am. Student Assistance, 1982-84, sr. v.p., 1984-93, exec. v.p. 1993—; mem. faculty Harvard U., 1970-77; cons. Mass. Bd. Higher Edn., 1973-77. Bd. dirs. Rivers Country Day Sch., Weston, Mass., Simon's Rock Coll., Great Barrington, Mass., Wayland (Mass.) Fair Housing, Cambridge Mental Health Assn., Family Service Greater Boston, Concerts in Black and White, Mass. Higher Edn. Assistance Corp.; chmn. bd. dirs. North Shore Community Coll., 1986-88, mem. bd. dirs., 1985—; trustee and alumnae bd. dirs. Manhattanville Coll., 1986—. Mem. adv. com. Upward Bound, Chestnut Hill Boston Coll., 1972-74, Women in Politics Johm McCormack Inst., 1994—; Camp Chimney Corners, Becket, Mass., 1971-77; bd. dirs. Am. Cancer Soc., Mass., 1987-89, Boston Coll., 1990—, Merrimack Coll., 1992—, Mass. Found. for the Humanities, 1990-92, Mass. Bay United Way, 1990-94, Grimes King Found., 1992—, St. Elizabeta's Hosp., 1991; overseer Mt. Ida Coll., 1990—. Recipient Educator of the Year award Boston and Vicinity Club, 1989; named One of Ten Outstanding Young Leaders, Boston Jr. C. of C., 1971, Sojourner's Daughters: 25 African women who have made a difference, 1991; recipient Bicentennial medal Boston Coll., 1976; Achievement award Greater Boston YMCA, 1977, Human Rights award Mass. Tchrs. Assn., 1988, Pres'. award Mass Ednl. Opportunity Assn., 1988. Mem. Women in Politics, Nat. (exec. council 1973-75), Eastern (1st v.p. 1973) assns. financial aid officers, Coll. Scholarship Service Council, Links, (pres. local chpt. 1967-69), Nat. Inst. Fin. Aid Adminstrs. (dir. 1975-77), Jack and Jill Am. (pres. Newton chpt. 1972-74, Delta Sigma Theta, Delta Kappa Gamma (pres. 1988-90). Club: Manhattanville (pres. Boston 1966-68). Home: 3 Dean Rd Wayland MA 01778-5007 Office: 330 Stuart St Boston MA 02116-5229

SIMMS, AMY LANG, writer, educator; b. Bryn Mawr, Pa., Sept. 21, 1964; d. Eben Caldwell and Anna Mary L.; children: Harrison Lang, Maud Whittington. BA in French and Sociology, Bucknell U., 1986; postgrad., Sch. Museum of Fine Arts, 1988, Cambridge Ctr. Adult Edn., 1988, Bryn Mawr Coll., 1988, Vassar Coll., 1993, U. Pa., 1995—. Assoc. dir. pub. rels. Haverford (Pa.) Coll., 1995-96; copywriter, media and prodn. asst. DBM Assocs., Cambridge, Mass., 1986-88; teaching asst. sociology dept. Bucknell U., Lewisburg, Pa., 1989; staff reporter Lewisburg Daily Jour., 1989-92, asst. editor, 1991; asst. editor Milton (Pa.) Standard, 1991; co-founder, co-editor Lewisburg Holiday Herald, 1990; co-founder Environ. Advisor Newsletter, Lewisburg, 1990-91. Assoc. editor: Main Line Life; contbr. articles to profl. jours. Media corr. Elem. Related Arts Com., Lewisburg, 1989; mem. adv. bd. Union County Children and Youth Svcs., Lewisburg, 1991-92; trustee Sarah Hull Hallock Meml. Libr., Milton, N.Y., 1993-95. Recipient Hon. Speakers award Lewisburg Lions Club, 1990. Mem. AAUW. Home and Office: 606 Trowill Ln Wayne PA 19087

SIMMS, FRANCES BELL, elementary education educator; b. Salisbury, N.C., July 29, 1936; d. William Taft and Anne Elmira (Sink) Bell; m. Howard Homer Simms, June 24, 1966 (dec. Oct. 1993); 1 child, Shannon Lara. AB in English, U. N.C., 1958, MEd, U. Fla., 1962; postgrad., Boston U., 1963—, U. Va.; Queen's Coll., Cambridge, U.K. Playroom attendant dept. neurology Children's Hosp., Boston, 1958-60; reading clinician Mills Ctr., Inc., Ft. Lauderdale, Fla., 1960-61; reading/lang. arts tchr. Arlington (Va.) Pub. Schs., 1962—; adv. bd. mem. ad hoc com. Edn. Tech., Arlington, 1965-67; reading instr. Va. Poly. Inst. and State U., Arlington, 1974; prodr., dir. Barcroft Newsbag-CATV, Arlington, 1982—; chair self-study Elem. Sch., Arlington, 1987, 93; adv. bd. Reading is Fundamental of No. Va., Arlington, 1988—. Lay leader, choir mem. Cherrydale Meth. Ch., Arlington, 1976—; laborer Christmas in April, Arlington, 1990 ; tutor, vol. instr. Henderson Hall Marine Corps, Arlington, 1990—; organizer, instr. Better Beginnings, Arlington, 1994—, The Reading Connection, P.R., 1994—. Recipient Literacy award, Margaret McNamara award Reading is Fundamental of No. Va., 1994-95. Mem. Va. State Reading Assn. (mem. conf. coms.), Arlington Edn. Assn. (contbg. editor newsletter 1967-69), Greater Washington Reading Coun. (com. chairperson 1962—, Tchr. of Yr. 1995-96), Delta Kappa Gamma (Alpha Omicron former news writer, v.p., program chairperson, news editor). Home: 6110 23rd St N Arlington VA 22205-3414

SIMMS, KRISTINA MOORE, retired school counselor, author; b. Montezuma, Ga., Oct. 14, 1936; d. Sidney Leighton and Violet (Soderquist) Moore; m. James Carroll Simms (div. 1972); children: Claudia, Katherine Simms Bergwall. AB, Mercer U., 1956; MA, Stephen F. Austin State U., 1966. Counselor Macon County High Sch., Montezuma, Ga., 1976—. Author: Macon: Georgia's Central City, 1989, A Goose, A Goat, A Snow White Cat, 1994; author of poems. Democrat. Unitarian. Home: 710 Mason Terr Rd #40 Perry GA 31063

SIMMS, LAURIE ANN, vocational educational association administrator; b. Southampton, N.Y., July 17, 1958; d. Norman Monroe and Rita Onnellee (Boyer) Simms. BSW, Ashland U., 1980; M in Counseling Edn., Fla. Atlantic U., 1995. Cert. by Acad. of Cert. Baccalaureate Social Workers, cert. rehab. counselor. Edit dept. supr. Dept. Health and Rehabilitative Svcs., Riviera Beach, Fla., 1981-82, food stamp caseworker, 1983-84; food stamp supr. Dept. Health and Rehabilitative Svcs., Lakeworth, Fla., 1984-86, protective investigator, 1986-89; vocat. rehabilitation counselor Divsn. Vocat. Rehabilitation, Delray Beach, Fla., 1989-90; case mgr. Gulfstream Goodwill Industries, West Palm Beach, Fla., 1990-93, sr. case mgr., 1993-94, dir. vocat. programs, 1995—. Mem. Fla. Rehabilitation Assn. (pres. 1995—), West Palm Beach Profl. Jaycees. Democrat. Home: 431 Jupiter Lakes Blvd # 2110C Jupiter FL 33458 Office: Gulfstream Goodwill Ind 1715 Tiffany Dr E West Palm Beach FL 33407

SIMMS, LILLIAN MILLER, nursing educator; b. Detroit, Apr. 13, 1930; d. John Jacob and Mary Agnes (Knight) Miller; m. Richard James Simms, Feb. 2, 1952; children: Richard James Jr., Frederick William, Andrew Michael. BSN, U. Mich., 1952, MSN, 1966, PhD in Ednl. Gerontology, 1977. Program dir., assoc. prof. nursing health svcs. adminstrn. U. Mich., Ann Arbor, 1977-82, interim assoc. dir. nursing, asst. dean clin. affairs, 1981-82, assoc. prof. nursing adminstrn. and health gerontology, 1982-90, assoc. prof. nursing, 1990—; prof. emeritus, 1995; spkr., presenter in field; mem. spl. study sect. NIH, 1986; mem. adv. com., panel of judges for inquiry and practice of nursing svc. adminstr. Intra and Interdisciplinary Inviational Conf., 1990; series editor Delmar Pubs., Inc., 1991-93; mem. med. delegation People to People Citizen Amb. Program, Australia and New Zealand, 1982, People's Republic of China, Hong Kong and Korea, 1989; dir. China project that developed acad. relationships with schs. of nursing in People's Republic of China, 1991-94. Developer nursing concept of work excitement; co-author: Administracion de Servicios de Enfermeria, 1986, A Guide to Redesigning Nursing Practice Patterns, 1992, The Professional Practice of Nursing Administration, 2d edit., 1994; contbr. numerous articles to profl. publs.; reviewer for various publs. in field. Bd. dirs. Domino House Sr. Ctr., Ann Arbor, 1990—. Recipient Excellence in Nursing Edn. award Rho chpt. Sigma Theta Tau, 1995; grantee U. Mich., 1983-84, 84-87, 87-88, Presdl. Initiatives, 1990-92, W.K. Kellogg Found., 1991-93. Fellow Am. Acad. Nursing; mem. ANA, Am. Orgn. Nurse Execs., Midwest Nursing Rsch. Soc., Coun. on Grad. Edn. for Adminstrn. in Nursing (sec. 1986-88, chair publs. com. 1988-89), U. Mich. Nursing Alumni Assn., Sigma Theta Tau. Home: 1329 Wines Dr Ann Arbor MI 48103-2543 Office: U Mich Sch Nursing 400 N Ingalls St Rm 2174 Ann Arbor MI 48109-0482

SIMMS, MARIA ESTER, health services administrator; b. Bahia Blanca, Argentina; came to U.S., 1963; d. Jose and Esther (Guays) Barberio Esandi; m. Michael Simms, July 15, 1973 (Aug. 1993); children: Michelle Bonnie Lee Carla, Michael London Valentine, Matthew Brandon. Degree medicine, Facultad del Centenario, Rosario, Argentina, 1962; Physician Asst. Cert. (hon.), U. So. Calif., 1977. Medical diplomate. Pres. Midtown Svcs. Inc., L.A., 1973—. Chmn. bd. Am.'s Film Inst., Washington; chmn. bd. trustees World Film Inst. Nominated chairwoman of bd. trustees World Film Inst.

Fellow Am. Acad. Physicians' Assts.; mem. Bus. for Law Enforcement (northeast divsn.), Physicians for Social Responsibility, Mercy Crusade Inc., Internat. Found. for Survival Rsch., Noetic Scis. Soc., Inst. Noetic Scis., So. Calif. Alliance for Survival, Supreme Emblem Club of U.S., Order Eastern Star, Flying Samaritans, Shriners.

SIMON, CARLY, singer, composer, author; b. N.Y.C., June 25, 1945; d. Richard S.; m. James Taylor, 1972 (div. 1983); children: Sarah Maria, Benjamin Simon; m. James Hart, Dec. 23, 1987. Studied with Pete Seeger. Singer, composer, rec. artist, 1971—. Appeared in film No Nukes, 1980; albums include Carly Simon, 1971, Anticipation, 1972, No Secrets, 1973, Hotcakes, 1974, Playing Possum, 1975, The Best of Carly Simon, 1975, Another Passenger, 1976, Boys in the Trees, 1978, Spy, 1979, Come Upstairs, 1980, Torch, 1981, Hello Big Man, 1983, Spoiled Girl, 1985, Coming Around Again, 1987, Greatest Hits Live, 1988, My Romance, 1990, Have You Seen Me Lately?, 1990, Carly Simon, This Is My Life, 1992, Letters Never Sent, 1994; single records: Nobody Does It Better, 1977, Let the River Run, 1988 (Academy award best original song, 1989), (with Frank Sinatra) In the Wee Small Hours of the Morning, 1993; recipient Grammy award as best new artist 1971; TV appearance: Carly in Concert: My Romance, 1990; author: Amy the Dancing Bear, 1988, The Boy of the Bells, 1990, The Fisherman's Song, 1991, The Nightime Chauffeur, 1993; created opera Romulus Hunt, 1993. *

SIMON, CATHY JENSEN, architect; b. L.A., Sept. 30, 1943; d. Bernard Everett and Bitten Hanne (Smith) S.; m. Michael Palmer, Nov. 23, 1972; 1 child, Sarah Marina. B.A. Wellesley Coll., 1965; M. Arch., Harvard U., 1969. Registered architect, Calif. 1974, N.Y. 1988, Mass. 1988, Colo. 1995, Ariz. 1996. Architect Cambridge 7 Assocs., Mass., 1968-69, Building Systems Devel., San Francisco, 1970-72, Mackinlay Winnacker McNeil, Oakland, Calif., 1973-74; prin. Marquis Assocs., San Francisco, 1974-85; prin. Simon Martin-Vegue Winkelstein Moris, 1985—; sr. lectr. architecture U. Calif., Berkeley, 1982-85, vis. lectr., 1973-82; teaching coordinator Women's Sch. Planning and Arch., Santa Cruz, Calif., 1976; speaker ALA Nat. Conv., 1992, Les Grandes Bibliotheques de L'Avenin, Paris, 1991. Prin. works include Yerba Buena Gardens Retail and Entertainment Complex, San Francisco, Mus. N.Mex. Master Plan, Santa Fe, San Francisco Ballet Pavilion, Lick Wilmerding High Sch. Master Plan, San Francisco, Bothell Br. Campus, Bothell, Wash., San Francisco New Main Libr., Oceanside Water Pollution Control Project, San Francisco, Newport Beach (Calif.) Ctrl. Libr., Coll. 8 U. Calif., Santa Cruz, Olin Humanities Bldg. Bard Coll., N.Y., San Francisco Day Sch., Fremont (Calif.) Main Libr., Peter J. Shields Libr. U. Calif., Davis, Elena Baskin Visual Art Studios U. Calif., Santa Cruz, Primate Discovery Ctr., San Francisco Zoo, Braun Music Ctr., Stanford U. The Premier, La Jolla Colony, La Jolla, Calif. Mem. exec. com. San Francisco Mus. Modern Art; active Leadership Commn. Design Industry; mem. tech. assistance com., San Francisco Redevel. Agy., San Francisco, 1982—; mem. adv. panel Calif. Bd. Archtl. Examiners; bd. dirs. Golden Gate Nat. Park Assn. Recipient Calif. Preservation award Chambord Apartments, 1984, Adaptive Re-use award Engr. Offices, Am. Soc. Interior Designer, 1982, Commodore Sloat Sch. Honor award Nat. Sch. Bds. Assocs., 1980, Marcus Foster Mid. Sch. Honor award East Bay AIA, 1980; NEA grantee 1983. Mem. Orgn. Women Architects (founding 1972), San Francisco chpt. AIA, AIA (jury mem. nat. honor awards 1980, Los Angeles chpt. awards jury 1984). Home: 265 Jersey St San Francisco CA 94114-3822 Office: Simon Martin-Vegue Winkelstein Moris 501 2nd St # 701 San Francisco CA 94107-1431

SIMON, DOLORES DALY, copy editor; b. San Francisco, Nov. 18, 1928; d. Francis Edward and Jeannette (Cooke) Daly; m. Sidney Blair Simon, Aug. 24, 1952 (div. Nov. 1955); children: John Roderick, Douglas Brian. BA in Journalism, Pa. State U., 1950. County editor Centre Daily Times, State College, Pa., 1950-51; soc. editor Bradford (Pa.) Era, 1951-52; copy editor Harper & Bros., Pubs., N.Y.C., 1955-60; copy chief Harper & Row, Pubs., N.Y.C., 1960-88; freelance editor, copy editor Warwick, N.Y., 1988—. Co-author: Recipes into Type, 1993 (Best Food Reference 1994). Mem. James Beard Found., Phi Mu. Democrat. Office: Editl Svcs 63 Blooms Corners Rd Warwick NY 10990

SIMON, DORIS MARIE TYLER, nurse; b. Akron, Ohio, Jan. 24, 1932; d. Gabriel James and Nannie Eliza (Harris) Tyler; m. Matthew Hamilton Simon, Apr. 20, 1952; children: Matthew Derek, Denise Nanette, Gayle Machele, Doris Elizabeth. ADN, El Paso (Tex.) Coll. Media, 1969, El Paso Community Coll., 1976; BSPA in Health Care Adminstrn., St. Joseph's Coll., North Windham, Maine, 1991. RN, Tex. Med. asst. Dr. Melvin Farris, Akron, 1962-63, Dr. Samuel Watt, Akron, 1967-68, Drs. May, Fox and Buchwald, El Paso, 1972-76; head nurse, home dialysis and transplant coord. Hotel Dieu Med. Ctr., El Paso, 1977-87; nurse mgr., transplant coord. Providence Meml. Hosp., El Paso, 1987-94, nurse clinician neurology, 1994-96; transplant coord. Sierra Med. Ctr., El Paso, 1996—; med. asst. instr. Bryman Sch. Med. Assts., El Paso, 1970-72. Youth choir dir. Ft. Sill, Okla., 1964-67; choir dir. Ft. Sill area and Ft. Bliss, Tex., 1964-74; instr. in piano and music theory, Ft. Sill, 1964-67; leader Ft. Sill coun. Girl Scouts U.S., 1965-67; instr. Sch. for Handicapped, Lawton, Okla., 1965-67; nephrology nurse del. to People's Republic China Citizen Amb. Program, People to People Internat., 1988, to Russia and the Baltics Citizen Amb. Group Project Asst. Healthcare, 1992. Recipient Molly Pitcher award U.S. Army, 1963-67, Martin Luther King Jr. Share a Dream Svc. award, 1993, Delta Sigma Theta Outstanding Profl. of 1993 award; named One of 12 Outstanding Personalities of El Paso El Paso Times, 1993. Mem. ANA, Am. Med. Assts. Assn., Am. Nephrology Nurses Assn., Les Charmantes (Akron) (pres./sec. 1950-52), Links Inc. (pres. El Paso chpt. 1992—), Interclub Coun. (pres. 1992—), Donor Awareness Coalition 1992—. Baptist. Home: 8909 Parkland Dr El Paso TX 79925-4012 Office: Transplant Dept Sierra Med Ctr 1625 Medical Center Dr El Paso TX 79902

SIMON, EILEEN NUGENT, lawyer; b. N.Y.C., 1953. AB, Cornell U., 1975; JD, Bklyn. Law Sch., 1978. Bar: N.J. 1978, N.Y. 1979. Ptnr. Skadden Arps Slate Meagher & Flom, N.Y.C. Office: Skadden Arps Slate Meagher & Flom 919 3rd Ave New York NY 10022*

SIMON, FRANCOISE LOUISE, management consultant, researcher, educator; b. Cordemais, Loire, France, Dec. 27, 1946; came to U.S., 1969; d. Louis Joseph and Yvonne (David) S.; m. Vibert A. Miller, Dec. 29, 1975 (div. Apr. 1985). BA, Universite de Nantes, France, 1968, MA, 1969; MBA, Northwestern U., 1983; PhD, Yale U., 1980. Instr. Wellesley (Mass.) Coll./MIT, 1975-78; asst. prof. Northwestern U., Evanston, Ill., 1978-81; new product mgr. Abbott Labs., North Chicago, Ill., 1983-84; mgr. Cresap, McCormick & Paget, N.Y.C., 1985-86; prin. Ernst & Young, N.Y.C., 1986-89; dir. Arthur D. Little, Cambridge, Mass., 1990-91; prof. Columbia Bus. Sch., 1991—. Author: Europe and Latin America in the World Economy, 1995; contbr. articles to profl. jours. Yale U. fellow, 1985-86; grantee Northwestern U., 1980. Mem. Coun. on Fgn. Rels., Planning Forum, Strategic Mgmt. Soc. Roman Catholic. Office: Columbia Bus Sch 505 Oris Hall New York NY 10027

SIMON, JACQUELINE ALBERT, political scientist, journalist; b. N.Y.C.; d. Louis and Rose (Axelroad) Albert; m. Pierre Simon; children: Lisette, Orville. BA cum laude, NYU, MA, 1972, PhD, 1977. Adj. asst. prof. Southampton Coll., 1977-79; mng. editor Point of Contact, N.Y.C., 1975-76; assoc. editor, U.S. bur. chief Politique Internationale, Paris, 1979—; sr. resident scholar Inst. French Studies, NYU, 1980—, asst. prof. govt., 1982-83; assoc. Inst. on the Media for War and Peace; frequent appearances French TV and radio. Contbg. editor Harper's, 1984-92; contbr. numerous articles to French mags., revs., books on internat. affairs. Bd. dirs. Fresh Air Fund, 1984—. Mem. Women's Fgn. Policy Group, Overseas Press Club (bd. govs.), CWG (v.p.), Phi Beta Kappa. Home: 988 5th Ave New York NY 10021-0143

SIMON, JAMI LEA, actress; b. Ames, Iowa, Apr. 19, 1958; d. James Marvin and Letha Jane (Spillers) S. BA in Theater, BS in Dance, Iowa State U., 1981; MS in Dance, Ill. State U., 1983. Basketball pub. address announcer Ames, 1976-81, TV and radio spokesperson for theater and dance events, 1976-81; grad. teaching asst. Ill. State U., Normal, 1981-82; children's dance tchr., Ames, 1981, N.Y.C., 1992; co-founder Footfalls Dance Concert, Ames, 1979; choreographer various dance concerts, Ames, Normal, 1976-82. Appeared in TV shows including Ryan's Hope, Guiding Light, Reading Rainbow, 1983—; appeared in films including Teen TV Terrorist, The Oracle, 1983—; appeared in off-Broadway and children's theater prodns., music videos, commls., 1983—; author: Episodes and Other Works, 1982, (play) Like a Poet's Dream, 1993; contbr. feature stories to newspapers. Active Univ./Student/City Commn., Ames, 1976; vol. blood drive ARC, Ames, 1975-77; com. mem., co-chair Muscular Dystrophy Assn. Dance-a-thon, Ames, 1976-81. Recipient Achievement award in Writing Nat. Coun. Tchrs. English, 1975, Citizenship award Soroptimists Soc., 1976, Honorary Stars and Bars Internat. Thespian Soc., 1976, Bronze medal in social dance Brigham Young U., 1981, Writers Digest Honorable mention for playwriting, 1995. Mem. SAG, Actors Equity Assn., AFTRA, Phi Eta Sigma.

SIMON, JEANNE HURLEY, federal commissioner; m. Paul Simon; 2 children. BA, Barat Coll.; JD, Northwestern U. Legis. analyst Nat. Adv. Coun. Women's Ednl. Programs; mem. Ill. Gen. Assembly; chair Nat. Commn. Librs. and Info. Sci., Washington, 1993—; cons. women's initiative Am. Assn. Ret. Persons, Nat. Security Archive, Emeritus Found.; mem. adv. com. White Ho. Conf. Libr. and Info. Svcs., 1979. Mem. ALA, AAUW, LWV, Ill. Bar Assn., Women's Bar Assn., D.C. Bar Assn., Chgo. Bar Assn. Office: Nat Comm on Libraries 1110 Vermont Ave NW Ste 820 Washington DC 20005-3522

SIMON, JO ANN (JOANNA CAMPBELL), novelist; b. Norwalk, Conn., Nov. 2, 1946; d. Charles Lester and Josephine Fredrika (Berglund) Haessig; m. Kenneth William Campbell, Dec. 27, 1969 (div. 1976); children: Kimberly Ann, Kenneth William Jr.; m. Richard M. Simon (div. Jan. 1980); m. Ian R. Bruce, May 16, 1988. Student, Norwalk (Conn.) Cmty. Coll., 1964-65. Asst. to v.p. Hanson & Orth, Inc., Darien, Conn., 1972-81; owner, proprietor Time & Again Antiques, Rockport, Maine, 1983-85. Author: Love One in Passing, 1981, Thoroughbred, 1981, Hold Fast to Love, 1982 (West Coast Rev. of Books bronze Porgi), Secret Identity, 1982, Love Once Again (Romantic Times Best Time Travel Novel 1983), Love Notes, 19:3, The Caitlin Trilogy, 1984-85, Beloved Captain, 1988, Palm Beach Prep series, Bible and six outlines, 1988, A Horse of Her Own, 1988, Star, 1989, The Wild Mustang, 1989 (Maude Lovelace award), The Thoroughbred Series Books 1-4, 1991, Battlecry Forever!, 1992, Star of Shadowbrook Farm, 1992, The Thoroughbread Series Books 5-8, 1993, Books 9-13, 1994, Super Edits. 1, 2, 1995, Book 14, 1995. Active Environ. Def. Fund, Hopebuilders-Habitat for Humanity. Named Best Time Travel Novelist, Romantic Times, N.Y.C., 1984. Mem. AAUW, NOW, Romance Writers Am. (bd. dirs. 1982-84). Democrat. Home and Office: PO Box 426 43 John St Camden ME 04843

SIMON, KAREN MICHELE, clinical psychologist, educator; b. L.A., Nov. 18, 1953; d. Herbert and Miriam (Romanovsky) S. BA with honors, UCLA, 1975; PhD, Stanford U., 1979. Asst. prof. psychology U. Notre Dame, South Bend, Ind., 1979-81; postdoctoral fellow U. Pa., Phila., 1981-82; clin. asst. prof. Hahnemann U., Phila., 1984-87; clin. assoc. U. Pa., Phila., 1985-88, clin. asst. prof., 1988-92; dir. cognitive therapy CPC Santa Ana (Calif.) Hosp., 1992-93; dir. clin. ops. Ctr. for Cognitive Therapy, Newport Beach, Calif., 1993—; vis. asst. prof. Stanford U., 1980; cons., workshop leader Phila., 1982-92; cons. to numerous profl. jours. Co-author: Clinical Applications of Cognitive Therapy, 1990, Cognitive Therapy of Personality Disorders, 1990; co-editor: Depression in the Family, 1986, Comprehensive Handbook of Cognitive Therapy, 1989; contbr. articles to sci. and profl. jours. Mem. Am. Psychol. Assn., Assn. for Advancement of Behavior Therapy, Internat. Assn. Cognitive Psychotherapy, Calif. Psychol. Assn., Pi Gamma Mu. Office: Ctr for Cognitive Therapy 1101 Dove St Ste 240 Newport Beach CA 92660

SIMON, LOU ANNA KIMSEY, academic administrator. Provost Coll. Human Medicine Mich. State U. Office: Mich State U A-110 East Fee Hail East Lansing MI 48824*

SIMON, MARILYN WEINTRAUB, art educator, sculptor; b. Chgo., Aug. 25, 1927; d. William and Caroline Mabel (Bergman) Weintraub; m. Walter E. Simon, Mar. 19, 1950 (div. Sept. 1990); children: Nina Fay Simon-Rosenthal, Jacob Aaron, Maurine Joy Simon Rubinstein, Linda Gay Simon Shapiro. PhB, U. Chgo., 1947; MEd, Temple U., 1969. Cert. tchr., Pa. Bd. sec. Delaware Valley Smelting Corp., Bristol, Pa., 1957-89; art tchr. Calumet Sch. Dist., Ill., 1951-53; art tchr., chmn. elem. art program Cheltenham (Pa.) Sch. Dist., 1969—; real estate agt., Tullytown, Pa.; speaker in field; devel. dir., exec. bd. Art Forms, Manayunk, Pa. One woman show Hahn Gallery, Phila., 1985; permanent exhibits Elkins Park (Pa.) Libr., Univ. Hosp., Cleve.; also represented in med. offices, private collections; author publs. on using art reproductions in edn. Chmn. Phila. chpt. U. Chgo. Alumni Fund Assn., 1978-84. Recipient numerous art awards including 1st prize Doylestown Art League, 1986-87, Best Sculpture award Mummers's Mus. Phila., 1987, Juror's award Cheltenham Art Ctr., 1987-88, 3d prize Abington Art Ctr., 1988, 1st prize for sculpture Art Assn. of Harrisburg, 1989. Mem. Nat. Art Edn. Assn., Pa. Art Educators Assn. (regional rep. 1988-89, Outstanding Art Educator of Yr. award 1987), Oil Pastel Assn. N.Y.C. (invited mem.). Democrat. Jewish. Office: PO Box 29722 Elkins Park PA 19027-0922

SIMON, NORMA PLAVNICK, psychologist; b. Washington, Sept. 20, 1930; d. Mark and Mary Plavnick; m. Robert G. Simon, Dec. 18, 1949; children: Mark Allan, Susan. BA, NYU, 1952, cert. in psychoanalysis, 1977; MA, Columbia U., 1953, EdD, 1968. Diplomate Am. Bd. Profl. Psychology, 1988. Psychologist Queens Coll. Counseling Ctr., Flushing, N.Y., 1968-70, asst. dir., 1970-76, dir., 1976; gen. practice psychology N.Y.C., 1976—; faculty, supr. New Hope Guild, Bklyn., 1976—, dir. child and adolescent tng. prog., 1988—; adj. prof. clin. psychology Columbia U., N.Y.C., 1986—; supr. NYU Postdoctoral Prog. in Psychoanalysis, 1988—. Author: (with Robert G. Simon): Choosing a College Major: Social Science, 1981; mem. editorial bd. The Counseling Psychologist jour., 1986-89. Vice chairperson N.Y. State Bd. for Psychology State Edn. Dept., Albany, 1978-82, chairperson, 1982-88; bd. dirs. Pelham (N.Y.) Guidance Coun., 1980-83; pres.-elect Assn. State and Provincial Psychology Bds., 1990, pres., 1991. Recipient Karl Heiser award, 1993. Fellow APA (mem. bd. profl. affairs 1987-89, chair bd. profl. affairs 1989-90, policy and planning bd. 1991-93, mem. ethics com. 1995-98, vice chair ethics com. 1996—, John Black award 1994), Nat. Acads. of Practice (elected disting. practitioner). Office: 500A E 87th St # 5A New York NY 10128-7626

SIMON, SHEILA SANDRA, special education educator, administrator; b. N.Y.C., July 24, 1940; d. Leo and Frances (Wexler) Brown; children: Steven Marc, Scott Irwin, Sean Eric, Rebecca Shane. BA in Psychology, Lehman Coll., Bronx, 1974; MS in Spl. Edn., Coll. New Rochelle, N.Y., 1978; MS in Counseling, Loyola Marymount Coll., L.A., 1992; postgrad., UCLA, 1993—. Elem. tchr. spl. edn. N.Y.C. Pub. Schs., Bronx, 1974-79; tchr. spl. edn. Lincoln Spl. Sch., Palm Desert, Calif., 1979-83; tchr., chair dept. spel. edn. Mt. Vernon Jr. H.S. L.A. Unified Sch. Dist., 1983-86, resource specialist Revere Jr. H.S., 1986-91, outreach cons. Manual Arts H.S., 1991-94; exec. dir. spl. edn. commn. L.A. Unified Schs., 1994—. Mem. Los Angeles County Multicultural Collaborative, 1994, Los Angeles County Hate Crime Network, L.A. Roundtable for Children. Recipient Outstanding Sch. Svc. award Revere PTA, L.A., 1988. Mem. Coun. for Exceptional Children, Calif. Assn. of Resource Specialists, Calif. Assn. Counseling and Devel., Calif. Sch. Counselors, Kappa Delta Pi, Delta Kappa Gamma. Office: LA Unified Sch Dist Spl Edn Commn 450 N Grand Ave # H256 Los Angeles CA 90012-2100

SIMONDS, MARIE CELESTE, architect; b. Miami, Fla., Mar. 30, 1947; d. Hinton Joseph and Frances Olivia (Burnett) Baker; m. Albert Rhett Simonds, Jr., Oct. 9, 1974; children: Caroline Lamar, Frances Rhett. BA, U. Pa., 1968; BArch, U. Md., 1973. Registered architect, Va. Architect Harry Weese & Assocs., Washington, 1973-75; pvt. practice Alexandria, Va., 1976—. Com. chmn. Jr. Friends Alexandria YWCA, 1974-78; mem. Jr. League Washington, 1978—. NSF grantee, 1972; recipient Design award No. Va. Chpt. AIA, 1990. Mem. AIA (scholar 1971, Design award No. Va. 1990), Va. Soc. AIA, West River Sailing Club (Galesville, Md.), Sierra Club. Episcopalian. Home and Office: 624 S Lee St Alexandria VA 22314-3820

SIMONDS, PEGGY MUÑOZ, writer, lecturer, retired literature educator; b. New Rochelle, N.Y., Feb. 29, 1928; d. Francisco Javier Muñoz and Julia Pinckney Dunham; m. Roger Tyrrell Simonds, Nov. 21, 1956; children: Robin Pinckney, Martha Muñoz. BA in English, U. Del., 1949; MA in Creative Writing/Latin Am. Studies, U. of the Americas, Mexico City, 1956; PhD in Lit. and History of Art, Am. U., 1975. Journalist, arts critic Mexico City, 1949-55; tchr. English U. of the Ams., Mexico City, 1953-55; lectr. Greek drama Norfolk (Conn.) Music Sch. of Yale U., summer 1955; tchr. English Montgomery (Md.) Coll., 1966-88, prof. emerita, 1988—; ind. scholar, 1988—; lectr. and presenter in field. Author: Myth, Emblem, and Music in Shakespeare's "Cymbeline": An Iconographic Reconstruction, 1992, A Critical Guide to Iconographic Research in English Renaissance Literature, 1995; contbr. numerous articles to profl. jours. Recipient U. Del. Press award, 1990; NEH fellow, 1982. Mem. Assn. Lit. Scholars and Critics, Shakespeare Assn. Am., Internat. Shakespeare Assn., Renaissance Soc. Am., Southeastern Renaissance Soc., South Ctrl. Renaissance Soc., Internat. Soc. for Classical Tradition, Internat. Soc. for Emblem Studies, Internat. Assn. for Neo-Latin Studies, Phi Kappa Phi. Home and Office: 5406 Beech Ave Bethesda MD 20814

SIMONE, GAIL ELISABETH, research analyst; b. Boston, Dec. 3, 1944; d. Hugh Nelson and Louise Amelia (Shedrick) Saunders; m. Edburnne R. Hare, Sept. 7, 1968 (div. 1974); m. Joseph R. Simone, June 27, 1987. BA, The King's Coll., 1966; postgrad., Harvard U., 1976-77, N.H. Coll., 1991—. Placement dir. Boston Bar Assn., 1966-67; pub. relations Emerson Coll., Boston, 1967-69; asst. to v.p. Vance, Sanders, Inc., Boston, 1969-70; office mgr. Trans. Displays, Inc., Boston, 1970-71; seminar coordinator Assn. Trial Lawyers Am., Cambridge, Mass., 1971-74; writer, researcher Ednl. Expeditions Internat., Belmont, Mass., 1975-76; analyst United Brands Co., N.Y.C., 1976-80; analyst Mil. Sealift Commd., USN, Washington, 1980-84, legis. affairs officer, 1984-88; rsch. analyst Bath (Maine) Iron Works Corp., 1988—; free-lance writer, editor, Boston, 1970-73. Active Childreach, Warwick, R.I., 1986—; mem. Amnesty Internat., N.Y.C., 1987—, various other orgns. Mem. AAUW, NAFE. Office: Bath Iron Works 700 Washington St Bath ME 04530-2574

SIMONE, HEATHER ANN, management consultant; b. Hollywood, Fla., July 25, 1967; d. Paul John and Cathie Ann (Randle) S. A in Mgmt., Clayton State Coll., 1991; B in Mgmt., Ga. Tech., 1993. Software support tech. Peachtree Software, Norcross, Ga., 1992-93; tng. specialist XcelleNet, Atlanta, 1993; LAN adminstr. J.O. Patterson & Co., Atlanta, 1993-95; bus. application cons. Hewlett Packard, Atlanta, 1995—. Vol. Nat. Wildlife Fedn., 1992-93. Mem. Am. Mktg. Assn., Archtl. Com./Crossview. Republican. Lutheran.

SIMONE, SHARON MICHELLE, marketing professional; b. Balt., Aug. 31, 1966; d. Jerold H. and Lorryne R. Lane; m. John David Simone, Oct. 9, 1994. BA, U. Rochester, 1988; MBA, Rutgers U., 1994. Asst. media planner Rumrill-Hoyt Inc., Rochester, N.Y., 1989-90; media planner Saatchi & Saatchi Direct, N.Y.C., 1990-92; mktg. mgr. Franklin Mint, Franklin Ctr., Pa., 1994—. Recipient Honorable Mention Student Paper Contest Am. Assn. Pub. Opinion Rsch., N.Y.C., 1993. Mem. Beta Gamma Sigma. Office: Franklin Mint US Rte 1 Franklin Center PA 19091

SIMONES, JOYCE MARIE, nursing educator; b. St. Cloud, Minn., May 22, 1951; d. Lawrence John Rahm and Mary Lena Kline; m. Gregory Dean Simones, Sept. 11, 1976; children: David Allen, Thomas Gregory, Ann Elizabeth. ADN, St. Mary's Jr. Coll., 1972; BSN, U. Minn., 1976, MS, 1992. Cert. ACLS, CCRN, Minn. Staff nurse St. Mary's Hosp., Rochester, Minn., 1972-73; critical care nurse North Meml. Hosp., Mpls., 1973-76, Fairview Southdale Hosp., Mpls., 1976-86, St. Mary's Hosp., Rochester, 1986-89, St. Cloud (Minn.) Hosp., 1989—; asst. prof. Coll. of St. Benedict, St. Joseph, Minn., 1992—. Mem. Cen. Minn. Area Critical Care Nurse (treas. 1992-93). Home: 9379 County Road 6 Saint Cloud MN 56301-9406

SIMON-FEINBERG, SUSAN BARBARA, public information specialist; b. Chgo., Sept. 4, 1959; d. Harry and Karol (Silverstein) Simon; m. Mitchell Scott Feinberg, July 5, 1981; 1 child, Kerry Harnson. BJ, U. Mo., 1981. Reporter, editor The Watchman, Clinton, La., 1981-82; advt. and pub. rels. specialist Bank New Eng., Boston, 1982-84; dir., editor staff comm. Fed. Res. Bank N.Y., N.Y.C., 1984-88; freelance writer and editor Birmingham mag., Bus. Ala. mag.,, 1988-92, Houston Chronicle and Media Inc. Mags. Group, 1988-92; sr. pub. info. specialist Houston Lighting & Power Co., 1993—. Mem. mktg. com. Sheltering Arms, Houston, 1995-96. Mem. Pub. Rels. Soc. Am. (Best of Show and 1st place awards for speeches, Grand Excalibur award, gold Excalibur award 1995), Women in Comm. (bd. dirs. 1992—, Jobline chmn. 1992—, 1st and 2d place Matrix awards 1994, 95, 96), Internat. Assn. Bus. Communicators (bd. dirs. 1986-87, Bronze Quill award of excellence 1994, award of merit 1996, Silver Quill award of excellence regional awards competition 1995, 96), Houston Forum. Office: Houston Lighting & Power Co 1111 Louisiana Houston TX 77002

SIMON-GILLO, JEHANNE E., physicist; b. Liege, Belgium, Mar. 27, 1963; came to U.S., 1967; d. Nicolas Victor and Noelle Marie (Van Den Peereboom) Simon; m. Andrew James Gillo, June 9, 1990. BS, Juniata Coll., 1985; PhD, Tex. A&M U., 1991. Postdoctoral work Los Alamos (N.Mex.) Nat. Lab., 1991-94, staff mem., physicist, 1994—. Mem. Am. Chem. Soc., Am. Phys. Soc. Republican. Roman Catholic. Office: Los Alamos Nat Lab H846 LANL Los Alamos NM 87545

SIMON-PETER, REBEKAH ELLEN, pastor; b. El Paso, Tex., Apr. 19, 1961. BS, U. Vt., 1985; MDiv with honors, Iliff Sch. of Theology, 1995, postgrad., 1995—. Ordained deacon United Meth. Ch., 1995. Environ. technician Dept. of Water Resources, State of Vt., Montplier, 1982, 84-87; account exec. Intermountain Jewish News, Denver, 1987-90; spiritual dir. Denver, 1989-94; student chaplain St. Joseph's Hosp., Denver, 1994; intern assoc. pastor Scott United Meth. Ch., Denver, 1995—. Founder Colo. Jews and Christians in Dialogue, Denver, 1990—, women's Rosh Chudesh Group, Talmudic Rsch. Inst., Denver, 1982-91; founder, preacher Healing Svcs. Work Group, Denver, 1992—; homeless advocate, Denver, Vt., 1984—; mem. Green Mountain Club, Burlington, Vt., 1980-87. Scholarship Bohnett Meml. Fund, 1993, Iliff Sch. of Theology Master's Asst. scholarship, 1992-93. Democrat. United Methodist. Office: Scott United Meth Ch 2880 Garfield St Denver CO 80205

SIMONS, BARBARA M., lawyer; b. N.Y.C., Feb. 7, 1929; d. Samuel A. and Minnie (Mankes) Malitz; m. Morton L. Simons, Sept. 2, 1951; 1 child, Claudia. BA, U. Mich., 1950, JD, 1952. Bar: N.Y. 1953, U.S. Supreme Ct. 1963, U.S. Ct. Appeals (D.C. cir.) 1971, (5th cir.) 1992, (1st cir.) 1994. Ptnr. Simons & Simons, Washington, 1962—. Mem. Forest Hills Citizens Assn., Washington, Clean Air Project; past pres. D.C. chpt. U. Mich. Alumnae, Washington. Alumnae scholar U. Mich., 1946-50. Mem. Washington Coun. Lawyers, Women's Legal Def. Fund, Phi Beta Kappa, Phi Kappa Phi, Alpha Lambda Delta. Office: Simons & Simons 5025 Linnean Ave NW Washington DC 20008-2042

SIMONS, ELIZABETH R(EIMAN), biochemist, educator; b. Vienna, Austria, Sept. 1, 1929; came to U.S., 1941, naturalized, 1948; d. William and Erna Engle (Weisselberg) Reiman; B.Ch.E., Cooper Union, N.Y.C., 1950; M.S., Yale U., 1951, Ph.D., 1954; m. Harold Lee Simons, Aug. 12, 1951; children—Leslie Ann Mulert, Robert David. Research chemist Tech. Operations, Arlington, Mass., 1953-54; instr. chemistry Wellesley (Mass.) Coll., 1954-57; rsch. asst. Children's Hosp. Med. Center and Cancer Rsch. Found., Boston, 1957-59, rsch. assoc. pathology, 1959-62; research assoc. Harvard Med. Sch., 1962-66, lectr. biol. chemistry, 1966-72; tutor biochemical scis. Harvard Coll., 1971-94 (ret.); assoc. prof. biochemistry Boston U., 1972-78, prof., 1978—. Contbr. articles to profl. jours. Grantee in field. Mem. AAAS, Am. Chem. Soc., Am. Heart Assn., Am. Soc. Biol. Chemists, Am. Soc. Cell Biology, Am. Soc. Hematology, Assn. Women in Sci., Biophys. Soc., Internat. Soc. Thrombosis and Hemostasis, N.Y. Acad. Sci., Sigma Xi. Office: Boston U Sch Medicine 80 E Concord St Roxbury MA 02118-2307

SIMONS, HELEN, school psychologist, psychotherapist; b. Chgo., Feb. 13, 1930; d. Leo and Sarah (Shrayer) Pomper; m. Broudy Simons, May 20, 1956 (May 1972); children: Larry, Sheri. BA in Biol., Lake Forest Coll., 1951; MA in Clin. Psychology, Roosevelt U., 1972; D of Psychology, Ill. Sch. Profl. Psychology, 1980. Intern Cook County Hosp., Chgo., 1979-80; pvt.

practice psychotherapist Chgo., 1980—; sch. psychologist Chgo. Bd. Edn., 1974-79, 80—. Contbr. articles on psychotherapy of A.D.D. and P.T.S.D. children to profl. jours. Mem. APA, Nat. Sch. Psychologists Assn., Midwestern Psychol. Assn., Mental Health Assn. Ill., Ill. Psychol. Assn., Ill. Sch. Psychologists Assn., Chgo. Psychol. Assn., Chgo. Sch. Psychol. Assn. Home: 6145 N Sheridan Rd Apt 29D Chicago IL 60660-2883 Office: Brennemann Sch 4251 N Clarendon Ave Chicago IL 60613-1523

SIMONS, LYNN OSBORN, state education official; b. Havre, Mont., June 1, 1934; d. Robert Blair and Dorothy (Briggs) Osborn; BA, U. Colo., 1956; postgrad. U. Wyo., 1958-60; m. John Powell Simons, Jan. 19, 1957; children: Clayton Osborn, William Blair. Tchr., Midvale (Utah) Jr. High Sch., 1956-57, Sweetwater County Sch. Dist. 1, Rock Springs, Wyo., 1957-58, U. Wyo., Laramie, 1959-61, Natrona County Sch. Dist. 1, Casper, Wyo., 1963-64; credit mgr. Gallery 323, Casper, 1972-77; Wyo. state supt. public instrn., Cheyenne, 1979-91; sec.'s regional rep. region VIII U.S. Dept. Edn., Denver, 1993—; mem. State Bds. Charities and Reform, Land Commrs., Farm Loan, 1979-91; mem. State Commns. Capitol Bldg., Liquor, 1979-91; Ex-officio mem. bd. trustees U. Wyo., 1979-91; ex-officio mem. Wyo. Community Coll. Commn., 1979-91; mem. steering com. Edn. Commn. of the States, 1988-90; mem. State Bd. Edn., 1971-77, chmn., 1976-77; advisor Nat. Trust for Hist. Preservation, 1980-86. Bd. dirs. Denver Fed. Exec. Bd., 1995—. Mem. LWV (pres. 1970-71). Democrat. Episcopalian. Office: US Dept Edn 1244 Speer Blvd Ste 310 Denver CO 80204-3582

SIMONS, MARLENE J., state legislator, rancher; b. Deadwood, S.D., July 1, 1935; d. Royal B. Mills and Elsie M. Snook; m. Frank Simons, Sept. 24, 1951; children: Greg, Linda, Sully. Grad. high sch., Sundance, Wyo. Pres. Outdoors Unltd., Kaysville, Utah; mem. Wyo. Ho. of Reps., 1979-94, appropriation com., 1994—; mem. rules com., chmn. agrl. com., mem. appropriations com., mem. western legis. state conf. com., mem. water policy com.; vice chmn. Pub. Lands Adv. Coun., 1986—; stockgrower Farm Bur., Wyo., 1969—; rancher, outfitter. Pres. Wyo. Multiple Use Coalition, Ranch A Restoration Found.; sec. Black Hills Multi-Use Coalition; mem. Madison water steering com. Black Hills Hydrology Study; leader 4-H. Republican. Home: Windy Acres Ranch 5480 Hwy 14 Beulah WY 82712 Office: Outdoors Unltd PO Box 373 Kaysville UT 84037-0373

SIMONTACCHI, CAROL NADINE, nutritionist, retail store executive; b. Bellingham, Wash., July 6, 1947; d. Ralph Eugene and Sylvia Arleta (Tyler) Walmer; m. Bob Simontacchi, Oct. 3, 1981; children: Caryl Anne, Bobbie Anne, Melissa Anne, Laurie Anne. BS in Health and Human Svcs., Columbia Pacific U., 1996, postgrad., 1996—. Cert. nutritionist, Wash. CEO The Health Haus, Inc., Vancouver, Wash., 1985—; host radio program Back to the Beginning, Vancouver, 1990—; CEO The Natural Physician Ctr., Beaverton, Oreg., 1995—. Author: Your Fat is Not Your Fault, 1994, The Sun Rise Book: Living Beyond Depression, 1996, The Attention! Book, Living Beyond ADHD, 1996. Mem. Soc. Cert. Nutritionists (pres. bd. 1992-93), Nat. Nutritional Foods Assn. (chair edn. com., N.W. region legis. chair 1991—). Republican. Christian Ch. Office: The Health Haus Inc 101 E 8th St Ste 250 Vancouver WA 98660-3294

SIMPKINSON, ANNE ADAMCEWICZ, editor, administrator; b. Norwich, Conn., Oct. 22, 1950; d. Walter S. and Sophia (Brozyna) Adamcewicz; m. Charles Hoffman Simpkinson, Sept. 23, 1978. BA, Syracuse U., 1972; MA in Counseling, Lindenwood Coll., St. Charles, Mo., 1976. Prodn. asst. Army Times, Washington, 1972-73; editor Environ. Edn. Report, Washington, 1973-74; freelance writer and editor Washington, 1975-77; psychotherapist in pvt. practice Washington, also Olney, Md., 1977-83; editor Grace Commn., Washington, 1983; editor, adminstr. Common Boundary, Inc., Bethesda, Md., 1984—. Co-editor: Sacred Stories, 1993, Nourishing the Soul, 1995. Recipient Gen. Excellence award Utne Reader, 1995. Mem. Am. Soc. Mag. Editors, Women in Comms. Inc., Soc. Profl. Journalists, Assn. for Transpersonal Psychology (bd. dirs. 1991-96, sec. 1995). Home: 5272 River Rd Ste 650 Bethesda MD 20816-1405

SIMPSON, AGNES MONIKA, financial advisor; b. Vienna, Nov. 30, 1956; came to U.S., 1957; d. Jozsef and Katalin (Havasi) Toth; m. Michael E. Simpson, Nov. 29, 1986; 1 child, Kathryn. BS in Indsl. Econs., Union Coll., 1977, MBA, 1982. Cert. fin. planner. Oil and gas analyst The Ayco Co., LP, Albany, N.Y., 1980-83; pres. Rexco Energy Securities, Shreveport, La., 1984-87, v.p. mktg., 1983-87; dir. mktg. The Ayco Co., LP, Albany, 1987-88, dir. oil and gas adv. svc., 1988-92, assoc. account mgr., 1992-94, account mgr., ptnr., 1995—. Trustee Albany Acad. for Girls, 1992-95. Recipient Disting. Alumna award Albany Acad. for Girls, 1995. Mem. Albany Acad. for Girls Alumnae Assn. (treas. 1987-95). Office: The Ayco Co LP 2839 Paces Ferry Rd Ste 210 Atlanta GA 30339

SIMPSON, ALLYSON BILICH, lawyer; b. Pasadena, Calif., Feb. 5, 1951; d. John Joseph and Barbaran Rita (Bessolo) Bilich; m. Roland Gilbert Simpson, Aug. 11, 1979; children: Megan Elise, Erin Marie, Brian Patrick. BS, U. So. Calif., L.A., 1973, JD, 1976. Bar: Calif. 1976. Staff atty. Gen. Telephone Co., Thousand Oaks, Calif., 1978-79; group staff atty., dir. legis. compliance Pacific Mut. Life Ins. Co., Newport Beach, Calif., 1980-86; corp. counsel and sec. Amicare Ins. Co., Beverly Hills, Calif., 1986; assoc. Leboeuf, Lamb, Leiby & MacRae, L.A., 1986-87; from assoc. to ptnr. Musick, Peeler & Garrett, L.A., 1988-94; ptnr. Sonnenschein Nath & Rosenthal, L.A., 1994-95; sr. v.p., sec., gen. counsel Fremont Pacific Ins. Group, Glendale, Calif., 1995—; vis. pro. bus. law U. So. Calif., L.A., 1981. Trustee St. Anne's Maternity Home Found., L.A., 1991—; bd. dirs. St. Anne's Maternity Home, L.A., 1993—. Mem. Western Pension & Benefits Conf., Conf. of Ins. Counsel. Republican. Roman Catholic. Office: Fremont Pacific Ins Group 500 N Brand Blvd Glendale CA 91203

SIMPSON, ANDREA LYNN, energy communications executive; b. Altadena, Calif., Feb. 10, 1948; d. Kenneth James and Barbara Faries Simpson; m. John R. Myrdal, Dec. 13, 1986; 1 child, Christopher Ryan Myrdal. BA, U. So. Calif., 1969, MS, 1983; postgrad. U. Colo., Boulder Sch. Bank Mktg., 1977. Asst. cashier United Calif. Bank, L.A., 1969-73; asst. v.p. mktg. 1st Hawaiian Bank, Honolulu, 1973-78; v.p. corp. comm. BHP Hawaii, Inc. (formerly Pacific Resources, Inc.), Honolulu, 1978—. Bd. dirs. Arts Coun. Hawaii, 1977-81, Hawaii Heart Assn., 1978-83, Coun. Pacific Girl Scouts U.S., 1982-85, Child and Family Svcs., 1984-86, Honolulu Symphony Soc., 1985-91, Sta. KHPR Hawaii Pub. Radio, 1988-92, Kapiolani Found., 1990-95, Hanahauoli Sch., 1991—; bd. dirs., 2nd. v.p. Girl Scout Coun. Hawaii, 1994-96, adv. bd., 1996—; trustee Hawaii Loa Coll., 1984-86, Kapiolani Women's and Children's Hosp., 1988—, Hawaii Sch. For Girls at LaPietra, 1989-91, Kapiolani Med. Ctr. at Pali Momi, 1994—; commr. Hawaii State Commn. on Status of Women, 1985-87, State Sesquecentennial of Pub. Schs. Commn., 1990-91; bd. dirs. Hawaii Strategic Devel. Corp., 1991—, Children's DiscoveryCtr., 1994—, Pacific Asian Affairs Coun., 1994-96, adv. dir. Hawaii Kids at Work, 1991—, Hawaii Mothers Against Drunk Driving, 1992-96. Named Panhellenic Woman of Yr. Hawaii, 1979, Outstanding Woman in Bus. Hawaii YWCA, 1980, Outstanding Young Woman of Hawaii Girl Scouts Coun. of the Pacific, 1985, 86, Hawaii Legis., 1980. Mem. Am. Mktg. Assn., Pub. Rels. Soc. Am. (bd. dirs. Honolulu chpt. 1984-86, Silver Anvil award 1984, Pub. Rels. Profl. Yr. 1991, Silver Anvil award of excellence 1996), Pub. Utilities Communicators Assn. (Communicator of Yr. 1984), Honolulu Advt. Fedn. (Advt. Woman of Yr. 1984), U. So. Calif. Alumni Assn. (bd. dirs. Hawaii 1981-83), Outrigger Canoe Club, Pacific Club, Kaneohe Yacht Club, Rotary (pub. rels. chmn. 1988—, Honolulu chpt.), Alpha Phi (past pres., dir. Hawaii), Hawaii Jaycees (Outstanding Young Person of Hawaii 1978). Office: BHP Hawaii Inc 733 Bishop St Ste 2700 Honolulu HI 96813-4022

SIMPSON, CAROL LOUISE, investment company executive; b. Phila., Jan. 30, 1937; d. William Huffington and Hilda Agnes (Johnston) S. Student, Community Coll., 1985, 86, 87, U. Minn., 1986, 87, 88. Cert. Nat. Assn. Securities Dealers, Inc., Washington; registered options, mcpl. securities, gen. securities, fin. and ops. prin.; lic. life, accident, health ins. Exec. asst. Germantown Fed. Savs., Phila., 1954-67; asst. sec. Am. Med. Investment Co., Inc. (formerly Cannon and Co., Inc.), Blue Bell, Pa., 1967-91; also bd. dirs. Cannon & Co., Inc., 1986; v.p., sec. AMA Investment Advisers, Inc. (formerly Pro Svcs., Inc.), Blue Bell, Pa., 1967-91; also bd. dirs. AMA Investment Advisers, Inc. (formerly PRO Svcs., Inc.), Blue Bell, Pa., 1984-86; fin. svcs. compliance cons., 1991; exec. v.p., sec. Rutherford Fin. Corp., Phila., 1991—, Rutherford, Brown & Catherwood Inc., Phila., 1991—, Walnut Asset Mgmt. Inc., Phila., 1991—. Bd. dirs. VNA Cmty. Svc. Found., 1995—. Mem. World Affairs Coun., Investment Co. Inst. (fed. legis. com. 1984-91, investment advisers com. 1988—, compliance com. 1990—), Internat. Assn. Fin. Planners, Investment Women's Club, Nat. Notary Assn., Pa. Assn. Notaries, Nat. Soc. Compliance Profls. (assoc.), VNA Cmty. Svc. Found. (bd. dirs.), Whitemarsh Valley Country Club. Republican. Home: 7701 Lawnton St Philadelphia PA 19128-3105 Office: Rutherford Fin Corp 1617 John F Kennedy Blvd Philadelphia PA 19103

SIMPSON, CAROLYN MARIE, critical care nurse; b. Boise, Idaho, Mar. 1, 1950; d. Thomas Michael and Eva Lucille (Hieter) Sliman; m. Jon E. Simpson, Feb. 17, 1973; children: Christy Lynn, David Jon. Diploma, St. Elizabeth Sch. Nursing, 1971. Cert. utilization rev. and managed care ACLS, CCRN. Staff nurse St. Elizabeth's Hosp., Yakima, Wash., 1971-72, Vancouver Meml. Hosp., 1972-73; relief house supervisor Tri-State Meml. Hosp., Clarkston, Wash., 1973-75; charge nurse VA Hosp., Vancouver, 1975-84; charge nurse Bess Kaiser, Portland, Oreg., 1985-96, staff nurse, 1992—; med.-legal cons., lectr. Bess Kaiser, AACN; owner And All That Stuff. Leader Girl Scouts U.S., Portland. Mem. AACN, Oreg. Nurses Assn. (exec. com. 1988, gen. welfare 1989), Eagles Aux., Women of the Moose. Roman Catholic. Home: 5017 NE 139th Ave Vancouver WA 98682

SIMPSON, DIANE JEANNETTE, social worker; b. Denver, Sept. 20, 1952; d. Arthur Henry and Irma Virginia (Jordan) S.; 1 child, Shantè N. BS, Nebr. Wesleyan U., 1974; MSW, U. Denver, 1977. Asst. Mile Hi coun. Girl Scouts U.S.A., Denver, 1971-77; social worker asst. Denver Pub. Schs., 1974-75, social worker, 1977—; field instr. Grad. Sch. of Soc. Work, U. Denver, 1984—. Tour leader Kenyan Safari to Kenya, East Africa, 1988. V.p. United Meth. Women, Christ United Meth. Ch., Denver, 1989-91; chmn. Christian action com., 1985-88; active Girl Scouts U.S.A., 1959—; mem. collaborative decision making com. Denver Pub. Schs., 1993-95; mem. Shorter A.M.E. Ch., sr. usher bd. and edn. and scholarship com., 1996—. Mem. NASW. Democrat. Home: 6865 E Arizona Ave # D Denver CO 80224-1829 Office: Denver Pub Schs 900 Grant St Denver CO 80203-2907

SIMPSON, DONNA MONIQUE, mathematics educator; b. Jackson, Tenn., June 11, 1967; d. Arthur Edmond Simpson and Emma Lee (Dupree) Lundy. BS in Tchg. of Math., U. Ill., Chgo., 1989; M of Ednl. Adminstrn., Gov.'s State U., University Park, Ill., 1995. Tchr. math. Thomas Jr. H.S., Arlington Heights, Ill., 1989-90, NIKE, various, 1992—; tchr. math. Homewood-Flossmoor (Ill.) H.S., 1990-93, coord. math. dept., 1993—. Mem. ASCD, Nat. Coun. Supervisors of Math., Am. Assn. Cheerleading Coaches and Adivsors, Nat. Coun. Tchrs. Math., Ill. Coun. Tchrs. Math., Ill. Cheerleading Coaches Assn. (bd. dirs. 1992—), South Suburban Math. Supervisors, Math. Dept. Heads West Chgo. Suburbs, Alpha Kappa Alpha. Home: 4201 W 189th St Country Club Hills IL 60478 Office: Homewood Flossmoor HS 999 Kedzie Ave Flossmoor IL 60422

SIMPSON, ELIZABETH ANN, pharmacist, educator; b. Steubenville, Ohio, Nov. 11, 1941; d. Robert Thompson and Elizabeth Ann (Rogers) Lucas; m. James Lewis Simpson, Nov. 8, 1963; children: James L., Mary Elizabeth. BS in Pharmacy, W.Va. U., 1963; postgrad., U. Tex., 1986. Staff pharmacist, Mich., Pa., N.J.; staff pharmacist Mass., W.Va., 1964-80; staff pharmacist St. John Hosp. and Med. Ctr., Detroit, 1980-83, dir. pharmacy svcs. St. John Outpatient Corp., 1983-93; asst. dir. div. pharmacy svcs. St. John Health System, 1993—; adj. clin. instr. dept. pharmacy practice Coll. Pharmacy and Allied Health Professions, Wayne State U., Detroit, 1982—; presenter in field, 1986—; mem. pharmacy and therapeutics com. Georgian East Nursing Home, 1987-89. Contbr. articles to profl. jours. Pres. bd. dirs. Meml. Co-Op Nursery Sch., 1973-75; mem. various PTO coms. and bds. Grosse Pointe (Mich.) Sch. System, 1975-89; chmn. pub. affairs com. Jr. League Detroit, 1975-76, mem. exec. com., 1978-80; chmn. pub. affairs com. Jr. Leagues Mich., 1976-78; mem. adv. bd. Chesterfield Twp. Police, 1992-93; mem. zoning bd. appeals Chesterfield Twp., 1993—, chmn., 1996—; chmn. fin. com. Grace United Meth. Ch., Chesterfield, Mich., 1996—. Recipient Vol. of Yr. award Jr. League Detroit, 1976, Torch Drive Communication award United Found., 1985. Fellow Am. Coll. Cons. Pharmacists, Acad. Pharmacy Practice and Mgmt. (policy com. 1987, chmn. instnl. practice sect. 1990—, mem. edn. com. 1988-89); mem. Am. Soc. Hosp. Pharmacists, Am. Pharm. Assn. (ho. of dels. 1987—, William S. Apple program fellow 1986), Mich. Pharmacists Assn. (physician dispensing adv. com. 1988-91, chmn. profl. and pub. affairs com. 1987-90, chmn. pharm. care task force), Mich. Soc. Hosp. Pharmacists (profl. and legal affairs com. 1987-90), Southeastern Mich. Soc. Hosp. Pharmacists, Lambda Kappa Sigma. Republican. Home: 46978 Jans Dr Chesterfield MI 48047-5128 Office: St John Hosp and Med Ctr 22101 Moross Rd Grosse Pointe MI 48236-2148

SIMPSON, ELIZABETH ANN, reading and language arts educator; b. Collins, Miss., Oct. 20, 1940; d. Clyde C. and Edna L. (Lewis) McRaney; m. Arthur Thomas Simpson, Dec. 15, 1962; children: Lisa Bukovnik, Art, Cindy Simpson-Scharff, Sheri Lucas. BS, U. So. Miss., 1978, MEd, 1982. Tchr. Biloxi (Miss.) Pub. Schs., 1978—; conv. presenter Miss. Coun. Tchrs. of English, Jackson, 1992. Leader Girl Scouts Am., San Antonio, 1970, Biloxi, 1975; Sunday sch. tchr. Episcopal Ch. of the Redeemer, Biloxi, 1978. Fellow South Miss. Writing Project, 1991, 92. Mem. Internat. Reading Assn., Nat. Coun. Tchrs. of English, Nat. Coun. Tchrs. of Math., Miss. Reading Assn. (sec. Gulf Coast chpt. 1986), Phi Delta Kappa, Phi Kappa Phi. Home: 347 Saint Mary Blvd Biloxi MS 39531-3419 Office: Beauvoir Elem Sch 2003 Lawrence St Biloxi MS 39531-4106

SIMPSON, GAIL R., diabetes educator; b. Tuscaloosa, Ala., Feb. 3, 1953; d. James Carl and Julia Rachel (Bowling) Rutland; 1 child, Chris Simpson. BSN magna cum laude, U. Ala., 1986. Cert. diabetes educator, Nat. Cert. Bd. Diabetes Educators; cert. insulin pump trainer. Neurosurgery/orthopaedic nurse DCH Regional Med. Ctr., Tuscaloosa, 1987-88, Healthcare Staffing, Birmingham, Ala., 1988-89; psychiat. nurse, charge nurse West Ala. Hosp., Northport, 1989-92; diabetes educator, outpatient coord. Brookwood Med. Ctr., Birmingham, 1992-93; diabetes education program coord. Alacare Home Health, Birmingham, 1993-95; diabetes mgmt. specialist Cottondale, Ala., 1995—; mem. psychiat. steering com. U. Ala. Continuing Edn., Tuscaloosa, 1993—. Author patient edn. modules, diabetes nurse clinician course. Mem. Am. Assn. Diabetes Educators, Am. Diabetes Assn., Nat. League Nursing, Ala. Assn. Diabetes Educators (sec. 1994), Tuscaloosa Diabetes Adv. Coun. Home and Office: Diabetes Mgmt Svcs 15604 Peace Valley Rd Cottondale AL 35453

SIMPSON, JENIFER JANE, social services lobbyist; b. Essex, Eng., Nov. 29, 1955; came to U.S., 1966; d. John and Suzette (Goodchild) S.; m. Lawrence Chartienitz, Sept. 11, 1982 (div. Mar. 1992); 1 child, Joshua. BA, U. Mass., 1984. Arts adminstr. Cambridge (Mass.) Arts Coun., 1982-86; policy analyst United Cerebral Palsy Assns., Washington, 1989—; mem. personal assistance task force No. Va. Independence Ctr., Arlington, 1994—; prin. speech disability investigator universal access project Gallaudet U., Washington, 1995; mem. telecomms. adv. com. U.S. Access Bd., 1996—. Author, editor: (voting guide for persons with disabilities) Word from Washington, 1996; cons. editor, contbr. to weekly newsletter Washington Watch, 1995. Mem. parent adv. com. Hosp. for Sick Kids, Washington, 1995—; chair task force on telecomms., comms. access and tech. Coalition for Citizens with Disabilities, Washington, 1992—; mem. exec. bd. Mayor's Coun. on Developmental Disabilities, 1992—; block capt. Bloomingdale Civic Assn., 1988—. Mem. Ams. With Disabilities Vote (bd. dirs. 1996—). Episcopalian. Home: 48 Adams St NW Washington DC 20001 Office: United Cerebral Palsy Assns 1660 L St NW Washington DC 20036

SIMPSON, JOANNE MALKUS, meteorologist; b. Boston, Mar. 23, 1923; d. Russell and Virginia (Vaughan) Gerould; m. Robert H. Simpson, Jan. 6, 1965; children by previous marriage: David Starr Malkus, Steven Willem Malkus, Karen Elizabeth Malkus. B.S., U. Chgo., 1943, M.S., 1945, Ph.D., 1949; D.Sc. (hon.), SUNY, Albany, 1991. Instr. physics and meteorology Ill. Inst. Tech., 1946-49, asst. prof., 1949-51; meteorologist Woods Hole Oceanographic Instn., 1951-61; prof. meteorology UCLA, 1961-65; dir. exptl. meteorology lab. NOAA, Dept. Commerce, Washington, 1965-74; prof. environ. scis. U. Va., Charlottesville, 1974-76; W.W. Corcoran prof. environ. scis. U. Va., 1976-81; head Severe Storms br. Goddard Lab. Atmospheres, NASA, Greenbelt, Md., 1981-88, chief scientist for meteorology, 1988—; Goddard sr. fellow, earth scis. dir. Goddard Space Flight Ctr., NASA, 1988—; project scientist tropical rainfall measuring mission, 1986—; mem. Bd. on Atmospheric Scis. and Climate, NRC/NAS, 1990-93, Bd. on Geophys. and Environ. Data, 1993—. Author: (with Herbert Riehl) Cloud Structure and Distributions Over the Tropical Pacific Ocean; assoc. editor: Revs. Geophysics and Space Physics, 1964-72, 75-77; contbr. articles to profl. jours. Mem. Fla. Gov.'s Environ. Coordinating Coun., 1971-74. Recipient Disting. Authorship award NOAA, 1969, Silver medal Dept. Commerce, 1967, Gold medal, 1972, Vincent J. Schaefer award Weather Modification Assn., 1979, Cmty. Headliner award Women in Comm., 1973, Profl. Achievement award U. Chgo. Alumni Assn., 1975, 92, Lifetime Achievement award Women in Sci. Engring., 1990, Exceptional Sci. Achievement award NASA, 1982, William Nordberg award NASA, 1994; named Woman of Yr. L.A. Times, 1963; Guggenheim fellow, 1954-55, Goddard Sr. fellow, 1988—. Fellow Am. Meterol. Soc. (hon., coun. 1975-77, 79-81, exec. com. 1977, 79-81, commr. sci. and tech. activities 1982-88, pres.-elect 1988, pres. 1989, publs. commr. 1992—, Meisinger award 1962, Rossby Rsch. medal 1983, Charles Franklin Brooks award 1992), Am. Geophys. Union, NAE Oceanography Soc.; mem. Cosmos Club, Phi Beta Kappa, Sigma Xi. Home: 540 N St SW Washington DC 20024-4557 Office: NASA Goddard Space Flight Ctr Earth Scis Dir Greenbelt MD 20771

SIMPSON, JULIETTE RICH, elementary educator; b. Bainbridge, Ga., Jan. 9, 1944; d. Robert Lloyd Jr. and Juliette (Lane) Rich; m. Ralph Felward Simpson, Aug. 13, 1966; children: Juliette, Elena. AB in Elem. Edn., Wesleyan Coll., 1966. 2d grade tchr. Bibb County Sch. System, Macon, Ga., 1966-69; title I tchr. Tift County Sch. System, Tifton, Ga., 1974-77, 3d grade tchr., 1977—; mem. sci. curriculum writing com. Tift County Bd. Edn., Tifton, 1989-90, mem. lang. arts curriculum writing com., 1990-91, mem. social studies curriculum writing com., 1991-92. Alt. del. Nat. Rep. Conv., Houston, 1992, San Diego, 1996; mem. State Rep. Com., 1994—; 8th dist. Phil Gramm leadership chmn.; chmn. Tift County Rep. Party, 1994-96; co-pres. Tifton Cir. Bar Assn., 1990-91; active Annie Belle Clark Sch. PTO; v.p. Tifton Choral Soc., 1994-96, vice-chmn., 1995-96. Mem. Profl. Assn. Ga. Educators, Internat. Reading Assn., Tift County Found. for Ednl. Excellence (Outstanding Tchr. award), Ga. Coun. for Social Scis., Dogwood Garden Club. Presbyterian. Home: 1020 N College Ave Tifton GA 31794-3942 Office: Annie Belle Clark Sch 506 W 12th St Tifton GA 31794-3930

SIMPSON, KAREN CRANDALL, artist, educator; b. Newport, R.I., Mar. 31, 1944; d. Jack Conway and Elizabeth Ann (McLyman) Crandall; m. Donal Robertson Simpson, Mar. 30, 1968. BA, U. R. I., 1966; MFA, Tex. Womans U., 1992. Cert. Tchr. Pa., Md., Conn., R.I. Spl. issues editor Phoenix Times Newspaper, Bristol, R.I., 1975-81; newsletter editor Trinity Ch., Newport, R.I., 1980-83; pub. editor St. Matthews Episcopal Ch., Austin, Tex., 1984-86; exhibiting artist Dallas, 1988—; adj. faculty Mt. View Coll., Dallas, 1993-95; freelance writer, 1975-81, horticultural cons. DSA Architects, Newport, 1975-83; tchr. of record Tex. Womens U., 1990-92. One-woman shows include Brookhaven Coll., Farmers Branch, Tex., 1994, Sam Houston State U., 1995, others; exhibited in group shows including Eastfield Coll., Dallas, 1993, others; curator Mountain View Coll., Dallas, 1994, Handley-Hicks Gallery, Ft. Worth, 1996. Mem. Tex. Fine Arts Assn., Dallas Visual Art Ctr., Dallas Womens Caucus for Art (v.p. 1993, pres. 1994-95), Nat. Womens Caucus for Art, McKinney Ave Contemory. Episcopalian. Home: 6735 Bevington Rd Dallas TX 75248 Studio: 1700 Routh St Dallas TX 75201

SIMPSON, LINDA SUE, elementary educator; b. Rogers, Ark., Oct. 13, 1947; d. Richard Eugene and Shirley Joan (Kilpatrick) S. BS in Edn., Ohio State U., 1969, postgrad., 1989-91, MA in Edn., Ea. Ky. U., 1978. Cert. elem. tchr. Tchr. Conrad Sch., Newark, Ohio, 1969-71; tchr. 1-6 North Elem. Sch., Newark, 1971-89; tchr. K-3 Cherry Valley Elem., Newark, 1989—; adv. bd. Ohio Coun. of Social Studies, Columbus, 1994—; planning team Ctrl. Ohio Regional Profl. Devel., Columbus, 1994-95. Elder 1st Presbyn. Ch., Newark, 1990-93; tutor Licking County Children's Home, Newark, 1969-73. Jenning scholar Martha H. Found., 1987; named Newark Tchr. of the Yr., 1981; recipient Ashland Oil Tchg. award Ashland Oil Co., 1995. Mem. DAR (history and scholarship chair 1982—), Delta Kappa Gamma. Presbyterian. Home: 579 Manor Dr Newark OH 43055 Office: Cherry Valley Sch 1040 W Main St Newark OH 43055

SIMPSON, MARY MICHAEL, priest, psychotherapist; b. Evansville, Ind., Dec. 1; d. Link Wilson and Mary Garrett (Price) S. B.A., B.S., Tex. Women's U., 1946; grad. N.Y. Tng. Sch. for Deaconesses, 1949; grad., Westchester Inst. Tng. in Psychoanalysis and Psychotherapy, 1976; S.T.M., Gen. Theol. Sem., 1982. Missionary Holy Cross Mission, Bolahun, Liberia, 1950-52; mem. Order of St. Helena, 1952—; acad. head Margaret Hall Sch., Versailles, Ky., 1958-61; sister in charge Convent of St. Helena, Bolahan, 1962-67, novice dir., 1968-74; pastoral counselor on staff Cathedral St. John the Divine, N.Y.C., 1974-87, canon residentiary, canon counselor, 1977-87, hon. canon, 1988—; ordained priest Episcopal Ch., 1977; cons. psychotherapist Union Theol. Sem., 1980-83; dir. Cathedral Counseling Service, 1975-87; priest-in-charge St. John's Ch. Wilmot, New Rochelle, N.Y., 1987-88; pvt. practice psycholanalyst, 1974—; Bd. dirs. Westchester Inst. Tng. in Psychoanalysis and Psychotherapy, 1982 84; trustee Council on Internat. and Pub. Affairs, 1983-87; interim pastor St. Michael's Ch., Manhattan, 1992-94; cons. Diocese of N.Y., 1992—. Mem. Nat. Assn. Advancement of Psychoanalysis, N.Y. State Assn. Practicing Psychotherapists, N.Y. Soc. Clin. Psychologists. Author: The Ordination of Women in the American Episcopal Church: the Present Situation, 1981; contbg. author: Yes to Women Priests, 1978. Home and Office: 151 E 31st St Apt 8H New York NY 10016-9502

SIMPSON, VERONICA ANN, photographer, lab technician; b. Bethlehem, Pa., Feb. 21, 1955; d. Peter H. and Shirley A. (DeWalt) Ricci; m. Richard James Simpson, Sept. 29, 1984; children: Jesse, Jenna. Cert. photography, Northampton C.C., Bethlehem, Pa., 1980, cert. in fine and performing arts, 1981; attended, Bawm Sch. Art, Allentown, Pa. Lab. technician Ronn Studio, Bethlehem, 1978-82; lab. technician, photographer Sam Smith Studio, Allentown, 1980-85; pvt. photographer Nazareth, Pa., 1980—; owner pvt. shop Nazareth, 1995—. Sch. dir. Nazareth Area Sch. Bd., 1995—. Mem. Nazareth Area C. of C. Roman Catholic. Office: Unique Images by Ronnie 1 N Main St Nazareth PA 18064

SIMS, DEBBIE DEANN, psychotherapist; b. Ft. Wayne, Ind., Dec. 18, 1948; d. Richard and Helen (Becker) Brudi; m. Andrew J. Dodzik (div. 1983); children: Julie Kristine, Peter Allen, Stephanie Ann; m. Tom E. Sims, Oct. 5, 1985. RN, Parkview Sch. Nursing, Ft. Wayne, 1969; BA, Concordia Sr. Coll., 1976; MS, St. Francis Coll., 1979. Cert. clin. specialist in adult psychiat. and mental health nursing; cert. clin. social worker; cert. marriage and family therapist; lic. profl. clin. counselor. Staff nurse Parkview Meml. Hosp., Ft. Wayne, 1969-74, clin. supr., 1991-95; sr. psychotherapist, intake clinician Psychiat. Svcs., Inc., Ft. Wayne, 1974-91; ptnr. Psychiat. Care Inc., Ft. Wayne, 1995—; cons., therapist Parkview Sch. Nursing, Ft. Wayne, 1980-89. Mem. Am. Mental Health Counselor Assn., Am. Assn. Counseling & Devel. Roman Catholic. Home: 4814 Golfview Dr Fort Wayne IN 46818 Office: 1910 St Joe Center Rd Ste 25 Fort Wayne IN 46825

SIMS, JANETTE ELIZABETH LOWMAN, educational director; b. Lincolnton, N.C., July 21, 1934; d. Lee Hobson and Myrtle Elizabeth (Travis) Lowman; m. Mickey Ray Sims, Feb. 2, 1951; children: Carol Lee Sims Walden, Rickey Ray. BS, Lenoir-Rhyne Coll., 1968; MAT, U. N.C., 1973; EdD, U. N.C., Greensboro, 1989. N.C. "G" tchg. cert; cert. devel. edn. specialist. Quality control supr. Kiser Roth Hosiery, Inc., Maiden, N.C., 1959-63; 9th grade phys. sci. and math. tchr. Cherryville (N.C.) Jr. H.S., 1968; phys. sci., chemistry and astronomy tchr. Maiden (N.C.) H.S., 1968-75; dir. studies lab. coord. Catawba Valley C.C., Hickory, N.C., 1975-79; physics, chemistry, math. and computer sci. instr. Catawba Valley C.C., Hickory, 1979-90, dir. developmental studies and learning assistance ctr., 1990—; trustee Catawba County Assn. for Spl. Edn., Conover, 1978-79, Catawba Valley Found., Hickory, 1993-96, chair, 1996; apprentice program instr. Meredith/Burda Corp., Newton, N.C., 1979-88; chairperson devel. math. com. N.C. Math. Assn. Two-Yr. Colls. Devel. Math. Com., N.C., 1991-93, sec., 1996—. Coun. mem., choir mem., tchr. Faith Luth. Ch., Conover, 1980—. Mem. NEA, N.C. Assn. Educators (local unit pres.), Nat. Assn. Developmental Educators, N.C. Assn. Developmental Educators (regional chair 1990), Atlantic Assn. Physics Tchrs. (chair nominations com. 1992), Am. Legion Aux., Delta Kappa Gamma. Home: 300 Parlier Ave Conover NC 28613-9312 Office: Catawba Valley CC 2550 Us Highway 70 SE Hickory NC 28602-8302

SIMS, KONSTANZE OLEVIA, social worker; b. Dallas, Dec. 20, 1944; d. Kenneth Winn and Odie Lee (Wells) S. Student, U. Dallas, 1963-64; BA, U. Tex., Arlington, 1968; MEd, U. North Tex., 1972. Sec. Stillman Coll. Regional Campaign Fund, Dallas, 1969; employment interviewer Zale Corp., Dallas, 1969-71; sch. counselor Bishop Dunne High Sch., Dallas, 1973-78; dir. guidance Notre Dame High Sch., Wichita Falls, Tex., 1978-81; taxpayer svc. rep. IRS, Dallas, 1981-83, acct. analyst, 1983-88; freelance Dallas, 1989-90; social worker Tex. Dept. Human Svcs., Dallas, 1991-96, Tex. Workforce Commn., 1996—. Reader, North Tex. Taping & Radio for the Blind, Dallas, 1991—; mem. choir St. Peter the Apostle Cath. Ch.; mem. Whale Adoption Project; mem. Union Chorale. Mem. AAUW, Am. Counseling Assn., Nat. Specialty Merchandising Assn., Am. Multicultural Counseling Assn., Am. Bible Tchrs. Assn., Tex. Counseling Assn., Tex. Multicultural Counseling Assn., Assn. Rsch. and Enlightenment, Inc., Assn. for Spiritual, Ethical, and Religious Values in Counseling, U. Tex Arlington Alumni Assn., U. North Tex. Alumni Assn. Office: Tex Workforce Commn 4533 Ross Ave Dallas TX 75204-8417

SIMS, MARCIE LYNNE, English language educator, writer; b. Monrovia, Calif., Feb. 22, 1963; d. Charles Eugene and Delores May (Wonert) S.; m. Douglas Todd Cole; 1 child, Marcus Anthony Cole. BA in English, Calif. State Poly., 1986; MA in English, San Diego State U., 1990. Page U.S. Senate, Washington, 1979; instr. Calif. Conservation Corps, San Diego, 1990; instr. in English Shoreline C.C., Seattle, 1990-94, Seattle Ctrl. C.C., 1990-94, Green River C.C., Auburn, Wash., 1994—; founder Wild Mind Women Writers Workshop, Seattle, 1992—. Author: Soul-Making: John Keats and the Stages of Death, 1990; contbg. author Moms on Line, 1996; co-editor: The Great Tchrs. Almanac, 1988-90. Vol. cons. Camp Fire, Wash., 1994-96. Mem. Am. Fedn. Tchrs., The Keats-Shelley Orgn., Wash. Fed. Tchrs. (exec. bd. mem. 1993-94), Phi Kappa Phi, Sigma Tau Delta. Democrat. Office: Green River CC 12401 SE 320th St Auburn WA 98092-3699

SIMS, REBECCA GIBBS, accountant, certified fraud examiner; b. Houston, Mar. 13, 1951; d. Shelton P. Gibbs and Elizabeth Gill Bisby; m. Morris Raymond Sims (div. 1977); children: Diana Elizabeth, Aaron Redding. BFA, U. Houston, 1977. Cert. fraud examiner. V.p. Lexley U.S.A., Inc., Houston and Mexico City, 1977-81; acct. self-employed, Houston, 1982-87, journalist/investigator, 1987—, fin. fraud investigator, 1991—; mng. ptnr. Boynton & Assocs., 1996—. Editor, rschr.: Maria, CIA and George Bush, 1992; screenwriter; journalist Bilanz mag., Switzerland, 1989-91; author article. Childbirth instr. Houston Orgn. Parent Edn., Houston, 1974-77. Mem. Investigative Reporters and Editors, Nat. Writers Union, Mensa. Democrat. Office: 440 Louisiana Ste 1720 Houston TX 77002

SIMS, TERRE LYNN, insurance company executive; b. Madison, Wis., Dec. 26, 1951; d. Roy Charles and Ruth Marie (McCloskey) Pierstorff; m. Gary Peter Paul Laufenberg, Feb. 15, 1969 (div.); children: Amie, Monte, Tawna; m. Perry Allen Sims, May 3, 1994. Sales agt. Bankers Life and Casualty, Madison, 1977-80, asst. mgr., 1981-84; br. mgr. Bankers Life and Casualty, Peoria, 1984-91; co-owner Complete Ins. Svcs., Inc., Madison, Wis., 1991—; owner, operator Ohio Tavern, Madison, 1993—. Office: Complete Ins Svcs Inc 6400 Gisholt Dr Madison WI 53713-4800

SIMSON, BEVLYN ANN, artist; b. Columbus, Ohio, Sept. 9, 1917; d. Amon and Fannie Florence (Gilbert) Thall; m. Theodore Richard Simson, Mar. 25, 1938; children: Sherran Blair, Douglas A. BFA, Ohio State U., 1969, MFA, 1972. One woman shows include J.B. Speed Art Mus., Louisville, 1970, Huntington Gallery, Columbus, Ohio, 1970, 73, United Christian Ctr., Columbus, 1970, Bodley Gallery, N.Y., 1971, 74, Gilman Galleries, Chgo., 1971, Gallery 200, Columbus, 1972, Hopkins Hall Gallery, Ohio State U., Columbus, 1972, Meth. Theol. Sch., Delaware, Ohio, 1973, Columbus Pub. Libr., 1973, Garfinkels, Washington, 1973, City Hall, Mayor's Office, Columbus, 1974, 82, Capital U., Bexley, Ohio, 1977, Hillel Found., Ohio State U., 1978, Motorists Gallery, Columbus, 1978, Columbus Tech. Inst., 1979, Springfield (Ohio) Art Mus., 1980, Peace Luth. Ch., Gahanna, Ohio, 1981, Franklin U. Gallery, Columbus, 1981, Columbus Mus. Art, Collectors Gallery, 1983; exhibited in group shows at Columbus Mus. Art-Columbus Art League, 1968, 70, 71, 73, 74, 75, 77, 78, 79, 80, 86, Ohio Statehouse and State Office Tower, Columbus, 1968-78, Battelle Meml. Inst., Columbus, 1969-73, 75, 78, 81-82, Schumacher Gallery, Capital U., Columbus, 1969-85, 87, 88, Salles d'Exposition, Paris, 1969, Am. Cultural Ctr., Kyoto, Japan, 1970, Cin. Art Mus., 1970, J.B. Speed Art Mus. Collector's Gallery, Louisville, 1970-85, Studio San Guiseppe, Mt. St. Joseph Coll., Cin., 1971, Mansfield (Ohio) Art Ctr., 1971, Collector's Showroom, Chgo., 1971-82, Gov.'s Mansion State of Ohio, 1972, 74, Western Ill. U., 1972, Albatross Gallery, Rome, 1972, Palazzo Dell Exprizioni, Rome, 1972, Place-Allrich Gallery, San Francisco, 1973-75, Chautauqua Assn., N.Y., 1973, Butler Inst. Am. Art, Youngstown, Ohio, 1973, 76, Huntington Gallery, Columbus, 1973, 74, Gallery 200, Columbus, 1972-76, Ainsworth Gallery, Boston, 1973-84, Columbus C. of C., 1974, 75, Zanesville (Ohio) Art Ctr., 1976, Columbus Inst. Contemporary Art, 1978, Nationwide Ins. Gallery, Columbus, 1980, Nationwide Plaza Gallery, Columbus, 1980, Franklin U., Columbus, 1980, Columbus Art League, 1987, Jeffrey Mansion, Bexley, Ohio, 1996; represented in permanent collections Columbus Mus. Arts, J.B. Speed Art Mus., Louisville, Capital U., Bexley, Fordham U., N.Y.C., Kyoto City U. Fine Arts, Springfield Art Mus., Tyler (Tex.) Mus. Art, Wichita (Kans.) Mus. Art, Zanesville Art Ctr., Ohio State U., Columbus, Meth. Theol. Sch., Delaware, Ohio, Yerke Morgtgage Co., Columbus, Marcorp, N.Y., Kresge Co., Detroit, IBM, Columbus, Chase Manhattan Bank, N.Y.C., Chase Bank of Ohio, Am. Bancorp., Columbus, Ohio Nat. Bank Plaza, Columbus, Pan Western Life Ins. Co., Columbus, First Investment Co., Columbus, Redwood Bank, San Francisco, Children's Hosp., Phila., Franklin County Crippled Children's Ctr., Columbus, Zenith East, N.Y.C., First Cmty. Bank, Columbus, Ronald McDonald House, Columbus, Columbia Gas of Ohio, Columbus, Midland Title Security Co., Columbus, Huntington Nat. Bank Ctr., Columbus, Price Waterhouse Co., Columbus, Lehman Bros., N.Y.C., Columbus Sch. for Girls, Grand Prix Assocs., Inc., Columbus, Grant Hosp. Med. Ctr., Columbus; represented in pvt. collections. Mem. Nat. League Am. Pen Women, Artists Equity Assn., Bexley Area Art Guild, Columbus Mus. Art, Columbus Art League (bd. dirs. 1965-96, treas., sec., pres. 1977), Ohio State U. Alumni Assn., Winding Hollow Country Club, Phi Sigma Sigma. Studio: First Cmty Bank Bldg 4300 E Broad St Columbus OH 43213

SIMSON, JO ANNE, anatomy and cell biology educator; b. Chgo., Nov. 19, 1936; d. Kenneth Brown and Helen Marjorie (Pascoe) Valentine; m. Arnold Simson, June 1961 (div.); 1 child, Maria; m. Michael Smith, Nov. 10, 1971 (div.); children: Elizabeth Smith, Briana Smith. BA, Kalamazoo Coll., 1959; MS, U. Mich., 1961; PhD, SUNY, Syracuse, 1969. Postdoctoral fellow Temple U. Health Sci. Ctr., Phila., 1968-70; asst. prof. Med. U. S.C., Charleston, 1970-76, assoc. prof., 1976-83, prof. anatomy and cell biology, 1983—; featured in Smithsonian exhibit, Sci. in Am. Life, 1994—. Contbr. articles to profl. jours.; author short stories and poems. Active adult edn. Unitarian Ch., Charleston, 1973-75, social action, 1990-92. Grantee NSF, 1959-60, NIH, 1966-67, 72-87, 91-95. Mem. Am. Assn. Anatomists, Am. Soc. Cell Biology, Histochem. Soc. (sec. 1979-82, exec. com. 1985-89), Fogarty Internat. Fellowship Bioctr. (Basel, Switzerland, 1987-88), Amnesty Internat. (newsletter editor Group 168 1982-86), Phi Beta Kappa. Home: 1760 Pittsford Cir Charleston SC 29412-4110 Office: Med U SC Anatomy 171 Ashley Ave Charleston SC 29425-0001

SIMUNICH, MARY ELIZABETH HEDRICK (MRS. WILLIAM A. SIMUNICH), public relations executive; b. Chgo.; d. Tubman Keene and Mary (McCamish) Hedrick; m. William A. Simunich, Dec. 6, 1941. Student Phoenix Coll., 1967-69, Met. Bus. Coll., 1938-40. Exec. sec. sales mgr. Sta. KPHO radio, 1950-53; exec. sec. mgr. Sta. KPHO-TV, 1953-54; account exec. Tom Rippey & Assos., 1955-56; pub. rels. dir. Phoenix Symphony, 1956-62; co-founder, v.p. Paul J. Hughes Pub. Rels., Inc., 1960-65; owner Mary Simunich Pub. Rels., Phoenix, 1966-77; pub. rels. dir. Walter O. Boswell Meml. Hosp., Sun City, Ariz., 1969-85; pub. rels. cons., 1985—; pres. DARCI PR, Phoenix, 1994—, Cityscape, Inc. (formerly Citynet, Inc.), 1994—; instr. pub. rels. Phoenix Coll. Evening Sch., 1973-78. Bd. dirs. Anytown, Ariz., 1969-72; founder, sec. Friends Am. Geriatrics, 1977-86. Named Phoenix Advt. Woman of Year, Phoenix Jr. Advt. Club, 1962; recipient award Blue Cross, 1963; 1st Pl. award Ariz. Press Women, 1966. Mem. NAFE, Women in Comm., Internat. Assn. Bus. Communicators (pres. Ariz. chpt. 1970-71, dir.), Pub. Rels. Soc. Am. (sec., dir. 1976-78), Am. Soc. Hosp. Pub. Rels. (dir. Ariz. chpt. 1976-78), Nat., Ariz. Press Women. Home: 4133 N 34th Pl Phoenix AZ 85018-4771 Office: DARCI Group 2425 E Camelback Ste 450 Phoenix AZ 85016-4236

SINANIAN, LINDA MARIE, violinist, educator; b. L.A., Nov. 18, 1961; d. Loris Roy and Peggy (Gavin) Sinanian; m. Jeffrey James Forden, Oct. 12, 1991. BMus, Converse Coll., Spartanburg, S.C., 1983; postgrad., New Eng. Conservatory, Boston, 1988-89; MMus, Manhattan Sch. Music, 1985; PhD of Mus. Arts, SUNY, Stony Brook, 1996. Violinist, concermaster Manhattan Chamber Orch., N.Y.C., 1982-87; violinist Jupiter Symphony Orch., N.Y.C., 1982-87; prin. 2d violin L'Opera Lyrico Sperimentale, Spoleto, Italy, 1984; violinist Portland (Maine) Symphony Orch., 1987-89, Opera Co. of Boston, 1987-89, Boston Philharmonic Orch., 1987-89, Atlanta Opera Orch., 1991-92, The St. Jude Ensemble, Atlanta, 1991—, L.I. Chamber Players, 1995—; solo violinist concert tour throughout Italy, 1995; faculty Clayton State Coll., Morrow, Ga., 1991-92; condr. Chinese Chamber Orch., Stony Brook, 1992-93; violin instr. The Stony Brook Sch., 1995—; pvt. studio Rocky Point and Stony Brook, 1992—; artistic dir., founder St. Jude Ensemble, 1991; co-founder Manhattan Chamber Orch., 1982. Coach, condr. Greater Boston Youth Symphony Orch. Urban Outreach Program, 1988. Recipient 1st place prize New Eng. Conservatory Concert Competition, 1988, Pro Music Young Artists competition, 1985, Converse Coll. Concerto competition, 1982. Roman Catholic. Home and Office: 174 Broadway Rocky Point NY 11778

SINAY, DEBORAH J., broadcast professional; m. Charles Kravetz; two children: Sasha, Jessica. Grad., Baypath Coll.; grad. intensive exec. sales mgmt. program, Harvard U. Former broadcast media dir. Smith Patterson Advt. divsn. Jordan Marsh Dept. Stores, New Eng.; from acct. exec. in sales to v.p., sales mgr. WCVB-TV, Needham Heights, Mass., 1976-84, v.p., gen. sales mgr., 1984—; tchr. Boston U. Sch. Comms.; guest lectr. Boston-area colls. and univs.; part-time instr. comms. Grahm Jr. Coll., Boston, 1973-76. Mem. exec. bd. Scleroderma Rsch. Fund; mem. comms. com. Patriot's Trail Girl Scouts U.S. Coun. of Greater Boston, Anti-Defamation League. Named Citizen of Yr., Norwich, Conn. C. of C., 1984; recipient YMCA Women of Achievement in Bus. award West Suburban Boston, 1985; named one of the area's Ten Outstanding Young Leaders, Boston Jaycees, 1986. Mem. NOW, LWV. Office: WCVB-TV 5 TV Place Needham Heights MA 02194-2303

SINCLAIR, BARBARA, political scientist, educator. BA, Rice U., 1962; PhD, U. Rochester, 1970. From asst. prof. to prof. U. Calif. Riverside, 1970-96; Marvin Hoffenberg prof. Am. Politics UCLA, 1996—; v.p. Am. Polit. Sci. Assn., 1987-88, Fenno prize 1990; pres. We. Polit. Sci. Assn., 1992-93. Author: Congressional Realignment, 1982, Majority Leadership in the U.S. House, 1983, The Transformation of the U.S. Senate, 1989, Legislators, Leaders and Lawmaking, 1995. Recipient D.B. Hardeman prize LBJ Found., 1990. Office: Univ Calif Dept Polit Sci Los Angeles CA 90024

SINCLAIR, CAROLE, publisher, editor, author; b. Haddonfield, N.J., May 13, 1942; d. Earl Walter and Ruth (Sinclair) Dunham; 1 child, Wendy. Student, U. Florence, Italy, 1963; BA in Polit. Sci., Bucknell U, 1964. Advt. copywriter BBD&O Advertising, N.Y.C., 1966-67; sales promotion mgr. Macmillan Pub. Co., N.Y.C., 1967-71; mktg. mgr. Doubleday & Co., Inc., N.Y.C., 1972-74, promotion dir., 1974-76, advt. mgr., sales and promotion, chmn. mktg. com., 1976-80; v.p. mktg., editorial dir. Davis Pubs., N.Y.C., 1980-83; founder, pub., editorial dir., sr. v.p. Sylvia Porter's Personal Fin. Mag., N.Y.C., 1983-90; pres. The Sylvia Porter Orgn., Inc., N.Y.C., 1980-91; founder, pres. Sinclair Media Inc., N.Y.C., 1990—; mktg. dir. Denver Pub. Inst., summers 1975-78; lectr. Columbia U. Bus. Sch. and Sch. of Journalism, 1976; host nationally syndicated TV show, Sylvia Porter's Money Tips, syndicated daily radio show, Sylvia Porter's Personal Fin. Report, audio cassette series on fin. topics. Author: Keys for Women Starting and Owning a Business, 1991, Keys to Women's Basic Professional Needs, 1991, When Women Retire, 1992; contbg. editor Pushcart Prize, 1977; contbr. The Business of Publishing, 1980. Renaissance Art Program fellow, Florence, Italy, 1963; White House intern, 1962. Mem. Women's Forum, Intercorp. Communications Group, Mag. Pubs.' Assn., Advt. Women in N.Y., Spence Sch. Parent's League. Presbyterian. Club: Pubs. Lunch.

SINCLAIR, DAISY, advertising executive, casting director; b. Perth Amboy, N.J., Mar. 22, 1941; d. James Patrick and Margaret Mary (McAniff) Nieland; m. James Pratt Sinclair, May 25, 1978; children: Duncan, Gibbons. BA, Caldwell Coll., 1962. Jr. copywriter Young & Rubican, N.Y.C., 1962-64; various positions in casting dept. Ogilvy & Mather, N.Y.C., 1964-90, sr. v.p., dir. casting, 1990—. Mem. Am. Assn. Advt. (talent agt. com. 1972—), Drama League N.Y. (3d v.p. 1982—), The Knickerbocker Greys (v.p.), Edgartown Yacht Club, Chapaquoit Yacht Club, The Tuxedo Club. Republican. Episcopalian. Home: 4 E 95th St New York NY 10128-0705 Office: Ogilvy & Mather Advt Worldwide Plz 309 W 49th St New York NY 10019-7316

SINCLAIR, SARA VORIS, health facility administrator, nurse; b. Kansas City, Mo., Apr. 13, 1942; d. Franklin Defenbaugh and Inez Estelle (Figenbaum) Voris; m. James W. Sinclair, June 13, 1964; children: Thomas James, Elizabeth Kathleen, Joan Sara. BSN, UCLA, 1965. RN, Utah; lic. health care facility adminstr.; cert. health care adminstr. Staff nurse UCLA Med. Ctr. Hosp., 1964-65; charge nurse Boulder (Colo.) Meml. Hosp., 1966, Boulder (Colo.) Manor Nursing Home, 1974-75, Four Seasons Nursing Home, Joliet, Ill., 1975-76; dir. nursing Home Health Agy of Olympia Fields, Joliet, Ill., 1977-79; dir. nursing Sunshine Terr. Found., Inc., Logan, Utah, 1980, asst. adminstr., 1980-81, adminstr., 1981-93; dir. divsn. health systems improvement Utah Dept. Health, Salt Lake City, 1993—; mem. long term care profl. and tech. adv. com. Joint Commn. on Accreditation Healthcare Orgns., Chgo., 1987-91, chmn., 1990-91; adj. lectr. Utah State U., 1991-93; mem. adj. clin. faculty Weber State U., Ogden, Utah; moderator radio program Healthwise Sta. KUSU-FM, 1985-93; spkr. Nat. Coun. Aging, 1993, Alzheimer's Disease Assn. Ann. Conf., 1993; del. White House Conf. on Aging, 1995; chmn. Utah Dept. of Health's Ethics, Instnl. Rev. Bd. Com., 1995—, Utah Dept. Health Risk Mgmt. Com., 1995—; exec. com. Utah Long Term Care Coalition, 1995; presenter in field. Contbg. author: Associate Degree Nursing and The Nursing Home, 1988. Mem. dean's adv. coun. Coll. Bus. Utah State U., Logan, 1989-91, mem. presdl. search com., 1991-92; chmn., co-founder Cache Cmty. Health Coun., Logan, 1985; chmn. bd. Hospice of Cache Valley, Logan, 1986; mem. Utah State Adv. Coun. on Aging, 1986-93; apptd. chmn. Utah Health Facilities Com., 1989-91; chmn. Bear River Dist. Adv. Coun. on Aging, 1989-91; chmn. health and human svcs. subcom. Cache 2010, 1992-93. Recipient Disting. Svc. award Utah State U., 1989. Fellow Am. Coll. Health Care Adminstrs. (presenter 1992-93, 95, presenter 1996 ann. convocation New Orleans, v.p. Utah chpt. 1992-94, convocation and edn. coms. 1992-93, region IX vice gov. 1994-96, bylaws com. 1996—); mem. Am. Healthcare Assn. (non-proprietary v.p. 1986-87, region v.p. 1987-89, presenter workshop conv. 1990-93, presenter ann. convocation 1995, exec. com. 1993), Utah Health Care Assn. (pres. 1983-85, treas. 1991-93, Disting. Svc. award 1991, Svc. award for long term care 1996), Utah Gerontol. Soc. (bd. dirs. 1992-93, 95—, chmn. nominating com. 1993-94, chmn. ann. conf. 1996, pres.-elect 1996), Cache C. of C. (pres. 1991), Logan Bus. and Profl. Women's Club (pres. 1989, Woman of Achievement award 1982, Woman of Yr. 1982), Rotary (Logan chpt., chair comty. svc. com. 1989-90). Office: Utah Dept Health Div Health Sys Improvement 288 N 1460 W Salt Lake City UT 84114-2851 also: PO Box 142851 Salt Lake City UT 84114-2851

SINCLAIR, STACY LYNN, elementary education educator; b. L.A., May 6, 1967; d. Harold Louis and Joan P. (Kline) Yeoman. BA, Bennington (Vt.) Coll., 1989; student, Calif. State U. Northridge, L.A., 1992; MS in Edn. and Adminsrv., Pepperdine U., L.A., 1995. Cert. tchr., archivist, Calif. Tchr., cons. on movement L.A. Unified Sch. Dist., 1991—. Author: Teaching School Curriculum through Dance, 1991. Recipient Gov.'s award Vt. State Gov., 1988; Calif. State U. Northridge Found. grantee, 1990. Mem. United Tchrs. L.A. Office: Millikan Mid Sch 5041 Sunnyslope Ave Van Nuys CA 91423

SINDEROFF, RITA JOYCE, property management company executive, real estate broker, mortgage broker; b. Bklyn., June 22, 1932; d. Joseph George and Mary (Cohen) Rothkopf; m. Arthur B. Schneider, Oct. 18, 1953 (div. Sept. 1973); children: Linda Ellen, Debra Carol. Degree in comml. art Pratt Inst., 1953; BA in Acctg., Bklyn. Coll., 1954. Contr. Central Funding Co., Bklyn., 1973-80; owner, contr. Riteway Mgmt. Inc., Coral Springs, Fla., 1980-86; realtor Riteway Internat. Realty Corp., Coral Springs, 1985-86, ERA Regal Internat. Realty Inc.; realtor, mortgage broker Regal Fin. Svcs. and LCAM Regal Assn. Svcs., Coral Springs, Fla., 1986-94; mortgage broker; cons. in field. Active Cancer Soc., Bklyn., 1954-73, March of Dimes, Bklyn., 1960-70. Recipient 1st art award City of N.Y., 1950. Mem. Nat. Bd. Realtors, North Broward Bd. Realtors, Fla. Assn. Mortgage Brokers, Nat. Real Estate Assn., Fla. Assn. Community Mgrs. (lic.), Community Assn. Inst. Democrat. Jewish. Avocations: reading, dancing, swimming.

SING, DORIS ANNE, music educator; b. Houston, Oct. 1, 1947; d. Theron Ponton Sr. and Anna Agnes (Dethlefsen) Spradley; m. William B. Sing, Sept. 1, 1967; children: Erin Elaine, Emily Elizabeth. BS in Edn. cum laude, U. Houston, 1970, BMus cum laude, 1990. Cert. tchr. elem. and spl. edn., Tex. Dir. children's choir St. Andrew's Presbyn. Ch., Houston, 1984-90; tchr. music St. Andrew's Presbyn. Sch., Houston, 1991-93; founder, dir. Arts a la Carte, Houston, 1993—. Elder St. Andrew's Presbyn. Ch., 1992-94. Mem. Early Childhood Music Assn., KinderMusik Educators Assn. (cert. tchr.), ORFF-Schulwerk Assn., Phi Kappa Phi, Kappa Delta Pi. Office: Arts a la Carte 3637 W Alabama Ste 490 Houston TX 77027

SINGER, BARBARA HELEN, photographer; b. N.Y.C., Jan. 29, 1927; d. Robert and Rose (Kaplowitz) S.; m. Nat Herz, Jan. 15, 1956 (dec. Nov. 1964); m. Melvin C. Zalkan, Sept. 7, 1983 (dec. Nov. 1993). BA in Biology, NYU, 1947; studied with Eli Siegel, 1944-76. Radiographer, 1951-90; instr. Meth. Hosp. Sch. Radiologic Tech., Bklyn., 1968-72; asst. to Benedict J. Fernandez & Lucien Clergue New Sch./Parsons, N.Y.C., N.Y., 1985-91; photographer N.Y.C., 1983-96. Group exhbns. include Associated Artists Gallery, Winston-Salem, N.C., 1985, Donnell Libr., N.Y.C., 1986, Lincoln Sq. Gallery, N.Y.C., 1990, Konica Plz., Tokyo, 1990, Nikon House, N.Y.C., 1990, St. Margaret's House, N.Y.C., 1991, Duggal Downtown, N.Y.C., 1994, Salmagundi Club, N.Y.C., 1994, Coll. New Rochelle, N.Y., 1994, Artists Talk on Art, N.Y.C., 1994, Gallery Cedar Hollow, Malvern, Pa., 1995, Columbia U., N.Y.C., 1995, Erector Sq. Gallery, New Haven, 1995, Hudson Pk. Libr., N.Y.C., 1996, Learning Alliance, N.Y.C., 1996, Lever House, N.Y.C., 1996, Severoceske Mus., 1996, Nat. Mus. Asian, African & Am. Cultures, Prague, Czech Republic, 1996, Time Life Bldg., N.Y.C., 1996, Wildlife Conservation Soc., N.Y.C., 1996; CD-ROM Urbane Photography, 1996; photography published in Profl. Women Photographers Newsletter, 1985, 95, Light and Shade, 1985, Best of Photography Annual 1990, Women of Vision, 1990, Tear Sheet, 1995. Photographers' Forum Finalist, 1990; recipient Photography award Beaux Arts Soc., 1994. Mem. Profl. Women Photographers, Pictorial Photographers Am., Artists Talk on Art, Soc. Media Photographers. Office: Madison Sq Sta PO Box 1150 New York NY 10159

SINGER, CECILE DORIS, state legislator. BA, Queens Coll. Past rep. Spl. Svcs. for Children, N.Y.C.; past exec. dir. N.Y. State Assembly Social Svcs. and Judiciary Coms., Joint Legis. Com. on Corps., Authorities and Commns.; past pub. rep. Yonkers (N.Y.) Emergency Control Bd.; past coord. Westchester County Assembly Dels.; past chief of staff for dep. minority leader; mem. N.Y. State Assembly, Albany, 1988—, leadership sec. Rep. Conf., mem. assembly children & families com., mem. various other coms.; bd. dirs. Hudson Valley Bank; past rep. Temp. Commn. to Revise Social Svcs. Law; mem. Presdl. Commn. on Privacy Conf., N.Y. State Senate Transp. Conf.; mem. task force on substance abuse Am. Legis. Exch. Coun., task force on econ. devel., crime victims' rights, hosp. crisis, women's issues, com. on mass transit; sec. Rep. Conf. Nat. Adv. Panel Child Care Action Campaign; dir. Hudson Valley Bank; chmn. Westchester County Commn. on Pub. Financing of Campaigns; chmn. Lower Hudson Valley Adv. Com. N.Y. State Divsn. for Women. Mem. adv. bd. Legal Awareness for Women, Big Bros. and Big Sisters, Westchester C.C. Found., Westchester 2000 Rsch., Womens Adv. Bd. Westchester County; mem. task force on certiorari Westchester County Sch. Bds. Assn.; sch. and cmty. chmn. Yonkers PTA; bd. dirs. Yonkers Gen. Hosp., Yonkers chpt. United Jewish Appeal. Recipient Jenkins Meml. award, Nat. PTA award; inducted Women's Hall of Fame, 1996, Sr. Citizens Hall of Fame, 1996. Mem. Mental Health Assn. (bd. dirs., mem. nominating and pub. affairs coms. Westchester County chpt.), Rotary. Home: 117 Cliffside Dr Yonkers NY 10710-3144 Office: 21 Scarsdale Rd Yonkers NY 10707

SINGER, DAVIDA, poet, jouranlist, educator; b. Burlington, Vt., Oct. 31, 1957; d. Benjamin Singerman and Lilyan (Ostrow) Fishman. BA in Writing, Columbia U., 1983; MA in Journalism, NYU, 1991. Instr. writing and ESL Baruch Coll., CUNY, 1993—; theater journalist The Villager newspaper, 1994—; freelance mag. writer, 1992—. Author: Shelter Island Poems, 1995; creator, prodr. (performance art piece) Khupe, 1996. Mem. Nat. Writers Union, Transp. Alternative, Jews for Racial and Econ. Justice. Jewish. Home and Office: 223 W 105th St Apt 3FW New York NY 10025

SINGER, DONNA LEA, writer, editor, educator; b. Wilmington, Del., Oct. 6, 1944; d. Marshall Richard and Sara Emma (Eppihimer) S. BA in English cum laude, Gettysburg Coll., 1966; postgrad., Montclair State Coll., 1972-73, U. Birmingham, Eng., 1977; M of Letters, Drew U., 1985. Asst. to dir. student activities Fairleigh Dickinson U., Madison, N.J., 1966-68; tchr., drama coach Morris Hills High Sch., Rockaway, N.J., 1968-84; free-lance editor Basic Books, Inc., N.Y.C., 1983-86; adj. instr. Fairleigh Dickinson U., Madison, 1986-87; free-lance writer, editor Visual Edn. Corp., Princeton, N.J., 1988—, Fact's on File, Bantam, Random House, Fodor's Travel Books, N.Y.C., 1990—, John Wiley & Sons, N.Y.C., 1990—; co-founder, co-dir. Traveling Hist. Troupe, Rockaway, 1976-78; tour leader Am. Leadership Study Groups, 1976, 78, 82; theatre studies participant Royal Shakespeare Co., Stratford, Eng., 1978, 79, 81; docent, lectr. acting co. Hist. Spanish Point, Osprey, Fla., 1989—. Contbg. author: (poetry) Chasing Rainbows, 1987, An American Heritage, 1994, (biographies) Past and Promise: Lives of New Jersey Women, 1990, American Cultural Leaders, 1993. Big sister Big Bros./Big Sisters, Sarasota, Fla., 1990—. Mem. Internat. Women's Writing Guild, Gulf Coast Writers Forum, Met. Mus. Art, Royal Shakespeare Company Assocs.

SINGER, ELEANOR, sociologist, editor; b. Vienna, Austria, Mar. 4, 1930; came to U.S., 1938; d. Alfons and Anna (Troedl) Schwarzbart; m. Alan Gerard Singer, Sept. 8, 1949; children: Emily Ann, Lawrence Alexander. BA, Queens Coll., 1951; PhD, Columbia U., 1966. Asst. editor Am. Scholar, Williamsburg, Va., 1951-52; editor Tchrs. Coll. Press, N.Y.C., 1952-56, Dryden-Holt, N.Y.C., 1956-57; rsch. assoc., sr. rsch. assoc., sr. rsch. scholar Columbia U., N.Y.C., 1966-94; rsch. scientist Inst. for Social Rsch. U. Mich., Ann Arbor, 1994—; editor Pub. Opinion Quar., N.Y.C., 1975-86. Author: (with Carol Weiss) The Reporting of Social Science in the Mass Media, 1988, (with Phyllis Endreny) Reporting On Risk, 1993; editor: (with Herbert H. Hyman) Readings in Reference Group Theory and Research, 1968, (with Stanley Presser) Survey Research Methods: A Reader, 1989; contbr. articles to profl. jours. Mem. Am. Assn. Pub. Opinion Research (pres. N.Y.C. chpt. 1983-84, pres. 1987-88), Am. Sociol. Assn., Am. Statis. Assn. Office: U Mich Inst Social Rsch Box 1248 Ann Arbor MI 48106

SINGER, JEANNE (JEANNE WALSH), composer, concert pianist; b. N.Y.C., Aug. 4, 1924; d. Harold Vandervoort and Helen (Loucks) Walsh; m. Richard G. Singer, Feb. 24, 1945 (dec.); 1 son, Richard V. BA magna cum laude, Barnard Coll., 1944; artist diploma Nat. Guild Piano Tchrs., 1954; student in piano Nadia Reisenberg, 1945-60, composition, Douglas Moore, 1942-44, PhD (hon.) in Music World U., 1984. Composer, concert pianist solo chamber ensembles N.Y., 1947—; tchr. piano Manhasset, N.Y., 1960—; found, dir. Musinger Players Chamber Ensemble, 1986—, over 100 concerts performed by this ensemble; lectr. in field. Recipient spl. award merit Nat. Fedn. Music Clubs, 1st prize in nat. competition Composers Guild, 1979, Grand prize Composers Guild, 1982, 1st prize Composers and Songwriters Internat., 1985, also various nat. awards; honored at all-Singer concert,

Bogotá, Colombia, 1980; N.Y. Council Arts grantee. Fellow Internat. Biog. Assn.; mem. ASCAP (awards 1978—), Am. Music Center, Nat. League Am. Pen Women (nat. music chmn.), Composers, Authors and Artists Am. (v.p. N.Y.C., music mag. editor 1972-80, nat. award 1981), Am. Women Composers, Internat. Alliance for Women in Music, L.I. Composers Alliance, Pen and Brush, Barnard Coll. Club, Bohemians, Phi Beta Kappa. Composed numerous instrumental, vocal works including: Summons (baritone), 1975, A Cycle of Love (4 songs with piano), 1976, Suite in Harpsichord Style, 1976, From The Green Mountains (trio), 1977, (choral work) Composers' Prayer, Nocturne for Clarinet, 1980, Suite for Horn and Harp, 1980, From Petrarch (voice, horn, piano), 1981, Grandmother's Attic, Quartet for Flute, Oboe, Violin, Cello, 1982, Recollections of City Island, 1984 (for viola, oboe, piano), Come Greet the Spring (choral), 1981, An American Vision (song cycle), 1985, Wry Rimes (voice and Bassoon), 1986, The Lost Garden (voice, piano, cello), 1988, To Be Brave Is All (orch. and voice), 1993; 23 art songs recorded on CD To Stir a Dream, 1991; performed Lincoln Center, radio, TV. Home and Office: 64 Stuart Pl Manhasset NY 11030-2620

SINGER, LINDA SUE ROLLET, elementary school principal; b. Glenwood, Iowa, May 14, 1949; d. Paul Anthony and Dorothy Louise (Singleton) Rollet; m. Rory Karl Singer, Sept. 11, 1976 (div. Apr. 1986). Student, Chapman Coll., 1969; BA in Speech Pathology, U. Redlands (Calif.), 1971, MS in Comm. Disorders, 1973; BS in Elem. Edn., U. Utah, 1977; adminstrv. cert., Utah State U., 1988. Speech and lang. specialist Ocean View Sch. Dist., Huntington Beach, Calif., 1972-75; with retail sales dept. RESOA, Park City, Utah, 1975-77; resource tchr. Park City Sch. Dist., 1977-83, prin., 1983—; mem. adj. faculty Westminster Coll., Salt Lake City, 1983-85; mentor prin. leader's prep. program Brigham Young U., Park City, 1988. Mem. ASCD, Utah ASCD, Nat. Assn. Elem. Sch. Prins. (bd. dirs. Utah chpt. 1985-87), Rotary Club (pres. 1994-95). Home: 2788 Holiday Ranch Loop Rd Park City UT 84060 Office: McPolin Elem Sch 2270 Kearns Blvd Park City UT 84060

SINGER, MAXINE FRANK, biochemist, think tank executive; b. N.Y.C., Feb. 15, 1931; d. Hyman S. and Henrietta (Perlowitz) Frank; m. Daniel Morris Singer, June 15, 1952; children: Amy Elizabeth, Ellen Ruth, David Byrd, Stephanie Frank. AB, Swarthmore Coll., 1952, DSc (hon.), 1978; PhD, Yale U., 1957; DSc (hon.), Wesleyan U., 1977, Swarthmore Coll., 1978, U. Md.-Baltimore County, 1985, Cedar Crest Coll., 1986, CUNY, 1988, Brandeis U., 1988, Radcliffe Coll., 1990, Williams Coll., 1990, Franklin and Marshall Coll., 1991, George Washington U., 1991, NYU, 1992, Lehigh U., 1992, Dartmouth Coll., 1993, Yale U., 1994, Harvard U., 1994; PhD honoris causa, Weizmann Inst. Sci., 1995. USPHS postdoctoral fellow NIH, Bethesda, Md., 1956-58; rsch. chemist biochemistry NIH, 1958-74; head sect. on nucleic acid enzymology Nat. Cancer Inst., 1974-79; chief Lab. of Biochemistry, Nat. Cancer Inst., 1979-87, rsch. chemist, 1987-88; pres. Carnegie Inst. Washington, 1988—; Regents vis. lectr. U. Calif., Berkeley, 1981; bd. dirs. Johnson & Johnson; mem. sci. coun. Internat. Inst. Genetics and Biophysics, Naples, Italy, 1982-86; mem. adv. bd. Chulabhorn Rsch. Inst., 1990—. Mem. editorial bd. Jour. Biol. Chemistry, 1968-74, Sci. mag., 1972-82; chmn. editorial bd. Procs. of NAS, 1985-88; author (with Paul Berg) 2 books on molecular biology; contbr. articles to scholarly jours. Trustee Wesleyan U., Middletown, Conn., 1972-75, Yale Corp., New Haven, 1975-90; bd. govs. Weizmann Inst. Sci., Rehovot, Israel, 1978—; bd. dirs. Whitehead Inst., 1985-94; chmn. Smithsonian Coun., 1992-93. Recipient award for achievement in biol. scis. Washington Acad. Scis., 1969, award for rsch. in biol. scis. Yale Sci. and Engring. Assn., 1974, Superior Svc. Honor award HEW, 1975, Dirs. award NIH, 1977, Disting. Svc. medal HHS, 1983, Presdl. Disting. Exec. Rank award, 1987, U.S. Disting. Exec. Rank award, 1987, Mory's Cup Bd. Govs. Mory's Assn., 1991, Wilbur Lucius Cross Medal for Honor Yale Grad. Sch. Assn., 1991, Nat. Medal Sci. NSF, 1992, Pub. Svc. award NIH Alumni Assn., 1995. Fellow Am. Acad. Arts and Scis.; mem. NAS (coun. 1982-85, com. sci., engring and pub. policy 1989-91), AAAS (Sci. Freedom and Responsibility award 1982), Am. Soc. Biol. Chemists, Am. Soc. Microbiologists, Am. Chem. Soc., Am. Philos. Soc., Inst. Medicine of NAS, Pontifical Acad. of Scis, Human Genome Orgn., N.Y. Acad. Scis. Home: 5410 39th St NW Washington DC 20015-2902 Office: Carnegie Inst Washington 1530 P St NW Washington DC 20005-1910

SINGER, NIKI, publishing executive, public relations executive; b. Rochester, N.Y., Sept. 10, 1937; d. Goodman A. and Evelyn (Simon) Sarachan; BA cum laude, U. Mich., 1959; m. Michael J. Sheets, 1973; children: Romaine Kitty, Nicholas Simon Feramorz. Mgr. advt. sales promotion Fairchild Publs., N.Y.C., 1959-67; account exec., account supr. Vernon Pope Co., N.Y.C., 1967-69, v.p., 1969-71; pres. Niki Singer, Inc., N.Y.C., 1971-93; sr. v.p. M. Shanken Comm., 1994—. Mem. Am. Inst. Wine and Food (bd. dirs.), Les Dames d'Escoffier. Home: 1035 5th Ave New York NY 10028-0135 Office: M Shanken Comm 387 Park Ave S New York NY 10016-8810

SINGER, SANDRA MARIA, forensic scientist; b. Wilkes-Barre, Pa., Sept. 9, 1964; d. Russell John and Anita Louise (Hovanec) S. BS in Chemistry, King's Coll., 1986; MS in Forensic Sci., George Washington U., 1989. Forensic analyst Collaborative Testing, Inc., Herndon, Va., 1988-89; forensic scientist Pa. State Police Crime Lab., Wyoming, 1990—. Mem. AAAS, Am. Acad. Forensic Sci., Am. Chem. Soc. Home: 203 Owen St Swoyersville PA 18704 Office: Pa State Police Wyoming Regional Crime Lab 479 Wyoming Ave Wyoming PA 18644

SINGER, SARAH BETH, poet; b. N.Y.C., July 4, 1915; d. Samuel and Rose (Dunetz) White; m. Leon Eugene Singer, Nov. 23, 1938; children: Jack, Rachel. B.A., NYU, 1934; postgrad., New Sch. Social Research, 1961-63. Tchr. creative writing Hillside Hosp., Queens, N.Y., 1964-75, Samuel Field YMHA, Queens, 1980-82. Author: Magic Casements, 1957, After the Beginning, 1975, Of Love and Shoes, 1987, The Gathering, 1992, contbr. poetry to anthologies, poetry mags. and quars. including: Am. Women Poets, 1976, Yearbook Am. Poetry, 1981, The Best of 1980, 81, Filtered Images, 1992, the Croton Rev., The Lyric, Bitterroot, Judaism, Encore, The Jewish Frontier, Yankee, Hartford Courant, Poet Lore, N.Y.Times, Christian Sci. Monitor, Voices Internat., The Round Table, Orphic Lute, Brussels Sprout, Poetry and Medicine Column Jour. AMA, The Shakespeare Newsletter, Midstream (N.Y.C. Jewish Rev.), The Penwoman; cons. editor Poet Lore, 1975-81. Recipient Stephen Vincent Benet award Poet Lore, 1968, 71, Dellbrook award Shenandoah Valley Acad. Lit. and Dellbrook-Shenandoah Coll. Writers' Conf., 1978, 79, C.W. Post Poetry award, 1979-80, award for best poem Lyric quar., 1981, biennial award for achievement in poetry Seattle br. Nat League Penwomen, 1988; award for traditional poetry Wash. Poets Assn., 1989, crit. of merit Muse mag.,1990, Editor's Choice award for Haiku Brussels Sprout, 1992, poem chosen for Met. Bus. Poetry Project, Seattle, 1992; poem Upon My Demise translated into Russian, recorded 1st rpize Marj McAllister award Voices Internat. 1993. Mem. PEN, Poets and Writers, Nat. League Am. Penwomen (poetry chmn. L.I. br. 1957-87, publicity chmn. 1990, sec. Seattle br. 1990, pres. 1992-94, v.p. 1994—, publicity chmn. State of Wash. 1992—, Marion Doyle Meml. award 1976, 1st prize nat. poetry contet 1976, Drama award 1977, Poetry award 1977, 1st prize modern rhymed poetry 1978, Lectr. award 1980, Sonnet award Alexandria br. 1980, 81, Catherine Cushman Leach award 1982; poetry award Phoenix br. 1983, Pasadena br. 1984, Alexandria br. 1985, 1st prize award Portland br. 1990, structured verse award Spokane br. 1992, Della Crowder Miller Meml. Petrarchan Sonnet award 1994, Honorable Mention Anita Marie Boggs Meml. award 1994, Owl award and Ann. award for achievement in poetry Seattle br. 1994, Poet's Choice award Portland br. 1995, 2d prize Internat. Poetry Contest, Palomar br., 1996), Poetry Soc. Am. (v.p. 1974-78, exec. dir. L.I., 1979-83, James Joyce award 1972, Consuelo Ford award 1973, Gustav Davidson award 1974, 1st prize award 1975, Celia Wagner award 1976). Address: 2360 43rd Ave E Apt 415 Seattle WA 98112-2703

SINGER, SHERI, broadcast executive; m. Steve White; 4 children. Grad., U. Okla. News prodr., reporter KOCO-TV, Oklahoma City; newswriter WLS-TV, Chgo.; writer, prodr. WMAQ-TV, Chgo.; exec. prodr. Columbia Pictures TV; with Embassy TV, v.p. for drama; sr. v.p. movies for TV Walt Disney TV; v.p. long form programming Lifetime Television, N.Y.C., 1994-95, v.p. movies and daram series, 1995—. Prodr.: Donahue; exec. prodr. (TV movies) Guilty of Innocence: The Lenell Geter Story, Cast the First Stone, 1989; prodr. (movies) A Mom for Christmas, She stood Alone. Recipient Emmy for Donahue.

SINGER, SHIRLEY, cultural organization executive; b. N.Y.C., Jan. 13, 1929; d. Sam and Dora (Schiff) Starer; m. Jack Singer; children: Sharon, Pauline, Elliott. Student, Bklyn. Coll., 1947-48. Exec. v.p. Emunah of Am., N.Y.C., 1964—. Del. Dem. Conv., Albany, N.Y., 1976. Mem. Conf. Pres. of Am. Jewish Orgns., Jewish Cmty. Rels. Coun., Inst. Pub. Affairs. Office: Emunah of Am 7 Penn Plz New York NY 10001

SINGER, SUZANNE FRIED, editor; b. N.Y.C., July 9, 1935; d. Maurice Aaron and Augusta G. (Ginsberg) Fried; m. Max Singer, Feb. 12, 1959; children: Saul, Alexander, Daniel, Benjamin. BA with honors, Swarthmore Coll., 1956; MA, Columbia U., 1958. Program asst. NSF, Washington, 1958-60; assoc. editor Bibl. Archaeology Rev., Washington, 1979-84, mng. editor, 1984-96, exec. editor, 1996—; mng. editor Bibl. Rev., Washington, 1985-94, exec. editor, 1994—; mng. editor Moment, Washington, 1990—. Mem. Am. Schs. Oriental Rsch., Soc. Bibl. Lit. Jewish. Office: Bibl Archaeology Soc 4710 41st St NW Washington DC 20016-1700

SINGLEHURST, DONA GEISENHEYNER, horse farm owner; b. Tacoma, June 19, 1928; d. Herbert Russell and Rose Evelyn (Rubish) Geisenheyner; m. Thomas G. Singlehurst, May 16, 1959 (dec.); 1 child, Suanna Singlehurst. BA in Psychology, Whitman Coll., 1950. With pub. rels. and advt. staff Lane Wells, L.A., 1950-52; staff mem. in charge new bus. Bishop Trust Co., Honolulu, 1953-58; mgr. Town & Country Stables, Honolulu, 1958-62; co-owner, v.p. pub. rels. Carol & Mary, Ltd., Honolulu, 1964-84; owner Stanhope Farms, Waialua, Hawaii, 1969—; internat. dressage judge, sport horse breeding judge Am. Horse Shows Assn.; sr. judge Can. Dressage Fedn. Chmn. ways and means com. The Outdoor Cir., Hawaii, 1958-64, life mem.; pres. emeritus Morris Animal Found., Englewood, Colo., 1988—, pres., 1984-88; bd. dirs., pres. Delta Soc., Renton, Wash., 1994—; mem. Jr. League of Honolulu. Recipient Best Friends award Honolulu Vet. Soc., 1986, Spl. Recognition award Am. Animal Hosp. Assn., 1988, Recognition award Am. Vet. Med. Assn. Mem. NAFE, Hawaii Horse Show Assn. (Harry Hutaff award 1985, past pres., bd. dirs.), Hawaii Combined Tng. Assn. (past pres. bd. dirs.), Calif. Dressage Soc., U.S. Dressage Fedn., U.S. Equestrian Team (area chmn. 1981-85), Hawaiian Humane Soc. (life), U.S. Pony Clubs (dist. commr. 1970-75, nat. examiner 1970-75), Pacific Club, Outrigger Canoe Club. Republican. Episcopalian. Home and Office: Stanhope Farms Waialua HI 96791

SINGLETARY, JULIE B., home healthcare administrator, pediatrics nurse; b. Denver, Mar. 4, 1959; d. Dewey Elroy Jr. and Mary Elizabeth (Mays) Brunner; m. Harold Kelzo Singletary, Jan. 21, 1984; children: Amanda, Jessica. BSN, Valdosta State U., 1982. RN, Ga. Staff RN John Archibold Meml. Hosp., Thomasville, Ga., 1982-83, Med. Ctr. Ctrl. Ga., Macon, 1983-84, Kennestone Hosp., Marietta, Ga., 1984; staff/charge RN Gwinnett Med. Ctr., Lawrenceville, Ga., 1984-88; staff RN Primedical Urgent Care, Norcross, Ga., 1988, Egleston Children's Hosp., Atlanta, 1988-89, Pediatric Svcs. of Am., Norcross, 1989, Kid's Med. Club, Atlanta, 1987-93; staff RN, case mgr. Hand In Hand Home Health, Cumming, Ga., 1993-95; clin. dir. Extended Cmty. Home Health of Atlanta, 1995—. Mem. Home Health Care Nurses Assn., Sigma Theta Tau, Kappa Delta. Republican. Baptist. Home: 1725 Lawrenceville Suwanee Rd Lawrenceville GA 30243-3587 Office: Extended Cmty Home Health Atlanta 4151 Memorial Dr Ste 223A Decatur GA 30032-1515

SINGLETON, CINTHIA, writer; b. Sonoma, Calif., Mar. 9, 1960; d. Robert Walter and Carol Ann (Foster) S. BFA, Bard Coll., 1982. Producer, dir. WBAI/Pacifica Radio, N.Y.C., 1992—; dir. Waterfront Ensemble, Hoboken, N.J., 1995—; author, co-prodr. (radio drama) Past the Rear View Mirror, 1994, co-author, co-prodr. Chanel-38, 1993, author, dir. Madeline, 1992, Miss Big Girl Lady; editor, N.Y.C., 1990-95. Mem. Workmen's Circle. Home and Office: Apt 9 239 Elizabeth St New York NY 10012

SINGLETON, LAVERNA, community health nurse; b. Friend, Nebr., Nov. 14, 1940; d. Lester and Frances Anna M. (O'Dea) S. Diploma, St. Elizabeth Hosp., Lincoln, Nebr., 1961; BAAS, Midwestern State U., Wichita Falls, Tex., 1988, MA in Pub. Adminstrn., 1990. Quality control coord. Bethania Regional Health Care Ctr., Wichita Falls, head nurse, orthopedics, 1969-77, asst. dir. nursing, 1977-90; regional rev. mgr. Tex. Peer Rev. Orgn., Tex. Med. Found., Dallas, 1991-93; quality mgmt. mgr. Vis. Nurse Assn. Tex., Dallas, 1993-96; dir. QA Compliance Conss. for the Home Care Industry, Garland, Tex., 1996—. Mem. NLN, Tex. League Nursing, Tex. Orgn. Nurse Execs., Pi Sigma Alpha.

SINGLETON, STELLA WOOD, educator and habilitation assistant; b. Moore County, N.C., Nov. 3, 1948; d. Jay and Thelma A. Wood; m. Tommy Singleton, Dec. 21, 1968; children: Jennifer, Mike. Diploma, Hamlet Hosp. Sch. Nursing, Hamlet, N.C., 1975; postgrad., Appalachian State U., Boone, N.C., 1990—. RN, N.C. Dir. Hospice of Boone (N.C.) Area, 1982-83; Hospice dir. Hospice of Avery County, Newland, N.C., 1983-85; DON Toe River Health Dist., Newland, N.C., 1983-84; mental health nurse II New River Mental Health, Newland, N.C., 1977-82, 85-95; beauty cons. Mary Kay Cosmetics, 1986—; habilitation asst. Devl. Disabilities Svcs., Boone, N.C., 1995—; instr. Mayland C.C., Spruce Pine, N.C. Co-facilitator Avery County Alzheimer's Support Group, group facilitator Cancer Support Group Svc.; rehab. chmn. Am. Cancer Soc. Recipient Gov's. award for administrv. vol. Mem. N.C. Biofeedback Soc. Home: PO Box 483 Crossnore NC 28616-0483 Office: Devel Disabilities Svcs 404 Oak Summit Boone NC 28607 also: Mayland CC PO Box 547 Spruce Pine NC 28777

SINGREEN, SHIRLEY ANN BASILE (MRS. HARRY VOSS SINGREEN), lawyer; b. New Orleans, Apr. 10, 1941; d. Dominick Joseph and Rose Aile (O'Reilly) Basile; m. Harry Voss Singreen, May 12, 1979; children: Michael Harry, Elizabeth Alexandra. AB, Loyola U., New Orleans, 1962, JD, 1964. Bar: La. 1964. Law clk. Civil Dist. Ct., 1964-65; assoc. Doyle, Smith & Doyle, New Orleans, 1965-66; staff counsel U.S. Ct. Appeals (5th cir.), New Orleans, 1966-68; assoc. Plaintiff's Personal Injury Firm, New Orleans, 1968-71; spl. cons. Henican, James & Cleveland, New Orleans, 1972-73; sr. law clk. 24th Jud. Dist. Ct., Jefferson Parish, La., 1973-76; appellate counsel, legal cons., trial analyst, New Orleans. Mem. La. State Bar Assn., New Orleans Notaries Assn., Phi Alpha Delta. Republican. Roman Catholic. Office: 260 Audubon Blvd New Orleans LA 70125-4125

SINKFORD, JEANNE CRAIG, dentist, educator; b. Washington, Jan. 30, 1933; d. Richard E. and Geneva (Jefferson) Craig; m. Stanley M. Sinkford, Dec. 8, 1951; children: Dianne Sylvia, Janet Lynn, Stanley M. III. BS, Howard U., 1953, MS, 1962, DDS, 1958, PhD, 1963; DSc (hon.), Georgetown U., 1978; DSc (Hon.), U. Med. and Dentistry of N.J., 1992. Instr. prosthodontics Sch. Dentistry Howard U., Washington, 1958-60, mem. faculty dentistry, 1964—, rsch. coord., co-chmn. dept. restorative dentistry, assoc. dean, 1968-75, dean, 1975-91, prof. Prosthodontics Grad. Sch., 1977-91; dean emeritus, prof. Sch. Dentistry Howard U.; spl. asst. Am. Assn. Dental Schs., 1991-93, dir. office women and minority affairs, 1993—; instr. rsch. and crown and bridge Northwestern U. Sch. Dentistry, 1963-64; cons. prosthodontics and rsch. VA Hosp., Washington, 1965—; resident Children's Hosp. Nat. Med. Ctr., 1974-75; cons. St. Elizabeth's Hosp.; mem. attending staff Freedman's Hosp., Washington, 1964—; adv. bd. D.C. Gen. Hosp., 1975—; mem. Nat. Adv. Dental Rsch. Coun., Nat. Bd. Dental Examiners; mem. ad hoc adv. panel Tuskegee Syphilis Study for HEW; sponsor D.C. Pub. Health Apprentice Program; mem. adv. coun. to dir. NIH; adv. com. NIH/NIDR/NIA Aging Rsch. Coun.; mem. dental devices classification panel FDA; mem. select panel for promotion child health, 1979-80; mem. spl. med. adv. group VA; bd. overseers U. Pa. Dental Sch., Boston U. Dental Sch.; bd. advs. U. Pitts. Dental Sch.; mem. anat. rev. bd. for D.C. NRC Gov. Bd.; cons. Food and Drug Adminstrn.; Nat. Adv. Rsch. Coun., 1993—; active Nat. Rsch. Coun. Governing Bd. Mem. editorial rev. bd. Jour. Am. Coll. Dentists, 1988—. Adv. bd. United Negro Coll. Fund, Robert Wood Johnson Health Policy Fellowships; mem. Mayor's Block Grant Adv. Com., 1982; mem. parents' coun. Sidwell Friends, 1983; mem. adv. bd. D.C., mem. Women's Health Task Force, NIH; bd. dirs. Girl Scouts U.S.A., 1993—. Louise C. Ball fellow grad. tng., 1960-63. Fellow Am. Coll. Dentists (sec.-treas. Wash. met. sect.), Internat. Coll. Dentists (award of merit); mem. ADA (chmn. appeal bd. coun. on dental edn. 1975-82), Am. Soc. for Geriatric Dentistry (bd. dirs.), Internat. Assn. Dental Research, Dist. Dental Soc., Am. Inst. Oral Biology, North Portal Civic League, Inst. Grad. Dentists (trustee), So. Conf. Dental Deans (chmn.), Wash. Coun. Adminstrv. Women, Assn. Am. Women Dentists, Am. Pedodontic Soc., Am. Prosthodontic Soc., Fed. Prosthodontic Orgn., Nat. Dental Assn., Inst. Medicine (coun.), Am. Soc. Dentistry for Children, N.Y. Acad. Scis., Smithsonian Assocs., Dean's Coun., Proctor and Gamble, Golden Key Honor Soc., Links Inc., Sigma Xi (pres.), Phi Beta Kappa, Omicron Kappa Upsilon, Psi Chi, Beta Kappa Chi. Address: 1765 Verbena St NW Washington DC 20012-1048

SINKIN, FAY MARIE, environmentalist; b. N.Y.C., Mar. 24, 1918; d. Joseph E. and Amelia (Kronish) Bloom; m. William R. Sinkin, May 31, 1942; children: Richard, Lanny. BA, Syracuse U., 1938. Pres. LWV, San Antonio, 1947-51; pres., organizer Vis. Nurse Assn., San Antonio, 1952-54; pres. Brandeis U. Women's Com., San Antonio, 1954-56; recruiter, cons. U.S. State Dept. (A.I.D.), Washington, 1963-67; pres. Aquifer Protection Assn., San Antonio, 1974-80, Portrait of Am. Women, San Antonio, 1976-82; chair Bexar County/Edwards Underground Water Dist., San Antonio, 1983-89; chairwoman Edwards Aquifer Preservation Trust, San Antonio, 1990. Editor (pamphlet) Is Applewhite Necessary?, 1978. Named Woman of Yr. Express New Publ., 1964, Sunday Woman San Antonio Light, 1965, Mother of Yr. Avance, 1988; recipient WICI award Women in Comm., 1989, Spirit of Giving award J.C. Penney, 1993; elected to Women's Hall of Fame, San Antonio, 1985. Mem. San Antonio 100, Tex. Internat. Woman's Forum. Democrat. Jewish. Home: 7887 Broadway St Apt 706 San Antonio TX 78209-2537

SINKINSON, DIANE WITHROW, hotel management educator; b. Champaign, Ill., Jan. 12, 1957; d. Phillip Brooks and Margaret Ellen (Huston) Withrow; m. Carl Pavia (div.); m. William Robert Sinkinson, Nov. 24, 1989; children: Brook and Megan (twins). BS in Criminal Justice, Ill. State U., 1977; postgrad., Dumas Pere, Glenview, Ill., 1983; MS in Hospitality, Fla. Internat. U., 1986. Apprentice chef Pump Room, Ritz Carlton, Chgo., 1979-80, Pump Room, Ritz Carleton, Chgo., 1980-83; charter chef, yacht deliveries Dromedary Yacht, 1983-88; property mgr. Vieques, P.R., 1988-91; lead instr. hotel restaurant/travel and tourism Mt. Aloyisius Coll., Cresson, Pa., 1991-93; lead instr. hotel-restaurant mgmt. Cape Fear C.C., Wilmington, N.C., 1993—; mem. Coun. on Hospitality, Restaurant and Instnl. Educators; cons. in field. Soup kitchen worker West Side Shelter, Chgo., 1982-83; host family Ctrl. Am. Student in Sign Lang., Mt. Aloyisius Coll., 1991-93; vol. Meals of Wheels, Wilmington, N.C., 1994. Democrat. Unitarian Universalist. Office: CFCC 411 N Front St Wilmington NC 28401

SINSABAUGH, KATHERINE ANNE, musician, educator; b. Danville, Ill., June 9, 1963; d. Arthur R. and Francine (Lewis) S.; m. Darryl G. Pellegrini, Mar. 31, 1989 (div. 1994). BA, Barnard Coll., 1985; MusB, Manhattan Sch. Music, 1985, MusM, 1991. Violist, founder Riverside Piano Quartet, N.Y.C., 1991-95; viola tchr. The Green Meadow Walforf Sch., Chestnut Ridge, N.Y., 1991—, SUNY, Purchase, N.Y., 1994—, The Breadley Sch., N.Y.C., 1995—. Violist with orchs. of musicals on Broadway including Metro, 1991, Kiss of the Spider Woman, 1992-94, Show Boat, 1994—. Mem. N.Y. Viola Soc., Musician's Union 802. Home: 325 Riverside Dr New York NY 10025

SIPE, DORIS ELAINE, college dean; b. Hickory, N.C., Aug. 20, 1942; d. Elmer Eugene and Beaulah Viola (Herman) Sipe. BS, Concordia Coll., 1964; MA, Appalachian State U., 1970; EdD, N.C. State U., 1988. Secondary sch. tchr. U.S. Peace Corps, Bentong, Pahang, Malaysia, 1964-66; elem. sch. tchr. Concordia Christian Sch., Conover, N.C., 1967-69; asst. prpof. Sacred Heart Coll., Belmont, N.C., 1970-81, dean adult edn., 1982-87; dir. adult degree program Belmont (N.C.) Abbey Coll., 1987-90; dean coll. continuing edn. Concordia U., River Forest, Ill., 1990—; faculty adv. com. Ill. Bd. for Higher Edn., Springfield, 1995—; cons., evaluator North Ctrl. Assn., Chgo., 1996—. Named Tchr./Adminstr. of the Yr., Sacred Heart Coll., 1986. Mem. LWV (chpt. pres. 1984), Am. Assn. Higher Edn., Assn. for Continuing Higher Edn., Ill. Coun. for Continuing Higher Edn. (program com. 1990—), Oak Park (Ill.) Rotary Club (bd. dirs. 1993—). Democrat. Lutheran. Home: 209 Augusta St Maywood IL 60153 Office: Concordia Univ 7400 Augusta St River Forest IL 60305

SIPER, CYNTHIA DAWN, special education educator; b. Bklyn., Apr. 16, 1965; d. Joel S. and Diana M. (Kessler) Rosenblatt; m. Alan Siper, Apr. 9, 1989; children: Rebecca Ruth, Daniel Louis. BS in Edn., SUNY, Plattsburgh, 1988; MEd, SUNY, New Paltz, 1992. Cert. K-12 spl. edn. tchr., N-6 elem. edn. tchr., N.Y. Tchr. spl. edn. Valley Cen. Sch. Dist., Montgomery, N.Y., 1988-90, Middletown (N.Y.) Enlarged City Sch. Dist., 1990—; spl. edn. tchr. rep. Coun. on Spl. Edn., Middletown, 1990—. Mem. Coun. for Exceptional Children, Middletown Tchrs. Assn., Kappa Delta Pi.

SIPPEL, FRANCINE ANN, psychological associate; b. Chgo., Nov. 23, 1966; d. John Nuzzo and Sandra Lee (Santarsiere) Halma; m. Marc A. Sippel, Dec. 23, 1990; 1 child, Camille Marlys. BS, Andrews U., Berrien Springs, Mich., 1988; MS, No. State U., Aberdeen, S.D., 1991; EdD, U. S.D., Vermillion, 1995. Lic. prof. counselpr; nat. cert. counselor; lic. marriage and family therapist. Therapist Northeastern Mental Health Ctr., Aberdeen, 1991-92, 1993-95, psychol. assoc., 1995—; mem. Children & Adolescent Svc. Sys. Planning Com., Aberdeen, 1991-92, 93—; mem. Juvenile Delinquency Prevention Policy Bd., Aberdeen, 1994—. Title V grantee Fed. Govt., Aberdeen, 1994-95. Mem. ACA, Chi Sigma Iota. Democrat. Home: PO Box 483 Groton SD 57445 Office: Northeastern Mental Health Ctr PO Box 550 Aberdeen SD 57401

SIPPEL, SANDRA LYNNE, industrial food broker; b. Charlotte, N.C., Sept. 16, 1947; d. Richard Oliver McCorkle and Norma Terry (Hardie) Howard; m. Nickie B. Penrod, Oct. 15, 1967 (div. June 1975); children: Debrah L., Richard P.; m. John H. Murray, July 4, 1981 (div. Sept. 1982); m. David Lee Sippel, Apr. 17, 1993. Student, U. S.C., 1966, Meramec Community Coll., St. Louis, 1971. Office clk. G.S. Suppiger Co., St. Louis, 1967-69, Comml. Printing Co., St. Louis, 1969-70; office mgr. St. Louis Food Sales, Inc., 1970-84, v.p., 1981-84; pres. Midwest Indsl. Food Sales, Inc., 1984-85, Indsl. Food Ingredients, Inc., Arnold, Mo., 1985—. Author: Great Poets of Today, 1987 (Golden Poet award 1987), World Poetry Anthology, 1987. Pres., bd. dirs. Jefferson County no. unit Am. Cancer Soc., 1989-92; vol. counselor women's shelter A Safe Place; sec. bd. dirs. Rocky Ridge Ranch Property Owner's Assn. Trustees, 1993-94; tutor Project Literacy, 1988-90. Recipient Cert. Recognition Mo. Ho. Reps., 1992. Mem. Arnold C. of C. (v.p. bd. dirs. 1993, office dir. 1985—, co-editor newsletter 1990-91, editor 1991-93, chmn. Easter program, v.p. bd. dirs. Arnold Days Parade com., v.p. 1993). Office: PO Box 467 Arnold MO 63010-0467

SIRIWARDANE, RANJANI VINITA, chemist; b. Matale, Sri Lanka, May 30, 1955; d. Buddhipriya and Kumari Wijesundera; m. Hema Jayalath Siriwardane, Feb. 10, 1977; children: Nishani Marcia, Emil Nuwan. BS Chemistry, U. Sri Lanka, 1977; MS Chemistry, Va. Poly. Inst. and State U., 1979, PhD Chemistry, 1981. Rsch. assoc. W. Va. U., Morgantown, 1981-84, rsch. asst. prof., 1987-88; rsch. fellow U.S. Dept. Energy, Morgantown, 1984-87, rsch. chemist, 1988—; lectr. in field. Contbr. articles to profl. jours. and publs.; patentee in field. Recipient award for Acad. Excellence in Grad. Studies, Atlantic Richfield Co., 1981. Mem. Am. Chem. Soc., Sigma Xi, Phi Kappa Phi, Phi Lambda. Office: US Dept Energy METC Collins Ferry Rd Morgantown WV 26505

SIRLIN, DEANNA LOUISE, artist; b. Bklyn., Mar. 7, 1958; d. Robert and Sylvia (Goldsmith) S.; m. Philip Auslander, Aug. 29, 1990. BA, SUNY at Albany, 1978; MFA, CUNY, 1980. bd. dirs. 20th Century Soc., High Mus. Art, Atlanta. One-woman shows include Fay Gold Gallery, 1993, 95, Cheekwood Fine Arts Ctr., 1995, Nexus Contemporary Arts Ctr., 1996; represented in permanent collections Macon (Ga.) Mus. of Arts and Scis., Ga. Pacific, United Airlines, Dulles Airport, CSX Corp., Egleston Hosp. Recipient Yaddo fellowship, 1983, Artist grant Artist's Space, 1987, Artist award Fulton County Arts Coun., 1994, Ga. Coun. for the Arts, 1994. Home and Office: 120 N Christophers Run Alpharetta GA 30201

SIRONEN, LYNN JANE, secondary school educator; b. London, Dec. 15, 1951; came to U.S., 1953; d. Harold Walter and Jane Adele Markham; m. Jan Steven Sironen, June 5, 1971; children: Karen, Christina, Steven. BA in Elem. Edn., U. R.I., 1973, MA in Sci. Edn., 1986. Elem. tchr. North

Kingstown (R.I.) Schs., 1973, 75, substitute tchr., 1974, 80, computer tchr., 1985-86, tchr. sci., 1986—; tchr. sci. Westerly (R.I.) Schs., 1981, The Wheeler Sch., Providence, 1981-82; grad. asst. U. R.I., Kingston, 1982-84, part-time instr., 1987. Mem., vice comdr., exec. bd. North Kingstown Ambulance Corps, 1975-87; pres. North Kingstown Band Parents, 1992-94. Mem. Nat. Sci. Tchrs. Assn., NEA of North Kingstown (sec. 1994-96), North Kingstown Bus. and Profl. Women's Club (treas. 1993-94) Rotary (Tchr. of Month 1993). Episcopalian. Home: PO Box 152 North Kingstown RI 02852-0152 Office: North Kingstown High School 150 Fairway Dr North Kingstown RI 02852-6202

SIROWER, BONNIE FOX, fundraising executive; b. Bklyn., Jan. 9, 1949; d. Stanley S. and Harriet (Fischer) Fox; m. Martin Alan Sirower, Sept. 20, 1970; children: Kenneth, Daniel. AB, Barnard Coll., 1970; MA, Columbia U., 1971. Tchr. United Cerebral Palsy, N.Y.C., 1970-73, Bergen County Bd. Spl. Svcs., Paramus, N.J., 1973-76; spl. events coord. Am. Heart Assn., Glen Ridge, N.J., 1979-81; dir. devel. Goodwill Industries, Astoria, N.Y., 1981-83; pres. Access Unltd., 1984-85; dir. devel. Cheshire Home, Inc., 1986-89, Barnert Hosp., Paterson, N.J., 1989-95; dir. devel. United Way Passaic County (N.J.), 1995-96, sr. v.p., 1996—. Commr. Paterson (N.J.) Coun. for Disabled, 1994; trustee YMCA of Paterson, 1991; founder Pride in Paterson, 1993—; chair Youth in Philanthropy, 1995—. Named Outstanding N.J. Fundraiser, Nat. Soc. of Fundraising Execs. of N.J., 1995. Mem. N.J. Soc. Fund Raising Execs. (bd. dirs. 1989, chmn. mentoring com., chmn. N.J. Conf. on Philanthropy 1994), Assn. Fund Raisers for Disabled (pres. 1981-83), N.J. Puzzlers' League (pres.), Barnard Coll. Class of '70 (pres. 1990—), Rotary Internat. (v.p. Paterson, pres., Outstanding fundraiser in N.J. 1995), Bergen Women of Accomplishment, Phi Beta Kappa. Jewish. Home: 69 Godfrey Ter Glen Rock NJ 07452-3510

SISEMORE, CLAUDIA, educational films and videos producer, director; b. Salt Lake City, Sept. 16, 1937; d. Darrell Daniel and Alice Larril (Barton) S. BS in English, Brigham Young U., 1959; MFA in Filmmaking, U. Utah, 1976. Cert. secondary tchr., Utah. Tchr. English, drama and writing Salt Lake Sch. Dist., Salt Lake City, 1959-66; tchr. English Davis Sch. Dist., Bountiful, Utah, 1966-68; ind. filmmaker Salt Lake City, 1972—; filmmaker-in-residence Wyo. Coun. for Arts and Nat. Endowment for Arts, Dubois, Wyo., 1977-78; prodr., dir. ednl. films Utah Office Edn., Salt Lake City, 1979-93, Canyon Video, 1993—. Prodr., dir. Beginning of Winning, 1984 (film festival award 1984), Dancing through the Magic Eye, 1986, Se Hable Espanol, 1986-87; writer, dir., editor (film) Building on a Legacy, 1988, (videos) Energy Conservation, 1990, Alternative Energy Sources, 1990, Restructuring Learning, 1991, Kidsercise, 1991, Traditional Energy Sources, 1992, A State Government Team, 1992, Problem Solving Using Math Manipulative, 1993, Canyon Video, 1993—; videos Western Mountains and Basins, 1994, Bikes, Boards and Blades, 1994, Fitness After 50, 1995, Timescape, 1996, Splash of Color, 1996; exhibited (abstract paintings) in group show Phillips Gallery; represented in numerous pvt. and pub. collections. Juror Park City (Utah) Arts Festival, 1982, Utah Arts Festival, Salt Lake City, 1982, Am. Film Festival, 1985-86, Best of West Film Festival, 1985-86; bd. dirs. Utah Media Ctr., Salt Lake City, 1981-87; mem. multi-disciplinary program Utah Arts Coun., Salt Lake City, 1983-87. Recipient award Utah Media Ctr., 1984, 85; Nat. Endowment for Arts grantee, 1978, Utah Arts Coun. grantee, 1980. Mormon.

SISK, CHARLOTTE SUE, secondary school educator; b. Elizabethton, Tenn., May 17, 1927; d. Lawrence David and Amelia Dove Brumit; divorced; children: Deborah, Trey. AA, St. Petersburg (Fla.) Jr. Coll., 1947; BS, East Tenn. State U., 1949; MEd, Stetson U., 1983; postgrad., U. So. Fla. Cert. lang. arts and social studies supr. and adminstr. Tchr. Claxton Elem., Anderson County, Tenn., 1949-50, Norwood Elem., Anderson County, Tenn., 1953-54, Clinton (Tenn.) H.S., 1951-63; tchr. Oak Grove Mid. Sch., Clearwater, Fla., 1964-93, dept. chmn., 1983-90. Neighborhood leader Am. Lung Assn., 1989-95. Mem. NOW, AAUW, NEA. Republican.

SISK, JANE ELIZABETH, economist, educator; b. West Reading, Pa., Sept. 23, 1942; 2 children. BA with honors, Brown U., 1963; MA, George Washington U., 1965; PhD, McGill U., Montreal, Que., Can., 1976. Cons. Nat. Planning Assn., Washington, 1976; scholar VA, Washington, 1978-81; rsch. dir. Office Tech. Assessment, U.S. Congress, Washington, 1976-78, sr. analyst, 1981-84, sr. assoc., 1984-91; vis. prof. Columbia U. Sch. Pub. Health, N.Y.C., 1990-91, prof., 1992—. Co-author: Toward Rational Technology in Medicine, 1981; mem. editl. bd. Internat. Jour. Tech. Assessment in Health Care, 1987—, vol. editor, 1990; asst. editor Am. Jour. Pub. Health, 1990-91; mem. editl. bd. Health Svcs. Rsch., 1994—; contbr. articles to profl. jours. Pres. Internat Soc. Tech. Assessment in Health Care, 1991-93, bd. dirs., 1987-95; mem. N.Y. State Task Force on Clin. Guidelines & Med. Tech. Assessment, 1994—. Elisah Benjamin Andrews scholar Brown U., 1961, 63; Bronfman fellow McGill U., 1971. Mem. Phi Beta Kappa. Office: Columbia U Sch Pub Health 600 W 168th St New York NY 10032

SISKIN, CARYL F., women's health primary care nurse practitioner; b. Louisville, June 2, 1939; d. Ralph E. and Esther Marian (Binder) Flumbaum; m. Michael Baggish, 1960 (div. 1983); children: Jeffrey Steven Baggish, Mindy Ann Baggish, Cindy Beth Baggish, Stuart Harrison Baggish; m. Robert S. Siskin, 1985. Diploma, St. Anthony Hosp. Sch. Nursing, 1960; student, Nazareth Coll., Johns Hopkins U.; BSN summa cum laude, U. Hartford, 1980. Cert. NCC, ob-gyn NP. Head nurse Womens Clinic Johns Hopkins Hosp., Balt.; clin. instr., ob-gyn. dept. Mt. Sinai Hosp., Hartford, Conn.; mem. internat. health care team S.E. Asia U.S. AID, 1973-74; ob-gyn. N.P. collaborative practice George Bacall, M.D., Hartford, 1984-90; pvt. practice Bloomfield, Conn., 1990-94. Vol. local soup kitchen; co-founder Rebekah's House, West Palm Beach, Fla. Mem. ANA, Nurses Assn. of Am. Coll. Ob-Gyn., Am. Acad. Nurse Practitioners, Assn. Reproductive Health Profls., Am. Fertility Soc., Jewish Arts Found., Temple Israel Sisterhood, Sigma Theta Tau (1st pres. Iota Upsilon chpt.). Home: 13677 Rivoli Dr Palm Beach Gardens FL 33410

SISKIN, SHARON VALERIE, art educator; b. Elkins Park, Pa., Feb. 22, 1955; d. Jack and Lora (Wexler) S.; m. John Christopher Lavine, Sept. 29, 1991. BFA, Tyler Sch. ARt, 1976; MFA, U. Calif., Berkeley, 1981; MA, U. N.Mex., 1979. Artist-in-residence Calif. Arts Coun., Bay Area, 1988—; instr. Chabot Coll., Hayward, Calif., 1988—, Contra Costa Coll., San Pablo, Calif., 1992—; adj. prof. John F. Kennedy U., Orinda, Calif., 1991—; lectr. in field. One-woman shows include Tyler Sch. Art, Elkins Park, Pa., 1976, U. Calif., berkeley, 1981, Pro Arts Gallery, Oakland, Calif., 1984, Gregory Ghent Gallery, San Francisco, 1987, Richard Reynolds Gallery, Stockton, Calif., 1991, Arts and Consciousness Gallery, Orinda, 1991, Addison St. Windows Installation Space, Berkeley, 1992, 93, Falkirk Cultural Ctr., San Rafael, Calif., 1994, Kennedy Art Ctr. Gallery, Oakland, 1995, Palo Alto (Calif.) Cultural Ctr., 1995-96, others; group shows include Teh Galleria, Albuquerque, 1978, Downtown Ctr. Arts, Albuquerque, 1979, 80, Univ. Art Mus., Berkeley, 1981, Univ. Gallery, Hayward, 1982, Richmond (Calif.) Art Ctr., 1983, Napa (Calif.) Valley Coll. Art Gallery, 1984, Irvine (Calif.) Art Ctr., 1985, Chabot Coll., Hayward, 1986, Mission Cultural Ctr., San Francisco, 1987, Berkeley Art Ctr., 1988, Sun Gallery, Hayward, 1990, Eddie Rhodes Gallery, San Pablo, Calif., 1991, Prieto Gallery, Oakland, 1992, The Drawing Ctr., N.Y.C., 1993, M.H. de Young Meml. Mus., San Francisco, 1994, Alternative Mus., N.Y.C., 1995, Bedford Gallery, Walnut Creek, Calif., 1996, others. Grantee Ford Found., 1978, 79, Calif. Arts Coun., Sacramento, 1988-91, 92-95, 96-97, John F. Kennedy U., Orinda, Calif., 1995, 96, Reva and David Logan Found., Chgo., 1991—, LEF Found., 1995, 96. Mem. Coll. Art Assn., Women's Caucus Art, Pro Art. Democrat. Jewish. Home: 2434 9th St Berkeley CA 94710 Studio: Nexus Inst 2701 8th St Berkeley CA 94710

SISKO, MARIE FERRARIS, fund raising executive; b. N.Y.C.; BA, Queens Coll., 1975; postgrad. Adelphi U., 1976; divorced; children: Warren Joseph, Robert Edward. Pers. dir. Daypac Inc., 1969-70; sales asst. Ponder & Best, 1971-73; sales adminstr. Ampacet Corp., 1973-75; mktg. rep. Better Bus. Bur., 1975-77; ast. dir. Leukemia Soc. Am., 1978-82; campaign dir. Ketchum, Inc., 1982-85; dir. maj. gifts Seton Hall U., 1985-88; program dir. Brakeley, John Price Jones, 1988-93; fund raising cons., 1990—. Mem. Nat. Soc. Fund Raising Execs., Queens Coll. Alumni Assn. (pres. Ace chpt. 1977-79). Lutheran. Home: 32 Center Dr Flushing NY 11357-1005

SISLEY, BECKY LYNN, physical education educator; b. Seattle, May 10, 1939; d. Leslie James and Blanche (Howe) S.; m. Jerry Newcomb, 1994. BA, U. Wash., 1961; MSPE, U. N.C., 1964, EdD, 1973. Tchr. Lake Washington High Sch., Kirkland, Wash., 1961-62; instr. U. Wis., Madison, 1963-65, U. Oreg., Eugene, 1965-68; prof. phys. edn. U. Oreg., 1968—, women's athletic dir., 1973-79, head undergrad. studies in phys. edn., 1985-92. Co-author: Softball for Girls, 1971; contbr. articles to profl. jours. Admitted to Hall of Fame, N.W. Women's Sports Found., Seattle, 1981, Honor award, N.W. Dist. Assn. for Health, Phys. Edn., Recreation and Dance, 1988, State of Oreg. Sports Hall of Fame, 1993; recipient Honor award Nat. Assn. for Girls and Women in Sports, 1995; U.S. record holder Age 50-54 Triple Jump, Javelin, High Jump, Age 55-50 Javelin, Pole Vault; world record holder Age 55-59 Pole Vault. Mem. AAHPERD, Oreg. Alliance Health, Phys. Edn., Recreation and Dance (hon. life mem.), Western Soc. for Phys. Edn. of Coll. Women (exec. bd. 1982-85), Oreg. High Sch. Coaches Assn., Nat. Softball Coaches Acad., N.W. Coll. Women's Sports Assn. (pres. 1977-78), Oreg. Women's Sports Leadership Network (dir. 1987—), Phi Epsilon Kappa, others. Office: University of Oregon Phys Activity & Recreation Svcs Eugene OR 97403

SISLEY, EMILY LUCRETIA, retired psychologist, medical writer; b. North Charleroi, Pa., May 7, 1930; d. Frederick William and Harriet Watkins (Litman) S. PhD in Clin. Psychology, L.I. U., 1972. Diplomate Am. Bd. Med. Psychotherapists. Mng. editor Med. Jours., Harper & Row, N.Y.C., 1960-67; freelance med. writer-editor N.Y.C., 1967-95; supervising psychologist, dept. psychiatry Roosevelt Hosp., N.Y.C., 1972-77; clin. instr. Columbia Univ. Coll. Physicians and Surgeons, N.Y.C., 1975-77; chief psychologist Gramercy Park Inst., N.Y.C., 1978-84; staff therapist MedcoBehavioral Care Sys., N.Y.C., 1984-95; ret., 1995; cons. Internat. Jour. Group Tensions, N.Y.C., 1968-72. Illustrator: You and Your Brain, 1963, Thomas Alva Edison award, 1963; co-author: The Vitamin C Connection, 1983; contbr. articles to profl. jours. Fellow Am. Bd. Med. Psychotherapists; mem. APA, N.Y. Acad. Scis. Democrat. Episcopalian.

SISLEY, NINA MAE, physician, public health officer; b. Jacksonville, Fla., Aug. 19, 1924; d. Leonard Percy and Verna (Martin) S.; m. George W. Fischer, May 16, 1962 (dec. 1990). BA, Tex. State Coll. for Women, 1944; MD, U. Tex., Galveston, 1950; MPH, U. Mich., 1963. Intern City of Detroit Receiving Hosp., 1950-51; resident in gen. practice St. Mary's Infirmary, Galveston, Tex., 1951-52; sch. physician Galveston Ind. Sch. Dist., 1953-56; dir. med. svcs. San Antonio Health Dept., 1960-63, acting dir., 1963-64; resident in pub. health Tex. Dept. Pub. Health, San Antonio, 1963-65; dir. community health svcs. Corpus Christi-Nueces County (Tex.) Health Dept., 1964-67; dir. Corpus Christi-Nueces County (Tex.) Dept. Pub. Health, 1987—; dir. Tb control region 5 Tex. Dept. Health, Corpus Christi, 1967-73; dir. pub. health region 11 Tex. Dept. Health, Rosenberg, 1978-87; chief chronic illness control City of Houston Health Dept., 1973-78; lectr. Incarnate Word Coll., San Antonio, 1963-64; adj. prof. U. Tex. Sch. Pub. Health, Houston, 1980—; guest lectr. Corpus Christi State U., 1987—; pvt. practice Galveston, Stockdale, Hereford and Borger, Tex., 1952-59; mem. adv. bd. N.W. Cmty. Adv. Coun., North Bay Longterm Health Adv. Coun. Bd. dirs. Coastal Bend chpt. ARC, Corpus Christi, 1990-94, pres., 1990-91; bd. dirs. United Way-Coastal Bend, Coastal Bend Coalition on AIDS, 1988-94, Coastal Bend chpt. Am. Diabetes Assn., 1990—; mem. Nuences County Child Fatality Rev. Com. Fellow Am. Coll. Preventive Medicine; mem. AMA, APHA, Tex. Med. Assn., Nuences County Med. Soc. (pres.-elect 1996—), Tex. Assn. Pub. Health Physicians, Tex. Pub. Health Assn. (pres. 1991-92). Episcopalian. Home: 62 Rock Creek Dr Corpus Christi TX 78412-4214 Office: Corpus Christi-Nueces County Dept Health 1702 Horne Rd Corpus Christi TX 78416-1902

SISSON, JEAN CRALLE, middle school educator; b. Village, Va., Nov. 16, 1941; d. Willard Andrew and Carolyn (Headley) Cralle; m. James B. Sisson, June 20, 1964 (div. Oct. 1994); 1 child, Kimberly Carol. BS in Elem. Edn., Longwood Coll., 1964; MA in Adminstrn. and Supervision, Va. Commonwealth U., 1979. Tchr. 2nd grade Tappahannock (Va.) Elem. Sch., 1964-67; tchr. 2nd and 4th grades Farnham (Va.) Elem. Sch., 1967-71; tchr. 6th grade Callao (Va.) Elem. Sch., 1971-81; tchr. 6th and 7th grades Northumberland Mid. Sch., Heathsville, Va., 1981—; sr. mem. Supt. Adv. Com., Heathsville, 1986-93. Author: My Survival, 1994; author of children's books, short stories and poetry. Lifetime mem. Gibeon Bapt. Ch., Village, Va., 1942—. Mem. NEA, ASCD, Aerobics & Fitness Assn. Am., Va. Mid. Sch. Assn., Exercise Safety Assn., Nat. Coun. of English Tchrs., Nat. Wildlife Fedn. Republican. Home: RR 1 Box 39A Callao VA 22435-9706 Office: Northumberland Mid Sch PO Box 100 Heathsville VA 22473-0100

SISSON, MARY WINIFRED, retired elementary education educator; b. Decatur, Ill., Oct. 8, 1919; d. Leland Eugene and Amy Gertrude (Chaplin) Jayne; m. Lewis Milton Sisson, June 30, 1962 (dec.). BS, Bradley U., 1948. Elem. tchr. Milford (Ill.) Sch., 1941-43, Pekin (Ill.) Douglas Sch., 1943-58, Lake Weston Sch., Orlando, Fla., 1958-60, various, San Jose, Calif., 1960-61, White Sch., Peoria, Ill., 1960-65, Blaine-Sumner Sch., Peoria, 1965-67; adult tutor Common Place, Peoria, 1985-89, 92-94; leader summer playgrounds, Pekin, Ill., 1954-58. Active Westminster Presbyn. Ch. travel activities. Recipient scholarships Ill. State U., Normal. Mem. DAR, Naomi Cir., Peoria Area Retired Tchrs. Assn., Ill. Retired Tchrs. Assn. Republican. Presbyterian. Home: 3507 N Molleck Dr Apt 317 Peoria IL 61604-1003

SITARZ, ANNELIESE LOTTE, pediatrics educator, physician; b. Medellin, Colombia, Aug. 31, 1928; came to U.S., 1935; d. Hans and Elisabeth (Noll) S. BA cum laude, Bryn Mawr (Pa.) Coll., 1950; MD, Columbia U., 1954. Diplomate Nat. Bd. Med. Examiners, Am. Bd. Pediatrics., Am. Bd. Pediatric Hematology and Oncology. With Columbia U., N.Y.C., 1957—, assoc. prof. clin. pediatrics, 1974-83, prof. clin. pediatrics, 1983—; cons. pediatrics, hematology and oncology Harlem Hosp., N.Y.C., 1967-72, Overlook Hosp., Summit, N.J., 1975—. Contbr. numerous articles to profl. jours. Pres. Mt. Prospect Assn., Summit, 1987—. Fellow Am. Acad. Pediatrics; mem. Am. Assn. Cancer Rsch., Am. Soc. Clin. Oncology, Am. Soc. Hematology, Internat. Soc. Hematology, Harvey Soc. Republican. Episcopalian. Office: Babies and Children's Hosp Harkness Pavilion 180 Ft Washington Ave New York NY 10032-1537

SITARZ, PAULA GAJ, writer; b. New Bedford, Mass., May 25, 1955; d. Stanley Mitchell and Pauline (Rocha) Gaj; m. Michael James Sitarz, Aug. 26, 1978; children: Andrew Michael, Kate Elizabeth. BA, Smith Coll., 1977; MLS, Simmons Coll., 1978. Children's libr. Thomas Crane Pub. Libr., Quincy, Mass., 1978-84; dir. Reader's Theatre Workshop Thomas Crane Pub. Library, Quincy Mass., 1985. Author: (book) Picture Book Story Hours: From Birthdays to Bears, 1986, More Picture Book Story Hours, 1989, The Curtain Rises: A History of Theater From Its Origins in Greece and Rome Through the English Restoration, 1991, The Curtain Rises Volume II: A History of European Theater from the Eighteenth Century to the Present, 1993; contbr. monthly column Bristol County Baby Jour., 1992—, South Shore Baby Jour., 1992—, First Tchr., 1993—. Mem. New Eng. Libr. Assn., Libr. Sci. Honor Soc., Smith Club of Southeastern Mass. (v.p. 1987-89, pres. 1989-91), Dartmouth (Mass.) Arts Coun., Beta Phi Mu. Roman Catholic. Home and Office: 25 Stratford Dr North Dartmouth MA 02747-3843

SIVE, REBECCA ANNE, public affairs company executive; b. N.Y.C., Jan. 29, 1950; d. David and Mary (Robinson) S.; m. Clark Steven Tomashefsky, June 18, 1972. BA, Carleton Coll., 1972; MA in Am. History, U. Ill., Chgo., 1975. Asst. to chmn. of pres.' task force on vocations Carleton Coll., Northfield, Minn., 1972; asst. to acquisitions librarian Am. Hosp. Assn., Chgo., 1973; rsch. asst. Jane Addams Hull House, Chgo., 1974; instr. Loop Coll., Chgo., 1975, Columbia Coll., Chgo., 1975-76; cons. Am. Jewish Com., Chgo., 1975, Ctr. for Urban Affairs, Northwestern U., Evanston, Ill., 1977, Ill. Consultation on Ethnicity in Edn., 1976, MLA, 1977; dir. Ill. Women's History Project, 1975-76; founder, exec. dir. Midwest Women's Ctr., Chgo., 1977-81; exec. dir. Playboy Found., 1981-84; v.p. pub. affairs/pub. rels. Playboy Video Corp., 1985; v.p. pub. affairs Playboy Enterprises, Inc., Chgo., 1985-86; pres. The Sive Group, Inc., Chgo., 1986—; guest speaker various ednl. orgns., 1972—; instr. Roosevelt U., Chgo., 1977-78; dir. spl. projects Inst. on Pluralism and Group Identity, Am. Jewish Com., Chgo., 1975-77; cons. Nat. Women's Polit. Caucus, 1978-80; bd. dirs. NOVA Health Systems, Woodlawn Community Devel. Corp.; trainer Midwest Acad.; mem. adv. bd. urban studies program Associated Colls. Midwest; proposal reviewer NEH. Contbr. articles to profl. jours. Commr. Chgo. Park Dist., 1986-88; mem. steering com. Ill. Commn. on Human Rels., 1976; mem. structure com. Nat. Women's Agenda Coalition, 1976-77; del.-at-large Nat. Women's conf., 1977; mem. Ill. Gov.'s Com. on Displaced Homemakers, 1979-81, Ill. Human Rights Com., 1980-87, Ill. coordinating com., Internat Womens Yr.; coord. Ill. Bicentennial Photog. Exhbn., 1977; mem. Ill. Employment and Tng. Coun.; mem. employment com. Ill. Com. on Status of Women; bd. dirs. Nat. Abortion Rights Action League and NARAL Found., Ill. div. ACLU, Midwest Women's Ctr. Recipient award for outstanding community leadership YWCA Met. Chgo., 1979, award for outstanding community leadership Chgo. Jaycees, 1988. Home: 3529 N Marshfield Ave Chicago IL 60657-1224 Office: The Sive Group 359 W Chicago Ave Ste 201 Chicago IL 60610-3025

SIZEMORE, BARBARA ANN, Black studies educator; b. Chgo., Dec. 17, 1927; d. Sylvester Walter Laffoon and Delila Mae (Alexander) Stewart; m. Furman E. Sizemore, June 28, 1947 (div. Oct. 1964); children: Kymara, Furman G.; m. Jake Milliones, Sept. 29, 1979 (div. Feb. 1992). BA, Northwestern U., 1947, MA, 1954; PhD, U. Chgo., 1979; LLD (hon.), Del. State Coll., 1974; LittD (hon.), Cen. State U., 1974; DHL (hon.), Bal. Coll. of Bible, 1975; D of Pedagogy (hon.), Niagara U., 1994. Tchr., prin., dir. Chgo. Pub. Schs., 1947-72; assoc. sec. Am. Assn. Sch. Adminstrs., Arlington, Va., 1972-73; supt. schs. D.C. Pub. Schs., Washington, 1973-75; ednl. cons. Washington and Pitts., 1975—; prof. Black studies U. Pitts., 1977-92; dean Sch. of Edn. DePaul U., Chgo., 1992—. Author: The Ruptured Diamond, 1981; bd. mem. Jour. Negro Edn., 1974-83, Rev. Edn., 1977-85. Candidate city coun. Washington, 1977; mem. NAACP. Recipient Merit award Northwestern U. Alumni Assn., 1974, Excellence award Nat. Alliance Black Sch. Educators, 1984, Human Rights award UN Assn., 1985; named to U.S. Nat. Com., UNESCO, 1974-77. Mem. Nat. Coun. for Black Studies, African Heritage Studies Assn. (bd. mem. 1972—), Nat. Alliance Black Sch. Educators, Delta Sigma Theta. Democrat. Baptist. Office: DePaul U Sch of Edn 2320 N Kenmore Ave Chicago IL 60614-3210

SIZEMORE, CAROLYN LEE, nuclear medicine technologist; b. Indpls., July 22, 1945; d. Alonzo Chester and Elsie Louise Marie (Osterman) Armstrong; m. Jessie S. Sizemore Sr., June 9, 1966; 1 child, Jessie S. Jr. AA in Nuclear Medicine, Prince George's Community Coll, Largo, Md., 1981; BA in Bus. Adminstrn., Trinity Coll., 1988. Registered technologist (nuclear medicine); cert. nuclear medicine technologist, Md.; lic. nuclear med. technologist. Nuclear med. technologist Washington Hosp. Ctr., 1981-88; chief technologist, mem. com. Capitol Hill Hosp., Washington, 1988-91; chief technologist, asst. radiation safety officer Nat. Hosp. Med. Ctr., Arlington, Va., 1991—; mem. Am. Registry of Radiologic Technologists Nuclear Medicine Exam. Com., 1990-93. Contbr. articles to profl. jours. Mem. com. Medlantic Rsch. Found., Washington, 1989-93; sec. Crestview Area Citizens Assn., 1994-95. Mem. Va. Soc. Radiol. Technologists, Potomac Dist. Soc. Radiol. Technologists, Med. Soc. Radiol. Technologsts, Med. Soc. Nuclear Medicine Technologists, Soc. Nuclear Medicine (chmn. membership 1983-85, sec. 1985-87, 88-89, co-editor Isotopics 1991, editor Isotopics 1992-96, nominating com. 1995-96), Nuclear Medicine Adv. Bd., Am. Legion Aux. (exec. com. 1975-76), Internat. Platform Assn., Crestview Area Citizens Assn. (sec. 1994-95). Republican. Lutheran. Home: 6700 Danford Dr Clinton MD 20735-4019

SIZER, REBECCA RUDD, performing arts educator, arts coordinator; b. Melrose, Mass., July 28, 1958; d. David William and Harriet Fay (Sart) Rudd; m. Theodore Sizer II, June 21, 1980; children: Caroline Foster, Lydia Catherine Rachel, Theodore Rudd. AB, Mount Holyoke Coll., 1980; MFA, Rochester Inst. Tech., 1983; postgrad., Eastman and Westminster Choir Coll. Cert. tchr. music and art K-12, N.J. Dir. music Christian Bros. Acad., Lincroft, N.J., 1991-93, Peddie Sch., Hightstown, N.J., 1993-94; chair dept. fine and performing arts, arts curriculum coord. Ranney Sch., Tinton Falls, N.J., 1994—; dir. after sch. art program Upstairs Youth Agy., Rochester, N.Y., 1984-85; music dir. Peninsula Opera Rep. Co., Rumson, N.J., 1986-88, local music. theatre, Red Bank, N.J., 1986—; freelance artist, musician. Illustrator: (books) China: A Brief History, 1981, Making Decisions, 1983. Joseph A. Skinner fellow Mt. Holyoke Coll., 1981, Dodge fellow Geraldine R. Dodge Found., 1993. Mem. Music Educators Nat. Conf., Local 399 Musicians Union. Home: 385 Branch Ave Little Silver NJ 07739

SJURSEN, HOPE BIANCHI, marketing professional; b. Arcadia, Calif., Mar. 8, 1959; d. John Ernest and Donna Shirlene (Gill) Bianchi; m. John Norman Sjursen V, Oct. 1, 1988; children: Lauren Michelle, John Norman VI. BS, Pepperdine U. Asst. dept. mgr. Bullock's Dept. Store, Century City, Calif., 1980; asst. buyer Bullock's Dept. Store, L.A., 1980-81; factory sales rep. Bianchi Internat., Temecula, Calif., 1981-85, sales mgr. western region, 1986-88, mktg. mgr., 1989-91, dir. mktg., customer svcs., 1991—. Mem. NRA (life, instr. women's personal protection 1993-95), NAFE, Am. Defense Preparedness Assn., Rally for Children (founder). Republican. Roman Catholic. Home: 3647 Katie Lendre Dr Fallbrook CA 92028 Office: Bianchi Internat 100 Calle Cortez Temecula CA 92590

SKAAR, SARAH HENSON, editor; b. Bryan, Tex., June 19, 1958; d. James Bond Henson and Evie Leone (Callihan) Miller; m. Kent Skaar, Apr. 7, 1990. BS, Wash. State U., 1983, M in Adult and Continuing Edn., 1986. Asst. prof. U. Idaho Coop. Extension System, 1984-91; editor Intermountain Horse and Rider, Idaho Falls, 1994—. Author: Risk Management: Strategies for Managing Volunteer Programs, 1988. Recipient Pub. Info. award Nat. Assn. County Agrl. Agts., 1989.

SKADDEN, NANCY LEE MACKEY, secondary education educator; b. River Falls, WI, May 18, 1939; d. Harold Elbert Mackey and Dorothy E. (Newville) Brand; m. William Stewart Skadden, July 11, 1958; children: Anita Joanne S. Pandolfe, William Harold Skadden. BA, U Wis., Green Bay, 1973. Cert. lang. arts tchr., secondary. Tchr. So. Door Middle Sch., Brussels, Wis., 1973-96; negotiator Wis. Edn. Assn., Madison, 1984-88; mediator farm mediation program Wis. Dept. Agr., Madison, 1992—. Dem. candidate for Wis. senate dist. 1, 1982; del. Dem. Nat. Conv., 1984, 88; mem. Lake Mich. Comml. Fishing Bd., 1985-89, Fed. Merit Selection Commn. Ea. Dist., Wis., 1986-88; mem. Door County Bd. Adjustment, Sturgeon Bay, 1990—, chair, 1993—. Mem. Wis. Edn. Assn. (bd. dirs. 1974-78, 80-83). Mem. United Ch. of Christ. Office: So Door Middle Sch Brussels WI 54204

SKAGGS, ARLINE DOTSON, elementary school educator; b. Houston, Sept. 10, 1935; d. Gordon Alonzo and Fannie Mae (O'Kelley) Dotson; m. May 24, 1958 (div. Dec. 1969); children: Fred Mack, Ray Gordon. BS, U. Houston, 1957. Recreation leader VA Hosp., Houston, 1957-59; 4th and 5th grade tchr. Houston Ind. Sch. Dist., 1967-91; ret., 1991—; sponsor Number Sense, 1975-87, Sci. Fair, 1984-85. Auditor PTA, 1985, 87, 88; treas. Mt. Olive Luth. Sch. PTO, 1967-68; pres. Gulfgate Lioness Club, 1966-67; mem. Delphian Soc., 1965, Ch. of Houston Bread Distbn. program, 1990-91; treas. Houston Night Chpt. Women's Aglow, 1982; tchr. Children's Ch., 1972, 83, 84; prayer ptnr. Trinity Broadcasting Network, 1989-90, Christian Broadcasting Network, 1982-83; Braves scorekeeper Braes Bayou Little League, 1969-71; mem. United Way Funding Com., Salvation Army, Star of Hope & United Svcs. Orgn., 1974-76. Winning sponsor Citywide Math. Competition, Houston Ind. Sch. Dist., 1982, N.E. Area Math. Competition, 1976, 78, 79, 81, 82, 83, Lockhart Math. Contest, 1987. Mem. NEA (del. 1974), Houston Tchrs. Assn. (sch. rep. 1968-77, exec. bd. 1972-74, dir. N.E. area 1972-74, by-laws chmn. 1976), Tex. State Tchrs. Assn. (life, del. convs. 1968-75). Home: 4437 Vivian St Bellaire TX 77401-5630

SKAGGS, SARAH JO, choreographer, dancer; b. St. Louis, Oct. 11, 1957; d. Jerome Donley and Demethra Joan (Glascock) S. BA in Theater Arts, Sweet Briar Coll., 1979. Vis. prof. dance Sweet Briar (Va.) Coll., 1980; artistic dir. Sarah Skaggs Dance, N.Y.C., 1992—; dance tchr. DTW Suitcase Fund, Prague, Czech Republic, 1993, USIA, Hong Kong, 1994. Choreographer/dancer Cross Cultural Studies, 1984, Deep Song Solo, 1991, Higher Ground, 1993, (group collaboration) Reeling, 1995. Bd. dirs. Danspace Project, St. Mark's Ch., 1992—; bd. dirs., v.p. MAD ALEX Arts Found., Inc., 1994—. NEA Choreographer's fellow, 1987—, N.Y. Found. for Arts Choreographer's fellow, 1987-92. Home: 246 Mott St New York NY 10012

SKAL, DEBRA LYNN, lawyer; b. Dayton, Ohio, Oct. 2, 1958; d. Lawrence and Anne Bernice (Cunix) S. BS with high distinction, Ind. U., 1986; JD, Duke U., 1989. Bar: Ga. 1989. Assoc. Powell, Goldstein, Frazer & Murphy, Atlanta, 1989—. Exec. editor: Alaska Law Rev., 1987-89. Mem. Lupus Found. Am., Atlanta, 1992—; coun. mem. Yes!Atlanta, 1990—; mem. Sjogren's Found., Port Washington, N.Y., 1992—. Mem. ABA, State Bar Assn. Ga., Atlanta Bar Assn., Beta Gamma Sigma. Office: Powell Goldstein Frazer & Murphy 191 Peachtree St NE 16th Fl Atlanta GA 30303

SKARI, LISA A., college administrator, educator; b. Missoula, Mont., Aug. 1, 1965; d. Carman Skari and Mora Christine (MacKinnon) Payne. B in Clothing and Textiles, Wash. State U., 1987; MBA, Pacific Luth. U., 1992. Cert. vocat. edn. instr., Wash. Area sales mgr. Lamonts, Federal Way, Wash., 1987-89; buyer Lamonts, Seattle, 1989-92; store mgr., buyer Morning Sun, Tacoma, Wash., 1992-94; adj. instr. Highline C.C., Des Moines, Wash., 1992-94, dir. cooperative edn., 1994—. Mem. Am. Vocat. Assn., Cooperative Edn. Assn., S. King C. of C. Office: Highline CC PO Box 98000 Des Moines WA 98198-9800

SKAURAS-OLDKNOW, MIMI SKANDALAKIS, religious organization administrator. Pres. Greek Orthodox Ladies Philoptochos Soc. Office: 345 E 74th St New York NY 10021*

SKED, MARIE JOSEPHINE, financial service owner, nurse; b. Stroudsburg, Pa., June 15, 1935; d. Newell Walter and Marjorie Frances (Keegan) Felton; m. Henry Daniel Kehr, Sept. 25, 1955 (div. Dec. 1972); children: Wendy Carol, John Francis, Newell Walter; m. Ogden Stanley Sked, Mar. 10, 1973. Student, Temple U., 1953-55; AAS in Nursing, Mercer County C.C., 1970; postgrad., Stockton State Coll., 1973-74. RN, Pa. LPN, emergency rm. and float nurse Zurbrugg Meml. Hosp., Riverside, N.J., 1964-67; LPN, staff nurse State of N.J. E.R. Johnstone Rsch. for Mentally Retarded, Bordentown, 1967-70, head nurse, 1970-71; asst. oper. rm. supr. Hamilton Hosp., Trenton, N.J., 1971-76; pvt. scrub nurse Dr. Ralph Ellis, Trenton, 1977-78; owner Income Tax Svc., Newfoundland, Pa., 1985—. Sec.-treas. Panther Lake Homeowner's Assn., 1984-94; mem. Pa. Hist. Mus. Commn. State of N.J. scholar, 1968. Mem. AARP (instr. for income tax vols. 1985—). Home: Pine Grove Rd PO Box 216 Newfoundland PA 18445

SKELTON, DOROTHY GENEVA SIMMONS (MRS. JOHN WILLIAM SKELTON), art educator; b. Woodland, Calif.; d. Jack Elijah and Helen Anna (Siebe) Simmons; BA, U. Calif., 1940, MA, 1943; m. John William Skelton, July 16, 1941. Sr. rsch. analyst War Dept., Gen. Staff, M.I. Div. G-2, Pentagon, Washington, 1944-45; vol. rschr. monuments, fine arts and archives sect. Restitution Br., Office Mil. Govt. for Hesse, Wiesbaden, German, 1947-48; vol. art tchr. German children in Bad Nauheim, Germany, 1947-48; art educator, lectr. Dayton (Ohio) Art Inst., 1955; art educator Lincoln Sch., Dayton, 1956-60; instr. art and art edn. U. Va. Sch. Continuing Edn., Charlottesville, 1962-75; rschr. genealogy, exhibited in group shows, Calif., Colo., Ohio, Washington and Va.; represented in permanent collections Madison Hall, Charlottesville, Madison (Va.) Ctr. Recipient Hon. Black Belt Karate Sch. of Culpeper, Va., 1992. Vol. art cons.; bd. dirs. Va. Rappahannock-Rapidan Vol. Emergency Med. Svcs. Coun., 1978—. Mem. Nat. League Am. Pen Women, AAUW, Am. Assn. Museums, Coll. Art Assn. Am., Inst. for Study of Art in Edn., Dayton Soc. Painters and Sculptors, Nat. Soc. Arts and Letters (life), Va. Mus. Fine Arts, Cal. Alumni Assn., Air Force Officers Wives Club. Republican. Methodist. Club: Army Navy Country. Chief collaborator: John Skelton of Georgia, 1969; author: The Squire Simmons Family, 1746-1986, 1986. Address: Lotos Lakes Brightwood VA 22715

SKIDMORE, LINDA CAROL, science and engineering program administrator, consultant; b. Salisbury, Md., July 15, 1948; d. David Donaldson Skidmore Sr. and Mabel Frances Matthews Shockley; m. Charles Raymond Dix, Sept. 13, 1969 (div. Dec. 1991); 1 child, Larisa-Rose. BA, Loyola Coll., Balt., 1972; MEd, Salisbury (Md.) State Coll., 1982. Advanced profl. Md. State Dept. Edn. Tchr. secondary schs. Balt., 1972-73; tchr. James M. Bennett Sr. High Sch., Salisbury, 1973-77, coord. English dept., 1978-81; adminstrv. asst. Commn. Human Resources Nat. Rsch. Coun., Washington, 1981-82; adminstrv. assoc. Office Sci. Engring. Pers. Nat. Rsch. Coun., Washington, 1982-84, adminstrv. officer, 1984-87, program officer, 1987-90, study dir., 1990-94; dir. com. on women in sci. and engring., 1994—; instr. English Salisbury State Coll., 1979; cons. leadership tng. program for women Md. State Tchrs. Assn., Balt., 1978-81, Anne Arundel County Pub. Schs., Annapolis, Md., 1982-90; prin. investigator Engring. Personnel Data Needs in the 1990's, Edn. and Employment Engrs., Minorities Sci. and Engring., Women Sci. and Engring.; staff officer Com. on the Internat. Exch. and Movement Engrs., Com. Engring. Labor-Market Adjustments, Com. on Scientists and Engrs. in Fed. Govt.; panel on gender differences in the career outcomes of PhD scientists and engrs.; presenter Computer Math. Sci. Fair, 1990—; lectr. in field. Editor: Women: Their Underrepresentation and Career Differentials in Science and Engineering, 1987, Minorities: Their Underrepresentation and Career Differentials in Science and Engineering, 1987, On Time to the Doctorate, 1989, (with Alan K. Campbell) Recruitment, Retention and Utilization of Federal Scientists and Engineers, 1990, (with Marsha Lakes Matyas) Science and Engineering Programs: On Target for Women?, 1992, Women Scientists and Engineers Employed in Industry: Why So Few?, 1994; author: Women and Minorities in Science and Engineering, 1989; contbr. articles to profl. jours. Original appointee Wicomico County Commn. Women, 1977-81; Sunday sch. tchr. Severna Park, Md. United Meth. Ch., 1985-91; mem. Heartfriends, 1987—, co-chmn., 1989-90. Recipient cert. of Appreciation Wicomico County Bd. Edn., 1980; named Outstanding Young Woman Wicomico County Jaycees, 1977. Mem. AAAS, AAUW (chair women's issues Severna Park, Md. br. 1990-92, 1st v.p. 1992-95), Am. Assn. Higher Edn., Assn. for Women in Sci., Commn. on Profls. in Sci. and Tech., Fedn. Orgns. for Profl. Women, Nat. Coun. for Rsch. on Women, N.Y. Acad. Scis., Scho. Sci. and Math. Assn., Am. Ednl. Rsch. Assn. (spl. interest group on women and edn.), Nat. Coalition for Women and Girls in Edn., Women in Engring. Program Adv. Network, Women in Tech. Internat., Am. Legion Aux., Nat. Mus. Women Arts (charter), Md. State Tchrs. Assn. (chair women's caucus 1977-78, human rights com. 1979-81, meritorious svc. 1978, 80), Wicomico County Edn. Assn. (pres. 1978-79), Sigma Delta Epsilon. Democrat. Home: 912 Winsap Ct Baltimore MD 21227 Office: NRC Office Sci and Engring Pers Rm TJ 2011 2101 Constitution Ave NW Washington DC 20418

SKIDMORE, MARGARET COOKE, fundraiser; b. N.Y.C., Sept. 10, 1938; d. M. Bernard and Mary Frances (Adams) Cooke; m. Louis Skidmore Jr., Sept. 10, 1960; children: Christopher, Elizabeth, Heather. BA, Chatham Coll., 1960; cert. Mgmt. Program, Rice U., 1986. Devel. asst. Yale U., New Haven, 1960-62, sec. French dept., 1963; devel. asst. Chgo. Symphony, 1976; dir. devel. Children's Meml. Hosp., Chgo., 1976-77, Mus. Fine Arts, Houston, 1978—. Adv. bd. mem. Cultural Arts Coun., Houston, 1990-96. Named Outstanding Women Am., 1971. Mem. Nat. Soc. Fund Raising Execs. (nat. bd. dirs. 1981-85, chpt. pres. 1982-83, bd. dirs. 1979-85, 88-91, cert., Outstanding Fundraising award 1980, 81, 82, Outstanding Fundraising Exec. award 1985), Art Mus. Devel. Assn. (pres. 1983). Episcopalian. Home: 302 Litchfield Ln Houston TX 77024 Office: Museum Fine Arts PO Box 6826 Houston TX 77265

SKIGEN, PATRICIA SUE, lawyer; b. Springfield, Mass., June 16, 1942; d. David P. and Gertrude H. (Hirschhaut) S.; m. Irwin J. Sugarman, May 1973 (div. Nov. 1994); 1 child, Alexander David. BA with distinction, Cornell U., 1964; LLB, Yale U., 1968. Bar: N.Y. 1968, U.S. Dist. Ct. (so. dist.) N.Y. 1969. Law clk. Anderson, Mori & Rabinowitz, Tokyo, 1966-67; assoc. Rosenman Colin Kaye Petschek Freund & Emil, N.Y.C., 1968-70; assoc. Willkie Farr & Gallagher, N.Y.C., 1970-75, ptnr., 1977-95; v.p., co-chair corp. fin. group legal dept. Chase Manhattan Bank, N.Y.C., 1995—; dep. supt., gen. counsel N.Y. State Banking Dept., N.Y.C., 1975-77, 1st dep. supt. banks, 1977; adj. prof. Benjamin Cardozo Law Sch. Yeshiva U., 1979. Contbr. articles to profl. jours. Cornell U. Dean's scholar, 1960-64, Regent's scholar, 1960-64, Yale Law Sch. scholar, 1964-68. Mem. ABA (corp. banking and bus. law sect.), Assn. of Bar of City of N.Y. (chmn. com. banking 1991-94, long range planning com. 1994—, audit com. 1995—), Phi Beta Kappa, Phi Kappa Phi. Office: Chase Manhattan Bank 270 Park Ave New York NY 10081

SKILBECK, CAROL LYNN MARIE, elementary educator and small business owner; b. Seymour, Ind., May 1, 1953; d. Harry Charles and Barbara Josephine (Knue) S.; div.; 1 child, Michael Charles. Postgrad., U. Cin., 1977, Wright State U., 1985-86, Northern Ky. U., 1995—. Cert. tchr., Ohio. Sec. Procter & Gamble, Cin., 1971-76; classified typist The Cin. Enquirer, Cin., 1976; tchr. St. Aloysius Sch., Cin., 1977-79, St. William Sch., Cin., 1979-82; legal sec. County Dept. Human Svcs., Cin., 1982-86; tchr. St. Jude Sch., Cin., 1986-91; educator, owner CLS Tutoring Svcs., Cin., 1991—; photographer Interstate Studio and Am. Sch. Pictures, 1994—; comm. edn. tchr. No. Ky. U., 1996; tchr. St. Martin Gifted Program, Cin., 1992-93, Oak Hills Schs. Community Edn., Cin., 1990—, Super Saturday Gifted Program, Cin., 1990—; adult leader antidrug program Just Say No, Cin., 1989-92. Author: Study Skills Workshop, 1993; writer, dir. Christmas play, 1993. Vol. interior designer for homeless shelter St. Joseph's Carpenter Shop, Cin., 1990; mem. LaSalle PTA, 1993—; vol. Habitat for Humanity. Mem. Nat. Tchrs. Assn. Democrat. Roman Catholic. Home and Office: 3801 Dina Ter Cincinnati OH 45211-6527

SKILLINGER, LUANNE, educator; b. Beaver Falls, Pa., Dec. 15, 1957; d. Richard Thurman and Marie Louise (George) S. Student, Delaware Tech., 1975-77, Salisbury State Coll., 1980; BS in Psychology, Northeastern U., Boston, 1983. Caseworker/juv. Key Program, Lawrence, Mass., 1983-84; bus. educator A.B. Inst., Boston, 1984-86; tech. instr. Unisys Corp., McLean, Va., 1986-88, project mgr., 1988-92, program mgr., 1992-94, edn. cons., 1994—. Vol. United Way Nat. Capital Area, Falls Church, Va., 1995—. Mem. Smithsonian Instn. Republican. Lutheran. Office: Unisys Corp 8008 Westpark Dr Mc Lean VA 22102

SKINNER, ANITA MARIER, talk show host, law enforcement official; b. Portland, Maine, Feb. 23, 1933; d. Rene Ernest and Eva (Boivin) Marier; m. Andrew Y. Skinner III, Jan. 17, 1953 (div. Aug. 1986); children: Drew, Dean Brien, Jamie. Student, Georgetown U., 1955-57. Cert. TV producer, camera operator. Exec. sec. Dept. Navy, Washington, 1951-57; dep. sheriff Tampa (Fla.) Sheriff's Office, 1985—; talk show host Jones Intercable, Inc., Tampa, 1985—, producer Personality Profiles, 1988—; pres. Anita Skinner Prodns., 1989—; freelance videographer, Tampa, 1990—; treas. Micah Prodns., 1987-91. Prodr. (videos) Medjugorje, Yugoslavia, 1988, Maine-Lobsters, 1989, (TV spl.) The Lamb That Was Slain, 1989 (Golden Cassette award, finalist for Home Town USA, 1990); prodr., camera operator (TV spls.) Person of Vision, 1989, Stamping Out Aids, 1989, America This Is What We Declare, 1989, Sing Noel, 1989, Russian Orthodox Divine Liturgy, 1990, Standing Room Only, 1990, Cheval Polo Tournament for LUPUS, 1990 (Golden Cassette award, 1990), Universal Studios Orland Grand Opening, 1990, Shake Rattle and Roll, 1990 (Golden Cassette award, 1990), Producers Three, The Entertainment Revue, (videos) Welcome Home Gen. H.N. Schwarzkopf & Troops, 1991, Queen Elizabeth's Arrival on the Britania, 1991, USA and USSR Athletes Exhbn., 1991; prodr., talk show host Personality Profile, 1992 (Golden Cassette award 1993). Mem. Fla. Motion Picture and TV Assn., Pub. Access (sec. 1987-90, membership treas. 1992). Democrat. Roman Catholic. Home: 815 Country Club Dr Tampa FL 33612-5629 Office: Jones Intercable Inc 1001 N B St Tampa FL 33606

SKINNER, HELEN CATHERINE WILD, biomineralogist; b. Bklyn., Jan. 25, 1931; d. Edward Herman and Minnie (Bertsch) Wild; m. Brian John Skinner, Oct. 9, 1954; children: Adrienne, Stephanie, Thalassa. BA, Mt. Holyoke Coll., 1952; MA, Radcliffe/Harvard, 1954; PhD, Adelaide (Australia) U., 1959. Mineralogist sect. molecular structure Nat. Inst. Arthritis and Metabolic Diseases, NIH, 1961-65; with sect. crystal chemistry Lab. Histology and Pathology Nat. Inst. Dental Rsch., NIH, 1965-66; lectr. dept. geology and geophysics Yale U., 1967-69, rsch. assoc. dept. surgery, 1967-72, sr. rsch. assoc. dept. surgery, 1972-75; Alexander Agassiz vis. lectr. dept. biology Harvard U., 1976-77; lectr. dept. biology Yale U., 1977-83; assoc. prof. biochemistry in surgery Yale U., New Haven, 1978-84, lectr. dept. orthopaedic surgery, 1972—, lectr., rsch. affiliate in geology and geophysics, 1967—; pres. Conn. Acad. Arts and Scis., 1986-94, publs. chair, 1994—; mineralogist AEC, summer 1953; master Jonathan Edwards Coll., Yale U., 1977-82; Alexander Agassiz vis. lectr. dept. biology Harvard U., 1976-77; vis. prof. sect. ecology and systematics dept. biology Cornell U., 1980-83; vis. disting. prof. geology Adelaide U., 1990-91; dental adv. com. Yale-New Haven Hosp., 1973-80; mem. faculty adv. com. Yale-New Haven Tchrs. Inst., 1983—; chmn. site visit team nat. Inst. Dental Rsch., 1974-75; mem. pubs. com. Am. Geolog. Inst., 1993-96. Author: (with others) Asbestos and Other Fibrous Materials: Mineralogy, Crystal Chemistry and Health Effects, 1988; co-editor: Biomineralization Processes of Iron and Manganese: Modern and Ancient Environments, 1992; contbr. over 50 articles to profl. jours.; tech. abstractor Geol. Soc. Am., 1961-65; sect. editor Am. Mineralogist, 1978-82. Mem. bd. edn. com. Conn. Fund for Environ., 1983-89, mem. sci. adv. com., 1989-92; founder, pres. Investor's Strategy Inst., New Haven, 1983-85; trustee Miss Porter's Sch., Farmington, Conn., mem. edn. com., 1986-88, mem. salaries and benefits com., 1988-91; treas. YWCA, New Haven, 1983-84. Fellow AAAS, Geol. Soc. Am., Mineral. Soc. Am. (mem. various coms., councilor 1979-81, Pub. Svc. award 1991); mem. Am. Soc. Bone and Mineral Rsch., Am. Assn. Crystal Growth, Am. Assn. Dental Rsch., Internat. Assn. Dental Rsch., Mineral Soc. Can. Home: PO Box 894 Woodbury CT 06798-0894 Office: Yale U Dept Geology Geophysics P O Box 208109 New Haven CT 06520-8109

SKINNER, LINDA SCOTT, lawyer; b. Jefferson City, Mo., Feb. 14, 1941; d. Frederick Donald and Lucille Mary (Meller) Scott; children: Gregory Skinner, Jeffrey Skinner, Evan Skinner. AA in Paralegal, Johnson County Coll., 1979; BA in Legal Asst., Avila Coll., 1982; JD, U. Mo. Kansas City, 1985. Bar: Mo. 1985, Kans. 1986. Ct. reporter transcriber B. Jackson Reporting, Kansas City, 1961-77; legal asst. E.A. McConwell Law Firm, Overland Park, Kans., 1977-82; law clk. Mo. Ct. Appeals, Kansas City, 1985-86; pvt. practice lawyer Overland Park, 1987-92, 94—; ptnr. Auston & Skinner, Overland Park, 1992-94; orientation chair Women's Law Caucus, Kansas City, 1984; mem. Avila Coll. Adv. Bd., Kansas City, 1987—; part-time judge Overland Park Mcpl. Ct., 1994—. Assoc. adminstrv. editor (law rev.) U. Mo. Kansas City Law Sch., 1983-84. Moot ct. judge U. Mo. Kansas City Law Sch., 1986—, mentor, 1987—; vol. attys. project Kansas City Met. Bar Assn., 1988—; committeewoman Rep. Party, Johnson County, 1988-89. Mem. Assn. for Women Lawyers (treas. 1989-90), Kans. Bar Assn., Mo. Bar Assn. (continuing edn. instr. 1988—, Johnson County Bar Assn. (ethics and impaired atty. assistance coms. 1994—), Johnson County Barristers (newsletter editor 1992-94), Johnson County Coll. Alumni Assn. (exec. bd.). Office: Ste 210 6701 W 64th Overland Park KS 66202

SKINNER, PATRICIA MORAG, state legislator; b. Glasgow, Scotland, Dec. 3, 1932; d. John Stuart and Frances Charlotte (Swann) Robertson; m. Robert A. Skinner, Dec. 28, 1957; children: Robin Ann, Pamela. BA, NYU, 1953. Mdse. trainee Lord & Taylor, N.Y.C., 1955-59; adminstrv. asst. Atlantic Products, N.Y.C., 1954-59; newspaper corr. Salem Observer, N.H., 1964-84; mem. N.H. Ho. of Reps., 1973-94, chmn. labor, human resources and rehab. com., 1975-86, House Edn. Com., 1987, chmn., 1989-94, exec. com. Nat. Conf. State Legislatures, 1987-90; chmn. N.H. Adv. Council Unemployment Compensation, 1984-94. Bd. dirs. chmn. Castle Jr. Coll., 1975, chmn. bd., 1988—; v.p. bd. Swift Water council Girl Scouts U.S., v.p. 1987-92; mem. chmn. coun. N.H. Voc-Tech. Coll., Nashua, 1978-83; trustee Nesmith Library, Windham, N.H., 1982—, chmn. bd. trustees, 1994. Mem. N.H. Fedn. Women's Clubs (parliamentarian, legis chmn. 1984—), N.H. Fedn. Republican Women's Clubs (pres. 1979-82). Christian Scientist. Club: Windham Woman's (pres. 1981-83). Lodge: Order Eastern Star.

SKINNER-LINNENBERG, VIRGINIA M., English language educator; b. Middletown, Ohio, Dec. 27, 1951; d. Bernard David and Joan Elizabeth (Koeppel) Skinner; m. Daniel M. Linnenberg, Aug. 22, 1975. BA, Bowling Green State U., 1974, PhD, 1993; MA, U. Louisville, 1983. New play reader Actors Theatre of Louisville, 1983-84; newspaper editor The Index, Dousman, Wis., 1985-87; coll. instr. Brescia Coll., Owensboro, Ky., 1987-88; coll. instr. Bowling Green State U., Ohio, 1988-89, tchg. fellow, 1989-92; coll. instr. U. Toledo, 1988-89; coll. prof. North Ctrl. Mich. Coll., Petoskey, 1992—; cons., Petoskey, Mich., 1992—; mem. adv. bd. PACE, Indian River, Mich., 1993—. Author short story and one-act plays; mem. rev. bd. St. Martin's Press, N.Y.C., 1995. Mem. MLA, AAUW (bd. dirs. 1994—), Nat. Conf. Tchrs. of English, Conf. on Coll. Composition & Comms. (mem. proposal rev. bd. 1995), Rhetoric Soc. Am. Episcopalian. Office: North Ctrl Mich Coll 1515 Howard St Petoskey MI 49770

SKIPPER, BECKY LOUISE, purchasing manager; b. Houston, July 14, 1967; d. James Maxwell and Ann Louise (Jones) S. BBA, U. Houston, 1989, MBA, 1993. Inside salesperson Dooley Tackaberry, Inc., Deer Pk., Tex., 1989-92, purchasing agt., 1992-94, purchasing mgr., 1994—. Precinct sec. Dem. Party, Houston, 1996; treas. Shadycrest Bapt. Ch., 1996. Mem. NOW, AAUW, Nat. Breast Cancer Coalition, Greater Houston Women's Found., Planned Parenthood of Houston and S.E. Tex. (Action Fund 1996—). Democrat. Baptist. Home: 10515 Sagevale Ln Houston TX 77089-2916

SKLADAL, ELIZABETH LEE, elementary school educator; b. N.Y.C., May 23, 1937; d. Angier Joseph and Julia May (Roberts) Gallo; m. George Wayne Skladal, Dec. 26, 1956; children: George Wayne Jr., Joseph Lee. BA, Sweet Briar Coll., 1958; EdM, U. Alaska, 1976. Choir dir. Main Chapel, Camp Zama, Japan, 1958-59, Ft. Lee, Va., 1963-65; choir dir. Main Chapel and Snowhawk, Ft. Richardson, Alaska, 1968-70; tchr. Anchorage (Alaska) Sch. Dist., 1970—. Active Citizen's Adv. Com. for Gifted and Talented, Anchorage, 1981-83; mem. music com. Anchorage Sch. Dist., 1983-86; soloist Anchorage Opera Chorus, 1969-80, Cmty. Chorus, Anchorage, 1968-80; mem. choir First Presbyn. Ch., Anchorage, 1971—, deacon, 1988—, elder, 1996—; participant 1st cultural exch. from Anchorage to Magadan, Russia with Alaska Chamber Singers, 1992; participant mission trip to Swaziland, Africa with First Presbyn. Ch., Anchorage, summer 1995. Named Am. Coll. Theater Festival winner Amoco Oil Co., 1974; recipient Cmty. Svc. award Anchorage U. Alaska Alumni Assn., 1994-95. Mem. AAUW, Anchorage Concert Assn. Patron Soc. (assocs. coun. of dirs.), Alaska Chamber Singers, Am. Guild Organists (former dean, former treas., mem.-at-large). Republican. Presbyterian. Home: 1841 S Salem Dr Anchorage AK 99508-5156

SKLAR, DORIS ROSLYN, conference planning executive; b. N.Y.C., Feb. 15, 1936; d. Philip and Anna (Donn) S. BA, Hunter Coll., 1957. Sec. GE Co., N.Y.C., 1957-69; exec. sec. Behavioral Sci. Applications, Inc., N.Y.C., 1969-72; conf. planning specialist GE Co., N.Y.C., 1972-76, conf. planning cons., 1976-82, mgr. conf. planning, 1982-96; pres. Sklar Worldwide Meeting Mgmt. Ltd., N.Y.C., 1996—; adj. asst. prof. mgmt. inst. Sch. Continuing Edn., NYU, 1988-91; speaker in field. Contbr. articles to profl. publs. Recipient Pacesetter award Hospitality and Mktg. Assn. Internat., 1995. Mem. Profl. Conv. Mgmt. Assn., Meeting Profls. Internat. (bd. dirs., Internat. 1976-1995, Planner of Yr. award 1988), Acad. Women Achievers, Internat. Assn. Conf. Ctrs.

SKLAR, HOLLY LYN, nonfiction writer; b. N.Y.C., May 6, 1955. BA, Oberlin Coll., 1977; MA in Polit. Sci., Columbia U., 1980. Researcher UN Ctr. Transnat. Corps., N.Y., 1978; writer, rschr. N. Am. Congress Latin Am., N.Y., 1981-82; exec. dir. Inst. New Communications, N.Y., 1982-84; writer, lectr. N.Y., Boston; review panelist Nat. Endowment Humanities, Washington, 1989; del. Soviet-Am. Women's Summit, N.Y., Washington, 1990. Author, co-author books including Trilateralism, 1980, Poverty in the American Dream: Women and Children First, 1983, Washington's War on Nicaragua, 1988, Streets of Hope: The Fall and Rise of an Urban Neighborhood, 1994, Chaos or Community? Seeking Solutions, Not Scapegoats for Bad Economics, 1995. Mem. adv. bd. Nationwide Women's Program, Am. Friends Svc. Com., The Progressive Media Project, Polit. Rsch. Assocs.; mem. steering com. Caribbean Basin Info. Project, 1982-85. Recipient Outstanding Book award Gustavus Myers Ctr. for Study Human Rights in U.S., 1988, Assocs. award Polit. Rsch. Assocs., Cambridge, 1991-96; fellow Columbia U. Grad. Sch. Arts and Scis., 1978-80. Mem. Nat. Writers Union, Acad. Polit. Sci., Latin Am. Studies Assn. Office: 97 Sheridan St Boston MA 02130-1857

SKLAR, KATHRYN KISH, historian, educator; b. Columbus, Ohio, Dec. 26, 1939; d. William Edward and Elizabeth Sue (Rhodes) Kish; m. Robert A. Sklar, 1958 (div. 1978); children: Leonard Scott, Susan Rebecca Sklar Friedman; m. Thomas L. Dublin, Apr. 30, 1988. B.A. magna cum laude, Radcliffe Coll., 1965; Ph.D., U. Mich., 1969. Asst. prof., lectr. U. Mich., Ann Arbor, 1969-74; assoc. prof. history UCLA, 1974-81, prof., 1981-88, chmn. com. to administer program in women's studies Coll. Letters and Sci., 1974-81; Disting. Prof. history SUNY, Binghamton, 1988—; Pulitzer juror in history, 1976; fellow Newberry Libr. Family and Community History Seminar, 1973; NEH cons. in women's studies U. Utah, 1977-79, Santa Clara U., 1978-80, Roosevelt U., 1980-82; hist. cons. AAUW; active Calif. Coun. for Humanities, 1981-85, N.Y. Coun. for Humanities, 1992—. Author: Catharine Beecher: A Study in American Domesticity, 1973 (Berkshire prize 1974); editor: Catharine Beecher: A Treatise on Domestic Economy, 1977, Harriet Beecher Stowe: Uncle Tom's Cabin, or Life Among the Lowly: The Minister's Wooing, Oldtown Folks, 1981, Notes of Sixty Years: The Autobiography of Florence Kelley, 1849-1926, 1984, (with Thomas Dublin) Women and Power in American History: A Reader (2 vols.), 1991, (with Linda Kerber and Alice Kessler-Harris) U.S. History as Women's History: New Feminist Essays, 1995; co-editor: The Social Survey Movement in Historical Perspective, 1992, Florence Kelley and the Nation's Work. The Rise of Women's Political Culture, 1830-1900, 1995; mem. editl. bd. Jour. Women's History, 1987—, Women's History Rev., 1990—, Jour. Am. History, 1978-81; contbr. chpts. to books. Fellow Woodrow Wilson Found., 1965-67, Danforth Found., 1967-69, Radcliffe Inst., 1973-74, Nat. Humanities Inst., 1975-76, Rockefeller Found. Humanities, 1981-82, Woodrow Wilson Internat. Ctr. for Scholars, 1982, 1992-93, Guggenheim Found., 1984, Ctr. Advanced Study Behavioral and Social Scis., Stanford U., 1987-88, AAUW, 1990-91; Daniels fellow Am. Antiquarian Soc., 1976, NEH fellow Newberry Library, 1982-83; Ford Found. faculty rsch. grantee, 1973-74; grantee NEH, 1976-78, UCLA Coun. for Internat. and Comparative Studies, 1983. Mem. Am. Hist. Assn. (chmn. com. on women historians 1980-83, v.p. Pacific Coast br. 1986-87, pres. 1987-88), Orgn. Am. Historians (exec. bd. 1983-86, Merle Curti award com. 1978-79, lectr. 1982—), Am. Studies Assn. (coun. mem.-at-large 1978-80), Berkshire Conf. Women Historians, Am. Antiquarian Soc., Phi Beta Kappa. Office: SUNY Dept History Binghamton NY 13902

SKLAR, LOUISE MARGARET, service executive; b. L.A., Aug. 12, 1934; d. Samuel Baldwin Smith and Judith LeRoy (Boughton) Nelson; m. Edwynn Edgar Schroeder, Mar. 20, 1955 (div. July 1975); children: Neil Nelson, Leslie Louise Schroeder Grandclaudon, Samuel George; m. Martin Sklar, Oct. 17, 1983. Student, U. So. Calif., 1952-54, UCLA, 1977-79. Acct. Valentine Assocs., Northridge, Calif., 1976-78, programmer, 1978-79; contr. Western Monetary, Encino, Calif., 1979-81; pres. Automated Computer Composition, Chatsworth, Calif., 1984—. Mem. Am. Contract Bridge League (bd. govs. 1993—, mem. nat. charity com. 1982, mem. nat. goodwill com. 1994—), Assn. Los Angeles County Bridge Units (bd. dirs. 1990—, sec. 1984-86), DAR, Conn. Soc. Genealogists, Ky. Hist. Soc., So. Calif. Asistance League, Heart of Am. Geneal. Soc., Chatsworth C. of C., Greater L.A. Zoo Assn., Zeta Tau Alpha. Republican. Office: Automated Computer Composition Inc 21356 Nordhoff St Chatsworth CA 91311-5818

SKLARIN, ANN H., artist; b. N.Y.C., May 21, 1933; d. Sidney and Revera (Myers) Hirsch; m. Burton S. Sklarin, June 29, 1960; children: Laurie Sklarin Ember, Richard, Peter. BA in Art History, Wellesley Coll., 1955; MA in Secondary Art Edn., Columbia U., 1956. Art tchr. jr. high sch. N.Y.C. Sch. System, 1956-61, chmn. art. dept. jr. high sch., 1957-61. One-woman shows include Long Beach (N.Y.) Libr., 1973, Silvermine Guild Ctr. Arts, New Canaan, Conn., 1986, Long Beach Mus. Art, 1986, Discovery Art Gallery, Glen Cove, N.Y., 1987—; exhibited in juried shows at Nassau C.C., Garden City, N.Y., 1970, Nassau County (N.Y.) John F. Kennedy Ctr. Performing Arts, 1970 (1st Pl. award 1970), Long Beach Art Assn., 1970 (1st Pl. award 1970), Gregory Mus., 1973-74, L.I. Arts 76, Hempstead, N.Y., 1976, 5 Towns Music and Art Found., Woodmere, N.Y., 1980 (1st Pl. award 1981, Honorable Mention award 1981), 83 (3d Pl. award 1983), 85, Long Beach Art Assn. and Long Beach Mus. Art, 1982 (1st Pl. award 1982), 84, 85 (3d Pl. award 1985), Silvermine Guild Arts, 1984 (Richardson-Vicks Inc. award 1985), 87 (Pepperidge Farm Inc. award 1987), Long Beach Mus. Art, 1985 (Best in Show-Grumbacher award 1985), Heckscher Mus., Huntington, N.Y., 1985, 87, Fine Arts Mus. L.I., Hempstead, 1985, 91, Long Beach Art League and Long Beach Mus. Art, 1986 (2d Pl. award 1986), Wunsch Arts

Ctr., Glen Cove, 1986, 87, Smithtown Twp. Arts Coun., St. James, 1989 (Honorable Mention award 1989); exhibited in group shows at Hewlett-Woodmere Libr., 1969, B.J. Spoke Gallery, Port Washington, N.Y., 1985, Shirley Scott Gallery, Southampton, N.Y., 1986, Smithtown Twp. Arts Coun., St. James, N.Y., 1988, 90, N.Y. Inst. Tech., Old Westbury, N.Y., 1989, Dowling Coll., Oakdale, N.Y., 1990, Discovery Art Gallery, 1992, 93, 94, 95, Silvermine Guild Arts Ctr., 1992, Sound Shore Gallery, Stamford, Conn., 1993, Krasdale Foods Gallery, N.Y.C., 1993. Mem. exec. bd. 5 Towns Music & Art Found., 1960—, pres., 1971-74. Mem. Silvermine Guild Artists, Discovery Gallery (artist mem.). Studio: 501 Broadway Lawrence NY 11559-2501

SKODRAS, VICKI HERRING, banker; b. South Bend, Ind., June 4, 1958; d. David Lee and Ruth Irene (Ross) Herring; m. Dan Peter Skodras, June 24, 1989; children: Jonathan David, Alexander Constantin. BS, Ball State U., 1981. Asst. br. mgr. ITT Fin. Svcs., Cin., 1982-83; br. mgr. Transam. Fin. Svcs., Atlanta, 1983-85; loan officer 1st Source Bank, South Bend, 1985-86, br. mgr., asst. v.p., 1986-88, br. mgr., bus. devel. mgr., 1988-90, asst. v.p., br. mgr. main office, 1990-92; asst. v.p., br. mgr. Roseland br. 1st Source Bank, 1992. Vol. United Way, 1985-87, 90, Jr. League, 1991—; parent aide Child Abuse and Neglect Coun., 1987-89; casa program Youth Svc. Bur., 1992—. Named Boss of Yr., Am. Bus. Woman's Assn., Potawotomi chpt., 1990-91. Mem. Jr. League South Bend. Home: 17570 Irongate Ct Granger IN 46530-6412

SKOLAN-LOGUE, AMANDA NICOLE, lawyer, consultant; b. Los Angeles, Feb. 19, 1954; d. Carl Charles and Estelle (Lubin) Skolan; m. James Edward Logue, Dec. 10, 1983. BS, U. Calif., Los Angeles, 1973; MBA, U. So. Calif., 1976; JD, Southwestern U., Los Angeles, 1982. Bar: Calif. 1982, U.S. Dist. Ct. (cen., no. and ea. dists.) Calif. 1982, N.Y. 1986. Sr. internal cons. Getty Oil Co., Los Angeles, 1976-80; atty. litigation ACLU of So. Calif., Los Angeles, 1982-83; corp. atty. Am. Can Co., Greenwich, Conn., 1983-86; assoc. Shereff, Friedman, Hoffman & Goodman, N.Y.C., 1986-88; region counsel Gen. Electric Capital Corp., Danbury, Conn., 1988—. Mem. ABA, N.Y. State Bar Assn. Republican. Home: 33 Musket Ridge Rd New Fairfield CT 06812-5101 Office: Gen Electric Capital Corp 44 Old Ridgebury Rd Danbury CT 06810-5107

SKOLFIELD, MELISSA T., government official; b. New Orleans, June 25, 1958; m. Frank W. Curtis. BA in Econ. and Behavioral Sci., Rice U., 1980; MA in Pub. Affairs, George Washington U., 1986. Account exec. McDaniel & Tate Pub. Rels., Houston, 1981-84; press sec. Rep. Michael Andrews of Tex., 1985-87; press. sec. Senator Dale Bumpers of Ark., 1987-93; dep. asst. sec. for pub. affairs for policy and strategy Dept. Health and Human Svcs., Washington, 1993-95, asst. sec. pub. affairs, 1995—. Press asst. Dem. Nat. Com., Dem. Nat. Conv., 1988, Clinton Pres. Campaign, Dem. Nat. Com., 1992. Mem. Senate Press Secs. Assn. (pres.), Assn. Dem. Press Assts., Pub. Rels. Soc. Am. Office: Dept Health & Human Svcs 200 Indendence Ave SW Washington DC 20201

SKOLNICK ROTHENBERG, BARBARA, elementary education educator; b. Greenfield, Mass., Nov. 8, 1952; d. Simon and Lililan (Margolskee) Skolnick; m. David Rothenberg, Dec. 23, 1978; children: Jeffrey, Sarah. BA in Elem. Edn., Fairleigh Dickinson U., 1974; MEd in Reading, U. Mass., 1980, CAGS in Edn., 1985. Cert. in elem. edn., spl. needs, prin., reading, supervision, Mass. Tchr. Amherst (Mass.) Pub. Schs., 1975—; presenter in field. Author, compiler: Songs We Sing, 1991. Choral dir. for children's choir Internat. Sunday, Amherst, 1991—; founder Amherst Cmty. theatre, 1993; founder children's choir Voices That Care, Amherst, 1989—. Recipient honorable mention UN World Children's Day Found., 1992; named World of Difference Tchr., Anti Defamation League, Boston, 1993, Walt Disney Am. Tchr., Walt Disney Co., 1994. Mem. NEA, Nat. Coun. for Social Studies (Tchr. of Yr. 1993), Mass. Tchrs. Assn. Home: 84 Grantwood Dr Amherst MA 01002-1536 Office: Fort River Elem Sch SE St Amherst MA 01002

SKRATEK, SYLVIA PAULETTE, mediator, arbitrator, dispute systems designer; b. Detroit, Dec. 23, 1950; d. William Joseph and Helen (Meskauskas) S.; m. John Wayne Gullion, Dec. 21,1984. BS, Wayne State U., 1971; MLS, Western Mich. U., 1976; PhD, U. Mich., 1985. Media specialist Jackson (Mich.) Pub. Schs., 1971-79; contract specialist Jackson County Edn. Assn., 1976-79; field rep. Mich. Edn. Assn., E.Lansing, 1979-81; contract adminstr. Wash. Edn. Assn., Federal Way, 1981-85, regional coord., 1985-88, program adminstr., from 1988; dir. mediation svcs. Conflict Mgmt. Inst., Lake Oswego, Ore., 1986-87; exec. dir. N.W. Ctr. for Conciliation, 1987-88; served in Wash. State Senate, 1990-94; tng. cons. City of Seattle, 1986—; trustee Group Health Coop. of Puget Sound, Wash., 1984-87; sole proprietor Skratek & Assocs., 1980—; pres. Resolutions Internat., 1990—; v.p. Mediation Rsch. and Edn. Project, Inc., 1990—. Contbr. articles to legal jours. Mem. Soc. for Profls. in Dispute Resolution, Indsl. Rels. Rsch. Assn.

SKROPANIC, JESSICA T., anthropology, archaeology and sociology educator; b. Louisville, Aug. 3, 1966; d. Jan Charles and Marilyn Lee (Hendrickson) Green; m. Zeljko Tomislav Skropanic, Jan. 6, 1990. Student, Miami U., Oxford, Ohio, 1984-85; BA in Anthropology with honors, Humboldt State U., 1989, MA in Anthropology/Sociology with honors, 1992. Archaeologist Miami U., 1985; rsch. asst. Humboldt State U., Arcata, Calif., 1986-89, rsch. asst. libr./archives, 1989-92, social sci. tutor, 1990-91, grad. tchg. asst., 1991; coord. vol. and docent programs Redding Mus. Art and History, Turtle Bay Pk. and Mus. Corp., 1994; sociology, social psychology, anthropology and archaeology tchr. Simpson Coll., Redding, Calif., 1992—. Lay eucharist minister, lay pastor All Sts. Episcopal Ch., Redding, 1993-94; vol. Humboldt Jour. Social Rels., 1986-89; vol., mem. various museums. Mem. Am. Anthropol. Soc., Swiss-Am. Hist. Soc., Phi Kappa Phi, Pi Gamma Mu. Office: Simpson Coll Social Sci Dept 2211 College View Dr Redding CA 96003-8601

SKURDENIS, JULIANN VERONICA, librarian, educator, writer, editor; b. Bklyn., July 13, 1942; d. Julius J. and Anna M. (Zilys) S.; A.B. with honors, Coll. New Rochelle, 1964; M.S., Columbia U., 1966; M.A., Hunter Coll., 1974; m. Lawrence J. Smircich, Aug. 21, 1965 (div. July 1978); m. 2d, Paul J. Lalli, Oct. 1, 1978; 1 adopted dau., Kathryn Leila Skurdenis-Lalli. Young adult librarian Bklyn. Pub. Library, 1964-66; periodicals librarian, instr. Kingsborough Community Coll., Bklyn., 1966-67; acquisitions librarian Pratt Inst., Bklyn., 1967-68; acquisitions librarian, asst. prof. Bronx (N.Y.) Community Coll., 1968-75, head tech. services, assoc. prof., 1975—, acting dir. Libr. Resource Learning Ctr., 1994—. N.Y. State fellow, 1960-66, Columbia U. fellow, 1964-66, Pratt Inst. fellow, 1965. Mem. AAUP, Library Assn. CUNY (chairwoman numerous coms.), Archaeol. Inst. Am. Author: Walk Straight Through the Square, 1976, More Walk Straight Through the Square, 1977; contbg. editor Internat. Travel News, 1989—; travel editor Archaeology mag., 1986-89; contbr. over 200 travel, hist., and archaeol. pieces. Avocations: archaeology, travel, travel writing. Office: CUNY Bronx CC University Ave Bronx NY 10453-6994

SKURNIK, JOAN IRIS, special education evaluator, educator, consultant; b. Bklyn., Apr. 14, 1935; d. Benjamin and Dorothy (Blum) Hessel; m. Maurice Skurnik, Sept. 1, 1955 (div. Jan. 1982); children: Jennifer, Jonathan. BA magna cum laude, CCNY, 1973; MA, Columbia U., 1975. Cert. tchr. nursery to 6th grade, N.Y. Pvt. practice remedial therapist, diagnostician N.Y.C., 1974—; ednl. cons. in learning disabilities The Calhoun Sch., N.Y.C., 1977-85, The Collegiate Sch., N.Y.C., 1984-87, Riverdale (N.Y.) Country Sch., 1989-90, Abraham Joshua Heschel Sch., N.Y.C., 1991—; cons. Holy Rosary Sch., Pitts., 1976; planning commn. mem. Ethical Culture Schs., N.Y.C., 1980-82; conf. and workshop coord. in field; presenter in field. Mem. NOW, Internat. Reading Assn., Orton Dyslexia Soc. (N.Y. br. bd. mem. 1985-88), Profl. Colleagues Group, Phi Beta Kappa, Planned Parenthood (N.Y.C.), Appalachian Mountain Club (N.Y.C.).

SKVARLA, LUCYANN M., college official; b. Kingston, Pa., Jan. 15, 1959; d. John T. and Sophie H. (Turel) S. AS, Lackawanna Jr. Coll., Wilkes-Barre, Pa., 1978; BS, King's Coll., Wilkes-Barre, 1992. Cert. profl. sec. Sec. King's Coll., Wilkes-Barre, 1978, sec./adminstrv. asst., 1978-87, asst. for instnl. rsch., 1987—; part-time instr. non-credit workshops King's Coll., 1994—; part-time instr. McCann Sch. Bus., Wyoming, Pa., 1989-91. Lector St. Hedwig's Ch., Kingston, Pa., 1983-92. Mem. Assn. for Instnl. Rsch. (participant in inst. at No. Ky. U. 1993), N.E. Assn. for Instnl. Rsch., Delta Mu Delta, Delta Epsilon Sigma, Alpha Sigma Lambda. Office: Kings Coll 133 N River St Wilkes Barre PA 18711

SKWIRA, RHONDA RENEE, accountant; b. Denver, May 30, 1965; d. Keith Allen and Linda Diane (Florea) Mitchell; m. Alex Richard Skwira, Aug. 23, 1986; 1 child, Morgan Ann. BA, Abilene Christian U., 1986; postgrad. in acctg., Kennesaw State Coll., 1994-95. Broadcaster KEAN-FM, Abilene, Tex., 1985-86; news dir. KACU, Abilene, Tex., 1986; asst. in pres.'s office Ralph Lauren Corp., N.Y.C., 1986-87, asst. to controller, 1987-89, retail analyst, 1989-90; acct. mgr. Ralph Lauren Corp., Atlanta, 1990-94; acct. Malgeri & Assocs., CPAs, Marietta, Ga., 1994-96, Branch & Assocs., Atlanta, Ga., 1996—; acct. Susan G. Komen Found., Atlanta, 1994—. Acct. Race for the Cure, Atlanta, 1995; participant spring fling Ronald McDonald House, Atlanta, 1994-95; treas. Home Owner's Assn., 1995—. Named one of 2000 Notable Am. Women, Am. Bibliographic Inst., 1996. Mem. NAFE, Alpha Epsilon Rho Honor Soc. (v.p. 1986). Home: 1438 Heritage Glen Dr Marietta GA 30068

SKY, ALISON, artist, designer; b. N.Y.C.. BFA, Adelphi U., 1967; student, Art Students League, 1967-69, Columbia U. Co-founder, v.p. Sculpture in the Environ./SITE, N.Y.C., 1969-91; co-founder, prin. SITE Projects, N.Y.C., 1970-91; adj. faculty mem. Parsons Sch. Design, N.Y.C., 1994-95, Cooper Union, N.Y.C., 1995; vis. artist Purchase Coll., SUNY, 1994-95; artist-in-residence Urban Glass, 1995; lectr. in field. Exhbns. include The Venice Biennale, 1975, The Pompidou Ctr. and Louvre, Paris, 1975, The Mus. Modern Art, N.Y.C., 1979, 84, Ronald Feldman Fine Arts, N.Y.C., 1980, 83, The Wadsworth Atheneum, Hartford, Conn., 1980, The Va. Mus. Fine Arts, Richmond, Va., 1980, Neuer Berliner Kunstverein, 1982, Castello Sforzesco, Sala Viscontea, 1983, Victoria and Albert Mus., London, 1984, Nat. Mus. Modern Art, Tokyo, 1985-86, The Triennale di Milano, Italy, 1985, Whitney Mus. Am. Art, N.Y.C., 1985-86, Grey Art Gallery, N.Y.C., 1987-88, Documenta 8, Kassel, Germany, 1987, Am. Craft Mus., N.Y.C., 1996; permanent collections include, Smithsonian Instns., Washington, Mus. Modern Art, N.Y.C., Avery Libr., Columbia U., N.Y.C., Formica Corp., N.J., GSA, Pharr, Tex.; projects include BEST Products, 1979-84, Williwear Ltd., N.Y.C. and London, 1982-89, SITE Studio, 1984, The Mus. Borough of Bklyn., N.Y.C., 1985, Laurie Mallet House Memories, N.Y.C., 1986, Hwy. 86, Vancouver, Can., 1986, Pershing Sq., L.A., 1986, MTV Sets, N.Y.C., 1988, SWATCH, N.Y.C. and Zurich, Switzerland, 1988-90, Rockplex, Music Complex, Universal City, Calif., 1989, Peace Garden, Washington, 1989, NASA Exhibit, Sevilla, Spain, 1990, N.Y.C. Pub. Libr., 1990, Franz Mayer, Munich, 1991, Robert Lehman Gallery, 1996; author: (series of Books) ON SITE, 1971-76, Unbuilt America, 1976; pub. numerous books on art, 1971-76. Artery Arts finalist, Boston, 1994-95, RTA Arts-in-Transit finalist, Cleve., 1994, Pub. Art Commn. finalist, Cleve., 1994; Design fellow NEA, 1984, 90, Pollock-Krasner Found. fellow, 1991, Fulbright Indo-Am. fellow, 1992. Fellow Am. Acad. Rome. Studio: 60 Greene St New York NY 10012-4301

SKYE, IONE, actress; b. London, Sept. 4, 1971; d. Donovan and Enid Karl; m. Adam Horovitz. Appeared in (films) River's Edge, 1987, Stranded, A Night in the Life of Jimmy Reardon, Say Anything..., The Rachel Papers, Mindwalk, The Color of Evening, Wayne's World, Gas Food Lodging, Samantha, Guncrazy, Four Rooms; (TV series) Covington Cross; (spls.) It's Called the Sugar Plum, Nightmare Classics. Office: care SAG 5757 Wilshire Blvd Los Angeles CA 90036*

SLACK, AMY ALLEN, counselor; b. McKinney, Tex., Aug. 29, 1956; d. Tom Wallace Jr. and Patsy Ruth (Paysinger) Allen; children: Emily, Allison. BS, North Tex. State U., 1978; MEd, U. North Tex., 1993. Lic. profl. counselor, Tex.; registered play therapist. Tchr. McKinney Ind. Sch. Dist., 1978-81, St. Peters Sch., McKinney, 1986-93; counselor CCA, McKinney, 1991—. Chmn. organ com. 1st Bapt. Ch., 1994—, asst. organist, 1986—, children's choir dir., 1976-96; numerous other civic and school coms. Named to Outstanding Young Women of Am., 1988. Mem. ACA, Tex. Assn. for Play Therapy, Assn. Play Therapy. Office: CCA 1216 N Central Mc Kinney TX 75070

SLADE, GEORGIANA ELIZABETH, museum educator; b. Mpls., Sept. 30, 1969; d. James William and Jenella Elliot (Randall) S. BA in Art History, Boston U., 1991. Family day assoc. Mpls. Inst. Arts, 1993-94, adult class and film assoc., 1994—. Mem. Juneteenth Film com. Juneteenth Festival, Mpls., 1995—; active Whittier Youth Employment Com. for disadvantaged youth in a lower income neighborhood. Mem. Nat. Art Edn. Assn., Am. Assn. Mus. Office: The Mpls Inst Arts 2400 3rd Ave S Minneapolis MN 55404

SLAGER, JOAN K., nurse midwife; b. Hastings, Mich., June 10, 1958; d. Richard E. and Pauline B. (First) Wolverton; m. Vernon R. Slager, Dec. 4, 1982; children: Michele E., Mark R., Meredith P. BS in Nursing cum laude, Nazareth Coll., 1980; cert in Nurse-midwifery, Frontier Sch. of Midwifery, Hyden, Ky., 1991; MS in Nursing, Case Western Reserve U., 1992. Staff nurse neonatal ICU Bronson Hosp., Kalamazoo, 1979-81; staff nurse Lehigh (Fla.) Acres Gen. Hosp., 1981; clinic nurse Kalamazoo County Health Dept., 1981-84; staff nurse birthing ctr. Borgess Med. Ctr., Kalamazoo, 1984-91; cert. nurse midwife Family Health Ctr. of Battle Creek, Mich., 1991-93; cert. nurse midwife Bronson Women's Svc., Kalamazoo, 1993—, dir. nurse-midwifery, 1995—; com. mem. Infant Mortality Rev. Com., Family Health Ctr., Battle Creek, 1992-93; guest speaker Sales Tng. Upjohn Co., Kalamazoo, 1992—. Mem. Am. Coll. of Nurse Midwives (cert. nurse midwife, sec. Region IV, chpt. XIII 1992-94, chpt. chair ACNM region IV chpt. XIII 1996). Home: 3681 S 26th St Kalamazoo MI 49001 Office: Bronson Women's Svc 252 E Lovell St Kalamazoo MI 49007-5316

SLATEN, PAMELA GAIL, artist; b. Winter Haven, Fla., May 9, 1964; d. L. Lee and Priscilla Jane (Phillips) Collins. Grad., Flint Tech. Inst., 1990. Artist The Pub., Senoia, Talbot, Ga., 1982-89, Thomaston, Ga., 1988-93; artist Bostwick Tigers, Thomaston, Ga., 1992-93; artist Thomaston Upson Arts Coun., 1993, Upson County Commrs., 1993. One-woman show Hightower Meml. Libr., Thomaston, 1995, 96; exhibited in group shows, including Cherry Blossom Festival, Macon, Ga., Thomaston-Upson Arts Coun.; represented in permanent collections Epilespy Found., Ga. State Capitol, Roosevelt Warm Springs Rehab. Ct., Hightower Meml. Libr., Presdl. Libr., Little Rock, also corp. collections. Vol. Epilepsy Found. Am., arts & crafts dept. Wal-Mart, 1994, St. Jude's Hosp., 1993, 94, Upson County Child Abuse Program, 1994. Reciient cert. of appreciation Pilot Club Mt. Atlanta, 1993, 94, hon. mention and bronze medal, 1994; cert. of appreciation Ga. State Capitol, 1994, Roosevelt Warm Springs Rehab. Ctr., 1995, Sister Kenny Inst., 1994. Mem. Nat. Mus. Women in Arts, Epilepsy Found. Am., Thomaston-Upson Arts Coun. Home: 368 Sheila Cir Thomaston GA 30286-9593

SLATER, DORIS ERNESTINE WILKE, business executive; b. Oakes, N.D.; d. Arthur Waldemar and Anna Mary (Dill) Wilke; m. Lawrence Bert Slater, June 4, 1930 (dec., 1960). Grad. high sch. Sec. to circulation mgr. Mpls. Daily Star, 1928-30; promotion activities Lions Internat. in U.S., Can., Cuba, 1930-48; exec. sec. parade and spl. events com. Inaugural Com., 1948-49; exec. sec. Nat. Capital Sesquicentennial Commn., 1949-50, Capitol Hill Assos., Inc., 1951, Pres.'s Cup Regatta, 1951; adminstrv. asst. Nat. Assn. Food Chains, 1951-60; v.p., sec.-treas. John A. Logan Assos., Inc., Washington, 1960—; v.p., sec.-treas. Logan, Seaman, Slater, Inc., 1962—; mng. dir. Western Hemisphere, Internat. Assn. Chain Stores, 1964—. With pub. relations div. Boston Met. chpt. ARC, 1941-42; mem. Nat. Cherry Blossom Festival Com., 1949—; mem. Inaugural Ball Com., 1953, 57, 65. Methodist. Lion. Home and Office: 2500 Wisconsin Ave NW Washington DC 20007-4501

SLATER, HELEN RACHEL, actress; b. N.Y.C., Dec. 15, 1963; d. Gerald and Alice Joan (Chrin) S. Stage appearances include Responsible Parties, 1985, Almost Romance, 1987; films: Supergirl, 1984, The Legend of Billie Jean, 1985, Ruthless People, 1986, The Secret of My Success, 1987, Sticky Fingers, 1988, Happy Together, 1989, City Slickers, 1991, Lassie, 1994; TV appearances include (series) Capital News, 1990, (movies) Chantilly Lace, 1993, 12:01, 1993. Office: Innovative Artists 1999 Ave of Stars Ste 2850 Los Angeles CA 90211*

SLATER, JILL SHERRY, lawyer; b. N.Y.C., Apr. 8, 1943. BA with distinction and honors, Cornell U., 1964; JD cum laude, Harvard U., 1968. Bar: Mass. 1968, Calif. 1971, U.S. Dist. Ct. (cen. dist.) Calif. 1971, U.S. Ct. Appeals (9th cir.) 1974, U.S. Dist. Ct. (so. dist.) Calif. 1977, U.S. Dist. Ct. (ea. dist.) Calif. 1984, U.S. Dist. Ct. (no. dist) Calif. 1985, U.S. Ct. Appeals (Fed. cir.) 1982, U.S. Supreme Ct. 1986, N.Y. 1988. Atty. Boston Redevel. Authority, 1968-70; from assoc. to ptnr. Latham & Watkins, N.Y.C., 1970—. Woodrow Wilson fellow, 1964. Mem. ABA., Phi Beta Kappa. Office: Latham & Watkins Ste 1000 885 Third Ave New York NY 10022-4802

SLATER, JOAN ELIZABETH, secondary education educator; b. Paterson, N.J., Aug. 27, 1947; d. Anthony Joseph and Emma (Liguori) Nicola; m. Francis Graham Slater, Nov. 16, 1974; children: David, Kristin, Kylie. BA in English, Montclair State Coll., 1968, MA in English, 1971. Cert. English, speech and theater arts tchr., N.J., Tex. Tchr. Anthony Wayne Jr. High Sch., Wayne, N.J., 1968-70, Wayne Valley High Sch., Wayne, N.J., 1970-74, Strack Intermediate Sch., Klein, Tex., 1987—; cons. Tex. Assessment Acad. Skills, Houston Post Newspaper, 1994—; adv. bd. Tex. Edn. Assn., winter 1993; sch. dist. rep. Southern Assn. Colls. and Schs., 1993; editor, advisor Pawprints Lit. Mag., 1989—. Co-author: Klein Curriculum for the Gifted and Talented, 1992-93. Com. chairperson Klein After-Prom Extravaganza, 1994-95; parent supporter Challenge Soccer Club, Klein, 1993—; mem. Rep. Nat. Com., Washington, 1994—; mem. Klein H.S. Girls Soccer Team Bd., 1995-96. Mem. North Harris County Coun. Tchrs. English (sec. 1992-95), Klein Edn. Assn., Nat. Coun. Tchrs. English, Tex. Mid. Sch. Assn., Internat. Reading Assn., Greater Houston Area Reading Coun., Nat. Charity League. Home: 6018 Spring Oak Holw Spring TX 77379-8833 Office: Strack Intermediate Sch 18027 Kuykendahl Rd Klein TX 77379-8116

SLATER, KRISTIE, construction company executive; b. Rock Springs, Wyo., Nov. 14, 1957; d. Fredrick Earl and Shirley Joan (McWilliams) Alexander; m. C. James Slater, May 11, 1992. A in Bus. Adminstrn., Salt Lake City Coll., 1978. EMT, Wyo. Cost engr., material coord. Project Constrn. Corp., LaBarge, Wyo., 1985; cost engr., scheduler Flour Daniel Constrn. Co., Salt Lake City, 1985-86, Bibby Edible Oils, Liverpool, Eng., 1986-87; cost engr., safety technician Sunvic, Inc./I.S.T.S., Inc., Augusta, Ga., 1987-88; cost engr. Brown & Root, Inc., Ashdown, Ark., 1988-89, Wickliffe, Ky., 1989; sr. cost engr. Brown & Root, Inc., Pasadena, Tex., 1989-90, LaPorte, Tex., 1990-91; project controls mgr. Yeargin Inc., Thousand Oaks, Calif., 1991-92; corp. controls mgr. Suitt Constrn. Co., Greenville, S.C., 1993-95. Pres. 4-H State Coun., Laramie, Wyo., 1976; mem. com. Houston Livestock Show and Rodeo. Mem. LDS Ch.

SLATER, MARILEE HEBERT, theatre administrator, producer, director, consultant; b. Laredo, Tex., Feb. 25, 1949; d. Minos Joseph and Eulalie (Fisher) Hebert; m. Stewart E. Slater, Dec. 3, 1972 (div. July 1978). BA, Baylor U., 1970, MA, 1972. Cert. secondary sch. tchr., Tex. Actress, dir., assoc. producer Everyman Players, Ky. and La., 1972-80; community rels. dir. Actors Theatre of Louisville, 1973-74, dir. children's theatre, lunchtime & cabaret theatre, 1974-76, dir., apprentice intern program, 1974-77, new play festivals coord., 1979-81, mgr. internat. touring, 1980—, assoc. dir., 1981—; guest dir. Louisville Children's Theatre, 1978; grants panelist Ky. Arts Coun., La. Arts Coun.; conf. lectr. Ky. Arts Coun., Va. Arts Commn., Southeastern Theatre Conf., S.W. Theatre Conf., So. Arts Fedn. Author: (play) Hey Diddle Diddle!, 1976. Pres. Ky. Citizens for Arts, 1985-86, 90-91; co-chmn. subcom. on arts Edn. Workforce, 1990-93; grad. Leadership Louisville, 1989, bd. dirs., 1992—; vice-chmn. Focus Louisville, 1994-96; chmn. Louisville Downtown Mgmt. Dist., 1996, Leadership Ptnrs., 1996—; mem. Downtown Devel. Implementation com., Louisville, 1991-93; Louisville Forum adv. coun., 1995-96; bd. dirs. Louisville Ctrl. Area, 1996; pres. Park IV Condo Assn., 1989-91, sec. Main St. Assn., 1992-96; staging dir., cons. Walnut St. Bapt. Ch., 1980—. Bingham fellow, 1995-96; recipient Ky. Commonwealth award 1996. Democrat. Baptist. Office: Actors Theatre Louisville 316 W Main St Louisville KY 40202-4218

SLATER, SHELLEY, document and training manager; b. Ogden, Utah, June 26, 1959; d. Lynn Russell and Darlene (Allen) Slater; m. Dale Thomas Hansen, Jan. 26, 1977 (div. Feb. 1979); 1 child, Thomas Arthur; m. Eugene Allan DuVall, Mar. 8, 1981 (div. Dec. 1985); 1 child, Gregory Allan; m. Steven Blake Allender, June 9, 1990 (div. May 1993). BBA cum laude, Regis U., 1992, postgrad., 1992—. Installation, repair technician MT Bell, Clearfield, Utah, 1977-81; ctrl. office technician MT Bell, Salt Lake City, 1981-83, engring. specialist, 1983-86; engring. specialist U.S. West Comm., Englewood, Colo., 1986-93; network analyst, documentation and tng. mgr. Time Warner Comm., Englewood, Colo., 1993—; bus. cons. Jr. Achievement, Denver, 1988-89. Day capt. AZTEC Denver Mus. of Natural History, 1992; loaned exec. Mile High United Way, 1993. Mem. Women in Cable and Telecomms., Soc. of Cable Telecomms. Engrs. (bd. dirs., v.p. Rocky Mt. chpt.). Democrat. Home: 9618 S Cordova Dr Highlands Ranch CO 80126-3788 Office: Time Warner Comm 160 Inverness Dr W Englewood CO 80112-5001

SLATER, VALERIE A., lawyer; b. Passaic, N.J., Oct. 13, 1952. BA magna cum laude, Allegheny Coll., 1974; JD, Catholic U. Am., 1977. Bar: D.C. 1977, U.S. Ct. Appeals (D.C. cir.) 1978, U.S. Dist. Ct. (D.C. dist.) 1982, U.S. Ct. Internat. Trade 1984, U.S. Ct. Appeals (fed. cir.) 1984. Mem. Phi Beta Kappa. Office: Akin Gump Strauss Hauer & Feld Ste 400 1333 New Hampshire Ave NW Washington DC 20036-1511*

SLATKIN, NORA, government official; b. Glen Cove, N.Y., May 5, 1955; d. Carl L. and Muriel (Breen) S.; m. Deral Willis, July 4, 1982; stepchildren: Nick, Lisa, Kelly. BA in Internat. Rels., Lehigh U., 1977; MS in Fgn. Svc., Georgetown U., 1979. Def. analyst Congl. Budget Office, Washington, 1977-84; mem. profl. staff House Armed Svcs. Com., Washington, 1984-93; asst. Sec. of Navy for rsch., devel., acquisition Washington, 1994—; exec. dir. CIA, Washington, 1995—; spl. asst. to under sec. of def. for acquistion Office Sec. Def., Washington, 1993. Grad. fellow Nat. Security Coun. Dept. State CIA. Mem. Phi Beta Kappa. Home: 36 Chesapeake Lndg Annapolis MD 21403-2615 Office: Asst Sec Navy Rsch Devel Acquisition 1000 Navy Pentagon Washington DC 20350-1000*

SLATTERY, MARILYN ELIZABETH, educational administrator; b. Weymouth, Mass., Feb. 3, 1954; d. Francis Edward and Marjorie Phyllis (Casna) S. BA, Suffolk U., 1972, MEd, 1983, postgrad., 1995. Tchr. reading Colegio Maria Alvarado, Lima, Peru, 1976-77; tchr. Spanish Arlington (Mass.) Cath. High Sch., 1977-84, chair fgn. lang., 1978-84; tchr. Spanish Archbishop Williams High Sch., Braintree, Mass., 1985-87, Weymouth (Mass.) South High Sch., 1987-90; tchr. Spanish, French Silver Lake Regional Jr. High Sch., Pembroke, Mass., 1990-92, Weymouth High Sch., 1992-93; facilitator human rels. Weymouth Pub. Schs., 1993-94; asst. prin. Adams Intermediate Sch., Weymouth, 1994—; founder South Shore Consortium on Violence Prevention, Weymouth, 1993-94; mem. Drug Free Cons., Weymouth, 1993-94. Park commr. Weymouth Pk. & Recreation, 1991—; town meeting mem. Town of Weymouth, 1992—, mem. Korean War Meml., 1993—. Democrat. Home: 64 Unicorn Ave East Weymouth MA 02189-1738 Office: East Weymouth Intermed Sch 89 Middle St East Weymouth MA 02189-1359

SLAUGHTER, CANDICE E., foundation administrator, consultant; b. Columbus, Ohio, Oct. 21, 1951; d. A.E. and Joy Elizabeth (Davis) S.; m. Jerome Bruce Warmke, June 5, 1982; 1 child, Katherine Slaughter Harrier. AAS, Ohio U., 1982; cert., Forrester Instituto, San Jose, Costa Rica. Dir. Salvation Army Domestic Violence Ctr., New Port Richey, Fla., 1982-83; exec. dir. Sunrise of Pasco County, Dade City, Fla., 1983-86; CEO Windmill Cons., New Port Richey, Fla., 1986-94; CEO, pres. Women's Peacepower Found., San Antonio, Fla., 1994—; chairperson Formerly Battered Women's Caucus, 1988-92, Women in Prison com., Fla., 1990-94; bd. dirs. Nat. Coalition Against Domestic Violence, Denver; adv. bd. dirs. Nat. Domestic Violene Hotline, Austin, Tex.; mem. Working Woman's Think Tank. Author: Guide to Operating a Rural Safe House Network for Battered Women, 1988. Candidate Pasco County Commr., Fla., 1986; mem. Arbor Bd. City of New Port Richey, Fla., 1989-90; vol. Super Playground,

New Port Richey, 1990. Recipient Every Woman award Fla. Coalition Against Domestic Violence, 1988, Giraffe award Giraff Project, 1991, JC Penney Golden Rule award, 1993, Gov.'s Peace at Home award, Fla., 1995, Outstanding Humanitarian award YWCA, Clearwater, Fla., 1996, Outstanding Woman award Melita Corp., 1996. Mem. NOW, Dade City Investment Women. Office: Women's Peacepower Found PO Box 1281 San Antonio FL 33576

SLAUGHTER, LOUISE MCINTOSH, congresswoman; b. Harlan County, Ky., Aug. 14, 1929; d. Oscar Lewis and Grace (Byers) McIntosh; m. Robert Slaughter, 1956; children: Megan Rae, Amy Louise, Emily Robin. BS, U. Ky., 1951, MS, 1953. Bacteriologist Ky. Dept. Health, Louisville, 1951-52, U. Ky., 1952-53; market researcher Procter & Gamble, Cin., 1953-56; mem. staff Office of the Lt. Gov. N.Y., Albany, 1978-82; state rep. N.Y. Gen. Assembly, Albany, 1983-86; mem. 100th-103rd Congresses from 30th (now 28th) N.Y. dist., Washington, D.C., 1987—; mem. Ho. Govt. Reform and Oversight com., Ho. Budget com. Del. Dem. Nat. Conv., 1972, 76, 80, 88, 92; mem. Monroe County Pure Water Adminstrn. Bd., Nat. Ctr. for Policy Alternatives Adv. Bd., League of Women Voters, Nat. Women's Polit. Caucus. Office: US Ho of Reps Office of House Mems 2347 Rayburn Bldg Washington DC 20515-0005

SLAVICK, ANN LILLIAN, art educator; b. Chgo., Sept. 29, 1933; d. Irving and Goldie (Bernstein) Friedman; m. Lester Irwin Slavick, Nov. 21, 1954 (div. Mar. 1987); children: Jack, Rachel. BFA, Sch. of Art Inst. of Chgo., 1973, MA in Art History, Theory, Criticism, 1991. Dir. art gallery South Shore Commn., Chgo., 1963-67; tchr. painting, drawing, crafts Halfway House, Chgo., 1972-73; tchr. studio art Conant H.S., Hoffman Estates, Ill., 1973-74; tchr. art history and studio arts New Trier H.S., Winnetka and Northfield, Ill., 1974-80; tchr. 20th century art history New Trier Adult Edn. Program, Winnetka, 1980-81; tchr. art adult edn. program H.S. Dist. 113, Highland Park, Ill., 1980-81; rschr., writer Art History Notes McDougall-Littel Pub., Evanston, Ill., 1984-85; tchr. art and art history Highland Park and Deerfield (Ill.) H.S., 1980—; tchr. art history Coll. of Lake County, Grayslake, Ill., 1986-88; faculty chair for visual arts Focus on the Arts, Highland Park H.S., 1981-85, faculty coord. Focus on the Arts, 1987—. One woman show Bernal Gallery, 1979, U. Ill., Chgo., 1983, Ann Brierly Gallery, Winnetka, 1984; exhibited paintings, drawings, prints and constrns. throughout Chgo. area; work represented by Art Rental and Sales Gallery, Art Inst. Chgo., 1960-87, Bernal Gallery, 1978-82; group shows at Bernal Gallery; work in pvt. collections in Ill., N.Y., Calif., Ariz., Ohio. Recipient Outstanding Svc. in Art Edn. award Ea. Ill. U., 1992, Mayors award for contbn. to the arts, Highland Park, 1995. Mem. Nat. Art Edn. Assn., Ill. Art Edn. Assn. Home: 5057 N Sheridan Rd Chicago IL 60640-3127 Office: Highland Park High Sch 433 Vine Ave Highland Park IL 60035-2044

SLAVIN, ALEXANDRA NADAL, artistic director, educator; b. Port-au-Prince, Haiti, Oct. 26, 1943; came to U.S., 1946; d. Pierre E. and Marie Therese (Clerié) Nadal; m. Eugene Slavin, Dec. 24, 1967; 1 child, Nicholas V. Grad. high sch., Chgo. Dancer Ballet Russe de Monte Carlo, N.Y.C., 1960-61, Chgo. Opera Ballet and N.Y.C. Opera Ballet, 1961-64, Am. Ballet Theatre, N.Y.C., 1965-66, Ballet de Monte Carlo, 1966-67, The Royal Winnipeg (Can.) Ballet, 1967-72; artistic dir. Ballet Austin, Tex., 1972-89; owner, dir. The Slavin Nadal Sch. Ballet, Austin, 1989—. Recipient Achievement in the Arts award Austin chpt. YWCA, 1987. Roman Catholic. Office: Slavin-Nadal Sch Ballet 5521 Burnet Rd Austin TX 78756-1603

SLAVIN, ARLENE, artist; b. N.Y.C., Oct. 26, 1942; d. Louis and Sally (Bryck) Eisenberg; m. Neal Slavin, May 24, 1964 (div. 1979); m. Eric Bregman, Sept. 21, 1980; 1 child, Ethan. BFA, Cooper Union for the Advancement of Sci. and Art, 1964; MFA, Pratt Inst., 1967. One woman exhbns. include Fischbach Gallery, N.Y., 1973,74, Brooke Alexander Gallery, N.Y., 1976, Alexander Milliken Gallery, N.Y.C., 1979, 80, 81, 83, U. Colo., 1981, Pratt Inst., N.Y.C., 1981, Am. Embassy, Belgrad, Yugoslavia, 1984, Heckscher Mus., Huntington, N.Y., 1987, Katherine Rich Perlow Gallery, 1988, Chauncey Gallery, Princeton, N.J., 1990, The Gallery Benjamin N. Cardoza Sch. Law, 1991, Norton Ctr. for Arts, Danville, Ky., 1992, Kavesh Gallery, Ketchum, Idaho, 1993; exhibited in group shows at Bass Mus. Art, Fla., Whitney Museum of Art, 1973, The Contempory Arts Center, Cinn., Oh., 1974, Indianapolis Museum of Art, 1974, Madison (Wis.) Art Ctr., Santa Barbara (Calif.) Mus., Winnipeg (Can.) Art Gallery, Gensler Assocs., San Francisco, 1986, Eliane Benson Gallery, Bridgehampton, N.Y., 1987, 89, 91, 93, City of N.Y. Parks and Recreation Central Park, N.YC. 1989, Benton Gallery, Southampton, N.Y., 1991, Parish Mus., Southampton, 1991, Michele Miller Fine Art, 1993 ; executed murals N.Y. Aquarium, Bklyn., 1982, Pub. Art Fund, N.Y.C., 1983, Albert Einstein Sch. of Medicine, Bronx, N.Y., 1983, Hudson River Mus., Yonkers, N.Y., 1983, Bellevue Hosp. Ctr., N.Y.C., 1986; represented in permanent collections at Met. Mus. of Art, N.Y.C, Bklyn. Mus., Fogg Art Mus., Cambridge, Mass., Hudson River Mus., Yonkers, N.Y., Hecksler Mus., Huntington, N.Y., Cin. Art Mus., Readers' Digest, Pleasantville, N.Y., Guild Hall, East Hampton, N.Y., Allen Meml. Art Mus., Oberlin, Ohio, Norton Mus., Palm Beach, Fla., Portland (Oreg.) Mus., Orlando (Fla.) Mus. Art, Neuburger Mus., Purchase, N.Y.; commd. work iron gates Cathedral St. John the Divine, N.Y.C., 1988, 55' steel fence Henry St Settlement, N.Y., 1992, metal work stairway De Soto Sch., N.Y. Sch. Art, 1994-95. Grantee Nat. Endowment for Arts, 1977-78, Threshold Found., 1991. Home and Studio: 119 E 18th St New York NY 10003-2107

SLAVIN, ROSANNE SINGER, textile converter; b. N.Y.C., Mar. 24, 1930; d. Lee H. and Rose (Winkler) Singer; student U. Ill.; divorced; children: Laurie Jo, Sharon Lee. Prodn. converter Doucet Fabrics, silk prints, N.Y.C., 1953-57; sales mgr., mdse. mgr. print div. Crown Fabrics, N.Y.C., 1957-65; owner Matisse Fabrics, Inc. printed fabrics (name now Hottmomma Inc.), N.Y.C., 1965—. Recipient Tommy award Am. Printed Fabrics Coun., 1978, 93; designated ofcl. printed fabric supplier for U.S. Olympic swimteam, 1984. Office: 1071 Ave of the Americas New York NY 10018

SLAVINSKA, NONNA, psychoanalyst, psychotherapist; b. Warsaw, Poland; came to U.S., 1953, naturalized, 1958; d. Paul and Nadezda (von Vetter) Slawinski; m. Vaclav L. de P. Holy, Feb. 22, 1970; 1 child, Alexander Levitsky. MS cum laude, L.I. U., 1957; PhD, NYU, 1967; cert. psychoanalysis and psychotheraphy, Postgrad. Ctr. Mental Health, 1971, cert. group psychotherapy, 1974, cert. supervision psychoanalytic process, 1975. Pvt. practice clin. psychology, 1957—; clin. psychologist N.J. Dept. Instns. and Agencies, Trenton, 1957-64; cons. spl. edn. Howell Twp. Bd. Edn., N.J., 1964-66, Monmouth County High Sch., N.J., 1966-68; cons. in psychology Dept. Labor and Industry, Newark, 1970-75; supr. Inst. Mental Health Edn., Engelwood, N.J., 1976-80; supr. faculty Payne-Whitney Clinic, N.Y. Hosp., Cornell Med. Ctr., N.Y.C., 1978-82; supr. Psychol. Ctr. CCNY, 1981-82; supr. Psychonanalytic Inst. Postgrad. Ctr. for Mental Health, N.Y.C., 1983—, sr. supr. group therapy dept., 1982—, faculty, 1972—, asst. supr. faculty group therapy dept., 1976—; supr. group and family studies div. Albert Einstein Coll. Medicine, Yeshiva U., N.Y.C., 1987—; founder, chairperson com. on mental health Kosciuszko Found., N.Y.C., 1982-88; founder, chairperson interdisciplinary psychology and mental health sect. Polish Inst. Arts and Scis., N.Y.C., 1984—; vis. prof. dept. psychiatry Jagiellonian U., Poland. Internat. editor GROUP Jour., 1983-86; internat. coord., cons. editor Internat. Jour. Group Psychotherapy, 1984-87. Recipient Five Yr. Service to N.J. award, 1963, Founder's Day award NYU, 1968, Cert. , Am. Group Psychotherapy Assn., 1981. Fellow APA (internat. rels. com., Am. Group Psychotherapy Assn. (internat. aspects com.); mem. Internat. Assn. Group Psychotherapy (bd. dirs. 198-386, founder, chairperson adv. com. on inquiry and rsch. 1984—), N.J. Psychol. Assn., Internat. Assn. Applied Psychology, Internat Div. 29 Am. Psychol. Assn. (chmn. com. on rsch. 1985—). Office: 9 E 96th St # 9B New York NY 10128-0778

SLAWSKY, DONNA SUSAN, librarian, singer; b. N.Y.C., Jan. 18, 1956; d. Samuel Slawsky and Lillian (Freizer) Alexander. BA, City Coll. N.Y., 1977. Coord. NYNEX Market Info. Ctr., White Plains, N.Y., 1985-87; libr. asst. NYNEX Info. Access Ctr., White Plains, N.Y., 1987-88; libr. and records mgr., exhbns. curator HarperCollins Pubs., N.Y.C., 1988—; singer N.Y.C., 1987—. Contbr. articles to profl. jours.; appeared in Mikado, Light Opera of Manhattan, 1989, Hercules, 1995, Magic Flute with Cantata Singers, 1996. Pres. Assn. HarperCollins Employees, N.Y.C., 1990-94; dir. Yellowstone Blvd. Tenants Assn., Forest Hills, N.Y., 1990-92, Tenants Assn., N.Y.C., 1994. Recipient Schubertiade Lieder Competition award 92d St. Y, N.Y.C., 1990. Mem. Assn. Records Mgrs. and Adminstrs., Spl. Librs. Assn., Profl. Women Singers Assn. (treas. 1992—). Home: 31 Jane St Apt 16G New York NY 10014 Office: HarperCollins Pubs 10 E 53d St New York NY 10022

SLAYMAKER, JILL BROOK, artist, educator; b. Youngstown, Ohio, Feb. 20, 1955; d. Gene Arthur and Martha Louise (Spitler) S.; m. Ned Paul Ginsburg, June 17, 1995. BA, Ind. U., 1979; MFA, Ea. Tex. State U., 1981; cert. tchr., Sch. Visual Arts, N.Y.C., 1995. student tchr. East Tex. State U., 1980-81, guest lectr., 1988; lectr. Mus. Modern Art, N.Y.C., 1990-91, asst. to assoc. dir. of internat. program, 1984-89; educator Bklyn. Mus., 1990-91; art tchr. Sch. Visual Arts, N.Y.C., 1995; guest lectr. William Paterson Coll., Wayne, N.J., 1995; tchr. OCCC Sch. Art, Demarest, N.J., 1995; art tchr. 92nd St. Y, 1996—; artist-in-residence N.Y.C. Pub. Schs., 1996—; co-coord. photo exhibit Covenant House/UNICEF, N.Y.C., 1983, Staff Union of the Mus. Modern Art and Bond Gallery, N.Y.C., 1988. One-woman shows East Tex. State U., Commerce, 1981, Nolo Contendere Gallery, N.Y.C., 1985, Wexler Gallery, N.Y.C., 1986, Jon Gerstad Gallery, N.Y.C., 1988, Alternative Space, N.Y.c., 1989, Gallery Juno, N.Y.C., 1994; group exhbns. include Electronic Cafe, Kassel, Germany, 1992, Brooke Alexander Gallery, N.Y.C., 1993, Columbia U., N.Y.C., 1994, Mus. Modern Art, N.Y.C., 1994, Artists Space, N.Y.C., 1995, Grey Art Gallery, N.Y.C., 1995, Richmond Art Mus., 1995, Maison des Arte, Creteil, France, 1996, others; represented in permanent collections SITE, N.Y.C., Bus. Internat., N.Y.C., The Kreisberg Group, N.Y.C., The Teaco Corp., Chgo., East Tex. State U., Commerce, Baricua Coll., Bklyn., U. Iowa, Iowa City, J.M. Boehm Co., New Orleans, Asian Am. Art Ctr., N.Y.C. Dir. art programs La Candelaria Cmty. Ctr. of East Harlem, N.Y., 1993-96, bd. dirs., 1995-96, CEO, 1995-96; adv. bd. mem. Nat. MS Soc.-Project Rembrandt and Grey Art Gallery, N.Y.C., 1995. Recipient Award Millay Colony, Austerlitz, N.Y., 1996. Mem. Femmes Vitale (founder). Buddhist. Home: 151 W 18th St New York NY 10011

SLAYMAN, CAROLYN WALCH, geneticist, educator; b. Portland, Maine, Mar. 11, 1937; d. John Weston and Ruth Dyer (Sanborn) Walch; m. Clifford L. Slayman; children—Andrew, Rachel. B.A. with highest honors, Swarthmore Coll., 1958; Ph.D., Rockefeller U., 1963; D.Sc. (hon.), Bowdoin Coll., 1985. Instr., then asst. prof. Case Western Res. U., Cleve., 1967; from asst. prof. to prof. genetics Yale U. Sch. Medicine, New Haven, 1967—, Sterling prof. genetics, 1991—, chmn. dept. genetics, 1984-95, dep. dean for acad. and sci. affairs, 1995—; chmn. genetic basis of disease rev. commn. NIH, 1981-85, nat. adv. gen. med. scis. coun., 1989-93; bd. dirs. J. Weston Walch Pub., Portland, Maine, The Perkin-Elmer Corp.; mem. sci. rev. bd. Howard Hughes Med. Inst., 1992—. Mem. editorial bd. Jour. Biol. Chemistry, 1989-94; contbr. articles to sci. jours. Trustee Foote Sch., New Haven, Conn., 1983-89, Hopkins Sch., New Haven, 1988-93; bd. overseers Bowdoin Coll., Brunswick, Maine, 1976-88, trustee, 1988—. Recipient Deborah Morton award Westbrook Coll., 1986. Mem. Am. Soc. Biol. Chemists, Genetics Soc. Am., Soc. Gen. Physiologists, Am. Soc. Microbiology, Phi Beta Kappa. Office: Yale U Sch Medicine Dept Genetics 333 Cedar St New Haven CT 06510-3206

SLEBODNIK, TRESSA ANN, retired elementary education educator; b. Belle Vernon, Pa., Nov. 11, 1931; d. Michael Ferdinand and Elizabeth (Skruber) Nusser; m. Thomas Patrick Slebodnik, June 6, 1953; children: Thomas, Anita, Eleanor, Edward, Charles, Kathleen, Linda. BS, California (Pa.) State Tchrs. Coll., 1953. Cert. tchr., Pa. Tchr. kindergarten Yough Sch. Dist., West Newton, Pa., 1969-76; tchr. first grade Yough Sch. Dist., Sutersville, Pa., 1976-80, Smithton, Pa., 1980-81; tchr. kindergarten Yough Sch. Dist., Smithton and Ruffsdale, Pa., 1981-82, Ruffsdale, 1982-96; ret., 1996; devel. Approach to Sci. and Health, Ruffsdale, 1990-96; grade level coord., mentor tchr. and curriculum coun. Pres. St. Edward Bowling League, Herminie, mem. curriculum coun.; active Altar-Rosary Soc., Herminie. Mem. NEA, Pa. State Edn. Assn., Keyston State Reading Assn., Yough Edn. Assn. (bldg. rep.), Westmorland County Reading Coun. Democrat. Roman Catholic. Home: RR 1 Box 200 Irwin PA 15642-9617

SLEPCHUK, JEWEL M., accountant; b. Springfield, Mass., May 25, 1955; d. Peter and Gloria Slepchuk. Degree in Bus. Adminstrn., U. Mass., 1977; MS in Taxation, U. Hartford, Conn., 1984. CPA, Mass., Conn. Staff acct. Ernest & Young, Hartford, Conn., 1977-78; real estate acct. Cigna Ins. Co., Bloomfield, Conn., 1978-80, tax supr., 1980-84; sr. tax acct. Coopers & Lybrand, Sprinfield, Mass., 1984-86; pvt. practice Sprinfield, Mass., 1986-89; tax ptnr. Polumbo & Ptnrs., CPA's, Sprinfield, Mass., 1989—. Mem. NOW, AICPA, Mass. Soc. CPAs, Springfield Bus. Profl. Women's Club. Office: 155 Maple St Ste 405 Springfield MA 01105-1828

SLEWITZKE, CONNIE LEE, retired army officer; b. Mosinee, Wis., Apr. 15, 1931; d. Leo Thomas and Amelia Marie (Hoffman) S. BSN, U. Md., Balt., 1971; MA in Counseling and Guidance, St. Mary's U., San Antonio, 1976. Commd. 1st lt. U.S. Army, 1957, advanced through grades to brig. gen., 1987; ret., 1987; chief dept. nursing Letterman Army Med. Ctr. U.S. Army, San Francisco, 1978-80; asst. chief nurse Army Nurse Corps U.S. Army, Washington, 1980-83; chief brigadier gen. U.S. Army, 1983-87; mem. Va. Adv. Com. on Women Vets. Contbr. articles to profl. jours. Decorated D.S.M., Legion of Merit, Bronze Star medal. Mem. ANA, Va. Nurses Assn., Alumni Assn. U.S. Army War Coll., Assn. U.S. Army, Women in Mil. Svc. for Am. Found. (v.p.), Am. Assn. for History of Nursing, Sigma Theta Tau.

SLIDER, DORLA DEAN (FREEMAN), artist; b. Tampa, Fla., Sept. 9, 1929; d. Samuel Manning and Ida Caroline (Heller) Weeks; m. James Harold Slider, July 8, 1951; 1 child, Cindi Darnel Slider Dvornicky. Studied with Dr. Walter Emerson Baum, Allentown, Pa., 1940-48. Profl. advisor Pottstown (Pa.) Area Artists Guild, 1967-94; mem. jury of selection Nat. Soc. Painters in casein and acrylic, N.Y.C., 1992, 95; juror selection and awards Fla. Keys Watercolor Soc., Key West, 1987-90; nat. art judge and juror nat. and regional art shows. Exhibited in group shows at Am. Watercolor Soc., The Nat. Acad. of Design, Allied Artists, Audubon Artists, KnickerbockerArtists, Nat. Arts Club, Nat. Soc. Painters in Casein and Acrylic, N.Y.C., Pa. Acad. Fine Arts, Phila. Mus. Art, William Penn Mus., Pa., Butler Inst. Am. Art, Ohio, Watercolor U.S.A., Mainstreams Nat., Ohio, The Salt Palace, Utah, others; represented in permanent collections Brandywine River Mus., Chadds Ford, Pa., Berman Art Mus., Collegeville, Pa. Recipient Doris Kennedy Meml. award, Audubon Artists N.Y., 1979, C.L. Wolfe Art Club Gold medal, N.Y.C., 1970; Best of Show award Miami Water Color Soc., 1984, Arjomari/Arches/Rives award Nat. Soc. Painters Acrylic, 1991, award of excellence Nat. League Am. Pen Women, Washington, 1996, top awards Mainstream Internat., Allentown Art Mus., Internat. Soc. Artists, Salmagundie Club, Nat. Soc Painters in Caseim and Acrylic, Marion F. Gourville award Bianco Gallery, 1996, others. Mem. Am. Watercolor Soc. (Herb Olsen award 1972), Nat. Soc. Painters in Casein and Acrylic, Knickerbocker Artists (gold medal 1977), Audubon Artists (Savoir Faire award 1993, Yarka award 1995), Am. Artist Profl. League N.Y., Artists Equity, Phila. Watercolor Club (bd. dirs. 1996—, Dawson Meml. award 1994). Home: 268 Estate Rd Boyertown PA 19512-1922

SLIKER, SHIRLEY J. BROCKER, bookseller; b. Irwin, Pa., Sept. 5, 1929; d. Robert John and Hannah Alberta (McGrew) Brocker; m. Alan Sliker, June 23, 1956; children: Mark Alan (dec.), William James, Barbara Louise Sliker-Seewer. BS, Syracuse U., 1951, MS, 1954. Owner Shirley's Book Svcs., Okemos, Mich., 1987—; tchr. evening coll. Mich. State U., East Lansing, 1988—; mgr. Book Burrow, Friends of Lansing (Mich.) Pub. Libr., 1985-86. Commr. Lansing Charter Commn., 1976-78. Mem. Mid-Mich. Antiquarian Bookdealers Assn., Interloc, Zonta (chmn. various coms. 1992—), Lansing Woman's Club. Office: Shirleys Book Services 4330 Hulett Rd Okemos MI 48864-2434

SLOAN, JENNIFER, artist; b. N.Y.C., Jan. 20, 1958; d. William J. and Gwen G. (Gregg) S. BA, SUNY, 1978; postgrad., U. Paris, 1977-79, Internat. Ctr. Photography, 1981-83. Audio-visual tech. Sarah Lawrence Coll., Bronxville, N.Y., 1980-81, Bklyn. Mus., 1980-82; free-lance photographer N.Y.C., 1981-92; instr. sequential art for kids Franklin Furnace, N.Y.C., 1993; instr. Bronx Mus. Arts, N.Y.C., 1993; exhbn. developer S.I. Childrens Mus., N.Y.C., 1993-96; exhbn. project mgr. Children's Mus. of Manhattan, N.Y.C., 1996—; curator The Self Portrait Show, N.Y.C., 1994. One-woman shows include Photographic Resource Ctr., Boston, 1989, Ctr. for Photography, Woodstock, N.Y., 1991, Art in Gen. Window Installation, N.Y.C., 1992, Artists Space, AIDS Forum, N.Y.C., 1994, Stockton Art Gallery, Pomona, N.J.; co-author: It's News to Me, 1995; editor: Adventures in Three Dimensions, 1995. Money for Women/Barbara Demming Meml. Fund grantee, 1991, Sculpture Space grantee, 1996. Money for Women/Barbara Demming Meml. Fund grantee, 1991. Mem. Internat. Sculpture Ctr., Art Initiatives, Art & Sci. collaborative. Democrat. Home: 105 Duane St #15C New York NY 10007

SLOAN, JULIA ANN, international management development consultant; b. Bryan, Ohio, July 3, 1956; d. Vernon C. and Carol B. (Breethauer) S. BS, Kent State U., 1979; MS, U. Ala., 1986; PhD, Columbia U., 1996. Tchr. music Anchorage Sch. Dist., 1982-86; dir. programs Fuji Xerox co. Ltd., Tokyo, 1986-92; human resources/personnel devel. cons. N.Y.C., 1992—. Mem. NAFE, Nat. Speakers Ass., Am. Soc. Tng. and Devel., Japan Soc. Tng. and Devel., Asia Soc. Tng. and Devel., Soc. Human Resource Mgmt. Office: 147 W 72d St # 3C New York NY 10023

SLOAN, ROSALIND, nurse, military officer; b. New Haven, Apr. 22, 1953; d. Paul and Blanche (Kopp) S. BSN, U. Conn., 1976; M of Ednl. Adminstrn., San Diego State U., 1993. Staff nurse Peter Bent Brigham Hosp., Boston, 1976-79; commd. officer USN, 1979, advanced through grades to comdr., 1988; staff nurse Portsmouth (Va.) Naval Hosp., 1979-83, Charleston (S.C.) Naval Hosp., 1983-85; charge nurse labor and delivery U.S. Naval Hosp., Subic Bay, Philippines, 1985-88; instr. Basic Hosp. Corps Sch.-Naval Sch. Health Scis., San Diego, 1988-90, asst. dir., 1990-91; asst. officer-in-charge, acad. officer Naval Sch. Dental Assisting and Tech., San Diego, 1991-92; dept. head command edn. and tng. Naval Med. Ctr., Oakland, Calif., 1993-96; mgr. rsch. and evaluation studies Bur. of Medicine & Surgery, Washington, 1996—. Recipient Naval Commendation medal USN, Subic Day, 1988, Naval Commendation medal Naval Sch. Health Scis., San Diego, 1991. Mem. ASTD, Nat. Nursing Staff Devel. Orgn., Nat. Holistic Nursing Assn., Women Officers Profl. Assn., Ret. Officers Assn., Phi Kappa Phi.

SLOAN, SANDRA MERNELL, nuclear engineer; b. Houston, Apr. 29, 1966; d. James Clinton and Mildred Mernell (Bell) S.; m. Robert Paul Martin, Oct. 13, 1990. BS in Nuclear Engring., Tex. A&M U., 1988, MS in Nuclear Engring., 1990. Prin. engr. Idaho Nat. Engring. Lab., Lockheed-Martin Idaho Techs., Idaho Falls, 1990—. Contbr. articles to sci. jours. Referee Am. Yough Soccer Orgn., Idaho Falls, 1995—. Nuclear engring. fellow Dept. Energy, 1988-90. Mem. Am. Nuclear Soc. (membership com., program com. thermal hydraulics divsn., sec. Idaho sect. 1993-94, bd. dirs. 1994-95), Tautphaus Park Zool. Soc., Tau Beta Pi, Phi Kappa Phi, Alpha Nu Sigma. Home: 1384 S Bellin Rd Idaho Falls ID 83402 Office: Lockheed-Martin Idaho Techs Idaho Nat Engring Lab PO Box 1625 Idaho Falls ID 83415-3895

SLOANE, BEVERLY LEBOV, writer, consultant; b. N.Y.C., May 26, 1936; d. Benjamin S. and Anne (Weinberg) LeBov; m. Robert Malcolm Sloane, Sept. 27, 1959; 1 child, Alison Lori Sloane Gaylin. AB, Vassar Coll., 1958; MA, Claremont Grad. Sch., 1975, doctoral study, 1975-76; cert. in exec. mgmt., UCLA Grad. Sch. Mgmt., 1982, grad. exec. mgmt. program., UCLA 1982; grad. intensive bioethics course Kennedy Inst. Ethics, Georgetown U., 1987, advanced bioethics course, 1988; grad. sem. in Health Care Ethics, U. Wash. Sch. Medicine, Seattle, summer 1988-90, 94; grad. Summer Bioethics Inst. Loyola Marymount U., summer, 1990; grad. Annual Summer Inst. on Teaching or Writing, Columbia Tchrs. Coll., summer 1990; grad. Annual Summer Inst. on Advanced Teaching of Writing, summer, 1993, Annual Inst. Pub. Health and Human Rights, Harvard U. Sch. Pub. Health, 1994, grad. profl. pub. course Stanford U., 1982, grad. exec. refresher course profl. pub. Stanford U., 1994; cert. Exec. Mgmt. Inst. in Health Care, U. So. Calif., 1995, cert. advanced exec. program Grad. Sch. Mgmt. UCLA, 1995; cert. in ethics corps tng. program, Josephson Inst. of Ethics, 1991, cert.; ethics fellow Loma Linda U. Med. Ctr., 1989; cert. clin. intensive biomedical ethics, Loma Linda U. Med. Ctr., 1989. Circulation libr. Harvard Med. Libr., Boston, 1958-59; social worker Conn. State Welfare, New Haven, 1960-61; tchr. English, Hebrew Day Sch., New Haven, 1961-64; instr. creative writing and English lit. Monmouth Coll., West Long Branch, N.J., 1967-69; freelance writer, Arcadia, Calif., 1970—; v.p. council grad. students, Claremont Grad. sch., 1971-72, adj. dir. Writing Ctr. Speaker Series Claremont Grad. Sch., 1993—, spkr., 1996; mem. adv. coun. tech. and profl. writing Dept. English, Calif. State U., Long Beach, 1980-82; mem. adv. bd. Calif. Health Rev., 1982-83; mem. Foothill Health Dist. Adv. Coun. L.A. County Dept. Health Svcs., 1987-93, pres., 1989-91, immediate past pres., 1991-92. Ann. Key Mem. award, 1990. Author: From Vassar to Kitchen, 1967, A Guide to Health Facilities: Personnel and Management, 1971, 2nd edit. 1977, 3d edit., 1992. Mem. pub. relations bd. Monmouth County Mental Health Assn., 1968-69; chmn. creative writing group Calif. Inst. Tech. Woman's Club, 1975-79; mem. ethics com., human subjects protection com. Jewish Home for the Aging, Reseda, Calif., 1994—, Santa Teresita Hosp., 1994—; mem. task force edn. and cultural activities, City of Duarte, 1987-88; mem. strategic planning task force com., campaign com. for pre-eminence Claremont Grad. Sch., 1986-87, mem. alumni coun., 1993-96, bd. dirs., governing bd. alumni assn., 1993-96, mem. alumni coun., mem. steering com. annual alumni day 1994-96, mem. alumni awards com., 1994-96, mem. alumni events com., 1994-96, mem. vol. devel. com., 1994-96; Vassar Coll. Class rep. to Alumnae Assn. Fall Coun. Meeting, 1989,, class corr. Vassar Coll. Quarterly Alumnae Mag., 1993—; co-chmn. Vassar Christmas Showcase New Haven Vassar Club, 1965-66, rep. to Vassar Coll. Alumnae Assn. Fall Coun. Meeting, 1965-66; co-chmn. Vassar Club So. Calif. Annual Book Fair, 1970-71; chmn. creative writing group Yale U. Newcomers, 1965-66, dir. creative writing group Yale U. Women's Orgn., 1966-67; grad. AMA Ann. Health Reporting Conf., 1992, 93; mem. exec. program network UCLA Grad. Sch. Mgmt., 1987—; trustee Ctr. for Improvement of Child Caring, 1981-83; mem. League Crippled Children, 1982—, bd. dirs., 1988-91, treas. for gen. meetings, 1990-91, chair hostesses com., 1988-89, pub. rels. com., 1990-91; bd. dirs. L.A. Commn. on Assaults Against Women, 1983-84; v.p. Temple Beth David, 1983-86; mem. cmty. rels. com. Jewish Fedn. Council Greater L.A., 1985-87; del. Task Force on Minorities in Newspaper Bus., 1987-89; cmty. rep. County Health Ctrs. Network Tobacco Control Program, 1991. Recipient cert. of appreciation City of Duarte, 1988, County of L.A., 1988; Coro Found. fellow, 1979; named Calif. Communicator of Achievement, Woman of Yr. Calif. Press Women, 1992. Fellow Am. Med. Writers Assn. (pres. Pacific Southwest chpt. 1987 89, dir. 1980-93, Pacific S.W. del. to nat. bd. 1980-87, 89-91, chmn. various conv. coms., chmn. nat. book awards trade category 1982-83, chmn. Nat. Conv. Networking Luncheon 1983, 84, chmn. freelance and pub. relations coms. Nat. Midyr. Conf. 1983-84, workshop leader ann. conf. 1984-87, 90-92, 95—, nat. chmn. freelance sect. 1984-85, gen. chmn. 1985, Asilomar Western Regional Conf., gen. chmn. 1985, workshop leader 1985, program co-chmn. 1987, speaker 1985, 88-89, program co-chmn. 1989, nat. exec. bd. dirs. 1985-86, nat. adminstr. sects. 1985-86, pres.-elect Pacific S.W. chpt. 1985-87, pres. 1987-89, immediate past pres. 1989-91, bd. dirs., 1991-93, moderator gen. session nat. conf. 1987, chair gen. session nat. conf., 1986-87, chair Walter C. Alvarez Meml. Found. award 1986-87, Appreciation award for outstanding leadership 1989, named to Workshop Leaders Honor Roll 1991); mem. Women in Comm. (dir. 1980-82, 89-90, v.p. cmty. affairs 1981-82, N.E. area rep. 1980-81, chmn. awards banquet 1982, sem. leader, speaker ann. nat. profl. conf., 1985, program adv. com. L.A. chpt. 1987, v.p. activities 1989-90, chmn. L.A. chpt. 1st ann. Agnes Underwood Freedom of Info. Awards Banquet 1982, recognition award 1983, nominating com. 1982, 83, com. Women of the Press Awards luncheon 1988, Women in Comm. awards luncheon 1988), Am. Assn. for Higher Edn., AAUW (legis. chmn. Arcadia br. 1976-77, books and plays chmn. Arcadia br. 1973-74, creative writing chmn. 1969-70, 1st v.p. program dir. 1975-76, networking chmn. 1981-82, chmn. task force promoting individual liberties 1987-88, named Woman of Yr., Woman of Achievement award 1986, cert. of appreciation 1987), Coll. English Assn., APHA, Am. Soc. Law, Medicine and Ethics, Calif. Press Women (v.p. programs L.A. chpt. 1982-85, pres. 1985-87, state pres. 1987-89, past immediate past state pres. 1989-91, chmn. state speakers bur. 1989—, del nat. bd. 1989—, moderator ann. spring conv., 1990, 92, chmn. nominating com. 1990-91, Calif. lit. dir. 1990-92, dir. state lit. com. 1990-92, dir. family literacy day Calif., 1990, Cert. of Appreciation, 1991, named Calif. Communicator of Achievement 1992), AAUP, Internat. Comm. Assn.,

N.Y. Acad. Scis., Ind. Writers So. Calif. (bd. dirs. 1989-90, dir. Specialized Groups 1989-90, dir. at large 1989-90, bd. dirs. corp. 1988-89, dir. Speech Writing Group, 1991-92), Hastings Ctr., AAAS, Nat. Fedn. Press Women, (bd. dirs. 1987-93, nat. co-chmn. task force recruitment of minorities 1987-89, del. 1987-89, nat. dir. of speakers bur. 1989-93, editor of speakers bur. directory 1991, cert. of appreciation, 1991, 93, Plenary of Past Pres. state 1989—, workshop leader-speaker ann. nat. conf. 1990, chair state women of achievement com. 1986-87, editor Speakers Bur. Addendum Directory, 1992, editor Speakers Bur. Directory 1991, 92, named 1st runner up Nat. Communicator of Achievement 1992), AAUW (chpt. Woman of Achievement award 1986, chmn. task force promoting individual liberties 1987-88, speaker 1987, Cert. of Appreciation 1987, Woman of Achievement-Woman of Yr. 1986), Internat. Assn. Bus. Communicators, Soc. for Tech. Comm. (workshop leader, 1985, 86), Kennedy Inst. Ethics, Soc. Health and Human Values, Assoc. Writing Programs, Authors Guild. Clubs: Women's City (Pasadena), Claremont Colls. Faculty House, Pasadena Athletic, Town Hall of Calif. (vice chair cmty. affairs sect. 1982-87, speaker 1986, faculty-instr. Exec. Breakfast Inst. 1985-86, mem. study sect. coun. 1986-88), Authors Guild. Lodge: Rotary (chair Duarte Rotary mag. 1988-89, mem. dist. friendship exch. com. 1988-89, mem. internat. svc. com. 1989-90, info. svc. com. 1989-90)

SLOAT, BARBARA FURIN, cell biologist, educator; b. Youngstown, Ohio, Jan. 20, 1942; d. Walter and Mary Helen (Maceyko) Furin; m. John Barry Sloat, Nov. 2, 1968; children: John Andrew, Eric Furin. BS, Denison U., 1963; MS, U. Mich., 1966, PhD, 1968. Lab. asst. U. Ghent, Belgium, 1964; teaching fellow, lectr. U. Mich., Ann Arbor, 1964-66, 68-70, asst. rsch. biologist Mental Health Rsch. Inst., 1972-74; vis. asst. prof., lectr. U. Mich., Ann Arbor and Dearborn, 1974-76; dir. women in sci. U. Mich., Ann Arbor, 1980-84, assoc. dir. honors, 1986-87, rsch. scientist, 1976—, lectr. Residential Coll., 1984—; assoc. Inst. Humanities U. Mich., Ann Arbor, 1991—. Author: Laboratory Guide for Zoology, 1979, Summer Internships in the Sciences for High School Women (CASE Silver medal, 1985, Excellence in Edn. award, U. Mich., 1993). Recipient Acad. Women's Caucus award, U. Mich., 1984, Grace Lyon Alumnae Award, Denison U., 1988; grantee NSF, U.S. Dept. Edcn., Warner Lambert Found., others. Mem. AAAS, Am. Soc. Cell Biology, N.Y. Acad. Scis., Nat. Assn. Women Deans, Adminstrs. and Counselors, Assn. for Women in Sci. (councilor 1988-90, pres. elect 1990, mentor of yr. award Detroit area chpt. 1994), Phi Beta Kappa, Sigma Xi. Home: 2010 Hall Ave Ann Arbor MI 48104-4816 Office: U Mich Residential Coll 216 Tyler East Quad Ann Arbor MI 48109-1245

SLOBIN, KATHLEEN OVERIN, sociology educator, researcher, consultant; b. Santa Ana, Calif., July 18, 1942; d. Courtenay Stuyvesant Overin and Janet Kathleen (Raitt) Church; m. Dan Isaac Slobin, May 21, 1969 (div. Sept. 1983); children: Heida Slobin Shoemaker, Shem. BA, Pomona Coll., 1964; MFA, Calif. Coll. Arts and Crafts, 1980; MPA, Calif. State U., Hayward, 1984; PhD, U. Calif., San Francisco, 1991. Instr. fine arts Indian Valley C.C., Novato, Calif., 1981-82; coord. edn. Nat. Energy Found., San Francisco, 1982; assoc. dir. continuing edn. dept. psychiatry U. Calif., 1983-86, rsch. asst., 1986-90, staff rsch. assoc., 1990; asst. prof. sociology N.D. State U., Fargo, 1991—; rschr., cons. West River Regional Med. Ctr., Hettinger, N.D., 1994—. Contbr. articles to profl. jours., chpt. to book. Rschr., cons. cmty. refugee agys., Fargo, 1993-95. Anthony fellow U. Calif., 1988, 89, grad. rsch. grantee, 1989. Mem. Am. Sociol. Assn., African Studies Assn., Soc. for Symbolic Interaction, Soc. for Women Sociologists. Democrat. Mem. Soc. of Friends. Office: ND State U Dept Sociology-Anthropology PO Box 5075 Fargo ND 58105

SLOCUM, ROSEMARIE R., physician management search consultant; b. Port Arthur, Tex., Dec. 19, 1948; d. Edly and Ella (McNeely) Raccard; m. James Rubenstein; 1 child, Blair Ashton. BS, La. State U., Baton Rouge, 1971. Cert. tchr., La. Edn. specialist La. Dept. Occupational Standards, Baton Rouge, 1971-74; account exec. Uarco, Inc., Baton Rouge, 1974-77; owner, broker Rosemarie Slocum Real Estate, Baton Rouge, 1977-91; physician recruiter MSI, New Orleans, 1985-86; assoc. dir. physician recruitment Physician Search, Inc., Fairfax, Va., 1986-88; spl. cons. Caswell/Winters Physician Search Cons., Milw., 1988-89; v.p. U.S. Med. Search, Inc. subs. of Caswell/Winters, Milw., 1988-89; dir. physician recruitment/mktg. East Range Clinics, Ltd., Virginia, Minn., 1989-91; pres. Rosemarie Slocum, Inc., Virginia, Minn., 1991—. Office: RSI 817 S 5th Ave Virginia MN 55792-2804

SLOM, JANET, artist; b. Johannesburg, Transuaal, South Africa, Jan. 29, 1952; d. Joseph Harold and Lily (Goldstuck) S.; m. Ashley John Schapiro, April 29, 1973; children: Gina Michelle, Daniel Jonathan. Attended, U. Witwatersrand, Johannesburg, 1970-73, Mass. Coll. Art, 1993-96, Art Students League, N.Y., 1988-93. Solo exhbns. include Nedbank Gallery, Rosebank, South Africa, 1973, Shambhala Gallery, Rivonia, Sandton, South Africa, 1976, Casa Bella Gallery, N.Y., 1982, Margaret Lipworth Gallery, Boca Raton, Fla., 1985, Kohn Pedersen Fox Gallery, N.Y., 1994, 95, Frank Pages Gallery, Baden-Baden, Germany, 1995, 96, Galleria Arte E Arte M. Granaro, Italy, 1995, 96; group exhns. include Broome Street Gallery, N.Y., 1993, Nat. Exhbn. Cooperstown (N.Y.) Art Assn., 1993, Cork Gallery, Lincoln Ctr., N.Y., 1994, 93, Women's Caucus For Art, 1994, Silvermine Guild Arts Ctr., New Canaan, Conn., 1994, 95, 96, Galeria Arte, Montecatini, Italy, 1994, 95, 96, U.N. 50 Yr. Celebration, 1995, Artplace, Southport, Conn., 1995, 96, Nat. Arts Club N.Y., 1996, numerous others; public collection include Housatonic Mus., Conn., Norwalk (Conn.) Cmty. Coll., Canaveral Internat., Miami, Ghandi Found., San Francisco, Shepard Steel, Hartford, Conn. Founder Seize the Day Found., Shambhala Project. Mem. N.Y. Soc. of Women Artists, Women's Caucus for Art (Conn. chpt.), Silvermine Guild of Artists, Art Place. Jewish. Home: 6 Apache Trl Westport CT 06880

SLONAKER, MARY JOANNA KING, columnist; b. Richmond, Ind., July 18, 1930; d. Claiborn F. and Carlyle (Diffendenfer) King; divorced; children: Mary Sue Hosey, Steven, Allis Ann. Student, Earlham Coll., 1948-49; BS, Ball State U., 1969; MA in Teaching, Ind. U., 1974. Cert. residential child care worker. Home econs. tchr. Lewisville (Ind.) Sch., 1978-79, Morton Meml. Sch., Knightstown, Ind., 1970-83; town coun. mem. Cambridge City, Ind., 1991-95. Recipient Kiwanis Cmty. award, 1983-84, 95, Appreciation award Am. Bus. Women, 1985, Appreciation award Waseda U. Japanese Exch. Program, 1986-88. Mem. AAUW, Ind. Univ. Alumni Club, Psi Iota Xi, Alpha Delta Kappa. Democrat. Presbyterian. Home: 36 W Church St Cambridge City IN 47327-1615 Office: 127 N Foote St Cambridge City IN 47327-1190

SLONE, SANDI, artist; b. Boston, Oct. 1, 1939; d. Louis and Ida (Spind) Sudikoff; children: Erric Solomon, Jon Solomon. Student, Boston Mus. Fine Arts Sch., 1970-73; BA magna cum laude, Wellesley Coll., 1974. Sr., grad. painting faculty Boston Mus. Fine Arts Sch./Tufts U., 1975—; instr. grad. program Sch. Visual Art, N.Y.C., 1989-90; lectr. painting Harvard U., Cambridge, Mass., 1982; vis. artist Triangle Artists Workshop, N.Y., 1982, 87, 90; co-founder, dir. Art/Omi Internat. Artists Found., N.Y.C., 1992—. Solo shows including ICA, Boston, 1977, Harcus Krakow Gallery, Boston, 1978, 79, 80, 82, 84, 86, Acquavella Contemporary Art, N.Y., 1977, 79, 80, 82, 84, Contemporary Art, N.Y., 1977, 79, 80, 82, 84, Stephen Rosenberg Gallery, N.Y., 1988, Levinson Kane Gallery, Boston, 1989, Smith Jariwala Gallery, London, 1990, Jersey City Mus., 1996, J.J. Brookings Gallery, San Francisco, 1996; group shows include at Mus. Fine Arts, Boston, 1977, Corcoran Gallery of Art 35th Biennale, Washington, 1977, Edmonton Art Gallery, 1977, 85, Hayden Gallery MIT, Cambridge, Mass., 1978, New Generation Andre Emmerich Gallery, N.Y., 1980-81, Am. Ctr., Paris, 1980-81, Amerika Haus, Berlin, 1980-81, Carpenter Ctr., Harvard U., Ctr. de la Cultura Contemporanea, Barcelona, 1987, Federated Union of Black Artists, Johannesburg, South Africa, 1989, Jan Weiss Gallery, N.Y., 1990, Olympia Internat. Art Fairs, London, 1991, Gallery Korea, N.Y., 1992, Klarfeld Perry Gallery, N.Y., 1994, Out of the Blue Gallery, Edinburgh, Scotland, 1994, Gallery One, Toronto, 1996; represented in permanent collections Mus. Modern Art, N.Y.C., Mus. Contemporary Art, Barcelona, Mus. Fine Arts, Boston, Hirshhorn Mus., Washington; artist-in-residence City Hall, Barcelona, 1987, 89. Mus. Fine Arts Boston fellow, 1977, 81; Ford Found. grantee, 1979. Studio: 13 Worth St New York NY 10013-2925

SLORAH, PATRICIA PERKINS, anthropologist; b. Williamson, W.Va., Oct. 3, 1940; d. Guy Bennett and Annie Lee (Carlton) Perkins; m. John Brander Slorah III, Apr. 19, 1960; 1 child, Heather Michelle Slorah Newkirk. AA, St. Pete Jr. Coll., Clearwater, Fla., 1969; BA, U. South Fla., 1971, MA, 1988, PhD, 1994. Cert. elem. tchr., Fla. Tchr. Belleair Montessori, Pinellas, Fla., 1964-68, Pinellas Elem. Schs., 1971-80; grad. asst. U. South Fla., Tampa, 1987-88; researcher Case Western Med. Longitudinal Study, Tampa, 1987, Tampa Bay Share, 1991; witness Spl.Com. on Aging, Washington, 1991. V.p., sec. Friends of the Libr., Tarpon Springs, Fla., 1982-86; pres. Local Polit. Club, Tarpon Springs, 1988-90; speaker Congressman Michael Bilirakis Speaker Bur., 9th Dist., 1988—; founder Grandparents Rights Adv. Movement, 1989; mem. adv. bd. Nat. Task Force of Grandparents United for Children's Rights, Madison, Wis., 1991-92; active Nat. Ctr. Sci. Edn., 1993, Fla. Ctr. Children & Youth, 1993—. Fellow Soc. for Applied Anthropology; mem. AAUW, Am. Anthropol. Soc., Gerontol. Soc. Am., Nat. Ctr. Sci. Edn., So. Gerontol. Soc., Assn. Gerontology and Anthropology, Phi Kappa Phi, Pi Gamma Mu, Phi Mu (chmn. recommendations com. 1986-88). Presbyterian. Home: 1225 N Florida Ave Tarpon Springs FL 34689-2003

SLOVIK, SANDRA LEE, art educator; b. Elizabeth, N.J., Mar. 22, 1943; d. Edward Stanley and Frances (Garbus) S. BA, Newark State Coll., 1965, MA, 1970. Cert. art tchr. Art tchr. Holmdel (N.J.) Twp. Bd. Edn., 1965—; computer art in-sv. tng. Holmdel Bd. Edn., 1990; computer art workshop Madison (N.J.) Bd. Edn., 1991. Charter supporter, mem. Statue of Liberty/Ellis Island Found., 1976—; charter supporter Sheriffs' Assn. N.J., 1993—; mem. PTA, Holmdel, 1965—. Recipient Curriculum award N.J. ASCD, 1992; grantee Holmdel Bd. Edn., 1989, 90, N.J. Bus., Industry, Sci., Edn. Consortium, 1990. Mem. NEA, Nat. Art Edn., Assn., N.J. Art Educators Assn., N.J. Edn. Assn., Monmouth County Edn. Assn., Holmdel Twp. Edn. Assn. (sr. bldg. rep. 1977-79). Office: Village Sch 67 McCampbell Rd Holmdel NJ 07733-2231

SLOVITER, DOLORES KORMAN, federal judge; b. Phila., Sept. 5, 1932; d. David and Tillie Korman; m. Henry A. Sloviter, Apr. 3, 1969; 1 dau., Vikki Amanda. AB in Econs. with distinction, Temple U., 1953, LHD (hon.), 1986; LLB magna cum laude, U. Pa., 1956; LLD (hon.), The Dickinson Sch. Law, 1984, U. Richmond, 1992; LL.D. (hon.), Widener U., 1994. Bar: Pa. 1957. Assoc., then ptnr. Dilworth, Paxson, Kalish, Kohn & Levy, Phila., 1956-69; mem. firm Harold E. Kohn (P.A.), Phila., 1969-72; assoc. prof., then prof. law Temple U. Law Sch., Phila., 1972-79; judge U.S. Ct. Appeals (3d cir.), Phila., 1979—, chief judge, 1991—; mem. bd. overseers U. Pa. Law Sch. Mem. S.E. region Pa. Gov.'s Conf. on Aging, 1976-79, Com. of 70, 1976-79; trustee Jewish Publ. Soc. Am., 1983-89; Jud. Conf. U.S. com. Bicentennial Constn., 1987-90, com. on Rules of Practice and Procedure, 1990-93. Recipient Juliette Low medal Girl Scouts Greater Phila., Inc., 1990, Honor award Girls High Alumnae Assn., 1991, Jud. award Pa. Bar Assn., 1994, U. Pa. James Wilson award, 1996, Temple U. Cert. of Honor award, 1996; Disting. Fulbright scholar, Chile, 1990. Mem. ABA, Fed. Bar Assn., Fed. Judges Assn., Am. Law Inst., Nat. Assn. Women Judges, Am. Judicature Soc. (bd. dirs. 1990-95), Phila. Bar Assn. (gov. 1976-78), Order of Coif (pres. U. Pa. chpt. 1975-77), Phi Beta Kappa. Office: US Ct Appeals 18614 US Courthouse 601 Market St Philadelphia PA 19106-1510

SLOYAN, SISTER STEPHANIE, mathematics educator; b. N.Y.C., Apr. 18, 1918; d. Jerome James and Marie Virginia (Kelley) S. BA, Georgian Ct. Coll., 1945; MA in Math., Cath. U. Am., 1950, PhD, 1952. Asst. prof. math. Georgian Ct. Coll., Lakewood, N.J., 1952-56, assoc. prof., 1956-59, prof., 1959—, coll. pres., 1968-74; lectr. Grad. Sch. Arts and Scis., Cath. U. Am., Washington, 1960-82. Mem. Math. Assn. Am. (bd. govs. 1988-91), Am. Math. Soc., Sigma Xi. Democrat. Roman Catholic. Office: Georgian Ct Coll Dept Math Lakewood NJ 08701

SLUTSKY, LORIE ANN, foundation executive; b. N.Y.C., Jan. 5, 1953; d. Edward and Adele (Moskowitz) S. BA, Colgate U., 1975; MA in Urban Policy and Analysis, New Sch. for Social Rsch., N.Y.C., 1977. Program officer N.Y. Cmty. Trust, N.Y.C., 1977-83, v.p., 1983-87, exec. v.p., 1987-89, pres., CEO, 1990—; former mem. and chmn. bd. Coun. on Founds., Inc., Washington, 1986-95. Trustee, chmn. budget com. Colgate U., Hamilton, N.Y., 1989—; vice chmn., bd. dirs. Found. Ctr., Inc., N.Y.C., United Way, N.Y.C.; bd. dirs. L.A. Wallace Fund for Metro. Mus. Art, N.Y.C., D. Wallace Fund for Meml. Sloan Kettering. Office: NY Community Trust 2 Park Ave New York NY 10016-5603

SMALL, ELAINE DOLORES, financial analyst; b. Trenton, N.J., Aug. 18, 1954; d. Moses and Hattie (Mitchell) S.; m. Richmond Akumiah, Dec. 1982 (div. Aug. 27, 1987). BS, Rochester Inst. Technol., 1976; MBA, Atlanta U., 1985. Mktg. rep. Mobil Oil Corp., 1976-77; mfg. analyst Reader's Digest, Pleasantville, N.Y., 1977-80; mgr. fin. instns. Am. Express, N.Y.C., 1980-83; sr. market analyst Ryder Systems Inc., Miami, 1985-86; dir. recruiting Atlanta U., 1986; cons. Consultants & Assocs., Washington, 1987-89; mgr. fin. analysis Blue Cross Blue Shield of Va., Roanoke, 1989-90; dir. group fin. reporting & analysis Blue Cross Blue Shield of Md., Owings Mills, 1990-93; sr. med. group analyst mid-Atlantic states region Kaiser Permanente, Rockville, Md., 1993-95; supr. budget, statistics Sch. Medicine Johns Hopkins U., Balt., 1995—. Named IBM scholar, 1983. Mem. NAFE, Md. New Directions (bd. dirs. 1994-96), Internat. Soc. Strategic Planners, Nat. Assn. MBA Execs. Democrat. Methodist. Home: 6741 Old Waterloo Rd Apt 107 Baltimore MD 21227-6706 Office: Johns Hopkins Sch Medicine Reed Hall B-102 1620 McElderry St Baltimore MD 21205

SMALL, ELISABETH CHAN, psychiatrist, educator; b. Beijing, July 11, 1934; came to U.S., 1937; d. Stanley Hong and Lily Luella (Lum) Chan; m. Donald M. Small, July 8, 1957 (div. 1980); children Geoffrey Brooks, Philip Willard Stanley; m. H. Sidney Robinson, Jan. 12, 1991. Student, Immaculate Heart Coll., Los Angeles, 1951-52; BA in Polit. Sci., UCLA, 1955, MD, 1960. Intern Newton-Wellesley Hosp., Mass., 1960-61; asst. dir. for venereal diseases Mass. Dept. Pub. Health, 1961-63; resident in psychiatry Boston State Hosp., Mattapan, Mass., 1965-66; resident in psychiatry Tufts New Eng. Med. Ctr. Hosps., 1966-69, psychiat. cons. dept. gynecology, 1973-75; asst. clin. prof. psychiatry Sch. Medicine Tufts U., 1973-75, assoc. clin. prof., 1975-82, asst. clin. prof. ob-gyn, 1977-80, assoc. clin. prof. ob-gyn, 1980-82; assoc. prof. psychiatry, ob-gyn U. Nev. Sch. Med., Reno, 1982-85; practice psychiatry specializing in psychological effects of bodily changes on women, 1969—; clin. prof. psychiatry U. Nev. Sch. Medicine, Reno, 1985-86, prof. psychiatry, 1986-95, clin. assoc. prof. ob-gyn, 1985-88, emeritus prof. psychiatry and behavioral scis., 1995—; mem. staff Tufts New Eng. Med. Ctr. Hosps., 1977-82, St. Margaret's Hosps., Boston, 1977-82, Washoe Med. Ctr., Reno, Sparks (Nev.) Family Hosp., Truckee Meadows Hosp., Reno, St. Mary's Hosp., Reno; chief psychiatry svc. Reno VA Med. Ctr., 1989-94; lectr. various univs., 1961—; cons. in psychiatry; mem. psychiatry adv. panel Hosp. Satellite Network; mem. office external peer rev. NIMH, HEW; psychiat. cons. to Boston Redevelopment Authority on Relocation of Chinese Families of South Cove Area, 1968-70; mem. New Eng. Med. Ctr. Hosps. Cancer Ctr. Com., 1979-80, Pain Control Com., 1981-82, Tufts Univ. Sch. Medicine Reproductive System Curriculum Com., 1975-82. Mem. editorial bd. Psychiat. Update Am. (Psychiat. Assn. ann. rev.), 1983-85; reviewer Psychosomatics and Hosp. Community Psychiatry, New Eng. Jour. of Medicine, Am. Jour. of Psychiatry Psychosomatic Medicine; contbr. articles to profl. jours. Immaculate Heart Coll. scholar, 1951-52; Mira Hershey scholar UCLA, 1955; fellow Radcliffe Inst., 1967-70. Mem. AMA, Am. Psychiat. Assn. (rep. to sect. com. AAAS, chmn. ad hoc com. Asian-Am. Psychiatrists 1975, task force 1975-77, task force cost effectiveness in consultation 1984—, caucus chmn. 1981-82, sci. program com. 1982-88, courses subcom. chmn. sci. program com. 1986-88), Nev. Psychiat. Assn., Assn. for Acad. Psychiatry (fellowship com. 1982), Washoe County Med. Assn., Nev. Med. Soc., Am. Coll.Psychiatrists (sci. program com. 1989-98). Home: 602 Alley Oop Reno NV 89509-3668 Office: 475 Hill St Reno NV 89501

SMALL, GLORIA JEAN, elementary school educator; b. Libertyville, Ill., Feb. 6, 1946; m. Lou G. Small, Jr., June 13, 1971; children: James, David, Andrea. BA, Carroll Coll., 1968; MA, Roosevelt U., Chgo., 1971. Elem. tchr. Libertyville Pub. Schs., 1967-76; presch. tchr. Barne Hage Presch., Washington Island, Wis., 1981-83; elem. tchr. Washington Island Sch., 1983—. Contbr. (newspaper) Observer. Mem. Washington Island Women's Club (program chair 1994-95). Lutheran. Home: RR 1 Box 141 Washington Island WI 54246-9744 Office: Washington Island Sch RR 1 Box 2 Washington Island WI 54246-9702

SMALL, JOYCE GRAHAM, psychiatrist, educator; b. Edmonton, Alberta, Can., June 12, 1931; came to U.S., 1956; d. John Earl and Rachel C. (Redmond) Graham; m. Iver Francis Small, May 26, 1954; children: Michael, Jeffrey. BA, U. Saskatchewan, Can., 1951; MD, U. Manitoba, Can., 1956; MS, U. Mich., 1959. Diplomat Am. Bd. Psychiatry and Neurology, Am. Bd. Electroencephalography. Instr. in psychiatry Neuropsychiat. Inst. U. Mich., Ann Arbor, 1959-60; instr. in psychiatry med. sch. U. Oreg., Portland, 1960-61, asst. prof. in psychiatry med. sch., 1961-62; asst. prof. in psychiatry sch. of medicine Washington U., St. Louis, 1962-65; assoc. prof. in psychiatry sch. of medicine Ind. U., Indpls., 1965-69, prof. psychiatry sch. of medicine, 1969—; mem. initial rev. groups NIMH, Washington, 1972-76, 79-82, 87-91; assoc. mem. Inst. Psychiat. Rsch., Indpls., 1974—. Editorial bd.: Quar. Jour. of Convulsive Therayp, 1984, Clin. Electroencephalography, 1990, and more than 150 publs. in field; contbr. articles to profl. jours. Rsch. grantee NIMH, Portland, Oreg., 1961-62, St. Louis, 1962-64, Indpls., 1967—, Epilepsy Found., Dreyfus Found., Indpls., 1965; recipient Merit award NIMH, Indpls., 1990. Fellow Am. Psychiat. Assn., Am. Electroencephalographic Soc. (councillor 1972-75, 1982); mem. Soc. Biol. Psychiatry, Cen. Assn. Electroencephalographers (sec., treas. 1967-68, pres. 1970, councillor 1971-72), Sigma Xi. Office: Larue D Carter Meml Hosp 1315 W 10th St Indianapolis IN 46202-2802

SMALL, LEILA DANETTE-MADISON, actress; b. Jacksonville, Fla., Aug. 23, 1909; d. Daniel Mays Madison and Leila (Joplin) Madison-Williams; m. Clarence Elias Small, Sept. 18, 1926. BS, Morgan State Coll.; MA, Md. U. Elem. tchr. City Bd. of Edn., Balt., 1932-42; speech specialist D.C. Bd. Edn., Washington, 1958-68; actress Actors Equity Assn., N.Y.C., 1968—. Mem. Actors Equity Assn., Screen Actors Guild, AFTRA. Democrat. Roman Catholic. Home: 484 W 43rd St # 8F New York NY 10036-6344

SMALL, NATALIE SETTIMELLI, pediatric mental health counselor; b. Quincy, Mass., June 2, 1933; d. Joseph Peter and Edmea Natalie (Bagnaschi) Settimelli; m. Parker Adams Small, Jr., Aug. 26, 1956; children: Parker Adams III, Peter McMichael, Carla Edmea. BA, Tufts U., 1955; MA, EdS, U. Fla., 1976; PhD, 1987. Cert. child life specialist. Pediatric counselor U. Fla. Coll. Medicine, Gainesville, 1976-80; pediatric counselor Shands Hosp.-U. Fla., Gainesville, 1980-87, supr. child life dept. patient and family resources, 1987—; adminstrv. liaison for self-dir. work teams, mem. faculty Ctr. for Coop. Learning for Health and Sci. Edn., Gainesville, 1988—, assoc. dir., 1996; cons. and lectr. in field. Author: Parents Know Best, 1991; co-author team packs series for teaching at risk adolescent health edn. and coop. learning. Bd. dirs. Ronald McDonald House, Gainesville, 1980—, mem. exec. com., 1991—; bd. dirs. Gainesville Assn. Creative Arts, 1994—; mem. health profl. adv. com. March of Dimes, Gainesville, 1986—, HIV prevention planning partnership, 1995. Boston Stewart Club scholar, Florence, Italy, 1955; grantee Jessie Ball Du Pont Fund, 1978, Children's Miracle Network, 1990, 92, 93, 94, 95; recipient Caring and Sharing award Ronald McDonald House, 1995. Mem. ACA, Nat. Bd. Cert. Counselors, Am. Assn. Mental Health Counselors, Assn. for the Care of Children's Health, Fla. Assn. Child Life Profls., Child Life Coun. Roman Catholic. Home: 3454 NW 12th Ave Gainesville FL 32605-4811 Office: Shands Hosp Patient and Family Resources PO Box 100306 Gainesville FL 32610

SMALL, REBECCA ELAINE, accountant; b. Meridian, Tex., Apr. 5, 1946; d. James Milford and Rosa Lee Elaine (Berry) Allen; m. Jay Austin Small, Sept. 16, 1964 (div.); children: Lashawn Renee, Jay Austin Jr.; m. Jerry Leon Cooper, Dec. 10, 1983 (div. Sept. 1985). Student Okla. Sch. Bus. and Banking, 1972; BS in Acctg. magna cum laude, Cen. State U., Edmond, Okla., 1977, MA in Exptl. Psychology summa cum laude, 1989; postgrad., U. Okla., 1991—. Staff acct. Robert A. Mosley, CPA, Moore, Okla., 1972-74, Robert Stewart, CPA, Edmond, 1974-75, Lowder & Co., Oklahoma City, 1975-81; pvt. practice acctg., Oklahoma City, 1981—. Fellow Nat. Inst. Mental Health, NIH; recipient Rsch. award Dept. Psychology Cent. State U., 1988. Mem. AICPA, Okla. Woman's Bus. Orgn. (chmn. 1982), Okla. Soc. CPAs, Am. Woman's Soc. CPAs, Nat. Assn. Accts. (hon.), Soc. of Neurosci., Alpha Lambda Delta, Alpha Chi, Psi Chi. Democrat. Avocations: writing poetry, horticulture, bicycling.

SMALL, SARAH MAE, volunteer; b. Salisbury, N.C., Nov. 16, 1923; d. Clint and Lillie Mae (Wilbourn) Evans; m. Jesse Small Sr., May 4, 1941; children: Jesse Jr., Jean Carol Small Bell. Cert., Cortez Bus. Sch., 1948. File clk. gen. acctg. office Fed. Govt., Washington, 1941-47; sec., stenographer CIA, Washington, 1948-52; adminstrv. asst. CIA, McLean, Va., 1952-65; ret. CIA, 1965; elected pres. Energetic Crusaders, Inc., 1993—. Pres. Youth Triumph Ch., Washington, Md., S.C. and Ga., 1965-76, The Energetic Crusaders, Inc., 1993; bd. dirs. ARC, Washington, 1986-87, Children's Edn. Found., Inc., 1989—; mem. adv. bd. D.C. Gen. Hosp., 1985-86. Recipient Outstanding and Dedicated Vol. Svc. award Kiwanis Club of Capital Centre, 1985, Plaque in Recognition of Dedicated and Outstanding Vol. Svc. to the Corps and Washington D.C., Community Jr. Citizen's Corps., 1989, Appreciation award for Outstanding and Dedicated Vol. Svc. to Corps, Jr. Citizens Corps., Inc., 1990, Appreciation award Jr. Citizens Corp., Inc., 1990, Community Svc. award for leadership and youth advocacy Bus. and Profl. Women's League, Inc., 1991, Vol. award achievement excellence svc. youths of Jr. Citizens Corps., Inc., 1992, others. Mem. Jr. Citizens Corps (life, pres. 1985—, Dedicated Community Svc. award 1983, Bus. and Community Svc. award 1986), Bus. and Profl. Women's League (treas. 1982-86), Women in Arts (chartered, pres. 1984—), Nat. Coun. Negro Women, World Affairs Coun. Washington, Agrl. Coun. Am., Exec. Travel Club Riverdale. Democrat. Baptist. Home: 2010 Upshur St NE Washington DC 20018-3244

SMALLEY, BARBARA MARTIN, English educator; b. Connersville, Ind., Apr. 20, 1926; d. Floyd Stanley and Esther Anna (Davis) Martin; m. Donald Arthur Smalley, Sept. 8, 1952. B.S., Ind. U., 1954; M.A. in French, U. Ill., 1965, Ph.D. in Comparative Lit., 1968. Asst. prof. comparative lit. and English Lit., U. Ill., Urbana, 1968-75, assoc. prof. English and comparative lit., 1975—. Author: George Eliot and Flaubert: Pioneers of the Modern Novel, 1974; editor: Ranthorpe (G.H. Lewes), 1974; (with others) Third Force: Psychology and the Study of Literature, 1986; contbr. articles to profl. jours. Mem. Am. Comparative Lit. Assn., MLA, AAUP, Can. Comparative Lit. Assn., Internat. Comparative Lit. Assn. Office: U Ill English Bldg 261 608 S Wright St Urbana IL 61801-4029

SMALLEY, DONNA WESSON, lawyer, educator; b. Ft. Sill, Okla., Oct. 8, 1955; d. Robert Eugene and Frances Marie (Yates) Wesson; m. Jack Smalley Jr., July 31, 1978 (div. Jan. 1987); 1 child, Jack Smalley III. BA in Journalism, U. Ala., 1975, JD, 1978; cert. instr. Nat. Inst. Trial Advocacy, U. Calif. Berkeley, San Francisco, 1994. Bar: Ala. 1978. State lobbyist U. Ala., Tuscaloosa, 1974-75; personal injury claims adjuster State Farm Mutual Auto Ins., Birmingham, 1978-82; assoc. Williams & Pradat, Tuscaloosa, 1982-83; legal clk., adminstrv. asst. Tuscaloosa County Dist. Ct., 1983-84; assoc. atty., ptnr. Gibson & Smalley, P.C., Tuscaloosa, 1984-88; pvt. practice Tuscaloosa, 1988-95; ptnr., gen. practitioner Smalley & Carr, L.L.C., Tuscaloosa, 1996—; adj. English instr. U. Ala., Tuscaloosa, 1988-91, adj. trial advocacy instr., 1991—; bd. mem. Ala. Lawyers for Children, Montgomery, 1993-96, Ala. Children's Trust Fund Bd., Montgomery, 1994—; cir. judge pro-tem Ala. Adminstrv. Office of Cts., Tuscaloosa, 1995; chair citizen's edn. Ala. State Bar Assn., Montgomery, 1995-96; spkr. in field. Paintings exhibited Jr. League, 1990 (3d place), Lawyers for Children Charitable Auction, 1996. Chair mediation com. Tuscaloosa County Bar, 1989-91; task force mem. Lt. Gov.'s Task Force-Juvenile Crime, Montgomery, 1993-96; exec. com. Ala. State Dem. Party, Birmingham, 1994—; parent-bd. liason Tuscaloosa Acad., 1994-95. Named Outstanding Young Businesswoman, Jaycees, Tuscaloosa, 1984, Outstanding Young Careerist, Bus. and Profl. Women, Tuscaloosa, 1985; recipient Outstanding Achievement-CLE award Ala. State Bar, Montgomery, 1994, 95. Fellow Am. Acad. Matrimonial Lawyers; mem. Ala. Trial Lawyers (exec. bd. 1994—). Methodist. Office: Smalley & Carr LLC Attys 601 Greensboro Ave Tuscaloosa AL 35401

SMALLEY, PENNY JUDITH, laser nursing consultant; b. Chgo., Feb. 20, 1947; d. Ernest Rich and Muriel L. (Touff) Brown; m. Ivan H. Smalley, Jan. 11, 1972; children: Cherie Ann, Michael John, Geoffry Paul. Grad., Evanston Hosp. Sch. Nursing, Ill., 1980. Cert. Am. Bd. Laser Surgery, 1989. Staff nurse Evanston Hosp., 1979-81, laser coord., 1981-83; office mgr. Women's Health Group, 1981; laser nurse specialist Cooper Lasersonics, various, 1983-86; pres., CEO Technology Concepts Internat., Inc., Chgo., 1986—; lectr., writer Sino Fgn. Laser Conf., People's Republic of China, 1987; bd. dirs. Laser Inst. Am. Contbg. author: Nursing Clinics of North America, 1990; editorial bd. Clin. Laser Monthly, Laser Nursing mag., 1989—, Minimally Invasive Surg. Nursing; contbr. articles to profl. jours. Mem. Am. Soc. Laser Medicine and Surgery (chmn. edn. com. 1987-90, standards of practice com. 1990, quality assurance com., nursing sect. chmn. 1992-94), award for Excellence in Laser Nursing 1993), Laser Inst. Am. (bd. dirs.), Am. Nat. Standards Com., Inst. Com. Lasers in Health Care (exec. com., nurse rep.), Brit. Med. Laser Assn. (course dir. first laser nursing conf. in U.K., 1990), Assn. Oper. Rm. Nurses (tchr. nat. seminars, spl. com. on internat. issues), Internat. Soc. Laser Surgery and Medicine (chmn. nursing 1988—). Democrat. Home and Office: 1444 W Farwell Ave Chicago IL 60626-3410

SMARR, MARY ANN, librarian; b. Sharon, S.C., Mar. 3, 1939; d. William Lawrence Jr. and Margaret (Smith) Hill; children: William Craig, Eric McMurray. BS, Winthrop U., 1961; M Librarianship, U. S.C., 1986. Asst. cataloger, reference libr. Clemson (S.C.) U., 1961-62; asst. to libr. Gardner-Webb Coll., Boiling Springs, N.C., 1962-63; v.p., treas. Pool Chem. and Supply, Greenville, S.C., 1976-84; libr. Rutledge Coll., Greenville, 1986; libr. I, Greenville County Libr., Greenville, 1987; libr. Spartanburg (S.C.) Tech. Coll., 1988-89, Greenville Tech. Coll., 1990—. Mem. ALA, S.C. Libr. Assn. Office: Greenville Tech Coll 506 S Pleasantburg Dr Greenville SC 29606

SMART, ANITA GRACE, small business owner; b. Denison, Tex., July 10, 1938; d. Paul Kikendall and Grace Irene (Brotherton) James; m. S.B. Smart Jr., July 20, 1958; 1 child, Bobby Gene. Grad. high sch. With Vareo, Garland, Tex., 1981; owner, truck driver IXS, Jackson, Miss., 1995—; art tchr. Methodist.

SMART, CAROLE ANNE, French language educator; b. Amesbury, Mass., July 2, 1953; d. Aime and Lucille Cécile (Roy) Lizotte; m. Charles Armand Smart, June 8, 1974; children: Charles Jared, Benjamin Roy. BA in French, Lowell State Coll., 1975; MEd in Adminstrn. and Supervision (hon.), U. N.H., 1993. Tchr. French and English Amesbury H.S., 1975-76; tchr. French Newmarket (N.H.) Jr./Sr. H.S., 1977—; advisor student couns., fgn. lang. clubs Newmarket H.S., mem. prin.'s adv. coun., 1992-93, chairperson dept. fgn. langs, 1992—, chairperson renaissance team; mem. evaulation team New Eng. Assn. Sch. Accreditation, 1989; mem. team exploring tracking of culture through lit. NEH, 1981. Sec./treas. Cub Scouts pact 201, Boy Scouts Am., Newmarket, 1989-95. Mem. ASCD, NEA (treas. chpt. 1980-83), Am. Assn. Tchrs. of French, N.H. Assn. Tchrs. of French. Home: 181 Grant Rd Newmarket NH 03857-2145

SMART, DEBORAH LYN, insurance company executive; b. Evanston, Ill., June 25, 1955; d. William H. and Patricia (Herman) S. BA in Polit. Sci., Drury Coll., 1977. Claim adjuster Liberty Mut., St. Louis, 1977-79; claim supr. Home Ins., Chgo., 1979-81; claim supt. Home Ins., St. Louis, 1981-83; ops. mgr. Home Ins., Chgo., 1983-86; claim cons. CNA, Chgo., 1986-90; claim dir. CNA, N.Y.C., 1990-93; claim v.p. CNA, Indpls., 1994-95, Brea, 1996—. Cons. Big Bros./Big Sisters, Cgho., 1986. Fellow Who's Who Am. Execs.; mem. NAFE, AAUW, Am. Mus. Nat. History (assoc.), Kappa Delta. Office: CNA Ins 3075 E Imperial Hwy Brea CA 92622

SMART, EDITH MERRILL, civic worker; b. N.Y.C., Sept. 10, 1929; d. Edwin Katte and Helen Phelps (Stokes) Merrill; student Smith Coll., 1947-49, Barnard Coll., 1949-50; m. S. Bruce Smart, Jr., Sept. 10, 1949; children—Edith Minturn Smart Moore, William Candler, Charlotte Merrill Smart Rogan, Priscilla Smart Schwarzenbach. Tchr. elem. schs., Gibson Island, Md., 1959-60; guide, instr. Mill River Wetlands Com., Fairfield, Conn., 1967-85; treas. Near and Far Aid Assn., Fairfield, 1970-75, v.p., 1975-77, pres., 1977-79; pres. Nature Ctr. of Environ. Activities, Westport, Conn., chmn., 1981-85; trustee Fairfield Univ., 1987-93; leader No. Cook County council Girl Scouts U.S.A., Kenilworth, Ill., 1962-64; chmn. Southport-Westport Antiques Show, 1974-76; trustee Conn. chpt. Nature Conservancy, 1981-91, Va. chpt., 1992—; guide Nat. Acquarium, 1985-90; dir. Piedmont Child Devel. Ctr., 1994—; vestryman St. Timothy's Ch., Fairfield, 1976-79. Republican. Episcopalian. Clubs: Sasqua Garden (Fairfield), Upperville Garden, Middleburg Tennis, MFH The Fairfax Hunt. Home: 20561 Trappe Rd Upperville VA 20184-9708

SMART, MARRIOTT WIECKHOFF, research librarian consultant; b. Memphis, Aug. 26, 1935; d. Gerhard Emil and Beatrice (Flanegan) Wieckhoff; m. John A. Smart, May 9, 1959; children: Denise, Holly. BS in Geology, U. Tex.-Austin, 1957; MLS, U. Pitts., 1976. Geophysicist Mobil Corp., New Orleans, 1957-59; geologist Hanson Oil Co., Roswell, N.Mex., 1959-62; info. specialist Gulf Corp., Pitts., 1977-79, library mgr., Denver, 1979-84, library cons. team, Pitts., 1984; supr. Library-Info. Ctr., Amoco Minerals Co., Englewood, Colo., 1984; dir. Library-Info. Ctr., Cyprus Minerals Co., 1985-92; cons. Ask Marriott, Littleton, Colo., 1992—. Choir mem. Grace Presbyn. Ch., Littleton, 1979—. Mem. Spl. Libraries Assn. (bull. bus. mgr. 1982, treas. petroleum and energy divsn. 1984-86, chmn. petroleum and energy divsn. 1987-88, pres. Rocky Mountain chpt. 1991-92), Colo. Info. Profls. Network, Women in Mining, Alpha Chi Omega. Home: 3337 E Easter Pl Littleton CO 80122-1910

SMART, MARY-LEIGH CALL (MRS. J. SCOTT SMART), civic worker; b. Springfield, Ill., Feb. 27, 1917; d. S(amuel) Leigh and Mary (Bradish) Call; m. J. Scott Smart, Sept. 11, 1951 (dec. 1960). Diploma, Monticello Coll., 1934; student, Oxford U., 1935; B.A., Wellesley Coll., 1937; M.A., Columbia U., 1939, postgrad., 1940-41; postgrad., N.Y. U., 1940-41; painting student, with Bernard Karfiol, 1937-38. Dir. mgmt. Cen. Ill. Grain Farms, Logan County, 1939—; owner Lowtrek Kennel, Ogunquit, Maine, 1957-73, Cove Studio Art Gallery, Ogunquit, 1961-68; art collector, patron, publicist, 1954—, cons., 1970—. Editor: Hamilton Easter Field Art Found. Collection Catalog, 1966; originator, dir. show, compiler of catalog Art: Ogunquit, 1967; Peggy Bacon-A Celebration, Barn Gallery, Ogunquit, 1979. Program dir., sec. bd. Barn Gallery Assocs., Inc., 1958-69, pres., 1969-70, 82-87, asst. treas., 1987-92, hon. dir., 1970-78, adv. trustee, 1992-94, v.p., 1994—; curator Hamilton Easter Field Art Found. Collection, 1978-79, curator exhbns., 1979-86, chair exhbn. com., 1987-94; mem. acquisition com. DeCordova Mus., Lincoln, Mass., 1966-78; mem. chancellor's coun. U. Tex., 1972—; mem. pres.'s coun. U. N.H., 1978—; bd. dirs. Ogunquit C. of C., 1966, treas., 1966-67, hon. life mem., 1968—; bd. overseers Strawbery Banke, Inc., Portsmouth, N.H., 1972-75, 3d vice chmn., 1973, 2d vice chmn., 1974; bd. advisors U. Art Galleries, U. N.H., 1973-89, v.p., bd. overseers, 1974-81, pres., 1981-89; bd. dirs. Old York Hist. and Improvement Soc., York, Maine, 1979-81, v.p., 1981-82; adv. com. Bowdoin Coll. Mus. Art Invitational exhibit, 1975, '76 Maine Artists Invitational Exhbn., Maine State Mus., Maine Coast Artists, Rockport, 1975-78, All Maine Biennial '79, Bowdoin Coll. Mus. Art juried exhbn.; mem. jury for scholarship awards Maine com. Skowhegan Sch. Painting & Sculpture, 1982-84; nat. com. Wellesley Coll. Friends of Art, 1983—; adv. trustee Portland Mus. Art, 1983-85, fellow, 1985—; mem. mus. panel Maine State Commn. on Arts and Humanities, 1983-86; adv. com. Maine Biennial, Colby Coll. Mus. Art, 1983; coun. advisors Farnsworth Libr. & Art Mus., Rockland, Maine, 1986—; collections com. Payson Gallery, Westbrook Coll., Portland, 1987-91; dir. Greater Piscataqua Cmty. Found., N.H. Charitable Fund, 1991—; mem. corp. Ogunquit Mus. Am. Art, 1988-90, 95—; mem. Maine Women's Forum, 1993—. Recipient Deborah Morton award Westbrook Coll., 1988, Friend of the Arts award Maine Art Dealers Assn., 1993. Mem. Mus. Modern Art, Springfield Art Assn., Jr. League Springfield, Western Maine Wellesley Club. Episcopalian. Address: 30 Surf Point Rd York ME 03909-5053

SMART, SUZANN LYNN, fund raising executive; b. Cleve., May 20, 1947; d. William Robertson and Avis Evelyn (Perkins) S.; m. Thomas L. Merklinger, Feb. 24, 1973; children: Robert William, David Thomas, John Christopher Merklinger. BFA, U. Rochester, 1969. Fund raiser N.H. Pub. TV, Durham, N.H., 1970-77, The Children's Mus., Indpls., 1977-97, Parsons Child and Family Ctr., Albany, N.Y., 1987-92; exec. dir. Ellis Hosp. Found., Schenectady, N.Y., 1992—; cons. N.Y. State Mus., Albany, Wesley Health Care Ctr., Saratoga Springs, N.Y. Mem. Jr. League Indpls., 1979-86, Albany-Schenectady, 1986-96; com. chair Cub Scout Pack 45, Clifton Park, N.Y., 1988-91; mem. sch. partnership team Skano Elem. Sch., Clifton Park, 1994-95. Mem. Nat. Soc. Fund Raising Execs. (bd. dirs. 1988-96, treas., Outstanding Fund Raising Exec. Hudson Mohawk chpt. 1995). Office: Ellis Hosp Found PO Box 1015 Schenectady NY 12301-1015

SMAYLING, LYDA MOZELLA, speech pathologist; b. Britton, Okla., Apr. 19, 1923; d. Miles and Evelyn (King) Maxwell; m. George F. Smayling, Sept. 12, 1944 (dec. 1985); children: Sally, Michael, Miles. BA magna cum laude, U. Wichita, Wichita, Kans., 1944; MA summa cum laude, U. Wichita, 1947. Dir., cons., assoc. U. Kans. Med. Ctr., Kans. City, 1947-56; cons. Westchester County Cerebral Palsy Assn., Bedford Village, N.Y., 1947-54; asst. dir. Inst. Logopedics, Wichita, 1957-68; instr. Wichita (Kans.) State U., 1957-68; cons. Wichita, 1957-68; pvt. practice Mpls., 1968—. Contbr. articles to profl. jours. V.p. PTA, Wichita, 1957-64, tchr. Unitarian Ch., Wichita, 1959-64;. Mem. Am. Speech-Lang. Hearing Assn., Kans. Speech-Lang. Hearing Assn. (v.p., bd. dirs., treas.). Unitarian Universalist. Home and Office: 3145 Dean Ct # 903 Minneapolis MN 55416-4390

SMEAL, CAROLYN A., community health nurse, educator; b. Guilford, N.Y., Jan. 30, 1930; d. Charles C. and Margaret C. (Wilson) Bloom; m. William C. Smeal, May 28, 1949; children: Dale, Sandra Smeal Barlow, Stacey (dec.), William M. Diploma, Millard Fillmore Hosp., Buffalo, 1950; BS, SUNY, Buffalo, 1967. Cert. community health nurse, sch. nurse-tchr. Staff nurse in oper. rm., emergency rm. Niagara Falls (N.Y.) Meml. Med. Ctr.; staff nurse Niagara Falls Air Base; sch. nurse tchr. Bd. Edn., Niagara Falls; community health nurse Niagara County Health Dept., Niagara Falls; retired, 1995. Bd. dirs. Ctr. for Young Parents, Cerebral Palsy Recreation Group. Mem. Assn. for Retarded Children (bd. dirs., past pres.). Home: 710 Chilton Ave Niagara Falls NY 14301-1008

SMEAL, JANIS LEA, operating room nurse, health facility administrator; b. Johnstown, Pa., Aug. 31, 1953; d. Charles Truman S. and Clara Belle (Smeal) Satterlee. RN, Mercy Hosp. Sch. Nursing, 1974; BS summa cum laude, U. Houston, 1996. ACLS, 1982; CNOR, 1988. Staff, relief chage nurse emergency room Mercy Hosp., Altoona, Pa., 1974-85; staff nurse operating room McAllen (Tex.) Med. Ctr., 1985-87, Rio Grande Regional Hosp., McAllen, Tex., 1987-88; co-owner Associated Hypnotherapy and Pain Mgmt. Svcs. Tex., Bellaire, 1991—; staff nurse operating room Meml. City Hosp., Houston, 1992—; co-owner, cons. J.L. Med. Svcs., McAllen, Tex., 1988-94. Recognition Golden Key Nat. Honor Soc., 1993, Phi Kappa Phi, 1994, Natural Sci. and Math. Scholars and Fellows, 1995. Mem. AORN, NOW, Golden Key, Phi Kappa Phi. Office: Assoc Hypnotherapy/ Pain Svc Ste 333 6300 W Loop So Bellaire TX 77401

SMEDLEY, ELIZABETH, researcher, codifier, consultant, historian, writer; b. Phila., Jan. 5, 1915; d. Elwood Quimby and Hazel deRemer (Ward) S. BA cum laude, Bryn Mawr Coll., 1936. Editor, rechr., writer Hist. Records Survey, Phila., 1939-43; rechr., writer U.S. Army Chief of Ordnance, Phila., 1943-45; local govt. specialist Bur. Mcpl. Affairs, Harrisburg, Pa., 1945-51; local govt. codifier, writer Penns Valley Pubs., State College, Pa., 1951-75; rschr., writer Pa. State Assn. Boroughs, Harrisburg, 1975-82; dir. codification, co-owner Century IV Codes, Inc., Hershey, Pa., 1982-95; owner, rechr. Century IV Codes, Inc., Hummelstown, Pa., 1995—; cons., writer Pa. State Assn. Boroughs, Harrisburg, 1962-65, Pa. Dept. Transp., Harrisburg, 1979-81. Author: Zion's Path of History, 1987, 1936: A 50 Year Perspective, 1986. Chmn. State College Govt. Study Commn., 1971-73. Mem. DAR, Daus. Am. Colonists. Republican. LDS. Home and Office: 54 Ridgeview Rd Hummelstown PA 17036-9721

SMETANA, E. BETH SEIDMAN, consulting company executive; m. Gerard C. Smetana; children—Susannah, Frederick. Student L'Institut des Etudes Politiques, Paris; B.A., Sarah Lawrence Coll.; M.S. in Journalism, Northwestern U.; postgrad. Loyola U., Chgo. C.P.A., Ill. Reporter, copy editor Hollister Publs., Wilmette, Ill., 1966-68; asst. editor The Trib, Chgo. Tribune, 1965-66; staff acct. Arthur Young & Co., Chgo., 1978-80; cash mgr. Electrographic Corp., Chgo., 1980-81; dir. employee benefits and risk mgmt. A.T. Kearney, Inc., Chgo., 1981—. Rep. for Sarah Lawrence Coll., Coll. Bd. of Chgo., 1972-75; mem. alumni bd. Francis W. Parker Sch., Chgo., 1973—. Mem. Am. Inst. C.P.A.s, Ill. Soc. C.P.A.s, Women in Communications, Alliance Francaise, Beta Alpha Psi. Clubs: Chgo. Press, River, Casino. Office: AT Kearney Inc 222 W Adams St Chicago IL 60606

SMIACH, DEBORAH, accountant, educator, consultant; b. Johnstown, Pa., Mar. 10, 1960; d. Frank Raymond and Pearl Lillian (Rudeck) S. BA in Acctg., U. Pitts., Johnstown, 1982; MBA, Katz Grad. Sch. Bus., Pitts., 1989, M of Info. Systems, 1991. CPA Pa., CGFM Va. Staff acct. C.E. Wessel & Co., Johnstown, Pa., 1982-84; sr. acct. Sickler, Reilly & Co., Altoona, Pa., 1984-86; assoc. prof. acctg. U. Pitts., Johnstown, 1986—, chmn. dept. bus., 1995—; cons. Cambria-Somerset Coun. for Health Profls., Johnstown, 1986—; internal inspector Walter Hopkins & Co., Clearfield, Pa., 1995, Wessel & Co., Johnstown, 1992—. Mem. bd. dirs. Bottleworks Ethnic Arts Ctr., Johnstown, Pa., 1993—, Am. Red Cross-Keystone chpt., 1995—, coun. mem. Our Lady of Mount Carmel, South Fork, Pa., 1993-95. Mem. AICPA, Pa. Inst. Cert. Pub. Accts., Pa. Bus. and Profl. Women (dist. 5 chair public relations com. 1993-95, chair woman of the yr. com. 1995-96), Johnstown Bus. and Profl. Women (pres., pres-elect, v.p., treas.). Democrat. Roman Catholic. Office: U Pitts Johnstown 104 Krebs Hall Johnstown PA 15904

SMILEY, CINDY YORK, psychotherapist educator; b. Pasadena, Tex., Oct. 6, 1956; d. Clem T. and Sharon G. (Mead) York; m. Richard E. Smiley, June 7, 1975 (div. Apr. 1989); 1 child, Matthew J.; Lee Allen Moore, Jr., May 22, 1993. AA in Bus. Adminstrn., San Jacinto Coll., 1986; BS in Psychology, U. Houston-Clear Lake, 1988, MA in Clin. Psychology, 1993. Lic. profl. counselor; cert. group therapist, mediator. Proprietor Custom Tinting, Pasadena, Tex., 1980-92; co-developer, founder Innovative Alternatives, Houston, 1986-92; coord., exptl. therapy Intracare Hosp., Houston, 1993-94, case mgr., therapist children and adult svcs., 1994-95; pvt. practitioner psychotherapy Cindy Y. Smiley, M.A., LPC, Houston, 1994—; dir. mediation and sexual abuse tng. programs Innovative Alternatives, Houston, 1995—; adj. prof. mediation U. Houston-Clear Lake, Houston, 1991-92; trainer, conflict resolution Innovative Alternatives, Houston, 1988—. Spkr., presenter for workshops and seminars, Houston, 1989—. Named to Nat. Dean's List, 1988. Mem. Am. Counseling Assn., Am. Assn. Specialist GroupWork, U.S. Assn. Victim/Offender Mediation. Home: 604 Yorkshire Pasadena TX 77503 Office: Innovative Alternatives 18301-A Egret Bay Houston TX 77058

SMILEY, JANE GRAVES, author, educator; b. L.A., Sept. 26, 1949; d. James La Verne and Frances Nuelle (Graves) S.; m. John Whiston, Sept. 4, 1970 (div.); m. William Silag, May 1, 1978 (div.); children: Phoebe Silag, Lucy Silag; m. Stephen Mark Mortensen, July 25, 1987; 1 child, Axel James Mortensen. BA, Vassar Coll., 1971; MFA, U. Iowa, 1976, MA, 1978, PhD, 1978. Asst. prof. Iowa State U., Ames, 1981-84, assoc. prof., 1984-89, prof., 1989-90, Disting. prof., 1992—; vis. asst. prof. U. Iowa, Iowa City, 1981, 87. Author: (fiction) Barn Blind, 1980, At Paradise Gate, 1981 (Friends of American Writers prize 1981), Duplicate Keys, 1984, The Age of Grief, 1987 (Nat. Book Critics Circle award nomination 1987), The Greenlanders, 1988, Ordinary Love and Goodwill, 1989, A Thousand Acres, 1991 (Pulitzer Prize for fiction 1992, Nat. Book Critics Cirle award 1992, Midland Authors award 1992, Amb. award 1992, Heartland prize 1992), Moo: A Novel, 1995; (non-fiction) Catskill Crafts: Artisans of the Catskill Mountains, 1987. Grantee Fulbright U.S. Govt., Iceland, 1976-77, NEA, 1978, 87; recipient O. Henry award, 1982, 85, 88. Mem. Author's Guild, Screenwriters Guild. Office: Iowa State U Dept English 201 Ross Ames IA 50011-1401*

SMILEY, JANICE MARIE, special education educator; b. Little Rock, Jan. 3, 1965; d. Thomas Thornton and Mary Charlene (Holt) George; m. Henry Thomas Smiley, June 4, 1988; 1 child, Matthew Thomas. BS in Edn., U. Ctrl. Ark., 1988, MS in Edn., 1990. Cert. tchr. spl. edn. Resource tchr. Enola (Ark.) Elem. Sch., 1988-89, Guy (Ark.)-Perkins Elem. Sch., 1989-96, Carl Stuart Middle Sch., Conway, Ark., 1996—. Bd. dirs. Arkansans for Drug Free Youth Faulkner County chpt., 1992-94, sec., 1993-94; orgnl. steering ocm. Habitat for Humanity Internat., Conway. Democrat. Baptist. Home: 2230 Remington Rd Conway AR 72032-2303 Office: Carl Stuart Middle Sch 2745 Carl Stuart Rd Conway AR 72032

SMILEY, LINDA CASE, financial planner; b. Harrisburg, Pa., Sept. 10, 1958; d. Paul Willis and Olive Blanche Case; m. Edward Barton Smiley, Oct. 20, 1984; children: Danielle Elizabeth, Michelle Lynn, Noelle Elise. Student, Albright Coll., 1975-76; AA, Harrisburg (Pa.) Area C.C., 1982; BS, Elizabethtown Coll., 1989; postgrad., Lebanon Valley Coll., 1993—. CFP. Clk. Pa. Pub. Utility Commn., Harrisburg, 1977-81; nuclear chemistry tech. GPU Nuclear Corp., Middletown, Pa., 1981-89; registered rep. John Hancock, Boston, 1989-90; dist. rep. Luth. Brotherhood, Mpls., 1990-95; fin. planner Nationwide Ins. Co., Lebanon, Pa., 1996—. Mem. AAUW, Nat. Assn. Life Underwriters, Million Dollar Round Table. Republican. Lutheran. Home: 276 Kokomo Ave Hummelstown PA 17036-1118 Office: Nationwide Ins Co Lebanon PA 17042

SMILEY, MARILYNN JEAN, musicologist; b. Columbia City, Ind., June 5, 1932; d. Orla Raymond and Mary Jane (Bailey) S. BS (State scholar), Ball State U., 1954; MusM, Northwestern U., 1958; cert., Ecoles d'Art Americaines, Fontainebleau, France, 1959; Ph.D. (Grad. scholar, Delta Kampa Gamma scholar), U. Ill., 1970. Public sch. music tchr. Logansport, Ind., 1954-61; faculty music dept. SUNY-Oswego, 1961—, Disting. Teaching prof., 1974—, chmn. dept., 1976-81; presenter papers at confs. Contbr. articles to profl. jours. Bd. dirs. Oswego Opera Theatre, 1978—, Oswego Orch. Soc., 1978—, Penfield Libr. Assocs., 1985—. SUNY Research Found. fellow, summers 1971, 72, 74. Mem. AAUW (br. coun. rep. dist. III, N.Y. State div. 1986-88, br. coun. coord. N.Y. State div. 1988-90, pres. Oswego br. 1984-86, N.Y. divsn. area interest rep. cultural interests 1990-92, grantee 1984, N.Y. divsn. diversity dir. 1993—), NEH (rsch. grantee 1990-91), Am. Musicological Soc. (chmn. N.Y. chpt. 1975-77, chpt. rep. to AMS Coun. 1993—, bd. dirs. N.Y. State-St. Lawrence chpt. 1993—), Medieval Acad. Am., Music Libr. Assn., Coll. Music Soc., Renaissance Soc. Am., Sonneck Soc. Am., Oswego County Hist. Soc., Heritage Found. of Oswego, Delta Kappa Gamma, Phi Delta Kappa, Delta Phi Alpha, Pi Kappa Lambda, Sigma Alpha Iota, Sigma Tau Delta, Kappa Delta Pi. Methodist. Office: SUNY Dept Music Oswego NY 13126

SMITH, ABBIE OLIVER, college administrator, educator; b. Augusta, Ga., Jan. 31, 1931; d. Rowland Sheppard and Abigail Seabrook (Hanahan) Oliver; m. William Parkhurst Smith, Jr., July 2, 1953; children: William Parkhurst Smith, III, Oliver Hamilton. BS, George Washington U., 1953, MEd, 1958, EdDin Higher Edn., 1986. Tchr. St. Mary's Acad., Monroe, Mich., 1954-55; tchr., coach Washington-Lee H.S., Arlington, Va., 1955-58; homemaker, cmty. vol. Bethesda, Md., 1959-64; asst. professorial lectr. George Washington U., Washington, 1965-69, adminstr. continuing edn., 1969-80, asst. dean, dir., 1981-89, acting dean divsn. continuing edn., 1989-93, asst. v.p., asst. to dean institutional advancement, 1993—; panelist t.v. series WETA, Washington; newsletter editor Tng. Officers Conf., 1989—, chair charter expansion 1992—. co-author: (workbook) Developing New Horizons for Women, 1975, Manual for Counselors for Developing New Horizons for Women, 1975. Mem. adv. bd. Washington Bd. Trade, 1975-77, women's branch adv. bd. State Nat. Bank, Bethesda, Md., 1978-81; collegiate adv. bd. Episcopal Diocese of Washington, 1977-79. Recipient Leadership in Adult Edn. award, 1976, GW award for outstanding contbn. to univ. life Office of GW Pres., 1991, Washington Women of Achievement, Washington Edn. TV Assn., 1980. Mem. Nat. U. Continuing Edn. Assn. (awards chair divsn. women's edn. 1977-78, nat. chair 1977-78, chair-elect divsn. part-time students program 1984-86, nat. chair 1984-86, chair coun. human resources 1985-86, nat. spl. com. on couns. and divsn. 1984-86, nat. exec. bd. 1984-86, nat. bd. dirs. 1984-98, nat. charters and bylaws coms. 1987-89, sec.-elect divsn. cert. and nontraditional degree programs 1987-89, chair-elect 1989-90, nat. chair 1990-91, nat. ann. planning coms. 1987, 92, sec. region II 1989-90, chair-elect, ann. conf. chair, single host instn. ann. conf. region II 1990-91, chair region II 1991-92, awards com. chair 1992, Walton S. Bittner Svc. Citation 1994, hon. mention for program catalog nat. divsn. mktg. 1988), Phi Delta Kappa Internat. (G.W. chpt., v.p. for programs 1995-96, pres. 1996-97). Democrat. Episcopalian. Home: 3751 Jocelyn St NW Washington DC 20015 Office: George Washington U 2134 G St NW Washington DC 20052

SMITH, ADA L., state legislator; b. Amherst County, Va.; d. Thomas and Lillian Smith. Grad., CUNY. Dep. clk. N.Y.C.; state senator N.Y. Legislature, Albany, 1988—; mem. various coms. N.Y. Legislature, ranking corp. commn. and authorities, 1994, minority whip; mem. Senate Dem. Task Force Women's Issues, Senate Dem. Task Force Financing Affordable Housing, Senate Dem. Task Force Child Care 2000, Sen. Dem. Task Force Affirmative Action and Econ. Devel., Senate Dem. Task Force Primary Health Care, Senate Minority Puerto Rican and Hispanic Task Force; chair Senate Minority Task Force on Privatization of Kennedy and Laguardia Airports. Trustee, life dir. Coll. Fund Baruch Coll. Recipient Outstanding Alumni award Baruch Coll. Mem. African Am. Clergy and Elected Ofcls., Inc. (treas.), N.Y. Assn. of State Black and Puerto Rican Legislators (vice chair), Baruch Coll. Alumni Assn. (pres., Disting. Svc. award, Outstanding Achievement award). Office: NY State Senate Rm 304 Legis Office Bldg Albany NY 12247 also: Queens Dist Office 116-43 Sutphin Blvd Jamaica NY 11434

SMITH, AGNES MONROE, history educator; b. Hiram, Ohio, Aug. 8, 1920; d. Bernie Alfred and Joyce (Messenger) Monroe; m. Stanley Blair Smith; children: David, Doris, Darl, Diane. BA, Hiram Coll., 1940; MA, W.Va. U., 1945; PhD, Western Res. U., 1966. Social sci. tchr. Freedom (Ohio) High Sch., 1940-44; instr. of history W.Va. U., Morgantown, 1945; instr. of social sci. Hiram Coll., 1946; inst. history and social sci. Youngstown (Ohio) State U., 1964-66, asst. prof. to prof. of history, 1966-84, prof. history emeritus, 1984—; vis. prof. history Hiram Coll., 1988-90. Co-editor: Bourgeois, San Culottes and Other Frenchmen, 1981; contbr. articles to profl. jours. Mem. Ohio Acad. History, Delta Kappa Gamma, Phi Alpha Theta, Pi Gamma Mu. Mem. Christian Ch. (Disciples of Christ). Home; 16759 Main Market Rd West Farmington OH 44491-9608

SMITH, ALICE MARIE, secondary school mathematics educator; b. Hagerstown, Md., June 2, 1969; d. Glenn Curtis and Martha Sue (Nofsinger) S. BA, Western Md. Coll., 1991, M in Adminstrn., 1993, cert. in Adminstrn., 1994. Math. tchr. Francis Scott Key H.S. Carroll County Bd. Edn., Union Bridge, Md., 1991—; freshmen basketball coach Francis Scott Key H.S., Union Bridge, 1992-93, jr. varsity, 1993-94, varsity, 1994—, jr. varsity volleyball, 1993—. Named Coach of Yr., Balt. Sun, 1995-96. Mem. ASCD, Nat. Coun. Tchrs. of Math., Md. State Tchrs. Assn., Carroll County Tchrs. Assn. Democrat. Roman Catholic. Home: 1106 Singer Dr Westminster MD 21157-5840 Office: Francis Scott Key HS Bark Hill Rd Union Bridge MD 21791

SMITH, ALICE MURRAY, civic worker, mathematician; b. Buffalo, Apr. 23, 1930; d. Robert Leslie and Alice Emma (Bennett) Murray; m. Robert Crellin Smith, Feb. 21, 1953 (div. 1988); children: William Stewart, Peter Crellin, Edward Bennett. AB, Smith Coll., 1951. Mathematician U.S. Govt., Las Cruces, N.Mex., 1951-52. Contbr. articles to profl. jours. Pres. Phoenix Rep. Women, 1967, Arizonans for Nat. Security, Phoenix, 1983-87, 89-91, Ariz. Coordinating Coun. Rep. Women, 1991-93; mem. Ariz. Rep. Com., 1992—; mem. curriculum com. All Saints Day Sch., Phoenix, 1968-71. Republican.

SMITH, ALMA DAVIS, elementary education educator; b. Washington, June 27, 1951; d. Wyatt Deeble and Martha Elizabeth (Lingenfelter) Davis; m. Perry James Smith, Jan. 1, 1979; children: Lauren, Hunter. BS, James Madison U., 1973; MEd, U. Va., 1978. Cert. elem. tchr. and prin., Va. Tchr. Robert E. Lee Elem. Sch., Spotsylvania, Va., 1973-79, Conehurst Elem. Sch., Salem, Va., 1979, Hopkins Rd. Elem. Sch., Richmond, Va., 1980-87; tchr. Reams Rd. Elem. Sch., Richmond, Va., 1987-95, asst. prin. summer sch., 1990; tchr. Crestwood Elem. Sch., Richmond, Va., 1995—. Bd. mem. PTA, 1994-95, life mem., 1995. Mem. NEA, Spotsylvania Edn. Assn. (numerous chair positions), Chesterfield Edn. Assn. Home: 2811 Ellesmere Dr Midlothian VA 23113-3800

SMITH, ANN MARIE, rehabilitation nurse; b. Columbus, Ohio, Sept. 23, 1965; d. Jerome Spangler and Josephine Anna (Wizemann) S.; m. Stephen

Kenneth Smith, Oct. 22, 1988. BS, Ohio State U., 1987, MS, 1988, PhD, 1995. RN, Ohio; CRRN. Staff nurse, weekend supr. Columbus Quality Care Nursing Ctr., 1987-88; staff nurse head injury rehab. Ohio State U. Med. Ctr., Columbus, 1988-95; patient care resource mgr. Ohio State U, Med. Ctr., 1995—; presenter in field. Contbr. articles to profl. publs., chpt. to book. Recipient Staff Nurse award Health South Corp., 1994, Malcom Maloof scholar 1995 nurse in Washington Internship, Mid Ohio Dist. Nursing Scholarship, 1995. Mem. ANA, Ohio Nurses Assn., Ohio Head Injury Found., Assn. Rehab. Nurses (founding bd. Ctrl. Ohio chpt., pres. 1993-94), Mortar Bd., Sigma Theta Tau. Home: 3356 Timber Oak Dr Columbus OH 43204-4100

SMITH, ANN MONTGOMERY, librarian, educator; b. Denver, Jan. 18, 1941; d. Kenneth Peyton and Jane Jewell (Williams) Montgomery; m. Whitney Smith Jr., Sept. 9, 1962 (div. 1976); children: Adrian, Austin. BA in Romance Langs. and Lit., Radcliffe Coll., 1963; MLS, Simmons Coll., 1969; MA in Edn., U. Conn., 1994. Reference libr. Winchester (Mass.) Pub. Libr., 1969-76, Nat. Ctr. for Assessment and Dissemination of Bilingual Edn., Cambridge, Mass., 1976-79; cons. for svcs. to physically handicapped Mass. Bd. Libr. Commrs., Boston, 1980-83; dir. librs., curator spl. collections Wentworth Inst. Tech., Boston, 1983-95; interpreter/guide U.S. State Dept., Washington, 1993, 94; pres., mem. Fenway Librs. Online, Boston, 1984-95; acad. specialist USIA Projects, Chile and Peru, 1994; library dir. New Britain (Conn.) Pub. Libr., 1995—. Contbr. articles to Bilingual Jour. Mem., pres. Oficina Hispana de la Communidad, Boston, 1986-95, Spanish Speaking Ctr., New Britain, 1996—; mem. Town Meeting, Winchester. ALA Libr. fellow, Peru, 1992. Mem. ALA, Am. Soc. for Engring. Edn. (chair awards com. 1986-89, historian 1984-95). Office: New Britain Pub Libr 20 High St New Britain CT 06051-2206

SMITH, ANNA DEAVERE, actress, playwright; b. Balt., Sept. 18, 1950; d. Deavere Young and Anna (Young) S. BA, Beaver Coll., Pa., 1971, hon. doctorate; MFA, Am. Conservatory Theatre, 1976; hon. doctorate, U. N.C. Ann O'Day Maples prof. arts and drama Stanford U. Playwright, performer one-woman shows On the Road: A Search for American Character, 1983, Aye, Aye, Aye, I'm Integrated, 1984, Piano, 1991 (Drama-Logue award), Fires in the Mirros, 1992 (Obie award 1992, Drama Desk award 1992), Twilight: Los Angeles 1992 (Obie award, 2 Tony award nominations, Drama Critics Cir. spl. citation, Outer Critics Cir. award, Drama Desk award, Audelco award, Beverly Hills, Hollywood NAACP theatre awards); writer libretto for Judith Jamison, performer Hymn, 1993; other appearances include (state) Horatio, 1974, Alma, the Ghost of Spring Street, 1975, Mother Courage, 1980, Tartuffe, 1983, (TV) All My Children, 1983, (films) Soup for One, 1982, Dave, 1993, Philadelphia, 1993, The American President, 1995. Named One of Women of Yr., Glamour mag., 1993; fellow Bunting Inst., Radcliffe Coll. Office: 1676 Dolores St San Francisco CA 94110 also: Stanford Univ Dept of Drama Memorial Hall Stanford CA 94305

SMITH, ANNE BOWMAN, academic administrator, editor; b. Craigsville, Va., Dec. 17, 1934; d. Joseph Benjamin and Louise Frances (Smith) Bowman; m. William Jerry Smith, June 29, 1957; children: Stacey Anne, Joan Elizabeth. Student, Madison Coll., 1951-54, Old Dominion U., 1979-82; BA, Cath. U. Am. Reporter The Richmond (Va.) Times-Dispatch, 1955-56, The Miami (Fla.) Herald, 1965-68, 70-72, The Virginian-Pilot, Norfolk, 1968-70, 72-78; Portsmouth-Chesapeake city editor The Virginian-Pilot, 1978, govt. editor, 1978-80, asst. met. editor, 1980-82; dir. pub. info. Cath. U. Am., Washington, 1982-84, exec. dir. pub. affairs, 1984—; editor in chief Cath. U. Am. mag., 1989—; lectr. journalism, pub. rels. Cath. U. Am., Washington, 1988-92. Editor: Century Ended, Century Begun, 1990. Bd. dirs. Summer Opera Theatre Co., Washington, 1990—. Recipient numerous awards including Va. Press Assn., Va. Press Women, Nat. Fedn. Press Women, Cath. Press Assn. Mem. Soc. Profl. Journalists, Cath. Press Assn., Coun. Advancement and Support of Edn., Assn. Am. Univs., Coll. News Assn. Office: Cath U Am Washington DC 20064

SMITH, ANNICK, writer, producer; b. Paris, May 11, 1936; d. Stephen and Helene Deutsch; m. David James Smith (dec. 1974); children: Eric, Stephen, Alex, Andrew. Student, Cornell Univ., 1954-55, U. Chgo., 1955-57; BA, U. Wash., 1961. freelance filmmaker, producer, arts administrator, writer, Mont., 1974—; devel. dir. Hellgate Writers, Inc., 1985-93; past H.S. tchr., cmty. organizer, environ. worker. Exec. prodr. Heartland, 1981; co-prodr. A River Runs Through It, 1992; co-editor: (with William Kittredge) The Last Best Place; author: Homestead, 1994; contbr. to anthologies including Best Am. Short Stories, 1992. Recipient Western Heritage award Cowboy Hall of Fame, 1981; Mont. Humanites award Mont. Com. for Humanities, 1988. Mem. Trout Unlimited, Blackfoot Challenge. Democrat. Office: Box 173 Star Route Bonner MT 59823*

SMITH, ARIANE, playwright; b. Hunterdon, N.J., Aug. 9, 1963; d. Felix and Elisabeth (Carroll) S. BS in Theatre and Dance, Skidmore Coll., 1983. Performer, writer Avignon (France) Theatre Festival, 1987; repertory performer Chanticleer Theatre, London, 1988, Ho. of Candles Theatre, N.Y.C., 1989; performer, producer Toon Theatre, N.Y.C., 1991-94; owner Ariane's Animal Krakers, N.Y.C., 1986—. Performer Phantom of the Opera, 1990; performer, producer The Laughing Gargoyles, N.Y.C., 1991-92; author: (plays) Venus of Willendorf "Part I" The Venus Cycle, 1995, Venus at LEspugue "Part II", 1996 Venus in Tanabata "Part III", 1997. Emerging Artist grantee The Field, N.Y.C., 1993. Home and Office: 27 Commerce St New York NY 10014

SMITH, BARBARA ANN, elementary education educator; b. Peoria, Ill., Dec. 21, 1933; d. Gerald Clyde and Kathryn Jane Smith. BS, Taylor U., Ft. Wayne, Ind., 1959; MS, St. Francis Coll., Ft. Wayne, 1967. Tchr. freshman phys. edn. Taylor U., 1957-58; tchr. James H. Smart Sch., Ft. Wayne, 1959-67, Southwick Elem. Sch., Ft. Wayne, 1967-95, Meadowbrook Elem., 1995—; chair Young Authors, Ft. Wayne, 1990-92; chair Coalition of Essential Schs., Ft. Wayne, 1992-94; mem. coun. Region 8 Dept. Edn., Ind., 1992-94; chairperson Performance Based Assessment Climate Com., 1992-94; facilitator Ind. 2000, 1993-95; chair Parent/Staff Adv. Coun., Ft. Wayne, 1994-95; title I Home/Sch. Coord., 1995. Campaign worker Rick Hawks for Congress, Ft. Wayne, 1990. Recipient various teaching awards. Mem. NEA, Ind. Profls., Internat. Reading Assn. (sec. 1993-94, Fort Wayne chpt. Elem. Tchr. of Yr. 1993), East Allen Tchrs., Ind. State Tchrs. Assn. Republican. Home: 2803 Cherokee Run New Haven IN 46774-2917

SMITH, BARBARA ANNE, healthcare management company consultant; b. N.Y.C., Oct. 10, 1941; d. John Allen and Lelia Maria (De Silva) Santoro; m. Joseph Newton Smith, Feb. 5, 1961 (div. Sept. 1984); children: J. Michael, Robert Lawrence. Student, Oceanside/Carlsbad Coll. Real estate agt. Routh Robbins, Inc., Washington, 1973-75; gen. mgr. Mall Shops, Inc., Kansas City, Kans., 1975-80; regional mgr. FAO Schwarz, N.Y.C., 1980-84; clin. adminstr. North Denver Med. Ctr., Thornton, Colo., 1984-88; adminstrv. dir. Country Side Ambulatory Surgery Ctr., Leesburg, Va., 1989-91; pres. SCS Healthcare Mgmt. Inc., Washington, 1991—; bd. dirs. Franz Carl Weber Internat., Geneva, 1982-84. Pres. Am. Women Chile, 1968; v.p. Oak Park Assn., Kansas City, 1977-78, pres., 1978-79; vol. Visitor Info. and Assn. Reception Ctr. program Smithsonian Instn., Washington. Mem. NAFE, Network Colo., Profl. Bus. Women Assn., Med. Group Mgmt. Assn., Federated Ambulatory Surgery Assn.

SMITH, BARBARA BARNARD, music educator; b. Ventura, Calif., June 10, 1920; d. Fred W. and Grace (Hobson) S. B.A., Pomona Coll., 1942; Mus.M., U. Rochester, 1943, performer's cert., 1944. Mem. faculty piano and theory Eastman Sch. Music, U. Rochester, 1943-49; mem. faculty U. Hawaii, Honolulu, 1949—; assoc. prof. music U. Hawaii, 1953-62, prof., 1962-82, prof. emeritus, 1982—; sr. fellow East-West Center, 1973; lectr., recitals in Hawaiian and Asian music, U.S., Europe and Asia, 1956—; field researcher Asia, 1956, 60, 66, 71, 80, Micronesia, 1963, 70, 87, 88, 90, 91, Solomon Islands, 1976. Author publs. on ethnomusicology. Mem. Internat. Soc. Music Edn., Internat. Musicol. Soc., Am. Musicol. Soc., Soc. Ethnomusicology, Internat. Coun. for Traditional Music, Asia Soc., Am. Mus. Instrument Soc., Coll. Music Soc., Soc. for Asian Music, Music Educators Nat. Conf., Pacific Sci. Assn., Assn. for Chinese Music Rsch., Phi Beta Kappa, Mu Phi Epsilon. Home: 581 Kamoku St Apt 2004 Honolulu HI 96826-5210

SMITH, BARBARA JEAN, marketing director; b. Palmer, Nebr., July 19, 1948; d. Alphonse E. and Helen (Dubas) Kozak; m. James Smith, Nov. 11, 1967; children: Ken, Allen, Shane, Mark. Student, Platte Coll., 1981. Owner Smith & Wigington Market, Columbus, Nebr., 1983-85; mgr. 1st Cable Advt., Columbus, 1985-89, Columbus TV Advt., 1989—; nurse, phys. therapist, 1973-83, presch. tchr., 1976—. Mem. Big Pal Little Pal; bd. dirs. local ch. Mem. Optimist Internat. (pres. local club 1992-93, bd. dirs.), Altar Soc., Toastmasters (sec.), Extenstion Club. Democrat. Roman Catholic. Home and Office: 309 Colombo Calle Columbus NE 68601

SMITH, BARBARA JEAN, real estate broker; b. Miami, Fla., Aug. 13, 1950; d. Hyman and Rose (Braun) Katz; m. David Thomas Smith, Mar. 15, 1975; children: Lindsey Rose, Wesley Harris. BA in Tchg., U. Fla., 1972; MEd in Guidance and Counseling, U. Miami, 1974. Registered real estate broker, Fla. Prof. U. Marietta, Ga., 1975-80; psychologist Cmty. Mental Health Ctr., Rome, Ga., 1980-85; pvt. practice psychology Rome, 1980-85; broker assoc. Smith and Assocs. Investment Co., Realtors, Tampa, Fla., 1985—; real estate instr. Greater Tampa Assn. Realtors, 1985—. Vol. Children's Aux., Tampa., 1980; gardener Stoney Point Garden Club, Tampa, 1982; mem. booster club St. Mary's Episcopal Day Sch. PTA, Tampa, 1984—; mem. booster club, and PTA, Plant H.S., Tampa, 1993—. Recipient Sales Achievement award Riverhills Arvida Cmty., 1993. Mem. Nat. Assn. Realtors, Fla. Assn. Realtors. Republican. Methodist. Home: 4808 W Estrella St Tampa FL 33629 Office: Smith and Assocs 3801 Bay to Bay Blvd Tampa FL 33629

SMITH, BARBARA LYNN, clinical psychologist, nurse; b. St. Louis, Oct. 12, 1953; d. Martin Ralph Smith and Louise Smith Wall; m. Dejan Jadric, Dec. 9, 1994. AB in Psychology, U. Calif., Berkeley, 1977; BSN, St. Louis U., 1979; PhD in Clin. Psychology, Washington U., St. Louis, 1993. RN, Mo. RN emergency dept. Washington U. Med. Ctr., St. Louis, 1981-83; field officer ICRC, Aranyaprathet, Thailand, 1981; pub. health nurse Internat. Res. Com., Malaysia, 1979, Somalia, 1983, Sudan, 1984-85; country dir. Internat. Res. Com., Lilongwe, Malawi, 1987-88; emergency coord. Internat. Res. Com., N.Y.C., 1992-93; mental health program dir. Internat. Res. Com., Sarajevo, Bosnia-Herzegovina, 1993-94; dir. health programs Internat. Res. Com., N.Y.C., 1994-96, v.p. overseas programs, 1996—; Bd. dirs. Women's Commn. for Refugee Women and Children, N.Y.C.; expert mem., advisor UN Crime Br., Vienna, Austria, 1995. Author: International Responses to Traumatic Stress, 1995, Public Health and War, 1996. Recipient Outstanding Svc. award Am. Nat. Red Cross, 1981, Heart of Gold award ANA, 1985. Office: Internat Rescue Com 122 E 42nd St New York NY 10036

SMITH, BARBARA MARTIN, art educator; b. St. Louis, Feb. 3, 1945; d. Charles Landon and Mary Louise (Nolker) Martin; m. Timothy Van Gorder Smith, Nov. 27, 1976; children: Brian Eliot, Marjorie Van Gorder. BA, Lawrence U., 1967; MFA, So. Ill. U., 1975. Cert. tchr., Mo. Art instr. Horton Watkins High Sch., Ladue, Mo., 1968-76; leader Experiment in Internat. Living, Brattleboro, Vt., 1974; art tchr. Michigan City (Ind.) Ctr. for the Arts, 1979-80, Cleve. Mus. of Art, 1981-83; art instr. Villa Duchesne, St. Louis, 1986—; edn. dir. Dunes Art Found., Michigan City, 1979; co-chmn. Internat. Wives Group, Cleve. Coun. on World Affairs, 1982-84; bd. dirs. Webster Groves (Mo.) Sch. Found., 1992. Exhibited in shows at Art Inst. of Chgo., 1979, So. Ill. U. Alumnae Exhibit, 1982, Focus Fiber, Cleve. Mus. of Art, 1982, Nova, Wearable Art, Kuban Gallery, Cleve., 1983, Drawings & Prints, St. Louis Artist's Guild, 1986. Recipient Grad. Fellowship Ann. Grad. award So. Ill. U., 1975; named Artist in Residence/ Artist in Schs. Ind. Arts Commn./NEA, 1978-79; named to Honors Seminar for Advancement of Art Edn., R.I. Sch. of Design, 1988, Mem. Art Edn. Delegation to Japan, 1992. Mem. Nat. Art Edn. Assn., Internat. Soc. for Edn. through Art, St. Louis Art Mus., St. Louis Artist Guild. Home: 135 Jefferson Rd Webster Grv MO 63119-2934 Office: Villa Duchesne Oak Hill Sch 801 S Spoede Rd Des Peres MO 63131-2606

SMITH, BERT KRUGER, mental health services professional, consultant; b. Wichita Falls, Tex., Nov. 18, 1915; d. Sam and Fania (Feldman) Kruger; m. Sidney Stewart Smith, Jan. 19, 1936; children: Sheldon Stuart, Jared Burt (dec.), Randy Smith Huke. BJ, U. Mo., 1936; MA, U. Tex., 1949; DHL (hon.), U. Mo., 1985. Soc. and entertainment editor Wichita Falls Post, 1936-37; freelance writer Juneau, Alaska, 1937; assoc. pub. Coleman Daily Dem. Voice, 1950-51; assoc. editor Jr. Coll. Jour., Austin, Tex., 1952-55; spl. cons., exec. Hogg Found. for Mental Health, Austin, 1952—; chmn. bd. Austin Groups for the Elderly, 1985—. Author: No Language But A Cry, 1964, Your Non-Learning Child, 1968, A Teaspoon of Honey, 1970, Insights for Uptights, 1970, Aging in America, 1973, The Pursuit of Dignity, 1977, Looking Forward, 1983; contbr. numerous articles to profl. jours. Bert Kruger Smith professorship Sch. Social Work U. Tex., 1982; recipient Disting. Svc. award City of Austin, 1988, Cert. of Appreciation, Tex. Dept. Human Svcs., 1989, Ann Bert Smith award Sr.'s Respite Svc., 1989, S.W. Found. Founders' Spirit award, 1990, Tex. Leadership award Ann. Tex. Joint Conf. on Aging, 1992, Tex. Leadership award Tex. Dept. on Aging, 1992; named to Tex. Women's Hall of Fame, 1988. Mem. Women in Comm. (Lifetime Achievement award 1994), Am. Fedn. for Aging Rsch., Adult Svc. Coun. (bd. dirs. 1970—, Family Elder Care Guardian Angel award 1996), Family Eldercare (bd. dirs. 1979—), Authors Guild, Nat. Assn. Sci. Writers, Hadassah, B'nai B'rith Women, Delta Kappa Gamma (hon). Jewish. Home: 5818 Westslope Dr Austin TX 78731-3633 Office: Hogg Found Mental Health PO Box 7998 Austin TX 78713-7998 also: U Tex Austin Austin TX 78713

SMITH, BETHANY RAE, accountant; b. Middletown, N.Y., Jan. 4, 1972; d. Walter Vincent Poharski and Linda Joy Diffendale Ovitt. BS in Acctg., SUNY, Plattsburgh, 1993. Svc. ctr. assoc. Hannaford Bros., Amsterdam, N.Y., 1988-90; bookkeeper Hannaford Bros., Plattsburgh, N.Y., 1990-93; bookkeeper, asst. office mgr. Hannaford Bros., Troy, N.Y., 1994—; bus. assurance assoc. Coopers & Lybrand L.L.P., 1994—. Recipient N.Y. State Soc. CPAs award, 1993. Democrat. Episcopalian. Home: 459 Summer St #22 Schenectady NY 12306 Office: Coopers & Lybrand LLP 80 State St Albany NY 12207

SMITH, BETTY, writer, nonprofit foundation executive; b. Bonham, Tex., Sept. 16; d. Sim and Gertrude (Dearing) S. Student, Stephens Coll.; BJ, U. Tex. Women's editor Daily Texan; pres. Hope Assocs. Corp., N.Y.C., 1948-50; pres., owner Betty Smith Assocs., N.Y.C., 1950—. Author: A Matter of Heart, 1969. Pres. Melchior Heldentenor Found., N.Y.C., 1987—, Gerda Lissner Found., 1994—; v.p. Herman Lissner Found., 1990—. Mem. Author's Guild. Home: 322 E 55th St New York NY 10022-4157 Office: care Lissner Found 135 E 55th St New York NY 10022-4049

SMITH, BETTY DENNY, county official, administrator, fashion executive; b. Centralia, Ill., Nov. 12, 1932; d. Otto and Ferne Elizabeth (Beier) Hasenfuss; m. Peter S. Smith, Dec. 5, 1964; children: Carla Kip, Bruce Kimball. Student, U. Ill., 1950-52; student, L.A. City Coll., 1953-57, UCLA, 1965, U. San Francisco, 1982-84. Freelance fashion coordinator L.A., N.Y.C., 1953-58; tchr. fashion Rita LeRoy Internat. Studios, 1959-60; mgr. Mo Nadler Fashion, L.A., 1961-64; showroom dir. Jean of Calif. Fashions, L.A., 1965—; freelance polit. book reviewer for community newspapers, 1961-62; staff writer Valley Citizen News, 1963. Bd. dirs. Pet Assistance Found., 1969-76; founder, pres., dir. Vol. Services to Animals L.A., 1972-76; mem. County Com. To Discuss Animals in Rsch., 1973-74; mem. blue ribbon com. on animal control L.A. County, 1973-74; dir. L.A. County Animal Care and Control, 1976-82; mem. Calif. Animal Health Technician Exam. Com., 1975-82, chmn., 1979; bd. dirs. L.A. Soc. for Prevention Cruelty to Animals, 1984-94, Calif. Coun. Companion Animal Advocates, 1993—; dir. West Coast Regional Office, Am. Humane Assn., 1988—; CFO Coalition for Pet Population Control, 1987-92; mem. Calif. Rep. Cen. Com., 1964-72, mem. exec. com., 1971-73; mem. L.A. County Rep. Cen. Com., 1964-70, mem. exec. com., 1966-70; chmn. 29th Congl. Cen. Com., 1969-70; sec. 28th Senatorial Cen. Com., 1967-68, 45th Assembly Dist. Cen. Com., 1965-68; mem. speakers bur. George Murphy for U.S. Senate, 1970; campaign mgr. Los Angeles County for Spencer Williams for Atty. Gen., 1966; mem. adv. com. Moorpark Coll., 1988—; mem. adv. bd. Wishbone Prodn., 1995—. Mem. Internat. Platform Assn., Mannequins Assn. (bd. dirs. 1967-68), Motion Picture and TV Industry Assn. (govt. rels. and pub. affairs com. 1992—), Lawyer's Wives San Gabriel Valley (bd. dirs. 1971-74, pres. 1972-73), L.A. Athletic Club, Town Hall. Home: 1766 Blufffhill Dr Monterey Park CA 91754

SMITH, BETTY ELAINE, geography educator; b. Paterson, N.J., Oct. 28, 1949; d. Robert Francis and Elaine Gertrude (Buchholz) Clough; m. Harrison John Smith, Sept. 6, 1975. BA in Geography, U. Calif., Davis, 1971; MA in Geography, Calif. State U., Chico, 1987; PhD in Geography, SUNY, Buffalo, 1994. Asst. planner City of Sacramento, Calif., 1973-75; real estate broker Sun Realty, Redding, Calif., 1976-88, Medley Realty, Redding, 1976-88; rsch./tchg. asst. SUNY, Buffalo, 1991-94, instr., 1993-94; lectr. U. Wis., Oshkosh, 1994-95; asst. prof. Ea. Ill. U., Charleston, 1995—. Contbr. articles to profl. jours. Mem. Assn. Am. Geographers, Conf. Latinamericanist Geographers, Regional Sci. Assn. Internat., Sigma Xi (assoc.). Office: Ea Ill U Dept Geology and Geography Charleston IL 61920

SMITH, BETTY MALLETT, philosopher, educator; b. Tulsa, Dec. 4, 1924; d. James L. and Eula (Gravitt) Mallett; m. Myron Chawner Smith, Aug. 28, 1948; children: Marston, Shelley, Shonti. BA, William Jewell Coll., 1947; MA, Brown U., 1949. Instr. philosophy Baylor U., Waco, Tex., 1950-51, Santa Monica (Calif). Coll., 1968-69; lectr. philosophy Mt. St. Mary's Coll., L.A., 1963-64, 66-67, Calif. Luth. U., Thousand Oaks, 1969-73; tchr. C.G. Jung Inst., L.A., 1974—; founder, dir. Poiesis, Malibu, Calif., 1966—; lectr. in field. Mem. LWV. Marston scholar Brown U., 1947-48. Mem. AAUW, C.G. Jung Club L.A. Democrat. Quaker.

SMITH, BEVERLY ANN, community health nurse; b. Chgo., Oct. 18, 1950; d. Edmond and Mary Ollie (Dominique) Joseph; m. Paul Ike, May 4, 1974. Diploma in Nursing, Good Samaritan Hosp., 1973; BSN, Xavier U., 1984. RN, Ohio. Staff nurse Univ. Hosp., Cin., 1974—, ambulatory adminstrv. nurse, 1981-82, chairperson ambulatory clin. ladder com., 1986-89, 89-90, 1994-95, chairperson outpatient customer svc. com., 1993—, diabetes resource nurse, 1982—, clin. nurse II, 1984-92, clin. nurse III, 1993-96, clin. nurse III unit 1, 1993—; mem. ambulatory quality improvement com. Univ. Hosp., 1992—. Instr. for smoking cessation classes Black Nurses Assn., Cin., 1991—. Mem. ANA, Southwestern Ohio Nurses Assn. (nominating com. 1992-93), Diabetes Educator, Sigma Theta Tau Internat. Honor Soc. Roman Catholic. Home: 1382 Forester Dr Cincinnati OH 45240-1102 Office: Univ Hosp 234 Goodman St Cincinnati OH 45219-2364

SMITH, BONNIE BEATRICE, corporate communications executive; b. Dayton, Ohio, July 22, 1948; d. Joseph Edward and Phyllis Jean (Shook) S. BS in Journalism, Ohio U., 1970. Accredited bus. communicator. Reporter Piqua (Ohio) Daily Call, 1970-71; asst. dir. pub. rels. Bethesda Hosps., Cin., 1971-76; dir. communication St. Joseph's Hosp., Ft. Wayne, Ind., 1976-81; publs. editor E. Ohio Gas Co., Cleve., 1981-88, coord. customer communications, 1988-90; mgr. employee communication Picker Internat., Inc., Highland Heights, Ohio, 1990-96; mgr. internal comm. Prudential Healthcare, Roseland, N.J., 1996—; speaker, seminar leader various hosps., bus. and profl. orgns., 1975—. Outreach vol. Cleve. Children's Mus., 1986-88, co-chmn. outreach program, mem. speaker's bur., 1988-89, mem. pub. rels. task force, 1989-92. Recipient numerous awards Ohio Hosp. Assn., Ohio Press Women, Acad. Hosp. Pub. Rels., Cin. Editors Assn., also others. Mem. Internat. Assn. Bus. Communicators (dir. mem. svcs. internal communications coun. 1985-88, chmn. directory mktg. coun. 1988-90, dir. examiners accreditation bd. 1986-88), numerous awards 1975—). Home: 1700 E 13th St Apt 22S Cleveland OH 44114-3238 Office: Prudential Healthcare 56 Livingston Ave Roseland NJ 07068-1790

SMITH, BRENDA JOYCE, author, editor, social studies educator; b. Washington, Jan. 2, 1946; d. William Eugene and Marjorie (Williams) Young; m. Duane Milton Smith, Aug. 4, 1978. BA in History and Govt. cum laude, Ohio U., 1968, postgrad. in Am. and European History, 1972. Tchr. Jr. High Sch., Lancaster, Ohio, 1968-69, Reynoldsburg (Ohio) Mid. Sch. and High Sch., 1970-71; grad. teaching asst. Ohio U., Athens, 1969-70, 71-72; polit. speech writer Legis. Reference Bur., Columbus, Ohio, 1972-74; pub. rels. writer Josephinum Coll., Columbus, 1976-78; social studies editor Merrill Pub. Co., Columbus, 1979-91; freelance author/editor social studies Columbus, 1991—. Project editor: Human Heritage: A World History, 1985, 89, World History: The Human Experience, 1992; author: The Collapse of the Soviet Union, 1994, Egypt of the Pharaohs, 1995; writer-editor African Am. history series, 5th grade; writer of 3 Am. history books. Del. 1st U.S.-Russia Joint Conf. on Edn., 1994. Mem. Nat. Coun. Social Studies, Ohio Coun. Social Studies, Freelance Editl. Assn. Office: 3710 Harborough Dr Gahanna OH 43230-4037

SMITH, CAROLE DIANNE, legal editor, writer, product developer; b. Seattle, June 12, 1945; d. Glaude Francis and Elaine Claire (Finkenstein) S.; m. Stephen Bruce Presser, June 18, 1968 (div. June 1987); children: David Carter, Elisabeth Catherine. AB cum laude, Harvard U., Radcliffe Coll., 1968; JD, Georgetown U., 1974. Bar: Pa. 1974. Law clk. to Hon. Judith Jamison Phila., 1974-75; assoc. Gratz, Tate, Spiegel, Ervin & Ruthrouff, Phila., 1975-76; freelance editor, writer Evanston, Ill., 1983-87; editor Ill. Inst. Tech., Chgo., 1987-88; mng. editor LawLetters, Inc., Chgo., 1988-89; editor ABA, Chgo., 1989-95; product devel. dir. Gt. Lakes divsn. Lawyers Coop. Pub., Deerfield, Ill., 1995-96; product devel. mgr. Midwest Market Ctr., Thomson Legal Pub. (formerly Lawyers Coop. Pub.), Deerfield, Ill., 1996—. Author Jour. of Legal Medicine, 1975, Selling and the Law: Advertising and Promotion, 1987; (under pseudonym Sarah Toast) 61 children's books, 1994-96; editor The Brief, 1990-95, Criminal Justice, 1989-90, 92-95 (Gen. Excellence award Soc. Nat. Assn. Pubs. 1990, Feature Article award-bronze Soc. Nat. Assn. Pubs. 1994), Franchise Law Jour., 1995; mem. editl. bd. The Brief, ABA Tort and Ins. Practice Sect., 1995—. Dir. Radcliffe Club of Chgo., 1990-93; mem. parents council Latin Sch. Chgo., 1995-96. Mem. ABA, Chgo.-Lincoln Inn of Ct. Office: Thomson Legal Pub 155 Pfingsten Rd Deerfield IL 60015

SMITH, CATHY DAWN, administrator; b. Northampton, Pa., Feb. 6, 1954; d. Russell W. and Edna (Kleckner) Seidel; m. Ronald James Smith, Nov. 1, 1975; 1 child, Ronald James Jr. Grad. high sch., Slatington, Pa. Fiscal asst. Ctr. for Humanistic Change, Inc., Bath, Pa., 1985—. Sec. Parkland Sch. dist. Drug Free Schs. Bd., Orefield, Pa., 1989—; mem. comty. action com. Alert-Partnership for a Drug Free Valley, Lehigh Valley, Pa., 1992-94; program coord. Parkland Alliance for Youth, Pa., 1977-85; explorer advisor Explorers Officer Assn., 1994—; mem. Minsi Trails coun. Boy Scouts Am., 1976—; 1st v.p. Catasaugua Suburban North YMCA, 1993. Mem. Chapel of Four Chaplains, Lehigh Valley Kennel Club. Democrat. mem. United Ch. Christ. Office: Ctr for Humanistic Change Inc 7574 Beth Bath Pike Bath PA 18014-8967

SMITH, CECE, venture capitalist; b. Washington, Nov. 16, 1944; d. Linn Charles and Grace Inez (Walker) S.; m. John Ford Lacy, Apr. 22, 1978. B.B.A., U. Mich., 1966; M.L.A., So. Meth. U., 1974. C.P.A., Tex. Staff accountant Arthur Young & Co. (C.P.A.s), Boston, 1966-68; staff accountant, then asst. to controller Wyly Corp., Dallas, 1969-72; controller, treas. sub. Univ. Computing Co., Dallas, 1972-74; controller Steak and Ale Restaurants Am., Inc., Dallas, 1974-76; v.p. fin. Steak and Ale Restaurants Am., Inc., 1976-80, exec. v.p., 1980-81; exec. v.p. Pearle Health Services, Inc.,, 1981-84, pres. Primacare div., 1984-86; gen. ptnr. Phillips-Smith Specialty Retail Group, 1986—; pres. Le Sportsac Dallas, Inc., 1981-87; bd. dirs. Henry Silverman Jewelers, Inc., Lil Things, Inc., Hot Topic, Inc.; chmn. Fed. Res. Bank of Dallas, 1994—. Former co-chmn. pres.'s rsch. coun. U. Tex. S.W. Med. Ctr. Dallas; mem. vis. com. U. Mich. Grad. Sch. Bus.; former exec. bd. So. Meth. U. Cox Sch. Bus.; former v.p., bd. dirs. Jr. Achievement Dallas, past pres. Charter 100; past treas. Dallas Assembly; former bd. dirs. Taco Villa, Inc., BizMart, Inc., A Pea in the Pod, Inc. Mem. Tex. Soc. CPAs (former dir.). Home: 3710 Shenandoah St Dallas TX 75205-2121 Office: 5080 Spectrum Dr Ste 700 W Dallas TX 75248-4658

SMITH, CHARLOTTE REED, retired music educator; b. Eubank, Ky., Sept. 15, 1921; d. Joseph Lumpkin and Cornelia Elizabeth (Spenser) Reed; m. Walter Lindsay Smith, Aug. 24, 1949; children—Walter Lindsay IV, Elizabeth Reed. B.A. in Music, Tift Coll., 1941; M.A. in Mus. Theory, Eastman Sch. of Music, 1946; postgrad. Juilliard Sch., 1949. Asst. prof. theory Okla. Bapt. U., 1944-45, Washburn U., 1946-48; prof. music Furman U., Greenville, S.C., 1948-92; chmn. dept. music, 1987-92. Editor: Seven Penitential Psalms with Two Laudate Psalms, 1983; author: Manual of

Sixteenth-Century Contrapuntal Style, 1989. Mem. Internat. Musicological Soc., Am. Musicological Soc., Soc. for Music Theory, AAUP (sec.-treas. Furman chpt. 1984-85), Nat. Fedn. Music Clubs, Pi Kappa Lambda. Republican. Baptist.

SMITH, CHRISTINE, small business owner; b. Bklyn., Feb. 8, 1961; d. Veronica (Bronner) S.; life ptnr. Charlotte Cannella Poole. BA, SUNY, Stony Brook, 1982. Scenic artist Disney Co., Lake Buena Vista, Fla., 1990-94, finisher, 1991-94; pres. K.I.S.S. inc., home maintenance, Orlando, Fla., 1994—. Chmn. S.E. Woman to Woman, Orlando, 1995.

SMITH, CHRISTINE JEAN, secondary school educator; b. Manchester, N.H., June 11, 1960; d. Frederick C. and Evelyn F. (Hofer) Caton; m. Leonard A. Smith, July 29, 1990. BA in French, St. Anselm Coll., 1982; MA in English, Rivier Coll., 1991, postgrad. Cert. English and French tchr., N.H. English tchr. Pelham (N.H.) H.S., 1984—, Rivier Coll., Nashua, N.H., 1992; summer sch. English tchr. Haverhill (Mass.) H.S., 1987-92. Mem. Nat. Coun. Tchrs. English, New Eng. Assn. Tchrs. English, N.H. Assn. Tchrs. English, New Eng. Assn. Tchrs. Fgn. Langs., Phi Delta Kappa. Republican. Roman Catholic.

SMITH, CLARA JEAN, retired nursing home administrator; b. Berwick, Pa., Aug. 31, 1932; d. Barton Fredrick and Evelyn Miriam (Bomboy) Hough; RN, Williamsport (Pa.) Hosp., 1953; B.S. in Nursing Edn., Wilkes Coll., Wilkes-Barre, Pa., 1960; M.S. in Edn., Temple U., Phila., 1969; m. Robert W. Smith, June 7, 1958. From staff nurse to dir. nursing Retreat State Hosp., Hunlock Creek, Pa., 1953-80; dir. long term care facility Danville (Pa.) State Hosp., 1980-82; ret., 1982; dir. accrediatation coordination and quality assurance Nursing Home Adminstrs., 1980—; speaker, instr. in field. Author tng. and ednl. programs. Mem. Pa. State Employees Retirement Assn. (pres. Luzerne/Columbia County chpt., regional v.p. northeastern Pa.), Williamsport Hosp. Sch. Nursing Alumni, Sunshine Club, Town Hill Hobby Group, Town Hill Over 50 Group. Methodist. Home: PO Box 999 Berwick PA 18603-0699

SMITH, CORRINE GEORGIA, artist, art educator; b. Rock Island, Ill., Aug. 30, 1957; m. Stephen Michael Smith, Oct. 4, 1980; children: Dillon, Jenna. BA with honors, U. Southern Ill., 1979; MFA, U. Ky., 1983. Layout artist Eagles Advt. Dept., Rock Island, Ill., 1975; freelance advt. artist Ill., Iowa, 1977-95; tchr. Kaleidoscope/Augustana Coll., Rock Island, Ill., 1994—; staff mem. kaleidoscope program Augustana Coll., Rock Island, Ill., 1994, 95—; spkr. WVIK radio, Rock Island, 1995. One-woman shows include Studio 15 Gallery, Davenport, Iowa, 1994, Performing Arts Hair Salon and Art Gallery, Davenport, 1995, and others; two-women shows include Quad City Arts Gallery, Rock Island, Ill., 1991; group shows include Hauberg Art and Craft Show, Rock Island, 1991, 93, Quad City Times Riverssance, Davenport, 1993 (merit award 1993, 94, 95), Studio 15 Gallery, Davenport, 1994, 95, Left Bank Art League's 38th Ann. Invitational Fine Arts and Craft Show, 1994, Beaux Arts Fine Arts Festival, Davenport, 1994, 7th Ann. Riverssance Festival Fine Arts, Davenport, 1994, Blue Cat Brew Pub, Rock Island, 1994, 95—, 19th Ann. Rock Island Fine Arts Exhibition, Rock Island, 1995, Beaux Arts Festival, 1995, Left Bank Art League's 39th Ann. Invitational Fine Arts and Craft Show, Moline, Ill., 1995, Trinity West Med. Ctr., Rock Island, 1995—, Quad City Arts, Rock Island, 1995—, and numerous others; represented in permanent collections at Quad City Arts Gallery, Rock Island, 1991—, Iowa Artisans Gallery, Iowa City, 1993—. Chmn. Cultural Arts Day, Rock Island, 1995. Recipient honorable mention 17th Ann. Rock Island Fine Arts Exhibition, 1993. Mem. Rock Island Art Guild (chmn. 1993—), Left Bank Art League, Studio 15 Gallery. Home: 3119 24th St Rock Island IL 61201

SMITH, CYNTHIA TURNER, gifted education educator; b. Lenoir, N.C., Mar. 24, 1960; d. Johnny Mack and Jeantte (Campbell) Turner; m. James Dwight Smith, May 6, 1989. BS in Middle Sch. Social Studies, Appalachian State U., 1982, BS in Cross Categorical Spl. Edn., 1985, MA in Gifted Edn., 1986. Tchr. 8th grade social studies McDowell County Schs., Marion, N.C., 1983; tchr. spl. edn. and academically gifted Caldwell County Schs., Lenoir, 1983-91, tchr. academically gifted, 1991—; mem. Academically Gifted Challenge Com., Lenoir, 1994-95. Bd. dirs. Blueridge Cmty. Action, Lenoir, 1989-93. Mem. NEA, N.C. NEA, Caldwell County NEA (newsletter editor 1988-89), Am. Needlepoint Guild. Democrat. Baptist. Home: 316 Hazel Lee St NW Lenoir NC 28645-3943

SMITH, DANI ALLRED, sociologist, educator; b. Natchez, Miss., Dec. 12, 1955; d. Paul Hollis and Mary Frances (Byrd) Allred; m. Ronald Bassel Smith, Aug. 9, 1980. BS in Social Sci., Lee Coll., 1977; MA in Sociology, U. Miss., 1980; postgrad., U. Tenn., 1989—. Staff writer Natchez Dem., 1977; secondary tchr. Natchez Pub. Schs., 1977-78; instr. sociology U. Miss., 1980-81, 82, rsch. assoc., instr. mgmt. info. systems, 1982-87; secondary tchr. Coffeeville (Miss.) Schs., 1981-82; asst. prof. sociology Lee Coll., Cleveland, Tenn., 1988—; workshop speaker Ch. of God Prison Conf., Cleveland, 1993, 94, 95; speaker Bradley County Law Enforcement Tng. Assn., Cleveland, 1992; advisor Lee Collegian, 1988-93. Contbr. articles to profl. jours. and newspapers. Advisor Sociology Club, Alpha Kappa Delta, Soc. for Law and Justice. Mellon Appalachian fellow, 1993-94; named one of Outstanding Young Women Am., 1981. Mem. Am. Sociol. Assn., So. Sociol. Assn., Christian Sociol. Assn., Am. Soc. Criminology, Nat. Audubon Soc., Cumberland-Harpeth Audubon Soc., The Nature Conservancy, Am. Mus. Natural History, Gt. Smoky Mountains Natural History Assn., Am. Hiking Soc., Phi Kappa Phi, Alpha Chi, Alpha Kappa Delta. Home: 430 20th St NE Cleveland TN 37311-3949 Office: Lee Coll 1120 N Ocoee St Cleveland TN 37311-4458

SMITH, DARLENE KAY, middle school educator; b. Wauseon, Ohio, Feb. 22, 1947; d. Harold and Marie (Schwab) Vollmer; m. Tommy L. Smith, Apr. 13, 1968; children: Jody, Jeff. BA, Adrian Coll., 1969. Cert. elem. tchr., Fla. 3d grade tchr. Britton (Mich.) Pub. Sch., 1968-69, Birmingham (Mich.) Pub. Sch., 1979-81, Hudson (Ohio) Pub. Schs., 1971-73; presch. tchr. First Presbyn. Ch., Naples, Fla., 1977-79; kindergarten tchr. Collier County Schs., Naples, 1980-81, 5th grade tchr., 1981-86, 6th grade tchr., 1986—; mem. textbook evaluation com. Collier County Schs., 1990; chmn. lang. dept., chmn. curriculum and instrn. Golden Gate Mid. Sch., 1994. Pres. PTO, Naples, 1981-82. Mem. Internat. Reading Assn., Fla. Reading Assn. Home: 2660 14th St N Naples FL 33940-4536

SMITH, DEBBIE JANE, telecommunications manager; b. Fairfield, Ala., Oct. 21, 1957; d. Samuel Adams and Patsy H. (Walker) S. BA in Bus. Adminstrn., Birmingham So. Coll., 1981; MBA, Samford U., 1984. Keypunch operator Mortgage Corp. of the South, Birmingham, Ala., 1976-77, shipping clk., 1977-78; keypunch operator Ala. Power, Birmingham, 1978-79; white page directory clk. South Ctrl. Bell Telephone Co., Birmingham, 1979-83; dispatch clk. BellSouth Advanced Sys., Birmingham, 1983-87, sys. facility adminstr., 1987, supr. telecomm. adminstrn. ctr., 1987-89; staff mgr.-technical support BellSouth Comm. Sys., Birmingham, 1989-93; mgr. telecomm. sys. BellSouth Telecomm., Birmingham, 1993—. Presch. choir dir. 1st Bapt. Ch. Pelham, Ala., 1992-94, 1st Bapt. Ch. Midfield, Ala., 1982-90, coord., worker children's dept., 1990, mem. fin. com., pers. com., benevolence com., 1982-90. Recipient Nat. Cmty. Leadership and Svc. award U.S. Achievement Acad., Lexington, Ky., 1984. Republican. Home: 123 Stratshire Ln Pelham AL 35124-2711 Office: BellSouth Telecomm 3196 Highway 280 S Rm 206N Birmingham AL 35243-4183

SMITH, DEBORAH KILCREASE, elementary education educator; b. Montgomery, Ala., May 22, 1953; d. George Edward and Evelyn Gertrude (Nix) Kilcrease; m. L. Lowell Smith, Mar. 1, 1975; 1 child, Jamison Wesley. BS in Elem. Edn., Troy (Ala.) State U., 1974, MS in Elem. Edn., 1981. Cert. elem. tchr., Ala. Tchr. Samson (Ala.) City Schs., 1974-75, Opp (Ala.) City Schs., 1975—. Mem. Opp Edn. Assn. (past treas.), Delta Kappa Gamma (v.p. 1990-91, chmn. world scholarship 1992-94). Baptist. Home: RR 1 Box 144 Opp AL 36467-9801 Office: South Highlands Elem Sch 503 Brown St Opp AL 36467-3043

SMITH, DEBORAH S., maternal and women's health nurse; b. Seneca, S.C., Aug. 25, 1957; d. Charles Robert and Emmy Lou (Jones) S.; m. Michael E. Smith, Aug. 12, 1977; children: Ashley Leigh, Jennifer Michelle, Lindsey Elizabeth. ADN, Clemson U., 1977. RN, S.C. Office nurse Dr. Perry B. Deloach, Clemson, S.C., 1986; nurse St. Francis Community Hosp., Greenville, S.C., 1977-78; nursing supr. Oconee Meml. Hosp., Seneca, 1983-85; new mother educator Pediatric Assocs., P.A., Seneca; prenatal educator for an ob-gyn. physician Seneca, 1992-95; newborn nursery nurse, labor and delivery nurse Oconee Meml. Hosp., Seneca, 1979-83; labor and delivery nurse Bapt. Med. Ctr., Easley, S.C., 1995—.

SMITH, DENISE GROLEAU, data processing professional; b. Worcester, Mass., Feb. 7, 1951; d. Edmond Laurence and Audrey Mildred (Paquin) Groleau; m. Wayne Marshall Smith, Apr. 17, 1976; 1 child, Andrew. BSBA, Fitchburg State U., 1983. Bindery worker Atlantic Bus. Forms, Hudson, Mass., 1969-73; proofreader New Eng. Bus., Townsend, Mass., 1974-75; computer operator New Eng. Bus., Groton, Mass., 1975-80, adminstrv. asst. bus. systems, 1980-82, adminstrv. asst. info. ctr., 1982-85; info. ctr. analyst Wright Line Inc., Worcester, 1985-88; personal computer coord. Thom McAn Shoe Co., Worcester, 1988-91; cons. personal computer Buckingham Transp., Groton, 1987-96, Software Edit. Moppet Sch., 1993—. Mem. NAFE. Home: 14 Cedar Cir Townsend MA 01469-1336

SMITH, DENTYE M., library media specialist; b. Atlanta, July 21, 1936; d. William Harry and Gladys Magdalene (Bruce) S. AB, Spelman Coll., 1958; MLM, Ga. State U., 1975. Cert. Libr., media specialist. Tchr. English Atlanta Pub. Schs., 1961-82, supr. tchr., 1968-69, tchr. journalism, 1975-80, libr. media specialist, 1982-94; media specialist West Fulton High Sch., 1982-92, West Fulton Mid. Sch., 1992, Booker T. Washington Comprehensive High Sch., Atlanta, 1992-94; leader jur. gt. books Archer and West Fulton high schs.; coord. Atlanta Pub. Schs. reading cert., program West Fulton H.S.; vol. liaison Atlanta-Fulton Pub. Libr., 1987-94, local arrangements com. Atlanta Libr. Assn., 1990-91; seminar presenter in field; coord. study skills seminars Morris Brown Coll.'s Summer Upward Bound Program, 1993, 94, 95; mem. High Mus. of Art, Atlanta, Atlanta Hist. Soc., Ga. Pub. TV. Contbr. articles to profl. jours. Named to Acad. Hall of Fame, Atlanta Pub. Schs., 1990; recipient Tchr. of Yr. award West Fulton H.S., Atlanta, 1974, acad. achievement incentive program award in media APS, 1990. Mem. ALA, NEA, Nat. Ret. Tchrs. Assn., Nat. Coun. Tchrs. English, Am. Assn. Sch. Librs., Soc. Sch. Librs. Internat., Ga. Assn. Educators, Atlanta Assn. Educators, Ga. Libr. Assn., Ga. Libr. Media Assn., Nat. Alumnae Assn. Apelman Coll., Ga. State U. Alumni Assn., Nat. Trust Hist. Preservation, Ga. Trust Hist. Preservation, Atlanta Ret. Tchrs. Assn., Atlanta Hist. Assn., Ga. Ret. Tchrs. Assn., the Smithsonian Assocs., Libr. of Congress Assocs.

SMITH, DIANNE LOUISE, military officer, historian; b. Lincoln, Nebr., Jan. 17, 1948; d. Fay William Smith and Clara Louise (Lostroh) Smith Weiland. BA in History, U. Nebr., Lincoln, 1970; MA in History, U. Calif., Davis, 1971, PhD in History, 1989; diploma, U.S. Army War Coll., 1995. Spl. agt. U.S. Army Counterintelligence Spl. Ops. Detachment, Munich, 1977-79; asst. prof. Russian history USMA, West Point, N.Y., 1979-82; chief counterintelligence Combined Field Army, Uijongbu, Korea, 1983-84; chief strategic studies bur. Allied Forces Cen. Europe, Netherlands, 1986-90; chief soviet/strategic studies bur. Defense Intelligence & Security Sch., Ashford, Kent, England, 1990-92; team chief Ctrl. Asia, Defence Intelligence Agy., Washington D.C., 1992-95; strategic rsch. analyst Strategic Studies Inst., USAWC, Carlisle, Pa., 1995—. Mem. Friends of Battlefield Parks at Gettysburg, Pa., 1994—. Mem. Am. Hist. Assn., Am. Assn. Advancement Slavic Studies, Western Front Assn., Fortress Study Group, Women in Internat. Security. Office: Strategic Studies Inst USAWC Carlisle Barracks Carlisle PA 17013

SMITII, DOLORES MAXINE PLUNK, dancer, educator; b. Webster City, Iowa, Dec. 22, 1926; d. Herschel Swanson and Kathryn (Wilke) Hassig; m. Del O. Furrey, Aug, 26, 1945 (div. Feb. 1960); children: Bob H. Furrey, Jon B. Furrey, Kathryn E. Furrey; m. Dewey Pechota, 1962 (div. 1963); m. Leon Plunk, 1965 (div. 1966); m. Harold Burdick, 1974 (div. 1977); m. Floyd E. Smith, July 13, 1985. BS in Edn., Black Hills Tchrs. Coll., 1962; MA, Tex. Woman's U., 1964, PhD, 1974. Owner, operator pvt. dance studios, S.D., 1953-62; tchr. rural schs. Rosebud Reservation, S.D., 1945-49; tchr. Mellette County Pub. Schs., White River, S.D., 1958-60, St. Francis Indian Day Sch., 1960-61, Converse County (Wyo.) High Sch., 1961-62; grad. asst. Tex. Woman's U., Denton, 1962-64, 71; asst. prof. dance Sam Houston U., Huntsville, Tex., 1964-65; prof. Ctrl. Mo. State U., Warrensburg, 1965—; judge dance contest Kansas City Dance Theatre Co., 1987, 88, World Dance Assn., 1988, Mo. State Fair, 1989; judge Miss Am. Co-ed Pageants, 1991-93; dir. Dance Partisans Assn., Ctrl. Mo. State U., 1982—, cmty. children's gymnastics program, 1982—, tchr. cmty. dance program, 1988—, dir. show dance team, 1991—; dance coord. Internat. Coun. Health, Phys. Edn., Recreation, Sport and Dance, 1991—; presenter Japanese Asia Dance Events, Malaysia, 1994, Dance Edn. Conf., Mich. State U., 1994. Contbr. articles to profl. jours. Bd. dirs. Kansas City Dance Theatre Co.; dir. Commn. on Dance, 1991-96, co-dir., 1994-96. Coun. for Health, Phys. Edn., Recreation, Sport and Dance scholar, 1995. Mem. Dance Masters Am. (sec. 1985-87, chmn. Mr. and Miss Dance Contest 1985, scholarships com. 1988-90), AAHPERD (honors award cen. dist. chpt., cen. dist. presentor 1991-92, dance chair, coll. chair, dance performance chair 1989-90, v.p. dance edn. 1991-93), Mo. Assn. Health, Phys. Edn., Recreation and Dance (pres. 1972, svc. award), Nat. Dance Assn. (v.p. dance edn. 1991-93, chmn. Heritage luncheon 1968, 78, 87, Heritage award com. 1988-89, mem. ad hoc spl. svcs. com. 1989—, pub. Spotlight 1989-90), Mid-Am. Dance Network (on-site coord. choreographers/dancers workshop 1992, bd. dirs., sec. 1992-94), Mo. Art Coun. Basic Arts Edn. (basic arts edn. task force higher edn.), Dance and Child Internat. (display chair, presider 1991), Asian Pacific Conf. Arts Edn. (presenter 1989), Assn. Supervision and Curriculum Devel., Internat. Congress Health, Phys. Edn. and Recreation Presenters (congress dels. representing dance, presenter 1991, 93), Internat. Phys. Edn. and Sports for Girls and Women, Phys. Edn. and Recreation, Mo. Alliance for Arts Edn. Home: 130 SW 400th Rd Warrensburg MO 64093-8109 Office: Ctrl Mo State U Dept Physical Education Warrensburg MO 64093

SMITH, DOLORES SNYDER, real estate rehabilitator; b. Martinsburg, W.Va., Nov. 27, 1937; d. Edward Lee and Elsie (Unger) Snyder; m. Gerald F. Smith, May 2, 1959 (div. May 1985); children: Gerald F. Jr., Michael A. Student, Strayer Coll., Washington D.C., 1956. Sec. to pres. Thieblot Aircraft Co., Martinsburg, W.Va., 1956-58; legal sec. various attys., Winchester, Va., 1959-72; v.p. Valley Proteins, Inc., Winchester, 1972-82; real estate rehabilitator Winchester, 1982—. Democrat. Baptist. Office: Holiday Apts 1605 S Braddock St Winchester VA 22601-3149

SMITH, DORIS CORINNE KEMP, retired nurse; b. Bogalusa, La., Nov. 22, 1919; d. Milton Jones and Maude Maria (Fortenberry) Kemp; m. Joseph William Smith, Oct. 13, 1940 (dec.). BS in Nursing, U. Colo., 1957, MS in Nursing Adminstrn., 1958. RN, Colo. Head nurse Chgo. Bridge & Iron Co., Morgan City, La., 1941-45, Shannon Hosp., San Angelo, Tex., 1945-50; dir. nursing Yoakum County Hosp., Denver City, Tex., 1951-52; hosp. supr. Med. Arts Hosp., Odessa, Tex., 1952-55; dir. insvc. edn. St. Anthony Hosp., Denver, 1961-66; coord. Sch. Vocat. Nursing, Kiamichi Area Vocat.-Tech. Nursing Sch., Wilburton, Okla., 1969-77; supr. non-ambulatory unit Lubbock (Tex.) State Sch., 1978-85, ret., 1985; mem. steering com. Western Interstate Commn. on Higher Edn. for Nurses, Denver, 1963-65; mem. curriculum and materials com. Okla. Bd. Vocat.-Tech. Edn., Stillwater, 1971-76; mem. Invitational Conf. To Plan Nursing for Future, Oklahoma City, 1976-77; mem. survey team to appraise Sch. of Vocat.-Tech. Edn. Schs. for Okla. Dept. Vocat.-Tech. Edn., 1975-76. Author, editor: Survey of Functions Expected of the General Duty Nurse, State of Colorado, 1958; co-editor: Curriculum Guides; contbr. numerous articles to profl. jours. Recipient citation of merit Okla. State U., 1976; named Woman of Yr. Sunrise chpt. Am. Bus. Women's Assn., 1994-95. Mem. AAAS, ANA, AAUW (life), Nat. League for Nursing, Tex. League for Nursing, Tex. Nurses Assn., Dist. 18 Nurses Assn., Tex. Employees Assn. (v.p. 1984-85), U. Colo. Alumni Assn., Am. Bus. Women's Assn. (pres. Lubbock chpt. 1986-87, rec. sec. 1989-90, edn. chair 1994-95, hospitality chair 1995-96), Bus. and Profl. Women's Assn. (sec. 1992-95), Chancellor's Club U. Colo., Pi Lambda Theta (sec. local chpt. 1957-58). Republican. Home: 2103 55th St Lubbock TX 79412-2612

SMITH, DORIS VICTORIA, educational agency administrator; b. N.Y.C., July 5, 1937; d. Albin and Victoria (Anderson) Olson; m. Howard R. Smith, Aug. 21, 1960; children: Kurt, Steven, Andrea. BS in Edn., Wagner Coll., 1959; MA in Edn., Kean Coll., 1963, cert., 1980; EdD, Nova Southeastern U., 1995. Cert. adminstr., tchr. elem. edn., N.J. Thorough and efficient coord. East Hanover (N.J.) Twp. Sch. Dist., 1977-79; ednl. specialist N.J. State Dept. Edn., Morristown, 1979—, ednl. planner, 1982-87, ednl. mgr., 1987—; pres. N.E. Coalition Ednl. Leaders, Inc.; founding mem. Morris County Curriculum Network. Author: Affirmative Action—Rules and Regulations, 1982, Supervising Early Childhood Programs, 1984. Past pres. bd. trustees Florham Park Libr.; founding mem. Morris Area Tech. Alliance; founding mem., pres. Calvary Nursery Sch.; bd. of trust office N.J. Coun. Edn.; pres. bd. trustees Madison/Chatham Adult Sch.; trustee Morris County Children's Svcs. Tchr. insvc. grantee; recipient Disting. Svc. award N.E. Coalition Ednl. Leaders, 1991, Disting. Svc. award Morris County Prins. and Suprs. Assn., Outstanding Educator award N.J. ASCD, 1995. Mem. N.J. Coun. Edn., N.J. Schoolmasters Assn., Phi Delta Kappa.

SMITH, DOROTHY OTTINGER, jewelry designer, civic leader; b. Indpls.; d. Albert Ellsworth and Leona Aurelia (Waller) Ottinger; student Herron Art Sch. of Purdue U. and Ind. U., 1941-42; m. James Emory Smith, June 25, 1943 (div. 1984); children: Michael Ottinger, Sarah Anne, Theodore Arnold, Lisa Marie. Comml. artist William H. Block Co., Indpls., 1942-43, H.P. Wasson Co., 1943-44; dir. Riverside (Calif.) Art Center, 1963-64; jewelry designer, Riverside, 1970—; numerous design commns. Adviser Riverside chpt. Freedom's Found. of Valley Forge; co-chmn. fund raising com. Riverside Art Ctr. and Mus., 1966-67, bd. dirs. Art Alliance, 1980-81, Art Mus.; mem. Riverside City Hall sculpture selection panel Nat. Endowment Arts, 1974-75; chmn. fund raising benefit Riverside Art Ctr. and Mus., 1973-74, trustee, 1980-84, chmn. permanent collection, 1981-84, co-chmn. fund drive, 1982-84; chmn. Riverside Mcpl. Arts Commn., 1974-76, Silver Anniversary Gala, 1992; juror Riverside Civic Ctr. Purchase Prize Art Show, 1975; mem. pub. bldgs. and grounds subcom., gen. plan citizens com. City of Riverside, 1965-66; mem. Mayor's Commn. on Civic Beauty, Mayor's Commn. on Sister City Sendai, 1965-66; bd. dirs., chmn. spl. events Children's League of Riverside Community Hosp., 1952-53; bd. dirs. Crippled Children's Soc. of Riverside, spl. events chmn., 1952-53; bd. dirs. Jr. League of Riverside, rec. sec., 1960-61; bd. dirs. Nat. Charity League, pres. Riverside chpt., 1965-66; mem. exec. com. of bd. trustees Riverside Arts Found., 1977-91, fund drive chmn., 1978-79, project rev. chmn., 1978-79; juror Gemco Charitable and Scholarship Found., 1977-85; mem. bd. women deacons Calvary Presbyn. Ch., 1978-80, elder, 1989-92; mem. incorporating bd. Inland Empire United Fund for Arts, 1980-81; bd. dirs. Hospice Orgn. Riverside County, 1982-84; Art Awareness chmn. Riverside Arts Found.; mem. Calif. Coun. Humanities, 1982-86. Recipient cert. Riverside City Coun., 1977, plaque Mayor of Riverside, 1977. Mem. Riverside Art Assn. (pres. 1961-63, 1st v.p. 1964-65, 67-68, trustee 1959-70, 80-84, 87-92), Art Alliance of Riverside Art Ctr. and Museum (founder 1964, pres. 1969-70). Recipient Spl. Recognition Riverside Cultural Arts Coun., 1981, Disting. Service plaque Riverside Art Ctr. and Mus., Jr. League Silver Raincross Community Svc. award, 1989, Cert. Appreciation Outstanding Svc. to the Arts Community Riverside Arts Found., 1990. Address: 3979 Chapman Pl Riverside CA 92506-1150

SMITH, ELAINE DIANA, foreign service officer; b. Glencoe, Ill., Sept. 15, 1924; d. John Raymond and Elsie (Gelbard) S. BA, Grinnell Coll., 1946; MA, Johns Hopkins U., 1947; PhD, Am. U., 1959. Commd. fgn. service officer U.S. Dept. State, 1947; assigned to Brussels, 1947-50, Tehran, Iran, 1951-53, Wellington, N.Z., 1954-56; assigned to Dept. State, Washington, 1956-60, Ankara, Turkey, 1960-69, Istanbul, Turkey, 1969-72; assigned to Dept. Commerce Exchange, 1972-73; dep. examiner Fgn. Service Bd. Examiners, 1974-75; Turkish desk officer (Dept. State), Washington, 1975-78; consul gen., Izmir, Turkey, 1978—. Author: Origins of the Kemalist Movement, 1919-1923, 1959. Recipient Alumni award Grinnell Coll., 1957. Mem. U.S. Fgn. Svc. Assn., Phi Beta Kappa. Home: The Plaza 800 25th St NW Apt 306 Washington DC 20037-2207

SMITH, ELEANOR JANE, university chancellor; b. Circleville, Ohio, Jan. 10, 1933; d. John Allen and Eleanor Jane (Dade) Lewis; m. James L. Banner, Aug. 10, 1957 (div. 1972); 1 child, Teresa M. Banner Watters; m. Paul M. Smith Jr. BS, Capital U., 1955; PhD, The Union Inst., Cin., 1972. Tchr. Columbus (Ohio) Pub. Schs., 1956-64, Worthington (Ohio) Pub. Schs., 1964-72; from faculty to administrator U. Cin., 1972-88; dean Smith Coll., Northampton, Mass., 1988-90; v.p. acad. affairs, provost William Paterson Coll., Wayne, N.J., 1990-94; chancellor U. Wis.-Parkside, Kenosha, 1994—; dir. Afrikan Am. Inst., Cin., 1977-84; adv. bd. Edwina Bookwalter Gantz Undergrad. Studies Ctr., Cin. Spl. Arts Night Com., Northampton, 1988-89. Named career woman of achievement YWCA, Cin., 1983. Mem. Nat. Assn. Women in Higher Edn., Am. Assn. for Higher Edn., Leadership Am. (bd. dirs., treas. 1993-95), Nat. Assn. Black Women Historians (co-founder, co-dir. 1979-82), Am. Coun. on Edn. (mem. com. on internat. edn. 1994—, bd. dirs. 1995—), Am. Assn. State Colls. and Univs. (mem. com. on policies and purposes 1994—). Home: 40 Harborview Dr Racine WI 53403-1098 Office: U Wis Parkside 900 Wood Rd Kenosha WI 53141-2000

SMITH, ELISE FIBER, international non-profit development agency administrator; b. Detroit, June 14, 1932; d. Guy and Mildred Geneva (Johnson) Fiber; m. James Frederick Smith, Aug. 11, 1956 (div. 1983); children: Gregory Douglas, Guy Charles. BA, U. Mich., 1954; postgrad., U. Strasbourg, France, 1954-55; MA, Case Western Res. U., 1956. Tchr. U.S. Binat. Ctr., Caracas, Venezuela, 1964-66; instr. English Am. U., 1966-68; prof. lang. faculty Catholic U., Lima, Peru, 1968-70; coord. English lang. and culture program, lang. faculty El Rosario U., Bogota, Colombia, 1971-73; lang. specialist, mem. faculty Am. U., English Lang. Inst., 1975-78; exec. dir. OEF Internat. (name formerly Overseas Edn. Fund), Washington, 1978-89, bd. dirs.; dir. Leadership Program, Winrock Internat. Inst. for Agrl. Devel., 1989—; v.p., bd. dirs. Pvt. Agys. Collaborating Together, N.Y.C., 1983-89; trustee Internat. Devel. Conf., Washington, 1983—, mem. exec. com., 1985-90; mem. hon. com. for Global Crossroads Nat. Assembly, Global Perspectives in Edn., Inc., N.Y.C., 1984, Washington, 1984-92, mem. gen. assembly, 1992; mem. nat. com. Focus on Hunger '84, L.A.; sec. bd. dirs. U.S. Binat. Sch., Bogota, Colombia, 1971-73; ofcl. observer UN Conf. on Status Women, 1980, 85, 95; mem. mental health adv. com. Dept. State, 1974-76; U.S. del. planning seminar integration women in devel. OAS, 1978; participant Women, Law and Devel. Forum; mem. exec. com., co-chair commn. advancement women Interaction (Am. Coun. for Vol. Internat. Action), 1994; bd. dirs. Sudan-Am. Found.; mem. adv. bd. Global Links Devel. Edn., Washington, 1985-86; adv. coun. Global Fund for Women, 1988-93. Co-editor: Toward Internationalism: Readings in Cross-cultural Communication, 1979, 2d edit. 1986. Bd. dirs. Internat. Ctr. Rsch. on Women, 1992—; mem. adv. com. on vol. fgn. aid U.S. AID, 1994—. Rotary Internat. fellow Strasbourg, France, 1954-55; grantee Dept. State, 1975. Mem. Soc. Internat. Devel., Assn. Women in Devel., Soc. Intercultural Edn. Tng. and Rsch., Coalition Women in Internat. Devel. (co-founder 1979, chair 1993—), Pvt. Agys. in Internat. Devel. (co-chmn. 1980-82, pres. 1982-85), Nat. Assn. Fgn. Student Affairs (grantee 1975), U. Mich. Alumni Assn., Women's Fgn. Policy Group, Rotary Internat. (mem. global com. Women in Future Soc. 1996). Unitarian. Home: 4701 Connecticut Ave NW Apt 304 Washington DC 20008-5617 Office: Winrock Inst 1611 N Kent St Ste 600 Arlington VA 22209-2111

SMITH, ELIZABETH PATIENCE, oil industry executive, lawyer; b. N.Y.C., June 21, 1949; d. Harry Martin and Frances (Blauvelt) S.; m. Kwan-Lan Mao, Apr. 1, 1989. BA cum laude, Bucknell U., 1971; JD, Georgetown U., 1976. Atty. Texaco Inc., White Plains, N.Y., 1976-84, dir. investor rels., 1984-89, v.p. corp. communications div., investor rels., 1989-92, v.p. investor rels. and shareholder svcs., 1992—. Mem. bd. trustees Marymount Coll., Tarrytown, N.Y.; bd. dirs. Westchester Edn. Coalition, Texaco Found. Mem. Petroleum Investor Rels. Assn., Nat. Investor Rels. Inst., Investor Rels. Assn., N.Y. Bar Assn. Office: Texaco Inc 2000 Westchester Ave White Plains NY 10650-0001

SMITH, ELIZABETH SHELTON, art educator; b. Washington, Feb. 12, 1924; d. Benjamin Warren and Sarah Priscilla (Harrell) Shelton; m. John Edwin Smith, Aug. 16, 1947 (dec. July 1992); children: Shelley Hobson, Dale Henslee, John Edwin Jr.; m. Headley Morris Cox Jr., Dec. 30, 1994. BA in Art, Meredith Coll., 1946; MEd in Supervision and Adminstrn., Clemson U., 1974. Youth dir. St. John's Bapt. Ch., Charlotte, N.C., 1946-47; art tchr.

Raleigh (N.C.) Pub. Schs., 1947-49, East Mecklenberg H.S., Charlotte, 1968-69, D. W. Daniel H.S., Central, S.C., 1970-86; art instr. U. S.C., Columbia, 1966-68; adj. prof. Clemson (S.C.) U., 1991-93; artist-in-residence edn. program S.C. Arts Commn., Columbia, 1991—. Exhibited in numerous one and two person shows and in group exhibits, 1946—. Vol. worker, editor newsletter Pickens County Habitat for Humanity, Clemson, 1981—; vol. art tchr. St. Andrew's Elem. Sch., Columbia, 1962-68. Named S.C. Tchr. of Yr., S.C. Dept. Edn. and Ency. Britannica, 1976, Citizen of Yr. Clemson Rotary Club, 1979, Disting. Alumna award Meredith Coll., 1996. Mem. S.C. Art Edn. Assn. (pres. 1978, Lifetime Svc. award 1990, Lifetime Achievement in Art Edn. award 1995), Nat. Art Edn. Assn. (ret. art educator affiliate, pres. 1994, Disting. Svc. award 1995), S.C. Watercolor Soc., Upstate Visual Artists (Best in Show award). Baptist. Home: 1604 Six Mile Hwy Central SC 29630-9483

SMITH, ELSIE CHASTAIN, lawyer; b. Lavonia, Ga., Feb. 4, 1940; d. Gordon Ray and Lettie Ruth (Cole) Chastain; m. Emory Harwell Smith, June 23, 1962. BA, Emory U., 1962, MA, 1964; JD, Nashville Sch. of Law, 1988. Rsch. analyst Tenn. Comptr. of Treasury, Nashville, 1968-74; chief engrossing clk. Tenn. State Senate, Nashville, 1974-89, staff atty., 1989-94; asst. commr., gen. counsel Dept. Gen. Svcs. State of Tenn., Nashville, 1994—. Contbr. Sta. WPLN, Nashville, 1970—, Internat. Rescue Com., N.Y.C., 1980—; chmn. Adv. Com. Purchases from the Blind and Other Severely Handicapped, Nashville, 1995—. Mem. Nat. Assn. State Purchasing Ofcls., Tenn. Govt. Exec. Inst., Tenn. Bar Assn., Nashville Bar Assn. Home: 1010 Barnes Rd Antioch TN 37013 Office: Dept Gen Svcs 312 8th Ave N Nashville TN 37243-0532

SMITH, ELSKE VAN PANHUYS, retired university administrator; b. Monte Carlo, Monaco, Nov. 9, 1929; came to U.S., 1943; d. Johan Abraham AE and Vera (Craven) van Panhuys; m. Henry J. Smith, Sept. 10, 1950 (dec. June 1983); children: Ralph A., Kenneth A. BA, Radcliffe U., 1950, MS, 1951, PhD, 1956. Rsch. assoc. Sacramento Peak Observatory, Sunspot, N.Mex., 1955-62; rsch. fellow Joint Inst. for Lab. Astrophysics, Boulder, Colo., 1962-63; assoc. to prof. U. Md., College Park, 1963-80, asst. provost, 1973-78, asst. vice chancellor, 1978-80; dean, coll. humanities and scis. Va. Commonwealth U., Richmond, 1980-92, interim dir. environ. studies, 1992-95; ret., 1995; cons. NASA, Greenbelt, Md., 1964-76, reviewer, Washington, 1970's, NSF, Washington, 1970's, 86; vis. com. Assn. of Univ.'s for Rsch. in Astronomy, Tucson, 1975-78. Author: (with others) Solar Flares, 1963, Introductory Astronomy and Astrophysics, 1973, 3d edit., 1992; also numerous articles. Mem. various environ. orgns. Rsch. grantee Rsch. Corp., 1956-57, NSF, 1966-69, 90, NIH, 1981-90, NASA, 1974-78; program grantee Va. Found. for Humanities, 1985, NEH, 1987, Assn. Am. Colls., 1987. Fellow AAAS; mem. Am. Astron. Soc. (counselor 1977-80, vis. prof. 1975-78), Internat. Astron. Union (chief U.S. del. 1979, U.S. Nat. com.), Coun. Colls. of Arts and Scis. (bd. dirs. 1989), Phi Beta Kappa. Democrat. Home: 68 Old Stockbridge Rd Lenox MA 01240

SMITH, ERIN ELYSA, nurse; b. Charleston, S.C., May 27, 1957; d. Douglass Warren and Mary Anne (Lauterbach) S.; m. Kevin Kenneth Scheer, Feb. 22, 1985 (div. 1992). BA, U. Fla., 1980, BSN, 1982; MA, Webster U., 1990. Cert. Med. Surg. Nurse. Comd. 2d lt. USAF, 1983; advanced through grades to maj. Wilford Hall Med. Ctr., 1995; staff nurse Wilford Hall Med. Ctr., San Antonio, 1983-89; asst. charge nurse 3d Med. Ctr. Elmendorf, Anchorage, 1989-93; staff devel. officer 95th Med. Group, Edwards AFB, 1993-95; tutor Laubach Literacy Internat., 1990-95. Maj. USAF, 1993-95. Mem. ANA, Air Forces Assn. Office: 95th Med Group 10 Hospital Rd Edwards AFB CA 93524

SMITH, ESTHER THOMAS, editor; b. Jesup, Ga., Mar. 13, 1939; d. Joseph H. and Leslie (McCarthy) Thomas; m. James D. Smith, June 2, 1962; children: Leslie, Amy, James Thomas. BA, Agnes Scott Coll., 1962. Staff writer, Sunday women's editor Atlanta Jour.-Constn., 1961-62; mng. editor Bull. of U. Miami Sch. Medicine, 1965-66; corr. Atlanta Jour.-Constn. and Fla. Times-Union, 1964, 67-68; founding editor Bus. Rev. of Washington, 1978-81; founding editor, gen. mgr. Washington Bus. Jour., 1982; pres., bd. dirs. Tech News, Inc., 1986—, ceo, 1995—; editor-at-large Washington Tech., 1986—, Tech. Transfer Bus. Mag., 1992-95; bd. dirs. MIT Enterprise Forum of Washington/Balt., 1981-82, TechNews, Inc., 1986—; mem. Greater Washington Board of Trade, Internat. Task Force, Women's Forum, Washington, 1981—; mem. No. Va. Bus. Round Table (exec. com.); mem. adv. bd. Va. Math Coalition, 1991-94; bd. trustees Ctr. for Excellence in Edn., 1993—. Mem. Assn. Tech. Bus. Couns. (chmn. bd. advisors 1989-94), Pres.'s Forum, Mid-Atlantic Venture Assn., No. Va. Tech. Coun. (mem. exec. com., bd. dir.), Suburban Maryland High Tech. Coun. Office: 8500 Leesburg Pike Ste 7500 Vienna VA 22182-2409

SMITH, ETHEL CLOSSON (MRS. JOHN GRIER PARKS), soprano, educator; b. Germantown, Pa., Dec. 8, 1921; d. Harry Framer and Mary (Closson) S.; m. John Grier Parks. Student, Westminster Choir Coll., Princeton, N.J., 1939-41; BMus in Edn., Wheaton Coll., 1943; MMus in Edn., Temple U., 1945; postgrad., N.Y. Theol. Sem., 1946-47, Juilliard Sch. Music, 1948, Princeton Theol. Sem., 1950-51, Union Theol. Sem., N.Y.C., 1951-52; MusD, Ind. U., 1968; student, Mozarteum, Salzburg, Austria, 1969, U. Florence, Italy, 1969, Goethe Inst., Prien am Chiemsee, Germany. Dir. ch. choir and Christian edn. 3d Presbyn. Ch., Chester, Pa., 1953-54; asst. prof. music Ind. State U., Terre Haute, 1962-65, assoc. prof. music, 1965-71, prof. music, 1971-87; mem. faculty Ind. U. Continuing Studies, 1989—; with Presbyn. students Westminster Found. Temple U., U. Pa., 1950-51; mem. faculty summer tng. inst. Presbyn. Ch., Wooster, 1953-54; prof. vocal pedagogy, vocal diction, song lit and pvt. voice, 1962-1987. Soloist various chs., N.Y.C., Phila., 1946-59; performed various concerts and recitals, 1946-59, including Radio City Music Hall, 1949, Silver Bay, N.Y., 1951, Chautauqua, N.Y., 1955, Ind. U. Opera performances, 1960, Ind. State U. Faculty solo and chamber recitals. Bd. dirs. Ind. U. Soc. of Friends of Music, 1973-95; assoc. Nat. Coun. Met. Opera, Ctrl. Opera Svc. Mem. AAUP, AAUW, Nat. Assn. Tchrs. Singing (pres. Ind. chpt. 1965-66, lt. gov. Ind. 1970-72, nat. sec.-treas. 1990-92, nat. historian 1993-95), Internat. Assn. Rsch. in Singing, Voice Found. Internat. Congress Voice Tchrs. (assoc.), Music Tchrs. Nat. Assn., Ind. Music Tchrs. Assn., Nat. Soc. Arts and Letters (pres. Bloomington chpt. 1990-92), Ind. U. Alumni Assn. (mem. exec. coun., mem. music alumni bd. 1994-96), Pi Kappa Lamda, Delta Kappa Gamma, Sigma Alpha Iota. Home: Windermere 1205 Pickwick Pl Bloomington IN 47401 also: 435 Overstreet Dr Destin FL 32541

SMITH, FERN M., judge; b. San Francisco, Nov. 7, 1933. AA, Foothill Coll., 1970; BA, Stanford U., 1972, JD, 1975. Bar: Calif. 1975. m. F. Robert Burrows; children: Susan Morgan, Julie. Assoc. firm Bronson, Bronson & McKinnon, San Francisco, 1975-81, ptnr., 1982-86; judge San Francisco County Superior Ct., 1986-88, U.S. Dist. Ct. for Northern Dist. Calif., 1988—; mem. U.S. Jud. Conf., Adv. Com. Rules of Evidence, 1993—; mem. hiring, mgmt. and pers. coms., active recruiting various law schs. Contbr. articles to legal publ. Apptd. by Chief Justice Malcolm Lucas to the Calif. Jud. Coun.'s Adv. Task Force on Gender Bias in the Cts., 1987-89; bd. visitors Law Sch. Stanford U. Mem. ABA, Queen's Bench, Nat. Assn. Women Judges, Calif. Women Lawyers, Women's Forum West/Internat. Women's Forum, Bar Assn. of San Francisco, Fed. Judges Assn., 9th Cir. Dist. Judges Assn., Am. Judicature Soc., Calif. State Fed. Judicial Coun., Phi Beta Kappa.*

SMITH, FREDA L., retired elementary education educator; b. Birds, Ill., Oct. 3, 1923; d. Loney W. and Mattie A. (Perrott) Thomas; m. Lloyd Preston, May 18, 1947 (dec. 1991); 1 child, Thelma. BS, U. Western Ky., 1959. Tchr. Jefferson Sch., Robinson, Ill., 1953-54, Franklin County (Tenn.) Sch., 1954-56, Muhlenberg (Ky.) Pub. Schs., 1956-58, Livingston County Pub. Schs., Salem, Ky., 1958-61, Custer (S.D.) Elem. Sch., 1961-64, Chugwater (Wyo.) Elem. Sch., 1964-87. Vol. Headstart, Wheatland, Wyo., 1991—, Lauback Internat., Kingman, Ariz., 1987-91. With WAVES, 1944-46. Mem. AAUW (pres. 1980-81), NEA, Chugwater Edn. Assn. Episcopalian. Home: PO Box 731 Wheatland WY 82201-0731

SMITH, FREDRICA EMRICH, rheumatologist, internist; b. Princeton, N.J., Apr. 28, 1945; d. Raymond Jay and Carolyn Sarah (Schleicher) Emrich; m. Paul David Smith, June 10, 1967. AB, Bryn Mawr Coll., 1967; MD, Duke U., 1971. Intern, resident U. N.Mex. Affiliated Hosps., 1971-73; fellow U. Va. Hosp., Charlottesville, 1974-75; pvt. practice, Los Alamos, N.Mex., 1975—; chmn. credentials com. Los Alamos Med. Ctr., 1983—, chief staff, 1990; bd. dirs. N.Mex. Physicians Mut. Liability Ins. Co., Albuquerque. Contbr. articles to med. jours. Mem. bass sect. Los Alamos Symphony, 1975—; mem. Los Alamos County Parks and Recreation Bd., 1984-88, 92—, Los Alamos County Med. Indigent Health Care Task Force, 1989—; mem. ops. subcom. Aquatic Ctr., Los Alamos County, 1988—. Fellow ACP, Am. Coll. Rheumatology; mem. N.Mex. Soc. Internal Medicine (pres. 1993—), Friends of Bandelier. Democrat. Office: Los Alamos Med Ctr 3917 West Rd Los Alamos NM 87544-2222

SMITH, GLADYS VANDETTA, career officer; b. Ft. Lee, Va., June 24, 1955; d. Sutton and Roberta (Scales) Smith. BS, Va. State U., 1978; student, Command and Gen. Staff Coll., 1991; MS in Gen. Adminstrn., Ctrl. Mich. U., 1996. Commd. 2nd lt. US Army, 1979, advanced through grades to capt., 1984; BDE asst. adjutant 4th tng. brigade US Army, Ft. Leonard, Mo., 1979-80, tng. officer 3rd and 5th bn., 1980-81, co. commdr. B co. 3rd bn. 4th brigade, 1981-82; mech. maint. officer 8th maint. bn. US Army, Hanau, Germany, 1983-84, co. commdr. 81st maint. co., 1984-85, force modernization officer 8th maint. bn., 1985-86; instr., writer Engr. Sch. US Army, Ft. Belvoir, Va., 1986-90; bn. S3 plans and opers. 193d support bn. US Army, Ft. Clayton, Panama, 1991-92, bn. exec. officer 193d support bn., 1992-93; chief logistics opers. 41st area support group US Army, Corozal, Panama, 1993-94; ammunition staff officer army material command US Army, Alexandria, Va., 1994—. Mem. NAFE. Home: 5903 Mount Eagle Dr Unit #605 Alexandria VA 22303

SMITH, HEATHER LYNN, psychotherapist, recreational therapist,; b. Modesto, Calif., May 31, 1956; d. Gary Fremont and Marilyn Rae (Brown) S. BS, Calif. State U., Fresno, 1979; MA, U. San Francisco, 1989. Lic. marriage, family and child counselor, Calif. Recreational therapist Casa Colina Rehab. Hops., Pomona, Calif., 1979-82; evaluator developmentally delayed, coord. family edn. Cath. Charities, Modesto, 1982-87; bereavement counselor Hospice, Modesto, 1983-87; high risk youth counselor Ctr. Human Svcs., Modesto, 1987-90; pvt. practice, family therapist Modesto, 1993—; program dir. chemically dependent treatment program Stanislaus County Juvenile Hall, 1990—. Named Outstanding Young Woman of Stanislaus County, 1986, Citizen of Yr., Civitan, 1986, Outstanding Individual award Stanislaus County, 1992. Mem. Calif. Assn. Marriage and Family Therapists, Kappa Kappa Gamma. Republican. Episcopalian. Home: 806 Claratina Ave Modesto CA 95356-9610 Office: Bldg A Ste 2 250 S Oak Ave Oakdale CA 95361 also: 1015 12th St Ste 8 Modesto CA 95354-0838

SMITH, HEATHER SUE, elementary education educator; b. Anderson, Ind., Jan. 1, 1967; d. L. Keith and Wanda L. (Wildermuth) S. BA in Elem. Edn., Wheaton Coll., 1989. Tchr. grades 5 & 6 Orozco Cmty. Acad., Chgo., 1989-92; tchr. trainer Cup of Cold Water Ministries, La Paz, Bolivia, 1992-93; tchr. grades 6 & 7 Irving Park Middle Sch., Chgo., 1993—; cons. Uptown Bapt. Ch., Chgo., 1993-95, summer intern supr., 1990-94. Tchr. rep. Local Sch. Coun., Chgo., 1991-92. Grantee Chgo. Found. for Edn., 1993-94, Oppenheimer Family Found., 1995; recipient Reading award Rochelle Lee Fund, 1994-95. Mem. Nat. Sci. Tchrs. Assn. Baptist. Office: Irving Park Middle Sch 3815 N Kedvale Ave Chicago IL 60641-3113

SMITH, HELEN CASAREZ, educator; b. Roswell, N.Mex., Jan. 22, 1949; d. Rosendo and Emma Casarez; m. Michael Lee Smith, July 21, 1978; children: Sara Marisa, Amanda Lee. BS, N.Mex. State U., 1970; MA, Pepperdine U., 1976. Tchr. elem. sch. San Antonio Ind. Schs., 1971-72, Chino (Calif.) Unified Schs., 1972-74, Rowland Heights (Calif.) Unified Schs., 1974-76, Roswell (N.Mex.) Pub. Schs., 1977-85, Gadsden Ind. Sch. Dist., Anthony, N.Mex., 1985-88, Las Cruces (N.Mex.) Pub. Schs., 1988—; mem. Las Cruces Tchrs. Ctr. Adv. Bd., 1992-94; presenter in field. Mem. Nat. Sci. Tchrs. Assn. (mem. com. on presch.-elem. sci. teaching), Nat. Coun. Tchrs. Math., Coun. for Elem. Sci. Internat., N.Mex. S.W. Region Systemic Initiative in Math and Sci. Edn. (Tchr. Leadership Cadre). Roman Catholic. Home: 1105 Sharon Cir Las Cruces NM 88001 Office: Las Cruces Pub Schs 505 S Main Las Cruces NM 88001

SMITH, HELEN DIBELL, executive assistant; b. Ellwood City, Pa., Apr. 9, 1941; d. Nicholas J. and Helen (Pintea) Savu; m. David L. Dibell, July 8, 1961 (div. 1986); children: Marta, Todd, Troy, Mark; m. Gordon H. Smith, Apr. 9, 1991. Student, Geneva Coll., Beaver Falls, 1959-61, U. Ill., 1962. Payroll acct. Babcock & Wilcox Steel Corp., Beaver Falls, Pa., 1960-62; admininstrv. asst. U. Ill., Urbana, 1962-63, Lockheed Missiles & Space Co., Vandenberg AFB, Calif., 1963-64; acct. tng. Vanda Beauty Counselor, N.Y., 1964-78; adminstrv. asst. Okaloosa Walton Jr. Coll., Niceville, Fla., 1977-78; adminstrv. asst. Tex. Instruments, Va., 1978-79; exec. asst. Allied Signal Bendix Aerospace, Arlington, 1979-89, Orion Group Ltd., Dr. Richard DeLauer and Matra Aerospace Inc., Arlington, 1988-89; asst. to bd. dirs. Fairchild Space and Def. Corp., Germantown, Md., 1989-91; cons. Meridian Strategies, Inc., Fullerton, Calif., 1991-93, ret., 1995; with Assistance League of Fullerton, 1996—. Mem. Women Def., Army Assn., Am. Def. Preparedness Assn., Air Force Assn. Republican. Presbyterian. Home and Office: 956 W Rancho Cir Fullerton CA 92835-3337

SMITH, HELEN ELIZABETH, retired military officer; b. San Rafael, Calif., Aug. 11, 1946; d. Jack Dillard and Marian Elizabeth (Miller) S. BA in Geography, Calif. State U., Northridge, 1968; MA in Internat. Rels., Salve Regina, Newport, R.I., 1983; MS in Tech. Comm., Rensselaer Poly. Inst., 1988; postgrad., Naval War Coll., 1982-83. Commd. ensign USN, 1968, advanced through grades to capt., 1989; adminstrv. asst. USN Fighter Squadron 101, Key West, Fla., 1969-70; adminstrv. officer Fleet Operational Tng. Group, Mountain View, Calif., 1970-72; leader human resource team Human Resource Ctr., Rota, Spain, 1977-79; adminstrv. officer Pearl Harbor (Hawaii) Naval Sta., 1979-80; dir. Family Svc. Ctr., Pearl Harbor, 1980-82; officer-in-charge R&D lab. Naval Ocean Systems Ctr., Kaneohe, Hawaii, 1983-85; exec. officer Naval ROTC, assoc. prof. Rensselaer Poly. Inst., Troy, N.Y., 1985-88; comdg. officer Navy Alcohol Rehab. Ctr., Norfolk, Va., 1988-90; faculty mem., commanding officer Naval Adminstrv. Command, dean adminstrv. support, comptr. Armed Forces Staff Coll., Norfolk, Va., 1990-93; ret., 1993; exec. dir. Calif. for Drug-Free Youth, 1995-96. Author: (walking tour) Albany's Historic Pastures, 1987; composer (cantata) Night of Wonder, 1983. Chair Hawaii State Childcare Com., Honolulu, 1981-82; coun. mem. Hist. Pastures Neighborhood Assn., Albany, N.Y., 1985-88; mem. working group Mayors Task Force on Drugs, Norfolk, 1989-90; chair, bd. dirs. Va. Coun. on Alcoholism, 1989-92, Calif. for Drug Free Youth, 1995-96; singer North County Baroque Ensemble. Mem. AAUW, Waves (nat. unit 126), Kiwanis. Republican. Presbyterian.

SMITH, ILEENE A., book editor; b. N.Y.C., Jan. 21, 1953; d. Norman and Jeanne (Jaffe) S.; m. Howard A. Sobel, June 3, 1979; children: Nathaniel Jacob, Rebecca Julia. BA, Brandeis U., Waltham, Mass., 1975; MA, Columbia U., 1978. Editorial asst. Atheneum Publishers, N.Y.C., 1979-82; sr. editor Summit Books, N.Y.C., 1982-91, lit. editor, 1991-92; edit. cons. The Elie Wiesel Found. for Humanity, 1993—; editl. cons. Marsalis on Music; cons. editor Paris Rev., N.Y., 1987—. Author introductory scripts for Met. Opera Telecasts, 1987-93. Jerusalem fellow, 1987; recipient Tony Godwin Meml. award, 1982, PEN/Roger Klein award for editl. excellence, 1988, Contbg. to Prodn. of Aida cert. NATAS, 1990.

SMITH, JAMESETTA DELORISE, author; b. Chgo., Jan. 26, 1942; d. James Gilbert and Ora Mae (Roberts) Howell; m. Leroy Smith, June 2, 1962; children: Leroy, Darryll Keith. Student, Oxford Bus. Coll., Chgo., 1961-62. Office clerk Justice of the Peace, Gary, Ind., 1966-69; bookkeeper, office mgr. Jones Electric, Gary, Ind., 1971-85. Author: How Strong is Strong, 1988; contbr. articles to profl. jours., newspapers. Treas., bd. dirs. N.W. Ind. Lupus Found., Gary, 1988-92; co-founder, pres. Ark. chpt. Lupus Found., 1993—, mem., race organizer, 1995; facilitator Gary Meth. Hosp. for Lupus Found., 1991-92; pastor's aide Bible study leader Greater St. Paul Bapt. Ch., 1995, sec. ch. food com., 1994, ch. trustee, 1994; Bible enrichment instr., 1996—; pastor's aide sec. Clark Rd. M.B. Ch., 1990-92. Named Vol. of Yr., Ark. chpt. Lupus Found., 1995. Mem. Jones Electric Gary Ind. (Sec. 1986). Democratic. Baptist.

SMITH, JANE WARDELL, historian, philanthropist, entrepreneur; b. Detroit, Aug. 9, 1943; d. John Slater and Lucille Maude (Hoskins) Beck; m. marshall Smith, Oct. 31, 1964 (div. 1972); children: Aaron Wardell, Gerald Allen. Student, Detroit Bus. Coll., Cass Sch. Tech. Exec. sec. Wayne County Cir. Ct. 7th Dist., 1968-72, Wayne County Friend of Ct., Detroit, 1968-72; with exec. mgmt. City Detroit Pers. Dept., 1972-79; fin. analyst City of Detroit, 1979-82, Merlite Industries, N.Y.C., 1994—; salesperson Mason Shoe Co., Chippewa Falls, 1968-72; fin. analyst A. J. Valenci, Salem, W.Va., 1968-72; examiner Mich. State Dept., Detroit, 1972-79. Critic various consumer groups. Vol. Richard Austin polit. campaign, Grand River, Mich., 1975, John Conters polit. campaign, Livernois, Mich., 1980; mem. Mayor's Com. for Human Resources, Detroit, 1979; active local drama and theater clubs, Detroit, 1980—, local Bapt. Ch., 1984—. Recipient numerous awards, honors and achievements. Democrat.

SMITH, JANET L. BASS, pianist, teacher, performer; b. Cheyenne, Wyo., Jan. 11, 1936; d. Ellwood Aven and Clara Anna (Hahn) B.; m. Charles Warren Smith, Aug. 24, 1957; children: Randall Allan, Bradley Taylor, Bryan Keith, Roger Andrew. BMus, U. Wyoming, 1957; advanced study, Eastman Sch. of Music, Rochester, N.Y., 1967-68; MMus in Piano Performance, U. N.C., 1972; D in Musical Arts (Piano Performance), U. Mo. Conservatory, Kansas City, 1987. Piano instr. Salem Coll. (prep. dept.), Winston Salem, N.C., 1969-70; instr. in music U. N.C., Greensboro, 1970-72; asst. prof. of music Livingstone Coll., Salisbury, N.C., 1972-75; piano instr. (part time) S.E. Mo. State U., Cape Girardeau, Mo., 1975-89; dir. music prep. program S.E. Mo. State U., Cape Girardeau, 1985-89; co-dir. of music and organist St. Andrew LUth. Ch., Cape Girardeau, 1980-89; pianist, teacher, performer, lectr. pvt. practice, Bowling Green, Ky., 1951—; park ranger (docent) Mammoth Cave, Ky., summers 1993—. Author: (book) The Golden Portion of the Published Solo Piano Music of Vincent Persichetti, 1987; (pamphlet) Scholarship Programs in Member Preparatory Schools within Colleges and Universities. Recipient Theodore Pressor Found. scholarship U. Wyoming, 1954; grantee Cashman and Stubbs Charitable Trust, Women's Coun. Univ. of Mo., 1986. Mem. Music Tchrs. Nat. Assn. (cert. master tchr.), Ky. Music Tchrs. Assn. (sec. 1990-92, v.p. 1992-94, pres. 1994-96), Ind. Music Tchrs. Assn. (pres. 1991-93, sec. 1995-97; S.E. Mo. Music Tchrs. Assn. (organizer, pres. 1980-89), Beethoven Soc. fo Pianists. Home: 2737 Utah Dr Bowling Green KY 42104

SMITH, JANET MARIE, professional sports team executive; b. Jackson, Miss., Dec. 13, 1957; d. Thomas Henry and Nellie Brown (Smith) S. BArch, Miss. State U., 1981; MA in Urban Planning, CCNY, 1984. Draftsman Thomas H. Smith and Assocs. Architects, Jackson, 1979; mktg. coord. The Eggers Group, P.C. Architects and Planners, N.Y.C., 1980; program assoc. Ptnrs. for Livable Places, Washington, 1980-82; coord. asst. Lance Jay Brown, Architect and Urban Planner, N.Y.C., 1983-84; coord. architecture and design Battery Park City Authority, N.Y.C., 1982-84; pres., chief exec. officer Pershing Sq. Mgmt. Assn., L.A., 1985-89; v.p. stadium planning and devel. Balt. Orioles Oriole Park at Camden Yard, 1989-94; v.p. sports facilities Turner Properties, Atlanta, 1994—; v.p. planning and devel. Atlanta Braves, Braves, 1994—; bd. dirs. Assn. Collegiate Schs. Architecture, Washington, 1979-82, Assn. Student Chpts. AIA, Washington, 1979-82. Guest editor: Urban Design Internat., 1985; assoc. editor: Crit, 1979-82; contbr. articles to profl. jours. Named Disting. Grad., Nat. Assn. State Univs. and Land Grant Colls., 1988, One of Outstanding Young Women of Am., 1982; recipient Spirit of Miss. award, Sta. WLBT, Jackson, 1987. Mem. AIA (assoc.), Urban Land Inst. Democrat. Episcopalian. Office: Turner Properties Inc 1 CNN Center Ste 275 Atlanta GA 30303

SMITH, JANET SUE, systems specialist; b. Chgo., Jan. 15, 1945; d. Curtis Edwin and Margaret Louise (Yost) Smith; B.A., Ind. U., 1967. Sales mgr. Marshall Field & Co., Chgo., 1968-70, programmer, 1970-72; sr. programmer, analyst Trailer Train Co., Chgo., 1972-75; mgr. data base and systems devel. Railinc-Assn. Am. R.R., Washington, 1975-85, asst. v.p., corp. sec., 1985-93, asst. v.p. strategic systems, 1994—. Nat. student v.p. YWCA, 1966-67; bd. dirs., v.p. planning and fin. Guide Internat., Friends of the Nat. Zoo; advisor Jr. Achievement. Mem. Am. Council R.R. Women, Ind. U. Alumni Assn. (life), Women's Transp. Seminar. Home: 2000 N St NW Washington DC 20036-2336 Office: 50 F St NW Washington DC 20001-1530

SMITH, JANICE SELF, family nurse practitioner; b. Marietta, Ga., Nov. 8, 1942; d. Robert Dewey and Dovia Evelyn (Seay) Self; m. Charles William Smith, Nov. 9, 1963; children: Scott, Stephanie, Suzanne. Diploma, Piedmont Hosp. Sch. Nursing, 1963; Cert. Family Nurse Practitioner, Ga. State U., 1981; BSN, West Ga. Coll., 1994. RN, Ga.; cert. family nurse practitioner, Ga. Staff nurse Gordon Hosp., Calhoun, Ga., 1963-69; pub. health nurse Gordon County Health Dept., Calhoun, Ga., 1977-80; family nurse practitioner Gordon Primary Care Unit, Calhoun, Ga., 1982—; rep. health dept. Child ABuse Coun., Calhoun, 1986; led effort to implement Good Touch-Bad Touch program, Calhoun, 1986. Chmn. pub. edn. Am. Cancer Soc., Calhoun, 1971, bd. chmn., 1973, chmn. patient svcs., 1974-79; sec. commn. on missions 1st United Meth. Ch., Calhoun, 1994. Named Gord County Vol. of the Yr., 1979; Ingram scholar West Ga. Coll., 1994. Mem. ANA, Ga. Pub. Health Assn. (sec. nursing sect. 1994-95, vice chair nursing sect. 1995-96, chair nursing sect. 1996—), Ga. Nurses Assn. (treas. 1995-96), Nurses Honor Soc. West Ga. Coll. Methodist. Home: 141 Derby Ln Calhoun GA 30701-2023 Office: Gordon County Health Dept 310 N River St Calhoun GA 30701

SMITH, JEAN, interior design firm executive; b. Oklahoma City; d. A. H. and Goldy K. (Engle) Hearn; m. W. D. Smith; children: Kaye Smith Hunt, Sidney P. Student Chgo. Sch. Interior Design, 1970. v.p. Billco-Aladdin Wholesale, Albuquerque, 1950-92, v.p. Billco Carpet One of Am, 1970. Pres. Opera Southwest, 1979-83, advisor to bd. dirs.; active Civic Chorus, 1st Meth. Ch.; pres. Inez PTA, 1954-55, life mem.; hon. life mem. Albuquerque Little Theater, bd. dirs. Republican. Clubs: Albuquerque County, Four Hills Country, Daus. of the Nile (soloist Yucca Temple). Home: 1009 Santa Ana Ave SE Albuquerque NM 87123-4232 Office: Billco-Aladdin Wholesale 7617 Menaul Blvd NE Albuquerque NM 87110-4647

SMITH, JEAN KATHERINE MARTIN, English language educator, department chairperson; b. Richmond, Va., Apr. 5, 1946; d. William Patrick and Doris Ruth (Garf) Martin; m. Colin Frank Smith, Apr. 15, 1972 (div. Oct. 1981); 1 child, Andrea Megan Smith. BA in English, Averett Coll., Danville, Va., 1978; MA in Humanities, Hollins Coll., Roanoke, Va., 1993. Cert. tchr., Va. Tchr. English Martinsville (Va.) H.S., 1978-87; tchr. English, journalism, dept. chair Carlisle Sch., Martinsville, 1987—; adj. instr. English Patrick Henry Cmty. Coll., Martinsville, 1993—. Contbr. poems to anthologies, chpt. to book. Recipient Shakespeare Workshop grantee U. Va., 1990, Ind. Study fellow, 1992. Mem. ACLU, Nat. Coun. Tchrs. English, Va. Assn. Tchrs. English, Amnesty Internat. Democrat. Home: 1016 Jefferson Cir Martinsville VA 24112 Office: Carlisle Sch Carlisle Rd Martinsville VA 24112

SMITH, JEAN WEBB (MRS. WILLIAM FRENCH SMITH), civic worker; b. L.A.; d. James Ellwood and Violet (Hughes) Webb; B.A. summa cum laude, Stanford U., 1940; m. George William Vaughan, Mar. 14, 1942 (dec. Sept. 1963); children: George William, Merry; m. William French Smith, Nov. 6, 1964. Mem. Nat. Vol. Svc. Adv. Coun. (ACTION), 1973-76, vice chmn., 1974-76; dir. Beneficial Standard Corp., 1976-85. bd. dirs. Cmty. TV So. Calif., 1979-93; mem. Calif. Arts Commn., 1971-74, vice chmn., 1973-74; bd. dirs. The Founders, Music Ctr., L.A., 1971-74; bd. dirs. costume coun. L.A. County Mus. Art, 1971-73; bd. dirs. United Way, Inc., 1973-80, Hosp. Good Samaritan, 1973-80, L.A. chpt. NCCJ, 1977-80, Nat. Symphony Orch., 1980-85, L.A. World Affairs Coun., 1990, L.A. chpt. ARC, 1994-95; bd. fellows Claremont Univ. Ctr. and Grad. Sch., 1987—; bd. dirs. Hosp. Good Samaritan, 1973-80; mem. exec. com., 1975-80; mem. nat. bd. dirs. Boys' Clubs Am., 1977-80; mem. adv. bd. Salvation Army, 1979—; bd. overseers The Hoover Instn. on War, Revolution and Peace, 1989-94; mem. President's Commn. on White House Fellowships, 1980-90, Nat. Coun. on the Humanities, 1987-90; bd. govs. Calif. Cmty. Found., 1990—; bd. regents Children's Hosp. L.A., 1993—. Named Woman of Yr. for cmty. svc. L.A. Times, 1958; recipient Citizens of Yr. award Boy Scouts Am., L.A. coun., 1982, Life Achievement award Boy Scouts Am., L.A. coun., 1985. Mem. Jr. League of L.A. (pres. 1954-55, Spirit of Volunteerism award 1996), Assn. Jr. Leagues of Am. (dir. Region XII, 1956-58, pres. 1958-60),

Phi Beta Kappa, Kappa Kappa Gamma. Home: 11718 Wetherby Ln Los Angeles CA 90077-1348

SMITH, JENNIFER C., insurance company executive; b. Boston, Nov. 3, 1952; d. Herman J. and Margaree L. S.; B.A. in English, Union Coll., 1974; M.A., Fairfield U., 1982. Claim rep. Travelers Ins. Co., Boston, 1974-75, supr., N.J., 1976-78, regional asst., account exec., Hartford, Conn., 1979-81, tng. adminstr., 1981, asst. dir. casualty and property depts., 1981-83, sec. casualty and property depts., 1983-85; personnel dir. City of Hartford, 1984-85, asst. city mgr., 1985-87; dir. mktg. Travelers Cos., 1987; asst. v.p. corp. human resources, Aetna Life and Casualty Co., 1987-88, v.p. pers., 1990, v.p. corp. mktg., 1991; v.p., chief of staff Aetna Health Group, 1992-93; v.p., chief oper. officer Aetna Profl. Mgmt. Co., 1993-94; v.p. Occupl. Managed Care Aetna, 1994—; claim rep. Sentry Ins. Co., N.J., 1975-76. Bd. dirs. Hartford Stage Co., exec. com., nominating com.; bd. dirs. Boys Club Hartford; trustee St. Joseph's Coll., Martin Luther King Jr. Scholarship Fund, U. Conn. Contbr. articles to Conn. Bus. Times. Office: Aetna Life and Casualty Co Aetna Health Plans RE 6K 151 Farmington Ave Hartford CT 06156-0001

SMITH, JENNIFER CAROL, primary school educator; b. Key West, Fla., Sept. 3, 1968; d. Tommy Joe and Carolyn Ruth (Spaulding) S. BS, Berea (Ky.) Coll., 1990; MS, Ea. Ky. U., 1994. Cert. tchr. early elem. edn., Ky. Primary tchr. Broughtontown Elem. Sch., Crab Orchard, Ky., 1992-94, Crab Orchard Elem. Sch., 1994—. Home: 125 Harness Ridge Rd Crab Orchard KY 40419-9720

SMITH, JENNIFER LYNN, secretary; b. Dallas, May 7, 1967; d. Wayne Cecil and Shirley Ann (Williams) Jones; m. Raymond Eugene Smith, Sept. 9, 1989. Studetn, Lon Morris Jr. Coll., Jacksonville, Tex., 1985-86. Tech. sec. Black & Marsh Corp., Sylvania, Ohio, 1987-90; exec. sec. Air-Ride Inc., Swanton, Ohio, 1990-91; asst. to pres. P.E. Black Corp., Holland, Ohio, 1992—. Methodist. Home: 213 W Airport Hwy Swanton OH 43558

SMITH, JOAN LOWELL, writer, public relations consultant; b. Orange, N.J., June 20, 1933; d. William Jr. and Katherine Margaret (Macpherson) Lowell; m. John A. Nave, Dec. 14, 1957 (div. May 1961); children: Deborah Lowell, Nancy Lowell; m. Warren W. Smith, July 19, 1969. Student, Lasell Coll., 1951-52, Drake Bus. Sch., N.Y.C., 1952-53. Exec. sec. Amb. Ernest A. Gross, N.Y.C., 1954-57; adminstrv. asst./v.p. J.B. Williams Co. (Geritol), Clark, N.J., 1966-74; pub. rels. dir. N.J. State Opera, Newark, 1974-78; talk show host-radio WJDM (AM) WFME (AM-FM), Elizabeth and West Orange, N.J., 1974-82; exec. dir. Chamber of Commerce, Westfield, N.J., 1976-79; legis. aide Assemblyman C. Hardwick, N.J., 1980-82; exec. dir. Alzheimer's Disease Fund, Westfield, N.J., 1986-87; pub. rels. dir. Children's Specialized Hosp., Mountainside, N.J., 1993-94; pres./owner Media Mgmt., Westfield, 1974—. Contbr. articles to various jours. and newspapers. Recipient 11 awards N.J. Press Woman, 1991—. Mem. DAR (regent 1985-89), Assn. Children with Learning Disabilities (chmn. bd. dirs. 1980-82), Westfield Day Care Ctr. (bd. dirs.), Geneal. Soc. of West Fields (bd. dirs. 1984-88), Daus. of Cin. Republican. Presbyterian. Office: Media Mgmt 1739 Boulevard Westfield NJ 07090

SMITH, JUDITH ANN, academic administrator; b. Springfield, Mo., Jan. 1, 1950; d. Harley Jr. and Barbara Jean (Anderson) Cozad; m. Robert Eugene Smith, July 11, 1969. BS in Edn., S.W. Mo. State U., 1973, MA in English, 1976. Cert. tchr. (life), Mo. Tchr. R-12 Schs., Springfield, 1973-83; program/communications mgr. Performing Arts Ctr. Trust, Tulsa, 1983-84; gen. mgr. Springfield Symphony Assn., 1984-86; assoc. dir. devel., dir. planning giving S.W. Mo. State U., 1986-89, dir. devel. alumni rels., 1989—; dir. Summerscape (gifted program), Springfield, 1980-82; mem. NCAA fiscal integrity com. S.W. Mo. State U., 1994-96. Vol. Springfield Symphony Guild, 1986—; vol. fundraising advisor First Night, Springfield, 1993—; appointee Greene County Hist. Sites Bd., 1994—, chair, 1995-96; bd. dirs. Springfield Area Arts Coun., 1995—, Discovery Ctr. of Springfield, 1994—; mem. Cmty. Cultural Plan, 1995-96. Named Outstanding Young Educator Springfield Jaycees, 1976, Mo. Jaycees, 1977. Mem. Coun. for Advancement and Support of Edn. (com. on women and minorities 1988-90, Merit and Excellence awards 1988, 89, 90), Leadership Springfield Alumni Assn., PEO, Rotary, Delta Kappa Gamma (past chpt. officer). Office: SW Mo State U 901 S National Ave Springfield MO 65804-0027

SMITH, JUDITH BERTENTHAL, psychology educator; b. N.Y.C., Mar. 5, 1949; d. Howard and Ida (Mazur) Bertenthal; m. Harry Ambrose Smith III, Mar. 21, 1970; children: Nathaniel, Samantha. BA, Case Western Res. U., Cleve., 1971; MS, W. Va. U., 1974, postgrad., 1983-85, 85-89. Lic. profl. counselor, W.Va. Hosp. librarian Cleve. Pub. Library, 1970-72; elem. tchr. Tucker County Bd. Edn., Parsons, W.Va., 1973; early childhood tchr. Randolph County Bd. Edn., Elkins, W.Va., 1973-76; lectr. psychology Davis & Elkins Coll., Elkins, 1977-85; lectr. psychology and edn. Davis & Elkins Coll., 1985-86, asst. prof. psychology and edn., 1986—; pvt. practice psychology Elkins Ctr. for Counseling & Devel., 1988—; child devel. cons. Youth Health Svc., Elkins, 1988-89. Bd. dirs. Women's Aid in Crisis, Elkins, 1984-90. Mem. ACA, Am. Play Therapy Assn., W.Va. Counseling Assn. Home: 26 Pinewood Dr Elkins WV 26241-9336 Office: Davis & Elkins Coll Dept Psychology Elkins WV 26211

SMITH, JUDY A., communications company executive. BS in Pub. Rels., Boston U., 1980; JD, Am. U., 1986. Congrl. liaison U.S. Atty., 1987-89; spl. counsel U.S. Atty., Washington, 1989-91; chief dept. press sec. Pres. George Bush, Washington, 1991-93; sr. v.p. corp. comms. NBC, N.Y.C., 1993—. Former exec. editor Law Rev., Washington Coll. of Law, Am. U. Recipient Fair Shake award, numerous comms. and leadership awards. Office: NBC Rockefeller Plaza New York NY 10112

SMITH, JULIA AMELIA, English language educator; b. San Antonio, Tex., Dec. 25, 1935; d. George Leon and Julia E. (Garcia) S. BA, Our Lady of the Lake, San Antonio, Tex., 1956; MA, U. Tex., 1958; postgrad., Harvard U., 1961; PhD, U. Tex, 1969. Elem. tchr. San Antonio (Tex.) Sch. Dist., 1956-57; instr. Laredo (Tex.) Jr. Coll., 1959-68; asst. prof. English, Tex. A&M U., Kingsville, 1969-72; assoc. prof. Tex. A&I U., Kingsville, 1972-78, prof., 1978—, chmn. dept., 1977-83. Contbr. articles to profl. jours. Organist St. Martin's Ch., Kingsville, Tex. Mem. Modern Language Assn., Nat. Council of Tchrs of English, Conf. of Coll. Tchrs. of English, Tex. Coll English Assn., Music Club of Kingsville, Audubon Soc., Delta Kappa Gamma, Kappa Nu. Democrat. Roman Catholic. Office: Tex A&M PO Box 162 Kingsville TX 78364-0162

SMITH, JULIA LADD, medical oncologist, hospice physician; b. Rochester, N.Y., July 26, 1951; d. John Herbert and Isabel (Walcott) Ladd; m. Stephen Slade Smith; 1 child. BA, Smith Coll., 1973; MD, N.Y. Med. Coll., 1976. Diplomate Am. Bd. Internal Medicine, Am. Bd. Med. Oncology. Intern in medicine N.Y. Med. Coll., N.Y.C., 1976-77; resident in medicine Rochester Gen. Hosp., 1977-79; internist Genesee Valley Group Health, Rochester, 1979-80; oncology fellow U. Rochester, 1980-82, asst. prof. oncology in medicine sch. medicine & dentistry, 1986—; oncologist Med. Ctr. Clinic, Ltd., Pitts., 1982-83; oncologist, internist Rutgers Community Health Plan, New Brunswick, N.J., 1983-86; med. dir. Genesee Region Home Care Assn./Hospice, Rochester, 1988—. Bd. dirs. Am. Cancer Soc., Monroe County, 1988-92. Nat. Cancer Inst. rsch. grantee, 1993-95. Mem. ACP, Am. Soc. Clin. Oncology, Acad. Hospice Physicians. Unitarian-Universalist. Address: Genesee Hosp 224 Alexander St Rochester NY 14607

SMITH, KARAN BARBEE, mathematics educator; b. Aiken, S.C., June 7, 1953; d. Ralph Lamuel and Jessie (Barbee) S. BA in Math., Clemson U., 1975; MBA, U. S.C., 1977, MS in Math., 1982, PhD in Math. Edn., 1991. Mgr. current planning/circuit provision bur. So. Bell, Columbia, S.C., 1977-80; teaching asst. dept. math., then lectr. U. S.C., Columbia, 1980-83, rsch. asst., mgr. statistics lab., 1987-88, instr. MBA - ETV program, 1988, instr. math., 1990-91; instr. div. sci., math. and engring. U. S.C., Sumter, 1989-90; instr. U. N.C., Wilmington, 1984-87, asst. prof. dept. math. sci., 1991-96, assoc. prof. dept. math. sci., 1996—; tchr. math. Cardinal Newman H.S., Columbia, 1983-84; rsch. in computer and calculator tech. for math. tchg. and curriculum reform. Mem. Nat. Coun. Tchrs. Math., Assn. Math. Tchr. Educators, Am. Ednl. Rsch. Assn., N.C. Coun. Tchrs. Math., Assn. Advancement of Computing in Edn., Phi Delta Kappa, Pi Mu Epsilon. Office: UNC Dept Math 601 S College Rd Wilmington NC 28403-3201

SMITH, KAREN ANN, chemist; b. Idaho Falls, Idaho, Aug. 30, 1958; d. Elmer Robert and Mildred Mae (Form) S.; m. Agustin P. Kintanar, Oct. 28, 1989; children: Ryan Agustin Kintanar, Dylan Robert Kintanar. BS, Penn State U., 1978; PhD, U. Ill., 1984. Sr. rsch. chemist Colgate-Palmolive, Piscataway, N.J., 1984-90; instr. Iowa State U., Ames, 1990, instrument specialist, 1990-95; dir. nuc. magnetic resonance facility U. N. Mex., Albuquerque, 1995—. Contbr. articles to profl. jours. Mem. Am. Chem. Soc., Am. Inst. Chemists, AAAS, N.Y. Acad. Sci. Home: 457 Camino de la Tierra Corrales NM 87048 Office: Dept Chemistry U N Mex Clark Hall Albuquerque NM 87131

SMITH, KAREN ANN, artist, graphic designer, educator; b. Trenton, N.J., May 25, 1964; d. James Roy and Clara Patricia (Walton) S. A in Graphic Design, Art Inst. Phila., 1984; BFA in Graphic Design and Art Therapy, U. Arts, Phila., 1989; grad. in graphic design, Basel Sch. for Design, 1991; MA in Expressive Therapies, Lesley Coll., 1993. Graphic designer Mercer County C.C., Trenton, 1984-86; mural painter, supr. Anti-Graffiti Network, Phila., 1988; tchr. drawing and set design Chestnut Hill (Mass.) Sch., 1995—; freelance graphic designer Swiss Fed. Rys., Bern, 1993-95; tchr. drawing Wentworth Inst. Tech., Boston, 1996—. One-woman show Contempo Galerie, Bern, Switzerland, 1994; exhibited in group shows including Boston Ctr. for Arts, 1994, Howard Yezerski Gallery, Boston, 1994, Kingston Gallery, Boston, 1995. Scholar Women in Graphic Arts, 1987-89; grantee Mystic Studios Trust, 1994—. Mem. Coll. Art Assn. Studio: 567 Tremont St Boston MA 02118

SMITH, KATHERINE ANNE, small business owner, consultant; b. Naperville, Ill., Aug. 21, 1966; d. Robert Frederick and Anita Grace (Knol) Smith; m. James Frank Hodonicky, 1995. Student, Coll. of DuPage, Glen Ellyn, Ill., 1984-86; grad., Mktg. Tng. Ctr., Elk Grove Village, Ill., 1987; student, San Francisco City Coll., 1990. dir. F&G Publs., Lisle, Ill., 1991—. English tutor Literacy Vols. Am., Naperville, 1993-96; election judge DuPage County Election Bd., Wheaton, Ill., 1992-94; vol. Ronald McDonald's Children's Charities, Oak Brook, Ill., 1993, 94; bd. dirs. Recycled Clothing, Lisle, 1993—. Mem. Nat. Assn. Realtors, Ill. Assn. Realtors, DuPage Assn. Realtors, Literacy Vols. Am. Home: 2745 Bristol Dr # 103 Lisle IL 60532

SMITH, KATHERINE ANNE, secondary school English educator; b. Aurora, Ill., Dec. 13, 1957; d. Jared K. Pickell and Sylvia A. (Tullar) Pickell Wagner; m. Jack T. Smith, June 22, 1991; children: Sean M. Hamann, Michael T. Smith. BA, Ind. U., 1980; MEd, Nat.-Louis U., 1992. English and German tchr. St. Xavier H.S., Louisville, 1980-83; English tchr. Purcell-Marian H.S., Cin., 1984; English tchr. Addison (Ill.) Trail H.S., 1987—, Integrated Studies coord., 1993—; cons., presenter at various confs. in field. Contbr. articles to profl. jours. Judge, tchr. Nat. Baton Twirling Assn. Mem. ASCD, AAUW, Nat. Coun. Tchrs. English, Internat. Reading Assn., Ill. Fedn. Tchrs. (ho. of reps. local 571 1994-96). Office: Addison Trail HS 213 N Lombard Rd Addison IL 60101

SMITH, KATHLEEN DANA, principal, consultant; b. Fargo, N.D., June 24, 1947; d. Dana Eugene and Georgia Caroline (Cook) S.; m. Thomas Donald Gash, June 7, 1980; children: Caroline, Kathryn. BA in Polit. Sci. and History, U. Denver, 1969, MA in Counseling and Guidance, 1970; EdD in Leadership and Mgmt., U. No. Colo., 1985. Cert. tchr., Colo.; lic. counselor, Colo. Tchr., counselor Denver Pub. Schs.-East High Sch., 1969-71; counselor, tchr. Cherry Creek Schs.-Cherry Creek High Sch., Englewood, Colo., 1971-77, chair counseling dept., 1977-80, asst. to prin., 1980-81, adminstrv. asst. to dep. supt., 1982-83, dir. of pupil svcs., 1983-88; asst. prin. Cherry Creek Schs./Horizon Mid. Sch., Aurora, Colo., 1988-89, prin., 1989-93; prin. Cherry Creek High Sch., Englewood, Colo., 1993—; presenter in field; cons. in field; mem. faculty U. Phoenix, Denver, 1988—. Mem. Gov.'s Task Force for Better Air, Denver, 1984-86; mem., various chairs Jr. League Denver, 1983—; bd. dirs. Cerebral Palsy Ctr., Denver, 1991—; adv. com. Colo. Bd. Land Commrs., 1992—. Harvard U. fellow, 1989; Colo. Dept. of Edn. grantee, 1987. Fellow Inst. for Devel. Ednl. Activities; mem. ASCD, Nat. Assn. Secondary Sch. Prins., Phi Delta Kappa. Roman Catholic. Office: Cherry Creek High Sch 9300 E Union Ave Englewood CO 80111-1306

SMITH, KATHLEEN MARIE, health facility administrator; b. Grand Rapids, Mich., Oct. 17, 1940; d. Albert Edward and Ila Melissa (Thorp) Andrews; m. John J. Smith, June 5, 1965; children: Lisa, Debra, Richard. BS, Aquinas Coll., 1965; postgrad., Mich. State U., 1969-70. Med. technologist St. Mary's Hosp., Grand Rapids, 1960-61, Holy Family Hosp., Des Plaines, Ill., 1962-64, Blodgett Meml. Hosp., Grand Rapids, 1964-65, St. Joseph's Hosp., Denver, 1965-66, Porter Meml. Hosp., Englewood, Colo., 1966-67, Ionia County Meml. Hosp., Ionia, Mich., 1967-73; med. technologist, sect. chief Clinton Meml. Hosp., St. Johns, Mich., 1974-80; lab. mgr. Clinton County Med. Ctr., St. Johns, 1980-95; owner, pres. KMS Computer Svcs., St. Johns, 1991—; tchr. Cath. edn., 1969-74, 88-90. Mem. singing group Me and My Friends, 1974-84. Mem. NAFE, Am. Soc. Clin. Pathologists (cert.), Am. Soc. Med. Technologists, Mich. Soc. Med. Technologists. Home: 600 Circle Dr Saint Johns MI 48879-2006

SMITH, KATHLEEN TENER, bank executive; b. Pitts., Oct. 19, 1943; d. Edward Harrison Jr. and Barbara Elizabeth (McCormick) Tener; m. Roger Davis Smith, May 30, 1970 (dec.); children: Silas Wheelock, Jocelyn Tener, Luke Ewing Taft. BA summa cum laude, Vassar Coll., 1965; MA in Econs., Harvard U., 1968. Rsch. assoc. Harvard U. Grad. Sch. Bus., Cambridge, Mass., 1967-69; assoc. economist Chase Manhattan Bank, N.Y.C., 1969-70, asst. treas., 1971, 2d v.p., 1972, v.p., 1973—, sec. asset liability mgmt. com., 1985-90, treas. Global Bank, 1990-91, divsn. exec. structured investment products, 1991-93, global mktg. and comms. exec. Global Risk Mgmt. Sect., 1993-94, global mktg. and comms. product devel. exec., 1994-96, global asset mgmt. and pvt. bank mktg., 1996—. Editor: Commodity Derivatives and Finance, 1996. Trustee Vassar Coll., Poughkeepsie, N.Y., 1979-91, mem. exec. com., 1987-91; mem. subcom. on edn. Chase Manhattan Found., N.Y.C., 1985-90. NSF fellow, 1965-67. Mem. Am. Fin. Assn., Am. Econ. Assn., Fin. Mgmt. Assn., Yale Club. Republican. Episcopalian. Home: 454 State Route 32 N New Paltz NY 12561-3040 Office: Chase Manhattan Bank 1211 Avenue of the Americas New York NY 10036

SMITH, KATHRYN (KAY SMITH), watercolor artist; b. Vandalia, Ill., Feb. 27, 1923; m. William Smith (dec.); 1 chld, Julia. BA in Fine Arts, Sch. of Art Inst. of Chgo. Watercolor artist, 1970—. Exhibited in group shows St. John's Uihlein-Peters Gallery, Milw., World's Women On-Line Network, UN 4th World Conf. on Women, Beijing, Richard J. Daley Civic Ctr., Chgo., Vis.'s Ctr. of Valley Forge (Pa.) Nat. Park, Olivet Nazarene U., Kankakee, Ill., Benton & Bowles, N.Y.C., Lansing (Mich.) City Ctr., Am. Nat. Bank, Chgo., Yorktown (Va.) Victory Ctr., The Exec. Mansion, Springfield, Ill., Northwestern Military & Naval Acad., Wis., Three Arts Club, Chgo., Millikin U., Ill., Harry S. Truman Libr. & Mus., Mo., Ill. Inst. Tech. Hermann Hall Art Ctr., Ill.; represented in permanent collections R.R. Donnelly & Sons, Truman Libr., Independence, Mo., Playboy Found., Union League Club Chgo., Amoco Corp., also pvt. collections; commd. for 6 paintings for Daley Civic Ctr., Chgo. Artist laureate State of Ill., 1994. Recipient medal Freedom Found. of Valley Forge, award Mcpl. Art League of Chgo., 1991, Cert. of Achievement, Ill. Sec. of State, 1992. Mem. Chgo. Artists Coalition, Arts Club Chgo. Home: 2239 N Burling Chicago IL 60614

SMITH, KATHRYN ANN, advertising executive; b. Harvey, Ill., Mar. 30, 1955; d. Kenneth Charles and Barbara Joan (Wise) Smith; m. Christopher A. Erwin, July 16, 1994; stepchildren: Brian, Courtney, Misty. Student Art Inst. Chgo., 1973. Advt. salesperson Calumet Index, Inc., Riverdale, Ill., 1974-77, Towne & Country Ind., Hammond, 1977-78; owner, sales person Ad-Com, Merrillville, Ind., 1978-92, pres., Crown Point, Ind., 1978-92, corp. pres., chief exec. officer, 1993; pres. Smith-Halcomb Advt., Chgo., 1993; pres., owner Smith-Leonard & Assocs. Advt., Des Plaines, Ill., 1993—. Dir., producer cable TV comml., 1982; dir., producer TV comml., 1987-88. Recipient Silver Microphone award, 1987, 90; named Am. On Line Spl. Interest Forum Leader, 1991. Mem. Advt. Agy. Owners Assn. (chair 1985-88), Merrillville C. of C. Avocations: painting, fishing, antiques, computers, travel.

SMITH, LANA KAY, social services specialist; b. Hicksville, Ohio, Oct. 30, 1958; d. Lloyd Lorrell Smith and Beverly Jean (Walkenstine) Rioux; m. Larry G. Loyster, Aug. 14, 1981 (div. Aug. 1983); 1 child, Lana Angelina Louise. BA in Pub. Rels., Miami U., Oxford, Ohio, 1981; MS in Sys. Mgmt., U. So. Calif., 1988. Commd. USAF, 1981, advanced through grades to capt.; base-level pers. officer USAF, Dyess AFB, Tex., 1982-84, Yokota AB, Japan, 1984-88; pers. staff officer USAF, Scott AFB, Ill., 1988-92; manpower adminstr., pers. specialist USAF, Yokota AB, 1992; transition assistance specialist Pascagoula Navy Family Svc. Ctr., Gautier, Miss., 1993-95; relocation assistance specialist 81 MSS/DPF, Keesler AFB, Miss., 1995—; asst. chair Relocation Assistance Coord. Com., Keesler AFB, 1995; adminstrv. asst. So. Region Mil. Job Fair Com., Jackson, Miss., 1993—. Editor, author newsletter Single Parents Support Group, 1988-92. Troop leader Girl Scouts Am., Ocean Springs, Miss., 1993—; mem. choir 1st Presbyn. Ch., Ocean Springs, 1993—. With USAFR, 1992—. Mem. Am. Bus. Women's Assn. (Woman of Yr. 1990, editor, author newsletter 1989-90). Republican. Presbyterian. Home: 115 Roberts Cir Ocean Springs MS 39564 Office: 81 MSS/DPF 500 Fisher St Rm 111 Keesler AFB MS 39534

SMITH, LAUREL SUE, physical education educator, coach; b. Port Jefferson, N.Y., July 5, 1954; d. Frederick Irving and Billie Sue (Wade) S. BS in Edn., SUNY, Cortland, 1976; MS, Emporia State U., 1978. Cert. physical edn. tchr., N.C. Sports info. dir., coach Emporia (Kans.) State U., 1978-79; substitute coach McGraw (N.Y.) H.S., 1979-80; instr., coach Salem (W.Va.) Coll., 1980-89; coach, asst. prof. St. Andrews Presbyn. Coll., Laurinburg, N.C., 1989-91; coach, instr. Polk C.C., Winter Haven, Fla., 1991—. Percussionist Bartow (Fla.) Adult Cmty. Band, 1993—; outfielder Illusions Softball Team, Winter Haven, 1993—. Mem. AAHPERD, Am. Volleyball Coaches Assn., Nat. Softball Coaches Assn., Nat. Assn. Intercollegiate Athletics-Softball Coaches Assn. (sec. 1983-84, 2d v.p. 1982-83, 1st v.p. 1983-84, pres. 1984-85). Republican. Methodist. Home: 222 Grant Cir Davenport FL 33837 Office: Polk Cmty Coll 999 Avenue H NE Winter Haven FL 33881-4256

SMITH, LEANNE SUSAN, psychotherapist, consultant; b. Homestead, Fla., June 6, 1966; d. Lester Blair and Martha Lee (Davis) Smith. BS, Fla. State U., 1988; MA, U. Ctr. Fla., Orlando, 1990; PhD, Walden U., Mpls., 1994. Lic. psychotherapist. Therapist Glenbeigh Hosp. of Orlando, 1990-92, psychometrician, 1990-92; therapist Cen. Fla. Psychol. Svcs., Sanford, Fla., 1990—; abuse coord., supr. Project III of Cen. Fla., Fla., 1991-94; dir. residential programs Children's Home Soc., Daytona Beach, Fla., 1994-96; psychotherapist Columbia Med. Ctr.-Peninsula, 1996—. Mem. Orlando Women's Rep. Club, 1993. Mem. ACA, Am. Mental Health Counselors Assn., Fla. Counseling Assn., Fla. Mental Health Counselors Assn., Kappa Delta Pi, Phi Delta Phi. Republican. Methodist. Home: 878 Westchester Dr Deland FL 32724

SMITH, LEILA HENTZEN, artist; b. Milw., May 20, 1932; d. Erwin Albert and Marian Leila (Austin) Hentzen; m. Richard Howard Smith, Sept. 12, 1959; 1 child, Jennie. BFA, Miami U., 1955; cert., Famous Artists Schs., 1959. Quilting tchr. Milw. Pub. Schs., 1975-79. One-woman shows include Boerner Bot. Gardens, Whitnall Park, Wis., 1995; 2-woman show West Bend (Wis.) Gallery Fine Arts, 1963, Mapledale Sch. Gallery, Bayside Wis., 1981; exhibited in group shows, Including Milw. Art Ctr., 1961, Mustum Mus. Art, Racine, Wis., 1966, 77, Artist's World Gallery, Cedarburg, Wis., 1975, Ozaukee Art Ctr., Cedarburg, 1982-86, 93, John Michael Kohler Arts Ctr., Sheboygan, Wis., 1984, 87, 89-96, Cedarburg Cultural Ctr., 1988-96, West Bend Gallery Fine Arts, 1993, 96, Rahr-West Art Mus., Manitowoc, Wis., 1994, Gallery 110 North, Plymouth, Wis., 1996; represented in permanent collections Milw. County Art Commn., Wheaton Franciscans. Women's aux. vol. Salvation Army, Milw. Recipient Honorable Mention for painting Bayshore Merchants Assn, 1969, Delta Gamma Art Fair, 1981, Best of Show for painting John Michael Kohler Arts Ctr., 1988. Mem. AAUW, Cedarburg Artists Guild, Wis. Watercolor Soc., Seven Arts Soc. Milw. (pres. 1967-68, painters group chmn. 1962-63), Wis. Watercolor Soc., DAR (Milw. chpt. Holiday Folk Fair chmn. 1965-76, libr. historian 1974-77, corr. sec. 1977-80, dir. 1983-86, rec. sec. 1992-95, regent 1995—, Outstanding Jr. Mem. 1966), Wis. Soc. Daus. of Founders and Patriots of Am. (pres. 1964-66, 2d v.p. 1966-68, 70-73, corr. sec. 1976-79), Wis. Ct. Assts., Nat. Soc. Women Descendants Ancient and Hon. Artillery Co. Boston, Wis. Soc. Mayflower Descendents, Delta Zeta. Congregationalist. Home and Studio: 9966 N Corey Ln Mequon WI 53092-6207

SMITH, LEONORE RAE, artist; b. Chgo.; d. Leon and Rose (Hershfield) Goodman; m. Paul Carl Smith, Apr. 17, 1945; children: Jill Henderson, Laurie Christman. Student, Chgo. Art Inst., 1935-40, U. Chgo., 1939—. performer in many Broadway shows, with Met. Opera Quartet, Carnegie Hall, nat. concerts; portrait landscape painter; signature artist Oil Painters of Am., Chgo., 1992-96; ofcl. artist U.S. Coast Guard, Washington, 1989-95; cert. artist Am. Portrait Soc., Huntington Harbor, Calif., 1985; nat. adv. bd. The Portrait Club, N.Y.C., 1983. Pres. Pacific Palisades Rep. Women, Calif. Recipient Best of Show awards Salamagundi U.S. Coast Guard, N.Y.C., 1989, Pacific Palisades Art Assn., 1987, 1st prize in oils Greater L.A. Art Competition, Santa Monica, Calif., 1995, prize The Artist's Mag., 1995, Internat. Soc. Artists, 1977, 1st Pl. The Artists Mag. Internat. Dream Studies Competition, 1996. Mem. Salmagundi Club, Pacific Palisades Art Assn. (past pres.), Calif. Art Club, Oil Painters of Am., Am. Portrait Soc.

SMITH, LINDA A., congresswoman, former state legislator; m. Vern Smith; children: Sheri, Robi. Office mgr.; former mem. Wash. State Ho. of Reps.; mem. Wash. State Senate; congresswoman, Wash. 3rd Dist. U.S. House Reps., Washington, D.C., 1995—. Republican. Home: 10009 NW Ridgecrest Ave Vancouver WA 98685-5159 Office: 1217 Longworth Washington DC 20515*

SMITH, LINDA H., mathematics educator; b. Birmingham, Ala., May 16, 1963; d. Edward H. and Mattie L. (Ellison) H.; m. James A. Smith Jr., Dec. 23, 1988; children: Jimmy, Kaytie. BS in Math., U. So. Miss., 1989, BS in Secondary Edn., 1989. Math. tchr. So. Jones H.S., Ellisville, Miss., 1989-90, West Ouachita H.S., West Monroe, La., 1990-94. Address: 5633 Northglenn Dr Johnston IA 50131-1293

SMITH, LINDA LOU, city official; b. Fullerton, Ky., Jan. 26, 1943; d. James Oliver and Ethel Lucille (Stewart) Newman; m. Richard Glenn Smith, Aug. 28, 1959; children: Richard Jr., Janet Smith Sparks, Robert Orin. Student, Wayne County C.C., 1979, Detroit Bus. Inst., 1985; cert. mcpl. clk., Mich. State U., 1992. Sec. Brownstown (Mich.) Twp., 1976-85, apptd. dep. clk., 1988, elected clk., 1988-92, 1992—. Bd. dirs. Downriver Comty. Conf., Southgate, Mich., 1988-92; sec., vice-chair Downriver Comty. Alliance, Southgate, 1992-95; mem. Wayne County Election Scheduling Bd., Detroit, 1988—; mem. dist 16 Mich. Dem. Party, Wayne, 1988-93; elected Brownstown Precinct Del., 1992—. Recipient Spl. Svc. award Downriver Human Svc. Ctr., 1984. Mem. LWV (dir. 1988—), Internat. Inst. Mcpl. Clks. (cert. mcpl. clk., advanced acad. edn.), Mich. Mcpl. Clks. Assn., Wayne County Clks. Assn., South Wayne County C. of C., Jaycees (v.p. 1974, 77, pres. 1975, 78, Key Woman), Kiwanis. Home: 24781 Pamela Brownstown MI 48134 Office: Charter Twp Brownstown 21313 Telegraph Rd Brownstown MI 48183

SMITH, LISA ANN PETER, nursing administrator; b. Greenwich, Conn., Mar. 15, 1960; d. Erich Carl and Angela Louise (Petti) Peter; m. Robert John Smith, Oct. 23, 1983; children: Melissa Marie, Michael Robert, Matthew Erich. BSN, Fairfield U., 1982. RN, Conn., PALS. Psychiat. nurse Stamford (Conn.) Hosp., 1982-86; pediatric nurse Greenwich (Conn.) Hosp., 1987-92, home care case mgr., 1992-95, clin. nurse supr., 1995—; cons. Glenbrook Cmty. Ctr., Stamford, 1991-93. Roman Catholic. Home: 77 Hirsch Rd Stamford CT 06905 Office: Greenwich Hosp Perryridge Rd Greenwich CT 06830

SMITH, LISA CATHERINE, agricultural economist; b. Kenosha, Wis., Jan. 30, 1964; d. Steve Sigmund Smith and Hilde Iris (Schneider) Betonte. BA summa cum laude, U. Calif. San Diego, La Jolla, 1986; PhD,

U. Wis., 1995. Rsch. asst. dept. agrl. economy Land Tenure Ctr.-U. Wis., Madison, 1988-91; founding fellow West African Rsch. Assn., Burkina Faso, 1991-92; intern Internat. Food Policy Rsch. Inst., Washington, 1991-92; rsch. ast. internat. agrl. programs U. Wis., Madison, 1992-93, family policy fellow Law Sch., 1993-95; diplomacy fellow AAAS, Washington, 1995—. Mem. AAAS, Am. Agrl. Econ. Assn., African Studies Assn., Phi Beta Kappa, Gamma Sigma Delta. Office: US Agy for Internat Devel PPC/PHD Rm 3881 320 21st St NW #6 Washington DC 20523

SMITH, LIZ (MARY ELIZABETH SMITH), newspaper columnist, broadcast journalist; b. Ft. Worth, Feb. 2, 1923; d. Sloan and Sarah Elizabeth (McCall) S. B.J., U. Tex., 1948. Editor Dell Publns., N.Y.C., 1950-53; assoc. producer CBS Radio, 1953-55, NBC-TV, 1955-59; assoc. on Cholly Knickerbocker newspaper column, N.Y.C., 1959-64; film critic Cosmpolitan mag., 1966; columnist Chgo. Tribune-N.Y. Daily News Syndicate (now Tribune Media Services), 1976-91, New York Newsday, L.A. Times Syndicate, 1991—, Family Circle mag., 1993—; TV commentator WNBC-TV, N.Y.C., 1978-91; commentator Fox-TV, N.Y.C., 1991—; freelance mag. writer, also staff writer Sports Illus. mag.; commentator Gossip Show E! Entertainment, 1993—. Author: The Mother Book, 1978. Office: N Y Newsday 2 Park Ave New York NY 10016-5603*

SMITH, LOIS ANN, real estate executive; b. Chgo., Jan. 1, 1941; d. Alburn M. and Ruth A. (Beaver) Beaudoin; m. Dickson K. Smith, Mar. 24, 1962 (div. May 1982); children: Michelle D., Jeffrey D. BA, U. Utah, 1962; MBA, Marquette U., 1972. Asst. mgr. prodn. Northwestern Mut. Life Ins. Co., Milw., 1979-83, asst. mgr., asset mgr., 1983-88; assoc. dir., asset mgmt. Asset Mgmt., 1988-89; dir. asset mgmt. Northwestern Mut. Life Ins. Co., Milw., 1990-95, dir. real estate equities, 1995—. Cons. Girl Scouts Am., Milw., 1986, YWCA, Milw., 1986, bd. dirs. YWCA, 1981-87; bd. dirs. Wis. Rep. Orgn., 1985-87. Mem. Internat. Council Shopping Ctrs., Profl. Dimensions, Beta Gamma Sigma. Unitarian. Home: 21N W 25090 Cir E Pewaukee WI 53072 Office: Northwestern Mut Life Ins Co 720 E Wisconsin Ave Milwaukee WI 53202-4703

SMITH, LOIS COLSTON, secondary school educator; b. Edgewater, Ala., Aug. 3, 1919; d. Roy Minnie and Rebecca (Hayes) Colston; children: Linnie Ree Colston Carter, Lois Louise Colston Smith, Jessie Mae Colston Smith, Johnniza Colston Purifoy, Johnny Colston, Dorothy Dean Colston Cottingham, Lillian Dolly B. Colston Tarver. BS, A&M U., 1939; MA, N.Y.U., 1957. Vocat. Home Econ. Edn. 3rd and 4th grade tchr. Sulligent, Ala., 1957-61; elem. prin. Millport, Ala., 1962-67; 11th grade sci. and social studies tchr. Vernon, Ala., 1967-70; 7th-9th grade gen. vocat. home econ. tchr. Tuscaloosa, Ala., 1970-80, 7th grade gen. and voca. home econ. tchr., 1980-92; ret., 1995. Chmn. Voters registration, Tuscaloosa, Ala., 1980; troop leader Girl Scouts Am., Tuscaloosa, Ala., 1967-92; mem. bd. dirs. Shelter State Community Coll. Wellness Coun., 1993. Recipient Tombigbee Girl Scout 15 yr. svc. pin, Cert. Appreciation, Valuable Svc. award, Girl Scouts; named Zeta of Yr., Beta Eta Zeta chpt., Stillman Coll., 1983, Golden Cert. of Appreciation and Admiration Ala. A&M U., Huntsville, 1993. Mem. Ala. Edn. Assn., NEA, Order of Eastern Star, Ala. Vocat. Assn., AAUW, Beta Eta Zeta. Democrat. Baptist. Home: 3238 18th Pl Tuscaloosa AL 35401-4102

SMITH, LOLA CAROL, auto dealership administrator, beauty salon owner; b. Devils Lake, N.D., Apr. 8, 1937; d. Howard Merton and Jeannette (Oliver) Rice; m. Lawrence John Smith, Mar. 24, 1958; children: Mary Kay Brown, Jeannette Burrier, Bert Smith. Student, Aakers Bus. Coll., Grand Forks, N.D., 1957. Sec. Law office, Grand Forks, 1956; exec. sec. City of Grand Forks, 1956-57; acct. Forx Motor Co., Grand Forks, 1957-58, No. Mont. Hosp., Havre, 1967-76; adminstrv. mgr. G and B Motors, Inc., Havre, 1976—; owner Golden Belle Beauty Shoppe, Havre, 1982—. Mem. Soroptimist Internat. Am. of Havre (treas., v.p., pres.), Cath. Daughters Am. (vice regent, fin. sec., regent), Coun. Cath. Women (sec., treas., pres.). Roman Catholic.

SMITH, LORETTA MAE, contracting officer; b. Washington Twp., Pa., May 25, 1939; d. Irvin Calvin and Viola Mary (Deibler) Shambaugh; 1 child, Miriam Estella Smith. B in Humanities, Pa. State U., 1984. Bookkeeper Harrisburg (Pa.) Nat. Bank, 1957-62; contract specialist USN, Mechanicsburg, Pa., 1987—; founder Telecare, Harrisburg, Pa., 1972-82. Active ARC, instr. CPR, 1982—; active Girl Scouts U.S., trainer, 1972—. Recipient Hemlock award Hemlock coun. Girl Scouts U.S., Harrisburg, 1981; Merit scholar Hall Found., 1982. Mem. Nat. Contract Mgmt. Assn., Mensa.

SMITH, LUCY, intercultural communication specialist; b. Krakow, Poland, June 15, 1933; came to U.S., 1968; d. Henryk Kreisler and Mina Grunhut; divorced; 1 child, Daniel. MFA equivalent, Acad. Fine Arts, Warsaw, Poland, 1959; postgrad., Sorbonne, Paris, 1961-65, l'Acad. Grande Chaumiere, 1963. Cert. ESL trainer Minn. Literacy Coun. Rschr. Spanish art Doubleday, Spain, 1963; comty. faculty mem. Met. State U., St. Paul, 1970-79; media coord. St. Paul Open Sch., 1979; costume designer Penumbra Theater, St. Paul, 1979; interculturalist, 1980—; speaker on Holocaust, Nat. Conf., The Jewish Hist. Soc., Omaha, 1989, Jewish Comty. Rels. Coun. of Minn. and the Dakotas, 1989—; intercultural presenter Nat. Tchrs. ESL Conf., St. Paul, 1990; spkr. on status of women in Poland, Internat. Women's Rights Watch, The Humphrey Inst., U. Minn., 1990; intercultural workshop leader Internat. Soc. for Intercultural Edn., Tng. and Rsch., Internat. Congress, Banff, Can., 1991, Internat. Congress, Montego Bay, Jamaica, 1992; intercultural presenter Minn. Assn. of Continuing Adult Edn., St. Paul, 1992, 93, 94; intercultural workshop leader Nat. Laubach Literacy Confs., Raleigh, N.C., 1992, Little Rock, 1994; trainer Minn. Alts. to Violence Program, 1991—. Pub. art: Une Experience d'Orientation/Esprit mag., Paris, 1966, (textbook) Every Woman Has a Story, 1982; editor: (newsletters) The Citizen, 1980-82, AVP Matters, 1995—; contbr. to profl. publs. Chair The Ethiopian Jewry Com., The Jewish Comty. Rels. Coun. of Minn. and the Dakotas, 1988-90; conceived program for mut. exch. of Spanish and Am. cultures, St. Paul YWCA. Recipient 2d prize for story St. Paul Jewish Comty. Ctr., 1985. Mem. NOW (bd. dirs. Minn. chpt. 1994—). Home: 1747 Randolph Saint Paul MN 55105-2154

SMITH, DAME MAGGIE, actress; b. Ilford, Eng., Dec. 28, 1934; d. Nathaniel and Margaret (Hutton) S.; m. Robert Stephens, 1967 (div. 1974); m. Beverley Cross, 1974. Grad., Oxford High Sch. Girls; D.Litt. (hon.), St. Andrews, 1971; DLitt (hon.), Oxford U., 1994. dir. United British Artists, 1982—. Stage and film actress, 1952—; stage appearances include: New Faces, debut N.Y.C., 1956, Share My Lettuce, 1957, The Stepmother, 1958, Rhinoceros, 1960, Strip The Willow, 1960, The Rehearsal, 1961, The Private Ear and The Public Eye, 1962, Mary, Mary, 1961; appearances at Old Vic, 1959-60, Nat. Theatre, London, 1963—; productions at Nat. Theatre include Private Lives, 1972, Othello, Hay Fever, Master Builder, Hedda Gabbler, Much Ado About Nothing, Miss Julie, Black Comedy, Stratford Festival, Ont., Can., 1976, 77, 78, 80, Antony and Cleopatra, Macbeth, Three Sisters, Richard III, Night and Day, London and N.Y.C., 1979-80, Virginia, London, 1981, Way of the World, Chichester Festival, London, 1984-85, Interpreters, London, 1985-86, Lettice and Lovage, 1988, also in N.Y., 1990, The Importance of Being Earnest, 1993, Three Tall Women, 1994; films include Othello, 1966, The Honey Pot, 1967, Oh What a Lovely War, 1968, Hot Millions, 1968, The Prime of Miss Jean Brodie, 1968 (Acad. award for best actress), Love and Pain and The Whole Damn Thing, 1971, Travels With My Aunt, 1972, Murder by Death, 1976, Death on the Nile, 1977, California Suite, 1978 (Acad. award for best supporting actress), Quartet, 1978, Clash of the Titans, 1981, Evil under the Sun, 1981, The Missionary, 1982, A Private Function, 1984 (best actress award Brit. Acad. of Film & TV Arts, 1985), Lily in Love, 1985, A Room With a View, 1985, The Lonely Passion of Judith Hearn, 1987 (Brit. Acad. of Film & TV Arts award, 1989), Paris By Night, 1988, Hook, 1991, Sister Act, 1992, The Secret Garden, 1993, Richard III, 1995, The First Wives Club, 1996; TV films include Memento Mori, 1992, Suddenly Last Summer, 1993 (Lead Actress-Miniseries Emmy nominee, 1993); BBC-TV appearance Bed Among the Lentils, 1988. Recipient Best Actress award Eve. Std., 1962, 70, 82, 85, 94, Best Film Actress award Soc. Film and TV Arts U.K., 1968, Film Critics Guild, 1968, Taomina Gold award, 1985, Antoinette Perry award (Tony), 1990, Shakespeare prize, 1991; decorated Dame Brit. Empire, 1989; named Actress of Yr., Variety Club, 1963, 72, Brit. Acad. Best Screen Actress, 1985; Brit. Film Inst. fellow, 1992, Theater Hall of Fame, 1994. Office: Write on Cue, 15 New Row 3d Fl, London WC2N 4LA, England*

SMITH, MARA A., small business owner, artist; b. Houston, July 31, 1945; d. Charles Parker and Mary Lee (Langford) S. BS, Tex. Woman's U., 1969, MFA, 1980. Owner, pres. Archtl. Murals in Brick, Seattle, 1977—; lectr. in field. Executed murals in brick Loew's Anatole Hotel, Dallas, 1978, 83, Am. Bank and Trust Co. Bldg., Reading, Pa., 1983, Pacific N.W. Bell Ctr., Seattle, 1985, One Bethesda Ctr., Bethesda, Md., 1986, Dragon Hill Hotel, U.S. Army, Seoul, Republic of Korea, 1989, Tarleton State U. (Tex. A&M U.), Stephenville, Tex., 1994, Small Mammal Reptile Pavilion Lincoln Park Zoo, Chgo., 1996, others; contbr. articles to profl. jours. Mem. NOW (co-director). Named one of Outstanding Young Women of Am., 1978, Disting. Alumna, Tex. Woman's U. Mem. Internat. Sculpture Ctr., Artist Trust. Office: 339 NW 82nd St Seattle WA 98117-4033

SMITH, MARCIA JEAN, accountant, tax specialist, financial consultant; b. Kansas City, Mo., Oct. 19, 1947; d. Eugene Hubert and Marcella Juanita (Greene) S. Student, U. Nebr., 1965-67; BA, Jersey City State Coll., 1971; MBA in Taxation, Golden Gate U., 1976, postgrad., 1976-77; MS in Acctg., Pace U., 1982; Cert. of completion, Cours Commerciaux de Geneve, 1985-86. Legal intern Port Authority, N.Y., N.J., N.Y.C., 1972; legis. aide to Senator Harrison A. Williams Washington, 1973; tax accountant Bechtel Corp., San Francisco, 1974-77; sr. tax accountant Equitable Life Assurance Soc. U.S., N.Y.C., 1977, sec., 1977-79; tax sr. Arthur Andersen & Co., N.Y.C., 1979-82; pres. M.J. Smith Co., N.Y.C., 1983-85; prin. owner MJS Cons. Svcs. Internat. Tax Cons., Boston, Mass., 1988-93; gen. auditor dept. fin. Fulton County Govt., Atlanta, 1993-95; auditor State of Georgia, Dept. Med. Assistance, 1995—; cons. U.N., specialized agys., Geneva, 1985-87; asst. sec. Equico Lessors, Inc., Mpls., 1977-78, Equitable Gen. Ins. Group, Ft. Worth, 1977-79, Heritage Life Infield Assurance Co., Toronto, Ont., Can., 1978-79, Informatics, Inc., L.A., 1978-79; sec. Equico Capital Corp., N.Y.C. 1977-79, Equico Personal Credit, Inc., Colorado Springs, Colo., 1978-79, Equico Securites, Inc., N.Y.C., 1977-79, Equitable Environ. Health, Inc., Woodbury, N.Y., 1977-79; tax cons., real estate salesperson. Spl. advisor U.S. Congl. Adv. Bd.; human rights chmn. YWCA, Lincoln, Nebr., 1966-67; mem. Atlanta Women's Network. Spl. advisor U.S. Congl. Adv. Bd.; human rights chmn. YWCA, Lincoln, Nebr., 1966-67; mem. Atlanta Women's Network. Mem. AAAS, AAUW, NAA (Swiss Romande chpt.), Am. Mgmt. Assn., Nat. Soc. Pub. Accts., Inst. Mgmt. Accts., Am. Acctg. Assn., Internat. Assn. Fin. Planners, Internat. Fin. Mgmt. Assn., Am. Women's Club of Geneva, Nat. Assn. Women Bus. Owners, Am. Assn. Individual Investors, Inst. Internal Auditors, N.Y. Acad. Scis., Nat. Hist. Soc., Nat. Assn. Tax Practitioners, Assn. Managerial Economists, Postal Commemorative Soc., Am. Mus. Natural Nistory, Nat. Trust Historic Preservation, Ga. Govt. Fin. Officers Assn., Internat. Tax Inst., Ga. Soc. CPAs, Ill. CPA Soc., Assn. Cert. Fraud Examiners, Assn. Govt. Accts., Am. Econs. Assn., UN Assn. USA, EDP Auditors Assn., Mass. Soc. Ind. Accts., Acad. Legal Studies in Bus., Am. Bus. Law Assn., Internat. Platform Assn., U.S. Senatorial Club. Office: State of Ga Dept Med Assist Ste 502 1430 W Peachtree St NW Atlanta GA 30309-2936

SMITH, MARGARET ANN, health care executive; b. Marshall, Ark., May 17, 1951; d. Vernon J. and Helen M. (Talbert) Sorensen; m. Rodney J. Smith, Aug. 24, 1969 (div.); children: Shannon Denette, Rodrick Cannon. Cert. patient accounts mgr. Coord. cen. registration Community Gen. Osteo. Hosp., Harrisburg, Pa., 1979-83; supr. patient accounts The Gettysburg (Pa.) Hosp., 1983-84; dir. patient accounts Polyclinic Med. Ctr., Harrisburgh, 1984-87; sr. cons. Arthur Young & Co., Washington, 1987-89; asst. v.p. bus. svc. Regional Healthcare Systems, Inc., Brooksville, Fla., 1989—. Mem. Soc. of Patient Accounts Mgmt., Am. Guild of Patient Accounts Mgmt., Nat. Assn. Hosp. Admitting Mgrs., Keystone Assn. Patient Accounts Mgrs. (Outstanding Mem. 1985-87). Republican. Home: 1506 June Ave Brooksville FL 34601-3929 Office: Regional Healthcare Sys Brooksville FL 34601

SMITH, MARGARET BRAND, insurance executive, lawyer; b. Chattanooga, Okla., June 29, 1911; d. William August and Flora May (Davis) Brand; m. Harry Eben Smith, July 24, 1937 (dec. 1970). LLB, Jefferson Sch. Law, Dallas. Pvt. practice, also ins. cos. atty. Dallas, 1937-57; exec. v.p. Union Bankers Ins. Co., Dallas, 1957-62, pres., chief exec. officer, 1962-68, vice chair, 1968-73; pres., chief exec. officer United Gen. Ins. Co., Dallas, 1973-76; chmn. bd. Dallas Gen. Life Ins. Co., Dallas, 1980—. Pres. Dallas Girl Scouts, 1952; bd. dirs., pres. Presbyn. Children's Home, Waxahachie, Tex., 1970-76; elder North Park Presbyn. Ch., Dallas, 1972-76. Recipient Top Hat award Nat. Assn. Bus. and Profl. Women, Chgo., 1963, Award of Excellence Dallas Bus. and Profl. Women, 1964, Mature Woman award Altrusa Club, 1965, Woman of Awareness B'nai B'rith, 1965, Outstanding Svc. award North Dallas Bus. and Profl. Women, 1969. Mem. State Bar of Tex., Dallas Bar Assn. Republican. Presbyterian.

SMITH, MARGARET PHYLLIS, editor, consultant; b. Plymouth, Pa., Aug. 24, 1925; d. Harold Dewitt and Mae Elmira (Bittenbender) S. AB magna cum laude, Bucknell U., 1946, AM, 1947; postgrad., U. Pa., summer 1951-54. Instr. English Bucknell U., Lewisburg, Pa., 1947-52, asst. prof., 1952-55; personnel asst. RCA Labs., Princeton, N.J., 1955-58, staff writer pub. affairs dept., 1958-76, adminstr. communications, 1976-87; editor spl. projects David Sarnoff Rsch. Ctr. (formerly RCA Labs.), Princeton, 1987-92, contbg. editor, 1992—; mng. editor Vision mag. David Sarnoff Rsch. Ctr., 1987—, editor UPDATE newsletter, 1969—. Editor: 1942-67 Twenty-five Years at RCA Laboratories, 1968. Mem. corp. communications com. United Way, Princeton, 1976-88. Mem. AAUW, N.J. Press Women (publicity dir. 1985-86), Internat. Assn. Bus. Communicators. Episcopalian. Office: David Sarnoff Rsch Ctr 201 Washington Rd Princeton NJ 08540-6449

SMITH, MARGARET RILEY, accountant, systems analyst; b. Rochester, N.Y., June 10, 1960; d. James Michael and Katherine Persis (Baker) R. AAS in Acctg., Community Coll. Finger Lakes, Canandaigua, N.Y., 1980; BA in Acctg., St. John Fisher Coll., Rochester, 1982; MBA, U. Rochester, 1992. Cert. mgmt. acct., cash mgr. Contr. Carpet Clearance Outlet Stores, Rochester, 1984-86; cost acct. Comstock Foods div. Curtice Burns Foods Inc., Rochester, 1986-87, acctg. systems coord. parent co., 1987-88, asst. mgr. corp. acctg., 1988-92; fin. analyst Corning (N.Y.) Asahi Video, 1992-94; instr. Elmira Bus. Inst., 1995—. Vol. Rochester Area Multiple Sclerosis Assn., 1987-91; treas. Chemung Valley Multiple Sclerosis Soc. Assn.; sr. resource assoc. Compeer, Rochester, 1988-91. Mem. Nat. Assn. Accts. (assoc. bd. dirs. 1987, assoc. dir. 1989, dir. 1990-91), Inst. Mgmt. Accts. (pres. 1996—). Republican. Roman Catholic. Office: Elmira Bus Inst 180 Clemens Ctr Pkwy Elmira NY 14901

SMITH, MARGHERITA, writer, editor; b. Chgo., May 24, 1922; d. Henry Christian and Alicia (Koke) Steinhoff; m. Rufus Zartman Smith, June 26, 1943; children: Matthew Benjamin, Timothy Rufus. AB, Ill. Coll., 1943. Proofreader Editorial Experts, Inc., Alexandria, Va., 1974; mgr. proofreading div. Editorial Experts, Inc., Alexandria, 1978-79, mgr. publs. div., 1979-81, asst. to pres., 1980-81; freelance editor, cons. Annandale, Va., 1981—; instr. proofreading and copy editing, George Washington U., Washington, 1978-82; presenter workshops on proofreading for various profl. orgns., 1981—. Author: (as Peggy Smith) Simplified Proofreading, 1980, Proofreading Manual and Reference Guide, 1981, Proofreading Workbook, 1981, The Proof Is In the Reading: A Comprehensive Guide to Staffing and Management of Typographic Proofreading, 1986, Mark My Words: Instructions and Practice in Proofreading, 1987, rev. edit., 1993, Letter Perfect: A Guide to Practical Proofreading, 1995; contbr. articles to revs. to various publs. Recipient Best Instrnl. Reporting award Newsletter Assn. Am., 1980, Disting. Achievement award for excellence in ednl. journalism Ednl. Press Assn. Am., 1981, Disting. Citizen award Ill. Coll., 1992. Home and Office: 9120 Belvoir Woods Pky # 110 Fort Belvoir VA 22060-2722

SMITH, MARIE THERESE, home health agency; b. Bklyn., Oct. 22, 1928; d. Edwin Lyden Smith and Marie Byrne. BS, St. John's U., 1955, MS, 1965. RN, N.Y. Head nurse Kings County Hosp. Ctr., Bklyn., 1963-66; supr. in svc. edn. Long Island Coll. Hosp., Bklyn., 1963-66; asst. exec. dir. Cath. Med. Ctr. Bklyn. and Queen, Inc., 1966-84; adminstrn. home health program Flushing Hosp. & Med. Ctr., Flushing, N.Y., 1984-88; home health agy. adminstrn., dir. patient svc. Brookdale Hosp. Med. Ctr., Bklyn, 1988-90; home health cons., 1990-94, Cmty. Health Accrediting Program, Inc., N.Y.C., 1994—. Mem. Girling Health Care, Doonan Drake Disable. Roman Catholic. Home: 553 Argyle Road Brooklyn NY 11230

SMITH, MARILYN PAULETTE, guidance counselor; b. Okla. City, Okla., Feb. 18, 1950; d. Paul Eugene Hoffman and Ramona Jean (Satterlee) Davidson; m. Douglas Alan Smith, Dec. 12, 1977; children: Zachary, Matthew. Cert. libr. sci., Northeastern Okla. State U., 1975; BA in Sociology, Northeastern State Coll., 1973; MS in Counseling Psych., Northeastern State U., 1994. Shelter mgr. Help in Crisis, Tahlequah, Okla., 1990-93, rape responder, 1990—, counselor, 1994-95; psych asst. Wagoner (Okla.) County Guidance Ctr., 1995—; crisis line vol. Help in Crisis, 1986-93. Bd. mem. Opportunity House Bill Willis Mental Health, 1994-96. Democrat.

SMITH, MARJORIE AILEEN MATTHEWS, museum director; b. Richmond, Va., Aug. 19, 1918; d. Harry Anderson and Adelia Charlotte (Howland) Matthews; m. Robert Woodrow Smith, July 23, 1945 (dec. Mar. 1992). Pilot lic., Taneytown (Md.) Aviation Svc., 1944, cert. ground sch. instr., 1945. Founder, editor, pub. Spinning Wheel, Taneytown, 1945-63; v.p. Antiques Publs., Inc., Taneytown, 1960-68; pres. Prism Inc., Taneytown, 1968-78; mus. dir. Trapshooting Hall of Fame, Vandalia, Ohio, 1976—, sec., 1993—. Co-author: Handbook of Tomorrow's Antiques, 1954; contbr. articles to profl. publs. Sec. Balt. area coun. Girl Scouts USA, 1950. Named to All-Am. Trapshooting team Sports Afield mag., 1960, 61. Mem. Nat. League Am. Pen Women, Amateur Trapshooting Assn. (life), Am. Contract Bridge League, Internat. Assn. Sports Mus. and Halls of Fame (bd. dirs. 1993-94). Lutheran. Office: Trapshooting Hall of Fame 601 W National Rd Vandalia OH 45377-1036

SMITH, MARSHA ELLEN, secondary education educator; b. Austin, Tex., Nov. 26, 1963; d. Robert Hadley and Betty Ann (Bullock) Smith. BA in Spanish, U. Tex., 1986, BS in Secondary Edn., 1988; MEd, Tex. Tech U., 1995. Cert. tchr., Tex. Tchr. mid. sch. Northside Ind. Sch. Dist., San Antonio, 1988-90; tchr. h.s. Eagle Mt.-Saginaw Ind. Sch. Dist., Saginaw, Tex., 1990-92, New Deal (Tex.) Ind. Sch. Dist., 1992-96. ESL tchr. Hyde Pk. Bapt. Ch., Austin, 1987-89. Mem. NOW, Children Internat. Democrat. Episcopalian.

SMITH, MARSHA H., state agency administrator, lawyer; b. Boise, Idaho, Mar. 24, 1950; d. Eugene F. and Joyce (Ross) Hatch; m. Terrell F. Smith, Aug. 29, 1970; 2 children. BS in Biology/Edn., Idaho State U., 1973; MLS, Brigham Young U., 1975; JD, U. Wash., 1980. Bar: Idaho, U.S. Dist. Ct. Idaho, U.S. Ct. Appeals (9th cir.), U.S. Ct. Appeals (D.C. cir.). Dep. atty. gen. Bus./Consumer Protection Divsn., Boise, 1980-81; dep. atty. gen. Idaho Pub. Utilities Commn., Boise, 1981-89, dir. policy and external rels., 1989-91, commr., 1991—, pres., 1991-95; mem. Harvard Electricity Policy Group, Nat. Coun. on Competition and The Electric Industry. Legis. dist. chair Ada County Democrats, Idaho, 1986-89. Mem. Nat. Assn. Regulatory Utility Commrs. (chair electric strategic issues subcom.), Idaho State Bar, Western Conf. Pub. Svc. Commrs. Office: Idaho Pub Utilities Commn PO Box 83720 Boise ID 83720-0074

SMITH, MARTHA VIRGINIA BARNES, elementary school educator; b. Camden, Ark., Oct. 12, 1940; d. William Victor and Lillian Louise (Givens) Barnes; m. Basil Loren Smith, Oct. 11, 1975; children: Jennifer Frost, Sean Barnes. BS in Edn., Ouachita Bapt. U., 1963; postgrad., Auburn U., 1974, Henderson State U., 1975. Cert. tchr., Mo. 2d and 1st grade tchr. Brevard County Schs., Titusville and Cocoa, Fla., 1963-65, 69-70; 1st grade tchr. Lakeside Sch. Dist., Hot Springs, Ark., 1965-66, Harmony Grove Sch., Camden, 1972-76; 1st and 5th grade tchr. Cumberland County Schs., Fayetteville, N.C., 1966-69; kindergarten tchr. Pulaski County Schs., Ft. Leonard Wood, Mo., 1970-72; 3d grade tchr. Mountain Grove (Mo.) Schs., 1976—; chmn. career ladder com. Mountain Grove Dist., 1991-96. Children's pastor 1st Bapt. Ch., Vanzant, Mo., 1984-88. Mem. NEA (pres.-elect Mountain Grove chpt. 1995—), Kappa Kappa Iota. Office: Mountain Grove Elem Sch 320 E 9th St Mountain Grove MO 65711

SMITH, MARTHE ELISABETH, retired pathologist; b. N.Y.C., Apr. 17, 1928; d. Glenn Waldo and Frankie Ernestine (Faul) S. BA, U. Oreg., 1948; MS, U. Oreg. Med. Sch., 1951, MD, 1951. Diplomate Am. Bd. Nuclear Medicine, Am. Bd. Anatomic and Clin. Pathology. Dir. cytology lab. U. Calif. Med. Sch., San Francisco, 1956-58; assoc. pathologist St. Luke's Hosp., San Francisco, 1957-87; ret., 1987; asst. clin. prof. U. Calif. Med. Sch., 1958—. Mem. Medicare utilization rev. com. for extended care facility San Francisco Med. Soc., 1970-75. Mem. Marin Ski Club (corr. sec. 1970—, historian, trophy 1960, Gold medal Triway race 1987, Blue Ribbon 1986), 4th Thursday Salmon Fishing Club (numerous awards).

SMITH, MARY ALICE See ALICE, MARY

SMITH, MARY ELINOR, retired dean, mathematics educator, counselor; b. Louisville, Dec. 18, 1913; d. Harry Robert and Susan Magdalene (Corrigan) S. AA, Sacred Heart Jr. Coll., Louisville, 1933; BA, Nazareth Coll., 1935; postgrad., U. Minn., summers 1937-39; MA, Cath. U. Am., 1951; student NDEA Inst., Mich. State U., 1967-68. Tchr. math. Jefferson County Schs., Medora, Ky., 1935-36; substitute tchr. Louisville Pub. Schs., 1936-37, tchr. math., 1937-44; hosp. staff aide ARC, 1944-45; caseworker Jefferson County Children's Home, Louisville, 1946-48; dean women, lectr. Quincy (Ill.) Coll., 1950-52; dean women, lectr. Cath. U., Washington, 1952-71, assoc. dean counseling and svcs., 1971-79; ret., 1979; scholarship evaluator AAUW, Washington, 1975-79, Youth for Understanding, Washington, 1980-86; conf. lectr. Barry U., Miami Shores, Fla., 1990. Chair Task Force on AIDS, Spalding U., Louisville, 1988-89; bd. trustees Ursuline Campus Schs., Inc., Louisville, 1990-92; mem. St. Francis of Assisi Parish, 1986—. Recipient Cert. of Appreciation, Black Students of Cath. U., 1977, Frank A. Kunz Alumni award Cath. U., 1978, Outstanding Svc. Appreciation award Undergrad. Student Govt., Cath. U., 1978-79, Citation, Nat. Assn. Women Deans, Adminstrs., Counselors, 1979, Citation, Pres. and Bd. Trustees of Cath. U., 1952-79; Mary Elinor Smith Community Svc. award, 1980—, Caritas award Spalding U., 1985. Mem. APA, Women's Overseas Svc. League (treas. 1991-92), Ky. Ch. Myasthenia Gravis Found., Louisville Geneal. Soc. (city/county chair 1989-90), Spalding U. Alumni Assn., Ursuline Acad. Alumnae Assn., Filson Club, Veritas Soc. Democrat. Roman Catholic. Home: 2126 Village Dr Apt 2 Louisville KY 40205-1940

SMITH, MARY HELENA, artist, author; b. Kansas City, Mo., Jan. 15, 1930; d. Edwin Jennings and Mary Pauline (Remington) Anderson; m. Robert Alan Smith, Dec. 14, 1957 (div. 1978); 1 child, Susanah Mara Smith Malara. BA, Ottawa (Kans.) U., 1950; postgrad., U. Kans., 1951, Kansas City Art Inst. Artist animation dept. Walt Disney Prodns., Burbank, Calif., 1954-58; pvt. cartoonist Calif., 1977-92; tchr. Mira Costa Coll., Calif., 1991, So. Oreg. State Coll., 1993; freelance cartoonist, caricaturist, Calif. Author: Long Ago Elf, 1968, Crocodiles Have Big Teeth All Day, 1970. Mem. Rogue Gallery. Office: 1345 W Jones Creek Rd Grants Pass OR 97526

SMITH, MARY HILL, volunteer; b. Dallas, Jan. 14, 1943; d. Wendell Tennyson and Laura Leta (Massey) Hill; m. Andrew Jeptha Kincannon Smith, July 10, 1965; children: Emily Catherine, Andrew III, Bradley Tennyson. BA with Volunteer Adminstrn. Cert., Metro. State U., 1987. Pres., mem. Raggedy Ann chpt. Children's Health Ctr. Assn., Mpls., 1972-83; pres. exec. com. Jr. League Mpls., 1973-84; dir. 75th Anniversary bd. Minn. Orchestral Assn., Mpls., 1977-78; dir. Guthrie Theater Bd., Mpls., 1979-83; bd. dirs. YWCA, 1981-82; pres. Wayzata (Minn.) Cmty. Edn. Bd., 1981-83; mem. adv. bd. N. Hennepin C. C., Brooklyn Center, Minn., 1982-84; chair, sec. Wayzata Sch. Bd., 1984-92; chair Minn. Women's Polit. Caucus, St. Paul, 1984-92; bd. dirs. Hennepin Tech. Coll., Plymouth, Minn., 1985-92; chair, bd. dirs. Art Ctr. Minn., Orono, 1985-92; mem. Metro. Coun., St. Paul, 1993—. Chmn. transp. com. Twin West Chamber Leadership com., Minnetonka, Minn., 1992; mem. State Ethical Practice Bd., St. Paul, 1986-91, Gov. Carlson's Re-election com., 1994-95, State Adv. Coun. on Metro Airports, St. Paul, 1995; del. Orono (Minn.) Rep. Party, 1992; active Hennepin County Libr. Found., 1996—, Sheltering Arms Found., 1996—. Republican. Episcopalian. Home: 515 N Ferndale Wayzata MN 55391 Office: Metro Coun 230 E 5th St Saint Paul MN 55101

SMITH, MARY HOWARD HARDING, business consultant; b. Washington, Jan. 24, 1944; d. John Edward Harding and Sonja (Karlow) Harding Mulroney. AB, Duke U., 1965; MPA, Cen. Mich. U., 1975. With U.S. Army, 1968-91; dir. program mgmt. systems devel. agy. U.S. Army, Washington, 1987-91, dep. dir. program analysis and evaluation, 1987-91; dep. dir. def. info. Office Sec. Def., Arlington, Va., 1991-94; pres. Enterprise Opportunities, Inc., Arlington, Va., 1994—. Contbr. numerous articles to profl. jours. Bd. dirs. Army Family Action Symposiu, Washington, 1982. Mem. Am. Soc. Mil. Comptrollers, NAFE. Home and Office: 1805 24th St S Arlington VA 22202-1534

SMITH, MARY JACKSON, elementary education educator; b. Uvalde, Tex., Mar. 21, 1947; d. William Eaton and Nell (Thomas) Jackson; m. Dewey Nelson Smith, Aug. 19, 1967; children: Nancy Nell, Mary Meighan. Student, Sullins Jr. Coll., Bristol, Va., 1965-66, Tex. Tech. U., 1966-68; BS cum laude, U. Tex. Edinburg, 1976. Cert. tchr., Tex. Tchr. elem. Rio Grande City (Tex.) Ind. Sch. Dist., 1974-75, Edinburg Consol. Ind. Sch. Dist., 1976-79, St. Matthews Episc. Day Sch., Edinburg, 1979-83, St. Mary's Hall, San Antonio, 1983-87, Comal Ind. Sch. Dist., Bulverde, Tex., 1992—. Bd. dirs. The Canterbury Sch., McAllen, Tex., 1981-83. Alamo Writing Project fellow Trinity U., 1986. Mem. AAUW, NOW. Democrat. Episcopalian. Office: Bulverde Elem Sch 1715 E Ammann Rd Bulverde TX 78163

SMITH, MARY LEVI, academic administrator; b. Jan. 30, 1936. Pres. Ky. State U., Frankfort. Office: Kentucky State U Office of President Frankfort KY 40601

SMITH, MARY LOU, librarian; b. Huntington, Ind., Mar. 8, 1927; d. Harry Martin and Birtha (Fox) Bowers; m. Donald Eugene Smith, Oct. 2, 1948; children: Larry Wayne, Samuel Lee, Lynn Ellen Smith Worch, Michael Ray. BS in Edn., Huntington Coll., 1971; MS in Edn., Ball State U., 1973, MLS, 1973. Cert. tchr.; cert. libr.; cert. audio visual. Profl. musician Ft. Wayne (Ind.) Civic Symphony, 1942-45, Philharmonic Orch., Ft. Wayne, 1945-57, Civic Symphony, Chgo., 1947-49; owner M.L. Smith Reed Co., Huntington, Ind., 1950-65; libr., audio-visual specialist Huntington Sch. Systems, 1971-75; libr. Huntington Coll., 1975-77, Warsaw (Ind.) High Sch., 1978-85, Pub. Libr., Port Isabel, Tex., 1994-95; area coord. Am. Inst. Fgn. Study, Greenwich, Conn., 1978-85. Head ladies dept. YMCA, Huntington, 1966-70; bd. dirs., sec.-treas. Outdoor Resorts, Port Isabel, 1986-92; swimming instr. ARC, 1966-69; mem. Rosary Sodality, Huntington. Mem. AAUW, Ind. Sch. Libr. Assn. (sec. 1973-75), Ind. Sch. Libr. Assn., Ind. Ret. Tchrs. Assn., Altrusa Internat. (editor Warsaw chpt. 1983-86), Sigma Phi Gamma. Roman Catholic. Home: 950 S Garcia St Unit 53 Port Isabel TX 78578-4010 Home (summer): 901 Evergreen Ave Huntington IN 46750-4026 Office: Port Isabel Libr 213 N Yturria St Port Isabel TX 78578-4602

SMITH, MARY LOUISE, real estate broker, salesperson; b. Eldorado, Ill., May 29, 1935; d. Joseph Henry Smith and Opal Marie (Shelton) Hungerford; m. David Lee Smith, June 18, 1961; children: Ricky Eugene, Brenda Sue Smith Millsap. Student, So. Ill. U., 1954-56, 57-58. Cert. substitute tchr., Mo.; cert. real estate broker/salesman, Mo. With acctg. dept. Cen. Hardware Co., St. Louis, 1958-61; mgr. income tax office Tax Teller Inc., St. Louis, 1967-69, H&R Block Co., St. Louis, 1970-76, 83, 92-96; with acctg. dept. Weis Neumann Co., St. Louis, 1976-79; broker/salesperson Century 21 Neubauer Realty Inc., St. Louis, 1980-83, 88-90; sales assoc. John R. Green Realtor, Inc., St. Louis, 1983-85; sales assoc. Century 21 Action Properties, St. Louis, 1985-88, real estate broker/salesperson, 1986-88; real estate broker/salesperson Century 21 Neubauer Realty, Inc., St. Louis, 1988-90, L.K. Wood Realtors, 1992-96; substitute tchr. St. Louis Pub. Schs.; security officer Reliance Security; substitute tchr., St. Louis Bd. Edn., 1967—; security officer Reliance Security Co., 1995—. Younger children's dir. Lafayette Park Bapt. Ch., St. Louis, 1981-95. Mem. Am. Fedn. of Tchrs., St. Louis Realtors. Home: 4558 Adkins Saint Louis MO 63109

SMITH, MARY LOUISE, politics and public affairs consultant; b. Eddyville, Iowa, Oct. 6, 1914; d. Frank and Louise Anna (Jager) Epperson; BA, U. Iowa, 1935; LHD (hon.), Drake U., 1980; LLD (hon.), Grinnell Coll., 1984; m. Elmer Milton Smith, Oct. 7, 1934; children: Robert C., Margaret L., James E. Mem. Eagle Grove (Iowa) Bd. Edn., 1955-60; Republican precinct committeewoman, Eagle Grove, 1960-62, vice-chairwoman, Wright County, Iowa, 1962-63; mem. Rep. Nat. Com., 1964-84, mem. exec. com., 1969-84, mem. conv. reforms com., 1966, vice-chairwoman Steiger com. on conv. reform, 1973, co-chmn. nat. com., 1974, chmn. Com., 1974-77; vice-chairwoman U.S. Commn. on Civil Rights, 1982-83; vice-chairwoman Midwest region Rep. Conf., 1969-71; del. Rep. Nat. Conv., 1968, 72, 76, 80, 84, alt. del., 1964, hon officer, 1988, 92, organized and called to order, 1976; vice-chairwoman Iowa Presdl. campaign, 1964; nat. co-chmn. Physicians Com. for Presdl. Campaign, 1972; co-chairwoman Iowa Com. to Reelect the Pres., 1972; mem. Nat. Commn. on Observance Internat. Women's Year, 1975-77, del. Internat. Women's Yr. Conf., Houston, 1977; vis. fellow Woodrow Wilson Fellowship Found., 1979. Mem. U.S. del. to Extraordinary Session of UNESCO Gen. Conf., Paris, 1973; mem. U.S. del. 15th session population commn. UN Econ. and Social Council, Geneva, 1969; mem. Pres.'s Commn. for Observance of 25th Anniversary of UN, 1970-71; mem. Iowa Commn. for Blind, 1961-63, chairwoman, 1963, mem. Iowa Gov.'s Commn. on Aging, 1962; trustee Robert A. Taft Inst. Govt., 1974-84, Herbert Hoover Presdl. Libr. Assn., Inc., 1979-91. Pres. Eagle Grove Cmty. Chest; bd. dirs. Mental Health Center North Iowa, 1962-63, YWCA of Greater Des Moines, 1983-87, Orchard Place Resdl. Facility for Emotionally Disturbed Children, 1983-88, Learning Channel, cable TV, 1984-87, Iowa Peace Inst., 1985-90, Planned Parenthood of Greater Iowa, 1986-92, U. Iowa Found., 1987—; trustee Drake U., 1990—; bd. dirs. U.S. Inst. Peace, 1990—, Chrysalis Womens Found., 1994—; bd. dirs., nat. co-chair Rep. Mainstream Com.; bd. dirs. Alliance for Arts and Understanding, 1993-96; mem. adv. coun. U. Iowa Hawkeye Fund Women's Program, 1982-87, co-founder Iowa Women's Archives, 1991; chairperson UN Day for Iowa, 1987; polit. communication ctr. conf. U. Okla., 1987; disting. vis. exec. Coll. Bus. Asminstrn. U. Iowa, 1988; co-chmn. select com. on drug abuse City of Des Moines, 1989-90; mem. Des Moines Human Rights Commn., 1995—; hon. chmn. Iowa Student/Parent Mock Election, 1995-96. Named hon. col., mil. staff Gov. Iowa, 1973; Iowa Women's Hall of Fame, 1977; named to Iowa City H.S. Hall of Fame, 1995; recipient Disting. Alumni award U. Iowa, 1984, Hancher Medallion award, 1991; Cristine Wilson medal for equality and justice Iowa Commn. on Status of Women, 1984, Elinor Robson award Coun. for Internat. Understanding, 1992, Pres. award Midwest Archives Conf., 1994; Mary Louise Smith award named in her honor, YWCA, 1988; Mary Louise Smith endowed chair in Women and Politics, Iowa State U., 1995; Brotherhood/Sisterhood award Iowa region NCCJ, 1996. Mem. Women's Aux. AMA, UN Assn., Nat. Conf. Christians and Jews, Nat. Women's Polit. Caucus (adv. bd. 1978—), PEO, Kappa Alpha Theta. Address: 654 59th St Des Moines IA 50312-1250

SMITH, MARYA JEAN, writer; b. Youngstown, Ohio, Nov. 12, 1945; d. Cameron Reynolds and Jean Rose (Sause) Argetsinger; m. Arthur Beverly Smith Jr., Dec. 30, 1968 (div. 1996); children: Arthur Cameron, Sarah Reynolds. BA, Cornell U., 1967. Editorial asst. Seventeen Mag., N.Y.C., 1967-68; promotion writer U. Chgo. Press, 1968-70; asst. account exec. Drucilla Handy Co., Chgo., 1970-72; feature writer various mags. Chgo., 1972-74; freelance writer Cornell U., Ithaca, N.Y., 1975-76, lectr., 1976-77; playwright Playwrights' Ctr. Prodn., Chgo., 1978; humor columnist various jours. Chgo., 1979-81, freelance writer, 1982—. Author: Across the Creek, 1989, Winter-Broken, 1990, Danish edit., 1991; contbr. poetry Primavera, Ariel VI and VIII, 1974, 87, 89; contbr. articles to mags. and papers, 1984—. Vol. reading tutor Literacy Vols. Western Cook County, Oak Park, Ill., 1988-89, Oak Park Pub. Libr. Reading Program, 1990-94. Recipient 1st Pl. for News Writing Associated Ch. Press, 1986, Poetry award Poets and Patrons, 1986, Triton Coll. Salute to Arts, 1987, 89. Mem. Nat. Writers Union, Soc. Children's Book Writers, Author's Guild, Chgo. Women in Pub., Children's Reading Round Table. Roman Catholic.

SMITH, MERILYN J., art teacher; b. Royston, Ga., Jan. 5, 1943; d. William W. and Ruth E. (Johnson) Johnson; m. W. Calvin Smith, Sept. 6, 1964; children: Kymberley Louise Smith, Aimee Elizabeth Smith. Student, Emory U., 1960-62, Ga. State U., 1962-64; BA, La Grange Coll., 1967; MA, U. S.C., 1978. Design and layout artist Farm Record Book Co., Chapel Hill, N.C., 1968-71; art tchr. North Augusta (S.C.) H. S., 1972-76, Aiken H.S., 1977-80, S. Aiken H.S., 1980—; co-dir., co-creator Gateway (Gifted and Talented Edn. Artist Youth), Aiken, S.C., 1985—; tchr. seminar Nat. Gallery Art, Washington, 1993, tchr. intern program S.C. Gov. Sch. Arts, Greenville, S.C., 1982, 84. Contbr. article to profl. jour. One person show Etheredge Ctr., Aiken, S.C., 1995. Fullbright exchange tchr. USA Info. Agy., 1986-87. Mem. Nat. Edn. Assn., Nat. Art Edn. Assn., S.C. Art Edn. Assn. (secondary coord. 1978-79), S.C. Edn. Assn., Aiken County Edn. Assn. Democrat. Episcopalian. Home: 2073 Dibble Rd Aiken SC 29801 Office: S Aiken H S 232 E Pine Log Rd Aiken SC 29803

SMITH, MERILYN ROBERTA, art educator; b. Tolley, N.D., July 24, 1933; d. Robert Coleman and Mathilda Marie (Staael) S. BA, Concordia Coll., Minn., 1953; MA, State U. of Iowa, Iowa City, 1956, MFA, 1966. Tchr. Badger (Minn.) High Sch., 1954; instr. in art Valley City (N.D.) State Tchrs. Coll., 1957, 58; instr. in art U. Wis., Oshkosh, 1967, asst. prof. art, 1969, assoc. prof., 1977-91, prof., 1991-93, prof. emeritus, 1993—; represented by Miriam Perlman Gallery, Chgo.; counselor Luth. Student Ctr., U. Iowa, 1959-65, rsch. asst. in printmaking, 1960-65; owner, dir. James House Gallery, Oshkosh, 1972-77; dir. Allen Priebe Gallery, U. Wis., Oshkosh, 1975. Exhibited in group shows at N.W. Printmakers Internat., Seattle and Portland, Oreg., 1964, Ultimate Concerns 6th Nat. Exhbn., Athens, Ohio, 1965, 55th Nat. Exhbn., Springfield, Mass., 1974, 11th An. So. Tier Arts and Crafts, Corning, N.Y., 1974, Soc. of the Four Arts, Palm Beach, Fla., 1974, Appalachian Nat. Drawing Competition, Boone, N.C., 1975, Rutgers Nat. Drawing Exhbn., Camden, N.J., 1975, 8th and 9th Biennial Nat. Art Exhibit, Valley City, N.D., 1973, 75, Clary-Miner Gallery, Buffalo, 1988, Nat. Art Show, Redding, Calif., 1989, Internat. Printmaker, Buffalo, 1990, Westmoreland Nat. Juried Competition, Youngwood, Pa., 1990, Ariel Gallery, Soho, N.Y., 1990, Grand Prix de Paris Internat., Chapelle De La Sorbonne, Paris, 1990, Nat. Juried Exhbn., Rockford, Ill., 1991, Nat. Invitational Exhbn., Buffalo, 1991, East Coast Artists Nat. Invitational Art Exhbn., Havre de Grace, Md., 1991, Ariel Gallery, Soho, N.Y., 1991, N.Y. Art Expo, 1991, Milw. Art for AIDS Auction, 1991, 92, 94. Mem. Winnebago Hist. Soc., Oshkosh, 1987—. Lutheran. Home: 226 High Ave Oshkosh WI 54901-4734 Office: U Wis Dept Art Oshkosh WI 54901

SMITH, MICHELE, lawyer; b. Ogden, Utah, Feb. 12, 1955; d. Max S. and Grace B. (Gerstman) Smith; m. Philip A. Turner, Aug. 25, 1985. BA, SUNY, Buffalo, 1976; JD, U. Chgo., 1979. Law clk. U.S. Ct. Appeals (7th cir.), Chgo., 1979-81; asst. atty. no. dist. U.S. Atty's Office, Chgo., 1981-89; assoc. gen. counsel Navistar Internat. Transportation Corp., Chgo., 1989—. Mem. Am. Corp. Counsel Assn., Phi Beta Kappa. Office: Navistar Internat Transp Corp 455 N Cityfront Plaza Dr Chicago IL 60611-5503

SMITH, MICHELE, softball player; b. June 21, 1967. Grad., Okla. State U., 1990. Pitcher Redding (Calif.) Rebels, 1993-95. Recipient Gold medal Women's World Challenger Cup, 1992, Intercontental Cup, 1993, South Pacific Classic, 1994, ISF Women's World Championship, 1994, Pan Am. Games, 1995, Superball Classic, 1995, Atlanta Olympics, 1996, Bertha Tickey award, 1990, 93-95; named MVP Women's Major Fast Pitch Nat. Championship Am. Softball Assn., 1995, Sportswoman of Yr. Am. Softball Assn., 1990, 94, All-Am. team. Office: Amateur Softball Assn 2801 NE 50th St Oklahoma City OK 73111-7203*

SMITH, MILDRED CASSANDRA, systems engineer; b. Rocky Mount, N.C.; d. Naaman and Mildred (Laws) Foster; m. Edward B. Smith III, July 22, 1967 (div. 1976); children: Camille Eileen, Regina Dar. BA, Howard U., 1966; MS, Georgetown U., 1973, PHD, 1979. Cert. computer programmer. Programmer IBM Corp., Gaithersburg, Md., 1966-76; asst. prof. Howard U., Washington, 1976-80; engr./analyst VITRO Corp., Silver Spring, Md., 1980-82; analyst U.S. Dept. Agriculture, Washington, 1983-86; systems engr. MITRE Corp., McLean, Va., 1986—; pres., founder MLF, Inc., 1995—. Contbr. article to Software Reengring. Vol. D.C. Pub. Schs., 1978-80; judge Alice Deal Jr. High Sci. Fair, Washington, 1987; mentor corp. engring. enrichment program T.C. Williams High Sch., 1991. Named one of Outstanding Young Women Am., 1977, 78. Mem. D.C. Assn. for Computing Machinery (chmn. local interest group on mgmt. of data 1989—), Assn. for Computing Machinery, Assn. for Computational Linguistics. Democrat. Presbyterian.

SMITH, NANCY DUVERGNE, editor, writer, educator; b. Meridian, Miss., Mar. 22, 1951; d. Frank Gordin and Edna Henley (Brogan) S.; m. Mark Michael Sirdevan, Oct. 25, 1980; 1 child, Mei Smith Sirdevan. BFA, Tulane U., 1973; M in Liberal Arts, Harvard U., 1989. Newspaper reporter The Meridian (Miss.) Star, 1975-77, 81-82; mng. editor New Age mag., Brookline, Mass., 1978-80; English tchr. Am. Cultural Inst., Alexandria, Egypt, 1981; editorial dir. pub. affairs office Wellesley (Mass.) Coll., 1983-95, lectr. writing program, 1989—, editl. cons., 1992—. Paintings exhibited at Musee des Beaux Arts, 1981; editor NWU Databook, 1988; contbr. articles to mags. Chair adv. bd. Boston Writers Rm., 1990-92; bd. dirs. Artists Found. Mem. AAUP, Boston Women Communicators, Nat. Writers Union (sec.-treas. 1985-89, nat. bd. dirs.), Coun. for Advancement and Support of Edn. (conf. speaker 1988, 89, 92), Nat. Writers United Svcs. Orgn. (sec.-treas.). Democrat. Home: 298 Derby St Newton MA 02165

SMITH, NANCY GIBBONS, mathematics and computer educator; b. Washington, Aug. 2, 1941; d. Leonard Harold and Marie (Cadell) Gibbons; m. Howard Thomas Smith, Aug. 24, 1963; children: Bruce Edward, Angela Marie. BS in Edn., Salisbury (Md.) State Coll., 1963; MEd, Salisbury (Md.) State U., 1971. Tchr. math., student coun. advisor Pocomoke City, Md., 1963-68; tchr. math. Wicomico Sr. H.S., Salisbury, 1968-69; tchr. math., coach math. league and computer faire Caravel Acad., Bear, Del., 1980-82; tchr. math. and computers, math. league and computer faire coach St. Mark's H.S., Wilmington, Del., 1982—, supervising tchr. student tchrs., 1992—; tchr. summer sch. Christiana Sch. Dist. and Brandywine Sch. Dist., 1980—; advisor F.E.A., 1993—. Softball mgr., coach Suburban Little League, New Castle, Del., 1985-90; mgr., coach All-Star Softball Team, Suburban Softball, 1988-89. Mem. ASCD, Nat. Coun. Tchrs. Math., Del. Coun. Tchrs. Math., Future Educators Am., Phi Delta Kappa (Del. chpt.). Office: St Marks HS Pike Creek Rd Wilmington DE 19808

SMITH, NANCY HOHENDORF, sales and marketing executive; b. Detroit, Jan. 30, 1943; d. Donald Gerald and Lucille Marie (Kopp) Hohendorf; m. Richard Harold Smith, Aug. 21, 1978 (div. Jan. 1984). BA, U. Detroit, 1965; MA, Wayne State U., 1969. Customer rep. Xerox Corp., Detroit, 1965-67; mktg. rep. Univ. Microfilms subs. Xerox Corp., Ann Arbor, Mich., 1967-73, mktg. coord., 1973-74, mgr. dir. mktg., 1975-76; mgr. mktg. Xerox Corp., Can., 1976-77; major account mktg. exec. Xerox Corp., Hartford, Conn., 1978-79, New Haven, Conn., 1979-80; account exec. State of N.Y. Xerox Corp., N.Y.C., 1981; N.Y. region mgr. customer support Xerox Corp., Greenwich, Conn., 1982, N.Y. region sales ops. mgr., 1982; State of Ohio account exec. Xerox Corp., Columbus, 1983; new bus. sales mgr. Xerox Corp., Dayton, Ohio, 1983, major accounts sales mgr., 1984; info. systems sales and support mgr., quality specialist Xerox Corp., Detroit, 1985-87, new product launch mgr., ops. quality mgr., 1988, dist. mktg. mgr., 1989-91, major accounts sales mgr., 1992—. Named to Outstanding Young Women of Am., 1968, Outstanding Bus. Woman, Dayton C. of C., 1984, Women's Inner Circle of Achievement, 1990. Mem. NAFE, Am. Mgmt. Assn., Women's Econ. Club Detroit, Detroit Inst. Arts Founders' Soc., Detroit Hist. Soc., Greater Detroit C. of C. Republican. Roman Catholic. Home: 23308 Reynard Dr Southfield MI 48034-6924 Office: Xerox Corp 300 Galleria Officentre Southfield MI 48034-4700

SMITH, NANCY LYNNE, journalist, real estate agent, public relations consultant; b. San Antonio, July 31, 1947; d. Tillman Louis and Enid Maxine (Woolverton) Brown; m. Allan Roy Jones, Nov. 28, 1969 (div. 1975); 1 dau., Christina Elizabeth Woolverton Jones. BA, So. Meth. U., 1968; postgrad. So. Meth. U., 1969-70, Vanderbilt U., 1964, Ecole Nouvelle de la Suisse Romande, Lausanne, Switzerland, 1962. Tchr. spl. edn. Hot Springs Sch. Dist. (Ark.), 1970-72; reporter, soc. editor Dallas Morning News, 1974-82; soc./celebrity columnist Dallas Times Herald, 1982—; owner, pub. High Soc., Soc. Fax; realtor, Ebby Halliday Realtors; stringer Washington Post, 1978; contbg. editor Ultra mag., Houston, 1981-82, Tex. Woman mag., Dallas, 1979-80, Profl. Woman mag., Dallas, 1979-80; mem. bd. advisors Ultra Mag., 1985—; owner Nancy Smith Pub. Rels. Appeared on TV series Jocelyn's Weekend, Sta. KDFI-TV, 1985. Bd. dirs. TACA arts support orgn., Dallas, 1980—, asst. chmn. custom auction, 1978-83; judge Miss Tex. USA Contest, 1984; bd. dirs. Am. Parkinson Disease Assn. (Dallas chpt.), mem. adv. bd. Cattle Baron's Ball Com., Dallas Symphony Debutante presentations; hon. mem. Dallas Opera Women's Bd., Northwood Inst. Women's Bd., Dallas Symphony League; mem. Friends of Winston Churchill Meml. and Library, Dallas Theatre Ctr. Women's Guild, Childrens' Med. Ctr. Auxiliary; hon. mem. Crystal Charity Ball Com.; mem. Community Council Greater Dallas Community Awareness Goals Com. Impact '88, 1985—; co-chmn. Multiple Sclerosis San Simeon Gala, 1988; celebrity co-chmn. Greer Garson Gala of Hope 1990-91; gala chmn. Greer Garson Gala of Hope for Am. Parkinson's Disease Assn., 1991-93; chmn. gala benefit Northwood U., 1994; co-chmn. star studded stomp Mar. Dimes, 1994; mem. Femmes du Monde spl. activities com., com. Dallas Coun. World Affairs. Mem. Soc. Profl. Journalists (v.p. communications 1978-79), Nat. Press Club, Dallas Press Club, DAR, Daus. of Republic of Tex. (registrar 1972), Dallas So. Memorial Assn., Dallas County Heritage Soc., Dallas Mus. Art League, Dallas Opera Guild. Club: Argyle (sec. 1983-84), The 500 (Dallas), Energy. Home: 6324D Bandera Ave Dallas TX 75225-3614 Office: 8333 Douglas Ste 100 Dallas TX 75225

SMITH, NANCY MICHALAK, computer systems manager, software engineer; b. Chgo., Dec. 23, 1963; d. Arthur Allen and Marilyn Angela (Banaszak) Michalak; m. Ronald Bruce Smith, Sept. 20, 1990; children: Blake Allen, Allison Nicole. Student, U. Mo.-Rolla, 1982-83; BS, Southwest Mo. State U., 1986. Systems analyst E.I. DuPont de Nemours, Savannah River Site, Aiken, S.C., 1986-88, sr. software engr., 1988-90; mgr. mgmt. info. systems, reactor divsn. Westinghouse Savannah River Co., Aiken, S.C., 1990-91, mgr. control systems, reactor divsn., 1991-93, mgr. tech. computing stds., engring./constrn. svcs. divsn., 1993-94, mgr. computer systems, defense waste processing facility, 1994—; site liaison DOE Nuclear Weapons Complex Software Quality Assurance Com., 1993-95; site rep. IEEE Software Engring. Stds., 1994—. Presenter in field. Mem. IEEE, IEEE Computer Soc., Delta Sigma Pi (chancellor 1986). Home: 120 Coventry Circle North Augusta SC 29841 Office: Westinghouse Savannah R Co Savannah R Site MS 704-S Aiken SC 29808

SMITH, NONA COATES, academic administrator; b. West Grove, Pa., Apr. 1, 1942; d. John Truman and Elizabeth Zane (Trumbo) Coates; m. David Smith, Oct. 12, 1968 (div. May 1986); children: Kirth Ayrl, Del Kerry, Michael Sargent, Sherri Lee. BA, West Chester (Pa.) U., 1988; postgrad., Temple U., 1989—. Legal sec. Gawthrop & Greenwood, West Chester, 1968-73, MacElree, Gallagher, O'Donnell, West Chester, 1981-84; social sec. Mrs. John B. Hannum, Unionville, Pa., 1975-81; rsch. asst. West Chester U., 1984-88, cons., 1988; dir. faculty grants Bryn Mawr (Pa.) Coll., 1989—, chair rsch./tchg. evaluation, 1993-95. Treas. Kennett Vol. Fire Co., Kennett Square, Pa., 1984-86. Recipient Scholastic All-Am. award U.S. Achievement Acad., 1988, Rsch. award Truman Libr., 1992, Goldsmith Rsch. award Harvard U., 1993. Fellow Phi Alpha Theta; mem. AAUW, Am. Hist. Assn., Soc. Historians of Am. Fgn. Rels., Nat. Coun. Univ. Rsch. Adminstrs. (mem. nat. conf. com. 1995-96). Republican. Presbyterian. Home: Box 239 Unionville PA 19375 Office: Bryn Mawr Coll 101 N Merion Ave Bryn Mawr PA 19375

SMITH, NORMA JANE, elementary education educator; b. N.Y.C., Aug. 19, 1933; d. Raymond and Thelma (Kavares) Schneider; m. Thomas Edward Smith; children: Robyn, Sharon, Ilene. BA, CUNY, 1955; cert. in art, N.Y. Inst. Tech., 1986; postgrad., L.I. U., 1990. Cert. tchr., N.Y. Tchr. grade 1 Plainedge (N.Y.) Pub. Schs., 1956-59; tchr., reading specialist Half Hollow Hills Schs., Dix Hills, N.Y., 1969-70, tchr. grade 4, 1970-95, tng. and supervision of student tchrs., 1972-93, drama dir., 1982-95, social studies coord., 1982, 83, sci. coord., 1988, 89; instr. in-svc. tchr. edn. courses Half Hollow Hills, 1989, 90, 91; advisor Math Olympiads, Chestnut Hills, 1994-95. Author: The Queen's Mirrors, 1973, Pot Pourri, 1984, Spelling Pizazz, 1992, A Fish Named Willie Blue, 1992. Bd. dirs. San Remo (N.Y.) Civic Assn., Half Hollow Hills Active Ret. Tchrs. Recipient award for 20 yrs. of dedicated svc. to children of Chestnut Hill, Chestnut Hill PTA, 1990. Mem. ASCD, Half Hollow Hills Tchrs. Assn. (rep. 1974-79, newsletter publ. 1996—), Soc. of Children's Book Writers and Illustrators. Home: 17 Acacia Rd Kings Park NY 11754

SMITH, PATRICIA ANN, middle school educator; b. N.Y.C., Apr. 21, 1947; d. James and Ursula (Wedhorn) Mentesane; m. Ted Holton Smith, June 28, 1968; children: Monica Marie, Elizabeth Christine, Stephanie Nicole. BA, U. South Fla., 1968; MA in Tchg., Oklahoma City U., 1973. Cert. elem. K-8, reading specialist, jr. h.s. math, sci., social studies tchr., Okla., elem. and secondary adminstrn. Tchr. Oklahoma City Schs., 1970-74, Putnam City Schs., Oklahoma City, 1975-76, Hennessey (Okla.) Pub. Schs., 1976-88, Norman (Okla.) Pub. Schs., 1988—; field experiences supr. U. Okla., 1991-95. Vol. Norman Regional Hosp., 1994—, Habitat for Humanity, Norman, 1995, St. Joseph's Cath. Ch., Norman. 1st lt. U.S. Army, 1968-70. Mem. NEA, Nat. Coun. Tchrs. Math., Okla. Edn. Assn., Profl. Educators Norman, Kappa Alpha Theta. Republican. Roman Catholic. Home: 613 Riverwalk Ct Norman OK 73072 Office: Norman Pub Schs 2000 W Brooks Norman OK 73069

SMITH, PATRICIA ANNE, special education educator; b. West Chester, Pa., Aug. 19, 1967; d. William Richard and Carol Anne (Benn) S. BS in Spl. Edn. cum laude, West Chester U., 1989; postgrad., Immaculata Coll., 1993—. Cert. mentally and physically handicapped tchr., Pa. Learning support tchr. Chester County Intermediate Unit, Downington, Pa., 1989-90, early intervention tchr., 1990-92; autistic support tchr. Coatesville (Pa.) Area Sch. Dist., 1992—, event coord. WOYC workshops, 1993—; workshop presenter ann. conf. Pa. Assn. of Resources for People with Mental Retardation, Hershey, 1994, co-presenter ARC, 1996; presenter info. sessions ann. conf. Del. Valley Assn. for Edn. of Young Children, Phila., 1994, Lions, Downingtown, Pa., 1992, early childhood conf. Capital Area Assn. for Edn. of Young Children, Harrisburg, Pa., 1995, vols. Caln Athletic Assn. Challenger League, 1995—; mentor West Chester U., 1995—. Mem. recreation adv. bd. dirs. Assn. for Retarded Citizens, Exton, Pa., 1993—, Daisy Girl Scout Leader, 1995—; vol. tutor Chester County Libr. Adult Literacy Program, 1995—. Recipient Outstanding Svc. award Coatesville Area Parent Coun., 1994, 96, Vol. award Friendship PTA, 1993, 96, Pa. Early Childhood Edn. Assn. Workshop presenter award, 1993; grantee Pa.Dept. Edn., 1993, Coatesville Area Sch. Dist., 1990. Mem. ASCD, Nat. Assn. for the Edn. of Young Children, Autism Soc. Am., Kappa Delta Pi. Republican. Roman Catholic. Home: 501 Clover Mill Rd Exton PA 19341-2505 Office: Friendship Elem Sch 296 Reeceville Rd Coatesville PA 19320

SMITH, PATRICIA GASKINS, school administrator; b. Florence, S.C., June 21, 1951; d. Carlton Jackson and Audrey (Keefe) Gaskins; m. E.Z. Smith III, June 28, 1975; children: Audrey Lee, E.Z. IV. BA in Elem. Edn., U. S.C., 1972, M in Spl. Edn., 1973, M in Elem. Adminstrn., 1976; EdD, Nova Southeastern U., Ft. Lauderdale, Fla., 1995. Cert. tchr., S.C., Fla., N.C. Spl. edn. tchr. Swansea (N.C.) Mid. Sch., 1973-74, Swansea H.S., 1974-75, Wardlaw Mid. Sch., Columbia, S.C., 1975-76, Baker County H.S., Macclenny, Fla., 1976-77; tchr. 3d grade Baker County Elem. Sch., Macclenny, 1977-80; remedial tchr. Concord (N.C.) H.S., 1981-88; asst. prin. Wolf Meadow Elem. Sch., Concord, 1988—. Chair Elem. Sch. Safety Coun., Cabarrus County, N.C., 1993-94; chair Forest Hill Meth. Playsch., Concord, 1990—. Mem. ASCP, Internat. Reading Assn., Nat. Assn. Elem. Sch. Prins. Home: 300 Rosemont Ave SE Concord NC 28025-3816

SMITH, PATRICIA GRACE, government official; b. Tuskegee, Ala., Nov. 10, 1947; d. Douglas and Wilhelmina (Griffin) Jones; m. J. Clay Smith, Jr., June 25, 1983; children—Eugene Douglas, Stager Clay, Michelle L., Michael L. B.A. in English, Tuskegee Inst., 1968; postgrad. Auburn U., 1969-71, Harvard U., 1974, George Washington U., 1983; cert. sr. exec. service 1987; exec. mgmt. tng. devel. assignments Dept. Def., 1986, U.S. Senate Commerce Com., 1987. Instr. Tuskegee Institute, Ala., 1969-71; program mgr. Curber Assocs., Washington, 1971-73; dir. placement Nat. Assn. Broadcasters, Washington, 1973-74, dir. pub. affairs, 1974-77; assoc. producer Group W Broadcasting, Balt., 1977, producer, 1977-78; dir. affiliate relations and programming Sheridan Broadcasting Network, Crystal City, Va., 1978-80; dep. dir. policy, assoc. mng. dir. pub. info. and reference svcs., FCC, Washington, 1992-94, acting assoc. mng. dir., pub. info. and reference svcs., 1994; dep. dir. Office Pub. Affairs, 1994—; chief of staff office assoc. adminstr. for comml. space transp., FAA, U.S. Dept. Transp., 1994-96, dep. assoc. adminstr. office assoc. adminstr. for comml. space transp., 1996—. vice chmn. Nat. Conf. Black Lawyers Task Force on Communications, Washington, 1975-87. Mem. D.C. Donor Project, Nat. Kidney Found., Washington, 1984—; trustee, mem. exec. com., nominating com., youth adv. com. Nat. Urban League, 1976-81; mem. communications com. Cancer Coordinating Council, 1977-84; mem. Braintrust Subcom. on Children's Programming, Congl. Black Caucus, 1976—; mem. adv. bd. Black Arts Celebration, 1978-83; mem. NAACP; mem. journalism and communications adv. council Auburn U., 1976-78; mem. Washington Urban League, 1985—; bd. dirs. Black Film Rev., 1989-91; mem D.C. Commn. on Human Rights, 1986-88, chmn. 1988-91; mem. adv. coun. Nat. Insts. Health, 1992—; mem. bd. advisors The Salvation Army, 1993—. Named Outstanding Young Woman of Yr., Washington, 1975, 78; recipient Sustained Superior Performance award FCC, Washington, 1982-94. Mem. Women in Communications, Inc. (mem. nat. adv. com.), Lambda Iota Tau. Club: Broadcasters (bd. dirs. 1976-77). Democrat. Baptist. Avocations: writing, swimming. Home: 4010 16th St NW Washington DC 20011-7002 Office: DOT/OCST 400 7th St SW Rm 5415 Washington DC 20590-0001

SMITH, PATRICIA J., educational consultant; b. Chgo., Aug. 19, 1946; d. Joseph Peter and Jean Gloria (Sturmer) S. BA in English, Siena Heights Coll., 1970; MA in Spl. Edn., Eastern Mich. U., 1972. Cert. elem., spl. edn. tchr., Mich. Tchr. St. Theresa Sch., Detroit, 1970-71, Wayne County Child Devel. Ctr., Northville, Mich., 1971-73, Detroit Pub. Schs., 1981-82; tchr., advisor Met. State Hosp., Waltham, Mass., 1973-78; ednl. supr. Children's Friend and Svcs., Warwick, R.I., 1978-81; recruiter Mgmt. Support Svcs., Southfield, Mich., 1982-86; cognitive therapist Rehab. Resources, Inc., Southfield, 1985-86; ednl. coord. Fedn. Girls' Homes, Detroit, 1986-87, Davenport Shelter, Spectrum Youth Svcs., Highland Park, Mich., 1987-92; ednl. cons. Beverly Hills, Mich., 1988—; tchr. Detroit House of Corrections, Plymouth, Mich., 1971-73. Mem. Mich. Assn. Tchrs. of Emotionally Disturbed Children, Networks of Educators and Therapists Working in Orgns. for Rehab., Corrections and Spl. Edn. (sec. 1989—).

SMITH, PATRICIA JOAN MCADAM, legislative and political organizer; b. Miami, Sept. 19, 1945; d. Richard G. and Lilyan (Dolazinski) McA.; m. James Lee Smith (div. 1981); 1 child, Bradley James Smith. BA, Marymount Coll., 1968; MA, U. Okla., 1973. Cert. tchr. of secondary English. Tchr. St. Mary's of the Angels, Chgo., 1968-69, Patrick Henry Elem., Chgo., 1969-70, Tinker Air Force Base, Midwest City, Okla., 1971-75, Crooked Oak Jr. H.S., Oklahoma City, 1970-73, Moore (Okla.) Ctrl. Mid-High, 1973-85; legis., polit. organizer Okla. Edn. Assn., Oklahoma City, 1985—; English dept. chair Moore Ctrl. Mid-High, 1977-79, coord. renaissance Shakespeare festival, 1977-78, coord. Civil War festival, 1978-79; pres. Moore Assn. of Classroom Tchrs., 1979-80. Precinct chair Cleve. County Dem. Party, Moore, 1983—, precinct co-chair, 1981-82; state/dist. del. Dem. Party of Okla., 1981-94, nat. del., N.Y.C., 1992. Named Tchr. of Yr. Moore Assn. of Classroom Tchrs., 1980, Secondary Project of the Yr. Moore Pub. Schs. News, 1978. Mem. AAUW, Okla. Profl. Staff Orgn., Nat. Staff Orgn. Democrat. Roman Catholic. Home: 821 Windemere Dr Moore OK 73160 Office: Okla Edn Assn 323 E Madison Ave Oklahoma City OK 73105

SMITH, PATRICIA KATHRYN, computer literacy and mathematics educator; b. Crockett, Tex., July 4, 1952; d. Alfred Wilson and Mildred (Walker) Ormand; m. Roy Clarence Smith, Dec. 21, 1975; children: Russell Casey, Jerrell Glenn. BS in Edn., Stephen F. Austin U., 1974; postgrad. in Math., Counseling, Computer, various univs., 1979-85. Cert. elem., secondary math., computer literacy tchr. 3d grade tchr. Garland (Tex.) Ind. Sch. Dist., 1974-75; 1st grade tchr. Arlington (Tex.) Ind. Sch. Dist., 1976, 3d grade tchr., 1976-78, 4th grade tchr., 1978-81, 2d grade tchr., 1981-83, 8th grade tchr. math., 1983-85, computer literacy tchr., 1985—; 8th grade math. level leader Workman Jr. H.S., Arlington, 7th grade math. level leader, 1994-95, math. dept. head, 1995—; computer tech. trainer Arlington Ind. Sch. Dist., 1995—; exec. bd. parliamentarian J.B. Little, 1987-88, exec. bd. spl. projects, 1995-96. Co-author Arlington Ind. Sch. Dist. Computer Literacy Curriculum Guide, 1994. Mem. edn. com. St. Barnabas United Meth. Ch., 1993-95. Mem. Assn. Tex. Profl. Educators, Alpha Delta Kappa (chaplain 1994-95). Office: Arlington Ind Sch Dist Workman Jr HS 701 E Arbrook Blvd Arlington TX 76014

SMITH, PATRICIA LYNNE, visual artist; b. Camden, N.J., Nov. 3, 1955; d. Thomas Patrick Connelly and Elizabeth Jean (Swope) Shober; m. William Clarence Smith, Nov. 30, 1973 (div. June 1980); children: Travis Smith, Taryn Smith. BA, Rutgers U., Camden, N.J., 1980; MFA, Rutgers U., New Brunswick, N.J., 1984. Adj. instr. Rutgers U., New Brunswick, N.J., 1983-84, Trenton State Coll., 1989-90. Solo exhbns. include: Walt Whitman Ctr. for the Arts & Humanities, Camden, N.J., 1982, Rutgers U., New Brunswick, N.J., 1984, Piezo Electric Gallery, N.Y.C., 1986, bOb, N.Y.C., 1993, Saint Peter's Ch., N.Y.C., 1994, A.I.R. Gallery, N.Y.C., 1994, S.O.M.A. Gallery, Berlin, Germany, Croxhapox Gallery, Gent, Belgium, 1995, Black & Herron Gallery, N.Y.C., 1996; group exhbns. include The Brecht Forum, N.Y.C., 1990, 148 Duane Gallery, N.Y.C., 1991, Whitehall Gallery, N.Y.C., 1992, Tribeca 148 Gallery, N.Y.C., Herron Test-Site, Bklyn., 1992, Loft Lawyers, N.Y.C., 1992, Art in General, N.Y.C., 1992, AlleyCat Gallery, N.Y.C., 1993, PDG Gallery, N.Y.C., 1994, Times Square Hotel, N.Y.C., 1994, Tourniquet, N.Y.C., 1994, 450 Broadway Gallery, N.Y.C., 1994, Sauce Gallery, Bklyn., 1994, Eighth Floor, N.Y.C., 1995, Gallery Super Nova, N.Y.C., 1995, Galerij De Witte Beer Brugge, Belgium, 1996, Art Exch. Fair, N.Y.C., 1996, numerous others. Recipient Stedman Purchase prize Rutgers U., 1980, Garden State fellow, 1982-84, Exhbn. grantee Artist's Space, 1988, 90. Home & Studio: 7 Dutch St # 1 New York NY 10038

SMITH, PATRICIA TAYLOR, utilities/energy executive. Sr. v.p., gen. counsel Pub. Svc. Co. Colo., Denver. Office: Pub Svc Co Colo 1225 17th St Denver CO 80202-8533*

SMITH, PAULA MARIE, medical technologist; b. Meadville, Pa., July 22, 1964; d. William Paul and Mary Frances (Siegel) S. BS in Applied Sci., Youngstown State U., 1988. Cert. specialist in blood banking ARC Blood Svcs., No. Ohio Region, 1992-93, med. technologist with specialization in blood bank certification. Med. technologist St. Joseph Health Ctr., Warren, Ohio, 1988-92; blood bank supr. St. Joseph Health Ctr., Warren, 1993—. Active Rainforest Action Internat. Network, Cleve. Metroparks Zoo, 1993. Youngstown Found. scholar Youngstown State U., 1984, 85. Mem. NOW, Am. Soc. Clin. Pathologists, Am. Assn. Blood Banks, Ohio Assn. Blood Banks. Home: 2936 Red Fox Run Dr NW Warren OH 44485 Office: St Joseph Health Ctr Lab 667 Eastland Ave Warren OH 44484

SMITH, QUINN ROXANNE, special education educator; b. Richmond, Va., Oct. 2, 1969; d. Paul Holcombe and Martha Jeanne (Wilcox) Scott; m. Daniel Hubbard Smith, Nov. 24, 1990; (div. Oct., 1991); 1 child, Kyle. BS in Spl. Edn., Jacksonville State U., 1992; postgrad. studies in spl. edn., Ga. State U., 1994—. Cert. spl. edn. tchr. for mentally retarded, behavioral disorders, orthopedic impairments, Ga. Spl. edn. resource tchr. Walker County Lafayette (Ga.) H.S., 1993; spl. edn. tchr. for orthopedic impairment Catoosa County, Ringgold, Tigar Crest Elem. Schs., Ringgold, Ga., 1993-94, Bartow County Hamilton Crossing Elem. Sch., Cartersville, Ga., 1994—. Mem. NEA, Coun. for Exceptional Children, Kappa Delta Epsilon. Episcopalian. Home: 2 Raspberry Rd Rome GA 30165 Office: Hamilton Crossing Elem Sch Hamilton Crossing Rd Cartersville GA 30120

SMITH, REBECCA BEACH, federal judge; b. 1949. BA, Coll. William and Mary, 1971; postgrad., U. Va., 1971-73; JD, Coll. William and Mary, 1979. Assoc. Wilcox & Savage, 1980-85; U.S. magistrate Ea. Dist. Va., 1985-89; dist. judge U.S. Dist. Ct. (ea. dist.) Va., Norfolk, 1989—; exec. editor Law Review, 1978-79. Active Chrysler Mus. Norfolk, Jean Outland Chrysler Libr. Assocs., Va. Opera Assn., Friends of the Zoo, Friends of Norfolk Pub. Libr., Ch. of the Good Shepherd. John Marshall Soc. fellow; recipient Acad. Achievement and Leadership award St. George Tucker Soc.; named one of Outstanding Women of Am., 1979. Mem. ABA, Va. State Bar Assn., Fed. Bar Assn. Supreme Ct. Hist. Soc., Fourth Cir. Judicial Conf., The Harbor Club, Order of Coif., Phi Beta Kappa. Office: US Dist Ct US Courthouse 600 Granby St Ste 358 Norfolk VA 23510-1915*

SMITH, REBECCA MCCULLOCH, human relations educator; b. Greensboro, N.C., Feb. 29, 1928; d. David Martin and Virginia Pearl (Woodburn) McCulloch; m. George Clarence Smith Jr., Mar. 30, 1945; 1 child, John Randolph. BS, Woman's Coll., U. N.C., 1947, MS, 1952; PhD, U. N.C., Greensboro, 1967; postgrad., Harvard U., 1989. Tchr. pub. schs., N.C. and S.C., 1947-57; instr. U. N.C., Greensboro, 1958-66, asst. prof. to prof. emeritus human devel. and family studies, 1967-91, adj. prof. emeritus, 1991-94, dir. grad. program, 1975-82; adj. prof. ednl. cons. depts. edn. N.C., S.C., Ind., Ont., Man.; vis. prof. N.W. La. State U., 1965, 67, U. Wash., 1970, Hood Coll., 1976, 86. Named Outstanding Alumna Sch. Home Econs., 1976; recipient Sperry award for service to families N.C. Family Life Coun., 1979. Mem. Nat. Coun. Family Rels. (exec. com. 1974-76, treas. 1987-89, Osborne award 1973), U. N.C. at Greensboro Alumni Assn. (chair membership recruitment com. 1994-96). Author: Teaching About Family Relationships, 1975, Klemer's Marriage and Family Relationships, 2d edit., 1975, Resources for Teaching About Family Life Education, 1976, Family Matters: Concepts in Marriage and Personal Relationships, 1982; co-author: History of the School of Human Environmental Sciences: 1892-1992, 1992, assoc. editor Family Relations (Jour. Applied Family and Child Studies), 1980-90; ednl. cons. Current Life Studies, 1977-84. Home: 1212 E Ritters Lake Rd Greensboro NC 27406-7816 Office: U NC Dept Human Devel Sch Human Environ Scis Greensboro NC 27412

SMITH, ROBERTA HAWKING, plant physiologist; b. Tulare, Calif., May 3, 1945; d. William Brevard and Freda Lois (Kessler) Hawkins; m. James Willie Smith Jr., Sept. 17, 1968; children: James Willie III, Cristine Lois. BS, U. Calif., Riverside, 1967, MS, 1968, PhD, 1970. Postdoctoral fellow dept. plant sci. Tex. A&M U., College Station, 1972-73, asst. prof. dept. plant sci., 1974-79, assoc. prof. dept. plant sci., 1979-85, prof. dept. soil and crop sci., 1985—; asst. prof. Sam Huston State U., Huntsville, Tex., 1973-74. Editl. bd. In Vitro Cellular and Dev. Biology, 1991-96, Jour. Plant Physiology, 1994—; assoc. editor Jour. Crop Sci., 1995—. Mem. Crop Sci. Soc. Am. (chmn. C-7 divsn. 1990-91), Internat. Crops Rsch. Inst. Semi-Arid Tropics (bd. govs. 1989-95), Faculty of Plant Physiology (chmn. 1987-89), Soc. In Vitro Biology (chmn. plant divsn. 1983-86, pres. 1994-96). Republican. Methodist. Home: RR 1 Box 701 Hearne TX 77859-9734 Office: Tex A&M Univ Dept Soil And Sci College Station TX 77843

SMITH, RONA, finance company executive; b. N.YC., Dec. 10, 1944; d. Harry and Edith (Stern) Silberman; m. Barry Martin Smith, Aug. 29, 1965; children: David Evan, Letty Chandra. BA, CUNY, 1965; MA, NYU, 1968, PhD, 1977. Asst. prof. CUNY, 1970-77; cons. N.Y.C., 1977-80; broker Douglas Elliman Gibbons & Ives, N.Y.C., 1980-85; mng. dir. 1st London Properties Fund, N.Y., London, 1985-91, 1st London Group, N.Y., London, 1988-92; with Equitable Fin. Cos., N.Y.C., 1992-95. Mem. Reform Club, Sloane Club (London). Home: 290 W End Ave New York NY 10023-8106

SMITH, RUTH LILLIAN SCHLUCHTER, librarian; b. Detroit, Oct. 18, 1917; d. Clayton John and Gertrude Katherine (Kastler) Schluchter; m. Thomas Guilford Smith, Sept. 28, 1946; 1 son, Pemberton, III. AB, Wayne State U., Detroit, 1939; AB in Libr. Sci., U. Mich., Ann Arbor, 1942. Libr. Detroit Pub. Libr., 1942-43; rsch. asst. Moore Sch. Elec. Engring. U. Pa., Phila., 1946-47; libr. Bethesda (Md.) Meth. Ch. Libr., 1955-61; reference libr., chief reader svcs. Inst. Def. Analyses, Arlington, Va., 1961-65, chief unclassified libr. sect., 1965-67, head libr., 1967-75, mgr. tech. info. svcs., 1975-81; dir. office customer svcs. Nat. Tech. Info. Svc., 1981-88, cons., 1988—; leader ch. libr. workshops, 1960—; speaker profl. meetings; founder, chmn. Com. Info. Hang-ups, 1969-86; mem. Depository Libr. Coun. to Pub. Printer, 1975-78, Def. Tech. Info. Ctr. Resource Sharing Adv. Group, 1980-82; chmn. edn. working group Fed. Libr. and Info. Ctr. Com., 1984-88, cons., 1988—. Author: Publicity for a Church Library, 1966, Workshop Planning, 1972, (with Claudia Hannaford) Promotion Planning, 1975, Getting the Books off the Shelves, 1975, rev. edit., 1985, 2nd rev. edit., 1991, Cataloging Made Easy, 1978, rev. edit., 1986, Setting up a Library: How to Begin or Begin Again, 1979, rev. edit., 1987, 2nd rev. edit., 1994, Running a Library, 1982; contbr. articles to library and religious jours. Mem. ALA, Am. Soc. Info. Sci., Ch. and Synagogue Library Assn. (founding mem., life mem., pres. 1967-68), Fedn. Info. Users (v.p. interactive affairs 1973-75), Spl. Libraries Assn. (chmn. aerospace div. 1975-76, chmn. library mgmt. div. 1978-79, chmn. div. cabinet 1980-81, John Cotton Dana award 1979, SLA Fellow award 1987, Hall of Fame award 1988). Republican. Methodist. Home: 5304 Glenwood Rd Bethesda MD 20814-1406

SMITH, SALLY ELAINE BECKLEY, veterinary technician; b. Oneonta, N.Y., July 28, 1959; d. Clyde Allen Beckley and Doris Robinson; m. David Michael Smith, Apr. 17, 1983. AS, SUNY, Delhi, 1979. Lic. vet. technician; cert. kennel operator. Vet. technician Am. Animal Hosp., Mt. Freedom, N.J., 1979-81, hosp. adminstrs., 1981-87; dir. Golub Animal Hosp./Animal Inn, Ledgewood, N.J., 1987—; pres., cons. Companion Pet Enterprises, Blairstown, N.J., 1994—; bd. dirs. Airborne Animals, Inc., Ledgewood; spkr. and cons. in field. Mem. Am. Boarding Kennels Assn. (regional dir. 1995—, chair edn. com. 1989—, Nat. Appreciation award 1989, Golden Scoop 1994), N.J. Vet. Technicians (sec. 1985-88), Ind. Pet & Animal Transp. Assn. (sec. 1994—). Republican. Office: Animal Inn PO Box 425 Ledgewood NJ 07852

SMITH, SALLY LYON, portrait artist; b. Pitts., Oct. 31, 1919; d. Prescott Langworthy and Mary Louise (Steele) Lyon; m. Robert E. Smith, Jan. 5, 1942 (dec. 1992); children: Prescott Lyon, Robert E., Samuel Thayer. Grad. h.s., Phila. Cert. Am. Portrait Soc. Portrait artist Old Sacramento, Calif., 1974-77, Sacramento, 1977-80, Folsom, Calif., 1980-95, Carmichael, Calif., 1995—. One woman shows Casa de Los Ninos, 1985, 88, 89, 92, Midtown Gallery-Sacramento, 1995, 96, Dr. Patrick McMenamin-Sacramento Office Complex, 1995; groups exhibitions include Calif. Arts League, 1980-96, Soc. of Western Artists, 1980, 91, 95, Pastels Soc. of the West Coast, 1987, 88, 89, 91, 93, 95; represented in permanent collections. Bd. dirs. Gateway Ho., Sacramento, 1965-75, guild mem. 1975-85, founder 1965. Recipient numerous awards. Mem. Pastel Soc. of West Coast (sec. 1986-87), Soc. of Western Artists, Calif. Arts League. Republican. Episcopalian. Home and Studio: 3939 Walnut Ave #325 Carmichael CA 95608

SMITH, SALLYE WRYE, librarian; b. Birmingham, Ala., Nov. 11, 1923; d. William Florin and Margaret (Howard) Wrye; m. Stuart Werner Smith, Sept. 20, 1947 (dec. June 1981); children: Carol Ann, Susan Patricia, Michael Christopher, Julie Lynn, Lori Kathleen. BA, U. Ala., 1945; MA, U. Denver, 1969. Psychometrician U.S. Army, Deshon Gen. Hosp., Butler, Pa., 1945-46, U.S. Vet. Adminstrn. Vocat. Guidance, U. Ala., Tuscaloosa, 1946; clin. psychologist U.S. Army, Walter Reed Gen. Hosp., Washington, 1946-47, U.S. Army, Fitzsimons Gen. Hosp., Denver, 1948, U.S. Vets. Adminstrn., Ft. Logan, Colo., 1948-50; head sci.-engring. libr. U. Denver, Colo., 1969-72; instr., reference libr. Penrose Libr., U. Denver, 1972-80, asst. prof., reference libr., 1980-90, interim dir., 1990-92; vis. prof. U. Denver Grad. Sch. Libr. Info. Mgmt., 1975-77, 83; info. broker Colo. Rschrs., Denver, 1979—; cons., presenter The Indsl. Info. Workshop Inst. de Investigaciones Tecnologicas, Bogota, Colombia, 1979, LIPI-DRI-PDIN workshop on R&D mgmt., Jakarta, Indonesia, 1982; mem. BRS User Adv. Bd., Latham, N.Y., 1983-86. Indexer: Statistical Abstract of Colorado 1976-77, 1977. Recipient Cert. of Recognition, Sigma Xi, U. Denver chpt., 1983. Mem. ALA, Spl. Libr. Assn., Colo. Libr. Assn., Phi Beta Kappa, Beta Phi Mu.

SMITH, SANDRA GRACE, fine art educator, artist; b. Rochester, N.Y., Jan. 25, 1950; d. Eugene Frank and Grace Anna (Karweick) Garvey; m. Scott Kellogg Smith, June 23, 1973; children: Alexander, Margaret. BS, Hartwick Coll., 1972; postgrad., Russell Sage Coll., 1973-79, Ea. Conn. State Coll., 1973-79, Skidmore Coll., 1985. Permanent cert. tchr. Art tchr. Webster Sch. Dist., Rochester, N.Y., 1972-73, Gloversville (N.Y.) Sch. Dist., 1973—; adj. tchr. Fulton-Montgomery C.C., Gloversville, 1978-80; pres. SmithWorks, Gloversville, 1973-82; juror Schenectady (N.Y.) Mus. Craft Show, 1977. Recipient 1st Pl. award N.Y. State Tchr.'s Union Design, 1980, Elsie M. Birch award Cooperstown Nat. Art Exhbn., 1992; N.Y. State Stipend grantee N.Y.S.F.A. and Rensselear Coun. for Arts, 1993, N.Y. State mini grantee, 1977. Republican. Office: Kingsborough Sch 172 Baird Rd Gloversville NY 12078

SMITH, SELMA MOIDEL, lawyer, composer; b. Warren, Ohio, Apr. 3, 1919; d. Louis and Mary (Oyer) Moidel; 1 child, Mark Lee. Student U. Calif., 1936-39, U. So. Calif., 1939-41; JD, Pacific Coast U., 1942. Bar: Calif. 1943, U.S. Dist. Ct. 1943, U.S. Supreme Ct. 1958. Gen. practice law; mem. firm Moidel, Moidel, Moidel & Smith. Field dir. civilian adv. com. WAC, 1943; mem. nat. bd. Med. Coll. Pa. (formerly Woman's Med. Coll. Pa.), 1953—, exec. bd., 1976-80, pres., 1980-82, chmn. past pres. com., 1990-92. Decorated La Orden del Merito Juan Pablo Duarte (Dominican Republic). Mem. ABA, State Bar Calif. (servicemen's legal aid com., conf. com. on unauthorized practice of medicine, 1964, Disting. Svc. award 1993), L.A. Bar Assn. (psychopathic ct. com., Outstanding Svc. award 1993), L.A. Lawyers Club (pub. defenders com.), Nat. Assn. Women Lawyers (chmn. com. unauthorized practice of law, social commn. UN, regional dir. western states, Hawaii 1949-51, mem. jud. adminstrn. com. 1960, nat. chmn. world peace through law com. 1966-67, liaison to ABA sr. lawyers divsn. 1996—), League of Ams. (dir.), Inter-Am. Bar Assn., So. Calif. Women Lawyers Assn. (pres. 1947, 48), Women Lawyers Assn. L.A. (chmn. Law Day com. 1966, subject of oral hist. project, 1986), Coun. Bar Assns. L.A. County (charter sec. 1950), Calif. Bus. Women's Coun. (dir. 1951), L.A. Bus. Women's Coun. (pres. 1952), Calif. Pres.'s Coun. (1st v.p.), Nat. Assn. Composers U.S.A. (dir. 1974-79, ann. luncheon chmn. 1975), Nat. Fedn. Music Clubs (nat. vice chmn. for Western region, 1973-78), Calif. Fedn. Music Clubs (state chmn. Am. Music 1971-75, state conv. chmn. 1972), Docents of L.A. Philharm. (v.p. 1973-83, chmn. Latin Am. community rels. 1972-75, press and pub. rels. 1972-75, cons. coord. 1973-75), Assn. Learning in Retirement Orgns. in West (pres. 1993-94, exec. com. 1994-95, Disting. Svc. award 1995), Euterpe Opera Club (v.p. 1974-75, chmn. auditions 1972, chmn. awards 1973-75), ASCAP, Iota Tau Tau (dean L.A., supreme treas.), Plato Soc. of UCLA (Toga editor, 1990-93, sec. 1991-92, chmn. colloquium com. 1992-93, discussion leader UCLA Constitution Bicentennial Project, 1985-87, moderator UCLA extension lecture series 1990, Exceptional Leadership award 1994). Composer of numerous works including Espressivo-Four Piano Pieces (orchestral premiere 1987, performance Nat. Mus. Women in the Arts 1989). Home: 5272 Lindley Ave Encino CA 91316-3518

SMITH, SHANNON KAY, consultant; b. Jacksboro, Tex., June 3, 1967; d. Charles Thomas and Loretta (Robinson) S. BA in History and Polit. Sci., Texas Tech U., 1991; MA in Am. Studies/Hist. Preservation, U. Hawaii at Manoa, 1996. Data control supr. Lubbock County Courthouse, Lubbock, Tex., 1985-91; mgmt. asst. Oahu Consol. Family Housing, Ft. Shafter, Hawaii, 1993-94; computer application specialist Dohinen Capital Rsch. Inst., Inc., Honolulu, 1994-95; pres., owner SS Cons., Honolulu, 1995—; pres. SS Cons./Kahala Mandrin Hotel, Honolulu, 1996; pres., owner SS Cons./Med. Practice Mgmt., Honolulu, 1995—. Vol. Spl. Olympics, Honolulu, 1993-96. Mem. Nat. Trust for Hist. Preservation, Am. Studies Assn., Alpha Delta Pi (chpt. pres. 1986-91). Home: 2048 Clement St Honolulu HI 96822

SMITH, SHARRON WILLIAMS, chemistry educator; b. Ashland, Ky., Apr. 3, 1941; d. James Archie and May (Waggoner) Williams; m. William Owen Smith, Jr., Aug. 16, 1964; children: Leslie Dyan, Kevin Andrew. BA, Transylvania U., 1963; PhD, U. Ky., 1975. Chemist, Procter & Gamble, Cin., 1963-64; tchr. sci. Lexington pub. schs., Ky., 1964-67; chemist NIH, Bethesda, Md., 1974-75; asst. prof. chemistry Hood Coll., Frederick, Md., 1975-81, assoc. prof., 1981-87, prof. 1987—, chair dept. chemistry, physics and astronomy, 1982-86, 95—, acting dean grad. sch. 1989-91, Whitaker prof. Chemistry, 1993—. NDEA fellow, 1967-70, Dissertation Yr. fellow U. Ky., Lexington, 1970-71; grantee Hood Coll. Bd. Assocs., 1981, 85, 91, Beneficial-Hodson faculty fellow Hood Coll., 1984, 92; grantee NSF, 1986. Mem. AAAS, Am. Chem. Soc., Middle Atlantic Assn. Liberal Arts Chemistry Tchrs. (pres. 1984-85). Democrat. Office: Hood Coll Dept Chemistry Frederick MD 21701

SMITH, SHEILA DIANE, medical transcriptionist; b. Caribou, Maine, Aug. 20, 1965; d. Melvin and Flora Jane (Michaud) Kennard; m. John Philip Smith, Aug. 25, 1984; children: Daniel Craig, Janelle Marie. Cert. legal asst., Hillcrest Inst., Portland, Maine, 1993; cert med. transcriptionist, At-Home Professions, Ft. Collins, Colo., 1993; cert. in fin. statement analysis, payroll I & collections, Am. Inst. Profl. Bookkeepers, 1995. Lic. occupl. sec., Fla. Sec., data entry processor Aroostook County Courthouse, Caribou, Maine, 1983; typist, adminstrv. asst. Continental Contracting Co., Mascoutah, Ill., Houston, 1986-87; sales assoc. AAFES Main Exch., Torrejon AB, Spain, 1990-91; family daycare provider MWR (USAF), Torrejon AB, Spain, 1991; med. clk., adminstrv. asst. 401st Hosp. (USAF), Torrejon AB, Spain, 1991-92; med. transcriptionist, sec. Bridgeway Ctr., Inc., Ft. Walton Beach, Fla., 1993-94; owner, med. transcriptionist, billing specialist Smith's Bus. Svcs., Eglin AFB, Fla., 1994—. Vol. Girl Scouts Am., Eglin AFB, 1994-95; mem. nat. steering com. Clinton/Gore '96 Campaign, Washington, 1995-96. Mem. AAUW, NAFE, Am. Inst. Profl. Bookkeepers, Smithsonian Inst. (assoc.). Roman Catholic. Office: Smith's Bus Svcs 102-D Fir St Eglin AFB FL 32542

SMITH, SHELAGH ALISON, public health educator; b. Oak Ridge, Tenn., June 3, 1949; d. Nicholas Monroe and Elizabeth (Kimbrough) S.; m. Milton John Axley, 1991; 1 child, Elizabeth Claire. BS in Edn., U. Tenn., 1971, AS in Dental Hygiene, 1974; MPH in Health Svcs. Adminstrn., Johns Hopkins, 1979. Lic., cert. health edn. specialist, 1989. Social sci. rsch. analyst Dept. Health and Human Svcs., Health Care Fin. Adminstrn., Balt., 1980-85; pub. health educator, evaluator Nat. Cancer Inst.-NIH, Bethesda, Md., 1985-90; sr. policy analyst NIMH, Rockville, Md., 1990-92; pub. health advisor Ctr. Mental Health Svcs., Rockville, Md., 1992—. Recipient adminstr.'s citation Health Care Fin. Adminstrn., 1981, dir.'s award Nat. Cancer Inst., 1989; Gen. Alumni scholar U. Tenn., 1973. Mem. APHA (pub. health edn. sect., chmn. fin. and reimbursement for prevention svcs. com. 1987-89, 96), Md. Pub. health Assn. (governing coun. 1996—, membership chmn. 1980, treas. 1981), Md. Women's Health Coalition, Planned Parenthood Md., Soc. Pub. Health Edn. (governing bd. and ho. of dels. 1993-95, legis. co-chmn. 1990-91, nat. capital area exec. bd., profl. devel. chair 1996, chpt. pres. 1996-97), Phi Kappa Phi. Democrat. Home: 14106 Heathfield Ct Rockville MD 20853-2760 Office: SAMHSA Ctr Mental Health Svc 5600 Fishers Ln Rockville MD 20857-0001

SMITH, SHELLEY MERRIFIELD, writer, non-profit organization administrator; b. Louisville, Ky., Sept. 24, 1950; d. Lucien Lyne and LaVerne (Weare) S. BA with honors, Ind. U., 1972. Missionary to India, India, 1978—; founder, pres., dir. Kailashananda Mission of Am., Inc.,, Watkinsville, Ga., 1981—; behavioral therapist Kailashananda Mission Am., Inc., Lexington, Ky., 1981—, Colo., 1989—. Author: Mother Light, 1994, The Journey of Being, 1996; contbr. articles to profl. jours. Organizer, dir. Oconee County Alliance for Literacy, Watkinsville, 1992—; vol., dir. Oconee County Libr., 1990—, dir. literacy program, 1991—; active Oconee Adolescence Orgn., 1993—, Oconee County 2000 for Literacy, 1993—. Recipient award of recognition for outstanding vol. svc. Athens Regional Libr., 1993. Mem. Watkinsville C. of C. (mem. edn. com. 1992—). Roman Catholic. Home: 1500 Broadlands Dr Watkinsville GA 30677-2148

SMITH, SHERYL VELTING, elementary school executive director; b. Grand Rapids, Mich., Apr. 5, 1946; d. Louis and Martha (Kamminga) Velting; children: Laura, Paul. BA in Elem. Edn., Western Mich. U., Kalamazoo, 1968; MA in Adminstrn. and Supr./Edn., Akron U., 1980. Cert. edn. adminstr. and supr. Elem. tchr. Northview Pub. Schs., Grand Rapids, Mich., 1968-69, Ft. Knox (Ky.) Dependent Schs., 1969-70, Dept. of Def., Okinawa, 1970-71, Jefferson County Schs., Louisville, 1971-76, Hudson (Ohio) Local Schs., 1976-80; dir., preschool tchr. The Treehouse Preschool, 1981-83; exec. dir. High Meadows Sch., Roswell, Ga., 1993—; regional conf. bd. Assn. Gifted Children, Akron, Ohio, 1979; chairwomen bd. dirs. Friends of High Meadows, Roswell, Ga., 1990-94; mem. adv. bd. Mt. Pisgah Christian Schs., Alpharetta, Ga., 1991-92; mem. North Fulton Cmty. Found. Bd., 1996—. Office: High Meadows Sch 1055 Willeo Rd Roswell GA 30075-4131

SMITH, SHIRLEY, artist; b. Wichita, Kans., Apr. 17, 1929; d. Harold Marvin and Blanche Carrie (Alexander) S. BFA, Kans. State U., 1951; postgrad., Provincetown (Mass.) Workshop, 1962-66. One woman exhbns. 55 Mercer St. Gallery, N.Y.C., 1973, Wichita Art Mus, 1978, Stamford Mus. and Nature Ctr., Conn., 1987, Aaron Gallery, Washington, 1987, 88, Joan

Hodgell Gallery, Sarasota, Fla., 1987; group exhbns. include Chrysler Mus., Provincetown, 1964, The Va. Mus., Richmond, 1970, Whitney Mus. Am. Art, 1971, Colo. Springs Fine Art Ctr., 1972, Everson Mus., Syracuse, N.Y., 1976-80, Nat. Acad. Design, N.Y.C., 1986, One Penn Pla., N.Y.C., 1987, 88, Am. Acad., Inst. Arts and Letters, N.Y.C., 1990, 91; permanent collections Whitney Mus. Am. Art, N.Y.C., U. Calif. Art Mus., Berkeley, Phoenix Art Mus., The Aldrich Mus. Contemporary Art, Ridgefield, Conn., Ulrich Mus., Wichita, Everson Mus., Syracuse, South County Bank collection, St. Louis, Prudential Life Ins., Newark, N.J., King Features Syndicate, N.Y.C., Chase Manhattan Bank Collection, N.Y.C., Senator Nancy Kassabaum Russel Senate Bldg., Washington. Recipient Grumbacher Cash award for mixed media New Eng. Exhibition, Silvermine, Conn., 1967, Acad. Inst. award Am. Acad. Arts and Letters, N.Y.C., 1991. Mem. Artist Equity. Democrat. Presbyterian. Home: 141 Wooster St New York NY 10012-3163

SMITH, STEPHANIE ZAHAROUDIS, producer; b. Washington, May 12, 1958; d. Angelo Constantine and Sally (Laliotis) Zaharoudis; m. John Dorrance Smith, Sept. 15, 1990. BS, U. Md., 1980. Asst. editor Bus. Aviation Weekly, Washington, 1980-81; copy aide, free-lance writer Washington Post, 1980-83; assoc. producer Satellite News Channel, Washington, 1982-83; assignment editor, assoc. producer Sta. WJLA-TV, Washington, 1983-84; assoc. producer weekend news Sta. ABC-TV, Washington, 1984-86, producer weekend news, 1986-89, producer Pentagon, 1989-93; producer World News Tonight, 1993—. Recipient Joan Barone award House Radio-TV Gallery, Washington, 1988. Office: ABC News 1717 Desales St NW Washington DC 20036-4401

SMITH, SUE FRANCES, newspaper editor; b. Lockhart, Tex., July 4, 1940; d. Monroe John Baylor and Myrtle (Krause) Mueck; m. Michael Vogtel Smith, Apr. 20, 1963 (div. July 1977); 1 child, Jordan Meredith. B. Journalism, U. Tex., 1962. Feature writer, photographer Corpus Christi Caller Times, 1962-64; feature writer, editor Chgo. Tribune, 1964-76; features editor Dallas Times Herald, 1976-82; sales assoc. Bumpas Assocs., Dallas, 1982-83; asst. mng. editor for features Denver Post, 1983-84, assoc. editor, 1984-91; asst. mng. editor in charge of Sunday paper Dallas Morning News, 1991-94, asst. mng. editor Lifestyles, 1994-96, dep. mng. editor Lifestyles, 1996—; active Coun. Pres., 1993. Mem. Am. Assn. Sunday and Feature Editors (pres. 1993), Newspaper Features Coun. (bd. dirs., sec., treas.), Tex. Associated Press Mng. Editors (bd. dirs.), Delta Gamma. Home: 6060 Jereme Trl Dallas TX 75252-5130 Office: 508 Young St Dallas TX 75202-4808

SMITH, SUSAN ARLENE, nursing educator; b. Columbia, S.C., Dec. 16, 1953; d. Gibson and Eva Mae (Sharpe) Lawson; m. John Earl Smith, May 14, 1977; 1 child, Nancy Michelle. BSN, U. S.C., 1976, MSN, 1979. RN, S.C.; cert. HIV/AIDS educator ARC. Proofreader, sec. Vogue Press Printing, Columbia, 1972-74; nursing asst. Bapt. Med. Ctr., Columbia, 1974-76, staff nurse obstetrics, 1976-78; staff nurse, program nurse specialist for child health Ctrl. Midlands Health Dist., Columbia, 1978-80; prof. nursing U. S.C., Columbia, 1981-83; staff nurse ob/gyn. surgery Lexington Med. Ctr., West Columbia, S.C., 1981-86; prof. pediatrics nursing and HIV/AIDS edn. Midlands Tech. Coll., Columbia, 1986—; CEO HIV/AIDS ednl./support network Tomorrow's Hope, 1993—; mem. adv. bd. S.C. AIDS Tng. Network, Columbia, 1994—; presenter in field. Co-author: HIV Disease/AIDS: Curriculum for Allied Health Students, 1991; contbr. articles to profl. publs.; author manual in field. Founder, facilitator support group for HIV/AIDS patients, West Columbia, 1992—, HIV/AIDS Care Team, West Columbia, 1992—, HIV/AIDS Peer Edn. Program, Columbia, 1994; mem. nat. AIDS task force So. Bapt. Conv., 1994—; mem. Nat. AIDS Task Force, 1995—; mem. AIDS care team, mem. pers. com., pres. sanctuary choir, Sunday sch. tchr. Trinity Bapt. Ch.; vol. March of Dimes, Arthritis Found.; fundraiser AIDS Walk, 1994; spkr. on health careers Davis Elem. Sch. Named Outstanding Faculty Mem. So. Region Assn. C.C. Trustees, 1993, Tchr. of Yr., Midlands Tech. Coll., 1992, Faculty Mem. of Yr., 1993. Mem. Bapt. Nursing Fellowship (chair nominating com. 1992—), Sigma Theta Tau. Home: 116 Longleaf Dr Cayce SC 29033-1912 Office: Midlands Tech Coll PO Box 2408 Columbia SC 29202-2408

SMITH, SUSAN ELIZABETH, guidance director; b. Phila., Mar. 24, 1950; d. E. Burke Hogue and Janet Coffin Hogue Ebert; m. J. Russell Smith, June 17, 1972 (div. June 1989); 1 child, Drew Russell. BS in Elem. Edn., E. Stroudsburg Coll., 1972; MEd in Counseling, U. Okla., 1974, postgrad., 1976-77; postgrad., Trenton State Coll., 1989-90; EdM in Devel. Disabilities, Rutgers U., 1992, postgrad., 1994—. Cert. elem. tchr., N.C.; cert. elem. tchr., early childhood edn. tchr., guidance and counseling, Okla.; cert. elem. tchr., guidance and counseling, tchr. of handicapped, psychology tchr., supr. instrn., dir. student pers. svcs., N.J. Elem. tchr. Morton Elem. Sch. Onslow County Schs., Jacksonville, N.C., 1971-72; instr. U. Isfahan, Iran, 1974-76; guidance counselor Moore (Okla.) Pub. Schs., 1976-77; counselor Johnstone Tng. Ctr. N.J. Divsn. Devel. Disabilities, Bordentown, 1988-90; spl. edn. tchr. Willingboro (N.J.) Schs., 1990-91; guidance counselor Haledon (N.J.) Pub. Schs., 1991-92; spl. edn. adj. tchr. Gateway Sch., Carteret, N.J., 1991-93; guidance counselor Bloomfield (N.J.) Pub. Schs., 1992-94; dir. guidance Somerville (N.J.) Pub. Schs., 1994-95; adj. prof. in spl. edn. Essex County (N.J.) Coll., 1994; guidance Ft. Lee (N.J.) Schs., 1995—; cons., seminar and workshop presenter on behavior mgmt., parenting skills, and behavior modification techniques; cons. N.J. Fragile X Assn. Author: Motivational Awards for ESL Students, 1993, Parent Contracts to Improve School Behaviors, 1996; contbr. articles to profl. jours. Leader Boy Scouts Am., Oklahoma City, 1983-87, com. chmn., Redmond, Wash., 1987-88. Recipient Rsch. award ERIC/CAPS, 1992, Svc. award N.J. Fragile X Assn., 1993. Mem. ACA, Am. Sch. Counselor Assn. (grantee 1992), N.J. Counseling Assn., N.J. Sch. Counseling Assn., Assn. for Multicultural Counseling and Devel., AAUW, Assn. for Counselor Edn. and Supervision, N.J. Assn. for Counselor Edn. and Supervision, N.J. Prins. and Suprs. Assn., Nat. Assn. Coll. Admissions Counselors (grantee 1995), Alpha Omicron Pi. Episcopalian. Home: 13 Yale St Nutley NJ 07110-3386

SMITH, SUSAN GEORGE, occupational health nurse; b. Summit, N.J., Feb. 24, 1954; d. William Joseph and Irma May (Shallcross) George; m. Jerome Smith, June 19, 1976 (div. May 1988); children: Lisa Maureen, Abigail Carolyn. BSN, Georgetown U., 1976; MA, Fairleigh Dickinson U., 1988. RN, N.J., N.Y.; cert. occupational health nurse; cert. hearing conservation, BLS instr., cert. Respiratory Surveillance. Staff nurse pediatrics Overlook Hosp., Summit, N.J., 1976-80; staff nurse Summit Med. Group, P.A., 1982-87; staff nurse Immedicenter, Bloomfield, N.J., 1987-88, program dir. high risk obesity clinic, 1988-90; cons. employee health svcs. Ciba-Geigy Pharma Div., Summit, 1986-92, adminstr./clin. supr. employee health svcs., 1992-94, mgr. nursing, wellness and workers compensation, 1994—, dir. edn. programs, 1995—. Art in the Classroom docent elem. schs. Jefferson and Washington Schs., Summit, 1987-90; asst. leader, co-leader Girl Scouts U.S., Summit, 1987-89; mem. adminstrv. bd. cmty. health affairs Meth. Ch., chair, 1995. Mem. Tri-County N.J. Assn. Occupl. Health Nurses (dir. edn. com. 1996—). Republican. Home: Unit 7 800 Old Springfield Ave Summit NJ 07901-1129 Office: Ciba-Geigy Corp Pharm Divsn 556 Morris Ave D1038 Summit NJ 07901

SMITH, THELMA TINA HARRIETTE, gallery owner, artist; b. Folkston, Ga., May 5, 1938; d. Harry Charles and Malinda Estelle (Kennison) Causey; m. Billy Wayne Smith, July 23, 1955; children: Sherry Yvonne, Susan Marie, Dennis Wayne, Chris Michael. Student, U. Tex., Arlington, 1968-70; studies with various art instrs. Gen. office worker Superior Ins. Corp., Dallas, 1956-57, Zanes-Ewalt Warehouse, Dallas, 1957-67; bookkeeper Atlas Match Co., Arlington, 1967-68; sr. acct. Automated Refrigerated Air Conditioner Mfg. Corp., Arlington, 1968-70; acct. Conn. Gen. Life Ins. Corp., Dallas, 1972-74; freelance artist Denton, Tex., 1974—; gallery owner, custom framer Tina Smith Studio-Gallery, Mabank, Tex., 1983—. Painting in pub. and pvt. collections in numerous states including N.Y., Fla., Ga. and N.D.; editor Cedar Creek Art Soc. Yearbook, 1983—. Treas. Cedar Creek Art Soc., 1987-88, 89—; mem. com. to establish state endorsed Arts Coun. for Cedar Creek Lake Area, Gun Barrel City, Tex. Recipient numerous watercolor and pastel awards Henderson County Art League, Cedar Creek Art Soc., Cmty. Svc. award Mayor Wilson Tippit, Gun Barrel City, Tex., 1986. Mem. Southwestern Watercolor Soc. (Dallas), Pastel Soc. of the S.W. (Dallas), Cedar Creek Art Soc. (Gun Barrel City) (v.p. 1983-86, treas.), Profl. Picture Framers Assn. Baptist. Office: Tina Smith Studio-Gallery 139 W Main St Gun Barrel City TX 75147

SMITH, TINA ASHBY, special education educator; b. Tremtonton, Utah, Sept. 15, 1953; d. LaMar J. and Julene (Winter) Ashby; m. Dale Keith Smith, Sept. 18, 1970; children: Jeffery, Jennifer, Ryan. BS cum laude, Utah State U., 1991. Cert. tchr., Utah. Spl. edn. tchr. kindergarten and 1st grade Lincoln Elem. Sch., Ogden (Utah) City Schs., 1992-95; tchr. Ogden Preschool, 1995—; mem. com. Ptnrs. for Success, Ogden, 1991-92. Mem. NEA, Utah Edn. Assn., Ogden City Edn. Assn., Coun. for Exceptional Children, Golden Key. Office: Ogden Preschool 1950 Monroe Ogden UT 84401

SMITH, TONI COLETTE, government official, social worker; b. Columbus, Ohio, Oct. 31, 1952. BA, Ohio State U., Columbus, 1974, postgrad., 1975-76; postgrad., Ohio State U., Columbus, 1978-90; MS in Edn., U. Dayton, 1993. Lic. social worker, Ohio. Cons. Ohio Dept. Human Svc., Columbus, 1974-75; mgr. Fisher Body Div., Columbus, 1977-78; with Franklin County Human Svc., Columbus, 1975—, supr., 1979-86, adminstr., 1986-91, asst. dep. dir., 1991-95, dep. dir., 1996—; pub. speaker human svcs. program Franklin County Human Svc., 1988—; instr., human svc. devel. Columbus State C.C., 1990—; grad. United Way Project Diversity Leadership Program. Mem. adv. bd. Columbus City Comprehensive Plan, 1989—, pres. Syntaxis Group Home, Columbus, 1989—; Informed Neighbors Com., 1989—, Berwick Civic Assn., Columbus (v.p. 1990-92, pres. 1992—); trustee Mental Health Assn., Columbus. Mem. AAUW (corr. sec. Columbus Chpt. 1988—), NAFE, LWV, Columbus Women's Network, Berwick Civic Assn. (pres. 1992-94). Democrat. Roman Catholic. Home: 2665 Mitzi Dr Columbus OH 43209-3263 Office: Franklin County Dept Human Svc 80 E Fulton St Columbus OH 43215-5127

SMITH, VALENE, anthropology educator; b. Spokane, Wash., Feb. 14, 1926; d. Ernst Frank and Lucy (Blachly) S.; m. Edwin Chesteen Golay, June 7, 1970 (dec. June 1980; m. Stanley George McIntyre, Nov. 26, 1983. BA in Geography, U. Calif., 1946, MA in Geography, 1950; PhD in Anthropology, U. Utah, 1966. Prof. earth sci. L.A. City Coll., 1947-67; prof. anthropology Calif. State U., Chico, 1967—; cons. World Tourism Orgn., Madrid, 1987. Editor: Hosts and Guests: The Anthrop, 1989, Tourism Alternatives: Potentials and Problems in the Development of Tourism, 1992. Mem. Internat. Acad. for Study Tourism, Anthrop. Soc. Wash., Cert. Travel Counselors, Am. Anthrop. Assn., AAUW, Canyon Oaks Country Club, Soroptimists. Republican. Office: U Calif Dept Anthropology Chico CA 95929

SMITH, VALERIE GAY, school counselor; b. Austin, Tex., Oct. 31, 1947; d. James Griffin and Ida Mae (Routon) Black; m. James David Smith, July 20, 1993. BA in English, McMurry Coll., 1969; MEd in Counseling, U. North Tex., 1974. Lic. profl. counselor, Tex.; cert. sch. counselor, Tex. Tchr. Nimitz H.S., Irving, Tex., 1969-71; tchr. MacArthur H.S., Irving, Tex., 1971-74, counselor, 1974-79; counselor Ditto Elem. Sch., Arlington, Tex., 1989-94, Withers Elem. Sch., Dallas, 1994—. Mem. ACA, Am. Sch. Counselor Assn., Tex. Sch. Counselor Assn. (elem. v.p. 1990-92, senator 1988-90, sec. 1986-88, Rhosine Fleming Outstanding Counselor award 1987, pres.-elect 1992-93, pres. 1993-94), Tex. PTA (life), Tex. Counseling Assn. (region 4 dir. 1990-93, pres.-elect 1995-96, pres. 1996-97), Phi Delta Kappa. Home: 2120 Nob Hill Carrollton TX 75006 Office: Withers Elem Sch 3959 Northaven Dallas TX 75229

SMITH, VANGY EDITH, accountant, consultant, writer, artist; b. Saskatoon, Sask., Can., Dec. 17, 1937; d. Wilhelm and Anne Ellen (Hartshorne) Gogel: m. Clifford Wilson, May 12, 1958 (de. Dec. 1978); children: Kenneth, Koral, Kevin, Korey, Kyle; m. Terrence Raymond Smith, Dec. 14, 1979. Student, Saskatoon Tech. Collegiate Inst., 1956, BBA, 1958, MBA, 1987, PhD in English with honors, 1988. Prin. Vangy Enterprises, Springfield, Oreg., 1960—; accounts payable clk. Maxwell Labs., Inc., San Diego, 1978; invoice clk. Davies Electric, Saskatoon, 1980-81; office mgr. Ladee Bug Ceramics, Saskatoon, 1981-87, Lazars Investments Corp., Eugene, Oreg., 1987; bookkeeper accounts payable Pop Geer, Eugene, Oreg., 1987; office mgr., bookkeeper Willamette Sports Ctr., Inc., Eugene, Oreg., 1985-89; clk. I Lane C.C., 1992—; self-employed Vangy Enterprises, 1992—; circulation mgr. Nat. WCTU, 1990-92, UN rep. for World WCTUm 1989-91, appointed mem. Parliament for the U. for Peace, Holland, 1991. Contbr. articles to scholarly jours. (recipient doctoral award 1987). Counselor Drug and Rehab. Ctr., Eugene, 1970-88; trustee Children's Farm Home, Corvallis, Oreg., 1989-91, 3d v.p., 1989-90; mem. Found. Christian Living; pres. Oreg. State Christian Temperance Union, 1989-90; mem. pub. safety adv. com. City of Eugene, 1989-90; co-pres. Lane County UN Assn., 1989-90; mem. artist Nat. Bd. Edn., 1989, 90; mem. adv. com. Dept. Pub. Safety for City of Eugene, 1990; exec. dir. H.E.L.P., 1993—; pres. Lane County Coun. of Orgns., 1994—; treas. Cascade/Coast chpt. Alzheimers Assn., 1994. Recipient 3d and 4th place artists' awards Lane County Fair, 1987, 1st and 2d place awards Nat. Writing Contest, 1987, 88, 89, 90, 91. Mem. WCTU (life, pres., state bd. dirs. projection methods circulation 1987-90, Appreciation award 1982, Presdl. award 1985, Lane County Euenge Woman of Yr. 1990), Am. Soc. Writers, Alzheimers Assn. (treas. Cascade/Coast chpt. 1994), Noble Grand-Rebekah Lodge, Rebekkah Juanita Lodge, Lions (sec. 1994). Democrat.

SMITH, VERONICA LATTA, real estate corporation officer; b. Wyandotte, Mich., Jan. 13, 1925; d. Jan August and Helena (Hulak) Latta; m. Stewart Gene Smith, Apr. 12, 1952; children: Stewart Gregory, Patrick Allen, Paul Donald, Alison Veronica, Alisa Margaret Lyons, Glenn Laurence. BA in Sociology, U. Mich., 1948, postgrad., 1948. Tchr. Coral Gables (Fla.) Pub. Sch. System, 1949-50; COO Latta Ins. Agy, Wyandotte, 1950-62; treas. L & S Devel. Co., Grosse Ile, Mich., 1963-84; v.p. Regency Devel., Riverview, Mich., 1984—. Active U. Mich. Bd. Regents, 1985-92, regent emeritus, 1993—; mem., pres. Martha Cook Bd. Govs., U. Mich., 1972-78, 76-78; del. Rep. County Conv., Wayne County, Mich., 1988—, Rep. State Conv., Grand Rapids, Mich., 1985, 87, 89, 91, 92, 94, Detroit, 1986, 88, 90, 92; mem. pres. adv. com. Campaign for Mich., 1992—, mem. campaign steering com., 1992—. Mem. Mich. Lawyers Aux. (treas. 1975, chmn. 1976, 77, 78, 79), Nat. Assn. Ins. Women (cert.), Faculty Women's Club U. Mich. (hon.), Radrick Farms Golf Club (Ann Arbor), Pres.'s Club U. Mich., Investment Club (pres. 1976, sec. 1974-75, treas. 1975-76), Alpha Kappa Delta. Home: 22225 Balmoral Dr Grosse Ile MI 48138-1403

SMITH, VIRGINIA BROWN, classical musician; b. Nashville, July 24, 1954; d. Jordan Stokes and Annie Frances (Sory) Brown; m. Mark Brampton Smith, Feb. 28, 1976 (div. 1986); 1 child, Evelyn Anne. MusB, Eastman Sch. Music, 1976; MusM, U. Mich., 1979. Dir. music Good Shepherd United Meth. Ch., Dearborn, Mich., 1977-81, Westminster Presby. Ch., Ann Arbor, Mich., 1981-84; instr. voice Schoolcraft Coll., Livonia, Mich., 1986-89; pvt. practice voice instr. Ann Arbor, 1976—; adj. instr. Albion (Mich.) Coll., 1991-95; solo recitals, performances Ann Arbor, Detroit, Mpls., Nashville, Washington, 1977—. Soprano soloist Christ Ch. Cranbrook, Bloomfield Hills, Mich., 1984—, U. Mich. Early Music Ensemble, 1994-96, Ann Arbor Cantata Singers, 1981-89, Ars Musica Choir, Ann Arbor, 1984-85, Vocal Arts Ensemble, 1995-96. Mem. Nat. Assn. Tchrs. Singing (bd. dirs. Mich. chpt.), Music Tchrs. Nat. Assn. (nat. profl. cert. 1989), Acad. for Study and Performance Early Mus. (bd. dirs. and sec. 1994), Early Mus. Am., Mich. Music Tchrs. Assn. (bd. dirs., cert. 1988, state voice chairperson 1989-95), Ann Arbor Piano Tchrs. Guild (treas. 1983-85), Livonia Area Piano Tchrs. Forum (pres. 1991-93), Detroit Musicians League, Pi Kappa Lambda, Sigma Alpha Iota. Democrat. Epsicopalian. Home: 3730 Burns Ct Ann Arbor MI 48105

SMITH, VIRGINIA DODD (MRS. HAVEN SMITH), congresswoman; b. Randolph, Iowa, June 30, 1911; d. Clifton Clark and Erville (Reeves) Dodd; m. Haven N. Smith, Aug. 27, 1931. A.B., U. Nebr., 1936; hon. degree, Nebr. U., 1987, Chadron State Coll., 1988. Nat. pres. Am. Country Life Assn., 1951-54; nat. chmn. Am. Farm Bur. Women, 1954-74; dir. Am. Farm Bur. Fedn., 1954-74, Country Women's Council; world dep. pres. Asso. Country Women of World, 1962-68; mem. Dept. Agr. Nat. Home Econs. Research Adv. Com., 1960-65; bd. dirs. Norwest Bank Cmty. Bd., Property Owners and Residents Bd., Sun Health Corp. Bd., Recreation Ctrs. Sun City West, sec., mem. gov. bd.; bd. dirs. Del Webb Hosp. Mem. Crusade for Freedom European inspection tour, 1958; del. Republican Nat. Conv., 1956, 72; bd. govs. Agrl. Hall of Fame, 1959—; mem. Nat. Livestock and Meat Bd., 1955-58, Nat. Commn. Community Health Services, 1963-66; adv. mem. Nebr. Sch. Bds. Assns., 1949; mem. Nebr. Territorial Centennial Commn., 1953, Gov.'s Commn. Status of Women, 1964-66; chmn. Presdl. Task Force on Rural Devel., 1969-70; mem. appropriations com., ranking minority mem. agrl. appropriations subcom., appropriations subcom. on energy and water devel. 94th-101st Congresses from 3d dist. Nebr.; v.p. Farm Film Found., 1964-74, Good Will ambassador to Switzerland, 1950. Apptd. adm. Nebr. Navy; bd. dirs. Shepherd of the Hills Meth. Ch. Recipient award of Merit, DAR, 1956; Disting. Service award U. Nebr., 1956, 60; award for best pub. address on freedom Freedom Found., 1966; Eyes on Nebr. award Nebr. Optometric Assn., 1970; Internat. Service award Midwest Conf. World Affairs, 1970; Woman of Achievement award Nebr. Bus. and Profl. Women, 1971; selected as 1 of 6 U.S. women Govt. France for 3 week goodwill mission to France, 1969; Outstanding 4H Alumni award Iowa State U., 1973, 74; Watchdog of Treasury award, 1976, 78, 80, 82, 83, 84, 86, 88; Guardian of Small Bus. award, 1976, 78, 80, 82, 84, 86, 88; Nebr. Ak-Sar-Ben award, 1983, Agrl. Achievement, Nebr. U., 1987; named Favorite Community Leader, Sun City West, 1994. Mem. AAUW, Delta Kappa Gamma (state hon. mem.), Beta Sigma Phi (internat. hon. mem.), Chi Omega, PEO (past pres.), Eastern Star. Methodist. Club: Business and Professional Women. Address: 13828 W Terra Vista Dr Sun City West AZ 85375-5432

SMITH, VIRGINIA LYNN, law librarian; b. Winston-Salem, N.C., Mar. 26, 1952; d. Vernon W. and Virginia Evelyn (Erwin) S. BA, La. State U., 1974, MLS, 1976, JD, 1984. Bar: La. 1984. Libr. Jefferson Parish Pub. Libr., Metairie, La., 1977, New Orleans Pub. Libr., 1977-78, La. State U. Med. Ctr. Libr., New Orleans, 1978-81; lawyer New Orleans City Attys. Office, 1984-86, Borello, Huber & Dubuclet, Metairie, 1986-91; law clk. Disciplinary Bd. La. State Bar Assn., New Orleans, 1992-93; law libr. Chaffe, McCall, Phillips, Toler & Sarpy, New Orleans, 1993—; sec. New Orleans Bar Assn. Exec. Com., 1991-92. Vol. LA/SPCA, New Orleans, 1995—. Mem. Am. Assn. Law Librs., La. State Bar Assn. (chair bridging the gap com. 1988, 89), New Orleans Assn. Law Librs. (sec. 1995-96, v.p., pres.-elect 1996-97). Office: Chaffe McCall Phillips Toler & Sarpy 1100 Poydras St Ste 2300 New Orleans LA 70163

SMITH, VIRGINIA WARREN, artist, writer, educator; b. Atlanta, Mar. 7, 1947; d. Ralph Henry and Dorothy Jane (Kubler) S. AB in Philosophy, Ga. State U., 1976, M Visual Art in Art and Photography, 1978. dir. The Upstairs Artspace, Tryon, N.C., 1984-86; mng. editor Art Papers, Atlanta, 1986-88; art critic Atlanta (Ga.) Jour./Constn., Atlanta, 1987-92; adj. faculty Atlanta (Ga.) Coll. Art, 1991—, Ga. State U., Atlanta, 1991—. Author, photographer: Scoring in Heaven: Gravestones and Cemetery Art in the American Sunbelt States, 1991, Alaska: Trail Tails and Eccentric Detours, 1992; exhbns. include High Mus. Art, Atlanta, 1972, 78, 80, 81, 82, 84, 88, 89, Nexus Contemporary Art Ctr., Atlanta, 1986, 87, 91, Sandler Hudson Gallery, Atlanta, 1987, 89, 92, Jackson Fine Art, Atlanta, 1988, 91, 93, Aperture Found., N.Y.C., 1989, MS Found., N.Y.C., 1991, Albany (Ga.) Mus. Art, 1991, Montgomery (Ala.) Mus. Art, 1992, Bernice Steinbaum Gallery, N.Y.C., 1992, Wyndy MoreLead Gallery, New Orleans, 1991, 92, U.S. Info. Agy., Washington, 1994, Chatahouchee Valley Art Mus., Lagrange, Ga., 1994, others; works in permanent collections including Mus. Modern Art, N.Y.C., Mus. Fine Arts, Boston, High Mus. of Art, Atlanta, New Orleans Mus. Art, Harvard U., Rochester Inst. Tech., N.Y., U. N.Mex., Ctr. for Study of So. Culture U. Miss., Oxford, Miss., Columbia (S.C.) Mus. Art and Sci., Ringling Sch. Art, Sarasota, Fla., City of Atlanta, Franklin Furnace, N.Y.C. Bd. mem. Art Papers, Atlanta, 1983-88; adv. bd. memd. Arts Festival Atlanta, Ga., 1990-93. Mem. Coll. Art Assn., Soc. for Photog. Edn., Photography Forum of the High Mus. Art (v.p. 1994-95). Democrat. Home and Office: PO Box 1110 Columbus NC 28722

SMITH, VME (VERNA MAE EDOM SMITH), sociology educator, freelance writer, photographer; b. Marshfield, Wis., June 19, 1929; d. Clifton Cedric and Vilia Clarissa (Patefield) Edom; children: Teri Freas, Anthony Thomas. AB in Sociology, U. Mo., 1951; MA in Sociology, George Washington, 1965; PhD in Human Devel., U. Md., 1981. Tchr. Alcohol Safety Action Program Fairfax County, Va., 1973-75; instr. sociology No. Va. C.C., Manassas, 1975-77, asst. prof., 1977-81, assoc. prof., 1981-84, prof., 1984-94, prof. emerita, 1995; coord. coop. edn. No. Va. Community Coll., Manassas, 1983-89; Chancellor's Commonwealth prof. Manassas, 1991-93; freelance writer, editor and photographer, 1965—; co-dir. Clifton C. Edom Truth With a Camera (photography seminars); asst. producer history of photography program Sta. WETA-TV, Washington, 1965; rsch. and prodn. asst., photographer, publs. editor No. Va. Ednl. TV, Sta. WNVT, 1970-71; cons. migrant div. Md. Dept. Edn., Balt., summer 1977; researcher, photographer Roundabout presch. high sch. series on Am. Values Sta. WNVT, 1970-71. Author, photographer: Middleburg and Nearby, 1986; co-author: Small Town America, 1993; contbr. photography to various works including Visual Impact in Print (Hurley and McDougall), 1971, Looking Forward to a Career in Education (Moses), 1976, Child Growth and Development (Terry, Sorrentino and Flatter), 1979, Photojournalism (Edom), 1976, 80, Migrant Child Welfare, 1977, (Cavenaugh), Caring for Children, 1973 (5 publs. by L.B. Murphy), Dept. Health, Edn. and Welfare, Nat. Geog., 1961, Head Start Newsletter, 1973-74. Mem. ednl. adv. com. Head Start, Warrenton, Va. Recipient Emmy Ohio State Children's Programming award; Fulbright-Hays Rsch. grantee, 1993. Mem. Va. Assn. Coop. Edn. (com. mem.). Democrat.

SMITH, WENDY HAIMES, federal agency administrator; b. Amarillo, Tex.; d. Ernest A. and Fannie Haimes; m. Jay L. Smith, 1983. BA in Econs., U. Mich.; postgrad., Ohio State U., Am. U., Washington Studio Sch. Cert. real estate agt. Office mgr. Haimes Travel Agy., Ohio, 1972-73; mgmt. intern U.S. Dept. Commerce, 1973-75, country specialist for Korea, 1973, spl. asst. to dep. asst. sec. for internat. commerce, 1973-74, project officer, maj. projects divsn., 1974-75, project mgr. indsl. sys., maj. projects divsn., 1975-77, country specialist for Brazil, 1978, project mgr., hydrocarbons and chem. process plants, maj. export projects divsn., 1977-79, exec. asst. to dep. asst. sec. of commerce for export devel. and staff dir. Pres. Export Coun., 1979-81, dir. Pres. Export Coun., 1981-92, acting dir. Office Planning and Coordination, 1988-89, dir. adv. coms. and pvt. sector programs Internat. Trade Adminstrn., 1992—. Author, editor: U.S. Trade in Transition: Maintaining the Gains, 1988; co-author, editor: The Export Imperative, 1980, Coping with the Dynamics of World Trade in the 1980s, 1984. Active Smithsonian Instn., Washington Studio Sch., Washington Opera Guild. Mem. Alpha Epsilon Phi (pres. Pi chpt. 1971). Office: Dept of Commerce Rm H2015B 14th and Constitution Ave NW Washington DC 20230

SMITH, WENDY JEAN, physical education educator; b. Havertown, Pa., Jan. 7, 1961; d. Hubert Bell and Elaine L. (David) S. BS, Jacksonville U., 1982. Substitute tchr. Marple Newtown Sch. Dist., Newtown Square, Pa., 1983-87; softball coach West Chester (Pa.) U., 1984; phys. edn. tchr. St. Barnabas Sch., Phila., 1987-90; lacrosse coach Marple Newtown Sr. High Sch., Newtown Square, 1985-91, basketball coach, 1984-93, field hockey coach, 1983—; softball coach Akiba High Sch., Bala Cynwyd, Pa., 1992—; camp dir. Tiger Field Hockey Camp, Newtown Square, 1987—; phys. edn. tchr., athletic dir. Solomon Schechter Day Sch., Bala Cynwyd, 1990—; bd. dirs. Newtown Square Softball, 1987-93, pres. 1994; cons. phys. edn. Marple Newtown Sch. Dist., 1989-92. Recipient Svc. and Appreciation award Solomon Schechter Student Coun., 1991-92, Svc. award Newtown Square Softball, 1994. Mem. AAHPERD, Pa. Field Hockey Coaches. Office: Solomon Schechter Day Sch Old Lancaster Highland Ave Bala Cynwyd PA 19004

SMITH, WENDY JEANE MARIE, medical association administrator; b. Fulton, N.Y., Apr. 11, 1964; d. Michael Charles and Sally Jeane (Ingison) S. BS, Rutgers U., 1988; MPH, Johns Hopkins U., 1994. Pharmacoepidemiologic rsch. assoc. Health Info. Designs, Inc., Arlington, Va., 1989-90; disease control specialist divsn. communicable diseases and vector-borne disease Prince George's County Health Dept., Cheverly, Md., 1990-93; assoc. dir. dept. profl. svcs. Soc. Nuclear Medicine, Reston, Va., 1994—; commr. commn. for animal control Prince George's County Govt., Hyattsville, Md., 1990-93; mem. acad. ethics com. Johns Hopkins U. Sch. Hygiene and Pub. Health, Balt., 1993-94. Editor-in-chief, contbr. Soc. Nuclear Medicine newsletter, 1994—. Mem. Am. Soc. Assn. Execs., Am.

Assn. Med. Soc. Execs. Am. Pub. Health Assn. Greater Washington Soc. Assn. Execs. (mem. govt. rels. com. 1995-96). Democrat. Home: 2819-B S Wakefield St Arlington VA 22206

SMITH, WENDY L., foundation executive; b. Chgo., Sept. 12, 1950; d. John Arthur and Dolores Mae (Webb) Rothenberger; m. Alan Richard Smith; children: Angela Fuhs, Erica Smith. Ed., Oakton C.C., Des Plaines, Ill., 1986, Mundelein Coll., 1990. Purchasing clk. AIT Industries, Skokie, Ill., 1975-76; purchasing agt. MCC Powers, Skokie, 1976-78; office mgr. Spartan Engring., Skokie, 1978-80, Brunswick Corp., Skokie, 1980—; successively sr. sec., coord. indsl. rels., dir. Brunswick Found., Lake Forest, Ill., 1982-89; pres. Brunswick Found., Lake Forest, 1989—; asst. sec. Brunswick Pub. Charitable Found., Lake Forest, 1989—; mem. adv. com. Found. for Ind. Higher Edn., Stamford, Conn., 1989—, Coun. Better Bus. Burs., Arlington, Va., 1988-90; bd. dirs. Associated Colls. of Ill., 1991—; bd. dirs., mem. trustees com., mem. compensation and benefits com. Donors Forum of Chgo., 1988-93. Bd. dirs. INROADS/Chgo., Inc., 1994—; mem. steering com. Dist. 57 Edn. Found., Mt. Prospect, Ill., 1996—. Recipient Pvt. Sector Initiative Commendation, U.S. Pres., 1987-89. Mem. Donors Forum Chgo. (treas. 1988-91, bd. dirs., mem. exec. com., chairperson audit and fin. com., mem. trustees com. 1992—), Coun. on Founds., Ind. Sector Suburban Contbns. Network (chairperson 1987-89), Women in Philanthropy Corp. Founds. (mem. cmty. rels. com. 1985-87), Chgo. Women in Philanthropy. Office: Brunswick Found 1 N Field Ct Lake Forest IL 60045-4810

SMITH, YVONNE CAROLYN, therapist; b. Lockport, N.Y., June 12, 1923; d. William Louis and Bertha (Zoss) S. BA, Valparaiso U., 1948; M in Social Sci. Adminstrn., Case-Western Res. U., Cleve., 1955. Cert. social worker. Caseworker Niagara County Welfare Dept., Lockport, 1950-53, Luth. Children's Aid, Cleve., 1954, Luth. Family Svc., Chgo., 1955-56, Family Svc. Soc., Buffalo, 1956-62; therapist, dir. Child & Family Svcs., Buffalo, 1962-88; ret. Child & Family Svcs., Cheetowaga, N.Y., 1988; field instr. social work SUNY, 1962-80; cons. Genesee County Social Svcs., Batavia, 1975-85, cons. Seneca County Social Svcs. Waterloo, 1988. Bd. dirs. Luth. Svc. Soc., Buffalo, 1979-85, 88-93, 95-96, mem. family svc. com., 1993—; speaker United Way of Buffalo, 1956-88; mem. edn. com. ea. dist. Luth. Ch. Mo. Synod, 1991—. Mem. AAUW, Internat. Human Learning Resources Network, Nigara County Hist. Soc., Kenmore Art Soc. Republican. Home: 401 Englewood Ave Apt 3 Buffalo NY 14223-2809

SMITH-ANSOTEGUI, SUSAN COONLEY, elementary school educator; b. Tokyo, Aug. 14, 1951; d. Franklin Leonard and Hanako (Kondo) Coonley; m. R. Michael Ansotegui, June 28, 1993; children: Johana, Ashley. BS in Elem. Edn., U. Nev., Reno, 1973; postgrad., Lesley Coll., 1995—. Home sch. tchr. Calvert Sch., Kauai, Hawaii, 1977-80; tchr. 1st grade Northside Elem. Sch., Fallon, Nev., 1973-77, 80-81; tchr. reading and history Minnie P. Blair Mid. Sch., Fallon, 1981-88; tchr. 6th grade E.C. Best Elem. Sch., Fallon, 1988-96, Numa Elem. Sch., Fallon, 1996—; tchr. trainer in math. Nev. Dept. Edn., Carson City, 1990—. Named County Tchr. of the Yr., Churchill County, 1994, Minnie P. Blair PTA Tchr. of the Yr., 1986. Mem. ASCD, Nat. Assn. of Gifted and Talented, Nat. Coun. Tchrs. Math., Churchill County Edn. Assn. (sec. 1986—, disting. svc. award 1996), Nev. Math. Coun. (sec. 1995—). Home: 2677 Rice Rd Fallon NV 89406-7445 Office: Churchill County Sch Dist 545 E Richards St Fallon NV 89406-3022

SMITHART, DEBRA L., food service executive. Exec. v.p., CFO Brinker Internat., Dallas. Office: Brinker Internat 6820 LBJ Frwy Dallas TX 75240*

SMITH-CARROLL, MYRTLE, civic worker, former journalist; b. N.Y.C., July 16, 1926; d. John Leo and Violet Jane (Robertson) Reilly; m. Charles Jackson Smith Jr., Sept. 21, 1946 (div. Aug. 1962); children: Charles Jackson III, Lynda Maureen Smith Necker, Robert William, Raymond Gerard, Rosemary Rita, Walter Alfred; m. Charles F. Carroll, Mar. 17, 1979. BA in English, Hunter Coll., 1947. Columnist Midland News, S.I., N.Y., 1960-63, Amsterdam News, N.Y.C., 1963-66; editor religious sect. St. Petersburg (Fla.) Times, St. Petersburg, Fla., 1972-73; diocesan reporter, photographer Fla. Cath., St. Petersburg, 1973-76; columnist, photographer Pinellas Dem., St. Petersburg, 1974-76; reporter Sta. WTSP-TV, St. Petersburg, 1975-76; talk show host Sta. WTSP, St. Petersburg, 1977-90; media specialist St. Petersburg Fire Dept., 1983-88; cons. Pinellas County Emergency Med. Svc., Clearwater, Fla., 1987-88, St. Petersburg Jr. Coll., 1992. Asst. prodr.: (TV show) Link to a Lifeline, 1986; prodr.: (child's puppet show) Fire Station 911, 1989; author, prodr.: (theatrical prodn.) Book of Newteronomy, 1995. St. Petersburg rep. on trip to China, 1983; cons. Juvenile Welfare Bd., St. Petersburg, 1992, bd. dirs., 1994—; bd. dirs. Brookwood, St. Petersburg, 1992-94, ACLU, St. Petersburg, 1994—; state committeewoman Pinellas County Dems., St. Petersburg, 1992—; Dem. nat. committeewoman, 1994—; sec. women's polit. caucus Dem. Nat. Com., 1994—; coord. women's network Fla. Dem. Party, 1995—. Recipient Susan B. Anthony award NOW, Pinellas County, 1980. Mem. Suncoast Tiger Bay Club. Democrat. Home: 330 Belleair Dr NE Saint Petersburg FL 33704

SMITHERS, RUTH ANNE HALL, educator, consultant; b. Phoenix, Nov. 17, 1928; d. Frank Ernest and Anne Marie (Diechelbohrer) Hall; m. Charles F. Smithers Jr., May 21, 1955 (div. Apr. 1993); children: Charles F. III, Claire Hall, Bonnie Louisa Smithers de Falla. BA, Tex. Woman's U., 1949; MAT, Manhattanville Coll., 1977; postgrad., Hertford Coll., Oxford, Eng., 1985. Loan closer So. Abst. & Title Co., Houston, 1949-55; pvt. tutor learning disabled, pvt. practice ednl. cons. New Canaan, Conn., 1977—; pvt. tutor learning disabled Harvey Sch., Katonah, N.Y., 1978-80. Active various polit. campaigns Dem. Party, New Canaan, 1965—; vice chmn. Dem. Town Com., New Canaan, 1982-84, chmn., 1990-92; candidate 1st selectman Town of New Canaan, 1995. Mem. Orton Soc., Elem. Sch. Bldg. Com. Roman Catholic. Home and Office: 25 Kimberly Pl New Canaan CT 06840

SMITHEY, MARGARET WALKER, education educator; b. Nashville, Tenn., Mar. 22, 1942; d. Zeb Lee and Margaret Ford (George) Walker; m. James Larry Smithey; children: Lee, David. BA, Belmont U., Nashville, 1964; MA, Peabody Coll., Nashville, 1967; PhD, Vanderbilt U., 1991. Asst. prof. Belmont U., Nashville, 1988-93; sr. lectr. Peabody Coll./Vanderbilt U., Nashville, 1993—, co-dir. mentor project, 1992—, dir. internship, 1993—. Mem. Svcs. Acad. Selection com. for Congressman Bob Clement, 1992-96. Mem. ASCD, Am. Ednl. Rsch. Assn., Mid-South Ednl. Rsch. Assn., Kappa Delta Pi. Office: Vanderbilt Univ Peabody Coll Box 330 Nashville TN 37203

SMITH-FLEMING, LINDA, advertising sales executive; b. San Antonio, Apr. 10, 1952; d. Vernon Russell and Alice Mary (Lucas) Smith; m. Michael Fleming, Aug. 12, 1995. Grad., St. Mary's H.S., Rutherford, N.J., 1970. Lic. realtor, N.J. Adminstr., pers. sec. Maxell Corp., 1981-83; adminstrv. asst. Craig Corp., 1983-84; coor. car audio divsn. JVC Co., 1984-86; mem. sales and tech. support staff Meadowlands Electronics, 1986-93; advt. account rep. Happi Mag., Superconductor Industry Mag. Rodman Pub. Co., Ramsey, N.J., 1993—. Mem. Cosmetic Exec. Women, Cosmetic Industry Buyers and Suppliers, Women in Packaging. Office: Rodman Pub Co PO Box 555 17 S Franklin Tpk Ramsey NJ 07446-0555

SMITH-LEINS, TERRI L., mathematics educator; b. Salina, Kans., Sept. 19, 1950; d. John W. and Myldred M. (Hays) Smith; m. Larry L. Leins, May 26, 1984. BS, Ft. Hays (Kans.) U., 1973, MS, 1976; AA, Stephen Coll., Columbia, Mo., 1970. Math tchr. Scott City (Kans.) Jr. H.S., Howard (Kans.) Schs.; instr. math. Westark C.C., Ft. Smith, Ark. Contbr. articles to profl. jours., chpts. to books. Mem. AADE, ASCD, Nat. Assn. Devel. Edn. (state sec. 1986-88, computer access com. 1980-85), Phi Delta Kappa (Kappan of Yr. 1985), Delta Kappa Gamma (state chairperson women in art 1993-95). Home: PO Box 3446 Fort Smith AR 72913-3446

SMITH-MEYER, LINDA HELENE (LINDA SMITH), artist; b. Manhattan, Nov. 18, 1947; d. Murray and Beatrice Victory (Waters) S.; m. Charles Emil Meyer, Oct. 28, 1995. BFA, SUNY, 1969; MFA, NYU, 1973. One-woman shows include Sushi Gallery, West Hollywood, Calif., 1983, The Ivey Gallery, L.A., 1987, Schwartz Cierlak Gallery, Santa Monica, Calif., 1990; group shows include Cicchinelli Gallery, N.Y.C., 1981, Proteus Gallery, Beverly Hills, Calif., 1981, Elizalde Gallery Internat., Laguna Beach, Calif., 1981, 82, Gallery Helene, West Hollywood, 1982, Factory Place Gallery, L.A., 1983, 84, The Ivey Gallery, 1986, Ratliff-Williams Gallery, Sedona, Ariz., 1990-91, Spago Restaurant, Hollywood, Calif., 1985—, others; represented in permanent collections at Peter Selz, Berkeley, Calif., Cedars-Sinai Med. Ctr., L.A., Martin Blinder/Barry Levine-Martin Lawrence Galleries, L.A., Ms. Found. for Women, N.Y.C., also pvt. collections; contbr. articles to profl. jours. Home: 1228 S Highland Ave Los Angeles CA 90019

SMITH-OLSON, BEVERLY DENISE, artist, educator; b. Manitowoc, Wis., June 19, 1952; d. Gene Edward and Doris Ethel (Kiekhaefer) Walker; m. Donald Dana Olson, June 18, 1981 (div. 1993). BS in Art, Western Oreg. State Coll., 1979; MFA, U. Wash., 1982. Studio artist Port Orchard, Wash., 1982—; art prof. Olympic C.C., Bremerton, Wash., 1991—; mentor, tchr. art workshops and pvt. study, 1983-95. Represented in permanent collections at Steel Case Corp. and Stowe and Davis Corp. Sarah Denny Grad. fellowship U. Wash., 1982; recipient Awards Ann. Pacific N.W. Arts Show, 1987, 93. Democrat. Home: 7368 King Rd SE Port Orchard WA 98366 Office: Olympic CC 1600 Chester Ave Bremerton WA 98337-1699

SMITH-ROMER, HELENE BONNIE, artist, educator; b. Chgo., July 6, 1948; d. Julius and Annie (Kaminsky) Smith; m. Eric R. Romer. BFA, Columbia Coll., 1984; MFA, U. Ill., Chgo., 1990. Photog. editor, writer Culture Mag., Chgo., 1982-83; gallery asst. Edwyn Houk Gallery, Chgo., 1983-84; inst. art and photography Jewish Cmty. Ctr.- Summer of the Arts, Skokie, Ill., 1984-85; instr. photography Truman Coll., Chgo., 1984-90; instr. computer graphics, exptl. images, multi-media Columbia Coll., Chgo., 1991—; curator, coord./curator vis. artist program I Due Art 4 You Mus., Chgo., 1993, 95—; curator Ukranian Inst. Modern Art, 1986, U. Ill., 1988, Art Inst. Chgo., 1990. Author: Conversations with Elmer, 1983, 4 Women Scrapbook, 1990, Confession of A Space Rider, 1993, Letters From Home, 1996. Recipient scholarship Albert P. Weisman, 1981, 82, 83; Ragdale Artist residency; grant Chgo. Coun. on Fine Arts, 1990-91, Photgraphy grant Ill. Arts Coun., 1992. Mem. Women Caucus for Arts (vis. artist/curator 1994—), Soc. for Photog. Educators. Home: 7348 N Ridge Blvd Chicago IL 60645

SMITH WILLIAMS, CRISTINA DE ANDRADE, non profit administrator; b. Salvador, Bahia, Brazil, Jan. 30, 1967; d. Richard Kelley and Maria Luiza (Navarro de Andrade) Smith; m. John L. Williams, Sept. 30, 1994. AAS in Mktg., Tulsa (Okla.) Jr. Coll., 1987; BA in Comm., U. Tulsa, 1992. Program dir. Tulsa Global Alliance, 1992—. Mem. Young Dems., Tulsa, 1988-93. Mem. Women in Comm. (chair youth chpt. 1996—), Tulsa Assn. for Vol. Adminstrs. (com. mem. 1995—). Democrat. Home: 3120 E 3rd Tulsa OK 74104 Office: Tulsa Global Alliance S Boston #401 Tulsa OK 74119

SMITS, HELEN LIDA, physician, administrator, educator; b. Long Beach, Calif., Dec. 3, 1936; d. Theodore Richard Smits and Anna Mary Wells; m. Roger LeCompte, Aug. 28, 1976; 1 child, Theodore. BA with honors, Swarthmore Coll., 1958; MA, Yale U., 1961, MD cum laude, 1967. Intern, asst. resident Hosp. U. Pa., 1967-68; fellow Beth Israel Hosp., Boston, 1969-70; chief resident Hosp. U. Pa., 1970-71; chief med. clinic U. Pa., 1971-75; assoc. adminstr. for patient care svcs. U. Pa. Hosp., 1975-77; v.p. med. affairs Community Health Plan Georgetown U., Washington, 1977; dir. health standards and quality bur. Health Care Financing Adminstrn., HHS, Washington, 1977-80; sr. rsch. assoc. The Urban Inst., Washington, 1980-81; assoc. prof. Yale U. Med. Sch., New Haven, 1981-85; assoc. v.p. for health affairs U. Conn. Health Ctr., Farmington, 1985-87; prof. community medicine U. Conn. Sch. Medicine, Farmington, 1985-93; hosp. dir. John Dempsey Hosp., Farmington, 1987-93; dep. adminstr. Health Care Financing Adminstrn., Washington, 1993-96; pres., med. dir. Health Right, Inc., Meriden, Conn., 1996—; commr. Joint Com. on Accreditation Hosps., Chgo., 1989-93, chair, 1991-92. Contbr. numerous articles to profl. jours. Bd. dirs. The Ivoryton Playhouse Fedn., Inc., 1990-92, The Connecticut River Mus., 1990-93, Hartford Stage, 1990-93; mem. Dem. Town Com., Essex, Conn., 1982-89. Recipient Superior Svc. award HHS, Washington, 1982; Royal Soc. Medicine Found. fellow, London, 1973; Fulbright scholar, 1959-60. Mem. ACP (master, regent 1984-90), Phi Beta Kappa, Alpha Omega Alpha. Episcopalian. Home: 81 Main St Ivoryton CT 06442-1032 Office: Health Right Inc 184 State St Meriden CT 06450

SMOCK, JUDITH NORDER, elementary school educator; b. Corry, Pa., Mar. 26, 1942; d. Carl Emmanuel and Kathrine Maria (Thomson) Norder; m. Philip Emerson Smock, Nov. 25, 1967; children: Philip Edward, Carl Arthur, Eileen Siobhan, Timothy Paul. BS in Elem. Edn., Edinboro State Coll., 1962, MEd, 1965. Cert. tchr., Pa. 1st grade tchr. Harbor Creek (Pa.) Sch. Dist., 1962-65, kindergarten tchr., 1965-88, 4th grade tchr., 1988-89, transitional tchr., 1989—. Mem. Delta Kappa Gamma (projects chmn. Alpha Iota chpt. 1994-96). Home: 8120 E Lake Rd Erie PA 16511-1635

SMOLENSKI, LISABETH ANN, family practice physician; b. Pitts., Oct. 1, 1950; d. Anthony Edward and Betty Jean (Gross) S.; m. William Ward Daniels, May 24, 1980; 1 child, Kathryn Elizabeth. BA, Carlow Coll., 1972; MD, Hahnemann U., 1982. Diplomate Am. Bd. Family Practice. Resident in family practice West Jersey Health Sys., Voorhees, N.J., 1982-85; pvt. practice, Somerville, Tenn., 1985-90, Memphis, 1990—; sec. exec. com. med. staff Meth. Hosp. Somerville, 1988-90. Fellow Am. Acad. Family Physicians. Republican. Office: Health First Med Group 5240 Poplar Ave Memphis TN 38119

SMOOT, HAZEL LAMPKIN, retired piano teacher, poet; b. Kamiah, Idaho, Oct. 17, 1916; d. Albert Chuning and Cora Benson (Buckland) Weaver; m. Daniel Joseph Smoot, Feb. 18, 1939 (div. 1960); children: Daniel Jerome, David Reed. AA, Sacramento City Coll., 1937; student, Linfield Coll., 1938. Contbr. poetry to anthologies published by World of Poetry, also to Vantage Press and The Golden Treasury of Great Poems, Great American Poetry Anthology. Scholar Linfield Coll.; recipient Golden Poetry awards World of Poetry, 1987, 88, 89, Best Poems of 1996 award Nat. Libr. of Poetry, 1996, A Sea of Treasures award Nat. Libr. of Poetry, 1996.

SMOOT, SKIPI LUNDQUIST, psychologist; b. Aberdeen, Wash., Apr. 10, 1934; d. Warren Duncan and Miriam Stephen (Bishop) Dobbins; m. Harold Richard Lundquist, June 2, 1951 (div. Mar. 1973); children: Kurt Richard, Mark David, Ted Douglas, Blake Donald; m. Edward Lee Smoot, June 14, 1975. BA in Psychology, Coll. of William and Mary, 1978; MA, Pepperdine U., 1980; PhD, Calif. Sch. of Profl., Psychology, San Diego, 1985. Lic. clin. psychologist, Calif.; lic. marriage and family therapist, Calif. Owner, operator McDonald's Restaurants, San Pedro and Torrance, Calif., 1965-76, Williamsburg, Va., 1965-76; psychotherapist Coll. Hosp., Cerritos, Calif., 1979-81, Orange County Child Guidance, Laguna Hills, Calif., 1981-82; psychotherapist Calif. State Police, Costa Mesa, 1982-83, Anaheim, 1983-84; psychologist Orange County Mental Health, Santa Ana, Calif., 1984-85, Psychol. Ctr., Orange and El Toro, Calif., 1985-91; clin. dir. Career Ambitions, Irvine and Laguna Hills, 1991-94, Psychol. Decisions, Irvine-Laguna Hills, Calif., 1991-94; psychol. cons. seminars and workshops for bus., Irvine and Laguna Hills, 1991-94. Mem. APA, Calif. Psychol. Assn., Calif. Assn. Marriage and Family Therapists. Democrat. Office: Psychol Decisions Career Ambitions Unltd 23161 Lake Ctr Dr Ste 124 Lake Forest CA 92630

SMUCKER, BARBARA CLAASSEN, former librarian, writer; b. Newton, Kans., Sept. 1, 1915; dual citizen U.S. and Can.; d. Cornelius Walter and Addie (Lander) Claassen; m. Donovan Ebersole Smucker, Jan. 21, 1939; children: Timothy, Thomas, Rebecca. BS, Kans. State U., 1936; postgrad., Rosary Coll., 1963-65; LittD (hon.), U. Waterloo, 1986; DHL (hon.), Bluffton Coll., 1989. English tchr. Harper (Kans.) High Sch., 1937-38; reporter Evening Kansan Republican, Newton, 1939-41; tchr. Ferry Hall Sch., Lake Forest, Ill., 1960-63; children's librarian Kitchener (Ont.) Public Library, 1969-77; reference librarian, head librarian Renison Coll., U. Waterloo, Ont., 1977-82, sr. fellow Renison Coll., 1982—; writer Am. Educator Ency., Lake Bluff, Ill., 1960-63; convocation speaker U. Waterloo, Ont., 1986. Author: Henry's Red Sea, 1955, Cherokee Run, 1957, Wigwam in the City, Susan, 1970, Underground to Canada, 1977, Runaway to Freedom, 1977, Under Jorden Til Canada, 1977, Les Chemins Secrets de la Liberte, 1978, Folge dem Nordstern, 1979, Days of Terror, 1980, June Lilly, 1981, Amish Adventure, 1983, Huida al Canada, 1983, Nubes Negras, 1984, Dagen Van Angst, 1985, White Mist, 1985, Jacob's Little Giant, 1987 (selected as gift to Prince Harry by govt. Ont.), Incredible Jumbo, 1990, (I.O.D.E. award 1991), Racc to Freedom, 1994, Selina and The Bear Paw Quilt, 1995, Selina and Shoo-Fly Pie, 1996; (oratorio, libretto) The Abiding Place, 1984, Garth and the Mermaid, 1992; (interpretation) Oxford Companion to Canadian Literature, 1985, Michelle Landsberg's Guide to Children's Books, 1986; illustrator (autobiography) Something About the Author, 1991. Recipient prizes Can. Council, 1980, Ruth Schwartz Found., 1980, Disting. Service award Kans. State U., 1980, Brotherhood award NCCJ, 1980; $2000 Vicki Metcalf prize for outstanding contbn. to Can. children's lit. Can. Authors Assn., 1988, Kitchener award, 1990. Mem. AAUW, Canadian Assn. Univ. Women, Canadian Soc. Children's Authors, Illustrators and Performers, Children's Reading Round Table, Chgo. Home: 20 Pinebrook Dr Bluffton OH 45817-1145

SMUTNY, JOAN FRANKLIN, academic director, educator; b. Chgo.; d. Eugene and Mabel (Lind) Franklin; m. Herbert Paul Smutny; 1 child, Cheryl Anne. BS, Northwestern U., MA. Tchr., New Trier High Sch., Winnetka, Ill.; mem. faculty, founder, dir. Nat. High Sch. Inst., Northwestern U. Sch. Edn., Chgo.; mem. faculty, founder dir. high sch. workshop in critical thinking and edn., chmn. dept. communications Nat. Coll. Edn., Evanston, Ill., exec. dir. high sch. workshops, 1970-75, founder, dir. Woman Power Through Edn. Seminar, 1969-74, dir. Right to Read seminar in critical reading, 1973-74, seminar gifted high sch. students, 1973, dir. of Gifted Programs for 6, 7 and 8th graders pub. schs., Evanston, 1978-79, 1st-8th graders, Glenview (both Ill.) 1979—; dir. gifted programs Nat.-Louis U., Evanston, 1980-82, dir. Center for Gifted, 1982—; dir. Bright and Talented and Project 1986—, North Shore Country Day Sch., Winnetka, 1982—; dir. Job Creation Project, 1980-82; dir. New Dimensions for Women, 1973, dir. Thinking for Action in Career Edn. project, 1974-77 , dir. Individualized Career Edn. Program, 1976-79, dir. TACE, dir. Humanities Program for Verbally Precocious Youth, 1978-79; co-dir., instr. seminars in critical thinking Ill. Family Svc., 1972-75 . Writer ednl. filmstrips in Lang. arts and Lit. Soc. for Visual Edn., 1970-74 ; mem. speakers bur. Counc. Fgn. Rels., 1968-69 ; mem. adv. com. edn. professions devel. act U.S. Office Edn., 1969—; mem. state team for gifted, Ill. Office Edn., Office of Gifted, Springfield, Ill., 1977; writer, cons. Radiant Ednl. Corp., 1969-71 ; cons. ALA, 1969-71 , cons., workshop leader and speaker in area of gifted edn., 1971—; coord. of career edn. Nat. Coll. Edn., 1976-78, dir. Project 1987—, dir. Summer Wonders, 1986—, Creative Children's Acad., bd. dirs., Worlds of Wisdom and Wonder, 1978—; dir. Future Tchrs. Am. Seminar in Coll. and Career, 1970-72; cons. for research and devel. Ill. Dept. Vocat. Edn., 1973—; cons. in career edn. U.S. Office Edn., 1976—; evaluation cons. DAVTE, IOE, Springfield, Ill., 1977, mem. Leadership Tng. Inst. for Gifted, U.S. Office Edn., 1973-74; dir. workshops for high sch. students; cons., speaker in field; dir. Gifted Young Writer's and Young Writer's confs., 1978, 79; dir. Project '92 The White House Conf. on Children and Youth; mem. adv. bd. Educating Able Learners, 1991—; chmn. bd. dirs. Barbereux Sch., Evanston, 1992—; asst. editor, mem. editl. bd. Understanding Our Gifted, 1994—. Mem. AAUP, Nat. Assn. for Gifted Child (nat. membership chmn. 1991—, co-chmn. schs. and programs, co-editor newsletter early childhood divsn.), Nat. Soc. Arts and Letters (nat. bd., 1st and 3d v.p. Evanston chpt., dir. 1983-92, pres. Evanston chpt. 1990-92), Mortar Bd., Outstanding Educators of Am. 1974, Pi Lambda Theta, Phi Delta Kappa (v.p. Evanston chpt., rsch. chmn. 1990-92). Author: (with others) Job Creation: Creative Materials, Activities and Strategies for the classroom, 1982, A Thoughtful Overview of Gifted Education, 1990, Your Gifted Child - How to Recognize and Develop the Special Talents in Your Child from Birth to Age Seven, 1989, paperback, 1991, Education of the Gifted: The Young Gifted Child: An Anthology, 1990, Potential and Promise: The Young Gifted Child, 1996; contbg. editor Roepper Review, 1994—; asst. editor Understanding a Gift, 1995—; editor, contbr. Maturity in Teaching; writer ednl. filmstrips The Brother's Grimm, How the West Was Won, Mutiny on the Bounty, Dr. Zhivago, Space Odessey 2001, Christmas Around the World; editor Jour. for Gifted, Ill., 1984—, Ill. Coun. Gifted Jour., 1985-93; contbg. editor Roeper Review, 1994—; editor IAGC Jour. for Gifted, 1994—; contbg. editor numerous books in field; contbr. articles to profl. jours. including Chgo. Parent Mag. Reviewer of Programs for Gifted and Talented, U.S. Office of Edn., 1976-78. Home: 633 Forest Ave Wilmette IL 60091-1713

SMYER, MYRNA RUTH, drama educator; b. Albuquerque, June 10, 1946; d. Paul Anthony and Ruth Kelly (Klein) S.; m. Carlton Weaver Canaday, July 5, 1980. BFA, U. N.Mex., 1969; MA, Northwestern U., 1971. Pvt. practice drama instr. Albuquerque, 1974-78; dir. drama Sandia Preparatory Sch., Albuquerque, 1977—, chmn. dept. fine arts, 1980—; dialect coach, dir. Chgo. Acting Ensemble, 1969-71; lectr., performer Albuquerque Pub. Schs. and various civic orgns., Albuquerque, 1974—; writer, dir., performer Arts in the Pks., Albuquerque, 1977-80; performer, crew various indsl. videos, 1981-86; instr. workshops and continuing edn. U. N.Mex. 1977-80. Writer, dir., designer children's plays including May The Best Mammal (Or Whatever) Win, 1977, A Holiday Celebration, 1977, Puppets on Parade, 1978, A Witch's Historical Switches, 1979, Once Upon a Rhyme, 1987— (Outstanding Contbn. Arts in Edn. Bravo award Albuquerque Arts Alliance 1995), Little Red Riding Hood, 1987, Goldilocks and The Three Bears, 1988, Cinderella, 1989, Hansel and Gretel, 1990, Rumpelstiltskin, 1991, The Dancing Princesses, 1992, The Three Pigs, 1994, Sleeping Beauty, 1996; dir. numerous other children and adult plays. Instr., writer, dir. various community theatres including Albuquerque Little Theatre, Corrales Adobe Theatre, Kimo Theatre, Albuquerque Civic Light Opera, Now We Are Theatre; mem. Albuquerque Cable TV Adv. Bd.; mem. task force on the arts for children Albuquerque Little Theatre. Recipient 1st Pl. award for quality in edn. N.Mex. Rsch. and Study Coun., U. N.Mex., 1989-90, Albuquerque Acad. grant (children theatre), 1993, 95, Neighborhood Appreciation award Four Hills, 1993. Mem. Am. Alliance for Theatre and Edn., Theater N.Mex., Albuquerque Arts Alliance. Office: Sandia Preparatory Sch 532 Osuna Rd NE Albuquerque NM 87113-1031

SMYTH, ADRIENNE CHARLENE, preschool educator; b. Balt., Feb. 16, 1965; d. Nobile Guy and Dorothy Perkins (Coleman) Costantine; m. David Ralph Smyth, May 24, 1985. AA, Hillsborough C.C., 1986; BA in Psychology/Early Childhood Edn., Shippensburg U., 1995. Group leader Lutz (Fla.) Bapt. Daycare, 1983-86; site mgr. Latchkey Svcs. for Children, Pasco County, Fla., 1988-89; lead tchr. Hand in Hand Daycare, Lambertville, N.J., 1989-91; instr. Pa. State Coll. Tech., Wellsboro, 1989; parent educator childcare Migrant Child Devel., Chambersburg, Pa., 1993; group supr. Mt. Rock Care & Share, Shippensburg, Pa., 1991-95; exec. dir. Fulton County Ctr. for Families, 1995—. Continuing Edn. scholar Keystone U. Rsch. Corp., Erie, Pa., 1994; recipient Ctr. award Latchkey Svcs., Pasco County, 1988. Mem. ASCD, Nat. Assn. for Edn. of Young Children, Assn. Childhood Edn. Internat. Home: PO Box 478 Shippensburg PA 17257-0478 Office: Fulton County Ctr for Families PO Box 461 Mc Connellsburg PA 17233

SMYTHE, SHEILA MARY, academic dean and administrator; b. N.Y.C., Nov. 1, 1932; d. Patrick John and Mary Catherine (Gonley) S. Student, Creighton U., 1952; BA, Manhattanville Coll., 1952; MS, Columbia U., N.Y.C., 1956; LHD (hon.), Manhattanville Coll., 1974. From rsch. assoc. to asst. dir. of rsch. and planning Blue Cross Assn., Chgo., 1957-63; exec. asst. to pres. Empire Blue Cross & Blue Shield, N.Y.C., 1963-72, v.p., 1972-74, sr. v.p., 1974-78, exec. v.p., 1978-82, pres., chief oper. officer, 1982-85; health fin. and mgmt. cons. N.Y.C. and Washington, 1986-87; chief health policy advisor GAO, Washington, 1987-95, cons., exec. v.p., 1995—; dean grad. sch. health scis. N.Y. Med. Coll., N.Y.C., 1990—; adj. asst. prof. Grad. Sch. Pub. Health, Columbia U., 1980-86; bd. dirs. Mut. of Am., product & mktg. com. 1991-93, nominating com., 1992-94, audit com., 1993—, strategic planning com., 1994—; bd. dirs. Nat. Health Coun., Inc., mem. fin. com., 1987-94; bd. dirs. Hudson Valley Health Sys. Agy., sec., 1993-94, 1st v.p., 1994-95, pres., 1995—; active N.Y. State Hosp. and Rev. Planning Coun., 1994—. Chmn. bd. Manhattanville Coll., Purchase, N.Y., 1994—, trustee affairs, acad. affairs, exec. coms.; bd. dirs. Cath. Charities-U.S.A., 1989-95, mem. exec. pers. coms.; bd. dirs. March of Dimes Birth Defects Found., 1989—, vice chair, mem. fin. com., chair pub. affairs com., dir. Greater N.Y. March of Dimes, 1985-89. Recipient Elizabeth Cutter Morrow award YWCA, N.Y., 1977, Disting. Alumni award Manhattanville Coll., 1981, Excellence in Leadership award Greater N.Y. March of Dimes, 1989. Mem. Nat. Arts Club N.Y.C. Roman Catholic. Office: NY Med Coll Grad Sch Health Scis Valhalla NY 10595

SNAPP, ELIZABETH, librarian, educator; b. Lubbock, Tex., Mar. 31, 1937; d. William James and Louise (Lanham) Mitchell; BA magna cum laude, North Tex. State U., Denton, 1968, MLS, 1969, MA, 1977; m. Harry Franklin Snapp, June 1, 1956. Asst. to archivist Archive of New Orleans Jazz, Tulane U., 1960-63; catalog librarian Tex. Woman's U., Denton, 1969-71, head acquisitions dept., 1971-74, coord. readers svcs., 1974-77, asst. to dean Grad. Sch., 1977-79, instr. libr. sci., 1977-88, acting Univ. libr., 1979-82, dir. librs., 1982—, univ. historian, 1995—; chair-elect Tex. Coun. State U. Librs., 1988-90, chmn., 1990-92; mem. adv. com. on libr. formula Coordinating Bd. Tex. Coll. and Univ. System, 1981-92; del. OCLC Nat. Users Council, 1985-87, mem. by-laws com., 1985-86, com. on less-than-full-svcs. networks, 1986-87; trustee AMIGOS Bibliographic Coun., Inc., 1994—, sec. bd. trustees, 1996—; project dir. NEH consultancy grant on devel. core curriculum for women's studies, 1981-82; chmn. Blue Ribbon com. 1986 Gov.'s Commn. for Women to select 150 outstanding women in Tex. history; project dir. math./sci. anthology project Tex. Found. Women's Resources. Co-sponsor Irish Lecture Series, Denton, 1968, 70, 73, 78. Sec. Denton County Dem. Caucus, 1970. Recipient Ann. Pioneer award Tex. Women's U., 1986. Mem. AAUP, ALA (standards com. 1983-85), Tex. Libr. Assn. (program com. 1978, Dist. VII chmn. 1985-86, archives and oral history com. 1990-92, co-chair program com. Tex. Libr Assn. Ann. Conf. 1994, mem. Tall Texan selection com. 1995-96, treas. exec. bd. 1996—), Tex. Hist. Commn. (judge for Farenbach History prize 1990-93), Women's Collecting Group (chmn. ad hoc com. 1984-86), AAUW (legis. br. chmn. 1973-74, br. v.p. 1975-76, br. pres. 1979-80, state historian 1986-88), AAUW Ednl. Found. (rsch. and awards panel 1990-94), So. Conf. Brit. Studies, Tex. Assn. Coll. Tchrs. (pres. Tex. Woman's U. chpt. 1976-77), Alliance Higher Edn. (chair coun. libr. dirs. 1993-95), Woman's Shakespeare Club (pres. 1967-69), Beta Phi Mu (pres. chpt. 1976-78; sec. nat. adv. assembly 1978-79, pres. 1979-80, nat. dir. 1981-83), Alpha Chi, Alpha Lambda Sigma (pres. 1970-71), Pi Delta Phi. Methodist. Club: Soroptimist Internat. (Denton) (pres. 1986-88). Asst. editor Tex. Academe, 1973-76; co-editor: Read All About Her! Texas Women's History: A Working Bibliography, 1995; contbg. author: Women in Special Collections, 1984, Special Collections, 1986; book reviewer Library Resources and Tech. Services, 1973—. Contbr. articles to profl. jours. Home: 1904 N Lake Trl Denton TX 76201-0602 Office: TWU Sta PO Box 424093 Denton TX 76204-2093

SNAVELY, SHARON MARTIN, interior designer; b. Columbus, Ohio, July 31, 1946; d. John William and Patricia Mary (Mantel) Martin; m. Charles William Isaly, Nov. 5, 1966 (div. May, 1989); children: Jeffrey, Bradley; m. Donald Snavely, 1994. BA in Liberal Arts, No. Ariz. U., 1967. Interior designer John Martin Construction, Phoenix, 1967-73; v.p., owner Martin Constrn., Missoula, Mont., 1973-80; pres., owner SMI Interiors, Ariz., Mont., and Calif., 1980-92; constrn. adminstr. Trittipo & Assoc., Carlsbad, Calif., 1989-91; owner, ptnr. Design Group, Missoula, 1992-96; pres., owner Sharon Snavely, ASID, Missoula, 1996—. Mem. adv. bd. Florence Crittendon, Helena, Mont., 1994—, Missoula Symphony Bd., 1990—; pres. Symphony Guild; mem. action bd. Young Reps., Mont., 1994; bd. dirs. Extended Families, Missoula, 1994-96. Mem. Am. Soc. Interior Designers, Am. Inst. Archs., Gen. Contractors Assn., Art Assocs. (pres.), Women in Art San Francisco, Missoula C. of C. Redcoats, Rotary. Home: 2020 W Greenough Dr Missoula MT 59802 Office: 201 N Higgins Missoula MT 59802

SNAY, JOYCE ELAINE, association administrator; b. Hutchinson, Kans., Dec. 21, 1943; d. Howard F. and Merna L. (Chance) S.; m. Kenneth W. Laflin, Dec. 20, 1963 (div. 1977); 1 child, Kendra Laflin. BS, Colo. State U., 1966; MS, U. North Tex., 1976, EdD, 1978. Registered mcpl. clk., Tex. Tchr., coach Unified Sch. Dist. #369, Burrton, Kans., 1966-67, Tombstone (Ariz.) H.S., 1967-68, Englewood (Colo.) Ind. Sch. Dist., 1968-70, Ferris (Tex.) H.S., 1970-72; teaching fellow U. North Tex., Denton, 1972-78; educator, coach U. Sci. & Arts, Chickasha, Okla., 1978-79; mgr., buyer Voertman's Inc., Denton, 1985-92; exec. dir. Tex. Mcpl. Clks. Assn., Inc., Denton, 1994—. Vol., treas., v.p. MADD, Denton, 1971—, leader victim's impact panel, 1994—. Mem. Tex. Mcpl. Clks. Assn. Inc. Methodist. Home: 2007 Westwood Denton TX 76205 Office: Tex Mcpl Clks Assn Inc Chilton Hall UNT Denton TX 76203

SNEAD, LYNN GRABENSTEIN, social services administrator; b. Pitts., Nov. 30, 1948; d. Earl Kenneth and Eileen (Kohl) Grabenstein; divorced; children: Libbeth, Erik, Sean. BSW summa cum laude, U. Pitts., 1988, MSW, 1990. Lic. social worker, Pa. Administr. Carnegie-Mellon U., Pitts., 1975-78; dir. tng. program devel. facilitation group workshops Effective Research, Pitts., 1978-92; exec. dir. Alle-Kiski Area Hope Ctr., Pitts., 1992—; part-time mem. faculty Creative Problem Solving Inst. SUNY, Buffalo, 1988—. Vol. Crisis Ctr. North, Allison Park, Pa., 1987—. Merit scholar U. Pitts., 1987-88, scholar N. Hills Jr. Women's Club, 1988. Mem. Nat. Assn. Social Workers, Am. Soc. Engring. Edn., Creative Problem Solving Inst. Alumni Assn., Golden Key. Democrat. Roman Catholic. Office: Alle-Kiski Area Hope Ctr PO Box 67 Tarentum PA 15084

SNEARLY, PATRICIA MEARA, art educator; b. Muncie, Ind., Oct. 22, 1944; d. John William and Edith Augusta (Beyer) Meara; m. Ward Dean Snearly, Mar. 12, 1966; children: David, Allison. BA, Purdue U., 1981, MA, 1984. Cert. tchr., Ind. Mgr. resource libr. dept. visual art Purdue U., West Lafayette, Ind., 1981-88; designer Walcott Weavers, Lafayette, Ind., 1988-90; tchr. Delphi (Ind.) Middle and High Schs., 1990-91, Harrison High Sch., West Lafayette, 1991-94, Frankfort (Ind.) Middle Sch., 1994—; coach Acad. Superbowl and Acad. Decathlon Delphi, 1990-91, West Lafayette, 1991-94; chairperson steering com. performance based accreditation Delphi and West Lafayette. Arts grantee Ind. Dept. Edn., 1992, 93. Mem. Nat. Art Edn. Assn., Wabash Artist Alliance, Greater Lafayette Mus. Art. Home: 329 N Marish Rd Frankfort IN 46041

SNEDAKER, CATHERINE RAUPAGH (KIT SNEDAKER), editor; b. Fargo, N.D., Apr. 2; d. Paul and Charity (Primmer) Raupagh; B.A., Duke U.; m. William Brooks; children—Eleanor, Peter William; m. 2d, Weldon Snedaker. Pub. relations exec. United Seamen's Service, 1950-57; promotion mgr. sta. WINR-TV and WNBF-TV, Binghamton, N.Y., 1957-60; TV editor, feature writer Binghamton Sun, 1960-68; mem. staff Los Angeles Herald Examiner, 1968—, food editor, 1978—, restaurant critic, 1978-80, food and travel editor, 1980-86; editor The Food Package. Author: The Great Convertibles; contbr. numerous articles on food and travel to nat. mags. and newspapers; guest editor Mademoiselle mag., 1942. Recipient 3 awards Los Angeles Press Club, VISTA award, 1979. Mem. Soc. Am. Travel Writers, Travel Journalist's Guild. Democrat. Home: 140 San Vicente Blvd Apt A Santa Monica CA 90402-1533

SNELL, LINDA HARNER, women's health nurse, educator; b. Brockport, N.Y., July 28, 1953; d. Roy Seymour and Helen Belle (Dowden) Harner; m. Alden H. Snell, June 14, 1975; children: Alden II, Christopher. BSN, Roberts Wesleyan Coll., Rochester, N.Y., 1975; MS, SUNY, Buffalo, 1985; DNS, 1996. RN, N.Y.; cert. ob-gyn. nurse practitioner. Staff nurse Lankenau Hosp., Phila., 1975-78, Carthage (N.Y.) Area Hosp., 1981-82, Lockport (N.Y.) Meml. Hosp., 1982-83; clin. instr. SUNY Buffalo Sch. Nursing, 1985-88; nurse practitioner Health Care Plan, Buffalo, 1990—; asst. prof. nursing D'Youville Coll., Buffalo, 1992—. Recipient Alumni award SUNY at Buffalo Sch. Nursing, 1985; Sigma Theta Tau rsch. grantee, 1992. Mem. Nurse Practitioner Assn. Western N.Y., Assn. Women's Health, Obstet. and Neonatal Nurses (sect. chair 1991-96). Office: D'Youville Coll 320 Porter Ave Buffalo NY 14201-1032

SNELL, LINDA WAGES, counselor; b. Wilspoint, Tex., July 13, 1956; d. Homer Junior and Patsy Ruth (Simmons) Wages; m. Jere W. Snell, Feb. 2, 1975; children: Wesley, Stephen. BA, Northwestern State U., 1985; MEd, Stephen F. Austin State U., 1994. Tchr. F.L. Moffett Primary Sch., Center, Tex., 1985—; counselor Center (Tex.) Ind. Sch. Dist. primary/elem., 1995—. Mem. Beta Sigma Phi (v.p. 1995—). Baptist. Office: F L Moffett Primary Sch Rt 3 Box 1480 Center TX 75935

SNELL, MICHELLE LOUISE, elementary education educator; b. Mascoutah, Ill., Feb. 25, 1970; d. Charles Edward Snell and Karen Louise (Squier) Benson. BA, Simpson Coll., 1992. Substitute tchr. grades K-6 Murray (Iowa) Cmty. Schs., 1992—, Clarke Cmty. Schs., Osceola, Iowa, 1992—, East Union Schs., Afton, Iowa, 1993—. Democrat. Home: 313 S Lincoln St Osceola IA 50213-1553

SNELL, PATRICIA POLDERVAART, librarian, consultant; b. Santa Fe, Apr. 11, 1943; d. Arie and Edna Beryl (Kerchmar) Poldervaart; m. Charles Eliot Snell, June 7, 1966. BA in Edn., U. N.M., 1965; MSLS, U. So. Calif., 1966. Asst. edn. libr. U. So. Calif., L.A., 1966-68; med. libr. Bedford (Mass.) VA Hosp., 1968-69; asst. law libr. U. Miami, Coral Gables, Fla., 1970-71; acquistions libr. U. N.Mex. Law Sch. Libr., Albuquerque, 1971-72; order libr. Los Angeles County Law Libr., 1972-76, cataloger, 1976-90; libr. Parks Coll., Albuquerque, 1990-92; records technician Technadyne Engring. Cons. to Sandia Nat. Labs., 1992-93; instr. libr. sci. program Coll. Edn. U. N.Mex., Albuquerque, 1991—, libr. Tireman Learning Materials Ctr., 1993—. Ch. libr.. Beverly Hills Presbyn. Ch., 1974-90, ch. choir libr., 1976-90. Southwestern Library Assn. scholar 1965. Mem. ALA, N.Mex. Libr. Assn., Pi Lambda Theta. Office: U N Mex Coll Edn EM/LS Program Tireman Libr Albuquerque NM 87131

SNELLING, BARBARA W., state official; b. Fall River, Mass., Mar. 22, 1928; d. Frank Taylor and Hazel (Mitchell) Weil; m. Richard Arkwright Snelling, June 14, 1947 (dec. Aug. 1991); children: Jacqueline, Mark, Diane, Andrew. AB magna cum laude, Radcliffe Coll., 1950; D of Pub. Svc. (hon.), Norwich U., 1981. V.p. U. Vt., 1974-82; pres. Snelling and Kolb, Inc., 1982-95; lieut. gov. State of Vt., 1993—; chmn. bd. dirs. Chittenden Bank Corp., 1990—. Trustee Radcliffe Coll., 1990-95; bd. dirs. Vt. Community Found., 1986-94, Shelburne Mus., 1988—; mem. Vt. Ednl. Partnerships, 1992—; v.p. for devel. and external affairs U. Vt., 1974-82; mem. Vt. State Bd. Edn., 1971-77; trustee Champlain Coll., 1971-74; mem. Vt. Alcohol and Drug Rehab. Commn., 1970-73, Shelburne Sch. Bd., 1958-73, chmn. 1965-73; mem. Vt. Edn. Adv. Coun., 1968-71, Vt. Tchr. Edn. Adv. Com., 1968-70, Bd. of Sch. Dirs., Champlain Valley Union High Sch., 1962-69, chmn. 1962-68, others. Recipient Fanny G. Shaw award for Disting. Community Svc., Burlington Community Coun., 1972, Laymen's award Vt. Edn. Assn., 1965. Office: Office of Lieutenant Governor State House Montpelier VT 05633*

SNELLING, NORMA JUNE, retired music educator, English educator; b. Brooten, Minn., June 1, 1928; d. Harold Melvin and Mabel Olga (Markuson) Hellickson; m. Douglas Howard Snelling, June 27, 1953; children: Julie Marie, Mary Merced, Steven Douglas. BA, Concordia Coll., Moorhead, Minn., 1949. Cert. tchr., Minn. Tchr. Wolverton (Minn.) Sch. Dist., 1949-51, Kimball (Minn.) Sch. Dist., 1951-52, Benson (Minn.) Sch. Dist., 1952-53, Belgrade (Minn.) Sch. Dist., 1953-57, Hutchinson (Minn.) Sch. Dist., 1964-66, Litchfield (Minn.) Sch. Dist., 1966-92; mem. staff edn. liaison 2d Congl. Dist. Minn., Litchfield, 1992—. Assoc. chairperson county level, del. Dem. Farmer Labor Party, Minn., 1992—, chair 1994; del. to Dem. Nat. Conv., 1984; co-chairperson Concert Series, Litchfield, 1962, Cancer Dr., Litchfield, 1960; dir. Choralaires, Eden Valley, Minn., 1976—; dir. music Zion Luth. Ch., Litchfield, 1962-85, poet ch. pubs., dedications, etc., also Big Grove Luth. Ch.; speech coach Litchfield Jr. H.S., 1972-77; mem. VFW Aux., Am. Legion Aux. 94m. NEA (life, congl. contact person 1985-90), Minn. Edn. Assn. (govtl. rels. uniserve chairperson, Leadership award medal 1986), Ret. Educators Minn. (legis. chairperson 1993—), Internat. Platform, Sons of Norway (musician, pres. Vannland Lodge 1993-94, Bronze medal 1993-94), Gen. Fedn. Women's Study Clubs, Halling Laget, Delta Kappa Gamma. Home: 621 W Crescent Ln Litchfield MN 55355-1830

SNETRO, PAMELA CIABURRI, stockbroker, financial executive; b. New Haven, Feb. 28, 1958; d. Joseph V. and Mary Grace (Calandro) Ciaburri; m. David M. Snetro, Sept. 29, 1989; 1 child, Derek M. BA in Econs., Fairfield U., 1980. Lic. series 7. V.p. Shearson Lehman Hutton, Westport, Conn., 1984-96; account v.p. investments Paine Webber, Fairfield, Conn., 1996; spkr. in field; tchr. investment classes, Fairfield County. Contbr. monthly investment article Fairfield County Bus. Jour. Mem. Omicron Delta Epsilon. Home: 37 Eagle Dr Fairfield CT 06430

SNIBBE, PATRICIA MISCALL, advertising agency executive; b. Hackensack, N.J., June 1, 1932; d. Jack and Margaret Lois (Drake) Miscall; m. Richard Wilson Snibbe, Sept. 8, 1962; stepchildren: John Robinson, Paul Clor. BFA, R.I. Sch. Design, 1954; postgrad., New Sch. for Social Rsch., 1975-80, U. London, 1989. Art dir., film producer Peckham Prodns., N.Y.C., 1960-64; dir. art, ptnr. Stallman and Snibbe, N.Y.C., 1964-66; dir. art Shevlo Advt., N.Y.C., 1966-72, Bernard Hodes Advt., N.Y.C., 1972-77; owner, creative dir. Designstuff, N.Y.C., 1978-88; creative dir. Archtl. Film Libr., N.Y.C., 1980—; pres. Crommelin and Bliss, Parfumier, 1988—. Author and artist: Feminist Funnies, 1981—. Recipient Golden Cir. award Affiliated Advt. Agys. Internat., 1975-77, Creativity award of Distinction, 1978. Mem. NOW (bd. dirs. N.Y.C. 1983-84), Graphic Artists Guild (steering com. Cartoonists Guild div. 1984-85), NATAS, Archael. Inst. Am. Home: 139 E 18th St New York NY 10003-2470

SNIDER, MARIE ANNA, syndicated columnist; b. Croghan, N.Y., Aug. 9, 1927; d. Nicholas and Dorothy (Moser) Gingerich; m. Howard Mervin, Nov. 27, 1954; children: Vada Marie, Conrad Howard. BS, Goshen Coll., 1949; M in Religious Edn., Mennonite Bibl. Sem., 1957; MS, Kans. State U., 1980. High sch. tchr. Rockway Collegiate, Kitchener, Ont., Can., 1949-53; free-lance writer, 1953-54; pub. rels. Goshen Coll., Ind., 1955-57; free-lance writer, homemaker, 1957-67; info. editor Prairie View, Inc., Newton, Kans., 1967-76; dir., pub. info. & edn. Prairie View, Inc., Newton, 1976-85, dir. communications, 1985-91; freelance writer, columnist North Newton, 1991—; syndicated columnist "This Side of 60", 1992—; bd. dirs. Health Systems Agy. of S.E. Kans., 1981-86, v.p., 1986-87; workshop presenter Nat. Coun. of Community Mental Health Ctrs., Atlanta, 1980, N.Y., 1982, 89, Miami, 1987. Editor: Media and Terrorism--The Psychological Impact, 1976; columnist: This Side of 60. pres. City Council, N Newton, 1977-79, pres. 1980. Recipient 1st Pl. MacEachern award Assn. of Hosp. Pub. Rels., 1981, 1st Pl. Media award Nat. Coun. Community Mental Health Ctrs., 1977, 84, runner-up Pub. Rels. award Nat. Assn. Pvt. Psychiat. Hosps., 1980. Mem. Nat. Soc. Newspaper Columnists. Democrat. Home and Office: PO Box 332 North Newton KS 67117-0332

SNIDER, RUTH ATKINSON, retired counselor; b. Louisville, Jan. 7, 1930; d. Ellis Orrell and Fanola Blanche (Miller) Atkinson; m. Arnold Wills Snider, Feb. 17, 1950; children: Yvonne Marie, Ray Wills, Mark Alan. Student, Centre Coll., 1947-48; BS, Spalding U., 1965, MEd, 1970; rank I, Western Ky. U., 1981. Cert. sch. psychometrist, sch. prin., supr. of instrn. Tchr. Shelby County (Ky.) Bd. Edn., 1949-50, Louisville Pub. Schs., 1956-57; tchr. Jefferson County Pub. Schs., Louisville, 1965-67, counselor, 1967-92; vol. co-chairperson for mentor program Spalding U., Louisville, 1991. Vol. Ky. Ctr. for Arts, 1989, 90, 91, Actors Theatre of Louisville, 193-94, 95, 96, Klondike Elem. Sch. Libr., 1994-95; pub. chair World Day of Prayer, 1996; sec. adv. com. Beechwood Bapt. Ch. Mem. ACA (del.), Am. Sch. Counselors Assn. (del. nat. conf.), Ky. Assn. Counseling and Devel., Ky. Sch. Counselors Assn. (conf. chairperson), Spalding Soc. (pres. 1995-96), Spalding Alumni Assn. (sec. 1994-96, Caritas award), Jefferson County Ret. Tchrs. Assn., Christian Women's Club. Home: 2428 Chattesworth Ln Louisville KY 40242-2849

SNIERSON, LYNNE WENDY, communications executive; b. Laconia, N.H., Feb. 28, 1952; d. Bernard Irwin and Muriel Stella (Goldberg) S. BA, Duke U., 1975. Reporter, prodr. WMUR-TV, Manchester, N.H., 1981-83; sportswriter Boston Herald, 1983-87, Miami (Fla.) News, 1987-89, St. Louis Sun, 1989-90; contbg. reporter KMOX Radio, St. Louis, 1990-93; sportswriter The Racing Times, N.Y.C., 1991-92; dir. comm. Arlington Internat. Racecourse, Arlington Heights, Ill., 1992-95; dir. comm. and mktg. Rockingham Park, Salem, N.H., 1995—. Reporter (tv show) Arlington Weekend, 1993-94; contbr. articles to publs. Recipient Best Sports Story award New Eng. Womens Press Assn., 1986, award of excellence New Eng. Womens Press Assn., 1986; named one of 10 most powerful women in NFL, Coll. and Pro Football Weekly, 1988. Mem. Profl. Football Writers of Am., Nat. Turf Writers Assn., New Eng. Turf Writers Assn. (sec.-treas. 1995-96, v.p. 1996—), Fla. Turf Writers Assn., Turf Publicists of Am., Assn. for Women in Sports Media, NOW, Nat. Abortion Rights Action League, N.H. Women's Lobby. Democrat. Office: Rockingham Park Rockingham Park Blvd Salem NH 03079

SNITOW, VIRGINIA LEVITT, secondary school educator; b. N.Y.C., Apr. 9, 1911; d. Louis and Tania (Rosenberg) Levitt; m. Charles Snitow; children: Ann, Alan. BA in English, Hunter Coll., 1931; postgrad., Columbia U., 1932-35. Cert. secondary English tchr. English tchr. Wadligh H.S., N.Y.C., 1932-44, Seward Park H.S., N.Y.C., 1944-46; v.p. U.S. World Trade Fair, 1956-66; nat. pres. Nat. A. J. Congress Women's Divsn., 1964-70; chair leadership conf. Nat. Jewish Women's Orgn., N.Y.C., 1970-73, Hunter Hall of Fame, 1977; bd. dirs. Hunter Coll. Found., 1991—. Contbr. articles to profl. jours. NGO rep. UN, N.Y.C., 1960-62; del. Dem. Nat. Convention, Chgo., 1968, Miami, 1972; mem. N.Y. State Coord. com. Internat. Women's Yr., 1977-78; founder, hon. chair U.S./Israel Women to Women, 1978—; founding mem. Legal Awareness Women, 1979—. Recipient Woman for Our Time award Am. Jewish Congress, 1971, Louise Waterman Wise Laureate, 1979, Pres. Merit award Haifa U., 1991, Susan B. Anthony award NOW, 1992. Office: 4 Sniffen Ct New York NY 10016

SNODGRASS, LOUISE VIRGINIA, state legislator, dental assistant; b. Balt., June 28, 1942; d. Peter Francis and Mary Frances (Gelwicks) Kramer; m. Franklin P. Snodgrass III, Sept. 9, 1962; children: Anne, Mark. Cert. dental asst., U. Md., Balt. Lic. dental asst. Dental asst., 1966—; mem. Md. Ho. of Dels. from Dist. 3, 1995—; mem. Commerce and Govt. Matters Subcom. Md. Ho. of Dels., mem. Subcom. on Procurement, Unfunded Mandates Task Force. Elected liaison Md. State Bd. Dental Examiners; mem. Frederick County (Md.) Ctrl. Com., 1986-94, past vice chair, past sec., 1986-90; bd. dirs. Md. Mayors Assn., 1991-94, hon. mem., 1994; past pres. Frederick County Coun. Govt., 1991, 92, 93; liaison to transp. svcs. adv. com. Md. Mcpl. League, 1990-94, chmn. state conv., 1991, legis. mem., 1991-94, appointed to subcom. on annexation, 1992, legis. chmn., 1993-94, past pres., v.p., sec.-treas. Frederick chpt.; Mayor Middletown, Md., 1986-94; active J. Elmer Harp Med. Ctr., Inc. Assn., Frederick Meml. Hosp. Aux., Frederick County Rep. Men's Club; life mem. Middletown Hist. Soc. Named Outstanding Legislator of Yr., Md. Mcpl. League, 1995, cert. appreciation, 1996. Mem. Md. Dental Assts. Assn. (past pres.), Am. Dental Assts. Assn. (trustee). Office: Md Ho of Dels House Office Bldg Rm 324 Annapolis MD 21401

SNOW, KIMBERLEY, editor, writer; b. Greenwood, S.C., Nov. 10, 1939; d. Kimberley and Louise (Hodges) Hartzog; m. Barry Spacks, Feb. 25, 1987; children: Kimberley Harrison, Simms Teramoto. PhD, U. Ky., 1979. Tchr. U. Calif., Santa Barbara, 1980-90; editor Chagdud Gonpa Found., Junction City, Calif., 1990—. Author: Writing Yourself Home, 1990, Keys to the Open Gate, 1994, (play) Multiple, 1986 (Jacksonville U. Ann. Playwrights award 1987). Vol. Dawn Hospice, Weaverville, Conn., 1995—. Buddhist. Home: 1111 Bath St Santa Barbara CA 93101

SNOW, MARINA SEXTON, author; b. Boston, Apr. 9, 1937; d. Charles Ernest Snow and Katherine Alice Townsend; m. Richard DeVere Horton, Aug. 30, 1958 (div. 1968); children: Heather Kertchem, James Horton; m. Charles A. Washburn, Jan. 7, 1978 (div. 1979). BA, U. Iowa, 1958; MA in Speech Pathology, N.Mex. State U., 1967; MA in Librarianship, San Jose State U., 1976; MA in Theatre Arts, Calif. State U., Sacramento, 1979. Cert. clin. competence Am. Speech and Hearing Assn. Tchr. ESL Inst. Colombo-Americano, Cali, Colombia, 1958-59; tchr. Las Cruces (N.Mex.) Pub. Schs., 1964-66; speech therapist Sutter County Schs., Yuba City, Calif., 1967-72; reference libr. Calif. State U. Libr., Sacramento, 1976-95. Contbr. articles to profl. jours.; author 2 plays: Apricot Coffee, Alkali Flat. Pres. Alkali Flat Neighborhood Assn., Sacramento, 1987-94, Sacramento Old City Assn., 1979—. Mem. Sacramento Old City Assn.

SNOW, REBECCA, lawyer; b. Boulder City, Nev., Dec. 7, 1960. BA summa cum laude, Brigham Young U., 1983; JD cum laude, Harvard U., 1986. Bar: Nev. 1986, D.C. 1987. Legis. aide U.S. Dept. Interior Office Legis. Counsel, Washington, 1982-83; ptnr. Covington & Burling, Washington, 1994—. Co-author: Superfund Law and Procedure, 1992. Office: Covington & Burling PO Box 7566 1201 Pennsylvania Ave NW Washington DC 20044-7566*

SNOWDEN, BARBARA BLYTHE, secondary education educator; b. Charlotte, N.C., Jan. 9, 1945; d. James Frank and Louise (Lackey) Blythe; m. Wilson Walker, Sept. 13, 1970, 1 child, Beth. BA, Mars Hill (N.C.) Coll.; MEd, Ea. Carolina U., 1992. Tchr. Curritack County Schs., Curritack, N.C., 1967-70, 77—. Editor: Heritage of Curritack Heritage, Jour. of Hist. Soc., 1976. Trustee Mus. of Albemarle, Elizabeth City, N.C., 1992-96, chmn., 1995-96; mem. adv. bd. Outer Banks History Ctr., Manteo, N.C., 1991—, exec. coun. Maritim History Coun., Raleigh, 1991—; bd. dirs. N.C. CSS, 1990, Whaleshead Preservation in Trust (trustee 1992), vice chmn.; pres. Curritack Hist. Soc., 1976, 90-92. Home: Courthouse Rd Curritack NC 27929 Office: Curritack County Sch Star Rt Barco NC 27917

SNOWDEN, BERNICE RIVES, former construction company executive; b. Houston, Mar. 21, 1923; d. Charles Samuel and Annie Pearl (Rorex) Rives; grad. Smalley Comml. Coll., 1941; student U. Houston, 1965; m. Walter G. Snowden; 1 dau., Bernice Ann Ogden. With Houston Pipe Line Co., 1944-45; clk.-typist Charles G. Heyne & Co., Inc., Houston, 1951-53, payroll asst., 1953-56, sec. to pres., also office mgr., 1956-62, sec. to pres., also controller, 1962-70, sec.-treas., 1970-77, chief fin. officer, also dir. Mem. Women in Constrn., Nat. Assn. Women in Constrn. (past pres.), San Leon C. of C. Methodist. Club: Lord and Ladies Dance. Home: 6611 Kury Ln Houston TX 77008-5101

SNOWDEN, LYNN, magazine editor, writer; b. Norfolk, Va., May 26, 1958; d. Robert and Valerie (Opshinsky) S. BFA, Va. Commonwealth U., 1979. Freelance photographer Richmond, Va., 1978-79; model Prestige/Elite Modeling Agy., N.Y.C., 1980-84; staff writer Spy Mag., N.Y.C., 1986-87; contbg. editor N.Y. Woman Mag., N.Y.C., 1989-92, Harper's Bazaar Mag., N.Y.C., 1994—, Mademoiselle, N.Y.C., 1996—; online host America Online, 1996—; guest panelist Politically Incorrect with Bill Mahr TV show, 1994—. Contbr. articles to Spin, Esquire, Vogue, Glamour, Working Woman, Cosmopolitan, Premiere, Outside, New York Times; author: Nine Lives - From Stripper to Schoolteacher: My Yearlong Odyssey in the Workplace, 1994.

SNOWDON, JANE LOUISE, industrial engineer; b. Ann Arbor, Mich., July 17, 1959; d. John Colin and Anne Joy (Vickery) S. BS in Indsl. Engring., Pa. State U., 1981; MS in Indsl. Engring., U. Mich., 1982; PhD in Indsl. Engring., Ga. Inst. Tech., 1994. Semiconductor cost engring. coordinator IBM Corp., Hopewell Junction, N.Y., 1982-85; engagement mgr. IBM Corp., Boca Raton, Fla., 1990-95; mem. rsch. staff T.J. Watson Rsch. Ctr. IBM Corp., Yorktown Heights, N.Y., 1996—. Contbr. articles to profl. jours. Mem. Inst. Indsl. Engrs. (sr., Mid-Hudson chpt. devel. officer 1984-85, sec. 1983-84, N.Y.-Pa. Inst. Indsl. Engrs. scholar 1980, v.p. West Palm Beach chpt. 1991-93), Inst. Ops. Rsch. and Mgmt. Scis., Soc. Women Engrs. (Union Carbide scholar 1978), English Speaking Union, Pi Mu Epsilon, Alpha Pi Mu, Alpha Lambda Delta, Tau Beta Pi, Phi Mu (Mary King Shepardson scholar 1981, Lowe scholar, 1986, 88), Sigma Xi. Republican. Episcopalian. Home: 44 Northfield St Greenwich CT 06830

SNOWE, OLYMPIA J., senator; b. Augusta, Maine, Feb. 21, 1947; d. George John and Georgia G. Bouchles; m. John McKernan. BA, U. Maine, 1969; LLD (hon.), U. Maine, Machias, 1982, Husson Coll., 1981, Bowdoin Coll., 1985, Suffold U., 1994. Businesswoman; mem. Maine Ho. of Reps., 1973-76, Maine Senate, 1976-78; mem. 96th-103d Congresses from 2d Maine Dist., 1979-94; mem. budget com., mem. commerce sci. and transp. com., chmn. fgn. rel.subcom. on internat. ops. US Sen. from Maine; co-chair Congl. Caucus for Women's Issues; dep. Republican whip, U.S. senator from Maine, 1995—; corporator Mechanics Savs. Bank. Republican. Greek Orthodox. Club: Philoptochos Soc. Office: US Senate 495 Russell Senate Bldg Washington DC 20510-1903

SNYDER, ALLEGRA FULLER, dance educator; b. Chgo., Aug. 28, 1927; d. R. Buckminster and Anne (Hewlett) Fuller; m. Robert Snyder, June 30, 1951 (div. Apr. 1975, remarried Sept. 1980); children: Alexandra, Jaime. BA in Dance, Bennington Coll., 1951; MA in Dance, UCLA, 1967. Asst. to curator, dance archives Mus. Modern Art, N.Y.C., 1945-47; dancer Ballet Soc. of N.Y.C. Ballet Co., 1945-47; mem. office and prodn. staff Internat. Film Found., N.Y.C., 1950-52; editor, dance films Film News mag., N.Y.C.,

1966-72; lectr. dance and film adv., dept. dance UCLA, 1967-73, chmn. dept. dance, 1974-80, 90-91, acting chair, spring 1985, chair of faculty Sch. of the Arts, 1989-91, prof. dance and dance ethnology, 1973-91, prof. emeritus, 1991—; pres. Buckminster Fuller Inst., Santa Barbara, Calif.; vis. lectr. Calif. Inst. Arts, Valencia, 1972; co-dir. dance and TV workshop Am. Dance Festival, Conn. Coll., New London, 1973; dir. NEH summer seminar for coll. tchrs. Asian Performing Arts, 1978, 81; coord. Ethnic Arts Intercoll. Interdisciplinary Program, 1974-73, acting chmn., 1986; vis. prof. performance studies NYU, 1982-83; hon. vis. prof. U. Surrey, Guildford, Eng., 1983-84; cons. Thyodia Found., Salt Lake City, 1973-74; mem. dance adv. panel Nat. Endowment Arts, 1968-72, Calif. Arts Commn., 1974-91; mem. adv. screening com. Coun. Internat. Exch. of Scholars, 1979-82; mem. various panels NEH, 1979-85; core cons. for Dancing, Sta. WNET-TV, 1988—. Dir. film Baroque Dance 1625-1725, in 1977; co-dir. film Gods of Bali, 1952; dir. and wrote film Bayanihan, 1962 (named Best Folkloric Documentary at Bilboa Film Festival, winner Golden Eagle award); asst. dir. and asst. editor film The Bennington Story, 1952; created films Gestures of Sand, 1968, Reflections on Choreography, 1973, When the Fire Dances Between Two Poles, 1982; created film, video loop and text Celebration: A World of Art and Ritual, 1982-83; supr. post-prodn. film Erick Hawkins, 1964, in 1973. Also contbr. articles to profl. jours. and mags. Adv. com. Pacific Asia Mus., 1980-84, Festival of the Mask, Craft and Folk Art Mus., 1979-84; adv. panel Los Angeles Dance Currents II, Mus. Ctr. Dance Assn., 1974-75; bd. dirs. Council Grove Sch. III, Compton, Calif., 1976-81; apptd. mem. Adv. Dance Com., Pasadena (Calif.) Art Mus., 1970-71, Los Angeles Festival of Performing Arts com., Studio Watts, 1970; mem. Technology and Cultural Transformation com., UNESCO, 1977. Fulbright research fellow, 1983-84; grantee Nat. Endowment Arts, 1981, Nat. Endowment Humanities, 1977, 79, 81, UCLA, 1968, 77, 80, 82, 85; recipient Amer. Dance Guild Award for Outstanding Achievement in Dance, 1992. Mem. Am. Dance Therapy Assn., Congress on Rsch. in Dance (bd. dirs. 1970-76, chmn. 1975-77, nat. conf. chmn. 1972), Coun. Dance Adminstrs., Am. Dance Guild (chmn. com. awards 1972), Soc. for Ethnomusicology, Am. Anthrop. Assn., Am. Folklore Soc., Soc. Anthropology of Visual Comm., Soc. Humanistic Anthropology, Calif. Dance Educators Assn. (conf. chmn. 1972), L.A. Area Dance Alliance (adv. bd. 1978-84, selection com. Dance Kaleidoscope project 1979-81), Fulbright Alumni Assn. Home: 15313 Whitfield Ave Pacific Palisades CA 90272-2548 Office: Buckminster Fuller Inst Ste 224 2040 Alameda Padre Serra Santa Barbara CA 93103

SNYDER, ANNE GIBSON, artist, marketing consultant; b. Albuquerque, Nov. 30, 1949; d. Joseph Edward and Mary Louise (Dize) S.; m. Michael Edward Stovall, Jan. 27, 1976; 1 child, Jesse Edward Stovall. BA in Studio Art, Mary Washington Coll., 1971. Cert. tchr., Va. Chair art dept. Frederick (Md.) H.S., 1971-73; owner Catepetl Art Gallery, Frederick, 1973-90, Catepetl Art Collectors, Braddock Heights, Md., 1990-94; owner, artist Catepetl Studio, Braddock Heights, Md., 1995—; mktg. rep. Stone Manor, Middletown, Md., 1996—; juror Newark (Del.) Parks & Recreation Dept., 1995; arts bd. mem. Mayors Adv. Bd., Frederick, 1987; art cons. AT&T, Tysons Corner, Va., 1990-93; guest curator Delaplaine Visual Arts Ctr., Frederick, 1994. Artist, designer Women's History Trail map, 1995; artist, set painter Gondoliers Lancaster Opera Co., 1992. 1st chair In the St., Frederick, 1983; chair visual arts Frederick Festival Arts, 1988; display designer Washington County Mus., Hagerstown, Md., 1991-95. Recipient Jurors award Washington County Mus., 1993, People's Choice award Frederick County Commn. Women, 1995, Poster award Frederick City Holiday Com., 1995. Mem. Nat. Mus. Women Arts. Office: Catepetl Studio Braddock Heights MD 21714

SNYDER, CAROLYN ANN, university dean, librarian; b. Elgin, Nebr., Nov. 5, 1942; d. Ralph and Florence Wagner; m. Barry Snyder, Apr. 24, 1969. Student, Nebr. Wesleyan U., 1960-61; BS cum laude, Kearney State Coll., 1964; MS in Librarianship, U. Denver, 1965. Asst. libr. sci. and tech. U. Nebr., Lincoln, 1965-67, asst. pub. svc. libr., 1967-68, 70-73; pers. libr. Ind. U. Librs., Bloomington, 1973-76, acting dean of univ. librs., 1980, 88-89, assoc. dean for pub. svcs., 1977-88, 89-91, interim devel. officer, 1989-91; adminstrv. army libr. Spl. Svcs. Agy., Europe, 1968-70; dean libr. affairs So. Ill. U., Carbondale, 1991—; team leader Midwest Univs. Consortium for Internat. Activities-World Bank IX project to develop libr. system and implement automation U. Indonesia, Jakarta, 1984-86; libr. devel. cons. Inst. Tech. MARA/Midwest Univs. Consortium for Internat. Activities Program in Malaysia, 1985. Contbr. chpt. to book and articles to profl. jours. Mem. Humane Assn. Jackson County, 1991—, Carbondale Pub. Libr. Friends, 1991—. Recipient Cooperative Rsch. grant Coun. on Libr. Resources, Washington, 1984. Mem. ALA (councilor 1985-89, Bogle Internat. Travel award 1988, H.W. Wilson Libr. Staff devel. grantee 1981), Libr. Adminstrn./Mgmt. Assn. (pres. 1981-82), Com. on Instnl. Coop./Resource Sharing (chair 1987-91), Coalition for Networked Info. (So. Ill. U. at Carbondale rep. 1991—), Coun. Dirs. State Univ. Librs. in Ill. (chair 1992-93), Ill. Assn. Coll. and Rsch. Librs. (chair Ill. Bd. Higher Edn. liaison com. 1993-94), Ill. Network (bd. dirs.), Ind. Libr. Assn. (chair coll./univ. divsn. 1982-83), U.S. Grant Assn. (bd. dirs. 1992—), Ill. Libr. Computer Sys. Orgn. (policy coun. 1992-95), Nat. Assn. State Univs. and Land-Grant Colls. (commn. on info. tech. and its distance learning bd. 1994—), NetIllinois (bd. dirs. 1994—), OCLC Users Coun. (elected rep. 1995—). Office: So Ill U Morris Libr Carbondale IL 62901-6632

SNYDER, DEBORAH ANN, press secretary; b. Lancaster, Pa., Sept. 10, 1966; d. Irvin Lloyd and Beatrice Jane (Bowers) Bossler; m. Paul Franklin Snyder III, Oct. 10, 1992. BS, Oral Roberts U., 1988. Assignment editor Sta. WITF-TV-FM, Harrisburg, Pa., 1988-91; pub. rels. dir. Liberty Prodns., Harrisburg, 1991; pub. rels. coord. Pa. Internat. Air Show, Harrisburg, 1991, 92; ops. coord. Radio Pa. Network, Harrisburg, 1991-93; press sec. Dept. Revenue, Commonwealth of Pa., Harrisburg, 1993—; publicity coord. Clyde Dupin Crusade, Carlisle, Pa., 1995. Mem. Old Neighborhood League, Carlisle, 1992—. Mem. Pa. Pub. Rels. Soc. Home: 201 E Pomfret St Carlisle PA 17013

SNYDER, JAN LOUISE, administrative aide; b. Warrington Twp., Pa., Sept. 15, 1935; d. Wilbert Adam and Alice (Myers) March; divorced; children: Steven Michael Krone, David Sylvan Snyder. Grad. high sch., Dover, Pa. With McCrory Stores Divsn. McCrory Corp., York, 1966, receptionist exec. buying divsn. Active Northwestern region York Hosp. Aux., 1979—, York Symphony Assn., 1990—, membership com., 1992—; active York chpt. Am. Cancer Soc. Am., 1990—, York Chorus, 1988-90; mem. Ch. of the Open Door of Shiloh, 1956—, Dover Twp. Fire Co. Aux. for Women, 1975—, Harrisburg Jr. League Lectr. Series, 1980-95, York Jr. League Lectr. series, 1989—. Mem. Am. Bus. Womens Assn. (pres. Colonial York charter chpt. 1980, mem. adv. bd. 1980-89), Nat. Trust for Historic Preservation. Democrat. Home: 2823 Grandview Ave York PA 17404-3905

SNYDER, JANE MCINTOSH, retired classics educator; b. Champaign, Ill., July 25, 1943; d. Harold Ray and Mary Jane (McIntosh) S. BA, Wellesley Coll., 1965; PhD, U. N.C., 1969. Prof. classics Ohio State U., Columbus, 1968-95, prof. emeritus, 1995—, assoc. dean Coll. Humanities, 1986-88. Author: Puns and Poetry in Lucretius, 1980, The Woman and the Lyre: Women Writers in Classical Greece and Rome, 1989 (first prize in reference/scholarly books Chgo. Women in Pub. 1989); co-author: Stringed Instruments of Ancient Greece, 1989 (Nicholas Bessaraboff prize Am. Musical Instrument Soc. 1991). Recipient Grant-in-Aide, Am. Coun. Learned Socs., 1972. Mem. Phi Beta Kappa. Office: Dept Greek and Latin 414 University Hall Ohio State Univ Columbus OH 43210

SNYDER, JILL, museum director; b. Trenton, N.J., June 28, 1957; d. Barry and Arline (Gellar) S. BA, Wesleyan U., Middletown, Conn., 1979. Exec. assoc. Guggenheim Mus., N.Y.C., 1983-88, edn. assoc., 1989-91; dir./curator Freedman Gallery, Albright Coll., Reading, Pa., 1993-95; dir. The Aldrich Mus. of Contemporary Art, Ridgefield, Conn., 1995—; mem. curatorial rev. panel Abington Art Ctr., Jenkintown, Pa., 1995; staff lectr. Mus. of Modern Art, N.Y.C., 1989-94, Guggenheim Mus., 1988-92; adj. faculty N.Y. Sch. Interior Design, 1988-92. Author: Caring for Your Art, 1991, In the Flesh (catalogue), 1996, Impossible Evidence: Contemporary Artists View the Holocaust (catalogue), 1994, Against the Stream: Milton Avery, Adolph Gottlieb and Mark Rothko in the 1930s (catalogue), 1994. Bd. dirs. Forum for U.S.-Soviet Dialogue, Washington, 1990-91. Milton and Sally Avery Found. fellow, 1990, Shelby and Leon Levy fellow, 1988. Mem. Art Table, Am. Assn. Mus., Coll. Art Assn. Office: Aldrich Mus Contemp Art 258 Main St Ridgefield CT 06877

SNYDER, JO ANNA W., cartographer, computer graphics designer; b. Atlanta, July 10, 1961; d. Joseph Hans Werner and Ruby Lee (Patty) Horton; m. Edward H. Snyder, Feb. 4, 1992. Grad. high sch., Ooltewah, Tenn., 1979; cert. computer drafting and design specialist, Charter Coll., Anchorage, 1994. Freelance graphics designer; typesetter, artist Printer's Workshop, Anchorage, 1984-85, Pip Printing, Anchorage, 1985-87; computer graphics designer BP Exploration (Alaska) Inc., Anchorage, 1987-92, cartographer, 1990-92; owner desktop pub. firm Graphics Alaska; freelance graphics designer, Wasilla, Alaska, 1989-94; CAD technician, then mktg. specialist New Horizons Telecom., Inc., Palmer, Alaska, 1994-96. Editor: Alaska Parenting Mag., 1996—. Checker Iditarod Trail Sled Dog Assn., Wasilla, 1990-91. Mem. NAFE, nat. Contract Mgmt. Assn., Nat. Computer Graphics Assn., Computer Graphics Network (founder, chmn. 1989-91). Home: HC 89 Box 330 Willow AK 99688-9704

SNYDER, KAROLYN JOHNSON, education educator; b. Mpls., Mar. 2, 1938; d. Wade Leslie and Helen (Allen) Johnson; m. T. Richard Snyder, Aug. 22, 1959 (div. 1978), 1 child, Kristen Michele Snyder Wolf; m. Robert H. Anderson, Jan. 24, 1979. BA, Wheaton Coll., 1960; MEd, Temple U., 1945; EdD, Tex. Tech. U., 1977. Tchr. Elem. Schs. in N.J., Pa., Brazil, 1959-68; founder and dir. Project Learn Sch., Phila., 1968-71; house leader and unit leader Hightstown (N.J.) Schs., 1972-75; instr. Tex. Tech. U., Lubbock, Tex., 1975-76; programs adminstr. Pedamorphosis, Inc., Lubbock, 1977-83; v.p. Pedamorhosis, Inc., Lubbock, Tampa, Fla., 1977—; prof. edn. U. S. Fla., Tampa, 1984—. Author: (book) Managing Productive Schools, 1986; (tng. sys.) Managing Productive Schs., 1986; co-author: (ednl. tools) Schools in Transition to Quality, 1994, Diagnostic System, 1994; co-editor: Clinical Supervision; chief editor ASCD Jour., 1987-91; co-editor Wingspan, 1982—. Recipient Gov.'s award, Minn., 1988. Pres COPIS, 1995-96. mem. ASCD, Coun. of Profs. of Instructional Supervision, Am. Edn. Rsch. Assn. Home: 13604 Waterfall Way Tampa FL 33624-6907 Office: Univ S Fla Fowler Ave Tampa FL 33620

SNYDER, MARIAN H., nursing educator and administrator; b. Webster, S.D., June 10, 1942; d. Harry C. and Helen L. (Potter) Walker; 1 child, Susan Marin. BSN, U. Conn., 1964; MS in Nursing, U. Ky., 1977; PhD, Marquette U., 1987. Staff nurse USAF, San Antonio, 1965-67; instr. Norton-Children's Hosp., Louisville, 1967-77; faculty Columbia Coll., Milw., 1977-81; dean, chief exec. officer Carroll-Columbia Coll. Nursing, Milw., 1981—. 1st lt. Nurses Corps, USAF. Mem. ANA, NLN, Sigma Theta Tau. Office: Columbia College 2121 E Newport Ave Milwaukee WI 53211-2952

SNYDER, NANCY MARGARET, translator, language services company executive; b. Detroit, Sept. 24, 1950; d. Estle M. and Noreen V. (Woodruff) S.; m. P. W. Denton, July 15, 1972 (div. Feb. 1980); 1 child, Virginia. BA in German, Mich. State U., 1972; cert. in programming and ops., Control Data Inst., 1984. Office mgr. Detroit Translation Bur., Southfield, Mich., 1980-82; bilingual sec. Volkswagen Am., Troy, Mich., 1984-85, translator, 1985-88; owner, operator Tech. Lang. Svcs., Birmingham, Mich., 1988—; guest speaker Kent State U. Inst. Applied Linguistics, 1992, Ferndale (Mich.) High Sch., 1992. Contbr. articles to profl. jours. Stadium usher Olympic Games, Munich, 1972; mem., worker Cass Corridor Food Coop., Detroit, 1986-90. Mem. S.E. Mich. Translators and Interpreters Network (newsletter editor 1993), Am. Translators Assn. (accredited German to English translator), Chgo. Area Translators Assn., Am. Mensa Ltd., Amherst Block Club. Office: Tech Lang Svcs 600 S Adams Rd Ste 210 Birmingham MI 48009-6863

SNYDER, NANCY SUSAN, reading specialist; b. East Stroudsburg, Pa., Sept. 15, 1950; d. Robert Milton and Elinor Ackerly (Smith) Richards; m. William Robert Snyder, July 2, 1973. BSEdn., East Stroudsburg U., 1973, MEd, 1979, Reading Specialist, 1983. Cert. tchr. elem. edn., reading specialist. Office worker, supr. Burnley Workshop of Poconos, East Stroudsburg, 1969-73; remedial tchr. Colonial Northampton Intermediate Unit #20, Easton, Pa., 1973—; mem. Act 178 Professional Devel. Com., Easton, 1985—. Mem. Nat. Coun. Tchrs. Math., Internat. Reading Assn., Colonial Intermediate Unit #20 Edn. Assn. 9sec. 1973—), Keystone Reading Assn. Republican. Home: Rte 2 Box 2030A Stroudsburg PA 18360 Office: Colonial Northampton Int 20 6 Danforth Dr Easton PA 18042

SNYDER, ROSALYN GRAHAM, editor; b. Rock Hill, S.C., Oct. 13, 1947; d. Plesant Gradford and Nina Pope (Kitchens) Graham; m. Wesley Edwin Snyder, Aug. 25, 1968; children: Kathryn Irene Snyder Schwarting, Graham Edwin, Robert Wesley. BA, U. S.C., 1968; MS in Journalism, U. Ill., 1973. Secondary sch. tchr. vol. U.S. Peace Corps, Kusungu, Malawi, 1968-69; pub. info. specialist State N.C., Raleigh, 1977-79; freelance writer/editor Raleigh, 1980-87; mng. editor IEEE Robotics and Automation Soc., Raleigh, 1987—; pres. Comm. Unltd., Raleigh, 1986-92. Leader Girl Scouts Am., Raleigh, 1980; chair Raleigh United Neighborhoods, 1982-83. Mem. IEEE (assoc.), Women in Comm., Inc. (treas. Triangle chpt. 1995—), U.S. PTA. Democrat. Presbyterian.

SNYDER, SUSAN BROOKE, retired English literature educator; b. Yonkers, N.Y., July 12, 1934; d. John Warren and Virginia Grace (Hartung) S. BA, Hunter Coll., CUNY, 1955; MA, Columbia U., 1958, PhD, 1963. Lectr. Queens Coll., CUNY, N.Y.C., 1961-63; instr. Swarthmore Coll., Pa., 1963-66, asst. prof. English lit., 1966-70, assoc. prof., 1970-75, prof., 1975-93, Eugene M. Lang research prof., 1982-86, Gil and Frank Mustin prof., 1990-93; ret.; prof. emeritus Swarthmore Coll., 1993—; rschr. Folger Shakespeare Libr. Author: The Comic Matrix of Shakespeare's Tragedies, 1979; editor: Divine Weeks and Works of Guillaume de Saluste, Sieur du Bartas, 1979, Othello: Critical Essays, 1988, All's Well that Ends Well, 1993; mem. editl. bd. Shakespeare Quar., 1972—. Folger Library sr. fellow, 1972-73; Nat. Endowment for Humanities fellow, 1967-68; Guggenheim Found. fellow, 1980-81; Huntington Library summer grantee, 1966, 71; Folger Library grantee, 1969; Nat. Endowment for Humanities grantee, 1970; Nat. Endowment for Humanities summer grantee, 1976. Mem. Renaissance Soc. Am. (coun. 1979-81), Shakespeare Assn. Am. (trustee 1980-83).

SNYDER, SUSAN LEACH, science educator; b. Columbus, Ohio, Nov. 25, 1946; d. Russell and Helen Marie (Sharpe) Leach; m. James Floyd Snyder, June 18, 1988. BS in comprehensive sci. edn., Miami U., 1968; MS in entomology, U. Hawaii, 1970. Gen. and health sci. tchr. Columbus Pub. Schs., 1971-73; life, earth & physical sci. tchr. Upper Arlington (Ohio) Schs., 1975—; ednl. cons. Innovation Alliance, Columbus, 1990—. Author: The Ocean Environment, 1992; co-author: Focus on Earth Science, 1987, 89, 96, Merrill Earth Science, 1993, 95; mem. author team: Science Interactions, 1993, 95; contbr. articles to profl. jours. Trustee N.Am. Astrophys. Obs., Delaware, Ohio, 1983—; pres. Consortium of Aquatic and Marine Educators Ohio, 1983-84; sec. Ohio chpt. Nat. Tchrs. of Yr., 1993-95. Named Outstanding Earth Sci. Tchr. of State of Ohio and East Cen Sect. Nat. Assn. Geology Tchrs., 1983, Ohio Tchr. of Yr. Ohio State Dept. Edn., 1986, Finalist Nat. Tchr. of Yr. Coun. of Chief State Sch. Officers, 1986; Pres. award for Excellence in Sci. and Math Teaching Nat. Sci. Tchrs. Assn., 1992, Outstanding Tchr. award Geological Soc. Am., 1992. Mem. Nat. Sci. Tchrs. Assn. (Exemplary Earth Sci. Teaching Team 1983, 84, 85, conf. workshop presenter 1985), Nat. Marine Educators Assn. (Nat. Outstanding Marine Sci. Tchr. 1984, bd. mem., conf. workshop presenter 1984), Sci. Edn. Coun. Ohio, NEA, Great Lakes Educators of Aquatic and Marine Educators. Home: 1361 Marlyn Dr Upper Arlington OH 43220 Office: Jones Middle Sch 2100 Arlington Ave Upper Arlington OH 43221

SNYDERMAN, SELMA ELEANORE, pediatrician, educator; b. Phila., July 22, 1916; d. Harry Samuel and Rose (Koss) S.; m. Joseph Schein, Aug. 4, 1939; children: Roland M. H., Oliver Douglas. AB, U. Pa., 1937, MD, 1940. Diplomate Am. Bd. Pediatrics, Am. Bd. Clin. Nutrition. Intern Einstein Med. Ctr., Phila., 1940-42; resident Bellevue Hosp., N.Y.C., 1944-45; fellow NYU Med. Ctr., N.Y.C., 1945-46; instr. pediat. NYU Sch. Medicine, N.Y.C., 1946-50, assoc. prof., 1950-57, 1957-67, prof., 1967-95; assoc. prof. U. Tex. Med. Br., Galveston, 1952-53; attending physician Bellevue Hosp., 1947—; dir. Pediatric Metabolic Disease Ctr. Bellevue Med. Ctr., 1965-95; attending physician Tisch Hosp., N.Y.C., 1947-95; prof. human genetics and pediat., attending physician Mt. Sinai Med. Ctr., N.Y.C., 1995—, dir. Metabolic Disease Ctr., 1995—; mem. nutrition study sect. NIH, Bethesda, Md., 1973-77. Contbr. numerous med. articles to profl. jours. Named career scientist Health Rsch. Coun., 1961-75. Fellow Am. Acad. Pediatrics (Borden award 1975); mem. Am. Inst. Nutrition, Am. Pediatric Soc., Soc. for Pediatric Rsch., Am. Soc. Clin. Nutrition, Soc. Inherited Metabolic Disorders (v.p. 1978, pres. 1979, bd. dirs. 1980-83), Soc. Parenteral and Enteral Nutrition, Soc. for Study of Inborn Errors of Metabolism, Phi Beta Kappa. Jewish. Office: Mount Sinai Med Ctr Dept Human Genetics Fifth Ave & 100th St New York NY 10029

SO, CONNIE CHING, ethnic studies educator; b. Kowloon, Hong Kong, June 12, 1964; d. Ka Chick and Big Yin (Woo) So; m. Brett Edward Eckelberg, Aug. 31, 1991. BS, U. Wash., 1987; MPA, Princeton U., 1989; postgrad., U. Calif., Berkeley, 1989—. Reader U. Wash., Seattle, 1986-87; minority affairs advisor Princeton (N.J.) U., 1988-89; instr. U. Calif., Davis, 1991-92, Berkeley, 1989-93; lectr. U. Wash., Seattle, 1990—; cons. Wing Luke Asian Mus., Seattle, 1993—, Asian Am. Commn., Seattle, 1995-96, Wash. State Hist. Sites, Seattle, 1991-92, Nat. Com. on U.S. China Rels., N.Y.C., 1988; spkr. in field. Contbr. articles, essays to profl. publs. Advisor, asst. treas. Campaign Connections, Seattle, 1989; cons., panelist Asian Pacific Am. Leadership Conf., Seattle, 1995—; trustee N.W. Asian Am. Theater, Seattle, 1986-87; del. Wash. Dem. Com., Seattle, 1984. Fellow Alfred P. Sloan Found., 1985, U.S. Info. Agy., 1988, U. Calif.-Berkeley, 1989-95. Democrat. Home: 5432 Beacon Ave S Seattle WA 98108 Office: U Wash Am Ethnic Studies Seattle WA 98108

SOARES, VALESKA CORREA, visual artist; b. Belo Horizonte, Brazil, Mar. 2, 1957; d. Britaldo Silveira and Terezinha (Correa) S.;m. Rodrigo Pereira Cardoso, 1992. BA in Architecture, Universidade Santa Ursula, Brazil, 1987; MFA, Pratt Inst., N.Y., 1992; postgrad., NYU, N.Y.C. One-woman shows include Centro Cultural Sergio Porto, Rio de Janeiro Art Found., 1991, Centro Cultural Sao Paulo (Brazil), Sao Paulo Art State Found., 1992, Galeria Camargo Vilaca, Sao Paulo, 1994, Info. Gallery, N.Y.C., 1994, Galeria Camargo Vilaca, Sao Paulo, 1996, Laumelar Sculpture Park, St. Louis, Christopher Grimes Gallery, Santa Monica, Calif., 1996; exhibited in group shows at Espaco Cultural Sergio Porto, Rio de Janeiro, 1991, IV Biennial of Havanna, Cuba, 1991, Galeria Casa Triangulo, Sao Paulo, 1991, Mus. Modern Art, Rio de Janeiro, 1991, Nat. Found. Arts, Rio de Janeiro, 1991, Mus. Art, Curitiba, Brazil, 1991, Art Mus. Sao Paulo, 1991, Galeria Camargo Vilaca, Sao Paulo, 1992, Paco das Artes, Sao Paulo, 1992, Sidney Mishkin Gallery, N.Y.C., 1993, The Bronx (N.Y.) Mus., 1993, Mitchell Mus., Mt. Vernon, Ill., 1993, Valenzuela Klenner Galeria, Bogota, Colombia, 1993, Stux Gallery, N.Y.C., 1993, Museu de Arte Contemporanea de Sao Paulo, 1993, XXII Internat. Biennial of Sao Paulo, 1994, Info. Gallery, N.Y.C., 1994, Centro Cultural Sao Paulo, 1994, Mus. Modern Art, Sao Paulo, 1991, 94, Parque Lage, 1991, Paco Imperial, Rio de Janeiro, 1994, New Mus. Contemporary Art, N.Y.C., 1995, Stark Gallery, N.Y.C., 1995, Haus Der Kulturen Der Welt, Berlin, 1995, White Columns, N.Y.C., 1995, Site Sante Fe, N.Mex., 1995, Centro Cultural Banco do Brazil, Rio de Janeiro, 1995, Galeria Luis Serpa, Lisbon, Portugal, 1996, Galleria Marabini, Bologna, Italy, 1996, New Impulses in Decorative Arts, Art in Gen., N.Y.C., 1996, Hospicio Cabanas, Guadalara, Mexico, 1996, others. Recipient Acquisition award Nat. Found. for Arts, Brazil, 1989, FIAT award for visual arts, Brazil, 1990, Internat. Grant for art Edn. Ministry, Brazil, 1991, Arts and Sci. Ministry, Brazil, 1994, Simon Guggenheim fellow, 1996. Home and Office: 474 Degraw St Brooklyn NY 11217

SOAVE, ROSEMARY, internist; b. N.Y.C., Jan. 23, 1949. BS, Fordham U., 1970; MD, Cornell Med. Coll., 1976. Diplomate Am. Bd. Internal Medicine, Subspecialty Bd. in Infectious Diseases. Intern, resident N.Y. Hosp., N.Y.C., 1976-79; chief med. resident Meml.-Sloan Kettering Cancer Ctr., N.Y.C., 1979-80; fellow infectious diseases N.Y. Hosp., N.Y.C., 1980-82, asst. prof. medicine, 1982-89, assoc. prof. medicine and pub. health, 1989—; speaker in field; mem. NIAID-ARRE Study Sect. Contbr. numerous articles to profl. jours., chpts. to books, reviews and abstracts to profl. jours. Recipient Mary Putnam Jacobi fellowship for rsch., 1981-82, Leopold Schepp Rsch. fellowship, 1983-84, Nat. Found. for Infectious Diseases Young Investigator Matching Grant award, 1984-85; NIH grantee, 1986-89, 83-86, 87-90. Fellow Am. Coll. Physicians, Infectious Diseases Soc. Am.; mem. AAAS, Am. Fedn. Med. Rsch., N.Y. Acad. Scis., Infectious Diseases Soc. Am., Am. Soc. for Microbiology, Harvey Soc., Sigma Xi. Office: NY Hosp Cornell Med Ctr 1300 York Ave New York NY 10021-4805

SOBCZAK, DARLENE MARIE, police officer; b. Chgo., Nov. 17, 1956; d. Richard and Marilyn (Fuesting) Dvorak; children: Christopher B., Gina K. A of Criminal Justice, Morton Coll., 1991; B in Criminal Justice, U. Ill., Chgo., 1993. Police officer Town of Cicero, Ill., 1984—; field tng. officer Cicero Police Dept., 1989—, detective, 1992-95, sgt., 1995—; bd. dirs. Cicero Police Pension Bd. Active PTA, Cicero, 1984—. Fellow Ill. Police Assn., Fraternal Order Police; mem. Cicero Police Benevolent Assn. (pres. 1985—), Cicero Police Pension Bd. (bd. dirs. 1992—).

SOBCZAK, JUDY MARIE, clinical psychologist; b. Detroit, Dec. 28, 1949; d. Thaddeus Joseph and Bernice Agnes (Sowinski) Gorski; m. John Nicholas Sobczak, Aug. 17, 1974. BE cum laude, U. Toledo, 1971; postgrad., Ea. Mich. U., 1980-82; PhD, U. Toledo, 1987. Lic. psychologist. Tchr. Ottawa (Ohio)-Glandorf Schs., 1971-73; prin., tchr. St. Mary Sch., Assumption, Ohio, 1973-77; tchr. Our Lady of Perpetual Help Sch., Toledo, 1978-79; staff psychologist Outer Dr. Hosp., Lincoln Park, Mich., 1987-90; psychologist Adult/Youth Devel. Svcs., Farmington, Mich., 1991-95, Davis Counseling Ctr., Farmington Hills, Mich., 1996—; with Northwestern Cmty. Svcs., Livonia, Mich., 1996—, Orchard Hills Psychiat. Ctr., Plymouth, Mich., 1996—; adj. asst. prof. Madonna U., Livonia, Mich., 1987-94. Eucharistic minister St. Anthony Cath. Ch., Belleville, Mich., 1991—, parish coun. 1993-96; Cath. Svc. Appeal co-chmn., 1993—; sec. bd. dirs. Children Are Precious Respite Care Ctr., 1995. Fellow Mich. Women Psychologists (charter; newsletter editor 1987-92, treas 1989-93, Plaque of Appreciation 1992-96, sec. 1993—); mem. Mich. Psychol. Assn., Phi Kappa Phi. Home: 41498 Mckinley St Belleville MI 48111-3439 Office: Davis Counseling Ctr 37923 W Twelve Mile Rd Farmington Hills MI 48331

SOBEL, LAUREN B., lawyer; b. Oceanside, N.Y., Mar. 16, 1964. BA cum laude, Union Coll., 1966; JD, George Washington U., 1989. Bar: N.Y. 1990, D.C. 1990. Ptnr. Anderson Kill Olick & Oshinsky, N.Y.C. Mem. ABA, D.C. Bar Assn., N.Y. State Bar Assn. Office: Anderson Kill Olick & Oshinsky 1251 Ave of the Americas New York NY 10020-1182*

SOBELL, NINA R., artist; b. Patchogue, N.Y., May 4, 1947; d. Jack and Helen Ruth (Rosenberg) S.; m. Christopher Rogers Shearer, Sept. 8, 1982 (div. Mar. 1987); 1 child, Jacqueline Corianne. BFA, Temple U., 1969; MFA, Cornell U., 1971. Cert. educator N.Y. Vis. artist Calif. Inst. of the Arts, Valencia, 1975, Sch. of Architecture, London, 1976; vis. lectr. dept. art Reading (Eng.) U., 1976-77; vis. lectr. dept. design & sculpture UCLA, 1979, assoc. prof. electronic imagery, 1984-85; artist-in-residence interactive telecomm. program NYU, N.Y.C., 1991-92, artist-in-residence Ctr. Digital Multimedia, 1994—; instr. video prodn. Sch. Visual Arts, N.Y.C., 1992-93; dir. tech. integration Aux. Svc. High Schs., N.Y.C. Bd. Edn., 1994—; artist-lectr. Documenta VII, Kassel, Germany, 1977; juror U.S. Film and Video Festival, L.A., 1984; juror media arts divsn. N.Y. State Coun. on the Arts, N.Y.C., 1994; artist-presenter Siggraph, New Orleans, 1996. Prin. works include installation Interactive Brainwave Drawings, 1974—, interactive installation Videophone Relay, 1977-79; artist/dir. HIV-INFO Interactive Call-In TV Show, Manhattan Pub.-Access Cable, 1992, ParkBench Pub-Access Web Kiosks, 1994—; curriculum designer Online Art Network for At-Risk Youth, N.Y.C. Bd. Edn., 1996; represented in permanent collection Mus. Modern Art, N.Y.C., Whitney Mus. Art Whitney Web Site. Installation/Lecture grantee Found. Art Resources, 1981; Installation grantee N.Y. State Coun. Arts, 1981. Mem. Art and Sci. Collaborations, Inc., Coll. Art Assn., Assn. Ind. Video and Filmmakers, United Fedn. of Tchrs. Democrat. Jewish. Home: 190 Eldridge St # 3S New York NY 10002 Office: NYU Ctr Digital Multimedia 719 Broadway 12th Fl New York NY 10013

SOBERANO, CAROL ANN, speech and language pathologist; b. Barberton, Ohio, June 8, 1946; d. Edgar J. and Gertrude A. (Weiand) Weaver; m. Reynaldo M. Soberano; children: Mark, Gina. BS in Spl. Edn.,

Kent (Ohio) State U., 1968; MA in Speech Pathology, U. Akron, 1980. Lic. speech pathologist, pre-kindergarten and early edn. of handicapped tchr., Ohio. Speech pathologist Head Start, Barberton, Ohio, 1968, 69, 70, St. Augustine Sch., Barberton, 1970-71, Akron (Ohio) Pub. Schs., 1968-70, 71-72, Barberton Pub. Schs., 1972—; presch. speech pathologist Barberton Schs., 1990—, speech pathologist supr., 1990—. Treas. St. Monica Altar Soc., 1992-96. Mem. Ohio Speech and Hearing Assn. (legis. councilor 1984-85, 95-96, conv. chair 1984, 90, contbg. author to Hearsay mag. 1995), Ohio Sch. Speech Pathologist and Audiology Coalition (conv. co-chair 1995, 96), Akron Regional Speech Hearing Assn. (sch. rep. 1977-78, pres. 1983-84, Honors of Assn. 1988), Delta Kappa Gamma (pres. Beta Xi chpt., pres. joint coun.). Democrat. Roman Catholic.

SOBERON, PRESENTACION ZABLAN, state bar administrator; b. Cabambangan, Bacolor, Pampanga, Philippines, Feb. 23, 1935; came to U.S., 1977, naturalized, 1984; d. Pioquinto Yalung and Lourdes (David) Zablan; m. Damaso Reyes Soberon, Apr. 2, 1961; children: Shirley,Sherman, Sidney, Sedwin. Office mgmt., stenography, typing cert. East Cen. Colls., Philippines, 1953; profl. sec. diploma, Internat. Corr. Schs., 1971; student Skyline Coll., 1979, LaSalle Ext. U., 1980-82; AA, cert. in Mgt. and Supervision, Diablo Valley Coll. With U.S. Fed. Svc. Naval Base, Subic Bay, Philippines, clerical, stenography and secretarial positions, 1955-73, adminstrv. asst., 1973-77; secretarial positions Mt. Zion Hosp. and Med. Center, San Francisco, 1977, City Hall, Oakland, Calif., 1978; secretarial positions gen. counsel div. and state bar court divsn., State Bar of Calif., San Francisco, 1978-79, adminstrv. asst. fin. and ops. div., 1979-81, office mgr. sects. and coms. dept., profl. and pub. svcs. div., 1981-83, appointment adminstr. office of bar rels., 1983-86; adminstr. state bar sects. bus. law sect., estate planning, trust and probate law sect., labor and employment law section, office of bar rels., 1986-89, adminstr. antitrust and trade regulation law sect., labor and employment law sect., workers' compensation sect., edn. and meeting svcs., 1989-96, criminal law sect., 1996—, labor and employment sect., 1996—, internat. law sect., 1996—, workers' compensation sect., 1996—, edn. and meeting svcs., 1996—; disc jockey/announcer Philippine radio stas. DZYZ, DZOR and DWHL, 1966-77. Organizer Neighborhood Alert Program, South Catamaran Circle, Pittsburg, Calif., 1979-80. Recipient 13 commendation certs. and outstanding pers. monetary awards U.S. Fed. Svc., 1964-77, 20 Yr. U.S. Fed. Svc. pin and cert., 1975; Nat. 1st prize award for community svc. and achievements Nat. Inner Wheel Clubs Philippines, 1975; several plaques and award certs. for community and sch. activities and contbrns. Olongapo City, Philippines. Mem. NAFE, Am. Soc. Assn. Execs., N.Y.C. Olongapo-Subic Bay Assn. No. Calif. (Pittsburg rep. 1982-87, bus. mgr. 1988—, pub. rels. officer 1993-94), Castillejos Assn. of No. Calif. Roman Catholic. Home: 207 S Catamaran Cir Pittsburg CA 94565-3613 Office: State Bar of Calif 555 Franklin St San Francisco CA 94102-4456

SOCHACKI, TINA MARIE, secondary education educator; b. Evergreen Park, Ill., July 10, 1967; d. Alex Wayne and Judith Anne (Zicha) Spirakes; m. Matthew Zygmunt Sochacki, June 18, 1993. BA in French and Spanish Edn., U. Ill., 1989; postgrad., Gov.'s State U., University Park, Ill., 1994-96. Cert. 6-12 tchr., Ill.; Ill. type 75 cert. Tchr. fgn. lang. Bremen H.S., Midlothian, Ill., 1989-90, Acad. of Our Lady H.S., Chgo., 1990-91, Evergreen Park H.S., 1991—. Mem. ASCD, Am. Assn. Tchrs. French, Ill. Coun. on Tchg. Fgn. Langs., U. Ill. Alumni Assn., Golden Key. Office: Evergreen Park HS 9901 S Kedzie Ave Evergreen Park IL 60805

SOCHEN, JUNE, history educator; b. Chgo., Nov. 26, 1937; d. Sam and Ruth (Finkelstein) S. B.A., U. Chgo., 1958; M.A., Northwestern U., 1960, Ph.D., 1967. Project editor Chgo. Superior and Talented Student Project, 1959-60; high sch. tchr. English and history North Shore Country Day Sch., Winnetka, Ill., 1961-64; instr. history Northeastern Ill. U., 1964-67, asst. prof., 1967-69, assoc. prof., 1969-72, prof., 1972—. Author: The New Woman, 1971, Movers and Shakers, 1973, Herstory: A Woman's View of American History, 1975, 2d edit., 1981, Consecrate Every Day: The Public Lives of Jewish American Women, 1981, Enduring Values: Women in Popular Culture, 1987, Cafeteria America: New Identities in Contemporary Life, 1988, Mae West: She Who Laughs Lasts, 1992; editor: Women's Comic Visions, 1991; contbr. articles to profl. jours. Nat. Endowment for Humanities grantee, 1971-72. Office: Northeastern Ill U 5500 N Saint Louis Ave Chicago IL 60625-4625

SODER-ALDERFER, KAY CHRISTIE, counseling administrator; b. Evanston, Ill., Oct. 25, 1949; d. Earl Eugene and Alice Kathryn (Lien) Soder; m. David Luther Alderfer, May 15, 1976. BSE, No. Ill. U., 1972; postgrad., Luth. Sch. Theology, Phila., 1973; MA, Gov.'s State U., University Park, Ill., 1978; PhD, Walden U., 1985. Consecrated deaconess Luth. Ch., 1974. News reporter Suburban Life Newspaper, La Grange Park, Ill., 1972; counselor various orgns. Ill. & Pa., 1973—; parish worker Luth. Ch., De Kalb, Ill., 1973-74; pub. rels. asst. Luth. Ch. Women, Phila., 1974-76; editor Luth. Ch., Chgo., 1979—; spiritual dir. Gentle Pathways, Downers Grove, Ill., 1988—, counseling psychologist, 1990—, also bd. dirs.; cons. Evang. Luth. Ch. in Am., Chgo., 1988—, Lehigh Valley Hosp. Assn., Allentown, Pa., 1986. Author: Gentle Journeys, 1993, With Those Who Grieve, 1995, Help! There's a Monster in My Head, 1996; editor Entree, 1988-93, Multicultural Jour., 1992—; graphic designs exhbn. Franklin Mus., Phila., 1981. Spokeswoman Progressive Epilepsy Network, Phila., 1980-85; chair spiritual life com. Luth. Deaconess Cmty., Gladwyne, Pa., 1990-92; founder Teens with Epilepsy and Motivation, 1995; vol. March of Dimes, Ill., 1991-93; amb. of goodwill Good Bears of the World, 1993-94; spiritual dir. Evang. Luth. Ch. in Am. Recipient Silver award Delaware Valley Neographics Soc., 1981; 50th anniversary scholar Luth. Deaconess Community, 1983. Mem. AAUW, APA (div. women and psychology, div. psychology and the arts, div. psychology and religion). Office: Gentle Pathways 1207 55th St Downers Grove IL 60515-4810

SOECHTIG, JACQUELINE ELIZABETH, telecommunications executive; b. Manhasset, N.Y., Aug. 12, 1949; d. Alvin Hermann and Regina Mary (Murphy) Venzke; m. James Decatur Miller, July 4, 1976 (div. Oct. 1982); M. Clifford Jon Soechtig, Oct. 19, 1983. B.A. cum laude, Coll. of New Rochelle (N.Y.), 1974; M.A. summa cum laude, U. So. Calif., 1979. Computer operator IBM, White Plains, N.Y., 1970-72, ops. job scheduler, 1972-74, various spl. assignments, 1974-75, mktg. rep., Bethesda, Md., 1975-76, Charleston, W. Va., 1979-81, adv. regional mktg. rep. Dallas, 1981-82; dist. mgr. Am. Speedy Printing Co., Dallas, 1982-83, nat. sales devel. mgr., Detroit, 1984; regional mgr. major and nat. accounts MCI Telecommunications, Southfield, Mich., 1984-85, dir. nat. accounts, 1985-86, v.p. nat. accounts, 1987-88, v.p. mktg. and customer svc., 1988-89, v.p. consumer segment, 1989-90; v.p. integrated telecommunications solutions Sprint United, Atlanta, 1990-92; pres., chief exec. officer Precision Systems, 1992-94; pres., chief exec. officer, chmn. Lasergate Sys. Inc., 1994—; interviewer, Sergio Segre, Bolonga, Italy, 1977, Radio Free Europe, Brussels, 1978, World Health Program, Rome, 1978, ITT, Brussels, 1977, Franz Josef Strauss, 1978. Recipient Golden Circle Achievement award IBM, 1980, Quar. Recognition award, 1980, 81; named New Bus. Pacesetter, 1980, 81. Republican. Club: German Am. Women's (v.p. Stuttgart, W.Ger. 1977-78). Office: Lasergate Syss Inc 28050 US 19 N Ste 502 Clearwater FL 34621

SOEHREN, SHARON KAYE, school district administrator; b. Reeder, N.D., Jan. 28, 1943; d. Orville W. and Marian (Rose) Honeyman; m. Marvin D. Soehren, Aug. 11, 1964; children: Shannon, Shawn. BA, Dickinson State U., 1963; BS Elem. Edn., U. Mary, 1982. Tchr. Bowman (N.D.) Sch., 1963-65, Reeder (N.D.) Sch., 1966—; prin. Reeder Sch., 1987—, dist. adminstr., 1993—; mem. State Health Curriculum, Bismarck, N.D., 1993—; tchr., trainer HIV/AIDS Dept. Pub. Instrn., Bismarck, 1992—. Eucharistic minister Sacred Heart Ch., Reeder, 1994. Named tchr. of yr. Farm Bur., Hettinger, N.D., 1993. Mem. NEA, N.D. Edn. Assn., Nat. Elem. Sch. Prins., N.D. Elem. Sch. Prins. Home: 206 2d Ave E Reeder ND 58649 Office: Reeder Pub Sch N Main St Reeder ND 58649

SOETAERT, PAMELA JOYCE, journalist, editor; b. Victorville, Calif., May 25, 1953; d. Theodore John and Ruby Ester (Spitzenberger) Ogrodnik; m. Gerald Robert Soetaert, Sept. 15, 1974. Degree in graphic design, NEAK Tech. Sch., Aichison, Kans., 1973; fellow, U. Md., College Park, 1995. Layout, graphic artist Neff Printing, Mission, Kans., 1973-74, Clester Comms., Belle Plaine, Kans., 1979-81, 83-85; editor Southern View Mag., Haysville, Kans., 1985-88; staff writer Winfield (Kans.) Daily Courier, 1988-91; editor Table Rock Gazette, Kimberling City, Mo., 1991—; editor Lifelines Mo. Press Women, 1994-95, mktg. dir., 1994-95, outside mktg. dir., 1995-96; mem. Harbor Lights Women's Crisis, Kimberling City, 1995-96. V.p. Kimberling Area Merchants Assn., 1993-96. Recipient numerous awards in field. Mem. Kimberling City Rotary Club (pub. rels. chair 1994, 95, internat. chair 1996). Office: The Table Rock Gazzette PO Box 432 Kimberling City MO 65686

SOETEBER, ELLEN, journalist, newspaper editor; b. East St. Louis, Ill., June 14, 1950; d. Lyle Potter and Norma Elizabeth (Osborn) S.; m. Richard M. Martins, Mar. 16, 1974. BJ, Northwestern U., 1972. Edn. writer, copy editor Chgo. Today, 1972-74; reporter Chgo. Tribune, 1974-76, asst. met. editor, 1976-84, assoc. met. editor, 1984-86, TV and media editor, 1986, met. editor, 1987-89, assoc. mng. editor for met. news, 1989-91, dep. editor editorial page, 1991-94; mng. editor Ft. Lauderdale (Fla.) Sun-Sentinel, 1994—; fellow journalism U. Mich., Ann Arbor, 1986-87. Office: The Sun-Sentinel 200 E Las Olas Blvd Fort Lauderdale FL 33301-2248

SOFFER, ROSEMARY S., community health nurse, consultant, educator; b. N.Y.C., June 29, 1953; d. E.F. Harvey and Paula L. Show. Diploma, Hosp. U. Pa. Sch. Nursing, 1975; BSN, Neumann Coll., 1980; postgrad., Temple U./Beh Sci, 1983—, Neumann Coll., 1994—. RN, Pa., Del.; cert. CPR instr. Educator nursing sch., consulting nurse practitioner, educator Ambilikkai Village Health Clinic, India; program devel., nurse cons. Anglican Ch. India, 1995; charge nurse Hosp. of U. Pa., Phila., audit ventricular tachycardia, 1980; community nurse Community Nursing Svc., Chester, Pa.; program devel. nurse cons. Anglican Ch. India, Phila./Delaware County, Pa., 1995; ind. nurse contractor, 1994, 95; spkr. in field at Neumann Coll., chs. and orgns.; presenter numerous seminars on internat. nursing issues; exec. dir. Christian Ministry Internat. Author: The Real Rambo, 1989, Coping Mechanism of the Chronically Ill During Separation, 1983, Opened Eyes, 1990. Exec. com. Rambo Co., Inc. Sight for Curable Blind; bd. dirs. Ecumenical Caring Coalition-Chester Food Cupboard; elder Yeadon Presbyn. Ch., 1990-93; pres., dir. Ministry Internat., 1995—. Named one of Outstanding Young Women of Am., nominated by Dept. Atty. Gen. Harrisburg, 1991-92, Professionalism award Yeaden High Sch., 1971. Mem. Internat. Nursing Soc., Pa. Med. Missionary Soc. (bd. dirs. 1990-95), Sigma Theta Tau.

SOH, CHUNGHEE SARAH, anthropology educator; b. Taegu, Korea, May 1, 1947; came to U.S., 1970; d. Sang Yung and Ock Yun (Choi) S.; m. Jerry Dee Boucher. BA summa cum laude, Sogang U., 1971; postgrad., U. Calif., Berkeley, 1971; MA in Anthropology, U. Hawaii, 1983, PhD in Anthropology, 1987. Staff instr. English Korean Air Lines, Edn. & Tng. Ctr., Seoul, 1978-79; instr. anthropology Ewha Womans U., Seoul, 1985; asst. prof. U. Hawaii, 1990; asst. prof. anthropology Southwest Tex. State U., San Marcos, 1991-94; asst. prof. anthropology San Francisco State U., 1994-96, assoc. prof. anthropology, 1996—; guest lectr. Chaminade U. Honolulu, 1988; vis. asst. prof. anthropology U. Ariz., 1990-91; cons. in field. Author: Women in Korean Politics; contbr. articles to profl. jours. Recipient East-West Ctr. grantee, 1981-87, NSF Dissertation Rsch. grantee, 1985-86; Korea Found. fellow, 1993. Fellow Am. Anthrop. Assn.; mem. Am. Ethnological Soc., Soc. Psychol. Anthropology, Assn. Asian Studies (exec. bd. Com. Women Asian Studies), Western Social Sci. Assn., Korean Assn. Womens Studies, Royal Asiatic Soc. Korean Br. Office: San Francisco State U Dept Anthropology 1600 Holloway Ave San Francisco CA 94132-1722

SOHL, JOYCE D., religious organization administrator; m. Lowell Sohl (dec.); children: John, Stephen. BA, Westmar Coll., 1957; MA, U. Nebr., 1959; MDA, Fordham U., 1984. Math. tchr. Jr. H.S., 1959-61, Sr. H.S., 1961-64; assoc. treas. gen. bd. global ministries women's divsn. United Meth. Ch., White Plains, N.Y., 1976-90, dep. gen. sec. gen. bd. global ministries women's divsn., 1991—; Author: (book) Managing Our Money, Workbook on Women and Finance; (videos) Giving: A Gift of God's Grace, Called to Mission, 1994, Managing Our Money, 1990, Count Me In; columnist: monthly column Responsively Yours, in Response, 1991—; also articles in ch. publs. and program materials for program book of Women's Soc. of World Svc. and United Meth. Women. Past mem. bd. trustees, treas. Meml. United Meth. Ch., White Plains, current lay del. to ann. conf., mem. pastor/parish rels. com., adminstrv. bd., substitute organist; mem. investments com. Riverdale United Methodist Home; mem. adv. com. United Seminary, Dayton; bd. dirs. Scarritt-Bennett Ctr.; trustee Bennett Coll., Greensboro, N.C. Mem. NAFE, Am. Mgmt. Assn. Office: Gen Bd Global Ministried United Meth Ch 475 Riverside Dr New York NY 10115

SOHN, JEANNE, librarian; b. Milton, Pa.; d. Robert Wilson and Juliette Lightner (Hedenberg) Gift; m. Steven Neil Sohn, Nov. 23, 1962. BA, Temple U., 1966; MSLS, Drexel U., 1971. Lit. bibliographer Temple U., Phila., 1971-75, chief of collection devel., 1975-81; asst. dean for collection devel. U. N.Mex., Albuquerque, 1981-86, assoc. dean for libr. svcs., 1986-89; dir. libr. svcs. Cen. Conn. State U., New Britain, 1989—; cons. New Eng. Assn. Schs. and Colls., Winchester, Mass., 1991—. Mem. editorial bd. Collection Mgmt., 1984—; contbr. articles to profl. jours. Mem. Gov.'s Blue Ribbon Commn. on the Future of Libraries, 1994—. Mem. ALA, New Eng. Libr. Assn., Conn. Libr. Assn., Assn. Coll. and Rsch. Librs., Beta Phi Mu. Home: 1820 Boulevard West Hartford CT 06107-2815 Office: Cen Conn State Univ Elihu Burritt Libr New Britain CT 06050

SOHNEN-MOE, CHERIE MARILYN, business consultant; b. Tucson, Jan. 2, 1956; d. D. Ralph and Angelina Helen (Spiro) Sohnen; m. James Madison Moe, Jr., May 23, 1981. BA, UCLA, 1977. Rsch. asst. UCLA, 1975-77; ind. cons. L.A., 1978-83; cons. Sohnen-Moe Assocs., Tucson, 1984—. Author: Business Mastery, 1988, 2d edit., 1991; contbr. to Compendium mag., 1987-90, Massage Mag., 1992-94, 96—, Am. Massage Therapy Assn. Jour., 1989—. Vol. Am. Cancer Soc., Tucson, 1984—; mem. Ariz. Sonora Desert Mus., Tucson; pres. Women in Tucson, 1989. Recipient Outstanding Instr. award Desert Inst. of Healing Arts, 1992. Mem. NOW, ASTD (dir. mem. svcs. 1988, Achievement award 1987, Disting. Svc. award 1988, dir. mktg.), Nat. Fed. Independent Bus., Internat. Assn. Ind. Pubs., Pubs. Mktg. Assn., New Age Pub. and Retailing Alliance, Sierra Club, Nat. Fedn. of Ind. Bus. Office: Sohnen-Moe Assocs 3906 W Ina Rd # 200-348 Tucson AZ 85741-2295

SOILEAU, DOROTHY JOANNA JUMONVILLE, educator, counselor; b. New Orleans, June 29, 1943; d. Harry Nicholas and Dorothy (Hubert) Jumonville; m. Joseph Veazey Soileau, Nov. 18, 1967; children: Colette S. Hamilton, Marc Nicolas. BA, U. New Orleans, 1965; MS summa cum laude, Loyola U., 1991. Cert. tchr., La. Tchr. Orleans Parish Pub. Sch., New Orleans, 1965-68, Woodridge Acad., Pearl River, La., 1981-92, St. Tammany Pub. Schs., 1992-93, Our Lady of Lourdes Sch., Slidell, La., 1993—; counselor Tulane U., New Orleans, 1991-92; evaluator woodridge Acad., 1990-92. Den mother Cub Scouts Am., New Orleans, 1977-79. Mem. Chi Sigma Iota, Alpha Sigma Nu. Roman Catholic. Home: 806 Lake D Cote Ct Slidell LA 70461-3602

SOJKA, SANDRA KAY, investor; b. Ames, Iowa, Jan. 22, 1942; d. Clyde Burdette and Helen Rae (Daley) Smith; m. Gary Allan Sojka, Aug. 5, 1962; children: Lisa Kay, Dirk Allan. BS in Bus. Mgmt. with acad. honors, Ind. U., 1968, MS in Counseling-Guidance with honors, 1979, MS in Coll. Student Pers. with honors, 1979. Asst. to vet. extension office Purdue U., Lafayette, Ind., 1962-67; CPA asst. Geo. Greene & Co., Bloomington, Ind., 1975-76; office mgr., bldg. supr. Univ. Ministries, 1973-75; counselor, adminstrv. asst. dept. athletics Ind. U., Bloomington, 1977-84; first lady Bucknell U., Lewisburg, 1984-95, coord. univ./cmty. activities for pres.'s office, 1984-95, asst. sec. to bd. trustees, 1989-95; mem. Susquehanna Valley program adv. com. Pub. TV and Radio Sta. WVIA and FM90, 1994-95; mem. steering com. cmty. health assessment Evang. Cmty. Hosp./Sun Home Health Svcs., 1995—; mem. formation com. Bucknell in Action, 1990-91; mem. leadership adv. group for capital campaign WVIA/TV, 1994. Coauthor: Job Readiness Training Guide, 1977, Graduate Course Design and Evaluation Module, 1979. Bd. dirs. Evang. Cmty. Hosp., Lewisburg, 1984-91, Bloomsburg Theatre Ensemble, 1986-89; trustee Coe Coll., Cedar Rapids, Iowa, 1988-95, chmn. nominating com., 1992-95; bd. dirs. Assn. for Arts Bucknell U., 1984—; adv. bd. Four County Mental Health/Mental Retardation Orgn., Danville, Pa., 1986-94, pres., 1991-93; fundraising com. Camp Victory for Disabled Children, Millville, Pa., 1988-91. Recipient Disting. Svc. award Four County Mental Health/Mental Retardation Orgn., 1993. Mem. AAUW (bd. dirs. 1989-90), Bucknell U. Campus Club (pres. 1985-87), Lewisburg Aux. to Evang. Cmty. Hosp., Union County Hist. Soc., Lewisburg Garden Club (chair social program com. 1987-88, 94-95, chair nominations com. 1990-91, program spkr./presenter 1995-96, 96-97), Civic Club Lewisburg, Lewisburg Federated Womens Club, Alpha Xi Delta, Beta Gamma Sigma.

SOKALSKI, DEBRA ANN, computer systems developer, programming consultant; b. Paterson, N.J., June 27, 1959; d. John Michael and Cecelia Ann (O'Brien) S. Computer program cert., Electronic Computer Prog.Inst., Paterson, 1978; student, Montclair State Coll., 1988. Programmer trainee Numerax, Inc., Paramus, N.J., 1978-79, programmer, 1979-82, programming supr., 1982-83, mgr. programming, 1983-84, mgr. data processing, 1984-88; dir. system devel. Numerax/McGraw-Hill, Inc., 1989-90; sr. programmer analyst ADP, Roseland, N.J., 1990-92, lead programmer analyst, 1992-93; lead tch. analyst, 1993—; programming cons. Leslie Co., Parsippany, N.J., 1979-80. White House Fellowship nominee, 1994-95. Mem. NAFE. Democrat. Roman Catholic. Home: 174B Main St Little Falls NJ 07424-1421 Office: ADP 1 ADP Blvd # B337 Roseland NJ 07068-1728

SOKOLOVE, ROXANE N., lawyer; b. Newark, Dec. 10, 1955. BA magna cum laude, Am. Univ., 1976; JD, U. Balt., 1979. Staff atty. Bd. Immigration Appeals, 1979-80; trial atty. Organized Crime and Racketeering Sect. U.S. Dept. Justice, 1980-83; asst. U.S. atty. Dist. Columbia, 1983-87; ptnr. Aiken, Gump, Strauss, Hauer & Feld, L.L.P., Washington, 1987—. Mem. D.C. Bar, Bar of Commonwealth of Pa. Office: Akin Gump Strauss Hauer & Feld Ste 400 1333 New Hampshire Ave NW Washington DC 20036-1511*

SOKOLOW, ISOBEL FOLB, sculptor; b. Bklyn.; d. Henry Folb and Betty Forshaw; m. Gilbert Sokolow; children: Helene, Cheryl. Student, Silvermine Coll. Art, 1965-68, Art Students League, Nat. Acad. Design, Westchester C.C., N.Y., Ednl. Alliance Art Sch. Tchr., art therapist Jewish Guild for the Blind, Yonkers, N.Y., 1974-76; dir. Westchester Art & Culture Assn., Ardsley, N.Y., 1984-86; coord. sculpture workshops Pietrasanta, Italy, 1984-86; coord. summer workshop Pratt U., Venice, Italy, 1987; artist in residence Nat. Woman's Com., Brandeis U., 1995. One-woman shows include Bell Gallery, Greenwich, Conn., 1977, River View Gallery, Dobbs Ferry, N.Y., 1978, No. Shore Sculpture Ctr., Great Neck, N.Y., 1980, Harkness House, N.Y.C., 1981, Musavi Art Ctr., N.Y.C., 1984, Atlantic Gallery, N.Y.C., 1988, 90, 92, 94, Sara Lawrence Coll., 1995-96; exhibited in group shows at Monmouth Mus. Art, Red Bank, N.J., 1990, Westbeth Gallery, N.Y.C., 1991, Capital Bldg. Gallery, Tallahassee, 1991, Atlantic Gallery, N.Y.C., 1991, N.Y. Acad. Sci., N.Y.C., 1991, Broome St. Gallery, N.Y.C., 1991, Gallery Stendahl, N.Y.C., 1991, Raleigh Gallery, Dania, Fla., 1993, Casa d'arte Gadiva Gallery, Forte dei Marmi, Italy, 1993, Bigi Art Gallery, Florence, Italy, 1993, Living Arts Gallery, Milan, Italy, 1994, Steiner Gallery, Bal Harbor, Fla., 1995, Amb. Gallery, 1995; selected exhibits include Yonkers Art Assn., 1978, Audubon Artists Guild, 1978-80, N.J. Painters and Sculptors, 1980, Sculptors Allicance, 1982, Nat. Assn. Women Artists, 1984, N.Y. Soc. Women Artists, 1986, Am. Soc. Contemporary Artists, 1992; spl. exhibits include Dancer II, GM Bldg., N.Y.C., 1978-79, Torso, Schulman Realty Group, N.Y.C., 1983-85, Dancer I, Westchester C.C., Valhalla, N.Y., 1982-92, Dancer Reborn, Roosevelt H.S., Yonkers, N.Y., 1992—. Recipient Silver medal Audubon Artists, 1978, Sculpture award Mamaroneck (N.Y.) Artists Guild; Tres Jolle des Arts award Nat. Assn. Women Artists, 1984, Best in Show award, 1993. Mem. Am. Soc. Contemproary ARtists (v.p.), Artists Equity (past bd. dirs., past v.p.), Art Students League, Atlantic Gallery. Home and Studio: 498 Winding Rd N Ardsley NY 10502-2702

SOLA, JANET ELAINE, secondary school educator; b. New Britain, Conn., Oct. 23, 1935; d. Walter Andrew and Helen (Mandl) Sinkiewicz; m. Raymond Albert Sola,. BS, Cen. Conn. State U., 1957; MS, So. Conn. State U., 1962; postgrad., U. Conn, 1969. Tchr. bus. Amity Regional High Sch., Woodbridge, Conn., 1957-60; bus. instr. Stone Coll., New Haven, 1962; instr. Manpower Devel. and Tng. Act, New Britain, 1970-74; instr. So. Ctrl. C.C., New Haven, 1977, lectr., 1987; mgmt. lectr. II, Quinnipiac Coll., Hamden, Conn., 1981-87; mayor's aide Town of Hamden, 1987-89, recycling coord., 1989-92; tchr. bus. edn. Hamden High Sch., 1992—, coord. coop. work experience and diversified occupations, 1992—; assessor credit for life Quinn Coll., Hamden, 1986-89. Author: (poetry) Flights of Fancy, 1991, Recycled Thoughts, 1992; contbr. poetry to Contemporary, The Hamden Chronicle, Treasured Poems of Am., Nat. Arts Soc. Campaigner Sola for Town Clk. Com., Hamden, 1981; community liaison Carusone for Mayor Com., Hamden, 1981-87; v.p., Am. Legion Aux. Unit 88, Hamden, 1985—. Mem. ASCD, NAFE, AAUW, Nat. Bus. Educators, Ctrl. Conn. State U. Alumni Assn. (bd. dirs.), Internat. Platform Assn., Internat. Soc. Poetry (disting. mem.), Hamden Liions Internat. Home: 50 Vernon St Hamden CT 06518-2825 Office: Hamden HS 2040 Dixwell Ave Hamden CT 06514-2404

SOLBERG, ELIZABETH TRANSOU, public relations executive; b. Dallas, Aug. 10, 1939; d. Ross W. and Josephine V. (Perkins) Transou; m. Frederick M. Solberg, Jr., Mar. 8, 1969; 1 son, Frederick W. BJ, U. Mo., 1961. Reporter, Kansas City (Mo.) Star, 1963-70, asst. city editor, 1970-73; reporter spl. events, documentaries Sta. WDAF-TV, Kansas City, Mo., 1973-74; prof. dept. journalism Park Coll., Kansas City, Mo., 1975-76, advisor, 1976-79; mng. ptnr. Fleishman-Hillard, Inc., Kansas City, Mo., from 1979, now exec. v.p., sr. ptnr., gen. mgr. Kansas City br.; pres. Fleishman-Hillard/Can. Mem. Kansas City Commn. Planned Indsl. Expansion Authority, 1974-91; mem. long-range planning com. Heart of Am. council Boy Scouts Am., 1980-82, bd. dirs., 1986-89; mem. Clay County (Mo.) Devel. Commn., 1979-88; bd. govs. Citizens Assn., 1975—; mem. exec. com. bd. Kansas City Area Devel. Coun., 1989-96, co-chair, 1991-93; trustee Pembroke Hill Sch., 1987-93, U. Kansas City, 1990—, exec. com., 1992—, Midwest Rsch. Inst., 1995—; bd. dirs. Greater Kansas City Cmty. Found. and Affiliated Trusts, 1996—, Starlight Theatre, 1996—; regent Rockhurst Coll., 1984-96; active Bus. Coun., Nelson Gallery Found., Nelson-Atkins Mus. Art, 1990—; bd. dirs. Civic Coun. Greater Kansas City, 1992—. Recipient award for contbn. to mental health Mo. Psychiat. Assn., 1973, Arthur E. Lowell award for excellence in orgn. comm. Kansas City/IABC, 1985, Kansas City Spirit award Gillis Ctr., 1994. Mem. Pub. Relations Soc. Am. (nat. honors and awards com., co-chmn. Silver Anvil com. 1983, Silver Anvil award 1979-82, chair nat. membership com. 1989-91, assembly del.-at-large 1995-96), Counselor's Acad. (exec. com. 1991-92), Mo. C. of C. Pub. Relations Council, Greater Kans. City C. of C. (chair 1994-95, bd. exec. com.), Pi Beta Phi. Clubs: Jr. League, River Kansas City, Carriage, Central Exchange. Office: Fleishman Hillard Inc 2405 Grand Blvd Ste 700 Kansas City MO 64108-2519

SOLBRIG, INGEBORG HILDEGARD, German literature educator, author; b. Weissenfels, Germany, July 31, 1923; came to U.S., 1961, naturalized, 1966; d. Reinhold J. and Hildegard M.A. (Ferchland) S. Grad. in chemistry, U. Halle, Germany, 1948; BA summa cum laude, San Francisco State U., 1964; postgrad., U. Calif., Berkeley, 1964-65; MA, Stanford U., 1966, PhD in Humanities and German, 1969. Asst. prof. U. R.I., 1969-70, U. Tenn., Chattanooga, 1970-72, U. Ky., Lexington, 1972-75; assoc. prof. German U. Iowa, 1975-81, prof., 1981-93, prof. emerita, 1993—. Author: Hammer-Purgtall und Goethe, 1973; main editor Rilke Heute, Beziehungen und Wirkungen, 1975; translator, editor; (bilingual edit.) Reinhard Goering: Seeschlacht/Seabattle, 1977, Orient-Rezeption, 1995; contbr. numerous articles, revs. and transls. to profl. jours., chpts. to books. Mem. Iowa Gov.'s Com. on 300th Anniversary German-Am. Rels. 1683-1983, 1983. Recipient Hammer-Purgstall Gold medal Austria, 1974; named Ky. col., 1975; fellow Austrian Ministry Edn., 1968-69, Stanford U., 1965-66, 68-69; Old Gold fellow Iowa, 1977; Am. Coun. Learned Socs. grantee; German Acad. Exch. Svc. grantee, 1980; sr. faculty rsch. fellow in the humanities, 1983; NEH grantee, 1985; May Brodbeck fellow in the humanities, 1989; numerous summer faculty rsch. grants. Mem. MLA (life), Internat. Verein fur Germanische Sprach und Lit. Wiss., Goethe Gesellschaft, Deutsche Schiller Gesellschaft, Am. Soc. for 18th Century Studies, Can. Soc. for 18th Century Studies, Goethe Soc. N.Am., Inc. (founding mem.), Internat. Herder Soc. Prin. Rsch. Interest: contact of eastern and western cultures. Home: 1126 Pine St Iowa City IA 52240

SOLÉ, MARIA JESUS (XUSCA SOLÉ), visual artist; b. Torredembarra, Spain, May 24, 1960; d. Ventura and Josefa (Ceballos) S. MFA, U. Barcelona, Spain, 1986; postgrad., Am. Leadership Coll., 1993-94, NYU, 1994, Pratt Manhattan Inst., 1994. Info. searcher La Generalitat, Barcelona, Spain, 1982-83; dir. Art Difusion, N.Y.C., 1989-93; advt. Riomar and Riazor, N.Y.C., 1988-96; gallery's artist Jadite Gallery, N.Y.C., 1990-96; author, tchr. Author: (graphic book) Sun and Moon, 1995, Electric Light, 1995, Different Perception of the World, 1995. Mem. Dialectic Reality, Tarragona, Spain, 1976-79; vol. N.Y.C. Sch. Vol. Program, N.Y.C., 1995. Grantee Madrid's Ministry of Edn. and Sci., 1981-86, 83-84, 85-86, Basic Programmation, 1985. Fellow Spanish Profls. in Am.; mem. N.Y. Found. for the Arts, The Technology Assn.

SOLES, ADA LEIGH, former state legislator, government advisor; b. Jacksonville, Fla., May 19, 1937; d. Albert Thomas and Dorothy (Winter) Wall; B.A., Fla. State U., 1959; m. James Ralph Soles, 1959; children—Nancy Beth, Catherine. Mem. New Castle County Library Adv. Bd., 1975-80, 95—, chmn., 1975-77; chmn. Del. State Library Adv. Bd., 1975-78; mem. Del. State Ho. Reps., 1980-92; sr. advisor Gov. of Del., 1993-94; mem. U. Del. Libr. Assocs. Bd., 1995—. Adminstrv. asst. U. Del. Commn. on Status of Women, 1976-77; acad. advisor U. Del. Coll. Arts and Scis., 1977-92. Mem. LWV (state pres. 1978-80), Phi Beta Kappa, Phi Kappa Phi, Mortar Bd., Alpha Chi Omega. Episcopalian.

SOLESKI, SUSAN MARIE, elementary school educator; b. San Diego, Sept. 6, 1963; d. Richard Leslie and Judith Francis (Harring) Hennig; m. Scott William Soleski, June 19, 1987; 1 child, Kaitlin Leslie. BA, St. Norbert Coll., 1985. 5th grade tchr. St. Joseph Sch., Grafton, Wis., 1985-86; 4th and 5th grade tchr. All Sts. Sch., Denmark, Wis., 1986-89; 2d grade tchr. Green Bay (Wis.) Area Schs., 1989-90, 4th grade tchr., 1990-94, 5th grade tchr., 1994—; mem. tchr. adv. com. NEWIST, Green Bay, 1988, 89; mem. galaxy classroom demonstration Hughes Aircraft, 1992-94. Recipient Tchr. of Distinction/Golden Apple award Ptnrs. in Edn. (Green Bay Area C. of C., 1995. Mem. NEA, Wis. Edn. Assn., Green Bay Edn. Assn. (mem. PAC 1993, Disting. Svc. award 1991, 93, 96, elections com. 1996), Greater Bayland Reading Coun. (editor newsletter 1991). Home: 2320 Constellation St Green Bay WI 54303-6572 Office: Christa McAuliffe Sch 2071 Holl Dr Green Bay WI 54311-5013

SOLIS, PATTI, federal official; b. Chgo., Aug. 23, 1965; d. Santiago and Alejandrina (Ortega) S. BA in Comm., Northwestern U., 1990. Asst. to treas. City of Chgo., 1989-91; dir. of scheduling for Hilary Rodham Clinton Clinton-Gore Campaign, Little Rock, 1991-92, Clinton Transition Team, Little Rock, 1992-93; spl. asst. to Pres., dir. of scheduling for First Lady The White House, Washington, 1993—. Roman Catholic. Office: Presdl Scheduling & Advance 1600 Pennsylvania Ave NW Washington DC 20500

SOLIS-KLEIN, RUTH ELIZABETH, foreign language educator; b. Oberlin, Ohio, July 28, 1935; d. Bertram James and Ruth Langworthy (Brown) Smyth; m. Guillermo Abel Solis-Bonilla, Sept. 14, 1963; children: Roselia Ruth, Bertram Oliver; m. Charles B. Klein, Jr., Nov. 20, 1993. BA, Coll. of Wooster, 1957; MA, U. Kans., 1960; PhD, U. Akron, 1990. Cert. secondary tchr., Kans. Teaching asst. U. Kans., Lawrence, 1957-60; instr. Hiram (Ohio) Coll., 1960-62; asst. instr. Case Western Res. U., Cleve., 1962-64; from. instr. to prof. fgn. langs. Cuyahoga C.C., Cleve., 1964-93; ret., 1993; lectrice Ecole de Commerce, Clermont-ferrand, France, 1958-59; dir. courses Inst.-Guatemalteco, Guatemala City, Guatemala, 1979-80. Author: Curriculum Development, 1990; executed sculpture (1st Place award 1961). Deaconess 1st Christian Ch., Hudson, Ohio, 1988—. Recipient Innovator of Yr. award, 1991; Cuyahoga Community Coll. grantee, 1968, 88. Mem. AAUP, AARP, Nat. Inst. of Staff and Orgnl. Devel., Ohio Fgn. Lang. Assn., Akron Univ. Women's Club, Order of Eastern Star, Phi Sigma Iota (pres. 1956-57), Pi Lambda Theta, Phi Delta Kappa. Democrat.

SOLLID, FAYE EISING, volunteer; b. Milw., Aug. 31, 1913; d. George Walter and Jessie Belle (Davey) Eising; m. Erik Sollid, Aug. 1, 1936 (dec. Mar. 1977); 1 child, Jon Erik. BA in Journalism, U. Wis., 1936; postgrad., U. Denver, 1947. Asst. in basic communications U. Denver, 1947. Editor Am. Hindi cookbook for Am. Woman's Club New Delhi, 1956; mem. Clearwater (Fla.) Libr. Bd., 1981-89, liaison between Libr. Bd. and Friends of Libr. Bd., 1984-89; mem. Clearwater Beautification Com., 1989-92. Recipient Citation of Sincere Appreciation for pub. svc. as mem. libr. bd. 1981-89 Mayor City of Clearwater, 1989. Mem. AAUW, Internat. Graphoanalysis Soc., Nat. Mus. Women in Arts, Upper Pinellas African Violet Soc. (v.p. 1973-74, pres. 1974-75), Sovereign Colonial Soc. Ams. Royal Descent, Plantagenet Soc., Soc. Descs. Most Noble Order Garter, Order of Crown Charlemagne in U.S.A., Colonial Order of the Crown, Suncoast Magna Charta Dames (rec. sec. 1980-83), Nat. Soc. Colonial Dames XVII Century (v.p. 1983-85, 89-93).

SOLLIE, VIOLET JOHNSON, lawyer, statistician, researcher; b. Mpls., Jan. 18, 1907; d. Claus August and Priscilla (Jones) Johnson; m. Allen Nicholas Sollie Feb., 11, 1944 (dec. Jan., 1987). BA, Hamline U., 1928; MA, U. Minn., 1929; LLB, William Mitchell Coll., Mpls., 1957. Bar: Minn., 1957. Rschr. Minn. League of Municipalities, Mpls., 1928-30, Gov.'s Office State of W. Va., Charleston, 1930, U. Minn. Bus. Sch., Mpls., 1931-32; statistician income tax divsn. Minn. Tax Dept., St. Paul, 1933-39; part time organizer, part time rschr. Office Employees Union Local 12, Mpls., 1940-42; asst. statistician Dept. Commerce divsn. census bur., Washington, 1942-43; labor investigator Minn. Dept. of Labor, St. Paul, 1943-51; analyst and exec. asst. Wage Stabilization Bd., Mpls., 1951-53, 58-72; lawyer pvt. practice Mound, Minn., 1953-73, Mpls., 1958-72. Co-author (with R.G. Blakely) State Income Taxes, 1942; contbr. articles on Taxes to various publs., 1941-81. Recipient Clara Ueland fellowship U. Minn., Mpls., 1930-31. Mem. ABA (sr.), Hennepin County Bar Assn. (exec. bd. 1963-67, sec. atty.'s referral), Minn. Hist. Soc., LWV (state bd. dirs. 1930-31). Home: 2855 Cambridge Ln Mound MN 55364

SOLO, JOYCE R., volunteer; b. Buffalo, N.Y., Feb. 14, 1924; d. Jay Harry and Rose (Maisel) Rubenstein; m. Richard D. Solo, Jan. 6, 1946; children: Harry Jay Solo, Eleanor Solo, Sally Solo. BA, Wellesley Coll., 1945. Pres. LWV, Sarasota County, Fla., 1990-92; healthcare com. chair, 1988-90, 92—; sec. Sarasota County Health Care Coord. Adv. Coun., 1993-95; active Planned Approach to Cmty. Health/Healthy Sarasota 2000; chair sr. adv. com. Sarasota Meml. Hosp.; vol. Reach to Recovery Breast Cancer Task Force, Manatee County Am. Cancer Soc.; pres. Beth Israel Women Bd., Temple Beth Israel, numerous others health and civic orgn. activities.

SOLOMON, AMELIA KROLL, artist; b. Zwenigo Rodka-Kiev, Russia, Nov. 24, 1908; d. Abraham Krugliak Kroll and Nora Pipco; m. Herman Lampert Solomon, July 31, 1931 (dec. 1989); children: Ernest, Suzon, Semyon T., Sheba S. Studied with Ralph Stackpole, 1947; attended, Patri Sch. Fine Art, 1960, Foothill Coll., 1969, San Miguel de Allenda Art Inst., 1970; BA magna cum laude, San Jose State U., 1979, MFA, 1986. Lectr. in field. Solo shows include Stanford (Calif.) U., 1982, 83, Oakland (Calif.) Art Assn., 1985, Open Studio, San Jose, 1989, 90, Rosicrucian Egyptian Mus., San Jose, 1989, Metro Contemporary Art Gallery, Foster City, Calif., 1989, Koret Gallery, Palo Alto, Calif., 1992; group shows include Palo Alto Art Club, 1966, 69, San Mateo Floral Fiesta, 1970, Livermore (Calif.) Art Assn., 1979, San Francisco Women Artists, 1980, 81, Ana Gardner Gallery, 1980, Soma Gallery, San Francisco, 1980, Open Studio, 1986, Fenwick's Estate Art Show, Los Altos Hills, Calif., 1987, San Jose Inst. Contemporary Arts, 1987, 94, Gallery III, San Jose, 1990, Olive Hyde Gallery, Fremont, Calif., 1990, San Jose Art League, 1993, Los Gatos (Calif.) Tait Mus., 1993, Gallery Tanantzin, San Juan Bautista, 1993. Syntex Gallery, Palo Alto, 1993, Synopsis Gallery, Mountain View, Calif., 1993, Tait Mus., Los Gatos, 1994, Solomon Dubnick Gallery, Sacramento, 1994, Seippe Gallery, Palo Alto, 1994, Koret Gallery, 1995, many others. Mem. San Jose State U. Sculptors Guild (treas. 1977-95), League Nat. PEN Women, Womens Caucus for Arts, Internat. Sculpture Ctr.

SOLOMON, GWEN LOIS, government official, author; b. N.Y.C., Apr. 25, 1944; d. Richard and Helen (Simon) Wolff; m. Stan Solomon, July 3, 1966; 1 child, Deborah. BA in English, CCNY, 1965, MA in English, 1970; advanced cert. adminstrn., SUNY, New Paltz, 1981. Tchr. N.Y.C. Pub. Schs./Taft, Bronx, 1965-81, dir. project Etc., 1981-84; tech. coord. N.Y.C. Pub. Schs., Bronx, 1984-90; dir. Sch. of Future N.Y.C. Pub. Schs., 1990-93; coord. instrnl. tech. planning N.Y.C. Bd. Edn., 1993-94; sr. analyst U.S. Dept. Edn., Washington, 1994—. Author: Teaching Writing with Computers, 1986, Connect Online, 1996; (computer software) Success with Writing, 1989; contbr. articles to profl. jours. Mem. Internat. Soc. Tech. Edn. (bd. dirs. 1992), Consortium Sch. Networking (chair 1990). Office: US Dept Edn 600 Independence Ave SW Washington DC 20202

SOLOMON, MARCIA IRMA, bookkeeper, writer; b. Bklyn., Apr. 24, 1941; d. Myer and Leah Claire (Jacobson) Solomon; m. Luther Leroy Craig, July 21, 1959 (div. May 1976); children: Brett Craig, David Craig. BA in English, U. N.C., Charlotte, 1978, postgrad., 1982-86. Estimator, project mgr., sales B&B Contracting Co., Charlotte, 1979-83; outside sales Design Materials, Raleigh, N.C., 1982-86; owner, mgr. Tile Gallery, Charlotte, 1986-89; bookkeeper Leah's Bookkeeping and Taxes, Charlotte, 1989—, Lesesne & Connette, Charlotte, 1993—; mem. Profl. Estimators, Charlotte, 1979-83. Bd. dirs. P-Flag, Charlotte, 1988-94, Diversity Coun. Carolinas, Charlotte; pres. Charlotte Interfaith Network for Gay and Lesbian Equality; workshop coord. OUT Charlotte Arts Festival, 1995. Mem. Leadership Devel. Democrat. Jewish. Home: 2417 Elkwood Cir Charlotte NC 28205 Office: Leah's Bookkeeping 2417 Elkwood Cir Charlotte NC 28205

SOLOMON, MARILYN KAY, educator, consultant; b. Marshall, Mo., Oct. 16, 1947; d. John W. and Della M. (Dille) S. BS, Ctrl. Mo. State U., 1969; MS, Ind. U., 1974. Cert. in early childhood and nursery sch. edn., Mo., Ind. Tchr. Indpls. Pub. Schs., 1969-74; dir. Singer Learning Ctrs., Indpls., 1974-78; v.p. ECLC Learning Ctrs., Inc., Indpls., 1978-95; pres., CEO, owner Early Learning Ctrs., Inc., Indpls., 1995—; owner, pres., CEO, Solomon Antique Restoration, Inc., Indpls., 1996—; mem. OJT tng. task force Dept. Labor, Washington; mem. nat. task force for parenting edn. HEW, Washington; cons. to numerous corps. on corp. child care. Co-author curricula. Founding bd. dirs. Mid City Pioneer, Indpls., 1977; mem. adv. bd. Zone Small Bus. Incubator, Indpls., 1995—; founding bd. dirs. Family Support Ctr., Indpls., 1983, pres. bd. dirs., 1985-87. Recipient Outstanding Leadership award Ind. Conf. on Social Concerns, 1975, 76, 77, Children's Mus. Edn. award, 1974; named to Outstanding Young Women of Am., 1984. Mem. Indpls. Mus. Art, Ind. Lic. Child Care Assn. (v.p. 1992, pres. 1974, 75), State of Ind. Quality and Tng. Coun. (chair 1992), Step Ahead-Marion County (rep. for child care 1992—), Ind. Alliance for Better Child Care (bd. dirs. 1992), Order Eastern Star, Indpls. Zool. Soc. (charter). Office: Early Learning Ctrs Inc 1315 S Sherman Dr Indianapolis IN 46203-2210

SOLOMON, MARSHA HARRIS, draftsman, artist; b. Tulsa, Oct. 21, 1940; d. Ruel Sutton and Anna May (Fellows) Harris; m. Robert E. Collier, Aug. 13, 1960 (div. Dec. 1968); 1 child, Craig Robert Collier; m. Louis G. Solomon, Sept. 5, 1984. Student, U. Tex., 1958-61; BFA, U. Houston, 1966. Chief draftsman Internat. Paper, Petroleum & Minerals Divsn., Houston, 1985—; artist, ptnr. Archway Gallery, Houston, 1994. Mem. Nat. Mus. Women in Art (charter). Mem. Watercolor Art Soc. Houston (bd. dirs. 1984-91, treas. 1987-89, pres. 1990-91), N.Mex. Watercolor Soc. (signature mem.). Home: 5832 Valley Forge Dr Houston TX 77057-2248

SOLOMON, MILDRED ZELDES, health services researcher, educational psychologist; b. Chgo., Apr. 7, 1949. BA in English, Smith Coll., 1971; postgrad., U. Mass., 1973-74; MA, U. Newcastle-upon-Tyne, Eng., 1978; EdD, Harvard U., 1991. Lang. arts tchr. Gateway Regional Sch. Dist., Huntington, Mass., 1971-73; tchr. educator U.S. and U.K., 1974-76; tchr. trainer Scotland and Eng., 1975-76; dir. curriculum devel. Edn. Devel. Ctr., Inc., Newton, Mass., 1976-82, project dir., 1982-86, sr. assoc. for devel., 1984-86, sr. scientist, 1987—; project dir. Teenage Health Tchg. Modules, 1982; prin. investigator Sexually Transmitted Disease Project, 1983-86, Decisions Near the End of Life, 1987—; dir. Ctr. for Applied Ethics and Effective Practice, 1996—; presenter, lectr. in field. Contbr. articles to profl. publs., newspapers, mags., chpts. to books; author curriculum materials in field; author audiovisual prodns. A Question of Burning, 1977, Regardless of Sex, 1979, It Just Happens Sometimes, 1984, So They Gave Me These Pills, 1986, Let's Do Something Different, 1986. Recipient Silver award Houston Internat. Film Festival, 1986, Finalist award Info. Film Prodrs. Am., 1979, Cindy award Audio-Visual Communicators Am., 1986, John R. Hogness award Lectureship, Assn. Acad. Health Ctrs., 1994. Mem. APHA, Am. Soc. Law, Medicine and Ethics, Assn. for Health Svcs. Rsch. Office: Edn Devel Ctr 55 Chapel St Newton MA 02158-1060

SOLOMON, PHYLLIS LINDA, social work educator, researcher; b. Hartford, Conn., Dec. 6, 1945; d. Louis Calvin and Annabell Lee (Nitzberg) S. BA in Sociology, Russell Sage Coll., 1968; MA in Sociology, Case Western Res. U., 1970, PhD in Social Welfare, 1978. Lic. social worker, Pa. Rsch. assoc. Inst. Urban Studies Cleve. State U., 1970-71; program evaluator Cleve. State Hosp., 1971-74; project dir. Ohio Mental Health and Mental Retardation Rsch. Ctr., Cleve., 1974-75; rsch. assoc. Psychiat. Rsch. Found. of Cleve., 1975; project dir. Ohio Mental Health and Mental Retardation Rsch. Ctr., 1977-78; rsch. assoc. dirs. rsch. and mental health planning Fedn. for Community Planning, 1978-88; prof. dept. mental health scis., dir. sect. mental health svcs. and systems research Hahnemann U., Phila., 1988-94; prof. Sch. Social Work U. Pa., Phila., 1994—; secondary appointment Prof. Social Work in Psychiatry U. Pa. Sch. Medicine; adj. prof. dept. psychiatry Allegheny U. Author: (with others) Community Services to Discharged Psychiatric Patients, 1984; co-editor: New Developments in Psychiatric Rehabilitation, 1990, Psychiatric Rehabilitation in Practice, 1993; editorial adv. bd. Community Mental Health Jour., 1988—; contbr. articles to profl. jours. Trustee Cleve. Rape Crisis Ctr., 1981-84, CIT Mental Health Svcs., Cleve., 1985-88; mem. citizen's adv. bd. Sagamore Hills (Ohio) Children's Psychiat. Hosp., 1984-88. Named Evaluator of the Yr., Ohio Program Evaluators Group, 1987; recipient Ann. award Cuyahoga County Community Mental Health Bd., 1988. Mem. Internat. Assn. Psychosocial Rehab. Svcs. Jewish. Home: 220 E Mermaid Ln Apt 186 Philadelphia PA 19118-3215 Office: U Pa Sch Social Work 3701 Locust Walk Philadelphia PA 19104-6214

SOLOMON, RISA GREENBERG, video software industry executive; b. N.Y.C., June 22, 1948; d. Nathan and Frances (Guttman) Greenberg; m. Philip Howard Solomon, June 21, 1970; children: Elycia Beth, Cynthia Gayle. BA, NYU, 1969, MA, 1970. Asst. editor Redbook Mag., N.Y.C., 1969-70; assoc. editor Greenwood Press, Westport, Conn., 1970-71; mng. editor Dushkin Pub., Guilford, Conn., 1971-72; freelance editor Yale U. Press, New Haven, Conn., 1972-75; v.p. ops. Videoland, Inc., Dallas, 1980-82; v.p. Video Software Dealers Assn., Cherry Hill, N.J. and Dallas, 1981-83; pres. Videodome Enterprises, Dallas, 1983—; cons. Home Recording Rights Coalition, Washington, 1983-84. Contbr. articles to video mags. Bd. dirs. Congregation Anshai Emet, Dallas, 1985-86. Mem. Video Software Dealers Assn. (founder, dir. 1981-82). Democrat. Jewish. Office: Videodome Enterprises 11420 St Michaels Dr Dallas TX 75230-2436

SOLON, HELEN LISA, artist; b. Bklyn., May 16, 1960; d. George and Helen Solon; m. Philip U. Tremmel, Oct. 23, 1992. BA in Journalism, NYU, 1981, MBA in Fin., 1985. Mgr. personal computer facilities NYU, N.Y.C., 1981-87; v.p. Salmon Bros. Inc., N.Y.C., 1987-92; pvt. practice artist Bloomfield, N.J., 1992—; artist-in-residence Newark Mus., 1996. Artist (artist book) Edition VI: Icons, 1994, Edition VII: Parallels, 1995. Recipient first prize N.E. Art Festival/Caldwell (N.J.) Coll., 1993, Welsh award So. Vt. Art Ctr., Manchester, 1993, first prize annual exhbn. Watchung (N.J.) Arts Ctr., 1994, first prize works on paper exhbn. N.Y. Inst. Tech., Old Westbury, 1994. Office: PO Box 8145 Glen Ridge NJ 07028

SOLON, MELVA JUNE, mental health nurse; b. Streator, Ill., Mar. 12, 1943; d. Melvin L. and Vincentina J. (Verdiramo) Chalfant; m. Thomas P. Solon, July 25, 1964; children: Thomas P. (dec.), Susan Denise. Diploma, St. Charles Hosp. Sch. Nursing, 1964; BSN, Gov.'s State U., University Park, 1981; MSN, Ind. U.-Purdue U., Indpls., 1996. RN, Ill., Ind.; cert. mental health nurse. Night supr. Chastain's Nursing Home & Convalescent Ctr., Highland, Ill.; staff charge nurse night shift Norman (Okla.) Mcpl. Hosp., Wesley Meml. Hosp., Chgo.; staff nurse, night charge nurse Danville (Ill.) VA Med. Ctr. Mem. AAUW (charter), Am. Psychiat. Nurses Assn. (charter), Ill. Psychiat. Nurses Assn. (charter), Sigma Theta Tau (charter). Home: 1644 N Franklin St Danville IL 61832-2364

SOLÓRZANO, SHARON LOUISE, secondary education educator; b. Ft. Belvoir, Va., Feb. 5, 1968; d. Donald Louis and Rita Marie (Reilly) Siebenaler. Student, U. Muenster, Germany, 1988-89; BA, Coll. William & Mary, 1990; MEd, Marymount U., 1992. Cert. secondary tchr., Va. Tchr. Social Studies Arlington (Va.) Pub. Schs., 1992—; forensics coach Arlington Pub. Schs., 1993—; mem. Social Studies assessment com., Arlington Pub. Schs., 1993-95, restructuring com., Wakefield H.S., Arlington, 1993-95. Coauthor: (sch. manual) Program Overview Grade 9 World History, 1993. Pres. Off Campus Student Coun., Williamsburg, 1989-90. Recipient grad. assistantship Marymount U., 1990-91. Mem. NEA, Nat. Coun. for Social Studies, Nat. Orgn. Women.

SOLOWAY, ROSE ANN GOULD, clinical toxicologist; b. Plainfield, N.J., Apr. 19, 1949; d. George Spencer Jr. and Rose Emma (Frank) Gould; m. Irving H. Soloway, Dec. 13, 1979. BSN, Villanova U., 1971; MS in Edn., U. Pa., 1976. Diplomate Am. Bd. Applied Toxicology. Staff nurse Hosp. of U. Pa., Phila., 1971-73; asst. clin. instr. Hosp. of U. Pa. Sch. Nursing, Phila., 1973-77; staff devel. instr. Hosp. of Med. Coll. Pa., Phila., 1977-78; dir. Emergency Nurse Tng. Program Ctr. for Study of Emergency Health Svcs., U. Pa., Phila., 1979-80; edn./comms. coord. Nat. Capital Poison Ctr. Georgetown U. Hosp., Washington, 1980-94; clin. toxicologist Nat. Capital Poison Ctr. George Washington U. Med. Ctr., Washington, 1994—; adminstr. Am. Assn. Poison Control Ctrs., Washington, 1994—; mem. Clin. Toxicology and Substance Abuse Adv. Panel, U.S. Pharmacopeial Conv., Inc., Washington, 1990-95, 95—; bd. dirs. Am. Bd. Applied Toxicology. Contbr. articles to profl. publs. Mem. APHA, Am. Assn. Poison Control Ctrs. (co-chmn. pub. edn. com. 1985-90), Poison Prevention Week Coun. (vice chmn. 1988-91, chair 1991-93). Office: Am Assn Poison Control Ctrs 3201 New Mexico Ave NW Ste 310 Washington DC 20016-2756

SOLSVIG, SARAH JANE, public relations professional; b. Edina, Minn., June 29, 1968; d. Richard Robert and Betty Jean (Fogel) Busch; m. Keith Arthur Solsvig, Nov. 12, 1994. BA in Comm. Arts, U. Wis., Eau Claire, 1990; MA in Indsl. Rels., U. Minn., 1991. Asst. account exec. Henry Comm., Inc., Mpls., 1990-92; pub. rels. and devel. specialist Little Bros.-Friends of the Elderly Nat., Chgo., 1992-93; account exec. Bev Kennedy and Co., Chgo., 1993-94, LaBreche & Murray Pub. Rels., Mpls., 1994—; venue media chief Internat. Spl. Olympics, Mpls., 1991; media rels. dir. Taste of Lincoln Ave., Chgo., 1992-93. Author, editor: Wisconsin in Scotland Student Handbook, 1988; writer feature stories Reader, 1993-94; columnist feature stories Chicagoland Sr. News, 1992-94. Jr. bd. dirs. Jane Addam's Hull House, Chgo., 1992-93; vis. vol. Little Bros. Friends of the Elderly, Chgo., 1992-94; vol. Am. Cancer Soc., Chgo., 1993; co-chair Welcome Ministries, Wayzata Cmty. Ch., 1995—. Scholar Edina (Minn.) Women's Club, 1986. Mem. Pub. Rels. Am. (monthly meeting planner 1995, classics awards judge 1995), Jr. League Mpls. (Gala media mgr.), Job's Daus. (hon. queen 1979-86), Delta Zeta Sorority (pres. 1986-90). Home: 316 Walker Ave North Wayzata MN 55391 Office: LaBreche Murry Pub Rels 801 Nicollet Mall #1750 Minneapolis MN 55402

SOLTIS, KATHERINE, editor; b. Pitts., Apr. 15, 1950; d. John Andrew and Katherine (Hnidec) Goidich; m. Patrick T. Soltis, July 27, 1973 (div. 1996). BA, Mich. State U., 1972; MA in English/Linguistics, Case Western Res. U., 1982. Part time clk. Case Western Res. U., Cleve., 1974-83; lexicographer Webster's New World Dictionaries Macmillan/Simon & Schuster, Cleve., 1983—. Editor: Webster's New World Vest Pocket Dictionary, 2nd edit., 1994. Trustee Cleve.- Volgograd Ptnr. Cities, 1990—; pres. Women Speak Out for Peace & Justice/Women's Internat. League for Peace & Freedom, 1993-95, chair program com., 1995—; orgn. rep. Cleve. Coalition Against the Death Penalty; supporter/advocate Ariz. death row inmate, 1981—. Mellon fellow Case Western Res. U. Mem. Am. Dialect Soc., Dictionary Soc. North Am., City Club, Phi Beta Kappa. Mem. Soc. of Friends. Home: 896 Englewood Rd Cleveland Heights OH 44121

SOLYMOSY, HATTIE MAY, writer, publisher, storyteller, educator; b. Kew Gardens, N.Y., Apr. 1, 1945; d. Julius and Sylvia Becky (Glantz) Fuld; m. Richard Milk, June 30, 1966 (div. Feb. 1974); 1 child, Jared Marc Milk.; m. Abraham Edward Solymosy, Apr. 21, 1974. BA, Queens Coll., 1966, MS in Edn., 1973. Cert. tchr., N.Y.C. and N.Y. Actress, model, 1950-60; elem. tchr. N.Y.C. Bd. of Edn., 1966—; owner Ultimate Jewelry, N.Y.C., 1976-80; tutor N.Y.C., 1983-91; children's writer N.Y., 1991—, romance writer, 1993—; owner Hatties' Tales, Cedarhurst, N.Y., 1993; storyteller Mo. flood victims, Okla. Fed. Bldg. bombing victims, various children's hosps.; exec. Hamajama Gifts. Author: (sound recs.) Delancy Dolphin, 1993, Thaddius Thoroughbred, 1993, Willie's War, 1993, Noodles-An Autobiography, 1993, (with Jared Marc Milk) Trapped With The Past, 1993, Thick Slick Tangled Webs, 1993, Cinderella Cockroach, 1993, A Christmas Tale, 1993, Chanukah Tale, 1993, Doc Simon, 1995, Mr. Music, 1996, Women on Film, 1996, Buying a Dream, 1996, Rock and Roll, 1996; owner Cigar Box Factory. Social sec., fundraiser Children's Med. Ctr., N.Y.C., 1969-79; aux. mem. St. John's Hosp., N.Y., 1987—; contbr. children's stories Okla. Bombing, Mo. Flood Victims, Children's Hosps.; assoc. mem. Mus. Natural History. Mem. Romance Writers of Am., Soc. of Children's Writers and Illustrators, Simon Wiesenthal Ctr., World Jewish Congress. Democrat. Jewish. Home: 470 W Broadway Cedarhurst NY 11516-1531 Office: Hatties' Tales PO Box 24 Cedarhurst NY 11516-0024

SOMAN, SHIRLEY CAMPER, writer, journalist, columnist, consultant, social worker; b. Boston; d. David and Fannie (Apteker) Isenberg; m. Frederic R. Camper (dec.); children: Frederic D., Frances A.; m. Robert O. Soman (dec.). BA, U. Wis.; M in Social Sci., Smith Coll. Sch. social worker Bur. Child Guidance N.Y.C. Bd. Edn.; assoc. editor My Baby mag., Shaws Market News, N.Y.C.; family life cons. Family Svc. Assn. Am., N.Y.C.; v.p., ptnr. Associated Film Cons., N.Y.C.; columnist Springfield (Mass.) Union-News, 1991-93; pres., CEO Acorn to Oak Pub. Co., N.Y.C., 1991—; cons. White House Conf. Children and Youth, Washington, 1980, Child Welfare League Am., Washington, 1989; adj. prof. child advocacy and children's rights CUNY, 1976, 77. Author: How to Get Along With Your Child, Let's Stop Destroying Our Children, 1974, Preparing for Your New Baby, 1982; syndicated columnist; contbr. numerous articles to jours., newspapers. Panelist 1st USA Conf. on Human Rights Amnesty Internat.; founder, chair Parents for Carter-Mondale, N.Y., 1976; bd. dirs. Pub. Action Coalition for Toys, N.Y., 1976-82, Creative Arts Rehab. Ctr., N.Y., 1977-82, Childsavers, Inc., Washington, 1992—; chair First Nat. Child Advocacy Symposium, 1974; founder Fin. Friends, 1994; lectr. social and family issues numerous orgns. Recipient award Women in Communications, 1986. Mem. NATAS, Am. Soc. Journalists and Authors, Nat. Assn. Sci. Writers, Nat. Assn. Social Workers, Acad. Cert. Social Workers (cert. N.Y. State), N.Y. Acad Sci., Soc. Profl. Journalists, Authors Guild and League. Home and Office: 142 W End Ave New York NY 10023-6103

SOMERFELD, ESTHER, physician, educator; b. Chgo., July 2, 1901; d. Emanuel and Matilda (Lustgarten) S.; m. Eugene Ziskind, Nov. 10, 1927 (dec. Nov. 1993); 1 child, Emile Jacobson. SB, U. Chgo., 1923; MD, Rush Med. Coll., 1925; MA in Psychology, UCLA, 1934. Diplomate Am. Bd. Neurology and Psychiatry. Intern L.A. County Gen. Hosp., 1925-26, attending physician, 1928-96; rsch. fellowship Santa Barbara (Calif.) Cottage Hosp., 1926; med. resident L.A. Children's Hosp., 1927; chair psychiatry dept. Cedars of Lebanon Hosp., 1956-65; prof. psychiatry, then emeritus USC Med. Sch., L.A., 1960—. Contbr. articles to profl. jours. Recipient Rsch. award Calif. Med. Assn., 1932, Hon. award So. Calif. Psychiat. Soc., 1985, L.A. Soc. Neurol. Scis., 1995. Fellow AMA (life), Am. Psychiat. Assn. (discuss chmn. 1970), Am. Group Psychotherapy Assn.; mem. Group Psychotherapy Assn. of So. Calif. (pres. 1955—), L.A. Soc. Neurology and Psychiatry (pres. 1960), Severance Club (pres. 1978-80).

SOMERS, ANNE RAMSAY, medical educator; b. Memphis, Sept. 9, 1913; d. Henry Ashton and Amanda Vick (Woolfolk) Ramsey; m. Herman Miles Somers, Aug. 31, 1946; children: Sara Ramsay, Margaret Ramsay. BA, Vassar Coll., 1935; postgrad., U. N.C., 1939-40; DSc (hon.), Med. Coll. Wis., 1975. Ednl. dir. Internat. Ladies Garment Workers Union, 1937-42; labor economist U.S. Dept. Labor, 1943-46; rsch. assoc. Haverford Coll., 1957-63; rsch. assoc. indsl. rels. sect. Princeton U., 1964-84; prof. U. Medicine and Dentistry of N.J.-R. Wood Johnson Med. Sch. (formerly Rutgers Med. Sch.), 1971-84, adj. prof., 1984—; adj. prof. geriat. medicine U. Pa. Sch. Medicine, 1990—; mem. Nat. Bd. Med. Examiners, 1983-86; cons. in health econs., health edn., geriats., gerontology, realted areas. Author: Hospital Regulation: The Dilemma of Public Policy, 1969, Health Care in Transition: Directions for the Future, 1971, (with H.M. Somers) Workmen's Compensation: The Prevention, Rehabilitation and Financing of Occupational Disability, 1954, Medicare and the Hospitals, 1967, Doctors, Patients and Health Insurance, 1961, Health and Health Care: Policies in Perspective, 1977, (with N.L. Spears) The Continuing Care Retirement Community: A Significant Option for Long Care?, 1992; editor: (with D.R. Fabian) The Geriatric Imperative: An Introduction to Gerontology and Clinical Geriatrics, 1981. Mem. bd. visitors. Duke U. Med. Ctr., 1972-77, U. Tex. Health Scis. Ctr., Houston, 1980-86. Recipient Elizur Wright award Am. Risk and Ins. Assn., 1962; named to Health Care Hall of Fame, 1993. Fellow Am. Coll. Hosp. Adminstrs. (hon.), Coll. Physicians Phila. (hon.); mem. Inst. Medicine of NAS, Soc. Tchrs. of Family Medicine (hon.). Home: Pennswood Vlg # G-205 Newtown PA 18940

SOMERS, KATHY JO, home economics educator, consultant; b. Elkin, N.C., Sept. 13, 1953; d. Edward Roan and Kathleen (Cochrane) Snyder. BS in Home Econs. Edn., U. N.C., 1975, MEd in Home Econs. Edn., 1976. Program coord. title VII nutrition program for elderly High Point (N.C.) Housing Auth., 1976-78; food preparation, culinary arts instr. Weaver Edn. Ctr., Greensboro, N.C., 1978—, classroom and lab. instr., dept. chair, 1978-95; summer sch. instr. Weaver End. Ctr., Greensboro, N.C., 1979-89, night sch. instr., 1983-93, Sat. enrichment program instr., 1987, Job Tng. Placement Act instr., 1990-93; continuing edn. instr. microwave cooking Gulford Tech. C. C., Jamestown, N.C., 1984-88; dir. Sat. enrichment program Guilford County Schs., N.C., 1995; chpt. adv. Future Homemakers of Am., Inc., 1985-96, adv. to event winners, 1987-96, regional co-adv., regional leadership coun. mem., regional adv., coord. state proficiency events tabulation, 1990-95, mem. state proficiency events handbook writing project, 1988, coord. state leadership tng. workshop, 1995, mem. state mgmt. team, 1989-96, mem. nat. membership com., 1987, evaluator, Students Taking Action Recognition Events, 1987, mem. scholarship selection nat. com., 1987, 90, mem. adult editl. bd. Teen Times, The Adviser, 1988, nat. cons. Leaders at Work in Food Svc., 1990, 96; asst. instr. food svc. course N.C. Dept. Pub. Instrn., 1985, mem. textbook adoption com., 1986, leader for commercial foods VoCATS State Team, 1990-92, mem. Com. Practitioners Carl D. Perkins Act, equipment stds. review com., 1993; mem. tchg. fellows screening com. Greensboro (N.C.) Pub. Schs., 1987; mem. adv. bd. culinary arts Guilford Tech. C.C.; spkr., presenter in field. Mem. disaster action team Greensboro (N.C.) chpt. ARC, 1989-95, Greensboro Youth Coun. Toys for Tots, 1992; neighborhood chair Easter Seals Soc. N.C., 1990-94; mem. ladies auxiliary Southeast Vol. Fire Dept., 1979-95; flotilla staff officer, pub. affairs USCG auxiliary, Belews Lake, N.C., 1992, 93, vice commdr. flotilla, 1993, bd. dirs. divsn. XVIII, 1993-95, commdr. flotilla, 1994, 95; mem. Elkin Presbyn. Ch. Named Oustanding Young Educator Weaver Edn. Ctr. nominee N.C. Jaycees, 1984; nominee Am. Tchg. award Walt Disney Company, 1992. Mem. Am. Vocat. Assn. (del. nat. conv. 1989-90, 90-91, host President's reception, Region II Outstanding Vocat. Tchr. of Yr. 1994, Nat. Outstanding Tchr. of Yr. 1994), Nat. Assn. Vocat. Home Econs. Tchrs. (attendee nat. conv., N.C. contact person), N.C. Vocat. Assn. (attendee summer conf. 1984-95, profl. devel. com. 1988-89, v.p. divsn. 1989, 90, bd. dirs. 1989-90, 90-91, program work com. 1989-90, exec. com. 1990-91, membership com. 1990-91, awards com. 1991-92, bd. dirs., chair ways and means com. 1992-95, Family and Consumer Scis. Edn. divsn. voting del. assembly of dels. 1988-95, mem. com. chari. conv. com. 1988-89, pres., chair program of work com., 1989-90, pres., chair, newsletter editor membership com., 1990-91, pres., chair awards com. 1991-92, chair pub. info. com. 1992-93, Outstanding Vocat. Tchr. of Yr. 1993), U. N.C. Home Econs. Alumni Assn. (pres. 1984-85). Presbyterian. Home: 4605 Rosemary Dr Greensboro NC 27406 Office: Weaver Edn Ctr 300 South Spring St Greensboro NC 27401

SOMERS, LEONORA PATIÑO, psychotherapist; b. N.Y., Mar. 28, 1927; d. Carlos Eduardo and Marie Catherine Czerwinski Patino; m. Bernard Joseph Somers (div. 1984); children: Bianca Somers Ohle, Evan Carlos Somers. BS, M. Stewart Internat. U., 1976; MA, Goddard Coll., 1977. Lic. marriage, family and child therapist, Calif. Founding area reference person Re-Evaluation Counseling, L.A., 1970-77; guest instr. psychology L.A. County Dept. Healt Svcs., 1978-82; dimension faculty mem. Sierra U., Santa Monica, Calif., 1980-87; mental health care provider Blue Shield, L.A., 1986-96, Prunetwork, L.A., 1990-96; pvt. practice L.A., 1978—; mem. internat. reference com., Re-Evaluation Counseling, Seattle, 1971-75, regional reference person, 1973-75; mem. advisory bd. Sierra U., Santa Monica, 1980-87; guest. lectr. U. So. Calif., L.A., 1982-85. Author: (book) Emotional Freedom, 1996; contbr. articles to profl. jours. Founding area reference person Co-Counseling, L.A., 1972; pres. L.A. chpt. Nat. ParaPlegia Found., 1979-81; so. Calif. chair SANE, L.A., 1967-69; mem. Californians for Liberal Reps., L.A., 1968-70. Mem. Calif. Assn. Marriage and Family Therapists, Am. Assn. Counseling and Devel., U. Calif. L.A. Alumni Assn. Democrat. Home and Office: 3565 Tilden Ave Los Angeles CA 90034

SOMERS, MARION, gerontologist, retirement specialist; b. N.Y.C.; d. John Joseph and Lottie (Kramer) Strahl; children: Lynne Caryl, Randy Mass., Craig Caryl, Matthew Somers. BA, CUNY, 1976; MS, Lehman Coll., 1980; PhD, The Fielding Inst., 1988. Lic. nursing home adminstr., N.Y. Activities dir. Wartburg Luth. Nursing Home, N.Y.C., 1980-82; prof. Lehman Coll., N.Y.C., 1982-84; pres. Mrion Somers, N.Y.C., 1985—; chief recreation therapist Kingsbrook Jewish Med. Ctr. and Rutland Nursing Home, 1989-91; adminstr. in tng. Hebrew Home for the Aging, Palisades Nursing Home, Riverdale, N.Y., 1991-92; grant reader HHS, Washington, 1980—; observer White House Conf. on Aging, 1982; bd. dirs. Sr. Action in Gray Environ., 1980-84. Author viewer's guide for ABC-TV prodn. The Shell Seekers, Last Wish, The Home, for art jour. Creative Exit, 1994; exhibited watercolors, poetry and photography, 1996. Advisor Sen. A. D'Amato, N.Y., 1981-82. Recipient Profl. award Met. Recreation & Pk. Soc., N.Y.C., 1985. Mem. Gerontol. Soc. Am., Nat. Coun. on Aging, Nat. Recreation and Pk. Assn. (Presdl. award 1984), N.Y. State Therapeutic Recreation Soc. (chair 1983-84, pres. 1984-85), Am. Therapeutic Recreation Soc., Nat. Assn. Retirement Profls., Internat. Soc. Retirement Planning. Office: 601 7th St Brooklyn NY 11215-3708

SOMERS, SUZANNE, actress, singer; b. San Bruno, Calif., Oct. 16, 1946; divorced; 1 child; m. Alan Hamel. Student, Lone Mountain Sch., San Francisco Coll. for Women; studies with Charles Conrad. Actress: (feature films) Yesterday's Hero, 1979, Bullitt, 1968, Daddy's Gone a Hunting, 1969, Fools, 1970, American Graffitti, 1973, Magnum Force, 1973, Nothing Personal, 1980, Serial Mom, 1994, Seduced By Evil, 1994; (TV films) Sky Heist, 1975, It Happened at Lakewood Manor, 1977, Zuma Beach, 1978, Keeping Secrets, 1991, Rich Men, Single Women, 1990, Exclusive, 1992; (TV series) Three's Company, 1977-81, She's the Sheriff, 1987, Step by Step, 1991—, The Suzanne Somers Show, 1994; (TV mini-series) Hollywood Wives, 1985; performer Las Vegas (Nev.) Hilton, MGM Grand, Las Vegas, Sands Hotel, Atlantic City, USO, various TV comms.; author: Touch Me Again, 1973, Some People Live More than Others, Keeping Secrets, 1988. Office: Chasin Agy 8899 Beverly Blvd Ste 716 Los Angeles CA 90048*

SOMERSTEIN, AURORA ABRERA, preschool administrator, educator; b. Manila, Feb. 17, 1943; d. Bernardo Paez and Rosalia (Sityar) Abrera; m. Jules Leon Somerstein, Dec. 10, 1967 (div. July 1995); children: Joseph, Sandra, Marc. BA in English, U. Philippines, Manila, 1964; MA in English Edn., NYU, 1978, MA in Elem. Edn., 1987; postgrad., U. Pitts., Oxford (Eng.) U., 1964-66, 86. Cert. tchr., N.Y. Instr. U. Pitts., 1965-66, U. of the East, Manila, 1968-69; tchr. Am. Internat. Sch., Manila, 1966, Domenec High Sch., Pitts., 1967-68; substitute tchr. Lakeland and Peekskill Sch. Dist., N.Y., 1975-77; exec. dir. Internat. Pre-Sch. Ctr., Inc., N.Y.C., 1977—; instr. Bd. Coop. Ednl. Svcs., N.Y.C., 1989—; exec. sec. Ctr. Ednl. TV, Manila, 1964; sec. NYU, 1973-74, UN, N.Y.C., 1975; producer, interviewer Continental Cablevision, N.Y.C., 1984—; child devel. adviser Westchester County, N.Y.C., 1989—; cons. Hudson Valley Export-Import, Inc., N.Y.C., 1988-92. Vol. Philippine Band of Mercy, Manila, 1963-93. Mem. Nat. Child Care Assn., Nat. Assn. Edn. Young Children, Nat. Coun. Tchrs. English, N.Y. Child Care Assn., Assn. Childhood Edn. Internat., Child Care Coun. Westchester, Manitoga, Peekskill/Cortlandt C. of C. (bd. dirs. 1989-92). Democrat. Office: Internat Pre-Sch Ctr Inc PO Box 187 Buchanan NY 10511-0187

SOMERVILL, BARBARA ANN, small business owner; b. New Rochelle, N.Y., July 28, 1948; d. Harold Phillip and Hope Agatha (Hayden) Klesius; m. Michael O. McWilliams, June 10, 1972 (div. June 1986); children: Scott, Matthew; m. Charles Forrest Somervill, June 30, 1990; children: Seth, Taylor. BA, St. Lawrence U., 1970. Chmn. dept. writing techniques Pinewood Pvt. Sch., Los Altos, Calif., 1980-86; mgr. corp. comm. Karastan Bigelow, Greenville, S.C., 1986-88; editor Monarch Edge, food mag., Greenville, 1988-94; pres. Somervill Inc., Simpsonville, S.C., 1994—; mem. adv. bd. Local advt. rev. bd. Better Bus. Bur., Greenville, 1989-93; mem. adv. bd. Pearce Young Angel/Monarch Health Care, Greenville, 1990-93. Bd. dirs. Christmas Is For Kids, Greenville, 1989-94, Greenville Soup Kitchen, 1994—. Mem. NAFE, Women in Comm., Greenville Duplicate Bridge Club (bd. dirs. 1994—). Episcopalian. Home and Office: 103 Rainwood Dr Simpsonville SC 29681

SOMERVILLE, CAROLYN JOHNSON, principal; b. Parkersburg, W.Va., Mar. 11, 1942; d. George Hughes and Nellie Maude (Cather) Johnson; m. Ron D. Somerville, Aug. 22, 1965 (div. 1981); children: Jennifer Nicole Somerville Moon, Ron Dean. BS, Asbury Coll., 1963; MEd, Ohio U., 1966. Cert. elem. prin., Okla. Tchr. jr. high Prince George County Schs., Md., 1963-64; grad. asst. Ohio U., Athens, 1964-65; social worker W.Va. Dept. of Welfare, Huntington, 1965-67; counselor jr. high Wood County Schs., Parkersburg, W.Va., 1972-78, tchr. jr. high, 1979-81; substitute tchr. Yukon (Okla.) Schs., 1982-83; asst. prin. elem. Western Heights Schs., Oklahoma City, 1983-85, Skyview Elem. Sch., 1985—; presenter workshops; cons. in field. Mem. adv. bd. Planned Parenthood, Parkersburg, W.Va., 1974-77; counselor, speaker Gov. Com. on Crime and Delinquency, Parkersburg, 1974-77; tchr. Sunday sch. Trinity Bapt. Ch., Yukon, 1982-83; sponsor Alateen, 1988-93. Named Adminstr. of Yr. Dist. 11A, 1995. Fellow Nat. Prins. Assn., State of Okla. Prins. Assn.; mem. ASCD, Okla. Assn. Elem. Sch. Prins. (com.), Coop. Coun. Okla. Sch. Adminstrn., Yukon Curriculum Coun. Home: 113 W Vail Dr Yukon OK 73099-5829 Office: Skyview Elem Sch 2800 Mustang Rd Yukon OK 73099

SOMERVILLE, DAPHINE HOLMES, elementary education educator; b. Clinton, N.C., Jan. 19, 1940; d. George Henry and Mamie Estelle (Streeter) Holmes; m. Kalford Burton Somerville, Dec. 26, 1970 (div. Sept. 1992); 1 child, Daria Lynn. AA, Blackburn Coll., 1959, BA, 1961; MS in Edn., Hofstra U., 1967; postgrad., Columbia U., 1971. Permanent teaching cert. common br. subjects grades 1-8. Tchr. East Islip (N.Y.) Sch. Dist., 1961—; mem., instr. Outcome Based/Mastery Learning/Excellence in Learning Com., East Islip, 1984-89; mentor East Islip Sch. Dist., 1987-88, mem. sch. improvement team, 1989-91, staff devel. com., 1992—. Co-author: (booklet) Baptist Training Union Study Guide, 1976; founder, co-author: (tutoring program) Adopt-A-School Child/Family, 1990. Mem. Bay Shore (N.Y.) Civic Assn. and Bay Shore Pub. Schs. Task Force for the Advancement of Equality of Ednl. Opportunity, 1967-69; sec. Islip Town NAACP, Bay Shore, 1965-90; mem. First Bapt. Ch., Bay Shore, 1951—, trustee, 1972-90; dir. Bapt. Tng. Union, 1974-81. Recipient Cmty. Svc. award Town Bd.-Town of Islip, Suffolk County, 1982, Br. Recognition award Islip Town NAACP, 1987, Disting. Svc. award L.I. Region NAACP, 1993, Dedicated Svc. award Ptnrs. in Edn. First Bapt. Ch. of Bayshore, 1995. Mem. Nat. Coun. Negro Women (life, ednl. involvement award 1993), East Islip Tchrs. Assn. (past bldg. rep.), N.Y. State United Tchrs. Democrat. Home: 130 Carman Rd Dix Hills NY 11746-5648 Office: J F Kennedy Elem Sch Woodland Dr East Islip NY 11730

SOMERVILLE, DIANA ELIZABETH, author; b. Lincoln, Nebr., June 12, 1942; d. Edward John and Eunice Louise (Johnson) Wagner; m. Dale Springer Johnson, Aug. 7, 1961 (div. 1971); children: Carlyle Johnson Lee, Kelmie Blake. BA in English Lit., Centenary Coll., 1967. Dir. info. office Nat. Ctr. Atmospheric Rsch., Boulder, Colo., 1969-81; mgr. info. svcs. RDD Cons., Boulder, 1981-82; sci. writer U. Colo., Boulder, 1983-87; mgr. comm. Optoelectronic Computing Sys. Ctr., Boulder, 1987-88; columnist Daily Camera, Boulder, 1992—; lectr. U. Colo., 1996—. Editor: Optimum Utilization of Human Knowledge, 1983, Artful Meditation, 1995; contbr. numerous articles to mags. including New Scientist, Earth mag. and in World Book Ency. Mem. women's caucus AAAS, 1969-75; mem. com. on pub. info. Am. Geophys. Union, 1977-78; mem. ednl. programs com. Am. Meteorol. Soc., 1978-80; mem. Turning the Wheel dance/theatre co. Recipient Exceptional Achievement award Coun. for the Advancement and Support of Edn., Gold medal, 1986, Gold Pick award Pub. Rels. Soc. Am., 1985, Gold Quill award Internat. Assn. Bus. Comms., 1985. Mem. Nat. Writers Union, Nat. Assn. Sci. Writers, Am. Soc. Journalists and Authors, Boulder County Healthy Communities Initiative.

SOMERVILLE, MARY ROBINSON, library director; b. Fairfield, Ala., Aug. 16, 1941; d. E. Bryce Robinson, Jr. and Margaret Allen m. Ormond Somerville, July 10, 1964 (d. 1976). BA in English with honors in Writing, U. N.C., 1963; MA in English, U. Colo., 1965; MLS, U. Okla., 1971. Youth svcs. adminstr. Lincoln City (Nebr.) Librs., 1973-78; youth svcs. mgr. Louisville (Ky.) Free Pub. Libr., 1978-88, proj. dir. automation, 1985-86, grants adminstr., 1986-87, mgr. employee rels., 1987-88; youth svcs. adminstr. Broward County Libr., Ft. Lauderdale, Fla., 1988-90; youth svcs. adminstr. Miami-Dade Pub. Libr., 1990-91, asst. dir. branches and spl. svcs., 1991-93, interim dir., 1993-94, dir., 1994—. Named Outstanding Alumnus Sch. Libr. and Info. Studies U. Okla., 1995. Mem. ALA (spkr., lectr. 22 states, pres. Assn. for Libr. Svc. to children 1987-88, mem. 5 person del. to former Soviet Union 1989, cons. U.S. Dept. Edn. 1988, chair nominating com. 1992, planning and budget assembly 1992, coun. 1992, mem. exec. bd. 1993-95, pres. 1996-97, initiator projects that won H.W. Wilson Staff Devel. award and 4 John Cotton Dana awards), Phi Beta Kappa, Beta Phi Mu. Home: 800 West Ave # 735 Miami Beach FL 33139 Office: Miami Dade Pub Libr System 101 W Flagler St Miami FL 33130-1523

SOMERVILLE, VIRGINIA PAULINE WINTERS, executive assistant; b. Jo Daviess County, Ill., Jan. 14, 1936; d. Roy and Effie Stadel Winters; m. Thomas C. Somerville, June 8, 1957; children: Tod Andrew, Ian Winter. BMus magna cum laude, U. Dubuque, 1957; MMus with honors, Roosevelt U., 1964. Music tchr. pub. sch. Jessup, Iowa, 1959-60; music tchr. pvt. sch. P.R., 1960-61; prof. music St. Andrews Presbyn. Coll., Laurinburg, N.C., 1966-71; pvt. music tchr. Glendale, Calif., 1976-86; exec. asst. to sr. min. First Congl. Ch. L.A., 1986—; workshop and seminar leader Chapman Coll. Ch. Sec.'s Seminar, Orange, Calif., 1991, 92. Performer one-woman musical shows. Active PTA, Canoga Park, Calif., Glendale, 1972-84, Glendale Assistance League, 1975—. Recipient Citizen Appreciation award PTA-Verdugo Woodlands, Glendale, 1980, various music awards. Mem. Nat. Exec. Secs., Nat. Assn. Tchrs. of Singing. Office: First Congl Ch LA 540 S Commonwealth Ave Los Angeles CA 90020-1298

SOMMA, BEVERLY KATHLEEN, medical and marriage educator; b. Bayonne, N.J., June 13, 1938; d. Leroy and Isabelle (Lysaght) Latourette; m. Louis Anthony Somma, Nov. 24, 1973; children: Francis, Keith. AS, Ocean County Coll., 1973; BA, Georgian Ct., 1977; MAT, Monmouth Coll., 1978; postgrad., U. Pa., 1980-85, 88-89. Nurse's aide Community Meml. Hosp., Toms River, N.J., 1971-72; with marriage coun. dept. psychiatry U. Pa. Sch. Medicine, Phila., 1993—; with Helene Fuld Med. Ctr. Edn., 1993—; ednl. cons. Ctr. for Cognitive Edn., Yardley, Pa., 1990—, tng. program Archdiocese Phila., Penn Found., Inc., 1993; lectr. Marriage Coun. of Phila. dept. psychiatry, sch. medicine U. Pa., 1993—; with Helene Fuld Med. Ctr. Edn., 1993—. Voter svc. chmn. LWV, Toms River, N.J., 1971-72; contact rep. Pro Life Coalition, Phila.; vol. nursing tutor Ocean County Coll., Toms River, 1972; vol. tchr.'s aide St. Michael the Archangel, Levittown, Pa., 1987-88; vol. VITA; counselor Bucks County Coun. Alcoholism and Drug Dependence, Inc., 1984-93; active World Affairs Coun. Phila. All Am. scholar; recipient U.S. Achievement Acad. Nat. award. Mem. Nat. Soc. for Fund Raising Execs., Alumni Assn. Georgian Ct. Coll., Ocean County Coll., Bucks County C.C., Sigma Tau Delta. Republican. Methodist. Home: 1506 Kathy Dr Yardley PA 19067-1717

SOMMER, ANNEMARIE, pediatrician; b. Königsberg, Prussia, Federal Republic Germany, Jan. 1, 1932; came to U.S., 1955; d. Heinrich Otto and Maria Magdalena (Kruppa) S. BA, Wittenberg U., Springfield, Ohio, 1960; MD, Ohio State U., 1964. Diplomate Am. Bd. Pediat., Am. Bd. Med. Genetics. Intern Grant Hosp., Columbus, Ohio, 1964-65; resident in pediat. Children's Hosp., Columbus, 1965-67; NIH fellow in med. genetics, 1968-70; asst. prof. pediatrics Coll. Medicine Ohio State U., Columbus, 1975-80, assoc. prof., 1980—, chief genetics div., 1984—; mem. adv. bd. Heinzerling Found., Columbus, 1980—; bd. dirs. Regional Genetics Ctr., Columbus. Contbr. articles to profl. jours. Com. mem. Ohio Prevention MR/DD Coalition, Columbus, 1987; bd. dirs. Franklin County Bd. Health, Columbus, 1985—. Fellow Am. Acad. Pediatrics, Am. Bd. Med. Genetics, Am. Coll. Med. Genetics (founder); mem. Am. Med. Women's Assn., Cen. Ohio Pediatric Soc., Midwest Soc. for Pediatric Research, Dublin (Ohio) Hist. Soc. Lutheran. Home: 4700 Brand Rd Dublin OH 43017-9530 Office: Ohio State Coll of Medicine Chief Sect of Genetics 700 Childrens Dr Columbus OH 43205-2666

SOMMER, PHYLLIS AYN, women's health nurse; b. Chgo., Sept. 5, 1954; d. Dave C. and Adele H. (Ebner) Goldstein; m. Mark Sommer, Aug. 16, 1981; children: Ariel, Everett, Adrian, David. Diploma, Wesley-Passavant Sch. Nursing, 1978; BSN, U. Wash., 1985; MSN, U. Ill. RN, Ill. Vol Peace Corps, Niger, West Africa, 1978-81; staff nurse labor & delivery Virginia Mason Hosp., Seattle, 1982-85; staff nurse out-patient chemotherapy The Mason Clinic, Seattle, 1981-85; staff nurse labor & delivery Springbranch Meml. Hosp., Houston, 1989-91, W. Houston Med. Ctr., 1989-91; nurse clinician in birth ctr. Ill. Masonic Med. Ctr., Chgo., 1992—. Contbr. article to jour. in field. Mem. Am. Coll. Nurse-Midwives, Sigma Theta Tau. Democrat. Home: 933 Aspen Dr Buffalo Grove IL 60089-1316

SOMMERFELD, MARIANNA, retired social worker, writer; b. Frankfurt, Germany, Jan. 25, 1920; d. Martin and Helene (Schott) S. BA, Smith Coll., 1940; MA, Radcliffe Coll., 1946; MSW, Simmons Coll., 1957. Lic. ind. social worker. Tchr. Latin, German, English Burnham Sch. Girls, Northampton, Mass., 1940-43; German translator Yale Inst. Human Rels., New Haven, 1943-44; tchr. Northfield (Mass.) Sch. Girls, 1944-45; psychiat. social worker McLean Hosp., Belmont, Mass., 1957-59, Gaebler Children's Unit/Met. State Hosp., Waltham, Mass., 1959-62, Boston U./Boston City Hosp., 1962-67, New Eng. Med. Ctr., Boston, 1967-71; pvt. practice Cambridge, Mass., 1962-68; supr. clin. social work Erich Lindeman Health Ctr., Boston, 1971-90; writer, 1991—. Author: Marianna Sommerfeld: Diary of a Single Woman, 1991. Vol. Cambridge Sch., 1993. Mem. NOW, AFL-CIO, Planned Parenthood, So. Poverty Law Ctr., Nat. Writers Union, Women's Nat. Book Assn., PEN New Eng., Profl. Writers Cape Cod.

SOMMERS, MAXINE MARIE BRIDGET, writer, educator, publisher; b. Crystal Falls, Mich., May 7, 1932; d. Francis Ernest and Irene Catherine (Raher) Munns; m. Clemens Struve, June 10, 1952 (div. 1975); children: Stephen, Joseph; m. Norval Isom Sommers (dec. 1989). Student, Milw. Downer Coll. for Women, 1948-49, U. Tex. Med. Br., Galveston, 1949-50, St. Mary's Hosp., 1950-51. Owner, operator Pound Sterling Publ., 1982—, Pound Sterling Media Svc., 1983—. Author: A Texan on the Road Again to the Far East, 1992; author 28 books and mini-books on cuisine, and travel, also children's books. Pres. Corpus Christi Symphony Guild, 1967-69, Tex. Assn. Symphony Orchestras, 1969; bd. dirs. Corpus Christi Symphony Soc., 1975—, South Tex. Health Syss. Agy., 1982-85; bd. dirs., pvt. svc. trainer Tex. divsn. Am. Cancer Soc., 1974-94; pres. Tex. Coastal Bend Mental Health Assn., 1976-78. Recipient cert. of award Byliners Tex. Wide Writers, 1992, Bus. Assoc. Night award Am. Bus. Women's Assn., 1992, cert. merit Corpus Christi Symphony Guild, 1969, cert. recognition Tex. Women's Assn. Symphony Orchestras, 1969, various awards Am. Cancer Soc. Mem. Byliners, Austin Writers League, Internat. Platform Assn. Home: 4270 Ocean Dr Corpus Christi TX 78411-1283

SOMMERVILLE, JEAN L., financial company executive, banker, accountant. BSBA, U. Redlands; MBA, UCLA. CPA, Calif. Various positions to sr. mgr. fin. svcs. industry group Price Waterhouse, L.A., 1977-92; sr. v.p. ops. analysis Gt. Western Fin. Corp., Chatsworth, Calif., 1992—, Gt. Western Bank subs. Gt. Western Fin. Corp., Chatsworth, 1992—. Mem. AICPA, Inst. Internal Auditors, Fin. Mgrs. Soc., Am. Woman's Soc. CPA's, Calif. Soc. CPA's (chmn. com. on depository instns.). Office: Gt Western Fin Corp 9200 Oakdale Ave Chatsworth CA 91311

SOMVILLE, MARILYN F., university dean. Dean Mason Gross Sch. Arts, New Brunswick, N.J. Office: Rutgers U Mason Gross Sch Arts New Brunswick NJ 08903

SONDERBY, SUSAN PIERSON, federal bankruptcy judge; b. Chgo., May 15, 1947; d. George W. and Shirley L. (Eckstrom) Pierson; m. James A. De Witt, June 14, 1975 (dec. 1978); m. Peter R. Sonderby, Apr. 7, 1990. AA, Joliet (Ill.) Jr. Coll., 1967; BA, U. Ill., 1969; JD, John Marshall Law Sch., 1973. Bar: Ill. 1973, U.S. Dist. Ct. (cen. and so. dists.) Ill. 1978, U.S. Dist. Ct. (no. dist.) Ill. 1984, U.S. Ct. Appeals (7th Cir.) 1984. Assoc. O'Brien, Garrison, Berard, Kusta and De Witt, Joliet, 1973-75, ptnr., 1975-77; asst. atty. gen. consumer protection div., litigation sect. Office of the Atty. Gen., Chgo., 1977-78; asst. atty. gen., chief consumer protection div. Office of the Atty. Gen., Springfield, Ill., 1978-83; U.S. trustee for no. dist. Ill. Chgo., 1983-86; judge U.S. Bankruptcy Ct. (no. dist.) Ill., Chgo., 1986—; adj. faculty De Paul U. Coll. Law, Chgo., 1986; spl. asst. atty. gen., 1972-78; past mem. U.S. Trustee adv. com., consumer adv. coun. Fed. Res. Bd.; past sec. of State Fraudulent I.D. com., Dept. of Ins. Task Force on Improper Claims Practices. Mem. Fourth Presbyn. Ch., Art Inst. Chgo.; past mem. Westminster Presbyn. Ch., Chgo. Coun. of Fgn. Rels.; past bd. dirs. Land of Lincoln Coun. Girl Scouts U.S.; past mem. individual guarantors com. Goodman Theatre, Chgo.; past chmn. clubs and orgns. Sangamon County United Way Capital campaign; past bd. dirs., chmn. house rules com. and legal subcom. Lake Point Tower; past mem. Family Svc. Ctr., Aid to Retarded Citizens, Henson Robinson Zoo. Master Abraham Lincoln Marovitz Inn of Ct.; fellow Am. Coll. Bankruptcy; mem. Nat. Conf. Bankruptcy Judges (legis. outreach com.), Am. Bankruptcy Inst., Comml. Law League Am. (exec. coun. bankruptcy and insolvency sect., bankruptcy com., past vice chmn. U.S. Trustee Rev. com., edn. com.), Law Club of Chgo., Legal Club of Chgo. (hon.), Nordic Law Club. Office: US Bankruptcy Ct 219 S Dearborn St Ste 638 Chicago IL 60604-1704

SONDOCK, RUBY KLESS, retired judge; b. Houston, Apr. 26, 1926; d. Herman Lewis and Celia (Juran) Kless; m. Melvin Adolph Sondock, Apr. 22, 1944; children: Marcia Cohen, Sandra Marcus. AA, Cottey Coll., Nevada, Mo., 1944; BS, U. Houston, 1959, LLB, 1961. Bar: Tex. 1961, U.S. Supreme Ct. 1977. Pvt. practice, Houston, 1961-73, 89—; judge Harris County Ct. Domestic Rels. (312th Dist.), 1973-77, 234th Jud. Dist. Ct., Houston, 1977-82, 83-89; justice Tex. Supreme Ct., Austin, 1982; of counsel Weil Gotshal and Manges, 1989-93, Houston Ctr., 1993—. Mem. ABA, Tex. Bar Assn., Houston Bar Assn., Houston Assn. Women Lawyers, Order of Barons, Phi Theta Phi, Kappa Beta Pi, Phi Kappa Phi, Alpha Epsilon Pi. Office: 2650 Two Houston Ctr 909 Fannin Houston TX 77010

SONES, ROSALIE T., elementary education educator; b. N.Y.C.; m. Richard M. Sones; 2 children. BS in Elem. Edn., St. John's U., 1966; MA in Elem. Edn., Adelphi U., 1988. Cert. tchr., N.Y. 5th and 6th grade tchr. Hicksville (N.Y.) Pub. Schs., 1966-92, middle sch. math. tchr., 1992—; profl. devel. com. Hicksville Pub. Schs., 1986-90. Leader Girl Scouts Am., Island Trees, N.Y., 1980-84. Mem. NEA, N.Y. NEA (Long Island regional coun. del.), Nat. Coun. Tchrs. Math., Hicksville Congress Tchrs. (1st v.p., negotiator). Office: Hicksville Pub Schs Jerusalem Ave Hicksville NY 11801

SONES, SHARI CAROLYN, counselor, educator; b. Warner Robins, Ga., May 3, 1966; d. Jon Chalmers and Eleanor Jean (Spaulding) Niemeyer. BS, Brenau Coll., 1988; MS, Ga. State U., 1991. Cert. Nat. Bd. for Cert. Counselors, Inc.; lic. profl. counselor. Asst. tchr. Hi Hope, Lawrenceville, Ga., 1988; counselor Anxiety Disorder Inst. Atlanta, 1991-94; pvt. practice Atlanta, Ga., 1994—; tchr. Oglethorpe U., Atlanta, 1993; clin. dir. Trauma and Abuse Resource Program, 1994—. Vol. group leader Ga. Counsel on Child Abuse, Atlanta, 1991-92. Mem. ACA, Nat. Assn. Alcoholism and Drug Abuse Counselors. Office: Anxiety Disorders Inst 1 Dunwoody Pk Ste 112 Atlanta GA 30338

SONI, MARIA HABIB, controller; b. Kahale, Beirut, Lebanon, July 27, 1956; came to U.S., 1979; d. Habib Hanna and Sadie (Zeghondy) Abi-Khalil; divorced; 1 child, Jean-Noel. M in Child Psychology and Math, U. Lyon, 1975; BA, Beirut Bus. Sch., 1977; BA in Acctg. Tchr. Dominican Sisters,

Beirut, 1974-78; adminstr. Daoud Engring., Beirut, 1978-79; v.p. Sa-Beers Jewelry, 1979-83; v.p., exec. adminstr. Gaylin Buick, Union, N.J., 1986-91; adminstr., treas., contr. Ruckstuhl USA, Union, N.J., 1992—; cons. in field. Mem. Rotary (bd. dirs. 1995—, dir. 1995—, reporter mag. 1995—), Interact Club (chmn.). Republican. Home: 2243 Morris Ave Union NJ 07083 Office: Ruckstuhl USA Ltd 1480 Ridgeway St Union NJ 07083

SONI, POONAM, child psychiatrist; b. India, Jan. 24, 1959; came to U.S., 1959; d. Raj Pal and Kusum (Kapila) S. AB, U. Chgo., 1981; MD, U. Tenn., 1986. Bd. cert. adult psychiatry, bd. cert. child and adolescent psychiatry. Staff psychiatrist Valley Mental Health, Salt Lake City, 1991—; asst. prof. psychiatry, adj. asst. prof. pediats. U. Utah, Salt Lake City, 1994—; dir. psychiat. svcs. and child protection team Primary Children's Med. Ctr., Salt Lake City, 1994—; cons. Shriners Hosp., Salt Lake City, 1994—. Mem. APSAC (bd. dirs. 1994-96), Intermountain Acad. Child and Adolescent Psychiatry (pres. 1994-95, del. 1996—). Office: ARTEC/Valley Mental Health 3809 W 6200 S Kearns UT 84118

SONIAT, KATHERINE THOMPSON, English educator, poet; b. Washington, Jan. 11, 1942; d. Raymond Webb Thompson and Katherine Lenox (Hayward) Claiborne; children: Shelton, Ashton. BA n History, Newcomb Coll., New Orleans, 1964; MA in English, Tulane U., 1983. Asst. prof. English Hollins Coll., Roanoke, Va., 1989-91; assoc. prof. English Va. Poly. Inst. and State U., Blacksburg, 1991—. Poet: Notes of Departure, 1984 (Camden Poetry prize), Winter Toys, 1990, Cracking Eggs, 1991, A Shared Life, 1993 (Iowa prize). Mem. steering com. Second Harvest Foodbank, Roanoke, 1994-95; local organizer Share Our Strength, Washington, 1995. Recipient Camden (N.J.) Poetry award Walt WhitmanCtr. for Arts, 1984, fellowship, scholarship Breadloaf Writers Conf., Middlebury Coll., Vt., 1985, 89, Va. Prize for poetry Va. Coun. for Arts, Richmond, 1989, Edwin Ford Piper award U. Iowa Press, Iowa City, 1993, Ann Stanford prizes U. Soc. Calif., L.A., 1993, 95. Mem. Associated Writing Programs. Office: Va Tech English Dept Williams Hall Blacksburg VA 24061-0112

SONNE, MAGGIE LEE, sales executive; b. Pasadena, Calif., July 14, 1958; d. Roscoe Newbold Jr. and Ann Miriam (Vierhus) S.; m. Donald Alan Blackburn, Sept. 8, 1979 (div. 1983). AS, Oreg. Inst. Tech., 1981, BS, 1983. Sales trainee NCR Corp., Dayton, Ohio, 1983-84; sales rep. NCR Corp., Portland, Oreg., 1984-86; account mgr. NCR Corp., Seattle, 1986-87; sr. account mgr. NCR Corp., Portland, 1987-88; sr. account rep. Wang Labs., Portland, 1988-91; account exec. Tandem Computers, Portland, 1991-94; sr. acct. exec. Fin. Svcs., L.A., 1994-96; pres. Travel Club Adventures, Surfside, Calif., 1996—. Active Emily's List, Project Vote Smart, Ams. for Change, Presdl. Task Force, Pres. Coun., Tandem Computers, Inc. Mem. Soc. Advancement Mgmt., Costeau Soc., Alpha Chi. Home & Office: PO Box 323 Surfside CA 90743-0323

SONNENFELDT, MARJORIE HECHT, public relations executive, consultant; b. Balt., Feb. 8, 1931; d. Stewart Emanuel and Sylvia (Cahn) Hecht; m. Helmut Sonnenfeldt, Oct. 4, 1953; children: Babette Sonnenfeldt Lubben, Walter H., Stewart H. AB with honors magna cum laude, Smith Coll., 1952. Adminstr. U.S. Dept. State, Washington, 1952-54; rschr./writer Dem. Nat. Com., Washington, 1954-56, Robert L. Spivack, Journalist, Washington, 1956-59; writer, editor Com. Nat. Trade Policy, Washington, 1959-63; freelance writer, cons., editor Washington, 1964-69; mem. coun. staff Montgomery County Coun., Rockville, Md., 1970-71; community rels. adviser Montgomery County Planning Bd., Silver Spring, Md., 1971-73; chmn. Montgomery County Bd. Appeals, Rockville, 1973-81; exec. dir. Consumers World Trade, Washington, 1978-80; dir. internat. govt. affairs, v.p. Hill and Knowlton Inc., Washington, 1981-87; v.p. Fleishman-Hillard, Inc., Washington, 1987—. Bd. dirs. D.C. chpt. Am. Jewish Com., 1982—; bd. dirs. Lourie Ctr. Infants & Young Children, Rockville, 1993—. Office: Fleishman-Hillard Inc 1301 Connecticut Ave NW Washington DC 20036-1815

SONS, LINDA RUTH, mathematics educator; b. Chicago Heights, Ill., Oct. 31, 1939; d. Robert and Ruth (Diekelman) S. AB in Math., Ind. U., 1961; MS in Math., Cornell U., 1963, PhD in Math., 1966. Teaching asst. Cornell U., Ithaca, N.Y., 1961-63, instr. math., summer 1963, rsch. asst., 1963-65; asst. prof. No. Ill. U., De Kalb, 1965-70, assoc. prof., 1970-78, prof., 1978—; presdl. tchg. prof. No. Ill. U., DeKalb, 1994—; vis. assoc. prof. U. London, 1970-71; dir. undergrad. studies math. dept. No. Ill. U., 1971-77, exec. sec. univ. coun., 1978-79; chair faculty fund No. Ill. U. Found., De Kalb, 1982—. Author: (with others) A Study Guide for Introduction to Mathematics, 1976, Mathematical Thinking in a Quantitative World, 1990; contbr. articles to profl. jours. Mem. campus ministry com. No. Ill. Dist. Luth. Ch./Mo. Synod, Hillside, 1977—; mem. ch. coun. Immanuel Luth. Ch., De Kalb, 1978-85, 87-89; pres. Luth. Women's Missionary League, 1974-87; bd. dirs., treas. De Kalb County Migrant Ministry, 1967-78. NSF Rsch. grantee, 1970-72, 74-75; recipient 1988 Award for Disting. Svc. of Ill. Sect. of the Math Assn. Am., 1991 Award for Excellence in Coll. Teaching of Ill. Coun. Tchrs. Math. Mem. Am. Math. Soc., Assn. for Women in Math., Math. Assn. Am. (mem. nat. bd. govs. 1989-92, mem. com. undergrad. program in math. 1990-96, Disting. Svc. to Ill. Sect. award 1988, Disting. Coll. or U. Tchg. of Math. award 1995), Ill. Math. Assn. (v.p. sect., pres.-elect, pres., then past pres. 1982-87, bd. dirs. 1989-92), London Math. Soc., Phi Beta Kappa (pres. No. Ill. assn. 1981-85), Sigma Xi (past. chpt. pres.). Office: No Ill U Dept Math Scis De Kalb IL 60115

SONSTEBY, KRISTI LEE, healthcare consultant; b. Anoka, Minn., Nov. 16, 1958; d. Glenn and Rosella (Rebischke) S. Charge nurse Baylor U. Med. Ctr., Dallas, 1980-81; clin. nurse specialist ARA Living Ctrs., Houston, 1981-86; pres., owner KristiCare Inc., Dallas, 1986-89; healthcare cons. SDG Ent., Inc., Austin, Tex., 1989-90; pres., owner NursePlus Inc., Mpls., 1991—; judge Provider Mag., Washington, 1988; cons. in field; lectr. in field; conductor workshops in field. Patentee and patent pending in field; author: Handbooks for Nurses, Vols. I-X, 1991; contbr. articles to profl. jours. Vol. to elderly various civic orgns. Office: Nurse Plus Inc 716 Highway 10 NE Ste 163 Minneapolis MN 55434-2389

SONTAG, SUSAN, writer; b. N.Y.C., Jan. 16, 1933; m. Philip Rieff, 1950 (div. 1958); 1 son, David. BA, U. Chgo., 1951; MA in English, Harvard U., 1954, MA in Philosophy, 1955. Instr. English U. Conn., Storrs, 1953-54; editor Commentary, N.Y.C., 1959; lectr. philosophy City Coll., N.Y.C., 1959-60, Sarah Lawrence Coll., Bronxville, 1959-60; instr. dept. religion Columbia U., N.Y.C., 1960-64; writer in residence Rutgers U., 1964-65. Author: (novels) The Benefactor, 1963, Death Kit, 1967, The Volcano Lover: A Romance, 1992; (plays) Alice in Bed: A Play in Eight Scenes, 1993; (stories) I, etcetera, 1978, The Way We Live Now, 1991; (essays) Against Interpretation, 1966 (Mat. Book award nomination 1966), Styles of Radical Will, 1969, Trip to Hanoi, 1969, On Photography, 1977 (Nat. Book Critics Circle award for criticism 1978), Illness as Metaphor, 1978, Under the Sign of Saturn, 1980, AIDS and Its Metaphors, 1989; (anthology) A Susan Sontag Reader, 1982; screenwriter, dir.: (films) Duet for Cannibals, 1969, Brother Carl, 1971; dir.: (films) Promised Lands, 1974, Unguided Tour, 1983; editor, author of introduction: Antonin Artaud: Selected Writings, 1976, A Roland Barthes Reader, 1982, Danilo Kis's Homo Poeticus: Essays & Interviews, 1995. Guggenheim fellow, 1966, 75, Rockefeller Found. fellow, 1965, 74, MacArthur fellow, 1990-95; recipient George Polk Meml. award, 1966, Ingram Merrill Found. award in lit. in field of Am. Letters, 1976, Creative Arts award Brandeis U., 1976, Malaparte prize, 1992; named Officier de l'Ordre des Arts et des Lettres, France, 1984. Mem. Am. Acad. Arts and Scis. (elected 1993), Am. Acad. Arts and Letters (Arts and Letters award 1976), PEN (pres. Am. Ctr. 1987-89). Address: 470 W 24th St New York NY 10011

SOPER, ANNE MARIE, psychologist; b. Indpls., Feb. 19, 1951; d. William and Helen (Starost) Speicher; m. Dan Allen Soper, Nov. 19, 1978; children: Thomas, Mark, Elise. Student, Butler U., 1969-70; BA summa cum laude, Mich. State U., 1973; MA, Ball State U., 1977; MEd, Harvard U., 1982; EdD, Boston U., 1990. Cert. sch. psychologist, Ind. Sch. psychologist Logansport (Ind.) Pub. Schs., 1977-78, Indpls. Pub. Schs., 1978-80; vocat. rehab. counselor Morgan Meml. Goodwill, Boston, 1980-81; psychology intern Simmons Coll., Boston, 1982-83, West-Ros-Park Mental Health, Boston, 1984-86; counselor Resolve, Arlington, Mass., 1986-90; psychology intern South End. Cmty. Health, Boston, 1995-96; psychologist Metrowest Mental Health, Marlborough, Mass., 1995—, Tri City Mental Health, Medford, Mass., 1995—; tchg. asst. Boston U., 1983-84. Butler U. scholar, 1969. Mem. APA, Mass. Psychol. Assn., Phi Beta Kappa.

SOPER, VICKI MARIE, English educator; b. Wewoka, Okla., Apr. 5, 1954; d. Wilbur Thomas and Peggy Ann (Ledbetter) Butler; m. Dana Leon Soper, Aug. 6, 1971; children: Jeremy Scott, Bridget Leigh Soper Cress, Kyle Thomas. AA, Western Tex. Coll., Snyder, 1985; BA, Eastern N.Mex. U., 1989, MA, 1991. Instr. Eastern N.Mex. U., Portales, 1989-91; adj. faculty Coll. of Southwest, Hobbs, N.Mex., 1992-94, asst. prof. English, 1994—. Contbr. poetry and fiction to various lit. mags. Mem. Hobbs Booster Club, 1994-96. Mem. MLA, AAUW, Nat. Coun. Tchrs. of English, Phi Alpha Theta, Sigma Tau Delta. Republican. Church of Christ. Home: 123 W Wolfcamp Dr Hobbs NM 88240 Office: College of the Southwest 6610 Lovington Hwy Hobbs NM 88240

SOPHER, VICKI ELAINE, museum director; b. Streator, Ill., May 22, 1943; d. Donald Bird and Thelma Elsie (Saxton) Watson; m. Terry Ray Sr., Jan. 20, 1962 (div. Aug. 1982); 1 child, Terry Ray Jr. AA, No. Va. Community Coll., 1973; BA, Am. U., 1976; MS, Bank State Coll. Edn., 1986. Adminstrv. asst. Decatur & Wilson House, Washington, 1977-81; asst. dir. Decatur House/Nat. Trust for Hist. Preservation, Washington, 1981-84, dir., 1984-95; exec. dir. Hammond-Harwood House Assn., Annapolis, Md., 1996—; cons. curator Monmouth Mus., Freehold, N.J., 1978-80; founder, pres. Historic House Mus. Metropolitan Wash. Mem. Am. Assn. Museums, Mid-Atlantic Assn. Museums, Am. Assn. for State and Local History, Victorian Soc. Am. (bd. dirs.). Home: 2621 12th St S Arlington VA 22204-4819 Office: Hammond Harwood House 19 Maryland Ave Annapolis MD 21401

SOREFF, HELEN NONIDES, artist; b. Bklyn.; d. Athan Nonides; m. Stephen M. Soreff, Nov. 13, 1960; children: Alexander, Zachery. BFA, U. Ga.; postgrad., Atlanta Art Inst., NYU; MA, L.I. U., 1972. Tchr. U. Wash., Seattle, 1969; tchr. spl. programs Hofstra U., Hempstead, N.Y., 1971-72; vis. artist Skidmore Coll., Saratoga Springs, N.Y., 1987; tchr. liberal studies Parsons Sch. Design, N.Y.C., 1988—; resident N.Y. Found. for Arts, 1982; artist-in-residence Altos de Chavon, La Romana, Dominican Republic, 1982, Dorland Mountain Art Colony, Temecula, Calif., 1992. One-person shows at Phoenix Gallery, N.Y.C., 1963, Pace U. Gallery, N.Y.C., 1968, Richard White Gallery, Seattle, 1970, Benson Gallery, Bridgehampton, 1975, Lamagna Gallery, N.Y.C., 1975, L.I. U., Brookville, N.Y., 1976, Fifty Five Mercer Gallery, N.Y.C., 1977, Bertha Urdang Gallery, N.Y.C., 1977, 78, Condeso-Lawler Gallery, N.Y.C., 1983, M-13 Gallery, N.Y.C., 1988, 89, 91, 93, 95, Guild Hall Mus., East Hampton, N.Y., 1989, Islip (N.Y.) Fine Art Mus., 1990; exhibited in group shows at M-13 Gallery, N.Y.C., 1988, 93, N.Y. Inst. Tech., Westbury, 1989, 55 Mercer Gallery, N.Y.C., 1989, Blum-Helman Gallery, N.Y.C., 1989, Artists of Springs Invitational, East Hampton, 1990, 91, Benton Gallery, Southampton, N.Y., 1992, 93, Guild Hall Mus., East Hampton, 1992, 95, N.J. State Mus., Trenton, 1992, 94, Stark Gallery, N.Y.C., 1992, Ulrich Mus., Wichita, Kans., 1992, Marymount Coll., N.Y.C., 1993, Springs (N.Y.) Invitational, 1994, Peconic Gallery, Suffolk (N.Y.) U., 1994, S.W. Tex. U., San Marcos, 1994, Bujese Gallery, East Hampton, 1994, 95, Parrish Mus., Southampton, 1994, Noyes Mus., Oceanville, N.J., 1994, Broward Coll., Ft. Lauderdale, Fla., 1995, others; represented in permanent collections at Sally Serkin Found., L.A., N.J. State Mus., Trenton, Guild Hall Mus., Islip Mus. Fine Arts, East Islip, N.Y., others; organizer, curator Women in Arts Exhbn., L.I. U. C.W. Post Campus, 1972, Womens Interard Ctr. Group Exhbn., 1976. Recipient awards Cite Des Artistes Internat., Paris, 1978, Va. Ctr. for Creative Arts, Mount San Angelo, Va., 1984, 86, grant award Adolph and Esther Gottlieb Found., N.Y.C., 1986, Painting awards N.Y. Found. for Arts, N.Y.C., 1987, Richard A. Florsheim Fund, Tampa, 1991, painting fellow The Elizabeth Found. for Arts, N.Y.C., 1995. Mem. Am. Abstract Artists. Home: 79 Mercer St New York NY 10012

SOREL, CLAUDETTE MARGUERITE, pianist; b. Paris; d. Michel M. and Elizabeth S. Grad. with top honors, Juilliard Sch. Music, 1947, postgrad., 1948; student of, Sigismund Stojowski, Sari Biro, Olga Samaroff Stokowski, Mieczyslaw Horszowski, Rudolf Serkin; ensemble with, Felix Salmond; musicology with, Dr. Robert Tangeman; music history with, Marian Bauer; grad., Curtis Inst. Music, 1953; B.S. cum laude in Math., Columbia U., 1954. music faculty, vis. prof. Kans. U., 1961-62; assoc. prof. music Ohio State U., 1962-64; prof. music, head piano dept. SUNY Fredonia, 1964—, Disting. Univ. prof., 1969—, univ. artist, 1969—, faculty exchange scholar, 1976—; mem. internat. jury Van Cliburn Internat. Piano Competition, Tex., 1966, Que. and Ont. Music Festivals, 1967, 75; chmn. music panel Presdl. Scholars in Arts Program, 1979—; juror numerous nat. and internat. music competitions; cons. Ednl. Testing Service, Princeton. Author: Compendium of Piano Technique, 1970, 2d edit., 1987, Japanese edit., 1987, Mind Your Musical Manners - Off and On Stage, 1972, 3d revised edit., 1995, The 24 Magic Keys, 3 vols., 1974, The Three Nocturnes of Rachmaninoff, 1974, 2d edit., 1975, 3d edit. with cassette in compact disc, 1988, Fifteen Smorgasbord Studies for the Piano, 1975, 2d edit., 1995, 17 Little Piano Studies, 1995, Arensky Piano Etudes, 1976; spl. editor: Music Insider; painter of oil portraits; contbr. articles to profl. mags.; compiler: The Modern Music of Today, 1974, Serge Prokofieff - His Life and Works, 1947, The Ornamentations in Mozart's Music, 1984; debut at Town Hall, N.Y.C., 1943; since appeared in leading cities of U.S.; performed with N.Y. Philharm., London Philharm., Zurich, Boston, San Antonio, Milw., NBC, Phila., New Orleans and Cin. symphony orchs., Youth Orch. of Am., 200 others; appeared at Aspen, Berkshire, Chautauqua, other festivals, European concert tours, 1956, 57, 58, to Eng., Sweden, Holland, Germany, Switzerland, France; appeared on various radio, TV programs; made recs. for RCA Victor Rec. Co., Monitor Records, Mus. Heritage; compact disc MacDowell Piano Concerto #2 with N.Y. Philharm. Orch., 1993; 2000 solo appearances, U.S. and Europe. Bd. dirs. Olga Samaroff Found.; Jr. com. aux. bd. N.Y. Philharmonic Symphony Orch., N.Y. State Nat. Fedn. Music Clubs; mem. adv. bd. Univ. Library Soc.; pres. Shelton Apartments, Inc. Fulbright fellow, 1951; Ford Found. Concert grantee, 1962; winner Phila. Orch. Youth Auditions, 1950, to appear with orch. under direction of Eugene Ormandy; U.S. Senatorial Bus. Adv. Com. Fulbright scholar, 1951; recipient Harry Rosenberg Meml., Frank Damrosch prizes, 1947, Nat. Fedn. Music Clubs Young Artist award, 1951; citation svc. to Am. music Nat. Fedn. Music Clubs, 1966, citations Nat. Assn. Composers & Condrs., 1967, Mu Phi Epsilon, 1968, Freedom medal U.S. Senatorial Com., 1994; nominated Kyoto Japan Humanitarian award, 1989, 92; Claudette Sorel Scholarship for Women Ctr. in Music created by NYU. Mem. Nat. Music Coun. (dir. 1973—, chmn. performance com.), Nat. Arts Club, Music Critics Assn., Broadcast Music Incorp., Columbia Univ. Club (N.Y.C.), Nat. Arts Club, Pi Kappa Lambda, Mu Phi Epsilon (dir. Meml. Found., nat. chmn. Sterling Staff Concert Series, citation 1968). Home: 333 W End Ave New York NY 10023-8131

SORELL, KITTY JULIA, public relations executive; b. Vienna, Austria, Apr. 20, 1937; came to U.S. 1938; d. Bruno Alexander and Ilse (Fischl) Singerman. BA, Syracuse U., 1959. Lic. real estate salesperson. Spl. events coord. Gimbel's, N.Y.C., 1966-69; pub. rels./account exec. Hamra Assocs., N.Y.C., 1969-71; spl. events/pub. rels. dir. Stern Bros., Paramus, N.J., 1972; pub. rels. account exec. Zachary & Front, N.Y.C., 1972-76; dir. pub. rels. RSM&K Advt., N.Y.C., 1976-77; owner Kitty Sorell Pub. Rels., N.Y.C., 1977—; reporter Wisdom's Child, 1981-84, The Villager, 1986-88; lectr. in field. Contbg. editor Mktg. Maker mag., 1976. Fundraiser WNET-TV, N.Y.C., 1974-75; vol. pub. rels. Sheridan Sq. Triangle Assn., N.Y.C., 1984-89; pres. bd. dirs. Apt. House Coop., 1991—; bd. dirs. Greenwich Village Alliance, 1994—. Mem. Am. Soc. Profl. and Exec. Women, Publicity Club. Democrat. Jewish. Office: Kitty Sorell Pub Rels 250 W 57th St New York NY 10107

SORENSEN, ANGELA FLYNN, neuropsychologist; b. Champaign, Ill., Mar. 13, 1961; d. James Dunn and Joanne Eloise (Storer) F.; m. Michael J. Sorensen, Mar. 13, 1994. BS in Biology summa cum laude, Eastern Wash. U., 1984; MS in Clinical Psychology, Wash. State U., 1987, PhD in Clin. Psychology, 1990. Postdoctoral fellowship Medical Coll. of Wis., Milw., 1990-92; neuropsychologist Boulder Cmty. Hosp., Boulder, Colo., 1992-94; pvt. practice, 1995—. Contbr. articles to profl. jours. Recipient Rsch. grant Alcohol & Drug Abuse Program, 1988-89, Mary Wilson Shields scholarship Eastern Wash. Univ., 1984. Mem. APA, Internat. Neuropsychol. Soc., Nat. Register of Health Svc. Providers in Psychology, Nat. Acad. of Neuropsychology, Colo. Neuropsychol. Soc., Midwest Neuropsychology Group, Phi Kappa Phi.

SORENSEN, ELIZABETH JULIA, cultural administrator; b. Kenora, Ont., Can., Nov. 24, 1934; d. John Frederick and Irene Margaret (Dowd) MacKellar; m. O. Leo P. Sorensen, July 7, 1956 (div. 1963); children: Lianne Kim Sorensen Kruger. BA, Lakehead U., 1970; MA, Brigham Young U., 1972; Assoc. Royal Conservatory, U. Toronto, 1978; Assoc., Mt. Royal Coll., Calgary, AB, 1978. Sec. Canadian Med. Assn. Manitoba div., Winnipeg, 1956-59; legal sec. Filmore, Riley & Co., Winnipeg, 1961-63; tchr. Fort Frances (Ont.) High Sch., 1963-70; instr. drama, speech, English Lethbridge (Alta.) Community Coll., 1972-77; tchr. bus. edn. Henderson Coll. Bus., Lethbridge, 1978-80; supt. cultural svcs. City Medicine Hat, Alta., 1980—. Mem. Alta. Mcpl. Assn. for Culture (sec. 1982-87, treas. 1982-90, vice-chair 1990-92, chair 1992—), Can. Conf. Arts, World Leisure and Recreation Assn. Mormon. Office: City of Medicine Hat, 580 1 St SE, Medicine Hat, AB Canada T1A 8E6

SORENSEN, JACKI FAYE, choreographer, aerobic dance company executive; b. Oakland, Calif., Dec. 10, 1942; d. Roy C. and Juanita F. (Bullon) Mills; m. Neil A. Sorensen, Jan. 3, 1965. BA, U. Calif., 1964. Cert. tchr., Calif. Ptnr., Big Spring Sch. Dance, 1965; tchr. Pasadena Ave. Sch., Sacramento, 1968; founder, pres., choreographer Jacki's Inc., DeLand, Fla., 1990—; cons., lectr. on phys. fitness. Author: Aerobic Dancing, 1979, Jacki Sorensen's Aerobic Lifestyle Book, 1983; choreographer numerous dance exercises for records and videocassettes. Trustee Women's Sports Found. Recipient Diamond Pin award Am. Heart Assn., 1979, Individual Contbn. award Am. Assn. Fitness Dirs. in Bus. and Industry, 1981, Spl. Olympics Contbn. award, 1982, Contbn. to Women's Fitness award Pres.'s Coun. Phys. Fitness and Sports, 1982, Healthy Am. Fitness Leader award U.S. Jaycees, 1984, Lifetime Achievement award Internat. Dance Exercise Assn., 1985, New Horizons award Caldwell (N.J.) Coll., 1985, Legend of Aerobics award City Sports mag., 1985; Pres. Coun. award Calif. Womens' Leadership Conf., 1986, Hall of Fame award Club Industry mag., 1986, IDEA, 1992. Mem. AAHPERD, AFTRA, Am. Coll. Sports Medicine, Nat. Intramural and Recreation Assn. Office: Jacki's Inc PO Box 289 Deland FL 32721-0289

SORENSEN, MEREDITH JEAN, elementary school educator; b. Penn Yan, N.Y., May 23, 1940; d. Kenneth Edwin and Mary (Raiman) S. BA, Ottawa (Kans.) U., 1962; MA, No. Mich. U., 1976; postgrad., New Zealand Whole Lang. Mentorship Program, Hamilton, summer 1989. Cert. elem. tchr., elem. sch. prin. Tchr. Rochester (N.Y.) City Schs., 1962-63, Penfield (N.Y.) Cen. Sch., 1963-67, Marion (N.Y.) Cen. Sch., 1967—. Vol. (correctional facility) Industry (N.Y.) Sch., 1970-83, vis. dir., 1982—; bd. dirs. Ottawa U., 1970-74; mem. N.Y. State Legis. Adv. Com., Albany, 1977-92; bd. dirs. Fairport Apts. for sr. citizens, 1981-83; founder Swinging Singles Western Sq. Dance Club, Rochester, 1967. Named one of Outstanding Young Women Am., 1971. Mem. Am. Fedn. Tchrs., N.Y. State United Tchrs., Marion Tchrs. Assn. (treas., chair legis com. social and sunshine com., negotiations com.), N.Y. State Reading Assn., Genesee Valley Devel. Learning Group, Danish Sisterhood (Penn Yan), Phi Delta Kappa. American Baptist. Office: Marion Cen Sch 3863 N Main St Marion NY 14505-9579

SORENSEN, SARAH HEATHER, adult educator, health educator; b. Fayetteville, Ark., July 11, 1963. Cert. in Addictions Counseling, Coll. of DuPage, 1988; BA in Psychology summa cum laude, Northeastern Ill. U., 1990; MA in Philosophy, No. Ill. U., 1992, EdD (ABD), 1995. Counselor Camp Chippewa Bay, New Auburn, Wis., 1980, 81; custodian Mennonite Hosp., Bloomington, Ill., 1981-82; health food cook Under the Water Tower Cafe, Kirkville, Mo., 1982-84; activity asst. Adult Cmty. Care, Elmhurst, Ill., 1986; activity dir. Cmty. Adult Day Care, Downers Grove, Ill., 1986-87; addictions counselor Chem. Dependency Unit, Lakeside Cmty. Hosp., 1988-89; departmental tutor Psychology Dept. Northeastern Ill. U., Chgo., 1989-90; teaching asst. philosophy dept. No. Ill. U., De Kalb, 1990-92; health educator Univ. Health Svc. No. Ill. U., De Kalb, 1992—; grad. rep. Women's Studies Adv. Bd., No. Ill. U., De Kalb, 1994-95; presenter Midwest Am. Coll. Health Assn. Conf., Big. Rapids, Mich., 1994—, Leadership and Ednl. Policy Studies Rsch. Symposium, No. Ill. U., De Kalb, 1994. Housing coord. Women's Cultural Festival, De Kalb Area Women's Ctr., 1994-95. Mem. Am. Assn. of Adult and Continuing Edn., Nat. Womens Studies Assn., Soc. for Women in Philosophy. Feminist. Unitarian.

SORENSEN, SHEILA, state senator; b. Chgo., Sept. 20, 1947; d. Martin Thomas Moloney and Elizabeth (Koehr) Paulus; m. Wayne B. Slaughter, May, 1969 (div. 1976); 1 child, Wayne Benjamin III; m. Dean E. Sorensen, Feb. 14, 1977; (stepchildren) Michael, Debbie, Kevin, Dean C. BS, Loretto Heights Coll., Denver, 1965; postgrad. pediatric nurse practicioner, U. Colo., Denver, 1969-70. Pediatric nurse practicioner Pub. Health Dept., Denver, 1970-71, Boise, Idaho, 1971-72; pediatric nurse practicioner Boise (Idaho) Pediatric Group, 1972-74, Pediatric Assocs., Boise, 1974-77; mem. Idaho State Ho. Reps., 1987-92; mem. Idaho Senate, 1992—, chair senate health and welfare com., 1992-94, chair senate majority caucus, vice chair state affairs com., 1994—. Precinct committeeman Ada County Rep. Ctrl. Com., Boise, 1982-86, dist. vice chair, 1985-88; polit. chair Idaho Med. Assn. Aux., 1984-87, Ada County Med. Assocs., 1986-87; bd. dirs. Family Practice Residency Program, 1992—, Univ./Cmty. Health Sci. Assn., Bishop Kelly Found., 1993—; chair Senate Majority Caucus, 1995, vice chair state affairs com. Recipient AMA Nathan Davis award for Outstanding State Legislator, 1994. Mem. Nat. Conf. State Legislators, Nat. Orgn. Women Legislators (state chair), Am. Legis. Exch. Coun. Roman Catholic.

SORENSON, GEORGIA LYNN JONES, administrator; b. Abilene, Tex., Aug. 23, 1947; d. Wyly King and Olive M. (Sorenson) Jones; 1 child, Suzanna Simmonds Strasburg. BA, Am. U., 1974; MA, Hood Coll., 1976; PhD, U. Md., 1992. Social scientist Nat. Inst. Edn., Washington, 1978-79, U.S. Commn. Civil Rights, Washington, 1976-79; sr. policy analyst The White House, Washington, 1979-80; dir., faculty Ctr. Polit. Leadership and Participation U. Md., College Park, 1980—; adv. mem. W.K. Kellogg Found. Nat Fellows, Battle Creek, Mich., 1996—. Co-author: (with James MacGregor Burns) The Clinton Presidency; contbr. articles to profl. jours. Chair Md. Women's Polit. Caucus, 1991-94; mem. White House Productivity Coun., Washington, 1979; mem. V.P. Youth Employment Task Force, 1979-80. Mem. Am. Polit. Sci. Assn., Internat. Soc. Polit. Psychologists, A.K. Rice Inst. Office: U Md Ctr Political Leadership College Park MD 20742

SORENSON, JEANNE, nursing consultant; b. Longmont, Colo., July 11, 1941; d. Dell Edwin and Verna Elizabeth (Nelson) Waggener; m. Roy Everett Sorenson, Sept. 15, 1962; children: JoDee Sorenson Wells, Roy E. III. Student, Sacramento State U., 1959, Contra Costa C.C., 1959-61; diploma, Kaiser Found. Sch. Nursing, 1962; postgrad., Am. River C.C., 1982. RN, Calif.; cert. rehab. RN, case mgr. Charge nurse Roseville (Calif.) Hosp., 1962-64; float nurse Mercy Gen. Hosp., Sacramento, 1964-66; float nurse Am. River Hosp., Carmichael, Calif., 1966-67, admissions nurse, 1967-73; sr. coord. Greater Sacramento Profl. Stds. and Rev. Orgn., 1973-80; med. rev. specialist ComputerSci Corp., Sacramento, 1980-86; sr. case mgr. Blue Shield of Calif., Folsom, 1986-91; ind. RN cons. SorensonEtal, Inc., Carmichael, 1991—; presenter seminars in field; mem. adv. bd. Casa Colina Rehab. Ctr., Pomona, Calif., 1989—, No. Valley Rehab. Ctr., Chico, Calif., 1989—, Kangaroo Kids, Sacramento, 1987—. Bd. dirs. No. Calif. Girls Softball Assn., Carmichael, 1975-80, Del Campo Little League, Carmichael, 1982-84, Childrens' Respit Ctr., Sacramento, 1990—. Mem. Nat. Head Injury Found. (mem. pediatric task force 1991—), Assn. Rehab. Nurses, Am. Assn. Spinal Cord Injury Nurses, Case Mgmt. Soc. Am., Nat. Assn. Rehab. Profls. Home: 5119 Mckinney Way Carmichael CA 95608-0762 Office: SorensonEtal Inc PO Box 1147 Carmichael CA 95609-1147

SORENSON, LIANE BETH MCDOWELL, women's affairs director, state legislator; b. Chgo., Aug. 13, 1947; d. Harold Davidson McDowell and Frances Elanor (Williams) Daisey; m. Boyd Wayne Sorenson, June 30, 1973; children: Nathan, Matthew, Dana. BS in Edn., U. Del., 1969, M in Counseling with honors, 1986. Tchr. Avon Grove Sch. Dist., West Grove, Pa., 1969-70, Alexis I. duPont Sch. Dist., Wilmington, Del., 1970-73, Barrington

(Ill.) Sch. Dist., 1973-75; counseling intern Medill Intensive Learning Ctr.-Christina Sch. Dist., Newark, Del., 1985; counselor Family Violence Shelter CHILD, Inc., Wilmington, 1985, 86-87, dir. parent edn. programs, 1987-88; dir. Office Women's Affairs, exec. dir. Commn. on Status of Women U. Del., Newark, 1988—; mem. Del. Legislature, Dover, 1992—; chair Del. Ho. Edn. Com., 1992—; commr. Edn. Commn. State Del.; mem. tng. com. Nat. Conf. State Legislatures; mem. joint sunset com. Del. Legislature, Del. House of Reps., 1992-94, Del. Senate, 1994—, Del. Legis. Joint Fin. Com. Del. Legis., 1994—. Presenter papers various meetings & confs. Pres. bd. dirs. Nursing Mothers, Inc., 1980-81; trustee Hockessin Montessori Sch., 1982-84, enrollment chair, 1982-83; trustee Hockessin Pub. Libr., 1982-84, pres. bd., 1982-84; bd. dirs. Del. Coalition for Children, 1986-88; bd. dirs. Children's Bur. Del., 1984-87, sec., 1985-87; pres. Jr. League Wilmington, 1986-87, rsch. coun. v.p., 1985-86; bd. dirs. YWCA New Castle County, 1989-91; pres. Del. Women's Agenda, 1986-88; vice-chair Women's Leadership Ctr., 1992—; mem. Del. Work Family Coalition. Grantee Del. Dept. Svcs. to Children, Youth and Their Families, 1987-88, 1988, State of Del. Gen. Assembly, 1992. Mem. Am. Assn. for Higher Edn. (chair women's caucus 1991-92, program chair women's caucus 1990-91, pre-conf. workshop coord. women's caucus 1990 Ann. Conf.), Del. Greenway and Trails Coun., Rotary (charter mem. Hackessin Pike Creek club 1994—), Del. Alliance for Arts in Edn., Del. Family Law Commn. Republican. Methodist. Office: State of Delaware Legislative Hall Dover DE 19901

SORENSON, PATRICIA ANN, software engineer; b. Beverly, Mass., Oct. 14, 1955; d. Walter F. and Gloria D. (Mascioli) S. BS in Math., Salem State Coll., 1983. Computer operator Madico, Inc., Woburn, Mass., 1978-80, programmer, 1980-83; cons. Turning Point Systems, Inc., Beverly, 1983-85, project mgr., 1987-91, product mgr., 1991-95; programmer/analyst Daly Drug div. Cardinal Health, Peabody, Mass., 1985-87; project mgr. ISSC Corp divsn. IBM, Waltham, Mass., 1995—. Mem. Am. Mgmt. Assn., IEEE Computer Soc., Appalachian Mountain Club. Home: 10 Bentley St Salem MA 01970-5213

SORESE, DENISE POWERS, reading consultant, educator; b. N.Y.C., Sept. 11, 1945; d. Daniel Dennis and Frances Louise (Kruft) Powers; m. Vincent James Sorese, Aug. 12, 1967; children: Jaclyn, Lauren. BS in Edn., SUNY, Cortland, 1967; M of Reading, U. Bridgeport, 1970; cert. advanced study in adminstrn., Fairfield U., 1993. Tchr. early childhood N.Y.C. Bd. Edn., 1965-67; tchr. elem. sch. Greenwich (Conn.) Bd. Edn., 1967-72, reading specialist, 1972-77, 91—, learning facilitator, 1995—, mainstreaming assoc., 1986-91, adminstr. summer sch., 1993—; dir. summer acad. Convent of Sacred Heart Sch., 1994—; learning facilitator Hamilton Ave. Sch., Greenwich, Conn., 1995—; aftersch. adminstr. Hamilton Ave. Sch., Greenwich, 1993—; state assessor Conn. State Dept. Edn., Hartford, 1993—, tech. advisor, 1993—; presenter in field. Mem., project Charlie chmn. Jr. League Greenwich, 1989-92; bd. dirs. St. Pauls Day Sch., Riverside, Conn., 1981-92, PTA, Greenwich, 1984-93, St. Catherines Players, Riverside, 1993-94. Reading grantee State of Conn., 1973, 74. Mem. NEA, ASCD, Conn. Edn. Assn., Conn. Reading Assn. (bd. dirs., exemplary reading award, chairperson 1994—), Conn. Coun. Tchrs. English, Internat. Reading Assn., Delta Kappa Gamma. Roman Catholic. Office: Hamilton Ave Sch 184 Hamilton Ave Greenwich CT 06830-6113

SORGEN, ELIZABETH ANN, retired educator; b. Ft. Wayne, Ind., Aug. 21, 1931; d. Lee E. and Miriam N. (Bixler) Waller; m. Don DuWayne Sorgen, Mar. 8, 1952; children: Kevin D., Karen Lee Sorgen Hoeppner, Keith Alan. BS in Edn., Ind. U., 1953; MS in Edn., St. Francis Coll., Ft. Wayne, 1967. Tchr. East Allen County Schs., Monroeville, Ind., 1953-94, also bldg. rep. and math. book adoption rep., 1953-94. Founder nursery sch., choir mem. St. Marks Luth. Ch., Monroeville, 1960—; active Allen County Local Edn. Fund; vol. Sci. Ctrl. Recipient Golden Apple award East Allen County Schs., 1976, Monroeville Tchr. of Yr. award, 1993. Mem. AAUW, East Allen County Educators Assn., Buck and Dears Square Dance Club (sec. 1954), Ind. Two Steppers, Delta Kappa Gamma. Home: 25214 Lincoln Hwy E Monroeville IN 46773-9710

SORIA, REGINA ROSA ENRICA, English educator, author; b. Rome, Mar. 17, 1911; came to U.S., 1940; d. Comandante Angelo Levi and Marcella Malvano (Levi) Bianchini; m. Dion Charles Philip Soria, Jan. 12, 1936 (dec. 1975). LittD, U. Rome, 1933; cert. proficiency of English, London U., 1933. Cert. tchr. English, Italy. Instr. Coll. of Notre Dame of Md., Balt., 1942-61, prof. Italian, chmn. modern langs. dept., 1942-61, mem. adj. faculty, 1978-85; instr. Italian Summer Sch., Middlebury, Vt., 1949, 51-52; instr. summer sch. Cath. U. and Johns Hopkins U., 1940s; co-founder Circolo Culturale Italiano di Baltimorea, 1955-75. Author: Elihu Vedder American Visionary Artist in Rome (1836-1923), 1970, Dictionary of Nineteenth Century American Artists in Italy 1760-1914, 1979, American Artists of Italian Heritage 1776-1945, A Biographical Dictionary, 1993. Recipient Cavaliere Dell' Ordine Al Merito della Repubblica Italiana, 1986, Cornaro award Ausonia Soc., Sarasota, Fla., 1995. Mem. MLA, Am. Assn. Tchrs. Italian, Am. Italian Hist. Assn. Home: 4000 N Charles St Unit 805 Baltimore MD 21218-1736

SOROCA, BARBARA J., performing company executive. Exe dir Stamford Symphony Orchestra, Stamford, CT. Office: Stamford Symphony Orch 400 Main St Stamford CT 06901-3004*

SOROKIN, CHERYL A., bank executive. Group exec. v.p. Bank Am. Corp., San Francisco. Office: Bankamerica Corp 555 California St San Francisco CA 94104-1502*

SORRENTINO, RENATE MARIA, illustrator; b. Mallnitz, Carinthia, Austria, June 21, 1942; came to the U.S., 1962; d. Johann and Theresia (Kritzer) Weinberger; m. Philip Rosenberg, Nov. 22, 1968 (dec. 1982); m. Francis J. Sorrentino, Sept. 4, 1988. Grad. gold and silversmith artist, Höhere Technische Lehranstalt, Austria, 1961. Draftswoman Elecon Inc., N.Y.C., 1962-65; jr. designer Automatics Metal Prod. Corp., N.Y.C., 1965-70; designer, art dir. Autosplice, Inc., Woodside, N.Y., 1970-90; freelance artist Jupiter, Fla., 1990—. Patentee Quick Disconnect from Continuous Wire, 1977. Home: 2301 Marina Isle Way Apt 404 Jupiter FL 33477-9423 Office: Autosplice Inc 10121 Barnes Canyon Rd San Diego CA 92121-2725

SORSTOKKE, ELLEN KATHLEEN, marketing executive, educator; b. Seattle, Mar. 31, 1954; d. Harold William and Carrol Jean (Russ) S. MusB with distinction, U. Ariz., 1976; postgrad., UCLA Extension, 1979-83, L.A. Valley Coll., 1984-85, Juilliard Extension, fall 1987, U. Calif. Berkeley Extension, 1992-93. Pvt. practice music tchr. Music Land, Tucson, 1975-77; music tchr. Eloy (Ariz.) Elem. Schs., 1976-77, Whiteriver (Ariz.) Pub. Schs., 1977-78; svc. writer, acting svc. mgr., asst. svc. mgr. Alfa of Santa Monica, Calif., 1978-79; purchasing agt. Advance Machine Corp., L.A., 1979-80; asst. mgr. Atlantic Nuclear Svcs., Gardena, Calif., 1980-81; mgr. Blue Lady's World Music Ctr., L.A., 1981-83; instrument specialist Baxter-Northup Music Co., Sherman Oaks, Calif., 1983-85; dir. mktg. Mandolin Bros., Ltd., S.I., N.Y., 1985-89; product mgr. Gibson Guitar Corp., Nashville, 1989; sales mgr. Saga Musical Instruments, South San Francisco, Calif., 1990-91, mktg. dir., 1991-95; freelance mktg. cons., S.I., Foster City, 1986—; freelance music tchr., Tucson, L.A., N.Y.C., 1975-89; music cons. 20th Century Fox, L.A., 1984; freelance music copyist and orchestrator, Tucson, L.A., N.Y.C., 1972-89; freelance graphic designer and advt., Foster City, Calif., 1993—. campaign worker Richard Jones for Supr., Tucson, 1972; mem., program book designer Marina Del Rey-Westchester Symphony Orch., L.A., 1981-83; active Calif. Wind Ensemble, 1992—. Scholar U. Ariz., 1973-76, ASCAP scholar, 1980-81. Mem. Am. Fedn. Musicians, Soc. for the Preservation Film Music, Tucson Flute Club (publicity chmn. 1974-75, v.p. 1975-76). Republican.

SORSTOKKE, SUSAN EILEEN, systems engineer; b. Seattle, May 2, 1955; d. Harold William and Carrol Jean (Russ) S. BS in Systems Engring., U. Ariz., 1976; MBA, U. Wash., Richland, 1983. Warehouse team mgr. Procter and Gamble Paper Products, Modesto, Calif., 1976-78; quality assurance engr. Westinghouse Hanford Co., Richland, Wash., 1978-80; supr. engring. document ctr. Westinghouse Hanford Co., Richland, 1980-81; mgr. data control and adminstrn. Westinghouse Electric Corp., Madison, Pa., 1981-82, mgr. data control and records mgmt., 1982-84; prin. engr. Westinghouse Elevator Co., Morristown, N.J., 1984-87; region adminstrn. mgr. Westinghouse Elevator Co., Arleta, Calif., 1987-90; ops. rsch. analyst Am. Honda Motor Co. Inc., Torrance, Calif., 1990-95; project leader parts sys. Am. Honda Motor Co., Inc., Torrance, Calif., 1995—; adj. prof. U. LaVerne, Calif., 1991-92. Advisor Jr. Achievement, 1982-83; literacy tutor Westmoreland Literacy Coun., 1983-84, host parent EF Found., Saugus, Calif., 1987-88, Am. Edn. Connection, Saugus, 1988-89, 91; instr. Excell, L.A., 1991-92. Mem. Soc. Women Engrs., Am. Inst. Indsl. Engrs., Nat. Coun. Systems Engring., Optimists Charities, Inc. (bd. dirs. Acton, Calif. 1991-94). Republican. Methodist. Home: 2567 Plaza Del Amo Unit 205 Torrance CA 90503-8962 Office: Am Honda Motor Co Inc Dept Parts Quality and Systems 1919 Torrance Blvd Torrance CA 90501-2722

SORVINO, MIRA, actress; b. 1968; d. Paul S. AB, Harvard U., 1990. Appeared in films including Amongst Friends, 1993, The Second Greatest Story Ever Told, 1993, Quiz Show, 1994, Parallel Lives, 1994, Barcelona, 1994, Tarantella, 1995, Sweet Nothing, 1995, Mighty Aphrodite, 1995 (Oscar for Best Supporting Actress), The Dutch Master, 1995, Blue in the Face, 1995, Beautiful Girls, 1996, (TV) The Buccaneers, 1995, Norma Jean and Marilyn, 1996, Jake's Women, 1996; assoc. prodr. Amongst Friends, 1993. Office: The William Morris Agy 151 El Camino Dr Beverly Hills CA 90212

SOSNICK, FAY MAXINE, retired educator, volunteer; b. N.Y.C., June 25, 1914; d. Philip and Gussie (Cohen) Shapiro; m. Max Sosnick, Dec. 25, 1937 (dec. Sept. 1989); children: Renee Beth Bain, Janet Ruth Hughes. BA in Chemistry, Math. and Sci., Hunter Coll., 1934; MEd in Math., Fairleigh Dickinson U., 1964; AAS in Philosophy, Brookdale C.C., N.J., 1984. Auditor U.S. Fin. Office, 1943-46; acctg., analyst and payroll staff Quindar Electronics, N.J., 1955-68; exec. Inglemoor Nursing Homes, 1969-74. Creator, organizer Home Owners Assn., The Guardian-Newspaper Pub. Condo. Assn., 1973-76; creator, liaison Self-Help Groups in Arthritis, Fitness, Svcs. to Hosp., Freehold Boro Hosp., 1974—; vol. govtl. svc. Sr. Health Ins. N.J. State, 1976-80; with Brookdale C.C. Alumni Assn., N.J., 1983-87; mem. juvenile conf. com. Superior Ct. Chancery Divsn., N.J., 1985-89; others.

SOSSIADIS, KATINA, artist; b. Bethlehem, Pa., May 9, 1971; d. Emmanuel and Maria Stephanie (Skoutelas) S. BA, Moravian Coll., 1993, grad. with honors in art, 1993; MFA, U. Pa., 1996. Mus. tour guide Kemerer Mus. Decorative Arts, Bethlehem, 1990; fine arts asst. Allentown Art Mus., 1992; gallery asst. Payne Gallery, Bethlehem, 1992. One-woman shows include Payne Gallery, Bethlehem, 1993, pvt. gallery, Tarpon Springs, Fla., 1994, The Artisan, Bethlehem, 1995-96, Connexians, Easton, 1996, Touchstone Theater, Bethlehem, 1994, Java Jack's Cafe, Bethlehem, 1995; exhibited in group shows Moravian Coll., 1991, 92, Rotunda Gallery, Bethlehem, 1992, Geometrics Gallery, Bethlehem, 1994—, Open Space Gallery, 1994-95, U. Pa., 1994, 95, 96; art editor: Manuscript, 1991-93. Recipient Daniel W. Tereshko Meml. prize in studio art Moravian Coll., 1993, Best Painting award, 1992; Coll. Gen. Studies tchg. grantee U. Pa. Mem. Art Club of Moravian Coll. (sec. 1992, v.p. 1992-93), Kappa Pi. Democrat. Greek Orthodox. Home and Office: 228 Apollo Dr Bethlehem PA 18017

SOTIR, JUDITH S., educational technology consultant, researcher; b. Chgo., Nov. 18, 1951; 1 child, Heather Genevieve. BA, Elmhurst (Ill.) Coll., 1974. Sales mgr. Unicorn, Ltd., Chgo., 1982-86; lab. coord. Waubonsee Coll., Aurora, Ill., 1987-90; promotions mgr. MidAm. Savings Bank, Clavendon Hills, Ill., 1988-90; assessment coord. Waubonsee Coll., 1990-92, ESL coord., 1992-95, dir. innovative tech. design, 1992—; mem. editl. review bd. Nat. Ctr. on Adult Literacy, U. Pa., Phila., 1995—; mem. peer evaluation team No. Ill. U., Dekalb, Ill. 1995; presenter various workshops. Contbr. articles to profl. jours. dir. bd. edn. Indian Prarie Dist. 204, Naperville, Ill., 1983—; gov. bd. mem. Ill. Assn. Sch. Bds., Glen Ellyn, 1986-90; dir. Indian Prarie Ednl. Found., Naperville, 1988—; mem. ad-hoc com. edn. State Rep. Mary Lou Cowlishaw, Springfield, Ill., 1986—. Mem. Am. Assn. for Adult and Continuing Edn., Ill. Assn. for Adult and Continuing Edn., Ill. Computing Educators, Internat. Soc. Tech. Educators, Assn. for Curriculum and Devel. Republican. Roman Catholic. Home: 3698 Monarch Circle Naperville IL 60564 Office: Waubonsee Coll Innovative Tech Design Ctr 5 E Galena Blvd Aurora IL 60506

SOTO, RAMONA, training specialist; b. East Chicago, Ind., Apr. 14, 1963; d. Robert Rudy and Antonia (Perez) S. Student, Purdue U., 1982-86, U. Ill., Chgo., 1990, DePaul U., 1992-95. Salesperson The Gap, Inc., Ind., 1979-84; asst. mgr. The Gap, Inc., Ind. and Ill., 1984-88; tng. mgr. The Gap, Inc., Ill., 1988-90; tng. specialist Montgomery Ward & Co., Ill., 1990-93; temp. worker The Richard Michael Group, Chgo., 1993, Resort Travel Corp, Oakbrook Terrace, Ill., 1993; ind. tng. cons. Chgo., 1994—; tutor tng. mgr. The Cabrini Green Tutoring Program, Chgo., 1991-94, jr. asst. coord., 1995—, tutor Preparing An Attitude for Learning, Leadership and Success, 1991-94, jr. asst. advisor, 1995—. Mem. ASTD. Home: 3550 N Lake Shore Dr Chicago IL 60657-1916

SOTOMAYOR, SONIA, federal judge; b. N.Y.C., June 25, 1954; d. Juan Luis and Celina (Baez) S.; m. Kevin Edward Noonan, Aug. 14, 1976 (div. 1983). AB, Princeton (N.J.) U., 1976; JD, Yale U., 1979. Bar: N.Y. 1980, U.S. Dist. Ct. (ea. and so. dists.) N.Y. 1984. Asst. dist. atty. Office of Dist. Atty. County of N.Y., N.Y.C., 1979-84; assoc., ptnr. Pavia & Harcourt, N.Y.C., 1984-92; fed. judge U.S. Dist. Ct. (so. dist.) N.Y., N.Y.C., 1992—. Editor Yale U. Law Rev., 1979. Bd. dirs. P.R. Legal Def. and Edn. Fund, N.Y.C., 1980-92, State of N.Y. Mortgage Agy., N.Y.C., 1987-92, N.Y.C. Campaign Fin. Bd., 1988-92; mem. State Adv. Panel on Inter-Group Rels., N.Y.C., 1990-91. Mem. Phi Beta Kappa. Office: US Courthouse 500 Pearl St New York NY 10007

SOUCY, DONNA MARCELLE, state legislator; b. Manchester, N.H., Sept. 7, 1967; d. Charles Arthur and Lillian Estelle (Provost) S. BA, St. Anselm Coll., 1989. Polit. cons. Keefe for Congress, Manchester, N.H., 1990; mem. N.H. State Ho. of Reps., 1992—, mem. fin. com., 1991-92; campaign mgr. Machos for State Senate, Manchester, 1992; book seller. Ward clk. Dem. Party Manchester, 1987-91; chmn. Dem. ward com., 1989-92, vice chair, 1988—. Flemming fellow Ctr. Policy Alternatives. Democrat. Office: NH Ho of Reps Main St Concord NH 03301*

SOUDERS, JEAN SWEDELL, artist, educator; b. Braham, Minn., July 13, 1922; d. John Almond and Frances Johanna (Alm) Swedell; m. Robert Livingston Souders, Sep. 22, 1945 (dec. 1985). BA, Duluth (Minn.) State Coll., 1944; postgrad., Minn. Sch. of Art, 1944, Walker Sch. of Art, Minn., 1948; MA, U. Iowa, 1955, MFA, 1956. Instr. art St. Olaf Coll., Northfield, Minn., 1947-50; instr. craft U. Minn., 1951; prof. art history painting Calif. State U., Chico, Calif., 1957-74; prof. art history Calif. State U., Chico, 1959-60; faculty gen. studies Calif. State U., Chico, Calif., 1971-73. Exhbn. Creative Art Ctr., 1975, Des Moines Art Ctr., Crocker Mus. of Art, and various others. Mem. Nat. Archives, Mus. of Women in the Arts, Washington, Women Artists Assn. San Francisco. Lutheran.

SOULE, LUCILE SNYDER, pianist, music educator; b. Fargo, N.D., Sept. 21, 1922; d. Roy Henry and Gene (McGhee) Snyder; m. Leon Cyprian Soule Jr., Sept. 1, 1954 (dec. Dec. 1994); children: Robert Leon, Anne Lucile. MusB, MusB in Edn., U. Minn., Mpls., 1943; BA, Smith Coll., Northampton, Mass., 1945; postgrad. diploma, Juilliard Sch. Music, 1948. Organist various chs., Mont., La., and Ohio, 1935-68; instr. Smith Coll., Northampton, 1945-46; freelance pianist, accompanist Juilliard Sch. Music, also pvt. groups and individuals, N.Y.C., 1946-69; from instr. to asst. to assoc. prof. Newcomb Coll., Tulane U., New Orleans, 1949-51, 52-61; staff pianist, soloist New Orleans Symphony, 1954-61; guest artist Contemporary Music Festival La. State U., Baton Rouge, 1953-61; lectr. Lakewood br. Ohio State U., 1964-66; music tchr. East Cleveland (Ohio) Pub. Schs., 1969-85; music dir. East Cleveland Theater, 1985—; accompanist Zhao Rongchun, Cleve., 1995—; pres. New Orleans Music Tchrs. Assn., 1958-59; bd. dirs., publicity chair Rocky River (Ohio) Chamber Music Soc., 1963-67; v.p. Cleve. chpt. Am. Orff Schluwerk Assn., Cleve., 1974-75, presenter nat. conf., 1992. Mem. Citizens Adv. Group, East Cleveland, 1967-69. Woolley Found. fellow, 1950-51, tchg. fellow Case Western Res. U., 1967-68, tchg. fellow Smith Coll., 1943-45; scholar Juilliard Sch. Music, 1946-48. Mem. Darius Millhaud Soc. (bd. dirs. 1984—), Fortnightly Mus. Club (corr. sec. 1996—), Lecture Recital Club (bd. dirs. 1993-95), Mu Epsilon. Democrat. Christian Scientist. Home and Office: 15617 Hazel Rd East Cleveland OH 44112

SOULE, NANCY ELAINE, counselor; b. Portland, Maine, Apr. 19, 1945; d. Rufus Frederic and Marjorie A. (Andersen) S. BS in Edn., U. Maine, 1968, MEd, 1995. Cert. sch. counselor; registered counselor; cert. adult edn. dir., cert. tchr. Tchr. Union 60, Greenville, Main, 1968-86; sch. bus driver SAD 68, Union 60, 1989—; Greenville sch. bus transp. dir. Rowell's Garage, Dover-Forcroft, Maine, 1994—; owner Woodcarver's Shop & Sign Co., Greenville, 1988—; sch. counselor Forest Hills Sch., Jackman, Maine, 1995—; adult edn. dir. Union 60, Greenville, 1994—, sch. bd. dirs., 1988-92, chmn. safe and drug free schs. com., 1995—, chmn. dropout prevention com., 1987-90, mem. sch. sys. improvement team, 1994—, chmn. recreation com., 1984-90; dir. Moosehead Youth Collaborative, Greenville, 1994—. Coord. Jump Rope for Heart and Hoops and Heart, Greenville, 1987—; organizer Nat. Jr. Tennis League of Greenville, 1990—, Jackman, Maine, 1996. Mem. ACA, Am. Sch. Counselors assn., Maine Assn. of Health, Phys. Edn., Recreation and Dance, Maine Sch. Counselors Assn., Moosehead Rowers. Home: PO Box 59 Pritham Ave Greenville ME 04441 Office: Greenville Schs Adult Edn Pritham Ave PO Box 100 Greenville ME 04441

SOULE, SALLIE THOMPSON, retired state official; b. Detroit, May 13, 1928; d. Hayward Stone and Elizabeth Robinson Thompson; A.B., Smith Coll., 1950; M.A., U. Vt., Burlington, 1952; m. Gardner Northup Soule, July 26, 1958; stepchildren: Gardner Northup, Nancy Soule Brown; children: Sarah Goodwin, Trumbull Dickson. Sec. trade sales dept. Macmillan Pub. Co., N.Y.C., 1952-57; tech. writer sales svc. div. Eastman Kodak Co., Rochester, N.Y., 1957-58; feature writer Brighton-Pittsford Post, Pittsford, N.Y., 1958-68; v.p., gen. mgr. F. H. Horsford Nursery, Inc., Charlotte, Vt., 1968-76; ptnr., pres. Bygone Books, Inc., Burlington, Vt., 1978—; mem. Vt. Ho. of Reps., 1976-80, mem. ways and means com., 1976-80; mem. Vt. Senate, 1980-84, mem. appropriation com., energy and natural resources com. 1980-84; commr. Vt. Dept. Employment and Tng., Montpelier, 1985-88; chmn. Vt. Employment Security Bd., 1985-88.

SOULTOUKIS, DONNA ZOCCOLA, library director; b. Princeton, N.J., July 28, 1949; d. Peter Joseph and Josephine (Taraschi) Zoccola; m. Dimitrios Athanasios Soultoukis, July 26, 1980. AB, Georgian Ct. Coll., Lakewood, N.J., 1971; MS, Drexel U., 1976; Cert., Italian U. for Foreigners, Perugia, 1974. Libr. asst. Geology Libr. Princeton U., 1971-73; libr. Friends Hosp., Phila., 1976-86, dir. libr. svcs., 1986—; bd. dirs. Mental Health Materials Ctr., N.Y.C., 1996—; cons. Lower Bucks Hosp., Bristol, Pa., 1991-95. Vol. outreach program Old St. Joseph's Ch., Phila., 1992-95, sanctuary min., 1993—, mem. pastoral coun., 1995—. Mem. Med. Libr. Assn. (chair mental librs. divsn. 1991-93), Spl. Librs. Assn. (Phila. chpt. bd. dirs. 1985-88, pres. 1982-84, chmn. long-range planning 1993, mem. adv. bd. 1995—, chair profl. devel. com. Solo divsn., 1995—, mem. strategic planning com. Solo divsn.). Home: 290 Cinnabar Ln Yardley PA 19067 Office: Friends Hosp 4641 Roosevelt Blvd Philadelphia PA 19124-2399

SOUSA, CONSUELO MARIA, pediatrician; b. New Bedford, Mass., Aug. 5, 1931; d. Edward Rogers and Candida Helena (Rogers) S.; m. Timothy Leonard Stephens, July 7, 1959; children: Timothy Leonard III, Susan Ellen, Amy Louise. BS, Howard U., Washington, 1953, MD, 1958; MPH, Harvard U., 1962; MBA, Case Western Res. U., Cleve., 1983. Diplomate Am. Bd. Pediatrics. Intern St. Luke's Hosp., New Bedford, 1958; resident pediatrics Freedmen's Hosp., Washington, 1959-61; fellow dept. maternal and child health Harvard Sch. Pub. Health, Boston, 1961-62; instr. preventive medicine Boston U. Sch. Medicine, 1962-63; asst. physician home med. svc. Mass. Meml. Svc. Hosp., 1962-63; pvt. practice, assoc. attending staff St. Luke's Hosp., New Bedford, 1963-66; pediatrician Well Child Conf., Fairhaven, Mass., 1965-66; clin. instr. pediatrics Case Western Res. U., Cleve., 1967-94; mem. pediatric staff Rainbow Babes and Children's Hosp., Cleve., 1967-94; chief pediatrics Hough Norwood Family Health Care Ctr., Cleve., 1967-76; vis. asst. pediatrics Cleve. Met. Gen. Hosp., 1967-91; dir. health svcs. Buckeye Health Plan, Inc., Cleve., 1976-79, acting exec. dir., 1979, med. health svcs. dir., 1979-80; v.p., med. adminstr. Assocs. in Orthopaedics, Inc., Cleve., 1982—, cons., 1980-82; chmn. med. staff Health Hill Hosp., Cleve., 1982-84; mem. Headstart Health Adv. Com., Cleve., 1971-78, chmn., 1977-78. Contbr. articles to profl. jours. Mem. Citizens Adv. Bd. of Juvenile Ct. Cuyahoga County, 1975-90, chmn. bd., 1985-89; appointed commr. Cuyahoga Met. Housing Authority, 1990; mem. bd., founding trustee Harambee Svcs. to Black Families, Cleve., 1979-85; mem. adv. bd. Youth Svcs., Cuyahoga County, 1980-90. Named Outstanding American, Cape Verdean Am. Vets., New Bedford, 1972. Fellow Am. Acad. Pediatrics; mem. AMA, Nat. Med. Assn., No. Ohio Pediatric Soc. Home: 13475 N Park Blvd Cleveland OH 44118-4927 Office: Assocs in Orthopaedics Inc 11201 Shaker Blvd Ste 328 Cleveland OH 44104-3833

SOUTH, MARY ANN, pediatrics educator; b. Portales, N.Mex., May 23, 1933; d. John Anderson and Carrie (Schumpert) S.; m. Allard W. Loutherback, Dec. 29, 1983 (dec. June 1985); children: George Louie, Linda Lee Loutherback Putnam. Student, Baylor U., Waco, Tex., 1951-53; BA, Ea. N.Mex. U., 1955; MD, Baylor U., Houston, 1959. Diplomate Am. Bd. Pediatrics. Intern Presbyn. St. Luke's Hosp., Chgo., 1959-60, resident in pediatrics, 1960-62; fellow in infectious diseases Baylor U., 1962-64; fellow in immunology, instr. in pediatrics U. Minn., Mpls., 1964-66; asst. prof., assoc. prof. Baylor U. Coll. Medicine, 1966-73; assoc. prof. U. Pa., Phila., 1973-77; prof., chmn. dept. pediatrics Tex. Tech U. Health Scis. Ctr., Lubbock, 1977-79, rsch. prof., 1979-83; med. officer Nat. Inst. Neurol.-Communicative Disorders and Stroke, NIH, Bethesda, Md., 1982-85; vis. scientist Gallaudet Coll., Washington, 1984-85; prof. pediatrics Meharry Med. Coll., Nashville, 1986-89, W.K. Kellogg disting. prof., 1989—. Contbr. over 140 articles to med. jours., chpts. to books. Recipient Disting. Alumnus award Ea. N.Mex. U., 1969, rsch. career devel. award NIH, 1968-73. Fellow Infectious Diseases Soc. Am.; mem. Am. Pediatric Soc., Am. Assn. Immunology, Assn. for Gnotobiology, Am. Med. Women's Assn., Pediatric Infectious Diseases Soc., Alpha Omega Alpha. Home: 9479 New Hwy 96 W Franklin TN 37064 Office: Meharry Med Coll 1005 DB Todd Blvd Nashville TN 37208

SOUTHALL, VIRGINIA LAWRENCE, artist; b. Portsmouth, Va., Aug. 25, 1927; d. Malachi Ashley Lewis and Bessie (Oliver) Lawrence; m. Junius Nathan Southall, Apr. 18, 1959; children: Lawrence Nathan. Student Norfolk divsn., Va. State Coll., 1945-46. Sec. to dean sch. engring. Tuskegee (Ala.) Inst., 1949-51; passport clk., ID clk. dept. army The Pentagon, Washington, 1951-62; pers. clk. AID, Dept. State, Washington, 1963-67. Exhibited in group shows including U. Md. Coll. Arts Program Gallery, College Park, 1993, Prince Georges C.C., Marlboro Gallery, Largo, Md., 1993-94, Montpelier Cultural Art Ctr., Laurel, Md., 1996. Concert choir mem. Prince Georges C.C.; Chancel Choir mem. Ebenezer United Meth. Ch., vol. art tchr. for youth programs. Mem. Nat. Mus. Women in the Arts, Md. Choral Soc. Home: 9015 Wallace Rd Lanham MD 20706

SOUTHERLAND, WANDA MAE, newspaper editor; b. Fayetteville, Tenn., Sept. 26, 1948; d. Bennie Franklin and Jewell Katherine (Hall) Bennett; m. Howard Ewing Southerland, Dec. 6, 1969; children: Marlon Duane, Kathryn Michelle. Student, Draughons Coll of Bus., Nashville, 1967, Normandale C.C., Bloomington, Minn., 1984-87, David Lipscomb U., 1987. Reporter Eden Prairie (Minn.) News, 1987; reporter Chronicle of Mt. Juliet (Tenn.), 1989-91, editor, 1991-94, 1995-96; editl. asst. GCA Pub., Nashville, 1994-95, editor, 1995—; cons., writer Varallo & Assocs., Nashville, 1990; cons. D&H Electronics, Mt. Juliet, 1995—. Active West Wilson Rep. Women, Mt. Juliet, 1991-94, Lebanon (Tenn.) Rep. Women, 1992. Recipient Media award Tenn. Edn. Assn., 1992, Wilson County Edn. Assn., 1992; named Aide de Camp, Gov. State of Tenn., 1996. Mem. Mt. Juliet C. of C., Mt. Juliet Kiwanis. Mem. Ch. of Christ. Home: 911 Bay Dr Old Hickory TN 37138 Office: GCA Publishing Ste 219B 4004 Hillsboro Pike Nashville TN 37215

SOUTHERN, EILEEN (MRS. JOSEPH SOUTHERN), music educator; b. Mpls., Feb. 19, 1920; d. Walter Wade and Lilla (Gibson) Jackson; m. Joseph Southern, Aug. 22, 1942; children: April, Edward. A.B., U. Chgo., 1940, M.A., 1941; Ph.D., NYU, 1961; M.A. (hon.), Harvard U., 1976; D.A. (hon.), Columbia Coll., Chgo., 1985. Instr. Prairie View U., Hempstead, Tex., 1941-42; asst. prof. So. U., Baton Rouge, 1943-45, 49-51; tchr. N.Y.C. Bd. Edn., 1954-60; instr. Bklyn. Coll., CUNY, 1960-64, asst. prof., 1964-69;

assoc. prof. York Coll., CUNY, 1969-71, prof., 1972-75; prof. music Harvard U., Cambridge, Mass., 1976-87, chmn. dept. Afro-Am. studies, 1976-79, prof. emeritus, 1987—. Concert pianist, 1940-55; author: The Buxheim Organ Book, 1963, The Music of Black Americans: A History, 1971, 2d edit., 1983, Readings in Black American Music, 1971, 2d edit., 1983, Anonymous Chansons in MS El Escorial Biblioteca del Monasterio, IV a 24, 1981, Biographical Dictionary of Afro-American and African Musicians, 1982, African-American Traditions in Song, Sermon, Tale, and Dance, 1630-1920; An Annotated Bibliography, 1990 (with Josephine Wright); editor: The Black Perspective in Music (1973-90), Nineteenth Century African-American Musical Theater, 1994; contbr. articles to profl. jours. Active Girl Scouts U.S.A., 1954-63; chmn. mgmt. com. Queens Area YWCA, 1970-73. Recipient Alumni Achievement award U. Chgo., 1970, Deems Taylor award ASCAP, 1973, Peabody medal Johns Hopkins U., 1991; NEH grantee, 1979-83. Mem. NAACP, Internat. Musicol. Soc., Am. Musicol. Soc. (hon., bd. dirs. 1974-76), Sonneck Am. Music Soc. (bd. dirs. 1986-88), Renaissance Soc., Phi Beta Kappa (hon. Radcliffe Coll.), Alpha Kappa Alpha. Home: PO Box 1 Jamaica NY 11411-0001 Office: Harvard U Cambridge MA 02138

SOUTHGATE, (CHRISTINA) ADRIENNE GRAVES, lawyer; b. Biloxi, Miss., Feb. 26, 1951; d. James Henry Jr. and Helen Alvera (Mataya) Graves; m. Theodore John Southgate, June 26, 1972; children: Edward James Leyland, Colin Scott Christian. BA, Wellesley (Mass.) Coll., 1973; postgrad., Gordon-Conwell Theol. Sem., South Hamilton, Mass., 1973-75; JD, Wayne State U., 1978, postgrad. Bar: Mich. 1979, U.S. Ct. Appeals (6th cir.) 1980, U.S. Ct. Appeals (5th, 7th and 11th cirs.) 1982, U.S. Supreme Ct. 1982, U.S. Ct. Appeals (3d, 4th, 8th, 9th, 10th and D.C. cirs.) 1983, U.S. Ct. Appeals (1st, 2d and fed. cirs.) 1984, R.I. 1985. Law clk. to presiding justice Mich. Supreme Ct., Detroit, 1979-81; chief appellate counsel Charfoos, Christensen & Archer, P.C., Detroit, 1981-85; assoc. Carroll, Kelly & Murphy, Providence, 1985-87; asst. dir., chief legal counsel R.I. Dept. Environ. Mgmt., Providence, 1987-89; gen. counsel R.I. Pub. Utilities Commn., Providence, 1989—; adj. instr. legal writing Detroit Coll. Law, 1979-81; counsel exec. com. Emma Willard Sch., Troy, N.Y., 1985-90; cons. Jr. League of Providence, R.I., 1986-91; adj. prof. Vt. Law Sch., 1987-91. Contbr. articles to profl. jours. Vol. atty. R.I. Protection and Advocacy Services, Inc., Internat. Inst. R.I.; mem., chair fin. stewardship com. Episcopal Diocese R.I.; bd. dirs. alumnae fund and exec. coun. Emma Willard Sch.; bd. dirs. Big Sisters Assn. R.I., YMCA Greater Providence, South East New Eng. Cluster YMCAs; R.I. rep. east field com. YMCA U.S.A.; sr. warden St. Matthew's Episc. Ch.; local coord. World Learning Inc. Internat. H.S. Program; active Leadership R.I.; mem. R.I. bd. govs. external com. telecomm., 1994-95. Mem. ABA (editorial bd. gen. practice sect. 1982-93, various coms.), R.I. Bar Assn. (specialization com. 1985-86, adminstrv. law com. 1991—, young lawyers clerkship com. 1985-94), Fed. Energy Bar Assn., Fed. Bar Assn., Nat. Assn. Women Lawyers, Am. Judicature Soc., R.I. Women's Bar Assn., R.I. Wellesley Club. Republican. Home: 22 Rosedale Ave Barrington RI 02806 Office: R I Pub Utilities Comm 100 Orange St Providence RI 02903-2963

SOUTHWORTH, LINDA JEAN, artist, critic, educator; b. Milw., May 11, 1951; d. William Dixon and Violet Elsie (Kuehn) S.; m. David Joseph Roger, Nov. 16, 1985 (div. July 1989). BFA, St. John's U., Queens, N.Y., 1974; MFA, Pratt Inst., Bklyn., 1978. Printmaker, still life and portrait painter, collage artist, photographer self-employed, N.Y.C., 1974—; art critic Resident Publs., N.Y.C., 1993-95; adj. prof. art history St. Francis Coll., Bklyn., 1985-94; artist-in-residence Our Saviour's Atonement Luth. Ch., N.Y.C., 1993-95. Exhibited in solo shows at Galimaufry, Croton-on-Hudson, N.Y., 1977, Kristen Richards Gallery, N.Y.C., 1982, Gallery 84, N.Y.C., 1990, The Bernhardt Collection, Washington, 1991, The Netherland Club, N.Y.C., 1992, Chuck Levitan Gallery, Soho, 1996; group shows include Union St. Graphics, San Francisco, 1974, Nuance Gallery, Tampa, 1987, 88, Soc. Illustrators Ann. Drawing Show, N.Y.C., 1989, 90, Salmagundi Club, N.Y.C., 1991, 92, Henry Howells Gallery, N.Y.C., 1992, 93, Mus. Gallery, N.Y.C., 1994, Cavalier Gallery, Greenwich, Conn., 1995, Carib Gallery, N.Y.C., 1995, Chuck Levitan Gallery, N.Y.C., 1996; artist Christmas card/UNICEF, 1992. Home: 106 Cabrini Blvd Apt 5D New York NY 10033-3422

SOVIE, MARGARET DOE, nursing administrator, college dean, educator; b. Ogdensburg, N.Y., July 7, 1934; d. William Gordon and Mary Rose (Bruyere) Doe; m. Alfred L. Sovie, May 8, 1954; 1 child, Scot Marc. Student, U. Rochester, 1950-51; diploma in nursing, St. Lawrence State Hosp. Sch. Nursing, Ogdensburg, 1954; postgrad., St. Lawrence U., 1956-60; BS in Nursing summa cum laude, Syracuse U., 1964, MS in Edn., 1968, PhD in Edn., 1972; DSc (hon.), Health Sci. Ctr. SUNY, Syracuse, 1989; MSN, U. Pa., 1995. Cert. adult health nurse practitioner. Staff nurse, clin. instr. St. Lawrence State Hosp., Ogdensburg, 1954-55, instr. nursing, 1955-62; staff nurse Good Shepherd Hosp., Syracuse, 1962; nursing supr. SUNY Upstate Med. Ctr., Syracuse, 1963-65, insvc. instr., 1965-66, edn. dir. and coord. nursing svc., 1966-71, asst. dean Coll. Health Related Professions, 1972-84, assoc. prof. nursing, 1973-76, dir. continuing edn. in nursing, 1974-76, assoc. dean and dir. div. continuing edn. Coll. Health Related Professions, 1974-76; spl. assignment in pres.'s office SUNY Upstate Med. Ctr. and Syracuse U., 1972-73; assoc. dean for nursing U. Rochester, N.Y., 1976-88, assoc. prof. nursing, 1976-85, prof., 1985-88; assoc. dir. for nursing Strong Meml. Hosp., U. Rochester Med. Ctr., 1976-88; chief nursing officer Hosp. U. Pa., Phila., 1988-96, assoc. exec. dir., 1988-94, assoc. dean for nursing practice Sch. Nursing, 1988-96, Jane Delano prof. nursing adminstrn. Sch. Nursing, 1988—, chief nursing officer, 1988-96; sr. fellow Leonard Davis Inst. Health Econs. U. Pa., Phila., 1992—; trustee bd. U. Pa. Health Sys., Phila., 1993-96; nursing coord. and project dir. Cen. N.Y. Regional Med. Program, Syracuse, 1968-71; mem. edn. dept. State Bd. Nursing, Albany, N.Y., 1974-84, chmn., 1981-83, chmn. practice com., 1975-80, mem. joint practice com., 1975-80, vice chmn., 1980-81; mem. adv. com. to clin. nurse scholars program Robert Wood Johnson found., Princeton, N.J., 1982-88; adj. assoc. prof. Syracuse U. Sch. Nursing, 1973-76; mem. Gov.'s Health Adv. Panel N.Y. State Health Planning Commn., 1976-82, task force on health manpower policy, 1978, informal support networks sect. steering com., 1980; mem. health manpower tng. and utilization task force State N.Y. Commn. on Health Edn.and Illness Prevention, 1979; mem. task force on nursing personnel N.Y. State Health Adv. Coun., 1980; mem. adv. panel on nursing svcs. U.S. Pharm. Conv. Inc., Washington, 1985-90; cons. Nat. Ctr. for Svcs. Rsch. and Health Care Tech. Assessment, Rockville, Md., 1987; mem. nursing stds. task force Joint Commn. Accreditation Health Care Orgns., 1988-90; mem. various other adv. coms.; lectr. in field. Mem. editl. bd. Health Care Supr., 1982-87, Nursing Econs., 1983—, Best Practices and Benchmarking in Health Care, 1995—; manuscript rev. panel Nursing Outlook, 1987-91; mem. editorial bd. Seminars for Nurse Mgrs., 1994—; contbr. articles to profl. jours., chpts. to books. Mem. bd. visitors Sch. Nursing U. Md., Balt., 1984-89; mem. bd. mgrs. Strong Meml. Hosp., Rochester, 1983-88; bd. dirs. Monroe County Assn. for Hearing, Rochester, 1979-82, Vis. Nurse Svc., Rochester and Monroe County, 1978, Southeastern Pa. chpt. ARC, 1991—. Ann. Margaret D. Sovie lectureship inaugurated Strong Meml. Hosp. U. Rochester, 1989; spl. nurse rsch. fellow NIH, 1971-72; grantee various orgns.; recipient Dean's Outstanding Alumni award Coll. of Nursing, Syracuse U., 1994. Fellow Am. Acad. Nursing (program com. 1980-81, task force on hosp. nursing 1981-83, chair expert panel on quality health 1994—); mem. ANA (nat. rev. com. for expanded role programs 1975-78, site visitor to programs requesting accreditation 1976-78, cabinet on nursing svcs. 1986-90, cert. bd. nursing adminstrn. 1983-86, Ad Hoc com. on advanced practice 1992-95), Am. Orgn. Nurse Execs. (stds. task force 1987), N.Y. State Nurses Assn. (med. surg. nursing group, chmn. edn. com. dist. 4 1974-76, chmn. cmty. planning group for nursing dist. 4 1974-75, coun. on regional planning in nursing 1974-76, del. to conv. 1978, Nursing Svc. Adminstrn. award 1985), Inst. Medicine (com. design strategy for quality rev. and assurance in Medicare 1988-90), Sigma Theta Tau, Pi Lambda Theta. Republican. Roman Catholic. Office: U Pa Sch Nursing 420 Guardian Dr Philadelphia PA 19104-6096

SOVINEE, BONNIE CHRISTINE, small business owner; b. Somerset, N.J., Apr. 22, 1951; d. Rudolph William and Freda May Sovinee; m. Frank Levi Blair, Aug. 30, 1992. BS in Art Edn., Kutztown U., 1973. Owner Sovinee Blair Enterprises, Somerset, N.J.; adminstrv dir. Tourism and Conv. Coun., 1996—; advisor, contbg. mem. Nat. Jeweler Mag., 1992-95, Am. Jewelry Mfrs. Mag., 1988-91, Jewelers Circular Keystone, 1986-95. Graphic artist: (subscription brochure) Heritage Trail Assn., 1996, (logo design) Historic Bound Brook, Main St. Area Mchts. Assn. Pres., v.p., founding mem. Main St. Ave. Merchants Assn., Bound Brook, 1984-88; chair Historic Bound Brook Main St. Program, 1993-95; exec. dir. Miss Somerset County Scholarship Pageant, 1989-94; candidate State Senate, Dist. 16, N.J., 1991; sec., bd. dirs. Heritage Trail Assn. Somerset County, 1995-96. Mem. Jewelers of Am. (2d v.p., 3d v.p. affil. coun.), N.J. Jewelers Assn. (bd. dirs. 1984-94, pres. 1986-90), Jewelers Vigilance Com., Jewelry Industry Coun. (truth in pricing com. 1986-95), Somerset County C. of C. (mem. coun., charter, mem. tourism and conv. coun. 1993—, Outstanding Woman in Bus. 1989).

SOWALSKY, PATTI LURIE, author; b. Hartford, Conn., Oct. 16, 1940; d. Joseph Aaron and Mildred (Weisinger) Lurie; m. Jerome Saul Sowalsky, Oct. 22, 1961; children: Richard, John, Susan. Cert. dental hygiene, U. Pa., 1960. Author, publisher On Exhibit Fine Art Publs., Potomac, Md., 1992—. Author, publisher: (art travel guide) On Exhibit: The Art Lover's Travel Guide to American Museums, 1992-96. Docent Corcoran Mus., Washington, 1985-90; cert. in Braille, Libr. of Congress, Washington, Golden Circle mem. Kennedy Ctr., Washington, 1988—. Recipient Docent of Yr. award Corcoran Mus., Washington, 1989. Home: 8613 Chateau Dr Potomac MD 20854 Office: On Exhibit Fine Art Publs PO Box 59734 Potomac MD 20859

SOWDER, KATHLEEN ADAMS, marketing executive; b. Person County, N.C., Feb. 9, 1951; d. George W. and Mary W. (Woody) A.; BS, Radford Coll., 1976; MBA, Va. Poly. Inst., 1978; m. Angelo R. LoMascolo, Apr. 11, 1980 (div.); 1 child, Mary Jennifer; m. Terry Tetirick, Dec. 27, 1995. Asst. product mgr. GTE Sylvania, Waltham, Mass., 1978-79, product mgr. video products, 1979-80; comml. mktg. mgr. Am. Dist. Telegraph, N.Y.C., 1980-87; v.p. mktg. ESL, Hingham, Mass., 1987-91; pres. Q.B. Air dba Falcon Holdings, Summit, N.J., 1991—; exec. v.p. Falcon Detection Techs., Inc., Plymouth, Mass., 1991-94; v.p. mktg. Westec Security, Irvine, Calif., 1995—. Mem. Am. Mktg. Assn., Am. Soc. Indsl. Security (past chair standing com. on phys. security). Republican. Home: 2521 E Gelid Ave Anaheim CA 92806 Office: Westec 5 Mason Irvine CA 92618

SOWERS, MARGARET ANN, home economics, family and consumer science educator; b. Pitts., Apr. 4, 1946; d. Richard Conwell and Ruth Eleanor (Springer) Westermann; m. Christopher Herr Sowers, Sept. 20, 1969; children: Heather Ross. BS in home econs., Carnegie-Mellon U., 1968; MS in edn., Temple U., 1974. cert. family life educator, 1994. Sub. tchr. Lebanon (Pa.) Sch. Dist., 1981-87, home economics tchr., 1970-74, 84-85; home economics cons. Lebanon County Penn State Coop. Extension, 1986—; home economics tchr. Cedar Crest H.S., Lebanon, 1993—; acting extension home economist, 1988-89, Train the Trainer Pa. Dept. Edn., 1993—; cons. Hershey Foods Test Kitchens, 1995—; presenter at convs. in field. Bd. dirs. Am. Heart Assn., 1988-94, chairperson of Heart-At-Work Task Force, 1987-91, vice chairperson ctrl. program com., 1988-91, chairperson, 1991-94; co-chmn. Centennial Anniversary Celebration of Zion United Meth. Ch., Bible sch. tchr., mem. ch. choir, mem. bell choir; vol. Dietitian for Boost II, Lebanon, 1976-78. Recipient Educator's award Dept. Edn. Pa., 1985, Stds. for Excellence Sr. H.S. Home Econs. Program, 1995; named Vol. of Yr. Am. Heart Assn., 1991. Mem. ASCD, Am. Assn. Family and Consumer Scis., Pa. Assn. Family and Consumer Scis., Lebanon County Home Econs. Assn. (pres., v.p., treas.), Pa. Nutrition Coun., Nat. Assn. for Edn. Young Children, Nat. Coun. Family Rels., Family and Consumer Scis. Edn. Assn., Lebanon Valley Assn. Edn. Young Children (treas.), Phi Delta Kappa. Home: 1015 Franklin Ave Lebanon PA 17042-7112 Office: Cedar Crest H S Cornwall-Lebanon Sch Dist 115 E Evergreen Rd Lebanon PA 17042-7505

SOWLES, BETH A., secretary; b. Battle Creek, Mich., June 11, 1960. AS, Ferris State U., Big Rapids, Mich., 1981. Legal sec. Kidston-Peterson, P.C., Kalamazoo, Mich., 1981-82, Christovich & Kearney, New Orleans, 1982-84; sec. Cath. Family Svcs., Kalamazoo, 1984-87; sec. bldgs. dept. City of Kalamazoo, 1987-88, sr. sec. dept. transp. metro transit div., 1988—. Contbg. author Resource Ctr. Newsletter; editor monthly newsletter Women's Therapist Network. Organizing mem. Take Back the Night, Kalamazoo, 1990, Victories Over Violence, Kalamazoo, 1991; mem. Kalamazoo Area Legal Secs. Assn., 1981-83. Home: 133 E Candlewyck Dr # 110 Kalamazoo MI 49001 Office: City of Kalamazoo 530 N Rose St Kalamazoo MI 49007-3638

SOWLES, HOLLY MARGARET, artist, illustrator; b. Flagstaff, Ariz., Dec. 22, 1960; d. Kenneth M. and Louann J. (Johnson) S. BS in Interior Design, U. Ctrl. Okla., 1985; MA in Interdisciplinary Studies, Boise State U., 1996. With mktg. dept. Clinique Cosmetics, Oklahoma City, Portland, Oreg., 1982-87, NCH Corp., Portland, 1987-89, Wasasau Ins. Agys., Portland, 1989-91; gallery dir. Galos Fine Arts, Boise, Idaho, 1994-95; creative cons., Boise, 1995—; bd. dirs. Social Expressiions Inc., Boise. One-woman show Hemmingway Ctr., Boise, 1996; commd. Leukemia Soc., 1995; illustrator Coinciding Visions, 1994, Calypso Beans, 1993, Merry Christmas, 1995; represented in pvt. collections. Mem. Phi Omicron Upsilon, Gamma Phi Beta. Democrat.

SOYSTER, MARGARET BLAIR, lawyer; b. Washington, Aug. 5, 1951; d. Peter and Eliza (Shumaker) S. AB magna cum laude, Smith Coll., 1973; JD, U. Va., 1976. Bar: N.Y. 1977, U.S. Dist. Ct. (so. and ea. dists.) N.Y. 1977, U.S. Ct. Appeals (2nd cir.) 1979, U.S. Supreme Ct. 1981, U.S. Ct. Appeals (4th cir.) 1982, U.S. ct. Appeals (11th cir.) 1987, U.S. Ct. Appeals (7th cir.) 1991, U.S. Ct. Appeals (3d cir.) 1992. Assoc. Rogers & Wells, N.Y.C., 1976-84, ptnr., 1984—. Mem. ABA, Assn. of Bar of City of N.Y., Nat. Assn. Coll. and Univ. Attys., Phi Beta Kappa. Office: Rogers & Wells 200 Park Ave Ste 5200 New York NY 10166-0005

SPACEK, SISSY (MARY ELIZABETH SPACEK), actress; b. Quitman, Tex., Dec. 25, 1949; d. Edwin S. and Virginia S.; m. Jack Fisk, 1974; children: Schuyler Elizabeth, Virginia Madison. Student, Lee Strasberg Theatrical Inst. Motion picture appearances include Prime Cut, 1972, Ginger in the Morning, 1972, Badlands, 1974, Carrie, 1976 (Acad. award nomination for best actress 1976), Three Women, 1977, Welcome to L.A., 1977, Heartbeat, 1980, Coal Miner's Daughter, 1980 (Acad. award for best actress 1980), Raggedy Man, 1981, Missing, 1982 (Acad. award nomination for best actress), The River, 1984 (Acad. award nomination for best actress), Marie, 1985, 'Night Mother, 1986, Crimes of the Heart, 1986 (Acad. award nomination for best actress), Violets Are Blue, 1986, JFK, 1991, The Long Walk Home, 1990, Hard Promises, 1992, Trading Mom, 1994, The Grass Harp, 1995, Streets of Laredo, 1995, If These Walls Could Talk, 1996; TV movie appearances include The Girls of Huntington House, 1973, The Migrants, 1973, Katherine, 1975, Verna: USO Girl, 1978, A Private Matter, 1992, A Place for Annie, 1994, The Good Old Boys, 1995; guest host TV show Saturday Night Live, 1977; appeared in episode TV show The Waltons. Named Best Actress for Carrie, Nat. Soc. Film Critics, 1976, Best Supporting Actress, N.Y. Film Critics, 1977. Office: care Creative Artists 9830 Wilshire Blvd Beverly Hills CA 90212-1804*

SPACKS, PATRICIA MEYER, English educator; b. San Francisco, Nov. 17, 1929; d. Norman B. and Lillian (Talcott) Meyer; 1 child, Judith Elizabeth Spacks. BA, Rollins Coll., Winter Park, Fla., 1949, DHL, 1976; MA, Yale U., 1950; PhD, U. Calif., Berkeley, 1955. Instr. English Ind. U., Bloomington, 1954-56; instr. humanities U. Fla., Gainesville, 1958-59; from instr. to prof. Wellesley Coll., Mass., 1959-79; prof. English Yale U., New Haven, 1979-89, chmn. dept., 1985-88; Edgar F. Shannon prof. English U. Va., 1989—, chmn. dept., 1991—. Author: The Poetry of Vision, 1967, The Female Imagination, 1975, Imagining a Self, 1976, The Adolescent Idea, 1982, Gossip, 1985, Desire and Truth, 1990, Boredom: The Literary History of a State of Mind, 1995. Fellow Guggenheim Found., 1969-70, NEH, 1974, Am. Council Learned Socs., 1978-79, Nat. Humanities Ctr., 1982-83, 89. Mem. MLA (2nd v.p. 1992, 1st v.p. 1993, pres. 1994, mem. adv. com. 1976-80, mem. exec. coun. 1986-89), Am. Acad. Arts and Scis., Am. Coun. Learned Socs. (mem. bd. trustees 1992—, v.p. 1994—). Home: 1830 Fendall Ave Charlottesville VA 22903-1614 Office: U Va Dept English Bryan Hall Charlottesville VA 22903

SPAETH, BARBETTE STANLEY, classics educator; b. Chgo., Mar. 26, 1956; d. Harold Opie and Barbara Adeline (Yunker) Stanley; m. Robert Thomas Spaeth, June 24, 1978 (div. June 1990). BA summa cum laude, MA, Northwestern U., 1977; PhD, Johns Hopkins U., 1987. Lectr. European divsn. U. Md., Heidelberg, Germany, 1983-84, U. Md. Baltimore County, Catonsville, 1984; asst. prof. dept. classical studies Tulane U., New Orleans, 1987-94, assoc. prof., 1994—; excavator Sanctuary of Apollo, Kourion, Cyprus, summers 1982-83; trenchmaster Kommos (Crete, Greece) Excavations, summers 1984-85. Author: The Roman Goddess Ceres, 1996; contbr. articles to profl. jours. Chmn. program coun. 1st Unitarian-Universalist Ch., New Orleans, 1996. Jacob Hirsch fellow Am. Sch. Classical Studies, Athens, 1986-87, Oscar Broneer fellow Am. Acad. in Rome, 1990-91. Mem. Am. Philol. Assn., Archaeol. Inst. Am., Classical Assn. Mid. West and South. Democrat. Office: Tulane U Dept Classical Studies New Orleans LA 70118

SPAFFORD, MICHELLE, special education educator; b. New Kensington, Pa., June 7, 1964; d. Del John and Joan Elizabeth (Dunlap) S. BA in Therapeutic Recreation, Alderson-Broaddus Coll., Philippi, W.Va., 1986; M in Spl.Edn., Clarion (Pa.) U., 1991. Cert. tchr. mentally and physically handicapped, Pa. Resident care specialist Verland Found., Sewickley, Pa., 1986; child care specialist Luth. Youth and Family Svc., Pa., 1986-87; mental health therapist DuBois (Pa.) Regional Med. Ctr., 1987-90, recreational therapist, 1990-91; supr. Clearfield County Child & Youth Svcs., Clearfield, Pa., 1990-91; grad. asst. Clarion U., 1990-91; spl. edn. tchr. DuBois Area Sch. Dist., 1992—; recreational therapist The Golden Age, DuBois, 1994-95; mem. Perkins participatory planning com. Jefferson Tech., DuBois, 1994—; mem. Sandy Twp. Recreation Bd., 1995—. Tchr. pioneer club Christian Missionary Alliance, DuBois, 1993; tchr., coach Spl. Olympics, DuBois, 1991; advisor Environ. Club, DuBois Area H.S., 1994—. Mem. Council for Exceptional Children, Pa. Therapeutic Recreation Assn., The Wilderness Soc. Republican. Baptist. Home: 1229 Treasure Lk Du Bois PA 15801-9029 Office: Du Bois Area Sch Dist Liberty Blvd Du Bois PA 15801

SPAFFORD-DAVIS, DARLA, healthcare professional; b. Rochester, N.Y., Aug. 5, 1971; d. David Gates and Darlene Ann (LaDue) Spafford; m. Alfred Scott Davis, June 17, 1994. BS in Psychology, Brigham Young U., 1993; postgrad., SUNY, Buffalo. Residential treatment specialist Monroe County ARC, Rochester, 1993-94, staff trainer, 1994-95, treatment specialist, 1995—. Friend So. Poverty Law Ctr., Birmingham, Ala., 1994—. Mem. NOW. Home: # 1 300 Meigs St Rochester NY 14607 Office: Monroe County ARC 1000 Elmwood Ave Rochester NY 14620

SPAGNUOLO, PASQUALINA MARIE, rehabilitation nurse; b. Phila., Jan. 21, 1942; d. Charles and Lena (Damiano) Caruolo; children: Louis, Charles, Jason. Lic. practical nurse diploma, Salem (N.J.) Community Coll., 1985; BSN, Widener U., Chester, Pa., 1989. Lic. practical nurse, Del., N.J., Pa.; RN, Del., N.J., Pa. Practical nurse A.I. Dupont Rehab. Hosp., Wilmington, Del.; med. sec. Underwood Meml. Hosp., Woodbury, N.J., nurse's aide; pvt. duty nurse, Mt. Ephraim, N.J. Merit scholar Widener U., 1985-86, Charlotte Newcomb scholar, 1986-87; recipient Eleanore O. Dower award, 1988.

SPAIN, JOYCE HICKS, nurse; b. Benton, Ky., Dec. 29, 1954; d. Ralphly Howell and Irene (Eldridge) Hicks; m. John Conrad Spain, Mar. 11, 1978; children: John Matthew, Timothy Joseph, Adam William. BS, Bethel Coll., McKenzie, Tenn., 1977; ASN, Union U., Jackson, Tenn., 1983. RN, Tenn. Staff nurse Jackson-Madison County Gen. Hosp., 1983-85, Home Health Care, Inc., Huntingdon, Tenn., 1985-88, Meth. Home Health, McKenzie, 1988-90, Meth. Hosp., McKenzie, 1990-91; nurse, team leader HomeCare Helath Svcs. (formerly TriCounty Home Health), Huntingdon, 1991—; mem. disaster team ARC, Huntingdon, 1994. Den leader Boy Scouts Am., Huntingdon, 1991-93, Webelos asst. leader, 1994, Webelos den leader, 1993-95; treas. Huntingdon Band Boosters, 1994-95; leader TOPS #TN 175, McKenzie, 1994-95; mem. Huntingdon Fire Dept. Ladies Aux., 1994—. Mem. Ch. of Christ. Home: RR 2 Box 158-a Huntingdon TN 38344-9802

SPALDING, RITA LEE, artist; b. Pitts., Nov. 30, 1928; d. Clarence E. and Irene Francis (Israel) McEldowney; m. Willard Perkins Spalding, Sept. 15, 1956; children: Gregory Scott, Laura Lee Dooley. BA, Chatham Coll., 1950. Artist IDL, Inc., Pitts., 1950-56; tchr. West Pa. Sch. for Deaf, Pitts., 1970-82; dir. family daycare Beulah Presbyn. Ch., Pitts., 1983-87; sec. Penn Hills (Pa.) Arts Coun., 1989-91. Exhibited in many one-woman shows and group shows including Three Rivers Arts Festival, West Va. U., chatham Coll., Pitts. Ctr. for the Arts, Scaife Gallery, Westmoreland Mus. of Art, Studio Z. Elder, trustee Beulah Presbyn. Ch., Churchill, Pa., 1979-82, pres. deacons, 1976-79; vol. Meals on Wheels, Churchill, 1995—; judge of elections Penn Hills 5-5, 1993—. Recipient Jean Thoburn award Aqueous Open, 1979, Jurors award Pitts. Watercolor Soc., 1988, Merit award Westmoreland Art Nats., 1993, Awards Wilkins Art Festival, 1991-95, Awards Penn Hills Arts Festival, 1988—, many local awards. Mem. Pa. Art Assn. (bd. govs. 1994—, pres. 1989-94), Penn Hills Arts coun. (sec. 1991—), Associated Artists Pitts., Pitts. Print Group, Pitts. Watercolor Soc. (membership chair 1993—). Republican. Home: 611 Dixie Dr Pittsburgh PA 15235

SPALLONE, SHARON LEE, secondary education educator; b. Hazleton, Pa., Sept. 18, 1946; d. Joseph Raymond and Helen Irene (Purcell) Bergeron; m. Robert Charles Spallone, Dec. 26, 1970. BS, Bloomsburg (Pa.) State Coll., 1968; MA, Pa. State U., 1970; postgrad., U. Alaska, Carlow Coll., Ind. Wesleyan U., Coll. of St. Rose. Cert. comm. and speech tchr., Pa. Instr. speech Bloomsburg State U., 1970; tchr. comm. and English, Weatherly (Pa.) Area H.S., 1970—, mentor, 1987; adj. instr. Luzerne County C.C., Nanticoke, Pa., 1980. Author: Elephant Stew, 1972; contbr. poetry to various anthologies and mags. Mem. adv. com. Pocono Renaissance Fiare, Mt. Pocono, Pa., 1993, 94, Dem. Steering Com., 1995. Mem. NEA, Pa. Edn. Assn., Weatherly Area Edn. Assn. (chmn. publicity com.), Nat. Women's Mus. (charter).

SPANDORFER, MERLE SUE, artist, educator, author; b. Balt., Sept. 4, 1934; d. Simon Louis and Bernice P. (Jacobson) S.; m. Lester M. Spandorfer, June 17, 1956; children: Cathy, John. Student, Syracuse U., 1952-54; BS, U. Md., 1956. Mem. faculty Cheltenham (Pa.) Sch. Fine Arts, 1969—; instr. printmaking Tyler Sch. Art Temple U., Phila., 1980-84; faculty Pratt Graphics Ctr., N.Y.C., 1985-86. One woman shows include Richard Feigen Gallery, N.Y.C., 1970, U. Pa., 1974, Phila. Coll. Textiles and Sci., 1977, Ericson Gallery, N.Y.C., 1978, 79, R.I. Sch. Design, 1980, Syracuse U., 1981, Marian Locks Gallery, Phila., 1973, 78, 82, Temple U., 1984, Tyler Sch. Art, 1985, University City Sci. Ctr., 1987, Gov.'s Residence, 1988, Wenniger Graphics Gallery, Provincetown, Mass., 1989, Mangel Gallery, Phila., 1992, Widener U. Art Mus., 1995, Gloucester County Coll., 1996; group shows Bklyn. Mus. Art, 1973, San Francisco Mus. Art, 1973, Balt. Mus. Art, 1970, 71, 74, Phila. Mus. Art, 1972, 77, Fundacio Joan Miro, Barcelona, Spain, 1977, Del. Mus. Art, Wilmington, 1978, Carlsberg Glyptotek Mus., Copenhagen, 1980, Moore Coll. Art, Phila., 1982, Tyler Sch. Art, 1983, William Penn Meml. Mus., Harrisburg, Pa., 1984 Ariz. State U., 1985, Tiajin Fine Arts Coll., China, 1986, Beaver Coll., Phila., 1988, The Port of History Mus., Phila., 1987, Sichuan Fine Arts Inst., Chong Qing, People's Republic China, 1988, Glynn Vivian Mus., Swansea, Wales, 1989, Phila. Mus. Art, 1990, Fgn. Mus., Riga, Latvia, 1995; represented in permanent collections Met. Mus. Art, N.Y.C., Whitney Mus. Am. Art, N.Y.C., Mus. Modern Art, N.Y.C., The Israel Mus., Balt. Mus. (gov's prize and purchase award 1970), Phila. Mus. Art (purchase award 1977), Toyoh Bijutsu Gakko, Tokyo, Library of Congress, Temple U.; commd. works represented in U. Pa. Inst. Contemporary Art, 1991; co- author: Making Art Safely, 1993. Recipient award Balt. Mus. Art/Md. Inst. Art, 1971, Govs. prize and Purchase award Balt. Mus. Art, 1970, Outstanding Art Educators award Pa. Art Edn. Assn., 1982, Purchase award Berman Mus., 1995; grantee Pa. Coun. Arts, 1989. Mem. Am. Color Print Soc., Pa. Art Edn. Assn. Jewish. Studio: 307 E Gowen Ave Philadelphia PA 19119-1023

SPANEL, HARRIET ROSA ALBERTSEN, state senator; b. Audubon, Iowa, Jan. 15, 1939; m. Leslie E. Spanel, June 3, 1961; 3 children. BS in Math., Iowa State U., 1961. Rep. Wash. State, 1987-93, senator, 1993—. Home: 901 Liberty St Bellingham WA 98225-5632 Office: PO Box 40482 Olympia WA 98504-0482

SPANN, WILMA NADENE, educational administrator; b. Austin, Tex., Apr. 24, 1938; d. Jamison and Nadene (Burns) Jamison Plummer; m. James W. Spann II, Aug. 2, 1958; children: James III, Timothy, Terrance, Kemberly, Kelby, Elverta, Peter, Margo. BA, Marquette U., 1974; MS, U.

Wis., 1985. Sec. Spandagle Coop., Milw., 1969-89; tchr. adult basic edn. Milw. area Tech. Coll., Milw., 1975-80; tchr. Milw. Pub. Sch. System, 1975-90, adminstrv. intern, 1990-91; asst. prin. Clara Barton Elem. Sch., Milw., 1992-93; asst. prin. in charge Greenfield Montessori Sch., Milw., 1993-94, 1993-94, prin., 1993—; prin. Greenfield Montessori Sch., 1993—; del. Inter Group Coun. Contbr. articles to profl. jours. Dir. Vacation Bible Sch., Tabernacle Cmty. Bapt. Ch., Milw., 1977-80, bd. dirs. Christian edn., 1981-90; v.p. women's aux. Wis. Gen. Bapt. State Conv., 1985-95, pres. women's aux., 1995—; instr. Wis. Congress Christian Edn., 1982—; asst. dean Wis. Gen. Bapt. State Congress Christian Edn., 1985; mem. sr. retreat com. Nat. Bapt. Youth Camp; fin. sec. Interdenominational Min.'s Wives Wis. Recipient cert. of Recognition, women's auxiliary Wis. Gen. Bapt. State Conv., 1986, Bd. Edn. Tabernacle Bapt. Ch., 1990. Mem. NAACP, Internat. Assn. Childhood Edn. (sec. 1990-92), Met. Milw. Alliance Black Sch. Educators, Nat. Bapt. Conv. (life, del. intergroup coun., Myra Taylor shcolar com.), Marquette U. Alumni Assn., Assn. Childhood Edn. Internat. (sec. 1990-92), Interdenominational Alliance Minister's Wives & Widows of Wis. (fin. sec.), Assn. Women in Adminstrn., N.Am. Baptist Women's Union, Ch. Women United (life, del. to intergroup), Phi Delta Kappa, Eta Phi Beta. Democrat. Home: 1906 W Cherry St Milwaukee WI 53205-2046 Office: Greenfield Montessori Sch 1711 S 35th St Milwaukee WI 53215-2004

SPANO, RINA GANGEMI, sociology educator; b. Jersey City, Aug. 22, 1948; d. Joseph and Rose (Calabria) Gangemi; m. Domenico Spano, Sept. 12, 1971; children: Elisabeth, Cristina. BA, Caldwell Coll., 1970; MA in Teaching, Montclair State Coll., 1975, MA in Sociology, 1982; PhD in Sociology, CUNY, 1991. Cert. tchr. English grades K-12, N.J. Tchr. St. Cecilia's Sch., Kearny, N.J., 1972-77; instr. sociology Caldwell (N.J.) Coll., 1979-82, asst. prof., 1982-92, assoc. prof., 1992-96, prof., 1996—, chmn. dept., 1979-96; presenter in field. Mem. adv. bd. Trinity Acad. Mem. Am. Sociol. Assn., Ea. Sociol. Soc., N.J. Sociol. Soc., Nat. Orgn. Italian-Am. Women, Delta Epsilon Sigma, Kappa Gamma Pi, Pi Delta Epsilon. Roman Catholic. Home: 79 Evergreen Dr North Caldwell NJ 07006 Office: Caldwell Coll Dept Sociol 9 Ryerson Ave Caldwell NJ 07006-6109

SPARKMAN, LILA GILLIS, health care facility administrator; b. Cumby, Tex., Feb. 24, 1930; d. William Paul and Cora (Caviness) Gillis; m. Alton C. Sparkman, July 26, 1947; children: Claudia, Vivian, Alan. BS summa cum laude in Social Work, East Tex. State U., 1978, MA, 1980; postgrad. U. Tex., Tyler, 1982; PhD in Clin. Sociology, U. N. Tex. Cert. social worker, mental retardation diagnostic and evaluation specialist, mental retardational profl. Prof. sociology Paris (Tex.) Jr. Coll., 1980; coordinator geriatric services Sabine Valley Regional Mental Health-Mental Retardation Ctr., Marshall, Tex., 1980-82, adminstr. Mental Retardation Residential Homes, Longview, Tex., 1983—; clin. dir. Hunt County Family Svcs. Ctr., Greenville, Tex., 1987; pvt. clin. practice, Winnsboro, Tex., 1989—; sec.-treas. KAM Well Service, New London, Tex., 1981—; social work cons. Forest Acres, Longview, 1983. Author: Comparison of Traditional and Non-traditional Female Students and Their Perceived Reasons for University Attendance, 1980 co-author: Day Care Centers for the Elderly: An Alternative, 1983. Mem. Am. Sociol. Assn., Nat. Assn. Social Workers, Mid South Sociol. Assn., Pub. Health Assn., Alpha Kappa Delta, Alpha Chi, Cap and Gown. Democrat. Methodist. Lodge: Rebekah. Home: PO Box 529 Winnsboro TX 75494-0529

SPARKS, BETH K., financial planner; b. Columbus, Ohio, June 21, 1957; d. Harold E. and Ann E. (Loehnert) Kitzmiller; m. Robert E. Sparks, Aug. 4, 1979; children: Courtney E., Amy B. Student, Miami U., 1975-76, Ohio State U., 1976-79. CFP; lic. life/health ins., Ohio. Sign artist Kroge Co., Lancaster, Ohio, 1980-81; aerobics instr. YWCA, Lancaster, 1980-86; PR dir. YWCA/YMCA, Lancaster, 1982-83; prin. Beth K. Sparks, Lancaster, 1983-87; investment cons. The Ohio Co., Lancaster, 1986—; advisor investment clubs Blue Chips, Fairfield Women's Investors Group, 1988—; com. mem., vol. Bus. Partnership Program with County Schs., Lancaster, 1995—. Vol. Lancaster High Sch., 1985—, vol. girls golf coach, 1995—; co-chmn. Jon Myers State Rep. Reelection, Lancaster, 1994; active Citizens Com. for Children, Lancaster, 1996, Com. for Lancaster's Future, 1996. Named Club Champion, Lancaster County Club, 1990-96. Mem. DAR, Internat. Assn. CFP, Inst. CFP, Lancaster C. of C. (bd. dirs. 1989-95, chmn. women's divsn. 1995—), Columbus Stock and Bond Club, Ohio High Sch. Golf Coaches Assn. Republican. Presbyterian. Home: 1159 Stone Run Ct Lancaster OH 43130 Office: The Ohio Co 227 E Main St Lancaster OH 43130

SPARKS, CARMEN ELAINE, customer service representative; b. West Plains, Mo., Apr. 1, 1953; d. Thomas Clennon and Susie Ann (Renfro) Holloway; children: Julia, Heather, Carissa. Student, Big Bend C.C., Moses Lake, Wash., 1978-93. Sec. Ill. Coll., Jacksonville, 1971-72; driver sch. bus Royal City and Moses Lake (Wash.) Sch. Dists., 1980-83; legal sec. Moberg Law Firm, Moses Lake, 1982-83; customer svc. rep. Grant County PUD, Moses Lake, 1983—. Mem. Silhouette Gun Club, South Campus Athletic Club. Home: 2136 W Neppel St Moses Lake WA 98837

SPARKS, DENISE RENE, flooring contractor; b. Peoria, Ill., July 9, 1959; d. William Edward Sparks and Bette June (Lohman) Lawrence. Cert. water damage restoration technician. Exec. sec. Atlas, St. Louis, 1979-91; pres. Metro-Area Enterprises, Inc., Alton, Ill., 1993—; cons. Alton Park & Recreation, 1991, 93, 94. Coach safety tng. ARC, Alton, 1993-94, water safety instr., 1994—. Mem. Internat. Inst. Carpet and Rug Cleaners. Lutheran. Office: Metro-Area Enterprises Inc 605 Main Alton IL 62002

SPARLING, MARY LEE, biology educator; b. Ft. Wayne, Ind., May 20, 1934; d. George Hewson and Velmah Evelyn (McClain) S.; m. Albert Alcide Barber, Sept. 1, 1956 (div. Jan. 1975); children: Bonnie Lee Barber, Bradley Paul Barber. BS, U. Miami, Coral Gables, Fla., 1955; MA, Duke U., 1958; PhD, UCLA, 1962. Lectr. UCLA, 1962-63; asst. prof. Calif. State U., Northridge, 1966-72, assoc. prof., 1972-76, prof., 1976—; statewide acad. senator Calif. State U., 1996—. Contbr. articles to profl. jours. NSF grantee Calif. State U., Northridge, 1971-72, 81-83, 89, NIH grantee Calif. State U., Northridge, 1987-89. Mem. AAUP (pres. 1981-82), Am. Soc. Cell Biology, Soc. for Devel. Biology, Am. Soc. Zoologists, Sigma Xi (bd. dirs. Research Triangle, N.C. 1974-91). Home: 8518 White Oak Ave Northridge CA 91325-3940 Office: Calif State U Biology Dept Northridge CA 91330

SPARNON, DEBORAH A., librarian; b. Leesville, La., Feb. 20, 1952; d. John Patrick and Marilyn Margaret (Dougherty) Oates; m. John Sparnon, July 6, 1974; children: Jeffrey, James. BA, William Paterson Coll., 1974, MEd, 1982. Cert. tchr., ednl. media specialist, N.J. Libr. Upsala U., Wantage, N.J., 1990-93; libr., media specialist Marian E. McKeown Sch., Newton, N.J., 1980—; adj. instr. Rutgers U., New Brunswick, N.J., 1990—. NEH grant, 1994; Geraldine R. Dodge Found. fellow, 1994. Mem. N.W. Jersey Reading Coun. (v.p., pres.-elect, pres.), N.J. Reading Assn., N.J. Edn. Assn., Sussex County Sch. Media Assn., Ednl. Media Assn. N.J., Hampton Twp. Edn. Assn. (sec. 1994-95). Office: Marian E McKeown Sch One School Rd Newton NJ 07860

SPARTZ, ALICE ANNE LENORE, retired retail executive; b. N.Y.C., May 14, 1925; d. John Francis and Alice Philomena (Murray) Rattenbury; m. George Eugene Spartz, Oct. 29, 1949; children: Mary Elizabeth, James, Barbara, Anne, Thomas, William, Michael, John, Matthew, Clare, Robert, Richard. Student, Wright Coll., 1945-47, No. Ill. U., 1950; AA, Triton Coll., 1987. Svc. rep. Ill. Bell Tel., Chgo., 1945-46; stewardess United Airlines, Denver, 1947-49; ret. mgr. Family Life League Resale Shop, Oak Park, Ill., 1987-95; retired, 1995. Mem. Cicero (Ill.) Cmty. Coun., 1967-69; mem. Park Dist. Oak Park Com., 1973-74; active Ill. Right to Life Com., Chgo., 1971—, Com. Pro-Life Caths., Chgo., 1992—; former bd. dirs. Ill. Pro-Life Coalition, Family Life League; vol. canteen workers ARC, Chgo., 1942-45. Mem. St. Edmunds Womens Club. Democrat. Roman Catholic. Office: 226 N Ridgeland Oak Park IL 60302

SPATTA, CAROLYN DAVIS, education consultant; b. Gauhati, Assam, India, Jan. 20, 1935; d. Alfred Charles and Lola Mildred (Anderson) Davis; m. John Robert Spatta, June 2, 1957 (div. Feb. 1964); children: Robert Alan, Jennifer Lynn Spatta-Harris; m. S. Peter Karlow, July 25, 1981. AB, U. Calif., Berkeley, 1964; MA, U. Mich., 1968, PhD, 1974. Rsch. asst. U. Calif., Berkeley, 1963-65; instr. Schoolcraft Coll., Livonia, Mich., 1968-74; corp. sec. Oberlin (Ohio) Coll., 1974-78; pres. Damavand Coll., Tehran, Iran, 1978-79; cons. pvt. practice, Washington, 1979-80; v.p., adminstr. E. Mich. U., Ypsilanti, Mich., 1980-81; Dir. Inst. grants programs, and adv. svc. Assn. Am. Colls., Washington, 1982-84; v.p., adminstrn. and bus. affairs Calif. State U., Hayward, 1984-92, prof. geography and environ. studies, 1992-94; ind. mediator, cons. higher edn., 1995—; vis. lectr. E. Mich. U. Ypsilanti, 1969, 1970; mem. accreditation team Western Assn. Schs. Colls.; Fulbright scholar, Malaysia, 1994. Contbr. articles to profl. jours. Bd. dirs. Wellness, Inc.; mem. Trinity Parish, Menlo Pk., Calif. (pers., bldg. coms.), U. Mich. Alumni Assn., St. John's Episc. Ch. (pastoral care commn.), Chevy Chase, Md., Oberlin Open Space Com., Tenaya Guild, John Muir Hosp., Walnut Creek, Calif. (pres.), steering com. Ann Arbor Citizens for Good Schs.; trustee Pacific Sch. of Religion, 1992—. Recipient fellowship Nat. Defense Foreign Lang., 1966-68; Fulbright scholar, Malaysia, 1994—. Mem. Am. Assn. Higher Edn., Asian Studies on Pacific Coast, Assn. Asian Studies, Assn. Am. Geographers, Assn. Pacific Coast Geographers.

SPAULDING, KARLA RAE, lawyer; b. Breckenridge, Mich., Feb. 22, 1954; d. Donald Hugh and Shirley Ann (Federspiel) S. BA magna cum laude, Western Mich. U., 1975; JD, Northwestern U., 1980. Bar: Ohio 1980, Fla. 1987. Vis. prof. Grand Valley State Colls., Allendale, Mich., 1975-76; assoc. Baker & Hostetler, Cleve., 1980-83; asst. U.S. atty. U.S. Atty. Office, Tampa, Fla., 1983-88, Grand Rapids, Mich., 1988-89; chief maj. drug trafficking sect. Mid. Dist. Fla. U.S. Atty. Office, Tampa, 1989-90, chief appellate div. Mid. Dist. Fla., 1990-92; asst. U.S. atty. Organized Crime and Drug Enforcement Task Force, Tampa, 1992; chief fraud and econ. crime sect. So. Dist. Tex. U.S. Atty. Office, Houston, 1992-93; ptnr. Holland & Knight, Tampa, Fla., 1994, James, Hoyer & Newcomer, P.A., Tampa, 1994—. Bd. editors, dep. editor-in-chief Fed. Bar Jour., 1992-95; contbr. articles to profl. publs. Recipient Dir.'s award IRS, 1988. Mem. ABA, ATLA, Hillsborough County Bar Assn. Republican. Office: James Hoyer & Newcomer 4830 W Kennedy Blvd Tampa FL 33609-2564

SPAVONE, SANDRA ELLEN, parochial school educator; b. Fairmont, W.Va., Apr. 8, 1963; d. Glen McCoy and Eleanor Cora (Toothman) Waybright; m. Thomas Spavone, June 9, 1984; children: Thomas Glen, Christina Elizabeth. BS, Hyles Anderson Coll., 1985. English tchr. Riverdale Bapt. Sch., Upper Marlboro, Md., 1989-93, 94—, Bethlehem Bapt. Sch., Fairfax, Va., 1993-94. Sunday sch. jr. H.S. tchr., girls' minister Riverdale Bapt. Ch., Upper Marlboro, 1993—. Home: 2412 Oak Glen Way Forestville MD 20747-3705 Office: Riverdale Bapt Sch 1133 Largo Rd Upper Marlboro MD 20772-8619

SPEACH, ANNETTE, principal; b. Syracuse, N.Y., Feb. 28, 1958; d. Anthony John and Viola Catherine (Bellardini) S.; m. Bernard Hayes, Feb. 16, 1996. AA in Humanities, Onondaga C.C., Syracuse, N.Y., 1978; BS in Spl. Edn./Elem. Edn., Buffalo State Coll., 1980; MS in Learning Disabilities, Syracuse U., 1983; CAS Ednl. Adminstrn., SUNY, Oswego, 1994. Spl. edn. tchr. Sylvan-Verona Beach Common Sch. Dist., Sylvan Beach, N.Y., 1980-85; spl. edn. tchr. North Syracuse (N.Y.) Ctrl. Sch. Dist., 1985-94, elem. prin., 1994—; learning disabilities cons. Onondaga Cortland Madison Bd. Coop. Ednl. Svcs., Syracuse, 1989-95. Mem. North Syracuse Edn. Assn. (2nd v.p. 1991-94). Office: Cicero Elem Sch Rte 31 Cicero NY 13039

SPEAR, BARBARA L., state legislator; b. Alton, N.H., June 3, 1926; Widow; 4 children. BA, U. N.H., 1948. Ret. tchr. N.H.; mem. N.H. Ho. Reps., 1992—, mem. buget com., parks and recreation com., mem. econ. devel. com., ways and means com.; vice-chair edn. com.; chmn. Bd. of Selectmen, 1990—. Active in organizing child care ctr. Mem. Womens Club. Republican. Baptist. Office: NH House of Reps State Capitol Concord NH 03301

SPEAR, KATHLEEN KELLY, lawyer; b. Cinco Bayou, Fla., June 4, 1949; d. John Francis and Alma (Cancian) Kelly; m. Brian Blackburn Spear, June 17, 1972; children: Matthew, Olivia. AB magna cum laude, Smith Coll., 1971; MA, Brown U., 1973; JD cum laude, Northwestern U., 1979. Bar: Ill. 1979, U.S. Ct. Appeals (7th cir.) 1979, U.S. Dist. Ct. (no. dist.) Ill. 1979, U.S. Ct. Appeals (7th cir.) 1980, U.S. Ct. Appeals (8th cir.) 1982, U.S. Ct. Appeals (10th cir.) 1983. Assoc. Kirkland & Ellis, Chgo., 1979-84; antitrust and litigation counsel Kraft Inc., Glenview, Ill., 1984-85; sr. counsel bus. devel. and venture Kraft, Inc., Glenview, Ill., 1985-88, group counsel frozen foods, 1988-92, v.p., dep. gen. counsel, 1992—. Precinct capt. New Trier Dem. Orgn., Wilmette, Ill., 1980—. Mem. ABA, Ill. Bar Assn., Chgo. Bar Assn., Chgo. Council Lawyers, North Shore Smith Club. Roman Catholic. Office: Kraft Foods Inc 3 Lakes Dr Northfield IL 60093

SPEAR, LAURINDA HOPE, architect. BFA, Brown U., 1972; MArch, Columbia U., 1975. Registered architect, Fla., N.Y., Colo.; cert. Nat. Coun. Archtl. Registration. Founding prin. Arquitectonica, Coral Gables, Fla.; mem. faculty U. Miami; lectr. in field. Prin. works include Pink Ho., Miami, Fla., 1978, The Palace, Miami, 1982 (Honor award Miami chpt. AIA 1982), Overseas Tower (Honor award Fla. chpt. AIA 1982, Honor award Miami chpt. 1982), The Atlantis, Miami, 1982 (Miami chpt. AIA award 1983), The Sq. at Key Biscayne (Honor award Miami chpt. AIA 1982), The Imperial, Miami, 1983, Casa los Andes (Record Hos. award Archtl. Record 1986), North Dade Justice Ctr., Miami, 1987 (Honor award Miami chpt. AIA 1989), Rio, Atlanta, 1988 (Honor award Miami chpt. AIA 1989), Banco de Credito del Peru, Lima, 1988 (Honor award Miami chpt. AIA 1989), The Ctr. Innovative Tech., Herndon, Va., 1988 (Honor award Va. chpt. AIA 1989, Honor award Miami chpt. 1990, Merit award Fairfax, Va., County Exceptional Design Awards Program 1990), Sawgrass Mills (Merit award Miami chpt. AIA 1990, Honor award Fla. chpt. 1991), Miracle Ctr. (Honor award Miami chpt. AIA 1989), Internat. Swimming Hall of Fame, Ft. Lauderdale, Fla., 1991, Banque de Luxembourg, 1993, Disney All-Star Resorts, Orlando, Fla., 1994, Foster City (Calif.) Libr., 1994, U.S. Embassy, Lima, 1994, USCG Family Housing, Bayamon, P.R., 1994, Altamira Ctr., Caracas, Venezuela, 1994. Mem. beaux arts support group Lowe Art Mus., Miami; bd. dirs. Miami Youth Mus. Recipient Design Awards citation Progressive Architecture, 1975, 80, Rome Prize in Architecture, 1978, Award of Excellence, Atlanta Urban Design Commn., 1989. Fellow AIA. Office: Arquitectonica 426 Jefferson Ave Miami FL 33139

SPEARING, KAREN MARIE, physical education educator, coach; b. Chgo., Apr. 17, 1949; d. John Richard and Naomi (Allen) Miller; m. Edward B. Spearing III, Apr. 28, 1973. BS in Phys. Edn., U. Wis., Whitewater, 1972; MS in Outdoor Edn., No. Ill. U., 1978. Cert. phys. edn. tchr., Ill.; cert. CPR instr., hunter safety instr., boating safety instr., master snowmobile instr., Ill. Tchr., coach Glenside Mid. Sch., Glendale Heights, Ill., 1973—, athletic dir., 1981-92, 95—, dept. chairperson, 1992-93; hunter safety instr. State of Ill., 1988—, water safety instr., 1989—, snowmobile instr., 1990—, master snowmobile instr., 1995, CPR instr., 1996—. Awards chairperson U.S. Power Squadron, Chgo., 1987-93, mem. exec. com. DuPage br., 1993-96, edn. officer, 1996—; mem. com. Ill. Hunting and Fishing Days, Silver Springs State Pk., 1993—; amb. People to People Citizen Amb. Program, Russia and Belarus, 1993. Mem. AAHPERD, Ill. Assn. Health, Phys. Edn., Recreation and Dance, Ill. H.S. Assn. (volleyball referee). Office: Glenside Mid Sch 1560 Bloomingdale Rd Glendale Heights IL 60139

SPEARING, KAYE JEAN, elementary education educator; b. Cadillac, Mich., Dec. 21, 1942; d. Wendell Robert and Clara Elisa (Hatlem) Mellberg; children: Charles, Jennifer. B in Mus. Edn., Ctrl. Mich. U., 1964, M in Classroom Edn., 1990. Elem. and jr. high music tchr. Traverse City (Mich.) Pub. Schs., 1964-72; elem. and jr. high music tchr. Suttons Bay (Mich.) Pub. Schs., 1973-77, elem. classroom tchr., 1977—; steering com. chair North Ctrl. Accreditation, Suttons Bay, 1987-94; voice tchr., gifted/talented dir. Suttons Bay (Mich.) Schs., 1988-94. Singer: Song From a Summer Salon, 1994. Treas., soloist Traverse Chorale, Traverse City, Mich., 1964-70, Leelanau Choir, Suttons Bay, 1973-96, choir dir.; choir dir., soloist Trinity Ch., Northport, Mich., 1966—. Grantee Mich. State Dept. Edn., 1989, Traverse City (Mich.) Rotary, 1992. Mem. Suttons Bay Edn. Assn. (sec. 1976-77, Outstanding Person in Edn. award 1989), Delta Kappa Gamma. Mem. United Ch. of Christ. Home: 488 Stoney Pt Suttons Bay MI 49682

SPEARMAN, DIANE NEGROTTO, art/special education educator; b. New Orleans, Nov. 22, 1949; d. Allen Jules and Constance Lenora (Hinkel) Negrotto; m. Joe Dalton Spearman, June 26, 1971; children Brett Dalton, Eric Clayton, Scott Brandon. BS in Art Edn., La. State U., 1971, MA in Art Edn., 1991, Ed. Spl. Education, 1994. Cert. tchr. La. art, English, spl. edn., 1-12, supr. student tchrs. Art tchr. E. Baton Rouge (La.) Schs., 1971-72, 1973-78, 1981-83, spl. edn. art tchr., 1990-95; presenter state confs. gifted and spl. edn., Baton Rouge, 1985, 94; mem. com. to write art edn. curriculum Holmes Program La. State U., Baton Rouge, 1988, supr. student tchrs., 1992-96, cons. art and spl. edn., 1991-96. Products of students sold to fund program for spl edn. have been featured in newspaper and magazine articles. Leadership positions Cub Scouts Pack 37, Boy Scouts Troop 478, Boy Scouts Am., 1982-95; scoutmaster Troop 93 (handicapped boys), Baton Rouge, 1992-96. Named Arlington Tchr. of Yr. East Baton Rouge Parish Schs., 1993-94; grantee Arts Coun. of Greater Baton Rouge, Jr. League, 1991, 92, 93. Mem. Nat. Art Edn. Assn., La. Art Edn. Assn., Coun. for Exceptional Children, Arts Coun. Greater Baton Rouge (arts in edn. com. 1988-91), Am. Legion Auxiliary, Unit 288, New Orleans. Republican. Roman Catholic. Home: 14628 Bailey Dr Baton Rouge LA 70816 Office: Arlington Prep Acad 931 Dean Lee Dr Baton Rouge LA 70820

SPEARMAN, MAXIE ANN, financial analyst, administrator; b. Piedmont, S.C., Sept. 14, 1942; d. J. Mac and Margaret Cecille (Johnson) S. BS, U. S.C., 1965; postgrad., Ga. State U., 1985; student, U. Ga. Acct. Shell Oil Co., Atlanta, 1965-66; internal auditor Sears, Roebuck & Co., Atlanta, 1966-67; acct. Econ. Opportunity Atlanta, Atlanta, 1967-68; acct. City of Atlanta, 1968-78, fin. analyst, 1978-89, sr. fin. analyst planner, 1989—; investment cons., Atlanta, Conyers, Ga., 1980—. Mem. Rep. Presdl. Task Force, 1985—, U.S. Senatorial Club, Rep. Nat. Com., 1988—, Ga. Rep. Party, 1990—, Atlanta Safety Com., 1985—, Mayor's Spl. Events Task Force, 1990—; charter founder Ronald Reagan Rep. Ctr., 1988; del.-at-large Rep. Platform Planning Com., 1992, 94. Recipient safety award Atlanta City Govt., 1990, Presdl. Commn. Exec. Com. of Republican Party award, 1992; Order of Merit award Nat. Rep. Senatorial Com., 1996. Mem. NAFE, Am. Mgmt. Assn., Ga. Assn. Med. Victims, Inc. (sec., treas. 1985—), Nat. Trust for Historic Preservation. Methodist. Home: 1280 Vineyard Dr SE Conyers GA 30208-2466 Office: 55 Trinity Ave SW Ste 1450 Atlanta GA 30303-3531

SPEARMAN, MOLLY M., state legislator. Tchr. S.C.; mem. S.C. Ho. Reps., 1993—. Republican. Office: SC House of Reps State House Columbia SC 29211

SPEAR-OBERMILLER, MARY PATRICIA, sales and marketing executive; b. Sheridan, Wyo., May 4, 1954; d. Bradford Johnson and Patricia Ann (Brooder) S.; m. Kenneth Ray Gleason, June 3, 1972 (div. June 1982); children: Seth Kendy, Susan Michele; m. Rodney Dean Obermiller, Sept. 27, 1991. Grad. high sch., Dayton, Wyo. Bookkeeper Padlock Ranch, Ranchester, Wyo., 1972; ranch ptnr. Eagle Point Ranch, Busby, Mont., 1972-82; purchasing agt. Top Office Products, Inc., Sheridan, 1982-86, sales rep., 1985-87; nat. sales and mktg. dir. GeoLearning Corp., Sheridan, 1988-89, gen. mgr., 1990-93; mktg. dir. Antelope Butte Corp., Sheridan, 1993—; ski sch. instr. Antelope Butte Corp., Sheridan, 1986—, ski sch. dir., 1989—. Bd. dirs. Sch. Dist. 17K Big Horn County, Kirby, Mont., 1980-82. Recipient Outstanding Skiing award Sheridan C. of C., 1970; named 1st Runner-up Mother of Yr. Big Horn County, 1980. Fellow NAFE; mem. PEO (treas. chpt. T), Profl. Ski Instrs. Am., Kiwanis (v.p. local club 1989-90, pres. 1990-91), Future Farmers Am. Alumni Assn. (sec. 1988-90), Young Farmers and Ranchers Edn. Assn., Antelope Butte Ski Club (bd. dirs. 1991-92). Republican. Episcopalian. Home: PO Box 6 Dayton WY 82836-0006 Office: Antelope Butte Corp PO Box 460 Dayton WY 82836-0460

SPEARS, DIANE SHIELDS, fine arts coordinator, educator; b. Seattle, May 21, 1942; d. Richard Keene McKinney and Dorothy Jean (Shields) Thacker; m. Howard Truman Spears, Sept. 3, 1977; 1 child, Truman Eugene. BA in Art, English, Edn., Trinity U., 1964; MA in Christian Counseling, San Antonio Theol. Sem., 1986, D of Christian Edn., 1988. Cert. tchr. secondary edn., elem. edn. Instr. ESL Dliel-Geb (Def. Lang. Inst.), San Antonio, 1973-74, Ceta/Ace Bexar County Sch. Bd., San Antonio, 1975-78; tchr. elem. edn., art, music New Covenant Faith Acad., San Antonio, 1983-89; instr. ESL Jewish Family Svc., San Antonio, 1991; tchr. elem. art Edgewood Ind. Sch. Dist., San Antonio, 1992-93, dist. art specialist, 1993-95, fine arts coord., 1995—; owner, operator Art for Kings, San Antonio, 1985—; mem. adv. bd. Zion Arts Inst., San Antonio, 1995—. Illustrator teacher-created materials-lit. activities for young children, 1989-90; author: (art curriculum) Art for Kings, 1987; editor: (art curriculum) Edgewood Ind. Sch. Dist. Elem. Art Curriculum, 1993; exhibited in group shows Charles and Emma Frye Mus., Seattle, 1966, 68. Dir. intercessory prayer New Covenant Fellowship, San Antonio, 1980-90. Mem. NEA, Nat. Mus. for Women in Arts (charter), Colored Pencil Soc. Am. (charter), Tex. Art Edn. Assn. (1st pl. graphics divsn. 1995), San Antonio Art Edn. Assn. (1st pl. 1995), Hill Country Arts Found., Coppini Acad. Fine Arts. Republican. Home: 10314 Dreamland Dr San Antonio TX 78230 Office: Edgewood Ind Sch Dist Guerra Devel Ctr 1931 Herbert Ln San Antonio TX 78227

SPEARS, GEORGANN WIMBISH, marketing executive; b. Ft. Worth, Apr. 21, 1946; d. George Vardeman and Lela Ellon (Clifton) Wimbish; m. Richard Scarborough Spears, Dec. 31, 1981. BA in Govt. and History, Tex. Christian U., 1969. Cert. secondary govt. and history tchr., Tex. V.p., gen. mgr. Sports Today Mag., Arlington, Tex., 1982-83; editor corp. newsletter Amason Internat. Mktg., Dallas, 1983-85; supply mgr., dir. Am. Photocopy, Arlington, 1985-92; v.p. Mineral Wells (Tex.) Clay Products, Inc., 1993-96; v.p. mktg., chmn. bd. dirs. Educators Industries, Inc., Ft. Worth, 1993-95, chmn. bd., 1995—; v.p., vice chmn., bd. dirs. Superior Properties, Inc., 1995—. Features editor mag. Sports Today, 1982. Active Jewel Charity Ball, Ft. Worth, 1979—, Rep. Party of Tex., Austin, 1983—, PETA, 1992—; vol. ICU and CCU Arlington Meml. Hosp., 1983-86; vol. John Peter Smith Hosp., 1980-82. Mem. U. North Tex. Athletics (trustee 1994—), People for Ethical Treatment of Animals. Republican. Episcopalian. Home: 1909 Rockbrook Dr Arlington TX 76006-6615 Office: Educators Industries Inc 6633 Grapevine Hwy Fort Worth TX 76180-1523

SPEARS, JAE, state legislator; b. Latonia, Ky.; d. James and Sylvia (Fox) Marshall; m. Lawrence E. Spears; children: Katherine Spears Cooper, Marsha Spears-Duncan, Lawrence M., James W. Student, U. Ky. Reporter Cin. Post, Cin. Enquirer newspapers; rsch. Stas. WLW-WSAI, Cin.; tchr. Jiya Gakuen Sch., Japan; lectr. U.S. Mil. installations East Anglia, Eng.; del. State of W.Va., Charleston, 1974-80; mem. W.Va. Senate, Charleston, 1980-1993; mem. state visitors com. W.Va. Extension and Continuing Edn., Morgantown, 1977-91, W.Va. U. Sch. Medicine, 1992—. Chmn. adv bd. Sta. WNPB, 1992-94; congl. liaison Am. Pub. TV Stas. and Sta. WNPB-TV, 1992—; mem. coun. W.Va. Autism Task Force, Huntington, 1981-90; mem. W.Va. exec. bd. Literacy Vols. Am., 1986-90, 94—, pres., 1990-92; mem. Gov.'s State Literacy Coun., 1991—; bd. dirs. Found. Ind. Colls. W.Va., 1986—; mem. regional adv. com. W.Va. Gov.'s Task Force for Children, Youth and Family, 1989; mem. USS W.Va. Commn., 1989; mem. exec. com. W.Va. Employer Support Group for Guard and Res., 1989, mem. steering com., 1990—. Recipient Susan B. Anthony award NOW, 1982, nat. award Mil. Order Purple Heart, 1984, Edn. award Profl. Educators Assn. W.Va., 1986, Ann. award W.Va. Assn. Ret. Sch. Employees, 1985, Meritorious Service award W.Va. State Vets. Commn., 1984, Vets. Employment and Tng. Service award U.S. Dept. Labor, 1984, award W.Va. Vets. Council, 1984; named Admiral in N.C. Navy, Gov. of N.C., 1982, Hon. Brigadier Gen. W.Va. N.G., 1984. Mem. Bus. and Profl. Women (Woman of Yr. award 1978), Nat. League Am. Pen Women (Pen Woman of Yr. 1984), Nat. Order Women Legislators, DAR, VFW (aux.), Am. Legion (aux.), Delta Kappa Gamma, Alpha Xi Delta. Democrat. Home and Office: PO Box 2088 Elkins WV 26241-2088

SPEARS, MARIAN CADDY, dietetics and institutional management educator; b. East Liverpool, Ohio, Jan. 12, 1921; d. Frederick Louis and Marie (Jerman) Caddy; m. Sholto M. Spears, May 29, 1959. BS, Case Western Res. U., 1942, MS, 1947; PhD, U. Mo., 1971. Chief dietitian Bellefaire Children's Home, Cleve., 1942-53; head dietitian Drs. Hosp., Cleve., 1953-57; assoc. dir. dietetics Barnes Hosp., St. Louis, 1957-59; asst. prof. U. Ark., Fayetteville, 1959-68; assoc. prof. U. Mo., Columbia, 1971-75; prof., head dept. hotel, restaurant, instn. mgmt. and dietetics Kans. State U., Manhattan, 1975-89; cons. dietitian small hosps. and nursing homes; cons. dietetic edn. Author: Foodservice Organizations Textbook, 3d edit., 1995; contbr. articles to profl. jours. Mem. Am. Dietetic Assn. (Copher award

1989), Am. Sch. Foodsvc. Assn., Food Systems Mgmt. Edn. Coun., Soc. Advancement of Foodsvc. Rsch., Nat. Restaurant Assn., Coun. Hotel, Restaurant, Inst. Mgmt. Edn., Manhattan C. of C., Sigma Xi, Gamma Sigma Delta, Omicron Nu, Phi Kappa Phi. Home: 1522 Williamsburg Dr Manhattan KS 66502-0408 Office: Kans State U 105 Justin Hall Manhattan KS 66506-1400

SPECHT, ALICE WILSON, library director; b. Caracus, Venezuela, Apr. 3, 1948; (parents Am. citizens); d. Ned and Helen (Lockwood) Wilson; m. Joe W. Specht, Dec. 30, 1972; 1 child, Mary Helen. BA, U. Pacific, 1969; MLS, Emory U., 1970; MBA, Hardin-Simmons U., 1983. Libr. social scis. North Tex. State U., Denton, 1971-73; reference libr. Lubbock (Tex.) City and County Libr., 1974-75; system coord. Big Country Libr. System, Abilene, Tex., 1975-79; assoc. dir. Hardin-Simmons U., Abilene, 1981-88, dir. univ. librs., 1988—; apptd. Mayor's Task Force Libr. Svcs., 1995-96. Author bibliog. instrn. aids, 1981-90; editor; The College Man, For Pilots Eyes Only. Mem. mayor's task force Abilene Pub. Libr., 1995-96. Recipient Boss of Yr., Am. Bus. Women's Assn., 1994. Mem. ALA, Tex. Libr. Assn. (chair com. 1978-84, sec.-treas. coll. and univ. librs. divsn. 1993-94, legis. com. 1994—), Abilene Libr. Consortium (chair adminstrv. coun. 1990, 93, coord. nat. conf. 1991, 93), Rotary (chair com. 1989-90). Home: 918 Grand Ave Abilene TX 79605-3233 Office: Hardin-Simmons U PO Box 16195 2200 Hickory Abilene TX 79698-0001

SPECK, ROBIN ELLEN, emergency nurse; b. Englewood, N.J., May 13, 1951; d. Paul Bernard and Eleanore Roslyn (Schwarz) S.; m. Forrest William Kneisel, Sept. 27, 1980; children: Frederic Wayne, Benjamin Aaron, Rachael Victoria. BSN, Seton Hall U., 1976; MSN, George Mason U., 1993. RN, N.J.; cert. emergency nurse. From staff nurse to charge nurse Beth Israel Hosp., Passiac, N.J., 1976-78; head nurse nursery Baptist Med. Ctr., Columbia, S.C., 1983-84; agy. nurse Delta, San Antonio, 1984-85; sr. clin. nurse Walter Reed Army Med. Ctr., Washington, 1985-86; staff nurse Mt. Vernon Hosp., Alexandria, Va., 1990-94; patient care coord. Kuakini Med. Ctr., Honolulu, 1995—; instr. maternal/child health U. D.C., 1986; instr. maternal/child health Hawaii Pacific U., Honolulu, 1995—; counselor child abuse prevention Frankfurt Army Cmty. Svc., Germany, 1987-90. Merit badge counsellor Boy Scouts Am., Chantilly, Va., 1993-94; treas. Frankfurt Hosp. Aux., 1989-90; treas. Troop 621 Girl Scouts U.S., Honolulu, 1994-95. Cpt. U.S. Army, 1979-83. Mem. AACCN, Emergency Nurses Assn. Home: 280A Grewia Pl Honolulu HI 96818 Office: Kuakini Med Ctr 347 N Kuakini St Honolulu HI 96817

SPECTOR, ELEANOR RUTH, government executive; b. N.Y.C., Dec. 2, 1943; d. Sidney and Helen (Kirschenbaum) Lebost; m. Mel Alan Spector, Dec. 10, 1966; children: Nancy, Kenneth. BA, Barnard Coll., 1964; postgrad. sch. pub. adminstrn., George Washington U., 1965-67; postgrad sch. edn., Nazareth Coll., 1974. Indsl. investigator N.Y. State Dept. Labor, White Plains, 1964-65; mgmt. intern Navy Dept., Washington, 1965, contract negotiator, 1965-68, contract specialist, 1975-78, contracting officer/br. head, 1978-82, dir. div. cost estimating, 1982-84; dep. asst. sec. def. for procurement Washington, 1984-91; dir. Def. Procurement, Washington, 1991—; advisor Nat. Contract Mgmt. Assn., 1984—. Recipient Def. Meritorious Civilian Svc. medal, 1986, 93, Meritorious Svc. Presdl. award, 1989, 94, Disting. Civilian Svc. medal, 1991, 94, Presd. award 1990, Def. Disting. Civilan Svc. Office: Office Under Sec Defense Acquisition & Technology 3060 Def Pentagon Rm 3E144 Washington DC 30301-3060

SPECTOR, JOHANNA LICHTENBERG, ethnomusicologist, former educator; b. Libau, Latvia; came to U.S., 1947, naturalized, 1954; d. Jacob C. and Anna (Meyer) Lichtenberg; m. Robert Spector, Nov. 20, 1939 (dec. Dec. 1941). DHS, Hebrew Union Coll., 1950, MA, Columbia U., 1960. Rsch. fellow Hebrew U., Jerusalem, 1951-53; faculty Jewish Theol. Sem. Am., N.Y.C., 1954—, dir., founder dept. ethnomusicology, 1962-85, assoc. prof. musicology, 1966-70, Sem. prof., 1970-85, prof. emeritus, 1985—. Author: Ghetto-und Kzlieder, 1947, Samaritan Chant, 1965, Musical Tradition and Innovation in Central Asia, 1966, Bridal Songs from Sana Yemen, 1960; documentary film The Samaritans, 1971, Chicago International, 1973, Middle Eastern Music, 1973, About the Jews of India: Cochin, 1976 (Cine Golden Eagle 1979), The Shanwar Telis or Bene Israel of India, 1978 (Cine Golden Eagle 1979), About the Jews of Yemen, A Vanishing Culture, 1986 (Cine Golden Eagle 1986, Blue Ribbon, Am. Film Festival 1986), 2000 Years of Freedom and Honor: The Cochin Jews of India, 1992, Margaret Mead, 1992, Columbus International, 1993; religious and folk recs. number over 10, 000; contbr. articles to encys., various jours.; editorial bd. Asian Music. Fellow Am. Anthrop. Assn.; mem. Am. Ethnol. Soc., Am. Musicol. Soc., Internat. Folks Music Coun., World Assn. Jewish Studies, Yivo, Asian Mus. Soc. (v.p. 1964—, pres. 1974-78), Soc. Ethnomusicology (sec.-treas. N.Y.C. chpt. 1960-64). Home: 400 W 119th St New York NY 10027-7125

SPECTOR, ROSE, state supreme court justice. BA, Columbia U.; JD, St. Mary's Sch. Law, 1965. Judge County Ct. at Law 5, 1974-80, 131st Dist. Ct., 1980-92; justice Tex. Supreme Ct., 1993—. Office: Capital Station PO Box 12248 Austin TX 78711

SPEECE, KAREN A. See MARKS, KAREN ANNETTE SPEECE

SPEECE, SUSAN PHILLIPS, biology educator; b. Chgo., Aug. 13, 1945; d. George Truman and Patricia Carrie (Harrity) Phillips; m. Joseph Morris Speeece, June 10, 1967 (div. July 1989); children: Ryan Joseph, Nicole Suzanne. BS, Purdue U., 1967, MS, 1971; EdD, Ball State U., 1978; postgrad., Ind. U./Purdue U., Indpls., 1993. Cert. tchr., Ind. Sci. tchr., chair dept. Gosport (Ind.) Schs., 1967-68, Wes Del H.S., Gaston, Ind., 1971-76; instr. Purdue U., West Lafayette, Ind., 1968-70; instr. Anderson (Ind.) U., 1977-78, dir. tchr. edn., 1978-81, prof., chair dept. biol. scis., 1984-95; adj. faculty grad. sch. Ball State U., Muncie, Ind., 1978-84; dean math., sci. and engring. Fresno (Calif.) City Coll., 1995—; cons. Ind. Acad. Comp., 1985-88, NSF, 1987-90, Ind. Dept. Edn., 1991-92, Field Mus., Chgo., 1992-93; presenter in field; chair adv. coun. Nat Sci. Edn. and Assessment Stds. NAS/NRC, 1993—; guest seminar to grad. faculty Wright State U., 1991; mem. AIDS adv. panel State of Ind., 1990. Contbr. articles to profl. publs. Mem. Ind. Pesticide Rev. Bd., 1988—. Grantee Commn. on Higher Edn., 1987, 89, 90, Lilly Found., 1988, 92, Anderson U., Ball Bros.' Found., 1992; recipient citation for excellence in sci. edn. Calumet Area Sci. Tchrs., Disting. Svc. award Hoosier Assn. Science Tchrs., Inc., 1989, Gov.'s citation for outstanding leadership Corp. for Sci. and Tech., 1987. Mem. AAAS (nominating com. 1993—), Nat. Sci. Tchrs. Assn. (mem. exec. bd. 1989, Cert. of Recognition 1987-90), Hoosier Assn. Sci. Tchrs., Inc., Colo. Biology Tchrs. Assn., Nat. Assn. Biology Tchrs. (nat. sci. stds. rev. com. 1993, dir. at large 1992—), Am. Inst. Biol. Sci., Ind. Acad. Sci., Internat. Soc. for AIDS Edn., Nat. Assn. for Rsch. in Sci. Tchg., Phi Delta Kappa. Home: 2682 W Robinhood Ln Fresno CA 93711 Office: Fresno City Coll 1101 E University Ave Fresno CA 93741

SPEED, BILLIE CHENEY (MRS. THOMAS S. SPEED), retired editor, journalist; b. Birmingham, Ala., Feb. 21, 1927; d. John J. and Ruby (Petty) Cheney; m. Thomas S. Speed, July 7, 1968; children: Kathy Lovell Windham Williams, Donna Lovell Adams, Melanie Lovell Wright. Grad., W.Ga. Coll. Reporter, sports writer Birmingham News, 1945; sports writer, gen. assignment reporter, ch. editor Atlanta Jour., 1947-53, with promotion dept., 1955-57, religion editor, 1965-89; feature editor Coach and Athlete Mag., 1958, So. Outdoors, 1958. Recipient Sharp Tack award Cumberland dist. Seventh Day Adventists; Spl. Service award Christian Council of Metro Atlanta, 1974, award for outstanding personal ministry, 1986, personal service award, 1986; Arthur West award for religious feature writing United Meth. Ch., 1977; Alumni Achievement award West Ga. Coll., 1985; Trustee award Protestant Radio & TV Ctr., 1986; Faith & Freedom award Religious Heritage of Am., 1986. Fellow Religious Pub. Relations Council; mem. Nat. Religion Newswriters Assn., Nat. Fedn. Press Women, Theta Sigma Chi. Methodist. Home: 559 Rays Rd Stone Mountain GA 30083-3142

SPEER, GLENDA O'BRYANT, middle school educator; b. Uvalde, Tex., Mar. 30, 1956; d. Harvey Glen and Mary (Miller) O'Bryant; m. Weldon Michael Speer, July 12, 1975; children: Janena Lea, Jon Michael. BS, Sul Ross State U., Alpine, Tex., 1978; MA, U. Tex., San Antonio, 1984. Tchr. math. Jackson Middle Sch., San Antonio, 1978-82; tchr. math., computers Bradley Middle Sch., San Antonio, 1982-86, chmn. dept. math., 1986—; computer edn. tchr. trainer N.E. Ind. Sch. Dist., San Antonio, 1984—; acad. pentathlon coach Bradley Middle Sch., 1988-92; software reviewer Nat. Coun. Tchrs. Math., Reston, Va., 1994. Editor Math Matters newsletter, 1989—; writer curriculum guide: Computer Literacy Guide for Teachers, 1992. Black belt Karate and self-defense instr. Tang So Do Karate Assn., San Antonio, 1994—. Recipient Supt.'s award N.E. Ind. Sch. Dist., 1990, 92, 93, Red Apple Tchrs. award St. Mary's U., San Antonio, 1992. Mem. Nat. Coun. Tchrs. Math., Tex. Coun. Tchrs. Math., Bradley Middle Sch. PTA. Office: Bradley Middle Sch 14819 Heimer Rd San Antonio TX 78232-4528

SPEGAL, KATHIE MARIE, organization executive; b. Tillamook, Oreg., Nov. 29, 1943; d. Carl Joseph and Margaret Eileen (Eastin) Zoeller; m. William Leslie Spegal, Feb. 11, 1967 (div. Feb. 1983); children: Beth Ann Eades, Julia Morris, Patrick. BA, U. Ky., 1965; MEd, Miami U., 1967. Cert. Girl Scout exec. dir. Substitute tchr. grades K-12 Ohio, 1968-79; dir. pub. rels. and tng. Treaty Line Girl Scout Coun., Richmond, Ind., 1979-86; dir. program and membership Land of Lincoln Girl Scout Coun., Springfield, Ill., 1986-90; exec. dir., CEO Green Meadows Girl Scout Coun., Urbana, Ill., 1990—. Presenter bd. roles and responsibilities United Way Vol. Ctr., Champaign, Ill., 1995, 96, U. Ill. Alumni Assn., Champaign, 1996; mem. mktg. com. United Way Champaign County, 1992-95; bd. dirs. Va. Theater Group, Champaign, 1996—. Mem. Bus. and Profl. Women (sec.-treas. 1991-97, sec. dist. XII 1995-96), Rotary Internat. (vice-chair longterm youth exch. dist. 6490 1991-96), Assn. Girl Scout Exec. Staff (bd. dirs. pub. rels. membership 1987-96), Champaign-Urbana Sunrise Rotary (bd. dirs., pres. 1991-96, New Rotarian 1991, Rotarian of Yr. 1995). Office: Green Meadows Girl Scout Cn 1405 N Lincoln Ave Urbana IL 61801

SPEIER, K. JACQUELINE, state legislator; b. San Francisco, May 14, 1950; m. Steven K. Sierra, 1987 (dec. 1994); children: Jackson Kent, Stephanie Katelin. BA, U. Calif., Davis, 1972; JD, U. Calif., 1976. Legal coun., legis. asst. to Leo J. Ryan U.S. Rep. of Calif., 1973-78; mem. San Mateo County Bd. Supr., Calif., 1981-86, chairwoman, 1985; mem. Calif. State Assembly, 1986-96, majority wip, 1987-95, mem. health commn., mem. judiciary commn., mem. fin. and ins. commn., chair consumer protection com., 1991-95. Democrat. Roman Catholic. Office: 3151 State Capitol Sacramento CA 95814

SPEIER, KAREN RINARDO, psychologist; b. New Orleans, Aug. 19, 1947; d. William Joseph Rinardo and Shirley Eva (Spreen) Christensen; m. Joe Max Sobotka, Nov. 27, 1970 (div. 1972); m. Anthony Herman Speier, May 29, 1982; children: Anthony Herman III, Austin Clay. Student, Vanderbilt U., 1965-67; BA, La. State U., New Orleans, 1969; MS, U. New Orleans, 1974; PhD, La. State U., 1985. Lic. psychologist, La. Tchr. spl. edn. Huntsville (Ala.) Achievement Sch., 1970-72; instr. neurology La. State U. Med. Ctr., New Orleans, 1972-78; clin. assoc. Dawson Psychol. Assocs., Baton Rouge, 1979-81; tchr. asst. dept. psychology La. State U., Baton Rouge, 1979-81; psychol. examiner La. Sch. for Deaf, Baton Rouge, 1979-80; psychology intern VA Med. Ctr., Martinez, Calif., 1981-82; psychology extern East La. State Hosp., Jackson, 1982-83; clin. assoc. Baton Rouge Psychol. Assocs., 1983-86, pvt. practice clin. psychology, 1986—; sr. neuropsychologist Rehab. Hosp. of Baton Rouge, 1995-96; sec. bd. dirs. Baton Rouge Employment Devel. Svcs., 1987-89; mem. psychology cons. com. Meadow Wood Hosp., Baton Rouge, 1987-89; mem. psychology adv. com. Parkland Hosp., Baton Rouge, 1989-92; clin. neuropsychologist Baton Rouge Gen. Med. Ctr., 1996—. Contbr. articles to profl. publs. Mem. steering com. Baton Rouge Stepfamily Support Group, 1983-90; tchr. St. James Episcopal Sunday Sch., Baton Rouge, 1984-86, 90-91, 92—). Mem. Orton Dyslexia Soc. (bd. dirs., pres. La. br.), Nat. Head Injury Found., Agenda For Children, Baton Rouge Area Soc. Psychologists, La. Psychol. Assn., Am. Psychology Assn., Internat. Soc. Child Abuse and Neglect, Mental Health Assn. La. Office: Ctr Psychol Resources 4521 Jamestown Ave Ste 2 Baton Rouge LA 70808-3234

SPEIGHT, VELMA RUTH, alumni affairs director; b. Snow Hill, N.C., Nov. 18, 1932; d. John Thomas and Mable Lee (Edwards) S.; m. Howard H. Kennedy, 1953 (div. 1961); 1 child, Chineta. BS, N.C. A&T U., 1953; MEd, U. Md., 1965, PhD, 1976. Cert. counselor, tchr., Md. Tchr. math., French Kennard High Sch., Centreville, Md., 1954-60; counselor Kennard High Sch., Centreville, 1960-66; coord. guidance dept. Queene Anne's County High Sch., Centreville, 1966-69; adv. specialist in civil rights Md. State Dept. Edn., Balt., 1969-72, supr. guidance, 1972-76, dep. asst. state supt., 1976-82, asst. state supt., 1982-86; dir. EEO recruitment U. Md., College Park, 1972; coord. guidance and counseling U. Md. Ea. Shore, Princess Anne, 1986-87; assoc. prof. counselor edn. East Carolina U., Greenville, 1989; chmn. dept. edn., coord. grad. prog. guidance and counseling U. Md., Eastern Shore, Greenville, 1989-93, chmn. dept. edn., 1990-94; dir. alumni affairs N.C. A&T U., Greensboro, 1993—; adj. prof. Loyola U., Balt., 1976-80, Johns Hopkins U., Balt., 1980; cons., 1987—; speaker numerous seminars. Mem. Nat. Coalition for Chpt. I Parents, Washington, 1980-87, Human Rights Commn., Howard County, Md., 1987—; chmn. Gov.'s com. Studying Sentencing Alternatives for Women, Annapolis, Md., 1987; founder, chmn. Mothers to Prevent Dropouts, Centreville. Recipient Early Childhood Edn. award Japanese Govt., 1984, Md. State Tchrs.' Assn. Minority award Black Chs. for Excellence in Edn.; Fulbright Hayes scholar, 1991. Mem. Am. Counseling Assn., Nat. Alliance Black Educators, Assn. for Supervision and Curriculum Devel., Assn. Tchr. Edn., Md. Assn. Coll. Tchr. Edn., Md. Counseling Assn., N.C. A&T U. Alumni Assn. (nat. pres. 197983, Excellence award 1983), Tchr. Edn. and Profl. Standards Bd. Democrat. Presbyterian. Club: Community Action (Centreville). Home: 11 Carissa Ct Greensboro NC 27407-6366 Office: NC A&T State U Off of Dir Alumni Affairs Greensboro NC 27411

SPEIGHTS, JULIA L., mathematician, educator; b. Birmingham, Ala., Feb. 22, 1945; d. Thomas Burt and Lenora (Colvin) Long; m. John Angelo Speights III, July 19, 1975; children: Alice, Rhea, Jaclyn. BS, U. Ala., 1967, MA, 1973, postgrad., 1984-87. Tchr. math. Shaw H.S., Mobile, Ala., 1967-68, Stillman Coll., Tuscaloosa, Ala., 1968-72, Kendrich H.S., Columbus, Ga., 1972-78, Shaw H.S., Columbus, 1978-80, Auburn U., Montgomery, Ala., 1982-87, Lee H.S., Montgomery, 1987—. Leader Girl Scouts U.S., Montgomery, 1983—; com. mem. Ala. Dance Theatre, 1992—. Baptist. Home: 4667 Chrystan Rd Montgomery AL 36109-4029

SPEILLER-MORRIS, JOYCE, English composition educator; b. Utica, N.Y., Nov. 11, 1945; d. Arnold Leonard Speiller and Sybil (Sall) McAdam; m. Joseph Raymond Morris, Mar. 17, 1984. BS, Syracuse U., 1968; MA, Columbia U., 1969. Cert. tchr., N.Y., Fla. Chmn. upper sch. social studies dept., tchr. grade 6 social studies and English Cathedral Heights Elem. Sch., N.Y.C., 1969-74; adj. prof. Broward Community Coll., Hollywood, Davie and Pompano, Fla., 1982-90, Biscayne Coll., Miami, Fla., 1983, Miami-Dade Community Coll., 1983, Nova U., Miami and Davie, 1983-84; adj. prof., semester lectr. U. Miami, Coral Gables, 1985—; master tchr. U. Miami, 1990, 92, 94, faculty fellow, 1990-94, mem. curriculum devel., 1991-94; contbr. presentation to Fla. Coll. English Assn., 1991-92, Wyo. Conf. English, 1991; guest spkr. in field of svc.-learning, 1992-94; cons. svc.-learning curriculum design, 1994; acad. advisor U. Miami, 1994, 95, 96. Reviewer textbook McGraw Hill, 1993; contbr. instr.'s manual of textbook, 1994; contbr. poetry to revs., articles to profl. jours. Founder, dir. Meet the Author program, Coral Gables, 1989—. Recipient V.P. award U. Miami, 1992, cert. recognition West Palm Beach, Fla., TV sta., 1992; grantee Fla. Office for Campus Vols., 1992, Dade Community Found., 1992. Mem. MLA, Nat. Soc. Experiential Edn., Fla. Coll. English Assn., Coll. English Assn., Nat. Coun. Tchrs. English, Fla. Chpt. of Tchrs. of English to Spkrs. of Other Langs. (spkr. conf. 1992), Am. Correctional Assn., Phi Delta Kappa, Phi Lambda Theta. Home: Tower 200 Apt 806 19101 Mystic Pointe Dr North Miami Beach FL 33180 Office: U Miami Office English Composition PO Box 248145 Coral Gables FL 33124-8145

SPELLER-BROWN, BARBARA JEAN, pediatric nurse practitioner; b. Windsor, N.C., Feb. 8, 1958; d. Thomas Franklin and Esther Lee (Bond) Speller; m. Samuel Brown Jr., Nov. 16, 1985; children: Samuel, Shaun, Shea, Shanele. BSN, Howard U., 1981; MSN, U. Utah, 1993. Cert. pediatric nurse practitioner. Charge nurse Rosebud (S.D.) Indian Health Facility, 1981-82, Carl Albert Indian Health Facility, 1982-83; asst. head nurse Pitt County Meml. Hosp., Greenville, N.C., 1984-85; staff nurse St. Bernardine's Hosp., San Bernardino, Calif., 1986, San Bernardino Cmty. Hosp., 1986-87; staff nurse/charge nurse Gorgas Army Hosp., Republic of Panama, 1987-90; charge nurse Humana Hosp. Davis North, Layton, Utah, 1990-93; staff nurse Primary Children's Med. Ctr., Salt Lake City, Utah, 1990-93; pediatric nurse practitioner Cmty. Health Care Inc., Capital Heights, Md., 1994—, Our Kids Ctr., Nashville, 1995; clin. preceptor Community Health Care, Capitol Heights, 1995. Treas. Word of God Bapt. Ch. Nurses Guild, Washington, 1995, mem. parents assn., 1995. 1st lt. USPHS, 1981-83. Named Outstanding Young Woman Am. Delta Sigma Theta. Mem. Nat. Assn. Pediatric Nurse Practitioners and Assns., Am. Profl. Soc. on the Abuse of Children, Sigma Theta Tau, Phi Kappa Phi. Home: 705 Wabash Pl Nashville TN 37221

SPELMAN, NANCY LATTING, psychologist, consultant; b. Oklahoma City, Sept. 13, 1945; d. Trimble Baggett and Patience Francelia (Sewell) Latting; m. Douglas Gordon Spelman, June 21, 1970; children: Brooke Patience, Erin Latting. BA in Polit. Sci., Boston U., 1967; MA in Psychology, Bucknell U., 1972; PhD in Psychology, U. Hong Kong, 1987. Developmental psychologist. Tour guide UN, N.Y.C., summer 1966; tchr. emotionally disturbed and retarded pre-sch. children Mass. Dept. Mental Health, Boston, 1968-70; coord. vols. campaign for mayor Patience Latting, Oklahoma City, 1971; lectr. psychology Petaling Jaya Community Coll., Kuala Lumpur, Malaysia, 1987-88, George Mason U., Fairfax, Va., 1989; interactive skills observer, facilitator mgmt. programs Xerox Corp. Edn. and Tng., Leesburg, Va., 1989-91; pers. officer Am. Inst. in Taiwan, Taipei, 1993-95; demonstrator (tutor) psychology U. Hong Kong, 1996—. Bd. dirs. Internat. Sch. Kuala Lumpur, 1986-87, sec., 1987-88; bd. dirs. Golf Course Square Cluster, Reston, Va., 1991; com. mem. Hong Kong Soc. for Disabled, 1976-77. Democrat.

SPENCE, BARBARA E., publishing company executive; b. Bryn Mawr, Pa., July 8, 1921; d. Geoffrey Strange and Mary (Harrington) Earnshaw; m. Kenneth M. Spence Jr., June 29, 1944; children: Kenneth M. III, Christopher E., Hilary B. Grad. high sch. Movie, radio editor Parade Mag., N.Y.C., 1941-45; with Merchandising Group, N.Y.C., 1946-47; exec. dir. Greenfield Hill Congl. Ch., Fairfield, Conn., 1958-74, dir. religious edn., 1968-74; assoc. Ten Eyck-Emerich Antiques, 1974-76; personnel dir. William Morrow & Co., Inc., N.Y.C., 1976-91; ret., 1991. Chmn. pub. relations, bd. dirs. ARC, 1951-56, Family Service Soc., Fairfield, 1956-57, 61-63; chmn. pub. relations Citizens for Eisenhower, 1952, Fairfield Teens Players, 1968-71; bd. dirs. Fairfield Teens, Inc., 1965-70, Planned Parenthood of Greater Bridgeport, 1969-75, chmn. pub. affairs, 1971-72, chmn. personnel, 1972-73, chpt. vice chmn., 1973-75; pres. steering com. Am. Playwrights Festival Theatre, Inc., Fairfield, 1969-70, v.p., bd. dirs., 1971—; bd. govs. Unquowa Sch., Fairfield, 1963-69; bd. dirs. Fairfield U. Playhouse, 1971-73, Downtown Cabaret Theatre, Bridgeport, 1975-76. Mem. AAP (compensation survey com.), Fairfield Women's Exch. (bd. dirs. 1993). Home: 101 Twin Brook Ln Fairfield CT 06430-2834

SPENCE, CARMA PATRICIA, writer; b. Santa Rosa, Calif., Aug. 26, 1966; d. Vernon Charles Spence and Dolores Antoinette (Gonzales) Delgado. BA in Biology, U. Calif., Santa Cruz, 1988; MA in Journalism, U. Md., 1993. Coord. Santa Cruz (Calif.) Ops., 1988-91; writer Md. Agrl. Experiment Sta., College Park, 1992-93, City of Hope, Duarte, Calif., 1994—; asst. account exec. Gracelyn and Burns, Santa Rosa, Calif., 1994. Mem. Am. Soc. for Health Care Mktg. and Pub. Rels., Healthcare Pub. Rels. and Mktg. Assn., Nat. Assn. Sci. Writers, Internat. Assn. Bus. Communicators, Pub. Rels. Soc. Am. Home: 648 S Glendora # D West Covina CA 91790 Office: City of Hope 1500 E Duarte Rd Duarte CA 91010

SPENCE, DIANNA JEANNENE, software engineer, educator; b. Mountain View, Calif., June 5, 1964; d. Ronald Kenneth and Susan (Durham) S.; m. James Paul Blyn. BA, Coll. William and Mary, 1985; MS, Ga. State U., 1996. Tchr. math. and computers Woodward Acad., College Park, Ga., 1985-90; software engr. Computer Comm. Specialists, Inc., Norcross, Ga., 1990—; tutor, 1994—. Mem. Pi Kappa Phi, Pi Mu Epsilon. Universalist.

SPENCE, JANET BLAKE CONLEY (MRS. ALEXANDER PYOTT SPENCE), civic worker; b. Upper Montclair, N.J., Aug. 17, 1915; d. Walter Abbott and Ethel Maud (Blake) Conley; m. Alexander Pyott Spence, June 10, 1939; children: Janet Blake Spence Kerr, Robert Moray, Richard Taylor. Student, Vassar Coll., 1933-35; cert., Katharine Gibbs Sch., 1936. formerly active Jr. League, Neighborhood House, ARC, Girl Scouts U.S.A.; active various community drives; chmn. Darien (Conn.) Assembly, 1955-56; sec., chmn. Wilton Jr. Assembly, 1961-63; subscription chmn. Candlelight Concerts Wilton, Conn., 1963-65; rec. sec. Pub. Health Nursing Assn. Wilton Bd., 1964-67; corr., rec. sec. Royle Sch. Bd., Darien, 1952-55; fund raiser Vassar Class of 1937; mem. Washington Valley Community Assn.; mem. N.J. Symphony Orch. League, treas. Morris County br. 1978-83, corr. sec. 1982-83, pres. 1985-89, acting pres. 1989—, state coun. mem. 1985-89, acting pres. Morris br. 1989-90; docent Macculloch Hall Historica Mus., Morristown, N.J., 1992—. Mem. Vassar Alumni Assn., Dobbs Alumni Assn., Jersey Hills Vassar Club (ann. fund raiser), Wilton Garden Club (life), Washington Valley Cmty. Assn. (life corr. sec. 1977-82, pres. 1982-84, v.p. 1984-85, co-pres. 1985-86, chmn. membership com. 1987-89, mem. archives com. 1988—, treas. 1990—), Washington Valley Home Econs. Club. Congregationalist. Home: 168 Washington Valley Rd Morristown NJ 07960-3333

SPENCE, MARY LEE, historian; b. Kyle, Tex., Aug. 4, 1927; d. Jeremiah Milton and Mary Louise (Hutchison) Nance; m. Clark Christian Spence, Sept. 12, 1953; children: Thomas Christian, Ann Leslie. BA, U. Tex., 1947, MA, 1948; PhD, U. Minn., 1957. Instr., asst. prof. S.W. Tex. State U., San Marcos, 1948-53; lectr. Pa. State U., State College, 1955-58; mem. faculty U. Ill., Urbana-Champaign, 1973—, asst. prof., assoc. prof., 1973-81, 81-89, prof. history, 1989-90, prof. emerita, 1990—. Editor (with Donald Jackson) The Expeditions of John Charles Fremont, 3 vols., 1970-84, (with Clark Spence) Fanny Kelly's Narrative of Her Captivity Among the Sioux Indians, 1990, (with Pamela Herr) The Letters of Jessie Benton Fremont, 1993; contbr. articles to profl. jours. Mem. Children's Theater Bd., Urbana-Champaign, 1965-73. Grantee Nat. Hist. Pub. and Records Commn., Washington, 1977-78, 87-90, Huntington Libr., 1992; recipient Excellent Advisor award Liberal Arts and Sci. Coll./U. Ill., 1986. Mem. Western History Assn. (pres. 1981-82), Orgn. Am. Historians, Phi Beta Kappa (exec. sect. Gamma chpt. 1985-89, pres. 1991-92), Phi Alpha Theta. Episcopalian. Home: 1107 S Foley St Champaign IL 61820-6326 Office: U Ill Dept History 810 S Wright St Urbana IL 61801-3611

SPENCE, PATRICIA DUFFY, evaluation specialist; b. Plainfield, N.J., Feb. 2, 1951; d. James F. and Joan Lilian (Sweeney) Duffy; m. Verne Edgar Spence, Aug. 1, 1975; 1 child, Cynthia Lee. BA, U. Ctrl. Fla., 1979, MEd, 1988; PhD, U. Fla., 1996. Tchr. Volusia County Schs., DeLand, Fla., 1979-90, 93-94; rsch. intern U. Fla., Gainesville, 1989-90; project dir. Psychol. Corp., San Antonio, Tex., 1991-92; evaluation specialist State of Fla., Orlando, 1994—; adj. prof. U. Ctrl. Fla., Orlando, 1992—; cons. in field. Mem. adv. com. DeLand Mid. Sch., 1987; mem. state bd., educator St. Peter's Ch., DeLand, 1983-84. Rsch. fellow State of Fla. Dept. Edn., 1989-90. Mem. ASCD, Am. Ednl. Rsch. Assn., NAt. Coun. Measurement Edn. Democrat. Roman Catholic. Home: 597 E Oakwood Ave Orange City FL 32763-4212 Office: Fla Dept Edn 5404 Diplomat Cir Orlando FL 32810-5603

SPENCE, SANDRA, professional administrator; b. McKeesport, Pa., Mar. 25, 1941; d. Cedric Leroy and Suzanne (Haudenshield) S. BA, Allegheny Coll., 1963; MA, Rutgers U., 1964. With Pa. State Govt., Harrisburg, 1964-68, Appalachian Regional Commn., Washington, 1968-75; legis. rep. Nat. Assn. Counties, Washington, 1975-77; fed. rep. Calif. Dept. Transp., Washington, 1977-78; dir. congl. affairs Amtrak, Washington, 1978-81, corp. sec., 1981-83; dir. computer svcs. Nat. R.R. Passenger Corp., Washington, 1983-84; co-owner Parkhurst-Spence Inc., 1985; owner The Spence Group, 1986-90; v.p. Bostrom Corp., Washington, 1990-92; exec. dir. Soc. Glass and Ceramic Decorators, 1992—; chmn. legis. com. Womens Transp. Seminar, 1977-79, dir., 1982-83, v.p., 1983-84, chmn. edn. com., 1982-83; com. on edn. and tng. Transp. Rsch. Bd., 1982-85. Contbr. articles to profl. jours. Commr., sec. D.C. Commn. for Women, 1983-88; del. Ward III Dem. Com., 1982-90, 1st vice chmn., 1987-88. Fellow Eagleton Inst. Politics, 1963-64;

recipient Achievement award Transp. Seminar, 1982, 83. Mem. Greater Washington Soc. Assn. Execs. (vice-chair law and legis. com. 1989-90, chmn. 1990-91, chmn. scholarship com. 1992-93, bd. dirs. 1993-96, Rising Star award 1989, Chmn.'s award for Govt. Rels. 1991), Am. Soc. Assn. Execs. (mgmt. cert. 1987), Phi Beta Kappa. Home: 3701 Appleton St NW Washington DC 20016-1807 Office: Soc Glass and Ceramic Decorators 1627 K St NW Ste 800 Washington DC 20006-1702

SPENCER, BARBARA BURTON, therapist; b. N.Y.C., Oct. 18, 1943; d. John and Sylvia (Carlin) Burton; m. Gary Spencer; children: David, Elizabeth, Steven, Abby. BS, Boston U., 1966; MN, U. Fla., 1972; PHD, Calif. Coast U., 1983. RN, Mass. Nurse Children's Hosp., Boston; instr. U. Fla., Gainsville, 1972-73, BOCES, Syracuse, N.Y., 1976; asst. prof. Syracuse U., 1973-79, SUNY, Morrisville, 1980-81; pvt. practice Syracuse, 1979—. Mem. Nat. Assn. Alcoholism and Drug Counselors (clin. mem.), Am. Assn. Marriage and Family Therapists (corr. sec. 1982—). Home: 4325 Hepatica Hill Rd Manlius NY 13104 Office: 719 E Genesee St Syracuse NY 13210

SPENCER, CAROL BROWN, association executive; b. Normal, Ill., Aug. 26, 1936; d. Fred William and Sorado (Gross) B.; m. James Calvin Spencer, Dec. 18, 1965 (div. July 1978); children: James Calvin Jr., Anne Elizabeth. BA in English, Calif. State U., Los Angeles, 1964, MA in Pub. Adminstrn., 1986. Cert. secondary edn. tchr., Calif. Tchr. English Seneca Vocat. High Sch., Buffalo, 1966-70; pub. info. officer City of Pasadena, Calif., 1979-90, City of Mountain View, Calif., 1990-93; exec. dir. Calif. Assn. for the Gifted, 1993—; owner PR to Go, 1994—. Sec., bd. dirs. Calif. Music Theatre, 1987-90; bd. dirs. Pasadena Beautiful Found., 1984-90, Pasadena Cultural Festival Found., 1983-86, Palo Alto-Stanford Heritage, 1990-93; mayoral appointee Strategic Planning Adv. Com., Pasadena, 1985-86. Mem. NOW, Pub. Rels. Soc. Am., Calif. Assn. Pub. Info. Ofcls. (exec. bd., Paul Clark Achievment award 1986, award for mktg. 1990), City/County Comms. and Mktg. Assn. (bd. dirs. 1988-90, Savvy award for mktg. 1990), Nat. Assn. for Gifted Children. Democrat. Episcopalian. Home: 426 Escuela Ave Apt 19 Mountain View CA 94040-2022

SPENCER, CAROL DIANE, consulting company executive; b. Pitts., Mar. 12, 1952; d. Louis John and Elinor Edwinna (Clark) Kacinko; m. Dirk Victor Spencer, May 12, 1993; children: Erick Jon Powell, Tiffani Dawn Showalter. AS in Computer Sci., C.C. Allegheny County, 1974; BSBA, U. Pitts., 1979. Data base adminstr. Beckwith Machinery, Murrysville, Pa., 1974-78; systems analyst Mode Inc., Irwin, Pa., 1978-80; supr. data base Tex. Instruments, Dallas, 1980-83, E-Systems Melpar, Falls Church, Va., 1983; dep. dir. Vanguard Techs., Fairfax, Va., 1983-85; mgr, data base Siecor, Hickory, N.C., 1985-86; sr. cons. Computer Task Group, Raleigh, N.C., 1986-88; prin. cons., mgr. Tex. Instruments, 1988-94; pres. Kacinko Consulting, Reston, Va., 1994—; speaker Computer Assocs., Atlanta, 1994. Mem. Digital Users Group, DB2 Users Group. Home and Office: 12608 Bridoon Ln Herndon VA 22071-2827

SPENCER, CONSTANCE MARILYN, secondary education educator; b. New York, Jan. 2, 1942; d. Edward Bennett and Blanche Lloyd (Miller) Asbury; m. Robert William Spencer, Dec. 30, 1966; children: Keane Thomas, Keith Lyle. BA, U. Calif., Santa Barbara, 1964; MA in English, U. West Fla., 1974. Cert. lang. devel. specialist, preliminary adminstr. Tchr. Valley Stream (N.Y.) N. H.S., Workman Jr. H.S., Pensacola, Fla., Imperial Beach (Calif.) Elem. Sch.; substitute tchr. South Bay Union Sch., Imperial Beach; mgr. Geni, Inc., Pasadena, Calif., Avon Products, Inc., Pasadena; tchr. Walnut (Calif.) H.S., 1985—; pres. Am. Computer Instrn. Inc., Upland, Calif.; grant writer Walnut Valley Unified Sch. Dist., 1986-94, mentor tchr., 1988-97; accreditation co-chair Walnut H.S., 1993-94. Mem., sec. Toastmistress, Ontario, Calif., 1977-86. Grantee Calif. Dept. Edn., 1987, Walnut Valley Unified Sch. Dist., 1988, Diamond Bar (Calif.) Rotary, 1994. Republican. Roman Catholic. Home: 2238 Coolcrest Way Upland CA 91784-1290 Office: Walnut HS 400 Pierre Rd Walnut CA 91789-2535

SPENCER, CYNTHIA JEAN, artist, ceramics educator; b. Seoul, Korea, June 21, 1958; d. Frank L. and Willa S. (Haines) Spencer; m. Patrick Langdon Hadlock. BA, Willamette U., 1979. Computer operator Ga.-Pacific Corp., Portland, 1979-81; adminstrv. asst. Springfield (Oreg.) Utility Bd., 1981-85, Old Mill Sch., Corvallis, Oreg., 1985-95; artist Corvallis, Oreg., 1985—; pottery instr. Linn Benton C. C., 1990-95; Presenter Nat. Coun. Edn. Ceramic Arts Conf., New Orleans, 1994. Exhbns. include daVinci Days Arts Festival, 1992 (sculpture award), Am. Craft Coun., San Francisco, 1994, 95, Arts in Oreg. Show, Salem, 1994 (best of show), Willamette U., 1995, Salem (Oreg.) Art Festival, 1995, Am. Craft Coun., Balt., 1996. Juror Salem (Oreg.) Art Festival, 1995; mem. bd. Fall Festival, Corvallis, Oreg., 1995. Mem. Am. Craft Coun., Corvallis (Oreg.) Arts Ctr. (vol. 1985—), Women's Art Caucus Nat., Willamette Ceramics Guild (newsletter editor 1990-95, pres. 1987-90), Oreg. Potters Assn. (chair membership 1993-95). Home: 1105 NW 30th Corvallis OR 97330

SPENCER, ELIZABETH, author; b. Carrollton, Miss., 1921; d. James Luther and Mary James (McCain) S.; m. John Arthur Blackwood Rusher, Sept. 29, 1956. BA, Belhaven Coll., 1942; MA, Vanderbilt U., 1943; LittD (hon.), Southwestern U. at Memphis, 1968; LLD (hon.), Concordia U. at Montreal, 1988; LittD (hon.), U. of the South, 1992. Instr. N.W. Miss. Jr. Coll., 1943-44, Ward-Belmont, Nashville, 1944-45; reporter The Nashville Tennessean, 1945-46; instr. U. Miss., Oxford, 1948-51, 52-53; vis. prof. Concordia U., Montreal, Que., Can., 1976-81, adj. prof., 1981-86; vis. prof. U. N.C., Chapel Hill, 1986-92. Author: Fire in the Morning, 1948, This Crooked Way, 1952, The Voice at the Back Door, 1956, The Light in the Piazza, 1960, Knights and Dragons, 1965, No Place for an Angel, 1967, Ship Island and Other Stories, 1968, The Snare, 1972, The Stories of Elizabeth Spencer, 1981, Marilee, 1981, The Salt Line, 1984, Jack of Diamonds and Other Stories, 1988, (play) For Lease or Sale, 1989, On the Gulf, 1991, The Night Travellers, 1991; contbr. short stories to mags. and anthologies. Recipient Women's Democratic Com. award, 1949, recognition award Nat. Inst. Arts and letters, 1952, Richard and Hinda Rosenthal Found. award Am. Acad. Arts and Letters, 1957; Guggenheim Found. fellow, 1953, 1st McGraw-Hill Fiction award, 1960, Henry Bellamann award for creative writing, 1968; Award of Merit medal for the short story Am. Acad. Arts and Letters, 1983, Salem award for lit., 1992, Dos Passos award for fiction, 1992; Kenyon Rev. fellow in fiction, 1957; Bryn Mawr Col. Donnelly fellow, 1962; Nat. Endowment for Arts grantee in lit., 1983, Sr. Arts Award grantee Nat. Endowment for Arts, 1988, N.C. Gov.'s award for lit., 1994. Mem. Am. Acad. Arts and Letters, Fellowship of So. Writers (charter; vice chancellor 1993—). Home: 402 Longleaf Dr Chapel Hill NC 27514-3042

SPENCER, IOLANTHA ESTELLA, academic affairs administrator; b. Tuskegee Institute, Ala., Dec. 25, 1953. BS, Tuskegee Inst., 1975, MEd, 1980. Cert. fundraiser. Clk., typist Sch. Vet. Medicine Tuskegee U., Tuskegee Inst., 1975-81, grants specialist Office Devel., 1981-84, recruiter, coord. Sch. Nursing & Allied Health, 1984-87, instr., 1987-90, dir. learning ctr., 1987-90, asst. dir. provost office, 1990-93, instr. acad. affairs, 1993—, asst. Title III coord. acad. affairs provost office, 1993—; exec. dir. Tuskegee U. Nat. Athletic Assn., 1987—; mem. adv. coun. Macon County Cmty. Decision Making Coun., Tuskegee Institute, 1995-96, leadership com. Tuskegee/Macon County Town & Gown, 1995—. Mem. Macon County Dem. Club, Tuskegee, 1994; steering com. Campaign to Build City Police Dept., Tuskegee, 1995, Campaign to Elect Sheriff, Tuskegee, 1994. Mem. AAUW, NAACP, Continental Socs. Inc. (v.p. 1993-95, pres. 1995—), Alpha Kappa Alpha (editor newsletter 1993-95, chair stds. 1995—, Vol. Svc. award 1992, Outstanding Svc. award 1995). Baptist. Home: 2814 Azalea St Tuskegee Institute AL 36088 Office: Tuskegee U Office of Provost Kresge Ctr Tuskegee Institute AL 36088

SPENCER, ISABEL BRANNON, editor; b. Tryon, N.C., Nov. 10, 1940; d. George Smith and Isabel (Ducharme) B.; m. F. Gilman Spencer, July 3, 1965; 1 child, Isabel Caroline. BA, Bryn Mawr Coll., 1962. Reporter Main Line Times, 1962, Delaware County Daily News, 1963-65, The Trentonian, 1965-67, The Frentonian, 1969-76, Phila. Inquirer, 1976-77; city editor The News Jour., Wilmington, Del., 1979-84; asst. city editor The Star Ledger, Newark, 1984-88; editor The Daily Jour., Elizabeth, N.J., 1988-90; mng. editor The Denver Post, 1990—. Home: 1133 Race St Denver CO 80206-2836 Office: The Denver Post 1560 Broadway Denver CO 80202-5133

SPENCER, KATHELEN V., insurance company executive; m. Tracy Spencer; 3 children. BA in Polit. Sci., Emory U.; JD, U. Ga., 1982. Bar: Tex., Ga. Lawyer pvt. practice Columbus, Ga., 1983-85; assoc. counsel AFLAC, Columbus, Ga., 1985-87; dep. counsel AFLAC, Columbus, 1987-89, v.p., dir. pub. rels., 1989-92, sr. v.p., dep. counsel, dir. corp. comm., 1992—; bd. dirs. Columbus Bank and Trust Co.; mem. AFLAC Donations Com., dir. shareholder svcs. dept. Trustee Brookstone Sch., Columbus Coll. Found., Pastoral Inst., Columbus Mus; mem. adv. bd. Emory U. Sch. of Pub. Health; past pres. Jr. League Columbus; alumna Leadership Ga. Office: AFLAC Inc 1932 Wynnton Rd Columbus GA 31999

SPENCER, LONABELLE (KAPPIE SPENCER), political agency administrator, lobbyist; b. Owatonna, Minn., Aug. 3, 1925; d. Reuben Alvin and Florence Elizabeth (Wells) Kaplan; m. Mark Rodney Spencer, Sept. 14, 1947 (dec. May 1986); children: Gregory Mark, Gary Alan, Carol Ann (Spencer) Glumac, Dane Kaplan. BA, Grinnell Coll., 1947. State bd. legis. chair Am. Assn. Univ. Women, Des Moines, Iowa, 1978-82; nat. legis. com. Am. Assn. Univ. Women, Washington, 1980-83, nat. bd. legis. chair, 1982-83, nat. legis. and program coms., 1985-89, nat. bd. dir. for women's issues, 1985-89; founder, dir. Nat. Gender Balance Project, Sarasota, Fla., 1988—; bd. dirs., nat. steering com. Nat. Women's Political Caucus, Washington, 1992—; lobbyist, cmty. activist state legis. and congress, Fla. Iowa, Washington, 1974—; pub. policy cons. women's orgns., nationwide, 1978—; rep. Fla. women's pol. caucus ERA summit, Washington, 1992—. Author: (pub. policy manuals) Don't Leave It All to the Experts, 1965, It's a Man's World Unless Women Vote, 1983, Woman Power: It's a Capitol Idea, 1995, Gender Balance Project-USA: Politics and Decision Making, 1995; exhibitor, presenter in field. U.S. rep. World Assn. Girl Guides Girl Scouts U.S., Acapulco, Mex., 1965, bd. dirs. Moincona Coun. Girl Scouts U.S., 1965-75; Rep. candidate Iowa senate, Des Moines, 1976; del., workshop presenter Internat. Fedn. Univ. Women, Netherlands, New Zealand, Finland, Sweden, 1983, 86, 89, workshop presenter U.S./China Joint Conf. on Women's Issues, Beijing, China, 1995, Nongovernmental Orgn. Forum, Huairou, China, 1995; trustee Grinnell (Iowa) Coll., 1993—; Iowa del. to Nat. Women's Conf., 1977. Recipient Girl Scout awards Moingona Girl Scout Coun., Des Moines, 1969, 73, 78, Christine Wilson medal for Equality and Justice, Iowa Women's Hall of Fame, Des Moines, 1990; named gift honoree Am. Assn. Univ. Women, Des Moines and Sarasota, Fla. branches, Iowa and Vt. divsns., 1980, 82, 87, 92. Mem. AAUW (leader corps, various coms. 1075—), UN Fund for Women (UNIFEM), Nat. Assn. Commns. for Women, Vet. Feminists of Am., Women in Senate and House WISH-LIST (founder 1992—), Fla. Women's Consortium (founder, bd. dirs. 1989—). Republican. Home: 3735 Beneva Oaks Way Sarasota FL 34238

SPENCER, MARGARET GILLIAM, lawyer; b. Spokane, Wash., Aug. 30, 1951; d. Jackson Earl and Margaret Kathleen (Hindley) Gilliam; m. John Bernard Spencer, Feb. 21, 1993. BA in Sociology, U. Mont., 1974, MA in Sociology, 1978, JD, 1982. Bar: Mont. 1982, Colo. 1982. Assoc. Holland & Hart, Denver, 1982-84; assoc. Roath & Brega, P.C., Denver, 1984-88, shareholder, dir., 1988-89; spl. counsel Brega & Winters, P.C., Denver, 1989; corp. counsel CH2M Hill, Inc., Denver, 1989—. Democrat. Episcopalian. Office: CH2M Hill Inc PO Box 22508 Denver CO 80222-0508

SPENCER, MARIA E., construction engineering administrator; b. Binghamton, N.Y., Aug. 17, 1966; d. Paul P. and Mary V. (Hanzalik) Rusnak; m. Michael R. Spencer, Aug. 18, 1990. A in Liberal Arts, Broome C.C., Binghamton, N.Y., 1987; B in Profl. Studies in Architecture, U. Buffalo, 1989; student, SUNY, Binghamton, 1992. Arch. intern JHL Design, Hornell, N.Y., 1989-92; asst. project mgr. Morse Deisel Internat., Oneonta, N.Y., 1992-94; project mgr. L.C. Whitford Cons. Co., Wellsville, N.Y., 1994-95; project engr. Ruscilli Cons. Co., Columbus, 1995—. Home: 111B Beaufort Ln Columbus OH 43214 Office: Ruscilli Cons Co 2041 Arlingate Ln Columbus OH 43228

SPENCER, MARY MILLER, civic worker; b. Comanche, Tex., May 25, 1924; d. Aaron Gaynor and Alma (Grissom) Miller; 1 child, Mara Lynn. BS, U. North Tex., 1943. Cafeteria dir. Mercedes (Tex.) Pub. Schs., 1943-46; home economist coordinator All-Orange Dessert Contest, Fla. Citrus Commn., Lakeland, 1959-62, 64; tchr. purchasing sch. lunch dept. Fla. Dept. Edn., 1960. Clothing judge Polk County (Fla.) Youth Fair, 1951-68, Polk County Federated Women's Clubs, 1964-66; pres. Dixieland Elem. Sch. PTA, 1955-57, Polk County Council PTA's, 1958-60; chmn. public edn. com. Polk County unit Am. Cancer Soc., 1959-60, bd. dirs., 1962-70; charter mem., bd. dirs. Lakeland YMCA, 1962-72; sec. Greater Lakeland Community Nursing Council, 1965-72; trustee, vice chmn. Polk County Eye Clinic, Inc., 1962-64, pres., 1964-82; bd. dirs. Polk County Scholarship and Loan Fund, 1962-70; mem. exec. com. West Polk County (Fla.) Community Welfare Council, 1960-62, 65-68; mem. budget and audit com. Greater Lakeland United Fund, 1960-62, bd. dirs., 1967-70, residential chmn. fund drive, 1968; mem. adv. bd. Polk County Juvenile and Domestic Relations Ct., 1960-69; worker children's services div. family services Dept. Health and Rehab. Services, State of Fla., 1969-70, social worker, 1970-72, 74-82, social worker OFR unit, 1977-81, with other pers. svcs., 1981-82; supr. OFR unit 1982-83, pub. assistance specialist IV, 1984-89; with other pers. svcs. Emergency Fin. Assistance Housing Program, 1990-96. Mem. exec. com. Suncoast Health Council, 1968-71; mem. Polk County Home Econs. Adv. Com., 1965-71; sec. bd. dirs. Fla. West Coast Ednl. TV, 1960-81; bd. dirs. Lake Region United Way, Winter Haven, 1976-81; mem. Polk County Community Services Council, 1978-88. Mem. Nat. Welfare Fraud Assn., Fla. Congress Parents and Tchrs. (hon. life; pres. dist. 7 1961-63, chmn. pub. relations 1962-66), AAUW (pres. Lakeland br. 1960-61), Polk County Mental Health Assn., Fla. Health and Welfare Council, Fla. Health and Social Service Council, U. North Tex. Alumni Assn. Democrat. Methodist. Lodge: Order of Eastern Star. Home and Office: PO Box 2161 Lakeland FL 33806-2161

SPENCER, MURIEL HEATHER, artist; b. Fortuna, Calif., Feb. 7, 1936; d. Charles Orliff and Lennette Merdene (Williams) Pedrotti; m. Leslie Raymond Spencer, Sept. 23, 1961; children: Leslie Tisha Spencer McCrigler, Brian Raymond. BA in Edn., Calif. Coll. Arts and Crafts, 1958; postgrad., U. Hawaii, 1960, Immaculate Heart Coll., 1960. Art tchr. Wm. S. Hart Jr./Sr. High Sch., Newhall, Calif., 1958-60; adult edn. art tchr. Eureka (Calif.) High Sch., Fortuna Union High Sch., 1970's; arts and crafts tchr. Coll. of Redwoods, Eureka, 1980-88; owner, designer a stuffed animal portrait bus. Spencer's Zoo, Rio Dell, Calif., 1982—; craft cons. Canadian Govt. for N.W. Territories Devel. Corp., Taloyoak, 1993. Contbg. editor S.W. Crafts, 1991. Sunday sch. supt. Rio Dell Ch. of Christ, 1992—, Sunday sch. tchr., 1988—. Mem. Soc. Craft Designers, Fortuna Art Coun. (pres. 1993), Soc. Decorative Painters. Home: 715 Walnut Dr Rio Dell CA 95562

SPENCER, SHEILA MARIE, guide dog trainer; b. Wichita, Kans., Jan. 22, 1961; d. James Blaine and Theresa Marie S.; m. Thomas Joseph Sherman, Nov. 7, 1992; 1 child, Justine Marie. BA cum laude, Wichita State U., 1991. Lic. guide dog instr., Calif. Vet. asst. Pottorff Animal Hosp., Wichita, Kans., 1976-79; audio engr. KAKE-TV, Wichita, Kans., 1983-91; guide dog instr. Guide Dogs for the Blind, Inc., San Rafael, Calif., 1991—; pvt. dog tng., San Rafael, 1991—; team leader Guide Dogs for the Blind, Ind., San Rafael, 1995—. Mem. NOW, World Wildlife Fund, Human Soc. of U.S. Office: Guide Dogs for the Blind 32901 SE Kelso Rd Boring OR 97009

SPENCER, TRICIA JANE, wholesale manufacturing executive; b. Springfield, Ill., Dec. 8, 1952; d. Frank Edward and LaWanda (Edwards) Bell; m. Mark Edward Spencer, Aug. 21, 1982. Student pub. schs. Instr., Falcons Drum & Bugle Corps, Springfield, 1969-72; concert, stage, TV, film performer, 1970-82, part-time 1982—; guest dir. Sing out Salem, Ohio, 1973; contbg. writer Saddle Tramps Wild West Revue, 1977—; legal sec. to pvt. atty., Tustin, Calif., 1980-82; owner Am. Dream Balloons & Svcs., Orange, Calif., 1982-89; founder, corp. pres. Am. Dream Limousine Svc., Inc., Orange, 1983-90; founder, pres., designer Am. Dream Creations Co., Inc., Irvine, Calif., 1988—; founder Am. Dream Bride's Mus., 1992. Songwriter; designer greeting cards, T-shirts and wedding related gifts; one-of-a-kind automobile; producer, dir. mus. stage shows, 1974-82; author: TIPS - The Server's Guide to Bringing Home the Bacon, 1987, There's a Bunny in the House, 1992, Real Rabbitts Don't Eat Lettuce, 1992, Elysium, 1996. Performer, Up With People, 1972-73; organizer Bicentennial Com. Springfield, 1976; mediator Limousine and Chauffeur Council, Orange County, 1984—; vol. Orange County Performing Arts Soc., 1985—. Recipient Appreciation, Achievement awards Muscular Dystrophy Assn., 1977-79, Transp. Partnership award, 1988, 7 songwriting and vocal performance awards Music City Song Festival, 1989, Outstanding Booth Display award Chgo. Gift Show, 1991; named one of top 100 Bridal Companies Assn. Bridal Consultants. Mem. Am. Entrepreneurs Assn., Internat. Platform Assn., Nat. Limousine Assn., So. Calif. Limousine Owners Assn., Nat. Assn. Female Execs., Nat. Bridal Assn., Orange County C. of C., Greenpeace, Doris Day Animal League, People for Ethical Treatment of Animals. Republican. Avocations: guitar, piano, writing. Office: Am Dream Creative Enterprises Co 634 N Poplar St Ste K Orange CA 92668-1026

SPENCER, WINIFRED MAY, art educator; b. Tulsa, Oct. 7, 1938; d. Len and Madge (Scofield) S. BA in Comml. Art, U. Tulsa, 1961, Cert. in Tchg., 1962. Cert. comml. art, K-12 art, English/journalism tchr. Freelance comml. artist Tulsa, 1962-63; art/sci. educator Pleasant Porter Elem. Tulsa Pub. Schs., 1963-65, art educator, supervising tchr. Kendall Elem., 1965-70, art educator, team leader pilot program Bunche Elem., 1970-75, art educator Carnegie Elem., 1975-81, art educator, fine arts dept. chair Foster Jr. High, 1982-83, art educator, fine arts dept. chair Foster Mid. Sch., 1983—; judge Okla. Wildlife Arts Festival, Okla. Wildlife Arts Assn., Tulsa, 1988; supervising tchr., tchr. tng. U. Tulsa, 1965-70, Northeastern State U., Tahlequah, Okla, 1965-70; pres. Tulsa Elem. Art Tchrs., Tulsa Pub. Schs., 1967-68, curriculum writing/curriculum cons., 1970-75, 91—; coord. summer arts/artists in the schs. program Tchr. Adv. Bd., Summer Arts Tulsa Arts and Humanities Coun., 1986-94. Exhibited in group shows at Tulsa City-County Ctrl. Libr., 1989, Philbrook Art Mus., 1993, 94. Mem. Rep. Nat. Com., 1994-96; art adv. PTA, Tulsa, 1970—; ch. leader Christian Sci. Ch., Tulsa, 1960—; mem. city of Tulsa goals for tomorrow task force on cultural affairs, 1995—. Invited U.S. China Joint Conf. on Edn., Citizen Amb. Program People to People Internat., 1992, U.S. Spain Joint Conf. on Edn., Citizen Amb. Program People to People Internat., 1995. Mem. AAUW, NEA, ASCD, Okla. Edn. Assn., Tulsa Classroom Tchrs. Assn., Okla. Mid. Level Edn. Assn. (del. 1994), Nat. Art Edn. Assn. (del. 1992, 94, 96), Okla. Art Edn. Assn. Home: 439 S Memorial Dr Tulsa OK 74112-2203 Office: Foster Mid Sch 12121 E 21st St Tulsa OK 74129-1801

SPENCER-DAHLEM, ANITA JOYCE, medical, surgical and critical care nurse; b. Weirton, W.Va., Aug. 26, 1961; d. Carlas A. and Evelyn Faye (Miller) Spencer; m. Terry Dahlem. BS, Alderson-Broaddus Coll., Philippi, W.Va., 1984. Staff nurse, orthopedic unit Charleston (W.Va.) Area Med. Ctr., 1984-86; ICU staff nurse Ohio Valley Hosp., Steubenville, Ohio, 1986—; nurse on cardiac catheterization unit Ohio Valley Hosp., Steubenville, 1994—. Mem. Ohio Nurses Assn.

SPENGLER, MARGARET BURTON, music educator; b. Milford, Del.; d. Irwin G. and Maradel (Geuting) Burton; m. Gary Kenneth Spengler, July 2, 1992; 1 stepchild: Kristin E. Spengler. AA, Wesley Coll., 1975; BS, Lebanon Valley Coll., 1978; MMEd, West Chester U., 1982. Band dir. Milford Sch. Dist., 1978—; trombone player Dover (Del.) Jazz Lab. Band, 1989—, Swing City, Dover, 1994—. Home: 24 Saundra Ct Frederica DE 19946-9729 Office: Milford Sch Dist Lakeview Ave Milford DE 19963

SPERBER, MARILYN JANICE, special education educator; b. N.Y.C., Feb. 24, 1947; d. Max Schuman and Doris (Behr) Schuman Friedman; m. Mark Victor Sperber, Mar. 24, 1968; children: Dustin Cory, Jonathan Kyle. BS in Edn., SUNY, New Paltz, 1968, MS in Spl. Edn., 1976; postgrad., Fordham U., 1989-90. Cert. elem. tchr., K-12 spl. edn. tchr., N.Y. Elem. tchr. Mamaroneck (N.Y.) Ctrl. Sch., 1968-69, N.Y.C. Pub. Schs., 1969-70; edn. therapist Astor Day Treatment Ctr., Poughkeepsie, N.Y., 1976-80; spl. educator The Children's Annex, Kingston, N.Y., 1980-84; instr. Jr. Coll. of Albany, N.Y., 1984-87; spl. educator R.C.G. BOCES, Castleton, N.Y., 1984-87; asst. prof. Sullivan County C.C., Loch Sheldrake, N.Y., 1987-95; spl. educator resource rm. Benjamin Cosor Elem. Sch., Fallsburg, N.Y., 1987—. Grantee Fallsburg Ctrl. Schs., 1991, Hudson Valley Portfolio Project, 1993. Mem. Fallsburg Tchrs. Assn. (asst. treas. 1990—), Sullivan Reading Coun., N.Y. State Reading Coun., Phi Delta Kappa. Home: 204 Edwards Rd Monticello NY 12701-3400 Office: Benjamin Cosor Elem Sch Brickman Rd Fallsburg NY 12733

SPERLING, DORIS HYMAN, elementary education educator; b. Mt. Vernon, N.Y., June 12, 1931; d. Maxwell and Beatrice (Sandler) Hyman; m. Lawrence W. Sperling, June 13, 1953; children: Michael, Gene, Anne, Rick. BA in Design, U. Mich., 1953, MA in Edn., 1971. Cert. elem. tchr., secondary art tchr. Tchr. elem. art Ann Arbor (Mich.) Pub. Schs., 1959-70, tchr. elem., 1972-88, specialist classroom assessment, 1988-94; cons. classroom assessment Ann Arbor, 1994—; lectr. Ea. Mich. U., Ypsilanti, 1995. Contbr. articles to profl. jours. Bd. dirs. Young People's Theater, Ann Arbor, founder. Mem. Internat. Reading Assn. (conf. presenter), Learning Disabilities Am. (bd. dirs. 1985-90), Mich. Reading Assn. (presenter), Mich. Ednl. Rsch. Assn. (presenter). Home and Office: 1265 Lincolnshire Ln Ann Arbor MI 48103-2354

SPERO, JOAN EDELMAN, federal agency administrator; b. Davenport, Iowa, Oct. 2, 1944; d. Samuel and Sylvia (Halpern) Edelman; m. C. Michael Spero, Nov. 9, 1969; children: Jason, Benjamin. Student, L'Inst. d'Etudes Politiques, Paris, 1964-65; BA, U. Wis., 1966; MA, Columbia U., 1968, PhD, 1973. Asst. prof. Columbia U., N.Y.C., 1973-79; ambassador of U.S. to UN Econ. and Social Council, N.Y.C., 1980-81; v.p. Am. Express Co., N.Y.C., 1981-83, sr. v.p. internat. corp. affairs, 1983-89; treas., sr. v.p., 1989-91; exec. v.p. corp. affairs and communications Am. Express Co., 1991-93; under sec. for econ., bus. and agrl. affairs Dept. of State, Washington, 1993—; vis. scholar Fed. Res. Bank N.Y., 1976-77; mem. U.S.-Japan Bus. Coun., Washington, 1983—. Author: The Politics of International Economic Relations, 4th edit., 1990, The Failure of the Franklin National Bank, 1980; contbr. articles to profl. jours. Trustee Amherst Coll.; bd. dirs. French-Am. Found.; mem. Coun. Am. Ambassadors. Named to Acad. Women Achievers, YWCA, 1983; named Fin. Woman of Yr., Fin. Women's Assn., 1990; recipient George Washington Disting. Statesperson award, 1994; Woodrow Wilson fellow. Mem. Coun. on Fgn. Rels. (Internat. Affairs fellow), The Trilateral Commn., Svcs. Policy Adv. Com., Phi Beta Kappa. Democrat. Jewish. Office: US Dept State Econ Bus and Ag Affairs 2201 C St NW Washington DC 20520-7512

SPEVACEK, DONNA MUNSON, elementary education educator; b. La Crosse, Wis., July 22, 1939; d. Ernest and Agnes (Allan) Munson; m. John Edward Spevacek, Sept. 1, 1962; children: Michael, Jan, Chris. BS, U. Wis., La Crosse, 1961. Tchr. elem. Manitowoc (Wis.) Bd. Edn., 1961-64; tchr. elem. Mishicot (Wis.) Bd. Edn., 1964-95, ret., 1995. Mem. Delta Kappa Gamma (sec. 1985-87). Roman Catholic. Home: 132 Barthels Rd Two Rivers WI 54241-9626

SPEVACEK, JOANN MAXINE, state agency administrator; b. Port Huron, Mich., Dec. 2, 1935; d. Maxwell Claire and Josephine Louise (Borkowski) Cook; m. John David Spevacek, Oct. 5, 1957 (div. Mar. 1981); children: Jennifer J. Spevacek-Meyer, Vanessa Renee. BA, U. Iowa, 1961. Campaign coord. Atty. Gen. Campaign, Arlington, Va., 1972; fundraiser, cons. Gubernatorial Campaign, Annandale, Md., 1978; legis. aide Va. Ho. of Dels., Richmond, 1974-78, Va. Gen. Assembly, Richmond, 1978-80; govt. affairs rep. Planning Rsch. Corp., McLean, Va., 1980-86; campaign mgr. Va. State Senate Campaign, McLean, 1986-87; dir. legis. svcs. No. Va. Planning Dist. Commn., Annandale, 1987—; exec. dir. Va. Assn. Planning Dist. Commns., Annandale and Richmond, 1989-95; commr. U.S. Dept. Interior/Nat. Park Svc., 1992—. Mem. Fairfax County Social Svcs. Bd., 1974-89, Cmty. Action Agy. Adminstrv. Bd., Fairvax County, 1975-76, Fairfax County Child Abuse Task Force, 1987-88; del. Dem. Nat. Conv., N.Y.C., 1976; pres sec. 8th dist. Va. U.S. Congl. Campaign, 1977; dep. campaign mgr., conv. mgr. U.S. Senate Campaign, Va., 1978, 82; candidate for 40th dist. Va. Ho. of Dels., 1995. Mem. Women in Govt. Rels. Home: 9810 Lakepointe Dr Burke VA 22015

SPEWOCK, THEODOSIA GEORGE, reading specialist, educator; b. Canton, Ohio, Sept. 11, 1951; d. George Eleftherios and Despina George (Ilvanakis) Sideropoulos; m. Michael Andrew Spewock, Aug. 23, 1974. BS, Kent State U., 1974; MEd in reading, Pa. State U., 1978; cert. in early childhood edn., Ind. U. of Pa., 1989, cert. elem. prin., 1994. Tchr. Winnisquam Regional Sch. Dist., Tilton, N.H., 1974-77; reading specialist Tyrone (Pa.) Area Sch. Dist., 1978-80, home-sch. liaison, 1980—, title 1 coord., 1994—; chair adv. bd. Family Ctr., Tyrone, 1994; steering com. Altoona Reading Inst., Altoona, Pa., 1991—; chair state reading conf. Keystone Reading Assn., 1994-96. Creator and host (weekly radio story hour): Mrs. Spewock & Friends, 1990—; author: Just for Five's, 1995, Just for Four's, 1995, Just for Three's, 1995, Just for Two's, 1995, Just for One's, 1995, Just for Babies, 1995, Getting Ready to Read, 1996; contbr. articles to profl. jours. Assoc. contbr. Altoona Symphony Orch., 1994; mem. adv. bd. strategic planning Tyrone Area Sch. Dist., 1994; rep. Pa. in Washington D.C., 1992. Recipient Dist. Svc. award Tyrone Area Cmty. Orgn., 1992, Outstanding Employee award, 1989. Mem. Keystone State Reading Assn. (pres. 1995), Internat. Reading Assn., Blair County Reading Coun. (pres. 1986-88), Assn. Supervision and Curriculum Devel., Nat. Assn. Edn. Young Children, Pa. Assn. Elem. Sch. Prins., Phi Delta Kappa. Office: Tyrone Area Sch Dist 1317 Lincoln Ave Tyrone PA 16686-1415

SPICER, CAROL INGLIS, freelance writer; b. Detroit, June 8, 1907; d. William Inglis and Carolyn (Clay) Rittenhouse; m. Robert Walker Spicer, 1936;1 child, Susan. AB, U. Mich., 1930. Free lancer Ann Arbor, Mich. Contbr. articles to House Beautiful, McCall's, Parents, Yankee, Better Homes and Gardens, Vogue, L.A. Times, Newsday, Boston Globe, Toronto Star, Cleve. Plain Dealer, Washington Post, Saturday Evening Post, Country Living, Toronto Globe and Mail, Brit. Heritage. Mem. Midwest Travel Writers Assn. (Best Mag. Article award 1979, Best Newspaper Article award 1981), Detroit Women Writers. Home: 740 Green Hills Dr Ann Arbor MI 48105-2718

SPIEGEL, EVELYN SCLUFER, biology educator, researcher; b. Phila., Mar. 20, 1924; d. George and Helen (Laurantos) Sclufer; m. Melvin Spiegel, Apr. 16, 1955; children: Judith Ellen, Rebecca Ann. BA, Temple U., 1947; MA, Bryn Mawr Coll., 1951; PhD, U. Pa., 1954. Asst. program dir. for regulatory biology NSF, Washington, 1954-55; instr. in biology Colby Coll., Waterville, Maine, 1955-59; rsch. assoc. Dartmouth Coll., Hanover, N.H., 1961-74, rsch. assoc. prof. biology, 1974-78, rsch. prof. biology, 1978-91; rsch. prof. biology emerita, 1991—; vis. scholar Calif. Inst. Tech., Pasadena, 1964-65, U. Calif.-San Diego, La Jolla, 1970, Nat. Inst. for Med. Rsch., Mill Hill, Eng., 1971, NIH, Washington, 1975-76, U. Basel (Switzerland) Biocenter, 1979, 80, 81, 82, 85. Contbr. numerous articles to profl. jours., chpts. to books and book reviews. Mem. Soc. for Devel. Biology, Marine Biol. Lab. Corp. (trustee 1981-86, 88-92). Office: Dartmouth Coll Dept Biol Scis Hanover NH 03755

SPIEGEL, MARILYN HARRIET, real estate executive; b. Bklyn., Apr. 3, 1935; d. Harry and Sadie (Oscher) Unger; m. Murray Spiegel, June 12, 1954; children: Eric Lawrence, Dana Cheryl, Jay Barry. Grad. high sch., Bklyn. Exec. sec. S & W Paper Co., N.Y.C., 1953-54, Japan Paper Co., N.Y.C., 1954-58; salesperson Red Carpet Realtors, Los Alamitos, Calif., 1974-75, Coll. Park Realtors, Garden Grove, Calif., 1975-79; owner, broker S & S Properties, Los Alamitos, Calif., 1979—. Named Realtor of Yr., 1989. Mem. Calif. Assn. Realtors (bd. dirs. 1984—), West Orange County Bd. Realtors (bd. dirs. 1984—, 1st v.p. 1987, pres. 1988), Million Dollar Sales Club, Long Beach C. of C., Seal Beach C. of C., Orange County C. of C., Summit Orgn., Toastmasters (pres. founders group Garden Grove, Calif. 1990). Home: 1371 Oakmont Rd 150-D Seal Beach CA 90740-3035 Office: S & S Properties 3502 Katella Ave Ste 208 Los Alamitos CA 90720-3115

SPIEGEL, PHYLLIS, public relations consultant, journalist; b. Bronx, N.Y.; d. Bernard and Lillian (Horowitz) Finkelberg; m. Stanley Spiegel, Sept. 20, 1959 (div. 1981); children: Mark, Adam. BA, NYU. Feature writer various newspapers, pubs., 1960's-70's; dir. pub. rels. Mort Barish Assocs., Princeton, N.J., 1975-80; account exec. pub. rels. Keyes Martin, Springfield, N.J., 1980-84; pres. Phyllis Spiegel Assocs., Plainsboro, N.J., 1984—. Pub. rels. dir., founder Red Oak Coop. Nursery Sch., Middletown, N.J., 1960's, Matawan, N.J., Student Enrichment Program, 1960's-70's; pub. rels. cons., event organizer New Philharm. of N.J., Morristown, 1991-93; advocate Child Placement Rev. Bd. of Family Ct., Mercer County, N.J., 1994—. Recipient Commendation from Gov. N.J. for U. Med. and Dental of N.J. campaign, 1983, Commendation for N.J. Pharm. Assn. campaign Pub. Rels. News Assn., 1979. Mem. Soc. for Humanistic Judaism (bd. dirs. 1983-85). Office: Phyllis Spiegel Assocs PO Box 243 Plainsboro NJ 08536-0243

SPIEGEL, VANESSA ANN, mathematics educator; b. Port Arthur, Tex., Feb. 9, 1958; d. Eli and Zula (Duhon) Stelly; m. Carl B. Spiegel, Dec. 17, 1977; 1 child, Aaron Keat. BS, Lamar U., Beaumont, Tex., 1979; MEd, Lamar U., 1988. Tchr. math. Port Arthur Ind. Sch. Dist., 1979-80; tchr. math. Port Neches (Tex.) Ind. Sch. Dist., 1980—, team coach Mathcounts, 1983—; faculty math. Lamar U., Beaumont, 1994—; lead Tex. tchr. New Stds. for Econ. Devel., U. Pitts., 1992—; mem. Tex. Math. Rev. com., 1988—. Dist. advisor Bus. Partnership Initiative, Port Neches, 1992-93. Tex. Edn. Assn. Tech. Innovative grantee, 1994, Pt. Neches Grove Ind. Sch. Dist. Ednl. Found. grantee, 1996. Mem. Tex. Classroom Tchrs. Assn., Nat. Coun. Tchrs. Math., PTA (life), Delta Kappa Gamma (1st v.p.), Phi Kappa Phi. Roman Catholic. Home: 2211 Avenue L Nederland TX 77627-5437 Office: Port Neches Middle School 2031 Llano St Port Neches TX 77651-3701

SPIEGELBERG, EMMA JO, business education educator; b. Mt. View, Wyo., Nov. 22, 1936; d. Joseph Clyde and Dorcas (Reese) Hatch; BA with honors, U. Wyo., 1958, MEd, 1985; EdD Boston U., 1990; m. James Walter Spiegelberg, June 22, 1957; children: William L., Emory Walter, Joseph John. Tchr. bus. edn. Laramie (Wyo.) High Sch., 1960-61, 65-93, adminstr., 1993—. Bd. dirs. Cathedral Home for Children, Laramie, 1967-70, 72—, pres., 1985-88, Laramie Plains Mus., 1970-79. Author: Branigan's Accounting Simulation, 1986, London & Co. II, 1993; co-author: Glencoe Computerized Accounting, 1993, 2nd edit., 1995, Microcomputer Accounting: Daceasy, 1994, Microcomputer Accounting: Peachtree, 1994, Microcomputer Accounting: Accpac, 1994, Computerized Accounting with Peachtree, 1995, Glencoe Computerized Accounting: Peachtree, 1995. Named Wyo. Bus. Tchr. of Yr., 1982. Mem. Am. Vocat. Assn. (policy com. region V 1984-87, region V Tchr. of Yr. 1986), Wyo. Vocat. Assn. (exec. bd. 1978-80, pres. 1981-82, Outstanding Contbns. to Vocat. Edn. award 1983, Tchr. of Yr. 1985, exec. sec. 1986-89), Nat. Bus. Edn. Assn.(bd. dirs. 1987-88, 1991-96, Sec. Tchr. of the Yr. 1991), Mt. Plains Bus. Edn. Assn. (Wyo. rep. to bd. dirs. 1982-85, pres. 1987-88, Sec. Tchr. of the Yr. 1991, Leadership award 1992), Internat. Soc. Bus. Edn., Wyo. Bus. Edn. Assn. (pres. 1979-80), NEA, Wyo. Edn. Assn., Albany County Edn. Assn. (sec. 1970-71), Laramie C. of C. (bd. dirs. 1985-88), U. Wyo. Alumni Assn. (bd. dirs. 1985-90pres. 1988-89), Kappa Delta Pi, Phi Delta Kappa, Alpha Delta Kappa (state pres. 1978-82), Chi Omega, Pi Lambda Theta, Delta Pi Epsilon. Mem. United Ch. of Christ. Club: Zonta. Home: 3301 Grays Gable Rd Laramie WY 82070-5031 Office: Laramie High Sch 1275 N 11th St Laramie WY 82070-2206

SPIELMAN, BARBARA HELEN NEW, editor, consultant; b. Canton, Ohio, June 28, 1929; d. Arthur Daniel and Helen Barbara (Rickenmann) New; m. David Vernon Spielman, Nov. 24, 1956; children: Daniel Bruce, Linda Barbara. BS in English and History Edn. cum laude, Miami U., Oxford, Ohio, 1951. Cert. tchr., Ohio, Tex. Tchr. Canton Pub. Schs., 1951-53; vets. aide U. Tex., Austin, 1954-57; copy editor, mng. editor U. Tex. Press, Austin, 1964-91; ret., 1991; editorial cons. Chicago Manual of Style, 13th edit., 1975, Amon Carter Mus., Ft. Worth, 1970—, Ctr. for Mex. Am. Studies, Austin, 1980, Archer M. Huntington Art Gallery, Austin, 1975—, 64 Beds Project for Homeless and Hungry, Austin, 1989—; mem. search com. for dir., U. Tex. Press, 1991. Troop leader Girl Scouts Am., Austin, 1970-73; officer PTA, Austin, 1964-73. Mem. Am. Assn. Univ. Presses, Smithsonian Instn., Nat. Geog. Soc., Althenoi, Seton Med. Ctr. Aux., Phi Beta Kappa, Kappa Delta Pi, Sigma Sigma Sigma. Democrat. Presbyterian. Home: 3301 Perry Ln Austin TX 78731-5330

SPIELMANN, DIANE RUTH, research center public services development coordinator; b. N.Y.C., May 27, 1951; d. Elias and Walli (Mischkowski) S. BA magna cum laude, Queens Coll. CUNY, Flushing, 1973; MPhil, CUNY Grad. Sch., N.Y.C., 1979; PhD, CUNY, N.Y.C., 1987. Editl. asst. Harcourt, Brace, Jovanovich, N.Y.C., 1973-74; archivist Leo Baeck Inst., N.Y.C., 1976-92, pub. svcs. and devel. coord., 1992—; German instr., lectr. CUNY Grad. Sch., N.Y.C., 1976-78, Queens Coll. CUNY, Flushing, 1978-81; judge nation-wide jr. high sch. essay contest U.S. Holocaust Meml. Coun., Washington, 1991; guest lectr. on archives Assn. Jewish Librs. Conf., Livingston, N.J., 1987. Author in field. Chair Holocaust meml. com. Hillcrest Jewish Ctr., Flushing, 1988-91, lectr. in Holocaust history, 1988; bd. mem. PhD Alumni Assn. CUNY Grad. Sch., 1995—. Recipient prize for Excellence in Interpretation of German Lit., Lit. Soc. Found., 1973; Grad. U. fellow CUNY, N.Y.C., 1975, 78-79. Mem. MLA, Soc. Am. Archivists, German Studies Assn., Leo Baeck Inst., Phi Beta Kappa, Delta Phi Alpha. Jewish. Office: Leo Baeck Inst 129 E 73rd St New York NY 10021-3502

SPIER, LUISE EMMA, film editor, director; b. Laramie, Wyo., Aug. 22, 1928; d. Louis Constantine Cames and Vina Jane Cochran; m. John Spier, Sept., 1957 (div. 1962). Student, U. Wyo., 1947, U. Calif., Berkeley, 1948-53. Head news film editor Sta. KRON-TV, San Francisco, 1960-70, film editor, 1980—; freelance film editor, director San Francisco, 1970-80, 83—. Edited and directed numerous news specials and documentaries, including The Lonely Basque, Whaler, The American Way of Eating. Recipient numerous awards for film editing and directing, including Cine Golden Eagle, Best Med. Res. Film award John Muir Med. Found., Chris Statuette, Bronze and Silver Cindy awards Info. Film Producers Am.

SPIES, PHYLLIS BOVA, information services company executive; b. Syracuse, N.Y., Nov. 10, 1949; d. Ralph Anthony and Elizabeth Margaret (Caputo) Bova; m. John William Spies, June 28, 1980; children: Fletcher, Logan. BA in Art History, SUNY, Cortland, 1971; MLS in Libr. and Info. Sci., Syracuse U., 1972. Libr. systems analyst Ohio Coll. Library Ctr., Columbus, 1973-78; mgr. libr. systems analysis OCLC Online Computer Libr. Ctr., Dublin, Ohio, 1978-83, div. v.p., 1983-89, v.p. internat., 1989-92, v.p. mem. svcs., sales and internat., 1992—; v.p. mem. svcs., sales and internat. OCLC Online Computer LIbr. Ctr., Dublin, Ohio, 1994—; trustee Maps Micrographic Preservation Svc., Bethlehem, Pa., 1990—. Contbr. articles to profl. jours. Mem. Columbus Coun. World Affairs. Fellow The Gaylord Co., 1971. Mem. ALA, Internat. Fedn. Libr. Assns., Dublin Women in Bus. Office: OCLC Online Computer Libr Ctr 6565 Frantz Rd Dublin OH 43017-5308

SPIEWACK, MARTHA FRANCES, secondary school educator; b. Providence, Sept. 29, 1952; d. George and Genevieve (Murphy) Mulcahey; m. Richard Theodore Spiewak, May 21, 1977; children: Megan, Michael, Brendan. BA in Math. Edn., R.I. Coll., 1993. Math. tchr. S. Kingstown (R.I.) Jr. H.S., 1993-94, S. Kingstown (R.I.) H.S., 1994—; mem. math. task force S. KIngstown Sch. Dept., 1993—, sch. to work, S. Kingstown Sch. and So. R.I. Collaborative, 1994—. Mem. Nat. Coun. Tchrs. of Math., R.I. Math. Tchrs., Kappa Delta Pi, Pi Mu Epsilon. Home: 33 Schooner Dr Wakefield RI 02879

SPIKES, ROZELIA KATHERINE, author, speaker, poet, consultant; b. Eunice, La.; d. Dominic and Ozelia (Anderson) Simon; m. Isiah Spikes Jr., June 11, 1966 (div. 1985); children: Stacy G., Marcus A. BS in Instn. Mgmt., Grambling State U., 1966; MS, Tex. Women's U., 1977. Pres. R.K. Spikes Cons., Inc., Houston, 1978-92, R.K. Spikes Performance Mgmt. Cons., San Diego, 1992—; prof. bus. mgmt. U. Phoenix, San Diego, 1993—, Nat. U., San Diego, 1993—; prof. Internat. Bus. Exec. program San Diego State U., 1993; human resource devel. specialist Meth. Hosp., Hosuton, 1985-90; mgr. Baylor Coll. Medicine, Houston, 1981-85; exec. dir. African Am. Heritage Mus., Houston, 1989-90; cons. Ctr. for Creative leadership, San Diego, 1996; exec. dir., founder African Am. Bus. Network, San Diego, 1994. Author: Ultimate Partner, 1995, Winning at Relationships, 1995, Winning at Performance Reviews Through Partnering, 1995, Understanding the Power of Women: Words to Live By, 1996. Bd. dirs. Vista Hill Found., San Diego, 1995—, Land Eagle Project, San Diego, 1992-94; mem. cmty. outreach bd. La Jolla Playhouse, 1994. Mem. Nat. Coalition of 100 Black Women (bd. dirs. 1990, treas. 1988), Toastmasters (v.p. pub. rels. 1993, v.p. edn. Centre City chpt. 1993, Area 14 gov. 1994, pres. Communicators chpt. 1994, Outstanding Mentor Dist. 5 1994). Office: PO Box 124572 San Diego CA 92112-4572

SPIKOL, EILEEN, artist; b. Sarasota, Fla.; 1 child, Hannah. BA in Fine Arts, Fordham U., 1975; MFA in Sculpture, City Coll., N.Y., 1977. Supr. reproduction studio Am. Mus. Natural History, N.Y.C., 1971-78; tchr. painting and drawing grades 7-12 Fieldston Sch., Riverdale, N.Y., 1977-79; tchr. molding, casting, patina workshop Children's Mus. Manhattan, N.Y.C., 1979-80; tchr. art spl. edn. Sch. Visual Arts, N.Y.C., 1982; tchr. drawing, painting, sculpture, printmaking Studio in a Sch., N.Y.C., 1987-90; instr. Bronx (N.Y.) Mus. Arts, 1990-91; tchr. sculpture Md. Ctr. Arts Goucher Coll., Towson, 1986; adj. prof. art edn., spl. edn. Bkyln. (N.Y.) Coll., 1979-85, field supr.; adj. prof. fine arts St. Johns U., Queens, N.Y., 1991-93; artist in residence Found. Michel Karolyi, Vence, France, 1989; adj. prof. in art edn., spl. edn. Nat. History N.Y.C., 1979-85; lectr. in field. One woman exhbns. include Soho 20 Gallery, N.Y.C., 1974, 75, 77, 78, Maples Gallery Fairleigh Dickinson U., Teaneck, N.J., 1980, 84, Islip Art Mus., E. Islip, N.Y., 1986, Bronx (N.Y.) Mus. Arts, 1988; group exhbns. include One Hundred Acres Gallery, N.Y.C., 1972, Aldrich Mus., Ridgefield, Conn., 1974, New Britain (Conn.) Mus., 1974, Hera Gallery, Wakefield, R.I., 1976, Bronx (N.Y.) Mus. Arts, 1979, 1980, Landmark Gallery, N.Y.C., 1979, Nobe' Gallery, N.Y.C., 1979, Walnut St. Galleries, Phila., 1979, Blaffer Gallery U. Houston, 1980, Mus. Natural History, N.Y.C., 1982, The Fine Arts Ctr. SUNY, Stony Brook, 1982, Fed. Plz., N.Y.C., 1982, Freedman Gallery Albright Coll., Reading, Pa., 1982, The New Mus., N.Y.C., 1984, Henry Street Settlement, N.Y.C., 1986, Artspace Gallery, New Haven, Conn., 1992, Leopold-Hoesch-Mus., Duren, Ger., 1992, B4A Gallery, N.Y.C., 1993; featured in Arts Mag., Soho Weekly News, Womanart, The Nation, The Village Voice, Coll. Art Jour., N.Y. Times, Newsday, New Haven Register. Home: 175 W 72nd St New York NY 10023

SPILLENGER, RITA, civil liberties advocate, civil liberties union executive; b. N.Y.C., Apr. 4, 1960; d. Kenneth and Harriet (Bolotin) Sklar; m. Paul William Spillenger, June 17, 1989; 1 child, Franz David. BA, Hunter Coll., 1988; postgrad., Columbia U., 1988-89. Adminstrv. asst., rschr., special projects coord. ACLU, N.Y.C., 1990-91; exec. dir. ACLU of Ark., Little Rock, 1992—; bd. dirs. Ark. Coalition to Abolish the Death Penalty, Ark. Coalition for Choice. Office: ACLU of Ark 103 W Capitol Little Rock AR 72201

SPILLERS, DIANNE LYN, medical executive; b. Troy, Ohio, Jan. 12, 1961; d. Carl A. Spillers and Linda L. (Locke) Heaston; m. Charles B. Girton, Sept. 10, 1978 (div. Apr. 1988); children: Kerri Girton, Jeromy Girton, Larrin Girton. BS in Acctg., Ind. U. East, Richmond, 1996. Shift leader Goble's Dairy Queen, West Lafayette, Ind., 1980-84; acctg. mgr. F. Sys., Inc., Lynn, Ind., 1984-87; bus. mgr., collection mgr. Gen. Surgeons, Inc., Richmond, 1987—. Mem. Inst. Mgmt. Accts., Whitewater Valley Harley Owners Group (sec. 1995—). Home: PO Box 538 Lynn IN 47355-0538

SPILLMAN, JANE SHADEL, curator, researcher, writer; b. Huntsville, Ala., Apr. 30, 1942; d. Marvin and Elizabeth (Russell) Shadel; m. Don Lewis Spillman, Feb. 18, 1973; children: K. Elizabeth, Samuel Shadel. AB, Vassar Coll., 1964; MA, SUNY, 1965. Rsch. asst. Corning (N.Y.) Mus. Glass, 1965-70, asst. curator, 1971-73, assoc. curator Am. glass, 1974-77, curator, 1978—, head of curatorial dept., 1994—; cons. New Bedford (Mass.) Glass Mus., 1986, The White House Curator's Office, Washington, 1987-90. Author: Complete Cut and Engraved Glass of Corning, 1979, Knopf Collectors Guide to Glass, Vol. 1, 1982, Vol. 2, 1983, White House Glassware, 1989, Masterpieces of American Glass, 1990, The American Cut Glass Industry: T.G. Hawkes and His Competitors, 1996, also 6 other books, numerous articles. Mem. Am. Assn. Mus. (chairperson curators com. 1989-93), Nat. Early Am. Glass Club (bd. dirs. 1989-95), Glass Circle of London. Office: Corning Mus Glass 1 Museum Way Corning NY 14830-2253

SPILLMAN, MARJORIE ROSE, producer, dancer; b. Norfork, Va., Jan. 5; d. William Bert and Rose Marjorie (Naperski) S.; m. David E. Marks, Apr. 4, 1985; children: F. Oscar Marks, Miranda Rose. AS, Mt. Ida Jr. Coll., 1974; CT, Northeastern U., 1975; BS in Nursing, U. Mass., 1977. RN, Mass. Charge nurse VA Med. Ctr., Northampton, Mass., 1977-82; dancer N.E. Am. Ballet, Northampton, 1982, Ballet Theater Sch., Springfield, Mass., 1982-84, Smith Coll., Northampton, 1984—; sales rep. Winthrop Pharm., N.Y.C., 1982-94, Nycomed, N.Y.C., 1994-96; prin. dancer Project Opera, Northampton, 1984-86; dancer Polobulus East St. Dance, Hadley, Mass., 1985; dance and theatre reviewer Holyoke T. Telegram, 1991, 92; theater critic Daily Hampshire Gazette, 1993—. Dancer, creator part of Carmen in Carmen, 1985, Ruth St. Denis in the House of Ruth Ted and Martha, 1994; cancer, choreographer A Victorian Evening, 1986; dancer Nutcracker Ballet Pioneer Valley Ballet, 1988; creator, prodr. The Halloween House at Sunnyside, 1990, producing dir., 1991, 92; actor, author play Mary P. Wells Smith Narrates, 1987; founder, prodr., dir. Northampton Children's Theater, 1993—; prodr. Northampton's First Night Children's Parade, 1996. Democrat. Lutheran.

SPILMAN, PATRICIA, artist, educator; b. Charlottesville, Va., Oct. 3, 1930; d. Harry Franklin and Katherine Elizabeth (Alexander) Black; m. William Bruce Spilman, Feb. 3, 1951 (dec. May 1987); children: Rebecca, Elizabeth, Barbara, William; m. Alvin B. Marks Sr., Apr. 13, 1988. BA, Madison Coll., 1969, MEd, 1971. Art tchr. Stuarts Draft (Va.) H.S., 1969-86; artist in residence Augusta County Schs., Fishersville, Va., 1987—; pvt. tchr. art, Waynesboro, Va., 1986—; docent Shenandoah Valley Art Ctr., Waynesboro, 1986—. Elder Westminster Presbyn. Ch., 1995—; troop leader Girl Scouts U.S., 1958-66. Mem. Nat. Mus. Women in the Arts, Am. Inst. Fgn. Study (travel tchr. 1977-83), Va. Watercolor Soc., Shenandoah Valley Art Ctr., Capitol Hill Art League, Delta Kappa Gamma. Home: 1837 Cherokee Rd Waynesboro VA 22980

SPINDLER, JUDITH TARLETON, elementary school educator; b. Dayton, Tenn., Mar. 4, 1932; d. Frank Willson and Julia Elizabeth (Venable) S. BS in Edn., Longwood Coll., 1953; MA in Edn., Va. Commonwealth U., 1976. Tchr. Oceana, King's Grant Sch., Virginia Beach, Va., 1953-66, Ginter Park Elem. Sch., Richmond, Va., 1966-67, Bon Air Elem. Sch., Chesterfield County, Va., 1967-87; ret., 1987. Charter mem. Web of Hope sponsored by ARC (Humanitarian award). Recipient 1st, 2nd and 3rd pl. awards various knitting competitions, Best in Show award rosette competition. Mem. NEA, Va. Edn. Assn., Knitting Guild Am. (qualified tchr.), The Kitty Gritty, Knit Wit Guild. Home: 4103 Hyde Park Dr Chester VA 23831-4826

SPINWEBER, CHERYL LYNN, research psychologist; b. Jersey City, July 26, 1950; d. Stanley A. And Evelyn M. (Pfleger) S.; m. Michael E. Bruich, June 18, 1977; children: Sean Michael Bruich, Gregory Alan Bruich. AB with distinction, Cornell U., 1972; PhD in Exptl. Psychology, Harvard U., 1977. Lic. psychologist, Calif. Asst. prof. psychiatry Tufts U. Sch. Medicine, Medford, Mass., 1977-79; asst. dir. sleep lab. Boston State Hosp., 1973-79; dep. head dept. behavioral psychopharmacology Naval Health Research Ctr., San Diego, 1978-86, head dept. behavioral psychopharmacology, 1986-89; research asst. prof. dept. psychiatry Uniformed Svcs. U. of the Health Scis., Bethesda, Md., 1985—; lectr. workshop instr. U. Calif. San Diego, La Jolla, 1979-81, vis. lectr. 1979-86; assoc. adj. prof. Dept. Psychology, 1989-94, adj. prof., 1994—; courtesy clin. staff appointee dept. psychiatry Naval Hosp., San Diego, 1984-89, clin. dir. Sleep Disorders Ctr. Mercy Hosp., San Diego, 1991—; pediatric sleep specialist Children's Hosp., San Diego, 1992-95. Contbr. articles to profl. jours. Scholar Cornell U., Ithaca, N.Y., 1968-72, West Essex Tuition, 1968-72, Cornell U. Fedn. Women, 1917-72, Harvard U., 1972-73, 74-76, NDEA Title IV, 1973-74; postdoctoral associateship Nat. Research Council, 1978-80, Outstanding Tchg. award U. Calif. San Diego, 1994. Fellow Am. Sleep Disorders Assn., Clin. Sleep Soc., We. Psychol. Assn. (sec.-treas. 1986—); mem. Am. Men and Women of Sci., Sleep Rsch. Soc. (exec. com. 1986-89), Calif. Sleep Soc., Sigma Xi. Office: U Calif San Diego Dept Psychology 0109 La Jolla CA 92093

SPIRE, NANCY WOODSON (MRS. LYMAN SPIRE), civic worker; b. Wausau, Wis., May 6, 1917; d. Aytchmonde Perrin and Leigh (Yawkey) Woodson; B.S., Radcliffe Coll., 1939; postgrad. Syracuse U., 1957; m. Lyman J. Spire, June 29, 1940; children: Stephen Crittenden Woodson, Abigail Lyman. Vice pres. Woodson Fiduciary Corp., Wilmington, Del. Trustee Aytchmonde Woodson Found., pres., 1963—; trustee Corinthian Found., 1958-63, 68—, Syracuse Child and Family Service, 1957-62; trustee, sec. Crouse-Irving Meml. Hosp., Syracuse; trustee Syracuse Symphony Orch.; mem. exec. com. Syracuse U. Library Assos., 1958-63, trustee, 1958—. Bd. visitors N.Y. State Tng. Sch. for Girls; v.p. bd. dirs. Leigh Yawkey Woodson Art Mus. Mem. Syracuse Symphony Guild (treas. 1958-59), U.S. Trotting Assn. Republican. Universalist (trustee). Club: Virgin Islands Game Fishing. Office: Yawkey Lumber Co PO Box 65 Wausau WI 54402-0065 also: 707 Kimry Moor Fayetteville NY 13066-1834 also: Cowpet Bay W 24 Windward Way Saint Thomas VI 00802

SPIRER, JUNE DALE, marketing executive, clinical psychologist; b. N.Y.C., May 14, 1943; d. Leon and Gloria (Wagner) Spirer; BA, Adelphi U., 1965; MS, Yeshiva U., 1980, PhD in Psychology, 1984, postgrad. NYU, 1988. TV/radio buyer BBD&O, 1965-66, SSC&B, 1966-68; sr. media planner Norman, Craig & Kummel, N.Y.C., 1968-71; assoc. media dir. Ted Bates Co., 1971-72; v.p., account supt. C.T. Clyne Co., N.Y.C., 1972-74; dir. advt. Am. Express, 1974-75; corp. dir. advt. Del Labs., Farmingdale, N.Y., 1975-79; pres. J. Spirer & Assocs., Inc., N.Y.C., 1978-96; pres., CEO Media Placement Svcs., Inc., 1985-95, Tactics, Inc., 1988-95; CEO 75 Main St. Restaurant, Southampton, N.Y., 1990—; Mem. Am. Psychol. Assn. Home: PO Box 490 Southampton NY 11969-0490 Office: 2 Horatio St New York NY 10014-1608

SPIRES, DENISE TATE, secondary education educator; b. Oxford, Ala., Sept. 4, 1956; d. Robert Lanier and Mary Bernice (Ginn) Tate; m. Wesley Davis Spires, Mar. 3, 1984. BS in Secondary Math., Auburn (Ala.) U., 1979; MEd in Secondary Math., Ga. Southwestern State U., 1990; EdS in Secondary Math. Edn., Columbus Coll., 1995. Tchr. math. Crisp County H.S., Cordele, Ga., 1979—, chairperson dept., 1992—; mem. steering com. 10 yr. study Crisp County H.S., Cordele, 1992, student coun. advisor, 1988-93. Named STAR Tchr., 1985-86. Mem. Nat. Coun. Tchrs. Math., Page. Presbyterian. Home: 1972 Royal Rd Cordele GA 31015-9000 Office: Crisp County HS 2012 Frontage Rd Cordele GA 31015

SPIRES, ROBERTA LYNN, court clerk; b. Gary, Ind., Sept. 4, 1952; d. Merle Russell and Kathryn Dias (Felts) Harris; m. Richard John Badovinich, Aug. 16, 1975 (div. 1989); m. Patrick Robert Spires, Mar. 14, 1992; 1 child, Zachary Robert. Grad. high sch., Griffith, Ind. Dep. clk. U.S. Bankruptcy Ct., Gary, 1970-80; chief dep. clk. U.S. Bankruptcy Ct., 1980—. Mem. Fed. Ct. Clks. Assn., Fed. Bar Assn. (lectr., cert. 1984). Democrat. Roman Catholic. Home: 719 N Rueth Dr Griffith IN 46319-3817 Office: US Bankruptcy Ct 610 Connecticut St Gary IN 46402-2550

SPIRN, MICHELE SOBEL, communications professional, writer; b. Newark, Jan. 26, 1943; d. Jack and Sylvia (Cohen) Sobel; m. Steven Frederick Spirn, Jan. 27, 1968; 1 child, Joshua. BA, Syracuse U., 1965. Creative dir. Planned Communications Svcs., N.Y.C., 1966-72, EDL Prodns., N.Y.C., 1972-73; free-lance writer Bklyn., 1973-83; dir. pub. rels. Nat. Coun. Jewish Women, N.Y.C., 1983-90, dir. communications, 1990-95; freelance writer Bklyn., 1995—; adj. lectr. CUNY, Bklyn., 1977-81. Author: The Fast Shoes, 1985, The Boy Who Liked Green, 1985, The Know-Nothings, 1995; co-author: A Man Can Be..., 1981; editor, columnist Children's Entertainment Rev. mag., N.Y.C., 1982; columnist The Phoenix newspaper, Bklyn., 1983. Pres. Tenth St. Block Assn., Bklyn., 1989-91; vol. Model Media Program, Bklyn., 1985—. Recipient Silver medal for pub. svc. film N.Y. Internat. Film and TV Festival, 1972. Mem. Editl. Freelancers Assn., Soc. Children's Book Writers and Illustrators.

SPIRO, VANESSA GREEN, lawyer; b. Washington, May 17, 1964; d. Gary S. and Shia Toby (Riner) G.; m. Alexander Charles Stiefel Spiro, May 8, 1993. AB in Asian Studies, Vassar Coll., 1986; JD, Fordham U., 1989. Bar: N.Y., 1990, Washington, 1991. Atty. Sidley & Austin, N.Y.C., 1989-93, Shearman & Sterling, N.Y.C., 1993-95, Credit Lyonnais, N.Y.C., 1995—. Chair Vassar Coll. Ann. Fund, Class of '86, Poughkeepsie, N.Y., 1991-96. Louis B. Stein Law and Ethics fellow, Fordham U., 1988-89; recipient Am. Jurisprudence award, Am. Jurisprudence Pub. Co., 1988. Mem. ABA, Assn. of Bar of City of N.Y. Office: Credit Lyonnais 1301 Ave of the Americas New York NY 10019

SPISAK, SARA LOUISE, women's apparel retail business owner; b. Parma, Ohio, Mar. 11, 1966; d. Frank Eugene and Mary Louise (Babjak) S. AA in Applied Bus., Mgmt., Mktg., Cuyahoga Community Coll. West, Parma, Ohio, 1985. Exec. fashion buyer, merchandise mgr. Rosenblum's Inc., Cleve., 1986-92; owner Elegance for Less, North Royalton, Ohio, 1994—; adviser Parma 60+ Mall Fashion Shows, 1986-90; fashion coord., model AAA Travel Agy, Cleve. Fashion coord. for Rosenblum's Fashion, Parma Jr. League, 1990, fashion coord., narration writer, Parma Area Fine Arts Coun. Fashion Show, 1991; hon. judge Miss Parma Pageant, 1991. Recipient Scholastic Art awards, Cleve. Inst. Art, 1983. Mem. NAFE, Nat. Assn. Investors Corp., Phi Theta Kappa. Byzantine Catholic. Office: Elegance for Less 12871 State Rd Cleveland OH 44133

SPITTLER, JAYNE ZENATY, advertising executive; b. Chgo., July 24, 1948; d. Ernest Frederick and Mary Winifred (McEvilly) Zenaty; m. Joseph R. Spittler, Aug. 22, 1987; 1 child, Brian Joseph. BA, Clarke Coll., 1971; PhD, Mich. State U., 1980. Asst. dir. pub. rels. Clarke Coll., Dubuque, Iowa, 1974-76; asst. prof. dept. telecommunications Ind. U., Bloomington, 1979-81; supr. media rsch. Leo Burnett Co., Inc., Chgo., 1981-82, mgr. media rsch., 1982-84, v.p., dir. media rsch., 1985-95, sr. v.p., dir. media rsch., 1995—; guest lectr. Northwestern U., Evanston, Il., 1981—. Vol. ARC, McHenry County, Ill.; zoo parent Brookfield (Ill.) Zoo, 1975—. Named to Media Rsch. All Star Team, Media Decisions, N.Y., 1987; recipient Excellence in Teaching award, Mich. State U., 1979, grant broadcast ownership, FCC, 1979, grant VCR Usage, Corp. for Pub. Broadcasting, 1980. Mem. Advt. Rsch. Found. (chair video electronic media coun. 1990-94, mem. media comm. coun. 1986—, radio rsch. coun. 1988—), Chgo. Advt. Fedn. (bd. dirs. 1986-91), Am. Assn. Advt. Agys. (media rsch. com. 1984—), Mich. State U. Alumni Assn. (Disting. Alumna award 1994), Women's Advt. Club Chgo. (Advt. Woman of Yr. 1995). Roman Catholic.

SPITZER, MANDY, social worker, artist; b. St. Louis, Jan. 9, 1955; d. Robert S. and Becky B. Spitzer; m. Domenico Anatrone, Dec. 21, 1980; 1 child, Soledad. BA in art, Goddard Coll., 1979; student in glass art, lit., Inst. Allende, Mex., 1972; student in glass art, Rochester Inst. Tech., 1977, R.I. Sch. Design, 1978, San Jose (Calif.) State Coll., 1984-86; student in sculpture, archtl. design, Cabrillo Coll., 1987-90. Counselor NAACP, Santa Cruz, Calif., 1979; co-owner Traveling Video Show, Santa Cruz, Calif., 1980-87; shelter mgr. Women's Crisis Support, Santa Cruz, Calif., 1987-90; asst. dir. Casa Delle Donne, Bologna, Italy, 1990-93; vol. coord. Defensa de Mujeres, Watsonville, Calif., 1993-94; family advocate Healthy Start, Watsonville, Calif., 1994—; co-dir. Arte Latino, Santa Cruz, 1993—; co-leader Wen-Do, Bologna, 1991-93; bd. mem. Santa Cruz Dance Gallery, 1993-94, Santa Cruz Ethnic Arts Network, 1987-90. Exhbns. include Corning Mus. Glass, N.Y., 1976, 89, Goddard Coll., Vt., 1978, Cabrillo Coll., Santa Cruz, 1981, YWCA, Santa Cruz, 1981, San Jose State U., 1986, Primitivo Gallery, San Francisco, 1988, Santa Cruz Art League, 1988, 90, Compositions Gallery, San Francisco, 1988, 89, Banaker Gallery, Walnut Creek, Calif., 1988, Santa Cruz Metro Ctr., 1989, Artoptions Gallery, San Francisco, 1989, Boulder Creek (Calif.) Libr., 1989, Elaine Pottery Gallery, San Francisco, 1989, Open Studio '89, Santa Cruz, 1989, 94, Il Giardino Dell'Arte, Bologna, 1989, 91-93, Lumina Gallery, San Francisco, 1989, Del Mano Galleries, L.A. and Pasadena, Calif., 1990, Coco Gallery, Santa Cruz, 1990, Calif. State Fair, Sacramento, 1990 (artistic merit prize), ArteLatino Bookshop, Santa Cruz, 1994, Santa Cruz Dance Gallery, 1995, Santa Cruz Mus., 1995. Democrat. Office: Healthy Start Salsipuedes School 115 Casserly Rd Watsonville CA 95076

SPIVACK, EDITH IRENE, lawyer; b. N.Y.C., Apr. 19, 1910; d. Harry A. and Ethel Y. (Mantell) Spivack; m. Bernard H. Goldstein, Dec. 22, 1933; children: Rita Goldstein Christopher, Amy Goldstein Bass. BA, Barnard Coll., 1929; LLB, Columbia U., 1932; hon. doctorate St. John's U. Bar: N.Y. 1933, U.S. Dist. Ct. (so. dist.) N.Y. 1949, U.S. Cts. Appeals 1950, 75, U.S. Supreme Ct. 1969, U.S. Dist. Ct. (ea. dist.) Pa. 1973. Assoc. asst. Corp. Counsel's Office, City of N.Y., 1934-76, exec. asst., 1976—; ptnr. Tenzer, Greenblatt, Fallon & Kaplan, N.Y.C.; mem. panel to rev. qualifications for ea. dist. ct. bankruptcy judges; spl. master appellate div. 1st Dept., 1991, mem. com. on character and fitness, 1995—. Active Planned Parenthood, Legal Aid Soc.; Columbia Law Sch. rep. to Alumni Council, also past bd. dirs. Recipient William Nelson Cromwell award N.Y. County Law Assn., 1976, Fund for City of N.Y. Pub. Service award, 1975, Disting. Service award Mayor Koch, 1981, Columbia award for Conspicuous Service, 1975, NIMLO award for Outstanding Pub. Service, 1976, Disting. Alumnae award Barnard Coll., 1984, Disting. and Dedicated Corp. Counsel Service award, 1986. Fellow N.Y. Bar Found. (Community Service award); mem. Am. Bar Found., Assn. Bar City N.Y. (cts. and membership coms., judiciary com.), N.Y. State Bar Assn. (judiciary com., del., status of women in cts. com., Service plaque, Fifty-yr. Lawyer award 1984, 60 year dedicated svc. award), N.Y. County Lawyers Assn. (bd. dirs., fin. com., women's rights com., judiciary com.), N.Y. County Lawyers Found., Am. Judicature Soc., Columbia U. Law Sch. Alumni Assn. (medal for excellence com.). Democrat. Jewish. Club: Princeton (N.Y.C.). Home: 21 Colonial Rd Port Washington NY 11050 Office: Office Corp Counsel 100 Church St New York NY 10007-2601

SPIVACK, SHELLEY ROBIN, lawyer; b. Atlanta, June 2, 1954; d. Milton D. Spivack and Jacquelyn (Manning) Ciluffo; m. Patrick Hardin, Sept. 4, 1983; 1 child, Trevor Hayse Hardin. BA, Rutgers U., 1976; JD, Bklyn. Law Sch., 1980. Bar: N.J. 1981, N.Y. 1981, Mich. 1981. Staff atty. Legal Svcs. P.E. Mich., Flint, 1980-82; pvt. practice Flint, 1983—. Bd. dirs. Planned Parenthood East Cen. Mich., Flint, 1990—; dir. Flint Art Fair, 1990—. Named Person of Yr., NOW, 1988. Mem. ACLU (past co-chair), Women Lawyers Assn., Criminal Def. Attys. of Mich., Gem County Bar Assn. Democrat. Jewish. Office: 720 Church St Flint MI 98502

SPIVAK, HELAYNE, advertising agency executive; b. Queens, NY, June 12, 1952. Student, Parsons Sch. of Design, N.Y.C., Sch. of Visual Arts. Past sec. Della Femina, Travisano & Ptnrs., N.Y.C.; copywriter, then sr. v.p. and assoc. creative dir. Ally & Gorgano; v.p., assoc. creative dir., then sr. v.p. Ammirati & Puris, Inc. (name changed to Ammirati, Puris, Lintas), N.Y.C., 1986-88; vice chmn., chief creative officer Ammirati, Puris, Lintas, N.Y.C.; sr. v.p., exec. creative dir. Hal Riney & Ptnrs., Inc., N.Y.C., 1988-90; exec. v.p., creative dir. Young & Rubicam N.Y., N.Y.C., 1990—. Recipient Clio awards. Office: Ammirati Puris Lintas One Dag Hammarskjold Plz New York NY 10017*

SPIVEY, SHARON L., health facility administrator; b. Conway, S.C., Nov. 29, 1944; d. Joseph Carl and Ruby Opal (Mintz) Livingston; m. Larry Neal Spivey, Dec. 15, 1973. BA, Winthrop Coll., 1966; MSW, Fla. State U., 1969. Lic. social worker, S.C. Caseworker III Dept. Social Svcs., York, S.C., 1966-67; asst. dir. Greenville (S.C.) Mental Health Ctr., 1969—; clin. coord. disaster svcs. S.C. Dept. Mental Health, 1995—. Mem. Action Coun., Greenville Crisis Response Team; bd. dirs. S.C. Crisis Response Consortium. Recipient hon. outstanding support award Nat. Cross Cultural Conf., 1989, Otis A. Corbitt Leadership award, 1992. Mem. Internat. Assn. Trauma Counselors, Internat. Soc. for Traumatic Stress Studies, Greenville Mental Health Assn., Greenville Assn. Dirs. Social Agys. Home: 113 Suffolk Ct Greer SC 29650-2832 Office: Greenville Mental Health Ctr 715 Grove Rd Greenville SC 29605

SPOFFORD, SALLY HYSLOP, artist; b. N.Y.C., Aug. 20, 1929; d. George Hall and Esther (McNaull) Hyslop; m. Gavin Spofford, Mar. 11, 1950 (dec. Jan. 1976); children: Lizabeth Spofford Smith, Leslie Spofford Russell. Student, The China Inst., N.Y.C., 1949, The Art Students League, N.Y.C., 1950; BA with high honors, Swarthmore Coll., 1952. Instr. Somerset Art Assn., Peapack, N.J., 1978-95, Hunterdon Art Ctr., Clinton, N.J., 1985—; adv. bd., lectr. Apollo Muses, Inc., Gladstone, N.J.; bd. trustees Artshowcase, Inc. One-man show Riverside Studio, Pottersville, N.J., 1985, Morris Mus., Morristown, N.J. 1989, Schering-Plough Gallery, Madison, N.J., 1989, Phoenix Gallery, N.Y.C., 1990, Robin Hutchins Gallery, Maplewood, N.J., 1992, Berlex Labs. Corp. Office, Wayne, N.J., 1992, Hunterdon Art Ctr., Clinton, N.J., 1993; exhibited in group shows at Hickory (N.C.) Mus., 1983, Purdue U., 1983, Monmouth (N.J.), 1984, Nabisco Brands Gallery, E. Hanover, N.J., 1985, 89, Hunterdon Art Ctr., Clinton, N.J., 1988, 93, Schering-Plough Gallery, Madison, 1988, Morris Mus., Morristown, 1989, Montclair (N.J. State U., 1995; represented in permanent collections N.J. State Mus., Trenton, Newark Mus. Painting residency fellow Vt. Studio Ctr., 1992. Mem. Assoc. Artists N.J. (pres. 1985-87), N.J. Watercolor Soc., Federated Art Assns. of N.J. (panel mem. 1985, demonstrator 1991). Home: PO Box 443 Bernardsville NJ 07924-0443

SPOHN, JANICE, elementary education educator, consultant; b. Pitts., Jan. 12, 1952; d. James Arthur and Jean Edna (Smithyman) Rowan; m. Chester Michael Spohn II, Oct. 23, 1972; children: Chester M. III, Lisa Marie. BE, Clarion U., 1973; ME, Slippery Rock U., 1989; supervisory cert., Duquesne U., 1992. Cert. reading specialist, gifted edn., supervisor reading, Pa. Group supr. Butler County (Pa.) Children Ctr., 1974-87; temp. instr. Slippery Rock U., Slippery Rock, Pa., 1989; reading specialist North Allegheny Schs., Pitts., 1990—; coord. Pa. Framework Network, North Allegheny Schs., 1991—; inservice com. Allegheny Intermediate Unit, 1993—; Pa. Framework steering com. Allegheny Intermediate Unit, 1993—. Co-author/editor: (book) Pennsylvania Framework-Portfolio Implementation Guide, 1993. Mem. ASCD, Nat. Coun. Tchrs. of English, Internat. Reading Assn., Keystone State Reading Assn., Three Rivers Reading Coun., Butler County Reading Coun. Home: 520 Herman Rd Butler PA 16001-9157 Office: Peebles Elem N Allegheny Schs 8526 Peebles Rd Pittsburgh PA 15237

SPOLAR-BLUMER, ANNE MARIE, insurance purchasing specialist; b. Tigerton, Wis., Sept. 2, 1956; d. Anthony R. and Bernadine G. (Donder) Spolar; m. William F. Blumer. A in Police Sci., Fox Valley Tech. Inst., Appleton, Wis., 1976; grad., Gemol. Inst. Am., 1990, 95. Cert. gemologist. Salesperson Spolar's Jewelry, Appleton, Wis., 1976-85; asst. mgr. customer svc. Paradise Printing, Madison, Wis., 1985-88; gemology instr. Gemological Inst. Am., Santa Monica, Calif., 1989-93; purchasing specialist State Farm Ins. Co., Bloomington, Ill., 1993—. Mem. NAFE, Am. Gem Soc., Nat. Assn. Watch and Clock Collectors, Women's Jewelry Assn., Gemology Inst. Am. Alumni Assn. Office: State Farm Ins Co # B4 1 State Farm Plz Bloomington IL 61710-0001

SPOONAMORE, DORIS JEAN, artist; b. Akron, Ohio, Mar. 8, 1910; d. Frederick Marguaretta Ursula (Keun) Apel; m. Russell Spoonamore; children: Richard, Stephen. BA, U. Akron, 1933. Art tchr. Akron Pub. Schs., 1933-34, Cathedral Sch., Havana, Cuba, 1946-52, Coventry-Erwin w Jr. High Sch., Akron, 1953-73; owner, operator Spoonamore Studio, Akron, 1973-93; contbr. Channel 25, Cleve., 1977-89. Artist numerous paintings, collages and quilts. Tchr. elderhostle program U. Akron, 1979; cook, server Friendship Meals, Barberton, Ohio, 1986-93; vol. tchr.'s aide Portage Lakes Schs., 1975-93; vol. tchr.'s aide Portage Lake Schs., 1975, 85-87. Recipient Bronze medal N.Y. Great Am. Quilt Show, 1976, award Internat. Women's Art Festival, 1975-76, Honor awards Almond Tea Gallery, 1985-86, Honor award Stan Hywet, 1983, Honor award Ohio State Fair; named best of show Massillon Mus., 1981. Mem. Akron Soc. Artists (Honorable mention 1987), Whiskey Painters Am., Liturgical Art Guild, N. Coast Collage Soc., Women's City Club (little gallery bd.), Kappa Kappa Gamma (pres. local chpt. 1933). Home and Office: PO Box 61774 Phoenix AZ 85082-1774

SPORN, JUDITH BERYL, lawyer; b. N.Y.C., Mar. 3, 1951; d. Milton and Helen Florence (Berman) Shapiro; m. Robert C. Sporn, May 22, 1977; 1 child, David Benjamin. BA magna cum laude, SUNY, Buffalo, 1973; postgrad., Columbia U., 1973-74; JD, Loyola U., L.A., 1979. Bar: N.Y. 1979, Conn. 1982. Atty. firm Cohen & Tucker, N.Y.C., 1980-82, Barst & Mukamal, L.A., 1982-85; sole practice Westport, Conn., 1985—. Vol. atty. Vol. Lawyers for the Arts, N.Y.C., 1980-82, Los Angeles County Bar Pro Bono Immigration Project, L.A., 1983-85; bd. dirs. Women's Crisis Ctr., Norwalk, Conn., 1986. Mem. Fed. Bar Assn., Westport Bar Assn., Fairfield Women's Bar Assn., Am. Immigration Lawyers Assn. Office: 125 Main St Westport CT 06880-3303

SPRABERY, CAROL ANN, health facility administrator; b. North Island, Calif., July 6, 1945; d. Thomas Eugene and Dorothy Frances (Grimes) Forister; div.; children: Scott Ellis, Cynthia Anne. BS, U. Miss., 1967; MEd, Miss. State U., 1986, PhD, 1990. Lic. profl. counselor; cert. psychometrist, nat. counselor. Adolescent counselor Laurelwood Psychiat., Meridian, Miss.; counselor Lamar Sch., Meridian; tchr. counselor edn. Weems Cmty. Mental Health Ctr., Meridian, 1990-95; pvt. practice Glen Burnie, Md., 1995—; mem. adj. faculty Miss. State U., 1990—. Mem. ACA, Miss. Counselors Assn., Assn. Mental Health Counselors, Assn. Sch. Counselors, Lauderdale County Mental Health Bd. Office: Ste 409 1600 S Crain Hwy Glen Burnie MD 21061

SPRADLIN, VIRGINIA GOULD, accountant; b. Lafayette, Ind., Dec. 22, 1943; d. Thomas Landers and Marjorie Emma (Marquis) Gould; m. Norman A. Spradlin, July 11, 1964; children: Jill A. Olson, Lori D. BS in bus., Butler U., Indpls., 1966. CPA, Ind. Staff acct. M.S. Cassen & Co., Indpls., 1965-81; treas. Christian Ch. Found., Inc., Indpls., 1981—, v.p., 1987—. Elder Allisonville Christian Ch., 1991—. Mem. Ind. CPA Soc., Nat. Com. on Planned Giving. Office: Christian Ch Found Inc 130 E Washington St Indianapolis IN 46204

SPRAGGINS, PEGGY ANN, government representative; b. Cleve., Feb. 13, 1955; d. Donald W. and Viola A. (Tomaselli) Berteau; m. Lawrence A. Spraggins, Oct. 18, 1974; children: Kelly, Lisa, David. BA in Speech Pathology and Audiology, Cleve. State U., 1976; MPA, Kent State U., 1992. Cert. mcpl. clk., Advanced Acad. Edn. for Mcpl. Clks. Clk. of coun. City of Macedonia, Ohio, 1980-91, County of Summit, Akron, Ohio, 1991-94; field rep. Kent (Ohio) State U., 1994—; mem. adv. bd. Ctr. for Pub. Adminstrn. and Pub. Policy, Kent, 1989-90; mem. adv. bd. polit. sci. dept. Kent State U., 1995-96. Dem. precinct committeeman Summit County Dem., Akron, 1988-96; pres. Nordonia Hills Coun. PTA, Northfield, Ohio, 1989-91; bd. trustees Kids Voting Northeast Ohio, 1994-96. Mem. Am. Soc. Pub. Adminstrs. (bd. trustees 1994-96), Nordonia Hills Rotary (pres. 1996—). Methodist. Home: 508 Ledge Rd Macedonia OH 44056 Office: Kent State U PO Box 5190 Kent OH 44242

SPRAGUE, AMARIS JEANNE, real estate broker; b. Jackson, Mich., Feb. 18, 1935; d. Leslie Markham and Blanche Lorraine (Basnaw) Reed; student Mich. State U., 1952-53; B.S., Colo. State U., 1965; m. John M. Vetterling, Oct. 1985; children by previous marriage—Anthony John, James Stuart. Real estate sales Seibel and Benedict Realty, Ft. Collins, Colo., 1968-69; salesman Realty Brokers Exchange, Ft. Collins, 1969-72; broker, pres. Sprague and Assos., Inc., Realtors, Ft. Collins, 1972-80; broker assoc. Van Schaack & Co., Ft. Collins, 1980-86; broker ptnr. The Group, Inc., 1986—; dir. Univ. Nat. Bank. Mem. bus. adv. council Colo. State U., 1976-84, chmn. 1979-80, mem. adv. council Coll. of Engring., 1981. Cert. real estate broker. Mem. Nat. Assn. Realtors, Colo. Assn. Realtors, Ft. Collins Bd. Realtors, Ft. Collins C. of C. (bd. dirs. 1978-84, pres. 1982-83). Republican. Episcopalian. Home: PO Box 475 Fort Collins CO 80522-0475 Office: 401 W Mulberry St Fort Collins CO 80521-2839

SPRAGUE, GLENNA MAE, music educator; b. Gallipolis, Ohio, Apr. 12, 1953; d. William Ross and Emily Mae (Phillips) S. MusB magna cum laude, Capital U., Columbus, Ohio, 1975; MusM, Ohio U., 1977. Class piano tchg. asst. Ohio U., Athens, 1975-76, instr. class piano, 1976-78; instr. elem. music Meigs Local Sch. Dist., Pomeroy, Ohio, 1976-78; instr. music Oakton Coll., DesPlaines, Ill., 1978-81; asst. prof. music Oakton Coll., DesPlaines, 1981-85, assoc. prof. music, 1985-89, prof. music, 1989—, coord. music dept., 1987—; grant reviewer Ill. Arts Coun. Adv. Panel, Chgo., 1986-89; mem. Ill. Bd. Higher Edn., 1995; adjudicator Am. Music Scholarship Assn.-Internat. Festival, Cin., 1979, Chgo. Symphony Orch., 1990; performer, guest clinician Ill. Music Educators Assn. All-State Conf., 1988, Nat. Conf. on Piano Pedagogy, Schaumburg, Ill., 1992, Music Tchrs. Nat. Assn. Nat. Conv., Spokane, Wash., 1993, Ill. State Music Tchrs. Assn. State Conv., Northwestern U., 1994, Coll. Music Soc./Gt. Lakes Regional Conf., Mich. State U., 1996; performer Chgo. Civic Opera House, 1991; mem. various coms. Oakton Coll., Des Plaines, 1978—. Pianist Capital U. Wind Ensemble, 1972-73; accompanist Opera Workshop, Capital U., 1973, Summer Choir, Ohio U., 1976; keyboardist, piano and celeste Capital U. Symphony Orch., 1973-74; condr., performer Oakton Six Piano Ensemble, 1980—; guest pianist DePaul U., Chgo., 1984; rehearsal pianist/orch. keyboardist-synthesizer Three Penny Opera, Oakton Coll., 1987; guest pianist Chgo. Bar Assn. Revue, 1988; guest pianist, clinician for critical literacy conf. Holiday Inn Mart Plaza, Chgo., 1990; many others. Charles and Olivia Bash Meml. Scholarship award. Mem. Music Tchrs. Nat. Assn., Ill. State Music Tchrs. Assn., Music Educators Nat. Conf., Am. Music Scholarship Assn., Coll. Music Soc., Pi Kappa Lambda, Kappa Alpha Pi, Phi Beta. Home: 8541 Lotus Ave Skokie IL 60077-5100 Office: Oakton Coll 1600 E Golf Rd Des Plaines IL 60016-1234

SPRAGUE, JO ANN, state legislator; b. Nashville, Ind., Nov. 3, 1931; m. Warren G. Sprague; 6 children. BA, U. Mass., 1980. Mem. Mass. Ho. of Reps., Boston, 1980-92, mem. capital budget com., 1990-92; mem. Walpole Prison Adv. Com., 1979-92, Rep. Town Meeting, 1979—. Bd. trustees Walpole Scholar Found., 1990-92. 2d lt. U.S. Army, 1950-53. Mem. Walpole Vis. Nurses Assn. (bd. dirs. 1989-92), Walpole LVW, Norfolk Am. Legion (Post No. 335). Republican. Home: 305 Elm St Walpole MA 02081-1903 Office: Mass Ho of Reps State Capitol Boston MA 02133

SPRAGUE, MARY GABRIELLE, lawyer; b. Phila., Oct. 7, 1957. AB summa cum laude, Harvard U., 1979; JD, Yale U., 1983. Bar: Colo. 1984, D.C. 1992. Law clk. to Hon. Jim R. Carrigan U.S. Dist. Ct. Colo., 1984-85; law clk. to Hon. Byron R. White U.S. Supreme Ct., Washington, 1986-87; ptnr. Arnold & Porter, Washington. Mem. Phi Beta Kappa. Office: Arnold & Porter 555 12th St NW Washington DC 20004*

SPRAGUE-GOULD, CHRISTINE ANN, accountant; b. Watertown, N.Y., Sept. 12, 1967; d. Harland S. and Norma J. (Williams) Sprague; m. Bryan J. Gould, July 6, 1985; children: Jessica Lee, Cody Jay. AAS in Acctg., Jefferson C.C., Watertown, 1995. Purchasing agt. Rubbermaid Corp., Ft. Drum, N.Y., 1985; jr. acct. Kennard Enterprises, Inc., Fallbrook, Calif., 1986; acct. Pride-Air Mech., Escondido, Calif., 1987; jr. acct. Comprehensive Bus. Svcs., Fallbrook, 1988; sr. acct. Ewing Bus. Svcs., Fallbrook, 1988-90; v.p. Accurate Acctg. Svcs., Inc., Watertown, 1996. acct., vol. advocate for disabled Lasting Inclusion for Freedom of Edn., Watertown, 1995-96. Mem. Inst. Mgmt. Accts., Nat. Assn. Tax Practitioners, The Greater Watertown C. of C. Republican. Methodist. Office: Accurate Acctg Svcs Inc 21931 Sunset Ridge Watertown NY 13601

SPRATT, GEORGIA A. POTTERTON, children's educational director, parish administrator; b. Manchester, Conn., May 29, 1940; d. George Arthur and Barbara Fenn (Isham) Potterton; m. Edward N. "Jack" Spratt; children: John, Janina, Stephen. BS, U. Conn., 1962, MA in Edn., 1969. Cert. secondary tchr., Conn. Tchr. Bassick H.S., Bridgeport, Conn., 1962; tchr., head home econs. dept. Eastern Jr. H.S., Greenwich, Conn., 1962-71; home econs. instr. Mattatuck C.C., Waterbury, Conn., 1972-76; adminstrv. dir. Garden Edn. Ctr., Cos Cob, Conn., 1982-85, shop mgr., 1985-89, dir. children's programs, 1993—; lectr. in field. Parish adminstr. St. Saviour's Episcopal Ch., Old Greenwich, Conn., 1989—; vol. Greenwich chpt. ARC Blood Program. Mem. AAUW, DAR (local, state, and nat. chpts., past regent Putnam Hill chpt., state chaplain, state membership chmn., recording sec., mem. bd. dirs. Ellsworth Meml. Assn., nat. speaker's staff), Am. Assn. Family and Consumer Svcs. (life), Conn. Home Econs. Assn. (past pres.), Garden Club of Old Greenwich (rec. sec., past pres.), Federated Garden Clubs of Conn. (life), Navy League of U.S., Nat. Maritime Hist. Soc., Scott Family Assn., U. Conn. Alumni Assn. (life), Old Greenwich Yacht Club (life), State Officers' and Regents' Club (rec. sec.). Republican. Home: 11 Park Ave Old Greenwich CT 06870 Office: St Saviour's Episcopal Ch 350 Sound Beach Ave Old Greenwich CT 06870

SPRAUER, CYNTHIA CAROL, optometrist; b. Bridgeton, N.J., Apr. 11, 1962; d. Frederick Henry and Edna Catherine (Hepner) S. BS in Biology, Va. Tech., 1984; BS in Visual Sci., Pa. Coll. Optometry, 1988, OD, 1991. Tech. rep. Vineland (N.J.) Chem., 1984-87; optometrist Office of Drs. Klein & Schwab, Mays Landing, N.J., 1991-93, Nu Vision, Northfield, N.J., 1993—. Mem. Am. Optometric Assn., N.J. Optometric Assn., South Jersey Optometric Soc., Beta Sigma Kappa. Home: 3627 Whitehall Ct Mays Landing NJ 08330-3244

SPRAYBERRY, ROSLYN RAYE, secondary school educator; b. Newnan, Ga., June 29, 1942; d. Henry Ray and Grace (Bernhard) S. BA, Valdosta State Coll., 1964; MA in Teaching, Ga. State U., 1976, EdS in Spanish, 1988; EdD, Nova U., 1993. Cert. tchr., Ga. Tchr. history Griffin (Ga.) High Sch., 1964-65; tchr. 6th grade Beaverbrook Elem Sch., Griffin, 1965-66; tchr. Spanish, chair fgn. lang. dept. Forest Park (Ga.) High Sch., 1966-77; chair fgn. lang. dept. Spanish Forest Park (Ga.) High Sch., 1969-77; tchr. Spanish, chair fgn. lang. dept. Riverdale (Ga.) High Sch., 1977—; correlator Harcourt, Brace, Jovanovich, 1989; adv. bd. So. Conf. Lang. Teaching, 1992—; lectr. and speaker in field. Contbr. articles to The Ednl. Resource Info. Ctr. Clearinghouse on Langs. and Linguistics, Ctr. for Applied Linguistics, Washington; designed courses for the Gifted, Ga. Dept. of Edn. Cnvener Acad. Alliances-Atlanta II, Clayton County, Ga., 1982—; advisor, workshop leader Ga. Fgn. Lang. Camp, Atlanta, 1983; dir. Clayton County Fgn. Lang. Festival, 1990-91. Recipient STAR Tchr. award Ga. C. of C., 1982; Fulbright-Hays scholar, 1978; NEH grantee, 1977, 84. Mem. NEA, Am. Coun. Tchrs. Fgn. Langs., Am. Assn. Tchrs. Spanish and Portuguese, Ga. Assn. Educators, Fgn. Lang. Assn. Ga. (treas. 1977-85, assoc. editor jour. 1981-86, Tchr. of Yr. award 1976), Clayton County Edn. Assn., So. Conf. Lang. Teaching, KPS Leadership Specialists (co-founder 1993). Methodist. Home: 9261 Brave Ct Jonesboro GA 30236-5110

SPRECHMAN, DEBBY S., technical writer, computer programmer, analyst; b. Utica, N.Y., May 10, 1959; d. Kenneth Crawford Thomson Jr. and June A. Rutsehouser; m. David Sprechman, Oct. 4, 1980; children: Harrison, Eric. BA in Anthropology cum laude, SUNY, Binghamton, 1980; diploma in computer sci., Grumman Data Sys. Inst., 1981. Computer programmer Grumman Data Sys., Bethpage, N.Y., 1982-84, sr. programmer, 1984-87, programmer analyst, 1987-89; sr. programmer analyst Grumman Data Sys., Bethpage, $D, 1989-90; sr. programmer NaBanco, Sunrise, Fla., 1992-93; tech. writer Computer Solutions, Inc., Miami, 1995—. Puppet maker children's puppets, 1994—.

SPRESSER, DIANE MAR, mathematics educator; b. Welch, W.Va., Dec. 12, 1943; d. Paul Mack and Rachel Jean (DeMario) S. BS with honors, Radford U., 1965; MA, U. Tenn., 1967; postgrad., Ohio State U., summers 1970-72; PhD, U. Va., 1977. Math. instr. James Madison U., Harrisonburg, Va., 1967-68, asst. prof. math., 1968-77, assoc. prof. math., 1977-82, prof. math., 1982—, acting head dept. math., 1978-79, head dept. math. and computer sci., 1979-92, head dept. math., 1992-94; tchr. enhancement program dir. NSF, Arlington, Va., 1994—; mem. nat. question writing com. MathCounts, 1993-96. Reviewer Computing Revs. of Assn. for Computing Machinery, 1990—; contbr. articles to profl. jours. Organist Blessed Sacrament Ch., Harrisonburg, 1969-81. Mem. Am. Math. Soc., Math. Assn. Am., Assn. Women in Math., Nat. Coun. Tchrs. Math., Assn. for Computing Machinery, Va. Acad. Sci. (rsch. com. 1991-96). Roman Catholic. Office: NSF 4201 Wilson Blvd Rm 885 Arlington VA 22230-0001

SPRIESER, JUDITH A., food products company executive. BA in Linguistics, Northwestern U., MBA in Fin. CPA, Ill., 1982. Comml. banker Harris Bank, Chgo., 1974-81; dir. treasury ops. Esmark, 1981-84; asst. treas. Nalco Chem. Co., 1984-87; asst. treas. corp. fin. Sara Lee Corp., 1987-90; sr. v.p., CFO Sara Lee Bakery N.Am., 1990-93, pres., CEO, 1993-94; sr. v.p., CFO Sara Lee Corp., 1994—; bd. dirs. USG Corp. Bd. dirs. Hinsdale Hosp. Found.; trustee Northwestern U. Mem. AICPA, Chgo. Network, Young Pres. Orgn., Chgo. coun. Fgn. Rels., Econ. Club, Conf. Bd. Coun. Fin. Execs. Office: Sara Lee Corp Three First National Plz Chicago IL 60602

SPRING, NICOLE MARIE, legal nurse consultant; b. Cleve., Oct. 8, 1947; children: Jim, Mark. Diploma in nursing, St. Vincent Charity Hosp., Cleve., 1968. RN, Ohio; cert. geriatrics nurse. Staff nurse Center Cmty. Hosp., State College, Pa., 1968-70; office nurse D.E. Mulhatten, MD, State College, 1970-72; head nurse Sera-Tec Biologicals, State College, 1972-74; pediatric office nurse Euclid Clin. Found., Cleve., 1975-76; unit nurse Sagamore Hills Children's Psychiat. Hosp., Northfield, Ohio, 1976-80; supr. med. divsn. ICM Sch. Bus., Cleve., 1980-82; staff nurse St. Luke's Hosp., Cleve., 1982-88, Cleve. Clin. Found., 1988-90; home care supr. Interim Health Care, Shaker Heights, Ohio, 1989-94; supr. Preserve Home Health Care, Parma, Ohio, 1994-95; home care supr. Nurses Calling, Beachwood, Ohio, 1995.

Active Joining Together to Stop Sexual Abuse, Cleve., 1994—, Ohio Coalition on Sexual Assault. Recipient INTERIM award of Distinction for the Fiscal Yr., 1994.

SPRINGER, MARLENE, university administrator, educator; b. Murfreesboro, Tenn., Nov. 16, 1937; d. Foster V. and Josephine Jones; children: Ann Springer, Rebecca Springer. BA in English & Bus. Adminstrn., Centre Coll., 1959; MA in Am. Lit., Ind. U., 1963, PhD in English Lit., 1969. Chair English dept. U. Mo., Kansas City, 1980-81, acting assoc. dean grad. sch., 1982; Am. Coun. of Edn. Adminstrn. fellow U. Kans., Laurence, 1982-83; dean of grad. sch. U. Mo., Kansas City, 1983-84, assoc. vice chancellor for acad. affairs & grad. studies, 1985-89; vice chancellor for acad. affairs East Carolina U., Greenville, N.C., 1989-94; pres. CUNY Coll. S.I., 1994—. Author: What Manner of Woman: Essays, 1977, Thomas Hardy's Use of Allusion, 1983, Plains Woman: The Diary of Martha Farnsworth, 1986 (Choice award 1986), Ethan Frome: A Nightmare of Need, 1993. Huntington Libr. fellow, 1988. Mem. Am. Coun. on Edn. (profl. devel. com. 1991—, invited participant Nat. Forum 1984), Am. Assn. State Colls. & Univs. (exec. com. 1992-94), Acad. Leadership Acad. (exec. com. 1992-94), Assn. Tchr. Educators (chair 1992), Coun. Grad. Schs. (chair 1986-88). Office: Coll Staten Island 2800 Victory Blvd Staten Island NY 10314-6600

SPROAT, KEZIA VANMETER, communications executive, writer; b. Chillicothe, Ohio, Nov. 8, 1937; d. Joseph Vause and Helen Rose (Janes) Vanmeter; children: Cornelia Sisson Vanmeter, Eliza Bradford Delano. AB, Vassar Coll., 1959; MA, Ohio State U., 1963, PhD, 1975. Field dir. Miami Valley Campfire Girls, Dayton, Ohio, 1959-60; tchr. English Kingswood Sch. Cranbrook, Bloomfield Hills, Mich., 1960-61; grad. asst. Dept. English Ohio State U., Columbus, 1961-68, lectr. comparative lit., 1968-73, editor ctr. human resource rsch., 1979-85; dir. food for thought Univ. Ctr. Ministries, Columbus, 1978-79; pres. Sproat Comm., Inc., Columbus, 1985—; editor, writer Ross Labs., Columbus, 1987-91; dir. Vanmeter Farm, Inc., Piketon, Ohio, 1993—; pres., founder Highbank Farm Peace Edn. Ctr., Chillicothe, 1994. Author, editor: National Longitudinal Surveys: Bibliography, 1985; editor: Malnutrition: A Hidden Cost, 1993 (2 Addy awards 1994); editor 7 books; editor Peace Grows Bull., 1996—. Founder, co-chair Community Film Assn., Columbus, 1979—; publicist Peace Grows, Inc., Columbus and Akron, Ohio, 1990—; coord. South Ctrl. Ohio Preservation Soc., 1992—. Recipient Florence Howe award MLA, 1975, Mayor's award for vol. svcs Mayor of Columbus, 1980, Pres. award Abbott Labs., 1988; grantee Ohio Humanities Coun., 1977, 78. Mem. Women Comm., Inc., Physicians Human Rights, Women's Poetry Workshop. Office: Sproat Comm Corp 184 E Oakland Ave Columbus OH 43201-1209

SPROUL, JOAN HEENEY, elementary school educator; b. Johnstown, Pa., July 17, 1932; d. James L. and Grace M. (Dunn) Heeney; m. Robert Sproul, July 31, 1957; 1 child, Mary Claire. BS, Clarion U., 1954; MA, George Wash. U., 1963; postgrad., U. Va., 1966-88. Cert. tchr., Va. Kindergarten tchr. Jefferson Sch., Warren, Pa., 1954-55; primary grades tchr. Alexandria (Va.) Pub. Schs., 1955-64; elem. tchr. Fairfax County Schs., Springfield, Va., 1965—; math. lead tchr. West Springfield (Va.) Sch., 1987—. Contbr. (with others) Virginia History, 1988. Advisor Springfield Young Organists Assn., 1971-83; mem. Fairfax County Dem. Com., 1988-94, West Springfield Civic Assn., 1965—. Grantee Impact II, 1985-86. Mem. NEA, Nat. Fedn. Bus. and Profl. Women (pres., dir., dist. VIII 1984—, Woman of Yr. 1985, 88), Delta Kappa Gamma (2d v.p. Va. chpt. 1963—), Phi Delta Kappa. Episcopalian. Home: 8005 Greeley Blvd West Springfield VA 22152-3036 Office: West Springfield Elem Sch 6802 Deland Dr Springfield VA 22152-3009

SPROULE, BETTY ANN, computer industry strategic planning manager; b. Evanston, Ill., Dec. 30, 1948; d. Harold Fletcher and Lois (Reno) Mathis; m. J. Michael Sproule, Mar. 3, 1973; children: John Harold, Kevin William. BS, Ohio State U., 1969, MS, 1970, PhD, 1972. Mem. tech. staff Bell Telephone Labs., Columbus, Ohio, 1973-74; asst. prof. U. Tex., Odessa, 1974-77; analyst bus. systems Maj. Appliance Bus. div. GE, Louisville, 1977-78; dir. forecasting and analysis Brown and Williamson Tobacco, Louisville, 1978-86; strategic planning mgr. Hewlett-Packard Co., Santa Clara, Calif., 1986—. Contbr. articles to profl. jours.; patentee in field. Sr. mem. IEEE, Soc. Women Engrs. Home: 4135 Briarwood Way Palo Alto CA 94306-4610 Office: Hewlett-Packard Co 5301 Stevens Creek Blvd Santa Clara CA 95052

SPROULL, BARBARA LYNN, secondary education educator; b. Tarentum, Pa., July 20, 1943; d. Paul David and Bernadette A. (Rassau) Adams; m. James F. Sproull, Aug. 20, 1966; children: Kevin, Jennifer. BS, Indiana (Pa.) State Coll., 1965; MEd, Pa. State U., 1970. Tchr. math. Gateway Sch. Dist., Monroeville, Pa., 1965-67, State College (Pa.) Area Sch. Dist., 1967-71, Freeport (Pa.) Area Sch. Dist., 1984-89, Aiken County Pub. Schs., Aiken, S.C., 1989—. Mem. Nat. Coun. Tchrs. Math., S.C. Coun. Tchrs. Math. Home: 118 Aberdeen Dr Aiken SC 29803-7100

SPROUSE, EARLENE PENTECOST, educational diagnostician; b. Hopewell, Va., Apr. 23, 1939; d. Earl Paige and Sophia Marlene (Chairky) Pentecost; m. David Andrew Koren, July 3, 1957 (div. Jan. 1963); children: David Andrew Jr., Elysia Marlene, Merri Paige; m. Wayne Alexender Sprouse, Sept. 2, 1964; 1 child, Michael Wayne. AS, Paul D. Camp C.C., Franklin, Va., 1973; BS in Comm. Disorders, Old Dominion U., 1975, MEd in Spl. Edn., 1977. Tchg. cert. with endorsement in speech lang. pathology, learning disabilities and emotional disturbance, Va. Speech lang. pathologist Southampton County Schs., Va., 1975-76; learning disabled tchr. itinerant Franklin (Va.) City Pub. Schs., 1976-78, emotionally disturbed/learning disabled tchr., 1978-85, speech lang. pathologist, 1986-91, ednl. diagnostician, 1992—; com. mem. The Childrens Ctr., Franklin, 1986—, Early Childhood Coun., Franklin, 1992—; needs assessment com. Juvenile Domestic Rels. Ct., Franklin, 1993—; project leader curriculum guide Listening and Lang. Processing Skills, 1990-91. Com. mem. Dem. Com., Suffolk, Va., 1985-92, Family Fair, Franklin, 1993—. Recipient Excellence in Edn. award C. of C., Hampton Roads, Va., 1988-89; grantee Va. Edn. Assn., Richmond, 1994—, Project UNITE Dept. Edn., Richmond, 1994—. Mem. ASCD, Coun. for Exceptional Children (com. mem.), Speech and Hearing Assn. Va., Franklin City Edn. Assn. (pub. rels. com., pres. 1980, 91), Orton Dyslexia Soc. Presbyterian. Home: 319 Gray's Creek Ln Surry VA 23883 Office: Franklin City Pub Schs 800 W 2nd Ave Franklin VA 23851-2162

SPROUSE, SUSAN RAE MOORE, human resources specialist; b. Amsterdam, N.Y., Feb. 23, 1948; d. Charles Franklin and Alice Rae (Lawson) Moore; m. Richard D. Sprouse, May 5, 1973; children: Jennifer Lynn, Melinda Rae. BS, U. So. Miss., 1970, MBA, 1971. Spl. non-exempt employee rels. GE Co., Owensboro, Ky., 1972-74; from instr. entry level tng. to spl. profl. rels. and EEO GE Co., Chgo., 1974-78; from employee rels. clk. to material control specialist GE Co., Ft. Smith, Ark., 1978-82; employee rels. rep. Mason Chamberlain Inc., Stennis Space Ctr., Miss., 1982-90; human resource specialist Inst. for Naval Oceanography, Stennis Space Ctr., Miss., 1990-92; program coord. Ctr. for Ocean and Atmospheric Modeling, Stennis Space Ctr., Miss., 1992-95; human resources specialist Computer Scis. Corp., Stennis Space Ctr., Miss., 1995—; co. rep. Jr. Achievement, Owensboro, 1972-74. Libr., Am. flag chair DAR, Picayune, Miss., 1967-92; bd. dirs. Picayune On Stage, v.p., sec., 1982—. Named Outstanding Jr. Mem. DAR, Picayune, 1970; profiled in Picayune Item, 1988. Mem. Nat. Soc. Magna Charta Dames, Sigma Sigma Sigma, Phi Delta Rho. Republican. Church of Christ. Office: CSC Bldg 3205 Stennis Space Ctr Bay Saint Louis MS 39529

SPRUILL, LOUISE ELAM, retired secondary educator; b. Mecklenburg County, Va., Aug. 17, 1918; d. William Llewellyn and Lillie Clayton (Puryear) Elam; m. Jacob Sipe Fleming, Aug. 12, 1941 (dec. Nov. 1957); 1 son, James Sipe Fleming; m. Edward Muse Spruill, Nov. 6, 1968; 1 stepdaughter, Florence Spruill Mackie. BA, East Carolina U., 1939, MA, 1961. cert. secondary tchr. Tchr. Washington County Bd. Edn., Plymouth, N.C., 1957-69; chmn. math. dept. Plymouth High Sch., 1965-69; treas. Washington County Hosp. Aux., 1991-93, v.p., 1993—. Mem. Plymouth City Coun., 1980-87; trustee Pettigrew Regional Libr., 1983-88; mem. Washington County Libr. Bd., 1983-92, chmn., 1985-88; mem. Bd. of Adjustments, Plymouth, 1989—; sec. Grace Ch., 1981-84, vestry, 1981-84, 95—. Named Outstanding Woman in Washington County, Washington County Coun. on Status of Women, 1988. Mem. N.C. Ret. Sch. Pers., Washington County Hist. Soc. (bd. dirs. 1987—), Fortnightly Lit. Club of Chase City, Va. (pres. 1978-79), Delta Kappa Gamma (v.p. chpt. 1968-70, corr. sec. chpt. 1986-88). Democrat. Episcopalian.

SPRUNG, SHARON LISA, artist, educator; b. Bklyn., June 16, 1953; d. Jack Sprung and Ruthann (Silverman) Shaffer; m. William Peter Astwood, June 10, 1979; 1 child, Jesse Jack Astwood. Student, Cornell U., 1971-72, Art Students League, 1972-75, Nat. Acad. Sch. Fine Arts, 1972-75. Instr. figure drawing and figure painting Sch. Fine Arts, Nat. Acad. Design, N.Y.C., 1983—; represented by Gallery Henoch, N.Y.C., 1994—. Represented in permanent collections at Chase Manhattan Bank, N.Y.C., AT&T, Orlando, Fla., Sherman & Sterling, N.Y.C., Scott Bennett, Inc., N.Y.C. Grantee Greenshields, 1979, Stacey Found., 1984, 86; recipient Fitzgerald Meml. award Allied Artists Am., 1979, Advancement of Art award Allied Artists Am., 1981. Home and Studio: 394 Atlantic Ave Brooklyn NY 11217

SPRY, KAREN LYNN, nurse; b. St. Louis, May 30, 1956; d. Jeremiah Joseph and Marilyn Ann (Winkler) F.; divorced; children: Jennifer Lynn, Jacqueline Leigh. ADN, St. Louis C.C., 1976; BSN, St. Louis U., 1981; postgrad., Webster U. RN, Mo. Staff nurse St. Louis Univ. Hosp., 1977-79; oper. rm. staff nurse Deaconess Health System, St. Louis, 1979-86; oper. rm. instr. Deaconess Health System, 1994—; oper. rm. staff nurse Tarpon Springs (Fla.) Gen. Hosp., 1986-88; med.-surg. instr. Sanford Brown Coll., St. Louis, 1995—. BLS instr. Am. Heart Assn., St. Louis, 1994—; girl scout leader Girls Scouts U.S., 1986-93. Mem. AORN (CNOR, chmn. rsch. com. 1994—). Roman Catholic. Office: Deaconess Health System 530 Des Peres Rd Saint Louis MO 63131

SPUDIS, BARBARA C., lawyer; b. Rochester, Minn., Nov. 12, 1955. AB, Duke U., 1978; JD, U. Va., 1981; LLM in Taxation, IIT, 1986. Bar: Calif. 1981, Ill. 1983. Ptnr. Baker & McKenzie, Chgo. Office: Baker & McKenzie 130 E Randolph Dr Chicago IL 60601*

SPUNGIN, JENNIFER BARBARA, secondary education educator; b. Princeton, N.J., Apr. 21, 1969; d. Gardner Mawney and Susan Joy (King) S. BA, Skidmore Coll., 1991; postgrad., SUNY, Albany, 1991-93. Editor Gardner Press, Inc., N.Y.C., 1986-94, Verbal Images Press, Rochester, N.Y., 1992-93; publishing cons. Image, Rochester, 1993-95; English tchr. Nazareth Acad., Rochester, 1993-95. Editor Folio, Saratoga, N.Y., 1987-91, 13th Moon, Albany, N.Y., 1992-93. Recipient Disting. Writer award Skidmore Coll., 1992. Mem. Nat. Coun. Tchrs. of English, Poets and Writers, U.S. Combined Tng. Assn. Presbyterian. Home: 221 W 82d St New York NY 10000 Office: Nazereth Acad 1001 Lake Ave Rochester NY 14613

SPURRIER, MARY EILEEN, investment advisor, financial planner; b. Mpls., Sept. 16, 1943; d. Charles Joseph and Ruth Eileen (Rowles) Dickman; m. Joseph Leo Spurrier, Jan. 16, 1965 (div. Aug. 1976); 1 child, Christopher Jude; m. Gary Albert Gutfrucht, July 8, 1988. BS, U. Minn., 1965. CFP; registered prin., registered investment advisor. Rsch. fellow, libr. Sch. Bus. Adminstrn. U. Minn., Mpls., 1965-68; exec. dir. Zero Population Growth, N.Y., 1972-76; fin. cons. Merrill Lynch, Rochester, N.Y., 1977-84, Shearson/Smith Barney, 1984-89; investment cons. CitiCorp, Rochester, 1989-91; assoc. v.p. Essex Investment, Rochester, 1991-95; pres. M. Spurrier Fin. Svcs., Rochester, 1995—; cons. Fund Devel. Rochester Women's Network, 1995—, Women's Coun. C. of C., Rochester, 1992—; spkr. in field. Contbr. articles to newspapers. Chair YWCA Endowment Campaign, Rochester, 1994—; mentor Wilson Commencement Park, Rochester, 1993—; v.p., bd. dirs. N.Y. State Environ. Planning Lobby, 1973-75; bd. dirs. N.Y. State Family Planning Coalition, 1973-75; fin. dir. LWV, Rochester, 1989-90. Recipient Eminent Rochester Women award Upstate Mag., 1974. Mem. NAFE (spkr. 1990-95), Women's Network, Rochester Women's Network, Women's Coun. C. of C., Nat. Assn. Women Bus. Owners. Office: 315 Westminster Rd Rochester NY 14607

SQUAZZO, MILDRED KATHERINE (MILDRED KATHERINE OETTING), corporate executive; b. Bklyn., Dec. 22; d. William John and Marie M. (Fromm) Oetting; student L.I. U. Sec.-treas., Stanley Engring., Inc. and v.p. Stanley Chems., Inc., 1960-68; founder, pres. Chem-Dynamics Corp., Scotch Plains, N.J., 1964-68; gen. adminstr., purchasing dir., Richardson Chem. Co., Metuchen, N.J., 1968-69; owner Berkeley Employment Agy. and Berkeley Temp. Help Service, Berkeley Heights, N.J., 1969-91, Berkeley Employment Agy., Morristown, N.J., 1982-91, Bridgewater, N.J., 1987-91; pres. M.K.S. Bus. Group, Inc., Berkeley Heights, 1980-91; mgmt. cons.; personnel fin.; lectr. Served with Nurse Corps, U.S. Army, 1946-47. Mem. Nat. Bus. and Profl. Women's Club. Home and Office: 16 Heather Ln Warren NJ 07059-5258

SQUIER, PRUDENCE ANN, journalist; b. Renton, Wash., May 9, 1942; d. Clifford Benjamin and Mae (Baker) Bergman; m. Roy Stacy, 1964 (div. 1966); m. Robert Dave Squier, Jan. 15, 1977. BA in Spanish Lit., George Washington U., 1964. Social worker L.A. County, 1966-70; stewardess TWA, N.Y.C., 1970-74; journalist People Mag., 1982—, Washington Post, 1982—, Travel & Leisure, 1982—, European Travel & Life, 1982—, Southern Accents, 1982—. Bd. dirs. Concern Hotline, Winchester, Va., 1993, Bethel Inc., Berryville, Va., 1989—, Grafton Sch., Berryville, 1983, Belle Grove, Berryville, 1988, 92. Democrat. Home: 673 Dream Island Rd Longboat Key FL 34228-1502

SQUIRE, LAURIE RUBIN, media consultant; b. N.Y.C., Jan. 30, 1953; d. Daniel and Ruth Thelma (Deutsch) Rubin; m. Herbert E. Squire Jr., Aug. 6, 1975; children: Amy Ruth, Julie Wynn. BA cum laude (scholar), Finch Coll., 1974; MA, NYU, 1976; postgrad., Columbia U., 1977—. Actress TV commls., 1960-65; arts editor Finch/Metro newspaper, N.Y.C., 1970-74; co-editor Finch Alumnae mag., 1971-72; intern producer Sta. WBAI-FM, N.Y.C., 1973; music prodn. coord. Ballet Theatre spl. Sta. WNET-TV, 1973; coll. bd. writer Mademoiselle mag., 1973; intern asst. pub. affairs dir. N.Y. Cultural Ctr., 1974; mdse. coord. Sta. WOR-AM, N.Y.C., 1974-76, contbg. writer Bob and Ray's Mary Backstage serial, contbr. nostalgia features Joe Franklin Show, producer Jean Shepherd Show and sydicated markets, 1975-77, producer Bernard Meltzer What's Your Problem, 1977-80; broadcast stage mgr. Texaco Met. Opera, 1976—; dance critic Show Bus., theatre newspaper; bd. dirs. publicity and advt. L.I. Playhouse, 1982—; press rep. Great Neck Pla. Contbg. writer Newsday, North Shore Today, Can. Publs. Publicity cons. Nassau County Mus. Fine Art; v.p. pub. rels. United Community Fund. Recipient commendations for Leukemia Radiothons Peabody Broadcasting citation, 1983. Mem. Internat. Radio and TV Soc., Great Neck Hist. Soc. Home and Office: 892 Middle Neck Rd Great Neck NY 11024-1400

SQUIRE, MOLLY ANN, organizational psychologist; b. Highland Park, Mich., Aug. 18; d. George Edward and Dorothy Laura (Molteni) Squirrell; m. Arthur Bruce Hanson, June 23, 1990; 1 child, Mark Arthur. AA, NYU, 1978; BS cum laude, U. LaVerne, 1980; MA, Claremont (Calif.) Grad. Sch., 1982; PhD, Pacific-Western U., 1991. Cert. Profl. Cons. to Mgmt. Health svcs. adminstr. health care delivery orgns., 1978-82; nat. dir. Huntington's Disease Rsch. Project, Calif., 1981-82; CEO Claremont Mgmt. Cons. (name now Squire Cons.), Malibu, Calif., 1982—; past statis. analyst to pres. L.A. City Coll.; past part-time instr.L.A. Trade Tech.; part-time instr. Glendale C.C., 1994-96. Founding editor LASER; editor BEACON newsletter, 1989-96; past editor Benezet Gazette, (yearbook) So. Calif. Com. to Combat Huntington's Disease; contbr. articles to profl. jours.; patentee bus. and health care products. Past officer and sci. liaison So. Calif. Huntington's Disease Com.; magic performer various charitable benefits. Decorated knight Templar of Jerusalem, Internat. Br. Netherlands; recipient Cert. of Appreciation City of Ukiah, Calif., 1984, Western Square Dance Assn., 1986, Am. Heart Assn., 1990, So. Calif. Skeptics, 1987, Pacific-Bell, 1990, Achievement award No. Am. Women's Inner Circle, 1991, Cert. of Appreciation, L.A. City Coll., 1995; grad. fellow Claremont Grad. Sch., 1980-82; established Krauthamer & Squire 'Thelma & Louise' Women's Scholarship, L.A. City Coll., 1993. Mem. APA, Nat. Bur. Profl. Cons. to Mgmt., Soc. Indsl. and Orgnl. Psychologists, Soc. Am. Magicians (Zinger award, Certs. of Appreciation, award of Merit 1991, 94, named Best Character Act 1994, Peller Meml. trophy 1994), Internat. Brotherhood Magicians (past pres. #254, sec., Best Mentalist trophy 1987, Cert. of Appreciation), Pacific Coast Assn. Magicians (golden circle mem. 1994), Soc. of Am. Magicians (life), Arthurian Soc. Arthuret (hon. life, U.K.), Mensa (proctor). Presbyterian. Office: PO Box 41633 Los Angeles CA 90041

SQUIRES, BONNIE STEIN, fundraising consultant; b. Phila., May 12, 1940; d. Joseph and Lillian (Ponnock) Stein; children: Deborah Rose, David Abram; m. Sami Ouahada. BE, U. Pa., MA. Various positions Temple U., Phila., 1983-89, exec. dir. capital campaign, 1992-94; asst. exec. dir. Pa. Edn. Assn., Harrisburg, 1989-92; v.p. for devel. Phila. Geriatric Ctr., 1994-95; pres. Squires Consulting, Wynnewood, Pa., 1995—. Author: (poetry) New Eden, 1977; editor: (poetry) This Land of Fire, 1988, (student essays, poems and photos) A New Nation, 1976. Mem. Fedn. Jewish Agys., Citizens' Crime Commn., Ctr. UN Reform Edn.; bd. dirs. Phila. com. Am. Jewish Congress, Phila. Mus. Art, Am. Friends Hebrew U., Harrisburg Jewish Community Rels. Coun.; del. Israel's Prime Minister's Solidarity Conf., 1989, Pres. Bush's regional Edn. Summit, 1989; pres. Pa. region Am. Jewish Congress; v.p. Pa. Breast Cancer Coalition. Recipient Torch award and Lillian Alpers award Am. Friends Hebrew U., Louise Waterman award Am. Jewish Congress. Mem. AAUW (del. Beijing UN Conf. Women), LWV. Home: 11 Arthurs Round Table Wynnewood PA 19096-1202

SRACIC, KAREN K., librarian; b. Sharon, Pa., Sept. 16, 1955. BFA, Pa. State U., 1977; postgrad., Ill. State U., 1978-80; MLS, Clarion U., 1991, postgrad., 1991—. Grad. teaching asst. art Ill. State U., Normal, 1978-80; libr. tech. asst. III, cataloging, Milner Libr., 1980-88, work-study libr. tech. svcs. dept. Pub. Libr. of Youngstown (Ohio) and Mahoning County, 1988-91; catalog and ref. libr., instr. McGill Libr. Westminster Coll., New Wilmington, Pa., 1991-93; union catalog liaison INFOHio Project, Youngstown, 1996—. Contbr., reviewer: Plays for Children and Young Adults: An Evaluative Index and Guide, 1991. Mem. ALA, Assn. for Libr. Collections and Tech. Svcs., Pa. State U. Alumni Assn., Beta Phi Mu.

SRUOGIS, ELAINE SMOLLIN, cultural organization administrator; b. Lincoln, R.I., May 15, 1953; m. Saulius Sruogis, Aug. 30, 1992. MFA, Pratt Inst., Bklyn., 1975, BFA, 1981. Cert. archaeol. field technician. Archaeologist African Burial Ground Site, N.Y.C., 1991-92; rsch. assoc. Rsch. Ctr. Lithuanian Castles, Vilnius, Lithuania, 1992—; exec. dir. Ledig House Internat. Writers' Colony, Ghent, N.Y., 1993—; dir. Am.- Baltic Anthrop. Rsch., Ghent and Vilnius, 1995—; exec. dir. Fellowship Ctrl. Asian Writers, 1995—. Activist, adminstr. Opportunities for Citizens in Newly Independent States, Ghent, 1990—. Draftsmanship grantee NEA, 1986; MacDowell fellow, 1980, 81, 85. Home and Office: Ghent NY 12075-0033

STABENOW, DEBORAH ANN, state legislator; b. Gladwin, Mich., Apr. 29, 1950; d. Robert Lee and Anna Merle (Hallmark) Greer; children: Todd Dennis, Michelle Deborah. BS magna cum laude, Mich. State U., 1972, MSW magna cum laude, 1975. With spl. svcs. Lansing (Mich.) Sch. Dist., 1972-73; county commr. Ingham County, Mason, Mich., 1975-78; state rep. State of Mich., Lansing, 1979—. Founder Ingham County Women's Commn.; co-founder Council Against Domestic Assault; mem. Dem. Bus. and Profl. Club, Mich. Dem. Women's Polit. Caucus, Grance United Meth. Ch. (past lay leader, chair Social Concerns Task Force, Sunday Sch. music tchr., Lansing Boys' Club, profl. adv. com. Lansing Parents Without Ptnrs., adv. com. Ctr. Handicapped Affairs, Mich. Council Family and Divorce Mediation Adv. Bd., Nat. Council Children's Rights, Big Bros./Big Sisters Greater Lansing Adv. Bd., Mich. Child Study Assn. Bd. Advisors, Mich. Women's Campaign Fund. Recipient Service to Children award Council for Prevention of Child Abuse and Neglect, 1983, Disting. Service to Mich. Families award Mich. Council Family Relations, 1983, Outstanding Leadership award Nat. Council Community Mental Health Ctrs., 1983, Snyder-Kok award Mental Health Assn. Mich., Awareness Leader of Yr. award Awareness Communications Team Developmentally Disabled, 1984, Communicator of Yr. award Woman in Communications, 1984, Lawmaker of Yr. award Nat. Child Support Enforcement Assn., 1985, Disting. Service award Lansing Jaycees, 1985, Disting. Service in Govt. award Retarded Citizens of Mich., 1986; named One of Ten Outstanding Young Ams. Jaycees, 1986. Mem. NAACP, Lansing Regional C. of C., Delta Kappa Gamma. Home: 2709 S Deerfield Ave Lansing MI 48911-1783*

STABILE, JANE SANFORD, tax consultant, enrolled agent; b. N.Y.C., Dec. 8, 1952; d. George Robert Sanford and Barbara Joan (Hendrick) Hugus; m. Lawrence Anthony Stabile, July 26, 1975; children: Marianne Sanford, Paula Sanford, Kimberly Sanford. BA in psychology, Wellesley Coll., Wellesley, 1973; MBA, Boston U., Boston, 1978. Asst. admin. for ambulatory care U. Hosp., Boston, 1978-81, mgr. evening ops., 1981-83; pvt. practice enrolled agent, tax cons. Wayland, Mass., 1991—. Chair, governing bd. First Parish Ch., Wayland, Mass., 1996—. Mem. AAUW (treas. 1995—, v.p. membership 1993-95), Cochituate Preservation Assn. (steering com. 1985—), Nat. Tax Practice Inst., Wayland Bus. Assn. (trustee Wayland Town house, 1982-90; chair Wayland Fin. Com 1993-94; commr. Wayland Park & Recreation Com., 1995—). Home: 120 Commonwealth Rd Wayland MA 01778

STACHOWSKI, MARIA VANESSA, college health nurse; b. Ossining, N.Y., Nov. 3, 1953; d. Joaquim Alfonse and Maria Thomas (de Aquino) Pires; m. Thomas Carrol Pownall, Jul. 28, 1972 (div. Sept. 1988); children: Nathan Sean Pownall, Kristian Michael Pownall; m. Dennis Valentine Stachowski, Aug. 19, 1989. A in applied sci., Alfred State Coll. Cert. Coll. Health Nurse. Staff med./surg. nurse Cuba (N.Y.) Meml. Hosp., 1984-86, adminstr. coord., 1986-87, emergency dept. coord., 1987-90; coll. health nurse Alfred (N.Y.) State Coll., 1990—; clinical instr. Bd. of Coop. Edn., Olean, N.Y., 1992—; nurse adv. bd. mem. Western Reg. Emergency Svcs., Buffalo, N.Y., 1987-90. Shop steward Pub. Employees Fedn. Alfred State Coll., 1994—; bd. dirs. Am. Heart Assn., 1988—; active Lioness, Cuba, 1989—. Mem. N.Y. State Coll. Health Assn. Democrat. Episcopalian. Home: 5677 Whittier Rd Belmont NY 14813 Office: SUNY Alfred Health Svcs Brooklyn Ave Wellsville NY 14895

STACISHIN, ELIZABETA QUEIROZ (LIZA STACISHIN), architect, landscape architect; b. Recife, Brazil, June 12, 1946; came to U.S., 1986; d. Romeu Valente and Elizabeta Babier (Stacishin) de Queiroz; m. Roberto Countinho de Moura, Dec. 31, 1965 (div. Apr. 1973); children: Elizabeta Stacishin-Moura, Liliane Stacishin Moura; m. Robert Alexander Riggs, Aug. 10, 1993. BA in Architecture, U. Fed. de Pernambuco, Recife, 1970; M in Landscape Architecture, Utah State U., 1993. Apprentice Borsoi Arquitetos Associados Ltda, Recife, 1970-73; ptnr. Arquitetura 4, Recife, 1973-81; prin., ptnr. Arquitetura 4 Arquitetos Associados, Recife, 1981-86; bldg. designer Sun Studio Designs, La Grande, Oreg., 1993—; architect Arquitetur 4 Return Partnership, 1996—. Home: 708 4th St La Grande OR 97850 Address: Arquitetur 4 Return Partnership, R Cap Rebelinho 388, LEP 51011-010 Recife PE Brazil

STACK, MAY ELIZABETH, library director; b. Jackson, Miss., Nov. 10, 1940; d. James William and Irene Thelma (Baldwin) Garrett; m. Richard Gardiner, Apr. 15, 1962; children: Elinor, Harley David. BS, Miss. State Coll. for Women, 1962; MBA, Western New Eng. Coll., 1981; MLS, So. Conn. State U., 1989. Clk. Western New Eng. Coll., Springfield, Mass., 1965-66; acquisitions staff Western New Eng. Coll., Springfield, 1966-72, cataloger, 1972-84, asst. dir., 1984-89, acting dir., 1989-90, dir., 1990—; chair Ctrl./Western Mass. Automated Resource Sharing Collection Devel. Com., Paxton, Mass., 1993-95, exec. bd., 1993-96. mem. East Longmeadow (Mass.) Hist. Soc., 1989-92. Mem. ALA, Mass. Libr. Assn., Assn. Coll. and Rsch. Librs., Libr. and Mgmt. Assn., Libr. Info. and Technology Assn. Methodist. Office: Western New Eng Coll D'Amour Libr 1215 Wilbraham Rd Springfield MA 01119-2654

STACK, RUTH HOEKSTRA, management consultant; b. St. Anne, Ill., Aug. 11, 1929; d. Simon and Maude (Tallman) Hoekstra; m. Walter O. Stack, Apr. 12, 1952; children: Scott, Mari, Debra, Rebecca, Tamara. RN, Wesley Med. Sch. of Nursing, Chgo., 1949; BS, U. Minn., 1952. Assoc. dir. Twin City Health Care Devel. Project, Mpls., 1972-73, exec. dir., 1973-76; exec. dir. Nat. Assn. Employers on Health Maintenance Orgns., Mpls., 1976-80, Nat. Assn. Employers Health Care Action, Mpls., 1980-87; pres. Nat. Assn. Employers Health Care Action, Key Biscayne, Fla., 1987-92, Stack Mgmt. Group, Inc., Boca Raton, Fla., 1992—. Author: HMO Fact Book for Employers, 1976, PPO Fact Book for Employers, 1980. V.P. Citizens Com. on Pub. Edn., Mpls. 1971, League of Women Voters, Mpls., 1965-67;

chmn. Minn. Commn. of Status of Women, St. Paul, 1970-71. Mem. Am. Soc. Assn. Execs. (cert. assn. exec. recognition 1989), Fla. Soc. Assn. Execs. (bd. dirs. 1992-94).

STACK, TERESA MARIE, publishing executive; b. Barberton, Ohio, June 12, 1962; d. Roy Edward and Dorothy Ann (Faix) S. BA, Pa. State U., 1984. Asst. fulfillment mgr. Fairchild Publs., N.Y.C., 1985-86; asst. promotion mgr. Faichild Publs., N.Y.C., 1986-87, circulation mgr., 1987-90, corp. circulation dir., 1990-93; v.p. The Nation, L.P., N.Y.C., 1993-96, assoc. publisher, 1996—; freelance copywriting and graphic design, N.Y.C., 1986—. Companion to elderly Village Vis. Neighbors, N.Y.C., 1989—. Mem. NOW. Office: The Nation LP 72 Fifth Ave New York NY 10011

STACY, FRANCES H., judge. BA, Baylor Univ., 1977; JD, Baylor Law Sch., 1979. With U.S. Atty.'s Office (Tex. so. dist.) Criminal Divsn., 1980, Civil Rights Divsn., 1980-81, Land and Resources Divsn., 1981-87, Civil Divsn., 1987-88, Appelate Divsn., 1988-90; magistrate judge U.S. Dist. Ct. (Tex. so. dist.), 5th circuit, Houston, 1990—. Author: Federal Civil Procedure Before Trial, Lawyers Cooperative Practice Guide. Mem. Tex. Bar Found. Office: Fed Bldg 515 Rusk St Ste 7727 Houston TX 77002-2604*

STAFFIER, PAMELA MOORMAN, psychologist; b. Passaic, N.J., Dec. 7, 1942; d. Wynant Clair and Jeannette Frances (Rentzsch) Moorman; B.A., Bucknell U., 1964; M.A. in Psychology, Assumption Coll., Worcester, Mass., 1970, C.A.G.S., 1977; Ph.D., Union Inst., 1978; m. John Staffier, Jr., Apr. 5, 1975; children—M. Anthony, C. Matthew. Psychologist, Westboro (Mass.) State Hosp., 1965, prin. psychologist, also asst. to supt., 1973-76; psychologist Moriarty Mental Health Clinic; psychiat. cons. local gen. hosp.; research psychologist Wrentham (Mass.) State Sch., 1966, Cushing Hosp., Framingham, Mass., 1967; prin. psychologist, also asst. to supt. Grafton (Mass.) State Hosp., 1967-72; dir. Staffier Psychol. Assocs., Inc., 1978—. Mem. Am. Psychol. Assn. (assoc.), Am. Psychol. Practitioners Assn. (founding mem.), Mass. Psychol. Assn., Nat. Register Health Service Providers in Psychology. Research, publs. on state hosp. closings, biochem. basis of Schizophrenia. Home: 68 Adams St PO Box 1103 Westborough MA 01581 Office: 57 E Main St Westborough MA 01581-1464

STAFFIN, ALLISON BETH, secondary education educator; b. Phila., Nov. 12, 1968; d. Bernard Hirsch and Frances Yetta (Lindenberg) Staffin. BA, Glassboro State Coll., 1991. Cert. in elem. and secondary edn. Gifted & talented tchr. Eastern Regional H.S., Voorhees, N.J., 1992; social studies tchr. Cherry Hill (N.J.) High Schs., 1992—; group leader Great Times Day Camp, Winslow, N.J., summer 1992-95; cheerleading coach, Cherry Hill H.S. East, 1993—. Adv. Amnesty Internat., Cherry Hill H.S. West, 1994-96. Mem. Libr. Congress, Nat. Geographic Soc., History Book Club, Phi Alpha Theta. Office: Cherry Hill High Sch West 2101 West Chapel Ave Cherry Hill NJ 08034

STAFFORD, BARBARA MARIA, art history educator; b. Vienna, Austria, Sept. 16, 1941; came to U.S., 1946; naturalized.; d. K.S. and Ingeborg Anna Davis; m. Fred E. Stafford, Aug. 24, 1963. BA, Northwestern U., 1963, MA, 1966; postgrad., Warburg Inst., 1968, 70; PhD, U. Chgo., 1972. Asst. prof. to assoc. prof. art history U. Del., Newark, 1973-81; prof. art history U. Chgo., 1982-95, William B. Ogden Disting. Svc. prof. art history, 1995—. Author: Symbol and Myth: Humbert de Superville's Essay on Absolute Signs in Art, 1979, Voyage into Substance: Art, Science, Nature, and the Illustrated Travel Account, 1760-1840, 1984, Body Criticism: Imaging the Unseen in Enlightenment Art and Medicine, 1991, Artful Science: Enlightenment Entertainment and the Eclipse of Visual Education, 1994, Good Looking (essays), 1995; contbr. articles to profl. jours. Recipient Excellence-in-Tchg. award U. Del., 1976, Millard Meiss Pub. award CCA, 1983; NEH fellow, 1979-80, Ctr. for Advanced Study in Visual Arts fellow, 1981-82, Woodrow Wilson Internat. Ctr. for Scholars fellow Smithsonian Inst., 1984-85, Guggenheim fellow, 1989-90, Humboldt Sr. fellow, 1989-91, U. Calif. Humanities Rsch. Inst. fellow, 1991; Getty scholar, 1995-96. Mem. Am. Soc. for Eighteenth-Century Studies (pres. 1995—, Clifford prize 1979). Office: Univ of Chicago Dept of Art 5540 S Greenwood Ave Chicago IL 60637-1506*

STAFFORD, BETH GILLIES, social worker; b. Greensboro, N.C., Aug. 12, 1950; d. David Benbow and Maude Gillies (Phillips) S.; m. Frank R. Huff, June 2, 1979. BA, U. Wis., Stevens Point, 1972; MSW, U. Tenn., Nashville, 1982. Cert. social worker, lic. clin. social worker, Acad. Cert. Social Workers. Social worker Babcock Ctr., Columbia, S.C., 1973-76; social svc. supr. Babcock Ctr., Columbia, 1976-80; interim social worker Middle Tenn. Mental Health Inst., Nashville, 1981, psychiatric social worker, 1982-83; coord. state linkages Tenn. Children's Svc. Commn., Nashville, 1983-84, child welfare, legis. specialist, 1984-86; social worker Ea. State Hosp., Lexington, Ky., 1986-89; program specialist Ea. State Hosp., Lexington, 1989-90, program supr., 1990-92, program dir., chief social worker, 1990—; orgnl. rep. Hospitality House Bd., Lexington, 1994-96. rep. from Ohio Valley to yearly meeting Friends World Com. Consultation, Chavakali, Kenya, 1991, sect. of Ams. office, Phila., 1991—; foster parent Fayette Co. Dept. Social Svcs., Lexington, 1995—. Mem. NASW (Bluegrass rep. 1995—). Mem. Soc. of Friends. Office: Ea State Hosp 627 W 4th St Lexington KY 40508

STAFFORD, EMILY-MAE, former assistant news editor; b. Haverhill, Mass., Dec. 11, 1934; d. Charles Gilbert and Leona May (Stout) S. BS, Tex. Woman's U., 1956; postgrad, U. Tex., 1961-65. News bur. supr. Tex. Woman's Univ., Denton, Tex., 1957-61; researcher/instr. U. Tex., Austin, Tex., 1961-66; asst. news editor Fort Worth Star-Telegram, Ft Worth, 1966-94; ret., 1994. Bd. trustees Shakespeare in the Park, Ft. Worth, 1989-95. Mem. Women in Communications, Inc. (newsletter editor 1967-94), Tex. Woman's Univ. Alumni Assn. (Denton, bd. dirs. 1986—), Woman's Club Ft. Worth (newsletter editor 1985-87, 94-96), Woman's Shakespeare Club. Republican. Methodist. Home: PO Box 424804 Denton TX 76204-4804

STAFFORD, JOSEPHINE HOWARD, lawyer; b. San Antonio, July 27, 1921; d. Joseph and Olive Maeblume (Goodson) Howard; m. Harry B. Stafford (div. 1958); 1 child, Julie. BA, U. N.C., 1942, LLB, 1952. Bar: N.C. 1952, Fla. 1953, U.S. Dist. Ct. (mid. dist.) Fla. 1954, U.S. Ct. Appeals (11th cir.), U.S. Ct. Appeals (5th cir.); lic. real estate broker; cert. arbitrator, Hillsborough County Cir. Ct. Assoc. Fowler, White, Gillen, Yancey and Humkey, Tampa, Fla., 1952-54; pvt. practice Tampa, 1954-57, 69-72; exec. dir., atty. Legal Aid Bur., Tampa, 1957-69; atty. City of Tampa, 1972—; instr. U. South Fla., Tampa, 1971-72; adj. prof. Hillsborough Community Coll., Tampa, 1980-86; lectr. U. South Fla., Tampa, 1973, U. Tampa, U. Fla., Gainesville, 1959; atty. Housing Authority City of Tampa, 1970-72; substitute judge mcpl. ct., 1958-71, interim mcpl. ct. judge, 1971-72; mem. Grievance Com. "13C". Author: Amendments to Search Warrant Law; Tax Laws, Agencies and Divorce, 1979; author Mayor's Proclamation Commemorating D-Day, 1994. Precinct committeewoman Hillsborough County Dem. Exec. Coun., Tampa, 1991, co-chmn., 1970; bd. mem., past pres., chmn. com. Travelers Aid Soc., Tampa, 1971-93, life mem., 1994; bd. mem., fin. com. Girl Scouts Am., Tampa, 1991-95; bd. mem., exec. com., past pres. Police Athletic League, Tampa, 1984-88, 90—; mem. Fla. Commn. on Status of Women; co-chmn. Selective Svc. System, 1971-76; bd. dirs. ARC, Tampa chpt., 1964-79, Am. Cancer Soc., Hillsborough County unit, 1982-84. Recipient Svc. to Mankind award Sertoma Internat., Tampa, 1969, Outstanding Bus. and Profl. Woman of Yr. award Bus. and Profl. Women, Tampa, 1959, 69, Women Helping Women award Soroptimist Club, Tampa, 1979, Excellence award Hillsborough County Dem. Women's Club, 1991. Mem. ABA (Nat. Conf. Lawyers and Social Workers, Nat. Conf. Lawyers and Realtors, Standing Com. on Nat. Conf. Groups), Fla. Bar assn. (chmn., legal aid com.), Tampa and Hillsborough County Bar Assn. (dir. 1958-63, chmn. elder law com. 1991-93, mem Liberty Bell award com. 1996), Nat. Legal Aid and Defender Assn. (nat. bd. dirs.), Fla. Assn. Women Lawyers (pres.), Tampa Assn. Women Lawyers (pres., named Outstanding Women Lawyers of Achievement 1993), Fla. Fedn. Social Workers (pres. Hillsborough County chpt. 1964, pres. state bd. 1969), Tampa Legal Sec. Assn., U.S. Navy League. Democrat. Methodist. Home: 3402 S Gardenia Dr Tampa FL 33629-8208 Office: City of Tampa Legal Dept 315 E Kennedy Blvd Tampa FL 33602-5211

STAFFORD, REBECCA, academic administrator, sociologist; b. Topeka, July 9, 1936; d. Frank C. and Anne Elizabeth (Larrick) S. AB magna cum laude, Radcliffe Coll., 1958, MA, 1961; PhD, Harvard U., 1964. Lectr. dept. sociology Sch. Edn., Harvard U., Cambridge, Mass., 1964-70, mem. vis. com. bd. overseers, 1973-79; assoc. prof. sociology U. Nev., Reno, 1970-73, prof., 1973-80, chmn. dept. sociology, 1974-77, dean Coll. Arts and Scis., 1977-80; pres. Bemidji (Minn.) State U., 1980-82; exec. v.p. Colo. State U., Ft. Collins, 1982-83; pres. Chatham Coll., Pitts., 1983-91, Monmouth U., West Long Branch, N.J., 1993—; bd. dirs. First Fidelity Bancorp, N.J. Contbr. articles to profl. jours. Trustee Monmouth Med. Ctr.; bd. dirs. Univ. Presbyn. Hosp., 1985-93, Pitts. Symphyony, 1984-93, Winchester-Thurston Sch.; chmn. Harvard U. Grad. Soc. Coun., 1987-93. Recipient McCurdy-Rinkle prize for rsch. Eastern Psychiat. Assn., 1970; named Man of Yr. in Edn., City of Pitts., 1986, Woman of Yr. in Edn., YWCA Tribute to Women, 1989; grantee Am. Coun. Edn. Inst. Acad. Deans, 1979, Inst. Ednl. Mgmt., Harvard U., 1984. Mem. Harvard U. Alumni Assn. (bd. dirs. 1985-87), Phi Beta Kappa, Phi Kappa Phi. Office: Monmouth University West Long Branch NJ 07764

STAFINSKI, RUTH LOUISE, shop owner; b. Worcester, Mass., June 26, 1956; d. Alexander W. and Martha E. (Sanford) S. AS, Quinsigamond Coll., 1977; BS, Worcester State U., 1982. Owner The Englishwomans' Garden, Millbury, Mass., 1980—. Conservation chmn. Fedn. of Womans Clubs, Millbury, 1984-89. Mem. Am. Rose Assn., Tower Hill Botanical Assn., Mass. Descendants of the Mayflower. Republican. Protestant.

STAGE, GINGER ROOKS, psychologist; b. Allentown, Pa., Sept. 23, 1946; d. John Myers Rooks and Catherine Estelle (Graser) Rooks Bistritz; m. Robert Roy Stage, Aug. 23, 1969; 1 child, Stephen. BA in Psychology magna cum laude, Moravian Coll., 1968; MA in Psychology, Temple U., 1969. Lic. psychologist, Pa. Instr. Beaver campus Pa. State U., Monaca, 1969-74; staff psychologist St. Francis Community Mental Health Ctr., Pitts., 1974-83; pvt. practice family therapy Coraopolis, Pa., 1977—; mem. Greenstein Family Therapy Consultation Group, Pitts., 1981—; mem., speaker Human Sexuality Alliance, Pitts., 1989-91; speaker on marital, family and parenting issues. Mem. Am. Psychol. Assn., Greater Pitts. Psychol. Assn., Western Pa. Family Ctr. Episcopalian. Home: 112 Wessex Hills Dr Coraopolis PA 15108-1021 Office: 409 Mill St Coraopolis PA 15108-1607

STAGEN, MARY-PATRICIA HEALY, marketing executive; b. Ridgewood, N.J., Apr. 4, 1955; d. Bernard Patrick and Mary Patricia (O'Connor) Healy; m. Daniel A. Stagen, Oct. 31, 1987. BA in History, lic. in secondary edn.-libr. sci., Elms Coll., Chicopee, Mass., 1977; MBA in Mktg. and Info. Svcs., Rutgers U., 1994. Adminstrv. asst. to meeting dir. Am. Inst. Chem. Engrs., N.Y.C., 1980-81, meetings coord., 1981-84, mgr. spl. projects to exec. dir., 1984-89; v.p. mktg. Wall St. Rsch. Svcs., Inc., Clifton, N.J., 1990—; with Equifax Svcs., East Rutherford, N.J., 1992-96; meeting planner Am. Assn. Engring. Socs., Washington, 1984-85. Mem. NAFE, Assn. of MBA Execs., Am. Mktg. Assn. Republican. Roman Catholic. Home: 86 Boulevard Passaic NJ 07055-4706

STAHL, ALICE SLATER, psychiatrist; b. Vienna, Austria, Jan. 28, 1913; came to U.S., 1938; d. Sam and Helen (Bluman) Slater; widowed; chidlren: Kenneth Lee, June Audrey. Baccalaureate, Gymnasium, Vienna, 1932; Med. Dr., U. Vienna Med. Sch., 1938. Intern Williamsport (Pa.) Gen. Hosp., 1939-40; resident in psychiatry Gallinger Mcpl. Hosp., Washington, 1940-41, Independence State Hosp., 1941-42; resident in psychiatry Bellevue Hosp., N.Y.C., 1942-43, attending psychiatry, 1945-48; staff psychiatrist Jewish Bd. of Guardians, N.Y.C., 1943-45; attending psychiatrist Jamaica Hosp., Queens, N.Y., 1948-52; dir. adolescent psychiatry Hillside Hosp., Glen Oaks, N.Y., 1954-62, attending staff psychiatrist, 1962—; supervising psychiatrist Bergen Pines County Hosp., Paramus, N.J., cons. psychiatrist, 1988—; asst. prof. clin. psychiatry Yeshiva U. Med. Sch., 1978—. Fellow AMA (life), Am. Psychiat. Assn. (life); mem. Am. Psychoanalytic Assn. (life), Am. Soc. for Adolescent Psychiatry (life). Home and Office: 305 Joan Pl Wyckoff NJ 07481 2818

STAHL, ARLEEN MARIE, nursing educator; b. Joliet, Ill., Mar. 19, 1947; d. Joseph Ralph and Mary Margaret (Starina) Dusa; m. Robert John Stahl, Aug. 23, 1969; children: Jennifer, Erika, Alicia, Raymond. Diploma in nursing, Little Co. of Mary Hosp., 1968; BS in Profl. ARts, Coll. St. Francis, 1975; BSN, No. Ill. U., 1980, MSN, 1984. RN, Ill. Staff/charge nurse critical care units St. Joseph Med. Ctr., Joliet, 1968-73, 77-80, instr. nursing Sch. Nursing, 1973-76, 80-88; tchg. asst. No. Ill. U., Dekalb, 1992-93, rsch. asst., 1994-95; asst. prof. nursing St. Joseph Coll. Nursing, Joliet, 1989—; mem. patient edn. task force Open Heart Surgery Com., St. Joseph Med. Ctr., Joliet, 1989; textbook cons. J.B. Lippincott Co., Phila., 1991-92; com. mem. Joliet Area Cmty. Hospice Edn. Com., Joliet, 1991-92. Rsch. grantee NIH, 1995, 96. Mem. Sigma Theta Tau (Beta Omega chpt.), Phi Sigma Soc. (Beta Epsilon chpt.). Home: 1013 Windsor Dr Shorewood IL 60431 Office: St Joseph Coll Nursing 290 N Springfield Ave Joliet IL 60435

STAHL, DIANE IRENE, parochial school educator; b. Ridgewood, N.Y., May 2, 1952; d. Frederick Martin and Stanislava Mary (Halunka) S. BS in Edn., Wagner Coll., 1974. 6th grade tchr. St. Mark's Luth. Sch., Bklyn., 1975-79, 8th grade tchr., asst. prin., 1979-81, 8th grade tchr., acting prin., 1981-82, 8th grade tchr., asst. prin., 1982-84; 6th grade tchr. Redeemer Luth. Sch., Glendale, N.Y., 1984-87, 8th grade tchr., 1987—. Named Tchr. of Yr. Luth. Schs. Assn., 1985. Home: 64-40 Catalpa Ave Ridgewood NY 11385 Office: Redeemer Luth Sch 69-26 Cooper Ave Glendale NY 11385

STAHL, KATHLEEN JOANN, insurance company executive; b. Grand Haven, Mich., Jan. 27, 1950; d. Lawrence W. and Mary Helen (Nowacki) Berg. BS, U. Mich., 1980. Claim supr. Washington Nat. Ins., Evanston, Ill., 1981-83; asst. dir. Gallagher Bassett, Rolling Meadows, Ill., 1983-85; claim supr. Fort Dearborn Life Ins., Chgo., 1985-86, internal auditor, 1986-88, mgr. policyowner svc., 1988-89; claim cons. Northshore Internat., Salem, Mass., 1990-94; v.p. ops. Interra Reinsurance Group, Indpls., 1994-96, v.p. adminstrn. & audit, 1996—. Office: Interra Reinsurance Group Ste 150 9449 Priority Way West Dr Indianapolis IN 46240

STAHL, LESLEY R., journalist; b. Lynn, Mass., Dec. 16, 1941; d. Louis and Dorothy J. (Tishler) S.; m. Aaron Latham; 1 dau. BA cum laude, Wheaton Coll., Norton, Mass., 1963. Asst. to speechwriter Mayor Lindsay's Office, N.Y.C., 1966-67; rschr. N.Y. Election unit CBS News, 1967-68; rschr. London-Huntley Brinkley Report, NBC News, 1969; producer, reporter WHDH-TV, Boston, 1970-72; news corr. CBS News, Washington, from 1972; White House corr. CBS News, 1979-91; moderator Face the Nation, 1983-91; co-editor, corr. CBS News, 60 Minutes, 1991—. Trustee Wheaton Coll. Recipient Tex. Headliners award, 1973, Dennis Kauff award for lifetime achievement in journalism, Fifth Estate award Broadcasting Mag. Hall of Fame, 1992, Fred Friendly First Amendment award, 1996; named Best White House Corr., Washington Journalism Rev., 1991. Office: CBS News 60 Minutes 555 W 57th St New York NY 10019-2925*

STAHL, MARGO SCHNEEBALG, marine biologist; b. Coral Gables, Fla., June 24, 1947; d. Martin and Rose (Osman) Schneebalg; m. Glenn Stahl, Aug. 17, 1969 (div. June 1988); 1 child, Shaina Flori Georgina. BS in Biology, U. Miami, 1969, MS in Marine Biology, 1973. Fish and wildlife aide Calif. Dept. Fish and Game, Long Beach, 1973; assoc. rsch. engr. So. Calif. Edison Co., Rosemead, 1973-75; rsch. assoc. in urban and regional planning U. Hawaii, Honolulu, 1975-76, Hawaii Inst. Marine Biology, Kaneohe, 1975-77, Anuenue Fisheries Rsch. Ctr., Honolulu, 1977-79; aquatic biology Hawaii Dept. Land and Natural Resources, Honolulu, 1979-83; instr. sci. U. Hawaii Windward C.C., Kaneohe, 1985-88; ecologist U.S. Army C.E., Honolulu, 1988-93; supervisory fish and wildlife biologist U.S. Fish and Wildlife Svc., Honolulu, 1993—; pres. Mermaid Aquatic Cons., Honolulu, 1979-81, 84-88; mem. Hawaii Water Quality Tng. Interagy. Com., Honolulu, 1991-93. Contbg. author: Taste of Aloha, 1983 (Jr. League award 1985); contbr. articles to profl. jours. Project mgr. Kokokahi Aquaculture Model, Kaneohe, 1978-80; mem. adv. bd. Windward C.C., 1982-83; hon. coord. RESULTS Hunger Lobby, Honolulu, 1989. Recipient Stoye award in icythyology Am. Soc. Ichtyologists and Herpetologists, 1972, Career Woman award Sierra Mar dist. Calif. Bus. and Profl. Womens Club, 1975, Comdr's award for exceptional performance U.S. Army C.E., Ft. Shafter, Hawaii, 1990. Mem. Nat. Assn. Environ. Profls. (cert. environ. profl., chmn. cert. com. 1992-93, C.E.P. award 1991), Assn. for Women in Sci. (bd. dirs. 1985), Hawaii Assn. Environ. Profls. (bd. dirs. 1991-93, pres.-elect 1993-94), World Mariculture Soc. (bd. dirs. 1981), Am. Fisheries Soc., Western Soc. Naturalists. Home: 46-436 Holopeki St Kaneohe HI 96744-4227 Office: US Fish and Wildlife Svc Honolulu HI 96850

STAILEY, HEATHER ANN, health facility administrator; b. Shreveport, La., Feb. 19, 1953; d. Raymond Lenard and Shirley (Thomas) S. BSN, Pacific Luth. U., 1975; MBA in Health Care Adminstrn., City U., Bellvue, Wash., 1995. Pediatric nurse Mary Bridge Children's Hosp., Tacoma, 1975-76, 79-88; pediatric office nurse Western Clinic, Tacoma, 1976-79; pediatric spl. care nurse Children's Hosp., San Diego, 1988-91; mgr. patient care svcs. Tacoma Family Medicine, 1992—; instr. critical care St. Mary's Hosp., Long Beach, Calif., 1991. Named to Outstanding Young Women of Am., 1986. Mem. AACN (cert.). Home: 3725 N 25th St Tacoma WA 98406-5315 Office: 521 Martin Luther King Jr Way Tacoma WA 98405-4238

STAILEY, JANIE RUTH, occupational health nurse; b. DeRidder, La., Nov. 23, 1946; d. James Raynie and Betty Lou (Bolding) Whiteley; m. Claude Perry Spicer (div. 1992); 1 child, Cherie Suzanne; m. Ronald Ira Stailey, 1993; stepchildren: Melissa Elliott, Ron, Bobby. Diploma in Nursing, Confederate Meml. Med. Ctr., Shreveport, La., 1968; BS, St. Joseph's Coll., Windham, Maine, 1991. RN, La.; cert. occupl. health nurse specialist. Head nurse Merryville (La.) Gen. Hosp., 1970-79; employee health coord., indsl. hygiene technician, hazard comm. coord. Westvaco Corp., DeRidder, La., 1980—; health care cons. So. Insulation, DeRidder, 1989—, JM&M Constrn., DeRidder, 1988—, Ron Williams Constrn., 1995—. Sec. Beauregard Parish chpt. Am. Cancer Soc., DeRidder, 1988-91, Beauregard Cmty. Concerns, DeRidder, 1988-91. Named La. Occupl. Health Nurse of Yr., Schering Pharm./La. Assn. Occupl. Health Nurses, 1989, Beauregard Parish Woman of the Yr., 1994. Mem. ANA, S.W. La. Dist. Nurses Assn. (Occupl. Health Nurse of Yr. 1989), La. State Nurses Assn., VFW Ladies Aux. (v.p. 1994-95), Am. Assn. Occupl. Health Nurses (bd. dirs. 1989-94, rep. nurse in Washington intership 1993), La. Assn. Occupl. Health Nurses (treas., bd. dirs. 1986—), S.W. La. Assn. Occupl. Health Nurses (pres., v.p.), Beta Sigma Phi. Home: 1124 Elm Rd Deridder LA 70634 Office: Westvaco Corp 400 Crosby Rd Deridder LA 70634

STAINER, MARGARET GAYLE, artist, educator, art gallery curator; b. South Weymouth, Mass., Aug. 29, 1942; d. Michael Harunkiewiecz and Margaret Rose (Frazier) Wingate; m. Fred Sebastion Stainer, Apr. 7, 1960; c child, Leighanne. BA in Art History, San Jose State U., 1973, BA in Art and Painting, 1980, MFA, 1984. Dir. art gallery Ohlone Coll., Fremont, Calif., 1986-89, 96—; gallery curator Works/San Jose, San Jose, Calif., 1979-82; art tchr. City of Fremont, 1984-86; adj. art prof. Ohlone Coll., Fremont, 1984—; art prof. Acad. of Art Coll., San Francisco, 1986-89, art prof., gallery dir., 1990; co-chair annual nat. symposium Women's Caucus for Art, 1989. Author, curator: (research art catalog) Agnes Pelton, 1989; contbr. drawings to book Bitter Fruit, 1993; contbr. articles and drawings to gallery catalogues and newspapers. Mem. Non Profit Art Gallery Assn., Women's Caucus for Art (bd. dirs. 1985-93, Author Recognition 1990), Adjunct Faculty Union. Office: Ohlone Coll Fine Arts Dept 43600 Mission Blvd Fremont CA 94538

STALERMAN, RUTH, civic volunteer, poet; b. N.Y.C., Mar. 18, 1919; d. Samuel and Minnie (Weckstein) Kosson; m. Joseph Stalerman, June 5, 1949 (dec. Aug. 1986); children: Helene, Enid. Student, Modern Machines Bus. Sch. Various bookkeeping positions, to 1951. Poetry pub. Am. Anthology Contemporary Poetry, Nat. Libr. Poetry, A Far Off Place, Songs on the Wind, Tears of Fire, numerous other pubs. and jours. Co-editor, then editor newsletter PTA; dist. dir. Girl Scouts U.S., 1958-62; pres. White Plains chpt. B'nai B'rith, cons. on membership, programming; mem. White Plains Hosp. Aux., mem. instnl. rev. bd. Recipient Editor's choice awards for outstanding achievement in poetry, 1994, 95, 96. Mem. Jewish War Vets. (chaplain, contbr. to newsletter), Internat. Soc. Poets. Home: 30 Lawrence Dr North White Plains NY 10603

STALEY, DAWN, basketball player; b. Phila., May 4, 1970. Grad., U. Va. Basketball player USA Women's Nat. Team. Scholar U. Va.; named 1994 USA Basketball Female Athlete of Yr. Office: USA Basketball 5465 Mark Dabling Blvd Colorado Springs CO 80918-3842

STALKER, JACQUELINE D'AOUST, academic administrator, educator; b. Penetang, Ont., Can., Oct. 16, 1933; d. Phillip and Rose (Eaton) D'Aoust; m. Robert Stalker; children: Patricia, Lynn, Roberta. Teaching cert., U. Ottawa, 1952; tchr. music, Royal Toronto Conservatory Music, 1952; teaching cert., Lakeshore Tchrs. Coll., 1958; BEd with honors, U. Manitoba, 1977, MEd, 1979; EdD, Nova U., 1985. Cert. tchr. Ont., Man., Can. Adminstr., tchr., prin. various schs., Ont. and Que., 1952-65; area commr. Girl Guides of Can., throughout Europe, 1965-69; administr., tchr. Algonquin Community Coll., Ottawa, Ont., 1970-74; tchr., program devel. Frontenac County Bd. Edn., Kingston, Ont., 1974-75; lectr., faculty advisor dept. curriculum, edn. U. Man., Can., 1977-79; lectr. U. Winnipeg, Man., Can., 1977-79; cons. colls. div. Man. Dept. Edn., 1980-81, sr. cons. programming br., 1981-84, sr. cons. post secondary, adult and continuing edn. div., 1985-88, dir. post secondary career devel. br. and adult and continuing edn. br., 1989; asst. prof. higher edn., coord. grad. program in higher edn. U. Man., 1989-92, assoc. prof., coord. grad. program in higher edn., 1992-95; cons. lectures, seminars, workshops throughout Can. Contbr. articles to profl. jours.; mng. editor Can. Jour. of Higher Edn., 1989-93. Mem. U. Man. Senate, 1976-81, 86-89, bd. govs., 1979-82; Can. rep. Internat. Youth Conf., Garmisch, Fed. Republic of Germany, 1968; vol. Can. Cancer Soc.; mem. Assn. RN Accreditation Coun., 1980-85; chair Child Care Accreditation Com., Man., 1983-90; chair Task Force Post-Secondary Accessibility, Man., 1983; vol. United Way Planning and Allocations; provincial dir., mem. nat. bd. Can. Congress for Learning Opportunities for Women. Recipient award for enhancing the Outreach activities of the univ. U. Man., 1994. Mem. Can. Soc. Study Higher Edn., Man. Tchrs. Soc., U. Man. Alumni Assn., Women's Legal Edn. and Action Fund, Am. Assn. Study Higher Edn. Home: 261 Baltimore Rd, Winnipeg, MB Canada R3L 1H7

STALLARD, G. ANN, printing company executive, association executive; b. Kingsport, Tenn., Nov. 15, 1946; d. James Carter and Helen (McClelland) S. BA in Edn. and Art, U. Ky., 1969. Comml. artist Clarkson-Stallard, Atlanta, 1969-76; with sales dept. Graphic Comm. Corp., Atlanta, 1976-80, v.p., 1980-84, exec. v.p., 1984—; logo and materials designer Women and the Constitution, 1988; cons. Nat. Coop. League, Washington, 1972-74, Artisan's Craft Coop., Chaddsford, Pa., 1974-76; gov.'s com. Post Secondary Edn., 1980; rep. women bus. owners in Ga., SBA Women in Bus. Owners Conf., 1984, 85, 86. Bd. dirs. YWCA of the U.S.A., 1976-88, chair nat. pub. rels. com., 1981-84, chair racial justice com., 1985-88, pres. bd. dirs., 1991—, nat. pres. 1992—; v.p. Northwest Ga. Girl Scout Coun., Inc., 1988-91; active White House Nat. Initiative on Women's Bus. Ownership Task Force, 1985; founding mem., treas. Vote Choice Ga. Polit. Action Com., 1989—; bd. dirs. United Way of Greater Atlanta, 1993—. Recipient Nat. honor for Display Honoring Hidden Heroines, Girl Scouts U.S., 1977, Willing Svc. award Sta. WSB, Atlanta, 1977, Outstanding Community Svc. award YWCA of Greater Atlanta, 1982, Image Maker award Atlanta Profl. Women's Directory, 1982, Good Guy award Bus. Coun. Ga., 1987, Torchbearer award Women Bus. Owners Atlanta, 1990; named one of ten Outstanding Young Women, Atlanta Jaycees, 1976, Women in Bus. Advocate for Ga., SBA, 1985, Woman of Achievement, Atlanta, 1994; named to Racial Justice Hall of Fame, East Dallas Pub. Schs., 1984;. Mem. Leadership Atlanta (exec. com. 1991—), Atlanta C. of C. (task force on small bus.), Gwinnett C. of C., Women Bus. Owners of Atlanta (bd. dirs. 1981-84, v.p. 1983, pres. 1988-89). Episcopalian. Home: 1231 Fairview Rd NE Atlanta GA 30306-4661 Office: Graphic Comm Corp 394 N Clayton St Lawrenceville GA 30245-4817

STALLINGS, VIOLA PATRICIA ELIZABETH, systems engineer, educational systems specialist; b. Norfolk, Va., Nov. 6, 1946; d. Harold Albert and Marie Blanche (Welch) S.; m. (div. Oct. 1984); 1 child, Patricia N.P. Stallings. BS in Psychology, Va. State U., 1968; MBA with distinction, U. Pa., 1975; postgrad., Temple U., 1972-74, Calif. State U., San Francisco, 1973; EdD with specialization in tech., Nova Southeastern U., Ft. Lauderdale, Fla., 1996. Tchr., supr. Peace Corps, Liberia, West Africa, 1968-71; tchr. Day Care Ctr., disruptive h.s. students Tioga Comm. Youth Ctr., 1972-73; tchr.

Phila. Sch. Dist., 1972-76; bus. cons. Phila., 1976; sr. sys. engr./sr. industry svcs. specialist, project mgr. IBM/K-12 Edn., Mt. Laurel, N.J., 1976—; bd. dirs. Woodrock, Inc., Phila., 1974-84, 87-95; mem. nat. edn. rsch. fund com.; task force leader IBM Corp., 1990-91. Bd. dirs., v.p. Unity Ch. of Christ, 1993-95. Recipient Outstanding Svc. award IBM Black Workers Alliance, Washington, 1984. Mem. AAUW, Assn. for Ednl. Comm. and Tech., Beta Gamma Sigma. Baptist. Home: 105 Burnamwood Ct Mount Laurel NJ 08054-3106 Office: IBM EduQuest 1000 Atrium Way Mount Laurel NJ 08054

STALLONE, DIANNA R., lawyer; b. Bklyn.; d. Joseph and Elaine (Lundgren) S.; 1 child, Briana Colette Sexton-Stallone. BA, U. Minn., 1981; JD, William Mitchell Coll. Law, 1985. Bar: Minn. 1985, Mass. 1987. Assoc. Meagher, Geer, Markham, Anderson, Adamson, et al, Mpls., 1985-87, Burns & Levinson, Boston, 1987-88, Powers & Hall, P.C., Boston, 1989-92; pvt. practice Northampton and Boston, 1992—. Author: The Secret Path, 1995. Commr. Mpls. Commn. on Civil Rights, 1985-87; bd. dirs. Lawyers Internat. Human Rights Com., Mpls., 1985-87. Recipient Am. Jurisprudence award, 1982. Mem. NOW. Office: 160 Main St Ste 31 Northampton MA 01060

STALLWORTH, ALMA GRACE, state legislator. Grad., Highland Park Community Coll., 1956; student, Wayne State U., 1956. Mem. Mich. Ho. of Reps., Lansing, 1970-74, 81—; dep. dir. Hist. Dept. City of Detroit, 1975-78, job developer, 1978-79; mem. exec. com. Nat. Conf. State Legislatures, 1986-89. Commr. Wayne County Charter, Detroit, 1978-79, Martin Luther King Commn., Detroit, 1987; chairperson bd. dirs. task force on infant mortality Mich. Legislature, 1987; pres. Nat. Black Child Devel. Inst., Detroit; vol. United Negro Coll. Fund, 1987—; founder, adminstr. Black Caucus Found. of Mich., 1987—. Recipient cert. of appreciation Mich. Dept. Edn., 1986, Advs. award Mich. Health Mothers, Health Babies Coalition, 1987; named Woman Leader in Pub. Health, Mi ch. Assn. Local Pub. Health, 1987, Woman of Yr., Minority Women's Network, 1988. Mem. NAACP, Nat. Conf. State Legislators (exec. commr. 1986), Nat. Black Caucus State Legislators, (sec. women's caucus), Mich. Legis. Black Causus (chair 1987), Alpha Kappa Alpha. Democrat. Clubs: Cameo, Top Ladies of Distinction. Home: 19793 Sorrento Detroit MI 48235 Office: Mich Ho of Reps State Capitol Lansing MI 48909

STALLWORTH, ANNE NALL, writer, writing educator; b. Birmingham, Ala., Sept. 30, 1935; d. John Martin and Lida Lucille (Crump) Nall; m. Clarke J. Stallworth Jr., Mar. 23, 1925; children: Carole Anne Stallworth, Clarke J. Stallworth III. Student, Birmingham-So. Coll., 1952-53. Tchr. U. Ala., Birmingham; tchr. Birmingham. Author: This Time Next Year, 1972 (Best Fiction award), Where the Bright Lights Shine, 1977, Go, Go, Said the Bird, 1984 (movie rights pending); (short story) Waiting (McCall's mag.), 1976. All had fgn. publ. Editor Found. for Women's Health newsletter, Birmingham; publicity dir. Birmingham Music Club. Recipient Best Fiction award Ala. Libr., 1972. Home: 4316 Wilderness Rd Birmingham AL 35213-2411

STALLWORTH-BARRON, DORIS A. CARTER, librarian, educator; b. Ala., June 12, 1932; d. Henry Lee Carter and Hattie Belle Stallworth; m. George Stallworth, 1950 (dec.); children: Annette LaVerne, Vanzette Yvonne; m. Walter L. Barron, 1989. BS, Ala. State U., 1955; MLS, CUNY, 1968; postgrad., Columbia U., St. John's U., NYU. Cert. supr. and tchr. sch. libr. media, N.Y. Libr. media specialist N.Y.C. Bd. Edn.; head libr. Calhoun County High Sch., Hobson City, Ala.; cons. Libr. Unit, N.Y.C. Bd. Edn.; cons. evaluator So. Assn. Secondary Schs., Ala.; supr., adminstr., liason rep. Community Sch. Dist. #24 N.Y.C. Sch. System; previewer libr. media Preview Mag., 1971-73; mem. ednl. svcs. adv. coun. Sta. WNET, 1987-89; mem. coun. N.Y.C. Schs. Libr. System, 1987-90; turn-key tchr. trainer N.Y. State Dept. Edn., 1988; spl. guest speaker and lectr. Queens Coll., City U., Community Sch. Dist. #24, PTA, N.Y. City Sch. System, Libr. unit, 1980-90; curriculum writer libr. unit N.Y.C. Bd. Edn., 1985-86. Contbr. articles to ednl. publs. Mem State of Ala. Dem. Exec. Com., 1994—; active A+ for Kids. Mem. NAFE, ALA, Am. Assn. Sch. Librs. (spl. guest speaker and lectr. for conv. 1987), Am. Sch. Libr.'s Assn., Nat. Assn. Black Pub. Adminstrs., N.Y. State Libr. Assn., N.Y.C. Sch. Librs. Assn., Nat. Forum for Black Pub. Adminstrs., N.Y. Coalition 100 Black Women, Lambda Kappa Mu Sorority, Inc., Alpha Kappa Alpha Sorority.

STAMATAKIS, CAROL MARIE, state legislator, lawyer; b. Canton, Ohio, Apr. 27, 1960; d. Emmanuel Nicholas and Catherine Lucille (Zam) S.; m. Michael Charles Shklar, Mar. 23, 1985. BA in Criminology and Criminal Justice, Ohio State U., 1982; JD, Case Western Res., 1985. Bar: N.H. 1985, U.S. Dist. Ct. N.H. 1985. Atty. Law Office Laurence F. Gardner, Hanover, N.H., 1985-87, Law Office William Howard Dunn, Claremont, N.H., 1987-90, Elliott, Jasper & Stamatakis, Newport, N.H., 1990-93; state rep. N.H. State Legislature, 1988-94; of counsel Law office of Michael C. Shklar, Newport, 1994—; staff atty. N.H. Dept. Health and Human Svcs., Keene, 1994—; instr. Am. Inst. Banking, Claremont, 1987-88, 91-92, 95. Asst. editor: (jours.) Health Matrix: The Jour. of Health Services Mangement, 1983-85. Treas., mem. Town of Lempster N.H. Conservation Commn., 1987—; bd. dirs. Orion House, Inc., Newport, N.H., 1987-91; town chair N.H. Dem. Party, 1987—; mem. Town of Lempster Recycling Com., 1988—, Community Task Force on Drug and alcohol Abuse, 1988. Mem. N.H. Bar Assn., Sierra Club, Upper Valley Group (former vice chair and solid waste chair). Home: PO Box 807 Newport NH 03773-0807

STAMBERG, SUSAN LEVITT, radio broadcaster; b. Newark, Sept. 7, 1938; d. Robert I. and Anne (Rosenberg) Levitt; m. Louis Collins Stamberg, Apr. 14, 1962; 1 child, Joshua Collins. BA, Barnard Coll, 1959; DHL (hon.), Gettysburg Coll., 1982, Dartmouth Coll., 1984, Knox Coll., U. N.H., SUNY, Brockport. Editorial asst. Daedalus, Cambridge, Mass., 1960-62; editorial asst. The New Republic, Washington, 1962-63; host, producer, mgr., program dir. Sta. WAMU-FM, Washington, 1963-69; host All Things Considered Washington, 1971-86; host Weekend Edition Nat Pub. Radio, Washington, 1987-89; spl. corr. Nat. Pub. Radio, 1990—; bd. dirs. AIA, Washington, 1983-85, PEN/Faulkner Fiction Award Found., 1985—. Author: Every Night at Five, 1982, The Wedding Cake in the Middle of the Road, 1992, Talk: NPR's Susan Stamberg Considers All Things, 1993. Recipient Honor award Ohio U., 1977, Edward R. Murrow award Corp. for Pub. Broadcasting, 1980; named Woman of Yr., Barnard Coll., 1984; fellow Silliman Coll. Yale U., 1984—; inducted Broadcasting Hall of Fame, 1994. Office: Nat Pub Radio 635 Massachusetts Ave NW Washington DC 20001-3752

STAMMER, DAPHNE S., art educator, artist; b. Little Falls, N.Y., May 14, 1941; d. Elwyn A. and Jeanette (Laurie) Nellis; m. Jack E. Stammer, Oct. 6, 1973; 1 child, Alicia. AA, Yakima Valley Coll., 1961; BA, Coll. of Idaho, 1963; MA, Sacramento State U., 1969. Art tchr. Wenatche (Wash.) H.S., 1963-64; art tchr. Cordova H.S., Rancho Cordova, Calif., 1964-92, art dept. chmn., 1964-85; docent Crocker Art Mus., Sacramento, 1992—. Exhibited in group shows at The Art Works, 1990-92, Lincoln Arts Ctr., 1990, Am. Acad. Equine Art, 1989-90, Catherine Lorillard Wolfe Ann. Open, 1988, 91, Sacramento Fine Arts Ctr., 1981—, Pogan's Art Gallery, 1992, Hummingbird Originals, 1993—, Calif. Arts League, 1981—, Crocker Art Mus., 1979, Watercolor Artists Sacramento Horizons, 1993—, East Bay Watercolor Soc., 1994, North Valley Art League Nat., 1993, 96, U. Club, Davis, 1994, Women Artists the West, 1990—, Pastel Soc. the West Coast, 1992—, Soc. Western Artists, 1992, Draft Horse Classic, 1991-92, Sierra Western Artists, 1992, Cassatt Pastel Soc., 1988—. Mem. Women Artists of West, Calif. Arts League, Pastel Soc. West Coast.

STAMSTA, JEAN F., artist; b. Sheboygan, Wis., Nov. 2, 1936; d. Herbert R. and Lucile Caroline (Malwitz) Nagel; m. Duane R. Stamsta, Aug. 18, 1956; children: Marc, David. BS, BA, U. Wis., 1958. guest curator Milw. Art Mus., 1986; resident artist Leighton Artist Colony, Banff, Alta., Can., 1987. One-woman shows Am. Craft Mus., N.Y.C., 1971, Winona (Minn.) State U., 1986, Lawrence U., Appleton, Wis., 1990, Walkers Point Ctr. Arts, Milw., 1990, U. Wis. Ctr., Waukesha, 1995; exhibited in group shows, incuding Cleve. Mus. Art, 1977, Milw. Art Mus., 1986, 88, Nat. Air and Stace Mus., Smithsonian Instn., Washington, 1986, Madison (Wis.) Art Ctr., 1987, 90, Paper Press Gallery, Chgo., 1988, North Arts Ctr., Atlanta, 1990, Dairy Barn Cultural Arts Ctr., Athens, Ohio, 1991, Paper Arts Festival, Appleton, 1992, Fine Arts Mus., Budapest, Hungary, 1992, Tilburg Textile Mus., The Netherlands, 1993, U. Wis. Union Gallery, 1994, Holland Area Arts Coun. Gallery, U. Mich., Ann Arbor, 1996. NEA craftsman fellow, 1974. Home and Studio: 9313 Center Oak Rd Hartland WI 53029

STANAITIS, SANDRA LEE, nurse; b. Chester, Pa., Dec. 27, 1958; d. Leon David and Margaret (Sharpless) S. BA in Psychology, Widener U., 1980; BS in Biology, SUNY, Albany, 1983; postgrad., East Carolina U., 1984; BSN, West Chester U., 1993. RN, Del., N.J., Pa.; cert. in venipuncture, perioperative nursing. Instr. biology lab. East Carolina U., Greenville, N.C., 1987-88, tutor math. and sci., 1986-88, technician biol. lab. Sea Grant Program, 1987, adj. lectr. biology, 1987-88; tutor math. and sci. Vocat. Rehab., Greenville, 1987-88; technician environ. lab. Weyerhauser Pulp Mill, New Bern, N.C., 1987-88; insp. pharm. quality control Burroughs-Wellcome, Greenville, 1988; clin. data asst. Wyeth Labs., Radnor, Pa., 1988-89; rep. customer svc. Met. Pers., Wayne, Pa., 1989-92, Bayada Nurses Home Health Care Specialist, 1993—; charge nurse subacute care ctr. Genesis Health Ventures, Suburban Woods, Norristown, Pa., 1994—; instr. med.-surg. clin. nursing Delaware County C.C., 1995. James McDaniel Meml. scholar East Carolina U., 1986-88, Army Nurse Corps scholar, 1991-93, U. N.C. Inst. Nutrition scholar, 1985-87. Mem. U.S. Figure Skating Assn., Recreation Skating Inst. Am., Skating Club Wilmington, West Chester U. Nursing Honor Soc., Sigma Xi, Sigma Theta Tau. Office: Suburban Woods 2751 DeKalb Pike Norristown PA 19403

STANBERRY, DOSI ELAINE, English literature educator, writer; b. Elk Park, N.C.; m. Earl Stanberry; 1 child, Anita St. Lawrence. Student in Bus. Edn., Steed Coll. Tech., 1956; BS in Bus. and English, East Tenn. State U., 1961, MA in Shakespearean Lit., 1962; EdD, East Tex. State U., 1975; postgrad., North Tex. State U., U. South Fla., NYU, Duke U., U. N.C. Prof. Manatee Jr. Coll., Bradenton, Fla., 1964-67, Dickinson State U., N.D., 1967-81; retired, 1981. Author: Poetic Heartstrings, Mountain Echoes, Love's Perplexing Obsession Experienced by Heinrich Heine and Percy Bysshe Shelley, Poetry from the Ancients to Moderns: A Critical Anthology, Finley Forest, Chapel Hill's Tree-lined Tuck, (plays) The Big Toe, The Funeral Factory; contbr. articles, poetry to jours., mags. Recipient Editor's Choice award Nat. Libr. Poetry, 1988, 95, Distinguished Professorof English Award, Dickinson State U., 1981; included in Best Poems of 1995. Mem. Acad. Am. Poets, N.C. Writers Network, N.C. Poetry Soc. (Carl Sandburg Poetry award 1988), Poetic Page, Writers Jour., Poets and Writers, Friday-Noon Poets, Delta Kappa Gamma. Home: Finley Forest 193 Summerwalk Cir Chapel Hill NC 27514-8642

STANCIL, IRENE MACK., family counselor; b. St. Helena Island, Sept. 29, 1938; d. Rufus and Irene (Wilson) Mack; m. Nesby Stancil, Dec. 29, 1968; 1 child, Steve Lamar. BA, Benedict Coll., 1960, CUNY, 1983; MA, New World Bible Coll., 1984; SSD, United Christian Coll., 1985. Supr. City of New York; tchr. local bd. edn., S.C. Mem. Am. Ctr. for Law & Justice.

STANDER, LORENE E., personnel coordinator; b. San Jose, Calif., Aug. 16, 1967. AA, Fla. State U., Tallahassee, 1987, BS, 1989. Asst. mgr. Alden Merrell, Boca Raton, Fla., 1985-86, Las Casas Inn, Tallahassee, 1988-91; pers. coord. Adia Pers. Svcs., Tallahassee, 1993—. Home: 302 E Sinclair Rd Tallahassee FL 32312

STANDFAST, SUSAN J(ANE), state official, research, consultant, educator; b. Callicoon, N.Y., July 2, 1935; m. Theodore P. Wright Jr., 1967; children: Henry S., Margaret S., Catherine B. AB in Biology and Chemistry, Wells Coll., 1957; MD, Columbia U., 1961; MPH In Epidemiology, U. Calif., Berkeley, 1965. Cert. Am. Bd. Preventive Medicine. Intern King County Hosp., Swedish Hosp, Seattle, 1961-62; pediatric resident U. Wash., Seattle, 1963; sr. resident in epidemiology N.Y. State Health Dept., 1965-67; instr. dept. community health Albany (N.Y.) Med. Coll., 1965-67, asst. prof. dept. preventive and community medicine, 1968-72, cons. in epidemiology, 1968-72, adj. asst. prof. preventive and community medicine, 1975-80, adj. assoc. prof., 1980-91, cons. preventive medicine dept. family practice, 1983-91; research physician bur. cancer control, div. epidemiology N.Y. State Dept. Health, Albany, 1975-83, dir. cancer surveillance unit cancer control sect. bur. chronic disease prevention, 1983-85, asst. to dir. div. epidemiology, 1985-86, dir. injury control program div. epidemiology, 1986-90; physician pub. health Albany, 1983-95; retired, 1995, dir. disability prevention program, 1988-91; cons. epidemiologist div. family health N.Y. State Dept. Health, Albany, 1991-95; vis. lectr. G.S. Med. Coll., Bombay, 1969-70, London Sch. Hygiene, 1974-75, Coll. Community Medicine, Lahore, Pakistan, 1991; cons. in epidemiology Bombay Cancer Registry Tata Meml. Hosp., Albany, 1968-72; cons. inifectious diseas sect. VA Med. Ctr., Albany, 1979; mem. ad hoc task force on data resource devel. for dir. epidemiology and biometry rsch. program Nat. Inst. Child Health and Human Devel., Bethesda, Md., 1979-80; assoc. prof. epidemiology Sch. Pub. Health, SUNY, 1987—, co-dir. master's pub. health program, 1991—; lectr. in field. Contbr. numerous articles to profl. jours. Mem. med. adv. bd. Hudson-Mohawk chpt. Nat. Found. SIDS, 1976-84; mem. med. adv. bd coun. on human sexuality Planned Parenthood, Albany, 1971-88; mem. Physicians for Social Responsibility, 1984—, Doctors Ought to Care, 1984—, also numerous pub. health task forces and coms.; bd. dirs. Eddy Cmty. Care, Troy, N.Y. Recipient Disting. Alumnae award Wells Coll., 1994. Fellow Am. Coll. Preventive Medicine, Am. Coll. Epidemiology; mem. APHA, Am. Assn. for Automotive Medicine. Home: 27 Vandenburg Ln Latham NY 12110-1190

STANDIFER, SABRINA, state legislator; m. Brad Barkley. Mem. Kans. Ho. of Reps., 1993—; self-employed computer cons. Democrat. Home: 317 W 41st St N Wichita KS 67204-3203 Office: Kans Ho of Reps State Capitol Topeka KS 66612*

STANDIFORD, NATALIE ANNE, writer; b. Balt., Nov. 20, 1961; d. John Willard Eagleston and Natalie Elizabeth Standiford; m. Robert Craig Tracy, Apr. 29, 1989. BA, Brown Univ., 1983. Clerk Shakespeare and Co. Bookstore, N.Y.C., 1983; editl. asst. Random House, N.Y.C., 1984-85, asst. editor books for young readers divsn., 1985-87; freelance writer N.Y.C., 1987—. Author: The Best Little Monkeys in the World, 1987, The Bravest Dog Ever: The True Story of Balto, 1989 (Puffin award Alaska Assn. Sch. Libr. 1992), The Headless Horseman, 1992, Brave Maddie Egg, 1995, Space Dog and Roy, 1990, Space Dog and the Pet Show, 1990, Space Dog in Trouble, 1991, Space Dog the Hero, 1991 (Fifty Books of Yr. citation Fedn. Children's Book Groups 1992), The Power #2: The Witness, 1992, The Power #4: The Diary, 1992, The Power #7: Vampire's Kiss, 1992, (picture book) Dollhouse Mouse, 1989, (as Emily James) Fifteen: Hillside Live!, 1993, Jafar's Curse, 1993, (picture book) Santa's Surprise, 1992, The Mixed-Up Witch, 1993, Astronauts are Sleeping, 1996. Reader, N.Y.C. Author Read-Aloud Program, 1992—. Mem. Soc. Children's Book Writers and Illustrators, Author's Guild, Authors League Am. *

STANDING, KIMBERLY ANNA, educational researcher; b. Hagerstown, Md., Mar. 24, 1965; d. Thomas Townsend and Ruth Annadeane (Powell) Stone; m. Christopher G. Standing, May 20, 1989; 1 child, Iain Christopher. BA in Math., St. Mary's Coll., 1988; MA in Higher Edn. Adminstrn., George Washington U., 1996. Rsch. analyst Westat, Inc., Rockville, Md., 1988—. Mem. Am. Ednl. Rsch. Assn., Assn. Study Higher Edn. Home: 11545 Brundidge Ter Germantown MD 20876-5500 Office: Westat Inc 1650 Research Blvd # TB243 Rockville MD 20850-3129

STANDRIDGE, KIM DIANE, accountant; b. Santa Ana, Calif., Apr. 26, 1957; d. Howard Vernon and Mary Louise (Countryman) Horner; m. Roger Odell Standridge, Jan. 7, 1978 (div. Aug. 1983). BSBA, Okla. State U., 1984; cert. in music ministry Bible Sch., Tulsa, 1993. CPA, Okla. Acct., Kerr-McGee Corp., Oklahoma City, 1980-82, Warren Petroleum Co., Tulsa, 1983, Occidental Petroleum Co., Tulsa, 1985-89, Phillips Petroleum Co., Bartlesville, 1990-92, Amoco Prodn. Co., Tulsa, 1994—; owner Multinet Internat., 1988—; auditor Ernst & Young, Tulsa, 1984-85. Vol. med. missions team to Nigeria, 1990, Bulgaria, 1991, Latvia, 1993; mem., min. music Charismatic Ch. Mem. AICPA, NAFE, Okla. Soc. CPA's, Nat. Assn. Accts., Toastmasters, Phi Kappa Phi, Beta Gamma Sigma, Beta Alpha Psi. Republican. Avocations: singing and performing in musicals, snow and water skiing, sailing, softball. Home: 3319 E 8th St Tulsa OK 74112 Office: Amoco Prodn Co PO Box 591 Rm FP 1190 Tulsa OK 74102

STANEK, GENA STIVER, critical care clinical nurse specialist; b. Washington, Feb. 9, 1958; d. William Earl and Norma A. (Cull) Stiver; m. Andrew Henry Stanek, July 1, 1984; children: Amiel Benjamin, Alyssa Anna. BSN, U. Md., 1980, MS, 1985. RN, Md. Clin. nurse specialist Johns Hopkins Hosp., Balt.; clin. nurse critical care Shock Trauma Ctr. U. Md. Med. System, Balt.; rsch. cons.. U. Md., Balt.; clin. nurse specialist shock trauma U. Md. Hosp., Balt. Mem. AANN, AACCN, ASPEN, U. Md. Sch. of Nursing Alumni Assn., Phi Kappa Phi, Sigma Theta Tau. Home: 5217 Lynngate Ct Columbia MD 21044-1437

STANFIELD, ALYSON BLAIR, curator/curator of education; b. Great Falls, Mont., Feb. 3, 1963; d. E. Neil and Barbara Joan (Pannage) S. Student, U. Wyo., 1981-83; BA in Art History, U. Okla., 1985; MA in Art History, U. Tex., 1991. Asst. curator Oklahoma City Art Mus., 1991-92, curator, 1992-95—; curator of edn. Fred Jones Jr. Mus. of Art, U. Okla., Norman, 1995—. Author: Quilts Now: The Art of the Craft, 1994. Public issues advocate Jr. League Oklahoma City, 1994; trustee Carepoint, Inc., 1995—. Mem. Nat. Art Edn. Assn., Am. Assn. Mus. (edn. com.), Coll. Art Assn., Mountain Plains. Mus. Assn., Okla. Mus. Assn., Okla. Conf. Art Historians, Individual Artists of Okla., Okla. Visual Arts Coalition. Democrat. Office: Fred Jones Jr Mus Art Univ Okla 410 W Boyd St Norman OK 73019-0525

STANFORD, AMELIA JEAN, elementary education educator; b. Eudora, Miss., Oct. 29, 1940; d. Charles Loyd and Thelma Adelaide (Shelton) Sexton; m. Carl Dennis Stanford, June 30, 1961; children: Carla, Lesa, Dennis. Student, N.W. Jr. Coll., 1960; BS, Memphis State U., 1967. Cert. elem. edn. educator 1-6, Miss. 5th-6th grade tchr. Miss Lee's Sch., Memphis, 1962-63; 6th grade tchr. St. Paul Sch., Memphis, 1965; 3d grade tchr. Southaven (Miss.) Sch., 1965-68; 2d grade tchr. Sacred Heart Sch., Walls, Miss., 1968—. Co-editor: (filmstrip) Helping Children with Homework, 1977. Active Coalition Christian Voters, DeSoto County, Miss., 1993—; Sunday sch. tchr. Glenn's Chapel, Lake Cormorant, Miss., 1963—, Bible sch. dir., 1963—, children's ch. dir., 1990—. Mem. Nat. Cath. Edn. Assn. Methodist. Home: 291 Highway 301 N Lake Cormorant MS 38641-9657 Office: Sacred Heart Sch PO Box 96 Walls MS 38680-0096

STANGER, ILA, writer, editor; b. N.Y.C.; d. Jack Simon and Shirley Ruth (Nadelson) S. B.A., Bklyn. Coll., 1961. Feature and travel editor Harpers Bazaar, N.Y.C., 1969-75; exec. editor Travel and Leisure mag., N.Y.C., 1975-85; editor in chief Food and Wine Mag., N.Y.C., 1985-89, Travel and Leisure mag., N.Y.C., 1990-93; contbg. editor Town and Country and Quest mag., 1993—; writer on arts, features and travel; consulting editor Internat. Masters Pubs., London. Mem. N.Y. Travel Writers., Am. Soc. Mag. Editors. Home and Office: 115 W 71st St New York NY 10023-3838

STANIAR, LINDA BURTON, insurance company executive; b. Glen Ridge, N.J., July 6, 1948; d. Harold Burton and Helen (Kintzing) Staniar; m. William Glasgow Bergh, Jan. 21, 1978; 1 child, Courtney Christian Bergh. BA, Briarcliff Coll., 1970; MA, NYU, 1974. Pub. rels. asst. N.Y. Life Ins. Co., N.Y.C., 1977-78, pub. rels. assoc., 1978-80, dir., 1981-84, asst. v.p., 1984-86, corp. v.p., 1986-88, v.p. pub. rels. and advt., 1988-93, v.p. corp. comms., 1993-96, sr. v.p. corp. comm., 1996—. Mem. Advt. Women of N.Y. Office: NY Life Ins Co 51 Madison Ave New York NY 10010-1603

STANKEWICH, KIMBERLY JO, elementary and special education educator; b. New London, Conn., Apr. 17, 1972; d. Joseph P. and Linda Marie (D'Agostino) S. BA magna cum laude, Providence Coll., 1994. Playground dir. Town of Groton (Conn.) Parks/Recreation, 1990-96, gymnastics instr., 1989—; latch key site leader Town of Groton, 1994-95, day care provider, 1994—; substitute tchr. Town of Ledyard, Conn., 1994; tchr. Waterford Country Sch., 1994—. Participant Habitat for Humanities, Providence, 1990-94; tutor Vols. in Providence, 1990-94; entertainer Smith Hill House, Providence, 1990-94. Mem. Coun. Exceptional Children, Kappa Delta Pi (v.p. 1993-94). Home: 17 Affeldt Dr Groton CT 06340-4801

STANLEY, CHERYL LYNNE, computer professional; b. Rochester, N.Y., May 1, 1968; d. Bertram Russell and Joanne Emma (Tauro) S. AS in Comm. and Media Arts, Monroe C.C., 1989; BS in Criminal Justice, Rochester Inst. Tech., 1991; postgrad., U. San Francisco, 1991. Delicatessen clk. Wegmans Food Markets, 1987-91; vol. intern Monroe County Dist. Atty.'s Office, 1990; jud. intern RIT Criminal Justice Program, 1991; legal referral staff Calif. Lawyers for the Arts, San Francisco, 1992; info. security analyst Xerox Corp., 1993, network telecom. analyst, 1994; network telecom. analyst Electronic Data Sys., 1994, tech. support ctr. staff, 1994—. Sec. Bigala, San Francisco, 1992; instr. Harp Karate, 1986-91, 95—. Office: 2210 Monroe Ave Rochester NY 14618

STANLEY, DENISE ROSE, secondary school educator; b. Norton, Va., June 15, 1970; d. Gary Duane and Tina Leigh (O'Dell) Rose; m. Kenneth Darrell Stanley Jr., May 31, 1991; 1 child, Andrew Kenneth Lee. BA in English, Clinch Valley Coll., 1992. Cert. tchr. English, secondary sch., Va. Instr. English J.J. Kelly H.S., Wise, Va., 1992-93; English, speech and drama instr. Ervinton H.S., Nora, Va., 1993—; forensic and drama coach Ervinton H.S., Nora, 1993—; co-chair media cluster writing com., tech. prep comm. arts S.W. Va. C.C. Consortium, Richlands, 1994—; mem. tech. com. Dickenson County Sch. System, Clintwood, Va., 1994; facilitator for reading to learn in-svc. project Dickenson County Schs., 1995. Dir. Miss EHS Pageant, 1994, 95, 96; admissions/pub. rels. asst. SVCC, 1995. Mem. NEA, Dickenson County Edn. Assn. Republican. Methodist. Home: Rt HC05 Box 427 Coeburn VA 24230 Office: Ervinton HS PO Box 406 Nora VA 24272

STANLEY, ELLEN MAY, historian, consultant; b. Dighton, Kans., Feb. 3, 1921; d. Delmar Orange and Lena May (Bobb) Durr; m. Max Neal Stanley, Nov. 5, 1939; children: Ann Y. Stanley Epps, Janet M. Stanley Horsky, Gail L. Stanley Peck, Kenneth D., Neal M., Mary E. Stanley McEniry. BA in English and Journalism, Ft. Hays (Kans.) State U., 1972, MA in History, 1984. Pvt. practice local/state historian, cons., writer local history Dighton, 1973—, cons. genealogy, 1980—; vice chmn. State Preservation Bd. Rev., Kans., 1980-87; area rep. Kans. State Mus. Assn., 1978-84. Author: Early Lane County History: 12,000 B.C.—A.D. 1884, 1993 (cert. of commendation Am. Assn. State and Local History), Cowboy Josh: Adventures of a Real Cowboy, 1996; contbr. articles to profl. jours. Precinct woman com. Alamota Township, Kans., 1962-86; mem. Dem. State Affirmative Action Com., 1975. Recipient hon. mention for photography Ann. Christian Arts Festival, 1974, Artist of Month award Dane G. Hansen Mus., 1975. Mem. Kans. State Hist. Soc. (pres. 1990-91), Lane County Hist. Soc. (sec. 1970-78). Methodist. Home: 100 N 4th Dighton KS 67839 Office: 116 E Long St Dighton KS 67839

STANLEY, FRANCES LUCILLE, human resources manager, fire commissioner; b. Bklyn.; d. Vito C. and Rose Lamia; m. Gilbert James Stanley, Oct. 28, 1962 (dec. Aug. 1984). Student, CCNY, 1967; hon., Drake Bus. Sch., N.Y.C., 1980. Adminstrv. asst. N.Y. Hosp./Cornell Med. Ctr., N.Y.C., 1957-59; personnel asst. Inst. Muscle Disease, MDA, N.Y.C., 1959-62; sr. personnel asst., human resources Meml. Sloan-Kettering Cancer Ctr., N.Y.C., 1962-88; owner My Mother's Cookies, Hartsdale, N.Y., 1990—. Composer, singer Off-Broadway musical Collateral, 1995; USO soloist, N.Y.C., 1960's; poetry pub. (anthology) The Voice Within, 1996. Fire Commr. (elected) Hartsdale Fire Dist., 1984—; fundraiser N.Y. Heart Assn., United Cerebral Palsy, N.Y. Assn. for the Blind, MDA; mem. Ann. Appeal com. Soc. Meml. Sloan-Kettering Cancer Ctr., including orgn. and direction of choral group to sing for patients, 1963-73, also entertaining N.Y. Hosp. Cornell Med. Ctr. and The Hosp. for Special Surgery, N.Y.C., 1972. Mem. Antique Automobile Club of Am., Assn. Fire Dists. County of Westchester (N.Y.), Westchester County Assn. Fire Chiefs. Roman Catholic. Home: 64 Pinewood Rd Hartsdale NY 10530

STANLEY, IVY V., motel owner; b. Syracuse, N.Y., Mar. 3, 1949; d. Richard G. and Charlett M. (Coorer) Dow; m. Samuel T., James T., Richard S., Mark S., Marzella C. Self-employed sec. Peabody, Mass., 1968-96; motel owner and mgr. Sams Pl. Motel, Attleboro, Mass., 1996—. Vol. United Way, Attleboro. Home and Office: 46 Washington St South Attleboro MA 02703

STANLEY, KAREN FRANCINE MARY LESNIEWSKI, human resources professional; b. Amsterdam, N.Y., Oct. 10, 1948; d. Francis Raymond and Genievive Mary (Klementowski) Lesniewski; m. Mark Anthony Stanley, Nov. 11, 1972. BA, Alliance Coll., 1970; MA, The Coll. St. Rose, 1976, CAS, 1987. English tchr. Middle Country Sch., Centereach, N.Y., 1970-71; English and social studies tchr. Mt. Carmel, Gloversville, N.Y., 1971-72; English tchr. Bishop Scully H.S., Amsterdam, 1972-80, Shenendehowa Ctrl., Clifton Park, N.Y., 1980-82; English tchr., head dept. Broadalbin (N.Y.) Ctrl. Sch., 1982-86; adminstrv. intern Saratoga Springs (N.Y.) City Sch. Dist., 1986-87, dir. for human resource svcs., 1987—; bd. dirs. N.Y. State Staff Devel. Coun., 1990-92. Mem. Am. Soc. for Human Resource Mgrs., N.Y. State Assn. Women Adminstrs., Nat. Assn. Schs., Colls. and Univs., Nat. Assn. Ednl. Negotiators, Soroptimist Internat. (sec. Saratoga County chpt. 1991-92, del. Dist. I 1992-93, 96-97, asst. treas. 1994-95, treas. 1995-96), Ednl. Adminstrn. Assn./Coll. St. Rose (bd. dirs., sec. 1986-89, pres. 1989-92). Republican. Roman Catholic. Office: Saratoga Springs City Schs 5 Wells St Saratoga Springs NY 12866-1205

STANLEY, KAREN GWENEITH, vocational nurse; b. Malvern, Ark., Oct. 4, 1943; d. Raybon and Gwendolyn (Smith) Kindrick; m. Lewis Frank Stanley, Aug. 31, 1962; children: Mark Steven, Catherine Leigh, James Lawson. Cert. vocat. nurse, Med. Arts Clinic Hosp., 1964; student, Jefferson County C.C., Louisville, 1973. Surg. scrub tech. Louisville Gen. Hosp.; vocat. nurse Med. Arts Clinic Hosp., Big Spring, Tex., 1965, So. Clinic, Texarkana, Tex., 1965-66, Rome (N.Y.) City Hosp., 1966-67, Geriat. Hosp., Louisville, 1969, St.'s Mary and Elizabeth Hosp., Louisville, 1971-76, Louisville Gen. Hosp., 1976-78, Quality Care Nursing Svc., Louisville, 1978-79, Wesley Manor Nursing Home, Louisville, 1979-84, Collom and Carney Clinic, Texarkana, 1984—. Mem. NOW. Democrat. Humanist.

STANLEY, LANETT LORRAINE, state legislator; b. Atlanta, Nov. 5, 1962; d. Archie and Ethel Francis (Dixon) S. BS, U. Tenn., 1985; postgrad., Carver Bible Coll., Atlanta, 1991—. Children's reporter Sta. WXIA-TV, Atlanta, 1979-80; model, sales clk. Rich's Dept. Store, Atlanta, 1979-83; copy clk. Knoxville (Tenn.) Jour., 1984-85; reporter Atlanta Daily World, 1986; intern Sta. WTBS-TV, Atlanta, 1986; adminstrv. aide Bd. Commrs. Fulton County, Atlanta, 1986-87; mem., sec to the caucus Ga. Ho. of Reps., Atlanta, 1987—; ind. mktg. cons., 1991—; mem. Nat. and Ga. Legis. Black Caucus, 1987. Bd. dirs. West End Med. Ctrs., Inc., 1988—, Southside Youth Athletic Acad. Assn., 1991—. Democrat. Baptist. Office: Ga Gen Assembly Ga State Capitol Atlanta GA 30318*

STANLEY, MARGARET KING, performing arts administrator; b. San Antonio, Tex., Dec. 11, 1929; d. Creston Alexander and Margaret (Haymore) King; children: Torrey Margaret, Jean Cullen. Student, Mary Baldwin Coll., 1948-50; BA, U. Tex., Austin, 1952; MA, Incarnate Word Coll., 1959. Tchg. cert. 1953. Elem. tchr. San Antonio Ind. Sch. Dist., 1953-54, 55-56, Arlington County Schs., Va., 1954-55, Ft. Sam Houston Schs., San Antonio, 1955-57; art, art history tchr. St. Pius X Sch., San Antonio, 1959-60; tchr. Trinity U., 1963-65; designer-mfr., owner CrisStan Clothes, Inc., San Antonio, 1967-73; founder, exec. dir. San Antonio Performing Arts Assn., 1976-92, founder Arts Council of San Antonio, 1962; founding chmn. Joffrey Workshop, San Antonio, 1979; originator, founding chairwoman Student Music Fair, San Antonio, 1963; radio program host On Stage, San Antonio, 1983—. Originator of the idea for a new ballet created for the City of San Antonio, "Jamboree," commd. from the Joffrey Ballet, world premiere in San Antonio, 1984. Pres. San Antonio Symphony League, 1971-74; v.p. Arts Council of San Antonio, 1975; bd. govs. Artists Alliance of San Antonio, 1982; v.p. San Antonio Opera Guild, 1974-76, founder Early Music Festival, San Antonio, 1990; mem. adv. bd. Hertzberg Circus Mus. Recipient Outstanding Tchr. award Arlington County Sch. Dist., 1954, Today's Woman award San Antonio Light Newspaper, 1980, Woman of Yr. in Arts award San Antonio Express News, 1983, Emily Smith award for outstanding alumni Mary Baldwin Coll., 1973, Erasmus medal The Dutch Consulate, 1992, Mary Baldwin Sesquicentennial medallion, 1992; named to Women's Hall of Fame, San Antonio, 1984, Disting. Alumnae, St. Mary's Hall, 1995; teaching fellow Trinity U., San Antonio, 1964-66. Mem. Internat. Soc. for the Performing Arts (regional rep. 1982-85, bd. dirs. 1991—), Met. Opera Nat. Coun., Assn. Performing Arts Presenters, Women in Comm. (Headliner award 1982, San Antonio chpt.), Jr. League of San Antonio, Battle of Flowers Assn., S.W. Performing Arts Presenters (chmn. 1988-92). Avocations: traveling, reading.

STANLEY, MARLYSE REED, horse breeder; b. Fairmont, Minn., Sept. 19, 1934; d. Glenn Orson and Lura Mabel (Ross) Reed; m. James Arthur Stapleton, 1956 (div. 1976); 1 child, Elisabeth Katharene; m. John David Stanley, Oct. 22, 1982. BA, U. Minn., 1957. Registered breeder Arabian horses in Spain, 1976-94. Chmn. bd. dirs. Sitting Rock Spanish Arabians, Inc., Greensboro, N.C., 1978-81; pres. Sitting Rock Spanish Arabians, Inc., Hollister, Calif., 1981-91, Stanley Ranch, Yerington, Nev., 1991—; bd. dirs. Glenn Reed Tire Co., Fairmont, Minn. Author Arabian hunter/jumper rules Am. Horse Shows Assn.; contbr. articles to horse jours. Named Palomino Queen of Minn., 1951, Miss Fairmont, 1954, Miss Minn., 1955. Mem. AAUW, Arabian Horse Registry Am., Internat. Arabian Assn. (bd. dirs. region 10, Minn. and Wis. 1973-76, nat. chmn. hunter-jumper com. 1976-81), Minn. Arabian Assn. (bd. dirs. 1972-75), Am. Paint Horse Assn. (nat. bd. dirs. 1967-70), Assn. Española de Criadores de Caballos Arabes (Spain), World Arabian Horse Assn., Alpha Xi Delta. Republican. Episcopalian.

STANLEY, MELINDA LOUISE, mental health nurse, oncology researcher; b. Tyler, Tex., July 13, 1971; d. Jerry Luther and Joyce Louise (Kinard) S. ADN, Tyler Jr. Coll., 1992; BSN magna cum laude, U. Tex., Tyler, 1995, postgrad., 1995—. RN, Tex. Staff nurse East Tex. Med. Ctr. Hosp., Tyler, 1991-92, Tyler Rehab. Hosp., 1993-96, East Tex. Med. Ctr. Behavioral Health, Tyler, 1996—; presenter, lectr. on cmty. cancer awareness, prevention of breast cancer, Tyler, 1994—. Mem. ANA, Tex. Nurses Assn., Profl. Women's Assn., U. Tex. Alumni Assn., Sigma Theta Tau (Alpha Chi Honor Soc.).

STANLEY, PAMELA AURELIA, state legislator; b. Mar. 13, 1956; 2 children. Student, Ga. Tech., Ga. State, Morris Brown Coll. Former clk. U.S. Postal Svc.; mem. Ga. Ho. of Reps., 1992—; mem. game, fish & parks, ins. and state planning and cmty. affairs coms. Democrat. Baptist. Home: 706 Foundry St NW Atlanta GA 30314-4004 Office: Ga Ho of Reps 512 Legislative Office Bldg Atlanta GA 30334

STANLEY, PATRICIA GRADY, rural letter carrier; b. Halls, Tenn., Nov. 23, 1945; d. Daniel Lee and Hester E. (Rhoads) Grady; m. Mack Bryant Stanley, Aug. 27, 1962; 1 child, Alesia. Student, Dyersburg (Tenn.) State Coll., 1971, 84. From machine operator to payroll clk. Allen-Stone Boxes Inc., Halls, 1967-71; sec., bookkeeper Lauderdale County Bd. Edn., Halls, 1971-85; rural carrier substitute U.S. Postal Svc., Halls, 1980-85, rural letter carrier, 1985—. Various offices Halls First United Meth. Ch., 1955—. Mem. Tenn Rural Letter Carriers (chmn. bd. 1995, sec. 1994), West Tenn. Rural Letter Carriers, Dyersburg Lions Coub (pub. rels. chair 1992—). Democrat. Home: 311 Oakleigh Dr Dyersburg TN 38024-5259 Office: US Postal Svc 215 Sharp St Halls TN 38040-9998

STANLEY, PAULA HELEN, counseling educator, psychotherapist; b. Whiteville, N.C., May 22, 1952; d. Rhodes Brooks Stanley and Lenora Helen (Hardie) Stanley Campbell. AA in Liberal Arts, Southeastern Community Coll., Whiteville, 1972; BA in Psychology, Appalachian State U., 1974, MA in Counseling, 1975; PhD in Counseling, U. N.C., Greensboro, 1991. Nat. cert. counselor; lic. profl. counselor, Va. Instr. psychology Surry Community Coll., Dobson, N.C., 1975-87; teaching and rsch. asst. U. N.C., 1987-91; asst. prof. counseling Radford (Va.) U., 1991-95, assoc. prof., 1995—. Co-author: Invitational Teaching, Learning and Living, 1991, The Inviting School Treasury, 1994; editor Invitational Edn. Forum newsletter, 1988—, Current Trends newsletter; assoc. editor Chi Sigma Iota newsletter, 1989—; mem. editl. bd. Jour. Humanistic Edn. and Devel. Mem. ACA, VCA, AERA, AACD, Internat. Alliance for Invitational Edn. (exec. sec. 1988-91, membership chmn. 1991—), Chi Sigma Iota (fellow 1989). Office: Radford U Dept Counselor Edn PO Box 6994 Radford VA 24142

STANLEY, SADIE L., computer science educator; b. Houston. BS in Math., Lamar U., 1962; MS in Mgmt. Computer Sys., Houston Bapt. U., 1993. Programmer IBM, Houston, 1962-69, mgr. projects, 1970-78, sales rep., 1979-92; instr. Tex. Luth. Coll., Seguin, 1993—; pres. Stanley Assocs. Consulting, Inc., Sequin, 1992. Mem. ASTD, Assn. Quality and Participation (Alamo chpt. dir. 1993).

STANLEY, SHIRLEY DAVIS, artist; b. Mt. Vernon, N.Y., Dec. 5, 1929; d. Walter Thompson and Elsie Viola (Lumpp) Davis; m. Charles B. Coble Jr., June 11, 1951 (div. 1968); children: Jennifer Susan Farmer, Charles B. Coble III; m. Marvin M. Stanley, Dec. 18, 1983 (dec.). BA in Home Econs. and Gen. Sci., Greensboro Coll., 1951; grad., Real Estate Inst., 1962. Tchr. Dryher H.S., Columbia, S.C., 1951-52, Haw River (N.C.) Sch., 1954-56, Alexander Wilson Sch., Graham, N.C., 1957-58; guest essayist for news Mebane (N.C.) Enterprise, 1955-56; pres. Shirley, Inc., Burlington, N.C., 1962-94; artist, 1956—. One woman show Art Gallery Originals, Winston-Salem, 1976, Olive Garden Gallery, 21st Century Gallery, Williamsburg, Va., numerous galleries in Fla., N.C. Bd. dirs. Girl Scouts Am., Burlington, 1961; life mem. Rep. Inner Cir., Washington, 1990—; active Salvation Army; vol. fund raiser Physicians for Peace; com. mem. York County Rep. Party, 1995; vol. disaster & blood banks ARC, 1990—; founding mem. Am. Air Force Mus. Recipient Rep. Medal of Freedom, 1994. Mem. AAUW, Am. Watercolor Soc. (assoc.), Va. Watercolor Soc., Nat. Soc. Amateur Dancers, Sierra Club, Williamsburg Bibliophiles. Episcopalian. Home and Studio: 103 Little John Rd Williamsburg VA 23185-4907

STANLEY-SMITH, LISA ANN, public relations specialist; b. Concord, N.H., Jan. 23, 1965; d. Richard Arnold and Marion Laura (Barrett) S.; m. David A. Smith II, Apr. 29, 1989. BA, Pembroke (N.C.) State U., 1986, M in English Edn., 1990. Asst. mgr. Nautilus Conditioning Ctr., Lumberton, N.C., 1983-86; pub. rels. specialist, bd. dirs. Sta. WECT-TV, Lumberton, 1986-91; legis. producer, reporter N.C. Ctr. for Pub. TV, 1991; mgr., mktg. dir. Biggs Park Mall, 1991-95; assoc. exec. dir. Lumberton Area C. of C. and Visitor's Bur., 1996—; bd. dirs. Sta. WECT-TV Internship Program, Lumberton; pub. speaker, 1987—. Bd. dirs. ARC, Lumberton, 1988—. Mem. Zeta Tau Alpha (pres. 1987). Democrat. Roman Catholic. Home: 4140 Manchester Ln Lumberton NC 28358-9057

STANSBERRY, JUDITH OVERTON, mental health counselor, educator; b. Franlinville, N.Y., Apr. 5, 1947; d. Wilson Burney and Miriam Emily (Card) Overton; m. Tony Lee Stansberry, Sr., may 10, 1968 (div. 1982); Tony Lee, Jr., Judith Christa. BA, U. Tenn., 1988, MS, 1993. Cert. Nat. Bd. for Cert. Counselors, Spl. in Criminal Justice. Gen. med. tech. Morristown (Tenn.) Hamblen Hosp., 1972-76; med. tech blood bank Fort Sanders Regional Med. Ctr., Knoxville, 1976-82, E. Tenn. Children's Hosp., Knoxville, 1982-85; med. tech. supr. Blount Meml. Hosp., Maryville, Tenn., 1985-92; case mgr. Knox County Sherriff, Knoxville, 1992-93; residential counselor Reflection Treatment Agy., Knoxville, 1993-94; adj. faculty U. Tenn., Knoxville, 1995; mental health coord. Cmty. Alterative to Prison, Knoxville, 1993—. Coord. of Cedar Mission St. Marks United Meth. Ch., Lakeshore Mental Hosp., Knoxville, 1994-95, Tenn. Vol. Adv. Bd., 1995—. Mem. Am. Counseling Assn., Assn. of Spl. in Group Work, Tenn. Conf. of Social Welfare, Tenn. Cmty. Correction Assn., Nat. Assn. of Forensic Counselors. Presbyterian. Home: 1029 Tranquilla Dr Knoxville TN 37919 Office: Cmty Alternatives to Prison Program 1209 Euclid Ave Knoxville TN 37921-6732

STANTON, CAROL MARIE, special education educator; b. Casper, Wyo., Dec. 12, 1953; d. Ronald Lee and Mina Jo (Jones) Schooler; div.; children: Andrew, Lucian, Rita. BS in Motion Pictures, U. Miami, 1992, MS in Spl. Edn., 1993. Cert. tchr., Fla. Tchr. learning disabilities Dade County Pub. Schs., Miami, Fla., 1993-94; tchr. pre-kindergarten Bay County, Youngstown, Fla., 1994-96; mem. tech. com. School-Waller Elem., Youngstown. Mem. Phi Kappa Phi, Phi Lambda Pi. Home: 660 Stanton Dr Chipley FL 32428

STANTON, ELIZABETH MYNATT, primary education educator; b. Florence, S.C., Nov. 9, 1949; d. George Rubin and Frances Elizabeth (Wylie) Mynatt; m. Carson Michael Stanton, Oct. 26, 1968; children: Carson Michael Jr., Bethany Lynne. Student, U. Tenn., 1967-71; BS, Ga. State U., 1973; MEd, West Ga. Coll., 1986. Tchr. grade 2 Cobb County Sch. Dist., Marietta, Ga., 1973-77; tchr. grades kindergarten and 1 Cobb County Sch. Dist., Marietta, 1977-88; tchr. grade 1 Baldwin County Sch. Dist., Milledgeville, Ga., 1988-90, Clarke County Sch. Dist., Athens, Ga., 1990-95; tchr. grade 2 Westwood Sch., Dalton, Ga.; math. cons. Ga. Pub. TV, 1995-96; vis. com. mem. So. Assn. Colls. and Schs., 1988, 90, 91; textbook adv. com. math. Ga. Dept. Edn., Atlanta, 1994; curriculum writing team The Atlanta (Ga.) Com. for the Olympic Games, 1994. Recipient Presdl. award for excellence in math. tchg. NSF, 1993. Mem. Nat. Coun. Tchrs. of Math., Ga. Coun. Tchrs. Math. (Ga. math.-sci. roundtable award 1994, 95). Methodist. Home: 406 Rosewood Ln Cartersville GA 30120 Office: Westwood Sch Dalton GA 30721

STANTON, JEANNE FRANCES, retired lawyer; b. Vicksburg, Miss., Jan. 22, 1920; d. John Francis and Hazel (Mitchell) S.; student George Washington U., 1938-39, BA, U. Cin., 1940; JD, Salmon P. Chase Coll. Law, 1954. Admitted to Ohio bar, 1954; chief clk. Selective Svc. Bd., Cin., 1940-43; instr. USAAF Tech. Schs., Biloxi, Miss., 1943-44; with Procter & Gamble, Cin., 1945-84, legal asst., 1952-54, head advt. svcs. sect. legal div., trade practices dept., 1954-73, mgr. advt. svcs., legal div., 1973-84, ret., 1954. Team capt. Community Chest Cin., 1983; mem. ann. meeting com. Archaeol. Inst. Am., 1983; trustee, asst. corr. sec., statutory agt. Friends of Bronze Age Archaeology in the Aegean area, 1987—. Mem. ABA (chmn. subcom. D of com. 307 copyright sect. 1987-88, 89, 90), Ohio Bar Assn. (chmn. uniform state laws com. 1968-70), Cin. Bar Assn. (sec. law day com. 1965-66, chmn. com. on preservation hist. documents 1968-71), Vicksburg and Warren County Hist. Soc, Cin. Hist. Soc., Intercontinental Biog. Assn., Lawyers Club Cin. (exec. com. 1979—, pres. 1983), Cin. Women Lawyers (treas. 1958-59, nominating com. 1976), Terrace Park Country Club. Personal philosophy: Most people are good and honest. If a person does the honorable thing, that is its own reward. Home: 2302 Easthill Ave Cincinnati OH 45208-2608

STANTON, SARA BAUMGARDNER, retired secondary school educator; b. Johnstown, Pa., Sept. 11, 1930; d. Emmanuel Boyd and Ethel Leora (Shaffer) Baumgardner; m. George Welles Stanton, June 20, 1953; children: David Mark, Frederick George. BS in Edn., Bucknell U., 1952. Tchr. Adams-Summerhill High Sch., Sidman, Pa., 1952-53, Waymart (Pa.) High Sch., 1953-55, Honesdale (Pa.) High Sch., 1955-57; substitute tchr. Wayne County Sch. Dist., 1957-77; tchr. Honesdale High Sch., 1977-90; ret., 1990; leadership instr. Pa. Assn. Hosp. Auxs., Harrisburg, Pa., 1976—. Den mother Cub Pack 104, 1965-69; bd. dirs. Health Systems Agy., Wilkes-Barre, Pa., 1983-86, Pa. State U.-Scranton Campus, 1977-85, Wayne County Meml. Hosp., Honesdale, 1974-86. Recipient Leader's Fellowship award Nat. Bd. YMCA, 1964, B'nai B'rith Citizenship Citation, 1974 (co-recipient with husband). Mem. AAUW (br. pres. 1980-81), Pa. Assn. Hosp. Auxs. (mem. leadership tng. team 1975-80, 91—, chmn. state ann. conv. 1985, pres. 1986-88), Pa. Assn. Sch. Retirees, Hosp. Assn. Pa. (mem. cmty. concerns com. 1974-75, ex officio 1986-88), Wayne County Hist. Soc. (bd. dirs. 1991-92, 95-99, sec. 1995-96), Woman's Club Honesdale (pres. 1958-60). Republican. Methodist. Home: 1512 West St Honesdale PA 18431-1764

STANTON, SUSAN M., retail executive. Pres., COO Payless Cashways, Inc., Kansas City, Mo., 1994—. Office: Payless Cashways Inc Box 419466 2300 Main St Kansas City MO 64108*

STAPF, GLENDA FAY, nursing educator; b. Antlers, Okla., Dec. 11, 1948; d. Aubrey Ellis Rhine and Edith Marie Hawkins; m. James Lowell Stapf, Jan. 29, 1972; children: Charvet Stoneking Stapf, Troy Stapf. BSN in Pub. Health Nursing, Holy Names Coll., 1991; MSN in Advance Practice High Risk Populations, Samuel Merritt Coll., 1994. RN, Calif.; cert. school tchr., Calif. Educator New Haven Unified, Union City, Calif., 1982—; pub. health nurse Cmty. Health Ctr., Hayward, 1990-91. CPR-First Aid instr. ARC, Union City, 1985—; mem. Calif. Regional Occupl. Program, 1990—; vol.-nurse San Jose (Calif.) Sch. Health Adminstrn. Office, 1990-91, San Jose Health Ctr., 1993-94. Mem. Calif. Assn. Health Career Educators, Sigma Theta Tau. Democrat. Office: James Logan High Sch 1800 H St Union City CA 94587-3321

STAPLES, ALICE MARIE, elementary education educator; b. Onsted, Mich., Aug. 26, 1935; d. Faye Walter and Bernice Belle (Matthews) Barrows; m. Charles Albert Staples, Jr., Mar. 8, 1952; children: Linda Joan Staples Bird, Patricia Suzanne Staples Buwalda. BS in Edn., Siena Heights Coll., Adrian, Mich., 1971, MA in Edn., 1975; student in spl. edn., U. Toledo, 1988. Cert. tchr., Mich. Elementary sch. tchr. Tecumseh (Mich.) Pub. Schs., 1971—. Chair, diaconate First Bapt. Ch., Tecumseh, 1994—, adult Sunday Sch. instr., 1990—. Mem. Tecumseh Edn. Assn. (nom. com. 1980-95), Lenawee Reading Assn. (pres., v.p., sec. 1972-80), Phi Delta Kappa (nom. com. 1989). American Baptist. Home: 1202 Shady Lane Tecumseh MI 49286

STAPLES, MAVIS, singer; b. Chgo., 1940; d. Roebuck "Pops" and Oceloa S. Singer Staple Singers, 1951—; represented by United, 1954, Vee Jay Label, 1956, CBS/Epic, 1964, Stax, 1968, Curtom, 1975; opened for Prince's overseas tour, 1990; provided back-up vocals for Ray Charles, Kenny Loggins, Marty Stuart and others. Albums include Only for the Lonely, 1970. Single "Uncloudy Day" reached number one on gospel charts; single "I'll Take you There" reached number one on gospel and rythym and blues charts, 1993. Office: Paisley Park Records 1999 Ave of the Stars Ste 3150 Los Angeles CA 90067*

STAPLETON, CLAUDIA ANN, city official; b. Memphis, July 14, 1947; m. Mark Phillip Stapleton, Sept. 18, 1985. Student, Tex. Tech. U., 1976-77; AS, Amarillo Coll., 1990; student, West Tex. A&M U., 1990—. Code enforcement officer City of Lubbock, Tex., 1975-85; owner, operator Claudia Stapleton Consulting, Amarillo, Tex., 1985—; code enforcement officer City of Amarillo, 1990—; cons. in field. Mem. NAFE, Nat. Elec. Sign Assn., Tex. Assn. Legal Secs., Tex. Heritage, Am. Bus. Women's Assn., Code Enforcement Assn. of Tex. (2d v.p.), Beta Sigma Phi. Republican. Methodist. Home: 3321 Lenwood Dr Amarillo TX 79109-3345 Office: City of Amarillo 509 E 7th Ave Amarillo TX 79101-2539

STAPLETON, JEAN (JEANNE MURRAY), actress; b. N.Y.C.; d. Joseph E. and Marie (Stapleton) Murray; m. William H. Putch (dec.); 2 children. Student, Hunter Coll., N.Y.C., Am. Apprentice Theatre, Am. Actors Co., Am. Theatre Wing; student with, Harold Clurman; LHD (hon.), Emerson Coll.; hon. degree, Hood Coll., Monmouth Coll. Opera debut in Candide with Balt. Opera Co.; appeared in The Italian Lesson with Balt. Opera; first N.Y. stage role in The Corn is Green, Equity Library Theatre; starred as mother in Am. Gothic, Circle-in-the-Sq.; Broadway debut with Judith Anderson In The Summer House; also appeared on Broadway in Damn Yankees, Bells Are Ringing, Juno, Rhinoceros and Funny Girl; first major break in comic ingenue role as Myrtle Mae with Frank Fay in Harvey on-tour; played with nat. tour of Come Back, Little Sheba starring Shirley Booth; starred in tour of Morning's at Seven, The Show-Off, Daisy Mayme; appeared in motion pictures including Damn Yankees, 1958, Bells Are Ringin, 1960, Up the Down Staircase, 1967, Cold Turkey, 1971, The Buddy System, 1984, Klute; appeared in numerous TV shows including Studio One, Naked City, Armstrong Circle Theatre, The Defenders, Jackie Gleason show, PBS-TV appearances Grown-ups, Trying Shakespeare Co. D.C., 1994, Night Seasons, Signature Theatre N.Y., 1994, Blithe Spirit, Costa Mesa, Calif.; guest star Grace Underfire (Emmy nomination); stepmother in N.Y.C. Opera's Cinderella, 1995. U.S. commr. to Internat. Woman's Yr. Commn. and Nat. Conf. Women, Houston, 1977; bd. dirs. Women's Rsch. and Edn. Inst.; trustee Actors' Fund Am. Recipient Emmy award for best performance in comedy series 1970-71, 71-72, 78, Golden Globe awards Hollywood Fgn. Press Assn. 1972, 73, Obie award, 1990. Mem. AFTRA, SAG, Actors Equity Assn. Office: care Bauman & Hiller 5757 Wilshire Blvd Los Angeles CA 90036*

STAPLETON, JEAN, journalism educator; b. Albuquerque, June 24, 1942; d. James L. and Mary (Behrman) S.; m. John Clegg, Apr. 15, 1965 (dec. Sept. 1972); m. Richard Bright, Jan. 13, 1973 (div. 1985); children: Lynn, Paul; m. William Walter Farrah, Nov. 9, 1996. BA, U. N.Mex., 1964; MS in Journalism, Northwestern U., 1968. Reporter Glenview (Ill.) Announcements, 1967-68, Angeles Mesa News Advertiser, L.A., 1968-69, City News Svc., Radio News West, L.A., 1969-71; press sec. polit. campaign, 1972; instr. journalism East L.A. Coll., 1973-75, prof., dept. chair, 1975—. Author: Equal Marriage, 1975, Equal Dating, 1979; co-editor Star, Am. Yankee Assn., 1987-88. Mem. NOW (pres. L.A. chpt. 1973-74), Women in Comm., Soc. Profl. Journalists, Ninety Nines. Democrat. Methodist. Home: 3232 Philo St Los Angeles CA 90064-4719 Office: East LA Coll 1301 Avenida Cesar Chavez Monterey Park CA 91754-6001

STAPLETON, KATHARINE HALL (KATIE STAPLETON), food broadcaster, author; b. Kansas City, Mo., Oct. 29, 1919; d. William Mabin and Katharine (Hall) Foster; m. Benjamin Franklin Stapleton, June 20, 1942; children: Benjamin Franklin, III, Craig Roberts, Katharine Hall. BA, Vassar Coll., 1941. Cookbook reviewer Denver Post, 1974-84; producer, writer, host On the Front Burner, daily radio program Sta. KOA-CBS, Denver, 1976 79, Sta. WGN, Portland, Maine, 1979-81, Cooking with Katie, live one-hour weekly, Sta. KOA, 1979-88; guest broadcaster Geneva Radio, 1974, London Broadcasting Corp., 1981, 82; tour leader culinaries to Britain, France and Switzerland, 1978-85. Eng., 1978. Chmn. women's div. United Fund, 1955-56; founder, chmn. Denver Debutante Ball, 1956, 57; hon. chmn. Nat. Travelers Aid Assn., 1952-56, 93-96; commr. Denver Centennial Authority, 1958-60; trustee Washington Cathedral, regional v.p., 1967-73; mem. world service council YWCA, 1961-87; trustee, Colo. Women's Coll., 1975-80; sole trustee Harmes C. Fishback Found. Decorated chevalier de L'Etoile Noire (France); recipient People-to-People citation, 1960, 66, Beautiful Activist award Altrusa Club, 1972, Gran Skillet award Colo./Wyo. Restaurant Assn., 1981, Humanitarian of Yr. award Arthritis Found., 1995, Disting. Woman of Yr. award Rocky Mountain News, 1996; named Chevalier du Tastevin, 1989, Outstanding Vol. Fundraiser Nat. Philanthropy Day, 1995, Disting. Woman of Yr., Rocky Mountain News. Republican. Episcopalian. Clubs: Denver Country, Denver. Author: Denver Delicious, 1980, 3d. edit., 1983; High Notes, 1984. Home: 8 Village Rd Cherry Hills Village CO 80110

STAPLETON, MAUREEN, actress; b. Troy, N.Y., June 21, 1925; d. John P. and Irene (Walsh) S.; m. Max Allentuck, July 1949 (div. Feb. 1959); children: Daniel, Katharine; m. David Rayfiel, July, 1963 (div.). Student, Siena Coll, 1943. Debut in Playboy of the Western World, 1946; toured with Barretts of Wimpole Street, 1947; plays include Anthony and Cleopatra, 1947, Detective Story, The Bird Cage, Rose Tattoo, 1950-51, The Sea Gull, Orpheus Descending, The Cold Wind and the Warm, 1959, Toys in the Attic, 1960-61, Plaza Suite, 1969, The Gingerbread Lady, 1970 (Tony award 1970), 27 Wagons Full of Cotton, Country Girl, 1972, Secret Affairs of Mildred Wild, 1972, The Gin Game, 1977-78, The Little Foxes, 1981; motion pictures include Lonely Hearts, 1959, The Fugitive Kind, 1960, A View from the Bridge, 1962, Bye Bye Birdie, 1963, Trilogy, 1969, Airport, 1970, Plaza Suite, 1971, Interiors, 1978, The Runner Stumbles, 1979, Reds, 1981 (Oscar award as best supporting actress), The Fan, 1981, On the Right Track, 1981, The Electric Grandmother, 1982, Mother's Day, 1984, Johnny Dangerously, 1984, Cocoon, 1985, The Money Pit, 1986, Nuts, 1987, Made in Heaven, 1987, Cocoon: The Return, 1990, Passed Away, 1992, Trading Mom, 1994, The Last Good Time, 1995; TV films include Tell Me Where It Hurts, 1974, Cat On a Hot Tin Roof, 1976, All the King's Men, 1958, For Whom the Bell Tolls, 1959, Save Me a Place at Forest Lawn, 1966, Mirror, Mirror, Off the Wall, 1969, Queen of the Stardust Ballroom, 1975, The Gathering, 1977, Part II, 1979, Letters From Frank, 1979, Little Gloria ... Happy at Last, 1982, Sentimental Journey, 1984, Private Sessions, 1985, Liberace: Behind the Music, 1988, Last Wish, 1992, Miss Rose White, 1992. Recipient Nat. Inst. Arts and Letters award, 1969. *

STAPP, OLIVIA BREWER, opera singer; b. N.Y.C., May 31, 1940; d. Henry and Jean Brewer; m. Henry Stapp III; 1 child, Henry. BA, Wagner Coll; studied with, Marjorie Mayer Steen, Ettore Campogalliani, Rodolfo Ricci and Oren Brown; Dr. honoris causa, Wagner Coll., 1988. Appeared as leading soprano in Truandot, Idomeneo at La Scala, Milano; Tosca, Elektra, Macbeth, Tabarro at Met. Opera, N.Y.C.; Erani, Macbeth, Il Tabarro at Liceo Barcelona; Macbeth, Madame Butterfly, Tosca, Aida, Fanciulla del

West, Lohengrin at Deutche Oper Berlin; Vespre Sciciliani at Grand Theater, Geneva; Nabucco, Attila, Macbeth at Zurich Oper; Salome at The Colon Theater, Buenos Aires; Cavalleria Rusticana, Anna Bolena, Tosca, Nabucco at San Francisco; Elektra Cavalleria Rusticana at Vienna Staatsoper; Idameneo at Munich Staatsoper; Carmen, The Consul, Ariadne auf Naxos, Anna Bolena, Roberto Deveraux, Cavalleria Rusticana at City Opera, N.Y.C.; Lady Macbeth, Nabucco, Turandot at Hamburg Staatsoper; Fanciulla el West, Aida, Nabucco, Turandot at the Arena de Verona; Turandot at Seoul, Korea; Turandot in N.H.K. Tokyo; Norma in Winnipeg, Edmonto, Montreal and Vancouver, Can.; Lady Macbeth in Chatelet Theater, Paris, others. Recipient Puccini award Vissi d'Arde, 1991; Fulbright scholar. Address: Columbia Artist Mgmt Inc Zemsky Green Div 165 W 57th St New York NY 10019-2201*

STAR, GLORIA GAY, astrologer, writer, educator, consultant; b. Abilene, Tex., Sept. 6, 1948; d. Jess Jerl and Frances Louise (Watts) Franklin; m. Richard Gordon Brownd, July 1967 (div. 1974); 1 child, Taletha Brownd; m. Jack Miller, Aug. 1980 (div. Mar. 1983); 1 child, Christopher Miller; m. Richard H. Roess, Jan. 25, 1991. Student, N.W. Tex. Hosp. Sch. Nursing, 1968-69, West Tex. State U., 1967-70, U. Okla., 1975-80. Rsch. assoc. dept. family practice Okla. U. Heath Sci. Ctr., Oklahoma City, 1971-76, ednl. liaison dept. family practice, 1976-78; owner/mgr. The Earth Natural Foods, Norman, Okla., 1979-82; astrological counselor, Norman, San Diego, Clinton, Conn., 1974—; faculty United Astrology Congress, Inc., L.A., 1986—. Author: Optimum Child, 1987, The Sun Sign Book (annually), 1990—, Llewellyn's Moon Sign Book Personal Forecasts, 1995, 96, 97; contbg. author: How to Measure and Manage Crisis, 1993; feature writer The Mountain Astrologer mag., 1995—; editor Assn. for Astrological Networking newsletter, 1990—. Mem. Assn. for Astrological Networking (advisor, sec. 1990-92, newsletter comm. dir. 1992-95), Nat. Coun. for Geocosmic Rsch. (adv. bd. 1989—). Democrat.

STARCHER, LISA DAWN, arts association administrator, writer; b. Wheeling, W.Va., Aug. 7, 1965; d. Millard Glenn and Nelva June (Griffin) S. Attended, Ohio U., Athens, 1982, Mountain State Coll., Parkersburg, W.Va., 1987-88, W.Va. U., Parkersburg, 1988-89; Cert. Arts Adminstrn., U. Mass., Amherst, 1990. Reporter Ravenswood (W.Va.) News, 1982-83; reporter, photographer Humboldt Sun, Winnemucca, Nev., 1985; arts edn. coord. Artsbridge, Inc., Parkersburg, 1987-89, devel. dir., 1989-91; exec. dir. Harrison Arts Coun., Clarksburg, W.Va., 1991-93, Artsbridge, Inc., Parkersburg, 1993—; mem. bd. dirs. W.Va. Arts Advocacy Com., 1994—, Alliance of Ohio C,ty. Arts Agys., 1994—, Blennerhassett Hist. Soc., Parkersburg, 1995—. Contbr. articles to profl. jours. Recipient Leadership award W.Va. C. of C., 1990-91, Young Careerist award Bus. & Profl. Women, 1992; Arts Adminstrn. fellow NEA, 1991. Mem. Nat. Soc. Arts & Letters, W.Va. Arts Assembly (conf. chair 1995), Leadership W.Va. (chair arts & culture section 1992—), Wood Co. Econ. Roundtable, Rotary Club of Parkersburg. Democrat. Office: Artsbridge Inc 935 Market St Parkersburg WV 26101

STARCZEWSKA-MURRAY, ROMA, retired radio announcer, producer, artist; b. Warsaw, Apr. 22, 1935; came to US, 1964; d. Karol and Stefania (Bartos) Kucinski; m. Philip G. Murray, Sr. Student in Fgn. Trade Economy, Warsaw U., 1963. Announcer, prodr. Polish Svc. Voice of Am., Washington, 1967-95; ret., 1995. One woman exhbns. include Rocky Mount (N.C.) Art Ctr., 1982, Polish-Am. Congress, Stevens Point, Wis., 1983, George Mason Lib., Annandale, Va., 1987, Clin. Ctr. Art Gallery NIH, Bethesda, Md., 1989, Nat. Mus. Wome in the Arts, 1991, N.C. Mus. Art, Raleigh, 1993; group exhbns. include Am. U., Washington, 1973, George Mason U., Fairfax, Va., 1974, 1983, The Hecht Co., Washington, 1974, Thomas Jefferson Lib., Fairfax, Va., 1974, Martha Washington Lib., Alexandria, Va., 1974, City Hall, Washington, 1974, Scarab Club, Detroit, 1975, Md. Fedn. Art, Annapolis, 1975, Polish-Am. Academia Club, Chgo., 1975, The Art League-Torpedo Factory, Alexandria, Va., 1975, Cath. U. Am., Washington, 1975, Nekoosa Paper, Inc., Wisconsin Rapids, Wis., 1975, Lewes (Del.) Hist. Soc., 1976, Dundalk (Md.) C. C., 1976, Johns Hopkins U., Balt., 1977, Rehoboth Art League, Inc., Rehoboth Beach, Del., 1977, Arlington (Va.) Art Ctr., 1979, 80, U. Wis., Stevens Point, 1979, Corner Gallery, Inc., Hastings-Upon-Hudson, N.Y., 1979, The Warsaw Gallery, Inc., Alexandria, Va., 1980, Europa Imports, Inc., Balt., 1981, Treasury fo Nations Gallery, Bethesda, Md., 1993, Strathmore Hall Arts Ctr., Rockville, Md., 1993; featured in Polish Daily News, The Washington Post, The Chicago Tribune, The Sun, others; appeared in Real to Reel, Am. U. Radio Station, CBS Sunday Morning News, others. Hon. Citizenship Mayor William Donald Schaefer, Balt., 1978. Home: 518 N Paxton St Alexandria VA 22304

STARFIELD, BARBARA HELEN, physician, educator; b. Bklyn., Dec. 18, 1932; d. Martin and Eva (Illions) S.; m. Neil A. Holtzman, June 12, 1955; children: Robert, Jon, Steven, Deborah. AB, Swarthmore Coll., 1954; MD, SUNY, 1959; MPH, Johns Hopkins U., 1963. Teaching asst. in anatomy Downstate Med. Ctr., N.Y.C., 1955-57; intern in pediatrics Johns Hopkins U., 1959-60, resident, 1960-62, dir. pediatric med. care clinic, 1963-66, dir. community staff comprehensive child care project, 1966-67, dir. pediatric clin. scholars program, 1971-76, prof. health policy, joint appointment in pediatrics, 1975—, disting. univ. prof., 1994—; mem. Nat. Com. Vital Stats., 1994—; cons. DHHS; mem. nat. adv. coun. Agy. for Health Care Policy and Rsch., 1990-94; adv. subcom. on Health Systems and Svcs. Rsch. Pan Am. Health Orgn., 1988-92, 1995—; cons. Health Care Fin. Adminstrn., 1980—. Editorial bd. Med. Care, 1977-79, Pediatrics, 1977-82, Internat. Jour. Health Svcs.,1 978—, Med. Care Rev., 1980-84; contbr. articles to profl. jours. Recipient Dave Luckman Meml. award, 1958; HEW Career Devel. award, 1970-75, Am. Pub. Health Assn. Martha May Eliot award, 1995, Disting. Investigator award, Assn. for Health Svcs. Rsch., 1995, 1st Primary Care Achievement award, Pew Charitable Trust Fund, 1994, 1st Annual Rsch. award of Ambulatory Pediatric Assn., 1990. Fellow Am. Acad. Pediat.; mem. APHA (Martha May Eliot award 1995), NAS Inst. Medicine (governing coun. 1981-83), Am. Pediat. Soc., Soc. Pediat. Rsch., Internat. Epidemiologic Assn., Ambulatory Pediat. Assn. (pres. 1980), Sigma Xi, Alpha Omega Alpha. Office: Johns Hopkins Sch Hygiene 624 N Broadway Baltimore MD 21205-1901

STARHAWK, MIRIAM SIMOS, writer, educator; b. St. Paul, June 17, 1951; d. Jack and Bertha Claire (Goldfarb) Simos; m. Edwin Walter Rahsman, Jan. 22, 1975 (div. Oct. 31, 1982); m. David John Miller, June 13, 1992. BA, UCLA, 1972; MA, Antioch U. West, San Francisco, 1982. Writer, lectr., tchr., workshop leader Calif., 1979—; lectr. Inst. for Culture, Oakland, Calif., 1983-95, Antioch U. West, San Francisco, 1983-87. Author: The Spiral Dance: A Rebirth of the Ancient Religion of the Great Goddess, 1979, 89, Dreaming the Dark: Magic, Sex, and Politics, 1982, Truth or Dare: Encounters with Power, Authority and Mystery, 1987 (Media Alliance Meritorious Achievement award for nonfiction 1988), The Fifth Sacred Thing, 1993 (Lambda award 1994); cons. (films) Goddess Remembered, The Burning Times. Mem. Pagan/Jewish Ch. Home: PO Box 410187 San Francisco CA 94110

STARK, AGNES GORDON, artist, educator; b. Balt., June 9, 1938; d. Alexander Gordon and D'Arck (Hilles) Young; m. James Edward Stark, May 8, 1965; children: Gordon Metcalf. BFA, Carnegie Mellon U., 1962. Prodn. asst. The Peterborough (N.H.) Players, 1958-60; asst. to designer Westport County Playhouse, Conn., 1961; lighting designer North Shore Music Theatre, Beverly, Mass., 1962; asst. to designer John Drew Theatre, Hampton, N.Y., 1963, Arena Stage, Washington, 1963-64, Front St Theatre, Memphis, 1964-65; artist, potter Memphis, 1970—; crafts adv. panelist Tenn. Arts Commn., Nashville, 1970; adv. Memphis Arts Coun., 1989, judge, 1990—. Exhbns. include Ark. Arts Ctr., Little Rock, 1968, 70, 73, 77, 84, La. Crafts Coun. Juried Show, 1970, Memphis Brooks Mus. Art, 1973-77, Theatre Memphis, 1975, 78-95, Old Tyme Commissary Gallery, Greenwood, Miss., 1976, Memphis Area C. of C., 1977, Nat. Bank of Commerce, Memphis, 1978, 80, 84, Memphis Botanic Garden, 1978, 79, Dallas Market Show, 1981, Balt. Winter Market, 1982, Turner Clark Gallery, Memphis, 1982, Rhodes Coll., Memphis, 1985, Univ. of Memphis, 1985, Ferguson Gallery, Memphis, 1995. Bd. dirs. Art Today-Memphis Brooks Mus., 1985-91. Mem. Am. Crafts Coun., Tenn. Assn. Craft Artists (v.p. 1986), Memphis Assn. Craft Artists (pres. 1972-76). Republican. Episcopalian. Home: 3598 Cowden Ave Memphis TN 38111

STARK, DIANA, public relations and promotion executive; b. N.Y.C., July 1; d. Benjamin and Sara (Zelasny) S.; BA, Hunter Coll. Promotion mgr. TV Guide mag., N.Y.C., 1950-61; promotion mgr. Show Bus. Illustrated, N.Y.C., 1961-62; broadcast specialist Young & Rubicam, N.Y.C., 1962-69; pres. Stark Communications, Inc., N.Y.C., 1969-76; pub. svc. publicity account exec. Y & R E, N.Y.C., 1976-77; pres. Stark Communications, Internat., N.Y.C., 1978—; pub. rels. workshop leader Chgo. Econ. Devel. Corp., 1973-76; cons. to Asahi Shimbun for English Language Newsletter. 1991-92. Columnist Host mag., 1960-65; writer, producer programs for women's TV shows, 1962—; coord. We Have Arrived, Portraits at Ellis Island, Augustus Sherman Photographs 1902-1924; book developer Ellis Island: The First Experience With Liberty, 1991. Mem. Pub. Rels. Soc. Am., Nat. Acad. T.V. Arts and Scis. (trustee 1974-78, publicity com. chmn., chpt. gov. 1972-76, 82—, editor N.Y. TV Directory 1987—), Internat. Radio and TV Soc., Fgn. Policy Assn.

STARK, ELIZABETH ANN, home health nurse; b. Wharton, Tex., Apr. 14, 1952; d. Ardell William and Mary Elizabeth (Thomas) Staggs; 1 child, Candice Ann Petersen. BSN cum laude, N.E. La. U., 1989. RN, La.; cert. med.-surg. nurse, home health nurse, ANA. Co-owner, mgr. Staggs Auto Parts, West Monroe, La., 1973-89; weekend nursing supr. Richland Nursing Home, Delhi, La., 1990; PRN staff gyn. clinic Dr. James Truly M.D., West Monroe, 1991; PRN contract work/supplemental staffing Advantage Nursing Svcs., Shreveport, La., 1991-92; staff nurse/charge nurse med.-surg. diabetes unit Glenwood Regional Med. Ctr., West Monroe, 1989-90, charge nurse med.-surg., diabetes unit, 1990-93; case mgr., asst. clin. dir. AlphaCare Home Health Inc., Monroe, 1993-94; DON Med-Care Home Health Inc., Ruston, La., 1994-96; asst. DON Today's Home Health, Inc., Monroe, 1994—. Mem. Strauss Playhouse, Monroe Symphony Orch. Concert Series; flutist Twin City Concert Band; vol. ARC, Monroe, 1994-95. Mem. ANA, La. State Nurses Assn., Nat. Assn. Health Care Quality, Monroe Dist. Nurses Assn. ARC, Am. Diabetes Assn., Med.-Surg. Nurses Assn., Sigma Theta Tau (Lambda Mu chpt.). Home: 117 Davis Ln West Monroe LA 71291 Office: Todays Home Health 810 N 29th St Monroe LA 71201

STARK, JANICE ANN, elementary education educator; b. Oelwein, Iowa, July 25, 1940; d. Wilbert Goerge and Martha Isabelle (Bulgur) Brown; widowed; children: Stephanie, Brad. BA, U. No. Iowa, 1962; MA, St. Thomas U., 1991. Lic. tchr. Tchr. 5th grade Roseville (Minn.) Schs., 1962-63; tchr. 4th grade Iowa City Schs., 1963-64, Calumet City (Ill.) Schs., 1964-65; tchr. 3d grade, substitute tchf. 6th grade Robbinsdale (Minn.) Schs., 1965-69, 74-78; tutor, W.I.S.E. vol. Mpls. Pub. Schs., 1969-72, 79-86, tchr. grades 3-5 Putnam Elem., 1986-92, tchr. 4th grade Hamilton Elem., 1992-93; with Tchr. Inst., Minn. Humanities Commn., 1995; tchr. Burroughs Elem. Sch., Mpls., 1995—; mem. City-Wide Tchr. Adv. Com., 1987-89; bldg. contact rep. Lang. Arts and Social Studies, 1986-89; mem. Site Coun. Leadership Team, 1989-92; N.E. Mplw. tchr. contact person Whole Lang., 1991-92; mem. Mpls. Pub. Schs. Profl. Devel. Com., 1992-93, Local 59 Leadership Consortium, 1992-93. Mem. AAUW. Home: 8317 34th Ave N New Hope MN 55427 Address: 3 200 Beaconsfield Parade, 3206 Melbourne Victoria, Australia

STARK, JOAN SCISM, education educator; b. Hudson, N.Y., Jan. 6, 1937; d. Ormonde F. and Myrtle Margaret (Kirkey) S.; m. William L. Stark, June 28, 1958 (dec.); children: Eugene William, Susan Elizabeth, Linda Anne, Ellen Scism; m. Malcolm A. Lowther, Jan. 31, 1981. B.S., Syracuse U., 1957; M.A. (Hoadly fellow), Columbia U., 1960; Ed.D., SUNY, Albany, 1971. Tchr. Ossining (N.Y.) High Sch., 1957-59; free-lance editor Holt, Rinehart & Winston, Harcourt, Brace & World, 1960-70; lectr. Ulster County Community Coll., Stone Ridge, N.Y., 1968-70; asst. dean Goucher Coll., Balt., 1970-73; asso. dean Goucher Coll., 1973-74; assoc. prof., chmn. dept. higher postsecondary edn. Syracuse (N.Y.) U., 1974-78; dean Sch. Edn. U. Mich., Ann Arbor, 1978-83, prof., 1983—; dir. Nat. Ctr. for Improving Postsecondary Teaching and Learning, 1991-96. Editor: Rev. of Higher Edn., 1991-96; contbr. articles to various publs. Leader Girl Scouts U.S.A., Cub Scouts Am.; coach girls Little League; dist. officer PTA, intermittently, 1968-80; mem. adv. com. Gerald R. Ford Library, U. Mich., 1980-83; trustee Kalamazoo Coll., 1979-85; mem. exec. com. Inst. Social Research, U. Mich., 1979-81; bd. dirs. Mich. Assn. Colls. Tchr. Edn., 1979-81. Mem. Am. Assn. for Higher Edn., Am. Ednl. Rsch. Assn., Assn. Study Higher Edn. (dir. 1977-79, v.p. 1983, pres. 1984, Rsch. Achievement award 1992), Assn. Innovation Higher Edn. (nat. chmn. 1974-75), Assn. Instl. Rsch. (disting. mem.), Assn. Colls. and Schs. Edn. State Univs. and Land Grant Colls. (dir. 1981-83), Acctg. Edn. Change Commn., Phi Beta Kappa, Phi Kappa Phi, Sigma Pi Sigma, Eta Pi Upsilon, Lambda Sigma Sigma, Phi Delta Kappa, Pi Lambda Theta. Office: Univ Mich 2002 Sch of Edn Ann Arbor MI 48109-1259

STARK, MARY CULBERTSON, art educator; b. Plainfield, N.J., June 2, 1953; d. Robert Warren and Betty Love (MacFarlane) Culbertson; m. Gary Stephen Stark, Dec. 10, 1977. BFA, U. S.C., 1975; MEd in Art Edn., U. Pitts., 1979. Art instr. K-12 Bethel Park (Pa.) Sch. Dist., 1975—, chmn. art dept., 1992—; art instr. K-12 Peters Twp. Mid. Sch., 1987; team leader apprenticeship program Associated Artists of Pitts., Bethel Park, 1994—; cons. Pitts. Fund for Art Edn., 1990—, The Carnegie Mus., Pitts., 1994—; artist liaison Pitts. Cultural Trust, 1993—; edn. cons. Master Visual Artists of Pitts., 1995—. One woman shows, Pitts., 1984-96; exhibited in numerous group shows, 1984—; (paintings) Ascension of Lisa Steinberg, 1989 (1st pl. award), (illustration work) Theos Foundation Publications, 1991, (sculpture) Hoyt Inst. of Art Regional Exbhn. (Award of Distinction 1995). Art dir. Art Rm. Gallery, 1986, Nat. Student Coun. Conf., 1985; art cons. Pitts. Commn. for Women Exhbn., 1989-90; cons., speaker Hugh O'Brien Leadership Found., 1993; cons. Mid. States Evaluation, 1993. Recipient Distinctive Svc. award Nat. Student Coun., 1985, Thanks to Tchrs. award Sta. KDKA-TV, Giant Eagle, 1991, 3 Commendations for Excellence in Art Edn., Pa. House and Senate. Mem. Nat. Art Edn. Assn., Associated Artists of Pitts. (assoc. bd. mem., com. mem. 1992-94, com. chair 1986-94, Svc. award 1988, Distinction award 1988, workshop presenter 1993—), Exec. Women's Coun. Pitts. (com. chair 1992—), South Hills Art League, Pitts. Watercolor Soc. (selection com. 1989—), Pitts. Print Group, Pa. Art Edn. Assn. (workshop presenter interdisciplinary studies). Office: Bethel Park Sr H S 309 Church Rd Bethel Park PA 15102-1607

STARK, NELLIE MAY, forest ecology educator; b. Norwich, Conn., Nov. 20, 1933; d. Theodore Banjamin and Dorothy Josephine (Pendleton) Beetham; m. Oscar Elder Stark, Oct. 1962 (dec.). BA, Conn. Coll., 1956; AM, Duke U., 1958, PhD, 1962. Botanist Exptl. Sta., U.S. Forest Svc., Old Strawberry, Calif., 1958-66; botanist, ecologist Desert Rsch. Inst., Reno, Nev., 1966-72; prof. forest ecology Sch. Forestry, U. Mont., Missoula, 1972-92; pvt. cons. Philomath, Oreg.; pres. Camas Analytical Lab., Inc., Missoula, 1987-92. Contbr. articles to profl. jours. Named Disting. Dau. Norwich, Conn., 1985; recipient Conn. award Conn. Coll., 1986, 54 grants. Mem. Ecol. Soc. Am. (chair ethics com. 1974, 76), Soc. Am. Foresters (taskforce 1987-88).

STARK, PATRICIA ANN, psychologist, educator; b. Ames, Iowa; d. Keith C. and Mary L. (Johnston) Moore. BS, So. Ill. U., Edwardsville, 1970, MS, 1972; PhD, St. Louis U., 1976. Counselor to alcoholics Bapt. Rescue Mission, East St. Louis, 1969; researcher alcoholics Gateway Rehab. Center, East St. Louis, 1972; psychologist intern Henry-Stark Counties Spl. Edn. Dist. and Galesburg State Research Hosp., Ill., 1972-73; instr. Lewis and Clark Community Coll., Godfrey, Ill., 1973-76, asst. prof., 1976-84, assoc. prof., 1984, coordinator child care services, 1974-84; mem. staff dept. psychiatry Meml. Hosp., St. Elizabeth's Hosp., 1979—; supr. various workshops in field, 1974—; dir. child and family services Collinsville Counseling Center, 1977-82; clin. dir., owner Empas-Complete Family Psychol. and Hypnosis Services, Collinsville, 1982—; cons. community agys., 1974—; mem. adv. bd. Madison County Council on Alcoholism and Drug Dependency, 1977-80. Mem. Am. Psychol. Assn., Ill. Psychol. Assn., Midwestern Psychol. Assn., Nat. Assn. Sch. Psychologists, Am. Soc. Clin. Hypnosis, Internat. Soc. Hypnosis. Office: 2802 Maryville Rd Maryville IL 62062

STARKEY, LUCILLE A., music educator; b. East Liverpool, Ohio; d. William Oscar and Goldie May (Cline) Mansfield; m. James Richard, Apr. 6, 1968; 1 child, Karen Michelle. BA, Northland Coll., 1966. Tchr. 1st grade Monroe Local Sch., Graysville, Ohio, 1967-68; tchr. music Caldwell (Ohio) Ex Village, 1969-71, Switzerland of Ohio, Woodsfield, 1971—. Home: 45518 Henthorn Rd Woodsfield OH 43793-9705 Office: Woodsfield Elem 118 N Paul St Woodsfield OH 43793-1151

STARKMAN, BETTY PROVIZER, genealogist, writer, educator; b. Detroit, July 18, 1929; d. Jack and Rose (Bodenstein) Provizer; m. Morris Starkman, Dec. 25, 1952; children: Susan Lynn Starkman Rott, Robert David Starkman. AB, Wayne State U., 1951; postgrad., U. Wis., 1949; MA, Wayne U., 1954. Cert. social worker. Social worker Wayne County Social Aid, Detroit, 1951-54, B'nai B'rith Youth Orgn., Detroit, 1951-54; genealogist, historian Birmingham, Mich., 1979—; tchr. Midrasha Coll., Southfield, Mich., 1986-88, Coll. Jewish Studies, Birmingham, 1986-88; lectr. Jewish Cmty. Ctr., West Bloomfield, Mich., 1986-89. Editor jour. Generations, 1986; contbr. articles to Jwish News, Generations, Search, others. Bd. dirs. Anti Defamation League,Detroit, 1980—, Jewish Cmty. Coun., Southfield, 1980—, Tribute Fund, Detroit, 1979-85; v.p. Maimonides, Detroit, 1966-67; bd. dirs. Am. Mogen David for Israel, Mich. br.; del. 1st conf. Jewish of Old China, Harvard U., 1992; mem. archives com. Jewish Welfare Fedn. Mich., 1993—. Recipient 8 Gold Keys for debate and oratory Wayne U., 1947-51; Humanitarian award State of Israel Bonds, 1980, Helping Hand award, Israel Red Cross, 1980, Humanitarian award, 1991. Mem. Jewish Genealogy Soc. Mich. (founder, pres. 1984-86, bd. dirs. 1995—), Jewish Genealogy Soc. Ill., Jewish Genealogy Soc. Inc., Jewish Hist. Soc. (Mich. bd. dirs. 1986-88), Jewish Genealogy Soc. L.A., Jewish Genealogy Soc. Phila., Jewish Genealogy Soc. Washington, Jewish Genealogy Soc. Toronto, Polish Genealogy Soc. Mich. Home and Office: 1260 Stuyvessant Rd Bloomfield Hills MI 48301-2141

STARKS, FLORENCE ELIZABETH, retired special education educator; b. Summit, N.J., Dec. 6, 1932; d. Edward and Winnie (Morris) S. BA, Morgan State U., 1956; MS in Edn., CUNY, 1962; postgrad., Fairleigh Dickinson U., 1962-63, Seton Hall U., 1963, Newark State Coll. Cert. blind and visually handicapped and social studies tchr., N.J. Tchr. adult edn. Newark Bd. of Edn.; ret., 1995; tchr. N.Y. Inst. for Edn. of the Blind, Bronx; developer first class for multiple handicapped blind children in pub. sch. system, Newark, 1960; ptnr. World Vision Internat. Mem. ASCD, AFL-CIO, AAUW, Coun. Exceptional Children, Nat. Assn. Negro Bus. and Profl. Women's Club Inc., N.J. Edn. Assn., Newark Tchrs. Assn., Newark Tchrs. Union-Am. Fedn. Tchrs., World Vision Internat. (ptnr.). Home: 4 Park Ave Summit NJ 07901-3942

STARKWEATHER, ALEEN MARY, retired computer systems engineer, artist, environmentalist; b. Chgo., June 13, 1928; d. Floyd William and Opal Dea (Davis) S.; m. Donald E. Bolinger, 1947 (div. 1952); 1 child, Larry Stark. Student, Columbia U., 1954-57; BA, Friends World Coll., 1978. Cert. data processor. Computer prog. & acct. DeLeuw, Cather & Co., Chgo., 1964-66; computer sys. programmer Computer Tech. Inc., Chgo., 1966-70; computer sys. engr. KRAFTCO, Glenview, Ill., 1972-74; computer cons. on budget rev. sys. U.S. Senate Computer Ctr., Washington, 1982-86; computer sys. cons. Computer Data Sys. Inc., Rockville, Md., 1986-90, Orkand Corp., Silver Spring, Md., 1990-92; ret., 1992. One-woman shows include Martinsburg (W.Va.)-Berkeley County Pub. Libr., 1992, 95; two-person show Founders Rm., Old Opera House, Charles Town, W.Va., 1993; works exhibited in group shows Mansion House Gallery, Hagerstown, Md., 1992-95, Entler Hotel and Becketts Gallery, Shepherdstown, W.Va., 1992-94, Boarman Arts Ctr., Martinsburg, 1992, Vintage House Gallery, Funkstown, Md., 1993, Cliffside Inn, Harpers Ferry, W.Va., 1994; newsletter editor Goose Creek Friends Meeting, Lincoln, Va., 1992-94; newsletter editor, publicity chmn. LWV of Jefferson County, W.Va., 1989-94; newsletter editor, chmn. Sierra Eastern Panhandle Group, W.Va., 1993-95. Bd. dirs. William Penn House, Washington, 1982-87; chmn. Friends in Unit with Nature, 1991—; co-chmn. Outdoor Friends Com., 1995; treas. Olney HELP, Md., 1996—. Mem. LWV of Md. (Patuxent unit adminstr. 1996—), Olney Art Assn., Sierra Club of Md. Mem. Soc. of Friends.

STARKWEATHER, TERESA MADERY, artist, educator; b. L.A., June 12, 1950; d. Earl and Maureen Madery; m. Lee A. Starkweather, May 29, 1977; children: Ashley, Chelsea. Student, Art Ctr. Coll. Design, L.A., 1970-72; BFA, Atlanta Coll. Art, 1973; credential, Calif. State U., Northridge, 1994-96. artist Chaleur, Torrance, Calif., 1991, Prestige Graphics, L.A., 1993-95; artist, designer Zarah Co., Topanga, Calif., 1991-95. Artistic dir. Echoes Cards, Topanga, Calif., 1991-94. Contbg. artist Am. Artist Mag., spring 1991, The Best of Watercolor, 1995, Splash 4 The Splendor of Light, 1996; exhibited Madison Nat. Watercolor, Edgewood Coll., Wis., 1988, Woodstock Artists Assn., Hudson River Regional Watercolor, 1989, Lankershim Arts Ctr., Calif., 1990, L.A. City Hall, 1990, Orlando Gallery, Sherman Oaks, Calif., 1991, Watercolor West Nat. Exhbn., Calif., 1991, Century Gallery, L.A., 1992, L.A. Mcpl. Art Gallery, 1993, Artspace Gallery, L.A., 1993, Springfield Art Mus., Mo., 1994, Foothills Art Ctr., Colo., 1994, Orlando Gallery, Sherman Oaks, 1996. Recipient Bronze medal Art Calif. Mag. Discovery Awards, 1992, 93, First Place award Valley Watercolor Assn., Artspace Gallery, L.A., 1993, Patron Purchase award Watercolor U.S.A., Springfield, Mo., 1994.

STARLING, DEIDRA ANN, secondary education educator; b. Houston, Feb. 18, 1957; d. William Victor and Betty Bob (Kennedy) Rhodes; m. Terry Edwin, July 5, 1957; children: Garett, Brandon, Travis. BS in Edn., S.W. Test State U., 1978; MA in Edn., Western Ky. U., 1981. Cert. secondary tchr. Educator Sring Br. Ind. Sch. Dist., Houston, 1978-79, Hallettsville (Tex.) Ind. Sch. Dist., 1981-85, Yoakum (Tex.) Ind. Sch. Dist., 1985-86, Cuero (Tex.) Ind. Sch. Dist., 1990—. Bd. dirs. Am. Cancer Soc., 1988-91; mem. Yoakum Heritage Mus., 1994—, Friends of the Libr., Yoakum, 1990—; cubmaster Boy Scouts Am., Yoakum, 1989—. Mem. Tex. Classroom Tchrs. Assn., Nat. Coun. Tchrs. of Math., Delta Kappa Gamma (fin. com. chmn., v.p. Alpha Phi chpt. 1983—). Republican. Office: Cuero High Sch 401 Park Heights Dr Cuero TX 77954

STARNER, BARBARA KAZMARK, marketing executive; b. Detroit, Sept. 2, 1940; d. Eugene Anthony and Lucille Ann (Marcinkowski) Kazmark; m. G. Frederick Starner, June 30, 1962; 1 child, Natasha Lucienne. BA with honors, U. Mich., 1962; BS, Ohio State U., 1965. Art tchr. Columbus (Ohio) Pub. Schs., 1965-68, Mt. Olive Pub. Schs., Budd Lake, N.J., 1968-71; stained glass designer Barbara Designs, LaCrosse, Wis., 1975-87; from trade show mgr. to v.p. advt., mktg., export sales Kart-A-Bag (divsn. Remin), Joliet, Ill., 1978-96; advt., mktg. cons. Starner Mktg., L.A., 1987-95. Mem., pres. East Bank Artists, LaCrosse, 1979-86; co-founder, dir. crafts Great River Traditional Music & Crafts Festival, LaCrosse, 1975-87; chmn. bd. dirs. Spiritual Frontiers Fellowship, Mpls., 1979-85, 85-87; chmn. Spiritual Sci. Fellowship, 1985-87. Mem. NOW, Emily's List. Democrat. Mem. Universalist Ch. Office: Kart-A-Bag 510 Manhattan Rd Joliet IL 60433

STARNES, DEBRA L., petrochemical company executive; b. Beaumont, Tex.; m. David Lindsay. BSChemE, U. Miss.; MBA, So. Ill. U. Process engr. petrochem. plan Lyondell Petrochem. Co. (divsn. ARCO until 1989), Channelview, Tex., 1975-81; coord. feedstock and product volume Lyondell Petrochem. Co. (divsn. ARCO until 1989), Phila., 1981-85; mgr. comml. mktg. Lyondell Petrochem. Co. (divsn. ARCO until 1989), Houston, 1985-86; planning mgr. all chem., refining and mktg. ops. Lyondell Petrochem. Co. (divsn. ARCO until 1989), L.A., 1986-89; dir. planning Lyondell Petrochem. Co. (divsn. ARCO until 1989), Houston, 1989-91, v.p. corp. planning and bus. devel., 1991-92, v.p. petrochems. bus. mgmt. and mktg., 1992-94, sr. v.p., 1994-95, sr. v.p. polymers, 1995—. Office: Lyondell Petrochem Co One Houston Ctr 1221 McKinney St Ste 1600 Houston TX 77010

STARNES, SUSAN SMITH, elementary education educator; b. Grinnell, Iowa, Oct. 8, 1942; d. Edwin Fay Smith Jr. and Miriam Jane (Spaulding) Smith Simms; m. Wayman J. Starnes, Apr. 25, 1964; children: Michele Ann Starnes Hoffman, Mary Shannon Starnes. BS in Edn. summa cum laude, Mo. Bapt. Coll., 1991. Cert. early childhood tchr., elem. tchr. 1-8. Adminstr. Presbyn. Ch. in Am. Hist. Ctr., St. Louis, 1985-90; tchr. 3rd grade Ctrl. Christian Sch., St. Louis, 1991—; chapel com. Ctrl. Christian Sch., St. Louis, 1991—. Children's dir. Canaan Bapt. Ch., St. Louis, 1991—, mission trip vol., 1992, 93; camp counselor Youth for Christ, Kansas City, 1992, 93.

STARR, CYNTHIA HOPE, editor, pharmacist; b. Jersey City, Dec. 4, 1956; d. Arnold and Nancy B. (Camche) S.; m. Jonathan Brian Hauptman, June 14, 1992; children: Emily Aliza and Wesley Drew (twins). BS in Pharmacy, Rutgers U., Piscataway, N.J., 1979; MS in Drug Info., L.I. U., 1994. Registered pharmacist, N.J. Pharmacist, asst. mgr. Thrift Drugs, various locations, 1977-81; pharmacist, mgr. State Vitamin, Lansing, Mich., 1981-83, Betty Lee Pharmacy, Bergenfield, N.J., 1983-87; sr. assoc. editor Drug Topics mag., Montvale, N.J., 1987-89, sr. editor, 1989-93; sr. editor Patient Care Med. Econs. Co., Montvale, 1993—. Contbr. articles to profl. jours. Recipient Don L. Berg award for excellence in writing, 1991, 1st prize award N.Y. Bus. Press Editors, 1992, others. Mem. Am. Pharm. Assn., Am. Soc. Cons. Pharmacists, Am. Med. Writers Assn., Am. Soc. Health-Sys. Pharmacists, Rho Chi. Office: Patient Care Med Econs Co 5 Paragon Dr Montvale NJ 07645-1742

STARR, CYNTHIA SUE, accountant; b. Bellevue, Wash., Oct. 16, 1970; d. Frank Huston and Shirley Jane (Sleeper) S. SB in Econs., MIT, 1992. CPA, Wash.; cert. mgmt. acct., Wash. Cons. Columbia Bank, Bellevue, Wash., 1992; acct. Objective Med. Assessments Corp., Seattle, 1992-93, Cmty. Sector Sys. Inc., Seattle, 1993—. Mem. Inst. Mgmt. Accts., Wash. CPA Assn., MIT Alumni Assn., Mensa, Order of Omega (founder, pres. 1991-92), Sigma Kappa (founder, social chmn. 1988-92). Home: 6730 Division Ave NW Seattle WA 98117 Office: Cmty. Sector Systems Inc Suite 5500 700 5th Ave Seattle WA 98104

STARR, ILA MAE, educator; b. La Grande, Oreg., Dec. 27, 1917; d. Samuel Fulmer Andrew and Ida Luella Perry; m. James Marion Starr, Mar. 2, 1940; children: Jacqueline Ann Starr Brandon, James Steven Starr. BA, U. Wash., 1939; BS, Eastern Oreg. Coll., LaGrande, Oreg., 1960, Tchr. Cert. Oreg., 1940. Cert. Wash. 1962, Calif. 1974. Mus. tchr. La Grande (Oreg.) Pub. Schs., 1939-40; girl scout exec. Girl Scouts of Am., Grand Coulee, Wash., 1940-41; Elem. Sch. Tchr. Centralia (Wash.) Pub. Schs., 1954; elem. sch. tchr. Wenatchee (Wash.) Pub. Schs., 1956-64, Lancaster (Calif.) Pub. Schs., 1964-68, Marysville (Calif.) Pub. Schs., 1968-79; pvt. mus. tchr., Seattle, Grand Coulee and Wenatchee, Wash., 1940—. Bd. dirs. Community Concert Assn., Yuba City, Calif., 1986-88; inspiration chmn. Republican Women, Yuba City, 1986-88. Recipient Hon. Pub. Sch. Award, Masonic Lodge 437, Lancaster, 1966; Nominee for Tchr. of Yr., Marysville Pub. Schs., 1978. Mem. Am. Assn. U. Women (program v.p. 1976; Grant Honoree 1977), PTA (hon. life mem. 1965), The Seminar Club (program chmn.), Innerwheel Club (pres. 1985-86). Mem. LDS Ch.

STARR, JUNE O., law educator; b. Cin., Apr. 1, 1934; d. M. Herbert and Jane (Rauh) Oettinger; m. George A. Starr, Mar. 23, 1958 (div. 1968); 1 child, Stephen Z. BA, Smith Coll., 1956; MA, Columbia U., 1961; PhD, U. Calif., Berkeley, 1970; MSL, Yale U., 1990; JD, Stanford U., 1992. From asst. prof. to prof. anthropology SUNY, Stony Brook, 1970-93, dir. sociol. studies, 1983-87, 93-94; assoc. prof. law Ind. U., Indpls., 1994—; Fulbright prof. Indian Law Inst., New Delhi, 1979, Ankara (Turkey) Law Sch., 1989; vis. scholar Stanford Law Sch., Palo Alto, Calif., 1992-93, Socio-Legal Ctr., Oxford U., 1981-82. Mem. Assn. Law Schs., Am. Anthropol. Assn., Turkish Studies Assn., Law and Soc. Assn. (trustee 1976-79, 89-92), Assn. Polit. and Legal Anthropologists. Home: 8935 Woodacre Ln Indianapolis IN 46234 Office: Ind U Sch Law 735 New York St Indianapolis IN 46234

STARR, NANCY BARBER, pediatric nurse practitioner; b. Carlsbad, N.Mex., Dec. 7, 1954; d. John Thomas and Janet Lee (Fleehart) B. BSN cum laude, Tex. Christian U., 1976; MS, U. Colo., 1980. Cert. pediatric nurse practitioner; RN, Colo., Tex. Staff nurse/team leader The Children's Hosp., Denver, 1976-79, clin. nurse specialist, 1980-83; pediatric nurse practitioner Nancy Byrd, M.D., P.C., Houston, 1984-89, Aurora (Colo.) Pediatric Assocs., 1989—; interim dir. edn. Nat. Assn. Pediat. Nurse Assocs. & Practitioners, Cherry Hill, N.J., 1995-96. Author: Pediatric Primary Care Textbook; dept. editor Jour. Pediat. Health Care, 1994—; contbr. articles to profl. jours. Deacon, mem. outreach steering com. Greenwood Cmty. Ch., Denver, 1991-94; tchr. Bethel Ind. Ch., Houston, 1985-89; mem., leader Bible Study Fellowship, Houston and Denver, 1985-91, 94-95. Fellow Nat. Assn. Pediatric Nurse Assocs. and Practitioners (program chair 1989-93, Rocky Mt. chpt. AAP liaison 1989-95, Houston area chpt. pres. 1988-89); mem. Colo. Nurses Assn., Sigma Theta Tau. Office: Aurora Pediatric Assocs 830 Potomac Cir Unit 105 Aurora CO 80011-6751

STARR, SHARON DIANE, elementary education educator; b. Newton, Kans., Aug. 1, 1953; d. Warner Grey and Dorothy Louise (Schlup) Williams; m. Fredric Ross Starr, oct. 8, 1976; children: Caleb, Kristi. BS Elem. Edn., BS History, Coll. of the Ozarks, 1975. Elem. tchr. Tulsa (Okla.) Christian Acad., 1975-78; tchr. kindergarten La Petite Acad., Tulsa, 1979-81; tchr. first and second grades Tulsa Christian Sch., 1985-91, Trinity Christian Sch., Broken Arrow, Okla., 1991; tchr. first grade Southpark Christian Sch., Tulsa, 1991—. Numerous activities at Eastland Bapt. Ch., Tulsa, including: Sunday Sch. tchr., children's choir dir., ch. organist, vocalist, ch. camp counselor, Vacation Bible Sch. tchr. Republican. Home: Rte 6 Box 406 Claremore OK 74017 Office: Southpark Christian Sch 10811 E 41st St Tulsa OK 74146

STARRELS, CAROL SILVER, foreign language educator; b. Phila., Feb. 26, 1946; d. Milton A. and Frances R. (Rosenberg) Silver; m. Michael E. Starrels, Aug. 5, 1967; children: Jennifer, Joanna, Jill. BA, Wellesley Coll., 1968; MA, U. Pa., 1970, PhD, 1973. Lectr. Haverford (Pa.) Coll., 1970-71; French and German tchr. Solebury Sch., New Hope, Pa., 1982-85; prof. fgn. lang. Bucks County C.C., Newtown, Pa., 1985—, fgn. lang. coord., 1988—; mem. adv. bd. Bucks County Intermediate Unit, Doylestown, Pa., 1991—. Tchr. Art Goes to School, Central Bucks, Pa., 1982-87; pres. sisterhood Temple Judea of Bucks County, Doylestown, 1985-87. Mem. MLA, MLA of Phila. and Vicinity, Assn. Tchrs. of Fgn. Lang. in Bucks County (founder, pres. 1989—), Am. Assn. Tchrs. of German (testing chair 1992-94), Am. Coun. Tchg. Fgn. Lang. Office: Bucks County CC Dept Lang and Lit Newtown PA 18940

STARRETT, ELIZABETH ANN, secondary education educator; b. Heidelburg, Germany, May 9, 1969; d. Lawrence William and Karen Ann (Sherman) N.; m. Joseph Edward Starrett, May 22, 1993. BS in English Edn., Ohio State U., 1992. Cert. English tchr., Ohio. Advisor to flag corps Olentangy Sch. Dist., Delaware, Ohio, 1989-94; subsitute tchr. Columbus (Ohio) Cath., Dublin (Ohio) Schs., 1992-93; tchr. St. Paul Sch., Westerville, Ohio, 1993—. Mem. Cath. Diocese Educators Assn. Roman Catholic. Home: 3231 Kellingsworth Way Dublin OH 43017 Office: St Paul Sch 61 Moss Rd Westerville OH 43081

STARRETT, JENNIFER WEBER, nurse, consultant; b. San Francisco, Jan. 11, 1968; d. Robert Theodore and Yvonne (Kahl) Weber; m. Andrew Kemp Michael Starrett, Jan. 1, 1994. ADN, Regent's Coll., 1992; BSN, Barton Coll., 1995. Staff nurse critical care unit Cape Fear Valley Med. Ctr., Fayetteville, N.C., 1993-94; nurse cons. Ft. Bragg, N.C., 1994-95; adj. faculty mem. 91C (LPN) Sch., Ft. Bragg, 1994-95. With USAF, 1987-92. Mem. AAUW, Altrusa, Alpha Chi, Sigma Theta Tau. Republican. Lutheran. Home: 203 Laketree Blvd Spring Lake NC 28390 Office: Womack AMC Fort Bragg NC 28307

STARRETT, PAMELA ELIZABETH, symphony executive director, violinist, conductor; b. Concord, N.H., July 15, 1962; d. John Frederick and Nancy Elizabeth (Garland) S.; m. John Peter Ingalls, May 14, 1988; children: Hugh Starrett Ingalls, Edmund Starrett Ingalls. B of Mus. Arts, U. Mich., 1984, MusM, MBA, 1988. Orch. mgr. Ann Arbor (Mich.) Symphony Orch., 1987-88, asst. condr., 1988; mktg. dir. Kalamazoo Symphony Orch., 1988-90; music dir. Battle Creek (Mich.) Youth Orch., 1989-91; exec. dir. Battle Creek Symphony Orch., 1990—. Chair young artists competition Kalamazoo Bach Festival, 1989-90; co-founder Cmty. Music Sch. Battle Creek Symphony Orch. Mem. Mich. Orch. Assn. (trustee 1990-91, 93—). Home: 153 Laurel Dr Battle Creek MI 49017-4666 Office: Battle Creek Symphony Orch 25 Michigan Ave W Ste 1206 Battle Creek MI 49017-7012

START, JOANNE E., human resources executive; b. Detroit, 1944. Grad., Nazareth Coll., 1967, Wayne State U., 1975. Sr. v.p. human resources Kelly Svcs., Troy, Mich. Mem. Am. Soc. Employers (bd. dirs.), Soc. Human Resource Mgmt. Office: Kelly Svcs Inc 999 W Big Beaver Rd Troy MI 48084-4716*

STASHOWER, SARA ELLEN, advertising executive; b. Cleve., Sept. 6, 1954; d. David Lippmann and Sally Carol (Weiss) S. BA cum laude, Macalester Coll., 1976; MEd, Harvard U., 1982. Lower sch. instr., curriculum supr. St. Paul Acad., 1976-81; cons. 3M Co., St. Paul, 1979-81; promotions dir. Robinson Broadcasting, Cleve., 1982-83; account exec. Liggett-Stashower Advt., Cleve., 1984-89, v.p., account supr., 1989-94, sr. v.p., 1994—; sr. v.p., gen. mgr. Liggett Stashower Consulting, Cleve., 1994; cons. Ctr. for Contemporary Art, Cleve., 1993-94. Trustee Playhouse Square Found., Cleve., 1993—, Cleve. Film Soc., 1990-96, Cleve. Children's Mus., 1996—; trustee, com. chair Montefiore Home, Cleve., 1991—; co-founder, co-chair exec. com. Playhouse Square Ptnrs., 1990-93; trustee New Orgn. for Visual Arts, 1991-96; Ohio co-chair, alumni rep. Macalester Coll. Alumni Admissions, 1981—. Recipient Achievement award No. Ohio Live Mag., 1992, 93; named one of Outstanding Young Women in Am., 1986. Mem. Cleve. Advt. Club (instr. 1990—), Jr. League Cleve. (community advisor 1990-94). Jewish. Home: 16300 Van Aken Blvd Shaker Hts OH 44120 Office: Liggett-Stashower Advt 1228 Euclid Ave Cleveland OH 44115-1831

STASKO, NANCY LEE EASTERLY, volunteer educator; b. Phila., Sept. 27, 1952; d. Wallace Hayes and Margaret Eva (Omrod) Easterly; m. Michael John Stasko, June 8, 1974; children: Michael Wallace, Laura Easterly. BA in Psychology, Rutgers U., 1974. Houseparent Bancroft Sch., Haddonfield, N.J., 1974; interviewer N.J. State Employment Svc., Camden, Burlington, Woodbury, 1975-77, counselor, 1977-80; human resources specialist Cigna, Voorhees, N.J., 1981-84; baker Riverton (N.J.) Country Club, 1980; baker Hiller's Meat Market and Victorian Thymes, Cinnaminson, N.J., 1984-88, Riverton, 1984-85; substitute tchr. K-12 Cinnaminson Schs., 1994—. Columnist Courier Post newspaper, 1979-80. Vol. Ranicocas Nature Ctr., N.J. Audubon Soc., Mt. Holly, 1990-94; tchr. field explorers After Sch. Program, Cinnaminson, 1990-94. Recipient Pres.'s award Internat. Assn. Pers. Employment Security, 1978. Mem. AAUW (pres. 1989-91, chmn. book and author luncheon 1994-96), N.J. chpt. Internat. Assn. Pers. Employment Security (pres. 1978-79), Riverton Writers, Outdoors Club South Jersey. Presbyterian. Home: 313 Cleveland Ave Cinnaminson NJ 08077

STATEN, DONNA KAY, elementary art educator; b. Temple, Tex., Apr. 17, 1958; d. Paul James and Doris Mary (Kleypas) Hoelscher; 1 child, Ryan. BS in Edn., U. Mary Hardin-Baylor, Belton, Tex., 1980. Cert. tchr. in art, elem. edn., health, phys. edn. and recreation, Tex. Art tchr. Meridith Magnet Sch., Temple, 1980-84; bank officer mktg. Tex. Am. Bank, Houston, 1985-88; self employed art tchr. and designer, Houston, 1989; tchr. ESL Aldine Ind. Sch. Dist., Houston, 1990; art tchr. Meridith Magnet Sch., 1991—; exec. dir. Visual Arts Friends of the Cultural Activities Ctr., Temple, 1993-95, Temple Sister Cities Corp., Temple, 1994—; chmn. fine arts team Meridith Campus, 1993—. Curator Internat. Children's Art Exhbn., 1996, art exhibit From Russia with Love, 1993—. Mem. The Contemporaries, Temple, 1994—; singer St. Luke's Ch. Choir, Temple, 1991—, mem. St. Luke's Women's Soc., 1993—; treas. Oaks Homeowners Assn., Temple, 1994—. Recipient honorable mention in Christmas Decorating Contest Women's Day mag., 1989, cert. of recognition Crayola/Binney & Smith, 1993-94, 95-96. Mem. ASCD, AAUW, Fine Arts Network, Internat. Soc. for Edn. Through Art, Nat. Art Assn., Tex. Classrm. Tchrs. Assn., Am. Craft Coun., Soc. Craft Designers, Tex. Computer Edn. Assn., Tex. Fine Arts Assn., Tex. Art Edn. Assn., Nat. Mus. of Women in the Arts, Cultural Activities Ctr., Temple Assn. for the Gifted, Electronic Media Interest Group, Tex. Alliance Edn. and the Arts., Friends of the Temple Libr. Roman Catholic. Home: 3927 River Oaks Cir Temple TX 76504-3566 Office: Meridith Magnet Sch 1717 E Avenue J Temple TX 76501-8414

STATMAN, JACKIE C., career consultant; b. Kingman, Kansas, June 15, 1936; d. Jack Carl and Dorothy E. (Kendall) Pulliam; m. Jerome Maurice Statman, Dec. 29, 1959; children: David Alan, Susan Piotrowski. BA, U. Kans., 1958. Reg. music therapist Topeka State Hosp., Kans., 1958-59; caseworker Child Welfare, Pensacola, Fla., 1960-61; devel. rsch. tester The Children and Youth Project, Dallas, 1973-74; middle sch. counselor The Hockaday Sch., Dallas, 1981-84; career cons. Career Design Assocs., Inc., Garland, Tex., 1984-86; owner Career Focus Assocs., Plano, Tex., 1987—; pres. Assn. Women Entrepreneurs of Dallas, Inc., 1991-93; mem. career edn. adv. com. Plano Ind. Sch. Dist., 1993—. Author: (newspaper column) "Career Forum", 1991-92. With Cmty. Svcs. Commn., City of Plano, 1993—; mem. Leadership Plano Alumnae Assn., 1990—; mem. bd. dirs. Mental Health Assn. in Tex., 1989-93; founding pres. Mental Health Assn. Collin County, 1988-90. Recipient Child Advocacy award Mental Health Assn. of Greater Dallas, 1985, Golden Rule award JC Penney Comp., Inc., 1986, Humanitarian Vo. of the Yr. award Vol. Ctr. Collin County, 1990. Mem. Am. Counseling Assn., Nat. Assn. Women Bus. Owners (mem. Dallas/Ft. Worth bd. dirs. 1992-93), Nat. Career Devel. Assn., Plano C. of C. Office: Career Focus Assocs 1700 Coit Rd Ste 220 Plano TX 75075-6138

STATOM, LAURENA EDITH, special education educator; b. Winter Haven, Fla., Jan. 10, 1927; d. James Alphonso and Rodella Berry Thompson; m. William Lee Statom, Feb. 3, 1944; children: William, Therman, Deborah, Maria. BS, Coppin State Coll., 1984. Cert. spl. edn. tchr. Tchr./coord. The Nursery-Nannie Helen Burroughs Sch., 1984-96; tchr. People to People Exch. Programs: U.S. China. Conf. on Edn., 1992, People to People Exch. Programs: U.S./Russia/Poland Conf., 1992. Mem. Young Women's League, Inc. (pres. 1984-92), Washing and Vicinity Fedn. of Women's Clubs (chmn. exec. bd. 1992-94, pres. 1994-96), Irene McCoy Gaines Community Club (pres. 1987-96). Home: 7828 Orchid St NW Washington DC 20012-1132

STATON, CYNTHIA CHARLENE, elementary school educator; b. Man, W.Va., Nov. 23, 1965; d. Thomas Guy and Stella Virginia (Toler) Walls; m. Larry Paul Staton, Aug. 11, 1990. BS in Elem. Edn., Concord Coll., Athens, W.Va., 1987; MA in Reading Edn., W.Va. Grad. Coll., Institute, 1993. Tchr. music Wyoming County Bd. Edn., Pineville, W.Va., 1989-91, Chpt. I reading/math. tchr., 1991—. Mem. Nat. Coun. Tchrs. Math. (session spkr. regional conf. 1994), Wyoming County Reading Coun. (sec., honor coun. chair), W.Va. Reading Coun., Internat. Reading Assn. Democrat. Baptist. Home: PO Box 1631 Oceana WV 24870-1631

STATON, SHAWNA YEOMANS, lawyer; b. Sea Level, N.C., Aug. 11, 1966; d. Clifton Vaughn and Evelyn Gail (Piner) Yeomans; m. Thomas E. Staton, Jr., Aug. 4, 1990. AA, Peace Coll., 1986; BA, U. N.C., 1988, JD, 1991. Bar: N.C. 1991. Assoc. Toms & Assocs., Cary, N.C., 1991—; adj. instr. Meredith Coll., Raleigh, N.C., 1996. Chair by-laws com. Wake County Am. Cancer Soc., 1993-95. Mem. ABA, Am. Bankruptcy Inst., N.C. State Bar Assn. (bankruptcy sect.), Wake County Bar Assn. Office: Frederic E Toms & Assocs 103-A Kilmayne Dr Cary NC 27511

STAUB, TINA MARIE CROMER, primary education educator; b. Newberry, S.C., Oct. 15, 1966; d. James Thomas and Terri (McCarty) Cromer; m. Kevin Nichols Staub, July 9, 1988; children: Ryan Brynn, Evan Brooke. BA in Early Childhood Edn., U. S.C., 1988; MA in Reading Edn., Clemson U., 1993. Presch. tchr. Early Childhood Learning Ctr., Columbia, Md., 1988-90; tchr. kindergarten Anderson Sch. Dist. 1, Williamston, S.C., 1990-94, elem. tchr., 1994-96, chmn. sch. improvement coun., 1990-93. Chmn. Bunny Hop Fundraiser, 1993. Grantee Govt. of S.C., 1993, 94. Republican. Methodist. Office: Concrete Primary Sch 535 Powdersville Main Easley SC 29642

STAUBER, MARILYN JEAN, secondary and elementary school; b. Duluth, Minn., Feb. 5, 1938; d. Harold Milton and Dorothy Florence (Thompson) Froelich; children: Kenneth D. and James H. Atkinson; m. Lawrence B. Stauber Sr., Jan. 11, 1991. BS in K-6 Edn., U. Minn., Duluth, 1969, MEd in Math., 1977. Cert. elem. and secondary reading tchr., remedial reading specialist, devel. reading tchr., reading cons. Sec. div. vocat. rehab. State Minn., Duluth, 1956-59; sec. Travelers Ins. Co., Duluth, 1962-66; lead tchr. Title 1 reading and math. Proctor, Minn., 1969—. Mem. choir, comm. coord. Forbes Meth. Ch., Proctor. Mem. NEA, Internat. Reading Assn., Nat. Reading Assn., Minn. Arrowhead Reading Coun., Elem. Coun. (pres. 1983-84, 86-87), Proctor Fedn. Tchrs. (recert. com. 1980—, treas. 1981-86), Proctor Edn. Assn. Home: 6713 Grand Lake Rd Saginaw MN 55779-9782

STAUDER, CYNTHIA, counselor; b. Covington, Ind., June 2, 1948; d. Jack Kenneth and Lorraine Jeanette (Allen) Gerard; m. Phillip James, Aug. 31, 1968; children: Melissa Ann Coomer, Matthew John. BS in Elem. Edn., Ind. State U., 1971; MA, Trevecca Nazarene Coll., 1993. Tchr. Bapt. Elem. Sch., Danville, Ill., 1979-88; tchr. Metro Schs., Nashville, Tenn., 1990-94, elem. counselor, 1994—. Tchr. Jr. ch. Beacon Bapt. Ch., Nashville, 1990-95; pres. PTA, Nashville, 1995. Mem. Tenn. Counselors Assn., Nat. Coun. of Tchrs. of Math., Tenn. Edn. Assn., Sjorgrens Syndrome Found.

STAUDTE, DIANE ELAINE, rehabilitation and medical-surgical cardiac nurse; b. Springfield, Mo., Apr. 5, 1962; d. Carl E. and Estelle A. (Block) Richter; m. Mark A. Staudte, Dec. 28, 1985; children: Shaun M., Sarah K., Rachel E. ADN, St. John's Coll., Winfield, Kans., 1985; BA, Southwestern Coll., Winfield, 1986. RN, Kans, Mo.; cert. rehab. nurse. Staff nurse med. surg. ICU William Newton Meml. Hosp., Winfield, Kans.; staff nurse med.-surg. Olsten, Inc., Prairie Village, Kans.; charge nurse, nephrology, CCU Menorah Med. Ctr., Kansas City, Mo.; staff nurse Mid Am. Rehab. Hosp., Overland Park, Kans.; staff nurse rehab. unit Springfield (Mo.) Cmty. Hosp.; nurse contractor Supplemental Staffing, Leawood, Kans.; staff nurse Integral Staffing, Overland Park. Mem. ARN, AACN. Home and Office: 2444 W Page St Springfield MO 65802-4938

STAUFFER, JOANNE ROGAN, steel company official; b. Coatesville, Pa., Oct. 15, 1956; d. Joseph Chester and Anne Mary (Kauffman) Rogan; m. Robert Lee Marvin Stauffer, Oct. 15, 1988. AS in Bus. Adminstrn., Harrisburg Area Community Coll, 1979, postgrad., 1986-88. Store acct. Giant Foods, Harrisburg, Pa., 1977-79; payroll clk. Bethlehem Steel (name changed to Pa. Steel Techs.), Steelton, Pa., 1980-83, material and cost acct., 1983-86, cost analyst, 1986-96, bus. mgr. for gen. mech. dept., 1996—. Adult vol. River Valley Riders 4H Club. Mem. Internat. Platform Assn., Am. Bus. Women's Assn. (corr. sec. Rainbow Valley charter chpt. 1991-92, v.p. 1992-93, pres. 1993-94), Steelton Plant Engrs. Club (sec. 1982-85, v.p. 1985-86, pres. 1986-87). Republican. Roman Catholic. Home: 401 Sheetz Rd Halifax PA 17032-9695

STAUFFER, KATHLEEN, editor, author; b. Pottstown, Pa., Feb. 7, 1963; d. Willard Henry and Margaret Mary (Henry) S. BA in Journalism, Point Park Coll., 1985. Intern The Pitts. Press, 1983, Reader's Digest, Pleasantville, N.Y., 1984, Prevention Mag., Emmaus, Pa., 1985; asst. editor Cath. Digest, St. Paul, 1986-89, assoc. editor, 1989-93, mng. editor, 1993—. Co-author: Womansport: The Women's Sports Bible, 1994, Facing Life's Challenges, 1996; cartoonist Minn. NOW Times, 1994—. Coord. Police-Cmty. Storefront, St. Paul, 1995—; phone vol. Minn. AIDS Project, Mpls., 1995—. Mem. NOW, Cath. Press Assn. (lidge 1995), Soc. Profl. Journalists. Office: Cath Digest PO Box 64090 Saint Paul MN 55164

STAUFFER, LOUISE LEE, retired educator; b. Altoona, Pa., Mar. 31, 1915; d. William Thomas and Mary Hall (Schroyer) Lee; m. John Nissley Stauffer, Aug. 20, 1938 (dec. Sept. 1983); children: Thomas Michael, Nancy Kay, John Lee, Donald David. BA, Juniata Coll., 1936; postgrad., Columbia U., U. Pa., Pa. State U. Tchr. Latin, Middletown (Pa.) High Sch., 1936-41; tchr. English and Latin, Roosevelt Jr. High Sch., Springfield, Ohio, 1949-57; tchr. French, North High Sch., Springfield, 1957-63; ret., 1963. Mem. Moorings Property Owners Assn., Naples, Fla., 1983—; sec. King's Port, Inc., Naples, 1990-96, Emmanuel Luth. Ch., Naples, 1980—; bd. dirs., editor newsletter, membership chmn., rec. sec., corr. sec., parliamentarian Naples Cmty. Hosp. Aux., 1985—. Mem. AAUW, Am. Assn. Ret. Persons, Women's League (Juniata Coll.), Founders Club (Juniata Coll.), Moorings Country Club.

STAUTBERG, SUSAN SCHIFFER, communications executive; b. Bryn Mawr, Pa., Nov. 9, 1945; d. Herbert F. and Margaret (Berwind) Schiffer; m. T. Aubrey Stautberg, Jr., Dec. 10, 1979. BA, Wheaton Coll., 1967; MA, George Washington U., 1970. Nat. TV corr., Washington, 1970-74; White House fellow, 1974-75; dir. communications U.S. Consumer Products Safety Commn., Washington, 1976-78, McNeil Consumer Products Co., 1978-80; v.p. Fraser/Assos., Washington, 1980; exec. asst. to pres. Morgan Stanley & Co., N.Y.C., 1980-82; dir. communications Deloitte & Touche, N.Y.C., 1982—. pres. MasterMedia Ltd., 1986—; bd. dirs. States, Inc.; Author: Making It in Less Than an Hour, 1976, Pregnancy Nine to Five: The Career Woman's Guide to Pregnancy and Motherhood, 1985, The Pregnancy and Motherhood Diary: Planning the First Year of your Second Career, 1988, Managing it All, 1989, Balancing Act, 1992. Mem., nat. chmn. adv. coun. Ctr. for Study of the Presidency, 1976—; mem. Phila. Regional Panel for Selection White House Fellows; bd. dirs. Schiffer Pub., The Berwind Found.; mem. Reagan-Bush Presdl. Transition Team; mem. Commn. Presdl. Scholars; State Dept. speaker various countries. Selected as one of Wheaton's 10 Most Outstanding Grads., Alumnae Assn., Wheaton Coll., 1982. Mem. Pub. Rels. Soc. Am. (bd. dirs.), Pub. Affairs Profls., Nat. Soc. Colonial Dames, Acorn Club, City Tavern Club, Cosmopolitan Club, Colony Club, Radnor Hunt Club. Office: Mastermedia 9 W 57th St Fl 20 New York NY 10019

STAVES, SUSAN, English educator; b. N.Y.C., Oct. 5, 1942; d. Henry Tracy and Margaret (McClernon) S. AB, U. Chgo., 1963; MA, U. Va., 1964, PhD, 1967. Woodrow Wilson intern Bennett Coll., Greensboro, N.C., 1965-66; from asst. prof. to prof. Brandeis U., Waltham, Mass., 1967—, Paul Proswimmer prof. of Humanities, 1993—; dept. chair Brandeis U., Waltham, 1986-89, 95—; Clark prof. UCLA, 1989-90. Author: Players' Scepters: Fictions of Authority in the Restoration, 1979, Married Women's Separate Property in England, 1660-1833, 1990; co-author: (with John Brewer) Early Modern Conceptions of Property, 1994; also articles in Modern Philology, 18th-Century Studies, Studies in Eng. Lit., Studies in Eighteenth Century Culture, Law and History, Prose Studies, others; co-editor: (with Cynthia Ricciardi) E. Griffith, The Delicate Distress, 1996. Assoc. mem. Belmont (Mass.) Dem. Town Com.; mem. ACLU, 1967—. Woodrow Wilson fellow, 1963-64, Woodrow Wilson Dissertation fellow, 1966-67, Harward Liberal Arts fellow, 1980-81, John Simon Guggenheim fellow, 1981-82. Mem. MLA (exec. com. div. on late-18th century English lit. 1984-86), Am. Soc. for 18th-Century Studies (exec. bd. 1987-90), Am. Soc. for Legal History, AAUP, English Inst. Episcopalian. Office: Brandeis U Dept English Waltham MA 02254

STAVROPOULOS, ROSE MARY GRANT, community activist, volunteer; b. Decatur, Ill.; d. Walter Edwin and Ora Lenore (Kepler) Grant; m. Stan Stavropoulos; children: Becky Ann Stavropoulos Betian, Stephanie Diane. BS, Ea. Ill. U., 1954. Cert. elem. edn. Tchr. 2nd grade Garfield Sch., Decatur, 1954-55; bd. dirs. Wilmot Sch. Bd. PTA, Deerfield, 1971-73, Moraine Girl Scout Coun., Deerfield, 1968-75; also bd. dirs. Moraine Girl Scout Coun., Deerfield, Ill., 1984-89; chmn. Human Rels. Commn., Deerfield, 1975-84; mem. sr. citizen adv. com. Deerfield Park Dist., 1984-89; pres. Lake County (Ill.) LWV, 1979-81; chmn. Deerfield Village Caucus, 1980-82; pres. Caring For Others, Inc., Deerfield, 1986-88, Deerfield Area LWV, 1989; bd. mem. Deerfield Area United Way, 1976-93, pres., 1991-93; Mem. Deerfield Village Caucus Adv. Coun., 1980-81, 92—. Recipient Deerfield Human Rels. Humanitarian award, 1984, Lerner Life's Citizen of Month, 1987. Mem. Deerfield Area Hist. Soc., Highland Park Hosp. Aux, Delta Zeta. Home: 1629 Village Green Ct Deerfield IL 60015-2638

STAVROPOULOS, YVETTE, writing and English literature educator, editor; b. West Chester, Pa., June 17, 1964; d. Vasilios and Era (Havelos) S. BA, West Chester (Pa.) U., 1986, MA, 1991. Corr. The Mercury, Pottstown, Pa., 1986-87, staff reporter, 1987-88; lectr. in English Pa. State U., Media, 1992—; adj. instr. English Widener U., Chester, Pa., 1992—; bus. writing tutor, textbook editor Ins. Inst. Am., Malvern, Pa., 1994—. Recipient Phila. Pres. Assn. award, 1989. Mem. Hellenic U. Club of Phila. Greek Orthodox.

STAY, BARBARA, zoologist, educator; b. Cleve., Aug. 31, 1926; d. Theron David and Florence (Finley) S. A.B., Vassar Coll., 1947; M.A., Radcliffe Coll., 1949, Ph.D., 1953. Entomologist Army Research Center, Natick, Mass., 1954-60; vis. asst. prof. Pomona Coll., 1960; asst. prof. biology U. Pa., 1961-67; asso. prof. zoology U. Iowa, Iowa City, 1967-77; prof. U. Iowa,

1977—. Fulbright fellow to Australia, 1953; Lalor fellow Harvard U., 1960. Mem. Am. Soc. Zoologists, Am. Inst. Biol. Scis., Am. Soc. Cell Biology, Entomol. Soc. Am., Iowa Acad. Scis., Sigma Xi. Office: U Iowa Dept Biological Scis Iowa City IA 52242

STEAD, FRANCESCA MANUELA LEWENSTEIN, natural health care consultant, massage therapist; b. Bklyn., May 2, 1949; d. Robert Gottschalk Lewenstein and Shirley Winifred (Goodman) Lewenstein Ozgen; m. Thomas David Stead, May 28, 1975; children: Chandra Dharani, Thomas Robert. Student, Case Western Res. U., 1967-69; BA in Govt. cum laude, Ohio U., 1973; cert. in Massage Therapy, Cen. Ohio Sch. Massage, Columbus, 1978. Lic. massage therapist; cert. sports massage therapist. Youth service coordinator Adams-Brown Community Action Agy., Decatur, Ohio, 1973; child welfare worker Scioto Children's Services, Portsmouth, Ohio, 1975-77; project dir. youth services Scioto County Community Action Agy., Portsmouth, Ohio, 1978-79; co-owner Stead Enterprises, Otway, Ohio, 1978—; self employed massage therapist Portsmouth, Ohio, 1979—; owner Total Health Care Cons., Portsmouth, 1985-95, Jade Star Sys., Otway, Ohio, 1995—; drug and alcohol counselor Coun. on Alcoholism, West Union, Ohio, 1982; instr. Yoga, Cradtal, Shawnee State U., Portsmouth, 1985—; staff mem. Area Psychiatric and Psychotherapy Group, Health Ctr. One, Huntington, W.Va., 1986-90; instr. summer career edn. prog. Shawnee State U., 1986; reimbursement officer Ohio Dept. Mental Health, Columbus, 1982-85; cons. Portsmouth Dept., 1977; cons. drug abuse Aberdeen Sch., Ohio, 1982; Yoga instr. YMCA, Portsmouth, 1979-80, 85-87. Dem. campaign worker Ohio, 1968—; organizer So. Ohio Task Force on Domestic Violence, 1976; organizer campus ministry Shawnee State U., Portsmouth, 1976-77; organizer Portsmouth Food Coop., 1975. Flora Stone Mather scholar Case Western Res. U., 1967. Mem. Portsmouth Area Women's Network (adv. bd. 1988—), Am. Massage Therapy Assn. (govt. affairs com. Nat. Sports Massage Team Ohio chpt. 1990—, Ohio del. nat. conv. 1991, 93, sports massage team strategic planning com. 1995—), Women in Networking, Pi Gamma Mu. Democrat. Kagyupa Buddhist. Home and Office: 4140 Mt Unger Rd Otway OH 45657-9515

STEADMAN, LYDIA DUFF, elementary school educator, symphony violinist; b. Hollywood, Calif., Dec. 31, 1934; d. Lewis Marshall and Margaret Seville (Williams) Duff; m. John Gilford Steadman, Apr. 14, 1961 (dec.). Student, Pepperdine U., 1952-55; BA in Music Edn., U. So. Calif., 1957. Cert. spl. secondary music, edn. tchr., Calif. Instrumental music tchr. Lancaster (Calif.) Sch. Dist., 1957-62; instrumental music tchr. Simi Sch. Dist., Simi Valley, Calif., 1962-70, elem. tchr., 1970—; tchr. Polynesian culture, dances, games, 1970—; hist. play wright for elem. grades, organizer elem. sch. dance festivals; dir. All Dist. Orch., Lancaster, Simi Valley Schs., 1957-70; compile Japanese Culture Study Unit for elem. grades Ventura County. 1st violinist San Fernando Valley Symphony, Sherman Oaks, Calif., 1962-75, Conejo Valley Symphony, Thousand Oaks, 1975-81, tour concert mistress, 1980; 2d violinist Ventura County Symphony, 1981-95. Pres. San Fernando Cmty. Concerts, Van Nuys, Calif., 1982-94; free lancing with pit orch. Cabrillo Music Theatre, Conejo Players Theater; organizer ann. sch. Jump Rope-a-Thon for Am. Heart Assn., Nat. Geog. Geography Bee; bd. dirs. East Ventura County Cmty. Concert Assn. Mem. AAUW, NAFE, Bus. and Profl. Women of Conejo Valley (pres. Golden Triangle chpg. 1988-90, 95-96, issues and mgmt. chair 1990, ways and means chair Coast chpt. 1990, editor Golden Triangle newsletter 1988-90, treas. 1992-93, sec. 1993-94, v.p. 1994—), Pacific Asia Mus., Armand Hammer Mus., Sigma Xi. Republican. Mem. Ch. of Christ. Home: 32016 Allenby Ct Westlake Village CA 91361

STEARNS, CHERYL ANN, commercial airline pilot; b. Albuquerque, July 14, 1955; d. William Paul and Joan Reid (Meyers) S. AA, Scottsdale (Ariz.) C.C., 1975; BS Aviation Adminstrn. magna cum laude, Embry-Riddle Aero. U., 1978, MS of Aero. Sci., 1985. Pilot Raeford (N.C.) Aviation, 1975-77; instr. aerobatics Duane Cole Sch. Aerobatics, Burleson, Tex., 1980-81; pilot Fla. Med. AirEvac, Orlando, 1981-82, Henson Airlines, Salisbury, Md., 1985-86, Piedmont Airlines, Winston-Salem, N.C., 1986-88, US Air, Charlotte, N.C., 1988—. Sgt. U.S. Army, 1977-80, 82-85, staff sgt. USAR. Recipient Diplome Leonardo da Vinci Fedn. Aeronautique Internat., 1990; recipient numerous nat. and internat. championship awards in skydiving. Mem. Internat. Soc. Women Airline Pilots, U.S. Parachute Assn. (Ruby Expert Parachutist Wings, Penta Diamond Freefall Badge). Office: US Air Charlotte Douglas Airport PO Box 19004 Charlotte NC 28219

STEARNS, SHEILA MACDONALD, academic administrator; b. Ft. Snelling, Minn., Aug. 30, 1946; d. Colin Alexander and Marie Kristine (Peterson) MacD.; m. Hal Stearns, June 22, 1968; children: Scott, Malin. BA, U. Mont., 1968, MA, 1969, EdD, 1983. English and history tchr. Wiesbaden (West Germany) Jr. High Sch., 1969-72; libr. media specialist Missoula Pub. Schs., 1975-77; dir. alumni rels. U. Mont., Missoula, 1983-87, v.p. univ. rels., 1987-93; chancellor Western Mont. Coll., Dillon, 1993—; legis. liaison Mont. U. System, 1988—; bd. dirs. Bank of Mont. Contbr. articles to profl. publs. Internat. Women's Forum, chair gov. bd. dirs. St. Patrick Hosp., Missoula, 1991-93; mem. Mayor's Adv. Bd., Missoula. Mem. Missoula C. of C. (v.p. exec. com.), Rotary (bd. dirs.) Alpha Phi (Chi chpt.), Phi Delta Kappa. Roman Catholic. Office: U Mont Western Mont Coll 710 S Atlantic St Dillon MT 59725-3598*

STEARNS, SUSAN TRACEY, lighting design company executive, lawyer; b. Seattle, Oct. 28, 1957; d. Arthur Thomas and Roberta Jane (Arrowood) S.; m. Ross Alan De Alessi, Aug. 11, 1990; 1 child, Chase Arthur. AA, Stephens Coll., 1977, BA, 1979; JD, U. Wash., Seattle, 1990. Bar: Ct. Appeals (9th cir.) 1990, U.S. Dist. Ct. (no. dist.) Calif 1990, U.S. Dist. Ct. (we. dist.) Wash. 1991. TV news prodr. KOMO, Seattle, 1980-86; atty. Brobeck, Phleger & Harrison, San Francisco, 1990-92; pres. Ross De Alessi Lighting Design, Seattle, 1993—. Author periodicals in field. Alumnae Assn. Coun. Stephens Coll., Columbia, Mo., 1995—. Named Nat. Order of Barristers U. Washington, Seattle, 1990. Mem. ABA (mem. state labor and employment law subcom.), Wash. State Bar Assn. (mem. bench-bar-press com.), State Bar Calif., King County Bar Assn., Bar Assn.San Francisco, Wash. Athletic Club. Office: Ross De Alessi Lighting Design 2815 2nd Ave Ste 280 Seattle WA 98121-1261

STEBBINS, VRINA GRIMES, elementary school educator, counselor; b. Columbus, Ohio, Aug. 24, 1939; d. Marion Edward and Vrina Elizabeth (Davis) Grimes; m. Gary Frank Stebbins, Dec. 23, 1959; 1 child, Gregory Gary. Student, Ohio U., 1957-59; BS in Edn., Miami U., Oxford, Ohio, 1965; MS in Edn., St. Francis Coll., 1971; Counseling Endorsement, Ind.-Purdue U., Ft. Wayne, 1988. Cert. elem. classroom educator K-6, sch. counselor, social worker, Ind. 1st grade tchr. Greenville (Ohio) Pub. Schs., 1963-68; elem. educator East Allen County Schs., New Haven, Ind., 1969-84; elem. sch. counselor East Allen County Schs., New Haven, 1984—; presenter at Ind. profl. orgns., 1985-92, 1st Presbyn. Ch., Ft. Wayne, 1984—, Project 2000, Ft. Wayne, 1992—; participant Bus.-Edn. Exchange, Ft. Wayne C. of C., 1993. Mem. ACA, Ind. Counseling Assn. (com. mem. 1992-93, Ind. Elem. Counselor of Yr. 1991), East Allen Educators' Assn. (chair com. 1989—, East Allen County Schs. Elem. Educator of Yr. 1989), Arts United, Phi Delta Kappa, Delta Kappa Gamma (participant leadership mgmt. seminar 1993, 1st v.p. Ind. state 1993-95, Ind. state pres. 1995—). Democrat. Presbyterian. Home: 5712 Sandra Lee Ave Fort Wayne IN 46819-1118 Office: Village Elem Sch 4625 Werling Dr Fort Wayne IN 46806-3410

STECKLER, PHYLLIS BETTY, publishing company executive; b. N.Y.C.; d. Irwin H. and Bertha (Fellner) Schwartzbard; m. Stuart J. Steckler; children: Randall, Sharon Steckler-Slotky. BA, Hunter Coll.; MA, NYU. Editorial dir. R.R. Bowker Co., N.Y.C., Crowell Collier Macmillan Info. Pub. Co., N.Y.C., Holt Rinehart & Winston Info. Systems, N.Y.C.; pres., CEO Oryx Press, Scottsdale, Ariz., 1973-76, Phoenix, 1976—; adj. prof. mktg. scholarly publs. Ariz. State U., Tempe. Past chmn. Info. Industry Assn.; pres. Ariz. Ctr. for the Book; bd. dirs. Contemporary Forum of Phoenix Art Mus., Phoenix Pub. Libr. Friends; past pres. Friends of the Librs., U.S.A.; mem. edn. adv. coun. Senator John McCain; mem. Ariz. Women's Forum. Recipient Women Who Make a Difference award The Internat. Women's Forum, 1995; elected to Hunter Coll. Hall of Fame. Mem. ALA, Spl. Librs. Assn., Am. Soc. Info. Soc., Ariz. Libr. Assn., Univ. Club of Phoenix (bd. dirs.). Home: 6711 E Camelback Rd Unit 32 Scottsdale AZ 85251-2065 Office: Oryx Press 4041 N Central at Indian School Rd Phoenix AZ 85012

STECKLING, ADRIENNE See **ADRI**

STEDGE, JOYCE, retired clergywoman; b. Spring Valley, N.Y., Mar. 2, 1926; d. Sidney and Lila Mae (Joyce) Kearsing; m. Leland Stedge, Sept. 4, 1948 (div. Apr. 1978); children: Leland Jr., Deborah Stedge-Stroud, David, Donald, Claudia, Douglas; m. Joseph Charles Fowler, June 23, 1985. B Liberal Arts, U. Iowa, 1947; MDiv, Union Theol. Sem., N.Y.C., 1973. Ordained to ministry Presbyn. Ref. Ch. in Am., 1973; cert. elem. tchr., N.Y. Elem. tchr. Ramapo I Sch. Dist., Suffern, N.Y., 1966-68, Ramapo II Sch. Dist., Spring Valley, 1968-69; pastor Rochester Ref. Ch., Accord, N.Y., 1973-76; NIMH clin. pastoral intern in mental health St. Elizabeths Hosp., Washington, 1976-77, clin. pastoral resident in supervision and consultation, 1977-79; pastor-at-large New Castle Presbytery, Wilmington, Del., 1979-82; interim pastor coop. parish St. George's, Port Penn, Del. City, Pencader Presbyn. chs., 1980; interim pastor 1st and Olivet Presbyn. Ch., Wilmington, 1980, Hanover Presbyn. Ch., Wilmington, 1981, Ocean City (Md.) Presbyn. Ch., 1982; pastor Christ Presbyn. Ch., Martinsville, N.J., 1982-85; min. to elderly United Presbyn. Ch., Plainfield, N.J., 1985-91; ret., 1991; chaplain Robert Wood Johnson Health Care Ctr., Plainfield, 1985-91; cons., clin. pastoral educator and therapist, 1975-95; mem. task force on abortion Nat. Coun. Chs., 1970-73, mem. Commn. on Women in Ministry, 1973-80, mem. women's ecumenical coordinating group, 1973-79; mem. justice for women com. Elizabeth Presbytery, 1982—, mem. social issues com., 1986-91, moderator, 1991-92, mem. gen. coun., 1990-91, mem. pers. com., 1991-95; del. to Gen. Assembly, Presbyn. Ch. (U.S.A.), 1985, 91. Former leader Rockland County coun. Girl Scouts U.S.A.; former treas., fin. chmn., bd. dirs. LWV; com. mem. Water, Sewer and Fign. Policy Rockland County Study, 1955-73; former program chmn. Women's Assn., former adult edn. chmn. Spring Valley Ref. Ch.; former mem. coun. and edn. chmn. Ctrl. Rockland Ecumenical Witness, Spring Valley. Democrat. Home: 1352 New Brunswick Ave Piscataway NJ 08854-2081

STEDING, KATY, basketball player; b. Lake Oswego, Oreg., Dec. 11, 1967; d. Mide and Patricia (Huntley) S.; m. John Jueb. Basketball player USA Womens Nat. Team; founder, owner girls basketball camps 3-Point, Inc., Portland. Office: USA Basketball 5465 Mark Dabling Blv Colorado Springs CO 80918-3842

STEEDMAN, DORIA LYNNE SILBERBERG, advertising agency executive; b. L.A.; d. Mendel B. and Dorothy H. (Howell) Silberberg; m. Richard Cantey Steedman, Feb. 19, 1966; 1 child, Alexandra Loren. BA summa cum laude, UCLA. Producer EUE/Screen Gems, N.Y.C., 1963-66, Jack Tinker & Ptnrs., N.Y.C., 1966-68, Telpac Mgmt., N.Y.C., 1968-72; v.p. broadcast prodn. Geer DuBois Advt., N.Y.C., 1973-78, account mgr., dir. ops., 1979-92; exec. v.p., dir. creative devel. Partnership for a Drug-Free America, N.Y.C., 1992—. Recipient Andy award Art Dirs. Club, 1968, 71; named one of 100 Best and Brightest Women in Advt., Advt. Age mag., 1988. Mem. Advt. Women N.Y. (pres. 1993-95, Advt. Women N.Y. Found. (pres. 1994—), Phi Beta Kappa. Office: Partnership for a Drug-Free Am 405 Lexington Ave New York NY 10174

STEEL, DANIELLE FERNANDE, author; b. N.Y.C., Aug. 14, 1947; d. John and Norma (Stone) Schuelein-Steel. Student, Parsons Sch. Design, 1963, NYU, 1963-67. Vice pres. pub. relations and new bus. Supergirls Ltd., N.Y.C., 1968-71; copywriter Grey Advt., San Francisco, 1973-74. Author novels Going Home, 1973, Passion's Promise, 1977, Now and Forever, 1978, The Promise, 1978, Season of Passion, 1979, Summers End, 1979, To Love Again, 1980, The Ring, 1981, Loving, 1980, Love, 1981, Remembrance, 1981, Palomino, 1981, Once in a Lifetime, 1982, Crossings, 1982, A Perfect Stranger, 1982, Thurston House, 1983, Changes, 1983, Full Circle, 1984, (non-fiction) Having A Baby, 1984, Family Album, 1985, Secrets, 1985, Wanderlust, 1986, Fine Things, 1987, Kaleidoscope, 1987, Zoya, 1988, Star, 1988, Daddy, 1989, Message from Nam, 1990, Heartbeat, 1991, No Greater Love, 1991, Jewels, 1992, Mixed Blessings, 1992, Vanished, 1993, Accident, 1994, The Gift, 1994, Wings, 1994, Lightning, 1995, Five Days in Paris, 1995, Malice, 1996; (children's) Martha's Best Friend, Martha's New School, Martha's New Daddy, Max's New Daddy, Max and The Babysitter, Max's Daddy Goes To The Hospital; contbr. poetry to mags., including Cosmopolitan, McCall's, Ladies Home Jour., Good Housekeeping. Home: PO Box 1637 New York NY 10156-1637 Office: care Dell Publishing 1540 Broadway New York NY 10036*

STEEL, DAWN, motion picture producer; b. N.Y.C., Aug. 19; m. Charles Roven; 1 child, Rebecca. Student in mktg., Boston U., 1964-65, NYU, 1966-67. Sportswriter Major League Baseball Digest and NFL, N.Y.C., 1968-69; editor Penthouse Mag., N.Y.C., 1969-75; pres. Oh Dawn!, Inc., N.Y.C., 1975-78; v.p. merchandising, cons. Playboy mag., N.Y.C., 1978-79; v.p. merchandising Paramount Pictures, N.Y.C., 1979-80; v.p. prodn. Paramount Pictures, L.A., 1980-83, sr. v.p. prodn., 1983-85, pres. prodn., 1985-87; pres. Columbia Pictures, 1987-90; formed Steel Pictures (with Touchstone Pictures and Walt Disney Film & TV), 1990-94, Atlas Entertainment, 1994; mem. dean's adv. bd. UCLA Sch. Theater, Film, TV, 1993. First woman studio pres.; prodns. for Paramount include Flashdance, Footloose, Top Gun, Star Trek III, Beverly Hills Cop II, The Untouchables, The Accused, Fatal Attraction, 1985-87; prodns. for Columbia include Ghostbusters II, Karate Kid III, When Harry Met Sally, Look Who's Talking, Casualties of War, Postcards from the Edge, Flatliners, Awakenings; prodr. Steel Pictures for Disney: Honey, I Blew Up the Kid, 1992, Cool Runnings, 1993, Sister Act 2, 1993; prodr. (benefit concert) For Our Children, Pediatric AIDS Found., 1992; author: They Can Kill You, But They Can't Eat You, 1993. Appointeee Presdl. Commn. Scholars, 1993; mem. L.A. Mayor Richard Riordan's Transition Team, 1993, U.S. Del. to Winter Olympics, 1994; chair Mayor's Entertainment Industry Task Force, 1993; bd. dirs. Hollywood Supports, 1993. Recipient Women Film Crystal award Women in Film, 1989. Mem. Acad. Motion Picture Arts and Scis. Office: Atlas Entertainment 9169 W Sunset Blvd Los Angeles CA 90069-3129

STEEL, GAYLA RUTH, writer; b. Perry, N.Y., July 20, 1933; d. Robert Ledlie and Margaret Ruth (Splatt) Moag; m. Paul Kent Steel, Oct. 12, 1957; children: Marla Ruth Steel Clement, Esther Elizabeth Steel Barclay, David Kent Steel. BA in English summa cum laude, No. Ill. U., 1978, MA in English with distinctions, 1980, PhD, 1991. Instr. English No. Ill. U., DeKalb, 1979-87, lectr. English dept., 1983-87; pvt. tutor Geneva, Ill., 1994—; mem. scoring team No. Ill. U., DeKalb, 1982, Scholastic Testing Svc., Carol Stream, Ill., 1983. Author: Sexual Tyranny in Wessex: Hardy's Witches and Demons of Folklore, 1993; contbr. poems to poetry jours. Mem. AAUW, MLA, Midwest Modern Lang. Assn., Nat. Mus. Women Arts. Republican.

STEELE, ANA MERCEDES, government official; b. Niagara Falls, N.Y., Jan. 18, 1939; d. Sydney and Mercedes (Hernandez) S.; m. John Hunter Clark, June 2, 1979. AB magna cum laude, Marywood Coll., 1958. Actress, 1959-64; sec. Nat. Endowment for Arts, Washington, 1965-67, dir. budget and research, 1968-75, dir. planning, 1976-78, dir. program coordination, sr. exec. service, 1979-81, assoc. dep. chmn. for programs, dir. program coordination, sr. exec. service, 1982-93, acting chmn., acting sr. dep. chmn., 1993, sr. dep. chmn., sr. exec. svc., 1993-96; dep. chmn. for mgmt. and budget, sr. exec. svc., 1996—; guest lectr. George Washington U., 1987; trustee Marywood Coll., 1989—. Author, editor report: History of the National Council on the Arts and National Endowment for the Arts During the Johnson Administration, 1968; editor: Museums USA (Fed. Design Council award of Excellence 1975), 1974; National Endowment Arts 1965-1985: A Brief Chronology of Federal Involvement in the Arts, 1985. Former reader Rec. for the Blind, N.Y.C.; former tutor Future for Jimmy, Washington. Named Disting. Grad. in Field of Arts, Marywood Coll., 1976; recipient Sustained Superior Performance award Nat. Endowment for Arts, Washington, 1980, Disting. Service award, 1983, 84, 85, 89, 92. Mem. Actors' Equity Assn., Screen Actors Guild, Delta Epsilon Sigma, Kappa Gamma Pi. Office: Nat Endowment for Arts Nancy Hanks Ctr 1100 Pennsylvania Ave NW Washington DC 20004-2501

STEELE, BARBARA SCHUMACHER, elementary school educator; b. Augusta, Ga., Oct. 31, 1946; d. Albert W. and Mary Jane (Napier) Schumacher; m. Thomas H. Steele, Feb. 24, 1968; children: Katherine E., Grayson H. BA in Edn., U. Fla., 1967; MEd, Kennesaw State Coll., 1994. Cert. tchr., Ga. Tchr. Richmond County Bd. Edn., Augusta, Ga., 1968-69, New Hanover County Bd. Edn., Wilmington, N.C., 1970-71, Mt. Ida Schs. (Ark.) Bd. Edn., 1973-74, Buffalo Valley (Okla.) Schs., 1976; tchr. W.C. Abney Elem. Sch. Paulding County Bd. Edn., Dallas, Ga., 1981—, grade chair, chair student support team, 1989—, chair student recognition com., 1989-91. Mem. numerous leadership coms. First Presbyn. Ch., Marietta, Ga., 1980—, Second Union Ch., San Juan, P.R., 1976-79. Mem. Profl. Assn. Ga. Educators, Internat. Reading. Assn. Home: 2092 Breconridge Dr Marietta GA 30064 Office: WC Abney Elem Sch 1635 Dallas Acwonh Rd Dallas GA 30132

STEELE, ELIZABETH MEYER, lawyer; b. San Mateo, Calif., Jan. 12, 1952; d. Bailey Robert and Kathryn Steele (Horrigan) Meyer; m. Gene Dee Fowler, Aug. 9, 1975 (div. Apr. 1985); 1 child, Steele Sternberg. BA, Kirkland Coll., 1974; JD, U. N.Mex., 1977. Counsel U.S. Dept. Energy, Los Alamos, N.Mex., 1977-78; law clk. to judge Howard C. Bratton U.S. Dist. Ct., Albuquerque, 1978-80; assoc. Davis, Graham & Stubbs, Denver, 1980-84, ptnr., 1985-87; v.p., gen. counsel Jones Intercable, Inc., Englewood, Colo., 1987—. Office: Jones Intercable Inc 9697 E Mineral Ave Englewood CO 80112-3408

STEELE, HILDA BERNEICE HODGSON, farm manager, retired home economics supervisor; b. Wilmington, Ohio, Mar. 24, 1911; d. George Sanders and Mary Jane (Rolston) Hodgson; m. John C. Steele, Jan. 10, 1963 (dec. Jan. 1973). BS, Wilmington Coll., 1935; MA, Ohio State U., 1941; postgrad., Ohio U., 1954, Miami U., Oxford, Ohio, 1959. Cert. elem. and high sch. gen. tchr. and vocat. supr., Ohio. Part-time tchr. Wilmington Pub. Schs., Midland Elem. Sch., 1931-32; tchr. Brookville (Ohio) Pub. Schs., 1932-37, Dayton (Ohio) Pub. Schs., Lincoln Jr. High Sch., 1937-40; tchr. practical arts, coord. home econs. Dayton Pub. Schs., 1940-45, supr. home econs., 1945-81; mgr. Steele's Farm, Xenia, Ohio, 1972—; mem. home econs. adv. com. Cen. State U., Wilburforce, Ohio, 1941-92, Miami Valley Hosp. Nursing Sch., Dayton, 1951-63; mem. adv. bd. Dayton Sch. Practical Nursing, 1951-92. Mem. adv. com. Montgomery County ARC, Dayton, 1940-80; mem. town and country career com. Miami Valley Br. YMCA, Dayton, 1948-59; mem. Ohio Electrification Com., Dayton, 1964-66; mem. corp. com. United Way, Dayton, 1970-96; bd. dirs. Ohio Future Homemakers of Am.-Home Econs. Related Occupations, Columbus, 1979-81; chmn. home econs. adv. com. Ohio Vets. Children Home, 1987-95. Recipient Outstanding Contbns. award Girls Scouts U.S., 1987, Appreciation award Dayton Practical Nursing Program, 1989; named Ohio Vocat. Educator of the Yr., 1981. Mem. NEA, Ohio Edn. Assn., Am. Home Econs. Assn. (Appreciation award 1990), Am. Vocat. Assn., Ohio Home Econs. Assn. (various coms., Friend of Family award 1994), Ohio Vocat. Assn. (life), Ohio Dist. C Home Econs. Assn., Ohio Ret. Tchrs. Assn. (life), Montgomery County Ret. Tchrs. Assn., Dayton Pub. Schs. Adminstrv. Assn., Met. Home Econs. Assn. (pres. 1949-50, 60-61), Greene County Landmark Assn., Electric Womens Roundtable Assn. (Dayton-Cin. chpt. 1951-72, mem.-at-large 1972—), U.S. C. of C., Phi Upsilon Omicron (hon.), Ea. Star, Zonta (pres. Dayton chpt. 1950-52). Mem. Ch. of Christ. Home: 1443 State Route 380 Xenia OH 45385-9789

STEELE, JUDITH MCCONNELL, writer; b. Lamar, Colo., Oct. 5, 1945; d. Taylor and Elva June (Buchtel) McC.; m. Richard M. Steele, Nov. 14, 1975. BA, Cornell Coll., 1967; MA, Northwestern U., 1972. Vol. Peace Corps, Sergipe, Brazil, 1968-70; translator office Project Hope, Rio Grande do Norte, Brazil, 1972; adminstrv. asst. Northwestern U., Evanston, Ill., 1972-74; nursery/kindergarten tchr. Wilmette (Ill.) Pub. Schs., 1974-75, La Pepiniere, Lausanne, Switzerland, 1975-77; reporter, columnist The Idaho Statesman, Boise, 1978-93; freelance writer fiction, poetry Boise, 1993—; chair young writers competition IJA Prodns., Boise, 1994. Author: Stories From Home, 1989, More Stories From Home, 1993. Mem. Snake River Writers, Log Cabin Literary Ctr. (spl. events).

STEELE, KAREN KIARSIS, state legislator; b. Haverhill, Mass., Sept. 26, 1942; d. Victor and Barbara (McFee) Kiarsis; m. Edward E. Steele, Apr. 16, 1966; children: Shawn Robert, Gretchen Garvey. BA, U. Vt., 1964. Tchr. Waterbury Sch. System, 1964-65, Burlington (Vt.) Sch. System, 1965-67; legislator State of Vt., Montpelier, 1982—. Trustee Ctrl. Vt. Hosp., Berlin, Woodridge Nursing Home, Berlin. Mem. Am. Legis. Exch. Coun. (nat. chmn. health and human svcs. task force). Republican. Home: RR 2 Box 796 Waterbury VT 05676-9713 Office: State House Montpelier VT 05602

STEELE, KATHLEEN FRANCES, federal official; b. Kansas City, Mo., Oct. 28, 1960; m. Steve Danner, Jan. 18, 1996. Admissions counselor N.E. Mo. State U., Kirksville, 1980-83, assoc. dir. admissions, 1983-86, programming coord. dept. pub. svcs., 1986-87; Iowa, N.H. dir. Gephardt for Pres., St. Louis, 1987-88; mem. Mo. Ho. of Reps., Jefferson City, 1988-94; state dir. Clinton for Pres., 1991-92; regional dir. U.S. Dept. Health and Human Svcs., Kansas City, Mo., 1994—; chair Freshman Dem. Caucus, 1989, chair sci., tech. and critical issues com. Bd. dirs. Adair County chpt. ARC, 1987. Recipient Young Careerist award Kirksville Bus. and Profl. Women, 1988. Mem. Nat. Order Women Legislators, Women Legislators of Mo. (pres. 1989-92). Roman Catholic. Home: 6 Nantucket Ct Smithville MO 64089-9605 Office: US Dept Health and Human Svcs 601 E 12th St Ste 210 Kansas City MO 64106-2808

STEELE, LILLIAN JANE, historian, scholar; b. Salisbury, N.C., Apr. 27, 1955; d. Abner Randolph and Jimmie Lou (Tabor) S. BA in Edn., Livingstone Coll., 1977; MLS, NCCU, 1980, MA in History, 1986. Cert. grad. tchr., N.C. Libr. media asst. South Rowan Sr. H.S., China Grove, N.C., 1977-78; reference libr. Barber Scotia Coll., Winston-Salem, N.C., 1980; libr. II, Forsyth County Pub. Libr., Winston-Salem, N.C., 1981-84; libr. Forsyth Co. Pub. Libr., 1981-84; grad. asst. dept. history NCCU, Durham, 1985; bldg. guide Old Salem, Inc., Winston-Salem, 1986—; hist. cons., Mocksville, N.C., 1992—. Author: African-American Business in Winston-Salem, N.C., 1869-1950, 1990; author, prodr. Afro-Am. tour, Old Salem, 1989. Vol. VA. Paient and Med. Libr., Salisbury, 1987, N.C. Pub. TV, Research Triangle Park, 1995, 96, Central Intercollegiate Athletic Assn. Basketball Tour, Winston-Salem, 1996. Music scholar Livingston Coll., 1973-77, spl. talents scholar NCCU, 1985; HEW libr. fellow NCCU, 1978-79. Mem. Phi Gamma Mu. Democrat. Home: 1565 US Hwy 601S Mocksville NC 27028 Office: Dept Ednl Programs Old Salem Inc Drawer F Salem Station NC 27101

STEELE, NANCY EDEN ROGERS, educator; b. Elgin, Ill., Aug. 18, 1946; d. Vance Donald and Barbara Marie (Yarwood) Rogers; m. James Frederick Steele, Apr. 12, 1976; children: Justin Vance Jabari, Barbara Marie Noni. BS, Centenary Coll., 1968; MA, U. Nebr., 1971. Program asst. Head Start & Follow Through, Lincoln, Nebr., 1971-74; K-12 resource tchr. Nantucket (Mass.) Pub. Schs., 1975-77; kindergarten lead tchr. Parkville Sch., Guaynabo, P.R., 1977-79; instr. in gen. psychology L.A. C.C., Sebana Seca, P.R., 1978-79; lang. arts and parent edn. tchr. Sweetwater Union H.S. Dist., Chula Vista, Calif., 1980-86; upper grade team leader park View Elem. Sch., Chula Vista, 1986-91; upper grade tchr. Clear View Elem. Sch., Chula Vista, 1991-94; mentor tchr. Chula Vista Elem. Sch. Dist., 1990-94; acad. dir. Nat. Civilian Cmty. Corps, San Diego, 1994-96; asst. prin. Harborside Elem. Sch., Chula Vista, 1996—; cons. in field. Author: Peace Patrol: A Guide for Creating a New Generation of Problem Solvers, 1994; co-author: Power Teaching for the 21st Century, 1991 (Golden Bell award 1993). Mem. Friends of Odawara, Japan, 1994-96. Recipient Peacemaker of Yr. award San Diego Mediation Ctr., 1993, Champion for Children award Children's Hosp. and San Diego Office of Edn., 1994. Mem. NEA, ASCD, Calif. Edn. Assn., Nat. Coun. for Social Studies, Chula Vista Aquatics Assn. (v.p. bd. dirs. 1986-96), Optimist Club (bd. dirs. 1991-96). Home: 1551 Malibu Point Ct Chula Vista CA 91911

STEELE, SANDRA ELAINE NOEL, nursing educator; b. Warren, Pa., May 8, 1939; d. Cecil Harry Johnson and Romaine Mae (Goodwin) Hamblin; children: Lynne Cerise, William Leslie. Diploma in nursing, Allegheny Gen. Hosp., 1961; postgrad., City U., Bellevue, Wash., 1988-89, Bus. Computer Tng. Inst., 1994. RN, Wash.; CNOR. Staff nurse oper. rm. Allegheny Gen. Hosp., Pitts., 1961-62, Dr.'s Hosp., Seattle, 1962-66; staff nurse immunization clinic Snohomish County Health Dept., Everett, Wash., 1969-77; staff nurse oper. rm. Gen. Hosp. Med. Ctr., Everett, 1977-82, clin.

educator surg. svcs., 1982-93; patient coord. Cascade Regional Eye Ctr., Marysville, 1993-94; nursing educator Cascade Valley Hosp., Arlington, Wash., 1994-96, dir. hosp. edn., 1996—; cons. Reed, McClure, Moceri, Thonn and Moriarty Legal Firm, Seattle, 1989—. Pres. Tulalip Elem. Sch. PTSA, Marysville, Wash., 1974-76, pres. Marysville PTSA Coun., 1976-80; leader Campfire Girls, Marysville, 1972-76; bd. dirs. N.W. Laser Network, Seattle, 1988-90. Recipient Outstanding Svc. award Washington State PTSA, 1974, Goledn Acorn award Marysville PTSA Coun., 1979, People Taking Significant Action award Marysville PTSA, 1978. Mem. Assn. Oper. Rm. Nurses, Nat. Nursing Staff Devel. Lutheran. Home: 418 Priest Point Dr NW Marysville WA 98271-6823

STEELMAN, SARA GERLING, state legislator; b. Wichita, Kans., Apr. 24, 1946; d. Paul Henry and Amy (Gessner) Gerling; m. John Henry Steelman; 1 child, Amy. BS in Zoology, U. Chgo., 1967; PhD in Behavior Genetics, Stanford U., 1976. Instr. dept. psychology No. Ill. U., DeKalb, 1974-75; instr. Fullerton (Calif.) Jr. Coll., 1976-80; postdoctoral fellow dept. psychobiology U. Calif., Irvine, 1976-80; asst. prof. dept. biology Skidmore Coll., Saratoga Springs, N.Y., 1980-83; freelance copy editor Saratoga, N.Y., 1983-86; staff writer Saratogian, Saratoga Springs, 1983-86; freelance copy editor Indiana, Pa., 1987-90; contbg. writer Indiana Gazette, 1987-93; elected mem. Pa. Ho. of Reps., Harrisburg, 1990—. Contbr. articles to sci. publs. Co-chair com. on women in politics Pitts. Inst. Politics, 1993—. Rsch. fellow Nat. Inst. Aging, 1979-80. Mem. AAUW (notable Woman 1991), Indiana Symphony Soc. (bd. dirs. 1992—), LWV, Zonta. Democrat. Office: The Atrium 665 Philadelphia St Indiana PA 15701-3941

STEEN, ANN ELIZABETH, mathematics educator; b. Cin., Nov. 26, 1949; d. William Johnston and Marguerite (Gruenwald) Montgomery; m. William Richard Steen, Dec. 19, 1984; children: Wilson, Matthew, Elizabeth. BA cum laude, U. Cin., 1972, MS, 1973. Adj. instr. U. Pa., Phila., 1973; math. instr. Germantown Friends Sch., Phila., 1973-76; math. prof. Santa Fe C.C., Gainesville, Fla., 1976—. Guild mem. Gainesville Chamber Orch., 1986-90. Recipient scholarship for grad. studies NSF, 1972, Project CALC Duke U., 1993; Instrumentation and Lab. Improvement grantee, 1994. Mem. Math. Assn. of Am., Am. Math. Assn. Two Yr. Colls., Fla. Two-Yr. Coll. Math. Assn. (pres. 1978-79), Kappa Delta Pi. Home: 2065 NW 11th Rd Gainesville FL 32605-5204 Office: Santa Fe Community Coll 3000 NW 83rd St Gainesville FL 32606-6210

STEEN, CAROL J., artist; b. Highland Park, Mich., Nov. 6, 1943; d. David and Jean (Cohen) S.; m. Carter R. Jones, Jr., Sept. 26, 1988. B.A., Mich. State U., 1965; M.F.A., Cranbrook Acad. Art, 1971. Solo exhbns. include: Detroit Inst. Art, 1973, Hundred Acres Gallery, N.Y.C., 1975, Little Gallery, Birmingham, Mich., 1975, Gallery 7, Detroit, 1976, 55 Mercer, N.Y.C., 1978, 81, 82, 85, 87, 89, 91, 95; Sill Gallery, Eastern Mich. U., 1979, Cade Gallery, Royal Oak, Mich., 1988; exhibited in group shows: DeCordova Mus., Lincoln, Mass., 1974, U. Mich. Alumni Mus., 1975, Willis Gallery, Detroit, 1976, Cranbrook Mus., 1976, Mus. Contemporary Crafts, Finch Coll., N.Y.C., 1975-77, Ctr. for Creative Studies, Detroit, 1977, The Detroit Inst. Art, 1977, 55 Mercer, 1978, Nobe Gallery, N.Y.C., 1978, Arte Fiore, Bologna, Italy, 1978, P.S. 1, L.I.C., 1979, Contemporary Art Mus., Chgo., 1981, Stonybrook Campus Gallery, 1981, A.I.R. Invitational, N.Y.C., 1982, 84, 85, 55 Mercer, 1983, Damon Brandt Gallery, N.Y.C., 1983, 84, City Gallery, N.Y.C., 1985, Galveston Art Ctr., Tex., 1985, Fed. Res. Bank, N.Y.C., 1986, Drew U., Madison, N.J., 1986, A.I.R. Gallery, N.Y.C., 1989, Brody's Gallery, Washington, 1989, Cranbrook Acad. of Art, Bloomfield Hills, Mich., 1990, Phila. Mus. Art, 1990, B4A Gallery, N.Y.C., 1991, Joel Starkman Gallery, Toronto, 1992, Cleve. Inst. Arts, 1992, Charles A. Wustum Mus., Racine, Wis., 1992, The Art Center on First, Jersey City, 1993, Kouros Gallery, N.Y.C., 1995; represented in permanent collections: Robert McLaughton Gallery, Oshawa, Ont., Can., Printmaking Workshop, N.Y.C., Detroit Inst. Art, Smithsonian Archives of Am. Art, Am. Craft Mus., N.Y.C., V.A.R.S., Slide File, N.Y.C.; dir. 55 Mercer, 1983. MacDowell Colony fellow, 1980; Printmaking Workshop guest artist, N.Y.C., 1983-85; vis. artist U. Mich., Ford Found., 1975; fellow N.Y. Found. for Arts, 1986-87, Materials For the Arts, 1987. Address: 39 Bond St New York NY 10012-2427

STEEN, NANCY, artist; b. Denver, Feb. 7, 1949; d. John and Petrita (Pino) Ciddio; m. Charles A. Steen, Nov. 13, 1968 (div. June 1976); children: Monica Lee Steen, Charles A. Steen III; m. Ben Q. Adams, Dec. 31, 1985. BA cum laude, Gonzaga U., 1973; postgrad., N.Mex. State U., 1973-74, U. N.Mex., 1974-76. Pub., owner New Leaf Press, Walnut Creek, Calif., 1974-79, The Leaf Press, Santa Monica, Calif., 1974-79, New Leaf Press, Albuquerque, 1974-79; rsch. adminstr. Taos Editions, Albuquerque, 1981-89; asst. dir. Western Graphics, Albuquerque, 1983—, R.C. Gorman pub., 1983-91. Author: R.C. Gorman: The Graphic Works, 1988, Who is R.C. Gorman?: An Insiders Portrait, 1996; exhibited in one-woman and group shows including Art Outdoors, Albuquerque, 1980, Mus. of Art, Albuquerque, 1980, 81, Susanne Brown, Scottsdale, Ariz., 1981, Mus. of Art, Santa Fe, 1982, Am. Design, Dallas, 1983, Phoenix Art Mus., 1983, Nabisco World Headquarters, East Hanover, N.J., 1984, Gallery One, Dallas, 1986, Gallery One, Denver, 1986, 87, Gallery Mach, Seattle, 1988, Mus. of the Permain Basin, Odessa, Tex., 1989, Silver City (N.Mex.) Mus., 1990, Santa Fe Style, Madison, Wis., 1990, Denver Art Mus., 1993, Dartmouth Street Gallery, 1994, Fiesta Del Carazon Creative Response to AIDS, Albuquerque, 1994, Live at the KIMO, Albuquerque, 1994; exhibited in numerous permant collections include L.A. County Mus. of Art, Oakland Mus. of Art, San Jose Mus. of Art, Phoenix Art Mus., U. Nev., Koofenay Sch. of Art, U. Calgary, U. Wash., N.Mex. State U., Maderia Sch., Tamarind Inst., Crocker Gallery, Western Graphics Collection, Mus. of Fine Art, Monterey Peninsula Mus. of Art, many others. Chairperson NAMES Project-Quilt Dis., Albuquerque, 1994; bd. dirs. NMAPLA-N.Mex. Assn. of People Living with AIDS, Albuquerque, 1993-94; fundraiser Make A Wish, Denver, 1994, Am. Heart Assn., Honolulu, Albuquerque, 1994-96. Grantee N.Mex. State U., 1973. Mem. Pi Beta Phi. Democrat. Roman Catholic. Home: PO Box 373 Corona NM 88318 Office: Western Graphics Workshop 2428 Baylor SE Albuquerque NM 87106

STEEN, PATRICIA, technology educator; b. Chgo., Aug. 7, 1950; d. Vincent Michael and Evelia (Izzi) Sosnowski; m. Ronald James Steen, Sept. 26, 1974; children: Jacquelin, Karen. BS in Edn., Northern Ill. U., 1972; MA in Edn., Gov.'s State U., University Park, Ill., 1982. Cert. secondary edn., reading specialist. Remedial reading tchr. Tinley Park, Ill., 1983-87, chpt. I reading tchr., 1987-92; reading tchr., computer cons. Consolidated Sch. Dist. 146, Tinley Park, Ill., 1992-94, dist. tech. coord., 1994—; presenter Internat. Reading Assn., Atlanta, 1990, Chpt. I ESEA State Conf., Chgo., 1993, 10th Great Lakes Regional Reading Conf., 1993, Computer Parent Workshop, Tinley Park, Ill., 1993, Am. Forum for Global Edn., Silver & Gold Bridges to the Future Conf., 1995. Contbr. (poem) New American Poetry Anthology, 1988; contbr. articles to profl. jours. Named Those Who Excel, Ill. State Bd. Edn., 1994. Mem. Internat. Reading Assn., South Suburban Reading League, Internat Soc. for Tech. in Edn. Office: Cmty Consolidated Sch Dist 146 17316 Oak Park Ave Tinley Park IL 60477-3404

STEENBURGEN, MARY, actress; b. Newport, Ark., Feb. 8, 1953; m. Malcolm McDowell, 1980 (div. 1990); children: Lilly, Charlie; m. Ted. Danson, Oct. 7, 1995. Student, Neighborhood Playhouse. Films: Goin' South, 1978, Time After Time, 1979, Melvin and Howard, 1980 (Academy Award, Best Supporting Actress), Ragtime, 1981, A Midsummer Night's Sex Comedy, 1982, Cross Creek, 1983, Romantic Comedy, 1983, One Magic Christmas, 1985, Dead of Winter, 1987, End of the Line, 1987 (also exec. prodr.), The Whales of August, 1987, Miss Firecracker, 1989, Parenthood, 1989, Back to the Future III, 1990, The Long Walk Home, 1990 (narrator), The Butcher's Wife, 1991, Philadelphia, 1993, What's Eating Gilbert Grape, 1993, Clifford, 1994, It Runs in the Family, 1994, Pontiac Moon, 1994, Powder, 1995, Nixon, 1995, My Family, 1995, The Grass Harp, 1995; appeared in Showtime TV's Faerie Tale Theatre prodn. of Little Red Riding Hood and (miniseries) Tender Is the Night, 1985, Gulliver's Travels, 1996; TV series: Ink, 1996; TV films: The Attic: The Hiding of Anne Frank, 1988; theater appearances include: Holiday, Old Vic, London, 1987, Candida, Broadway, 1993. Office: William Morris Agy Inc 151 S El Camino Dr Beverly Hills CA 90212-2704*

STEENECK, REGINA AULTICE, information systems specialist; d. Albert M. Aultice and Hilda M. (Fields) Smith; m. Lee R. Steeneck; children: Bradley, Darren. BA, Va. Poly. Inst., 1970. Programmer AT&T Long Lines, White Plains, N.Y., 1970-71, So. New Engl. Telephone Co., New Haven, 1971-72; systems specialist Aetna Life and Casualty, Hartford, Conn., 1972-76; systems analyst and programmer Bayer (Miles Labs.), West Haven, Conn., 1976-77; cons. Blue Cross/Blue Shield Conn., North Haven, 1978-79; account mgr. AGS Computers, Inc., Mountainside, N.J., 1977-79; systems cons. Comm. Design Corp., Stamford, Conn., 1986-89; sr. CICS programmer Westinghouse Comm. Software, Stamford, Conn., 1989-90, systems cons., 1990-92; sys. cons. Comware Sys. Inc., Stamford, 1993-94; systems cons. RAS Assocs., Trumbull, Conn., 1979—; co-owner Sunshine Flowers, 1980-81; Conn. regional co-chair campaign for Va. Tech., 1995—. Bd. dirs., fin. sec., chmn. computer com., vacation Bible Sch. supt., memls. com. chmn., women's soc. sec. Holy Cross Luth. Ch., 1979—; bd. dirs., dist. coord. Fairfield Prep. Bellarmine Guild, 1996—. Mem. Trumbull Parents Children with Spl. Needs (mem. adv. bd. 1992—), Conn. Assn. for Children with Learning Disabilities (bd. dirs., treas. 1993—), Fairfield Network Exec. Women (bd. dirs., treas. 1992-94), Assn. Computing Machinery, Trumbull Jr. Woman's Club (bd. dirs. 1980-88, 1st v.p., newspaper editor, other coms.), Conn. Jr. Women's Club (bd. dirs., newsletter editor, Dist. VIII rep.). Lutheran. Home: 211 Putting Green Rd Trumbull CT 06611-2504

STEERE, ANNE BULLIVANT, retired student advisor; b. Phila., July 27, 1921; d. Stuart Lodge and Elizabeth MacCuen (Smith) B.; m. Richard M. H. Harper Jr., Nov. 14, 1942 (div. Oct. 1967); children: Virginia Harper Kliever, Richard M. H. Harper III, Patricia Harper Flint, Stuart Lodge Harper, Lucy Steere, Grace Steere Johnson; m. Bruce Middleton Steere, July 5, 1968. BS in Sociology, So. Meth. U., 1978, M in Liberal Arts, 1985. Asst. to dir. Harvard Law Sch. Fund, Cambridge, Mass., 1958-68; advisor to older students So. Meth. U., Dallas, 1976-85. Contbr. articles to profl. jours. Trustee, Pine Manor Coll., Chestnut Hill, Mass., 1983—; bd. dirs. Planned Parenthood, Dallas, 1975-85. Mem. New Eng. Hist. and Geneal. Soc., Alpha Kappa Delta. Episcopalian. Clubs: Chilton (Boston); Jr. League. Avocations: reading, needlepoint, sailing. Home (winter): 1177 N Lake Way Palm Beach FL 33480-3245

STEFANCICH, DONNA LEE, information security specialist; b. West Islip, N.Y., Jan. 13, 1961; d. Stanley Frank and Irene Eleanor (Soullard) S. AAS in Archtl. Tech., SUNY, Farmingdale, 1981; BS in Computer Sci. summa cum laude, NY Inst. of Tech., 1985, postgrad., 1993—. Programmer, analyst Fairchild Republic Co., Farmingdale, N.Y., 1985-87; sr. computer security analyst Grumman Data Systems, Bethpage, N.Y., 1987-94; mgr. data security and controls Nationar, Woodbury, N.Y., 1994-95; mgr. network security Cablevision Systems Corp., Woodbury, 1995—. Mem. Nat. Computer Security Assn., Computer Security Inst., Nu Ypsilon Tau. Home: 17 Taca Blvd Deer Park NY 11729 Office: Cablevision Systems Corp 150 Crossways Park Dr W Woodbury NY 11797

STEFANEC, TAMARA CHRISTINE, entrepreneur; b. Lakewood, Ohio, Mar. 28, 1963; d. John Stefanec and Christina (Shibley) Caputo. BBS, Cleve. State U., 1989, MBA, 1991. Prin. Stefanec's Barber Shop, Cleve., 1983-95; pres. Adventure Sailing Inc., Lakewood, 1995—; cons. CSU/SBA, Cleve., 1990-91. Bd. dirs. Harbour Light Condominiums, N. Royalton, 1980's. Mem. World Wildlife Fedn., Edgewater Yacht Club. Office: Adventure Sailing 1364 Bonnieview Ave Lakewood OH 44107

STEFANICS, ELIZABETH T. (LIZ STEFANICS), state legislator. BA, Eastern Ky. U.; MS, U. Wis.; PhD, U. Minn. Mem. N.Mex. Senate; mem. conservation com., judiciary com., chmn. health and human svcs. com., adminstr. health and human svcs. Democrat. Address: PO Box 10127 Santa Fe NM 87504-6127 Office: N Mex State Senate State Capitol Santa Fe NM 87503*

STEFANIK, JANET RUTH, realtor; b. Harrisville, W.Va., Apr. 25, 1938; d. John Jackson Davis Jr. and Helen Virginia (Waller) D.; m. Robert John Stefanik, Oct. 13, 1956 (div. Apr. 1977); children: Robert Mark, Deborah Ruth, Perry Wayne, David Lee, Susan Irene. Grad., Midview High Sch., Grafton, Ohio; student, Lorain County Community Coll., Elyria, Ohio, 1982, 85, 90-91. Salesperson Demby Real Estate, Elyria, 1970-71, Schwed Real Estate, Elyria, 1971-93; mem. women's coun. Lorain County Bd. Realtors, 1971-74, past pres., 1974. Toll collector Ohio Turnpike Commn., 1975. Mem. Gibson Girls Variety Chorale Group, Nat. Arbor Day Found., AARP. Mem. Women of the Moose, United Electrical Radio & Machine Workers of Am. (treas.). Republican. Roman Catholic. Home: PO Box 1556 Elyria OH 44036-1556

STEFANSKI, SUSAN LEE, cardiovascular nurse; b. Boston, Sept. 26, 1961; d. Peter B. and Louise Helen (Sylvester) Borriello; m. Mark Adam Stefanski, Apr. 29, 1995. BSN, Boston Coll., 1983; postgrad., Northeastern U., 1994—. RN, Mass.; cert. BLS, ACLS. Clin. nurse gen. med. unit Mass. Gen. Hosp., Boston, 1983-85, clin. nurse med. ICU/CCU, 1985-89; clin. nurse III educator cath lab. Beth Israel Hosp., Boston, 1989-94; DON, Biocardia Diagnostics, Inc., Brookline, Mass., 1994—. Mem. Coun. Cardiovascular Nurses, Am. Heart Assn., 1992—. Mem. AACN, Nat. League for Nursing, Boston Coll. Nurses Assn., Sigma Theta Tau. Home: 15 Boardman St Salem MA 01970

STEFFEL, SUSAN ELIZABETH, English language and literature educator; b. Muskegon, Mich., Feb. 9, 1951; d. Sherman Burgess and Geraldine (Westerman) Bos; m. Andrew John Steffel, July 12, 1975. BA, Hope Coll., 1973; MA in English, Mich. State U., 1978, PhD in English, 1993. Tchr. secondary English Maple Valley Schs., Vermontville, Mich., 1973-91; asst. prof. English Ctrl. Mich. U., Mt. Pleasant, 1991—; supr. secondary student tchrs. dept. English Ctrl. Mich. U., 1991—, vice-chair profl. educators, 1994-95, chair profl. educators coun., 1995—. Co-author: High School English: A Process for Curriculum Development, 1985, 20th Century Children's Authors, 1994. Recipient Excellence in Edn. award Lansing Regional C. of C., 1985, 86, 88, 89, 90, Excellence in Teaching award Ctrl. Mich. U., 1996. Mem. ASCD, AAUW, Am. Assn. Colls. for Tchr. Edn., Am. Ednl. Rsch. Assn., Nat. Coun. Tchrs. English (guest reviewer 1993—), Mich. Coun. Tchrs. English (mem. steering com. 1985—, asst. editor jour. 1993—), Assembly Lit. for Adolescents, Conf. English Edn., Golden Key Honor Soc. (hon.), Phi Kappa Phi, Phi Delta Kappa (sec. 1995—). Office: Ctrl Mich U 242 Anspach Hall Mount Pleasant MI 48859

STEFFEN, PAMELA BRAY, secondary school educator; b. Bessemer, Ala., Mar. 9, 1944; d. James Ernest and Margaret Virginia (Parsons) Bray; m. Ted N. Steffen, June 17, 1972; children: Elizabeth, Thor. BA, U. Louisville, 1966; MA, Spalding U., 1975. Cert. tchr., gifted tchr., Ky. Tchr. English and German Louisville (Ky.) Pub. Schs., 1967-73; tchr. English to fgn. students Internat. Ctr., U. Louisville, 1970-78; bookkeeper T.N. Steffen PSC, Louisville, 1978-85; tchr. of adults Jefferson County Pub. Schs., Louisville, 1985-87, tchr. English and German, 1987—; network participant, bd. dirs. Foxfire, Louisville, 1990—; spokesperson Coalition Essential Schs., Providence, 1990—, Ctr. for LEadership in Sch. Reform, Louisville, 1990—; group leader AAUW, Louisville, 1983-88; presenter seminars; 94 AATG summer Austrian Inst. Graz; participant Austrian Landeskunde Internat., 1994. Bd. dirs. Jefferson County Med. Soc. Aux., Louisville, 1984-88, Highland Community Ministries, Louisville, 1980-87, Highland Ct. Apts. for Elderly, Louisville, 1984-87; nat. v.p. Deafness Rsch. Found. Aux., 1984-88; mem. vestry and rector search com. St. Andrew's Episcopal Ch., Louisville, 1985-88; active Louisville Fund for Arts campaign, 1980-93; Louisville Orch. Assn. fundraiser. Fulbright fellow Goethe Inst., Munich, 1969; grantee Ky. Arts Coun., 1991-92, artist-in-residence, 1992—; grantee Ky. Humanities Coun. CES, 1993, fall forum presenter; named to Ky.'s Commonwealth Inst. Tchrs. and Vis. Tchrs. Inst.; selected for Landeskunde in Österreich, 1994; sumer study scholar Freiberg, Germany. Mem. ASCD, Nat. Coun. Tchrs. English, Coalition Essential Sch., Nat. Coun. Tchrs. English, Greater Louisville Coun. Tchrs. English, Am. Assn. Tchrs. German. Home: 2404 Park Boundary Rd Louisville KY 40205-1620 Office: Fairdale High Sch 1001 Fairdale Rd Fairdale KY 40118-9731

STEFFEN, TINA MARIE, journalist, home economist; b. Amarillo, Tex., Apr. 10, 1958; d. Lynn Troy and Mary Lou (Odell) Bavousett; m. Gary Edgar Steffen, June 6, 1981; children: Christopher Michael, Erin Marie. Student, Sam Houston State U., 1976-78; BS in Home Econs., Tex. Tech U., 1981. Cert. home economist; cert. in family and consumer scis. Lifestyle writer Big Spring (Tex.) Herald, 1981-82, lifestyle editor, 1982-85, dir. creative svcs., 1985-86; reporter edn. beat Daily Ardmoreite, Ardmore, Okla., 1987; freelance writer home econs. reference books and curriculum guides Tex. Edn. Agy. and Tex. Tech U. Home Econs. Curriculum Ctr., Lubbock, Tex., 1987-89; feature writer, fashion editor, Lifestyle writer Lubbock Avalanche-Jour., 1989-91; communications writer Ft. Worth Ind. Sch. Dist., 1991-92; asst. editor spl. features Fort Worth Star-Telegram, 1992—; editor Abode mag. Impact Publs., Ft. Worth, 1993-94. Author: Hospitality Services, 1990; co-author: Apparel and Textiles Production, Management and Services, 1990; contbr. numerous articles to newspapers and mags. Mem. Am. Assn. Family and Consumer Scis., Soc. Profl. Journalists, Tex. Profl. Comm. (treas. dist. 14 1990-91, state scholarship dir. 1991-93, numerous writing awards), Nat. Fedn. Press Women (1st Pl. Writing award 1990), Women in Comms., Inc. (chair freedom of info com. 1990-91, Communicator of Yr. 1991). Mem. Christian Ch. Home: 6316 Whitman Ave Fort Worth TX 76133-3421 Office: Ft Worth Star-Telegram 400 W 7th St Fort Worth TX 76102-4701

STEFFENS, ANNIE LAURIE, sign language educator, interpreter; b. N.Y.C.; d. Robert William and Irene Marie (Hoecker) S. Certificate, U. Ariz., Tucson, NYU, Gallaudet U., Washington D.C. Cert. sign lang. interpreter; cert. Am. sign lang. educator. Sign language interpreter high sch., Brattleboro, Vt., Longmeadow, Mass.; tchr. sign language pvt. sch., Putney, Vt., Main Street Arts, Saxtons River, Vt., Cmty. Coll., Greenfield, Mass., Cheshire Hosp., Keene, N.H., YMCA, Keene, Brattleboro Sr. Ctr., Brattleboro Recreation Ctr.; self employes new Am. Sign lang.; sign lang. choir Gallaudet U., NYU; poetry educator Main Street Arts. Author: (poem) Down Peaceful Paths. advocate for women Women's Shelter, Brattleboro; counselor Vt. respite care project Mental Health of Southeastern Vt., Brattleboro. Mem. Nat. Assn. Deaf, Sign Instrs. Guidance Network. Home: 14 Spruce St Brattleboro VT 05301

STEFFENS, DOROTHY RUTH, political economist; b. N.Y.C., May 5, 1921; d. Saul M. and Pearl Y. (Reiter) Cantor; m. Jerome Steffens, Nov. 19, 1940; children: Heidi Sue, Nina Ellen. BBA, CCNY, 1941; MEd, Temple U., 1961; PhD, Anthony U., 1981. Economist Nat. War Labor Bd., Washington, 1941-44, United Elec. Radio Machine Workers, Phila., 1944-46; instr. group dynamics Temple U., Phila., 1955-57; seminar program dir. Soc. Friends, Washington, 1958-61; tng. dir. Nat. Coun. Negro Women, Washington, 1967-68; edn. cons. Peace Corps, Nigeria, 1969-70; exec. dir. Women's Internat. League for Peace and Freedom, Phila., 1971-77, Fund for Open Info. and Accountability, Inc., 1978-80; conf. dir. Haverford Coll., 1980-84; exec. sec. Nigerian Women's Com., 1968-69; del. African Women's Seminar UN, Accra, Ghana, 1969; mem. Africa panel Am. Friends Svc. Com., 1976-88, mem. internat. divsn. exec. com., 1977-84; resource lectr. Internat. Women's Seminar, Lillehammer, Norway, 1991. Author: The Day after Summer, 1966; editorial bd. The Churchman, 1977—; mem. nat. bd. Gray Panthers, 1989-91; contbr. articles to profl. jours., newspapers, mags. N.Y. C. of C. scholar, N.Y. State Regents scholar CCNY, 1941. Quaker.

STEFFY, MARION NANCY, state agency administrator; b. Fairport Harbor, Ohio, Sept 23, 1937; d. Felix and Anna (Kosaber) Jackopin; 1 child, Christopher C. BA, Ohio State U., 1959; postgrad. Butler U., 1962-65, Ind. U., 1983. Exec. sec. Franklin County Mental Health Assn., Columbus, Ohio, 1959-61; caseworker Marion County Dept. Pub. Welfare, Indpls., 1961-63, supr., 1963-66, asst. chief supr., 1966-73; dir. div. pub. assistance, Ind. Dept. Pub. Welfare, Indpls., 1973-77, asst. adminstr., 1977-85; regional adminstr. Adminstrn. Children and Families Ill. Dept. Health and Human Svcs., Chgo., 1985—; lectr. Ball State U., Lockyear Coll., Ind. U. Grad. Sch. Social Work; mem. Ind. Devel. Disabilities Coun., 1979-81, Ind. Cmty. Svc.s Adv. Coun., 1978-81; Ind. Child Support Adv. Coun., 1976-82, Welfare Svc. League, 1968—; chmn. rules com. Ind. Health Facilities Coun., 1974-81. Chmn. Lawrence Twp. Roundtable, 1983—. Mem. Nat. Assn. State Pub. Welfare Adminstrs., Am. Pub. Welfare Assn., Network of Women in Bus. Roman Catholic. Office: Adminstrn for Children & Families 105 W Adams St Chicago IL 60603-6201

STEGALL, MARBURY TAYLOR, psychiatric, mental health nurse; b. Madison, Wis., June 23, 1948; d. Eldon Gordon and Dorothy Elaine (Lanzendorf) Hall; m. Richard Steven Taylor, 1968 (div. 1973); m. Raymond Hance Stegall, June 1, 1982; 1 child, Eldon Gordon. AS, DeKalb C.C., Clarkston, Ga., 1973; BS, Ga. State U., Atlanta, 1976; MN, Emory U., 1978. RN, Ga.; cert. clin. specialist in adult psychiat. mental health nursing. Adult psychiat. mental health clin. nurse specialist Grady Health Sys., Atlanta, 1968—, Ctr. for Interpersonal Studies, P.A., Smyrna, Ga., 1981-84; pvt. practice psychotherapy Riverdale, Ga., 1981—; clin. instr. Clayton State Coll., Morrow, Ga., 1995—; temporary clin. instr. Ga. Bapt. Coll. Sch. Nursing, 1993, 94; peer reviewer mental health peer rev. sys. Am. Psychiat. Assn., Washington, 1986-90; spkr. in field. Asst. den leader North Atlanta dist. Boy Scouts Am., 1993-95, commr., 1994-95; mem. Inman Park Neighborhood Assn., Atlanta, 1980—, sec., 1982. NIMH tng. grantee Emory U., 1977-78. Mem. ANA (nominating com. coun. on psychiat.-mental health 1984-85), Ga. Nurses Assn. (del. ann. meeting 1994), Am. Psychiat. Nurses Assn., Metro Atlanta Advanced Practice Nurse Group (founding, pres. 1986-89), Am. Soc. Law, Medicine and Ethics, Soc. for Edn. and Rsch. in Psychiat. Nursing, Emory U. Alumni Assn., Ga. State U. Alumni Assn., Sigma Theta Tau. Home: 62 Spruce St NE Atlanta GA 30307-2430 Office: Bldg 700 Ste D 8455 Georgia Hwy 85 Riverdale GA 30274

STEGER, MARTHA TRUITT, college official; b. Logansport, La., Mar. 22, 1948; d. Garvin and Lucille (Daw) Truitt; m. Eric K. Steger, June 7, 1969; 1 child, Jill Ellen. BS, Stephen F. Austin State U., Nacogdoches, Tex., 1969; MEd, East Ctrl. U., Ada, Okla., 1976, 86; EdD, Okla. State U., 1990. Cert. elem. tchr. and prin., psychometrist, learning disability tchr., Okla. Elem., secondary and spl. edn. tchr. pub. schs., Royce City, Tex., 1969-70, Sasakwa, Okla., 1972-73, 74-76, Jonesboro, La., 1973-74, Ada, 1976-80; instr. East Ctrl. U., 1983, 85-86; grad. asst. Okla. State U., Stillwater, 1987-89; pvt. tutor, Ada, 1980-85; dir. acad. assistance Seminole (Okla.) Jr. Coll., 1989—; organizer spl. interest group Okla. Assn. for C.C.'s. County and dist. campaign chmn. nat. presdl. campaign, Ada, 1984; mem. adb. bd. Christian Family Counseling Ctr., United Meth. Ch., Seminole, 1994—; mem. exec. bd. Big Bros. and Big Sisters, Shawnee, Okla., 1995—; county coord. PUSH bd., Okla. Commn. for Children, Seminole, 1994—; chmn. planning com. Youth Speak-Out, Seminole, 1995; nat. del. Nat. Dem. Conv., 1984; former mem. bd. dirs., officer Battered Women's Shelter, Ada; co-chmn. Ada Task Force for Passage ERA, 1981-82. Recipient Women Helping Women award Soroptimists, Ada, 1985. Mem. Okla. Assn. for Improvement Devel. Edn. (a founder, pres.-elect 1996), Assn. for Learning Disabled, Phi Delta Kappa. Office: Seminole Jr Coll 2701 Boren Blvd Box 351 Seminole OK 74868

STEGGE, DIANE FAYE, counselor; b. Cedar Rapids, Iowa, Jan. 21, 1948; d. Ivor and Anna Ella Matilda (Wardenburg) Mumm; married; children: Joseph, James. BS, Iowa State U., 1970; MS, Drake U., 1990. Tchr. Havelock (Iowa)-Plover Community Sch., 1973-77, Ayrshire (Iowa) Consolidated Sch., 1977-81; tchr. Sioux Valley Community Sch., Peterson, Iowa, 1981-90, elem. counselor, 1990—. Mem. AAUW, ACA, Am. Sch. Counseling Assn., Iowa Counseling Assn., Iowa Sch. Counseling Assn., Iowa Girls High Sch. Athletic Assn (ofcl.). Democrat. Lutheran. Office: Sioux Ctrl Cmty Sch 401 3rd St Peterson IA 51047

STEIDLE, KATHLEEN ANN, elementary school educator; b. Rockville Center, N.Y., Oct. 2, 1968; d. Peter A. and Ann Elizabeth (O'Connor) Steidle; m. Chris N. Soulias, July 19, 1996. BS in Bus. and Fin., Marist Coll., Poughkeepsie, N.Y., 1990; MS in Reading, Elem. Edn., Dowling Coll., Oakdale, N.Y., 1992. Cert. elem. tchr. N-6, reading K-12. Elem. reading specialist Parliament Place Elem. Sch. North Babylon (N.Y.) Unified Sch. Dist., 1992-94; kindergarten/reading recovery tchr. Lee Road Elem. Sch./Levittown (N.Y.) Unified Sch. Dist., 1994—; mem. Reading Recovery Coun. N.Am. Dowling Coll. grad assistantship, 1990-92; Marist Coll. Presdl. scholar, 1986. Mem. Internat. Reading Assn., Nassau Reading Coun., Nat. Coun. Tchrs. English, Alpha Upsilon (Alpha Beta chpt. sec. 1992—). Office: 901 Lee Rd Wantagh NY 11793

STEIGER, BETTIE ALEXANDER, information industry specialist; b. Spirit Lake, Idaho, Jan. 27, 1934; d. Walter and Velma Esteline (Williamson) Alexander; m. Donald Wayne Steiger, Nov. 10, 1956; children: Craig Alexander Scott, Ann Alexander Carla. BS in Polit. Sci., Wash. State U., 1956, postgrad., 1957; AMP, Harvard U., 1987. V.p. Gartner Group, Inc., Stamford, Conn., Reference Tech. Inc.; exec. dir. Assn. for Info and Image Mgmt., Silver Spring, Md.; dir. to prin. Worldwide Mktg. Xerox Corp., McLean, Va.; prin. tech. and market devel. v.p. Xerox Graphic Sys., Palo Alto, Calif.; founder online system The Source; bd. dirs. Wall Data, Inc. Founder Army Family Symposium, 1979; class sec. Harvard Bus. Sch., 1987—; bd. dirs. Internat. Sch. Info. Mgmt. Recipient Outstanding Alumni award Wash. State U., 1988. Mem. Internat. Women's Forum, Women's Forum West, Army Officers Wives (pres. Greater Washington Area 1976), Wash. State U. Found. (bd. regents), Info. Industry Assn., Videotex Industry Assn. (bd. dirs.), Am. Women's Club (pres. 1971), Pi Beta Phi (pres. alumnae prov. 1965). Republican. Presbyterian. Home: 1370 Trinity Dr Menlo Park CA 94025-6680

STEIGER, JANET DEMPSEY, government official; b. Oshkosh, Wis., June 10, 1939; 1 child, William Raymond. BA, Lawrence Coll., 1961; postgrad., U. Reading, Eng., 1961-62, U. Wis., 1962-63; LLD (hon.), Lawrence U., 1992. Legis. aide Office of Gov., Wis., 1965; v.p. The Work Place, Inc., 1975-80; commr. Postal Rate Commn., Washington, 1980-89, acting chmn., 1981-82, chmn., 1982-89; commr. FTC, Washington, 1989—; U.S. del. OECD, Paris, 1989—. Author: Law Enforcement and Juvenile Justice in Wisconsin, 1965; co-author: To Light One Candle, a Handbook on Organizing, Funding and Maintaining Public Service Projects, 1978, 2d edit., 1980. Chmn. Commn. on Vets. Edn. Policy, 1987-90. Woodrow Wilson scholar; Fulbright scholar, 1961. Mem. Phi Beta Kappa. Office: FTC Office of Chmn 6th & Pennsylvania Ave NW Washington DC 20580-0002

STEIGERWALD, BEVERLY, sculptor, educator; b. Akron, Ohio, Nov. 15, 1934; d. Benjamin Wilford and Marion Eleanor (Ion) Betz; m. James Carl Steigerwald, June 21, 1958 (dec. 1988); children: Mary Jo, Michael, James, Denise, Michelle, Suzanne, Beth. Attended, Cleve. Inst. Art, 1952-54. Sculpture tchr. Art Students League, Denver, 1995—; chmn. organizing com. Foothills Art Ctr., N.Am. Sculpture Exhbn., Golden, Colo., 1985-92; presenter Interfaith Forum on Religion, Art and Architecture, Brno, Czechoslovakia, 1992; presenter Exposition des Artistes Americains, Auvillar, France, 1996; lectr. Cath. City Women's Club, Akron, 1995. Prin. works include life-size bronze figures St. Michael the Archangel Ch., Aurora, Colo., 1990, 15 relief bronze plaques St. Patrick Ch., Colorado Springs, Colo., 1991, bronze relief figure and wall Mercy Hosp. Chapel, Denver, 1992, outdoor life-size bronze Queen of Peace Ch., Aurora, Colo., 1993. Vol. Foothills Art Ctr., 1976—. Recipient Excaliber Bronze award Catherine Lorillard Wolfe Art Club, 1986, Roman Bronze award Pen and Brush, 1987, Internat. Visual Arts Citation award Interfaith Forum on Religion, Art and Architecture, 1991. Home and Office: 782 South Emporia Denver CO 80231

STEIGERWALDT, DONNA WOLF, clothing manufacturing company executive; b. Chgo., Apr. 2, 1929; d. Harry Hay and Donna (Curry) Wolf; m. William Steigerwaldt, Dec. 31, 1969; children: Debra, Linda. BA, U. Colo., Colo. Springs, 1950, LHD (hon.), 1987. Ins. broker Conn. Mut. Life Ins. Co., Chgo., 1950-53; vice chmn. Jockey Internat., Inc., Kenosha, Wis., 1978-80, chmn., chief exec. officer, 1980—. Pres. Donna Wolf Steigerwaldt Found., Inc.; mem. Infant Welfare Soc., Evanston Hosp.-Glenbrook Hosp. Corp., N.W. Cmty. Hosp. Aux., Aid to Animals No. Ill., Inc.; vice chmn. Carthage Coll., 1982-92, chmn., 1992—; bd. dirs. Century Club Sarasota Meml. Hosp. Paul Harris fellow, Rotary, 1984. Mem. Am. Apparel Mfrs. Assn., Navy League U.S., Glenview Hist. Soc., Exec. Women Internat. (hon.), Rotary (Paul Harris fellow 1984). Republican. Episcopalian. Clubs: North Shore Country, Plaza, Valley Lo Sports; Meadows Country (Sarasota, Fla.). Office: Jockey Internat Inc 2300 60th St Kenosha WI 53140-3822

STEIGMAN, CARMEN KAY, pathologist; b. Dallas, May 14, 1956; d. Walter Benjamin and Margaret Louise (Patton) S. BS, N.E. La. U., 1977; MD, La. State U., 1983; MPH, St. Louis U., 1994. Diplomate Am. Bd. Pathology; cert. anatomic, clin. and pediatric pathology. Pathology resident Fairfax Hosp., Falls Church, Va., 1983-87; pediatric pathology fellow Children's Hosp. of Phila., 1987-89; pathologist Sparrow Hosp., Lansing, Mich., 1989-90; asst. prof. pathology St. Louis U. Sch. Medicine, 1990—; pathologist Cardinal Glennon Childrens Hosp., 1990-96; dir. Pub. Health Lab. City of St. Louis Dept. Health & Hosps., 1996—. Fellow Coll. Am. Pathologists; mem. Soc. for Pediatric Pathology, Am. Assn. Clin. Chemistry, Am. Coll. Physician Execs., Am. Pathology Found. Office: Pub Health Lab 634 N Grand Blvd Saint Louis MO 63104

STEIN, ANNE MADELINE, secondary education educator, consultant; b. Phila., Sept. 5, 1935; d. Graignor Franklin and Anne Mary (Fay) S.; (div. Dec. 1993); children: William Reagan, Brian Reagan, Antonia Tellis. BA, Calif. State U., Sacramento, 1965; MA, Calif. State U., Northridge, 1969. Cert. tchr. secondary and jr. coll. English and social studies. Tchr. Tamalpais (Calif.) H.S. Dist., 1970-87; tutor, ednl. cons. Marin County, Calif., 1992-95. Organizer slide show and lectures History of Women Artists, Northern Calif. Coun. Nat. Mus. Women in the Arts; founding mother Women on the Move, Marin County, Calif., 1971-75, Redwood Child Devel. Ctr., Marin County, 1971-75, Kids Without Support, Marin County, 1975-77. Mem. Educators in Pvt. Practice, 1991-95.

STEIN, CHERYL DENISE, lawyer; b. N.Y.C., Nov. 3, 1953; d. Arthur Earl and Joyce (Weitzman) S. BA magna cum laude, Yale U., 1974; postgrad., U. Chgo., 1974-75; JD, Yale U., 1977. Bar: D.C. 1978, U.S. Dist. Ct. D.C. 1983, U.S. Dist. Ct. Md. 1995, U.S. Ct. Appeals (D.C. cir.) 1988. Atty. advisor CAB, Washington, 1978-79; assoc. Cohn & Marks, Washington, 1979-82; pvt. practice Washington, 1982—. Vol. reader radio reading svc. for the blind Washington Ear, Silver Spring, Md., 1982-91; vol. tutor Friends of Tyler Sch., 1992-95; pvt. vol. tutor, 1995—. Mem. Nat. Assn. Criminal Def. Lawyers, D.C. Assn. Criminal Def. Lawyers, George Washington Am. Inn of Ct. Democrat. Jewish. Office: 705 8th St SE Ste 100 Washington DC 20003-2856

STEIN, ELEANOR BENSON, playwright; b. New Haven, Conn., Feb. 18, 1922; d. Harry Lorin and Bertha Adeline (Schwolow) Benson; m. Louis Stein; children: Eleanor Smith, Patrice Forgues, Mary Kelly, Paul Stein. Student, Rockland C.C., Suffern, N.Y., 1966-67, S.D. State U., 1969-70, Mesa Coll., 1975, S.D. City Coll., 1976. Office mgr. Thatcher & Hurst Attys., San Diego, Calif., 1968-73. Author: (plays) Squeeze, 1989, Emily Dickinson, 1996; (poetry) Journey's End, 1985, Muggsy McGrew Looks After the Zoo, 1985, others. Bd. dirs. local theater groups. Recipient Clara Barton Roll of Honored Women Unitarian Universalist Women's Fedn., 1978, Aurelia Reinhardt Roll of Honored Women, 1983, Unitarian Universalist award for cmty. svc. First Universalist Ch., 1990, Woman of Achievement So. Regional Conf. Women, 1991. Mem. Nat. League Am. Pen Women, Nat. Womens Polit. Caucus, Dramatists Guild, Scripteasers, Poets in Profile. Home and Office: 4870 1/2 Old Cliffs Rd San Diego CA 92120

STEIN, ELLYN BETH, mental health services professional; b. Chgo.. BS, Ariz. State U., 1988, M of Counseling, 1991. Cert. profl. counselor, Ariz. Rsch. asst. Ariz. State U., Tempe, 1985, 87, practicum, 1990, grad. asst., 1990, 91; residential counselor/supr. Wayland Family Ctrs., Phoenix, Ariz., 1988-91; intern St. Luke's Behavioral Health, Phoenix, 1991, Phoenix Adolescent Recovery Ctr., 1991; intake specialist II ComCare, Phoenix, 1991-94; needs assessment and referral coord. Charter, Chandler, Ariz., 1993—; clin. case mgr. Contact, Tempe, 1994—; vol. crisis counselor Terros, Phoenix, 1989-95; vol. warm line ComCare, Phoenix, 1995—. Mem. Valley of the Sun Active 20/30 Club, Phoenix, 1993—; vol. Make-A-Wish Found., Phoenix, 1995—. Mem. Am. Counseling Assn., Am. Mental Health Counselors Assn., Phi Beta Kappa (2nd v.p. 1994—).

STEIN, JO-AN ZIMMERMAN, financial advisor, securities trader, insurance agent; b. Attica, Ohio, Feb. 7, 1927; d. Darrel Daniel and Alta (Rogers) Zimmerman; m. William George Stein, Sept. 9, 1950; children: Barbara J. Hellwig, Robert W., Diane E. Glidden, William D. BS, Heidelberg Coll., 1948; MS, Purdue U., 1950. Cert. fin. planner. Instr. chem. lab. Heidelberg Coll., Tiffin, Ohio, 1948-49, 51-53; rsch. asst. Purdue U., W. Lafayette, Ind., 1949-50; dir. rsch. Linde Air Products, Lackawanna, N.Y., 1950-51; instr. chem. lab. U. Toledo (Ohio), 1952-56; substitute tchr. Churchville (N.Y.) Ctrl. Sch., 1968-78; fin. planner, sr. fin. adv. Am. Express, Rochester, N.Y., 1978—. Contbr. articles to profl. jours. Bd. trustees YWCA, Rochester, N.Y., 1980-83. Mem. Livonia (N.Y.) C. of C. (bd. dirs. 1979-83), Gates C. of C. (bd. dirs. 1979-83). Presbyterian. Office: Am Express Fin Advs 300 Canal View Blvd Ste 300 Rochester NY 14623

STEIN, MARY KATHERINE, writer, editor, communications executive; b. Denver, Sept. 7, 1944; d. Robert Addison and Minta Mary (MacDonald) Dunlap; m. Lawrence Bronstein, June 29, 1970 (div. 1974); m. Donald L. Stein, Aug. 16, 1982. BS in Journalism, U. Kans., 1966. Sr. editor Am Family Physician mag., Kansas City, Mo., 1967-78; editor-in-chief Current Prescribing mag., Oradell, N.J., 1978-79; sr. editor Diagnosis mag., Oradell, 1979-83; mng. editor Advances in Reproductive Medicine, Bolton, Conn., 1983-85; pres. MD Comm., Tucson, 1983—. Author: Child Abuse, 1987, Caring for the AIDS Patient, 1987, Lifetime Weight Control, 1988, Substance Abuse, 1988, An Overview of HIV Infections and AIDS, 1989, Cardiovascular Disease: Evaluation and Prevention, 1989; mng. editor: Eating Disorders Rev., 1990—; editor Nutrition and the M.D., 1992-95; contbr. articles to mags. Mem. Women in Comm. (pres. Greater Kansas City chpt. 1977-78, pres. Orange County chpt. 1990-92), Am. Med. Writers Assn. Democrat. Lutheran. Office: MD Comm 302 S Pinto Pl Tucson AZ 85748-6902

STEIN, PAULA NANCY, psychologist, educator; b. N.Y.C., Aug. 23, 1963; d. Michael and Evelyn (Graber) S.; m. Andreas Howard Smoller, Sept. 2, 1991; 1 child, Rebecca Leigh Smoller. BA, Skidmore Coll., 1985; MA with distinction, Hofstra U., 1986, PhD, 1989. Lic. clin. psychologist, N.Y.; cert. in sch. psychology, N.Y. Intern NYU Med. Ctr.-Rusk Inst., N.Y.C., 1988-89; instr. Mt. Sinai Med. Ctr., N.Y.C., 1989-93, asst. prof. rehab. medicine, 1993—; chief psychologist Fishkill (N.Y.) Consultation Group, 1991—. Contbr. chpt. to book, articles to profl. jours. Kraewic scholar Skidmore Coll., 1985. Mem. APA, Am. Congress Rehab. Medicine (subcom. on tng.), Assn. for Advancement of Behavior Therapy, Hudson Valley Psychol. Assn., Phi Beta Kappa. Jewish. Office: Fishkill Consultation Group Box 446 90 Main St Fishkill NY 12524

STEIN, SANDRA LOU, educational psychologist, educator; b. Freeport, Ill., Oct. 6, 1942; d. William Kenneth and Marien Elizabeth Stein. BS, U. Wis., Madison, 1964; MS in Edn., No. Ill. U., 1967, EdD, 1969. Tchr. English Rockford (Ill.) Sch. Dist., 1964-65; tchr. Russian Jefferson County Sch. Dist., Lakewood, Colo., 1965-66; asst. prof. edn. U. S.C., Columbia, 1969-71, No. Ill. U., DeKalb, 1971-72, Rider U., Lawrenceville, N.J., 1972-75; assoc. prof. edn. Rider Coll., Lawrenceville, N.J., 1975-81, prof. edn., 1981—, dept. chair, 1983-91; cons. on measurement and evaluation, women's edn., 1973—. Contbr. articles to ednl. publs. Treas. Lawrenceville Men's Breakfast Club, 1983-85; deacon Presbyn. Ch. Lawrenceville, 1984-87; contest judge N.J. Fedn. Bus. and Profl. Women, 1989; vol. Habitat for Humanity, Trenton, N.J., 1989. Recipient Disting. Teaching award Rider Coll. and Lindback Found., 1981. Mem. AAUP (Outstanding Achievement award Rider Coll. chpt. 1988), Am. Ednl. Rsch. Assn., Am. Psychol. Assn., Phi Delta Kappa (chpt. pres. 1986-87, Svc. Key award 1991, faculty advisor 1994—). Office: Rider U 2083 Lawrenceville Rd Trenton NJ 08648-3001

STEINBERG, DEBRA BROWN, lawyer; b. Nashville, May 16, 1954. AB, Smith Coll., 1976; JD, Boston Coll., 1979. Bar: N.Y. 1980, U.S. Dist. Ct. (so. and ea. dists.) N.Y., 1981, U.S. Ct. Appeals (2d cir.) 1987. Ptnr. Cadwalader, Wickersham and Taft. Office: Cadwalader Wickersham & Taft 100 Maiden Ave New York NY 10006*

STEINBERG, DEVORAH JILL, social worker, educator; b. N.Y.C., June 3, 1964; d. Alan M. Steinberg and Harriet (Bush) Gerstenfeld. BA, U. Vt., 1986; MSW, Simmons Coll., 1991. Lic. social worker. Intake coord., counselor Habit Mgmt. Inc., Boston, 1988-89; social worker Jewish Big Bros./Sister of Boston, 1991-94; social worker, bereavement counselor Good Samaritan Hosp., Boston, 1994-95; psychotherapist, pvt. practice Brookline, Mass., 1994—; co-founder Grief & Healing Assocs., Newton, Mass., 1995—; workshop leader The Wellness Cmty., Newton, 1993—, cmty. coord., 1995—; presenter Dana Farber Cancer Inst. Conf., Boston, 1994, Ann. Mass. Hospice Fedn. Conf., Marlboro, Mass., 1995, Beth Israel Hosp., 1996, Boston U. Sch. Social Work, 1996. Mem. NASW, Social Work Oncology Group. Democrat. Jewish.

STEINBERG, IRMA FRANCES (IRMA F. BLOOMBERG), retired lawyer; b. Bklyn., July 25, 1928; d. Berry and Mollie Bloomberg; m. Joseph Steinberg; children: Margo Bader, Roberta. BA magna cum laude, St. John's U., Bklyn., 1949, JD cum laude, 1951. Bar: N.Y. 1951. Ptnr. Lesser & Bloomberg, N.Y.C., 1951-52; pvt. practice N.Y.C., 1952-63; ptnr. Bloomberg & Steinberg, N.Y.C., 1963-89; ret., 1989. Bd. dirs. Temple Shalom, Bklyn. Democrat. Jewish. Home: 21452 Juego Cir Boca Raton FL 33433

STEINBERG, JANET ECKSTEIN, journalist; b. Cin.; d. Charles and Adele (Ehrenfeld) Eckstein; m. Irvin S. Silverstein, Oct. 22, 1988; children: Susan Carole Steinberg Somerstein, Jody Lynn Steinberg Lazarow. BS, U. Cin., 1964. Free-lance writer; guest appearances Braun and Co., Sta.-WLW-TV, Sta. WMKV-TV; guest lectr. Tri State Travel Sch., 1994—; travel cons., 1994—; Contbr. numerous articles to newspapers, mags. and books, U.S., Can., Singapore, Australia, N.Z.; travel columnist Cin. Post, 1978-86, Ky. Post, 1978-86, Cin. Enquirer, 1986-94; travel editor S. Fla. Single Living, 1988-92; contbr. Singles Scene and Cin. Mag., 1980—; travel columnist Eastside Weekend Mag., 1994—; contbg. editor Travel Agt., 1986-88, Birnbaum Travel Guides, 1988—, The Writer, 1988-92, Entree, 1986—; travel columnist Northeast mag., 1986-88, South Fla. Single Living, 1984-92. Recipient Lowell Thomas travel journalism award, 1985, 86, 91, Henry E. Bradshaw Travel Journalism award, 1st place, best of show, 1988, Buckeye Travel award Ohio Divsn. Travel & Tourism, 1992. Mem. Am. Soc. Journalists and Authors, Soc. Am. Travel Writers (1st place award for best newspaper story 1981, 3d place award for best mag. story 1981, 91, 1st place award for best newspaper article award 1984, 91, best mag. article 1985, 2d place award best pathos article, 1984, 88, 2d place award specific category, 1989, 1st place award best mag. series, 2d place best mag. article), Midwest Travel Writers Assn. (Best Mag. Story award 1981, 95, Best Series award 1981, 84, 94, 96, Cipriani award 1981, 1st place award best article 1989, 2d place award for best article 1982-84, 89, 95, 3d place award best article 1992, Mark Twain award 1992, best mag. series), Am. Soc. Journalists and Authors, Soc. Am. Travel Writers, Midwest Travel Writers Assn., Soc. Profl. Journalists, Losantiville Country Club, Travelers Century Club, Circumnavigators Club. Home: 900 Adams Crossing # 9200 Cincinnati OH 45202-1666

STEINBERG, JOAN EMILY, retired middle school educator; b. San Francisco, Dec. 9, 1932; d. John Emil and Kathleen Helen (Montgomery) S. BA, U. Calif.-Berkeley, 1954; EdD, U. San Francisco, 1981. Tchr., Vallejo (Calif.) Unified Sch. Dist., 1959-61, San Francisco Unified Sch. Dist., 1961-93, elem. tchr., 1961-78, tchr. life and phys. sci. jr. high sch., 1978-85, 87-93, sci. cons., 1985-87; lectr. elem. edn. San Francisco State U., 1993-94; ind. sci. edn. cons., 1993—. Contbr. articles to zool. and edn. books and profl. jours. Fulbright scholar U. Sydney (Australia), 1955-56; recipient Calif. Educator award, 1988, Outstanding Educator in Teaching award U. San Francisco Alumni Soc., 1989. Mem. ASCD, San Francisco Zool. Soc., Exploratorium, Astron. Soc. Pacific, Am. Fedn. Tchrs., Calif. Acad. Scis., Calif. Malacozool. Soc., Nat. Sci. Tchrs. Assn., Elem. Sch. Sci. Assn. (sec. 1984-85, pres. 1986-87, newsletter editor 1994—), Calif. Sci. Tchrs. Assn., Sigma Xi. Democrat.

STEINBERG, MARCIA BEVERLY, microbiologist; b. Phila., Sept. 20, 1950; d. David and Ruth (Greenfield) S. BS, Rutgers U., 1972, MBA, 1984. cert. pathologist. Med. tech. Cooper Med. Ctr., Camden, N.J., 1972-76, Children's Hosp., Phila., 1976-80; from microbiologist to specialist mktg./tech. EM Diagnostic Sys., Gibbstown, N.J., 1980-88; from microbiologist to supervisor Whitehall/Robins Labs., Hammonton, N.J., 1988-95; mgr. microbiol. control CIBA Self-Medication, Ft. Washington, Pa., 1995—. Mem. Am. Soc. Clin. Pathologists, Am. Soc. Microbiology. Jewish. Office: CIBA Self-Medication 500 Virginia Dr Fort Washington PA 19034-8727

STEINBERG, SYBIL JOAN, editor; b. Bridgeport, Conn., May 3, 1933; d. Marcus Leon and Ann (Backer) Schless; m. Harold Steinberg, Nov. 28, 1954; children: Jonathan, Peter, Richard. BA, Smith Coll., 1954; MA, Fairfield U., 1975. Contbg. editor Pubs. Weekly, Westport, Conn., 1976-79, assoc. editor, 1979-83, editor Pubs. Weekly interviews, 1982—, editor Fiction Forecast, 1983—; bd. dirs. Carolina Pub. Inst., Chapel Hill, N.C. Editor: (book) Writing for Your Life vol. I, 1992, vol. II, 1995. Founder, co-dir. Coun. Pre-Sch. for Disadvantaged Children, Westport, 1965-69. Mem. Nat. Book Critics' Cir. (bd. dirs. 1989-92), Women's Media Group, Phi Beta Kappa. Office: Publishers Weekly 249 W 17th St Westport CT 06880

STEINEGER, MARGARET LEISY, non-profit organization officer; b. Newton, Kans., Feb. 8, 1926; d. Ernest Erwin and Elva Agnes (Krehbiel) L.; m. John Francis Steineger, Dec. 2, 1949; children: John Steineger III, Cindy Blair, Melissa, Chris. B., So. Meth. U., 1947; M. in Social Work, U. Kans., 1949. County vice-chair United Way, Kansas City, Kans., 1960-61; bd., sec., treas. Wyandotte County Bar Aux., Kans., 1960-63; bd. Jr. League of Kansas City, 1962-66, County Coun. PTA, Wyandotte County, 1963-66, KCK Friends of the Arts, Kansas City, 1974-77; pres. Grinter Place Mus. Friends, Kans., 1977-78; bd. Kaw Valley Arts Coun., Kansas City, 1982-86; commr. Landmarks Commn., Kansas City, 1985-87; bd. Arts with the Handicapped, Wyandotte County, 1986—; bd. dirs. Kans. Arts Adv. Bd., Grinter Place Friends, Kans., Tri-County Tourism Coun., Kans. V.p. Kans. Legis. Wives, Topeka, 1975-76; bd. dirs. KCK Friends of the Libr., Kansas City, 1984—, Shepherd's Ctr., 1996—; founder Wyandotte County Libr., 1963-64, Creative Experiences, Kansas City, 1967; commr. Kans. Arts Commn., 1965-85; mem. Kaw Valley Arts and Humanities Bd., 1988-92; mem. adv. bd. Parents as Tchrs., 1992—; mem. KCK C.C. Endowment Bd., 1989—. Recipient Humanities award Kans. Com. for the Humanities, 1989; named Citizen of Yr. Kansas City, Kans., 1978. Democrat. Methodist. Home: 6400 Valleyview St Kansas City KS 66111-2013 Office: Security Bank Building Ste 600 Kansas City KS 66101

STEIN EIRICH, GENEVIEVE THERESA, reading specialist, elementary school educator; b. Sheboygan, Wis., Oct. 26, 1945; d. Alfred A. and Irene E. (Bonde) Stein; m. Stephen E. Eirich, Dec. 23, 1967; children: Michelle Ann, Sharon Marie. BA, U. Wis., 1975; MA, Carthage Coll., 1981. Cert. tchr. elem. edn. 1-8, reading K-12, reading specialist K-12. Elem. tchr. Milw. Archdiocese, Sheboygan, 1965-72, Kenosha (Wis.) Unifed Schs., 1975-88; reading specialist Kenosha (Wis.) Unified Schs., 1988—; coord. beginning tchrs./mentors Kenosha Unified Schs., 1994-95, talent devel. com., site-based village partnership, dimensions of learning action team, staff com., bldg. level team, multi-age sub., task force for dist. implementation of inclusion, staff devel. coun., lang. arts com., site-based com. for staff devel. Mem. parish coun. St. Mary's Catholic Ch., Kenosha, 1990-93, 96-99, liturgy com., 1989—. Recipient Herb Kohl award Herb Kohl Edn. Found., 1994. Mem. ASCD, NEA, Internat. Reading Assn., Nat. Staff Devel. Coun., Assn. for Early Childhood, Wis. Reading Assn., Nat. Coun. Tchrs. English, Racine-Kenosha Reading Coun., Staff Devel. Coun., Kenosha Edn. Assn. (bd. dirs. 1980—), Phi Delta Kappa. Office: Kenosha Unified Sch Dist 3600 52nd St Kenosha WI 53144-2664

STEINEM, GLORIA, writer, editor, lecturer; b. Toledo, Mar. 25, 1934; d. Leo and Ruth (Nuneviller) S. BA, Smith Coll., 1956; postgrad. (Chester Bowles Asian fellow), India, 1957-58; D. Human Justice, Simmons Coll., 1973. Co-dir., dir. ednl. found. Ind. Rsch. Svc., Cambridge, Mass. and N.Y.C., 1959-60; contbg. editor Glamour Mag., N.Y.C., 1962-69; co-founder, contbg. editor New York Mag., 1968-72; feminist lectr., 1969—; co-founder, editor Ms. Mag., 1971-87, columnist, 1980-87, cons. editor, 1987—; Active various civil rights and peace campaigns including United Farmworkers, Vietnam War Tax Protest, Com. for the Legal Def. of Angela Davis (treas., 1971-72); active polit. campaigns of Adlai Stevenson, Robert Kennedy, Eugene McCarthy, Shirley Chisholm, George McGovern; Co-founder, bd. dirs. Women's Action Alliance, 1970—; convenor, mem. nat. adv. com. Nat. Women's Polit. Caucus, 1971—; co-founder, pres. bd. dirs. Ms. Found. for Women, 1972—; founding mem. Coalition of Labor Union Women, 1974; mem. Internat. Women's Year Commn., 1977; editorial cons., Conde Nast Publications, 1962-69, Curtis Publishing, 1964-65, Random House Publishing, 1988—, McCall Publishing. Author: The Thousand Indias, 1957, The Beach Book, 1963, Wonder Woman, 1972, Outrageous Acts and Everyday Rebellions, 1983, Marilyn: Norma Jeane, 1986, Revolution from Within: A Book of Self-Esteem, 1992, Moving Beyond Words, 1994; contgb. corr. NBC Today Show, 1987-88; contbr. to various anthologies. Pres. Voters for Choice, 1979—. Recipient Penney-Missouri Journalism award, 1970, Ohio Gov.'s award for Journalism, 1972, Bill of Rights award ACLU of So. Calif., 1975; named Woman of the Yr. McCall's mag., 1972; Woodrow Wilson Internat. Ctr. for Scholars fellow, 1977; inducted into Nat. Women's Hall of Fame, 1993. Mem. NOW, AFTRA, Nat. Press Club, Soc. Mag. Writers, Authors' Guild, Phi Beta Kappa. Office: Ms Magazine 230 Park Ave Fl 7 New York NY 10169-0799*

STEINER, BETSY DAVIES, equestrian, trainer, public speaker, commentator, author; b. Cleve., Feb. 2, 1951; d. John E. and June A. (Davies) McMillan; m. Uwe Steiner, Feb. 14, 1970 (separated); children: Jessie L., Devon R. Student, Reitinstitut von Neindorff, Karlsruhe, Germany, 1969-71. Examiner for cert. instrs. U.S. Dressage Fedn. Team mem. Concours Dressur Internat. U.S. Equestrian Team, Toronto, Can., 1986; team mem. U.S. Equestrian Team, Lusanne, Switzerland, 1988; individual Am. Horse Show Assn., U.S. Equestrian Team, Aachen, Germany, 1990; U.S. Equestrian Team mem. World Equestrian Games, Stockholm, 1990; team mem. Olympic Sports Festival, L.A., 1991; coach, chef d'equipe young rider, Ill., Calif., 1991-95; mem. Athlete's Adv. Coun. to U.S. Olympic Com., 1995—. Contbr. articles to profl. jours. Recipient Tiffany award for most elegant rider Tiffany Jewelers, Delmar, Calif., 1994. Mem. U.S. Equestrian Team (bd. dirs. 1992-93, chmn. active riders com. 1992—), Am. Horse Show Assn. (bd. dirs. 1992—). Home: 2764 Borchard Rd Newbury Park CA 91320 Office: Dressage Classic Internat 933 W Potrero Thousand Oaks CA 91361

STEINER, CLARA, artist, educator, curator; b. Annapolis, Md., July 10, 1924; d. Nathan and Minnie (Feldstein) Swead; m. Hans Steiner, Aug. 24, 1966. Cert. Fine Arts, Cooper Union, 1947; student, S.W. Hayter's Printmaking Workshop, 1947-48, Brooklyn Mus. Art Sch., 1953-55; BS in Art Edn., NYU, 1969; MS in Art Edn., Pratt Inst. Art specialist Alzheimers Day Care Ctr. Herricks (N.Y.) Schs., 1992—; curator Manhasset (N.Y.) Libr. Gallery, 1990—; art specialist h.s. divsn. N.Y.C. Pub. Schs., 1968-80; instr. fine arts divsn. continuing edn. Hofstra U. One woman exhbns. Sunken Meadow Gallery, Smithtown, N.Y., 1963, Cooper Union Alumni Gallery, N.Y.C., 1974, Manhasset (N.Y.) Libr. Gallery, Gallery 84, N.Y.C., 1980, Port Washington (N.Y.) Gallery; group exhbns. include City Ctr. Gallery, N.Y.C., 1960, Elaine Starkman Gallery, N.Y.C., 1986, Gayle Wilson Gallery, Southampton, N.Y., 1991, Erector Sq. Gallery, New Haven, Conn., 1992, Artemisia Gallery, Chgo., 1993, Audubon Artists, N.Y.C, 1994, Shirley Goodman Gallery FIT, N.Y.C., 1995, The Print Club, Phila., Brooklyn (N.Y.) Mus. Student Gallery, Mus. Modern Art, N.Y.C., Soc. Am. Graphic Artists, C.W. Post, Brookville, N.Y., Penn's Landing Mus., Phila., Mills Pond House, St. James, N.Y., Firehouse Gallery Nassau Cmty. Coll., Fibre Forum, Sands Point, N.Y., New Print U.S.A. U. Minn., Mpls., New Prints Northeast Binnewater Arts Ctr., N.Y., Windows on White St., N.Y.C., Castillo Gallery, N.Y.C., Elaine Benson Gallery, Bridgehampton, N.Y.C., Graphic Eye Gallery, Port Washington, N.Y., Westbeth Gallery, N.Y., Shelter Rock Art Gallery, Manhassett, N.Y., Gallery North, Setauket, N.Y., Ann Harper Gallery, Amagansett, N.Y., Harper Collins Exhbn. Space, N.Y.; permanent collections Shelter Rock Art Gallery, Unitarian Universalist Ch.; featured in N.Y. Times Long Island Sect. Art Review. Home: 14 4th St Manhasset NY 11030

STEINER, DONNA FORBES, minister, consultant; b. Pierson, Iowa, Sept. 8, 1937; d. Dewey Wainwright and Veda Mae (Vannorsdel) Forbes; m. Paul David Steiner, Sept. 21, 1974; children: David Paul, Jonathan L., Ethan Greg. BA in Music Edn., Drake U., 1959; MA in Religious Edn., Bethany Theol. Seminary, Ill., 1964. Ordained to ministry, 1974. Tchr. English and music Brethren Vol. Svc. Ch. of the Brethren, Jos, Nigeria, 1960-62; min. of edn. Ch. of the Brethren, Palmyra, Pa., 1964-68; adminstrv. asst. Mid-Atlantic Ch. of the Brethren, Ellicott City, Md., 1968-69; mgr. theol. bookstore Bethany Sem. Ch. of the Brethren, Oak Brook, Ill., 1969-70; assoc. min.

York Ctr. Ch. of the Brethren, Lombard, Ill., 1969-74; co-pastor Ch. of the Brethren, Union Bridge, Md., 1976-82; congregation cons. Mid-Atlantic Ch. of the Brethren, Ellicott City, 1982-85; ministry cons. Ch. of the Brethren, Union Bridge, 1985—; min. Christian edn. St. Paul's United Ch. of Christ, Westminster, Md., 1987-95; spkr. Ch. of the Brethren Conf., Dayton, Ohio, 1975, retreat leader, Ohio, Pa., Va., Md., 1996; theol. tchr. Ch. of the Brethren Mid-Atlantic Dist., Frederick, Md., moderator Mid-Atlantic dist., 1994; co-chmn. Nat. Coun. Chs. Comm. Ch./Ministries in Edn., Cin., 1984—; mem. devel. coun. Jubilee Anabapt. Curriculum, 1986-92. Author: (study resource) Partners in Learning, 1991. Mem. AAUW (v.p. membership, ednl. found. chair 1985—), Ch. of the Brethren assn. of Christian Educators (charter, pres. 1978—). Democrat. Home and Office: 4791 Bark Hill Rd PO Box 518 Union Bridge MD 21791-0518

STEINER, GLORIA LITWIN, psychologist; b. Newark, Oct. 21, 1922; d. David Milton and Minna (Krasner) Litwin; m. Charles Steiner, Aug. 29, 1942; children: Charles Jr., Susan Steiner Sher, Jeanne. BA, U. Pa., 1944; MS, CCNY, 1956; EdD, Columbia U., 1965. Psychologist St. Michael's Hosp. and Mt. Carmel, Newark, 1956-62; chief psychologist Children's Hosp., Newark, 1965-78; prof. psychology, dir. psychol. svc. Child Study Ctr., Kean Coll., Union, N.J., 1971-78; vis. assoc. prof. grad. sch. applied and profl. psychology Rutgers U., Piscataway, N.J., 1976-94; clin. assoc. prof., former dir. psychology tng. U. Medicine and Dentistry N.J.-N.J. Med. Sch., Newark, 1978—; psychology cons. Nat. Pediatric HIV Resource Ctr., 1991-94. Co-author: Traumatic Abuse/Children, 1980; co-editor: Children, Families and HIV/AIDS: Psychosocial and Psychotherapeutic Issues, 1995; contbr. articles to profl. jours.; mem. editl. bd. Jour. Psychotherapy, 1981-96. Mem. N.J. State Task Force on AIDS, 1986-89, N.J. State Bd. Psychol. Exam., 1978-84, Regional Health Planning Coun., N.J., 1984-85, child adv. com. Mental Health Assn., N.J., 1974-80; trustee, founder N.J. Acad. Psychology, 1978-83, bd. trustees, 1994—. Grantee tng. health care workers Regional AIDS Edn. and Tng. Ctr. U. Medicine and Dentistry N.J., Newark, 1990, Nat. Pediat. HIV Resource Ctr., Newark, 1991-94. Fellow Am. Orthopsychiat. Assn.; mem. N.Y. Acad. Scis., N.J. Assn. for the Advancement Family Therapy (vice-chmn. 1979-81), Am. Psychol. Assn. Home and Office: 35 Sequoia Dr Watchung NJ 07060-6113

STEINER, HOPE ELIZABETH, school counselor; b. St. Louis, Feb. 24, 1952; d. William Frank and Antonette (Liolios) Speros; m. Jeffrey Jay Steiner, July 23, 1977; children: Sarah Elizabeth, Laura Antonette. BS, U. Mo., 1973, MEd, 1974. Lic. profl. counselor, Mo.; nat. cert. counselor. Counselor, dir. counseling Cowley County C.C., Arkansas City, Kans., 1974-82; dir. counseling svcs. St. Louis C.C.- Meramec, 1982-93, counselor, assoc. prof., dept. chair, 1993-96, counselor, prof., 1996—; mem. campus coms. Wellness, AIDS Awareness, Instrnl. Coun., St. Louis C.C.- Meramec, 1982—; developer, organizer mental health seminars students and cmty., 1990—, clin. dir. screening depression and eating disorders, 1995, 96; pvt. practice counselor St. Louis Ctr. Healing Arts, 1993-95. Co-chair cookie sales Girl Scouts, 1988-90; vol. counselor to Flood '93 victims ARC, 1993; active citizen's adv. com. Parkway Sch. Dist., St. Louis, 1994-96, exec. com. PTO Southwest Middle Sch., St. Louis, 1995-96, adv. coun. Valley Park Sch. Dist.- A-Plus Sch. Grant, St. Louis, 1995—. Recipient cert. Leadership, YWCA, St. Louis, 1984; named for Outstanding Merit in the Area of Continuing Edn., Nat. Bd. Certified Counselors, 1990-94, scholastic judge Jr. Miss, South St. Louis County, 1994. Mem. Am. Coll. Counseling Assn., Mo. Coll. Counseling Assn., Kans. Coll. Counseling Assn. (pres. 1976), Mo. C.C. Assn., St. Louis Counseling Assn. (pres.-elect 1995-96), St. Louis Psychol. Assn. Office: St Louis CC-Meramec 11333 Big Bend Blvd Saint Louis MO 63122

STEINER, MARY ANN, nursing administrator, consultant; b. Spokane, Wash., Nov. 12, 1946; d. John Anthony and Mildred Ann (Costello) S. Vacat. nurse (cum laude), Coll. San Mateo, 1970; RN, NYU, 1980. Staff nurse Mills Meml. Hosp., San Mateo, Calif., 1970-73; charge nurse emergency dept. Grande Ronde Hosp., LaGrande, Oreg., 1973-76; charge nurse CCU, SCU Mills Meml. Hosp., San Mateo, 1976-90; pres. Maids, Etc., San Mateo, 1990-92; supr. advice nurse Mills-Peninsula Homecare, Burlingame, Calif., 1992-94; home health nursing educator Age Ctr. Alliance, Burlingame, 1992-94; home health nurisng educator Age Ctr. Alliance, Menlo Park, Calif., 1993—; nurse mgr. telemedicine dept. MidPeninsula Homecare & Hospice, Mountainview, Calif., 1994—; pub. speaker League of Women Voters, San Mateo, 1985-95, Calif. State dir. of speakers No. On Prop. 128, Burlingame, 1990, telemedicine cons. Hosp. Consortium of San Mateo Co., Burlingame, 1993—. Bd. dirs. League of Women Voters, San Mateo, 1985-95, vice chair Libertarian party, San Mateo, 1995—. Roman Catholic. Home: 815 N Humboldt San Mateo CA 94401

STEINER, SHARI YVONNE, publisher, editor, journalist; b. Colorado Springs, Colo., Mar. 3, 1941; d. Evan Keith and Blanche Marie (Ketzner) Montgomery; m. Clyde Lionel Steiner, June 24, 1962; children: Vienna Kay, Marco Romano. BA, Adams State Coll., 1962; cert. in sociology, London Sch. Econs., 1978; postgrad., U. Calif., Berkeley, 1988—. Lic. real estate broker, Calif. Freelance journalist various publs., 1964—; owner, mgr. SREI Group, San Francisco, 1985-87; tng. design developer loan div. 1st Nationwide Bank, San Francisco, 1987—; pub., editor Ind. Info. Publs., San Francisco, 1990—; pres. The SREI Group, San Francisco; feature writer Internat. Herald Tribune, Rome, 1964-79; acct. exec. Allen, Ingersol & Weber, Rome, 1970-72; gen. ptnr. Greenhaven Park, Sacramento, 1990—, Port Chicago Indsl., Concord, Calif., 1991—. Author: The Female Factor: A Report on Women in Europe, 1972, 2d edit., 1978, Steiners' Complete How to Move Handbook, 1996; editor The Bottom Line newsletter, 1985—; assoc. editor The Semaphore, 1990—. Coord. urban reforestation Friends of Urban Forest, San Francisco, 1989; co-founder New Sch. for Internat. Elem. Students, Rome, 1970. Recipient internat. journalism award Guida Monaci, 1970, award of merit Lotus Club, N.Y.C., 1975; corr. in archives Am. Heritage Ctr., U. Wyo. Mem. Nat. Assn. Realtors (multiple listing svc. selection com. 1986, 91, investment real estate group 1991), Comml. Real Estate Women (editor, bd. dirs. 1985—), Am. Soc. Journalists and Authors, PEN Internat., Employee Relocation Coun.

STEINER-HOUCK, SANDRA LYNN, interior designer; b. Columbia, Pa., May 29, 1962; d. Howard Jr. and Mary Louise Steiner; m. Paul Harry Houck, Sept. 14, 1990; children: Brandon Paul, Brittany Leigh. AA in Interior Design, Bauder Fashion Coll., 1981. Cert. kitchen designer. Designer Bob Harry's Kitchen Ctr., Inc., York, Pa., 1982-87, Leggett, Inc., Camp Hill, Pa., 1987-90, Mother Hubbard's Kitchen Ctr., Mechanicsburg, Pa., 1990-93; owner ind. design svc., 1994—. Designer: Bath Industry Technical Manuals Vol.3, 1993; contbr. designs to profl. jours. Recipient 1st pl. award and Best of Show Resdl. Bath Design, 1986, Showroom Design, 1989, 3d pl. award Resdl. Kitchen, 1992, Resdl. Bath Design, 1992, Heritage Custom Kitchens Mfr.'s Design award, 1986, 94, 3 Nat. Design. awards Resdl. Kitchen, 1994, Kasmar Kitchen Design award 1994, 95, 96. Mem. Am. Soc. Interior Design, Soc. Cert. Kitchen Designers. Home and Office: 515 Mockingbird Dr Columbia PA 17512

STEINFELS, MARGARET O'BRIEN, editor; b. Chgo., July 28, 1941; m. Peter Steinfels, Aug. 31, 1963; 2 children: Gabrielle, John Melville. BS, Loyola U., Chgo., 1963; MA, NYU, 1971. Editor Hastings Ctr. Report, 1974-80; social sci. editor Basic Books, 1980-81; bus. mgr., later exec. editor Christianity and Crisis, 1981-84; founding editor Church mag., dir. publs. Nat. Pastoral Life Ctr., 1984-87, dir. publications; editor Commonweal mag., 1988—. Author: Who's Minding the Children: The History and Politics of Day Care in America, 1974. Office: Commonweal 15 Dutch St New York NY 10038-3719*

STEINHAUER, GILLIAN, lawyer; b. Aylesbury, Bucks, Eng., Oct. 6, 1938; d. Eric Frederick and Maisie Kathleen (Yeates) Pearson; m. Bruce William Steinhauer, Jan. 2, 1960; children: Alison (Humphrey) Eric, John, Elspeth. AB cum laude, Bryn Mawr (Pa.) Coll., 1959; JD cum laude, U. Mich., 1976. Bar: Mich. 1976, Mass. 1992, U.S. Dist. Ct. (ea. dist.) Mich. 1976, U.S. Ct. Appeals (6th cir.) 1982. Assoc. Miller, Canfield, Paddock & Stone, Detroit, 1976-82, sr. ptnr., 1983-92; dir. Commonwealth of Mass. Workers' Compensation Litigation Unit, Boston, 1992—; mem. Atty. Gen.'s Task Force to Reduce Waste, Fraud and Abuse in the Workers' Compensation System, 1992—. Chancellor Cath. Ch. St. Paul, Detroit, 1976-83, 91; pres. bd. trustees Cath. Cmty. Svcs. Inc., 1989-92; bd. dirs. Spaulding for Children, 1991-92, Davenport House, 1992—, chair 1995-96, mem. Vestry St. Michael's Ch., Marblehead, Mass., 1994—. Mem. Mich. State Bar Found. (life), Fed. Jud. Conf. 6th Cir. (life). Home: 510 Hale St Prides Crossing MA 01965 Office: 100 Cambridge St Rm 1801 Boston MA 02202-0044

STEINHAUSER, JANICE MAUREEN, university administrator, artist; b. Oklahoma City, Okla., Apr. 3, 1935; d. Max Charles and Charlotte (Gold) Glass; m. Stuart Z. Hirschman, Dec. 30, 1954 (div. 1965); children: Shayle, David, Susan; m. Sheldon Steinhauser, May 2, 1965; children: Karen, Lisa Steinhauser Hackel. BFA, U. Colo., Denver, 1972; student, U. Mich., 1953-55. Community affairs adminstr. United Bank Denver, 1973-76; dir. visual arts program Western States Arts Found., Denver, 1976-79; exec. dir. Artreach, Inc., Denver, 1980-82; v.p. mktg. Mammoth Gardens, Denver, 1982-83; dir. pub. rels. Denver Ctr. for Performing Arts, 1983-86; founder, pres. Resource Co., Denver, 1986-88; dir. liberal studies div. Univ. Coll. U. Denver, 1992—. Bd. dirs. Met. Denver Arts Alliance, 1982-85, Denver Internat. Film Festival, 1983-86, Colo. Nat. Abortion Rights Action League, 1991-95. Mem. Women's Forum Colo., Internat. Women's Forum, Colo. New Music Assn. (bd. dirs. 1987-91), Asian Performing Arts Colo. (bd. dirs. Mizel Mus. of Judaica, 1995—), Phi Beta Kappa, Kappa Delta Phi. Democrat. Jewish.

STEINKE, BETTINA, artist; b. Biddeford, Maine, June 25, 1913; d. William and Alice Mary (Staples) S.; m. Don Blair, Mar. 21, 1946. Student, Sch. Fine Arts, Newark, 1930, Cooper Union, 1931-33, Phoenix Art Sch., 1934-35. Represented in permanent collections Indpls. Mus., Ft. Worth Mus., Nat. Cowboy Hall of Fame and Western Heritage; artist original drawings of Toscanini, 1938, Paderewski, 1939 (both now in Smithsonian Inst.); charcoal portraits NBC book on Toscanini and Orch., 1938; many portraits of well known personalities; retrospective shows Palm Springs Desert Mus., Gilcrease Mus., Tulsa, Okla., Nat. Cowboy Hall of Fame, 1995; subject of biography Bettina. Pres. bd. dirs. Harwood Found. U. N.Mex.; exec. bd. Nat. Cowboy Hall of Fame and Western Heritage. Recipient Gold and Silver medals Nat. Cowboy Hall of Fame, Oklahoma City, 1973-89, Gold medal award for Outstanding Contbn. to Painting, 1995, N.Mex. Gov.'s award, 1996, John Singer Sargant award Portrait Soc. (East Coast), 1996, others; scholar Phoenix Art Sch., N.Y.C., 1934-35. Mem. Nat. Acad. Western Artists (Prix de West award, Cowboy Hall of Fame). Home: PO Box 2342 Santa Fe NM 87504-2342

STEINKELLNER, CHERI, television producer. Exec. prodr. TV sitcom "Hope & Gloria" Warner Bros. TV, L.A., 1995—. Office: Warner Bros TV 4000 Warner Blvd Burbank CA 91522*

STEINMAN, JOAN ELLEN, lawyer, educator; b. Bklyn., June 19, 1947; d. Jack and Edith Ruth (Shapiro) S.; m. Douglass Watts Cassel, Jr., June 1, 1974 (div. July 1986); children: Jennifer Lynn, Amanda Hilary. Student U. Birmingham, Eng., 1968; AB with high distinction, U. Rochester, 1969; JD cum laude, Harvard U., 1973. Bar: Ill. 1973. Assoc., Schiff, Hardin & Waite, Chgo., 1973-77; asst. prof. law Chgo.-Kent. Coll. Law Ill. Inst. Tech., 1977-82, assoc. prof., 1982-86, prof., 1986—, interim dean, 1990-91; cons. in atty. promotions Met. Dist. Greater Chgo., 1981, 85. Contbr. articles to law jours. Coop. atty. ACLU Ill., Chgo., 1974, Leadership Coun. for Met. Open Cmtys., Chgo., 1975, Better Govt. Assn., 1975; arbitrator Better Bus. Bur. Met. Chgo., 1987; appointee bd. arbitrators Nat. Assn. Security Dealers, 1989; appointed to Ill. Gov.'s Grievance Panel, 1987; bd. dirs. Pro Bono Advocates, 1995-96. Norman and Edna Freehling scholar Chgo.-Kent Coll. Law., 1989-93. Mem. ABA, Am. Law Inst. (adviser Fed. Jud. Code project 1996, complex litigation project 1990-93, restatement of the law, third, torts, products liability, 1993), Soc. Am. Law Tchrs., Chgo. Coun. Lawyers, AAUW (legal advocacy network 1987-96), Chgo.-Lincoln Am. Inn of Ct. (master 1991), Order of the Coif, Phi Beta Kappa. Democrat. Jewish. Office: Chgo Kent Coll Law 565 W Adams St Chicago IL 60661-3601

STEINMAN, LISA MALINOWSKI, English literature educator, writer; b. Willimantic, Conn., Apr. 8, 1950; d. Zenon Stanislaus and Shirley Belle Malinowski; m. James A. Steinman, Apr. 1968 (div. 1980); m. James L. Shugrue, July 23, 1984. BA, Cornell U., 1971, MFA, 1973, PhD, 1976. Asst. prof. English Reed Coll., Portland, Oreg., 1976-82, assoc. prof., 1982-90, prof., 1990—, Kenan prof. English lit. and humanities, 1993—; cons. NEH, Washington, 1984-85. Author: Lost Poems, 1976, Made in America, 1987, All That Comes to Light, 1989, A Book of Other Days, 1992, Ordinary Songs, 1996; editor Hubbub Mag., 1983—; editl. bd. Williams Rev., 1991—, Stevens Jour., 1994—; contbr. articles to profl. jours. Fellow Danforth Found., 1971-75, NEH, 1983, 96, Oreg. Arts Commn., 1984-84, Nat. Endowment for Arts, 1984; Rockefeller Found. scholar, 1987-88; recipient Pablo Neruda award, 1987, Oreg. Inst. Lit. Arts award, 1993. Mem. MLA, Poets and Writers, PEN (N.W. chpt., co-founder, officer 1989-93). Home: 5344 SE 38th Ave Portland OR 97202-4208 Office: Reed Coll Dept English 3203 SE Woodstock Blvd Portland OR 97202-8138

STEINMETZ, KAYE H., state legislator; m. Bob Steinmetz; children: Mark, Steven, Richard, Stacey. Grad., Columbia Coll.; postgrad., U. Mo. Mem. Mo. Ho. of Reps., chmn. children, youth and families com., mem. social svc. and Medicaid com., edn. com., appropriations com. for social svc. and corrections, others. Alt. del. Nat. Conf. State Legis.; bd. dirs. Nat. Order Women Legislators, Mo. State Jr. Miss Scholar Progam; mem. Gov. Conf. Edn., 1976, Gov. Conf. Children and Youth, White House Conf. Aging, Mo. State Adv. Bd. Sch. Nurses and Parents as 1st Tchrs., Adv. Bd. Ct. App. Spl. Advocates, Planning Coun. United Way Greater St. Louis, Mo. PTA. Recipient Woman of Achievement award, 1975, Dem. Meritorious Svc. award St. Louis Globe; named to 10 Best Legislators List by Mo. Times. Address: 1814 Kilmory Dr Florissant MO 63031-1054 Office: Mo Ho of Reps State Capitol Building Jefferson City MO 65101-1556*

STELLA, CONCETTA AMELIA, medical administrator, consultant; b. Bklyn., Nov. 22, 1940; d. Joseph Domenick and Maria (Savino) S. BA in Biology, Bklyn. Coll., 1963; MPH, N.Y. U., 1981; cert. in alcoholism counseling, Marymount Coll., 1989; postgrad., New Sch. for Social Rsch., 1991—. Coord. neurosurgery N.Y. U. Med. Ctr., N.Y.C., 1961-83; adminstr. pediatric primary care St. Lukes-Roosevelt Med. Ctr., N.Y.C., 1983-86; program coord. radiology Coll. Physicians and Surgeons, Neurol. Inst., N.Y.C., 1986-87; mgr. MRI radiology N.Y. U. Med. Ctr., N.Y.C., 1987-88; mgr. KBDI, 1988-89; adminstr., gen. mgr. Corinthian Diagnostic Radiology, N.Y.C., 1989—; cons. Physician Offices for Reimbursement and Coding, N.Y.C., 1990—; lectr. in field; panelist Jr. League Drugs and Alcohol, 1989. Active Planned Parenthood, 1987—, Episcopal Soc. Ministry on Aging, 1988—, Diocese N.Y. commn. on Drug and Alcohol Abuse, 1989—, Partnership for Homeless, 1990—; del. People to People Ambassadorship Program, China, South Africa. Mem. NAFE, Nat. Health Care Radiology Adm., Health Care Fin. Assn. (Advanced standing), Magnetic Resonance Mgrs. Soc., Women's City Club N.Y., N.Y.S. Pub. Health Assn., N.Y.C. Ambulatory Care Assn., Med. Group Mgmt. Assn. (radiology assembly), NYU Grad Sch. Pub. Adminstr. Alumni, Radiology Bus. Mgrs. Soc. Democrat. Episcopalian. Office: Corinthian Diagnostic Radiology 345 E 37th St Ste 204 New York NY 10016-3217

STELLWEG, CARLA M., gallery owner; b. Bandung, Indonesia, June 8, 1942; came to U.S., 1981; d. Carl August and Toos (de Iongh) Stellweg; m. W. Roger Welch; 1 child, George G. Stellweg. BA, Lyceum/Gymnasium, The Hague, Netherlands, 1958; MA in Art History, U. of Ams., Mexico City, 1964; postgrad., Nat. Inst. History/Anthrop., Mexico City, 1965-67. Art cons., 1985-87; curator Mus. of Cont. Hispanic Art, N.Y.C., 1987-88; owner Carla Stellweg Gallery, N.Y.C., 1989—. Co-author: Frida Kahlo: The Camera Seduced, 1992, Havana Biennal, Cuba (catalog), 1994. Adv. bd. YWCA, N.Y.C., 1995—. Fellow in Humanities Rockefeller Found., 1996—. Mem. Art Table. Office: Carla Stellweg Gallery 87 E Houston St New York NY 10012

STENDAHL, BRITA KRISTINA, educator, cultural organization administrator; b. Stockholm, Jan. 10, 1925; came to U.S., 1954; d. Johan Victor and Ingeborg (Normann) Johnsson; m. Krister Stendahl, Sept. 7, 1946; children: Johan, Anna, Dan. Cand. Theology, Uppsala (Sweden) U., 1949, can. Philosophy, 1954, PhD (hon.), 1981. Hist. and lit. tchr. Gymnasium, Uppsala, Sweden, 1949-54; hist. and lit. tchr. extension program Harvard U., Cambridge, Mass., 1956-59, hist. and lit. tchr. freshman program, 1964-74; hist. and lit. tchr. seminar program Radcliffe Coll., Cambridge, 1976-84; cultural sec. Ch. of Sweden, Stockholm, 1984-88; retired, 1990; mem. Govt. Coun. for Coord. and Planning of Rsch., Stockholm, 1985-88. Author: (monographs) Søren Kierkegaard, 1976, The Education of a Self-Made Woman, Fredrika Bremer, 1801-1865, 1994; (autobiography) Sabbatical Reflections, 1978; co-author: The Force of Tradition, 1984. Co-chair Fellowship in Israel for Arab-Jewish Youth, Boston, 1972-84, 88—; bd. dirs. The Abraham Fund, N.Y.C., 1996—. Bunting fellow, Radcliffe Coll., Cambridge, Mass., 1972-84; assoc. fellow Henry A. Murray Ctr. at Radcliffe, 1981-82; recipient Myron B. Bloy award The Assn. for Religion and Intellectual Life, 1993. Mem. Arstasallskapet for Fredika Bremer-Studier (chmn. 1985—), Assn. Concerned With Devel. in Third World (bd. dirs. 1985—). Mem. Democratic Party. Lutheran. *

STENGE, LYNDA ANN, independent music tour coordinator; b. Newport Beach, Calif., Nov. 16, 1967; d. Ronald David Stenge and Diane Margret (Chapman) Swarts; m. Herbert Dwight Raymond IV, Sept. 17, 1994. Diploma, Richards Beauty Sch., Hollywood, Calif., 1985. Club coord. JFK Prodn., Hollywood, 1985-90; music mgr. Smash Pop, Studio City, Calif., 1990-94, Q Mgmt., L.A., 1994-95; ind. tour coord. L.A., 1995—. Prodr.: Rockin Little Runaways, 1993, Rock Against Rape, 1994; co-prodr.: Benefit for Children, L.A., 1992. Mem. Planned Parenthood, Rock for Choice. Mem. ASPCA. Democrat. Home and Office: 10800 Hartsook St North Hollywood CA 91601

STENGER, JUDITH ANTOINETTE, middle school educator; b. Camp Blanding, Fla., Dec. 20, 1942; d. Jack Joseph DiSalvo and Judith Lorraine (Donnelly) DiSalvo-Kohser; m. Harry Richard Stenger, Feb. 4, 1967; children: Scott Joseph, Christopher Richard. BS in Art Edn., Indiana U. Pa., 1965; postgrad., Trinity Coll., 1983-84, Western Md. Coll., 1983-84. Tchr. art elem. sch. Elizabethtown (Pa.) Schs., 1965, Freedom (Pa.) Area Schs., 1966; tchr. art elem. and mid. schs. Carroll County (Md.) Schs., 1967-69; spl. educator Montgomery County (Md.) Schs., 1980-92, tchr. art mid. sch., 1992—; co-leader Md. Student Assistance Program (drug intervention), Rockville, 1995—, mem., 1993—. Represented in 17 group shows. Named Outstanding Tchr. Coun. Exceptional Children, 1986. Mem. NEA, Md. State Tchrs. Assn., Montgomery County Tchrs. Assn., Nat. Art Edn. Assn., Nat. Artists Equity, Md. Art Edn. Assn., Rockville Arts Place. Office: Montgomery County Pub Schs Parkland Mid Sch 4610 W Frankfort Dr Rockville MD 20853-2721

STENGER, NANCY RENE, emergency room nurse; b. Bradenton, Fla., Apr. 2, 1962; d. Edward Joseph and Sue Carolyn (Sherbert) S. BSN, Med. Coll. Ga., 1985. RN, Ga.; CEN; cert. ACLS, BLS, BTLS and PALS; cert. TNCCP. Intermediate care nursery RN Med. Coll. Ga., Augusta, 1985-86; ICU nursery RN U. Hosp., Augusta, 1986-88, RN, emergency rm. staff nurse, 1988-91; RN, emergency rm. staff nurse East Ala. Med. Ctr., Opelika, 1991-92; RN staff nurse Ga. Bapt. Urgent Care, Fayetteville, 1992-93, Stockbridge, 1993-94; RN, emergency rm. staff nurse Peachtree Regional Hosp., Newnan, Ga., 1994—. Recipient scholarship Atlanta Aux. to AMA, 1984, first recipient Emergency Rm. Nurse of Quarter, Sterling Emergency Physicians, 1995. Roman Catholic. Home: 310 Everdale Rd Peachtree City GA 30269

STENMARK, JEAN KERR, mathematics educator; b. Davis, Calif., Aug. 25, 1922; d. Norman and Rachel Minerva (Bledsoe) Kerr; m. Roy M., Aug. 24, 1952, (div. July 1975); children: Ruthann, John, Jane. BA, U. Calif., Berkeley, 1942; MS, Calif. State U., Hayward, 1978. Cert. elem. tchr., Calif. With civil svc. U.S. Navy-Aviation Supply, Oakland, Calif., 1942-45; acct. various acctg. firms, San Francisco, 1945-56; tchr. Oakland Unified Sch. Dist., 1969-80; maths. specialist EQUALS and Family Math. Programs U. Calif., Berkeley, 1980-95; cons. Calif. Assessment Program, Sacramento, 1975-92, New Standards Assessment Project, Oakland, Calif., 1991—. Editor: 101 Short Problems, 1995, Mathematics Assessment: Myths, Models, Good Questions and Practical Suggestions, 1991; author: Assessment Alternatives in Mathematics, 1989; co-author: Family Math, 1986, Math for Girls and Other Problem Solvers, 1981. Mem. Nat. Coun. Tchrs. Maths., Calif. Maths. Coun., Math/Sci. Network, PTA (hon. life mem.). Democrat. Protestant. Home and Office: 1201 Brickyard Way Apt 408 Point Richmond CA 94801-4143

STENSLAND, LINDA L., state senator; 3 children. Student, Sioux Falls Coll., Augustana Coll. Mem. S.D. State Senate from 14th dist.; pres. Environ. Consulting Co. Author: Ground Water Protection Act, Comprehensive Recycling Act. Mem. edn. and job tng. com. State Fed. Assembly of Nat. Conf. State Legislatures; bd. dirs. Nat. Recycling Coalition, Washington. Democrat. Lutheran. Home: 1800 E Otonka Rdg Sioux Falls SD 57103-4565 Office: SD Senate Pierre SD 57501*

STEORTS, NANCY HARVEY, international management consultant; b. Syracuse, N.Y., Nov. 28, 1936; d. Frederick William and Josephine Elizabeth (Jones) Harvey; 1 dau., Deborah Joan. BS, Syracuse U., 1959. Asst. buyer, public relations coordinator Woodward & Lothrop, Washington, 1958-61; home economist Washington Gas Light Co., 1961-64; sales assoc. real estate Summit, N.J., 1967-68; survey specialist Dept. Agr., Washington, 1968-69; chmn. U.S. Consumer Product Safety Commn., Washington, D.C., 1981-85; pres., CEO Nancy Harvey Steorts & Assocs., Dallas, 1985-88, Nancy Harvey Steorts Internat., Washington and Dallas, 1988—; cons. Exec. Reorgn. Govt., Washington, 1971; nat. dir. women's speakers' bur. Com. Re-elect Pres., Washington, 1971-72; dir. candlelight dinners Presdl. Inaugural Commn., 1972-73, 81; expns. dir. Dept. Commerce, Washington, 1973; spl. asst. for consumer affairs to sec. agr., 1973-77; pres. Nancy Harvey Steorts & Assocs., 1977-81; disting. lectr., Strom Thurmond Inst. Govt. and Pub. Affairs, Clemson U.; mem. adv. coun. to bd. dirs., Adolph Coors Co.; mem. U.S. Dept. of Commerce Nat. Adv. Com. Tex., Nat. Adv. Com., Dist. Export Coun. Tex., Nat. Adv. Com. Export Now; mem. working com. on standards between U.S. and Russia; U.S. del. NAFTA Com. on environ. standards; bd. govs. Nat. Consumers adv. com. Fed. Reserve, 1990-93; U.S. del. to COPOLCO, Am. Nat. Standards Inst., The Hague, The Netherlands, NAFTA Del. on Environ. Standards; dir. People to People Trade Mission to Spain, 1987; del. Japan-Tex. Trade Mission, Tokyo, Osaka, Japan, Moscow, Kiev, Leningrad, U.S.-Russia Bus. Devel. Com. on Stds.; chmn. Dallas del. to meet with Prince Charles; mem. nat. consumer adv. coun. Fed. Res. Bd.; official U.S. rep. to 4th Pub. Health, Med. Equipment and Drugs Expn. Moscow USSR; speaker U.S. Seminar Soviet Health Care Exhbn., Moscow; bd. dirs., corp. adv. bd. Sch. Mgmt., Syracuse U.; mem. nat. consumer adv. com. Am. Nat. Standards Inst., nat. bd. dirs., exec. com.; bd. dirs. Mission Investment Trust Co., Tuscon; chmn. U.S. Delegation to COPOLCO, Geneva; chmn. consumer interest coun. Am. Nat. Inst.; official U.S. Delegation on Standards to ASEAN countries; internat. lectr. and keynote speaker in field. Producer, host syndicated TV show spl. Trustee Food Safety Council Conf. Consumer Orgn.; bd. dirs. Women's Inst. Am. U.; bd. advisers Coll. Human Devel., Alumnae Assn., Syracuse U., nat. bd. dirs.; commr. Montgomery County Commn. Women; pres. Welcome Wagon Clubs from 1986, Dallas Citizens Council, 1986—; bd. dirs. Council of Better Bus. Burs.; bd. adv. Am. U. Women's Inst.; bd. dirs. Med. Coll. Pa., Tex. Women's Alliance; bd. dirs., vice-chmn. regional devel. Nat. Assn. Women Bus. Owners; mem. internat. com. Com. 2000; bd. dirs. Jr. Achievement, United Way, Dallas, Goals of Dallas, Internat. Mayor's Ball; internat. del. 1st Women's Internat. Trade Mission to Europe for Women Entrepeneurs; chairwoman Trade Mission of Women Leaders to Taiwan, 1988; del. to USSR Internat. Women's Forum Mission; mem. adv. coun. to So. Meth. U. Dept. Economics; co-chmn. fundraising, Dallas Symphony; nat. dir., coord. bicentennial presdl. inaugural dinners, 1989; pres. Dallas Citizens' Coun., 1986-88; chmn. Afternoon with Oprah Winfrey Fundraising Benefit; chmn. Women Leaders Delegation to Taiwan; mem. corp. bd. dirs. Ariz. Rehab. Systems; mem. nat. bd. overseers U.S. Dept. Commerce; mem. Am. Nat. Standards Inst., chmn.; Nat. Consumer Adv. Coun.; chmn. Mayor's Glass Ceiling Commn., Dallas; bd. dirs. Nat. Women's Econ. Alliance Found., I Have a Dream Found.; chmn. Dallas Glass Ceiling Commn.; bd. overseers Tex. Quality Bd.; consumer safety expert TV network news shows; host Nat. Consumer Safety, satelitte cable show. Recipient George P. Arents Pioneer medal Syracuse U., 1979, spl. award for consumer concern Nat. Diet Workshop, Malcolm Baldridge award, Bd. of Overseers; named one of five outstanding pub. servants Gallagher Report, 1984. Mem. Nat. Bd. Dirs., Am. Home Econs. Assn., AAUW. Nat. Consumers League, Am. Women in Radio and TV, Exec. Women in Govt. (chmn.), Nat. Conf. Consumer Orgns., Syracuse U. Alumni Assn. (bd. dirs.). Office: 4689 S Versailles Ave Dallas TX 75209-6017

STEPHAN, HOPE, editor; b. Mt. Pleasant, Pa., Apr. 1, 1952; d. John P. and Dorothy (Bertram) S. BS, Slippery Rock State Coll., 1974; MA, Pa. State U., 1977. Reporter Mt. Pleasant Jour., 1977-79, Latrobe (Pa.) Bull., 1979, Connellsville (Pa.) Courier, 1979-81; prodn. coord. Barash Advt., 1982-83; reporter, copyeditor Tribune Chronicle, 1983-86, features editor, regional editor, 1986-89, asst. metro editor, 1989-93, spls. editor, 1993-95; editor The Meadville (Pa.) Tribune, 1995—; part-time instr. dept. English, Youngstown (Ohio) State U., 1987-94, advisor campus newspaper, fall 1993. Journalism fellow Rotary Internat. Found., 1981-82. Mem. AP Mng. Editors, Pa. Soc. Newspaper Editors, Soc. Newspaper Design. Office: The Meadville Tribune 947 Federal Ct Meadville PA 16335

STEPHANI, NANCY JEAN, social worker, journalist; b. Garden City, Mich., Feb. 19, 1955; d. Ernest Helmut Schulz and Margaret Mary Fowler Thompson; m. Edward Jeffrey Stephani, Aug. 29, 1975; children: Edward J., Margaret J., James E. AA, Northwood Inst., Midland, Mich., 1975; student in theology, Boston Coll., 1991; BS summa cum laude, Lourdes Coll., Sylvania, Ohio, 1992; MSW, Ohio State U., 1995. Lic. social worker. Profl. facilitator Parents United, Findlay, Ohio, 1989-94; contbg. writer Cath. Chronicle, Toledo, 1988-95; mem. ministry formation faculty Cath. Diocese of Toledo, 1992-96, mem. accreditation com., ministry formation program, 1996-97; crisis intervention specialist John C. Hutson Ctr., 1994—; social work clinician Family Svc. Hancock County, Blanchard Valley Home Health Social Svc.; trustee, bd. dirs. Hope House for the Homeless, Findlay, 1990—, v.p. 1996-97; adult edn. coord. St. Michael Parish, Findlay, 1986-93, mem. strategic plan core com., 1989-91, v.p., pres. parish coun., 1985-89; program planning com. Family Life Conf., Cath. Diocese, 1994-95, mem. accreditation com. ministry formation dept.; profl. facilitator Hope Plus Program through Hancock County Common Pleas Ct., 1996—. Founder Food Coop., MPBA, Findlay, 1981; founding mem. Chopin Hall, Findlay, 1983; mem. Hancock County AIDS Task Force, 1994—; strategic planning com. mem., co-chair goal setting com. Findlay Pub. Schs., 1994. Nat. Inst. Food Svcs. grantee, 1974; Diocese of Toledo grantee, 1991; Ohio State U. Coll. Social Work grantee, 1994. Mem. NOW, NASW, Am. Assn. on Child Abuse, Transpsychol. Assn., Friends of Creation Spirituality, Cognitive/Behavioral Profl. Soc., Call to Action, Pax Christi. Home: 2615 Goldenrod Ln Findlay OH 45840-1025

STEPHANICK, CAROL ANN, dentist, consultant; b. South Amboy, N.J., Feb. 5, 1952; d. Edward Eugene and Gladys (Pionkowski) S. BS, Rutgers U., 1974; MS, Med. Coll. Pa., 1980; DMD, Temple U., 1984. Lic. dentist, Pa., N.J., Vt. Med. technologist Jersey Shore Med. Ctr., Neptune, N.J., 1975-76, South Amboy Meml. Hosp., 1976-78, Smith-Kline Clin. Labs., King of Prussia, Pa., 1981; instr. dept. biology St. Peter's Coll., Jersey City, 1976-78; instr., edn. coord. Coll. Allied Health, Hahnemann U., Phila., 1978-80; instr. dept. oral radiology Sch. Dentistry, Temple U., Phila., 1984-87; assoc. dentist Personal Choice Dental Assocs., South Amboy, 1985-86, Marcucci and Marcucci, P.C., Phila., 1986-90, Gwynedd Dental Assocs., Springhouse, Pa., 1990-92; spl. events coord. Liberty Dental Conf., Phila., 1990—. Neighbor patrol Sprague St. Neighbors Town Watch, Phila., 1986-93. Named to Legion of Honor, Chapel of Four Chaplains, 1987. Mem. ADA, Pa. Dental Assn., Philadelphia County Dental Soc. (publicity coord. 1990—, pub. info. coord. 1991, semi-finalist judge sr. smile contest 1990—, com. on concerns of women dentists, select com. 1988—), Delaware Valley Assn. Women Dentists, Am. Assn. for Functional Orthodontics, Am. Soc. Clin. Pathologists (med. technologist), Delta Sigma Delta. Roman Catholic. Home: PO Box 386 Haddonfield NJ 08033-0310 Office: 777 White Horse Pike S Hammonton NJ 08037-2029

STEPHENS, ALICE ELIZABETH (ALICE WANKE STEPHENS), artist; b. Portland, Oreg., Feb. 2, 1926; d. A.E. and Elfrieda I. (Strauch) Wanke; m. Farrold Franklin Stephens, Feb. 2, 1950; children: Scott, Lynn, Todd. Student, Oreg. State U., 1944-46; BA, Stanford U., Palo Alto, Calif., 1948. bd. dirs., cons. Wanke Cascade, Portland. Exhibited in numerous one-woman shows including Thor Gallery, Louisville, 1971, Unitarian Ch., Portland, 1976, George Fox Coll., Newberg, Oreg., 1987, Beaverton (Oreg.) Arts Commn., 1988, Clackamas C.C., Oreg. City, 1988, World Forestry Ctr., 1989, 94, West Hills Unitarian Fellowship, Portland, 1991, First United Meth. Ch., Portland, 1991, Japanese Garden Pavilion, Portland, 1991, Auditor's Office Portland City Hall, 1990, 95; represented at Rental Sales Gallery, Portland Art Mus. bd. dirs. Portland Womens Union. Mem. Oreg. Soc. Artists, Cap and Gown of Stanford U., City Club Portland, Pi Beta Phi. Democrat. Mem. Disciples of Christ. Home: 2323 SW Park Pl Apt 805 Portland OR 97205-1039

STEPHENS, CYNTHIA LOZANO, secondary school Spanish educator; b. Washington, Dec. 17, 1952; d. Oscar F. and Stella (Seale) Lozano; m. Thomas L. Stephens Jr., June 14, 1975. BA in Spanish, Va. Tech. Inst. and State U., 1975; MA in Curriculum and Instrn., Va. Inst. Tech. and State U., 1991. Spanish tchr. Christiansburg (Va.) H.S., 1975-77, Blacksburg (Va.) H.S., 1977-81, Roanoke (Va.) Cath. H.S., 1981-83, Salem (Va.) H.S., 1983—. Va. Edn. Assn. grantee, 1992; recipient cert. of recognition Richmond U., 1993. Fellow Nat. Writing Project; mem. Am. Assn. Tchrs. of Spanish. Office: Salem HS 400 Spartan Dr Salem VA 24153-3202

STEPHENS, DEBORAH LYNN, health facility executive; b. Newton, Iowa, May 30, 1952; d. Clarence Harry and Nancy Elizabeth (Gass) Wright; m. David K. Brender, Dec. 18, 1971 (div.); m. Michael E. Stephens, May 21, 1988 (div.). BS, U. Iowa, 1974; postgrad., U. Wis., Milw., 1978-80, U. Calif., Berkeley, 1987. Asst. to dean of fin. U. Iowa Coll. Medicine, Iowa City, 1975-77; contract audit acct. Miller Brewing Co., Milw., 1977-79; asst. controller Unicare Health Facilities, Milw., 1979-81; v.p. fin. Sacred Heart Rehab. Hosp., Milw., 1981-84; exec. v.p., chief operating officer Sacred Heart Rehab. Hosp., Med. Rehab. Inst., Milw., 1984-88; prin. founding mem., pres., chief exec. officer Behavioral Health Systems, Birmingham, Ala., 1989—, also bd. dirs.; cons. on rehab., fin., multi-corp. planning and zero-base budgeting, Birmiingham, 1988; founding mem. Am. Rehab. Network, Inc., Washington, 1986-87; mem. oral exam. bd. City of Milw., 1984-86, Jefferson County, Ala., 1995; mem. prospective payment adv. com. HHS, Washington, 1986; nat. presenter on zero-base budgeting, cor. reorgns., managed care, and planning. Contbr. articles to profl. jours. Mem. health-care cost containment com. Bus. Coun. Ala., Rotary Club of Birmingham. Named One of Top 5 Thriving Bus. Women in Birmingham, Bus. to Bus., 1995; featured in Healthwatch, Open Minds, Birmingham Post Herald, Birmingham News. Mem. Hosp. Fin. Mgmt. Assn. (governing bd. 1981-88), Nat. Forensic League (life), Nat. Assn. Accts., Nat. Assn. Rehab. Facilities (prospective payment adv. bd. 1986-88, com. on med. oriented facilities 1983-88), Ga. Managed Care Assn. (bd. dirs. 1995), Birmingham C. of C. (Small Bus. Person of Yr. award 1995), Venture Club, Kappa Kappa Gamma. Office: Behavioral Health Systems 2 Metroplex Dr Ste 503 Birmingham AL 35209-6827

STEPHENS, DELIA MARIE LUCKY, lawyer; b. Temple, Tex., Aug. 2, 1939; d. James Richard and Mattie (Barfield) Lucky; m. Billy C. Stephens, 1962 (div. 1983); children: William Carl, James Kelley. BA, U. Mary Hardin-Baylor, 1961; JD, Thurgood Marshall Sch. Law, Houston, 1981. Bar: Tex. 1981, U.S. Dist. Ct. (so. dist.) Tex. 1981. Pvt. practice law Houston, 1981—. Writer feature stories The Jour. Newspapers, 1976-79. Elder, trustee Clear Lake Presbyn. Ch., Houston, 1985—; founding dir. East-West Cultural Inst., 1991—; bd. dirs. Palmer Drug Abuse Coun., 1986-90. Mem. AAUW, Tex. State Bar Assn., Houston Bar Assn., Houston Rose Soc., Am. Rose Soc., Houston Mus. Fine Arts, U. Mary Hardin-Baylor Alumni Assn. (nominating com. 1973), Coastal Bend Mary Hardin-Baylor Club (pres. 1972), Clear Lake Area C. of C., Houston Outdoor Nature Club. Democrat. Presbyn. Home: 482 Lost Rock Dr Webster TX 77598-2608 Office: 17000 El Camino Real Ste 104 Houston TX 77058-2632

STEPHENS, ELISA, art college president, lawyer. Pres. Acad. Art Coll., San Francisco. Office: Acad Art Coll Office of President 79 New Montgomery St San Francisco CA 94105-3410

STEPHENS, GAIL, music educator, flutist; b. Buffalo, N.Y., June 23, 1959. BS in Fine Arts, Nazareth Coll. of Rochester, 1984. Freelance flutist, 1980—; instr. Older Adult Svc. and Info. System, Rochester, N.Y., 1992—; pvt. flute tchr. Rochester, N.Y., 1993—; instr. Brighton Ctrl. Schs. Continuing Edn. Dept., Rochester, N.Y., 1995—. Adv. com. Genesee Transp. Coun. Bicycle and Pedestrian, 1994—; libr. Rochester Bicycling Club, 1995—; sec. Finger Lakes Conf., Geneva, N.Y., 1995—.

STEPHENS, GAY, public administrator; b. Aurora, Ill., Sept. 29, 1951; d. Benjamin Mark Jr. and Joyce Audrey (Sinclair) S. BA magna cum laude, George Williams Coll., 1973, MS summa cum laude, 1975. Clin. dir. Village of Downers Grove (Ill.) Dept. Health and Human Svcs., 1975-78; exec. dir. Villages of Bloomingdlae (Ill.) Police Program, 1978-81, Family Support Ctr., Aurora, 1981-83; devel. dir. Family Svc. & Mental Health Ctr. of Oak Park, Ill., 1983-88; mgmt. cons. United Way of Chgo., 1988-89; exec. Office of Inspector Gen. Ill. Dept. Mental Health and Devel. Disabilities, Chgo., 1989-96; exec. office inspector gen. Ill. Dept. Pub. Aid, 1996—. Mem. Unitarian Ch. of Naperville, 1973—; vol. Girl Scouts U.S. of DuPage County, Naperville, 1973-77; bd. dirs. Horizons, 1991-92. Mem. Nat. Soc. Fundraising Execs., Women in Mgmt., Chgo. Area Runners Assn., Kappa Delta Phi. Democrat.

STEPHENS, GAYLE LEE, elementary education educator; b. Houston, Dec. 23, 1948; d. George W. Combs and Ruby Ruth (Ebel) Scarborough; m. Alexander Michael Stephens, May 20, 1972; children: Kyle, Kimberly. BS, Stephen B. Austin U., 1972; MEd, Lamar U., 1989. Tchr. Gilmer (Tex.) Elem. Sch., 1972-73, Kountze (Tex.) Ind. Sch. Dist., 1973—; workshop presenter Region V Svc. Ctr., Beaumont, 1992-94. Bd. dirs. Kountze Pub. Libr., 1992—, chmn., 1994-96. Mem. ASCD, Nat. Coun. Tchrs. of English, Tex. Coun. Tchrs. of English, Tex. Classroom Tchrs. Assn. (dist. 5 dir. 1996—), Kountze Classroom Tchrs. Assn. (pres. 1992-94), Woman's Club of Kountze (sec. 1986-88, pres. 1992-94). Home: PO Box 846 520 Maplewood Kountze TX 77625

STEPHENS, JENNIFER SUE, law librarian; b. Denton, Tex., June 5, 1964; d. Elvis Clay and Joyce (Perkins) S. BBA, U. North Tex., 1986; MLS, Tex. Woman's U., 1990. Clk. Voertmans, Inc., Denton, 1985-86, U. North Tex., Denton, 1986-87; student asst. libr. Tex. Woman's U., Denton, 1988-89, grad. asst. libr., 1989-90; law libr. Dresser Industries, Inc., Dallas, 1990—. Mem. Am. Assn. Law Librs., Dallas Assn. Law Librs. (chair tech. sect. 1993-95), Southwestern Assn. Law Librs. Independent. Methodist.

STEPHENS, MARTHA, psychiatrist; b. Phila., Feb. 21, 1927; d. Elmer Martin and Mary (Corwin) S. BA, Wells Coll.; MD, N.Y. Med. Coll.; MSc, Columbia U. Diplomate Am. Bd. Psychiatry and Neurology; diplomate Am. Bd. Pediat. Mem. Am. Psychiat. Assn., N.Y. State Med. Soc. Office: Jewish Guild for Blind 15 W 65 St New York NY 10023

STEPHENS, MARTHA FOSTER, advertising executive; b. Lansing, Mich., Dec. 4, 1961; d. Richard Bailey and Gretchen (Meyer) Foster; m. Mark Burgis Stephens, Apr. 11, 1987; children: Emily Kaitlynn, Matthew Foster, Holly Holbrook. BA in English, Mich. State U., 1984; postgrad., Wayne State U. Mem. editorial staff Better Investing, Royal Oak, Mich., 1986-88; with communications Holtzman and Silverman, Farmington Hills, Mich., 1988-89; tech. writer, intern Unisys, Plymouth, Mich., 1989; dir. corp. svcs. and advt. Nat. Assn. Investors Corp., Royal Oak, 1989—. Mem. Nat. Investor Rels. Inst. (sec. 1991-92, v.p. mem. 1992-93, v.p. programs 1993-94, pres. 1994-95, bd. dirs. 1995—). Office: Nat Assn Investors Corp PO Box 220 Royal Oak MI 48068-0220

STEPHENS, MARTHA LOCKHART, art educator; b. Corpus Christi, Tex., Jan. 3, 1940; d. Hugh Rairdon and Amelia Virginia (McRee) Lockhart; m. David George Hmiel, June 10, 1961 (div. Oct. 1969); m. William Melvin Stephens Jr., June 2, 1971. BA in English Lit., Colo. Coll., 1961; MA in English Lit., U. Ariz., 1967; BFA in Drawing, U. Tex., San Antonio, 1989. Cert. tchr., Tex. English tchr. Colo., Ala., N.Y., Va. and Calif. pub. schs., 1961-68, San Antonio Ind. Sch. Dist., 1968-73; English tchr. North East Ind. Sch. Dist., San Antonio, 1973-82, level chmn. English, 1974-82, chmn. English lit. selection com., 1977, art and creative writing tchr., 1981-85, art tchr., head dept., 1986-94; presenter in field; cons., tour guide, presenter workshops San Antonio Mus. Art, 1983-86; cons., docent McNay Art Mus., San Antonio, 1987; mem. adv. bd. San Antonio Coun. Tchrs. English, 1980. One woman show Art Ctr. Gallery, 1988; two-person show Chapman Grad. Ctr., Trinity U., 1979; numerous group exhbns. including Tex. Soc. Sculptors, 1979, NOW Art Show, San Antonio, 1980, Alternate Space Gallery, San Antonio, 1983, United Bank of Austin, 1985, U. Tex., San Antonio, 1986, N.E. Ind. Sch. Dist., 1986, others; contbr. articles to profl. pubs.; authorized biographer Dorothy Dehner. Sponsor/recipient Gold Crown award Columbia Sch. Press Assn., 1992, citation for excellence Scholastic Art and Writing Awards, 1992, State Champion award Tex. H.S. Press Assn., 1990, 91, 92. Mem. NEA, Tex. State Tchrs.' Assn. (pres. Tchrs. of English sect. region 10 1979), North East Tchrs.' Assn., Nat. Art Edn. Assn., Tex. Art Edn. Assn. (regional rep. 1989-93, Merit award 1986, rep. region V 1989-93, capt. region V 1991-93), San Antonio Art Edn. Assn. (pres. 1990-92, Svc. award 1993, adv. bd. 1988-93). Democrat. Episcopalian. Home: 10935 Whisper Valley St San Antonio TX 78230-3617

STEPHENS, MARY EVELYN, banquet manager; b. Tuscaloosa, Ala., Aug. 8, 1966; d. George Harold and Evelyn (Mosely) S. BFA, Atlanta Coll. of Art, 1990. Banquet mgr. Hyatt Hotels, Atlanta, 1990—. Mem. Downtown Restaurant Assn. (exec. com. 1994—). Home: 132 Cityline Ave NE Atlanta GA 30308

STEPHENS, PATRICIA ANN, marketing professional; b. Gulfport, Miss., Feb. 1, 1945; d. James Marshall and Edna Mathilda (Hogan) S. BA, St. Louis U., 1967; MA, Memphis State U., 1971. Lic. secondary educator speech, theatre, English, religion. Exec. v.p. Prodns. Unltd., Memphis, 1971-73; chairperson speech dept. Southaven (Miss.) High Sch., 1973-77; instr. speech N.W. Jr. Coll., Southaven, 1974-76; pub. rels. dir., instr. St. Agnes Acad., Memphis, 1977-78; religion and English instr. Memphis Cath. High Sch., 1978-82; resource tchr. communications Mobile (Ala.) City Schs., 1982-84; mktg. devel. specialist/mktg. mgr. Prime Health Ala., Mobile, 1984-85; mktg. mgr. Blue Cross Blue Shield Fla./Health Options, Lakeland and Orlando, Fla., 1986-92; ind. agt., 1992-94; nat. mktg. and svc. coord. Delta Care, PMI, Tampa, 1994—. Bd. mem. Red Balloon Players, Memphis, 1971-73, Downtown Dream Machine, Memphis, 1980-82, Cir. Playhouse/Playhouse on the Square, Memphis, 1980-82. Newspaper Fund fellow Wall St. Jour. Newspaper Fund, U. Oreg., 1968, writing fellow Greater Memphis Writing Project, Memphis State U., 1980, part-time masters fellow Memphis State U., 1981-82; recipient Pres.'s Club BCBSF/Health Options Sales Mgr. award Health Options of Polk County, 1987. Democrat. Roman Catholic. Home: 4128 Sunny Land Dr Lakeland FL 33813-3946 Office: Deltacare Delta Dental Ste 300 9501 Princess Palm Ave Tampa FL 33619

STEPHENS, SYLVIA A., accountant; b. Detroi, Feb. 14, 1946; d. Edison and Adell Pearline (Espy) Carter; m. Mar. 1965 (dec. Mar. 1972); children: Reginal, Dion. BA in Bus. Adminstrn., Marygrove Coll., Detroit, 1986, MA in Human Resources, 1988. Cashier A & P Tea Co., Detroit, 1964-66; supt.'s clk. Chrysler Corp., Detroit, 1969-82; tech. aide, jr. acct., semi-sr. acct. Civic Ctr. dept. City of Detroit, 1988-93, sr. acct. transp. dept., 1993-95, prin. acct. housing dept., 1995—. Precinct del. Detroit Dem. Com., 1992—. Baptist. Home: 18477 St Louis St Detroit MI 48234

STEPHENS, WANDA BREWER, social services administrator, investor; b. Bolckow, Mo., Nov. 6, 1932; d. Perry Clark and Mary Carolyn (Fisher) Brewer; m. Lloyd Wesley Stephens, June 19, 1954; children: Ruth Ann, Susie Jo, John Allen, Donna Lynn. BS in home econs., U. Ark., 1954, MS, 1958. Cert. secondary edn. Home economics tchr. West Fork (Ark.) High Sch., 1954-58; pres. Devel. Child Care Assn., Fayetteville, Ark., 1971-74; pres., founding bd. Infant Devel. Ctr., Fayetteville, Ark., 1972-75, treas., 1975-81; edn. chmn., fin. com., admin. bd. Cen. United Meth. Ch., Fayetteville, Ark., 1976-79; pres. League of Women Voters, Fayetteville, Ark., 1979-83, Nat. Orgn. Women, Fayetteville, Ark., 1983-89; state legis. v.p. NOW, Fayetteville, 1985-90, 93-96; state pres. Nat. Orgn. Women Ark., Fayetteville, 1991-93; bd. sec., headstart Econ. Opportunity Agy., Fayetteville, 1969-70; treas. Mama's Milk Investment Club, 1970-72. Co-author: Bylaws for Economic Opportunity Agy., 1969; co-editor: Washington County, Ark., 1982. Fundraiser United Fund, 1972-75; polit. organizer NOW, 1986; treas. Washington County Dem. Women, 1990-92; organizer/staff/fund Women's Libr., 1982-91; cons./organizer Ctrl. Child Care Ctr., 1977-78. Recipient Internat. 4-H Youth Exch., 1953-54, Infant Devel. Ctr. Founders Plaque Univ. Ark., 1987; named Lay Person of Yr., Ctrl. United Meth. Ch., 1977. Mem. Mental Health Assn. (Community Svc. award 1972), AAUW (pres. 1975-77, treas. 1996—, Edn. Found. fellow 1984), ACLU (Susan B. Anthony award 1985), Ark. Women's Polit. Caucus (Uppity Woman award 1987, 92). Democrat. Methodist. Home: 1177 E Ridgeway Dr Fayetteville AR 72701-2612

STEPHENSON, ANN WATZ, artist; b. Fayetteville, W.Va., June 30, 1933; d. George W. and Eva J. (Weatherford) Booth; m. Roger Allen Stephenson, July 19, 1958 (div. May 1993); 1 child, David. AA, Ctrl. Acad. Art, Cin., 1955. Fashion artist Mabley & Carew, Cin., 1957-61, Shillto's Dept. Store, Cin., 1961, Gidding/Jenny, Cin., 1964; head fashion artist McAlpin's Dept. Store, Cin., 1964-77; art dir., dir. phtography Rogers Dept. Store, Grand Rapids, Mich., 1977-95; art dir., owner Ann Stephenson Designs, Charleston, W.Va., 1996—. Author, artist: Introduction to Fashion Art, 1981; fine art watercolor exhibits, 1992, 94. Recipient five Addy awards, 1975, 78. Mem. Nat. Mus. Women Arts, Rivertown Artist Guild (historian 1992). Home: 1577 Lee St E Charleston WV 25311

STEPHENSON, BARBERA WERTZ, lawyer; b. Bryan, Ohio, Dec. 10, 1938; d. Emerson D. and Beryl B. (Barber) Wertz; m. Gerard J. Stephenson Jr., June 22, 1960; 1 child, Thomas. Student, Smith Coll., 1956-57; BSEE, MIT, 1961; JD, U. N.Mex., 1981. Bar: N.Mex. 1981. Electronic engr. Digital Equipment Corp., Maynard, Mass., 1960-66; logic analyst Librascope, Glendale, Calif., 1966; electronic engr. Md. Dept. of Def., Ft. Meade, 1966-68; mem. tech. staff Xerox Data Systems, Rockville, Md., 1968; pvt. practice cons., Silver Spring, Md., 1969-78; pvt. practice law, Albuquerque, 1981—. Author: Financing Your Home Purchase in New Mexico, 1992; patentee analog to digital converter, kitchen calculator. Mem. N.Mex. Bar Assn. Office: 4221 Silver Ave SE Albuquerque NM 87108-2720

STEPHENSON, DOROTHY MAXINE, volunteer; b. Hanna, Ind., July 16, 1925; d. William John and Inez Louisa (Werner) Hunsley; m. Orville Lee Stephenson, Mar. 10, 1945 (dec. Oct. 1985). Grad. high sch., Hanna. Postal clk. U.S. Post Office, Hanna, 1943-44; bookkeeper LaPorte Co Farm Bur. Coop Assn., Hanna, 1944-45; news correspondent Hanna, Ind., 1950—; organist Wanatah (Ind.) United Meth. Ch., 1959-60, Bethel Presbyn. Ch., Union Mills, Ind., 1960—. Compiler: Werner-Wentz Connections, 1982, Inez Scribblins/Dot's Jottings, 'N Nibblins, 1986, abstractions Hanna H.S. Alumni records, 1990, record books II, III and IV for Bethel Presbyn. Ch., 1992; compiler, pub. Poetry, Music of the Soul, 1995. Publicity person Am. Heart Assn. (Ind. affiliate), LaPorte, 1982-85, LaPorte County Geneal. Soc., 1984—. Recipient Golden Poet award World of Poetry, 1988, hon. mention, 1987-88, Editor's Choice award Nat. Libr. of Poetry, Best Poems of 90's and the 1990 Nat. Anthology award, Echoes of Yesterday, 1994; Voices of America by Sparrowgrass Poetry anthologies, 1989, 90, 91, 92, Amherst Soc. anthologies, 1990, 92, Iliad Press anthologies, 1992, 93, Quill Books, 1993, Outstanding Poets of Am. anthology, 1994, Distinguished Poets of America anthology, 1993. Mem. Merry Prairie (treas. 1964—), Order Ea. Star (worthy matron 1953, 85-90). Democrat. Presbyterian. Home and Office: 12805 S Hunsley Rd Hanna IN 46340-9736

STEPHENSON, IRENE HAMLEN, biorhythm analyst, consultant, editor, educator; b. Chgo., Oct. 7, 1923; d. Charles Martin and Carolyn Hilda (Hilgers) Hamlin; m. Edgar B. Stephenson, Sr., Aug. 16, 1941 (div. 1946); 1 child, Edgar B. Author biorhythm compatibilities column Nat. Singles Register, Norwalk, Calif., 1979-81; instr. biorhythm Learning Tree Open U., Canoga Park, Calif., 1982-83; instr. biorhythm character analysis 1980—; instr. biorhythm compatibility, 1982—; owner, pres. matchmaking svc. Pen Pals Using Biorhythm, Chatsworth, Calif., 1979—; editor newsletter The Truth, 1979-85, Mini Examiner, Chatsworth, 1985—; researcher biorhythm character and compatibility, 1974—, biorhythm columnist Psychic Astrology Horoscope, 1989-94, True Astrology Forecast, 1989-94, Psychic Astrology Predictions, 1990-94, Con Artist types, 1995, Pedophile (child molester) types, 1995, Personality types, 1996; author: Learn Biorhythm Character Analysis, 1980, Do-It-Yourself Biorhythm Compatibilities, 1982, Con Artist Types, 1995, Pedophile (child molester) Types, 1995, Personality Types, 1996; contbr. numerous articles to mags.; frequent guests clubs, radio, TV. Office: PO Box 3893-ww Chatsworth CA 91313

STEPHENSON, JUDITH BURKE, lawyer; b. Washington, Apr. 1, 1944; d. James Bastion and Eleanor Margaret (Dwyer) B.; m. Thomas F. Stephenson, May 18, 1968 (div. 1984); children: Tenley, Cameron, Anne; m. L. Scott Harshbarger, July 11, 1987. BA, Cornell U., 1966; JD, Northeastern U., 1988. Bar: Mass. Computer sys. analyst Dept. Navy, Washington, 1966-67; stewardess Flying Tiger Airlines, 1967-68; mgmt. analyst NASA Rsch. Ctr., Cambridge, Mass., 1968-69; asst. dir. Cornell U. Pub. Affairs, Wellesley, Mass., 1977-80; founder, pres. Advantage, Inc., Boston, 1981-85; dep. fin. dir. Dukakis for Gov., Boston, 1981-82; asst. pers. dir. Office of Gov., Boston, 1983; state fin. dir. Mondale for Pres., Boston, 1984; law clk. Superior Ct. of Mass., Boston, 1988-89; atty. Middlesex County Dist. Atty., Cambridge, 1992—. Bd. dirs. Crittendon/Hastings House, Boston, 1991—, Children's Trust Fund, Boston, 1992—. Mem. AAUW, ABA, Boston Bar Assn., Cornell U. Alumni Assn. (mem. leadership coun. 1991—). Home: 439 Sandy Valley Rd Westwood MA 02090

STEPHENSON, LINDA F., public relations executive. With Zigman Joseph Skeen, 1964-69, v.p., 1985-87, exec. v.p., 1987-89; pres., CEO Zigman Joseph Stephenson, 1989—. Office: 100 E Wisconsin Ave Ste 1000 Milwaukee WI 53202-4107*

STEPKA, DARCY D., secondary education educator, librarian; b. Santa Barbara, Calif.; d. Dean R. and Louise McIntyre; m. J. Allen Stepka; 1 child, Rachel Dianne. BA in Spanish, San Diego State U., 1977, MA in Secondary Edn. Curriculum, 1984. Cert. tchr. single subject Spanish credential life; multiple subjects profl. clear. Bilingual tour guide Sea World, San Diego, 1976-78; tchr. Clairemont Christian Sch., San Diego, 1978-87; spl. edn. aide Santa Barbara (Calif.) Sch. Dists., 1987-89; tchr. ESL Goleta (Calif.) Union Sch. Dist., 1989; libr., Spanish tchr. Bishop Garcia Diego H.S., Santa Barbara, 1989—, head fgn. lang. dept., 1994—; freelance translator Sea World, San Diego, 1977. Mentor Youth at Risk, Jr. League, Santa Barbara, 1991-93; parent vol. Am. Lung Assn., Santa Barbara, 1992—; mem. adv. bd. Santa Barbara (Calif.) Sch. Dists., 1992—; cmty. outreach coord. Allergy and Asthma Network/Mothers of Asthmatics, Inc., Santa Barbara, 1994—. Mem. ALA, Assn. Librs., Calif. Sch. Librs., Nat. Cath. Educators. Republican.

STEPNIAK, NINA ARNY LAIRD, mathematics educator; b. Stoneham, Mass., Dec. 15, 1966; d. Jon Asgeir and Beverly June (Allen) Asgeirsson; m. Michael John Stepniak, May 26, 1991. BA, Atlantic Union Coll., 1989; MEd, Harvard U., 1991. Math. tchr. Parker Mid. Sch., Reading, Mass., 1991-92; band dir., brass ensemble dir. Atlantic Union Coll., South Lancaster, Mass., 1991-92; math. tchr. The Bromfield Sch., Harvard, Mass., 1992-94, John Hersey H.S., Arlington Heights, Ill., 1994—; choir dir. The Bromfield Sch., 1992-94. Choir mem. Millar Chapel Choir at Northwestern U., Evanston, Ill., 1994—; band mem. Northshore Concert Band, Wilmette, Ill., 1994—. Mem. Nat. Coun. Thcrs. of Maths. Democrat. Adventist. Address: 7641 Carroll Ave #1 Takoma Park MD 20912

STEPP, LAURA SESSIONS, journalist; b. Ft. Smith, Ark., July 27, 1951; d. Robert Paul Sessions and M. Rae Barnes; m. Carl Sessions Stepp; children: Ashli, Amber, Jeffrey. BA, Earlham Coll., 1973; MA, Columnia U., 1974. Reporter Palm Beach Times, West Palm Beach, Fla., 1974; MA Columbia U., Phila., 1975; projects editor The Charlotte (N.C.) Observer, 1979-81, asst. editorial page editor, 1981-82; Md. editor The Washington Post, 1982-86, religion editor, 1987-92, writer Style sect., 1992—. Bd. advisors U. Md. Casey Journalism Ctr. Children and Families, College Park. Recipient Nat. Reporting award Religion Writers Am., Feature Writing award AAUW, 1994. Mem. Investigative Reporters and Editors (bd. dirs.

1986-90). Office: Washington Post Co 1150 15th St NW Washington DC 20071-0001

STEPP, WENDY WYELS, special education educator; b. Waynesburg, Pa., Apr. 8, 1951; d. George Irwin Jr. and Wilma Dale (Davis) Wyels; m. John Phillips Nelson Stepp, June 30, 1973; children: Jason Robert, Michelle Renee. BS in Edn., California U. Pa., 1988. Cert. spl. edn., early childhood tchr., Pa.; cert. in crisis intervention. Travel counselor West Pa. AAA, Pitts., 1970-72; supr. ctrl. file 1st Nat. Bank, Washington, Pa., 1972-73; child alert tchr. Intermediate Unit I, Uniontown, Pa., 1989-91; learning support tchr. Bethelehem Ctr. Sch. Dist., Fredericktown, Pa., 1991—; dir., tchr. TRIAD, McMurray, Pa., 1990—. Recipient Gift of Time award, 1993, 96. Mem. Pa. Edn. Assn., Bethlehem Ctr. Edn. Assn. (bldg. rep. 1993), Bus. and Profl. Women's Club. Democrat. Methodist. Home: Box 289 1214 Hill St Marianna PA 15345

STEPS, BARBARA JILL, lawyer; b. Springfield, Mo., June 19, 1945; d. Louis Edward and Margaret Pearl (Stiver) Bredeman; m. Robert William Steps, Dec. 21, 1968; children: Rebecca Harper, Aaron Andrew, Jessica Anne. BA in Psychology, St. Louis U., 1966; JD, U. Mo., 1969; MBA, U. Conn., 1983. Atty. Ralston Purina Co., St. Louis, 1969; law clerk U.S. Dist. Ct., St. Louis, 1969-72; assoc. Stone, Keck & Staser, Evansville, Ind., 1973-75, Cline & Callahan, Indpls., 1975-77, Law Office, Herbert V. Camp, Ridgefield, Conn., 1978-81; comml. counsel Framatome Connectors (formerly Burndy Corp.), Norwalk, Conn., 1981-82, domestic counsel, 1982-86, corp. counsel, 1986-89, corp. counsel, sec., 1989-93, v.p., counsel & sec., 1993—. Mem. ABA, Am. Corp. Counsel Assn., Conn. Bar Assn., Corp. Bar Assn. of Westchester & Fairfield (co-chair bus. & comml. law com. 1990-92, dir. 1993—). Home: 6 Mulberry St Ridgefield CT 06877-3706 Office: Framatome Connectors USA Inc 51 Richards Ave Norwalk CT 06854-2309

STEPTOE, MARY LOU, lawyer; b. Washington, July 15, 1949; d. Philip Pendleton and Irene (Hellen) S.; m. Peter E. Carson, Sept. 1986; children: Elizabeth Maud, Julia Grace. BA, Occidental Coll., 1971; JD, U. Va., 1974. Bar: Va., 1974, Supreme Ct., 1987. Staff atty., Bur. of Competition FTC, Washington, 1974-79, atty. advisor to commr., 1979-86, exec. asst. to chmn., 1988-89, assoc. dir., Bur. of Competition, 1989-90, dep. dir., 1990-92, acting dir., 1992-95, dep. dir., 1995-96; attorney Skadden Arps Slate Meagher & Flom, Washington, D.C. *

STERBA, WENDY ELLEN, German literature and culture educator, film and media educator; b. Kansas City, Kans., May 26, 1955; d. Richard Ludwig Anton and Betty Lynn (Hunt) S.; m. Don Stafford Renshaw Jr. BA in German, Reed Coll., 1978; MA in German, Rice U., 1987, PhD in German, 1988. H.s. German tchr. AWTY Internat. Sch., Houston, 1984; teaching asst. Rice U., Houston, 1984-88; assoc. prof. Coll. St. Benedict/St. John's U., St. Joseph, Minn., 1988—; dir. modern studies humanities adv. coun. St. John's U., 1993—; dir. Salzburg (Austria) Study Abroad program, 1994. Contbr. articles to profl. jours. Dir., exec. com. Dem. Party, Stearns County, 1992-94. DAAD scholar, 1975, 85; rsch. grantee Bremer Found., 1989. Mem. NAACP, MLA, Am. Assn. Tchrs. German, Minn. MLA, SCMLA (sect. organizer 198 9-94), Women in German. Mem. Soc. of Friends. Office: Coll St Benedict 37 S College Ave Saint Joseph MN 56374

STERK, GWENDOLYN J., lawyer, educator; b. Hammond, Ind., May 6, 1965; d. Henry and Carol (Osenga) S.; m. Frederick M. Smithhart, Oct. 24, 1992. BS, Liberty U., 1985; MA, Loyola U., Chgo., 1988, JD, 1988. Bar: Ill., Ind. Assoc. Goldstine, Skrodzki, Russian, Nemec & Hoff, Summit, Ill., 1991—; prof. Trinity Internat. U., Deerfield, Ill., 1991—. Mem. Ind. State Bar, Chgo. Bar Assn. Home: PO Box 5396 Lansing IL 60438

STERKOVSKY, JULIA ELLEN, activist, organizer; b. Toledo, Ohio, Aug. 30, 1960; D. William Thomas and Jacquelyn Agnes (Swick) Lester; m. Brian Keith Culkowski Sterkovsky, Feb. 11, 1984. BA in Psychology, U. Toledo, 1982; MA in Social Scis., U. Chgo., 1986. Patient advocate, trainer Ctr. for Choice II, Toledo, 1986-88; dir. Collingwood Springs Redevel. Corp., Toledo, 1986-88, Coalition for People, New Haven, Conn., 1988-89; vol. coord. Anawim Homeless Shelter for Men, New Haven, Conn., 1990; organizational facilitator Domestic Violence Tng. Project, New Haven, 1990-91; dir. New Haven Women's Liberation Ctr., 1989-91, Women's Ctr. Miami U., Oxford, Ohio, 1991—; student cons. Dwight Hall at Yale U., New Haven, 1990; faculty cons., Winona (Minn.) State U. Women Studies, 1994; cons. Fla. Internat. U., 1994-95, Wright State U. Women's Ctr., Dayton, Ohio, 1995-96; presenter confs. on women's issues., 1992—. Named Hon. Woman of Color, Creative Women's Collective, New Haven, Conn., 1991; recipient Lila Wallace Internat. Artist's award, Lila Wallace Reader's Digest, N.Y.C., 1994, Disting. Svc. award, Miami U. Ctr. for Black Culture, Oxford, Ohio, 1995, Alumna Achievement award U. Toledo, 1995. Mem. AAUW, NOW, Nat. Assn. Women in Edn., Juno Network (founding mem.), Butler County Alliance for Women (founding mem., steering com.), Nat. Assn. Women's Ctrs. (internal coord. 1992-94, officer). Office: Miami U Womens Ctr Oxford OH 45056

STERLING, COLLEEN, artist; b. Sterling, Ill., Dec. 17, 1951; d. Gordon Dennis and Ruth Mary (Lendman) McKee. Student, Mundelein Coll., Chgo., 1970-72, Sch. of the Art Inst., Chgo., 1973-74, U. Cin., 1974, Mass. Coll. Art, Boston, 1980, 85. Mem. staff Mus. of the Art Inst., Chgo., 1973-74, Mus. Fine Arts, Boston, 1974-76, Visual Comm. Network, Cambridge, 1984-89; owner, operator Sterling Graphics, Blairsville, Ga., 1989-92; visual artist Blairsville, 1989—; dir. Studio Epona, Cambridge, 1980-83. One-woman shows include Amarillo (Tex.) Art Ctr. and Mus., 1993, Bur. Cultural Affairs, Atlanta, 1996; group shows include Telfair Mus. Art, Savannah, Ga., 1995, Vanderbilt U., Nashville, 1995. Mem. Ga. Citizens for the Arts, Atlanta, 1995—, Calif. Lawyers for the Arts, San Francisco, 1994-95, Nat. Mus. for Women in the Arts; bd. dirs. S.A.F.E. House, Blairsville, 1996—. Recipient 2d pl. Howard Hunter award Boston Ctr. for the Arts, 1989; individual visual artists grantee Ga. Coun. for Arts, Atlanta, 1995. Democrat. Home: 3529 Mason Rd Blairsville GA 30512

STERLING, KENDALL WILLS, medical editor, writer, small business owner; b. Radford, Va., July 22, 1957; d. Willie Blanton and Myrtle Ross (Nolen) Wills; m. William Edward Sterling, Sept. 3, 1983. BA summa cum laude, U. Richmond, 1979; specialty cert. in Editing/Writing and Pharm. Writing, Am. Med. Writers Assn., 1992. Manuscript editor C.V. Mosby Co., St. Louis, 1980-81; editor, freelance coord. William Byrd Press, Richmond, Va., 1981-89; pres., mng. editor Sterling Comm. Svcs., Richmond, 1989—; cons. Schering-Plough, Madison, N.J., 1993. Editor: (report to U.S. Congress) The Contribution of Pharmaceutical Cos.: What's at Stake for America, 1993; 60 medical or allied health books including: Alzheimer's Disease: Treatment and Management, The Breast: Comprehensive Management of Benign and Malignant Diseases, Atlas of Pediatric Surgery, Cutaneous Surgery, Pediatric Arrhythmias: Electrophysiology and Pacing; article and issue editor: 25 med. and tech. jours including: Current Therapeutics Rsch., Am. Jour. Hosp. Pharmacy, Trauma Quarterly, Clin. Therapeutics. Mem. steering com. Campaign for Richmond, U. Richmond, 1991-93. Recipient David E. Howard Journalism scholarship U. Richmond, 1978-79. Mem. Am. Med. Writers Assn., Bd. Editors in Life Scis. (cert. editor in life scis., subcom. on member and pub. rels. 1992—), Coun. Biology Editors (authors editors com. 1993-95), European Assn. Sci. Editors, N.Y. Acad. Scis., Soc. Tech. Comm. Home and Office: Sterling Comm Svcs 2605 Mallards Xing Richmond VA 23233-2163

STERLING, SHIRLEY FRAMPTON, artist, educator; b. L.A., Oct. 9, 1920; d. James Alexander and Elizabeth Mary (Herman) F.; m. Edwin Leigh Sterling, Mar. 26, 1942; children: Michael Leigh, Marianne. BA, Occidental Coll., 1942; postgrad., La. Tech. U., 1979-89. Cert. tchr. Tchr. Glendale, Calif., 1942-45; artist, tchr. Watercolor Art Soc., Houston, Pasadena, Kemah, Tex., 1973—; lectr., demonstrator various art socs. Active as Gray Lady Internat. Red Cross, Wiesbaden, Fed. Republic Germany, 1960-61, Honolulu, 1968-69. Mem. Nat. Watercolor Soc.(elected signature mem.), Knickerbocker Artists, Southwestern Watercolor Soc., Tex. Watercolor Soc. (Patron of Arts award), So. Watercolor Soc., Watercolor Art Soc.-Houston, Western Fedn. Watercolor Soc., Phi Beta Kappa. Republican. Home: 4011 Manorfield Dr Seabrook TX 77586-4209

STERN, FLO, union organizer; b. N.Y.C., May 8, 1949; d. Ralph and Edna (Kleiman) S.; life ptnr. Nancy de Prosse; children: Michael, Natasha, Jaye-Jaye. AAS, Bronx C.C., 1970; BA, MA, Columbia U., 1978. RN, N.Y.; cert. employee assistance profl. Staff nurse Montefiore Hosp., Bronx, N.Y., 1970-71; head nurse Jacobi Hosp., Bronx, 1971-76; staff nurse Halifax Hosp., Daytona Beach, Fla., 1978-79; psychiat. nurse therapist Fedn. Employment and Guidance Svc., N.Y.C., 1979-93; pres. local 215 Am. Fedn. State, County and Mcpl. Employees, 1989-93; dir. local 285 Svc. Employees Internat. Union, Boston, 1993-94; assoc. dir. Mass. Nurses Assn., Canton, 1996—; adj. faculty mem. Hofstra U., N.Y.C., 1980, Cornell U., N.Y.C., 1989-93; staff mem. Univ. and Coll. Labor Edn. Assn. Summer Inst. for Union Women, N.E. region, 1984—. Mem. Town Meeting, Amherst, Mass., 1996—. Mem. Pride at Work (steering com. 1994-95), Amherst Gay, Lesbian and Bisexual Parents Network (co-chair 1995—). Jewish. Home: 120 Pulpit Hill Rd Amherst MA 01002

STERN, GAIL FRIEDA, historical association director; b. Atlantic City, May 18, 1950; d. Herbert and Faith (Beldegreen) Stern; m. Irwin Allen Popowsky (div.); m. Shawn Paul Aubitz, Sept. 20, 1987; 1 child, Jonathan. Student, Brown U., 1972; postgrad., U. Pa., 1973. Asst. in decorative arts Phila. Mus. Art, 1972-75; asst. curator Wheaton Mus. Glass, Millville, N.J., 1973-74; assoc. dir. Pa. Humanities Coun., Phila., 1976-79; mus. curator The Balch Inst. for Ethnic Studies, Phila., 1979-83, mus. dir., 1984-93; dir. Hist. Soc. Princeton, N.J., 1993—; chair Pa. Task Force on Folk Arts and Culture, 1981-82; vice chmn. crafts panel Pa. Coun. on the Arts, Harrisburg, 1988-89; chair cultural conservation com., Pa. Heritage Affairs Commn., Harrisburg, 1990-92; participant Internat. Partnership in Mus., Singapore, 1991. Mem. Mus. Coun. Phila. (v.p. 1982-83), Am. Assn. Mus./Internat. Coun. Mus. (bd. dirs.), N.J. Mus. Assn. (mem. bd. dirs.), Am. Assn. for State and Local History Awards (N.J. chair 1994-95). Home: 131 E Maple Ave Morrisville PA 19067-6235 Office: Hist Soc Princeton 158 Nassau St Princeton NJ 08542-7077

STERN, GRACE MARY, former state legislator; b. Holyoke, Mass., July 10, 1925; d. Frank McLellan and Marguerite M. (Nason) Dain; m. Charles H. Suber, June 21, 1947 (div. 1959); children: Ann, Peter, Thomas, John; m. Herbert L. Stern, May 13, 1962; stepchildren: Gwen, Herbert III, Robert. Student, Wellesley Coll., 1942-45; LLD (hon.), Shimer Coll., 1984. Asst. supr. Deerfield Twp., Lake County, Ill., 1967-70; county clk. Lake County, Ill., 1970-82; mem. Ill. Ho. of Reps., Springfield, 1984-92, Ill. State Senate, 1993-95. Author: With a Stern Eye, 1967, Still Stern, 1969. Candidate lt. gov. State of Ill., 1982. Democrat. Presbyterian. Home: 291 Marshman Ave Highland Park IL 60035-4732 Office: 540 W Frontage Rd Ste 1000 Northfield IL 60093-1201

STERN, JEANNETTE ANNE, secondary school educator; b. Bklyn., June 13, 1948; d. Samuel and Rosalie (Presler) Beckerman; m. William D. Stern, Aug. 10, 1974; children: Susan Rachel, Diana Lynne. BA, SUNY, Albany, 1970; MA, Hofstra U., 1972; MEd, Tchrs. Coll., N.Y.C., 1993, EdD, 1994. Cert. tchr. social studies 7-12, Spanish 7-12, adminstrn. and supervision. Tchr. Spanish Wantagh (N.Y.) Pub. Schs., 1970-73, tchr. social studies, 1973-92, chmn. dept. social studies, 1992—; regional dir. N.Y. State Middle Sch. Assn., 1990—; cons. in field. Contbr. articles to profl. jours. Chairperson sch. bd. Congregation B'nai Israel, Freeport, N.Y., 1989—. Recipient Faculty Svc. award Am. Legion, 1983, PTA Svc. award, Wantagh, 1988. Mem. Nat. Middle Sch. Assn., Wantagh United Tchrs., Am. Fedn. Tchrs., SUNY at Albany Alumni Assn. (bd. dirs. 1970-73), Holocaust Mus. (charter), Phi Delta Kappa. Home: 17 Florence Ave Freeport NY 11520-5823 Office: Wantagh Pub Schs 3301 Beltagh Ave Wantagh NY 11793-3365

STERN, JOAN NAOMI, lawyer; b. Phila., Mar. 7, 1944; d. Clarence J. and Diana D. (Goldberg) S. BA, U. Pa., 1965; JD, Temple U., 1977. Bar: Pa. 1977. Assoc. Blank, Rome, Comisky & McCauley, Phila., 1977-83, ptnr., 1983—, co-chair pub. fin. group, 1983-92, chair pub. fin. group, 1993, chair pub. fin. dept., 1994—; cons. counsel Phila. Charter Commn., 1993-94. Contbr. articles to profl. jours. Mem. Sch. Dist. Task Force on Regulatory Reform, Phila., 1987, Tax Policy and Budget Com., Phila., 1989, Phila. Mayor's Fiscal Adv. Com., 1990; chair Sch. Dist. of Phila. Task Force on Alternate Financing Strategies, 1995; bd. mgrs. Moore Coll. Art and Design, Phila., 1993—, vice chair bd. mgrs., 1995—; bd. dirs. Police Athletic League, Phila., 1994—. Fellow Am. Bar Found.; mem. ABA, Nat. Assn. Bond Lawyers, Phila. Bar Assn., Phila. Bar Assn. (chmn. mcpl. govt. com. 1983—), Pa. Assn. Bond Lawyers. Office: Blank Rome Comisky & McCauley 4 Penn Center Plz Philadelphia PA 19103-2521

STERN, KATE MACOMBER, writer, educator; b. Iowa City, Iowa, Aug. 19, 1952; d. Richard Gustave and Ruth Gay (Clark) S.; m. Jeffrey Jay Baron, Dec. 27, 1980; children: Liza Cady, Alexander Macomber. BA in English, Washington U., St. Louis, 1973; MA in English, U. Iowa, 1976; PhD in English, Loyola U., Chgo., 1983. With sch. dept. Holt, Rinehart and Winston, N.Y.C., 1973-74; press sec. Congressman Clarence Long, Washington, 1979; legis. corr. Senate Fin. Com., Washington, 1980; lectr. Georgetown U., Washington, 1983-85. Author: Christina Stead's Heroine, 1989; contbr. book rev. to literary jours. Mem. MLA, Am. Assn. Australian Lit. Studies. Home: 5513 Mckinley St Bethesda MD 20817-3729

STERN, LYNN SOLINGER, photographer; b. N.Y.C., Mar. 31, 1942; d. David Morris and Hope Alva (Gimbel) Solinger; m. Robert A. M. Stern, May 22, 1966 (div. 1977); 1 child, Nicholas; m. Jeremy Pollard Lang, Dec. 3, 1980. BA cum laude, Smith Coll., 1964. Apprentice editor Ross-Gaffney Films, N.Y.C., 1965-66; photographic archivist Stern & Hagmann Archs., N.Y.C., 1968-77; photographer N.Y.C., 1978—. Author, photographer: Unveilings, 1989, Dispossession, 1995 (Ernst Haas award 1995). Mem. nat. coun. Environ. Def. Fund, N.Y.C., 1991—; dir. Bernard F. & Alva B. Gimbel Found., 1988—. Democrat. Home and Office: 101 Central Park W New York NY 10023

STERN, MADELEINE BETTINA, rare books dealer, author; b. N.Y.C., July 1, 1912; d. Moses Roland and Lillie (Mack) S. BA, Barnard Coll., 1932; MA, Columbia U., 1934. Tchr. English N.Y.C. High Schs., 1934-43; ptnr. Leona Rostenberg Rare Books, N.Y.C., 1945—, Leona Rostenberg and Madeleine B. Stern Rare Books, N.Y.C., 1980—; lectr. history of book, feminism, pub. history, lt. Author: The Life of Margaret Fuller, 1942, Louisa May Alcott, 1950, new edit., 1996, Purple Passage: The Life of Mrs. Frank Leslie, 1953, Imprints on History: Book Publishers and American Frontiers, 1956, We the Women: Career Firsts of Nineteenth Century America, 1962, new edit., 1994, So Much in a Lifetime: The Story of Dr. Isabel Barrows, 1965, Queen of Publishers' Row: Mrs. Frank Leslie, 1966, The Pantarch: A Biography of Stephen Pearl Andrews, 1968, Heads and Headlines: The Phrenological Fowlers, 1971, Books and Book People in 19th-Century America, 1978, Antiquarian Bookselling in the United States: A History from the Origins to the 1940s, 1985, Nicholas Gouin Dufief of Philadelphia Franco-American Bookseller, 1776-1834, 1988, The Life of Margaret Fuller: A Revised Second Edition, 1991; (with Leona Rostenberg) Old and Rare: Forty Years in the Book Business, 1974, rev. edit. 1988, Between Boards: New Thoughts on Old Books, 1978, Bookman's Quintet: Five Catalogues about Books, 1980, Quest Book-Guest Book: A Biblio-Folly, 1993, Connections: Our Selves-Our Books, 1994; editor: Women on the Move, 4 vols., 1972, Victoria Woodhull Reader, 1974, Louisa's Wonder Book-An Unknown Alcott Juvenile, 1975, Behind a Mask: The Unknown Thrillers of Louisa May Alcott, 1975, new edit., 1995, Plots and Counterplots: More Unknown Thrillers of Louisa May Alcott, 1976, Publishers for Mass Entertainment in 19th-Century America, 1980, A Phrenological Dictionary of 19th-Century Americans, 1982, Critical Essays on Louisa May Alcott, 1984, A Modern Mephistopheles and Taming a Tartar by Louisa May Alcott, 1987, Louisa May Alcott Unmasked: Collected Thrillers, 1995, Modern Magic: Five Stories by Louisa May Alcott, 1995, The Feminist Alcott: Stories of a Woman's Power, 1996; co-editor: Selected Letters of Louisa May Alcott, 1987, A Double Life: Newly Discovered Thrillers of Louisa May Alcott, 1988, The Journals of Louisa May Alcott, 1989, Louisa May Alcott: Selected Fiction, 1990, (co-editor) Freaks of Genius: Unknown Thrillers of Louisa May Alcott, 1991, From Jo March's Attic: Stories of Intrigue and Suspense, 1993 (Victorian Soc. award), The Lost Stories of Louisa May Alcott, 1995. Guggenheim fellow, 1943-45; recipient Medalie award Barnard Coll., 1982, Victorian Soc. award. Mem. Antiquarian Booksellers Assn. Am. (gov. 1966-68, 78-80), Internat. League Antiquarian Booksellers, MLA, Am. Printing History Assn. (co-recipient award 1983), Authors League, Manuscript Soc. (former trustee), Phi Beta Kappa. Jewish. Home: 40 E 88th St New York NY 10128-1176 Office: Rare Books 40 E 88th St New York NY 10128-1176

STERN, MARCI ANN, English educator; b. Plainview, N.Y., May 27, 1968; d. Jeffrey Ellner and Janet (Zeichner) Stark; m. David Emanuel Stern, Aug. 13, 1995. BA in English Lit., SUNY, New Paltz, 1990; MS in English Edn., L.I. U., 1996. Retail asst. mgr. Merry Go Round Enterprises, Woodbridge, N.J., 1990; graphic artist Getting To Know You, Westbury, N.Y., 1991-92; adminstrv. asst. data mgmt. FI Serv, Melville, N.Y., 1992; photographer, studio mgr. Moto Photo, Inc., New Hyde Park, N.Y., 1992; pub. rels. asst. Sumner Rider & Assoc. Inc., N.Y.C., 1992-93; pub. rels. mgr. adminstrv. asst. Greenville Baker Boys and Girls Club, Locust Valley, N.Y., 1993; English educator Commack (N.Y.) Mid. Sch., 1995, Dawnwood Mid. Sch., Centereach, N.Y., 1995—; dir. musical theatre Dawnwood Mid. Sch., 1995—, cons. computers in edn., 1995-96, coord. spelling bee, 1995-96. Letter writing campaign organizer Commack Mid. Sch., 1995; actor, singer Glen Players, Glen Cove, N.Y., 1993. Mem. Nat. Coun. of Tchrs. of English (local pub. rels. rep. 1995—), Internat. Reading Assn., Libr. of Congress, Internat. Soc. of Poets. Democrat. Jewish. Office: Dawnwood Middle Sch 10 43rd St Centereach NY 11720

STERN, MARGARET LESLIE, public relations counselor; b. N.Y.C., May 14, 1941; d. Michael D. and Estelle R. (Goldstein) S. BA, Syracuse U., 1961. Asst. acct. exec. Fred Rosen Assocs., N.Y.C., 1965-68; adminstrv. asst. Congressman Edward I. Koch, N.Y.C., 1968-69; account supr. Bell & Stanton, N.Y.C., 1969-72; v.p. dir. pub. rels. Schieffelin & Co., N.Y.C., 1972-79, brand mgr., 1977-79; v.p. dir. external affairs The Wine Spectrum/Coca-Cola Co., Atlanta, 1979-83; v.p., dir. pub. rels. Seagram Wine Co., N.Y.C., 1983-84; v.p., dir. mktg. Frederick Wildman & Sons, N.Y.C., 1984-87; v.p. pub. rels. The Buckingham Wile Co., Lake Success, N.Y., 1987-90; pres. Stern Comm., N.Y.C., 1990—. Home and Office: Stern Comm Ste 22A 100 West 57th St New York NY 10019-3327

STERN, MARILYN BETH, picture editor, photographer, writer; b. Detroit, Nov. 8, 1953; d. Julian and Phyllis S. BA, Brown U., 1976. Photographer's asst. N.Y.C., 1976-82, freelance photographer, 1976—; tchr. photography pvt. practice, N.Y.C., 1980-83; freelance writer N.Y.C., 1985—; picture editor Across the Board mag., N.Y.C., 1990—. Photographer/organizer: (book) Masked Culture: The Greenwich Village Halloween Parade, 1994; author/photographer: Kval! Die Waldanger der Lofoten, 1990; represented in permanent collection Detroit Inst. Arts. Travel Study grantee Royal Norwegian Consulate to Norway in the U.S., 1987, Am.-Scandinavian Found., 1986. Jewish. Office: The Conference Bd 845 3rd Ave New York NY 10022-6679

STERN, PAULA, international trade advisor; b. Chgo., Mar. 31, 1945; d. Llooyd and Fan (Wener) Stern; m. Paul A. London; children: Gabriel Stern London, Genevieve Stern London. BA, Goucher Coll., 1967; MA in Middle Eastern Studies, Harvard U., 1969; MA in Internat. Affairs, Fletcher Sch. of Law and Diplomacy, 1970, MA in Law and Diplomacy, 1970, PhD, 1976; D of Comml. Sci. (hon.), Babson Coll., 1985; LLD (hon.), Goucher Coll., 1985. Legis. asst., then sr. legis. asst. U.S. Sen. Gaylord Nelson, Washington, 1972-74, 1976; guest scholar Brookings Inst., Washington, 1975-76; policy analyst Pres. Carter-V.P. Mondale Transition Team, Washington, 1977-78; internat. affairs fellow Council on Fgn. Relations, Washington, 1977-78; commr. Internat. Trade Commn., Washington, 1978-87, chairwoman, 1984-86; sr. assoc. Carnegie Endowment for Internat. Peace, Washington, 1986-88; pres. The Stern Group, 1988—; sr. fellow The Progressive Policy Inst., 1993—; bd. dirs. Westinghouse Corp., Harcourt Gen., Duracell Internat., Wall-Mart; holder Howard W. Alkire chair in internat. bus. and econs. Hamline U., 1994—; sr. adviser to Clinton campaign; mem. Pres.'s Adv. Com. for Trade Policy and Negotiations; chair adv. com. U.S. Export-Import Bank, working chair transatlantic adv. com. on stds., cert. and regulatory policy; mem. Trilateral Commn., Commn. for Econ. Devel. Author: Water's Edge--Domestic Politics and the Making of American Foreign Policy, 1979; author numerous articles and chpts. on internat. affairs. Recipient Journalism award Alicia Patterson Found., 1970-71. Mem. Coun. Fgn. Rels., Inter-Am. Found. (bd. dirs. 1980-81). Democrat. Jewish. Office: The Stern Group Inc 3314 Ross Pl NW Washington DC 20008

STERN, ROSLYNE PAIGE, magazine publisher; b. Chgo., May 26, 1926; d. Benjamin Gross and Clara (Sniderman) Roer; m. William E. Weber, May 3, 1944 (div. Mar. 1956); m. Richard S. Paige, June 28, 1958 (div. Apr. 1978); children: Sandra Weber Porr, Barbara Paige Kaplan, Elizabeth Paige (dec.); m. Robert D. Stern, June 5, 1978. Cert., U. Chgo., 1945. Profl. model, singer, 1947-53; account exec. Interstate United, Chgo., 1955-58; sales mgr. Getting To Know You Internat., Great Neck, N.Y., 1963-71, exec. v.p., 1971-78; pub. After Dark Mag., N.Y.C., 1978-82; assoc. pub. Dance Mag., N.Y.C., 1978-85, pub., 1985—; pres., 1996—; bd. dirs. Rudor Consol. Industries, Inc., N.Y.C., AGC/Sedgwick, Inc., Princeton, N.J. Founding pres. Dance Mag. Found., N.Y.C., 1984-86; life mem. nat. women's com. Brandeis U., Waltham, Mass., 1958—. Mem. Pub. Relations Soc. Am., LWV, Am. Theatre Wing, Nat. Arts Club. Democrat. Jewish. Home: 2 Imperial Lndg Westport CT 06880-4934 Office: Dance Mag Inc 33 W 60th St 10th Fl New York NY 10023-7905

STERN, RUTH, business executive, artist; b. Bronx, N.Y., Oct. 14, 1929; d. Albert and Margaret (Karl) Nussbacher; student Hunter Coll., N.Y.C., 1947; cert. writing UCLA, 1988; BFA, Calif. Inst. of Arts, 1994, postgrad., 1995—; m. Martin Szold, Apr. 10, 1949 (div. Sept. 1978); children—Lauren, Terry; m. James C. Stern, Aug. 22, 1982. Exec. legal sec. to sr. partner firm Paul, Weiss, Rifkind, Wharton & Garrison, N.Y.C., 1958-62; asst. to pres. M.E. Green & Co., brokerage co., N.Y.C., 1962-65; demonstrator and cons. for various cosmetic cos., 1965-85; founder, pres. Ruth Szold Promotional Models, N.Y.C., 1968-84, Cosmetic Art, Inc., cosmetic and theatrical workshops, N.Y.C., 1979-85; founder, pres., designer, promoter cosmetic line Cosmetic Art, 1979-85; columnist Fire Island News, Ocean Beach, N.Y., 1985-89; asst. to pres., chief exec. officer Gladden Entertainment, L.A., 1989-90; exec. adminstr. C&O of Cogent Light and Techs., 1990-91; demonstrator-lectr. for TV, also video tapes; condr. cosmetic workshops for N.Y. Salute to Fashion Industries, 1981; chmn. earthquake com. Fountainview Assn., 1989—; cons. in field. Mem. council Girl Scouts U.S.A., 1964-69; bd. dirs. Bleecker Tower Tenants Corp., N.Y.C., 1979-80, chmn. architecture and design com., 1979-80, chmn. maintenance, 1980-85, pres., 1981-82; mem. Hunger Project, Financial Family; lectr., mem. panel Am. Women's Econ. Devel. Corp., 1981. Recipient Gold medal Deborah Fund Raising Dinner, 1955. Mem. Foragers of Am., Nat. Retail Mchts. Assn., Fragrance Found., Cosmetic Exec. Women. Clubs: Brandeis U., Hadassah. Home: 8455 Fountain Ave Apt 515 Los Angeles CA 90069-2543

STERN, S(EESA) BEATRICE, executive secretary, registered nurse; b. Atlantic City, Feb. 13, 1919; d. Max and Gussie (Thierman) Rosen; m. Francis H. Stern, June 29, 1958 (dec. Feb. 1973); m. Bernard N. Abelson, Dec. 5, 1973 (div. Feb. 1992). AA, Miami-Dade C.C., Fla., 1982, AS in Nursing, 1982. Sec. Highway Dept., Trenton, N.J., 1938-41; columnist N.J. Herald, Trenton, N.J., 1939-41; sec. U.S. Army, various locations, 1941-46; legal sec. Gus Feuer, Atty. at Law, Miami, 1946-47; exec. sec. to pres. and office mgr. Pharms., Inc., N.Y.C., 1947-58; med. sec. Phila., 1958-72; RN Mt. Sinai Med. Ctr., Miami Beach, Fla., 1982-83, Atlantic City Med. Ctr., 1983-84. Vol. Hollywood Med. Ctr., 1992-96, Aventura Med. Ctr., 1992-96. Mem. Brith Sholom (bd. govs. 1970-96), Brith Sholom Women (nat. pres. 1970-72), Phi Theta Kappa. Democrat.

STERN, SHARON ANN, freelance writer, editor; b. N.Y.C., Oct. 2, 1945; d. Isidor Isaac and Gertrude Zahava (Aronson) S. BA, Empire State Coll., 1976. Tutor N.Y.C., 1967—; editor Belsom Mgmt., N.Y.C., 1980-85. Contbr. poetry to numerous small mags., essays and stories to small mags. Bd. dirs. Comty. Bd., N.Y.C., 1975; with gracious living and productive with Respiratory Quadriplegia, N.Y.C., 1954—; mem. Food and Water, Washington, 1990, Sane/Freeze, N.Y.C., 1985, People for Ethical Treatment of Animals, N.Y.C., 1982. Mem. Life Scribes, Jour. Writing Network, Crystal Quilt. Home: # 1008 540 Main St New York NY 10044

STERNGLASS, MARILYN SEINER, English literature educator; b. Pitts., Aug. 21, 1932; d. Harry and Eva (Price) Seiner; m. Ernest J. Sternglass, Sept. 21, 1957; children: Daniel, Susan. BS, Carnegie-Mellon U., 1954, MA, 1967; PhD in Linguistics, U. Pitts., 1973. Instr. Carnegie-Mellon U., Pitts., 1967-72, asst. prof. English, 1973-75; assoc. prof. English Indiana U. Pa., 1975-79, Ind. U., Bloomington, 1979-85; assoc. prof. English City Coll. of CUNY, 1985-87, prof., 1987-96, prof. emerita, 1996—. Author: The Presence of Thought, 1988, Reading, Writing and Reasoning, 1991, 92, 93; contbr. articles to profl. jours. Profl. Staff Congress/CUNY rsch. grantee, 1991, 93, 94, Nat. Coun. Tchrs. English grantee, 1992, 93. Jewish. Home: 4601 Fifth Ave Apt 824 Pittsburgh PA 15213

STERNHAGEN, FRANCES, actress; b. Washington, Jan. 13, 1930. Student, Vassar Coll., Perry-Mansfield Sch. of Theatre; studied with Sanford Meisner, N.Y. Tchr. Milton Acad., Mass.; actress Arena Stage, Washington, 1953-54. Debut Thieves Carnival, N.Y., 1955; plays include The Carefree Tree, The Admirable Bashville (Clarence Derwent award, Obie award), Ulysses in Night Town, Red Eye of Love, Misalliance, The Return of Herbert Bracewell, Laughing Stock, The Displaced Person, The Pinter Plays (Obie award); Broadway shows include The Skin of Our Teeth, Viva Madison Avenue, Great Day in the Morning, The Right Honorable Gentleman, The Cocktail Party, Cock-a-Doddle Dandy, Playboy of the Western World, The Sign in Sidney Brustein's Window, The Good Doctor (Tony award 1973), Equus, Angel, On Golden Pond (Drama League award), The Father, Grownups, Summer, You Can't Take It With You, Home Front, Driving Miss Daisy, Remembrance, A Perfect Ganesh, The Heiress (Tony award 1995); actress films including Up The Down Staircase, Starting Over, 1979, Outland, 1981, Independence Day, 1983, Romantic Comedy, 1983, Bright Lights, Big City, 1988, See You in the Morning, 1989, Communion, 1989, Misery, 1990, Doc Hollywood, 1991, Raising Cain, 1992; (TV series) Love of Life, The Doctors, Secret Storm, Cheers, Golden Years, Under One Roof, The Road Home; (TV movies) Who Will Save Our Children?, 1978, Prototype, 1982, Resting Place, 1986, Follow Your Heart, 1990, She Woke Up, 1992, Labor of Love: The Arlette Schweitzer Story, 1993, Reunion, 1994, Tales from the Crypt, Outer Limits. *

STERNITZKE-HOLUB, ANN, elementary school educator; b. Oklahoma City, Okla., May 5, 1952; d. James Francis and Doris Josephine (Lahr) Sternitzke; m. James Robert Holub, Apr. 4, 1987. AA, Golden West Coll., Huntington Beach, Calif., 1972; BS, Calif. State U., Fullerton, 1975, postgrad., 1976. Cert. secondary multiple subject, phys. edn. and English tchr. grades kindergarten-12, Calif.; life cert. educator Calif. Cmty. Colls. Phys. edn. and fencing instr. Fullerton Coll., 1976-82; fencing instr. Golden West Coll., Huntington Beach, 1977-83, Calif. State U., Fullerton, 1983-86; elem. phys. edn. specialist Placentia-Yorba Linda (Calif.) Unified Sch. Dist., 1989-93, elem. tchr. Bryant Ranch Sch., 1993—; puppeteer Adventure City Amusement Park, Anaheim, Calif. Mem. support staff 1984 Olympics, Long Beach, 1984; entertainer Stagelight Family Prodns., Brea, Calif., 1993—. Grantee Disneyland, 1993, 94, 95, 96. Mem. AAHPERD, U.S. Fencing Assn., U.S. Olympic Soc., U.S. Fencing Coaches Assn., Calif. State U. Alumni Assn. Republican. Office: Bryant Ranch Sch 24695 Paseo De Toronto Yorba Linda CA 92687-5116

STERNLIGHT, JEAN RENEE, lawyer; b. Bklyn., Oct. 30, 1958; d. Peter Donn and Lenore (Frane) S. BA, Swarthmore (Pa.) Coll., 1979; JD, Harvard U., 1983. Bar: N.Y. 1984, Pa. 1985, U.S. Dist. Ct. (ea. dist.) Pa. 1985, U.S. Ct. Appeals (3d cir.) 1985. Law clk. Hon. Marilyn Hall Patel, U.S. Dist. Ct., San Francisco, 1983-84; assoc. Samuel & Ballard, P.C., Phila., 1984-89; mem., v.p. Samuel & Ballard, P.C., 1989-91, 1989—; asst. prof. Fla. State U. Coll. of Law, Tallahassee, 1991—; dir. edn. and rsch., Fla. Dispute Ctr., 1994—. Editor in chief Harvard Civil Rights-Civil Liberties Law Rev., 1982-83. Office: Fla State U Coll Law Tallahassee FL 32306

STERRENBERG-ROSE, MARILYN SUE, lawyer; b. Birmingham, Ala., Oct. 13, 1954; d. Kenneth George and Elsie Marie (Wright) Sterrenberg; m. Brian Hugh Rose, July 8, 1978; 1 child, Benjamin Hugh. BA, Lawrence U., 1976; JD with high honors, Ill. Inst. Tech., Chgo., 1981. Bar: Colo. 1982, U.S. Dist. Ct. Colo. 1982, U.S. Ct. Appeals (10th cir.) 1995. Casualty underwriter Hartford Accident and Indemnity Co., Chgo. and Joliet, Ill., 1976-78; assoc. Hall & Evans, Denver, 1982-89, mem., 1990—; Denver area placement coordinator Ill. Inst. Tech., 1984—. Recipient Corpus Juris Secundum award Am. Jurisprudence Awards, 1980. Mem. ABA, Colo. Bar Assn., Colo. Def. Lawyers Assn., Def. Rsch. and Trial Lawyers Assn., Profl. Liability Underwriting Soc., Nat. Assn. Women Bus. Owners, Denver Bar Assn., Presbyterian. Office: Hall & Evans LLC 1200 17th St Denver CO 80202-5817

STERRETT, JANE EVELYNE, illustrator, artist; b. N.Y.C., Jan. 3, 1942; d. Anthony H. and Frances S. Sterrett. Student, with Oskar Kokoschka, Salzburg, Austria, 1962; BFA, R.I. Sch. Design, 1963; MFA, Yale U., 1965. Chairperson art dept. Milton (Mass.) Acad./Girls Sch., 1965-68; instr. Parsons Sch. Design, N.Y.C., 1974-80; prin. Jane Sterrett Studio, N.Y.C., 1970—, freelance illustrator, 1970—; adj. prof. Pratt Inst., Manhattan, N.Y., 1972—. Free lance illustrator for various publs., corp. and advt. agys. Recipient numerous awards. Mem. Soc. Illustrators, Graphic Artists Guild. Office: 160 5th Ave New York NY 10010-7003

STERRITT, JANET ROBINSON, engineering executive; b. Lower Merion, Pa., Aug. 2, 1956; d. George and Helen (Kerswell) Robinson; m. James A Sterritt, II, Feb. 19, 1983; children: James Robinson, John George. BSEE, U. Rochester, 1978. Engr. Xerox Corp., Rochester, N.Y., 1978-87, program mgr., 1982-84, sys. integration mgr., 1984-85, diagnostics mgr., 1985-86, sys. mgr., 1986-87; mgr. r & d Hollis Automation, Nashua, N.H., 1987-90, dir. r & d, 1990-92; dir. imaging DuPont Imagitex, Nashua, N.H., 1992—; dir. med. imaging Howtek, Inc., Hudson, N.H., 1994—. Co-author: Solder Joint Reliability, 1990; contbr. articles to profl. jours.; patentee in field. Home: 31 Irene Dr Hollis NH 03049 Office: Howtek Inc 21 Park Dr Hudson NH 03051

STETSER, CAROL LINDA, editor; b. Syracuse, N.Y., Apr. 11, 1948; d. Dana George and Virginia (Masland) S.; m. Ronald E. Berenbeim (div.); m. Jimmy M. King. Student, Smith Coll., Northampton, Mass., 1966-68; BS, Emerson Coll., Boston, 1970. Founder, editor Padma Press, Sedona, Ariz., 1976—. Author: (photography books) Black and White, 1977, Chopping Wood, Carrying Water, 1978, Continuum, 1979; 16 artists books including Hierograms, 1988, Currents, 1992; (compilations) Fashion: Spring Collection '86, 1986, Fall Collection '90, 1990. Book repairer, book binder Sedona Pub. Libr., 1995. Mem. Internat. Soc. Copier Artists. Home and Office: Padma Press PO Box 20081 Sedona AZ 86341

STETTER, DEBRA LYNN, lawyer; b. Evanston, Ill., Nov. 17, 1962; d. Rolf Henry and Clarice Lucille (Young) S. AB in Econs., Bryn Mawr Coll., 1984; MBA, U. Chgo., 1987; JD, Northwestern U., Chgo., 1992. Bar: Ill. 1992. Budget analyst Rotary Internat., Evanston, 1984-85; econ. rsch. analyst The No. Trust Co., Chgo., 1985-86; dir. strategic devel. Med. Mgmt. Am., Chgo., 1987-89; atty. Schiff Hardin & Waite, Chgo., 1992—. Mem. Women's Bar Assn. (Achievement scholar 1991), Chgo. Bar Assn., Order of Coif. Office: Schiff Hardin & Waite 7200 Sears Tower Chicago IL 60606

STEUER, KAREN L., legislative staff member; b. Reading, Pa., Apr. 29, 1953. BA, Goddard Coll., 1989. With Aetna Life & Casualty, Hartford, Conn., 1979-85; prin. investigator, dir. conservation and ednl. programs Ctr. for Coastal Studies, 1991-93; profl. staff mem. com. on merchant marine and fisheries, 1991-93; mem. legis. staff com. resources House of Reps., 1994—. Office: 522 O'Neill House Office Bldg Washington DC 20515*

STEURY, ELLEN HOCHSTEDLER, criminal justice educator and researcher; b. Angola, Ind., Oct. 20, 1952; d. Richard McLouth and Winona (Fields) Hochstedler; m. Steven R. Steury, Jan. 30, 1988; stepchildren: Steven N. Steury, Rachel D. Steury, Jill H. Steury. AB, Ind. U., 1973; MA, SUNY, Albany, 1976, PhD, 1980; JD, U. Wis., 1996. Asst. prof. criminal justice U. Wis., Milw., 1979-84, assoc. prof., 1984-93, prof., 1993—; vis. prof. law Nihon (Japan) U., Tokyo, 1991, Haudong U. Inst. of Politics and Law, 1996—. Author: Criminal Court Process, 1996; editor: Corporations as Criminals, 1983; contbr. articles to profl. jours. Bd. dirs. ACLU, Milw., 1984-88.

STEVENS, ALICE THERESE ALLGAIER, writer, administrator; b. Chgo., Feb. 4, 1949; d. Joseph Michael and Alice Romayne (Roche) Allgaier; m. Robert Skeens, Apr. 27, 1979 (div. Dec. 1981); 1 child, Christopher Skeens; m. Richard Street Stevens, June 24, 1989. BA, U. Ill., Chgo., 1971, MA, 1974. Editor bibliographies Ency. Brit., Chgo., 1971-72; instr., dir. writing lab. St. Louis C.C., 1974-76; asst. editor health care Hosps. mag., Chgo., 1977-80; tech. writer Zenith Data Systems, Chgo., 1981; creator, dir. documentation dept. Kemper Fin. Svcs., Chgo., 1982-87, Chgo. Rsch. & Trading, 1987-92, Interface, Chgo., 1982-95; in mktg. comms. Technology Solutions Co., Chgo., 1996—. Contbr. poetry to The Oyez Rev., Black Maria, others. Founding mem. Women's Studies Collective, U. Ill., Chgo., 1973-74; regional coord., regional rep. New Am. Movement, Chgo., 1977; area precinct organizer Harold Washington for Mayor, Chgo., 1982-83; precinct captain Carol Mosely Braun for Senate, Chgo., 1992; sr. mem. Dem. Socialists of Am., 1974—. Mem. Soc. for Tech. Communicators (sr.). Democrat. Home: 302 Main St Evanston IL 60202

STEVENS, BARBARA HELEN, economist; b. Ft. Knox, Ky., Mar. 24, 1952; d. Edgar C. and Marguerite Florence (Nordburg) S.; m. Michael Kent Robertson, June 16, 1973. BA, So. Ill. U., 1974; MA, No. Ill. U., 1977. Coord. natural resources Ill. Dept. Transp., Springfield, 1985-88, socio-economic analyst, 1989-92, socio-economic specialist, 1993—; adj. faculty St. Mary of the Woods (Ind.) Coll., 1982-84; rsch. panel mem. Transp. Rsch. Bd., Washington, 1992, 95; peer review com. Fed. Hwy. Adminstrn., Washington, 1993. Mem. AAUW, Am. Econ. Assn., Midwest Econs. Assn. Home: 2250 N 400 East Rd Rochester IL 62563 Office: Ill Dept Transp 2300 S Dirkson Pky Springfield IL 62764

STEVENS, BRENDA ANITA, psychologist, educator; b. N.Y.C., Oct. 23, 1949; d. Henry Stevens and Frances Marie (Russo) Incorvaia; m. Edwin Randall Trinkle, Feb. 21, 1976 (div. 1987); m. John Alexander Czaja, Sept. 10, 1994; 1 child, Peter A. BS, Boston U., 1971, MEd, 1971, CAGS, 1973; PhD in Edn., U. Tenn., 1991. Nat. cert. sch. psychologist. Sch. adjustment counselor Dedham (Mass.) Pub. Schs., 1972-73; testing specialist Children's Hosp. Med. Ctr., Boston, 1973-74; sch. psychologist North Middlesex Regional Schs., Townsend, Mass., 1974-78; grad. asst. U. Tenn., Knoxville, 1978-79, 89-90, program evaluator, 1983-84, clinic coord., 1989-90; psychology assoc. Cherokee Mental Health Ctr., Morristown, Tenn., 1985; asst. prof. U. Nebr., Kearney, 1990-93, Miami U., Oxford, Ohio, 1993—; psychol. cons. Roane County Pub. Schs., Kingston, Tenn., 1978-89; cons., adminstrv. intern Knox County Pub. Schs., Knoxville, 1984-85; sch. psychologist Jefferson County Pub. Schs., Dandridge, Tenn., 1986-88, Oak Ridge (Tenn.) Pub. Schs., 1989; cons. Psychol. Corp., 1994-96. Commr.'s appointee Mass. State Coun. for Hearing Impaired, Boston, 1976-78; bd. dirs. Luth. Social Ministries Tenn., Knoxville, 1989; exec. bd. Luth. Community Svcs., Knoxville, 1987-89; cons. Mass. State Dept. Edn., Boston, 1974-78. Head Start grantee, 1991-94, Project One to One grantee Dawson County, 1991; Trustee scholar Boston U., 1968-71; recipient Women of Achievement award Commn. Women, 1983. Mem. Am. Psychol. Assn., Nat. Assn. Sch. Psychologists, Phi Kappa Phi, Pi Lambda Theta, Ohio Sch. Psychologists Assn, Phi Delta Kappa. Office: Miami U Dept Ednl Psychology 201 McGuffey Oxford OH 45056

STEVENS, CAROLE ANN, historian; b. Bklyn., Feb. 26, 1944; d. Frederic and Teresa (Palagano) S. BA in English, Utica (N.Y.) Coll., 1968; MA, Ga. State U., 1994. Historian Ga. Hist. Commn., Atlanta, 1972-75, DeKalb Hist. Soc., Decatur, Ga., 1976-80; enumerator U.S. Census Bur., Atlanta, 1980; historian Nat. Park Svc., Atlanta, 1982-83; archivist Ga. State U., Atlanta, 1986. Editor: Life in Dixie, 1862-65, 1978; co-author: (pamphlet) Robert A. Alston Papers, 1976. Vol., rschr. DeKalb Hist. Soc., 1994, 95-96. Mem. Phi Alpha Theta. Home: 2460 Peachtree Rd NW #613 Atlanta GA 30305

STEVENS, DIANA LYNN, elementary education educator; b. Waterloo, Iowa, Dec. 12, 1950; d. Marcus Henry and Clarissa Ann (Funk) Carr; m. Paul John Stevens; 1 child, Drew Spencer. BS, Mid Am. Nazarene Coll., 1973; M in Liberal Arts, Baker U., 1989. Elem. tchr. Olathe (Kans.) Sch. Dist. #233, 1975—. Artwork appeared in traveling exhibit ARC/Nat. Art Edn. Assn., 1968. Mem. Cedarhouse Aux., Olathe, 1986—; pres. Artists' League, Olathe, 1990—. Mem. NEA, Kans. Edn. Assn., Olathe Edn. Assn. (social com.), Nat. Art Edn. Assn., Delta Kappa Gamma (profl. affairs com. mem.), Coll. Ch. of the Nazarene. Home: 217 S Montclaire Dr Olathe KS 66061-3828

STEVENS, ELISABETH GOSS (MRS. ROBERT SCHLEUSSNER, JR.), writer, journalist; b. Rome, N.Y., Aug. 11, 1929; d. George May and Elisabeth (Stryker) Stevens; m. Robert Schleussner, Jr., Mar. 12, 1966 (dec. 1977); 1 child, Laura Stevens. B.A., Wellesley Coll., 1951; M.A. with high honors, Columbia U., 1956. Editorial assoc. Art News Mag., 1964-65; art critic and reporter Washington Post, Washington, 1965-66; free-lance art critic and reporter Balt., 1966—; contbg. art critic Wall Street Jour., N.Y.C., 1969-72; art critic Trenton Times, N.J., 1974-77; art and architecture critic The Balt. Sun, 1978-86. Author: Elisabeth Stevens' Guide to Baltimore's Inner Harbor, 1981, Fire and Water: Six Short Stories, 1982, Children of Dust: Portraits and Preludes, 1985, Horse and Cart: Stories from the Country, 1990, The Night Lover: Art & Poetry, 1995; contbr. articles, poetry and short stories to jours., nat. newspapers and popular mags. Recipient A.D. Emmart award for journalism, 1980, Critical Writing citation Balt.-Washington Newspaper Guild, 1980, fiction awards Md. Poetry Rev., 1992, 93, 94, 2d prize Lite Circle, 1994, 1st prize in fiction Lite Circle, 1995, 96, award Balt. Writers Alliance, 1994, Balt. Writers Alliance Play Writing Contest award, 1994; art critics' fellow NEA, 1973-74, fellow MacDowell Colony, 1981, Va. Ctr. for Creative Arts, 1982-85, 88-90, 92, 93, 95, Ragdale Found., 1984, 89, Yaddo, 1991, Villa Montalvo, 1995; Work-in-Progress grantee for poetry Md. Art Coun., 1986, Creative Devel. grantee for short fiction collection Balt. Mayor's Com. on Art and Culture, 1986. Mem. Nat. Press Club Washington, Coll. Art Assn., Balt. Bibliophiles, Authors Guild, Am. Studies Assn., Poetry Soc. Am. Home: 6604 Walnutwood Cir Baltimore MD 21212-1213

STEVENS, HELEN JEAN, retired elementary school educator, musician; b. Nevada, Iowa, July 11, 1934; d. Paul Ellison and Helen Margaret (Ives) S. MusB, U. So. Calif., L.A., 1956. Cert. secondary music tchr., Calif. Tchr. San Francisco Sch. Dist., 1956-58; prin. oboist Marin Symphony Orch., San Rafael, Calif., 1956-94, Santa Rosa (Calif.) Symphony, 1956-86; tchr. Santa Venetia Mid. Sch., San Rafael, 1958-83; asst. prof. music Sonoma State Coll., Rohnert Park, Calif., 1963-76; tchr. Davidson Mid. Sch., San Rafael, 1984-89; tchr. oboe students; oboist Debut TV Show, L.A., 1954-55, Carmel (Calif.) Bach Festival, 1955-82; prin. oboist Light Opera Curren Theatre, San Francisco, 1966-67, Marin Opera Co., San Rafael, 1980-84. active Sonoma County 4-H Guide Dog Project Leader, Guide Dogs for the Blind, Inc., 1974-87. Recipient Svc. award PTA, 1974, Golden Bell award Marin County Office of Edn., 1984; named Outstanding Tchr., Marin Edn. Found., 1986, Continuing Svc. award Calif. Congress Parents, Tchrs. and Students, Inc, 1989. Mem. German Shepherd Dog Club Am. Democrat. Presbyterian. Home: 8555 Kirk Dr Colorado Springs CO 80908-2910

STEVENS, JUDITH, special education educator; b. Ephrata, Pa., Feb. 18, 1938; d. Robert Bucher and Virginia Anna (Bare) Witmyer; m. Gordon Appleton Stevens, Apr. 1, 1964 (dec. May 1994); 1 child, Friedrich Menckhen. BS, Bloomsburg State Tchrs. Coll., 1960; MEd, Millersville State Coll., 1979. Cert. spl. edn. tchr., Pa. Classroom tchr. Devereux Found., Devon, Pa., 1960-66, Lancaster-Lebanon Intermediate Unit # 13, East Petersburg, Pa., 1969—. Edn. chairperson Emmanuel United Meth. Ch., Brownstown, Pa., 1985—; sec. West Earl Fire Co. Aux., Brownstown, 1990—. Mem. NEA, Pa. Edn. Assn., Lancaster-Lebanon Intermediate Unit Edn. Assn. (local sec. 1990—), Coun. for Exceptional Children (chair campership com. 1972-94), Am. Assn. on Mental retardation (life). Republican. Methodist. Home: 240 E Main St PO Box 323 Brownstown PA 17508

STEVENS, JUDITH ANN, minister, theology educator; b. Greenville, S.C., Aug. 3, 1951; d. Leonard Earle and Ruth Doris (Joyner) Stevens. BA in Econs. and Bus. Adminstrn., Furman U., 1982; MDiv, Southeastern Sem., Wake Forest, N.C., 1985, ThM, 1987, MPhil, Union Theol. Sem., 1991. Assoc. min. First Bapt. Ch., Rock Hill, S.C., 1983-85; New Testament fellow, rsch. asst. Southeastern Sem., 1985-87; head tchr. Wake Tch. Coll., Raleigh, N.C., 1985-87; tchg. asst. Union Theol. Sem., N.Y.C., 1988-94; clergy mem. United Meth. Ch., Sloatsburg, N.Y., 1991—; dir. Women's Ctr., Union Theol. Sem., 1994-95, adv. bd. faculty search com., 1992-93, com. on status and role of women, 1994—. Chaplain's asst., Trauma Ctr. and Hospice, Greenville, 1980-82; mem. Hunger Prevention Task Force, Rockland County, N.Y., 1993—. Mem. AAUW, NOW, Am. Acad. Religion, Soc. of Biblical Lit., Clergywomen Caucus of United Meth. Ch., Meth. Fedn. for Social Action. Democrat. Methodist. Office: United Methodist Church 93 Orange Turnpike Sloatsburg NY 10974

STEVENS, JULIE ANN, peri-operative nurse; b. Normal, Ill., June 3, 1961; d. James E. and Janice J. (Richey) S. BSN with honors, Baylor U., 1984. RN, Tex.; cert. CNOR, CNRN. Nurse intern operating rm. Parkland Meml. Hosp., Dallas, 1984-85, staff nurse, 1985-89; charter employee, staff nurse Zale Lipshy U. Hosp. at Southwestern Med. Ctr., Dallas, 1989-92, clin. coord. neurosurgery, 1992-96; staff nurse Med. City Dallas Hosp., 1996—. Recipient Interlocking Circle of Caring award Delta Airlines, Dallas, 1986, Divisional Achievement award Zale Lipshy U. Hosp., 1994. Mem. Assn. Oper. Rm. Nurses, Am. Assn. Neurosci. Nurses, DAR, Internat. Order of Job's Daus (past Honored Queen). Methodist. Home: 1913 Bachman Ct Plano TX 75075-6162 Office: Med City Dallas Hosp 7777 Forest Lane Dallas TX 75230

STEVENS, LEOTA MAE, retired elementary education educator; b. Waverly, Kans., Mar. 27, 1921; d. Clinton Ralph and Velma Mae (Kukuk) Chapman; m. James Oliver Stevens, Nov. 7, 1944 (dec.); children: James Harold, Mary Ann Hooker Tibbits. BA, McPherson Coll., 1954; MS, Emporia U., 1964, postgrad., 1969-77; postgrad., Wichita U., 1977. Educator Pleasant Mound Sch., Waverly, 1940-41; prin. educator Halls Summit Sch., Waverly, 1941-42; educator Waverly Grade Sch., 1942-43, Ellinwood (Kans.) Jr. H.S., 1943-45, Hutchinson (Kans.) Grade Sch., 1945-48, Lincoln Sch., Darlow, Kans., 1948-49; educator prin. Mitchell-Yaggy Consol. Sch., Hutchinson, 1949-57; educator elem. Hutchinson Sch. Dist. 308, 1957-85, ret., 1985; v.p. Reno County Tchrs. Assn. Hutchinson, 1956-57, pres. Assn. Childhood Edn. Internat., 1978-79. Author of numerous poems; compiler The Alexander-Kukuk Descendants: 1754 to 1990. Mem. Worker ARC Blood Mobile, 1986—, Hutchinson Cmty. Concerts 1970—; ch. sch. tchr. Trinity United Meth. Ch., 1959-71. (attendance chair, 1994); historian Women's Civic Ctr., 1988-92, art com. chmn., 1992-96; den mother Cub Scouts, 1963-66, leader Girl Scouts Ellinwood, 1944-45. Mem. AAUW (news reporter 1984-87, legis. chmn. program com. 1991—, 2d v.p., 1994—), Ret. Nation State and Local Edn. Assn., Reno County Tchrs. Assn. (v.p. 1956-57), Assn. Childhood Edn. Internat. (pres. 1978-79), Reno County Extension Homemaker Coun. (rep. 1987—), Rainbow Extension Club (pres. 1986-92), Hutchinson Area Ret. Tchrs. Assn. (historian 1996—), Am. Legion Aux., Friends of Preservation, Delta Kappa Gamma (sec., v.p. 1972-80, grant chmn. 1980-88, publicity com. 1990-93, legis. chmn. 1994—). Republican. Home: 805 W 23rd Ave Hutchinson KS 67502-3765

STEVENS, LINDA GALE BISSON, public utilities executive; 1 child, Teresa Adrienne Paulinet. BA in History, U. N.H., 1972; MBA, Simmons Coll., Boston, 1980. Cert. utility regulation studies, Mass., Mich. Law sch. admissions dir. Franklin Pierce Law Ctr., Concord, N.H., 1978-79; v.p., co-founder BCI Geonetics, Inc., Santa Barbara, Calif., 1981-87; commr. Pub. Utilities Commn., Concord, N.H., 1987-93; exec. dir. NE Conf. Pub. Utilities Commrs., Inc., Providence, 1993—; adj. faculty bus. Daniel Webster Coll., Nashua, N.H., 1986-87; vice-chmn. Def. Adv. Com. on Women in the Svcs., D.C.; del. 1st Japan-Am. Grassroots Summit; with NARUC; chmn. Com. on Water, subcom. on Conservation., bd. advs. U.S. Naval War Coll., Newport, R.I. Trustee New Eng. Coll., fin. com.; bd. dirs., chmn. Def. Issues Task Force, WESG; trustee The Nature Conservancy, N.H.; incorporator N.H. Charitable Fund; adv. bd. mem. MIT Energy Lab., NH DRED Econ. Adv. Group; pub. coun. mem. Am. Water Works Assn. Rsch. Found.; admissions coun. mem. Simmons Coll. GSM; mem. U.S.M.C. Scholarship Found. Com.; active numerous nat. and local regulatory agys. RJR Nabisco Fellow Harvard U. Kennedy Sch. Govt.; recipient Rappaport Achievement award Simmons Coll., 1990. Mem. Am. Water Works Assn. (mem. pub. adv. forum), Univ. N.H. Alumni Assn. (nat. pres., bd. dirs.), Rotary Internat., Army and Navy Club, Bald Peak Colony Club, Ida Lewis Yacht Club. Home: PO Box 356 Newport RI 02840-0003

STEVENS, LYDIA HASTINGS, community volunteer; b. Highland Park, Ill., Aug. 2, 1918; d. Rolland T.R. and Ruth Shotwell (Beebe) Hastings; m. George Cooke Stevens, Nov. 2, 1940; children: Lydia Stevens Gustin, Priscilla Stevens Goldfarb, Frederick S., Elizabeth Stevens MacLeod, George H., Ruth Stevens Stellard. BA, Vassar Coll., 1939. State rep. 151st Dist. of Conn., Greenwich, 1988-92; cons. Nat. Exec. Svc. Corps, N.Y.C., 1985. Pres. Greenwich YWCA, 1971-74, Greenwich Housing Coalition, 1982-86; v.p. planning Greenwich United Way, 1973-76; sr. warden Greenwich Christ Episcopal Ch., 1981-86; chmn. rev. commn. Episcopal Diocese of Conn., 1985-87; bd. dirs. Greenwich Libr., 1985-93; chmn. Greenwich Commn. Aging, 1986-88; pres., bd. dirs. Greenwich Broadcasting Corp., 1977-79; bd. dirs. Fairfield County Cmty. Found., 1992, United Way of Greenwich. Recipient Golden Rule award J.C. Penney, 1987, President's award Greenwich YWCA, 1992. Republican. Episcopalian.

STEVENS, MARILYN RUTH, editor; b. Wooster, Ohio, May 30, 1943; d. Glenn Willard and Gretchen Elizabeth (Ihrig) Amstutz; BA, Coll. Wooster (Ohio), 1965; MAT, Harvard U., 1966; JD, Suffolk U., 1975; m. Bryan J. Stevens, Oct. 11, 1969; children: Jennifer Marie, Gretchen Anna. Bar: Mass. 1975. Tchr., Lexington (Mass.) Public Schs., 1966-69; in various editorial positions Houghton Mifflin Co., Boston, 1969—, editorial dir. sch. depts., 1978-81, editorial dir. math. and scis. Sch. Div., 1981-84, mng. editor sch. pub., 1984—. Mem. LWV, Mass. Bar Assn. Office: Houghton Mifflin 222 Berkeley St Boston MA 02116-3748

STEVENS, MARY ANN, state legislator; b. West, Miss.; m. A.J. Stevesn, III; 1 child, Elizabeth Ann. Grad., West H.S. Mem. Miss. Ho. of Reps., 1981—, chmn. ins. com., mem. appropriations com., jud. com., juvenile justice com.; former banker, landowner; project dir. West Primary Health Care Clinic. Former mayor, former alderman Town of West. Mem. West Garden Club (past pres.), Miss. Women's Club. Democrat. Methodist. Office: Miss State Senate State Capital PO Box 1018 Jackson MS 39215-1018*

STEVENS, PHYLISS ELIZABETH, fine art dealer, consultant, publisher, lecturer; b. Balt., Dec. 30, 1953; d. Lawrence and Frances Elizabeth Stevens. BS, Va. Commonwealth U., 1977. Gallery dir. KenWest Gallery, L.A., 1979-84; fine art cons. La Mirage Gallery, L.A., 1984-86; gallery dir. West 43rd St. Gallery, L.A., 1986-89; pres. Vibrant Fine Art, L.A., 1990—; pres., founder, organizer Art in Pub. Places, L.A., 1984-86; creative dir. The Black Child/Art, L.A., 1986-88; art cons. NBC-TV Segment Series, Hill St. Blues, Hollywood, Calif., 1982. Editor Art Forum, 1984, American Black Artists Newsletter, 1988. Recipient Top Cons. Design Workshop award West Coast Art Stars, 1978, Community Involvement In the Arts award Founder's Women Club, 1980. Mem. NAFE, Am. Artist Club (pres. 1986-88). Democrat. Office: Vibrant Fine Art Los Angeles CA 90016

STEVENS, ROSEMARY A., academic dean, public health and social history educator; b. Bourne, Eng.; came to U.S., 1961, naturalized, 1968; d. William Edward and Mary Agnes (Tricks) Wallace; m. Robert B. Stevens, Jan. 28, 1961 (div. 1983); children: Carey, Richard; m. Jack D. Barchas, Aug. 9, 1994. BA, Oxford (Eng.) U., 1957; Diploma in Social Adminstrn., Manchester (Eng.) U., 1959; MPH, Yale U., 1963, PhD, 1968. Various hosp. adminstrv. positions Eng., 1959-61; rsch. assoc. Med. Sch. Yale U., 1962-68, asst. prof. Med. Sch., 1968-71, assoc. prof. Med. Sch., 1971-74, prof. pub. health Med. Sch., 1974-76; master Jonathan Edwards Coll., 1974-75; prof. dept. health systems mgmt. and polit. sci. Tulane U., New Orleans, 1976-78; chmn. dept. health systems mgmt. Tulane U., 1977-78; prof. history and sociology of sci. U. Pa., Phila., 1979—, chmn. dept., 1980-83, 86-91, UPS Found. prof., 1990-91, dean Sch. Arts and Scis., Thomas S. Gates prof., 1991—; vis. lectr. Johns Hopkins U., 1967-68; guest scholar Brookings Instn., Washington, 1967-68; acad. visitor London Sch. Econs., 1962-64, 1973-

74. Author: Medical Practice in Modern England: The Impact of Specialization and State Medicine, 1966, American Medicine and the Public Interest, 1971, In Sickness and in Wealth: American Hospitals in the Twentieth Century, 1989, (with others) Foreign Trained Physicians and American Medicine, 1972, Welfare Medicine in America, 1974, Alien-Doctors: Foreign Medical Graduates in American Hospitals, 1978. Bd. dirs. Milbank Meml. Fund; chmn. bd. dirs. Ctr. for Advancement of Health. Fellow Am. Acad. Arts and Scis.; mem. Inst. Medicine of Nat. Acad. Sci., History of Sci. Soc., Am. Assn. for History of Medicine, Coll. Physicians of Phila., Cosmopolitan Club. Home: 1900 Rittenhouse Sq # 18 A Philadelphia PA 19103-5735 Office: U Pa Office of Dean 116 College Hall Philadelphia PA 19104-6377

STEVENS, RUTH STEPHENS, county clerk; b. Muskegon, Mich., Mar. 21, 1940; d. John Logan and Viola Florence (Anderson) Stephens; m. C. Leigh Stevens, Oct. 8, 1960; children: Elizabeth Ann, Paul Max. Student, U. Mich., 1959-60, Coffeyville Jr. Coll., 1960; BA, Grand Valley U., 1972. Asst. mgr. Stephens-Hayes Co., Coffeyville, Kans., 1964-65, Logan-Ames Co., Kingfisher, Okla., 1967-68; city councilman Norton Shores, Mich., 1974-78; chief dep. county clk. County of Muskegon, Mich., 1980-82; county clk. County of Muskegon, 1984—. Mem. Muskegon C. of C. (mem. women's divsn. 1972—, pres. women's divsn. 1980-81), Bus. and Profl. Women's Club (officer, bd. dirs. 1982—, pres. 1994-96). Congregational. Office: County of Muskegon 990 Terrace Muskegon MI 49442

STEVENS, SANDY (AMANDA STEVENSON), document examiner; b. Bklyn., Oct. 24, 1943; d. Haakon and Grace Svendsen; m. James W. Moseley, 1962 (div. 1965); children: Elizabeth B. Moseley, Lawrence Harmon. Grad., Bay Ridge H.S., Bklyn., 1961. Cert. document examiner. Pvt. practice Pitts., 1967—; lectr. Jersey City State Coll., John Jay Coll. of Criminal Justice, N.Y.C., Mcpl. Credit Union, N.Y.C.; cons. numerous lawfirms. Co-author: How to Raise an Emotionally Health, Happy Child, 1964; designer forms for document examination; composer, librettist (mus.) Nellie Bly. Mem. AEA, Dramatists Guild, Songwriters Guild. Mem. Nat. Assn. Document Examiners. Democrat. Unitarian. Home and Office: 1473 Mervin Ave Pittsburgh PA 15216-2028

STEVENS, SHEILA MAUREEN, teachers union administrator; b. Glendale, Calif., Nov. 1, 1942; d. Richard Chase and Sheila Mary (Beatty) Flynn; m. Jan Whitney Stevens, Sept. 12, 1964; children: Ian Whitney, Bevin Michelle. AA in Liberal Arts, Monterey Peninsula Coll., Calif., 1963; BA in Anthropology, Calif. State U., Long Beach, 1969; postgrad. studies in Edn., U. Guam, 1976-77. Tchr. U.S. Trust Territory of the Pacific, Koror, Palau Island, 1968-72, Kolonia, Ponape Island, 1972-76; tchr. Dept. Edn., Agana, Guam, 1976-79; newspaper editor Pacific Daily News (Gannett), Agana, 1979-83; comm. dir. Guam Fedn. of Tchrs., Agana, 1983-84, exec. dir., 1984-85; exec. dir. Alaska Fedn. Tchrs., Anchorage, 1985-87; labor rels. specialist N.Y. State United Tchrs., Watertown, 1987-93; regional staff dir. N.Y. State United Tchrs., Potsdam, 1993—; mem. Gov.'s Blue Ribbonn Panel on Edn., Agana, Guam, 1983-85; leadership devel. coord. Am. Fedn. Tchrs., Washington, 1983—; trainer positive negotiations program Situation Mgmt. Sys., Hanover, Mass., 1988—. Author, editor: Pacific Daily News, 1981-83 (Guam Press Club awards 1981, 82, 83); contbr. articles to mag. and jours. Mem. task force on labor policy, com. on self determination, Govt. of Guam, Agana, 1984-85, Adult Basic Edn. Planning Com., 1985; mem. labor studies adv. bd., Anchorage, Alaska, 1989, regional compact coalition N.Y. State Edn. Dept., Albany, 1994. Named Friend of Edn., Carthage (N.Y.) Tchrs. Assn., 1990. Mem. NOW, ACLU, ASCD, Am. Fedn. Tchrs. Comm. Assn. (Best Editorial award 1984). Democrat. Methodist. Office: NY State United Tchrs 12 Elm St Potsdam NY 13676-1812

STEVENS, SUZANNE DUCKWORTH, artist, educator; b. Richmond, Ind., Feb. 1, 1946; d. Delbert Raymond and Virginia (Grosvenor) Duckworth; married, 1970 (divorced 1979); 1 child, Neil D. Stevens. BA in Painting and Drawing, Fla. State U., 1968; MA in Painting and Drawing, Goddard Coll., Plainfield, Vt., 1978. Substitute counselor Crisis Intervention Home, Virginia Beach, Va., 1978-85; art instr. Virginia Beach Ctr. for Arts, 1979—; pvt. art instr. and artist Fine Art Studio, Virginia Beach, 1978—; artist in residence Virginia Beach Sch. Sys., 1991, 93; curator student shows Virginia Beach Ctr. for Arts, 1990—; instr. Va. Marine Sci. Mus., Virginia Beach, 1993—. One-person shows at Decker Studios, Virginia Beach, 1986, Virginia Beach Ctr. for Arts, 1987, 89, Commons Gallery, Norfolk, Va., 1990, Waterworks Visual Arts Ctr., Salisbury, N.C., 1991, Artists at Work Gallery, Virginia Beach, 1992; exhibited in group shows at Peninsula Fine Arts Ctr., Newport News, Va., 1982, 83, 84, Virginia Beach Ctr. for Arts, 1986, 88, 94, 95, 96, Maritime Mus., Virginia Beach, 1988, Gallery 32, Virginia Beach, 1989, Seashore State Park, Virginia Beach, 1992, Mulligen Gallery, Virginia Beach, 1995; represented in permanent collections at Chrysler Mus., Norfolk; featured in Visions Mag. for Arts & Gallery, Virginia Beach, 1996—. Recipient Outstanding Tchr. award Gov.'s Sch. for Visual and Performing Arts, U. Richmond, Va., 1990, 93. Mem. Women in the Arts Mus., Classics Plus Dance Orgn., Tadems Dance Orgn. Democrat. Home and Studio: 202 81st St Virginia Beach VA 23451

STEVENSON, AMANDA See STEVENS, SANDY

STEVENSON, CYNTHIA, actress; b. Oakland, Calif., Aug. 7, 1963. Appearances include: (films) The Player, The Gun in Betty Lou's Handbag, Watch It, Forget Paris, Home for the Holidays, (TV series) My Talk Show, Hope and Gloria, (theater) Ladies Room. Office: care NBC 3000 W Alameda Blvd Burbank CA 91523*

STEVENSON, FRANCES KELLOGG, museum program director; b. Boston; d. Charles Summers and Alice deGueldry (Stevens) S.; m. James Richard Wein, 1971 (div. 1989). BA, Wells Coll., Aurora, N.Y., 1967; MA, Oxford U., 1972; MBA, U. Pa., 1992. Cert. personal trainer, Aerobics and Fitness Assn. Am. News editor Sierra Club, San Francisco, 1970-71; copy editor Oxford (United Kingdom) U. Press, 1972-73; from editor to publs. officer Smithsonian Instn., Washington, 1974—. Co-editor: Abroad in America: Visitors to the New Nation, 1976; compiler: (book) National Portrait Gallery Permanent Collection Illustrated Checklist, 1982. James E. Webb fellow Smithsonian Instn., 1988-89. Mem. Sulgrave Club. Home: 2724 Ordway St NW Apt 4 Washington DC 20008-5047 Office: Smithsonian Instn Portrait Gallery 8th and F Sts NW Washington DC 20560

STEVENSON, JANET ATLANTIS, writer; b. Chgo., Feb. 4, 1913; d. John Carter and Atlantis Octavia (Mcclendon) Marshall; m. Philip E. Stevenson, Oct. 14, 1940 (div. Sept. 1963); children: Joseph, Edward P.; m. Benson Rotstein, Sept. 11, 1964 (dec. Aug. 1970). BA magna cum laude, Bryn Mawr Coll., 1933; MFA in Drama, Yale U., 1935; postgrad., U. Chgo., 1934. Author: (plays) Streak of Pink, 1937 (Bur. of New Plays award), (with Philip Stevenson) Declaration, 1949, The Innocent Bystander, 1952, But Yet a Woman, 1952 (John Golden fellowship, Nat. Arts of the Theatre award 1963), The Third President, 1977 (Internat. Bicentennial Playwriting prize 1973), Sarah Ann, 1986, (novels) Weep No More, 1959, paperback edit., 1971 (Friends of Am. Writers Hon. Mention award 1952), The Ardent Years, 1962, Sister and Brothers, 1961, Departure, 1985, (non-fiction) Woman Aboard, 1967, paperback edit., 1981, (biography: The Undiminished Man: A Political Biography of Robert Walker Kenny, 1980, (books for young readers) John James Audubon, 1961, Marian Anderson, 1963, Archibald Grimke, 1969, Pioneers in Freedom, 1969, Soldiers in the Civil Rights War, 1971, The Montgomery Bus Boycott, 1971, The First Book of Woman's Rights, 1972, The School Segregation Cases, 1973; librettist Kumana, 1952, Lysistrata, 1970; contbr. articles to mags. and newspapers; prodr. weekly radio program Feminist Agenda, 1987-89. Founding mem. Women's Strike for Peace, L.A., 1960; mem. Home Rule Charter Drafting Com., Clatsop County; founding mem., pres. North Coast Women's Polit. Caucus, 1984, 94; mem. adv. bd. Lives in Transition program Clastsop C.C.; mem. exec. bd. Clatsop County Econ. Devel. Coun., 1987-94, chair, 1991-92; mem. governing bd. Clastop County Hist. Soc., 1987-92. Recipient White Rose award March of Dimes, 1985, Charles Erskine Scott Wood award Oreg. Inst. Lit. Arts, 1988, Women of Achievement award State of Oreg. Commn. for women, 1994, Disting. Svc. award LWV, 1995. Home and Office: 783 5th Ave Hammond OR 97121

STEVENSON, JENNIFER E., accountant; b. Mt. Pleasant, Mich., Aug. 13, 1967; d. James J. Rush and Ida G. (Frosh) Shields; m. Peter R. Stevenson, Aug. 15, 1992. BA in History, U. Mich., 1989; postgrad., Mich. State U., 1991. CMA; CPA, Mich. Cost analyst Lear Plastics Corp., Mendon, Mich., 1991-92; cost acct. The Harter Group, Sturgis, Mich., 1992-93; cost analyst L Perrigo Co., Allegan, Mich., 1993-94, 1994-96, bus. process redesign team mem., 1996—. Mem. Inst. Mgmt. Accts. (assoc. dir. corp. devel. 1994-95, dir. corp. devel. 1995—), Mich. Assn. CPAs. Office: L Perrigo Co 117 Water St Allegan MI 49010

STEVENSON, JO ANN C., federal bankruptcy judge; b. 1942. AB, Rutgers U., 1965; JD cum laude, Detroit Coll. Law, 1979. Bar: Mich. 1979. Law clk. to Vincent J. Brennan, Mich. Ct. Appeals, Detroit, 1979; law clk. to Cornelia G. Kenendy, U.S. Ct. Appeals for 6th Cir., Detroit, 1980; assoc. Hertzberg, Jacob & Weingarten, P.C., Detroit, 1980-87; judge U.S. Bankruptcy Ct., Grand Rapids, Mich., 1987—. Office: US Bankruptcy Ct PO Box 3310 712 Ford Fed Bldg Grand Rapids MI 49503*

STEVENSON, LOUISE, history educator; b. Glen Cove, June 11, 1948; d. Mary Louise (Lord) S.; m. Apr. 26, 1981; children: Katherine L. Zimmerman, Lila S. Zimmerman. BA in Am. Studies, Barnard Coll., 1970; MA in History, NYU, 1973; PhD Am. and New Eng., Boston U., 1981. Vis. lectr. dept. history U. N.H., Durham, 1981-82; asst. prof. dept. history and Am. studies program Franklin and Marshall Coll., Lancaster, Pa., 1982-89, assoc. prof. dept. history and Am. studies program, 1989-96, prof. dept. history and Am. studies program, 1996—; Mem. Merle Curti award com. Orgn. Am. Historians, 1985-91. Author: Scholarly Means to Evangelical Ends: The New Haven Scholars and the Transformation of Higher Learning in America, 1830-90, 1986, Miss Porter's School: A History in Documents, 1987, The Victorian Homefront: American Thought and Culture, 1860-1880, 1991, Women's History: Selected Reading Lists and Course Outlines form American Colleges and Universities, 3rd edit. 1992;mem. editl. bd. History of Education Quarterly, 1994—; contbr., reviewer numerous articles to profl. jours. Trustee com. acad. oversight Tatnall Sch., Wilmington, Del., 1992-93; trustee James Madison Meml. Fellowship Found., 1995—, Lancaster LWV, 1996—. Andrew W. Mellon Fellow, Lib. Co. Phila., 1994; H.F. DuPont Scholar Winterthur Mus. and Gardens, 1988; grantee Spencer Found., 1989, 94; recipient Bradley Franklin & Marshall R. Dewey award scholarship and tchg., 1992. Mem. Am. Antiquarian Soc. (adv. com. history of the book 1991-96, also bd. overseers), Am. Studies Assn. (sec.-treas. mid-Atlantic chpt. 1984—), Am. Hist. Assn., Orgn. Am. Historians, History of Edn. Soc., Intellectual History Group (mem. editl bd. newsletter 1985-91), Soc. on History of Authorship, Reading, Pub. Office: Franklin and Marshall Coll Dept History & Am Studies Box 3003 Lancaster PA 17604

STEVENSON, RUBY VIRGINIA, special education educator; b. Hollister, Calif., July 26, 1943; d. Vernon Keith and Dorothy Josephine (Hooton) Stone; m. Dennis Alan Stevenson, June 15, 1962; children: Steven Neil, Callie Lois, April Dawn. BA in Elem. Edn., We. State Coll., 1986; MA in Spl. Edn., U. Colo., 1991. Cert. tchr. elem. K-6, spl. edn., early childhood spl. edn. Tchr., cons. infant stimulation Cmty. Options Inc., Montrose, Colo., 1980-90; cons. early childhood spl. edn. Montrose Sch. Dist., 1990-94; tchr. elem. spl. edn. Mesa County Schs., Grand Junction, Colo., 1994—; dir., tchr. pre-sch. Children ETC, Delta, Colo., 1980-82; tchr., coord., dir. Montrose Children's Mus., 1989—, Mus. of Natural History, Grand Junction, Colo., 1989—, bd. dirs. 1985-94. Grantee Norwest Banks, 1994, GeoTech, 1994. Mem. NEA, Coun. Exceptional Children, Nat. Assn. Young Children. Republican. Baptist.

STEVES, GALE C., editor-in-chief; b. Mineola, N.Y., Dec. 20, 1942; d. William Harry and Ruth (May) S.; m. David B. Stocker, Mar. 31, 1972 (div. Apr. 1978); m. Philip L. Perrone, Aug. 14, 1983. BS, Cornell U., 1964; MA, NYU, 1966. Editorial asst. Ladies Home Jour., N.Y.C., 1966-69; seafood consumer specialist U.S. Dept. Commerce, N.Y.C., 1969-73; editor food Homelife mag., N.Y.C., 1973-74; editor food and equipment Co-Ed mag., N.Y.C., 1974-76, Am. Home mag., N.Y.C., 1976-78; editor kitchen design and equipment Woman's Day mag., N.Y.C., 1979-83; editor-in-chief Woman's Day Spls., N.Y.C., 1983-91; v.p., editor-in-chief Home Mag. Group, N.Y.C., 1991—; bd. dirs. Les Dames d'Escoffier, N.Y.C., Council of Sr. Ctrs. and Services of N.Y.C.; mem. editorial bd. Sr. Summary, N.Y.C., 1982-88. Author: Game Cookery, 1974, The International Cook, 1980, Creative Microwave Cooking, 1981, (with Lee M. Elman) Country Weekend Cooking. Chmn. alumni adv. bd. Coll. Human Ecology, Cornell U., mem. univ. coun., 1996—, mem. pres.;s coun. for Cornell women, 1992—. Mem. NAFE, Internat. Furnishings and Design Assn., Am. Soc. Mag. Editors, Garden Writers Assn. Am., Acad. of Women Achievers at YWCA of N.Y.C. Office: Home Magazine Group 1633 Broadway New York NY 10019-6708

STEWART, ALLISON, artist, educator; b. Chgo., May 30, 1941. BS in Biology, Spring Hill Coll., 1963; MFA, U. New Orleans, 1980. Instr. U. New Orleans, 1980-90; asst. prof. Loyola U., New Orleans, 1991; instr. Acad. Fine Arts, New Orleans, 1988—; v.p. arts policy com. Contemporary Arts Ctr., New Orleans. Solo exhbns. includeArthur Roger Gallery, New Orleans, 1982, 84, 88, 93, 94, Gallery 291, Atlanta, 1985, Barbara Gillman Gallery, Miami, 1986, 94, Winfield Gallery, Gulfport, Miss., 1990, Pensacola (Fla.) Jr. Coll.,1991, Mario Villa Gallery, Chgo., 1991, 92, 94, 96, Broadway Art Gallery, Asheville, N.C., 1992, 94, State Street Gallery, Sarasota, Fla., 1995, Southeastern La. State U., Hammond, La., 1995; group exhbns. include Lauren Rogers Mus. of Art, Laurel, Miss., 1984, Galerie Melancon, Lake Charles, La., 1986, Contemporary Art Ctr., New Orleans, 1987, Island Gallery, Vero Beach, Fla., 1988, 90, Masur Mus., Monroe, La., 1988, 95, Historic New Orleans Collection, 1989, Arthur Roger Gallery, N.Y., 1991, 94, Contemporary Arts Ctr., New Orleans, 1992, Barbara Gillman Gallery, Miami, 1993, Savannah (Ga.) Nat., 1993, Kurts Bingham Gallery, Memphis, 1994, Mobile Mus. of Art, Ala., 1995, Slidell (La.) Art Ctr., 1995, New Orleans Acad. Fine Art, 1991, 93, 94, 96; commd. artist. Recipient grant Mary Freeman Wisdom Found., New Orleans, 1995, ITT Sheraton Pub. Art Project award for artwork in lobby space Sheraton Hotel, New Orleans. Office: 1301 Marengo St New Orleans LA 70115

STEWART, ARLENE JEAN GOLDEN, designer, stylist; b. Chgo., Nov. 26, 1943; d. Alexander Emerald and Nettie (Rosen) Golden; m. Randall Edward Stewart, Nov. 6, 1970; 1 child, Alexis Anne. BFA, Sch. of Art Inst. Chgo., 1966; postgrad., Ox Bow Summer Sch. Painting, Saugatuck, Mich., 1966. Designer, stylist Formica Corp., Cin., 1966-68; with Armstrong World Industries, Inc., Lancaster, Pa., 1968-96, interior furnishings analyst, 1974-76, internat. staff project stylist, 1976-78, sr. stylist Corlon flooring, 1979-80, sr. exptl. project stylist, 1980-89, sr. project stylist residential DIY flooring floor divsn., 1989-96, master stylist DIY residential tile, 1992-96; creative dir. Stewart Graphics, Lancaster, Pa., 1996—. Exhibited textiles Art Inst. Chgo., 1966, Ox-Bow Gallery, Saugatuck, Mich., 1966. Home: 114 E Vine St Lancaster PA 17602-3550 Office: Stewart Graphics 114 E Vine St Lancaster PA 17602

STEWART, BARBARA DEAN, writer, musician, educational consultant; b. Rochester, N.Y., Sept. 17, 1941; d. George Adgate and Louise (Griswold) Dean; children: Allison, Whitney. AB, Cornell U., 1962; MS, Simmons Coll., 1964; diploma with honors in flute, prep. dept. Eastman Sch. Music, 1958; MFA in playwriting Columbia U. 1993. Asst. law libr. CornScell U., 1963-64; writer/performer Kazoophony, Rochester, N.Y., 1972—; pres. Stewart Assocs. Ednl. Systems Group, Rochester, 1979-85; pres. SmartWriters, Inc., 1985—; flutist La Jolla Civic Orch., 1966-68; exec. assoc. Nat. Actors Co., N.Y.C., 1991, co. dramaturg, asst. to artistic dir., 1992-93. Founding chmn. jr. devel. U.S. Squash Racquets Assn.; pres. bd. dirs. Rochester Chamber Orch.; bd. dirs. Rochester chpt. English Speaking Union, 1982-85. Fellow Yale Sch. Drama, 1989-90. Author: How to Kazoo, Squash Racquets: Pro & Khan. Winner 68 nat. championships and 2 world championships in 20 different masters track and field events, holder 14 Am., 6 world records; recipient 5 MAC Achievement award Met. Athletics Congress, N.Y.C., 1987, 88, 90. Mem. ASCAP. Am. Fedn. Musicians, Dramatists Guild, Cornell U. Athletic Hall of Fame. Home: 11 W Church St Fairport NY 14450

STEWART, BARBARA ELIZABETH, free-lance magazine editor, artist; b. Ft. Dodge, Iowa, June 26, 1923; d. Warren Wheeler and Christine (Hubbard) Pickett; m. Charles Crombie Stewart, Sept. 2, 1943; 1 child, Charles Crombie IV. Student, Mt. Holyoke Coll., 1940-41, Wayne State U., 1941-42, So. Conn. State U., 1944-45; AA, Mercer County Community Coll., 1970; BA, Trenton State Coll., 1972. Cert, K-12 art tchr. Copywriter Fed. Dept. Stores, Goodwin's, Detroit, 1942-43; dept. coord. Sears, Roebuck & Co., Trenton, N.J., 1944; sec., writer Yale U., New Haven, Conn., 1945, 46; contbg. editor Mercer Bus. Mag., Trenton, 1980—. Oil and acrylic artist. Chmn. Stokes Sch. PTA, Trenton, 1952-58; pres. Rutgers Coop. Extension Mercer County, Trenton, 1970-82; chmn., mem. Hillcrest Civic Assn., Trenton, 1956-83; bd. dirs. Trenton YWCA, 1975-77; chmn. women's study fellowship Covenant Presbyn. Ch., Trenton, 1990-96; vol. Art Goes to Sch. program, 1992. Mem. Nat. Art Edn. Assn., N.J. Art Edn. Assn., AAUW (local chmn. 1965, 67), Torch Club (ofcl. del. 1985-88, tchr./vol. Art Goes to Sch. Programs, Pa./N.J. chpt.). Democrat. Home: Pennswood Village L101 1382 Newtown-Langhorne Rd Newtown PA 18940-2401

STEWART, BARBARA LYNNE, geriatrics nursing educator; b. Youngstown, Ohio, May 10, 1953; d. Carl Arvid and Margaret (Ashton) Swanson; m. James G. Stewart, Mar. 17, 1973; children: Trevor J., Troy C. AAS, Youngstown State U., 1973, BS, 1982. Cert. gerontol. nurse, ANCC. Asst. dist. office supr. divsn. quality assurance Bureau of Healthcare Stds. and Quality; supr., dir. nursing svcs. Peaceful Acres Nursing Home, North Lima, Ohio; nurse repondent Health Sci. Ctr. U. Colo., Denver; charge nurse Westwood Rehab. Med. Ctr., Inc., Boardman, Ohio, Park Vista Health Care Ctr., Youngstown, Ohio; dir. nursing Rolling Acres Care Ctr., North Lima, Ohio; primary instr. Alliance (Ohio) Tng. Ctr., Inc.; asst. dist. office supr. divsn. of quality assurance Bureau Healthcare Stds. and Quality, Akron, Ohio. Former instr. CPR, ARC. Mem. Tri County Dir. Nurses Assn., Nat. Gerontol. Nursing Assn. (nomination com.), Youngstown State U. Alumni Assn.

STEWART, CAROL ANN, graphic arts professional; b. Cleve., Oct. 28, 1940; d. Joseph Chapman and Dorothy Jeanne (Page) Bronson; m. Claude Henry Wenner, Apr. 2, 1986 (dec.); m. Robert Ogden Stewart, Sept. 1, 1989. AA in Print Prodn. Mgmt., Graphic Arts Assn. of, Delaware Valley, Phila., 1973; BSBA cum laude, Villanova U., 1980, MBA, 1985. Film libr. Wyeth-Ayerst Labs., Radnor, Pa., 1963-67, prodn. asst., 1967-74, supr. promotion prodn., 1974-86, mgr. graphic arts, 1986—. Sec. Daylesford Hills Civic Assn., Berwyn, Pa., 1973-75; pres. Bear Creek Lakes Civic Assn., Jim Thorpe, Pa., 1985-87, bd. dirs., 1983-88. Recipient Capitol award Nat. Leadership Coun., 1991. Mem. NAFE, Execs. Club Graphic Arts (v.p. 1990-91, pres. 1991-93). Republican. Home: 543 Marietta Ave Swarthmore PA 19081-2416 Office: Wyeth-Ayerst Labs PO Box 8299 Philadelphia PA 19101-0082

STEWART, CARRIE LYNN, community activist, volunteer; b. Detroit, Feb. 2, 1959; d. Samuel B. Jr. and Barbara J. (Morrison) Stewart; m. Frederick S. Ditmars II, Sept. 5, 1993; 1 child, Frederick Stewart Ditmars. AB, Smith Coll., 1981; postgrad., Northeastern U., 1985-90, Rutgers U., 1994-96. Legal asst. Burns and Levinson, Boston, 1981-82, 84-85, Sloane and Walsh, Boston, 1982-84, Sullivan and Worcester, Boston, 1985-87, Digital Equipment Corp., Maynard, Mass., 1987-90, Vedder, Price, Kaufman and Kamholz, Chgo., 1990-91, Stryker, Tams & Dill, Newark, 1992-93, LeBoeuf, Lamb, Greene and Macrae, Newark, 1993-95. Bd. dirs., chair racial justice task force YWCA, Plainfield, N.J., 1994-96; bd. dirs., chair denominational affairs 1st Unitarian Soc. Plainfield, 1995-96; mem. diversity com. Resource Ctr. for Women, Summit, N.J., 1994-96; mem., past chair North Plainfield (N.J.) Jr. Women's Club, 1992-96; mem., facilitator Mothers Ctr. of Ctrl. N.J., 1996. Mem. Smith Club Watchung Hills. Democrat. Home: 11202 Tanya Trail Austin TX 78726

STEWART, CLAUDETTE SUZANNE, small business owner, author; b. East Orange, N.J., Jan. 23, 1948; d. Michel Fred and Helen Alberta (Margerum) Mautor; children: Shaun R., Michael B. BS, Rollins Coll., 1980. Bus. mgr. Wometco, Orlando, Fla., 1978-80; acctg. mgr. CNA, Orlando, 1980-81; fin. mgr. Martin Marietta Data Sys., Orlando, 1981-83; owner, operator Yellow Mountain Flower Farm, Leicester, N.C., 1983—; rschr., contbr. Lark Books, Asheville, N.C., 1988, 89, 91; rsch. writer Rodale Press, Emmaus, Pa., 1991. Author: Living with Potpourri, 1988, Everlasting Floral Gifts, 1990, Nature at Ground Level, 1993; author numerous poems. Vol. counselor Youth Programs, Inc., Orlando, 1981-83; vol. instr. Jr. Achievement, Orlando, 1981-83; vol. mountain search and rescue Asheville Area Rescue Squad, 1990-92; vol. Leicester Vol. Fire Dept., 1990—, Nat. Hug-A-Tree and Survive, 1996, N.C. Assn. Rescue and Emergency Med. Svcs., 1992—. Mem. N.C. Herb Assn. Office: Yellow Mountain Flower Farm 57 Davidson Gap Rd Leicester NC 28748

STEWART, DORIS MAE, biology educator; b. Sandsprings, Mont., Dec. 12, 1927; d. Virgil E. and Violet M. (Weaver) S.; m. Felix Loren Powell, Oct. 8, 1956; children: Leslie, Loren. BS, Coll. Puget Sound, 1948, MS, 1949; PhD, U. Wash., 1953. Instr. U. Mont., Missoula, 1954-56, asst. prof., 1956-57; asst. prof. U. Puget Sound, Tacoma, 1957-58; head sci. dept. Am. Kiz Lisesi, Istanbul, Turkey, 1958-62; rsch. asst. prof. U. Wash., Seattle, 1963-67, rsch. assoc. prof., 1967-68; assoc. prof. Cen. Mich. U., Mt. Pleasant, 1970-72; assoc. prof. U. Balt., 1973-81, prof., 1981-95, prof. emeritus, 1995—. Contbr. numerous articles to profl. jours. Mem. Am. Physiol. Soc., Sigma Xi. Home: 1103 Frederick Rd Baltimore MD 21228-5032

STEWART, EILEEN ROSE, real estate broker; b. Indpls., Oct. 20, 1942; d. Burgess Charles and Flora Clara (Schott) S.; m. Richard Michael Grindle, Feb. 12, 1966 (div. 1977). BS, Ind. U., 1965, MS, 1972; postgrad., Walden U., Naples, Fla., 1995-96, Liberty Retreat Yoga Tng. Sch., Boulevard, Calif., 1996. Lic. real estate broker, Ind., Fla. Tchr. pub. schs. various locations, Ind., Fla., 1965-72; sales rep. UARCO Bus. Forms, Ft. Lauderdale, Fla., 1972-74; staff trainer Palm Beach County Comprehensive Employment Tng. Act program, West Palm Beach, Fla., 1975-77; pres. Untapped Resources, Inc., West Palm Beach, 1978-80; mgmt. cons. Profl. Mgmt. Assocs., Silver Spring, Md., 1980-82; sales rep. The St. George's Club, Washington, 1983-84; real estate broker Mascari Realty, Indpls., 1985-89; pres. Stewart Manor, Inc., Indpls., 1987-89; sales mgr. Charles Hotel Condominium, Miami Beach, Fla., 1990-92; sales assoc. Infinity Realty, Miami Beach, 1992-93, Real Estate Enterprises, 1993—; gen. mgr. Charles Hotel Condominiums, 1994—; cons. Planned Parenthood, West Palm Beach, 1976-78, Jim Stewart Tire Co., Indpls., 1985-89; chair adv. bd. Palm Beach County Displaced Homemakers Ctr., Lake Worth, 1977-78. Mem. Women's Bus. Initiative, Indpls. Bus. Network, Ind. Bed and Breakfast Assn. (cen. regional coord. 1989), NOW (past officer South Palm Beach County chpt., asst. state coord. Fla. sect. 1978, nat. bd. dirs. 1978-79, newsletter editor 1976-77), Women of Miami Beach (pres. 1993-95), Miami Beach Devel. Corp. (bd. dirs. 1994-95). Democrat. Home: 569 Cielo Vista Ct Greenwood IN 46143-1712

STEWART, GAIL WOODSON, lawyer; b. Tulsa, May 10, 1958. BA summa cum laude, Baylor U., 1980, JD, 1983. Bar: Tex. 1983. Ptnr. Baker & Botts LLP, Houston. Mem. ABA, Order of Barristers, Moot Ct. Soc., Houston Bar Assn., State Bar Tex. Office: Baker & Botts 1 Shell Plz Houston TX 77002*

STEWART, GEORGIANA LICCIONE, author; b. Mount Vernon, N.Y., May 18, 1943; d. Arthur Alfred and Grace Marie (Zuzzolo) Liccione; m. William Lawrence Stewart, July 18, 1975. BA, Columbia U., 1971; MA, Columbia Tchr.'s Coll., N.Y.C., 1973; MAT, Manhattanville Coll., 1973. Author, cons. Kimbo Ednl., Long Branch, N.J., 1970—; spl. edn. tchr. Tuckahoe (N.Y.) High Sch., 1989-; cons. NAEYC, SACUS, 1975-89, Pres.'s Coun. on Physical Fitness, 1979-81. Author 58 children's musical activity records and books including: Adaptive Motor Learning, 1982, Bean Bag Activities, 1983, Preschool Aerobic Fun, 1989, Children of the World, 1991, Multicultural Rhythm Stick Fun, 1992, Toddlerific, 1993. Mem. AAHPERD, Nat. Assn. for Edn. of Young Children, So. Assn. for Children Under Six, Assn. for Retarded Citizens, Columbia Club, Women's Nat. Rep. Club. Home: 81 Pondfield Rd #328 Bronxville NY 10708-0625 Office: Kimbo Ednl PO Box 477 Long Branch NJ 07740-0477

STEWART, JANICE MAE, judge; b. Medford, Oreg., Feb. 13, 1951; d. Glenn Logan and Eathel Mae (Jones) S.; m. F. Gordon Allen III, Aug. 10, 1975; children—Benjamin Stewart, Rebecca Mae. AB in Econs., Stanford U., 1972; JD, U. Chgo., 1975. Bar: Ill. 1976, Oreg. 1977, U.S. Dist. Ct. Oreg. 1977, U.S. Ct. Appeals (9th cir.) 1978. Assoc. Winston & Strawn, Chgo., 1975-76, McEwen, Gisvold Rankin & Stewart, Portland, Oreg., 1976-81, ptnr., 1981-93; U.S. magistrate judge, Portland, 1993—. Mem. Multnomah County Profl. Responsibility Com., Portland, 1979-82, Oreg. Profl. Responsibility Bd., 1982-85, Oreg. State Bar Practice and Procedure Com., 1985-88, Profl. Liability Fund Def. Panel, Portland, 1985-93, Multnomah County Judicial Selection com., 1985-87, Oreg. State Bar Professionalism Com., 1989-92, Multnomah County Professionalism Com., 1995—, Coun. Ct. Procedures, 1991-93, lawyer rep. 9th Cir. Jud. Conf., 1990-93. Mem. ABA, Am. Arbitration Assn. (arbitrator 1990-93), Oreg. Bar Assn., Multnomah County Bar Assn. (dir. 1990-93), Phi Beta Kappa. Democrat. Office: 608 US Courthouse 620 SW Main St Portland OR 97204

STEWART, JOANNE, secondary school educator; b. Vancouver, Wash., Mar. 10, 1944; d. Edward Charles and Claudine Marie (Meilleur) Spencer; m. William Lemley Stewart, Sept. 2, 1966 (dec. June 1983); children: Amy Diane, Nicholas William. BS, Wash. State U., 1966, MA, 1973. Cert. tchr., Mont., Idaho, Wash., Calif. Tchr. foods Seaside High Sch., Monterey, Calif., 1966-67; tchr. home econs. Marysville (Wash.) High Sch., 1967-68, Palouse (Wash.) High Sch., 1968-73, Ennis (Mont.) High Sch., 1973-76, Genesee (Idaho) High Sch., 1976-77; instr. young family Missoula (Mont.) County High Sch., 1983-84; tchr. home econs. Woodman Sch., Lolo, Mont., 1985-86; travel cons. Travel Masters, Missoula, 1984-87; ticketing mgr. Blue Caboose Travel, Missoula, 1987-91; tchr. family and consumer scis. Victor (Mont.) High Sch., 1991—. Co-pres. Lolo PTO, 1980-81; v.p. Lolo Community Ctr., 1981; sec. Lolo Mosquito Control Bd., 1988—; mem. telecommunications com. Conrad Burns & Gov. Racicot. Marysville Edn. Assn. scholar, 1962, Future Homemakers Am. scholar, 1962. Mem. AAUW (sec. 1986, program chmn. 1987), Forestry Triangle (pres. 1981, editor cookbook 1982), Future Homemakers Am. (hon. advisor), Am. Family and Consumer Scis. Assn., Mont. Family and Consumer Scis. Assn. (bylaws chair 1994, pres. 1996—, pres. elect 1995-96), Mont. Vocat. Tchrs. Assn. (returning Rookie of Yr. 1992, Am. Federated Tchrs., Mont. Vocat. Family and Consumer Scis. Tchrs. (v.p. 1993-94, pres. 1994-95). Republican. Methodist. Home: 1200 Lakeside Dr Lolo MT 59847-9705 Office: Victor High Sch Family and Consumer Scis 425 4th Ave Victor MT 59875-9468

STEWART, KAREN MEYER, pediatrics nurse, nursing manager; b. Bryn Mawr, Pa., June 7, 1957; d. William Stanford and Ruth May (Schrumpf) Meyer; m. James Allen Stewart, Sept. 1, 1979; children: Karrie, Matthew. BSN, U. Mich., Ann Arbor, 1979; MS, U. Minn., 1994. Grad. nurse Pediatrics Mott Children's Hosp., Ann Arbor, Mich., 1979; staff nurse, charge nurse, pediatric ICU Saint Mary's Hosp., Rochester, Minn., 1979-84; asst. head nurse pediatric ICU, 1984-89; nurse mgr., pediatric ICU, pediatric transport team Mayo Med. Ctr., Rochester, Minn., 1989—; instr. pediat. Mayo Med. Sch., Rochester, Minn., 1994—. Mem. AACN, Minn. Nurses Assn., Assn. for Care Children's Health, Minn. Orgn. Leaders in Nursing, Soc. Critical Care Medicine, Phi Kappa Phi, Sigma Theta Tau. Home: 5812 Glencroft Ln SW Rochester MN 55902 Office: Mayo Eugenio Litta Children's Hosp Pediat ICU 1216 Second St SW Rochester MN 55902

STEWART, KATHERINE LEE, secondary education educator; b. Lubbock, Tex., Nov. 3, 1958; d. Jim Louis and Velma Waldine (Wells) Walker; m. Roger Elwin Stewart, June 6, 1981; children: Heidi, Noah. BA, Austin Coll., 1981. Tchr. North Lamar Ind. Sch. Dist., Paris, Tex., 1986—. Mem. Nat. Coun. Tchrs. Math., Sci. Tchrs. Assn. Tex., Delta Kappa Gamma. Republican. Baptist. Office: North Lamar High Sch 3201 Lewis Ln Paris TX 75462-2017

STEWART, LEA P., communication educator; b. Cleve., May 27, 1951; d. Hans R. and Jean Barbara (Melichar) Pestel; m. Alan D. Stewart, Nov. 23, 1973. BA in Psychology, Allegheny Coll., 1973; MA in Comms., Purdue U., 1977, PhD in Comms., 1979. Asst. prof. U. Hartford, Conn., 1979-81; asst. prof. Rutgers U., New Brunswick, N.J., 1981-87, assoc. prof., 1987-93, prof., 1993—, dir. PhD program in comms., info. and libr. studies, 1993—; cons. AT&T Sch. Bus., Somerset, N.J., 1995-96. Author: Communication and Gender, 1996; contbr. articles to profl. jours. Pres. Orgn. for Study of Comm., Lang. and Gender, 1985-86. Fellow Tchg. Excellence Ctr., Rutgers U., 1992-93. Mem. AAUW, Nat. Coun. for Rsch. on Women, Speech Comm. Assn. (chair ethics commn. 1990-92), Internat. Comm. Assn. (Outstanding Mem. award 1990), Acad. Mgmt., Eastern Comm. Assn. (Past Pres. award). Office: Rutgers U 4 Huntington St New Brunswick NJ 08901

STEWART, LEORA KLAYMER, textile artist, educator; b. Jerusalem, June 5, 1943; came to the U.S., 1952; d. Errol and Reva (Svirsky) Klaymer. BFA, Art Inst. Chgo., 1962, MFA, 1968. Asst. prof. Tyler Sch. Art, Phila., 1970-72, New Sch. Parsons, N.Y.C., 1974-77; prof. art Baruch Coll., N.Y.C., 1977-96, Fashion Inst. Tech., N.Y.C., 1987—; textile designer LLAMA Studios, Bklyn., 1990—; lectr. Textile Conservation Group, fall 1988; guest artist Textile Study Group N.Y., 1992, Textile Arts Conf., Chgo., 1993, Textile Conservation Group, 1990; juror/curator of numerous exhbns. One-woman exhibits include Hadler/Rodriguez Galleries, N.Y.C., 1976, 79; two-person shows include Gayle Wilson Gallery, Southampton, L.I., N.Y., 1988; group exhibits include Gayle Wilson Gallery, Southampton, 1993-94, Pres.'s Office-FIT, N.Y., 1993-94, Colonial House Gallery, N.Y., 1994, Faculty Exhbn.-FIT Galleries, N.Y., 1994-95, Acad. of the Arts, Easton, Md., 1996, many others; archtl. commn. Knoll Internat. Showrooms, World Trade Ctr., Dallas, Gotaas-Larsen Shipping Corp., N.Y.C., Bank of Hong Kong, World Trade Ctr., N.Y.C., Bullock's Corp., Christown Mall, Phoenix; represented in permanent collections Prudential Life Ins., Chase Manhattan Bank, Continental Wheat and Grain Corp., S.E. Banking Corp., Becton-Dickson Pharm. Corp. Travel grantee Art Inst. Chgo., 1968-69; craftsman fellow Nat. Endowment for the Arts, Washington, 1972-73, 76-77. Fellow N.Y. Textile Soc. Group, Textile Conservation. Office: Fashion Inst Tech 27th St & 7th Ave New York NY 10001

STEWART, LINDA, accountant, controller; b. Dallas, Apr. 17, 1948; d. Robert Lewis and Helen (Stell) Lowrance; m. Carroll Ray Stewart, Jr., July 7, 1973; children: Robert Sean, Stephen Ray. BA in Microbiology, U. Tex., 1970; MBA in Fin., U. Houston, 1978. Bacteriologist Houston Health Dept., 1971-74; rsch. asst. Baylor Coll. Medicine, Houston, 1974-78; fin. analyst Coastal Corp., Houston, 1978-79; supr. pediatric endocrinology lab. U. Tex. Med. Br., Galveston, 1987-90; dir. acctg. and data processing Meml. Med. Ctr., Port Lavaca, Tex., 1991-94, asst. contr., 1994—. Mem. Tex. Assn. for Hosp. Fin. Adminstrn., Pilot Internat. (sec. 1991-96). Office: Meml Med Ctr 815 N Virginia St Port Lavaca TX 77979

STEWART, LYN VARN, critical care nurse; b. Charleston, S.C., July 3, 1957; d. Allen Hamilton and Merilyn (Windsor) Varn; m. James Milton Stewart Jr., May 26, 1979; children: Kevin James, Sean Allen. BA in History, Clemson U., 1979; ADN, U. S.C., 1983. Cert. BLS, ACLS. Staff RN med.-surg. units Piedmont Med. Ctr., Rock Hill, S.C., 1983-85, staff nurse progressive care unit, 1985-94, RN, asst. head nurse progressive care unit, 1991-92, preceptor coord., 1991-93, quality improvement rep. progressive care unit, 1991-92; office nurse, cardiac stress testing Carolinas Med. Group-Shiland, Rock Hill, 1995—; preceptor coord., quality improvement rep. progressive care unit Piedmont Med. Ctr., Rock Hill, 1991-92; office RN cardiac stress testing Carolinas Med. Group-Shiland, Rock Hill, 1995—. Bd. dirs. Westminster Christian Sch., Rock Hill., 1991-93, mem. yearbook staff, 1991-93, mem. PTO bd., 1992-93, coach Westminster Little Tigers soccer team, 1992-93, asst. coach Westminster Lions soccer team, 1992-93; bd. trustees Westminster Catawba Christian Sch., Rock Hill, 1993-94, mem. PTO bd., 1993-95, newsletter editor, 1992—, co-coord. sch. soccer program, 1992-95, asst. coach under-10 & under-12 soccer team, 1994—; sec. Westminster Catawba Christian Sch. Athletic Booster Club, 1994—; founding mem. Spirit Soccer League, Rock Hill, 1996—. Mem. S.C. Assn. Nurses Endorsing Transplantation. Home: 603 Greenbriar Ave Rock Hill SC 29730-3301

STEWART, MARTHA KOSTYRA, editor-in-chief, lecturer, author; b. Jersey City; d. Edward and Martha (Ruszkowski) Kostyra; m. Andy Stewart, July 1, 1961 (div. 1990); 1 child, Alexis. BA in European History and Archtl. History, Barnard. Former model; former stockbroker N.Y.C.; former profl. caterer, mag. owner, editor-in-chief; mag. owner, editor-in-chief Martha Stewart Living, 1990—; lifestyle cons. for K-Mart Corp. Author: (with Elizabeth Hawes) Entertaining, 1982, Weddings, 1987; Martha Stewart Hors d'Oeurvres: The Creation and Presentation of Fabulous Finger Food, 1984, Martha Stewart's Pies and Tarts, 1985, Martha Stewart's Quick Cook Menus: Fifty-two Meals You Can Make in Under an Hour, 1988, The Wedding Planner, 1988, Martha Stewart's Gardening: Month by Month, 1991, Martha Stewart's New Old House: Restoration, Renovation, Decoration, 1992, Martha Stewart's Christmas, 1993, Martha Stewart's Menus for Entertaining, 1994, Holidays, 1994; appears in semi-monthly cooking segment on Today Show. Office: Martha Stewart Living 10 Saugatuck Ave Westport CT 06880 also: care Susan Magrino Agy 167 E 73rd St New York NY 10021-3510*

STEWART, NORMA JUNE, secondary mathematics educator; b. Punxsutawney, Pa., July 5, 1948; d. Earl Bryan Blystone and Mildred Inez (Henderson) Bair; m. James M. Stewart, Aug. 12, 1943; children: Shannon, Michael. AA summa cum laude, Truett McConnell Coll., Toccoa, Ga., 1990; BS in Edn., U. Ga., 1993. Cert. secondary tchr., Ga. Subsitutute tchr. Stephens County Ga. Mid. Sch., Toccoa, 1984—. Sec. Karate Club, 1985-89; pres., v.p. theater bd., Toccoa, 1988-90. Gov.'s Office State of Pa. scholar, 1966. Mem. Nat. Guard Spouses Assn. (treas. 1994), Band Boosters. Home: PO Box 833 Toccoa GA 30577-0833

STEWART, PAMELA L., lawyer; b. Bogalusa, La., Mar. 13, 1953; d. James Adrian and Patricia Lynn (Wood) Lloyd; m. Steven Bernard Stewart, Aug. 31, 1974 (div. July 1980); 1 child, Christopher. BA, U. New Orleans, 1986; JD, U. Houston, 1990. Intern La. Supreme Ct., New Orleans, 1984, Councilman Bryan Wagner, New Orleans, 1984-85; legal asst. Clann, Bell & Murphy, Houston, 1988-89, Tejas Gas Corp., Houston, 1989-90; atty. Law Offices of Pamela L. Stewart, Katy, Tex., 1991—. Bd. dirs. Alliance for Good Govt., New Orleans, 1983-84, Attention Deficit Hyperactivity Disorder Assn. Tex., 1989-90; vol. Houston Vol. Lawyers Program, Houston, 1992—. Innsbruck scholar, U. New Orleans, 1985. Fellow Inst. Politics; mem. ABA, Am. Bankruptcy Inst., Tax Freedom Inst., Nat. Assn. Consumer Bankruptcy Attys. (co-chair ethics com.), Houston Bar Assn., Houston Bankruptcy Conf., Nat. Assn. of Chpt. 13 Trustees (assoc.), Katy Bar Assn., Houston Assn. Debtors Attys. (pres.), Am. Acad. Estate Planning Attys. Methodist. Home: 22415 N Rebecca Burwell Ln Katy TX 77449-2908 Office: Law Offices of Pamela L Stewart Ste 219 One West Loop South Houston TX 77027

STEWART, PATRICIA ANN, bank executive; b. Phoenix, Nov. 3, 1953; d. Travis Delano and Ann Helen (Lopez) Hill. BS, Ariz. State U., 1975. Programmer, analyst Victor Comptometer Corp., Phoenix, 1975-77, Lewis & Roca, Attys., Phoenix, 1977-79; data processing mgr. Central Mgmt. Corp., Phoenix, 1979-80; corp. systems cons. S.W. Forest Industries, Phoenix, 1981-87; human resources system mgr. Western Savs. and Loan, Phoenix, 1987-90; asst. v.p., loan and deposit systems mgr. Bank of Am., Ariz., 1990-91; application mgr. Data Line S.W. div., 1991-93; v.p. Bank of Am. Ariz., 1993—; ptnr. Abacus Group, 1981-83. Troop leader Ariz. Cactus Pine Coun. Girl Scouts U.S., membership registrar Paradise Vally Neighborhood. Mem. Data Processing Mgmt. Assn. (pres. Phoenix chpt. 1982), Ariz. HP Users Group (mem. dir. 1987). Home: 15849 N 20th Pl Phoenix AZ 85022-3405 Office: Bank of Am Ariz 101 N 1st Ave Phoenix AZ 85003-1902

STEWART, PATRICIA CARRY, foundation administrator; b. Bklyn., May 19, 1928; d. William J. and Eleanor (Murphy) Carry; m. Charles Thorp Stewart, May 30, 1976. Student U. Paris, 1948-49; BA, Cornell U., 1950. Fgn. corr. Irving Trust Co., N.Y.C., 1950-51; with Janeway Rsch. Co., N.Y.C., 1951-60, sec., treas., 1955-60; with Buckner & Co. and successor firms, N.Y.C., 1961-73, ptnr., 1962-70, v.p.-treas., 1970-71, pres.-treas., 1971-73; pres., treas. Knight, Carry, Bliss & Co., Inc., N.Y.C., 1971-73; pres., treas. G. Tsai & Co., Inc., 1973; v.p. Edna McConnell Clark Found. Inc., 1974-92; dir., vice chair Cmty. Found. Palm Beach and Martin Counties; bd. dirs. Melville Corp., Banker Trust Co., Bankers Trust N.Y. Corp., Trans World Airlines, 1973-85, Borden Inc., 1976-95, Continental Corp., 1976-95, Morton Norwich Inc., 1979-84; allied mem. N.Y. Stock Exch., 1962-73; past mem. nominating com. Am. Stock Exch., N.Y. Stock Exch., N.Y.C. Fin. Svcs. Corp.; dir. emeritus, past chmn. Investor Responsibility Rsch. Ctr. Trustee emerita, vice-chair Cornell U., bd. life overseers Cornell Med. Coll.; vis. com. Grad. Sch. Bus., Harvard U., 1974-80; bd. dirs. NOW Legal Def. and Edn. Fund, 1984-92, Women in Founds./Corp. Philanthropy 1980-86; vice chmn. Community Found. Palm Beach and Martin Counties, 1993—; v.p. fin. com. Women's Forum, 1982-90; vice chmn. CUNY, 1976-80; bd. dirs. United Way of Tri-State, 1977-81, Inst. for Edn. and Rsch. on Women and Work; voting mem. Blue Cross and Blue Shield Greater N.Y., 1975-82; trustee N.Y. State 4-H Found., 1970-76, Internat. Inst. Rural Reconstruction, 1974-79; mem. N.Y.C. panel White House Fellows, 1976-78; mem. bus. adv. coun. The Hosp. Chaplaincy. Recipient Elizabeth Cutter Morrow award YWCA, 1977, Catalyst award Women Dirs. in Corps., 1978, Trustee medal CUNY, 1983, Accomplishment award Wings Club N.Y., 1984, Women's Funding Coalition Innovators for Women$hare award, 1986, Banking Industry Achievement award Nat. Assn. Bank Women, 1987, Cert. Disting. Accomplishments Barnard Coll., 1989; named to YWCA Acad. Women Achievers. Mem. Fin. Women's Assn. N.Y., NOW (bd. dirs.), Coun. Fgn. Rels., Pi Beta Phi. Clubs: Country Club of Fla. (bd. dirs.), University (N.Y.C.); Gullane Golf (Scotland), The Glen (Scotland). Home and Office: 2613 N Ocean Blvd Delray Beach FL 33483-7367 also: Halfland Barns, North Berwick EH395PW, Scotland

STEWART, PATRICIA RHODES, retired clinical psychologist, researcher; b. Vallejo, Calif., Feb. 11, 1910; d. Butler Young Rhodes and Sarah Virginia (Ryan) Rhodes; m. John Kenneth Stewart (div.); children: John K., Nancy Bowditch. AB summa cum laude, Stanford U., 1930; MA, San Jose State U., 1959; PhD, U. London, 1963. Tchg. asst. San Jose State U., 1959-60; staff psychologist Napa State Hosp., 1964-77; pvt. practice in psychotherapy Berkeley, Calif., 1978-94; pvt. rsch. in adolescent deviance Berkeley, 1979-85; staff psychologist Westwood Mental Health Facility, Fremont, Calif., 1985-88. Author: Children in Distress: American and English Perspectives, 1976. Chair criminal justice com. No. Calif. region Am. Friends Svc. com., San Francisco, 1977-80, chair exec. com. 1970-74, 80-83, bd. dirs., 1980-83; bd. dirs. Friends Com. on Legis., Sacramento, 1985-88, No. Calif. Ecumenical Coun., Oakland, Calif., 1989-95. Mem. APA, Soc. Friends, Phi Beta Kappa. Home: 1225 Monterey Ave Berkeley CA 94707-2718

STEWART, PENNY MORRIS, secondary school educator; b. Glendale, Calif., Sept. 30, 1949; d. C. Harold and Margaret (Nelson) Morris; m. Paul D. Finocchiaro, Apr. 9, 1996; children from previous marriage: E. Pierce III, Hailey M. BA in Speech and English, Muskingum Coll., New Concord, Ohio, 1971; MA in Edn., Nat. U., Sacramento, 1991. Cert. multiple and single subject tchr., Calif. Assoc. prod. Alhecama Players, Santa Barbara (Calif.) C.C. Dist., 1972-86; docent Santa Barbara Mus. Art, 1975-86; importer Cambridge Place Corp., Santa Barbara, 1974-86; with promotions and fund raising depts. Stewart-Bergman Assocs., Nevada City, Calif., 1986-89; travel columnist The Union, Grass Valley, Calif., 1987-90; tchr. drama and English Bear River H.S., Grass Valley, 1991—, dept. chair visual and performing arts, 1993—. Art docent coord. Deer Creek Sch., Nevada City, 1986-90, pres. Parent Tchr. Club, 1987-88. Recipient award for valuable contbn. to schs. Nevada City Sch. Dist., 1990, Dir.'s award Santa Barbara C.C., 1982. Mem. Ednl. Theatre Assn., Calif. Ednl. Theatre Assn., No. Calif. Ednl. Theatre Assn. Home: 230 Fairmont Dr Grass Valley CA 95945-9709 Office: Bear River HS 11130 Magnolia Rd Grass Valley CA 95949-8366

STEWART, SALLY, public relations consultant; b. Phoenix, Mar. 1, 1955; d. Biven and Nancy Sue (Spurlock) S.; children: Padraic Haines, Colin Haines. BS in Broadcast Journalism, Ariz. State U., 1977, BA in Edn., 1980. Staff writer, media rep. Salt River Project, Phoenix, 1979-81; copy editor Mesa (Ariz.) Tribune, 1981-82; mktg. adminstrv. asst. Phoenix chpt. ARC, 1983; pub. info. asst. City of Scottsdale, Ariz., 1983-84; bus. editor, asst. city editor Scottsdale Progress, 1984-86; comms. mgr. Mesa Conv. and Visitors Bur., 1986-90; mgmt. asst. Neighborhood Improvement and Housing Dept., City of Phoenix, 1990-92, Pub. Info. Office, City of Phoenix, 1992-93; comm. cons. Ariz. Pub. Svc., Phoenix, 1993—. Mem. com. Fiesta Bowl, Phoenix, 1987-89; mem. pub. rels. com. Juvenile Diabetes Found., Phoenix, 1990; mem. pub. rels. com. Children's Garden Ground Breaking, Phoenix, 1993. mem. Pub. Rels. Soc. Am. (accredited, bd. dirs. 1991-93, assembly del. 1993-95, pres. Valley of the Sun chpt. 1997). Office: Ariz Pub Svc 2 Arizona Ctr 400 N 5th St Phoenix AZ 85004-3902

STEWART, SALLY ANNE, mathematics educator; b. Portland, Maine, Jan. 3, 1956; d. Peter Paul and Mary Elizabeth (Welch) Joyce; m. Wilson Westervelt Stewart, July 25, 1981; children: Michael, William. BS, U. Orono, Maine, 1978. Tchr. math., mem. dist. math. com. Kingswood Regional Mid. Sch., Wolfeboro, N.H., 1978—; math. tutor, Wolfeboro, 1988—, Tuftonboro, N.H., 1988—; girls basketball coach Kingswood Regional Mid. Sch., Wolfeboro, 1978-85, curriculum writing, summer 1984, dir. summer math. program, summer 1986. Mem. Nat. Coun. Tchrs. Math., New Eng. League Mid. Schs. Home: 174 Middle Rd Center Tuftonboro NH 03816-9710 Office: Kingswood Regional Mid Sch Main St Wolfeboro NH 03894

STEWART, SALLY BEAL, pilot; b. Englewood, N.J., Apr. 10, 1955; d. Peter Coakley and Betty (Meyer) Van de Water. BS, Northwestern U., 1977. Lic. airline transport pilot, flight engr., flight instr., jumpmaster, skydiving. Sr. tech. rep. Xerox, Milw., 1979-81; flight instr. Capital Aviation, Milw., 1981-82; DC-3 pilot Air Charter/Mr. Douglas, De Leon Springs, Fla., 1982; capt. Mueller Pipeliners, New Berlin, Wis., 1982, Aero Taxi, Rockford, Ill., 1982; skydiver Hi Sky Promotions, Milw., 1980-82; capt., 1st officer Simmons Airlines, Marquette, Mich., 1983-84; capt. Am. Cen. Airlines, Dubuque, Iowa, 1984; first officer Boeing 747-400 Northwest Airlines, Mpls., 1984—; model John Casablancas, Berg Talent Agy., Tampa, Fla., 1991—. Pilot TV spl. Wide World of Sports, 1982; skydiver, interviewee TV spl./video Flight of the Dream Team, 1988. Holder world record for 60 woman freefall formation, Deland, Fla., 1986, world record for 120 person freefall formation, Quincy, Ill., 1986, world record for 144 person formation, Quincy, 1988. Mem. Air Line Pilots Assn., U.S. Parachute Assn. Home and Office: PO Box 7399-101 Breckenridge CO 80424

STEWART, SANDRA RAE, security marketing professional; b. East Liverpool, Ohio, Sept. 23, 1969; d. Charles Bruce and Rita Janet (Groff) S. BA, U. Tampa, 1990. Info. advisor Army Inst. of Rsch. in Mgmt., Info. and Comm. Systems, Atlanta; contract audit specialist Def. Contract Audit Agy., Marietta, Ga., 1990-92; pers. actions specialist Heidelberg Regional Civilian Pers. Office; manpower info. specialist 7th Med. Command, Heidelberg, 1992-94; asst. dir. Karlsruhe (Germany) Child Devel. Ctr., 1994-95; asst. to the venue/village security mgrs. Atlanta Com. for the Olympic Games, 1995—; security mgmt. specialist Olympic Venue Security, 1995—; assoc. Environ. Solutions, Richmond, 1995; mem. adv. bd. Karlsruhe Child Devel., 1994-95; sr. advisor 44th Signal Batt./7th Signal Brigade Wives Club, 1992-95. Model UN chairperson Harvard Nat. Model UN, 1987-90. Mem. NAFE, Sigma Phi Epsilon, Kappa Kappa Psi. Republican. Home: 3534 Kennesaw Station Dr Kennesaw GA 30144 Office: ACOG Security 250 Williams St Atlanta GA 30301

STEWART, SUE S., lawyer; b. Casper, Wyo., Oct. 9, 1942; d. Fraizer McVale and Carolyn Eliabeth (Hunt) Stewart; BA, Wellesley Coll., 1964; postgrad. Harvard U. Law Sch., 1964-65; JD, Georgetown U., 1967; m. Arthur L. Stern, III, July 31, 1965 (div.); children—Anne Stewart, Mark Alan; m. John A. Ciampa, Sept. 1, 1985 (div.). Admitted to N.Y. bar, 1968; clk. to Judges Juvenile Ct., Washington, 1967-68; mem. firm Nixon, Hargrave, Devans & Doyle, Rochester, N.Y., 1968-74, ptnr., 1975—; lectr. in field; trustee Found. of Monroe County (N.Y.) Bar, 1976-78. Sec., dir. United Community Chest of Greater Rochester, 1973-87, 92—; trustee, sec. Internat. Museum Photography at George Eastman House, Rochester, 1974—, Genesee Country Mus., Mumford, N.Y., 1976—; bd. dirs. Ctr. for Govtal. Research; trustee, chmn. United Neighborhood Ctr. of Greater Rochester Found., 1991—. Mem. Am. (chmn. task force on charitable giving, exempt orgns. com. tax sect. 1981—), N.Y. State (exec. com. tax sect., 1974-76, chmn. com. exempt orgns. 1975-76), Monroe County Bar Assn. (trustee 1974-75), BNA Portfolio, Pvt. Found. Distbns. Author: Charitable Giving and Solicitation. Office: Nixon Hargrave Devans & Doyle PO Box 1051 Clinton Sq Rochester NY 14603-1051

STEWART, TERESA ELIZABETH, elementary school educator; b. Cheverly, Md., Nov. 26, 1966; d. Richard Lynn and Sandra Lois (O'Neill) S. BS in Elem. Edn. cum laude, Bowie State U., 1988, MEd in Elem. Edn., 1996. Cert. elem. tchr., Md. Asst. tchr. Tom Thumb Day Care, Bowie, Md., 1989; elem. tchr. Berwyn Bapt. Sch., College Park, Md., 1989-95, Berkshire Elem. Sch., Forestville, Md., 1995—. Dir. vacation Bible sch., youth group leader Bowie United Meth. Ch., 1988—, sec. adminstrv. coun., 1993—, chairperson pastor parish rels. com., 1996, sec. membership com., 1993—; tchr. children's Bible class University Park Ch. of Brethren, 1990-94; instr., judge Belle-Aires Twirling Corp., Bowie, 1986—; mem. Md. Bato n Coun. Koonz, McKinney & Johnson Law Firm scholar, 1986-88. Mem. Huntington Heritage Soc., Kappa Delta Pi, Delta Kappa Gamma. Democrat. Home: 13126 11th St Bowie MD 20715-3726 Office: Berkshire Elem Sch 6201 Surrey Square Ln Forestville MD 20747

STEWART-PÉREZ, RENICE ANN, writer; b. Milw., Jan. 2, 1947; d. Fredrick and Lucia (Stewart) Fregin; children: Jennifer Jean, Whitney Susan; m. Robert Anthony Pérez, Dec. 21, 1995. BA, U. San Diego, 1988, MA, 1990. Pres. Chubby Bumpkins, Inc., Houston, 1980-82; contracts adminstr. Gulf States Computer Svcs., Houston, 1980-82; pres. RAM Prodns., Houston, 1981-82, Pizza Internat., Inc., Houston, 1982-84; contracts adminstr. First Alliance Corp., Houston, 1982-85; freelance pub. rels. cons. San Diego, 1985—. Tutor U. San Diego Writing Ctr., 1987-89; founder, dir. pub. rels.-tng. Montgomery County (Tex.) Crisis Action Line, Houston, 1979-84; founder, v.p., bd. dirs. Montgomery County Rape Crisis Coalition, 1982-84, speaker, 1982-84; speaker Rape Trauma Coalition, 1982-84; mem. prodn. com. community Women Together, Montgomery County, 1980-82; pres. Living Arts Coun., Houston, 1980-81. Named Woman of Yr. YWCA, 1981, 82. Mem. Am. Assn. Bus. Women (dir. activities Houston chpt. 1983-84), Bus. Women's Forum (bd. dir. community awareness Houston chpt. 1982-83), Assn. Women Bus. Owners, Lions (hon.), Phi Alpha Delta.

STICK, ALYCE CUSHING, information systems consultant; b. N.J., July 13, 1944; d. George William and Adele Margaret (Wilderotter) Cushing; m. James McAlpin Easter, July, 1970 (div. Aug. 1986); m. T. Howard F. Stick, June, 1989. AA, Colby-Sawyer Coll., 1964; student, Boston U., 1964-65, Johns Hopkins U., 1972-74; cert., Control Data Inst. and Life Office Mgmt. Assn., 1976. Claims investigator Continental Casualty Co., Phila., 1967-69; data processing coord. Chesapeake Life Ins. Co., Balt., 1970-72; sr. systems analyst Comml. Credit Computer Corp., Balt., 1972-80; v.p. Shawmut Computer Systems, Inc., Owings Mills, Md., 1980-85; pres. Computer Relevance, Inc., Gladwyne, Pa., 1985—; cons. Siani Hosp., Balt., 1982-85, AT&T, Reading, Pa., 1987-88, Dun and Bradstreet, Allentown, Pa., 1988, Arco Chem. Co., Newtown Square, Pa., 1990-91, Rohm and Haas Co., Phila., 1992-96. Designer/author: (computer software systems) Claim-Track, 1977, Property-Profiles, 1979, Stat-Model, 1989; co-designer/author: Patient-Profiles, 1983. Treas. Balt. Mus. Art, Sales and Rental Gallery, 1984. Mem. Assn. for Systems Mgmt., Data Processing Mgmt. Assn., Ind. Computer Cons. Assn., Merion Cricket Club (Haverford, Pa.). Republican. Office: Computer Relevance Inc 1501 Monticello Dr Gladwyne PA 19035-1206

STICKELER, CARL ANN LOUISE, professional parliamentarian; b. Plant City, Fla., Dec. 26, 1930; d. Carl Ulysses and Marian Lucille (Churchill) Sangster; m. Nickolas Joseph Stickeler, May 14, 1949; children: Nickolas J., Juliann E., Carl A., John C., Katherine M. Profl. registered parliamentarian. Bus. mgr. Kendall Automobile Sales, Inc., Miami, 1967-82; parliamentarian Stickeler & Assocs., P.A., Miami, 1982-88, Ocala, Fla., 1988—. Editor: The Answer, 1983-89, The Florida Parliamentarian, 1983-87. Recipient Internat. Woman of Distinction Beta Sigma Phi Internat., 1980, Order of the Rose award Beta Sigma Phi Internat., 1969. Mem. Internat. Platform Assn., Nat. Assn. Parliamentarians (bd. dirs. 1979-83, 91-93, v.p. 1983-89, pres. 1989-91), Acad. Parliamentary Procedure and Law (bd. dirs. 1979—, pres. 1985-87), Gen. Fedn. Women's Clubs, Fla. Fedn. of Women's Clubs (parliamentarian 1992—), DAR, Beta Sigma Phi. Republican. Roman Catholic. Office: Stickeler & Assocs 102 Almond Rd Ocala FL 34472-8634

STICKNEY, JESSICA, former state legislator; b. Duluth, Minn., May 16, 1929; d. Ralph Emerson and Claudia Alice (Cox) Page; m. Edwin Levi Stickney, June 17, 1951; children: Claudia, Laura, Jeffrey. BA, Macalester Coll., St. Paul, Minn., 1951; PhD (hon), Rocky Mtn. Coll., Billings, Mont., 1986. Rep. State of Mont., 1989-92; mem. Gov.'s Commn. on Post-Sec. Edn., Mont., 1973-75. Mem. Sch. Bd. Trustees, Miles City, Mont., 1968-74; mem., chmn. zoning bd., Miles City, 1975-89; mem. Govt. Study Commn., Miles City, 1974-76, United Ch. Christ Bd. Homeland Ministries, 1975-81;

chmn., conf. moderator United Ch. Christ Bd. Mont.-Northern Wyo. Conf., 1980-82; chmn. Town Meeting on the Arts, Mont., 1980; mem., chmn. Miles Community Coll. Bd., 1975-89, chmn. 1978-80. Mem. Mont. Arts Coun. (chmn. 1982-85), Western States Arts Found. (vice chmn. 1984), Nat. Assembly State Arts Agys. (bd. dirs. 1982-88), AAUW (pres. 1964-66). Democrat.

STIDD, LINDA MARIE, rehabilitation nurse; b. Martins Ferry, Ohio, Mar. 20, 1947; d. Stephen George and Helen Jane (Cupryk) Mularcik; m. William Leroy Stidd, May 4, 1968; 1 child, Christopher Alan. Diploma, Ohio Valley Gen. Hosp., 1968; BSN, Ohio U., 1995. CRRN; RN cert. in gerontology. Staff nurse Ohio Valley Gen. Hosp., Wheeling, W.Va., 1968-69, 73-79; supr. Woodland Acres Nursing Home, St. Clairsville, Ohio, 1971-73; staff nurse Ohio Valley Med. Ctr., Wheeling, 1973-79, head nurse rehab., 1981-91; nurse mgr. OVMC Rehab. at Woodsdale, Wheeling, 1991-92; nurse mgr. for skilled care/rehab. Peterson Rehab. Hosp. and Geriatric Ctr., Wheeling, 1991-95. Mem. Assn. Rehab. Nurses, W.Va. Assn. Rehab. Nurses, W.Va. Orgn. Nurse Execs., Nat. Disting. Svc. Registry Med. and Vocat. Rehab. Democrat. Roman Catholic. Office: Peterson Rehab Hosp and Geriatric Ctr Homestead Ave Wheeling WV 26003-6697

STIDMAN, EDITH (JANET) SCALES, parliamentarian; b. Balt., Sept. 19; d. Joseph Edward and Edith Morris (Caulk) Scales; m. Herbert Jean Silcox, May 18, 1944 (dec. Mar. 1945); m. John Charles Stidman, Sept. 27, 1947; children: Janet Stidman Eveleth, John Scales Stidman. BS in Instn. Mgmt., U. Md., 1944. With Cen. Club for Nurses, N.Y.C., 1944-45; dietitian, trouble shooter Studio Club YWCA, N.Y.C., 1944-45; food svc. supr. AT&T, N.Y.C., 1946-47; parliamentarian, tchr., lectr., spk. and cons. in field. Editor (newsletter) Govans Guidepost, 1959-62, Md. Parent Tchr., 1960's, The Pen Woman, 1992-96, Md. Assn. Capsule Epistle, 1991-93, editor-in-chief, 1995—; editor-in-chief Nat. Parliamentation, 1987-89; contbr. articles to profl. jours. Vice-chmn., chmn. Grace United Meth. Ch., adminstrn. bd., fin., nominating, edn., pastor/parish rels., worhip com., lay mem. to conf.; tchr., jr. dept. supt., counseling tchr., pres. Grace United Meth. Women, 1984-88, 89-90; recording sec. Md. Congress of Parents & Tchrs., Inc., 1965-68, dist. v.p., 1962-65, bd. dirs., 1960-68; trustee William Lemmel Scholarhip Fund and Screening Com., 1960's, The Boy's Latin Sch. Md., 1969-70; charter mem. jr. bd. and sec. Florence Crittenden Home, 1948-50; coord. Cub Scout pack Boy Scouts Am., bd. dirs. Safety Coun. of Md., 1968—, v.p. 3 divsns., 1969-75; pres. Legisl. Clearing Hosue of Md., 1971-75; corr. sec. Balt. City PTA Coun. pres., 1959-61; pres. Govans PTA, 1959-61, Northern H.S. PTA, 1965-67; hon. life mem. Md. PTA, Nat. PTA; past pres. Md. Coun. on Edn.; parliamentarian Woman's Club Roland Park, Balt., 1978—, 1st v.p., 1994-96, pres. elect, 1996—, judge parliamentary performance contests H.S. teams statewide for State Dept. Edn., Md., 1993—; bylaws chmn. Union Meml. Hosp. Aux., 1990-92, parliamentarian, 1973—. Recipient Vol. Svc. cert. Balt. City Health Dept. 1957, Generous Svc. and Committment to Bus. Edn. cert. Balt. County Bd. Edn., 1983, Recognition of Svc. to Blue Ridge Region cert. Internat. Toastmistress Orgn., 1983, Appreciation cert. Howard Vocat. Tech. Sch., 1983, Towson State U., Profl. Secs. Internat., Future Bus. Leaders Am., Spl. Mission Recognition award United Meth. Women, 1981. Mem. AAUW (parliamentarian Md. chpt. 1973-75), Nat. Assn. Parrliamentarians (pres. 1987-89), Md. Assn. Parliamentarians (pres. 1973-75, 95—), Am. Inst. Parliamentarians, Internat. Platform Assn., Nat. League Am. Pen Women (parliamentarian 1992-96, 5th v.p. 1994, 4th v.p. 1994-96), U. Md. Alumni Assn. (life, recunion com. 1995), Md. Assn. Hosp. Aux. (parliamentarian 1973—), Edith S. Stidman Unit (pres. 1984-87, pres. parliamentary edn. unit 1971-73, pres. M.W. Wneelock unit 1976-79), Md. Reigstered Parliamentarians (pres. unit 1993-94), Morgan State Univ. Unit, Nat. Parks and Conservation Assn., Women's Civic League. Republican. Methodist. Home and Office: 606 Cedarcroft Rd Baltimore MD 21212-2703

STIEBER, TAMAR, journalist; b. Bklyn., Sept. 15, 1955; d. Alfred and Florence (Spector) S. Student, Rockland C.C., 1972-75, Rockland C.C., 1972-75, West London (Eng.) Coll., 1973-74; BA in Film cum laude, U. Calif., Berkeley, 1985, postgrad., 1985-86; grad. police reserve academycum laude, Napa Valley Coll., 1988. Office mgr., confidential sec. AP, San Francisco, 1981-83; stringer Daily Californian, Berkeley, Calif., 1983-84; film rsch. teaching asst. U. California, Berkeley, 1984-86; libr. and rsch. asst. Pacific Film Archive, Berkeley, 1984-86; intern San Francisco Examiner, 1984; reporter Sonoma (Calif.) Index-Tribune, 1987-88, Vallejo (Calif.) Times-Herald, 1988-89, Albuquerque Journal, 1989-94. Recipient Pulitzer prize for specialized reporting, 1990, first place pub. svc. divsn. N.Mex. Press Assn., 1990, pub. svc. award Albuquerque Press Club, 1990; first place newswriting N.Mex. Press Assn., 1991; honorable mention Assn. Press Managing Editors, 1994. Mem. AAUW, Soc. Profl. Journalists, Investigative Reporters and Editors, N.M. Found. Open Govt., Internat. Platform Soc., Phi Beta Kappa. Home: PO Box 9835 Santa Fe NM 87504-9835

STIEFEL, SUSAN CAROL, legal services firm human resources executive; b. N.Y.C., Apr. 25, 1945; d. Michael and Judith (Kleinman) Dronsick; m. Lloyd Mark Haffner, Apr. 3, 1966 (div. 1980); children: Jessica Lynn, Meredith Paige; m. Alan lee Stiefel, Oct. 7, 1984; stepchildren: Suzanne Leigh, Jennifer Lynne. BA in Sociology, SUNY, Binghamton, 1966; MBA with honors, Lake Forest Grad. Sch. Mgmt., 1984. Researcher Child Welfare League Am., N.Y.C., 1966-68; pers. asst. Solo Cup Co., Highland Park, Ill., 1979-80, employment mgr., 1980-83; pers. rep. Denticon/Sybron Corp., Evanston, Ill., 1983-84, mgr. human resources, 1984-86; dir. human resources Medserv Corp., Lake Forest, Ill., 1986-87; v.p. for human resources Medserv Corp., Marietta, Ga., 1988-93; dir. human resources Kilpatrick & Cody, Atlanta, 1993—. Campaign worker Lake County (Ill.) Dem. Cen. Com., 1980. Mem. NAFE, Soc. for Human Resource Mgmt., Assn. Legal Adminstrs., Lake Forest Grad. Sch. Mgmt. Alumni Assn. (v.p. bd. dirs. 1986-88). Jewish. Office: Kilpatrick & Cody 1100 Peachtree St NE Ste 2800 Atlanta GA 30309-4528

STIEFVATER, PAMELA JEAN, chiropractor; b. Utica, N.Y., Oct. 16, 1956; d. Kenneth Carl and Henriette Ramona (Billick) S. BS cum laude, SUNY, Oswego, 1977; D of Chiropractic cum laude, Palmer Coll., 1984. Lic. chiropractor, N.Y., Mass.; diplomate Nat. Bd. Chiropractic Examiners. Sci. tchr. Altmar, Parish, Williamstown High Sch., Parish, N.Y., 1978-80; chiropractor, owner Bayside Chiropractic, South Dennis, Mass., 1986—. Mem. Am. Chiropractic Soc., Mass. Chiropractic Soc., Cape Code Chiropractic Soc. Office: Bayside Chiropractic 430 Old Bass River Rd South Dennis MA 02660-2724

STIEHL, ELAINE MARIE, mental health nurse; b. Boston, Aug. 19, 1948; d. Philip and Rose Marie (Katula) Vaccaro; m. Walter Alan Stiehl, Dec. 28, 1974; 1 child, Walter Daniel. BSN, Boston Coll., 1970, MS in Med.-Surg. Nursing, 1975, postgrad., 1988. RN, Mass.; cert. in psychiat./cmty. mental helath nurse, adult nurse practitioner. Staff and charge nurse Tufts New Eng. Med. Ctr., Boston, 1970-72; staff nurse med. dept. MIT, Cambridge, 1972-75; adult nurse practitioner Harvard Cmty. Health Plan, Cambridge, 1975-88; preceptor for nurse practitioner students Boston U., 1983-87, clin. assoc. of nursing, 1986-87; on-call nurse practitioner Beth Israel Hosp., Boston, 1988-93; crisis nurse, supr. crisis stabilization program Tri-City Cmty. Mental Health & Retardation Ctr., Medford, Mass., 1988-91; psychiatric liaison nurse Lawrence Meml. Hosp., Medford, 1991-93; adult nurse practitioner Harvard U., Cambridge, 1993—; psychiatric clin. specialist Youville Hosp. and Rehab. Ctr., Cambridge, 1993-96; program mgr. nursing home program Vinten Corp., Cambridge, 1995—; psychopharmacology nurse clin. specialist nursing home program McLean Hosp., Belmont, Mass., 1996—, Bay Colony Health Svcs., Inc., Cambridge, 1996—. 1st aid coord. Greater Boston Walk for Hunger, Boston, 1986-89. Mem. Sigma Theta Tau (chairperson fin. com. 1977-78, chairperson publicity/mailings 1978-79). Office: Bay Colony Health Svcs Inc 800 W Cummings Pk Woburn MA 01801

STIEHLER, DOREEN ANN, mechanical engineer; b. Poughkeepsie, N.Y., Jan. 5, 1947; d. Robert John and Evelyn Theresa (Fee) S. BA in English, SUNY, Buffalo, 1970, BS in Engring. Sci., 1978. Tchr. math. Buffalo Bd. of Edn., 1970-75; structural analysis engr. United Tech. Optical Sys., West Palm Beach, Fla., 1978-83; mfg. supr. Motorola, West Palm Beach, Fla., 1983-92; project engr., mgr. United Tech. Optical Sys., Boynton Beach, Fla., 1993-95; mfg. supr. Motorola, Plantation, Fla., 1995-96; structural analysis engr. United Engrs., West Palm Beach, 1996—. Mem. NAFE, Soc. Women Engrs. Home: 421 Northlake Dr North Palm Beach FL 33408

STIENMIER, SAUNDRA KAY YOUNG, aviation educator; b. Abilene, Kans., Apr. 27, 1938; d. Bruce Waring and Helen E. (Rutz) Young; m. Richard H. Steinmier, Dec. 20, 1958; children: Richard, Susan, Julia, Laura. AA, Colo. Women's Coll., 1957; student, Temple Buell Coll., U. Colo., 1959, 69; ed., Embre Riddle Aviation U., Ramstein, Germany. Cert. FAA pilot. Dir. Beaumont Gallery, El Paso, Tex., 1972-77; mem. grad. studies faculty Embre Riddle Aviation U., 1979-80; mgr. Ramstein Aero Club, USAF, 1977-80, Peterson Flight Tng. Ctr., Peterson AFB, Colo., 1980—. Named Outstanding S.W. Artist. Mem. AAUW, Order Eastern Star, Scottish Soc. Pikes' Peak, Scots Heritage Soc., Internat. Women Pilots Assn., Beta Sigma Phi, Delta Psi Omega, Aircraft Owners and Pilots Assn., Nat. Pilots Assn., Colo. PilotsAssn., Soc. Arts and Letters, 99's Club. Office: PO Box 14123 Colorado Springs CO 80914-0123

STIKNA, DOROTHY J., municipal official; b. Paterson, N.J., July 21, 1954; d. Richard E. and Agnes J. (Hoey) Allen; m. Steven M. Stikna, June 19, 1976; 1 child, Sharon. BA, Glassboro (N.J.) State Coll., 1976; postgrad., Fairleigh Dickinson U., 1992—. Cashier Twp. W. Caldwell (N.J.), 1976-79; auditor Dickinson, Vrabel & Cassells, PA, Denville, N.J., 1979-85; CFO Twp. of Bernards, Basking Ridge, N.J., 1985—; treas. CFO Borough of Far Hills (N.J.), 1992-95, Bernards Twp. Bd. Edn., Basking Ridge, N.J., 1995—. Co-leader Girl Scouts Am., Morris Area, N.J., 1992-94. Mem. Govt. Fin. Officers Assn. N.J. (mem. exec. bd. 1992—), Tax Collectors and Treas. Assn. N.J. Roman Catholic. Home: 58 Meadowbrook Blvd Randolph NJ 07869 Office: Twp of Bernards One Collyer Ln Basking Ridge NJ 07920

STILES, MARY ANN, lawyer; b. Tampa, Fla., Nov. 16, 1944; d. Ralph A. and Bonnie (Smith) S. AA, Hills Community Coll., 1973; BS, Fla. State U., 1975; JD, Antioch Sch. Law, 1978. Bar: Fla. 1978. Legis. analyst Fla. Ho. of Reps., Tallahassee, 1973-74, 74-75; intern U.S. Senate, Washington, 1977; v.p., gen. counsel Associated Industries Fla., Tallahassee, 1978-81, gen. counsel, 1981-84, spl. counsel, 1986—; assoc. Deschler, Reed & Crichfield, Boca Raton, Fla., 1980-81; founding ptnr. Stiles, Taylor & Metzler, Tampa, Fla., 1982—; shareholder and dir. Stiles Taylor & Metzler, P.A., Six Stars Devel. Co. of Fla., Inc.; with 1st Trust, Inc.; shareholder First Comml. Bank of Tampa. Author: Workers' Copmenstaion Law Handbook, 1980-94 edit. Bd. dirs., sec. Hillsborough C.C. Found., Tampa, 1985-87, 94-96; bd. dirs. Hillsborough Area Regional Transit Authority, Tampa, 1986-89, Boys and Girls Club of Tampa, 1986—; mem. Bay Area chpt. Nat. Women's Polit. Caucus, 1993—, The Spring, 1992-93, What's My Chance, 1992-94; mem. Gov.'s Oversite Bd. on Workers' Compensation, 1989-90, Workers Comp. Rules Com., Fla. Bar, 1990-95, Workers Comp. Exec. Counsel Fla. Bar, 1990-95Jud. Nominating Commn. for Workers' Compensation Cts., 1990-93, trustee Hillsborough Cmty. Coll., 1994—, vice-chair, 1995-96, chair, 1996—. Mem. ABA, Fla. Bar Assn., Hillsborough County Bar Assn., Hillsborough Assn. Women Lawyers, Fla. Assn. Women Lawyers, Fla. Women's Alliance, Hillsborough County Seminole Boosters (past pres.). Democrat. Baptist. Club: Tiger Bay (Tampa, past pres., sec.). Office: 315 S Plant Ave Tampa FL 33606-2325 also: 111 N Orange Ave Ste 850 Orlando FL 32801-2381 also: 317 N Calhoun St Tallahassee FL 32301-7605 also: 200 E Las Olas Blvd Ste 1760 Fort Lauderdale FL 33301-2248

STILLER, MARGARET M., secondary education educator; b. El Dorado, Ark., Jan. 1, 1951; d. Eugene and Faye (Gunnels) McNeely; m. Bill Stiller, Dec. 18, 1971; children: Sha, Neely. BS in Math. Edn., La. Tech. U., 1972; postgrad. in Secondary Edn., U. Nebr., Omaha, 1993—. Cert. tchr., Tex., Nebr. Math. tchr. Plattsmouth (Nebr.) H.S., 1993—. Home: 2818 Century Rd Bellevue NE 68123 Office: Plattsmouth HS 1724 8th Ave Plattsmouth NE 68048

STILLMAN, ANDREA L., state legislator; b. N.Y.C.. BA, Calif. State U., Northridge. Mem. Conn. Ho. of Reps., 1993—. Rep. town meeting, 1980-83; mem. Bd. Fin., 1984-92; bd. dirs. Conn. Resource Recovery Authority, 1988-92, Conn. Low Level Radioactive Waste Adv. Coun., 1992; mem. Waterford Dem. Town Com., Waterford Hist. Soc., Citizen's Task Force on Substance Abuse, 1996. Mem. AAUW, LWV, Nat. Women's Political Caucus, Nat. Assn. Women, Lions Club. Democrat. Jewish. Address: 5 Coolidge Ct Waterford CT 06385-3309 Office: Conn Ho of Reps State Capitol Hartford CT 06106

STILLMAN, ANNE WALKER GWATHMEY, fashion designer; b. Amsterdam, The Netherlands, Apr. 15, 1951; came to U.S., 1953; d. Edmund and Mary (Gwathmey) S. Student Barnard Coll., 1968-72. Pres., designer Sofia & Anne, Ltd., Bethel, Conn., Stratford, Conn. and N.Y.C., 1978-90; designer Sofia & Anne Sportknit, 1983-90, Sofia & Anne Children's Wear, 1985-90, Go Cashmere for L'Zinger by Sofia & Anne, 1986; pres., designer Anne Stillman, Ltd., Bethel, Stratford, N.Y.C., 1990-94; designer Anne Stillman Knitwear, 1996—; cons. Conn. Trust Hist. Preservation, 1994—. Co-Author exhbn. catalog: Between Fences, 1996; editor Historic Properties Exchange, 1995—; contbg. editor Conn. Preservation News, 1995—. Office: 940 Whitney Ave Hamden CT 06517-4002

STILLMAN, ELINOR HADLEY, lawyer; b. Kansas City, Mo., Oct. 12, 1938; d. Hugh Gordon and Freda (Brooks) Hadley; m. Richard C. Stillman, June 25, 1965 (div. Apr. 1975). BA, U. Kans., 1960; MA, Yale U., 1961; JD, George Washington U., 1972. Bar: D.C. 1973, U.S. Ct. Appeals (10th cir.) 1975, U.S. Ct. Appeals (9th cir.) 1976, U.S. Ct. Appeals (2d cir.) 1976, U.S. Ct. Appeals (5th cir.) 1983, U.S. Ct. Appeals (4th cir.) 1985, U.S. Supreme Ct. 1976. Lectr. in English CUNY, 1963-65; asst. editor Stanford (Calif.) U. Press., 1967-69; law clk. to judge U.S. Dist. Ct. D.C., Washington, 1972-73; appellate atty. NLRB, Washington, 1973-78; asst. to solicitor gen. U.S. Dept. Justice, Washington, 1978-82; supr. appellate atty. NLRB, Washington, 1982-86, chief counsel to mem. bd., 1986-88, 94—, chief counsel to chmn. bd., 1988-94. Mem. ABA, D.C. Bar Assn., Order of Coif, Phi Beta Kappa. Democrat. Office: Nat Labor Rels Bd 1099 14th St NW Washington DC 20005-3419

STILLMAN, JOYCE L., artist, educator, writer, illustrator, consultant; b. N.Y.C., Jan. 19, 1943; d. Murray W. and Evelyn (Berger) Stillman. BA, NYU, 1964; student, Art Students League, 1965, Pratt Inst., 1972; MFA, L.I. U., 1975; postgrad., Calif. Inst. Integral Studies, 1994—. Tchr. N.Y.C. Pub. Schs., 1964-71; artist Cen. Hall Gallery, Port Washington, N.Y., 1974-76, Louis K. Meisel Gallery, N.Y.C., 1975-84, Tolarno Gallery, Melbourne, Australia, 1976—, Allan Stone Gallery, N.Y.C., 1990—; vis. assoc. prof. Towson State U., 1982; tchr. Women in Art, Tompkins Cortland C.C., 1988; lectr. Cornell U., 1990; founder Ithaca Women Artists Salon. One-person shows include Cen. Hall Gallery, Port Washington, 1975, Tolarno Gallery, Melbourne, 1976, Louis K. Meisel Gallery, N.Y.C., 1977, 80, 81, 82, Heckscher Mus., Huntington, N.Y., 1980, Holtzman Gallery, Towson (Md.) State U., 1982, Roslyn Oxley Gallery, Sydney, 1976, 82, Tomasulo Gallery, Union College, N.J., 1983, Stages, Keuka Coll., Keuka Park, N.Y., 1985, New Visions, Ithaca, N.Y., 1989, Herr-Chambliss, Hot Springs, Ark., 1990, Artist on the Lake, Hector, N.Y., 1992, Mus. Modern Art Christmas Card Collection, 1994; designer Mus. Modern Art Christmas Collection, 1978-81, 94, Time-Life Poster, 1978; exhibited in over 75 group shows, corp. and mus. collections. Recipient Flower Painting award Artist's Mag., 1986, Art Dir.'s Club 58th Annual Distinctive Merit award, 1979, N.Y. State Creative Artist's Pub. Svc. grant, 1979. Mem. AAUW, Nat. Assn. Women Artists, Allan Stone Gallery N.Y.C. Home and Studio: PO Box 662 Montour Falls NY 14865 also: 203 S Genesse St Montour Falls NY 14865

STILLMAN, NINA GIDDEN, lawyer; b. N.Y.C., Apr. 3, 1948; d. Melvin and Joyce Audrey (Gidden) S. AB with distinction, Smith Coll., 1970; JD cum laude, Northwestern U., 1973. Bar: Ill. 1973, U.S. Dist. Ct. (no. dist.) Ill. 1973, U.S. Dist. Ct. (ea. dist.) Wis. 1979, U.S. Dist. Ct. (no. dist. trial bar) Ill. 1983, U.S. Ct. Appeals (7th cir.) 1974, U.S. Supreme Ct. 1981, U.S. Dist. Ct. (ctrl. dist.) Ill. 1994. Assoc. Vedder, Price, Kaufman & Kammholz, Chgo., 1973-79, ptnr., 1980—; mem. adv. bd. occupational health and safety tng. program U. Mich., Ann Arbor, 1980-83; adj. faculty Inst. Human Resources and Indsl. Rels., Loyola U., Chgo., 1983-86, mem. bd. advisors, 1986—. Author: (with others) Women, Work, and Health: Challenge to Corporate Policy, 1979, Occupational Health Law: A Guide for Industry, 1981, Employment Discrimination, 1981, Personnel Management: Labor Relations, 1981, Occupational Safety and Health Law, 1988; contbr. articles to profl. jours. Legal advisor, v.p. Planned Parenthood Assn. Chgo., 1979-81; sec. jr. governing bd. Chgo. Symphony Orch., 1983. Recipient Svc. award Northwestern U., 1994. Mem. ABA (occupational safety and health law com. 1978—), Chgo. Bar Assn. (chmn. labor and employment law com. 1986-87), Human Resources Mgmt. Assn. Chgo. (officer, bd. dirs. 1986-88), Am. Inns of Ct. (v.p. Wigmore chpt. 1988-89), Northwestern U Sch. Law Alumni Assn. (pres. 1991-92), Coun. of 100, Smith Coll. Club Chgo. (pres. 1972), Law Club, Econ. Club Chgo., The Chgo. Com. Office: Vedder Price Kaufman & Kammholz 222 N La Salle St Chicago IL 60601-1003

STILTNER, MARSHA DIAZ, mathematician, educator; b. Montgomery, W.Va., Apr. 18, 1953; d. Marshall Leonard and Thelma Jean (Hudson) Diaz; m. Dean Stiltner, June 24, 1978. BA in Math. Edn., Marshall U., 1975, MA in Elem. Edn., 1980; post grad., W.Va. Grad. Coll., 1993. Tchr. math. Oak Hill (W.Va.) H.S., 1975—. Named Favorite Educator, W.Va. Govs. Honors Acad., 1990, 92, 94. Mem. NEA, Nat. Coun. Tchrs. Math., W.Va. Coun. Tchrs. Math., W.Va. Edn. Assn. (del. to assembly 1979-87), Fayette County Edn. Assn. (membership chair 1979-82), Delta Kappa Gamma. Democrat. Methodist. Office: Oak Hill HS Oyler Ave Oak Hill WV 25901

STILWELL, CHARLOTTE FINN, vocational counselor; b. San Francisco, Oct. 31, 1947; d. Frederick William and Helen Carolyn (Watson) Finn; Bobby Gene Stilwell, Dec. 17, 1937; children: Robert, Shelley, James, Joel. AA, St. Petersburg Jr. Coll., 1967; BS, Fla. State U., 1969; MA, U. South Fla., 1971; attended, U. S.C., 1972. Nat. cert. counselor; cert. sch. counselor. Dir. tutorial program Hillsborough County Schs., Tampa, Fla., 1971-72, tchr., counselor, 1972-73, h.s. counselor, 1973-77; vocat. counselor Pinellas County Schs., Clearwater, Fla., 1977—; dist. coord. Counseling for High Skills Kans. State, 1992—. Vol. Suicide & Crisis Ctrs., Tampa, St. Vincent DePaul's Soup Kitchen, St. Petersburg, Fla., 1993, Toy Shop, 1994-95, Spl. Olympics, 1996. General Electric Found. fellow. Mem. Am. Counseling Assn., Am. Sch. Counselor Assn. (Am. Sch. Counselor of Yr. 1995), Fla. Counseling Assn., Fla. Sch. Counselor Assn. (v.p. post secondary 1993-95), Phi Delta Kappa (historian 1993—), Pinellas Sch. Counselor Assn. (pres. 1991-95). Republican. Office: PTEC Clearwater 6100 154th Ave Clearwater FL 34620

STIMPSON, CATHARINE ROSLYN, English language educator, writer; b. Bellingham, Wash., June 4, 1936; d. Edward Keown and Catharine (Watts) S. A.B., Bryn Mawr Coll., 1958; B.A., Cambridge U., Eng., 1960, M.A., 1960; Ph.D., Columbia U., 1967. Mem. faculty Barnard Coll., N.Y.C., 1963-80; prof. English, dean of grad. sch., vice provost grad. edn. Rutgers U., New Brunswick, N.J., 1980-92, Univ. prof., 1991—; chmn. bd. scholars Ms. Mag., N.Y.C., 1981-92; dir. fellows program MacArthur Found., 1994—. Author: Class Notes, 1979, Where the Meanings Are, 1988; founding editor: Signs: Jour. Women in Culture and Society, 1974-81; book series Women in Culture and Society, 1981; columnist Change Mag., 1992-93. Chmn. N.Y. Council Humanities, 1984-87, Nat. Council Research on Women, 1984-89 ; bd. dirs. Stephens Coll., Columbia, Mo., 1982-85; trustee Bates Coll., 1990—. Hon. fellow Woodrow Wilson Found., 1958; Fulbright fellow, 1958-60; Nat. Humanities Inst. fellow New Haven, 1975-76; Rockefeller Humanities fellow, 1983-84. Mem. MLA (exec. coun., chmn. acad. freedom com., 1st v.p., pres. 1990), PEN, AAUP, NOW, Legal Def. and Edn. Fund (bd. dirs. 1991—), PBS (bd. dirs. 1994—). Democrat. Home: 62 Westervelt Ave Staten Island NY 10301-1432 Office: Rutgers U 172 College Ave New Brunswick NJ 08901-1157

STIMSON, GRACE HEILMAN, editor; b. Wyndmoor, Pa., Dec. 25, 1907; d. Edgar James and Mary Alice (Bechtold) Heilman; m. Claude William Stimson, Feb. 7, 1953 (dec. June 1973). AB cum laude, Wilson Coll., Chambersburg, Pa., 1929; MA in History, U. Pa., Phila., 1937, PhD in History, 1949. Tchr. math. Linden Hall, Lititz, Pa., 1929-35; libr. Hist. Soc. Del., Wilmington, 1940-42; rsch. asst. Haynes Found., L.A., 1946-53; rsch. asst., free-lance editor Bur. Bus. and Econ. Rsch., UCLA, 1953-54; assoc. editor U. Calif. Press, UCLA Office, 1954-73; free-lance editor U. Calif. Press and U. Wash. Press, Seattle, 1973—. Editor: Calendar of Joel R. Poinsett Papers, 1941; co-author: Production Cost Trends in Selected Industrial Areas, 1948; author: Rise of Labor Movement in Los Angeles, 1955. Precinct worker Adlai Stevenson, Dem. party, 1952. Lt. USNR, 1942-46. Wilson Coll. Alumnae fellow, 1935-38, Moorefellow U. Pa., 1938-39; recipient scholarship U. Pa., 1936-37, prize Am. Hist. Assn., 1955. Mem. Phi Beta Kappa. Home and Office: 2661 Tallant Rd # 713 Santa Barbara CA 93105-4838

STINE, CATHERINE MORRIS, artist; b. Roanoke, Va., Jan. 12, 1953; d. Richard Dengler and Dorothy Geraldine (Cornog) S.; m. Norris Jewett Chumley, Oct. 22, 1983; children: Jack H.M., Nathaniel B. BFA, Mus. Sch. Fine Arts, Boston, 1975. Art dir. Ear Mag., N.Y.C., 1980-83; asst. art dir. Jacmel Jewelry, N.Y.C., 1984-88; textile designer Style Coun., N.Y.C., 1989-90, Ruvetta Designs, N.Y.C., 1990—; curator Bratton Gallery, N.Y.C., 1989. One-woman shows include Plant Factory, Boston, 1974, Sixth Sense Gallery, N.Y.C., 1986, Pinnacle Awards/Am. Women in Radio and TV, N.Y.C., 1987, Limelight Club, N.Y.C., 1987, Parker-Bratton Gallery, N.Y.C., 1987, Bratton Gallery, N.Y.C., 1988, Carol Getz Gallery, Miami, Fla., 1990, Sunnen Gallery, N.Y.C., 1993, 94, Galley B.A.I., N.Y.C., 1996; group shows include Mus. Fine Arts Gallery, Boston, 1974, Williamsburg, Bklyn., 1982, ABC No Rio, N.Y.C., 1983, 85, City Without Walls Gallery, Newark, 1984, 85, Parsons Gallery, N.Y.C., 1985, author, illustrator: The Halcyon, 1984, Hudson Valley Exhbn., Poughkeepsie, 1985, Parker-Bratton Gallery, N.Y.C., 1986, Bratton Gallery, 1989, Neo Persona, N.Y.C., 1990, Tribeca 148, N.Y.C., 1991, Helio Gallery, N.Y.C., 1991, S. Bitter Larkin, N.Y.C., 1992, Sarah Rentschler Gallery, N.Y.C., 1992, Dooley-Le Cappellaine, N.Y.C., 1993, NYU Law Sch., 1994; represented in permanent collections Art Mus. Western Va., Paramount Pictures, others. Clk. religious edn. com. Fifteenth St. Quaker Meeting, N.Y.C. Curatorial grantee Artist Space, N.Y.C., 1989. Home: 264 East 7th St New York NY 10009

STINE, JEANNE M., mayor, educator; b. Detroit, June 18, 1929; d. William Lyle and Eleanor Laura (Abele) Goodwin; m. Cornelius Robert Powers, Oct. 3, 1952 (div. Feb. 1956); 1 child, Sheila Maureen Powers; m. John Follett Stine, Feb. 1962. BS in Edn., Wayne State U., 1960, MA in Edn., 1965. cert. K-8 Elem. edn., K-12 counseling. Telephone operator Mich. Bell, Detroit, 1946-51; clerk typist McGregor Meml. Conf., Detroit, Detroit Pub. Libr., 1950-52; display advertiser Daily Tribune, Royal Oak, Mich., 1952-54; elem. sch. tchr. Guardian Angels Sch., Clawson, Mich., 1958; elem. sch. tchr. Clawson Pub. Schs., 1959-66, middle sch. counselor, 1966-92; sec. Clawson Edn. Assn., 1960-63; pres. Clawson Youth Assist., 1968-74. initiator Troy youth bur. Police Dept., 1977; pres. Troy Youth Svcs. Activities Commn., 1977-80; v.p. Troy Profl. Women's Club, 1978-84, pres. Troy Youth Svcs. Forum, 1980-84, chair Troy Consortium on Drug and Alcohol Abuse; city councilwoman City of Troy, 1976-92; pres. Troy Vol. Firefighters Women's Aux., 1989-92; mayor City of Troy, 1992—; mem. bd. dirs. Boys and Girls Club of Troy, Traffic Improvement Assn. Oakland County. Recipient Dist. Citizen award Troy C. of C., 1985, Community Svc. award Clawson-Troy Elks, 1985. Mem. Nat. League of Cities (mem. transp. steering com. 1978-86, trans. policy com. 1989-92), Am. Legion Aux., Mich. Mcpl. League (chmn. region IV transp. and pub. works 1990, meritorius svc. award 1988), Mich. Assn. Mayors (bd. dirs.), Tri County Mayors Assn. (mem. steering com.), Zontas. Republican. Roman Catholic. Home: 1915 Boulan Dr Troy MI 48084-1512 Office: 500 W Big Beaver Rd Troy MI 48084-5254

STINE, PAMELA MOHLER, special education educator; b. Beckley, W.Va., June 20, 1951; d. Robert S. and Ethel (Edwards) Mohler; m. Jeffrey Stine (div. 1986); 1 child, Michael J.M. MA in Spl. Edn., Ariz. State U., 1976. Lang. devel. specialist. Tchr. Apache Junction (Ariz.) Schs., 1973-76; catering mgr. Durfey Hotels, San Mateo, Calif., 1976-78; diagnostic tchr. State Diagnostic Sch. State of Calif., 1977-82; resource specialist RCSD, Redwood City, Calif., 1984-90; presch. learning specialist Redwood City (Calif.) Sch. Dist., 1990—; cons. for preschs. Redwood City, 1992—; workshop presenter on self-esteem and child devel., Peninsula, No. Calif., 1988—. Accelerated Schs. Project, Stanford U., 1989; v.p. PTA, 1994—. Office: Roosevelt Sch 2223 Vera Ave Redwood City CA 94061

STINN, DEBRA ANN, upper elementary and middle school educator; b. Oskaloosa, Iowa, July 12, 1953; d. Gilbert Charles and Lucille Frances (Scott) Anderson; m. Glen Fredrick Stinn, July 22, 1978; 1 child, Kevin Edward. BS in Elem. Edn., Peru (Nebr.) State Coll., 1975. Cert. tchr., Nebr. Tchr. 5th grade Dunlap (Iowa) Cmty. Schs., 1975-78, Colo (Iowa) Cmty. Schs., 1978-81; substitute tchr. Columbus (Nebr.) Pub. Schs., 1981-83; ednl. cons. Achilles Hostel, Columbus, 1983-84; substitute tchr. Bellevue (Nebr.) Pub. Schs., 1989-92; math./computer tchr. Cardinal Spellman Sch., Omaha, 1992—. Vol. coord. Birchcrest PTA, Bellevue, 1993-96. Mem. Nat. Coun. Tchrs. Math., Nat. Cath. Edn. Assn., Omaha Archdiocese Math. Commn., United Meth. Women. Democrat. Methodist. Home: 1210 W 15th Ave Bellevue NE 68005-3821 Office: Cardinal Spellman Sch 12210 S 36th St Omaha NE 68123

STINSON, SUSAN ELIZABETH, director, writer; b. Amarillo, Tex., Oct. 17, 1960; d. Billy Ray and Mollie Elizabeth (Jordan) S. BA, U. Colo., Boulder, 1983. Dir. devel. Ctr. for Popular Econs., Amherst, Mass., 1990—; mem. Valley Lesbian Writers Group, Northampton, Mass., 1987-95; editor Orogeny Press, Northampton, 1992—. Author: Belly Songs, 1993, Fat Girl Dances with Rocks, 1994, Martha Moody, 1995, Gracious Flab/Gracious Bone (video), 1995, (Mass. arts lottery grant, 1993). Fiction fellow The Millay Colony, Austerlitz, N.Y., 1991, Helene Wurlitzer Found., Taos, N.M., 1991, Blue Mountain Ctr., Blue Mountain Lake, N.Y., 1994; fiction grant Ludwig Vogelstein Found., N.Y.C., 1992. Mem. Nat. Assn. to Advance Fat Acceptance. Home: PO Box 433 Northampton MA 01061 Office: Ctr for Pop Economics PO Box 785 Amherst MA 01004

STIPEK, KATHLEEN, reference librarian; b. Oakland, Calif., Nov. 14, 1946; d. William Antone and Geraldine Catherine (Cullen) S. BA, Fla. Atlantic U., 1967; MLS, Fla. State U., 1982. Clerical/secretarial positions U. Fla., Gainesville, 1968-81; dir. Haines City (Fla.) Pub. Libr., 1982-86; adult svcs. coord. Ctrl. Fla. Regional Libr., Ocala, 1986-89; reference libr. Hernando County Libr. Sys., Brooksville, Fla., 1989; freelance writer and editor, 1989-91; reference libr. Alachua County Libr. Dist., Gainesville, 1991—. Contbr. chpt. to book, articles to profl. jours. Higher Edn. Act Title IIB fellow, 1981-82. Mem. ALA, Fla. Libr. Assn., Fla. Pub. Libr. Assn., Am. Mensa. Office: Alachua County Libr Dist 401 E University Ave Gainesville FL 32601

STIRITZ, MARETTE MCCAULEY, English language educator, consultant; b. Center Point, Ark., Dec. 9, 1931; d. Edrie Delos and Lucyle Virginia (Dautrieve) McCauley; m. Charles Wayne Jackson, July 1, 1950 (dec. June 1986); children: Charles, Retta, Shelia; m. John David Stiritz, Dec. 3, 1992. BSE, Ark. State U., 1962; MA, U. Ark., 1965, PhA, 1986. Tchr. elem. Plum Bayou (Ark.) Pub. Schs., 1950-52; tchr. Laura Connor H.S., Augusta, Ark., 1955-59, Swifton (Ark.) Elem. Sch., 1959-60, Swifton H.S., 1962-63; prof. English So. Ark. U., Magnolia, 1965-78, U. Cen. Ark., Conway, 1978—; cons. high schs., Conway, Morrilton, Vilonia, 1983—, Ark. Dept. Edn., Little Rock, 1982, 84; lectr. U. Chile, Santiago, 1989, Moscow Pedagogical U., 1991, 92, Academica Inst. Chileno-Norteamericano, Santiago, 1994; speaker 8th Bi-ann. Conf. Profs. Fgn. Langs., Chile, 1992, 9th Conf., Chile, 1994. Contbr. articles to profl. jours.; book reviewer Ark. Elem. Coun., 1980—. Del. Faulkner County Dems., Conway, 1984; exec. sec., founder Columbia Tchrs. Eng., Magnolia, 1974-78. Mem. Ark. Coun. Tchrs. English (pres. 1979-80, bd. dirs. 1989-93), Ark. Philol. Assn., Nat. Coun. Tchrs. English, Ark. Coll. Tchrs. English (pres. 1992-93), Conway Rotary Internat. Breakfast Club (charter), Alpha Chi (region II v.p. 1992-93. Democrat. Methodist. Home: 3414 Rhonda Ct Conway AR 72032-9168

STIRLING, ELLEN ADAIR, retail executive; b. Chgo., June 21, 1949; d. Volney W. and Ellen Adair (Orr) Foster; m. James P. Stirling, June 6, 1970; children: Elizabeth Ginevra, Diana Leslie, Alexandra Curtiss. Student, U. Chgo., 1970-71; BA, Wheaton Coll., Norton, Mass., 1971; postgrad., U. London, 1974. Pres., CEO, The Lake Forest Shop, 1986—; bd. dirs. Lake Forest Bank and Trust. Founder, v.p. aux. bd. Art Inst. Chgo., 1972-91; dir. Friends of Ryerson Woods, 1992—; mem. women's bd. Lyric Opera, Chgo., 1992—, Lake Forest Coll., 1989—; mem. costume com. Chgo. Hist. Soc. Mem. Onwentsia Club, Racquet Club. Office: The Lake Forest Shop 165 E Market Sq Lake Forest IL 60045

STIRLING, MICHELLE DIANNE, tax specialist, accountant; b. Buffalo, N.Y., Dec. 8, 1975; d. Ian Scott and Dianne Louise (Garland) S. BBA in Acctg., Niagara U., 1996. Acct. asst. N.Am. Adminstrs., Amherst, N.Y., 1993-96; tax preparer Michael Greenberg & Assocs., Inc., North Tonawanda, N.Y., 1996—; acct. Heritage Ctrs., Buffalo, 1996—; tax preparer Vol. Income Tax Assistance, Niagara Falls, 1995. Vol. United Way, Niagara Falls, N.Y., 1987—, World Univ. Games, Niagara Falls, 1993, Niagara U. Cmty. Action Program, Niagara Falls, 1995—, Niagara Hospice, Niagara Falls, 1995—. Scholar Niagara U., 1993—. Mem. Inst. Mgmt. Accts., Niagara Univ. Acctg. Soc., Delta Epsilon Sigma. Home: 3801 Pine Ave Niagara Falls NY 14301

STITELER, CINDY GAYLE, property and financial manager; b. Long Beach, Calif., Aug. 24, 1947; d. Gilbert Eugene and Sara Jane (Wallace) Burress; m. Stephen Ernest Stiteler, Sept. 20, 1970 (div. 1982); children: Kier R., Sheppard K. BA in Art, U. Calif., Irvine, 1970. Childbirth educator Bradley Method, Orange County, Calif., 1971-82; co-owner art gallery Emerald City, Santa Barbara, Calif., 1973-75; co-owner soft sculpture bus. Champagne Ltd., Santa Barbara, 1976-78; property and fin. mgr. Siegel Properties, Santa Barbara, 1977-79, Taos, N.Mex., 1979—; co-trustee Richard B. Siegel Trust, L.A., 1991—; treas. Richard B. Siegel Found., L.A., 1991—. Treas. Hands-on-Elders, Taos, 1992—. Office: Siegel Properties Box 2707 Taos NM 87571

STITES, SUSAN KAY, human resources consultant; b. Colorado Springs, Colo., Sept. 20, 1952; d. William Wallace and Betty Jane (Kosley) Stites; m. Gerald Frederick Simon, Aug. 14, 1988. BA, Wichita State U., 1974; MA, Northwestern U., 1979. Benefits authorizer Social Security Adminstrn., Chgo., 1974-77; trainer Chgo. Urban Skills Inst., 1977-79; human resources mgr. Montgomery Ward, Chgo., 1979-83; mgr. tng. Lands' End, Dodgeville, Wis., 1983-87; dir. human resources Cen. Life Assurance, Madison, Wis., 1988-90; owner Mgmt. Allegories, Madison, Wis., 1987—. Author: Delegating for Results, 1992, Business Communications, 1992, Managing with a Quality Focus, 1994, Training and Orientation for the Small Business, 1994, Powerful Performance Management, 1994, Safety Management Techniques, 1995, Teaching First Aid and CPR, 1995, Alive at 25, 1995, Strategic Thinking and Planning, 1995, Teaching Alice at 25, 1996, Fundamendals of Industrial Hygiene, 1996, Recruiting, Developing, and Retaining Volunteers, 1996. Vol. tutor Japanese Students in English, Evanston, Ill., 1977-80; read to blind Chgo. Coun. for the Blind, 1974-76. Named Outstanding Woman of the Yr. Wichita State U., 1974. Mem. ASTD (chpt. pres. 1988, v.p. membership 1986, region V awards chair 1992), Soc. Applied Learning Tech., Madison Area Quality Improvement Network, Assn. for Quality and Participation, Rotary (vol. fund raiser), Mendota Yacht Club (treas. 1990-94). Home: 3788 Highridge Rd Madison WI 53704-6206 Office: Mgmt Allegories 3788 Highridge Rd Madison WI 53704-6206

STITH, BEVERLY JEAN, paralegal; b. Washington, Mar. 27, 1949. Assoc. Degree in Transp. Mgmt., LaSalle U., 1977; Environ. Sci. Diploma, Calif. State U., 1993, Thomas Edison State Coll., 1993; BS/MBA-Bus. Adminstrn., Chadwick U., 1995. Transp. asst. Interstate Commerce Commn., Indpls., 1977-79; paralegal specialist Interstate Commerce Commn., Washington, 1979-84; legal staff asst. Armed Svcs. Bd. of Contract Appeals, Falls Church, Va., 1987-89; paralegal specialist Mil. Sealift Command, Far East, Yokohama, Japan, 1989-94, Def. Fin. and Acctg. Svc. (former Spouse Divsn.), Cleve., 1994—. Author: Prevention of Sexual Harassment in the Workplace, 1992. Decorated Navy Unit Commendation Cert./Mil. Sealift Command, (Desert Shield/Desert Storm), Yokohoma. Mem. Nat. Paralegal Assn., Nat. Environ. Health Assn. Republican. Baptist. Home: 5146 Arch St Maple Heights OH 44137-1506 Office: Def Fin Acctg Svc Code L 1240 E 9th St Cleveland OH 44199-2001

STITH, CHERYL DIANE ADAMS, elementary school educator; b. Birmingham, Ala., Oct. 15, 1950; d. Mack Jones and Joan (Logan) Adams; m. Hugh P. Stith, III, Jan. 7, 1972; children: Jennifer Dawn, Kristy Michelle. BS cum laude, U. Ala., Birmingham, 1986, MA in Edn., 1992, EdS, 1994. Cert. ednl. specialist, Ala. Substitute tchr. Homewood City (Ala.) Schs., 1986-87; tchr. Robert C. Arthur Elem. Sch., Birmingham, 1987-95; instrnl. support specialist Edgewood Elem. Homewood City Schs., 1995—; mem. summer enrichment program U. Ala.-Birmingham, 1993; mem. State of Ala. Textbook Com., Montgomery, 1995; lectr. in field. Vol. Birmingham Soup Kitchens, 1988—, Habitat for Humanity, Birmingham, 1992—; spkr. Ala. Kidney Found., Birmingham, 1992—; vol. U. Ala.-Birmingham's Young Author's Conf., 1986-92; mem. Robert C. Arthur Elem. Sch. PTO. Named Tchr. of the Yr., Birmingham Pub. Schs., 1993-94, Outstanding Tchr., 1994; Beeson fellow Samford U. Writing Project, 1990; Ala. Ret. Tchrs. Found. scholar, 1994. Mem. NEA, Ala. Edn. Assn., Birmingham Edn. Assn., Internat. Reading Assn. (S.E. regional conf. presider and vol.), Ala. Reading Assn., Birmingham Reading Coun., Birmingham Tchrs. Applying Whole Lang., Nat. Coun. Tchrs. English, Phi Kappa Phi, Kappa Delta Pi. Methodist. Home: 1034 Greystone Ct Birmingham AL 35242

STITT, DOROTHY JEWETT, journalist; b. Houston, Sept. 4, 1914; d. Harry Berkey and Gladys (Norfleet) Jewett; m. James Wilson Stitt, Feb. 14, 1939; children: James Harry, Thomas Paul. AB, Rice U., 1937; MS, Columbia U., 1938. Reporter Houston Post, 1936-38, asst. city editor, 1938; editor of publs. Jewett Family of Am., 1971-94, editor emeritus, 1994—; spl. asst. to pub. Jewett Genealogy Vols. III and IV, 1995—; Jewett family Dir.-for-Life, 1995—; gen. chmn. Jewett Family Reunion, 1996. Author, editor: The 100th Anniversary Yearbook and History of the George Taylor Chapter, DAR, 1895-1995, 1994, Easton Red Cross Fiftieth Anniversary Booklet and History—Fifty Years of Service, 1967. Mem. adv. bd. Easton Salvation Army, pub. chmn., 1956—, chmn. bd. dirs., 1964, bd. treas., 1981; bd. dirs., pub. chmn. ARC, 1952-67, organizing chmn., vol. Lehigh chpt., 1995-96; pres. Easton JC wives, 1950-53; mem. fin. com. Little Stone House Mus. Assn., 1974-76, 80, organizing bd. dirs. sec. and pub. chmn., 1974-91; bd. dirs. Easton United Cmty. Chest/United Way, 1957-60, active in publicity for 1st campaign, 1960; active Easton Civil Def. Comms., 1956-60; mem. pub. bd. Montgomery County Pa. Girl Scouts USA, 1946-48, initiator and editor county newsletter; den mother cub scouts Easton Boy Scouts Am., 1948-55; capt. renovation campaign area YWCA, 1956; mem. March Sch., mem. Easton PTA, 1948-57, sec., 1952-54, v.p., 1954-56, bylaws chmn., 1953, Easton H.S., 1954-61, membership chmn., 1955-57, 59-60; bd. dirs. Easton Young Woman's Christian Assn., 1965-68, publicity chmn. Y-Teen com., 1953-68. Recipient plaques Salvation Army, 1982, 91, Jewett Family of Am., 1993, Cert. for Outstanding Svcs., Easton chpt. ARC, 1967, citation Hist. and Geneal. Soc. Northampton County for outstanding svc. in restoration and pub. of Little Stone House Mus., 1993, citation United Way of Easton, 1960, Molly Pitcher gold medal of appreciation, SAR, 1980. Mem. AAUW (treas. Easton br. 1950-52, newsletter initiator and editor 1951-60, rep. of br. to UN N.Y.C. conf. 1961-68, internat. rels. chmn.), UDC (Jefferson Davis chpt.), DAR (George Taylor chpt. regent 1974-80, 89-95, vice regent 1980-83, historian 1971-74, 95—, pub. chmn. 1969—; Penn. state chmn. vol. svcs. 1995—), PEO (chpt. AF Houston), Easton Tavern House Soc., World Affairs Coun. Phila., Woman's Club of Easton (pres. 1961-64, bd. dirs. 1959—, pub. chmn. 1952-68, 70-82, 92—, parliamentarian 1984-92, spl. fin. chmn. 1969-78, legis. chmn. 1996—, internat. affairs chmn. 1996—, Outstanding Woman of Yr. 1992, Gold Medal of Honor 1992), Northampton Country Club (Niners' Golf chmn. 1957-91), Women's Golf Assn. (constn. and bylaws chmn., parliamentarian 1960-92). Republican. Episcopalian. Home: 110 Upper Shawnee Ave Easton PA 18042-1356

STIVER, PATRICIA ABARE, elementary education educator; b. Plattsburgh, N.Y., Nov. 17, 1941; d. Joseph LaBarge and Janet Marcella (Downs) Abare. BA, SUNY, Fredonia, 1964; MS, SUNY, Albany, 1988. Cert. elem. educator N.Y. Tchr. elem. Randolph (N.Y.) Ctrl. Sch., 1964-66; tchr. elem. Schoharie (N.Y.) Ctrl. Schs., 1966-86, asst. elem. math. coord., 1986—, remedial math. tchr., 1986—, coord. elem. computer assisted instrn., 1986-90. Mem. ASCD, Nat. Coun. Tchrs. Math., Assn. Math. Tchrs. of N.Y. State, N.Y. State United Tchrs. and Affiliates. Democrat. Home: 107 Brookside Pl PO Box 121 Schoharie NY 12157-0121 Office: Schoharie Ctrl Sch Main St Schoharie NY 12157

STIVERSON, MARY ELLEN, elementary education educator; b. Bklyn., Dec. 31, 1943; d. Thomas and Helen (Goss) Hancock; 1 child, Anna Jorgensen Edwards. BA in Elem. Edn./Remedial Reading, U. No. Iowa, Cedar Falls, 1979; MS in Adminstrn., Creighton U., 1989. Tchr. 8th and 9th grade math. Edison Jr. H.S., Council Bluffs (Iowa) Pub. Schs., 1979-80; tchr. 7th and 8th grade math., sci. and reading Immaculate Conception Sch., Omaha, 1980-85; tchr. reading Bryan Jr. High Omaha Pub. Schs., 1985-86; tchr. 5th-6th grades and chpt. I reading Belvedere Elem. Sch., 1986-93; tchr. 6th grade Rosehill Elem. Sch. Omaha Pub. Schs., 1993-96; cons. Ready-Let's Read, Omaha, 1994; mem. assessment team Nebr. Math./Sci. Frameworks, Lincoln, 1994; cons. test validation bd. for profl. tchg. stamdards Nat. Profl. Standards Bd., Charlottesville, Va., 1994; membership chair, bd. dirs. Met. Reading Coun., 1986-90; adminstrv. intern Benson W. Elem. Sch., 1996—. Vol. Nebr. Dem. Party, 1990—. Recipient Pres.'s award Internat. Reading Assn., 1989. Mem. NEA (assembly rep.), Nebr. Edn. Assn. (del.), Omaha Edn. Assn. (bd. dirs. 1993-95, chair OEA/PAC 1992-95), Kappa Kappa Iota (Iota state sec. 1994-96). Roman Catholic. Office: Benson West Elem Sch 6652 Maple St Omaha NE 68104

STIX, SALLY ANN, lawyer; b. Cin., Jan. 1, 1950; d. Charles Nathan and Marjory Ann (Hauenstein) S.; m. Michael F. McDermott, May 4, 1985; 1 child, Emily. BA, U. Wis., Madison, 1974; JD, Ill. Inst. Tech., Chgo., 1979. Bar: Ill. 1979, U.S. Supreme Ct. 1990, Wis. 1993. Pvt. practice Chgo., 1980-93, Madison, 1993—. Pres. Mazomanie (Wis.) Barracudas Swim Team, 1995-96. Mem. Nat. Employment Lawyers Assn., Nat. Lawyers Guild, State Bar Wis., Legal Assn. for Women, AFL-CIO Lawyers Coordinating Coun. Office: 122 W Washington Ste 804 Madison WI 53703

STOCK, ANN, federal official; m. Stuart C. Stock; 1 child. Grad., Purdue U. Dep. press sec. to V.p. Walter F. Mondale, 1980, 84; regional dir. pub. rels. Bloomingdales Dept. Stores, 1982-85, dir. br. stores, 1986-87, v.p. pub. rels., 1988-93; spl. asst. to Pres. and Social Sec. The White House, Washington, 1993—. Mem. Capital Children's Mus. (co-founder), The Women's Forum, N.Y. Fashion Group (former program chmn.), Washington Woman Roundtable (founder), "Race for the Cure" (co-founder). Office: Office of the First Lady 1600 Pennsylvania Ave NW Washington DC 20500

STOCK, MARGOT THERESE, nurse, anthropologist, consultant, educator; b. Toronto, Ont., Can., Aug. 10, 1936; Arrived in US 1967.; d. Karl Dwight and Marguerite Anne (Lafitte) K.; m. Philip Anthony, Jan. 11, 1946; children: Dwight, Scott, Kayler, Travis & Anthony (twins) Sean. AAS, Suffolk County Com. Coll., Selden, N.Y., 1981; BS in Nursing, U. S. Fla., Ft. Myers, Fla., 1983; MS in Nursing, U. Tex., 1984; DPhil in Social Anthropology, U. Oxford, England, 1989. Nurse Sarasota Meml. Hosp., Fla., 1981-82, LW Blake Meml. Hosp., Bradenton, Fla., 1982-83, Med. Center Del Oro, Houston, 1983-85, Pitt County Meml. Hosp., Greenville, N.C.; asst. prof. E. Carolina U., Greenville, N.C., 1985-89; Cons. Gerontol. Nursing Network Greensboro N.C. Designer Game and Software (computer), Nursing Math Made Easy, Understanding Mgmt., Teaching Nursing Theory 1984; Author (with others) Book Clinical Pharmacology & Nursing 1987, Poetry Evolution Lycidas Jaso 1980-87. Mem. AAUW, Sigma Theta Tau, Sigma Kappa Found. (Houston Sigma Kappa award), Phi Theta Kappa (pres. 1981). Roman Catholic. Home: 118 Old London Rd Greenville NC 27834-8833 Office: East Carolina U Sch of Nursing Greenville NC 27858-4353

STOCK, MAXINE, sculptor, librarian, art therapist; b. Benton Harbor, Mich., June 17, 1933; d. Laurence James and Gertrude Frances (Drake) S.; m. Allen Neil Kimmerly, Aug. 25, 1951 (div. Sept. 1976); children: Melissa, Allen Neil II, Eliza, Christopher Stock. Diploma, U. Chgo., 1951; BS in Art Edn., Andrews U., 1970; MFA, U. Notre Dame, 1975; MSLS, Atlanta U., 1986. Cert. libr., Ga.; cert. art tchr. grades K-12, Ga., Mich. Supportive svcs. art therapy Martin Luther King Elem., Benton Harbor, 1970-72; tchg. asst. studio art and art history U. Notre Dame, Ind., 1973-75; exec. dir. Southeastern Sch. Creative Edn., Tifton, Ga., 1977-81; art therapist, cons., pvt. practice 6 Ga. Psychoedn. Ctrs., 1978-85; regional circulation libr. Brunswick (Ga.)-Glynn Regional Libr., 1984-93; ext. svcs. libr. Okefenokee Regional Libr. Sys., Waycross, Ga., 1993—; art therapist, bibliotherapy Artshouse, St. Simons Island, Ga., 1981—; artist-in-residence Mich. Fine Arts Coun., 1976, Ga. Coun. for the Arts, 1979; studio pottery tchr., therapist Coastal Ctr. for the Arts, St. Simons Island, 1981—. One-woman shows include St. Marys Coll., South Bend, Ind., 1974, Okefenokee Heritage Ctr., Waycross, 1994; groups shows Avery Fisher Hall, Womenart Gallery, N.Y.C., 1979. Intern Program grantee Nat. Endowment for the Arts, 1977. Mem. Am. Art Therapy Assn., Beta Phi Mu. Bahai. Office: Okefenokee Regional Libr Sys 401 Lee St Waycross GA 31501

STOCK, PEGGY A(NN), college president, educator; b. Jan. 30, 1936; married; 5 children. BS in Psychology, St. Lawrence U., 1957; MA in Counseling, U. Ky., 1963, EdD, 1969. Lic. psychologist, Ohio. Instr., research asst. dept. psychology and spl. edn. U. Ky., Lexington, 1958-59, 63-67, staff psychologist Med. Ctr., 1964-66; dir. edn. United Cerebral Palsy of the Bluegrass, Lexington, 1959-61; exec. dir. Community Council for Physically Handicapped and Mentally Retarded, Lexington, 1962-64; dir. clin. program No. Ky. Regional Community Mental Health Ctr., Covington, 1969-71; pres. Midwest Inst. Tng. and Edn., Cin., 1971-76; assoc. prof., counseling psychologist Mont. State U., Bozeman, 1975-77, asst. dean Office of Student Affairs and Service, 1977-79; spl. asst. to pres. U. Hartford, Conn., 1979-80, assoc. prof. Coll. of Edn., 1980-85, v.p. adminstrn., 1981-86; prof., pres. Colby-Sawyer Coll., New London, N.H., 1986-95; pres. Westminster Coll. of Salt Lake City, 1995—; vis. prof. dept. sociology and edn. Thomas Moore Coll., Fort Mitchell, Ky., 1970-71; panelist Nat. Inst. Edn., 1985; cons. and lectr. in field. Contbr. chpts. to books, articles to profl. jours. Mem. coun. N.H. Coll. and Univ.; nat. bd. dirs. Med. Coll. Pa.; mem. New London Bus. Adv. Bd.; active numerous other civic orgns. Recipient Disting. Alumna award St. Lawrence U., 1989; grantee in field, most recent George I. Alden Trust, Helen Fuld Health Trust, Surdna, Cogswell, U.S. Dept. Edn., 1981-89, numerous others; fellow U. Ky., 1966-68, Am. Council Edn., 1979-80, United Jewish Com., 1981. Mem. Am. Coun. on Edn., Am. Assn. for Higher Edn., Advancement Women in Higher Edn. Office: Westminster Coll Salt Lake City 1840 South 1300 East Salt Lake City UT 84105-3597

STOCKAR, HELENA MARIE MAGDALENA, artist; b. Bratislava, Czechoslovakia, Mar. 22, 1933; came to the U.S., 1968; d. Arnost J. and Helen R. (Strakova) Kubasek; m. Ivo J. Stockar, Oct. 31, 1959; children: David, Laura Bates. Diploma, Graficka Skola, Prague, 1952, Music Conservatory, Prague, 1954. Piano tchr. Music Sch., Prague, 1954-68; company pianist State Ballet/Breacrest Sch., R.I., 1968-74; piano tchr. Music Tchr. Assn., R.I., 1968-86. One-woman shows include Warwick Mus., R.I., 1986, Brown U., Providence, 1987, Westerly Art Gallery, R.I., 1987, Westerly Art Gallery/Morin-Miller, 1988, 89, Galerie Horizon, Paris, 1989, others; two-woman exhibit R.I. State Com. of Nat. Mus. of Women in the Arts, Triboro Studio, R.I., 1995; exhibited in group shows at World Congress of Czechoslovak Soc. of Art and Sci., Washington, 1988, Morin-Miller Internat., N.Y.C., 1989, Ariel Gallery, Soho, N.Y.C., 1989, Art Expo N.Y.C., 1989, R.I. State Com. Nat. Mus. Women Arts, 1995, Providence Art Club, 1996, others; represented in permanent collections around the world; featured on numerous TV shows. Recipient Second prize Nat. Competition of Children's Book Illustration, Prague, 1965; named finalist Internat. Art Competition, L.A., 1984. Mem. Nat. Mus. of Women in the Arts (R.I. state com.), Czechoslovak Soc. of Art and Sci., Music Club Providence, Chopin Club Providence, Schubert Club Providence, Chaminade Club Providence. Office: PO Box 7282 Warwick RI 02887-7282

STOCKBAR, LINDA LOUISE, counselor; b. Joliet, Ill.; d. John Joseph and Lillian Lucille (Long) S. BS in Edn., Ea. Ill. U., 1968, MS in Edn., 1974. Educator Kankakee (Ill.) Sch. Dist., 1969—. Bd. dirs. Kankakee Valley Theater, 1970—; past v.p. Kankakee Cmty. Arts Coun., 1976. Mem. ASCD, Am. Fedn. Tchrs., Ill. Counseling Assn. Home: 25 Old Farm North Ct Bradley IL 60915-1438 Office: Kankakee HS 1200 W Jeffery St Kankakee IL 60901-4667

STOCKDALE, KAY LITTLE, librarian; b. Ft. Jackson, S.C., Nov. 3, 1942; d. Edward Earl and Hazel Appie (Price) Little; m. Dennis LeRoy Stockdale, June 27, 1965; 1 child, Lee. BA, Barton Coll., 1965; MLS, U. Ala. Tuscaloosa, 1972; postgrad., U. N.C. Greensboro. Tchr. English North Johnston H.S., Kenly, N.C., 1965-66, Greene Ctrl. H.S., Snow Hill, N.C., 1966-68, Druid H.S., Tuscaloosa, Ala., 1968-69; dir. Ridgecrest area program U. Ala. Tuscaloosa, 1969-71; tchr. English Stillman Coll., Tuscaloosa, Ala., 1971-72; libr. Hist. Found. Presbyn. Ch. U.S., Montreat, N.C., 1972-88; libr. C.D. Owen H.S., Swannanoa, N.C., 1988-91, Accelerated Learning Ctr., Asheville, N.C., 1994—. Contbr. articles to profl. jours. Mem. AAUW (pres. Tuscaloosa chpt. 1970-72, v.p. Ala. divsn. 1972, bd. dirs. N.C. divsn. 1975-80), NEA, N.C. Assn. Educators, N.C. Libr. Assn., Sierra Club. Home: 33 Rainbow Ridge Swannanac NC 28778 Office: Accelerated Learning Ctr 441 Haywood St Asheville NC 28806

STOCKER, BEATRICE, speech pathologist; b. N.Y.C., Nov. 20, 1909; d. Tobias and Ida (Weinstein) Klipstein; m. Jule E. Stocker, Mar. 26, 1932; children: Maida Stocker Abrams, Michael. BA, Barnard Coll., 1931; MA, Columbia U., 1937. Adminstrv. asst. Speech and Hearing Ctr. Queens Coll. CUNY, 1949-78, lectr., 1968-78; pvt. practice N.Y.C., 1978—; cons. in field. Author: Stocker Probe Technique for Diagnosis and Treatment of Stuttering in Young Children, 1976, rev. 3rd edit. (with Robert Goldfarb), 1995. Axe-Houghton Found. grantee, 1973, CUNY Rsch. Found. grantee, 1971—. Mem. AAUP, Am. Speech, Lang. and Hearing Assn. (cert. clin. competence in speech and audiology), N.Y. State Speech, Lang. and Hearing Assn. (honoree 1994), N.Y.C. Speech, Lang. and Hearing Assn. (honoree 1990). Home and Office: 17 W 54th St New York NY 10019-5412

STOCKER, JOYCE ARLENE, retired secondary school educator; b. West Wyoming, Pa., May 13, 1931; d. Donald Arthur and Elizabeth Mae (Gardner) Saunders; m. Robert Earl Stocker, Nov. 26, 1953; children: Desiree Lee Stocker Stackhouse, Rebecca Lois Stocker Genelow, Joyce Elizabeth Stocker Scrobola. Grad. cum laude, Coll. Misericordia, Dallas, 1953; Master's equivalency diploma, Pa. Dept. Edn., 1991. Cert. tchr., Pa. Tchr. music and lang. arts West Pittston (Pa.) Sch. Dist., 1953-60; tchr. music and choral Wyoming Area Sch. Dist., Exeter, Pa., 1970-78, tchr. English composition, 1978-93, chmn. lang. arts dept., 1982-90, dir. nat. history day activities, 1982-93; state cons. Nat. History Day, 1996—. Organist, choir dir. United Meth. Ch., Wyo., 1958—; choir dir. Wyo. Centenial Choir, Wyo., 1983; mem. com., sec. Continuing Profl. Devel. Com. Pa., Exeter, 1988-93, Long Range Plan Wyo. Area Sch. Dist., Exeter, 1990-91; tutor, judge Nat. History Day; judge regional, state, and nat. events for Nat. History Day. Recipient DAR Tchr. of Yr. award, 1992-93, Wilkes U., 1990; named Outstanding Educator, Times Leader, 1993. Mem. NEA, Pa. Edn. Assn., Wyo. Edn. Assn., N.E. Pa. Writing Coun., Nat. Coun. Tchrs. English, Women Educators Internat., Orgn. Am. History, Pa. Music Educators Assn., Music Educators Nat. Coun., Nat. Coun. Social Studies, Pa. Assn. Sch. Retirees, Pa. Sch. Employees Retirement Sys., Pa. Retired Pub. Sch. Employees Assn. (Luzerne-Wyoming counties chpt.), Pa. Coun. Social Studies, Delta Kappa Gamma (recording sec. 1991—), Phi Mu Gamma. Methodist. Office: Wyoming Area Sch Dist 20 Memorial St Exeter PA 18643-2659

STOCKLIN, ALICE MARLENE, author, retired nurse; b. Mt. Vernon, Wis., June 1, 1919; d. Nicklas and Katherine (Thoni) Engelbert; m. Walter Lincoln, Nov. 14, 1942 (dec. May 1974). 3-yr. nurse's diploma, Wis. Med. Sch., Madison, 1938. Pvt. nurse various pvt. patients, various cities, 1939-42. Author: My Stroke, My Blessing, 1990; co-author: Road Ahead, 1988; contbr. articles, stories and poems to various jours. Vol. nurse 1942-72. Republican. Home: Canterbury Gardens #159 11265 E Mississippi Ave Aurora CO 80012

STOCKLIN, ALMA KATHERINE, retired public relations consultant; b. New London, Conn., May 9, 1926; d. Stephen Sullivan and Theresa Catherine (Flynn) Sheehan; m. Philip L. Stocklin, Jan. 28, 1950 (div. 1984); children: Brian, Christopher, Virginia Katherine, Walter, Stephen. Student, U. Conn., 1945-46, Conn. Coll., 1946; cert., Sch. Modern Photography, N.Y.C., 1948; AA, Charter Oak Coll., 1979; BA cum laude, Eastern Conn. State U., 1981. Advt. photographer GE, Bridgeport, Conn., 1948-49; chmn. Conn. PTA State Juvenile Protection, 1959; pub. rels. cons. Norwich and Groton, Conn., 1983-86; asst. to dean Ea. Conn. State U., Willimantic, 1984-91, ret., 1991; adminstr. br. office U.S. Submarine Base Ea. Conn. State U.,

Groton, 1984-91; pub. rels. cons., 1994—; coord. videotape courses for submarines, New London, 1984-91. Founder, chmn. bd. dirs. Newport (R.I.) Holiday for Sr. Citizens, 1972, Uncas on Thames Conn. State Hosp. Aux., 1978; mem. Norwich Harbor Day Com., 1982-83, Catchment Area coun. 11 S.E. Coun. Mental Health Bd., 1989-90, Norwich Regional Mental Health Adv. Bd., 1987-90, Norwich Stae Hosp. Adv. Bd., 1987-89; vice chair Ea. Conn. Regional Mental Health Bd., 1988-89; founder, chmn. Norwich Nuclear Freeze Com., 1982; bd. dirs. Ea. Conn. Symphony Orch., New London, 1984-87, Friend of the Symphony, 1987-90, Laurel Glen, Groton, 1984-91; co-founder, bd. dirs. Newport Ch. Cmty. Housing Corp., 1969-72; founder, chmn. Holiday for Sr. Citizens, Newport R.I., 1972; chair Conn. State PTA Juvenile Protection, 1957; founder, pres. Cath. Mother's Cir., Dorset, Eng., 1962; exec. sec. Overnight Shelter, Loughborough, Eng., 1973-74; founder, chair Bicycle Paths for Schoolchildren, Loughborough, 1974; bd. dirs. Friends of the Fairfield County Dist. Libr., Lancaster, Ohio, 1994—; mem. St. Bernadette's Parish Coun., 1994—. Recipient award for outstanding svc. in founding the Newport Holiday for Sr. Citizens, City of Newport, 1972, award for outstanding svc. Pres. of Conn. PTAs. Mem. Fairfield County (Conn.) Respiratory Disease and TB Assn. (bd. dirs. 1991-95), Friends of Libr. Assn. Fairfield County Dist. (bd. dirs. 1994—), Nat. Alliance for the Mentally Ill, Phi Beta Phi, Conn. Alpha Pi Beta Phi. Democrat. Roman Catholic.

STOCKWELL, CATHERINE (KAY STOCKWELL), lawyer; b. Virginia Beach, Va., Aug. 18, 1967. BA cum laude, Duke U., 1989; JD, U. Va., 1992. Bar: N.Y. 1993, U.S. Dist. Ct. (so. and ea. dists.) N.Y. 1993, D.C. 1994. Ptnr. Anderson Kill Olick and Oshinsky, P.C., N.Y.C. Mem. ABA, N.Y. State Bar Assn., D.C. Bar Assn. Office: Anderson Kill Olick & Oshinsky PC 1251 Ave of the Americas New York NY 10020-1182*

STOCKWELL, VIVIAN ANN, nursing educator; b. Hardy, Ark., Apr. 26, 1943; d. Belvin L. and Armilda L. (Langston) Cooper; m. R.D. Sneed, Mar. 16, 1963 (div. Jan. 1981); m. Homer E. Stockwell, Jan. 6, 1990; 1 child, Sherilyn. Diploma, St. Luke's Sch. Nursing, Kansas City, Mo., 1964; BS in Nursing summa cum laude, Avila Coll., Kansas City, 1987. Staff nurse operating rm. North Kansas City (Mo.) Hosp., 1972-76; pvt. scrub nurse Van M. Robinson, MD, North Kansas City, 1976-81; instr. health occupations Independence (Mo.) Pub. Schs., 1981-85; instr. Park Coll., Parkville, Mo., 1987-89, asst. to dir. dept. nursing, 1989-90. Ch. sch. tchr. Independence Blvd. Christian Ch., 1976-87, deacon, 1979-88, elder, 1988—; pres. Christian Women's Fellowship, 1994—; mem. adult adv. bd. NCK Assembly, Internat. Order of Rainbow for Girls, 1983-94. Mem. Assn. Operating Rm. Nurses, Am. Vocat. Assn., Mo. Vocat. Assn., Order Eastern Star, Sigma Theta Tau, Kappa Gamma Pi, Delta Epsilon Sigma.

STODDARD, SANDOL, writer; b. Birmingham, Ala., Dec. 16, 1927; d. Carlos French and Caroline (Harris) S.; m. Felix M. Warburg (div. 1966); children: Anthony, Peter, Gerald, Jason; m. Peter R. Goethals, May 1, 1984. BA magna cum laude, Bryn Mawr Coll., 1959. Author 26 books including: Growing Time, 1971, The Doubleday Children's Bible, 1983 (Lewis citation 1983), The Hospice Movement: Updated and Expanded Edition, 1992, Prayers, Praises and Thanksgivings, 1992. Bd. dirs., co-founder Hospice of Kona, Kailua-Kona, Hawaii, 1985; co-founder Kona Theol. Inst., 1990; bd. dirs. Choice in Dying, N.Y.C. Recipient Humanitarian Svc. award Forbes Health System, 1979, Notable Book award Am. Libr. Assn., 1964. Mem. AAUW, Nat. Writer's Guild, Cosmpolitan Club. Democrat. Episcopalian. Home and Office: 78-6646 Mamalahoa Hwy Holualoa HI 96725-9734

STODDART, VERONICA GOULD, periodical editor-in-chief; b. Bogotá, Colombia, Nov. 1, 1948; d. Juan Benedict Gould and Rose Arlene (Wall) Rodman; married (div. Jan. 1995); children: Shauna Irene, Kyra Theresa, Kristin Anna. BA, Wellesley Coll., 1970. Stringer Time-Life News Svc., Niamey, Niger, West Africa, 1970-71; rsch. asst. Harvard U., Cambridge, Mass., 1971-72; publs. asst. Ptnrs. of the Americas, Washington, 1973-74; assoc. editor Americas Mag., OAS, Washington, 1974-82, travel and art editor, 1982-85; consulting editor Nat. Geographic Soc., Washington, 1985-86; editor-in-chief Caribbean Travel & Life, Inc., Silver Spring, Md., 1986-96. Recipient Citation nomination, Magazine Week, N.Y.C., 1990, Publishing Excellence award, 1991; recipient Silver award Best Mag. Cover, Folio Mag., N.Y., 1992, Bronze award Best Mag. Design, 1992, Marcia Vickery-Wallace award for Excellence in Travel Journalism, 1996. Mem. Am. Soc. Mag. Editors, Soc. Am. Travel Writers (Ben Carruthers award 1986, Lowell Thomas award 1984, 88, 89, 90, 91, 92, 93. Office: Caribbean Travel & Life 8403 Colesville Rd #830 Silver Spring MD 20910

STOECKL, SHELLEY JOAN, marketing professional; b. Buffalo, Feb. 24, 1951; d. Joseph T. and Joan (Carriere) S. AAS in Bus. Adminstrn., Bryant-Stratton Bus. Inst., 1978; cert. in gen. banking, Am. Inst. Banking, 1982; cert. in pers. & human resource mgmt., Canisius Coll., 1983; postgrad., Empire State Coll. Cert. profl. sec. Sr. sec. Mfrs. Hanover Trust Co., Buffalo, 1974-79, exec. sec., 1979-82, pers. asst., 1982-84, pers. mgr., 1984-87; account coord. Computer Task Group Direct Mktg. Svcs., Buffalo, 1987-89; project mgr. ANCOR Info. Mgmt., Inc., Buffalo, 1989-91; account mgr. IMPCO Integrated Mktg. Ptnrs., Buffalo, 1991—. Co-author: (presentation) Go For the Gold: CPS, 1983—; coord.: 60 Minutes: A Look Inside the Inst. for Certifying Secs., 1991, Marketing Your Credentials to Management, 1992. Co. coord. United Way, Buffalo, 1980-87; vol. Jack Kemp for Congress, Buffalo, 1970. Recipient scholastic award Buffalo Clearing House Assn., 1982. Fellow Cert. Profl. Secs. Acad.; mem. NAFE, Profl. Secs. Internat. (bd. dirs. 1980-82, v.p. 1982-83, corr. sec. 1983-85, pres. 1986-87), Cert. Profl. Secs. Soc. N.Y. State (pres. 1987-88), Inst. for Cert. (rep. N.E. dist. 1988-94), Toastmasters. Conservative. Roman Catholic. Home: 239 Wimbledon Ct Buffalo NY 14224-1955 Office: IMPCO Integrated Mktg Ptnrs 29 Depot St Buffalo NY 14206-2203

STOHLMAN, CONNIE SUZANNE, obstetrical gynecological nurse; b. Tucson, Sept. 27, 1960; d. Irvin Wendell and Betty Jo (Stewart) Holmes; m. Bruce R. Stohlman, Sept. 14, 1991. BSN, Bishop Clarkson Coll. Nursing, 1987; BA, U. Nebr., 1982; cert. med. asst., Omaha Coll. Health Careers, 1983. Primary nurse I U. Md. Med. System, Balt., 1987-90; staff nurse St. Joseph Hosp., Omaha, 1990—; mem. quality assurance task force U. Md. Med. System, 1987-90; mem. quality assurance com. St. Joseph Hosp., 1992—. Named to Outstanding Young Women of Am., 1986.

STOHS, DEBRA ANN, primary education educator; b. Smith Center, Kans., Aug. 18, 1953; d. Oren M. and Velda N. (Johnson) Christy; m. Dave E. Stohs, Mar. 26, 1978; children: Michel, Jennifer, Andrea. BS in Edn., Fort Hays State U., 1974, MS in Spl. Edn., 1977. Cert. elem. edn., spl. edn., educable mentally handicapped, trainable mentally handicapped, behavior disorders, reading specialist. Spl. edn. trainable mentally handicapped Twin Lakes Ednl. Coop., Clay Center, Kans., 1975-81; tchr. grades 1 and 2 Bremen (Kans.) Luth. Sch., 1981-83, 85-86; title I reading tchr. USD #364, Marysville, Kans., 1983-84; tchr. grade 3 inclusion classroom USD #364, Marysville, 1986—. Mem. NEA, Nat. Coun. Tchrs. English, Coun. for Exceptional Children, Internat. Reading Assn. Home: 867 2nd Rd Bremen KS 66412-8630 Office: USD #364 1010 Carolina St Marysville KS 66508-1680

STOKELY, JOAN BARBARA, elementary school educator; b. Cleve., May 6, 1945; d. Paul Warner and Florence Leona (Sorensen) S. BS, Lamar U., 1967, M Elem. Edn., 1970. Cert. tchr., adminstr., Tex. 4th grade tchr. Vidor (Tex.) Ind. Sch. Dist., 1967-74, 88-94, 5th grade tchr., 1974-77, 7th and 8th grade tchr., 1979-88; grad. equivalency diploma tchr. Beaumont Ind. Sch. Dist., Vidor, 1977-81. Pres. Vidor Tchrs. Fed. Credit Union, 1985—; mem. troop com. Boy Scouts Am., Vidor, 1972-83; tchr. Roman Cath. Chs., Beaumont, Tex., 1967-87. Mem. AAUW, DAR, Am. Bus. Women Assn. (Vocat./Woman of Yr., chmn. 1977-78), Tex. State Tchrs. Assn. (pres. Vidor chpt. 1990-94, chmn. uniserve adv. coun. region 15 1991-92, sec. region 15 1993—), Tex. Computer Edn. Assn., Colonial Dames. Office: Oak Forest Elem Sch 2400 Highway 12 Vidor TX 77662-3403

STOKES, (GLADYS) ALLISON, pastor, researcher, religion educator; b. Bridgeport, Conn., Aug. 17, 1942; d. Hugh Vincent and Mildred Roberta (Livengood) Allison; m. Jerome Walter Stokes, June 1, 1964 (div. 1977); children: Jonathan Jerome, Anne Jennings. BA, U. N.C., 1964; MPhil, Yale U., 1976, PhD, 1981, MDiv, 1981. Ordained to ministry United Ch. of Christ, 1981. Acting univ. min. Wesleyan U., Middletown, Conn., 1981; assoc. pastor Orange Congl. Ch., Conn., 1981-82; chaplain, asst. prof. religion Vassar Coll., Poughkeepsie, N.Y., 1982-85; assoc. univ. chaplain Yale U., New Haven, 1985-87; pastor Congl. Ch., West Stockbridge, Mass., 1987—; rsch. assoc. Hartford (Conn.) Sem., 1987-92; founding dir. Women's Interfaith Inst. in the Berkshires, 1992—; bd. dirs. Dutchess Interfaith Coun., Poughkeepsie, 1984-85; clk., bd. dirs. Gould Farm, Monterey, Mass., 1992—. Author: Ministry after Freud, 1985; co-author: Defecting in Place, 1994, Women Pastors, 1995, Finding Time, Finding Energy, 1996; contbr. articles to profl. jours. Kanzer Fund Psychoanalysis and Humanities grantee, 1977; AAUW fellow, 1978, Merrill fellow Harvard Div. Sch., 1994. Mem. Am. Acad. Religion, Berkshire Conf. Women Historians, Kiwanis. Home: PO Box 422 Housatonic MA 01236-0422 Office: Conregational Church 45 Main St West Stockbridge MA 01266

STOKES, ANNE DOROTHY, retired education professional; b. Elyria, Ohio, Nov. 29, 1928; d. Edgar Pier and Dorothy Anne (Day) Gates; m. Kenneth Irving Stokes, June 30, 1951; children: Alan, Randall, Bradley, Harlan. BA, Oberlin (Ohio) Coll., 1950; MEd, U. Fla., 1970, EdS, 1974, EdD, 1977. Cert. K-12 tchr., Minn.; lic. parent educator. Kdg. tchr. Elyria Pub. Schs., 1950-51, Hamden (Conn.) Pub. Schs., 1951-53; owner, tchr. Lads N Lassies Kdg., Glen Ellyn, Ill., 1961-65; trainer, cons. Head Start, Bradford and Putnam Cty., Fla., 1968-69; instr. U. Fla., Gainesville, 1968-72, curriculum developer, 1972-73; edn. dir. Palmer King Day Care, Gainesville, 1971-72; interim prof. U. Minn., Mpls., 1977-78, Concordia Coll., St. Paul, 1986; coord. early childhood family edn. St. Louis Park (Minn.) Schs., 1979—; sec. evaluation com. Minn. State Family Edn. Resources of Minn., Dept. Edn., 1986—; cons., spkr. schs. and chs.; bd. dirs. Bell Nursery Sch. Project, Gainesvvile, 1970-73; mem. ethics com. Minn. Coun. of Family Rels., 1991—. Author: The Thinking Parent, 1993, Career Education Manual for Teachers and Supervisors, 1976; contbr. articles to profl. jours. Informal lobbyist Early Childhood Family Edn., Minn. State Capitol. Career Growth fellowship Bush Found. U. Minn., 1983; fellowship U. Fla., 1969. Mem. ASCD, Assn. for Childhood Edn. Internat., Minn. Coun. on Family Rels., Nat. Assn. for Edn. of Young Children, Phi Kappa Phi, Pi Lambda Theta. Mem. United Ch. of Christ. Home: 9709 Rich Rd Bloomington MN 55437-2025

STOKES, DEBORAH ANN, special education educator, consultant; b. Boulder, Colo., Nov. 14, 1951; m. Robert D. Stokes, July 27, 1978; children: Tamsen, Jay. BS, U. No. Colo., 1973, Masters, 1976. Juvenile counselor Araphahoe Youth Ctr., Denver, 1973-74; spl. edn. tchr. Jefferson County Schs., Golden, Colo., 1976-90, Evergreen, Lakewood, Colo., 1991-92; ednl. cons. Jefferson County Schs., Arvada, Colo., 1992—; advisor Regis U., Denver, 1994. Cons. (pamphlet) Parent to Parent, 1993. Mem. Coun. of Exceptional Children, Internat. Reading Assn.

STOKES, ROBERTA ANNE, clinical nurse specialist, manager; b. Phila.; d. Robert Thomas and Anne Louise (Kurtz) Park; children: Tracey Jane, Suzanne Lee. ADN, Lakeland Community Coll., Mentor, Ohio, 1972; BSN, Ursuline Coll. Ctr. for Nursing, 1983; MSN, Case Western Res. U., 1987. Cert. clin. specialist gerontology nursing ANCC; cert. hemodialysis nurse Bd. Nephrology Examiners; cert. nephrology nurse Nephrology Nursing Cert. Bd. With Cleve. Clinic Found., 1972—, clin. instr. acute hemodialysis, 1985-87, nurse educator transition care, 1987-93; clin. faculty Frances Payne Bolton Sch. Nursing Case Western Res. U., Cleve., 1990—; del. nephrology nursing del. Citizen Amb. Program, Berlin, Budapest, Hungary, Prague, Czech Republic, Moscow, 1991; mem. advanced practice coun. divsn. patient care ops. Cleve. Clinic Found., 1994—; presenter in field of nephrology nursing topics. Author: Competency-Based Orientation Manual for Hemodialysis Nursing, 1991; editor Cleve. Clinic Nurse jour. Cleve. Clinic Found., 1992-94, mem. editl. bd., 1994-95; contbr. articles to profl. jours., chpt. to books. Recipient Emma Barr Excellence in Clin. Practice award, 1990; Stewart fellow, 1991-92; Fenn scholar Greater Cleve. Citizens League for Nursing, 1970-71, 71-72, 82-83. Mem. ANA, Ohio Nurses Assn. (Vol. Recognition awards 1989, 91, 93, 95), Greater Cleve. Nurses Assn., Am. Nephrology Nurses Assn. (AMGEN Ednl. scholar 1990, 1st pl. writing award 1991, chpt. coord. elect North Ctrl. Region 1992-93, chpt. coord. 1993-94, continuing edn. approval bd. 1990-93, manuscript rev. panel jour. 1993-95, asst. editor 1995—, program com. clin. concerns 1995), Sigma Theta Tau (Alpha Mu chpt. 1987—, corr. sec. 1988-90, newsletter editor 1989-92, Iota Psi chpt. 1988-94, Media Print award 1990). Home: 246 Hawthorne Dr Chagrin Falls OH 44022-3326 Office: Cleve Clinic Found 9500 Euclid Ave Cleveland OH 44195-0001

STOKES, ROSA, educational administrator; 1 child from previous marriage, Kellé Marie; m. James Milton Stokes. BS in Sociology and Social Work, Morgan State U., Balt., 1971; MS in Spl. Edn., Coppin State U., Balt., 1983; postgrad., Johns Hopkins U., 1992—. Cert. in advanced studies, evaluation, group process and leadership advanced proficiency, Md. Med. social worker Balt. City Hosp., 1971-73; salesperson Equitable Life Assurance Soc., Balt., 1977-79; tchr. Balt. City Pub. Schs., 1985-92, asst. prin. J. Briscoe Sch., 1992—, coord. Project Respond, 1992-94, exec. dir. Project Respond, 1994—; mem. adv. bd. Project Succeed, Balt., 1990-92, Project Raise, Morgan State U., 1991-92; cons. Family Preservation Initiative, Balt., 1994—. Coord. bicentennial N.W. Area Ctrl. Md., Girl Scouts U.S.A., Balt., 1976; sec. Jack and Jill, Balt., 1991-93; advisor Balt. State U.-Friends Sch., 1992-94. Mem. ASCD, NEA, Pub. Sch. Tchrs. Am., Balt. City Internat. Reading Assn., NAACP, Phi Delta Kappa.

STOLL, LOUISE FRANKEL, federal official; b. N.Y.C., June 6, 1939; d. Abraham H. and Ruth C. (Flexo) Frankel; m. Marc H. Monheimer, Dec. 22, 1978; children: Miriam F., Malaika S., Abraham D. BA, MA in Philosophy with honors, U. Chgo., 1961; PhD, U. Calif., Berkeley, 1978. High sch. English tchr. Nairobi, Kenya, 1964-65; trustee Berkeley Unified Sch. Dist., 1971-78; mgr. govt. affairs Clear Water Program San Francisco, 1978-80, budget dir. Pub. Utilities Commn., 1980-85; sr. v.p., No. Calif. regional mgr. O'Brien-Kreitzberg and Assoc., Inc., San Francisco, 1985-93; CFO and asst. sec. budget and programs Office of Sec. Dept. Transp., Washington, 1993—; mem. Nat. Legal Affairs Com., Mid. East Com. of Anti-Defamation League of B'nai B'rith. Active Anti-Defamation League of B'nai B'rith. Recipient Mayor's Fiscal Adv. award, City of San Francisco, 1984. Jewish. Office: Office of Sec Dept Transp 400 7th St SW Rm 10101 Washington DC 20590

STOLLDORF, GENEVIEVE SCHWAGER, media specialist; b. Ames, N.Y., July 17, 1943; d. Herbert Blakely and Genevieve Agnes (Alessi) Schwager; m. John G. Stolldorf, June 25, 1972; 1 child, Nathan Schwager. AA, Auburn (N.Y.) C.C., 1963; BS, Murray State U., 1967; MA in Edn., Seton Hall U., 1975. Cert. libr. media specialist, social studies tchr. grades 7-12. Libr. So. Orangetown Schs., Orangeburg, N.Y., 1967-70; libr. media specialist Nanuet (N.Y.) Pub. Schs., 1970-78; tchr. social studies grade 9 Monroe (N.Y.)-Woodbury, 1978-80; libr. media specialist Nyack (N.Y.) Pub. Schs., 1981—. Reviewer Libr. Jour., 1981-90. Kykuit guide Hist. Hudson Valley, 1994—; active Friends of the Nyacks, Nyack. Mem. N.Y. Libr. Assn., N.Y. State United Tchrs., Sch. Libr. Media Specialists Southeastern N.Y., Nyack Tchr. Assn. (editor newsletter 1982-84), Tri-Town League Women Voters, C. of C. of the Nyacks (hon.). Office: Valley Cottage Elem Sch Lake Rd Valley Cottage NY 10989

STOLLER, PATRICIA SYPHER, structural engineer; b. Jackson Heights, N.Y., Dec. 16, 1947; d. Carleton Roy and Mildred Vivian (Ferron) Sypher; m. David A. Stoller Sr.; children: Stephanie Jean, Sheri Lynn. BSCE, Washington U., St. Louis, 1975; M in Mgmt., Northwestern U., 1989. R&D engr. Amcar div. ACF Industries, St. Charles, Mo., 1972-79; project engr. Truck Axle div. Rockwell Internat., Troy, Mich., 1979-81; sr. engr. ABB Impell, Norcross, Ga., 1981-83; supervising mgr., client mgr., div. mgr. ABB Impell, Lincolnshire, Ill., 1983—; dir. bus. devel., v.p. VECTRA (formerly ABB Impell), Lincolnshire, 1991-94; pres., CEO ASC Svcs. Co., LLC, Chgo., 1994—; Author computer program Quickpipe, 1983; numerous patents in field. Mem. CREW, YPO, ASCE, NAFE, Soc. Women Engrs., Am. Nuclear Soc. (exec. bd. Chgo. sect. 1991-93). Office: ASC Svcs Co LLC 300 W Washington St Ste 200 Chicago IL 60606-1720

STOLTMANN, NINA LAURETTA, marketing professional; b. Milw., Dec. 28, 1953; d. James Russell and Lola Margery (DeBruin) Von S.; m. John William Callahan, Feb. 14, 1995. Attended, MaComb County Coll., Warren, Mich., 1976; BA, U. Detroit, 1992. Cert. EMT. A/V technician Booth Cable, Birmingham, Mich., 1986-87; media svcs. tech., graphic artist U. of Detroit, 1987-90, adminstrv. asst., 1990-95; sr. mktg. rep. Danka Bus. Sys., Detroit, 1995—. Pub. rels. mgr. NOW, Detroit, 1994—; bd. dirs. PAC, 1995, ACLU, Mich., 1995—, Wayne County Women's Polit. Caucus. Mem. Detroit Prodrs. Assn., Alpha Sigma Nu. Home: 1300 E Lafayette # 1712 Detroit MI 48207 Office: Danka Bus Sys 1211 Trumbull Ave Detroit MI 48216

STOLZENBERG, PEARL, fashion designer; b. N.Y.C., Oct. 9, 1946; d. Irving and Anna (Shenkman) S. Student, Fashion Inst. Tech., 1964-66. Textile stylist, designer Forum Fabrics Ltd., N.Y.C., 1966-68; freelance ceiling designer Maxwell's Plum, N.Y.C., 1968; dir. styling Beauknit Corp., N.Y.C., 1969-74; stylist, designer Mi-Bru-San Co., Inc., N.Y.C., 1983-84; gen. mgr. Laissez-Faire Inc., N.Y.C., 1984-85; merchandiser prodn. The Clothing Acad. Inc., N.Y.C., 1986-87; v.p. String of Pearls Knitwear, Inc., N.Y.C., 1988—; pres. Pearl's Cutting Ltd., N.Y.C., 1994—; cons. Tam O'Shanter Textile Ltd., Montreal, 1974-79, Mitsui, Osaka, Japan, 1976-79, Sergio Valente English Town Sportswear, N.Y.C., 1980-84; cons. merchandiser The Fashion Acad., Hollywood Crossing, Inc., N.Y.C.; owner Josu Cutting Inc., Bklyn. Democrat. Jewish. Home: 8340 Austin St Apt 1E Jamaica NY 11415-1827 Office: Pearl's Cutting Ltd 410-W 16th St New York NY 10011-5891

STOMFAY-STITZ, ALINE MARIA, education educator; b. Newark, N.J.; d. Adolph and Irene (Badowska) Wegrocki; m. Emery Stomfay-Stitz; children: Peter, John, Robert. BA, Barnard Coll.; MA, Case Western Reserve U.; EdD, No. Ill. U., 1984. Asst. prof. Coll. St Scholastica, Duluth, Minn., 1984-85, St. Leo (Fla.) Coll., 1985-87, Nicholls State U., Thibodaux, La., 1989-91; assoc. prof. edn. Christopher Newport U., Newport News, Va., 1991-96; vis. assoc. prof. U. No. Fla., Jacksonville, 1996—; asst. editor Joun. Early Childhood Tchr. Edn. Author: Peace Education in America 1828-1990, 1993; author (book chpt.): Toward Education That is Multicultural, 1992, Multicultural Education for the 21st Century, 1993; contbr. articles to profl. jours. Mem. Am. Ednl. Rsch. Assn., Am. Psychological Assn., Consortium for Peace, Rsch. Edn. & Devel., Internat. Peace Rsch. Assn.

STONE, BONNIE M., artist, educator; b. Chgo., May 14, 1939; d. Laurence Joseph and Ruth (Brodsky) Melnick; m. M. Lee Stone; children: Barrie A., Rachel Stone Arriola, Benjamin J. BFA, U. Ill., 1960. Art tchr. Maine Twp. West H.S., Des Plaines, 1960-64, Ft. Riley (Kans.) Officer Wives Club, 1966-67, Grandin-Miller Sch., San Jose, Calif., 1968-69; vol. Congress Springs Sch., Saratoga, Calif., 1977-78; docent De Saisset Mus., Santa Clara (Calif.) U., 1986-88; vol. after sch. program Grandin-Miller Sch., San Jose. Illustrator: The Yiddish Alphabet Book, 1979, 88, Nathan the Needle and Other Stories, 1994, Memories from a Russian Kitchen, 1996. Recipient Juror's award NYU, 1984, Cal Labrun award Jewish Family Svc., 1989. Mem. Nat. League Am. PEN Women Arts. Jewish. Home: 19212 Shubert Dr Saratoga CA 95070

STONE, CAROLINE FLEMING, artist; b. N.Y.C., Mar. 26, 1936; d. Ralph Emerson and Elizabeth (Fleming) S.; m. Oakleigh B. Thorne, June 1956 (div. 1969); children: Oakleigh, Henry. Student, Art Students' League, 1954-57, 71-72, Pratt Graphics, 1973-74. One-woman shows include Washington Art Assn., Conn., Ella Sharp Mus., Mich., 1980, San Diego Pub. Library, 1981, Trustman Gallery Simmons Coll., Boston, 1985, Mary Ryan Gallery, N.Y.C., 1989, Boston Pub. Libr., 1994, Messiah Coll., 1995; two-person shows include Mary Ryan Gallery, 1985, Katonah Gallery, N.Y., 1986, Davidson Gallery, Seattle, 1990, The Millbrook (N.Y.) Gallery, 1993; juried shows include Silvermine Nat. Printmaking, Conn., 1978, Print Club, Phila., 1981, Trenton State (Nat. Print Exhibn. Purchase award), 1982, Minot State Coll., N.D., 1985, Boston Printmakers (Jurors Commendation), 1986; group shows include Mus. N.Mex., 1984, De Cordova and Dana Mus., Nat. Acad. Art, N.Y.C., Boston Pub. Library, Mus. Contemporary Hispanic Art, N.Y.C., 1987, World Print Exhbn., San Francisco, Smith Coll. Gallery, Northampton, Mass., Mary Ryan Gallery, 1988, 91, Virginia Lynch Gallery, R.I., 1989, 91, Accent on Paper, Lintas, N.Y., 1991, Women Printmaker's Nat. Touring Show, Boston Pub. Libr. 1991, The Tenth Anniversary Show Original Lynch Gallery, 1993; represented in permanent collections Art Inst. Chgo., Mid-West Mus. Am. Art, Ind., Mus. N.Mex., Nat. Mus. Am. Art, Boston Pub. Library, U. Chgo., U. Mich., Exxon Corp. Chase Manhattan Bank, IBM, Mellon Bank, The Portland Art Mus. Mem. The Kitchen (pres., bd. dirs.). Mem. Reformed Church. Home and Office: C Stone Press 80 Wooster St New York NY 10012-4347

STONE, DEBRA LYNN (DEBBIE STONE), elementary education educator; b. Washington, Ind., Aug. 18, 1956; d. Gerald Leo and Agnes Ilene (Wade) Mangin; m. Richard Brice Stone, June 10, 1978; children: Jonathan, Christopher. AS in Elem. Edn., Vincennes U., 1976; BS, Ind. State U., 1978, MS, 1984. Cert. K-6 tchr., 7-8 tch., Ind. Sec. Ind. U., Bloomington, 1978-79; Chpt. I tchr. reading and math. Barr Reeve Intermediate Sch., Montgomery, Ind., 1979-80; 3d grade tchr. Ind. U., 1980—; chmn. faculty Ellettsville Elem. Sch., 1990-94, 86-88, mem. tchr. assistance team, 1992—. Mem. bd. edn. St. John's Cath. Ch., Bloomington, 1988-89; band parent Edgewood Jr. H.S., Ellettsville, 1993-95; treas. PTA Ellettsville Elem. Sch., 1994-95. Mem. Alpha Delta Kappa (pres. Beta Zeta chpt. 1994-96). Home: 4855 W Woodland Dr Bloomington IN 47404 Office: Ellettsville Elem Sch 200 E Association St Ellettsville IN 47429-1511

STONE, E. LOUISE, adult educator education; b. Buffalo, Apr. 3, 1947; d. Robert Clark and Eugenia Loretta (Funk) S. BA, Radford Coll., 1969; MA, Ea. Ky. U., 1972. Soc. worker Norfolk (Va.) Soc. Svcs. Bur., 1969-71; counselor Florence Crittenton Home, Lexington, Ky., 1972-73; dir. student svcs. coll. nursing U. Ky., 1973-80, dir. experiential edn., 1980—; cons. U. Ky., 1980—, trainer Myers-Briggs, Learning Styles, Self Esteem, Teams, Assertiveness, 1980—. Contbr. articles to profl. jours. Mem. A.C.L.U. Lexington, 1989-91, Chrysallis House, Lexington, 1980-82, Lexington Rape Crisis Ctr., 1992-94. Recipient Servant Leader award Nat. Soc. for Experiential Edn., 1988, Outstanding Profl. Coop. Edn. Assoc. of Ky., 1988. Mem. Nat. Soc. for Experiential Edn., U. Ky. Women's Forum, Lexington Profl. Womens Forum. Democrate. Episcopal. Office: U Ky Office For Experiential Edn 206 Mathews Lexington KY 40506-0047

STONE, ELAINE MURRAY, author, composer, television producer; b. N.Y.C., Jan. 22, 1922; d. H. and Catherine (Fairbanks) Murray-Jacoby; m. F. Courtney Stone, May 30, 1944; children: Catherine Gladnick, Pamela Webb, Victoria. Student, Juilliard Sch. Music, 1939-41; BA, N.Y. Coll. Music, 1943; licentiate in organ, Trinity Coll. Music, London, 1947; student, U. Miami, 1952, Fla. Inst. Tech., 1963; PhD (hon.), World U., 1985. Organist, choir dir. St. Ingatius Episc. Ch., 1940-44; accompanist Strawbridge Ballet on Tour, N.Y.C., 1944; organist All Saints Episc. Ch., Ft. Lauderdale, 1951-54, St. John's Episc. Ch., Melbourne, Fla., 1956-59, First Christian Ch., Melbourne, 1962-63, United Ch. Christ, Melbourne, 1963-65, piano studio, Melbourne, 1955-70; editor-in-chief Cass Inc., 1970-71; dir. continuity radio Sta. WTAI, AM-FM, Melbourne, 1971-74; mem. sales staff Engle Realty Inc., Indialantic, Fla., 1975-78; v.p. pub. relations Consol. Cybertronics Inc., Cocoa Beach, Fla., 1969-70; writer, producer Countdown News, Sta. KXTX-TV, Dallas, 1978-80; assoc. producer Focus News, Dallas, 1980; host producer TV show, Focus on History, 1982-94, Epsic. Digest, 1984-90; judge Writer's Contest sponsored Brevard Cmty. Coll., 1987; v.p. Judges Fla. Space Coast Writer's Conf., 1985—, chmn., 1987. Author: The Taming of the Tongue, 1954, Love One Another, 1957, Menéndez de Avilés, 1968, Bedtime Bible Stories, Travel Fun, Sleepytime Tales, Improve Your Spelling for Better Grades, Improve Your Business Spelling, Tranquility Tapes, 1970, The Melbourne Bi-Centennial Book, 1976, Uganda: Fire and Blood, 1977, Tekla and the Lion, 1981 (1st Place award Nat. League Am. PEN Woman), Brevard County: From Cape of the Canes to Space Coast, 1988, Kizito, Boy Saint of Uganda, 1989 (2nd Place award Nat. League Am. PEN Woman 1990), Christopher Columbus: His World, His Faith., His Adventures, 1991 (1st Place award Nat. League Am. PEN Woman 1992), Elizabeth Bayley Seton: An American Saint, 1993 (3d Place award Nat. League Am. PEN Women 1994), Dimples The Dolphin, 1994 (1st Place award Fla. Space Coast Writer's Guild, 1994), Brevard at The Edge of Sea and Space, 1995, Carter G. Woodson Father of Black History, 1996, Maximilian Kolbe: Saint of Auschwitz, 1996; composer: Christopher Columbus Suite, 1992 (1st Place award PEN Women Music Awards 1992, 2d Place award 1993), Florida Suite for cello and piano, 1993; contbr. articles to nat. mags., newspapers including N.Y. Herald Tribune, Living Church, Christian Life; space corr. Religious News Service, Kennedy Space Ctr., 1962-78. Mem. exec. bd. Women's Assn., Brevard Symphony, 1967—; mem. heritage com. Melbourne Bicentennial Commn.; mem. Evangelism Commn. Episc. Diocese Cen. Fla., 1985-94; v.p. churchwomen group Holy Trinity Episcopal Ch., Melbourne, 1988-89, Stephen minister, 1988—, pres. churchwomen group, 1989—; bd. dirs. Fla. Space Coast Council Internat. Visitors, Fla. Space Coast Philharm., 1989—, Aid for the Arts, 1994. Recipient 1st place for piano Ashley Hall, 1935-39, S.C. State Music Contest, 1939, 1st place for piano composition Colonial Suite, Constitution Hall, Washington 1987, 88, 89, 3d place for vocal composition, 1989, honorable mention for article, 1989, 2nd place for piano composition, 1989, award lit. contest Fla. AAUW, 1989, 1st place award Fla. State PEN Women, 1990, 1st Place award Nat. Black History Essay Contest, 1990, Disting. Author of Yr. plaque Fla. Space Coast Writers Guild, 1992; numerous other awards. Mem. AAUW, ASCAP, Nat. League Am. PEN Women (1st place awards Tex. 1979, v.p. Dallas br. 1978-80, organizing pres. Cape Canaveral br. 1969, pres. 1988-90, 96—), Women Communications, DAR (Fla. state chmn. music 1962-63), Colonial Dames Am. (organizing pres. Melbourne chpt. 1994), Nat. Soc. DAR (organizing regent Rufus Fairbanks chpt. 1981-85, vice regent 1987—, historian 1989—), Children Am. Revolution (past N.Y. state chaplain), Am. Guild Organists (organizing warden Ft. Lauderdale), Space Pioneers, Fla. Press Episc. Home: 1945 Pineapple Ave Melbourne FL 32935-7656

STONE, ELIZABETH CAECILIA, anthropology educator; b. Oxford, Eng., Feb. 4, 1949; d. Lawrence and Jeanne Cecilia (Fawtier) S.; m. Paul Edmund Zimansky, Nov. 5, 1976. BA, U. Pa., 1971; MA, Harvard U., 1973; PhD, U. Chgo., 1979. Lectr. anthropology SUNY, Stony Brook, 1977-78, asst. prof., 1978-85, assoc. prof., 1985—; participated archaeol. in Eng., Iran, Iraq, Afghanistan; dir. archaeol. projects Ain Dara, Syria,, Tell Abu Duwari, Iraq. Author: Nippur Neighborhoods, 1987; co-author: (monograph) Old Babylonian Contracts from Nippur 1, 1976, Adoption in Old Babylonian Nippur and the Archive of Mannum-meshu-lissur, 1991; co-editor: The Cradle of Civilization: Recent Archaeology in Iraq-Biblical Archaeologist, 1992, Velles Paraules: Ancient Near Eastern Studies in Honor of Miguel Civil on the Occasion of His 65th Birthday, 1991; mem. editl. bd. Bull. Am. Schs. Oriental Rsch., 1993-95; contbr. articles to profl. jours. Assoc. trustee Am. Schs. of Oriental Rsch., 1983-90. Fulbright fellow, 1986-87; rsch. grantee Ford Found., 1974, Nat. Geog. Soc., 1983, 84, 88, 90, Am. Schs. of Oriental Rsch., 1987, 88, NSF, 1989-92, NEH, 1989-93. Office: SUNY Dept Anthropology Stony Brook NY 11794

STONE, ELIZABETH WENGER, retired dean; b. Dayton, Ohio, June 21, 1918; d. Ezra and Anna Bess (Markey) Wenger; m. Thomas A. Stone, Sept. 14, 1939 (dec. Feb. 1987); children: John Howard, Anne Elizabeth, James Alexander. A.B., Stanford U., 1937, M.A., 1938; M.L.S., Catholic U. Am., 1961; Ph.D., Am. U., 1968. Tchr. pub. schs. Fontana, Calif., 1938-39; asst. state statistician State of Conn., 1939-40; libr. New Haven Pub. Librs., 1940-42; dir. pub. relations, asst. to pres. U. Dubuque, Iowa, 1942-46; substitute libr. Pasadena (Calif. Pub. Libr. System), 1953-60; instr. Cath. U. Am., 1962-63, asst. prof., asst. to chmn. dept. libr. sci., 1963-67, assoc. prof., asst. to chmn., 1967-71, prof., asst. to chmn., 1971-72, prof., chmn. dept., 1972-80, dean Sch. Libr. and Info. Scis., 1981-83, prof. and dean emeritus, 1983—, lectr., 1990; libr. cons. U.S. Inst. of Peace, 1988-90; libr. Nat. Presbyn. Ch. and Ctr., Washington, 1991—, archivist, 1994—; founder, exec. dir. Continuing Libr. Edn. Network and Exchange, 1975-79; founder Nat. Rehab. Info. Ctr., 1977, project mgr., 1977-83; co-chmn. 1st World Conf. on Continuing Edn. for the Libr. and Info. Sci. Professions, 1984-85, 2nd World Conf., Barcelona, 1993. Author: Factors Related to the Professional Development of Librarians, 1969, (with James J. Kortendick) Job Dimensions and Educational Needs in Librarianship, 1971, (with R. Patrick and B. Conroy) Continuing Library and Information Science Education, 1974, Continuing Library Education as Viewed in Relation to Other Continuing Professional Movements, 1975, (with F. Peterson and M. Chobot) Motivation: A Vital Force in the Organization, 1977, American Library Development 1600-1899, 1977, (with others) Model Continuing Education Recognition System in Library and Information Science, 1979, (with M.J. Young) A Program for Quality in Continuing Education for Information, Library and Media Personnel, 1980, (with others) Continuing Education for the Library Information Professions, 1985, The Growth of Continuing Education, 1986, Library Education: Continuing Professional Education, 1993, (with others) ALA World Encyclopedia of Library and Information Science, 3d edit., 1993; author, editor: Continuing Professional Education for Library and Information Science Personnel: Papers from Seminar at Matica Slovenska, Martin Czechoslovakia, 1989; editor: D.C. Libraries, 1964-66; contbr. articles to profl. jours. Mem. Pres.'s Com. on Employment of Handicapped, 1972-88, Establishment of Elizabeth W. Stone Annual Lectureship Cath. U. Am., 1990—; pres. D.C. chpt. Am. Mothers, Inc., 1984-86, nat. v.p., 1989-91. Recipient Presdl. award Cath. U. Am., 1982, Spl. Librs. Profl. award, 1988, DCLA Ainsworth Rand Spofford Pres.'s award, 1990, Hon. Life Mem. 1994, Alumni Achievement award in libr. and info. sci. Cath. U. Am., 1990; named D.C. Mother of Yr., 1980. Mem. ALA (coun. 1976-83, v.p. 1980-81, pres. 1981-82, chmn. Nat. Libr. Week, 1983-85; founder ALA Nat. Ptnrs. for Librs. and Literacy 1984, Lippincott award 1986, Hon. Life award 1986), Assn. Libr. Info. and Sci. Edn. (pres. 1974), Am. Soc. Assn. Execs., Am. Assn. Adult and Continuing Edn., Internat. Fedn. Libr. Assns. and Instns. (chmn. Continuing Profl. Edn. Roundtable 1986-93), D.C. Libr. Assn. (hon. life, pres. 1966-67, hon. chair centennial com. 1992-94, hon. life 1994), Spl. Librs. Assn. (hon. life, pres. D.C. chpt. 1973-74), Cath. Libr. Assn. (hon. life), Continuing Profl. Edn. Libr. and Info. Sci. Pers., Soc. Am. Archivists, Cosmos Club, Phi Sigma Alpha, Beta Phi Mu, Phi Lambda Theta. Presbyterian. Home: 4000 Cathedral Ave NW # 15B Washington DC 20016-5249 Office: Cath U Am Sch Lib & Info Scis Washington DC 20064

STONE, GAIL MARIA, community health nurse; b. N.Y.C., Mar. 27, 1950; d. Louis and Florence Christina (Green) S.; m. David Bunch, Sept. 27, 1968 (div. Mar. 1972); children, David, Cerise. BS, Lehman Coll., 1978; MA, Webster U., 1986. CCRN, CNOR. Pub. health nurse Vis. Nurse of N.Y., N.Y.C., 1978-81; Capt. U.S. Army, USAF, 1981-89; oper. room nurse U.S. Army, San Antonio, 1981-84; oper. room nurse supr. USAF, Caribou, Maine, 1985-89; critical care nurse Lenox Hill Hosp., N.Y.C., 1989-90, Gotham Registry, N.Y.C., 1990-93; oper. room nurse VA Med. Ctr., Atlanta, 1993-95; home care nurse Olsten Kimberely, Marietta, Ga., 1996—. Home: 2102 Whitfield Ln Lawrenceville GA 30243-6364

STONE, JEANETTE BARBARA, secondary school educator; b. Oklahoma City, Nov. 13, 1953; d. Robert R. and Elizabeth R. (Klein) Ruyle; m. May 12, 1972; children: Jennifer, Jon, Jacey, Jake. BS in Edn., Southwestern Okla. State U., 1989. Tchr. math. Clinton (Okla.) Pub. Schs., 1990—. Leader, advisor 4-H, Custer County, Okla., 1983—. Named to Outstanding Young Women of Am., 1982. Mem. Nat. Coun. Tchrs. Math. Democrat. Roman Catholic. Home: RR 1 Box 3385 Clinton OK 73601-9324

STONE, JUDITH ELISE, artist, English educator; b. Boston, Sept. 15, 1940; d. Morris Joseph and Frances (Maletz) Tissenbaum; m. Donald Ivan Promish; m. Edward Johnson Stone, Aug. 24, 1964 (div. Mar. 1974); children: David Benjamin, Sylvia Beth. BA magna cum laude, Vassar Coll., 1962; MA in Tchg., Harvard U., 1965; MFA, U. Colo., Boulder, 1977. Adj. prof. Temple U., Phila., 1979-87, St. Joseph's U., Phila., 1983—, Coll. of Textiles, Phila., 1984—; tchr. Temple U., Japan, 1986-87; lectr. various colls., univs. and confs. Contbr. articles to profl. jours.; one-person shows include Grimaldis Gallery, Balt., 1985, Hinoki Gallery, Tokyo, 1987, University City Sci. Ctr. Gallery, Phila., 1983, 89, Lancaster (Pa.) Mus. of Art, 1996; exhibited in group shows at Denver Mus. of Art, 1977, Boulder (Colo.) Fine Arts Ctr., 1978, Sebastian Moore Gallery, Denver, 1979, U. Colo. Art Galleries, Boulder, 1979, Allentown (Pa.) Mus., 1986, Pa. State Mus., Harrisburg, 1994, Stephen F. Austin U., Nacogdoches, 1995, Phila. Mus. Art, 1995, 100 Women/100 Works, Rochester, N.Y., 1996, San Diego Art Inst. (Grand prize); represented in permanent collections at University City Sci. Ctr., Phila., St. Joseph's U., Phila., Balt. Gulf and Electric, Toyoda Internat. Sales, Inc., Tokyo, Design Studios, Tokyo, Idaho Nat. Bank, Boise. MacDowell colony resident fellow, 1992. Mem. AAUP. Democrat. Jewish. Home: 126 Rockland Ave Merion PA 19066 Office: St Josephs U Dept Fine & Performing Arts 5600 City Line Ave Philadelphia PA 19131

STONE, JUDITH IDA, public TV executive; b. Union City, Tenn., Oct. 29, 1949; d. Cecil Alexander and Katherine Janice (Nethery) S.; m. K. Mark Weaver, Jan. 19, 1985; step-children: John Benjamin Weaver, Chemaine Weaver Butner. AB, U. Ala., Tuscaloosa, 1971; MA, U. Mich., Ann Arbor, 1973. Prodr., dir. Montgomery (Ala.) Public TV, 1973-75, Pensacola (Fla.) Jr. Coll., 1976-77; wire editor Montgomery (Ala.) Advertiser, 1978; staff writer Ala. Power Co., Birmingham, 1978-79; asst. program dir. Univ. Television Series, Tuscaloosa, 1979-82; dir. Univ. Television Svcs., Tuscaloosa, 1982-88; asst. dean Coll. Communication U. Ala., Tuscaloosa, 1984-88; exec. dir. Ala. Public Television, Birmingham, 1989—; mem. bd. dirs. PBS, Alexandria, Va., 1991-97, vice chair, 1993-95; chair So. Ednl. Comms. Assn., Columbia, S.C., 1993-94; vice chair Orgn. State Broadcast Execs., Columbia, 1995-97. Mem. class IV Leadership Ala., 1994; treas. Am. Cancer Soc., 1994-96. Recipient Outstanding Alumna award Dept. Speech Communication U. Ala., 1988, Outstanding Communicator award Ala. Media Profls., 1990. Mem. Ala. Media Profls. Methodist. Office: Ala Pub TV 2112 11th Ave S Ste 400 Birmingham AL 35205

STONE, LESLEY, elementary education educator; b. Stoke-on-Trent, Eng., Dec. 17, 1945; came to the U.S., 1970; d. Norman and Beryl (Smallwood) Ellerton; m. Arthur James Stone, July 16, 1968; children: Mark, Gary. BS, William Cary on the Coast, 1984, MEd, 1990. Cert. reading tchr., Miss. RN British Army, 1963-67; 6th grade tchr. Harrison County, Woolmarket, Miss., 1984-85; kindergarten tchr. North Bay Elem. Sch., Bay St. Louis, Miss., 1985-90, 1st grade tchr., 1990—; tchr. cons. South Miss. Writing Inst., Gulfport, 1994—. Named tchr. of mo. Bay Waveland Rotary Club, 1995. Mem. Nat. Coun. Tchrs. English (presenter), PTA, ASCD. Baptist. Home: 21240 Torries Rd Saucier MS 39574-9172 Office: North Bay Elem Sch 740 Dunbar Ave Bay Saint Louis MS 39520-2921

STONE, MARY BETH See FISHTEIN, ELIZABETH

STONE, MINNIE STRANGE, retired automotive service company executive; b. Palatka, Fla., Mar. 10, 1919; d. James Arrious and Pansy (Thomas) Strange; student Massey Bus. Coll., 1938-39; m. Fred Albion Stone, Nov. 30, 1939; children: Fred Albion, James Thomas, Thomas Demere. Sec., bookkeeper Sears, Roebuck & Co., Jacksonville, Fla., 1939-41; fin. sec. U.S. Army, Macon, Ga., 1941, Atlanta, 1942; sec., bookkeeper Raleigh Spring & Brake Sv., Inc. (name changed to Stone Heavy Vehicle Specialist) (N.C.), 1953-84, sec.-treas. corp., 1960-84, dir., sec. Vol. Wake County Mental Health, 1970-80; pres. YWCA, Wake County, 1973-76, bd. dirs., 1966-76; bd. dirs. Urban Ministry Ctr. Raleigh, 1983-89, mem. adv. bd., 1989—; bd. trustees Bapt. Children's Homes N.C.; former mem. subcom. Gov. Coun. Older Adult Fitness. Mem. N.C. Mus. of History Assocs., N.C. Art Soc., Monthly Investors Club, Coley Forest Garden Club. Republican. Baptist. Home: 920 Runnymede Rd Raleigh NC 27607-3108

STONE, PEG ANN, systems administrator; b. Clinton, Mass., May 28, 1962; d. Hayward Max and Mary Phyllis (Galliano) S. AA, Quinsigamond C.C., 1986; BSBA, Nichols Coll., 1994; MEd, Cambridge Coll., 1995. From elec. inspector to instrnl. designer Digital Equipment Corp., Maynard, Mass., 1981-96; project mgr. Sys. Documentation, Inc., Nashua, N.H., 1996—. Mem. Northeast Human Resource Assn. Democrat. Roman Catholic. Home: 40 Lyman Rd Berlin MA 01503 Office: Sys Documentation 61 Spit Brook Rd Nashua NH 01503

STONE, RUBY ROCKER, state legislator; b. Portal, Ga., Feb. 6, 1924; d. Eddie Lee and Della (Taylor) Rocker; widowed; children: Dianne Carolyn Stone Milhollin, Raymond Edward Stone. Office mgr., dental asst. to Dr. Richard W. Collins, 1962-68; asst. to mgr. Am. Machine & Foundry Spl. Missile project Vandenberg AFB, 1959-60; sec. Idaho House State Affairs, 1970; aide to Gov. Don Samuelson, 1970-71; senate jour. clk. Idaho Ho. Reps., 1971-84, mem., 1986—, chmn. local govt. com., 1991—. Active ARC, and numerous other cmty. projects and cmty. vol. orgns. Recipient Sportsmanship award Idaho State Women's Amateur Golf Tournament, 1980, Plantation Ladies Golf Assn., Outstanding Woman award, 1992; inducted into Idaho Sports Hall of Fame, 1993, Idaho New Agenda Hall of Fame, 1993; named Republicn Outstanding Legislator-House, 1994. Mem. Nat. Orgn. Women Legislators, U.S. Golf Assn. (mem. jr. girls championship com. 1981—), Idaho Golf Assn. (bd. dirs. 1975-87), Plantation Golf Club, Gowen Field Officers Club, Gowen Field Officers Wives Club, Daus. of Nile, El Korah Honored Ladies Club, Elks. Republican. Protestant. Home: 6604 Holiday Dr Boise ID 83709-2022

STONE, SHARON, actress; b. Meadville, Pa., Mar. 10, 1958; d. Joe and Dorothy S; m. Michael Greenburg, 1984 (div. 1987). Student, Edinboro U. Model Eileen Ford Modeling Agy. Appeared in films Stardust Memories, 1980, Deadly Blessing, 1981, Irreconcilable Differences, 1984, King Solomon's Mines, 1985, Allan Quatermain and the Lost City of Gold, 1986, Cold Steel, 1987, Police Academy 4, 1987, Action Jackson, 1988, Above the Law, 1988, Total Recall, 1990, He Said/She Said, 1991, Scissors, 1991, Basic Instinct, 1991, Where Sleeping Dogs Lie, 1992, Sliver, 1993, Intersection, 1994, The Specialist, 1994, (also co-prodr.) The Quick and the Dead, 1995, Casino, 1995 (Golden Globe award for best actress in film 1996, Acad. award nominee for best actress 1996), Diabolique, 1996; TV appearances include Not Just Another Affair, 1982, Bay City Blues, 1983, Calendar Girl Murders, 1984, The Vegas Strip Wars, 1984, War and Remembrance, 1988, (guest) The Larry Sanders Show, 1994; narrator: Harlow: The Blond Bombshell, 1993. Office: PMK care Heidi Schaeffer Los Angeles CA 90048*

STONE, SHERRI LYNN, newsletter editor; b. Greenville, N.C., Aug. 4, 1963; d. Edgar W. Stone Jr. and Jeanne Everett-Black. BA in Polit. Sci., N.C. State U., 1986; MA in Polit. Sci./Internat. Studies, Am. U., 1993. Staff asst., legis. asst. Small Bus. Subcom. U.S. Ho. of Reps., Washington, 1987-89, profl. staff mem. Com. on Sci., Space and Tech., 1989-95; legis. asst. Capital Assocs., Inc., Washington, 1995; assoc. editor Online Banking Newsletter, Weber World Media, Arlington, Va., 1996—; bd. mem. Ho. Legis. and Asst. Assn., Washington, 1993. Contbr. articles to profl. publs.

STONE, SUSAN RIDGAWAY, marketing educator; b. Coronado, Calif., Oct. 30, 1950; d. Lester Jay and Marguerite Ridgaway (King) Stone; m. Martin Zachary Sipkoff, Oct. 27, 1984; 1 child, Benjamin. AB, Wilson Coll., 1977; MBA, Shippensburg U., 1980; DBA, George Washington, U., 1992. Assoc. prof. mgmt. and mktg. Shippensburg (Pa.) U., 1983—; dir. mktg. VSP Wastewater Tech., Gettysburg, Pa., 1982; mktg. cons. Svcs. Unltd., Gettysburg, 1975—; lectr. in field. Author: (with Stephen J. Holoviak) Managing Human Productivity: People are Your Best Investment, 1987; contbr. articles to profl. jours.; asst. editor mag. USN Acad. Alumni Assn., 1973-74; pres. Shippensburg U. Press. Former land use chair League of Women Voters, Gettysburg; mem. fund raising com. for local candidates; pers. chair, bd. dirs. Survivors', Inc. Am. Mktg. Assn. fellow, 1986. Mem. Acad. Mktg. Sci., Am. Mktg. Assns., Mensa, Adams County Literacy Coun., Beta Gamma Sigma, Kappa Kappa Gamma. Democrat. Episcopalian. Office: Shippensburg Univ 1871 Old Main Dr Shippensburg PA 17257

STONEBURNER, DOROTHY STERETT, writer, artist; b. Pasadena, Calif., Aug. 1, 1927; d. Lester Gahan and Margaret Esther (Beck) Sterett; m. Jack Stoneburner, Sept. 10, 1949 (dec. Nov. 1994); children: Dean Warren, Jeanne Somers, James Douglas. BA in Art and Theater, UCLA, 1950, MA, 1970. Writer/novelist Orinda, Calif., 1955—; instr, art and theater L.A. Pierce C.C., L.A., 1970-77; dir. Shoestring Theatre L.A. Pierce Coll., 1970-77; dir., founder Shoestring Theater Workshop, Canoga Park, Calif., 1960-70; tchr. mentally gifted minor programs L.A. City Schs., Ventura County Schs., L.A. C.C., others, 1960-70; cons. Camp Fire, Inc., L.A., 1975-76, L.A. City Schs., 1960-65, So. Calif. Automobile Assn., L.A., 1960-64; freelance photographer, tchr. Calif. State Coll., Northridge, State Farm Ins., L.A., 1960-65. Author: (novels) The Jerusalem Cross, 1980, The Last Hostage, 1996; illustrator: Physical Anthropology (Stein and Rowe) edits. 1-4, 1976; contbr. articles and editorials to publs. Safety svcs. chmn. ARC, San Fernando Valley, Calif., 1960-65; safety edn. activities L.A. City Schs., 1960-65; leader/trainer Camp Fire, Inc., L.A., 1960-75. Recipient Wakan award Camp Fire, Inc., 1975, Svc. award ARC, L.A., 1965. Mem. Nat. Writers Club (pres. 1990, bd. dirs. 1985-90), Nat. Assn. Fine Artists, AAUW, Calif. PTA (local pres. 1961-62). Home: 22 White Oak Dr Lafayette CA 94549

STONER, OLIVIA HATCHETT, lawyer, financial planner; b. Phila., Oct. 2, 1947; d. Haywood and Vivian (Helton) Hatchett; m. Charles Timothy Stoner, Aug. 6, 1977; children: Tesha Nashan, Brenden Charles. BS, Wilberforce U., 1970; MA in Tchg., Antioch Putney Coll., 1971; JD, U. Pitts., 1978. Bar: Pa. 1983; CFP, 1992. Tchr. math. Sch. Dist. Phila., 1970-71; sales agt. Met. Life Ins. Co., Phila., 1971; juvenile probation officer Phila. Common Pleas Ct., Phila., 1972-75; trust and estate adminstr. investment mgmt. & trust dept. PNC Bank, Phila., 1980—; CFO Synergy Devel. Group, Phila., 1990—. Mem. bd. mggrs., chmn. nominating com. YMCA, Phila., 1991-93. Mem. Pa. Bar Assn., Philadelphia County Bar Assn., Urban Bankers Assn. (treas. 1995-96), Delaware Valley Soc. CFP's (bd. dirs. 1994-96), Phila. Astrological Soc. (treas. 1992—). Democrat. Presbyterian. Home: 3213 Wallace St Philadelphia PA 19104

STONESIFER, PATTY, information systems executive. Degree, 1982. Editor-in-chief Que Corp., Indpls.; sr. mgr. Microsoft Press, 1988-89; gen. mgr. Microsoft Can., 1989-90; gen. mgr., then v.p. product support svcs. consumer divsn. Microsoft Corp., Redmond, Wash., 1990-93, sr. v.p. consumer divsn., 1993—. Office: Microsoft Corp 1 Microsoft Way Redmond WA 98052-6399

STOODT, BARBARA DERN, education educator, magazine editor; b. Columbus, Ohio, June 12, 1934; d. Millard Fissel and Helen Lucille (Taes) Dern; divorced; children: Linda Stoodt Neu, Susan Stoodt Price. BS in Edn., Ohio U., 1956; MA in Edn., Ohio State U., 1965; PhD, 1970; post-grad., U. Chgo., 1967. Tchr. North Charleston (S.C.) Schs., 1956-57, Cleveland Heights (Ohio) U., 1957-58, Mansfield (Ohio) Bd. Edn., 1958-59, 65-68; dir. reading, 1968; teaching assoc. Ohio State U., 1968-70; prof. edn. U. Akron, Ohio, 1970-77, U. N.C., Greensboro, 1977—; vis. prof. No. Ky. U. and U. Cin. Author: Reading Instruction, 1981, 2d edit., 1989, Teaching Language Arts, 1988; co-author: Secondary School Reading Instruction, 1987, 5th edit., 1994, Children's Literature: Discovery for a Lifetime, 1996, Riverside Reading Program. U.S. Office Edn. research grantee, 1970. Mem. Nat. Conf. on Research in English, Internat. Reading Assn. (Outstanding Dissertation award), Am. Ednl. Research Assn., Nat. Council Tchrs. English (outstanding research award 1971), Assn. for Supervision and Curriculum Devel., Assn. for Childhood Edn. Internat. Methodist. Home: PO Box 9630 Cincinnati OH 45209-0630 Office: Learning Mag 1607 Battleground Ave Greensboro NC 27408-8005

STOOPS, JULIA MARY, artist, educator; b. Western Samoa, 1965; d. Denis Hector Stoops and Colleen Margaret (O'Neill) Sibelman; m. Thomas James Martin, Apr. 20, 1991. BFA, Corcoran Sch. Art, Washington, 1986; BA, U. Auckland, New Zealand, 1990; cert. adult tchg., Auckland Inst. Tech., 1992; postgrad., Portland State U., 1994—. Rsch. asst. Auckland (New Zealand) City Art Gallery, 1991; lectr. Auckland Inst. Tech., 1992-93, ASA Sch. Art, Auckland, 1992-93; asst. prof. Pacific N.W. Coll. Art, Portland, Oreg., 1994—; cons. ASA Sch. Art, 1992. One woman shows include Beast, Auckland, 1987, Artspace Alternative Space, Auckland, 1987, Workplace Gallery, Portland, 1995; group shows include Anton Gallery, Washington, 1986, Washington Women's Art Ctr., 1986, Strathmore Arts Ctr., Md., 1986, New Art Ctr., Washington, 1986, Star Art Gallery, 1987, Olshonsky Gallery, Washington, 1991, Stanley St. Art Ctr., Auckland, 1993, ASA Gallery, Auckland, 1993, Workplace Gallery, Portland, 1994-95, Pacific Northwest Coll. Art, Portland, 1995, Elizabeth Leach Gallery, Portland, 1995. Office: Pacific NW Coll Art 1219 SW Park Ave Portland OR 97205

STOOPS, LOUISE, information services administrator; b. Honolulu; d. Robert Earl and Ethel Louise (Saunders) S. BA in Liberal Arts/English, U. Ariz.; MLS, Simmons Coll., 1952. Chief libr. Baker, Weeks & Co., N.Y.C., 1972-77; libr. mgr. Lehman Bros., Kuhn Loeb, N.Y.C., 1977-84; mgr. info. svcs. Bessmer Trust Co., N.Y.C., 1985—. Vol. dept. edn. Met. Mus. N.Y., 1985—. mem. Fin. Women's Assn. N.Y. (mem. internat. com. 1990-91), Spl. Librs. Assn., Chi Omega. Office: Bessmer Trust Co 630 Fifth Ave New York NY 10111-0100

STOORZA GILL, GAIL, corporate professional; b. Yoakum, Tex., Aug. 28, 1943; d. Roy Otto and Ruby Pauline (Ray) Blankenship; m. Larry Sttorza, Apr. 27, 1963 (div. 1968); m. Ian M. Gill, Apr. 24, 1981; 1 child, Alexandra Leigh. Student, N. Tex. State U., 1961-63, U. Tex., Arlington, 1963. Stewardess Cen. Airlines, Ft. Worth, 1963; advt. and acctg. exec. Phillips-Ramsey Advt., San Diego, 1963-68; dir. advt. Rancho Bernardo, San Diego, 1968-72; dir. corp. communications Avco Community Developers, San Diego, 1972-74; pres. Gail Stoorza Co., San Diego, 1974—, Stoorza, Ziegaus & Metzger, San Diego, 1974—; CEO Stoorza, Ziegaust, Metzger, Inc., 1993—; chmn. Stoorza/Smith, San Diego, 1984-85, Stoorza Internat., San Diego, 1984-85; CEO ADC Stoorza, San Diego, 1987—, Franklin Stoorza, San Diego, 1993—. Trustee San Diego Art Found.; bd. dirs. San Diego Found. for Performing Arts, San Diego Opera, Sunbelt Nursery Groups, Dallas. Names Small Bus. Person of Yr. Selest Com. on Small Bus., 1984, one of San Diego's Ten Outstanding Young Citizens San Diego Jaycees, 1979; recipient Woman of Achievement award Women in Communications Inc., 1985. Mem. Pubs. Soc. Am., Nat. Assn. Home Builders (residential mktg. com.), COMBO. Methodist. Clubs: Chancellors Assn. U. Calif. (San Diego), Pub. Relations, San Diego Press. Home: PO Box 490 Rancho Santa Fe CA 92067-0490 Office: Franklin Stoorza 225 Broadway Ste 1800 San Diego CA 92101*

STORB, URSULA BEATE, molecular genetics and cell biology educator; b. Stuttgart, Germany, July 6, 1936; came to U.S., 1966; d. Walter M. Stemmer and Marianne M. (Kämmerer) Nowara. MD, U. Freiburg, Fed. Republic Germany, 1960; Germany. Asst. prof. dept. microbiology U. Wash., Seattle, 1971-75, assoc. prof., 1975-81, prof., 1981-86, head. div. immunology, 1980-86; prof. dept. molecular genetics and cell biology U. Chgo., 1986—. Mem. editl. bd. Immunity, Current Opinion in Immunology, Internat. Immunology; contbr. articles to sci. jours. Grantee NIH, NSF, Am. Cancer Soc., 1973—. Fellow Am. Acad. Arts and Scis.; mem. Assn. Women in Sci., Am. Assn. Immunology, Am. Soc. Cell Biology. Office: U Chgo 920 E 58th St Chicago IL 60637-1432

STORER, MARYRUTH, law librarian; b. Portland, Oreg., July 26, 1953; d. Joseph William and Carol Virginia (Pearson) Storer; m. David Bruce Bailey, Jan. 1, 1981; children: Sarah, Allison. BA in History, Portland State U., 1974; JD, U. Oreg., 1977; M in Law Librarianship, U. Wash., 1978. Bar: Oreg. 1978. Assoc. law librarian U. Tenn., Knoxville, 1978-79; law librarian O'Melveny & Myers, Los Angeles, 1979-88; dir. Orange County Law Library, Santa Ana, Calif., 1988—. Mem. Am. Assn. Law Libraries, So. Calif. Assn. Law Libraries (pres. 1986-87), Coun. Calif. County Law Librs. (sec.-treas. 1990-94, pres. 1994—). Democrat. Episcopalian. Office: Orange County Law Library 515 N Flower St Santa Ana CA 92703-2354

STOREY, M. KARYL, insurance consultant; b. Dover, N.J., Mar. 7, 1945; d. Richard F. and Stephanie (Slatuik) Storey; m. Richard R. Watkins, June 10, 1967 (div. 1985); children: Sara S., Peter S.; m. Jimmy W. Broomhall, Nov. 17, 1990. BA, U. Denver, 1967. CLU, chartered fin. cons. Tchr. Denver pub. schs., 1967-75; rep. The Equitable Life Assurance Co., Denver, 1981-92; sales mgr. Lincoln Nat., 1992-95; acct. mgr. Acacia Fin. Group, Englewood, Colo., 1996—. Spl. events chmn. Coalition Against Fin. Abuse of Srs., Denver, 1989—; 2nd v.p. League Women Voters, Denver, 1977-81; dir. parish coun. Ch. of the Risen Christ, Denver, 1982-85. Fellow Life Underwriting Tng. Coun., 1995; recipient Career Devel. award GAMA, 1994. Mem. Nat. Assn. Life Underwriters, Equitable Nat. Leaders Corps, Million Dollar Round Table, Women's life Underwriters (charter mem. program chmn., bd. dirs. 1984-88), Centennial Life Underwriters Assn. (pres. elect 1996—), Lions, (found. bd. v.p.), Phi Gamma Mu. Office: Acacia Fin Ctr 7340 E Caley Ave #220 Englewood CO 80111

STOREY, PHOEBE REED, artist; b. Newton, Mass., Apr. 16, 1945; d. Dale C. and Barbara (Thurman) Reed; m. Roger Alan Storey, Feb. 3, 1967; children: Alan Matthew, Jeffrey Todd, Julia Loraine, Adrienne Reed. BA in Fine Arts, Hollins Coll., 1967. Artist Davis, Calif., 1989—; represented by Artistic Touch Gallery, Davis; tchr. Davis (Calif.) Art Ctr., 1993, Munroe Ctr. for the Arts, Lexington, Mass., 1995—. Commd. painting U.S. Fish and Wildlife Svc.; work selected for ann. ltd. edit. print Yolo County Arts Coun; exhibited in group show at New Eng. Watercolor Soc., 1994, 95 (hon.

mention award, 1995). Bd. mem. LWV, Eureka, Calif., 1970-72, 75-80, Glendale, Calif., 1973-74. Recipient award of merit Calif. State Fair, 1992. Home and Studio: 80 Franklin St Arlington MA 02174-3214

STOREY, VICKIE LEE, tax collector; b. Brookville, Pa., Dec. 10, 1952; d. John Robert and Miriam Elaine (Conrad) Garner; m. Donald C. Storey, Aug. 6, 1977; children: Robert, Adam. Tax collector Brookville Borough, 1990—. instr. for merit badges Boy Scouts Am., Brookville, 1995-96; mem. fundraiser bd. ARC, Brookville, 1994-95; mem. adv. coun. Area Agy. on Aging, Brookville, 1996. Mem. Pa. Tax Collectors Assn., Jefferson County Tax Collectors Assn. (sec./treas. 1992, 93, v.p. 1994-96). Republican. Presbyterian. Home: 55 Rebecca St Brookville PA 15825 Office: 91 Pickering St Brookville PA 15825

STORK, JANET KENNEDY, chemist; b. Flint, Mich., July 17, 1959; d. Robert Neal and Patsy Etta (Thompson) Kennedy; m. John Eric Stork, Sept. 1, 1984; children: Eric Robert, Sean Patrick, Donal Bryan. BS in Chemistry, U. Mich., Flint, 1982. Chemist Encotec, Ann Arbor, Mich., 1983-85, Brighton Analytical, Highland, Mich., 1986-89, GM Corp., Milford, Mich., 1990—; mem. emergency response team GM, Milford, 1991—, mem. hazardous comm. com., 1994—. Pres. Greater Flint Area Mothers of Multiples, 1990, 92. Presbyterian. Home: 645 N Adelaide Fenton MI 48430 Office: GM Vehicle Emission Lab 1 GM Rd Milford MI 48380-3726

STORRS, ELEANOR EMERETT, research institute consultant; b. Cheshire, Conn., May 3, 1926; d. Benjamin Porter and Alta Hyde (Moss) S.; m. Harry Phineas Burchfield, Jr., Nov. 29, 1963; children: Sarah Storrs, Benjamin Hyde. B.S. with distinction in Botany, U. Conn., 1948; M.S. in Biology, NYU, 1958; Ph.D. in Chemistry, U. Tex., 1967. Asst. biochemist Boyce Thompson Inst. for Plant Research, Yonkers, N.Y., 1948-62; research scientist Clayton Found. Biochem. Inst., U. Tex., Austin, 1962-65; biochemist Pesticides Research Lab., USPHS, Perrine, Fla., 1965-67; dir. dept. biochemistry Gulf South Research Inst., New Iberia, La., 1967-77; adj. prof. chemistry U. Southwestern La., Lafayette, 1974-77; research prof. biology, dir. comparative mammalogy lab. Fla. Inst. Tech., Melbourne, 1977-94; ret., cons. on leprosy-armadillo programs, 1975-94, mem. Faculty Senate, 1979-84; cons. in rehab. and prevention deformities leprosy Pan Am. Health Orgn., WHO, Venezuela, Argentina, Brazil, Mex., 1972-90; dep. v.p. Coll. Hansenology in Endemic Countries, 1980-85. Author: (with H.P. Burchfield) Biochemical Applications of Gas Chromatography, 1962, (with Burchfield, D.E. Johnson) Guide to the Analysis of Pesticide Residues, 2 vols, 1965; also articles, book chpts. Grantee NIH, 1968-88, CDC, 1969-73, WHO, 1973-93, Leprosy Program, 1978-93, German Leprosy Relief Assn., 1973-78, Nat. Coun. Episc. Ch., 1975-77, Brit. Leprosy Relief Assn., 1981-88; recipient plaque La. Health Dept., 1972, Disting. Alumni award U. Conn., 1975, Gold award Am. Coll. Pathologists and Am. Soc. Clin. Pathologists, 1974, Gerard B. Lambert award for spl. recognition, 1975. Fellow AAAS, N.Y. Acad. Scis.; mem. AAUW, Interant. Leprosy Assn., Am. Soc. Mammalogy, Am. Assn. Lab. Animal Sci. (Charles A. Griffin award 1975), East Coast Zool. Soc. (bd. dirs. 1989-92), Am. Recorder Soc., Early Music Assn., Sigma Xi. Episcopalian (vestryman). Clubs: Appalachian (Boston); Green Mountain (Bear Mountain, N.Y.); Mystik Krewe of Iberians (mem. ct. 1972, queen 1974). Home: 72 Riverview Ter Melbourne FL 32903-4640

STORY, ELLEN, state legislator; m. Ronald Story; 2 children. BA, U. Tex.; attended, U. Wis., SUNY, Stony Brook; MA, Cambridge Coll. Asst. county coord. Family Planning Coun. Western Mass., 1973, county coord., 1974, asst. exec. dir., 1981, assoc. exec. dir., 1984—; mem. Mass. Ho. of Reps., 1992—, mem. criminal justice com., edn. com., ethics and election laws com. Founding mem. Hampshire County Human Svcs., Mass., 1974, former mem. prof. adv. com.; organizer Western Mass. Dems. and Independents for Frank Hatch for Gov., 1978; chmn. Barbara Griffith for Amherst Selectbd., 1982; coord. Evelyn Murphy for Lt. Gov., 1982; mem. Amherst Town Meeting, Mass.; former del. Women, Infants and Children Avd. Coun. Mass.; pres., bd. dirs. Hampshire County Coun. Social Agencies, Mass.; bd. dirs. Hampshire Youth 2000 Coalition; charter mem. Friends of Amherst Recreation; co-founder, dir. Concerned Citizens for Quality Edn. Recipient Spl. Recognition award Hampshire County Coun. Social Agencies, 1991. Mem. Amherst Club (sec.). Democrat. Office: Mass Ho of Reps State House Rm 167 Boston MA 02133*

STORY, MARCIA REED STEVENS, retired Engish educator, artist; b. Waynesboro, Pa., July 14, 1934; d. Alfred Ludlow and Florence Louise (Reed) Stevens; m. William E. Story, Jan. 28, 1962 (div. 1968); 1 child, Pamela Dawn. B Edn. Arts, U. Nev., Reno, 1969, MA, 1971. Cert. tchr., Nev. English and social studies tchr. Clark County Sch. Dist., Las Vegas, Nev., 1971-96. Artist, illustrator, designer Nev. Lit. Map, 1992 (included in Libr. of Congress); contbr. articles to profl. publs. Mem. Nat. Coun. Tchrs. English (nat. chair slate 1992-96, cons., guest spkr. 1992—), So. Nev. Tchrs. English (pres. 1986-90), Nev. State Coun. Tchrs. English (pres. 1990-92). Republican. Methodist.

STORY, MARTHA VANBEUREN, librarian; b. Morristown, N.J., Mar. 6, 1940; d. John Mohlman and Jane de Peyster vanB.; m. William Ferguson Story, Oct. 19, 1963; children: Jessica, Alexandra. BA, Wellesley Coll., 1962; MLS, U. Md., 1975. Libr. Dewberry & Davis, Fairfax, Va., 1976-77, 80-84, Ashley Hall, Charleston, S.C., 1977-80, 85-86; cataloger Norfolk (Va.) Pub. Libr., 1987-90; dir. Mathews (Va.) Meml. Libr., 1990—. Publicity chmn. Mid. Peninsula Cmty. Concert Assoc., Gloucester, Va., 1993—; mem. Main St. Com., Mathews, Va., 1994—. Mem. Tidewater Area Libr. Dirs. Coun., Va. Libr. Assoc. Home: Holly Cove Cricket Hill Rd PO Box 117 Hudgins VA 23076 Office: Mathews Meml Libr Main St PO Box 980 Mathews VA 23109

STORY, SUE, transcriber, filmmaker; b. Bklyn., June 5, 1943; d. Abraham and Beatrice (Frost) Yermanok; m. Dwain Story, Dec. 26, 1969 (div. Jan. 1971). AS in Comm., Ulster County C.C., Stone Ridge, N.Y., 1979; BS in Radio, TV, Film, U. Tex., 1982. Advt./pub. rels. exec. various agencies, Miami Beach, Fla., 1963-69; waitress/bartender various restaurants, Woodstock, N.Y., 1970-79; film editor Dallas, 1983-86; film electrician/gaffer L.A., 1986-93; owner/operator CompuType, Shokan, N.Y., 1993—. Mem. Women in Film Dallas (bd. dirs 1984-86). Home and Office: 67 Ridge Rd Shokan NY 12481

STOSKUS, JOANNA JORZYSTA, computer information systems educator; b. Newark, Feb. 10, 1947; d. Joseph B. and Anna Mary (Stopa) Jorzysta; m. Joseph Thomas Stoskus, Jr., Oct. 25, 1969; 1 child, Caryn Judith. BA in Math., Kean Coll. N.J., 1968; MA in Computer Sci., Montclair State U., 1985. Programmer, analyst Prudential Ins. Co., Newark, 1968-70, Bell Labs., Murray Hill, N.J., 1970-72; adj. instr. Middlesex County Coll., Edison, N.J., 1974-77; chairperson, prof. County Coll. of Morris, Randolph, N.J., 1977—; mem. Whippany Park's Prin.'s Adv., Whippany, N.J., 1988-90; mem. Morris Area Tech. Alliance, Morristown, 1993—, N.J. State Computer Adv., Aberden, N.J., 1993—, Sussex County Vo-Tech. Adv., Sparta, N.J., 1994—. Mem. Data Processing Mgmt. Assn., N.J. C.C. Computer Consortium, Bucknell Partents Orgn. Republican. Office: County Coll Morris 214 Center Grove Rd Randolph NJ 07869-2007

STOTLER, ALICEMARIE HUBER, judge; b. Alhambra, Calif., May 29, 1942; d. James R. and Loretta M. Huber; m. James Allen Stotler, Sept. 11, 1971. BA, U. So. Calif., 1964, JD, 1967. Bar: Calif. 1967, U.S. Dist. Ct. (no. dist.) Calif. 1967, U.S. Dist. Ct. (cen. dist.) Calif. 1973, U.S. Supreme Ct., 1976; cert. criminal law specialist. Dep. Orange County Dist. Atty.'s Office, 1967-73; mem. Stotler & Stotler, Santa Ana, Calif., 1973-76, 83-84; judge Orange County Mcpl. Ct., 1976-78, Orange County Superior Ct., 1978-83, U.S. Dist. Ct. (cen. dist.) Calif., L.A., 1984—; assoc. dean Calif. Trial Judges Coll., 1982; lectr., panelist, numerous orgns.; standing com. on rules of practice and procedure U.S. Jud. Conf., 1991—, chair, 1993-96; mem. exec. com. 9th Cir. Jud. Conf., 1989-93, Fed. State Jud. Coun., 1989-93, jury com., 1990-92, planning com. for Nat. Conf. on Fed.-State Judicial Relationships, Orlando, 1991-92, planning com for We. Regional Conf. on State-Fed. Judicial Relationships, Stevens, Wash., 1992-93; chair dist. ct. symposium and jury utilization Ctrl. Dist. Calif., 1985, chair atty. liason, 1989-90, chair U.S. Constitution Bicentennial com., 1986-91, chair magistrate judge com., 1992-93; mem. State Adv. Group. on Juvenile Justice and Delinquency Prevention, 1983-84, Bd. Legal Speciliazations Criminal Law Adv. Commn., 1983-84, victim/witness adv. com. Office Criminal Justice Planning, 1980-83, U. So. Calif. Bd. Councilors, 1993—; active team in tng. Leukemia Soc. Am., 1993, 95; legion lex bd. dir. U. So. Calif. Sch. Law Support Group, 1981-83. Winner Hale Moot Ct. Competition, State of Calif., 1967; named Judge of Yr., Orange County Trial Lawyers Assn., 1978, Most Outstanding Judge, Orange County Bus. Litigation Sect., 1990; recipient Franklin G. West award Orange County Bar Assn., 1985. Mem. ABA (jud. adminstrn. divsn.and litigation sect. 1984—, nat. conf. fed. trial judges com. on legis. affairs 1990-91), Am. Law Inst., Am. Judicature Soc., Fed. Judges Assn. (bd. dirs. 1989-92), Nat. Assn. Women Judges, U.S. Supreme Ct. Hist. Soc., Ninth Cir. Dist. Judges Assn., Calif. Supreme Ct. Hist. Soc., Orange County Bar Assn. (mem. numerous coms., Franklin G. West award 1984), Calif. Judges Assn. (mem. com. on judicial coll. 1978-80, com. on civil law and procedure 1980-82, Dean's coll. curriculum commn. 1981), Calif. Judges Found. Office: US Dist Ct PO Box 12339 751 W Santa Ana Blvd Santa Ana CA 92701-4509

STOTLER, EDITH ANN, grain company executive; b. Champaign, Ill., Oct. 11, 1946; d. Kenneth Wagner and Mary (Odebrecht) S. Student, Mary Baldwin Coll., 1964-66; BA, U. Ill., 1968. Asst. v.p. Harris Trust and Savs. Bank, Chgo., 1969-83; mgr. Can. Imperial Bank of Commerce, Chgo., 1983, sr. mgr., 1983-85, asst. gen. mgr. group head, 1985-88, v.p., dir. utilities, 1988-90; ptnr. Stotler Grain Co., Champaign, Ill., 1990—; pres. Homer Grain Co., 1990—; bd. dirs., mem. exec. compensation com., nominating com. Southeastern Mich. Gas Enterprises, Inc. Mem. investment com. 4th Presbyn. Ch.; past pres. liberal arts and scis. constituent bd. U. Ill., mem. pres.' coun.; mem. Friends of Libr. Bd., U. Ill. Mem. U. Ill. Found., Champaign Country Club, Art Club. Home: 900 N Lake Shore Dr Apt 2106 Chicago IL 60611-1523

STOTT, ANNETTE, art historian, educator; b. Madison, Wis., May 29, 1955; d. Peter Hadley and Huldah Jean (Hyers) Pierce; m. Don W. Stott, Aug. 2, 1980. BA summa cum laude, Concordia Coll., Moorhead, Minn., 1977; MA, U. Wis., 1980; PhD, Boston U., 1986. Asst. prof. U. Maine, Orono, 1986-87, Winthrop Coll., Rock Hill, S.C., 1987-91; asst. prof. Denver U., 1991-94, assoc. prof., 1994—. Essayist: Gari Melchers: A Retrospective, 1990, Katwijk In De Schilderkunst, 1995; contbr. articles to profl. jours. Fulbright fellow, The Netherlands, 1983-84; Andrew Mellon Faculty fellow Harvard U., 1989-90; travel grantee Am. Coun. Learned Socs., Oxford, Eng., 1995. Mem. Am. Studies Assn., Assn. Historians Am. Art, Nineteenth Century Studies Assn., Coll. Art Assn. Office: Univ Denver Sch Art and Art History 2121 E Asbury Denver CO 80210

STOTT, DIANA ELLEN, social services advocate; b. Cedarville, Calif., Apr. 14, 1934; d. I.A. and Lois A. (Tyeryar) Barber; m. Norman K. Stott, June 29, 1956; children: Charlotte, Russell. BA, U. Calif., Berkeley, 1956; BS in Metaphysics, Am. Inst. Holistic Theology, Berkeley, 1996, Am. Inst. Holistic Theology, 1996; BA in Holistic Theology, Am. Inst. Holistic Theology, 1996. Cert. pre-sch., elem., adult edn. Tchr. Tsuda Sch., Tokyo, 1956, Colegio Americano, Durango, Mex., 1968, Mt. Diablo Schs., Concord, Calif., 1964-74; founder, owner Sunbonnet Sue Templates, Willits, Calif., 1970-89; owner, operator 3T Sheep Ranch, Willits, 1974-89; founder, dir. Animal Crackers PreSch., Willits, 1979-89; dir. of shelter svcs. CATRL, Kimberling City, Mo., 1992—; co-founder Harbor Lights Shelter Svcs., Stone County, Mo., 1994; com. Mo. Coalition Against Domestic Violence, 1992—, Nat. Coalition Against Domestic Violence; sch./cmty. organizer for drug and alcohol prevention, 1993—. Editor newsletter The Quilting Room, 1974-80. Patron Friends of the Libr., Kimberling City, Mo., 1989-94; legis. chmn. Bus. & Profl. Women, Tri-Lakes Area, 1993-94; publicity chmn. Welcome Wagon, Tri-Lakes Area, 1992. Recipient quilting awards Guild of Quilters, 1975-76, Premium Wool award Mendocino County Fair, 1986-88. Mem. AAUW (founder, chmn. Tri-Lakes 1993-94), Bus. and Profl. Women's Club (Woman of Yr. 1996), Kimberling Area C. of C. (rep. 1993-96), Phi Mu, Pi Lambda Theta. Mem. Unity Ch. Office: Christian Assocs of Table Rock Lake Country Club Shopping Ctr Kimberling City MO 65686

STOUFER, RUTH HENDRIX, community volunteer; b. Pitts., June 21, 1916; d. Walter Willits and Frances (Ponbeck) Hendrix; m. William Kimball Stoufer, Sept. 8, 1937 (dec.); children: Walter Hendrix, Frances Elizabeth Stoufer Waller (dec.). BS, Iowa State U., 1937. Trustee Marcus J. Lawrence Meml. Hosp., 1989—; devel. chairperson Sedona-Verde Valley Am. Heart Assn., 1988-91; mem. adv. bd. L.A. chpt. Freedom's Found., 1965-78; mem. coord. med. adv. bd. U. Ariz., 1986—; founding chairperson Muses of the Mus. No. Ariz., 1984-85, pres., 1986-87, mem. Sinagua Soc., 1983—; bd. dirs. Nat. Charity League, L.A., 1963, Found. for Children, L.A., 1964, 65, 66; pres. Panhellenic adv. bd. U. So. Calif. 1964; key adv. U. So. Calif. chpt. Beta Alpha of Gamma Phi Beta, 1960-63. Named Woman of Yr., Inter-city Coun., Gamma Phi Beta, 1963. Home: 87 Doodlebug Knoll Sedona AZ 86336-6422

STOUGHT, CYNTHIA MARIE, psychiatric nurse; b. Connellsville, Pa., Jan. 24, 1953; d. Matthew J. and Veronica Marie (Hertznell) Kremposky; m. Richard C. Stought, Apr. 26, 1975; children: Adam, Jeffrey. Diploma, Shadyside Hosp., 1973; BSN, Lebanon Valley Coll., 1981, postgrad., 1993—. RN, Pa.; cert. psychiat./mental health nurse. Staff nurse Holy Spirit Hosp. Cmty. Mental Health Ctr., Camp Hill, Pa., 1977-94; case mgr. State Employee Assistance Program, Harrisburg, 1994-95; gen. mgr. Global Vision, Inc., Harrisburg, Pa. Bd. dirs. Capital Area Share, 1988; active Jr. League of Harrisburg, 1982-93, bd. dirs., 1991-92, sustaining mem., 1993—.

STOUT, ELIZABETH WEST, foundation administrator; b. San Francisco, Mar. 4, 1917; d. Claudius Wilson and Sarah (Henderson) West; m. Bruce Churchill McDonald, Mar. 19 1944 (dec. 1952); children: Douglas, Anne; m. Charles Holt Stout, Oct. 27, 1958 (dec. 1992); stepchildren: Richard, George (dec.), Martha Stout Gilweit. Student, U. Nev., 1934-37; grad., Imperial Valley Coll., 1990. Cashier, acct. N.Y. Underwriters, San Francisco, 1937-42; sec. supply and accounts USN, San Francisco, 1942-44. Contbr. articles to profl. jours. Mem. adv. bd. Anza-Borrego Desert, Natural History Assn., 1974-84; founder Stout Paleontology Lab., Borrego Springs, Calif., 1982; found. trustee Desert Rsch. Inst., Reno, 1989—; active Black Rock Desert Project, 1989, Washoe Med. Ctr. League, 1953—, St. Mary's Hosp. Guild, 1953—. Named Disting. Nevadan U. Nev., 1993. Mem. Anza-Borrego Desert Natural History Assn. (dir. emeritus 1984), Soc. Vertebrate Paleontology, De Anza Desert Country Club, Kappa Alpha Theta. Republican. Episcopalian.

STOUT, HELEN OLIVIA, artist, writer; b. York, Yorkshire, Eng., May 6, 1910; d. Bruno and Margaret Naomi (Ward) Lasker; m. Aron S. Gilmartin, 1934 (div. 1960); children: David Gilmartin, Alice (dec.), Peter Ward Gilmartin; m. John E. Stout, 1968 (dec. 1988). AB, Smith Coll., 1931; MA, U. Chgo., 1940. Social worker various social aid orgns. in midwest 1940-55, Children's Home Soc., Seattle, 1955-74. Author: with others (taped poetry and memoirs of seniors) The Crystal Set, 1980; illustrator (poetry book) Daughter, 1986; author and illustrator 6 self-published books; artist: numerous performances and exhibitions of paintings, prints in Seattle, N.Y.C., Austin, Tex., Boulder, Colo., 1970—. Mem. ACLU, Sch. Program Involving City's Elderly, 1974—, Planned Parenthood, various programs to help AIDs patients. Recipient hon. mention and two firsts in art shows, Northwest region. Unitarian.

STOUT, JANIS P., English educator; b. Ft. Worth, May 4, 1939; d. Kenneth C. and Helean B. (Minshew) Pitts; m. Bob J. Stout, Oct. 27, 1956 (div. Aug. 1981); children: Douglas, Alan, Richard, Steven; m. Loren D. Lutes, May 15, 1982; stepchildren: Dan, David, Laura, Rebekah. BA, Lamar State Coll., 1966, MA, 1968; PhD, Rice U., 1973. Lectr. Bryn Mawr (Pa.) Coll., 1972-74; asst. prof. Haverford (Pa.) Coll., 1974-75; lectr. Lamar Coll., Orange, Tex., 1975-76; dir. grad. programs, lectr. Rice U., Houston, 1977-87; assoc. dean, prof. Tex. A&M U., College Station, 1987-94, prof., 1994—; acting assoc. dean Auburn (Ala.) U., 1992-93. Author: Sodoms in Eden: The City in American Fiction Before 1860, 1976, The Journey Narrative in American Literature: Patterns and Departures, 1983, Strategies of Reticence: Silence and Meaning in the Works of Jane Austen, Willa Cather, Katherine Anne Porter, and Joan Didion, 1990, Katherine Anne Porter: A Sense of Time, 1995, (novels) A Family Likeness, 1982, Eighteen Holes, 1984, Home Truth, 1992; contbr. articles to profl. jours., chpt. to books, short stories to jours. Vol. Houston Area Food Bank, 1985-87. Mem. MLA, AAUP, Katherine Anne Porter Soc. (co-organizer, sec. 1992—), Western Lit. Assn., Soc. for Study of So. Lit., PEN. Office: Tex A&M U Dept English College Station TX 77843-4227

STOUT, JUANITA KIDD, judge; b. Wewoka, Okla., Mar. 7, 1919; d. Henry Maynard and Mary Alice (Chandler) Kidd; m. Charles Otis Stout, June 23, 1942. BA, U. Iowa, 1939; JD, Ind. U., 1948, LLM, 1954; LLD (hon.), Ursinus Coll., 1965, Ind. U., 1966, Lebanon Valley Coll., 1969, Drexel U., 1972, Rockford (Ill.) Coll., 1974, U. Md., 1980, Roger Williams Coll., 1984, Morgan State U., 1985, Russell Sage Coll., 1966, Fisk U., 1988, Del. State Coll., 1990. Bar: D.C. 1950, Pa. 1954. Tchr. pub. schs. Seminole and Sand Springs, Okla., 1939-42; tchr. Fla. A&M U., Tallahassee, 1949, Tex. So. U., Houston, 1949; adminstrv. asst. to judge U.S. Ct. Appeals (3d cir.), Phila., 1950-54; pvt. practice law Turner & Stout, Phila., 1954-55; chief of appeals Dist. Atty.'s Office City of Phila., 1955-59, judge mcpl. ct., 1959-69; judge Ct. Common Pleas, Phila., 1969-88, sr. judge, 1989—; justice Supreme Ct. Pa., Phila., 1988-89; sitting as sr. judge Ct. Common Pleas. Recipient Jane Addams medal Rockford Coll., 1966, Disting. Svc. award U. Iowa, 1974, MCP/Gimbel award for humanitarianism, 1988, 89—, John Peter Zenger award John Peter Zenger Soc., 1994; named to Hall of Fame of Okla., Okla. Heritage Soc., 1981, Disting. Svc. award U. Okla. Alumni Assn. and U. Okla., 1995; Disting. Alumni svc. award Ind. U., Bloomington, 1992; named Disting. Dau. of Pa., 1988. Mem. ABA, Pa. Bar Assn., Phila. Bar Assn. (Sandra Day O'Connor award 1994), Nat. Assn. Women Judges, Nat. Assn. Women Lawyers. Democrat. Episcopalian. Home: Logan Sq E # 1803 2 Franklin Town Blvd Philadelphia PA 19103-1231

STOUT-PIERCE, SUSAN, marketing specialist; b. Denver, June 6, 1954; d. Joseph Edward and Esther Mae (Miller) Hull; m. Jerry Lee Stout, Nov. 3, 1979 (div. Aug. 1984); m. Gary Myron Pierce, Nov. 21, 1987. AS, Denver Community Coll., 1975; BS, Met. State Coll., 1986. Cert. Radiologic Technologist, Calif., Am. Registry Radiologic Technologists. Radiologic technologist The Swedish Med. Ctr., Englewood, Colo., 1975-79, The Minor Emergency Clinic, Lakewood, Colo., 1979-80, The Children's Hosp., Denver, 1980-86, Merit Peralta Med. Ctr., Oakland, Calif., 1986-87, Am. Shared Hosp. Svcs., Oakland, 1987, HCA South Austin (Tex.) Med. Ctr., 1987-88, U. Calif., San Francisco, 1988-89; clin. imaging specialist OEC-Diasonics, Salt Lake City, 1989-92; software applications specialist Cemax, Inc., Fremont, Calif., 1992-93; mktg. specialist ADAC Healthcare Info. Systems, Houston, Tex., 1993—. Mem. NAFE, Am. Bus. Women's Assn. Home: 264 Rachael Pl Pleasanton CA 94566-6228

STOVALL, CARLA JO, state official, lawyer; b. Hardner, Kans., Mar. 18, 1957; d. Carl E. and Juanita Jo (Ford) S. BA, Pittsburg (Kans.) State U., 1979; JD, U. Kans., 1982. Bar: Kans. 1982, U.S. Dist. Ct. Kans. 1982. Pvt. practice, Pittsburg, 1982-85; atty. Crawford County, Pittsburg, 1984-88; gov. Kans. Parole Bd., Topeka, 1988-94; attorney general State of Kansas, Topeka, 1995—; lectr. law Pittsburg State U. 1982-84; pres. Gilston Internat. Mktg., Inc., 1988—. Bd. dirs., sec. Pittsburg Family YMCA, 1983-88. Mem. ABA, Kans. Bar Assn., Crawford County Bar Assn. (sec. 1984-85, v.p. 1985-86, pres. 1986-87), Kans. County and Dist. Attys. Assn., Nat. Coll. Dist. Attys., Pittsburg State U. Alumni Assn. (bd. dirs. 1983-88), Pittsburg Area C. of C. (bd. dirs. 1983-85, Leadership Pitts. 1984), Bus. and Profl. Women Assn. (Young Careerist 1984), Kans. Assn. Commerce and Industry (Leadership Kans. 1983), AAUW (bd. dirs. 1983-87). Republican. Methodist. Home: 3561 SW Mission Ave Topeka KS 66614-3637 Office: Atty Gen Office Kansas Judicial Ctr 2nd Fl Topeka KS 66612*

STOVALL, CAROL ELIZABETH, communications specialist; b. Jacksonville, Fla., May 6, 1949; d. William Earl and Grace Elizabeth (Rung) S. BS in Advt., U. Fla., 1971; MA in Theology, U. Notre Dame, 1986. Cert. tchr., Fla.; joined Sisters of St. Joseph, Roman Cath. Ch., 1976. Staff sec. WJKS-TV, Jacksonville, 1971-72, mem. prodn. staff, 1972-73, promotion coord., 1973-74; promotion coord., pub. svc. dir. WJXT-TV, Jacksonville, 1974-76; diocesan dir. comms. Diocese of St. Augustine, Jacksonville, 1981-86; religion tchr. Bishop Kenny H.S., Jacksonville, 1986-90; cmty. rels. specialist Mercy Hosp., Miami, Fla., 1990-92; dir. comms. Diocese of Palm Beach, Palm Beach Gardens, Fla., 1992-96; srs. coord. Intracoastal Health Syss. Good Samaritan Hosp., W. Palm Beach, Fla., 1996—. Editor Palm Beach edit. The Fla. Cath. newspaper, 1992-94. Mem. Am. Women in Radio and TV, Pub. Rels. Soc. Am. (treas. Palm Beach chpt. 1994—). Office: Intracoastal Health Syss Good Samaritan Hosp 1309 N Flagler Dr W West Palm Beach FL 33401

STOVALL, FRANCES MIDDAGH, community leader; b. Lawrenceville, Ill., Dec. 7, 1921; d. John Judy and Rebecca (Fowler) Middagh; m. Jack N. Stovall, Aug. 16, 1941; children: Richard Middagh Stovall, Frances Judy S. Upchurch, John Fowler, Susan Calvert S. Carter. Student, McMurry Coll., 1938-41. Woman's Page editor Odessa (Tex.) News Times, 1937-40; reporter Abilene (Tex.) Reporter News, 1938-41. Author: Clear Springs and Limestone Ledges, A History of San Marcos and Hays County, 1986; editor: Cottage Kitchen Cookbook, 1983, Cottage Kitchen, Second Helping, 1986, Twenty Years In Cottage Kitchen, 1996; columnist San Marcos Daily Record, 1988-96. founder Heritage Assn. San Marcos, 1975, bd. dirs., 1975-96, hon. life mem., 1989—; chmn. City of San Marcos Bicentennial Commn., 1972-76, Hays County Hist. Commn., 1987-91; mem. Main St. Adv. Bd., San Marcos, 1989; founder Preservation Assocs., Inc., Friends of Hays County Hist. Commn., 1990-95. Named Woman of Yr. Beta Sigma Phi, San Marcos, 1976, 96, Vol. of Yr., Rotary Club San Marcos, 1995; recipient Tex. award for hist. preservation Tex. Hist. Commn., Austin, 1990, John Ben Shepperd Leadership award Tex. Hist. Commn., Austin, 1991, Lifetime Achievement award Tex. Hist. Commn., Austin, 1993. Mem. DAR, Nat. Trust for Hist. Preservation, Tex. Hist. Found., Tex. State Hist. Assn., Spring Lake Garden Club, Magna Charta Dames. Home: 20 Timbercrest Cir San Marcos TX 78666

STOVALL, SHEILA L., elementary education educator, computer analyst; b. Charleston, W.Va., July 12; d. Lester N. and Clara Lee (Whaley) Gibbs; m. Irl Thomas Stovall II, June 2, 1967; children: Irl Thomas III, Charles Benjamin. BA in Edn., U. South Fla., Tampa, 1978. Cert. in elem., childhood and gifted edn., Fla. Tchr. Genesis Elem. Sch., New Port Richey, Fla., 1979-83, Richey Elem. Sch., New Port Richey, 1983-87, Seven Springs Sch., New Port Richey, 1987-90, Gulfside Elem. Sch., Holiday, Fla., 1990—; tchr. Ridgewood H.S. Adult Edn., New Port Richey, 1989-90; tutor, 1979—; pres. Stovall & Assocs., New Port Richey, 1990—. Author: (books) Just Let Me. . ., 1993, Former Students and Other Criminals I Have Known, 1996, (poetry) Herald, 1975. With Spl. Olympics Orgn., New Port Richey, 1983-87. Mem. Fla. Assn. Computers in Edn. (v.p. 1990-91). Methodist. Home: 5524 Ridgewood Dr New Port Richey FL 34652-4315

STOVER, CAROLYN NADINE, middle school educator; b. Martinsburg, W.Va., May 30, 1950; d. Norman Robert and Garnet Agnes (Zombro) Whetzel; m. James Stenner Stover Sr., Nov. 20, 1971; children: Heather N., James S. Jr. BA in Home Econs., Shepherd Coll., 1972; cert. in advanced studies, W.Va. U., 1978; cert. in tchg. methods, Marshall U., 1973; cert. in spl. edn., Shippensburg Coll., 1972. Cert. tchr., W.Va., N.Mex.; reg. EMT. Substitute tchr. Berkeley County Schs., Martinsburg, W.Va., 1972, adult edn. instr., 1972-77, home econs. instr., 1973-83; substitute tchr. Ruidoso (N.Mex.) Mcpl. Schs., 1984-90, child find coord. Region 9 edn. coop., 1990, life skills and at-risk educator, 1991—, coord. coun., 1991-93, mem. budget com., 1993. Elder First Presbyn. Ch., Ruidoso, 1984-90, 94—; sponsor Acad. Booster Club, Ruidoso, 1993—; instr. CPR, 1980. Named Outstanding Young Women of Am., 1981. Mem. NEA, Nat. Middle Sch. Assn., Ruidoso Edn. Assn., Rotary (youth leadership councilor 1991—). Democrat. Home: Box 7837 1007 Hull Rd Ruidoso NM 88345 Office: Ruidoso Mid Sch 100 Reese Dr Ruidoso NM 88345-6016

STOVER, ELLEN SIMON, health scientist, psychologist; b. Bklyn., Nov. 21, 1950; d. Ralph and Charlotte (Tulchin) Simon; m. Alan B. Stover, June 3, 1973; children: Elena Randall Simon, Randall Alan Simon, Samantha Anne Simon. BA with honors, U. Wis., 1972; PhD, Catholic U., 1978. Cons. NIMH, Rockville, Md., 1972-74, spl. asst. to assoc. dir. extramural programs, 1976-77, chief, small grants program, 1977-79, asst., acting & chief rsch. resources br., 1980-85, dep. dir., div. basic scis., 1985-88, dir. office on AIDS, 1988—; exec. sec., drug abuse rsch. rev. com. Nat. Inst. on Drug

Abuse, Rockville, 1974-76; co-chmn. AIDS rsch. behavioral coordinating com. NIH, 1993—. Recipient Superior Svc. award USPHS, 1987, 92, 93, Dir.'s award NIH, 1996. Mem. APA, Am. Psychol. Soc. Office: NIMH 5600 Fishers Ln # 10-75 Rockville MD 20857-0001

STOVER, LYNN MARIE, nurse educator; b. Kittanning, Pa., June 23, 1967; d. Randolph John and Joan Patricia (Hillgrove) S. BSN, U. Ala., Birmingham, 1989, MSN, 1993, postgrad., 1995—. RN cert. pediatric nurse, ANCC. Nursing asst. U. Ala. Hosp., Birmingham, 1988-89; staff nurse III Children's Hosp. of Ala., Birmingham, 1989-93; grad. teaching asst. U. Ala., Birmingham, 1991-93; instr. nursing Capstone Coll. Nursing U. Ala., Tuscaloosa, 1993—; comty. infant care instr. DCH Regional Med. Ctr., Tuscaloosa, 1994—; faculty advisor U. Ala. Assn. Nursing Students, Tuscaloosa, 1994—; camp nurse Camp Winnataska, Pell City, Ala., 1992—; unit-level staff nurse orientation chmn. Children's Hosp. Ala., Birmingham, 1991-93. Contbr. articles to nursing jours. instr. religious edn. St. Francis Cath. Ch., Tuscaloosa, 1994—; vol. Crestwood Hosp., Huntsville, Ala., 1981-85, ARC, Huntsville and Birmingham, 1981-88; leader Girl Scouts Am., Birmingham, 1990-91. Recipient Best Student Paper award Ala. Acad. Sci., 1993; faculty summer rsch. grantee U. Ala., 1994. Mem. ANA, Nat. League Nursing (advocacy mem.), Nat. Student Nurse's Assn. (sustaining mem.), Ala. State Nurse's Assn. (treas. dist. III 1994-96, Outstanding New Mem. 1991), Sigma Theta Tau (Epsilon Omega chpt., publicity chmn., newsletter editor 1994—), Omicron Delta Kappa. Republican. Roman Catholic. Home: 4709 Cypress Creek Ave E # 106 Tuscaloosa AL 35405-4441 Office: U Ala Box 870358 Tuscaloosa AL 35487

STOWE, ALEXIS MARIANI, accountant, consultant; b. Binghamton, N.Y., May 3, 1950; d. Albert Joseph and Gilda Ann (DiNardo) Mariani; m. Dennis James Stowe, June 3, 1972 (dec. Nov. 1988); children: Cort Andrew, Derek Anthony, Jilda Ann. Student, Le Moyne Coll., 1968-70; BS in Acctg., SUNY, Buffalo, 1972; MS in Acctg., SUNY, Albany, 1974; MS in Taxation, Southeastern U., 1980. CPA, N.Y., Va.; cert. fraud examiner; cert. govt. fin. mgr., cert. info. sys. auditor. In-charge acct. Ernst & Young, CPA's, Buffalo, 1973-74; sr. corp. acct. Moog, Inc., East Aurora, N.Y., 1974-76; auditor U.S. Gen. Acctg. Office, Washington, 1976-78, 79-80; tax law specialist IRS, Washington, 1978-79; pvt. practice CPA Woodbridge, Va., 1980-87; v.p., contr. M.T. Hall, Ltd., Woodbridge, 1987-91; audit mgr. U.S. Dept. Health and Human Svcs., Washington, 1991-93; oversight mgr. Resolution Trust Corp., Washington, 1993-94; v.p., prin. Gardiner, Kamya, CPA's, Washington, 1994—; trustee pension plan M.T. Hall, Ltd., Woodbridge, 1987-90; team leader CFO task force Pres.'s Coun. on Integrity and Efficiency, Washington, 1991-93; instr. Inspector Gen. Auditor Tng. Inst., Ft. Belvoir, Va., 1992—; mem. task force on grants Govtl. Acctg. Stds. Bd., Norwalk, Conn., 1992—; mem. faculty Assn. Cert. Fraud Examiners, 1995—. Contbr. articles to profl. jours. N.Y. Regents scholar, 1968-72. Mem. AICPA, Va. Soc. CPAs, Assn. Govt. Accts. (vice chair pubs. 1994—, Author's award 1991), Assn. Cert. Fraud Examiners, Info. Sys. Audit Control Assn., Cath. Daus. of Am., Chi Omega, Beta Gamma Sigma. Roman Catholic. Home: 6013 Wheeler Ln Broad Run VA 22014-2201 Office: Gardiner Kamya & Assocs CPA 1717 K St NW Ste 601 Washington DC 20006-1501

STOWE, MADELEINE, actress; b. L.A., Aug. 18, 1958; m. Brian Benben. Films: Stakeout, 1987, Worth Winning, 1989, Revenge, 1990, The Two Jakes, 1990, Closetland, 1991, Unlawful Entry, 1992, The Last of the Mohicans, 1992, Another Stakeout, 1993, Short Cuts, 1993, China Moon, 1993, Blink, 1994, Bad Girls, 1994, Twelve Monkies, 1995; TV movies: The Gangster Chronicles: An American Story, The Nativity, Beulah Land, Black Orchid (miniseries). Office: care UTA 9560 Wilshire Blvd Fl 5 Beverly Hills CA 90212-2401*

STOWELL, MARY SAVAGE, psychotherapist, occupational therapist; b. Honolulu, Dec. 12, 1947; d. John Richard and Mary Van Dusen (Rogers) Savage; m. Franklin D'Olier Stowell, Aug. 26, 1972; children: Elspeth Amelia, Emily Esty Savage. BA, Vassar Coll., 1970; MS, Columbia U., 1973; PhD with distinction, Saybrook Inst., 1995. Registered occupl. therapist, Am. Occupl. Therapy Assn. Dir. activities therapies Southwood Mental Health Ctr., Chula Vista, Calif., 1974-75; occupl. therapist San Diego VA Med. Ctr., La Jolla, Calif., 1975-79; coord. day treatment Grossmont Dist. Hosp., La Mesa, Calif., 1979-80, sr. liaison occupl. therapist, 1981-82; coord. child activity program Children's Hosp. and Health Ctr., San Diego, 1982-83; intern in psychology Olympic Mental Health Assocs., Bremerton, Wash., 1990-92, assoc., 1992-95, resident in psychology, 1995—; cons. occupl. therapy, Bainbridge Island, Wash., Bremerton, 1986-92; vol. art therapy program Fred Hutchinson Cancer Rsch. Ctr., Seattle, 1985-87. Mem. editl. bd. Occupl. Therapy in Mental Health jour., 1975—. Bd. dirs. Helpline House, Bainbridge Island, 1995—. Recipient Eileen Garrett Scholarship grant Parapsychology Found., 1993. Mem. APA, Am. Soc. for Psychical Rsch., Soc. for Psychical Rsch., Am. Soc. for Clin. Hypnosis. Office: Olympic Mental Health Assoc 237 Sixth St Bremerton WA 98337

STRAAYER, CAROLE KATHLEEN, elementary education educator; b. Jackson, Mich., Jan. 4, 1934; d. Joseph and Maude Vivian (Whitney) Kerr; m. Richard Lee Straayer, Feb. 1, 1958; children: Steven Jay, Susan Kay Straayer Maxson. A, Jackson Community Coll., Mich., 1953; BS, Ea. Mich. u., 1957, MA, 1961. Cert. elem. tchr., Mich. Tchr. Napoleon (Mich.) Sch. Dist., 1954-56, Waterford (Mich.) Twp. Sch. Dist., 1957, Jackson (Mich.) Pub. Schs., 1957—. Mem. choir 1st Presbyn. Ch., Jackson, 1983—. Jackson Citizen Patriot scholar, 1971. Mem. NEA, AAUW (group leader 1989-92), Mich. Assn. Supervision and Curriculum Devel. (region 3 rep. 1989-90), Mich. Edn. Assn. (ret.), Jackson Edn. Assn. (blg. rep., chairperson tenure com. 1974-80, mem. negotiating team 1995), Jackson/Hillsdale Profl. Devel. (rep. 1988-90), Delta Kappa Gamma (Beta Beta chpt. pres. 1986-88). Home: 2220 Pioneer Dr Jackson MI 49201-8900

STRACHAN, GLADYS, religious organization executive; b. N.Y.C., Dec. 10, 1929; d. Jacob Allen and Annie Mae (Alston) McClendon; m. Eugene S. Callender (div. 1963); 1 child, Renee Denise; m. John R. Strachan (dec. 1982). Student, NYU, 1947-49. Dep. asst. Presbyn. Ch. of East Africa, Nairobi, Kenya, 1964-67; assoc. for women's program Presbyn. Ch. of U.S., N.Y.C., 1970-83; exec. dir. United Presbyn. Women, N.Y.C., 1983—; cons. Peace Corps, Nairobi, 1964-67, Operation Crossroads Africa, Nairobi, 1964-67, Afro-Am. Ednl. Inst., Teaneck, N.J., 1977-79, various women's orgns. in Asia, Australia, Europe, Africa. V.p. Addicts Rehab. Ctr. Bd., N.Y.C., 1957—; mem. N.Y. Coalition of 100 Black Women, N.Y.C., 1972—; v.p., bd. dirs. La. Internat. Cultural Ctr. Recipient Cert. of citation borough pres. N.Y.C., 1977, Harlem Peacemaking award Harlem Peacemaking Com., 1983. Mem. La. C. of C., River City Assn. Bus. and Profl. Women. Office: Presbyn Women 100 Witherspoon St Louisville KY 40202-1396

STRADA, CHRISTINA BRYSON, educator, librarian; b. Dunoon, Argyll, Scotland; d. Alexander Paul and Mary (Spencer) Bryson; m. Joseph Anthony Strada (dec.); children: Michael, David, Elaine, Mary Margaret. AB, SUNY, Fredonia, 1968, MS, 1970; MLS, U. Buffalo, 1973. Library media specialist. Tchr. English Dunkirk (N.Y.) H.S., 1969-70, Cardinal Mindzenty H.S., Dunkirk, 1970-71; tchr. English Lake Shore Cen. H.S., Angola, N.Y., 1971-72, libr., tchr., 1973-77; libr. dir. Darwin R. Barker Libr. and Mus., Fredonia, 1977-86; tchr., libr. Cassadaga (N.Y.) Valley Sch. Dist., Fredonia, 1990—; instr. English composition, English lit., libr. rsch. Empire State Coll. N.Y., State Univ. Coll., Fredonia; cons. Friends of Barker Libr. and Mus., 1986—. Author short stories. Organizer Fredonia Hist. Preservation Soc., 1986—. Mem. N.Y. state Library Assn., N.Y. State Tchr. Assn., AAUW (chmn. telephone and reservations com. 1969—), LWV, Fredonia Shakespeare Club (v.p. 1988-89), Zonta Internat. (corr. sec., membership chmn. 1981-82). Republican. Roman Catholic. Home: 15 Carol Ave Fredonia NY 14063-1207

STRADER, MARLENE KNOCKS, nursing educator; b. St. Louis; d. Charles Joseph and Julia (Motykaitys) Knocks; m. Timothy James Shocklee, Feb. 2, 1957 (div. Oct. 1974); children: Ellen Marie, Timothy James Jr.; m. Richard P. Strader, Nov. 6, 1974. ADN, Meramec C.C., St. Louis; BS in Nursing, St. Louis U., MS in Nursing, PhD. RN, Mo., Fla.; cert. health care risk mgr., Fla. Mem. nursing faculty So. U., Edwardsville, Ill., 1981-88, U. Mo., St. Louis, 1988-93; field rep., mem. faculty Joint Commn. on Accreditation of Health Care Orgns., Oakbrook Terrace, Ill., 1993-96; mem. adv. bd. CompreHealth, St. Louis, 1985—; cons. hosps. Ohio, Md., Fla., 1985—; nurse rschr. Midwest Nursing Rsch. Soc., St. Louis, 1988-91. Author: Role Transition to Patient Care Management, 1995. NIH grantee Nat. Ctr. for Nursing Rsch., Washington, 1990. Mem. ANA, Am. Nurses' Found. (grant 1988), Nursing Consortium St. Louis,Fla. Nurses' Assn., Sigma Theta Tau (grant 1988), Phi Kappa Phi. Home: 6600 Sunset Way # 119 Saint Petersburg Beach FL 33706

STRADER, MELINDA ANN AMASON, nursing consultant; b. Amarillo, Tex., Apr. 13, 1955; d. Robert Daniel Amason and MaryLou Ivy Amason Jordan; m. Dan M. Strader, June 12, 1976; children: Aaron, Ashley. Diploma, Meth. Hosp., 1976. RN, Tex.; cert. in audiometric screening, CPR. Staff nurse nursery HCA Med. Ctr., Plano, Tex., 1982-83; pediatrics nurse for pvt. physician Plano, 1983-87; nurse auditor Blue Cross/Blue Shield, Dallas, 1987-90; nurse cons. Genex Svcs. (formerly Gen. Rehab.), Dallas, 1990-95; case mgmt. supr. S.W. divsn. Sullivan Health mgmt., Plano, 1995—, dir. S.W. region. Mem. ICMA, CMSA, Nat. Assn. Rehab. Profls. in Pvt. Sector, Tex. Assn. Rehab. Profls. in Pvt. Sector, Tex. Nurses Assn. Office: Sullivan Health Mgmt 5757 Alpha #615 Dallas TX 75240

STRAHAN, JULIA CELESTINE, electronics company executive; b. Indpls., Feb. 10, 1938; d. Edgar Paul Pauley and Pauline Barbara (Myers) Shawver; m. Norman Strahan, Oct. 2, 1962 (div. 1982); children: Daniel Keven, Natalie Kay. Grad. high sch., Indpls. With EG&G/Energy Measurements, Inc., Las Vegas, Nev., 1967—; sect. head EG&G Co., 1979-83, mgr. electronics dept., 1984—. Recipient award Am. Legion, 1952, Excellence award, 1986. Mem. NAFE, Am. Nuclear Soc. (models and mentors), Internat. Platform Assn. Home: 5222 Stacey Ave Las Vegas NV 89108-3078 Office: EG&G PO Box 1912 Las Vegas NV 89125-1912

STRAHAN, NATALIE KAY, chiropractor; b. Indpls., Sept. 16, 1965; d. Norman Nathan and Julia Celestine (Pauley) S. BS in Psychology, So. Utah U.; BS in Biology, L.A. Coll. Chiropractic, PhD. Chiropractor Thropay Chiropractic, Downey, Calif., 1992-93, Skyline Chiropractic, Long Beach, Calif., 1993-94, Back Pain Ctr., Long Beach, Calif., 1994—. Sec. Soroptimist, Lakewood, Calif., 1994. Mem. Am. Chiropractic Assn., Christian Chiropractic Assn. Home: 404 Hillcrest St El Sigundo CA 90245 Office: Back Pain Ctr 532 Redondo Ave Long Beach CA 90814

STRAIT, VIOLA EDWINA WASHINGTON, librarian; b. El Paso, Tex., Aug. 29, 1925; d. Leroy Wentworth and Viola Edwina (Wright) Washington; m. Freeman Adams, Mar. 6, 1943; 1 child, Norma Jean (Mrs. Louis Lee James); m. Clifford Moody, Jan. 8, 1950; 1 child, Viola Edwina III (Mrs. Paul M. Cunningham); m. Amos O. Strait, Dec. 9, 1972. Bus. cert., Tillotson Coll., 1946, BA, 1948; MS in Libr. Sci., U. So. Calif., 1954. Substitute tchr. El Paso Pub. Schs., 1948; sec., bookkeeper U.S.O.-YWCA, El Paso, 1948-50; libr. asst. Spl. Svcs. Libr., Ft. Bliss, Tex., 1950-53, libr., 1954-71; equal employment opportunity officer Ft. Bliss, 1971-72; dep. equal employment opportunity officer Long Beach (Calif.) Naval Shipyard, 1972-85; with Temp. Job Mart, Torrance, Calif., 1986-87; substitute tchr. Ysleta Ind. Sch. Dist., 1988-89; profl. libr. Eastwood Hts. Elem. Sch., 1989-90; sec. Shiloh Bapt. Ch., El Paso, 1991-92; br. mgr. El Paso Pub. Libr., 1992—. Sec. Sunday sch. Bapt. Ch., 1956-66, min. music, 1958-72, supr. young adult choir, 1966-72, pres. sr. choir, 1969-71; disc jockey Sta. KELP, El Paso, 1970-72; host radio show Sta. KTEP, U. Tex., El Paso, 1994—. Mem. ALA, Border Region Libr. Assn. (chmn. scholarship com. 1970), NAACP (sec. 1996), Alpha Kappa Alpha. Democrat. Baptist. Home: 1667 Nancy Lopez Ln El Paso TX 79936-5410 Office: El Paso Pub Libr Vets Park Br 5303 Salem Dr El Paso TX 79924-1801

STRAITS, BEVERLY JOAN, gynecologist; b. Aurora, Ill., Jan. 29, 1939; d. Ernest Joseph and Mildred Betty (Shobe) S.; children: Kell Donald, Jill Elizabeth. BA, Carleton Coll., 1961; MD, Northwestern U., 1965. Diplomate in gynecology and obstetrics. Intern Passavant Hosp., Chgo., 1965-66; residency Lutheran Hosp., Milw., 1966-69; pvt. practice Wheat Ridge, Colo., 1969—. Fellow Am. Coll. Obstetrics & Gynecology. Office: 7855 W 38th Ave Wheat Ridge CO 80033-6109

STRAKOSCH, KATHERINE WENTON, executive recruiter; b. N.Y.C., Oct. 4, 1933; d. William J. and Elsie G. (Sullivan) Wenton; m. Raymond D. Strakosch, Nov. 10, 1956 (div. May 1977); children: Joanne, Mark, Gregory, Karen. B.A. cum laude, Coll. Mt. St. Vincent, 1955. Cert. personnel cons. Vice pres. Dunhill of Greater Stamford, Inc., Wilton, Conn., 1976-80, pres., 1980-93; mem. Town of Wilton Personnel Policies Com., 1983-93. Pres. bd. dirs. Wilton Playshop, 1971-73, vice chmn. bd. trustees, 1982-86, chmn. 1986-87; mem. Democratic Town Com., Wilton, 1976-79; pres. Surrey Search Group, 1994—. Mem. Conn. Assn. Personnel Consultants (sec. 1979, mem. ethics com. 1981-93, newsletter editor 1980), Nat. Assn. Pers. Cons., Women in Sales (v.p. membership Fairfield County chpt. 1989-90), Women in Mgmt. (opportunity com. 1991-92). Roman Catholic. Avocations: tennis, travel, reading. Home and Office: Surrey Search Group 60 Surrey Ln East Falmouth MA 02536-4943

STRALEY, RUTH A. STEWART, government administrator, small business owner; b. Tanner, W.Va., May 31, 1949; d. Robert Sherwood Sr. and Reta Virginia (Frymier) Stewart; m. Charles Edward Straley, Aug. 17, 1968. BS magna cum laude, U. Md., 1982. Sec. W.Va. U., Morgantown, 1968-70; certification asst. Prince Georges County Bd. Edn., Upper Marlboro, Md., 1970-71; clerical asst. Def. Intelligence Agy., Washington, 1971-72; budget asst. Naval Weather Svc. Command, Washington, 1972-76; budget analyst Navy Recruiting Exhibit Ctr., Washington, 1976-78, Navy Regional Data Automation Command, Washington, 1978-80; hdqrs. budget officer Naval Facilities Engring. Command, Alexandria, Va., 1980-83; fin. mgr. Naval Res. Readiness Command Region 8, Naval Air Sta., Jacksonville, Fla., 1983-93; owner, pres. Horizons Unltd. Planning Svcs., Orange Park, Fla., 1989—; comptr. Naval Pers. Support Activity Europe, Naples, Italy, 1993-94; comptroller U.S. Naval Sta., San Diego, 1994—. Treas. Eagle Bay Homeowners Assn., Orange Park, 1989-93. Named Woman of Yr., Fed. Women's Program, 1983. Mem. NAFE, Am. Soc. Mil. Comptrs. (sec. 1984-89, v.p. 1990-91, 95-96, pres. 1989-90, 91-93), Profl. Housing Mgmt. Assn. Republican. Methodist. Home: 432 C Ave Coronado CA 92118-1823 Office: Horizons Unltd Planning Svc PO Box 181611 Coronado CA 92178-1611

STRAND, MARION DELORES, social service administrator; b. Kansas City, Mo., Dec. 19, 1927; d. Henry Franklin and Julia Twyman (Noland) Pugh; m. Robert Carmen Scipioni, Aug. 2, 1947 (dec. 1984); children: Mark, Brian, Roberta, Laura, Steven, Mary,Angela, Julie, Victor, Robert, Lawrence; m. Donald John Strand, Sept. 1, 1985. BA, U. Kans., 1948; MS, SUNY, Brockport, 1975. Counselor N.Y. Dept. Labor, Rochester, 1971-75, 77-79; regulatory adminstr. N.Y. Dept. Social Svcs., Rochester, 1976-77, 79-81; pres. Greater Rochester Svcs., Inc. (doing bus. as Scribes & Scripts), 1982—; founder Ctr. for Law Access and Document Preparation. Columnist, local newspaper. Active polit. campaigns for women candidates, 1981—; UN envoy Unitarian Ch., Rochester, 1988-92; fin. chair William Warfield Scholarship Com., Rochester, 1988-90; chair bd. govt. affairs Genesee Valley Arthritis Found., Rochester, 1988-90; mem. parade com. 95/75 Celebration of Monroe County, 1995; mem. Lyell Av. Revitalization Com. Mem. NOW (pres. child care com. Greater Rochester sect. 1987-88, chair family issues task force), AAUW (bd. dirs., cmty. rep. Greater Rochester br.), DAR (Irondequoit chpt.), Greater Rochester C. of C. (legis. com., small bus. coun. 1987—, bd. dirs. women's coun. 1981-91, pres. 1989-90), Susan B. Anthony Rep. Women's Club (program com., 1st v.p. 1994, co-chair Greater Rochester Coalition for Choice 1994-95) Golden Girls Investment Club (founder), Phi Beta Kappa, Psi Chi. Home and Office: Greater Rochester Svcs Inc 105 Elmwood Ter Rochester NY 14620-3703

STRANDBERG, REBECCA NEWMAN, lawyer; b. Ft. Smith, Ark., Apr. 22, 1951; d. Russell Lynn and Doris Jean (Lindsey) Newman; m. Jeffrey Eugene Strandberg, Nov. 23, 1979; children: Lindsey Katherine, Russell Jeffrey. BA, Tex. Christian U., 1973; JD, So. Meth. U., 1976. Bar: Tex. 1976, Md. 1981, D.C. 1983. Field atty. NLRB, New Orleans, 1976-79; legis. asst. Senator Dale Bumpers, Washington, 1979-81; pvt. practice, Montgomery County, Md., 1981-92; ptnr. Carlin & Strandberg PA, Bethesda, Md., 1992-96; prin. Rebecca Strandberg & Assocs. PA, 1996—; mem. nominators commn., 1996—. Vice-pres. bd. dirs. Share-A-Ride Corp., Montgomery County, 1984; bd. mgrs. Woodside Meth. Ch., 1989-92; mem. Holy Cross Community Hosp Quality Evaluation Com., 1989—; CLE chmn. Montgomery County Bar: Am. Inns of Ct., 1990-92. Named Chmn. of Yr. Montgomery County Bar, 1992-93. Mem. ABA (litigation, labor and employment law sect. 1985—), Md. State Bar (bd. govs. 1992—, spl. com. devel. guidelines for prevention of sexual harassment 1994—, co-chair centenial pub. svc. project subcom.), Silver Spring C. of C., Montgomery County Women's Bar Assn. (chmn. membership 1982-83), Md. Women's Bar Assn., Silver Spring Bus. and Profl. Women (pres. 1984-85), SBA Women in Bus. (advocate 1982), Women's Bar D.C. Office: Rebecca Strandberg & Assocs PA 4405 E West Hwy Ste 402 Bethesda MD 20814-4537

STRANDJORD, MARY JEANNINE, telecommunications executive; b. Kansas City, Mo., Dec. 21, 1945; d. Vincent Stanley and Clara Lucille (Aylward) Kerwin; m. David Christian Strandjord, June 24, 1978; 1 child, Katie Marie. BSBA, Kans. U., 1968; postgrad., U. Mo., Kansas City, 1976. CPA, Mo. Mem. audit staff Enrst & Whinney, Kansas City, 1968-71; with Kansas City Power & Light, 1971-81, dir., asst. controller, 1979-81; dir., asst. controler Macy's Midwest, 1981-82, v.p. acctg., budget and expense, 1982-85; v.p. fin. and ops. Americsource subs. United Telecomm., Inc., Westwood, Kans., 1986, v.p., treas., 1986—. Treas. St. Health Ctr. Found., Kansas City, 1986—; mem. exec. com., acct. adv. coun. Kans. U., Lawrence, 1989—,. Named Woman of Yr., YMCA, 1987. Mem. AICPA, Fin. Exec. Inst., Blue Hills Country Club. Roman Catholic. Home: 908 W 121st Kansas City MO 64145-1013*

STRANG, RUTH HANCOCK, pediatric educator, pediatric cardiologist, priest; b. Bridgeport, Conn., Mar. 11, 1923; d. Robert Hallock Wright and Ruth (Hancock) S. BA, Wellesley Coll., 1944, postgrad., 1944-45; MD, N.Y. Med. Coll., 1949; MDiv, Seabury Western Theol. Sem., 1993. Diplomate Am. Bd. Pediat.; ordained deacon Episc. Ch., 1993, priest, 1994. Intern Flower and Fifth Ave. Hosp., N.Y.C., 1949-50, resident in pediatrics, 1950-52; mem. faculty N.Y. Med. Coll., N.Y.C., 1952-57; fellow cardiology Babies Hosp., N.Y.C., 1956-57, Harriet Lane Cardiac Clinic, Johns Hopkins Hosp., Balt., 1957-59, Children's Hosp., Boston, 1959-62; mem. faculty U. Mich., Univ. Hosp., Ann Arbor, 1962-89, prof. pediatrics, 1970-89, prof. emeritus, 1989—; priest-in-charge St. Johns Episcopal Ch., Howell, Mich., 1994—; dir. pediatrics Wayne County Gen. Hosp., Westland, Mich, 1965-85; mem. staff U. Mich. Hosps.; mem. med. adv. com. Wayne County chpt. Nat. Cystic Fibrosis Rsch. Found., 1966-80, chmn. med. adv. com. nat. found., Detroit, 1971-78; cons. cardiology Plymouth (Mich.) State Home and Tng. Sch., 1970-81. Author: Clinical Aspects of Operable Heart Disease, 1968; contbr. numerous articles to profl. jours. Mem. citizen's adv. coun. to Juvenile Ct., Ann Arbor, 1968-76; mem. med. adv. bd. Ann Arbor Continuing Edn. Dept., 1968-77; mem. Diocesan Com. for World Relief, Detroit, 1970-72, Am. Heart Assn. Mich. (v.p. 1989, pres. 1991); trustee Episcopal Med. Chaplaincy, Ann Arbor, 1971—; mem. bishop's com. St. Aidan's Episc. Ch., 1966-69, sec., 1966-68, vestry, 1973-76, 78-80, 84-86, 90-91, sr. warden, 1975, 76, 78, 80, 86, 90; del. Episc. Diocesan Conv., 1980, 91; bd. dirs. Livingston Cmty. Hospice, 1995—. Mem. AMA, Am. Acad. Pediatrics, Am. Coll. Cardiology, Mich. Med. Soc., Washtenaw County Med. Soc., N.Y. Acad. Medicine, Am. Heart Assn., Women's Rsch. Club (membership sec. 1966-67), Ambulatory Pediatric Assn., Am. Assn. Child Care in Hosps., Am. Assn. Med. Colls., Assn. Faculties of Pediatric Nurse Assn./Practitioners Programs (pres. 1978-81, exec. com. 1981-84), Episc. Clergy Assn. Mich., Northside Assn. Ministries (pres. 1975, 76, 79-80). Home: 4500 E Huron River Dr Ann Arbor MI 48105-9335

STRANG, SANDRA LEE, airline official; b. Greensboro, N.C., Apr. 22, 1936; d. Charles Edward and Lobelia Mae (Squires) S.; BA in English, U. N.C., 1960; MBA, U. Dallas, 1970. With American Airlines, Inc., 1960—, mgr. career devel. for women, N.Y.C., 1972-73, dir. selection and tng., 1974-75, sr. dir. selection, tng. and affirmative action, 1975-79, sr. dir. compensation and benefits, Dallas/Ft. Worth, Tex., 1979-84, dir. passenger sales tng. and devel., 1984—; regional sales mgr. Rocky Mountain Region, Denver, 1985—; pres. The SLS Group, Inc., (DBAs) Sales Leadership Seminars, Inc., Sr. Leadership Svcs., Inc., Svc. Leadership Seminars, Inc., Speakers, Lectrs., and Seminars, Inc, 1988—. AARP, Mem. Am. Mgmt. Assn., Assn. Advancement of Women into Mgmt., Am. Soc. Tng. and Devel., Am. Compensation Assn., Internat. Platform Assn. Home: 3493 E Euclid Ave Littleton CO 80121-3663

STRANGE, FRANCES RATHBUN, financial aid administrator, therapist; b. Wichita Falls, Tex., Aug. 14, 1949; d. Willie and Viola Gertrude (Loesby/Jarrell) Rathbun; m. Douglas William Strange, 1967 (div. Apr. 1992); children: Chad Douglas, Cameron Todd, Cooper Lane, Chance (dec.). B of Behavioral Sci., Hardin-Simmons U., 1988, MEd, 1992; M of Human Rels., U. Okla., 1990. Lic. profl. counselor. Bus. officer Hardin-Simmons U., Abilene, Tex., 1983-85; admissions office Hardin Simmons U., Abilene, Tex., 1986-88, asst. fin. aid dir., 1989-93, fin. aid dir., 1993—; grant coord. fin. aid Baylor U., Waco, Tex., 1985-86; social worker Dept. Human Svcs., Duncan, Okla., 1988-89; contract counselor Harmony Family Svcs., Abilene, 1992—. Mem. APA, ACA, Alpha Chi. Baptist. Home: 84 CR 529 Baird TX 79504

STRASSER, ROSE LOUISE, dance and physical education educator; b. Buffalo, Apr. 5, 1907; d. Ferdinand and Louisa (Hermann) S. BS in Edn., U. Mich., 1929, MS, 1933; student, Bennington Sch. Dance, 1939, U. Calif., 1940. Cert. tchr. health, physical edn. Tchr., physical edn. Rochester (Mich.) Pub. Schs., 1929-31; instr., physical edn. Keuka Coll., Keuka Park, N.Y., 1931-33; tchr., elem. physical edn. Buffalo Elem. Schs., 1933-35; tchr., health physical edn. Buffalo High Schs., 1935-46; dance div. health physical edn., recreation SUNY, Brockport, 1946-66; dir. student teaching, health, physical edn., recreation SUNY, chmn., dance dept., 1966-70; lectr. U. Buffalo, 1935—, St. Joseph's Tchrs. Coll., Buffalo, 1938—; vis. prof. NYU, Internat. Dance Camps, 1964-65; sec. Assn. Women Physical Edn., Albany, N.Y., 1939-41, v.p. 1941-42, pres. 1942-43. Contbr. articles to profl. jours. and mags. Dance specialist Internat. Inst., Buffalo, 1944-52; dance cons. N.Y. State Dirs. Health Physical Edn. Recreation, Albany, 1964-66, 68, Girl Scouts Am., Rochester & Monroe County, N.Y., 1962-65; judge square dancing N.Y. State Fair, Syracuse, 1965, 66, 67; judge folk dancing, square dancing Pa. State Fair, Harrisburg, 1967, 68, 69. Recipient Heritage award, 1989; grantee, 1968, 69. Fellow AAHPERD (sec. dance sect. 1964-66, Cert. of Appreciation 1985); mem. AAUP, Nat Dance Assn. (archivist, historian 1973-87), Am. Dance Guild (citation 1974), Am. Assn. Emeritii, N.Y. State Dance Tchrs. Higher Edn., Folk Dance Fedn. Calif., Nat. Folk Orgn. U.S., Soc. Folk Dance Historians, Arizonans Cultural Devel., We. Monroe Hist. Soc., Congress Rsch. Dance, U. Mich. Alumni Phoenix, Delta Kappa Gamma. Republican. Home: 5060 E Florian Ave Mesa AZ 85206-2830

STRASSER, SUSAN, historian, researcher, writer; b. Pitts., Mar. 27, 1948; d. Alexander and Maxine Harriet (Hochberg) S.; m. Robert Elliott Guldin, May 9, 1992. BA, Reed Coll., 1969; MA, SUNY, Stony Brook, 1971, PhD, 1977. Mem. faculty Evergreen State Coll., Olympia, Wash., 1975-88; lectr. Princeton (N.J.) U., 1989; dir. univ. honors program, assoc. prof. history George Washington U., Washington, 1990-92; rsch. fellow German Hist. Inst., Washington, 1993-95; cons. Smithsonian Instn., Washington. Author: Never Done, 1982 (Sierra award 1983), Satisfaction Guaranteed, 1988; mem. bd. editors Am. Quar., 1993-95; also numerous articles. Fellow Woodrow Wilson Found., 1969-70, Smithsonian Instn., 1973-75, Am. Coun. Learned Socs., 1984-85, Bunting Inst., 1984-85, Harvard U. Bus. Sch., 1985-86, Guggenheim Found., 1992-93. Mem. Am. Hist. Assn., Orgn. Am. Historians. Home and Office: 7309 Willow Ave Takoma Park MD 20912

STRASSMEYER, MARY, newspaper columnist; b. Cleve., Aug. 5, 1929; d. Frederick H. and Katherine (Mullally) S. A.B., Notre Dame Coll., 1951; postgrad., Toledo U., 1952; J.D., Cleve. Marshall Coll. Law, Cleve. State U., 1981. Bar: Ohio 1983. Reporter Cleve. News, 1956-60; contbr. Cleve. Plain Dealer, 1957-60, feature writer, 1960-65, beauty editor, 1963-65, travel writer, 1963—, society editor, 1965-77, 85—; columnist, 1977—; co-creator syndicated cartoon Sneakers; co-owner Gerry's Internat. Travel Agy., Cleve., 1991—. Author: Coco: The Special Delivery Dog, 1979. Mem. Soc. Am. Social Scribes (founder, 1st pres.), Notre Dame Coll. Alumnae Assn., Women in Comm. Club: Press (Cleve.) (inducted into Hall of Fame 1994). Home: 2059 Broadview Rd Cleveland OH 44109-4145 Office: The Plain Dealer 1801 Superior Ave E Cleveland OH 44114-2107

STRATAKI, ANASTASIA See STRATAS, TERESA

STRATAS, TERESA (ANASTASIA STRATAKI), opera singer, soprano; b. Toronto, Ont., Can., May 26, 1938. Student, of Irene Jessner, 1956-59; grad., Faculty Music, U. Toronto, 1959; LLD (hon.), McMaster U., 1986, U. Toronto, 1994. Winner Met. Opera auditions, 1959; major roles in opera houses throughout world include: Mimi in La Bohème; Tatiana in Eugene Onegin; Susanna in The Marriage of Figaro; Nedda in Pagliacci; Marenka in The Bartered Bride; Three Heroines in Il Trittico; Violetta in La Traviata; title role in Rusalka; Jennie in Mahagonny; created title role in completed version of Lulu (Alban Berg), Paris Grand Opera, 1979; film appearances Kaiser von Atlantis, Seven Deadly Sins; Zefirelli's La Traviata, Salome, Lulu, Paganini, Zarewitsch, Eugene Oregin; Broadway debut in Rags, 1986; creator the role of Marie Antoinette Ghosts of Versailles world premiere Met. Opera, 1992; sang both female leading roles Il Tabarro, Pagliacci double bill opening Met. Opera, 1994, numerous recs. including Richard Strauss' Salomé, Songs of Kurt Weill. Decorated Order of Can.; recipient 3 Grammy awards, Emmy award, Drama Desk award, 1986, 3 Grammy nominations, Tony nomination, 1986, Tiffany award, 1994; named Performer of Yr., Can. Music Council, 1979. Office: care Met Opera Co Lincoln Center Plz New York NY 10023 also: Vincent & Farrell Associates 157 W 57th St Ste 502 New York NY 10019-2210*

STRATE, JAN NICOLE (NIKI STRATE), contractor; b. Bassett, Nebr., Nov. 21, 1944; d. Howard Weir and Marian Evelyn (Wiese) Thompson; m. Paul Dean Peister, July 20, 1969 (div. Feb. 1984); children: Justin Paul, Jordan Nicole; m. James Richard Strate, Aug. 31, 1985. BA in Speech and Drama, Wayne State Coll., 1972, MS in Counseling magna cum laude, 1977. Clk. Meadowlark Gifts, Kearney, Nebr., 1965-66, Ransom House Gifts, Norfolk, Nebr., 1966-69; tchr. Norfolk Pub. Schs., 1970-84, Northeat C.C., Norfolk, 1970-84; supr. customer svc. Merchants Corp. Am., Buena Park, Calif., 1985-87; owner, v.p. Cal-Best Constrn. Co., Anaheim, Calif., 1987—. Republican. Episcopalian. Home: 6519 Joshua Tree Ave Orange CA 92667

STRATTON, ELAINE AUDREY, small business owner, writer; b. Flint, Mich., Apr. 27, 1925; d. Victor William and Eva Jane (Moore) Miller; m. Olin W. Stratton, Dec. 25, 1946 (dec. Sept. 1991); children: Candace, Jeffrey, John. BS in Education, So. Ill. U., 1946, MS, 1966; Adminstrv. cert., So. Ill. U., Edwardsville, 1976. Cert. sch. adminstrn. Tchr. Coulterville (Ill.) Sch., 1946-47; libr. Highland (Ill.) Cmty. Sch., 1948-80; dir. librs. Highland Cmty. Unit #5, 1970-80; dir., Fed. Elem. Writing Program WRITE ON, Highland, 1980-82; book reviewer KMOX, St. Louis, 1986; pub. Swiss Village Book Store, St. Louis, 1985-88, owner, 1978-94; cons. Libr. Book Selection Svc., Bloomington, Ill., 1975-82; oral historian, Ill. 1972-77; cons. in field. Author, editor, pub.: St. Louis and the River - a "Lite" History, 1988; editor, pub.: Illinois Sketches (Roscoe Misselhorn), 1985. Chairperson Bicentennial Rsch. & Dissemination Com. (developed and produced bicentennial calendar sent to Smithsonian), 1975-76; oral historian, 1975-77; mem. Friends of Louis Latzer Meml. Libr.; program dir., Sch. Vol. Program, 1978-82, Highland, Ill.; vol. St. Louis Visitors and Conv. Ctr., 1995; bd. dirs. Highland Hist. Assn.; sec. Historyonics Theatrical Co., St. Louis, 1992—. Recipient Ill. Bicentennial Com. award, 1976; grantee WRITE ON project, 1980-82. Mem. ALA (chairperson libr. media skills com. 1981-83), Nat. Assn. Women Bus. Owners, Am. Bookman's Assn. Office: Swiss Village Book Store Lacledes Landing 707 N 1st St Ste 107 Saint Louis MO 63102-2552

STRATTON, EVELYN JOYCE, judge, lawyer; b. Bangkok, Thailand, Feb. 25, 1953; came to U.S., 1971; d. Elmer John and Corrine Sylvia (Henricksen) Sahlberg; m. R. Stephen Stratton, June 16, 1973; children: Luke Andrew, Tyler John. A.A., U. Fla., 1973; B.A., Akron U., 1975; J.D., Ohio State U., 1978. Bar: Ohio 1979, U.S. Dist. Ct. (so. dist.) Ohio 1979, U.S. Ct. Appeals (6th cir.) 1983. Teaching asst. history LeTourneau Coll., Longview, Tex., 1973-74; law clk. Knepper, White, Columbus, 1978-79, Crabbe & Brown, Columbus, 1977-79; assoc. Hamilton, Kramer, Myers & Cheek, Columbus, 1980-85; ptnr. Wesp, Osterkamp & Stratton, 1985-88, judge Ct. Common Pleas, 1989—; assoc. justice Ohio State Supreme Ct.; trustee Linc Resources, Columbus, 1980-86, chmn. bd. dirs., 1984-86; speaker legal seminars. Worker Rep. Party Campaign, Columbus, 1983—; mem. Women's Rep. Rountable, 1984—; bd trustees Ohio affiliate Nat. Soc. to Prevent Blindness, 1989—; vice chmn. fund drive United Way Columbus, 1984; fundraiser Easter Seal Telethon, 1986, Columbus Mus. Art, 1986; bd. sec. Columbus Countywide Devel. Corp., 1987-88; mem. women's bd. Cen. Ohio Lung Assn., 1989—, Columbus Area Women's Polit. Caucus, 1987—, League Against Child Abuse, 1989. Recipient Gold Key award LeTourneau Coll., Gainesville, Fla., 1974, Service commendation Ohio Ho. of Reps., 1984. Mem. ABA, Columbus Bar Assn. (com. chmn. 1982-84, bd. govs. 1984-88), Ohio Bar Assn., Columbus Bar Found. (trustee 1985—, officer, sec. 1986-87, v.p. 1987-88), Nat. Assn. Women Judges, Ohio Common Pleas Judges Assn., Women Lawyers Franklin County, Phi Delta Phi (pres. 1982-83), Nat. Women's Polit. Caucus, Greater Franklin County Rep. Lawyers Club, Women's Rep. Club of Ohio, Civitan (trustee 1982-83), Univ. Club, Exec. Club of Columbus (bd. dirs. 1986—), Chairman's Club. Office: 30 E Broad St 3rd Fl Columbus OH 43215-3414*

STRATTON, MARIANN, retired naval nursing administrator; b. Houston, Apr. 6, 1945; d. Max Millard and Beatrice Agnes (Roemer) S.; m. Lawrence Mallory Stickney, nov. 15, 1977 (dec.). BSN, BA in English, Sacred Heart Dominican Coll., 1966; MA in Mgmt., Webster Coll., 1977; MSN, U. Va., 1981. Cert. adult nurse practitioner. Ensign USN, 1966, advanced through grades to rear adm., 1991; patient care coord. Naval Regional Med. Ctr., Charleston, S.C., 1981-83; nurse corps plans officer Naval Med. Command, Washington, 1983-86; dir. nursing svcs. U.S. Naval Hosp., Naples, Italy, 1986-89, Naval Hosp., San Diego, 1989-91; chief pers. mgmt. Bur. Medicine & Surgery, Washington, 1991-94; dir. USN Nurse Corps, Washington, 1991-94; ret. Oct. 1, 1994 USN, 1994. Decorated Disting. Svc. medal, Meritorious Svc. medal with two stars, Naval Achievement medal. Mem. ANA, Assn. Mil. Surgeons of U.s., Interagy. Inst. of Fed. Health Car Execs.

STRATTON-WHITCRAFT, CATHLEEN SUE, critical care, pediatrics nurse; b. Jackson, Mich., Jan. 14, 1964; d. Ronald Alfred and Shirley Anne (Wickham) Stratton; m. David R. Whitcraft, Aug. 14, 1988. BSN magna cum laude, SUNY, Brockport, 1985. Cert. critical care nurse, ACLS. Student clin. asst. Yale-New Haven Hosp., 1984; charge nurse Walter Reed Army Med. Ctr., Washington, 1990; clin. nurse, critical care med. ICU and pediatric ICU SRT-Med. Staff Agy., Springfield, Va., 1985-88; asst. head nurse Sinai Hosp., Balt., 1988-90; charge nurse surg. SICU ICU VA Med. Ctr., Balt., 1991—. 1st lt. U.S. Army Nurse Corps, 1985-88, Res., 1988-93. Recipient Cert. of Achievement, Elizabeth Dole.

STRAUS, HELEN LORNA PUTTKAMMER, biologist, educator; b. Chgo., Feb. 15, 1933; d. Ernst Wilfred and Helen Louise (Monroe) Puttkammer; m. Francis Howe Straus II, June 11, 1955; children: Francis Howe III, Helen E, Christopher M., Michael W. AB magna cum laude, Radcliffe Coll., 1955; MS in Anatomy, U. Chgo., 1960, PhD in Anatomy, 1962. With U. Chgo., 1964—, asst. prof. anatomy, 1967-73, dean of students, 1971-82, assoc. prof., 1973-87, dean of admissions, 1975-80, prof. anatomy and biol. scis., 1987—; bd. govs. U. Chgo. Internat. House, 1987—. Trustee Radcliffe Coll., Cambridge, Mass., 1973-83. Recipient Quantrell Award for Excellence in teaching, U. Chgo., 1970, 87, Silver medal Case Outstanding Tchr. Program, 1987. Mem. AAAS, NCAA (acad. requirements com. 1986-92, chmn. 1990-92, rsch. com. 1996—), Nat. Sci. Tchrs. Assn., Am. Assn. Anatomists, Harvard U. Alumni Assn. (bd. dirs. 1980-83), Phi Beta Kappa (sec., treas. U. Chgo. chpt. 1984—). Home: 5642 S Kimbark Ave Chicago IL 60637-1606 Office: U Chgo 5845 S Ellis Ave Chicago IL 60637-1404

STRAUSER, CAROL ANN, small business owner; b. Oak Ridge, Tenn., Sept. 3, 1947; d. Wilbur Alexander and Lois Irene (Carter) S. Student, U. Md. Salesperson Hecht Co., Bethesda, Md.; sec. Bricklayers, Washington, U.S. Govt., Rockville, Md. Mem. NOW, NAFE, AAUW, DAR, Mus. Women Arts. Home and Office: Carol A Strauser Inc 155 Skyline Dr California PA 15419

STRAUSS, CAROL KAHN, institute executive director, editor, consultant; b. N.Y.C., Sept. 21, 1944; d. Alfred and Lotte (Landau) K.; m. Peter Mathes, Dec. 1977 (div. 1980); m. Peter Strauss, June 1989. BS, Columbia U., 1970; MS, Hunter Coll., 1973. Asst. book editor Council on Fgn. Relations, N.Y.C., 1972-79; sr. editor, dir. pub. affairs Hudson Inst., Indpls., 1984-89; sr. editor, cons. 20th Century Fund, N.Y.C., 1990-94; exec. dir. Leo Baeck Inst., N.Y.C., 1994—; cons., writer, editor Ford Found., 20th Century Fund, Mayoral Task Forces, Kidder Peabody & Co., N.Y. Holocaust Commn. Editor: (books) The Coming Boom, 1982, Thinking About the Unthinkable in the 1980's, 1984; editor, co-author articles for profl. publs. Pres. Congregation Habonim, N.Y.C., 1984-92; trustee Self-Help, Inc., N.Y.C., 1986-93; v.p. Fedn. Jews from Ctrl. Europe, 1990—. Jewish. Club: Atrium (N.Y.C.). Home: 870 5th Ave New York NY 10021-4953 Office: Leo Baeck Inst 129 E 73d St New York NY 10021-3502

STRAUSS, DOROTHY BRANDFON, marital, family, and sex therapist; b. Bklyn.; d. Marcus and Beatrice (Wilson) Brandfon; widowed; 1 child, Josette E. MacNaughton. BA, Bklyn. Coll., 1932; MA, NYU, 1937, PhD, 1963. Diplomate Am. Bd. Sexology. Instr. Hunter Coll. CUNY, 1960-63; prof. Kean Coll., Union, N.J., 1963-77; pvt. practice and clin. supervision Bklyn. and, N.J., 1970—; clin. assoc. prof. psychiatry Downstate Med. Ctr., SUNY, Bklyn., 1974—; assoc. dir. Ctr. for Human Sexuality, 1974-82; mem. NIMH rsch. team U. Pa., 1973-82. Contbr. articles on gerontology and sexual dysfunctions to profl. jours. Fellow Am. Assn. Clin. Sexologists (founding); mem. Am. Psychol. Assn., Am. Assn. for Marital and Family Therapy (clin. mem. 1971—, supr. 1981—), Am. Assn. Sex Therapists, Counselors and Educators (chairperson task force on supervision 1984-86, chairperson supr. cert. com. 1986-93, chair cert. steering com. 1992—), Kappa Delta Pi. Home and Office: 1401 Ocean Ave Brooklyn NY 11230-3971

STRAUSS, HARLEE SUE, environmental consultant; b. New Brunswick, N.J., June 19, 1950; d. Robert Lemuel and Helene (Marcus) S. BA, Smith Coll., 1972; PhD, U. Wis., 1979. Postdoctoral fellow dept. biology MIT, Cambridge, 1979-81; congrl. sci. fellow U.S. House of Reps., Washington, 1981-83; spl. asst. Am. Chem. Soc., Washington, 1983-84; spl. cons. Environ. Corp., Washington, 1984-85; rsch. assoc. Ctr. for Tech., Policy and Indsl. Devel. MIT, Cambridge, 1985-86, rsch. affiliate, 1986—; sr. assoc. Gradient Corp., Cambridge, 1986-88; pres. H. Strauss Assocs., Inc., Natick, Mass., 1988—; pres., exec. dir. Silent Spring Inst., Inc., 1994-95; adj. assoc. prof. Sch. Pub. Health, Boston U., 1990-94; lectr. Sch. Medicine, Tufts U., Boston, 1988—; mem. steering com. Boston Risk Assessment Group, 1986-95. Co-editor, author: Risk Assessment in Genetic Engineering, 1991; author: Biotechnology Regulations, 1986; author book chpts. in field. Active Instl. Biosafety Com., Army Rsch. Lab., Natick, 1989—, Army Sci. Bd., 1994—. Mem. AAAS, Am. Chem. Soc., Am. Soc. Microbiology, Assn. for Women in Sci. (chmn. com. New England chpt. 1986-88, co-chmn. legis. com. 1985—), Biophys. Soc. (chmn. com. 1983-84, Congl. Sci. fellow 1981-83), Soc. for Risk Analysis (pres. New England chpt. 1991-92). Jewish. Office: H Strauss Assocs Inc 21 Bay State Rd Natick MA 01760-2942

STRAUSSER, BETH ANNE, grants officer; b. Norristown, Pa., Sept. 26, 1969; d. Jan Edwin and Josephine May (Seyfert) S. AB, Bryn Mawr Coll., 1991. Cert. grants officer level I U.S. Govt. Mgr. libr. publs. Bryn Mawr (Pa.) Coll. Libr., 1987-91; intern, asst. to Rep. Sam Morris Pottstown, Pa., 1988, 90; franchise mgr. Coll. Pro Painters, Valley Forge, Pa., 1989; pers. mgmt. specialist NSF, Arlington, Va., 1991-93; grants officer NSF, Arlington, 1993—. Mem., advocate Arlington/Alexandria Coalition for Homeless, 1991—; fundraiser Bryn Mawr Coll. Ann. Fund, 1991—; mem. Alexandria Singers, sect. leader, soloist, 1992-96, dance capt., 1996; mem. Vocal Express, Fairlington Ch. Choir, 1991-96. Democrat. Methodist. Home: 9138 Blarney Stone Dr Springfield VA 22152-2145

STRAVALLE-SCHMIDT, ANN ROBERTA, lawyer; b. N.Y.C., Jan. 2, 1957. Grad. cum laude, Phillips Exeter Acad., 1975; student, Occidental Coll., 1975-78, Oxford Coll., Eng., 1976-77; BS cum laude, Boston Coll., 1980; JD, Boston U., 1987. Bar: Conn. 1987, U.S. Dist. Ct. Conn. 1988, U.S. Supreme Ct. 1993. Consulting staff Arthur Andersen, Boston, 1980-82; supr. CID ops. Aetna Life & Casualty, Hartford, Conn., 1982-84; summer intern U.S. Atty.'s Office, Boston, 1985; jud. clk. Hon. Judge Thayer III N.H. Supreme Ct., 1987-88; trial lawyer Day, Berry & Howard, Hartford, 1988-91; sr. lawyer comml. litigation and appellate practice Berman & Sable, Hartford, 1991-96; asst. dir. The Traveler's Indemnity Co./Aetna Surety and Casualty Co., Hartford, 1996—; brief judge Nat. Appellate Advocacy Competition, 1996. Mem. editorial bd. Conn. Bar Jour., 1990—; contbr. articles to profl. jours. Mem. Hebron Dem. Town Com.; mem. Hebron Bd. Fin., 1995—; justice of the peace. Mem. ABA, Conn. Bar Assn. (founder, chair appellate practice com. litigation sect. 1994—, mem. exec. com. litigation sect.), Hartford Bar Assn., Hartford Assn. Women Attys. Home: 51 Elizabeth Dr Hebron CT 06248 Office: Travelers Indemnity Co/ Aetna Surety and Casualty One Tower Sq Hartford CT 06183-6016

STRAWN, FRANCES FREELAND, real estate executive; b. Waynesville, N.C., Nov. 18, 1946; d. Thomas M. and Jimmie (Smith) Freeland; m. David Updegraff Strawn, Aug. 30, 1974; children: Kirk, Trisha. AA, Brevard C.C., Cocoa, Fla., 1976; postgrad. U. Cen. Fla., 1976-77, Grad. Realtor Inst. Cert. real estate brokerage mgr., residential specialist. Acting sr. buyer Brevard County Purchasing Bd. of County Commns., Titusville, Fla., 1971-75; rsch. analyst Brevard C.C., Cocoa, 1977-78; realtor assoc., Orlando, Fla., 1979-82; realtor, broker, pres. Advance Am., Inc., Orlando, 1982-89; assoc. Ann Cross, Inc., Winter Park, Fla., 1988—. Contbr. articles to Fla. Realtor, 1993, Communique, 1994. Bd. dirs. Vol. Ctr. of Cen. Fla. (rec. sec. 1989), Cen. Fla. Zool. Pk., 1989-92; co-chmn, fundraiser Black Tie Walk on the Wild Side, 1992; program chmn. Young Rep. Women, Orlando, 1983; coord. Congressman Bill Nelson's Washington Internship Program; co-ticket chmn. Art and Architecture Orlando Regional Hosp.; mem. steering com. Fla. Heritage Homecoming, Orlando, 1987; sec. Mayor's Wife's Campaign Activities, Orlando, 1986-87; vice chmn. Horizon Exec. Bd., 1987-89, chmn., 1989; recording sec. Women's Bus. Edn. Council, 1988, mem. adv. bd. , 1987, bd. dirs. 1988-90; active calendar com. Women's Resource Ctr., bd. dirs. 1989-90; lectr. Jr. Achievement., 1988-93; mem. steering com. scholarship dinner Crummer Bus. Coll. Rollins Coll., 1992. Mem. Orange County Bar Aux. (bd. dirs. 1986-88, corr. sec. 1987), Creative Bus. Ownership for Women (adv. bd. 1986-88, grievance vice chmn. 1989), Nat. Assn. Realtors, Orlando Bd. Realtors (grievance com. 1985-91), Orlando Area Bd. Realtors (membership com. 1980-84, profl. standards com. 1983-84, lectr. Success Series 1988—), Women's Coun. of Realtors, Women's Exec. Coun., Citrus Club (Orlando, social com. 1987-88, bd. dirs 1990-95). Episcopalian. Avocations: travel, needlepoint, canoe trips, skiing. Home: 105 NW Ivanhoe Blvd Orlando FL 32804-5958 Office: Ann Cross Inc 233 W Park Ave Winter Park FL 32789-4343

STRAWN, KAREN MICHAL, county auditor; b. Sigourney, Iowa, June 21, 1951; d. Richard John and Myra Arlene (Appleget) Peiffer; m. Willis G. Strawn II, Nov. 6, 1971; children: Willis G. III, Laura Beth. BS, Iowa State U., 1975. Clk. Buena Vista County Auditor's Office, Storm Lake, Iowa, 1980-87; county auditor Buena Vista County, Storm Lake, 1987—; mem. Sec. of State's Elections Task Force, Des Moines, 1995-96. Mem. Iowa State Assn. County Auditors (sec. 1991, 2d v.p. 1992, 1st v.p. 1993, pres. 1994), Order Ea. Star (worthy matron), Storm Lake Bus. and Profl. Women (pres. 1986-88), HyNoon Kiwanis. Republican. Presbyterian. Home: 303 E Lakeshore Dr Storm Lake IA 50588 Office: Buena Vista County PO Box 220 215 E 5th St Storm Lake IA 50588

STRAWN, SUSAN HEATHCOTE, medical administrator; b. Pasadena, Calif., Feb. 10, 1940; d. Edward McNair and Ann Heathcote (Stevens) McNair; m. Harvey G. Holtz, June 24, 1960 (div. June. 1974); children: Christopher, Edward, David. AS, Butte Coll., 1973; lifetime tchg. credential, Calif. State U., Chico, 1987. Cert. respiratory therapist, 1974, cardiovascular tech., 1985. Respiratory therapist Feather River Hosp., Paradise, Calif., 1973-87; instr. respiratory therapy Butte Coll., Chico, 1982-87, instr. cardiovascular tech., 1987-95; cardiovasc. technologist Chico Cardiology, 1987-90; dir. cardiopulmonary dept. Oroville (Calif.) Hosp., 1990—; mem. adv. bd. Butte Coll., Chico, 1982—. Author 2-yr. cardiovasc. tech. program for Butte Coll., 1987. Mem. NOW, Am. Assn. Respiratory Care, Cardiovasc. Internat., Echo Soc., Calif. Soc. for Respiratory Care. Democrat. Episcopalian. Home: 32 Humpyback Rd Oroville CA 95965 Office: Oroville Hosp 2767 Olive Hwy Oroville CA 95966

STRAZDON, MAUREEN ELAINE, marketing and research director; b. Elizabeth, N.J., Aug. 6, 1948; d. Bruno H. and Leona E.(Sheehan) S.; m. Victor A. Bary, May 17, 1985. BA, Douglass Coll., New Brunswick, N.J., 1970; MLS, Rutgers U., New Brunswick, 1971; MBA, Drexel U., Phila., 1978; CLU, Am. Coll., Bryn Mawr, Pa., 1982. Bus., reference librarian Drexel U., Phila., 1971-78; head librarian Am. Coll., Bryn Mawr, Pa., 1978-82, Pa. State U., Abington, 1982-85; asst. dir. rsch. and devel. Am. Internat. Group, N.Y.C., 1985-93; dir. rsch. and planning CIGNA Property/Casualty, Phila., 1993-94; dir. market analysis Am. Internat. Underwriters, N.Y.C., 1994—. Editor Index, Database Ins. Periodicals Index, 1983—; author contbr. articles in profl. jours. 1979—. Named Outstanding Young Women Am. Mem. NAFE Women's Found. (awards luncheon com.), Beta Gamma Sigma. Office: Am Internat Underwriters 15th Fl 70 Pine St New York NY 10270-0002

STREEP, MERYL (MARY LOUISE STREEP), actress; b. Madison, N.J., June 22, 1949; d. Harry Jr. and Mary W. Streep; m. Donald J. Gummer, 1978. BA, Vassar Coll., 1971; MFA, Yale U., 1975, DFA (hon.), 1983; DFA (hon.), Dartmouth Coll., 1981. Appeared with Green Mountain Guild, Woodstock, Vt.; Broadway debut in Trelawny of the Wells, Lincoln Center Beaumont Theater, 1975; N.Y.C. theatrical appearances include 27 Wagons Full of Cotton (Theatre World award), A Memory of Two Mondays, Henry V, Secret Service, The Taming of the Shrew, Measure for Measure, The Cherry Orchard, Happy End, Wonderland, Taken in Marriage, Alice in Concert (Obie award 1981); movie appearances include Julia, 1977, The Deer Hunter, 1978 (Best Supporting Actress award Nat. Soc. Film Critics), Manhattan, 1979, The Seduction of Joe Tynan, 1979, Kramer vs. Kramer, 1979 (N.Y. Film Critics' award, Los Angeles Film Critics' award, both for best actress, Golden Globe award, Acad. award for best supporting actress), The French Lieutenant's Woman, 1981 (Los Angeles Film Critics award for best actress, Brit. Acad. award, Golden Globe award 1981), Sophie's Choice, 1982 (Acad. award for best actress, Los Angeles Film Critics award for best actress, Golden Globe award 1982), Still of the Night, 1982, Silkwood, 1983, Falling in Love, 1984, Plenty, 1985, Out of Africa, 1985 (Los Angeles Film Critics award for best actress 1985), Heartburn, 1986, Ironweed, 1987, A Cry in the Dark, 1988 (named Best Actress N.Y. Film Critics' Circle, 1988, Best Actress Cannes Film Festival, 1989), She-Devil, 1989, Postcards From the Edge, 1990, Defending Your Life, 1991, Death Becomes Her, 1992, The House of the Spirits,1994, The River Wild, 1994, The Bridges of Madison County, 1995 (Acad. award nominee for best actress 1996); TV film The Deadliest Season, 1977; TV mini-series Holocaust, 1978 (Emmy award); TV dramatic spls. Secret Service, 1977, Uncommon Women and Others, 1978;TV (narrator) The Velveteen Rabbit, 1985, A Vanishing Wilderness, 1990. Recipient Mademoiselle award, 1976, Woman of Yr. award B'nai Brith, 1979, Woman of Yr. award Hasty Pudding Soc., Harvard U., 1980, Best Supporting Actress award Nat. Bd. of Rev., 1979, Best Actress award Nat. Bd. of Rev., 1982, Star of Yr. award Nat. Assn. Theater Owners, 1983, People's Choice award, 1983, 85, 86, 87. Office: Creative Artists Agy 9830 Wilshire Blvd Beverly Hills CA 90212-1804

STREET, PATRICIA LYNN, secondary education educator; b. Lillington, N.C., May 3, 1940; d. William Banks and Vandalia (McLean) S.; m. Col. Robert Gest, June 2, 1962 (div. 1985); children: Robert, Roblyn Renee. BS, Livingstone Coll., 1962; MEd, Salisbury State U., 1974; postgrad., various, 1968—. Tchr. Govt. of Guam Marianas Island, Agana, Guam, 1962-64; sec., typist USAF, Glasgow AFB, Mont., 1964-65, Syracuse (N.Y.) U. AeroSpace Engring., 1966-67; tchr. Syracuse (N.Y.) City Sch. System, 1967-69; lectr. U. of Md., Eastern Shore, Princess Anne, Md., 1970-72; tchr. Prince George's County Pub. Schs., Upper Marlboro, Md., 1973—; instr. U. Guam, Anderson AFB, 1963, U.S. Armed Forces Inst., Anderson AFB, 1963, Yorktowne Bus. Inst., Landover, Md., 1987-90, Cheseapeake Bus. Inst., Clinton, Md., 1983-89; asst. advisor student tchrs. U. Md. Ea. Shore, Princess Anne, 1972; adj. instr. Bowie State U., 1990—; conv. speaker. Mem. AAUW, NEA, ASCD, Am. Vocat. Assn., Md. Bus. Edn. Assn. (pres.-elect 1987-88, pres. 1988-89, Educator of Yr. 1989), Md. Vocat. Assn. (regional rep. 1986-89, audit chmn. 1987-89, Vocat.-Tech. Educator of Yr. 1989), Ea. Bus. Edn. Assn. (co-editor newsletter 1990-91, secondary exec. dir. 1991-94), Md. State Tchrs. Assn., D.C. Bus. Edn. Assn., Nat. Bus. Edn. Assn., Data Processing Mgmt. Assn., Internat. Soc. for Bus. Edn., Md. Bus. Edn. Com., Prince George's County Edn. Assn. Democrat. Baptist. Home: 10107 Welshire Dr Upper Marlboro MD 20772 Office: Prince George's Pub Sch Upper Marlboro MD 20772

STREET, PICABO, Olympic athlete; b. Triumph, Idaho, 1971. Silver medalist, women's downhill alpine skiing Olympic Games, Lillehammer, Norway, 1994; downhill skier U.S. Ski Team, 1994—. Named World Cup Downhill Women's Champion, 1995. Office: US Olympic Com 1750 E Boulder St Colorado Springs CO 80909-5724

STREISAND, BARBRA JOAN, singer, actress, director; b. Bklyn., Apr. 24, 1942; d. Emanuel and Diana (Rosen) S.; m. Elliott Gould, Mar. 1963 (div.); 1 son, Jason Emanuel. Grad. high sch., Bklyn.; student, Yeshiva of Bklyn. N.Y. theatre debut Another Evening with Harry Stoones, 1961; appeared in Broadway musicals I Can Get It for You Wholesale, 1962, Funny Girl, 1964-65; motion pictures include Funny Girl, 1968, Hello Dolly, 1969, On a Clear Day You Can See Forever, 1970, The Owl and the Pussy Cat, 1970, What's Up Doc?, 1972, Up the Sandbox, 1972, The Way We Were, 1973, For Pete's Sake, 1974, Funny Lady, 1975, The Main Event, 1979, All Night Long, 1981, Nuts, 1987; star, prodr. film A Star is Born, 1976; prodr., dir., star Yentl, 1983, The Prince of Tides, 1991; exec. prodr.: (TV movie) Serving in Silence: The Margarethe Cammermeyer Story, 1995; TV spls. include My Name is Barbra, 1965 (5 Emmy awards), Color Me Barbra, 1966; rec. artist on Columbia Records; Gold record albums include People, 1965, My Name is Barbra, 1965, Color Me Barbra, 1966, Barbra Streisand: A Happening in Central Park, 1968, Barbra Streisand: One Voice, Stoney End, 1971, Barbra Joan Streisand, 1972, The Way We Were, 1974, A Star is Born, 1976, Superman, 1977, The Stars Salute Israel at 30, 1978, Wet, 1979, (with Barry Gibb) Guilty, 1980, Emotion, 1984, The Broadway Album, 1986, Til I Loved You, 1989; other albums include: A Collection: Greatest Hits, 1989, Just for the Record, 1991, Back to Broadway, 1993, Concert at the Forum, 1993, The Concert Recorded Live at Madison Square Garden, 1994, The Concert Highlights, 1995. Recipient Emmy award, CBS-TV spl. (My Name Is Barbra), 1964, Acad. award as best actress (Funny Girl), 1968, Golden Globe award (Funny Girl), 1969, co-recipient Acad. award for best song (Evergreen), 1976, Georgie award AGVA 1977, Grammy awards for best female pop vocalist, 1963, 64, 65, 77, 86, for best song writer (with Paul Williams), 1977, 2 Grammy nominations for Back to Broadway, 1994; Nat. Acad. of Recording Arts & Sciences Lifetime Achievement Award, 1994. Office: Creative Artists Agy care Fred Spector 9830 Wilshire Blvd Beverly Hills CA 90212-1804*

STREJCEK, ELIZABETH GEIERMAN, reading specialist, educator; b. Chgo., Dec. 7, 1948; d. Aloysius Herman and Lillian Elizabeth (Cowan) Geierman; m. George Joseph Strejcek, Jan. 27, 1971; children: James Edwin, Theodore Eliot. BA in History, U. Ill., Chgo., 1971, MA in Ednl. Leadership, 1981. Cert. reading specialist, Ill. Subs. tchr. pub. schs., Berwyn, Ill., 1972-74; tchr. reading grades 5-8 South Berwyn Pub. Sch., Berwyn, 1974-77; tchr. reading lab. grades 9-12 Bolinbrook (Ill.) High Sch., 1979-83; tchr. reading grades 7-8 Westview Mid. Sch., Romeoville, Ill., 1983-84, tchr. grades 6-8, 1984-85; chpt. I reading tchr. grades K-5 Northview Elem. Sch., Bolingbrook, 1985-91; tchr. grades 9-10 Morton East H.S., Cicero, 1991—, tchr. spl. program on attendance, chpt. I-title I tchr., 1991, 94, tchr. truancy and attendance program, 1993—, mem. various coms., 1991—; presenter lectures, demonstrations on reading and writing and using technology in classroom, 1989—. Mem. AAUW, Internat. Reading Assn., Ill. Reading Coun. (bd. dirs. 1994-95), Ill. Computing Educators, Nat. Coun. Tchrs. English, Vlasta Vraz chpt. Czechoslovak Nat. Coun. Am., Secondary Reading League (pres. 1993-95). Office: J Sterling Morton HS 2423 S Austin Blvd Cicero IL 60650-2627

STRELAU, RENATE, historical researcher, artist; b. Berlin, Feb. 1, 1951; came to U.S., 1960; d. Werner Ernst and Gerda Gertrud (Bargel) S. BA, U. Calif., Berkeley, 1974; cert. Arabic lang. proficiency, Johns Hopkins U., 1976; MA, Am. U., 1985, MFA, 1991. Rsch. asst. Iranian Embassy, Washington, 1976-80. One-woman shows include Cafe Espresso, Berkeley, Calif., 1973, Riggs Bank, Arlington, Va., 1994-95; represented in permanent collections at C. Law Watkins Meml. Collection, Am. U. Mem. Am. Hist. Assn., Orgn. Am. Historians, Soc. for Historians Am. Fgn. Rels. (life). Home: 1021 Arlington Blvd Apt E-1041 Arlington VA 22209-2212

STREMSTERFER, MARIANNE, artist, secondary education educator; b. Springfield, Ill., Dec. 6, 1949; d. Anthony Joseph Sr. and Margaret Mary (Burg) Kohlrus; m. Gary W. Stremsterfer, Aug. 16, 1969; children: Sara, John, Lara. AA, Springfield Coll., 1969; BA, Sangamon State U., 1975. Cert. tchr., Ill. Tchr. reading, math. St. Aloysius Sch., Springfield, Ill., 1975-77; tchr. art St. Aloysius Sch., Springfield, 1977—; prof. art Springfield Coll., 1990—; bd. dirs. Scholastic Art Awards, Springfield, workshop dir. 1993-95. Recipient Those Who Excel award of merit Ill. State Bd. Edn., 1991-92. Mem. Rembrandt Soc. (workship dir. 1995), Ill. Art Edn. Assn., Springfield Area Arts Coun., Ill. Arts Alliance. Roman Catholic. Home: 2063 Marland Springfield IL 62702 Office: St Aloysius Sch 2125 N 21st St Springfield IL 62702

STRETTON, ANN ELIZABETH, artist; b. Racine, Wis., June 30, 1961; d. Francis Edward and Mary Rose (Kaplan) S.; m. Stanley Lewis Starbuck, Feb. 12, 1988. BFA, Colo. State U., 1984; MFA, U. Wis., 1993. Macintosh artist Kinko's Copies, Ft. Collins, Colo., 1985-89, The Wright Life, Ft. Collins, Colo., 1988-89; desktop pub. Impressions, Madison, Wis., 1989-96; freelance computer design and illustrator, Madison, 1995—. One-woman shows include Neville Pub. Mus., 1996; exhibited in group shows at No. Nat. Art Exhibit, 1993 (Patrons award), Wis. Painters and Sculptors Juried Show, 1993 (Herb Kohl award), Appleton Art Ctr., 1995, Anderson Art Ctr., Kenosha, Wis., 1996. Tracy Noah Meml. scholar, 1983-84, Edith L. Gilbertson scholar, 1992-93. Mem. Wis. Painters and Sculptors, Wis. Women in The Arts. Home: 2125 Winnebago St Madison WI 53704

STREVA, LINDA TALBOT, elementary education educator; b. Franklin, La., Jan. 10, 1948; d. Oscar Lewis and Juanita Theresa (Blanchard) Talbot; m. August Anthony Streva, Nov. 21, 1970; children: Elizabeth Mary, Jennifer Leigh. BS in Psychology, U. Southwestern La., 1970; MEd in Guidance and Counseling, Nicholl's State U., 1980. Cert. tchr. elem. edn., La. Tchr. St. Mary Parish Schs., Morgan City, La., 1970-71, Holy Cross Elem., Morgan City, 1970-81, 87—; guidance counselor Holy Cross Elem., 1982-87. Mem. Nat. Cath. Edn. Assn., Krewe of Hephaestus. Democrat. Roman Catholic. Office: Holy Cross Elem 2100 Cedar St Morgan City LA 70380-1720

STREVER, MARTHA MAY, mathematics educator; b. Rhinebeck, N.Y., Oct. 27, 1939; d. Louis Grant and Marguerite Hazel (Irwin) S. BS, New Paltz (N.Y.) State U., 1961, MS, 1966. Cert. tchr. math. and sci., N.Y. Tchr. math. and sci. Red Hook (N.Y.) Ctrl. Sch., 1961-72, tchr. math., 1961—, chairperson dept. math., 1972—, jr. high computer coord., 1984-92, math/computer instrn. dept. chair, 1992—. Mem. choir, sec.-treas. Rhinebeck (N.Y.) Ref. Ch., 1974—, deacon and elder, 1976-80, Women's Guild edn. chmn., various yrs., pres., 1984-86, 89-90, 92-95, sec., 1996—. Summer Math and Sci. scholar New Paltz State U., 1962. Mem. ASCD, N.Y. State United Tchrs., Dutchess County Math. Tchrs. Assn., Nat. Coun. Tchrs. Math., N.Y. Assn. Math. Suprs., Assn. of Math. Tchrs. N.Y. State, Agonian Alumni Assn., Internat. Soc. for Tech. in Edn., N.Y. State Assn. for Computers and Tech. in Edn., Kappa Delta Pi, Delta Kappa Gamma, Alpha Zeta (1st v.p. 1978-80, pres. 1980-82, music chmn. 1982—). Home: 940 NY Route 9G Hyde Park NY 12538 Office: Red Hook Ctrl H S 63-73 West Market St Red Hook NY 12571

STRIBLIN, LORI ANN, critical care nurse, medicare coordinator, nursing educator; b. Valley, Ala., Sept. 23, 1962; d. James Author and Dorothy Jane (Cole) Burt; m. Thomas Edward Striblin, Oct. 26, 1984; children: Natalie Nicole, Crystal Danielle. AAS in Nursing, So. Union State Jr. Coll., Valley, Ala., 1992. RN, Ala.; cert. ACLS and BLS. Surg. staff nurse East Ala. Med. Ctr., Opelika, 1992-93, surg. charge nurse, 1993-95, critical care ICU staff nurse, 1993-95; RN case mgr. East Ala. Home Care, Opelika, 1995-96; staff devel. coord., medicare coord. Lanett (Ala.) Geriatric Ctr., 1996—; clin. instr. educator So. Union C.C., Valley, 1994—. Mem. AACN, Ala. State Nurses Assn. Baptist. Home: 268 Lee Rd 913 Valley AL 36854-6655 Office: Lanett Geriatric Center Lanett AL 36863

STRICHARTZ, INA LEE, lawyer; b. Oakland, Calif., Mar. 9, 1952; d. Richard and Beatrice (Zeesman) S.; m. Giles David Morris; 1 child, David Morris. BA, U. Mich., 1973; JD, U. So. Calif., 1976. Bar: Calif. 1976, D.C. 1976. Law clk. U.S. Ct. Appeals, D.C., 1976-77; asst. U.S. atty. D.C., 1978-85; trial atty. Dept. Justice, D.C., 1985—.

STRICK, SADIE ELAINE, psychologist; b. Masontown, Pa., May 5, 1929; d. Michael and Mary (Oziemblowski) Wierzbicki; m. John Mackovjak, Dec. 31, 1947 (dec. Mar. 1972); children: Deborah, Susan; m. Ellis Strick, Aug. 11, 1974. BSW, U. Pitts., 1975, MEd, 1977, PhD, 1981. Lic. psychologist; fellow, diplomate Am. Bd. Med. Psychotherapists. Psychologist I Mayview State Hosp., Bridgeville, Pa., 1984-87; owner Counseling & Behavior Specialists, P.C., Pitts., 1981—; mem. C.G. Jung Edn. Ctr., Pitts., 1980—; guest speaker Compassionate Friends, Pitts., 1986—, Womens Career Conv., Pitts., 1982. Bd. dirs. OAR/Allegheny, Pitts., 1981-82. Fellow Pa. Psychol. Assn.; mem. Am. Psychol. Assn., Pitts. Assn. for Theory and Practice of Psychoanalysis. Home: 2160 Greentree Rd Apt 605 Pittsburgh PA 15220-1437 Office: Counseling and Behavior Specialists PC 429 Forbes Ave Ste 1614 Pittsburgh PA 15219-1604

STRICKLAND, ANITA MAURINE, retired business educator, librarian; b. Groom, Tex., Sept. 24, 1923; d. Oliver Austin and Thelma May (Slay) Pool; m. LeRoy Graham Mashburn, Aug. 12, 1945 (dec. Mar. 1977); 1 child, Ronald Gene; m. Reid Strickland, May 27, 1978. BBA, West Tex. State U., 1962, MEd, 1965; postgrad. in library sci., Tex. Women's U., 1970. Cert. tchr., Tex.; cert. librarian. Employment interviewer Douglas Aircraft Co., Oklahoma City, 1942-45; cashier, bookkeeper Southwestern Pub. Services, Groom and Panhandle, Tex., 1950-58; acct. Gen. Motors Outlet, Groom, 1958-62; tchr. bus., lang. arts Groom Pub. Schs., 1962-68; bus. tchr., librarian Amarillo (Tex.) Pub. Schs., 1968-81. Vol. Amarillo Symphony, 1980—, Amarillo Rep. Com., 1981—, Lone Star Ballet, 1981-92; docent Amarillo Mus. Art, 1987—, sec., 1987-90, 93-94, Amarillo Art Alliance, 1989-93, 1989—, sec., 1989-90. Mem. AAUW (legis. com. 1986-88, sec. 1989-90, bd. dirs. 1989-91), Amarillo C. of C. (vol. women's divsn. 1981-86), Amarillo Christian Women's Club (asst. prayer advisor 1989-90, treas. 1995-96). Baptist. Home: 6513 Roxton Dr Amarillo TX 79109-5120

STRICKLAND, N(ANCY) KATHLEEN, lawyer, educator; b. Mobile, Ala., Dec. 12, 1949. Student, U. Vienna, 1969-70; BS, Spring Hill Coll., 1971; JD, U. San Diego, 1974. Bar: Calif. 1975, D.C. 1976, U.S. Dist. Ct. D.C. 1976, U.S. Ct. Appeals (D.C. cir.) 1976, U.S. Dist. Ct. (so. and ctrl. dists.) Calif. 1987, (no. and ea. dists.) Calif. 1988, Tex. 1994. Staff atty., office opinions and rev. FCC, Washington, 1974-76; asst. dist. atty. San Francisco Dist. Atty.'s Office, 1977-84; assoc. Burnhill, Morehouse, Burford, Schofield & Schiller, Walnut Creek, Calif., 1984-86; ptnr. Hassard, Bonnington, Rogers & Huber, San Fransisco, 1987-95, Carroll, Burdick & McDonough, San Fransisco, 1995—; adj. prof. Hastings Coll. Law, U. Calif., San Francisco, 1987-92; pro tem judge Contra Costa County Superior Ct., Martinez, Calif., 1987—; lectr. U. San Francisco, Harvard U., Stanford U., C.E.B. Basketball coach Lafayette-Moraga Youth Assn., 1986—. Mem. ABA (lectr. environ. law), San Francisco Bar Assn. (bd. dirs. environ. law assn.), Contra Costa Bar Assn., Calif. Women Lawyers. Roman Catholic. Office: Carroll Burdick & McDonough Ste 400 44 Montgomery St San Francisco CA 94104

STRICKLAND, NELLIE B., library program director; b. Belmont, Miss., Dec. 12, 1932. BS, Murray State U., 1954; MLS, George Peabody Coll., 1971. Ref. libr. Murray State Coll., Murray, Ky., 1954; asst. libr. Dept. Army, Ft. Stewart, Ga., 1955-56; field libr. U.S. Army, Japan, 1957-59; area libr. U.S. Army, Europe, 1960-66; staff libr. U.S. Army So. Command, C.Z., 1966-67; area libr. U.S. Army, Vietnam, 1967-68, staff libr., 1971-72; chief libr. U.S. Army, Ft. Benning, Ga., 1970-71; dir. library program U.S. Army Pacific, 1973-74; dir. Army libr. program Washington, 1974-94. Recipient Outstanding Performance award Ft. Benning, 1970, Armed Forces Achievement citation, 1982, 94, Order of the White Plume; Dept. of Army Tng. grantee, 1971; Dept. of Army decoration for Exceptional Civil Svc., 1994. Mem. ALA, Kappa Delta Phi, Alpha Sigma Alpha. Home: 203 S Yoakum Pky Apt 614 Alexandria VA 22304-3716

STRICKLIN, ALIX, publishing executive, writer; b. Knoxville, Tenn., Nov. 11, 1959; d. William Joseph and Alice Carolyn (West) S.; m. Joseph Paul Chiarello, May 17, 1980 (div. May 29, 1988); 1 child, Mary Conner. BS, Rutgers U., 1987; MBA, St. Joseph's U., 1989. Fin. analyst Macmillan Pub. Co., Inc., Riverside, N.J., 1985-86; acctg. mgr. Macmillan Pub. Co., Inc., Riverside, 1986-88; bus. mgr. W.B. Saunders Co., Harcourt Brace Jovanovich, Inc., Phila., 1988-89, dir. bus. mgmt. and fin. adminstrn., 1989-91; dir. artist royalty EMI-CMG, Brentwood, Tenn., 1991-94; contr. CB of Nashville, 1994-96, Boomerang Prodns., Nashville, 1996—; bd. dirs. PHCA, Inc.; vis. scholar Russian studies internat. program Rutgers U., 1987. Contbr. articles to profl. jours. Mem. Palmyra Twp. Planning Bd., 1991-92; com. chmn. Young Rep. Assn. South Jersey, Mt. Holly, 1989-91, officer, 1991; mem. Davidson Young Reps. Mem. AFTRA, DAR, Nashville Film/Video Assn., Mid. Tenn. Hunter Jumper Assn. (Menefee Combined Equitation award), Am. Horse Show Assn., New Eng. Women, Colonial Daus. 17th Century, Delta Zeta. Republican. Presbyterian.

STRIDER, MARJORIE VIRGINIA, artist, educator; b. Guthrie, Okla.; d. Clifford R. and Marjorie E. (Schley) S. BFA, Kansas City Art Inst., 1962. Mem. faculty Sch. Visual Arts, N.Y.C., 1970—; artist-in-residence City U. Grad. Ctr. Mall, N.Y.C., 1976, Fabric Workshop, Phila., 1978, Grassi Palace, Venice, Italy, 1978. One-woman shows of sculpture, drawings and/or prints include Pace Gallery, N.Y.C., 1963-64, Nancy Hoffman Gallery, N.Y.C., 1973-74, Weather Spoon Mus., U.N.C., Chapel Hill, 1974, City U. Grad. Center Mall, 1976, Clocktower, N.Y.C., 1976, Sculpture Center, N.Y.C., 1983, Steinbaum Gallery, N.Y.C., 1983, 84, Andre Zarre Gallery, 1993, 95; one-woman travelling shows to numerous mus. across USA; exhibited in group shows The Sculpture Center, N.Y.C., 1981, Drawing Biennale, Lisbon, Portugal, 1981, Newark Mus., 1984, William Rockhill Nelson Mus., Kansas City, 1985, Danforth Mus., Framingham, Mass., 1987, Delahoyd Gallery, N.Y.C., 1992; represented in permanent collections Guggenheim Mus., N.Y.C., U. Colo., Boulder, Albright-Knox Mus., Buffalo, Des Moines Art Center, Storm King (N.Y.) Art Center, Larry Aldrich Mus., Ridgefield, Conn., City U. Grad. Center, N.Y.C., Hirschhorn Mus. and Sculpture Garden, Washington, Santa Fe (N. Mex.) Mus. of Art, also pvt. collections. Nat. Endowment for Arts grantee, 1973, 80, Longview Found. grantee, 1974, Pollock-Krasner Found. grantee, 1990, Florsheim Art Fund grantee, 1991; Va. Ctr. for Creative Arts fellow, 1974, 92, Millay Colony for Arts fellow, 1992, Yaddo Colony, 1996.

STRIEFSKY, LINDA A(NN), lawyer; b. Carbondale, Pa., Apr. 27, 1952; d. Leo James and Antoinette Marie (Carachilo) S.; m. James Richard Carlson, Nov. 3, 1984; children: David Carlson, Paul Carlson, Daniel Carlson. BA summa cum laude, Marywood Coll., 1974; JD, Georgetown U., 1977. Bar: Ohio 1977. Assoc., Thompson, Hine and Flory, Cleve., 1977-85, ptnr., 1985—. Loaned exec. United Way of Northeast Ohio, Cleve., 1978; trustee Cleve. Music Sch. Settlement. Mem. Am. Bar Found., ABA (mem. real estate fin. com. 1980—, vice-chair lender liability com. 1993—), Am. Coll. Real Estate Lawyers bd. govs. 1994—), Internat. Coun. of Shopping Ctrs., Nat. Assn. Office and Indsl. Parks, Urban Land Inst., Cleve. Real Estate Women, Ohio State Bar Assn. (bd. govs. real property sect. 1985—), Greater Cleve. Bar Assn. (chmn. bar applicants com. 1983-84, exec. coun. young lawyers sect. 1982-85, chmn. 1984-85, mem. exec. coun. real property sect. 1980-84, Merit Svc. award 1983, 85), Pi Gamma Mu. Democrat. Roman Catholic. Home: 2222 Delamere Dr Cleveland OH 44106-3204 Office: Thompson Hine and Flory PLL 3900 Society Ctr 127 Public Sq Cleveland OH 44114-1216

STRIEGEL, PEGGY SIMSARIAN, advertising executive; b. Phila., July 12, 1941; d. Robert Ernest Samuel and Margaret (Miller) Thompson; m. James P. Simsarian, Sept. 4, 1965 (div. Sept. 1976); children: Catherine Ann, Sheila Thompson; m. Louis E. Striegel, Sept. 14, 1976 (div. June 1984); m. Andrew H. Schmeltz Jr., Dec. 4, 1991. BA, Sarah Lawrence Coll., 1963. Asst. editor Oxford U. Press, N.Y.C., 1963-64; picture editor Western Pub. Co., N.Y.C., 1964-66; art editor Houghton-Mifflin, Inc., Boston, 1966-68; pres. Peggy's Graphics, McLean, Va., 1968-78, Striegel Advt. and Graphics, Inc., Broken Arrow, Okla., 1978—. Lower Merion (Pa.) area coord. Shapp for Congress, Phila., 1970; area coord. and graphic designer Phillips for U.S. Congress, McLean, 1972; pres. bd. dirs. Gatesway Found., Broken Arrow, 1987-89; chair, Cmty. Playhouse Broken Arrow, 1979-81; mktg. bd. chair Tulsa Philharmonic, 1985-95, exec. com., bd. dirs. 1993—; active internet radio talk show Women of the Roundtable. Recipient numerous advt. awards including several Addies and citations Tulsa Advt. Club, 1990-91, Gold Quill, 1990, cert. Merit Printing Industries Am., 1983, award of Excellence Am. Inst. Graphic Arts, 1983, Am. Corp. Identity Graphics award, 1994. Mem. Advt. Fedn. Tulsa, Bus. and Profl. Advt. Assn. (Gold Ring award 1986, 87), Women in Communications (prog. chmn. 1991), Met. Tulsa C. of C., Broken Arrow C. of C., Bus. Profl. Advt. Assn., Jr. Achievement of Tulsa (bd. dirs. 1990-94). Democrat. Presbyterian. Club: Art Directors. Home: 6110 S 221st East Ave Broken Arrow OK 74014-2017 Office: 716 S Main St Broken Arrow OK 74012-5527

STRINGER, MARY EVELYN, art historian, educator; b. Huntsville, Mo., July 31, 1921; d. William Madison and Charity (Rogers) S. A.B., U. Mo., 1942; A.M., U. N.C., Chapel Hill, 1955; Ph.D. (Danforth scholar), Harvard U., 1973. Asst. prof. art Miss. State Coll. for Women (now Miss. U. for Women), Columbus, 1947-58; asso. prof. Miss. State Coll. for Women (now Miss. U. for Women), 1958-73, prof., 1973-91, prof. emeritus, 1991—; regional dir. for Miss., Census of Stained Glass Windows in Am., 1840-1940. Bd. dirs. Mississippians for Ednl. Broadcasting; mem. Miss. com. Save Outdoor Sculpture, 1992-93. Fulbright scholar W.Ger., 1955-56; Harvard U. travel grantee, 1966-67; NEH summer seminar grantee, 1980. Mem. AAUW, Coll. Art Assn., Southeastern Coll. Art Conf. (dir. 1975-80, 83-89, Disting. Svc. award 1992, Miss. Hist. Soc. (award of merit, 1995), Internat. Ctr. Medieval Art, Audubon Soc., The Nature Conservancy, Sierra Club, Phi Beta Kappa, Phi Kappa Phi. Democrat. Episcopalian. Office: Dept Art Miss U for Women Columbus MS 39701

STRINGFIELD, SHERRY, actress. BFA, SUNY, Purchase, 1989. Theater appearances include Goose and Tom Tom, Hurly Burly, Devil's Disciple, A Dream Play, Hotel Baltimore, The Kitchen, Tom Jones; appeared in (TV series) Guiding Light, 1989-92, NYPD Blue, 1993, ER, 1994— (Emmy nominee Outstanding Lead Actress in a Drama Series, 1995). Office: care Michaels Wose & Tencer 9350 Wilshire Blvd Beverly Hills CA 90210 also: United Talent Agy 9560 Wilshire Blvd Beverly Hills CA 90212

STRIPLING, LANA, therapist, counselor; b. Houston, June 17, 1941; d. Frank and Hanna (Griffin) Feagin; m. Bob Stripling, Aug. 18, 1962; children: Sheryl, William. BA, Baylor U., 1963; MA, So. Meth. U., 1967. Lic. profl. counselor, Tex. Tchr. Dallas Ind. Sch. Dist., 1963-65, St. Monica Sch., Dallas, 1974-76; acad. lang. therapist and DMHP therapist Shelton Sch., Dallas, 1976-96; pvt. practice in counseling Dallas, 1994—; ednl. cons. various schs., 1985-95. Author 5 books on developmental motor and handwriting program. Pres. PTA, Lakewood Elem., Dallas, 1972-73. Mem. Acad. Lang. Therapist (v.p. 1993-96), Orton Dyslexia Soc. (bd. dirs. 1993-96), Acad. Lang. Therapy Assn. (program chmn., v.p. 1993-96), Dallas Orton Dyslexia Soc. (program chair 1993-96, chair of Hot Line 1994-96), Baylor Alumni Assn., So. Meth. U. Alumni Assn., Chi Omega. Baptist. Home: 4133 Allencrest Dallas TX 75244

STRISOWER, SUZANNE, clinical hypnotherapist, counselor; b. San Francisco, Oct. 27, 1956; d. Edward Herman and Beverly Gene (Boutell) S. BFA, JFK U., Orinda, Calif., 1988; MA, Pacifica Grad. Inst., 1994. Cert. clin. hypnotherapist; cert. counselor. Wallcovering installer Orinda, Calif., 1974-82; interior designer Lyons, Hill & Ruga Inc., Pleasant Hill, Calif., 1983-85; project mgr. Wayne Ruga Inc., Martinez, Calif., 1985-88; exec. dir. Nat. Symposium for Healthcare Interior Design, Martinez, 1986-88; treatment counselor Youth Homes Inc., Walnut Creek, Calif., 1988-93; clin. hypnotherapist The Inner Journey, Walnut Creek, Calif., 1991—, marriage, family and child counselor, 1994-95; aide and community liaison to supr. Contra Costa County Dist. II, 1995——; tchr. Acalanes Adult Edn. Ctr., Walnut Creek, 1992—; lectr. in field. Child advisor, vice chairperson Contra Costa County Mental Health Commn., 1991-93; pres. Orgn. of Youth Svcs., 1991-94; mem. Juv. Justice Delinquency Prevention Commn. Contra Costa County, 1988-95, mem. family and children's trust com., mem. juv. sys. planning adv. com. Mem. Am. Coun. Hypnotist Examiners. Home: 4143 Chaucer Dr Concord CA 94521

STROBEL, SHIRLEY HOLCOMB, magazine editor, educator, non-profit organization writer; b. Hastings, Nebr., May 8, 1929; d. Dent Z. and Helen (Spiegel) Holcomb; m. Howard Austin Strobel, Aug. 26, 1953; children: Paul Austin, Gary Dent, Linda Susan Strobel Helgeson. BS, Northwestern U., 1951; MA, Duke U., 1953. Cert. counselor, N.C.; tchr., N.C. English tchr. Salem Acad., Winston-Salem, N.C., 1952-53; tchr. Durham city schs., N.C., 1954-55, Durham County schs., 1967-90; editor Ch. Tchrs. mag. Nat. Tchrs. Edn. Project, Durham, 1986-89; editor Ch. Tchrs., Harper Collins, San Francisco, 1990-93; part-time instr. Program in Edn. Duke U., Durham, 1991-93; chmn. dept. English Jordan High Sch., Durham, 1967-75; reader Nat. Coun. Tchrs. English, 1969-71; mem. accreditation team Duke U. Edn. Program, 1985; judge mag. competition for Episcopal Communicators Conf., 1992-94. Co-author: Advanced Placement English, 1983; author: The Brothers Karamazov Curriculum Unit, 1995. Founder, pres. Threshold Clubhouse for Mentally Ill, Durham, 1985-86, chmn. capital campaign, 1988-91, chmn. ways and means com., 1992-96; active Area Bd. Mental Health, Durham, 1990-92; mem. state bd. N.C. Alliance for the Mentally Ill, 1994—, pres.-elect 1996. Democrat. Baptist. Home: 1119 Woodburn Rd Durham NC 27705-5737

STROJAN, LINDA JEWELL, guidance counselor; b. Shreveport, La., Mar. 27, 1949; d. Robert Burnett and Helen Louise (Pflug) Jewell; m. Carl Lee Strojan, Apr. 10, 1976; 1 child, Christopher Robert. BA, U. Colo., 1971; MA, UCLA, 1981. Cert. counselor, social studies tchr. grades 7-12, S.C. Tchr. social studies Scotch Plains (N.J.) Fanwood H.S., 1971-76, Regis Jesuit H.S., Denver, 1981-86; counselor North Augusta (S.C.) H.S., 1986—; chair, bd. mem. Robert B. and Helen P. Jewell Scholarship Found., Lexington, Ky., 1988—; pres., bd. mem. Mental Health Assn. in Aiken (S.C.) County, 1992—; v.p., bd. mem. Planned Parenthood East Ctrl. Ga., Augusta, 1994—. Bd. mem. Aiken (S.C.) Preparatory Sch., 1995—. Fulbright grantee, Cairo, Egypt, 1976. Mem. S.C. Counseling Orgn., Phi Beta Kappa, Phi Delta Kappa, Phi Alpha Theta. Home: 202 Englewood Rd Aiken SC 29841

STROMAN, SUSAN, choreographer; d. Charles and Frances S. Grad., U. Del. Dancer: Chicago, 1977-78, Whoopee!, 1979, Richard III, 1980, Peter Pan, 1983; asst. dir., asst. choreographer: (off-Broadway) Musical Chairs, 1980; co-conceiver: Trading Places, Equity Library Theatre Informals, 1983; dir., co-conceiver: (off-Broadway) Living Color, 1986; choreographer: (off-Broadway) Broadway Babylon, 1984, Sayonara, 1987, Flora, the Red Menace, 1987, Shenandoah, 1988, Slasher, 1988, Rhythm Ranch, 1989, The Roar of the Greasepaint-The Smell of the Crowd, 1990, Gypsy, 1991, And the World Goes 'Round, 1991 (Outer Critics' Circle award 1991), A Christmas Carol, 1994; (Broadway) Crazy for You, 1992 (Tony award best choreography 1992, Drama Desk award 1992, Outer Critics' Circle award 1992, Laurence Olivier award 1993), Picnic, 1993, Show Boat, 1994 (Tony award best choreography 1995, Astaire award Theatre Development Fund 1995); (New York City Opera) Don Giovanni, 1989, A Little Night Music, 1990, 110 in the Shade, 1992; (other) Liza Minnelli: Stepping Out at Radio City Music Hall, 1991 (Emmy award nomination for HBO presentation), (mus.) Big Broadway, 1996; dir.: (TV spl.) A Evening with the Boston Pops-A Tribute to Leonard Bernstein, 1989; co-conceiver, choreographer: (TV spl.) Sondheim-A Celebration at Carnegie Hall, 1992.

STROMBERG, JEAN WILBUR GLEASON, lawyer; b. St. Louis, Oct. 31, 1943; d. Ray Lyman and Martha (Bugbee) W.; m. Gerald Kermit Gleason, Aug. 28, 1966 (div. 1987); children: C. Blake, Peter Wilbur; m. Kurt Stromberg, Jan. 3, 1993; 1 child, Kristoffer Stromberg. B.A., Wellesley Coll., 1965; LL.B. cum laude, Harvard U., 1968. Bar: Calif. 1969, D.C. 1978. Assoc. Brobeck, Phleger & Harrison, San Francisco, 1969-72; spl. counsel to dir. div. corp. fin. SEC, 1972-76, assoc. dir. div. investment mgmt., 1976-78; of counsel Fulbright & Jaworski, Washington, 1978-80; ptnr. Fulbright & Jaworski, 1980-96; dir. fin. instns. and market issues U.S. Gen. Acctg. Office, Washington, 1996—; mem. adv. panel on legal issues GAO, NASD select com. on Nasdaq, 1994-96. Mem. ABA (chmn. subcom. on securities and banks, corp. laws com., bus. sect.), D.C. Bar Assn. (chmn. steering com. bus. sect. 1982-84), Fed. Bar Assn. (chair exec. coun., securities com. 1993-95), Am. Bar Retirement Assn. (bd. dirs. 1986-90, 94—), Phi Beta Kappa. Home: 3411 Woodley Rd NW Washington DC 20016-5030 Office: US Gen Acctg Office 441 G St NW Washington DC 20548

STROMBOM, CATHY JEAN, transportation planner, consultant; b. Bremerton, Wash., Nov. 4, 1949; d. Paul D. and Carolyn (Snitman) Powers; m. David Glen Strombom, June 17, 1972; 1 child, Paul Davis. BA summa cum laude, Whitman Coll., 1972; M in City and Regional Planning, Harvard U., 1977; postgrad., U. Wash., 1982-84. Urban planner Harvard Inst. for Internat. Devel., Tehran, Iran, 1977; sr. transp. planner Puget Sound Coun. Govts., Seattle, 1978-84; mgr. transp. planning/prin. profl. assoc. Parsons Brinckerhoff Quade and Douglas, Inc., Seattle, 1984—; v.p. Women's Transp. Seminar, Seattle, 1988-90 (Woman of Yr. 1989). Contbr. articles to profl. jours. Vol. U.S. Peace Corps, Marrakech, Morocco, 1973-75. Mem. Am. Inst. Cert. Planners (cert.), Am. Planning Assn., Inst. Transp. Engrs., Phi Beta Kappa. Home: 2580 W Viewmont Way W Seattle WA 98199-3660 Office: Parsons Brinckerhoff Quade and Douglas Inc 999 3rd Ave Ste 801 Seattle WA 98104-4001

STROMMER, ANNE ELIZABETH RIVARD, librarian; b. Columbus, Ohio, Dec. 24, 1940; d. Edwin Kenneth Rivard and Alda Nathan (Olin) Rivard Willis; m. Mathias Adolf Strommer, Jan. 3, 1965; children: Elisabeth Anne, Mathias Edwin. BA, Kent (Ohio) State U., 1962; MA in Libr. Sci., U. MIch., 1964. Reference libr. Detroit Pub. Libr., 1962-65, Ft. Knox (Ky.) Mil. Libr., 1968-69; reference libr. Houston Pub. Libr., 1978-80, branch mgr., 1980-81; tech. svcs. libr. North Harris County Coll., Houston, 1981-85, coord. tech. svcs., 1985-89, coord. tech. and automation svcs., 1990-93, coord. automated libr. svcs., 1993-96; dir. automated libr. svcs., 1996—. Mem. ALA, NAFE, Tex. Libr. Assn., Freedom to Read Found. Home: 20718 Greymoss Ln Houston TX 77073-3108 Office: N Harris Montgomery CC Dist 250 N Sam Houston Pky E Houston TX 77060-2000

STRONG, BARBARA HILLMAN, art history and anthropology educator; b. Berkeley, Calif., Aug. 1, 1946; d. Ray S. and Elizabeth R. (Brown) S. BA, U. Calif., Santa Barbara, 1969, MA, 1973. Tchg. asst. U. Calif., Santa Barbara, 1970-72; art history and anthropology instr. Coll. of The Sequoias, Calif., 1973—; divsn. chair Coll. of The Sequoias, 1991-92, art dept. chair, 1992—, v.p. acad. senate, 1990-93, chair equivalency com., 1990-93. Author: A Handbook of Precolumbian Art and Culture, 1994; author (software) Pentimento, An Art Hist. Game, 1995, Maya Resource Companion, 1994, Women in Art History. Recipient grants Coll. of The Sequoias, 1976, 93, 94. Mem. Coll. Art Assn. Democrat. Home: PO Box 278 Three Rivers CA 93271 Office: Coll of The Sequoias Dept Art Visalia CA 93277

STRONG, KARIN HJØRT, artist, educator; b. N.Y.C., Jan. 30, 1956; d. Corrin Peter and Mette Hjørt (Matthiesen) S. BA, Boston U., 1981; AA, Pratt U., 1985. Art tutor Hampshire Coll., Amherst, Mass., 1977; co-founder, mgr., tchr. Poland Springs (Maine) Cmty. Program, 1977-79; tchr. Southampton Cultural Ctr., 1989-96; tchg. asst. master workshop on art L.I. Univ., Southampton, N.Y., 1990; bd. mem. Catharine Lorillard Wolfe Art Club, Inc., N.Y.C., 1989-96; painting judge Pen and Brush Club, Inc., N.Y.C., 1995; art show judge J.L.C. Art Ctr., Inc., Stony Brook, N.Y., 1995. Artist represented by Gallery East, Images Gallery, Lizan Tops Gallery, others. Vol. coord. Appalachian Mountain Club, Boston, 1981; monkey trainer to aid quadreplegics Boston U., 1981; spkr., event M.C. CLWAC, Nat. Arts Club, N.Y.C., 1992-95; spkr., lectr. Jimmy Ernst Artist Alliance, East Hampton, N.Y., 1993, Southampton Artists, 1994. Mem. Soc. Animal Artists, Southampton Artists (bd. mem., exhbn. chair, publicity com. 1988-90), Catharine Lorillard Wolfe Art Club, Inc. (pres. 1992-95).

STRONG, SARA DOUGHERTY, psychologist, family and custody mediator; b. Phila., May 30, 1927; d. Augustus Joseph and Orpha Elizabeth (Dock) Dougherty; m. David Mather Strong, Dec. 21, 1954. BA in Psychology, Pa. State U., 1949; MA in Clin. Psychology, Temple U., 1960, postgrad., 1968-72; cert. in Family Therapy, Family Inst. Phila., 1978. Lic.

psychologist, Pa. Med. br. psychologist Family Ct. Phila., 1960-85, asst. chief psychologist, 1985-88, chief psychologist, 1988-92; retired, 1992; pvt. practice Phila., 1992—; cons. St. Joseph's Home for Girls, Phila., 1963-84, Daughters of Charity of St. Vincent De Paul, Albany, N.Y., 1965-90. Mem. APA (assoc.), Am. Assn. Marriage and Family Therapists, Pa. Psychol. Assn., Nat. Register of Health Svc. Providers in Psychology, Family Inst. Phila. Democrat.

STRONG, SUSAN CLANCEY, communication consultant; b. Cin., Nov. 10, 1939; d. William Power and Elizabeth (Browne) Clancey; m. Oliver Swigert, 1957 (div. 1972); children: Silvia, David Mack; m. Richard Devon Strong, 1977. BA, Northwestern U., 1965; MA, U. Calif., Berkeley, 1972, PhD, 1979. Tchr. Helen Bush Parkside Sch., Seattle, 1965-66, Taipei (Taiwan) Lang. Inst., 1967-68; acting instr. U. Calif., Berkeley, 1972-78, teaching fellow, 1979, lectr., 1979-84; lectr. St. Mary's Coll., Moraga, Calif., 1982-85; pvt. practice Orinda, Calif., 1985-90; sr. rsch. assoc. Ctr. for Econ. Conversion, 1990-96; mem. Contra Costa County Conflict Resolution Panels, Calif., 1987—; affiliate Support Ctr./CTD, San Francisco, 1987—; del. UN Conf. on Econ. Conversion, Moscow, 1990; co-founder Who's Counting Project?, 1996. Author poetry, columnist, book reviewer, 1986—; author: (booklet) The GDP Myth: How It Harms Our Quality of Life and What Communities Are Doing About It, 1995; editor: (booklets) Deficit Delirium, 1993, Shaping A New Conversion Agenda, 1995. Mem. Bay Area Global Tomorrow Com., 1986; co-founder Peace Economy Working Group, 1988; co-author Peace Economy Campaign, 1988; mem. Peace Action Nat. Strategy Com., 1989-95, co-chair strategy com., 1992-93; conf. co-chmn. Nat. Sane/Freeze Congress, 1989-90, rep. nat. bd. advisors Nat. Peace Action, Washington, 1989-95; mem. bd. advisors Peace and Environ. Project, San Francisco, 1986-88; chmn. No. Calif. Sane Freeze, San Francisco, 1985-89; co-founder Who's Counting Project, 1996. Mem. Phi Beta Kappa. Democrat. Episcopalian.

STRONG, SUSAN RUMSEY, academic administrator; b. Buffalo, Apr. 24, 1944; d. Dexter Phelps and Kathryn Lovell (Skinner) Rumsey; m. Paul Strong, Mar. 31, 1964; children: Michael, Amy. BA, U. Wis., 1969; MLS, SUNY, Geneseo, 1973; PhD, U. Rochester, 1995. Cataloging asst. SUNY, Potsdam, 1969-71, Alfred (N.Y.) U., 1975-77; reference libr. NYSCC at Alfred U., 1973-77, art reference libr., 1977-90, art. reference libr., coll. archivist, 1981-90, asst. dean, 1986-88, acting dean, 1988-90; assoc. provost Alfred U., 1990—; mem. adv. bd. SUNY Women's Study Coun., 1987—; steering com. Mid. States Assn., 1984—. Author: History of American Ceramics An Annotated Bibliography, 1983, Charles Fergus Binns, Sesquicentennial, 1985. Mem. Am. Coun. Edn., Nat. Identification Program, Am. Ceramic Soc., Art Librs. Soc. N.Am. (travel award com. 1986—), Nat. Coun. Edn. for Ceramic Arts (archivist), Nat. Career Women's Assn. (adv. bd. 1987—), Soc. Am. Archivists, Phi Beta Kappa, Phi Kappa Phi. Office: Alfred Univ Saxon Dr Alfred NY 14802

STRONSKI, ANNA MARIA NIEDŹWIEDZKA, language professional; b. Starachowice, Poland, Aug. 17, 1940; came to U.S., 1954; d. Antoni Niedzwiedzki and Wanda Gluszkiewicz; divorced; 1 child, Alexandra Joanna Paszkowski. BA, Wayne State U., 1963, MA, 1972. Cert. secondary edn. tchr., Mich. Tchr. French and Spanish Ford Mid. Sch., Highland Park, Mich., 1965-66; tchr. fgn. lang. dept. Highland Park Cmty. H.S., 1966—, head fgn. lang. dept., 1968-70, 73-78, lang. arts facilitator, 1991-94; owner, founder Horizons-Internat., Grosse Pointe Park, Mich., 1993—; dist.-wide lang. cons./coord. Highland Park Pub. Schs., 1994—; ind. contractor/cons. Langs. and Svcs. Agy., 1993—; assessor, field study, tchr. performance lang. arts Nat. Bd. Profl. Tchg. Stds., Mich., 1994; scorer writing proficiency assessments Mich. Dept. Edn., 1994-95, trainer of tchrs., 1995; mem. instrnl./profl. devel. task force Mid. Cities Assn., Lansing, Mich., 1995—; mem. North Ctrl Accreditation Evaluations Teams, 1970—. Advisor: (high sch. yearbook) Polar Bear, 1985-86 (Big E award Josten's Printing Divsn. 1986); editor: (newsletter) Happenings, 1977-79, Mich. Writing Assessment News, 1994—. Bd. dirs. French Inst. Mich., Southfield, 1985—, Friends of Polish Art, Mich., 1995—. Recipient cert. appreciation for participation in Classrooms of Tomorrow program, Mich. Gov., 1990. Mem. Alliance Francaise: Detroit/Grosse Pointe, AAUW. Roman Catholic. Home: 790 Middlesex Blvd Grosse Pointe MI 48230-1742 Office: Horizons Internat 790 Middlesex Blvd Grosse Pointe Park MI 48230-1742

STROSCHEIN, SHARON MARIE, political campaign worker; b. Aberdeen, S.D., Sept. 20, 1944; d. William A. and Ethel L. (McAllen) Raetzman; m. Larry L. Stroschein, June 26, 1965; children: Amy Lynne Stroschein Mitchell, Ryan William, Lon Edward, Allyson Kaye. AA, No. State U., 1964, BS in Elem. Edn., 1984, M Sch. Adminstrn., 1986. Tchr. Northwestern Sch. Dist., Mellette, S.D., 1964-65; tchr. Warner (S.D.) Sch. Dist., 1966-68, tchr. music, 1971-74; field rep. U.S. Rep. Tim Johnson, Aberdeen, S.D., 1987—; dir. adv. bd. Resource Ctr. for Women, Aberdeen, 1988—. Chair combined fed. campaign United Way, 1993—, elected to United Way Exec. Bd.; mem. campaign staff Herseth for Gov., Aberdeen, 1986; mem. S.D. Dem. exec. bd., 1984—; S.D. committeewoman Dem. Nat. Com., 1984—, Midwest caucus sec., 1988—; chair Brown County Dems., Aberdeen, 1978-80; mem. adv. bd. Resource Ctr. for Women. Recipient McGovern Grassroots aard S.D. Dem. party, 1984; named Dem. Woman of Yr., S.D. Fedn. Dem. Women, 1992. Mem. AAUW (chair woman's work/worth com. 1988), Philanthropic Ednl. Orgn. (chair continuing edn. com. 1989), Nat. Farmers Orgn. (publicity dir. 1976—). Lutheran. Office: Dist Office 20 Sixth Ave SW Aberdeen SD 57401-6014

STROSSEN, NADINE, law educator, human rights activist; b. Jersey City, Aug. 18, 1950; d. Woodrow John and Sylvia (Simicich) S.; m. Eli Michael Noam, Apr. 25, 1980. AB, Harvard U., 1972, JD magna cum laude, 1975. Jud. clk. Minn. Supreme Ct., St. Paul, 1975-76; assoc. Lindquist & Vennum, Mpls., 1976-78, Sullivan & Cromwell, N.Y.C., 1978-83; prof. clin. law, supervising atty. Civil Rights Clinic, Sch. Law, NYU, 1984-88; prof. law N.Y. Law Sch., N.Y.C., 1988—. Editor Harvard Law Rev., 1975; contbr. book chpts., articles to profl. jours.; author: In Defense of Pornography: Free Speech and the Fight for Women's Rights, 1995. Bd. dirs. The Fund for Free Expression, 1990—. Recipient Outstanding Young Person award Jaycees Internat., 1986, Outstanding Contbn. to Human Rights Jour. Human Rights, N.Y. Law Sch., 1989; named one of Ten Outstanding Young Ams., U.S. Jaycees, 1986. Mem. ACLU (exec. com. 1985—, gen. counsel 1986-91, pres. 1991—), Nat. Coalition Against Censorship (bd. dirs. 1989—), Coalition to Free Soviet Jews (bd. dirs. 1984—), Human Rights Watch (exec. com. 1989-91), Asia Watch (vice chair 1989-91), Mid. East Watch (bd. dirs. 1989-91), Harvard Club (N.Y.C.). Home: 450 Riverside Dr # 51 New York NY 10027-6821 also: Sedgewood Club RR 12 Carmel NY 10512-9812 Office: NY Law Sch 57 Worth St New York NY 10013-2926*

STROTHERS, MARTINA HELEN, elementary school educator; b. Washington, Mar. 15, 1967. BA in Early Childhood and Elem. Edn., George Washington U., 1990. Cert. tchr. early childhood and elem. Intern Nat. Assn. for Edn. Young Children, Washington, 1988-89; student tchr. Montgomery County Pub. Sch. System, Silver Spring, Md., 1989; from student tchr. to tchr. D.C. Pub. Sch. System, Washington, 1990—. Troop leader, treas. Girl Scouts of U.S., Washington, 1993—. Mem. ASCD, Washington Tchrs. Union (in-house advisor). Home: 1227 Girard St NE Washington DC 20017-2424 Office: DC Pub Schs Mildred E Gibbs Elem Sch 19th and E Sts NE Washington DC 20002

STROUP, ELIZABETH FAYE, librarian; b. Tulsa, Mar. 25, 1939; d. Milton Earl and Lois (Buhl) S. BA in Philosophy, U. Wash., 1962, MLS, 1964. Intern Libr. of Congress, Washington, 1964-65; asst. dir. North Cen. Regional Libr., Wenatchee, Wash., 1966-69; reference specialist Congl. Reference div. Libr. of Congress, Washington, 1970-71, head nat. collections Div. for the Blind and Physically Handicapped, 1971-73, chief Congl. Reference div., 1973-78, dir. gen. reference, 1978-88; city libr., chief exec. officer Seattle Pub. Libr., 1988—; cons. U.S. Info. Svc., Indonesia, Feb. 1987. Mem. adv. bd. KCTS 9 Pub. TV, Seattle, 1988—; bd. visitors Sch. Librarianship, U. Wash., 1988—; bd. dirs. Wash. Literacy, 1988—. Mem. ALA (pres. reference and adult svcs. div. 1986-87, div. bd. 1985-88), Wash. Libr. Assn., D.C. Libr. Assn. (bd. dirs. 1975-76), City Club, Ranier Club. Office: Seattle Pub Libr 1000 4th Ave Seattle WA 98104-1109

STROUP, KALA MAYS, state education official. BA in Speech and Drama, U. Kans., 1959, MS in Psychology, 1964, PhD in Speech Comm. and Human Rels., 1974. V.p. acad. affairs Emporia (Kans.) State U., 1978-83; pres. Murray State U., Ky., 1983-90, S.E. Mo. State U., Cape Girardeau, 1990-95; commr. of higher edn. State of Mo., Jefferson City, 1995—; pres. Mo. Coun. on Pub. Higher Edn.; mem. pres.'s commn. NCAA; cons. Edn. Commn. of States Task Force on State Policy and Ind. Higher Edn.; adv. bd. NSF Directorate for Sci. Edn. Evaluation; adv. com. Dept. Health, Edn. and Welfare, chair edn. com.; citizen's adv. coun. on state of Women U. S. Dept. Labor, 1974-76. Mem. nat. exec. bd. Boy Scouts Am., nat. exploring com., former chair profl. devel. com., mem. profl. devel. com., exploring com., Young Am. awards com., 1986-87, north ctrl. region strategic planning com., bd. trustees, nat. mus. chair; mem. Gov.'s Cabinet, Gov.'s Coun. on Workforce Quality, State of Mo.; bd. dirs. Midwestern Higher Edn. Commn.; chair ACE Leadership Commn.; mem. bd. visitors Air U.; v.p. Missourians for Higher Edn.; mem. bd. St. Francis Med. Ctr. Found., 1990-95, Cape Girardeau C. of C., 1990-95, U. Kans. Alumni Assn.; pres. Forum on Excellence, Carnegie Found.; adv. bd. World Trade Ctr., St. Louis; mem. Mo. Higher Edn. Loan Authority, 1995—, depts. econ. devel. & agrl. Mo. Global Partnership, 1995—, Mo. Tng. & Employment Coun., 1995—, Concordia U. Sys. Advancement Cabinet, State Higher Edn. Exec. Officers; bd. govs. Heartland Alliance Minority Participation, 1995—. ACE fellow; recipient Alumni Honor Citation award U. Kans. and U. Kans. Womans Hall of Fame. Mem. Am. Assn. State Colls. and Univs. (past bd. dirs., mem. Pres.'s Commn. on Tchr. Edn., Task Force on Labor Force Issues and Implications for the Curriculum), Mortar Board, Phi Beta Kappa, Omicron Delta Kappa, Phi Kappa Phi, Rotary (found. Ednl. awards com.). Office: Southeast Missouri State Univ 1 University Plz Cape Girardeau MO 63701

STROUPE, M. JEAN, goverment official; b. Sevierville, Tenn., Jan. 31, 1956; d. Hugh Melvin and Trula Mae (Williams) Dinkins. Cert. payroll profl. Clk., typist City of Knoxville, Tenn., 1974-76; facilities customer svcs. mgr. Tenn. Valley Authority, Knoxville, 1976—, facilitator, 1991—. Bd. dirs. Tenn. Valley Kennel Club, Knoxville, 1986—. Home: 154 Winddrift Way Walland TN 37886 Office: Tenn Valley Authority 400 W Summit Hill Dr Knoxville TN 37902

STROUSE, JEAN, writer; b. L.A., Sept. 10, 1945; d. Carl David and Louise (Friedberg) S. BA, Radcliffe Coll., 1967. Editl. asst. N.Y. Rev. of Books, 1967-69; freelance writer N.Y.C., 1969-72; editor Pantheon Books, N.Y.C., 1972-75; freelance writer N.Y.C., 1975-79; book critic Newsweek Mag., N.Y.C., 1979-83; freelance writer N.Y.C., 1983—; selection com. mem. J.S. Guggenheim Found., N.Y.C., 1995—, trustee, 1987-94, fellow, 1977, 86; exec. bd. mem. Soc. Am. Historians; exec. coun. mem. Authors Guild. Author: Alice James, A Biography, 1980; editor: Women and Analysis: Dialogues on Psychoanalytic Views of Femininity, 1974. Fellow NEH, 1976, 92; recipient Bancroft prize in Am. History and Diplomacy Columbia U., 1981. Mem. PEN, Harvard Club N.Y., Phi Beta Kappa (vis. scholar 1996-97).

STRUBEL, ELLA DOYLE, advertising executive; b. Chgo., Mar. 14, 1940; d. George Floyd and Myrtle (McKnight) D.; m. Richard Craig G'sell, Apr. 26, 1969 (div. 1973); m. Richard Perry Strubel, Oct. 23, 1976; stepchildren: Douglas Arthur, Craig Tollerton. BA magna cum laude, Memphis State U., 1962; MA, U. Ill., 1963. Staff asst. Corinthian Broadcasting Co., N.Y.C., 1963-65; dir. advt.& pub. rels. WANE-TV, Ft. Wayne, Ind., 1965-66; asst. dir. advt. WBBM-TV, Chgo., 1966-67, mgr. sales promotion, 1967-69, dir. advt. sales promotion & info. svcs., 1969-70; pres. Ctr. Pub. Rels., Chgo., 1970-73; dir. pub. rels. Walthaw Watch Co., Chgo., 1973-74; mgr. advt. promotion & pub. rels. WMAQ-TV, Chgo., 1974-76; v.p. corp. rels. Kraft, Inc., Glenview, Ill., 1985-87; sr. v.p. corp. affairs Leo Burnett Co., Inc., Chgo., 1987-92, exec. v.p., 1992—. Bd. dirs. Rehab. Inst. Chgo., Chgo. Pub. Libr. Found., Leadership Greater Chgo., Family Focus; pres. Women's Bd. Rehab. Inst., 1982-84; chair Chgo. Network, 1994-95. Named Outstanding Woman in Comms. in Chgo., YWCA, 1995, one of 100 Most Influential Women in Chgo., Crain's Chgo. Bus., 1996. Mem. Northwestern U. Associates, Casino Club. Democrat. Presbyterian. Home: 55 W Goethe St Chicago IL 60610-2276 Office: Leo Burnett Co Inc 35 W Wacker Dr Chicago IL 60601-1614

STRUCHEN, SHIRLEY WHIPPLE, church organization administrator; m. Donald E. Struchen. Grad., Announcers Tng. Sch., N.Y.C.; BA in Telecom., Oral Roberts U.; MA in Comm. and Religious Studies, Canisius Coll. Exec. dir. TV awareness tng. program Media Action Rsch. Ctr. Inc., 1976-85; with pub. media divsn. United Meth. Comm., N.Y.C., from 1976, interim nat. dir. TV and Telecom. Fund, 1987-88, dir. conf. svcs., comm. edn., and U.M. Teleconf. Connection, v.p.; past dir. comm. and newspaper editor Western N.Y. Ann. Conf., United Meth. Ch.; former assoc. prodr. Catch the Spirit weekly mag. cable TV series; past exec. prodr. Christian radio script svc. The Word & Music; past editor Pep Talk newsletter for prodrs. electronic media; former exec. prodr. Light for World, ABD-TV. Former mem. alumni bd. Oral Roberts U., Tulsa; mem. adv. bd. Celectration Shop, Inc.; chmn. media edn. com. Comm. Commn., Nat. Coun. Chs. of Christ. Mem. NAFE, Am. Women in Radio and TV, Assn. for Christian Comm. (past mem. steering com. N.Am. broadcast sect.), Religious Pub. Rels. Coun. (nat. pres.), United Meth. Assn. Communicators (steering com.). Office: United Meth Comm 475 Riverside Dr Ste 1901 New York NY 10115

STRUCHTEMEYER, CAROL SUE, elementary education educator; b. Kansas City, Mo., Apr. 21, 1954; d. Olin Carl and Anna Christine (Skou) Brookshier; m. Leland Leonard Struchtemeyer, May 26, 1973; children: Rhonda Sue, Thomas Leland. BS in Edn., Ctrl. Mo. State U., 1975, MS in Edn., 1981; ednl. resource tchr. tng., U. Mo., 1977. Cert. elem. tchr., spl. edn. tchr. Tchr. elem. Mayview (Mo.) R-7 Sch. Dist., 1975-76; tchr. learning disabilities Odessa (Mo.) R-5 Sch. Dist., 1976-78; tchr. 5th grade Lexington (Mo.) R-5 Sch. Dist., 1978—; sec. Leslie Bell Intervention Team, Lexington, 1992-94. Mem. Trinity United Ch. of Christ, Lexington, 1990—, Lexington Athletic Boosters, 1992—, Lexington Fine Arts Club, 1992—. Mem. NEA, Nat. Coun. Tchrs. Math., Mo. Edn. Assn., Mo. Coun. Tchrs. Math., Lexington Cmty. Tchrs. Assn. (sec. 1983-84, treas. 1985-86). Home: PO Box 58 501 Roncelli Rd Lexington MO 64067

STRUCK, NORMA JOHANSEN, artist; b. West Englewood, N.J., Feb. 17, 1929; d. Hans Christian and Amanda (Solberg) Johansen; m. H. Walter Struck, Aug. 21, 1955; children: Steven, Laurie. Student, N.Y. Phoenix Sch. Design, 1946-50; Art Students' League, N.Y.C., 1976-77. Staff artist Norcross, Inc., N.Y.C., 1950-60, free-lance artist, 1967-75; artist portraits, prints Scafa-Tornabene, Nyack, N.Y., 1976—; artist portraits, paintings U.S.N., U.S. Coast Guard, Washington, 1976—; com. bd. mem. Navy Art Coop. Liaison, N.Y.C., 1976-80, Coast Guard Art Program, N.Y.C., 1980--. One-woman shows include Nabisco Co., Fairlawn, N.J., 1987; exhibited in group shows Navy Hist. Mus., Washington, 1976, Navy Combat Art Gallery, Washington, World Trade Ctr., 1979, USCG, New Eng. Air Mus., Windsor Locks, Conn., 1984, Fed. Hall, N.Y.C., 1986, 93, 94, 95, Salmagundi Club, N.Y.C., Officers Club, Governor's Island, Hudson Valley Show, White Plains, N.Y.; represented in permanent collections U.S. Pentagon, Washington, Heinie-Onstad Mus., Oslo, World Figure Skating Hall of Fame and Mus., Colorado Springs. Recipient Louis E. Seley award, Navy Art Program, 1979; Grumbacher award, Catherine Lorillard Wolfe, Nat. Arts Club, N.Y.C., 1978; George Gray award Coast Guard Art Program, Governors Island, N.Y., 1983, 89. Mem. Art Students League (life), Hudson Valley Assn. (bd. dirs. 1985-88, M. Dole award 1980), Soc. Illustrators, Salmagundi Club, Am. Artists Profl. League (Pres.'s award 1979). Home: 910 Midland Rd Oradell NJ 07649-1904

STRUG, KERRI, gymnast, Olympic athlete; b. Tucson, Ariz., Nov. 19, 1977. Mem. Jr. Pacific Alliance Team, Indpl., 1989, Jr. Pan Am. Games Team, Tallahassee, Fla., 1990, World Gymnastics Championship Team, Indpls., 1991, U.S. Olympic Team, Barcelona, Spain, 1992, Hilton Challenge Team, L.A., Calif., 1993, Team World Championship Team, Dortmund, Germany, 1994, World Champion Team, Sabae, Japan, 1995, U.S. Olympic Team, Atlanta, 1996. Placed 1st all around Am. Classic, Calif., 1989, 2d all around Am. Classic, Tex., 1989, 2d uneven bars, balance beam Dutch Open, Holland, 1990, 1st vault U.S. Gymnastics Championships, Ohio, 1991, 1st vault U.S. vs. Romania, Tex., 1991, 1st vault, balance beam U.S. Gymnastics Championships, Ohio, 1992, 2d all around, floor exercise U.S. Gymnastics Championships, Ohio, 1992, 1st all around, uneven bars, balance beam, floor exercise Am. Classic/World Championships Trials, Utah, 1993, 1st uneven bars and 2d all around, balance beam, floor exercise U.S. Olympic Festival, Tex., 1993, 2d uneven bars Coca Cola Nat. Championships, Utah, 1993, 1st balance beam, 2d all around, McDonald's Am. Cup, Fla., 1993, 2d (with Waller) all around Reebok Internat. Mixed Pairs, 1993, 2d all around NationsBank World Team Trials, Va., 1994, 1st all around, uneven bars U.S. Olympic Festival, Colo., 1995, 1st all around, balance beam, floor exercise, 2d vault, uneven Bars McDonald's Am. Cup, Tex., 1996; recipient Silver medal World Championships, 1991, Olympic Bronze medal, 1992, Silver medal Team World Championships, 1994, Bronze medal World Championships, 1995, Olympic Gold medal, 1996. Mem. Karolyi's Gymnastics. *

STRUGGER, ROBERTA, secondary education educator; b. N.Y.C., Nov. 18, 1954; d. Bernard and Sara Katherine (Aboulafia) S.; 1 child, David Richard. BA in History, Lehman Coll., 1977, MA in Secondary Edn., 1991, BS in Health Edn. and Promotion cum laude, 1996. Cert. health edn. specialist; cert. AIDS educator, N.Y. History tchr. Bronx (N.Y.) Satellite Acad., 1978-82, Taft H.S., Bronx, 1984-90; tchr. econs. A.E. Stevenson H.S., Bronx, 1990—; dean, tchr. Gates Ext., Dist. 9, Bronx, 1983-84; coord. GED program CUNY, N.Y.C., 1984-85; adj. lectr. health edn. Bronx Lebanon Hosp., 1996. Vol. deliverer food to AIDS patients God's Love We Deliver, N.Y.C., 1994, 95. Mem. Am. Sch. Health Assn., Soc. Pub. Health Edn., Greater N.Y. Soc. for Pub. Health Edn. Jewish. Home: 3605 Sedgwick Ave Bronx NY 10463

STRUNK, BETSY ANN WHITENIGHT, education educator; b. Bloomsburg, Pa., May 28, 1942; d. Mathias Clarence and Marianna (Naunas) Whitenight; children: Robert J. Jr., Geoffrey M. BS in Edn., Bloomsburg U., 1964; MEd, West Chester U., 1969; cert. mentally/physically handicapped, Pa. State U., 1981; postgrad., Wilkes U., St. Joseph's U., Drexel U., Western Md. Coll. Cert. elem. edn., spl. edn.; cert. single engine pvt. pilot. Tchr. Faust Sch., Bensalem (Pa.) Twp., 1964, Eddystone (Pa.) Elem. Sch., 1964-66, Lima Elem. Sch., Rose Tree Media Sch. Dist., 1966-69, Rose Tree Media (Pa.) Sch. Dist., 1977—; adj. prof. Wilkes Coll., Wilkes-Barre, Pa., 1981-86; instr. Delaware C.C., Media, 1986; instr., dir. ground sch. edn. Brandywine Airport, West Chester, Pa., 1986-88; instr. Drexel U., Phila., 1989—, Performance Learning Systems, Inc., Emerson, N.J. and Nevada City, Calif., 1981—; rep. FAA, Phila., 1986-88; spl. edn. resource rm. specialist, tchr. cons. Media Elem. Sch., Rose Tree Media Sch. Dist., spl. edn. supervisory selection com.; curriculum designer pvt. pilot ground sch.; instr. introduction to flying and pilot companion course; chairperson profl. devel. com. Rose Tree Media Sch. Dist., 1992; mem. Insvc. Coun. of Delaware County, 1992—; mem. educator's adv. com. Phila. Franklin Inst., 1990-92, 95—; cons. ednl. programs, 1988—; owner, designer Betsy's Belts, Del., N.J., Pa., 1970-74; mem. gov. bd. Southeastern Tchr. Leadership Ctr. West Chester (Pa.) U.; learning support specialist Glenwood Elem. Sch., Media, Pa., 1994—; presenter State of Pa. Lead Tchr. Conf., 1994, Ind. Sch. Tchrs. Assn., 1995; project dir. video documentary Performance Learning Sys., Calif., 1994. Program dir. video documentaries including Learning Through Live Events and Teaching Skills for the 21st Century, 1995; contbr. articles to profl. jours. Mem. Middletown Free Libr. Bd., 1977-79; officer Riddlewood Aux. to Riddle Meml. Hosp., Media, 1973-78; chairperson Lima (Pa.) Christian Nursery Sch., 1973, March of Dimes, Middletown, 1973; pres. Roosevelt PTG (Elem. Sch.), Media, 1982; com. person, v.p. Middletown Twp. Dem. Com., 1974; capt. March of Dimes, Media, 1987-91, Diabetes Assn., Media, 1989-91; mem. Vietnamese refugee com. Media Presbyn. Ch., 1975, mem., 1967—; vol. Tyler Arboretum, Middletown Twp., 1980-82. Recipient 1st Pl. Color Divsn. Photography award Pa. Colonial Plantation PLS 500 Club award, 1st pl. Color Divsn. in Photography Bloomsburg State Fair, 1994; Fine Arts in Spl. Edn. grantee Pa. Dept. Edn., 1993-94. Mem. NEA, ASCD, Pa. ASCD, Rose Tree Media Edn. Assn. (profl. devel. com. chairperson 1992-93, profl. devel. com. rep. 1990-93, Exceptional Svc. award), Pa. State Edn. Assn., Nat. Staff Devel. Coun., Aircraft Owners and Pilots Assn., Tyler Arboretum, Media Soc. Performing Arts, Phila. Zoo. Democrat. Home: 203 Cohasset Ln West Chester PA 19380-6507 Office: Rose Tree Media Sch Dist Glenwood Elem Sch Pennell Rd Media PA 19063

STRUNZ, KIM CAROL, military officer; b. Caro, Mich., May 3, 1954; d. Herbert James and Geraldine (Elliott) S. AAS with honors, Delta Coll., 1974; BS with honors, Alma Coll., 1980; postgrad., Ctrl. Mich. U., 1978-80; MPA, U. Okla., 1989. Commd. 2d lt. U.S. Army, 1980, advanced through grades to maj.; telecomms. ctr. specialist 178th signal co. U.S. Army, Heidelberg, Germany, 1974-77; chief plans, ops., tng. and security med. dept. activity U.S. Army, Bremerhaven, Germany, 1980-82; ambulance platoon leader Co. C 47th med. bn. U.S. Army, Furth, Germany, 1982-83; exec. officer dental activity U.S. Army, Ft. Lee, Va., 1983-85; adjutant Kenner Army Comty. Hosp. U.S. Army, Ft. Lee, 1985; comdr. med. co. 47th Field Hosp. U.S. Army, Ft. Sill, Okla., 1986-88; chief pers. svcs. divsn. 121st Evac. Hosp. 18th med. command U.S. Army, Seoul, Korea, 1988-89; chief mil. pers. br. William Beaumont Army Med. Ctr., El Paso, Tex., 1990-92, comdr. troop command, 1992-93; career planning officer U.S. Total Army Personnel Command, Alexandria, Va., 1993-95; pers. policy analyst Office of the Army Surgeon Gen., Falls Church, Va., 1995—. Contbr. rsch. articles to profl. jours. Vol. Therapeutic Horsemanship Assn., El Paso, Alexandria Hosp.; mem. Highland Presbyn. Ch. Softball Team, El Paso. Mem. Am. Soc. Pub. Adminstrn., Assn. U.S. Army, Army Women's Profl. Assn. Presbyterian. Home: 801 N Howard St Apt 306 Alexandria VA 22304-5460

STUART, DOROTHY MAE, artist; b. Fresno, Calif., Jan. 8, 1933; d. Robert Wesley Williams and Maria Theresa (Gad) Tressler; m. Reginald Ross Stuart, May 18, 1952; children: Doris Lynne Stuart Willis, Darlene Mae Stuart Cavalletto, Sue Anne Stuart Peters. Student, Calif. State U., Fresno, 1951-52, Fresno City Coll., 1962-64. Artist, art judge, presenter demonstrations at schs., fairs and art orgns. Calif., 1962—. Editor, art dir. Fresno High School Centennial 1889-1989, 1989; art advisor Portrait of Fresno, 1885-1985; contbg. artist Heritage Fresno, 1975; exhibited in group shows, including M.H. De Young Mus., San Francisco, 1971, Charles and Emma Frye Mus., Seattle, 1971, Calif. State U.-Fresno tour of China, 1974. Mem. adv. com. Calif. State Ken Maddy Ctrl. Calif. Conf. on Women, 1989-96, Patrons for Cultural Arts, Fresno, 1987-92, bd. dirs., 1991-92. Recipient 53 art awards, 1966-84; nominated Woman of the Yr., Bus./Profl. of Fresno, 1990. Mem. Soc. Western Artists (bd. dirs. 1968-74, v.p. 1968-70), Fresno Womens Trade Club (bd. dirs. 1986-93, pres. 1988-90), Fresno Art Mus., Fresno Met. Mus., Native Daus. Golden West Fresno. Republican. Home and Office: 326 S Linda Ln Fresno CA 93727-5737

STUART, JANE ELIZABETH, film and video executive; b. N.Y.C., Dec. 15, 1947; d. Mark Abraham and Melba Rita (Goldstein) Stuart; m. Bernard Schmetterer, Jan. 9, 1972 (div. 1978). Student, Upsala Coll., East Orange, N.J., 1964-66. Lic. real estate broker, N.Y. Reporter The Bergen Record, Hackensack, N.J., 1966-71; polit. speech writer Town of Ramapo, N.Y., 1971-72; pub. rels. specialist Bergen County, N.J., 1972-74; reporter Times Herald Record, Middletown, N.Y., 1974-76; real estate broker, v.p. Elizabeth Gretsch Realty, Monroe, N.Y., 1976-81; v.p., gen. mgr Eventime Inc., N.Y.C., 1981-86; talent mgr. N.Y.C., 1986—; pres., CEO Big Picture Comm., Inc., N.Y.C., 1993—; gen. mgr. The Big Picture, Inc., N.Y.C., 1988-95; pres. Big Picture/Even Time Ltd., 1995—; ptnr. Hwy. Interactive, Inc., N.Y.C., 1994—; v.p. Internat. Post Ltd., 1995—. Office: Big Picture/Even Time Ltd 62 W 45th St New York NY 10036-6611 also: 10 Longwoods Ln East Hampton NY 11937

STUART, JOAN MARTHA, fund raising executive; b. Huntington, N.Y., June 2, 1945; d. Ervin Wencil and Flora Janet (Applebaum) S. Student, Boston U., 1963-67. Cert. fund raiser. Prodn. asst. Random House, N.Y.C., 1968-69; book designer Simon & Schuster, N.Y.C., 1969-71; feature writer Palm Beach (Fla.) Post, 1971-72; co-founder, comm. dir. Stuart, Gleimer & Assocs., West Palm Beach, 1973-84, pres., 1982—; fin. devel. dir. YWCA Greater Atlanta, 1984-86, Ctr. for the Visually Impaired, Atlanta, 1986-90; ea. divsn. dir. City of Hope, 1990-94; devel. dir. Jewish Family Svcs., Atlanta, 1994—; adj. prof. Kennesaw Coll. Contbr. articles to profl. jours. Mem. crusade com. Am. Cancer Soc. Bd., 1981—; bd. dirs. Theatre Arts Co., 1980-81; cmty. svcs. chmn., bd. dirs. B'nai B'rith Women, 1980-82; chmn. publicity Leukemia Soc. Atlanta Polo Benefit, 1983; com. chmn.

Atlanta Zool. Beastly Feast Benefit, 1984; mem. Atlanta Symphony Assocs.; chmn. Salute to Women of Achievement, 1987-90; founder, advisor Lauren's Run, 1992—. Recipient Nat. award B'nai B'rith Women, 1978, Regional award, 1979, cert. of merit Big Bros./Big Sisters, 1976. Mem. Nat. Soc. Fund Raising Execs. (cert.), Ga. Exec. Women's Network, Diabetes Assn. (bd. dirs. 1990—), Jerusalem House (bd. dirs. 1991-94), Parent to Parent (bd. dirs. 1993-95). Democrat. Jewish. Office: 4549 Chamblee Dunwoody Rd Atlanta GA 30338

STUART, KATHRYN HILLIARD, family therapist; b. Washington, Nov. 8, 1967; d. Robert Glenn and Heather Ann (Prevost) Hilliard; m. Eugene Washington Stuart Jr., Aug. 4, 1990. BA in Psychology, Davidson Coll., 1990; MEd with honors, The Citadel, Charleston, S.C., 1992. Cert. nat. counselor; lic. profl. counselor; cert. family therapist; credentialed clin. counselor; lic. mental health counselor; lic. marriage and family therapist. Intern Navy Family Svcs., Charleston, S.C., 1991-92, Family Counseling Ctr., Charleston, 1992; clin. counselor Wesley Ctr. Dept. Alcohol and Other Drug Abuse Svcs., Charleston, S.C., 1992-94; family therapist Family Counseling Ctr., Greenville, S.C., 1994-95; mental health counselor Family Counseling Svcs., Jacksonville, Fla., 1995—. Contbg. editor The Fla. Woman mag., 1996. Supr. Hotline Crisis Counseling, Charleston, 1990-93; active Jr. League, Jacksonville, Fla., 1995—; conf. leader United Ministries Homeless Shelter, Greenville, S.C., 1994-95. Mem. Am. Assn. Marriage and Family Therapists (clin.), Fla. Assn. Marriage and Family Therapy, Charleston Network Marriage and Family Therapy (v.p. 1993-94), Chi Sigma Iota. Office: Family Counseling Svcs 1639 Atlantic Blvd Jacksonville FL 32207

STUART, LILLIAN MARY, writer; b. Chgo., Nov. 7, 1914; d. Ira and Katherine (Tries) Daugherty; m. Robert Graham Stuart, Aug. 7, 1936 (dec. Sept. 1969); 1 child, Mary Leone. Asst. to pres. Weisberger Bros., South Bend, 1933-42; head TWX distbn. Davis-Monthan AFB, Tucson, 1946-48; artist and music tchr., 1945-55; interviewer-counselor Ariz. State Employment Commn., Tucson, 1955-70; residence dir. YWCA, Tucson, 1970-71; tax preparer Tucson, 1971-72; U.S. census taker U.S. Govt., N.Mex., 1976, 80; mng. Luna County Rep. Party, Deming, 1976; tchr. YWCA, Tucson, 1969, El Paso Coll. Bus., 1972; tutor math, English, 1981; travel lectr. various civic groups and clubs; radio reader Lighthouse for the Blind, El Paso, 1983-89; spkr. Internat. Women's Day Celebration, 1996. Contbr. stories to The Quarterly; author: (series of biographies) Lighthouse for the Blind; actress Studebaker Players, South Bend, 1936-42, South Bend Theatre, 1936-42, (film) Extreme Prejudice, 1986; writer Centennial Mus. at U. Tex., El Paso, 1992-95. Counselor, vol. Crisis Ctr., Deming, 1975-77. Recipient plaques and prizes for various pieces of writing. Mem. Mensa, Rosicrucians, Sisters in Crime. Episcopalian. Address: 2710 W Ashby Pl Apt 323 San Antonio TX 78201-5380

STUART, LORI AMES, public relations executive; b. Hempstead, N.Y., Oct. 23, 1957; d. Henry Aschner and Janet (Hackel) Goldman; m. John Robert Ames, Jan. 30, 1982 (div. July 1990); 1 child, Robert Walter Ames; m. Robert John Stuart, July 27, 1991. BA, Hofstra U., 1979. Publicist Jane Wesman Pub. Rels., N.Y.C., 1980-84, v.p., 1991—; publicist, publicity mgr. William Morrow & Co., N.Y.C., 1984-89, publicity dir., 1989-90; lectr., mentor NYU, 1994. Jewish. Office: Jane Wesman Pub Rels 928 Broadway Ste 903 New York NY 10010-6008

STUART, LUANN LEIGH, counselor; b. Ashland, Ohio, Feb. 26, 1966; d. Ronald Lee and Janet Mae (Whitmore) S.; 1 child, Douglas Ross Ashley. BA in Psychology, Ashland U., 1989; MA in Pastoral Psychology and Counseling, Ashland Theol. Sem., 1992. Lic. profl. clin. counselor. Counselor Marriage and Family Guidance Svcs., Ashland, 1991—; cons. Compassion Inc., Ashland, 1991—; bd. dirs. Well Child and Prenatal Care Clinic, Ashland, 1992—. Mem. ACA. Republican. Mem. Grace Brethren Ch. Home: 713 Ellis Ave Ashland OH 44805 Office: Sunrise Family Svcs 713 Ellis Ave Ashland OH 44805

STUART, SANDRA JOYCE, computer information scientist; b. Wheatland, Mo., Aug. 15, 1950; d. Asa Maxville and Inez Irene (Wilson) Friedley; m. John Kendall Stuart, Apr. 17, 1971; 1 child, Whitney Renee. Student, Cen. Mo. State U., 1968-69; AA (hon.), Johnson County Community Coll., 1980; BS in Bus. Adminstrn. cum laude, Avila Coll., 1992. Statis. asst. Fed. Crop Ins. Corp., Kansas City, Mo., 1978-83; mgr. Fed. Women's Program, Kansas City, 1979-80; mgmt. asst. Marine Corps Fin. Ctr., Kansas City, 1983-85, analyst computer systems, 1985-88; computer programmer analyst Corps. of Engrs., Kansas City, 1988-91; regional program mgr. FAA, Kansas City, 1991—. Author: The Samuel Walker History, 1983. Asst. supt. Sunday sch. Overland Park (Kans.) Christian Ch., 1979-80, supt., 1980-82. Mem. Wheatland High Sch. Alumni Assn. (pres. 1990-91).

STUART, SANDRA KAPLAN, federal official; b. Greensboro, N.C.; d. Leon and Renee (Myers) Kaplan; children: Jay Jr., Timothy. BA, U. N.C., Greensboro; JD, Monterey Coll. Law. Chief legis. asst. Rep. Robert Matsui, Washington, 1979-81; legis. dir., assoc. staff Ho. of Appropriations and Budget Coms., Washington, 1981-87; adminstrv. asst. Rep. Vic Fazio, Washington, 1987-89, chief of staff, 1990-93; asst. sec. def. legis. affairs Dept. Def., The Pentagon, Washington, 1993—. Office: Office Legis Affairs Dept Def The Pentagon Washington DC 20301-1300

STUBBLEFIELD, KAREN HOLT MCINTOSH, public relations and marketing professional; b. Houston, June 2, 1965; d. Thomas Shirley and Audrey (Jean) McIntosh. BA, Tex. A&M U., 1987; cert. in publ. specialization, George Washington U., 1990. Staff asst. Sec. U.S. Senate, Washington, 1987-88; fed. writer Education USA, Arlington, Va., 1988-90; asst. dir. community affairs Mother Frances Hosp., Tyler, Tex., 1990-94, dir. pub. rels., 1994—. Active mem. United Way Tyler/Smith County; bd. dirs. east Tex. chpt. Am. Heart Assn. Recipient Paul R. Ellis media award Am. Heart Assn., 1995. Mem. Tex. Soc. Hosp. Pub. Rels. and Mktg., East Tex. Advt. Fedn., Kappa Alpha Theta. Methodist. Home: 11923 County # 140W Flint TX 75762

STUBBS, JAN DIDRA, retired travel industry executive, travel writer; b. Waseca, Minn., June 19, 1937; d. Gordon Everett and Bertha Margaret (Bertsch) Didra; m. James Stewart Stubbs, Nov. 24, 1962; children: Jeffrey Stewart, Jacqueline Didra. BA in Speech/English, U. Minn., 1961; cert. travel counselor, Inst. Cert. Travel Agts., 1988. Sales agt. United Airlines, Mpls., 1961-64; interior decorator Lloyd and Assocs., St. Paul, 1964-66; v.p. Stubbs and Assocs., Textiles, St. Paul, 1966-83; account exec. Twin Cities Mag., Mpls., 1983-85; account exec. Internat. Travel Arrangers, St. Paul, 1985-86, asst. dir. sales, 1986-88; mgr. Dayton's Group Holidays, Mpls., 1988-96; writer for Mgmt. Assistance Project. V.p. Jr. Women's Assn. of Minn. Symphony Orch.; chairperson 60th anniversary Jr. League of St. Paul, sec., 1967—, sustaining mem.; deacon Ho. of Hope Presbyn. Ch., St. Paul, 1970; mem. Unied Way adv. bd. corporate giving Dayton Hudson Corp. Named Outstanding Alumni, Coll. Liberal Arts, U. Minn., 1995, Women of Yr. 1995-96 Minn. Exec. Women in Tourism. Mem. AAUW, Inst. Cert. Travel Agts., Am. Soc. Travel Agts., Minn. Exec. Women in Tourism (publicity com. 1987-88, by-laws chmn. 1989-90, sec. 1988-89, 90, fedn. dir. 1990—, v.p., 1993, pres. 1993-94), Internat. Fedn. Women in Travel (alt. gov. Mid-Am. region, standing com. dir. historian, gov. mid-Ams. area I 1994, 95), Jr. Assistance League, St. Paul Pool and Yacht Club, Alpha Omicron Pi (pres. 1958-59, alumni pres. 1962), Whitefish Chain Yacht Club (sec.), U. Minn. Alumni Assn. Republican. Home: 1575 Boardwalk Ct Saint Paul MN 55118-2747 Office: Dayton's Group Holidays 320 Plymouth Bldg 12 S 6th St Minneapolis MN 55402-1508

STUBBS, KATRINA CHILDS, business consultant; b. Atlanta, Feb. 10, 1964; d. Theodore Roosevelt Childs and Jacqueline Louise (Clark) Childs-Taylor; m. Lorenzo Durango Stubbs, Oct. 26, 1991; 1 child, Kayla Laranza. BS in Chemistry, Dillard U., 1985; MBA, Albany State Coll., 1991. Med. specialist U.S. Army Res., Chamblee, Ga., 1981-87; rsch. asst. Clark-Atlanta U., 1985-87; technologist/chemist Miller Brewing Co., Albany, Ga., 1987-93; bus. cons. UGA Bus. Outreach Svc., Albany, 1993—; minority student dir. UGA Bus. Outreach Svc., Albany, 1994-95; com. mem. AGE Fed. Credit Union, 1991-93; bd. mem. Albany-Dougherty Inner City Authority, 1994—. Named Vol. of Month, First Step Vol. Program, Albany, 1994. Mem. NAFE. Democrat. Baptist.

STUBBS, MARILYN KAY, education administrator; b. Great Bend, Kans., Mar. 21, 1950; d. John Calvin and Roseanna (Edler) Rapp; m. Stephen Richard Stubbs, Apr. 4, 1970; children: Adam Richard, Anna Elizabeth. BA in English, Kans. State U., 1972. Asst. instr. Kans. State U., Manhattan, 1972; educator All Saints Sch., Kansas City, Kans., 1973-74, Archdiocese of Kansas City, Mo., 1975-78; adminstrv. asst. Sherwood Ctr. for the Exceptional Child, Kansas City, Mo., 1979-89; assoc. dir. Sherwood Ctr. for the Exceptional Child, Kansas City, 1989—; cons., trainer N.W. Mo. Autism Consortium, Kansas City, 1993—, Mo. State Team on Positive Behavior Support, Kansas City, 1994—, Autism Team Tng. Project, Kansas City, 1995-96; trainer Jackson County (Mo.) Bd. Svcs., Kansas City, 1995-96. Writer (newsletter) Sherwood Chronicle, 1980-86; editor (newsletters) Sherwood Chronicle, 1986-96, Families Addressing Auditory Integration Training, 1993-95. Mem. spkrs. bur. United Way, Kansas City, Mo., 1982-96; mem. Assn. United Way Execs., 1989-96; advocacy com. mem. Met. Coun. on Devel. Disabilities, 1990-94. Named Parent of Yr., Sherwood Parents Assn., Kansas City, Mo., 1985. Mem. Autism Soc. Am. (sec. Western Mo. chpt. 1993), Assn. for Severly Handicapped, Am. Assn. on Mental Retardation, Astron. Soc. Kansas City, Divers Alert Network. Office: Sherwood Center 7938 Chestnut Kansas City MO 64132

STUBBS, SUSAN CONKLIN, statistician; b. Washington, July 26, 1935; d. Maxwell Robertson and Marcia (Nye) Conklin; m. LeRoy Carter Hostetter, May 20, 1975 (div. 1988); m. Joel Richard Stubbs, Sept. 20, 1992. BA, Pa. State U., 1957. Economist Bur. of Census, Suitland, Md., 1973-74; economist Bur. of Labor Statistics, Washington, 1974-78, supervisory economist, 1978-84; statistician IRS, Washington, 1984-95, chief rschr. stats. of income div., 1989-92, coord. for indsl. classification, 1994-95; ret., 1995. Contbr. articles to profl. jours. Leader, del., com. mem., chmn., v.p., bd. dirs., nominating com. Girl Scout Coun. Nation's Capitol, Washington, 1968-96; sec., treas. Middlesex Beach Assn., Bethany, Del., 1991-94; jobs editor Caucus for Women in Statistics, Washington, 1992-95; mentor Mentors Inc., Washington, 1992-94. Mem. Am. Statis. Assn., Tax Economist Forum, River's Bend Assn. (audit, covenants, and nominating coms.), Woman's Club Northumberland County (pres. 1996). Home: Rt 3 Box 65EA Heathsville VA 22473

STUBER, IRENE ZELINSKY, writer, researcher; b. Cleve., Nov. 1, 1928; d. Joseph Frank and Marian (Kulchar) Zelinsky; m. Joseph Francis Stuber, Apr. 9, 1948 (div. Aug. 1954); children: Catherine, Geraldine, William. Student, Cleve. Coll., 1946-48. Editor Cleve. Kegler, 1954-60; publs. dir. Miami (Fla.)-Dade C. of C., 1963-65; staff writer Hollywood (Fla.) Sun-Tattler, 1966-67; urban affairs writer Ft. Lauderdale (Fla.) News, 1967-74; tech. editor Bell Aerospace, New Orleans, 1977-78; owner Kulchar's Jewelry, New Orleans, 1974-83, Hot Springs, Ark., 1983-90. Rschr., writer (Internet newsletter) Women of Achievement and Her Story, 1994-96 (3 Stars Net Guide 1995-96, Magellan Best Site 1995-96, 1001 Best Site PC 1995-96); writer (Internet newsletter) Catt's Claws, 1995-96 (3 Stars Net Guide 1995-96, Magellan Best Site 1995-96, 1001 Best Site PC 1995-96); freelance writer Ark. Woman's Jour. of Rebel Mag. Mem. exec. com. Broward County (Fla.) Dem. Party, 1974, mem. exec. com. Garland County (Ark.) Dem. Party, 1993, 96—; newsletter editor, corr. sec. Va. Clinton Kelley Dem. Women's Club, Hot Springs, 1995-96. Recipient Pub. Svc. award City of Hollywood, 1967, Journalistic Excellence award AP, 1967, Recognition of Svcs. award Fla. Bar Assn., 1968. Mem. NOW (Ark. chpt. pres. 1993-94, Hot Springs chpt. pres. 1992-96). Home: PO Box 6185 Hot Springs AR 71902

STUCKEY, DONNA SUE, information services executive; b. Pittsburg, Kans., Oct. 20, 1960; d. Carl E. and Mary Ann (Bugni) Pintar; m. Donald Oris Stuckey, May 20, 1982 (div. Apr. 14, 1986); children: Banning W., Cassandra R., Heather D. BS in Math., B.S. in Computer Sci., Pittsburg State U., 1982. Asst. mgr. office info. svcs. Pittsburg State U., 1979-82, asst. office mgr. dept. computer sci., info. sci., 1979-82, coord. devel. info. svcs., 1988-92, dir. development info. svcs., 1992—; bus. analyst/programmer Getty Oil Co., Tulsa, 1982-84; office mgr., sales asst. State Farm Ins. Co., Pittsburg, 1986-87; loan officer 1st Fed. Savs. & Loan, Pittsburg, 1987-88; asst. to grad. students, Pittsburg, 1988—; freelance installer PCs, Pittsburg, 1995—. Asst. troop leader Boy Scouts Am. Ozark Trails Coun., Pittsburg, 1989—, asst. troop leader Girl Scouts Am. Ozark Area Coun., 1990—; pres. home and sch. assn. St. Mary's Grade Sch., Pittsburg, 1995—. Mem. Info. Tech. Adv. Coun., Pittsburg C. of C. (ambassador com. 1995—), Alpha Sigma Alpha, Omicron Delta Kappa, Kappa Mu Epsilon, Delta Mu Delta. Roman Catholic. Home: 707 N Highland St Pittsburg KS 66762 Office: Pittsburg State U Devel Info Svcs 401 E Ford Ave Pittsburg KS 66762

STUCKEY, HELENJEAN LAUTERBACH, counselor educator; b. Bushnell, Ill., May 17, 1929; d. Edward George and Frances Helen (Simpson) Lauterbach; m. James Dale Stuckey, Sept. 30, 1951; children: Randy Lee, Charles Edward, Beth Ellen. BFA, Ill. Wesleyan U., 1951; MEd, U. Ill., 1969. Cert. art tchr., guidance, psychology instr.; lic. clin. profl. counselor, Ill. Display designer Saks Fifth Ave., Chgo., 1951; interior designer Piper City, Ill., 1953-63; art tchr. Forrest (Ill.)-Strawn-Wing Schs., 1967-68; tchr., counselor Piper City Schs., 1969-74; counselor, art tchr. Ford Cen. Schs., Piper City, 1974-85; psychiatric counselor Community Resource Counseling Ctr., Ford County, Ill., 1985-87; history tchr., counselor Iroquois West High Sch., Gilman, Ill., 1987-88; spl. needs coord. Livingston County Vocat., Pontiac, Ill., 1988-93; ret., 1993; clin. profl. counselor, pvt. practice Piper City, 1995—. Job skills coord. Livingston Area Edn. for Employment, 1994. Mem. AACD, Ill. Counseling Assn., Ill. Mental Health Counselors Assn., Ill. Ret. Tchrs., Delta Kappa Gamma (v.p., sec., program chmn., pres.). Presbyterian.

STUCKEY, SUSAN JANE, perioperative nurse, consultant. Diploma in nursing, The Polyclinic Med. Ctr., 1971; BBA in Health Care Adminstrn., Pa. State U., 1985; cert., Del. County C.C., Media, Pa., 1988; MBA, Kutztown U., 1996. RN, Pa.; cert. operating rm. nurse; cert. RN first asst. Charge nurse Nightingale Nursing Home, Camp Hill, Pa., 1971-72; clin. educator oper. rm. svcs., staff nurse Harrisburg (Pa.) Hosp., 1972-80; adminstr., nursing coord. Hillcrest Women's Med. Ctr., Harrisburg, 1978-81; office mgr., pvt. scrub nurse Office Dr. Henry Train, Harrisburg, 1979-82; with Kimberly Nurses Med Temps, Cleve., 1982-84; sr. splty. nurse oper. rm. Harrisburg Hosp., Harrisburg, 1984-88, splty. supr. surg. svcs. dept., 1988-90; 1st asst. laser/abdominal endoscopy Women's Med. Assocs. P.C., Harrisburg, 1990-96; 1st asst., cons., owner PeriOperative Care Assocs., Harrisburg, 1996—; proprietor, first asst., cons. C.B. Laser Assocs. Inc., Camp Hill, Pa., 1990-96; faculty mem. Pa. Jr. Coll. Med. Arts. Contbr. articles to profl. jours. Mem. Assn. Oper. Rm. Nurses, Am. Assn. Gynecol. Laparoscopists, Am. Soc. for Laser Medicine and Surgery. Home: 68 Fairfax Village Harrisburg PA 17112-9556 Office: Peri Operative Care Assocs 68 Fairfax N Harrisburg PA 17112

STUDLEY, JAMIENNE SHAYNE, lawyer; b. N.Y.C., Apr. 30, 1951; d. Jack Hill and Joy (Cosor) S.; m. Gary J. Smith, July 14, 1984. BA magna cum laude, Barnard Coll., 1972; JD, Harvard U., 1975. Bar: D.C. 1975, U.S. Dist. Ct. D.C. 1978. Assoc. Bergson, Borkland, Margolis & Adler, Washington, 1976-80; spl. asst., sec. U.S. HHS, 1980-81; assoc. Weil, Gotshal & Manges, Washington, 1981-83; assoc. dean law sch. Yale U., New Haven, 1983-87; lectr. law, 1984-87; syndicated columnist Am. Lawyer Media, 1990-91; exec. dir. Nat. Assn. for Law Placement, Washington, 1987-90, Calif. Abortion Rights Action League, 1992-93; dep. gen. counsel U.S. Dept. Edn., 1993—; vis. scholar adj. faculty U. Calif., Berkeley, 1990-93. Pres. Conn. Women's Ednl. and Legal Fund, Hartford, 1986-87; mem. bd. advisors Nat. Assn. Pub. Interest Law Pub. Svc. Challenge. Mem. ABA (commn. on women in the profession 1991-94, chair editl. bd. Perspectives, chair coord. coun. legal edn. 1996—), D.C. Bar Assn., Bar Assn. San Francisco, Women's Bar Assn., Assn. Alumnae Barnard Coll. (bd. dirs. 1978-81), Barnard in Washington (pres. 1977-78), Phi Beta Kappa. Home: 5349 MacArthur Blvd Washington DC 20016 Office: Office of the Gen Coun Dept of Edn 600 Independence Ave SW Washington DC 20202-0004

STUEVER, NANCY LOUISE, nursing educator; b. Bklyn., Sept. 15, 1951; d. William F. and Maysie E. (Noseworthy) Wisnom; m. A. Lawrence Stuever, Aug. 18, 1973; children: Michael, Jennifer, Jonathon. BSN, Carlow Coll., Pitts., 1973; M of Nursing Edn., U. Pitts., 1978. RN, Calif. Staff nurse Med. Ctr. at Princeton, N.J., 1973-74, Presbyn.-Univ. Hosp., 1974-78; instr. Louise Suydam McClintic Sch. Nursing, 1978-79; urgent care staff nurse HealthAm., 1982-86; temporary clin. instr. Carlow Coll., Pitts., 1985-86; critical care staff nurse Los Alamitos (Calif.) Med. Ctr., 1987-89; nursing clin. specialist U. Phoenix, So. Calif. campus, Calif., 1993-94; nursing mgr. U. Phoenix, So. Calif. campus, 1994—. Trustee Ocean View Sch. Dist., Huntington Beach, Calif., 1992—. Mem. AACCN, NLN, Calif. Sch. Bds. Assn., Orgn. Nurse Execs. Calif., Orgn. Nurse Leaders., Calif. Nurse Execs. Coun., Hosp. Assn. So. Calif., Calif. League Nursing, U. Phoenix Nursing Honor Soc. Democrat. Lutheran. Home: 9144 Daffodil Ave Fountain Valley CA 92708 Office: U Phoenix 949 South Coast Dr Costa Mesa CA 92626

STUKEL, BARBARA JEAN, secondary education educator; b. Joliet, Ill., Oct. 26, 1941; d. Anthony Matthew and Agnes Marian (Karruckas) Marentic; m. James William Stukel, Aug. 13, 1963; 1 child, Kimberly A. Student, Portland State U., 1962; BA, Coll. of St. Francis, 1963; postgrad., U. Chgo., 1963, No. Ill. U., 1972-73, Lewis U., 1973-74, U. Ill., 1975-76; MA, Govs. State U., 1982. Cert. high sch. tchr. Tchr. German and social studies Lockport (Ill.) Township High Sch., 1963—. Sponsor Lockport High Sch. German Club, 1963-72, Lockport High Sch. Ski Club, 1977-90, Lockport High Internat. Club, 1995—; sponsor, leader Lockport High Ann. Morning Star Mission Collection, 1985—; mem. Will County Humane Soc., Joliet. Ill., 1973—. German Sch. scholar Portland State U., 1962. Mem. AAUW, MLA, Am. Assn. Tchrs. German, Ill. Coun. Tchg. Fgn. Langs., Goethe Inst., Lambda Iota Tau. Roman Catholic. Home: 307 Maple Ln Shorewood IL 60431 Office: Lockport Ctrl High Sch 1222 S Jefferson St Lockport IL 60441

STUMBO, HELEN LUCE, retail executive; b. Macon, Ga., Aug. 7, 1947; d. George Edgar and Willouise (Butts) Luce; m. Edward Paul Coppedge (div. Mar. 1980); 1 child, George Laurence; m. John Ellis Stumbo. BA, Fla. State U., 1969. With Rich's Design Studio, Atlanta, 1970-72; pres. Peachland Consortium, Inc., Ft. Valley, Ga., 1986-95, Camellia & Main, Inc., 1987—; bd. dirs. Inst. on Religion and Democracy. Dir. Peach County Hosp. Authority, Ft. Valley, 1986-95, also dir. capital campaign com., 1985-88; bd. dirs. Forum for Scriptual Christianity, Wilmore, Ky., 1972—; participant Leadership Ga. program, Bus. Coun. Ga., 1989, Nat. Coalition Against Pornography, 1993—, United Meth. for Faith and Freedom, 1994—; chairwoman, bd. dirs. Enough is Enough!, 1994—. Recipient Athena award Peach County C. of C., Ft. Valley, 1986, Resolution of Commendation Ga. Ho. of Reps., Atlanta, 1987. Methodist. Home and Office: 305 Knoxville St Fort Valley GA 31030-3485

STUMBO, JANET L., judge; b. Prestonsburg, Ky.; d. Charles and Doris Stanley S.; m. Ned Pillersdorf; children: Sarah, Nancee, Samantha. BA, Morehead State U., 1976; JD, U. Ky., 1980. Staff atty. to Judge Harris S. Howard Ky. Ct. Appeals; pvt. practice Turner, Hall & Stumbo, P.S.C.; asst. county atty. Floyd County; prosecutor Floyd Dist. Ct. and Juvenile Ct.; ptnr. Slumbo, DeRossett & Pillersdorf, 1989; judge Ct. Appeals, Ky., 1989-93, Supreme Ct. of Ky., 1993—; Bar: Ky. 1980, W. Va. 1982. Named to Morehead State U. Alumni Assn. Hall of Fame, 1990; recipient Justice award Ky. Women Advocates, 1991, Outstanding Just award Ky. Women Advocates, 1995, Bull's Eye award Women in State Govt. Network, 1995. Office: Ky Supreme Ct Capital Bldg Rm 325 700 Capital Ave Frankfort KY 40601*

STUMPF, MARY RITA, administrator, executive director; b. Bklyn., Apr. 15, 1951; d. George Valentine and Rita Josephine (Kunz) S. Nursing Diploma, St. Mary's Hosp. Sch. Nursing, 1971; BSN, SUNY, Albany, 1980; MSN, Hunter Coll., 1982; PhD in Health Adminstrn., LaSalle U., 1995. RN, N.Y.; cert. nurse adminstr. advanced. Staff nurse St. Mary's Hosp., Bklyn., 1971-73, head nurse, 1973-78; clin. nurse II Meml. Sloan Kettering Inst., N.Y.C., 1978-82; adminstrv. supr. St. Mary's Hosp., Bklyn., 1983-85, assoc. dir. nursing, 1985-94; exec. dir. CMC Profl. Registry, Inc., Queens, N.Y., 1994—; proctor, advisor St. Joseph's Coll., Windham, Maine, 1990-94; advisor SUNY, Albany, 1995—. Mem. Soc. for Nurse Execs., N.Y. State Nurses Assn., St. Mary's Hosp. Alumni Assn. Roman Catholic. Office: CMC Profl Registry Inc 95-25 Queens Blvd Rego Park NY 11374

STUMPF, SUZANNE ELIZABETH, classical musician; b. Syracuse, N.Y.; d. Norman and Dorothy Carol (Boone) S.; m. Daniel Robert Ryan, June 10, 1990. BA, Wellesley (Mass.) Coll., 1980; postgrad, Mozarteum, Salzburg, Austria. Chamber music coach Wellesley Coll., 1985—, concert mgr., 1985—; flute instr. New England Conservatory Ext. Divsn., Boston, 1989—; prof. of flute Clark U., Worcester, Mass., 1985-89, Coll. of Holy Cross, Worcester, 1985-88; artistic dir. Musicians of the Old Post Rd., Boston, 1989—; freelance flutist Boston Baroque, The N.Y. Bach Ensemble, Handel and Hayden Soc., 1982—. Flutist: (compact disc) The Virtuoso Double Bass, 1994. Recipient Mary Elvira Stevens Travelling fellow Wellesley Coll., 1984-85; Rsch. grantee Coll. of the Holy Cross, 1986. Mem. Boston Musicians Assn.

STUNJA, VALERIE ANN, aircraft dispatcher; b. Pitts., Aug. 3, 1956; d. Joseph Nicholas and Anna Jane (Mustatia) S. AAS, C.C. of Beaver County, Monaca, Pa., 1985; Aircraft Dispatcher, Kellmark Aeronautics, Miami, 1989. Comml. photographer Pitts., 1978-80; ops. officer U.S. Air, Pitts., 1980-89, dispatcher, 1989—; flt. instr. Stensin Aviation, Monaca, Pa., 1984-85; real estate salesperson Northwood Realty, Pitts., 1993-94; advanced ground instr. Beaver Aviation, Monaca, 1982, flt. instr., 1984, comml. pilot, 1984. Republican. Roman Catholic. Office: US Air Inc Ops Control Ctr 173 Industry Dr Pittsburgh PA 15275

STUP, JANET ANITA, state legislator; b. Washington, Mar. 8, 1945; d. Louis Fillmore Jr. and Janet Lenman (Plummer) Watkins; m. William R. Stup, June 21, 1972; children: Scott Alan, Mark Louis. Student, Montgomery Jr. Coll., Takoma Park, Md., 1963-65; AA (hon.), Frederick Community Coll., 1988. Stewardess United Air Lines, Washington, 1965-66; faculty sec. Columbus Sch. Law, Cath. U. Am., Washington, 1966-68; sec. Univ. Legal Svcs., Washington, 1968; legal sec. Tomes and Spragins, Silver Spring, Md., 1968-70, Jackson Brodsky, Rockville, Md., 1970-74; legal sec., legal asst. Klaven & Mannes, Rockville, 1972-74; office adminstr. Meyers, Wagaman, Corderman & Young, Hagerstown, Md., 1974-75; mem. Bd. County Commrs. for Frederick County, Frederick, Md., 1982-90, pres., 1986-90; mem. Md. Gen. Assembly, Annapolis, 1991—. Past mem. various coms. Frederick County Bd. Edn.; past chmn. govt. div. United Way; past mem. adv. bd. Cmty. Commons; past bd. dirs. Arthritis Found., Frederick Meml. Hosp.; past pres. Frederick Mid. Sch. PTA; hon. chmn. Big Bros.-Big Sisters; past mem. Religious Coalition Frederick County; hon. mem. bd. dirs. Heartly House; past mem. steering com. Way Sta., Elephant Club. Mem. DAR, Md. Assn. Elected Women, Phi Theta Kappa. Republican. Lutheran. Home: 587 Pumphouse Rd Frederick MD 21702-6092 Office: 324 Lowe House Office Buil Annapolis MD 21401 Address: 153 W Patrick St Frederick MD 21701-5586

STURDIVANT, LINDA LEE, psychotherapist; b. Pitts., Dec. 19, 1949; d. Matthew Lewis and Doris (Richardson) S.; m. James D. Chandler, Dec. 19, 1980. BS in Psychology, U. Pitts., 1981, MEd, 1982. Cert. employee assistance profl. Addictions therapist St. Francis Med. Ctr., Pitts., 1978-80; adolescent therapist U. Pitts., 1980-82; counseling cons. USX Corp., Pitts., 1982-86; employee counselor U. Pitts. Med. Ctr., 1986—; bd. dirs. Allegheny Valley Mental Health/Mental Retardation, New Kensington, Pa.; therapist Turtle Creek Mental Health/Mental Retardation, Pitts., 1986—. Bd. dirs. Pa. Orgn. Women in Early Recovery, Pitts., 1990—, United Way, Pitts., 1991—. Mem. Coalition for Addictive Diseases, Employee Assistance Profls. Assn. (pres. Pitts. chpt. 1989-92, bd. dirs. 1993—, chairperson women's issues com. 1993-94, nat. treas. 1994—). Democrat. Roman Catholic. Home: 620 Milltown Rd Kensington PA 15068-9330 Office: Univ Pitts Med Ctr-EAP 200 Lothrop St Pittsburgh PA 15213

STURTEVANT, JOY E., microbiologist, educator; b. Washington, Nov. 17, 1955; d. Eugene William and Lois Evelyn (Weber) S. BS, Colo. State U., 1977; PhD, Duke U, 1985. Zookeeper Jacksonville (Fla.) Zoo, 1977; rsch. tech. Scripps Clinic Rsch. Edn., LaJolla, Calif., 1978-81; postdocroral rsch. asst. Uppsala U., Sweden, 1986-88, U. Glasgow, Millport, Scotland, 1986-88, Pasteur Inst., Paris, 1988-92; rsch asst. prof. Georgetown U., Washington, 1992—; cons. Cassenne Lab., Paris, 1989-91, vis. sci. U. Pierre & Marie Curie, Paris, 1991. Contbr. articles to profl. jours. Mem. DNC, Washington, 1992—, vol. DC Cares, Washington, 1994—. Fellow Phillipe Found., 1991. Mem. AAUW, Am. Soc. Microbiol., Med. Mycology Soc. of Am. Democrat. Office: Georgetown U Med Ctr Microbiology Dept 3900 Reservoir Rd NW Washington DC 20007

STURZ, SARA ANN, small business owner; b. Phila., Dec. 27, 1962; d. Libby Kushner Sturz. AS, Harcum Jr. Coll., Bryn Mawr, Pa.; BFA cum laude, Moore Coll. of Art and Design, Phila. Environ. graphic designer Cope Linder Assocs., Phila., 1986-89; environ. graphic designer, MacIntosh computer specialist Shapiro Petrauskas Gelber, Phila., 1989-91; creative dir., Macintosh software trainer, founder MacTactix/Phila., 1991—; MacIntosh systems cons. Visual Sound., Broomall, Pa., 1993—; bd. dirs. Visual Sound, Graphic Arts Assn., Phila. Missionary vol. St. Francis Inn, Kensington/Phila., Pa., 1993—, Thea's Women's Ctr., Kensington/Phila., 1993—. Office: MacTactix-Philadelphia 552 Howe Rd Merion PA 19066-1129

STUZIN, MARILYN HYMSON, adult education educator; b. N.Y.C., June 19, 1940; d. Jack and Celia (Honen) Hymson; m. Theodore Donald Stuzin, Aug. 17, 1963; children: Randolph Arthur, Michelle Nancy. M Elem. Edn., Queens (N.Y.) Coll., 1969, M TESOL, 1986; profl. diploma, Bklyn. Coll., 1989. Tchr. ESOL Freeport (N.Y.) Pub. Schs., 1984-91, dir. adult continuing cmty. edn., 1991—. Home: 63 Keswick Ln Plainview NY 11803-6107 Office: PO Box 50 Freeport NY 11520

STYER, ANTOINETTE CARDWELL, middle school counselor; b. Martinsville, Va.; d. John E. Cardwell and I. Lois Cardwell Shelton; children: Yvette D., Christopher P. BA in Liberal Arts, Temple U., 1975; MEd in Elem./Secondary Sch. Counseling, Antioch U., Phila., 1980. cert. sec. prin., 1994. Sec. Edward S. Cooper, M.D., Phila., 1960-66; rsch. asst. Temple U., Phila., 1971-73; confidential sec. Sch. Dist. Phila., 1967-71, sec., 1974-76, social worker Child Care Ctr., 1976-86, sch. counselor elem. edn., 1986-89; secondary edn. counselor Sch. Dist. Phila. Roosevelt Mid. Sch., Phila., 1989—; sch. evaluator Mid. States Assn. of Colls. and Schs.; co-organizer Project Exposure: Bus.; chaperone student visit to colls., Atlanta; interviewee Nat. Opinion Rsch. Ctr., Phila., 1971-72; mgmt. trainee GSA divsn. U.S. Govt., Phila., 1987; del. leader People to People Student Amb. Programs, Australia, 1993, Russia and the Baltic States, 1994, U.K. and Ireland, 1995, South Africa, 1996. Past chair 75th anniversary com. Pinn Meml. Bapt. Ch., scholarship com., new mem. com., aides to first lady and women's support group; mem. bd. dirs. Day Care Com.; ann. vol. United Negro Coll. Fund Telethon, mem. small bus. fundraising com. Mem. Nat. Coun. Negro Women, Pa. Sch. Counselors Assn., Mid. States Assn. Colls. and Schs., Delta Sigma Theta (life, chpt. journalist, chair May Week, del. to regional conv., mem. scholarship com.), Phi Delta Kappa. Home: 925 E Roumfort Rd Philadelphia PA 19150-3215 Office: Sch Dist Phila Roosevelt Mid Sch Washington Ln Musgrave St Philadelphia PA 19144

STYLES, BEVERLY, entertainer; b. Richmond, Va., June 6, 1923; d. John Harry Kenealy and Juanita Russell (Robins) Carpenter; m. Wilbur Cox, Mar. 14, 1942 (div.); m. Robert Marascia, Oct. 5, 1951 (div. Apr. 1964). Studies with Ike Carpenter, Hollywood, Calif., 1965—; student, Am. Nat. Theatre Acad., 1968-69; studies with Paula Raymond, Hollywood, 1969-70; diploma, Masterplan Inst., Anaheim, Calif., 1970. Freelance performer, musician, 1947-81; owner Beverly Styles Music, Joshua Tree, Calif., 1971—; v.p. spl. programs Lawrence Program of Calif., Yucca Valley, Calif.; talent coord., co-founder Quiet Place Studio, Yucca Valley, 1994. Composer: Joshua Tree, 1975, I'm Thankful, 1978, Wow, Wow, Wow, 1986, (with lyricist Betty Curtis), Music for the Whispering, 1994, World of Dreams, 1996, Thank You God, 1996; piano arrangements include Colour Chords and Moods, 1995, (with lyricist Betty Curtis), Desert Nocturne, 1996; records include The Perpetual Styles Of Beverly, 1978; albums include The Primitive Styles Of Beverly, 1977; author: A Special Plan To Think Upon, The Truth As Seen By A Composer, 1978, A Special Prayer To Think Upon, 1983. Mem. ASCAP (Gold Pin award), Profl. Musicians Local 47 (life), Internat. Platform Assn. Republican. Office: PO Box 615 Joshua Tree CA 92252-0615

STYLES, TERESA JO, producer, educator; b. Atlanta, Oct. 19, 1950; d. Julian English and Jennie Marine (Sims) S. BA, Spelman Coll., 1972; MA, Northwestern U., 1973. Researcher CBS News, N.Y.C., 1975-80, producer, 1980-85; instr. mass communications, English Savannah (Ga.) State Coll., 1985-89, asst. prof. English, 1990; asst. prof. mass comm. and women studies dir. Bennett Coll., Greensboro, N.C., 1990-93; asst. prof. mass comm. N.C. A&T State Univ., Greensboro, 1993—. Researcher documentary CBS Reports: Teddy, 1979 (Emmy cert.); assoc. producer documentaries for CBS Reports: Blacks: America, 1979 (Columbia Dupont cert. 1979), What Shall We Do About Mother?, 1980 (Emmy cert.), The Defense of the U.S., 1980 (Columbia Dupont cert.). Adv. bd. Greensboro Hist. Mus., Eastern Music Festival, Women's Short Film Project. Mem. Writers Guild Am. (bd. dirs. east), Dirs. Guild Am. (bd. dirs. east), African Am. Atelier (Greensboro, N.C. bd. dirs.), Eastern Music Festival (bd. dirs.). Home: 4400 Suffolk Trail Greensboro NC 27407

STYNES, BARBARA BILELLO, wellness consultant; b. N.Y.C., Apr. 24, 1951; d. Sylvester Francis and Jacqueline Marie (Giardelli) Bilello; m. Frank Joseph Stynes, Aug. 24, 1969; children: Christopher Francis, Jeremy Scott. BA, Rutgers U., 1976; postgrad., Antioch U., 1994—. Mktg. rep. McNeil Consumer Products Co., Fort Washington, Pa., 1979-82, Met Path Inc., Des Plaines, Ill., 1982-85; mktg. coord. Life program Meml. Hosp. and YMCA, Chattanooga, 1986-91; mem. Chattanooga Area Wellness Council, 1986-91, Chattanooga Area Healthcare Coalition, 1986-91; dir. mktg. and comm., met. YMCA, Chattanooga, 1986-91, dir. internat. program, 1989-91; wellness cons., 1992—; fiber sculptor, 1975-77; weaver, 1976-79. Vol. comm. com. Am. Heart Assn., 1972-91, Spl. Olympics, Chgo., 1982-84; speaker Tenn. Safety Belt coalition, 1986-91; clinic leader Am. Lung Assn., Chattanooga, 1986-88, YMCA cert. fitness specialist, 1986, weight mgmt. specialist, 1987; chairperson fundraising, trustee Pine Grove Coop. Sch., New Brunswick, N.J., 1977-78; bd. dirs. Signal Mountain Newcomers Assn., Tenn., 1985-86; mem. sch. bd. Notre Dame High Sch., 1989-91. Mem. NAFE, Am. Bus. Womans Network Chattanooga (chair membership), Fiber Arts Guild, Assn. Profl. Dirs., Kiwanis (chair internat. rels. com. Chattanooga chpt., 1990-91, publicity dir.), Gen. Bd. Newcomers, North Columbus, Sustaining Bd. Choices). Roman Catholic. Avocations: health and wellness, art, music. Home: 7718 Chancel Dr Columbus OH 43235-1462

STYRON, ROSE BURGUNDER, human rights activist, poet, journalist; b. Balt., Apr. 4, 1928; d. Benjamin Bernei and Selma (Kann) Burgunder; m. William Styron, May 4, 1953; children: Susanna, Polly, Thomas, Alexandra. BA, Wellesley Coll., 1950; MA, Johns Hopkins U., 1952; LHD (hon.), Briarcliff Coll., 1976, SUNY, Purchase, 1991. Bd. dirs. Amnesty Internat., USA, N.Y.C., 1973-83, chair nat. adv. coun., 1984-94. Author: (poems) From Summer to Summer, 1965, Thieves' Afternoon, 1973, By Vineyard Light, 1995; co-author, translator: Modern Russian Poetry, 1972; contbr. editorials, profiles, articles, book revs. and poetry to maj. newspapers and mags. Chair, judge Robert F. Kennedy Meml. Human Rights Award, 1983—; mem. adv. bd. Reebok Found. for Human Rights, 1987—; mem. exec. bd. Human Rights Watch, N.Y.C., 1975-94; bd. dirs. Acad. of Am. Poets, 1995—, Equality Now, 1993—; chmn. adv. coun. Roxbury (Conn.) Libr., 1990-92; bd. dirs. N.Y. Found. for Arts, N.Y.C., 1986-94, Lawyers Com. for Human Rights, N.Y.C., 1981—, Rainforest Found., 1989-95, Assn. to Benefit Children, 1993—, Folger Shakespeare Libr., 1994—; bd. overseers NYU Faculty of Arts and Scis., 1994—. Mem. P.E.N. (chair freedom-to-write com. 1983-89, bd. dirs. 1983-93), Coun. Fgn. Rels., Vineyard Haven Yacht Club. Democrat. Home: 12 Rucum Rd Roxbury CT 06783-1906

SU, JUDY YA HWA LIN, pharmacologist; b. Hsinchu, Taiwan, Nov. 20, 1938; came to U.S., 1962; d. Ferng Nian and Chiu-Chin (Cheng) Lin; m. Michael W. Su; 1 child, Marvin. BS, Nat. Taiwan U., 1961; MS, U. Kans., 1964; PhD, U. Wash., 1968. Asst. prof. dept. biology U. Ala., Huntsville, 1972-73; rsch. assoc. dept. anesthesiology U. Wash., Seattle, 1976-77, acting asst. prof. dept. anesthesia, 1977-78, rsch. asst. prof., 1978-81, rsch. assoc. prof., 1981-89, rsch. prof., 1989—; mem. surg. anesthesiology & trauma study sect. NIH, 1987-91; vis. scientist Max-Planck Inst. Med. Rsch., Heidelberg, West Germany, 1982-83; vis. prof. dept. anesthesiology Mayo Clinic, Rochester, Minn., Med. Coll. Wis., 1988; editorial bd. cons. Jour. Molecular & Cellular Cardiology, London, 1987—, European Jour. Physiology, Berlin, Germany, Muscle & Nerve, Kyoto, Japan, 1989—, Anesthesiology, Phila., 1987—, Molecular Pharmacology, 1988—, Jour. Biol. Chemistry, 1989—, Am. Jour. Physiology, 1990—; mem. rsch. study com. Am. Heart Assn., 1992-95. Contbr. articles to profl. jours. Grantee Wash. Heart Assn., 1976-77, 1985-87, Pharm. Mfrs. Assn. Found., Inc., 1977, Lilly Rsch. Labs, 1986-88, Anaquest, 1987—, NIH, 1978—; recipient Rsch. Career Devel. award NIH, 1982-87; rsch. fellowship San Diego Heart Assn., 1970-72, Max-Planck Inst., 1982-83. Mem. AAAS, Biophys. Soc., Am. Soc. for Pharmacology and Exptl. Therapeutics, Am. Physiol. Soc., Am. Soc. Anesthesiologists. Home: 13110 NE 33rd St Bellevue WA 98005-1318 Office: U Wash Dept Anesthesiology Box 356540 Seattle WA 98195-6540

SUBER, ROBIN HALL, former medical, surgical nurse; b. Bethlehem, Pa., Mar. 14, 1952; d. Arthur Albert and Sarah Virginia (Smith) Hall; m. David A. Suber, July 28, 1979; 1 child, Benjamin A. BSN, Ohio State U., 1974. RN, Ariz., Ohio. Formerly staff nurse Desert Samaritan Hosp., Mesa, Ariz. Lt. USN, 1974-80. Mem. ANA, Sigma Theta Tau.

SUBKOWSKY, ELIZABETH, insurance company executive; b. New London, Conn., Feb. 17, 1949; d. Thomas and Matilda (Mastroianni) Logan; m. Robert A. Subkowsky, June 9, 1972. BA with honors and dist., U. Conn., 1971; MBA, DePaul U., Chgo., 1977. Dir. info. tech. CNA Ins., Chgo., 1973—. Bd. dirs. Highland Park (Ill.) Hist. Soc., 1991-96, 1st v.p., 1993-96. Fellow Life Office Mgmt. Assn. (award 1977); mem. Woman's Club Evanston (aux. officer 1985-87, 79-91). Office: CNA Ins CNA Plz 9-S Chicago IL 60685

SUBLETTE, JULIA WRIGHT, music educator, performer, adjudicator; b. Natural Bridge, Va., Sept. 13, 1929; d. Paul Thomas and Annie Belle (Watkins) Wright; m. Richard Ashmore Sublette, Oct. 18, 1952; children: C. Mark, Carey P., Sylvia S. Bennett, Wright D. BA in Music, Furman U., 1951; MusM, Cin. Conservatory, 1954; postgrad., Chautaugua Inst., N.Y., 1951-52; PhD, Fla. State U., 1993. Ind. piano tchr., 1953—; instr. music and humanities Okaloosa-Walton C.C., Niceville, Fla., 1978—; panelist Music Tchr. Nat. Conv., Milw., 1992; instr. art humanities Troy State U., Ala. Editor Fla. Music Tchr., 1991—; contbr. articles to profl. music jours. Mem. AAUW, Music Tchrs. Nat. Assn. (cert., chmn. so. divsn. jr. high sch. piano/instrumental contests 1986-88), Fla. State Music Tchrs. Assn., So. Assn. Women Historians, Southeastern Hist. Keyboard Soc., Friday Morning Music Club, Colonial Dames of 17th Century Am., Pi Kappa Lambda. Home: 217 Country Club Rd Shalimar FL 32579-2203

SUBRAMANIAN, DONNA RAE, crtical care nurse; b. Englewood, N.J., Dec. 27, 1956; d. Bernard Ramon and Dorothy Katherine (Munzing) Gordon; m. Sambamurthy Subramanian, June 17, 1989. Grad., Buffalo Gen. Hosp. Sch. Nursing, 1977; attended, U. Miami, Fla, 1993; BS in Psychology, Union Inst., 1996. RN, N.Y., Fla.; cert. addictions counselor. Staff nurse ICU Buffalo Children's Hosp., 1977-78, asst. head nurse ICU, 1978-82; staff nurse ICU, burn unit Sheehan Meml. Hosp., Buffalo, 1982-87. Active Big Bros., Big Sisters, Buffalo, 1975; tutor inner city children, Buffalo, 1975. Mem. ACA, Soc. Trauma Based Disorders, Alpha Lambda Delta. Republican. Roman Catholic. Home: 4420 N Bay Rd Miami FL 33140

SUBSTAD LOKENSGARD-SCHIMMELPFENNIG, KATHRYN ANN, small business owner, career consultant; b. Mpls., Dec. 4, 1941; d. Arnold Torger and Ardis Louise (Klanderud) Substad; m. Arvid Luther Lokensgard, Nov. 23, 1963 (div. July 1982); children: Sara Kathryn Lokensgard Dickinson, Sigurd Arvid Lokensgard, Laura Ann Lokensgard; m. Wesley Ernest Schimmelpfennig, Mar. 24, 1990. BA, St. Olaf Coll., 1963; postgrad., Pacific Luth. Theol. Sem., 1989. Tchr. Lookout Mountain (Tenn.) Elem. Sch., 1964-66; tchrs. aide Greenvale Elem. Sch., Northfield, Minn., 1974-76; substitute tchr. Inclin Village (Nev.) High Sch., 1978-80, asst. libr., 1980-82; fin. aid dir., fgn. student advisor Sierra Nevada Coll., Incline Village, 1982-85, asst. to pres., 1985-89; mgr., v.p. Paul Bunyan Co., Tahoe Vista, Calif., 1990—; owner Tahoe Christian Bookstore, Tahoe Vista, Calif., 1993—; substitute tchr., career cons., 1990-92; liaison to bd. Sierra Nevada Coll., 1985-88. Bd. dirs. ch. coun. Christ the King Luth. Ch., Tahoe City, 1986-89, local pub. TV sta., 1986-89; vol. tchr. ESL, 1991—; active Nev. Literacy Coalition, 1991—; bd. dirs. North Tahoe Reading Ctr.; deacon Incline Village Community Presbyn. Ch., 1992-95; trainer, leader Stephen Ministries, 1996—. Mem. PEO (social sec. 1988-89), AAUW, C. of C. (bd. dirs. 1988-89, Hospice 1991—, Citizen of Month 1989).

SUCHECKI, LUCY ANNE, elementary education educator; b. East Cleveland, Ohio, May 3, 1945; d. Ben and Adelaide V. (Maneri) Urban; m. Robert K. Suchecki, Aug. 19, 1972. BS, Bowling Green State U., 1967; MA, Oakland U., 1981. Cert. elem. tchr., Mich. Elem. tchr. L'Anse Creuse Pub. Schs., Mt. Clemens, Mich., 1967—; grade cons. (book) Michigan, 1991. Active Immaculate Conception Ch., 1969—, Anchor Bay Women's Pool League, 1972—. Mem. NEA, MEA, MEA-NEA (local 1), L'Anse Creuse Ednl. Assn. (sec. 1968—), New Baltimore Hist. Soc. Roman Catholic. Home: 8504 Anchor Bay Dr Clay MI 48001-3507 Office: Marie C Graham Elem Sch 25555 Crocker Blvd Harrison Township MI 48045-3443

SUCHY, SUSANNE N., nursing educator; b. Windsor, Ont., Can., Sept. 20, 1945; d. Hartley Joseph and Helen Viola (Derrick) King; m. Richard Andrew Suchy, June 24, 1967; children: Helen Marie, Hartley Andrew, Michael Derrick. Diploma, St. Joseph Sch. Nursing, Flint, Mich., 1966; BSN, Wayne State U., 1969, MSN, 1971. RN, Mich. Afternoon supr., staff nurse oper. and recovery rm. St. John Hosp., Detroit, 1966-70; nursing instr. Henry Ford Community Coll., Dearborn, Mich., 1972—, on leave 1988-90; CNS/case mgr. surg. nursing Harper Hosp., Detroit, 1988-89; CNS case mgr. oncology, 1989—; mem. Detroit Demonstration Site Team for defining and differentiating ADN/BSN competencies, 1983-87. Contbr. articles to profl. jours. Past bd. dirs., pres. St. Pius Sch. Mem. ANA, AACH, N.Am. Nursing Diagnosis Assn. (by-law com. chmn. 1992—), Mich. Nursing Diagnosis Assn. (pres. 1987-90, elected by-law chmn. 1991-92, treas. 1993—), NLN, Detroit Dist. Nurses Assn. (past chmn. nominating com., legis. com., sec. 1994-96), Oncology Nursing Soc. (gov. rels. chmn. 1992—, presenter abstract conf. 1991, 95, poster presentations ann. conf. 1991-93, 95, 96), Daus. of Isabella (internat. dir. 1992—, past regent 1992—, state recording sec. 1995—), Wayne State U. Alumni Assn., Sigma Theta Tau (nominating com. 1991-93). Roman Catholic. Home: 12666 Irene St Southgate MI 48195-1765 Office: Henry Ford CC 5101 Evergreen Rd Dearborn MI 48128-2407

SUCKIEL, ELLEN KAPPY, philosophy educator; b. Bklyn., June 15, 1943; d. Jack and Lilyan (Banchefsky) Kappy; m. Joseph Suckiel, June 22, 1973. A.B., Douglass Coll., 1965; M.A. in Philosophy, U. Wis., 1969, Ph.D. in Philosophy, 1972. Lectr. philosophy U. Wis., Madison, 1969-71; asst. prof. philosophy Fla. State U., Tallahassee, 1972-73; asst. prof. philosophy U. Calif., Santa Cruz, 1973-80, assoc. prof., 1980-95, prof., 1995—, provost Kresge Coll., 1983-89. Author: The Pragmatic Philosophy of William James, 1982, Heaven's Champion: William James's Philosophy of Religion, 1996, also articles, book introductions and chpts. Mem. Am. Philos. Assn., Soc. for Advancement Am. Philosophy. Office: U Calif Cowell Coll Santa Cruz CA 95064

SUDANOWICZ, ELAINE MARIE, government executive; b. Dorchester, Mass., Aug. 3, 1956; d. John Anthony and Helen Mary (Budzinski) S. Student, Fontbonne Acad., Milton, Mass., 1974; BA, Boston State Coll., 1978; MPA, Suffolk U., Boston, 1986; grad. Exec. Leadership Devel. Program, Dept. of Def., 1993. Cert. level 2 contractor, and level 3 in program mgmt., notary pub., Mass. Pub. relations office mgr. MacDonald & Evans Inc. Litho., Dorchester, Mass., 1974-78; research asst. Nat. Commn. Neighborhoods, Wash., 1978; pol. cons. Various Nat. State & Local, Pol. Campaigns, 1974-86; telephonist supr., cons. ARC, Boston, 1980-81; adminstrv. asst. Suffolk County Courthouse Commn., Boston, 1981-82; exec. asst. sheriff Suffolk County Sheriff's Office, 1982-86; presl. mgmt. intern ESD/PK Air Force Systems Command, Hanscom AFB, Mass., 1986-89; advanced copper CAP Air Force Systems Command, Andrews AFB, Md., 1989-90; contract negotiatior Hdqrs., Electronic Systems div., Joint STARS Program, Hanscom AFB, Mass., 1990-92; program mgr. Hdqrs., Electronic Sys. Ctr., EN-1, Hanscom AFB, 1992-95; asst. program dir. bus. acquisition re-engring. Elec. Sys. Ctr., Hanscom AFB, 1994-95; dep. commr. for transp. City of Boston Transp. Dept., 1995—. Author: Constitutional Vignette, Separation of Powers and Contracting in the Bureaucrat, 1987; contbr. PMInformer, 1989—; also articles; agt., cons Theatre Arts-Play 1988—. Vol., cons. City & State Pub. Agys.-Pub. Sector, Boston; literacy vol., 1988-89. Recipient Spl. Achievement award U.S. Dept. Transp., 1989, Outstanding Alumnus award Suffolk U., 1990. Mem. Am. Soc. Pub. Adminstrn. (coun. mem. 1996—, rep. region 1 nat. young profls. forum 1988—), Nat. Contract Mgmt. Assn. (bd. dirs. 1996—, photographer No. Va. chpt. 1989-90, cert. profl. contracts mgr., nat. chair program mgmt. spl. topics com.), Presdl. Mgmt. Alumni Group (nat. bd. dirs. 1989-90, n.E. field bd. dirs. 1990—, Outstanding Alumnus award 1990), Trustees of Reservations Mass., Sr. Profl. Women's Assn., Suffolk County Deptury Sheriff's Assn., Boston Network for Women in Govt. and Politics, World Affairs Coun. Boston, Appalachian Mountain Club, Pi Alpha Alpha (pres. Suffolk U. chpt.). Democrat. Roman Catholic. Home: 108 Alban St Dorchester MA 02124-3711 Office: Boston Transportation Dept City of Boston Boston City Hall Office 721 Boston MA 02201

SUDARKASA, NIARA, academic administrator, anthropologist; b. Ft. Lauderdale, Fla., Aug. 14, 1938; d. Alex Charlton and Rowena (Evans) Marshall; m. John L. Clark; 1 child, Michael Sudarkasa. Student, Fisk U., 1953-56; AB, Oberlin Coll., 1957; MA, Columbia U., 1959, PhD, 1964; hon. degrees, Fisk U., Oberlin Coll., 1988, Sojourner-Douglass Coll., 1989, Franklin and Marshall Coll., 1990, Susquehanna U., 1990. Asst. prof. anthropology NYU, 1964-67; asst. prof. U. Mich., Ann Arbor, 1967-70, assoc. prof., 1970-76, prof., 1976-87, dir. Ctr. AfroAm./African Studies, 1981-84, assoc. v.p. acad. affairs, 1984-87; pres. Lincoln (Pa.) U., 1987—. Author: Where Women Work, 1973; co-editor: Women and National Development, 1977;contbr. numerous articles on African women, trade and migration to profl. jours.; articles on higher edn. in Chronicle of Higher Edn., Bull. Am. Assn. Higher Edn., Academe, other jours. Chair spl. adv. com. on minority enrollment State of Mich. Dept. Edn., 1985-86; bd. dirs. Ford Found. Project on New Emmigrants and Established Residents, 1987—, Pa. Econ. Devel. Partnership, 1987—, The Barnes Found., 1989—. Fulbright sr. research scholar, Republic of Benin, 1982-83; Ford Found. grantee, 1983-84; NEH grantee, 1983-84; Ford Found. Middle East & Africa research fellow, 1973-74; Social Sci. Research Council African Studies fellow, 1973-74; Ford Found. fgn. area tng. fellow, 1960-63; recipient numerous awards including Outstanding Achievement tributes and awards from Alpha Kappa Alpha, 1976, Zeta Phi Beta, U. Mich., 1971, 84, Zeta Phi Beta, Phila., 1987, Mich. State Senate, 1986, Mich. State Ho. of Reps., 1986, Pa. State Senate, 1987, Pa. State House of Reps., 1987 1986; Dr. Niara Sudarkasa Day, Ft. Lauderdale, 1976, Borough of Mahattan, 1987, Atlantic City, Atlanta, Detroit, 1987; E. Luther Cunningham award, 1988, Frederick D. Patterson award, 1988; named one of Top 100 Bus. & Profl. Women Dollars & Sense mag., 1988; included in I Dream A World: Portraits of Black Women Who Changed America, 1989. Mem. Am. Anthropol. Assn. (exec. bd. 1972-75), Am. Ethnol. Soc., African Studies Assn., Am. Assn. Higher Edn., Coun. on Fgn. Rels. Office: Lincoln U Office of the President Lincoln University PA 19352*

SUDBRINK, JANE MARIE, sales and marketing executive; b. Sandusky, Ohio, Jan. 14, 1942; niece of Arthur and Lydia Sudbrink. BS, Bowling Green State U., 1964; postgrad. in cytogenetics Kinderspital-Zurich, Switzerland, 1965. Field rep. Random House and Alfred A. Knopf Inc., Mpls., 1969-72, Ann Arbor, Mich., 1973, regional mgr., Midwest and Can., 1974-79, Can. rep., mgr., 1980-81; psychology and ednl. psychology adminstrv. editor Charles E. Merrill Pub. Co. div. Bell & Howell Corp., Columbus, Ohio, 1982-84; sales and mktg. mgr. trade products Wilson Learning Corp., Eden Prairie, Minn., 1984-85; fin. cons. Merrill Lynch Pierce Fenner & Smith, Edina, 1986-88; sr. editor Gorsuch Scarisbrick Pubs., Scottsdale, Ariz., 1988-89; regional mgr. Worth Publs., Inc. - von Holtzbrinck Pub. Grp., N.Y.C., 1988—. Lutheran. Home and Office: 3801 Mission Hills Rd Northbrook IL 60062-5729

SUDDOCK, FRANCES SUTER THORSON, grief educator, writer; b. Estelline, S.D., Oct. 23, 1914; d. William Henry and Anna Mary (Oakland) Suter; m. Carl Edwin Thorson, July 6, 1941 (dec. Apr. 1976); children: Sarah Thorson Little, Mary Frances Thorson; m. Edwin Matthew Suddock, Aug. 7, 1982 (dec. Sept. 1986). BA, Iowa State Tchrs. Coll., 1936; postgrad., Syracuse U., 1940-41, U. Iowa, 1946; MA, Antioch U., San Francisco, 1981. Cert. tchr. Tchr. various high schs., Correctionville and Eagle Grove, Iowa, 1936-38, 38-40, 41-43, 45-47; chief clk. War Price and Rationing Bd., Eagle Grove, 1943-45; instr. (part time) Eagle Grove Jr. Coll., 1953-61; adminstr. Eagle Grove Pub. Library, 1961-77; facilitator Will Schutz Assocs., Muir Beach, Calif., 1987-88. Author: Whither the Widow, 1981. Vol. Nat. Trainer Widowed Persons Svc. Am. Assn. Retired Persons, 1989—, ret. sr. vol. program, Anchorage, 1988—; pres., bd. dirs. Anchorage Widowed Persons Svc., 1992-94; bd. dirs. North Iowa Mental Health Ctr., Mason City, 1959-76, Eagle Grove Cmty. Chest, 1960, Help Line, Inc., Ft. Dodge, Iowa, 1976-77; chmn. Cmty. Mental Health Fund, Eagle Grove, 1966-73; charter pres. Eagle Grove Concerned, Inc., 1973-77; active various civic orgns. Mem. AAUW (charter pres. Eagle Grove br. 1973-75), Am. Soc. on Aging, Alaska Assn. Gerontology (treas. 1992-94), Anchorage Woman's Club, P.E.O., Kappa Delta Pi. Home: 333 M St Apt 404 Anchorage AK 99501-1902

SUDDRETH, DIANA LYNN, mathematics educator; b. Morristown, N.J., Mar. 21, 1959; d. Ronald D. and Janice K. (Grein) Brumm; m. Michael L. Suddreth, June 13, 1981; children: Simone, Samantha, Ian. BS in History, Utah State U., 1980, MS in History, 1988. Cert. tchr., Utah. Tchr. history Rancho H.S., Las Vegas, Nev., 1980-81; tchr. math. Intermountain Intertribal, Brigham City, Utah, 1981-82, Logan (Utah) Mid. Sch., 1982-83, Logan H.S., 1983-86, Norte Vista H.S., Riverside, Calif., 1986-89, Gage Mid. Sch., Riverside, 1989-91; tchr. math., dept. head Dixie Mid. Sch., St. George, Utah, 1991—; mid. sch. task force Washington County Sch. Dist., St. George, 1992-93, dist.-state liaison, 1993—, insvc. leader, 1993—; conf. presenter T3 Calculator Conf., Salt Lake City, 1994, Chpt. I Regional Conf., St. George, 1994. Mem. bd. edn. Trinity Luth. Sch., St. George, 1992-95; leader Girl Scouts Am., 1995—. Presidential award finalist, 1995. Mem. Nat. Coun. Tchrs. Math. (presenter nat. conf. San Diego 1996), Utah Coun. Tchrs. Math. (regional rep. 1994-96, George Shell award 1994). Republican. Lutheran. Home: 388 N Meadow Dr Dammeron Valley UT 84783-5127 Office: Dixie Mid Sch 825 S 100 E Saint George UT 84770-5506

SUDNEKEVICH, ANNA, computer programmer; b. Angarsk, Russia, June 22, 1955; came to U.S., 1993; d. Matvey and Eugenia (Pistryakov) Poisik; m. Yuri Petrov, Oct. 24, 1976 (div. Feb. 1988); children: Veronika, Ilya; m. Reginald Lavelle Condra, Mar. 1, 1995. MS in Applied Math., Tartu State U., 1978. Programmer, dept. mgr. Ministry Fin., Tallinn, Estonia, 1978-88; software engr. Technion, Haifa, Israel, 1990; programmer Bank Leumi le Israel, Lod, 1991-93; team leader Amdocs Inc., St. Louis, 1993—. Inventor in field. Mem. Engring. Soc. Israel. Jewish. Home: 1008 Rue La Ville Wk Saint Louis MO 63141

SUDOL, BONNIE LEMLEY, reading specialist; b. Passaic, N.J., Oct. 3, 1951; d. Frank and Janet (Drew) Lemley; m. David P. Sudol, June 22, 1974. BA, William Paterson Coll., 1973, MEd, 1978. Cert. elem. tchr., ESL tchr., cert. prin., supr., N.J. Elem. tchr. Lincoln Park (N.J.) Bd. Edn.; compensatory edn. tchr. grades K-5, 9-12 Wayne (N.J.) Bd. Edn., 1978-81, ESL tchr., 1982-90, tchr. in charge, reading specialist, 1990—; adult edn. tchr. Bergen C.C., Hackensack, N.J., 1981-82; mem. site based mgmt. team, grant writing com. Lafayette Sch., Wayne, 1994—. Mayor's liaison Lincoln Park Libr. Bd., 1990—, v.p., 1994—; mem. Lincoln Park Bd. Edn., 1990—; mem. Mayor's Adv. Bd. for Solid Waste, Lincoln Park, 1990—; pres. Polit. Party Lincoln Park; trustee, bd. edn. N.J. Sch. Bd. Assn., 1990—. Mem. ASCD, Internat. Reading Assn., Nat. Coun. Tchrs. English, N.J. Reading Assn., Pi Lambda Theta.

SUDOR, CYNTHIA ANN, marketing and corporate sponsorship consultant; b. Hershey, Pa., June 11, 1952; d. Milan and Mary (Strahosky) Sudor. BS in Design, Drexel U., 1974. Various mktg. positions in advt., promotion and publicity Hersheypark, Hershey, Pa., 1975-85, dir. sales and mktg., 1985-90; dir. destination mktg. Hershey Entertainment and Resort Co., 1990-91, dir. corp. sponsorship, 1991; owner Cynthia A. Sudor Enterprises, Grantville, Pa., 1992—, mktg.. corp. sponsorship consulting, 1992—; freelance writer, spkr., seminar presenter. Contbr. to Apprise Mag., Harrisburg, Pa., 1994—, Funworld Mag., Alexandria, Va., 1987-90. Bd. dirs., mktg. chair Profiles In Excellence, Inc., Harrisburg, 1993—. Recipient Best Seminar award Internat. Assn. Amusement Parks and Attractions (IAAPA), Dallas, 1988. Mem. Women in Comms. Inc. Office: Cynthia A Sudor Enterprises 1205 Ridge Rd Grantville PA 17028-9135

SUELTENFUSS, SISTER ELIZABETH ANNE, academic administrator; b. San Antonio, Apr. 14, 1921; d. Edward L. and Elizabeth (Amrein) S. BA in Botany and Zoology, Our Lady of Lake Coll., San Antonio, 1944; MS in Biology, U. Notre Dame, 1961, PhD, 1963. Joined Sisters of Divine Providence, Roman Catholic Ch., 1939; tchr. high schs. Okla. and La., 1942-49; mem. summer faculty Our Lady of Lake U. (formerly coll.), 1941-49, mem. full-time faculty, 1949-59, chmn. biology dept., 1963-73, pres., 1978—; mem. adminstrv. staff to superior gen. Congregation Divine Providence, 1973-77. Author articles in field. Bd. dirs. Am. Cancer Soc., San Antonio chpt. ARC, Mind Sci. Found., YWCA, Alamo Pub. Telecomm. Bd., S.W. Rsch. Found., I Have a Dream Found., Inst. Ednl. Leadership, Trim and Swim, San Antonio Edn. Partnership; bd. dirs., chmn. San Antonio Pub. Libr. Recipient Achievement and Leadership awards U. Notre Dame, 1979, Svc. to Community award, 1991, Headliner award Women in Comms., 1980, Good Neighbor award NCCJ, 1982, Brotherhood award, 1992, Today's Woman award San Antonio Light, 1982, Outstanding Women award San Antonio Express-News, 1983, Spirit of Am. Woman award J.C. Penney, 1992, Lifetime Achievement award, 1993, Svc. to Edn. awrd Ford Found., 1993; named to San Antonio Women's Hall of Fame, 1985. Mem. AAUP, AAUW, San Antonio 100 Tex. Women's Forum, San Antonio Women's C. of C., Hispanic Assn. Colls. and Univs., Greater San Antonio C. of C. (past vice chmn.), San Antonio Coun. Pres. (past pres.), San Antonio Women's Hall of Fame (past pres.). Home and Office: Our Lady of the Lake U Office of Pres 411 SW 24th St San Antonio TX 78207-4689

SUGAR, SANDRA LEE, art consultant; b. Balt., May 18, 1942; d. Harry S. and Edith Sarah (Levin) Pomerantz; children: Gary Lee, Terry Lynn. BS in Edn. and English, Towson State U., 1965; MS in Edn. and Applied Behavioral Scis., Johns Hopkins U., 1986. Chairperson arts exhibit Balt. Arts Festival, 1979; med. interviewer Johns Hopkins Sch. of Hygiene, Balt., 1980-82; copy writer Concepts & Communications, Balt., 1984; instr. art history and world cultures Catonsville Community Coll., Balt., 1981-85; instr. English Community Coll. of Balt., 1981-85; instr. English and math. Info. Processing Tng. Ctr., Balt., 1985; info. specialist Info. of Md. New Directions for Women, Balt., 1986; trainer, job developer Working Solutions, Balt., 1987-88; art gallery dir. Renaissance Fine Arts Gallery, Bethesda, Md., 1988-93; art cons. Bethesda, 1994—; judge nat. high sch. sci. fiction contests. Author poetry collection, juried exhibition, 1979, 80; editor mus. guides' newsletter Guidelines, 1978; painter juried exhibitions, 1979, 80. Docent Balt. Mus. of Art, 1973-86; festival coordinator Internat. Brass Quintet Festival, Balt., 1986; chairperson spl. events Balt. PTA, 1978-82; bd. dirs. Citizens Planning and Housing Assn., Balt., 1980-82; mem. women's com., ctr. stage hand Balt. Ballet, 1979-84, Balt. Symphony, 1979-80. Recipient F.J. Bamberger scholarship, Johns Hopkins U., 1985, Mayoral Vol. of Yr. award Balt. Mus. Art, 1979.

SUGARMAN, MURIEL, psychiatrist; b. Phila., Mar. 7, 1936; d. Nathaniel B. and Minerva Rose (Lieberman) Moldawer; m. Leonard Sugarman, May 31, 1964; children: J. Duke, Julie Ann. BS, Pa. State U., 1957; MD, Harvard Med. Sch., 1961. Pvt. practice psychiatry Brookline, Mass., 1966—; assoc. in child psychiatry Beth Israel Hosp., Boston, 1973-77, asst. child psychiatrist, 1977-78; instr. psychiatry Harvard Med. Sch., Boston, 1973—; clin. assoc. in psychiatry Mass. Gen. Hosp., Boston, 1979-83, asst. in psychiatry, 1983—; cons. in psychiatry McLean Hosp., Belmont, Mass., 1993—. Mem. Am. Profl. Soc. on Abuse of Children, Mass. Profl. Soc. on the Abuse of Children (bd. dirs. 1991—, v.p. membership), Boston Inst. Devel. Infants and Parents (treas., v.p., co-pres. 1973—). Office: Mass Gen Hosp Dept Child Psychiatry ACC 725 15 Parkman St Boston MA 02114

SUGGARS, CANDICE LOUISE, special education educator; b. Pitts., Jan. 16, 1949; d. Albert Abraham and Patricia Louise (Stepp) S. BS in Elem. Edn., W.Va. U., 1972; MS in Spl. Edn., Johns Hopkins U., 1979, Cert. Advanced Studies, 1986. Clin. supr./head tchr. The Kennedy Kreiger Inst., Balt., 1974-80, inpatient coord., 1980-83, ednl. evaluator, 1980-85, spl. educator/pediatric rehab. team, 1985-86; spl. edn. cons. Charleston County (S.C.) Sch. Dist., 1986-90, spl. edn. pre-sch. tchr., 1990-95; pvt. tutor children with spl. needs and disabilities, Charleston, 1995—; spl. needs cons. U. S.C., 1996—; mem. adv. bd. S.C. Accelerated Schs. Project, Charleston, 1994-95. Contbg. author: Disadvantaged Pre-School Child, 1979, Leisure Education for the Handicapped Curriculum, 1984. Exhibitor ann. conv. S.C. State Sch. Bd. Assn., 1994. Mem. Coun. for Exceptional Children (hospitality chair 1987-89, publicity chair 1989-90), Nat. Assn. for Edn. of Young Children. Home: 29 Savage St Apt B Charleston SC 29401-2409

SUGGS, JOSEPHINE GREENWAY, controller; b. Lula, Ga., Dec. 19, 1946; d. Marvin W. and Lucille (Echols) Greenway; m. Ray M. Suggs, May 31, 1969; children: Jeffrey Ray, Martin Ryan. Cert. in computer programming, Lanier Tech. Inst., 1979; AA, Am. Inst. Profl. Bookkeepers, 1989. Contr. Hilb, Rogal & Hamilton Co., Gainesville, Ga., 1988—. Vol. ARC, 1979—, N.E. Ga. Med. Aux., 1993—. Mem. NAFE, Am. Bus. Women, Am. Inst. Profl. Bookkeepers, Nat. Assn. Ins. Women, Ins. Women Gainesville. Baptist. Home: 5906 Homer Hwy PO Box 364 Lula GA 30554

SUGINTAS, NORA MARIA, veterinarian, scientist, medical company executive; b. Evergreen Park, Ill., Mar. 12, 1956; d. George and Mary (Navickas) S. BS in Biol. Scis. with highest distinction, U. Ill., Chgo., 1978; DVM, U. Ill., 1982. Lic. veterinarian, Ill. Profl. hosp. specialist Abbott Labs., Detroit, 1983-87; anes./crit. care patient monitoring equipment acct. exec. Shiley, Inc., Detroit, 1987-91; anesthesia and critical care monitoring equipment sales exec. and cons. Ohmeda, Detroit, 1991-94; regional mgr. Criticare Systems, Detroit, 1994-95, nat. acct. dir., 1995-96; dir. corp. accounts Isolyser Health Care, 1996—. Journalist The Lithuanian World-Wide Daily Newspaper, 1975; author: The Production S-Adenosylmethionine by Saccharomyces cerevisiae and Candida utilis. Troop leader Girl Scouts Lithuanian, Chgo., 1972-77, camp dir., 1977. Recipient Louis Pasteur award for Academic Excellence in the Biol. Scis. and Ind. Rsch. U. Ill., 1978. Mem. NAFE, Econ. Club Detroit, Phi Beta Kappa. Republican. Office: 6284 Aspen Ridge West Bloomfield MI 48322-4433

SUGRUE, BERNADETTE, principal; b. Detroit, Nov. 5, 1952; d. Felix Anthony and Irene Mary (Piwowarski) Tomasik; m. Dennis Patrick Sugrue, June 11, 1976; children: Dennis PAtrick II, Sean Michael-Francis. BA, Madonna U., 1974; MA, Ea. Mich. U., 1980, postgrad., 1995—. Tchr. St. Frances Cabrini Elem. Sch., Allen Park, Mich., 1974-90, prin., 1990—; jr. high sect. head St. Frances Cabrini Parish, Allen Park, 1976-77, elem. sect. head, 1977-78, jr. high coord., 1985-90; mem. sch. edn. team Archdiocesan of Detroit, 1980; mem. Mich. Nonpub. Sch. Accreditation Team, D1992-95. Mem. ASCD, Nat. Coun. Tchrs. Math., Nat. Cath. Edn. Assn., Kappa Gamma Pi. Roman Catholic. Office: St Frances Cabrini Elem Sch 15300 Wick Rd Allen Park MI 48101-1555

SUHL, AMY LYNN, electrical engineer; b. St. Louis, Mar. 21, 1964; d. Howard Lee and Bonita Faye (Altmna) Fitter; m. Mickey M. Suhl, Mr.a 24, 1991. BSEE, Tex. A&M U., 1986; MBA in Fin., Houston Bapt. U., 1994. Engr. Hewlett-Packard, Dallas, 1984, Colorado Springs, Colo., 1985; engr. Shell Oil Co., Houston, 1986-88, comm. engr., 1988-92; comm. supr. Shell Oil Co., Deer Park, Tex., 1992-95; sr. planning engr. Shell Chem. Co., Deer Park, 1995—. Office: Shell Chem Co 5900 Hwy 225 E Deer Park TX 77536

SUHM, MARY KATHERINE, municipal official; b. Beaumont, Tex., Jan. 3, 1947; d. James Hayden and Margaret Ann (Hodges) Moore; m. Victor C. Suhm, May 4, 1989; m. Robert Powell Tod, Aug., 24, 1968 (div. May 1983); children: Robert Gabriel Tod, Joshua Alton Tod. BS, Lamar U., Beaumont, 1968; MLS, U. North Tex., 1975, MBA, 1984. Biology tchr. Carrollton (Tex.) Independent Sch. Dist., 1968-69, Allen (Tex.) Independent Sch. Dist., 1969-70; dir. Allen Pub. Libr., 1972-78; mgr. branch librs. Dallas Pub. Libr., 1978-81, mgr. Urban Info., 1981-84; asst. to mayor City of Dallas, 1985-87, asst. to City Mgr., 1987-88, dir. of court svcs., 1988-90; exec. asst. dir. of Police Dallas Police Dept., 1990-93; asst. city mgr. City of Dallas, 1993—; sec., bd. dirs. City Employees Credit Union, Dallas, 1982-86. Facilitator Goals for Dallas, 1982; active Leadership Dallas, 1986, Vol. Ctr. Bd., 1987-90; mem. Cmty. Svcs. Bd. YMCA, 1990-94. Recipient Linda Keithley award for Women in Pub. Mgmt., 1995. Mem. Internat. Cith Mgmt. Assn. Office: City of Dallas 1500 Marilla 4/D/N Dallas TX 75201

SUI, ANNA, fashion designer; b. Dearborn Heights, Mich., 1955; d. Paul and Grace S. Grad., Parsons Sch. Design. Founder, designer Anna Sui, 1988—; opened outlet SoHo dist., 1992, N.Y.C.; designer Sui Anna Sui, 1995—. First runway show, 1991. Recipient Perry Ellis award new fashion talent Coun. Fashion Designers Am., 1992. Address: care Keeble Cavaco & Duka care Jill Nicholson 853 7th Ave Apt 10A New York NY 10019-5226

SUJAN, MEGAN NALINI, human resources manager; b. New Delhi, India, July 16, 1968; d. Shyam Ghanshyam and Mary Eugenia (Townsend) S. BA in Economics, Bucknell U., 1990. Fin. mgr. AT&T, Mesa, Ariz., 1990-91, Manassas, Va., 1991-92; human resources mgr. AT&T, Morristown, N.J., 1991-94, Basking Ridge, N.J., 1994—; guest lectr. U. Penn., 1995, Coll. of St. Elizabeth, Madison, N.J., 1994; sec., pub. rels. officer Asian Am. Assn. AT&T, 1993—. Editor Billboard newsletter, 1992-94, Globe newsletter, 1995. Active program devel. com. Urban League of Morris County, N.J., 1994.

SUJANSKY, EVA BORSKA, physician, educator; b. Bratislava, Slovak Republic, Feb. 14, 1936; d. Stefan and Terezia (Kaiserova) Borsky; m. Eduard Sujansky, Apr. 2, 1960 (dec. 1979); children: Paul, Walter. MD, Comenius U., Bratislava, Czechoslovakia, 1959. Diplomate Am. Bd. Pediats., Am. Bd. Med. Genetics. Resident in pediats. U. Iowa, Iowa City, 1971-73; fellow in human genetics Mt. Sinai Sch. Medicine, N.Y.C., 1973-74; clin. genetist Beth Israel Hosp., N.Y.C., 1973-74; dir. clin. genetics Sch. Medicine, U. Colo., Denver, 1974-90, assoc. prof. pediats., biochemistry, biophysics and genetics, 1981—; co-dir. divsn. genetic svcs. The Children's Hosp., U. Colo., Denver, 1990—. Contbr. articles to profl. jours. Fellow Am. Acad. Pediats., Am. Soc. Human Genetics, Am. Coll. Med. Genetics (founding fellow). Office: U Colo Med Ctr 1056 E 19th Ave Denver CO 80218-1007

SULC, JEAN LUENA (JEAN L. MESTRES), lobbyist, consultant; b. Worcester, Mass., Mar. 17, 1939; d. Emilio Beija and Julia (Bulan) Luena; m. Lee Gwynne Mestres, Oct. 9, 1965 (div. Dec. 1973); m. Lawrence Bradley Sulc, Nov. 4, 1983. BS in Psychology, Tufts U., 1961; M in Urban and Regional Planning, U. Colo., 1976. Lic. real estate, Va.; lic. pvt. pilot. Mem. staff U.S. fgn. svc. Dept. State, Washington, 1962-65; intern Adams County Planning Dept., Brighton, Colo., 1974-75; cons. office policy analysis City and County of Denver, 1976; program dir. Coun. Internat. Urban Liaison, Washington, 1976-79; asst., dir. internat. Cities Svc. Oil & Gas Corp., Washington, 1980-81; govt. affairs rep. Cities Svc., OXY USA Inc., Washington, 1982-89; mgr. fed. rels. OXY USA Inc., Washington, 1990-95; pres. EdgeSystem.XXI, Washington, 1996—; chmn. govt. affairs com. L.P. Gas Clean Fuel Coalition, Irvine, Calif., 1990-92. Author, editor: (newsletter) Dayton Climate Project, 1979-80; contbr. articles to newsletters. Vol. Reagan/Bush and Bush/Quayle Presdl. Campaigns and Inaugural Coms., Washington, 1984-89; pres. Hale Found., Nathan Hale Inst., Washington, 1984-85; mem. nat. panel consumer arbitrators Better Bus. Burs., Va., 1991—. Recipient Presdl. citation Nat. Propane Gas Assn., 1992; Minority Intern grantee Denver Regional Coun. Govts., 1974-76. Mem. ASTD, ABA (assoc., arbitration sect.), Am. League Lobbyists (chmn. energy sect., bd. dirs. 1994—, sec. 1996—), Women in Govt. Rels., Assn. Image Cons. Internat., Psi Chi. Episcopalian. Office: EdgeSystemXII 927 15th St NW Ste 1000 Washington DC 20005

SULEIMAN GONZALEZ, LAYLA PATRICIA, state official; b. Bogota, Colombia, Feb. 4, 1967; came to U.S., 1977; d. Subhi Ismael and Maria Dilia (Gonzalez) S. BS, Loyola U., Chgo., 1986, MA, 1990, postgrad, 1996—. Sr. policy analyst Commn. on Latino Affairs, Chgo., 1985-87; rsch. cons. Chgo., 1987-90; vis. instr. Loyola U., Chgo., 1990-93; rsch. cons. U. Chgo., 1993—; assoc. dir. Family Resource Coalition, 1994-95; U.S. Burgos Consent Decree Monitor Ill. Dept. Children & Family Svcs., 1995—; mem. Nat. Latino Child Welfare Advocacy Group, 1995—; mem. rsch. adv. group Family Impact Seminar, 1996—. Recipient grad. fellowship NSF, 1987, child welfare and family policy fellowship Chapin Hall Ctr. for Children, 1993. Mem. APA, Soc. Rsch. Child Devel., Soc. Psychol. Study Social Issues, Coun. Latino Execs. (Midwest chair 1994—).

SULLENBARGER, PEGGY ANN, nurse manager, rehabilitation consultant; b. St. Louis, Feb. 21, 1954; d. Arthur Ernst and Betty Alice (Smith) Koenig; divorced; children: Kristina Robyn, Sean David; m. Stuart Sullenbarger, De. 5, 1992. BSN, U. Tex., Arlington, 1977; postgrad., Wright State U., Dayton, Ohio, 1986—. RN, Ohio; cert. rehab. cons., case mgr., rehab. RN. Primary nurse Hospice of Dayton, 1982-86, Miami Valley Hosp., Dayton, 1986-89; grad. teaching asst. Wright State U., 1986; ind. rehab. nurse cons., 1987—; mgr. employee health svcs. Emery Worldwide., 1993—. Contbr. short stories and poems to various publs. Chmn. pub. info. Am. Cancer Soc., 1987-88, chmn. pub. issues, 1988—. Mem. NAFE, Assn. Rehab. Nurses, Ohio Nurses Assn. (alt. 1989), LWV. Office: One Emory Plz Vandalia OH 45377

SULLENBERGER, ARA BROOCKS, mathematics educator; b. Amarillo, Tex., Jan. 3, 1933; d. Carl Clarence and Ara Frances (Broocks) Cox; m. Hal Joseph Sullenberger, Nov. 2, 1952; children: Hal Joseph Jr., Ara Broocks Sullenberger Switzer. Student, Randolph-Macon Woman's Coll., 1951-52, So. Meth. U., 1952, U. Tex., Arlington, 1953, Amarillo Coll., 1953-54; BA in Math., Tex. Tech. U., 1955, MA, 1958; postgrad., Tex. Christian U., 1963-67, U. N. Tex., 1969-80, Tarrant Jr. Coll., Fort Worth, Tex., 1972-83. Cert. tchr., Tex. Math. tchr. Tom S. Lubbock (Tex.) High Sch., 1955-56; instr. math. Tex. Tech U., Lubbock, 1956-63; teaching fellow math. Tex. Christian U., Ft. Worth, 1963-64; chmn. dept. math. Ft. Worth Country Day Sch., 1964-67; instr. math. Tarrant County Jr. Coll.-South, Ft. Worth, 1967-70, asst. prof. math., 1970-74, assoc. prof. math., 1974-95; prof. emeritus, 1995—, ret., 1995; cons. Project Change, Ft. Worth, 1967-68; math. scis. advisor Coll. Bd., Princeton, N.J., 1979-83; math. book reviewer for vaarious pub. cos. including Prentice-Hall, McGraw Hill, D.C. Health, Prindle, Weber & Schmidt, MacMillan, Harcourt, Brace Jovanovich, West, Worth, Saunders, Wadsworth. Contbr. article, book revs. to profl. publs.; author book supplement to Intermediate Algebra, 1990. Active mem. Jr. League of Ft. Worth, 1954-73, sustaining mem., 1973—; editor newsletter Crestwood Assn., Ft. Worth, 1984, 86, 91, membership sec., 1985, 90, 91, 95, pres., 1988-89, crime patrol capt., 1993, v.p., 1993, treas. 1987, 96. Recipient award for excellence in teaching Gen. Dynamics, 1968. Mem. Math. Assn. Am. (life), Nat. Coun. Tchrs. Math. (life), Am. Math. Assn. Two-Yr. Colls. (life), Tex. Math. Assn. Two-Yr. Colls. (charter), Tex. Jr. Coll. Tchrs.' Assn., Pi Beta Phi. Republican. Episcopalian. Home: 600 Eastwood Ave Fort Worth TX 76107-1020

SULLIVAN, ADDIE LOUISE, trade association project assistance administrator; b. Chgo., July 7, 1942; d. Fred and Jimmie Sophie (Lacey) S. AA, Kennedy-King Coll., Chgo., 1973. Waitress Moon's Restaurant, Chgo., 1962; sec. Zenith Corp., Chgo., 1963-65; sec., collector Household Fin., Chgo., 1965-68; sec. temporary agencies, Chgo., 1968-70, Chgo. Housing Authority, 1973-75, 78-80, Cook County Hosp., Chgo., 1975-80; libr., membership rep. U. Chgo., 1980—; steward Internat. Brotherhood Teamsters Local 743, Chgo., 1984—, counselor Local743, Chgo., 1993—. Mem. Teamster Black Caucus, Washington, 1990, Coalition of Black Unionists, Chgo., 1991, Labor Party Advs., Chgo., 1995. Named Steward of Yr., Internat. Brotherhood Teamsters, 1989, Alpha Lambda chpt. ETA Phi Beta, 1994. Mem. Order of Ea. Star, Prince Hall Affiliation (past matron 1986, 89). Apostolic. Home: 5631 S Cottage Grove Chicago IL 60637

SULLIVAN, CELA MARIE, assistant principal; b. Nevada, Mo., Apr. 1, 1958; d. Marion Howard and Germaine Frances (Vogel) McKee; m. John Vincent Sullivan, Aug. 14, 1986. BA in Edn., U. Mo., Columbia, 1980; MA in Edn., U. Mo., Kansas City, 1987, EdS in Adminstrn., 1990, postgrad. Cert. prin. grades 4-12, cert. tchr. social studies grades 7-12, Mo. Tchr. social studies grade 7 New Mark Mid. Sch., Kansas City, 1980-84, tchr. social studies grade 8, 1984—, asst. prin. grades 6-8, 1995—; tutoring coord. New Mark Mid. Sch., 1989-96, mentor to 1st-yr. tchr., 1989, 96; mem. drug awareness com., 1992-96; scholarship advisor Nat. Jr. Honor Soc., New mark Mid. Sch., 1993-96. State incentive grantee, Mo., 1989. Mem. NEA, AAUW, ASCD, Mo. Mid. Sch. Assn., Kappa Kappa Gamma. Roman Catholic.

SULLIVAN, CLAIRE FERGUSON, marketing educator; b. Pittsburg, Tex., Sept. 28, 1937; d. Almon Lafayette and Mabel Clara (Williams) Potter; m. Richard Wayne Ferguson, Jan. 31, 1959 (div. Jan. 1980); 1 child, Mark Jeffrey Ferguson; m. David Edward Sullivan, Nov. 2, 1984. BBA, U. Tex., 1958, MBA, 1961; PhD, U. North Tex., 1973; grad., Harvard Inst. Ednl. Mgmt., 1991. Instr. So. Meth. U., Dallas, 1965-70; asst. prof. U. Utah, Salt Lake City, 1972-74; assoc. prof. U. Ark., Little Rock, 1974-77, U. Tex., Arlington, 1977-80, Ill. State U., Normal, 1980-84; prof., chmn. mktg. Bentley Coll., Waltham, Mass., 1984-89; dean sch. bus. Met. State Coll. Denver, 1989-92, prof. mktg., 1992—; cons. Denver Partnership, 1989-90, Gen. Tel. Co., Irving, Tex., 1983, McKnight Pub. Co., Bloomington, Ill., 1983, dental practitioner, Bloomington, 1982-83, Olympic Fed., Berwyn, Ill., 1982, Denver Partnership Econ. Devel. Adv. Coun., 1989-91; mem. African-Am. Leadership Inst. Gov. Bd. Contbr. mktg. articles to profl. jours. Direct Mktg. Inst. fellow, 1981; Ill. State U. rsch. grantee, 1981-83. Mem. Am. Mktg. Assn. (faculty fellow 1984-85), Beta Gamma Sigma. Republican. Methodist. Home: 408 E 10th Ave Salt Lake City UT 84103 Office: Met State Coll Dept Mktg MSCD Box 79 PO Box 173362 Denver CO 80217-3362

SULLIVAN, COLLEEN ANNE, physician, educator; b. Lucknow, India, Feb. 11, 1937; came to U.S., 1961; d. Douglas George and Nancy Irene (MacLeod) S.; m. Alexander Walter Gotta, July 17, 1965; 1 child, Nancy Colleen. MB ChB, U. St. Andrews, Scotland, 1961. Diplomate Am. Bd. Anesthesiology, Am. Coll. Anesthesiologists. Rotating intern Nassau Hosp., Mineola, N.Y., 1961-62; clin. instr. Cornell U., N.Y.C., 1962-64; resident in anesthesiology N.Y. Hosp./Cornell U., 1962-64; fellow in anesthesiology Meml. Sloan-Kettering Cancer Ctr., N.Y.C., 1964-67, asst. prof. Cornell U. Med. Coll., 1978-79; assoc. dir. anesthesia St. Mary's Hosp.-Cath. Med. Ctr., Bklyn., 1968-78; clin. assoc. prof. SUNY, Bklyn., 1979-90, clin. prof. anesthesiology, 1990—, clin. dir. anesthesia, 1990-93; clin. dir. anesthesia Kings County Hosp., Bklyn., 1983-90, med. dir. ambulatory surg. unit, 1993—. Author numerous chpt. in anesthesiology textbooks; contbr. articles to profl. jours. Mem. N.Y. State Soc. Anesthesiologists (ho. of dels. 1983—, asst. editor Sphere 1990-95, com. sci. program 1990—). Republican. Roman Catholic. Office: Kings County Hosp Dept Anesthesia 450 Clarkson Ave Brooklyn NY 11203-2012

SULLIVAN, CONNIE CASTLEBERRY, artist, photographer; b. Cin., Jan. 8, 1934; d. John Porter and Constance (Alf) Castleberry; m. John J. Sullivan, June 6, 1959; children: Deirdre Kelly, Margaret Graham. BA, Manhattanville Coll., 1957. spl. lectr. Cin. Contemporary Art Ctr., 1984, Toledo Friends of Photography, 1991, U. Ky. Art Mus., 1993, Dennison U. Sch. Art, 1993, El Instituto de Estudios Norte Americanos, Barcelona, 1994. One-woman shows include Contemporary Art Ctr. Cleve., 1982, Cin. Contemporary Arts Ctr., 1983, Fogg Art Mus., Cambridge, Mass., 1983, 90, Camden Arts Ctr., London, 1987, Jean-Pierre Lambert Galerie, Paris, 1988, 96, David Winton Bell Gallery, Brown U., Providence, 1989, Toni Burckhead Gallery, Cin., 1989, Rochester Inst. Tech., 1991, Fotomus. im Münchner Stadtmus., Munich, 1992, U. Ky. Art Mus., Lexington, 1993, Internat. Photography Hall, Kirkpatrick Mus. complex, Oklahoma City, 1993, Institut d'Estudios Fotografics de Catalunya, Barcelona, Spain, 1994, Cheekwood Art Mus., Nashville, 1994, Museo Damy di Fotografia Contemporanea, Brescia, Italy, 1995, Photography Gallery U. Notre Dame, Ind., 1995, Louisville Visual Art Assoc., Watertower, Louisville, KY, 1995; exhibited in numerous group shows including Dayton (Ohio) Art Inst., 1987, J.B. Speed Art Mus., Louisville, 1988, Ohio U., Athens, 1989, Centre Nat. Photographie, Paris, 1989, Cleve. Ctr. for Contemporary Art, 1991, Tampa Mus. Art, 1991, 93, Images Gallery, 1991, Dayton Art Inst./Mus. Contemporary Art Wright State U., Dayton, 1992, Bowling Green State U. Sch Art, 1992, Carnegie Arts Ctr., Covington, Ky., 1993, Cin. Art Mus., 1993, POLK Mus. Art, Lakeland, Fla., 1993, Tampa (Fla.) Mus. Art, 1993, Adams Landing Fine Art Ctr., Cin., 1995, Cheekwood Mus. Art, Nashville, 1995, Photo Forum Gallery, 1995, Jean-Pierre Galerie, 1996, Soros Ctr. Contemporary Art, Kiev, Ukraine, 1996, Dom Khudozhnikiv, Kharkiv, Ukraine, 1996; represented in numerous permanent collections Tampa Mus. of Art, Münchner Stadt Mus., Munich, Germany, Museo Damy, Brescia, Italy, Ctr. Creative Photography, Tucson, Detroit Inst. Arts, Biblioteque National, Paris, Internat. Photography Hall of Fame and Mus., Kirkpatrick Ctr. Mus. Complex, Okla. City, Nelson Gallery-Atkins Mus., Kansas City, Ctr. for Photography, Bombay, Milw. Art Mus., Mus. Photography Arts, San Diego, Musee Nat. D'Art Modern, Centre Georges Pompidou, Paris, Denver Art Mus., Boston Mus. Fine Arts, Stanford U. Mus. Art, Palo Alto, Indpls. Art Mus., New Orleans Mus. Art, Fogg Mus., Cambridge, Mass., numerous others; also pvt. collections; author: Petroglyphs of the Heart, Photographs by Connie Sullivan, 1983; work represented in numerous publs. Trustee Images Ctr. for Fine Photography, Cin., 1986-94. Arts Midwest fellow NEA, 1989-90; recipient award Toledo Friends Photography Juried Show, 1986, Best of Show award, 1988, Images Gallery, 1986, Pres.'s Coun. for Arts award Manhattanville Coll., 1991, Treasure of the Month award Mus. Fine Arts St. Petersburg, Fla., 1995; Aid to Individual Artists grantee Summerfair, 1987; named Hyde Park Living Person of Yr., 1996. Mem. McDowell Soc. Home and Studio: 9 Garden Pl Cincinnati OH 45208-1056

SULLIVAN, EILEEN MARIE, English/communications educator; b. Washington, Sept. 23, 1958; m. James Francis Sullivan III, Aug. 20, 1983; children: James, Grace, Amy. BA in English Lit., St. Louis U., 1980; MA, U. S.D., 1992. Asst. editor Arts of St. Louis, 1983-84, St. Louis Weekly, 1984-85; columnist, staff writer Observer, Yankton, S.D., 1985-87; legal sec., writer Kabieseman Law Office, Yankton, S.D., 1988-89; contbg. editor Bishop's Bulletin, S.D. Mag., Yankton, 1994; mktg. cons. Valley State Bank, Yankton, 1994; editorial cons. Press and Dakotan Daily Newspaper, Yankton, 1995-96; asst. prof. English, communications Mt. Marty Coll., Yankton, 1989-96; instr. comm. U. S.D., Vermillion, 1996—; adj. prof. communications U. S.D., Vermillion, 1994. Author of short stories, plays, editorials and poems; mem. editorial bd. PRess and Dakota, 1995. Campaign chair Kathleen Piper-Yankton County Dems., 1990, 94, press dir., 1989. Recipient S.D. Press Assn. awards, 1985-87, Golden Apple awards, 1987. Mem. AAUW.

SULLIVAN, ELIZABETH MARIE, lawyer; b. Silver Spring, Md., Aug. 16, 1943; d. James Finn and Ellen Kathleen Fitzpatrick; m. Robert Joseph Sullivan, Aug. 22, 1965; children: Theresa Ann Miller, Thomas Michael, Susan Christine, William Patrick. BA, Boston U., 1964; JD, U. Md., Balt., 1973. Bar: Md. 1973, D.C. 1974. Assoc. Weissbard, Conner, Cox, Balt., 1973-79, ptnr., 1979-83; ptnr. Sullivan, Brown, Dame & Werik, Towson, Md., 1983—. Treas. Pub. Justice Ctr., Balt., 1987—. Mem. ABA, Md. Bar Assn., Balt. Bar Assn. Office: Sullivan Brown Dame & Werik 6600 York Rd Ste 105 Baltimore MD 21212

SULLIVAN, ELIZABETH QUAY, English educator; b. Washington, Dec. 12, 1945; d. Richard Roberts and Marjorie Rebecca (Brownlee) Quay; m. Richard Joseph Sullivan, June 20, 1970; children: Naomi Rebecca, Nora Elizabeth, John Brownlee. BA, Wellesley Coll., 1967; MA, Rutgers U., 1970, PhD in Arts and Sci., English, 1975. Tchg. asst., NDEA fellow Rutgers U., New Brunswick, N.J., 1967-74; asst. prof. English George Mason U., Fairfax, Va., 1975-77, Fivetowns Coll., L.I., N.Y., 1978-80; asst. prof. English SUNY, Old Westbury, 1980-86, Farmindale, 1986—; faculty rep. SUNY Faculty Access to Computing Tech. Conf., 1995—. Contbr.: Jewish American Women Writers, 1994; contbr. articles to profl. mags. and encys. Recipient grant NEH, 1989, 90, Travel grant PDQWL, 1989. Mem. Nat. Coun. Tchrs. of English in 2-yr. Colls. (nominating com. N.E. regional chpt. 1993). Home: 588 Park Ave Huntington NY 11743 Office: SUNY Farmingdale Melville Rd Farmingdale NY 11735

SULLIVAN, IRENE A., lawyer; b. Bklyn., 1945. AB, Mount Holyoke Coll., 1967; MA, NYU, 1970; JD cum laude, Fordham U., 1975. Bar: N.Y. 1976. Ptnr. Skadden, Arps, Slate, Meagher & Flom. Mem. Phi Beta Kappa. Office: Skadden Arps Slate Meagher & Flom 919 3rd Ave New York NY 10022*

SULLIVAN, JERI LYNETTE, speech language pathologist; b. Port Arthur, Tex., Mar. 30, 1959; d. Jerry Joseph and Mary Helen (LeMire) Boudreaux;

m. Donald Lee Sullivan, Sr., July 20, 1980; children: Donald Lee Jr., Ryan Patrick. BS in Speech, Lamar U., 1981, MS in Speech Pathology, 1987. Cert. speech lang. pathologist, Tex. State Bd. Examiners for Speech Lang. Pathology and Audiology; cert. Am. Speech Hearing Assn.; cert. speech therapist Tex. Edn. Agy. Speech lang. pathologist Port Arthur Ind. Sch. Dist., 1986-87, Port Neches (Tex.) Groves Ind. Sch. Dist., 1987—, Theratx Rehab. Co., Port Arthur, 1993—; externship supr./pub. sch. Lamar U., Beaumont, Tex., 1994—, externship supr. Theratx Rehab., 1994—; clin. fellowship yr. supr. Theratx, Port Arthur, 1993—. Mem. PTA; asst. cub scout leader Boy Scouts Am., Groves, Tex., 1988-91, co-chmn. Boy Scout com., Port Arthur, 1993-94, com. chmn. Troop 75, Port Arthur, 1995-96. Mem. Am. Speech Hearing Lang. Assn., Tex. Speech Hearing Lang. Assn. (legis. liaison 1993-94), Tex. Classroom Tchrs. Assn.

SULLIVAN, KAREN LAU, real estate company executive, campaign consultant, federal commissioner; b. Honolulu, Jan. 21, 1948; d. Ralph Karn Yee and Beatrice (Loo) Lau; m. Paul Dennis Sullivan, Apr. 24, 1976. BA, Whittier Coll., 1970; MA, U. Hawaii, 1987. Staff asst. to Congresswoman Patsy Mink U.S. Ho. Reps., Washington, 1974, staff asst. subcom. mines and mining, 1975-77, legis. asst. to Congressman Cec. Heftel, 1977-79; spl. asst. to asst. to Pres. for policy and women's affairs The White House, Washington, 1979; spl. asst. office of sec. of transp. U.S. Dept. Transp., Washington, 1979-81; regional dir. mid-Atlantic states Mondale-Ferraro Presdl. Campaign, Washington, 1984; dep. nat. field dir. Paul Simon Presdl. Campaign, Washington, 1987-88; Ill. dir. forum inst. Martin & Glantz Polit. Cons., San Francisco, 1988; regional dir. western states Clinton-Gore Presdl. Campaign, Little Rock, 1992; dep. dir. for pub. outreach Office of Pres.-Elect Bill Clinton, Little Rock/Washington, 1992-93; v.p. Hoaloha Ventures, Inc., Honolulu, 1981—. U.S. alt. rep. South Pacific Commn., 1995-96. Mem. Carter/Mondale Alumni Fund, The Carter Ctr. Home and Office: 810-K N Kalaheo Ave Kailua HI 96734

SULLIVAN, KATHERINE MCGURK, lawyer; b. Holyoke, Mass., Oct. 2, 1949; d. John Joseph and Mary Helen (Knightly) McGurk; m. Thomas Christopher Sullivan, Aug. 18, 1973; 1 child, Thomas McGurk Sullivan. B.A., Regis Coll., Weston, Mass., 1971, J.D. cum laude, Georgetown U., 1988. Aide to Rep. Silvio O. Conte, U.S. Congress, Washington; Am. Bar Assn., Washington, 1973-85; chief of staff Aetna Life and Casualty Co., Hartford, Conn., 1988-94; sr. v.p., gen. counsel Conn. Mut. Life Ins. Co., 1994-96, Travelers Life Ins. Co., Hartford, 1996—. Mem. ABA, Coalition for Justice, Am. Alliance of Rights and Responsibilities (bd. dirs.), Individual Investors Com. of the N.Y. Stock Exchange. Democrat. Roman Catholic. Office: Travelers Life Ins Co 1 Tower Sq Hartford CT 06156

SULLIVAN, KATHIE JEAN, library director, researcher, writer; b. Burlington, Vt., Mar. 6, 1955; d. Eugenia Lucille (Hayes) S. BS in Edn., U. Vt., 1977; MLS, SUNY, Albany, 1986. Cert. secondary English tchr., Vt. Tchr. English, Fair Haven (Vt.) Union H.S., 1977-80, Middlebury (Vt.) Union H.S., 1981-82; unit sec. Med. Ctr. Hosp. Vt., Burlington, 1980-81; tchr. lang. arts Castleton (Vt.) Jr. H.S., 1982-84; adult edn. tutor Southwestern Vt. Adult Basic Edn., Rutland, 1984-85; libr. dir. McNamee, Lochner, Titus & Williams, P.C., Albany, 1986—. Contbr. articles and book revs. to profl. jours. Mem. Am. Assn. Law Librs. (editor newsletter column 1993-96, coun. chmn. 1994-95, com. chmn. 1995-96), Spl. Librs. Assn., Law Librs. New Eng., Assn. Law Librs. Upstate N.Y. (pres. 1994-95). Office: McNamee Lochner Titus Et Al PO Box 459 75 State St 12th Fl Albany NY 12201

SULLIVAN, KATHRYN ANN, librarian, educator; b. Elmhurst, Ill., Jan. 22, 1954; d. Joseph Terrence and Rose Marie (Wright) S. Student, Triton Jr. Coll., 1972-73; BA, No. Ill. U., 1975, MLS, 1977; D of Sci. in Info. Sci., Nova U., 1991. Chief periodicals clk. No. Ill. U., Dekalb, 1976-77; periodicals librarian West Chgo. (Ill.) Pub. Library, 1977-78, Winona (Minn.) State U., 1978—. Contbr. articles to profl. jours. Grantee Winona State U., 1986, 88, 92, 94. Mem. ALA, Minn. Libr. Assn., Libr. and Info. Tech. Assn., N.Am. Serials Interest Group. Home: 670 Winona St Winona MN 55987-3353 Office: Winona State U Maxwell Libr Winona MN 55987

SULLIVAN, KATHRYN MEARA, telecommunications company executive; b. Schenectady, N.Y., Sept. 20, 1942; d. Vincent Thomas and Agnes (Pendergast) Meara; m. Paul William Sullivan, Feb. 8, 1964; children: Mary Margaret, Paul Hammond, Patricia Eileen. BS in Physics, Bucknell U., 1964; MBA, Fairleigh Dickinson U., 1981. Software developer GE Corp., Phila., 1964-65; account exec. Honeywell Corp., Phila., 1975-77; regional sales mgr. Nicolet Instrument Corp., Northvale, N.J., 1977-81; mktg. mgr. AT&T, Basking Ridge, N.J., 1981-83; bus. devel. mgr. AT&T, Berkeley Heights, N.J., 1983-86; pres. AT&T-Pixel Machines, Somerset, N.J., 1986-90; dir. sales ops. and support AT&T Computer Sys., Morristown, N.J., 1990-91; dir. sales transition AT&T Computer Sys., Parisppany, N.J., 1991-92; dir. info. svcs. AT&T Bus. Comm. Svcs., Parsippany, 1992-93; dir. bus. applications and info. svcs. AT&T, Bedminster, N.J., 1993-95, dir. cross market product mgmt., 1995—; mem. charter adv. bd. Rothman Inst. for Entrepreneurial Studies, Fairleigh Dickinson U., 1989—. Chairperson career options for women com. YWCA, Plainfield, N.J., 1989-91. Recipient Anthony Gervino award Fairleigh Dickinson U., 1989, Pinnacle award, 1991. Mem. Nat. Computer Graphics Assn. (treas., exec. com. bd. dirs. 1989—).

SULLIVAN, LAURA PATRICIA, lawyer, insurance company executive; b. Des Moines, Oct. 16, 1947; d. William and Patricia (Kautz) S. BA, Cornell Coll., Iowa, 1971; JD, Drake U., 1972. Bar: Iowa 1972. Various positions Ins. Dept. Iowa, Des Moines, 1972-75; various legal positions State Farm Mut. Auto Ins. Co., Bloomington, Ill., 1975-81, sec. and counsel, 1981-88, v.p., counsel and sec., 1988—; v.p., sec., dir. State Farm Cos. Found., 1985—; sec. State Farm Lloyd's, Inc., 1987—; v.p., counsel and sec. State Farm Fire and Casualty Co., 1988—; v.p., counsel and sec. State Farm Gen. Ins. Co., 1988—, also bd. dirs.; v.p. counsel, sec., dir. State Farm Life and Accident Assurance Co.; v.p. counsel, sec. State Farm Annuity and Life Assurance Co., State Farm Life Ins. Co.; dir. State Farm Indemnity Co., Bloomington, Ill., 1995—; bd. dirs. Ins. Inst. for Hwy. Safety, Nat. Conf. Ins. Guaranty Funds, chmn., 1995—. Trustee John M. Scott Indsl. Sch. Trust, Bloomington, 1983-86; bd. dirs. Scott Ctr., 1983-86, Bloomington-Normal Symphony, 1980-85, YWCA of McLean County, 1993-95; chmn. Ins. Inst. for Hwy. Safety, 1987-88. Mem. ABA, Iowa State Bar Assn., Am. Corp. Counsel Assn., Am. Soc. Corp. Secs. Office: State Farm Mut Automobile Ins Co 1 State Farm Plz Bloomington IL 61710-0001

SULLIVAN, LILA ELAINE, education administrator; b. Matoon, Ill., Feb. 26, 1948; d. Ralph M. Horn and Eula E. (Phipps) Rodgers. BS in Edn., Eastern. Ill. U., 1969, MA in English, 1973, EdS in Adminstrn., 1984; EdD in Adminstrn., Ill. State U., 1992. Cert. adminstrn., English, history, Ill. Tchr. English Grayslake (Ill.) H.S., 1969-72; tchr. lang. arts, social studies Jefferson Jr. H.S., Mattoon, Ill., 1973-74; tchr. English Mattoon H.S., 1974-85, asst. prin., 1985-88; asst. prin. Lyons Twp. H.S., Western Springs, Ill., 1989-90; prin. Lyons Twp. H.S., Western Springs, 1990-94, Centennial H.S., Champaign, Ill., 1994—; adj. prof. Eastern Ill. U., Charleston, 19880-95; instr. Coll. of DuPage, Glen Ellyn, Ill., 1989-94. Mem. ASCD, Ill. Prins. Assn. (past bd. dirs.), Ill. Assn. for Supervision and Career Devel., Nat. Assn. Secondary Prins., Kiwanis Club Champaign, Kappa Delta Pi, Epsilon Sigma Alpha (past pres. Alpha Rho chpt.). Roman Catholic. Home: 809 Ramblewood Ct # B Savoy IL 61874-9568 Office: Centennial HS Office of the Principal Champaign IL 61821

SULLIVAN, MARGARET M., university program administrator; b. N.Y.C., Dec. 29, 1953; d. Joseph Aloysius and Margaret Patricia (Demarest) S.; m. Richard D. Lawrence. BA, Marymount Manhattan Coll., 1975; MA, U. Ill. Curatorial fellow Solomon R. Guggenheim Mus., N.Y.C., 1978-79; lectr. Coll. Fine and Applied Arts U. Ill., Champaign-Urbana, 1979-84, rsch. curator Krannert Art Mus., 1979-84; dir. sponsored rsch. Purchase Coll. SUNY, 1985-92, v.p. external affairs and devel. Purchase Coll., 1992—. Contbr. articles to profl. jours. Active Children's Ctr. at Purchase Coll., 1991-95; trustee Purchase Coll. Found., 1992—. Recipient Profl. Excellence award United Univ. Professions N.Y. State Labor Mgmt., Albany, 1991. Mem. Nat. Soc. Fundraising Execs., Coun. for Advancement and Support of Edn. (Circle of Excellence for Fundraising award 1995). Office: Purchase Coll SUNY 735 Anderson Hill Rd Purchase NY 10577

SULLIVAN, SISTER MARIE CELESTE, health care executive; b. Boston, Mar. 18, 1929; d. Daniel John and Katherine Agnes (Cunniff) S. BBA, St. Bonaventure U., 1965. Joined Order Franciscan Sisters Roman Cath. Ch., 1952; bus. mgr. St. Joseph's Hosp., Providence, 1954-62; asst. adminstr. St. Joseph's Hosp., Tampa, Fla., 1965-70, adminstr., 1970-83, chief exec. officer, 1983-93; pres., chief exec. officer Allegany Health Sys., Tampa, Fla., 1994—; coord. health affairs Diocese of St. Petersburg, 1980-93; mem. Fla. Cancer Control and Research Adv. Bd., 1980-90; bd. dirs. First Fla. Bank, N.A., Barnett Bank of Tampa; gen. councillor Franciscan Sisters of Allegany, 1984-92. Contbr. articles to profl. jours. Trustee St. Francis Med. & Health Ctr., Miami Beach, Fla., 1986-92; bd. dirs. local chpt. Am. Cancer Soc. Recipient Humanitarian award Judeo-Christian Health Clinic, Tampa, 1977, Athena award Fla. West Coast chpt. Women in Communications, 1978, Exec. Woman of Yr. award Tampa Bay chpt. Network Exec. Women, 1987. Fellow Am. Coll. Health Care Execs. (life); mem. Fla. Hosp. Assn. (trustee 1983-87), Am. Mgmt. Assn., Greater Tampa C. of C. (bd. govs. 1982-87). Democrat. Club: Centre (Tampa) (founding bd. govs.). Home: 2924 W Curtis St Tampa FL 33614-7102 Office: Allegany Health Sys 6200 Courtney Campbell Causeway Tampa FL 33607

SULLIVAN, MARISSA M., elementary school educator; b. Butte, Mont., Nov. 4; d. Walter M. and Gerry T. (Sullivan) S. BA in Biology and Sociology, Gonzaga U., 1984, MA, 1993. Cert. tchr., Wash. 3d grade tchr. Ea. Hoffsetter Sch., Colville, Wash., 1986-87; tchr. grade 2-3 Bemiss, Spokane, 1987-88; kindergarten tchr. Adam Sch., Spokane, Wash., 1988-89; 4th grade tchr. Arlington Elem. Sch., Spokane, Wash., 1989-90; 3d grade tchr. Arlington Elem. Sch., Spokane, 1990-92, 2d grade tchr., 1992-94; 2d grade tchr. Whitman Elem. Sch., Spokane, 1994—; mem. Dist. 81 Assessment Adv. Com., Spokane, 1992-93, Report Card Rev. Com., Spokane, 1993-94; spkr. N.W. Math. Conf., Victoria, B.C., 1994, Seattle, 1993. Mem. Nat. Tchrs. Math.

SULLIVAN, MARY ANN, school psychologist; b. Salina, Kans., Feb. 8, 1937; d. Alfred Vesper and Helen Margaret (Bozarth) Haerer; m. Robert Emmett Sullivan, Aug. 29, 1961. BS, U. Nebr., 1959, MEd, 1965, PhD, 1979. Nationally cert. sch. psychologist. Secondary edn. tchr. San Bernardino (Calif.) Pub. Schs., 1959-60; spl. edn. tchr. Lincoln (Nebr.) Pub. Schs., 1960-76, sch. psychologist, 1976—. Vol. Haydon Art Gallery, Lincoln, 1994—. Mem. Nat. Assn. Sch. Psychologists (state del. 1988-92, co-chair pub. info. com. 1991-93), Nebr. Sch. Psychologists Assn. (pres. 1985-86, outstanding sch. psychologist 1991, founders award 1994), PEO Roundtable of Lincoln (pres. 1976-77), PEO (Nebr. chpt. GD, pres. 1968-69, 81-82). Home: 1201 Piedmont Rd Lincoln NE 68510 Office: Lincoln Pub Schs 5901 O St Lincoln NE 68510

SULLIVAN, MARY E., secondary school educator, former state legislator; b. June 29, 1932; m. Charles M. Sullivan; children: Charles M. Jr., Ethel M., Mary E., Kathleen M., Mark C., Ursula M. AB, Regis U., 1954; MA, Boston Coll., 1955. Asst. prof. stats. Bentley Coll., Waltham, Mass., 1966-72; asst. prof., registrar Husson Coll., 1973-79; mem. staff Maine Dept. Manpower Affairs Rsch., 1980-81; math. tchr. John Bapst Meml. H.S., 1981—; also mem. Maine Ho. of Reps., 1992-94. City councilor City of Bangor, Maine, 1985—, mayor, 1988-89. Mem. Maine Munic Assn. (past pres.). Democrat. Address: 81 Grant St Bangor ME 04401-3821

SULLIVAN, MARY E., controller; b. Kingsville, Tex., Nov. 21, 1956; d. C. David and Patricia R. (McCall) Yates; m. Michael J. Sullivan, Sept. 3, 1977; 1 child, Michael Jr. BS in Math., Corpus Christi (Tex.) State U., 1979, MBA, 1981, MS in Computer Science, 1982. CPA, CFA, CMA, CISA. Statistical analyst Central Power & Light, Corpus Christi, 1979-80, internal auditor, 1980-81, acctg. supr., 1981-83, mgr. acctg. svcs., 1983-88, treas., 1988-92; budget analyst City of Corpus Christi, 1993; controller Am. Chrome & Chemicals, Corpus Christi, 1993—. Mem. bd. dirs. Food Bank of Corpus Christi, 1990—, Paisano Girl Scout Coun., Corpus Christi, 1991—. Mem. AICPA, Tex. Soc. CPAs, Inst. Mgmt. Acctg., Inst. Chartered Fin. Analysts, EDP Auditor's Assn. Office: Am Chrome & Chemicals PO Box 9912 Corpus Christi TX 78469

SULLIVAN, MARY JANE, elementary school educator; b. Mason City, Iowa, Nov. 23, 1947; d. Lawrence Wesly and Elizabeth Barbara (Steinbach) Kohler; m. Mark Jay Sullivan, June 26, 1993. BS, Mankato (Minn.) State U., 1970; MS, Iowa State U., 1982. Cert. tchr. K-9, coach K-12, Iowa. Tchr. 5th grade Keokuk (Iowa) Cmty. Sch., 1970-77, West Bend (Iowa) Cmty. Sch., 1977-80; tchr. 6th grade North Mahaska Cmty. Sch., New Sharon, Iowa, 1980—. Author: (poetry teaching book) Poetry Pals, 1982. Mem. Regional telecomms. Coun., Des Moines, 1994—; treas. New Sharon Activities Com., 1988—; mem. Iowa Pub. TV, Des Moines, Iowa Heritage Assn., Des Moines. Named County Sci. Tchr. of Yr., Mahaska County Conservation Bd., Oskaloosa, Iowa, 1992; sci. grantee Ctrl. Coll., Iowa Dept. Edn. Mem. NEA, ASCD, Iowa State Edn. Assn. (exec. bd. negotiations), Nat. Staff Devel. Coun. (mem. 1st acad.), Kappa Delta Pi, Phi Delta Kappa (v.p. 1990-91). Roman Catholic. Office: N Mahaska Elem Sch 204 W Maple New Sharon IA 50207

SULLIVAN, MARY JEAN, elementary school educator; b. Cambridge, Mass., May 13, 1956; d. Joseph Leo and Jean Marie (Isaac) S. BA, Flagler Coll., 1978; postgrad., U. No. Fla., 1980—, Fla. State U., 1992, Okla. State U., 1992. Cert. elem. educator, Fla. Tchr. grade 2 St. Agnes Sch., St. Augustine, Fla., 1978-79; tchr. grades 1 through 5 Evelyn Hamblen Elem. Sch., St. Augustine, 1979-91; tchr. grade 5 Osceola Elem. Sch., St. Augustine, 1991—, chair math./ sci.; adv. Sci. Club; chairperson, St. John's County Tchr. Edn. Coun., 1985—, SACS Evaluation Team, Duval County Schs., 1988, 89, 90; rep. tchr. edn. coun.; sch. improvement co-chair, 1994-95; trainer coll. intern students. Developer tchr. edn. coun. tng. handbook for State of Fla. Active PTO, past pres., Cub Scouts Am., past asst. program dir., Cathedral-Basilica Ch., United Child Care After Sch. Program, 1988-89; coord. summer recreation Evelyn Hamblen Sch., St. Augustine, 1987-90; dir. tournament Pam Driskell Meml. Paddle Tennis Scholarship Fund, 1986, 87, 88, 89. Grantee Fla. Coun. Elem. Edn., 1981-82, Summer Enhancement, 1988-89, Fla. Inst. Oceanography, 1994, St. John's County Horizon award mini-grantee, 1994, Fla. Assn. for Computer Edn., 1994, Fla. Humanities Coun., 1995; recipient Human Rels. award State of Fla., 1992, NEWEST award, 1992, award Geography Summer Inst., 1992; named Kiwanis Tchr. of Month, 1993. Mem. NEA, Nat. Sci. Tchrs. Assn., Fla. Teaching Profession, Fla. Assn. Staff Devel., Fla. Geographic Alliance, Fla. Assn. Computer Edn., St. John's Educator Assn., Fla. Assn. for Sci. Tchrs., ASCD. Office: Osceola Elem Sch 1605 Osceola Elem Sch Rd Saint Augustine FL 32095

SULLIVAN, MELANIE MOREL, minister; b. New Orleans, Sept. 28, 1952; d. Warren Valentine and Verna C. (Collo) Morel; m. Stephen Martin Sullivan, Aug. 1982 (div. 1992); 1 child, Stephen Warren George. Student, St. Mary's Dominican Coll., 1970-74, Loyola U., New Orleans, 1992. Ordained min. Unitarian Universalist Ch., 1993. Fashion model New Orleans, Southampton, Eng., 1971-76; asst. store mgr. Godchaux's, New Orleans, 1977-81; store mgr. Laura Ashley Shop, New Orleans, 1983-87; adminstr. 1st Unitarian Universalist Ch., New Orleans, 1987-90; student min. Our Home Universalist Ch., Ellisville, Miss., 1992-93; parish min. Unitarian Universalist Ch., Chattanooga, 1993—; faculty mem. Southwest Leadership Sch. Unitarian Universalist, Dallas, 1992—; bd. dirs. Mountain Unitarian Universalist Camp and Conf. Ctr., Highlands, N.C. Contbr. articles to profl. jours. Mem. ACLU (bd. dirs. Tenn. chpt. 1994-96), Unitarian Universalist Mins. Assn., Southeast Unitarian Universalist Min. Assn. (sec. 1995-96), Unitarian Universalist Christian Fellowship, Ministerial Sisterhood Unitarian Universalist, Chattanooga Interfaith Clergy Assn. Democrat. Office: Unitarian Universalist Ch 3224 Navajo Dr Chattanooga TN 37411

SULLIVAN, NELL INKLEBARGER, administrative secretary, counselor assistant; b. Charleston, Ark., Jan. 27, 1932; d. Hubert Huel and Maybelle (Heather) Inklebarger; m. J.W. Miller, June 10, 1950 (div. 1973); children: Allan Evan Miller, Sandy Miller Hays-Lusted, Elizabeth Kay Speer, Judith Lynelle Miller; m. Nathan Doyal Sullivan Sr., 1973. AA in Journalism, Westark Coll., Ft. Smith, Ark., 1986. Clk. U.S. Postal Svc., Lavaca, Ark., 1959-73; co-owner, operator, photographer Nell Miller Studio, Lavaca, 1960-75; office supr. U.S. Postal Svc., Ft. Smith, 1972-75; computer specialist Westark Coll., Ft. Smith, 1984-86, assoc. editor coll. newspaper, 1985-87; adminstrv. asst. BDM, Inc., Ft. Chaffee, Ark., 1987-89; counselor asst. Ark. Rehab. Svc., Ft. Smith, 1990-94. Recipient journalism scholarship Westark Coll., 1984-86. Mem. YWCA (bd. dirs. Ft. Smith 1986-93), Nat. Rehab. Assn., Ark. Rehab. Svcs., Ark. State Employees Assn., Nat. Assn. Rehab. Secs., 4-H Alumni Assn. (life), Phi Beta Lambda. Office: Ark Rehab Svc Essex Pl 1115 S Waldron Rd Ste 207 Fort Smith AR 72903-2588

SULLIVAN, NOLA DE JONG, art educator; b. Salt Lake City, Nov. 3, 1924; d. Gerrit and Rosabelle (Winegar) de Jong; m. Clyde E. Sullivan, May 1, 1944; children: Noel Clyde, Michael Gerrit, Kim Sullivan-Stevens. Student, Brigham Young U., 1942-45, Coll. Arts & Crafts, Oakland, Calif., 1954, Sch. Visual Arts, N.Y.C. Tchr. of handicapped children Richmond, Calif., 1948-58, Walnut Creek, Calif., 1958-60; tchr. of handicapped children Elwyn Sch., Media, Pa., 1961-64, White Plains, N.Y., 1972-75; pvt. practice watercolor tchr. Provo, 1983—; demonstrator of watercolor painting in field. One-person shows include Springville Mus. Art, Brigham Young U., Utah Valley Art Guild, Water Color Soc. shows, others; represented in permanent collections Nat. Mus. of Women in Arts, Washington. Vol., docent Springville (Utah) Art Mus., 1981-93, Brigham Young Univ. Art Mus., Provo, 1993-94; mem. Mayors Planning Commn., Provo, 1990-93. Mem. Utah Watercolor Soc., Utah Valley Art Guild (numerous positions including pres.). Mem. LDS Ch. Home: 2955 N Foothill Dr Provo UT 84604

SULLIVAN, PATRICIA A., academic administrator; b. S.I.; m. Charles Sullivan. Grad., St. John's U.; MS in Biology, NYU, PhD in Biology. Tchg. fellow, NIH pre-doctoral fellow NYU; post-doctoral fellow in cell biology Upstate Med. Ctr., Syracuse, N.Y.; vis. fellow Cornell U., 1976; tchr. Wells Coll., N.Y.; dir. biology honors program Tex. Woman's U., 1979-81; dean Salem Coll., Winston-Salem, 1981-87; v.p. acad. affairs Tex. Woman's U., 1987-94, interim pres., 1993-94; chancellor U. N.C., Greensboro, 1995—; pres. Assn. Tex. Colls. and Univs. Acad. Affairs Officers, Assn. So. Colls. for Women, N.C. Assn. Chief Acad. Officers; active numerous coms. Tex. Higher Edn. Coordinating Bd.; lectr. in field. Contbr. articles to profl. jours. Office: U N C 303 Mossman Bldg Greensboro NC 27412-5001

SULLIVAN, PATRICIA ANAYA, educational program director; b. Albuquerque, Jan. 10, 1961; d. Jose Miguel and Mary Magdelina (Sandoval) Anaya; m. Robert Patrick Sullivan, May 12, 1984; children: Brendan Patrick, Jordan Christine. BS, N.Mex. State U., 1983. Rsch. tech. SUMMA Med. Corp., Albuquerque, 1983; asst. program coord. N.Mex. State U., Border Rsch. Inst., Las Cruces, 1983-85, program dir., 1985-89, asst. dir., 1989-91, assoc. dir., 1991—; bd. dirs. Enchantment Land Cert. Devel. Corp., Albuquerque. Mem. NAFE, Nat. Assn. Small Bus. Internat. Trade Educators, Border Trade Alliance, N.Mex. Indsl. Devel. Execs. Assns. Democrat. Roman Catholic. Office: NMex State Univ Border Rsch Institute Las Cruces NM 88003*

SULLIVAN, PATRICIA CLARE, hospital administrator; b. Cortland, Nebr., July 2, 1928. R.N. diploma, Mercy Hosp. Sch. Nursing, Denver, 1954; B.S.N., Coll. St. Mary, Omaha, 1955; M.H.A., St. Louis U., 1971, cert. for internal resources for renewal, 1971; cert. in gerontology, U. Nebr., Omaha, 1976. Instr. Mercy Hosp. Sch. Nursing, Des Moines, 1955-58; dir. Mercy Hosp. Sch. Nursing, 1960-64; nursing supr. pediatrics Mercy Hosp., Des Moines, 1955-58; adminstr. Mercy Hosp., 1977-93; pres. Mercy Health Ctr. of Central Iowa, 1982-93, Mercy Hosp. Med. Ctr., 1993—, Mercy Found., Mercy Health & Human Services, Mercy Properties, ShareCare Ltd, Mercy Geriatric Services; coordinator rural hosp. nursing, nursing supr. obgyn Mercy Hosp., Durango, Colo., 1958-60, nursing supr., Williston, N.D., 1964-65; adminstr. St. Joseph's Mercy Hosp., Centerville, Iowa, 1965-69, resident Peter Bent Brigham Hosp., Boston, 1970-71; dir. Cen. Nat. Bancshares, First Interstate Bank Corp. Des Moines (formerly Bancshares), 1979—; in organizational renewal Province of Omaha, 1971-74; dir. community relations Archbishop Bergan Mercy Hosp., Omaha, 1974-77; mem. Province of Omaha Health Services Council, 1958—; provincial chpt. del. Province Omaha, 1970-74. Dir. film depicting tornado strike to Archbishop Bergan Mercy Hosp., 1975, numerous showings, including at Congl. hearing at Pentagon. Del. Mercy Gen. Chpt., 1981—; bd. dirs. Mercy Hosp., Devils Lake, N.D., 1972-81, Sub-Area IV, Iowa Health Systems Agy., 1977—, NCCJ, 1979-85, Health System of Mercy, 1979-83, Grand View Coll., Des Moines, 1982-87, Des Moines Better Bus. Bur., 1983-85; regional rep. Diocesan Pastoral Council, 1978-80; mem. Mercy Health Conf., 1979-83, Iowa Network Mercy Hosps. 1979—, IHA Coun. on Profl. Affairs, 1980—; bd. dirs. Convalescent Home for Children, 1980-84, Health System of Midlands, Omaha, 1984-86, Greater Des Moines Com., 1987—; chair Iowa Caucus Project, 1987-88; mem. pres.'s coun. Iowa State U., 1988—. Recipient Leadership award NCCJ, 1984, People of Vision award Iowa Soc. to Prevent Blindness, 1985; named Adminstr. of Yr. Des Moines Consortium of Family Practice Physicians, 1980-81; named to Iowa Women's Hall of Fame Iowa Commn. on Status of Women, 1988, Equestrian Order of Holy Sepulchre of Jerusalem, 1989. Mem. Nat. League for Nursing, Iowa League for Nursing (pres. 1966-69), Iowa Assn. Bus. Industry, Am. Acad. Med. Adminstrs. (pres. Iowa chpt. 1986-87, Adminstr. of Yr. 1984), Omaha League for Nursing (dir. 1976-77), Am. Hosp. Assn., Iowa Hosp. Assn., Soc. Advancement Mgmt., Des Moines C. of C. (bd. dirs.), Cath. Health Assn. (bd. dirs. 1987-93), Trendleaders of Ryan Club (advisor to chief exec. officers). Office: Mercy Health Ctr Ctrl Iowa 411 Laurel St Ste 3265 Des Moines IA 50314-3005

SULLIVAN, PATRICIA G., maternal, child and women's health nursing educator; b. Denver, June 26, 1948; d. Dale F. and Wilma (Fritz) Greb; m. Michael T. Sullivan, Sept. 10, 1971; children: Nicholas O., Matthew Alexander, Adam Michael. BS, Loretto Heights Coll., 1971; MS, U. Colo., 1976. Cert. bereavement svcs. counselor. Clin. instr. Loretto Hts. Coll., 1977-81; instr. pathophysiology U. Denver, summers 1983, 84; coord. women's health edn. Swedish Med. Ctr., Englewood, Colo., 1985-86; coord. childbirth edn. Med. Ctr. Hosp., Odessa, Tex., 1986-88; instr. nursing Midland (Tex.) Coll., 1990—; cons. Mosby's Med. Nursing & Allied Health Dictionary. Reviewer: Basic Nursing and Practice 3rd edit. 1995. Counselor RTS Bereavement Svcs., 1996. Mem. AWHONN, Tex. Nurses Assn., Tex. Jr. Coll. Tchrs. Assn., Sigma Theta Tau. Home: 2803 Douglas Ave Midland TX 79701-3831 Office: Midland Coll 3600 N Garfield St # 213 Midland TX 79705-6329

SULLIVAN, PEGGY (ANNE), librarian; b. Kansas City, Mo., Aug. 12, 1929; d. Michael C. and Ella (O'Donnell) S. A.B., Clarke Coll., 1950; M.S. in L.S, Cath. U. Am., 1953; Ph.D. (Tangley Oaks fellow, Higher Edn. Act Title II fellow), U. Chgo., 1972. Children's public librarian Mo., Md., Va., 1952-61; sch. library specialist Montgomery County (Md.) public schs., 1961-63; dir. Knapp Sch. Libraries Project, ALA, 1963-68, Jr. Coll. Library Info. Ctr., 1968-69; asst. prof. U. Pitts., 1971-73; dir. Office for Library Personnel Resources, ALA, Chgo., 1973-74; dean of students, assoc. prof. Grad. Library Sch., U. Chgo., 1974-77; asst. commr. for extension services Chgo. Public Library, 1977-81; dean Coll. Profl. Studies, No. Ill. U., DeKalb, 1981-90; dir. univ. librs. No. Ill. U., 1990-92; exec. dir. ALA, 1992-94; assoc. Tuft & Assocs., 1995—; dean Grad. Sch. Libr. and Info. Sci. Rosary Coll., 1995—; instr. several grad. libr. edn. programs, 1958-73, UNESCO cons. on sch. librs., Australia, 1970; trustee Clarke Coll., 1969-72; sr. ptnr. Able Cons., 1987-92. Author: The O'Donnells, 1956, Impact: The School Library and the Instructional Program, 1966, Many Names for Eileen, 1969, Problems in School Media Management, 1971, Carl H. Milam and the American Library Association, 1976, Opportunities in Library and Information Science, 1977, Realization: The Final Report of the Knapp School Libraries Project, 1968; (with others) Public Libraries: Smart Practices in Personnel, 1982. Mem. ALA, Cath. Libr. Assn. Roman Catholic. Home: 2800 N Lake Shore Dr Apt 816 Chicago IL 60657-6202 Office: Rosary Coll Grad Sch Libr and Info Sci 7900 W Division St River Forest IL

SULLIVAN, PENELOPE DIETZ, computer consulting and software development company executive; b. Roanoke, Va., Dec. 29, 1939; d. Joseph Budding and Katherine Dietz; m. Thomas F. Sullivan, Sept. 7, 1963 (div. Mar. 1975); children: Courtney, Todd; m. Paul B. Hill, Mar. 31, 1990. BA, Colby Coll., 1961. Claims examiner Blue Cross/Blue Shield of D.C., Washington, 1961-66; self employed maker slipcovers and upholstery Springfield, Va., 1966-75; ins. sales Met. Life Ins. Co., Arlington, Va., 1975-76, Med. Pers. Pool Inc., Alexandria, Va., 1976-77; mktg. rep. IBM Corp., Washington, 1977-88; program mgr. Advanced Workstations IBM Corp., Somers, N.Y., 1988-92; sales cons. IBM Open Sys., Washington, 1992-93; co-founder

Open Sys. Assocs., Inc., Reston, Va., 1993—. Office: Open Sys Assocs Inc Ste 400 1801 Robert Fulton Dr Reston VA 22091-4347

SULLIVAN, RUTH ANNE, librarian; b. Portland, Maine, Jan. 15, 1955; d. Lawrence P. and Mary Louise (Gilman) S.; m. Charles H. Sullivan, May 1, 1982; children: Nora J., Ian J. BA, Wheaton Coll., 1979; MLS, U. Ariz., 1980. Serials ref. Mass. Bay Community Coll., Wellesley, 1980-81; asst. dir. Bristol Community Coll., Fall River, Mass., 1981-86, chief libr., 1986—. Office: Bristol Community Coll 777 Elsbree St Fall River MA 02720-7307

SULLIVAN, SARAH LOUISE, management and technology consultant; b. Wilmington, Del., Sept. 24, 1954; d. Frederick William III and Ruth (Swavely) S. BS, Bowling Green U., 1975; MS, Ill. Inst. Tech., 1986, PhD, 1990. Programmer Computer Sci. Corp., Langley AFB, Va., 1975-77; sr. systems programmer JPLRCC, Perrysburg, Ohio, 1977-80; sr. systems engr. Kraft Inc., Glenview, Ill., 1980-83; project leader Siemens Gammasonics, Des Plaines, Ill., 1983-85; sect. mgr. Zenith Electronics, Glenview, Ill., 1985; mem. tech. staff AT&T Bell Labs., Naperville, Ill., 1986-87; cons., trainer Sarah L. Sullivan & Assocs., Morton Grove, Ill., 1987-90; instr. Ill. Inst. Tech., Chgo., 1988; asst. prof. dept. computer sci. North Cen. Coll., Naperville, 1988-89, Ind.-Purdue U., Ft. Wayne, 1990-94; prin. engr. Boeing Info. Svcs., Dayton, Ohio, 1995-96, Rockwell Collins, Cedar Rapids, Iowa, 1996—; presenter in field. Mem. IEEE, Assn. for Computing Machinery, Oasis Ctr. for Human Potential.

SULLIVAN, SHELLY M'LISSE, elementary education educator; b. El Paso, Tex., June 6, 1953; d. Charles Burrell and Marjorie Deloris (Foster) Romney; m. D. Carl Sullivan, May 26, 1985; children: Shanna Monique, Sheri Marie, Staci Monae, Stephanie Michelle. BS in Edn., N.Mex. State U., 1991. Office mgr. Romney Equipment Co., Las Cruces, N.Mex., 1971-91; tchr. 1st grade Berino Elem. Sch., Anthony, N.Mex., 1991—; mem. adv. bd. Berino Elem. Year Round Edn., Anthony, 1991—. Sec. Onate High Sch. Band, Las Cruces, 1994-95. Recipient Outstanding Achievement award Legis. State of N.Mex., Santa Fe, 1994. Mem. Internat. Reading Assn. (bldg. rep. 1994-95). Republican. Mem. LDS Ch. Home: 1700 Palo Verde Ave Las Cruces NM 88001-1525 Office: Berino Elem Sch 455 Shrode Rd Anthony NM 88021

SULLIVAN-HANLEY, CAROL ANN, education educator; b. Boston, June 24, 1956; d. James Edward and Marian Louise (Cameron) Sullivan; m. P.J. Hanley, Jr., July 28, 1984. AA, Mt. Ida Coll., Newton, Mass., 1976; BS, Wheelock Coll., Boston, 1978; MEd, Lesley Coll., 1986. Lead tchr. day care Tufts U., Medford, Mass., 1978-80; lead tchr. Children's Village, Inc., Cambridge, Mass., 1980-85, Chestnut Hill Sch., Newton, 1980-95; lead tchr., mem. faculty Mt. Ida Coll., 1989-95; mem. early childhood faculty Quincy (Mass.) Coll., 1995-96; mem. grad. faculty Lesley Coll., Cambridge, 1989—. Class officer Mt. Ida Coll., 1976—; mem. alumni bd. Wheelock Coll., 1989—; mem. alumni coun. Lesley Coll., 1990—; pres., bd. dirs. LWV, Scituate, Mass., 1987-95, mem. Mass. bd. dirs., Boston, 1995-97; tutor Literacy Vols. Am., Quincy, 1994—; vol. Rosie's Place, 1994—. Mem. Mass. Soc. Prevention of Cruelty to Animals. Democrat. Roman Catholic. Home: 79 Turner Rd Scituate MA 02066

SULLIVAN-WEST, DAWN LORREEN, deputy sheriff; b. Chgo., Mar. 29, 1953; d. Gene and Lorraine Myrtle (O'Day) Sullivan. Student, Loop Coll., Chgo., 1971-72; grad., Tidewater Acad., Hampton, Va., 1984. Asst. pub. Capricorn Music, Ltd., Chgo., 1972-73; mdse. mgr. TV Radio Features, Chgo., 1973-76; continuity CBS, Chgo., 1976-77; account exec. Cradle Democracy Broadcasting, Yorktown, Va., 1977-80; account rep. Hampton Roads Cablevision, Newport News, Va., 1979-81; owner Broomhilda Svcs., Newport News, 1980-83; coord. C.U.E. Group, Newport News, 1994—; owner First Dawn & Assocs., Newport News, 1994—; dep. sheriff/bailiff Newport News Sheriff's Office, 1983—. Host, coord. students BEC Fgn. Exch. Program, France/Eng., 1994. Recipient Svc. award City of Newport News, 1994. Mem. Va. State Sheriffs Assn. Home: 853 Garrow Rd Newport News VA 23608

SULTAN, TERRIE FRANCES, curator; b. Asheville, N.C., Oct. 28, 1952; d. Norman and Phyllis Ellen (Galumbeck) Sultan; m. Christopher French, June, 1988. BFA, Syracuse U., 1973; MA, John F. Kennedy U., 1985. Exhbn. dir. Source Gallery, San Francisco, 1982-83; adj. curator Oakland (Calif.) Mus., 1984-85; dir. pub. affairs and pub. programs New Mus. Contemporary Art, N.Y.C., 1986-88; curator contemporary art Corcoran Gallery of Art, Washington, 1988—. Author: Representation and Text in the Work of Robert Morris, 1990, Redefining The Terms of Engagement: The Art of Louise Bourgeois, 1944; also exhbn. catalogues. Mem. Am. Assn. Museums, Coll. Art Assn., ArTable. Democrat. Office: The Corcoran Gallery Art 17th St New York Ave NW Washington DC 20006

SULTANA, NAJMA, psychiatrist; b. Nirmal, Andhra, India; July 22, 1948; came to U.S. 1973; d. Khaja Moinuddin and Mujib (Unnisa) Begum; m. Khaja Mohiuddin, July 8, 1971 (div. 1978); m. M. Rashid Chaudhry, Oct. 16, 1981. M.B.B.S. Gandhi Med. Coll., Hyderaba, India, 1973. Resident in psychiatry SUNY/Kings County Hosp. Ctr., Bklyn., 1976-78, fellow child psychiatry, 1978-80; asst. clin. physician S. Beach Psychiat. Ctr., S.I., N.Y., 1980-81; asst. clin. prof. SUNY Downstate Med. Ctr., N.Y.C., 1981-94; attending psychiatrist King's County Hosp., Bklyn., 1981-94, Creedmore Psychiatric Ctr., 1994—. Exec. bd. mem. Balkan Rape Response Team; co-pres. Coalition for Intervention Against Genocide in Bosnia; pres. Am. Fedn. of Muslims from India, v.p.; founding mem. G.O.P.I.O.; bd. dirs. T.O.U.C.H. Recipient Non-Resident Indian Internat. Women's award, 1992. Mem. Am. Psychiat. Assn. Democrat. Muslim.

SUMMERS, LORRAINE DEY SCHAEFFER, librarian; b. Phila., Dec. 14, 1946; d. Joseph William and Hilda Lorraine (Ritchey) Dey; m. F. William Summers, Jan. 28, 1984. B.A., Fla. State U., 1968, M.S., 1969. Extension dir. Santa Fe Regional Library, Gainesville, 1969-71; pub. library cons. State Library of Fla., Tallahassee, 1971-78, asst. state librarian, 1978-84; dir. adminstrv. services Nat. Assn. for Campus Activities, Columbia, S.C., 1984-85; asst. state librarian State Library of Fla., Tallahassee, 1985—; cons. in field. Contbr. articles to profl. jours. Del. Pres.'s Com. on Mental Retardation Regional Forum, Atlanta. 1975; del. Fla. Gov.'s Conf. on Library and Info. Services, 1978, 90. Mem. ALA (orgn. com. 1979-83, council 1982-84, 93—, resolutions com. 1983-85, mem. legislation com. 1993-95, nominating com. 1996), Assn. Specialized and Coop. Library Agys. (dir. 1976-82, chmn. planning and orgn. com. 1976-80, chmn. nominating com., 1980-81, chmn. by laws com. 1985-86, exec. bd. state library agy sect. 1983-86, pres. 1987-88, chmn. standards rev. com. 1990-92), Southeastern Library Assn. (exec. bd. 1976-80, v.p., pres.-elect 1994-96, pres. 1996—), Fla. Library Assn. (sec. 1978-79, dir., 1976-80), Zonta (dir. 1992-95). Democrat. Methodist. Office: State Library Fla Ra Gray Bldg Tallahassee FL 32399

SUMMERSELL, FRANCES SHARPLEY, organization worker; b. Birmingham, Ala.; d. Arthur Croft and Thomas O. (Stone) Sharpley; m. Charles Grayson Summersell, Nov. 10, 1934. Student U. Montevallo, Peabody Coll.; LHD (hon.) U. Ala., 1996. Ptnr., artist, writer Assoc. Educators, 1959—. Vice chmn. Ft. Morgan Hist. Commn., 1959-63; active DAR, Magna Charta Dames, U. Women's Club (pres. 1957-58), Daus. Am. Colonists (organizing regent Tuscaloosa 1956-63). Recipient Algernon Sidney Sullivan award U. Ala., 1994. Mem. Tuscaloosa County Preservation Soc. (trustee 1965-78, svc. award 1975), Birmingham-Jefferson Hist. Soc., Ala. Hist. Assn. (exec. bd. Ala. Review 1991—), XXXI Women's Hon. Soc., Omicron Delta Kappa, Iota Circle, Anderson Soc. Clubs: University (Tuscaloosa). Co-author: Alabama History Filmstrips, 1961; Florida History Filmstrips, 1963; Texas History Filmstrips, 1965-66; Ohio History Filmstrips, 1967 (Merit award Am. Assn. State and Local History 1968); California History Filmstrips, 1968; Illinois History Filmstrips, 1970. Home: 1411 Caplewood Dr Tuscaloosa AL 35401-1131

SUMMINS, TRINA MICHELLE, small business owner; b. Tuscola, Ill., May 7, 1958; d. Andrew Lee and Vonda Belle (Branham) Flanigan; m. Drew Anthony Summins, Oct. 22, 1987; children: Christopher Nicholas, Eric John. BSBA, Calif. State U., Fresno, 1982. Partner, founder Vonda's, Fresno, 1977-87; bridal dir. R.H. Macy Co., Atlanta, 1988-94; pres. Summins Enterprises (doing bus. as Through Looking Glass), Atlanta, 1994—; florist The White House, Washington, 1980. Republican. Presbyterian. Office: Through the Looking Glass 3802 Roswell Rd Atlanta GA 30342

SUMMITT, ALIXANDRA PABLITA, art educator; b. Detroit, Mar. 11, 1943; d. Edmond Walter and Helene Marie (Zapytowski) Greniewicki; m. Hans Peter Jorgensen, July 2, 1964 (div. Mar. 1981); 1 child, Inger Nova. BA, Mich. State U., 1965, MS in Ednl. Systems Devel., 1981, PhD in Adult and Continuing Edn., 1990. Coord. art edn. Bath (Mich.) Consolidated Schs., 1967-68; instr. cmty. svcs. Northwestern Mich. Coll., Traverse City, 1975-78; tchr. art Alan Sch., Lansing, Mich., 1980-81; rsch. asst. Mich. State U. Dept. Pediatrics, East Lansing, 1981-82; supr. media ctr. Mich. State U. Coll. Osteo. Medicine, East Lansing, 1982-86; instr. Lansing C.C., 1983—, faculty curriculum rep. Ctr. for Teaching Excellence, 1996—; CEO Options in Art, East Lansing, 1990—; pres. Alixandra Summit Cons., Inc., Okemos, Mich., 1995—. dir. Summitry Prodns., Okemos, 1996—; art cons. Getty Improving Art Edn., L.A., 1991—; chair, founder Connections Collective Women Artists, East Lansing. Charter mem. Mich. Women's Hall Fame and Hist. Ctr., com. chair 1982—, award design 1983; charter mem. Nat. Mus. Women in Arts, 1991-96, Shri Hearthstone, Inc., 1995—, logo design, 1996; precinct del. Nat. Dem. Party, East Lansing, 1980, commr. Lansing Women's Commn., 1984-85, taskforce on women in poverty , 1985; v.p. Mid-Mich. Assn. Woking Artists, Lansing, 1978-79. Mem. Working Women Artists, Phi Delta Kappa (bd. dirs. 1991—, editor 1994). Home: 1856 Hamilton C-9 Okemos MI 48864 Office: Lansing C C 419 N Capitol Ave Lansing MI 48901

SUMPTER, NANCY HELEN, nurse; b. Balt., July 8, 1954; d. Daniel Henry and Shirley Virginia (Lee) Chetelat; m. Charles Edward Geyer Jr., June 7, 1975 (div. Oct. 1981); 1 child, Patricia Lee; m. Robert Paul Sumpter, Aug. 16, 1986; 1 child, Amanda Lee. AA, Essex C.C., 1974; BSN, Towson State U., 1990. Staff nurse JHH, Balt., 1974-75, Bapt. Med. Ctr., Pensacola, Fla., 1975-76; head nurse Driscoll Children's Hosp., Corpus Christi, Tex., 1977; charge nurse Guam Meml. Hosp., Guam, 1977-79, Jacksonville (Fla.) Children's Hosp., 1979-81; nurse practitioner Johns Hopkins Bayview Med. Ctr., Balt., 1982—, Franklin Square Hosp., Balt., 1991—; instr. neonatal resuscitation provider course, 1991—. Vol. parish nurse St. Peter's Luth. Ch., Balt., 1992-94, pres. sch. bd., 1990-94, mem. ch. coun., 1989-91, col. chmn. pub. rels., 1990—; vol. sch. nurse St. Peter's Christian Sch., Balt., 1991—. Mem. Nat. Assn. Neonatal Nurses, West-East Coast Assn. Neonatal Nurses. Home: 9415 Perglen Rd Baltimore MD 21236-1617 Office: Franklin Square Hosp Franklin Sq Dr Baltimore MD 21237

SUNDERLAND, JACKLYN GILES, former alumni affairs director; b. Corpus Christi, Tex., Oct. 21, 1937; d. Elbert Jackson and Mary Kathryn (Garrett) Giles; m. Joseph Alan MacInnis, Nov. 24, 1963 (div. Feb. 1982); children: Mary Kendall, Jackson Alan; m. Lane Von Sunderland, June 12, 1988. BA, U. Tex., 1960. Editor's asst. House & Garden mag., N.Y.C., 1962; reporter Corpus Christi Caller-Times, 1960, Home Furnishings Daily, Fairchild Publs., N.Y.C., 1961, Houston Post, 1963; writer, rschr. Saudi Press Agy., Washington, 1980; writer/rschr. for V.P. U.S. White House, Washington, 1982-84; dir. pub. affairs President's Com. on Mental Retardation, Washington, 1984-85; dir. speakers bur. Commn. on Bicentennial U.S. Constn., Washington, 1985-87; speechwriter Sec. of HHS, Washington, 1987-88, U.S. Sec. of Labor, Washington, 1989; dir. alumni affairs Knox Coll., Galesburg, Ill., 1990-92. Campaign chmn. Am. Cancer Soc., Corpus Christi, 1961; liaison Am. Embassy, Copenhagen, 1965-68; docent, tchr. art Nat. Gallery and Smithsonian Mus., Washington, 1970-73; vestrywoman Grace Episcopal Ch., Galesburg, 1991; mem. Jr. League Washington, 1963—. Recipient Continental Marine citation for community svc., Camp Pendleton, Calif., 1977. Republican. Home: 185 Park Ln Galesburg IL 61401

SUNDERLAND, KIMBERLY ANN, editor; b. Annapolis, Md., Feb. 10, 1961; d. William Richard and Elizabeth Edith (Rabe) S.; children: Murphy, Taylor and Casey. BA in Comm., George Mason U., 1988. Freelance writer The Fairfax Connection, Va., 1987-88; staff writer Washington Bus. Jour., Vienna, Va., 1988-89, Roanoke Times & World News, Christiansburg, Va., 1989-92, Washington Bus. Jour., Arlington, Va., 1992-94; editor Telecom Pub. Group, Alexandria, Va., 1994, mng. editor, 1994-95, exec. editor, 1995—. Sec. Second Cardinal Glen Home Owners Assn., 1994—; writer Fairfax County Mothers of Multiples Newsletter, 1994—. Mem. Nat. Press Club, Newsletter Pub. Assn. Office: Telecom Pub Group 1101 King St Ste 444 Alexandria VA 22314

SUNDERMAN, DEBORAH ANN, clothing designer and manufacturer; b. Detroit, Feb. 21, 1955; d. Eugene Wayne Sunderman and Nancy May (Reams) Sunderman-Elert. BS magna cum laude, No. Mich. U., 1978. Design instr. Newbury Coll., Boston, 1978-82, 92-93; asst. to designers Clothware, Boston, 1978-82; designer, ptnr. Toute Nue Swimwear, Boston, 1982; designer Mast Industries, The Limited, Woburn, Mass., 1982-83; designer, founder Deborah Mann & Co., Boston, 1983—; instr. fashion Mt. Ida Coll., Newton, Mass., 1991. Designer garment The Fiberarts Design Book, 1980. Organizer Neighborhood Crime Watch Group, Rossmore Rd., Boston, 1989-90. Recipient 2d Pl. award Peter White Art Exhibit, Marquette, Mich., 1978, Fresh Start award Self Mag., Washington, 1985; named one of Boston's Most Interesting Women, Boston Woman Mag., 1990. Mem. Ft. Pointe Arts Cmty., Fashion Group of Boston (bd. dirs.). Office: Deborah Mann & Co 1691B Massachusetts Ave Cambridge MA 02138-1842

SUNDQUIST, LEAH RENATA, physical education specialist; b. El Paso, Tex., July 22, 1963; d. Dominic Joseph and Patricia Ann (Manley) Bernardi; m. David Curtis Sundquist, June 23, 1990. AA, N.Mex. Mil. Inst., 1983; BS, U. Tex., El Paso, 1986; MEd in Curriculum & Instrn., City U., Bellevue, Wash., 1996. Field exec. Rio Grande Girl Scout Coun., El Paso, 1983-84; customer teller M-Bank, El Paso, 1984-85; soccer coach St. Clements Sch., El Paso, 1985; substitute tchr. El Paso Sch. Dist., 1986; commd. 2nd lt. U.S. Army, 1983, advanced through grades to capt., 1990-91; plans/exercise officer U.S. Army, Ft. Lewis, Wash., 1990; ops. officer U.S. Army, Ft. Lewis, 1990-1991; comdr. hdqs. Hdqs. Co. 141st Support Bn. U.S. Army N.G., 1996—; dir. Childrens World Learning Ctr., Federal Way, Wash., 1992-94; phys. edn. specialist, tchr. K-6 Kent (Wash.) Elem. Sch., 1995—. Coord. Nat. Conf. Christians and Jews, El Paso, 1979-81; v.p. Jr. Achievement, El Paso, 1980-81; adult tng. vol. Girl Scout Coun., bd. dirs. Pacific Peaks coun., 1993—, chair nominating com., 1996, jr. troop Girl Scout leader totem Girl Scout Coun., 1996; bd. dir. Jr. League Tacoma, 1993, 94. 3rd Res. Officer Tng. Corps scholar, 1981-83, H.P. Saunder scholar, 1982; recipient Humanitarian Svc. medal Great Fires of Yellowstone, U.S. Army, 1988, Gold award Girl Scouts U.S.A., 1981; decorated Nat. Def. Svc. medal Desert Storm; meritorius Svc. medal, 1991. Mem. NEA, Wash. Edn. Assn., Assn. U.S. Army, Air Def. Artillery Assn., Fellowship Christian Athletes, Zeta Tau Alpha (sec. 1983-85, house mgr. 1984-86). Republican. Roman Catholic. Home: 2905 N 14th St Tacoma WA 98406-6905

SUPPA-FRIEDMAN, JANICE DESTEFANO, secondary school educator; b. Morristown, N.J., Apr. 27, 1943; d. Eugene Arthur and Isabella Vienna (Bottiglia) DeS.; m. Dennis Ralph Suppa, June 28, 1964 (div. May 1994); children: Julie Ann, Chad Dennis; m. Michael Jac Friedman, Oct. 7, 1995. BS in Edn., Bowling Green State U., 1964; MA in Edn., Va. Poly. Inst. & State U., 1977, postgrad., 1990—. Cert. secondary tchr., Va. Tchr. English and reading Northwood (Ohio) Jr. High Sch., 1964-66; tchr. English and history Canaseraga (N.Y.) Ctrl. Schs., 1966-67; tchr. English and reading Marstellar Jr. High Sch., Manassas, Va., 1967-72; tchr. English Taylor Jr. High sch., Warrenton, Va., 1973-74; tchr. English and reading, writing specialist, dept. head, lead tchr. Brentsville Dist. Mid.-Sr. High Sch., Nokesville, Va., 1975—; cons. to coll. bd.; reader for advanced placement literature and composition exam, 1996. Editor newsletter Spinning Wheel, 1991-94; contbr. articles to profl. jours. Va. Comm. of the Arts grantee, 1994-95, grantee Edn. Found., 1995—. Mem. ASCD, NATE (pres. 1992-94), Nat. Coun. Tchrs. English (coord. Va. state Achievement in Writing awards 1995—), Va. Assn. Tchr. English (exec. bd., Svc. award 1993), Phi Delta Kappa. Office: Brenstville Dist Mid-Sr HS 12109 Aden Rd Nokesville VA 22123-2340

SURBECK-HARRIS, JOYCE ANNETTE, special education administrator; b. Jacksonville, Ill., July 21, 1947; d. Myrl Guy and Audrey G. (Black) Surbeck; m. Andrew O. Harris. BS in Edn., Ill. State U., 1974, EdD, 1992; MS in Edn., So. Ill. U., 1976. Cert. tchr.and adminstr., Ill. Program specialist 4 Rivers Spl. Edn., Jacksonville, 1976-79; instr. MacMurray Coll., Jacksonville, 1979-80; program coord. Macon-Piatt Spl. Edn., Decatur, Ill., 1981-83; tchr. Jacksonville Pub. Schs., 1983-84; edn. coord. Family Svcs. and Vis. Nurses Assn. Project Head Start, Alton, Ill., 1984-87; mgr. Ill. State Bd. Edn., Springfield, Ill., 1987-88; state coord. deaf-blind Minn. Dept. of Edn., St. Paul, 1989—, cons., 1990—; adj. prof. Ill. Coll., Jacksonville, 1980-87; owner Surbeck & Assocs., St. Paul, 1987—; cons. in field. Author: Implemting SLD Criteria, 1992; co-author: Behavior Disorders in Ealry Childhood, 1986; producer tng. video tapes. Developer various parent support programs, Ill, 1973—, Children Linking Families, Minn., 1990. U.S. Office of Edn. grantee, 1989, 90, 91, 92. Mem. Coun. for Exceptional Children, Coun. for Admisntrs. Spl. Edn.

SURGENT, SUSAN PEARL, benefits consultant; b. Binghamton, N.Y., Jan. 6, 1963; d. Victor J. and Joan A. (Linville) Courtney; m. David M. Surgent, Sept. 7, 1985. AAS in Bus., Broome C.C., Binghamton, 1982; BS in Applied Social Sci magna cum laude, Binghamton U., 1993. Notary pub., N.Y. Mktg. asst. Johnson Camping, Inc., Binghamton, 1982-84; employment asst. CAE-Link Corp., Binghamton, 1984-85, adminstr. facility benefits, 1985-90, adminstr. corp. benefits, 1990-94; regional sales mgr. Prepaid Health Plan, Binghamton, N.Y., 1994—. Vol. educator Sch. and Bus. Alliance, Broome and Tioga counties, 1992—. Mem. Internat. Soc. Employee Benefit Profls., Golden Key, Phi Theta Kappa. Democrat. Episcopalian. Home: 93 Albany Ave Johnson City NY 13790-1503 Office: Prepaid Health Plan 49 Court St Binghamton NY 13901-3236

SURIANO, PHYLLIS, paralegal; b. Phoenixville, Pa., June 14, 1955; d. Peter Anthony and Esther Rita (Eagano) S.; m. Samuel Glen Murphy (div. Sept. 1980); 1 child, Samuel G., Jr.; m. James Francis Carney, Nov. 23, 1982. Cert., Mainline Paralegal Inst., Wayne, Pa., 1981. Lic. real estate agt., Pa. Real estate agt. Re/Max, Norristown, Pa., 1987-90; scheduler Montgomery County Ct. Common Pleas, Norristown, 1991-96, family ct. supr., 1996—. Active Dem. Com., Chester County, Pa., 1981; legis. dir. LWV, Lansdalec Pa., 1988; vol. literacy tutor. Republican. Home: 217 E Poplar St Norristown PA 19401 Office: Montgomery County Ct Common Pleas Ct House Norristown PA 19404

SURLES, CAROL D., university president; b. Pensacola, Fla., Oct. 7, 1946; d. Elza Allen and Versy Lee Smith; divorced; children: Lisa Surles, Philip Surles. BA, Fisk U., 1968; MA, Chapman Coll., 1971; PhD, U. Mich., 1978. Personnel rep. U. Mich., Ann Arbor, 1973-78; vice chancellor-adminstrn. U. Mich., Flint, 1987-89; exec. asst. to pres., assoc. v.p. for human resources U. Ctrl. Fla., Orlando, 1978-87; v.p. acad. affairs Jackson State U., Miss., 1989-92; v.p. adminstrn. and bus. Calif. State U., Hayward, 1992-94; pres. Tex. Woman's U., Denton, Dallas, Houston, 1994—. Trustee Pub. Broadcasting Ch. 24, Orlando, 1985-87; bd. dirs. First State Bank, Denton, Tex., Tex.-N.Mex. Power Co., TNP-Enterprise. Recipient Outstanding Scholar's award Delta Tau Kappa, 1983. Mem. AAUW, Am. Assn. Colls. and Univs., Golden Key Honor Soc., Mortar Bd. Soc., Dallas Citizens' Coun., Dallas Women's Found., Coun. of Pres. (Austin, Tex.), Phi Kappa Phi, Alpha Kappa Alpha. Methodist.

SURMA, JANE ANN, secondary education educator; b. Chgo., Dec. 11, 1947; d. John James and Genevieve (Buettner) S. BS, Barry U., Miami, Fla., 1969; MST, U. Ill., 1974. Tchr. phys. edn. Little Flower H.S., Chgo., 1969-72; tchr. English, phys. edn. and health, coach Oak Lawn (Ill.) Cmty. H.S., 1974—. Named Coach of Yr. Southtown Economist, 1992, Boy's Volleyball Ill. State Championship Coach, 1994, Fred Parks Coach of Yr., 1995. Mem. AAHPERD, Ill. H.S. Coaches Assn., Ill. H.S. Assn., Nat. Coun. Tchrs. English. Roman Catholic. Office: Oak Lawn Cmty HS Oak Lawn IL 60453

SURPRENANT, KATHRYN WHEELER, special education educator; b. Seattle, Wash., Feb. 7, 1958; d. Lyle Duane and Patricia Ann (Willey) Wheeler; m. James John Surprenant, Apr. 12, 1980; children: Andrew, Aimee, Eric. BA, U. So. Fla., 1980, postgrad., 1996. Cert. tchr., Fla. Sales rep. Allstate Ins., Englewood, Fla., 1989-92; tchr. Charlotte County Schs., Port Charlotte, Fla., 1994—. Author: portfolio of spl. edn., 1995. Tchr. Englewood United Meth. Ch., 1990-92. Scholar Englewood United Meth. Ch., 1994. Mem. Phi Kappa Phi.

SURPRISE, JUANEE, chiropractor, nutrition consultant; b. Gary, Ind., Apr. 28, 1944; d. Glenn Mark and Willia Ross (Vasser) Surprise; m. Peter E. Coakley, Feb. 12, 1966 (div. Jan. 1976); children: Thaddeus, Mariah, Darius; m. Robert T.Howell, Feb. 24, 1984. RN, Phila. Gen. Hosp. Sch. Nursing, 1965; DrChiropractic summa cum laude, Life Chiropractic Coll, Marietta, Ga., 1981. Diplomate Nat. Bd. Chiropractic Bd. Nutrition, Am. Acad. Pain Mgmt.; cert. clin. nutritionist; cert. in acupuncture, Thompson technique, Nimmo receptor tonus technique. Staff nurse Children's Hosp., Balt., 1966-67; charge nurse Melrose (Mass.)-Wakefield Hosp., 1967-68; hosp. adminstr. Animal Hosp. of Wakefield, Mass., 1967-79; chiropractor Chiropractic Clinic of Greenville, N.C., 1982-84, Chiropractice Rehab. Clinic, Denton, Tex., 1984—. Mem., chmn. Cmty. Planning Commn., North Reading, Mass., 1976-79; chmn. bldg. com. Immaculate Conception Ch., Denton, 1987-90, parish coun., 1990-92. Mem. ACA Coun. on Nutrition (sec.-treas.), Internat. and Am. Assns. Clin. Nutritionists, Internat. Assn. Pain Mgmt., Am. Chiropractic Assn., Am. Chiropractic Bd. on Nutrition (pres.), Tex. Chiropractic Assn., Tex. Chiropractic Assn. Coun. on Nutrition (sec.-treas.), Pi Tau Delta. Republican. Roman Catholic. Office: Chiropractic Rehabs Clinic 1100 Dallas Dr Denton TX 76205-5153

SUSANKA, SARAH HILLS, architect; b. Bromley, Kent, England, Mar. 21, 1957; d. Brian and Margaret (Hampson) Hills; m. Lawrence A. Susanka, July 4, 1980 (div. May 1984); m. James Robert Larson, Sept. 4, 1988. BArch, U. Oreg., 1978; MArch, U. Minn., 1983. Registered architect. Prin. Mulfinger, Susanka, Mahady & Ptnrs., Mpls., 1983—; Contbr. articles to profl. jours. Mem. AIA Minn. Home: 70 Upper Afton Ter Saint Paul MN 55106 Office: Mulfinger Susanka Mahady & Ptnrs 43 Main St SE Minneapolis MN 55414-1029

SUSKI, SHERRIE LEIGH, human resources specialist; b. Clearwater, Fla., June 29, 1960; d. H. Mark and Sandy Ann (Tyler) Sherwood; m. Edward Daniel Suski, Apr. 16, 1988. BS in Psychology cum laude, U. Calif., Irvine, 1982; MS in Psychology, Calif. State U., 1985. Human resources positions including staffing, employee rels., tng. and compensation, benefits Silicon Systems, Tustin, Calif., 1983-93; dir. human resources SmartFlex Systems, Tustin, Calif., 1993—. Mem. ASTD, Pers. and Indsl. Rels. Assn., Am. Compensation Assn., Phi Beta Kappa, Alpha Lambda Delta. Office: SmartFlex Systems 14312 Franklin Ave Tustin CA 92680-7028

SUSKO, CAROL LYNNE, lawyer, accountant; b. Washington, Dec. 5, 1955; d. Frank and Helen Louise (Davis) S. BS in Econs. and Acctg., George Mason U., 1979; JD, Cath. U., 1982; LLM in Taxation, Georgetown U., 1992. Bar: Pa. 1989, D.C. 1990; CPA, Va., Md. Tax acct. Reznick Fedder & Silverman, P.C., Bethesda, Md., 1984-85; sr. tax acct. Pannell Kerr Forster, Alexandria, Va., 1985; tax specialist Coopers & Lybrand, Washington, 1985-87; supervisory tax sr. Frank & Co., McLean, Va., 1987-88; editorial staff Tax Notes Mag., Arlington, Va., 1989-90; adj. faculty Am. U., Washington, 1989—; tax atty. Marriott Corp., Washington, 1993-94; tax mgr. Host Marriott Inc., Washington, 1994—. Mem. ABA, AICPAs, Va. Soc. CPAs, D.C. Soc. CPAs, D.C. Bar Assn., Women's Bar Assn. of D.C., Am. Assn. Atty.-CPAs. Office: Host Marriott Dept 910 10400 Fernwood Rd Washington DC 20058

SUSSE, SANDRA SLONE, lawyer; b. Medford, Ma., June 1, 1943; d. James Robert and Georgie Coffin (Bradshaw) Slone; m. Peter Susse, May 10, 1969 (div. May 1993); 1 child, Toby. BA, U. Mass., 1981; JD, Vt. Law Sch., 1986. Bar: Mass. 1986, U.S. Dist. Ct. Mass. 1988, U.S. Ct. Appeals (1st cir.) 1995. Staff atty. Western Mass. Legal Svcs., Springfield, 1986—. Mem. ABA, Mass. Bar Assn., Women's Bar Assn. Mass. Office: Western Mass Legal Svcs 145 State St Springfield MA 01103

SUSSMAN, DEBORAH EVELYN, designer, company executive; b. N.Y.C., May 26, 1931; d. Irving and Ruth (Golomb) S.; m. Paul Prejza, June 28, 1972. Student Bard Coll., 1948-50, Inst. Design, Chgo., 1950-53, Black Mountain Coll., 1950, Hochschule für Gestaltung Ulm, Fed. Republic

Germany, 1957-58. Art dir. Office of Charles and Ray Eames, Venice, Calif., 1953-57, 61-67; graphic designer Galeries Lafayette, Paris, 1959-60; prin. Deborah Sussman and Co., Santa Monica, Calif., 1968-80; founder, pres. Sussman-Prejza and Co., Inc., Santa Monica, 1980-90, Culver City, Calif., 1990—; spkr., lectr. UCLA Sch. Architecture, Archtl. League N.Y.C., Smithsonian Inst., Stanford Conf. on Design, Am. Inst. Graphic Arts Nat. Conf. at MIT, Design Mgmt. Inst. Conf., Mass.; spl. guest Internat. Design Conf., Aspen, Colo., Fulbright lectr., India, 1976; spkr. NEA Adv. Coun., 1985, Internat. Coun. Shopping Ctrs., 1986, USIA Design in Am. seminar, Budapest, Hungary, 1988; one-woman shows include Visual Arts Mus. Sch. Visual Arts, N.Y.C., 1995; participant exhbn., Moscow, 1989, Walker Art Ctr., Mpls., 1989. Mem. editl. adv. bd. Arts and Architecture Mag., 1981-85, Calif. Mag., Architecture Calif. Fulbright grantee Hochschule für Gestaltung Ulm, 1957-58; recipient numerous awards AIA Nat. Inst. Honors, 1985, 88, Am. Inst. Graphic Arts, Calif. Coun. AIA, Comms. Arts Soc., L.A. County Bd. Suprs., Vesta award Women's Bldg. L.A. Fellow Soc. Environ. Graphic Design; mem. AIA (hon.), Am. Inst. Graphic Arts (bd. dirs. 1982-85, founder L.A. chpt., chmn., 1983-84, numerous awards), Am. Ctr. Design (hon.), L.A. Art Dirs. Club (bd. dirs., numerous awards), Alliance Graphique Internat. (elect. mem.), Architects, Designers and Planners Social Responsibility, Calif. Women in Environ. Design (adv. bd.), Trusteeship (affiliate Internat. Women's Forum, chmn.'s circle Town Hall). Democrat. Jewish. Avocation: photography. Office: Sussman/Prejza & Co Inc 3960 Ince Blvd Culver City CA 90232-2635

SUTCLIFFE, MARION SHEA, writer; b. Washington, July 29, 1918; d. James William and Ida (Hewitt) Shea; m. James Montgomery Sutcliffe, Aug. 23, 1941; 1 child, Jill Marion. BMus, Boston Conservatory Music, 1956-60; EdM, Boston State Coll., 1969. Cert. music, English, psychology and reading tchr., Mass. Tchr. Milford (Mass.) Pub. Schs., 1966-70; tchr. music Worcester (Mass.) Pub. Schs., 1970-71; reading tchr. Natick and Newton (Mass.) Pub. Schs., 1971-73; real estate developer Sutcliffe Family Trust, South Dennis, Mass., 1969—; developer Delray Beach Club, Dennisport, Mass.; mfr. A&A Assocs., South Dennis, 1989—; dir., sec. bd. mgrs. The Soundings Resort, Dennisport, Mass., 1990—. Songwriter Diablo, 1954. Founder, mgr. Boston Women's Symphony, 1962-66. Fuller grantee New England Conservatory, 1957, grantee State Mass., 1957. Mem. AAUW, DAR, Nat. Am. Theatre Organ Soc., Ea. Mass. Am. Theatre Organ Soc. (bd. dirs. 1989-92), Organ-Aires (v.p. 1991—), West Dennis Garden Club, Amateur Organists Assn. Internat. Episcopalian. Home: 145 Cove Rd South Dennis MA 02660-3515 Office: 60 Macarthur Rd Natick MA 01760-2938

SUTCLIFFE, MARY OGDEN, clinical social worker; b. Chgo., June 9, 1928; d. Dana Presley and Vera Marie (Gassman) Ogden; m. Herbert Alfred Sutcliffe, Oct. 30, 1963; children: Stephen, Timothy, James, Penney Stahl. AA, Colby/Sawyer Coll., 1948; BS in Journalism, Syracuse U., 1950; MSW, Howard U., 1967. Cert. clin. social worker. Asst. editor House & Garden Mag., N.Y.C., 1949-51; reporter Bay News, East Meadow, N.Y., 1956-58; chief social worker Cmty. Mental Health Clinic, Manassus, Va., 1967-72, Children & Youth Health Ctr., Exeter, N.H., 1978-82, Rockingham Child and Family Svc., 1982-88; assoc. prof. psychology Garrett Coll., Oakland, Md., 1989-93; clin. social worker pvt. practice, Bethesda, Md., 1972-78, Durham, N.H., 1978-88, Oakland, Md., 1988—. Sec. Rep. Club, Port Washington, L.I., N.Y., 1972; v.p. Garrett County Alliance for Mentally Ill. Mem. AAUW (pres. 1961), Toastmasters (v.p. 1988), Pi Beta Phi. Home: 392 Lake Shore Dr Oakland MD 21550 Office: PO Box 635 Mc Henry MD 21541

SUTER, ANNE SNELL, information specialist, writer, editor; b. Brookings, S.D., June 20, 1945; d. Floyd Franklin and Mary Helen (Hagen) Snell; m. Glen Hunter Suter, Apr. 13, 1967 (div. Oct. 1982); children: Laura Anne, Andrea Kay. BS in Liberal Arts, U. Iowa, 1967, MA in Libr. Sci., 1971; EDS in Media, U. Ga., 1976; MBA, Pepperdine U., 1990. Instr. libr. sci. Albany (Ga.) State Coll., 1971-72; sys. media coord. Worth County Bd. Edn., Sylvester, Ga., 1972-76; fed. programs coord. County Bd. Edn., Social Circle, Ga., 1976-78; adminstrv. mgr. Northrop Svcs. Inc., San Jose, Calif., 1979-93; info. specialist, assoc. Boster, Kobayashi & Assocs., Livermore, Calif., 1994—; owner, mgr. Write Words, Pleasanton, Calif., 1993—. Bd. dirs. Keystone Adult Learning Ctr., Pleasanton, 1991-93; pres. Libr. League, Pleasanton, 1986; founder Nursing Home Vols., Sylvester, 1974-76; vol. Girl Scouts, Ga., Calif., 1973-81. Mem. NAFE, Spl. Libr. Assn. Home: 4424 Del Valle Pky Pleasanton CA 94566

SUTER, PEGGY JEAN, library director; b. Wilburton, Okla., July 18, 1937; d. Henry Paul and Violet Jessie Eads; m. James William Suter, May 15, 1954; children: Pauline Jeanette Owens, Jo Lavonne Ahlm. Grad., Hartshorne (Okla.) H.S., 1955. Cert. grade I libr., N.Mex. Piano tchr. Lovington, N.Mex., 1968-72, Eunice, N.Mex., 1973-88; kindergarten music tchr. First Meth. Ch., Lovington, 1970-73; substitute sch. tchr. Eunice Pub. Schs., 1978-81; libr. dir. Eunice Pub. Libr., 1981—. Organist First Meth. Ch., Eunice, 1982—. Mem. Am. Libr. Assn., N.Mex. Libr. Assn. (community Svc. award 1992), Lea County Libr. Assn. (v.p. 1982, pres. 1983, treas. 1984). Democrat. Methodist. Office: Eunice Pub Libr Corner of 10th and Ave Eunice NM 88231

SUTHERLAND, ELIZABETH ANN, artist, painter; b. Takoma Park, Md., Apr. 4, 1954; d. William Harrison and Betsy Hart (McCann) S.; m. Paul Henry Daniel Kaplan, June 8, 1981; 1 child, Daniel Robert. BFA in Painting, Boston U., 1979; MFA in Painting, Tyler Sch. of Art, 1981. Instr. painting Tyler Sch. of Art, Phila., 1981; instr. painting Wake Forest U., Venice, Italy, 1984, Winston-Salem, N.C., 1982, 83, 87; instr. painting SUNY, Purchase, 1993; pres. Artworks Gallery, Winston-Salem, 1987-88. One woman show includes Hanes Art Gallery, U. N.C., 1988; exhibited in group shows at N.C. Mus. of Art, 1987, Cork Gallery Lincoln Ctr., 1990, Marymount Manhattan Coll. 1996. Recipient Secca 7 XII fellow, 1988; grad. sch. fellowships Tyler Sch. of Art, 1980-81, 79-80. Democrat.

SUTHERLAND, JULIA KATHERINE, public relations executive; b. Galax, Va., July 11, 1956; d. Horace Fulton and Edna Earl (Rickman) S. AB in Govt., Sweet Briar Coll., 1978. Paralegal Hall & Hall, Richmond, Va., 1980-81; dept. press sec. Va. Gov. Charles S. Robb, Richmond, 1982-85; policy analyst Va. Dept. Commerce, Richmond, 1985-86; dir. comms. Va. Dept. Health Regulatory Bds., Richmond, 1986, Democratic Party of Va., Richmond, 1986-88; pres. sec. Robb for U.S. Senate Campaign, Richmond, 1988, U.S. Senator Charles S. Robb, Washington, 1989-90; v.p. Fleishman-Hillard, Washington, 1990-93; sr. v.p. Powell Tate, Washington, 1993—. Vol. Robb for Gov. Campaign, Richmond, 1981; fund agent class of 1978 Sweet Briar Coll., 1988-93, reunion gift com. co-chair, 1993. Mem. Senate Press Secs. Assn., Richmond Sweet Briar Alumnae Club (treas. 1979), Washington Sweet Briar Almnae Club. Democrat. Presbyterian. Office: Powell Tate 700 13th St NW # 1000 Washington DC 20005

SUTHERLAND, LISA JO, legislative staff member; b. Dayton, Ohio, Nov. 29, 1956; d. George H. and Gerene R. (Koepke) O.; m. Scott A. Sutherland, Aug. 29, 1987. BA, Drake U., Des Moines, 1979; JD, U. Wash., 1987. Assoc. Birch, Horton, Bittner and Perkins Cole, Anchorage, Alaska, 1986; legis. aid Alaska Rep. Steven Roger, Juneau, 1986; legis. aid, asst. majority leader U.S. Senate; legis. dir. U.S. Senator Ted Stevens, Washington, chief staff; cons. Bristol Bay Native Corp., Anchorage, 1984. V.p. Courtland Civic Assn., Arlington, Va., 1994-95. Republican. Lutheran. Home: 1209 N Danville St Arlington VA 22201 Office: US Senator Ted Stevens 522 Hart Senate Office Bldg Washington DC 20510

SUTHERLAND, REBEKAH ERNST, academic administrator; b. Kingsport, Tenn., Apr. 10, 1954; d. Philip F. III and Jeree Gayle (Leeper) Ernst; m. James M. Sutherland, Aug. 6, 1976; children: Timothy, Jeremy. B of Biology, Emory and Henry Coll., 1976; MEd, U. S.C., 1995. Cert. postgrad. profl. tchr. Sci. tchr. Bristol (Tenn.) H.S., 1976-78; transcriptionist J. E.--Ct. Reporter, Abingdon, Va., 1978-87; computer cons. Cherry Tree Software, Bristol, Va., 1987-89; human resources profl. Gen. Physics, Aiken, S.C., 1990-91; tchr. sci. and health St. Mary's Sch., Aiken, 1991-94; evening supr. U. S.C., Aiken, 1994-96; dir. A Better Choice Sch., Aiken, 1994—. Patentee Soft Smock, 1989; composer, performer: (mus. rec.) Husbands and From Fetus Flown, 1987. Bryan Foods Ednl. grantee Bryan Foods, Inc., 1993. Mem. NAFE, Nat. Sci. Tchrs. Assn. Republican. Office: ABCS PO Box 5482 Aiken SC 29804-5482

SUTHERLAND, SUSAN J., lawyer; b. Canton, Ohio, 1957. BA, Denison Coll., 1979; JD, NYU, 1982. Bar: N.Y. 1983. Ptnr. Skadden, Arps, Slate, Meagher & Flom, N.Y.C. Office: Skadden Arps Slate Meagher & Flom 919 3d Ave New York NY 10022*

SUTHERLAND, YVETTE FAUSTINA, emergency room nurse; b. Biabou St. Vincent, W.I., Nov. 13, 1944; came to U.S., 1976; d. Enos Regisford and Rosilda Imelda Sutherland. BS, Coll. St. Francis, Joliet, Ill., 1985. Cert. ACLS, BLS, emergency nurse, Ill.; RN, Ind.; cert. midwife, Eng., Wales; cert. mobile intensive care nurse. Nurse Queen Victoria Hosp., Sussex, Eng., 1967-69, Farnborough Hosp., Kent, Eng., 1970-72; postgrad. psychiat. nurse St. Clement's Hosp., London, 1972; midwife Farnborough Hosp., Kent, Eng., 1973-75; emergency dept. nurse St. Andrew's Hosp., London, 1975-76; emergency dept. staff nurse Northwest Family Hosp., Gary, Ind., 1976—, acting head nurse, 1985-86; planner/presenter workshop: Child Sexual Abuse, 1985; presenter workshop: Sudden Infant Death Syndrome, 1985; lectr. in field. Hosp. rep. Sexual Abuse Task Force, Gary, 1984-86; mem. Northwest Hosp. Choir, Gary, 1988—; mem. Episcopal Cmty. Svcs., Gary, 1994; sponsor mother World Vision, Calif.-Haiti, 1986—. Mem. Emergency Nurses Assn. Home: PO Box 4315 Gary IN 46404-0315

SUTHERLAND-SMITH, PATRICIA JEAN, mathematics educator secondary level; b. Bryn Mawr, Pa., Sept. 3, 1956; d. Robert Lyle and Mary Louise (Prutton) Sutherland; m. Allan David Smith, Sept. 15, 1984. BA in Polit. Sci., Pa. State U., 1979; cert. of completion, U. Paris Sorbonne, France, 1981; MS in Internat. Rels., Pub. Adminstrn., U. So. Calif., 1982; MEd in Math., Widener U., 1985. Instr. English Bourghiba Inst. Langs., Tunis, Tunisia, 1981-82; adminstrv. asst. Societé Arabfact, Paris, 1983; math. tchr. Dallastown (Pa.) Area Sch. Dist., 1985-87, Pennsbury Sch. Dist., Fairless Hills, Pa., 1987—; mem. Pennsbury H.S. site based mgmt. team, Fairless Hills, 1993-96, chmn. 1995-96. Treas. Langhorne Manor (Pa.) Sewer Authority, 1990—. Mem. NEA, Pa. State Edn. Assn., Pennsbury Edn. Assn. (sec. 1994-97), Nat. Coun. Tchrs. of Math., Pa. Coun. Tchrs. of Math., Bucks County Coun. Tchrs. of Math. Office: Pennsbury HS 705 Hood Blvd Fairless Hills PA 19030-3115

SUTLIN, VIVIAN, advertising executive; b. Chgo.; d. Samuel E. and Doris (Weinberg) S. BA, Roosevelt U. V.p. creative group head Grey North Advt., Inc., Chgo.; v.p. creative dir., founder Pilot Products, Inc., Chgo.; TV writer, producer Grey Advt., Inc., N.Y.; sr. writer Young and Rubicam, Inc., N.Y.; v.p. creative dir. Dodge and Delano, N.Y.; pres. Vivian Sutlin Advt., new products and consumer packaged goods specialist with full svc. TV and print, domestic and internat. ops.; creative supr. William Douglas McAdams, Inc., N.Y., Grey Med. Advt., Inc., N.Y.; pres. Vivian Sutlin Comm.; cons. Consumer and Med./Pharm. Advt.; pres. Signature Products East, N.Y.C. Co-author: Industry Women Speak Out. Recipient Chgo. Fedn. Advt. Clubs award, Am. TV Commls. Festival award, TV award Art Dirs. Club Chgo., Triangle award Med. Advt. Print, Internat. Broadcasting award, Best of Decade award RX Club, Guacaipuro TV award.

SUTPHEN, MARTHA RUSK, English language educator; b. St. Louis, Mo., May 17, 1930; d. Howard A. and Gladys (Houx) Rusk; m. Preston L. Sutphen, Oct. 9, 1953 (dec. May 1996); children: Susan Sutphen Slowinski, Lucy Sutphen, Mary Sutphen, Ann Sutphen. BA in French Lit., Smith Coll., Northampton, Mass., 1951; MS in Edn., Fordham U., N.Y.C., 1993. Cert. tchr., N.Y.C., N.Y.S. Case officer CIA, Washington, D.C., 1951-53; devel. dir. The Buckley Sch., N.Y.C., 1972-78; dir. Intersch. Program, N.Y.C., 1978-84; English tchr. Julie Richman H.S., N.Y.C., 1985-93, Talent Unlimited H.S., N.Y.C., 1994—; trustee Spence Sch., N.Y.C., 1968-78. Dir. Maternity Assn. Dir., N.Y.C., 1976-86, Yorkville Civic Commn., N.Y.C., 1982-94. Home: 49 E 96th St PHA New York NY 10125 Office: Talent Unlimited HS 300 E 68th St New York NY 10021

SUTTON, AMY CATHERINE, graphic artist; b. Bishop, Calif., June 26, 1978; d. Michael Robert and Catherine Anne (Reynolds) S. Student, Kent State U., 1995—. Activities editor Spark, West Chester, Ohio, 1993-94, mng. editor, 1994-95; graphic artist Burr, Kent, Ohio, 1995—, on-line editor, 1996; graphic artist Daily Kent Stater, 1995—, graphics editor, 1996. Pub., editor Lakota H.S. PTO, West Chester, 1994-95, Ohio Prins.' Ctr., West Chester, 1994-95. Helen Carringer Honors scholar, 1995-96, 96-97. Mem. Women in Comms., Inc. (v.p. newsletter 1995—). Home: 7777 E Whitehall Cir West Chester OH 45069

SUTTON, BETTY SHERIFF, elementary education educator; b. Orangeburg, S.C., Jan. 16, 1933; d. Luther Doyle and Mattie (White) Sheriff; m. William Bryan Nunn, June 19, 1954; 1 child, Lisbeth Sheriff Nunn (Mrs. William Reid Clark); m. James Carlton Sutton, Dec. 28, 1979. Student, Columbia Coll., 1949-52; BS, U. S.C., 1953. Tchr. grade 4 State of S.C. Pub. Sch., Blackville, 1953-54; tchr. grade 2 Dream Lake Elem. Sch., Apopka, Fla., 1954-64; tchr. spl. edn. Leon County Sch., Tallahassee, Fla., 1965-66; page mother Fla. Ho. Reps., Tallahassee, 1966-67; tchr. grade 3 Timberlane Elem. Sch./Leon County Schs., Tallahassee, 1967-71; tchr. grades 3 and 4 Golfview Elem. Sch./Brevard County Schs., Rockledge, Fla., 1972-86; tchr. grade 1 Cambridge Elem. Sch./Brevard County Schs., Cocoa, Fla., 1987—; pres. Bits of Brevard, Inc., Rockledge. Chmn. Democrats for Conner, 1988, Keep Brevard Beautiful, 1990; active Brevard Symphony Orch. Guild, Brevard Mus. Guild, 1973—, Brevard Heritage Coun., Inc., Episcopal, St. Marks Guild. Recipient S.C. Forestry award State of S.C. Forestry Commn., 1977; ART grantee J. Paul Getty Ctr. for Edn. in the Arts, 1990. Mem. AAUW (pres. 1968-70), Apopka Woman's Club (pres. 1960-62), Apopka Garden Club, Brevard Reading Coun. (v.p. 1980-82), Am. Mothers, Inc., Columbia Coll. Column Club, Columbia Coll. Alumni Club. Ctrl. Fla., U. S.C. Alumni Club (life), Country Club of Rockledge, Delta Kappa Gamma (pres. 1992-94). Home: 1807 Rockledge Dr Rockledge FL 32955-4909

SUTTON, BEVERLY JEWELL, psychiatrist; b. Rockford, Mich., May 27, 1932; d. Beryl Dewey and Cora Belle (Potes) Jewell; m. Harry Eldon Sutton, July 7, 1962; children: Susan, Caroline. MD, U. Mich., 1957. Diplomate Am. Bd. Pediatrics, Am. Bd. Psychiatry and Neurology. Rotating intern St. Joseph Mercy Hosp., Ann Arbor, Mich., 1958; resident in child psychiatry Hawthorne Ctr., Northville, Mich., 1958-62; resident in pediatrics U. Hosp./U. Mich. Med. Ctr., Ann Arbor, 1959-61; resident in psychiatry Austin (Tex.) State Hosp., 1962-64, dir. children's svc., 1964-89, dir. psychitric residency program, 1989—, dir. tng. and rsch., 1993—; cons. in field. Contbr. articles to profl. jours. Active numerous civic orgns. Recipient Outstanding Achievement award, YWCA, 1989, Jackson Day award, Tex. Soc. Child and Adolescent Psychiatry, 1989, Showcase award, Tex. Dept. Mental Health/Mental Retardation,1990, Disting. Svc. award, Tex. Soc. Psychiatric Physicians, 1990. Fellow Am. Acad. Child and Adolescent Psychiatry, Am. Psychiatric Soc., Am. Pediatric Assn.; mem. Tex. Soc. Child and Adolescent Psychiatry (pres. 1979-80), Tex. Soc. Psychiatric Physicians, AMA, Tex. Med. Soc., Am. Genetics Soc. Office: Austin State Hospital 4110 Guadalupe St Austin TX 78751-4223

SUTTON, DOLORES, actress, writer; b. N.Y.C.. BA in Philosophy, NYU. Appeared in plays including Man With the Golden Arm, 1956, Career, 1958, Machinal, 1960, Rhinoceros, Liliom, She Stoops to Conquer, Hedda Gabler, Anna Karenina, Eccentricities of a Nightingale, Brecht on Brecht, Young Gifted and Black, Luv, The Friends, The Web and the Rock, The Seagull, Saturday, Sunday, Monday, The Little Foxes, What's Wrong With This Picture, The Cocktail Hour, My Fair Lady (Broadway revival), 1994, My Fair Lady (nat. tour), 1993-94; films include The Trouble With Angels, Where Angels Go, Trouble Follows, Crossing Delancey, Crimes and Misdeameanors, Tales of the Darkside: TV appearances include Studio One, Hallmark Hall of Fame Prodn. An Wilderness, Theatre Guild of the Air: Danger, Suspense, Gunsmoke, Valiant Lady, General Hospital, From These Roots, As the World Turns, Edge of Night, F. Scott Fitzgerald in Hollywood, Patty Hearst Story, All in the Family, Bob Newhart Show, All My Children, others; TV writer Lady Doc, The Secret Storm, Loving; playwright: Down at the Old Bull and Bush, The Web and the Rock, Company Comin', Born Yesterday, 1995, A Perfect Ganesh, 1995, Detail of a Larger Work, 1995, The Front Page, 1996. Mem. League of Profl. Theatre Women (bd. dirs.), Ensemble Studio Theatre (bd. dirs.).

SUTTON, JOYCE ELAINE, medical records director; b. Chillicothe, Mo., Aug. 28, 1946; d. William Stanley and Helen Louise (Ashlock) Henderson; m. Ferold Rodrick Vermilyea, Jr., Feb. 7, 1964 (div. Aug. 1973); m. Ronald Eldon Sutton, Jan. 15, 1978; children: Sherra Wood, Janae Nezerka, Michael Sutton, Brian Sutton, Marcia Sandner. Accredited record technician. Ward clk. Heartland West Hosp. (formerly Meth. Med. Ctr.), St. Joseph, Mo., 1970-73; ward clk. Hedrick Med. Ctr., Chillicothe, 1973-74; med. records clk. Hedrick Med. Ctr., 1974-75, A.R.T. trainee, 1975-77, med. transcriber, 1977-82, asst. supr., 1982-85, med. records supr., 1985-89, med. records dir., 1989—, quality assurance cons., 1989-92, also med. staff sec., treas., coord.; dir. med. records Pershing Meml. Hosp., Pershing Regional Hosp., Brookfield-Marceline, Mo., 1992—, dir. admissions dept.; cons. Brookfield (Mo.) Nursing Ctr., 1987—, Excelsior Springs (Mo.) City Hosp., 1988—; dir. outpatient program, Hedrick Med. Ctr., Chillicothe, 1987—, dir. quality assurance/risk mgmt., 1988—. Mem. local civic orgns., Chillicothe, 1987—. Mem. Hedrick Med. Ctr. Aux. (life), Am. Med. Records Assn., Mo. Med. Records Assn., Kansas City Area Med. Records Assn. Republican. Baptist. Home: PO Box 114 Meadville MO 64659-0114 Office: Pershing Meml Hosp 130 E Lockling St Brookfield MO 64628-2337

SUTTON, JULIA SUMBERG, musicologist, dance historian; b. Toronto, Ont., Can., July 20, 1928; d. Samuel L. and Anne R. (Rubin) Sumberg. AB summa cum laude, Cornell U., 1949; MA, Colo. Coll., 1952; PhD, U. Rochester, 1962. Instr. music history New Sch. for Social Research, 1962-63; instr. music Queens Coll., CUNY, 1963-66; chmn. dept. music history and musicology New Eng. Conservatory Music, 1971-90, chmn. faculty senate, 1971-73; prof. emerita New England Conservatory Music, 1992; vis. asst. prof. George Peabody Coll. for Tchrs., 1966-67; instr. NYU, summers 1963, 64; pvt. tchr. piano, 1949-65; lectr., rsch. dir. in musicology, music as related to the dance; presenter numerous workshops and summer insts. on Renaissance dance. Dance dir. N.Y. Pro Musica prodn. An Entertainment for Elizabeth, Caramoor, N.Y., Saratoga, N.Y., U. Ariz., Stanford U., UCLA, 1969, nationwide tours, 1970-1973; dance dir. Descent of Rhythm and Harmony, Colorado Springs, Colo., 1970, Renaissance Revisited, Phila., 1972, An Evening of Renaissance Music and Dance, York U., Toronto, 1974; author: Jean Baptiste Besard's Novus Partus 1617, 1962; editor: Thoinot Arbeau: Orchesography 1588, 1967; translator, editor: Fabritio Caroso: Nobiltà di dame 1600, 1986, rev. 1995; producer, co-dir. (tng. video) Il Ballarino, 1991; contbr. articles and book revs. to profl. jours. and encys. Mem. Am. Musicological Soc., Coun. of Rsch. in Dance, Soc. of Dance History Scholars, Phi Beta Kappa.

SUTTON, LINDA KAY, elementary school educator, union representative; b. Fort Wayne, Ind., Dec. 4, 1942; d. Harold Eldon and Bethelene A. (Crawford) L.; m. Robert Eugene Sutton, June 22, 1962. BS, Ind. U., Fort Wayne, 1971, MS, 1974. Treas. Little Turtle Internat. Reading Assn., Columbia City, 1980-82, 93-95, Whitley County Tchrs. Assn., Columbia City, Ind., 1980-85; bargaining team rep. Whitley County Tchrs. Assn., Columbia City, 1989—, v.p., 1993—; rep. Ind. State Tchrs. Assn. Bargaining Conf., Indpls., 1989—, Ind. State Tchrs. Assn. Rep. Assembly, Indpls., 1994—. Music dir. Vacation Bible Sch., Columbia City, 1970-90, Oak Grove Ch. of God, Columbia City, 1975-83; Sunday sch. tchr. Oak Grove Ch. of God, 1990. Mem. Philomathean Literary Orgn. (pres. 1984-85, treas. 1989-91, sec. 1991-92), Delta Kappa Gamma (parliamentarian 1990-92, mem. meml. com. 1990—). Democrat. Home: 520 E 400 S Columbia City IN 46725-9605 Office: Columbia Twp Sch 35 E 200 S Columbia City IN 46725-9778

SUTTON, MARCELLA FRENCH, interior designer; b. Prague, Czechoslovakia, Sept. 4, 1946; came to U.S., 1952, naturalized, 1956; d. Eugen E. and Frances V. (Pruchovia) French; BS in Profl. Arts, Woodbury U., 1971; m. Michael D. Sutton, Feb. 11, 1978; 1 child, Kevin Christopher. Mgr. design dept. W. & J. Sloane, Beverly Hills, Calif., 1972-76; project dir. Milton I. Swimmer, Beverly Hills, 1977-78; owner, interior designer Marcella French Designs, Woodland Hills and La Crescenta, Calif., 1969-94; owner designer project mgr., constrn. and design Marcella French Designs, 1994—, prin. designer; property mgmt. coord., interior designer Home Savs. and Loan., State of Calif., L.A., 1979-82; regional premises officer, asst. v.p. regional hdqrs. Bank Am., L.A., 1981-86; v.p. M.D. Sutton Ins. Agy.; cons. pvt. residences, comml. bldgs., office and banks. Project mgr., 1st v.p. fundraising Shephard of the Valley Sch., 1989-90, enrichment chmn., 1990-91, mem. enrichment program pub. sch. calendar, 1991; active Young Reps., Vinyard Ch.; treas. West Hills Baseball Aux., 1989-91; arcades coord. Theatre Arts Festival for Youth, Agoura, 1992-94, co-chmn. ways and means RTRWF, 1992-94, 1st v.p., 1995-96; treas. Taxpayers United for Fairness, 1994—; co-organizer 9th Grade Parent Network Orgn. & Found., Chaminade, 1994-95. Recipient various scholarships.

SUTTON, ROBERTA HARRISON, elementary education educator; b. Williamston, N.C., Sept. 20, 1940; d. Issac Jessup and Estelle (Lilley) Harrison; m. Hubbard Morris, Aug. 19, 1962; 1 child, Robert Morris. BS, East Carolina U., 1962; MEd, Va. Commonwealth Univ., 1982. 7th grade tchr. Cople Elem. Sch., Hague, Va., 1962-64; 3rd grade tchr. Waverly (Va.) Elem. Sch., 1966-67; 5th grade tchr. Grange Hall Elem., Moseley, Va., 1984—. Mem. Nat. Coun. of Tchrs. of Math., Greater Richmond Area Tchrs. of Math., Richmond Area Reading Coun. Methodist. Office: Grange Hall Elem Sch 19301 Hull Street Rd Moseley VA 23120-1412

SUTTON, SHARON JEAN, surgical nurse; b. Salisbury, N.C., Nov. 3, 1947; d. Archie Moody and Colleen (Bowers) S. ASN, St. Petersburg Jr. Coll., Clearwater, Fla., 1979; student, Clearwater Cmty. Hosp., 1990-91, St. Petersburg Jr. Coll., 1991. Cert. surg. asst.; RN. Flight nurse Fromhagen Aviation Air Ambulance, Clearwater, 1970-75; nurse mgr. Women's Med. Ctr., Clearwater, 1983—, operating rm. supr., 1991—. Mem. Assn. Oper. Rm. Nurses. Office: Womens Medical Ctr 1745 S Highland Ave Clearwater FL 34616-1852

SUTTON, SHARON MARIE, medical and surgical nurse; b. Niskayuna, N.Y., Dec. 16, 1952; d. John Arthur Bond Sutton and Marie Regina Healey Coyle; m. Jeffrey Glenn Schneider, Jan. 13, 1972 (div. Mar. 1975); 1 child, David Matthew. AAS in Nursing, Hudson Valley C.C., Troy, N.Y., 1973; BA in Polit. Sci./Econs., Union Coll., Schenectady, N.Y., 1988. RN, N.Y. Staff nurse/nursing supr. Hallmark Nursing Ctr., Schenectady, 1974-78; staff nurse St. Clares Hosp., Schenectady, 1977-84, Albany (N.Y.) Med. Ctr., 1985, Tri-Cities Nurses Registry, Latham, N.Y., 1985-87; gen. staff nurse Ellis Hosp., Schenectady, 1987-95, assoc. nurse mgr., 1995—; mktg. cons., 1988—. Co-chair Schenectady County AIDS Task Force, 1994—; vol. Talking with Kids About HIV/AIDS, Schenectady County/Cornell Coop., 1994—, bd.dirs.,1996; polit. activist/lobbyist. Mem. YWCA. Methodist. Home: 941 Vischer Ave Rotterdam NY 12306-3913 Office: Ellis Hospital 1101 Nott St Schenectady NY 12309

SUTTON-JONES, SUE, quality systems executive; b. Charlotte, N.C., Aug. 4, 1952; d. Henry Marion and Betty Joane (McKee) Sutton; m. Thomas Buckner Jones, Aug. 3, 1975; children: Anne Buckner, Sara Lynch, Thomas Buckner, Margaret Pearman. BA in Biochemistry, Queens Coll., 1974; student, Temple U., 1985-86, U. Wis., 1991, George Washington U., 1992. Tech. B level Med. Coll. Va., Richmond, 1975-76; sr. tech. Baxter-Travenol Labs., Round Lake, Ill., 1981-82; quality assurance validation supv. Micromedic Sys., Horsham, Pa., 1986-88; quality assurance assoc., mgr. Cintichem, Inc., Tuxedo, N.Y., 1988-90; sr. corporate quality assurance auditor, mgr. quality tech. Pfizer Hosp. Products Group, N.Y., 1990-92; v.p. quality sys. divsn. Biometric Rsch. Inst., Arlington, Va., 1992-94; v.p. regulatory affairs and quality assurance Telectronics Pacing Sys., Denver, 1994-96; v.p. West Coast ops. regulatory and quality allaince Biometric Rsch. Inst., Arlington, Va., 1996—. Mem. Am. Soc. Quality Control (cert. auditor 1989, cert. engr. 1990), Regulatory Affairs Profls. Soc., Parenteral Drug Assn. Republican. Roman Catholic. Office: Biometric Research Inst 1300 N 17th St Arlington VA 22209-3801

SUTTON-RAMSPECK, BETH, English language educator; b. Suffern, N.Y., July 9, 1954; d. Homer Lee and Mildred (Robinowitz) Sutton; m. Doug Ramspeck, Nov. 23, 1981; 1 child, Lee Audrey. BA, Kenyon Coll.,

1976; MA, U. Calif., Irvine, 1978; PhD, Ind. U., 1995. Tchg. asst. in English U. Calif., Irvine, 1976-78; instr. English S.W. Tex. State U., San Marcos, 1979-82, Va. Tech., Blacksburg, 1982-87; asst. instr. in learning skills, English, women's studies Ind. U., Bloomington, 1987-93, instr. English, 1994-95; asst. prof. English Millikin U., Decatur, Ill., 1995—; Hardy Disting. prof. in English Millikin U., 1996—. Coll. of Arts and Scis. Dissertation Rsch. fellow Ind. U., 1994, faculty fellow Millikin U., 1996. Mem. MLA, Nat. Coun. Tchrs. English, Midwest Victorian Studies Assn., Womens Caucus for Modern Langs., Edith Wharton Soc. Democrat. Office: Millikin U Dept English Decatur IL 62522

SVADLENAK, JEAN HAYDEN, museum administrator, consultant; b. Wilmington, Del., Mar. 4, 1955; d. Marion M. and Ida Jean (Calcagni) Hayden; m. Steven R. Svadlenak, May 26, 1979. BS in Textiles and Clothing, U. Del., 1977; MA in History Mus. Studies, SUNY, Oneonta, 1982; postgrad., U. Calif., Berkeley, 1982. Curatorial asst. The Hagley Mus., Wilmington, 1976-77; curator of costumes and textiles The Kansas City (Mo.) Mus., 1978-82, chief curator, 1982-84, assoc. exec. dir. for collection and exhibits mgmt., 1984-86, interim pres., 1986-87, pres., 1987-89; researcher, guest curator N.Y. State Hist. Assn., Cooperstown, 1980; grant reviewer Inst. for Mus. Svcs., 1985-89; ad hoc faculty U. Kans., 1991—, U. Mo., Kansas City, 1992—. Mem. Am. Assn. Mus. (surveyor mus. assessment program 1985-89, mem. accreditation vis. com. 1990—), Am. Assn. State and Local History, Costume Soc. Am., Heritage League Kansas City (bd. dirs. 1987-89), Midwest Mus. Conf. (coun. 1992-94), Mo. Mus. Assocs. (pres. 1992-94, com. on mus. profl. tng. 1993—, 2d v.p. 1994-96). Home: 624 Romany Rd Kansas City MO 64113-2037

SVALDI, MYRTHIA MOORE, financial advisor; b. Norwalk, Conn., Mar. 13, 1961; d. George L. III and Tirsa A. (Kinney) Moore; m. Michael John Svaldi, Oct. 11, 1987; children: Jason, Brian. Degree in fin. and econs., Harvard U., 1983. Fin. analyst banking industry; fin. and sales mgr. U.S. duty free market and Latin Am. Porsche Design; corp. fin. cons. Cellular One; fin. and estate analysis, ins., investments, group benefits Charter Fin. and Ins. Group, Inc., Miami, Fla., fin. and estate analysis, ins. investments. Bd. dirs. Voices for Children; mem. planned giving com. Am. Cancer Soc. Mem. Mercy Hosp. Found., Internat. Assn. Fin. Planners, Miami Assn. Life Underwriters, C. of C. Office: Charter Fin & Ins Group Inc 6161 Blue Lagoon Dr Ste 300 Miami FL 33126-2047

SVEC, SANDRA JEAN, state official; b. Evanston, Ill., Dec. 11, 1947; d. Joseph Francis and Martha Marjorie (Randau) Svec; m. Terry L. Yonker, June 28, 1969 (div. 1990). BS in Meteorology, U. Wis., Madison, 1969. Sec., sales asst. Moore Bus. Forms Inc., Lansing, Mich., 1970-72; rsch. asst. Mich. Dept. Social Svcs., Lansing, 1972-74; adminstrv. analyst Mich. Pub. Svc. Commn., Lansing, 1974-79, supr. orgn. devel., 1980-84; program mgr. Gov.'s Energy Awareness Adv. Com., Lansing, 1979-80; labor rels. rep. Mich. Dept. Agr., Lansing, 1984-87, acting personnel dir., 1987-89, asst. to chief dep. dir., 1989-93, dir. EEO/affirmative action office, 1991—. Bd. dirs. Lansing Area Advocates for Choice, 1991-93, Downtown Neighborhood Assn., Lansing, 1990—, v.p., 1992-95; vol. reader Radio Talking Book, East Lansing, Mich., 1974-93; active Stratford (Ont., Can.) Shakespearean Festival, 1974—; Marshal vol. co-chair Oldsmobile Classic Ladies PGA event, East Lansing, 1993-96; mem. Covenant Assn. United Ch. of Christ, Church and Ministry Com., 1992-96, chair, 1996. Mem. Am. Bus. Women's Assn. (chpt. Woman of Yr. 1977), Am. Assn. for Affirmative Action, State Assn. Accts., Auditors and Bus. Adminstrs., Nat. Wildlife Fedn., Friday Frolics. Home: 617 W Genesee St Lansing MI 48933-1010 Office: Mich Dept Agr PO Box 30017 Lansing MI 48909-7517

SVEDA-UNCAPHER, SUSAN, artist, educator; b. Antigo, Wis., Aug. 4, 1967; d. Frank and Joyce Ann (Nemcicky) Sveda. Student, U. Wis., Superior, 1990-92; BFA cum laude, U. Wis., Eau Claire, 1994. Cartographer Owen Ayres and Assocs., Eau Claire, 1989; gallery docent U. Wis., Eau Claire, 1992; illustrator U.S. Army, various locations, 1986-94; youth art instr. Dept. Parks and Recreation, Eau Claire, 1992-96; artist Regional Arts Ctr., Eau Claire, 1992-95, U. Wis., Eau Claire, 1992-94, L.E. Phillips Pub. Meml. Libr., Eau Claire, 1993-95, local businesses, Eau Claire, 1994-95; visual arts com. Regional Arts Ctr., Eau Claire. Exhbns. include Spirits of the Water: A Series of Environmental Stations Along the Little Niagra, 1994, Veiled Conclusions, 1994, First Words, 1995, HIV Vision, 1995. Artist United Way, Eau Claire, 1994, Chippewa Valley Theatre Guild, Eau Claire, 1991, 96. With U.S. Army, 1986-88. U. Wis. scholar, 1993-94; Bush Artist fellow, 1996. Home: 1618 Birney St #3 Eau Claire WI 54701

SVEINSON, PAMELA J., human resources executive. BA in Sociology, Whitman Coll., 1974; M in Indsl. Rels., U. Minn., 1980. Social worker Mont. State Dept. Social & Rehab. Svcs., 1975-77; behavior therapist Spl. Tng. Exceptional People, Billings, Mont., 1977; asst. mgr. manpower planning Burlington Northern, St. Paul, 1978-80; sr. human resources planner Morrison-Knudsen Co., Inc., Boise, Idaho, 1980-83; asst. v.p. human resources 1st Bank System, 1983-84, v.p., 1984-88, sr. v.p., 1988-90; v.p. human resources Star Tribune and Cowles Media Co., Mpls., 1990—; pres. Human Resources Exec. Coun., 1995-96. Mentor Minn. 100; mem. Mpls. Inst. Arts. Mem. Nat. Human Resources Planning Soc., Minn. Human Resources Planning Soc. (bd. dirs.), Horseman's Benevolent & Protective Assn., Park Ave. Meth. Ch. Home: 101 Meadow Ln Golden Valley MN 55416 Office: Cowles Media Co 329 Portland Ave Minneapolis MN 55415-1112

SVENDSEN, JOYCE R., real estate company executive; b. Bayonne, N.J.; d. Peder and Rita Agnes (Bogert) S.; m. Stephen G. Takach, June 22, 1968; 1 child, Mark Stephen. Lic. real estate broker. Sales dir. M.L. Levine Real Estate, Clifton, 1985-91; head Luxury Homes divsn. Nicholas Real Estate, Clifton, 1992—. Mem. N.J. Assn. Realtors (million dollar sales club 1986-95), Passaic County Bd. Realtors (assoc.), Sons of Norway. Republican. Unitarian Universalist. Office: Nicholas Real Estate 1624 Main Ave Clifton NJ 07011-2112

SVETLIK, BONNIE OLSON, elementary education educator; b. Bedford, Ohio, Apr. 18, 1944; d. George Olaf and Elva (Wise) Olson; m. Clevis Tvl Svetlik, June 17, 1967; children: Susan Elizabeth, Sharon Ann. BSEd., Baldwin Wallace Coll., 1966. Cert. elem. edn. and music tchr., Ohio. Tchr. Harrison Sch., Lakewood, Ohio, 1966-67, Noble Sch., Cleveland Hts., Ohio, 1967-68, Heskett Sch., Bedford, Ohio, 1968-69; substitute tchr. Chagrin Falls (Ohio) Schs., 1983-85; tchr. Our Lady of Peace Sch., Cleve., 1987-93, St. Mary Sch., Bedford, 1993—; sci. fair coord. St. Mary Sch., 1993—; prin. flutist Suburban Symphony Orchestra. Named Musician of Yr., Suburban Symphony Orchestra, Beachwood, Ohio, 1987. Mem. Suburban Symphony Orchestra Assn. (pres., steering com. chmn.), Cecilian Musical Club (pres.), Fortnightly Musical Club (festival chmn. 1986), Zeta Tau Alpha (pres./v.p.). Methodist. Home: 2545 Brainard Rd Pepper Pike OH 44124

SVETLOVA, MARINA, ballerina, choreographer, educator; b. Paris, May 3, 1922; came to U.S. from Australia, 1940; d. Max and Tamara (Andreieff) Hartman. Studies with Vera Trefilova, Paris, 1930-36, studies with L. Egorova and M. Kschessinska, 1936-39; studies with A. Vilzak, N.Y.C., 1940-57; D honoris causa, Fedn. Francaise de Danse, 1988. Ballet dir. So. Vt. Art Ctr., 1959-64; dir. Svetlova Dance Ctr., Dorset, Vt., 1965—; prof. ballet dept. Ind. U., Bloomington, 1969-92, prof. emeritus, 1992—, chmn. dept., 1969-78; choreographer Dallas Civic Opera, 1964-67, Ft. Worth Opera, 1967-83, San Antonio Opera, 1983, Seattle Opera, Houston Opera, Kansas City Performing Arts Found. Ballerina original Ballet Russe de Monte Carlo, 1939-41; guest ballerina Ballet Theatre, 1942, London's Festival Ballet, Teatro dell Opera, Rome, Nat. Opera, Stockholm, Sweden, Suomi Opera, Helsinki, Finland, Het Nederland Ballet, Holland, Cork Irish Ballet, Paris Opera Comique, London Palladium, Teatro Colon, Buenos Aires, others; prima ballerina Met. Opera, 1943-50, N.Y.C. Opera, 1950-52; choreographer: (ballet sequences) The Fairy Queen, 1966, L'Histoire du Soldat, 1968; tours in Far East, Middle East, Europe, S.Am., U.S.; performer various classical ballets Graduation Ball; contbr. articles to Debut, Paris Opera. Mem. Am. Guild Mus. Artists (bd. dirs.), Conf. on Ballet in Higher Edn., Nat. Soc. Arts and Letters (nat. dance chmn.). Office: 2100 E Maxwell Ln Bloomington IN 47401-6119 also: 25 W 54th St New York NY 10019-5411

SVILAR, LORRAINE EVA, educator; b. Bklyn., Dec. 14, 1946; d. Matthew and Dorothea Augusta (Langbehn) S.; children: Daniel W. Smith III, Matthew L. Smith. BA, Goucher Coll., Towson, Md., 1985; MS, Western Md. Coll., Westminster, 1992. Tchr. Bel Air (Md.) H.S., 1985—, advisor to newspaper, 1985—, coord., dir. mentoring program for women, 1994—. Mem. AAUW. Home: 514 Lee Way Bel Air MD 21014 Office: Bel Air HS 100 Heighe St Bel Air MD 21014

SVOBODA, TERESE, poet, novelist, filmmaker; b. Ogallala, Nebr., Sept. 5, 1950; d. Frank B. Svoboda and Anne Marie Walsh; m. Stephen Medaris Bull, July 18, 1981; children: Deng Breidenbach-Svoboda, Felix Bull, Franklin Bull. BFA, U. B.C., Vancouver, Can., 1973; MFA, Columbia U., 1978. Prodr. Voices and Visions, N.Y.C., 1980-82, Cast Iron TV, N.Y.C., 1988-92; tchr. U. Hawaii, 1992, Sarah Lawrence, N.Y.C., 1993-94, New Sch., N.Y.C., 1996—; mem. adv. bd. Poets House, N.Y.C., 1986-96. Author: (novel) Cannibal, 1995 (Bobst GLCA award 1995), Cleaned the Crocodile's Teeth; (translations) Mere Mortals (poetry) Laughing Africa, 1990 (Iowa prize) All Aberration, 1985. Recipient New TV award for Margaret Sanger documentary PBS, 1993; grantee Appleman Found., 1994, NEH, 1978, Jerome Found., 1990, N.Y. Found. for Arts, Creative Artists in Pub. Svc., 1982, 89.

SWAIN, DIANE SCOTT, principal; b. Atlantic City, N.J., July 13, 1946; d. Letha Noble; m. Raymond L. Swain Jr., Dec. 26, 1970; 1 child, Sean Scott Swain. BS, Hampton U., 1968; MEd, Lynchburg Coll., 1978; postgrad., U. Va., 1987—. Tchr. Lynchburg (Va.) City Schs., 1968-86, instructional coord., 1986-87, asst. prin., 1987-89, elem. prin., 1989—. Bd. dirs. Cen. Va. Speech and Hearing Ctr., Va. Bapt. Hosp., Lynchburg, 1990—. Mem. Lynchburg Assn. Elem. Prins. (pres. 1991—), Jack and Jill Inc. (v.p. Lynchburg chpt. 1989-90), Delta Sigma Theta Inc. (pres. Lynchburg alumnae chpt. 1982-84). Baptist. Home: 115 Yorkshire Cir Lynchburg VA 24502-2756 Office: Sheffield Elem Sch 115 Kenwood Pl Lynchburg VA 24502-2119

SWAIN, JOYE RAECHEL, writer; b. Oklahoma City, Jan. 1, 1940; d. Enos Gerald and Opal Cowan (Boulton) Garland; m. Dwight Vreeland Swain, Feb. 12, 1969 (dec. Feb. 1992); children: Rocio, Antonia, Ronald (dec.), Jenny, Jefferson, Dayane, Mike. BS in Math., Oklahoma City U., 1960; MA in Romance Langs., U. Okla., 1963. Freelance writer, lectr. Norman, Okla., 1965—; instr. French U. Okla., Norman, 1962-65; assoc. prof. French U. Sci. and Arts of Okla., Chickasha, 1965-68; coord. Spanish lang. program Instituto Allende, San Miguel de Allende, Guanajuato, Mex., 1971-74; tchr. French George Lynn Cross Acad., Norman, 1982-83; tchr. ESL U. Okla., Norman, 1990-93; exec. dir. Okla. Profl. Writers Hall of Fame. Co-author: Scripting for Video and AV, 1981, Film Scriptwriting, 1988. Mem. Mystery Writers Am., World Sci. Fiction (Liaison with Latin Am.), Okla. Writers' Fedn., Inc. (pres. 1992-93), Okla. Pen Woman (pres. 1988-90), Norman Galaxy of Writers (pres. 1991-92). Home: 1409 Quail Hollow Dr Norman OK 73072

SWAIN, MELINDA SUSAN, elementary education educator; b. Sacramento, Oct. 30, 1944; d. William A. and Maxine (Wickberg) S. BA, Aurora U., 1967; MA, U. N.Mex., 1981. Cert. early adolescence/generalist Nat. Bd. Profl. Tchg. Standards, 1995. Tchr. 1st grade Crownpoint (N.Mex.) Elem. Sch., 1968-69, tchr. English as second lang., 1969-71; tchr. English as second lang. Church Rock (N.Mex.) Elem. Sch., 1971-72; tchr. kindergarten Sky City Elem. Sch., Gallup, N.Mex., 1972-73; program specialist Gallup-McKinley County Schs., 1973-82, OCR program compliance officer, 1996—; tchr. 5th grade Lincoln Elem. Sch., Gallup, 1982-96; mem. Dist. Task Force, Gallup, 1989—. Columnist N.Mex. Jour. Reading, 1991—. Recipient N.Mex. World Class Tchrs. Project award, 1994-95. Mem. N.Mex. Coun. Internat. Reading Assn. (pres. 1984, state coord. 1991—), Gallup Reading Coun. of Internat. Reading Assn. (pres., membership dir. 1977—). Home: 1000 Country Club Dr Gallup NM 87301 Office: Gallup-McKinley County Schs PO Box 1318 Gallup NM 87305-1318

SWAIN, SUSAN MARIE, communications executive; b. Phila., Dec. 23, 1954; d. Samuel B. Swain and Marie (Baeder) Paget. BA in Communications magna cum laude, U. Scranton, Pa., 1976. Reporter Sta. WDAU-TV, Scranton, 1975-76; pub. relations staff Up With People, Inc., Tuscon, 1976-78; supr. Raytheon Service Co., Cambridge, Mass., 1978-80; research assoc. Nat. Counsel Assocs., Washington, 1980-82; producer C-SPAN Cable Network, Washington, 1982-83, dir. pub. relations, 1983-87, v.p. corp. communications, mem. exec. mgmt. com., 1987-89, sr. v.p., 1989—; speaker in field. Moderator (TV program) C-SPAN Viewer Call-In, 1982—. Recipient Alumni award U. Scranton, 1976, Disting. Achievement award, 1991. Mem. Cable TV Pub. Affairs Assn. (bd. dirs. 1986-90, sec. 1988-89), Washington Cable Club, Alpha Sigma Nu. Roman Catholic. Office: C-SPAN 400 N Capitol St NW Ste 650 Washington DC 20001-1511*

SWAINE, FRANCES MARGARET, special education educator; b. Chgo., May 30, 1964; d. Thomas Lawrence and Anne Rose (Wrobel) S. BA, Columbia Coll., 1988. Floor supr. Glenkirk, Northbrook, Ill., 1988-89; program mgr. Glenkirk CRA Home, Mt. Prospect, Ill., 1988-90; case mgr. Healthcare for Homeless, Chgo., 1990; floor supr. Little Friends, Downers Grove, Ill., 1992-94; tng. counsellor Builders of Skills, Niles, Ill., 1994—; tchr. Experanza Cmty. Svcs., Chgo., 1996—. Vol. BUILD, Chgo., 1983-88, Blind Svc. Assn., Chgo., 1993. Home: 1650 W Erie St Chicago IL 60622 Office: 520 Marshfield Chicago IL 60622

SWAN, BETH ANN, nursing administrator; b. Phila., Nov. 11, 1958; d. John H. and Elizabeth A. Jenkins; m. Eric J. Swan, Apr. 11, 1987. BSN, Holy Family Coll., Phila., 1980; MSN, U. Pa., 1983, PhD in Edn., 1996. RN, Pa.; cert. adult nurse practitioner ANCC. Nursing dir. admission evaluation ctr. Hosp. of U. Pa., Phila., 1980—. Mem. ANA, Pa. Nurses Assn., Am. Acad. Nurse Practitioners, Am. Acad. Ambulatory Nursing Adminstrn., Sigma Theta Tau.

SWAN, JOYCE ANN, comptroller; b. San Antonio, June 11, 1964; d. Richard Bronaugh II and Carolyn Ann (Gerhardt) Harn; m. Jesse G. Swan, June 3, 1983 (div. Dec. 1992). BBA in Acctg., U. Tex., San Antonio, 1986. Bookkeeper Gerhardts Paint and Wallpaper Co., San Antonio, 1976-84, Ike Neumann & Assocs., San Antonio, 1983-86, Patrician Properties, San Antonio, 1984-86; gen. mgr. San Antonio Hermann Sons Home Assn., 1982-86; comptroller Courtesy Chevrolet Co., Phoenix, 1986-91; CFO various orgns., Phoenix, 1992; human resources/customer rels., fin. mgr. Buick Co., Phoenix, 1993; office mgr. World Car Mazda, New Braunfels, Tex., 1993-94; comptr. Moretti's Fine Jewelry, San Antonio, Tex., 1995—. Mem. auditor bd. evaluators Valley of Sun United Way, Phoenix, 1988—, Chandler (Ariz.) Planning and Zoning Commn., 1990-92, Valley Forward Assn.; treas. com. re-elect Coy Payne for mayor City of Chandler; precinct com. person dist. 30 Dem. Nat. Com., 1991—; state com. person Ariz. Dem. Com., 1991-92; cmty. adv. bd. KLRN Pub. TV, 1995—; mem. spkrs. bur. Am. Cancer Soc., 1996—. Mem. Inst. Mgmt. Accts. (bd. dirs. Scottsdale chpt. 1988-89, v.p. edn. 1989-90, pres. 1990-91, mem. nat. contr.'s coun., scholarship sect. com. 1991-92, chmn. nominating com. 1991-92, bd. dirs., employment dir. San Antonio chpt. 1994—), Am. Soc. Women Accts. (com. Mesa East Valley chpt.), Am. Soc. Assn. Execs., Internat. Credit Assn. Greater Phoenix, Retail Fin. Execs. Ariz., Ariz. Cash Mgmt. Assn., Am. Inst. Individual Investors, Ariz. Automotive Accts. Assn. (founding pres., organizer 1991-92), Exec. Bus. and Profl. Women's Club (sec. Phoenix chpt. 1986-88, auditor 1986-87, 88-89, pres. 1991-92, Woman of Yr. award 1991), Friends of Libr., Alamo City Tall Club, U. Tex. at San Antonio Alumni Assn.

SWAN, KAREN PERRY, instructional technology educator; b. N.Y.C., June 30, 1948; d. Carroll J. and Margaret P. (deRaismes) S.; m. Marco J. Mitrani, Nov. 15, 1988; children: Sam Mitrani, Darby Brigham, Gillian Brigham. BA in Philosophy, U. Conn., 1972; MEd in Curriculum and Instrn., Keene State Coll., 1983; EdM in Instnl. Tech., Columbia U., 1985, EdD in Instnl. Tech., 1989. Childcare coord. Women's Crisis Ctr., Brattleboro, Vt., 1981-83; dir. gifted edn. Wheelock Elem. Sch., Keene, N.H., 1982-83; dir. computer sci. edn. BiCultural Day Sch., Stamford, Conn., 1984-88; rsch. asst. CITE Tchrs. Coll. Columbia U., N.Y.C., 1986-88; assoc. prof. instnl. tech. Sch. Edn. SUNY, Albany, 1988—, dir. Learning Techs. Lab., 1989—; prin. investigator Computer Pilot Project, N.Y.C., 1987-90, Elem. Sch. CA Project, N.Y.C., 1994-95; project dir. multimedia and lit. project Nat. Ctr. for Rsch. in Lit. Tchg. and Learning, Albany, 1993-95; project dir. electronic literacy and literate reasoning project Nat. Ctr. for Rsch. on Student Learning and Achievement in English, Albany, 1996—; ; cons. scholar IBM, Milford, Conn., 1992-94; design cons. Interactive Generation, Seattle, 1991—; mem. adv. panel New Sch. Visions, Hyde Park, N.Y., 1992-94; rsch. cons. N.Y.C. Bd. Edn., 1987—. Author: Set on Freedom: The American Civil Rights Movement, 1994; editor, author: Social Learning From Broadcast Television, 1996; contbr. articles to profl. publs. Computer tchr. Neighborhood Sch. House, Brattleboro, 1990—; pres. Parents & Friends Com., Marlboro, Vt., 1991-94; vice chair Dem. Party, Marlboro, 1992—. Mem. Am. Ednl. Rsch. Assn. (program chair, mem. media-culture and curriculum spl. interest group 1988—), Assn. for Advancement of Computing in Edn. (program com. 1992—), Internat. Soc. for Tech. in Edn., Assn. for Ednl. Comms. and Tech. Baptist. Home: Box 183 Standing On End Rd Marlboro VT 05344 Office: SUNY Albany ED114A Dept Edn Theory & Practice Albany NY 12222

SWAN, MARTHA LOUISE, retired educator; b. Chadron, Nebr., May 6, 1912; d. Neal Watterson and Sarrah Abbie (Brower) Cook; m. Earle Jameson Swan; (dec. 1970); children: Judith Louise, Linda Camille, Calvin Lawrence, Noreen Adell. BA, Conn. Coll. for Women, New London, 1937; MEd, Lewis & Clark Coll., Portland, Oreg., 1964. Tchr. Norwich (Conn.) Free Acad., 1937-38; music-art tchr. Milwaukie (Oreg.) Sch. Dist., 1947-48; music tchr. Skyline Elem. Sch., Washington County, Oreg., 1951-52, Vancouver (Wash.) Sch. Dist., 1952-53, 57-58; tchr. Portland (Oreg.) Sch. Dist., 1958-64, French and Spanish tchr., 1965-72; ret., 1972; pvt. tchr. piano and voice, 1938-92; lectr. on cut glass. Author: (book) American Cut and Engraved Glass: The Brilliant Period in Historical Perspective, 1986, 2d edit., 1994; contbr. articles and poems to numerous publs. Winthrop scholar Conn. Coll. for Women, 1936. Mem. AAUW (antiques chpt. Portland), R.I. Honor Soc., Am. Cut Glass Assn., Order Eastern Star (program chair 1938-40), Phi Beta Kappa. Home: Unit 62 3930 SE 162d Ave Portland OR 97236-7006

SWAN, SHARON L., sytems engineering manager, business consultant; b. Wilkes-Barre, Pa., June 22, 1944; d. Edward and Alice (Phoenix) Johnson; m. Charles Wesley Swan, Aug. 9, 1969; children: Simone Y., Charles W. Jr. BS in Chemistry, Howard U., 1966. Lab technician Sloan Kettering Meml., N.Y.C., 1966; chemist FDA, Washington, 1967-70; lab technician Gen. Analine and Film, Easton, Pa., 1970-71; from systems engr. to mktg. support rep., systems engr. mgr., project mgr. IBM, Scranton, Pa., Denver, Dallas, 1972-93; bus. cons. Swan & Assocs., Ltd., 1993—. IBM liaison mgr., chmn. adv. com. Job Tng. Ctr. Urban Leauge, Tampa, 1987—; spkr. outreach program, Tampa, 1989-90; judge Odyssey of Mind, Tampa, 1990; citizens adv. com., pres. U. South Fla., 1992. Corp. Vol. award Urban League, 1988-89. Jehovah's Witness.

SWANBERG-MEE, ANN MARIE, environmental engineer; b. Jacksonville, Fla., July 30, 1965; d. Clifford Duane and Margaret Mary (Spillane) Swanberg; m. Michael Sullivan-Mee, Feb. 28, 1995. BS in Mech. Engring., U. Ky., 1989; MSCE, U. N.Mex., 1996. Engr.-in-tng., Ariz. Sr. field engr. Indian Health Svc., Many Farms, Ariz., 1992—. Contbr.: Kenya and Northern Tanzania, 1992. Vol. U.S. Peace Corps, Nairobi, Kenya, 1989-91. Mem. ASCE, Soc. Ret. Peace Corps Vols. Home: 704 Cherokee Dr Henderson KY 42420 Office: Indian Health Svc PO Box 694 Many Farms AZ 86538

SWANEY, CYNTHIA ANN, sales executive, management consultant; b. Garfield Heights, Ohio, Feb. 25, 1959; d. Peter John and Juanita Catherine (Crowle) Christ; m. C. Keith Swaney, Aug. 4, 1984; children: Jason Scott, Samantha Jean. Grad. high sch., Pepper Pike, Ohio. With Park View Fed. S&L, Cleve., 1975-79; customer svc., teller, trainer Park View Fed. S&L, 1977-79; exec. sec., ops. mgr. Majestic Steel Svc., Solon, Ohio, 1979-84; v.p. adminstrn. Datashare Corp., Chagrin Falls, Ohio, 1984-94, pres., 1994—; owner, med. mgmt. cons. Oasis Health Svcs., 1994—; cons. Stenciler's Emporium, Hudson, Ohio, 1988—, Deep Springs Trout Club, Chardon, Ohio, 1988—, Hiram House Camp, Moreland Hills, Ohio, 1990—; numerous med. offices, 1986—. Trustee Hiram House Camp, 1991—. Office: Datashare Corp 17800 Chillicothe Rd Chagrin Falls OH 44023

SWANK, ANNETTE MARIE, software designer; b. Lynn, Mass., Nov. 9, 1953; d. Roland Paterson and Rita Mary (Edwards) S. BSEE and Computer Sci., Vanderbilt U., 1975; postgrad., Pa. State U., 1992—. Lead programmer GE, Phila., 1975-80; system analyst SEI Corp., Wayne, Pa., 1980-82; mgr., designer Premier Systems, Inc., Wayne, Pa., 1982-85, dir., 1985-88, tech. advisor, 1988-90, tech. architect, 1990-92; tech. architect Funds Assocs. Ltd., Wayne, 1992—. Designer: (programming lang. and data dictionary) Vision, 1985. Treas. Master Singers, Plymouth Meeting, Pa., 1987-88. Mem. Assn. for Computing Machinery, Gamma Phi Beta (com. chmn. alumna Phila. 1986-87). Home: 136 Pinecrest Ln King Of Prussia PA 19406-2368 Office: Funds Assocs Ltd 440 E Swedesford Rd Wayne PA 19087-1820

SWANN, BARBARA, lawyer; b. N.Y., Sept. 15, 1950; d. George Arthur. BA summa cum laude, Montclair State U., 1988; JD, Rutgers Law, 1992. Bar: N.J. 1992, D.C. 1994, N.Y. 1995, U.S. Dist. Ct. N.J. 1992, U.S. Ct. Appeals (3rd cir.) 1994. Correspondent The Associate Press, Newark, N.J., 1974-80; reporter, bureau chief The Hudson Dispatch, Union City, N.J., 1973-80; editorial page editor The Paterson (N.J.) News, 1980-81; v.p., acct. supr. Gerald Freeman, Inc., Clifton, N.J., 1981-86; pres. LePore Assoc., Inc., West Caldwell, N.J., 1986-89; law clk. to Hon. Robert N. Wilentz N.J. Supreme Ct., 1992-93; law clk. to Hon. Leonard I. Garth U.S. Ct. Appeals (3rd cir.), 1993-94; assoc. Cahill, Gordon & Reindel, N.Y., 1994—. Editor-in-chief: Rutgers Computer & Technology Law Jour., 1991-92. Founding trustee Ctr. for Children's Advocacy, Riverdale, N.J. 1994—. Mem. ABA, Assn. of the Bar of the City of New York, N.J. State Bar Assn., D.C. Bar Assn. Office: Cahill Gordon & Reindel 80 Pine St New York NY 10005

SWANSEN, DONNA MALONEY, landscape designer, consultant; b. Green Bay, Wis., July 8, 1931; d. Arthur Anthony and Ella Marie Rose (Warner) Maloney; m. Samuel Theodore Swansen, June 27, 1959; children: Jessica Swansen Bonelli, Theodor Arthur Swansen, Christopher Currie Swansen. AS in Integrated Liberal Studies, U. Wis., 1956; AS in Landscape Design, Temple U., 1982. Bridal cons. Richard W. Burnham's, Green Bay, 1951-54, 57-58; asst., buyer Shreve Crump & Low, Boston, 1958-59; buyer Harry S. Manchester, Madison, Wis., 1959-62; ptnr. Corson Borie & Swansen, Ambler, Pa., 1976, Swansen & Borie, Ambler, 1977-82; owner, operator Donna Swansen/Design, Ambler, 1983—; v.p. Energy Islands Internat. Inc., East Troy, Wis., 1963-94. Editor: Internat. Directory Landscape Designers, 1993. Mem. search com. for chair dept. landscape architecture and horticulture Temple U., 1987, curriculum rev. com., 1993; mem. Gwynedd (Pa.) Monthly Meeting of Friends (Quakers), 1974—; Dem. candidate for judge elections, 1988; co-founder Friends of Rising Sun, Ambler, Ambler Area Arts Alliance, 1975-76; founder, 1st pres. Plant Ambler, 1973-83; mem. adv. com. Green Bay Bot. Garden, 1993—; chair Temple U. Exhibit, Do It, Dig It. Recipient Key to the Borough, Borough of Ambler, 1972; winner urban beautification project Roadside Coun. Am., Ambler, 1975, award of Distinction Assn. Profl. Landscape Designers, 1996, Athena award Wissahickon Valley C. of C., 1996; entry named Best in Show Pa. Hort. Soc., Phila., 1987. Mem. Assn. Profl. Landscape Designers (cert., co-founder, 1st pres. 1989-91, bd. dirs. 1989-95, 1st pres. Landscape Design Network Phila. 1978-85), Sigma Lambda Alpha. Home and Office: 221 Morris Rd Ambler PA 19002

SWANSON, CHERYL ANN, small business owner, nurse; b. L.A., Feb. 17, 1967; d. Donald Herbert Cox and Mary Rosalie (Bowlds) Hook; m. Timothy Howard Swanson, Feb. 28, 1982 (div. Sept. 1987); 1 child, Christopher Michael. BSN magna cum laude, U. Ariz., 1995. RN, Ariz.; CCRN. Sales mgr. Double M Gem, Pocatello, Idaho, 1987-89, Desert Gem, Tucson, 1990-93; owner, mgr. AAA Loan & Jewelry, Tucson, 1993—; critical care nurse St. Joseph's Hosp., 1995. Scholar Idaho State U., 1988-89, M.B. and C.J. O'Connel scholar U. Ariz., 1995. Mem. ANA, Nat. League for Nursing, Golden Key, Sigma Theta Tau, Phi Kappa Phi. Democrat. Roman Catholic. Office: AAA Loan & Jewelry 1902 S Craycroft Tucson AZ 85711

SWANSON, DARLENE MARIE CARLSON, speech therapist, educator, speaker, writer; b. Boone, Iowa, Aug. 8, 1925; d. Arvid Wilhelm and Edith Marie (Peterson) Carlson; m. Reuben Theodore Swanson, Aug. 8, 1948; children: Conrad T., Joyce Marie Swanson Jobson. BA, Augustana Coll., 1947; postgrad., U. Chgo., 1949, Creighton U., 1972; student, Joslyn Art Mus., Omaha, 1975. Cert. tchr., Ill., Nebr. Speech therapist Rock Island and Rockford (Ill.) Pub. Sch. System, 1946-51, Omaha (Nebr.) Pub. Sch. System, 1963-64; ch. organist Calvary Luth. Ch., Moline, Ill., 1944-46; asst. organist Augustana Luth. Ch., Omaha, 1956-63; mortuary organist Swanson-Golden Mortuary, Omaha, 1956-63; freelance lectr., 1960—; freelance writer, 1960—; chalk artist lectr. and pub. speaker, retreat leader; observer Luth. World Fedn. Assembly, Budapest, Hungary, 1984. Sunday sch. tchr. Kountze Mem. Luth. Ch., Omaha, 1964-74; Sunday sch. supr. St. Andrew's Luth. Ch., West Hemstead, N.Y., 1951-54; sec. Omaha PTA, 1968-70; mem. adv. coun. Cen. High Sch., Omaha, 1971-74, Omaha Pub. Schs., 1971-74; bd. dirs., sec. Luth. Summer Music Program, 1990—; active Met. Opera Guild, 1986-90, Omaha Opera Guild, 1990—, Omaha Symphony Guild, 1990—; bd. dirs. Bethpage Mission Gt. Britain, sec., 1994—; bd.dirs. Omaha Symphony Assn., 1996—. Named Vol. of Yr. Omaha Head Start Program, 1965. Address: PO Box 37448 Omaha NE 68137-0448

SWANSON, DAWN ROBIN OLMSTED, librarian; b. Flint, Mich., July 9, 1969; d. Thomas James and Kathleen Lynn (Fournier) Olmsted; m. Jeffrey David Swanson, Jan. 19, 1991; 1 child, Thomas Jeffrey Swanson. BA, U. Mich., Flint, 1990; MLS, Wayne State U., Detroit, 1994; MLIS. Page Genesee Dist. Library, Flint, Mich., 1986-90; retrospective conversion technician Baker Coll. Library, Flint, 1990-94, librarian, 1994; automation specialist Mott Cmty. Coll. Library, Flint, 1990-95; technical svcs. librarian GMI Engring. & Mgmt. Inst. Library, Flint, 1995—; owner Info Finders, Flint, 1994—. Recipient Gloria A. Francis award Wayne State U., 1993, Book Collecting Contest award, 1994. Home: 2318 Missouri Ave Flint MI 48506 Office: GMI Engring & Mgmt Inst Library 1700 W 3d Ave Flint MI 48504

SWANSON, ELIZABETH SUE, art educator; b. Atlanta, Ga., Jan. 9, 1955; d. Edward Marion S. and Elizabeth Winningham Cellar Wales. BA in Art History, U. N. Fla., 1982, BA in Art Edn., 1982; MEd in Edn. Leadership, U. Ctrl. Fla., 1991. Cert. ednl. leadership, art K-12. Art tchr. The Bolles Sch., Jacksonville, Fla., 1983-85, Orange County Pub. Schs., Orlando, Fla., 1985—. Mem. PTA. Recipient Disting. Citizen's award WVOJ radio station, 1991, Innovative Classrooms Practices Orange County Schs., 1991, commendation Edn. Commn. State of Fla., 1990. Mem. Assn. Curriculum and Suprvsn., Nat. Edn. Assn., Phi Delta Kappa, Phi Kappa Phi.

SWANSON, EMILY, state legislator; b. Oak Park, Ill., Jan. 12, 1947; m. Tim Swanson; 2 children. BA, Bennington Coll.; MA, U. Calif., Berkeley. Mem. Mont. Ho. of Reps. Home: 15042 Kelly Canyon Rd Bozeman MT 59715-9625 Office: Mont Ho of Reps State Capitol Helena MT 59620*

SWANSON, KARIN, hospital administrator, consultant; b. New Britain, Conn., Dec. 8, 1942; d. Oake F. and Ingrid Lauren Swanson; m. B. William Dorsey, June 26, 1965 (div. 1974); children: Matthew W., Julie I., Alison K.; m. Sanford H. Low, Oct. 14, 1989. BA in Biology, Middlebury Coll., 1964; MPH, Yale U., 1981. Biology tchr. Kents Hill (Maine) Sch., 1964-66; laboratory instr. Bates Coll., Lewiston, Maine, 1974-78; asst. to gen. dir. Mass. Eye and Ear Infirmary, Boston, 1979-80; v.p. profl. services Portsmouth (N.H.) Hosp., 1981-83; v.p. Health Strategy Assn. Ltd., Chestnut Hill, Mass., 1983-85; v.p. med. affairs Cen. Maine Med. Ctr., Lewiston, 1986-89; health care mgmt. cons. Cambridge, Mass., 1989-91; CEO Hahnemann Hosp., Brighton, Mass., 1991-94; adminstr. Vencor Hosp., Boston, 1994-95; pres., CEO The Laser Inst. New Eng., Newton, Mass., 1996—. Mem. Phi Beta Kappa. Home: 198 Glen St Natick MA 01760-5606

SWANSON, KRISTY, actress; b. Mission Viejo, Calif., 1969. Appeared in films Pretty in Pink, Ferris Bueller's Day Off, Deadly Friend, Flowers in the Attic, Diving in, Mannequin Two On the Move, Hot Shots, Highway to Hell, Buffy the Vampire Slayer, The Program, The Chase, Getting In (Student Body), Higher Learning; appearances in tv shows include Dreamfinders, Knots Landing, Nightingales; appearances in made-for-tv movies include Miracle of the Heart: A Boys Town Story, Not Quite Human. Office: care Creative Artists Agy 9830 Wilshire Blvd Beverly Hills CA 90212*

SWANSON, LORNA ELLEN, physical therapist, athletic trainer, researcher; b. Bridgeport, Conn., July 22, 1954; d. Harold Carl and Marna Ellyn (French) S.; m. James M. Kelley, Oct. 16, 1993; 1 child, Ellen Elizabeth Kelley. BFA in Dance, So. Meth. U., 1975, MFA in Dance, 1978; BS in Phys. Therapy, U. Tex., Dallas, 1984; PhD in Exercise Sci., U. Tenn., 1994. Lic. phys. therapist, Tenn. Mem. faculty Brookhaven Coll., Dallas, 1982-84; staff therapist St. Mary's Med. Ctr., Knoxville, Tenn., 1984-85, Ft. Sanders Regional Med. Ctr., Knoxville, 1985-86, Knoxville Sports Therapy, 1991-92; program dir., mem. faculty Roane State C.C., Harriman, Tenn., 1987-92; clin. specialist Ft. Sanders Ctr. for Sports Medicine, Knoxville, 1992-93, mgr., 1994-96; clin. specialist Ft. Sanders Therapy Ctr. West, Knoxville, 1996—; grad. asst. athletic dept. U. Tenn., Knoxville, 1989-91; reviewer Jour. Orthopedic and Sports Phys. Therapy, 1993, 94; adj. faculty Pellissippi State Tech. C.C., 1994.; instr. East Tenn. Acad. Performing Arts, 1995-96; speaker at state and nat. profl. confs. Contbr. chpt. to book and articles to profl. jours. Ballet mistress Victoria Bolen Dance Theatre, Knoxville, 1986-88; mem. bd. of trust Appalachian Ballet Co., 1995—. Helen B. Watson dissertation rsch. awardee U. Tenn. Mem. Am. Phys. Therapy Assn. (bd. content experts 1990-93), Tenn. Phys. Therapy Assn., Nat. Athletic Tng. Assn. (cert. athletic trainer), Tenn. Athletic Tng. Assn., Nat. Strength and Conditioning Assn. (cert. specialist), Neurodevel. Treatment Assn. (nominating com. 1987-89). Democrat. Lutheran. Office: Ft Sanders Therapy Ctr West 200 Fort Sanders W Blvd Ste 204 Knoxville TN 37922-3355

SWANSON, NORMA FRANCES, federal agency administrator; b. Blue Island, Ill., Oct. 24, 1923; d. Arnold Raymond and Bessie Oween (Bewley) Brown; m. George Clair Swanson, Mar. 18, 1948; 1 child, Dane Craig. AB, Asbury Coll., 1946; BS cum laude, Eastern Nazarene Coll., Wollaston, Mass., 1970; MA cum laude, Ind. Christian U., 1986. Confidential asst. dep. undersec. interagy. intergovt. affairs U.S. Dept. Edn., Washington, 1981—; pres. Window to the World, Inc., Schroon Lake, N.Y., 1985—; asst. dir. edn. Commn. Bicentennial U.S. Constn., Washington, 1987—; dir. Horizons Plus Values Program Hampton Roads Va. Detention Homes; dir. Project Fresh Start Washington D.C. Pub. Sch., 1993-96; cons. Conf. Industrialized Nations, Williamsburg, Va., 1982, Nellie Thomas Inst. Learning, Monterey, Calif., 1981-82. Author: Dear Teenager, A Teen's Guide to Correct Social Behavior, 1987, A Constitution is Born, A Teacher's Guide to Resource Materials, 1987, Sunlights and More, Bright Beginnings, 1993, Vol. II, 1996, The Ones that Count and Other Stories with Values to Live By, 1994, A Think and Write Journal Sunlights and More Vol. II, 1996; editor: (anthology) Horizons Plus; developer ednl. materials; theorem artist Early Life mag., 1974. Bd. regents Ind. Christian U., 1986—; program dir. Tidewater (Va.) Outreach, 1992; dir. project Fresh Start, Washington Pub. Sch., 1993-94; dir. youth outreach with values program U.S. Dept. Juvenile Justice, 1992-93. Recipient J.C. Penney award for volunteerism, 1993, Precision Tune awrd for svc. tto Washington Inner-City Schs. Republican. Baptist. Address: 11 Cross Manor Rd #D Saint Inigoes MD 20684-3003

SWANSON, PATRICIA K., university official; b. St. Louis, May 8, 1940; d. Emil Louis and Patricia (McNair) Klick; 1 child, Ivan Clatanoff. BS in Edn., U. Mo., 1962; postgrad., Cornell U., 1963; MLS, Simmons Coll., 1967. Reference librarian Simmons Coll., Boston, 1967-68; reference librarian U. Chgo., 1970-79, sr. lectr. Grad. Library Sch., 1974-83, 86-88, head reference service, 1979-83, asst. dir. for sci. libraries, 1983-93, acting asst. dir. for tech. svcs., 1987-88, assoc. provost, 1993—; project dir. Office Mgmt. Svcs., Assn. Rsch. Librs., 1982-83; speaker in field; cons. on libr. mgmt., planning and space. Author: Great is the Gift that Bringeth Knowledge: Highlights from the History of the John Crerar Library, 1989; contbr. articles to profl. jours. Office: U of Chicago Office of the Provost 5801 S Ellis Ave Rm 501 Chicago IL 60637-1404

SWANSON, PEGGY EUBANKS, finance educator; b. Ivanhoe, Tex., Dec. 29, 1936; d. Leslie Samuel and Mary Lee (Reid) Eubanks; m. B. Marc Summers, Nov. 10, 1993. BBA, U. North Tex., 1957, M. Bus. Edn., 1965; MA in Econs., So. Meth. U., 1967, PhD in Econs., 1978. Instr. El Centro Coll., Dallas, 1967-69, 71-78, bus. div. chmn., 1969-71; asst. prof. econs. U. Tex., Arlington, 1978-79, asst. prof. fin., 1979-84, assoc. prof., 1984-86, chmn. dept. fin. and real estate, 1986-88, prof. fin., 1987—; expert witness various law firms, primarily Tex. and Calif., 1978—; cons. Internat. Edn. Program, 1992—; curriculum cons. U. Monterrey, Mexico, 1995. Contbr. articles to profl. jours. Vol. Am. Cancer Soc., Dallas, Arlington, 1981—, Meals on Wheels, Arlington, 1989—; mem. adv. bd. Ryan/Reilly Ctr. for Urban Land Utilization, Arlington, 1986-88. Mem. Fin. Exec. Inst. (chmn. acad. rels. 1987-88), Internat. Bus. Steering Com. (chmn. 1989-91), Am. Fin. Assn., Am. Econ. Assn., Fin. Mgmt. Assn. (hon. faculty mem. Nat. Honor Soc. 1985-86), Southwestern Fin. Assn. (program com. 1987-88, 96), Acad. of Internat. Bus. (program com. 1992-95), Phi Beta Delta (membership com. 1987-89). Republican. Episcopalian. Home: 4921 Bridgewater Dr Arlington TX 76017-2729 Office: U Tex at Arlington UTA Box 19449 Arlington TX 76019

SWANSON-SCHONES, KRIS MARGIT, developmental adapted physical education educator; b. Mpls., Mar. 22, 1950; d. Donald Theodore Swanson and Alice Alida (Swanson) Suhl; m. Gary Wallace Suhl, Apr. 6, 1974 (div. Aug. 1985); m. Gregory Edward Schones, Dec. 30, 1989. BA, Augsburg Coll., 1972. Cert. devel. adapted phys. edn. tchr., phys. edn. tchr., health tchr., coach/corrective therapist. Devel. adapted phys. edn. tchr. St. Paul Schs., 1972—, adapted athletic dir., 1989—; mem. adapted athletics adv. bd. Minn. State H.S. League, 1992—. Author: On the Move, 1979. Chmn. hospitality Tanbark Club, Lakeville, Minn., 1992—, mem. show cmty., 1991—; mem. outreach com. Spl. Olympics, Minn., 1989-94. Recipient Nutrition Edn. grant Fed. Govt., 1978-79, Christmas Album grant Spl. Olympics, 1989, Internat. Spl. Olympics Coach award Minn. Spl. Olympics, 1991. Mem. NEA, AAHPERD, Minn. Edn. Assn., Minn. Assn. Adapted Athletics (exec. bd. 1989—, sec. exec. bd. 1990—). Home: 16280 Webster Ct Prior Lake MN 55372-9772 Office: St Paul Schs Bridgeview 360 Colborne St Saint Paul MN 55102-3228

SWANTON, SUSAN IRENE, library director; b. Rochester, N.Y., Nov. 29, 1941; d. Walter Frederick and Irene Wray S.; m. Wayne Holman, Apr. 12, 1969 (div. June 1973); 1 child, Michael; life ptnr. James Donald Lathrop; children: Kathryn, Kristin. AB, Harvard U., 1963; MLS, Columbia U., 1965. Libr. dir. Warsaw (N.Y.) Pub. Libr., 1963-64, Gates Pub. Libr., Rochester, N.Y., 1965—. Pres. Drug and Alcohol Coun., Rochester, 1985-91, mem. adv. coun., 1992-94; bd. dirs., co-chairperson info. svcs. Rochester Freenet, 1995—. Mem. Gates-Chili Coun. Rochester Met. C. of C. (pres. 1982, sec. 1990-94, Citizen of Yr. 1995), Harvard Club of Rochester (mem. adv. bd.). Office: Gates Pub Libr 1605 Buffalo Rd Rochester NY 14624-1637

SWARNER, DEBRA EILEEN, university administrator; b. Carlisle, Pa., Oct. 6, 1963; d. Marlin L. and Janet A. (Weary) S. BA, Messiah Coll., 1986; MA, Ea. Coll., 1995. Sales coord. Best Western, Carlisle, Pa., 1986-92; housing and vol. coord. Ea. Mennonite U., Harrisonburg, Va., 1995—. Vol. Miss Cumberland Valley Scholarship Pageant of Miss Pa./Miss Am., 1990-95. Mem. ACA, Assn. of Coll. and Univ. Housing Officers, Assn. of Christians in Student Devel. Office: Ea Mennonite Univ 1200 Park Rd Harrisonburg VA 22801-2462

SWART, BONNIE BLOUNT, artist; b. Shreveport, La., May 19, 1939; d. Jonathan Prescott and Alice Florence (Crawford) Blount; m. Carter Eaton Swart; children: Kathleen Anne Nelson, Nancy Laurie Michel, Sherry Colleen Swart. Student, U. Calif., Davis. Exhibited in group exhibitions at Am. Acad. Equine Art, Nat. Mus. of the Horse, Lexington, Ky., Ceres Western Art Show, Calif., 1995, 96, Pastel Soc. of the West Coast, Sacramento, 1995, 96, Eight Annual Exhbn. on Animals in Art, La. State U., Baton Rouge, 1995, 96, Art At the Dog Show, Wichita, Kans., 1995, 96, Harness Tracks of Am., Lexington, 1994, 96, Am. Acad. of Equine Art, Louisville, 1992, 93, 96, Arabian Jockey Club Art Aucion, Delaware Park, Del., 1991, Equine Rsch. Benefit, Morvin Park, Leesburg, 1991, Arabian Horse Trust Art Auction, Scottsdale, 1990, Women Artist's of the West, Louisville, 1989, Internat. Arabian Horse Assn., Ky. Horse Park, Louisville, 1989, Arabian Horse Trust Mus. Exhibit, Westminster, 1987-89, Internat. Arabian Horse Show Art Auction, Oklahoma City, 1987; represented in pvt. collections. Mem. Am. Acad. Equine Art (assoc.), Knickerbocker Artists, Pastel Soc. West Coast. Home: 191 Church Tree Rd Crescent City CA 95531

SWARTZ, CAROL I., academic administrator; b. Providence, Dec. 15, 1950; d. Leo L. and Lillian (Gordon) S. BA, U. R.I., 1973; MSW, Portland State U., 1977. Cert. social Worker, 1978. Social worker Children's Friend and Svcs., Providence, 1973-75; counselor S.E. Youth Svcs. Ctr., Portland, Oreg., 1975-77; dir. treatment Mt. Hood Treatment Ctr., Sandy, Oreg., 1977-79; coord. child devel. svcs. Corbett (Oreg.) Sch. Dist., 1978-80; clinician Homer (Alaska) Cmty. Mental Health Ctr., 1980-82; adj. instr. psychology and sociology U. Alaska, Kachemak Bay campus, Homer, 1984-86, dir., 1986—; founding dir. So. Peninsula Women's Svcs., Homer, 1981 83; mgmt. cons. 1984-86; Alaska guardian ad litem, 1984-86. Trustee Homer Found., 1993—; mem. Homer Sister City Assn., 1992—; bd. dirs. Pratt Mus., Homer, 1992-94, Homer Coun. of Arts, 1993-95. Mem. Nat. Assn. of Higher Edn., Nat. Assn. Women in Edn., Nat. Assn. Women in C.C., Rotary Internat., Homer C. of C. (Citizen of Yr. nominee 1983, 86). Home: PO Box 2748 Homer AK 99603

SWARTZ, ROSLYN HOLT, real estate investment executive; b. Los Angeles, Dec. 9, 1940; d. Abe Jack and Helen (Canter) Holt; m. Allan Joel Swartz, June 2, 1963. AA, Santa Monica (Calif.) Coll., 1970; BA summa cum laude, UCLA, 1975; MA, Pepperdine U., 1976. Cert. community coll. instr., student-personnel worker, Calif. Mgr. pub. relations Leader Holdings, Inc., L.A., 1968-75, pres., 1991—; sec., treas. Leader Holdings, Inc., North Hollywood, Calif., 1975-81, pres., 1981-91; chief exec. officer Beverly Stanley Investments, L.A., 1979—; pres. Leader Properties, Inc., The Leader Fairfax, Inc., Leader 358, Inc., Leader 359, Inc., Leader Ventura, Inc., 1996—. Condr. An Oral History of the Elderly Jewish Community of Venice, Calif. at Los Angeles County Planning Dept. Library, 1974. Mem. Hadassah (life), Friends of the Hollywood Bowl; bd. dirs. Am. Friends of Haifa Med. Ctr. L.A., West L.A. Symphony; capital patron Simon Wiesenthal Ctr. Fellow Phi Beta Kappa (bicentennial); mem. NAFE, AAUW, Am. Soc. Profl. and Exec. Women, Nat. Women's Hall of Fame, Am. Pub. Health Assn., Am. Pharm. Assn., Women in Comml. Real Estate, L.A. World Affairs Coun., Town Hall (life), Century City C. of C., UCLA Alumni Assn. (life), UCLA Founders Circle, Women's Coun. Women's Guild Cedars-Sinai Med. Ctr., UCLA Prytanean Alumnae Assn., Santa Monica Coll. Alumni Assn. (life), Phrateres Internat., Order of Eastern Star, Phi Alpha Theta, Alpha Gamma Sigma, Alpha Kappa Delta, Phi Delta Kappa, Pi Gamma Mu. Office: PO Box 241784 Los Angeles CA 90024-9584

SWARTZBURG, SUSANNA GARRETSON, librarian; b. Summit, N.J., Aug. 26, 1938; d. Edwin Porter and Elsa Susanna (Heiland) Garretson; Marshall Swartzburg, Feb. 23, 1963; 1 child, Mark Ellis. BA in Philosophy, Wells Coll., 1960; MA in English Lit., NYU, 1962; MLS, Simmons Coll., 1966. Bibliog. rschr. U. Mich. Libr., Ann Arbor, 1963-64, N.Y. Pub. Libr., N.Y.C., 1964-65; project libr. Yale U. Libr., New Haven, Conn., 1966-71, preservation libr., 1971-72; dir. Alexander Libr. Rutgers U., New Brunswick, N.J., 1972-74, dir. art libr., 1974-75, preservation/gifts libr., 1975-85, asst. libr. collection mgmt., 1985—; mem. adv. bd. Northeast Doc. Cons. Ctr., Andover, Mass., 1979-86, 93—, Wells Coll. Book Arts Ctr., Aurora, N.Y., 1993—; mem. state libr. adv. com. preservation & access, 1988—. Author: Preserving Library Materials, 1980, 2d edit., 1995, Libraries and Archives, Design and Production, 1991; editor: Conservation in the Library, 1983. Mem. ALA, Am. Inst. Conservation, Am. Printing History Assn., Internat. Fedn. Libr. Assns. & Instns., Guild Book Workers, Art Libr. Soc., Soc. History Authorship, Reading & Pub. Home: 1050 George St #4L New Brunswick NJ 08901 Office: Rutgers U 169 College Ave New Brunswick NJ 08903-5062

SWARTZEL, MARY ELIZABETH, psychotherapist; b. Akron, Ohio, Apr. 10, 1952; d. John Douglas and Ethel Ada (Wise) Milne; m. Jeffrey Kyle Swartzel, Aug. 23, 1975; children: Richard John-Kyle, Devin Robert. BA, Ohio No. U., 1974; MS, St. Francis Coll., 1984; postgrad., Wright State U. Lic. social worker, Ohio. Crisis counselor Northwest Ctr. for Human Resources, Lima, Ohio, 1975-76; caseworker Shelby County Children Svcs. Bd., Sidney, Ohio, 1976-78; psychotherapist Mercer County Mental Health Ctr., Coldwater, Ohio, 1978-89, 93-95, exec. dir., 1989-93; social worker Otterbein-St. Mary's (Ohio) Nursing Facility, 1996—. Sec. Joint Coordinating Coun., Celina, Ohio, 1978-81; den leader Cub Scouts Pack 96, Coldwater, 1991-92; choir dir. for presch. Coldwater United Meth. Ch., 1990-95; active Red Cross Bd., Celina, 1990-92. Recipient 15 Yr. award for svc. Tri County Bd., 1994. Mem. ACA, Mercer County Mental Health Assn. (sec. 1989-93), Kiwanis. Home: 906 Mary Charles Ln Coldwater OH 45828

SWARTZMILLER, MILDRED M., art gallery owner; b. Flint, Mich., June 23, 1924; d. John and Anna Eva (Hrabinec) Chludil; m. John M. Bila, June 25, 1945 (div. June 1970); children: David, Sharon, Marsha; m. Joseph F. Swartzmiller, Nov. 5, 1987 (dec. Mar. 1996). Grad. h.s., Muskegon Heights. Sec. Swartzmiller Lumber, Chesaning, Mich.; treas. Chesaning Area Arts; part-owner Artist's Alley, Chesaning, 1994—. Contbr. poetry to anthologies. Vol. Chesaning Garden Club, 1984-94. Recipient Best Writing award AAUW, 1942. Home: 319 S Wood St Chesaning MI 48616

SWASY, ALECIA, newspaper editor; b. Indiana, Pa., Aug. 25, 1963; d. John and Maribel S. BA in Journalism, Pa. State U., 1985. Reporter Lexington (Ky.) Herald-Leader, 1986-87; reporter St. Petersburg (Fla.) Times, 1988, bus. editor, 1996—; reporter The Wall Street Jour., Pitts., 1988-91, Atlanta, 1993-94. Author: Soap Opera: The Inside Story of Procter & Gamble, 1993. Mem. Penn State Coll. Comm. Alumni Soc. Bd. (sec. 1995-96).

SWATERS, CHERIE LYNN BUTLER, nurse; b. Warrenton, Mo., Aug. 17, 1954; d. Thomas Pershing and Dorothy Fredrika (Wulff) Butler; m. James Louis Swaters, Jr., July, 20, 1974; children: Bradley Thomas, Rebecca Lynn. Diploma, St. Luke's Hosp. Sch. Nursing, Kansas City, Mo., 1979; BSN, Webster U., 1988. RN; cert. neonatal advanced life support. Staff nurse St. Luke's of Kansas City (Mo.), 1979-80, Menorah Med. Ctr., Kansas City, 1985-87, 87-89, North Kansas City (Mo.) Meml. Hosp., 1987, Liberty (Mo.) Hosp., 1989-96; perinatal continuing edn. program coord. Liberty Hosp., 1994-96. Sch. vol. PTA for Davidson Elem. Sch., Kansas City, 1985-92; sch. vol. Liberty Middle Sch., Ridgeview Elem. Sch., Liberty, Mo., 1992-93; facilitator of Grief Recovery Support Group for Liberty United Meth. Ch. Methodist.

SWATZELL, MARILYN LOUISE, nurse; b. Johnson City, Tenn., July 31, 1942; d. Dallas Fred and Minnie Thelma (Clark) S. BS cum laude, East Tenn. State U., 1966, MS, 1967; BSN, U. Tenn., 1974. Chmn. pediatric nursing Meth. Hosp. Sch. Nursing, Memphis, 1978-80; head nurse Le Bonheur Children's Med. Ctr., Memphis, 1981-83; dir. maternal child nursing Jackson (Tenn.) Madison County Gen. Hosp., 1985-88; staff nurse Vanderbilt U. Hosp., Nashville, 1988-90; supr. Meth. Hosp. Lexington, Tenn., 1990—. Contbr. articles on care plans to profl. jours. Mem. ANA, Tenn. Nurses Assn., Tenn. Orgn. Nurse Execs. Home: 231 Law Ln Lexington TN 38351-6048

SWAYZE, KATHLEEN CAROLYN, secondary school educator; b. Bethesda, Md., Sept. 19, 1967; d. Richard Dennis and Elaine Marian (Madden) Heenan; m. Mark Douglas Swayze, Jan. 13, 1990. B of Music Edn., Ind. U., 1989; M in Music Edn., Butler U., 1991. Artist intern Indpls. Pub. Schs., 1990-91; tchr. orch., music Pike Twp. Schs., Indpls., 1991-92, Washington Twp. Schs., Indpls., 1992—; sect. viola player Danville (Ill.) Symphony Orch., 1992—. Mem. Am. Fedn. Musicians, Am. String Tchrs. Assn., Music Educators Nat. Conf. Home: 3118 Brotherwood Ct Indianapolis IN 46268 Office: Westlane Mid Sch 1301 W 73rd St Indianapolis IN 46260-3919

SWAZEY, JUDITH POUND, institute president, sociomedical science educator; b. Bronxville, N.Y., Apr. 21, 1939; d. Robert Earl and Louise Titus (Hanson) Pound; m. Peter Woodman Swazey, Nov. 28, 1964; children: Elizabeth, Peter. AB, Wellesley Coll., 1961; PhD, Harvard U., 1966. Rsch. assoc. Harvard U., 1966-71, lectr., 1969-71, rsch. fellow, 1971-72; cons. com. brain scis. NRC, 1971-73; staff scientist neuroscis. rsch. program MIT, Cambridge, 1973-74; assoc. prof. dept. socio-med. scis. and community medicine Boston U., 1974-77, prof., 1977-80, adj. prof. Schs. Medicine and Pub. Health, 1980—; exec. dir. Medicine in the Pub. Interest, Inc., Boston and Washington, 1979-82, 89-93; pres. Coll. of the Atlantic, Bar Harbor, Maine, 1982-84, Acadia Inst., Bar Harbor, 1984—; mem. Army Sci. Bd., 1987-92. Author: Reflexes and Motor Integration, the Development of Sherrington's Integrative Action Concept, 1969, (with others) Human Aspects of Biomedical Innovation, 1971, (with R. C. Fox) The Courage to Fail, a Social View of Organ Transplants and Hemodialysis, 1975, rev. edit., 1978 (hon. mention Am. Med. Writers Assn., C. Wright Mills award Am. Sociol. Assn.), Chlorpromazine in Psychiatry, a Study of Therapeutic Innovation, 1974, (with K. Reeds) Today's Medicine, Tomorrow's Science, Essays on Paths of Discovery in the Biomedical Sciences, 1978; editor: (with C. Wong) Dilemmas of Dying, Policies and Procedures for Decisions Not to Treat, 1981, (with F. Worden and G. Adelman) The Neurosciences: Paths of Discovery, 1975, (with R. C. Fox) Spare Parts, Organ Replacement in American Society, 1992; assoc. editor IRB: A Jour. of Human Subjects Rsch., 1979—; mem. editl. bd. Sci. and Engring. Ethics, 1994—; contbr. articles to profl. jours. Mem. Maine Dept. Human Svcs. Bioethics Adv. Com. (chair 1991-94); mem. Commn. on Rsch. Integrity, 1994-95; bd. dirs. Maine Bioethics Network, 1994—. Wellesley Coll. scholar, 1961; Wellesley Coll. Alumnae fellow Harvard U., 1966, NIH predoctoral fellow, 1966, Radcliffe Coll. Coll. grad. fellow, 1966. Mem. AAAS (sci. freedom and responsibility com. 1986-89), Inst. Medicine NAS (mem. health scis. policy bd. 1986-89), Grad. Record Exam. (bd. dirs. 1987-91), Sherrington Soc., Phi Beta Kappa, Sigma Xi. Office: Acadia Inst PO Box 43 Bar Harbor ME 04609

SWEASY, JOYCE ELIZABETH, government official, military reserve officer; b. Key West, Fla., Apr. 25, 1948; d. James Alfred and Josephine Mary (Fassel) Messick. BFA, Phila. Coll. Art, 1971; A in Bus. Adminstrn., Howard County Community Coll., 1985; grad., Army Command and Gen. Staff Co, 1988. Commd. 1st lt. U.S. Army, 1978, advanced through grades to lt. col., 1996; contract specialist U.S. Army, Adelphi, 1978-84, analyst procurement Lab. Command,, 1984-85; appointed command competition adv. Sec. of the Army, Adelphi, 1985-91; dep. chief of staff procurement, 1991-92, div. chief small bus. adminstrn., 1992-94; chief constrn. and arch. engring. contracting NIH, Bethesda, Md., 1994—; owner, operator Hand Made 'N Ellicott City, Md., 1983—; owner, gen. mgr. Data Solutions. Contbr. numerous articles to profl. jours. Mem. Font Hill Citizens Orgn., Ellicott City, 1987—. Mem. U.S. Army Res. Officers Assn, Nat. Contract Mgrs. Assn., Am. Def. Preparedness Assn. Republican. Roman Catholic. Home: 4008 Arjay Cir Ellicott City MD 21042-5608 Office: NIH Bethesda MD 20892

SWEED, PHYLLIS, publishing executive; b. N.Y.C., Dec. 6, 1931; d. Paul and Frances (Spitzer) S.; m. Leonard Bogdanoff (dec. Oct. 1975); children: Patricia Romano (dec.), James Alan. BA, NYU, 1950. Asst. buyer Nat. Bellas Hess, N.Y.C., 1950; assoc. editor Fox-Shulman Pub., N.Y.C., 1951-57; products editor McGraw-Hill Pub., N.Y.C., 1957-61; mng. editor Haire Pub., N.Y.C., 1962-66; editor Gifts & Decorative Accessories Mag., 1966-78; sr. v.p. Geyer-McAllister Pub., N.Y.C., 1978—, editor, co-pub., 1978-95, editor-in-chief, co-pub., 1995—. Bd. dirs. Frances Hook Scholarship Fund, 1989-96. Recipient Editorial Excellence award Indsl. Mktg., 1964, Nat. Assn. Ltd. Edit. Dealers award, 1993, 96, MagWek Excellence award, 1992, Dallas Mkt. Ctr. award, 1969, 80, 82. Mem. Nat. Assn. Ltd. Ed. Dealers (assoc.), Internat. Furnishings and Design Assn. Home: 505 Laguardia Pl New York NY 10012-2001 Office: Geyer-McAllister Publs 51 Madison Ave New York NY 10010-1603

SWEENEY, JEAN MARIA, lawyer; b. N.Y.C., July 2, 1956; d. John Joseph and Rita Valerie (Colleran) Sweeney; m. David Thomas Maloof, Aug. 11, 1990; 1 child, Julia Jean Maloof. BA in English Lit., Coll. of the Holy Cross, Worcester, Mass., 1978; JD, St. John's U., Jamacia, Queens, 1982. Bar: N.Y. 1983; Supreme Ct. State of N.Y., 1983; U.S. Dist. Ct. (so. dist.)

N.Y., 1983. Assoc. atty. First Investers Corp., N.Y.C., 1983-86; assoc. Emmet, Marvin & Martin, N.Y.C., 1986-92; v.p. to first v.p. Shearson Lehman Brothers, N.Y.C., 1992-93; first v.p. Smith Barney, Inc., N.Y.C., 1993—. Democrat. Roman Catholic. Office: Smith Barney Inc 388 Greenwich St New York NY 10013-2375*

SWEENEY, JUDITH L., newspaper publishing executive. V.p., pres. Orange County edit. L.A. Times. Office: LA Times Times Mirror Sq Los Angeles CA 90012*

SWEENEY, LUCY GRAHAM, psychologist; b. Davenport, Iowa, Nov. 14, 1946; d. B. Graham and Dorothy (Lawson) S.; m. Richard N. Tiedemann, Dec. 2, 1978 (div. 1989); 1 child, Susan Lee. AA, William Woods Coll., 1966; BA with honors, U. Denver, 1968; MA in Devel. Psychology, Columbia U., 1977; PsyD, Rutgers U., 1990. Cert. family therapist. Profl. actress, 1968-73; dir. therapeutic play and recreation program St. Luke's Med. Ctr., N.Y.C., 1973-78; child life coord. St. Francis Hosp., Hartford, Conn., 1978-80; clinician Resolve Community Counseling Ctr., Scotch Plains, N.J., 1981-84; staff psychologist women's inpatient unit Lyons (N.J.) VA Med. Ctr., 1990; psychologist women's treatment program Fair Oaks Hosp., Summit, N.J., 1990-92; cons. Kessler Inst. for Rehab., East Orange, N.J., 1992-94, Resolve Community Counseling Ctr., Scotch Plains, N.J., 1992—; pvt. practice Westfield, N.J., 1993—. Contbr. articles to profl. jours. Recipient John Weyandt award for Outstanding Student in Theatre U. Denver, 1968. Mem. APA, N.J. Psychol. Assn., Phi Theta Kappa. Home: 21 Harwich Ct Scotch Plains NJ 07076-3165

SWEENEY, ROSEMARIE, medical association administrator; b. Fall River, Mass., Sept. 2, 1950; d. John Francis and Phyllis (Field) S.; m. Edmund Burke Rice, Feb. 24, 1978; 1 child, Jonathan Field Rice. Student, Hillsdale Coll., 1968-69; BA, Am. U., 1972, MPA, 1978. Profl. staff mem. Office of Rep. Margaret Heckler, Washington, 1972-74; staff assoc. fed. agy. affairs Am. Osteo. Assn., Washington, 1974-78, govt. affairs rep., 1978-79; dir. Washington office Am. Acad. Family Physicians, Washington, 1979-82; v.p. socioeconomic affairs and policy analysis, 1992—; mem. family practice adv. com. George Washington U., Washington, 1990—. Vol. Montgomery County Sexual Assault Svc., Rockville, Md., 1984-93; mem. Glen Echo Fire Dept., Bethesda, Md., 1986-92, Victim Svcs. Adv. Bd., Md., 1987-93; chmn. victim svc. adv. bd. Montgomery County, Md., 1991-93; bd. dirs. Westmoreland Children's Ctr., Bethesda. Recipient Outstanding Svc. award Montgomery County Crisis Ctr., Md., 1986, Outstanding Performance award Montgomery County Sexual Assault Svc., Md., 1987, Recognition award Soc. Tchrs. Family Medicine, Kansas City, Mo., 1990, Govs.' Sixth Annual Victim Assistance award, Balt., 1991. Mem. Women in Govt. Rels. Office: Am Acad Family Physicians 2021 Massachusetts Ave NW Washington DC 20036-1011

SWEENEY, VONNY HILTON, promotion company executive; b. Brownsville, Pa., Aug. 24, 1947; d. James and Ann Hilton; divorced; 1 child, Howard Hilton. AA, Am. River Coll., 1971; BA, Calif. State U., Sacramento, 1974. Nat. promotion coord. Sussex Records, L.A., 1974; adminstr. asst. promotion and pub. rels. Playboy, L.A., 1974-76; mgr. Polydor rec. artists Alton McClain & Destiny, L.A., 1976-80; mgr. Polygram rec. artists Lace Wing, L.A., 1985-90; pres. James Brown West, Inc., Hollywood, Calif., 1990—; cons., publicist James Brown Prodns., Augusta, Ga., 1974—; founder, chair Annual Pre-Grammy Gala, L.A., 1980—. Asst. producer Ebony Music Awards, L.A., 1975. Fundraiser various politicians, L.A. and Sacramento, 1974—; mem. com. Miss Black L.A., 1990. Mem. Nat. Acad. Recording Arts and Scis., Am. Film Inst. Office: PO Box 691354 West Hollywood CA 90069-9354

SWEET, CYNTHIA KAY, business administrator; b. Highland, Kans., Feb. 21, 1949; d. Jack Wendull and Ruthanna (Dittemore) Hedrick; m. Roger Keith Alexander, 1968; children: Karen Joyce, Melinda Ruth Anne; m. Erich Christian Sweet, Oct. 31, 1990. Student, U. Kans., 1968, North Peralta Coll., 1973-74, U. Colo., 1976-79; BS in Bus. Tech., Empire State Coll., 1984. Computer operator Computer Ctr. U. Colo., Boulder, 1977-79; subscription coord. Inst. Arctic & Alpine Rsch., Boulder, 1979; computer operator Computer Ctr. Rensselaer Poly. Inst., Troy, N.Y., 1979-80, dir. devel. info. svcs., 1982-85; rsch. analyst N.Y. State Mus., Albany, 1979-80, project mgr., 1980-82; product mgr. Info. Assocs., Rochester, N.Y., 1985-89, sr. program mgr., 1990-92; applications mgr. Claris Corp., Santa Clara, Calif., 1989-90; custom programming mgr. Datatel, Fairfax, Va., 1992-94; exec. dir. advancement solutions TRG, Phoenix, 1994—, dir. devel. USA group, 1996—; freelance fundraising cons., Albany and Rochester, 1984-89. Contbr. articles to profl. jours. Activity coord. Info. Assocs./United Way, Rochester, 1985-89, 91-92; mem. festival staff meml. Art Gallery, Rochester, 1987-89; bd. dirs. Draper Dance Theatre, Rochester, 1988-92. Mem. NAFE, ACLU, Am. Assn. Mus., Nat. Soc. for Fundraising Execs., Coun. for Advancement and Support of Edn., Project Mgmt. Inst., Sierra. Office: USA Group TRG 4343 E Camelback Rd Phoenix AZ 85018

SWEETING, LINDA MARIE, chemist; b. Toronto, Ont., Can., Dec. 11, 1941; came to U.S., 1965, naturalized, 1979; d. Stanley H. and Mary (Robertson) S. BSc, U. Toronto, 1964, MA, 1965; PhD, UCLA, 1969. Asst. prof. chemistry Occidental Coll., L.A., 1969-70; asst. prof. chemistry Towson (Md.) State U., 1970-75, assoc. prof., 1975-85, prof., 1985—; guest worker NIH, 1976-77; program dir. chem. instrumentation NSF, 1981-82; vis. scholar Harvard U., 1984-85; contractor U.S. Army MRICD, 1991-93. Bd. dirs. Chamber Music Soc. Balt., 1985-91. Exec. com. Exptl. NMR. Conf. 1985-87, local arr. chair 1986. Mem. Md. Acad. Scis. (mem. sci. council 1975-83, 89-94), Assn. for Women in Sci. (treas. 1977-78, Woman of Yr. 1989), Am. Chem. Soc. (mem. women chemists Com. 1983-89), AAAS, Nature Conservancy, Sierra Club, Sigma Xi (sec. TSU Club 1979-81, 95—, Towson chpt. pres. 1987-88, 91-92, sec. 1995—, mid-Atlantic nominating com. 1987-90, regional dir. 1988-89, nat. nominating com. 1991-94). Office: Towson State U Dept Chemistry Baltimore MD 21252-7097

SWEETLAND, ANNETTE FLORENCE (ANNIE SWEETLAND), special education educator; b. Dallas; d. George R. and Odessa (Donnhue) S.; children: George William Davison, James Erron Davison; m. Ralph J. Guinn. BS in Edn., U. Okla., 1988, MS in Edn., 1992. Lic. profl. counselor. Tchr. multi-handicapped students Noble (Okla.) Pub. Sch., 1988-90; child-find S.E.A.R.C.H. coord. and preschool handicap tchr. Shawnee (Okla.) Pub. Sch., 1989-93; regional coord. Sooner Start Okla. Dept. Edn., Norman, 1993-94; case mgr. II Developmental Disabilities Scv. Divsn./DHS, State of Okla., Oklahoma City, 1994-95; spl. educator Okla. Youth Ctr., 1995—; mgr. group home Able Group Homes, Norman, Okla., 1989-90; dir. returning adult program St. Gregory's Coll., Shawnee, 1990-91. Mem. ARC, ACA, Coun. for Exceptional Children, Okla. Edn. Assn.

SWEETSER, SUSAN W., state legislator, lawyer, advocate; b. Dec. 13, 1958; d. Robert Joseph and Lucretia Rose (Donnelly) Williams. BA in Polit. Sci./Environ. Adminstrn. with high honors, Johnson (Vt.) State Coll., 1982; JD magna cum laude, Vt. Law Sch., 1985. Bar: N.Y. 1986, Vt. 1986, U.S. Dist. Ct. Vt. 1989; CLU, ChFC. Confidential law clk. Appellate div. N.Y. Supreme Ct., Albany, 1985-86; assoc. Gravel & Shea, Burlington, Vt., 1986-90; atty. Nat. Life Ins. Co., Montpelier, Vt., 1990—; now mem. Vt. State Senate; victims rights adv. Essex Junction, Vt., 1980—; adj. prof. bus. law St. Michael's Coll., Winooski, Vt., 1991—, Johnson State Coll., 1995—; justice of peace Town of Essex, 1991-95; chair judiciary com.; former mem. Health and Welfare Com.; mem. Housing and Conservation Trust Fund Study Com., Civil Rights Study Com., Adoption Law Reform Study Com., Appropriations Com. Author articles on victims rights. Trustee Vt. State Colls., Waterbury, 1979-81, Univ. Health Ctr., 1992-94; mem. ethics com. Fanny Allen Hosp., Winooski, Vt., 1989-92; v.p. Lyric Theatre, Burlington, 1989—; mem. Vt. Rep. State Com., Montpelier, chmn. Rep. State Conv., 1988, 92; founder, pres. Survivors of Crime, Inc. Recipient Achievement award Vt. Law Enforcement Coordinating Com., 1990, Vt. Ctr. for Prevention and Treatment of Sexual Abuse and The Safer Soc. Program, 1991, Nat. recognition for victims rights work The Giraffe Project, 1991, award Nat. Found. for Improvement of Justice, 1993; named 754th Point of Light by former Pres. George Bush, 1992, Am. Heroine Ladies Home Jour., 1991, Legislator of Yr. Nat. Rep. Legislators Assn., 1995. Fellow AAUW; mem. Vt. Bar Assn., N.Y. State Bar Assn., Internat. Assn. Fin. Planners (chmn. legis. affairs Greater Vt. chpt. 1988-91). Roman Catholic. Office: Survivors of Crimes Inc PO Box 8304 Essex VT 05451-8304

SWENSEN, JOAN LINDA, educator; b. Ida Grove, Iowa, Jan. 5, 1948; d. Melvin August and Virginia Ann (Lindskoog) Schmidt; m. Dwain Donald Swensen, Aug. 6, 1977; children: Jennifer Ann, Jodie Lynn. BA, U. Northern Iowa, 1970. Elem. edn. tchr. Webster City (Iowa) Cmty. Schs., 1970-72, Morrison Acad., Taichung, Taiwan, Republic of China, 1973-75, Ida Grove (Iowa) Cmty. Schs., 1976-77, Odebolt (Iowa) Cmty. Schs., 1978—. Vol. children's groups Kiron Bapt. Ch., Kiron, Iowa, 1977—. Mem. Quint-County Reading Coun. (corresponding sec. 1982-83, treas. 1985-86), Iowa Reading Assn., Internat. Reading Assn., Kappa Delta Pi. Home: 1231 290th St Kiron IA 51448 Office: Odebolt-Arthur Cmty Sch 600 S Maple Odebolt IA 51458

SWENSEN, MARY JEAN HAMILTON, graphic artist; b. Laurens, S.C., June 25, 1910; d. Elvin A. and Della (Brown) Hamilton; m. Oliver Severn Swensen, Mar. 3, 1943 (dec.). BS, Columbia U., 1956, MA, 1960; Cert. Notable, U. Madrid, Spain; postgrad., Ariz. State U., 1974-80. mem. 1st USSA sr. internat. cross-country skiing team. One person shows at Colo. Fed. Savs. and Loan Assn., Denver, 1978, Panoras Gallery, N.Y.C., 1963; exhibited in group shows at Soc. Western Artist, M.H. de Young Mus., San Francisco, 1964, Nat. Art Roundup, Las Vegas, 1965, Fine Arts Bldg., Colo. State Fair, Pueblo, 1965, Duncan Gallery, Paris, 1974, Colo. Fed. Savs. & Loan Assn., Denver, 1978; graphics arts in pub. collections at Met. Mus. Art, N.Y.C., Nat. Graphic Arts Collection, Smithsonian Inst., Laurens (S.C.) Pub. Libr., N.Y.C. Pub. Libr. Assoc. Libr. of Congress, Archael. Inst. Am., Smithsonian Instn., Johns Hopkins. Recipient Duncan Gallery Prix de Paris, 1974, Notable award M.H. de Young Mus., 1964, YWCA of U.S.A. Gold Medal as most admired athlete of yr., 1977, USSA Nat. Vets. X-Country Racing Team Gold, Silver and Bronze medals for downhill, giant slalom, slalom, and cross-country sr. citizen and vet. races, 1963-79. Mem. Internat. Platform Assn., Am. Mensa, Columbia Club N.Y., Delta Phi Delta.

SWENSON, HOLLY ANN, software developer; b. Gladstone, Mich., Dec. 20, 1963; d. William A. and Juanita F. (Holmberg) S. BA, No. Mich. U., 1987. Programmer Intercontinental Fin. Group, Chgo., 1988-90; analyst programmer Rand McNally, Skokie, Ill., 1990-93, sys. adminstr., 1993-94, programmer, analyst, 1994-96, tech. cons., 1996—. Bd. dirs. Ctrl. Bennett East Coop., Evanston, Ill., 1993—. Mem. No. Mich. U. Alumni Assn., Order Ea. Star, Job's Daus., Job's Daus. Alumni Assn. (founding). Lutheran.

SWENSON, MARY ANN, bishop. Bishop Rocky Mountain Conf., Denver. Office: Rocky Mountain Conference 2200 S University Blvd Denver CO 80210-4708

SWENSON, SUSAN ANN, engineering recruiting company executive; b. Lansing, Mich., July 30, 1948; d. Milton Cecil and Dorothy Frances (Manuel) Taylor; m. John William Deutschmann, Apr. 17, 1982 (div. Oct. 1995); 1 child, Danielle Cecile. BA in Sociology, U. Wis., 1971; MSW, Mich. State U., 1974. Cert. social worker. Vocat. rehab. counselor Portland, Oreg., 1982-88; recruiter rschr. Corp. Builders, Portland, 1989; engring. recruiter Fran Low, Ltd., Portland, 1989-91; owner Swenson & Assocs., Scottsdale, Ariz., 1991—; social and rehab. svcs. trainee U.S. Govt. Mich. State U., East Lansing, 1972-73, 73-74. Asst. coach Arcadia Scottsdale United Soccer Club, 1995; soccer player N.W. United Women's Soccer, 1980-93; soccer player, mgr. Misfits Soccer Team, 1993-95. Mem. AAUW, Nationwide Interchange Svc., Inc., Ariz. Assn. Pers. Svcs. Democrat. Home and Office: Swenson & Assocs 8502 E Cholla St Scottsdale AZ 85260

SWERDLOW, AMY, historian, educator, writer; b. N.Y.C., Jan. 20, 1923; d. Joseph and Esther (Rodner) Galstuck; m. Stanley H. Swerdlow, Nov. 27, 1949 (dec. Sept. 1991); children: Joan Swerdlow-Brandt, Ezra, Lisa Thomas. BA, NYU, 1963; MA, Sarah Lawrence Coll., 1973; PhD, Rutgers U., 1984. Prof. emerita Sarah Lawrence Coll., Bronxville, N.Y., 1981-95, dir. grad. studies in women's history, 1983-95, dir. women's studies program, 1983—; mem. adv. bd. Feminist Press, 1973—. Editor, co-author: Families in Flux, 1980, reprint, 1989; author: Women Strike for Peace: Traditional Motherhood and Radical Politics in the 1960s, 1993; editor Feminist Perspective on Homework and Childcare, 1978; co-editor: Class, Race and Sex: The Dynamics of Control, 1983, Rethinking Women's Peace Studies, 1995; contbr. Sights on the Sixties: Reflections on a Critical Time, Women and Militarism: Essays in Hisotyr, Politics and Social Theory, Give Peace A Chance, The Abolitionist Sisterhood: Women's Political Culture in Antebellum America, 1994, American History as Women's History, 1994. Mem. nat. bd. conf. Pease Rsch. in History. Rutgers U. fellow, 1977-81, Woodrow Wilson Dissertation fellow, 1980. Mem. Am. Hist. Assn., Orgn. Am. Historians (coord. working com. of women in the hist. profession), Berkshire Conf. in Women's History. Home: 150 Claremont Ave Apt 4C New York NY 10027-4679

SWERDLOW, GERTRUDE KATZ, economist, educator; b. Chgo., June 14, 1915; d. Osias and Ethel (Apfelberg) Katz; m. Irving Swerdlow; children: Paul (dec.), Joel L., JoBetty. BA, Roosevelt Coll., 1942; MA, Syracuse (N.Y.) U., 1962. Cons. Dept. of Edn., Nor. Mariana Islands, 1976-77; cons. dept. of edn. Trust Ter. of the Pacific Islands, 1976-77, dir. vocat. edn., 1978; prof. econs. Onondaga C.C., Syracuse, N.Y., 1963-83; exec. dir., co-founder Families Against Cancer Terror, Syracuse, 1985—; textbook cons. McGraw Hill, Allyn Press. Trustee Onondaga C.C., Syracuse, 1984-93; exec. dir. vocat. adv. coun. Trust ter. of the Pacific Islands; vol. educator St. Michael's Sch. for the Blind, Rangoon, Burma; lectr. Rohtak Ctr. of Coll. Studies, Haryana, India, India and the Lahore Coll. for Women, Pakistan; co-founder FACT-A, Syracuse, 1985—; mem. program com. nat. coalition Cancer Rsch., Washington, 1993—; mem. tobacco edn. and advocacy coalition, N.Y.; mem. Fulbright Hart awards com. of N.Y. state; bd. trustees Ctrl. UN, World Affairs Assn. of Ctrl. N.Y. Recipient Merit award SUNY, Trustees Disting. Svc. award, Nat. award Joint Coun. on Econ. Edn. Mem. AAUW, Nat. Coalition for Cancer Rsch. Home: 521 Hillsboro Pkwy Syracuse NY 13214 Office: Families Against Cancer PO Box 588 De Witt NY 13214

SWETCHARNIK, SARA MORRIS, artist; b. Shelby, N.C., May 21, 1955; d. William Monroe and Nydia (Early) Morris; m. William Norton Swetcharnik. Grad., Schuler Sch. Fine Arts, Balt., 1978, postgrad., 1978-79; student, Art Students League, N.Y.C., 1979-81. Monitor for Robert Beverly Hale Art Students League, N.Y.C., 1979-81; instr. Frederick (Md.) Acad. Arts, 1981-82; workshop instr. Landon Sch., Washington, 1991-96. One-person exhbns. include Catepetl Gallery, Frederick, 1977, Holly Hills Country Club, Frederick, 1991, Landon Sch. Gallery, Washington, 1992, Frederick Cmty. Coll. Art Gallery, 1993, Weinberg Ctr. Arts., Frederick, 1994, 96, The Reptile House, Nat. Zool. Park, Washington, 96; two person exhbns. include Genesis Arts, Frederick, 1977, 78, 79, 80, Eikon Fine Arts, Frederick, 1979, Weinberg Ctr. Arts, 1980, Mt. St. Mary's Coll., Emmitsburg, Md., 1981, Christ Ch., Tarrytown, N.Y., 1982; exhibited in group shows at Catepetl Gallery, 1975-79, Jaffae Gallery, Balt., 1979-81, Harbor Gallery, Cold Spring Harbor, N.Y., 1982-84, Foxhall Gallery, 1982-85, Carroll Cmty. Coll. Gallery, 1992, Colorado Springs Coll. Art Gallery, 1994, Towson Unitarian Ch. Gallery, Balt., 1994, The 2d Gallery, Frederick, 1994, Nat. Zool. Park, Washington, 1994, Franklin Mint Mus., Franklin Square, Pa., 1994, Wesleyan U. Gallery, Ill., 1995, Nat. Sculpture Soc. Gallery, N.Y.C., 1995, Am. Numismatic Mus., Colorado Springs, 1995, Delaplaine Visual Arts Ctr., Frederick, 1995, 96, The Dog Mus., St Louis, 1996; competitive shows include Pastel Soc. of Am., N.Y.C., Miniature Painters, Sculptors and Gravers Soc., Washington; represented in pub. collections Haussner's Restaurant, Balt. Art Student League fellow 1981, IIE Fulbright fellow 1987-88, 1988-89, residency fellow Va. Ctr. Creative Arts, Sweet Briar, 1990, residency fellow Am. Numismatic Assn. Conf., 1994; recipient 1st Place sculpture award, Miniature Soc. of Sculptors, Painters, and Gravers, Washington, 1976, 1st Place sculpture award Allegheny Internat. Miniature Art Exhibit, 1989. Home and Studio: 7044 Woodville Rd Mount Airy MD 21771-7934

SWETNAM, RUTH E. DANGLADE, curriculum director; b. Marion, Ind., Jan. 27, 1940; d. Harold Davis and Elizabeth (Lake) Neel; m. James K. Danglade, Sept. 2, 1961 (div. Nov. 1979); children: Annette, John, Douglas, Adam, Matthew; m. Gary L. Swetnam, June 19, 1993. BS, Ball State U., 1961, MA, 1964. Cert. elem., secondary bus., spl. edn. and speech pathology tchr., Ind. Tchr. orthopedically handicapped Muncie (Ind.) Community Schs., 1961-67, tchr. of multiply handicapped, 1969-74, tchr. learning disabled, 1976-79; spl. edn. instr. Ball State U., Muncie, 1974-79; asst. dir. spl. edn. Delaware County Spl. Edn. Coop., Muncie, 1979-91; dir. curriculum Muncie Community Schs., 1991—; sci. curriculum cons. NSF, Muncie, 1976-78; learning disabilities cons. Ball State U., 1974-80. Bd. dirs. Delaware County Easter Seal Soc., Minnetrista Cultural Found., Inc.; chairperson adv. coun. Ball State U. Coll. Bus., 1985-90; mem. adminstrv. bd. High St. United Meth. Ch., Muncie, 1984-88, youth coord., 1985-88; mem. adv. bd. Delaware County 4-H. Mem. ASCD, Ind. ASCD, Assn. for Children with Learning Disabilities, Coun. Exceptional Children (pres. Delaware County chpt. 1977-78), Pi Lambda Theta, Phi Delta Kappa, Pi Beta Phi. Methodist. Office: Muncie Community Schs 2501 N Oakwood Ave Muncie IN 47304-2376

SWIENER, RITA ROCHELLE, psychologist, educator; b. Pitts., July 31, 1941; d. Julius D. and Rose (Sheinbein) Swiener; 1 child, Samuel L. Schuff. BA, U. Mo., St. Louis, 1970; MA in Psychology, So. Ill. U., Edwardsville, 1973. Prof. Psychology State Cmty. Coll., East St. Louis, Ill., 1972—; pvt. practice St. Louis, 1972—; adj. faculty St. Louis C.C., Meramac, 1993—; pres. Ill. C.C. Faculty Assn., 1979-80; trustee State Univs. Retirement Sys., 1990; pres. local 3912 IFT-AFT, East St. Louis, 1989-92; chairperson social and behavior panel Ill. C.C. Bd. and Bd. of Higher Edn. Articulation Initiative, 1992—. Pres. Call-for-Help, Inc., Edgemont, Ill., 1990-92, 94—; pres. and founder Santa's Helpers, Inc., St. Louis, 1966—; mem., founder Joy E. Whitener scholarship com. U. Mo. at St. Louis, 1990—. Recipient Outstanding C.C. Faculty Mem. award Ill. C.C. Trustees Assn., 1985, David Erikson award for Outstanding Leadership Ill. C.C. Faculty Assn., 1988, Hometown Hero award KPLR-TV, Suburban Jour., Hardees, St. Louis, 1994, Christmas Spirit award KSD-TV, John Pertzborn, St. Louis, 1990. Mem. APA, U. Mo. St. Louis Psychology Alumni Assn. (treas. 1989-91, Disting. Alumni award 1992), St. Louis Women Psychologist, Mo. Psychol. Assn. Jewish. Home: 7832 Balson Ave Saint Louis MO 63130-3624

SWIFF, KELLY, small business owner, civic volunteer, author. Student, Cordon Bleu Cookery Sch., London, LaVarenne Cookery Sch., Paris, Burgundy, France. Model The Dialing for Dollars, Good Morning Houston; co-owner Creative Mfg. Inc.; now coord. Makk Family Charitable Exhbns.; dir. ops. La Colombe d'Or Hotel and Restaurant; chef participant Beaujolais Wine Festival; instr. self-esteem courses, modeling courses, culinary courses, gala fund-raising. Author: Music Theory with F, A & C, Harp Theory with F, A & C, Take A Look Inside Yourself, Gala Fund Raising Fundamentals; contbr. articles to profl. publs. Founder, chair Woodlands Literary Gala for South Montgomery County; founder, pres. South Montgomery County Libr. Guild; founder Savoir-Faire Etiquette Program, Houston Fire Mus. Gala; past pres., Argonauta Women's Group; founder Neartown Bicycle Tour benefitting Houston Police Dept.; trustee Houston Fire Mus., founding chairperson Houston Fire Mus. Gala.; founder Houston Fire Mus. Gala. Recipient Women of Distinction award; named Top 94 Citizen, People Scene mag. Office: 3410 Montrose Blvd Houston TX 77056

SWIFT, EVANGELINE WILSON, lawyer; b. San Antonio, May 2, 1939; d. Raymond E. and Josephine (Woods) Wilson; 1 child, Justin Lee. Student So. Meth. U., 1956-59; LL.B., St. Mary's U., San Antonio, 1963. Bar: Tex. 1963, U.S. Ct. Appeals (5th cir.) 1972, D.C. 1976, U.S. Dist. Ct. D.C. 1976, U.S. Supreme Ct. 1980, U.S. Ct. Appeals (11th cir.) 1981, U.S. Ct. Appeals (10th cir.) 1982, U.S. Ct. Appeals (D.C. cir.) 1982, U.S. Ct. Appeals (fed. cir.) 1983. Atty.-adv. ICC, Washington, 1964-65; staff atty. Headstart Program, OEO, Washington, 1965; exec. legal asst. to chmn., spl. asst. to vice chmn. EEOC, Washington, 1965-71, chief decisions div., 1971-75, asst. gen. counsel, 1975-76; cons. to sec. Employment Standards Adminstrn., Dept. Labor, Washington, 1977-79; ptnr. Swift & Swift, P.C., Washington, 1977-79; gen. counsel Merit Systems Protection Bd., Washington, 1979-86, mng. dir., 1986-87, dir. policy and evaluation, 1987—; bd. govs. U.S. Ct. Appeals (fed. cir.) Bar Assn., 1984-93, treas., 1987-89, sec., 1989-90, pres. elect, 1990; Fed. Cir. Bar Assn. (pres. 1992); guest lectr. Drake U., U. Pa., MIT; mem. U.S. del. 23d Sessions UN Commn. on Status of Women, Geneva, 1970. Recipient Meritorious Service award Fed. Govt., 1967, Fed. Women's award, 1975, Performance award Merit Systems Protection Bd., 1981-86, 92, 93, 94, Gold award 1986, Presdl. CFC award, 1984, 86, 94, EEO award Merit Systems Protection Bd., 1985, 94, 96, Theodore Roosevelt award, 1988, Elmer B. Staats award NCAC, Am. Soc. Pub. Adminstrn., 1994, Mary D. Pinkard Leader in Fed. Equity award, Fed. Employed Women, 1995. Methodist. Office: Merit System Protection Bd Office of Policy and Evaluation 1120 Vermont Ave NW Washington DC 20419-0001

SWIFT, ISABEL DAVIDSON, editorial director; b. Tokyo; d. Carleton Byron and Mary Howard (Davidson) S.; m. Steven C. Phillips. BA, Harvard U., 1976. Asst. editor Pocket Books, Simon & Schuster, N.Y.C., 1979-81; assoc. editor, editor, sr. editor, editorial mgr. Silhouette Books, N.Y.C., 1981-91, editorial dir., 1991—; internat. speaker on romance genre. Contbr. articles to profl. jours. Recipient RITA award Romance Writers Am., 1992, 94. Mem. N.Y. Women's Found. Office: Silhouette Books 300 E 42nd St New York NY 10017-5947

SWIFT, JANE MARIA, state senator; b. North Adams, Mass., Feb. 24, 1965; d. John Maynard and Jean Mary (Kent) S.; m. Charles T. Hunt III, Feb. 19, 1994. BA in Am. Studies, Trinity Coll., Hartford, Conn., 1987. Exec. mgmt. trainee G. Fox. & Co., Hartford, 1987-88; adminstrv. aide Sen. Peter C. Webber, Boston, 1988-90; mem. Mass. State Senate, Boston, 1991—; 3d asst. minority leader, 1993—. Republican. Roman Catholic. Office: Massachusetts State Senate 8 Bank Row Pittsfield MA 01201 also: Jane Swift for Congress PO Box 551 5 North St Pittsfield MA 01202

SWIFT, JILL ANNE, industrial engineer, educator; b. Memphis, Nov. 12, 1959; d. Gary Green and Sharon (Willoughby) Brown; m. Fredrick Wallace Swift, June 12, 1987; children: Andrew, Samantha. BS, Memphis State U., 1981, MS, 1982; PhD, Okla. State U., 1987. Registered profl. engr., Fla.; cert. quality engr. Design engr. DuPont Co., Glasgow, Del., 1982-83; head dept. physics Coll. Boca Raton, Fla., 1983-87; asst. prof. indsl. engring. U. Miami, Coral Gables, Fla., 1987—; vis. scholar Air Force Inst. Tech., Wright-Patterson AFB, Ohio, 1988; cons. A. T. Kearney, Amman, Jordan, 1990; quality liaison U. Miami Inst. Study of Quality in Mfg. and Svc., 1988—; cons., spkr. in field. Author: Introduction to Modern Statistical Quality Control and Management, 1995; contbr. articles to profl. publs. Mem. IIE (chpt. dir. 1988-90, Christmas toy dr. coord. 1989, 90), Am. Soc. Engring. Edn., Am. Soc. Quality Control, Phi Kappa Phi, Alpha Pi Mu (faculty adviser 1988—), Tau Beta Pi. Republican. Office: Univ Miami 268 McArthur Bldg Coral Gables FL 33124

SWIFT, MARY LOU, art dealer, financial consultant; b. Syracuse, N.Y., July 25, 1942; d. Andrew G. Swift and E.R. Ensle. BA, Sarah Lawrence Coll., Bronxville, N.Y., 1964; postgrad. U. Pa., 1964-66, NYU Bus. Sch., 1967-69, N.Y. Inst. Finance, 1967-69. Reg. stockbroker. Adminstrv. head of syndicate dept. Drexel Harriman Ripley, N.Y.C., 1966-71; product mgr. Fieldcrest Mills, N.Y.C., 1971-74; acct. supr. advtg. Rosenfeld Sirowitz Lawson, N.Y.C., 1974-76, BBDO, N.Y.C., 1976-78, Cavalieri, Kleier, Pearlman, N.Y.C., 1978-79; bus., mktg. cons. Mary Lou Swift & Co., N.Y.C., 1979-81; instnl. stockbroker Mabon Securities, N.Y.C., 1981-91; Gerard Klauer Mattison, N.Y.C., 1992-93; pvt. art dealer internat. modern and contemporary art Mary Lou Swift Fine Arts, N.Y.C., 1994, 95. Recipient Undergraduate Fellowship (2) Am. Mus. Nat. History, 1962, 63. Office: Mary Lou Swift Fine Arts 41 White St New York NY 10013

SWIG, ROSELYNE CHROMAN, art advisor; b. Chgo., June 8, 1930; m. Richard Swig, Feb. 5, 1950; children—Richard, Jr., Susan, Marjorie, Carol. Student, U. Calif.-Berkeley, UCLA; MFA with honors, San Francisco Art Inst., 1976, DFA (hon.), 1988. Pres. Roselyne C. Swig Artsource, San Francisco, 1977-94; apptd. by President Clinton as dir. Art in Embassies program U.S. Dept. of State, 1994—. Trustee San Francisco Mus. Modern Art, U. Art Mus., Berkeley, Calif., Mills Coll., Oakland, Calif., United Jewish Appeal; ex officio bd. mem. Jewish Mus. San Francisco; bd. dirs. Am. Jewish Joint Distbn. Com.; vice chair panel Fed. Res. Sys.; past past pres., bd. dirs. Jewish Cmty. Fedn. San Francisco, the Peninsula,

Marin and Sonoma Counties; past commr. San Francisco Pub. Libr.; past bd. dirs. San Francisco Opera, Am. Coun. for Arts, KQED Broadcasting Sys.; past. pres. Calif. State Summer Sch. Arts, San Francisco Art Inst., San Francisco Arts Commn.; past nat. v.p. Am./Israel Pub. Affairs Com.

SWIGER, ELINOR PORTER, lawyer; b. Cleve., Aug. 1, 1927; d. Louie Charles and Mary Isabelle (Shank) Porter; m. Quentin Gilbert Swiger, Feb. 5, 1955; children: Andrew Porter, Calvin Gilbert, Charles Robinson. BA, Ohio State U., 1949, JD, 1951. Bar: Ohio 1951, Ill. 1979. Sr. assoc. Robbins, Schwartz, Nicholas, Lifton & Taylor, Ltd., Chgo., 1979—. Author: Mexico for Kids, 1971, Europe for Young Travelers, 1972, The Law and You, 1973 (Literary Guild award), Careers in the Legal Professions, 1978, Women Lawyers at Work, 1978, Law in Everday Life, 1977. Mem. Northfield Twp. (Ill.) Bd. Edn., 1976-83; mem. Glenview (Ill.) Fire and Police Commn., 1976-86; chmn. Glenview Zoning Bd. Appeals, 1987—. Mem. ABA (chmn. pub. edn. com. urban, state and local govt. sect. 1982-85), Ill. Bar Assn. (chmn. local govt. sect. 1986-87, chmn. legal edn. sect. 1991-92), Ill. Coun. Sch. Attys. (chmn.), Women Bar Assn. Ill., Chgo. Bar Assn. (chmn. legis. exec. com. 1990-92), Soc. Midland Authors. Republican. Home: 1933 Burr Oak Dr Glenview IL 60025 Office: Robbins Schwartz Nicholas Lifton & Taylor 29 S La Salle St Ste 860 Chicago IL 60603-1505

SWIGER, ELIZABETH DAVIS, chemistry educator; b. Morgantown, W.Va., June 27, 1926; d. Hannibal Albert and Tyreeca Elizabeth (Stemple) Davis; m. William Eugene Swiger, June 2, 1948; children: Susan Elizabeth Swiger Knotts, Wayne William. BS in Chemistry, W.Va. U., 1948, MS in Chemistry, 1952, PhD in Chemistry, 1964. Instr. math. Fairmont (W.Va.) State Coll., 1948-49, instr. math. and phys. sci., 1956-57, instr. chemistry, 1957-60, asst. prof. chemistry, 1960-63, assoc. prof. chemistry, 1964-66, prof. chemistry, 1966—, chmn., div. sci., math, and health careers, 1991-92; NSF fellow rsch. W.Va. U., Morgantown, 1963-64; prof. emeritus, 1992; advisor Am. Chem. Soc. student affiliates, 1965-88. Author: Morton Family History, 1984-94, Davis-Winters Family History, 1994, Civil War Letters and Diary of Joshua Winters, 1991; contbr. articles to profl. jours. Bd. dirs. Prickett's Fort Meml. Found., Fairmont, 1988—, chmn. elect, 1990-92, chair., 1992—, Blacks Chapel Meml. Found., 1993—, rep. adv. coun. to Bd. Regents, Fairmont State Coll., Charleston, 1977-78, rep. instl. bd. advisors, Fairmont, 1990-92. NSF grantee, 1963; named Outstanding Prof. W.Va. Legislature, Charleston, 1990. Mem. Am. Chem. Soc. (sec. chmn. North W. Va. 1975, 83), W.Va. Acad. Sci. (pres. 1978-79, exec. com. edn. chmn. 1990-93), The Nature Conservancy (bd. dirs. W.Va. chpt. 1970-86, chmn. 1980-82), AAUW. Republican. Methodist. Home: 1599 Hillcrest Rd Fairmont WV 26554-4807 also: 382 Laird Dr Freeport FL 32439

SWINDLE, PATRICIA F., women's health nurse; b. Poplarville, Miss., July 29, 1952; d. Carl Preston and Velma (Seals) Frazier; m. Jimmy C. Swindle, Jan. 11, 1969; children: Michele Swindle Penton, Jimmy Delane Swindle, Nicola Diane Swindle. LPN, Miss. Delta C.C., 1975; ADN, N.W. C.C., 1978. Staff LPN North Panola Hosp., Sardis, Miss., 1975-76; staff LPN South Panola Hosp., Batesville, Miss., 1976-78, staff RN, 1978-81, RN, DON, 1982-86; LPN instr. N.W. C.C., Senatobia, Miss., 1981-82; RN supr., nursing mgr., ob. edn. dir., nursing exec. Crosby Meml. Hosp., Picayune, Miss., 1986-92; nurse mgr. ob., labor and delivery nursing The King's Daus. Hosp., Greenville, Miss., 1991-95; dir. women/children's svcs. Lakeview Regional Med. Ctr., Covington, La., 1995—; adv. com. Pearl River C.C., Poplarville, Miss., 1988-92, Miss. Delta C.C., 1994-95; RN adv. com. South Panola Health Dept., Batesville, 1983-86. Donator United Way, Greenville, 1992-95, Am. Cancer Soc., 1992-95. Mem. Assn. Women's Health, Obstet. and Neonatal Nursing, Miss. Nurses Assn. (treas./del. 1994-95), LPN Assn. (del. 1974-75). Pentecostal. Office: Lakeview Regional Med Ctr Hwy 190 at Fairview Covington LA 70433

SWING, MARCE, producer, publisher; b. Wichita, Kans., Dec. 3, 1943; d. Eldon Derry and Ruth (Biddle) S. Bus. mgr. Old Westport Med. Assn., Kansas City, Mo., 1972-73; dept. chmn., instr. Ft. Bragg (N.C.) Nursery and Kindergarten, 1965-66, Luth. Schs., Tex. Dist., Irving, 1966-68, Kansas City (Kans.) Sch. Dist. 500, 1973-78, Extension Dept. U. Calif., Northridge, 1979-82, Pima Coll., Tucson, 1983-84, Kinder Care, Lake Buena Vista, Fla., 1989-90; TV/motion picture exec. producer, dir., writer Swing Prodns., Orlando, Fla., 1989—; owner, pres. Swing Enterprises/Swing Prodns., Orlando, 1978—, Living for Edn., Inc., Orlando, 1994—; exec. mgmt., acctg. andmktg. cons. to major internat. corps.; lectr., seminar instr., guest speaker, anchorperson, moderator, panelist. Exec. producer, dir., writer, featured talent on-air live and taped programming for networks, network affiliates and cable, feature motion picture, TV series, mini series, 30 celebrity profiles, 36 documentaries, 14 televents, 45 pub. svc. spots, 30 minute infomat, 12-hour entertinment Christmas Eve project; developer entertainment informational, ednl. and indsl. TV programs and videos; contbr. articles to profl. jours. Corp. adminstr., TV exec. producer, dir., fundraiser nat. hdqrs. March of Dimes, White Plains, N.Y., 1984-86, Arthritis Found., Atlanta, 1985; ofcl. hostess Seattle World's Fair; mem. Nat. Task Force for Child Care, Nat. Task Force for Youth Suicide, Nat. Task Force for Child Abuse; mem. Ariz. Commn. on Arts. Recipient local, regional and nat. art and craft awards. Mem. NEA, NAFE, AAUW, Am. Mgmt. Assn., Nat. Assn. Women Artists, Profl. Assn. Producers and Dirs., Nat. Printmaker's Assn., Nat. Thespian Soc., Thousand Oaks Art Assn., Show of Hands Gallery, Nat. Youth Camps. Lutheran.

SWINNEY, JOAN ELAINE RATZLAFF, school administrator, secondary level; b. Saskatoon, Sasktchwan, Can., Jan. 25, 1944; came to U.S., 1951; d. Peter Harold and Mathilda Ageneta (Boese) Ratzlaff; m. Frank Chick Swinney, June 3, 1967; 1 child, Erik Frank. BA in English, U. Okla., 1966; MA of Teaching in English, Lewis and Clark Coll., Portland, Oreg., 1975; EdD in leadership, Portland State U., 1991. Lic tchr., prin. supt., Oreg. Tchr. English Wichita (Kans.) Pub. Schs., 1966-69; tchr. English, journalism, photography Portland (Oreg.) Pub. Schs., 1971-77; exec. dir. AIA, Portland, 1978-81; writer, organizational cons. pvt. practice, Portland, 1980—; systems administr., tchr. English, journalism Portland Pub. Schs., 1987-94; acad. dean, vice prin. for academics St. Mary's Acad., Portland, 1994—; mem. bd. dirs. Architecture Found., Portland, 1983-87, chair comm. com., 1983-84, treas., 1984-85, pres. elect, 1985-86, pres. 1986-87; chair rsch. com. City Club of Portland, 1981-83. Author: (book) Going Public on International Markets, 1987; editor: The Oregon Entrepreneur, 1984, Strategic Planning, 1983; presenter Human Rels. Tng., 1991. Bd. dirs. Oreg. Ballet Co., 1983-85, bd. trustees Lewis & Clark Coll., Portland, 1986-87. Recipient Outstanding Profl. Svc. award Peat Marwick Internat., Portland, 1985, 87, Outstanding Alumni award Lewis and Clark Coll., 1988, Grad. fellowship award Can. Embassy, Ottawa, 1989-91, Commendation for Outstanding Contbn. to Multicultural/Multiethnic Understandings in Edn., Oreg. Alliance Black Sch. Educators, 1992; grantee Oreg. Coun. for Humanities, 1980, 81. Mem. ASCD, Am. Ednl. Rsch. Assn. (presenter at ann. meeting 1991), Coalition of Essential Schs., Assn. for Canadian Studies in U.S., Am. Ednl. Rsch. Assn.

SWINNEY, PHYLLIS MARIE, elementary education educator; b. Weimar, Tex., Oct. 27, 1950; d. Albert Frederick and Mary Ann (Potthast) Janecka; m. William Albert Swinney Jr., June 28, 1975; 1 child, Sarah Noelle. BS, U. Tex., 1973; M in Curriculum & Instrn., U. Tex., San Antonio, 1983, reading specialist cert., 1983; bilingual cert., Trinity U., San Antonio, 1976. Cert. elem. edn., bilingual edn., supervision and curriculum, reading specialist. Elem. tchr. Austin (Tex.) Ind. Sch. Dist., 1973-75, San Antonio (Tex.) Ind. Sch. Dist., 1975-77, Comal Ind. Sch. Dist., Bulverde, Tex., 1977-80; substitute tchr. Comal Ind. Sch. Dist., Bulverde, 1980-83; reading specialist St. Mary's Hall, San Antonio, 1983—; dir. Summer Reading Camp, San Antonio, 1988-95; instr. U. Tex., San Antonio, 1991, 92. Sunday sch. tchr. St. Joseph's Ch., Bulverde; vol. Raul Jimenez Thanksgiving Dinner for Srs., San Antonio, 1994; vol. various polit. campaigns; chairperson Battered Women's Shelter Project. Grantee Holt-Dupont Co., San Antonio, 1985, 87, 89, 95. Mem. Internat. Reading Assn., Tex. State Reading Assn., Alamo Reading Coun. (vol. Reading in the Mall 1983-92), Neuropsychol. Issues Group, History Spl. Interest Group, Parents and Reading (com. sect., treas., chairperson). Office: St Marys Hall 9401 Starcrest Dr San Antonio TX 78217-4162

SWINSON, ANGELA ANTHONY, physician; b. Washington, Nov. 5, 1960; d. Edgar and Phosia Lee (Hanna) Anthony; m. Kevin Lamont Swinson, June 28, 1986; 1 child, Erik Alan. BA, Johns Hopkins U., 1983, MPH, 1991; MD, Georgetown U., 1987. Phlebotomist Georgetown U. Hosp., Washington, 1984; med. resident Homewood Hosp. Ctr., Balt., 1987-88; clinic physician Ea. Chest Clinic, Balt., 1990-91; resident in preventive medicine Johsn Hopkins Sch. Hygiene and Pub. Health, Balt., 1990-92; asst. med. dir. Occupl. Med. Svc., NIH, Bethesda, Md., 1992—; mem. workgroup Prince George's County, Cheverly, Md., 1991-92. Contbr. articles to profl. jours. Sr. leader Girl Scouts Cen. Md., Balt., 1981-83; mem. inspirational choir Faith African Meth. Episcopal Ch., Laurel, Md., 1993—, mem. mass choir, 1993—, mem. scholarship com., 1995—, instr. vacation Bible sch., 1995; bd. dirs. Nat. Consortium for African Am. Children, Inc., 1995—. Grantee Nat. Med. Fellowships, 1983-85. Mem. APHA, Am. Coll. Occupl. and Environ. Medicine, Delta Sigma Theta (Golden Life, co-chair phys. & mental health com., Columbia, Md. alumnae chpt. treas., Mu.Psi chpt. 1980-82, pres. Mu Psi chpt. 1982-83, Minerva award 1981, chpt. award 1983). Office: NIH Occupl Med Svc Bldg 10 Rm 6C-306 10 Center Dr Bethesda MD 20892

SWIRE, EDITH WYPLER, music educator, musician, violist, violinist; b. Boston, Feb. 16, 1943; d. Alfred R. Jr. and Frances Glenn (Emery) Wypler; m. James Bennett Swire, June 11, 1965; 1 child, Elizabeth Swire-Falker. BA, Wellesley (Mass.) Coll., 1965; MFA, Sarah Lawrence Coll., Bronxville, N.Y., 1983; postgrad., Coll. of New Rochelle, 1984-85. Tchr. instrumental music, viola, violin The Windsor Sch., Boston, 1965-66; tchr., dir. The Lenox Sch., N.Y.C., 1967-76; music curriculum devel. The Nightingale-Bamford Sch., N.Y.C., 1968-69; head of fine arts dept. The Lenox Sch., N.Y.C., 1976-78, head of instrumental music, 1978-80; founder, dir., tchr. of string sch. Serpentine String Sch., Larchmont, N.Y., 1981—; mem. founding com. Inter Sch. Orch., N.Y.C., 1972, trustee, 1976—; panelist Nat. Assn. Ind. Sch. Conf., N.Y.C., 1977. Mem. music and worship com., Larchmont Ave. Ch., 1978-82, 88. Mem. Westchester Musicians Guild, N.Y. State Music Tchrs. Assn., Music Tchrs. Nat. Assn., Music Tchrs. Coun. Westchester (program com.), Violin Soc. Am., Wellesley in Westchester, Am. String Tchrs. Assn., The Viola Soc. of N.Y. Home and Office: 11 Serpentine Trl Larchmont NY 10538-2618

SWIRSKY, JUDITH PERLMAN, arts administrator, consultant; b. Bklyn., Oct. 31, 1928; d. Samuel and Rose (Klein) Perlman; m. Leo Jerome Swirsky, June 26, 1949; 1 child, Marjorie Ann Swirsky Zelner. BA, NYU, 1947; postgrad., Columbia U., 1947-48. Rsch. asst. The Bklyn. Mus., 1947-49, vol. coord., 1983-89; exec. dir. Grand Cen. Art Galleries Edn. Assn., N.Y.C., 1988-90; freelance curator Genest Gallery, Lambertville, N.J., 1990; dir. vol. resources Snug Harbor Cultural Ctr., S.I., 1992-95, dir. spl. events, 1994-95; dir. art sales and rental Gallery The Bklyn. Mus., 1974-77; del. Vol. Com. of Art Mus., Balt., 1973, panelist, 1979; mem., co-founder Vol. Program Adminstrs., N.Y.C., Cultural Inst., 1984—; ind. curator travelling exhbn. Relatively Speaking: Mothers and Daus. in Art, 1994—, Memory and Desire, Paintings and Watercolors by Harriet Shorr, Charles Parness: A Different View of Life and the World. Co-author: On Exhibit, 1993-96. Pres. Community Com. for the Bklyn. Mus., 1969-70; bd. dirs. Greater N.Y. Girl Scouts U.S., 1965-71; founder Children's Sch. Time Program and Women's League, Bklyn. Acad. Music, 1961-64; chmn. Bklyn. Guild for Opera, 1966-77; bd. dirs. Arthritis Found. Greater N.Y., 1969-79; trustee Bklyn. Home for Children, 1961-70, Julia Bernstein League of the Free Nurses Inst., 1952-60. Mem. Am. Assn. Mus., Assn. Vol. Adminstrn. (cert., editor region II newsletter), Am. Assn. Mus. Vols., Civitas. Home and Office: 57 Montague St Brooklyn NY 11201-3374

SWIST, MARIAN IRENE, emergency nurse; b. Pottsville, Pa., Oct. 26, 1941; d. Thomas Francis and Marian C. (Munster) Moran; m. John J. Swist, Aug. 3, 1963 (dec.); children: Christine M. Swist Mullen, Robert J. Diploma in nursing, Reading (Pa.) Hosp., 1962. RN, Pa.; cert. emergency nursing pediatric course. Staff nurse Reading Hosp. Med. Ctr., 1962-65; staff nurse emergency dept. Pottstown Meml. Med. Ctr., 1971—. Mem. Alumni Assn. Reading Hosp. Sch. Nursing.

SWITAJ, CARMEN MARIE, administrative assistant; b. Thompson Falls, Mont., Oct. 6, 1948; d. Donald L. Grende and Mary Joeda (Collogan) Brownell; m. Steven Anthony Switaj, Aug. 30, 1975; children: Stephanie Marie, Diana Lee. Grad. high sch., Whitefish, Mont. Typist to cartographers U.S. Army Topographic Command, Washington, 1970-71; sec. dept. installment loan Valley Bank, Kalispell, Mont., 1971-74; typist to civil engr. USAF, Lakeside, Mont., 1974-77; acct. Mel Dutcher, CPA, Caseville, Mich., 1979-80; customer svc. rep. Ann Arbor (Mich.) Trust, 1980-82; with dept. investments Valley Bank, Clarkston, Wash., 1984-86; office mgr. D & S Electric, Inc., Clarkston, 1986-87; mgr. ops. Sta. KLSR-TV, Eugene, Oreg., 1987-90, program dir., 1990-93; administry. asst. engring. dept. Hilton Waikoloa Village, Kamuela, Hawaii, 1994—; facilitator Sta. KLSR-TV, Eugene, 1987-92. Dist. head judge Thanks to Tchrs., Eugene, 1991-93. Mem. Nat. Assn. TV Program Execs., Mu Alpha Theta. Republican. Lutheran. Office: Hilton Waikoloa Village Engring Dept Kamuela HI 96743

SWOOPES, SHERYL, basketball player; d. Louis Swoopes; m. Eric Jackson. Student, South Plains Jr. Coll., Tex., Tex. Tech. Basketball player USA Women's Nat. Team; mem. 1995 Pan Am. Games Womens Basketball Team. Recipient bronze medal as mem. 1994 World Championship Team, gold medal as mem. 1994 Women's Goodwill Games Team; named 1993 Nat. Player of the Yr., MVP 1993 NCAA Final Four, 1992 and 1992 SWC Player of Yr., 1992 SWC Newcomer of the Yr.; Nike basketball shoe named in her honor. Address: 908 E Felt St #111 Brownfield TX 79316

SWOPE, DENISE GRAINGER, lawyer, educator; b. Columbia, S.C., Apr. 27, 1966; d. Thomas Dayton and Faye (Amerson) Grainger; m. William Koatsworth Swope, May 19, 1990. BA cum laude, U. S.C., 1986, JD, 1990. Bar: S.C. Asst. solicitor Charleston County (S.C.) Solicitor, 1991-92; pvt. practice Charleston, 1992—; instr. Inst. for Legal Edn., Columbia and Greenville, S.C., 1993—, Charleston So. U., 1994—. Atty., S.C. Bar Pro Bono Program, Columbia, 1991-95. U. S.C. Sch. Law Recruitment scholar, 1987, Outstanding Handicapped Law Student scholar, 1989. Mem. ABA, S.C. Bar Assn., Golden Key. Office: 1133 Hillside Dr # 2B Charleston SC 29407

SYDNEY, DORIS S., sports touring company executive, interior designer; b. N.Y.C., Feb. 18, 1934; d. Morris and Frances (Terrace) Steinman; m. Herbert P. Sydney, Oct. 20, 1957; children: Madeleine Jane, Peter Samuel. Student, Vassar Coll., 1950-52; BS, Columbia U., 1952-55; postgrad., NYU, 1956-57, N.Y. Sch. Interior Design, 1974. Cert. documentor Equitable Life Ins. Co., N.Y.C, 1955-57; researcher Fairchild Publs., N.Y.C., 1957-58; furniture sales Steinman's Inc., N.Y.C., 1958-60; interior designer, prin. Doris S. Sydney Interiors, Armonk, N.Y., 1975; exec. asst. Tennis Europe Inc., Conn., 1984--. Pres. Coman Hill Sch. PTA, 1971-72, Byram Hills High Sch. PTA, 1977-79, also chmn.; pres. Byram Hills Scholarship Fund, 1980-82, Non-partisan Nominating Com., 1982-84; coun. del. Vassar Coll. Alumni Assn., Poughkeepsie, N.Y., 1973-77; chmn. Fred Caruolo Meml. Fund, 1979-81; pres. bd. trustees North Castle Pub. Libr., 1981-90; v.p. Friends North Castle Pub. Libr., 1993—; treas., pres. Armonk Hadassah, 1980—. Republican. Jewish. Home: 65 Windmill Rd Armonk NY 10504-2833

SYDNEY, LAURIN JILL, newscaster; b. N.Y.C., Aug. 6, 1956. BA in Music, Harvard U., 1978. Tchr. music North Miami, 1978-79; host Epcot Mag. Walt Disney Co., 1979-80; hostess quiz show CBS T.V., N.Y.C., 1980-81; weathercaster Sta. WXIA, Atlanta, 1981; spokesperson Showtime Network, N.Y.C., 1982-85; reporter CNN T.V., N.Y.C., 1985-88, anchor Show Biz Today; 1988—. Bd. dirs. N.Y. Host Com., N.Y.C., 1992, Greentrees, N.Y.C., 1994, Crimebusters, N.Y.C., 1994; v.p. E.S.S.A., N.Y.C., 1994; active Make A Wish Found., God's Littlest Angels. Recipient ACE award-T.V. Assn. Cable Executives, 1984, Cambridge Honors, Cambridge Civic Soc., 1978, award CEBA, 1991; fellow John J. McCabe fellow CEBA, 1990. Mem. AFTRA, SAG, Am. Found. AIDS Rsch., Am. Cancer Soc., Am. Heart Assn., Women in Cable. Office: CNN Showbiz Today 5 Penn Plz Fl 21 New York NY 10001-1810*

SYKES, PAULA MARIE, school counselor; b. Somers Point, N.J., July 6, 1954; d. Richard Issac and Eleanor Marie (Landry) Cressey; m. Joseph William Sykes Jr., July 10, 1981; children: Kristina Marie, Teighan Marie. BA in Elem. Edn., Glassboro State Coll., 1978, MA in Student Pers. Svcs., 1981. Cert. tchr., N.J.; cert. sch. counselor, N.J. 3d grade tchr. Egg Harbor Twp. (N.J.) Bd. Edn., 1978-81, sch. counselor, 1981—, mem. pupil assessment com., 1994, chairperson pupil intervention com., 1989-94, coord. presdl. acad. fitness award com., 1987-96, coord. Children are People com., 1990-96, coord. peer leadership tng., 1994-96. Mem. Absecon PTO, past assembly com., past tchr.-of-yr. com.; vol. Atlantic City Med. Ctr., 1986-87; bd. dirs. Egg Harbor Twp. Cmty. Ctr., 1995. Mem. Alpha Delta Kappa (altruistic chairperson 1990). Republican. Roman Catholic. Home: 605 Chelsea Rd Absecon NJ 08201-1618 Office: Egg Harbor Twp Bd Edn EHT Intermediate Sch 25 Alder Ave Pleasantville NJ 08232-5315

SYKES, RUTH RAINEY, elementary educator; b. Portsmouth, Va., Sept. 14, 1940; d. Perry Hubert and Irene (Davis) Rainey; m. Mathew Joseph Sykes, Nov. 19, 1967. BA, Fla. State U., 1962; MA, U. Fla., 1967. Elem. tchr. Freedom 7, Cocoa Beach, Fla., 1962-67; curriculum coord. Cape View Elem. Sch., Cape Canaveral, Fla., 1967-70; varying exceptionalities tchr. Cole Elem. Sch., Nashville, 1970-77, 1st grade tchr., 1977-82; primary, multi-age tchr. Haywood Elem. Sch., Nashville, 1982—. Contbr. articles to profl. jours. Recipient Pencil Found. award Hosp. Corp. Am., 1986; Annette Eskind grantee, 1987. Mem. NEA, Tenn. Edn. Assn., Nashville Edn. Assn., Internat. Reading Assn., Tenn. Reading Assn. (exec. bd. 1981-90, treas. 1986-90), Mid. Tenn. Reading Assn. (pres. 1981-82), Tchrs. Applying Whole Lang., Delta Kappa Gamma (corr. sec. Beta chpt. 1986-88). Office: Haywood Elem Sch 3790 Turley Dr Nashville TN 37211-4964

SYLKE, LORETTA CLARA, artist; b. Parkston, S.D., Nov. 4, 1926; d. Jacob and Maria Magdelin (Frey) Sprecher; m. Arthur C. Sylke, Apr. 26, 1961; children: Michael Arthur, Patricia, Constance, Sharon, Catherine, Charles (dec.). Grad. H.S., Chgo. Represented by Becca Gallery Berlin, Wis. Works have appeared at N.Mex. Art League, Albuquerque, 1991, El Dorado Gallery, Colorado Springs, Mont. Miniature Show, Billings, The New Eng. Fine Art Inst., The N.E. Trade Ctr., Woburn, Mass., 1993, El Dorado Gallery, Colorado Springs, 1993, 20th Annual Am. Nat. Miniature Show, Laramie, Wyo., Art in the Park, Lenexa, Kans., Gov.'s office, Madison, Wis., Custer County Art Ctr., Miles City, Mont., 1995, Laramie (Wyo.) Miniature Show, 1995; juried exhibns., Beloit, Wis., Minature Show: Custer County Art Ctr., Miles City, Mont., 1995, 96; represented in pvt. collections. Recipient Masco award Madison Art Supply, 1982. Mem. Nat. Mus. Women in the Arts, Soc. Exptl. Artists, Wis. Women in the Arts, Catherine Lorillarr Wolfe Art Club (N.Y.C.). Home: N4392 Wicks Landing Princeton WI 54968-8508 Office: 1714 Studio Princeton WI 54968

SYLVESTER, LYNDA JOANN, product designer; b. Chgo., Apr. 30, 1950; d. Kenna (Gunderson) S. Student, U. Wis., Boston Mus. Fine Arts, Parsons Sch. of Design. Owner Kegonsa Gen. Store, Madison, 1969-75, Windward Specialties, Captiva Island, Fla., 1975-80, Lynda Sylvester Designs, N.Y.C., Sag Harbor, N.Y., 1980—; pres. C.L. Weekends (now Sylvester & Co.), Sag Harbor, 1987—; owner Harbor Mercantile, Sag Harbor, 1993—. patentee in field. Mem. Village Planning Bd., Sag Harbor, 1993—. Democrat. Home: PO Box 1192 Sag Harbor NY 11963-0039

SYLVESTER, NANCY KATHERINE, speech educator, management consultant; b. Evansville, Ind., July 17, 1947; d. Leonard Nicholas and Marjoire (Moore) Jochim; m. James Andrew Sylvester, Aug. 21, 1971; children: Marcy Dee, Holly Nicole. BS, Ind. State U., 1969; MA, U. Mich., 1970. Registered profl. parliamentarian; cert. prof. parliamentarian; team/meeting mgmt. specialist. Assoc. prof. speech Rock Valley Coll., Rockford, Ill., 1970—; co-owner Jimmy's Frozen Custard, 1996—; bd. dirs. First Fed. Savs. Bank, Belvidere, Ill. Author: Basics of Parliamentary Procedure, 1983, Handbook for Effective Meetings, 1993; contbr. articles to profl. jours. Bd. dirs. Jr. League Rockford, 1974-78, Rock River Homeowners Assn., 1990-91; pres. Children's Devel. Ctr. Aux. Bd., Rockford, 1984-85; parliamentarian Winnebago County Dem. Caucus, 1991; vice-chmn. Commn. on Am. Parliamentary Practice, 1989-90, chmn., 1990-91; nat. parliamentarian Girl Scouts U.S., 1996—, bd. dirs. Rock River coun., 1979-81. Recipient Jardene medal Ind. State U., 1969, RVC Faculty of Yr. award, 1994; Rockham scholar U. Mich., 1969-70. Mem. Am. Inst. Parliamentarians, Am. Soc. Women Accts. (parliamentarian 1980—), Am. Women Soc. CPAs (parliamentarian 1991—), Nat. Coun. State Bds. Nursing (parliamentarian 1992—), Ill. Assn. Parliamentarians, Nat. Assn. Ins. Women (parliamentarian 1983-91), Nat. Assn. Parliamentarians, Assn. Quality and Participation, Speech Commn. Assn., Coun. Better Bus. Burs. (parliamentarian 1993), Nat. League Nursing (parliamentarian), Rockford C. of C. (ex-officio bd. dirs.), Phi Rho Pi (region 4 v.p. 1972-73, nat. v.p. 1973-74), Am. Soc. Pain Mgmt. Nurses (nat. parliamentarian 1994—), Ind. Accts. Assn. Ill. (parliamentrian 1990—), Info. Sys. Audit and Control Assn. (parliamentarian 1994—). Roman Catholic. Home: 4826 River Bluff Ct Rockford IL 61111-5836

SYLVESTRE, VICTORIA ELIZABETH, educator, artist; b. Milw., Jan. 9, 1966; d. Edward Koelling and Marylou Elizabeth (Sernau) Higgins; m. Marc Edward Sylvestre, Nov. 18, 1989. BFA in Ceramics, East Carolina U., 1987, BFA in Art Edn., 1988, MFA in Ceramics, 1991. Educator visual arts East Carolina U., Greenville, N.C., 1988-91, Spirit Square Ctr. for Arts, Charlotte, N.C., 1991, North Stanly H.S., New London, N.C., 1991—; sponsor Nat. Art Honor Soc., New London, 1995—, Art Club, New London, 1995—; dir. color Stony Gap Pottery, Albemarle, N.C., 1992—, mktg. cons., 1992—. Artwork exhibited in various nat. shows, 1990—. Mem. Nat. Art Edn. Assn., Am. Craft Coun., N.C. Art Edn. Assn. Democrat. Home and Office: 40592A Stony Gap Rd Albemarle NC 28001-9178

SYMINGTON, TERRI DIANNE, designer, small business owner; b. Indpls., Sept. 4, 1953; d. Larry Dittimore Ribble and Carole Joy (Coonse) Hamblet; m. James Hanley Symington, Oct. 25, 1986; children: James H. Jr., Margot D., Lawrence A. Student, U. Houston, 1971-72, U. Tex., 1972-74, So. Meth. U., 1975-77; Assoc. in Interior Design, El Centro Coll., 1986; postgrad., Otis Parson's Sch. Design, Pasadena, Calif., 1991-92. Cert. interior designer, Calif. Design and layout artist J.C. Penny, Dallas, 1976-77; fashion illustrator Houston, Dallas, 1977-78; art dir., designer, illustrator Weiner's Dept. Stores, Houston, 1978-80; art dir., designer The Horchow Collection, Dallas, 1980-83; art dir., graphic and interior designer Dallas, 1983-86; interior designer, dir. accessory dept. Carole Eichen Interiors, Santa Ana, Calif., 1986-88; interior designer L.A., 1988-89; sr. interior designer Pink Ladies Design, Calabasas, Calif., 1989-90; pres. Symington Designs, L.A., Mass., 1991-94, Personal Stock Inc., Pepperell, Mass., 1995—; design cons. for low income housing City of L.A., 1992-94. Edn. grantee The Horchow Collection, 1983 (turned down). Mem. Worcester Women's Network, Calif. Coun. Interior Design (cert.). Episcopalian. Office: Personal Stock Inc PO Box 1075 Pepperell MA 01463

SYMON-GUTIERREZ, PATRICIA PAULETTE, dietitian; b. Orange, N.J., Jan. 21, 1948; d. Michael and Aneilia (Jablonski) Symon; m. Alfonso Pelayo Gutierrez, Jan. 20, 1990. Dietetic cert., N.Y. Inst. Dietetics, 1967; BS in Dietetics, Ga. Coll., 1978; MS in Nutrition and Dietetics, Finch U. Health Scis., Chgo., 1996. Lic. dietitian, Fla. Staff dietitian Landmark Learning Ctr., Opa-Loka, Fla., 1982-86; food svc. dir., dietitian Palm Ct. Nursing and Rehab. Ctr., Wilton Manors, Fla., 1986-87; food svc. dir. Canteen Co.-Dade County Juvenile Ctr., Miami, Fla., 1987-88; food svc. dir., dietitian Manor Care-Boca Raton, Fla., 1988-90, Manor Care-Plantation, Fla., 1990-92; dir. dietary svcs., dietitian Menorah House, Boca Raton, 1992—. Mem. Am. Dietetic Assn., Phi Sigma, Phi Upsilon Omicron. Episcopalian. Home: 8991 Sunset Strip Sunrise FL 33322-3737

SYMS, HELEN MAKSYM, educational administrator; b. Wilkes Barre, Pa., Nov. 12, 1918; d. Walter and Anna (Kowalewski) Maksym; m. Louis Harold Syms, Aug. 16, 1947; children: Harold Edward, Robert Louis. BA, Hunter Coll., 1941; MS, Columbia U., 1947; teaching credentials, Calif. State U., Northridge, 1964. Statis. clk. McGraw Hill Pub. Co., N.Y.C., 1941-42; acct. Flexpansion Corp., N.Y.C., 1943-47, Oliver Wellington & Co., N.Y.C., 1947-48, Broadcast Measurement Bur., N.Y.C., 1948-51; tchr. Calif. State U., Northridge, 1964, Burbank (Calif.) Unified Sch. Dist., 1964-79; chmn. bus. edn. dept. Burbank High Sch., 1974-79; docent, acct. arts coun. Calif. State U., Northridge, 1979—; tchr. M.E.N.D. (Meet Each Need with Dignity) Learning Ctr., Pacoima, Calif., 1987-89, assoc. dir., 1989-96. Mem. Phi Beta Kappa, Delta Kappa Gamma (pres. 1972-74, treas. Xi chpt. 1982-90,

92—, treas. area IX 1975-78). Home: 9219 Whitaker Ave Northridge CA 91343-3538

SYNNOTT, MARCIA GRAHAM, history educator; b. Camden, N.J., July 4, 1939; d. Thomas Whitney and Beatrice Adelaide (Colby) S.; m. William Edwin Sharp, June 16, 1979; children: Willard William Sharp, Laurel Beth Sharp. AB, Radcliffe Coll., 1961; MA, Brown U., 1964; PhD, U. Mass., 1974. History tchr. MacDuffie Sch., Springfield, Mass., 1963-68; instr. U. S.C., Columbia, 1972-74, asst. prof., 1974-79, assoc. prof. history, 1979—, dir. grad. studies history dept., 1990-92. Author: The Half-Opened Door, 1979; mem. editl. bd. History of Edn. Quar., 1996—; contbr. essays to books. Fulbright scholar, 1988; Am. Coun. Learned Socs. grantee, 1981. Mem. Am. Hist. Assn., So. Hist. Assn., Orgn. Am. Historians (membership com. 1990-93), S.C. Hist. Assn. (pres. 1994-95), History of Edn. Soc. (mem. editl. bd. 1996—). Office: U SC Dept History Columbia SC 29208

SYTEK, DONNA P., state legislator; b. Haverhill, Mass., Dec. 14, 1944; m. John Sytek; 1 child. AB, Regis Coll., 1966, MA. Mem. rules com., chmn. corrections & criminal justice com. N.H. Ho. of Reps., Concord; chmn. N.H. Rep. Com., 1982-84; pres. Nat. Rep. Legislators Assn., 1992-93; del. to Rep. Nat. Conv., 1980, 84, 88, 84 Const. Conv., Assembly on the Legislature, chmn., 1991-92; mem. exec. com. NCSL, 1990—, Coun. State Govt., 1989-92. Mem. Salem-BPW Club (pres. 1978-79), Crimeline (bd. dirs. 1985—), Dist. Nursing Assn. (bd. dirs. 1989—), Boys and Girls Club (bd. dirs. 1989—). Roman Catholic. Home: 9 Garrison Rd Salem NH 03079-3911 Office: NH Ho of Reps State House Concord NH 03301*

SZABAN, MARILYN C., small business owner; b. Palmer, Mass., Dec. 24, 1942; d. Joseph J. and Sophie V. (Duda) Martowski; m. Richard J. Szaban, June 9, 1962 (dec. 1993); children: Gregory John, Deborah Ann, Michael John. BFA summa cum laude, U. So. Maine, 1986; student, Notre Dame Coll., 1983. Owner, pres. Automotive Parts and Supply Co., Inc., Ramsdell & Van Dyke, Worcester, Mass., 1977—; co-owner, pres. Plymouth (N.H.) Auto Supply Co., Inc., 1980—; owner, pres. Transfigurations, Worcester, 1996—; bd. dirs. Apsco, Worcester, Pasco, Plymouth; art tchr. Jewish Comm. Ctr., Worcester, 1991, 92. Designer for Transfigurations, 1996; artist Portland Rev. of the Arts, 1986. Bd. dirs., art tchr. gallery com., Art Guild of Farmington, Conn., 1988-90. Recipient hon. mention Manchester Inst. Arts & Scis., 1981, 82, recognition award, 1983, Nat. Competition Juried Art Shows, Northeast and Mid-Atlantic States, 1981—. Mem. Plymouth C. of C. Home: 30 Olde Colony Dr Shrewsbury MA 01545 Office: Transfigurations 100 W Boylston St Worcester MA 01606 also: Automotive Parts & Supply Co Inc Ramsdell & Van Dyke Inc 98 W Boylston St Worcester MA 01606

SZEGO, CLARA MARIAN, cell biologist, educator; b. Budapest, Hungary, Mar. 23, 1916; came to U.S., 1921, naturalized, 1927; d. Paul S. and Helen (Elek) S.; m. Sidney Roberts, Sept. 14, 1943. A.B., Hunter Coll., 1937; M.S. (Garvan fellow), U. Minn., 1939, Ph.D., 1942. Instr. physiology U. Minn., 1942-43; Minn. Cancer Research Inst. fellow, 1943-44; rsch. assoc. OSRD, Nat. Bur. Standards, 1944-45, Worcester Found. Exptl. Biology, 1945-47; rsch. instr. physiol. chemistry Yale U. Sch. Medicine, 1947-48; mem. faculty UCLA, 1948—, prof. biology, 1960—. Named Woman of Year in Sci. Los Angeles Times, 1957-58; Guggenheim fellow, 1956; named to Hunter Coll. Hall of Fame, 1987. Fellow AAAS; mem. Am. Physiol. Soc., Am. Soc. Cell Biology, Endocrine Soc. (CIBA award 1953), Soc. for Endocrinology (Gt. Britain), Biochem. Soc. (Gt. Britain), Internat. Soc. Rsch. Reprodn., Phi Beta Kappa (pres. UCLA chpt. 1973-74), Sigma Xi (pres. UCLA chpt. 1976-77). Home: 1371 Marinette Rd Pacific Palisades CA 90272-2627 Office: U Calif Dept Molecular Cell & Devel Biology Los Angeles CA 90095-1606

SZEREMETA-BROWAR, TAISA LYDIA, endodontist; b. Geneva, N.Y., Mar. 21, 1957; d. Swiatoslaw Bohdan and Stefania (Melnyk) Szeremeta; m. Andrew Wolodymyr Browar, Sept. 19, 1981. BS in Dentistry, Case Western Res. U., 1978, DDS, 1980; cert. specialty endodontics magna cum laude, U. Ill., Chgo., 1982. Pvt. practice Hinsdale (Ill.) Periodontics and Endodontics, 1982—; asst. clin. prof. Northwestern U. Dental Sch., Chgo., 1986—. Counselor, mem. Plast-Ukrainian Scouting, 1963—; presenting team Worldwide Marriage Encounter, Chgo., 1985-94; mem. parish coun. Sts. Volodymyr and Olha, Chgo., 1985-94. E. Wach rsch. grantee U. Ill., Chgo., 1980. Mem. ADA, Am. Assn. Endodontists, Am. Coll. Stomatologic Surgeons, Ukrainian Med. Assn. (chair membership 1983-88), Ill. Assn. Endodontists (pres. 1990-91), Ill. State Dental Soc., Chgo. Dental Soc. (sec. table clinic 1990, vice chair 1991, chair 1992), Hinsdale C. of C. Ukrainian Catholic. Office: Hinsdale Periodontics & Endodontics 40 S Clay St Ste 111W Hinsdale IL 60521-3257

SZMANDA, LUCILLE MARIE, vocational school educator; b. Mishicot, Wis., Apr. 27, 1924; d. Walter Jacob and Clara Mary (Heinzen) Dirkmann; m. Robert Louis Szmanda, June 5, 1943; children: Robert Louis, William, Donald, Jeffery, Mary Clare, Timothy, Thomas, Margaret Ann. Student, Waukesha County Tech. Coll., 1967, LaSalle U., Chgo., 1970. Owner Park Upholstery & Decorating, East Troy, Wis., 1966-77; instr. upholstery program Gateway Tech. Coll., Kenosha, Wis., 1970-77; instr. upholstery diploma program Waukesha Tech. Coll., Pewaukee, Wis., 1973-77, Milw. Area Tech. Coll., 1977—; advisor Vocat. Indsl. Clubs Am., Milw., 1978-84; chair subcom. Task Force for Diversity, Milw., 1989—. Mem. Milw. Vocat. Assn. (mem. award com. 1992—, named Tchr. of Yr. 1990). Roman Catholic. Home: Unit 112 5253 N Lovers Lane Rd Milwaukee WI 53225-3039

SZOSTAK, M. ANNE, bank executive; b. London. Student, Colby Coll., 1972, Husson Coll., 1992. Chmn., pres., CEO Fleet Bank of Maine, Portland; sr. v.p. Fleet Fin. Group; bd. dirs. Maine Med. Ctr. Office: Fleet Bank of Maine 1 City Ctr Portland ME 04101-4004*

SZYMANSKI, EDNA MORA, rehabilitation psychology and special education educator; b. Caracas, Venezuela, Mar. 19, 1952; came to U.S., 1952; d. José Angel and Helen Adele (McHugh) Mora; m. Michael Bernard, Mar. 30, 1973. BS, Rensselaer Poly. Inst., 1972; MS, U. Scranton, 1974; PhD, U. Tex., 1988. Cert. rehab. counselor. Vocat. evaluator Mohawk Valley Workshop, Utica, N.Y., 1974-75; vocat. rehab. counselor N.Y. State Office Vocat. Rehab., Utica, N.Y., 1975-80; sr. vocat. rehab. counselor N.Y. State Office Vocat. Rehab., Utica, 1980-87; rsch. assoc. U. Tex., Austin, 1988-89; asst. prof. U. Wis., Madison, 1989-91, assoc. prof., 1991-93, assoc. dean sch. edn., 1993—, dir. rehab. rsch. and tng. ctr., 1993-96, prof. rehab. psychology and spl. edn., 1993—; cons. Rsch. Assocs. Syracuse, N.Y., 1988-90. Co-author various book chpts.; co-editor: Rehabilitation Counseling Basics and Beyond, 1992; co-editor Work and Disability, 1996, Rehabilitation Counseling Bull., 1994—; contbr. articles to profl. jours. Mem. Pres.'s Com. on Employment of People with Disabilities, Washington, 1987—. Recipient Rsch. award Am. Assn. Counselor Edn. and Supr., 1991. Mem. ACA (chair rsch. com. 1992-94, Rsch. awards 1990, 93, 95), Am. Rehab. Counseling Assn. (pres. 1985-86, Rsch. award 1989, 94), Coun. Rehab. Edn. (chair rsch. com. 1990-95, v.p. 1993-95), Nat. Coun. Rehab. Edn. (chair rsch. com. 1992—, Rehab. Edn. Rschr. of Yr. 1993, New Career in Rehab. Edn. award 1990). Office: U Wis Dept Rehab Psychology and Spl Edn 432 N Murray St Madison WI 53706-1407

SZYMONIAK, ELAINE EISFELDER, state senator; b. Boscobel, Wis., May 24, 1920; d. Hugo Adolph and Pauline (Vig) Eisfelder; Casimir Donald Szymoniak, Dec. 7, 1943; children: Kathryn, Peter, John, Mary, Thomas. BS, U. Wis., 1941; MS, Iowa State U., 1977. Speech clinician Waukesha (Wis.) Pub. Sch., 1941-43, Rochester (N.Y.) Pub. Sch., 1943-44; rehab. aide U.S. Army, Chickasha, Okla., 1944-46; audiologist U. Wis., Madison, 1946-48; speech clinician Buffalo Pub. Sch., 1948-49, Sch. for Handicapped, Salina, Kans., 1951-52; speech pathologist, audiologist, counselor, resource mgr. Vocat. Rehab. State Iowa, Des Moines, 1956-85; mem. Iowa Senate, Des Moines, 1989—. Mem. Des Moines City coun., 1978-88; bd. dirs. Nat. League Cities, Wahsington, 1982-84, Girl Scouts U.S., Civic Ctr., House of Mercy, Westminster House, Iowa Leadership Consortium, Coun. on Internat. Understanding, Iowa Commn. on Status of Women, Young Christian Assn.; chairperson Greater Des Moines Coun. for Internat. Understanding, United Way, 1987-88, Urban Dreams, Iowa Maternal and Child Health com. Named Woman of Achievement YWCA, 1982, Visionary Woman, Young Women's Resource Ctr. Mem. Am. Speech Lang. and Hearing Assn., Iowa Speech Lang. and Hearing Assn. (pres. 1977-78), Nat. Coun. State Legislators (fed. state com. on health, adv. com. on child protection), Women's Polit. Caucus, Nexus (pres. 1981-82). Home: 2116 44th St Des Moines IA 50310-3011 Office: State Senate State Capitol Des Moines IA 50319

TABAK, VALERIE, sociology educator, consultant; b. Chgo., Mar. 18, 1946; d. William Lieberman and Mary Louise Whitesell; divorced Aug. 1965; 1 child, Holly. BA, Govs. State U., University Park, Ill., 1976, MA, 1977. Assoc. dir. county planning commn. Kankakee County, Ill., 1979-83; dir. bus. and career sills ctr. South Suburban Coll., South Holland, Ill., 1983-86; program coord. South Cook Ednl. Svc. Ctr., Flossmoor, Ill., 1985-89; spl. asst. to bd. dirs. Residential Energy Loan Fund, Chgo., 1986-90; sociology instr. Moraine Valley C.C., Palos Hills, Ill., 1991—. Trade mission rep. to Japan and Korea, State of Ill., 1986; judge for Ill. Sci. Acad. Nominated Part-time Faculty Mem. of Yr., 1992, 94, 95. Office: Moraine Valley CC 10900 S 88th Ave Palos Hills IL 60465

TABER, CAROL A., magazine publisher. AA, Green Mountain Coll., 1965. Network mgr. Media Networks, Inc., 1970-74; N.Y. advt. mgr. Ladies' Home Jour., 1974-79; assoc. pub., advt. dir. Working Woman, N.Y.C., 1979-83, pub., 1984-94; pub. Working Mother, N.Y.C., 1994—; exec. v.p., group pub. Working Woman and Working Mother mags., 1989. Office: Working Mother 230 Park Ave Fl 7 New York NY 10169-0799*

TABER, DEBORAH KAY, state agency professional; b. Greencastle, Ind., Nov. 19, 1952; d. Abner Eugene and Dorothy Jean (Hammond) T. Sec.-adminstrv. med. degree, Ind. Vocat. Tech. Coll., 1984. Farmer Gosport, Ind., 1967—; asst. assessor Owen County, Spencer, Ind., 1981-83; sec. Ind. U. Sch. Law, Bloomington, 1984-85; clk. U.S. Postal Svc., Bloomington, 1985—; adv. bd. clk., mem. Harrison Twp. Owen County, Gosport, 1984-85. Mem., ch. treas., typist, youth dir. Quincy (Ind.) Bapt. Ch., 1963—. Mem. DAR. Republican. Home: RR 1 Box 456 Gosport IN 47433

TABER, LYNN SULLIVAN, education educator; b. Warren, Ohio, Feb. 21, 1947; d. James Wesley and Madelyn Jane (Nicholas) Sullivan; m. Robert Clinton Taber, June 12, 1992. BA in Psychology and English, Kent State U., 1968; MA in Coll. Student Pers., U. Colo., 1973; M in Mktg., Northwestern U., 1985; PhD in Ednl. Adminstrn., U. Tex., 1995. Cert. Laubach Literacy Action tutor, 1989. Counselor, instr. Laramie County C.C., Cheyenne, Wyo., 1973-76; dir., asst. dean, assoc. dean Triton Coll., River Grove, Ill., 1976-86; assoc. v.p., v.p. Fla. C.C., Jacksonville, 1986-92; W.K. Kellogg rsch. fellow U. Tex., Austin, 1992-95; adminstrv. intern asst. to pres. C.C. Denver, Colo., 1993; asst. prof. higher edn. adminstrn. U. Ala., Tuscaloosa, 1996—; mem. Ill. Coun. C.C. Admintrs., 1976-86, sec., 1985; cons. in field. Co-author: The Company We Keep-Collaboration in the Community College, 1995. Study team mem. Jacksonville (Fla.) Cmty. Coun., Inc., 1986-92; 1st v.p., bd. mem. Learn to Read, Inc., Jacksonville, 1988-90; chmn., CEO, bd. mem. Pine Castle, Inc., Jacksonville, 1990-92; co-facilitator INSIGHT-A Cmty. Visioning Process, Jacksonville, 1992. Roueche scholar in C.C. leadership U. Tex., Austin, 1994. Mem. Am. Ednl. Rsch. Assn., Am. Assn. C.C. (presenter 1981—), Phi Kappa Phi, Kappa Delta Phi. Office: U Ala Higher Edn Adminstrn Prog Box 87231 210 Wilson Hall Tuscaloosa AL 35487-0231

TABLER, SHIRLEY MAY, retired librarian, artist; b. Washington, Mar. 18, 1936; d. Howard Leon and Ella May (Miles) Bosley; m. Edward Charles Sepelak, July 30, 1954 (div. 1965); children: David Edward, Linda May, William Bryan; m. Carlton Byard Tabler, June 27, 1968 (dec. May 1993); stepchildren: Roger Byard, Charlotte Virginia. BS in Art Edn., U. Md., 1977, BA in Libr. Sci., 1978, MA in Art Edn., 1981, MLS, 1990. Sec. Nat. Capital Housing Authority, Washington, 1954-55; clk. Vitro Corp., Silver Spring, Md., 1956-57; hostess, cashier Hot Shoppes, Wheaton, Md., 1960-63; new accounts sec. State Nat. Bank, Bethesda, Md., 1966-68; media aide, art tchr. Montgomery County Pub. Schs., Rockville, Md., 1968-86, libr., cataloguer, computer tech., 1986-93. Exhibitions in group shows include Arts Club, Washington, 1990, 91, 92, 93, 94, 95, Rockville Mcpl. Gallery, 1992, 93, 94, 95, Sugar & Fricht Gallery, 1994, 95, Ten. Oaks Gallery-Clarksville, 1994, 95, Town Ctr. Gallery, 1994, Kensington Gallery, 1994, 95, 96; one person shows include Rockville Mcpl. Gallery, 1989, Landon Gallery, Bethesda, Md., 1990, Washington Printmakers Gallery, 1994. Leader, advisor Girl Scouts Am., Rockville, Md., 1964-82. Mem. ALA, Soc. Librs. Internat., Am. Art League, League Am. Pen Women (past pres. Chevy Chase), Md. Printmakers, Washington Printmakers Gallery, , Miniature Painters, Sculptors and Gravers Soc., D.C., Fla. Miniature Soc., Cider Painters Am., Art Gallery of Fells Point, Miniature Art Soc. Fla., Olney Art Assn. (newsletter editor 1984-91, show chmn. 1993, libr. show chmn. 1992-94, program chmn. 1995), Rockville Art League, Phi Kappa Phi. Democrat. Methodist. Home and Studio: 123 Charles St Rockville MD 20850-1510 Office: Genevieve Roberts Studio 17521 Shenandoah Ct Ashton MD 20861-9774

TABNER, MARY FRANCES, secondary school educator; b. Rochester, N.Y., Dec. 11, 1918; d. William Herman and Mary Frances (Willenbacher) Arndt; m. James Gordon Tabner, June 27, 1942; 1 child, Barbara Jean. BA, SUNY, Albany, 1940, MA, 1959; postgrad., U. Rochester, N.Y., 1944, 45, Northwestern U. (John Hay fellow), 1963-64, U. Manchester (Eng.), 1971-72. Tchr. history pub. schs. Mattituck, N.Y., 1940-43, Gorham, N.Y., 1943-46; tchr. pub. schs. Waterford, N.Y., 1949-55; tchr. social studies Shaker High Sch., Latham, N.Y., 1959-83, also dir., 1959-83, ret., 1983; tchr. ch. history Our Lady of Assumption Ch., Latham; dir. seminar in Russian Studies; tchr. Shaker Heritage. Author bibliographies on Russian history, Am. studies. Mem. Citizens Exch. Coun. N.Y. State Regents independent study grantee, 1966. Mem. AAUW, Nat. Coun. Social Studies, N.Y. State United Tchrs. Assn., Advancement Slavic Studies, SUNY Albany Alumni Assn., Albany Inst. History and Art, Capital Dist. Coun. Social Studies, Shaker Heritage Soc. (trustee, guide, tchr.), Nat. Trust Historic Preservation, English Speaking Union, Am. Assn. Retired Persons. Republican. Roman Catholic. Home: 557 Columbia St Cohoes NY 12047-3807

TABOR, BEVERLY ANN, elementary school educator; b. Dallas, Feb. 12, 1943; m. Charles W. Tabor, Aug. 22, 1964; children: Shawn, Josh. BS in Edn., U. N. Tex., 1964, MEd in Guidance, Counseling, 1970. Cert. tchr. elem. art, guidance and counseling, supr., Tex. Elem. tchr. Ft. Davis (Tex.) Ind. Sch. Dist., 1964-65, Mesquite (Tex.) Ind. Sch. Dist., 1965-69, '71—; counselor Amarillo (Tex.) Ind. Sch. Dist., 1970-71; mem. ins. adv. com. Tchr. Retirement Sys. of Tex., Austin, 1986—; chmn. site based mgmt. com. Tosch Elem. Sch., Mesquite, 1992-94, mentor for new tchrs., student tchrs., H.S. students considering the tchg. profession. Life mem. Tosch Elem. PTA, 1985—. Named to Apple Corps, 1995. Mem. Tex. State Tchrs. Assn. (life), Mesquite Edn. Assn., Alpha Delta Kappa (past pres. Mesquite). Home: 5321 Meadowside Dr Garland TX 75043-2733 Office: Tosch Elem Sch 2424 Larchmont Dr Mesquite TX 75150-5233

TABORN, JEANNETTE ANN, real estate investor; b. Cleve., June 9, 1926; d. Ralph Mason and Catherine MArie (Mitchell) Tyler; m. Albert Lorenzo Taborn, Oct. 4, 1947 (dec. 1994); children: Wesley Orren, Annette Loren, KAren Faye, Albert Lorenzo II, Thomas Tyler. Student, Ohio State U., 1944-47. Real estate agt. and investor Cleve., 1947-61; tech. proofreader Sass-Widder Tech Writers, Port Hueneme, Calif., 1961-66, Upjohn Co., Kalamazoo, Mich., 1966-84; mktg. rep. pvt. practice, Kalamazoo, Mich., 1984—; regional mgr. Primerica, 1994; co-facilitator Healing Racism Series. Pres. Kalamazoo County Parent Tchr. Student Assn., 1975; active YWCA, 1981, NAACP, 1983; Kalamazoo Pub. Sch. bd., 1978; Greater Kalamazoo Arts Coun., 1979, Mich. sch. bd. vocat./Edn., Liberty com. C. of Com.; pres. Loy Norrix Trustee Fund, 1983; trustee Kalamazoo Intermediate Sch.; regional mgr. Al Williams. Recipient Cmty. Medal of Arts. Mem. So. West Mich. Alzheimer's Assn. (bd. mem.), Delta Sigma Theta (Mary McLeod Bethune award). Mem. Bahai Faith. Office: PO Box 50853 Kalamazoo MI 49005

TABRISKY, PHYLLIS PAGE, physiatrist, educator; b. Newton, Mass., Aug. 28, 1930; d. Joseph Westley and Alice Florence (Wainwright) Page; m. Joseph Tabrisky, Apr. 23, 1955; children: Joseph Page, Elizabeth Ann, William Page. BS, Douglass Coll., 1952; MD, Tufts U., 1956. Cert. phys. medicine and rehab. Intern U. Ill. Hosp., Chgo., 1956-57; phys. medicine and rehab. residency U. Colo. Sch. Medicine, Denver, 1958-60; gen. med. officer dept. pediatrics and medicine Coco Solo Hosp., Panama Canal Zone, 1961-62; staff physician dept. pediatrics Ft. Hood (Tex.) Army Hosp., 1963; instr. dept. rehab. medicine Boston (Mass.) U. Sch. Medicine, 1964-66; asst. prof. phys. medicine and rehab. U. Colo. Sch. Medicine, Denver, 1966-68; staff physician VA Med. Ctr., Long Beach, Calif., 1968-71; acting chief phys. medicine and rehab. VA Med. Ctr., Long Beach, 1971-73, asst. chief rehab. med. svcs., 1973-91, chief phys. medicine & rehab. svc., 1992—; asst. clin. prof. phys. medicine and rehab. U. Calif. Coll. Medicine, Irvine, 1970-75, assoc. clin. prof., 1975-80, prof., 1980—, vice chair dept. phys. medicine and rehab., 1985—, dir. residency tng., 1982—. Fellow Am. Acad. Phys. Medicine and Rehab. (mem. accreditation coun. grad. med. com. 1993—); mem. Am. Congress Rehab. Medicine, Assn. Acad. Physiatrists (bd. trustees 1995-97), Alpha Omega Alpha. Republican. Episcopalian. Office: VA Med Ctr 5901 E 7th St Long Beach CA 90822-5201

TACHA, ATHENA, sculptor, educator; b. Larissa, Greece, Apr. 23, 1936; came to U.S., 1963; MA, Nat. Acad. Fine Arts, Athens, Greece, 1959; MA in Art History, Oberlin Coll., 1961; PHD, U. Paris, 1963. Curator modern art Allen Art Mus., Oberlin, Ohio, 1963-73; prof. art Oberlin Coll., 1973—. One-woman shows include Zabriskie Gallery, N.Y., 1979, 81, Max Hutchinson Gallery, N.Y., 1984, High Mus. Art, Atlanta, 1989, Franklin Furnace, N.Y., 1994, and many other exhibits throughout the world, 1966—; prin. pub. commns. include sculptures at Dept. Environ. Protection, Trenton, N.J., Case-Western Res. U., Cleve., U. South Fla., Ft. Myers, Low Water Dam Riverfront Pk., Tulsa, Dept. of Transp., Hartford, Conn., City of Sarasota, Fla.; collections include Hirshhorn Mus., Washington, Mus. Fine Arts, Houston, Nat. Coll. Fine Arts, Washington, Cleve. Mus. Art, Allen Art Mus., Oberlin; author: (as A. T. Spear) Rodin Sculpture in the Cleveland Museum of Art, 1967, Brancusi's Birds, 1969; contbr. articles to profl. jours. Recipient 1st prize May Show, Cleve. Mus. Art, 1968, 71, 79; NEA grantee, 1975. Home: 291 Forest St Oberlin OH 44074-1509

TACHA, DEANELL REECE, federal judge; b. Jan. 26, 1946. BA, U. Kans., 1968; JD, U. Mich., 1971. Spl. asst. to U.S. Sec. of Labor, Washington, 1971-72; assoc. Hogan & Hartson, Washington, 1973, Thomas J. Pitner, Concordia, Kans., 1973-74; dir. Douglas County Legal Aid Clinic, Lawrence, Kans., 1974-77; assoc. prof. law U. Kans., Lawrence, 1974-77, prof., 1977-85, assoc. dean, 1977-79, assoc. vice chancellor, 1979-81, vice chancellor, 1981-85; judge U.S. Ct. Appeals (10th cir.), Denver, 1985—. Office: US Ct Appeals 10th Cir 4830 W 15th St Ste 100 Lawrence KS 66049-3846

TACKWELL, ELIZABETH MILLER, social worker; b. Caney, Kans., Mar. 14, 1923; d. Jesse Winfield and Mattie (Shuler) Miller; m. Joseph J. Tackwell, Dec. 13, 1946 (dec. Mar. 1988); children: Steven, Tiana Tackwell David, Christy Tackwell Reyner. BA, U. Okla., 1953, MSW, 1962. Bd. cert. diplomate Am. Bd. Examiners in Clin. Social Work; lic. social worker, Okla. Social worker Dept. Pub. Welfare, Tulsa/Cleve./Okla. County, Okla., 1958-59; med. social analyst Dept. Pub. Welfare, Okla., 1960-61; assoc. John Massey M.D. Clinic, Oklahoma City, 1964-69; clin. asst. prof. Okla. U. Sch. Social Work, Oklahoma City, 1964—; asst. prof., clin. instr. dept. psychiatry/behavioral scis. Okla. U. Health Scis. Ctr., Oklahoma City, 1963—; psychiat. social worker VA Med. Ctr., Oklahoma City, 1961—, chief mental health sect., 1976—, adminstrv. dir. day treatment ctr., 1993—; pvt. practice Oklahoma City, 1971—; VA Med. Ctr.; psychiat. surveyor Health Care Fin. Adminstrn., Dept. Human Svcs., Washington, 1985—. Recipient Svc. Commendation award DAV, 1980, Chi Omega Scholastic award, Awards Am. Ex-Prisoners of War, 1994, 95, 96. Mem. NASW (diplomate in clin. social work, pres. Okla. chpt. 1971-73, Social Worker of the Yr. Western Okla. chpt. 1975), Acad. Cert. Social Workers, Okla. Health and Welfare Assn. (conf. chmn. 1975—), Pi Gamma Mu. Home: 1328 Tarman Cir Norman OK 73071-4846 Office: Vets Affairs Med Ctr 921 NE 13th St Oklahoma City OK 73104-5007

TADDEI, LOIS ANNETTE, artist, decorator; b. Phila., Sept. 17, 1935; d. Frank Rue Magowan and Grace Gloria (Valentino) Weinstein; m. Robert Matthew Taddei, May 21, 1960; 1 child, Robyn Grace. Degree, Pierce Bus. Sch. One-woman shows include Pa. Hort. Soc., Phila, La Grande Gallery, Moorestown, N.J., Camden County Libr.; group shows include Art at Armory, Phila, Great Galleries, New Hope, Pa., Hardcastle Gallery, Wilmington, Del., Hockessin, Del., Gallery I, Chadds Ford, Pa., Rhoads Gallery, Gwynedd Valley, Pa., Festival Arts, Cape May, N.J., Ocean City (N.J.) Arts Festival; designer Vassar Designers Showcase House, 1991-92, Haddonfield Design Showcase House, 1992, Barry Decorators Haddonfield & Cherry Hill, Interiors by Marilouise, West Chester, Pa., Rocco Marianni & Assoc. Interior Design, Haddonfield. Mem. Graphic Artist Guild, United Visual Artists. Home: 1 Coventry Ct Cherry Hill NJ 08002

TADIAN, LUANNE F. B., financial analyst, consultant, researcher; b. Colorado Springs, Colo., Mar. 29, 1965; d. Carlos Solomon and Josie Dolores (Vigil) C'DeBaca; m. Nishan Thaddeus Tadian, Dec. 30, 1985; children: Joshua Abel, Zachary Solomon. BS in Psychology and Biology, U.N.Mex., 1988; MBA, Calif. State U., L.A., 199. Lic. in real estate law, series 6 and 63, Nat. Assn. Securities Dealers. Jr. v.p. prodn. Sentry Mortgage, Albuquerque, 1988-89; rsch. cons., L.A., 1991-93; account mgr. Beverly Hills Group Fin. Mgmt. Specialists, L.A., 1993—; customer support account rep. Mid Atlantic and Eastern Seaboard Daylight Transport. Bd. dirs., chmn. vol. recognition, mem. pub. rels. and resource devel. coms. Calif. Litracy, San Gabriel, 1993—; del. Rep. Planning Com. Mem. NAFE, Nat. Assn. Women Bus. Owners, Nat. Assn. Life Underwriters, Beta Gamma Sigma. Republican. Roman Catholic. Home: House C 269 S Walnut Grove San Gabriel CA 91776

TADYCH, RENITA, English eduator; b. Manitowoc, Wis., Aug. 5, 1934; d. Zenon S. and Anita (Broecker) T. BA, Silver Lake Coll., Manitowoc, Wis., 1960; MA, U. Dayton, 1972; PhD, Indiana U. of Pa., 1992. Life cert. tchr., Wis.; joined Franciscan Sisters of Christian Charity, 1948. Elem. tchr. Dioceses of Steubenville (Ohio), Green Bay & LaCrosse (Wis.), Dioceses of Gaylord (Mich.) and L.A., 1952-66; secondary tchr. Dioceses of Chgo., Omaha, Milw. and Green Bay, 1967-84; assoc. prof. Silver Lake Coll., Diocese of Green Bay, Manitowoc, Wis., 1984—; mem. adv. bd. Collegiate Press, Alta Loma, Calif., 1994-95; supr. honors program Roncalli H.S., Manitowoc, 1984—. Mem. Nat. Coun. Tchrs. English, Wis. Coun. Tchrs. English (coll. and univ. com. 1993-96). Roman Catholic. Home and Office: Silver Lake Coll 2406 S Alverno Rd Manitowoc WI 54220-9319

TAECKENS, PAMELA W., bank executive; b. Oklahoma City, June 2, 1959; d. L. Gregory and Carolyn S. (Pace) Webb; m. Douglas R. Taeckens, Sept. 29, 1984. BS, U. Ariz., 1980; postgrad., Northwestern U., Evanston, Ill., 1989, 91. Audit analyst NBD Bank, Flint, Mich., 1985-88, trust adminstr., 1988-90, trust officer, 1990-92, asst. v.p., 1993—; Active membership com. YWCA of Greater Flint, 1990-94, fin. com., 1994—. Mem. Fin. Women Internat. Republican. Methodist. Office: NBD Bank G-2413 S Linden Rd Ste 7 Flint MI 48532

TAEUBER, WENDY KIM, film producer; b. Madison, Wis., June 7, 1971; d. Karl Ernst and Alma (Ficks) T. BFA, NYU, 1992. Asst. Scott Rudin Prodns., N.Y.C., 1992-93, story editor, 1993-94, dir. devel., 1994-96; v.p. The Kennedy Marshall Co., L.A. Exec. on project (film) Clueless, 1995. Vol. GMHC, N.Y.C., 1993, APLA, L.A., 1995. Mem. NOW. Democrat.

TAFT, FRANCES PRINDLE, art history educator; b. New Haven, Dec. 12, 1921; d. William Edwin and Mildred (Bradley) Prindle; m. Seth Chase Taft, June 19, 1943; children: Frederick Irving, Thomas Prindle, Cynthia Bradley, Seth Tucker. BA, Vassar Coll., 1942; MA, Yale U., 1948. Rsch. asst. Yale Med. Sch., New Haven, 1942; instr. comms. USN Officer Sch., Northampton, Mass., 1943-45; tchr. anatomy and art The Gateway Sch., New Haven, 1943-44; prof. art history Cleve. Inst. Art, 1950—; bd. trustees Cleve. Mus. Art, mem. women's coun., lectr., 1950—; bd. trustees Karamu Art Ctr., Cleve., 1949-65; mem., bd. dirs. Vassar Art Gallery, Poughkeepsie, N.Y., 1972—. Chmn. bd. Overseers Case Western Res. U., Cleve., 1984-86, bd. trustees Michelson-Morley Ctr., 1986-87; mem. adv. com. Martha Holden Jennings Found., Cleve., 1973-91; pres. alumni/alumnae Assn. Vassar Coll., Poughkeepsie, 1966-72. Lt. (j.g.) USN, 1942-45. Named Career Woman of Achievement, Cleve. YWCA, 1993; recipient Cleve. Arts prize, 1995. Mem. Coll. Art Assn., Soc. Artchtl. Historians (pres. local chpt.), Cleve. Archaeol. Soc. (pres.), Print Club Cleve. Home: 6 Pepper Ridge Rd Cleveland OH 44124

TAFT, TRACY L., special education educator; b. Denver, July 10, 1970; d. Donald E. and Lila Lee (Ehrbright) T. BS in Spl. Edn., U. N.C., Greensboro, 1992; postgrad., Mankato State U., 1992—. Cert. spl. edn. tchr., Minn. Spl. edn. tchr. Sch. Dist. 719, Prior Lake, Minn., 1993-94, Minn. River Valley Spl. Ednl. Coop., New Prague, 1994—. Mem. Minn. Edn. Assn., Coun. for Exceptional Children. Home: 3425 Spruce Trail Prior Lake MN 55372 Office: Westwood Elem Sch Plus Program 5370 Westwood Dr PO Box 539 Prior Lake MN 55372

TAGER, ROBERTA KAY, counselor; b. N.Y.C., June 24, 1937; d. Leslie Louis and Ethel Nellie (Glassburg) Kay; m. Michael George Tager, July 4, 1959; children: Jacqueline Hallie, Elizabeth Stacy, Suzanne Kim. BA, Queens Coll., 1958; MS, U. Bridgeport, 1984. Tchr. Meadowbrook Pub. Schs., L.I., N.Y., 1958-59, Rudyard (Mich.) Pub. Schs., 1960-61, Kimcheloe AFB, Kinross, Mich., 1962-63; tytor Rochester (Minn.) Pub. Schs., 1963-65; adult educator Westport (Conn.) Pub. Schs., 1980-90; counselor, therapist Wellness Health Counseling Therapy, Westport, 1984—; counselor Open Line, Westport, 1977-78, George Washington Carver C.C., Norwalk, Conn., 1983-84. Vol. Norwalk Hosp., 1995—, Westport Women's Club, 1995—; membership chair O.R.T., Westport, 1966-68; campaign chair Am. Heart Assn., Fairfield County, 1972-73. Mem. Am. Internat. Reiki Assn., New England Assn. Specialists in Group Work, Conn. Homeopathic Assn., Assn. Rsch. and Enlightenment, Inst. Noetic Sci., Assn. Religious and Phys. Rsch., The Ro-hun Profl. Assn., Ctr. Attitudinal Healing. Office: Wellness Health Counseling & Therapy 104 Imperial Ave Westport CT 06880

TAGGART, LOUISE ELIZABETH COOK, educator; b. nr. Lincoln, Nebr., Nov. 30, 1900; d. William Baker and Isabella Louisa (Cross) Cook; m. Paul Ferdinand Taggart, July 16, 1924 (dec. July 1979); children: J. Mark, Donna Louise Taggart McKinney. BS in Edn., U. Nebr., Lincoln, 1926; student, Washington Sch. Gemology, 1956. Cert. univ. tchr., Nebr. Tchr. high schs., Nebr., 1922-26; substitute tchr. pub. high schs., Denver, 1944-46, Montgomery County (Md.) high schs., 1952-57; gemstone tchr. in pvt. practice Bethesda, Md., 1963-71; tchr. gemstone classes for adult edn. Montgomery County Pub. Schs., 1971—; profl. book reviewer in dramatic style, 1930-45; guest speaker in gemology, 1960—. Organizer, host German-Am. women's discussion group, Bonn, Germany, 1957-62; organizer, instr. Mineral and Gemstone Club, Bonn, 1960-62; co-organizer, pres. German-Am. Women's Club, Stuttgart, Germany, 1947-52. Recipient Grand award of Honor, Internat. Gem. and Jewelry Show, Washington, 1991, Supt.'s Svc. award Montgomery Pub. Schs., 1988, Outstanding Tchr. award Adult Edn. Montgomery County, 1978. Mem. Gem, Lapidary, Mineral Soc. (Ednl. awrd 1995), Bead Soc. Greater Washington, PEO (pres. 1940-42).

TAGGART, SONDRA, financial planner, investment advisor; b. N.Y.C., July 22, 1934; d. Louis and Rose (Birnbaum) Hamov; children: Eric, Karen. BA, Hunter Coll., 1955. Cert. fin. planner; registered investment advisor; registered prin. Nat. Assn. Securities Dealers. Founder, dir., officer Copyright Svc. Bur., Ltd., N.Y.C., 1957-69; dir., officer Maclen Music, Inc., N.Y.C., 1964-69, The Beatles Ltd., 1964-69; pres. Westshore, Inc., Mill Valley, Calif., 1969-82; investment advisor, securities broker, chief exec. officer The Taggart Co. Ltd., 1982—. Editor: The Red Tapes: Commentaries on Doing Business With The Russians and East Europeans, 1978. Mem. Internat. Assn. Fin. Planners, Registry Fin. Planning Practitioners. Republican. Club: Bankers. Office: 9720 Wilshire Blvd Ste 205 Beverly Hills CA 90212-2006

TAGGE, ANNE KATHERINE, not-for-profit organization administrator; b. Waltham, Mass., Oct. 20, 1954; d. Raymond Carl and Anne (Weller) T. BA, Wellesley Coll., 1977. Pres., founder Susan Lee Campbell Inst., Wellesley, Mass., 1986—; hon. adv. bd. Ctr. for Am. Studies; pres. Fulbright Assn. Mass. chpt.; speaker in the field. Contbr. to newspapers, mags., jours. and books. Scholar Town of Wellesley, Fulbright, Salzburg Seminar, French Min. Fgn. Affairs; recipient US/UNEP Achievement award, honoree Rolex Awards for Enterprise. Fellow E. European Rsch. Ctr.; mem. Explorers Club. Home: Moshup Trail Martha's Vineyard MA 02535 Office: 37 Avon Rd Wellesley MA 02181-4618

TAGIURI, CONSUELO KELLER, child psychiatrist, educator; b. San Francisco; d. Cornelius H. and Adela (Rios) Keller; m. Renato Tagiuri; children: Robert, Peter, John. BA, U. Calif.-Berkeley; MD, U. Calif.-San Francisco. Diplomate Am. Bd. Psychiatry and Neurology. Resident psychiatry Mass. Gen. Hosp., Boston; staff psychiatrist Children's Hosp., Boston, 1951-59; med. dir. Gifford Sch., Weston, Mass., 1965-85; chief psychiatrist Cambridge (Mass.) Guidance Ctr., 1961-84; mem. faculty dept. psychiatry Harvard Med. Sch., Cambridge, 1965—; cons. early childhood program Children's Hosp., 1985—. Contbr. articles in field to books. Fellow Am. Orth. psychiat. Assn., Mass. Med. Soc., New Eng. Council Child Psychiatry.

TAHIR, MARY ELIZABETH, retail marketing and management consultant; b. Greenwood, Miss., Dec. 14, 1933; d. Mahmoud Ibrahim and Mary Constance (Ollie) T. Student, U. Miss., 1951-53. Cert. Profl. Cons., Acad, Profl. Cons. and Advisors. Mgmt. trainee Neiman-Marcus Co., Dallas, 1954-56; asst. buyer D.H. Holmes Co. Ltd., New Orleans, 1956-58, buyer, 1958-65, assoc. divisional mdse. mgr., 1965-67, divisional v.p., 1969-79, corp. v.p., gen. mdse. mgr., 1979-89; pres. Liz Tahir & Assocs., New Orleans, 1990—. Author: Mexico's Cosmetic and Fragrance Market: Past, Present and Future Opportunities, 1991, The Changing World of Mexican Retail Opportunities, 1991, Mexico: Window of Opportunity, 1991, Art of Negotiating, 1993, Negotiating More Profitable with Your Suppliers, Customers and Employees, 1994. Bd. dirs. Vieux Carre Property Owners Assn., New Orleans, 1990, YWCA, 1996—. Recipient Role Model award YWCA, 1990. Mem. Women's Profl. Coun. (chmn. New Choices 1989), World Trade Ctr., Fashion Group Internat. (Alpha award 1987-88, Lifetime Achievement award 1993), Nat. Spkrs. Assn., Am. Mktg. Assn. (bd. dirs. 1996—), Am. Assn. Profl. Cons., Am. Mgmt. Assn., Fgn. Rels. Assn. (bd. dirs. 1992—, pres. bd. dirs. 1994-96), Nat. Retail Fedn. Home: 817 Esplanade Ave New Orleans LA 70116-1940 Office: Liz Tahir & Assocs 201 Saint Charles Ave Ste 2500 New Orleans LA 70170-1000

TAI, JULIA CHOW, chemistry educator; b. Shanghai, China, Dec. 15, 1935; came to U.S., 1957; d. Fei-chen and Jean-tson (Liao) Chow; m. Hung-Chao Tai, Aug. 14, 1960; children: Eve, Helen, Michael. BS in Chemistry, Nat. Taiwan U., 1957; MS in Chemistry, U. Okla., 1959; PhD in Chemistry, U. Ill., 1963. Rsch. assoc. Wayne State U., Detroit, 1963-66, 67-68; vis. assoc. prof. Nat. Taiwan U., Taipei, Republic of China, 1968-69; asst. prof. U. Mich., Dearborn, 1969-73, assoc. prof., 1973-79, prof. chemistry, 1979—. Contbr. articles to sci. jours. Mem. Am. Chem. Soc., Quantum Chemistry Program Exch., Mich. Coll. Chemistry Tchrs. Assn. Office: Univ Mich Dearborn 4901 Evergreen Rd Dearborn MI 48128-2406

TAIBI, JOSEPHINE ROSE, bookkeeper; b. N.Y.C., Apr. 9, 1948; d. Filippo and Calogera (Butera) T. AS, Borough of Manhattan C.C., N.Y.C., 1976. Bookkeeper Raven Press, N.Y.C., 1976-85; pres. Budgetwise Bookkeeping, N.Y.C., 1986—; treas. Heritage of Pride, N.Y.C., 1988-90; bd. mem. Greater Gotham Bus. Coun., N.Y.C., 1990-92. Mem. N.Y. Bankers Group, Stonewall Bus. Assn., Lesbian Avengers, Pride Agenda.

TAJIMA, RENEE ELIZABETH, filmmaker, writer; b. Chgo., Sept. 11, 1958; d. Calvin and Marie (Ujiiye) Ta.; m. Armando de la Peña, Sept. 30, 1994. BA in East Asian Studies and Sociology, Harvard-Radcliffe Coll., 1980. Dir. Asian Cine-Vision, N.Y.C., 1980-82; editor Bridge: Asian Am. Perspectives Quar., N.Y.C., 1980-83; exec. producer Film News Found., N.Y.C., 1983-92; film critic The Village Voice, N.Y.C., 1989-91; commentator Nat. Pub. Radio, 1989-93; mem. competition jury Sundance Film Festival, Park City, Utah, 1993; mem. adv. bd. PBS Nat. Program Svc., Alexandria, Va., 1991-92; bd. govs. N.Y. Found. for the Arts, N.Y.C., 1990-91; v.p. bd. dirs. Media Alliance, N.Y.C., 1987-88. Producer, dir., writer films The Best Hotel on Skid Row, 1991 (Mannheim award 1991), My America. . .or Honk if You Love Buddha, 1996; sr. producer TV prodn. Declarations: All Men Are Created Equal?, 1993; producer, dir. film Who Killed Vincent Chin?, 1988 (Oscar nominee 1989). Mentor Puente, so. Calif., 1995. Recipient George Peabody award U. Ga., Dupont-Columbia award Columbia U., 1989. Mem. Nat. Asian Am. Telecomms. Assn. (bd. dirs. 1982-83), Internat. Documentary Assn., Film Arts Found., Asian Am. Journalists Assn., Assn. Ind. Video and Film. Office: 11507 Mississippi Ave Los Angeles CA 90025

TAJON, ENCARNACION FONTECHA (CONNIE TAJON), retired educator, association executive; b. San Narciso, Zambales, Philippines, Mar. 25, 1920; came to U.S., 1948; d. Espiridion Maggay and Gregoria (Labrador) Fontecha; m. Felix B. Tajon, Nov. 17, 1948; children: Ruth F., Edward F. Teacher's cert., Philippine Normal Coll., 1941; BEd, Far Eastern U., Manila, 1947; MEd, Seattle Pacific U., 1976. Cert. tchr., Philippines. Tchr. pub. schs. San Narciso and Manila, 1941-47; coll. educator Union Coll. Manila, 1947-48; tchr. Auburn (Wash.) Sch. Dist., 1956-58, Renton (Wash.) Sch. Dist., 1958-78; owner, operator Manila-Zambales Internat. Grill, Seattle, 1980-81, Connie's Lumpia House Internat. Restaurant, Seattle, 1981-84; founder, pres. Tajon-Fontecha, Inc., Renton, 1980—, United Friends of Filipinos in Am. Found., Renton, 1985—; founder Labrador Fontecha and Baldovi-Tajon Permanent Scholarship Fund of The Philippine Normal U., 1990; co-founder The United Filipino-Am. Coll. Fund for the USA and the Philippines, 1995; bd. mem. World Div. of the Gen. Bd. of Global Ministries of the United Meth. Ch., 1982-84, Ch. Women United Seattle Chapt.; mem. advisory bd Univ. Wash. Burke Mus., 1991—; mem. King TV Asian Am. Adv. Forum, 1993. Editor bull. Renton 1st United Meth. Ch., 1994. Bd. dirs. women's divsn. Gen. Bd. Global Ministries United Meth. Ch., 1982-84, Renton Area Youth Svcs., 1980-85, Girl's Club Puget Sound, Ethnic Heritage Coun. Pacific N.W., 1989—; mem. Mcpl. Arts Commn., Renton, 1980—; chairperson fundraising steering com. Washington State Women's Polit. Caucus, 1985-89; governing mem. nat. steering com. state coun. Nat. Women's Polit. Caucus, 1990—; mem. vol. action, 1990 Goodwill Games, Seattle; vol. worker Native Am. Urban Ministries, 1990—; mem. adv. bd. Renton Cmty. Housing Devel.; mem. cmty. adv. bd. U. Wash. Thomas Burke Meml. Mus., 1990—; mem. program com. UN, 1992—; mem. Asian Pacific task force Ch. Coun. Greater Seattle, 1993—; mem. Renton-Rainier area planning com. 1996 World Day of Prayer; coord. establishment and devel. Seattle-Renton area United Filipino-Am. Coll. Fund, 1995, coord. internat. buffet dinner United Filipino-Am. Coll. Fund for U. Wash., Filipino Youth Empowerment Project and Mentor's Child Sponsoring Program; emeritus bd. mem. Ethnic Heritage Coun. Pacific N.W., 1993—; co-chmn. Ann. Filipino and Filipino Am. youth Activities Pres.'s Day Spelling Bee Greater Seattle and Vicinity, 1990-96; coord. Ecumenical World Cmty. Day celebration luncheon Greater Seattle unit Ch. Women United, 1994. Recipient spl. cert. of award Project Hope, 1976, U.S. Bicentennial Commn., 1976, UNICEF, 1977, Spirit of Liberty award Ethnic Heritage Coun. Pacific Northwest, 1991; named Parent of Yr. Filipino Community of Seattle, Inc., 1984, One of 500 Seattle Pacific U. Centennial "Alumni of a Growing Vision", 1991. Mem. NEA, Wash. State Edn. Assn. (bd. dirs. 1990-92), Am. Assn. Ret. Persons, Nat. Ret. Tchrs. Assn., Renton Ret. Tchrs. Assn., U. Wash. Alumni Assn. (life), U. Wash. Filipino Alumni Assn. (pres. Wash. state chpt. 1985-87), Renton Hist. Mus. (life), Internat. Platform Assn., United Meth. Women, Pres.'s Forum, Alpha Sigma, Delta Kappa Gamma. Democrat. Home and Office: 2033 Harrington Pl NE Renton WA 98056-2303

TAKACS, KRISTY B., educator; b. Anaheim, Calif., Jan. 30, 1968; d. John A. and Karen A. T. BA in English, UCLA, 1990. Tchr. independent study, ESL Fullerton (Calif.) Unified H.S. Dist., 1991-93; tchr. English Don Bosco Tech. Inst., Rosemead, Calif., 1993—. L.A. Archdiocese grantee, 1994.

TAKAHASHI SCHUCHARDT, JACKLYN JOY, operating room nurse, consultant; b. Lodi, Calif., May 1, 1951; d. Jack Noburu and Evelyn Toshi (Honda) Takahashi; m. Michael Schuchardt, Apr. 18, 1993. Nursing diploma, S. Merritt Hosp Nursing Sch., Oakland, Calif., 1973; BS in Nursing, Calif. State U., Sacramento, 1978; MS in Nursing, San Francisco State U., 1988. RN, Calif. Cert. operating rm. nurse Nat. Certification Bd., cert. pub. health nurse, Calif., lic. nurse, Calif. Staff nurse surgery Samuel Merritt Hosp., Oakland, 1973-80, operating rm. edn. coord., 1980-91; operating rm., clin. nurse specialist edn. coord. Merrit Peralta Hosp., Oakland, 1991-92; surgical svcs. clin. nurse specialis Summit Med. Ctr., Oakland, 1992-93; surgical svcs. staff developer John Muir Med. Ctr., Walnut Creek, Calif., 1993-94; surgical svcs. clin. nurse specialist, educator John Muir Med. Ctr., Walnut Creek, 1994—; ptnr. Katana cons., Clayton, Calif., 1996—. Author: (with others, book) Reading and Reviewing Research, 1989; contbr. articles to Nursing handbooks and jours. Sponsor Manat Pankong Christian Childrens' Fund, Bangkok, Thailand, 1987—. Mem. Am. Assn. Operating Rm. Nurses (bd. dirs., pres., v.p., treas., Alameda County chpt., nat. chmn. edn. com., mem. many coms.), NAFE, Med. Legal Cons., Sigma Theta Tau. Democrat. Episcopalian. Office: Katana Cons PO Box 114 Clayton CA 94517

TAKAMURA, JEANETTE CHIYOKO, state agency administrator; b. Honolulu, Aug. 1, 1947; d. Jiro and Jane Chiseko (Ishida) Chikamoto; m. Carl Takeshi Takamura, May 17, 1974; 1 child, Mari Leigh. BA, U. Hawaii, 1969, MSW, 1972; PhD, Brandeis U., 1985. Program dir. Moiliili Community Ctr., Honolulu, 1972-74; instr. sch. medicine and social work U. Hawaii, Honolulu, 1975-78, asst. prof., 1982-86; dir. exec. office on aging Office of Gov., Honolulu, 1987-94; dep. dir. State Dept. of Health, 1995—; ptnr. Browne/Takamura, Honolulu, 1985-86. Contbr. articles to profl. jours. and chpts. to books; editorial bd.: Aging Today, 1991—. V.p. Moiliili Community Ctr., 1977. Grantee NIMH, 1982-84, U.S. Dept. HHS, 1985, 86, 89-90, 91. Mem. Nat. Assn. State Units on Aging (2d v.p. 1991-92), Am. Soc. on Aging (program planning com. 1992-93, exec. com. 1996—, nat. adv. bd. White House Conf. on Aging, 1995), Gerontology Soc. Am., Futurist Soc. Congregationalist. Office: Dept Health 1250 Punchbowl St Honolulu HI 96813

TALBOT, ARDITH ANN, editor; b. Superior, Nebr., Mar. 11, 1933; d. Charles Howard and Dollie Eunice (Ryan) Snell; m. Richard Charles Talbot, Oct. 17, 1954; children: Richard Daryl, Robert Charles. BA in Edn., U. Nebr., 1956. Recorded Friends min., 1993. Tchr. high sch. Pub. Schs., Juniata, Nebr., 1957-59, Hudson, Iowa, 1962-68, New Providence, Iowa, 1968-71; owner Retail Bookstore, Sutherland, Iowa, 1971-72, Marshalltown, Iowa, 1972-74, Mason City, Iowa, 1974-89; mgr. book store Friends United Mktg., Richmond, Ind., 1986-89; mgr., editor Friends United Press, Richmond, Ind., 1989—. Republican. Home: Box 343 Lynn IN 47355 Office: Friends United Meeting 101 Quaker Hill Dr Richmond IN 47374-1926

TALBOT, DEBORAH L., bank executive. Exec. v.p. global payment and treasury svcs. Chase Manhattan Bank, Bklyn. Office: Chase Manhattan Bank 4 Chase Metrotech Ctr Brooklyn NY 11245*

TALBOT, PAMELA, public relations executive; b. Chgo., Aug. 10, 1946. BA in English, Vassar Coll., 1968. Reporter Worcester, Mass. Telegram and Gazette, 1970-72; account exec. Daniel J. Edelman, Inc., Chgo., 1972-74, account supr., 1974-76, v.p., 1976-78, sr. v.p., 1978-84, exec. v.p., gen. mgr., 1984-90; pres. Edelman West, Chgo., 1990—; Consumer Worldwide, 1995.

TALBOT, PHYLLIS MARY, reading educator; b. Chgo., Mar. 14, 1949; d. James Joseph Watson and Sylvia (Slyk) Parker; m. Laurel Curtis Talbot, Oct. 6, 1967; children: Bill, Dennis, Mary, Anna, Tim. BS, Northwest Mo. State U., 1991, MEd, 1993, EdD, 1994. Cert. early childhood, elem., reading K-12, elem. adminstrn., adult basic edn. Literacy coord. Northwest Mo. Literacy Coun., Maryville, 1994-95; Title I reading tchr. St. Clair Sch. Dist., Appleton City, Mo., 1995—. Mem. AAUW, MSTA, Internat. Reading Assn. Roman Catholic. Home: 409 W Miller St Appleton City MO 64724 Office: Appleton City Elem Sch 408 W 4th Appleton City MO 64724

TALBOT-KOEHL, LINDA ANN, dancer, ballet studio owner; b. Fremont, Ohio, July 22, 1956; d. Donald Ray and Doris Ann (Opperman) Talbot; m. James G. Koehl, July 30, 1983. Student, U. Akron, 1974-76; BA in Psychology, Heidelberg Coll., 1984. Owner, instr. BalleTiffin, Inc., Tiffin, Ohio, 1987—; choreographer Heidelberg Summer Theater, Tiffin, 1986, Singing Collegians, 1993; choreographer Calvert H.S. Theater, Tiffin, 1986-88, Swing Choir, 1987-89, 91-92. Appeared (ednl. film) Rights on the Job, State of Ohio Dept. Edn., 1986. Mem. Dance Masters Am., Nat. Multiple Sclerosis Soc., The Ritz Players (choreographer 1985, 88-89, 96, make-up designer, advisor 1989-92, sound booth operator 1993—). Home and Office: BalleTiffin Inc 449 Melmore St Tiffin OH 44883-3628

TALBOTT, MARY ANN BRITT, secondary education educator; b. Augusta, Ga., Nov. 29, 1945; d. Charles Hubert and Mary Ann (Day) Britt; m. Lonnie Loyd Talbott, Oct. 20, 1978. AB, U. Ga., 1967, EdS, 1981, Cert. in Adminstrn./Supervision, 1989; MEd, Augusta Coll., 1975. Cert. tchr. support specialist. Tchr. English Hilsman Jr. H.S., Athens, Ga., 1967-68; tchr. English, chmn. dept. Tubman Jr. H.S., Augusta, Ga., 1969-73, Aquinas H.S., Augusta, 1973-79; tchr. English Winder (Ga.)-Barrow H.S., 1979-82; tchr. remedial writing/reading/math, career planning, Latin Morrow (Ga.) H.S., 1982-91, tchr. English, 1982-93; tchr. English Brunswick (Ga.) H.S., 1993—, mem. discipline task force, 1995-96; instr. English Clayton State Coll., Morrow, 1991-92, Ga. Mil. Coll., Ft. Gordon, 1975-77; instr. staff devel. Clayton County Bd. Edn., Jonesboro, Ga., 1985-91. Elder Stockbridge (Ga.) Presbyn. Ch., 1989-92; active Am. Cancer Soc., Augusta Choral Soc., Athens Choral Soc.; mem. Evangel. Luth. Ch. Resurrection, Augusta, Ga., 1995—. Recipient Psi Achievment award, 1979-81. Mem. Delta Kappa Gamma (pres. 1978-80, chmn. music com. 1985-87, 89-91, chair Psi State Achievement Award Com. 1979-81, dist. dir. 1981-83, scholar 1980, 87, Golden Gift award 1984), Alpha Lambda Delta, Kappa Delta Sigma, Phi Delta Kappa (Tchr. of Yr. 1989). Lutheran. Home: PO Box 13163 Jekyll Island GA 31527-3163 Office: Brunswick High Sch Habersham St Brunswick GA 31520

TALCOTT, JULIA MEANS, illustrator, artist; b. Evanston, Ill., Oct. 17, 1958; d. Hooker and Jane (McCurrach) T.; m. James Benjamin Meigs, Aug. 24, 1985; children: Ramsey, Stoddard, Isabel. BFA, Williams Coll., 1980; MFA, Cranbrook Acad. Art, Bloomfield Hills, Mich., 1984. Tchr. English NIC English Co., Osaka, Japan, 1980-81; designer Children's Mus., Boston, 1981-83; illustrator Boston, 1985—; tchr. Art Inst. Boston, 1990, 91. Illustrator: (book) Pilgrims, 1992, U.S. Postal Svc. Christmas stamps, 1996. Recipient Best Logo Design award Print Mag., 1993. Mem. Graphic Artists Guild (co-chair illustration com. 1988). Democrat. Episcopalian. Home: 74 Elmhurst Rd Newton MA 02158

TALESE, NAN AHEARN, publishing company executive; b. N.Y.C., Dec. 19, 1933; d. Thomas James and Suzanne Sherman (Russell) Ahearn; m. Gay Talese, June 10, 1959; children: Pamela Frances, Catherine Gay. B.A., Manhattanville Coll. of Sacred Heart, 1955. Fgn. exchange student 1st Nat. City Bank, London and Paris, 1956; editorial asst. Am. Eugenics Soc., N.Y.C., 1957-58, Vogue mag., N.Y.C., 1958-59; copy editor Random House Pub., N.Y.C., 1959-64; assoc. editor Random House Pub., 1964-67, sr. editor, 1967-73; sr. editor Simon & Schuster Pubs., N.Y.C., 1974-81; v.p. Simon & Schuster Pubs., 1979-81; exec. editor, v.p. Houghton Mifflin Co., N.Y.C., 1981-83, v.p., editor-in-chief, 1984-86, v.p., pub., editor-in-chief, 1986-88; sr. v.p. Doubleday & Co., N.Y.C., 1988-90; pres., pub., editorial dir. Nan A. Talese Books, 1990—. Home: 109 E 61st St New York NY 10021-8101

TALIAFERRO, NANCY ELLEN TAYLOR, artist; b. Richmond, Va., Feb. 16, 1937; d. Samuel Beryl and Nancy Loomis (Brinton) Taylor; m. Charles Mitchell Taliaferro, July 3, 1958; children: Chester Parsons, Nancy Brinton. BFA, Va. Commonwealth U., 1959. Comml. artist, illustrator, 1959-63, drawings, pastel portraits, 1963—, oil paintings, 1978—. Exhbns. include The Chrysler Mus., Norfolk, Va., 1994, Du Pont Art Gallery, Washington and Lee U., Lexington, Va., 1993, Uptown Gallery, Richmond, 1992-96, The Art Gallery, Ashland, Va., 1992-96, Va. Gen. Assembly and State Capitol Bldgs., 1989, 91, 93, Jacob Javits Fed. Bldg., N.Y.C., 1986, Women's Resource Ctr., U. Richmond, 1985. Recipient award The Artists Mag., 1992. Mem. Nat. Assn. Women Artists (Medal of Honor 1995, Audrey Hope Shirk Meml. award 1995), Uptown Gallery (charter mem.), James River Art League, U. Painters. Republican. Methodist. Home: 6724 Forest Hill Ave Richmond VA 23225-1802 Studio: 8413 Forest Hill Ave Richmond VA 23235-3125

TALLET, MARGARET ANNE, theatre executive; b. Binghamton, N.Y., Feb. 14, 1953; d. George Francis and Wilma Ann (Wagner) T.; m. Peter A., Myks, July 6, 1991. BA, St. Mary's Coll., 1975; MBA, SUNY, 1979. Asst. dir. Parrish Art Mus., Southampton, N.Y., 1979-87; assoc. dir. devel. Detroit Inst. Arts Founders Soc., 1981-92; v.p. Franco Pub. Rels. Group, Detroit, 1992-96; pres. Music Hall Ctr. for the Performing Arts, 1992-96. Bd. dirs. Aid for AIDS Rsch., 1987-92, Detroiters at Heart, 1992—; mktg. com. Mich. Career Found., Detroit, 1992—. Mem. Pub. Rels. Soc. Am. Roman Catholic. Office: Music Hall Ctr for Performing Arts 350 Madison Ave Detroit MI 48226

TALLEY, JANE, artist, educator; b. Spur, Tex., Oct. 17, 1929; d. Marshall Herff and Louise (Winfield) Applewhite; m. Oran Kent Talley, Feb. 28, 1948; children: Carleen Dolan, Linda Oldham. Attended, U. Tex., 1946-48. Gallery artist Top of the Line Gallery, Ft. Worth, 1980-89, Moralcs Gallery, Nags Head, N.C., 1985-91, Artenegies Gallery, Ft. Worth, 1988—, Tarbox Gallery, San Diego, 1990-92, Riuer Gallery, Reno, Nev., 1992-94; Castleberry Gallery, Arlington, Tex., 1992—; gallery artist Richelle Gallery, Bedford, Tex., 1993-94; art tchr. Imagination Celebration, Ft. Worth, 1993; demonstrator various workshops. Recipient Merit award Nat. Watercolor Okla., 1987, Citation award Tex. Fine Arts Assn., 1988. Mem. Soc. Watercolor Artists (bd. dirs., Pres. award 1994), Tex. Watercolor Soc. (Merit award 1982), Southwestern Watercolor Soc. Home: 8255 Carrick Fort Worth TX 76116

TALLEY, JEANNINE ELIZABETH, English educator, writer; b. Lakeland, Fla., Oct. 26, 1937; d. Joseph Wilson Talley and Annetta Jewel (Shellhouse) Rigsby. B in Music Edn., Fla. State U., 1960; MA in Folklore and Mythology, UCLA, 1967, PhD in Germanic Langs., 1977. Lectr. in folklore, mythology UCLA, 1976-80; sr. editor Oriental Healing Arts, L.A., 1980-85; asst. prof. English U. Guam, Mangilao, 1992—. Author: Women at the Helm, 1990, Capsized in the Coral Sea, 1992; co-editor: Belief and Superstition in Utah, 1984. Nat. Def. Fgn. Lang. fellow, UCLA, 1965-67. Mem. AAUW, Internat. Women Writers Guild. Office: CAS Divsn English U Guam Mangilao GU 96923

TALLEY, LINDA JEAN, food scientist, dietitian; b. Hearne, Tex., July 15, 1948; d. Roy Wesley and Dorothy Louise (Allen) Dugger; m. Thomas James Talley, May 15, 1970; children: John Paul, Jo Ann. BS in Food Tech., Tex. A & M U., 1969, MS in Food Sci. and Tech., 1979, PhD in Food Sci. and Tech., 1981. Registered dietitian Am. Dietetic Assn.; registered sanitarian; lic. dietitian, Tex. Technician I soil and crop scis. dept. Tex. A & M U., College Station, 1969-72; technician I in horticulture scis. Tex. A&M U., College Station, 1977-78, grad. asst., 1978-81; quality assurance mgr. food products divsn. Southland Corp., Ft. Worth, 1972-73; pub. health inspector Ft. Worth Pub. Health Dept., 1973-74; dir. quality assurance plant sanitation and product devel. Kimbell Foods, Inc., Mfg. Divsn., Ft. Worth, 1974-75; profl. cons. Ft. Worth, 1975-76; v.p., cons. TALCO, Dallas, 1981-91; sr. food scientist Enersyst Devel. Ctr., Inc., Dallas, 1990—; presenter in field. Contbr. articles to profl. jours. Mem. Inst. Food Techs., Sigma Xi, Phi Tau Sigma. Home: 3706 Oak Ridge Dr Bryan TX 77802-3426 Office: Enersyst Devel Ctr 2051 Valley View Ln Dallas TX 75234-8920

TALLMAN, KATHLEEN HINEY, special education educator; b. North Towanda Twp., Pa., Sept. 10, 1935; d. John Altgeld and Catherine (Zuzel) Hiney; m. Rodney Mack Tallman, Jan. 28, 1958 (dec. Feb. 1993); children: William Edward, Heather Ann. BA in History and Speech, Nazareth Coll., Rochester, N.Y., 1957; MS in Spl. Edn., Nat. U., San Diego, 1995. Cert. tchr., tchr. of learning handicapped, Calif. Substitute tchr. San Juan Sch. Dist., Carmichael, 1964-65; tchr. Grant Unified Sch. Dist., Sacramento, 1965-66; substitute tchr. Mount Diablo Unified Sch. Dist., 1972-93, resource tchr., 1993-94; spl. edn. tchr. Mt. Diablo Unified Sch. Dist., Concord, T, 1994—; mem. citizens adv. bd. Tracy Nat. Bank, Concord, 1991—. Active Republican Party, 1972—. The Exploratorium grantee, San Francisco, 1995. Mem. AAUW, Grant St. Assn., Mt. Diablo Edn. Assn. Home: 2055 Risdon Rd Concord CA 94518 Office: Mt Diablo HS 2450 Grant St Concord CA 94520

TALLY, LURA SELF, state legislator; b. Statesville, N.C., Dec. 9, 1921; d. Robert Ottis and Sara (Cowles) Self; A.B., Duke U., 1942; M.A., N.C. State U., Raleigh, 1970; m. J.O. Tally, Jr., Jan. 30, 1943 (div. 1970); children: Robert Taylor, John Cowles. Tchr., former guidance counselor Fayetteville (N.C.) city schs.; mem. N.C. Ho. of Reps. from 20th Dist., 1971-83, chmn. com. higher edn., from 1975, also 1980-83, vice chmn. com. appropriations for edn., 1973-86; state senator from 12th Dist. N.C., 1983-95; chmn. N.C. Senate Com. of Natural Resources, Community Devel. and Wildlife, 1987, Environment and Natural Resources, 1989-94. Past pres. Cumberland County Mental Health Assn., N.C. Historic Preservation Soc.; trustee Fayetteville Tech. Inst., 1981-94; mem. Legis. Research com. Mem. Am. Personnel and Guidance Assn., Fayetteville Bus. and Profl. Women's Club, Kappa Delta, Delta Kappa Gamma. Methodist. Club: Fayetteville Woman's (past pres.). Office: W Jones St Raleigh NC 27601

TALMADGE, MARY CHRISTINE, nursing educator; b. Monticello, Ga., Nov. 6, 1940; d. Herbert Pope and Margaret (Allen) T.; m. Larry Benson, Aug. 10, 1962 (div. 1975). Diploma, Crawford W. Long Hosp. Sch. of Nursing, Atlanta, 1961; BSN, U. Dayton, 1966; MPH, U. Hawaii, 1971, PhD, 1989. RN; cert. Family Life Edn. Staff charge nurse Crawford W. Long Hosp., Atlanta, 1961-62; instr. LPN program Dayton (Ohio) Bd. Edn., 1963-66; instr. Miami Valley Hosp. Sch. of Nursing, Dayton, 1967-69; clin. nurse specialist Hawaii State Hosp., Kaneohe, 1970-77, dir. nursing, 1978-80; adminstrv. asst. to dir. health Hawaii State Dept. of Health, Honolulu, 1977-78; clin. nurse specialist Windward Community Counseling Ctr., Kaneohe, 1980-83; asst. prof. U. Hawaii, 1983-85; assoc. prof. Hawaii Loa Coll., Kaneohe, 1987-89; assoc. prof., acting dept. head Ga. So. U., Statesboro, 1990-93; prof., chair dept. nursing Calif. State U., Long Beach, 1993—; cons. Tokyo Women's Med. Coll. Sch. of Nursing, 1988-90; local and internat. healthcare orgns. Sec., mem. Gov.'s Commn. on Mental Health and Criminal Justice, Honolulu, 1978-80; mem., chmn. Windward Oahu Svc. Area Bd. on Mental Health and Substance Abuse, Honolulu, 1985-86; candidate Neighborhood Bd. Kaneohe, 1988; bd. dirs. New Beginnings for Children; chair nursing task force, health com. Statesboro C. of C. Recipient Cmty. Svc. award African-Am. Caucus, Ga. So. U., 1993. Mem. Nat. League Nursing, Sigma Theta Tau, Phi Kappa Phi (faculty 1995). Democrat. Methodist. Home: 105 Lancaster Pt Statesboro GA 30458-6238 Office: Calif State Univ Long Beach CA 90802

TALUS, DONNA J., educator; b. Salem, Oreg., Sept. 13, 1931; d. Ralph V. and Estella R. (Barber) Sebern; m. Hank M. Talus, June 5, 1955 (dec.); children: Dottie Hofford, Steve, Stacy. BA in PE, Willamette U., 1953. Cert. ARC First Aid instr., travel agent. Secondary tchr. Langlois (Oreg.) H.S., Oreg., 1953-54, Heppner H.S., 1954-55; tchr. Stanfield (Oreg.) H.S., Oreg., 1955-57, Riverside (Oreg.) H.S., 1960; also bd. mem. Oreg.; secondary tchr. Myrtle Creek (Oreg.) H.S., 1960-67; caseworker Grant County Ctrl. Sch. Dist., John Day, Oreg., 1967-68; tchr. Prairie City (Oreg.) H.S., 1968-69; secondary tchr. Grant Union H.S., John Day, Oreg., 1969-75, Mt. Vernon (Oreg.) H.S., 1975-86, North Marion H.S., Aurora, Oreg., 1992-94; water fitness instr. Salem (Oreg.) Family YMCA, 1990—. Pres. PTA, Myrtle Creek, Oreg., 1966-67; Camp Fire guardian, Roseburg-John Day, Oreg., 1966-79; den mother Boy Scouts Am.; tchr. Meth. Ch. Sch. Camp, Oreg. Mem. NEA, AAUW (del. UN seminar 1982, pres. Oreg. State 1983-85). Republican. Methodist. Home: 29650 SW Courtside Dr # 22 Wilsonville OR 97070

TAMADA, JANET AYAKO, biomedical engineer; b. Seattle, Sept. 15, 1962; d. Henry Shiyoso and Katsuko T. BS in Chem. Engring., Caltech., 1984; PhD in Chem. Engring., U. Calif., Berkeley, 1989. Postdoctoral fellow MIT, Cambridge, Mass., 1989-91; rsch. scientist, sr. scientist Cygnus Inc., Redwood City, Calif., 1991—. Contbr. articles to profl. jours. Grad. fellow NSF, U. Calif., Berkeley, 1984; NIH Postdoctoral fellow, MIT, 1989. Mem. AIChE, Am. Chem. Soc., Controlled Release Soc. Democrat.

TAMAREN, MICHELE CAROL, special education educator; b. Hartford, Conn., Aug. 2, 1947; d. Herman Harold and Betty (Leavitt) Liss; m. David Stephen Tamaren, June 8, 1968; 1 child, Scott. BS in Elem. Edn., U. Conn., 1969; MA in Spl. Edn., St. Joseph Coll., West Hartford, Conn., 1976. Cert. elem. and spl. edn. tchr., Conn., Mass. Tchr. N.Y. Inst. for Spl. Edn., Bronx, 1971-74; ednl. cons. Renbrook Sch., West Hartford, 1975-78; grad. instr. St. Joseph Coll., 1978; elem. tchr. Acton (Mass.) Pub. Schs., 1969-70, tchr. spl. edn., 1978-94; learning specialist and writer Educators Pub. Svc., Cambridge, Mass., 1994-96; inclusion and behavioral specialist Acton (Mass.) Pub. Schs., 1996—; ednl. cons. to schs., parents, orgns., pubs., 1980—; internat. and nat. lectr. on bldg. self-esteem in classroom, 1988—. Author: I Make a Difference!, 1992; also articles. Bd. dirs. United Way of Acton-Boxborough. Horace Mann grantee Mass. Dept. Edn., 1987, 88, Mass. Gov.'s Alliance Against Drugs, 1992. Mem. Coun. for Exceptional Children, Learning Disabilities Assn., Orton Dyslexia Soc., Nat. Ctr. Learning Disabilities, Nat. Coun. for Self-Esteem, Internat. Platform Assn., Phi Kappa Phi, Kappa Delta Pi. Home: 15 Willis Holden Dr Acton MA 01720-3208

TAMÁS, KLÁRA See MISKOLCZI, ELISABETA

TAMBURRO, GIOVANNA M., artist; b. Corona, N.Y., Nov. 6; d. Carlo and Grace (Emanuela) Parente; m. americo M. Tamburro; children: Luana, Robert, Lisa. Assoc. in Fine Arts, Nassau C.C., 1977; postgrad., N.Y. Tech. Inst., 1982-83. Chiropractic asst. Office of Dr. Robert Tamburro, Hicksville, N.Y., 1985—; art tchr. to deaf children, Westbury and Hicksville, N.Y., 1974; health and wellbeing contbr. low fat diet Nassau County Med. Ctr., N.Y. State Coll. Human Ecology, Cornell U., Ithaca, N.Y. Exhibited in shows at Firehouse Gallery, 1973 (1st prize in graphics), Stix-Port Washington Libr., Stix-L.I. Black Artist Assn., 1977, N.Y. Tech. Inst., 1982-83, Huntington Art League (award 1990), East Islip Art League, 1990 (award), Jean Paris/Blossom Show (award), Graphic Eye Gallery, Port Washington, 1992; contbr. poems to Nat. Libr. Poetry, The Poet Band Co. Va., Kent Publs., Nat. Soc. Poets. Recipient award Internat. Soc. Poets, 1994. Mem. Trustees of Nat. Mus. of Women in ARts (assoc.).

TAMEN, HARRIET, lawyer; b. Yonkers, N.Y., May 17, 1947; d. Saul and Lily (Balglau) T. A.B., Bryn Mawr Coll., 1969; J.D., George Washington U., Washington, 1973. Bar: N.Y. 1974, U.S. Dist. Ct. (so. dist.) N.Y. 1975. Atty., W.T. Grant, N.Y.C., 1974-76; atty. City of N.Y. Office Econ. Devel., Div. Real Property, N.Y.C., 1977-81; atty. Credit Lyonnais Bank, N.Y.C., 1981-86, Chase Manhattan Bank, 1986-89; v.p., counsel internat. corp. fin. Citibank, 1989-92, partner, Claugus Tamen & Orenstein, 1992-93; pvt. practice, N.Y.C., 1994—. Bd. dirs. Dromenon Theatre, N.Y., 1980-86, Nat. Dance Inst., N.Y., 1982, chmn. bd. dirs., 1984-87; chmn. bd. dirs. Theatre & Dance Alliance, 1989-90; del. exch. program Women in Law, South Am., 1987—; mem. campaign staff Ed Koch for Mayor, N.Y.C., 1977, steering com. Soviet Am. Banking Law Working Group, 1991—; guest lectr. Moscow Conf. on Banking, 1992, Ulaan Baatar, Mongolia, 1993-94, 96, Harriman Inst. of Columbia U., 1994; co-chair N.Y. Lawyers Com. for Clinton-Gore. Mem. ABA, Assn. Bar City N.Y.

TAMEZ, MYRIAM, poet; b. Pontiac, Mich., Sept. 25, 1969; d. Homero Tamez and Angelica Zambrano. Student, Ohio State U., 1989; BA in English and Music, Albion Coll., 1991; postgrad., U. Tex.-Pan-Am., Edinburg, 1991-93, Bennington Coll., 1993. English tchr. Donna (Tex.) Ind. Sch. Dist., 1991-92, Weslaco (Tex.) Ind. Sch. Dist., 1992-93; poet, 1991—. Contbr. poems to profl. publs. Mem. First Spanish-Am. Bapt. Ch., Pontiac, 1974-95. Home and Office: 274 W Columbia Pontiac MI 48340

TAMM, ELEANOR RUTH, retired accountant; b. Hansell, Iowa, July 20, 1921; d. Horace Gerald and Sibyl (Armstrong) Wells; m. Roy C. Tamm, Oct. 18, 1941 (dec. Jan. 1980); children: Larry LeRoy, Marilyn Ruth Tamm-Schmitt. Grad., Am. Soc. Travel Agts., Inc., 1970; student, Iowa Cen. C.C., 1983, 85; grad., Inst. Children's Lit., 1994. Tchr. Howard County Rural Sch., Riceville, 1939-41; bookkeeper, cashier Cen. States Power and Light Co., Elma, Iowa, 1941-42; office supr. J.C. Penney Co., Goldsboro, N.C., 1942-44; bookkeeper J.C. Penney Co., West Palm Beach, Fla., 1945; head teller Iowa State Bank, Clarksville, Iowa, 1955-69; office and group mgr. Allen Travel Agy., Charles City, Iowa, 1969-81; tour conductor, tour organizer and planner Allen Travel Agy., Charles City, 1971-81; office mgr. Arora Clinics, P.C., Fonda, Iowa, 1986-90; freelance collaborator on children's books Clarksville, 1989—. Leader Girl Scouts U.S.A., Clarksville, 1946-47; tchr. St. John Luth. Ch., Clarksville, 1946-66, ch. sec., 1954-66, sec.-treas. Altar Guild, 1993-94; United Fund sec.-treas. Clarksville Cmty. Fund, 1956-66; sec.-treas. Clarksville Band Boosters, 1964-66. Lutheran. Home: 408 E 3rd St Fonda IA 50540-0425

TAN, AMY RUTH, writer; b. Oakland, Calif., Feb. 19, 1952; d. John Yuehhan and Daisy Ching (Tu) T.; m. Louis M. DeMattei, Apr. 6, 1974. BA in Linguistics and English, San Jose (Calif.) State U., 1973, MA in Linguistics, 1974; LHD (hon.), Dominican Coll. San Rafael, 1991. Specialist lang. devel. Alameda County Assn. for Mentally Retarded, Oakland, 1976-80; project dir. M.O.R.E. Project, San Francisco, 1980-81; free-lance writer, 1981-88. Author: The Joy Luck Club, 1989 (Nat. Book Critics Circle award for best novel nomination 1989, L.A. Times Book award nomination 1989, Gold award for fiction Commonwealth Club 1990, Bay Area Book Reviewers award for best fiction 1990), The Kitchen God's Wife, 1991, The Moon Lady, 1992, The Chinese Siamese Cat, 1994, The Hundred Secret Senses, 1995; also numerous short stories and essays; screenwriter, prodr.: (film) The Joy Luck Club, 1993. Recipient Best Am. Essays award, 1991. *

TAN, COLLEEN WOO, communications educator; b. San Francisco, May 6, 1923; d. Mr. and Mrs. S.H. Nq Quinn; m. Lawrence K.J. Tan; children: Lawrence L., Lance C. BA in English/Am. Lit., Ind. U., 1950, MA in English, 1952; MA in Speech Arts, Whittier Coll., 1972; postgrad., U. Calif. Berkeley, 1952-53. Cert. secondary edn. tchr., K-12, community coll., Calif. Tchng. aide English U. Calif., Berkeley, 1952-53; tchr. English and Social Studies Whittier (Calif.) High Sch., 1957-60; prof. speech comms. Mt. San Antonio Coll., Walnut, Calif., 1960-94; dir. forensics, 1969-80; sen. acad. senate Mt. San Antonio Coll., Walnut, Calif., 1982-90, faculty rep., 1990—; mem. numerous collegiate coms., campus advisor to Chinese Club and Asian Students Assn. Recipient Woman of Achievement Edn. award San Gabriel Valley, Calif. YWCA, 1995; named Outstanding Prof. Emeritus, Mt. San Antonio Coll. Found., 1994. Mem. AAUW (pres. Whittier Br. 1982, cultural interests chair Calif. state divsn. 1985-87, Fellowship award 1973-74, Las Distinguidas award 1992), Calif. Asian-Am. Faculty Assn., Delta Kappa Gamma, Phi Beta Kappa (Outstanding Educator of Am. award 1972). Roman Catholic. Home: 13724 Sunrise Dr Whittier CA 90602-2547 Office: Mt San Antonio 1100 N Grand Ave Walnut CA 91789-1341

TAN, SINFOROSA G., mathematics educator; b. Lugait, The Philippines, July 7, 1943; came to U.S., 1969; d. Eh Bon and Le Eng Tan; m. William H.P. Kaung, July 21, 1973. BSChemE, U. San Carlos, The Philippines, 1965; MST, Cornell U., 1970; PhD, Syracuse U., 1975. Cert. secondary tchr., N.Y. H.s. maths. tchr. Iligan High Sch., The Philippines, 1965-68; resident asst. Crouse-Irving Meml. Hosp., Syracuse, N.Y., 1970-73; grad. asst. Syracuse U., 1973-75; cons. math. Mt. Vernon (N.Y.) Bd. Edn., 1975-76; dir. metric program Bronx (N.Y.) Community Coll., 1976-77; prof. math. Westchester Community Coll., Valhalla, N.Y., 1977—, dir. math. computer lab., 1989—; adj. faculty Manhattanville Coll. Grad. Sch., 1996—; chair numerous faculty coms.; tutorial coord. Project Succeed, 1978-80; co-dir. Project Select, 1985-89; co-advisor Far Eastern Club, 1982—; advisor Calculator & Computer Club, 1992—; adj. prof. Mercy Coll., Dobbs Ferry, N.Y., 1976-78; prof. chemistry Iligan Capitol Coll., 1965-68. Contbr. chpts. to books including WCC Self-Study for Re-Accreditation, 1985, WCC Periodic Review Report, 1990, others; contbr. articles to profl. jours.; author: (monographs) Calculators in Education: A Survey of Calculator Technology in the Westchester/Putnam High Schools, 1995. Vol. Literacy Vols. Am., Mt. Vernon, 1976-77; mem. choir Our Lady Perpetual Help Ch., Pelham Manor, N.Y., 1987—, U.S.A. Chorus, 1995; coord. The Philippines Libr. Materials Project Found., Westchester County, 1988—; mem. coll. bd. Scholastic Aptitude Test com., 1990-93, ACCU Placer Math. Test Devel. com., 1994-96; mem. steering com. Westchester Alliance for Learning Techs., 1994-95; mem. math/sci. task force Westchester Tchr. Edn. Group, 1994-95; del. Balikturo Project, Assn. Filipino Tchrs. of Am., 1996—. Recipient The Found. for Westchester Community Coll. Medallion award, 1993, Chancellor's Excellence in Teaching award SUNY, 1983, Nat. Teaching Excellence award U. Tex. Study, 1989, Outstanding Advisor award Westchester Community Coll., 1987, Outstanding Alumni award U. San Carlos, 1993, Excellence in Tchg. award Found. for Westchester C.C., 1996; Vocat. Edn. grantee, 1989—. Mem. Nat. Coun. Tchrs. Math., Am. Math. Assn. Two Yr. Colls., N.Y. State Math. Assn. Two-Yr. Colls. (exec. bd. 1981-83, newsletter editor 1982-83, campus rep. 1993—, spkr. and workshop leader), Pi Lambda Theta (sec. 1983-85, 1st v.p. 1985-89, pres. 1989-91, regional rep. 1991-96, internat. extension com. 1994-95, Westchester adv. bd. 1996—, workshop leader and spkr., Disting. Svc. award 1985, Region 1 Outstanding Educator award for Teaching Excellence 1994). Office: Westchester Community Coll 75 Grasslands Rd Valhalla NY 10595-1636

TAN, VERONICA Y., psychiatrist; b. Manila, The Philippines, Oct. 8, 1944; came to U.S., 1970; children: Terrence, Kristine. MD, U. St. Thomas, Manila, 1969. Diplomate Am. Bd. Psychiatry and Neurology. Intern U. Ill. Hosp., Chgo., 1970-71; resident Lafayette Clinic and Children's Hosp., Detroit, 1971-775; child and adolescent psychiatrist Bon Secours Hosp., Grosse Pointe, Mich., 1993—. Author: The Gifted Child, 1970.

TANCK, CATHERINE ANN, lawyer; b. Canton, S.D., Aug. 28, 1957; d. Charles H. and Betty J. (Bothe) T. BA, Augustana Coll., 1979; JD, U. S.D., 1987. CPA, S.D. Intern IRS, Sioux Falls, S.D., 1977-79; tax mgr. McGladrey, Hendrickson & Pullen, Sioux Falls, S.D., 1979-85; law clk. to cir. judge U.S. Ct. Appeals (8th cir.), Pierre, S.D., 1987-88; atty. Davenport Evans Hurwitz and Smith, Sioux Falls, S.D., 1988—. Editor S.D. Law Rev., 1986-87. Recipient West Pub. Award West Pub. Co., 1985, 87; McKusick scholar U. S.D. Found., 1985-86, Law Found. scholar U. S.D. Found., 1986-87. Mem. ABA, Am. Inst. CPA's, S.D. Soc. CPA's, State Bar Assn. S.D., Sterling Honor Soc. Lutheran.

TANDY, JEAN CONKEY, art educator; b. Reese, Mich., May 17, 1931; d. Samuel Hall and Christine Margaret (Walker) Conkey; m. Norman Edward Tandy, Jan. 25, 1952; children: Michelle Tandy Ryan, Kristen, Peter Spence. BA, Mich. State U., 1962, MA in Fine Arts, 1965. Instr. French French Bath (Mich.) Cmty. Schs., 1961-62, designer program art curriculum, instr., 1962-67; instr. art Mahar Regional Schs., Orange, Mass., 1966-67, Athol (Mass.)-Royalston Regional Schs., 1967-68; invited designer, developer art curriculum Mt. Wachusett C.C., Gardner, Mass., 1968, chair art dept., 1968—, prof. art, 1968—. Watercolors and clay exhibited on regular basis, 1950—. Mt. Wachusett C.C. grantee, 1970-96, Fed. Govt. grantee, 1968. Mem. Am. Crafts Coun., Mass. C.C. Coun., Women in Arts, Teaching Faculty Assn. (v.p. 1979-80, pres. 1980-82, grievance officer 1981-82). Independent. Home: 539 Whipple Hill Rd PO Box 2 Winchester NH 03470

TANE, SUSAN JAFFE, retired manufacturing company executive; b. N.Y.C.; d. Irving and Beatrice (Albert) J.; m. Irwin R. Tane; children by previous marriage: Robert Wayne, Stephen Mark. BS, Boston U., 1964; postgrad., Hofstra U., C.W. Post U. Elem. sch. tchr. Long Beach, N.Y., 1964-67; pres. Fashions by Appointment, Glen Cove, N.Y., 1967-71; adminstrv. asst. Peerless Sales Corp., Elmont, N.Y., 1967-71; sales mgr., then mktg. dir. United Utensils Co., Inc., Port Washington, N.Y., 1973-78; v.p. ops. and control United Molded Products div. United Utensils Co., Inc., Port Washington, 1978-80; v.p. mktg. Utensco, Port Washington, 1980-88; bd. dirs. Peerless Aerospace Corp. Co-inventor plastic container and handling assembly. Trustee, sr. v.p. Am. Jewish Congress; mem. Dirs. Circle, Folger Shakespeare Libr.; life mem. Hadassah, Ronald McDonald House; mem. Friends of the Arts-L.I. U., Inner Circle-Nassau County Mus. Art; friend N.Y. Pub. Libr. Mem. Boston U. Alumni Assn. Home: 249 12th Ave Sea Cliff NY 11579-1021 Office: PO Box 735 Glenwood Landing NY 11547-0735

TANENBAUM, LEORA, writer, editor; b. Bronx, N.Y., June 3, 1969; d. Saul Martin and Sheila (Siegel) T.; m. Jonathan Ari Lonner. BA in Modern Culture and Media, Brown U., 1991. Rsch./editl. asst. author Gail Sheehy, N.Y.C., 1991-94; assoc. editor Hadassah Women's Zionist Orgn. Am., N.Y.C., 1995—; contbt. writer Boston Phoenix, 1994—. Contbr. numerous articles to profl. publs. Vol. Big Bros./Big Sisters N.Y.C., 1995—. Mem. Nat. Writers' Union, Phi Beta Kappa. Democrat.

TANG, DEBORAH, broadcast executive; b. Chgo., July 19, 1947; d. Edward Preston and Mildred Russell Canada; m. Roger Tang, Aug. 1979 (div.). Student, U. D.C., Chgo. State U., Chgo. Loop Jr. Coll. Prodr. KXAS-TV, Dallas, Ft. Worth, 1978-80, WRC-TV, Washington, 1980-82, WJLA-TV, Washington, 1982-83, WTTG-Fox TV, Washington, 1983-84; sr. prodr. WETA-TV, Washington, 1984-86; news dir. Black Entertainment TV, Washington, 1986-92, v.p. news and pub. affairs, 1992—, v.p. entertainment, children and sports programming, 1994—. Recipient Emmy award, 1983, CEBA award, 1990, NABJ award, 1991. Mem. Nat. Assn. Black Journalists, Capital Press Club. Office: Black Entertainment TV One BET Plz 1900 W Pl NE Washington DC 20018-1211*

TANGMAN, RUTH S., educational administrator; b. Cin., Mar. 3, 1944; d. George Trowbridge and Georgiana (Hollingworth) Strong; m. Edward P. Tangman, Mar. 27, 1971 (div. June 1993); children: David James, Michael Dennis, Elena Pilar. BS in Social Welfare, George Mason U., 1973; MSEd, Va. Polytech. Inst., 1977; postgrad. in edn., U. N.Mex., 1991—. Program analyst Nat. Adv. Coun. on Vocat. Edn., Washington, 1974-77; assoc. dir. employment and tng. Nat. Gov.'s Assn., Washington, 1977-78; dir. vocat. rsch. Westinghouse Nat. Issues Ctr., Arlington, Va., 1978-79; dir., sole propr. Inst. for Program Assistance, Santa Fe, 1979-82; exec. dir. N.Mex. Vocat. Assn., Santa Fe, 1981-83; work program coord., adminstrv. asst. to cabinet sec. Human Svcs. Dept., Santa Fe, 1983-87; dir. occupl., adult, and continuing edn. U. N.Mex., Los Alamos, 1987-89; assoc. v.p. for instrn. Albuquerque Tech.-Vocat. Inst., 1989—; instl. rep. Leadership Coun., Character Counts, Albuquerque, 1995—, exec. bd. mem. Teach and Learn Ednl. TV Channel, Albuquerque, 1993-95; cons. Cornell Coop. Extension, L.I., 1995; founding mem. N.Mex. Lit. Coalition, 1990. Contbr. articles to profl. jours. Mgmt. com. Albuquerque Bus.-Edn. Compact, 1989—; appointed commr. Albuquerque Goals Commn., 1990-93; co-chair Greater Albuquerque C. of C., bus. growth and devel. divsn., 1992; mem. Work-Force Devel. Task Force, Albuquerque, 1995—. Recipient Leadership Recognition award, Tech.-Vocat. Inst. Dir. Outreach and Transition, 1994; named Master Tchr., Nat. Inst. for Staff and Orgn. Devel., Austin, Tex., 1993; recipient Achievement award Greater Albuquerque C. of C., 1992. Mem. Am. Assn. Cmty. Colls., Nat. Coun. of Instrnl. Adminstrs., Nat. Coun. on Cmty. Svcs. and Continuing Edn., Nat. Tech. Prep Network, Albuquerque Sch.-to-Work Steering Com. Democrat. Office: Albuquerque Tech Voc Inst 525 Buena Vista SE Albuquerque NM 87106

TANINGCO, CORA MARIE DE GUZMAN, medical and surgical nurse, researcher, administrator; b. Manila, Philippines, Mar. 13, 1959; came to U.S., 1984; d. Bernabe Carbonell and Felipa (De Guzman) T. BSN, Manuel V. Gallego Found. Coll., Philippines, 1980. RN, N.J., N.Y., Calif., Oreg. Staff nurse ICU U. Philippines-PGH Med. Ctr., 1981-84; charge nurse ICU North Gen. Hosp., N.Y.C., 1984-88; program rev. assoc. Island Peer Rev. Orgn., Flushing, N.Y., 1988-89; rev. coord. Axiom Rev., Milburn, N.J., 1989-90; rev. coord. quality assurance North Gen. Hosp., N.Y.C., 1990-91, Lenox Hill Hosp., N.Y.C., 1991—; charge nurse Rockefeller U. Hosp., N.Y.C., 1991-93; nurse mgr. pediat. unit North Gen. Hosp., 1993—, star product coord. clin. area. Mem. editl. staff Nursing Pathway to Excellence Newsletter, 1996. Mem. ANA, Assn. Nurse Execs., Philippine Nurses Assn., Jaycees Toastmaster Club (asst. treas. 1991—), Philippine N.Y. Jaycees, Jaycees Internat., Toastmaster Internat. Home: 31-20 28 Rd Astoria NY 11102

TANNEN, DEBORAH FRANCES, writer, linguist; b. Bklyn., June 7, 1945; d. Eli S. and Dorothy (Rosen) T. BA, SUNY, Binghamton, 1966; MA, Wayne State U., 1970, U. Calif., Berkeley, 1976; PhD, U. Calif., 1979. Instr. Greek-Am. Cultural Inst., Heraklion, Greece, 1966-67; instr. in English as fgn. lang. Hellenic Am. Union, Athens, Greece, 1967-68; English instr. Detroit Inst. Tech., 1969, Mercer County C.C., Trenton, N.J., 1970-71; lectr. in acad. skills CUNY, Bronx, N.Y., 1971-74; asst. prof. Georgetown U., Washington, 1979-85, assoc. prof. linguistics, 1985-90, prof. linguistics, 1989-91, univ. prof., 1991—; McGraw disting. lectr. in writing Coun. for Humanities and dept. anthropology Princeton U., fall 1991; visitor Inst. for Advanced Study, Princeton, spring 1992; fellow Ctr. for Advanced Study in Behavioral Scis., Stanford, Calif., 1992-93. Author: Lilika Nakos, 1983, Conversational Style: Analyzing Talk Among Friends, 1984, That's Not What I Meant!: How Conversational Style Makes or Breaks Your Relations With Others, 1984, Talking Voices: Repetition, Dialogue and Imagery in Conversational Discourse, 1989, You Just Don't Understand: Women and Men in Conversation, 1990, Gender and Discourse, 1994, Talking From 9 to 5: How Women's and Men's Conversational Styles Affect Who Gets Heard, Who Gets Credit, and What Gets Done at Work, 1994; editor: Analyzing Discourse: Text and Talk, 1982, Spoken and Written Language: Exploring Orality and Literacy, 1982, Coherence in Spoken and Written Discourse, 1984, Perspectives on Silence, 1985, Linguistics in Context, 1986, Linguistics in Context: Connecting Observation and Understanding, 1988, Gender and Conversational Interaction, 1993, Framing In Discourse, 1993. Rockefeller Humanities fellow, 1982-83; grantee NEH, 1980, 85, 86; recipient Elizabeth Mills Crothers prize U. Calif., 1976, Dorothy Rosenberg Meml. prize U. Calif., 1977, Joan Lee Yang Meml. Poetry prize U. Calif., 1977, Shrout Short Story prize, 1978, Emily Chamberlain Cook prize, 1978. Office: Georgetown U Linguistics Dept Washington DC 20057

TANNENBAUM, JUDITH E., museum curator; b. N.Y.C., Oct. 26, 1944; d. Harold S. and Jeannette (Fuchs) T. AB in English, Rutgers U., 1966; MA in Art History, CUNY, 1973. Editor-in-chief Noyes Art Books, N.Y.C., 1975-77; curatorial rschr. Guggenheim Mus., N.Y.C., 1977-78; curator Mus. Contemporary Art, Chgo., 1978-79; contbg. editor Arts Mag., N.Y.C., 1973-81; dir. Freedman Gallery Albright Coll., Reading, Pa., 1981-86; assoc. dir., curator Inst. Contemporary Art, Phila., 1986—. Author: New York Art Yearbook, 1976, also exhbn. catalogs; contbr. articles and revs. to jours. and mags. Mem. adv. panel Pa. Coun. on Arts, Harrisburg, 1983-85; bd. dirs. Phila. Vol. Lawyers for Arts, 1987-93, Citizens for Arts in Pa., 1989—; chair adv. coun. Art in City Hall, Phila., 1993—; panelist Phila. Culture Fund, 1993—. Recipient Samuel S. Fleisher Founders award Phila. Mus. Art, 1991. Mem. Am. Assn. Mus., Coll. Art Assn. Am. (mus. com. 1995—). Office: U Pa Inst Contemporary Art 118 S 36th St Philadelphia PA 19104

TANNENWALD, LESLIE KEITER, educational administrator; b. Boston, May 5, 1949; d. Irving Jules and Barbara June (Caplan) Keiter; m. Robert Tannenwald. BA, Brandeis U., 1971, MA, 1976; MAT in Social Studies, Simmons Coll., Boston, 1972. Cert. Social Worker, Tchr., Mass. Sr. assoc. Combined Jewish Philanthropies of Greater Boston, 1977-84; interim dir., asst. dir. Cambridge (Mass.) Community Svcs., 1984-85; ednl. cons. Bur. Jewish Edn., Boston, 1985-87; ednl. dir. Congregation Shalom Emeth, Burlington, Mass., 1987-92, Congregation Temple Aliyah, Needham, Mass., 1992-93; religious sch. dir. Falmouth (Mass.) Jewish Congregation, 1993—; cons. Selected Ednl. Orgns. Boston 1972. Author: Curriculum, Male and Female, 1979 (Honors award 1971), Understanding the Holocaust, 1990, Awakening: Alternative Creative Learning Techniques, 1995. Officer, bd. dirs. Combined Jewish Philantropies of Greater Boston 1972—; mem. Am. Jewish Congress, Boston 1976—. Recipient Leadership award Inst. Leadership Devel. and Fund Raising. Mem. Nat. Alliance Profl. & Exec. Women, Alumni Assn. Benjamin S. Hornstein Program of Jewish Communal Svc., Assn. Jewish Community Personnel. Democrat. Home: 6 Clifton Rd Newton MA 02159-3147

TANNER, ALTHEA CLAIRE, artist; b. New Orleans, Aug. 3, 1918; d. Tabor Orme and Rose Janette (McTogue) Dodson; m. Warren Tanner, Mar. 1948 (div. 1955). Student, Augustine Bus. Sch., New Orleans, 1939. Sales person Sears, Roebuck & Co., New Orleans, 1939-41; layout Metairie (La.) Herald; furniture artist, lettering Barnett's, New Orleans, 1954-62; lettering artist Motion Picture Advt., New Orleans, 1964-72; typing, filing, lettering art T. Smith & Son Stevedoring Co., New Orleans, 1972-82. One-woman show Aerial Gallery, N.Y.C., 1992; exhibited in Winners Circle Gallery, Van Nuys, Calif., 1984, Arts Council of New Orleans, 1992; represented in permanent collection Old State Capitol, Baton Rouge, 1992. Contbr. donated art works WYES, channel 12, 1980-95, Arts for Aids, 1986-95, Contemporary Arts Ctr., 1992, Pops Found. 1995-96; active seminars Arts Coun. of New Orleans, 1992. Mem. Nat. Mus. of Women in the Arts, La. Women's Caucus for Art, Nat. Watercolor Soc., Nat. Watercolor Soc., New Orleans Mus. of Art, Arts Coun. of New Orleans, Contemporary Art Ctr. of

New Orleans. Republican. Roman Catholic. Home: 513 Arlington Dr Metairie LA 70001-5515

TANNER, ESTELLE NEWMAN, oral historian; b. Chgo., Sept. 2, 1936; d. Albert Hardy and Sylvia (Laff) Newman; m. Harold Tanner, July 6, 1957; children: David Allen, James Michael, Karen Tanner Allen. BA, Wellesley Coll., 1957. Cert. oral history tchr. Trustee Wellesley (Mass.) Coll., 1982—, Assn. of Governing Bds. of Univs. and Colls., Washington, 1985-94; trustee N.Y. State Archives Partnership Trust, Albany, 1994—, Ctr. Study of Philanthropy; dir. oral history project United Jewish Appeal Fedn., Jewish Philanthropists, N.Y., 1981—. Contbr.: Women as Donors, Women as Philanthropists, 1993. Trustee Colonial Williamsburg (Va.) Found., 1991—, WNYC Found., N.Y.C., 1985—. Mem. Cosmopolitan Club, Harmonie Club. Home: 775 Park Ave New York NY 10021-4253

TANNER, GLORIA, state legislator; b. Atlanta, July 16, 1935; d. Marcellus and Blanche Arnold Travis; m. Theodore Ralph Tanner, 1955 (dec.); children: Terrance Ralph, Tanvis Renee, Tracey Lynne. BA, Met. State Coll., 1974; MUA, U. Colo., 1976. Office mgr. Great Western Mfg. Co., Denver, 1965-67; writer Rage mag., 1969-70; reporter, feature writer Denver Weekly News, 1970-75; dir. East Denver Cmty. Office, 1974—; also real estate agt.; mem. Colo. Ho. of Reps., 1985-94; mem. from dist. 33 Colo. Senate, 1994—; minority caucus chairwoman; mem. appropriations, bus. affairs, labor coms. Dist. capt. Denver Dem. Com., Colo., 1973-75; chairwoman Senatorial Dist. 3 Dem. Com., 1974-82; adminstrv. aide Colo. State Senator Regis Groff, Denver, 1974-82; alt. del. Dem. Nat. Conv., 1976, del., 1980; commr. Colo. Status of Women, 1977—; chairwoman Colo. Black Women for Polit. Action, 1977—; exec. asst. to Lt. Gov., 1978-79; mem. adv. bd. United Negro Coll. Fund, Colo. State Treas. Served USAF, 1952-55. Recipient Outstanding Cmty. Leadership award Scott's Meth. Ch., 1974, Tribute to Black Women award, 1980; named Woman of Yr., Colo. Black Women Caucus, 1974. Mem. Colo. Black Media Assn. (pub. dir. 1972—), Reginas' Civic Club (founder, first pres. 1959—, Outstanding Woman of Yr. 1975), Nat. Assn. Real Estate Brokers. Roman Catholic. Democrat. Home: 2150 Monaco Pky Denver CO 80207-3951 Office: State Senate 200 E Colfax Ave Denver CO 80203*

TANNER, HELEN HORNBECK, historian; b. Northfield, Minn., July 5, 1916; d. John Wesley and Frances Cornelia (Wolfe) Hornbeck; m. Wilson P. Tanner, Jr., Nov. 22, 1940 (dec. 1977); children: Frances, Margaret Tanner Tewson, Wilson P., Robert (dec. 1983). AB with honors, Swarthmore Coll., 1937; MA, U. Fla., 1949; PhD, U. Mich., 1961. Asst. to dir. pub. rels. Kalamazoo Pub. Schs., 1937-39; with sales dept. Am. Airlines Inc., N.Y.C., 1940-43; teaching fellow, then teaching asst. U. Mich., Ann Arbor, 1949-53, 57-60, lectr. extension svc., 1961-74, asst. dir. Ctr. Continuing Edn. for Women, 1964-68; project dir. Newberry Libr., Chgo., 1976-81, rsch. assoc., 1981-95, sr. rsch. fellow, 1995—; dir. D'Arcy McNickle Ctr. for Indian History, 1984-85; cons., expert witness Indian treaties; mem. Mich. Commn. Indian Affairs, 1966-70. Author: Zespedes in East Florida 1784-1790, 1963, 89, General Green Visits St. Augustine, 1964, The Greenevelle Treaty, 1974, The Territory of the Caddo Tribe of Oklahoma, 1974, The Ojibwas, 1992; editor: Atlas of Great Lakes Indian History, 1987, The Settling of North America: An Atlas, 1995. NEH grantee, 1976, fellow, 1989; ACLS grantee, 1990. Mem. Am. Soc. Ethnohistory (pres. 1982-83), Am. Hist. Assn., Conf. Latin Am. History, Soc. History Discoveries, Orgn. Am. Historians, Chgo. Map Soc., Fla. Hist. Soc. Home: 5178 Crystal Dr Beulah MI 49617-9618 Office: The Newberry Libr 60 W Walton St Chicago IL 60610-3305

TANNER, LAUREL NAN, education educator; b. Detroit, Feb. 16, 1929; d. Howard Nicholas and Celia (Solvich) Jacobson; m. Daniel Tanner, July 11, 1948; m. Kenneth J. Rehage, Nov. 25, 1989. BS in Social Sci, Mich. State U., 1949, MA in Edn., 1953; EdD, Columbia U., 1967. Pub. sch. tchr., 1950-64; instr. tchr. edn. Hunter Coll., 1964-66, asst. prof., 1967-69; supr. Milw. Pub. Schs., 1966-67; mem. faculty Temple U., Phila., 1969—, prof. edn., 1974-89, prof. emerita, 1993—; prof. edn. U. Houston, 1989-96; vis. professorial scholar U. London Inst. Edn., 1974-75; vis. scholar Stanford U., 1984-85, U. Chgo., 1988-89; curriculum cons., 1969—; disting. vis. prof. San Francisco State U., 1987. Author: Classroom Discipline for Effective Teaching and Learning, 1978, La Disciplina en la enseñanza y el Aprendizaje, 1980; co-author: Classroom Teaching and Learning, 1971, Curriculum Development: Theory into Practice, 1975, 3d edit., 1995, Supervision in Education: Problems and Practices, 1987, (with Daniel Tanner) History of the School Curriculum, 1990; editor Nat. Soc. Study Edn. Critical Issues in Curriculum, 87th yearbook, part 1, 1988. Faculty rsch. fellow Temple U., 1970, 80, 81; recipient John Dewey Rsch. award, 1981-82, Rsch. Excellence award U. Houston, 1992; Spencer Found. rsch. grantee, 1992. Mem. ASCD (dir. 1982-84), Soc. Study Curriculum History (founder, 1st pres. 1978-79), Am. Edn. Rsch. Assn. (com. on role and status of women in ednl. R & D 1994—), Profs. Curriculum Assn. (Factotum 1983-84, chair membership com. 1994-95), Am. Ednl. Studies Assn., John Dewey Soc. (bd. dirs. 1989-91), Alumni Coun. Tchrs. Coll. Columbia U.

TANOUS, JUDITH ANGELA, municipal official; b. Atlanta, Feb. 18, 1948; d. Michael Teresa and Dorothy Alene (Dudley) Cafagno; m. Robert Basil Tanous, July 17, 1971 (div. 1988); 1 child, Angela Alene. LLB, Atlanta Law Sch., 1975, LLM, 1976. Ct. clk. City Ct. Atlanta, 1967-91, ct. adminstrv. supr., 1991-94, law clk., 1994-95, asst. ct. dir., 1995—; assoc. supr. Employee Assistance Program, Atlanta, 1991—, trauma response coord., 1995—; agy. coord. Fulton County Emergency Mgmt. Assn., Atlanta, 1993—. Worksite supr. Atlanta Pub. Schs., 1991-95; vol. fingerprint technician Clayton County Sheriff's Dept., Jonesboro, Ga., 1985-87; exercise instr. Clayton County YMCA, 1980-90. Recipient Appreciation cert. Clayton County Sheriff's Dept., 1985-86, Pvt. Industry Coun. Atlanta, 1991-94, Disting. Supporter award VFW, 1996. Mem. NOW, Nat. Assn. Ct. Mgmt. Republican. Home: 265 Merrydale Dr Fayetteville GA 30215 Office: City Court of Atlanta 104 Trinity Ave Atlanta GA 30335

TANUR, JUDITH MARK, sociologist, educator; b. Jersey City, Aug. 12, 1935; d. Edward Mark and Libbie (Berman) Mark; m. Michael Isaac Tanur, June 2, 1957; children: Rachel Dorothy, Marcia Valerie. BS, Columbia U., 1957, MA, 1963; PhD, SUNY, Stony Brook, 1972. Analyst Biometrics Rsch., N.Y.C., 1955-67; lectr. SUNY, Stony Brook, 1967-71, from asst. prof. to prof. sociology, 1971-94, disting. teaching prof., 1994—; cons. NBC, N.Y.C., 1976-89, Lang. of Data Project, Los Altos, Calif., 1980-89, Inst. for Rsch. on Learning, 1994-95; mem. Com. on Nat. Stats. of NAS, 1980-87; trustee NORC, U. Chgo., 1987—. Editor: Statistics: A Guide to the Unknown, 1972, Internat. Encyclopedia of Statistics, 1978, Cognitive Aspects of Survey Methodology, 1984, Questions About Questions, 1991; editor Internat. Ency. of Social Scis., N.Y.C., 1963-67; contbr. articles to sci., statis. and social sci. jours. Bd. dirs. Vis. Nurse Svc., Great Neck, N.Y., 1970—; bd. govs. Gen. Soc. Survey, Chgo., 1989-92. Sr. rsch. fellow, Am. Statis. Assn./NSF/Bur. Labor Statistics, 1988-89. Fellow, AAAS, Am. Statis. Assn.; mem. Internat. Statis. Inst., Phi Beta Kappa. Home: 17 Longview Pl Great Neck NY 11021-2508 Office: SUNY Dept Sociology Stony Brook NY 11794

TANZER, JAN P., marketing professional; b. Denver, June 21; d. Ben J. and Rose (Wenner) Pfefer; m. Herb Alan Tanzer; children: Fred, Greg, Josh. BA, U Wis.; MA, Wash. U., St. Louis. Mgr. sales promotion, mktg. Sprint, Kansas City, Mo., 1984-89, mgr. product mktg., 1989-93; mgr. product devel. divsn. video svcs. Bell Atlantic, Reston, Va., 1993-95; mktg. and product devel. mgr. new media and internet divsn. large bus. svcs. Bell Atlantic, Arlington, Va., 1994—; pres. Tech. Writers Kansas City, Mo., pres. Kans. NEA-Blue Valley. bd. dirs. Unicorn Theater, Kansas City, Mo., Woolly Mammoth Theater, Washington. Mem. Women's Ctr., Heart Am. Shakespeare Aux. (events chair). Democrat. Office: Bell Atlantic 1310 N Court House Arlington VA 22201

TANZI, CAROL ANNE, interior designer; b. San Francisco, Apr. 9, 1942; d. Raymond Edward and Anne Marie Giorgi. BA, U. San Jose, Calif., 1966. Teaching credential, Calif.; cert. interior designer, Calif. Home furnishings coord. R.H. Macy's, San Francisco, 1966-72; owner, pres. Carol A. Tanzi & Assocs., Burlingame, Calif., 1972—; instr. interior design Recreational Ctrs., Burlingame/Foster City, Calif., 1972-85; design cons. Am. Cancer Soc., San Mateo, Calif., 1994-95; mem. adv. com. for interior design students Coll. San Mateo, 1984-87; head designer San Mateo Battered Women's Shelter Pro Bono, 1993. Interior designer mags. Sunset, 1982, House Beautiful, 1992, 1001 Home Ideas, 1983; monthly cable TV program Interior Deesign by Tanzi, 1994—. Pres. Aux. to Mission Hospice, Burlingame, 1988-89, Hist. Soc. Burlingame, 1992-93; v.p. Cmty. for Edn., Burlingame, 1993-94, pres., 1996; mem. adv. com. Breast Ctr./Mills Peninsula Hosp., 1994—; mem. Oaks His. Adv. Bd., 1993-94; commr., pres. San Mateo County Commn. on Status of Women, 1990-95. Recipient Recogniton of Outstanding Performance Rotary Club of Burlingame, 1988—, Congl. Recognition U.S.A., Burlingame, 1994, Commendation Bd. Suprs., County of San Mateo, 1994, Recognition Calif. Legis. Assembly, Burlingame, 1994; named Superior Interior Designer Bay Area San Francisco Examiner, 1991, Woman of Distinction Soroptimist Internat., Burlingame/San Mateo, 1994. Mem. Am. Soc. Interior Designers (v.p. 1988, Presdl. Citation for disting. svc. 1986, 87, 88, Calif. Peninsula Chpt. Design award 1995), Burlingame C. of C. Women's Forum (chair 1986-95), Rotary Club of Burlingame (sec. 1988—). Home: 1528 Columbus Ave Burlingame CA 94010-5512 Office: Carol A Tanzi & Assocs PO Box 117281 Burlingame CA 94011-7281

TAO, CHIA-LIN PAO, humanities educator; b. Soochow, Kiangsu, China, July 7, 1939; came to U.S., 1961; d. Tsung-han and Hoi-chin Pao; m. Jingshen Tao, Aug. 22, 1964; children: Rosalind, Jeanne, Sandy. BA, Nat. Taiwan U., Taipei, 1961; MA, Ind. U., 1963, PhD, 1971. Assoc. prof. Nat. Taiwan U., Taipei, 1969-76, 78-79; vis. assoc. prof. U. Ariz., Tucson, 1976-78, 79-85, assoc. prof., 1989—; v.p. Hist. Soc. for 20th Century China in N.Am., 1992-93, pres., 1993-94. Editor, author: Studies in Chinese Women's History 4 vols., 1979-95. Mem. Tucson-Taichung Sister-City Com., Tucson, 1984—; sec. Ariz. Asian Am. Assn., 1989, dir., 1989-93. Rsch. grantee Nat. Sci. Coun., Taipei, 1971-72, 73-74, Harvard-Yenching Inst., Cambridge, Mass., 1972-74, Pacific Cultural Found., Taipei, 1984-85. Mem. Assn. for Asian Studies (pres. Western conf. 1994), Am. Assn. for Chinese Studies, Hist. Soc. for Gender Studies, Tucson Chinese Am. Profl. Soc. (pres. 1996), Tucson Chinese Assn. (bd. dirs.). Democrat. Office: Dept East Asian Studies Univ Ariz Tucson AZ 85721

TAPP, MAMIE PEARL, university official; b. Aiken, S.C., July 20, 1955; d. Willie Lee and Nancy (Madison) Garrett; m. Anthony Karl Tapp, Aug. 13, 1983; children: Anthony K. II, Barry Garrett, Myles Jarvis. BA, CUNY, 1977; MA, New Sch. for Social Rsch., 1984; postgrad., Nova Southeastern U., 1994—. Flight attendant Capitol Airlines, Jamaica, N.Y., 1976-81; pers. assoc. Cmty. Svc. Soc., N.Y.C., 1982-83; pers. specialaist Marriott Hotel, Tampa, Fla., 1983-84; dir. placement Tampa Coll., 1984-86, facility coord., 1986-87, compliance officer, 1987-88; career counselor Alpha House, Tampa, 1988-91; career specialist U. Tampa, 1991—, adj. prof., 1992-93. Author: Resumes, 1992, Cover Letters, 1991, Thank You Letters, 1992. Bd. dirs. Children's Mus. Tampa, 1992-94; com. mem. United Way, Tampa, 1994-95; mem. bd. St. Peter Claver Cath. Sch., Tampa, 1995—, exec. com. Glee Club, 1995. Recipient Outstanding Bus. Woman award Am. Bus. Women's Assn., Tampa, 1987, Cmty. Svc. award Tampa Connections, 1993. Mem. AAUW, Am. Vocat. Assn., Fla. Assn. Women in Edn. Roman Catholic. Office: U Tampa 401 W Kennedy Blvd Tampa FL 33606

TAPPER, JOAN JUDITH, magazine editor; b. Chgo., June 12, 1947; d. Samuel Jack and Anna (Swoiskin) T.; m. Steven Richard Siegel, Oct. 15, 1971. BA, U. Chgo., 1968; MA, Harvard U., 1969. Editor manuscripts Chelsea House, N.Y.C., 1969-71, Scribners, N.Y.C., 1971; editor books Nat. Acad. Scis., Washington, 1972-73; assoc. editor Praeger Pubs., Washington, 1973-74; editor New Rep. Books, Washington, 1974-79; mng. editor spl. pubs. Nat. Geog. Soc., Washington, 1979-83; editor Nat. Geog. Traveler, Washington, 1984-88; editor-in-chief Islands (internat. mag.), Santa Barbara, Calif., 1989—. Recipient Pacific Asia Travel Assn. Journalist of the Yr. award, 1995. Mem. Am. Soc. Mag. Editors, Soc. Am. Travel Writers (editors' coun.), Channel City Club. Democrat. Jewish. Home: 603 Island View Dr Santa Barbara CA 93109-1508 Office: Islands Mag 3886 State St Santa Barbara CA 93105-3112

TAPPERT, TARA LEIGH, art historian, archivist, researcher; b. Detroit, Jan. 9, 1950; d. Herman Henry and Carol Louise (Zannoth) T.; m. Clarke Foster Dilks, Oct. 18, 1975 (div. Apr. 9, 1980). BA in History, Hope College, 1973; MSLS in Libr. and Archives Adminstrn., Wayne State U., 1976; PhD in Am. Civilization, George Washington U., 1990. Law libr. U.S. Dist. Ct. (ea. dist.), Detroit, 1973-77, Sullivan & Cromwell, Washington, 1977-83; editor Am. Studies Internat. George Washington U., Washington, 1983-85; curatorial asst., researcher Nat. Mus. Am. Art, Washington, 1987; curatorial asst. Nat. Portrait Gallery, Washington, 1988-90, guest curator, 1990-96; curator exhbns. and collections Roanoke (Va.) Mus. Fine Arts, 1990; guest curator Borghi & Co., N.Y.C., 1991-93; rsch. assoc. Am. Craft Mus., N.Y.C., 1992-95; pvt. practice Roanoke, Va., 1990—; libr. cons. Nat. Press Club Libr., Washington, 1984-85; fine arts bibliographer Nat. Trust Brit. Libr., Cambridge, Mass., 1985-86; fine arts cons. Pa. Acad. Fine Arts, Phila., 1987; curatorial researcher, writer Detroit Inst. Arts, 1995. Author: (exhbn. catalogue) The Emmets: A Generation of Gifted Women, 1993, (exhbn. catalogue) Craft in the Machine Age: 1920-45, 1995, (exhbn. catalogue) Cecilia Beaux and the Art of Portraiture, 1995. Archivist, editor Roanoke Network for Profl. and Managerial Women, Roanoke, Va., 1992-93; founder women's reading group, Roanoke, 1995. Libr. Congress fellow George Washington U., 1985-86, Smithsonian pre-doctoral fellow, 1986-87, Beverly R. Robinson doctoral fellow Winterthur Mus., 1988. Mem. Am. Assn. Mus., Am. Studies Assn. (student 1985-87), Assn. Ind. Historians of Art, Coll. Art Assn., Mid-Atlantic Archives Conf. (local arrangements 1991), Women's Caucus for Art. Democrat. Mem. Soc. of Friends. Home and Office: 2408 Longview Ave SW #3-B Roanoke VA 24014

TARAKI, SHIRLEE, librarian; b. Chgo., Apr. 25, 1922; d. Frank and Leah (Simon) Heda; m. Mohamed Rasul Taraki, June 3, 1944 (dec. Aug. 1972); children: Lisa, Yosuf. BA in Psychology, U. Chgo., 1943, MA in Edn., 1947. Instr. English, Ministry of Edn., Kabul, Afghanistan, 1947-65; materials technician Ministry of Edn., Kabul, 1965-72; libr. asst. Northwestern U., Evanston, Ill., 1973-90; libr. Ctr. for Women's Health St. Francis Hosp., Evanston, 1990-95. Producer slide presentation An American Woman in Afghanistan, 1974—. Election judge Democrats of Evanston, 1991—, voting registrar, 1992—; vol. Wagner Health Ctr., Evanston, 1993—, vol. tutor Evanston Township H.S., 1990—. Mem. NOW (Evanston-North Shore chpt., founder), Circle Pines Ctr., Human Rights in Afghanistan Com. (cochair), Afghan Women's Task Force (founder, chair), Amnesty Internat., Phi Beta Kappa. Home: 1864 Sherman Ave #7 NW Evanston IL 60201

TARANTINI, MARY JEAN DELYCURE, secondary education educator; b. Wilkes-Barre, Pa., May 4, 1943; d. Michael Basil and Mary Dolores (Krempacky) Delycure; m. David John Tarantini, May 4, 1963; children: David Michael, Maria Elizabeth. BA, Coll. Misericordia, Dallas, 1964; MS, U. Scranton, Pa., 1970. Tchr. Swoyersville (Pa.) Sch. Dist., 1964-66; tchr. world culture Wyoming Valley West Schs., Plymouth, Pa., 1966—; advisor, mem. adv. com. dept. edn. Wilkes U., Wilkes-Barre, Pa., 1990—; cons. Pa. Framework: Social Studies, 1992—; advisor Wyoming Valley West History Day Team, 1980—. Named Pa. History Day Tchr. of Merit, Nat. History Day, 1992, Pa. History Day Outstanding Sch./Sr. Divsn., 1988, 90-91, 94, 95, 96. Mem. NEA, Pa. State Edn. Assn., Wyoming Valley West Edn. Assn., Plymouth Hist. Soc., Wyoming Hist. and Geol. Soc. (bd. dirs. 1993). Roman Catholic. Office: Wyoming Valley West HS Wadham St Plymouth PA 18651

TARCAI, ELSIE RENEE, lawyer; b. Budapest, Hungary, May 9, 1909; came to U.S., 1911; d. Louis and Mary (Berthal) T. BS, Ohio State U., 1934; LLB, John Marshall Sch. of Law, 1942. Bar: Ohio 1942, U.S. Dist. Ct. (no. dist.) Ohio 1948. Pvt. practice Cleve., 1942—. Mem. Cleve. Bar Assn., Cuyahoga County Bar Assn., Cleveland Marshall Law Alumni Assn. (life). Office: 925 Euclid Ave # 1598 Cleveland OH 44115

TARDOS, ANNE, artist, composer, writer; b. Cannes, France, Dec. 1, 1943; d. Tibor and Berthe (Steinmetz) T.; m. Oded Halahmy, Nov. 6, 1976 (div. Dec. 1979); m. Jackson Mac Low, Jan. 20, 1990; step-children: Mordecai-Mark Mac Low, Clarinda Mac Low. Attended, Akademie für Musik und Darstellende Kunst, Vienna, Austria, 1961-63, Art Students League of N.Y., 1963-69. guest tchr. Sch. Visual Arts, N.Y.C., 1974, 87, SUNY, Albany, 1986, U. Calif., San Diego, 1990, Schule für Dichtung in Wien, Vienna, Austria, 1992-94. Author: (book) Cat Licked the Garlic, 1992, Mayg-shem Fish, 1995; composer: (CD) Chance Operation: Tribute to John Cage, 1993, Open Secrets, 1993, Museum Inside the Telephone Network, 1991, (cassette) Gatherings, 1980; exhbns. include Jack Tilton Gallery, N.Y.C., 1989, Mus. of Modern Art, Bolzano, Italy, 1989, Venice Biennale, Venice, Italy, 1990, Galerie 1900-2000, Paris, 1990, Mus. of Modern Art, N.Y.C., 1993; (radio plays) Westdeutscher Rundfunk, Cologne, Germany, 1986, 96, Among Men, 1996.

TARGOS, JULIE DIANA, marketing company executive; b. Rib Lake, Wis., July 21, 1944; d. Stephen Josef and Gladys Louise (Maziarczyk) T. AA in Gen. Bus. and Acctg., Macomb County C.C., Warren, Mich., 1981; BA in Comm., U. Detroit, 1984. Managerial asst. Parke Davis & Co., Detroit, 1962-79; editor, office mgr. Brooks & Perkins, Inc., Southfield, Mich., 1979-81; account exec., art dir., writer G & D Comm., Inc., Troy, Mich., 1981-85; account exec., coord. spl. projects Mktg. Assocs., Inc., Bloomfield Hills, Mich., 1985-89; owner, pres. JDT Assocs., Inc., Rochester Hills, Mich., 1989-94, Nonpareil Comm., Inc., Clarkston, Mich., 1993—. Mem. publicity com. Scared Stiff/Safety and Survival, Rockville, Md., 1987—. Scholar U. Detroit Jesuit Founders, 1981. Mem. Am. Mktg. Assn., Am. Advt. Fedn., Mktg. Rsch. Assn., Women in Comm., Adobe Tech. Exch., Adcraft Club Detroit, Greater Detroit C. of C. (polit. action com. 1992-94), Greater Rochester C. of C. (polit. action com. 1990-94), World Trade Club. Mem. Ch. of Christ. Office: Nonpareil Comm Inc 8862 Nepahwin Dr Clarkston MI 48348-3336

TARGOW, JEANETTE GOLDFIELD, clinical social worker; b. Chgo., May 21, 1910; d. Isadore and Rebecca Covici Goldfield; children—Patricia Skinner, Richard Targow. Ph.B., U. Chgo., 1930; M.S.W., UCLA, 1953. Social worker U. So. Calif. Psychology Clinic, Los Angeles, 1953-55; clin. social worker Psychol. Service Center, Los Angeles, 1955-60; pvt. practice clin. social work, Los Angeles, 1960—; instr. Calif. Sch. Profl. Psychology; mem. faculty dept. psychology Loyola-Marymount Coll., 1981-83; supr. Didi Hirsch Mental Health Center, Culver City, Calif., 1977-81. Fellow Am. Group Psychotherapy Assn. (chmn. task force on womens' issues 1983-86), Group Psychotherapy Found. (bd. dirs.), Soc. for Clin. Social Work; mem. Los Angeles Group Psychotherapy Soc., Nat. Assn. Social Workers, Nat. Acad. Practice in Social Work, ACLU. Democrat. Jewish. Home: 1835 N Doheny Dr West Hollywood CA 90069-1150 Office: 648 N Doheny Dr Los Angeles CA 90069

TARITAS, KAREN JOYCE, telemarketing executive; b. Ft. Wayne, Ind., June 5, 1957; d. George and Patricia Louise (Smith) T. BS, Purdue U., 1988; AAS, Ind. U., 1980. Billing rep., experience analyst Lincoln Nat. Life Ins. Co., Ft. Wayne, 1974-82; customer svc. rep., underwriting asst. K&K Ins. Co., Ft. Wayne, 1984-86; telemarketing mgr. Stanley Steemer Carpet Cleaner, Ft. Wayne, 1990—. Mem. Am. Mus. Nat. History, Smithsonian Instn., Libr. Congress, Purdue U. Alumni Club, Ind. U. Alumni Club, Delta Sigma Pi. Home: 4414 S Hanna St Fort Wayne IN 46806 Office: Stanley Steemer Carpet Clnr 5109 Industrial Rd Fort Wayne IN 46825

TARR-WHELAN, LINDA, policy center executive; b. Springfield, Mass., May 24, 1940; d. Albert and Jane Zack; m. Keith Tarr-Whelan; children: Scott, Melinda. BSN, Johns Hopkins U., 1963; MS, U. Md., 1967. Program dir. AFSCME AFL-CIO, Washington, 1968-74, union area dir., 1974-76; adminstrn. dir. N.Y. State Labor Dept., Albany, N.Y., 1976-79; dep. asst. to pres. Carter White House, Washington, 1979-80; dir. govt. rels. NEA, Washington, 1980-86; CEO, pres. Ctr. for Policy Alternatives, Washington, 1986—, bd. dirs., 1985—; apptd. U.S. rep. UN Commn. on Status of Women, 1996—. Bd. dirs. Benton Found., Adv. Inst., Ind. Sector; pres. State Issues Forum; mem. Freddie Mac Affordable Housing Adv. Bd. Recipient Disting. Grad. award Johns Hopkins U., 1981, Breaking the Glass Ceiling award, 1996; leadership fellow Japan Soc., 1987-88. Democrat. Home: 3466 Roberts Ln Arlington VA 22207-5335 Office: Ctr for Policy Alternatives 1875 Connecticut Ave NW Washington DC 20009-5728

TARTER, BARBARA JANE, entertainment executive; b. New Rochelle, N.Y., Nov. 27, 1946; d. Andrew Lewis and Dorothy (Bailey) Smith; m. Fred Barry Tarter, Apr. 12, 1969; children: Scott Andrew, Heather Michelle, Megan Elisabeth. V.p., owner Deerfield Communications, N.Y.C., 1973-85; v.p. The Rainbow Group, Ltd., N.Y.C., 1985—; v.p. Boardwalk Entertainment, N.Y.C., 1990—. Republican. Episcopalian. Office: The Rainbow Group Ltd 210 E 39th St New York NY 10016-0911

TASKER, GRETA SUE, English as second language educator; b. Wichita, Kans., May 29, 1944; d. Cecil Tipton Gray and Neva Nancy (Rounds) Gray-Jones; m. David Byron Tasker, Dec. 19, 1964; children: Jack Weston, Richard Wade. BS in Edn., Emporia State U., 1966; MA, U. Kans., 1984. Spanish tchr. Hawaii State Dept. Edn., Honolulu, 1967-70; ESL tchr., coord. Olathe (Kans.) Dist. Schs., 1981—. Named Kans. Bilingual Tchr. of Yr. Kans. Assn. Bilingual Edn., 1989-90. Mem. TESOL, Kans. TESOL, Kans. Assn. Bilingual Edn., Mid.-TESOL.

TASSANI, SALLY MARIE, communications executive, marketing consultant; b. Teaneck, N.J., Dec. 30, 1948; d. Peter R. and Marie Irene (Sorbello) T. BA, Am. U., 1970. Elem. sch. tchr., Washington, 1970-73; asst. prodn. and promotion mgr. First Nat. Bank of Chgo., 1973-74; exec. dir. Jack O'Grady Graphics, Inc., Chgo., 1974-76; creative dir. Dimensional Mktg., Inc., Chgo., 1976-78; CEO, founder Tassani & Paglia, Inc. (formerly Tassani Comm., Nexus, Inc.), Chgo., 1978—; mem. adv. bd. Heizer Entrepreneurship Rsch. Ctr. Northwestern U. J.L. Kellogg Grad. Sch. Mgmt., U.Ill. Urbana-Champaign Coll. Commerce and Bus. Adminstrn. Elected to Com. of 200; hon. bd. dirs. Girl Scouts Chgo. Named one of Ad Age's Best and Brightest Women in Advt., Top Women Entrepreneur Crain's Chgo. Bus., Top Entrepreneurs poll USA Today, Who's Who in Chgo. Bus. 1990-93, Top Woman-Owned Firms 1990-92, Entrepreneur of Yr. women's category INC, 1990; named to Nat. Women's Hall Fame. Mem. Alliance, The Art Inst. Chgo., Chgo. Coun. on Fgn. Rels. (Chgo. com.), Old Town Triangle Assn, Entrepreneur of Yr. Inst., Internat. Assn. of Bus. Communicators (Spectra award 1987, guest speaker 1988), Women's Advt. Club of Chgo. (hon., bd. dirs., Advt. Woman of Yr. 1994), Young Pres.' Orgn., Econ. Club, Chgo. Advt. Fedn., The Chgo. Network, The Execs. Club Chgo. Avocations: power walking, sailing, photography, American crafts, graphic design. Home: 1735 N Orleans St Chicago IL 60614-5719

TASSELL, DIANNA LEE, former school nurse; b. Albuquerque, Jan. 14, 1955; d. Melvin Lee and Julia Dell (Gladish) Lane; m. Steven Joseph Tassell, Jan. 18, 1975; children: Amy, Julie. LPN, Sandusky Sch. Nursing, 1988. LPN, Ky. Staff nurse geriatrics Erie County Care Facility, Huron, Ohio, 1988-90, Elkins (W.Va.) Regional Convalescent, 1990-94; sch. nurse, instructional asst. spl. edn. Silver Hills Elem. Sch., Salt Lake City, Utah, 1994-95. Republican. Baptist. Home: 140 Miller Rd Hodgenville KY 42748-9703

TASSINARI, MELISSA SHERMAN, toxicologist; b. Lawrence, Mass., Sept. 26, 1953; m. R. Peter Tassinari; children: Michael, Emily, Sara. AB, Mt. Holyoke Coll., 1975; postgrad., U. St. Andrews, Scotland, 1973-74; PhD, Med. Coll. Wis., 1979. Diplomate Am. Bd. Toxicology. Rsch. asst. in orthopedic surgery., Lab. Human Biochemistry Children's Hosp. Med. Ctr., Boston, 1981-83; rsch. affiliate in toxicology Toxicology Dept. Forsyth Dental Ctr., Boston, 1983-86, staff assoc., 1986-89; asst. prof. cell biology U. Mass. Med. Ctr., Worcester, 1989-91; mgr. reproductive toxicology Pfizer Ctrl. Rsch., Groton, Conn., 1991—; rsch. fellow oral biology Harvard Sch. Dental Medicine, Boston, 1978-81, instr. oral biology and pathophysiology, 1981-83; asst. prof. biol. scis. Wellesley Coll., Mass., 1983-86, cons. teratology Arthur D. Little, Inc., Cambridge, Mass., 1985-91; asst. prof. biology Simmons Coll., Boston, 1986-87. Contbr. abstracts, articles to profl. jours. Mem. Teratology Soc., Neurobehavioral Teratology Soc., Mid Atlantic Reproduction and Teratology Assn. (steering com. 1994), Soc. Toxicology. Office: Pfizer Central Research Eastern Point Rd Groton CT 06340

TASSONE, GELSOMINA (GESSIE TASSONE), metal processing executive; b. N.Y.C., July 8, 1944; d. Enrico and A. Cira (Petriccione) Gargiulo; children: Ann Marie, Margaret, Theresa, Christine; m. Armando Tassone, Mar. 20, 1978. Student, Orange County Community Coll., 1975-79, Iona Coll., 1980—. Head bookkeeper Gargiulo Bros. Builders, N.Y.C., 1968-72;

pres., owner A&T Iron Works, Inc., New Rochelle, N.Y., 1973—. Recipient Profl. Image award Contractors Coun. Greater N.Y.C., 1986; named Businesswoman of Yr., Contractors Coun. Greater N.Y.C., 1985, N.Y. State Small Bus. Person of Yr., 1988, Entrepreneur of Yr. Inc. mag., 1990; company named a Successful Small Bus. Co. Westchester County C. of C./BSBA, 1986-88. Mem. Nat. Ornamental and Miscellaneous Metal Assn., Builders Inst. Westchester and Putnam County, Westchester Assn. Women Bus. Owners, Profl. Women in Constrn., Westchester C. of C. Office: A&T Iron Works Inc 25 Cliff St New Rochelle NY 10801-6803

TATE, DIANNE EVANS, program coordinator; b. Rockwood, Tenn., Apr. 1, 1947; d. Tom Harper and Myrle Lena (Marrs) Evans; m. James Barry Tate. BS in Edn., Kennesaw State Coll., 1988. Cert. tchr., Ga. Art tchr. Monroe County Schs., Madisonville, Tenn., 1968-69; dir. student ctr. Sanford U., Birmingham, Ala., 1969-73; sec. Cobb County Sch., Marietta, Ga., 1974-85; asst. state dir. vols. Ga. Dept. Corrections, Atlanta, 1988-92; JTPA coord. North Metro Tech., Acworth, Ga., 1992—; mem. Peach Bd., Cartersville, Ga., 1992—. Block capt. Neighborhood Watch, Catersville, 1995; bd. dirs. YWCA, Marietta, 1981-87. Mem. AAUW, Etonal Hist. Soc. (preservation chair 1992-95, chair tour of homes 1994). Home: 402 W Main Cartersville GA 30120 Office: North Metro Tech 5198 Ross Rd Acworth GA 30102

TATE, EVELYN RUTH, real estate broker; b. Ottumwa, Iowa, Sept. 21; d. Frank Edward and Ella Belle (Smith) Ross; student public schs., Huntington Park, Calif.; m. William Tate (dec.); 1 son, William. Owner, mgr. Evelyn R. Tate Realty Co., Sherman Oaks, Calif., 1943-53, Beverly Hills, Calif., 1942—; owner, mgr. Evelyn Tate Fine Arts, San Francisco, 1976—; mgr. Beverly Hills Galleries, Hyatt Regency Hotel, San Francisco, 1979—; mgr. art gallery Fairmont Hotel; owner, mgr. Tate Gallery, St. Frances Hotel, San Francisco, Hyatt Regency Hotel San Francisco, Fairmont Hotel, Dallas, Ritz Carlton Hotel, San Francisco. Home: 999 Green St Apt 1003 San Francisco CA 94133-3649

TATE, SARAH TUCKER, counselor; b. Rome, Ga., May 30, 1940; d. Henry Quigg Tucker and Lucy (Dent) Patton; m. Lee Tate, Mar. 18, 1967; children: David, Susan. AB, U. Ga., 1962; grad. psychological studies, Inst. Ga. State Univ., 1991, MS, 1991. Lic. profl. counselor. Counselor Alphacare Therapy Svcs., Atlanta, 1993-94; dir., profl. counselor Stone Mountain Christian Counseling Svcs., Inc., Stone Mountain, Ga., 1991—; support group coord. Stone Mountain Cmty. Ch., 1991—. Fellow Am. Bd. Cert. Managed Care Providers; mem. Christian Assn. Psychological Studies, Am. Assn. Christian Counselors, Am. Counseling Assn. Protestant. Home: 2579 Dunhaven Glen Shellville GA 30278 Office: Stone Mountain Christian Counseling Svcs Inc 1000 Main St Ste E Stone Mountain GA 30083

TATE, SHARON SUE, special events and catering executive; b. Gainesville, Tex., Sept. 21, 1949; d. Lucien Harvey and Ollie Pauline (Insel) T. AA, Cooke County Coll., 1972; postgrad., U. North Tex., 1973-74, So. Meth. U., 1984. Credit collections cons. J.C. Penney, Dallas, 1978-80; exec. v.p. Orville McDonald Assocs., Dallas, 1980-86; conf. coord. Plaza Ams. Hotel, Dallas, 1986-92; spl. events and catering mgr. dani' Foods at the Dallas Mus. Art, 1992-95; pres. Orville McDonald Assocs., Dallas, 1995—. Republican. Home: 8780 Park Ln Apt 1017 Dallas TX 75231-5504 Office: Orville McDonald Assocs PO Box 823185 Dallas TX 75382-3185

TATE, SHEILA BURKE, public relations executive; b. Washington, Mar. 3, 1942; d. Eugene L. and Mary J. (Doherty) Burke; m. William J. Tate, May 2, 1981; children: Hager Burke Patton, Courtney Paige Patton. BA in Journalism, Duquesne U., 1964; postgrad. in mass communications, U. Denver, 1975-76. former chairperson bd. dirs. Corp. for Pub. Broadcasting. Rsch. asst. Westinghouse Air Brake Co.; asst. account exec. Falhgren and Assos.; copywriter Ketchum, MacLeod and Grove, 1964-66; account exec. Burson-Marsteller Assocs., Pitts., 1967; sr. v.p. Burson-Marsteller Assocs., Washington, 1985-87; public rels. mgr. Colo. Nat. Bank, Denver, 1967-70; account exec. Hill and Knowlton, Inc., Houston, 1977-78; v.p. Hill and Knowlton, Inc., Washington, 1978-81; dep. to the chmn. Hill and Knowlton Inc., Washington, 1987-88; press sec. to First Lady White House, Washington, 1981-85; press sec. George Bush for Pres. Campaign, 1988; press sec. to Pres.-elect George Bush, 1988-89; vice chmn. Cassidy and Assocs. Pub. Affairs, Washington, 1989-91; pres. Powell Tate, Washington, 1991—; bd. dirs. Corp. for Pub. Broadcasting, vice chmn., 1990-92, chmn., 1992-94. Mem. civilian pub. affairs adv. bd. U.S. Mil. Acad.; mem. adv. bd. Ronald Reagan Inst. Emergency Medicine, George Washington U. Hosp., Washington. Mem. Nat. Press Club, Nat. Press Found. (bd. dirs.). Clubs: Duquesne U. Century, F Street, Washington Golf and Country, Farmington Country Club. Office: Powell Tate 700 13th St NW Ste 1000 Washington DC 20005-3960

TATE, SONDRA (SANDY TATE), retired business owner, typesetter; b. N.Y.C., Jan. 12, 1935; d. Marshall and Ruth (Bystock) Ruben. Owner, typesetter Sandy Tate Assocs., L.A., 1966-75; owner Feminist Horizons, L.A., 1975-84; computer operator various orgns. L.A., 1984-89. Contbr. articles to profl. jours. and newspapers. Treas. L.A. NOW, 1972-73. Mem. Old Lesbians Organizing for Change. Jewish.

TATE, STEPHANIE LOU, transportation company administrator, journalist; b. Twin Falls, Idaho, Mar. 3, 1966; d. Dennis Armfield and Blanche Laurel (Harper) T. BA in Comm., U. Wash., 1995. Reservations agt. Gray Line of Seattle, 1986-87, lead airport agt., 1987-90, sales and svc. agt., 1990-96, charter coord., 1996—. Contbr. articles to newspapers. Collective mem. Left Bank Collective, Seattle, 1990-95. Mem. ACLU (writer, vol. 1995). Office: Gray Line of Seattle 720 S Forest St Seattle WA 98134

TATE, VIRGINIA MARIE, computer scientist, consultant; b. Chgo., Oct. 19, 1947; d. Thomas Edgar and Delilar E. (Hawkins) Powell; children: Michelle Marie, Christina Dorothy. BS, Chgo. State U., 1968; MEd, Loyola U., Chgo., 1980, PhD, 1990. Cert. math. and computer sci. tchr., Ill. Tchr. Chgo. Bd. Edn., 1969-95; dir. tech. Energy Masters Corp., Overland Park, Kans., 1995—; mem. adv. bd. Mus. Sci. and Industry, Chgo. Author: video) Manual for State Chapter II, 1992, (tng. manual) Software Applications for Teachers, 1995. Bd. dirs. Kohl Mus., Wilmette, Ill., 1990—. Recipient Those Who Achieve award Ill. Inst. Tech., 1983, Internat. Tchr. award Kohl Mus., 1993. Mem. Ill. Soc. Bus. Educators (adv. bd. 1994—, Those Who Excel award 1994), Ill. Computer Edn. Soc. (sec. 1994-95). Democrat. Office: Energy Masters Corp 1400 E Touhy Ave Des Plaines IL 60018

TATHAM, JULIE CAMPBELL, writer; b. N.Y.C., June 1, 1908; d. Archibald and Julia deFres (Sample) Campbell; student pvt. schs., N.Y.C.; m. Charles Tatham, Mar. 30, 1933; children—Charles III, Campbell. Author more than 30 juvenile books including: The Mongrel of Merryway Farm, 1952; The World Book of Dogs, 1953; To Nick from Jan, 1957; author Trixie Belden series, 1946—, Ginny Gordon series, 1946—; co-author Cherry Ames and Vicki Barr series, 1947—; author: The Old Testament Made Easy, 1985; many series books transl. into fgn. langs.; contbr. numerous mag. stories and articles to popular publs., 1935—; free-lance writer, 1935—; contbr. numerous articles to Christian Sci. publs., including Christian Sci. Monitor, 1960—. Address: 1202 S Washington St Apt 814 Alexandria VA 22314-4446

TATNALL, ANN WESLAGER, reading educator; b. Uniontown, Pa., June 1, 1935; d. Clinton Alfred and Ruth Georgia (Hurst) Weslager; m. George Gress Tatnall, Oct. 8, 1954; children: Peggy Ann, George Richardson. BS in Edn., U. Del., 1967; MA in Edn., Glassboro State Coll., 1978. Cert. reading specialist, N.J.; cert. supr., N.J.; cert. elem. tchr., N.J. Tchr. reading Oldmans Twp. Bd. of Edn., Pedricktown, N.J., 1972-78, reading specialist, 1978-95, reading supr., 1981-95; mem. N.J. Dept. of Edn. Minimum Basic Skills Test Devel. Com., Trenton, N.J., 1981-82; mem. Quad-Dist. Reading Coordination Com., Salem County, N.J., 1987-95; chairperson Adminstrv. Com. of Oldmans Twp. Schs., Pedricktown, N.J., 1993-95. Chairperson Woodstown (N.J.) Candlelight House Tour, 1983—; pres. Pilesgrove-Woodstown Hist. Soc., 1994—; v.p. Pilesgrove Libr. Assn., 1994—; sec. Hist. Preservation Commn., Woodstown, 1989—; mem. Jr. Bd. of Wilmington (Del.) Med. Ctr., 1969—, treas. Thrift Shop, 1970-75. Recipient Gov.'s Tchr. Recognition Program award Gov. of N.J., 1988; selected Hands Across the Water, Russian/USA Tchr. Exchange, 1990-91. Mem. AAUW, Internat. Reading Assn., N.J. Reading Assn., Woman's Club of Woodstown. Home: 209 N Main St Woodstown NJ 08098

TATUM, L. KAY, lawyer; b. Houston, Feb. 2, 1951. BA summa cum laude, Tulane U., 1972; MA, Rice U., 1976, PhD, 1978; JD cum laude, U Houston, 1980. Ptnr. Akin, Gump, Strauss, Hauer & Feld, Washington. Mem. ABA. Office: Akin Gump Strauss Hauer & Feld LLP 1333 New Hampshire Ave NW Washington DC 20036*

TATUM, MELANIE GARNETT, reporter; b. Martinsville, Va., June 25, 1969; d. David Moore and Barbara Lucille (Martin) T. BA in English, BA in Internat. Studies, Coll. William and Mary, 1991. Radiotelephone lic. FCC. Radio announcer WLOE-AM, Eden, N.C., 1989; historic interpreter Jamestown Settlement, Williamsburg, Va., 1991; editor U.S. Army Intelligence and Security Command, Fort Belvoir, Va., 1991-93; layout editor Stevens Pub., Washington, 1993-95, reporter, 1995; reporter Saudi Press Agy., Washington, 1996—; vol. radio announcer, reporter WCWM-FM, Williamsburg, Va., 1988-91; freelance editor, cons., Arlington, Va., 1995—. Mem. Nat. Press Club, The Actors' Ctr., The Nature Conservancy. Home: 5619 N 6th St Arlington VA 22205

TAUBMAN, JANE ANDELMAN, Russian literature educator; b. Boston, Oct. 23, 1942; d. Hyman M. and Esther (Rosenthal) Andelman; m. William Chase Taubman; children: Alexander, Phoebe. BA, Radcliffe Coll., 1964; MA, Yale U., 1968, PhD, 1972. Instr. Russian Smith Coll., Northampton, Mass., 1968-72; asst. prof. Russian Amherst (Mass.) Coll., 1973-83, assoc. prof. Russian, 1983-89, prof. Russian, 1989—. Author: A Life Through Poetry: Marina Tsvetaeva's Lyric Diary, 1989; co-author: Moscow Spring, 1989; co-editor: Marina Tsvetaeva: One Hundred Years, 1994; contbr. articles to profl. jours. Woodrow Wilson Found. fellow, 1964—, Am. Coun. Learned Socs.-SSRC, 1974, trustee-faculty fellow Amherst Coll., 1978, fellow Nat. Def. Title VI, 1965-68; grantee Am. Philos. Soc., 1975, Amherst Coll., 1991, 94, IREX grantee USSR, 1988. Mem. AAUP, Modern Langs. Assn., Am. Assn. Tchrs. Slavic and East European Langs., Am. Assn. Slavic Studies, Am. Coun. Tchrs. of Russian, Am. Assn. Tchrs. of Slavic and East European Langs. Office: Amherst Coll Dept Russian Amherst MA 01002

TAUNTON, KATHRYN JAYNE, accountant; b. Thomaston, Ga., Nov. 3, 1953; d. Mack Doudal and Martha Jayne (Goolsby) T. AA, Cypress Coll., 1973; BA in Accounting, Calif. State U., 1977. Circulation clk. Buena Park Library Dist., Buena Park, Calif., 1973-76; account supr. ORCO State Employees Credit Union, Santa Ana, Calif., 1977-78, Santa Ana City Credit Union, 1978-79; self employed Reliable Credit Union Service, Buena Park, 1979-95.

TAUNTON, ROMA LEE, nurse educator. Diploma, Ida V. Moffett Sch. Nursing, 1959; BS In Nursing, U. Ala., 1963; M in Nursing, Emory U., 1965; PhD in Ednl. Psychology, U. Kans., 1983. Chief nurse children & youth project U. Ala. Med. Ctr., Birmingham, Ala., 1967-68; coord. children & youth project U. Ark. Med. Ctr., Little Rock, 1968-69; coord. pediatric nursing Grady Meml. Hosp., Atlanta, 1970-74; dir. pediatric nurse practitioner project Am. Nurses Assn., 1974-76; dir. nursing practice dept. Am. Nurses Assn., Kansas City, Mo., 1976-79; assoc. prof. Sch. Nursing U. Kans. Med. Ctr., Kansas City, 1983-92, prof., 1992—; cons. in field. Contbr. numerous articles to profl. jours. Recipient Cert. Outstanding Svc. in Nursing and Health Programs Met. chpt ARC, 1973, Mable Korsell award, 1975, Outstanding Young Women Am. award, 1974, Investigator Recognition award U. Kans. Med. Ctr., 1989, Dean's Rsch. award U. Kans. Sch. Nursing, 1989, Am. Jour. Nursing Books of the Yr. award, 1986, 88, 89, Chancellor's award for Outstanding Teaching, 1992; rsch. grantee Am. Nurses Found., NIH. Fellow Am. Acad. Nursing; mem. ANA, ANA Coun. Nurse Researchers, Midwest Nursing Rsch. Soc., Acad. Mgmt., Assn. for Health Svcs. Rsch., Coun. for Grad. Edn. for Adminstrn. in Nursing, Am. Orgn. Nurse Execs, Sigma Theta Tau (rsch. grantee). Home: 4417 Wyoming St Kansas City MO 64111-4370 Office: U Kans Med Ctr Sch Nursing 39th Rainbow Blvd Kansas City KS 66160-7503

TAURIAC-LEMELLE, YVONNE, education educator; b. New Iberia, La., Oct. 20, 1935; d. Anthony and Florence (Broussard) Tauriac;m. Wilbert John Lemelle, June 14, 1958; children: Patrice, Wilbert Jr., Gerald, Edward. BS in Biology, Grambling (La.) State U., 1960; MA in Biology Edn., U. Denver, 1963; MS in Mgmt., U.S. Internat. U., Nairobi, Kenya, 1979; PhD in Edn., Fordham U., N.Y.C., 1992. Sci. tchr. Ossining (N.Y.) Sch. Sys., 1966-69; instr. biology U.S. Internat. U., Nairobi, 1971-73; rschr. microbiology U. Nairobi, 1972-73; sr. fellow Phelps-Stokes Fund, N.Y.C., 1992—. Mem. AAUW, ASCD, Phi Delta Kappa, Kappa Delta Pi. Home: 57 Elizabeth Rd New Rochelle NY 10804-3211 Office: Phelps Stokes Fund 10 E 87th St New York NY 10128-0501

TAUSER, TERRI ANNE, English educator; b. Paterson, N.J., Feb. 12, 1965; d. William Paul and Margaret Anna (Cervine) Hauser; m. Joseph Raymond Tauser, oct. 21, 1989; 1 child, Margaret Alexandra. BA, St. Louis U., 1987, cert. bus. adminstrn., 1987; MEd in Secondary Curriculum, U. Mo., 1994. Cert. tchr., Mo. Pub. affairs libr. Gen. Dynamics Corp., Clayton, Mo., 1987-88; exploring exec. St. Louis area coun. Boy Scouts Am., 1988-90; tchr. secondary English Rockwood Sch. Dist., Eureka, Mo., 1992—; asst. Inroads Comm. Project, St. Louis, 1991; tchr. Access to Success Saturday Acad., St. Louis, 1992; coach speech/debate team Eureka (Mo.) H.S., 1992-94, Rockwood Summit H.S., Fenton, Mo., 1994-95. Day leader Elderly Vis. Program, St. Louis, 1983-89. Recipient Blue Vase award St. Louis Area Coun., Boy Scouts Am. 1980, acad. scholarship St. Louis U., 1983-87, leadership grant St. Louis U., 1986-87. Mem. Nat. Coun. Tchrs. English, Greater St. Louis English Tchrs. Assn. Roman Catholic. Home: 3512 S Spring Ave Saint Louis MO 63116 Office: Rockwood Summit HS Hawkins Rd Fenton MO 63026

TAVON, MARY E., public relations, marketing and communications executive; b. Montreal, Apr. 4, 1958. Student, Marianopolis Coll. Lit. and Langs., 1977; BA in English, Theatre and Film, McGill U., 1980. Mktg. analyst Korea Trade Promotion Assn., 1980-82; advt., pub. rels. asst. Ann Taylor, 1983-84; acct. exec. Michael Klepper Assocs., N.Y.C., 1984-86, acct. supr., 1986-88, v.p., 1988-89, pres., exec. prodr., 1989. Recipient cert. merit Chgo. Internat. Film Festival, 1990. Office: Michael Klepper Assoc Inc 805 3rd Ave New York NY 10022-7513

TAWNEY, LOIS GRIFFIN, systems analyst; b. Gasaway, W. Va., Oct. 1, 1963; d. David Linden and Nellie Ann (Loyd) Griffin; m. David Allen Tawney, Oct. 15, 1988; children: Christopher Allen, Nathan Griffin. BS in Computer Sci., W. Va. U., 1986. Programmer Westat, Inc., Rockville, Md., 1987-89; programmer, analyst Aspen Syss., Inc., Rockville, Md., 1989-90; sr. programmer, analyst Digital Ins. Syss. Corp., Columbus, 1990-91; project leader Victoria's Secret Stores, Columbus, 1991—; cons. Westat, Inc., Rockville, Md., 1989, Digital Ins. Syss. Corp., 1991. Methodist. Office: Victoria's Secret Stores P O Box 16586 Columbus OH 43216

TAYAG, CATHERINE EVANGELISTA, physician, educator; b. Manila, Philippines, May 20, 1965; Came to the U.S., 1991; d. Avelino Urquico and Concepcion Banzon (Evangelista) T. BS in Biology cum laude, U. Philippines, 1985, MD, 1990; intern pediatrics, Mount Sinai Svcs.-Elmhurst (N.Y.) Hosp. Ctr., 1991-92; resident pediatrics, North Shore U. Hosp.-Cornell Med. Coll., Manhasset, N.Y., 1992-94, chief resident pediatrics, 1994-95. Reg. physician N.Y., 1995; cert. Am. Bd. Pediatrics, 1994. Clin. assoc. in pediatrics Cornell U. Med. Ctr., N.Y., 1992-94, sr. clin. assoc. in pediatrics, 1994-95; chief resident pediatrics North Shore U. Hosp., Manhasset, 1994-95; attending pediatrician St. John's Episcopal Hosp., Far Rockaway, N.Y., 1995—, in charge in-patient svcs. pediatrics, 1995—. Mem. Am. Acad. Pediatrics, Am. Bd. Pediatrics, Am. Bd. Med. Specialties, Am. Coll. Physicians, Nassau Pediatric Soc., Phi Kappa Phi. Roman Catholic. Home: 2244 Dogwood Ln Westbury NY 11590 Office: St Johns Episcopal Hosp 327 Beach 19th St Far Rockaway NY 11691

TAYLOR, ANN LOUISE, marketing executive; b. Fairmont, Minn., Aug. 8, 1937; d. Eugene and Celia Ethel (Fulton) Lundahl; m. James Harold Taylor, May 23, 1959; children: Kimberly Taylor Locey, Jayme K. BA in Edn., U. Minn., 1959; postgrad., Am. Inst. Banking, 1985-87. Tchr. Nokomis Jr. High Sch., Mpls., 1959-61, Helen Keller Mid. Sch., Easton, Conn., 1973-75; photojournalist Suburban & Wayne Times, Berwyn, Pa., 1975-80; cons. pub. relations Fla. Internat. Bank, Miami, Fla., 1981-84; v.p. Fla. Internat. Bank, Miami, 1984-94; employee rels. mgr. Am. Bankers Ins. Group, Miami, 1994-96; freelance writer, pub. rels. cons., 1996—. Contbr. articles to profl. jours. Mem. women's adv. coun. Bapt. Hosp. of Miami, 1991—. Mem. Women in Comms. (pres. Greater Miami chpt. 1987-88, v.p. so. region 1989-92, v.p. fin. 1993-94, nat. pres. elect 1994-95, nat. pres. 1995-96), Greater South Dade-South Miami C. of C. (bd. dirs. 1987-94, pres.-elect 1989—, chmn. 1991-92), Founders of South Dade (pres. 1987-88). Republican. Lutheran.

TAYLOR, ANNA DIGGS, federal judge; b. Washington, Dec. 9, 1932; d. Virginius Douglass and Hazel (Bramlette) Johnston; m. S. Martin Taylor, May 22, 1976; children: Douglass Johnston Diggs, Carla Cecile Diggs. BA, Barnard Coll., 1954; LLB, Yale U., 1957. Bar: D.C. 1957, Mich. 1961. Atty. Office Solicitor, Dept. Labor, W, 1957-60; asst. prosecutor Wayne County, Mich., 1961-62; asst. U.S. atty. Eastern Dist. of Mich., 1966; ptnr. Zwerdling, Maurer, Diggs & Papp, Detroit, 1970-75; asst. corp. counsel City of Detroit, 1975-79; U.S. dist. judge Eastern Dist. Mich. Detroit, 1979—. Hon. chair, United Way Cmty. Found., S.E. Mich. Found. Soc., Detroit Inst. Arts, Greater Detroit Health Coun., Eastern Region Henry Ford Health Sys.; co-chair, vol. Leadership Coun. for S.E. Mich. Mem. Fed. Bar Assn., State Bar Mich., Wolverine Bar Assn. (v.p.), Yale Law Assn. Episcopalian. Office: US Dist Ct 740 US Courthouse 231 W Lafayette Blvd Detroit MI 48226-2719

TAYLOR, ANNE, judge, lawyer; b. Columbus, Ohio, Jan. 26, 1951; d. Gardner Brice and Donna M. (Kelly) T.; m. Steven Lee Smith, Oct. 21, 1994. BS, Ohio State U., 1973; JD, Capital U., 1979. Bar: Ohio 1979. Atty. Ohio State Legal Svcs. Assn., Columbus, 1979-81; pvt. practice Columbus, 1981-92; judge Franklin County Mcpl. Ct., Columbus, 1992—; bd. dirs. criminal laws procedure com. Ohio Jud. Conf., bd. dirs. civil law and procedure com. Bd. dirs. Columbus AIDS Task Force, 1993—. Reginald Heber Smith Comty. Lawyer fellow Legal Svcs. Assn., 1979-82; named one of Ten Outstanding Young Citizens, Columbus Jaycees, 192. Mem. Am. Inns Ct. (pres. Franklin chpt. 1995—), Spl. Ties (chair 1992—). Democrat. Office: Franklin County Mcpl Ct CTRM 15D 375 S High St Columbus OH 43215

TAYLOR, BARBARA ANN, insurance company executive; b. Newark, Feb. 19, 1950; d. Walter B. and Alice (Schwarz) Blumberg; m. C.W. Taylor Jr., Jan. 24, 1988. BS cum laude, Ohio U., 1972. Trainer, writer Am. States Ins., Indpls., 1976-79, tng. devel. supr., 1979-81, quality commitment cons., 1981-86, quality commitment mgr., 1986—, asst. v.p., 1987-94; asst. v.p., dir. employee devel. Lincol Nat. Corp., Fort Wayne, 1994—; instr. in ins. Am. States Ins., Indpls., 1979-86; ins. textbook reviewer Ins. Inst. Am., Malvern, Pa., 1985, 90. Big sister Big Sisters of Indpls., 1980-82; tchr. adult literacy Greater Indpls. Literacy League, 1985-94; bd. dirs. Arts Ind., Inc., Indpls., 1988-94, Friends of Herron Gallery and Sch. Art, Indpls., 1990-94, Greater Indpls. Literacy League, 1993-94, Ft. Wayne Mus. of Art, 1995—, Ind. Civil Liberties Union, 1995—. Mem. ASTD, Human Resource Planning Soc., Assn. Quality and Participation, Quality and Productivity Mgmt. Assn. Office: Lincoln Nat Corp 1300 S Clinton St Fort Wayne IN 46802-3506

TAYLOR, BARBARA ANN, educational consultant; b. St. Louis, Feb. 8, 1933; d. Spencer Truman and Ann Amelia (Whitney) Olin; m. F. Morgan Taylor Jr., Apr. 5, 1954; children: Frederick M. III, Spencer O., James W., John F. AB, Smith Coll., 1954; M of Mgmt., Northwestern U., 1978, PhD, 1984; LHD, U. New Haven, 1995. Mem. faculty Hamden (Conn.) Hall Country Day Sch., 1972-74; cons. Booz, Allen & Hamilton, Inc., Chgo., 1979; program assoc. Northwestern U., Evanston, Ill., 1982; co-founder, exec. dir. Nat. Ctr. Effective Schs. Rsch. & Devel., Okemos, Mich., 1986-89, rsch. assoc., 1987; cons. on effective schs. rsch. and reform Nat. Ctr. Effective Schs. R&D, U. Wis., Madison, 1990-96; pres. Excelsior! Found., Chgo., 1994—; mem. exec. com. Hudson Inst., New Am. Schs. Devel. Corp. Design Team, 1990—; Danforth Disting. lectr. U. Nebr., Omaha, 1993. Co-author: Making School Reform Happen, 1993, Keepers of the Dream, 1994, The Revolution Revisited: Effective Schools and Systemic Reform, 1995; editor: Case Studies in Effective Schools Research, 1990; contbr. articles to profl. jours. Pres. Jr. League of New Haven, 1967-69; pres. NCCJ, New Haven, 1971-73; co-chair Coalition Housing and Human Resources, Hartford-New Haven, 1970-73; co-chair steering com. Day Care Comn., Hartford, 1971-73; bd. dirs. U. New Haven, 1961-71, Smith Coll., Northampton, Mass., 1984-90, Lake Forest Coll., 1996—. Recipient Humanitarian award Mt. Calvary Bapt. Ch., 1988, Outstanding Alumna award John Burroughs Sch., 1994. Mem. ASCD, Nat. Commn. Citizens Edn. (bd. dirs. 1980-86), Nat. Staff Devel. Coun., Phi Delta Kappa. Episcopalian. Office: Nat Ctr Effective Schs Rsch & Devel 222 E Wisconsin Ave Ste 301 Lake Forest IL 60045-1723

TAYLOR, BARBARA J., writer; b. Louisville, Sept. 15, 1946; d. Charles Allen and Marjorie Ozie (Meador) T.; m.; Richard C. Taylor (wid.); children: Geoff, Christopher, Rachael; m. John McCafferty, nov. 15, 1982 (div. July 1993). BA, U. Louisville, 1980. Author: (pen name Taylor McCafferty/fiction books) Pet Peeves, 1990, Ruffled Feathers, 1992, Bed Bugs, 1993, Thin Skins, 1994, Hanky Panky, 1995, (pen name Tierney McClellan) Heir Condition, 1995, Closing Statement, 1995, A Killing in Real Estate, 1996; co-author: (with Beverly Taylor Herald) Double Murder, 1996. Mem. Mystery Writers of Am., Sisters in Crime. Office: care Richard Parks Agy 138 E 16th St # 5B New York NY 10003

TAYLOR, BARBARA JO ANNE HARRIS, government official, librarian, educator, civic and political worker; b. Providence, Sept. 9, 1936; d. Ross Cameron and Anita (Coia) Harris; m. Richard Powell Taylor, Dec. 19, 1959; 1 child, Douglas Howard. Student, Tex. Christian U., 1952, Salve Regina Coll., 1952-53; Student, Our Lady of the Lake Coll. and Convent, 1953-54, St. Mary's U., 1954, Incarnate Word Coll., 1954-55, Georgetown U., 1956-59, 62-63; BS cum laude, Georgetown U., 1963. Adminstrv. asst. profl. devel. and welfare NEA, Washington, 1956-59; asst. to dir. Georgetown U., Washington, 1956-59; exec. asst. All Am. Conf. to Combat Communism, Washington, 1960; spl. legis. asst. mil. affairs to chmn. mil. R & D subcom. U.S. Senate Armed Svcs. Com., 1971-72; U.S. nat. commr. UNESCO, 1982—, mem. exec. com. U.S. nat. commn., 1983—, sr. advisor 22d gen. conf., 1983; speaker in field. Contbr. articles to profl. jours. Del. numerous internat. confs.; U.S. commr. Nat. Commn. Librs. and Info. Sci., 1985-96, mem. various coms.; gen. chmn. George Bush for Pres. Md. State Steering Com., 1987-88; co-chmn. Md. del. Rep. Nat. Conv., 1988, 92; dep. chmn. Md. Victory '88, Bush-Quayle Campaign; mem. Nat. Fin. Com. Reagan for Pres., 1980, Reagan-Bush, 1984; state fin. chmn. Md. Rep. Party, 1980; mem. Nat. Rep. Club; mem. exec. bd. Salvation Army Aux., Washington, 1967-75, chmn. membership com., 1969-70, chmn. fund-raising com., 1968-69, mem. exec. com. of exec. bd., 1970-75, treas., mem. fin. com., 1970-71, v.p., 1971-72, historian, 1972-73, editor newsletter, 1968-69, chmn. nominating com., 1974-75, spl. awards for exceptional vol. svc., 1969, 72; mem. exec. bd. Welcome to Washington Internat., 1969-74, bd. advisers, 1969-74, dir. workshop, 1969-74; exec. bd. Am. Opera Sch. Soc., Washington, 1970—, v.p., 1974—; mem. Episc. Ch. Home for Aged Women's Aux., 1970-75, Episc. Ctr. for Emotionally Disturbed Children Women's Aux., 1970-75; exec. bd. St. David's Episc. Ch. Aux., 1970-72, 73-74; bd. dirs., treas. Spanish-Portuguese Study Group, 1970-72; mem. exec. bd. League Rep. Women D.C., 1964-67, 75-77, treas., 1964-67; mem. nat. coun. Women's Nat. Rep. Club, N.Y.C., 1969—, chmn. Washington-Md.-Va. legis. com., 1970-75; mem. Nat. Fedn. Rep. Women, 1964—; mem. nat. fin. com. Reagan for Pres., 1979-80; mem. governing bd. Capital Speakers Club, 1973-75, chmn. by-laws com., 1973-74; mem. exec. bd. Nat. Vols. in Action, 1975-77; mem. adv. com. Rock Creek Found. Mental Health, 1982-87; mem. 50th anniversary com. Save the Children; mem. fund-raising com. Washington Choral Arts Soc., 1982-84; state fin. chmn. Reagan-Bush campaign Md. Rep. Com., 1980; Md. coord. Nat. Inaugural Com., 1981, 85; trustee Crossnore Sch., Inc., N.C., 1983—, vice chmn. bd.; trustee Kate Duncan Smith DAR Sch., Grant, Ala., 1983-86, Tamassee (S.C.) DAR Sch., 1983-86; adviser Bacone Am. Indian Coll., Inc., Muscogee, Okla., 1983-88. Mem. ALA, Spl. Librs. Assn., Coun. on Libr. Resources (commn. on preservation and access), Am. Libr. Trustees Assn., Libr. Adminstrn. and Mgmt. Assn., Assn. Coll. and Rsch. Librs., Am. Antiquarian Soc., Internat. Platform Assn., Spanish-Portuguese Study Group, Nat. Lawyers' Wives, Nat. Capital Law League, Nat. Soc. DAR (chmn. nat. resolutions com. 1980-83, chmn. nat. Nat. Soc.

DAR sch. com. 1983-86; state historian 1978-80, mem. state bd. mgmt. 1973—, Nat. Soc. DAR libr. gen., mem. exec. com. and nat. corp. bd. mgmt. 1986-89, chmn. nat. commemorative events com. 1992-95, chmn. nat. Nat. Soc. DAR libr. centennial com. 1995—), Nat. Soc. Children Am. Revolution (sr. nat. asst. registrar 1978-80, mem. sr. nat. bd. mgmt. 1978-80, sr. nat. exec. com. 1978-80), Nat. Assn. Parliamentarians, World Affairs Coun., League of Rep. Women, Md. Fedn. Rep. Women, Women's Nat. Republican Club, Nat. Fed. Rep. Women, Commn. on Preservation and Access, Lit. Vols. Am. (Washington Met. area affiliate), Exec. Women in Govt., Am. News Women's Club, Internat. Club, Capital Hill Club, Univ. Club Washington, Washington Club, Congl. Country Club (Potomac, Md.).

TAYLOR, BEVERLY LACY, stringed instrument restorer, classical guitarist; b. Denver, Mar. 1, 1928; d. Frederick Thurlow and Ruth (Rogers) Lacy; m. Arthur D. Taylor, Mar. 18, 1967. BA, Wheaton Coll., Norton, Mass., 1949; postgrad., U. Denver, 1951-53, U. Colo., 1953. Scene designer, tech. dir. Piper Players, Idaho Springs, Colo., 1949-51; art instr. Denver Art Mus., 1952; craft and speech instr. Wallace Sch., Denver, 1953; illustrator dept. native art Denver Art Mus., 1954-56; designer, owner The Art Studio, Santa Fe, 1956-58; instr., owner Classic Guitar Studio, Santa Fe, 1959—; instr. classical guitar Santa Fe Conservatory of Music, 1966-67, Coll. Sante Fe, 1971-72; stringed instrument restorer Lacy Taylor Studio, Santa Fe, 1967—. One-woman shows of mosaic panels include Mus. N.Mex., Santa Fe, 1959; exhibited in group shows at Mus. New Mex., 1962, 63; executed mosaic panels Denver Art Mus. Recipient Miriam Carpenter Art prize Wheaton Coll., 1949, prize N.Mex. State Fair, 1959, 61. Mem. Guild Am. Luthiers, Assn. String Instrument Artisans. Home: 1210 Canyon Rd Santa Fe NM 87501-6128

TAYLOR, CAROLE JAN HUDSON, insurance company administrator; b. Port Arthur, Tex., May 17, 1949; d. Henry and Vivian Corine (Duncan) Hudson. BBA, Stephen F. Austin U., 1971. Claim rep. The Travelers Ins. Co., Houston, 1971-73, asst. supr., 1973-78, sr. rep., 1978-87, regional gen. adjuster, 1987-93, exec. gen. adjuster, 1993—. Author software program Business Interruption, 1988. Mem. Women for Reagan, Houston, 1983. Recipient cert. of achievement Am. Ednl. Inst., 1974, G.A.B. Bus. Interruption, 1988. Mem. NAFE, Ford's of 50's (treas. 1981-82). Republican. Baptist. Office: Travelers Ins Co 10800 Richmond Houston TX 77042

TAYLOR, CELIANNA ISLEY, information systems specialist; b. Youngstown, Ohio; d. Paul Thornton and Florence (Jacobs) Isley; divorced; children: Polly, Jerry, Jim. BA in Philosophy, Denison U., 1939; MLS, Western Res. U., 1942. Worked in several pub. librs. and univ. librs., 1939-50; head Libr. Cataloging Dept. Battelle Mem. Inst., Columbus, Ohio, 1951-53; head pers. office, assoc. prof. libr. adminstrn. Ohio State U. Librs., Columbus, 1954-65; coord. info. svcs., assoc. prof. libr. adminstrn. Nat. Ctr. for Rsch. in Vocat. Edn., Ohio State U., Columbus, 1966-70; sr. rsch. assoc., adminstrv. assoc., assoc. prof. libr. adminstrn. dept. computer and info. sci. Ohio State U., Columbus, 1970-86; assoc. prof. emeritus Univ. Librs. dept. computer and info. sci. Ohio State U., Columbus, 1986—; mem. Task Force on a Spl. Collections Database, Ohio State U. Librs., Columbus, 1988-89, comm. systems and recs. coord. Ohio State U. Retirees Assn., Columbus, 1992-93; cons. for several profl. orgns. including Ernst & Ernst CPA's and Oreg. State Sys. of Higher Edn., 1961-82. Author: (with J. Magisos) book, Guide for State Voc-Tech Edn. Dissemination Systems 1971, (with A.E. Petrarca, and R.S. Kohn) book, Info. Interaction 1982; several articles for profl. jours.; designer: info. systems, CALL System, 1977-82, Channel 2000 Proj. Home Info. Svc., 1980-81, Continuing Education Info. Ctr., 1989-90, Human Resources (HUR) System, 1976-77,1979-82, DECOS, 1975-86, Computer-asst. libr. System, Optical Scan System, 1972-73, ERIC Clearinghouse for vocat. edn., 1966-70. Bd. dirs. Columbus Reg. Info. Svc., 1974-78, Cmty. Info. Referral Svc., Inc. 1975-81; chmn. subcom. on design, info. and ref. com. Columbus United Cmty. Coun., 1972-73; dir. Computer Utility for Pub. Info. Columbus, 1975-81; acct. coord. Greater Columbus Free-net, 1994—. Mem. ALA, Assn. Computing Machinery (Ctrl. Ohio chpt.), Am. Soc. Info. Sci.,Assn. Faculty and Profl. Women Ohio State U., Columbus Metro Club, Coun. for Ethics in Econs., Olympic Indoor Tennis Club. Home and Office: 3471 Greenbank Ct Columbus OH 43221-4724

TAYLOR, DEBRA JO, musician; b. Point Pleasant, N.J., Mar. 12, 1960; d. Joseph Owen and Virginia (Conboy) T. Student, Boston U., 1978-80; BMus, Curtis Inst. Music, Phila., 1984. Second trombonist Fla. Symphony Orchestra, Orlando, 1986-87; prin. trombonist Taipei Philharmonic Festival Orchestra, Taiwan, 1990, San Diego (Calif.) Symphony Orchestra, 1993-94; second trombonist Santa Fe (N.Mex.) Opera Orchestra, summers 1995—; second/asst. prin. trombonist Grant Park Symphony Orchestra, Chgo., summers 1986—; prin. trombonist N.Mex. Symphony Orchestra, Albuquerque, 1989—; clinician and soloist Edwards Instruments, 1992—; guest artist Santa Fe Chamber Music Festival, 1995, N.Y. Trumpet Ensemble, Carnegie Hall, N.Y.C., 1983; soloist and clinician Internat. Brassfest, Long Beach, Calif., 1996, Internat. Trombone Assn. Workshop, Las Vegas, 1995, N.Mex. Symphony, 1996; soloist Women's Internat. Trombone Choir/Internat. Trombone Assn. Workshop, Detmold, Germany, Ill. Chamber Orchestra, Springfield, Ill., 1989; Faculty Roosevelt U., Chgo., 1988-89. Musician: (CD recordings) Millar Brass Ensemble, 1988, San Diego Symphony, 1994-95, Santa Fe Chamber Music Festival, 1995. Vol. organizer, producer Benefit Brass Ensemble Concert, Albuquerque, 1991; sec., bd. trustees Turquoise Trail Arts Coun., Albuquerque, 1990-93. Mem. Internat. Trombone Assn., Toastmasters Internat., Evolutionary Trombonists (co-founder, v.p. 1995—). Democrat.

TAYLOR, DIANE R., director alumni relations program; b. Aug. 1, 1960; m. Roger S. Taylor III, Apr. 23, 1983; children: Stephanie, Kevin, Matthew. BS, Kutztown (Pa.) U., 1982. Claims analyst AON Corp., Trevose, Pa., 1982-83; pers. recruiter AON Corp., 1983-87; alumni coord. Trenton (N.J.) State Coll., 1987-91; dir. alumni rels. Holy Family Coll., Phila., 1991—. Mem. Walt Disney PTO, Levittown, Pa., 1991—, Pennsbury Sch. Dist. After Sch. Childcare Task Force, Fallingston, Pa., 1990-91, Coun. for Advancement/Support of Edn.; Brownie scout leader Girl Scouts U.S.A., Valley Forge, Pa., 1991-95. Mem. Nat. Soc. Fundraising Execs. Roman Catholic. Office: Holy Family Coll Grant & Frankford Aves Philadelphia PA 19114

TAYLOR, DONNA BLOYD, vocational rehabilitation consultant; b. Louisville, Ky., July 15, 1958; d. Donald Ray Bloyd and Georgia Carmen (Bryant) Whitehead; 1 child, Stephanie Micah Taylor; m. Douglas A. Garner, June 6, 1992. BS, U. Louisville, 1981, MEd, 1982. Lic. profl. counselor, qualified rehab. provider, Ohio; cert. rehab. counselor U.S. Dept. Labor; qualified rehab. coord., Ky.; cert. disability mgmt. specialist; cert. case mgr., vocat. evaluator, nat. counselor; diplomate Am. Bd. Vocat. Experts; qualified mental retardation profl.; cert. vocat. evaluator, RAS. Program coord. Hazelwood ICF-MR, Louisville, 1981-83; lead vocat. therapist Rehab. Ctr. Southeastern Ind., Clarksville, 1983-85; regional supr., vocat. cons. Rehab. Coords., Inc., Louisville, 1985; asst. mgr., rehab. cons. Nat. Rehab. Cons., Cin., 1985-88; dist. mgr., vocat. cons. Recovery Unlimited, Inc., Cin., 1988-92; pvt. practice, Lawrenceburg, Ind., 1992—; vocat. expert Social Security Adminstrn. Co-author: (with Timothy Field and others) Study Guide to the CIRS Exam, 1992, The St. Thomas Resource on Certification, Ethics and Training for Private Sector Rehabilitation, 1993, CCM Study Guide, 1994. Vol. Am. Cancer Soc., mem. Rape Crisis Intervention Team. Mem. Nat. Assn. Rehab. Profls. in Pvt. Sector (past pres. Ky. chpt., SCRB com., co-chair internat. affairs divsn.), Nat. Rehab. Assn., Nat. Forensic Ctr., Nat. Disting. Svc. Registry, Individual Case Mgmt. Assn., U. Louisville Alumni Assn., Disability Network Ohio-Solidarity, Rehab. Referral Network, Rehab. Internat., Phi Kappa Phi. Democrat. Methodist. Office: 15 Mary St Lawrenceburg IN 47025-1900

TAYLOR, DONNA LYNNE, adult education coordinator; b. Balt., July 1, 1944; d. Noel Leroy and Dorothy Anna (Henry) Welsh; 1 child, Tom A., Jr. BS, Okla. State U., 1965, EdD, 1992; MS, Phillips U., 1984. Cert. vocat. bus. and trade and indsl. edn. tchr., prin., supt., vocat. adminstr., Okla. Retail sales Tulsa, 1961-62; secretary Okla. State U. Coop. Extension Svc., Stillwater, 1965-67; secondary instr. social studies Waller Jr. High, Enid, Okla., 1967-69; substitute instr. Autry Tech. Ctr., Enid, 1971-78, instr. vocat. bus. part-time, 1978-84, instr. vocat. bus. full time, 1984-94, coord. adult edn., 1994—; small bus. owner Lynne's Country Crafts, Enid, 1975-85; coord. adult edn. Autry Tech. Ctr., Enid, 1994—; adult educator Sch. Continuing Edn., Enid, 1981-85; mem. strategic planning com. and policy and procedures com. Staff Devel. Affirmative Action, Enid, 1989—; presenter ann. confs. and meetings Okla. State Dept. Vocat. Tech., Stillwater, 1991-92; coord., chair Articulation Agreement Com., Enid, 1991—; advisor FBLA/Phi Beta Lambda, Enid, 1990-94; mem. North Ctrl. Accreditation Steering Com., 1992-93, staff devel. chair, 1993-94. Bd. dirs. Sch. Continuing Edn., Enid, 1975-85; mem. vol. YWCA, March of Dimes, Am. Heart Assn., MS Soc., Am. Diabetes Assn., Enid Art Assn., 1985—; deacon Christian Ch., Enid, 1986-88, elder, 1988-92, 95—; active Leadership Greater Enid. Recipient Women of Achievement award March of Dimes, 1992; named Okla. Bus. Tchr. of Yr., 1994. Mem. ASCD, Am. Vocat. Assn., Okla Vocat. Assn., Mountain Plains Bus. Edn. Assn., Okla. Bus. Edn. Assn., Nat. Bus. Edn. Assn., Nat. Assn. Classroom Bus. Educators, Vocat. Bus. and Office Edn., Enid C. of C. (edn. com. 1991-92), Phi Delta Kappa (sec. 1992—), PEO. Republican. Home: 2110 Appomattox Enid OK 73703-2008 Office: Autry Tech Ctr 1201 W Willow Rd Enid OK 73703-2506

TAYLOR, DOROTHY KARL, elementary education educator; b. Newark, June 21, 1949; d. Edward H. and Margaret H. (Miller) Karl; divorced; children: Patrick Leonard, Brian Edward. BA, Coll. Notre Dame, 1971. Tchr. elem. sch. Ridgewood (N.J.) Pub. Schs., 1971-77, Assumption Sch., Morristown, N.J., 1986—; tutor Suburban Tutoring Svc., Springfield, N.J., 1986—; mgr. Stardust Recreation Assn., Morris Twp., N.J. Cub scout leader Boy Scouts Am., Randolph, N.J., 1986—, Boy Scout merit badge counselor, 1992—. Mem. Assn. Children with Learning Disabilities (sch. liaison 1993—), Nat. Cath. Edn. Assn., Delta Kappa Gamma (parliamentarian 1977-94). Independent. Roman Catholic. Home: 7 N Star Dr Randolph NJ 07869-4779 Office: Assumption Sch 63 Macculloch Ave Morristown NJ 07960-5231

TAYLOR, ELINOR ZIMMERMAN, state legislator; b. Norristown, Pa., Apr. 18, 1921; d. Harold I. and Ruth A. (Rahn) Zimmerman; m. William M. Taylor, 1947; 1 child, Barbara. BS, West Chester State Tchrs. Coll., 1943; student, Columbia U., 1944, U. Del., 1955; MEd, Temple U., 1958. Tchr. Ridley Park (Pa.) H.S., 1943-46, West Chester (Pa.) H.S., 1946-50; prof. West Chester State Coll., 1955-68, adminstr., 1968-76, now. prof. emeritus; mem. Pa. Ho. of Reps., 1977—; chmn. subcom. on higher edn.; sec. Rep. Caucus; bd. dirs. Pa. Higher Edn. Assistance Agy.; active Gov. Commn. on Funding Higher Edn., Women; in Politics and Polit. Action Com.; Rep. chmn. Health and Welfare Com.; trustee Charles S. Swope Found.; founding trustee Bd. Chester County Edn. Found. Councilwoman Borough of West Chester, Pa., 1974-77, mem. recreation com., 1974-77. Named West Chester Citizen of Yr., 1985, Legislator of Yr. Pa. Assn. Home Health Agys., 1993; recipient Hon. award Pa. State Assn. for Health, Phys. Edn. and Recreation, 1962, Hon. Umpires award U.S. Field Hockey Assn., 1967, Disting. Alumni award West Chester State Coll., 1977, alumni award Temple U., 1982, Love of Children of Greater West Chester Golden Heart award, Achievement cert. Pa. Fedn. of Bus. and Profl. Women's Club, George Washington Honor award Valley Forge Freedom Found., Guardian of Small Bus. award, 1993-94, cert. of appreciation Am. Legion, 1995, Margaret Hoover Brigham award Chester County Emergency Med. Svc., 1995, Police Athletic League award, 1995; named to Henderson H.S. Hall of Fame, 1994. Mem. AAUW (former pres.), Nat. Assn. Women Legislators, Chester County Art Assn., Pa. Paramedice Assn. (hon.). Republican. Presbyterian. Home: 859 Spruce Ave West Chester PA 19382 also: 13 W Miner St West Chester PA 19382-3213 Office: Pa Ho of Reps House Box 20202 Harrisburg PA 17120-2020*

TAYLOR, ELISABETH COLER, secondary school educator; b. N.Y.C., Jan. 24, 1942; d. Gerhard Helmut and Judith (Horowitz) C.; m. Billie Wesley Taylor II, Jan. 27, 1960; children: Letitia Rose, Billie Albert. Student, Wilmington Coll., 1959-60; BS, Wayne State U., Detroit, 1969; MS, The Ohio State U., 1980; postgrad., Wright State U., Dayton, Ohio, 1989—. Cert. home economist. H.s. tchr. home econs., computer sci., lang. arts Dayton (Ohio) City Schs., 1972—. Bd. mem. Camp Fire Girls, 1970-71, vol. Detroit Mus. of Art, 1970-71, group leader Camp Fire Girls, Boy Scouts, Detroit, 1968-74. Mem. AAUW (life), NEA, Ohio Edn. Assn., Dayton Edn. Assn. Home: 131 Snow Hill Ave Dayton OH 45429-1705

TAYLOR, ELIZABETH ANN (BETH TAYLOR), advertising and marketing executive; b. New Orleans, Oct. 14, 1954; d. Eddie M. and Rita Joy (Bova) T.; divorced. BS in Journalism, La. State U., 1977. Polit. cons. La. Rep. Party, New Orleans, 1972-75; gen. assignment reporter The Times-Picayune, New Orleans, 1975-76; asst. news dir. WRBT-TV, Baton Rouge, 1976-78; sports anchor/reporter WDAM-TV, Hattiesburg, Miss., 1978-85; bur. chief WDAM-TV, Hattiesburg, 1985-86, assignments editor, 1986-89; dir. admissions/mktg. Pine Grove Psychiat. Hosp., Hattiesburg, 1989-91; owner, CEO Letter B Prodns., Hattiesburg, 1991—; facility adv. coun. mem. Miss. Vocat.-Rehab. Dept., Laurel, Miss., 1988-89; mem. adv. com. Miss. Blood Svcs., Laurel, 1986-88; mem. women's adv. bd. Forrest Gen. Hosp., Hattiesburg, Miss., 1988-90; rsch. bd. adv. Am. Biog. Inst., 1991—. Author, creator video/mktg. promotions. Mem. comm. bd. United Way of Pine Belt Region, Laurel, 1985-88, United Way of S.E. Miss., Hattiesburg, 1988-90; mem. adv. bd. Hattiesburg Edn. Literacy Project, Hattiesburg, 1989-95; bd. dirs. Domestic Abuse Family Shelter, Laurel, 1988-95. Recipient 2nd and 3rd pl. documentary prodn. Miss. A.P. Assn. Broadcasters, 1986. Mem. Ad Fedn. South Miss., Pub. Rels. Assn. Miss., Miss. Broadcasters Assn. (assoc., Cert. of Excellence 1980, Silver cert. 1990), Ad Fedn. South Miss. (Addy award 1994, 2 Citations of Excellence 1994, 3 Citations of Excellence 1995, award of distinction, Nat. Comms. award, 2 Hon. Mention awards 1996, 1 Citation of Excellence, 1995, 3 Citations of Excellence, 1996, 1 Nat. Communicator award, 2 Honorable Mentions, 1995, 1 Nat. Communicator award, 1 Honorable Mention, 1996, 2 Silver Microphone Nat. Finalist awards 1996). Office: Letter B Prodns 2009 Hardy St Box C Hattiesburg MS 39401

TAYLOR, ELIZABETH ROSEMOND, actress; b. London, Feb. 27, 1932; d. Francis and Sara (Sothern) T. Student, Byron House, Hawthorne Sch., Metro-Goldwyn-Mayer Sch. Motion pictures include There's One Born Every Minute, 1942, Lassie Come Home, 1943, The White Cliffs of Dover, 1944, Jane Eyre, 1944, National Velvet, 1944, Courage of Lassie, 1946, Cynthia, 1947, Life with Father, 1947, A Date with Judy, 1948, Julia Misbehaves, 1948, Little Women, 1950, Conspirator, 1950, The Big Hangover, 1950, Father of the Bride, 1950, Father's Little Dividend, 1951, A Place in the Sun, 1951, Callaway Went Thataway, 1951, Love Is Better Than Ever, 1952, Ivanhoe, 1952, The Girl Who Had Everything, 1953, Elephant Walk, 1954, Rhapsody, 1954, Beau Brummel, 1954, The Last Time I Saw Paris, 1954, Giant, 1956, Raintree County, 1957, Cat on a Hot Tin Roof, 1958, Suddenly Last Summer, 1959, Scent of Mystery, 1960, Butterfield 8, 1960 (Acad. award best actress), Cleopatra, 1963, The V.I.P.'s, 1963, The Sandpiper, 1965, Who's Afraid of Virginia Woolf?, 1966 (Acad. award best actress), The Taming of the Shrew, 1967, The Comedians, 1967, Reflections in a Golden Eye, 1967, Dr. Faustus, 1967, Boom!, 1968, Secret Ceremony, 1968, The Only Game in Town, 1970, Under Milkwood, 1971, X, Y and Zee, 1972, Hammersmith Is Out, 1972, Night Watch, 1973, Ash Wednesday, 1973, That's Entertainment, 1974 (guest star), The Driver's Seat, 1974, Blue Bird, 1975, Winter Kills, 1977, A Little Night Music, 1977, The Mirror Crack'd, 1980, Young Toscanini, 1988, The Flintstones, 1994; TV appearances include Divorce His/Divorce Hers, 1973, Victory at Entebbe, 1977, Return Engagement, 1979, Between Friends, 1982, Hotel (series), 1984, Malice in Wonderland, 1986, North and South (miniseries), 1986, There Must Be a Pony, 1986, Poker Alice, 1987, Sweet Bird of Youth, 1989; theatre appearances in The Little Foxes, 1981 (Broadway debut), Private Lives, 1983; narrator film documentary Genocide, 1981; author: (with Richard Burton) World Enough and Time, poetry reading, 1964, Elizabeth Taylor, 1965, Elizabeth Taylor Takes Off: On Weight Gain, Weight Loss, Self Esteem and Self Image, 1988; lics. (fragrances) Elizabeth Taylor's Passion, Passion for Men, White Diamonds/Elizabeth Taylor, Elizabeth Taylor's Diamonds & Emeralds, Diamonds & Rubies, Diamonds & Sapphires, (jewelry) The Elizabeth Taylor Fashion Jewelry Collection for Avon. Active philanthropic, relief, charitable causes internationally, including Israeli War Victims Fund for the Chaim Sheba Hosp., 1976, UNICEF, Variety Children's Hosps., med. clinics in Botswana; initiated Ben Gurion U.-Elizabeth Taylor Fund for Children of the Negev, 1982; supporter AIDS Project L.A., 1985; founder, nat. chmn. Am. Found. for AIDS Rsch. (AmFAR), 1985—, internat. fund, 1985—; founder Elizabeth Taylor AIDS Found., 1991—. Named Comdr. Arts Letters (France), 1985; recipient Legion of Honor (France), 1987 (for work with AmFAR), Aristotle S. Onassis Found. award, 1988, Jean Hersholt Humanitarian Academy award, 1993 (for work as AIDS advocate), Life Achievement award Am. Film Inst., 1993; honored with dedication of Elizabeth Taylor Med. Ctr. Whitman-Walker Clinic, Washington, 1993. Address: care Chen Sam & Assocs Inc 506 E 74th St Ste 3E New York NY 10021-3486

TAYLOR, ELLEN BORDEN BROADHURST, civic worker; b. Goldsboro, N.C., Jan. 18, 1913; d. Jack Johnson and Mabel Moran (Borden) Broadhurst; student Converse Coll., 1930-32; m. Marvin Edward Taylor, June 13, 1936; children: Marvin Edward, Jack Borden, William Lambert. Bd. govs. Elizabethan Garden, Manteo, N.C., 1964-74; mem. Gov. Robert Scott's Adv. Com. on Beautification, N.C., 1971-73; mem. ACE nat. action com. for environ. Nat. Coun. State Garden Clubs, 1973-75; bd. dirs. Keep N.C. Beautiful, 1973-85; mem. steering com., charter mem. bd. dirs. Keep Johnston County (N.C.) Beautiful, 1977-92; life judge roses Am. Rose Soc.; chmn. local com. that published jointly with N.C. Dept. Cultural Resources: An Inventory of Historic Architecture, Smithfield, N.C., 1977; co-chmn. local com. to survey and publish jointly with N.C. Div. Archives and History: Historical Resources of Johnston County, 1980-91; charter life mem. N.C. Mus. History Assocs., 1994; charter mem. founder's circle New Mus. History Bldg., Raleigh, 1994. Mem. Nat. Coun. State Garden Clubs (life; master judge flower shows), Johnston County Hist. Soc. (charter), Johnston County Arts Coun. (Spl. award for 1987 projects of Pub. Libr. Johnston County & Smithfield 1965-87), N.C. Geneal. Soc. (charter), Johnston County Geneal. Soc. (charter), Hist. Preservation Soc. N.C. (life), N.C. Art Soc. (life). Democrat. Episcopalian. Clubs: Smithfield (N.C.) Garden (charter; pres. 1969-71), Smithfield Woman's (v.p. 1976), DAR (organizing vice-regent chpt. 1976), Gen. Soc. Mayflower Descs. (life), Descs. of Richard Warren, Nat. Soc. New Eng. Women (charter mem. Carolina Capital chpt.), Colonial Dames Am. (life), Magna Charta Dames, Nat. Soc. Daus. of Founders and Patriots Am. Home: 616 Hancock St Smithfield NC 27577-4008

TAYLOR, ELOUISE CHRISTINE, artist; b. Berkeley, Calif., Sept. 17, 1923; d. Charles Vincent and Lola Lucile (Felder) T.; m. P.S. Carnohan, Sept. 8, 1947 (div. 1982); children: Marcus Jay, Max Todd, Cecilia Ann. Student, Chgo. Opera Ballet Sch., Hollywood, Calif., 1941, San Francisco Opera Ballet Sc. Featured skater Sonja Henie Hollywood Ice Revue, 1941-51, Ctr. Theater, N.Y.; artist Reno, Nev.; instr. figure skating and painting. Oil paintings featured in numerous group and one-woman shows; portrait of Sonja Henie and several others in permanent collection at World Figure Skating Hall of Fame and Mus., Colorado Springs, Colo.; paintings exhibited local shows Los Altos, Calif., 1970-74, Santa Rosa, 1974-79, also Half Moon Bay-Shoreline Sta. Gallery & art shows, 1981, 82, Parklane Mall, Reno, Nev., 1993; numerous commd. paintings.

TAYLOR, GRACE ELIZABETH WOODALL (BETTY TAYLOR), lawyer, law educator, law library administrator; b. Butler, N.J., June 14, 1926; d. Frank E. and Grace (Carlyon) Woodall; m. Edwin S. Taylor, Feb. 4, 1951 (dec.); children: Carol Lynn Taylor Crespo, Nancy Ann Filer. AB, Fla. State U., 1949, MA, 1950; JD, U. Fla., 1962. Instr. asst. librarian U. Fla., 1950-56; asst. law librarian Univ. Libraries, U. Fla., 1956-62; dir. Legal Info. Ctr., 1962—, prof. law, 1976—; Clarence J. TeSelle prof. of law U. Fla., 1994—; trustee Nat. Ctr. for Automated Rsch., N.Y.C., 1978-96; past chmn. joint com. on LAWNET, Am. Assn. Law Librs., Am. Assn. Law Schs. and ABA, 1978—; cons. to law librs., 1975—; mem. adv. com. N.E. Regional Data Ctr., U. Fla., 1990—. Co-author: American Law Publications, 1986, 21st Century: Technology's Impact, 1988, Law in the Digital Age: The Challenge of Research in Legal Information Centers, 1996, also articles. Recipient 1st Disting. Aluni award Fla. State U. Libr. Sch., 1983; Lewis Scholar Fla. Legislature, 1947-50; grantee NEH, 1981-82, Coun. Libr. Resources, 1984-86. 96Mem. ABA (Law Libr. Congress facilities com. 1991—), Am. Assn. Law Librs. (exe bd. 1981-84), Am. Assn. Law Schs. (accreditation com. 1978-81), OCLC Users Coun. (pres. 1983-86), Phi Beta Kappa (v.p. U. Fla. chpt. 1994-95, pres. 1995-96—), Beta Phi Mu Democrat. Methodist. Office: U Fla Legal Info Ctr Gainesville FL 32611

TAYLOR, HELEN S., civic worker; b. Bloomington, Ind., Nov. 27, 1922; d. Lester Howard Shields and Mary Margaret (Galyan) Shields-Fleener; m. Richard R. Hurst, July 29, 1945 (div. Feb. 1959); children: Pamela Hurst Hayes, Richard S.; m. Clyde Leon Taylor, Dec. 2, 1961; 1 child, John P. AA, Coll. Sequoias, 1975; BA, Calif. State U., Fresno, 1979. bd. dirs. Taylor Machinery, Inc., Visalia, Calif. Author: Japanese Invasion of the Philippines, 1977, Russia Today, 1979. Sponsor Town Hall, Inc., Fresno, 1990-96; past pres. Tulare County Symphony, Visalia, Meth. Women, Visalia, 1952-96; mem. Ice House Theatre, Visalia, 1980-96. Mem. AAUW (grantee 1979), U.S. Fgn. Policy Assn. (co-chair 1986-96), Alpha Gamma Sigma. Democrat. Home: 1545 S Chinowth St Visalia CA 93277 Office: Taylor Machinery Inc 4146 W Mineral King Visalia CA 93291

TAYLOR, JACQUELINE ANN, systems administrator; b. Chgo., May 11, 1950; d. John R. and Edna Madigan; m. Richard LaVern Taylor, Aug. 19, 1972; children: Kristen Nicole, John William. BS in Math., No. Ill. U., 1972. Cert. Novell adminstr. Systems adminstr., acct. Am. Roofing Supply, Evansville, Ind., 1986-88; sr. acct. Challenge Dairy Products, Dublin, Calif., 1988-89; systems adminstr., asst. acctg. mgr. Semco, Carlsbad, Calif., 1989-90; systems adminstr., acting mgr. La Jolla (Calif.) Surgi Ctr. Carson M. Lewis, M.D., 1990-92; systems adminstr., collections adminstr. Coleman Floor Co., Rolling Meadows, Ill., 1993-95; systems adminstr., EDP specialist Village of Glen Ellyn, Ill., 1995—; pres. Oblis Consultants, Barrington, Ill., 1994—. Mem. NAFE. Democrat. Roman Catholic. Home: 205 Rue Touraine Barrington IL 60010

TAYLOR, JANET WINONA MILLS, secondary school educator; b. Shelby, N.C., Aug. 3, 1948; d. Robert Lee Sr. and Janet Elizabeth (Plair) Mills; m. Bernard D. Taylor, Dec. 31, 1983; 1 child, Adam Jason. BS in Health Edn., Morgan State Coll., 1974; MS in Ednl. Leadership, Morgan State U., 1986, EdD in Ednl. Adminstrn., 1994. Md. State Dept. Edn. Advanced Profl. cert. for supt., supr., secondary prin., health and gen. sci. tchr. grades 5-12. Tchr. Baltimore (Md.) City Pub. Schs., 1973-78; health educator Morgan State Coll., Balt., 1978-79; tchr. Montgomery County Pub. Schs., Rockville, 1979—; tech. writer, cons. The Assignment Group, Rockville, Md., 1990—; rsch. cons., rsch. assoc. Inst. for Urban Rsch., Morgan State U., 1992-93; libr. adv. bd. mem. Morgan State U., Balt., 1993—; grant cons. United Missionary Bapt., Inc., Balt., 1993—; GED test adminstr. Md. State Dept. Edn., Balt., 1993-94; co-dir. for grants and proposals United Missionary Bapt. Devel. Corp. Md., Balt., 1993—; mem. selection and evaluation adv. com. Montgomery County Pub. Schs., Rockville, 1993—. Editor (monthly jour.) The Doorkeeper, 1987-88. Dir. youth ministry Mt. Hebron Bapt. Ch., Balt., 1990-94; co-dir. children's ministry Bapt. Congress Christian Edn., Balt., 1992-94; corr. sec. Bapt. Congress Christian Edn., Balt., 1993—. Sgt. USAR, 1975-80. Mem. AERA, Zeta Phi Beta. Baptist. Home: 1822 Wadsworth Way Baltimore MD 21239-3109

TAYLOR, J(OCELYN) MARY, museum administrator, zoologist, educator; b. Portland, Oreg., May 30, 1931; d. Arnold Llewellyn and Kathleen Mary (Yorke) T.; m. Joseph William Kamp, Mar. 18, 1972 (dec.). B.A., Smith Coll., 1952; M.A., U. Calif., Berkeley, 1953, Ph.D., 1959. Instr. zoology Wellesley Coll., 1959-61, asst. prof. zoology, 1961-65; assoc. prof. zoology U. B.C., 1965-74; dir. Cowan Vertebrate Mus., 1965-82, prof. dept. zoology, 1974-82; collaborative scientist Oreg. Regional Primate Research Ctr., 1983-87; prof. (courtesy) dept. fisheries and wildlife Oreg. State U., 1984—; dir. Cleve. Mus. Nat. History, 1987—; adj. prof. dept. biology Case Western Res. U., 1987—. Assoc. editor Jour. Mammalogy, 1981-82. Contbr. numerous articles to sci. jours. Trustee Benjamin Rose Inst., 1988-93, Western Res. Acad., 1989-94, U. Circle, Inc., 1987—, The Cleve. Aquarium, 1990-93, Cleve. Access to the Arts, 1992—; corp. bd. Holden Arboretum, 1988—. Fulbright scholar, 1954-55; Lalor Found. grantee, 1962-63; NSF grantee, 1963-71; NRC Can. grantee, 1966-84; Killam Sr. Research fellow, 1978-79. Mem. Soc. Women Geographers, Am. Soc. Mammalogists (1st v.p. 1978-82, pres. 1982-84, Hartley T. Jackson award 1993, Lake County environ. award 1996), Australian Mammal Soc., Cooper Ornithol., Assn. Sci. Mus. Dirs. (v.p. 1990-93), Rodent Specialist Group of Species Survival Commn. (chmn. 1989-93), Sigma Xi. Episcopalian. Office: Cleve Mus Natural History 1 Wade Oval Dr Cleveland OH 44106-1701

TAYLOR, JUDITH ANN, sales executive; b. Sheridan, Wyo., July 9, 1944; d. Milo G. and Eleanor M. (Wood) Rinker; m. George I. Taylor, Sept. 15, 1962; children: Monte G., Bret A. Fashion dept. mgr. Montgomery Ward, Sheridan, 1968-73; pers. mgr., asst. mgr. Dan's Ranchwear, Sheridan, 1973-80; sales/prodn. coord. KWYO Radio, Sheridan, 1981-83; sales mgr., promotions coord. KROE Radio, Sheridan, 1984—; mng. editor BOUNTY Publ., 1993—; notary pub. State of Wyo., 1985—; lectr., instr. BSA Merit U.; lectr. acad. achievement LVA Adv. Bd., 1993—, instr. Tongue River Middle Sch. Academic Enrichmen t Program, 1994-95; S.C. Ambs., 1980—, pres., 1995—. mng. editor BOUNTY Publ., 1993—. Sec.-treas. Sheridan County Centennial Com., 1986-89; local sec.-treas. Wyo. Centennial Com., Sheridan, 1986-90; exec. dir. Sheridan-Wyo. Rodeo Bd., 1983—; bd. dirs. Sheridan County Fair Bd., 1991—, treas., 1995—; bd. dirs. "Christmas in April" Sheridan County, 1992—; mem. WJTP Coun., Cheyenne, 1990-92; mem. adv. coun. Tutor-Literacy Vols. of Am., 1993—; Mrs. Santa Claus for local groups; vol. coord. AIDS Quilt. Mem. Wyo. Assn. Broadcasters, S.C. C. of C. (dir. 1988—, pres. 1989-91), UMWA Aux. (pres. 1982-89), Kiwanis (v.p. 1992—, pres.-elect 1993, pres. 1994), S.C. Ambassadors (pres. 1995—), Ft. Phil Kearney/Bozeman Trail (bd. dirs. 1995—). Democrat. Christian Ch. Home: 98 Decker Rd Sheridan WY 82801-9612 Office: KROE AM PO Box 5086 Sheridan WY 82801-1386

TAYLOR, JUDITH ANNE, librarian; b. Bklyn., July 21, 1937; d. Edward S. and Ida (Osterland) Weber; m. Arnold H. Taylor, July 17, 1960; children: Beth Allison, Lynn Erica. BA, Barnard Coll., 1959; MS, Columbia U., 1960, postgrad., 1960-62; postgrad., L.I. U., 1970-72, U. Colo., 1980, 81. Cert. tchr., N.Y.; pub. libr., N.Y. Reference libr. CUNY, 1960-61; rsch. libr. Barnard Coll., N.Y.C., 1961-63; edn. libr. CUNY, Flushing, 1963-68; reference libr. Plainview (N.Y.)-Old Bethpage Pub. Libr., 1968-70; libr. media specialist Plainview-Old Bethpage Schs., 1970-72, Manhasset (N.Y.) Jr. High Sch., 1972-95; adj. prof. grad. program in libr. info sci. Palmer Libr. Sch. C.W. Post Univ., 1995—; bd. dirs. tchr. Resource Ctr., Manhasset Schs., 1986-90, dist.-wide and county wide tech. coms.; presenter workshops ALA, N.Y. Libr. Assn.; cons., presenter Nassau Sch. Libr. System. Author: Great Paperback Contest, 1980, newsletter Link Up, 1988-90; contbr. articles to profl. jours. Triviathon organizer, participant United Cerebral Palsy, Roosevelt, N.Y., 1989-95; bd. trustees Internat. Brotherhood Elec. Workers Scholarship Alumnae, 1985—. Mem. ALA, N.Y. Libr. Assn. (sch. libr. media sect.), N.Y. State United Tchrs., L.I. Sch. Media Assn., Nassau Sch. Libr. Assn. (rep. sys. coun. 1989-92, cluster leader 1987-92, liaison 1988-95), Manhasset Edn. Assn., Barnard Coll. Alumnae Assn. (class corr. 1984-89, coun. 1984-89). Jewish. Home: 90 Virginia Ave Plainview NY 11803-3626

TAYLOR, KAREN A., film company executive. Sr. v.p. fin. Carolco Pictures, L.A. Office: Carolco Pictures 8800 Sunset Blvd Los Angeles CA 90069*

TAYLOR, KAREN ANNETTE, mental health nurse; b. Kinston, N.C., Oct. 7, 1952; d. Emmett Green and Polly Ann (Taylor) Tyndall; m. Paul Othell Taylor Jr., June 24, 1979; 1 child, Clarissa Anne. AA, Lenoir C.C., Kinston, 1972; Diploma, Lenoir Meml. Hosp. Sch. of, Nursing, 1984; student, St. Joseph's Coll., Windham, Maine, 1993-94. RN, N.C. Staff nurse Lenoir Meml. Hosp., 1984-86; staff nurse, relief patient care dir. Brynn Marr Hosp., Jacksonville, N.C., 1987-90; staff nurse, quality assurance Naval Hosp., Camp Lejeune, N.C., 1990-92. Recipient Meritorious Unit Commendation Am. Fedn. of Govt. Employees, 1992. Baptist.

TAYLOR, KATHERINE LYNN, ecologist; b. Urbana, Ill., July 27, 1965; d. Max Daryl and Kay Ellen (Howard) T. BS, Western Wash. U., 1986, MS, 1988; PhD, La. State U., 1992. Teaching asst. dept. chemistry Western Wash. U., Bellingham, 1985-86, teaching asst. dept. biology, 1986-88; Bd. Regents Grad. fellow dept. botany La. State U., Baton Rouge, 1988-92; asst. prof. biology Coastal Carolina U., Conway, S.C., 1992-94; dir. Columbia River Estuary Study Task Force, Astoria, Oreg., 1996—; pvt. practice botany cons., Seattle, 1987. Contbr. articles and abstracts to profl. jours. Recipient Environ. Ednl. grant EPA. Mem. AAUW, LWV, Ecol. Soc. Am., Bot. Aos. Am., Am. Inst. Biol. Scis., Soc. Wetland Scientists, Sigma Xi (Grant-in-Aid of Rsch. 1989). Office: CREST 750 Commercial St Rm 205 Astoria OR 97103

TAYLOR, KAY, artist; b. Birmingham, Ala., Oct. 12, 1966; d. James Herbert and Alfreda Kay Taylor; m. Carey Phillips Williams. BFA, U. Ala., Birmingham, 1991, MA, 1995. Exhibited in group shows at Birmingham Art Assn. exhbns., 1987—, U. Ala., Birmingham, 1991, Art Students League, Tuscaloosa, 1992, Monty Stabler Galleries, 1993-96, La Gallerie, Shayne, Montreal, Quebec, Canada, Affinity Gallery, Grayton Beach, Fla.; selected to make Christmas ornament White House Christmas Tree through U. Ala., Birmingham, 1994; corporate collections include Woodward & Williams, Birmingham, B.E. & K., Birminham, U. Ala., Birmingham Med. Group. Art tchr. underprivileged children Jefferson County Housing Authority, Birmingham, 1993; mem. Ballet Guild, 1991—, Shipmates, 1987—, Nat. Mus. of Women in the Arts. Recipient Phi Mu Purchase award Art Students League exhbn., 1992, Emerging Artist award Magic City Art Connection, 1990, Award of Distinction, 14th Juried Student Ann. Exhbn., Birmingham, 1990. Birmingham Art Assn. Methodist.

TAYLOR, L. ANN, financial analyst; b. N.Y.C., Apr. 10, 1965; d. Robert Lee Taylor and Margaret Lena Gray. BS, Cornell U., 1986; postgrad., Simmons Coll., 1995—. Human resources mgr. Shearson Lehman, N.Y.C., 1986-87; database mgr. Thomson Fin./Securities Data, Newark, 1987-91; asst. treas. Bankers Trust, N.Y.C., 1991-92; nat. adminstr. NAACP Econ. Devel., Balt., 1992-94; analyst U.S. Trust, Boston, 1994—. V.p. Cornell Black Alumni Assn., N.Y.C., 1992-93. Office: US Trust 40 Court St Boston MA 02108

TAYLOR, LESLI ANN, pediatric surgery educator; b. N.Y.C., Mar. 2, 1953; d. Charles Vincent Taylor and Valene Patricia (Blake) Garfield. BFA, Boston U., 1975; MD, Johns Hopkins U., 1981. Diplomate Am. Bd. Surgery. Surg. resident Beth Israel Hosp., Boston, 1981-88; rsch. fellow Pediatric Rsch. Lab. Mass. Gen. Hosp., Boston, 1984-86; fellow pediatric surgery Children's Hosp. of Phila., Phila., 1988-90; asst. prof. pediatric surgery U. N.C., Chapel Hill, 1990—. Author: (booklet) Think Twice: The Medical Effects of Physical Punishment, 1985. Recipient Nat. Rsch. Svc. award NIH, 1984-86. Fellow Am. Coll. Surgeons; mem. AMA, Am. Acad. Pediatrics, Am. Pediat. Surg. Assn.

TAYLOR, LILI, actress; b. Chgo., 1967. Appeared in films Mystic Pizza, Say Anything, Born on the Fourth of July, Bright Angel, Dogfight, Watch It, Household Saints, Short Cuts, Rudy, Arizona Dream, Mrs. Park and the Vicious Circle, Ready to Wear, The Addiction, Cold Fever, I Shot Andy Warthol; broadway plays include What Did He See, Aven U Boys; regional plays include Mud, The Love Talker, Fun. Office: care William Morris Agy 151 El Camino Beverly Hills CA 90212*

TAYLOR, LINDA RATHBUN, investment banker; b. Rochester, N.Y., May 25, 1946; d. Leis Standish and Elizabeth Florence (Hunt) Rathbun; m. Donald Gordon Taylor, Mar. 1, 1975; children: Alexander Standish, Abigail Elizabeth, Elizabeth Downing. BA, Vasser Coll., 1968; MBA, Harvard U., 1973. Chartered fin. analyst. Assoc. corp. fin. Donaldson, Lufkin & Jenrette, N.Y.C., 1973-75; cons. IBRD, Washington, 1975; fin. analyst U.S. Treas. Dept., Washington, 1976-78; chief investment officer United Mine Workers Fund, 1978-85; investment mgr. Cen. Pension Fund Internat. Union Oper. Engrs., Wahington, 1985-86; investment banker Saranow Co., 1986-89; pvt. investor, 1990—; pres. Pony Prodns., Inc. Trustee Montgomery County (Md.) Employees' Retirement Sys., 1987-93, Washington Internat. Horse Show, bd. dirs., 1995—; com. mem. Vassar Coll. Endowment Fund, 1992—; elder Bradley Hills Presbyn. Ch., 1992—; bd.pensions Presbyn. Ch. U.S.A., 1996—, dir. bd. pensions, 1996— . Contbr. articles to profl. jours. Mem. Jr. League Washington, Washington Soc. Investment Analysts (bd. dirs. 1984-85), Fin. Analyst Fedn. Republican.

TAYLOR, LINNEA BERGUND, secretary; b. Princeton, Minn., Sept. 20, 1938; d. Harold William and Lenora (Mitchell) Berglund. Student, San Francisco Art Inst., 1965-66. Sec. to v.p. Crocker Bank, San Francisco, 1963—; sec. adminstrv. officer Fed. Housing Adminstrn., San Francisco, 1966—. Mem. NOW, Multnomah County (Oreg.) Hon. Sheriff's Assn., Police Assn. Booster. Democrat. Presbyterian. Home: 731 SW Salmon St Portland OR 97205

TAYLOR, MARETTA MITCHELL, state legislator; b. Columbus, Ga., Jan. 25, 1935. BS, Albany State, 1957; MS, Ind. U., 1966. Mem. Ga. Ho. of Reps., 1991-92, 93—; mem. edn., retirement, state planning and cmty. affairs coms.; co-owner, mgr. Designers Ltd., 1987—. Democrat. Baptist. Home: 1203 Bunker Hill Rd Columbus GA 31907-6718 Office: Ga House of Reps State Capitol Atlanta GA 30334*

TAYLOR, MARGARET ALEXANDER, newspaper publisher; b. Magnolia, Ark., June 12, 1926; d. Sam Pickering and Louie Maye (Falkner) Alexander; m. Joe Wayne Taylor, Sept. 12, 1948 (dec. Feb. 1978); children: Deborah Ann Taylor Starks, Timothy Wayne. AA, Magnolia A&M Coll., 1946; BS in Home Economics, Oklahoma A&M Coll., 1948. Pub./editor The Davis News, Davis, Okla., 1978-92; retired, 1992. Mem. Okla. Press Assn. (bd. dirs. 1983-92, pres. 1990-91), Order of Eastern Star, Akomda Club, Omicron Nu, Phi Kappa Phi. Democrat. Baptist. Home and Office: The Davis News Inc 1008 S 5th St Davis OK 73030-3317

TAYLOR, MARGARET TURNER, clothing designer, economist, writer, planner; b. Wilmington, N.C., May 7, 1944. A.B. in Econs., Smith Coll., 1966; M.A. in Econ. History, U. Pa., 1970, now Ph.D. candidate in City and Regional Planning. Tchr. Jefferson Jr. High Sch., New Orleans, 1966-69; instr. econs. U. Tex.-El Paso, 1974-75; adj. prof. econs., Salisbury State U., Md., 1976-78; prin. mgr., designer Margaret Norriss, women's clothing, Salisbury, Md., 1980-95; owner Functional Design Ideas, Inc., 1995—; planner at Wharton Ctr. Applied Research, Phila., 1985-86; planning cons., writer.

TAYLOR, MARGARET WISCHMEYER, retired English language and journalism educator; b. Terre Haute, Ind., Aug. 5, 1920; d. Carl and Grace (Riehle) Wischmeyer; m. John Edward Taylor, Sept. 5, 1942 (dec. 1988); children: Deborah Ann, Tobin Edward, Mary Leesa. BA magna cum laude, Duke U., Durham, 1941; MA, John Carroll U., Cleve., 1973. Feature writer Dayton Daily News, Dayton, 1945-53; freelance writer Cleve., 1953—; asst. to Dr. Joseph B. Rhine Duke U. Parapsychology Lab., Durham, 1941; asst. prof. English and journalism Ea. Campus, Cuyahoga C.C., Cleve., 1973-92, prof. emeritus, 1992—, advisor campus newspaper, 1973-84, dir. Writers Conf., 1975-90; writing cons., editor various cos. and pubs., Cleve., 1973—; founder, operator Grammar Hot Line, 1987-92. Author: Crystal Lake Reflections, 1985, English 101 Can Be Fun, 1991, The Basic English Handbook, 1995. Recipient top state honors Ohio Newspaper Women's Assn., 1947, award for best ednl., best overall stories Am. Heart Assn., 1970, Besse award for teaching excellence, 1980, Nat. Teaching Excellence award Coun. for Advancement and Support of Edn., 1989; named Ohio Outstanding Citizen, Ohio Ho. Reps., 1987, 89, Innovator of Yr., League for Innovations in C.C.s, 1988. Mem. Mensa, Phi Beta Kappa. Presbyterian. Home: 27900 Fairmount Blvd Cleveland OH 44124-4616

TAYLOR, MARY ALICE, delivery service executive; b. West Point, Miss., Feb. 11, 1950; d. James and Mary Alice (Talbot) Wooten; m. Robert Glenn Taylor, Apr. 28; children: Mary Carole, Emily Cristen. BA in Bus., Miss. State U., 1971; LHD (hon.), So. Coll. Optometry, 1994. Sr. acct. Shell Oil Co., New Orleans, 1971-73; contr. Cook Industries, Memphis, Tenn., 1973-77; fin. planning mgr. Northern Telecom., Memphis, 1977-80; sr. mgmt. info. systems Fed. Express Corp., Memphis, 1980-82, mgr. fin., 1982-83, mng. dir. bus. svc. ctr. divsn., 1983-85, v.p. logistics, 1985-88, v.p. so. region ground ops., 1988-91, sr. v.p. ctrl. support svcs., 1991-94, sr. v.p. U.S. and Can., 1994—; bd. dirs. Perrigo Co., Allegan, Mich., Autodesk, San Rafael, Calif., Allstate Corp., Chgo. Exec. dir. Chikasaw Coun. Boy Scouts Am., Memphis; mem. external rsch. adv. com. Miss. State U., exec. adv. bd. Transp. Studies MIT. Roman Catholic.

TAYLOR, MARY ANN BURNS, municipal official; b. Butler, Pa., Nov. 8, 1932; d. Arthur Roscoe and Mary Aleene (Stewart) Burns; m. Robert Gates Taylor, Dec. 27, 1955 (dec. Mar., 1970); children: Mary Annette, Robert Arthur, Melissa Beth. BS, U. Pitts., 1954; postgrad. studies, Lehigh U., 1954-55. From monitor to program dir. weatherization monitor Butler (Pa.) County, 1974-77; program analyst Pa. Dept. Comty. Affairs, Harrisburg, 1977-93; elected supr. S. Middleton Twp, Boiling Springs, Pa., 1994—. Pres., Butler Br. AAUW, 1969-70, Nixon Area Rep. Women, Butler, 1969-70, Boiling Springs Civic Assn., 1990. Mem. Boiling Spring Lions Club (bd. dirs.). Presbyterian. Home: PO Box 337 Boiling Springs PA 17007

TAYLOR, MARY ELIZABETH, retired recreation administrator, retired dietitian; b. Medina, N.Y., Dec. 10, 1933; d. Glenn Aaron and Viola Hazel (Lansill) Grimes; m. Wilbur Alvin Fredlund, Apr. 12, 1952 (div. Jan. 1980); 1 child, Wilbur Jr.; m. Frederick Herbert Taylor, Mar. 15, 1981; children: Martha Dayton, Jean Grout, Beth Stern, Cindy Hey, Carol McLellan, Cheryl Dearborn, Robert. BS in Food and Nutrition, SUCB, Buffalo, 1973; MEd in Health Sci. Edn. and Evaluation, SUNY, 1978. Registered dietitian, 1977. Diet cook Niagara Sanitorium, Lockport, N.Y., 1953-56; cook Mount View Hosp., Lockport, N.Y., 1956-60, asst. dietitian, 1960-73, dietitian, food svc. dir., 1973-79, cons. dietitian, 1979-81; instr. Erie Community Coll., Williamsville, N.Y., 1979-81; sch. lunch coord. Nye County Sch. Dist., Tonopah, Nev., 1982-93; retired Nye County Sch. Dist., 1993; food svc. mgmt. cons., fin. mgmt. advisor pvt. practice, 1994—; activity dir. Preferred Equity Corp. Recreation Vehicle Resort, Pahrump, Nev., 1993-95; ret., 1996; cons. dietitian Nye Gen. Hosp., Tonopah, 1983-88; adj. instr. Erie Community Coll., Williamsville, 1978-79; nutrition instr. for coop. extension Clark County Community Coll., 1990—; cons. Group Purchasing Western N.Y. Hosp. Adminstrs., Buffalo, 1975-79, vice-chmn. adv. com., 1976-78; cons. BOCES, Lockport, 1979-81. Nutrition counselor Migrant Workers Clinic, Lockports, 1974-80; mem. Western N.Y. Soc. for Hosp. Food Svc. Adminstrn., 1974-81; nutritionist Niagara County Nutrition Adv. Com., 1977-81. Recipient Outstanding Woman of the Yr., YWCA-UAW Lockport, 1981, Disting. Health Care Food Adminstrn. Recognition award Am. Soc. for Hosp. Food Svc. Adminstrs., 1979, USDA award Outstanding Lunch Program in Nev. and Western Region, 1986, 91. Mem. Am. Assn. Ret. Persons, Am. Sch. Food Svc. Assn. (bd. dirs. 1987, 92-93, cert. dir. II 1987, 5-yr. planning com. 1990, mem. ann. confs. 1988-93), Am. Dietetic Assn. (nat. referral system for registered dietitians 1992-93), So. Nev. Dietetic Assn. (pres. 1985-86), Nev. Food Svc. Assn. (participant ann. meetings 1990-93), Nutrition Today Soc., Nev. Sch. Food Svcs. Assn. (dietary guidelines com. 1991-93). Republican. Baptist. Home: 481 N Murphy PO Box 656 Pahrump NV 89041-0656

TAYLOR, MARY ROSS, artistic administrator; b. Pine Bluff, Ark., Jan. 26, 1945; d. Pinchback Taylor Jr. and Betty (Strickland) Abbott. BA, Vanderbilt U., 1967; MA, U. Tenn., 1969; postgrad., U. Tex., 1969-72; MA, John F. Kennedy U., Orinda, Calif., 1995. Propr., mgr. The Bookstore, Houston, 1973-83; project dir. Through the Flower Corp., Benicia, Calif., 1983-85, exec. dir., 1985-90; exec. dir. Lawndale Art and Performance Ctr., Houston, 1991—; mem. adv. bd. Nat. Mus. Women in Arts, Washington, 1991—. Mem. Tex. Gov.'s Commn. on Women, 1991-93. Mem. Leadership Am. Assn. (pres. 1989). Home: 1816 Kipling Houston TX 77098 Office: 4912 Main St Houston TX 77002

TAYLOR, MILDRED D., author. Vol., tchr. English and history Peace Corps, Ethiopia; then recruiter Peace Corps, U.S.; study skills coord. black edn. program U. Colo. Author: (children's fiction) Song of the Trees, 1975, Roll of Thunder, Hear My Cry, 1976, Let the Circle Be Unbroken, 1981, The Gold Cadillac, 1987, The Friendship and Other Stories, 1987, Mississippi Bridge, 1990, The Road to Memphis, 1990, The Well, 1995. Address: care Dial Books For Young Readers 375 Hudson St New York NY 10014-3658*

TAYLOR, NANCY MURRELL, management executive; b. Lansing, Mich., Aug. 16, 1954; d. Edward Charles and Josephine Ann (Mc Donald) Murrell; m. John Cameron Taylor, Aug. 21, 1977. BA, Mich. State U., 1976. Market analyst Ned Lloyd Swire, Sydney, Australia, 1979-80; exec. dir. Calhoun County Reps., Battle Creek, Mich., 1981-83; program dir. Cmty. Action Coun., Burnsville, Minn., 1983-85; from adminstrv. asst. to asst. exec. Rep. caucus Mich. Ho. Reps., Lansing, 1985-91, dir. comms., 1991-95, dir. office of clk. of house, 1995—; oversight com. Exec. Info. Sys., Lansing. Legis. liaison Williamston (Mich.) Elem. PTA, 1996. Mem. Am. Soc. Legis. Clks. & Secs. Office: Office of Clk Mich Ho Reps State Capitol 2d Fl Lansing MI 48913

TAYLOR, PAMELA S., special education educator; b. Conway, Ark., Jan. 9, 1969; d. Ben and Della Mae (Trammell) T. AA Gen. Edn., N. Ark. C.C., 1989; BS in Edn., U. Ctrl. Ark., 1992. Cert. tchr., Ark. Spl. edn. tchr. Witts Spring (Ark.) Sch., 1993—; ednl. trainer Ark. Pediatric Facility, North Little Rock, 1993. Mem. Coun. for Exceptional Children, Order of Eastern Star. Republican. Baptist. Home: Rte 2 Box 18 Saint Joe AR 72675

TAYLOR, PATRICIA KRAMER, nurse; b. Kempton, Germany, Nov. 20, 1948; came to U.S., 1950; d. Claude John and Dorothy Ruth (Carpenter) Kramer; m. Robert Lemuel Taylor Sr., Oct. 8, 1971; children: Robert Lemuel Jr., John Barden, William Russell. BSN, Duke U., 1971. RN, N.C.; cert. post anesthesia nurse; cert. ACLS, BLS Instr., PALS, TNCC. Staff nurse Duke U. Med. Ctr., Durham, N.C., 1971-73; office nurse Drs. Proctor, Gaddy & Johnston, Raleigh, N.C., 1973; clin. staff nurse Wake Med. Ctr., Raleigh, N.C., 1973-74, surg. staff nurse, 1974-78, staff nurse PACU, 1978—. Den, pack leader Boy Scouts Am., Knightdale, N.C., 1981-90; pres. Phillips H.S. PTA, 1994-95. Mem. Triangle Assn. Post Anesthesia Nurses, N.C. Assn. Post Anesthesia Nurses (treas. 1995—), Am. Soc. Post Anesthesia Nurses, N.C. Assn. Perianesthesia Nurses (treas. 1995-97). Home: PO Box 646 Knightdale NC 27545-0646 Office: Wake Med Ctr Post Anesthesia Care Unit PO Box 14465 Raleigh NC 27620-4465

TAYLOR, ROSEMARY, artist; b. Joseph, Oreg.; d. Theodore and Sarah A. (Lambright) Resch; student Cleve. Inst. Art, 1937-40, NYU, 1947; m. Robert Hull Taylor; children: Barbara Taylor Ryalls, Robert H. Tchr. pottery Rahway (N.J.) Art Center, 1950-55; one-woman shows: Paterson (N.J.) Coll., 1964, Westchester (Pa.) Coll., 1970, Gallery 100, Princeton, N.J., 1967, George Jensen's, N.Y.C., 1972, Artisan Gallery, Princeton, 1974, Am. Crafts (Ohio), 1979-94, Guild Gallery, 1986-91, Little Art Gallery, N.C., 1985-94, 95, Olde Queens Gallery (N.J.), 1987, N.J. Designer Craftsmen, 1990 (bd. dirs. 1986-87, standard chmn., 1994), Creative Hands, 95, Princeton, 1994; group shows include: Mus. Natural History, N.Y.C., Newark Mus., Trenton (N.J.) Mus., Montclair (N.J.) Mus., Phila. Art Alliance, Pa. Horticulture Soc., 1988, Nat. Design Center, N.Y.C., Michener Mus., Pa., 1996; represented in permanent collection Westchester Coll.; pottery cons. McCalls Mag., 1962-72. Bd. dirs. Solebury Community Sch.; mem. Fulbright award com., 1982, 83. Mem. LWV (pres. Plainfield, N.J. chpt.). Mem. Am. Craft Council, N.J. Designer-Craftsmen, Phila. Craft Group, Bucks County (Pa.) C. of C., Visual Artists and Galleries Assn., Nat. Assn. Am. Penwoman, Michener Mus., Doylestown, Pa., Women in the Arts (charter). Democrat. Unitarian. Home: PO Box 46 Lumberville PA 18933-0046 Office: PO Box 282 Stockton NJ 08559-0282

TAYLOR, SANDRA JEAN, artist; b. Webster, Mass., Dec. 29, 1957; d. Carl Alfred and Frances Thelma (Houlberg) T. BA, Anna Maria Coll. Art dir. Rotman's, Worcester, Mass., 1982-85; designer Neon Jungle, Worcester, Mass., 1986-90; from artist to dir. preproduction Heinrich Ceramic Decal, Worcester, Mass., 1990—. Editor: Liquid Lovers, 1989. Mem. Pastel Soc. Am., Digital Printers Instn., Worcester Computer Soc. Office: Heinrich Ceramic Decal 150 Goddard Meml Dr Worcester MA 01603

TAYLOR, SHERRILL RUTH, management educator; b. Endwell, N.Y., July 9, 1943; d. Wallace Bixby and Lillie Mary (Sprague) Ingalls; m. William Leon Taylor, July 18, 1964; children: Mark William, Tammie Ann. BBA, Tex. Women's U., 1983, MBA, 1986. Cert. profl. human resources. Pers. rep. Tex. Women's U., Denton, Tex., 1986-87; fleet upgrade coord. Xerox Corp., Oakland, Calif., 1987-88; with Sun Diamond Growers, Pleasanton, Calif., 1988-90; mgmt. lectr. Tex. Women's U., 1990—, dir. Small Bus. Inst., 1993—. Mem. Denton Pers. Assn., Small Bus. Inst. Dirs. Assn., Southwestern Small Bus. Inst. Assn., Internat. Credit Assn. Denton County (sec. 1995), Job Svc. Employers Com. Methodist. Office: Tex Women's U Dept Bus PO Box 425738 Denton TX 76204

TAYLOR, SHIRLEY MAUDEAN, healthcare administrator; b. Black Oak, Ark., June 3, 1939; d. Willia Mathis and Maymie Lele (Osborne) Jones; m. Larry E. Taylor, Sept. 18, 1959 (div. Aug. 1992); children: Mickey Lynn Taylor Mustin, Tine Rose Taylor Bass, Larry E. II. Cert. nurse asst., IRCC Coll., 1987. Owner, adminstr. assisted homes Shirley Taylor Retirement Homes, Port St. Lucie, Fla., 1990—. Mem. Coun. on Aging, Okeechobee, Fla., 1977-80. Mem. Fla. Assisted Living Assn. (pres. 1994—, Appreciation award 1994), St. Lucie County C. of C. (bd. dirs. 1995). Republican. Home: 686 SW Lucero Dr Port Saint Lucie FL 34983

TAYLOR, SUZANNE MARIE, art educator; b. Walnut Creek, Calif., Jan. 20, 1963; d. Frederick Ronald and Maryan Ruth (Nelson) Jessen; m. Robert William Taylor, Mar. 27, 1988; 1 child, Alexander Jason. BS, Loma Linda U., 1994. Cert. art educator, Alaska, Calif. Substitute tchr. Long Beach (Calif.) Unified Sch. Dist., 1985-87, So. Calif. Conf. of Seventh-day Adventists, Glendale, Calif., 1982-88; sec., asst. treas. Long Beach Seventh-day Adventist Ch., 1981-89; art tchr. L.A. Unified Sch. Dist., 1989-93, Delta Greely Sch. Dist., Delta Junction, Alaska, 1993—; chairperson art curriculum com. Delta Junction, 1994-96; participant The Calif. Arts Project, Northridge, Calif., 1993. Artist (sculptures): Anasazi Pueblo, 1986, Hugo, 1995, (watercolor) Sitka Waterfowl, 1991. Art advisor Festival of Lights com., Delta Junction, 1994. Recipient Visual and Performing Arts grant State of Calif., L.A., 1991. Mem. Delta Greely Edn. Assn. (sec. 1994-96). Republican. Seventh-day Adventist. Home: PO Box 1418 Delta Junction AK 99737 Office: Delta High Sch Pouch 1 Delta Junction AK 99737

TAYLOR, SUZANNE ROCHELLE, educational specialist; b. Houston, Dec. 12, 1963; d. Roy Wright and JoAnn (Rochelle) T. AA, Wharton County Jr. Coll., Wharton, Tex., 1983; BS, S.W. Tex. State U., San Marcos, 1985; postgrad., U. Tex., Houston. Cons. Gulf Coast Regional Blood Ctr., Houston, 1990-93; health edn. coord. Tex. Children's Hosp., Houston, 1993-95; program mgr. Cable Healthcare, Austin, Tex., 1995; ednl. specialist U. Tex./M.D. Anderson Cancer Ctr., Houston, 1995—; cons. Children's Med. Mus., Houston, 1995, Tex. Children's Cancer Ctr., Houston, 1994-95. Vol. Am. Cancer Soc., Houston, 1988-91, Lupus Found. Am., Houston, 1994-95. Mem. Patient Edn. Coun. Methodist.

TAYLOR, TERRY R., editor, educator; b. Valley Forge, Pa., Oct. 4, 1952; d. Thomas R. and Anna P. (Bystrek) T. BA in Journalism, Temple U., 1974. Reporter gen. assignments, sch. news Charlotte (N.C.) News, 1974-77; supr., writer AP, Phila., 1977-81; supr., writer sports desk AP, N.Y.C., 1981-85, asst. editor sports, 1985-87, dep. editor sports, 1987-91, asst. chief bur., 1991-92, editor sports, 1992—; asst. editor sports N.Y. Times, 1991; assoc. in journalism Columbia U., N.Y.C., 1991-95; adv. bd. Honda Awards, 1996—. Recipient John A. Domino Meml. award St. Bonaventure U., 1996. Roman Catholic. Office: AP Sports 50 Rockefeller Plz New York NY 10020-1605

TAYLOR, THERESA EVERETH, registered nurse, artist; b. Carthage, N.Y., Aug. 9, 1938; d. Michael Patrick and Angelina (Cerroni) Evereth; m. James Edgar Taylor II, Mar. 12, 1966; children: Britt, Priscilla, Blackwell. Diploma in nursing, House of Good Samaritan Sch. Nursing, Watertown, N.Y., 1959; BFA summa cum laude, Ursuline Coll., 1992, postgrd., 1996—. RN, N.Y., Ohio. Home health nurse DON Brason's Willcare, Cleve., 1995—. Exhbns. in group shows. Pres. Wasmer Gallery Coun., Pepper Pike, Ohio, 1992-96; clk. vestry St. Christophers by the River, Gates Mills, 1979-81; treas. Welcome Wagon, Chesterland, Ohio, 1984-85; vol. artist Cleve. Ctr. Contemporary Art, 1993—; hospice vol.; art therapy intern. Home: 12060 Caves Rd Chesterland OH 44026-2104 Office: 6151 Wilson Mills Highland Heights OH 44143

TAYLOR, VESTA FISK, real estate broker, educator; b. Ottawa County, Okla., July 15, 1917; d. Ira Sylvester and Judie Maude (Garman) Fisk; m. George E. Taylor, Aug. 17, 1957 (dec. Oct. 1963); stepchildren: Joyce, Jean, Luther. AA, Northeastern Okla. A&M, 1931; BA, N.E. State U., Tahlequah, Okla., 1937; MA, Okla. State U., 1942. Life cert. Spanish, English, history, elem. Tchr. rural sch. grades 1-4 Ottawa County, Okla., 1931-33; tchr. rural sch. grades 1-8 Ottawa County, 1933-38; tchr. H.S.

Spanish, English Wyandotte, Okla., 1938-42; tchr. H.S. Spanish, English, math. Miami, Okla., 1942-57; tchr. H.S. Spanish Jacksonville, Ill., 1960-65; tchr. H.S. Spanish, English Miami, 1965-79; owner, broker First Lady Realty, Miami, 1979—; tchr. real estate for licensing N.E. Okla. Vocat.-Tech., Afton, 1980—; radio spellmaster weekly-county groups Coleman Theater Stage, 1954-57, radio program weekly 4-H, Miami, 1953-57. Author: (poem) The Country School, 1994. Sec. Ottawa County Senior's Ctr., 1993—; restoration com. Friends of Theater, 1993—; mem. Friends of the Libr. Named Outstanding Coach Ottawa County 4-H Clubs, Miami, 1955, 67, Outstanding Alumnus All Yrs. H.S. Reunion, Wyandotte, Okla., 1992, Champion Speller N.E. Okla. Retirees, Oklahoma City, 1991. Mem. AAUW (pres. 1978-80, treas. 1994—), Ottawa County ret. Educators (treas. 1990—), Spanish Study Club (pres., instr. 1962-63), Miami Classroom Tchrs. (v.p. 1973-77), Tri-State travel Club (purser 1989—), Kappa Kappa Iota. Democrat. Baptist. Home: 821 Jefferson St Miami OK 74354-4910 Office: First Lady Realty 206 A St NW Miami OK 74354

TAYLOR, VIRGINIA S., lawyer; b. Quitman, Ga.; d. Allen Candler and Anne (Sanderson) Smith; divorced; children: Anne Taylor Hendry, Thomas Fielding. AB, Smith Coll., 1961; JD with distinction, Emory U., 1977. Bar: Ga. 1977, U.S. Dist. Ct. (no. dist.) Ga. 1977, U.S. Dist. Ct. (mid. dist.) Ga. 1979, U.S. Dist. Ct. (ea. dist.) Mich. 1988, U.S. Ct. Appeals (fed. cir.) 1982, U.S. Supreme Ct. 1981. Assoc. Kilpatrick & Cody, Atlanta, 1977-83, ptnr., 1983—. V.p. Olmstead Parks Soc., Atlanta, 1985-93; bd. dirs. Piedmont Park Conservancy, Atlanta, 1991—, YWCA Metro. Atlanta, 1989-92, Leadership Atlanta, 1990. Mem. Ga. State Bar (chair patent, trademark and copyright sect. 1985-86), Order of Coif, Lawyer's Club Atlanta, Internat. Trademark Assn. (mem. publs. bd. 1995-96, chair internat. forums subcom. 1992-95, bd. dirs. 1991-93, chair pub. com. 1988-90). Democrat. Methodist. Office: Kilpatrick & Cody 1100 Peachtree St NE Ste 2800 Atlanta GA 30309-4528*

TAYLOR-GRIGSBY, QUEENIE DELORES, minister, consultant; b. Oklahoma City, Aug. 21, 1948; d. Barnett C., Sr. and Bedell (Boles) Taylor; m. Walter Thomas White II, Nov. 26, 1966 (div. June 1976); children: Walter Thomas III, Robin Orlando; m. James O. Grigsby, Oct. 19, 1976 (dec. Dec. 1976); 1 child, James Jumaané. BS, Howard U., 1970. Ordained to ministry Ray Deliverance Found., 1989. Assoc. cons. Trust Inc., Richmond, Va., 1974-80, Orgnl. Devel. Cons., Richmond, 1980-82; cons., pres. Taylor & Co., Phoenix, 1974—; min. Man Child Ministries, Phoenix, 1988—; cons. MARTA Atlanta, 1980-82, Fredrick County, Md., 1974, Richmond Pub. Sch. System, 1977, Black Police Officers, Tulsa, 1986. Author poetess. Advocate child welfare Dept. of Corrections, Phoenix, 1990, advocate tchr. rights, 1991; active tchr. rights Phoenix Pub. Sch. System, 1992; supr. elections County Election Bd., Maricopa County, Ariz., 1987. Lucille McMahn scholar, 1965, Nellie Green scholar, 1965; recipient Danforth Leadership award, 1965, Golden Poet award, 1991. Mem. Soc. Tng. and Devel. (cert. housing specialist), Housing Specialist Inst. Office: Taylor & Co PO Box 9605 Phoenix AZ 85068-9605

TAYLOR-PICKELL, LAVONNE TROY, editor; b. Riverside, Calif., May 20, 1941; d. Troy Virgil Bradstreet and R. Victoria (Freeman) Chambers; m. Robert Martin Taylor, May 15, 1958 (div. 1975); children: Dana Freeman, Timothy Rene; m. Herman Pickell, Feb. 14, 1985; children: Marianne, Barry, David. Reporter Thousand Oaks (Calif.) Chronicle; with prodn. News Chronicle, Thousand Oaks, prodn. supr., 1979-81; with prodn. Ind. Jour., Thousand Oaks, Herald Examiner, L.A., L.A. Times; asst. mgr. Publ. Typography, Agoura, Calif., 1981-85; owner Excellence Enterprises, L.A., 1982—; sr. editor arts Glencoe/McGraw-Hill Sch. Pub., Mission Hills, Calif., 1987-96; speaker various writers clubs. Editor, pub. L.A. My Way, 1991, On the Wings of Song, 1994; mng. editor The BookWoman, 1991-93. Mem. pub. rels. com. Conejo Players Theatre, Thousand Oaks, 1970-75, Betty Mann for 38th Assembly Dist., Agoura, 1975-76. Mem. NAFE, Nat. Writers Club (pres. 1990-91, Merit Svc. award 1991), Women's Nat. Book Assn. (L.A. chpt. pres. 1992-93, newsletter editor, bd. dirs.).

TAYLOR-SCHRAN, ELEANOR SUSAN, art gallery owner; b. Warrenton, Va., Feb. 2, 1951; d. Charlie Gordon and Mary Elizabeth (Stevenson) Taylor; m. William Roger Schran, Aug. 25, 1979. BA in Am. Studies, Mary Washington Coll., 1975. Regional display supr. The Ltd. Stores, Phila., 1975-78; reference clk. U.S. Internal Revenue, Washington, 1978-79, U.S. Interstate Commerce, Washington, 1979-81; supr. photo lab. Skyline Color Labs., Manassas, Va., 1982-86; owner photo studio E.S. Taylor-Schran Fine Art Documentation, Manassas, 1986—; owner Ctr. St. Gallery, Manassas, 1989-93, Fishscale & Moosetooth, Manassas, 1993—; sec., bd. mem. Old Town Bus. Assn., Manassas, 1989—; v.p., bd. dirs., mem. Ctr. for the Arts, Manassas, 1990—; grants panel mem. Prince William County (Va.) Arts Coun., 1995—; career advisor Women's Ctr., Woodbridge, Va., 1995—; organizer art auction Prince William Free Clinic, 1993. Revitalization task force City Coun., Manassas, 1991-93; sec., mem. Manassas Bus. Coun., 1994—; tourism com. Historic Manassas, Inc., 1994-95, econ. devel. com., 1995—. Recipient Pres.'s awards Old Town Bus. Assn., 1991, 92, Supporting Ground award Manassas Art Guild, 1994. Office: Fishscale & Moosetooth 9406 Main St Manassas VA 22110

TAYLOR-STEWARD, ALICE, nursing administrator; b. Kingsport, Tenn., Feb. 19, 1966; d. Robert E. and Jane A. (Adams) T.; m. William Anderson Steward, June 12, 1990; children: Caitlyne Elizabeth, Christian Edward Taylor. BSN, Berea Coll., 1988. RN, Tenn.; cert. rehab. RN, neurosci. RN, ANCC. Staff nurse U. Ky. Chandler Med. Ctr., Lexington, 1988-89, Johnson City (Tenn.) Med. Ctr., 1989-90; staff nurse, charge nurse Ft. Sanders Regional Med. Ctr., Knoxville, Tenn., 1990-94; rehab. nurse educator Ft. Sanders Regional Med. Ctr.- Patricia Neal Rehab. Ctr., Knoxville, 1994-95, admissions coord., case mgr., 1995; unit leader care mgmt. Patricia Neal Rehab. Ctr., 1995—. Author: (pediatric coloring book) You're a Hero, 1994. Active edn. coun. New Vision Fellowship Assembly of God, Women's Ministry Orgn., leader Childrens Ministries New Vision Fellowship. Mem. Am. Assn. Rehab. Nursing, East Tenn. Assn. Rehab. Nursing, Nurses Christian Fellow. Home: 9041 Highbridge Dr Knoxville TN 37922-1440 Office: Patricia Neal Rehab Ctr 1901 Clinch Ave Knoxville TN 37916

TAYRIEN, DOROTHY PAULINE, retired nursing educator; b. Bartlesville, Okla., June 15, 1921; d. William Cyprian and Ida May (Bennett) Tayrien; student Bartlesville Coll. High Jr. Coll.; diploma in nursing St. John Hosp., Tulsa, 1945; BS, U. Colo., 1948; AM, U. Chgo., 1959; postgrad. U. S.C., 1980-81. Hosp. staff nurse Pawhuska City Hosp., 1945-48; tchg. fellow Vanderbilt U., 1948-49; instr. Sch. Nursing, U. Okla., Oklahoma City, 1948-50; instr. surg. nursing Fla. State U., Tallahassee, 1951-52; asst. prof. nursing fundamentals Northwestern State Coll., Natchitoches, La., 1950-51; asst. prof., dir. clin. edn. Monroe (La.) Div., 1952-54; asst. prof., asst. dean Sch. Nursing, Baylor U., Waco, Tex., 1954-55; asst. dir. nursing svc. Washington Meml. Hosp., Bartlesville, 1955-57; asst. prof. nursing fundamentals S.W. La. U., Lafayette, 1957-59; assoc. prof. med. surg. nursing E. Tenn. State U., Johnson City, 1960-65, So. Ill. U., Edwardsville, 1965-67, Forest Park Jr. Coll., St. Louis, 1967-68; prof., dir. assoc. degree nursing program Kankakee (Ill.) C.C., 1968-70; assoc. prof., dir. continuing edn. program Coll. Nursing, Med. U. S.C., Charleston, 1970-81; ret., 1981; dir. nursing Tallahassee chpt. ARC, 1951-52; cons. in nursing, Belleville (Ill.) Meml. Hosp., 1967-68; spkr. in field. Bd. dirs. Lewis & Clark C.C., Ill., 1968-70, Women and Children in Crisis, Bartlesville, 1986-90, La Quinta Preservation Found., 1986-91; active St. John Roman Cath. Ch. S.C. Regional Med. Program grantee, 1975-77. Mem. AAUW, Am. Assn. Ret. Persons, Allied Arts & Humanities Coun., Bartlesville Art Assn. Democrat. Contbr. articles to profl. jours.; initiated and established AAS Degree in Nursing Program, Kankakee (Ill.) C.C., 1968-70. Home: 6547 Clear Creek Loop Bartlesville OK 74006-8010

TAYSE, AUDREY, professional society administrator; m. Michael D. Haynes. B in Social Work, Spalding U.; MSW, U. Ky. Dir. human resource devel. Ky. Dept. Mental Health and Mental Retardation Svcs., 1986-89; exec. dir. Ky. Literacy Commn., 1989-93, Bus. and Profl. Women/USA, Washington, 1993—; presenter in field; owner restaurant, Frankfort, Ky. Gov.'s appointee Ky. Bd. Elem. and Secondary Edn.; trustee Ky. Sch. Bd. Assn. Found.; nat. steering com. Laubach Literacy/USA; Pres.'s appointee bd. dirs. Nat. Inst. Literacy. Mem. Ky. Women's Leadership Network, Ky. Women Advocates, Frankfort C. of C. Office: Bus and Profl Women/USA 2012 Massachusetts Ave NW Washington DC 20017*

TCHAIKOVSKY, LESLIE J., judge; b. 1943. BA, Calif. State Univ., Hayward, 1967; JD, Univ. of Calif., Berkeley, 1976. Law clk. to Hon. John Mowbray Nev. Supreme Ct., 1976-77; with Dinkelspiel, Steefel, Leavitt & Weiss, 1977-80, Gordon, Peitzman & Lopes, 1981, Dinkelspiel, Donovan & Reder, 1981-88; bankruptcy judge U.S. Bankruptcy Ct. (Calif. no. dist.), 9th circuit, Oakland, 1988—. Office: US Courthouse 1300 Clay St Oakland CA 94612-1425

TCHUDI, SUSAN JANE, English educator; b. Peoria, Ill., Jan. 19, 1944; d. Woodrow Arthur and Jane Hope (Dallam) Schmidt; m. Richard Earl Koch, June 6, 1969 (div. 1974); 1 child, Emily; m. Stephen Nelson Tchudi, June 3, 1978; 1 stepcild, Stephen; children: Michael, Christopher. BA, So. Meth. U., 1966; postgrad., U. Kans., 1967; MA, Mich. State U., 1971, PhD, 1976. Mem. faculty U. Kans., Lawrence, 1967-69; grad. asst. Mich. State U., East Lansing, 1970-74, 75-76; asst. prof. Ctrl. Mich. U., 1976-81, assoc. prof., 1981-85, prof., 1985-90; prof. English U. Nev., Reno, 1990—; tchr. summer acad. youth program Ctrl. Mich. U., 1985, 86; presenter workshops in field; mem. staff Lake Tahoe Writing Inst., U. Nev., 1summers 1991, 92; mem. task force com. on exit exam. in reading Nev. State Dept. Edn., 1994; mem. Washoe County English/Lang. Arts Curriculum Adv. Com., 1995—; co-dir. Washoe K-16 Coun. English/Lang. Arts Consortium, 1995-96; adv. mem. Selection Com. for State Reading Test Adoption, 1995; cons. 4th Grade Statewide Writing Test Design, 1995-96; mem. planning com. Nev. Humanities Com. Festival of Book, 1995-96; co-chair Women in Lit. Conf., 1992, 94, 96; mem. articulation task force UCCSN, 1993; coord., instr. young writers' workshop Beal City Elem. Sch., 1984; cons. spirit project Gardner Jr. H.S., 1975. Co-author: (with Stephen Judy) The English Teachers' Handbook, 1979, Gift of Writing, 1980, An Introduction to the Teaching of Composition, 1981, (with Stephen Tchudi) Teaching Writing in the Content Areas: Elementary School, 1983, Young Writer's Handbook, 1984, The English/Language Arts Handbook, rev. edit., 1991, (with Seymour and Joan Yesner and Stephen Tchudi, 1990; author: Teaching Integrated Language Arts in the Elementary School, 1994; author plays: (with William Helder) The Gingerbread Witch, 1986, (with William Helder and Richard Addesso) Witches' Brew, 1990, Witches' Gumbo, 1992; contbr. articles and monographs to profl. publs. VISTA vol. Anderson Park elem. Sch., Atlanta, 1967-68. Mem. NOW, Nat. Coun. Tchrs. English (commn. on curriculum 1985-87, mem. com. to rev. affiliate publs. 1985-88, trustee Rsch. Found. 1988-91), Nev. State Coun. Tchrs. English, No. Nev. Tchrs. English, Nat. Writing Project, Mich. Coun. Tchrs. English (lectr. alternatives com. 1972-74, regional coord. 1977-78, 2d v.p. 1978-79, state conf. chair 1980, pres.-elect 1979-80, pres. 1980-81, past pres. 1981-82). Home: 3735 Gibraltar Dr Reno NV 89509 Office: U Nev Dept English MS 098 Reno NV 89557

TEACHOUT, NOREEN RUTH, writer; b. Oak Park, Ill., July 12, 1939; d. Anselm Uriel and R. Lydia (Bagne) Asp; m. Willem Heyneker, Nov. 20, 1958 (dec. 1968); children: Carolyn Heyneker Fors, Diana Heyneker Olds; m. Richard Kenneth Teachout, Jan. 21, 1966 (div. 1982); children: Jill, Janelle. BS, U. Minn., 1965; postgrad., Am. Inst. Holistic Theology, 1996—. Tchr. Bloomington (Minn.) Pub. Schs., 1965-85; writer, pubr., CEO The Peace Curriculum, Mpls., 1986—; educator Stockton & Franks Chiropractors, Burnsville, Minn., 1986-92; edn. svcs. dept. coord. Dame Comms., Plymouth, Minn., 1990—; cons., workshop leader Dame Comms.; writer U. Calif., Berkeley, 1967, Environ. Sci. Ctr., Mpls., 1968-69; educator, presenter Women's World Peace Conf., Dallas, 1988, World Peace Conf., San Jose, Costa Rica, 1989, 92; sponsor Therapeutic Humor Inst. Minn., Colo., 1996; dir. Wellness NOW, A Learning Place, Colo., 1996. Author curriculum programs, health and revitalization programs.

TEAGUE, MARY ELIZABETH, small business owner; b. Mt. Vernon, Tex., Aug. 18, 1928; d. Jodie Felter and Martha Willie (Crafts) T. AAS, C.C. of Air Force, 1987. Advanced through grades to chief master sgt. USAF, 1950, retired, 1988. Lutheran. Home: 4027 Waterwood Pass Dr Elmendorf TX 78112-6024

TEAGUE, MARY KAY, realtor; b. Troy, Ohio, May 15, 1925; d. Carl Joseph and Laura Mae (Jones) Wack; m. Roger A. Teague, Apr. 29, 1944 (dec. Nov. 1980); children: Margaret Colleen, Barbara Lynn, Roger A. Jr., Mary P., Betty A., Howard J. Realtor Teague Real Estate, Hitchcock, Tex., 1962—. Chmn. Hitchcock Planning Bd., 1987-93; dir. Hitchcock Indsl. Devel. Bd., 1983—. Mem. Nat. Assoc. Realtors, Tex. Assn. Realtors, Texas City-LaMarque Bd. Realtors (dir. 1974-78, 81-87, sec. 1979, pres. 1980, 88, Realtor of Yr. award 1986), Women's Coun. Realtors (sec. 1988, pres. 1991, Golden Rule award 1983), Hitchcock C. of C. (bd. dirs. 1984-91). Republican. Roman Catholic. Home: 301 Greenwood Dr Hitchcock TX 77563-1413 Office: Teague Real Estate PO Box 21 Hitchcock TX 77563-0021

TEAS, MOLLY MAGUIRE, international educator planner; b. Mpls.; d. Daniel Henry and Patricia Ann (Maguire) T. BA, Lawrence U., 1979; MA, U. Wis., 1984; MEd, Harvard U., 1988, EdD, 1992. Edn. specialist The World Bank, Washington, 1991-95; dir. Russell E. Train edn. for nature program World Wildlife Fund, Washington, 1995—; lectr. Harvard U., Cambridge, Mass., 1995—. Mem. Am. Edn. Rsch. Assn. Office: World Wildlife Fund 1250 24th St NW Washington DC 20037-1175

TEASLEY, UNICE H., educator; b. Athens, Ga., Feb. 7, 1944; d. Henry T. and Grace L. (Mack) Bothwell. BA in Edn., Ohio State U., 1967, MA in Edn., 1972, PhD, 1996. Tchr. Columbus (Ohio) Pub. Schs., 1967-69, 70-89, Dept. Defense Dept. Sch., Yokosuka, Japan, 1969-70; teaching asst. Ohio State U., Columbus, 1989-90, 91-96; tchr. Columbus Pub. Schs., 1990-91; program evaluator Ohio Dept. Edn., Columbus, 1994-95. Mem. Am. Ednl. Rsch. Assn. Home: 980 King Ave 6-12 Columbus OH 43212 Office: Ohio State U 29 W Woodruff Columbus OH 43210

TEATER, DOROTHY SEATH, county official; b. Manhattan, Kans., Feb. 11, 1931; d. Dwight Moody and Martha (Stahnke) Seath; m. Robert Woodson Teater, May 24, 1952; children: David Dwight, James Stanley, Donald Robert, Andrew Scott. BS, U. Ky., 1951; MS, Ohio State U., 1954. Home econs. tchr. Georgetown (Ky.) City Schs., 1951-53; extension specialist Ohio Coop. Extension, Columbus, 1967-73; consumer affairs adminstr. City of Columbus, 1974-79, Bank One Columbus NA, 1980-85; councilmember Columbus City Coun., 1980-85; commr. Franklin County, Columbus, Ohio, 1985—; active Ohio Cmty. Corrections Adv. Bd., Columbus Met. Area Cmty. Action Orgn., Land Policy & Boom Bust Real Estate Markets, 1994, Lincoln Inst. Land Policy. Bd. dirs. BBB; mem. hon. adv. bd. Girl Scouts. Recipient Outstanding Alumnus award U. Ky., 1989, Women of Achievement award YWCA, 1995; named Disting. Alumni, Ohio State U., 1977. Mem. County Commrs. Assn. Ohio (pres. 1994), Columbus Met. Club. Republican. Methodist. Office: Franklin County Commrs 373 S High St Columbus OH 43215-4591

TEBBS, CAROL ANN, secondary education educator; b. Columbus, Ohio, Sept. 9, 1939; d. John Arthur and Ann Laurie (Wickham) Williams; m. Ronald Daniel Tebbs, Mar. 3, 1957; children: Kimberly Ann, Ronald Dan. BA in English, Whittier Coll., 1963, MA in English and Edn., 1972. Cert. tchr. k-12 (life), Calif. Tchr. of art and English Hacienda La Puente Unified Sch. Dist., Hacienda Heights, Calif., 1963-84; tchr. advanced placement English, acad. decathalon advisor Hacienda La Puente Unified Sch. Dist., Hacienda Heights, 1984—; mentor tchr. Hacienda La Puenta Sch. Dist., Hacienda Hghts., 1988-95. Writer (jour.) Kosmos, Mountain Astrologer, 1995. Mem. Internat. Soc. for Astrological Rsch. (pres. 1988—), United Astrology Congress (coord. 1992—), Delta Kappa Gamma (pres. 1972-76). Methodist. Home and Office: 3423 Budleigh Dr Hacienda Heights CA 91745

TEBEDO, MARYANNE, state legislator; b. Oct. 30, 1936; m. Don Tebedo; children: Kevin, Ronald, Linda, Thomas, Christine. Former mem. Colo. Ho. of Reps.; now mem. Colo. Senate; profl. parliamentarian. Republican. Office: Colorado State Senate State Capitol Bldg Denver CO 80203*

TECCA, CRYSTAL ANNETTE, market researcher; b. Houston, Aug. 19, 1971; d. Robert Lee and Georgia Nell (Aiken) Tecca; m. Jeff Lizan Mangahas, May 28, 1994. BA in Bus. Adminstrn., U. Wash., 1993. Asst. dir. new student programs U. Wash., Seattle, 1993-95; project coord. Healthcare Comms. Inc., Princeton, N.J., 1995—. Active Literacy Vols. of Am. Mem. Mortar Board. Office: HCI Inc CN 5273 Princeton NJ 08543-5273

TECCE, JACQUELINE, real estate administrator; b. N.Y.C., Apr. 23, 1956; d. Sam L. and Lee M. (Malandri) T.; children: Samantha Nicole, Nicholas Alexander, Max Anthony. BA in Pychology St. Francis Coll., Bklyn., 1978, AAS in Bus Adminstrn., 1978. Lic. real estate sales agent. Asst. dir. lease adminstrn. Brooks Fashion Stores, N.Y.C., 1979-81; coordinator info. services Richard Kove Assocs., N.Y.C., 1981-87; systems cons. J.T.F. Word Pros, 1988-92; real estate adminstr. Lysaght, Lysaght & Kramer, 1992—. Mem. Anti-Vivisection Soc., 1978—, Save Our Strays, Bklyn., 1978—; vol. Rusk Inst., N.Y.C., 1982; mem. Citizens to Replace LILCO, 1985—. Mem. NAFE, Ill. Mgmt. and Exec. Search Cons., Parent Resource Ctr., Psi Chi, Chi Beta Phi. Republican. Roman Catholic. Home: 3 Oak Valley Dr Glen Head NY 11545-1728 Office: Lysaght Lysaght & Kramer PC 1983 Marcus Ave Ste C100 New Hyde Park NY 11042-1016

TEDESCO, JUDITH ANN, controller; b. Detroit, Sept. 26, 1946; d. Edward C. and Henrietta M. Aretz; m. Paul E. Tedesco, May 26, 1967; 1 child, Lori A. Bowlen. BBA in Acctg., Ea. Mich. U., 1978; MPA, U. Tex., Dallas, 1995. From acctg. clk. to budget analyst Ea. Mich. U., Ypsilanti, 1970-82; sr. acct. Great Western Sugar Corp., Dallas, 1982-83, U. Tex. Health Sci. Ctr., Dallas, 1983; fixed assets mgr. City of Dallas-Contr., 1983-85; fin. analysis mgr. City of Dallas-Water, 1985-91; sr. fin. analyst City of Garland, Tex., 1994-95; contr. Monroe County Solid Waste Mgmt. Dist., Bloomington, Ind., 1995—. Mem. Assn. Govt. Accts. (cert. govt. fin. mgr.), Inst. Mgmt. Accts., Govt. Fin. Officers Assn., Kappa Kappa Kappa. Office: Monroe County Solid Waste Mgmt Dist 3400 Old State Rd 37 South Bloomington IN 47401

TEDESCO, SUSAN MARY, pharmacy technician; b. Chgo., Sept. 22, 1954; d. Edmund L. and Viola M. (Cote) T. BA, U. St. Thomas, Houston, 1976. Cert. pharmacy technician. Sr. pharmacy technician, intravenous specialist Children's Meml. Hosp., Chgo., 1978—; pres., cons. Aseptech, Inc., Chgo., 1989—; instr., pharmacy technician educator South Suburban Coll., 1993—. Mem. Ill. Coun. Health-System Pharmacists (rep. bd. dirs. 1984-88, voting mem. bd. dirs. 1990-92, Pres.'s award 1987). Home: 2245 N Magnolia Ave Chicago IL 60614-3103 Office: Children's Meml Med Ctr 2300 N Childrens Plz Chicago IL 60614-3318

TEDROW, CHERYL MARIE VITEK, accountant; b. Groton, Mass., Aug. 23, 1964; d. Edwin Lewis and Patricia Gail (Huey) Vitek; m. Richard Frederick Tedrow, July 25, 1992. BA in Acctg., Western Wash. U., 1989; MBA, Seattle U., 1996. Cert. mgmt. acct. Acctg. intern Fluke Corp., Everett, Wash., summer 1988, gen. acctg. assoc. acct., 1989-90, corp. acct., 1991-94, cash mgmt., 1992-94, cost acct., 1995—. Mem. Inst. Mgmt. Accts. Office: Fluke Corp PO Box 9090 m/s 259C Everett WA 98206-9090

TEEGUARDEN, PAMELA ALICE, tennis player; d. Jerry and Lillian Teeguarden; m. Alfred W. Lee, May 22, 1995. Student, U. Calif., Berkeley, UCLA. Champion U.S. Open Mixed doubles, French Open ladies doubles, Can., Austrian, Swedish, Argentine and Va. Slims tournament titles; rep. Beverly Hills Country Club. Appeared on TV commls., tennis commentary for Va. Slims, talk shows. Co-chmn. Cystic Fibrosis So. Calif.; bd. dirs. Monty Hall Diabetes Tennis Tournament. Voted most watchable player U.S. Open.

TEEL, JOYCE, supermarket and drugstore retail executive; b. 1930. Dir. Raley's, West Sacramento, 1950 ; co-chmn., 1991 . Office: Raley's 500 W Capitol Ave Broderick CA 95605*

TEELE, CYNTHIA LOMBARD, lawyer; b. Boston, Oct. 11, 1961; d. John Hughes and Patricia Jeanne (Linder) T. AB in Urban Studies magna cum laude, Brown U., 1983; JD, U. Va., 1986. Bar: Calif. 1986. Assoc. Lillick McHose & Charles, L.A., 1986-87, Wyman Bautzer Kuchel & Silbert, L.A., 1987-91; sr. atty. Paramount Pictures Corp.-TV Divsn., Hollywood, Calif., 1991-92, dir., legal, 1992-94, v.p., legal, 1994—. Office: Paramount Pictures Corp 5555 Melrose Ave Los Angeles CA 90038-3149

TEER, KAY STOLTZ, museum director; b. Southern Pines, N.C., July 30, 1947; d. John Wesley and Ellen Kathrine (Wheeless) Stoltz; m. William Stewart Teer, June 2, 1968; children: John Stewart, Marguerite Kathrine. BS, East Carolina U., 1969; postgrad., U. S.C., 1971-89, U. N.C., 1983. Tchr. English Sch. Dist. 17, Sumter, S.C., 1969-73; exec. dir. Sumter Gallery of Art, 1982-88; grants writer S.C. Arts Commn., Columbia, 1988-89; advocacy coord. S.C. Arts Alliance, Columbia, 1988-89; exec. dir. Sumter County Mus., 1989—. Bd. dirs. Sumter Sch. Dist. 17, 1978-94, S.C. Arts Alliance, 1985-88, Fine Arts Coun., Sumter, 1986-93. Mem. Am. Assn. Mus., S.C. Fedn. Mus. (sec. 1994—), Southwestern Mus. Conf., Sumter C. of C. (bd. dirs. 1979-81, 90-92), Rotary. Mem. Am. Assn. Mus., S.C. Fedn. Mus. (sec. 1994—), Southeastern Mus. Conf., Sumter C. of C. (bd. dirs. 1979-81, 90-92). Methodist. Home: 11 Snowden St Sumter SC 29150-3224 Office: Sumter County Mus PO Box 1456 Sumter SC 29151-1456

TEETER, SUSAN, university coach; b. Miami, Fla., June 21, 1959; d. Robert H. and Babe (Reynolds) Teeter. BFA, U. Tenn., 1981. Asst. women's swimming coach U. Tenn., Knoxville, 1978-82; head coach Starlit Aquatic Club, Fairfax, Va., 1982-83; asst. men's and women's coach Auburn (Ala.) U., 1983-84; head coach for women Princeton (N.J.) U., 1984—; asst. mgr. U.S. swimming team Pan Pacific Games, Tokyo, 1989; head mgr. U.S. swimming team World U. Games, Sheffield, Eng., 1991, World Championships, Rome, 1994, Olympic Games, Atlanta, 1996; mem. sports sci. com. U.S. Swim Team, chmn., 1995-96; mem. Olympic Internat. Ops. Com., 1996. Dir. learn to swim for deaf Deaf Sch. N.J., Princeton, 1995. Mem. World Swim Coaches Assn., Coll. Swim Coaches Assn. (bd. dirs. 1981—, contbn. award 1989), Ea. Women's Swim League (chmn. 1985-95). Office: Princeton U Women's Swimming Dept PO Box 71 Princeton NJ 08544-0071

TEETERS, NANCY HAYS, economist; b. Marion, Ind., July 29, 1930; d. S. Edgar and Mabel (Drake) Hays; m. Robert Duane Teeters, June 7, 1952; children: Ann, James, John. A.B. in Econs., Oberlin Coll., 1952, LL.D. (hon.), 1979; M.A. in Econs., U. Mich., 1954, postgrad., 1956-57, LL.D. (hon.), 1983; LL.D. (hon.), Bates Coll., 1981, Mt. Holyoke Coll., 1983. Tchg. fellow U. Mich., 1954-55, instr., 1956-57; instr. U. Md. Overseas, Germany, 1955-56; staff economist govt. fin. sect. Bd. Govs. of FRS, Washington, 1957-66; mem. bd. Bd. Govs. of FRS, 1978-84; economist (on loan) Coun. Econ. Advs., 1962-63; economist Bur. Budget, 1966-70; sr. fellow Brookings Instn., 1970-73; sr. specialist Congl. Rsch. Svc., Library of Congress, Washington, 1973-74; asst. dir., chief economist Ho. of Reps. Com. on the Budget, 1974-78; v.p., chief economist IBM, Armonk, N.Y., 1984-90; bd. dirs., trustee Prudential Mut. Funds, 1985—; bd. dirs. Inland Steel Industries; mem. Coun. on Fgn. Rels., Forum for World Affairs, Women in Mgmt. Author: (with others) Setting National Priorities: The 1972 Budget, 1971, Setting National Priorities: The 1973 Budget, 1972, Setting National Priorities: The 1974 Budget, 1973; contbr. articles to profl. publs. Recipient Comfort Starr award in econs. Oberlin Coll., 1952; Disting. Alumnus award U. Mich., 1980. Mem. Nat. Economists Club (v.p. 1973-74, pres. 1974-75, chmn. bd. 1975-76, gov. 1976-79), Am. Econ. Assn. (com. on status of women 1975-78), Am. Fin. Assn. (dir. 1969-71). Democrat. Home: 243 Willowbrook Ave Stamford CT 06902-7020

TEGOVICH, ELAINE A., elementary education educator; b. Woonsocket, R.I., May 29, 1958; d. Kosta Stereo and Ida Anastasia (Steve) T. Student, Columbus Internat. Coll., Sevilla, Spain, 1979; BE, Worcester (Mass.) State Coll., 1980; MA in Lang., Reading and Culture, U. Ariz., 1991, EdS in Lang., Reading and Culture, 1993. Cert. elem., bilingual tchr., Mass., elem., bilingual tchr., reading specialist, Ariz. English as 2d lang./bilingual tchr. West Boylston (Mass.) Schs., 1980-81; elem. tchr. Sahuarita (Ariz.) Schs., 1981-93; reading specialist Gilbert (Ariz.) Schs., 1993—. Contbr. articles to profl. jours. State treas. Ariz. Edn. Assn. Women's Caucus, 1992-95; membership co-chair Gilbert Edn. Assn., 1993-96—; bldg. rep. Sahuarita Edn. Assn., 1981-93; coach Am. Youth Soccer Orgn., Amado, Ariz., 1981-83. Mem. AAUW (Eleanor Roosevelt fellowship 1990-91), Internat. Reading Assn., Phi Delta Kappa, Delta Kappa Gamma. Eastern Orthodox.

Home: 2331 E Stottler Dr Gilbert AZ 85296 Office: Mesquite Elem 1000 E Mesquite Gilbert AZ 85296

TEHRANI, FLEUR TAHER, electrical engineer, educator, researcher; b. Tehran, Feb. 16, 1956; came to U.S., 1984; d. Hassan and Pourandokht (Monfared) T. BS in Elec. Engrng., Sharif U. of Tech., Tehran, 1975; DIC in Comm. Engrng., Imperial Coll. Sci. and Tech., London, 1977; MSc in Comm. Engrng., U. London, 1977, PhD in Elec. Engrng., 1981. Registered profl. engr., Calif. Comm. engr. Planning Orgn. of Iran, Tehran, 1977-78; lectr. A elec. engring. Robert Gordon's Inst. Tech., Aberdeen, U.K., 1982-83; lectr. II elec. engring. South Bank U., London, 1984; asst. prof. elec. engring. Calif. State U., Fullerton, 1985-91, assoc. prof. elec. engring., 1991-94, prof. elec. engring., 1994—; vis. assoc. prof. elec. engring. Drexel U., Phila., 1987-88; sys. cons. Telebit Corp., Cupertino. Calif., 1985; engring. cons. PRD, Inc., Dresher, Pa., 1989-92; mem. NASA/Am. Soc. Engring. Edn. summer faculty Jet Propulsion Lab., Calif. Inst. Tech., Pasadena, 1995, 96. Contbr. articles to profl. jours.; patentee in field. Recipient Best Ann. Rsch. Manuscript award Assn. for the Advancement of Med. Instrumentation, 1993, Outstanding Excellence in Rsch. Faculty award Calif. State U., 1993. Mem. IEEE, Women in Sci. and Engring. (chair Calif. State U. chpt. 1990-91), Assn. Profs. and Scholars of Iranian Heritage (pres. 1991-92), Sigma Delta Epsilon. Office: Calif State U Dept Elec Engring 800 N State College Blvd Fullerton CA 92831-3599

TEICHMAN, EVELYN, antiques appraiser, educator, estate liquidator; b. N.Y.C., Mar. 13, 1929; d. Bernard and Minnie (Goldenberg) Mensch; m. Milton Teichman, Jan. 16, 1949; children: David, Jeb, Sondra. Student, CUNY, 1946-49. Tchr. Bergen County Adult Schs., N.J., 1976—; freelance appraiser Paramus, N.J., 1978—; house contents and estate sale coord. Home: 56 Bush Pl Paramus NJ 07652-4004

TEICHNER, MARTHA ALICE, network television news correspondent; b. Traverse City, Mich., Jan. 12, 1948; d. Hans H. and Miriam G. (Greene) Teichner. BA in Econs., Wellesley Coll., 1969; postgrad., U. Chgo., 1976-77. Gen. assignment reporter, newscaster WJEF radio, Grand Rapids, Mich., 1971-72; gen. assignment, city hall reporter WZZM TV, Grand Rapids, 1972-73; gen. assignment reporter WTVJ TV, Miami, Fla., 1973-75, WMAQ-TV, Chgo., 1975-77; news corr. CBS News, Atlanta, 1977-80, London, 1980-84, Dallas, 1984-87, Johannesburg, South Africa, 1987-89, London, 1989, 93, 1989-94; corr. CBS News "Sunday Morning", N.Y.C., 1994—; Atlanta assignments include El Salvador (first woman corr. sent by CBS), Panama: the Shah in Exile, United Mineworkers Strike, Cuban Boatlift, numerous disasters; London, Lebanon War (first woman corr. sent to Beirut by CBS), No. Ireland hunger strikes, Royal Wedding (Charles and Diana), Iran Hostage release; Dallas, Collapse oil industry, real estate, banks, Challenger crash, numerous disasters; Johannesburg, Mozambique civil war, significant racial, polit. issues; London, coverage former Yugoslavia (Slovenia, Croatia, Bosnia), Gulf War, Kuwait war aftermath, Romanian Revolution, Mandela release, polit. changes Ea. Europe, Mid. East, Royals, Clinton inauguration; N.Y.C., host series Conversations With..., Spoleto Festival, U.S.A., 1995. Bd. mem., Simon Found., Chgo. Recipient Robert F. Kennedy Journalism award, Robert F. Kennedy Meml. Found., 1981, Breakthrough award Women, Men and Media, 1991, Emmy award Am. Acad. TV Arts and Scis., 1996. Mem. DAR (Walter Hines Page Chpt.), Internat. Womens Media Found., Reform Club London, N.Y. Women's Forum, Art Table. Office: CBS News 524 W 57th St New York NY 10019-2902

TEIPE, EMILY JANE, history educator; b. Balt., Oct. 7, 1940; d. Ralph Edward and Mildred May (DeVillbiss) Molesworth; m. William Austin Teipe, Feb. 10, 1962 (div. Aug. 1988); children: William, Stephen, Mark, Peter; m. Franklin Luberg Brown, July 29, 1994. BA in History, Calif. State U., Fullerton, 1982, MA in History, 1984; PhD, U. Calif., Riverside, 1996. Dir. edn. St. Anthony Claret Sch., Anaheim, Calif., 1976-81; assoc. prof. history Fullerton Coll., Calif., 1989—; presenter in field; cons., spkr. bur. Fullerton Coll.; cmty. pub. spkr., Fullerton, 1991—. Author: A Different Voice: The Experience of Women in America, 1996, Inventing the American: Teacher's Guide; reviewer, editor: Magill's Literary Ann., 1995; dir., prodr., writer TV series A Different Voice-Women in Am. History, 1996—; contbr. articles to profl. jours., chpts. to books. Bd. dirs. Friends of Fullerton Coll. Libr., 1995-96. Recipient assistantship Williamsburg Found., Tchg. assistantship U. Calif., Riverside, Grad. assistantship Calif. State U., Fullerton. Mem. AAUW, Am. Hist. Assn., Colonial Dames Am., Assoc. Inst. Early Am.-History and Culture, Nat. Coun. for Social Studies, Soc. Quaker Historians and Quaker History, Western Assn. Women Historians (presenter ann. conf. 1995, 96), Soc. History Edn., Phi Delta Kappa, Alpha Gamma Sigma, Phi Alpha Theta. Democrat. Mem. Soc. of Friends. Office: Fullerton Coll 321 E Chapman Fullerton CA 92635

TEITELBAUM, MARILYN LEAH, special education educator; b. Bklyn., June 12, 1930; d. Abraham and Fay (Ingis) Nober; m. Harry Teitelbaum, Nov. 7, 1953; children: Mark, David, Deborah. BA, Bklyn. Coll., 1953; MS, Queens Coll., 1968, L.I. U., 1982. Cert. tchr., N.Y. Elem. and spl. edn. tchr. Franklin Square, Franklin's Square, N.Y., 1955-57; elem. tchr. Manetto Hill Sch., Plainview, N.Y., 1968-70; elem. tchr. Northport (N.Y.) Sch. Dist., 1970-78, spl. edn. tchr., 1978-87; pvt. spl. edn. tchr. Laguana Niguel, Calif., 1988—. Author: Teachers as Consumers-What They Should Know About the Hearing Impaired Child, 1981. V.p. Friends of Libr., Laguna Niguel Pub. Libr., 1988—. Recipient award Northport PTA, 1987. Mem. NEA, Coun. Exceptional Children, United Tchrs. Northport, Orange County Dyslexic Soc. Home: 29562 Avante Laguna Niguel CA 92677-7949

TEJADA, AUDREY DOLAR, artist, writer; b. Manapla, Philippines, Dec. 29, 1957; came to U.S., 1961; d. Peter Infante and Mary Placentero (Dolar) T.; m. Joseph Yu, June 14,1986. BA in English, Cornell U., 1982; MS in Broadcast Journalism, Boston U., 1996. Intern Fgn. Svc. Diplomatic Corps, Washington, 1980, Bur. Pub. Affairs U.S. Dept. State, Washington, summers '80, 81. Prodr., writer, dir.: (film) Rage, 1981; author, photographer: Celebration Cuisine, Alpha en Afrique, 1991; work reviewed by Pentangle Films, 1981; writer, prodr. (CD ROM) Balikbayan, 1995; contbr. articles to internet mag. Bd. trustees Cornell U., Ithaca, N.Y.; officer Harvard U., Cambridge, Mass. Recipient Chase Manhattan Found. fellowship, 1982; hon. mention Glamour Mag. Top Ten Coll. Women Competition, 1981. Mem. Quill and Dagger Soc., Internat. Platform Assn., Asian Am. Journalists Assn., RTNDA. Home: 74 Auckland St Boston MA 02125-3327 also: Montevista # 114 6000 Shepherd Mountain Cv Austin TX 78730-4900

TEJEDA-BROWN, MARY LOUISE, artist; b. L.A., Jan. 11, 1921; d. Francisco Tejeda and Elizabeth (Kramis) Tejeda; m. William Reynold Brown, Oct. 26, 1946 (dec. 1991); children: Marie, Reynold, Franz, Elisa, Cristina, Regina, Marta, Mariane. Student, Frank Wiggens Trade Sch. Artist Raymond Advt. Co., L.A., 1938-40, No. Am. Aviation, Inglewood, Calif., 1941-46; freelance artist Whitney, Nebr., 1989—; represented by Univ. Pl. Art Gallery, Lincoln, Nebr., Elaine's Art Gallery, Alliance, Nebr., Dakota Art Gallery, Rapid City, S.D., Victoria's, Scottsbluff, Nebr., Steven Goyda, Marysville, Kans. Exhibited in shows at Gallery East, Loveland, Colo., 1991, Chadron (Nebr.) State Coll., 1989, 91, 93, West Nebr. Arts Ctr., 1992, 94, 95, Ft. Robinson Art Show, Nebr., 1991, 92, 93, Dakota Art Gallery, 1994, Agate Beds Nat. Monument, Nebr., 1994, Pastel Soc. Am., N.Y.C., 1994, Univ. Pl. Art Gallery, 1995, Gov.'s Mansion, Lincoln, 1995, Mus. of Nebr., 1995. Mem. Cassatt Pastel Soc., Pastel Soc. Am. (assoc.). Home and Studio: 379 Bethel Road Whitney NE 69367

TEJEDOR, BELKYS BARBARA, science educator; b. Habana, Cuba, Aug. 18, 1963; came to U.S. 1966; d. Mario and Julia V. Tejedor. BS in Biology, St. Peter's Coll., 1986, MA in Edn., 1991. Cert. tchr. biol. sci., supr. edn. Tchr. sci. St. Anthony H.S., Jersey City, 1989-91, Essex County Vocat. H.S., Newark, 1991-95, Kearny (N.J.) H.S., 1995—.

TELEKI, MARGOT WHITESON, marketing communications executive; b. Cleve., May 24, 1935; d. Milton D. and Ilon (Sarkany) Whiteson; grad. New Eng. Conservatory Music, 1952; student Radcliffe Coll., 1950-51, Harvard Extension U., 1950-51, Hunter Coll., 1951-52. Media exec. J. Walter Thompson Co., N.Y.C., 1958-60; media exec. Reach McClinton & Co., Inc., N.Y.C., 1960-62, media rsch. mgr., 1962; rsch. dir. Sta. WNEW, N.Y.C., 1963-64; sr. rsch. analyst Young & Rubicam, N.Y.C., 1964-65; media exec. N.W. Ayer & Son, Inc., Phila., 1965-68; sr. editor Media-Scope Mag., N.Y.C., 1968-70, also columnist, 1969—; pres. Teleki Assocs., Ltd., N.Y.C., 1970-82; pres. TAL Communications, Inc., Morristown, N.J., 1982—; pres., chief exec. officer TAL Internat. Mktg. Inc., Morristown, N.J., 1989—. Contbr. feature articles to various mags. and publs. Mem. Yale Club (N.Y.C.). Trustee St. Hubert's Giralda, Madison, N.J. Office: Tal Internat Mktg Inc 65 Madison Ave Morristown NJ 07960

TELENCIO, GLORIA JEAN, elementary education educator; b. Trenton, N.J., Sept. 3, 1955; d. John and Anne (Tymoch) T. BA cum laude, Georgian Ct. Coll., 1977. Cert. elem. edn. Math and sci. tchr. grade 8 St. Anthony's Grammar Sch., Trenton, 1977-78; elem. tchr. grade 7 St. Mary's Assumption Sch., Trenton, 1978-79; elem. tchr. grade 2 Hamilton Twp. Bd. Edn., Trenton, 1979-85, elem. tchr. grade 1, 1985—; sch. coord. Regional Curriculum Svc. Unit, Learning Resource Ctr.-Ctrl., 1990-95. Recipient State of N.J. Gov.'s Tchr. Recognition award State of N.J., 1991, Resolution of Commendation, Town Coun. of the Twp. of Hamilton, 1991; mini-grantee Bd. Edn., 1987-88. Mem. NEA, N.J. Edn. Assn., Hamilton Edn. Assn., Sunnybrae PTA (tchr. rep. exec. bd. 1981-91, co-chair PTA 25th Anniversary com. 1990-91), Kappa Delta Pi, Sigma Tau Delta, Pi Delta Phi, Delta Tau Kappa. Republican. Byzantine Catholic. Home: 31 Newkirk Ave Trenton NJ 08629 Office: Sunnybrae Elem Sch 166 Elton Ave Yardville NJ 08620

TELFAIR, TULA, artist, educator; b. Bronxville, N.Y., Nov. 30, 1961; d. Peter and Frances (Maloring) T. BFA in Painting, Moore Coll. Art, 1984; MFA in Painting, Syracuse U., 1986. With Syracuse U., N.Y., 1984-85; acad. coord. for fine arts curriculum, designer of studio arts facilities Columbia Greene C.C., 1988-89, lectr., 1987-89; asst. prof. Wesleyan U., 1989-96; assoc. prof. Wesleyan U., Middletown, Conn., 1996—; vis. artist, lectr. SUNY, Fredonia, 1988, Darmouth Coll., 1988, Westminster Coll., 1990, Cornell U., Ithaca, 1993, Syracuse U., 1993, Moore Coll. Art, Phila., 1995, Goucher Coll., Balt., 1995; spkr. in field. One-woman shows include Michael Rockefeller Gallery SUNY, Fredonia, 1988, Paula Allen Gallery, N.Y.C., 1988, 89, Five Points Gallery, East Chatham, N.Y., 1991, Sampson Art Gallery Thiel Coll., Greenville, Pa., 1992, Kirkland Fine Art Gallery Millikin U., Decatur, Ill., 1992, Zilkha Gallery Wesleyan U., Middletown, Conn., 1993, Synderman Gallery, Phila., 1993, 94, 95, Xerox Bldg., Chgo., 1994, Peter Miller Gallery, Chgo., 1994, Kavish Gallery, Sun Valley, Idaho, 1995, Rosenberg Gallery Goucher Coll., Balt., 1995, Tremaine Gallery Hotchkiss Sch., Conn., 1996; exhibited in group shows at Harrisburg Art Mus., Pa., 1978, State Capital Rotunda, Harrisburg, 1980, Paley/Levy Gallery, Phila., 1983, Cheltenham Gallery, Phila., 1984, Syracuse U., N.Y., 1986, Harvard U., Cambridge, Mass., 1986, U. Neb., Lincoln, 1986, Lowe Art Gallery Syracuse U., 1986, Michael Rockefeller Gallery SUNY, Fredonia, 1986, Paula Allen Gallery, N.Y.C., 1986, Mid-Hudson Sci and Art Ctr., 1987, The Alternative Mus., N.Y.C., 1987, Hopkins Art Ctr. Dartmouth Coll., Hanover, 1989, Valeur, Rhinebeck, N.Y., 1989, Holman Gallery Trenton State Coll., N.J., 1989, Dutchess County Armory, Poughkeepsie, 1989, Shore Art Gallery Abilene Christian U., Tex., 1989, Southwestern U., Georgetown, Tex., 1989, Dishman Art Gallery Lamar U., Beaumont, Tex., 1990, Cultural Activities Ctr., Temple, Tex., 1990, The Nave Mus., Victoria, Tex., 1990, Laguna Gloria Art Mus., Austin, 1990, Redding Mus. Art, Calif., 1990, 93, Westminster Coll. Art Gallery, New Wilmington, Pa., 1990, Graham Horstman Gallery, Denton, Tex., 1990, Erector Square Gallery, New Haven, Conn., 1991, Couturier Gallery, L.A., 1991, Newport Art Mus., R.I., 1991, Zilkha Gallery Wesleyan U., Conn., 1992, AIR Gallery, N.Y.C., 1992, Stedman Art Gallery Rutgers U., N.J., 1992, Peter Miller Gallery, Chgo., 1992, 93, 94, 95, 96, Coll. Art Gallery SUNY, New Paltz, 1992, Five Points Gallery, East Chatham, N.Y., 1993, Elizabeth Harris Gallery, N.Y.C., 1993, The Hammond Galleries, Lancaster, Ohio, 1993, State of the Art Gallery, Ithaca, N.Y., 1993, Eastern N.Mex. U., Portales, 1993, Bent F. Larsen Gallery Brigham Young U., Provo, Utah, 1993, Snyderman Gallery, Phila., 1994, 95, 96, Peter Joseph Gallery, N.Y.C., 1995; represented in permanent collections at Mastercard Corp., Redding Art Mus., Steelcase Corp., Trenton State Coll., Wesleyan U., Syracuse U., Moore Coll. Art, Ruth Chenvin Found., Russ Corp., City Phila. Dist. Atty.'s Office. Recipient fellowship Pa. Gov.'s Sch. for the Arts, 1978, Moore Coll. Art Travelling fellowship, 1983, MacDowell fellow, 1994; Pa. State Women's Caucus Art award, 1980, Marion Locks award, 1984; W.W. Smith Found. grant, 1980-84, Wesleyan U. Supplementary grant in support of scholarship, 1989, 90, 91, 92, 93, 94, 95. Mem. Nat. Drawing Soc., Coll. Art Assn. Office: Wesleyan U Middletown CT 06459

TELFER, MARGARET CLARE, internist, hematologist; b. Manila, The Philippines, Apr. 9, 1939; came to U.S., 1941; d. James Gavin and Margaret Adele (Baldwin) T. BA, Stanford U., 1961; MD, Washington U., St. Louis, 1965. Diplomate Am. Bd. Internal Medicine, Am. Bd. Hematology, Am. Bd. Oncology; lic. Ill., Mo. Resident in medicine Michael Reese Hosp., Chgo., 1968, fellow in hematology and oncology, 1970, assoc. attending physician, 1970-72, dir. Hemophilia Ctr., 1971—, interim dir. div. hematology and oncology, 1971-74, 81-84, 89—, attending physician, 1972—; asst. prof. medicine U. Chgo., 1975-80, assoc. prof. medicine, 1980-85, assoc. prof. clin. medicine, 1985-89; assoc. prof. medicine U. Ill., Chgo., 1990—; mem. med. adv. bd. Hemophilia Found. Ill., 1971, chmn., 1972-83, lectr. annual symposium, 1978-84; mem. med. adv. bd. State of Ill. Hemophilia Program; dir. hematology-oncology fellowship program Michael Reese Hosp., 1971-75, 81-84, lectr. and mem. numerous coms.; lectr. Cook County Grad. Sch. Medicine, 1980-85, U. Chgo., ARC. Contbr. articles to profl. jours. Fellow ACP; mem. Am. Soc. Clin. Oncology, Am. Assn. Med. Colls., Am. Soc. Hematology, World Fedn. Hemophilia, Blood Club (Chgo.), Thrombosis Club (Chgo.). Office: Michael Reese Hosp 29th & Ellis Rm 1200 RC Chicago IL 60616

TELLEM, SUSAN MARY, public relations executive; b. N.Y.C, May 23, 1945; d. John F. and Rita C. (Lietz) Cain; m. Marshall R.B.. Thompson; children: Tori, John, Daniel. BS, Mt. St. Mary's Coll., L.A., 1967. Cert. pub. health nurse; RN. Pres. Tellem Pub. Rels. Agy., Marina del Rey, Calif., 1977-80, Rowland Grody Tellem, L.A., 1980-90; chmn. The Rowland Co., L.A., 1990—; pres., CEO Tellem, Inc., L.A., 1992-93; instr. UCLA Extension, 1983—; speaker numerous seminars and confs. on pub. rels. Editor: Sports Medicine for the '80's, Sports Medicine Digest, 1982-84. Bd. dirs. Marymount High Sch., 1984-87, pres., 1984-86; bd. dirs. L.A. Police Dept. Booster Assn., 1984-87; mem. Cath. Press Coun.; mem. pres.'s coun. Mus. Sci. and Industry. Mem. Am. Soc. Hosp. Mktg. and Pub. Rels., Healthcare Mktg. and Pub. Rels. Assn., Pub. Rels. Soc. Am. (bd. dirs. 1994—), L.A. Counselors, PETA, Am. Lung Assn. (chair comm. com. L.A. chpt.) Soc. for Prevention of Cruelty to Animals (chair PetSet), Sports Club (L.A.). Roman Catholic. Office: Tellem Inc Museum Sq 5757 Wilshire Blvd Ste 655 Los Angeles CA 90036-3686

TELLER, PAULINE IVANCOVICH, artist; b. Ross, Calif., May 3, 1914; d. Baldo Aloysius and Marien Barron Ivancovich; m. Frederic de Peyster Teller II, Aug. 29, 1941; children: Joan Teller Coda, Peter Ivancovich, Anne Teller Wallace, Frederic de Peyster III. BFA, Dominican Coll., 1936. One-woman shows include San Francisco Mus. Modern Art, 1940, Dominican Coll. Libr., 1975, Ross Valley Clinic, 1976, Marin Civic Ctr. Adminstrn. Bldg Gallery, 1981, Mus. Mission San Juan Capistrano, 1987, Hobar Gallery, Santa Barbara, Calif., 1989; exhibites include San Francisco Art Assn., 1939, Fine Arts Bldg GGIE, 1940, San Francisco Women Artists, 1945, Marin Soc. Artists, 1936-85, Terra Linda Art Assn., 1936-85, Soc. Western Artists, 1936-85, Marin Art Guild, 1970-85, Calif. State Fair, Sacramento, 1970-85, Gilbert Gallery, San Francisco, 1970-85, Shorebirds Gallery, Tiburon, 1970-85, L.A. Design Ctr., 1987, Village Artistry, Carmel, Calif., 1988-89, Linda Vida Gallery, Ruidoso, N.Mex., 1988-89, Hobar Gallery, Santa Barbara, Calif., 1989-90, Vigil Gallery, Sonoma, Calif., 1990, Nevada City, Calif., 1990, Linda Lundeen Gallery, Las Cruces, N.Mex., 1991, Projects Gallery, San Rafael, Calif., 1991, Arlene Siegel Gallery, N.Mex.; represented in permanent collections at Mrs. J.H. Dollar, Hr., Kentfield, Dr. Gary Boero, San Rafael, Domonican Coll., Leafy Mayhew, Sacramento, Stanford (Calif.) U., San Domenico Sch. San Anselmo, Calif., Stanford U. Hosp., Saiter Packard Children's Hosp., Stanford, Calif., others. Mem. Nat. Mus. Women in Arts (charter). Home: 290 Harvard Dr Larkspur CA 94939

TELLER, SUSAN ELAINE, lawyer; b. San Diego, Calif., May 27, 1953; d. Jack and Joan (Mayer) T.; m. Donald F. Austin, July 6, 1980; children: Greg Austin, Cary Austin, Jack Austin. BA, Calif. State U., Sonoma, 1975; JD, Hastings Coll. of Law, 1979. Bar: Calif. 1980, Oreg. 1994, Wash. 1994. Assoc. Shapiro and Thorn, San Francisco, 1981-83; ptnr. Silverman and Teller, Alameda, Calif., 1983-93; assoc. Gevurtz, Menashe, et. al., Portland, Oreg., 1993-95; ptnr. Demary & Teller, Portland, 1995—. Bd. dirs. Bus. and Profl. Women, Alameda; pres. PTA, Alameda. Named Woman of the Yr. Bus. Owner, Alameda Bus. and Profl. Women, 1988. Mem. Soroptimist Internat., AAUW, Oreg. Women's Lawyers, Queen's Bench, Soroptimist Internat. (bd. dirs. 1989). Office: Demary & Teller 6720 SW Macadam Ave Portland OR 97219

TELLO, DONNA, tax strategist; b. Annapolis, Md., Mar. 23, 1955; m. Gregory Tello, July 5, 1975 (div. 1978); children: Jesse Elliott Timothy Tello, Kimberlle Shey Thommasson; m. Dennis R. Thompson, Apr. 1, 1987 (dec. Jan. 1994). Enrolled agt. Owner Tax Savers, San Diego, 1981—. Libertarian party candidate for state assembly, 1984; candidate Calif. State Senate, 1996. Mem. Inland Soc. Tax Cons. (sec. San Diego chpt. 1989, bd. dirs. 1990, 2d v.p. 1991, 1st v.p. 1992, pres. 1993, soc. chmn. govt. affairs 1991, 93, 94, soc. sec. 1992, soc. pres. 1995, 96), Nat. Taxpayers Union, Camelopard Club (co-founder, treas. 1988-90, pres. 1995-96), Toastmasters (v.p. edn. Liberty chpt. 1987). Office: 14168 Poway Rd Ste 109 Poway CA 92064-4938

TEMELES, MARGARET STEWART, psychiatrist; b. Somerville, Mass., May 29, 1922; d. Henry Malcolm Stewart and Margaret Louise Nuttall; m. Lawrence Temeles; children: Gretchen Lee, Ethan Joel, Daniel Stewart. BS, Tufts U., 1943, MD, 1948. Diplomate Nat. Bd. Med. Examiners. Psychiat. cons. Camden Youth Detention Ctr., Lakeland, N.J., 1952-53; asst. chief of staff (now emeritus) Phila. Psychiat. Ctr. (name changed to Belmont Ctr.), 1952—; sr. psychiat. cons. Bryn Mawr (Pa.) Coll., 1964-86; clin. assoc. prof. Hahnemann Med. Coll., Phila., 1966—; cons. Disability Det. Svcs., Augusta, Maine, 1986-95. Author: (with others) Frontiers of Infant Psychology, 1983, Vulnerable Child, vol. I, 1993; editor: Bemoaning the Lost Dream, 1984; contbr. articles to profl. jours. Rsch. grantee Bryn Mawr Coll., 1982. Mem. Am. Psychiat. Assn., Am. Assn. Psychoanalysis, Internat. Assn. Psychoanalysis, World Assn. Infant Psychiatry, Assn. Child Psychoanalysis (recorder Phila. area study group 1980-85), Phila. Assn. Psychoanalysis (child study group 1962-86, child and adult faculty 1967-86, editor jour. 1979-85). Home and Office: 206 E Pleasant St Amherst MA 01002

TEMELKOFF, VONDA LEE, counselor, therapist; b. Sharon, Pa., July 12, 1937; d. Edward Hopkins and Alberta (Hall; m. Thomas B. Temelkoff, Nov. 10, 1956; children: Linda Temelkoff Schuller, Thomas C., Timothy B., Todd A. BS in Edn., Youngstown State U., 1970, MS in Edn., 1986; postgrad., Kent State U., 1981, 90, 92, Akron State U., 1981, Mt. St. Joseph, Cin., 1987, Bowling Green State U., 1989, Ashland Coll., 1990, Drake U., 1990. Cert. sch. counselor, Ohio tchr., Ohio; nat. bd. cert. counselor; nat. bd. cert. sch. counselor; lic. profl. counselor, Ohio. Tchr. elem. Woodside Elem. Sch., Austintown, Ohio, 1971-84; tchr. Am. history Austintown Middle Sch., 1984-85; tchr. math. and sci. Frank Ohl Middle Sch., Austintown, 1986-87; guidance counselor five elem. schs. Austintown, 1987—; children's therapist Regional Assocs. in Counseling, Canfield, Ohio, 1987-91; presenter, trainer parent workshop Austintown Elem. Sch., winter 1989, 91; speaker Rotary and Kiwanis, 1987, 89; presentor, facilitator, speaker parenting and drug free schs. programs Communtiy Orgns. and Ohio Sch. Confs.; intern NEOUCOM Cancer Rsch. Ctr., Rootstown, summer 1986. Writer, prodr. (video) It's Your Choice, 1986. Youngstown State U. scholar, 1985-86, Jennings scholar, 1993-94. Mem. AAUW (bd. dirs. 1987, program v.p. 1988), NEA, Ohio Edn. Assn., Austintown Edn. Assn. (bldg. rep. 1978), Am. Counseling Assn., Ohio Assn. for Counseling and Devel., Internat. Reading Assn. (bd. dirs. membership com. 1989), Friends of Am. Art, Chi Sigma Iota, Delta Kappa Gamma Soc. Republican. Episcopalian. Home: 235 Topaz Cir Canfield OH 44406-9676

TEMIN, DAVIA BETH, marketing executive; b. Cleve., June 5, 1952; d. J.T. and Sylvia (Black) Temin; m. Walter T. Kicinski, Aug. 10, 1991. BA, Swarthmore Pa./Coll., 1974; MA, Columbia U., 1976. Cmty. svcs. specialist Commonwealth Mass., Boston, 1975; editor-in-chief, founder Hermes mag. Columbia U. Bus. Sch., N.Y.C., 1976-79, dir. publ. affairs, 1979-83; v.p., dir. mktg. Citicorp Global Investment Bank, N.Y.C., 1983-86; v.p., dir. corp. mktg. Scudder, Stevens & Clark, N.Y.C., 1986-89; pres. The Temin Group, 1989-90; v.p., dir. mktg. Schroder Wertheim & Co., Inc., 1990-96; corp. v.p.. head corp. mktg. GE Capital, Stamford, Conn., 1996—; exec. prodr. The Night & The Music Prodns., 1994—. Chmn., bd. dirs. Mark Taylor Dance Co., 1987—, bd. dirs. The Fin. Comm. Soc., 1994—; advisor to pres. Swarthmore Coll., 1994—, trustee, 1995—; bd. advisors Knight-Bagelot Fellowship Journalism Sch. Columbia U., 1995—. Recipient Meritorious Svc. award Commonwealth of Mass., 1976. Mem. Fgn. Policy Assn., Pub. Rels. Soc. (exec. com., bd. dirs.), Fin. Women's Assn., Columbia Bus. Sch. Club, Swarthmore Club, Princeton Club. Home: 530 E 90th St Apt 5K New York NY 10128-7860 Office: GE Capital 260 Long Ridge Rd Stamford CT 06927

TEMKIN, JUDITH CELIA, elementary school educator; b. N.Y.C., July 16, 1943; d. Samuel and Lucy Clara (Bogage) Olchak; m. Samuel Temkin, June 20, 1965; children: David, Michael. BA magna cum laude, Queens Coll., 1964. Cert. elem. tchr., N.Y., N.J., R.I. Tchr. Providence Pub. Schs., 1965-66, Highland Park (N.J.) Pub. Schs., 1967-68, 77-78; adult basic edn. tchr. Bound Brook (N.J.) Pub. Schs., 1972-74; kindergarten tchr. Rutgers Prep. Sch., Somerset, N.J., 1976-77; gifted tchr. Milltown (N.J.) Sch. Dist., 1978-83, elem. tchr., 1983—, early childhood edn. leader tchr., 1993-94; presenter workshops on techniques for tchg. gifted, Office of the County Supt., Middlesex County, N.J., 1979-82, Getting Children to Write, 1984. Chairperson desegregation com. Highland Park Bd. Edn., 1978-79, mem. long-range planning com., 1972-74; pres. Highland Park chpt. LWV, 1976-77, chairperson edn. com., 1967-74. Recipient Gov.'s Tchr. Recognition award, 1995-96. Mem. Internat. Reading Assn., N.J. Sci. Tchrs. Assn., Phi Beta Kappa. Home: 113 Graham St Highland Park NJ 08904-2131 Office: Parkview Sch Violet Ter Milltown NJ 08850

TEMKINA, MARINA Z., poet, scholar; b. Leningrad, Soviet Union, Feb. 24, 1948; arrived in U.S., 1979; d. Zalman and Sara (Komm) T.; m. Sergei N. Blumin, Oct. 8, 1966 (div. Oct. 1990); 1 child, Daniel S. Blumin; ptnr. Michael F. Gerard, Sept., 1989. Student, Leningrad State U., 1967-71, MA in History and Cultural Studies, 1977; postgrad. intern, Hermitage State Mus., Leningrad, 1976-77; postgrad., Vienna State U., 1978-79. Freelance journalist Russia divsn. The Voice of Am. Broadcasting, N.Y.C., 1982-85, Radio Free Europe, N.Y.C., 1986-87; translator, occulturation cons. N.Y. Assn. for New Ams., N.Y.C., 1988-94; freelance writer, lectr., 1985—. Author: (book of verses) Part of Part, 1985, (books of poems) In Reverse, 1989, Kalancha, 1995; co-author: (artist's book) Observatoire Geomnesique, 1990. Chmn., co-founder The Archive: Inst. for Russian Jews in Diaspora, N.Y.C., 1996—; interviewer Survivors of the Shoah, L.A., 1996. Recipient Pergamon Press award Djerassi Found., 1989, Young Critics award Union of Artists, 1977; grantee Nat. Endowment Arts, U.S. Fed. Agy., 1994. Mem. Am. Assn. for Advancement of Slavic Studies (mem. Women East-West), PEN Am. Ctr. (bd. dirs. silent voices com. 1982-83), Network of East-West Women. Jewish.

TEMPEL, JEAN C., venture capital company executive; married; 2 children. BA in Math., Conn. Coll., 1965; MS in Computer Sci., Rensselaer Poly. Inst., 1972; postgrad., Harvard U., 1979. Various sr. mgmt. positions Conn. Bank and Trust Co., 1965-80; mgr. strategic planning and mktg. Bank New Eng., 1980-82; with Boston Co., 1983-90, exec. v.p., COO, 1985-90; mgmt. cons. Tempel Ptnrs. Inc., Boston, 1991; pres., COO, bd. dirs. Safeguard Scis. Inc., Wayne, Pa., 1992-93; gen. ptnr. TL Ventures affiliate Safeguard Scis. Inc., Boston, 1991—; mem. info. strategy group Am. Express, 1983-90; founder, pres. Boston Safe Clearing Corp., 1983-90; bd. dirs. Cambridge Tech. Ptnrs. Inc., Centocor, Inc., Sonesta Internat. Hotels, Inc., XL Vision, Inc.; trustee Scudder Funds; bd. dirs., chmn. Iprax Corp. Trustee Conn. Coll., Huntington Theater Co.; bd. overseers Northeastern U.; mem. adminstrn. and fin. com. United Way Massachusetts Bay. Office: TL Ventures Ten Post Office Sq Ste 1325 Boston MA 02109-4603

TEMPERATO, SUSAN, mental health counselor, clinical supervisor; b. Buffalo, N.Y., Mar. 14, 1948; d. Anthony F. and Rose M. (Iraci) T. BA in Psychology, Daemen Coll. (Rosary Hill Coll.), Buffalo, N.Y., 1971; MS in

Counselor Edn., Canisius Coll., Buffalo, 1985. Cert. clin. mental health counselor, nat. counselor, hypnotherapist. Tchr. Psychology, Sociology Mount St. Joseph Academy, Buffalo, 1970-71; mgmt. trainee Adam, Meldrum & Anderson, Buffalo, 1971-72; child care social worker Tiny Tot Child Devel. Ctr., Buffalo, 1972-83; supportive advocate for rape and sexual assault Suicide Prevention and Crisis Svcs., Buffalo, 1985-87, emergency admissions designee, 1985-87; cert. clin. mental health counselor Horizon Human Svcs., Buffalo, 1987—; part time pvt. practice, 1989—; mental health del. to People's Rep. of China People to People Citizen Amb. Program, 1994. V.p. N.Y. State Mental Health Counselors Assn., 1987-89. Mem. Am. Counselor's Assn., Am. Mental Health Counselors Assn. (nat. membership chair 1991-92, Profl. Svc. award 1992), N.Y. State Assn. for Counseling and Devel., N.Y. State Mental Health Counselors Assn. Office: 699 Hertel Ave Ste 350 Buffalo NY 14207

TEMPLETON, FIONA, performance artist, writer. Performances include: Recognition, 1993, 94, 95, 96, She Held Her Peace: 'Twas Strange!, 1994, Realities/Metamorphosis, 1992, Articulate Architecture, 1992, Be Our Guest, 1992, Where on Earth, 1990, Delirium of Interpretations, 1990, 91, You-The City, 1988—, Strange to Relate, 1989, Experiments in the Destruction of Time, 1983, Thought/Death, 1980, Defense, 1982, Cupid and Psyche, 1981, Out of My Way, 1988, A/Version, 1985, Against Agreement, 1981-82, Under Paper Spells, 1981-82, The Seven Deadly Jealousies, 1981-82, There Was Absent Achilles, 1981-82, The Hypothetical Third Person, 1987, Out of the Mouths, 1984, The New Three-Act Piece, 1983; co-founder, Theatre of Mistakes, London, 1975; author: Elements of Performance Art, 1976, London, 1984, You-The City, 1990, Cells of Release, 1997, Delirium of Interpretations, 1996. Home: 100 St Marks Pl Apt 7 New York NY 10009-5846

TEMPO, HOLLY JANE, artist, educator, artists association executive; b. Mpls., Feb. 3, 1964; d. Mary Jane (Riley) Jacobs; m. John Charles Eichinger, June 27, 1987 (div. 1993). BA, Pitzer Coll., 1986; MFA, Claremont Grad. Sch., 1991. Lectr. Scripps Coll., Claremont, Calif., 1993-94; adminstrv. asst. D'Agnenica Angels Project, L.A., 1994; dir. Lucky Nun Gallery, L.A., 1994-95; art instr. Riverside (Calif.) C.C., 1995—, Mt. San Antonio Coll., Walnut, Calif., 1995—; lectr. Artsreach program UCLA, 1995; dir. Seeking It Through Exhibitions SITE, L.A., 1995—; guest artist, lectr. Pomona Coll., Claremont, Calif., 1994, Calif. State U., Fullerton, 1994; guest curator Aria Noir Gallery, Pomona, 1995, Da Gallery, Pomona, 1990. Exhbns. include Kohn Turner Gallery, 1994, William Turner Gallery Annex, 1995, Calif. State L.A., 1996. Organizer of exhibition for Coun. of Chs., Homeless Pomona-Inland Valley, 1994. Recipient Honorarium L.A. Contemporary Exhibitions, 1991; Elsie DeWolf Found. scholar, 1986. Mem. Support Assocs. Grad. Art (v.p. 1994-96). Home: 2200 Glendale Blvd Los Angeles CA 90039 Office: Seeking It Through Exhbns PO Box 64885 Los Angeles CA 90017

TENER, CAROL JOAN, retired secondary education educator; b. Cleve., Feb. 10, 1935; d. Peter Paul and Mamie Christine (Dombrowski) Manusack; m. Dale Keith Tener, Feb. 13, 1958 (div. Aug. 1991); children: Dean Robert, Susan Dawn. Student, Cleve. Mus. Art, 1948-53, Cleve. Art Inst., 1953-54; BS in Edn. cum laude, Kent State U., 1957; MS in Supervision, Akron U., 1974; postgrad., Kent State U., 1964, 81, 88-90, Akron U., 1975, 79, John Carroll U., 1982, 83, 85-86, Ohio U., 1987, Baldwin Wallace Coll., 1989. Cert. permanent K-12 tchr., Ohio. Stenographer Equitable Life Iowa, Cleve., 1953-54; tchr. elem. art Cuyahoga Falls (Ohio) Bd. Edn., 1957-58, 62-63, 1965-68, tchr. jr. h.s., 1968-69; tchr. h.s. Brecksville (Ohio)-Broadview Heights Sch. Dist., 1969-94; chmn. dept. art Brecksville-Broadview Heights (Ohio) H.S., 1979-94; ret., chmn. curriculum devel., 1982, 89; instr. for children Kent State U., 1956; advisor, prodr. cmty. svc. in art Brecksville Broadview Heights Bd. of Edn., 1969-94; former tchr. recreation and adult art edn. 1967-68, City of Cuyahoga Falls, 1967-68; com. mem. North Ctrl. Evaluation Com., Nordonia City, Ohio, 1978, Solon City, Ohio, 1989; chmn. north ctrl. evaluation com. Garfield Heights H.S., 1991; chair pilot program curriculum devel. com. in art/econs. Brecksville-Broadview Heights H.S., 1985, 86. Contbr. articles to newspapers, brochures, mags.; commd. artist for mural Brecksville City's Kids Quarters, 1994, Christopher Columbus/John Glen portraits in relief commemorating Columbus Day, 1961, Wooster (Ohio) Products Co. Chmn. Artmart Invitational Exhibit PTA, 1982-94; active Meals on Wheels, 1995-96, Brecksville Broadview, Cancer, 1993-95, Leukemia, 1995, Heart Disease collection, 1995, Stow-Glen Assisted Living Visitations, 1994-95, NCR Assisted Living transp. provision to hosps. and dr. in neighboring county; trustee Gettysburg Devel. Block Group Parma, 1995-96, Kids Quarters, 1994. Recipient Ohio Coun. on Econ. Edn. award, 1985-86, award for significant svc. to cmty. Retired and Sr. Vol. Program of USA, 1996; Pres.'s scholar Kent State U., 1954-57. Mem. ASCD, Nat. Art Edn. Assn., Ohio Ret. Tchrs. Assn., Internat. Platform Assn., Brecksville Edn. Assn., Acad. Econ. Edn., Cleve. Mus. Art, NAFE, Nat. Mus. Women in Arts, S.W. Area Retired Educators (program chair 1996—), Phi Delta Kappa Pi. Roman Catholic. Home: 7301 Sagamore Rd Parma OH 44134-5732

TENER, LISA C., housing program executive; b. N.Y.C., Apr. 2, 1963; d. Martin J. and Elizabeth C. (Berger) T. BS, Mass. Inst. Tech., 1984, MS, 1989. Fin. modeling analyst Pacific Gas & Electric, San Francisco, 1984-87; programming analyst Fidelity Investments, Boston, 1987-88; nat. acct. exec. AT&T, Boston, 1989-90; exec. dir. The Hospitality Program, Boston, 1990—; ednl. counselor Mass. Inst. Tech., Cambridge, 1991-96. Mem. Women in Devel. (newsletter com. 1990-93, mentor 1994). Home: 81 Toxteth St Brookline MA 02146 Office: The Hospitality Program 138 Tremont St Boston MA 02111

TENG, JULIET, artist; d. Teng Lenten and Ho Wai Yu; children: Brendan, Trish, Jamie, Stacy, Phaeleau. B Commerce, U. Rangoon. Programmer First Boston Corp., N.Y.C.; systems programmer Chase Manhattan, N.Y.C., Merrill Lynch, Pierce, Fenner & Smith, Inc., N.Y.C.; artist/painter, 1976—. Exhbns. include Nat. Arts Club, N.Y.C., Pastel Soc. Am., N.Y.C., Audubon Artists Soc., N.Y.C., Catherine Lorrilard Wolf Art Club, N.Y.C., Painters and Sculptors Soc. N.J., N.Y.C., Knickerbocker Artists Am. Soc., N.Y.C., Keene-Mason Galleries, N.Y.C., Nat. Art Ctr., N.Y.C., Hudson Valley Art Assn., Westchester, N.Y., Manchester Art Ctr., Vt., Five Point Gallery, East Chatham, N.Y., Connoisseur Gallery, Rhinebeck, N.Y., Ridgewood Art Inst., N.J., The New England Fine Art Inst., Boston, numerous others. Mem. Nat. Arts Club, Art Students League. Home: 34 Sesame St Old Chatham NY 12136

TENNEY, PATRICIA ANN, psychotherapist, nurse; b. Hartford, Conn., Oct. 15, 1942; d. Adam Edward Waite and Catherine Helen Russell; m. John Lawrence Tenney, Nov. 25, 1967; children: Jeffrey Russell, Kate Theresa. Grad. in nursing, Cooley Dickinson Hosp., Northampton, Mass., 1964; BS in Sociology cum laude, Bridgewater State Coll., 1987; MA in Rehab. Counseling, Assumption Coll., Worcester, Mass., 1990. RN cert., N.J.; cert. in adult psychiatry. Head nurse, acting supr. Medfield State Hosp., Harding, Mass., 1964-67; supr. Bridgewater (Mass.) State Hosp., 1967-90, asst. DON, 1990-93; pvt. practice psychotherapy, behavioral cons., Taunton, Mass., 1993—; ct. apptd. guardian, Taunton, 1993—; facilitator S.E. Lung Assn., Middleboro, Mass., 1993—. Pres. St. Mary's Guild, Taunton, 1989-91; elected nursing rep. to bd. dirs. Taunton Nursing Home. Mass. Mental Health Nurses Assn. scholar, 1994. Mem. Mass. Nurses Assn. (nursing practice com. dist. IIII 1967—, bd. dirs. 1992-95, pres. unit 7, 1990-93, del. to ANA conv. 1990-95), Mass. Mental Health Nurses Assn. (v.p. 1987—), Mass. Mental Health Orgn. (lic.), Marriage and Family Therapists (lic.), Taunton C. of C. Democrat. Roman Catholic. Home: 14 Evergreen Dr Taunton MA 02780 Office: Behavioral Cons 135 Washington St Taunton MA 02780

TENNIHILL, SALLY KAY, writer, music educator; b. Columbus, Feb. 14, 1941; d. Wayne Harris and Ruth Anne Downs; m. Jack Tennihill (dec.), Oct. 17, 1961; children: John, Ralph, Myrtle, Joe. BA in English, Northwest Mo. State U., 1985, MA in English, 1987. Tchr. piano Maryville, Mo., 1970—; cert. nurse asst. Nodaway Nursing Home, Maryville, Mo., 1982-84; grad. asst. Northwest Mo. State U., Maryville, Mo., 1985-86, tchg. asst., 1986-87; substitute tchr. St. Joseph (Mo.) Sch. Bd., 1988-93; stringer St. Joseph News-Press, 1988-92. Contbr. poems, short stories to books, anthologies; editor: (creative mag.) Envy's Sting, 1985-86; dir., actor Nodaway County Theatre Co., Maryville, 1991-96. Mem. Coalition Against Domestic Violence, Maryville, Mo., 1987-96, Prison Fellowship, Maryville, 1996, Willa Cather Found., Maryvielle, 1993-96; head Women's Resource Ctr. Northwest Mo. U., Maryville, 1984-87; pres. M.S. Support Group, Maryville, 1995-96; v.p. Nodaway County Civil War Roundtable. Recipient Mattie Dykes Creative Writer scholarship, Presdl. Scholar's scholarship. Mem. AAUW, Retired Tchrs. Maryville, Sons and Daus. of the Civil War. Home: 123 Park Ave Maryville MO 64468

TENPAS, KATHLEEN M., dairy farmer, poet; b. Wickford, R.I., Apr. 14, 1952; d. Harold R. and Verna Lee (White) Mason; m. Stanley L. Tenpas, July 16, 1971; children: Julia, Melissa. Attended, Empire State Coll., Saratoga Springs, N.Y., 1972-75; AA, Jamestown (N.Y.) C.C., 1984; student, Antioch U., Yellow Springs, Ohio, 1995—. Artist in residence Art-in-Edn. Arts Coun. Chautauqua Co., Jamestown, N.Y., 1986—; tchr. spl. studies Schs. Dept., Chautauqua (N.Y.) Instn., 1993—. Editor: (small press lit. mag.) Arachne, Inc., 1980-93; author: (book) Hill Farm, 1985 (award 1985), (play) Hill Farm, 1988. Recipient Fund For the Arts fellow Arts Coun. Chautauqua County, 1989, Poetry Contest Reader's award Three Rivers Arts Festival, 1990. Mem. Reformed Ch. Home: 7549 Rt 474 N Clymer Panama NY 14767

TENUTA, JEAN LOUISE, sports reporter, medical technologist; b. Kenosha, Wis., Apr. 12, 1958; d. Fred and Lucy Ann (Taylor) Tenuta; m. Robert Louis Bennett, Nov. 22, 1989. BS in Biology, U.Wis., 1979; BA in Journalism, Marquette U., 1983; MS in Print Journalism, Northwestern U., 1989. Sports reporter Kenosha News, 1978-84, Washington Post, 1984-86, Jour. Messenger, Manassas, Va., 1986, Jour. Times, Racine, Wis., 1988-89; med. technologist St. Therese Med. Ctr., Waukegan, Ill., 1980-83, 86-87, Suburban Hosp., Bethesda, Md., 1985-86, Group Health Assn., Washington, 1985-86, St. Francis Hosp., Milw., 1988-89; sports reporter Jour.-Gazette, Ft. Wayne, Ind., 1989-90; med. technologist Columbia Hosp., Milw., 1991; tech. assoc. Coll. Am. Pathologists, 1991—. Recipient 1st place in sports writing Capital Press Women, 1986, 87, Women's Press Club of Ind., 1990, 91, Nat. Fedn. Press Women, 1986, 91. Mem. Am. Assn. for Clin. Chemistry (tox/TDM sect.), Am. Soc. Clin. Pathologists, Assn. Women in Sports Media (Midwest region coord. 1990-95, v.p. adminstrn. 1995—), Nat. Fedn. Press Women (treas. Capital area 1985-87, 1st pl. in sports writing 1986, 91), Soc. Profl. Journalists, Women in Comms. (v.p., sec. Milw. chpt.), Nat. Writers Club, Midwest Assn. for Toxicology & Therapeutic Drug Monitoring (sec., treas. 1995—, newsletters editor 1995—), Italian Geneaol. Soc. of Am., DAR (publicity chmn. mag. chmn. Kenosha chpt. 1994—), Friends of Kenosha Pub. Libr. (life). Democrat. Home: 9110 32nd Ave Kenosha WI 53142-5426 Office: Coll Am Pathologists 325 Waukegan Rd Northfield IL 60093-2719

TEPLITZKY, ELLEN C., lawyer; b. Wilmington, Del., Sept. 17, 1956; d. James N. and Edna B. (Baylson) Chaikin; m. Bruce A. Teplitzky, Oct. 5, 1985; children: Hannah L., Sarah B. BA, Emory Coll., 1978; JD, Emory U., 1982; LLM, U. London, 1992. Bar: Del. 1983. Assoc. levin, Spiller & Goldlust, Wilmington, Del., 1982-83; dep. atty. gen. Del. Dept. of Justice, Wilmington, 1983-85; sr. asst. regional counsel U.S. EPA, Phila., 1985-90; asst. gen. counsel Environsafe Svcs. Inc., Horsham, Pa., 1993-94; corp. counsel cons. LEXIS-NEXIS, Phila., 1994—. Mem. Am. Corp. Counsel Assn., Del. Bar Assn. Home: 21 Edgewood Rd Yardley PA 19067 Office: LEXIS-NEXIS One Liberty Pl Ste 1650 1650 Market St Philadelphia PA 19103

TEPPER, AMANDA, bank executive; b. N.Y.C., July 17, 1963; d. Ronald and Nancy (Boxley) T.; m. Jeffrey David Kiker, Feb. 14, 1993. BA, Brown U., 1985; MBA, U. Pa., 1991. Music dir. Sta. WPLR-FM, New Haven, 1985-86; corp. bond marketer Mabon, Nugent & Co., N.Y.C., 1986-89; with sect. banking and fin. Chem. Bank, N.Y.C., 1991-92, banking and corporate fin. assoc., 1992-94, v.p. banking and corporate fin., 1995—; v.p. Corporate Fin. Chase Securities Inc., 1996—. Fishman-Davidson Ctr. Grant fellow Fishman-Davidson Ctr., U. Pa., 1990-91. Mem. Banking and corp. Fin. Assn., Phi Beta Kappa. Home: 21 W End Ave Summit NJ 07901-1213 Office: Chase Securities Inc 270 Park Ave Fl 10 New York NY 10017-2014

TEPPER, LYNN MARSHA, gerontology educator; b. N.Y.C., Mar. 16, 1946; d. Jack Mortimer and Ida (Golembe) Drukatz; m. William Chester Tepper, Aug. 27, 1967; children: Sharon Joy, Michelle Dawn. BS, SUNY, Buffalo, 1967; MA, Wayne State U., 1971; MS, Columbia U., 1977, EdM, 1978, EdD, 1980. Instr. John F. Kennedy Sch., Berlin, 1967-68, ednl. counselor, 1968-69; ednl. coordinator Army Edn. Ctr., Berlin, 1969-71; psychologist U.S. Dept. Def., Berlin, 1971-73; prof. Gerontology L.I. U., Dobbs Ferry, N.Y., 1979—, Columbia U., N.Y.C., 1982—; cons. NATO, Belgium, Naples, Italy, 1969-71, numerous nursing homes, N.Y.C., 1978—, Found. for Long Term Care, 1992—; prof. gerontology Mercy Coll., Dobbs Ferry, 1979—; dir. Gerontology Resource Ctr., Ctr. for Geriatrics and Gerontology, Columbia U., N.Y.C., 1980-85, dir. divsn. behavioral sci., 1982—; del. White House Conf. on Aging, 1980. Author: (textbooks) Long Term Care, 1993, Respite Care, 1993; contbr. articles to profl. jours. and textbooks. Advisor Office on Aging, State of N.Y., Albany, 1980—; dir. Mercy Coll., Inst. Gerontology, 1990—; trustee St. Cabrini Nursing Home, 1991—. Brookdale Inst. on Aging fellow, 1983. Fellow Gerontol. Soc. Am.; mem. Northeastern Gerontol. Soc., N.Y. Assn. Gerontol. Edn., Am. Psychol. Assn. Home: 50 Burnside Dr Hastings Hdsn NY 10706-3013 Office: Columbia U Med Campus Box 20 630 W 168th St New York NY 10032

TEPPER, PHYLLIS ANN, museum school registrar; b. N.Y.C., Feb. 21, 1930; d. Isidor and Mollie (Siegel) Schnipper; m. Stanley Raffalo, Sept. 15, 1963 (dec. Mar. 1964); m. Irving Tepper, Mar. 2, 1967; stepsons: Robert S., Brian L. BA, Queens Coll., 1951; MA, NYU, 1963. Tchr. L.A. Bd. Edn., 1951-52, Bd. Edn., South Plainfield, N.J., 1964-67; registrar mus. sch. Mus. Am. Folk Art, N.Y.C., 1985-94; mem. friends com. bd. Mus. Am. Folk Art, N.Y.C., 1984-88, dir. N.Y. Quilt Project, 1986-94, lectr., 1987-94, guest curator, 1994. Author: New York Beauties, 1992. Chmn. regional planning study LWV, Metuchen, N.J., 1964-66, mem. dir., chmn. urban problems, 5 Towns chpt. Nassau County, N.Y., 1967-77. Fellow Mus. Am. Folk Art; mem. AAUW, Brandeis Univ. Nat. Women's Com., Am. Quilt Study Group.

TER-ABRAMYANTS, LALA ABRAMOVNA, artist, educator; b. Myaundzha, Kolyma, USSR, Aug. 4, 1956; d. Abram Moiseevitch and Valentina Vasilevna (Shestakova) T.-A.; m. Vitaliy Alexandrovich Osminin, July 8, 1980 (div. Sept. 1988); 1 child, Veronika Osminina; m. Alex Korsunsky, Jan. 5, 1991; 1 child, Abram Korsunsky. Student, Art Inst. Moscow, 1990. Photo retoucher Armavir (Russia) Photo Studio, 1974-75; artist designer Rwy. Sta. Dept., Moscow, 1975-80; archivist Art Inst. Moscow, 1983-86; graphic artist Newspaper Pub. House, Moscow, 1986-87; visual artist Factory of Art Prodn., Moscow, 1987-90; silk painter Factory of Art Prodn., 1990-92; pvt. tchr. drawing and painting Bronx, N.Y., 1994—; instr. painting on silk Riverdale YM-YWHA, N.Y.C., 1995; batic textile artist OUS Co. Inc., 1993—. Exhibited in group shows at Moscow Textile Fabrics, Oslo, Norway, 1991, Ctrl. House of Painters, Moscow, 1992, Princeton, N.Y., 1992, Madison Sq., N.Y.C., 1992, NYANA, N.Y.C., 1993, L.I., N.Y., 1994, Lincoln Sq., N.Y.C., 1996. Home: 3871 Sedgwick Ave Apt 6J Bronx NY 10463

TERHORST, CHERYL ANN, journalist; b. Buffalo, Aug. 3, 1960; d. Paul Bernard and Mary Jean (McNab) terH.; m. Burt W. Constable, Mar. 26, 1988; 2 children. BS in Journalism, U. Ill., 1982. Editorial asst. Woman;s Day mag., N.Y.C., 1982-84; city reporter Daily Herald, Arlington Heights, Ill., 1984-85, edn. reporter, 1985-86, feature writer, 1987—. Vol. Community Response, Oak Park, Ill., 1992-94. Recipient Peter Lisagor award Soc. Profl. Journalists, 1991, 94. Office: Daily Herald PO Box 280 Arlington Heights IL 60006

TERHUNE, JANE HOWELL, legal assistant, educator; b. Newark, June 8, 1932; d. Charles Edwin and Audrey L. (Rogers) Howell; m. Richard N. Terhune, Dec. 22, 1951 (div. 1980); children: Richard C., Susan J., Carolyn A. Cert., Katherine Gibbs Sch., 1951. cert. legal asst. specialist, civil litigation. Legal sec. Howell, Kirby, et al, Jacksonville, Fla., 1954-56, Bidwell Adam, Gulfport, Miss., 1962-63; legal asst. Sinkler Gibbs & Simons, Charleston, S.C., 1963-77; sr. legal asst. Hall, Estill, Hardwick, Gable, Golden & Nelson, P.C., Tulsa, Okla., 1977—; adv. com. to legal asst. com. ABA, Chgo., 1978-85; adv. com. legal asst. program Tulsa Jr. Coll., 1978-85; trustee Okla. Sinfonia, Inc., Tulsa, 1984-92; speaker/faculty Cert. Legal Asst. Short Course, 1986—. Contbr. articles to profl. jours.; seminar speaker in field. Mem. Nat. Assn. Legal Assts. (charter pres. 1975-77, chmn. certifying bd. 1977-80, parl. 1988-90), Tulsa Assn. Legal Assts. (parl. 1987-89). Republican. Presbyterian. Home: 3164 S 101st East Ave Tulsa OK 74146-1437 Office: Hall Estill Hardwick Gable Golden & Nelson PC 320 S Boston Ave Ste 400 Tulsa OK 74103-3704

TERIO, ANNE DOROUGH LINNEMANN, foreign service contracting officer, nurse; b. Lafayette, Ga., May 10, 1946; d. Calvin Cummins and Adelia (Park) Linnemann; m. James Donald Moore, Aug. 18, 1963 (div. July 1976); children: Marianne Lea Moore Elbertson, Christopher Cummins; m. Charles John Terio III, June 4, 1987; 1 stepchild, Christopher John. BA in History, U. N.C., Greensboro, 1971; AD in Nursing with honors, Prince George Coll., 1976. RN, Md., Va.; cert. secondary history tchr., N.C. Tchr. history Grimsley H.S., Greensboro, N.C., 1971-72; nurse Drs. Hoeck, Smith & Guarinello, Pediatricians, Clinton, Md., 1977-82; contract specialist Gen. Svcs. Adminstrn. real property contracts div., Washington, 1984-86; contract adminstr. Dept Navy Military Sealift Command M-104, Washington, 1986-88; contract specialist Dept. Transportation Maritime Adminstrn., Washington, 1988-92, U.S. AID, Rosslyn, Va., 1992-94; joined Fgn. Svc., 1994; contracting officer U.S. AID, Cairo, 1994—. Mem. Nat. Contract Mgmt. Assn., Beta Sigma Phi (numerous offices, Xi Gamma Gamma chpt., pres. 1992-93). Republican. Baptist. Home: Unit 64902 APO AE 09839-4902 Office: USAID Cairo Unit 64902 APO AE 09839-4902

TERMINI, ROSEANN BRIDGET, lawyer; b. Phila., Feb. 2, 1953; d. Vincent James and Bridget (Marano) T. BS magna cum laude, Drexel U., 1975; MEd, Temple U., 1979, JD, 1985. Bar: Pa. 1985, U.S. Dist. Ct. (ea. dist.) Pa. 1985, D.C. 1986. Jud. clk. Superior Ct. of Pa., Allentown, 1985-86; atty. Pa. Power & Light Co., Allentown, 1986-87; corp. counsel food and drug law Lemmon Co., Sellersville, Pa., 1987-88; sr. dep. atty. bur. consumer protection plain lang. law Office of Atty. Gen., Harrisburg, Pa., 1988-96; prof. U. Villanova U. Sch. Law, 1996—; Contbr. articles to profl. jours., law revs.; spkr. continuing legal edn.-plain lang. laws, environ. conf.; adj. prof. Widener U. Sch. Law, 1993—. Contbr. articles to profl. jours, law revs.; speaker environ. conf. Active in Sr. Citizens Project Outreach, Hospice, 1986—; mem. St. Thomas More Law Bd. Named Outstanding Young Women of Yr., Dauphin County Bar Assn., 1987; Edn. fellow Temple U., 1978-79. Mem. ABA (various coms.), Bar Assn. D.C., Pa. Bar Assn. (ethics, exceptional children and environ. sects.), Temple U. Law Alumni Assn., Drexel U. Alumni Assn., Omicron Nu, Phi Alpha Delta. Home: 1614 Brookhaven Rd Wippewood PA 19096 Office: Villanova U Law Sch Villanova PA 17120

TERNBERG, JESSIE LAMOIN, pediatric surgeon; b. Corning, Calif., May 28, 1924; d. Eric G. and Alta M. (Jones) T. A.B., Grinnell Coll., 1946, Sc.D. (hon.), 1972; Ph.D., U. Tex., 1950; M.D., Washington U., St. Louis, 1953; Sc.D. (hon.), U. Mo., St. Louis, 1981. Diplomate: Am. Bd. Surgery. Intern Boston City Hosp., 1953-54; asst. resident in surgery Barnes Hosp., St. Louis, 1954-57; resident in surgery Barnes Hosp., 1958-59; research fellow Washington U. (Sch. Medicine), 1957-58; practice medicine specializing in pediatric surgery St. Louis, 1966—; instr., trainee in surgery Washington U., 1959-62, asst. prof. surgery, 1962-65, assoc. prof., 1965-71, prof. surgery in pediatrics, 1975—, prof. surgery, 1971—, chief div. pediatric surgery, 1972-90; mem. staff Barnes Hosp., 1974-90, pediatric surgeon in chief, 1974-90, mem. operating room com., 1971—, mem. med. adv. com., 1975—; mem. staff Children's Hosp., dir. pediatric surgery, 1972-90. Contbr. numerous articles on pediatric surgery to profl. jours. Trustee Grinnell Coll., 1984—. Recipient Alumni award Grinnell Coll., 1966, Faculty/Alumni award Washington U. Sch. Medicine, 1991, 1st Aphrodite Jannopaulo Hofsommer award, 1993. Fellow ACS, mem. AAAS, SIOP, Am. Pediatric Surg. Assn., We. Surg. Assn. (2d v.p. 1984-85), St. Louis Med. Soc., Soc. Surgery of the Alimentary Tract, Am. Acad. Pediatrics, Soc. Pelvic Surgeons (v.p. 1991-92), Brit. Assn. Paediatric Surgeons, Assn. Women Surgeons (disting. mem. 1995), Mo. State Surg. Soc., St. Louis Surg. Soc. (pres. 1980-81), St. Louis Pediatric Soc., Soc. Surg. Oncology, Pediatric Oncology Group (chmn. surg. discipline 1983—), St. Louis Childrens Hosp. Soc. (pres. 1979-80), St. Louis Met. Med. Soc. (councilor, trustee), Barnes Hosp. Soc., Phi Beta Kappa, Sigma Xi, Iota Sigma Pi, Alpha Omega Alpha. Office: St Louis Childrens Hosp 1 Childrens Pl Saint Louis MO 63110

TERNUS, ANNE MARIE, journalist; b. Phila., Nov. 21, 1967; d. Robert Arnold and Mary Francis (McAniff) T.; m. Byron Cornell Bellamy, May 29, 1993; 1 child, William Cahill. BS, Northwestern U., 1989. Capitol reporter The Daily Recorder, Sacramento, Calif., 1989-94, sr. staff writer, 1994—. Mem. Sacramento Press Club, Capitol Press Corps. Democrat. Home: 3224 Churchill Rd Sacramento CA 95864 Office: The Daily Recorder 1115 H St Sacramento CA 95814

TERNUS, MARSHA K., judge; b. Vinton, Iowa, May 30, 1951. BA, U. Iowa, 1972; JD, Drake U., 1977. Bar: Iowa. 1977. With Bradshaw, Fowler, Proctor & Fairgrave, Des Moines, Iowa, 1977-93; justice Iowa Supreme Ct., Des Moines, 1993—. Editor-in-chief Drake Law Rev., 1976-77. Mem. Iowa State Bar Assn. (bd. govs. 1985-89), Polk County Bar Assn. (pres. 1984-85), Phi Beta Kappa, Order of Coif. Office: Iowa Supreme Ct State Capital Des Moines IA 50319*

TERPENING, VIRGINIA ANN, artist; b. Lewistown, Mo., July 17, 1917; d. Floyd Raymond and Bertha Edda (Rodifer) Shoup; m. Charles W. Terpening, July 5, 1951; 1 child by previous marriage, V'Ann Baltzelle Dlatrick. Studies with William Woods, Fulton, Mo., 1936-37; student Washington U. Sch. Fine Arts, St. Louis, 1937-40. Exhibited in one-woman shows at Culver-Stockton Coll., Canton, Mo., 1956, Creative Gallery, N.Y.C., 1968, The Breakers, Palm Beach, Fla., 1976; others; exhibited in group shows Mo. Ann., City Art Mus., St. Louis, 1956, 65, Madison Gallery, N.Y.C., 1960; Ligoa Duncan Gallery, N.Y.C., 1964, 78, Two Flags Festival of Art, Douglas, Ariz., 1975, 78-79, Internat. Art Exhibit, El Centro, Calif., 1977, 78, Salon des Nations, Paris, 1985, UN World Conference of Women, Narobi, Kenya, 1985, William Woods Coll., Fulton, Mo., 1992-95, La Junta Coll. Art League Internat., 1992, 94, Coffret Musee, Paris, 1995; represented in permanent collection Nat. Mus. Women in Art, 1990; lectr. on art; jurist for selection of art for exhibits Labelle (Mo.) Centennial, 1972; chmn. Centennial Art Show, Lewiston, 1971, Bicentennial, 1976; dir. exhibit high sch. students for N.E. Mo. State U., 1974; supt. ann. art show Lewis County (Mo.) Fair, 1975-90; executed Mississippi RiverBoat, oil painting presented to Pres. Carter by Lewis County Dem. Com., Canton, 1979. Mem. Lewistown Bicentennial Hist. Soc.; charter mem. Canton Area Arts Coun. N.E. Mo. Recipient cert. of merit Latham Found., 1960-63, Mo. Women's Festival Art, 1974, Bertrand Russell Peace Found., 1973, Gold Medallion award Two Flags Festival Art, 1975, Safeco purchase award El Centro (Calif.) Internat. Art exhibit, 1977, 1st pl. award LaJunta (Colo.) Fine Arts League, 1981, diploma Universita Delle Arti, Parma, Italy, 1981, Purchase award Two Flags Art Festival, 1981, award Assn. Conservation and Mo. Dept. Conservation Art Exhbt., 1982, Purchase award Canton Area Arts Coun., 1988, Colorado Springs Art Festival, 1989; paintings selected for Competition '84 Guide by Nat. Art Appreciation Soc., 1984; 1st pl. award New Orlean Internat. Art Exhibit, 1984, with Am. Women Artists at United Nations Conf. on Women, Nairobi, Kenya, 1985, Two Flags Festival of Art, 1986, Sunflower Judges award Harlin Mus., West Plains, Mo., 1994; named artist laureate, Nepenthe Mondi Soc., 1984, cert. on Arts for the Parks Nat., 1987. Mem. Artist Equity Assn., Inc., Internat. Soc. Artists, Internat. Platform Assn., Nat. Mus. Women in Art (charter), Canton Area Art Coun. (Purchase award 1988), Animal Protection Inst. Mem. Disciples of Christ Ch.

TERPINSKI, EVA ANTONINA, pharmaceutical company executive; b. Warsaw, Poland, Jan. 17, 1946; came to U.S. 1983; d. Stanislaw and Marianna (Lis) Zajaczkowski; m. Jacek Terpinski, Jan. 22, 1972; children: Peter, Agatha. MSc in Chemistry, Poly. U., Warsaw, 1969, MSc in Chem. Engring., 1969, PhD in Chemistry, 1977. Asst. Poly. U., Warsaw, 1969-73, sr.

asst., 1973-78, asst. prof., 1978-83; lectr. Rutgers U., New Brunswick, N.J., 1983-84; sr. scientist Nat. Patent Co., New Brunswick, N.J., 1984-88; mgr. Nat. Patent Co., New Brunswick, 1988-90, dir., 1990—. Contbr. articles to profl. jours.; editor 5 books; patentee in field. Instr. Girl Scouts U.S.A., Perth Amboy, N.J., 1988—. Mem. AAAS, Am. Assn. Pharm. Scientists, Internat. Soc. Magnetic Resonance, Am. Chem. Soc. Office: Nat Patent Devel Co 783 Jersey Ave New Brunswick NJ 08901-3605

TERR, LENORE CAGEN, psychiatrist, writer; b. N.Y.C., Mar. 27, 1936; d. Samuel Lawrence Cagen and Esther (Hirsh) Cagen Raiken; m. Abba I. Terr; children: David, Julia. AB magna cum laude, Case Western Res. U., 1957; MD with honors, U. Mich., 1961. Diplomate Am. Bd. Psychiatry and Neurology. Intern Med. Ctr. U. Mich., Ann Arbor, 1961-62, resident Neuropsychiat. Inst., 1962-64, fellow Children's Psychiat. Hosp., 1964-66; from instr. to asst. prof. Med. Sch. Case Western Res. U., Cleve., 1966-71; pvt. practice Terr Med. Corp., San Francisco, 1971—; from asst. clin. prof. to clin. prof. psychiatry Sch. Medicine U. Calif., San Francisco, 1971—; lectr. law, psychiatry U. Calif., Berkeley, 1971—, U. Calif., Davis, 1974; bd. dirs. Am. Bd. Psychiatry and Neurology, Deerfield, Ill., 1988-96. Author: Too Scared to Cry, 1990, Unchained Memories, 1994; contbr. articles to profl. jours. Rockefeller Found. scholar-in-residence, Italy, 1981, 88; project grantee Rosenberg Found., 1977, 80-81, William T. Grant Found., 1986-87; recipient Career Tchr. award NIMH, 1967-69, Child Advocacy award, APA, 1994. Fellow Am. Psychiat. Assn. (Child Psychiatry Rsch. award 1984, Clin. Rsch. award 1987), Am. Coll. Psychiatrists (program chair 1991-92, Bowis award 1993), Am. Acad. Child and Adolescent Psychiatry (coun. 1984-87); mem. Group for Advancement Psychiatry (bd. dir. 1986-88), Phi Beta Kappa, Alpha Omega Alpha. Office: Terr Med Corp 450 Sutter St Rm 2534 San Francisco CA 94108-4204

TERRANOVA, LAURA ANDREA, small business owner; b. Bklyn., Dec. 21, 1960; d. Ben and Elsy (Palmieri) Cascio; m. Salvatore Terranova, Aug. 8, 1981; 1 child, Elizabeth. Grad., Katherine Gibbs Sch., 1980. Sec. Blue Cross and Blue Shield, N.Y.C., 1980-81; adminstrv. asst. Marine Midland Bank, N.Y.C., 1981-83; sec. Rooney Pace, N.Y.C., 1983-84; owner Cable Equipment Locators, Allison Park, Pa., 1992—. Recipient Gift of Time Tribute Pa. State Awards Com., 1993. Office: Cable Equipment Locators 24 Quail Run Estates Allison Park PA 15101

TERRAS, AUDREY ANNE, mathematics educator; b. Washington, Sept. 10, 1942; d. Stephen Decatur and Maude Mae (Murphy) Bowdoin. BS with high honors in Math., U. Md., 1964; MA, Yale U, 1966, PhD, 1970. Instr. U. Ill., Urbana, 1968-70; asst. prof. U. P.R., Mayaguez, 1970-71; asst. prof. Bklyn. Coll., CUNY, 1971-72; asst. prof. math. U. Calif.-San Diego, La Jolla, 1972-76, assoc. prof., 1976-83, prof., 1983—, vis. positions MIT, fall 1977, 83, U. Bonn (W.Ger.), spring 1977, Inst. Mittag-Leffler, Stockholm, winter, 1978, Inst. Advanced Study, spring 1984, Math. Scis. Rsch. Inst., Berkeley, Calif., winter 1992, spring 1995; dir. West Coast Number Theory Conf., U. Calif.-San Diego, 1976, AMS joint summer rsch. conf., 1984; lectr. in field. Author: Harmonic Analysis on Symmetric Spaces and Applications, Vol. I, 1985, Vol. II, 1988. Contbr. articles and chpts. to profl. publs. Woodrow Wilson fellow, 1964; NSF fellow, 1964-68; NSF grantee Summer Inst. in Number Theory, Ann Arbor, Mich., 1973; prin. investigator NSF, 1974-88. Fellow AAAS; mem. AAAS (nominating com. math. sect. project 2061), Am. Math. Soc. (com. employment and ednl. policy, com. on coms., council, transactions editor, com. for the yr. 2000), Math. Assn. Am. (program com. for nat. meeting 1988-90, chair joint com. Am. Math. Soc. and Math. Assn. Am. 1991), Soc. Indsl. and Applied Math., Assn. for Women in Math. (travel grants com. 1996), Assn. for Women in Sci. Research in harmonic analysis on symmetric spaces and number theory. Office: U Calif San Diego Dept Math La Jolla CA 92093-0112

TERRELL, DOMINIQUE LARA, dramatic soprano, actress, real estate and marketing executive; b. South Bend, Ind., Apr. 26; d. Harold J. Metzler and Margaret Terrell (Whiteman) Metzler Fogarty. BA, Ithaca Coll., 1960; diploma, Brown's Bus. Coll., Decatur, Ill., 1960; postgrad. in real estate sales, NYU, 1984. Lic. securities dealer, real estate salesperson. Exec. legal asst. Carb Luria Glassner Cook & Kufeld, N.Y.C., 1962-64; Exec. legal asst. Graubard Moskovitz McGoldrick Dannett & Horowitz, N.Y.C., 1964-79; opera and concert singer N.Y.C.; real estate salesperson Rosemary Edwards Realty, N.Y.C., 1985, Kenneth D. Laub & Co., Inc., N.Y.C., 1987-89, GSW Realty, Inc., N.Y.C., 1990-91, Kuzmuk Realty, Inc., 1992-94, Gala 72 Realty, Inc., 1994—; bd. dirs., singer Broadway-Grand Opera, 1992—; pres. Mystique of Dominique, Whiteman and Stewart Prodns., DharMacduff Publs.; corr. sec., bd. dirs. Community Opera, Inc., N.Y.C., 1984—. Mem. internat. affairs com. and other coms. Women's Nat. Rep. Club, N.Y.C., 1968-82; active Rep. County Vols., N.Y.C., 1976-82; mem. nominating com. Ivy Rep. Club, N.Y.C., 1983-87; bd. dirs. Am. Landmark Festivals, 1986—. Named Female Singer of Yr., Internat. Beaux Arts, Inc., 1978-79, Princess Nightingale, Allied Indian Tribes N.Am. Continent-Cherokee Nation, 1985. Mem. Wagner Internat. Instn. (dir. pub. rels. 1982-84), Navy League U.S. (life, mem. N.Y. coun.), Assn. Former Intelligence Officers (assoc.), Friends of Spanish Opera (bd. dirs. 1982—), Finlandia Found., Inc. (life), The Bohemians, Nat. Arts Club (music com. 1983-87), N.Y. Opera Club.

TERRELL, SHARON MARLENE, bank security director; b. Indpls., Mar. 5, 1950; d. Frederick and Martha Josephine (Cox) Ayers; m. Clark King Terrell, Oct. 23, 1993. BA in Sociology with distinction, Ind. U. S.E., 1995. Teller Liberty Nat. Bank, Louisville, 1969-71; teller First Nat. Bank, Louisville, 1971-78, asst. dir. of security, 1978-86; dir. security First Nat./Nat. City Bank, Louisville, 1986—; security commr. Bank Adminstrn. Inst., 1993-94. Mem. Am. Soc. for Indsl. Security (sec., treas. 1994—), Bus. and Profl. Women, Pride of Ky. Chorus (bus. mgr. 1991, 92, 95, 96, bd. dirs.). Home: 306 Ring Rd Louisville KY 40207

TERRELL, SUZANNE HAIK, lawyer; b. New Orleans, July 8, 1954; d. George Michel and Isabel (Saloom) Haik; m. Walter Lee, Apr. 23, 1976; children: Catherine Julie, Elizabeth Lee, Christine Alyce. BA in Art History, Tulane U., 1976; JD, Loyola U., New Orleans, 1984. Jud. law clk. La. 4th Cir. Ct. Appeals, New Orleans, 1984-85, 86-88, La. Supreme Ct., New Orleans, 1985-86; atty. Baldwin & Haspel, New Orleans, 1988-91, Wootan & Saunders, New Orleans, 1991-93; city coun. mem. City of New Orleans, 1994—; advisor Teen Ct. Project, New Orleans; legis. strategist La. Opthalmology Assn., New Orleans; adj. faculty mem. Univ. Coll. Tulane U., New Orleans. Trustee Metalrie Park Country Day Sch.; bd. dirs. Eye Found. Am., Met. Area Com., Charity Hosp. New Orleans. Recipient award Loyola Law Alumni Assn., 1983. Mem. ABA, Fed. Bar Assn., Assn. Women's Atty., Coun. Young Children, La. Bar Assn., Jr. League New Orleans, Young Leadership Coun.,. Republican. Home: 170 Audubon Blvd New Orleans LA 70112 Office: New Orleans City Coun Rm 2W80 1300 Perdido St New Orleans LA 70112

TERRELL MITCHELL, ALLISON ANN, marketing executive; b. Tampa, Fla., Sept. 1, 1962; d. John Lostin and Louise Marian (Hedrick) Terrell; m. Glenn Stokes Mitchell, Sept. 30, 1995. BA in Speech Comm., U. South Fla., Tampa, 1984. Corp. mktg. coord. Fla. Fed. Savs. & Loan, St. Petersburg, 1984-88; sales rep. Standard Register, Tampa, 1988-90; mktg. exec. Tampa Conv. Ctr., Tampa, 1990—. Vol. Fla. Orch., Tampa, 1996, Beach Clean-Up and Renourishment, St. Petersburg, 1990-96; active Young Reps., St. Petersburg, 1987-93, also treas. Named to Outstanding Young Women of Am., 1991. Mem. Am. Soc. for Assn. Execs., Internat. Assn. Exposition Mgrs., Tampa C. of C., Fla. Mus. Art, Gator Club, Alpha Delta Pi. Republican. Home: 3018 Harbor View Tampa FL 33611

TERRIS, LILLIAN DICK, psychologist, association executive; b. Bloomfield, N.J., May 5, 1914; d. Alexander Blaikie and Herminia (Doscher) Dick; BA, Barnard Coll., 1935; PhD, Columbia U., 1941; m. Louis Long, Apr. 22, 1935 (dec. Sept. 1968), 1 son, Alexander Blaikie Long; m. Milton Terris, Feb. 6, 1971. Instr. psychology Sara Lawrence Coll., Bronxville, N.Y., 1937-40; jr. pers. tech. SSA, Washington, 1941; sr. pers. clk. OWI, N.Y.C., 1941-43; dir. profl. examination svc. Am. Pub. Health Assn., N.Y.C., 1943-70, pres., 1970-79, pres. emeritus, 1979—. Assoc. editor Jour. Pub. Health Policy, 1979—. Life mem., bd. dirs. Profl. Exam. Svc.; chair bd. VNA Chittenden County, Vt., 1989, mem. hon. bd., 1993—. Recipient Nat. Environ. Health Assn. award, 1976, Cert. of Svc. award Am. Bd. Preventive Medicine, 1979. Diplomate Am. Bd. Examiners in Profl. Psychology. Fellow Am. Psychol. Assn.; mem. Am. Pub. Health Assn., N.Y. State Psychol. Assn., Am. Coll. Hosp. Adminstrs. (hon. fellow), Phi Beta Kappa, Sigma Xi. Contbr. articles in field to profl. jours. Home: 208 Meadowood Dr South Burlington VT 05403-7401 Office: 475 Riverside Dr New York NY 10115-0122

TERRY, KAY ADELL, marketing executive, management consultant; b. Portland, Oreg., July 11, 1939; d. Langdon Alcott and Emma Francis (Meyer) Howard; m. Frank F. Terry, Aug. 31, 1963 (div. Mar. 1988); 1 child, Kimberly Sue. CPC, CIPC. Office mgr. Merck Sharp & Dohme, Portland, 1959-63; asst. dir. admissions Seattle Pacific U., Seattle, 1963-66; owner United Personnel Svc., Seattle, 1966-86; pres., chief exec. officer Ram Force Cos., Seattle, 1986-91; pres. N.W. region Robert Half Internat., Seattle, 1991-93; pres., CEO Terry & Assocs., Seattle, 1993—; CEO and pres. Key Staff, LLC, 1996—; bd. dirs. Ram Force Cos., Seattle Acctg. Force, Inc., Seattle, Office Force, Inc., Seattle, Data Force, Inc., Seattle. Contbr. articles to profl. jours. Mem. Seattle C. of C., 1989; vol. Spl. Olympics, Seattle. Fellow Seattle Pacific U., 1989. Mem. Women Bus. Owners, Nat. Assn. Accts. (bd. dirs. 1985-87, Mem. Achievement award 1987, Disting. Svc. award 1987), Nat. Assn. Pers. Svcs. (vice chmn. 1993), Nat. Assn. Temp. Svcs., Pacific N.W. Pers. Mgmt. Assn., Wash. Athletic Club. Republican.

TERRY, MEGAN, playwright, performer, photographer; b. Seattle, July 22, 1932; d. Harold Joseph and Marguerite Cecelia (Henry) Duffy. Student, Banff Sch. Fine Arts, summers, 1950-52, 56, U. Alta., Edmondton, Can., 1952-53; B.Ed., U. Wash., 1956. Founding mem. Open Theater, N.Y.C., 1963; ABC fellow Yale U., 1966-67; founding mem., v.p. N.Y. Theatre Strategy, 1971; adj. prof. theatre U. Nebr., Omaha, until 1977; Hill prof. fine arts U. Minn.-Duluth, spring 1983; Bingham prof. humanities U. Louisville, 1981; mem. theatre panel, mem. overview panel Nat. Endowment Arts, 1976-86, mem. opera/music theatre panel, 1985, mem. advancement panel, 1987; mem. theatre panel Rockefeller Found., 1977-85; mem. performing arts panel Nebr. State Council for Arts, 1977; mem. Nebr. Com. for Humanities, 1983-86; mem. Gov.'s Com. on Film and Telecommunications, 1985-86; founding mem. N.Y. Open Theatre, 1963-73; judge playwriting competition Mass., Wis., Ohio, Oreg. states, So. Playwrights Competition; Nat. Endowment Arts vis. artist in residence U. Iowa, 1992. Dir. Cornish Players, Cornish Sch. Allied Arts, Seattle, 1954-56, founding dir. playwrights workshop, Open Theatre, N.Y.C., 1963-68, playwright-in-residence, literary mgr. Omaha Magic Theatre, 1974—; author plays including: Kegger, Comings and Goings, The Magic Realists, Sanibel & Captiva, The People vs. Ranchman, Kepp Tightly Closed in a Cool Dry Place, The Gloaming Oh My Darling, Approaching Simone, Viet Rock, Massachussetts Trust, The Tommy Allen Show, Calm Down Mother, Sleazing Toward Athens, Babes in the Big House, Ex Miss Copper Queen, Mollie Bailey's Traveling Family Circus, Goona-Goona, Retro, Hothouse, Dinner's in the Blender, Objective Love, Katmandu, Fifteen Million Fifteen Year Olds, Fireworks, The Trees Blew Down, Choose a Spot on the Floor, Future Soap, Brazil Fado, Pro Game., Amtrak, Headlights, Breakfast Serial, Do You See What I'm Saying?, The Snow Queen, India Plays, I Forgot How Much I Like You; editor, writer: plays including Sea of Forms, Nightwalk, 1001 Horror Stories of The Plains, Running Gag, Couplings and Groupings, Walking Through Walls, Babes Unchained, Cancel That Last Thought; or See The 270 Foot Woman in Spandex, X-Raydiate: E-Motion in Action, Body Leaks, Sound Fields, Belches on Couches, Star Path Moonstop; photographer/editor: Right Brain Vacation Photos: Production Photographs of Omaha Magic Theatre Productions, 1972-92; mem. performance ensemble Omaha Magic Theatre nat. and internat. performance tours Body Leaks, 1991, Body Leaks, 1992, Sound Fields, 1993, 94, Belches on Couches, 1993, 94; contbr. articles in field to profl. jours. Mem. Nebr. Artist-in-the Schs., 1987—. Recipient Stanley Drama award, 1965, Office of Advanced Drama Rsch. award, 1965, Obie award, 1970, Disting. Contbrn. To and Svc. in Am. Theatre Silver medal Amoco Oil Co., 1977; Dramatists Guild Com. of Women Ann. award, 1983, Nebr. Artist of Yr. 1992; Gov. award Nebr., 1992; Rockefeller grantee, 1968, 87; NEA Lit. fellow, 1973; Guggenheim fellow, 1978; NEA playwriting fellow, 1989, Lifetime Am. Theatre fellow, 1994. Mem. NEA (reporter and panelist for theatre program, 1975-85), Women's Theatre Coun. (founding 1971), Women's Forum (charter), Am. Theatre Assn. (co-chmn. playwriting program 1977, chmn. playwrights project com. 1978-79, C. Crawford playwriting judge of 1987), Theatre Comm. Group (bd. dirs. 1988-92), New Dramatists (alumni, judge nat. playwriting competition 1987-88), ASSISTEJ-USA (bd. dirs. 1986-91). Home: 2309 Hanscom Blvd Omaha NE 68105-3143 Office: E Marton Agy Rm 612 One Union Sq New York NY 10003-3303

TERRY, SANDRA ELEANOR, visual artist; b. Clifton Forge, Va., May 23, 1947; d. Robert B. and Grace J. (Amante) T. BA, Mary Baldwin Coll., 1990; MFA, Ind. State U., 1994; postgrad., New Sch. for Social Rsch., N.Y., 1995—. Cert. tchr., Ind. Substitute tchr. Seymour (Ind.) Pub. Sch. Sys., 1990; tchg. asst., instr. Ind. State U., Terre Haute, 1991-94, tutor humanities Student Acad. Svcs., 1992-95; lab aid Computer Instrn. Ctr. New Sch. Social Rsch., N.Y.C., 1995—; lectr. in field. One-woman shows include Arts Illiana Exhbn. Space, Terre Haute, 1993, Turman Gallery, Ind. State U., 1994; exhibited in group shows at Turman Gallery, 1991, 92, 94, Sheldon Swope Art Mus., Terre Haute, 1991, 92, 93, Bare-Montgomery Meml. Gallery, Ind. State U., 1992, Broad St. Gallery, New Castle, Ind., 1992, Coffee Grounds Gallery, Terre Haute, 1993, Saint Mary-of-the-Woods Coll., Ind., 1993, Shircliff Gallery of Art, Vincennes (Ind.) U., 1993; permanent collections include Bratislava Sch. Art, Slovakia, U. Manitoba, Winnipeg, Canada, Mary Baldwin Coll., Staunton, Va., Ind. State U., Terre Haute. Mem. Soc. Am. Graphic Artists.

TERRY, SHERRIE LYNN, marketing executive; b. Portland, Oreg., Nov. 21, 1957; d. Milton Dee and Jennie Lee (Gillman) Kingsland; m. Randall Keith Terry, May 14, 1983. BBA, Lewis & Clark Coll., 1980; MBA in Mktg., Memphis State U., 1984. With Dr. Scholl's Footcare, Memphis, 1980-86, assoc. product mgr., 1983, product mgr., 1984-85, sr. product mgr., 1985-86; sr. product mgr. ConAgra Frozen Foods, St. Louis, 1986-87; product mgr. Vlasic Foods, Inc., Farmington Hills, Mich., 1987-88, sr. product mgr., 1988-89, dir. mktg., 1989-91, sr. dir. mktg., 1991-92; dir. new product devel. Chiquita Brands Internat., Cin., 1992-93; dir. mktg. Chiquita Banana N.Am., Cin., 1993-96, v.p. mktg., 1996—. Mem. Beta Gamma Sigma, Alpha Nu Alpha, Phi Kappa Phi, Delta Mu Delta. Home: 11740 Park Ct Loveland OH 45140-1971

TERVO, DENISE ANN, psychologist, educator; b. Denver, Aug. 28, 1950; d. John Collin and Irene Geraldine (Schueth) T.; m. Paul Saenger, June 2, 1973 (div. June 1981); m. Michael Craig Clemmens, Aug. 7, 1982; children: Lindsey, Brenden. Student, U. Ga., 1968-70; BA in Sociology, U. N.C., 1972, MEd, 1975; PhD in Counseling, U. Pitts., 1988. Lic. in psychology, Colo. Ednl. cons. Ky. River Foothills Devel. Coun. Headstart Area Program, Richmond, Ky., 1976-80; liaison ednl. counselor Cen. Ky. Re-Edn. Program, Lexington, 1976-80; child devel. specialist Childrens Hosp., Pitts., 1980-84; ednl. cons., psychotherapist Comty. Human Svcs., Pitts., 1984-86; intern in psychology Psychol. Specialists Inc., Pitts., 1984-89; pvt. practice psycyology Pitts., 1989—; adj. faculty mem. Gestalt Inst. Cleve., 1994—; cons. Madison County Interagy. Group for Parents Anonymous, Richmond, 1978-80; adj. prof. Sch. Social Work Ea. Ky. U., Richmond, 1977-79. Mem. Pitts. Ctr. for ARts, 1994—, Pitts. Ballet, 1989—, Nat. History and Sci. Mus., Pits., 1987-94. Mem. NAFE, APA, ACA, Ky. Coun. Children with Behavioral Disorders (pres., state coord. 1978-79), Gestalt Inst. Cleve., Alpha Lambda Delta, Phi Beta Kappa. Office: 401 Shady Ave Ste 104A Pittsburgh PA 15206

TERWILLIGER, JULIA ANNE, art educator, artist; b. Orange, N.J., May 17, 1947; d. Walter William and Rosina Marie (Pepe) Klem; m. Bert Alan Terwilliger, Jan. 1981 (div. Apr. 1989); children: Stacie Lea, David James, Christie Lea. BA cum laude, U. South Fla., 1987, MFA, 1990. Asst. to curator Aljira Gallery, Newark, 1991-92; with Met. Mus. Art Bookstore, N.Y.C., 1991-92; studio asst. Elyn Zimmerman, sculptor, N.Y.C., 1991-92; prof. art Hillsborough C.C., Tampa, 1992-93; sabbatical replacement U. Ctrl. Fla., Orlando, 1992-93, adj. prof. art 1993—; exbhn. com. Fla. Ctr. Contemporary Art, Tampa, 1992; presenter in field. Groups exhibitions include Einstein-Forum, Potsdam, Germany, 1996, Dunedin (Fla.) Fine Art Ctr., 1995, Ruth Eckard Hall, Clearwater Fla., 1995, The Prince Street Gallery, N.Y.C., 1992, Snug Harbor Cultural Ctr., S.I., 1992; one-person shows include Theater Gallery - U. South Fla., The Centre Gallery; also exhibited in numerous private collections. Artist AIDS Outreach Program, Tampa, 1991-94; vol. Aljira Gallery, Newark, 1990-91. Project grantee New Forms Fla., 1994-95; emerging artist grantee County Arts Coun., Hillsborough, 1990-91; finalist Divsn. Cultural Affairs, Fla., 1992. Mem. Coll. Art Assn. Am., Women's Caucus for Art. Home: 16413 Lake Ln Lutz FL 33549 Office: U Ctrl Fla Coll Arts & Scis Orlando FL 32816-1342

TESLIK, SARAH ANNA BALL, association executive, lawyer; b. Oberlin, Ohio, July 31, 1953; d. George Hudson and Nancy Ann (Cronon) Ball; m. Kennan Teslik, Aug. 21, 1976; children: Lee, William. BA, Whitman Coll., 1974; BA, MA, Oxford (Eng.) U., 1976; JD, Georgetown U., 1983. Bar: D.C. 1983. Assoc. Stroock and Stroock and Lavan, Washington, 1983-85, Wilkie, Farr and Gallagher, Washington, 1985-88; head of Washington office Hiscock and Barclay, N.Y.C., 1988-91; exec. dir. Coun. Instl. Investors, Washington, 1988—; pvt. practice law Washington, 1992—. Office: Coun Instl Investors 1730 Rhode Island Ave NW Washington DC 20036

TESORO, GIULIANA CAVAGLIERI, chemistry research educator, consultant; b. Venice, Italy, June 1, 1921; came to U.S., 1939; d. Gino and Margherita (Maroni) Cavaglieri; m. Victor Tesoro, Apr. 17, 1943; children: Claudia, Andrew. PhD, Yale U., 1943. Rsch. chemist Am. Cyanamid Co., Boundbrook, N.J., 1943-44; asst. dir. rsch. Onyx Chem. Co., Jersey City, 1944-58, J. P. Stevens & Co., Inc., Garfield, N.J., 1958-68; dir. chem. rsch. Burlington Industries, Greenboro, N.C., 1968-72; sr. scientist, adj. prof. MIT, Cambridge, 1973-82; rsch. prof. Poly. U., Bklyn., 1982—; Mem. nat. materials adv. bd. NRC, Washington, 1979-82. Contbr. numerous articles to profl. publs.; patentee in field. Recipient Am. Dyestuff Reporter award, 1959, Achievement award Soc. Women Engrs., 1978. Fellow Textile Inst. Gt. Britain; mem. AAAS (co-chmn. polymer combustion and fire retardance conf. 1977), Am. Assn. Textile Chemists and Colorists (Olney medal 1963), Am. Chem. Soc., Am. Inst. Chemists, Info. Coun. Fabric flammability, N.Y. Acad. Sci., Textile Rsch. Inst. (editorial bd.jours.), Fiber Soc. (pres. 1974-75). Democrat. Home: 278 Clinton Ave Dobbs Ferry NY 10522-3007 Office: Poly U 333 Jay St Brooklyn NY 11201-2907

TESSMANN, CARY ANNETTE, controller; b. Wausau, Wis., Oct. 30, 1956; d. Orin Sidney Olson and Phyllis Olga (Radtke) O. AS, U. Wis., Waukesha, 1986; BBA in Acctg., U. Wis., Whitewater, 1989; MBA in Acctg., U. Wis., 1995. Cert. mgmt. acct., 1994; CPA 1995. Clk.-typist I, II, III Waukesha County Dept. Social Svc., 1974-83; acct. clk. I Northview Nursing Home, Waukesha, 1984; from acct. clk. II, adminstrv. asst.-fiscal mgmt. I, budget technician, sr. fin. analyst to bus. mgr. Waukesha County Health & Human Svcs. Dept., 1984-94; contr. Waukesha County Tech. Coll., Pewaukee, 1994—; mem. acctg. curriculum adv. com. Waukesha County Tech. Coll., 1993—; cons., Sussex, Wis., 1990-93. Vol. Wis. Lutheran Child & Family Svc., Milw., 1989—, Bargain Ctr.-WELS Synod, Milw., 1970-83, Milw. Women's Ctr., 1989-92; vol. tax preparer IRS, Pewaukee, 1989-93; mem. bd. Waukesha County Cmty. Housing Initiatives, 1995—. Recipient Certificate of Spl. Recognition from Christoph Meml. YWCA Women of Distinction Award Program, 1986. Mem. Inst. Mgmt. Accts. (del. Mid-Am. coun. 1992—, chair corp. & acad. devel. 1994-95, co-dir. mem. attendance 1989-90, v.p. comm. 1990-92, v.p. fin. & adminstrn. 1991-92, pres. 1992-93), Southeastern Wis. Fin. Mgrs. Assn. (planning com. 1987-94), Govt. Fin. Officers Assn. (budget reviewer 1994—, award of excellence 1996). Office: Waukesha County Tech Coll 800 Main St Pewaukee WI 53072-4601

TETA, ROSEMARIE FRANCES STACEY, communications company executive; b. Chester, Pa., July 4, 1955; d. Robert Francis and Sarah A. (Meer) Stacey; m. Nicholas C. Teta Sr., Aug. 5, 1978; children: Monica, Laura, Nicholas C. Jr. BS in Acctg. and Econs., Widener U., 1976. Cert. cash mgr. Staff auditor Touche Ross & Co., Phila., 1976-79; chief acct. Hay Assocs., Phila., 1979-80; tax mgr. Avtex Fibers Inc., Valley Forge, Pa., 1980-82; mgr. treasury ops. Avtex Fibers Inc., Valley Forge, 1982-85, dir. treasury ops., 1985-86; corp. cash mgr. Comcast Corp., Phila., 1986-92, dir. corp. cash mgmt., 1992—; acad. adv. bd. Widener U. Mem. Nat. Assn. Accts. (bd. dirs. 1976-80). Republican. Roman Catholic. Home: 1021 Wedgewood Ln West Chester PA 19382 Office: Comcast Corp 1500 Market St Philadelphia PA 19102

TETELMAN, ALICE FRAN, city government official; b. N.Y.C., Apr. 15, 1941; d. Harry and Leah (Markovitz) T.; m. Martin A. Wenick, Dec. 7, 1980. BA, Mt. Holyoke Coll., South Hadley, Mass., 1962. Rsch. and info. asst. Edn. and World Affairs, N.Y.C., 1963-67; legis. asst. U.S. Sen. Charles Goodell, Washington, 1968-70; land use and energy specialist Citizens Adv. Com. on Environ. Quality, Washington, 1973-74; sr. assoc. prog. mgr. Linton & Co., Washington, 1971-73, 75-76; pub policy cons. Washington, 1977-78; adminstrv. asst. U.S. Congressman Bill Green (N.Y.), Washington, 1978-81; cons. The Precious Legacy Project, Prague, Czechoslovakia, 1982-83; Rep. staff dir. Select Com. on Hunger, U.S. Ho. of Reps., Washington, 1984-85; dir. State of N.J. Washington Office, 1986-90; exec. dir. Coun. of Gov/'s Policy Advisors, Washington, 1991-94; dir. Washington Office The City of N.Y., 1994—. Bd. mem. Republican Women's Task Force, Nat. Women's Polit. Caucus, 1976-80. European Community grantee, 1975. Mem. Ripon Soc. (nat. exec. com. 1971-73). Republican. Office: City of NY Ste 350 1301 Pennsylvania Ave NW Washington DC 20004

TETRO, CATHERINE ANNE, shop owner; b. Fulton, N.Y., July 26, 1925; d. Sam and Florence Elizabeth (Corsoneti) Froio; m. John Ralph Tetro, Nov. 29, 1969. Grad. H.S., Fulton, N.Y., 1942. Clk. U.S. Post Office Substa., Fulton, N.Y., 1941-53; owner, operator Kay's Tot Shop, Fulton, N.Y., 1953-95. Sec. Fulton Merchants Assn., 1982; mem. parish coun., 1982-85, mem. choir. Mem. Fulton Women's Bowling Assn. (treas., mem. Women's Bowling Hall of Fame).

TETTEGAH, SHARON YVONNE, education educator; b. Wichita Falls, Tex., Jan. 14, 1956; d. Lawrence Guice and Doris Jean (Leak) Oliver; 1 child, Tandra Ainsworth; m. Joseph Miller Zangai, Dec. 22, 1978 (div. 1983); 1 child, Tonia Monjay Zangai; m. George Tettegah, Apr. 28, 1989; 1 child, Nicole Jennifer Tettegah. AA, Coll. Alameda, 1985; BA, U. Calif., Davis, 1988, teaching cert., 1989, MA, 1991; postgrad., U. Calif., Santa Barbara. Cert. elem. tchr., Calif. Clk. II Alameda County Mcpl. Ct., Oakland, Calif., 1976-77; acct. clk. Alameda County Social Svcs., Oakland, 1977-78, eligibility technician, 1978-82; supervising clk. Alameda County Health Care Svcs., Oakland, 1982-84; tchr. Davis (Calif.) Joint Unified Sch. Dist., 1988-89, L.A. Unified Schs., L.A., 1990-92; tchr. Oakland Unified Sch. Dist., Oakland, 1992—, tchr. sci. mentor, 1993—; teaching asst. U. Calif., Santa Barbara, 1993-94; adminstrv. intern Oxnard Unified Sch. Dist., 1994, U. Calif. Cultural Awareness Program, Santa Barbara, 1994—; rsch. cons. to vice chancellor students affairs, cons. tchr. edn. program, facilitor registrar's office U. Calif., Santa Barbara, 1995-96, rsch. asst. Grad. Sch. Edn., 1996—; cons. U. Calif. , Davis, 1988-89, Montessori Ctr. Sch., Santa Barbara, Calif., 1996; multicultural cons. Davis Unified Sch. Dist., 1988-89; edn. cons. Ednl. Testing Svc., Emeryville, Calif., 1994; chair diversity com. of Santa Barbara Village Charter Sch.; mem. academic senate com. undergrad enrollment and admissions U. Calif. Santa Barbara, 1995, tchr. cross-cultural interactions course, summer, 1995; mem. academic affairs affirmative action com. U. Calif. Santa Barbara, 1995-96, grad. sch. of edn., grad. affairs and affirmative action comms. U. Calif. Santa Barbara, 1995-96. Mem. U. Calif. Santa Barbara Acad. Senate Bd. Undergraduate Admissions and Records; co-chair Diversity Com. Montecito-Santa Barbara Charter Sch.; pres. African-Am. Grad. and Profl. Students Orgn., Davis, 1988-89. Recipient Charlene Richardson Acad. Honors award Coll. Alameda, 1985; Calif. State Acad. fellow, 1989-91, Grad. Opportunity Acad. Excellence fellow, 1994-95, Vice Chancellors Acad. Achievement fellowship U. Calif. Santa Barbara, 1995-96, Vice Chancellors Acad. Fellowship Grad. Divsn., 1995-96. Mem. Am. Ednl. Researchers Assn., Calif. Sci. Tchrs. Assn., Calif. Advocacy for Math and Sci., Calif. Tchrs. Assn., Calif. Media Libr. Educators Assn., PTA, Multicultural Curriculum Assn., Supervision and Curriculum Leadership Assn., Bay Area Sci. and Tech. Educators Corsortium, Pan-African Students Assn., Kappa Delta Pi. Address: PO Box 1782 Santa Barbara CA 93116-1782 Office: U Calif Santa Barbara Sch Edn/Ednl Psychology Santa Barbara CA 93106

TEYLER, SHARON MARIE, secondary educator; b. Lynwood, Calif., Oct. 27, 1951; d. Fred George and Norma Francis (Tredo) Mann; m. Joseph Charles Cherocci, Feb., 1979 (div. 1991); children: Casey, Rebecca; m. Robert Wayne Teyler, Mar. 21, 1992. AA, Fullerton Coll., 1975; BA in Social Studies, Calif. Poly. U., 1987. Cert. tchr., Calif., Oreg. Presch. tchr. City of Duarte, Calif., 1980-82, Christ Luth. Sch., West Covina, Calif., 1982-84; tchr. Baldwin Park (Calif.) Sch. Dist., 1984-92; life in Am. tchr. E.F. for Fgn. Study, Brighton, England, 1984-87, Mass., 1988, N.Y.C., 1989-91; edn. specialist Alternative Youth Activities, Coos Bay, Oreg., 1993-94; social studies tchr. Marshfield High Sch., Coos Bay, 1994—; cheerleader dir. Baldwin Park High Sch., 1985, dir. Operation Big Switch, 1990-92, sr. class advisor, 1990-91; cheerleader dir. Christ Luth. Sch., 1982-84. Active Baldwin Park Hist. Soc., 1986-87; pageant dir. Baldwin Park City, 1967, 69, 70, 80-84; Coos Bay Parks commr., 1995—; Oreg. Assn. for Alts. in Edn. rep., 1994-96; chaperone German exch. to Germany, 1996; chaperone Sister exch. to Choshi, Japan, 1996. Named Jr. Miss Baldwin Park, 1966, Miss Baldwin Park, 1969, Miss San Gabriel Valley, 1970, Club Woman of Yr. Baldwin Park Woman's Club, 1980; recipient Achievement awards U.S. Congressman Esteban Torres, 1990-91. Mem. Hist. Preservation Soc. Republican. Home: 1453 Cedar Ave Coos Bay OR 97420-1867 Office: Marshfield High Sch 10th and Ingersoll Coos Bay OR 97420

THALER-CARTER, RUTH E., writer, editor; b. Rochester, N.Y., Apr. 24, 1953; d. Otto F. and Elizabeth E. Thaler; m. Wayne O. Carter, May 27, 1989. Student, Ind. U., 1971-73, U. Mo., St. Louis, 1975-77, U. Mo., Columbia, 1978-79. Staff writer St. Louis Argus, 1977-79; newsletter editor Washington U., St. Louis, 1980; asst. editor R&D Mexico Mag., Washington, 1980-82; comm. mgr. Am. Nat. Metric Coun., Washington, 1982-85; cons., 1985-88, 90—; newsletter editor Am. Sociol. Assn., Washington, 1984-85; publs. editor Coun. on Social Work Edn., Washington, 1984-85; chief publs. D.C. Gen. Hosp., Washington, 1985-86. Writer, pub. (newsletter) Communication Central, 1988-90. Ford fellow Ford Found., 1978-79; recipient EFfie awards for writing and editing Editors Forum, Kansas City, Mo., 1988-92, APEX award for features APEX Comm., Washington, 1990. Mem. Internat. Assn. Bus. Communicators (newsletter editor 1980-85, 90-94, Silver Inkwell 1986, Winners Circle award 1986, Communicator of Yr. 1987), Soc. Nat. Assn. Publs. (newsletter contbr. 1988-92), Washington Ind. Writers (newsletter editor 1980-88), Women in Comm. Inc. (newsletter editor 1980-85). Office: Ste 217 301 Warren Ave Baltimore MD 21230

THANE, NANCY LITCHFIELD, special education educator; b. White Plains, N.Y., June 30, 1955; d. Kendall Duane and Carolyn (Stewart) Litchfield; m. Steven Francis Thane, Aug. 15, 1976; children: Kristen Rebecca, Gregory Francis. BS, SUNY Cortland, 1977; MS, Minot State U., 1979; postgrad., Ithaca Coll., 1980-81. Cert. tchr. nursery to grade 6, deaf and hearing impaired, speech and hearing handicapped, N.Y. Tchr. deaf and speech pathologist Sherburne (N.Y.)-Earlville Ctrl. Schs., 1980-83; speech pathologist Dryden (N.Y.) Ctrl. Schs., 1983-87; tchr. deaf T-S-T BOCES, Ithaca, N.Y., 1987—; cons. SUNY Cortland, 1995. Contbr. articles to profl. jours. Mem. Groton (N.Y.) Ctrl. Sch. Dist. Sch. Bd., 1994—. Mem. Support Svc. Pers. (conf. coord. 1993), Alexander Graham Bell Assn. Democrat. Presbyterian. Home: 186 Old Stage Rd Groton NY 13073 Office: T-S-T BOCES 555 Warren Rd Ithaca NY 14850

THARNEY, LAURA CHRISTINE, lawyer; b. New Brunswick, N.J., June 19, 1965; d. Thaddeus Raphael and Madeline Kay (Baumann) T. AA in Liberal Arts, Union County Coll., 1984; BA in History, Rutgers U., 1986, JD, 1991. Bar: N.J. 1991, U.S. Dist. Ct. N.J. 1991, N.Y. 1992. With Specialized Legal Svcs., N.Y. and N.J., 1991-96; dep. county counsel Office of Middlesex County Counsel, New Brunswick, 1992-94; assoc. Law Offices of Edward J. Buzak, Montville, N.J., 1994-95, Heine Assocs., P.A., Cherry Hill, N.J., 1995-96; pvt. practice Milltown, N.J., 1996—. Mem. ABA, N.J. State Bar Assn. (mentor 1994—), N.Y. Bar Assn., Morris County Bar Assn. (mentor, mediator 1994—), Middlesex County Bar Assn., Phi Alpha Theta. Office: 161 S Main St Ste 2 Milltown NJ 08850

THARP, KAREN ANN, insurance agent; b. Montpelier, Ohio, Sept. 24, 1944; d. Howard Wesley and Thelma (Myers) Skiles; children: Pamela Lyn Tharp Grasso, James Alan, Jennifer Ann. Grad. high sch., Edon, Ohio. Sales agt. Equitable Life, Delray Beach, Fla., 1978-79; owner, pres. Fin. Profiles, Inc., Coral Springs, Fla., 1980—. Mem. Nat. Assn. Life Underwriters, Million Dollar Round Table. Republican. Home: 12432 NW 17th Pl Coral Springs FL 33071-7892 Office: Fin Profiles Inc 10101A W Sample Rd Coral Springs FL 33065-3937

THARP, MARTHA PAPO, journalist; b. Detroit, Nov. 19, 1933; d. Moraciah and Eleanor (Krause) Papo; m. Kenneth L. Tharp, Nov. 9, 1958; children: James Micah, Ronald Wade, Anne-Lenore Moradian. BA, U. Mich., 1955; MA, U. Colo., 1989. Reporter Ann Arbor (Mich.) News, 1955-56, Pueblo (Colo.) Chieftan, 1956-58; free-lance writer The Denver Post, 1965-68; reporter Denver Cath. Register, 1969-71; staff asst. U.S. Senator Floyd Haskell, Denver, 1973-74, Gov. Richard Lamm, Denver, 1974-76; dir. pub. rels. Western Interstate Commn. Higher Edn., Boulder, Colo., 1976-78; rsch. asst. L.A. Times, Denver, 1978-81; mng. editor Littleton (Colo.) Ind., 1981-85; assoc. prof. Colo. State U., Ft. Collins, 1985—; lectr. S.D. State U., Brookings, 1984-85; cons. Ctr. Ind. Journalism, Bratislava, Slovakia, 1993-94. Named Woman of Achievement Women in Communications, 1990. Mem. Soc. Profl. Journalists (pres. Colo. chpt. 1991). Democrat. Unitarian. Office: Colo State U Dept Journalism Fort Collins CO 80523

THARP, TWYLA, dancer, choreographer; b. Portland, Ind., July 1, 1941; m. Peter Young (div.); m. Robert Huot (div.); 1 child, Jesse. Student, Pomona Coll.; BA in Art History, Barnard Coll., 1963; D of Performing Arts (hon.), Calif. Inst. Arts, 1978, Brown U., 1981, Bard Coll., 1981; LHD, Ind. U., 1987; DFA, Pomona Coll., 1987; studied with Richard Thomas, Merce Cunningham, Igor Schwezoff, Louis Mattox, Paul Taylor, Margaet Craske, Erick Hawkins. Dancer Paul Taylor Dance Co., 1963-65; freelance choreographer with own modern dance troupe and various other cos. including Joffrey Ballet and Am. Ballet Theatre, 1965-87; founder, choreographer Twyla Tharp Dance Found., N.Y.C., 1965-87; artistic assoc., resident choreographer Am. Ballet Theatre, N.Y.C., 1987-91; teaching residencies various colls. and univs. including U. Mass., Oberlin Coll., Walker Art Ctr., Boston U.; choreographer White Oak Dance Project. Choreographer: Tank Dive, 1965, Re-Moves, 1966, One Two Three, 1966, Forevermore, 1967, Generation, 1968, Medley, 1969, After Suite, 1969, Dancing in the Streets of London and Paris, 1969, The One Hundreds, 1970, The Fugue, 1970, The Big Pieces, 1971, Eight Jelly Rolls, 1971, The Raggedy Dances, 1972, Deuce Coupe, 1973, As Time Goes By, 1974, Sue's Leg, 1975, Ocean's Motion, 1975, Push Comes to Shove, 1976, Once More Frank, 1976, Mud, 1977, Baker's Dozen, 1979, When We Were Very Young, 1980, Nine Sinatra Songs, 1982, The Catherine Wheel, 1982, Bach Partita, 1984, The Little Ballet, 1984, (with Jerome Robbins) Brahms/Handel, 1984, At the Supermarket, 1984, In the Upper Room, 1987, Ballare, 1987, Stations of the Crossed, 1988, Everlast, 1989, Quartet, 1989, Bum's Rush, 1989, The Rules of the Game, 1990, Brief Fling, 1990, Grand Pas: Rhythm of the Saints, 1991, Deuce Coupe II, 1992, The Men's Piece, 1992, (with Mikhail Baryshnikov) Cutting Up, 1992-93, Demeter and Persephone, 1993, Waterbaby Bagatelles, 1994, Demeter and Persephone, 1994, Red, White & Blues, 1995, How Near Heaven, 1995, I Remember Clifford, 1995, Jump Start, 1995, Americans We, 1995; (film) Hair, 1979, Ragtime, 1981, Amadeus, 1984, White Nights, 1985, Valmont, 1989, I'll Do Anything, 1994; (video spls.) Making Television Dance, 1977, CBS Cable Confessions of a Corner Maker, 1980; (Broadway shows) Sorrow Floats, 1985, Singin' In The Rain, 1985; (TV) Baryshnikov by Tharp (Emmy award Outstanding Choreography 1985, Emmy award Outstanding Writing of Classical Music/Dance Programming 1985, Emmy award Outstanding Directing of Classical Music/Dance Programming 1985), The Catherine Wheel, 1982 (Emmy award nom. Outstanding Choreography 1982); author (autobiography): When Push Comes to Shove, 1992. MacArthur Found. Chgo. fellow, 1992; recipient Creative Arts award Brandeis U., 1972, Dance mag. award, 1981, Univ. Excellence medal Columbia U., 1987, Lions of the Performing Arts award N.Y. Pub. Libr., 1989, Samuel M. Scripps award Am. Dance Festival, 1990. *

THATCHER, LAURA GLOVER, lawyer; b. West Point, Ga., Aug. 3, 1955. BA cum laude, Hollins Coll., 1975; JD with distinction, Emory U., 1980. Bar: Ga. 1980. Ptnr. Alston & Bird, Atlanta. Mem. Atlanta Bar Assn., State Bar of Ga., Phi Delta Phi, Order of Coif, Moot Ct. Soc. Office: Alston & Bird 1201 W Peachtree St 1 Atlantic Ctr Atlanta GA 30309-3424*

THATCHER, SHARON LOUISE, medical educator; b. Seattle, Feb. 17, 1942; d. Ralph McDonald and Audra Joy (Clauson) Thatcher. AB, Ga. State Coll., Milledgeville, 1964; degree in med. tech., Spartanburg Gen. Hosp., 1965; MEd, Ga. State U., 1981, EdS, 1987. Technologist chemistry dept. Greenville (S.C.) Gen. Hosp., 1965-66, Emory U. Hosp., Atlanta, 1966; hematology and bone marrow technologist Office of Dr. Spencer Brewer Jr., Atlanta, 1966-67; asst. lab. supr. chemistry dept. Grady Hosp., Atlanta, 1967-69; lab. technologist Ga. Mental Health Inst., Atlanta, 1969-70; chief lab. technologist Habersham County Hosp., Clarksville, Ga., 1970-72; survey officer Ga. Dept. Human Resources, 1972-74; part owner, gen. mgr. Nolan Biology Labs., Stone Mountain, Ga., 1974-75; bacteriology dept. technologist Northside Hosp., Atlanta, 1975-76; sales rep. Curtin Mathison Sci. Products, Atlanta, 1976-78; night supr. labs. Decatur (Ga.) Hosp., 1978; dir., ednl. coord. med. lab. tech. and phlebotomy tech. programs DeKalb Tech. Inst., Clarkston, Ga., 1978—, chairperson dept. allied health, 1980-86; cons. Med. Lab. Cons., Atlanta, 1987—; mem. site survey team Nat. Accrediting Agy. for Clin. Lab. Scis., Chgo., 1980, 85, 91, site survey team coord., 1993, 94, 95, 96; speaker and presenter in field. Named Outstanding Speaker Am. Soc. for Phlebotomy Technicians, 1986. Mem. Am Soc. for Clin. Lab. Scientists (exhibit chair region III 1971-72), Am. Microbiology Soc., Ga. Soc. for Clin. Lab. Scientists (chair membership 1970-71, exhibit chair 1971-72, pres.-elect 1974-75, pres. 1975-76, bd. dirs. 1976-77, convention chair ann. state meeting 1989-90, Omicron Sigma award 1990, Gloria F. Gilbert achievement award 1993), Kappa Delta Pi. Office: DeKalb Tech Inst 495 N Indian Creek Dr Clarkston GA 30021-2359

THAYER, EDNA LOUISE, medical facility administrator, nurse; b. Madelia, Minn., May 21, 1936; d. Walter William Arthur and Hilda Engel Emily Ann (Geistfeld) Wilke; m. David LeRoy Thayer, Aug. 30, 1958; children: Scott, Tamara, Brenda. Diploma in nursing, Bethesda Luth., 1956; BS in Nursing Edn., U. Minn., 1960; MSN, Washington U., St. Louis, 1966; MS in Counseling, Mankato (Minn.) State U., 1972. Cert. nursing adminstr. advanced ANA. Nurse Bethesda Luth. Hosp., St. Paul, 1956-58, U. Minn. Hosp., Mpls., 1958; from nurse to asst. head nurse supr., edn. dir. Fairmont (Minn.) Community Hosp., 1959-63; instr. Alton (Ill.) Meml. Hosp., 1963-66; from nursing instr. to assoc. prof. and dean Sch. Nursing Mankato State U., 1966-77; asst. adminstr. Rice County Dist. One Hosp., Faribault, Minn., 1977-89; RN, adminstrv. supr. St. Peter (Minn.) Regional Treatment Ctr., 1990—; nurse surveyor Minn. Dept. Tech. Edn., St. Paul, 1980-93; mem. adv. co. LPN and MA programs Tech. Inst., Faribault, 1977—. Mem. Rice County Ext. Bd., Faribault, 1986-91, adult leader 4-H Club, Rice County and St. Paul, 1971—; advisor Med. Explorers, Faribault, 1977-89; mem. Rep. Rodosovich Health Com., Faribault, 1984-94; coun. mem. Our Savior's Luth. Ch., Faribault, 1984-87; mem. Rep. Boudreau Health Care Adv. Com., 1996—. Recipient alumni award Nat. 4-H Club, 1983, Disting. Friend of Nursing award Mankato State U., 1995. Mem. Minn. Orgn. Nurse Execs. (bd. dirs. 1987-89), Dist. F Nursing Svc. Adminstrs. (pres. 1980-82), Minn. Nurses Assn. (bd. dirs. 1982-87, Pres.'s award 1983, pres. 5th dist. 1974, 75, pres. 13th dist. 1984-86), AAUW, Sigma Theta Tau, Delta Kappa Gamma (pres. Pi chptr. 1982-84, Woman of Achievement award 1985), Hosp. Aux. Republican. Home: RR 1 Box 7B Elysian MN 56028-9731 Office: Saint Peter Regional Treatment Ctr 100 Freeman Dr Saint Peter MN 56082-2516

THAYER, JANE See WOOLLEY, CATHERINE

THAYER, JILL, artist, designer, art educator; b. Sacramento, Calif., Mar. 14, 1956; d. William George and Shirley Edythe (Weiner) T. AA, Bakersfield Coll., 1976; BA in Fine Arts, Calif. State U., Bakersfield, 1978; postgrad., Santa Reparata Graphic Art Ct., Florence, Italy, 1978. Cert. in com. design U. Calif. Santa Barbara, fine and applied arts tchr. Calif. Graphic designer Calif. State U., Bakersfield, 1981-90, instr. design and mktg., 1995—; graphic designer Kern High Sch. Dist., Bakersfield, 1989-91; owner, designer Jill Thayer Assocs., Bakersfield, 1991—; owner, gallery dir. Jill Thayer Galleries at the Fox, Bakersfield, 1994—; nat. design instr. Univ. T.V. Network, L.A., 1980—; design instr. Bakesfield Coll., 1982-94; faculty comm. dept. Calif. State U., Bakersfield, 1996—. Represented in permanent collections Reagan Presdl. Libr., U.S. Congl. Offices, Washington, D.C., Ventana Inn, Zond and Nestle Dairies; also numerous pvt. and pub. collections. Bd. dirs. Bakersfield Art Found., 1993-96, pres., 1991-93; bd. dirs. Kern County Ad Club, Bakersfield, 1993-94; exec. sec, trustee Bakersfield Mus. of Art, 1994-96, pres. Artists' Guild, 1993-96. Recipient Artistic Innovation in Fine Art and Design award Arts Coun. of Kern, 1994, ADDY/Awards of Excellence in Design Am. Advt. Fedn., 1990-95. Mem. Am. Diabetes Assn. (bd. dirs. Kern County chpt., 1994-96); Soc. for Calligraphy, Greater Bakersfield C. of C. (Crystal Camelia award 1991). Republican. Roman Catholic. Office: Jill Thayer Assocs 1626 19th St Ste 11 Bakersfield CA 93301-4329

THAYER, MARTHA ANN, small business owner; b. Santa Fe, N.Mex., May 8, 1936; d. Duren Howard and Lena Odessa (Fox) Shields; m. Norman S. Thayer Jr., Jan. 30, 1960; children: Murray Norman, Tanya Noelle. BS, U. N.Mex., 1960. Child welfare worker State of N.Mex., Farmington and Santa Fe, 1961-63; owner Baskets by Thayer, Albuquerque, 1975-83, Noelle's, Albuquerque, 1985-89; ptnr., co-owner Indian Originals, Albuquerque, 1989-94, Native Design, 1995-96; treas. DHS Properties, Inc., 1994—; agent for Elizabeth Akeyta, Adrian Quintana, Alexandria Rohschieb Albuquerque, 1995—; co. agent for Martha A. Thayer, 1995—; crafts instr. Village Wool, Continuing Edn., Albuquerque, 1975-78; trustee Shields Trust, 1994—. Contbr. articles, revs. to craft publs.; juried show, Mus. of Internat. Folk Arts, 1975; baskets exhibited in group shows at N.Mex. State Fair, 1980 (1st place award), Women's Show, 1983 (1st place award). Campaign mgr. Dem. Candidate for State Supreme Ct., Bernalilto County, N.Mex., 1970; founding mem. Women's Polit. Caucus, Bernalillo County; chmn. Mother's March of Dimes, Bernalilto County, 1974. Mem. AAUW, Hist. Preservation Soc., Petroleum Club, Genealogy Club of Albuquerque Pub. Libr., Mus. Albuquerque (assoc.).

THAYER-BACON, BARBARA JEAN, education educator; b. Lake Charles, La., Dec. 2, 1953; d. John Treadwell and Jean Eileen (Gross) T.; m. Robert Allen Morrill, Oct. 14, 1975 (div. Dec. 1982); children: Alex Jean, Thayer Stephen, Spencer Ray; m. Charles Samuel Bacon, Dec. 20, 1986; 1 child, Samuel. BA, Rutgers U., 1974; MA, San Diego State U., 1987; PhD, Ind. U., 1991. Tchr. elem. sch. The Growing Concern, Tannersville, Pa., 1981-84, Montessori Ctr. Sch., Santa Barbara, Calif., 1984-85, Old Mission Montessori Sch., San Luis Rey, Calif., 1985-87; substitute tchr. Ft. Wayne (Ind.) Cmty. Schs., 1987-88; asst. prof. Bowling Green (Ohio) State U., 1991—; adj. & vis. prof. Ind./Purdue U., Ft. Wayne, 1988-90; adj. faculty Ball State U., Muncie, Ind., 1990, Ind./Purdue U., Indpls., 1991; cons. in field. Ind. U. fellow, Bloomington, 1988-90, scholar, 1989-90. Fellow Philosophy Edn. Soc.; mem. AAUW, Am. Ednl. Studies Assn., Am. Philosophy Assn., Am. Edn. Rsch. Assn., Ohio Valley Philosophy Edn. Soc. (pres. 1996-97), John Dewey Soc., Pi Lambda Theta. Democrat. Unitarian. Office: Bowling Green State U Dept Ednl Founds Bowling Green OH 43403

THELIAN, LORRAINE, public relations executive; b. N.Y.C., Jan. 13, 1948; d. Anthony G. and Inez (Gelfo) Bufano. BA, Molloy Coll., 1969. Account coordinator Basford Pub. Rels., N.Y.C., 1969-71; from asst. account exec. through v.p. Paluszek & Leslie Assoc., N.Y.C., 1971-74; sr. v.p., assoc. dir. Ketchum Pub. Rels., Washington, 1985-91, exec. v.p., dir., 1991—, mem. pub. affairs coun., 1990—; bd. dirs. Ketchum Comm., Inc., Washington, 1994—; bd. dirs. Ketchum Comm., Inc., Washington; mem. Pub. Affairs Coun., 1990—; mem. Washington Bd. Trade, 1987—. Mem. Pub. Rels. Soc. Am. (accredited, chmn. accreditation com. Washington chpt. 1987), Washington Comms. Assn., Women in Pub. Rels. (adv. panel 1994, honoree Pub. Rels. Woman of Yr. 1993). Roman Catholic. Office: Ketchum Pub Rels 1201 Connecticut Ave NW Ste 300 Washington DC 20036-2605*

THERNSTROM, ABIGAIL (MANN), political scientist; b. N.Y.C., Sept. 14, 1936; d. Ferdinand and Helen (Robison) Mann; m. Stephan Thernstrom, Jan. 3, 1959; children: Melanie, Samuel. BA, Barnard Coll., N.Y.C., 1958; MA, Harvard U., 1961; PhD, 1975. Lectr. Harvard U., Cambridge, Mass., 1975-78; project dir. The Twentieth Century Fund, N.Y.C., 1981-86; vis. lectr. Harvard U., Cambridge, Mass., 1988-89, Boston Coll., 1990; stringer The Economist, London, 1988-92; adjunct prof. Sch. Edn. Boston U., 1991—; sr. fellow The Manhattan Inst., N.Y.C., 1993—; mem. domestic strategy group Aspen (Colo.) Inst., 1192—; mem. edn. policy com. Hudson Inst., 1994—; mem. bd. dirs. Inst. for Justice, Washington, 1993—; mem. adv. bd. Am. Friends of the Inst. for Justice, London, 1993—. Author: Whose Votes Count?: Affirmative Action and Minority Voting Rights, 1987, School Choice in Massachusetts, 1991; editor: A Democracy Reader, 1992; contbr. articles to profl. jours. Mem. Bd. Edn. Commonwealth of Mass., 1995—. Recipient Anisfield Wolf Book award, 1987, Am. Bar Assn. cert. merit, 1988, Best Policy Book award Polit. Studies Orgn., 1987, Benchmark Book award Ctr. for Judicial Studies, 1987. Am. Polit. Sci. Assn. Home and Office: 1445 Massachusetts Ave Lexington MA 02173-3810

THEVENET, PATRICIA CONFREY, social studies educator; b. Norwich, Conn., Apr. 16, 1924; d. John George and Gertrude Pauline (Doolittle) Confrey; m. Rubén Thevenet, Dec. 15, 1945 (dec. Mar. 1983); chldren: Susanne, Gregory, Richard, R. James. BS, U. Conn., 1944; AM, U. Chgo., 1945; EdM, Columbia U., 1992, EdD, 1994. Cert. elem. tchr., N.J. Counselor testing and guidance U. Chgo., 1945; home economist Western Mass. Electric Co., Pittsfield, 1946; tchr. Unquowa Sch., Fairfield, Conn., 1950-53, Alpine (N.J.) Sch., 1968-86; program asst. soc. studies Tchrs. Coll. Columbia U., N.Y.C., 1987-93; ret., 1993; historian Borough Northvale, N.J., 1987-94; participant summer seminar Smithsonian Instn., Washington, 1984. Del 2d dist. rep. Town Mtg., Trumbull, Conn., 1954-56; pres., trustee Northvale Pub. Libr. Assn., 1957-63; trustee Northvale Bd. Edn., 1963-72, pres. Northvale Bd. Edn., 1969-70; exec. bd. dirs. Bergen County (N.J.) County Bds. Edn., 1965-72; mem. Evening Sch. Comm. No. Valley Regional Dist., Bergen County, 1976-83. Mem. Am. Hist. Assn., Nat. Coun. Social Studies, Alumni Coun. Tchrs. Coll., Columbia U., Conn. Hist. Soc., Voluntown Hist. Soc., Friends of Slater Mus. (bd. dirs.). Home: 88 N Shore Rd # B Voluntown CT 06384-1719

THEX, ALBERTA HUGHES, mathematics educator; b. Havre, Mont., Jan. 25, 1949; d. Albert Patrick and Florence Evangeline (Moe) Hughes; m. Tim Houston Thex, Nov. 25, 1972; children: David Scott, Kelly Marie. BA, Mont. State U., 1972; MS, Oreg. State U., 1995. Cert. tchr., Oreg. Tchr. Umpqua C.C., Roseburg, Oreg., 1975, Roseburg Sch. Dist., 1975-76, Salem (Oreg.)-Keizer Sch. Dist., 1980-87, Archdiocese of Portland, Stayton, Oreg., 1987-94; speech dir. St. Mary Sch., Stayton, Oreg., 1987-95; tchr. Salem-Keizer Sch. Dist., 1995-96; tchr., L.A. dir. Falls City H.S., 1996—. Author: Flood of '96, 1996; editor (poetry) Am. Anthology of Poetry, 1996. Dir. talent show Schirle Elem. Sch., Salem, 1986; re-election com. Rep. Party, Salem, 1980-81; leader Girl Scouts Am., Salem, 1988-91; mem. com., band booster Sprague Band, Salem, 1991—. Recipient Pell grant Mont. State U., 1968-72, Eisenhower fellowship Oreg. State U., 1993-95, Speech Coach Recognition award Cathedral Sch., Portland, 1993. Mem. NEA, Nat. Coun. Math. Tchrs., Oreg. Edn. Assn., Oreg. Coun. Math. Tchrs., Oreg. Math. Edn. Coun., Oreg. Talented and Gifted Bd. (bd. dirs. 1989-92), Salem Edn. Assn., 21st Century Oreg. Assessment (coun. rep. 1995). Lutheran. Home: 595 Valleywood Dr SE Salem OR 97306 Office: Falls City High Sch 111 N Main Falk City OR 97344

THIBAUDEAU, MAY MURPHY, writer; b. Nasboro, Wis., May 8, 1908; d. Hugh Isadore and Laura (Brown) Murphy; m. Raymond Joseph Thibaudeau, June 16, 1941; children: Adele, Yvonne, Clairese, Camille, Valerie, Marguerete, Hugh. BS, U. Wis., Milw., 1973. Lic. tchr., Wis. Tchr. rural state graded Fond du Lac County, Wis., 1927-34; tchr. city graded City of Peshtigo (Wis.), 1934-42; tchr. grade 3 St. Mary's Parish, South Milwaukee, Wis., 1956-75; writer South Milwaukee, 1976—. Author: Life and Times of Frederick Layton, 1984, I Shall Not Die I Shall Live on in You, 1990 (State Assembly citation 1990), The Donkey Stayed in Ireland, 1980. Pres. Fond du Lac County Tchrs. Assn., 1933-34; mem. Wis. Edn. Assn., Madison, 1935-42, Nat. Cath. Edn. Assn., Washington, 1956-75, Common Cause, Washington, 1975—, LWV, Washington, 1985-90; leader Girl Scouts U.S., Milw., 1955-62. Mem. Wis. Regional Writers, Writers Ink, AAUW (Edn. Found. Name grantee 1990). Democrat. Roman Catholic. Home: 1212 N Chicago Ave South Milwaukee WI 53172-1633

THIBODEAU, BRENDA FLORA, middle school educator; b. Rocky Mount, N.C., Mar. 23, 1959; d. John Mark and Margaret Ruth (Smith) Flora; m. Steven Douglas Thibodeau, June 23, 1990. BS in Math. Edn. magna cum laude, Campbell U., 1981; MA in Edn., Pembroke (N.C.) State U., 1994. Cert. math., sci. and social studies tchr., N.C. 7th and 8th grade math., sci. and social studies tchr. Ctrl. Mid. Sch., Whiteville, N.C., 1981-84; 9th grade math. tchr. Nash Ctrl. Jr. H.S., Nashville, 1985-90; high sch. math. tchr. Scotland H.S., Laurinburg, N.C., 1990-94; 8th grade math. tchr. Martin Mid. Sch., Tarboro, N.C., 1994-95, curriculum coord., 1996—; coop. tchr. Scotland County Schs., Laurinburg, 1994. Mem. vis. com., recorder So. Assn. Colls. and Schs., Lumberton, N.C., 1993. Mem. ASCD, N.C. Home Educators, Christian Educators Assn. Internat., N.C. Tchrs. Math., Phi Delta Kappa, Epsilon Phi Eta, Omicron Delta Kappa. Republican. Baptist. Home: RR 4 Box 102 Rocky Mount NC 27801-9442

THIBODEAUX, LAURA ANN, accountant; b. New Orleans, La., May 20, 1970; d. Thomas A. and Hazel Marie (Landry) T.; 1 child, Katherine Davis. BS, Nicholls State Univ., 1993. Cashier Jubilee Exxon Food & Deli, Schriever, La., 1989-90, America's Best Carwash, Thibodaux, La., 1992-93; bookkeeper Morrison Mfg. Inc., Chackbay, La., 1993—. Democrat. Roman Catholic. Office: Morrison Mfg Inc 202 Hwy 20 Thibodaux LA 70301

THIEL, THELMA KING, foundation executive; b. East Orange, N.J., Feb. 12, 1926; d. Thaddeus and Elizabeth Clara (Fickert) King; m. Charles T. Thiel, Mar. 25, 1954 (div. 1976); children: Mark Douglas, Donna Kalani, Dean Alan (dec.). B.A. in Health Edn. and Sch. Nursing, Jersey City State Coll., 1973. Cert. health educator, N.J. Exec. dir. Am. Council for Healthful Living, East Orange, 1973-79; commr. Nat. Com. of Digestive Diseases, Bethesda, Md., 1977-79; founder, chair Dean Thiel Found., Cedar Grove, N.J., 1971—; vice chmn, exec. dir. Am. Liver Found., Cedar Grove, N.J., 1979-84, pres., COO, 1984-94; founder, chair, CEO Hepatitis Found. Internat., 1994—. active Nat. Digestive Diseases Adv. Bd.; advisor Nat. Digestive Diseases Edn. and Info. Clearinghouse; charter mem. Rutgers U. Sch. Communication, Info. and Library Studies Bd. of Adv. Assocs. Author: Foundation for Decision Making, 1978. Mem. AAUW, Digestive Diseases Nat. Coalition (chmn. 1985-90, chmn. Nat. Health Coun., nom. com. 1989-91), Am. Nursing Assn., Soroptimist Internat., Am. Assn. Occupational Health Nurses. Presbyterian (elder). Office: 30 Sunrise Ter Cedar Grove NJ 07009-1423

THIELE, GLORIA DAY, retired librarian, small business owner; b. Los Angeles, Sept. 4, 1931; d. Russell Day Plummer and Dorothy Ruby (Day) Plummer Thi.; m. Donald Edward Cools, June 13, 1953 (div.); children: Michael, Ramona, Naomi, Lawrence, Nancy, Rebecca, Eugene, Maria, Charles. MusB, Mt. St. Mary's Coll., L.A., 1953. Libr. asst. Anaheim (Calif.) Pub. Libr., 1970-73, head Biblioteca de la Comunidad, 1973-74, children's libr. asst., 1974-76, children's br. specialist, 1976-78, children's libr., 1978-81; head children's svcs. Santa Maria (Calif.) Pub. Libr., 1981-85; cons. Literature Continuum, Santa Maria Sch. Dist., 1981-85; cons. Organizational Ch.-Sch. Libr., L.A., 1980; guest lectr. children's lit. Allan Hancock Coll., Santa Maria, 1981-85; owner, founder Discovery Garden, Grass Valley, Calif., 1989-93. Libr. liaison Casa Amistad Community Svc. Group, Anaheim, 1973-74; mem. outreach com. Santiago Libr. System, Orange County, 1973-74, mem. children's svcs. com., 1971-81; mem. Community Svcs. Coordinating Council, Santa Maria, 1982-85; chairperson children's svcs. com. Black Gold Libr. System, 1983-84; cons. children's libr. programs, 1986—; profl. storyteller, 1989—; Allegro Alliance vol. for music in the mountains, 1994—. Contbr. poems to Amherst Soc.'s Am. Poetry Ann., 1988. Mem. So. Calif. Council Lit. for Children and Young People, Kiwanis (sec., publicity chair 1996—), Delta Epsilon Sigma. Republican. Roman Catholic.

THIELEMANN, BARBARA JANET J., library director; b. Cleve., Feb. 14, 1934; d. George William and Freda Leona (Jacobs) Joslin; m. Henry Otto Thielemann, July 27, 1957; children: William Brett, Roberta Thielemann Zmuda, Holly Thielemann McPheeters. AB, Washington U., St. Louis, 1956; MA in Edn., So. Ill. U., 1992. Tchr. Euclid (Ohio) Pub. Schs., 1956-57, Roxana (Ill.) Cmty. Unit Schs., 1957-94; dir. Gilpin County Pub. Libr.,

Black Hawk, Colo., 1995—; cons., adv. curriculum com. Gilpin County Schs., 1994-95. Planning commr. Central City (Colo.) Govt., 1995—; edn. chair St. James Meth. Ch., 1994—, vice chair Peak to Peak Chorale, 1994-96; chair schs. divsn. Peak to Peak Health Communities, 1995—. Democrat. Home: Box 7 101 H St Central City CO 80427-0007

THIELEN, CYNTHIA HENRY, lawyer, state legislator. Student, Stanford U., 1951-52, UCLA, 1952-53; BA with high honors, U. Hawaii, 1975, JD, 1978. Staff atty. Legal Aid Soc. Hawaii, 1979-84; staff atty. planning and zoning com. Honolulu City Coun., 1984-85; sr. litigation assoc. Brown, Johnston & Day, 1985-88; pvt. practice Honolulu, 1988—. Editor Windward Community Newspaper, 1969-71. Mem. State Ho. of Reps., 1990—, minority floor leader, 1992—; mem. State Hwy Safety Coun., 1977-81, State Environ. Coun., 1984-87, Nature Conservancy, Hist. Hawai'i; bd. dirs. Hanahauoli Sch., 1976-86, Hawaii Women's Polit. Action League, 1987—; candidate for lt. gov., Hawaii, 1986; v.p. State Helicopter and Tour Aircraft Adv. Bd., 1986-88, Kailua Neighborhood Bd., 1987-89; pres. Hawaii Children's Mus. Arts, Sci. and Tech., 1987-88, mem., 1987-90; chair Mayor's Adv. Task Force on the Environ., 1989-90. Sixth generation direct descendant of Patrick Henry. Mem. LWV, ABA, Hawaii Bar Assn., Hawaii Women Lawyers (chartered), Stanford Club. Office: State Capitol 415 S Beretania St Rm 443 Honolulu HI 96813

THIENES, CAROLINE SUZANNE, accounting specialist; b. St. Cloud, Minn., June 1, 1966; d. Lawrence Richard Thienes and Suzanne Marie (Day) James. BA in English Lit., U. St. Thomas, 1988; legal asst. cert., U. Wash., 1991; postgrad., Seattle U., 1995—. Notary pub., Wash. Tribunal adminstr. Am. Arbitration Assn., Mpls., 1988-89; database asst. Perkins, Coie, Seattle, 1990-92; orgnl. cons. Time Savers, Seattle, 1992-94; exec. asst. Unigard Security Ins. Co., Seattle, 1994-95, acctg. specialist, 1995—. Mem. AAUW, NOW, Albers Grad. Student Assn. (v.p. adminstrn. 1995—).

THIERMAN, CHERIE MARIE KRYSIAK, accountant; b. Erie, Pa., May 21, 1971; d. Gerald Robert and Mary Jane (Deptula) Krysiak; m. Terry J. Thierman, May 28, 1994. BS, Gannon U., 1993. Sr. acct. Schaffner, Knight, Minnaugh & Co, P.C., Erie, Pa., 1993—. Home: 2650 W 38 St Apt 2A Erie PA 16506-4566 Office: Schaffner Knight Minnaugh & Co PC 1315 G Daniel Baldwin Bldg Erie PA 16501

THIMMIG, DIANA M., lawyer; b. Germany, May 5, 1959. BA cum laude, John Carroll U., 1980; JD, Cleve. State U., 1982. Bar: Ohio 1983, U.S. Dist. Ct. (no. dist.) Ohio 1983, U.S. Ct. Appeals (6th cir.) 1983, U.S. Supreme Ct. 1983; cert. Am. Bankruptcy Bd. for Consumer and Bus. Bankruptcy. Ptnr. Arter & Hadden, Cleve. Contbr. articles to profl. jours. Hon. consul of Germany, 1988—. Mem. Women's City Club Cleve. (pres. 1994—). Office: Arter & Hadden 1100 Huntington Bldg 925 Euclid Ave Cleveland OH 44115-1475*

THIXTON, BRENDA COX, marketing consultant; b. Tacoma, Aug. 13, 1958; d. Charles Madison and Joyce Yvonne (Felps) Cox; m. John Michael Thixton, Mar. 21, 1992; 1 child, Morgan Brooke Malayeri. Student, La. Tech. U., 1976-78; BA in Journalism, La. State U., 1981; BA in Mktg., Mellen U., 1996. Lic. broadcaster, Tex. Mktg. dir. La. Assn. B. & Ind., Baton Rouge, 1979-81; pres. Malayeri & Co., Baton Rouge, 1981-87; v.p. mktg. Ind. Mfrs. Assn., Indpls., 1987-92; pres. Thixton & Co., Indpls., 1992—; bd. dirs. Starlight Musicals, Indpls., Save-One Life Found., Indpls.; cons. devel. ABC, Nat. Glass Assn. Recipient Devel. award Assoc. Builders and Contractors, 1994. Mem. Am. Soc. Assoc. Execs., Ind. Soc. Assoc. Execs., Ind. State C. of C., Indpls. C. of C. Republican. Home: 3720 N Delaware St Indianapolis IN 46205

THOMAS, ALTA PARKER, secondary school educator; b. Butte, Mont., Sept. 18, 1940; d. Charles Clayton and Sarah Elizabeth (Bennett) Parker Hopkins; m. Vivian William Thomas Jr., Aug. 19, 1962; children: Christine Michelle Thomas Walters, Tracyy Ann Thomas, Lisa Janine Thomas Julson. BS, Mont. State U., 1962; MEd, Walla Walla Coll., 1991. Cert. tchr., Wash. Rsch. chemist Dow Chem. Co., Midland, Mich., 1962-64; tchr. Granite Sch. Dist., Salt Lake City, 1964-65; home and hosp. tchr. Richland (Wash.) Schs., 1975-77; sci. tchr. Kennewick (Wash.) Sch. Dist., 1977-84, high sch. biology tchr., 1984—, sci. dept. chair, 1992-94; coord. Internat. Baccalaureate Kennewick Sch. Dist., 1994—, chmn. sci. curriculum com., 1987-89, rep. dist. circle com., 1991-93; coach sci. olympiad team Kennewick H.S., 1988-94, mem. staff devel. com., 1985-91, site coun., 1995. Patented oven cleaner formula; editor: Curnutt Family Cookbook, 1986. Founder acad. booster club Kennewick High Sch., 1985. REST fellow Battelle Pacific N.W. Lab., 1988. Mem. Nat. Assn. Biology Tchrs., NEA, Wash. Edn. Assn., Kennewick Edn. Assn. (rep., negotiator 1977—), Wash. Sci. Tchr. Assn., Delta Kappa Gamma (membership chair, polit. affairs chair 1984—). Presbyterian. Home: 4029 S Cascade St Kennewick WA 99337-5185 Office: Kennewick High Sch 500 S Dayton St Kennewick WA 99336-5640

THOMAS, BARBARA ANN, record company executive; b. Bklyn., Feb. 5, 1948; d. Wilfred Godfrey and Violet Rose (Howell) Swaby; m. Ronald L. Hannah (div.). Adminstrv. asst. Million Dollar Record Poll, College Park, Ga., 1985-86, Points East Records, College Park, 1986-87, Greer Booking Agy., Atlanta, 1986-87; pres. Gunsmoke Records, College Park, 1988—; v.p. Toroy Mercedes Records, 1994—; mgr. Jesse James, 1983—. Mem. NAFE, COPE, Blues Found., Atlanta Top Star Awards, Nat. Young Black Programmers (bd. dirs.), Nat. Club Owners, Promoters and Entertainment Assn. (bd. dirs. 1996). Democrat. Roman Catholic. Office: Gunsmoke Records 2523 Roosevelt Hwy Ste 3D Atlanta GA 30337-6243

THOMAS, BETTY, actress; b. St. Louis. BFA, Ohio U. Former sch. tchr.; co-star Hill St. Blues, from 1981; Joined Second City Workshop, Chgo.; appeared on Second City TV, 1984; appeared in after sch. spl. The Gift of Love, 1985, Prison of Children, 1986. Appeared in The Fun Factory game show, 1976; film: Troop Beverly Hills, 1989; in TV film Outside Chance, 1978, Nashville Grab, 1981, When Your Lover Leaves, 1983; star TV series Hill Street Blues, 1981-87 (Emmy nominations 1981, 82, 83); dir.: (TV) Dream On: "For Peter's Sake" (Emmy award, Outstanding Individual Achievement in Directing in a Comedy Series, 1993), 1993, (film) The Brady Bunch Movie, 1995. Emmy Best Supporting Actress, 1985. Office: care ICM c/o Richard Feldman 8942 Wilshire Blvd Beverly Hills CA 90211*

THOMAS, BEVERLY IRENE, special education educator; b. Del Rio, Tex., Nov. 12, 1939; d. Clyde Louis and Eve Naomi (Avant) Whistler; m. James Henry Thomas, Jan. 28, 1972; children: Kenneth (dec.), Wade, Robert, Darcy, Betty Kay, James III, Debra, Brenda, Michael. BM summa cum laude, Sul Ross State U., 1972, MEd, 1976, MEd in Counseling, 1992, MEd in Mid. Mgmt., 1996. Cert. music, elem. edn., music edn., learning disabilities, spl. edn. generic, ednl. diagnosis, ednl. counseling, spl. edn. counseling and mid. mgmt. Edn. diagnostician West Tex. State Sch., Tex. Youth Commn. Mem. AAUW, ASCD, NEA, MENSA, Assn. for Children with Learning Disabilities (local sec. 1974), Tex. State Tchrs. Assn. (treas. 1991-94), Tex. Ednl. Diagnosticians Assn., Tex. Profl. Ednl. Diagnosticians, Reeves County Assn. of Children with Learning Disabilities, Nat. Coun. Tchrs. of Maths., Nat. Coun. Tchrs. English, Learning Disabilities Assn., Learning Disabilities Assoc., Tex., Coun. for Exceptional Children, Tex. Counseling Assn., Alpha Chi, Kappa Delta Pi. Home: 2410 S Eddy St Pecos TX 79772-7514

THOMAS, CAROLE DOLORES, gerontologist; b. Huntington, Ind., Dec. 20, 1937; d. James Robert and Gladys Agnes (Walraven) Williams; m. Norman Day Thomas, Sept. 1, 1962 (separated); children: Diane Thomas Laucirica, Mark Alexander. BA in Polit. Sci., U. Ill., 1960; MA in Gerontology, U. South Fla., 1982. Human svcs. analyst Dept. Health and Rehab. Svcs., Tampa, Fla., 1987-94, adult protective investigator, 1994—; mem. Adult Protection Team, Tampa, 1990—, Bradenton, Fla., 1990—, Long Term Care Ombudsman Coun., Tampa, 1989—. Mem. Fla. Orch. Guild, Tampa, 1985—; guardian ad litem 13th Jud. Cir., Tampa, 1991—; vol. Performing Arts Ctr., Tampa, 1992—. Home: 14314 Diplomat Dr Tampa FL 33613-3107 Office: Dept Health & Rehab Svcs 4000 W Martin Luther King Blvd Tampa FL 33614-7012

THOMAS, CYNTHIA ELIZABETH, advanced practice nurse; b. Highland, Ind., Sept. 3, 1958; d. James William and Naomi Elizabeth (Rice) T. BS in Animal Sci., Purdue U., 1980; ADN, Purdue U. Calumet, 1986, BSN, 1988, MSN, 1990. RN, Ind.; cert. adult nurse practitioner, family nurse practitioner, clin. specialist in med.-surg. nursing. Med.-surg. open heart ICU/CCU staff nurse, charge nurse Porter Meml. Hosp., Valparaiso, Ind., 1986-94; advanced practice nurse Cmty. Health Ctrs. Koontz Lake, LaCrosse, North Judson, Starke Meml. Hosp., Ind., 1994-95; advanced practice nurse Cmty. Health Ctrs.-Koontz Lake, LaCrosse, Ind., 1994-95, Starke Meml. Hosp., Knox, Ind., 1994-95; nurse practitioner/office coord. Hanna Family Med. Ctr., LaPorte Hosp./Lakeland Area Health Svcs., 1995-96; nursing instr. Bethel Coll., Mishawaka, Ind., 1995-96; adult medicine/pulmonary nurse practitioner Arnett Clinic, Lafayette, Ind., 1996—; med.-surg. clin. instr. Purdue U., Westville, Ind., 1993-94; nursing instr. Bethel Coll., Mishawaka, Ind., 1995-96; adult medicine/pulmonary nurse practitioner, Arnett Clinic, Lafayette, Ind., 1996—. Mem. AACN, Am. Acad. Nurse Practitioners, Alpha Zeta. Office: Pulmonary Dept Arnett Clinic 1500 Salem St Lafayette IN 47904

THOMAS, CYNTHIA GAIL, public policy research executive; b. Tulsa, Jan. 26, 1956; d. Jack Marcy and Dorothy (Bergfors) T. BS summa cum laude, U. Minn., 1978, MA, 1981. Analyst Met. Coun., St. Paul, 1978; rsch. analyst Common Cause Minn., St. Paul, 1979, lobbyist, 1980, rsch. cons., 1982; adminstr. NBC, N.Y.C., 1980; researcher Minn. State Sen., St. Paul, 1983-85, rsch. dir., 1985-86; owner Thomas Rsch., Dallas and Roseville, Minn., 1986—; pub. policy advisor Rep. Party, St. Paul, 1986—; commr. Roseville Planning Commn., 1991-95; sr. fellow Tex. Pub. Policy Found., 1996—. Contbr. articles to profl. publs. Vol. Little Bros. of Poor, Mpls., 1987-94, YWCA, St. Paul, 1989-90; mem. Tex. Pub. Policy Found.; softball coach Girls Age 10-12 team St. Paul, 1988. Mem. Greater Dallas C. of C., Nature Conservancy, Amnesty Internat., Fraser Ins. Republican. Home and Office: Thomas Rsch 1137 Meadow Creek Dr #271 Irving TX 75038

THOMAS, ELAINE FREEMAN, artist, educator; b. Cleve., July 21, 1923; d. Daniel Edquard and Ellen Douglas (Wilson) Freeman; m. Frederick Lindel Thomas, June 28, 1943 (dec. May 1969); children: Janet Thomas Sullen, Frederick L. III. BS, Tuskegee (Ala.) U., 1945; MA, NYU, 1949; postgrad., U. Paris, 1966, U. Poona, India, 1973, Columbia U., 1970. Fellow Northwestern U., Evanston, Ill., 1944; Rosenwald fellow Black Mountain (N.C.) Coll., 1945; faculty, art dept. chair Tuskegee U., 1945-89; fellow Berea (Ky.) Coll., 1956, U. of Ams., Mexico City, 1956; curator George Washington Carver Mus., Tuskegee Inst., 1962-77; mem. Fulbright-Hays Faculty Rsch., Senegal and LaGambia, Africa, 1989; panelist expansion arts Nat. Endowment of Arts, Washington, 1977-79; fgn. svc. officer evaluator U.S. Dept. State, Washington, 1979; mem. exec. com. Ala. Coun. Arts, Montgomery, 1986-91; numerous TV appearances. One-woman exhbn. Hallmark Greeting Cards, Crown Ctr., Kansas City, Mo.; participant TV documentary, 1974, 77, 82, 85, 87, 91, 94; set up George Washington Carver Exhbn., White House. Chmn. nat. screening com. Fulbright Grad. Fellows in Design, Inst. Internat. Edn., N.Y.C.. Named A Woman of Distinction, Auburn (Ala.) U., Ms. Sr. Am. of Ala., 1994; recipient Disting. Svc. award U.S. Dept. Interior, Nat. Park Svc., Bicentennial award Pres. Gerald Ford, Resolution HR 274 award State of Ala. Ho. of Reps., Ms. Sr. Ala. award, 1994; named to 1995 Ala. Sr. Citizens Hall of Fame. Mem. Nat. Mus. of Women Artists, Optimists, Tau Beta Sigma, Delta Sigma Theta, Zeta Phi Beta (Woman of Yr. award 1978). Home: 202 Rush Dr Tuskegee AL 36083

THOMAS, ELIZABETH TRENT (BETSY TRENT THOMAS), ornithologist, writer; b. Johnstown, Pa., Aug. 3, 1923; d. Albert Leo and Eleanor (Beamensderfer) Trent; m. Robert Harry Thomas, Dec. 27, 1946 (Div. Apr. 1979); children: Nancy Louise Thomas, Margaret Ann Thomas. Attended, U. Mass., Amherst, 1968; BS in Art, Skidmore Coll., Saratoga Springs, N.Y., 1946. Draftsman Curtiss-Wright Aircraft Corp., Columbus, Ohio, 1943; engring. asst. Gen. Motors Corp., Detroit, 1944; graphic designer Concordia Gallia Corp., N.Y., 1946-47; owner Betsy Trent Handcrafts, Pa., W.Va., N.J., Mass., 1948-62; owner (ornithological tours) Thomas Enterprises, Caracas, Venezuela, 1968-81; field rschr. Va. Dept. Agr., Harrisonburg, 1989; ornithological rschr. Venezuela, 1972-95, Va., 1986—; rsch. assoc. Smithsonian Instn., Washington D.C., 1985-88; mem. bd. dirs. Internat. Coun. for Bird Preservation, 1987-94, sec. 1989-92; plenary speaker 2d Brazilian Ornithological Congress, Campo Grande, Brazil, 1992. Author: (book) Conoce Nuestras Aves, 1979; contbr. chpts. to books and articles to profl. jours.; artist: (book illustrations) The Ferns of Pennsylvania, 1946. Dir. Girl Scout Camp, Saigon, Vietnam, 1960; speaker numerous ornithological and conservation orgns., Venezuela, Canada, Fla., N.Y., Mass. Kans., N.Mex., Calif. Va., 1970—; founder Sociedad Conservacionista Audubon de Venezuela, 1971 (1st pres. 1972, 10th pres. 1982). Grantee Am. Mus. Natural History, 1978-79, Venezuelan Govt., 1978, Am. Orinthologist's Union, 1982, Smithsonian Instn., 1987-92. Mem. Am. Orinthologists Union, Va. Soc. Orinthology, British Orinthologist's Club, Cooper Orinthological Soc., Wilson Orinthological Soc. Home: 125 Harry Settle Rd Castleton VA 22716

THOMAS, ELLA COOPER, lawyer; b. Ft. Totten, N.Y.; d. Avery John and Ona Caroline (Gibson) C.; m. Robert Edward Lee Thomas, Nov. 22, 1938 (dec. Jan. 1985); 1 child, Robert Edward Lee Jr. Student, Vassar Coll., 1932-34, U. Hawaii, 1934-35, George Washington U., 1935-36; JD, George Washington U., 1940. Bar: U.S. Dist. Ct. D.C. 1942, U.S. Ct. Appeals (D.C. cir.) 1943, U.S. Supreme Ct. 1947, U.S. Tax Ct. 1973. Secret maps custodian U.S. Dist. Engrs., Honolulu, 1941-42; contbg. editor Labor Rels. Reporter, Washington, 1942; assoc. Smith, Ristig & Smith, Washington, 1942-45; law libr. George Washington Law Sch., Washington, 1946-53; reporter of decisions U.S. Tax Ct., Washington, 1953-75. Author: Law of Libel and Slander, 1949. Mem. Inter-Am. Bar Assn. (coun. mem. 1973—), D.C. Bar Assn.

THOMAS, EMILY DENISE, nurse; b. Tuscaloosa, Ala., Feb. 14, 1962; d. Mack and Loretta (Thomas) Wedgeworth. ADN, Shelton State Jr. Coll., 1982, Samford U., 1988; BS in Acctg., Miles Coll., 1995. RN, Ala.; cert. ACLS and BCLS instr. Sec., receptionist Shelton State Jr. Coll., Tuscaloosa, 1981-82; cashier Handy Dan/Handy City, Birmingham, Ala., 1984-86; RN Brookwood Med. Ctr. Montclair, Birmingham, 1986—, neonatal technician, 1989-91, acctg. intern, 1995; monitor technician Med. Ctr. East, Birmingham, 1990-92; RN Birmingham Vets. Adminstrn. Med. Ctr., 1991—. Vol. Jimmy Hale Mission, Birmingham, 1989-90, IRS, Birmingham, 1994-95. Mem. Inst. Mgmt. Accts. (sec. 1994-95, Scholar award 1995), Alpha Kappa Alpha (sec. 1988-89). Home: 127 Ski Lodge Dr #215 Homewood AL 35209

THOMAS, ESTHER MERLENE, elementary education educator; b. San Diego, Oct. 16, 1945; d. Merton Alfred and Nellie Lida (Von Pilz) T. AA with honors, Grossmont Coll., 1966; BA with honors, San Diego State U., 1969; MA, U. Redlands, 1977. Cert. elem. and adult edn. tchr. Tchr. Cajon Valley Union Sch. Dist., El Cajon, 1969—; sci. fair coord. Flying Hills Sch.; tchr. Hopi and Navajo Native Americans, Ariz, Utah, 1964-74, Goose and Gander Nursery School, Lakeside, Calif., 1964-66; dir., supt. Bible and Sunday schs. various chs., Lakeside, 1961-87; mem. sci. com., math coun. Cajon Valley Union Sch. Dist., 1990-91. Author: Individualized Curriculum in the Affective Domain; contbg. author: Campbell County, The Treasured Years, 1990, Legends of the Lakeside; songwriter for Hilltop Records, Hollywood, Calif; songs released Never Trouble Trouble, Old Glory, Jesus Is Our Lord, Daniel's Prayer; contbr. articles to profl. jours. and newspapers. Tem. U.S. Senatorial Club, Washington, 1984—, Conservative Caucus, Inc., Washington, 1988—, Ronald Reagan Presdl. Found., Ronald Reagan Rep. Ctr., 1988, Rep. Presdl. Citizen's Adv. Commn., 1989—, Rep. Platform Planning Com., Calif., 1992, at-large del. representing dist. #45, Lakeside, Calif., 1992, 1995—, Am. Security Coun., Washington, 1994, Congressman Hunter's Off Road Adv. Coun., El Cajon, Calif., 1994, Century Club, San Diego Rep. Century Club, 1995; mem. health articulation com. project AIDS, Cajon Valley Union Sch. Dist., 1988—, Concerned Women Am., Washington, Recruit Depot Hist. Mus., San Diego, 1989, Citizen's Drug Free Am., Calif., 1989—, The Heritage Found., 1988—; charter mem. Marine Corps Mus.; mem. Lakeside Centennial Com., 1985-86; hon. mem. Rep. Presdl. Task Force, Washington, 1986; del. Calif. Rep. Senatorial Mid-Term Conv., Washington, 1994; mus. curator Lakeside Hist. Soc., 1992-93. Recipient Outstanding Svc. award PTA, 1972-74; recognized for various contbns. Commdg. Post Gen., San Diego Bd. Edn., 1989. Mem. Tchrs. Assn., Calif. Tchrs. Assn., Nat. Trust for Hist. Preservation, Cajon Valley Educators Assn. (faculty advisor, rep. 1980-82, 84-86, 87-88), Christian Bus. and Profl. Women, Capitol Hill Women's Club, Am. Ctr. for Law and Justice, Internat. Christian Women's Club (Christian amb. to Taiwan, Korea, 1974). Republican. Home: 13594 Highway 8 Business Apt 3 Lakeside CA 92040-5235 Office: Flying Hills Elem Sch 1251 Finch St El Cajon CA 92020-1433

THOMAS, ETHEL COLVIN NICHOLS (MRS. LEWIS VICTOR THOMAS), counselor, educator; b. Cranston, R.I., Mar. 31, 1913; d. Charles Russell and Mabel Maria (Colvin) Nichols; Ph.B., Pembroke Coll. in Brown U., 1934; M.A., Brown U., 1938; Ed.D., Rutgers U., 1979; m. Lewis Victor Thomas, July 26, 1945 (dec. Oct. 1965); 1 child, Glenn Nichols. Tchr. English, Cranston High Sch., 1934-39; social dir. and adviser to freshmen, Fox Hall, Boston U., 1939-40; instr. to asst. prof. English Am. Coll. for Girls, Istanbul, Turkey, 1940-44; dean freshman, dir. admission Women's Coll. of Middlebury, Vt., 1944-45; tchr. English, Robert Coll., Istanbul, 1945-46; instr. English, Rider Coll., Trenton, N.J., 1950-51; tchr. English, Princeton (N.J.) High Sch., 1951-61, counselor, 1960-62, 72-83, coll. counselor, 1962-72, sr. peer counselor, 1986—. Mem. NEA, AAUW, Nat. Assn. Women Deans Adminstrs. and Counselors, Am. Assn. Counseling and Devel., Bus. and Profl. Women's Club (named Woman of Yr., Princeton chpt. 1977), Met. Mus. Art, Phi Delta Kappa, Kappa Delta Pi. Presbyn. Clubs: Brown University (N.Y.C.); Nassau.

THOMAS, FLORENCE KATHLEEN, retired military officer; b. Torrington, Conn., June 20, 1945; d. James Dudley and Nova Lee (Campbell) T. BA in Mass Comm., U. Tex.-El Paso, 1970; MA in Adminstrn. of Justice, Wichita State U., 1984.. Commd. 2d lt. U.S. Army, 1969, advanced through grades to lt. col., 1990; chief ops. tng. devels. U.S. Mil. Police Sch., Ft. McClellan, Ala., 1979-80; exec. officer criminal investigation div. Kaiserslautern, Germany, 1980-82; comdr. criminal investigation div. Nuernberg Field Office, Fed. Republic Germany, 1982-83; corrections officer Forces Command, Provost Marshal, Ft. McPherson, Ga., 1985; chief law enforcement mgmt. div., 1985-87, chief evaluations, exercise div., dir. ops., 1987-88; chief force deployment br. plans div. office of dir. for ops. HQ USAREUR & 7A, Heidelberg, Germany, 1988-92, ret., 1992; with K & S The Lawn Ranger, El Paso, Tex., 1992—. mil. cons. law enforcement activities, 1977—. Mem. NAFE, Assn. U.S. Army, U.S. Golf Assn., Sun Country Golf Assn., Emerald Springs Women's Golf Assn., Internat. Women's Vet's. Golf Assn., Intercity Women's Golf Assn. Avocation: golf, fishing, landscaping, gardening. Home: 15000 Ashford St Apt 12 El Paso TX 79927-6413

THOMAS, GEORGIE A., state official. B.A., Cornell U., 1965; M.B.A., Columbia U., 1973. Asst. portfolio mgr. Money Mgmt. dept. R.W. Pressprich & Co. Inc., N.Y.C., 1968-71; portfolio analyst Bache & Co., N.Y.C., 1971-72; with Exxon Corp., N.Y.C., 1973-76, consolidation analyst Treas. dept., 1975-76; treas. Penntech Papers Inc., N.Y.C., 1976-79; budget dir. Yankee Publishing Inc., Dublin, N.H., 1982-85; treas. State of N.H., Concord, 1985—; mem. econ. growth and productivity and tech. coms. Bus. Research Adv. Council of Bur. Labor Statistics, 1978-79; mem. alumni counseling bd. Columbia U. Bus. Sch., 1973-79. Editor: Jour. World Bus., Columbia Bus. Sch. Mem. Fin. Women's Assn. N.Y. (mem. exec. bd. 1977-78), Womens Econ. Roundtable. Club: Cornell of Fairfield County (Conn.). Home: Ashley Rd Antrim NH 03440 Office: State NH State House Annex Rm 121 Concord NH 03301*

THOMAS, GERALDINE P., personnel executive; b. Atlanta, Dec. 10, 1951; d. Arthur and Vivian (Spence) Perrimon; m. Ronald Floyd Thomas, June 21, 1970; children: Erinn Danielle, Erich Perrimon. BS in Human Resources, Ga. State U., 1985. Coord. NationBank, Atlanta, mgr. recruitment, mgr. employee rels., mgr. payroll, cons. human resources, mgr. personnel, 1989—, now sr. v.p., state pers. exec.; exec. com. Fin. Employee Rels. Study Group, Wharton Sch. Bus., Phila. Mem. NAACP. Named Best and Brighest Bus. Woman Dollars & Sense, Chgo., 1991; Outstanding Woman in Banking Success Guide, 1992. Mem. Am. Bankers Assn. (exec. com. human resources com.), Am. Inst. Banking (bd. dirs., Nat. Bankers Assn. (bd. dirs., pres., Trailblazer award), Atlanta Inst. Banking (bd. dirs.), Atlanta Urban League, Alpha Kappa Alpha. Baptist. Office: 600 Peachtree St NE 54th Fl Atlanta GA 30308*

THOMAS, HEATHER CHERIE, elementary education educator; b. N.Y.C., Aug. 25, 1970; d. Donald Ray and S. Charmaine (Murphy) T. BA in Liberal Studies, Azusa Pacific U., 1992, supplementary credential in English, 1992, multiple subject credentials, 1993. 3d grade tchr. Saratoga (Calif.) Union Dist., 1993—; faculty advisor student coun., grade level tech. com. rep., Argonaut Elem. Sch., Saratoga, Calif., 1994—; dir. 3d grade musical Salute to Am., 1993. Named Tchr. of Week, 1994, KEZR Radio, San Jose, Calif. Mem. ASCD, Calif. Tchrs. Assn., Santa Clara County Reading Coun., Saratoga Tchrs. Assn. (rep. coun. mem.). Republican. Baptist. Office: Argonaut Elem Sch 13200 Shadow Mountain Dr Saratoga CA 95070

THOMAS, HELEN A. (MRS. DOUGLAS B. CORNELL), newspaper bureau executive; b. Winchester, Ky., Aug. 4, 1920; d. George and Mary (Thomas) T.; m. Douglas B. Cornell. BA, Wayne U., 1942; LLD, Eastern Mich. State U., 1972, Ferris State Coll., 1978, Brown U., 1986; LHD, Wayne State U., 1974, U. Detroit, 1979; LLD, St. Bonaventure U., 1988, Franklin Marshall U., 1989, No. Michigan U., 1989, Skidmore Coll., 1992; Susquehanna U., 1993, Sage Coll., 1994, U. Mo., 1994; LLD, Northwestern U., 1995, Franklin Coll., 1995; Hon. degree, Mich. State U., 1996. With UPI, 1943—; wire svc. reporter UPI, Washington, 1943-74; White House bur. chief UPI, 1974—. Author: Dateline White House. Recipient Woman of Yr. in Comm. award Ladies Home Jour., 1975, 4th Estate award Nat. press Club, 1984; Journalism award U. Mo., Dean of Sch. Journalism award, Al Newharth award, 1990, Ralph McGill award, 1995. Mem. Women's Nat. Press Club (pres. 1959-60, William Allen White Journalism award), Am. Newspaper Women's Club (past v.p.), White House Corrs. Assn. (pres. 1976), Gridiron Club (pres. 1993), Sigma Delta Chi (fellow, Hall of Fame), Delta Sigma Phi (hon.). Home: 2501 Calvert St NW Washington DC 20008-2620 Office: UPI World Hdqrs 1400 I St NW Washington DC 20005-2208

THOMAS, HELEN DEAN, journalist; b. Holcomb, Miss., Mar. 2, 1960; d. Elmo and Maggie Lee (Harbin) Harris; m. Ernest Dwight Thomas, May 10, 1991; 1 stepchild, Chrystal R.; 1 child, Ernest D. Jr. Degree in bus. adminstrn., Fayetteville (N.C.) Tech. Inst, 1984; degree in data processing, Holmes Jr. Coll., Goodman, Miss., 1988. Staff writer The Daily-Sentinel-Star, Grenada, Miss., 1988—. Served in U.S. Army, 1981-84, Germany. Decorated achievement medal U.S. Army, 1982, commendation medal, 1984, good conduct medal, 1984. Democrat. Mem. Ch. Christ. Home: 1907 Sweethome Rd Grenada MS 38901 Office: The Daily-Sentinel-Star 159 Green St Grenada MS 38901

THOMAS, HILARY BRYN, telecommunications executive, interactivist, writer, speaker; b. Brignorth, U.K., Jan. 31, 1943; came to U.S., 1985; parents, Kenneth Bryn and Nancy Barbara Tench (Cullum) T. BSc with honors, U. Wales, 1965. Instr. U. Victoria, B.C., Can., 1967-73; rsch. asst. Communications Studies Group Univ. Coll., London, 1975-76; cons. Communications Studies & Planning, Ltd., London, 1976-80; v.p. CSP Internat., Inc., London and N.Y.C., 1980-82, Aregon Internat., London and N.Y.C., 1982-85, Videodial, Inc., N.Y.C., 1985-88; pres. Minitel USA, Inc., N.Y.C., 1988-92; pres., bd. dirs. Minitel Holdings, Inc., Del.; chmn. bd. dirs. Minitel Svcs. Co., 1988-92; pres. Interactive Telecommunications Svcs. Inc., Mountain Lakes, N.J., 1992—; pres., founder ISED Corp., Howell, N.J., 1992—; spkr. interactive svcs., electronic commerce, the Internet. Contbr. articles to industry publs. Mem. Interactive Svcs. Assn. (bd. dirs. 1985—, chmn. 1987-89; Disting. Svc. award 1989), Internat. Inst. Comm., World Inst. on Disability (bus. adv. coun.).

THOMAS, JACQUELYN MAY, librarian; b. Mechanicsburg, Pa., Jan. 26, 1932; d. William John and Gladys Elizabeth (Warren) Harvey; m. David Edward Thomas, Aug. 28, 1954; children: Lesley J., Courtenay J., Hilary A. BA summa cum laude, Gettysburg Coll., 1954; student U. N.C., 1969; MEd, U. N.H., 1971. Libr. Phillips Exeter Acad., Exeter, N.H., 1971-77, acad. libr., 1977—, chair governing bd. Child Care Ctr., 1987-91; chair Com. to

Enhance Status of Women, Exeter, 1981-84; chair Loewenstein Com., Exeter, 1982—; pres. Cum Laude Soc., Exeter, 1984-86; James H. Ottaway Jr. prof., 1990—. Editor: The Design of the Libr.: A Guide to Sources of Information, 1981, Rarities of Our Time: The Special Collections of the Phillips Exeter Academy Libr. Trustee, treas. Exeter Day Sch., 1965-69; mem. bd. Exeter Hosp. Vols., 1954-59; mem. Exeter Hosp. Corp., 1978—; mem. bldg. com. Exeter Pub. Libr., 1986-88; chair No. New Eng., Coun. for Women in Ind. Schs., 1985-87; chmn. Lamont Poetry Program, Exeter, 1984-86; dir. Greater Portsmouth Community Found, 1990—; active AAC&U, On Campus with Women, Wellesley Coll. Ctr. for Rsch. on Women. N.H. Coun. for Humanities grantee, 1981-82; NEH grantee, 1982; recipient Lillian Radford Trust award, 1989. Mem. ALA, Internat. Assn. Sch. Librs., New Eng. Libr. Assn., N.H. Edn1. Media Assn., New Eng. Assn. Ind. Sch. Librs., Am. Assn. Sch. Librs. (chmn. non-pub. sch. sect.), Phi Beta Kappa. Home: 16 Elm St Exeter NH 03833-2704 Office: Acad Libr Phillips Exeter Acad 20 Main St Exeter NH 03833-2438

THOMAS, JANE ANN, columnist; b. Bklyn., Aug. 20, 1951; d. Robert Alfred and Florence Agnes (Coyne) Keil; m. Robert Lamson Thomas, Apr. 22, 1996. AA, Tallahassee Cmty. Coll., 1986. Monthly columnis ReFUNdamentals, Mims, Fla., 1994-95. Publicity chmn. Lincoln H.S. Band, Tallahassee, 1995—. Contbr. poetry to profl. publs.; semi-finalist Nat. Libr. of Poetry contest. Mem. Tallahassee Writer's Assn. Democrat. Roman Catholic.

THOMAS, JEANETTE MAE, accountant; b. Winona, Minn., Dec. 19, 1946; d. Herbert and Arline (Shank) Harmon; m. Gerald F. Thomas, Aug. 9, 1969; children: Bradley, Christopher. BS, Winona State U., 1968; postgrad., Colo. State U.; CFP, Coll. for Fin. Planning, Denver, 1985. Enrolled agt.; cert. fin. planner; registered rep. NASD; registered investment advisor; accredited tax advisor. Tchr. pub. schs. systems Colo., N.Mex., Mich., 1968-72; adminstrv. asst. Bus. Men's Svcs., Ft. Collins, Colo., 1974-75; tax cons. Tax Corp. Am., Ft. Collins, Colo., 1972-80; chief acct. Jayland Electric, La Porte, Colo., 1981-90; pres., CEO Thomas Fin. Svcs. Inc., Ft. Collins, 1980—. Contbr. articles to newspapers and profl. newsletters. Bd. dirs. local PTO, 1984-85; treas. Boy Scouts Am., 1985-88; master food safety advisor coop. ext. Colo. State U., 1988—; spkr., steering com. AARP Women's Fin. Info. Program, 1988—; chair adv. bd. Larimer County Coop. Ext., Colo. State U.; quality rev. com., career edn. adv. bd. Poudre R-1 Schs. Mem. Internat. Assn. Fin. Planning (past officer), Am. Soc. Women Accts. (bd. dirs. 1984-86, 96-97), Pvt. Industry Coun. (chair 1994-95), Nat. Soc. Pub. Accts., Colo. Soc. Pub. Accts., Inst. CFPs, Am. Notary Assn., Ft. Collins C. of C. (red carpet com. bus. assistance coun. 1989—). Home: PO Box 370 Laporte CO 80535-0370 Office: 400 S Howes St Ste 2 Fort Collins CO 80521-2802

THOMAS, JENNIFER LEE, veterinarian; b. Mount Pleasant, Mich., June 7, 1962; d. Larry Lee and Judith Louise (Andrews) T. BS in Physiology, BA in Criminal Justice, Mich. State U., East Lansing, Mich., 1986, DVM Coll. Veterinary Medicine, 1992. Veterinarian Mich. Humane Soc., Westland/Auburn Hills, Mich., 1992-93; assoc. veterinarian Tawas (Mich.) Animal Hosp., 1993-94; veterinarian Pets Are People, Too, Atlanta, 1994-96. Vol. The Nature Conservancy, East Lansing, 1988-94. Mem. Am. Veterinary Med. Assn., Mich. Veterinary Med. Assn., Greater Atlanta Veterinary Med. Soc., Assn. Veterinarians for Animal Rights. Home: 330A Arizona Ave NE Atlanta GA 30307

THOMAS, JOSEPHINE BOGIE, community activist; b. Mt. Sterling, Ky., Apr. 25, 1921; d. Joseph Chenault and Emma (Cooper) Bogie; m. Joseph Burghard Thomas, Mar. 14, 1940; 1 child, Sandra Ann. Cmty. activist Iron Overload Diseases Assn., North Palm Beach, Fla., 1983—. Mem. DAR, Eastern Star, Ladies Oriental Shrine. Republican. Presbyn.

THOMAS, JUDITH ANN, radio executive; b. Detroit, Sept. 26, 1961; d. Arthur Thomas and Mary Ellen (Hinkle) Nelson; m. William E. Thomas, Jan. 6, 1989; 1 child, Sarah. BS, Oakland U., Rochester, Mich., 1983. CPA, Mich.; CMA. Staff acct. Oakland-Livingston Human Svcs., Pontiac, Mich., 1983-85; auditor Doeren Mayhew & Co., CPAs, Troy, Mich., 1985-87; asst. contr. Emmett Industries, Warren, Mich., 1987-88; contr. Creative World, Southfield, Mich., 1988-91; contr., bus. mgr. ABC Radio/Walt Disney Inc./WJR-WHYT Radio, Detroit, 1991—. Mem. AICPAs, Am. Women in Radio and TV (treas.), BCFM. Presbyterian. Home: 2793 Brady Ln Bloomfield Hills MI 48304

THOMAS, JUDITH BRANCH, music educator; b. Biltmore, N.C., Aug. 16, 1941; d. Herbert Leon and Hazle (Boyle) Branch; m. James Donald Thomas, May 16, 1964; children: Elizabeth Suzanne Thomas Woolwine, Blake Fleming Thomas. BS in Music, High Point U., 1963. Cert. tchr., Va. 8th grade tchr. Franklin County Pub. Schs., Rocky Mountain, Va., 1963-64; 3d grade tchr. Henry County Pub. Schs., Collinsville, Va., 1964-66, 4th grade tchr., 1967-71, music specialist, 1972—. Mem. NEA, Va. Edn. Assn., Henry County Edn. Assn., Fairystone Squares. Methodist. Office: Henry County Pub Schs King's Mountain Rd Collinsville VA 24078

THOMAS, KAREN P., composer, conductor; b. Seattle, Sept. 17, 1957. BA in Composition, Cornish Inst., 1979; MusM in Composition, Conducting, U. Wash., 1985. Condr. The Contemporary Group, 1981-85; condr., music dir. Wash. Composers Forum, 1984-86; artistic dir., condr. Seattle Pro Musica, 1987—. Conducting debut Seattle, 1987; composer: Four Delineations of Curtmantle for Trombone or Cello, 1982, Metamorphoses on a Machaut Kyrie for Strong Orch. or Quartet, 1983, Cowboy Songs for Voice and Piano, 1985, There Must Be a Lone Range for Soprano and Chamber Ensemble, 1987, Brass Quintet, 1987, Four Lewis Carroll Songs for Choir, 1989, (music/dance/theater) Boxiana, 1990, Elementi for Clarinet and Percussion, 1991, (one-act children's opera) Coyote's Tail, 1991, Clarion Dances for Brass Ensemble, 1993, Roundup for Sax Quartet, 1993, Three Medieval Lyrics for Choir, 1992, Sopravvento for Wind Quartet and Percussion, 1994, When Night Came for Clarinet and Chamber Orch. or Clarinet and Piano, 1994, also numerous others. Recipient Composers Forum award N.W. Chamber Orch., 1984, King County Arts Commn., 1987, 90, Artist Trust, 1988, 93, Seattle Arts Commn., 1988, 91, 93, New Langton Arts, 1988, Delius Festival, 1993, Melodious Accord award 1993; fellow Wash. State Arts Commn., 1991; Charles E. Ives scholar AAAL. Mem. Broadcast Music, Am. Music Ctr., Internat. Alliance for Women in Music, Soc. Composers, Chorus Am.

THOMAS, KATHRYN DIANE, engineer; b. Saint Augustine, Fla., Feb. 23, 1967; d. George William Wehrli and Dorothy Jean (Weeks) Fillyaw; m. Winton Russell Thomas Jr., Oct. 12, 1991; 1 child, Ryan Brantly. AS, Lake City C.C., 1987; BSEE, U. Fla., 1990. Registered profl. engr., Fla. Engr. I Fla. Dept. Transp., Lake City, 1990-92, engr. II, 1992-93, engr. III, 1993-95, profl. engr. II, 1995-96, design project mgr., 1996—. Office: Fla Dept Transp PO Box 1089 Lake City FL 32056

THOMAS, LAURA MARLENE, artist, private antique dealer; b. Chico, Calif., Apr. 29, 1936; d. Boyd Stanley Beck and Lois Velma (Behrke) Lyons; m. Charles Rex Thomas; children: Tracy Loraine, Jeffory Norris. AA in Fine Arts, Sacramento City Coll., 1978; BA in Fine Arts, Calif. State U., 1981. Tchrs. asst. Hanford Elem. Sch., Hanford, Calif., 1963-68; asst. dir. RSVP: Retired Sr. Vol. Program, Hanford, 1971-74; dir. of Art Bank Sacramento City Coll., Sacramento, 1976-78; pub. asst. Student Activities Calif. State Univ., Sacramento, 1978-81; antique dealer pvt. practice, Sacramento, 1981--, arts and crafts bus., 1976--; social worker Cath. Social Svcs., Sacramento, 1985--. Artist: weaving, Double Image, 1977, 2nd Place 1977; ceramic sculptor, Bird. Charter mem. YWCA, Sacramento, 1972, Folsum Hist. Soc., 1988. Cert. of appreciation, Carmellia City Ctr. Adv. Council, Sacramento, 1986. Mem. Statue of Liberty-Ellis Island Found., 1985, North Shore Animal League (Benefactors award 1985), Calif. State U. Alumni Assn., Hanford Sportsman Club (v.p. 1963-68). Republican. Protestant. Home: 2719 I St Apt 4 Sacramento CA 95816-4354

THOMAS, LEELAMMA KOSHY, women's health care nurse; b. Kerala, Kozhencherry, India, Feb. 10, 1936; naturalized Am. citizen, 1977; d. V.T. and Kunjamma (Koruth) Koshy; m. C.A. Thomas, Oct. 26, 1967; children: Linda Thomas Mathew, Lucie Thomas, John Thomas. BS in Nursing with honors, Coll. Nursing, Delhi, 1960; MA, Karnatak U., Dharwar Karnataka, Mysore, 1968. RN, Punjab, India, Tex.; RNC. PHN operational rsch. Nat. Tuberculosis Inst., Banglore, Mysore State, India, 1960-67; lectr. nursing Armed Forces Med. Coll., Maharstra State, India, 1971—; nurse labor and delivery U. Tex. Med. Br., nurse infant spl. care unit, nursing care coord. obgyn; head nurse U. Tex. Med. Br., Galveston, 1980-92, nurse clinician IV women and infants, 1993—; clin. instr. U. Tex. Sch. Nursing, Galveston, 1982—; presenter in field. Contbr. articles to profl. jours. Sunday sch. tchr. First Bapt. Ch., Galveston, Tex., 1982—. Recipient U. Tex. Med. Br. Maternal Health Coun. award, 1984; Am. Women's scholar. Mem. Sigma Theta Tau. Office: U Tex Med Br Ob-Gyn Nursing Svc Galveston TX 77550 also: U Tex Sch Nursing Galveston TX 77550

THOMAS, LEONA MARLENE, health information educator; b. Rock Springs, Wyo., Jan. 15, 1933; d. Leonard H. and Opal (Wright) Francis; m. Craig L. Thomas, Feb. 22, 1955; (div. Sept. 1978); children: Peter, Paul, Patrick, Alexis. BA, Govs. State U., 1982, MHS, 1986; cert. med. records adminstrn., U. Colo., 1954. Dir. med. records dept. Meml. Hosp. Sweetwater County, Rock Springs, Wyo., 1954-57; staff assoc. Am. Med. Records Assn., Chgo., 1972-77, asst. editor, 1979-81; statistician Westlake Hosp., Melrose Park, Ill., 1982-84; asst. prof. Chgo. State U., 1984—, acting dir. health info. adminstrn. program, 1991-92; acting dir. health info. Internat. Coll., Naples, Fla., 1994; dir. health info. adminstrn. program Chgo. State U., 1994—; chairperson Coll. Allied Health Pers., 1986-88; mem. rev. bd. network Newsletter of Assembly on Edn. Co-pres. Ill. Dist. 60 PTA, Westmont: liaison Ill. Trauma Registry, 1991; mem. adv. com. Health Info. Tech. Program Morraine Valley Cmty. Coll., Palos Hills, Ill., 1995—, Health Info. Tech. Program Robert Morris Coll., Orland Pk., Ill., 1995—, Wellness Ctr., Chgo. State U. Mem. Assembly on Edn., Am. Health Info. Mgmt. Assn., Am. Pub. Health Assn., Ill. Pub. Health Assn., Chgo. and Vicinity Med. Records Assn. (publicity com. 1989-90), Ill. Assn. Allied Health Profls., Gov.'s State Alumni Assn. Democrat. Methodist. Home: 6340 Americana Dr Apt 1101 Clarendon Hills IL 60514-2249 Office: Chgo State U Coll Nursin & Allied Health 95th at King Dr Chicago IL 60628

THOMAS, LISA ANN, art consultant, art dealer; b. Warren, Mich., Aug. 10, 1969; d. Ronald Anthony and Lois Ann (Merling) T. BA, Marymount U., 1991; Cert. A, Christie's N.Y., 1994. Classified sales rep. Congressional Quarterly, Inc., Washington, 1991-93; acting advtg. dir. New Republic, Washington, 1993; program assoc. Digital Network T.V., N.Y.C., 1995—; co-dir. Franklin Parrasch Gallery, N.Y.C., 1996—; viss. svcs. Bard Grad. Ctr. for Studies in the Decorative Arts, N.Y.C., 1995; vol. phone campaign leader Landmark Edn. Corp., N.Y.C., 1994-95; founder, pres. Marymount U. advtsg. club, Arlington, Va., 1990-91. Co-creator (documentary video) Project Culture Shell, 1995; prodn. asst. (video performance) The Laments, 1995, Guggenheim Mus. Mem. Exit Art/The First World, Mus. Modern Art. Home and Office: 251 W 89th St #5E New York NY 10024

THOMAS, LYDIA WATERS, research and development executive; b. Norfolk, Va., Oct. 13, 1944; d. William Emerson and Lillie Ruth (Roberts) Waters; m. James Carter Thomas (div. 1970); 1 child, Denee Marrielle. BS in Zoology, Howard U., 1965, PhD in Cytology, 1973; MS in Microbiology, Am. U., 1971. Pres., CEO Mitretek Sys., McLean, Va., 1996—; affiliate Ctr. Sci. and Internat. Affairs, Harvard U., Cambridge, Mass., 1990—; bd. dirs. Cabot Corp.; mem. Draper Labs., Inc. Author: Automation Impacts on Industry, 1983. Mem. Environ. Adv. Bd., U.S. C.E., 1980-82; expert witness, Senate, U.S. govt. pub. hearings, Washington, 1985; mem. adv. bd. INFORM, N.Y.C., George Wash. U. Va. Campus; mem. Supt.'s Bus./Industry Adv. Coun. Fairfax County Pub. Schs. Recipient Tribute to Women in Internat. Industry YMCA, 1986, EBONE Image award Coalition of 100 Black Women, 1990, Dean's award Black Engineer of the Year, 1991. Mem. AAAS, AIAA, Am. Def. Preparedness Assn., Am. Mgmt. Assn., Am. Soc. Toxicology, Am. Astronautical Soc., Nat. Energy Resources Orgn., Nat. Security Indsl. Assn., Teratology Soc., U.S. Energy Assn., Conf. Bd./Townley Global Mgmt. Ctr., Sigma Xi (steering com.), Alpha Kappa Alpha. Office: Mitretek Systems 7525 Colshire Dr Mc Lean VA 22101-7492

THOMAS, LYNN ANN, maketing professional, public speaker; b. Chgo., Sept. 22, 1964; d. Lawrence Edward and Rita Ann (Bogacki) Lindvig; m. Michael Patrick Thomas, May 24, 1992. BS in Advtg., U. Ill., Urbana, 1988; MA in Comm., U. Ill., Chgo., 1996. Advtg. sales prodn. asst. Am. Jour. of Ophthalmology, Chgo., 1989-92; grad. asst. Career Svcs. U. Ill., Chgo., 1992-93, asst. dir. Career Svcs., 1995—. Cons. editor: (jour.) The Creative Woman, 1989-91; editor: (newsletter) Earth Day Chgo., 1990-92; manuscript editor: (textbook) Marketing and Entrepreneurship, 1993. Mem. bd. dirs. Earth Day Chgo., 1990-91; mem. Common Cause, Washington D.C., 1995—. Recipient Disting. Svc. award YMCA, Champaign, Ill., 1988. Mem. Women Employed, Women in Communications. Unitarian/Universalist.

THOMAS, LYNN MARIE, artist, retired dude ranch owner, operator; b. L.A., Nov. 20, 1939; d. Eugene Leonard and Genevie Juanita (Hupp) Pfeiffer; m. Joe Glen Thomas, Dec. 2, 1969 (div.); children from previous marriage: Beverly Linda Hahn, Deborah Jean Hahn, Michelle Marie Hahn (dec.). Grad h.s., Henderson, Nev. One-woman shows include Bark Gallery, Boulder City, Nev., 1976, 78, Pa-Jo's Western Art Gallery, Pinedale, Wyo., 1976, 80, 89, Bank of Nev., Las Vegas, 1976, 78, Energy Rsch. & Devel. Adminstrn., Las Vegas, 1977, U. Nev., Las Vegas, 1979, Rock Springs (Wyo.) Fine Arts Ctr., 1988, 89, White Mountain Libr., Rock Springs, 1990, 92, Green River (Wyo.) Libr., 1990, 93; group exhbns. include Wyo. Artists Assn. (Best of Show, Artist's Choice, People's Choice, Pres.'s Choice, 4 1st pl., 14 misc. awards), Sweetwater County Art Guild Nat. (Best of Show, People's Choice, 2 1st pl. in profl. divsn., misc. other awards), Seven State Regional (3 awards for 3 pieces), Black Canyon Show (2 1st pl., 3 misc. awards), Cody Western & Wildlife Classic (Purple ribbon), Audubon Nat. Wildlife Art Show (2 1st in oil prizes), Women Artists of West (Artist's Artist, 1987, 1st pl. in oils, 10 misc. awards), Cheyenne Frontier Days Old West Mus. (Beanie Herzog award 1985), Am. Mothers (Sweepstakes award 1979, 83, several misc. awards), Las Vegas Elks Helldorado Show (1st pl. oils 1975, 84, 3 misc. awards), Sublett County Fair (36 1st pl. awards, 10 Best of Show awards, 6 Overall Champion awards, 23 Champion awards, 13 misc. awards), Daisy Patch Gallery, Casper, Wyo., 1996, Savage Gallery, Sioux Falls, S.D., 1996, High Desert Gallery, Rock Springs, Wyo., 1996, ; represented in permanent collections including Las Vegas Rev. Jour., 1st Wyo. Bank, Big Piney, Sublett County Wyo. Libr., Las Vegas Elks Western Art Collection, Rock Springs Fine Arts Ctr., Ft. Huachuca Post Cavalry Mus., Green River Valley Mus., Big Piney; contbr. art to numerous pubs. and profl. jours. Mem. Nat. Cowgirl Hall of Fame, Hereford, Tex., Cowboy Artists of Am. Mus., Kerrville, Tex., Mus. of the Mountain Man, Pinedale, Wyo., Wyo. Coun. on Arts, Flaming Gorge Natural History Assn., Sublette County Hist. Soc., Green River Valley Mus.; charter mem. Nat. Mus. for Women in the Arts, Washington, Nat. Mus. of the Am. Indian, Washington. Mem. Women Artists of the West (emeritus), Pinedale Fine Arts Coun., Sublette County Artists Guild, Mixed Media, Wyo. Artists Registry, Nev. Artists Register, Wyo. Artists Assn. Home and Studio: House on Muddy 105 Richie Rd Boulder WY 82923

THOMAS, MABLE, communications company executive, former state legislator; b. Atlanta, Nov. 8, 1957; d. Bernard and Madie Thomas. BS in Pub. Adminstrn., Ga. State U., 1982, postgrad., 1983—. With acctg. dept. Trust Co. Bank, Atlanta, 1977; recreation supr. Sutton Cmty. Sch., Atlanta, 1977-78; data transcriber Ga. Dept. Natural Resources, Atlanta, 1978-79; clk. U.S. Census Bur., Atlanta, 1980; laborer City of Atlanta Parks and Recreation, 1980-81; student asst. Ga. State U., Atlanta, 1981-82; mem. Ga. Ho. Reps., Atlanta, 1984-94; pres. Master Comms. Inc., Atlanta, 1994—; mem. exec. com. Ga. Legis. Black Census, Atlanta, 1985—. Mem. adv. youth coun. Salvation Army Bellwood Club, 1975; founder, pres. Greater Vine City Opportunities Program Inc., 1996; founder Vine City Cmty. improvement Assn., Atlanta, 1985; mem. neighborhood planning unit adv. bd. of comprehensive youth svcs. Ga. State U., 1988—; mem. Nat. Black Woman's Health Project, Ga. Housing Coalition; bd. dirs. Ga. Coalition Black Women, 1996, Am. Cancer Soc., 1988—. Recipient Bronze Jubilee award City of Atlanta Cultural Affairs, 1984, Disting Svc. award Grady Hosp., 1985, Human Svc. award for cmty. and polit. leadership for disadvantaged, 1986, Exceptional Svc. award Young Cmty. Leaders, 1986, Citizenship award Salvation Army Club, Leadership and Achievement award Ga. Breast Cancer Prevention Coalition, 1994, Adopt a Sch. Appreciation award Atlanta Pub. Schs., 1996; named Outstanding Freshman Legislator, 1986, one of Outstanding Young People of Atlanta, 1987. Mem. Nat. Polit. Congress Black Women (bd. dirs., Fannie Lou Hamer award Phila. chpt. 1995), Conf. Minority Pub. Adminstrn. (Outstanding Svc. award), Ga. Assn. Black Elected Ofcls. (mem. housing and econ. devel. com.). Democrat. Methodist. Home: PO Box 573 Atlanta GA 30301-0573

THOMAS, MARGARET JEAN, clergywoman, religious research consultant; b. Detroit, Dec. 24, 1943; d. Robert Elcana and Purcella Margaret (Hartness) T. BS, Mich. State U., 1964; MDiv, Union Theol. Sem., Va., 1971; DMin, San Francisco Theol. Sem., 1991. Ordained to ministry United Presbyn. Ch., 1971. Dir. rsch. bd. Christian edn. Presbyn. Ch. U.S., Richmond, Va., 1965-71; dir. rsch. gen. coun. Presbyn. Ch. U.S., Atlanta, 1972-73; mng. dir. rsch. div. support agy. United Presbyn. Ch. U.S.A., N.Y.C., 1974-76; dep. exec. dir. gen. assembly mission coun. United Presbyn. Ch. U.S.A., 1977-83; dir. N.Y. coordination Presbyn. Ch. (U.S.A.), 1983-85; exec. dir. Minn. Coun. Chs., Mpls., 1985-95; synod exec. Synod of Lakes and Prairies Presbyn. Ch. (U.S.A.), Bloomington, Minn., 1995—; mem. Permanent Jud. Commn., Presbyn. Ch. (U.S.A.), 1985-91, moderator, 1989-91, mem. adv. com. on constn., 1992—, moderator, 1996—; sec. com. on ministry Twin Cities Area Presbytery, Mpls., 1985-91, vice moderator, 1991-92, moderator, 1992-93; mem. joint religious legis. coalition, 1985-95; mem. Commn. on Regional and Local Ecumenism Nat. Coun. Chs., 1988-91, officer Ecumenical Networks, 1992-95, mem. Unity and Rels. unit, 1992-93; treas. Nat. Coun. of Chs., 1996—; mem. nat. planning com. Nat. Workshop on Christian Unity, 1992-95; bd. dirs. Franklin Nat. Bank, Mpls., 1987—. Contbr. articles to profl. jours. Mem. adv. panel crime victims svcs. Hennepin County Atty.'s Office, 1985-86, Police and Cmty. Rels. Task Force, St. Paul, 1986; mem. adv. panel Hennepin County Crime Victim Coun., 1990-93, chmn., 1990-93; bd. dirs. Minn. Foodshare, 1985-95, Minn. Coalition on Health, 1986-92, Minn. Black-on-Black Crime Task Force, 1988, Twin Cities Coalition Affordable Health Care, 1986-87, Presbyn. Homes of Minn., 1995—, Clearwater Forest, Deerwood, Minn., 1995—; co-chmn. Minn. Interreligious Com., 1988-95; bd. dirs. Abbott Northwestern Pastoral Counseling Ctr., 1988-91, chmn., 1990-91. Recipient Human Rels. award Jewish Community Rels. Coun./Anti-Defamation League, 1989, Gov.'s Cert. of Commendation for Women's Leadership, 1993. Mem. N.Am. Acad. Ecumenists, NOW (Outstanding Woman of Minn. 1986). Mem. Democrat-Farm-Labor Party. Office: Synod of Lakes and Prairies Presbyn Ch USA 8012 Cedar Ave S Bloomington MN 55425-1204

THOMAS, MARGARET LOUISE, rehabilitation nurse; b. Savannah, Ga., Nov. 27, 1953; d. Frederick William and Margaret Ann (Russell) T. AAS, County Coll. of Morris, 1982; BS, Kean Coll., 1988; BSN, Regents Coll. of N.Y. Cert. rehab. nurse, ACLS. Supr. Kessler Inst. for Rehab., West Orange, N.J.; staff nurse ICU Shepherd Spinal Ctr., Atlanta, 1988—. Recipient Pride in Heritage award DAV, 1981, 82, 86, 87, 89. Mem. Am. Assn. Spinal Cord Injured Nurses, Assn. Rehab. Nurses. Baptist. Home: 851 River Glen Pl Riverdale GA 30296-2784 Office: Shepherd Spinal Ctr 2020 Peachtree St NW Atlanta GA 30309-1402

THOMAS, MARGOT EVA, lawyer; b. Grass Valley, Calif., Apr. 28, 1943; d. Walter Frederick and Edith Louise (Clark) T.; m. R.A. Maloof; children: Matthew E. Albertson, Nicholas E. Albertson, Elizabeth R. Albertson. AB, Brown U., 1965; JD, Western New Eng. Coll., 1981. Bar: Mass. 1981. Field worker So. Christian Leadership Conf., Lisman, Ala., 1965-66; computer programmer Irving Trust Co., N.Y.C., 1966-67; social worker Phila. Dept. Welfare, 1968-70; field dir. Girl Scouts of Delaware County Pa., Upper Darby, 1971-73; project dir. Pioneer Valley Girl Scouts, Springfield, Mass., 1973-74; pvt. practice lawyer Northampton, Mass., 1981—. Pres. Northampton (Mass.) Girls Soccer Assn., 1985-91; chair Northampton (Mass.) City Dem. Com., 1989-91, Jessie's House Adv. Bd., Northampton, 1992-95. Mem. Nat. Lawyers Guild, Mass. Bar Assn., Hampshire County Bar Assn., Mass. Assn. Women Lawyers, Mass. Lesbian and Gay Bar Assn. Office: 78 Main St Northampton MA 01060-3111

THOMAS, MARIANNE GREGORY, school psychologist; b. N.Y.C., Dec. 10, 1945. BS, U. Conn., 1985; MS, So. Conn. State U., 1987. Cert. sch. psychologist, Conn., N.Y. Sch. psychology intern Greenwich (Conn.) Pub. Schs., 1986-87; sch. psychologist Hawthorne (N.Y.)-Cedar Knolls, U.F.S.D., 1987-88, Darien (Conn.) Pub. Schs., 1988—. Mem. AAUW, NASP (cert.), Conn. Assn. Sch. Psychologists. Home: 154 Indian Rock Rd New Canaan CT 06840-3117

THOMAS, MARILYN JANE, insurance company executive; b. Fremont, Ohio, Dec. 11, 1944; d. Myron Elwood and Elvira Evelyn (Plagman) Magsig; m. William E. Thomas, Jr., Nov. 7, 1992; stepchildren: Dana Lauren Thomas, Keira Anne Schwartz. BS in Edn., Capitul U., Columbus, 1966; postgrad., U. Calif., Irvine, Fullerton, 1969-70. Tchr. pub. schs., Ohio, Calif., La., 1966-71; underwriter Tenn. Life Ins. Co., Houston, Tex., 1971-73; supr., mgr. contracts adminstrn. Phila. Life Ins. Co. (merger with Tenn. Life Ins. Co.), Houston, 1973-80; systems analyst Phila. Life Ins. Co., Houston, 1980-84; dir. market research/product devel. Phila. Am. Life Ins. Co. (merger Phila. Life Ins. Co.), Houston, 1984-87; 2d v.p. mktg. Phila. Am. Life Ins., Houston, 1987—. Vol. Spl. Olympics, Houston; tchr. Project Business, 1981. Recipient Outstanding Woman award, Houston YWCA, 1984. Mem. Am. Bus. Women's Assn. (chmn. edn. com. 1987-88), Soc. Group Contract Analysts (chmn. com. 1977-80), Houston Assn. Health Underwriters. Republican. Lutheran. Office: Phila Am Life Ins 3121 Buffalo Speedway Houston TX 77098-1823

THOMAS, MARLO (MARGARET JULIA THOMAS), actress; b. Detroit, Nov. 21, 1943; d. Danny and Rose Marie (Cassanti) T.; m. Phil Donahue, May 21, 1980. Ed., U. So. Calif. Theatrical appearances in Thieves, Broadway, 1974, Barefoot in the Park, London, Social Security, Broadway, 1986, The Shadow Box, Broadway, 1994; star: TV series That Girl, 1966-71 (Golden Globe award Best TV actress, 1967); appeared in TV films: The Body Human: Facts for Girls (Emmy award Best Performer Children's Program), 1981, The Last Honor of Kathryn Beck, 1984 (also exec. prodr.), Consenting Adults, 1985, Nobody's Child, 1986 (Emmy Best Dramatic Actress), Held Hostage: The Sis and Jerry Levin Story, 1991, Ultimate Betrayal, 1994, Reunion, 1994, A Century of Women, 1994; guest star Friends, 1995; conceived book and record, starred in TV spl. Free to Be. . . You and Me, 1974 (Emmy for best children's show); films include Thieves, 1977, In the Spirit, 1991, Jenny, 1963; conceived book, record and TV spl. Free to Be A Family (Emmy Best Children's Show). Recipient 4 Emmys, Golden Globe award, George Foster Peabody award, Tom Paine award Nat. Emergency Civil Liberties Com. Mem. Ms. Found., Nat. Women's Polit. Caucus. Office: CAA 9830 Wilshire Blvd Beverly Hills CA 90212-1804*

THOMAS, MARY ELIZABETH, artist; b. Huntsville, Ohio, Aug. 1, 1937; d. Roe and Bertha Mae (Godwin) Cooke; m. Wilson Woodrow Thomas, Aug. 24, 1957; children: David Gail, Penny Joann, Phyllip Roe, Brent Arthur. Grad. high sch., Belle Ctr., Ohio, 1955. Exhibited in group shows at Ohio Assn. of Family and Cmty. Edn. State Meeting, 1991, (2d pl. award), 95 (1st pl. award), Hardin County Fair, 1992 (Res. Champion), 94 (Grand Champion). Mem. Lawrence Valley Grange Deaf activities (merit for report 1995), Ohio Assn. of Family and Cmty. Edn. (homemakers ext., v.p. local club, 1995), hosp. guild (sewing unit), Women's Assn. United Presbyterian Ch. Democrat. Presbyterian. Home: 14494 Twp Rd 21 Harrod OH 45850

THOMAS, MARY ELLA, elementary education educator, retired; b. Pasadena, Calif., Feb. 20, 1924; d. Willis and Nancy Frances (Griggers) Jernigan; m. Wiley L. Thomas Jr., Mar. 17, 1947; 1 child, Wiley L. III. BS, East Tex. State U., 1945, MS, 1950. 1st grade tchr. DeKalb (Tex.) Ind. Sch. Dist., 1945-46, Gladewater (Tex.) Ind. Sch. Dist., 1946-49; elem. tchr. White Oak (Tex.) Ind. Sch. Dist., 1950-86; ret., 1986; coord. Pre-Sch. Bible Class. Sec., treas., program PTA, White Oak, hon. life mem.; pres. White Oak Cmty. Club, 1991-96; tchr. Bible class. Mem. NEA (life), Tex. State Tchrs. Assn. (life, sec. 1950-86), Dalta Kappa Gamma (pres. 1986-88, chairperson 1994—, chpt. Achievement award). Mem. Ch. of Christ. Home: 501 W Brookwood Ln White Oak TX 75693

THOMAS, MELANIE, sales official; b. Carbondale, Pa., Apr. 28, 1964; d. John Joseph and Carol Rosalie (Le Van) T. BS, U. Scranton, 1986. Supr. lang. lab. U. Scranton, Pa., 1982-86; methods and procedures analyst Pa. Nat. Mut. Casualty Ins. Group, Harrisburg, Pa., 1986-87; account rep. Keystone Cellular, Mehanicsburg, Pa., 1988-90, Pa. Tel. Products, Lemoyne, Pa., 1990-91; dist. mgr. I.C. Sys., St. Paul, 1991; sales rep. Lorillard Tobacco Co., Mechanicsburg, 1992—. Republican. Home: 775 Sunset Ln Northumberland PA 17857

THOMAS, NADINE, nurse, legislator, state official; b. Fort Myers, Fla., May 14, 1952; d. Marvin Lee and Carrie Lee (North) Dixon; m. Jolivet Aurelious Thomas, Jan. 15, 1977 (div. 1982); children: Nadia Joli, Doris Silas, Dorothy Silas. A, Edison Community Coll., 1974; student, Ga. State U., 1978-82. RN, Ga. Nursing unit coord. Crawford Long Hosp., Atlanta, 1977-90; nursing supr. S.W. Hosp. and Med. Ctr., Atlanta, 1990-92; state senator Ga. Senate; chmn. Changed Living Recovery, Decatur, Ga., 1991-92; bd. dirs. Ctr. for Drug Rehab. Mem. DeKalb Dem. Party Exec. Com., Decatur, 1988-90; pres. Brookwood and Knollwood Community Assn., Atlanta, 1988-92; state rep. Ga. Ho. Reps., Atlanta, 1990-92; co-pres. Sky Haven Pres. PTA, Atlanta, 1991-92. Mem. ANA, Ga. Nurses Assn. (Nurse Excellence award 1991). Home: 1375 Town Country Dr SE Atlanta GA 30316-3919 Office: Ga State Senate Rm 304 Legislative Office Bldg Atlanta GA 30334*

THOMAS, PAMELA ADRIENNE, special education educator; b. St. Louis, Oct. 28, 1940; d. Charles Seraphin Fernandez and Adrienne Louise (O'Brien) Fernandez Reeg; divorced, 1977; m. Alvertis T. Thomas, July 22, 1981. BA in Spanish and EdS, Maryville Coll., 1962; Cert. EdS, U. Ky., 1966-67; MA in Edn., St. Louis U., 1974. Cert. learning disabilities, behavior disorders, educable mentally retarded, Spanish, Mo. Tchr. Pawnee Rock Kans. Sch., 1963-64; diagnostic tchr. Frankfort State Hosp. Sch., Ky., 1964-67; spl. edn. tchr. St. Louis City Pub. Schs., 1968-71, itinerant tchr., 1971-73, ednl. strategist, 1973-74, elem. level resource tchr., 1974-78, secondary resource tchr., dept. head, 1978—; head dept. spl. edn., 1978—; Co-author: Sophomore English Resource for Credit Curriculum Handbook, 1991. Co-author: Teaching Foreign Language to Handicapped Secondary Students, 1990. Pres. Council for Exceptional Children, local chpt. #103, 1982-83, Mo. Division of Mentally Retarded, 1985-87. Mem. Alpha Delta Kappa (St. Louis chpt. pres. 1982-84). Home: 4534 Ohio Ave Saint Louis MO 63111-1324 Office: Cen VAP High Sch 3616 N Garrison Ave Saint Louis MO 63107-2501

THOMAS, PATRICIA ANNE, retired law librarian; b. Cleve., Aug. 21, 1927; d. Richard Joseph and Marietta Bernadette (Teevans) T.; BA, Case Western Res. U., 1949, JD, 1951. Admitted to Ohio bar, 1951, U.S. Supreme Ct. bar, 1980; libr. Arter & Hadden, Cleve., 1951-62; asst. libr., then libr. IRS, Washington, 1962-78; libr. dir. Adminstrv. Office, U.S. Cts., 1978-93; ret. 1993. Mem. Am. Assn. Law Libraries, Law Librs. Soc. D.C. (pres. 1967-69), Soc. Benchers (Case We. Res. Law Sch.).

THOMAS, PEGGY RUTH, public contract and procurement consultant; b. Granite, Okla., Dec. 19, 1933; d. Sidney Durrell and Ruth Mae (Tuley) Coffman; m. Charles Donald Gustafson, Nov. 28, 1953 (dec. Apr. 1959); children: Gene L., Richard L.; m. Donald Edward Thomas. Student, U. Okla., 1951-52, Okla. S.W. State U., 1952-53. Cert. purchasing mgr. Nat. Assn. Purchasing Mgmt. Contracting/procurement officer Fed. Govt., various locations, 1953-87, U. Alaska, Anchorage, 1988-93; CEO XPRT Cons., Anchorage, 1985—. Mem. Mensa. Home and Office: XPRT Cons 9701 Brien St Anchorage AK 99516

THOMAS, REBECCA LYNNE, librarian, writer; b. Akron, Ohio, Oct. 21, 1951; d. Eugene Milton and Helen (Nesterovich) T. BA in English, Kent (Ohio) State U., 1973, MLS, 1974; PhD, Ohio State U., 1986. Libr. Shaker Heights (Ohio) City Schs., 1976—; cons., writer R.R. Bowker, New Providence, N.J., 1988—; adj. faculty Baldwin-Wallace Coll., Berea, Ohio, 1990—; vis. asst. prof. Kent state U., 1977-86. Author: Primaryplots 1: A Booktalk Guide for Use With Readers Ages 4-8, 1989, Primaryplots 2: A Booktalk Guide for Use With Readers Ages 4-8, 1993, Connecting Cultures: A Guide to Multicultural Literature for Children, 1996. Recipient Mary Karrer award Coll. Edn. Ohio State U., Columbus, 1989. Mem. ALA (1994 Caldecott Com. 1993-94, Putnam Grossett award com. 1994-98), Shaker Heights Tchrs. Assn. (exec. bd. 1990—), Delta Kappa Gamma, Beta Phi Mu. Democrat. Episcopalian. Home: 2464 Edgerton Rd University Heights OH 44118 Office: Shaker Heights City Schs 15600 Parkland Dr Shaker Heights OH 44120

THOMAS, RHONDA CHURCHILL, lawyer; b. 1947; m. J. Regan Thomas; children: Ryan, Aaron, Evan. BA, Drury Coll., 1969; JD, U. Mo., 1972, Yale U., 1973. Bar: Mo. 1973. Newswoman Sta. KFRU Radio, Columbia, Mo., 1969-70; law clk. to Hon. Robert E. Seiler Supreme Ct. of Mo., Jefferson City, 1973-74; asst. city counselor City of Columbia, 1974-76, city counselor, chief legal advisor to city coun., dept. heads, 1976-79; assoc. prof. law U. Mo., 1979-82; ptnr. Thompson Coburn, St. Louis, 1985—; past chmn. franchise com. Nat. Inst. Mcpl. Law Officers. Contbr. articles to profl. jours. Past chmn. Boone County Home Rule Charter Commn.; past pres. Boone County Indsl. Devel. Authority. Mem. ABA (local govt. law sect., taxation sect.), Mo. Bar Assn. (mem. edn. law com., mem. local govt. law com., mem. med.-legal rels. com., past mem. spl. com. on quality and methods of practice), St. Louis Bar Assn., Nat. Assn. Bond Lawyers, Mo. Mcpl. Attys. Assn. (past pres.). Office: Thompson Coburn 1 Mercantile Ctr Ste 3400 Saint Louis MO 63101-1623

THOMAS, ROZONDA, singer; b. Atlanta, Feb. 27, 1971. Singer, mem. TLC, 1991—. Recipient Grammy for Rhythm and Blue Vocal by a group or duo, for "Creep", 1995. Office: LaFace Records One Capital City Plz 3350 Peachtree Rd Ste 1500 Atlanta GA 30326-1040*

THOMAS, SANDRA ANN, songwriter, lyricist; b. Dayton, Ohio, Oct. 14; d. Joseph Burghard and Mary Josephine (Bogie) T. AA, Palm Beach Community Coll., Lake Worth, Fla.; BA, Fla. Atlantic U. Cert. English tchr. Pres. Lady Sabre Recording and Prodn. Co., Delray Beach, Fla., 1989—, Lady Sabre Publishing Co., Delray Beach, 1989—. Lyricist, singer (albums) Under a Strange Spell, 1988, , Sandra Thomas Sings Folk Music, 1989, Enchanted, 1990; composer (documentary soundtrack) First Breath, 1971, Life and Breath, 1990. Nat. dir. pub. edn. Iron Overload Diseases Assn., Inc., North Palm Beach, Fla., 1986—; mem. Gulf Stream (Fla.) Rep. Club, 1991, Jr. League Boca Raton. Recipient Awards for Composition Music City Song Festival, 1988-91. Mem. ASCAP (award for lyrics 1991), AFTRA, SAG, Am. Guild Variety Artists, Actors Equity Assn., Fla. Atlantic U. Alumnae Assn., DAR (2d v.p., vice regent), Daus. Am. Colonists, Daus. Colonial Wars, Colonial Dames Am., U.S. Daus. of 1812, Sons and Daus of Pilgrims, Order Ea. Star, Ladies Oriental Shrine N.Am., Jamestown Soc., Alpha Omicron Pi. Office: Lady Sabre Pub Co PO Box 6906 Delray Beach FL 33482-6906

THOMAS, SHIRLEY, author, educator, business executive; b. Glendale, Calif.; d. Oscar Miller and Ruby (Thomas) Annis; m. W. White, Feb. 22, 1949 (div. June 1952); m. William C. Perkins, Oct. 24, 1969. BA in Modern Lit., U. Sussex, Eng., 1960, PhD in Comm., 1967; diploma, Russian Fedn. Cosmonautics, 1995. Actress, writer, producer, dir. numerous radio and TV stas., 1942-46; v.p. Commodore Prodns., Hollywood, Calif., 1946-52; pres. Annis & Thomas, Inc., Hollywood, 1952—; prof. technical writing U. So. Calif., L.A., 1975—; Hollywood corr. NBC, 1952-56; editor motion pictures CBS, Hollywood, 1956-58; corr. Voice of Am., 1958-59; now free lance writer; cons. biol. scis. communication project George Washington U., 1965-66; cons. Stanford Rsch. Inst., 1967-68, Jet Propulsion Lab., 1969-70. Author: Men of Space vols. 1-8, 1960-68, Spanish trans., 1961, Italian, 1962; Space Tracking Facilities, 1963, Computers: Their History, Present Applications and Future, 1965; The Book of Diets, 1974. Organizer, chmn. City of L.A. Space Adv. Com., 1964-73, Women's Space Symposia, 1962-73; foudner, chmn. aerospace hist. com. Calif. Mus. Sci. and Industry; chmn. Theodore von Karman Postage Stamp Com., 1965—, stamp issued 1992. Recipient Aerospace Excellence award Calif. Mus. Found. 1991, Nat. Medal Honor DAR, 1992, Yuri Gagarin Medal Honor, 1995. Fellow Brit. Interplanetary Soc.; mem. AIAA, AAAS, Internat. Soc. Aviation Writers, Air Force Assn. (Airpower Arts and Letters award 1961), Internat. Acad. Astronautics, Nat. Aero. Assn., Nat. Asn. Sci. Writers, Soc. for Tech. Communications, Am. Astronautical Soc., Nat. Geog. Soc., Am. Soc. Pub. Adminstrn. (sci. and tech. in govt. com. 1972—), Achievement Awards for Coll. Scientists, Muses of Calif., Theta Sigma Phi, Phi Beta. Home: 8027 Hollywood Blvd Los Angeles CA 90046-2510 Office: U So Calif Profl Writing Program University Park Waite-Phillips Hall 404 Los Angeles CA 90089-4034

THOMAS, SONYA, accountant, consultant; b. Chgo., Oct. 23, 1969; d. Jerry Robert and Katie May (Young) T. Student, Southwestern U., 1987-88; BA in Acctg., Mich. State U., 1992. Cashier Burger King, Lansing, Mich., 1986-87; receptionist Southwestern U., Georgetown, Tex., 1987-88; child care provider King's Kids Ednl. Learning, Lansing, 1988-90; student asst. Mich. Dept. Commerce, Lansing, 1990-92; accounts payable asst. Manpower, Lansing, 1992; auditor Coleman & Williams, Milw., 1992-93; auditor intern for Blue Cross/Blue Shield Mich. Jawood Mgmt. Assocs., Sterling Heights, Mich., 1993; auditor Blue Cross/Blue Shield-Mich., East Lansing, 1993-94; acct. Mich. Dept. Pub. Health, Lansing, 1994—. Mem. Mayoral Neighborhood Adv. Bd., Lansing, 1995—; cons. Lansing Christian Ctr. Ch., Lansing, 1995—; active Big Bro./Big Sister, Lansing, 1995; project team leader AmeriCorps, Lansing, 1995-96. Mem. State Assn. Accts., Auditors & Adminstrs. Home: 900 Long Blvd #781 Lansing MI 48909

THOMAS, SUE, political science educator; b. Oceanside, N.Y., Mar. 26, 1957; d. Robert Joseph and June (Adelman) T. m. Charles Robert Tremper. BA, UCLA, 1980, MEd, 1981; PhD, U. Nebr., 1989. Project assoc. L.A. Unified Sch. Dist., 1981-82; legis. advocate NOW, Calif. Abortion Rights Action League, Sacramento, Calif., 1982-85; asst. prof. Georgetown U., Washington, 1989-94, assoc. prof., 1994—. Author: How Women Legislate, 1994; co-editor: The Year of the Woman, Myths and Realities, 1994. Lobbyist Calif. chpt. NOW, Sacramento, 1982-84, Calif. Abortion Rights Action League, Sacramento, 1984-85. Dissertation grantee NSF, 1988, Rsch. grantee Rutgers U., 1988. Mem. Am. Polit. Sci. Assn. (women's caucus 1986—), Midwest Polit. Sci. Assn. (women's caucus 1986—). Office: Georgetown U Dept Govt Washington DC 20057

THOMAS, SUSAN ELIZABETH, public relations professional, artist; b. Boonton, N.J., Sept. 2, 1968; d. Arthur A. and Joan (Pfister) T. AAS, County Coll. Morris, Randolph, N.J., 1990; BA in Comms. Studies, Montclair State U., 1994. Activity coord. Wayne (N.J.) view Care Ctr., 1992; pub. rels. asst. Am. Liver Found., Cedar Grove, N.J., 1993; freelance ghostwriter, publicist N.J. World Am. Orgn., Belleville, 1993-94; spl. events/fundraising cons. N.J. State Orgn. for Cystic Fibrosis, Wayne, 1993; pub. rels. asst. Hospitality Franchise Sys., Parsippany, N.J., 1993-94; freelance asst. Moonshine Grill Restaurant, Secaucus, N.J., 1994-95; conf. coord. UPS I.S. World Tech. Hdqs., Mahwah, N.J., 1994—; keynote spkr. N.J. State Orgn. Jaycees, N.J. Fedn. Women's Clubs, D.A.R.E. Programs of N.J., Lincoln Park Libr. Christian youth leader. Named one of Ten Outstanding Citizens of N.J., N.J. Jaycees, 1993-94, Miss 1993 New Jersey, Miss World, Inc., 1993-94. Mem. Lincoln Park Day Assn. (pub. rels. chairperson, entertainment chairperson), Women in Comms., Inc. (N.Y.C. chpt.), Delta Phi Epsilon (historian, social chairperson), Lambda Pi Eta (comms. leader). Home: 57 Mandeville Ave Pequannock NJ 07440 Office: UPS IS World Tech Hdqs 340 MacArthur Blvd Mahwah NJ 07430

THOMAS, SUZANNE WARD, public relations director, communications educator; b. Akron, Ohio, Sept. 21, 1954; d. Kendall Kramer and Margaret Ann (Owen) Ward; m. James Michael Thomas, Oct. 20, 1980; children: Seth Evin, James Kendall. BS in Edn., Miami U., Oxford, Ohio, 1977; MA in Communications, Regent U., Virginia Beach, Va., 1980. Writer, prodr. Sta. WVIZ, PBS, Cleve., 1980-82; dir. pub. rels. Sta. WOAC-TV, Canton, Ohio, 1982-83, hostess children's show, 1982-84; v.p. Thomas Video Prodns., Canal Fulton, Ohio, 1987-90; dir. pub. rels., instr. comm. Malone Coll., Canton, 1990—, editor Horizon, 1990—. Author: (children's book) The Miracles of Jesus, 1991, also manuals. Hostess pub. affairs program Community TV Consortium, Canton, 1987; subcom. chmn. Govt. Day, Leadership Canton, 1987; v.p. Right to Life Ednl. Found., Canton, 1990; chmn. pub. rels. Jr. League Canton, 1986-87, rec. sec., 1987-88; bd. dirs. PTO, 1989-90. Recipient Sparkler award Jr. League Canton, 1986, Pub. Rels. award, 1987, Addy awards Canton Advt. Club, 1992, 96. Mem. Sales and Mktg. Execs. (bd. dirs. Stark County chpt. 1989), Assn. Jr. Leagues Internat., Pub. Rels. Soc. Am. (accredited in pub. rels. 1995). Republican. Office: Malone Coll 515 25th St NW Canton OH 44709-3823

THOMAS, VERSIE LEE, nursing educator; b. Metter, Ga., Nov. 10, 1947; d. Roy Lee Wigfall and Elizabeth (Donaldson) McFadden; m. Willie Frank Thomas May 5, 1973 (dec. Apr. 8, 1989); 1 child, Tamara. ADN, Miami Dade C.C., 1969; BSN, Armstrong State Coll., 1979; MSN, Valdosta State U., 1990. RN Fla., Ga.; ACLS, BLS instr. ICU staff nurse Miami Heart Inst., Miami Beach, Fla., 1969-70; CCU charge nurse Miami Heart Inst., Miami Beach, 1970-72; ICU staff nurse Palmetto Gen. Hosp., Hialeah, Fla., 1973-76; MICU staff nurse Glynn Brunswick Meml. Hosp., Brunswick, Ga., 1976-77; asst. head nurse (telemetry unit), relief nursing supr. Glynn Brunswick Meml. Hosp., Brunswick, 1982-93; office nurse mgr., hosp. nurse David J. Griffin, MD, Brunswick, 1977-82; from instr. practical nursing to asst. prof. nursing Brunswick (Ga.) Coll., 1984-93; nursing supr. S.E. Ga. Regional Med. Ctr., Brunswick, 1993-94, dir. edn. & rsch., 1994—; mem. adv. bd. Glynn County Bd. Edn. Health Occupations, Brunswick, 1989—; site visitor accrediting com. Health Occupations So. Assn. Colls. & Schs., Brunswick, 1989—; mem. edn. com. Ga. Bd. Nursing, Atlanta, 1991—. Mem. Am. Diabetes Assn., Brunswick, 1986—, Dept. Family and Children's Svcs., Brunswick, 1989—, vice chair, 1993-94: adv. bd. Diabetes Metabolic Ctr., Brunswick, 1990—; I Can Cope facilitator Am. Cancer Soc., Brunswick, 1985-87, profl. svc. nursing coord. 1986, exec. com. mem. 1986-87.; sec. minority outreach com., Brunswick, 1992-93; trustee St. Andrew's CME Ch., 1986—, sr. usher bd., 1988—. Recipient award for poster presentation Grad. Rsch. Seminar, Med. Coll. Ga., 1991. Mem. ANA, Ga. Nurses Assn. (exec. bd. mem.), Phi Delta Kappa, Sigma Theta Tau, Inc. Methodist. Office: SE Ga Regional Med Ctr 3100 Kemble Ave Brunswick GA 31521-1518

THOMAS, VIOLETA DE LOS ANGELES, real estate broker; b. Buenos Aires, Dec. 21, 1949; came to U.S., 1962; d. Angel and Lola (Andino) de Rios; m. Jess Thomas, Dec. 23, 1974; 1 child, Victor Justin. Student, Harvard U. and U. Buenos Aires, 1967-73. Mgr. book div. Time-Life, N.Y.C., 1967-73; real estate broker First Marin Realty, Inc., Mill Valley, Calif., 1985-95; assoc. broker Trump Corp., N.Y.C., 1996—. Bd. dirs. Alliance Francaise, St. Louis, 1995-96, City of Tuburon, Calif., 1987-93, Art and Heritage Commn., Tiburon. Named Woman of Yr., City of Buenos Aires, 1977, Agt. of Yr., Marin County and San Francisco, 1987-92. Home: 721 Fifth Ave Apt 57 C New York NY 10022 Office: Trump Corp 725 Fifth Ave 15 Fl New York NY 10022

THOMAS, YVONNE LINDER, psychologist; b. L.A.; d. G. and L. Linder; m. M. Thomas. BA in Psychology cum laude, Calif. State U., Northridge, 1986; MA in Psychology, Calif. State U., L.A., 1987; PhD in Psychology, Calif. Grad. Inst., L.A., 1992. Licensed psychologist. Psychol. intern The Counseling Ctr. West Los Angeles, Calif., 1988-92; registered psychol. asst. The Beverly Hills (Calif.) Counseling Ctr., 1992-96, psychologist, 1996—; guest radio therapist KIEV-870 AM Radio, Glendale, Calif., summer 1993; guest TV psychologist Century Cable Pub. Access, Santa Monica, Calif., 1996. Mem. APA, Calif. Psychol. Assn., L.A. County Psychol. Assn. (mem. media com., multi-cultural diversity com.), Golden Key, Psi Chi. Office: The Beverly Hills Counseling Ctr 9570 W Pico Blvd Ste 200 Los Angeles CA 90035

THOMAS, YVONNE SHIREY, family and consumer science educator; b. Jenner Cross Roads, Pa., Dec. 1, 1938; d. Edward Merle and Orphabel (Shaffer) Shirey; m. William Edward Thomas, Dec. 23, 1961; children: Scott Forrest, Matthew David. BS, Indiana U. of Pa., 1960; MS, Hood Coll., 1987. Home econs. educator Bristol (Pa.) Jr. Sr. High Sch., 1960-64; elem. educator Barbers Point Elem. Sch., Ewa Beach, Hawaii, 1964-65; guidance counselor Workman Jr. High Sch., Pensacola, Fla., 1966-68; middle sch. educator Broadfording Christian Acad., Hagerstown, Md., 1973-76; home econs. educator Hancock (Md.) Jr. Sr. High Sch., 1986-88, Springfield Middle Sch., Williamsport, Md., 1988—; consumer affairs intern Citicorp Credit Svcs., Inc, Hagerstown, 1986; career day coord. Springfield Middle Sch., Williamsport, 1988-92. Bd. mem. Washington County Commn. for Women, Hagerstown, 1989-96, Cedar Rapids Ministries, Hagerstown, 1990-95, 96—. Recipient Judith Ruchkin Rsch. award Md. ASCD, Balt., 1987; named Washington County Home Econs. Tchr. of Yr., Md. Home Econs. Assn., Hagerstown, 1989, Women-on-the-Move, The Herald Mail Co., Hagerstown, 1991. Mem. AAUW (chair edn. fund 1989-90, v.p. membership 1990-92, grant 1992, pres.-elect 1992-93, pres. 1993-94, grantee 1994, chair Md. state edn. fund 1990-92, ednl. equity chair 1994—), NEA, Md. State Tchrs. Assn. (Dorothy Lloyd Women's Rights award 1996), Am. Assn. Family and Consumer Scis. (cert. family life educator 1990-98), Soroptimist Internat. (Women of Distinction award 1996, Regional Woman of Distinction 1996), Delta Zeta (pres. 1959-60). Republican. Grace Brethren. Home: 8134 Mountain Laurel Rd Boonsboro MD 21713-1830

THOMAS-JOHN, YVONNE MAREE, artist, interior designer; b. Leeton, New South Wales, Australia, Sept. 8, 1944; came to U.S., 1966; d. Percy Edward and Gladys May (Markham) Thomas; m. Michael Peter John, Aug. 20, 1966; children: Michael Christian, Stephen Edwin Dennis. Student, Buenaventura Coll., 1969, U. Calif., Santa Barbara, 1975; cert., United Design Guild, 1975; AA, Interior Design Guild, 1976; Diploma, Internat. Correspondence Sch., 1976. Designer Percy Thomas Real Estate, Leeton, 1960-66; cosmetologist, artist Bernard's Hair Stylists, Ventura, Calif., 1966-67, 74-73; cosmetologist Banks Beauty Salon, Chgo., 1968-69; owner, mgr. Yvonne Maree Designs, Ventura and Olympia, Wash., 1978—; owner, cosmetologist Mayfair Salon, Leeton, 1962-66; owner, mgr. Y.M. Boutique, Griffith, Australia, 1965-66. Contbr. numerous short stories and poems to newspapers; artist numerous pen and ink drawings; exhibited one-person show Royal Mus. Sydney, Australia, 1954; exhibited group shows Ventura County Courthouse, 1970, Wash. Women in Art, Olympia, 1990, Timberland Libr., Olympia, 1990, Maska Internat. Gallery, Seattle, 1991, Nat. Hqrs. of Am. Soc. Interior Designers, Washington, 1992, Michael Stone Collection, Washington, 1992, Mus. Modern Art, Bordeaux, France, 1993, UN Fourth World Conf. on Women, Beijing, China, 1995, others; 1st release of ltd. edit. prints, 1992; exhibited oil painting and drawing Hargis Unique Gallery, Pomona, Calif., 1994; works collected in Royal Mus. of Sydney, O'Toole Coll., Melbourne, Nat. Mus. of Women in Arts, Washington, Patterson Collection, Mich., Witherow Collection, Washington, Samaniego Collection, Calif., Ronald Reagon Collection, Calif. Artist Ventura County Gen. Hosp., 1970's. Recipient Cash and Cert. awards Sydney Newspapers, 1950's, Ribbon awards Sydney County Fairs, 1950's, 1st round winner painting Hathaway Competition, Ventura, Calif., 1970's. Mem. Am. Platform Assn. Office: Yvonne Maree Designs PO Box 2143 Olympia WA 98507-2143

THOMAS-MYERS, SUSAN JANE, executive sales representatives group; b. Marin County, Calif., Sept. 12, 1967; d. William Richard and Jane Dunning (Lasher) Thomas; m. Collin Allen Myers, Aug. 26, 1995. Student gen. edn., Mesa Coll., 1985-87; BA in Liberal Arts and Scis., San Diego State U., 1990. Asst buyer Robinson's Dept. Store, L.A., 1990-91; buyer Helen's Cycles Stores, Santa Monica, 1991-93; pres. Thomas Promotional Group, Manhattan Beach, Calif., 1993—; coord. sponsorship Manhattan Beach (Calif.) Grand Prix, 1995. Named Rookie of Yr. J&B Importers, Washington, 1993. Lutheran.

THOMASON, PAMELA DARLENE, administrator; b. Lewisburg, Tenn., Dec. 7, 1957; d. James Howard and Ida Mai (Reed) Haislip; m. William A. Thomason Jr.; children: Mindy Lynn, William A. III. Grad. high sch., Cornersville, Tenn.; student, Columbia State C.C. Adminstr. fin. Mead Containerboard, Lewisburg, Tenn., 1976—; rep. Ptnrs. in Edn., Cornersville, 1990-96. Author of poems. Sec., mem. Cancer Soc., Lewisburg, 1991-93, active Pilot Club, Lewisburg, 1991-94; mem. UGF Com., Lewisburg, 1993-94, 96. Named Miss Marshall County, Lewisburg, 1975, Miss Cornersville, 1975. Mem. Am. Mule and Donkey Soc. Mem. Ch. of Christ. Home: Snake Creek Farm 1731 Snake Creek Rd Belfast TN 37019 Office: Mead Containerboard 700 Garrett Pky PO Box 2037 Lewisburg TN 37091

THOMASSEN, PAULINE F., medical, surgical nurse; b. Cleve., Jan. 19, 1939; d. Henry Clifford and Mabel Pauline (Hill) Nichols; m. Ruben Thomassen, Nov. 10, 1979; children: Rhonda, Terry, Diana, Philipp, Jody, Barbara. AA in Nursing, So. Colo. State Coll., 1974, BA in Psychology with distinction, 1975; BSN magna cum laude, Seattle Pacific U., 1986. RN, Wash. Staff nurse III orthopedic unit, preceptor orientation RNs and student RNs Swedish Hosp. Med. Ctr., Seattle, 1975—; mem. planning task force and faculty National Nurses Conference, The Nurse and Spinal Surgery, Cleve. Author: Spinal Disease and Surgical Interventions. Mem. Nat. Assn. Orthop. Nurses.

THOMAS TOPP, MARGARET ANN, educational administrator, art educator; b. Waukesha, Wis., June 19, 1951; d. Melvin Michael and Elizabeth (Brewer) T.; 1 child, Michael. BA in Art Edn., Beloit Coll., 1974; MA in Art, U. Wis., Whitewater, 1981, MA in Ednl. Psychology, 1985; MS in Ednl. Adminstrn., U. Wis., 1995, PhD in Ednl. Adminstrn., Ednl. Psychology. Cert. K-12 art tchr., Wis., elem. and H.S. prin., curriculum dir. K-12, supt. Tchr. art Beloit (Wis.) Pub. Schs., 1974—; mem. staff Beloit Coll., 1992-93; muralist instr. Beloit Coll., summers, 1985-91, adj. prof., 1993—; adj. prof. Nat. Louis U., 1994—. Author: Effective Teachers; Effective Schools, 1989; contbr. articles to profl. jours. Bd. dirs. Wis.-Gate Found., 1985-87, Wis. Racquetball Assn., 1986-87, Wis. Future Problem Solving, 1986-87; pres. bd. dirs. YWCA, 1987-91; dir. Beloit and Vicinity Art Show, Beloit Coll., 1982-84, Rock Prairie Showcase Festival; founder Summer Explorers Beloit Coll. Mem. Wis. Coun. for Gifted and Talented (bd. dirs. 1984-87, v.p. 1985-86, pres. 1986-87). Home: 4421 Ruger Ave Janesville WI 53546

THOMERSON, ANNE SPACH, counselor; b. Recife, Brazil, July 17, 1953; d. Jule Christian and Nancy (Clendinin) Spach; m. E. Harvey Thomerson, July 23, 1976; children: Alexander, Julia. MEd, Ga. State U., Atlanta, 1992. Counselor The Walker Sch., Marietta, Ga., 1991—. Author: In Defense of the Wolf, 1979. Mem. ACA, ASCA, Phi Beta Kappa. Democrat. Presbyterian.

THOMI, DIANA KAY, oncology support organization administrator; b. McPherson, Kans., July 1, 1948; d. Glenn Earl and Lois Joy (Shultz) T. Diploma, Wesley Sch. Nursing, Wichita, Kans., 1970; BS, Grace U., Omaha, 1976; cert. in non-profit mgmt., Wichita State U., 1991. RN, Kans. Office nurse Internal Medicine Assocs., Wichita, 1973-75; clin. instr. Wesley Sch. Nursing, 1976-78; asst. head nursing Wesley Med. Ctr., Wichita, 1970-73, head nurse, 1978-86; clin. svcs. mgr. day surgery Wichita Clinic, 1986-87; adminstrv. dir. Victory in the Valley Inc., Wichita, 1987—; co-founder Victory in the Valley Inc., 1983, mem. bd. trustees, 1983—, pres. Co-editor (newsletter) Victory in the Valley News, 1986—. Recipient Nursing: The Heart of Healthcare award Sch. Nursing U. Kans., 1995; Point of Light honoree U.S. Pres. George Bush, 1991. Mem. Oncology Nursing Soc. (nat., local chpt.), Wesley Sch. Nursing Alumni Assn. (pres. 1980-90, Seven Who Care award 1986). Office: Victory in the Valley Inc 917 N Market St Wichita KS 67214-3521

THOMPSON, ANNE ELISE, federal judge; b. Phila., July 8, 1934; d. Leroy Henry and Mary Elise (Jackson) Jenkins; m. William H. Thompson, June 19, 1965; children: William H., Sharon A. BA, Howard U., 1955, LLB, 1964; MA, Temple U., 1957. Bar: D.C. bar 1964, N.J. bar 1966. Staff atty. Office of Solicitor, Dept. Labor, Chgo., 1964-65; asst. dep. public defender Trenton, N.J., 1967-70; mcpl. prosecutor Lawrence Twp., Lawrenceville, N.J., 1970-72; mcpl. ct. judge Trenton, 1972-75; prosecutor Mercer County, Mercer County, Trenton, 1975-79; judge U.S. Dist. Ct. N.J., Trenton, 1979—, now chief judge; vice chmn. Mercer County Criminal Justice Planning Com., 1972; mem. com. criminal practice N.J. Supreme Ct., 1975-79, mem. com. mcpl. cts., 1972-75; v.p. N.J. County Prosecutors Assn., 1978-79; chmn. juvenile justice com. Nat. Dist. Attys. Assn., 1978-79. Del. Democratic Nat. Conv., 1972. Recipient Black Women Lawyers award, 1976, Disting. Service award Nat. Dist. Attys. Assn., 1979, Gene Carte Meml. award Am. Criminal Justice Assn., 1980, Outstanding Leadership award N.J. County Prosecutors Assn., 1980, John Mercer Langston Outstanding Alumnus award Howard U. Law Sch., 1981; also various service awards; certs. of appreciation. Mem. Am. Bar Assn., Fed. Bar Assn., N.J. Bar Assn., Mercer County Bar Assn. Democrat. Office: US Dist Ct US Courthouse 402 E State St Trenton NJ 08608-1507

THOMPSON, ANNE MARIE, newspaper publisher; b. Des Moines, Feb. 7, 1920; d. George Horace and Esther Mayer Sheely; m. J. Ross Thompson, July 31, 1949; children: Annette McCracken, James Ross. BA, U. Iowa, 1940; postgrad. U. Colo., 1971. Co-pub. Baca County Banner, Springfield, Colo., 1951-54, Rocky Ford (Colo.) Daily Gazette, 1954-82, pub., 1982—. Editor Toastmasters, 1983-94. Mem. Otero Jr. Coll. Coun., 1987-93, Colo. Ho. of Reps., 1957-61; Colo. presdl. elector, 1972; chmn. Colo. adv. com. SBA, 1979-81. Recipient Community Service award Rocky Ford C. of C., 1975; named Colo. Woman of Achievement in Journalism, 1959, Colo. Bus. Person of Yr., Future Bus. Leaders of Am., 1981; elected to Colo. Community Journalism Hall of Fame, 1981. Mem. Nat. Fedn. Press Women (dir. 1971-81), Nat. Newspaper Assn. (Emma C. McKinney award 1984), Colo. Press Assn. (dir. 1981-83, Golden Make-Up award 1991) , Colo. Press Women, PEO, Bus. and Profl. Women's Club. Republican. Methodist.

THOMPSON, ANNIE FIGUEROA, academic director, educator; b. Río Piedras, P.R., June 7, 1941; d. Antonio Figueroa-Colón and Ana Isabel Laugier; m. Donald P. Thompson, Jan. 23, 1972; 1 child, John Anthony. BA, Baylor U., 1962; MSLS, U. So. Calif., 1965; AMD, Fla. State U., 1978, PhD, 1980. Educator Mayan Sch., Guatemala City, Guatemala, 1962-63; cataloger libr. system U. P.R., Río Piedras, 1965-67, head music libr., 1967-81, assoc. prof. librarianship, 1981-85; dir. grad. sch. libr. info. sci. U. P.R., Río Piedras, 1986-93; prof. U. P.R., Río Piedras, 1986—. Author: An Annotated Bibliography About Music in Puerto Rico, 1975; co-author: Music and Dance in Puerto Rico from the Age of Columbus to Modern Times, An Annotated Bibliography, 1991; contbr. articles to profl. jours.; performed song recitals Inst. of P.R. Culture and U. P.R. Artist Series, 1974-78; soloist with P.R. Symphony Orch., San Juan, 1978; performed in opera, on radio and TV, San Juan, 1968-81;. Sec. P.R. Symphony Orch League, San Juan, 1982-84; mem. pub. libr. adv. com. Adminstrn. for Devel. of Arts and Culture, P.R., 1982-84, Pub. Libr. Adv. Bd., 1989-94. Recipient Lauro a la Instrucción Bibliotecaria Sociedad de Bibliotecarios de P.R., 1985, Lauro a la Bibliografía Puertorriqueña, 1993. Mem. ALA, Assn. Libr. and Info. Sci., San Juan Rotary, Sociedad de Bibliotecarios de P.R. (pres. 1994-96), Music Libr. Assn., Sigma Delta Kappa, Mu Phi Epsilon, Beta Phi Mu. Episcopalian. Home: N-64 Acadia St Park Gardens Rio Piedras San Juan PR 00926 Office: Grad Sch Library & Info Sci U of PR PO Box 21906 Rio Piedras San Juan PR 00931-1906

THOMPSON, ARLENE RITA, nursing educator; b. Yakima, Wash., May 17, 1933; d. Paul James and Esther Margaret (Danroth) T. BS in Nursing, U. Wash., 1966, Masters in Nursing, 1970, postgrad., 1982—. Staff nurse Univ. Teaching Hosp., Seattle, 1966-69; mem. nursing faculty U. Wash. Sch. Nurses, Seattle, 1971-73; critical care nurse Virginia Mason Hosp., Seattle, 1973—; educator Seattle Pacific U. Sch. Nursing, 1981—; nurse legal cons. nursing edn., critical care nurse. Contbr. articles to profl. jours. USPHS grantee, 1969; nursing scholar Virginia Mason Hosp., 1965. Mem. Am. Assn. Critical Care Nurses (cert.), Am. Nurses Assn., Am. Heart Assn., Nat. League Nursing, Sigma Theta Tau, Alpha Tau Omega. Republican. Presbyterian. Home: 2320 W Newton St Seattle WA 98199-4115 Office: Seattle Pacific U 3307 3rd Ave W Seattle WA 98119-1940

THOMPSON, BARBARA LOUISE, marine engineer; b. Midland, Tex., July 28, 1959; d. Willis Herbert Thompson and Emma Louise (Seamans) Brown. BS, Tex. A&M U., 1981. Registered profl. engr., Tec. Staff engr. Seaflo Systems, Houston, 1982-83, Barnett & Cassarian, Inc., Houston, 1982-85; project mgr. Barnett & Cassarian, Inc., 1993—; project engr. Combustion Engrng., Houston, 1985-89; project cons. Houston, 1989-93. Patentee in field. Mem. Houston Profl. Rep. Women, 1991—; lector All Saints Cath. Ch., Houston, 1995. Mem. Soc. Naval Architects and Marine Engrs. (sec., treas. 1985-87), Internat. Ships and Offshore Structures (assoc.), Tau Beta Pi. Roman Catholic. Home: 1860 White Oak #357 Houston TX 77009

THOMPSON, BERTHA BOYA, retired education educator, antique dealer and appraiser; b. New Castle, Pa., Jan. 31, 1917; d. Frank L. and Kathryn Belle (Park) Boya; m. John L. Thompson, Mar. 27, 1942; children: Kay Lynn Thompson Koolage, Scott McClain. BS in Elem. & Secondary Edn., Slippery Rock State Coll., 1940; MA in Geography and History, Miami U., 1954; EdD, Ind. U., 1961. Cert. elem. and secondary edn. tchr. Elem. tchr., reading specialist New Castle (Pa.) Sch. System, 1940-45; tchr., chmn. social studies Talawanda Sch. System, Oxford, Ohio, 1954-63; assoc. prof. psychology and geography, chair edn. dept. Western Coll. for Women, Oxford, 1963-74; assoc. prof. edn., reading clinic Miami U., Oxford, 1974-78, prof. emeritus, 1978—; pvt. antique dealer, appraiser Oxford, 1978—. Contbr. articles to profl. jours. Mem. folk art com. Miami U. Art Mus., Oxford, 1974-76; mem. adv. com. Smith libr., Oxford Pub. Libr., 1978-81. Mem. AAUP, Nat. Coun. Geographic Edn. (exec. bd. dirs. 1966-69), Nat. Soc. for Study Edn., Assn. Am. Geographers, Soc. Women Geographers, Nat. Coun. for the Social Studies, Pi Lambda Theta, Zeta Tau Alpha, Pi Gamma Mu, Gamma Theta Upsilon, Kappa Delta Pi. Home: 6073 Contreras Rd Oxford OH 45056-9708

THOMPSON, CAROL CUTHBERTSON, artist; b. Cleve., Sept. 25, 1946; d. Thomas Edward and Ann (Puchalski) Cuthbertson; m. Arthur S. Thompson, June 19, 1968 (dec. Feb. 1975); 1 child, Nathan. BA in English, Wake Forest U., 1968; MEd, Duke U., 1976; MFA in Painting, Temple U., 1984. Asst. editor Duke U. Press, Durham, N.C., 1971-75; freelance editor, Durham and Phila., 1976-77, 84-86, 92; instr. art Carolina Friends Sch., Durham, 1987-92; advisor, instr. writing Delaware Valley Friends, Phila., 1993-94; instr. Phila. C.C., 1995—; freelance artist Durham & Phila., 1978—. One-woman shows include Galerie Taub, 1984, Temple U., 1983, 84, Duke U., 1985, 92, Print Club, Phila., 1994; dual show at Pitts. Filmmakers, 1996; group shows include numerous galleries, 1979—; author: (pamphlet) Tagore: An Artist, 1968; work pub. in Mahattan Arts Internat., Shots Photo Rev. Recipient N.C. Fiction Network award, 1990; Tyler-Temple U. scholar, 1983. Mem. Tchrs. of English to Speakers of Other Langs., Sierra Club, Nature Conservancy, Appalachian Mountain Club. Home: 6603 Morris Park Rd Philadelphia PA 19151

THOMPSON, CAROLINE WARNER, film director, screenwriter; b. Washington, Apr. 23, 1956; d. Thomas Carlton Jr. and Bettie Marshall (Warner) T.; m. Alfred Henry Bromell, Aug. 28, 1982 (div. 1985). BA summa cum laude, Amherst Coll., 1978. Author: First Born, 1983; screenwriter: (films) Edward Scissorhands, 1990, The Addams Family, 1991, Homeward Bound: The Incredible Journey, 1993, The Secret Garden, 1993, Tim Burton's The Nightmare Before Christmas, 1993; screenwriter, dir.: Black Beauty, 1994. Mem. Phi Beta Kappa. Office: William Morris Agency Inc 151 S El Camino Dr Beverly Hills CA 90212-2704*

THOMPSON, CHERLY ANN, rehabilitation professional; b. Berlin, Sept. 15, 1967; d. Edward Joseph and Kathleen (Snay) T. BS in Spl. Edn., Westfield (Mass.) State Coll., 1989; MEd, R.I. Coll., 1994. Spl. edn. tchr. Behavior Rsch. Inst., Providence, R.I., 1989-92, Boston Ctr. for Blind Children, 1993-94, Barnstable Pub. Schs., Hyannis, Mass., 1996—; day program supr. Residential Rehab. Ctrs. Inc., Brewster, Mass., 1994-96. Mem. Assn. for Persons with Severe Handicaps, Am. Assn. on Mental Retardation, Prader-Willi Syndrome Assn. Democrat. Roman Catholic. Home: PO Box 1247 365 Rt 6 Eastham MA 02642 Office: Residential Rehab Ctrs Inc PO Box 1879 1646 Rt 6A Brewster MA 02631

THOMPSON, CHRISTINE K., meeting planner, consultant; b. Takoma Park, Md.. AS magna cum laude, Piedmont Coll., 1986. Dir. confs. Assn. Investment Mgmt. and Rsch., Charlottesville, Va., 1985-92; pres. Choice Meeting Profls., Charlottesville, Va., 1992-96. Contbr. article to profl. jour. Outreach coun. Ch. Incarnation, Charlottesville, Va., 1994-95. Mem. Am. Mgmt. Assn., Meeting Profls. Internat. (chairwoman 1994-95, cert. meeting profl.).

THOMPSON, CLAIRE LOUISA, nurse, educator, administrator; b. Columbus, Ohio, Sept. 29, 1938; d. Harry Edgar and Clara Etta (Brackenbusch) McKeever; m. Roger Lee Thompson, Dec. 20, 1958 (div. 1988); children: Jeffrey, Michael. Diploma, Bethesda Hosp. Sch. Nursing, Cin., 1959; student, Ball State, 1970, Ind. U., 1981, Purdue U., 1982-83. RN, Ohio, Ind., Calif.; cert. ins. rehab. specialist, 1985, CCM case mgr., 1993. Oper. rm./emergency rm. nurse Greene Meml. Hosp., Xenia, Ohio, 1959-60; med.-surg. nurse, charge nurse Bethesda Hosp., 1960-64; med.-surg. nurse Porter Meml. Hosp., Valparaiso, Ind., 1965-66; staff and charge nurse Mercy Hosp., Elwood, Ind., 1968-74; gen. practice nurse W. A. Scea, MD, Elwood, 1970-74; exec. dir. Vis. Nurse Assn., Elwood, 1974-78; analyst Blue Cross/Blue Shield of Indpls., 1978; supr. Meth. Hosp. Clinic, Indpls., 1979-80; dir. nursing Upjohn Health Care, Indpls., 1980; staff nurse Americana Health Care Ctr., Indpls., 1981; instr. health occups. Washington Twp. Schs., Indpls., 1981-84; br. mgr. health & rehab. Crawford & Co., Indpls., 1984-88; regional med. svcs. advisor western region Crawford & Co., San Francisco, 1988-92; br. mgr. Crawford & Co., Health Care Mgmt., Modesto, Calif., 1992-94; ret., 1994; developer in case mgmt. nursing svcs., 1974-94. Founder Meals on Wheels, Elwood, 1975, Vis. Nurses Asn., Elwood, 1976. Mem. NLN, Assn. Rehab. Nurses (pres. Ind. chpt. 1987-88), Nat. Ins. Womens Assn., Case Mgmt. Soc. Am., San Francisco Ins. Womens Assn., Rehab. Ins. Nurses Group. Roman Catholic. Home: 1232 Whitney Ln Westerville OH 43081

THOMPSON, DAWNE, church secretary; b. Marshall, Tex., Oct. 11, 1953; d. Oscar L. and Irene H. (Hill) Thompson; m. Bob G. Washington, June 16, 1984 (div. Sept. 1996); 1 stepchild, Bobby Glenn. BA in Psychology, U. Tex., 1975. Costumer, makeup artist, choreographer Afro-Am. Players, Inc., Austin, 1976-80; with Mortgage Profl. Svcs., Austin, 1980-81; mortgage processor Comml. Credit, Austin, 1981-82, MV Mortgage Co., Austin, 1982-83, Heart O' Tex. Mortgage Co./S.W. Mortgage Investments, Austin, 1983-85; mortgage underwriter, processor Mullis Mortgage Co., Inc., Austin, 1985-86; ch. sec. Ebenezer Bapt. Ch., Austin, 1986—; ind. profl. beauty cons. Mary Kay Cosmetics, Inc., Austin, 1991—. Poll worker Dem. Ctrl. Com., Austin, 1972. Recipient Mattie B. White award Black Arts Alliance, 1983. Mem. Austin Assn. So. Bapt. Secs. (sec. 1994—). Home: 5209 Langwood Dr Austin TX 78754

THOMPSON, DAYLE ANN, aerospace company executive; b. Grand Forks, N.D., Jan. 6, 1954; d. Duane Theodore and anna Mae (Desautel) T.; m. Michael Gary Sciulla, Aug. 6, 1977 (div. Sept. 1980); m. Manfred Hans von Ehrenfried II, June 11, 1982. Secretarial degree, Aaker's Bus. Coll., Grand Forks, 1973; cert. of completion mgmt., George Washington U., 1979, Masters Cert. in Project Mgmt., 1995. Receptionist U.S. Rep. Norman F. Lent U.S. Ho. of Reps., Washington, 1973-74; office mgr., personal sec. U.S. Rep. Les AuCoin, U.S. Ho. of Reps., Washington, 1975-78; bus. mgr., bookkeeper Virgin Islands POST, St.Thomas, USVI, 1978; office and pers. mgr. Internat. Energy Assocs. Ltd., Washington, 1978-82; program support mgr. MSI Svcs. Inc., Washington, 1982-84; pres., treas., chief exec. officer Tech. and Adminstrv. Svcs. Corp., Washington, 1984—; Hosp. vol. ARC, Arlington, Va., 1987. Recipient Group Achievement award NASA, 1984, 93, Commendation Letter, NASA, 1985, 87, 88, 91, 93, 94, Small Bus. Prime Contractor of Yr. award Small Bus. Adminstrn. Region 3, 1994. Mem. Washington Space Bus. Roundtable (sponsor-benefactor 1990-92), Women in Aerospace. Republican. Roman Catholic. Home: 4250 42nd Ave S Saint Petersburg FL 33711-4231 Office: TADCORPS 400 Virginia Ave SW Ste 730 Washington DC 20024-2511

THOMPSON, DENISSE R., mathematics educator; b. Keesler AFB, Miss., Aug. 26, 1954. BA, BS, U. South Fla., 1976, MA, 1980; PhD, U. Chgo., 1992. Cert. tchr., Fla. Tchr. Hernando County Schs., Brooksville, Fla., 1977-82; instr. maths. Manatee C.C., Bradenton, Fla., 1982-87; asst. prof. U. South Fla., Tampa, 1991—; cons. in field. Author: Fundamental Skills of Mathematics, 1987, Advanced Algebra, 1990, 2d edit., 1996, (with others) Precalculus and Discrete Mathematics, 1992, Nat. Coun. Tchrs. of Math. Yearbook, 1991, 93, 94, 95. Recipient Carolyn Hoefer Meml. award Pi Lambda Theta, 1988. Mem. ASCD, Math. Assn. Am., Nat. Coun. Tchrs. Math., Nat. Coun. Suprs. Math., Assn. Women in Maths., Phi Delta Kappa, Phi Kappa Phi. Office: U South Fla College of Edn EDU208B Tampa FL 33620

THOMPSON, DIDI CASTLE (MARY BENNETT), writer, editor; b. Terre Haute, Ind., Feb. 7, 1918; d. Robert Langley Bennett and Marjorie Rose (Tyler) Castle; student U. Ill., Champaign, 1935-36, U. Ky., 1936-39; m. Jamie Campbell Thompson, Jr., June 24, 1939; children—Jamie III, Julia King Balko, Langley Stewart Ruede. News editor Glen-Echoes, Glencoe, Ill., 1930; columnist Ky. Kernel, U. Ky., Lexington, 1937-39; radio script writer Modern Am. Music, 1940-42; asst. pub. relations dir. Salem Coll., Winston-Salem, N.C., 1945; pub. relations chmn. Barrington (Ill.) Horse Show, 1959-67; staff writer, columnist Barrington Press Newspapers, 1958-84; editor ECHO, Defenders of the Fox River, Inc. newsletter, 1970-80; travel editor Barrington Press Newspapers, 1973-84; columnist The Daily Herald, Paddock Publs., 1984-86; columnist Rapid City (S.D.) Journal, 1990-95; freelance writer, 1943—. Past bd. mem. Barrington chpt. Lyric Opera Guild Chgo., Barrington Sr. Center, Infant Welfare Soc. Chgo., Art Inst. Chgo., Barrington Assos.; elected trustee Village of Barrington Hills, 1969-73, health, pub. relations chmn., 1969-73; mem. Barrington Hills Plan Commn., 1986. Mem. Women in Communications (past dir.), Citizens for Conservation (past dir.), Barrington Countryside Assn. (past dir.), Barrington Hist. Soc., Spring Creek Basset Hounds Club, Barrington Hills Riding Club (past dir.), Pan Hellenic Council, DAR, Chgo. Press Club, Chi Omega. Episcopalian. Address: 1827 Princess Ct North Naples FL 34110

THOMPSON, DOLORES ANN, special education educator; b. Talladega, Ala., Jan. 24, 1936; d. William Hurston and Alice Faustine (Guest) T. BS, Samford U., 1957; MA, U. Ala., 1961, AA, 1965. Tchr. spl. edn. Birmingham Bd. Edn., 1958—. U.S. Dept. Edn. fellow, 1963-65; named Outstanding Young Educator Jaycees, 1968. Mem. DAR (chaplain 1988—), United Daus. Confederacy, Ala. Symphonic Assn., Caledonia Soc. Republican. Baptist. Office: Banks Mid Sch 721 S 86th St Birmingham AL 35206

THOMPSON, DONNA SUE, family counselor; b. Memphis, Mar. 19, 1958; d. Ocie and Augusta Angie (Ivy) T. BS, U. Tenn., Knoxville, 1982; MS, U. Memphis, 1993. Practicum counselor Mississippi Blvd. Christian Ch., Memphis, 1992; counseling intern Family Link, Memphis, 1992-93; social worker de signeé St. Joseph Hosp., Memphis, 1993; family therapist Family Focus Program, Memphis, 1993—. Vol. Family Trouble Ctr., Memphis, 1991, Memphis Interfaith Assn., 1993—; mem. Mission on the Move, Olivet Bapt. Ch., Memphis, 1995, mentor Sister to Sister program, 1995. Mem. ACA, Internat. Assn. Marriage and Family Counselors. Democrat. Baptist. Home: 6535 Lake Valley Dr Memphis TN 38141 Office: Frayser Family Counseling 2150 Whitney Ave Memphis TN 38127

THOMPSON, DOREEN, public relations executive; b. Somerville, Mass., Mar. 26, 1955; 2 children. BA in Mass. Comm., U. N.H., 1977; MA in Speech Comm., Emerson Coll., 1982. Account exec. Arnold Pub. Rels., Boston, 1984-85; account exec., account supr., v.p. Ingalls, Quinn & Johnson Pub. Rels., Boston, 1985-88; v.p., then sr. v.p. The Weber Group, Cambridge, Mass., 1988—. Trustee Lasell Coll., Newton, Mass., 1990—; pro bono work Gang Peace, Boston, 1994. Recipient Regional award CIPPRA, 1993, Bellringer award Publicity Club, 1994. Office: The Weber Group 101 Main St Cambridge MA 02142-1519*

THOMPSON, DOROTHEA KATHLEEN, microbiology researcher; b. Bellefonte, Pa., May 25, 1963; d. Charles Carr and Deborah Ann (Eavenson) T. BA in English and Microbiology, U. Tenn., 1986; MS in Microbiology, Va. Polytechnic Inst./State U., 1989; MA in English, Pa. State U., 1992; postgrad., Ohio State U. Grad. rsch. asst. dept. anaerobic microbiology Va. Tech., Blacksburg, 1986-89; grad. tchg. asst./lectr. dept. English Pa. State, University Park, Pa., 1990-92; grad. rsch. and tchg. assoc. dept. microbiology Ohio State, Columbus, 1992—; tchg. asst. Howard Hughes Scholars Inst. in Genetics, University Park, 1992; vice-speaker Va. Tech. Grad. Student Assembly, Blacksburg, 1987-88; grad. student rep. Coun. on Rsch. and Grad. Studies, Columbus, 1993-94; departmental del. Ohio State Coun. Grad. Students, 1993-94. Contbr. articles to profl. jours. Mem. NOW, AAAS, Am. Soc. Microbiology, Phi Beta Kappa, Phi Kappa Phi. Home: 1360 Dublin Rd Apt # 8 Columbus OH 43215 Office: Ohio State U Dept Microbiology 484 West 12th Ave Columbus OH 43210

THOMPSON, DOROTHY BARNARD, elementary school educator; b. Flushing, N.Y., Aug. 14, 1933; d. Henry Clay and Cecelia Minnie Theresa (La Pardo) Barnard; m. Norman Earl Thompson, Aug. 12, 1956; children: Greg, Scot, Henry, Marc, Matthew. BSEd, SUNY, New Paltz, 1953; MS, Hofstra U., 1984. Cert. elem. tchr. K-6th grades, reading specialist K-12th grades, N.Y. Adjunct prof. Suffolk Community Coll., Brentwood, N.Y., 1987—, Nassau Community Coll., Uniondale, N.Y., 1986—; adjunct prof., instr. Ctr. for Acad. Achievement Long Island U., Greenvale, N.Y., 1984-92; tchr. reading, K-5th grades Long Beach (N.Y.) Pub. Schs., 1988—; mem. founding group Parent/Tchr., The Learning Tree, Garden City, N.Y., 1971; founder parent coop. Happy Day Nursery Sch., Bellmore, N.Y., 1975; parent-tchr. Commonwealth Sch., Bay Shore, Oakdale, 1976-82. Mem. NEA, Nassau Reading Coun., N.Y. State Tchrs. Assn., Assn. for Supervision and Curriculum Devel. Home: 2385 Warren Ave Bellmore NY 11710-2545 Office: 456 Neptune Blvd Long Beach NY 11561-2425

THOMPSON, ELEANOR DUMONT, nurse; b. Derry, N.H., May 26, 1935; d. Louis Arthur and Florence Berthae (Gendreau) D.; m. Carl Hugh Thompson, Aug. 22, 1959; children: Justine, Julie. Student, Dartmouth Hitchcock Nur. Sch., 1956; BA, New Eng. Coll., 1977; MS, Drake U., 1984. Registered art therapist. Pediatric instr. Hanover (N.H.) Sch. Practical Nursing, 1958-61; pub. W.B. Sanders Co., Phila., 1962—; pediatric instr. St. Joseph Hosp., Nashua, N.H., 1978-81; cert. clin. nurse specialist Mercy Hosp. Med. Ctr., Des Moines, 1987-90; clin. nurse specialist HCA Portsmouth (N.H.) Regional Hosp., 1991—; pvt. practice Silverman & Assoc., Inc., 1991-93; puppeteer St. Joseph's Hosp. Sch. Nursing, Nashua, 1981-82; created and conducted shows on hospitalization for children; nursing cons. Hospice Cen. Iowa, Des Moines, 1982-89. Author: Pediatric Nursing An Introductory Text, 1965, 6th edit., 1992, Introduction to Maternity and Pediatric Nursing, 1990, 2d edit., 1995. Vol. nurse Vietnam Vets. Ctr., Des Moines, 1985-87, Camp Apanda Childrens Cancer Camp Boone, Iowa, 1984-86; organist Holy Trinity Ch. Des Moines, 1982, St. Pius Ch., Des Moines, 1982. Mem. ANA, Am. Psychiat. Nurses Assn., Am. Art Therpy Assn., N.H. Art Therapy Assn., Drake Alumnae Assn., N.H. Nurses Assn. Democrat. Roman Catholic. Home: 13 Sherman Ave Brentwood NH 03833-6225

THOMPSON, ELIZABETH JANE, small business owner; b. Ithaca, N.Y., Jan. 11, 1927; d. Merle Godley and Nellie Gray (Trowbridge) T. AB, Syracuse U., 1948, MA, 1962, PhD, 1971. Writer, editor Cornell U., Ithaca, N.Y., 1950-53; dir. pub. rels. Taylor Ward Advt., Ithaca, 1953-54; account exec. Doug Johnson Assocs., Syracuse, N.Y., 1954-58; assoc. in community rels., Youth Devel. Ctr. Syracuse U., 1958-66, grad. asst., 1967-68; from asst. prof. to prof. sociology Shippensburg (Pa.) U., 1968-90, dir. Fashion Archives, 1980-90; owner Timelines & Hemlines Cons. Svc., Shippensburg, 1991—; lectr. on costume, fashion and sociology of dress to numerous civic and ednl. groups. Co-editor: Among the People: Studies of the Urban Poor, 1968; contbr. articles on sociology of dress to numerous publs. Mem. Costume Soc. Am., Am. Sociol. Soc. Dutch Reform. Home and Office: 19 S Prince St Shippensburg PA 17257-1919

THOMPSON, EMMA, actress; b. London, Apr. 15, 1959; d. Eric Thompson and Phyllida Law; m. Kenneth Branaugh, Aug. 1989. Student of English, Cambridge U., Eng. Performances include: (films) Henry V, 1989, The Tall Guy, 1989, Dead Again, 1991, Impromptu, 1991, Howard's End, 1992 (Acad. award for best actress 1993), Peter's Friends, 1992, Much Ado About Nothing, 1993, The Remains of the Day, 1993 (Acad. award nominee for best actress 1993), In the Name of the Father, 1993 (Acad. award nominee for best supporting actress 1993), My Father, the Hero, 1994, Junior, 1994, Carrington, 1995 (Best Actress award Nat. Bd. Rev. 1995), Sense and Sensibility, 1995 (Golden Globe award nominee for best actress in film 1996, Acad. award nominee for best actress 1996); (TV in Eng.) Al Fresco, Up For Grabs (a.k.a. Sexually Transmitted), Tutti Frutti, (miniseries) Fortunes of War, Thompson; (TV in Am.) Fortunes of War, Cheers, 1991; (London stage) Me and My Girl, Look Back in Anger; also writer screen adaptation: Sense and Sensibility (Jane Austin), 1995 (Best Screenplay award N.Y. Film Critics 1995, L.A. Film Critics 1995, Boston Film Critics 1995, Golden Globe award for best adapted screenplay 1996, Acad. award for best adapted screenplay 1996, BAFTA Best Actress award 1996). Active in Footlights Theatrical Group, Cambridge, Eng. Office: William Morris Agy 151 El Camino Beverly Hills CA 90212

THOMPSON, G. GAYE, lawyer; b. Greensboro, N.C., Sept. 15, 1945; d. O.C. and Jean (Esterak) T.; m. Alvis Layton Barrier, Jr., Aug. 28, 1965 (div. 1988); children: Breton Foster, Amé Rebecca. BA, Southwestern U., 1967; JD, St. mary's U., 1987. Bar: 1987, U.S. Ct. Appeals (5th cir.) 1991, U.S. Supreme Ct. 1991. Psychiat. caseworker Austin (Tex.) State Hosp., 1967-68; counselor, acting dir. counseling Meth. Mission Home Tex., San Antonio, 1968-70; co-therapist sex and marital therapy J. Franklin Stokes, M.D., San Antonio, 1976-78; pvt. practice sex therapy, marital counseling Seguin, Tex., 1978-83; assoc. Irvine & Dial, P.C., Attys. at Law, Seguin, 1987; 1st asst. county atty. Guadalupe County, Seguin, 1987-90; ptnr. Thompson & Tiemann LLP, Attys. and Counselors at Law, Austin, 1991—; sex therapist Am. Assn. Sex Educators, Counselors and Therapists, Washington, 1978-91; sex educator Am. Bd. Sexology, Washington, 1990-93. Pres., bd. dirs. Marywood Child and Family Svcs., 1995-96, Palmer Drug Abuse Program, Seguin, 1982; organizer, dir. Helping Hand program Sequin PTA, 1980; presenter sexuality workshops for teens and parents, various chs., Seguin, 1981-82; pres. bd. dirs. Family Eldercare, 1996-97. Fellow Am. Coll. Sexologists, Internat. Coun. Sex Edn. and Parenthood; mem. AAUW, Am. Bd. Sexology (diplomate), Am. Assn. Sex Educators, Counselors and Therapists, Travis County Bar Assn. (bd. dirs. probate and estate planning sect.), Tex. Dist. and County Attys. Assn., Tex. Guardianship Assn. (bd. dirs.), Capital Area Dem. Women (pres., bd. dirs.), Delta Delta Delta. Episcopalian. Home: PO Box 5459 Austin TX 78763-5459 Office: Thompson & Tiemann LLP Attys and Counselors at Law 1206 S Congress Ave Austin TX 78704-2422

THOMPSON, GENEVA FLORENCE, medical technologist, cytotechnologist; b. Zionsville, Ind., Apr. 5, 1915; d. Alfred Seymour and Grace Viola (Kutz) T. Cert. in cytotechnology, Ohio State U., 1964; BA, Ind. U./Purdue U., Indpls., 1972. Cert. Am. Soc. Clin. Pathologists. Med. technician Noblesville (Ind.) Hosp., 1948-52; med. technician Riverview Hosp., Noblesville, 1952-56, med. technologist, 1956-60; med. technologist Office of Robert Harris, M.D., Noblesville, 1960-64; cytotechnologist Office of Thornton, Haymond, Costin, Buehl & Bolinger, M.D., Indpls., 1965-78, ret., 1978. Active with local church; served with U.S. Army W.A.C., 1944-46. Mem. AAUW (chmn. literature study group), Ind. U. Women's Club of Indpls., Am. Soc. Clin. Pathologists, Noblesville Tourist Club (sec.), Sr. Citizens Orgn., Inc. Republican.

THOMPSON, JANE JOHNSON, retail executive; b. Charleston, W.Va., July 13, 1951; d. Robert Paul and Phyllis Jane (Judson) Johnson; m. T. Stephen Thompson, Aug. 28, 1976; children: Robert Baker, Catherine Brooke. BBA, U. Cin., 1973; MBA, Harvard Coll., 1978. Brand mgr. Procter & Gamble, Cin., 1973-77; prin., ptnr. McKinsey & Co., Inc., Chgo., 1978-88; v.p. Sears Specialty Merchandising div. Sears Roebuck & Co., Chgo., 1988-89; v.p. planning Sears Roebuck & Co., Chgo., 1989-90, v.p. corp. and mdse. group planning, mem. corp. mgmt. com., 1990-93; exec. v.p. credit, gen. mgr., mem. exec. com. Sears Merchandise Group, 1993-96, pres. home svcs., mem. exec. com., 1996—; bd. dirs. ConAgra, Inc. Bd. dirs. Lincoln Park Zoo Soc. Aux., 1988—; bd. dirs., exec. com., head strategic planning com. Boys and Girls Club of Chgo., 1992—. Baker scholar Harvard U., 1978. Mem. Chgo. Network, Econ. Club Chgo., Nat. Retail Fedn. (credit. coun., bd. dirs.), Internat. Credit Assn. (bd. dirs.). Office: Sears Mdse Group B6-133A 3333 Beverly Rd # B6-133A Hoffman Estates IL 60179*

THOMPSON, JANE LYNN, elementary education educator; b. Winston-Salem, N.C., Jan. 5, 1969; d. Harry L. and M. Irene (Dawson) T. BS, Radford U., 1991. Cert. tchr. K-8, math., social studies, English mid. grades. Tchr. Gladesboro Elem. Sch., Hillsville, Va., 1991—. Mem. Nat. Coun. Tchrs. Math., Va. Edn. Assn., Carroll Edn. Assn. Home: 119 Jett Ave Hillsville VA 24343-1300

THOMPSON, JANN MARIE, secondary school educator; b. Marshalltown, Iowa, July 12, 1953; d. Thomas Ronald and Evelyn Marie (Muckler) Thompson; m. Michael Alden Knight, Sept. 2, 1972 (div. July 1994); children: Amy Susanne, Kelly Michael, Aaron. BA, U. Iowa, 1975; MA in Edn., U. No. Iowa, 1992. Cert. reading specialist K-12, cert. secondary tchr., English and ESL. English tchr. Charles City (Iowa) Jr. H.S.,

1990-92, ESL tchr., 1991-92, reading specialist, 1992-93; coord., CLHS Carrie Lane H.S., Charles City, 1992—, grant coord., 1994-96; instr. developmental studies Hawkeye C.C., Waterloo, Iowa, 1996—; adj. prof. U. No. Iowa, Charles City, 1992—; adv. coun. mem. Workstart Adv. Coun., Des Moines, 1991-94; adv. com. Workstart Consortium Adv. Com., Marshalltown, Iowa; grand coord. Reading Connections Literacy Project, Charles City, 1994—. Grantee ComServ Iowa, 1994, Iowa Dept. of Health, 1995. Mem. ASCD, Iowa Assn. of Alternative Educators, Internat. Reading Assn., Alpha Upsilon Alpha, Phi Delta Kappa. Republican. Methodist. Home: 1003 W Boone St Marshalltown IA 50158 Office: Hawkeye Community College Waterloo IA 50701

THOMPSON, JEAN TANNER, retired librarian; b. San Luis Obispo, Calif., June 15, 1929; d. Chester Corey and Mildred (Orr) T.; 1 child, Anne Marie Miller. Student, Whitworth Coll., Spokane, Wash., 1946-49; A.B., Boston U., 1951; postgrad., U. Wis., Eau Claire, 1964-67; M.S.L.S., Columbia U., 1973; Ed.M., U. Va., Charlottesville, 1978. Asst. social sci. librarian Univ. Libraries Va. Polytechnic Inst. and State U., Blacksburg, 1973-77, head social sci. dept. Univ. Libraries, 1977-83; head reference dept. Meml. Library U. Wis., Madison, 1983-86, asst. dir. reference and info. svcs., 1986-91, ret. Contbg. editor: ALA Guide to Information Access, 1994; mem. editorial bd. RQ, 1984-89. Mem. ALA, Assn. Coll. and Research Libraries (edn. and behavioral sci. sect. vice chmn. 1985-86, chmn. 1986-87), Wis. Library Assn., Wis. Assn. of Acad. Librarians. Methodist. Home: 103 S Hunter Ln Troy AL 36081-8206

THOMPSON, JERETTA STEWART, intermediate school principal; b. Oklahoma City, Okla., June 4, 1936; d. Lumpkin R. and Lucy C. (Thompson) Stewart; div.; children: Kendra Thompson, Sonya Pannell. BS in Edn., Southwestern State U., 1957; MEd, Stephen F. Austin U., 1983, mid-mgmt. cert., 1986. Cert. elem.-secondary bus. life; cert. counselor, cert. mid-mgmt. H.s. bus. tchr. Lamesa (Tex.) Ind. Sch. Dist., 1957-59, Borger (Tex.) Ind. Sch. Dist., 1959-61, Irving (Tex.) Sch. Dist., 1961-64; cmty. liaison Carthage (Tex.) Ind. Sch. Dist., 1974-76; elem. math. tchr. Cathage (Tex.) Ind. Sch. Dist., 1976-81, elem. counselor, 1981-84, intermediate prin., 1985—; mem. state adv. panel State Bd. of Edn. Tex., Austin, 1981-82, 83-84; mem. Tex. Tchrs. Practice Commn., Austin, 1982-84; pres. Tex. Classroom Tchrs., 1984-85. Mem. Carthage Book Forum (v.p. 1990—), Panola County C. of C. (bd. dirs. 1990-93, pres. 1993-94), Delta Kappa Gamma (pres. 1994-96). Methodist. Home: 808 University Dr Carthage TX 75633-1338 Office: Carthage Ind Sch Dist 1 Bulldog Dr Carthage TX 75633-2370

THOMPSON, JOSIE, nursing administrator, nurse; b. Ark., Apr. 16, 1949; d. James Andrew and Oneda Fay (Watson) Rhoads; m. Mark O. Thompson, Feb. 14, 1980. Diploma, Lake View Sch. Nursing, 1970; student, Danville C.C., 1974-75, St. Petersburg Jr. Coll., 1979. RN, Ill., Wyo. Staff nurse St. Elizabeth Hosp., Danville, Ill., 1970-78, Osteopathetic Hosp., St. Petersburg, Fla., 1980-81, Wyo. State Hosp., Evanston, 1981-83; staff nurse Wyo. Home Health Care, Rock Springs, 1984—, adminstr., 1986-95; pres. Home Health Care Alliance Wyo., 1991-92; staff nurse Interim Health Care, 1996—. Mem. nursing program adv. bd. Western Wyo. Community Coll.; mem. Coalition for the Elderly, Spl. Needs Com. Sweetwater County, 1992-93. Home: 2704 S Greeley Hwy Cheyenne WY 82007

THOMPSON, JOYCE ELIZABETH, arts management educator; b. Pasadena, Tex., Aug. 15, 1951; d. James Little and Ruth Lake (Skinner) Wilkison; divorced; children: Christine Joy, Cassidy Jane. BA in Psychology, David Lipscomb Coll., 1974; MA in Speech, Theater, Murray State U., 1976; postgrad., U. Tex., 1978; MA in Arts Adminstrn., Ind. U., 1981. Asst. prof. speech Vincennes (Ind.) U., 1976-79; asst. dir. mktg. Hartford (Conn.) Ballet, 1981-82; touring dir. Hartford Ballet/Conn. Opera, 1982-84; exec. dir. Wyo. Arts Coun., Cheyenne, 1984-91, South Snohomish County Arts Coun., Lynwood, Wash., 1991-92; asst. prof. arts mgmt. U. Ill., Springfield, Ill., 1992—; adj. instr., Manchester (Conn.) Cmty. Coll., 1982-84, Chapman Coll., 1990—, Edmonds Cmty. Coll., 1992—; mem. selection com. Coca-Cola Coll., 1992—; mem. selection com. Coca-Cola Scholars Found., 1989, 90, 91, 95. Mem. adv. bd. Cheyenne Little Theatre Players, 1986, Cheyenne Civic Ctr., 1987-88; bd. dirs. Assembly of Ill. Cmty. Arts. Orgns., 1995—. Mem. Assn. Arts Adminstrn. Educators (sec.), Assn. Performing Arts Producers, Speech Comm. Assn., Western States Arts Fedn. (bd. dirs. 1984-91, chair performing arts com. 1985-87), Assn. Arts Adminstrn. Educators (bd. dirs. 1994—). Democrat. Home: 854 S Glenwood Ave Springfield IL 62704-2453 Office: U Ill PAC 370 Springfield IL 62794-9243

THOMPSON, JOYCE LURINE, information systems specialist; b. White Oak Twp., Mich., Mar. 5, 1931; d. Orla Jacob and Ethel Inita (Thayer) Sheathelm; m. Robert E. Thompson, Dec. 10, 1949 (div. 1972); children: Wendy, Robin, Kristen. Student, Mich. State U., 1972-78, Lansing (Mich.) Community Coll, 1976-77. Programmer, analyst Mich. State U., East Lansing, 1966-73; tech. programmer Mich. State Police, East Lansing, 1973-77; database coord. Mich. Dept. Treasury, Lansing, 1977-79; systems engr. 4-Phase Systems, Grand Rapids, Mich., 1979-81; mktg. rep. Motorola, Grand Rapids, 1981-84; data analyst Whirlpool Corp., Benton Harbor, Mich., 1984-88, data adminstr., 1988—; owner, propr. Thompson House, South Haven, Mich., 1994—. Activity chmn. Girl Scouts U.S.A., East Lansing; leader 4-H Clubs, East Lansing; vol. Stepping Stones South Haven, ADA Com., Lake Mich. Maritime Mus. Mildred Erickson fellow Mich. State U., EAst Lansing, 1974-78. Mem. Assn. Systems Mgmt. (sec. 1984), Data Adminstrn. Mgmt. Assn. Office: Whirlpool Corp 2000 N M 63 Hwy Benton Harbor MI 49022

THOMPSON, JUDITH ANN, quality control professional, graphic artist; b. Ridgway, Pa., Nov. 28, 1954; d. John Robert Sr. and Marie Anne (Merat) Miller; m. William James Thompson Sr., May 11, 1986: stepchildren: William Jr., Brandy May. AA in Specialized Tech., Art Inst. Pitts., 1972-74. Cert. statis. process control, Pa. Artist and printer Al's Sign Svc., Erie, Pa., 1974-77; printer Silk Screen Unlimited, Erie, 1977-79; quality control insp. Exotic Metals, Inc., Ridgway, 1979—, Masco Tech. Sintered Components Inc., Ridgway. Editor EMI ECHO, Ridgway, 1990-94.

THOMPSON, JUDITH KASTRUP, nursing researcher; b. Marstal, Denmark, Oct. 1, 1933; came to the U.S., 1951; d. Edward Kastrup and Anna Hansa (Knudsen) Pedersen; m. Richard Frederick Thompson, May 22, 1960; children: Kathryn Marr, Elizabeth Kastrup, Virginia St. Claire. BS, RN, U. Oreg., 1958, MSN, 1963. RN, Calif., Oreg. Staff nurse U. Oreg. Med. Sch., Eugene, 1957-58; staff nurse U. Oreg. Med. Sch., Portland, 1958-61, head staff nurse, 1960-61; instr. psychiat. nursing U. Oreg. Sch. Nursing, Portland, 1963-64; rsch. asst. U. Oreg. Med. Sch., Portland, 1964-65, U. Calif., Irvine, 1971-72; rsch. assoc. Stanford (Calif.) U., 1982-87; rsch. asst. Harvard U., Cambridge, Mass., 1973-74; rsch. assoc. U. So. Calif., L.A., 1987—. Contbg. author: Behavioral Control and Role of Sensory Biofeedback, 1976; contbr. articles to profl. jours. Treas. LWV, Newport Beach, Calif., 1970-74; scout leader Girl Scouts Am., Newport Beach, 1970-78. Named Citizen of Yr. State of Oreg., 1966. Mem. Soc. for Neurosci., Am. Psychol. Soc. (charter), ANA, Oreg. Nurses Assn. Republican. Lutheran. Home: 28 Sky Sail Dr Corona Del Mar CA 92625-1436 Office: U So Calif University Park Los Angeles CA 90089-2520

THOMPSON, JULIA ANN, physicist, educator; b. Little Rock, Mar. 13, 1943; d. Erwin Arthur and Ruth Evelyn (Johnston) T.; m. Patrick A. Thompson, Mar. 22, 1964 (div. 1974); 1 child, Diane E.; m. David E. Kraus, Jr., June 22, 1976; children: Vincent Szewczyk, Larry Lynch. BA, Cornell Coll., Mt. Vernon, Iowa, 1964; MA, Yale U., 1966, PhD, 1969. Research assoc. Brookhaven Lab., Upton, N.Y., 1969-71; research assoc./assoc. instr. U. Utah, Salt Lake City, 1971-72; asst. prof. physics U. Pitts., 1972-78, assoc. prof., 1978-85, prof., 1986—, dir. undergrad. rsch. program, 1992—; mem. users coms. Brookhaven Nat. Lab., 1983-86; condr. expts. Inst. Nuclear Physics, Novosibirsk, USSR, Ctr. Europeene Recherche Nucleaire, Switzerland, Brookhaven Natl. Lab., L.I.; spokesperson hyperon decay expt BNL, 1972-80. Contbr. articles to profl. jours. Bd. dirs. 1st Unitarian Ch., Pitts., 1980-83; zone councillor Soc. Physics Students, 1986-88; with Nat. Acad. Sci. Exch. to USSR, 1989-90. Woodrow Wilson fellow, 1964-65. Mem. Am. Phys. Soc. (com. on status of women in physics 1983-86, exec. com. forum on physics and soc. 1990—). Democrat. Unitarian. Avocations: promoting effective science education, hiking, reading, music. Achievements include research with W.E. Cleland and D.E. Kraus in optical triggering; with the collaboration with AFS and HELIOS expt. in direct photon and lepton production, leading to modified understanding of the gluon function, and limits on anomalous electron production; studies of rare and semi-rare kaon decays.

THOMPSON, LAVERNE ELIZABETH THOMAS, education administration educator; b. Bklyn., July 17, 1945; d. Roscoe Lee and Mary Elizabeth (Blackwell) Thomas. BA in English, Bluffton Coll., 1967; MS in Ednl. Adminstrn./Supervision, U. Dayton, 1977; PhD in Higher Edn., U. Toledo, 1991. Cert. sch. prin., Ohio; cert. secondary sch. supr., Ohio; cert. realtor, Ohio; cert. notary public, Ohio. Instr. English, speech Piqua (Ohio) Cen. High Sch., 1967-68; instr. Lima (Ohio) Sr. High Sch., 1968-77, Shawnee High Sch., Lima, 1977-86; grad. asst. U. Toledo, 1986-91, interim counselor/adminstr. Student Support Svcs., 1989, interim adminstrv. asst. Multicultural Student Devel., 1990; dir. urban tchr. program Wayne County C.C., Detroit, 1996—, program dir. urban tchr. program, 1996—; real estate agt. Alberta Lee Realty, Lima Ohio, 1978-82, Spacey Slonaker Realty , Lima, 1982-84, Gooding Co., Lima, 1985-90; former substitute English tchr., Maumee (Ohio) City Schs., 1996; adj. prof., acad. coord. alternative edn. Spring Arbor Coll., Lambertville, Mich., 1995-96. Editor Higher Edn. newsletter, 1987. Bd. dirs. Lima YWCA, 1971; co-chair Brotherhood Dinner Sr. High Sch., Lima, 1976; participant 17th annual Nat. Conf. on Citizenship, Washington, 1962. Mem. Va. Assn. New Homemakers Am. (state pres. 1962, nat. pres. 1963), Blackwell Family Assn., All God's Children Collectors' Club, Belleek Collectors' Internat. Soc., Sarah's Attic Forever Friends Collectors' Club, Phi Delta Kappa, others. Home: 1038 Valley Grove Dr Maumee OH 43537-3203

THOMPSON, LEA, actress; b. Rochester, Minn., May 31, 1961; m. Howard Deutch. Actress: (films) Jaws 3-D, 1983, All the Right Moves, 1983, The Wild Life, 1984, Red Dawn, 1984, Back to the Future, 1985, Howard the Duck, 1986, Space Camp, 1986, Some Kind of Wonderful, 1987, Casual Sex, 1988, The Wizard of Loneliness, 1988, Going Undercover, 1988, Back to the Future II, 1989, Back to the Future III, 1990, Article 99, 1991, Dennis the Menace, 1993, The Beverly Hillbillies, 1993, The Little Rascals, 1994, The Right to Remain Silent, 1996 (TV movies) Nightbreaker, 1989, Montana, 1990, Stolen Babies, 1993, The Substitute Wife, 1994, The Unspoken Truth, 1995 (TV series) Tales from the Cript, 1989, Robert Wuhl's World Tour, 1990, Caroline in the City, 1995—. Pa. Ballet Co. scholar, Am. Ballet Theatre scholar, San Francisco Ballet scholar. Office: care NBC 3000 W Alameda Blvd Burbank CA 91523 Office: care The Gersh Agency 222 N Cannon Dr Ste 202 Beverly Hills CA 90210*

THOMPSON, LILLIAN HURLBURT, communications company executive; b. Bennington, Vt., Apr. 27, 1947; d. Paul Rhodes and Evelyn Arlene (Lockhart) Hurlburt; m. Wayne Wray Thompson, June 28, 1969. BS, Skidmore Coll., 1969; MS, U. So. Miss., 1975; MBA, George Washington U., 1994. Comm. cons. Southwestern Bell Telephone, San Antonio, 1978-80; acct. exec. C&P Telephone, Washington, 1980-82, Am. Bell, Washington, 1983; staff mgr. AT&T Info. Systems, Rosslyn, Va., 1984; mgr. sales intermediary mktg. dept. Bell Atlantic Corp., Silver Spring, Md., 1984-89, mgr. product line mgmt. dept., 1989-92, mgr. product profitability system fin. dept., 1992-93, mgr. market planning and strategies large bus. svcs. dept., 1993-94; dir. Bell Atlantic Internat., Inc., Arlington, Va., 1994-96; dir. mktg. Belgacom, Brussels, 1996—. Home: 9203 St Marks Pl Fairfax VA 22031-3045 Office: Belgacom, Bd E Jacqmain 177, Brussels B-1030, Belgium

THOMPSON, LINDA SUE HAMILTON, educational counselor; b. Appalachia, Va., Sept. 16, 1950; d. Richard Thomas and Charmie Kate (Cooper) Hamilton; m. Ted Wayne Thompson, Feb. 9, 1973; children: Michelle, Nicole. BA, Clinch Valley Coll., Wise, Va., 1975; MS, Radford (Pa.) Coll., 1989. Cert. elem. and middle sch. counselor and early edn. Home visitor Dileno Wisco, NOrton, Va., 1972-74, early childhood specialist, 1974-75; tchr. Keokee (Va.) Elem. Sch., 1980-81; tchr. J.W. Adams Elem. Sch., Pound, 1981-94, counselor, 1994—. Mem. NEA, Am. Sch. Counselor Assn., Va. Edn. Assn., Va. Counselor Assn. Home: 2541 B Hamilton Pl Big Stone Gap VA 24219 Office: JW Adams Elem PO Box 767 Pound VA 24279

THOMPSON, LOIS JEAN HEIDKE ORE, psychologist; b. Chgo., Feb. 22, 1933; d. Harold William and Ethel Rose (Neumann) Heidke; m. Henry Thomas Ore, Aug. 28, 1954 (div. May 1972); children: Christopher, Douglas; m. Joseph Lippard Thompson, Aug. 3, 1972; children: Scott, Les, Melanie. BA, Cornell Coll., Mt. Vernon, Iowa, 1955; MA, Idaho State U., 1964, EdD, 1981. Lic. psychologist, N.Mex. Tchr. pub. schs. various locations, 1956-67; tchr., instr. Idaho State U., Pocatello, 1967-72; employee/orgn. devel. specialist Los Alamos (N.Mex.) Nat. Lab., 1981-84, tng. specialist, 1984-89, sect. leader, 1989-93; pvt. practice indsl. psychology and healthcare, Los Alamos, 1988—; sec. Cornell Coll. Alumni Office, 1954-55, also other orgns.; bd. dirs. Parent Edn. Ctr., Idaho State U., 1980; counselor, Los Alamos, 1981-88. Editor newsletter LWV, Laramie, Wyo., 1957; contbr. articles to profl. jours. Pres. Newcomers Club, Pocatello, 1967, Faculty Womens Club, Pocatello, 1968; chmn. edn. com. AAUW, Pocatello, 1969. Mem. APA, ACA, N.Mex. Psychol. Assn. (bd. dirs. divsn. II 1990, sec. 1988-90, chmn. 1990), N.Mex. Soc. Adlerian Psychology (pres. 1990, treas. 1991-95, bd. dirs. 1996—), Soc. Indsl. and Orgn. Psychology, Assn. for Adult Devel. and Aging. Mem. LDS Ch. Home and Office: 340 Aragon Ave Los Alamos NM 87544-3505

THOMPSON, LYNN KATHRYN SINGER, educational director; b. Ames, Iowa, Nov. 30, 1947; d. William Andrew and Virginia Preston (Russell) Singer. BA, Cornell Coll., Mt. Vernon, Iowa, 1970; MA in Edn., Ariz. State U., 1980; EdD, No. Ariz. U., 1990. Cert. tchr. and adminstr., Ariz. Tchr. Crane Elem. Dist., Yuma, Ariz., 1970-81, 86-90; coord. fed. programs Crane Elem Dist., Yuma, Azri., 1981-83, asst. prin., 1983-85, dir. lang. acquisition and fed. programs, 1990—. Bd. dirs. Zonta Internat., Yuma, 1991, Yuma Fine Arts Assn., 1982-84; mem. Ariz. State Com. Practitioners, Phoenix, 1994—. Recipient Golden Bell award Ariz. Sch. Bds. Assn., 1992; Delta Kappa Gamma scholar, 1987, 89. Mem. PEO Internat., Delta Kappa Gamma (pres. 1988-90), Phi Delta Kappa (bd. dirs., rsch. chair 1991-95). Office: Crane Elem Dist 4250 W 16th St Yuma AZ 85364-4031

THOMPSON, MARCIA GEHRING, art educator; b. Urbana, Ill., June 7, 1947; d. Duane Glen and Jeanette (Thomas) Gehring; m. Richard Charles Thompson, Dec. 16, 1967; children: Amanda Camille, Gunnar Charles. BS, Winona (Minn.) State U., 1976; MEd in Profl. Devel., U. Wis., LaCross, 1990. Art coord. LaCrescent (Minn.) Sch. Dist., 1977-80; art instr. West Salem (Wis.) Sch. Dist., 1980—, Viterbo Coll., LaCrosse, 1992—; cons. Wis. Arts Bd., Madison, 1993-95, Artist Tchr. Inst., Madison, 1994, various sch. dists., 1993-95. Exhibited in group exhbns. at Kappa Pi All Campus Art Show, 1976 (Best of Show 1976), Rochester Cmty. Coll. Fibers Exhibit, 1976, Wis. Art Edn. Juried Exhibit, 1994. Mem. West Salem Hist. Soc., 1981—. Mem. Wis. Art Edn. Assn. (mid. sch. rep. 1988-95), Nat. Art Edn. Assn., Wis. Assn. of Mid. Level Educators (grantee 1994). Home: W5380 Innsbruck Rd West Salem WI 54669 Office: West Salem Mid Sch 450 N Mark St West Salem WI 54669

THOMPSON, MARCIA SLONE, choral director, educator; b. Ary, Ky., June 30, 1959; d. Ray and Wevena (Hall) Slone; m. Randall C. Thompson, Sept. 22, 1979; children: Tiffany, Ashley, Brittany, Alicia, Jessica, Matthew. B in Music Edn., Pikeville Coll., 1981; M in Secondary Edn., Morehead State U., 1985. Cert. Rank I supervision, music edn. tchr. with endorsement, grades K-12. Guitarist Slone Family Band, 1970-77; pvt. practice Hindman, Ky., 1977-93; band, choral dir. Pike County Bd. Edn., Pikeville, Ky., 1981-82, Floyd County Bd. Edn., Eastern, Ky., 1982-87; choral dir. Knott County Bd. Edn., Hindman, 1987—, Knott County Central High, Hindman, Ky, 1987—; piano instr. guitar instr., Upward Bound program Pikeville Coll., Hindman, 1977. Albums include Appalachian Bluegrass, 1972, Ramblin' Round with Slone Family, 1977; appeared on the Grand Ole Opry, 1976. Band conductor jr. high divsn. Pike County All-County Festival, Pikeville, 1981; music chair Red White Blue Festival, Martin, Ky., 1982; music judge Floyd County All-County Band, Prestonsburg, Ky., 1982-87; band dir. Ky. Derby Festival Parade, Louisville, 1985; piano accompanist choir 1st Bapt. Ch., Hindman, 1990-91, nursery asst., 1990-93, dir. youth choir, 1992, choral dir. music makers (children's music), 1994, Bapt. young women's hospitality officer, 1995, mem. sch. com.; performer Senator Benny Bailey Salute, Prestonsburg, 1991, Gingerbread Festival, Hindman, 1992-95; active Bapt. Young Women, 1993-95; co-founder Knott County Fine Arts Day Celebration, 1992—, hospitality officer Hindman Baptist Ch. Young Women's Group, 1995. Mem. Nat. Educators Assn., Am. Choral Dirs. Assn., Ky. Educators Assn., Ky. Music Educators. Democrat. Home: PO Box 15 Hindman KY 41822-0015 Office: Knott County Ctrl High Sch Hindman KY 41822

THOMPSON, MARGARET LOUISE, elementary school educator, writer, consultant; b. Meridian, Okla., Jan. 11, 1945; d. Leroy Parrish and Erma Lee Smith; m. Albert Marion Thompson Jr., Nov. 26, 1966; children: Sean Lamar, Albert Marion III. BS in Edn., Langston U., 1966; MA in Elem. Edn., Vanderbilt U., 1973. Cert. early childhood edn. tchr., Ga. Home econs. tchr. Custer H.S., Milw., 1966-67; pre-sch. tchr. Demonstration and Rsch. Ctr. for Early Edn., Nashville, 1971-74; kindergarten tchr. Edward A. White Sch., Ft. Benning, Ga., 1975-82, Teasley Elem., Smyrna, Ga., 1982-86, East Side Elem. Sch., Marietta, Ga., 1986-90, Timber Ridge Elem. Sch., Marietta, Ga., 1990—; presenter ednl. leadership conf. Cobb County, Marietta, 1985; presenter kindergarten kaleidoscope Met. Coun. Early Childhood Edn., Atlanta, 1987-90; presenter early childhood conf. Ga. Assn. Educators of Young Children, Savannah, 1990; presenter Savannah-Chatham Pub. Schs., 1990; student tchr. supr. East Side Elem. Sch., Marietta, 1987-89. Author: A Game Plan for the Alphabet, 1989, Number Jamboree, 1990, A Little Smalltalk, 1991. Mem. Aux. to Atlanta Med. Assn., 1986-90; mem. North Suburban Atlanta chpt. of Jack and Jill, Marietta, 1985-93. Recipient 1st pl. Instrnl. Fair Cobb County, 1984-85. Mem. Ga. Coun. Tchrs. English (presenter 1990-94), Edn. Dealers and Suppliers Assn. Democrat. Baptist. Home: 4774 Hampton Lake Dr Marietta GA 30068-4305 Office: Timber Ridge Elem Sch 5000 Timber Ridge Rd Marietta GA 30068-1533

THOMPSON, MARGUERITE MYRTLE GRAMING (MRS. RALPH B. THOMPSON), librarian; b. Orangeburg, S.C., Apr. 23, 1912; d. Thomas Laurie and Rosa Lee (Stroman) Graming; m. Ralph B. Thompson, Sept. 17, 1949 (dec. Oct. 1960). BA in English cum laude, U. S.C., 1932, postgrad., 1937; BLS, Emory U., 1943. Tchr. English pub. high schs., S.C., 1932-43; libr. Rockingham (N.C.) High Sch., 1943-45, Randolph County (N.C.) Libr., Asheboro, 1945-48, Colleton County (S.C.) Libr., Walterboro, 1948-61; dir. Florence (S.C.) County Libr., 1961-78. Sec. com. community facilities, svcs. and instns. Florence County Resources Devel. Com., 1964-67; vice chmn. Florence County Coun. on Aging, 1968-70, exec. bd. 1968-82, bd. treas., 1973-75, bd. sec., 1976-77, bd. v.p., 1979; mem. Florence County Bicentennial Planning Com., 1975-76; mem. rels. and allocations com. United Way, 1979-80. Named Boss of Yr. Nat. Secs. Assn., 1971. Mem. ALA (coun. 1964-72), Southeastern Libr. Assn., S.C. Libr. Assn. (pres. 1960, chmn. assn. handbook revision com. 1967-69, 80, sect. co-chmn. com. standards for S.C. pub. librs. 1966-75, fed. rels. coord. 1972-73, planning com. 1976-78), Greater Florence C. of C. (women's div. chmn. 1969-70, bd. dirs. 1975-77), S.E. Regional Conf. Women in C. of C. (bd. dir. 1970-71), Florence Bus. and Profl. Women's Club (2d v.p. 1975-76, Career Woman of Yr. 1974, parliamentarian 1980-81, chmn. scholarship com. 1981-82), Delta Kappa Gamma (county chpt. charter pres. 1963-65, treas. 1966-70, chmn. com. on expansion 1977-80, 82-84, state chpt. chmn. state scholarship com. 1967-73, state 2d v.p. 1971-73, state 1st v.p. 1973-75, state pres. 1975-77, chmn. policy manual 1977-81, chmn. adv. coun. 1978-85, chmn. fin. com. 1981-83, parliamentarian 1987-91, adminstrv. bd. 1987—, chmn. nominations com. 1989-91, dir. S.E. Region 1978-80, coord. S.E. Regional Golden Anniversary Conf. 1979, internat. scholarship com. 1970-74, internat. exec. bd. 1975-77, 78-80, internat. adminstrv. bd. 1978-80, internat. constn. com. 1980-82, internat. achievement award com., 1986-88), Florence Literary Club (sec. 1964-66, 79-82, pres. 1970-72). Methodist (chmn. ch. libr. com. 1965-71, chm. ch. history, 1968-69, sec. adminstrv. bd. 1979-82). Home: 1000 Live Oaks Dr SW # 8B Orangeburg SC 29115-9600

THOMPSON, MARI HILDENBRAND, medical staff services professional; b. Washington, Apr. 26, 1951; d. Emil John Christopher Hildenbrand and Ada Lythe (Conklin) Hildenbrand-Kammer; m. R. Marshall Thompson, Sept. 27, 1970 (div. June 1981); 1 child, Jeremy Marshall. BA in Secondary Edn., Am. U., 1976, BA in Performing Arts, 1976. Cert. med. staff coord.; cert. profl. credentialing specialist. Employment interviewer Scripps Meml. Hosp., La Jolla, Calif., 1977-81; office mgr. Jacksina & Freedman Press Office, N.Y.C., 1982-83; staffing coord., med. staff asst. Am. Med. Internat. Clairemont Hosp., San Diego, 1983-85; adminstrv. asst. Am. Med. Internat. Valley Med. Ctr., El Cajon, Calif., 1985-88; med. staff coord. Sharp Meml. Hosp., San Diego, 1988-92; adminstrv. asst. Grossmont Hosp., La Mesa, Calif., 1992-93, coord. Sharp family practice residency program, 1993-94; ops. coord. Sharp Meml. Hosp. med. staff svcs., San Diego, 1994—; wardrobe mistress various community theatres, San Diego, 1978-79, actress, San Diego, 1979-81. Appeared N.Y.C. (N.Y.) Playreaders Group, 1981-83, N.J. Shakespeare Theatre, Madison, 1982, Good Humor Improv Co., N.Y.C., 1982-83; contbg. writer to Poetry Revival: An Anthology, 1994. Mem. NOW, 1995, World Wildlife Fedn., Calif., 1991, Greenpeace, Calif., 1991, Sierra Club, Calif., 1991, 92, Audubon Soc., Calif., 1991, 92, Internat. Wildlife Fedn., 1992, Smithsonian, 1993, 94, Dem. Nat. Com., 1996. Included in Outstanding Young Women of Am., 1986. Mem. NAFE, AFTRA, Nat. Assn. Med. Staff Svcs., Calif. Assn. Med. Staff Svcs., San Diego Assn. Med. Staff, Nat. Assn. Health Care Quality, Assn. Family Practice Adminstrs. Democrat. Home: 7951 Beaver Lake Dr San Diego CA 92119-2610

THOMPSON, MARY EILEEN, chemistry educator; b. Mpls., Dec. 21, 1928; d. Albert C. and Blanche (McAvoy) T. B.A., Coll. St. Catherine, 1953; M.S., U. Minn., 1958; Ph.D., U. Calif.-Berkeley, 1964. Math. and sci. tchr. Derham Hall High Sch., St. Paul, 1953-58; faculty Coll. St. Catherine, St. Paul, 1964—, prof., chmn. dept. chemistry, 1969-90; project dir. Women in Chemistry, 1984—. Contbr. articles to profl. jours. Mem. Am. Chem. Soc. (chair women chemists com. 1992-94), Coun. Undergrad. Rsch. (councilor 1991—), N.Y. Acad. Sci., Chem. Soc. London, AAAS, Sigma Xi, Phi Beta Kappa. Democrat. Roman Catholic. Achievements include research interests in Cr(III) hydrolytic polymers, kinetics of inorganic complexes, Co(III) peroxo/superoxo complexes. Office: Coll St Catherine 2004 Randolph Ave Saint Paul MN 55105-1750

THOMPSON, MARY KOLETA, sculptor, non-profit organization director; b. Portsmouth, Va., Dec. 27, 1938; m. James Burton Thompson, May 5, 1957; children: Burt, Suzan, Kate, Jon. BFA, U. Tex., 1982; postgrad., Boston U. Cert. fund raising exec. Pres. The Planning Resource People, Austin, Tex., 1990—; Tex. fin. devel. specialist ARC Tex., 1994—; devel. dir. Very Spl. Arts Tex., 1991-92; dir. devel. ARC, Austin, 1992-94; dir. Tex. Children's Mus., Fredericksburg, 1987-88, Internat. Hdqrs. SHAPE Command Arts and Crafts Ctr., 1985-86; com. chmn. Symposium for Encouragement Women in Math. and Natural Sci., U. Tex., Austin, 1990. Sculptor portrait busts. Bd. dirs. Teenage Parent Coun., Austin, 1990-92. Named U.S. Vol. of Yr., Belgium, 1986; grantee NEA, 1988. Mem. AAUW (life, pres. 1990-92), Women in Comm. (co-chmn. S.W. regional conf.), U. Tex. Ex-Student Assn. (life), Tex. Hist. Found. (life), Leadership Tex. (life), Leadership Tex. Alumnae Assn. (bd. dirs.), Raleigh Tavern Soc. (founder), Austin Antiques Forum (founder). Office: San Antonio Area Chpt ARC 3642 E Houston St San Antonio TX 78219-3818

THOMPSON, MILDRED COLLINS, retired educator; b. DeQuincy, La., Mar. 28, 1918; d. Thomas Avery and Cleo Deane (Boyd) Collins; m. William Carey Thompson Jr., Sept. 5, 1942; children: Barbara D. Pritchard, Marilyn L. Laville, William C. III, David T. BS in Edn., Pittsburg (Kans.) State Coll., 1939; MA in Counseling and Guidance, N.Mex. State U., 1964, cert. reading specialist, 1970. Home econs. tchr. Coats (Kans.) Pub. Sch., 1939, Pittsburg Pub. Schs., 1939-42; home econs. tchr. Artesia (N.Mex.) Pub. Schs., 1954-63, sch. counselor, 1963-66; sch. counselor Santa Fe (N.Mex.) Pub. Schs., 1966-70, reading specialist, 1970-80; French tapestry weaver Albuquerque, 1991—; tchr. French Aubusson tapestry weaving Village Wools, Albuquerque, 1993-95. Exhibited tapestries in one-person shows, including Tapestry Gallery, Madrid, N.Mex., 1993. Demonstrate tapestry making N.Mex. State Fair, Albuquerque, 1991-95; asst. tchr. weaving Albuquerque Pub. Schs., 1996; vol. Albuquerque Children's Mus., 1994-95, Am. Lung Assn., Am. Heart Assn., March of Dimes, Albuquerque, 1992-95. Mem. Intermountain Weaving Assn., Am. Tapestry Alliance, Nat. Mus. Women in

Arts (assoc.). Republican. Methodist. Home: 1829 Chandelle Loop NE Albuquerque NM 87112

THOMPSON, MILDRED PURNELL, adminstrative assistant; b. Balt., Sept. 27, 1933; d. Fernando Nicholas and Elsie Virginia (Coates) Madison; m. Ernest Leonard Thompson, Nov. 28, 1952 (dec. Jan 1994); children: Agnes, Mary, Ernest, Jerome, Karen, Fernando. AA in Early Childhood Edn., C.C. Balt., 1974. Cert. notary pub. Tchr.'s asst. Dept. Edn., Balt., 1968-74; sec. Citizens for Washington Hill, Balt., 1974-91, bookkeeper, 1991-96; adminstrv. asst. South East Cmty. Orgn. Head Start, Balt., 1991—. Election judge, Balt., 1968-92; vol. Balt. City Fair, 1971-84, Pier 6 Concert Pavilion, Balt., 1986-91; panel mem. Fund for Arts in Neighborhoods, Balt., 1979-84. Recipient Presdl. citation Balt. City Coun., 1991, Citizen's citation Balt. City, 1991, Mayor's citation Balt. City, 1992. Democrat. Baptist.

THOMPSON, NANCI CUSHING, accountant, charter boat captain; b. Weymouth, Mass., July 26, 1945; d. Karl Pyam and Yvonne Francoise (Taylor) Cushing; m. Clyde Carlisle Twitchell, Jr., Apr. 4, 1964 (div. Oct. 1986); children: Karl Pyam, Brian Kenneth; m. Michael Joseph Thompson, Feb. 15, 1992. Grad. high sch., Braintree, Mass. Owner Acctg. Etc., Elkton, Md., 1965—; co-owner Sol y Paz Charters, Elkton, 1993—. Chmn. Hull (Mass.) Pub. Safety Bldg. Adv. Com., 1987-91. Recipient plaque Cohasset (Mass.) Permanent Firefighters, 1989. Mem. Cecil County C. of C. Office: Acctg Etc 104 Mitchell St Elkton MD 21921

THOMPSON, NANCY JEAN, home furnishings executive; b. Stillwater, Okla., July 25, 1954; d. Ramon D. and Jean (Ward) Prohaska; m. Noel David Thompson, Sept. 1, 1976; children: Alexander, Maximilian. BFA, Skidmore Coll., 1976; multimedia design cert., NYU, 1995. Exec. trainee Saks Fifth Ave., N.Y.C., 1976-78; mgr. Saks Fifth Ave., Chgo., 1978-79; buyer Wieboldt's, Chgo., 1979-81, Marine Corps Exchange Svc., Quantico, Va., 1981-82; sales mgr. mil. and spl. markets Loew's Corp./Bulova, Woodside, N.Y., 1982-88; v.p. home div. R.C. Staff/Milan, N.Y.C., 1988-90; buyer Lynn Hollyn Madison Ave.-Itokin/Japan-Space Creation, N.Y.C., 1990-91; product devel. Am. Pacific, Enterprise, N.Y.C., 1991; prin. Nancy Thompson, Design, Licensing & Mktg., Ltd., N.Y.C., 1992—; cons. to textile, furniture, retail industries in product devel., licensing, multimedia mktg. Group leader Ridgewood-Glen Rock Coun. Boy Scouts Am. Mem. NAFE, DAR, Internat. Furnishings and Design Assn., Hoboken Creative Alliance, Fashion Group N.Y.C. Episcopalian.

THOMPSON, NOVELLA WOODRUM, college administrator, psychotherapist; b. Frankfort, Germany, Apr. 24, 1968; d. Gary Lynn and Kaye Yvonne (Hickman) Woodrum; m. Philip Drew Thompson, Nov. 12, 1994. BA, W.Va. Wesleyan Coll., Buckhannon, 1992; MA, W.Va. Grad. Coll., Institute, 1994. Counselor, parent educator The Family Ctr., Inc., Beckley, W.Va., 1993; counselor Women's Resource Ctr., Beckley, 1993-94; psychotherapist The Family Inst. of W.Va., Beckley, 1994-95; dir. Sch. Acad. Enrichment & Lifelong Learning Coll. W.Va., Beckley, 1995—; guest lectr. W.Va. Grad. Coll., 1994-95; vol. counselor Women's Resource Ctr., Beckley, 1992-93; cons. non-traditional programs Coll. WVa., Beckley, 1995; parent educator & lectr. The Family Ctr. Raleigh County Cmty. Alliance Assn., 1994—. Mem. bd. dirs. The Family Ctr., Beckley, 1993; panelist, speaker Stop Child Abuse Now (SCAN), Beckley, 1994. Recognized for Cmty. Svc., Register-Herald "A Celebration of Women." Mem. ACA, W.Va. Counseling Assn., W.Va. Assn. for Specialists in Group Work, Coun. for Adult and Exptl. Learning (state rep. 1996). Home: 1500 Harper Rd Beckley WV 25801 Office: Coll WVa PO Box AG Beckley WV 25802

THOMPSON, PATRICIA A., lawyer; b. Waco, Tex., Apr. 28, 1952; d. George R. and Thelma M. (Franco) T.; m. Neil H. Korbas, Apr. 23, 1993. BA, Wash. State U., 1974; JD, St. Mary's U., 1977. Bar: Wash. 1978. From juvenile dep. to dep. prosecuting atty. Spokane County, Wash., 1978—. Bd. dirs. Northeast Wash. Treatment Alternatives, Spokane, 1985—, Spokane County Domestic Violence Consortium, 1994—. Mem. Am. Bus. Women's Assn. (pres., sec. 1982—, woman of yr. 1986), Catholic Bus. & Profl. Women (sec. 1988—), Action Women's Exch. (treas. 1994—), Sacred Heart Parish Coun. Roman Catholic. Home: 4111 S Perry Spokane WA 99203 Office: Spokane County Prosecutor 1100 W Mallon Spokane WA 99260

THOMPSON, PATRICIA ANN, horse owner and breeder; b. Dayton, Ohio, July 16, 1934; d. Neil James and Esther Rita (O'Connor) Curry; m. James Francis Thompson, Dec. 27, 1958. BS, U. So. Calif., 1956. Horse owner and breeder Ridgeley Farm, San Jacinto, 1956—. Mem. Calif. Thoroughbred Breeders Assn. (dir. 1987-95, sec. 1988, v.p. 1989-90, sec. 1991, 95), Horseman's Benevolent and Protective Assn. (dir. 1986-88). Office: Ridgeley Farm 37167 Esplanade Ave San Jacinto CA 92582-3769

THOMPSON, PATRICIA RATHER, English educator, department chair; b. Houston, Nov. 27, 1939; d. Daniel Irvin and Veda Byrl (Page) R.; m. Bobby Dean Thompson, Sept. 3, 1960; children: Troy, Byron, Mark. BA, Sam Houston State U., 1962, MA, 1980. Tchr. Houston Ind. Sch. Dist., 1962-65; tchr., dept. chair Klein (Tex.) Ind. Sch. Dist., 1980—; tchr. North Harris Montgomery County C.C., Conroe, Tex., 1993-96; writing cons., Spring, Tex., 1990—. Contbr. poetry to profl. jours. Mem. ASCD, Tex. Gifted and Talented, Tex. State Tchrs. English, North Harris County Tchrs. English. Home: 210 Shannondale Spring TX 77388 Office: Klein High Sch 16715 Stuebner Airline Klein TX 77379

THOMPSON, PHYLLIS D., lawyer; b. Washington, Oct. 1, 1952. BA, George Washington U., 1974, JD with high honors, 1981; MA, Princeton U., 1976. Bar: D.C. 1981. Instr., lectr. Georgetown U., Washington, 1977-81; ptnr. Covington & Burling, Washington. Mem. D.C. Bar Assn. (steering com. affairs divsn.). Office: Covington & Burling 1201 Pennsylvania Ave NW PO Box 7566 Washington DC 20044-7566*

THOMPSON, PHYLLIS DARLENE, elementary education educator; b. West Milton, Ohio, May 21, 1934; d. Howard Luther and Dorothy Mae (Heisey) Yount; m. Joel Kent Thompson, Aug. 22, 1954 (div. Feb. 1981); children: George Kevin, Jolanna Renee, Howard Kraig. BS in Edn., Manchester Coll., 1956; MEd, LaVerne U., 1977. Cert. tchr., Ill. Tchr. Dist. 83, North Lake, Ill., 1956-59; missionary, tchr. Ambon (Indonesia) U., 1961-62; tchr. Dist. Unit 46, Elgin, Ill., 1969—; organizer Mother Goose Day Care Ctr., Elgin, 1970s. Choir mem. Highland Ave Ch. of the Brethren, Elgin, 1964—, bd. chairperson, 1980-83. Recipient Ednl. Excellence award State Bd. Edn., 1978. Mem. NEA, Ill. Edn. Assn., Elgin Tchrs. Assn. (bldg. rep. 1994-96), Alpha Delta Kappa (pres., v.p., sec. 1972—). Democrat. Home: 11 Kensington Loop Elgin IL 60123

THOMPSON, ROBYN SUE, investment company executive; b. Pitts., Jan. 15, 1964; d. James H. and Lois Ann (Cosgrove) T. BA cum laude, Bethany Coll., 1985. Internal sales Federated Investors, Pitts., 1986-87, acct. adminstr., 1987-88, sr. acct. adminstr., 1988-92, client cons., 1992-95, sr. product mgr., 1995—. Mem. Nat. Assn. Exec. Woman. Republican. Episcopalian. Home: 327 Murrays Ln Pittsburgh PA 15234 Office: Federated Investors 1001 Liberty Ave 23rd Fl Pittsburgh PA 15222

THOMPSON, RONELLE KAY HILDEBRANDT, library director; b. Brookings, S.D., Apr. 21, 1954; d. Earl E. and Maxine R. (Taplin) Hildebrandt; m. Harry Floyd Thompson II, Dec. 24, 1976; children: Clarissa, Harry III. BA in Humanities magna cum laude, Houghton Coll., 1976; MLS, Syracuse U., 1976; postgrad., U. Rochester, 1980, 81; cert., Miami U., 1990. Libr. asst. Norwalk (Conn.) Pub. Libr., 1977; elem. libr. Moriah Cen. Schs., Port Henry, N.Y., 1977-78; div. coord. pediatric gastroenterology and nutrition U. Rochester (N.Y.) Med. Ctr., 1978-81, cons., mem. pediatric housestaff libr. com., 1980-81; dir. Medford Libr. U. S.C., Lancaster, 1981-83; dir. Mikkelsen Libr., Libr. Assocs., Ctr. for Western Studies, mem. acad. computing com., libr. com. Augustana Coll., Sioux Falls, S.D., 1983—, mem. adminstrv. pers. coun., 1989-94; presenter in field. Contbr. articles to profl. jours. Mem. adv. com. S.D. Libr. Network, 1986—, chair, 1989-91, 94—; mem. Sioux Falls Community Playhouse, S.D. Symphony, Sioux Falls Civic Fine Arts Assn.; advisor Minnehana County Libr., pers. dept. City of Sioux Falls. Named one of Outstanding Young Women Am., 1983; Syracuse U. Gaylord Co. scholar, 1976; recipient YWCA leader award, 1991. Mem. ALA, AAUW, Assn. Coll. and Rsch. Librs. (nat. adv. coun. coll. librs. sect. 1987—), Mountain Plains Libr. Assn. (chair acad. sect., nominating com. 1988, pres. 1993-94), S.D. Libr. Assn. (chair interlibr. coop. task force 1986-87, pres. 1987-88, chair recommended minimum salary task force 1988, chair local arrangements com. 1989-90), S.D. Libr. Network (adv. coun. 1986—, exec. com. 1992—, chair adv. coun. 1994—). Office: Augustana Coll Mikkelsen Libr 29th & Summit Sioux Falls SD 57197

THOMPSON, SALLY ANN, newspaper editor; b. Hillsboro, N.D., Apr. 10, 1943; d. C. Hilman and Blanche E. (Bjerkan) Swenson; m. Arthur G. Thompson, July 1, 1965 (dec. Mar. 1990); 1 child, Laurie Kate Beth. Student, Concordia Coll., Moorhead, Minn., 1961-65. Reporter The Valley Journal, Halstad, Minn., 1979-84; contbg. editor Prairie West Publs., Wahpeton, N.D., 1982-84; editor Hillsboro Banner, Hillsboro, N.D., 1984-95, Plymouth Sun-Sailer, Minn. Sun Publs., Minnetonka, Minn., 1995—; lectr. Career Day Mayville State U., N.D., 1985-92. Mem. commns. com. Ea. N.D. Synod ELCA, 1990-93; bd. dirs. Traill County Hist. Soc., 1979-95, Hillsboro Forestry Bd., 1990-93. Recipient numerous journalism awards. Lutheran. Home: 1805 Hwy 101 N #203 Plymouth MN 55447 Office: Minn Sun Publs 4785 S Hwy 101 Minnetonka MN 55345

THOMPSON, SALLY ENGSTROM, state official; b. Spokane, Wash., Feb. 17, 1940; d. Logan C. and Ava Leigh (Phillips) Engstrom; m. Donald Edward Colcun, 1981; children: Lauri Thompson, Tom Thompson, Tami Thompson, Sheri Colcun Trumpfheller. BS magna cum laude, U. Colo., 1975. CPA, Colo. 1976, Kans. 1986. Audit mgr. and mgmt. cons. Touche Ross & Co., Denver, 1975-82; v.p., mgr. planning and fin. analysis United Bank, Denver, 1982-85; pres., chief oper. officer Shawnee Fed. Svgs., Topeka, 1985-90; treas. State of Kans., 1990—. Past editorial advisor New Accountant mag. Bd. dirs. Everywoman's Resource Ctr., Topeka, 1988-92, Community Svc. Found. Kans., Kids Voting Kans. (hon.); v.p., bd. dirs. Downtown Topeka Inc., YWCA, Topeka, 1986-93, Woman of Achievement award, 1984; mem. fin. com. Girl Scouts U.S., Kaw Valley, various coms., United Way of Greater Topeka; chmn. art auction com. KTWU-TV, summer concert, Topeka Civic Theatre. Recipient Disting. Community Leadership award Topeka Pub. Schs., 1989, Disting. Leadership award Nat. Assn. Community Leadership, 1991, 1991 Class Leadership Kans. Mem. AICPAs, Am. Soc. Women Accts., Kans. Soc. CPAs, Kansas C. of C. and Industry, Greater Topeka C. of C. (bd. dirs. 1989-92), Emporia State U. Bus. Sch. Adv. Bd., Nat. Assn. State Auditors, Controllers and Treas., Nat. Assn. State Treas. (v.p., Midwest regional chair), Women Execs. in Govt., Beta Alpha Psi. Democrat. Offices: Office State Treasurer Landon State Office Bldg 900 SW Jackson St Ste 201N Topeka KS 66612-1220*

THOMPSON, SANDY MARIA, health and staff development coordinator; b. Ballston Spa, N.Y., May 3, 1953; d. George Andrew and Dorothy (Cooper) Simpson; m. John Michael Thompson, Jr., June 10, 1972; children: John, Matthew, Katie. ADN, No. Va. C.C., 1974; BSN, George Mason U., 1985, MSN, 1990. RN, Va. Staff RN No. Va. Doctors Hosp., Arlington, Va., 1974-84; sch. nurse Alexandria (Va.) City Pub. Schs., 1985-89; health and staff devel. coord. City of Manassas (Va.) Pub. Schs., 1989—; planner for cmty. summit The Changing Manassas Cmty. Steering Com., 1994; chairperson health adv. bd. City of Manassas Sch., 1992-94, numerous other coms. Author: (with others) Virginia School Health Guidelines, 1992, (booklet) First Aid for School Emergencies, 1991. Recipient Nurses Make a Difference award Am. Orgn. of Nurse Execs. and Am. Hosp. Assn., 1988, Outstanding Contbn. award City of Manassas, 1994. Mem. Va. Sch. Nurse Assn. (sec. 1988-89, dir. area 1 1990-91). Roman Catholic. Home: 11951 Shenandoah Ct Woodbridge VA 22192-1308 Office: City of Manassas Pub Schs 9000 Tudor Ln Manassas VA 22110-5700

THOMPSON, SARAH, artist; b. Lake Charles, La., Nov. 27, 1954; d. John Roland and Doris Virginia (Harrell) T. BFA, La. State U., 1978; MFA, U. Wash., 1981; studied with Jacob Lawrence. Instr. painting and drawing U. Wash. Extension, Seattle, 1984-92; acting curator of edn. Tacoma (Wash.) Art Mus., 1990; artist-tchr. MFA in Visual Arts Program, Vt. Coll., Norwich, 1991-94; interpreter African Art Seattle Art Mus., 1995—; Solo exhbns. include Metropolis Contemporary Art Gallery, Seattle, 1995, Art Bar, Seattle, 1995, Take 2, Seattle, 1995, Merlino Art Ctr., Tacoma, 1991, Imogen Cunningham Gallery, U. Wash., 1989, Hartness/Schoos Galleries, Seattle, 1988, Elliot Bay Book Co., Seattle, 1987, King County Arts Commn. Gallery, Seattle, 1985, Pelican Bay Cooperative Gallery, Seattle, 1982, Foster Gallery, La. State U., 1978, 77; group exhbns. include Benjamin Falk Gallery, Napa, Calif., 1995, Metropolis Contemporary Art Gallery, 1994, Bumbershoot Arts Festival, 1993, N.W. Internat. Art Competitions/Whatcom Mus. of history and Art, 1987, 92, numerous others; work collected in The Weltzien Family Collection, Camano Island, Wash., The New Orleans Restaurant, Seattle, Washington State Art in Pub. Place Collection, Morehead State U. Sch. of Art, Morehead, Ky., Harborview Med. Ctr., Seattle, numerous others. Contbr. photos/art to profl. jours. and newspapers. Recipient Artist award Artist Trust Ann. Auction, Seattle, 1995, City of Renton Ann. awards, Wash., 1985, 87, 89, Artist award 42nd Pacific N.W. Arts and Crafts Fair, Bellevue Art Mus., 1988; fellow in painting, Vt. Studio Colony, Johnson, Vt., 1988; grantee Ford Found., U. Wash., 1979, 80, others. Mem. Coll. Art Assn. of Am., Pacific Northwest Arts Coun., Founds. in Art: Theory and Edn., Contemporary Art Coun./Seattle Art Mus. Democrat. Unitarian.

THOMPSON, SHIRLEY J., public relations executive. Co-founder Carl Thompson Assocs., Boulder, Colo., 1985, sr. account exec., 1989-90, v.p., 1990-91, sr. v.p., 1991, pres., 1991—. Recipient Golden Quill award IABC. Mem. NIRI. Office: Carl Thompson Assocs 75 Manhattan Dr Ste 205 Boulder CO 80303-4252*

THOMPSON, SUE WANDA, small business owner; b. Azle, Tex., Nov. 26, 1935; d. Weldon W. Beasley and Eula Mae Hardee; m. William Henry Clark, Feb. 20, 1952 (div. 1959); children: Gloria, Russ, Bonnie; m. Robert L. Thompson Jr., Sept. 20, 1963; stepchildren: Christene, Lee. Nurse Harris Hosp., Ft. Worth, 1960-62, Denton State Sch., 1962-63; owner, v.p. Dalworth Med. Labs., Ft. Worth, 1963-68; sales leader, trainer Home Interior and Gifts, Dallas, 1970-80; owner, pres. Thompson Enterprises, 1980—; mgr., trainer Jafra Cosmetics, West Lake Village, Calif., 1981-84, Jewels by Park Lane, Chgo., 1984-89, Just Am., Rutlerfordton, N.C., 1989-91; with sales Dyna Tech Nutritionals, Willston Park, N.Y., 1993-94. Dir. parks and recreation City Forest Hills, Tex., 1970. Mem. Beta Sigma Phi (treas. Eta Lambda chpt. 1971-72, pres. 1972-73, Girl of Yr. 1974). Republican. Mem. Ch. Nazarene. Home: 4717 Applewood Rd Fort Worth TX 76133-7435

THOMPSON, SUSAN ROBERTA, magazine publishing executive; b. Englewood, N.J., Mar. 14, 1949; d. Herbert Gustav and Sarah Jeanette (Black) Goeckel; m. Tommy Thompson, May 1, 1971; children: Jordan, Mark. BA in journalism, Ga. State U., 1979. Charter airline trip coord. Atlanta Skylarks, 1971-75; advt. exec. McDonald & Little Adv., Atlanta, 1980-84, Advantage Mktg., Atlanta, 1984-86; bus. owner, mag. pub. New South Pub., Atlanta, 1986—. Editor: Know Atlanta mag., 1989, Net News mag., 1992. Publicity mem. Gubernatorial campaign, Atlanta, 1989; publicity com. Decorator's Showhouse Atlanta Symphony Jr. Com., Atlanta, 1986-92. Mem. Ga. Mag. Assn. (pres. 1994-95), Metro Atlanta Relocation Coun. (pres. 1992), Atlanta C. of C., Greater Atlanta Home Builders Assn. (sales and mktg. coun., bd. dirs. 1988-93), Cob C. of C. Republican. Methodist. Home: 5071 Hampton Lake Dr Marietta GA 30068-4314 Office: New South Pub 7840 Roswell Rd Ste 328 Atlanta GA 30350-4889

THOMPSON, SUSANNAH ELIZABETH, lawyer; b. Fullerton, Calif., May 20, 1953; d. Harry Lowell and Susannah Elizabeth (Glover) Rupp; m. James Avery Thompson, Jr., May 16, 1987; 1 child, Sarah Mary Elizabeth Thompson. BA, Calif. State U., Fullerton, 1980; JD with hons., Am. Coll. of Law, 1989. Bar: Calif. 1989, U.S. Dist. Ct. (cen. dist.) 1989, U.S. Dist. Ct. (so. dist.) 1991. Legal asst. Minyard & Minyard, Orange, Calif., 1987-89; assoc. Simon & Simon, San Bernardino, Calif., 1989-91; pvt. practice Temecula, Calif., 1991—. Asst. editor Law Rev./Am. Coll. Law, Brea, Calif., 1989. Sec. student bar assn. Am. Coll. Law, 1987-88. Mem. ABA, Riverside County Bar Assn., Calif. Women Lawyers Assn., Inland Empire Bankruptcy Forum, Women Lawyers Assn. (chmn. mem. 1994—), Temecula C. of C. Republican. Office: Ste 201 41593 Winchester Rd Temecula CA 92590

THOMPSON, TINA LEWIS CHRYAR, publisher; b. Houston, Dec. 31, 1929; d. Joshua and Mary Christine (Brown) Thompson; m. Joseph Chryar, May 25, 1943; 1 child, Joseph Jr. Cosmetologist, Franklin Coll., Houston, 1950; student, Crenshaw Coll., L.A., 1961. Pubr., composer, author B.M.I., N.Y.C., 1964-74; pubr. ASCAP, N.Y.C., 1974-86, The Fox Agy., N.Y.C., 1986—, Tech. World, L.A., 1990—; v.p. music Asset Records, L.A., 1978—; music dir., v.p. Roach Records, L.A., 1968; music dir. Rendezvous Records, Hollywood, 1950; v.p. Assoc. Internat., L.A., 1973; bd. govs. ABI, Inc., 1994; pres. Cling Music Pub., Soprano Music; pub. processor music catalogs Broadcast Music Inc. Author: Soprano Poems, 1985; creator/designer Baby Napin brand form-fitting, no-leak, no pins baby diaper, 1967, Saver Belt, 1993; patentee/pub. Letter's Tech in Word, used by TV stas. to advertise, 1972. Recipient recognition award IBC, Cambridge, Eng., 1991, cert. of proclamation Internat. Woman of Yr., 1991-92, Merit award Pres. Ronald Reagan, 1986; named Most Admired Woman of Decade, ABI, 1993. Mem. AAUW, NARAS, NOW, ABI (bd. govs. 1994), Am. Soc. Authors and Composers, Nat. Mus. Pubs. Assn., Songwriters Guild Am. (Cert. of Ranks of Composers and Lyricists 1991), Am. Fedn. Label Co. Unions, Am. Theatre Assn. Broadcast Music Inc. (pres. Soprano Music Publ. 1968), Rec. Acad. Country Music Acad., Internat. Platform Assn., L.A. Women in Music. Home: PO Box 7731 Beverly Hills CA 90212-7731

THOMPSON, VICKI LYN, elementary school educator; b. Miles City, Mont., Aug. 16, 1969; d. Herbert John and LaVonne Darlene (Myrhe) Sackman; m. David Lee Thompson, June 27, 1992. BS, Mont. State U., 1991. Cert. tchr., Iowa. 3d grade classroom tchr. Natrona County Pub. Schs., Casper, Wyo., 1991-93; learning resource ctr. tchr. Dubuque (Iowa) Cmty. Pub. Schs., 1993—. Youth group leader First Presbyn. Ch.s, Casper and Dubuque, 1991—; summer camp dir. Presbytery of Wyo., 1992-93. Recipient First Yr. Tchr. award Sallie Mae, 1992. Mem. Internat. Reading Assn., Iowa Talented and Gifted Assn., Iowa Coun. Math. Home: 1704 2d Pl NE Jamestown ND 58401

THOMPSON, WYNELLE DOGGETT, chemistry educator; b. Birmingham, Ala., May 25, 1914; d. William Edward and Dollie Odessa (Ferguson) Doggett; m. Davis Hunt Thompson, Sept. 17, 1938; children: Carolyn Wynelle, Helen Hunt, Cynthia Carle, Davis Hunt, jr. BS summa cum laude, Birmingham Southern, 1934, MS, 1935; MS, U. Ala., 1956, PhD, 1960. From grad. lab. asst. to instr. chemistry Birmingham (Ala.) Southern Coll., 1934-36,39-44; tchr. Bd. Edn., Sheffield, Ala., 1936-37; jr. chemist Bur. Home Econs. USDA, Washington, 1937-38; instr. chemistry U. Ala. extension ctr., Birmingham, 1950-54; grad. asst. biochemistry U. Ala. Med. Coll., Birmingham, 1954-55; from asst. prof. chemistry to prof. emerita Birmingham (Ala.) Southern Coll., 1955-76; rsch. assoc. U. Ala. Dept. Biochemistry, Birmingham, 1965, 1968, 1969, Dept. Biophysics, 1976-78; adj. prof. chemistry New Coll. Tuscaloosa, Ala., 1980—. Contbr. articles to profl. jours. Bd. dirs. Cahaba Coun. Girl Scouts U.S. (vol. chmn. troop orgn., camping.). Grantee NSF, Appleton, Wis., Emory U., Atlanta; recipient disting. alumna award Birmingham So. Coll., 1976, medal of svc. award, 1994. Fellow Am. Inst. Chemists; mem. AAUW (bd. dirs., treas.), Am. Chem. Soc. (sec. 1942-44, 72-73, chmn.-elect 1966-67, chmn. 1967-68, 50-Yr. Mem. award 1992), Ala. Acad. Sci. (chmn. edn. sect. 1960-62), Phi Beta Kappa, Sigma Xi (sec. 1970-72), Theta Chi Delta, Delta Phi Alpha, Theta Sigma Lambda, Kappa Delta Epsilon, Delta Kappa Gamma, Kappa Mu Epsilon. Republican. Methodist. Home: 1237 Berwick Rd Birmingham AL 35242

THOMPSON-CAGER, CHEZIA BRENDA, literature educator, writer, performance artist; b. St. Louis, Sept. 8, 1951; d. James Henry and Emma Jean (Mack-Anderson) Thompson; m. Lawrence Chris Cager Jr., May 19, 1984; 1 child, Chezia. BA, Washington U., St. Louis, 1973, MA, 1975; ArtsD, Carnegie-Mellon U., 1984. Tchg. asst. Washington U., 1973-76; instr., asst. prof. St. Louis C.C., 1975-79; asst. prof. Clarion (Pa.) State U., 1980-82, U. Md., Catonsville, 1982-86; assoc. prof. Smith Coll., Northampton, Mass., 1986-89; vis. assoc. prof. Bowie (Md.) State U., 1989-90; sr. v.p. Park Heights Devel. Corp., Balt., 1990-92; cons. Balt. City Pub. Sch., Inst. Div., 1992-94; prof. lang. & lit. Md. Inst. Coll. Art, Balt., 1993—; Disting. scholar in residence U. Pa. Dept. Theatre, University Park, 1989; project dir. poetry enrichment program U. City Pub. Sch., 1972; performance artist Artscape, 1996. Author: Jumpin' Rope on the Axis, 1986, Power Objects, 1996 (Netscape Poetry Competition award 1996), The Presence of Things Unseen, 1996, Praise Song for Katherine Dunhain Artscape, 1996, numerous poems; dir. dramatic works including Narrator Vachel Lindsay's Congo Visits Langston Hughes, 1989, Jestina's Calypso, 1988, 7 Principles: or how I got ova, 1987, Tribute to Martin Luther King, 1985; contbr. lit. criticisms, articles to profl. jours, freelance for St. Louis Am. News., Pitts. Courier News, Balt. Sun News. Mem. adv. bd. Sexual Assault Recovery Ctr., Balt., 1989-93; site proj. evaluator Nat. Endowment Arts, Washington, 1984; mem. Heritage Art panel Md. State Coun. Arts, 1990-94; cons. Balt. Arrabers Documentation Project, 1992. Recipient Paul Robeson Black Artist award Washington U., 1972, W.E.B. DuBois Svc. award, 1973, Merit for Poetry award Mo. State Coun. Arts, 1974, Mayor's Citizen Citation Poetry award, 1996, Resolution for Literacy award City Coun. Balt., 1996; named Oyo Traditions Pan-African Cultural Innovator, 1996. Mem. Nat. Assn. Tchrs. English, Nat. Black Theater Network, African Lit. Assn., Assn. Theater Higher Edn. Office: Md Inst Coll Art Dept Lit and Langs 1300 Mount Royal Ave Baltimore MD 21217

THOMS, JEANNINE AUMOND, lawyer; b. Chgo.; d. Emmett Patrick and Margaret (Gallet) Aumond; m. Richard W. Thoms; children: Catherine Thoms, Alison Thoms. AA, McHenry County Coll., 1979; BA, No. Ill. U., 1981; JD, Ill. Inst. Tech., 1984. Bar: Ill. 1984, U.S. Dist. Ct. (no. dist.) Ill. 1984, U.S. Ct. Appeals (7th cir.) 1985. Assoc. Foss Schuman Drake & Barnard, Chgo., 1984-86; assoc. Zukowski Rogers Flood & McArdle, Crystal Lake and Chgo., 1986-92, ptnr., 1992—; bd. dirs. McHenry County Mental Health Bd., 1991—, pres., 1995—; arbitrator 19th Jud. Ct. Ill., 1991—; cert. mediator Acad. Family Mediators, Ill., 1992—. Mem. Women's Adv. Coun. to Gov., State of Ill. Mem. ABA, LWV, Ill. State Bar Assn., Chgo. Bar Assn., McHenry County Bar Assn., Am. Trial Lawyers Assn., Acad. Family Mediators, Women's Network, Phi Alpha Delta. Office: Zukowski Rogers Flood & McArdle 50 N Virginia Crystal Lake IL 60014 also: 100 S Wacker Dr Chicago IL 60600

THOMS, JOSEPHINE BOWERS, artist, illustrator; b. Lansing, Mich., Sept. 14, 1922; d. Raymon Lyon and Adele (Hammond) Bowers; m. Bert Thoms, June 4, 1945 (dec.); 1 child, Adele Lucile Thoms; m. Peter Blackford Lauck, May 10, 1983. BA, Hillsdale Coll., 1944; MA, Md. Inst. Coll. Art, 1977. Instr. modern dance Hillsdale (Mich.) Coll., 1943-44; artist-in-residence St. John's Coll., Annapolis, Md., 1953-55, 68-70; instr. art Washington and Jefferson Coll., Washington, Pa., 1956, Bethany (W.Va.) Coll., 1963-65; illustrator Md. Dept. Natural Resources, Annapolis, 1977-95; instr. Washington Art Assn., 1958-69; art dir. Md. Fedn. Art, Annapolis, 1970-72, pres., 1972-74. Illustrator: Federal Prose, 1947; executed murals: History of Electricity, Hillsdale, 1942, The Harbor at Annapolis, Crownsville, Md., 1989. Mem. Caritas Soc. at St. John's Coll., 1969—, Md. Peace Action, Annapolis, 1983—. Recipient 1st prize for Exhbn. of Nature-Related Art, Adkins Arboretum, Tuckahoe State Pk., Denton, Md., 1995. Mem. Md. Soc. Portrait Painters (cert., exhibits chairperson 1995—), Md. Hall Artists Coop. (exhibiting mem.), Annapolis Watercolor Club (1st prize 1993), Sierra Club. Democrat. Episcopalian. Home: 61 Southgate Ave Annapolis MD 21401

THOMSEN, LAURA ELISE, counselor; b. Cadillac, Mich., Aug. 28, 1962; d. Robert Gerald and Barbara Elizabeth (Zinn) Porter; m. Karl William Thomsen, June 2, 1984; children: Elise Marie, Erin Michelle. Lic. profl. counselor, Mich. Tchr. elem. Pine River Area Schs., LeRoy, Mich., 1984-94; registrar, counselor Baker Coll. of Cadillac, 1994-95; counselor mid. sch. Lake City (Mich.) Area Schs., 1995—. Entertainment chairperson Am. Cancer Soc., Cadillac, 1995—, concession chairperson, 1994-95. Mem. ACA, Am. Fedn. Tchrs., Mich. Edn. Assn., Mich. Counseling Assn., Mich. Sch. Counselors Assn. Democrat. Home: 220 Vick Cadillac MI 49601 Office: Lake City Mid Sch 5534 W Davis Lake City MI 49651

THOMSEN, RENAE LUVERL, speech pathologist; b. Sioux Falls, S.D., June 16, 1967; d. Erling James and Luverl Jean (Watne) T. BS in Comm. Disorders, U. S.D., 1990, MA in Speech Pathology, 1991. Speech pathologist Ednl. Svc. Unit #1, Wakefield, Nebr., 1991-94, South Sioux City Cmty. Schs., 1994—; adj. prof. Wayne (Nebr.) State Coll., 1992-93. Mem. Am. Speech, Hearing, Lang. Assn.

THOMSON, GRACE MARIE, nurse, minister; b. Pecos, Tex., Mar. 30, 1932; d. William McKinley and Elzora (Wilson) Olliff; m. Radford Chaplin, Nov. 3, 1952; children: Deborah C., William Earnest. Assoc. Applied Sci., Odessa Coll., 1965; extension student U. Pa. Sch. Nursing, U. Calif., Irvine, Golden West Coll. RN, Calif., Okla., Ariz., Md., Tex. Dir. nursing Grays Nursing Home, Odessa, Tex., 1965; supr. nursing Med. Hill, Oakland, Calif.; charge nurse pediatrics Med. Ctr., Odessa; dir. nursing Elmwood Extended Care, Berkeley, Calif.; surg. nurse Childrens Hosp., Berkeley; med./surg. charge nurse Merritt Hosp., Oakland, Calif.; adminstr. Grace and Assocs.; advocate for emotionally abused children; active Watchtower and Bible Tract Soc.; evangelist for Jehovah's Witnesses, 1954—.

THOMSON, GRETCHEN OSTERHOF, arts adminstrator, consultant; b. Rapid City, S.D., Jan. 27, 1940; d. Gerard Gordon and Adah Margaret (Dick) Osterhof; John Godfrey Thomson, Jun. 22, 1963 (div. 1990); children: Trevor Gordon, Gregory Dick. AB, Grinnell Coll., 1962; MMusic, U. Wis., 1967, MBA, 1989. Cert. K-12 music tchr., Iowa, Minn., Wis. Music tchr. Richfield (Minn.) Pub. Schs., 1963-65; choir dir. Unity Temple, Oak Park, Ill., 1972-77; music tchr. New Glarus (Wis.) Pub. Schs., 1978-82; dir. Monroe (Wis.) Arts & Activites Ctr, 1980-83; dir. cmty. and info. devel. Wis. Arts Bd., Madison, 1985-91; pres. Thomson Arts Mgmt. Svcs., Milw., 1991-96; dir. Wis. Dance on Tour, Milw., 1991—; gen. mgr. Milw. Chamber Orch., 1995—; exec. dir. Ten Chimneys Found., Genesee Depot, Wis., 1996—; founder, pres. Unity Temple Concert Series, Oak Park, 1972-77, bd. dirs. Green Lake Festival of Music, Ripon, Wis., 1979-84, Arts Wis., Madison, 1991-94, Historical Keyboard Soc. of Wis., Milw., 1992-94. Founder, mem. Restless Legs Syndrome Support Group, Milw., 1995. Democratic. Office: Thomson Arts Mgmt Svcs 144 East Wells St Milwaukee WI 53202

THOMSON, MABEL AMELIA, retired elementary school educator; b. Lancaster, Minn., Oct. 28, 1910; d. Ernest R. and Sophie Olinda (Rotert) Poore; m. Robert John Thomson, June 20, 1936; children: James Robert, William John. BS, U. Ill., 1933; MEd, Steven F. Austin Coll., Nacogdoches, Tex., 1959. Tchr. La Harpe (Ill.) Sch. Dist., 1930, Scotland (Ill.) Sch. Dist., 1934, Washburn (Ill.) Sch. Dist., 1935-36, Tyler (Tex.) Ind. Sch. Dist., 1959-76; ret., 1976; substitute tchr. Tyler (Tex.) Ind. Sch. Dist., 1976-86. Past pres. Woman's Soc. Christian Svc. of local Meth. Ch. Mem. AAUW (pres. Tyler chpt. 1947-48), Am. Childhood Edn. (pres. 1960-61), Alpha Delta Kappa (charter Tyler br.), Phi Mu (life). Republican. Methodist.

THOMSON, MARJORIE BELLE, sociology educator, consultant; b. Topeka, Dec. 4, 1921; d. Roy John and Bessie Margaret (Knarr) Anderson; m. John Whitner Thomson, Jan. 4, 1952 (div. June 9, 1963); 1 child, John Coe. Diploma hostess, Trans World Airlines, 1945; diploma, U.Saltillo, Mex., 1945; BS, Butler U., 1957; MS, Ft. Hays Kans. State U., 1966; postgrad., U. Calif., Santa Barbara, 1968, Kans. State U., 1972-73, Kans. U., 1973. Cert. elem. tchr., Calif., Colo., Ind., Kans., jr. coll. tchr. Tech. libr. N.Am. Aviation, Dallas, 1944-45; flight attendant TWA, Kansas City, Mo., 1945-50; recreation dir. U.S. Govt., Ft. Carson, Colo., 1951-52; elem. tchr. Indpls. Pub. Schs., 1954-57; jr. high tchr. Cheyenne County Schs., Cheyenne Wells, Colo., 1958-59; elem. tchr. Sherman County Schs., Goodland, Kans., 1961-62; lectr. Calif. Luth. U., Thousand Oaks, 1967-69; instr. Ft. Hays Kans. State U., 1969-71; dir. HeadStart Kans. Coun. of Agrl. Workers and Low Income Families, Inc., Goodland, 1971-72; supr. U.S. Govt. Manpower Devel. Programs, Plainville, Kans., 1972-74; bilingual counselor Kans. Dept. Human Resources, Goodland, 1975-82; leader trainee Expt. in Internat. Living, Brattleboro, Vt., 1967-71; cons. M. Anderson & Co., Lakewood, Colo., 1982—; participant Internat. Peace Walk, Moscow to Archangel, Russia, 1991, N.Am. Conf. on Ecology and the Soviet Save Peace and Nature Ecol. Collective, Russia, 1992; amb. internat. Friendship Force, Tiblisi, Republic of Georgia, 1991, Republic South Africa, 1995, Turkey, 1996; presenter State Conv. AAUW, Aurora, Colo., 1992, nat. conv. Am. Acad. Audiology, Denver, 1992; cons. Gov.'s Conf. in Libr. and Info. Svc., Vail, Colo., 1992; presenter annual conf. Nat. Emergency Number Assn., 1996. Docent Colo. Gallery of the Arts, Littleton, 1989; spkr., state resource com. mem. Internat. Self Help for Hard of Hearing People, Inc., state recreation resource com. for Self Help for Hard of Hearing People Internat. Conv., Denver, 1991; mem. Denver Deaf and Hard of Hearing Access Com., 1991—; spkr. Ret. Sr. Vol. Program, Denver, 1992—; dir. Holiday Project, Denver, 1992; mem. Lakewood Access Com., 1994—, Arvada Ctr.'s Women's Voices com., 1995—; participant women readers com. Rocky Mountain News, Denver, 1995; trustee Internat. Self Help for Hard of Hearing People, Inc., Bethesda, Md., 1995—; Deaf Panel spkr. for Deaf Awareness Week, Denver, 1995; program co-chairperson Lakewood Woman's Club, 1996; spkr. Nat. Emergency Number Assn. Conf., Denver, 1996. Grantee NSF, 1970, 71; recipient Svc. award Mayor of Lakewood, 1995, Honorable Mention Four Who Dare, Colo. Bus. and Profl. Women and KCNC Channel 4, 1995, J.C. Penney Nat. Golden Rule award for cmty. vol. svc., 1996. Mem. AAUW (life, v.p., program chairperson Lakewood br. 1996), AARP (pres. Denver-Grandview chpt. 1994), VFW Aux. (life), Sociologists for Women in Soc., Bus. and Profl. Woman's Club, Internat. Peace Walkers, Spellbinders, Denver Press Club, Lakewood Woman's Club, TWA Internat. Clipped Wings (cert.), Mile High Wings, Order Ea. Star (life), Sons of Norway (life), UNESCO, Pi Gamma Mu, Alpha Sigma Alpha (life). Democrat. Presbyterian. Home: 12313 W Louisiana Ave Lakewood CO 80228-3829 Office: M Anderson & Co 6941 W 13th Ave Lakewood CO 80215-5259

THOMSON, SHIRLEY LAVINIA, museum director; b. Walkerville, Ont., Can., Feb. 19, 1930; d. Walter Cull. BA in Art History with honors, U. West Ont., 1952; MA in Art History, U. Md., 1974; PhD in Art History, McGill U., 1981, Doctoris honoris causa, 1989; PhD (hon.), Ottawa U., 1989; D (hon.), Mt. Allison U., 1990, U. West Ont., 1990; PhD (hon.), U. Windsor, Ont., 1996. Editor conf. NATO, Paris, 1956-60; asst. sec.-gen. World Univ. Svc. WUSC, Toronto, 1960-63; asst. sec. gen. Can. Commn. for UNESCO, Ottawa, 1964-67; sec.-gen. Can. Commn. for UNESCO, Montreal, 1985-87; rsch. coord., writer Memoirs of Sen. Thérèse Casgrain, 1968-70; spl. coord. Largillière Exhbn., Mus. Fine Arts, Montreal, 1981; dir. McCord Mus., 1982-85, Nat. Gallery Can., Ottawa, 1987—; dir., dep. commr. UNESCO Pavilion Man and His World, Montreal, 1978-80. Officer Order of Can., 1994. Decorated Chevalier des Arts et Letters, France, 1977-78; recipient Can. Coun. doctoral award, 1978-79. Mem. Can. Soc. Decorative Arts (coun.), Can. Mus. Assn. (dir.). Office: Nat Gallery Can, 380 Sussex Dr, Ottawa, ON Canada K1N 9N4

THOMSON, THYRA GODFREY, former state official; b. Florence, Colo., July 30, 1916; d. John and Rosalie (Altman) Godfrey; m. Keith Thomson, Aug. 6, 1939 (dec. Dec. 1960); children—William John, Bruce Godfrey, Keith Coffey. B.A. cum laude, U. Wyo., 1939. With dept. agronomy and agrl. econs. U. Wyo., 1938-39; writer weekly column Watching Washington pub. in 14 papers, Wyo., 1955-60; planning chmn. Nat. Fedn. Republican Women, Washington, 1961; sec. state Wyo. Cheyenne, 1962-86; mem. Marshall Scholarships Com. for Pacific region, 1964-68; del. 72d Wilton Park Conf., Eng., 1965; mem. youth commn. UNESCO, 1970-71, Allied Health Professions Council HEW, 1971-72; del. U.S.-Republic of China Trade Conf., Taipei, Taiwan, 1983; mem. lt. gov.'s trade and fact-finding mission to Saudi Arabia, Jordan, and Egypt, 1985. Bd. dirs. Buffalo Bill Mus., Cody, Wyo., 1987—; adv. bd. Coll. Arts and Scis., U. Wyo., 1989, Cheyenne Symphony Orch. Found., 1990—. Recipient Disting. Alumni award U. Wyo., 1969, Disting. U. Wyo. Arts and Scis. Alumna award, 1987; named Internat. Woman of Distinction, Alpha Delta Kappa; recipient citation Omicron Delta Epsilon, 1965, citation Beta Gamma Sigma, 1968, citation Delta Kappa Gamma, 1973, citation Wyo. Commn. Women, 1986. Mem. N.Am. Securities Adminstrs. (pres. 1973-74), Nat. Assn. Secs. of State, Council State Govts. (chmn. natural resources com. Western states 1966-68), Nat. Conf. Lt. Govs. (exec. com. 1976-79). Home: 3102 Sunrise Rd Cheyenne WY 82001-6136

THOMSON-KANE, CAROLINE L., manufacturing engineer; b. Bristol, Va., Oct. 16, 1946; d. Vincent T. and Virginia S. (Spaw) Kane. AAS in Chem. Tech., Tex. State Tech. Coll., 1968; student, Tyler (Tex.) Jr. Coll., 1980-81, Richland (Tex.) C.C., 1988-91, Amber U., 1991-94. Analytical rsch. asst. Phillips Petroleum Co., Bartlesville, Okla., 1968-74; asst. rsch. chemist Merichem Co., Inc., Houston, 1974-80; sr. lab. analyst Phillips Coal Co., Tyler, Tex., 1980-82; environ. chemist, dir. advt. Platers' Equipment and Supply, Inc., Longview, Tex., 1982-83; water treatment ops. engring. supr., working foreman Tex. Instruments, Dallas, 1984-86, rsch. asst., 1986-88, failure analyst, 1988-95; process devel. tech. sem microscopist Tex. Instruments, Dallas, Tex., 1995—; SPC coord. Tex. Inst., Temple; mem. waste Minimization coun. Tex. Instruments, 1993-95, indsl. coop. com., 1989-95; chem. tech. adv. com. Tex. State Tech. Coll., 1987—. Vol. United We Stand, Dallas, 1992; vol. Guardian Angel program Green Oaks Hosp., Dallas, 1989-90; ptnrs. of conscience Amnesty Internat., 1993-94; mem. in standing Greenpeace, 1995—; mem. Temple Jr. League, 1995—, Temple Newscomers Club, newsletter editor, 1995—; vol. Ronald McDonald House, Temple, 1995—. Home: 3701 Robinhood #7B Temple TX 76502

THON, MELANIE RAE, writer; b. Kalispell, Mont., Aug. 23, 1957; d. Raymond Albert and Lois Ann (Lockwood) T. BA, U. Mich.; MA, Boston U., 1982. Instr. U. Mass., Boston, 1988-91, Emerson Coll., Boston, 1988-93, Harvard U., Cambridge, Mass., 1989-93; prof. Syracuse (N.Y.) U., 1993-96, Ohio State U., 1996—. Author: Meteors in August, 1990, Girls in the Grass, 1991, Iona Moon, 1993.

THON, PATRICIA FRANCES, pediatrics nurse, medical and surgical nurse; b. Portland, Oreg., Sept. 25, 1959; d. Anthony William and Catherine Mary (Scully) Brenneis; m. Eric Phillip Thon, Apr. 30, 1988. AS, Johnson County C.C., 1980; BSN, U. Kans., Kans. City, 1982; MA, Webster U., 1992; postgrad., Portland State U., 1977; grad., St. Louis U., 1994. Staff nurse in pediatrics and oncology St. Luke's Hosp., Kansas City, Mo., 1982-84; commd. nurse officer USAF, 1984, advanced through grades to maj., 1988; staff nurse USAF, Scott AFB, Ill., 1984-88; flight nurse USAF, Scott AFB, 1988-91, sr. staff nurse in pediatrics and orthopedics, 1992; head nurse, flight chief maternal/child health Pediatric Clinic, Altus AFB, Okla., 1994—. Office: 97 MDG/SGOB 301 N 1st St Altus AFB OK 73523-5005

THOR, LINDA MARIA, college president; b. L.A., Feb. 21, 1950; d. Karl Gustav and Mildred Dorrine (Hofius) T.; m. Robert Paul Huntsinger, Nov. 22, 1974; children: Erik, Marie. BA, Pepperdine U., 1971, EdD, 1986; MPA, Calif. State U., Los Angeles, 1980. Dir. pub. info. Pepperdine U., Los Angeles, 1971-73; pub. info. officer L.A. C.C. Dist., 1974-75, dir. comm., 1975-81, dir. edn. svcs., 1981-82, dir. high tech., 1982-83, sr. dir. occupl. and tech. edn., 1983-86; pres. West Los Angeles Coll., Culver City, Calif., 1986-90, Rio Salado C.C., Phoenix, 1990—; bd. dirs. Coun. for Adult and Experiential Learning, 1990—, Tech. Exch. Ctr., 1986—, Greater Phoenix Econ. Coun., 1994—. Editor: Curriculum Design and Development for Effective Learning, 1973; author: (with others) Effective Media Relations, 1982, Performance Contracting, 1987; contbr. articles to profl. jours. Active Am. Assn. Cmty. Coll. Commn. Acad. and Student Devel., 1995—, Continuous Quality Improvement Network for Cmty. Colls., 1991—, Am. Coun. Edn. Commn. on Leadership Devel., 1995—; mem. Ariz. Gov.'s Adv. Coun. on Quality, 1992; pres. Ariz. Cmty. Coll. Pres.'s Coun., 1995-96. Recipient Delores award Pepperdine U., 1986, Alumni Medal of Honor, 1987, Outstanding Achievement award Women's Bus. Network, 1989; named Woman of the Yr., Culver City Bus. and Profl. Women, 1988. Office: 2323 W 14th St Tempe AZ 85281

THORBURN, NICOLE LEE, cartographer; b. Portland, Oreg., Dec. 15, 1965; d. Mark Dan and Leona Catherine (Kollodge) Mindolovich; m. Matthew Andrew Thorburn, June 10, 1995. BA, U. Oreg., 1991. Field asst. U.S. Geolog. Survey, Vancouver, Wash., 1991-92; stereoplotter operator, editor David C. Smith & Assoc., Portland, Oreg., 1992-93; softplotter operator Spencer B. Gross Inc., Portland, Oreg., 1994—. Mem. Pi Gamma Mu. Roman Catholic. Home: 4073 N Massachusetts Portland OR 97227

THORINGTON, CAROLINE MILLER, artist; b. Phila., Mar. 2, 1943; d. Franklin Rush and Ellen (Newhall) Miller; m. Richard Wainwright Jr., June 3, 1967; children: Ellen Moffat, Katherine Kimball. BA, Kans. State U., 1965; student, Acad. Fine Arts, Munich, 1965-66; MFA, George Washington U., Washington, 1975. Adj. prof. Montgomery Coll., Rockville, Md., 1975—; owner Thorington Studio, Bethesda, Md., 1970—. One-woman shows at Smithsonian Instn., 1982, Albrecht Mus., St. Joseph, Mo., 1988, NIH Collection of Fine Arts, 1991, Jane Haslem Gallery, Washington, 1995. Recipient fellowship Kans. State U. and U. Munich, 1965-66; grantee Winfield (Kans.) Arts Ctr., Washington, 1982, Arts Coun. Montgomery County, Md., 1993, Honor Ture Bengz Meml. award Boston Printmakers, 1992; recipient Merit award Print Club of Albany, 1995. Mem. Md. Printmakers (bd. mem. 1992-93), Boston Printmakers, Print Club Phila., Soc. Am. Graphic Artists, So. Graphics Coun., L.A. Printmaking Soc. Home: 7714 Old Chester Bethesda MD 20817 Office: Montgomery Coll Manakee St Rockville MD 20850

THORINGTON, HELEN LOUISE, radio producer, performing arts company executive, writer, artist; b. Phila., Nov. 16, 1928; d. Richard Wainwright and Katherine Louise (Moffat) Thorington. BA, Wellesley Coll., 1950. Exec. dir. New Radio and Performing Arts, Inc., N.Y.C., 1981—; cons. Assn. Independents in Radio, Washington, 1991—. Composer for post-modern dancers, 1980-84; composer, performer New Music America, 1984, 86, 88; independent radio prodr., writer, composer; sound designer, composer for avant-garde film Whitney Bienniel, Berlin Film Festival, 1987, 89; exec. prodr., creator nat. radio art series New American Radio 1989—; lectr. on radio art, USA and Europe, 1990—; founder, creator World Wide Web artist's site Turbulence, 1995—; numerous radio installations, taped works for radio, including Terra dell'Immaginazione, 1990, Dracula's Wives, 1992, Going Between, 1993, Locomotive, 1991, Angels Have Been Sent to Me, 1991, Partial Perceptions, 1992, North Country, 1995. Recipient funding awards NEA, 1987, 91, 93, N.Y. State Coun. on the Arts, 1989, 90, 91, 92, 95; winner First Prize First International Conf. on Radio Art, Warsaw, 1993. Mem. Snug Harbor Civic Assn.

THORLAKSON BELL, ROSEMARY AHEARN, contract trauma nurse; b. Columbus, Ohio, July 12, 1947; d. Joseph Edmond and Elizabeth Sabrina (Morse) Ahearn; m. Robert E. Thorlakson, Dec. 29, 1969 (div. Oct. 1972); children: AmySue Elizabeth, Stephen Robert; m. Gary Lee Bell, May 13, 1993. AAS in Nursing, Germanna C.C., 1975; BSN, U. Va., 1976, MEd, 1986, postgrad. Cert. BLS/ACLS instr., CCRN, CEN, TNCC instr., PALS, NALS, ATLS, C-EMT instr., first aid instr., water safety instr., breast self exam instr., cold water rescue and recovery; RN, Va., 18 others. Night shift supr. emergency dept. Potomac Hosp., Woodbridge, Va., 1975-77; emergency rm. trauma and life flight nurse U. Va., Charlottesville, 1977-79; supr. emergency dept. Carbon County Meml. Hosp., Rawlins, Wyo., 1979-80; contract RN, 1980-89, 91—; supr. emergency dept. Minidoka Meml. Hosp., Rupert, Idaho, 1989-91; community educator Am. Heart Assn., N.Y., Va., Wyo, Idaho, 1972—, ARC, N.Y., Ky., Wyo., Idaho, 1972—; state steering com. State EMS, Idaho, 1990-91. Contbr. articles to profl. jours. Former v.p. MADD, 1991-72; vol. ARC, Idaho, Ky., Va., 1975—, Spl. Olympics, Idaho, 1991—. Capt. U.S. Army, 1967-70. Mem. VFW, Vietnam Vets. of Am., Vietnams Womens' Assn., Am. Legion, Am. Vets, Women in Svc. to Am., Beta Sigma Phi. Democrat. Roman Catholic.

THORN, ANDREA PAPP, lawyer; b. Greenwich, Conn., May 22, 1960; d. Laszlo G. and Judith (Liptak) Papp; m. Craig Thorn IV, Aug. 27, 1982; children: C. Alexander, Kelsey Amanda. BA, Dartmouth Coll., Hanover, N.H., 1982; JD, Harvard U., 1987. Bar: Mass. 1987, N.H. 1993. Assoc. Bingham Dana & Gould, Boston, 1987-89, Gaffin & Krattenmaker PC, Boston, 1989-90, Phillips, Gerstein & Holber, Haverhill, Mass., 1993-94; spl. asst. to sec. of N.Mex. Dept. of Environment, 1991-92. Mem. ABA, Mass. Bar Assn., N.H. Bar Assn. Home: Phillips Academy Andover MA 01810-4161

THORNBER, JUDY PAULENE, real estate developer, consultant, lawyer; b. Chgo., May 26, 1941; d. Paul and Irene (Swanson) Davis. BA, U. Chgo., 1963, MBA, 1969; JD, Harvard U., 1966. Bar: Ill. 1967. V.p. Rubloff Devel. Corp., Chgo., 1970-72; sr. v.p. Am. INVSCO, Chgo., 1975-76; pres. Thorndev Corp., Chgo., 1978—; v.p. Fogelson Properties, Chgo., 1989-90; adminstrv. v.p. Cen. Sta. Devel. Corp., Chgo., 1990-91; exec. v.p. INVSCO Group, Ltd., 1991-93. Founding mem. Com. of 200, Chgo.; bd. dirs. Wellspring Wellness Ctr., 1991. Mem. Chgo. Bar Assn., Chgo. Assn. Realtors, U. Chgo. Women's Bus. Group (chmn. entrepreneurship subcom. 1993), Chgo. Fin. Exch. (bd. dirs. 1984), Chgo. Coun. on Fgn. Rels., Harvard Club Chgo., Phi Beta Kappa (exec. com. Chgo. area chpt.). Home and Office: 5555 N Sheridan Rd Apt 412 Chicago IL 60640

THORNE, JOYE HOLLEY, special education administrator; b. Shreveport, La., Jan. 4, 1933; d. Lockett Beecher and A. Irene (McWilliams) Holley; m. Michael S. Thorne, July 24, 1953; 1 child, Michael S. Jr. BS, Centenary Coll., 1954; MEd, U. Houston, 1969, EdD, 1974. Cert. tchr., Tex. Tchr. Aldine Ind. Sch. Dist., Houston, 1959-66, curriculum cons., 1966-69, dir. spl. edn., 1969—; adj. prof. U. Houston, Clear Lake, Tex., 1974-83, U. St. Thomas, Houston, 1993-95; spl. edn. specialist Dept. Def. Dependent Schs., Washington, 1983-84. Recipient Pres.'s award Gulf Coast chpt. Coun. Exceptional Children, Austin, Tex., 1980. Mem. Coun. Exceptional Children (pres. Gulf Coast chpt. 1976-77, pres. Tex. fedn. 1982-83, Pres.'s award 1980), Tex. Coun. Adminstrs. Spl. Edn. (pres. 1985-86, Dir. of Yr. award 1993). Republican. Methodist. Office: Aldine Ind Sch Dist 1617 Lauder Rd Houston TX 77039-3025

THORNE, KATE RULAND, writer, publisher, editor; b. Del Norte, Colo., Dec. 15, 1937; d. Joseph Lydian Norman and Avis Frances Kiemsteadt; m. Edwin G. Ruland, Aug. 20, 1960 (div. 1984); children: Gregory, Jeanie, Rebecca. BA, So. Meth. U., 1976. Speech pathologist Shady Brook Sch., Dallas, 1960-61, Hillside Rehab., Grand Junction, Colo., 1962-72; pub. Thorne Enterprises Pub. Inc., Sedona, Ariz., 1989—; editor, pub. Thorne/Swiftwind Pub., Sedona, 1993—; lectr. in field. Author: Lion of Redstone, 1980, Experience Sedona: Legends and Legacies, 1990, (screenplay) Blood Oath; author, editor: Experience Jerome and the Verde Valley: Legends and Legacies, 1992, The Yavapai: People of the Red Rocks, 1993, The Legacy of Sedona Schnebly, 1994, Upon This Rock, 1995; editor, columnist Sedona Mag., 1986-87; columnist Art Talk, Directions Mag.; contbr. numerous articles to mags. and newspapers; 1st woman editor Sedona Red Rock News, 1987-88. Founder, pres., Ariz. Indian Living Treasures, 1990-91; founding mem., sec. Western Am. Week, 1990-94. Mem. Ariz. Small Pub. Assn. (founding mem.), Sedona Hist. Soc. (pres.). Home and Office: 149 Gambel Ln Sedona AZ 86336-7119

THORNLEY, WENDY ANN, educator, sculptor; b. Bolton, Lancashire, Eng., Feb. 28, 1948; came to U.S., 1953; d. Ronald Thornley and Joan Gladys (Hancock) Green. BS, So. Conn. State U., 1970, MS, 1979; MA, Wesleyan U., Middletown, Conn., 1991. Cert. tchr., Conn. Tchr. art New Canaan (Conn.) Pub. Schs., 1970-71, Bristol (Conn.) Pub. Schs., 1972—; adj. faculty Naugatuck Valley Cmty.-Tech. Coll., 1993—; profl. artists residency Oxbow Summer Sch. Art Inst. Chgo., 1994. Exhibited in nat. and regional juried shows, 1978—, including tour Nat. Assn. Women Artists, 1989; commns. include wall relief Reichhold Chem. Co., 1987, Aetna Ins. Co., 1988, Bank of Boston, 1989, Law Office of Halloran, Sage, Phelon and Hagerty, 1990, Pitney-Bowes, Stamford, Pitney-Bowes Corp., 1996. Summer fellow Skidmore Coll., 1986; recipient 1st prize for sculpture Homestead Show, Fairfield, Conn., 1996. Mem. Nat. Art Edn. Assn., Conn. Art Edn. Assn. (Outstanding Secondary Art Educator award 1995), Nat. Assn. Women Artists, Soc. Conn. Crafts (bd. dirs. 1981-88, Best-in-Show award 1982, 84, 91, Best in Fiber award 1990, Master Craftsman award 1994), Conn. Women Artists (Binney & Smith award 1985, First prize sculpture, Homestead, Fairfield 1996), New Eng. Sculptors Assn. Home: 97 Summit Rd PO Box 7094 Prospect CT 06712

THORNTON, ANNA VREE, pediatrics and medical-surgical nurse; b. Chgo., June 10, 1936; d. Edward and Elizabeth Vree; m. George Q. Thornton, June 19, 1982. BA in Edn. Psych., Barrington Coll., 1960; postgrad., NYU, 1960-62; ADN., Dutchess C.C., Poughkeepsie, N.Y., 1986. Tchr. Saugerties (N.Y.) Cen. Schs., 1960-64, Kingston (N.Y.) Consolidated Schs., 1964-66, 68-70; owner BeeVer House, Saugerties, 1970-76; ins. agt. Combined Life Ins. Co., Poughkeepsie, N.Y., 1976-82; staff nurse Putnam County Community Hosp., Carmel, N.Y., 1983-86; charge nurse Calloway County Community Hosp., Murray, Ky., 1986—; tchr. U.S. Peace Corps, Nigeria, 1966-68. Pres. Saugerties Busnessmen's Orgn., 1977. Baha'i'. Home: 4563 Kirksey Rd Kirksey KY 42054-9728 Office: Calloway County Comm Hosp 800 Poplar St Murray KY 42071-2566

THORNTON, CHRISTINE DIANE, hospice development director; b. San Diego, June 25, 1959; d. Donald Vernon and Regene Caroline (Bergersen) Norgaard; m. Jeff Thornton, Dec. 1989 (div. Nov. 1995). BSBA, San Diego State U., 1982. Sales exec. Sea World, San Diego, 1986-88; dir. mktg. Naval Tng. Ctr. USN, San Diego, 1988-90; dir. devel. Elizabeth Hospice, Escondido, Calif., 1990-95, Hospice of Seattle, 1995—. Bd. dirs. Am. Heart Assn., San Diego, 1992-94; jr. mem. Nat. Wine Competition, San Diego, 1994-95. Named Ms. Calif. USA Petite Woman, 1995. Mem. Nat. Soc. Fund Raising Execs. (bd. dirs. 1993-95). Republican. Office: Hospice of Seattle 425 Pontius Ave N #300 Seattle WA 98109

THORNTON, EARLENE HAIRSTON, newspaper editor. BA in Edn., Winston-Salem U.; MA in Reading and Spl. Edn., Va. State U.; student, U. Va., 1966-67, Syracuse U., 1969-71; EdD, George Washington U., 1989. Cert. Md. Advanced Profl., N.Y. Permanent Advanced Profl. Elem. and Mid. Sch. supr., elem. and mid. sch. prin., spl. edn., reading specialist, English tchr., counselor. Asst. dir. Coll. Reading Clinic Va. Union U., Richmond, 1966-67; lang. arts chairperson, reading specialist Elmira, N.Y., 1967-72; reading specialist Montgomery County Sch. System, Md., 1975-88, guidance counselor, 1988—; counselor county schs., Md., 1975-94; exec. editor The County Globe, Frederick, Md., 1990—; adj. coll. prof.; v.p. G.E.D. Corp.; title I evaluator N.Y. State Dept. Edn., 1971; instr. English Frederick C.C., 1976-81. Chmn. Frederick County Ethnic Festival, 1977-86; v.p. Patuxent Women, 1990-94; bd. dirs. Cmty. Living, Inc. Mem. NEA (edn. com. Frederick's Human Rels. Coun.), AAUW (past v.p.), Internat. Reading Assn. (past pres.), Md. Coun. Edn. Assn., Frederick Negro Bus. and Profl. Women, Frederick County's Human Rels. Coun. (chmn.), Delta Kappa Gamma (chmn. profl. affairs com., pres. Gamma chpt.), Phi Delta Kappa. Home: 5503 Hines Rd Frederick MD 21701-6885

THORNTON, MARIA ANGELA, interpreter, translator, educator, civic worker; b. Hampton, Va., Mar. 15, 1949; d. James Otis and Caterina Maria (Quarri) T. Assoc. Applied Arts, Bauder Coll.; BA, U. Akron, 1971; postgrad., U. Tex., Arlington, 1983, Am. U., Barcelona, Spain. Cert. tchr., Tex. Tchr. Benedict Sch. of Langs., Barcelona, Spain, 1972-73; interpreter, translator, assoc. v.p. adminstrn. O.S.V. di Ermanno Arbizzi, Modena, Italy, 1973-78; fgn. officer Autogru P.M., Modena, 1978-81; asst. pers. dir. Am. Marazzi Tile Co., Sunnyvale, Tex., 1984-89; Amnesty program coord.-dir. Ctr. for English Lang., Dallas, 1989-91; ESL tchr., freelance cons. Dallas, 1989—; tutor, lang. tchr., Italy, France, Spain, 1972-81. Vol. Dallas Com. for Fgn. Visitors, Dallas Pers. Assn., N.E. Dallas Pers. Assn., Animal Rehab. Ctr., Midlothian, Tex., 1989—, People for the Ethical Treatment of Animals, Washington, 1989—, Acad. Achievement Assn., Dallas, 1989—, Union Gospel Mission, Dallas, 1990—, Walden Inst. Human Potential Resource Ctr., Dallas, 1992. Recipient achievement award for outstanding mus. study Music Tchr.'s Assn. Ala. Mem. Am. Literary Translators assn., Italian Am. Coun. for Commerce and Culture, Internat. Women's Club Dallas, Soc. d'Honneur Francaise (alumni, v.p.), Soc. Nacional Hispanica (life), Dallas So. Meml. Assn., Dallas Genealogical Soc., Rosicrucian Order AMORC, DAR (Ellis Island restoration chpt. chmn. 1988-91, Americanism and DAR manual for citizenship chpt. chmn. Farmer's Branch, Tex. 1990-91, organizing mem. Peter's Colony chpt. 1990-91, chmn. motion picture, radio , TV, pub. rels. 1992), United Daus. Confederacy (adopt-a-momument com.), Kappa Delta Pi. Mem. Unity Ch. Home: 9628 Park Highlands Dr Dallas TX 75238-2958 Office: 600 Williamsburg Manor Arlington TX 76014

THORPE, HILDA SHAPIRO, artist; b. Balt., Dec. 1, 1919; d. Jacob and Miriam (Levy) Gottlieb; m. James Thorpe (dec. dec. 1991). Art instr. Mt. Vernon Jr. Coll. and Sem., Washington, 1970-80; adj. prof. art dept./sculpture The Am. U., Washington, 1980-90. One person shows include Watkins Gallery, Am. U., Washington, 1959, Jefferson Place Gallery, Washington, 1961-72, Inst. Contemporary Art, Lima, Peru, 1966, Mount Vernon Coll.,

Washington, 1967, No. Va. C.C., Annandale, 1973, Phillips Collection, Washington, 1975, Gallery 641, Washington, 1975, Chilmark Gallery, Martha's Vineyard, Mass., 1976, Barbara Fiedler Gallery, Washington, 1976-81, Washington's Women's Art Ctr., 1977, Wolfe Street Gallery, Washington, 1978, Plum Gallery 2, Washington, 1979-80, Gallery 4, Alexandria, Va., 1979-80, Addison-Ripley Gallery, Washington, 1983, Artist Space, Georgetown Ct., Washington, 1984, Loyola U., Chgo., 1986, Athenaeum, Alexandria, 1988, Franz Bader Gallery, Washington, 1989, Mahler Gallery, Washington, 1991, The Athen Mus., Va., 1995, Nat. Mus. of Women in the Arts, Washington, 1995; exhibited in group shows at Barnett-Aden Gallery, Washington, 1959, Howard U., Washington, 1961, Corcoran Gallery of Art, Washington, 1963, Smithsonian Inst., Washington, 1970, 84-85, Phillips Collection, 1976, The White House, Washington, 1977, Chuck Levitan Gallery, N.Y., 1978, Boulder (Colo.) Arts Ctr., 1979, Pensacola (Fla.) Mus. Art, 1981, Art Soc. Internat. Monetary Fund, Washington, 1982, SUNY Art Gallery, New Paltz, 1985, Pa. State U., Middletown, 1985; represented in permanent collections Nat. Mus. Am. Art, Washington, Corcoran Gallery of Art, Phillips Collection, USHHS, Washington, Smithsonian Inst., City of Rockville, Md., Roanoke (Va.) Hosp., Fairfax City Park Authority, Va., Am. U., Howard U., Loyola U., Mount Vernon Coll., Washington, Almouhit Cultural Assn. of Asilah Asilah, Morocco, No. Va. C.C., Internat. Monetary Fund; represented in pvt. collections. Mem. Artists Equity. Democrat. Jewish. Home: 811 Arcturus on the Potomac Alexandria VA 22308 Office: 105 S Lee St Alexandria VA 22308

THORPE, JANET CLAIRE, lawyer; b. Bklyn., Dec. 8, 1953; d. Burton Walter and Phyllis Claire (Read) T.; m. David Frank Palmer, Aug. 26, 1978 (div. Aug. 1988); children—Katherine Elaine, Jennifer Claire; m. James Francis Box, June 29, 1991; children: Melissa Richelle, Maergrethe Cashel. Student, Boston U., 1972-74; A.B. in Polit. Sci. and History with honors, Union Coll., 1975; postgrad. Western New Eng. Sch. Law, 1975-76; J.D., Emory U., 1978. Bar: Ga. 1978, U.S. Dist. Ct. (no. dist.) Ga. 1978, U.S. Ct. Appeals (5th and 11th cirs.) 1978, 80, Fla. 1987, U.S. Dist. Ct. (mid. dist.) Fla. 1987. Law clk. to judge U.S. Dist. Ct., Atlanta, 1978; regional atty. Comptroller of Currency, Atlanta, 1978-80; assoc. corp. counsel Trust Co. Ga., Atlanta, 1980-86 ; dir. Trusco Properties, Inc., Atlanta 1981-86; gen. counsel, corp. sec. SunTrust Banks of Fla., Inc., 1986—; bd. mem., corp. sec. SunTrust Bank Card N.A., 1993— ; gen. counsel SunTrust Bank, Ctrl. Fla., N.A., 1986—; group v.p. SunTrust Banks, Inc., 1995—. Mem. Council on Battered Women, Atlanta, 1983-86, bd. dirs., 1986; bd. visitors Cornell Mus. Fine Art, Rollins Coll., 1995—. Mem. Ga. Bar Assn., Fla. Bar Assn., Assn. Bank Holding Cos. (lawyers com. 1983-90), Am. Corp. Counsel Assn. (bd. dirs. ctrl. Fla. chpt. 1991-94), Am. Diabetes Assn. (bd. dirs. Fla. chpt. 1989—), Leadership Orlando. Democrat. Episcopalian. Avocations: gardening; child rearing; house renovation; photography. Office: SunTrust Banks Inc 200 S Orange Ave Orlando FL 32801-3410

THORSEN, MARGUERITE ABIGAIL, marketing professional, consultant; b. Framingham, Mass., Feb. 11, 1948; d. Robert M. and Rita A. (Giard) Ferrick; m. Brian K. Thorsen, Aug. 22, 1970 (div. 1994); children: Kathryn R., Robert C. BA, Simmons Coll., 1970; MBA, Babson Coll., 1985. Dept. mgr. Jordan Marsh Co., Framingham, Mass., 1970-72; retail advt. mgr. Middlesex News, Framingham, 1972-82; account exec. Evans Press, Ft. Worth, 1982-84; dir. advt. Worcester County Newspapers, Auburn, Mass., 1984-85; advt. mgr. Enterprise-Sun Newspapers, Marlborough, Mass., 1985-88; prin. Marguerite Mktg., Marlborough, Mass., 1988-93; dir. mktg. Credit Union League of Mass., Waltham, Mass., 1993—; adj. prof. Nichols Coll., Dudley, Mass., 1990-94. Mem. campaign cabinet United Way of Assabet Valley, Marlborough, 1991-93. Mem. Marlborough C. of C. (dir. 1986-95, vice chmn. 1989-91, Outstanding Mem. award 1991), Assabet Valley Home Health Assn. (bd. dirs. 1994-96), Greater Marlborough Bus. and Profl. Women, Simmons Coll. Alumnae Assn. (v.p. class of 1970), Marlborough Rotary Club (bd. dirs. 1995—). Office: Credit Union League Mass 85 River St Waltham MA 02254-9163

THORSEN, MARIE KRISTIN, radiologist, educator; b. Milw., Aug. 1, 1947; d. Charles Christian and Margaret Josephine (Little) T.; m. James Lawrence Troy, Jan. 7, 1978; children: Katherine Marie, Megan Elizabeth. B.A., U. Wis., 1969; M.B.A., George Washington U., 1971; M.D., Columbia U., 1977. Diplomate Am. Bd. Radiology. Intern, Columbia-Presbyn. Med. Ctr., N.Y.C., 1977-78, resident dept. radiology, 1978-81; fellow computed body tomography Med. Coll. Wis., Milw., 1981-82; asst. prof. radiology, 1982-87, assoc. prof., 1987-94, prof., 1994—; dir. mammography Waukesha Meml. Hosp. Contbr. articles to profl. jours. Mem. Am. Coll. Radiology, Radiol. Soc. N.Am.

THORSEN, NANCY DAIN, real estate broker; b. Edwardsville, Ill., June 23, 1944; d. Clifford Earl and Suzanne Eleanor (Kribs) Dain; m. David Massie, 1968 (div. 1975); 1 child, Suzanne Dain Massie; m. James Hugh Thorsen, May 30, 1980. BSc in Mktg., So. Ill. U., 1968, MSc in Bus. Edn., 1975; grad. Realtor Inst., Idaho, 1983. Cert. resdl. and investment specialist, fin. instr.; Designated Real Estate Instr. State of Idaho; accredited buyer rep. Personnel officer J.H. Little & Co. Ltd., London, 1969-72; instr. in bus. edn. Spl. Sch. Dist. St. Louis, 1974-77; mgr. mktg./ops. Isis Foods, Inc., St. Louis, 1978-80; asst. mgr. store Stix, Baer & Fuller, St. Louis, 1980; assoc. broker Century 21 Sayer Realty, Inc., Idaho Falls, Idaho, 1981-88, RE/MAX Homestead Realty, 1989—; speaker RE/MAX Internat. Conv., 1990, 94, RE/MAX Stars Cruise, 1993, RE/MAX Pacific N.W. Conv., 1994, Century 21 Austral-Asia, 1995, women's seminar Clemson U., 1996; real estate fin. instr. State of Idaho Real Estate Commn., 1994; founder Nancy Thorsen Seminars, 1995. Bd. dirs. Idaho Vol., Boise, 1981-84, Idaho Falls Symphony, 1982; pres. Friends of Idaho Falls Libr., 1981-83; chmn. Idaho Falls Mayor's Com. for Vol. Coordination, 1981-84; power leader Power Program, 1995. Recipient Idaho Gov.'s award, 1982, cert. appreciation City of Idaho Falls/Mayor Campbell, 1982, 87, Civitan Disting. Pres. award, 1990; named to Two Million Dollar Club, Three Million Dollar Club, 1987, 88, Four Million Dollar Club, 1989, 90, Top Investment Sales Person for Eastern Idaho, 1985, Realtor of Yr. Idaho Falls Bd. Realtors, 1990, Outstanding Realtors Active in Politics, Mem. of Yr. Idaho Assn. Realtors, 1991, Women of Yr. Am. Biog. Inst., 1991, Profiles of Top Prodrs. award Real Estate Edn. Assn.; named Western Region Power Leader, Darryl Davis Seminars. Mem. Nat. Spkrs. Assn., Idaho Falls Bd. Realtors (chmn. orientation 1982-83, chmn. edn. 1983, chmn. legis. com. 1989, 95—, chmn. program com. 1990, 91), Idaho Assn. Realtors (pres. Million Dollar Club 1988—, edn. com. 1990-93), So. Ill. U. Alumni Assn., Idaho Falls C. of C., Newcomers Club, Civitan (pres. Idaho Falls chpt. 1988-89, Civitan of Yr. 1986, 87, outstanding pres. award 1989), Idaho Real Estate Educators Assn. Office: RE/MAX Homestead Inc 1301 E 17th St Ste 1 Idaho Falls ID 83404-6273

THORSON, JUDITH ANN, academic administrator; b. Mpls., Apr. 23, 1947; d. Erwin G. and Ruth Homan; m. Jerald C. Thorson, June 28, 1972. BS in Edn., U. Minn., 1971; MPA, Ind. U., 1981. Registered sch. bus. administrator. Tchr. Mpls. Pub. Schs., 1972, Muskingum Vocat. Sch., Zanesville, Ohio, 1973; property mgr. Remanco, Chgo., 1973-76; adminstr. City of Hammond (Ind.), 1976-83; exec. dir. adminstrv. svcs. City Coll. of Chgo., 1983-89; v.p. bus. and fin., treas. to bd. Delta Coll., University Ctr., Mich., 1989—. Bd. mem. Good Neighbor Mission, Saginaw, Mich., 1992—. Recipient Disting. Budget award Gov. Fin. Officer Assn., Chgo., 1992, 93, 94. Mem. Cen. Assn. Coll. and Univ. Bus. Officers (bd. mem.), Nat. Assn. Coll. and Univ. Bus. Officers (2 yr. com. chair), Rotary (Bay City, Mich.), Torch Club, Saginaw Bay C. of C. Office: Delta Coll University Center MI 48710

THOYER, JUDITH REINHARDT, lawyer; b. Mt. Vernon, N.Y., July 29, 1940; d. Edgar Allen and Florence (Mayer) Reinhardt; m. Michael E. Thoyer, June 30, 1963; children: Erinn, Michael John. AB with honors, U. Mich., 1961; LLB summa cum laude, Columbia U., 1965. Bar: N.Y. 1966, D.C. 1984. Law libr. U. Ghana, Accra, Africa, 1963-64; assoc. Paul, Weiss, Rifkind, Wharton & Garrison, N.Y.C., 1966-75, ptnr., 1975—; mem. TriBar Opinion Com., 1995—. Mem. bd. visitors Law Sch. Columbia U., N.Y.C., 1991—; bd. dirs. Women's Action Alliance, N.Y.C., 1975-89, pro bono counsel, 1975—; mem. Women's Coun. Dem. Senatorial, mem. campaign com., 1993—; com. on career devel. and advancement of women lawyers Alumnae Columbia Law Sch., 1996—. Mem. N.Y. County Lawyers Assn. (mem. securities and exchs. com., spl. com. on mergers, acquisitions and corporate control contests 1996—), Assn. of Bar of City of N.Y. (mem. securities regulation com. 1976-79, mem. recruitment of lawyers com. 1980-82, mem. spl. com. on mergers, acquisitions and corp. control contests 1996—). Home: 1115 5th Ave Apt 3B New York NY 10128-0100 Office: Paul Weiss Rifkind Wharton & Garrison 1285 Avenue Of The Americas New York NY 10019-6028

THRAILKILL, FRANCIS MARIE, college president; b. San Antonio, Sept. 21, 1937; d. Franklin E. and Myrtle M. (Huggins) T. B.A. in History cum laude, Coll. New Rochelle, N.Y., 1961; M.A.in Sociology, Marquette U., Milw., 1969; Ed.D. in Higher Ednl. Adminstrn., Nova U., Ft. Lauderdale, Fla., 1975. Joined Ursuline Order of Sisters, Roman Catholic Ch., 1955; tchr. Ursuline Acad., Dallas, 1961-64; vice prin. Ursuline Acad., New Orleans, 1965-70; prin. Ursuline Acad., 1970-77; pres. Springfield (Ill.) Coll., 1978-87, Coll. of Mt. St. Joseph, Ohio, 1987—. Bd. dirs. Dan Beard Coun., Cin. Assn. for Blind, Joy Outdoor Edn. Ctr., Associated Bd. and Acordia, United Appeal, Wellness Cmty.; steering comm. Underground R.R. Freedom Mus. Mem. Nat. Assn. Ind. Colls. and Univs., Council Ind. Colls (bd. dirs.), Assn. Ind. Colls. and Univs. Ohio (exec. comm.), Ohio Found. Ind. Colls. and Univs. (bd. dirs.), Ohio Coll. Assn. (bd. dirs.), Ohio Tchr. Edn. and Certification Adv. Commn. (bd. dirs.), Greater Cin. Consortium Colls. and Univs., Campus Compact (exec. bd. dirs.). Office: Coll of Mt St Joseph Office of the President 5701 Delhi Rd Cincinnati OH 45233-1670

THRASHER, DIANNE ELIZABETH, mathematics educator, computer consultant; b. Brockton, Mass., July 11, 1945; m. George Thomas Thrasher, Jan. 28, 1967; children: Kimberly Elizabeth, Noelle Elizabeth. BA in Math., Bridgewater State Coll., 1967, postgrad. in computer sci., 1984-87. owner New Eng. Regional Kumon Ednl. Franchise, 1991-95; approved profl. point devel. provider for tchr. cert. State of Mass., 1996. Tchr. math. Plymouth/Carver Regional Schs., Plymouth, Mass., 1976-78, Alden Sch., Duxbury, Mass., 1980-82, Marshfield (Mass.) High Sch., 1982-84; computer cons. TC2I-Thrasher Computer Cons. and Instrn., Duxbury, Mass., 1988—; dir., owner Internat. Ednl. Franchise, 1991-95; owner Duxbury Math. Ctr. K-Adult, 1995—; owner New Eng. Regional Kumon Ednl. Franchise, 1991-95; Mass. State approved profl. point devel. provider for tchr. cert., 1996. Active U.S. Figure Skating Assn., Colorado Springs, 1978-85; 2d reader First Ch. Christ Scientist, Plymouth, 1971-73; bd. govs. Skating Club of Hingham, Mass., 1978-85, pres., 1983-85, dir. Learn to Skate program, 1983-85; mem. First Ch. Christ Scientist, Boston, 1964—; with New Eng. Regional Kumon Franchise Owners, 1991-95; charter mem. Nat. Adv. Coun. of the U.S. Navy Meml. Found., 1992. Recipient Ed Taylor Meml. Vol. Svc. award Skating Club Hagham, 1995. Mem. NAFE, AAUW, Nat. Coun. Tchrs. Math., Boston Computer Soc., Duxbury Bus. Assn. Home: 140 Toby Garden St Duxbury MA 02332-4945

THRASHER, ROSE MARIE, critical care and community health nurse; b. Urbana, Ohio, Jan. 19, 1948; d. Jesse and Anna Frances (Clark) T. Student, Mercy Med. Ctr. Sch. Med. Tech., 1966-67, Wittenberg U., 1969-70; BSN, Ohio State U., 1974, BA in Anthropology, 1994, postgrad., 1994—. RN, Ohio; cert. cmty. health nurse ANA; cert. provider BCLS and ACLS, Am. Heart Assn. Pub. health nurse Columbus (Ohio) Health Dept., 1977-78; critical care nurse VA Med. Ctr., San Francisco, 1981, Staff Builders Health Care Svc., Oakland, Calif., 1975-76, 81-85; supr., case mgr. home health nurse passport program and intermittent care program Interim Health Care (formerly Med. Pers. Pool), Columbus, 1976-77, 85—. Recipient numerous acad. scholarships Wittenberg U. and Ohio State U.; mem. Nat. Women's Hall of Fame. Mem. AACN, ANA (coun. cmty. health nursing), AAUW, Ohio Nurses Assn., Intravenous Nurses Soc., Ohio State U. Alumni Assn., Am. Anthropol. Assn., Ohio Acad. Sci., Ohio State U. Coll. of Nursing Alumni Soc.

THRIFT, JULIANNE STILL, academic administrator; b. Barnwell, S.C.; m. Ashley Ormand Thrift; children: Lindsay, Laura. BA, U. S.C., MEd; PhD in Pub. Policy, George Washington U. Formerly asst. exec. dir. Nat. Assn. Coll. and Univ. Attys.; ombudsman U. S.C.; exec. dir. Nat. Inst. Ind. Colls. and Univs., 1982-88; exec. v.p. Nat. Assn. Ind. Colls. and Univs., Washington, 1988-91; pres. Salem Acad. and Coll., Winston-Salem, N.C., 1991—. Office: Salem Coll Office of the President Winston Salem NC 27108-0548

THROCKMORTON, JOAN HELEN, direct marketing consultant; b. Evanston, Ill., Apr. 11, 1931; d. Sydney L. and Anita H. (Pusheck) T.; m. Sheldon Burton Satin, June 26, 1982. B.A. with honors, Smith Coll., 1953. Mktg. exec. Lawrence Chait & Co., N.Y.C., 1965; mktg. exec. Cowles Communications, Inc., N.Y.C., 1968-69; founder, chief exec. officer Throckmorton Assocs., Inc., N.Y.C., 1970-83; pres. Joan Throckmorton, Inc., N.Y.C., 1983—; lectr. in field; instr. Direct Mktg. Assn., Sch. Continuing Edn., NYU, N.Y.C., 1985. Author: Winning Direct Response Advertising, 1986, 2d edit., 1996. Trustee Halle Ravine Com. Nature Conservancy, 1985; mem. expetition com. Outward Bound, 1980-83. Named Direct Mktg. Woman of Yr., 1986. Mem. Women's Dir. Response Group (founding mem.), Dir. Mktg. Assn. (bd. dirs. 1971-77, exec. com. 1972-77, mem. long-range planning com. 1977-78), Women's Forum, Dir. Mktg. Idea Exchange, Dir. Mktg. Creative Guild (bd. dirs. 1984-85), Jr. League Mexico City, Jr. League N.Y.C., Phi Beta Kappa. Office: Joan Throckmorton Inc PO Box 452 Pound Ridge NY 10576-0452

THRONE, MARILYN ELIZABETH, English educator; b. Cleve., Oct. 24, 1939; d. Charles George and Clara Elizabeth (Kieffer) T.; m. James R. Woodworth. AB, Miami U. in Oxford, 1961, MA, 1962; PhD, Miami U. in Oxford, Ohio State, 1969. Instr. Miami U., Oxford, Ohio, 1964-69; asst. prof. Miami U., Oxford, 1969-79, assoc. prof., 1979-90, prof., 1990—. Author: Walter Havighurst: Novelist of the Heartland, 1979. Office: Miami U English Dept Oxford OH 45056

THROWER, ELLEN, academic administrator. BS in Bus. Adminstn., U. N.C., Greensboro, 1975, MBA, 1978; PhD, Ga. State U., 1981; postgrad., Harvard U., 1988. Asst. prof. ins. and risk mgmt. Fla. State U., Talahassee, 1981-84; assoc. prof. ins. Drake U., Des Moines, 1984-88, dir. ins. ctr., 1985-88; pres., CEO The Coll. of Ins., N.Y.C., 1988—; prof. risk mgmt. and ins. The Coll. of Ins., 1988—; bd. dirs. Pa. Nat. Ins. Cos., United Educators, Inc., SCOR, U.S., Excel, Ltd.; mem. editl. adv. bd. Risk Mgmt. mag., 1994—; mem. adv. bd. Bermuda Found. for Ins. Studies, Internat. Ins. Found. Contbr. numerous articles to profl. jours. Bd. dirs. N.Y.C. Coun. on Econ. Edn., 1992—, Ins. Edn. Found., 1988—. Named Ins. Woman of Yr. APIW, 1993; recipient Chmn.'s award Nat. Assn. Mut. Ins. Cos., 1994. Mem. Internat. Ins. Soc., Am. Risk and Ins. Assn., Am. Mgmt. Assn., Risk and Ins. Mgmt. Soc., Soc. for Ins. Rsch., So. Risk and Ins. Assn., Western Risk and Ins. Co., Fin. Women's Assn. N.Y., Consortium. Office: The Coll of Ins 101 Murray St New York NY 10007-2165

THUMA, GENEVIEVE EASTMAN, interior designer; b. Greenfield, Mass., Apr. 29, 1925; d. Howard Myron and Marion (Cranston) Eastman; m. Theodore E. Thuma, June 10, 1945; children: Judith E., Holly Diane. Student, Syracuse U., 1944-45, 1961. Interior designer Roth Bros. Manor House, Syracuse, N.Y., 1968-81; sr. interior designer L & J.G. Stickley Inc., Manlius, N.Y., 1981-91; free lance interior designer Fayetteville, N.Y., 1991—. Bd. dirs. home furnishings and decorating program/continuing edn. program Syracuse U., 1989-90. Mem. Interior Design Soc. (upstate N.Y. chpt. pres. 1980-81), PEO (chpt. pres. 1995-96), Suburban Garden Club (v.p.). Methodist. Home and Office: 217 Kittell Rd Fayetteville NY 13066

THUMMEL, ROSA, artist; b. Des Moines, Apr. 17, 1916; d. Sposeto Frank and Victoria Jaquinta; m. John W. Thummel-Senneich (dec. Mar. 1988); children: Randolph, Carl, Gabriella. Student, Drake U., U. Iowa. One woman shows include Swiss Ctr. Gallery, N.Y.C., 1975, Nat. Art Ctr., N.Y.C., 1979, Tosta Gallery, Coconut Grove, Fla., 1980-83, Corridor Gallery, Summit, N.J., 1981; exhibited in group shows at Montclair (N.J.) Pub. Libr., 1976, Summit Art Ctr., 1978, 80, 82 (Beth Born Portrait award 1978, Best in Show 1980, First prize 1982), Painters & Sculpters Soc., N.Y.C., 1976-79, N.J., 1980-83, Bergen County (N.J.) Artist Guild, 1980, Sheila Nussbaum Gallery, Millburn, N.J., Lever House, N.Y.C., 1984, others; represented in pvt. collections. Home: 72 Holton Ln Essex Fells NJ 07021

THURLOW, DONNA ELLEN, computer programmer, analyst; b. Putnam, Conn., Oct. 3, 1947; d. Nathan Albert and Phyllis Irene (Bushey) Rawson; divorced; children: Kerry Susan, Camiel Phyllis, Kevin Robert. BA, Ctrl. N.E. Coll., 1988. Computer operator Programmer Schott Fiber Optics, Southbridge, Mass., 1985-89; computer programmer, analyst Commerce Ins., Co., Webster, Mass., 1989—. Office: Commerce Ins 211 Main St Webster MA 01570

THURMAN, KAREN L., congresswoman; b. Rapid City, S.D., Jan. 12, 1951; d. Lee Searle and Donna (Altfillisch) Loveland; m. John Patrick Thurman, 1973; children: McLin Searl and Liberty Lee. BA, U. Fla., 1973. Mem. Dunnellon City Council (Fla.), 1974-82; mayor of Dunnellon, 1979-81; mem. Monroe Regional Med. Ctr. Governancy Com.; mem. Comprehensive Plan Tech. Adv. Com.; del. Fla. Dem. Conv.; Dem. Nat. Conv., 1980; mem. Regional Energy Action com.; mem. Fla. State Senate, 1982-1992; mem. 103rd-104th Congress from 5th Fla. dist., 1993—, ranking minority mem. govt. reform & oversight subcom. nat. security, internat. affairs & criminal justice, mem. com. on aging. Recipient Svc. Above Self award Dunnellon C. of C., 1980; Regional Planning Con. Appreciation for Svc. award. Mem. Dunnellon C. of C. (dir.), Fla. Horseman's Children's Soc. (charter). Episcopalian. Office: US Ho of Reps 130 Cannon House Office Bldg Washington DC 20515-0905*

THURMAN, UMA KARUNA, actress; b. Boston, Apr. 29, 1970; d. Robert and Nena (von Schlebrugge) T.; m. Gary Oldman (div.). Appeared in films Kiss Daddy Good Night, 1987, Johnny Be Good, 1988, Dangerous Liaisons, 1988, The Adventures of Baron Munchausen, 1989, Where the Heart Is, 1990, Henry and June, 1990, Final Analysis, 1992, Jennifer Eight, 1992, Mad Dog and Glory, 1993, Even Cowgirls Get the Blues, 1993, Pulp Fiction, 1994 (Acad. award nom. Best Supporting Actress), A Month By the Lake, 1995, The Truth About Cats and Dogs, 1996, Beautiful Girls, 1996; TV movies include Robin Hood, 1991. Office: care CAA 9830 Wilshire Blvd Beverly Hills CA 90212*

THURSTON, ALICE JANET, former college president; b. Milw., Mar. 20, 1916; d. Karl J. and Nellie Ann (Smith) Stouffer; children: Anne, Robert. B.A., Denison U., 1937; MA, Northwestern U., 1938; PhD, George Washington U., 1960. Mem. faculty dept. psychology, counselor, dean students Montgomery Coll., Takoma Park, Md., 1950-65; dir. counseling Met. Campus, Cuyahoga Community Coll., Cleve., 1965-66; dean of students Western Campus, Cuyahoga Community Coll., 1966-67; vis. lectr. U. Ill., 1968-69; dir. Inst. Research and Student Services Met. Jr. Coll. Dist., Kansas City, Mo., 1969-71; pres. Garland Jr. Coll., Boston, 1971-75, Los Angeles Valley Coll., Van Nuys, Calif., 1975-81; lectr. Pepperdine U., L.A., 1978-81, Calif. State U., Worthridge, 1984-95; mem. adv. com. grad. program student affairs Calif. State U., Northridge. Author works in field. Bd. dirs. New Dir. for Youth, Van Nuys, Calif.; mem. ministerial search com. Unitarian Ch., Studio City, Calif., 1991-92, chair caring com., 1994—. Recipient Disting. Alumnae award Denison U., 1987, Humanitarian award Juvenile Justice Connection Project, 1987. Mem. Kappa Alpha Theta, Mortar Bd. Democrat. Unitarian. Home: 13156 Crewe St North Hollywood CA 91605-4727

THURSTON, SALLY A., lawyer; b. Glen Falls, N.Y., 1961. BS, Cornell U., 1983; JD, Harvard U., 1987. Bar: N.Y. 1987. Ptnr. Skadden, Arps, Slate, Meagher & Flom, N.Y.C. Office: Skadden Arps Slate Meagher & Flom 919 3d Ave New York NY 10022*

TIBBS, ANNETTE, secondary education educator; b. San Antonio, Sept. 6, 1961; d. Clarence Gene Tibbs and Barbara MaryAnn (Crutchfield) Inge. BS in Elem. Edn. and Math., Jarvis Christian Coll., Hawkins, Tex., 1983. Cert. tchr., Tex. Tchr. math. Laney H.S., Augusta, Ga., 1986-88, Killeen (Tex.) H.S., 1988-89; tchr. basic skills Bellaire Elem. Sch., Killeen, 1989-90; tchr. Paul Knox Mid. Sch., North Augusta, S.C., 1990-92; tchr. math. Manor Mid. Sch., Killeen, 1992—. Home: 4402 Mountain View Dr Killeen TX 76543 Office: Manor Mid Sch 1700 S WS Young Dr Killeen TX 76542

TICE, CAROL HOFF, middle school educator, consultant; b. Ashville, N.C., Oct. 6, 1931; d. Amos H. and Fern (Irvin) Hoff; m. (div.); children: Karin E., Jonathan H. BS, Manchester Coll., North Manchester, Ind., 1954; MEd, Cornell U., 1955. Cert. tchr., Mich., N.Y., N.J. Tchr. Princeton (N.J.) Schs., 1955-60; tchr. Ann Arbor (Mich.) Schs., 1964—; dir. intergenerational programs Inst. for Study Children and Families Eastern Mich. U., Ypsilanti, 1985—; founder, pres. Lifespan Resources, Inc., Ann Arbor, 1979—; commr. U.S. Nat. Commn. Internat. Yr. of the Child, Washington, 1979-81; del. to White House Conf. on Aging, 1995. Innovator; program, Tch. Learning Intergenerational Communities, 1971; author: Guide Books and articles, Community of Caring, 1980; co-producer, Film, What We Have, 1976 (award, Milan, Italy Film Festival 1982). Trustee Blue Lake Fine Arts Camp, Twin Lake, Mich., 1975—; del. White House Conf. on Aging, 1995. Recipient Program Innovation award Mich. Dept. Edn., 1974-80, C.S. Mott Found. award, 1982, Nat. Found. Improvement in Edn. award, Washington, 1986, Disting. Alumni award Manchester Coll., 1979, A+ Break the Mold award U.S. Sec. of Edn., 1992; Ford Found. fellow, Ithaca, N.Y., 1955. Mem. AAUW (agt. 1979), Generations United (Pioneer award 1989), Optimist Club. Democrat. Presbyterian. Office: Scarlett MS 3300 Lorraine St Ann Arbor MI 48108-1970

TICER, TERRI JEAN, sales executive; b. Childress, Tex., Apr. 15, 1955; d. Jerry H. and J. Colene (Eudey) T. AA, Clarendon Jr. Coll., 1977; BS, W. Tex. State U., 1979. Human svcs. dir. S. Plains Coll., Plainview, Tex., 1979-81; sales rep. Avon Products, N.Y.C., 1981—. Editor Plainview Breakfast Newsletter, 1995—; contbr. articles to profl. jours. Vol. Hospice of Plains, Plainview, 1985—; mem. Faith in Sharing House, 1985-89, Friends of Libr., Plainview, 1986-91, Humane Soc., Plainview, 1987-92; bd. dirs. Big Bros./Big Sisters, 1986-88; chmn. Youth Group Reunion, 1990-91. Mem. AAUW (membership v.p. 1987-89, chmn. edn. found. 1989-92, hosp. aux. 1992—), Austin Writers' League, Plainview Writer's Guild (treas. 1993-96), Lions Club (newsletter editor 1995, treas. 1996). Home: 2503 W 13th St Apt 5 Plainview TX 79072-4869

TICKTIN, ESTHER KELMAN, psychologist; b. Vienna, Austria, Jan. 24, 1925; came to the U.S., 1940; d. Leo and Toni Lea (Pomeranz) Kelman; m. Max D. Ticktin, Nov. 25, 1945; children: Hannah, Deborah, Ruth. BA, Bklyn. Coll., 1947; cert., Washington Sch. Psychiatry, 1981; PhD, U. Chgo., 1980. Lic. psychologist, D.C. Psychologist Cmty. Mental Health Ctr., Washington, 1973-75, Children's Residential Treatment Ctr., Washington, 1978-80; pvt. practice psychotherapy Washington, 1980—. Contbr. articles to profl. jours. Mem. Fabrangen Jewish Cmty., B'not Esh Jewish Feminist Spirituality Group. Home: 2311 Connecticut Ave NW Washington DC 20008 Office: 3000 Connecticut Ave NW Washington DC 20008

TIDBALL, M. ELIZABETH PETERS, physiology educator, research director; b. Anderson, Ind., Oct. 15, 1929; d. John Winton and Beatrice (Ryan) Peters; m. Charles S. Tidball, Oct. 25, 1952. BA, Mt. Holyoke Coll., 1951, LHD, 1976; MS, U. Wis., 1955, PhD, 1959; MTS summa cum laude, Wesley Theol. Sem., 1990; ScD (hon.), Wilson Coll., 1973; DSc (hon.), Trinity Coll., 1974, Cedar Crest Coll., 1977; ScD (hon.), U. of South, 1978, Goucher Coll., 1979; DSc (hon.), St. Mary-of-The-Woods Coll., 1986; LittD (hon.), Regis Coll., 1980, Coll. St. Catherine, 1980, Alverno Coll., 1989; HHD (hon.), St. Mary's Coll., 1977, Hood Coll., 1982; LLD (hon.), St. Joseph Coll., 1983; LHD (hon.), Skidmore Coll., 1984, Marymount Coll., 1985, Converse Coll., 1985, Mt. Vernon Coll., 1986. Teaching asst. physiology dept. U. Wis., 1952-55, 58-59; research asst. anatomy dept. U. Chgo., 1955-56, research asst. physiology dept., 1956-58; USPHS postdoctoral fellow NIH, Bethesda, Md., 1959-61; staff pharmacologist Hazleton Labs., Falls Church, Va., 1961; assoc. in physiology George Washington U. Med. Ctr., 1960-62; cons. Hazleton Labs., 1962; asst. research prof. dept. pharmacology George Washington U. Med. Ctr., 1962-64, assoc. research prof. dept. physiology, 1964-70, research prof., 1970-71, prof., 1971-94, prof. emeritus, 1994—; asst. dir. M of Theol. Studies program Wesley Theol Sem., 1993-94; disting. rsch. scholar Hood Coll., Frederick, Md., 1994—; co-dir. Tidball Ctr. for Study of Ednl. Environments Hood Coll., 1994—; Lucie Stern Disting. vis. prof. natural scis. Mills Coll., 1980; scholar in residence Coll. Preachers, 1984, Salem Coll., 1985, Wesley Theol. Sem., 1992; Disting. scholar in residence So. Meth. U., 1985; vis. trustee prof. Skidmore Coll.,

1995; cons. FDA, 1966-67, assoc. sci. coord. sci. assocs. tng. programs, 1966-67; mem. com. on NIH tng. programs and fellowships Nat. Acad. Scis., 1972-75; faculty summer confs. Am. Youth Found., 1967-78; founder, dir. Summer Seminars for Women Am. Youth Found., 1987-95; cons. for instl. rsch. Wellesley Coll., 1974-75; exec. sec. com. on edn. and employment women in sci. and engrng. Commn. on Human Resources, NRC/NAS, 1974-75, vice chmn., 1977-82; cons., staff officer NRC/Nat. Acad. Scis., 1974-75; cons. Woodrow Wilson Nat. Fellowship Found., 1975—, NSF, 1974-91; bd. mentor Assn. Governing Bds. of Univs. and Colls., 1991—, Gale Fund for the Study of Trusteeship Adv. Comm., 1992—; cons. Assn. Am. Colls. Women's Coll. Coalition Rsch. Adv. Com., 1992—; Single Gender Schooling Working Group, U.S. Dept. Edn., 1992-94; rep. to D.C. Commn. on Status of Women, 1972-75; nat. panelist Am. Coun. on Edn., 1983-90; panel mem. Congl. Office of Tech. Assessment, 1986-87; mem. fellows selection com., fellows mentor Coll. Preachers, 1992—. Columnist Trusteeship, 1993—; mem. editl. bd. Jour. Higher Edn., 1979-84, cons. editor, 1984—; mem. editl. adv. bd. Religion and Intellectual Life, 1983—; contbr. sci. articles and rsch. on edn. of women to profl. jours. Trustee Mt. Holyoke Coll., 1968-73, vice-chmn., 1972-73, trustee fellow, 1988—; trustee Hood Coll., 1972-84, 86-92, exec. com., 1974-84, 89-92; overseer Sweet Briar Coll., 1978-85; trustee Cathedral Choral Soc., 1976-90, pres. bd. trustees, 1982-84, hon. trustee, 1991—; trustee Skidmore Coll., 1988—, mem. exec. com., 1993—; mem. governing bd. Coll. of Preachers, 1979-85, chmn., 1983-85; mem. governing bd. Washington Cathedral Found., 1983-85, mem. exec com., 1983-85; bd. vis. Salem Coll., 1986-93; ctr. assoc. Nat. Resource Ctr., Girls Clubs Am., 1983—. Shattuck fellow, 1955-56; Mary E. Woolley fellow Mt. Holyoke Coll., 1958-59; USPHS postdoctoral fellow, 1959-61; recipient Alumnae Medal of Honor Mt. Holyoke Coll., 1971, Award for Valuable Contbns. Gen. Alumni Assn. George Washington U., 1982, 87, Chestnut Hill Medal for Outstanding Achievement Chestnut Hill Coll., Phila., 1987; named Outstanding Grad. The Penn Hall Sch., 1988. Mem. AAAS, Am. Physiol. Soc. (chmn. task force on women in physiology 1973-80, com. on coms. 1977-80, mem. emeritus 1994—), Am. Assn. Higher Edn., Mt. Holyoke Alumnae Assn. (dir. 1966-70, 76-77), Histamine Club, Sigma Delta Epsilon, Sigma Xi. Episcopalian. Home: 4100 Cathedral Ave NW Washington DC 20016-3584

TIDWELL, ENID EUGENIE, sculptor, advocate; b. Farmington, N.Mex., Sept. 20, 1944; d. James Eugene and Eleanor Pynchon (Davenport) MacDonald; m. Thomas Russell Walker, May 12, 1963 (div. 1968); 1 child, Thomas Shawn; m. Roy Mc Tidwell, June 19, 1969; 1 child, Michael Eric. BA in English, Teaching cum laude, U. Ala., Huntsville, 1975. Sec. U. N.Mex., Albuquerque, 1964-66, Sandia Labs., Albuquerque, 1966-69; office mgr. Stanford Rsch. Inst., Kuwait, 1977-78; artist Calif., Va., 1978—; chmn., treas. Gallery House, Palo Alto, Calif., 1979-80. Exhibited in one person shows including Stanford U. Faculty Club, Palo Alto, Calif., 1979, Dominican Coll. Gallery, San Rafael, Calif., 1980, Zenith Gallery, Washington D.C., 1995, El Prado Gallery, Santa Fe, 1995; group shows include Quadrangle Devel. Corp., Washington, 1990, Artists Equity 3d Annual Memberhip Awards Exhibit, Washington, 1988, Allied Artists Am. 74th Annual Exhbn., N.Y.C., 1987, Hudson Valley '86, Poughkeepsie, N.Y., 1986, Washington Women's Art Ctr. Sculpture Show, 1982, 85, 86, Allied Artists Am. 71st Annual Exbn., N.Y.C., 1984, City Art 1981, Washington, 4th Annual Open Juried Non-Member Exbn. The Salmagundi Club, N.Y., 1981, Nat. Small Sculpture and Drawing Open Juried Competition Westwood Ctr. the Arts, L.A., 1981, Sculpture N.Mex., 1993, On-Site/Off-Site, Santa Fe, 1995, numerous others; represented in permanent collections including Ingersoll & Block, Walker Wire, Centennial Devel. Corp., Signet Bank, Fisher Group, others. Mem. Fairfax County (Va.) Cultural Facility Task Force, 1989-90; treas. Bluffs of Wolftrap Homeowners Assn., Vienna, Va., 1985-88; pres. Monte Sano Homeowners Assn., Huntsville, Ala., 1975-76; bd. dirs. Monte Sano Elem. PTA, Huntsville, 1970-72; active PTA, Ala., Calif., Va., 1969-89, Boy Scounts Am., Ala., Va., 1971-89. Mem. AAUW (pres. McLean br. 1988-90, Ednl. Found. grantee 1986, 91, program v.p. N.Mex. chpt. 1994-96), Allied Artists Am., N.Mex. Ednl. Found. (co-chair 1996—), Sigma Tau Delta. Home and Office: 5 E Sunflower Cir Santa Fe NM 87501-8523

TIDWELL, JANET ELIZABETH, adult education educator; b. Nashville, Oct. 17, 1941; d. Hudson Blair and Margaret Elizabeth (Patterson) Malone; m. John Edward Tidwell Jr., Sept. 15, 1962; children: Janet Blaire Tidwell Miller, Anne Elizabeth Tidwell Carey. BS in Elem. Edn., George Peabody Coll., 1962; postgrad., Miss. Coll., 1972, U. Tenn., 1978-79, 91, 94. Tchr. English & civics, jr. & sr. h.s. Lewis County Sch. System, Hohenwald, Tenn., 1963; tchr. 2d grade Alexandria (Va.) Sch. System, 1964; tchr., 1st & 3d grades Met. Nashville Sch. System, 1965-70; substitute tchr. Hinds County Sch. System, Jackson, Miss., 1974-78, Knox County Schs. System, Knoxville, Tenn., 1978-79; substitute tchr., tchrs. asst., tchr. 1st & 3d grade Wake County Sch. System, Raleigh, N.C., 1979-91; tchr. adult edn. Knox County Sch. System, 1991—. Docent Blount Mansion Assn., Knoxville, 1991—, McClung Mus., U. Tenn., Knoxville, 1993—, Confederate Meml. Hall, Knoxville, 1995—. Mem. Tenn. Assn. Women Hwy. Safety Leaders (Knox county rep. 1994-96), Tenn. Assn. Adult Continuing Edn., DAR (registrar 1996—), United Daus. of Confederacy (1st v.p. 1996—), U. Tenn. Faculty Women's Club, Alpha Delta Kappa. Baptist. Home: 3804 South View Cir Knoxville TN 37920-6167 Office: Knox County Sch System City County Bldg Knoxville TN 37901

TIDWELL, MARY ELLEN, risk/insurance coordinator; b. Liberty, S.C., June 25, 1940; d. William Robert and Ruby Irene (Trammell) Murphy; m. Howard Eugene Anderson, Sept. 8, 1956 (div. Jan. 1987); children: Howard Eugene Jr., Sterling Craig; m. Lear Tidwell, July 9, 1989. AS in Office Mgmt., Polk C.C., 1993. Sec. H. Lamar Stewart Ins. Agy, Frostproof, Fla., 1962-64; accounts payable clk. Ben Hill Griffin, Inc., Frostproof, 1964-65; agt. Bullard Ins. Agy., Inc., Lake Wales, Fla., 1966-79; risk/ins. coordinator Coca-Cola Foods, Auburndale, Fla., 1979—; dir. Fla. Girls State, Inc., Orlando, 1988-93. City chmn. March of Dimes, Frostproof, 1964; campaign worker Tom Wheeler for Sheriff, Winter Haven, Fla., 1988. Mem. Risk and Ins. Mgmt. Soc., Am. Legion, Order of Eastern Star. Democrat. Baptist. Office: Coca-Cola Foods PO Box 247 Auburndale FL 33823-0247

TIEFEL, VIRGINIA MAY, librarian; b. Detroit, May 20, 1926; d. Karl and June Garland (Young) Brenkert; m. Paul Martin Tiefel, Jan. 25, 1947; children: Paul Martin Jr., Mark Gregory. B.A. in Elem. Edn., Wayne State U., 1962; M.A. in Library Sci., U. Mich., 1968. Librarian Birmingham Schs., Mich., 1967-68; librarian S. Euclid-Lyndhurst Schs., Cleve., 1968-69; acquisitions-reference librarian Hiram Coll., Ohio, 1969-77; head undergrad. libraries Ohio State U., Columbus, 1977-84, dir. library user edn., 1978-95, faculty outreach coord., 1995—. Contbr. articles to profl. jours. Recipient Disting. Alumnus award U. Mich. Sch. Info. and Libr. Studies, 1993. Mem. ALA (v.p. Ohio sect. 1973-74, pres. 1974-75, Miriam Dudley Bibliographic Instrn. Librarian of Yr. 1986), Acad. Library Assn. Ohio (Outstanding Ohio Acad. Librarian 1984), Assn. Coll. and Research Libraries (chmn. bibliographic instrn. sect. com. on research 1983-84, chmn. com. on performance measures 1984-90). Lutheran. Home: 4956 Smoketalk Ln Westerville OH 43081-4433 Office: Ohio State U Libraries 1858 Neil Ave Columbus OH 43210-1225

TIEFENTHAL, MARGUERITE AURAND, school social worker; b. Battle Creek, Mich., July 23, 1919; d. Charles Henry and Elisabeth Dirk (Hoekstra) Aurand; m. Harlan E. Tiefenthal, Nov. 26, 1942; children: Susan Ann, Daniel E., Elisabeth Amber, Carol Aurand. BS, Western Mich. U., 1941; MSW, U. Mich., 1950; postgrad., Coll. of DuPage, Ill., 1988-90. Tchr. No. High Sch., Flint, Mich., 1941-44, Cen. High Sch., Kalamazoo, 1944-45; acct. Upjohn Co., Kalamazoo, 1945-48; social worker Family Svc. Agy., Lansing, Mich., 1948-50, Pitts., 1950-55; sch. social worker Gower Sch. Dist., Hinsdale, Ill., 1962-70; sch. social worker Hinsdale (Ill.) Sch. Dist. 181, 1970-89, cons., 1989—; sch. social worker Villa Park (Ill.) Sch. Dist. 45, 1989; addictions counselor Mercy Hosp., 1990-92; asst. prof. sch. social work, liaison to pub. schs. Loyola U., Chgo., 1990—; field instr. social work interns U. Ill., 1979-88; impartial due process hearing officer; mem. adv. com. sch. social work Ill. State Bd. Edn. approved programs U. Ill. and George Williams Coll.; speaker Nat. Conf. Sch. Social Work, Denver, U. Tex. Joint Conf. Sch. Social Work in Ill.; founder Marguerite Tiefenthal Symposium for Ill. Sch. Social Work Interns. Co-editor The School Social Worker and the Handicapped Child: Making P.L. 94-142 Work; sect. editor: Sch. Social Work Quarterly, 1979. Sec. All Village Caucus Village of Western Springs, Ill., mem. village disaster com.; deacon Presbyn. Ch. Western Springs, Sunday sch. tchr., mem. choir; instr. Parent Effectiveness, Teacher Effectiveness, STEP; trainer Widowed Persons Service Tng. Program for Vol. Aides AARP. Recipient Ill. Sch. Social Worker of Yr., 1982. Mem. Nat. Assn. Social Workers (chmn. exec. council on social work in schs.), Ill. Assn. Sch. Social Workers (past pres., past conf. chmn., conf. program chmn.), Sch. Social Workers Supervisors Group (del. to Ill. Commn. on Children), Programs. for Licensure of Social Work Practice in Ill., LWV, DKG, PEO. Home: 4544 Grand Ave Western Springs IL 60558-1545

TIEGS, CHERYL, model, designer. Profl. model, appearing in nat. mags., including, Time, Life, Bazaar, Sports Illustrated, Glamour; appeared weekly on ABC's Good Morning America; also appearing in TV commls., Cheryl Tiegs line of sportswear, Cheryl Tiegs nationally-distributed line of women's eyeglass frames, Cheryl Tiegs Collection of 14k Gold Jewelry, Fashion Watches, Shoes and Hosiery; author: The Way to Natural Beauty, 1980; Sports Illustrated video Aerobic Interval Training with Cheryl Tiegs. Address: care Barbara Shapiro 2 Greenwich Plz Ste 100 Greenwich CT 06830-6353

TIELEMANS, HENRIETTE A., lawyer; b. Antwerp, Belgium, May 6, 1953. Lic. Jur. magna cum laude, U. Antwerp, 1976; LLM, Harvard U., 1978. Bar: Brussels 1980. Vis. prof. Nat. U. Rwanda, 1979; asst. prof. law faculty U. Antwerp, 1976-77, 79-80; ptnr., resident Brussels office Covington & Burling, Washington. Contbr. articles to profl. jours. Fulbright fellow, 1978. Office: Covington & Burling PO Box 7566 1201 Pennsylvania Ave NW Washington DC 20044-7566*

TIEMAN, SUZANNAH BLISS, neurobiologist; b. Washington, Oct. 10, 1943; d. John Alden and Winifred Texas (Bell) Bliss; m. David George Tieman, Dec. 19, 1969. AB with honors, Cornell U., 1965; postgrad., MIT, 1965-66, Calif. Inst. Tech., 1971-72; PhD, Stanford U., 1974. Postdoctoral fellow dept. anatomy U. Calif., San Francisco, 1974-77; rsch. assoc. Neurobiology Rsch. Ctr. SUNY, Albany, 1977-90, sr. rsch. assoc., 1990—, assoc. prof. dept. biomed. scis., 1988-95, prof., 1995—, rsch. prof. dept. biol. scis., 1990—. Contbr. articles to profl. jours., chpts. to books in field. Rsch. grantee Nat. Eye Inst., SUNY, Albany, 1979-83, NSF, SUNY, 1983-86, 88-92, 92—; predoctoral fellow NSF, NIH, Stanford U., 1970-73, 73-74, postdoctoral fellow Nat. Eye Inst., U. Calif., San Francisco, 1974-77. Mem. AAAS, Soc. for Neurosci. (steering com. Hudson Berkshire chpt. 1980-81, pres. 1991-93), Assn. Rsch. in Vision and Ophthalmology, Am. Assn. Anatomists, Assn. Women in Sci., Fedn. Am. Socs. Exptl. Biology, Women in Neurosci., Nat. Audubon Soc., Nature Conservancy. Office: SUNY Neurobiology Rsch Ctr 1400 Washington Ave Albany NY 12222-0100

TIEMANN, MARGARET ANN, health educator; b. St. Louis, June 24, 1956; d. Herman T. and Margaret Ellen (Drury) Volkerding; m. Mark G. Tiemann, Nov. 4, 1978; children: Michelle, Jeffrey. Diploma in nursing, DePaul Hosp Sch. Nursing, St. Louis, 1978; BS in Bus. Adminstrn., Fontbonne Coll., 1991. RN, Mo. Staff nurse Christain Hosp. N.E., St. Louis, 1975-79; staff nurse ICU St. Joseph's Health Ctr., St. Charles, Mo., 1979-91; instr. St. Mary's Coll. of O'Fallon, Mo., 1987-88; asst. prof. St. Charles County C.C., St. Peters, Mo., 1988-96; adv. bd. mem. St. Charles County C.C. Health Info. Tech. Adv. Com., St. Peters, 1988—, faculty advisor, 1993-96; mem. self-evaluation com. St. Charles County C.C., St. Peters, 1988—; cons. Serenity Mgmt. and Cons., St. Louis, 1990. Mem. Ea. Mo. Health Info. Mgmt. Assn. (assoc.), St. Louis Met. Critical Care Soc., DePaul Hosp. Sch. Nursing Alumni. Roman Catholic.

TIERNEY, CATHERINE MARIE, librarian; b. Woodbury, N.J., July 11, 1947; d. William John and Marie Cecilia (Oakes) Morgan; m. Phillip A Tierney, Aug. 9, 1969. BA, Cardinal Stritch Coll., 1969; MLS, Kent State U., 1974. Reference libr. Akron (Ohio) Beacon Jour., 1974-76, chief libr., 1976—. Mem. Spl. Librs. Assn. Republican. Episcopalian. Office: Akron Beacon Jour 44 W Exchange St Akron OH 44328-0001

TIERNEY, ELAINE, neuropsychiatrist, educator; b. Boston, Mar. 7, 1962. BA in Art, U. Fla., 1984; MD, U. South Fla., 1989. Intern Cook County Hosp., Chgo., 1989-90; psychiatry resident Johns Hopkins U., Balt., 1990-92, pediats. psychiatry fellow, 1992-94, instr., 1994-95, asst. prof., 1995—, med. dir. Neurobehavioral Unit, 1996—. Mem. Am. Acad. Child and Adolescent Psychiatry, Am. Psychiat. Assn., Physicians for Social Responsibility, Physicians Forum. Office: Johns Hopkins U Kennedy Krieger Inst 707 N Broadway Baltimore MD 21205

TIERNEY, SUSAN FALLOWS, federal official; married; 2 children. BA, Scripps Coll., 1973; student, L'Institut d'Etudes Politiques, Paris; MA, Cornell U., 1976, PhD, 1980; LLD (hon.), Regis Coll. Asst. prof. U. Calif., Irvine, 1978-82; sr. economist Mass. Exec. Office Energy Resources, 1983-84; exec. dir. Mass. Energy Facilities Siting Coun., 1984-88; commr. Dept. Pub. Utilities, 1988-90, sec. environ. affairs, resources authority, 1991-93; asst. sec. energy, office of policy, planning and program evaluation Dept. Energy, Washington, 1993—; chmn. transmission task force New Eng. Gov.'s Conf. Power Planning Com.; mem. Keystone Project Electric Transmission Ind. Power Prodrs. Contbr. articles to profl. jours. Mem. New Eng. Conf. Public Utility Commrs., Nat. Assn. Regulatory Utility Commrs. (energy conservation gas com.), Electric Power Rsch. (adv. com.). Home: Dept Energy Policy 108 Hammond St Chestnut Hill MA 01267

TIETZE, PHYLLIS SOMERVILLE, retired media specialist; b. Bklyn., Aug. 5, 1941; d. Samuel Clark and Norma Helen (Vanderbeck) Somerville; m. Robert Morse Tietze, Dec. 22, 1962; children: Kevin North, Andrea Kristina. BS, U. Miami, 1962; ML, U. S.C., 1989. Rsch. asst. U. Miami Inst. Marine Sci., 1962-65; media specialist Pendleton (S.C.) High Sch., 1989—; ret. Mem. ALA, S.C. Assn. Sch. Librs., Anderson County Libr. Assn. Presbyterian. Home: 200 Hemlock Dr Highlands NC 28741 Office: Pendleton High Sch Hwy 187 Box 218 Pendleton SC 29670

TIGUE, BARBARA KUZMIAK, fitness trainer; b. Fairless Hills, Pa., May 9, 1967; d. Stephen and Joann (Weigle) Kuzmiak; m. Milton Tigue, Jr., Jan. 11, 1992. AA, U. Fla., 1987. Cert. personal trainer, fitness instr. Aerobic instr. Shapes Total Fitness, Tampa, Fla., 1980-90; personal fitness trainer Shapes Total Fitness, Tampa, 1992—; counselor Vitamin Storehouse, Tampa, 1989-92; fitness instr. Aerobic and Fitness Assn. of Am., Tampa, 1992—; personal trainer Am. Coun. on Exercise, Tampa, 1992—; personal fitness trainer Frank Calta's Co-ed Fitness, Tampa, 1993—; nutritional counselor Natural Food Outpost, Tampa, 1994—; personal fitness trainer World Gym, Carollwood, 1996—; aerobic instr. coord. Shapes Total Fitness, 1993—; nutritional seminar presentor Tampa Sports, 1994—; nutritional cons. Chuck's Natural Food Outpost, Tampa, 1994—. Nutrition/fitness presentor Tampa Sports Unltd., Tampa, 1994-96. Recipient U.S. Presdl. Sports award, 1995. Mem. Am. Coun. on Exercise (master mem.), Aerobic and Fitness Assn. of Am., Am. Coll. Sports Medicine, Woman's Sports Fedn., NIKE Instr. Network. Democrat. Office: Shapes Total Fitness Tampa FL 33618

TILBERIS, ELIZABETH, editor-in-chief; m. Andrew Tilberis, 1971. Student, Jacob Kramer Coll. Arts, Leeds, England; BA in Eng., Leicester (Eng.) Poly. Fashion asst. British Vogue, 1970, fashion editor, 1974, exec. fashion editor, 1984, sr. fashion editor, 1986, editor-in-chief, 1987; dir. Conde Nast Pubs., 1991; editor-in-chief Harper's Bazaar, N.Y.C., 1992—. Recipient 2 Nat. Mag. awards for design, photography, 1993, Coun. Fashion Designers of Am. award, 1994. Office: Harper's Bazaar 1700 Broadway New York NY 10019-5905 also: care Susan Magrino Susan Magrino Agency 167 E 73rd St New York NY 10021-3510*

TILDES, PHYLLIS LIMBACHER, author, illustrator, graphic designer; b. Bridgeport, Conn., Mar. 23, 1945; d. Philip Frederick and Olga Jennine (Chervenak) Limbacher; m. William J. Tildes, Apr. 6, 1968; 1 child, Jeffrey Carl. BFA, R.I. Sch. Design, 1967. Designer Hallmark, N.Y.C., 1965, 66; asst. art dir. Hopkins Art Ctr.-Dartmouth Coll., Hanover, N.H., 1967; graphic designer, illustrator William Wondriska Design, West Hartford, Conn., 1967-69, P.L. Tildes Design, Glastonbury, Conn., 1969—; design cons. Audubon Soc., Glastonbury, 1990—. Author, illustrator: (children's books) Counting on Calico, 1995, Calico Picks a Puppy, 1996, Animals Black and White, 1996. Apptd. mem. Glastonbury (Conn.) Fine Arts Com., 1977; founding mem. Glastonbury (Conn.) Conf. of Chs., 1980. Mem. Soc. Children's Book Writers and Illustrators. Democrat. Office: Charlesbridge Pub 85 Main St Watertown MA 02172

TILESTON, PEG BUELL, information specialist; b. Indpls., Nov. 28, 1931; d. Herbert J. and Georgia (Henry) Buell; m. Jules V., Aug. 14, 1954; children: Nancy, Anna, Gloria. BA, Earlham Coll., Richmond, Ind., 1954; student, U. Anchorage, 1972-74. Tchr. Danville (Ind.) Sch. System, 1954-56, Adams County Sch. Dist., Denver, 1957-59, 62-66, Montgomery County Sch. Dist., Silver Spring, Md., 1968-72; asst. dir. Alaska Ctr. for the Enviroment, Anchorage, 1976-80, exec. dir., 1980-81; pres. Environ. Rsch. and Info. Svc., Anchorage, 1981-84, Inform Alaska, Inc., Anchorage, 1985-91; owner Tileston & Assocs., 1992—; bd. dirs. Alaska Water Resource Bd., chairperson 1976-90; co-founder, treas. Alaska Common Ground, 1992—; mem. Alaska Oil & Gas Policy COun., 1996—. Editor for various newsletters. Co-founder, pres. Trustees for Alaska, Anchorage, 1975-81; treas., pres. Chagach Electric Assn., Anchorage, 1983-93, Alaska Conservation Found., 1980-86, 88—. Recipient Outstanding Svc. award Alaska Park & Recreation Assn., 1981, Sol Feinberg Environmental award, 1996, Celia Hunter Svc. award, 1988. Mem. Sierra (bd. dirs., treas. 1980-83). Democrat. Home and Office: 4780 Cambridge Way Anchorage AK 99503-7012

TILGER, JUSTINE THARP, research director; b. New Point, Ind., Sept. 11, 1931; d. Joseph Riley and Marcella Lorene (King) Tharp; m. Clarence A. Tilger II, Aug. 22, 1959 (div. Nov. 1972); children: Evelyn Mary, Clarence Arthur III, Joseph Thomas. AB, U. Chgo., 1951; BA, St. Mary's Coll., Notre Dame, Ind., 1954; MA, Ind. U., 1962, PhD, 1971. Mem. Sisters of the Holy Cross, Notre Dame, 1954-58; teaching fellow Ind. U., Bloomington, 1959-61; asst. editor Ind. Mag. History, Bloomington, 1962-64; bookkeeper Touche Ross, Boston, 1974-77; mgr. account services Harvard U., Cambridge, Mass., 1977-81; dir. research and records Bentley Coll., Waltham, Mass., 1982-84; dir. support services Sta. WGBH-TV, Boston, 1985; dir. research Tufts U., Medford, Mass., 1986—; cons. Laduke Assocs., Framingham, Mass., 1972-74, New Eng. Ballet, Sudbury, Mass., 1981-82. v.p. Potter Rd. Sch. Assn., Framingham, 1968-69; chmn. vols. St. Anselm's, Sudbury, 1970-71. Mem. Coun. for Advancement and Support Edn., Assn. Records Mgmt. Adminstrs., Am. Prospect Rsch. Assn., New Eng. Devel. Rsch. Assn., Mass. Bus. and Profl. Women (sec. 1981-82), Mensa. Roman Catholic. Home: 15 Auburn St # 6 Framingham MA 01701-4844 Office: Tufts U Dept of Research Pachard Hall Medford MA 02155

TILL, BEATRIZ MARIA, international business consultant, translator; b. Havana, Cuba, Sept. 27, 1952; came to U.S., 1961; d. Thomas Emanuel and Gladys Manuela (Loret de Mola) Alexander; m. John Edwin Till, Aug. 30, 1976. Student, U. Fla., 1970-71, 72-74, U. Ariz., 1988. Legal sec., translator-interpreter Norman Mopsik, Esquire, New Orleans, 1972; freelance translator and interpretor New Orleans, 1974-76; translating sales sec. Rozier Machinery, Tampa, Fla., 1976-78; legal sec., interpreter-translator Matias Blanco, Esquire, 1979; paralegal, interpreter-translator Barrs, Williamson and Levens, P.A., 1981-83; pres. Beatriz M. Till, Inc., 1983—; interpreter-translator Office of Worker's Compensation, State of Fla., Tampa, pvt. attys., 1979—; spl. advisor to Sec. of Commerce, State of Fla.; surveillance audio/video transcription specialist Fed. Ct. State of Fla. (middle dist.); also, expert witness on tape recording transcriptions and translations. Active Navy League of U.S. Mem. Internat. Platform Assn., Fla. C. of C., Tampa Bay Internat. Trade Coun.,Fla. Coun. Internat. Devel. Republican. Home: 12301 Pathway Ct Riverview FL 33569-4122 Office: Beatriz M Till Translations 12301 Pathway Ct Riverview FL 33569-4122

TILLEMA, SALLY JEAN, guidance counselor, coach, educator; b. Minot, N.D., July 10, 1963; d. James Eugene and Inez Delores (Koch) T. AA, U. N.D., Williston, 1983; BS, Valley City (N.D.) State U., 1986; MEd, N.D. State U., 1991. Asst. women's basketball coach Valley City State U., 1985-86; tchr. Fessenden (N.D.) H.S., 1986-89, athletic dir. boys'/girls' basketball, 1986-89, head girls' basketball coach, 1986-89, head boys' basketball coach, 1987-89; guidance counselor S.W. Jr. H.S., Forest Lake, Minn., 1991—, coach volleyball and basketball, 1991—; basketball camp counselor Lewis and Clark Basketball Camp, Williston, N.D., 1981-82, Valley City State U. Girls' Fundamental Camp, 1984, Big Players Specialty Camp, 1987-90; advisor to Karing Kids, 1991-96; mem. shared governance coun. Southwest Jr. H.S., 1993-96. Named Dist. Coach of the Yr., Fessenden, N.D., 1986; Bill Osmon scholar, 1985, N.D. State U. scholar, 1990-91. Mem. ACA, NEA, Am. Sch. Counselors Assn.

TILLER, DORA ELAINE, geriatrics services professional; b. Georgetown, Ohio, May 28, 1941; d. Walter and Beatrice (Campbell) Cremer; m. Robert Wells Tiller, Sept. 5, 1964; children: Nathan Michael, Caleb Matthew. BA, Transylvania U., 1963; MDiv, Yale U., 1967. Cert. clin. pastor. Student chaplain, recreation therapist Bellevue Hosp., N.Y.C., 1967-69; counselor, adminstr. Ednl. Opportunity Ctr., SUNY, Bklyn., 1972-80, project dir., 1973-74, acting coord. student pers. svcs., supr. career resource ctr., 1978-79; rsch. cons. Interfaith Conf. Met. Washington, summer 1980; dir. bereavement care program Hospice No. Va., Arlington, 1981-85; exec. dir. cmty. ministries program Bapt. Sr. Adult Ministries, Washington, 1985—; lectr., cons. in field. Contbr. articles to profl. jours., chpts. to books. Mem. Am. Soc. Aging (gov. coun. forum religion, spirituality and aging 1996—), Nat. Coun. Aging (bd. dirs. 1993—), Nat. Interfaith Coalition on Aging (chair bd. dirs. 1994—), So. Bapt. Assn. Ministries with the Aging (pres. 1993-94), Metro Share (past bd. dirs.), Grass Roots Orgn. Well-Being of Srs. (bd. dirs.), Cath. Charities USA (eldercare adv. com. 1995), Yale U. Divinity Sch. Alumnal Affairs Assn. Office: Bapt Sr Adult Ministries 1330 Massachusetts Ave NW Washington DC 20005

TILLER, MARTHA RUSSELL, public relations executive, consultant; b. Temple, Tex., Jan. 20, 1940; d. John Lafayette and Cleo (Davidson) Russell; m. David Clyde Tiller, Nov. 26, 1966; 1 child, John Russell. BFA cum laude, U. Tex., 1961; postgrad. Nat. U. Mex., 1962, Piaget Inst. of Tex. Christian U., 1970. With radio-TV prodns. dept. U. Tex. and Sta. KTBC-TV, Austin, 1959-61; asst. to producer CBS TV, N.Y.C., 1961-64; with Goodson Todman Prodns., N.Y.C., 1964-66; dir. publs. Tex. Fine Arts Commn., Austin, 1967-69; press and social sec. to Mrs. Lyndon B. Johnson, Austin, 1973-76, also spl. asst. to Pres. Lyndon B. Johnson, Office of the Former Pres., Austin, 1972; dir. pub. info. S.W. Ednl. Devel. Lab., Austin, 1976, media specialist, 1969-72, writer, 1967; dir. pub. affairs Glenn, Bozell & Jacobs, Inc., Dallas, 1977-78; dir. pub. affairs U.S. Dept. HEW Region XII, 1978-79; dir. pub. rels. Pla. of Ams. Hotel, Dallas, 1979-82; chmn., chief exec. officer Martha Tiller & Co. Pub. Rels. Counselors, Dallas, 1982—. Creator, producer award-winning video Basic Steps to Fire Safety, 1981. Mem. cultural activities task force Goals for Dallas; mem. Sta. KLRN-TV, Austin, Austin Symphony Orch. Soc., Town Lake Beautification Com. of Austin, Laguna Gloria Art Mus. and Guild, Austin; vice chmn. 8 Arts Ball, TACA Assn., 1981-82, bd. dirs., 1987-88; nat. gifts chmn. Worldwide USO Gala, 1985; vice chmn. James K. Wilson Luncheon, 1982; bd. dirs. Dallas Symphony Orch. League, 1986—, Grand Heritage Ball Commn., 1986, Dallas Opera Women, 1984, Girls Club of Dallas, 1987-89; mem. March of Dimes Women's Aux., Friends of LBJ Libr. (life), women's com. Dallas Civic Opera; bd. govs. Dallas Ballet, 1987-88, Dallas Opera, 1988—; mem. adv. coun. Austin Coll. Communications U. Tex., 1989—; pres. Dalla Summit, 1996; chair Dallas Opera Photogravure, 1996; mem. bd. Women's Issue Network, 1996—. Recipient Golden Key Pub. Rels. award Am. Hotel/Motel Assn., 1982; named Nation's Top Broadcasting Coed, Am. Women Radio and TV, 1959. Mem. Pub. Rels. Soc. Am., Tex. Pub. Rels., Internat. Women's Forum (mem. adv. coun. coll. of communicatoin found. U. Tex. at Austin), Tex. Pub. Rels. Assn. (Best of Tex. award 1981), Women in Communications, Austin Natural Sci. Assn., Mortar Bd., Alpha Epsilon Rho. Office: Martha Tiller & Co 3883 Turtle Creek Blvd Ste 118 Dallas TX 75204-2547

TILLER, OLIVE MARIE, retired church worker; b. St. Paul, Dec. 13, 1920; d. Otto William and Myrtle Alice (Brougham) Foerster; m. Carl William Tiller, June 21, 1940; children: Robert W., Jeanne L. Peterson. BS, U. Minn., 1940. Spl. edn. tchr. Prince Georges County, Md., 1955-63; spl. asst. for profl. svcs. Kendall Demonstration Elem. Sch., Gallaudet Coll., Washington, 1971-78; spl. asst. for program Ch. Women United, N.Y.C., 1979-80; exec. asst. to gen. sec. Nat. Coun. Chs. of Christ in U.S.A., N.Y.C., 1981-87; dep. gen. sec. for coop. Christianity Am. Bapt. Chs. of U.S.A., Valley Forge, Pa., 1987-88. Author: (with Carl W. Tiller) At Calvary, 1994. Mem.

Human Rels. Commn., Prince George's County, 1967-73; v.p. Am. Bapt. Chs. U.S.A., Valley Forge, 1976-77; bd. dirs. Am. Leprosy Missions, Greenville, S.C., 1981-95, Bapt. Peace Fellowship of N.Am., Memphis, 1984-95; mem. Nat. Interreligious Svc. Bd. for Conscientious Objectors, 1991—, treas., 1994—; mem. nat. coun. Fellowship of Reconciliation, 1985-88, 96—. Recipient Dahlberg Peace award Am. Bapt. Chs., 1991, Valiant Woman award Ch. Women United, 1978, Meeker award Ottawa U., 1995. Mem. Nat. Coun. Fellowship of Reconciliation. Baptist. Home: 100 Norman Dr Apt 283 Cranberry Township PA 16066-4235

TILLEY, CAROLYN BITTNER, technical information specialist; b. Washington, July 29, 1947; d. Klaud Kay and Margaret Louise (Hanson) Bittner; m. Frederick Edwin Dudley, June 18, 1985. B.S., Am. U., 1975; M.L.S., U. Md., 1976. With NIH, 1965-71; statis. research asst. Health Manpower Edn., Bethesda, Md., 1971-72; tech. info. specialist Nat. Libr. Medicine, Bethesda, Md., 1972-81, head medlars (med. lit. analysis and retrieval system) mgmt. sect., 1981—. Mem. editorial bd.: Med. Reference Services Quar. Mem. CENDI User Edn. Com., Nat. Fed. Abstracting and Info. Svc. Pub. Com. Recipient Merit award NIH, 1984, Rogers award Nat. Libr. Medicine, 1991. Mem. Med. Library Assn. Presbyterian. Office: Nat Libr Medicine 8600 Rockville Pike Bethesda MD 20894-0001

TILLMAN, ELIZABETH CARLOTTA, nurse, educator; b. Md., Aug. 31, 1929; d. Walter Monroe and Mozelle Virginia (Shugars) Brown; m. Lloyd A. Tillman, Apr. 16, 1949; children: Lloyd A. Jr., William L., Susan E. Tillman Chaires. Diploma, Md. Gen. Hosp. Sch. Nursing, 1950; student, Towson State U., U. Md., Loyola Coll., Balt., Howard C.C. RN. Psychiatric nurse Spring Grove Hosp. Ctr., Catonsville, Md., 1950; pvt. duty home health nurse Md., 1951-60; dir., tchr., nurse Doughoregan Manor Day Sch., Ellicott City, Md., 1960-80; med.-surg. nurse Woman's Hosp., Balt., 1964, Md. Gen. Hosp., Balt., 1980; nursing instr. Howard County Dept. Edn., Ellicott City, 1981-91; nursing educator Howard County Sch. Tech., 1981-91, Howard County Gen. Hosp., 1981-91; geriatric nurse Lorien Columbia (Md.) Nursing & Rehab. Ctr., 1981-91; home health nurse Md., 1992—. Mem. NEA, Md. State Tchrs. Assn., Md. Gen. Hosp. Alumni Assn., Am. Vocat. Assn., Health Occupations Educators, Md. Vocat. Assn., Phi Eta Sigma, Iota Lambda Sigma. Home: 10002 Reed Ln Ellicott City MD 21042-2238

TILLMAN, KAY HEIDT, real estate executive, commodity broker; b. Tampa, Fla., Jan. 24, 1945; d. Clarence Eugene and Doris (Tyson) Heidt; m. Thomas E. Barnes, Mar. 18, 1967 (div. 1972); children: Britton H., William H.; m. Herbert A. Tillman, Oct. 7, 1988. BA with honors, Rollins Coll., 1975, MS with honors, 1979. Lic. real estate sales person, Fla. Tchr. art Orange County Sch. Bd., Orlando, Fla., 1976-79; pres., owner Internat. Handcraft Ctr., Winter Garden, Fla., 1980-83, Decors Internat., Inc., Winter Garden, Fla., 1980-83, Mohamad & Barnes Investment Co., Orlando, Fla., 1983-89, Eagle Investment Properties, Orlando, 1985-89, Eagle-One Internat., Winter Garden, 1986—; pres., ptnr. Eagle Mktg. Group, Inc., Winter Garden, 1989—; cons. Nigerian Govt., Lagos, Nigeria, 1987-88, 93-94, Mid-East Investment Group, Orlando, Fla., 1986-89, 93-94. Pres. coun. Orlando C. of C., 1987-88; active recreation coun. Bapt. Ch., 1994; founder Loving Hands Outreach to Homeless, 1994. Miss. Fla., Am. Beauty Pageant, Long Beach, Calif., 1975. Mem. Am. Soc. Ind. Sec., Orlando Bd. Realtors, Alpha Chi Omega (v.p. 1966). Republican. Baptist. Home: 215 Valencia Shores Dr Winter Garden FL 34787-2619 Office: Eagle One Internat PO Box 770397 Winter Garden FL 34777-0397

TILLOTSON, CAROLYN, state legislator; m. John C. Tillotson. Mem. Kans. Senate, 1993—. Republican. Home: 1606 Westwood Dr Leavenworth KS 66048-6622 Office: Kans State Senate State Capitol Topeka KS 66612*

TILL-RETZ, ROBERTA, labor educator; b. San Diego, Feb. 4, 1940; d. Robert Clifton and Lela (Sessions) Till; m. Jae Carl Retz, Sept. 1, 1962; 1 child, Justine. BA, Brigham Young U., 1962; MA, Harvard U., 1964; PhD, U. Oreg., 1976, MA in Ind. Rels., 1980. Instr. Am. history European divsn. U. Md., Heidelberg, West Germany, 1964-69; rsch. assoc. women's studies Cornell U., Ithaca, N.Y., 1976-77; program assoc. Labor Edn. and Rsch. Ctr. U. Oreg., Eugene, 1979-80; dir. Labor Ctr. U. Iowa, Iowa City, 1984-93, program coord. Labor Ctr., 1980-84, 93—; mem. adv. bd. Pre-Vocat. Tng. Project, Iowa City, 1988-93; project dir. oral history project Iowa Fedn. Labor, AFL-CIO, Iowa City, 1981—; mem. adv. bd. Mayor's Youth Employment, Iowa City, 1993-95; mem. exec. bd. Iowa Fedn. Tchrs., 1985-90, 95-96. Author: Your Rights to Family and Medical Leave, 1994, Negotiating in a New Work Systems Environment, 1994; co-author: Labor Guide to Local Union Leadership, 1986; editor Class Issue Am. Fedn. Tchrs. # 716, 1993-96; book rev. editor Labor Studies Jour., 1987-96. Bd. dirs. Iowa Citizen Action Network, Iowa, 1990—; chair affirmative action com. Johnson County Dems., Iowa City, 1987-91, precinct chair, 1994-96. Fulbright-Hays dissertation fellow U.S. Govt., 1972-73; grantee German Marshall Fund Project Women, Trade Unions in 4 Countries, 1976-77, Occupational Health Edn. for Workers, Kellogg Found., 1986-90; Iowa Women in Workplace, Iowa Humanities Bd., 1986. Mem. Univ. and Coll. Labor Edn. Assn. (mem. exec. bd., Midwest instnl. rep. 1986-88, 91-93), Worker's Edn. Comm. Workers Am. Local 189 (Midwest rep. 1984-87, 90-94), Coalition Labor Union Women. Democrat. Home: 600 Manor Dr Iowa City IA 52246 Office: U Iowa Labor Ctr Oakdale Hall Iowa City IA 52242

TILLY, JENNIFER, actress. TV series include: Shaping Up, 1984, Bodyguard, 1990, Key West, 1993; TV movies include: Heads, 1994; films include: No Small Affair, 1984, Moving Violations, 1985, He's My Girl, 1987, Inside Out, 1987, Rented Lips, 1988, High Spirits, 1988, Johnny Be Good, 1988, Remote Control, 1988, The Fabulous Baker Boys, 1989, Let It Ride, 1989, Far From Home, 1989, Scorchers, 1991, Shadow of the Wolf, 1992, Made in America, 1993, At Home With the Webbers, 1993, Double Cross, 1994, Bullets Over Broadway, 1994 (Academy award nomination best supporting actress 1994), The Getaway, 1994, The Pompatus of Love, 1996, Liar, Liar, 1996, House Arrest, 1996, Edie & Pen, 1996, Bound, 1996. Home: Care Carrol Gettko 118 S Beverly Beverly Hills CA 90212*

TILLY, LOUISE AUDINO, history and sociology educator; b. Orange, N.J., Dec. 13, 1930; d. Hector and Piera (Roffino) Audino; m. Charles Tilly, Aug. 15, 1953; children: Christopher, Kathryn, Laura, Sarah. BA, Rutgers U., 1952; MA, Boston U., 1955; PhD, U. Toronto, 1974. From instr. to asst. prof. Mich. State U., East Lansing, 1972-75; from asst. prof. to prof. U. Mich., Ann Arbor, 1975-84; prof. history and sociology New Sch. for Social Rsch., N.Y.C., 1984-94, chair com. hist. studies, 1984—, Michael E. Gellert prof. history and sociology, 1994—; assoc. dir. studies Ecole des Hautes Etudes en Scis. Sociales, Paris, 1979, 80, 88; fellow Shelby Cullom Davis Ctr., Princeton (N.J.) U., 1978; vis. mem. Inst. for Advanced Study, Princeton, 1987-88; fellow Ctr. for Advanced Study Behavioral Scis., 1991-92; vis. scholar Russell Sage Found., 1994-95; bd. dirs. Social Scis. Rsch. Coun., N.Y.C., 1983-86. Author: Politics and Class in Milan, 1881-1901, 1992; co-author: The Rebellious Century, 1975, Women, Work and Family, 1978, rev. edit., 1987; co-editor, co-author: Class Conflict and Collective Action, 1981, Women, Politics and Change, 1990; co-editor: The European Experience of Declining Fertility: The Quiet Revolution, 1992; also articles. Active com. on women's employment and related social issues Nat. Acad. Scis., 1981-86, chmn., co-editor report Panel on Tech. and Women's Employment, 1984-86. Grantee Rockefeller Found., 1974-76, Am. Philos. Soc., 1977-78, 85-86, Russell Sage Found., 1985-86; Guggenheim Found. fellow, 1991-92. Mem. Am. Hist. Assn. (coun. 1985-87, pres. elect. 1992, pres. 1993), Social Sci. History Assn.(pres. 1981-82), Coun. on European Studies (exec. com. 1980-83), Berkshire Conf. Women Historians. Democrat. Home: 5 E 22nd St Apt 5K New York NY 10010-5321 Office: Com on Hist Studies 80 Fifth Ave 5th Fl New York NY 10011-8002

TILLY, MEG, actress; b. Long Beach, Calif., Feb. 14, 1960. Actress: (films) Fame, 1980, Tex, 1982, One Dark Night, 1983, The Big Chill, 1983, Psycho II, 1983, Impulse, 1984, Agnes of God, 1985 (Academy award nomination best supporting actress 1985), Off Beat, 1986, Masquerade, 1988, The Girl in a Swing, 1988, Valmont, 1989, The Two Jakes, 1990, Carmilla, 1990, Leaving Normal, 1992, Body Snatchers, 1994, Sleep with Me, 1994, Journey, 1996, (TV movies) In the Best Interest of the Child, 1990, Trick of the Eye, 1994, (TV series) Winnetka Road, 1993, Fallen Angels, 1993; author: Singing Songs, 1994. *

TILNEY, RACHEL GAWTRY, educational administrator; b. Boston, June 5, 1967; d. Lewis Gawtry and Mary Atkins (Spilhaus) T. Student, U. Konstanz, Germany, 1988; AB, Colby Coll., 1989; MA, Northwestern U., 1992. Resident counselor Salzburg (Austria) Internat. Prep. Sch., 1992-93; assoc. dir. admissions Westtown (Pa.) Sch., 1993—. Mem. Phi Beta Kappa. Home and Office: Westtown Sch PO Box 1799 Westtown Rd Westtown PA 19395-1799

TILSON, DOROTHY RUTH, word processing executive; b. Bloomsburg, Pa., Mar. 24, 1918; d. Roy Earl and Mary Etta (Masteller) Derr; m. Irving Tilson, Sept. 1949. BS, Bloomsburg U., 1940. Tchr. Madison Consol. Sch., Jerseytown, Pa., 1940-42; gage checker Phila. Ordinance Gage Lab., 1942-43; tabulating asst. Remington Rand, Phila., N.Y.C., 1943-46; copy writer Sears Roebuck, Phila., N.Y.C., 1946-48; statis. asst. Ford Internat., N.Y.C., 1949-56; word processing adminstrv. asst. Coopers & Lybrand, N.Y.C., 1956-91. Life mem. Rep. Senatorial Inner Circle, Washington, 1987—. Mem. Am. Movement for World Govt. (sec. 1991—), N.Y. Theosophical Soc. (libr. 1969—), UN Assn.-USA (mem. global policy project which includes internat. econ. governance and human rights). Home: 435 W 119 St 9G New York NY 10027-7102

TILSTON, MARY LOUISE, public health nurse; b. Ottawa, Ont., Can., May 14, 1950; d. Donald Patrick and Katherine Louise (Killam) McLauchlan; m. James Grant Tilston; 4 children. Bachelor of Nursing, Dalhousie U., 1971; cert. pub. health nurse, Calif. State U., Stanislaus, 1994; student, Chapman U., 1995—. RN, Calif. Staff nurse Izaak Walton Killam Hosp. for Children, Halifax, N.S., Can., 1971-72; pub. health nurse Wikwemikong Indian Reserve Health and Welfare, Can., 1972-74; instr. nursing Laurentian U., Sudbury, Ont., Can., 1974-76; pub. health nurse Sudbury and Dist. Health Unit, Sudbury, Ont., Can., 1980-81; supr. cmty. health nursing, asst. dir. Vegreville Health Unit, Alberta, Can., 1982; staff nurse obstetrics Madera Cmty. Hosp., Calif., 1987-93; cmty. health nurse in maternal child health Merced County Health Dept., Merced, Calif., 1989-91, cmty. health nurse, provider rels., 1991-92, pub. health nurse in AIDS case mgmt., 1992—; bd. dirs Ctrl. San Joaquin Valley HIV Care Consortium, Fresno, Calif., 1993—; mem. Merced County HIV Task Force, 1993—. Campaign worker New Democrats, Halifax, N.S., Can., 1968-70. Home: 1005 Lees Court Merced CA 95340

TIMBERLAKE, GRACE MARGARET, fundraiser; b. Royal, Ill., Sept. 14, 1938; d. William J. and Margaret T. (Grussing) Habben; m. John Butler Timberlake, Dec. 21, 1962; children: Rachael, David. BA, U. Ill., 1960; JD, Chgo.-Kent Coll. Law, 1980. Bar: Ill. 1980. Coder A.C. Nielson, Chgo., 1960-61; analyst Market Facts, Chgo., 1961-66; counsel Matteson-Richton Bank, Ill., 1980-81; trust counsel Harris Bank, Chgo., 1981-87; dir. gift planning NYU Med. Ctr., 1989—. Coord., fundraiser Bklyn. Heights Interfaith Shelter, 1988—. Mem. Planned Giving Group Greater N.Y. Home: 28 Cadman Plz W Th D Brooklyn NY 11201 Office: NYU Med Ctr 550 First Ave New York NY 10016

TIMBERMAN, BARBARA ANN, artist, educator; b. New Augusta, Ind., June 6, 1932; d. Fred Hugh and Bertha Jane (Adams) Bremerman; m. Walter M. Wolfe, Apr. 9, 1956 (div. 1966); children: W. Mark, Anne Gayle Wolfe Clark; m. Wayne A. Timberman, Dec. 1966 (dec.). BA, Rollins Coll., 1954; postgrad., Herron Sch. Art, Indpls., 1968-70; MA, Appalachian State U., Boone, N.C., 1979. Part-time instr. art Mayland C.C., Spruce Pine, N.C., 1979-85; adj. art instr. Lees-McRae Coll., Banner Elk, N.C., 1986—. One-woman shows include Hiddenite (N.C.) Ctr., 1986, Esceola Lodge, Linville, N.C., 1988, Lees McRae Coll., 1989, 93, 95, Carrol Reece Mus., Johnson City, Tenn., 1994, Jailhouse Gallery, Morganton, N.C., 1996; represented in permanent collections Bowman-Gray Med. Sch., Winston-Salem, N.C., Nationsbank, Banner Elk, N.C. Pres. Avery Arts Coun., Newland, N.C., 1976-86; trustee Mayland C.C., 1979-93. Named Woman of Yr., Avery County C. of C., 1979. Mem. Delta Kappa Gamma (pres. Alpha Gamma chpt. 1992-94). Roman Catholic. Home: 505 Wineberry Ln Newland NC 28657 Office: Divsn Humanities Lees-McRae Coll Banner Elk NC 28604

TIMINS, BONITA LEA, interior decorator; b. Scranton, Pa., Nov. 26, 1951; d. Edward Joseph and Mary Loretta (Lake) T. BS in Art Edn., Kutztown U., 1973; MA in Art Edn. magna cum laude, Marywood Coll., 1976, MA in Psychology magna cum laude, 1990; PhD in Metaphysics, Am. Internat. U., 1994. Art tchr. Scranton Sch. Dist., 1974-77; prodn. asst. Garan, Inc., N.Y.C., 1977-78, Marty Gutmacher, Inc., N.Y.C., 1979-81, R.R.J. Industries, N.Y.C., 1981-82; prodn. mgr. Double Dutch Sportswear, N.Y.C., 1982-84; MR/CLA supr. Allied Svcs., Scranton, 1984-86; home health care coord. Scranton, 1986-95; interior decorator Kurlancheek Furniture Gallery, Clarks Summit, Pa., 1995—; ind. curator, Scranton, 1992-94; chemistry tutor U. Scranton, 1994-95. Contbr. articles to profl. jours. Com. woman Dem. Party, Scranton, 1994; fundraiser Am. Cancer soc., Scranton, 1993; mem. Nat. Coun. for Geocosmic Rsch. Recipient Nightingale award Pa. Hosp. Assn., 1995, Outstanding Assoc. Mem. Cmty. Svc. award Lackawanna County Young Dems., 1996, Excellence award Sigma Theta Tau Internat. Nursing Soc., 1995. Mem. Art Student's League N.Y.C. (life), Psi Chi, Kappa Pi. Roman Catholic. Home: 2108 Jackson St Scranton PA 18504-1610

TIMMER, BARBARA, lawyer; b. Holland, Mich., Dec. 13, 1946; d. John Norman and Barbara Dee (Folensbee) T. BA, Hope Coll., Holland, Mich., 1969; JD, U. Mich., 1975. Bar: Mich. 1975, U.S. Supreme Ct. Assoc. McCrosky, Libner, VanLeuven, Muskegon, Mich., 1975-78; apptd. to Mich. Women Commn. by Gov., 1976-79; staff counsel subcom. commerce, consumer & monetary affairs Ho. Govt. Ops. Com., 1979-82, 85-86; exec. v.p. NOW, 1982-84; legis. asst. to Rep. Geraldine Ferraro, 1984; atty. Office Gen. Counsel Fed. Home Loan Bank Bd., 1986-89; gen. counsel Com. on Banking, Fin. and Urban affairs U.S. Ho. of Reps., Washington, 1989-92; asst. gen. counsel, dir. govt. affairs ITT Corp., Washington, 1992-96; with Alliance Capital, Washington, 1994-96; sr. v.p., dir. govt. rels. Home Savs. of Am., Irwindale, Calif., 1996—. Recipient Affordable Housing award Nat. Assn. Real Estate Brokers, 1990, Acad. of Women Achievers, YWCA, 1993. Mem. ABA (bus. law, exec. coun. adminstrv. law and regulatory practice sects.), Mich. Bar Assn., Fed. Bar Assn. (exec. coun. of banking law com.), Bar of Supreme Ct., Women in Housing and Fin. (bd. dirs. 1992-94, gen. counsel 1994—), Supreme Ct. Bar Assn., Supreme Ct. Hist. Soc. Episcopalian. Office: Home Savings of America 4900 Rivergrade Rd Irwindale CA 91706

TIMMER, MARGARET LOUISE (PEG TIMMER), educator; b. Osmond, Nebr., July 4, 1942; d. John Henry and Julia Adeline (Schilling) Borgmann; m. Charles B. Timmer, May 23, 1964 (div. June 1990); children: Jill Marie, Mark Jon. AA, N.E. Community Coll., Norfolk, Nebr., 1987; BA in Edn., K-12 art endorsement, Wayne (Nebr.) State U., 1988; MEd, Bank Street Coll./Parsons Sch. Design, N.Y.C., 1992. Cert. tchr., Nebr. Bookkeeper Goeres Electric, Osmond, 1960-61; tel. operator Northwestern Bell, Norfolk, 1961-64; with want advt. dept. Washington Post, 1964-65; saleswoman Jeannes Fashion Fabrics, Norfolk, 1970-72, Tripps, Norfolk, 1986-87; office and fin. mgr. Tim's Plumbing & Heating Inc., Norfolk, 1972-86; tchr. art Norfolk Cath. Schs., 1988—, mem. bd., 1985-88; instr. art history N.E. Community Coll., 1992—; mem. youth art bd. Norfolk Art Ctr., 1988—. One-woman show Uptown Restaurant, Norfolk, 1993, Norfolk Art Ctr., 1996; exhibited in group shows Sioux City (Iowa) Art Ctr., 1988, Columbus (Nebr.) Art Ctr., 1993. Mem. choir St. Mary's Cath. Ch., Norfolk, 1991—; mem. Norfolk Community Choir, 1991; bd. dirs. Norfolk Community Concerts Assn., 1984-87; treas. Norfolk Cath. Booster Club, 1985-86; leader 4-H, Madison County, 1973-78; judge art show Laurel (Nebr.) Women's Club, 1988. Named outstanding profl. vol. Norfolk Art Ctr., 1996. Mem. Nat. Art Edn. Assn. (presenter 1987), Nebr. Art Edn. Assn. (3d place award 1988). Home: Box 239 83729 Warnerville Dr Norfolk NE 68701-9758 Office: Norfolk Cath Schs 2300 Madison Ave Norfolk NE 68701-4456

TIMMONS, ANDREA CARROLL, publisher, public relations professional, paralegal, photographer, author; b. Lockesburg, Ark., Jan. 8, 1945; d. Jake Charles and Lola Evelyn (Hale) Carroll; m. Ronald William Jackson, Dec. 23, 1967 (div. Jan. 1978); m. Franklin Wayne Timmons, Aug. 3, 1991. B.S. in Edn., Henderson State U. cum laude, 1967; postgrad. in journalism La. State U., 1981-82; diploma Sch. Paralegal Studies, 1995; cert. corp. law and civil litig.; Phys. edn. tchr. Lamar Consol. Schs., Ark., 1967-68; field advisor Ark. Post coun. Girl Scouts U.S., Pine Bluff, 1969-74, pub. rels. dir. Ouachita coun., Little Rock, 1974-79; program and pub. rels. dir. Baton Rouge Area YWCA, 1979-81; editor Bayou Country Publs., Plaquemine, La., 1981-83; communications dir. Am. Lung Assn. of Ark., Little Rock, 1984-91; former owner, operator TLC Pet Care Svc.; editor: (tng. manual) Safe Homes Project for Battered Women, 1981; Ark. Women's Rights OURS newspaper, 1985-86, Ark. chpt. Sierra Club newspaper, 1988-90; mem. Dem. Nat. Com. Recipient Excellence in color slide photography awards Ouachita Girl Scout Coun. and Girl Scouts U.S., 1978, Feature Writing award Am. Pen Women, 1992; Outstanding Svc. award Baton Rouge Area YWCA, 1980. Mem. Mont. Assn. Legal Assts., Mem. Nat. Fedn. of Paralegal Assn. Ark. Press Women (feature writing awards, 2 in 1982, 3 in 1983, 2 interview awards 1984, 2 broadcast awards 1984, 87, writing editing and interviewing, 1985, 86), Lake County Humane Soc., The Nature Conservancy, Sierra Club. Avocations: movies, hiking, travel. Author: Concerned Citizens' Guide: How to Use the Media to Affect Public Opinion, 1991, Book Promotion Kit for Authors, 1993. Office: Piedalue Law Offices PC 283 W Front St Ste 302B Missoula MT 59802

TIMPANO, ANNE, museum director, art historian; b. Osaka, Japan, June 17, 1950; d. A.J. and Margaret (Smith) T. BA, Coll. William and Mary, 1972; MA, George Washington U., 1983. Program mgmt. asst. Nat. Mus. Am. Art, Washington, 1977-86; dir. The Columbus (Ga.) Mus., 1986-93, DAAP Galleries, U. Cin., 1993—; grant reviewer Inst. Mus. Svcs., Washington, 1988—, Ga. Coun. for Arts, Atlanta, 1988-91. Mem. 1992 Quincentenary Commn., Columbus, 1987-92. Recipient David Lloyd Kreeger award George Washington U., 1980. Mem. Am. Assn. Mus. (surveyor mus. assessment program), Assn. of Coll. and Univ. Mus. and Galleries, Coll. Art Assn., Midwest Mus. Conf. Roman Catholic. Home: 85 Pleasant Ridge Ave Fort Mitchell KY 41017 Office: U Cin PO Box 210016 Cincinnati OH 45221-0016

TIMPERMAN, TRACIE ANN, special education educator; b. Columbus, Ohio, Nov. 24, 1970; d. William Edward and Alice Kaye (Barker) T. BA in Spl. Edn., Purdue U., 1994. Cert. tchr. spl. edn. Rsch. asst., svcs. coord. Purdue U., West Lafayette, Ind., 1992-93; tchr. spl. edn. Pike Township Schs., Indpls., 1994—. Presenter in field. Coach Spl. Olympics, Indpls., 1994. Mem. Coun. Exceptional Children (Nat. conf. presenter 1995). Roman Catholic.

TIMS, RAMONA FAYE, medical/surgical nurse; b. Jackson, Tenn., Nov. 4, 1955; d. Willard Leon and Lois Ellen (Waldon) T. Assoc. Nursing, SUNY, Albany, 1987. LPN, RN; cert. BLS. Staff nurse neurol. ICU Jackson Madison County Gen. Hosp., 1976-88, clin. mgr., 1991—; nurse chemotherapy Jackson Clinic, P.A., 1988-91. Co-author: Oncology-Experience Counts. Republican. Baptist. Home: 43 Bemis Ln Jackson TN 38301

TINCHER, BARBARA JEAN, not for profit fund-raiser; b. Shawano, Wis., June 9, 1963; d. George William and Phyllis Jean (Albrecht) T. Student, Ripon Coll., 1983-84; BA, U. Minn., 1988. Cert. theatre adminstrn. Artistic and gen. adminstrv. asst. Pepsico Internat. Performing Arts Festival, Purchase, N.Y., 1986; programming and press asst. Riverside Studios, Hammersmith, England, 1987; club coord. Guthrie Theater, Mpls., 1986-88; devel. assoc. Huntington Theatre Co., Boston, 1988-89, coord. ann. fund, 1989-90; mgr. ann. fund L.A. (Calif.) Theatre Ctr., 1990, dir. devel., 1991; ind. fund raising cons. L.A., 1991; bd. devel. specialist AIDS Project L.A., Calif., 1991-94, dir. bd. rels., 1994-95; dir. leadership gifts Lawrence U., Appleton, Wis., 1995—; mem. Women in Devel. Greater Boston, 1989-90; del. Conf. About Vols. Regional Theatres, Milw., 1990; participant fall fund raising day Nat. Soc. Fund Raising Execs., L.A., 1990, Non-Profit Mgmt. Inst. Bd. Devel. Tng., San Diego, 1992, Nat. Ctr. for Non-Profit Bds. Annual Conf., 1994. Guest panelist AIDS Vision Cable Show, 1992, John Brown Planned Giving Conf., 1996, Conrad Teitell Philanthropy Tax Inst., 1996. Bd. dirs. Attic Theatre, 1996—. Mem. Alpha Xi Delta. Methodist. Home: 731 S Lynndale Dr Appleton WI 54914 Office: Lawrence U PO Box 599 Appleton WI 54912

TINDALL, JANICE CLOUGH, family physician; b. Glens Falls, N.Y., Feb. 7, 1945; d. Harold Arthur Clough and Carol Irene (McKernon) Smith; m. Robert Cook Tindall, June 18, 1966; children: Leslie Carol, Ami Catherine, Kelley Rae. BA in Biology, U. Rochester, 1966; BS in Edn., Pa. State U., 1968; MD, Hahnemann U., 1980. Lic. physician, Pa. Lab. rsch. asst. Pa. State U., State College, 1966-69; salesperson, mgr. Tupperware, Laramie, Wyo., 1971-75; mgr. Tupperware, Gap, Pa., 1975-76; resident family medicine Lancaster (Pa.) Gen. Hosp., 1980-83; family physician County Line Med. Ctr., Gap, 1983—; emergency "fast care" physician Lancaster Gen. Hosp., 1994—. Mem. vestry St. Johns Episcopal Ch., Gap. Mem. AMA, Am. Acad. Family Practice, Pa. Acad. Family Practice, Pa. Med. Soc., Lancaster City and County Med. Soc. Office: County Line Med Ctr 5275 Lincoln Hwy Gap PA 17527

TINER, DONNA TOWNSEND, nurse; b. Memphis, Dec. 14, 1947; d. Jack Edwin and Anne Coolidge (Burleigh) Townsend; m. Clinton William Matson, Aug. 30, 1969 (div. 1976); m. Dow David Tiner, Apr. 15, 1978; children: Jeffrey David, Cynthia Leigh, Catherine Renee. Grad., Bapt. Meml. Hosp. Sch. Nursing, Memphis, 1969. RN, Ark.; cert. ACLS. Nurse Bapt. Meml. Hosp., Memphis, 1969, 71-72, New Bern (N.C.) Surg. Assocs., 1970-71, Meml. Hosp., Little Rock, 1972-73, Bapt. Med. Ctr., Little Rock, 1974-87; practice nursing specializing in post-anesthesia care Little Rock, 1987-89; post-anesthesia care specialist Little Rock Surgery Ctr. (formerly Freeway Surgery Ctr.), 1989—. Instr., ARC, 1975—; leader Park Hill Bapt. Ch., 1986—. 1st. lt. U.S. Army Med. Unit 1976-79. Mem. Am. Soc. Post Anesthesia Nurses (chartered), Ark. Post Anesthesia Care Nurses, Alumnae Assn. Bapt. Hosp. Sch. Nursing. Republican. Home: 12 Knights Bridge Rd North Little Rock AR 72116-6535

TINGLE, KATHY CARTWRIGHT, school administrator; b. Lexington, Ky., May 25, 1961; d. Kenneth Cartwright and Marietta (Canter) Martin; m. M. Keith Tingle, July 12, 1980; children: Marshal Keith, Alexander Kenneth. BS, Georgetown Coll., 1984, MA in Edn., 1987; Adminstrv. Endorsement, Morehead State U., 1992. Cert. instrnl. supr. elem. and secondary schs., supt., elem. prin., mid. sch. prin., spl. edn. dir. Elem. tchr. Grant County Schs., Williamstown, Ky., 1984-89; early childhood tchr. Bath County Sch., Owingsville, Ky., 1990-92, dir. spl. edn. and early childhood programs, 1992-95; prin. Nicholasville (Ky.) Elem. Sch., 1995—; task force cert. of early childhood, Ky. Dept. Edn., Frankfort, 1993, assoc. Regional Svc. Ctr., 1993, early childhood cons., 1992—. Mem. Coun. for the Arts, Owingsville, 1991, Owingsville Homemakers, 1991; dir. Owingsville Community Choir, 1991—. Mem. Ky. Early Childhood Assn., So. Early Childhood Assn., ASCD, Nat. Mid. Sch. Assn., Ky. Assn. Sch. Adminstrs., Phi Delta Kappa. Democrat. Baptist. Home: 2445 Logana Rd Nicholasville KY 40356 Office: Nicholasville Elem Sch 414 W Maple St Nicholasville KY 40356

TINNER, FRANZISKA PAULA, social worker, artist, designer, educator; b. Zurich, Switzerland, Sept. 18, 1944; came to U.S., 1969; d. Siegfied Albin and Gertrude Emilie (Sigg) Maier; m. Rolf Christian Tinner, Dec. 19, 1976; 1 child, Eric Francis. Student, U. Del., 1973-74, Va. Commonwealth U., 1974; BFA, U. Tenn., 1984; BA of Arts, U. Ark., Little Rock, 1991, postgrad. Lic. real estate broker. Dominican nun Ilanz, Switzerland, 1961-67; waitress London, 1967-68; governess Bryn Mawr, Pa., 1969; saleswoman, 1970-90, model, 1983; artist, designer Made For You, Kerrville, Tex. and Milw., 1984—; realtor Century 21, Milw., 1987-91; intern Birch Community Ctr., 1992-93. Designer softsculptor doll Texas Cactus Blossom, 1984. Ombudsman Action 10 Consumerline, Knoxville, Tenn., 1983-84; foster mother, Powhatan, Va., 1976-81; vol. ARC, Knoxville, 1979, Va. Home for Permanently Disabled, 1975; vol., counselor Youth For Understanding-Fgn. Exch., Powhatan, Va., 1975-77; tchr. pager/archiving host, mentor, area expert on Am. On Line; vol. Interactive Ednl. Svc. Recipient Art Display award U. Knoxville, 1983, Prof. Choice of Yr. award, 1983, Outstanding Achievemnt award TV Channel 10, Knoxville, 1984, 1st place award for paintings and crafts State Fair Va., Tenn., 1st place award Nat. Dollmakers, 1985, finalist Best of Coll. Photography, 1991, Achievement award Coll. Scholar af Am., 1991, Achievement cert. in technique of anger therapy, 1993, Achievement cert. in crisis response team tng., 1994; named One of Outstanding 1000 Women, 1995, Woman of Yr., 1995. Mem. NASW, NAFE,

Milw. Bd. Realtors, Homemakers Club (pres. 1979-80), Newcomers Club, Bowlers Club (v.p.), Internat. Platform Assn.

TINOCO, JUDITH MARSHALL, food service executive; b. Copaigue, N.Y., June 18, 1959; d. Kenneth Clinton and Nancy (Rasmusson) Marshall; m. Porfirio Francisco Tinoco, Apr. 29, 1984 (div. 1990); children: Robert William, Angelina J. Student, Fla. Internat. U., 1983-86; degree in culinary arts, Inst. of South, 1987. Chef, gen. mgr. Maxfields of Boca Raton, Fla., 1974-81; mgr. Alfredo l'Originale di Roma, Lake Buena Vista, Fla., Bistro Internat. Inc., Miami, Fla., 1981-86; dir. ops. Bistro Internat. Inc., Miami, 1986-89; dir. career svcs. Restaurant Sch., Phila., 1989-91; dir. food svc. ops. Union League Club Phila., 1991-92; dir. ops. corp. foodsvc. div. Univest Corp., Washington, 1992-94; dir. facilities mgmt. divsn. Natcher Conf. Ctr./Encore Mgmt. Corp./NIH, 1995—; culinary instr. Main Line Sch. Night, Radnor, Pa., 1989-91; speaker in field. Vol. supr. Show Our Strength to Feed the Homeless, Phila., 1989-91; mem. community rels. bd. Bally's Grand, Atlantic City, N.J., 1989-91. Mem. Nat. Restaurant Assn., Phila./Del. Valley Restaurant Assn., NAFE, Womens Foodservice Forum, Roundtable for Women in Foodservice (bd. dirs. 1990—), Greater Phila. Restaurant and Purveyors Assn. (edn. com. 1991—), Pa. Restaurant Assn. Republican. Episcopalian.

TINSLEY, ADRIAN, college president; b. N.Y.C., July 6, 1937; d. Theodore A. and Mary Ethel (White) T. AB, Bryn Mawr Coll., 1958; MA, U. Wash., 1962; PhD, Cornell U., 1969. Asst. prof. English U. Md., College Park, 1968-72; dean William James Coll., Grand Valley State, Allendale, Mich., 1972-80; assoc. vice chancellor acad. affairs Minn. State U., St. Paul, 1982-85; exec. v.p., provost Glassboro (N.J.) State Coll., 1985-89; pres. Bridgewater (Mass.) State Coll., 1989—; coord. women higher edn. adminstrn. Bryn Mawr (Pa.) & Hers Summer Inst., 1977—. Editor: Women in Higher Education Administration, 1984. Office: Bridgewater State Coll Office of Pres Bridgewater MA 02325-0001

TINSMAN, MARGARET NEIR, state senator; b. Moline, Ill., July 14, 1936; d. Francis Earl and Elizabeth (Lourie) Neir; m. Robert Hovey Tinsman Jr., Feb. 21, 1959; children: Robert Hovey III, Heidi Elizabeth, Bruce MacAlister. BA in Sociology, U. Colo., 1958; MSW, U. Iowa, 1974. Health care coord. Community Health Care, Inc., Davenport, Iowa, 1975-77; assoc. dir. Scott County Info., Referal, and Assistance Svc., Davenport, Iowa, 1977-79; county supr. Scott County Bd. Suprs., Davenport, Iowa, 1978-89; senate State of Iowa, Des Moines, 1989—; asst. minority leader Iowa Senate, coms. appropriations, edn., human resources, human svcs. appropriations subcom., ranking mem., 1989—; chair Iowa adv. commn. on inter-govt. rels., 1982-84; U.S. county rep. to the German-Am. Symposium German Marshall Plan, 1983; commr. Iowa Dept. Elder Affairs, Des Moines, 1983-89. Chairperson Planning Com. Quad City United Way, Davenport; bd. dirs. Bi-State Met. Planning Commn., Davenport, 1981-89, Quad City Devel. Group, Davenport, 1988-90. Named Iowa Social Worker of Yr., NASW, 1978. Mem. Am. Lung Assn. (bd. dirs. 1989—), Davenport C. of C. (local/state govt. com. 1989—), Nat. Assn. Legislators, Nat. Assn. of Counties (bd. dirs. 1984-89, pres. Women Ofcl. 1984-89), Iowa State Assn. of Counties (bd. dirs. 1983-89, chair), Jr. League (sustaining mem. 1989), Vol. Action Ctr. (pres. 1989). Republican. Episcopalian. Home: 3055 Red Wing Ct Bettendorf IA 52722-2185 Office: c/o Twin State 3541 E Kimberly Rd Davenport IA 52807-2552*

TIPPETT, TERRI ELIZABETH, engineering administrator; b. Johnson City, Tenn., Aug. 27, 1955; d. Howard Dean Tippett and Mary Elizabeth Hunley Carr. BA in Human Svcs. summa cum laude, U. Tenn., Knoxville, 1983. Eligibility counselor Tenn. Dept. Human Svcs., Kingsport, 1978-81; tech. support Utility Cons., Atlanta, 1988-89; estimator Henderson Electric Co., Atlanta, 1989-90; cons. Geog. Info. Systems Internat. & Byers, Dublin, 1986, Codetel & Byers, Santo Domingo, Dominican Republic, 1986; project supr. Byers Engring., Atlanta, 1983-88, 90—. Active Human Resource Campaign Fund, Atlanta, 1994. Mem. ASTD, Soc. Women Engrs., Habitat for Humanity, The Dolphin Project, Nat. Wildlife Fedn. (supporter, educator), Sierra Club, Wilderness Club. Democrat. Home: 3046 Millstone Ct Austell GA 30001

TIPTON, KAREN, middle school educator; b. Junction City, Kans., Aug. 29, 1935; d. Clarence Calvert and Olive Ann (Bennett) T.; m. Merle Francis Channel, July 5, 1951 (div. Mar. 1983); children: Gloria Jeane Channel McKim, Steven Blair, Michael Curtis, Patrick Rock Channel. BS in Math., U. So. Colo., 1972; MA in Edn., Lesley Coll., 1990. Cert. tchr., Colo. Tchr. Pueblo (Colo.) Sch. Dist. 70, 1973—. Mem. NEA, AAUW, Pueblo County Tchrs. Assn., Elks, Eagles. Home: 316 W 21st St Pueblo CO 81003

TIPTON, KELLIE LYNN, occupational therapist, nurse; b. Asheville, N.C., Oct. 27, 1967; d. Brown Herman and Jodie Elizabeth (Russell) T. AAS in Occupational Therapy, Caldwell C.C., 1992. Cert. occupational therapist; LPN. LPN staff newborn nursery Spruce Pine (N.C.) Hosp., 1989-91; occupl. therapist asst. Mitchell County Schs., Bakersville, N.C., 1992—; sys.-wide assistive tech. project cons. Mitchell County Schs., 1994—; youth counselor Summer Retreat Program, Tricounty Area, N.C., 1989—. Mem. N.C. Occupational Therapy Assn. Free-Will Baptist. Office: Mitchell County Schs 115 School Rd Bakersville NC 28705

TIRELLA, THERESA MARY, special education educator; b. Worcester, Mass., Apr. 22, 1963; d. Samuel Louis and Cecilia Barbara (Trczinski) T. BS, Northeastern U., 1986, MEd, 1989. Acting supr., childcare worker Dr. Franklin Perkins Sch., Lancaster, Mass., 1983-84; sr. recreational counselor Friendly House Inc., Worcester, 1985; adult edn. educator Action for Boston Community Devel., 1986-87; spl. edn. educator Cotting Sch., Lexington, Mass., 1987—; cons. United Cerebral Palsy, Watertown, Mass., 1993, Spl. Needs Advocacy Network Newton, Mass., 1991-93; corrd, bd. dirs. Access Now, Boston, 1991-93. Vol. mem. program planning com. Ptnrs. for Disabled Youth, Boston, 1991-94; vol. tutor Bethel Bapt. Ch., Roxbury, Mass., 1991-92, mem. youth com., 1991-92, mem. choir, 1991-92. Mem. Assn. for Suprevision and Curriculum Devel., Northeastern Univj. Women's Alumni Club, Northeastern U. Alumni Assn. Home: 17 Seaverns Ave Jamaica Plain MA 02130-2874

TIRSCHWELL, KATHY ANN, veterinary hospital administrator; b. Hudson, Wis., Jan. 8, 1961; d. Walter Haskell and Doris Hilda (Dornfeld) T. DDS (hon.), Roth/Williams Ctr., 1993. Traffic dir. Sta. KRKC, King City, Calif., 1978-79; office mgr. Cable TV of King City/Greenfield, 1979-82; lead cashier Del Webb's High Sierra Hotel & Casino, Lake Tahoe, Nev., 1982-84; acctg. analyst Hyatt Hotels, Burlinghame, Calif., 1984-87; v.p., owner Computer Diagnostic Info Inc., Burlingame, Calif., 1987-93; exec. dir. Roth/Williams Ctr., Burlingame, Calif., 1990-93; event support mgr. Stuart Rental Co., Sunnyvale, Calif., 1994-96, Cheskin & Masten/ImageNet, Redwood Shores, Calif., 1996; adminstr. Bayshore Animal Hosp., San Mateo, Calif., 1996—. Pres. Jr. Fairboard, Salinas Valley Fair, King City, Calif., 1979-80. Office: Bayshore Animal Hospital 233 N Amphlett Blvd San Mateo CA 94401

TISCHLER, NANCY MARIE, English educator, program administrator; b. DeQueen, Ark., Mar. 20, 1932; d. Charles Edward and Phoebe Allene (Steel) Patterson; m. Charles Merle Tischler, Nov. 26, 1958; children: Carl Eric, Dale Grant. BS, Wilson Tchrs. Coll., 1952; MA, PhD, U. Ark., 1954, 56. Asst. prof. English George Washington U., Washington, 1956-62; assoc. prof. Susquehanna U., Selinsgrove, Pa., 1963-65; prof. English and Humanities Pa. State U., University Park, 1966—; pres. Conf. on Christianity and Lit., 1978-79, Assn. Univ. Summer Sessions, 1985-86, N.Am. Assn. of Summer Sessions, 1992-93. Author: Tennessee Williams: Rebellious Puritan, 1960, Black Masks, 1969, Legacy of Eve: Women in Scripture, 1977, Dorothy L. Sayers: A Pilgrim Soul, 1981, A Voice of Her Own, 1987. Fullbright fellow U.S. Govt., England, 1952-53. Mem. Kappa Delta Phi, Phi Beta Kappa (pres. Lambda chpt.). Republican. Presbyterian. Office: Pa State U Spruce Cottage University Park PA 16802

TISHNER, KERI LYNN, secondary education educator; b. Santa Ana, Calif., June 1, 1964; d. Albert John, Jr. and Barbara Ann (Milner) Geverink; m. David Jackson Tishner, Apr. 27, 1985. BA in Art with distinction, Calif. State U., Long Beach, 1988, tchg. credentials, 1991; postgrad. in edn.-instructional tech., Calif. State U., San Bernardino, 1994—. State D coaching license Calif. Youth Soccer Assn., 1993. High sch. art tchr. Apple Valley (Calif.) H.S., 1991—. Presenter in field of art. Participant in the Calif. Arts Project, San Bernardino, 1995. Mem. NEA, Nat. Art Edn. Assn., Calif. Tchrs. Assn., Calif. Art Edn. Assn., Los Angeles County Mus. Art, Norton Simon Mus. Art, Apple Valley Unified Tchrs. Assn., Kappa Delta Pi. Office: Apple Valley HS 11837 Navajo Rd Apple Valley CA 92308

TISINGER, CATHERINE ANNE, college dean; b. Winchester, Va., Apr. 6, 1936; d. Richard Martin and Irma Regina (Ohl) T. BA, Coll. Wooster, 1958; MA, U. Pa., 1962, PhD, 1970; LLD (hon.), Coll. of Elms, 1985. Provost Callison Coll., U. of Pacific, Stockton, Calif., 1971-72; v.p. Met. State U., St. Paul, 1972-75; v.p. acad. affairs S.W. State U., Marshall, Minn., 1975-76, interim pres., 1976-77; dir. Ctr. for Econ. Edn., R.I. Coll., Providence, 1979-80; v.p. acad. affairs Cen. Mo. State U., Warrensburg, Mo., 1980-84; pres. North Adams State Coll., Mass., 1984-91; dean arts and scis. Shenandoah U., Winchester, Va., 1991—; cons. North Cen. Assn. Colls. and Schs., 1980-84, New Eng. Assn. Schs. and Colls., 1978-79, 85—, Minn. Acad. Family Physicians, 1973-77; mem. adv. bd. First Agrl. Bank, North Adams, 1985-91; pres. No. Berkshire Cooperating Colls., 1986-91; v.p. Coll. Consortium for Internat. Studies, 1989-90. V.p. Med. Simulation Found., 1986-88; bd. dirs. Williamstown Concerts, 1988-91, Shawnee coun. Girl Scouts U.S., 1992-93. Mem. No. Berkshire C. of C. (bd. dirs. 1984-89, v.p. 1986-89). Avocations: fiber and textile arts, photography. Office: Shenandoah U 1460 College Dr Winchester VA 22601

TITILOYE, VICTORIA MOJIRAYO, pediatrics nurse; b. Okemesi Ekiti, Nigeria, Nov. 17, 1955; d. Ezekiel Ajiboye and Julianah Oyindaola (Atitebi) T. Diploma, Lagos U. Teaching Hosp., 1977; BS, SUNY, Bklyn., 1981; MA, NYU, 1983, PhD valedictory rep., 1988. Cert. occupational therapist, Nigerian nurse, RN. Asst. nursing supt. adult med. and surg. wards Wesley Guild Hosp., Unife-Complex, Ilesha, Oyo, 1977-78; sr. occupational therapist United Cerebral Palsy, Bklyn., 1982-85; occupational therapist con., Sch. for Multiply Handicapped Children, Vis. Therapist Assocs., Bklyn., 1985-89; rsch. assoc. NYU, N.Y.C., 1989-90; asst. dir. occupational therapy Cobble Hill Nursing Home, Bklyn., 1991-92; asst. prof. occupl. therapy SUNY Health Sci. Ctr., Bklyn., 1994—; dir. occupl. therapy dept. Sts. Joachim and Ann Residence, Bklyn., 1992-93; cons. drs. office occupl. therapy dept. U. Medicine and Dentistry N.J., 1993; clin. and rsch. cons. League Therapeutic Ctr., Bklyn., 1993—; rsch. cons. Kessler Inst. Rehab., East Orange, N.J., 1993—; adj. asst. prof. dept. life scis. N.Y. Inst. Tech., 1993-94; clin. and rsch. cons. League Therapeutic Ctr., Bklyn., 1993—; rep. NYU Sch. Edn., Health, Nursing and Arts Professions; reviewer articles and proposals for profl. jours. and confs. Contbr. articles to profl. jours. Food coord. Food Program for the Homeless, Sts. Ann and George, Bklyn.; reviewer conf. proposals. Recipient scholarships Nigerian govt., NYU Grad. Sch., Downstate Acad. Achievement. Mem. ANA, Am. Occupational Therapy Assn., Am. Soc. on Aging, N.Y. Acad. Scis., Nigerian Nurses Assn., MEDART Internat.

TITO, MAUREEN LOUISE, educational administrator; b. Long Beach, Calif., Mar. 14, 1946; d. Francis Bowen and Marie Louise (Hogan) Barrett; m. Jose D. Tito, July 4, 1971; children: Yvonne, Russell, Daryl, Nathan. AB in Polit. Sci., Holy Name Coll., Oakland, Calif., 1969; MA in Linguistics, Ateneo de Manila, Philippines, 1985. English lang. cons. Lang. Internat., Manila, 1975-89; English dept. coord. Maryknoll Coll. High Sch., Manila, 1981-85; edn. specialist Farrington Community Sch., Honolulu, 1985-91; English lang. cons. Job Preparation Program, Honolulu, 1990-91; project trainer U. Hawaii, Honolulu, 1989-90; edn. dir. Dept. of Pub. Safety, Honolulu, 1990-91, state dir. correctional edn., 1991—. Contbr. articles to profl. jours. Trainer AIDS for ARC, 1991—. Mem. AAUW, NAFE, Am. Assn. Adult and Continuing Edn., Hawaii Assn. Counseling and Devel., Correctional Edn. Assn., Nat. Assn. State Correctional Edn. Dirs. Home: PO Box 11958 Honolulu HI 96828-0958 Office: Dept Pub Safety 919 Ala Moana Blvd Honolulu HI 96814-4920

TITTLE, CAROLE JEAN, computer programmer; b. Temple, Tex., June 5, 1959; d. Lloyd Melvin Johnson and Shirley Faye (Bruss) Druley; m. Jerry Allen Tittle, Oct. 1, 1977; 1 child, James Adam. AA, NE Wis. Tech. Coll., 1988. Bookkeeper, sec. White House Music, Waukesha, Wis., 1976-77; acct. Lamplight Farms, Brookfield, Wis., 1979; prodn. clk. W.A. Krueger, Brookfield, Wis., 1979-80; data processing asst. Video Images, West Allis, Wis., 1980-85; adminstrn. asst. Jones Intercable, Brookfield, 1985; computer programmer Anamax Corp., Green Bay, Wis., 1988-89; quality assurance analyst Nielsen Mktg. Rsch., Green Bay, Wis., 1989; applications programmer N.E. Wis. Tech. Coll., Green Bay, 1990; programmer/analyst Fabry Glove & Mitten Co., Green Bay, 1995. Democrat. Roman Catholic. Office: Fabry Glove & Mitten Co PO Box 1477 1201 Main St Green Bay WI 54305-1477

TITUS, ALICE CESTANDINA (DINA TITUS), state legislator; b. Thomasville, Ga., May 23, 1950. AB, Coll. William and Mary, 1970; MA, U. Ga., 1973; PhD, Fla. State U., 1976. Prof. polit. sci. U. Nev., Las Vegas; mem. Nev. Senate, 1989—; alt. mem. legis. commn., 1989-91, mem., 1991-93; minority floor leader, 1993—; chmn. Nev. Humanities Com., 1984-86; mem. Eldorado Basin adv. group to Colo. River Commn.; active Gov. Commn. Bicentennial of U.S. Constn.; former mem. Gov. Commn. on Aging. Author: Bombs in the Backyard: Atomic Testing and American Politics, 1986, Battle Born: Federal-State Relations in Nevada during the 20th Century, 1989. Mem. Western Polit. Sci. Assn., Clark County Women's Dem. Club. Greek Orthodox. Home: 1637 Travois Cir Las Vegas NV 89119-6283 Office: Nev State Senate State Capitol Carson City NV 89710*

TITUS, CHRISTINA MARIA, lawyer; b. Phila., Oct. 31, 1950; d. George Herman and Frieda Anna (Szuchy) T.; m. Richard Christopher Daddario, Jan. 19, 1980; children: Alexandra Daddario, Matthew Daddario, Catharine Daddario. BA, NYU, 1972; JD, Georgetown U., 1977. Bar: N.Y. 1978, U.S. Dist. Ct. N.Y. (so. and ea. dists.) 1979. Assoc. Trubin Sillcocks Edelman & Knapp, N.Y.C., 1977-80; v.p., counsel Merrill Lynch, Hubbard, Inc., N.Y.C., 1980—. Recipient 1st prize Drexel Keyboard Competition, 1968. Mem. ABA, N.Y. State Bar Assn. (mem. com. on real estate financing and liens real property law sect.), Assn. of Bar of City of N.Y. Lutheran.

TITUS, LOIS ANN, middle school art educator; b. Galveston, Tex., July 5, 1944; d. Edward William Bradshaw and Velma (Smith) Bradshaw-Leavell; m. Lawrence George Ludington, June 11, 1966 (div. Nov. 1984); children: Laura Ann Ludington-Moeller, Alicia Bea Ludington; m. Jack Edward Titus Sr., Oct. 14, 1989. BS in Comml. Art, Lamar U., 1965; cert. in tchg., U. Houston, 1966, MA, 1994. Cert. tchr., Tex. Tchr. Pasadena (Tex.) Ind. Schs., 1966-68; libr. Donna Park Elem. Sch., Hurst, Tex., 1977-80; fundraiser Hurst Pub. Libr., 1980-84; asst. events dir. Galveston (Tex.) Hist. Found., 1984-88; tchr. Galveston Ind. Schs., 1990—. Editor, author: Friends & Celebrities Cookbook, 1983 (Mayor's award 1984). Bd. dirs. Galveston Attractions Assn., 1987-89, Strand Hist. Assn., Galveston, 1988-89; pres. Leadership Alumni Assn., Galveston, 1988-89. Mem. Tex. Art Educators Assn., Nat. Art Educators Assn., U.S. Soc. for Edn. Through Art, Galveston C. of C. (edn. com. 1986-87), Phi Kappa Phi, Kappa Pi. Home: 1517 Bayou Shore Dr Galveston TX 77551-4330

TITUS, SUSAN ANNE, association executive; b. L.A., Mar. 2, 1944; d. Clifford E. and Thelma A. (Chambers) T.; m. Philip M. Tuchinsky, Nov. 28, 1992. BA, U. N.C., 1965; MSW, Wayne State U., 1968. Asst. dir. Edgemont Cmty. Ctr., Durham, N.C., 1965-66; group activities specialist City of Detroit Parks and Recreation, 1968-70; program dir. Operation Friendship, Detroit, 1970-72; camping svcs. adminstr. Girl Scout Met. Detroit, 1972-74; adminstrv. asst. Detroit City Coun. Woman, 1974-77; exec. dir. Citizens for Better Care, Detroit, 1977—; mem. Mich. Dept. Social Svcs., 1973-80, adult cmty. placement adv. com., 1973-78, chairperson, 1976-78, chairperson, 1976-79, adult svcs. adv. com., 1976-80; mem. Comprehensive Health Planning Coun. of S.E. Mich., 1976-87, bd. dirs., 1977-87, plan implementation com., 1977-87, commn. to reduce excess hosp. capacity, 1978-87, vice chairperson, 1979-80; mem. Dept. Mental Health Adv. Com. on the Office of Recipient Rights, 1976-82, vice chairperson, 1977-80; part-time faculty dept. sociology and social work U. Detroit, 1978-79; part-time faculty Wayne State U. Sch. Social Work, Detroit, 1979-80; mem. New Detroit Health Com., 1979-93; mem. Fed. Emergency Mgmt. Adminstrn., U.S. Fire Adminstrn. Task Force on Fires in Boarding Homes, 1981-82; mem. adv. com. to med. dist. region 14 VA, 1983-86; apptd. mem. Mental Health and Aging Adv. Coun., 1990—; presenter in field. Mem., chairperson Mich. State Health Corod. Coun., 1978-87; mem. spkrs. bur. United Found. Met. Detroit, 1980—; mem., treas. Voight Park Neighborhood Security Com., 1988-90; mem. fin. com. Chateaufort Place Cooperative, 1990—. Recipient Demmy award United Found. Met. Detroit Spkrs. Bur., 1982, Disting. Recognition award Detroit City Coun., 1989, Spl. Tribute, Mich. State Ho. of Reps., 1989, Sidney Rosen Life Long Achievement award for cmty. svc. Detroit Area Agy. on Aging, 1995. Mem. ACLU (Mich. state bd. dirs. 1988-96, Met. Detroit br. bd. 1989-96, treas. 1990-92, NASW (cert., Detroit Met. chpt. bd. mem. at large 1967-70, v.p. 1971-73, pres. 1973-77, Mich. chpt. v.p. 1977-81, Met. Detroit area chpt. Social Worker of Yr. 1989), Nat. Citizens Coalition for Nursing Home Reform (nominating com. chairperson 1979-82, treas. 1984-86, v.p. 1986-88, 94—, pres. 1988-94, Advocacy Meml. award 1994), Coun. Exec. Officers (treas. 1990-96), Women Execs. (founder), Consumer Health Coalition (founder). Home: 1528 Chateaufort Pl Detroit MI 48207 Office: Citizens for Better Care 4750 Woodward Ave #410 Detroit MI 48201

TJARDA, JASMINE, nurse, artist; b. Rotterdam, The Netherlands. Grad. in gen. nursing, Rotterdam, The Netherlands, 1980; grad. in psychiatric nursing, Heiloo, The Netherlands, 1983; BA in Sculpture, San Francisco U., 1993. RN, Calif. With St. Anthony's Hosp., Amarillo, Tex., 1983, Golden Empire Convalescent Hosp., Grass Valley, Calif., 1984, Sierra Nevada Miners Meml. Hosp., Grass Valley, Calif., 1985, CPC Psychiatric Ctr., Sacramento, Calif., 1986, Sunrise Nurses, San Francisco, 1987, Home and Hosp. Help, Inc., San Mateo, Calif., 1988-93, DRG, San Francisco, 1992—; nurse, vis. nurse San Francisco, Marin, Calif., 1986—; founder, facilitator, owner Art's Yours, San Francisco, 1993—; treas. San Francisco Women Artists Gallery, 1994-95; nursing journalist Het Beterschap, The Netherlands, 1984-85; activist in trauma resolution and prevention through art and actions, 1991—; nursing cons. Sierra Nurses, San Carlos, 1991; career advisor San Francisco State U., 1995—. Exhibits include Marin Headlands, 1992, San Francisco Women's Artist Gallery, 1993, 94, 95, Somar Gallery, San Francisco, 1993, 94, Mandana House, Oakland, 1993, Simple Pleasures Cafe, San Francisco, 1994, Urban Art Retreat, Chgo., 1995, L'Arte Del Strada, San Francisco, 1995, others; prodr. video True Stories, 1995. Office: Arts Yours 4339 Balboa St San Francisco CA 94121

TKACZUK, NANCY ANNE, cardiovascular services administrator; b. Cambridge, Mass., Nov. 17, 1949; d. Ralph Aubrey and Eleanor Mae (Godding) Bedley; m. John Paul Tkaczuk, Apr. 9, 1977 (div. Apr. 1983); children: Timothy Aubrey, James Paul. AS in Social Svc., Endicott Coll., 1969; ADN, Clayton Coll., 1975. Coronary care nurse New England Meml. Hosp., Wakefield, Mass., 1975; cardiac cath lab nurse Saint Josephs Hosp., Atlanta, 1976-79; dir. cardiovascular svcs. Northside Hosp., Atlanta, 1979—; founder Mitral Valve Prolapse Support, Atlanta, 1986—; BCLS instr., trainer Am. Heart Assn., 1976—, instr. ACLS, 1990—, pub. spkr., 1975—. Author: Mitral Valve Prolapse, The Heart With A Different Beat, 1986. Mem. Am. Coll. Cardiovascular Adminstrs., Atlanta Health Care Alliance. Methodist. Home: 715 Cranberry Trail Roswell GA 30076 Office: Northside Hosp Cardiology Dept 1000 Johnson Ferry Rd NE Atlanta GA 30342

TOAL, JEAN HOEFER, lawyer, state supreme court justice; b. Columbia, S.C., Aug. 11, 1943; d. Herbert W. and Lilla (Farrell) Hoefer; m. William Thomas Toal; children: Jean Hoefer, Lilla Patrick. BA in Philosophy, Agnes Scott Coll., 1965; JD, U. S.C., 1968; LHD (hon.), Coll. Charleston, 1991; LLD (hon.), Columbia Coll., 1992. Bar: S.C. Assoc. Haynsworth, Perry, Bryant, Marion & Johnstone, 1968-70; ptnr. Belser, Baker, Barwick, Ravenel, Toal & Bender, Columbia, 1970-88; assoc. justice S.C. Supreme Ct., 1988—; mem. S.C. Human Affairs Commn., 1972-74; mem. S.C. Ho. of Reps., 1975-88, chmn. house rules com., constitutional laws subcom. house judiciary com.; mem. parish coun. and lector St. Joseph's Cath. Ch.; chair S.C. Juvenile Justice Task Force, 1992-94; chair S.C. Rhodes Scholar Selection Com., 1994. Mng. editor S.C. Law Rev., 1967-68. Bd. visitors Clemson U., 1978; trustee Columbia Mus. Art. Named Legislator of Yr. Greenville News, Woman of Yr., U. S.C.; recipient Disting. Svc. award S.C. Mcpl. Assn., Univ. Notre Dame award, 1991, Algernon Sydney Sullivan award U. S.C., 1991. Mem. John Belton O'Neill Inn of Ct., Phi Alpha Delta. Office: Supreme Ct SC PO Box 12456 Columbia SC 29211-2456

TOBACH, ETHEL, retired curator; b. Miaskovka, USSR, Nov. 7, 1921; came to U.S., 1923; d. Ralph Wiener and Fanny (Schechterman) Wiener Idels; m. Charles Tobach, 1947 (dec. 1969). BA, Hunter Coll., 1949; MA, NYU, 1952, PhD, 1957; DSc (hon.), L.I. Univ., 1975. Lic. psychologist, N.Y. Rsch. fellow Am. Mus. Natural History, N.Y.C., 1958-61, assoc. curator, 1964-69, curator, 1969-90, emerita curator; rsch. fellow NYU, N.Y.C., 1961-64; adj. prof. psychology CUNY, N.Y.C., 1964—. Co-editor: (series) T.C. Schneirla Conference Series, 1981, Genes & Gender, 1975; editor: International Jour. Comparative Psychology, 1987-93; assoc. editor: Peace and Conflict: Jour. of Peace Psychology, 1994—. Recipient Disting. Sci. Career, Assn. Women in Sci., 1974, Disting. Sci. Publ., Assn. for Women in Psychology, 1982, Kurt Lewin award Soc. for Psychol. Study of Social Issues, 1993. Fellow APA (pres. comparative psychology div. 1985); mem. Internat. Soc. Comparative Psychology (sec. 1988-92), Ea. Psychol. Assn. (pres. 1987), N.Y. Acad. Scis. (v.p. behavioral scis. 1973-76). Office: Am Mus Natural History Central Pkwy 79th St New York NY 10024-5192

TOBER, BARBARA D. (MRS. DONALD GIBBS TOBER), editor; b. Summit, N.J., Aug. 19, 1934; d. Rodney Fielding and Maude (Grebbin) Starkey; m. Donald Gibbs Tober, Apr. 5, 1973. Student, Traphagen Sch. Fashion, 1954-56, Fashion Inst. Tech., 1956-58, N.Y. Sch. Interior Design, 1964. Copy editor Vogue Pattern Book, 1958-60; beauty editor Vogue mag., 1961; dir. women's services Bartell Media Corp., 1961-66; editor-in-chief Bride's mag., N.Y.C., 1966-94; chmn. Am. Craft Mus.; pres. Acronym, Inc., N.Y.C., 1995—, The Barbara Tober Found., 1995—; dir. Gen. Brands Corp., sec.-treas.; adv. bd. Traphagen Sch.; coordinator SBA awards; Am. Craft Council Mus. Assoc., 1983—, benefit food com. chmn., 1984-87. Author: The ABC's of Beauty, 1963, China: A Cognizant Guide, 1980, The Wedding . . . The Marriage . . . And the Role of the Retailer, 1980, The Bride: A Celebration, 1984. Mem. Nat. Council on Family Relations, 1966; nat. council Lincoln Center Performing Arts, Met. Opera Guild; mem. NYU adv. bd. Women in Food Service, 1983; NYU Women's Health Symposium: Steering Com., 1983—. Recipient Alma award, 1968, Penney-Mo. award, 1972, Traphagen Alumni award, 1975, Diamond Jubilee award, 1983. Mem. Fashion Group, Nat. Home Fashions League (v.p., program chmn.), Am. Soc. Mag. Editors, Am. Soc. Interior Designers (press mem.), Intercorporate Group, Women in Communications (60 yrs. of success award N.Y. chpt. 1984), Nat. Assn. Underwater Instrs., Pan Pacific and S.E. Asia Women's Assn., Asia Soc., Japan Soc., China Inst., Internat. Side Saddle Orgn., Millbrook Hounds, Golden's Bridge Hounds, Wine and Food Soc., Chaines des Rotisseurs (chargée de press) (bd. dirs.), Dames d'Escoffier, Culinary Inst. Am. Home and Office: 620 Park Ave New York NY 10021-6591

TOBEY, MARGARET L., lawyer; b. Columbus, Ohio, June 27, 1949. BA, U. Iowa, 1974, MA, 1980, JD, 1980. Bar: Ohio 1980, U.S. Ct. Appeals (D.C. cir.) 1981, D.C. 1982, U.S. Dist. Ct. (D.C.) 1982, U.S. Supreme Ct. 1989. Law clk. Hon. Roger Robb, U.S. Ct. Appeals (D.C. cir.), 1980-81; ptnr. Akin, Gump, Strauss, Hauer & Feld, L.L.P., Washington, 1981—. Mem. ABA (adminstrv. law sect., forum com. on comms. law), Federal Comms. Bar Assn. (co-chair adjudicatory practice com. 1990-92, trustee found. 1991-95, chair 1993-95). Office: Akin Gump Strauss Hauer & Feld LLP 1333 New Hampshire Ave NW Ste 400 Washington DC 20036*

TOBIA, SUSAN J., reading educator; b. Providence, Nov. 21, 1946; d. Salvino Paul and Gertrude C. (LaRochelle) T. BA, Newton Coll. Sacred Heart, Mass., 1968; MEd, Temple U., 1970, PhD, 1988. Cert. in spl. edn., Pa. Tchr. educable retarded Phila. Pub. Schs., 1968-71; learning disabilities tchr. Nat. Regional Resource Ctr., King of Prussia, Pa., 1971-73, DeKalb County Schs., Decatur, Ga., 1973-74, Clarke County Schs., Athens, Ga., 1974-75, Mayfield City Schs., Cleve., 1975-77; reading instr. Temple U., Phila., 1977-80; reading specialist coord., program dir. Met. Collegiate Ctr., Phila., 1980-84; assoc. prof. reading/study skills C.C. Phila., 1984-93, coord. collaborative learning cmty., 1993—; curriculum design cons. Phila. Electric Co., 1985-87, Fellowship Commn., Phila., 1990, 92, 94; instr. Beaver Coll.,

Glenside, Pa., summer 1988; curriculum cons. Concerned Black Men, Phila., 1991-92. Author: (curriculum) Private Industry Council Transition Program, 1992; contbr. chpt. to book. Mem., exec. officer Citizens Com. on Pub. Edn. in Phila., 1985-94; mem. exec. team City Coun. Campaign, Phila., 1990-91, mem. team, 1994. Recipient Outstanding Contbn. to Spl. Programs and Support Svcs. award C.C. Phila., 1987. Mem. Internat. Reading Assn., Delaware Valley Reading Assn., Pa. Assn. for Devel. Educators. Office: CC of Phila 1700 Spring Garden St Philadelphia PA 19130-3936

TOBIAS, JUDY, university development executive; b. Pitts.; d. Saul Albert Landau and Bess (Previn) Kurzman; m. Seth Tobias (dec. May 1983); children: Stephen Frederic, Andrew Previn; m. Lewis F. Davis, 1990. Student Silvermine Artists Guild, 1951-55. Art cons. Westchester Mental Health Assn., White Plains, N.Y., 1968-69; cons. sch. social work NYU, 1973-74, devel. exec. 1976—; conf. coord. Today's Family: Implications for the Future, N.Y.C., 1974-75; cons. Playschools, Inc., N.Y.C., 1975; majority counsel mem. Emily's List, 1991—. Mem. Gov.'s Commn. on Continuing Edn., Albany, N.Y., 1968-70, Nat. Coun. on Children and Youth, Washington, 1974-75, Manhattan Inter-Hosp. Group on Child Abuse, 1975-76; chmn. N.Y. met. com. for UNICEF, 1976-77; mem. exec. com. Town Hall Found., N.Y.C., 1979—, vice chmn., 1986-90; founder, bd. dirs. N.Y. chpt. WAIF, Inc., 1961—, nat. pres., 1978-82, nat. bd. dirs. 1978—; pres. emeritus, 1993—; bd. dirs. Citizen's Com. for Children, City of N.Y., 1975—, v.p., 1983-90; bd. dirs. Am. br. Internat. Social Svc., 1965-80; bd. dirs. Andrew Glover Youth Program, 1986-89, mem. adv. coun. 1989—; bd. dirs. Goddard Riverside Cmty. Ctr., 1985—, Dance Mag. Found., 1986-92, St. John's Place Family Ctr., 1987-93, Capitol Hall Preservation Corp., 1989-93, chmn. bd. Inst. for Cult. Diversity, 1996—, Inst. for Social Complexity, 1996—. Recipient Nat. Humanitarian award WAIF, 1990. Mem. Child Study Assn. Am. (bd. dirs. 1963-71, pres. 1969-71, bd. dirs. Wel-Met Inc. 1972-85). Democrat.

TOBIAS, SHEILA, writer, educator; b. N.Y., Apr. 26, 1935; d. Paul Jay and Rose (Steinberger) Tobias; m. Carlos Stern, Oct. 11, 1970 (div. 1982); m. Carl T. Tomizuka, Dec. 16, 1987. BA, Harvard Radcliffe U., 1957; MA, Columbia U., 1961, MPhil, 1974; PhD (hon.), Drury Coll., 1994, Wheelock Coll., 1995. Journalist W. Germany, U.S. and Fed. Republic Germany, 1957-65; lect. in history C.C.N.Y., N.Y.C., 1965-67; univ. admintr. Cornell U., Wesleyan U., 1967-78; lect. in women's studies U. Calif., San Diego, 1985-92; lect. in war, peace studies U. So. Calif., 1985-88. Author: Overcoming Math Anxiety, 1978, rev. edit., 1994, Succeed with Math, 1987, Revitalizing Undergraduate Science: Why Some Things Work and Most Don't, 1992, Science as a Career: Perceptions and Realities, 1995; co-author: The People's Guide to National Defense, 1982, Women, Militarism and War, 1987, They're Not Dumb, They're Different, 1990, (with Carl T. Tomizuka) Breaking the Science Barrier, 1992. Chmn. bd. dirs. The Clarion newspaper. Mem. Am. Assn. Higher Edn. (bd. dirs. 1993—), Coll. Sci. Tchrs. Assn., Nat. Women's Studies Assn., Phi Beta Kappa.

TOBIASSEN, VIRGINIA HEGE, editor, author; b. Winston-Salem, N.C., Apr. 18, 1959; d. Frederick Pfohl and Dorothy Alice (Baker) Hege; m. William Edward Tobiassen, June 11, 1988; 1 child, Thor Hege Tobiassen. BA in English, U. N.C., 1981. Editor John F. Blair, Publisher, Winston-Salem, N.C., 1983-85, McFarland & Co., Inc. Publishers, Jefferson, N.C., 1988-89; asst. dir. for press activities Appalachian Consortium, Boone, N.C., 1989; freelance editor, author Boone, 1990-96; editor McFarland & Co., 1996—. Author: (book) Am I Glowing Yet?, 1995. Leader La Leche League, Boone, N.C., 1995—. Democrat. Moravian.

TOBIN, AILEEN WEBB, educational administrator; b. Milford, Del., July 9, 1949; d. Wilson Webster Webb and Dorothy Marie (Benson) Rust; m. Thomas Joseph Tobin, Jr., July 31, 1971. BA cum laude, U. Del., 1971, MEd, 1975, PhD, 1981. Cert. tchr. secondary edn., cert. reading specialist, cert. reading cons., Del. Dir. Del. Tutoring Ctr., Wilmington, 1971-74; grad. teaching asst. U. Del., Newark, 1974-81, instr. Coll. Edn., 1978-82; ednl. specialist U.S. Army Ordnance Ctr. & Sch., Aberdeen Proving Ground, Md., 1982-85, chief internal eval. br., 1985-88, chief evaluation div., 1988, chief standardization and analysis div., 1988-90, dir. quality assurance, 1990-94, dir. tactical support equipment dept., 1994—; cons. Dorchester County Sch. Dist., Dorchester County, Md., 1977-80; rsch. assoc., Ctr. for Ednl. Leadership, Newark, 1981-82; staff assoc., Rsch. for Better Schs., Inc., Phila., 1981-84. Author: (book chpt.) Approaches Informal Eval. of Reading, 1982, Dialogues in Literary Research, 1988, Cognitive & Social Perspectives for Literary Research & Instruction, 1989; contbr. articles to profl. jours. Recipient Silver award Fed. Exec. Bd., 1992, Comdr.'s award for Civil Svc. Dept. Army, 1994, Order of Samuel Sharpe award Ordnance Corps Assn., 1994, Superior Civil Svc. award Dept. Army, 1995. Mem. Internat. Reading Assn., Nat. Reading Conf., Am. Ednl. Rsch. Assn., Am. Evaluation Assn., Ordnance Corps Assn., Kappa Delta Pi. Methodist. Home: 4839 Plum Run Ct Wilmington DE 19808 Office: US Army Ordnance Ctr & Sch ATSL SB TSED Aberdeen Proving Ground MD 21005

TOBIN, JOAN ADELE, writer; b. N.Y.C., Nov. 24, 1930; d. William and Helen (Steinis) Butler; m. Oct. 15, 1950; children: Patricia, Michael, Eileen. Freelance editor Suffield, Conn., 1980-85; owner, pub. Paper Works, Suffield, Conn., 1984-92. Contbr. over 80 articles to Internat. Mensa Jour., OWL Nat. News, N.Y. Times, N.Y. Mensa, and others. Mem. Am. Mensa, NOW, Universalist-Unitarian Womens Fedn., Writers Group Mensa. Home: 32 Harmon Dr Suffield CT 06078-2062

TOBIN, MARGARET ANN, cardiac medical critical care nurse; b. Oakland, Calif., Dec. 10, 1959; d. William Leroy Jones and Barbara Kay (Rains) Carter; m. Wesley Vernon Keene, June 21, 1977 (div. June 1984); m. James Edward Tobin, Aug. 15, 1985; 1 child, Nicholas William. ADN, Ctrl. Tex. Coll., 1983; BSN, U. Mary Harden Baylor, 1994; postgrad., Tex. A&M U., Corpus Christi, 1994—. RN, Tex.; cert. med.-surg. nurse ANCC; cert. BCLS instr., ACLS. Grad. nurse surg. fl. Olin E. Teague VA Ctr., Temple, Tex., 1983-84, staff nurse cardiac med. ICU, 1984-95, nurse mgr. surg. ICU, 1995-96, nurse mgr. cardiac med. ICU, 1996—, clin. instr., 1996—. Mem. Tar Wars Kids Against Tobacco, Temple, 1993—. Mem. AACN (pres.-elect 1993-94, pres. 1994-95), Sigma Theta Tau. Baptist. Home: 101 S 43rd St Temple TX 76504-3914

TOCKLIN, ADRIAN MARTHA, insurance company executive, lawyer; b. Coral Gables, Fla., Aug. 4, 1951; d. Kelso Hampton and Patricia Jane (Crook) Cook Atkins; m. Gary Michael Tocklin, Nov. 23, 1974. BA, George Washington U., 1972; JD, Seton Hall U., 1994. Regional claim examiner Interstate Nat. Corp., St. Petersburg, Fla., 1973-74; branch supr. Underwriter's Adjusting Co. subs. Continental Corp., Tampa, Fla., 1974-77, asst. dir. edn. tng. adminstrn., N.Y.C., 1977, asst. regional mgr. adminstrn. ops., Livingston, N.J., 1977-78, br. mgr., Paramus, N.J., 1978-80, sr. v.p. mktg., N.Y.C., Piscataway, N.J., 1980-84, regional v.p., mgr., Livingston, N.J., 1984-86, exec. v.p., 1986-88, also bd. dirs.; sr. v.p. Continental Corp., 1988-92, exec. v.p. 1992-94, pres., N.Y.C., 1994-95; pres. diversified ops. CNA Ins., Chgo., 1995—; pres. bd. dirs. U.S. Protection Indemnity Agy., Inc., N.Y.C.; bd. dirs. Underwriters Adjusting Co., Arbitration Forums, Inc., Tarrytown, N.Y., Continental Ins. Co., Sonat Corp.; v.p. Continental Risk Services, Inc., Hamilton, Bermuda, 1983-86; editor-in-chief Profl. Ins. Bulletin Update, N.Y.C., 1977-79. Mem. YWCA Acad. Women Achievers. Mem. Nat. Assn. Ins. Women (Outstanding Ins. Woman in N.Y.C.), NOW. Democrat. Lutheran. Office: CNA Ins CNA Plz Chicago IL 60685

TODARO, PATRICIA ANNE, painter, singer; b. Rockville Centre, N.Y., Feb. 24, 1933; d. Russell Norman and Grace Ruth (Eyerman) Sheidow; m. Raymond Ashman, Feb. 6, 1958 (div.); children: Robert Ashman, Richard Ashman, Kathryn Ashman. Student, Sullins Coll., 1950-51, Art Students League, 1954, Susquehanna U., 1952-54, Coll. of William and Mary, 1982-84. With programming dept. ABC, 1954-55; with travel dept. Rand, Santa Monica, Calif., 1955-56; pres. Seltzer Gallery, N.Y.C., 1986, 87. One-woman shows include Seltzer Coll., 1985-87, Seltzer Gallery, Phoenix Visual Arts Ctr., 1988, Kerr Cultural Ctr., Scottsdale, Ariz., 1989, Williamsburg Duke of Glouster Show, 1984, Albert Einstein Med. Ctr., N.Y.C., 1987, Seltzer Gallery, represented in pvt. collections Albi-France, 1986, Leo House, N.Y.C., 1986-87, Shanti-AIDS Home, Phoenix, Ariz., 1988, Unipas Gallery, N.Y.C., 1991. Recipient Silver medal Salon D'Automne, Albi, France, 1986; scholar Am. Theatre Wing, 1954-58. Mem. Am. Fedn. Musicians.

TODD, JAN THERESA, counselor; b. Mobile, Ala., Mar. 20, 1961; d. Joseph Thomas and Lessie Grey (Sullivan) T. BA, U. Tex., San Antonio, 1983, MA, 1992. Cert. profl. counselor; cert. provisional tchr. English tchr. Bandera (Tex.) High Sch.-Bandera (Tex.) Ind. Sch. Dist., 1987-91; counselor Yorktown (Tex.) High Sch.-Yorktown (Tex.) Ind. Sch. Dist., 1992-93, John F. Kennedy High Sch.-Edgewood Ind. Sch. Dist., San Antonio, 1993-95, Lackland Jr./Sr. H.S., San Antonio, 1995—. Mem. ACA, Tex. Counselors Assn., South Tex. Counselors Assn., Assn. Tex. Profl. Educators. Home: 9415 De Sapin San Antonio TX 78250-6308 Office: Lackland Jr/Sr High School Bldg 8265 2460 Bong Ave San Antonio TX 78236-1244

TODD, JAN(ICE) SUFFOLK, physical education educator; b. Lock # 4, Pa., May 22, 1952; d. James Herbert Suffolk and Wilma (Yerty) White; m. Terry Todd, Nov. 16, 1973. BA in Philosophy and English, Mercer U., 1974, MEd, 1976; PhD in Am. Studies, U. Tex., 1995. English and history tchr. New Germany (Nova Scotia) Rural H.S., coach, 1979-84; founder Todd-McLean Phys. Culture Collection U. Tex., Austin, 1984—; chairperson Internat. Powerlifting Fedn.; head coach U.S. Men's and Women's Powerlifting Teams, 1981, 84. Pub., editor The Powerlifter, Iron Game History: The Jour. of Phys. Culture, 1990—; co-author: Lift Your Way to Youthful Fitness, 1985; contbr. articles to profl. jours. Named World's Strongest Woman, Sports Illustrated and Guiness Book of Records, 1977, 1st Woman inducted into Internat. Powerlifting Hall of Fame, 1982. Mem. AAHPERD, N.Am. Sport Libr. Info. Network (exec. com. 1992-95, exec. com. 1993-95), Nat. Strength and Conditioning Assn., Oldetime Barbell Assn. (Lifetime Achievement award 1993), N.Am. Soc. for Sport History (chmn. time and site com. 1992-95). Office: U Tex/Dept Kinesiology Todd-McLeon Phys Culture 217 Gregory Gym Austin TX 78712

TODD, KATHLEEN GAIL, physician; b. Portland, Oreg., Aug. 31, 1951; d. Horace Edward and Lois Marie (Messing) T.; m. Andrew Richard Embick, March 31, 1980; children: Elizabeth Todd Embick, Margaret Todd Embick. BA, Pomona Coll., 1972; MD, Washington U., St. Louis, 1976. Diplomate Am. Bd. Family Practice. Resident U. Wash. Affiliated Hosps., Seattle, 1976-79; pvt. practice Valdez (Alaska) Med. Clinic, 1980—; chief of staff Valdez Community Hosp., 1986—. Mem. AMA, AAFP, Am. Acad. Family Practice, Alaska State Med. Assn. (counselor-at-large 1986-87). Democrat. Episcopalian. Office: Valdez Med Clinic PO Box 1829 Valdez AK 99686-1829

TODD, LINDA MARIE, air traffic-weather advisor, nutritional researcher, financial consultant; b. L.A., Mar. 30, 1948; d. Ithel Everette and Janet Marie (Zito) Fredricks; m. William MacKenzie Cook, Jan. 11, 1982 (div. Oct. 1989); m. Robert Oswald Todd, Apr. 8, 1990; 1 child, Jesse MacKenzie Todd. BA in Psychology and Sociology, U. Colo., 1969; student Psychology Grad. work, U. No. Colo., 1970. Pilot lic., weather cert., FCC lic., Calif. life ins. lic., coll. teaching credential; registered with Nat. Assn. Securities Dealers. Counselor Jeffco Juvenile Detention Ctr., Golden, Colo., 1969-71; communications Elan Vital, Denver, 1971-81; legal sec. Fredman, Silverberg & Lewis, San Diego, 1980-82; escrow supr. Performance Mktg. Concepts, Olympic Valley, Calif., 1982-85; mgmt. commn. instr. Sierra Coll., Truckee, Calif., 1986-87; regional mgr. Primerica Fin. Svcs., Reno, 1987-91; air traffic, weather advisor Truckee (Calif.) Tahoe Airport Dist., 1986—; student tour leader, air show organizer Truckee (Calif.) Tahoe Airport; fin. cons. Primerica Fin. Svcs., Truckee, 1987-91; gen. agt. TTS Fin., 1992—; co-founder Todd Nutrition, 1995—. Editor: (newsletter) Communications, 1975. Sec. gen. Arapahoe H.S. Model UN, Littleton, Colo., 1965; del. State Model UN, Colo., 1966; conv. del. Elan Vital, The Ninety-Nines, Inc. Recipient Univ. scholarship Littleton (Colo.) Edn. Assn., 1966, flight scholarship The Ninety-Nines Inc., Reno, 1990; named Recruiter of Month, Al Williams Primerica, Reno, 1987. Mem. Elan Vital, Plane Talkers, The Ninety Nines, Planetary Soc. Home and Office: PO Box 1303 Truckee CA 96160-1303

TODD, LISA ANDERSON, judge; b. Summit, N.J., Mar. 2, 1942; d. Carl Magnus and Ida (Johnson) Anderson; m. David C. Todd, Sept. 6, 1986. BA, Cornell U., 1964; LLB, Stanford U., 1967. Bar: Calif. 1968, D.C. 1968, U.S. Ct. Claims 1970, U.S. Supreme Ct. 1973. Staff atty. United Planning Orgn., Washington, 1967-69; assoc. vomBaur, Coburn, Simmons & Turtle, Washington, 1970-73, Morgan, Lewis & Bockius, Washington, 1973-79; sole practice, Washington, 1979-83; adminstrv. judge, bd. contract appeals NASA, Washington, 1983-93, vice chmn., 1990-93, chmn., 1993; adminstrv. judge, Armed Svcs. Bd. of Contract Appeals, 1993—. Mem. ABA, Fed. Bar Assn., Bd. Contract Appeals Judges Assn. (bd. dirs. 1991-92, 94—), Nat. Assn. Women Judges (treas. 1987-88). Democrat. Lutheran. Home: 3811 Fulton St NW Washington DC 20007-1345 Office: 5109 Leesburg Pike Falls Church VA 22041-3208

TODD, MARGARET LOUISE, retired secondary education educator; b. Newport News, Va., Nov. 27, 1919; d. Preson Curtis and Lydia Emos (Diggs) Watson; m. Jesse Emerson Todd, Sr., Apr. 5, 1947; children: Frances Diggs, Jesse Emerson Jr. AB, Coll. William & Mary, Williamsburg, Va., 1943; MA, Hampton U., 1978. Elem. tchr. Newport News (Va.) Sch. System, 1943-45; newspaper reporter Times-herald, 1945-46; tchr. English Goerge Wythe Jr. High, 1946-47; tchr. English Bethel High Sch., Hampton, 1970-82, ret., 1982; speaker in field and tchr. workshops. Author: (with others) Hampton From the Sea to the Stars, 1985; author: (biograph) C. Alton Lindsay: Educator and Community Leader, 1994; contbr. articles to profl. jours. Cert. lay speaker United Meth. Ch., Peninsula, 1970s-95; judge Va Forensics Debate, 1970s-82; debate coach Bethe H.S., Hampton, 1971-82. Mem. AAUW (life), Va. Ret. Tchrs. Assn. (trustee Va. conf. UM Hist. Soc.), Nat. Assn. Parliamentarians, Great Books Group, Planned Parenthood (pres. 1967-68), Hampton Hist. Found., Nat. Blackstone Coll. Alumnae Assn. (pres. 1995—). Home: 909 Todds Ln Hampton VA 23666-1842

TODD, MARY PATRICIA, nursing administrator; b. Loogootee, Ind., Sept. 5, 1959; d. James Walter and Anna Margaret (Arvin) T. BS in Social Work, St. Mary of the Woods Coll., 1982; AS in Nursing, Tenn. State U., 1989; postgrad., Vanderbilt U., 1995—. Cert. disaster nursing ARC. Comty. organizer Rogers Park Tenants Com., Chgo., 1984-85; dir. Nashville Comys. Orgn. for Progress, Nashville, 1986-87, Tenn. Coun. Sr. Citizens, Nashville, 1987-89; staff nurse Nashville VA Med. Ctr., Nashville, 1989-90; charge nurse Hartsville (Tenn.) Convalescent Ctr., 1990-94; quality assurance coord. ABC Home Health, Hartsville, 1992-93; adminstr. ABC Home Health, Lafayette, Tenn., 1994-95; charge nurse Trousdale Med. Ctr., Hartsville, Tenn., 1995—; presenter rural health conf. Meharry Med. Sch., Nashville, 1994; spkr. Tenn. rural Health Assn., 1995. Contbr., pub.: Love Passed On, 1991; contbr.: Photographic History of Martin County, 1993, Voices from the Hills, 1995; organizer, author: (diaster plan) Caring When it Counts, 1994. Bd. dirs., chair membership com. Mid. Cumberland Cmty. Health Agy., Nashville, 1992—; mem. network, Washington, 1993—; organizer Trousdale County Cmty. Health Coun., Hartsville, 1992—; active Greenpeace, 1990-92; tchr. Confraternity of Christian Doctrine, Holy Family Cath. Ch., 1992, 94. Mem. ANA, Tenn. Nurses Assn., Tenn. Assn. for Home Care, Tenn. Rural Health Assn., Trousdale County C. of C., Amnesty Internat., Health Profls. Network, Rural Tenn. Women's Support Group (organizer 1994). Democrat. Home: 314 Church St Apt 22 Hartsville TN 37074-1713 Office: Trousdale Medical Center 500 Church St #22 Hartsville TN 37074

TODD, RUTH, artist; b. Sanford, N.C., Nov. 10, 1909; m. Judson Cornelius and Flora Thomas; m. Littleton Todd, May 19, 1934. Student, Anderson Coll., 1927-28, U. Miami, 1930-31, Colorado Springs Coll., 1954. One-woman shows Morris Gallery, N.Y.C., 1958, Bodley Gallery, N.Y.C., 1962, Internat. House, Denver, 1964, U. Colo., Boulder, 1968, Joseph Magnin Gallery, Denver, 1975, Merrill-Chase Galleries, Chgo., 1977, West End Gallery, Winston-Salem, N.C., 1979, also others; exhibited in numerous group shows, including Santa Fe Mus., Sweat Meml. Art Mus., Portland, Maine, Creative Galleries, N.Y.C., N.Y.C. Ctr. Gallery, N.C. State Mus. Art, Raleigh, Mulvane Art Ctr., Topeka, Denver Art Mus., U. N.Mex., Albuquerque, Colorado Springs (Colo.) Fine Arts Ctr., La Galléria Escondido, Taos, N.Mex.; represented in permanent collections Princeton U., NYU, also corp. and pvt. collections. Recipient awards for art including Soc. Four Arts Mus., Palm Beach, Fla., Nelson Adkins Gallery, Kansas City (Mo.) Mus., George Walter Vincent Smith Art Mus., Springfield, Mass., Joslyn Art Mus., Omaha, Okla. Fine Arts Ctr., Oklahoma City; 1st award Nat. Space Art Exhibit, 1969, 3d award, 1975. Episcopalian.

TODD, SHIRLEY ANN, school system administrator; b. Botetourt County, Va., May 23, 1935; d. William Leonard and Margaret Judy (Simmons) Brown; m. Thomas Byron Todd, July 7, 1962 (dec. July 1977). B.S. in Edn., Madison Coll., 1956; M.Ed., U. Va., 1971. Cert. tchr., Va. Elem. tchr. Fairfax County Sch. Bd., Fairfax, Va., 1956-66, 8th grade history tchr., 1966-71, guidance counselor James F. Cooper Mid. Sch., McLean, Va., 1971-88, dir. guidance, 1988-96; chmn. mktg. Lake Anne Joint Venture, Falls Church, Va., 1979-82, mng. ptnr., 1980-82. Del. Fairfax County Republican Conv., 1985. Fellow Fairfax Edn. Assn. (mem. profl. rights and responsibilities commn. 1970-72, bd. dirs. 1968-70), Va. Edn. Assn. (mem. state com. on local assns. and urban affairs 1969-70), NEA, No. Va. Counselors Assn. (hospitality and social chmn., exec. bd. 1982-83), Va. Counselors Assn. (exec. com. 1987), Va. Sch. Counselors Assn., Am. Assn. for Counseling and Devel., Chantilly Nat. Golf and Country Club (v.p. social 1981-82, Centreville, Va.). Baptist. Avocations: golf, tennis. Home: 6543 Bay Tree Ct Falls Church VA 22041-1001

TODD, SUSAN MARIE, geology department head; b. Evansville, Ind., July 6, 1946; d. Russell H. and Irene G. (Horn) Wiberg. BS, U. Tex., 1969, postgrad., 1986—; MA, U. Tex., Dallas, 1976. Tchr. Forest Oaks Mid. Sch., Ft. Worth, Tex., 1969-71, Browne Mid. Sch., Dallas, 1971-76; lectr. U. Tex., Dallas, 1977-78; geology dept. head Brookhaven Coll., Dallas, 1978—. Mem. editl. rev. bd. Jour. Coll. Sci. Tchg., 1984-87; contbr. articles to profl. jours. Maj. gifts chmn. Sta. KERA-TV Auction, Dallas, 1985-88; grad. Leadership Lewisville, Tex., 1989-90; v.p. Lewisville Edn. Found., 1989—; bd. dirs. Greater Lewisville Habitat for Humanity, 1995—. Recipient Master Tchr. award Nat. Inst. for Staff & Organizational Devel., 1987; Kellogg Found. fellow, 1988. Mem. Geol. Soc. Am., Lions (Balloon Festival com. chair 1991—, treas. 1992—), Delta Kappa Gamma. Home: 20 Horseshoe Dr Highland Village TX 75067-6714 Office: Brookhaven Coll 3939 Valley View Ln Dallas TX 75244-4906

TOENSING, VICTORIA, lawyer; b. Colon, Panama, Oct. 16, 1941; d. Philip William and Victoria (Brady) Long; m. Trent David Toensing, Oct. 29, 1962 (div. 1976); children: Todd Robert, Brady Cronon, Amy Victoriana; m. Joseph E. diGenova, June 27, 1981. BS in Edn., Ind. U., 1962; JD cum laude, U. Detroit, 1975. Bar: Mich. 1976, D.C. 1978. Tchr. English Milw., 1965-66; law clk. to presiding justice U.S. Ct. Appeals, Detroit, 1975-76; asst. U.S. atty. U.S. Atty.'s Office, Detroit, 1976-81; chief counsel U.S. Senate Intelligence Com., Washington, 1981-84; dep. asst. atty. gen. criminal div. Dept. Justice, Washington, 1984-88; spl. counsel Hughes Hubbard & Reed, Washington, 1988-90; ptnr. Cooter and Gell, Washington, 1990-91; ptnr., co-chmn. nat. white collar group Manatt, Phelps and Phillips, Washington, 1991-95; founding ptnr. diGenova & Toensing, Wasington, 1996—; mem. working group on corp. sanctions U.S. Sentencing Commn., 1988-89; co-chairperson Coalition for Women's Appts. Justice Judiciary Task Force, 1988-92; legal analyst for trial of O.J. Simpson, Am.'s Talking Network, 1995. Author: Bringing Sanity to the Insanity Defense, 1983, Mens Rea: Insanity by Another Name, 1984; contbg. author: Fighting Back: Winning The War Against Terrorism, Desk Book on White Collar Crime, 1991; contbr. articles to profl. jours. Founder, chmn. Women's Orgn. To Meet Existing Needs, Mich., 1975-79; chmn. Republican Women's Task Force, 1979-81; bd. dirs. Project on Equal Edn. Rights, Mich., 1980-81, Nat. Hist. Intelligence Mus., 1987-95, America's Talking Legal Analyst, 1995. Recipient spl. commendation Office U.S. Atty. Gen., 1980, agy. seal medallion CIA, 1986, award of achievement Alpha Chi Omega, 1992; featured on cover N.Y. Time Mag. for anti-terrorism work, April 1991. Mem. ABA (mem. standing com. on law and nat. security, mem. coun. criminal justice sect., mem. adv. com. complex crimes and litigation, vice chmn. white collar crime com., chmn. subcom. on corp. criminal liability).

TOEPFER, SUSAN JILL, editor; b. Rochester, Minn., Mar. 9, 1948; d. John Bernard and Helen Esther (Chapple) T.; m. Lorenzo Gabriel Carcaterra, May 16, 1981; children: Katherine Marie, Nicholas Gabriel. BA, Bennington Coll., 1970. Mng. editor Photoplay Mag., N.Y.C., 1971-72; freelance writer, N.Y.C., 1972-78; TV week editor N.Y. Daily News, N.Y.C., 1978-79, leisure editor, 1979-82, features editor, 1982-84, arts and entertainment editor, 1984-86, exec. mag. editor, 1986-87; sr. writer People Mag., 1987-89, sr. editor, 1989-91, asst. mng. editor, 1991-94, exec. editor, 1994—. Office: People Mag Time-Life Bldg Rockefeller Ctr New York NY 10020

TOFT, THELMA MARILYN, secondary school educator; b. Balt., Sept. 15, 1943; d. George Edward and Thelma Iola (Smith) Trageser; m. Ronald Harry Toft, Aug. 27, 1966; 1 child, Joanna Lynn. BS in Med. Tech., Mt. St. Agnes Coll., Balt., 1965; BSE, Coll. Notre Dame, Balt., 1972; MEd, Pa. State U., 1983. Recreation dir. Villa Maria, Balt., 1961-65; blood bank supr. Wayman Park NIH, Balt., 1965-68; tchr. Sacred Heart, St. Mary's Govan's, Balt., 1968-74, Lincoln Intermediate Unit # 12, Adams County, Pa., 1979-80, York (Pa.) City Sch. Dist., 1980—; curriculum dir. M.O.E.S.T. Pa. State U., 1991-93; mem. Pa. State Consortium-Pa. Team for Improving Math. and Sci.; grant writer, speaker in field; writer sch. to work curriculum. Active Girl Scouts USA, Hanover, 1988-92, leader, 1984-87; mgmt. bd. Agrl. Indsl. Mus. Mem. ASCD, AAUW, Nat. Ptnrs. in Edn., Am. Bus. Women's Assn. (edn. com. 1992, sec. 1993, Chpt. Woman of Yr. 1994, York County Woman of Yr. 1995), Phi Delta Kappa. Democrat. Roman Catholic. Home: 30 Panther Dr Hanover PA 17331-8888

TOKARCZYK, MICHELLE MARIANNE, English language educator; b. Bronx, N.Y., Jan. 2, 1953; d. Michael Andrew and Florence May (Roberts) T.; m. Paul John Groncki, Aug. 25, 1979. BA in English, Herbert Lehman Coll., 1975; MA in English, SUNY, Stony Brook, 1978, PhD in English, 1985. Asst. prof. English Hofstra U., Hempstead, N.Y., 1985-86, Rutgers U., New Brunswick, N.J., 1986-89; assoc. prof. Goucher Coll., Balt., 1989-95, 1995—; reader, cons. Ednl. Testing Svcs., Princeton, N.J., 1992—; cons. editor Belles Lettres, North Potomac, Md., 1986—; poetry editor Women's Quar. Rev., N.Y.C., 1983-86. Author: E.L. Doctorow: An Annotated Bibliography, 1988, (poems) The House I'm Running From, 1989; editor: Working-Class Women in the Academy, 1993. Chair arts com. Village Ind. Dems., N.Y.C., 1984-85. Mem. MLA, Nat. Coun. Tchrs. of English, Poetry Soc. Am., Am. Studies Assn. Home and Office: Goucher Coll 1021 Dulaney Valley Rd Baltimore MD 21204

TOKER, KAREN HARKAVY, physician; b. New Haven, Conn., Oct. 23, 1942; d. Victor M. and Nedra (Israel) Harkavy; m. Cyril Toker, Sept. 1, 1968; children: David Edward, Rachel Lee. BS in Chemistry, Coll. William and Mary, 1963; MD, Yale U., 1967. Diplomate Am. Bd. Pediatrics, 1974. Intern dept. pediatrics Bronx Mcpl. Hosp. Ctr., Albert Einstein Coll. Medicine, N.Y., 1967-68, asst. resident dept. pediatrics, 1968-69, sr. resident dept. pediatrics, 1969, 70-71, attending pediatrician, 1971-72, 73-76; pediatrician Montgomery Health Dept., Silver Springs, Md., 1976-83; pediatric cons. Head Start Program Montgomery County Pub. Schs., Rockville, Md., 1976-83; pvt. practice gen. pediatrics Rockville, 1983-89; pediatrician Nemours Children's Clinic, Jacksonville, Fla., 1991-95; med. dir. Pearl Plaza Pediatrics, Duval County Pub. Health Unit, 1995—; instr. pediatrics Albert Einstein Coll. Medicine, N.Y., 1971-74, asst. prof. pediatrics, 1974-76; clin. asst. prof. U. Fla., 1995—. Exec. bd. sec. Congregation Har Shalom, Potomac, 1989-91. Fellow Am. Acad. Pediatrics; mem. Fla. Med. Assn., Duval County Med. Soc., Ambulatory Pediatric Assn. Democrat. Jewish. Home: 6030 Oakbrook Ct Ponte Vedra Beach FL 32082-2052 Office: Pearl Plaza Pediatrics 5220 N Pearl St Jacksonville FL 32208

TOKOLY, MARY ANDREE, microbiologist; b. Manila, Dec. 4, 1940; (parents Am. citizens) d. Robert Francis Tokoly and Ruby Waunita (Shriner) Kaderli. BS, Tex. Woman's U., 1962, MS, 1964, PhD, 1974. Instr Victoria (Tex.) Coll., 1964-66; asst. prof. Kans. State Coll., Pittsburg, 1966-68, Kans. Newman Coll., Wichita, 1974-75; grad. teaching asst. Tex. Woman's U., Denton, 1968-74; microbiologist Nix Hosp., San Antonio, 1975-77, Met. Meth. Hosp., San Antonio, 1977—. Sec. Bexar County chpt. Czech Heritage Soc. Tex., San Antonio, 1988. Robert A. Welch Found. grantee, 1971, 72. Mem. AAUW, Am. Soc. Clin. Pathologists (registered microbiologist), Tex. Soc. Microbiology, South Tex. Assn. Microbiology Profls., Am. Soc. Med. Tech., N.Y. Acad. Scis., S.W. Assn. Clin. Microbiologists,

Sigma Xi. Roman Catholic. Office: Met Meth Hosp 1310 Mccullough Ave San Antonio TX 78212-5601

TOLAND, JOY E., marketing professional; b. Newark, Apr. 8, 1965; d. William D. Cartwright; m. Mark E. Toland, Sept. 10, 1988. BS, Montclair State U., 1987. Staff acct., acctg. clk., billing clk. Delta Dental Plan of N.J., Parsippany; support svc. mgr. PyMaH Corp., Flemington, N.J., 1996—; dir. mktg. Am. Multi-Svcs. Unltd., Inc., Manville, N.J. Mem. NAFE, N.J. Healthcare Cen. Svc. Assn., N.Y.C. Assn. for Cen. Svc. and Materials Mgmt. Pers., L.I. Intercounty chpt. Cen. Svc. Pers., Kiwanis (treas. Circle K 1983-84).

TOLBERT, NINA DIANNE, library technician; b. Washington, July 20, 1964; d. Alvin Joseph and Cleora Demetrice (Cato) T. BA cum laude, Marymount Coll., 1986. Libr. page Folger Shakespeare Libr., Washington, 1986-87; tech. editor Vitro Corp., Silver Spring, Md., 1987; sec. HAY Systems, Inc., Washington, 1988; proofreader ASCI Corp., Washington, 1989; sec. USAF, Washington, 1991-94; libr. technician Telesec, Gaithersburg, Md., 1995, Libr. Systems & Svcs., Washington, 1995—. D.C. Sch. Librs. scholar, 1982, Marymount Coll. scholar, 1983-84. Mem. Nat. Coun. Negro Women Inc., Nat. Mus. Women in Arts. Democrat. Baptist. Office: Dept Energy Libr 1000 Independence Ave Sw Washington DC 20585

TOLCHIN, JOAN GUBIN, psychiatrist, educator; b. N.Y.C., Mar. 10, 1944; d. Harold and Bella (Newman) Gubin; m. Matthew Armin Tolchin, Sept. 1, 1966; 1 child, Benjamin. AB, Vassar Coll., 1964; MD, NYU, 1972. Diplomate Am. Bd. Gen. Psychiatry, Am. Bd. Child Psychiatry. Rsch. asst. Albert Einstein Coll. Medicine, N.Y.C., 1964-68; instr. psychiatry med. coll. Cornell U., N.Y.C., 1977-78, clin. instr., 1978-86, clin. asst. prof., 1986—. Contbr. articles to profl. jours. Fellow Am. Acad. Child and Adolescent Psychiatry; mem. APA, Am. Acad. Psychoanalysis, N.Y. Coun. Child and Adolescent Psychiatry (bd. dirs. 1992-96, pres. 1994-95), Alpha Omega Alpha. Office: 35 E 84th St New York NY 10028-0871

TOLCHIN, SUSAN JANE, public administration educator, writer; b. N.Y.C., Jan. 14, 1941; d. Jacob Nathan and Dorothy Ann (Markowitz) Goldsmith; m. Martin Tolchin, Dec. 23, 1965; children: Charles Peter, Karen Rebecca. B.A., Bryn Mawr Coll., 1961; M.A., U. Chgo., 1962; Ph.D., N.Y.U., 1968. Lectr. in polit. sci. City Coll., N.Y.C., 1963-65, Bklyn. Coll., 1965-71; adj. asst. prof. polit. sci. Seton Hall U., South Orange, N.J., 1971-73; assoc. prof. polit. sci., dir. Inst. for Women and Politics, Mt. Vernon Coll., Washington, 1975-78; prof. pub. adminstrn. George Washington U., Washington, 1978—. disting. lectr. Industrial Coll. of the Armed Forces, 1994. Author: (book) The Angry American: How Voter Rage is Changing the Nation, 1996; co-author (with Martin Tolchin): To The Victor: Political Patronage from the Clubhouse to the White House, 1971, Clout-Womanpower and Politics, 1974, Dismantling America-The Rush to Deregulate, 1983, Buying Into America-How Foreign Money Is Changing the Face of Our Nation, 1988, Selling Our Security-The Erosion of America's Assets, 1992. Bd. dirs. Cystic Fibrosis Foun., 1982—; county committeewoman Dem. Party, Montclair, N.J., 1969-73. Dilthey fellow George Washington U., 1983, Aspen Inst. fellow, 1979; named Tchr. of Yr., Mt. Vernon Coll., 1978; recipient Founder's Day award NYU, 1968. Fellow Nat. Acad. Pub. Adminstrn.; mem. Am. Polit. Sci. Assn. (pres. Women's Caucus for Polit. Sci. 1977-78), Am. Soc. Pub. Adminstrn. (chairperson sect. Natural Resources and Environ. Adminstrn. 1982-83). Democrat. Jewish. Office: George Washington U Dept Pub Adminstrn Washington DC 20052

TOLER, ANN PATRICK, public relations executive; b. Washington, Oct. 7, 1948; d. William A. and Marie Violet (Tyer) Patrick; m. Ronald Aubrey Toler, July 4, 1970; 1 child, Bradley Neal. Student, East Carolina U., 1966-68; cert. bank mktg, U. Colo., 1989. Admiting clk. Beaufort County Hosp., Washington, N.C., 1966-69; receptionist then exec. sec. Flanders Filters, Washington, 1969-81; adminstrv. sec. Bank of Va., Richmond, 1981-85, personal svc. assoc., 1985-87; mktg. coord. Signet Bank, Richmond, 1987-89, mktg. officer, 1989-90, asst. v.p., 1990-93, regional pub. rels. exec., 1993-94, regional pub. rels. exec. Va. Cmty. Affairs, 1994—. Dir. tournament Signet Open Va., Richmond, 1986—; bd. dirs. Easter Seal Soc., Richmond, 1989—; co-chair spl. events com. United Way, Richmond, 1991, chair 1992 ; chair regional conf. Am. Heart Assn., Richmond, 1991; sec., bd. dirs. Christmas in Apr., Richmond. Mem. Bank Mktg. Assn. Methodist. Office: Signet Bank Ste 200 800 E Main St Richmond VA 23219-2512

TOLES, SYKIE REBECCA, elementary education educator; b. San Francisco, May 3, 1965; d. Wilson Ackley and Nikki Yvette (Storich) T. BA in Comm. summa cum laude, U. So. Maine, 1988; MA in Edn., Antioch U., 1994. Cert. tchr. K-8, Wash. Whitewater rafting guide Unicorn Rafting Expeditions, Brunswick, Maine, 1987-89; wilderness instr. Pacific Crest Outward Bound Sch., Portland, Oreg., 1990-92; elem. tchr. Seattle Pub. Schs., 1994—; v.p. Pathfinder Sch. Site Coun., Seattle, 1995-96. Mem. Seattle Edn. Assn., Can. Alpine Club. Democrat. Home: 7557 40th Ave NE Seattle WA 98115 Office: Pathfinder Sch 5012 SW Genesee Seattle WA 98102

TOLIA, VASUNDHARA K., pediatric gastroenterologist; b. Calcutta, India; came to U.S., 1975; d. Rasiklal and Saroj (Kothari) Doshi; m. Kirit Tolia, May 30, 1975; children: Vinay, Sanjay. MBBS, Calcutta U., 1968-75. Intern, resident Children's Hosp. Mich., Detroit, 1976-79, fellow, 1979-81; asst. prof. Wayne State U., Detroit, 1983-91, assoc. prof., 1991—; dir. pediat. endoscopy unit Children's Hosp. of Mich., Detroit, 1984-90, dir. pediat. gastroenterology and nutrition, 1990—; instr. pediatrics Wayne State U., 1981-83. Contbr. articles to profl. jours. Named Woman of Distinction, Mich. chpt. Crohn's and Colitis Found. Am., 1991. Fellow Am. Coll. Gastroenterology, Am. Acad. Pediats.; mem. Am. Gastroenterology Assn., N.Am. Soc. Pediat. Gastroenterology & Nutrition, Soc. Pediat. Rsch. Office: Children's Hosp of Mich 3901 Beaubien St Detroit MI 48201-2119

TOLIAS, LINDA PUROFF, music educator; b. Dearborn, Mich., Nov. 26, 1954; d. Nick Puroff and Milka Stoycheff; m. Peter Elias Tolias, June 26, 1988. MusB in Music Edn. with honors, U. Mich., 1976; MusM in Music Performance, Wayne State U., 1992. Tchr. music El Dorado (Ark.) Pub. Schs., 1976-77, Ferndale (Mich.) Pub. Schs., 1979-83; tchr. bands and orch. Dearborn Pub. Schs., 1983—; founder, condr. El Dorado Youth Symphony, 1976-77; instr. Oakland U. Summer Music Camp, Rochester, Mich., 1982-84; condr., string clinician Oakland U. Youth Orch., Rochester, 1982-84; string clinician Dearborn Pub. Schs., 1983-96, Farmington Pub. Schs., 1994-96. Sponsor City Beautiful Commn., Dearborn, 1983—. Mem. NOW, Mich. Educator's Nat. Conf., U. Mich. Alumni Assn. Democrat. Greek Orthodox. Home: 32267 Auburn Dr Beverly Hills MI 48025

TOLINO, ARLENE BECENTI, elementary education educator; b. Crownpoint, N.Mex., Dec. 26, 1942; d. Little Billie and Mary (Arviso) Becenti; m. Albert Ray Tolino, Nov. 23, 1963; children: Adrian, Nathaniel Ray, Bryan. BS, U. N.Mex., 1977; MA, No. Ariz. U., 1984. Cert. elem. tchr., N.Mex. Ednl. aide Bur. Ind. Affairs Ea. Agy., Crownpoint, 1966-77; elem. tchr. Bur. Ind. Affairs Ea. Agy., Mariano Lake, N.Mex., 1977-79; elem. tchr. Bur. Ind. Affairs Ea. Agy., Crownpoint, 1979—, adult edn. tchr., summer 1988; sch. curriculum trainer BeautyWay curriculum Navajo Tribe, Crownpoint, 1989; computer tchr. Crownpoint Community Sch., 1988-89; site coord. pilot project ICON, Crownpoint, 1986-87; mem. com., tutor Gifted and Talented Program, Crownpoint, 1989-91. Sch. coord. Girl Scouts Am., 1977-79; sec. Navajo Nation Chpt. Officers, Crownpoint, 1983-86; mem. St. Paul Parish Coun., Crownpoint, 1982—, sec., 1992—, chairperson edn. com. 1992—; pres. Crownpoint Community Sch. Staff Assn., 1992—. Recipient Appreciation award Chaparral coun. Girl Scouts U.S.A., 1978, Title I Outstanding Tchr. award Crownpiont Community Sch. Parent Action Com., 1981, Ea. Navajo Coun., 1988. Mem. Ea. Navajo Agy. Tchrs. (sch. rep. 1987-88). Democrat. Roman Catholic. Home: PO Box 344 Crownpoint NM 87313-0344 Office: Crownpoint Community PO Box Drawer H Crownpoint NM 87313

TOLKOFF, ESTHER PHYLLIS, writer, magazine editor; b. Bronx, N.Y., Nov. 13, 1947; d. Isadore and Muriel (Zimmerman) Tolkoff. BA, CCNY, 1968; MA in L.Am. Lit., U. Wis., 1969. Freelance writer various cities, 1969—; writer, TV and radio pub. affairs N.Y.C. Bd. Edn., 1970-73; adjunct instr. Spanish Lehman Coll., Bronx, 1971-73; writer Telegeneral Studios, N.Y.C., 1973-74, CUNY Courier, N.Y.C., 1974-76; publicity writer Yeshiva U., N.Y.C., 1977-79; assoc. editor, The New York Teacher N.Y. State United Tchrs., N.Y.C., then Albany, 1974-93; editor, The Communicator CCNY Alumni Assn., 1994-96, editor, The Alumnus Mag., 1995-96; steering com. mem. N.Y. local, Nat. Writers Union, 1994-95. Contbr. articles to periodicals, chpt. to book. Recipient recognition Best Feature Article, Internat. Labor Comm., Washington, 1989, Best Single Article, Met. Labor Press Coun., N.Y.C., 1990, Best Writing, 1981, 89. Mem. AFTRA (editl. bd. N.Y. local 1994-96), Internat. Mus. Theatre Alliance, Women in Comm., Coalition of Profl. Women in Arts and Media, Editl. Freelancers Assn., Comm. Alumni Group CUNY (bd. dirs. 1993—, editl. cons.). Democrat. Home: 315 E 21st St New York NY 10010

TOLL, ROBERTA DARLENE (MRS. SHELDON S. TOLL), clinical psychologist; b. Detroit, May 14, 1944; d. David and Blanche (Fischer) Pollack; married, Aug. 11, 1968; children: Candice, John, Kevin. B.A., U. Mich., 1966; M.S.W., U. Pa., 1971; PhD, 1990. Dir. counselors Phila. Family Planning, Inc., 1971-72; psychologist Lafayette Clinic, Detroit, 1972-73; social worker Project Headline, Detroit, 1973-75; pvt. practice clin. psychology, Bloomfield Hills, Mich., 1975—; adj. prof. U. Detroit, Oakland Community Coll. Past bd. dirs. Detroit chpt. Nat. Council on Alcoholism.; bd. dirs. Merill Palmer Inst., Child Abuse Coun.; pres. Mich. Women Psychologist. Cert. social worker, Mich. Fellow Masters and Johnson Inst.; mem. APA, Nat. Assn. Social Workers. Democrat. Club: Franklin Hills Country. Home and Office: 640 Lone Pine Hl Bloomfield Hills MI 48304-2822

TOLLEFSON-CONARD, MARGOT HELENA, statistician; b. Chgo., Sept. 1, 1951; d. Roy Melvin and Alice Marie (Titterud) T.; m. Clayton Gerard Conard, July 31, 1985. BA, Reed Coll., Porltand, Oreg., 1974; student, Northeastern U., 1979-80, Harvard U., 1980-83, MIT, 1982-83; MS, Iowa State U., 1985, PhD, 1992. Engring. aide Fed. Hwy. Adminstrn., Mapleton, Oreg., 1975-76; sci. aide EPA, Corvallis, Oreg., 1976; rodperson Boston Survey Cons., 1977-78; rsch. asst. Aerodyne Rsch., Bedford, Mass., 1979-80; rsch. assoc. MIT, Cambridge, 1981-83; rsch. and tchg. asst. Iowa State U., Ames, 1983-94; owner Vanward Statis. Cons., Stratford, Iowa, 1994—. Author 3 poems; contbr. articles to profl. jours. Platform com. Dem. Com., Boone, Iowa, 1990; group leader Ames Recovery Group, 1993—; sec. on healthcare and human svcs. platform subcom. State of Iowa. Mem. ACLU, NOW, Nat. Abortion Rights Action League, Internat. Soc. Astrological Rsch., Am. Statis. Assn., Iowa Assn. Energy Efficiency, Iowa Poetry Assn., Boone Amature Radio Klub, Mu Sigma Rho. Democrat. Home and Office: 612 Teneyck Ave Stratford IA 50249

TOLLETT, GLENNA BELLE, accountant, mobile home park operator; b. Graham, Ariz., Dec. 17, 1913; d. Charles Harry and Myrtle (Stapley) Spafford; m. John W. Tollett, Nov. 28, 1928; 1 child, Jackie J., 1 adopted child, Beverly Mae Malgren. Bus. cert., Lamson Coll. Office mgr, Hurley Meat Packing Co., Phoenix, 1938-42; co-owner, sec., treas. A.B.C. Enterprises, Inc., Seattle, 1942—; ptnr. Bella Investment Co., Seattle, 1962—, Four Square Investment Co., Seattle, 1969—, Warehouses Ltd., Seattle, 1970—, Tri State Partnership, Wash., Idaho, Tex., 1972—; pres. Halycon Mobile Home Park, Inc., Seattle, 1979—; co-owner, operator Martha Lake Mobile Home Park, Lynwood, Wash., 1962-73. Mem. com. Wash. Planning and Community Affairs Agy., Olympia, 1981-82, Wash. Mfg. Housing Assn. Relations Com., Olympia, 1980-84; appointed by Gov. Wash. to Mobile Home and RV Adv. Bd., 1973-79. Named to RV/Mobile Home Hall of Fame, 1980. Mem. Wash. Mobile Park Owners Assn. (legisl. chmn., lobbyist 1976-85, cons. 1984, pres. 1978-79, exec. dir. 1976-84, This is Your Life award 1979), Wash. Soc. of Assn. Execs. (Exec. Dir. Service award 1983), Mobile Home Old Timers Assn., Mobile Home Owners of Am. (sec. 1972-76, Appreciation award 1976), Nat Fire Protection Assn. (com. 1979-86), Aurora Pkwy. North C. of C.)sec. 1976-80), Fremont C. of C. Republican. Mormon. Home: 18261 Springdale Ct NW Seattle WA 98177-3228 Office: ABC Enterprises Inc 3524 Stone Way N Seattle WA 98103-8924

TOLLINGER, JANE, broadcast executive. Exec. v.p. Lifetime TV, Astoria, N.Y. Office: Lifetime 36-12 35th Ave Astoria NY 11106-1227*

TOLLIVER, EDITH CATHERINE, retired educator; b. Greenup, Ky., Sept. 6, 1925; d. Reece Madison and Nancy Elizabeth (Knipp) Bowling; m. Homer Tolliver, May 4, 1949 (dec. Nov. 1987); children: Gary M., Rodney D., James C., William H.; m. Robert O. Hutchins, July 7, 1990. BA, Morehead (Ky.) U., 1960; MA, Calif. State U., 1990. Cert. elem. tchr., Calif., Ky.; cert. reading specialist, Calif. Tchr. Fleming County Schs., Flemingsburg, Ky., 1943-48; factory worker Ecorse, Mich., 1948-49; tchr. Greenup County Schs., 1953-54, Carter County Schs., Olive Hill, Ky., 1954-62; 1st grade tchr. San Jacinto (Calif.) Elem. Sch., 1963-68, 72-87, mentor tchr., 1987-90; reading specialist Hyatt Elem., San Jacinto, 1968-72; 1 st grade tchr. DeAnza Elem., San Jacinto, 1987-95; ret., 1995, substitute tchr., 1995-96. Named Tchr. of Yr. San Jacinto Elem. Sch., 1982, 85. Mem. NEA, Calif. Tchrs. Assn., San Jacinto Tchrs. Assn. (sec. 1972, v.p. 1985, treas. 1995), Delta Kappa Gamma. Republican. Southern Baptist. Home: 26032 Amy Ln Hemet CA 92544-6230

TOM, GAIL, business educator; b. Rock Springs, Wyo., July 18, 1952; d. Edward Young and Ruby (Wong) T.; m. Calvin Tong, July 24, 1977; children: Ryan Tom Tong, Stephanie Tom Tong. BA, U. Calif., Davis, 1972, MS, 1974, PhD, 1978; MA, Calif. State U., Sacramento, 1973, U. Calif., Riverside, 1977. Grad. teaching asst. Calif. State U., Sacramento, 1973, prof., 1978—; rsch. asst. U. Calif., Davis, 1974-77, adj. prof., 1985—; s. U.S. Bankruptcy Ct., Sacramento, 1994-95, Calif. State Employment Devel. Dept., Sacramento, 1992-94, Silverado Broadcasting, Sacramento, Stockton, Calif., 1995—; reviewer Coll. Textbook Pubs., 1985—. Author: Applications of Consumer Behavior, 1982; contbr. articles to profl. jours. JC Penney Retail grantee Brigham Young U., 1994; Dir. Mktg. Assn. fellow, 1986, 96. Mem. Am. Mktg. Assn., Assn. Consumer Rsch., Western Mktg. Educators Assn. (bd. dirs. 1995—). Office: Calif State U Sch Bus 6000 J St Sacramento CA 95819

TOMA, DONNA M., psychologist, researcher; b. Belleville, N.J., Sept. 8, 1962; d. David and Patricia (D'Amore) T. BA, U. N.C., Charlotte, 1984; MA, Seton Hall U., 1986, Yeshiva U., 1990; PhD, Yeshiva U., 1993. Cert. crisis/suicide instr.; cert. in hypnosis, psychol. testing and evaluation. Liaison, therapist Union County Psychiat. Clinic, Plainfield, N.J., 1986-88; therapist individuals, families Sch. Based Youth Svc. Program, Plainfield, 1988-90; psychologist Spofford Maximum Security Facility Juvenile Offenders, Bronx, N.Y., 1990-91, Alliance for Recovery, Belleville, 1991—, Bergen County Spl. Svcs., Ridgewood, N.J., 1991—, Contemporary Counseling Psychotherapy Inst., Teaneck, N.J., 1994—; cons. substance abuse Da-Tom Enterprises, Clark, N.J., 1986-93; cons. psychologist to TV program, 1988—; cons., expert nat. TV talk shows. Contbr. articles to profl. jours. Vol. Children's Aid Soc., N.Y.C., 1992—, Gay Men's Health Crisis, N.Y./N.J., 1993—. Mem. APA, NOW (v.p. no. N.J. chpt.), Soc. Child Devel., Menninger Found., Orthopsychiat. Soc., C. Jung Inst., Kappa Delta Pi.

TOMA, PATTY JAN, financial systems accountant; b. Kansas City, Mo., Jan. 30, 1955; d. Donald Ray and M. Marie (Neth) Morris; m. Timothy Jon Toma. BS in Music Edn., William Jewell Coll., 1977; B of Gen. Sci., U. Mo., 1985. CPA, Mo. Instr. vocal music Pattonville Sch. Dist., Maryland Heights, Md., 1977-79; sec. Kellwood Co., Chesterfield, Mo., 1979-80, fin. sys. tech. asst., 1981-83, jr. fin. sys. specialist, 1983-85, fin. sys. specialist, 1985-89, supr. fin. sys., 1989—. Organist, choir mem., com. mem. 1st Bapt. Ch., Ellisville, Mo., 1980—. Mem. Mo. Soc. CPAs. Home: 15732 Plymton Ln Chesterfield MO 63017 Office: Kellwood Co 600 Kellwood Pkwy Chesterfield MO 63017

TOMAINO, LEAH KARRATOGLOU, artist; b. Denville, N.J., May 24, 1965; d. Peter Karratoglou and Edith (Dardick) Cefaloni; m. Francis Joseph Tomaino, Mar. 23, 1989; children: Francesca, Marcus. BFA, The Cooper Union, 1987; postgrad., Studio Art Sch. of the Aegean, Samos, Greece, 1987. One-person shows include The Atlantic Gallery, N.Y.C., 1994, 95, 96, The Randolph (N.J.) Twp. Free Pub. Libr., 1995; two-person shows include The West Wing Gallery, Ringwood, N.J., 1989; exhibited in group shows at Ringwood State Park, 1987, The Barn Gallery, Ringwood State Park, 1987, 88, Arts Coun. Gallery, Cobleskill, N.Y., 1993, The Atlantic Gallery, N.Y.C., 1993 , City Without Walls, Newark, 1994-95, New Work Corner, City Without Walls, Newark, 1995; represented in permanent collections Dover (N.J.) Mcpl. Bldg., Polizzotto & Polizzotto, Bklyn., various pvt. collections. Mem. The Atlantic Gallery (v.p. 1993—, exhbn. coord. 1994-95). Home: 12 Charles St Randolph NJ 07869

TOMAN, MARY ANN, federal official; b. Pasadena, Calif., Mar. 31, 1954; d. John James and Mary Ann Zajec T.; m. Milton Allen Miller, Sept. 10, 1988; 1 child, Mary Ann III. BA with honors, Stanford U., 1976; MBA, Harvard U., 1981. Mgmt. cons. Bain and Co., Boston, 1976-77; brand mgr. Procter & Gamble Co., Cin., 1977-79; summer assoc. E.F. Hutton, N.Y.C., 1980; head corp. planning The Burton Group, PLC, London, 1981-84; pres., founder Glendair Ltd., London, 1984-86; pres. London Cons. Group, London, Beverly Hills, Calif., 1987-88; mem. U.S. Presdl. Transition Team, Bus. and Fin., 1988-89; dep. asst. sec. commerce, automotive affairs, consumer goods U.S. Dept. Commerce, Washington, 1989-93; commr., chmn. L.A. Indsl. Devel. Authority, 1993-95; dep. treas. State of Calif., Sacramento, 1995—; bd. dirs. U.S. Coun. of Devel. Fin. Agencies, 1994—. Founder, chair Stanford U. Fundraising, London, 1983-88; chair Reps. Abroad Absentee Voter Registration, London, 1983-88; bd. dirs. Harvard Bus. Sch. Assn., London, 1984-87; vol. Bush-Quayle Campaign, 1988; trustee Bath Coll., Eng., 1988—; apptd. by Gov. Wilson to State of Calif. Econ. Devel. Adv. Coun., 1994—. Mem. Stanford Club U.K. (pres. 1983-88), Harvard Club N.Y., Harvard Club Washington. Roman Catholic. Home: 604 N Elm Dr Beverly Hills CA 90210-3421 Office: PO Box 71483 Los Angeles CA 90071

TOMASULO, VIRGINIA MERRILLS, retired lawyer; b. Belleville, Ill., Feb. 10, 1919; d. Frederick Emerson and Mary Eckert (Turner) Merrills; m. Nicholas Angelo Tomasulo, Sept. 30, 1952; m. Harrison I. Anthes, March 5, 1988. BA, Wellesley Coll., 1940; LLB (now JD), Washington U., St. Louis, 1943. Bar: Mo. 1942, U.S. Ct. Appeals (D.C. cir.) 1958, Mich. 1974, U.S. Dist. Ct. (ea. dist.) Mo. 1943, U.S. Supreme Ct. 1954, U.S. Tax Ct. 1974, U.S. Ct. Appeals (6th cir.) 1976. Atty. Dept. of Agr., St. Louis and Washington, 1943-48, Office of Solicitor, Chief Counsel's Office, IRS, Washington and Detroit, 1949-75; assoc. Baker & Hostetler, Washington, 1977-82, ptnr., 1982-89, of counsel, 1989, ret., 1989. Sec., S.W. Day Care Assn., Washington, 1971-73; mem. fin. com. Residents Assn. Village on the Green, Longwood, Fla. Mem. ABA, Mo. Bar, Fed. Bar, Village on the Green Residents Assn. (fin. com.), Wellesley Club (Ctrl. Fla.). Episcopalian. Home: 570 Village Pl Apt 300 Longwood FL 32779-6037

TOMASZESKI, JOSEPHINE GALLAS, retired nursing educator; b. Manchouli, Manchuria, China, Jan. 18, 1919; d. Paul Fedorovich Kislitzin and Barbara Matveevna (Borodeev) Kislitzin-Meisel; m. John Joseph Gallas, Jan. 22, 1953 (dec. Feb. 1966); m. Julian Stephen Tomaszeski, June 10, 1972; stepchildren: Julie Ann, Mary Jane, Wayne Michael, John William. Student, Mary Washington Coll., 1937; diploma, St. Mary's Coll. Nursing, 1941; BS in Pub. Health Nursing, Cath. U. Am., 1943; MSN, U. Calif., Berkeley and San Francisco, 1960. RN, Calif.; cert. pub. health nurse, tchr., Calif. Nurse, charge nurse Children's Hosp., Washington, 1941-43; pub. health nurse Dept. Pub. Health, Washington, 1943-45; dir. outpatient clinic, nurse instr. Mary's Help Hosp., San Francisco, 1946-49; nurse, pub. health nurse, nurse instr. VA Med. Ctr. and Gen. Clinics, San Francisco, 1949-54; nurse instr. St. Mary's Hosp., San Francisco, 1954-55; asst. prof. nursing U. San Francisco, 1954-72; medicine and treatment nurse Schutz Am. Sch., Alexandria, Egypt, 1972-73; newspaper corr. Representative, Calmar, Alta., Can., 1975-81; medicine and treatment nurse Hillhaven Convalescent Hosp., San Rafael, Calif., 1982. Vol. nurse County Health Dept., Sausalito, Calif., 1956-63; vol. pollworker City of Sausalito, 1962-65; vol. city coun. campaigns, Sausalito, 1962-65; vol. Santa Ventia Cmty. Orgn., San Rafael, Calif. Fed. Nursing grantee Cath. U. Am., 1942-43; Fed. scholar U. Calif., Berkeley, 1959-60. Mem. ANA, AAUP, Nursing Alumni Bd. U. San Francisco (voting vol. 1982-94), NLN (sec. 1956-60), Sigma Theta Tau, Alpha Phi Sigma. Republican. Roman Catholic. Home: 61 Labrea Way San Rafael CA 94903-3065 also: 5114 49th Ave, PO Box 444, Calmar, AB Canada T0C 0V0

TOMCISIN, THERESA ANN, public relations executive; b. Cleve., Jan. 12, 1960; d. George Tomcisin and Miyoko Oka; m. James D. Rosenthal, May 29, 1988. BA in Polit. Sci. cum laude, U. Dayton, 1982. Asst., corp. communications Playboy Enterprises, Inc., Chgo., 1984-85, coord., corp. communications, 1985-86, adminstr., corp. communications, 1986-88, mgr., corp. communications, 1988-90, dir., corp. communications, 1990—. Recipient acad. scholarship Univ. Dayton, 1978-82, Wright-Patterson Officers' Wives acad. scholarship, 1978. Mem. Nat. Investor Relations Inst., Chgo. Advt. Fedn., Internat. Assn. Bus. Communicators (Spectra award 1987, 90, Gold Quill Merit award 1991), Publicity Club of Chgo. (Silver Trumpet award 1987, 90, bd. dirs. arts bridge). Office: Playboy Enterprises Inc 680 N Lake Shore Dr Chicago IL 60611-4402

TOMEI, MARISA, actress; b. Bklyn., Dec. 4, 1964. TV appearances include (series) A Different World, 1987, (films) Parker Kane, 1990; film appearances include: The Flamingo Kid, 1984, Playing for Keeps, 1986, Oscar, 1991, Zandalee, 1991, My Cousin Vinny, 1992 (Acad. award best supporting actress 1993), Chaplin, 1992, Untamed Heart, 1993, Equinox, 1993, The Paper, 1994, Only You, 1994, The Perez Family, 1994, Four Rooms, 1995, Unhook the Stars, 1996; theatre appearances include Slavs! Thinking About the Longstanding Problems of Virtue and Happiness, 1994. Office: William Morris Agy 151 S El Camino Dr Beverly Hills CA 90212-2704*

TOMKIEL, JUDITH IRENE, small business owner; b. St. Louis, Nov. 4, 1949; d. Melvin Charles William and Mildred Neva (Kayhart) Linders; m. William George Tomkiel, Dec. 15, 1972; children: Soteara, William, Kimberli, Jennifer, Christopher. Order filler Baker & Taylor Co., Sommerville, N.J., 1972-74; owner, founder The Idea Shoppe, Garden Grove, 1983-90; seamstress, crafts person Cloth World, Anaheim, Calif., 1987-89; mgr. S.M.T. Dental Lab., San Clemente, Calif., 1990-94, pres., 1994—; Vol. Reading Is Fundamental Program, Garden Grove, 1988-89; freedom writer Amnesty Internat., Garden Grove, 1988-91. Author numerous poems; pub., editor (newsletter) Shoppe Talk, 1987-90; pub. Fakatale, 1988. Fellow World Literary Acad.; mem. NAFE, Nat. Writer's Club, Soc. Scholarly Pub., Dental LAb Owners Assn. (pres. S.M.T. Dental Lab., Inc. 1994).

TOMKINS, JOANNE KARK, health physicist, educator; b. Newark, Sept. 18, 1953; d. Jon Joseph and Anna Rose (Peters) Kark; m. Robert Norton McVey, Mar. 24, 1979 (div. Apr. 1980); m. Robin Joseph Tomkins, Mar. 6, 1992. BS, Villanova U., 1975; postgrad., Colo. State U., 1984-85. Cert. nuclear medicine technologist. Analytical chemistry technician SpectroChem Labs., Inc., Franklin Lakes, N.J., 1976-77; nuclear medicine technologist Albert Einstein Med. Ctr., Phila., 1977-79; biol. technician Oak Ridge (Tenn.) Nat. Lab., 1979-81, radiol. technician, 1981-84; nuclear safety health physicist Ill. Dept. Nuclear Safety, Glen Ellyn, 1986—; instr. radiation safety Oakton C.C., Des Plaines, Ill., 1989-91. Contbr. articles to profl. jours. Recipient program cert. of appreciation Suburban Bldg. Ofcls. Conf., 1988. Mem. Soc. Nuclear Medicine (assoc.), Health Physics Soc. (plenary treas. Midwest chpt. 1989, pub. info. com. 1989-92, chmn. legis. com. 1990-92). Roman Catholic. Office: Ill Dept Nuclear Safety 800 Roosevelt Rd Ste 200 Glen Ellyn IL 60137-5839

TOMKOW, GWEN ADELLE, artist; b. Detroit, May 16, 1932; d. Galen A. and Edythe Christine (Barr) Roberts; m. Michael Tomkow, Nov. 14, 1953; children: Eric Michael, Thomas Edward, Nikola Christine, Kit Adair. A of Bus., Detroit Bus. Inst., 1952; student, Birmingham Bloomfield Art, Assn., Mich., 1985-87, Visual Art Assn., Livonia, Mich., 1984-89. Tchr. watercolor Visual Art Assn., Livonia, 1989-96; tchr. workshop Ella Sharp Mus. Jackson Civic Art, Mich., 1996; tchr. watercolor workshop Village Fine Art Assn., Milford, Mich., 1996; slide lectr. Livonia Artist Club, 1995, Palette and Brush Club, Southfield, Mich., 1995, Pontiac (Mich.) Oakland Artists, 1995, Ea. Mich. U. Watercolor Soc., 1994; artist-in-residence Farmington Art Commn., Farmington Hills, 1988. Contbr. articles and photos to books, including: The Artistic Touch, 1994-95, The Artistic Touch 2, 1996, Splash 3, 1994-95, Splash 4, 1996, also Watercolor edit., Am. Artist Mag., 1991; represented in permanent collections E. Carothers Dunnegan Gallery of Art

Mus. Recipient Purchase awards U.S.A. Springfield (Mo.) Art Mus., 1990, 93, 94, 1st prize Helen de Roy Competition, Oakland C.C., Farmington, Mich., 1988, 92, Grumbacher Gold medal Farmington Artists Club, Farmington Hills, Mich., 1995. Mem. Mich. Watercolor Soc. (Meml. award 1992), Farmington Art Assn. (pres. 1987-89), Detroit Soc. Women Painters Sculptors (sec. 1994-95), Palette and Brush (v.p. 1982-83). Presbyterian.

TOMLIN, LILY, actress; b. Detroit, 1939. Student, Wayne State U.; studied mime with Paul Curtis, studied acting with Peggy Feury. Appearances in concerts and colls. throughout U.S.; TV appearances include Lily Tomlin, CBS Spls., 1973, 81, 82; 2 ABC Spls., 1975, Edithann Animated Specials, ABC, 1994, The Magic School Bus, 1994 (voice); formerly cast mem. The Music Scene, Laugh In; motion picture debut in Nashville, 1975 (N.Y. Film Critics award); also appeared in The Late Show, 1977, Moment by Moment, 1978, The Incredible Shrinking Woman, 1981, Nine to Five, 1980, All of Me, 1984, Big Business, 1987, Shadows and Fog, 1992, The Player, 1992, Short Cuts, 1993, The Beverly Hillbillies, 1993, And the Band Played On, HBO, 1993 (Best Supporting Actress Emmy nominee - Special, 1994), Getting Away with Murder, 1995, The Celluloid Closet, 1995, Blue in the Face, 1995, Flirting With Disaster, 1996; one-woman Broadway show Appearing Nitely, 1977 (Spl. Tony award), The Search for Signs of Intelligent Life in the Universe, 1985 (Drama Desk award, Outer Critics Circle award, Tony award 1986); recs. include This is a Recording, And That's The Truth, Modern Scream, On Stage. Recipient Grammy award 1971, 5 Emmy awards for CBS Spl. 1973, 81, Emmy award for ABC Spl. 1975. *

TOMLINSON, DONNA PARKS, mental health therapist; b. Oklahoma City, Oct. 2, 1951; d. Don Lee Parks and Patsy Ann (Davis) Stanley; m. Thomas Clayton Kemp, Oct. 31, 1971 (div. Aug. 1978); children: Lori, Melanie, Chad. BS, U. Ctrl. Okla., 1993, MEd., 1995. Cert. mediator. Dir. sales NW Investors, Hilton Inn, Oklahoma City, 1979-82, Quality Inn Cen., Oklahoma City, 1982-83; ptnr., exec. Hotel Connection, Oklahoma City, 1983—; owner Tomlinson Tour & Travel, Edmond, Okla., 1988—. Mem. APA, NAFE, North Am. Assn. Masters in Psychology, Country Music Assn., Hotel-Motel Assn. Democrat. Office: Ste 703 W 2601 NW Expressway St Oklahoma City OK 73112-7208

TOMLINSON, SUSAN WINGFIELD, social studies educator; b. Indpls., Apr. 11, 1956; d. George Emerson and Janet Wingfield (Murphy) Carlisle; m. Charles Everett Tomlinson, Aug. 14, 1976. BS, Ball State U., 1977, MA in Edn., 1982; cert. in gifted edn., Purdue U., 1985, 86. Cert. tchr. social studies and gifted edn., Ind. Tchr. social studies Justice Jr. H.S., Marion, Ind., 1977-79, Storer Mid. Sch., Muncie, Ind., 1979-80; lectr. global futures Burris Lab. Sch. Ball State U., Muncie, 1982-86; talented and gifted specialist Mannheim (Germany) Mid. & H.S., 1986-91; tchr. social studies Park Tudor Schs., Indpls., 1992; tchr. geography Franklin Twp. Mid. Sch., Indpls., 1992—; Ind. cadre cons. Ind. Dept. Edn., Indpls., 1983-86; mem. adv. com. Germany and the New Europe, Ohio Dept. Edn., Columbus, 1993-94; chair advisor com. Franklin Twp. Mid. Sch., Indpls., 1993-94. Contbr. articles to ednl. jours. Mem. PTA, Franklin Twp. Mid. Sch., Indpls., 1992—; vol. Salvation Army, Davenport, Iowa, 1993. Fulbright summer fellow People's Republic of China, 1990. Mem. Nat. Assn. for Gifted Children Germany (pres.-elect, pres., past pres. 1988-91), Ind. Coun. for Social Studies (presenter ann. convs. 1993, 94, 95, bd. dirs. 1996), Phi Delta Kappa (rsch. com. 1984). Office: Franklin Twp Mid Sch 6019 S Franklin Rd Indianapolis IN 46259-1319

TOMLINSON-KEASEY, CAROL ANN, university administrator; b. Washington, Oct. 15, 1942; d. Robert Bruce and Geraldine (Howe) Tomlinson; m. Charles Blake Keasey, June 13, 1964; children: Kai Linson, Amber Lynn. BS, Pa. State U., 1964; MS, Iowa State U., 1966; PhD, U. Calif., Berkeley, 1970. Lic. psychologist, Calif. Asst. prof. psychology Trenton (N.J.) State Coll., 1969-70, Rutgers U., New Brunswick, N.J., 1970-72; prof. U. Nebr., Lincoln, 1972-77; prof. U. Calif., Riverside, 1977-92, acting dean Coll. Humanities and Social Scis., 1986-88, chmn. dept. psychology, 1989-92; vice provost for academic planning and personnel U. Calif., Davis, 1992—. Author: Child's Eye View, 1980, Child Development, 1985; also numerous chpts. to books; articles to profl. jours. Recipient Disting. Tchr. award U. Calif., 1986. Mem. APA, Soc. Rsch. in Child Devel., Riverside Aquatics Assn. (pres.). Office: Office of Provost U Calif Davis Davis CA 95616

TOMLJANOVICH, ESTHER M., judge; b. Galt, Iowa, Nov. 1, 1931; d. Chester William and Thelma L. (Brooks) Moellering; m. William S. Tomljanovich, Dec. 26, 1957; 1 child, William Brooks. AA, Itasca Jr. Coll., 1951; BSL, St. Paul Coll. Law, 1953, LLB, 1955. Bar: Minn. 1955, U.S. Dist. Ct. Minn. 1958. Asst. revisor of statutes State of Minn., St. Paul, 1957-66, revisor of statutes, 1974-77; dist. ct. judge State of Minn., Stillwater, 1977-90; assoc. justice Minn. Supreme Ct., St. Paul, 1990—. Former mem. North St. Paul Bd. Edn., Maplewood Bd. Edn., Lake Elmo Planning Commn; bd. trustees William Mitchell Coll. Law, 1995—. Mem. Minn. State Bar Assn., Bus. and Profl. Women's Assn. St. Paul (former pres.). Office: Supreme Ct MN MN Judicial Ctr Rm 423 25 Constitution Ave Saint Paul MN 55155-1500

TOMMELEIN, IRIS DENISE, construction engineering and management educator, consultant; b. Brussels, Mar. 16, 1962; m. James Warren Lovekin, July 22, 1995. Grad. in Civil Engring., Free U. Brussels, 1984; MSCE, Stanford U., 1985, MS in Computer Sci., PhD in Civil Engring., 1989. Registered profl. engr., Belgium. Asst. prof. U. Mich., Ann Arbor, 1989-95, assoc. prof., 1995-96; acting assoc. prof. U. Calif., Berkeley, 1996—. Fellow Belgian Am. Ednl. Found.; mem. ASCE (assoc.), Sigma Xi, Xi Epsilon. Office: Univ Calif Berkeley 215 Mc Laughlin Hall # 1712 Berkeley CA 94720-1712

TOMPKINS, EILEEN, state legislator; m. Patrick Tompkins; 9 children. Attended, Inver Hills C.C., U. Minn., Coll. of St. Thomas. Mem. Minn. Ho. of Reps., 1984—; mem. health and human svcs. com., mem. local govt. com., mem. met. affairs com., mem. transp. and transit com. Home: 7734 133rd St W Apple Valley MN 55124-7623 Office: Minn Ho of Reps State Capital Building Saint Paul MN 55155-1606 also: 245 State Office Bldg Saint Paul MN 55155*

TOMPSON, MARIAN LEONARD, professional society administrator; b. Chgo., Dec. 5, 1929; d. Charles Clark and Marie Christine (Bernardini) Leonard; m. Clement R. Tompson, May 7, 1949 (dec. 1981); children: Melanie Tompson Kandler, Deborah Tompson Mikolajczak, Allison Tompson Fagerholm, Laurel Tompson Davies, Sheila Tompson Dorsey, Brian, Philip. Student public and parochial schs., Chgo. and Franklin Park, Ill. Co-founder La Leche League (Internat.), Franklin Park, 1956; pres. La Leche League (Internat.), 1956-80, dir., 1956—, pres. emeritus, 1990—; exec. dir. Alternative Birth Crisis Coalition, 1981-85; cons. WHO; bd. dirs. North Am. Soc. Psychosomatic Ob-Gyn, Natural Birth and Natural Parenting, 1981-83; mem. adv. bd. Nat. Assn. Parents and Profls. for Safe Alternatives in Childbirth, Am. Acad. Husband-Coached Childbirth; mem. adv. bd. Fellowship of Christian Midwives; mem. profl. adv. bd. Home Oriented Maternity Experience; guest lectr. Harvard U. Med. Sch., UCLA Sch. Public Health, U. Antioquia Med. Sch., Medellín, Columbia, U. Ill. Sch. Medicine, Chgo., U. W.I., Jamaica, U. N.C., Nat. Coll. of Chiropractic, Am. Coll. Nurse Midwives, U. Parma, Italy, Inst. Psychology, Rome, Rockford (Ill.) Sch. Medicine, Northwestern U. Sch. Medicine; mem. family com. Ill. Commn. on Status of Women, 1976-85; mem. perinatal adv. com. Ill. Dept. Pub. Health, 1980-83; mem. adv. bd. Internat. Nutrition Communication Service, 1980—; bd. cons. We Can, 1984—; exec. adv. bd. United Resources for Family Health and Support, 1985-86. Author: (with others) Safe Alternatives in Childbirth, 1976, 21st Century Obstetrics Now!, 1977, The Womanly Art of Breastfeeding, 3d edit., 1981, Five Standards for Safe Childbearing, 1981, But Doctor, About That Shot..., 1988, Breast Feeding, 5th edit., 1991; author prefaces and forwards in 10 books; columnist La Leche League News, 1958-80; columnist People's Doctor Newsletter, 1977-88, mem. adv. bd., cons., 1988-92; assoc. editor Child and Family Quar., 1967—; mem. med. adv. bd. East West Jour., 1980—; also articles. Recipient Gold medal of honor Centro de Rehabilitacao Nossa Senhora da Gloria, 1975, Night of 100 Stars III Achiever award Actors Fund Am., 1990. Mem. Nat. Assn. Postpartum Care Svcs. (adv. bd.), Chgo. Cmty. Midwives (adv. bd.). Office: 1400 N Meacham Rd Schaumburg IL 60173-4808

TOMS, KATHLEEN MOORE, nurse; b. San Francisco, Dec. 31, 1943; d. William Moore and Phyllis Josephine (Barry) Stewart. RN, AA, City Coll. San Francisco, 1963; BPS in Nursing Edn., Elizabethtown (Pa.) Coll., 1973; MS in Edn., Temple U., 1977; MS in Nursing, Gwynedd Mercy Coll. 1988; m. Benjamin Peskoff; children from previous marriage: Kathleen Marie Toms Myers, Kelly Terese Toms. Med.-surg. nurse St. Joseph Hosp., Fairbanks, Alaska, 1963-65; emergency room nurse St. Joseph Hosp., Lancaster, Pa., 1965-69, blood, plasm and components nurse, 1969-71; pres. F.E. Barry Co., Lancaster, 1971—; dir. inservice edn. Lancaster Osteo. Hosp., 1971-75; coord. practical nursing program Vocat. Tech. Sch., Coatesville, Pa., 1976-77; dir. nursing Pocopson Home, West Chester, Pa., 1978-80, Riverside Hosp., Wilmington, Del., 1980-83; assoc. Coatesville VA Hosp., 1983-89; chief Nurse, 1984-89; with VA Cen. Office; supr. psychiat. nursing Martinez (Calif.) VA Med. Ctr., 1989-94; assoc. chief nursing svc. edn. VA No. Calif. Sys. Clinics, Pleasant Hill, Calif., 1994—; trainee assoc. chief Nursing Home Care Unit, Washington; mem. Pa. Gov.'s Council on Alcoholism and Drug Abuse, 1974-76; mem. Del. Health Council Med.-Surg. Task Force, 1981-83; dir. Lancaster Cmty. Health Ctr., 1973-76; lectr. in field. Col. Nurse Corps, USAR. Decorated Army Commendation medals (5), Meritorious Svc. medals (2); recipient Cmty. Svc. award Citizens United for Better Public Relations, 1974; award Sertoma, Lancaster, 1974; Outstanding Citizen award Sta. WGAL-TV, 1975; U.S. Army Achievement award, 1983. Mem. Elizabethtown, Temple U. Alumni Assns., Pa. Nurses' Assn. (dir.), Sigma Theta Tau, Beta Gamma. Inventor auto-infuser for blood or blood components, 1971. Home: 208 Sea Mist Dr Vallejo CA 94591-7748 Office: VA No Calif System of Clinics 2350 Contra Costa Blvd Pleasant Hill CA 94523-3930

TOMS-BRONOWSKI, SUSAN, English and reading educator; b. Yonkers, N.Y., Dec. 24, 1948; d. John Skinner and Grace Elizabeth (Joyce) Toms; m. Carl W. Bronowski, June 12, 1981; children: Thomas Carl, Michael John. BA, Bridgewater (Mass.) State U., 1970; MST, U. Wis., Eau Claire, 1975; PhD, U. Wis., Madison, 1982. Cert. English, reading tchr., specialist. Reading specialist Eau Claire Acad., 1975-79, St. Francis De Sales H.S., Chgo., 1987-88; vis. prof. Governor's State U., University Park, Ill., 1985-88; asst. prof. reading U. Wis., Whitewater, 1989—; cons. in field. Mem. ASCD, Nat. Coun. Tchrs. English, Internat. Reading Assn., Wis. Reading Assn. (chair families and reading com. 1992-95). Office: University of Wisconsin 800 W Main St Whitewater WI 53190-1705

TONELLI, GIOVANNA MARIE, professional development consultant, social worker; b. Phila., Nov. 13, 1951; d. Peter Paul and Mary Rita (Campagna) T. AAS, Community Coll. of Phila., 1972; B of Social Work, Temple U., 1974, MSW, 1981. Lic. social worker, Pa. Med. social worker Bio-Med. Applications, Phila., 1976-79; with foster care program Tabor Children's Svcs., Doylestown, Pa., 1981; with adoption program, cons. Tabor Children's Svcs., Doylestown, 1982; social worker City of Phila., 1982; program dir. Italian Home for Children, Boston, 1983-87; trainer, cons. Temple U., Phila., 1987; social worker Support Ctr. for Child Advocates, Phila., 1987-88; trainer/ cons. profl. devel. Becoming, Phila., 1987—; mem. exec. bd. Today's Child, Boston, 1985-87 ; mem. network speakers USA, Inc., Pigeon Forge, Tenn., 1991; convenor Gathering Bus. Women in South Phila., 1991—. Vol. Boston Dept. Social Svcs., 1986-87; adv. Nat. Abortion Rights Action League, Phila. and Boston, 1974-89. Recipient Achiever award Success Motivation Inst., Inc., Waco, Tex., 1988. Mem. Nat. Assn. Social Workers (mem. child welfare task force 1984-87), NAFE, Bus. Women's Network. Home and Office: Becoming 905 Mountain St Philadelphia PA 19148-1117

TONELLO-STUART, ENRICA MARIA, political economist; b. Monza, Italy; d. Alessandro P. and Maddalena M. (Marangoni) Tonello; m. Albert E. Smith; m. Charles L. Stuart. BA in Internat. Affairs, Econs., U. Colo., 1961; MA, Claremont Grad. Sch., 1966, PhD, 1971. Sales mgr. Met. Life Ins. Co., 1974-79; pres., CEO, ETS R&D, Inc., Palos Verdes Peninsula, Calif., 1977—; dean internat. studies program Union U., L.A. and Tokyo; lectr. internat. affairs and mktg. UCLA Ext., Union U. Pub., editor Tomorrow Outline Jour., 1963—, The Monitor, 1988; pub. World Regionalism-An Ecological Analysis, 1971, A Proposal for the Reorganization of the United Nations, 1966, The Persuasion Technocracy, Its Forms, Techniques and Potentials, 1966, The Role of the Multinationals in the Emerging Globalism, 1978; developed the theory of social ecology and econsociometry. Organizer 1st family assistance program Langley FB Tractical Air Command, 1956-58. Recipient vol. svc. award VA, 1956-58, ARC svc. award, 1950-58. Mem. Corp. Planners Assn. (treas. 1974-79), Investigative Reporters and Editors, World Future Soc. (pres. 1974-75), Asian Bus. League, Chinese Am. Assn. (life), Japan Am. Assn., L.A. World Trade Ctr., Palos Verdes C. of C. (legis. com.), L.A. Press Club (bd. dirs.), Zonta (chmn. internat. com. South Bay), Pi Sigma Alpha.

TONEY, JUDITH H., personnel director; b. Phila., Oct. 28, 1946; d. John M. and Ruth A. (Work) Hesley; m. Paul David Toney, June 1, 1968; children: Ruth Holland, Amanda Hesley, Sarah Elizabeth. AB, Coker Coll., 1968. Tchr. Thomas Sumter Acad., Dalzell, S.C., 1968-69, Hillcrest Elem. Sch., Sumter, S.C., 1969-70; vocat. evaluator Stanly County Vocat. Workshop, Albemarle, N.C., 1971-72; exec. dir. Rutherford Vocat. Workshop, Spindale, N.C., 1972-94; personnel dir. County of Rutherford Govt., Rutherfordton, N.C., 1994 ; adv. bd. Gardner-Webb U., Billings Springs, N.C., 1990-92, Chase H.S., Forest City, N.C., 1990—. Pres. Rutherford Couny United Way, 1983, Pioneer coun. Girl Scouts U.S., Raleigh, N.C., 1992-94. Named citizen of yr. Kiwanis Club 1983. Mem. Internat. Personnel Mgrs. Assn., N.C. Assn. Rehab. Facilities (pres. 1990, 91). Methodist. Home: 278 Old Henrietta Rd Forest City NC 28043

TONJES, MARIAN JEANNETTE BENTON, education educator; b. Rockville Center, N.Y., Feb. 16, 1929; d. Millard Warren and Felicia E. (Tyler) Benton; m. Charles F. Tonjes (div. 1965); children: Jeffrey Charles, Kenneth Warren. BA, U. N.Mex., 1951, cert., 1966, MA, 1969; EdD, U. Miami, 1975. Dir. recreation Stuyvesant Town Housing Project, N.Y.C., 1951-53; tchr. music, phys. edn. Sunset Mesa Day Sch., Albuquerque, 1953-54; tchr. remedial reading Zia Elem. Sch., Albuquerque, 1965-67; tchr. secondary devel. reading Rio Grande High Sch., Albuquerque, 1967-69; rsch. asst. reading Southwestern Coop. Ednl. Lab., Albuquerque, 1969-71; assoc. dir., vis. instr. Fla. Ctr. Tchr. Tng. Materials U. Miami, 1971-72; asst. prof. U.S. Internat. U., San Diego, 1972-75; prof. edn. Western Wash. U., Bellingham, 1975-94, dir. summer study, 1979-94, prof. emerita, 1994—; dir. summer study at Oriel Coll. Oxford (Eng.) U., Bellingham, 1975-94; reading supr. Manzanita Ctr. U. N.Mex., Albuquerque, 1968; vis. prof. adult edn. Palomar (Calif.) Jr. Coll., 1974; vis. prof. U. Guam, Mangilao, 1989-90; speaker, cons. in field; invited guest Russian Reading Assn., Moscow, 1992; part-time prof. U. N.Mex., Albuquerque, 1995—. Author: (with Miles V. Zintz) Teaching Reading/Thinking Study Skills in Content Classrooms, 3d edit., 1992, Secondary Reading, Writing and Learning, 1991; contbr. articles to profl. jours. Tng. Tchr. Trainers grantee, 1975; NDEA fellow Okla. State U., 1969. Mem. Am. Reading Forum (chmn. bd. dirs. 1983-85), Adult and Adolescent Literacy Confs. (spkr. 1991-94), Internat. Reading Assn. (mem. travel, interchange and study tours com. 1984-86, mem. non-print media nd reading com. 1980-83, workshop dir. S.W. regional confs. 1982, mem. com. internat. devel. N.Am. 1991-96, Outstanding Tchrs. Educator 1988-90), U.K. Reading Assn. (spkr. 1977-93), European Conf. in Reading (spkr. Berlin 1989, Edinburgh 1991, Malmo 1993, Budapest 1995), European Coun. Internat. Schs. (The Hague, spkr. 1993), World Congress in Reading Buenos Aires (spkr. 1994), PEO (past chpt. pres.), Phi Delta Kappa, Delta Delta Delta.

TONKENS, REBECCA A., maternal women's health nurse; b. Searcy, Ark., Dec. 17, 1943; d. William T. and Velda M. (Goodloe) McAfee; m. Richard E. Morris, June 24, 1960 (div. Nov. 1980); children: Terri L. Morris Bomar, Toni L. Morris Carroll; m. Solvin W. Tonkens, Dec. 22, 1986. LPN, Area Vocat. Tech. Sch., Kansas City, Kans., 1973; ADN, Kansas City C.C., 1980; BSN, Webster U., 1992. RN, Kans., Mo. Area Vocat. Tech. Sch.; Staff nurse Providence-St. Margaret Hosp., Kansas City, 1973-80; indsl. nurse, office mgr. Kansas City Indsl. Clinic, 1980-81; staff nurse Bethany Med. Ctr., Kansas City, 1981—; active community rels. diabetes unit Bethany Med. Ctr., 1983-86. Officer, v.p., bd. dirs. Cambridge Townhouse Assn., Leawood, Kans., 1989-92; chaperone Rose Bud (Ark.) Band at Presdl. Inauguration, Washington, 1992; mem. adv. bd. Kansas City Kans. C.C. Day Care Ctr.; vol. Habitat for Humanity, Salvation Army, others. Recipient Cert. of Appreciation, Salvation Army, 1994. Mem. ANA, Am. Coll. Occupational and Environ. Medicine (aux.). Episcopalian. Home and Office: 12861 Cambridge Ter Leawood KS 66209-1634

TONSO, CHERYL JACKSON, retired secondary education educator; b. Denver, Jan. 12, 1934; d. James Homer and Virginia Isabelle (Anderson) Jackson; m. Jerome Peter Tonso, Mar. 2, 1957 (dec. May 1977); children: Tawlys Grace Tonso Kaufman, Trynis Marie Tonso Bradley. AA, Cottey Coll., 1954; BA, U. Colo., 1956. Classroom tchr. Mesa Valley Schs., Grand Junction, Colo., 1956-58; classroom tchr. Boulder (Colo.) Valley Pub. Schs., 1965-77, 80-87, organizational specialist, 1977-80, dean of students, 1987-92; pvt. bus. owner; real estate, property devel. specialist Colo., 1992—; cons. Denver Pub. Schs., 1979-80, Elizabeth (Colo.) Pub. Sch., 1979-80, St. Vrain Valley Pub. Sch., 1979-80. Collaborative author: Organization Development, 1977-90, Boulder Schools English Curriculum, 1987-89, Boulder Schools Junior High School Curriculum, 1969-73. Active Denver Mus. Natural History, Women of West Mus. Mem. NEA, P.E.O., AAUW (pres. 1969-71), Colo. Edn. Assn., Boulder Valley Edn. Assn. (several offices), Colo. North Ctrl. Assn. (state com. 1981-95, chmn. 1990-91), Western History Assn., Delta Kappa Gamma (pres. 1977-79), Phi Delta Kappa. Democrat. Home: 354 Eagle Pass Durango CO 81301

TOOHEY, MARGARET LOUISE, journal editor, researcher; b. Torrington, Conn., Mar. 18, 1925; d. Erwin Byron and Lucy Lucille (Duigou) Gabarée; m. John Michael Toohey, Nov. 25, 1950 (div. Jan. 1972); children: John Michael Jr., Michele Louise Toohey Parsons. BS, U. Rochester, 1974, MA in English, 1978, PhD in English, 1987. Rsch. asst. Sch. Medicine Psychiatry Dept. Yale U., New Haven, 1950-57; rsch. asst., adminstr. adult psychiatry NIMH, Bethesda, Md., 1957-71; data analyst coord. Psychiatry Dept., U. Rochester, 1973-74, rsch. assoc., 1977—; tech. editor Family Process, Vernon, N.J., 1986—, Family Systems Medicine, N.Y.C., 1990-95, Families, Systems & Health, Vernon, 1996—. Contbr. articles to profl. jours., books. Mem. MLA. Democrat. Office: U Rochester Dept Psychiatry Rm 1-9011 300 Crittenden Blvd Rochester NY 14642-8409

TOOLE, LINDA JERNIGAN, quality control technician, cosmetics company admininstrator; b. Smithfield, N.C., May 23, 1949; d. Jesse James Jernigan and Myrtle Irene Jernigan Brown; m. J.R. Toole; children: Rhonda Toole Griffin, Rodney, Scarlett. AAS, Johnston C.C., 1994. Cert. statis. process control technician. Line insp. GTE Sylvania, Smithfield, N.C., 1974-80; operator AP Parts, Goldsboro, N.C., 1982, insp., 1982-90, statis. process control tech., 1990-95; mng. dir. Luzier Personalized Cosmetics, Kansas City, Mo., 1990—; chief inspector B&M Machining and Fabrication, Smithfield, N.C., 1995—. Sunday sch. tchr. Yelverton Grove Ch., Smithfield, N.C., 1988—. Mem. Am. Soc. Quality Control, Phi Bata Lamba.

TOOMEY, JEANNE ELIZABETH, animal activist; b. N.Y.C., Aug. 22, 1921; d. Edward Aloysius and Anna Margaret (O'Grady) Toomey; m. Peter Terranova, Sept. 28, 1951 (dec. 1968); children: Peter Terranova, Sheila Terranova Beasley. Student, Hofstra U., 1938-40; student law sch., Fordham U., 1940-41; BA, Southampton Coll., 1976; postgrad., Monmouth Coll., 1978-79. Reporter, columnist Bklyn. Daily Eagle, 1943-52; with The Fitzgeralds, NBC Radio, N.Y.C., 1952-53; reporter, writer King Features Syndicate, N.Y.C., 1953-55; reporter, columnist N.Y. Jour.-Am., N.Y.C., 1955-61; newsman AP, N.Y.C., 1963-64; stringer; columnist News Tribune, Woodbridge, N.J., 1976-86; editor Calexico (Calif.) Chronicle, 1987-88; editor community sect. Asbury Park (N.J.) Press, 1988; pres., dir. Last Post Animal Sanctuary, Falls Village, Conn., 1991—. Author: Murder in the Hamptons, 1994. Named Woman of the Yr. N.Y. Women's Press Club, 1960. Mem. Newswomen's Club of N.Y., Overseas Press Club, N.Y. Press Club, Silurians. Roman Catholic. Home and Office: 95 Belden St Falls Village CT 06031-1113

TOOMEY, KATHRYN W., state legislator; b. Nashua, N.H., Feb. 3, 1942. Student, Nashua Bus. Coll. Mem. corrections & criminal justice com. N.H. Ho. of Reps., Concord. Democrat. Roman Catholic. Home: 10 Lantern Ln Nashua NH 03062-1364 Office: NH Ho of Reps State House Concord NH 03301*

TOOMEY, PAULA KATHLEEN, financial analyst, consultant; b. Framingham, Mass., July 15, 1959; d. Paul Joseph and Mary Theresa (Coronella) T. AB in Econs., Boston Coll., 1984; postgrad., Harvard U., 1993—. Office supr. ADIA, Cambridge, Mass., 1985-87; accounts receivable coord. WGBH Ednl. Found., Boston, 1987-88; fin. analyst Sta. WGBH-TV, Boston, 1988-91; unit mgr. Descriptive Video Svc. WGBH Ednl. Found., Boston, 1991—. Vol. cons. Grow Golphybhangyang, Nepal, 1993-95; vol. tchr. Jr. Achievement, Boston, 1987; vol. master's swim coach YMCA, Brighton, Mass., 1990-93; vol. Franciscan Children's Hosp., Brighton, 1991-93; active NOW. Mem. AAUW. Roman Catholic. Office: Sta WGBH Ednl Found 125 Western Ave Boston MA 02134

TOOMEY, SHEILA CRAWFORD, education educator, consultant; b. Beckley, W.Va., Mar. 1, 1943; d. Roger and Ruth (Ashworth) Crawford; m. Lloyd E. Johnston, June 4, 1966 (dec. Dec. 1988); 1 child, Jacqueline De Vries; m. James E. Toomey, Feb. 10, 1989. BA, Tenn. Tech. U., 1963; MA in Christian Edn., Seabury Western Theol. Sem., 1965; MS in Curriculum and Instrn., U. Tenn., Martin, 1989; EdD in Instrn. and Curriculum Leadership, U. Memphis, 1994; postgrad., San Jose State U., U. Calif., Berkeley, U. Utah, Tex. Woman's U. Cert. tchr., Tenn. Dir. Christian edn. St. Luke's Episcopal Ch., Rochester, Minn., 1965-66; elem. tchr. Santa Catalina Sch. Girls, 1967-69, Rowland-Hall St. Mark's Sch., Salt Lake City, 1968-69, Union City (Tenn.) Christian Sch., 1984-87; libr. Dept. Edn. U. Tenn. at Martin, 1987-89; rsch. asst. U. Memphis, 1989-92, adj. prof., 1996; prof., edn. dept. chair Lane Coll., Jackson, Tenn., 1992-94; reading tchr., drama club sponsor Ashland (Miss.) Mid. Sch., 1994-95; workshop presenter Jackson, Tenn., 1989—; ednl. cons. Masco, Jackson, 1995—; adj. prof. Shelby State C.C., 1995; tng. devel. coord. Delta Faucet Tenn., 1995-96; homebound tchr. Jackson-Madison County Schs., 1996; adj. prof. Shelby State C.C., 1995, U. Memphis, 1996; mem. campus All Stars, Honda, Jackson, 1992-93. Contbr. articles to profl. jours. Mem. Am. Counseling Assn., Tenn. ASCD, Assn. for Case Method Rsch., DAR, Nat. Libr. Assn., Ch. and Synagogue Libr. Assn., AAUW, Order Eastern Star (worthy matron 1980-89), Sigma Tau Delta, Kappa Delta Pi. Anglican. Home: 137-2 Birchwood Ln Jackson TN 38305-2508

TOOTE, GLORIA E. A., developer, lawyer, columnist; b. N.Y.C.; d. Frederick A. and Lillie M. (Tooks) Toote. Student, Howard U., 1949-51; J.D., NYU, 1954; LL.M., Columbia U., 1956. Bar: N.Y. 1955, U.S. Dist. Ct. (so. and ea. dists.) N.Y. 1956, U.S. Supreme Ct. 1956. With firm Greenbaum, Wolff & Ernst, 1957; mem. editorial staff Time mag., 1957-58; asst. gen. counsel N.Y. State Workmen's Compensation Bd., 1958-64; pres. Toote Town Pub. Co. and Town Sound Studios, Inc., 1966-70; asst. dir. Action Agy., 1971-73; asst. sec. Dept. HUD, 1973-75; vice chmn. Pres.'s Adv. Council on Pvt. Sector Initiatives, 1983-85; housing developer, 1976—; pres. Trea Estates and Enterprises, Inc.; newspaper columnist; chairperson The Policy Coun. Former bd. dirs. Citizens for the Republic, Nat. Black United Fund, Exec. Women in Govt., Am. Arbitration Assn., Consumer Alert; bd. overseers Hoover Inst., 1985-95; vice chair Nat. Polit. Congress of Black Women, 1984-92; former mem. Coun. Econ. Affairs, Rep. Nat. Com.; pres. N.Y.C. Black Rep. Coun.; exec. trustee Polit. Action Com. for Equality; mem. NYNEX Consumer Adv. Coun., 1995—. Recipient citations Nat. Bus. League, Alpha Kappa Alpha, U.S. C. of C., Nat. Assn. Black Women Attys. Mem. N.Y. Fedn. Civil Svc. Orgns., Nat. Assn. Real Estate Brokers, Nat. Fed. Mortgage Assn. (bd. dirs. 1992), Nat. Citizens Participation Coun., Nat. Bar Assn.,Delta Sigma Theta, others. Address: 282 W 137th St New York NY 10030-2439

TOOTHE, KAREN LEE, elementary and secondary school educator; b. Seattle, Dec. 13, 1957; d. Russell Minor and Donna Jean (Drolet) McGraw; m. Edward Frank Toothe, Aug. 6, 1983; 1 child, Kendall Erin. BA in Psychology with high honors, U. Fla., 1977, MEd in Emotional Handicaps and Learning Disabilities, 1979. Cert. behavior analysis Fla. Dept. Profl. Regulation. Alternative edn. self-contained tchr. grades 2 and 3 Gainesville Acad., Micanopy, Fla., 1979; emotional handicaps self-contained tchr. Ctr. Sch. Alternative Sch., Gainesville, Fla., 1979-80; learning disabilities resource tchr. grades 2 and 3 Galaxy Elem. Sch., Boynton Beach, Fla., 1980-81, learning disabilities self-contained tchr. grades 1-3, 1981, varying exceptionalities self-contained tchr. grades 3-5, 1981-83, chpt. one remedial reading tchr. grades 3 and 4, 1982-83; sec. and visual display unit operator Manpower, London, 1983-84; dir. sci./geography/social studies program Fairley House Sch., London, 1984-86, specific learning difficulties self-contained tchr. ages 8-12, dir. computing program, 1984-89; specific learning difficulties resource tchr. ages 8-16 Dyslexia Inst., Sutton Coldfield, Eng., 1990; behavior specialist, head Exceptional Student Edn. dept. Gateway High Sch., Kissimmee, Fla., 1990, behavior specialist, head ESE dept., 1991, resource compliance specialist, head ESE dept., 1991-93, tchr. summer youth tng. and enrichment program, 1993; tchr. summer youth tng. and enrichment program Osceola High Sch., Kissimmee, 1992; resource compliance specialist, program specialist for mentally handicapped, physically impaired, occupational and phys. therapy programs St. Cloud (Fla.) Mid. Sch., 1993-96, cmty.-based instrn., local augmentative/assistive tech. specialist, 1993-96; resource compliance specialist, program specialist physically impaired occupl. and phys. therapy programs, local augmentative/assistive tech. speciali st Hickory Tree Elem. Sch., 1996—; sch. rep. CREATE, Alachua County, Fla., 1979-80, Palm Beach County South Area Tchr. Edn. Ctr. Coun., 1980-83, chmn., 1982-83; mem. writing team Title IV-C Ednl. Improvement Grant, Palm Beach County, Fla., 1981; mem. math. curriculum writing team Palm Beach County (Fla.) Schs., 1983; mem., co-dir. Fairley House Rsch. Com., 1984-90; co-founder, dir. Rsch. Database, London, 1984-89; co-chmn. computer and behavior/social aspects writing teams Dyslexia Inst. Math., Staines, Eng., 1990; lectr., course tutor Brit. Dyslexia Assn., Crewe, Eng., 1990; mem. Vocat.-Exceptional Com., 1991-93; mem. Osceola Reading Coun., 1991—; mem. sch. adv. com. Gateway High Sch., 1991-93, St. Cloud Mid. Sch., 1993-96; presenter in field. Named Mid. Sch. Profl. of Yr. Osceola chpt. of Coun. Exceptional Children, 1995, 96. Mem. CEC (named local chpt. Mid. Sch. Profl. of Yr. 1995, 96), Fla. Soc. for Augmentative and Alt. Comm., Fla. Profl. Assn. Staffing Specialists, Phi Beta Kappa. Home: 2175 James Dr Saint Cloud FL 34771-8830 Office: Osceola Dist Schs 817 Bill Beck Blvd Kissimmee FL 34744-4492

TOOTLE, AMBER LEE, airline pilot; b. Claxton, Ga., Mar. 7, 1956; d. Robert H. and Hilda B. Tootle; m. James A. Murray, June 8, 1981 (div. July 1994). BA, Mercer U., 1976; MEd, Colo. State U., 1978. Recreation dir. Ga. Acad. for Blind, Macon, Ga., 1979; tchr. Wesleyan Coll., Macon, 1979-80, Ariz. Sch. for Deaf/Blind, Tucson, 1980-81; flight attendent United Airlines, Denver, 1984-87, pilot, 1988—.

TOPE, BARBARA CHANEY, retired school library media specialist; b. London, Ohio, May 18, 1934; d. Robert Lee and Georgiana (Emery) Chaney; m. James Marion Tope, Aug. 22, 1953; children: Raymond, Victor, Russell, Ronald. BS in Edn. cum laude, Ohio State U., 1973; media specialist cert., Wright State U., 1977; MEd in Supervision, Ashland U., 1988. Cert. comprehensive English edn., media specialist, supervision. News reporter, photographer Madison Press & Mt. Sterling Tribune, London, 1964-68; aide and tchr. title I Madison Plains Schs., London, 1968-71, English tchr., English dept. chair, 1973-78; receptionist Merit Plastics, Columbus, Ohio, 1978-79; cmty. employment and tng. act coord. Madison County Commrs., London, 1979-81; person-in-charge, clk. Ohio Bur. of Employment Svcs., London, 1981-84; libr./media specialist Madison Plains Middle Sch., London, 1984-88, Madison Plains H.S., London, 1988-96; ret., 1996; dist. libr. supr. Madison Plains Schs., London, 1991-96. Editor (newsletter and booklets) Madison County Hist. Soc., 1967-70, Ohio Assn. Hist. Socs. Newsletter, 1968-70 (award of achievement 1970), (jour.) Ohio Media Spectrum, 1993—. Pres. London (Ohio) Women's Club, 1960; chmn. Madison County Mental Health Bd., London, 1989-91. Mem. ALA, NEA, Ohio Edn. Assn., Madison Plains Edn. Assn., Assn. for Ednl. Computers and Tech., Ohio Ednl. Libr./Media Assn. (com. chair 1992-94, ctrl. region dir. 1996—, 2d v.p.-elect 1996, v.p. 1997). Home: 2740 State Route 323 Mount Sterling OH 43143-9617

TOPELIUS, KATHLEEN E., lawyer; b. July 15, 1948. BA, U. Conn., 1970; JD, Cath. U. Am., 1978. Bar: D.C. 1978, U.S. Supreme Ct. 1988. Atty. office of gen. counsel Fed. Home Loan Bank Bd., 1978-80; ptnr. Morgan, Lewis & Bockius, Washington, 1985-93, Bryan Cave, Washington, 1993—. Office: Bryan Cave 700 13th St NW Washington DC 20005-3960

TOPETE-STONEFIELD, LIZ, advertising marketing executive, public speaker; b. Mex. City, Dec. 8, 1955; d. Manuel Topete-Blake and Carmen Elizabeth (Vargas) Mills; m. DuWayne F. Stonefield, July 18, 1982. Diploma in classical ballet, Inst. Nacional de Bellas Artes, 1976; BA in Adv., Centro De Estudios En Ciencias De La Comunicacion, 1981. Cert. instr. Owner, dir. Ballet Liz Internat., Mex., 1975-79; freelance Mktg. and pub. rels., Mex., 1979-80; gen. mgr. Personal Eventual y Temp., Mex., 1981-82; owner, pres. Stonefield Spl. Events, Phoenix, 1984-85; pres., CEO Topete/Stonefield, Inc., Phoenix, 1985—; speaker for numerous orgn. Contbr. articles to profl. jours. Recipient numerous acknowledgements and awards, including Bert Getz Civic Leadership award, Ariz. Cmty. Found., 1991, Christina Small Leadership award, YWCA of Maricopa County, 1992, Women of Achievement award, Phoenix C. of C., 1993; named. Ad Person of Yr., 1993, Ad 2 Phoenix, and one of 10 Most Outstanding Women, Ariz. Woman Mag., 1992. Jehovah's Witness. Office: Topete/Stonefield Inc 325 W Encanto Blvd Phoenix AZ 85003

TOPETZES, FAY KALAFAT, retired school guidance counselor; b. Auburn, Ind., July 13, 1923; d. Alexander Christ and Andromache Basiliou Kalafat; m. Nick John Topetzes, Jan. 31, 1953; children: Andrea Topetzes Mann, John Nick, Sophia Angela. BS in Acctg. and English, Ind. U., 1945; cert. tchr., Marquette U., 1969, MS in Guidance and Counseling, 1973. Cert. tchr., Wis. Acct. Dana Corp., Auburn, Ind., 1945-47; mgr. theaters Kalafat Bros., Ind., 1947-53; tchr. Univ. Sch. of Milw., 1962-64, Spencerian Bus. Coll., Milw., 1959-62, Milw. Pub. Schs., 1962-69; counselor, dir. guidance West Allis (Wis.) Ctrl. H.S., 1969-86; ret., 1986. Bd. dirs. Gov.'s Tourism Coun. of Wis., Milw., 1990—, FLW Heritage Bd., Madison, Wis., 1990—; vol. for many charitable orgns.; active in ch., ednl., cultural and art orgns. Mem. APA, AAUW (past pres., pub. policy chairperson, Nat. award 1994-95), Wis. Pers. and Guidance Assn., Wis. Assn. Sch. Counselors, Milw. Found. for Women, Daus. of Penelope (dist. gov., nat. chmn. 1994-96), numerous Hellenic orgns. Home: 9119 N White Oak Ln Bayside WI 53217

TOPHAM, SALLY JANE, ballet educator; b. N.Y.C., June 2, 1933; d. William Holroyd Topham and Marian Phyllis (Thomas) Topham Halligan; m. Joseph Vincent Ferrara, Dec. 27, 1958 (div. 1977); children: Gregory Paul, Mark Edward. Student Ballet Theatre Sch., Royal Acad. Dancing, London; trained in Europe. Free-lance profl. dancer ballet, opera ballet, summer stock, 1956-59; founder, dir. Monmouth Sch. Ballet, N.J., 1963-83, 85—; founder Central Jersey Acad. Ballet, Red Bank, N.J., 1983-85 , also dir.; dir. Westfield sch. Ballet, N.J., 1976-77; tchr., dir. Mount Allison U. Summer Sch., New Brunswick, Can., 1973-77; prof. ballet Monmouth Coll., West Long Branch, N.J., 1981-83. Choreographer (ballet) Coppelia, 1981, 83; Shubert Songs, 1980; Homage to Bournonville, 1977; Nutcracker, 1985, Cinderella, 1988; staged many ballets and opera ballets. Bd. dirs. Monmouth Arts Found., Red Bank, 1972—, Shore Ballet Co., Red Bank, 1976—; founder, bd. dirs. Monmouth Civic Ballet, Red Bank, 1972-75. Mem. Royal Acad. Dancing (assoc., advanced tchr's. cert. 1979), English Speaking Union. Avocations: sailing, theater, music, books. Office: Shore Ballet Sch 31 E Main St Freehold NJ 07728

TOPINKA, JUDY BAAR, state official; b. Riverside, Ill., Jan. 16, 1944; d. William Daniel and Lillian Mary (Shuss) Baar; 1 child, Joseph Baar. BS, Northwestern U., 1966. Features editor, reporter, columnist Life Newspapers, Berwyn and LaGrange, Ill., 1966-77; with Forest Park (Ill.) Rev. and Westchester News, 1976-77; coord. spl. events dept. fedn. comm., AMA, 1978-80; rsch. analyst Senator Leonard Becker, 1978-79; mem. Ill. Ho. of Reps., 1981-84; mem. Ill. Senate, 1985-94; treas. State of Ill., Springfield, 1995—; former mem. judiciary com., former chmn. senate health and welfare com.; former mem. fin. instn. com.; former co-chmn. Citizens Coun. on Econ. Devel.; former co-chmn. U.S. Commn. for Preservation of Am.'s Heritage Abroad, serves on legis. ref. bur.; former mem. minority bus. resource ctr. adv. com. U.S. Dept. Transp.; former mem. adv. bd. Nat. Inst. Justice. Founder, pres., bd. dirs. West Suburban Exec. Breakfast Club, from 1976; chmn. Ill. Ethnics for Reagan-Bush, 1984, Bush-Quayle 1988; spokesman Nat. Coun. State Legislatures Health Com.; former mem nat. adv. coun. health professions edn. HHS; mem., GOP chairwoman Legis. Audit Commn of Cook County; chmn. Riverside Twp. Regular Republican Orgn., 1994—. Recipient Outstanding Civilian Svc. medal, Molly Pitcher award, Abraham Lincoln award, Silver Eagle award U.S. Army and N.G. Office: JR Thompson Ctr 100 W Randolph St Ste 15-600 Chicago IL 60601-3220

TOPP, SUSAN HLYWA, lawyer; b. Detroit, Oct. 9, 1956; d. Michael Leo and Lucy Stella (Rusak) Hlywa; m. Robert Elwin Topp, July 25, 1985; children: Matthew, Sarah, Michael and Jamie (triplets). BS in Edn. cum laude, Ctrl. Mich. U., 1978; JD cum laude, Wayne State U., Detroit, 1991. Bar: Mich. 1992, U.S. Dist. Ct. (ea. dist.) Mich. 1992. Conservation officer Mich. Dept. Natural Resources, Pontiac, 1980-88; environ. conservation officer Mich. Dept. Natural Resources, Livonia, 1988-93; pvt. practice law Gaylord, Mich., 1993; ptnr. Rolinski & Topp, PLC, Gaylord, 1993-95; assoc. Plunkett & Cooney, P.C., Gaylord, 1995—; ct. apptd. to represent abused children Probate Ct., Gaylord, 1993—. Recipient Am. Jurisprudence award Wayne State U., 1987, Trial Advocacy award, 1988. Mem. ABA (nat. resources and environ. law com.), Mich. State Bar Assn. (environ. law sect.), AAUW, Mich. C. of C. Roman Catholic. Office: Plunkett & Cooney PC Hidden Valley Exec Ctr PO Box 280 Gaylord MI 49735

TOPPAN, CLARA ANNA RAAB (MRS. FREDERICK WILLCOX TOPPAN), accountant; b. Cheyenne, Wyo., Nov. 9, 1910; d. Cornelius Emil and Gizella (Marczelly) Raab; m. Frederick Willcox Toppan, July 23, 1949 (dec. Nov. 1966). BS, U. Wyo., 1931. CPA, Wyo., D.C. Sec. Yellowstone Nat. Park, 1934, Nat. Park Svc., Washington, 1934-37; chief clk. Grand Teton Nat. Park, Moose, Wyo., 1937-42; acct. Cordle Raab & Roush CPA, Casper, Wyo., 1942-45; owner Clara Raab Toppan CPA, Jackson, Wyo., 1945-53; ind. part-time acct., 1954—; instr. acctg. U. Wyo., 1967. Treas. Community Bldg. Fund, Jackson, 1952-54, Teton County Libr. Fund, Jackson, 1950-53. Clara Raab Toppan Day proclaimed by Gov. of Wyo., 1990; named Outstanding Grad. Bus. Coll. U. Wyo., 1994-95. Mem. AICPA (hon., cert. commemorating 50 yrs. of membership), AAUW, Am. Women's Soc. CPA's, Wyo. Soc. CPA's (hon. life), Bus. and Profl. Women (organizer Jackson Hole), Jackson Hole C. of C. (an organizer), U. Wyo Alumni Assn., Jackson Hole Trap Club, Jackson Hole Golf and Country Club, Bradenton Country Club, Phi Gamma Nu. Republican. Home: 4525 N Fish Creek Rd Wilson WY 83014 Winter address: 3605 Sun Eagle Ln Bradenton FL 34210

TOPSY-ELVORD, DORIS LOUISE, municipal official; b. Vicksburg, Miss., June 17, 1931; d. Clyde Julius Walker and Mary Lee Rose; m. Urlee Topsy, Apr. 5, 1953; children: Gerald, Stanley, Stephen; m. Ralph Elvord, Dec. 29, 1984. BA in Social Welfare, Calif. State U., 1969; MA in Criminal Justice, Chapman Coll., 1981. Group supr. Calif. Youth Authority, 1956-59; procurement officer L.A. County Sheriff's Dept., 1961-66, recreation leader, 1966-69, dep. probation officer, 1969-88, civil svc. commr., 1988-92; mem. City Coun., Long Beach, Calif., 1992—; vice Mayor City of Long Beach, 1996—; v.p. Long Beacn Unified Sch. Dist. Pers. Commn., 1991-92. Bd. dirs. Pacific Hosp., Long Beach, 1991—, NCCJ, 1993—, NAACP; active Nat. Black Caucas, 1992—. Recipient Outstanding award McCobb Boys Home, 1984, Spl. award Dorothy Brown Sch., 1986. Mem. Nat. Coun. Negro Women, Eta Phi Beta (v.p. Kappa chpt. 1984-86, pres. 1986-88, Soror of Yr. 1982). Home: 2373 Olive Ave Long Beach CA 90806 Office: 333 W Ocean Blvd 14th Fl Long Beach CA 90802

TORAN, KAY DEAN, social services director; b. Birmingham, Ala., Nov. 21, 1942; d. Benjamin and Mary Rose Dean; children: Traci Rossi, John D. Toran. BA, U. Portland, 1964; MSW, Portland State U., 1970. Asst. prof. social work Portland (Oreg.) State U., 1971-76; mgr. Adult and Family Svcs., Salem, Oreg., 1976-79; asst. gov. Office of Gov., Salem, 1979-87; adminstr. purchasing divsn. Dept. Gen. Svcs., Salem, 1987-90; regional adminstr. Children's Svcs. Divsn., Portland, 1991-94, adminstr., 1994—; pres. Walker Inst., Portland, 1990-94, Portland chapter Links, Inc., 1990-92. Bd. trustees Catlin Gabel Sch., Portland, 1980-84, Portland State U. Found., 1980-87; bd. dirs. Oreg. Law Found., 1990-93. Office: Svcs to Childen & Families 500 Summer St NE Salem OR 97310-0101

TORBET, LAURA, graphic designer, author; b. Paterson, N.J., Aug. 23, 1942; d. Earl Buchanan and Ruth Claire (Ehlers) Robbins; B.A., B.F.A., Ohio Wesleyan U., 1964; m. Bruce J. Torbet, Sept. 9, 1967 (div. 1971); m. Peter H. Morrison, June 19, 1983 (dec. Nov. 1988); m. Salam Habibi, Aug. 23, 1995. Mng. editor Suburban Life mag., East Orange, N.J., 1964-65; asst. public relations dir. United Funds N.J., Newark, 1965-67; art dir. Alitalia Airlines, N.Y.C., 1967-69; propr. Laura Torbet Studio, N.Y.C., 1969-84; author: Macrame You Can Wear, 1972, Clothing Liberation, 1973, Leathercraft You Can Wear, 1975, The T-Shirt Book, 1976, The Complete Book of Skateboarding, 1976, How To Do Everything With Markers, 1977; (with Doug McLaggan) Squash: How to Play, How to Win, 1977; The Complete Book of Mopeds, 1978; (with Luree Nicholson) How to Fight Fair With Your Kids...and Win!, 1980; editor: Helena Rubenstein's Book of the Sun, 1979, The Encyclopedia of Crafts, 1980, (with George Bach) The Inner Enemy, 1982, A Time for Caring, 1982; (with Hap Hatton) Helpful Hints for Hard Times, 1982, The Virgin Homeowners Handbook, 1984, Helpful Hints for Better Living, 1984, (with James Braly) Dr. Braly's Optimum Health Program, 1985; (with Bernard Gittelson) Intangible Evidence, 1987; (with Harville Hendrix) Keeping the Love You Find, 1992, The Couples Companion, 1994, All Out Art; editor, ghost writer, co-author books. Bd. dirs. The Living/Dying Project. Mem. Boss Ladies. Home and Office: 1111 Butterfield Rd San Anselmo CA 94960-1181

TORBETT, JANICE G., bank officer; b. Weathers, Ark., June 8, 1950; d. Ira Randolph and Lillie Rose (Fields) Eaton; m. Eddie Carles Torbett, Oct. 5, 1978; children: Damon Jack, William Brett. Degree in Trust, So. Meth. U., 1983; Lic. Real Estate Broker, Ark. Real Estate Commn., 1985; BSBA in Fin. and Banking, U. Ark., 1990. Line worker Baldwin Piano Co., Fayetteville, Ark., 1968-69; filing/typist FBI, Washington, 1969-71; proof operator First Nat. Bank, Fayetteville, 1972-74, teller, 1974-77, trust sec., 1978-80, asst. trust officer AVP and trust office, 1980-86; trust officer The Bank of Fayetteville NA, 1987—; mem. adv. bd. Ark. Children's Hosp., Little Rock, 1992—. Mem. cmty. svc. com. Altrusa Internat., Fayetteville, 1987-93, treas., 1993; mem. Fayetteville C. of C., 1982-85. Mem. Rotary. Democrat. Baptist. Office: The Bank of Fayetteville NA 1 S Block PO Box 1728 Fayetteville AR 72702

TORCHIA, KARIN G., sports association administrator; b. Camp Springs, Md., June 28, 1969; d. John Anthony and Patricia Gail (Bernotas) DelBuono; m. Karl Victor Torchia, Aug. 7, 1993. BS in Sport Mgmt., W.Va. U., 1991, MS in Sports Adminstrn., 1993. Cert. coach. Asst. dep. polit. dir. GOPAC, Washington, 1990; sports comm. asst. W.Va. U. Athletic Dept., Morgantown, 1990-93; publicity dir. Tonya Knight Enterprises, Long Branch, N.J., 1993-94; asst. to the commr. Atlantic 10 Conf., Cranbury, N.J., 1993-95; dir. championship Metro Atlantic Athletic Conf., Edison, N.J., 1995—; games com. Metro Atlantic Athletic Conf., softball championship sel. com. Author, editor: The Total Student-Athlete, 1992; feature writer Ironman Mag., 1993, Fitness Mags., 1993. All-Am. scholar U.S. Achievement Acad., 1991. Mem. W.Va. Sport Mgmt. Assn. Roman Catholic. Office: Metro Atlantic Athletic Conf 1090 Amboy Ave Edison NJ 08837

TORDIFF, HAZEL MIDGLEY, education director; b. Columbia Station, Ohio, Sept. 24, 1920; d. Joseph and Mary Ceclia (Vitovec) Midgley; m. Joseph F. Tordiff, Nov. 13, 1946; children: Cathy, Joseph F. Jr., John C. BS, Kent State U., 1942; student, U. Va., 1968, Catholic U., 1975. Instr. Warren (Ohio) Bus. Coll., 1942-44; exec. sec. to plant mgr. GE, Warren, 1943-44; adminstrv. asst. Fgn. Svc., Dept. State, and Am. Embassy, Stockholm and Lisbon, Portugal, 1947-52; dir. tng. Washington Bus. Sch., Vienna, Va., 1969—. Leader Girls Scouts U.S., Bonn, Fed. Republic of Germany, 1960-64, den mother Cub Scouts Am., Bonn, 1962-66; scorekeeper Little League Baseball, Bonn and Vienna, 1960-70. Sgt. WAC, U.S. Army, 1944-47. Named Outstanding Bus. Tchr. in U.S., Assn. Ind. Schs. and Colls., 1984. Mem. Prof. Secs. Internat. (faculty sponsor 1981-84). Home: 1302 Ross Dr SW Vienna VA 22180-6724 Office: Washington Bus Sch 1980 Gallows Rd Vienna VA 22182-3913

TORELLO, JUDY S., corporate communications executive; b. Scranton, Pa., June 2, 1940; d. D. A. and Ann (Rogan) Santarsiero; m. Don Torello, May 19, 1974. Grad., U. Pitts., U. Scranton; BA in Polit. Sci. and English, Rosemont Coll. Publicist Sta. WOR-TV, N.Y.C., 1967-69, mgr. advt. and publicity, 1969-70; mgr. press info. Sta. WNET-TV, N.Y.C., 1970-72, Sta. WABC-TV, N.Y.C., 1972-80; v.p. media rels. Home Box Office, Inc., N.Y.C., 1980-87; sr. v.p. corp. commm. Backer Spielvogel Bates Worldwide, Inc., N.Y.C., 1987-96, exec. v.p. dir. corp. comm., 1996—. Recipient awards Ceba, Freedom Found., others. Office: Bates Worldwide Inc Chrysler Bldg 405 Lexington Ave New York NY 10174*

TORIANI, DENISE MARIA, legal administrator; b. Oakland, Calif., Dec. 30, 1954; d. David and Doris Elizabeth (Cantrell) Eirich; m. Dennis James Toriani, June 22, 1996, (div. 1976); children: Robert Justin, Shannon James; m. Oscar Quiroga DeLaRosa, May 1, 1983 (div. 1992). AAS, Truman Coll., 1983; BABA, DePaul U., 1987. Legal adminstr. Taylor, Miller, Sprowl, Hoffnagle & Merletti, Chgo., 1985-91, Leonard M. Ring & Assocs., Chgo., 1991-93, Boehm, Pearlstein & Bright, Ltd., Chgo., 1994-95, Purcell & Wardope Chartered, Chgo., 1995—; ESL tutor Literacy Vols., Chgo, 1985-86. Mem. ABA (assoc.), Ill. Bar Assn. (assoc.), Assn. Legal Adminstrs. Democrat. Roman Catholic. Office: Purcell & Wardope Chartered 300 S Wacker Dr Ste 800 Chicago IL 60606

TORKELSON, LUCILE EMMA, writer; b. Fond du Lac, Wis., Sept. 24, 1915; d. Joseph Michael Julka and Matilda (Elz) Pickart; m. Ivar John Torkelson, Sept. 24, 1945; children: Jean, David. PhB in Journalism, Marquette U., 1938; postgrad., U. Minn., 1950s. Reporter Fond du Lac Reporter, 1938-41, Milw. Jour., 1941-45; movie critic South Bend (Ind.) Tribune, 1945; editor LWV Mag., Mpls., 1961-62; office mgr. Midwest Bearing Corp., Milw., 1963-89; book features writer Milw. Sentinel, 1963-75, book reviewer, 1963—; freelance writer Wauwatosa, Wis., 1990—. Contbr. articles to popular jours., mags. Active LWV, Mpls., 1957-62. Mem. Women in Communications (50 Years of Svc. cert. 1988), Great Books Assn., Theta Sigma Phi. Republican. Roman Catholic. Home: 6511 Washington Cir Milwaukee WI 53213-2459

TORME, MARGARET ANNE, public relations executive, communications consultant; b. Indpls., Apr. 5, 1943; d. Ira G. and Margaret Joy (Wright) Barker; children—Karen Anne, Leah Vanessa. Student Coll. San Mateo, 1961-65. Pub. rels. mgr. Hoefer, Dieterich & Brown (now Chiat-Day), San Francisco, 1964-73; v.p., co-founder, creative dir. Lowry & Ptnrs., San Francisco, 1975-83; pres., founder Torme & Co. (now Torme & Kenney), San Francisco, 1983—; cons. in communications. Mem. Pub. Rels. Soc. Am., San Francisco C. of C. (outstanding achievement award for women entrepreneurs 1987), Jr. League (adv. bd.), Pub. Rsls Orgn. Internat. (v.p., dir.). Office: 545 Sansome St San Francisco CA 94111-2908

TORNATORE-MORSE, KATHLEEN MARY, pharmacy educator; b. Oneida, N.Y., Feb. 25, 1955; d. James Joseph and Concetta Barbara (Crimi) T.; m. Gene Morse; two children. BS in Pharmacy cum laude, Union U., 1978; PharmD, SUNY, Buffalo, 1981. Registered pharmacist, N.Y. Hosp. pharmacy residency U. Nebr. Med. Ctr., Omaha, 1978-79; pharmacist Health Care Plan, West Seneca, N.Y., 1979-80; lab. instr. Profl. Practice Lab. Sch. of Pharmacy SUNY, Buffalo, 1979-80, instr. in pharmacology nurse practitioner program, 1982-85, 87-91, clin. pharmacokinetics fellow, 1983-85, clin. instr. Sch. of Pharmacy, 1981-83, rsch. asst. prof. pharmacy Sch. of Pharmacy, 1985-87, asst. prof. pharmacy, 1987-90, clin. asst. prof. pharmacy, 1990-91, asst. prof. pharmacy, 1991-95; assoc. prof. pharmacy, 1995—; lectr. and presenter in field; pharmacokinetics cons. VA Med. Ctr., Buffalo, 1986-91; curriculum com. mem. Sch. of Pharmacy, SUNY, Buffalo, 1990-91, mem. Ctr. for Clin. Pharmacy Rsch., 1989—, mem. substance abuse com., 1990—, mem. Doctor of Pharmacy Student Rsch. com., 1987—, mem. curriculum com. Doctor of Pharmacy program, 1984-86, mem. policy and implementation com., 1984-86; quality assurance com. Buffalo Gen. Hosp. Corp., 1981-82, investigational rev. bd., 1982-83; mem. med. adv. com. West N.Y. Kidney Found., 1994—. Contbr. chpts. to Textbook of Pharmacology, 1991; contbr. numerous articles to profl. jours. including Transplantation, Clin. Pharmacology and Therapeutics, Clin. Nephrology, Clin. Transplantation, others. Recipient Outstanding Young Women of Am. award, 1984, Achievement award Albany Coll. Pharmacy, 1984; grantee Upjohn, 1984-86, 88, 90-91, 93, 95. Mem. AAAS, AAUW, Internat. Soc. Immunopharmacology, Am. Coll. Clin. Pharmacy, (mem. devel. and steering com. N.Y. state chpt. 1990-91, other coms. 1991-93), Am. Soc. Hosp. Pharmacists, Am. Assn. Colls. Pharmacy, Am. Fedn. Aging Rsch., Rho Chi. Office: SUNY Sch of Pharmacy Dept Pharmacy Practice 313 Cooke Hall Buffalo NY 14260-1200

TORNAY, CLAIRE JAEGER, psychotherapist; b. Brussels, Mar. 14, 1940; came to the U.S., 1946; d. Pincus and Adele (Goldblatt) Taffel; m. George F. Tornay Jr., Aug. 26, 1962; 1 child, Darrell Moss (dec. Feb. 1987). BA in Econ., Barnard Coll., 1960; MS in Ednl. Adminstrn., Pace U., 1971; MSW, Yeshiva U., 1993. Cert. social worker, N.Y. Classroom tchr. N.Y.C. Bd. Edn., 1961-85; pvt. practice psychotherapist N.Y.C., 1993—; psychiat. social worker Health Ins. Plan-Mental Health, N.Y.C., 1994—. Mem. NASW, AAUW, AARP, Orthopsychiat. Assn. Democrat. Jewish. Office: 710 Park Ave New York NY 10021

TORNEDEN, CONNIE JEAN, bank executive; b. Tonganoxie, Kans., Sept. 14, 1955; d. Byron Calvin and Edna Jeannette (Keck) Swain; m. Lawrence Dale Torneden, Sept. 18, 1976; 1 child, James Milton. Bus. cert., Kansas City C.C., Kans., 1974; student, Nat. Compliance Sch., Norman, Okla., 1984. Adminstrv. sec. to chmn. of bd., pres. First State Bank and Trust, Tonganoxie, 1974-80, asst. cashier, 1981-83, asst. v.p. and compliance officer, 1984—, bank security officer, 1989-95. Lobbyist, treas. 24-40 Hwy. Task Force, Leavenworth, Kans., 1989-91; bd. dirs., sec. Reno Cemetery Assn., Tonganoxie, 1986—; co-founder Tonganoxie Days, chmn., 1986, 88-93, 95-96; grad. So. Leavenworth County Leadership Devel., 1991; sec.-treas. Maple Grove Cemetery Assn., 1995—, Reno Twp. Fire Dept., 1996. Mem. Am. Bus. Women's Assn. (treas. 1986-87, Woman of Yr. award Twilight chpt. 1994), Mid-Am. Dairymen Assn. (sec. 1978-80), Nat. Assn. Old West Gunfighter Teams (nat. champions 1989, 90), Linwood Grange (5th and 6th degrees 1978), Tonganoxie C. of C. (sec. 1983-86, 92-94, pres. 1986, 88, 89, 96, v.p. 1995, Mem. of Yr. award 1990, 92), Tonganoxie Jaycees (sec. 1991). Democrat. Mem. Soc. of Friends. Office: First State Bank and Trust 4th and Bury PO Box 219 Tonganoxie KS 66086

TORNESE, JUDITH M., financial institution executive; b. Pitts., Aug. 26, 1942; d. Ilario and Rose Mary (Ali) T.; m. Jerrry E. Winters. Student, U. Pitts. CPCU. Various positions Transam Corp., San Francisco, 1971-81; dir. risk mgmt. TransAm. Corp., San Francisco, 1981-87, v.p. risk mgmt., 1987—. Dir. San Francisco Suicide Prevention, 1984-90; mem. Earthquake Ins. and Recovery Fin. Com. of Seismic Safety Commn., 1988-91. Named Risk Mgr. of Yr. Bus. Ins. Mag., 1992. Mem. Risk and Ins. Mgmt. Soc. (soc. dir. 1981—, chair nominating com. 1987-92), Mfr.'s Alliance Productivity anb Innovation (risk mgmt. coun. 1981—). Office: Transam Corp 600 Montgomery St San Francisco CA 94111-2702*

TORO, AMALIA MARIA, lawyer; b. Hartford, Conn., Nov. 6, 1920; d. Frederick and Maria (Casale) T. BA, U. Conn., 1942; JD, Yale U., 1944. Bar: Conn. 1944. Assoc. Wiggin & Dana, New Haven, 1944-46; atty., dir., chief elections div. Office Sec. of State, Conn., 1946-75; judge Ct. Common Pleas State of Conn., 1975; pvt. practice Hartford, Conn., 1975—; alt. pub. mem. Conn. Bd. Mediation and Arbitration, 1996—. Corporator St. Francis Hosp. & Med. Ctr., Hartford, 1984—; former mem. Ford Found Com. on Voting and Election Systems; mem. State Employees' Retirement Commn., 1956-75, past vice-chmn.; active Conn. State Employees Retirement Commn. Recipient AMITA award, 1970, Humanitarian award Columbus Day Celebration Com., 1986. Greater Hartford Bus. & Profl. Women (pres. 1989-91, Woman of the Yr. award 1969), Conn. Bar Assn. (Merit award), Conn. Assn. Mcpl. Attys. (past pres.), Greater Hartford U. Conn. Alumni Assn. (past pres.). Office: 234 Pearl St Hartford CT 06103-2113

TOROK, MARGARET LOUISE, insurance company executive; b. Detroit, June 22, 1922; d. Perl Edward Ensor and Mary (Seggie) Armstrong; m. Leslie A. Torok, Aug. 14, 1952; 1 child, Margaret Mary Ryan. Lic. Ins. Agy. Ins. agy. Grendel-Wittbold Ins., Southgate, Mich., 1961-68, corp.

officer, 1968-72; pres. of corp. Grendel-Wittbold Ins., Southgate, 1972--; bd. dirs. Ind. Ins. Agts. of Mich., Lansing, 1984-92, Ind. Ins. Agts. of Wayne County, Dearborn, 1979—, pres. 1978. Bd. dirs. So. Wayne County C. of C., Taylor, 1975, 1st vice chair, 1995; bd. dirs. City of Southgate Tax Increment Finance Authority Dist. and Econ. Devel. Commn.; leadership chmn. YMCA, Wyandotte, 1980—, Downriver Cmty. Alliance; lay chmn. Cath. Svc. Appeal for Archdiocese of Detroit, 1989; co-chair fundraiser Sacred Heart Ch.; mem. bd. MESC Employers Com., 1991—; mem. com., bd. New Workforce Devel. Com. (gov. appt., charter mem.). Recipient Capital award Ind. Ins. Agents of Mich., 1988, Amb. award, 1994, Woman of Yr. AAUW, 1994, Salute to Excellence award Downriver Coun. of Arts, 1993-94, Chmn. of Yr. award MESC Job Svc. Employers Com., 1991, Robert Stewart award Wyandotte Svc. Club Coun., 1994. Mem. Wyandotte Yacht Club, Soroptimist Club of Wyandotte Southgate Taylor (pres. 1984-86, Advancing Status Women award 1988, Soroptimist of Yr. award 1993-94). Roman Catholic. Office: Grendel Wittbold Agy Inc 12850 Eureka Rd Southgate MI 48195-1344

TORO-ZAMBRANA, WANDA, special education educator, researcher; b. Mayaguez, P.R., Sept. 6, 1963; d. Angel Toro and Flor Zambrana. BA in Spl. and Elem. Edn., U. P.R., Río Piedras, 1987, MA in Rehab. Counseling, 1991; postgrad., Purdue U., 1992-96. Cert. elem. and spl. edn. tchr., P.R. Elem. and spl. edn. educator various schs., P.R., 1987-88, 91; rehab. counselor Vocat. Rehab. Program, San Juan, 1990; teaching asst. spl. edn. Purdue U., West Lafayette, Ind., 1992, rsch. asst., 1992—, instr., 1993, 94, 96, project collaborator severe disabilities tng. program, 1993—, supr. spl. edn., 1993, 94; summer camp group coord. Asociacion de Padres Pro Bienestar de Ninos con Impedimentos, San Juan, 1990, 91, 92; cons. asst. Purdue U., 1994, 95. Co-author: Recognizing Choices in Community Settings by People with Significant Disabilities, 1994; contbr. articles to profl. jours. Active Verano Misionero, San Juan, 1987-92, Escuela de Lideres, San Juan, 1987-92; mem. social concerns br. St. Thomas Aquinas Cath. Ctr., West Lafayette, 1992—. Dissertation rsch. grantee Purdue Rsch. Found., 1995-96; fellow U.S. Dept. Edn., 1992-96; acad. scholar U. P.R., 1983-87, 89-91. Mem. Nat. Rehab. Assn. (multicultural rehab. concerns divsn.), Am. Assn. Mental Retardation, Assn. Behavior Analysis, Coun. Exceptional Children (career devel. and transition divsn., internat. spl. edn. and svcs. divsn., visually handicapped divsn., tchr. edn. divsn., divsn. for physical and health disabilities), Assn. for Persons with Severe Handicaps, Grad. Orgn. of Ednl. Studies. Home: 250 S Salisbury St Apt #3 West Lafayette IN 47906 Office: Purdue U Dept Ednl Studies LAEB 5163 Purdue University IN 47907

TORR, ANN M., state legislator; b. Rochester, N.H., Feb. 11, 1935; m. Franklin Torr; 3 children. RN, Notre Dame Sch. Nursing, Manchester, N.H., 1955; BA, New Eng. Coll., 1977. RN, N.H. Real estate agt. and nurse; mem. N.H. Ho. of Reps., 1985—; mem. legis. adminstrv. and ruls coms.; trustee Westworth Douglass Hosp., chmn., 1982—; vice chmn. bd. dirs. Health Cir. Inc. Del. N.H. Constnl. Conv., 1984; active Stafford County Exec. Com., 1984-90. mem. Stafford County Cmty. Action (bd. dirs., vice chmn. 1985-92), Northam Colonists Hist. Soc., C. of C., Dover Bus. and Profl. Women's Found. Republican. Roman Catholic. Home: One Old Littleworth Rd Dover NH 03820-4311 Office: NH Ho of Reps State House 107 N Main St Rm 312 Concord NH 03301*

TORRENCE, GWEN, Olympic athlete; b. Atlanta, June 12, 1965; m. Manley Waller Jr.; 1 child, Manley Waller III. 2d place NCAA 100, 1985; 7th place USA/Mobil 100, 1985; 5th place USA/Mobil 200, 1985; champion NCAA 100, 1987, NCAA 200, 1987; 5th place U.S. World Championships 200; winner of sprints World Univ. Games; winner Pan Am. Games 200, 1987; 3rd place in both 100 and 200 Olympic Trials, 1988; 2d place USA/Mobil 100, 1991; winner USA/Mobil 200, 1991; gold medalist 200 Meter, Barcelona, Spain, 1992; winner Mobil Grand Prix 100 meters, 1993; gold medalist 100 meters World Track & Field Championships, Gutenborg, Sweden, 1995; bronze medalist 100 meters Olympic Games, Atlanta, 1996, gold medalist 4x100 meters relay, 1996. Winner 100 meters, 200 meters USA/Mobil Track & Field Championships, 1995, 100 meters World Athletic Championships, 1995, Gold medal 100 meters, 200 meters Goodwill Games, 1995, Gold medal 4 x 100 meter relay Atlanta Olympics, 1996, Bronze medal 100 meters. *

TORRES, MARYANN, counselor; b. San Antonio, Oct. 9, 1969; d. José Acosta Torres and Patricia (Resch) Barnes; m. Larry James Hailey, Jr., Dec. 2, 1995. BS, Texas A&M U., 1991; MS, Texas A&I U., 1993. Lic. profl. counselor., Tex. Practicum counselor Tex. A&I U., 1992-93; counselor Navarro Coll., Kingsville, Tex., 1993—; practicum psychotherapist Spohn-Kleberg Psychiatric Ward, 1992. Mem. Am. Counseling Assn., Tex. Counseling Assn., Psi Beta (co-sponsor). Roman Catholic. Home: PO Box 1883 Corsicana TX 75151

TORRES, NORA ANGELA, electrical engineer, lawyer; b. N.Y.C., May 9, 1949; d. Edmund Rowan Blackadder and Sandra Felynna Tores; m. Miguel Jose Norte, Dec. 15, 1983; children: Carrie, Douglas, Sandra, Tyrus, Cyrus. BS, CCNY, 1970; MSEE, U. Minn., 1972; JD, John Marshall Law Sch., Chgo., 1993. Profl. engr., N.Y.; FCC radiotelephone lic. Engr. NASA, Houston, 1973-80, Bendix Field Engring., Greenbelt, Md., 1980-90; lawyer/engr. North Suburban Engring., Schaumburg, Ill., 1993—. Inventor electronic switching device used in microwave comm., 1982. Mem. NOW. Democrat. Office: North Suburban Engring 1613 Green River Dr Schaumburg IL 60194

TORRES-ULLAURI, MARIÁ ISABEL, banker; b. Valencia, Spain; d. José Manuel and Vicenta (Soriano) Mazás; m. Modesto Ignacio Torres-Ullauri. Student, U. Madrid; cert., Cambridge (Eng.) U.; BA, NYU; MBA, Adelphi U., 1977. Mgr. corp. banking Royal Bank Can., N.Y.C., 1975-85; v.p., rep. N.Am. Banque de la Soc. Financiere Europeenne, N.Y.C., 1986-90; v.p. pvt. banking Swiss Bank Corp., N.Y.C., 1990-93, dir., 1993—. Bd. dirs. Kennedy Child Study Ctr., N.Y.C., 1984-87; lectr. St. Patrick's Cathedral, N.Y.C., 1985—. Mem. Am. Mgmt. Assn., Univ. Club. Office: Swiss Bank Corp 10 E 50th St New York NY 10022-6831

TORREY, BARBARA BOYLE, research council administrator; b. Pensacola, Fla., Nov. 27, 1941; d. Peter F. and Elsie (Hansen) Boyle; m. E. Fuller Torrey, Mar. 23, 1968; children: Michael, Martha. BA, Stanford U., 1963, MS, 1970. Vol. Peace Corps, Tanzania, 1963-65; fiscal economist Office Mgmt. and Budget, Washington, 1970-80; dept. asst. sec. HHS, Washington, 1980-81; dir. Ctr. for Internat. Rsch., Census Bur., Washington, 1984-92; pres. Population Reference Bur., Washington, 1992-93; exec. dir. Commn. on Behavioral and Social Scis. and Edn., NRC, NAS, Washington, 1993—; bd. dirs. Luxembourg Income Study, 1984—. Co-editor: The Vulnerable, 1987, Population and Land Use, 1992; contbr. articles to profl. jours. Mem. Population Assn. Am. (bd. dirs. 1993—). Office: NRC 2101 Constitution Ave NW Washington DC 20418-0007

TORREZ, NAOMI ELIZABETH, copyright review editor, librarian; b. Scranton, Pa., July 3, 1939; d. Sterling E. and Naomi (Reynolds) Hess; m. Lupe F. Torrez, Dec. 23, 1961; children: Sterling Edward, Stanley Marshall. BA, U. Ariz., 1961; MA, U. Calif., Berkeley, 1964, MLS, 1970; DRE, Golden State Sch. Theology, Oakland, Calif., 1988; cert. in travel industry, Vista C.C., 1993. Libr. asst. Oakland Pub. Libr., 1966-67, U. Calif. Libr., Berkeley, 1967-70; tutor-cons. Sonoma State Hosp., Eldridge, Calif., 1973-77, libr. tech. asst., 1977-79; health scis. libr. Kaiser Hosp., Vallejo, Calif., 1979-87; copyright rev. editor Kaiser Dept. Med. Editing, Oakland, 1987—; former instr. Bay Cities Bible Inst., Oakland, Golden State Sch. Theology, Oakland; instr. Calif. Theol. Inst., 1996—; participant Statewide Latino Congress, 1994. Author: Not in My Pew, 1990, GSST Research Manual, 1990; contbr. to Co-op Low Cost Cookbook, 1965. Active Albany 75th Anniversary Com., 1983, Women's Health Initiative, 1995—; officer Ariz. Fedn. of the Blind, Calif. Coun. of the Blind, 1959-66. Woodrow Wilson fellow, 1961; winner Nat. Spelling Bee, 1953; Nat. Merit scholar, 1957-61. Mem. Kaiser Permanente Latino Assn., Kaiser Affirmative Action Com., Kaiser Health Edn. Com., K.P. Regional Librs. Group (chair 1988), Phi Beta Kappa, Phi Kappa Phi. Baptist. Home: 1009 Murrieta Blvd # 15 Livermore CA 94550-4134 Office: Kaiser Dept Med Editing 1800 Harrison St Fl 16 Oakland CA 94612-3429

TORRIANI, ANNA M., architect; came to U.S., 1980; d. Mario and Janet T. MArch, Eidgenossische Tech., 1978. Project architect Mario Botta, Switzerland, 1976, Paul Rudolph, N.Y.C., 1980; project mgr. Pasanella & Klein, N.Y.C., 1981-84, Prentice, Chan, Ohlhausen, N.Y.C., 1984-87; sr. project mgr. Beyer, Blinder, Belle, N.Y.C., 1987-90; prin. pvt. practice, N.Y.C., 1990—; v.p. Waterford Bd., N.Y.C., 1990—. One woman shows include Swiss Inst., 1990. Recipient 1st prize Mcpl. Art Soc. for N.Y. Waterfront, 1988. Mem. AIA, Swiss Inst. Architects and Engrs. Office: 300 E 93d St New York NY 10128

TORSEN, MARILYN JOANNE, counselor; b. Portland, Oreg., Feb. 26, 1937; d. Leighton Eugene and Dorris Mary (Scott) Roy; m. Ricahrd Morris Torsen, June 22, 1958; children: Michelle, Danielle, Chantelle. BS in Home Econs., Oreg. State U., 1964; MS in Counseling, Calif. State U., Hayward, 1989. Crisis intervention counselor Contact-Care, Lafayette, Calif., 1982-84; pregnancy counselor Planned Parenthood, Walnut Creek, Calif., 1984-87; counselor Family Counseling Svc., Walnut Creek, 1986-87; hospice team mem. Farmington Valley Hospice, Simsbury, Conn., 1988-90; youth svcs. coord. Town of East Granby, Conn., 1990-91; vol. coord. City of Oregon City, Oreg., 1993-94; co-chair Clackamas County Youth Issues and Planning Com., Oregon City, 1991—; steering com. Youth Gangs Task Force, Oregon City, 1992-94. Editor (newsletter) Focal Point, 1993-94 (2nd place 1994); author of poetry. Chair Status on Women, Concord, Calif., 1986; mem. Pub. Facilities Task Force, West Linn, Oreg., 1992, Recycling/Solid Waste Com., West Linn, 1996; group leader, mem. Vision Com., West Linn, 1992-93. Mem. AAUW (state diversity task force 1994-96). Home: 19685 Sun Circle West Linn OR 97068

TORZECKA-DANILEWICZ, MARZENA (MARLENA TORZECKA), artist representative, journalist; b. Warsaw, Jan. 29, 1956; came to the U.S., 1983; d. Wieslaw and Krystyna (Szczekocka) Mystek; m. Tadeusz Torzecki, Sept. 29, 1980 (div. Aug. 1986); 1 child, Michael Torzecki; m. Tomasz Danilewicz, Sept. 23, 1994. MA, Warsaw U., 1979. Journalist Sztandar Mtodych, Warsaw, 1979-81, Polish Daily Newspaper, Chgo., 1984-85, N.Y. Polish Daily, 1986-87; editl. asst. European Travel & Life Mag., N.Y., 1988-89; artist rep. Marlena Agy., N.Y., 1990-96, Princeton, 1996—. Home and Office: Marlena Agy 278 Hamilton Ave Princeton NJ 08540

TOSI, LAURA LOWE, orthopaedic surgeon; b. N.Y.C., Mar. 25, 1949; d. Jerome Richard T. and Deborah Thornton (Prouty) Rogers; m. David S.C. Chu, Apr. 1, 1978. BA, Boston U., 1971; MD, Harvard U., 1977. Orthopaedic surgeon Children's Nat. Med. Ctr., Washington, 1984—; asst. prof. orthopaedic surgery George Washington U., Washington, 1984—. Fellow Am. Acad. Cerebral Palsy and Devel. Medicine, Am. Acad. Orthopaedic Surgeons (bd. dirs. 1994-95); mem. Acad. Orthopaedic Soc., Pediatric Orthopaedic Soc. N.Am. (bd.dirs. 1990-91), Ruth Jackson Orthopaedic Soc. (treas. 1987-90, v.p. 1990-91, pres. 1991-92), Orthopaedic Rsch. & Edn. Found. (bd. trustees 1995—). Office: Children's Nat Med Ctr 111 Michigan Ave NW Washington DC 20010

TOSSELL, RENEE FAYHE, radiologic technology educator, consultant; b. District Heights, Md., Jan. 25, 1958; d. Donald Lee and Katharine Renate (Stahl) Keller; m. Larry James Tossell, Febr. 19, 1994. BS in Med. Radiography, No. Ariz. U., Flagstaff, 1979, MA in Vocat. Edn., 1987; postgrad., U. Ariz., 1994—. Cert. community coll. tchr.; diplomate Am. Registry of Radiologic Technologists; cert. in mammography and cardiovascular intervention. Staff technologist No. Ariz. Radiology P.C., Flagstaff, 1980-89; chief technologist Sells (Ariz) Indian Hosp., 1990-91; instr. Pima C.C., Tucson, 1991—; postgrad. educator sectional anatomy for computer tomography and magnetic resonance imaging correlation Pima C.C., 1993—; cons. Med. Radiologic Tech. Bd. Examiners, Tempe, Ariz., 1993—. Author articles. Recipient awards for essays and exhibits. Mem. Ariz. State Soc. Radiologic Technology (treas. 1987-88, v.p. 1988-89, pres.-elect Dist. II 1990-91), Assn. Collegiate Educators in Radiologic Technology (environ. health and safety 1992—, profl. devel. com. 1993—, think tank com. 1996—). Republican. Baptist. Office: Pima CC 2202 W Anklam Rd Tucson AZ 85709-0080

TOSTI, SALLY T., artist, educator; b. Scranton, Pa., Jan. 21, 1946; d. Ivan and Helen (Odell) Thompson; m. Robert Matthew Tosti, May 3, 1974; 1 child, Jennifer Marie. BS in Art Edn., Ind. (Pa.) U., 1967, postgrad., Tyler Sch. Art, 1969-70; MFA in Drawing and Painting, Marywood Coll., 1985. Art tchr. Bristol Twp. Schs., Levittown, Pa., 1967-69, Ctrl. Bucks Schs., Doylestown, Pa., 1971; adj. faculty Marywood Coll., Scranton, Pa., 1986-87; art coord. Keystone Coll., LaPlume, Pa., 1991-96, adj. faculty, 1995—. Exhbns. include San Diego Art Inst., 1993-94, Allentown (Pa.) Art Mus., Abercombie Gallerie, 1994, Lakeview Mus., 1995, U. Tex., Tyler, 1995-96, Linder Art Gallery, 1994—, State Mus. Pa., Harrisburg, 1994-96, Haggin Mus., Stockton, Calif., 1996, Fla. Printmakers Soc. Traveling Exhbn., 1995-96, So. Graphics Traveling Exbhn., 1996—. Active Countryside Conservancy, Waverly, Pa. Grantee Pa. Coun. Arts, 1995; F. Lammot Belin Arts scholar, 1996. Mem. Waverly Womans Club, Print Club Phila., So. Graphics Coun., Am. Print Alliance, Womens Studio Workshop, Everhart Mus. Democrat. Home: PO Box 776 Waverly PA 18471

TOTENBERG, NINA, journalist; b. N.Y.C., Jan. 14, 1944, d. Roman and Melanie (Shroder) T.; m. Floyd Haskell, Feb. 3, 1979. Student, Boston U.; LLD (hon.), Haverford Coll., Chatham Coll., Gonzaga U., Northeastern U., St. Mary's, SUNY; LHD, Lebanon Valley Coll., Westfield State Coll. Reporter Boston Record Am., 1965, Peabody Times, 1967, Nat. Observer, 1968-71, Newtimes, 1973, Nat. Pub. Radio, Washington, 1974—, Inside Washington, 1992—; reporter Nightline ABC, 1993—. contbr. articles to N.Y. Times Mag., Harvard Law Rev., Christian Sci. Monitor, N.Y. Mag., Parade. Recipient Alfred I. Dupont award Columbia U., 1988, George Foster Peabook award, 1991, George Polk award, 1991, Joan Barne award, 1991, Silver Gavel award ABA, 1991, Woman of Courage award Women in Film, 1991, Athena award, 1994. Mem. Sigma Delta Chi. Office: NPR 635 Massachusetts Ave NW Washington DC 20001-3753*

TOTER, KIMBERLY MROWIEC, nurse; b. Chgo., Apr. 22, 1956; d. A. Kenneth and Megan Dawson (Schiefer) Mrowiec; m. William Frank Toter, Dec. 16, 1978; children: William Kenneth, Kimberly Helen, Tod Frank, Matthew Jonathan, Haley Victoria, Toria Megan. BS in Biology, Millikin U., 1978; cert. sch. nursing, Decatur (Ill.) Meml. Hosp., 1978. RN, Ill.; cert. operating room nurse. Oper. room nurse Riddle Meml. Hosp., Media, Pa., 1979-89; pres., chief exec. officer Towic Med., Inc., Park Ridge, Ill., 1986—; staff nurse oper. room Luth. Gen. Hosp., Park Ridge, 1991; perioperative nurse, 1991—; instr. Delaware Community Coll., Media, 1986; reviewer, cons. Perioperative Nursing Care Planning; speaker laparoscopy seminar Luth. Gen. Hosp., 1992, 93. Contbg. author: Decision Making in Perioperative Nursing, 1987; also articles; patentee gastric drainage system. Cheerleading coach St. Paul of the Cross, 1993—. Recipient Young Alumnus of Yr. award Millikin U., 1991. Mem. Assn. Operat. Rm. Nurses (v.p. Southeast Pa. chpt. 1983-85, pres.-elect 1985-86, pres. 1986-87, ednl. chmn. 1983-85, chmn. bylaw and policy com. 1987—, bd. dirs. 1983-89, chmn. 1987-89, bd. dirs. NW suburban chpt. 1995—), Pa. Coun. Oper. Rm. Nurses, Am. Tech Mgmt. (bd. dirs. 1989—), Am. Reprographics Mgmt. (bd. dirs. 1989—), Pi Beta Phi. Roman Catholic.

TOTH, HEIDI MARIE, school nurse; b. Elizabeth, N.J., Aug. 6, 1962; d. Sandor and Gertrud Kertesz; m. Kenneth J. Toth, June 20, 1982; children: Kellie Marie, Brittany Suzanne. AAS, Middlesex County Coll., 1983; BSN, Monmouth Coll., 1990. Cert. infection control; cert. post anesthesia nurse; cert. ACLS. Staff nurse, team leader Alexian Bros. Hosp., Elizabeth, N.J., 1983-86; charge nurse, post anesthesia nurse Riverview Med. Ctr., Red Bank, N.J., 1986-88; infection control practitioner Riverview Med. Ctr., Red Bank, 1988-91, post anesthesia nurse, 1991-92, 93—, infection control coord., 1992-93; sch. nurse Carteret (N.J.) Pub. Schs., 1995-96, Red Bank Regional H.S., Little Silver, N.J., 1996—. Daisy co-leader Girl Scouts, Middletown, N.J., 1991; PTA mem. Lincroft Sch., Middletown, 1992—, nature tchr., 1994; rm. mother Lincroft and New Monmouth Schs., Middletown, 1993—. Monmouth Pk. scholar Monmouth Coll., West Long Branch, N.J., 1988-89. Mem. Nat. Soc. for Post Anesthesia Nurses, N.J. Soc. for Post Anesthesia Nurses (corr. sec. 1986-87), Nat. Assn. for Practitioners in Infection Ctrl., So. N.J. Chpt. Assn. for Practititioners in Infection Ctrl., Nat. Assn. for Sch. Nurses, N.J. Assn. for Sch. Nurses, Sigma Theta Tau (Delta chpt.). Roman Catholic. Office: Red Bank Regional HS 101 Ridge Ave Little Silver NJ 07739

TOTTEN, GLORIA JEAN (DOLLY TOTTEN), real estate executive, financial consultant; b. Port Huron, Mich., Sept. 23, 1943; d. Lewis Elmer and Inez Eugenia (Houston) King; m. Donald Ray Totten, Feb. 5, 1961 (div. Apr. 1981); children: D. Erik, Angela J. Totten Sales, Kymberly D. Totten DiVita. Student, Patricia Stevens Modeling Sch., Detroit, 1976-79, Gold Coast Sch., West Palm Beach, Fla., 1988; degree in mktg., St. Clair County Coll., Port Huron, Mich., 1979. Lic. real estate saleswoman, Fla., Mich. Demonstrator, saleswoman Hoover Co., 1969-75; instr., promoter Port Huron Sch. Bus., 1973-75; real estate borker Select Realty, Port Huron, 1979-81, Earn Keim Realty, Port Huron, 1981-83, Schweitzer's Better Homes and Gardens, Marysville, Mich., 1983-86, Coldwell Banker Property Concepts Corp., North Palm Beach, Fla., 1986-94; pres., broker, owner Dolly Totten Real Estate Inc., West Palm Beach, Fla., 1994—; model, instr. Patricia Stevens Modeling Sch., Troy, Mich., 1972-75; beauty cons. Mary Kay Cosmetics, 1982—. Grantee Mich. State U., 1972. Mem. Nat. Assn. Realtors, North Palm Beach Rd. Realtors, Million Dollar Club (Port Huron chpt.), Women's Coun. Realtors (co-founder Port Huron chpt.). Home and Office: 515 Evergreen Dr Lake Park FL 33403

TOTTEN, MARY ANNE, internist; b. Topeka, May 22, 1946; d. Frederick Eugene Totten and Mildred Roberta (Johnson) Black. BA in Microbiology, U. Kans., 1968, MD, 1972; MPH, Boston U., 1984. Am. Bd. Internal Medicine, Nat. Bd. Med. Examiners. Intern in internal medicine Hosp. of St. Raphael, New Haven, 1972-73; resident New Eng. Deaconess Hosp., Boston, 1973-75; fellow in endocrinology and metabolism Lahey Clinic Found., Burlington, Mass., 1975-76; fellow in diabetes Joslin Clinic, Boston, 1976-77; instr. medicine Boston U. Med. Ctr., 1977-83, asst. clin. prof., 1983-84; staff physician in gen. internal medicine Boston City Hosp., 1977-80; staff physician endocrinology Boston Hosp., 1977-84; dir. diabetes treatment and rehab. unit Mattapan (Mass.) Hosp., 1982-84; staff physician St. Joseph's Hosp., Parkersburg, W.Va., 1984—, chmn. dept. internal medicine, 1989-91, med. dir. skilled nursing unit, 1992—, pres. med. staff, 1995—; staff physician Camden Clark Meml. Hosp., Parkersburg, 1984—, chair diabetes mgmt. com., 1990-93; physician liaison advisor to Diabetes Care Task Force, 1994—, sec. to med. staff, 1994-95; mem. del. diabetes educators People to People Tour, USSR and People's Republic of China, 1987. Author, editor: Case Studies for Nurses and Nurse Practitioners, 1990; contbr. articles to med. jours. Bd. dirs., mem. YWA, Parkersburg, 1986-87. Recipient Physician Recognition award AMA, 1987, 90, Trailblazing Women of the Yr award YWCA and Altrusa, 1988, Leadership Devel. award Parkersburg C. of C., 1990. Fellow ACP (mem. Gov.'s Coun. W.Va. 1990-91); mem. Am. Diabetes Assn. (bd. dirs. W.Va. 1987-89), W.Va. Med. Assn., Parkersburg Area Diabetes Assn. (pres. 1988-90, bd. dirs. 1991-92), Parkersburg Acad. Medicine. Methodist. Office: Primary Health Care Inc Ste 303 600 18th St Parkersburg WV 26101-3235

TOUBORG, MARGARET EARLEY BOWERS, non-profit executive; b. Rome, N.Y., Aug. 12, 1941; d. George Thomas and Margaret Earley (Brown) Bowers; m. Jens Touborg, Sept. 9, 1961 (div. 1985); children: Margaret Earley, Anne Touborg Zimmer, Sarah Touborg Moyers, Peter Nicolai. AB magna cum laude, Radcliffe Coll., 1965; MEd, Harvard U., 1984. Asst. to pres. Radcliffe Coll., Cambridge, Mass., 1984-86, exec. asst. to pres., 1986-87, dir. corp. and found. relations, 1988-89; pres. U. Cape Town Fund, Inc., N.Y.C., 1989—; sr. project dir. Open Soc. Scholars Fund, N.Y.C., 1989—; bd. dirs. Technoserve, Inc. Trustee The Trinity Sch., N.Y.C., 1994—, Bemis Lectr. Series, Lincoln, Mass., 1982-85; nat. cons. Schlesinger Libr. on History of Women in Am., 1995—; assoc. chmn. edn. div. United Way Mass., 1986; mem. South African adv. com. New Eng. Bd. Higher Edn., 1987—. Mem. Harvard Club N.Y.C., Phi Beta Kappa (chmn. com. hon. membership 1976-94). Episcopalian. Office: 441 Lexington Ave New York NY 10017-3910

TOUBY, LINDA, artist; b. Bklyn.; d. Nat and Cele Touby; m. Barry Michael Schwartz, Dec. 24, 1964 (div. 1981); 1 child, Jaqueline. BFA, Pratt Inst., 1964; postgrad., Nat. Acad., N.Y.C., 1976, Art Students League, N.Y.C., 1990. Pvt. tchr. Art, N.Y.C., 1990—. Author, illustrator (children's books): Sasaphras, 1974, Up, Up and Away, 1980; illustrator. Glimmerings (Zack Ragow), 1978; one-woman shows: Alex Gallery, Washington, 1991, 95, Works in Progress Gallery, Delray, Fla., 1992, Tribeca Gallery, N.Y.C., 1992, 93, La Mama La Galleria, N.Y.C., 1993, 95, Novart Gallery, Madrid, 1996; exhibited in numerous group shows, including Ester Robinson Gallery, N.Y.C., 1986-87, Wetherholt Gallery, Washington, 1990, 91, Mus. Realism and Atheism, Lvov, Ukraine, 1990, La Mama Gallery, N.Y.C., 1991, Alex Gallery, 1991-95, Provincetown (Mass.) Art Assn. and Mus., 1992-95, Albert-Knox Art Gallery, Buffalo, 1995, Broome Street Gallery, N.Y.C., 1992, Tribeca Gallery, 1992, 93, Rice/Polak Gallery, Provincetown, 1992-95, Gallerie Roseg, St. Moritz, Switzerland, 1993, Eva Cohon Gallery LTD., Chgo., 1993, 94, Mus. Gallery, Boca Raton, Fla., 1993, Madelyn Jordon Gallery, N.Y.C., 1993, 94, Artspace/Virginia Miller Galleries, Coral Gables, Fla., 1994, 95, Goya Art Gallery, N.Y.C., 1995, Kouros Gallery, N.Y.C., 1995, Bill Hodges Gallery, N.Y.C., 1996; permanent collections: Lorimar Telepictures, Antonio Morales, Correo del Arte Publisher, Spain, Danforth Mus. of Fine Arts, Framingham, Mass. Grantee Change, Inc., 1995. Mem. Art Students League (life, Reilly scholar 1984). Studio: 500 W 52d St New York NY 10019

TOUCHSTONE, MARTHA JONES, retired public relations executive, volunteer; b. Detroit, Nov. 3, 1948; d. Robert Everett and Bess Alice (Johnson) Jones; m. John N. Touchstone, Jan. 24, 1987. Student, Williams Coll., 1969; BA, Vassar Coll., 1970. With radio and TV news dept. Burson Marsteller, N.Y.C., 1974; account exec. Hill & Knowlton, N.Y.C., 1975-78; dir. public relations and environ. affairs Fla. Phosphate Council, Lakeland, 1978-81; pres. Jones & Assocs., Lakeland, 1981-87, Houston, 1987-94. Apptd. commr. edn. Fla. Adv. Council on Sci. Edn., 1979, vice chmn., 1980-81, chmn., 1981-82; mem. Gov.'s Task Force on Phosphate-Related Radiation, 1979-80; trustee Learning Resource Ctr., Lakeland, 1979-82; bd. dirs. Campfire Inc., Lakeland, 1982-85; mem. Lakeland Young Life Council, 1985; del. Diocesan Conv., St. Stephen's Episcopal Ch., 1982-85, lay reader, 1983-86, mem. vestry, 1984-86; mem. adv. council Fla. Defenders of Environ., 1980, United Way, 1980, Hist. Lakeland, 1979-80, Fla. Assn. Sci. Tchrs., 1981; active Leadership Lakeland, 1985-86, Diana Wortham Theatre Star Chamber, Asheville, 1995-96, Pack Pl. Mktg. com., 1995—; master gardener vol., Asheville, 1996— . Recipient nat. 1st place Addy award Am. Advt. Fedn., 1978. Mem. Fla. Pub. Relations Assn. (bd. dirs. Polk chpt. 1983-84, Golden Image awards 1979-80, 82, Grand All Fla. award 1982), Leadership Lakeland, Lakeland C. of C., Jr. League Asheville, Country Club Asheville. Episcopalian. Home and Office: 51 Jump Cove Rd Weaverville NC 28787-9440 also: 1223 Augusta Dr Apt 21 Houston TX 77057-2232

TOUGAS, JENNIFER, massage therapist; b. Artesia, N.Mex., Sept. 19, 1956; d. Charles A. Tougas and Marilyn Eaton; m. Randal Williams (div. Mar. 1992). Massage therapist Amado, Ariz., 1978; asst. to chiropractor Green Valley, Ariz., 1980-81; asst. to dental lab. Amado, 1981-82; massage therapist Tubac, Ariz., 1979—. Basic flight instr. Flying W Ranch, Tubac, 1996—; Copperstate Ultralight chair divsn. Exptl. Aviation Assn., 1996, Chandler; singer, vol. Tubac Ctr. of Arts, 1983-96; mem., bd. dirs. Friends of Santa Cruz River, Tubac, 1993-96. Mem. Tucson Ultralight Club (newsletter editor 1988—), Tumbleweed Flying Club (sec.). Home: PO Box 32 Tumacacori AZ 85640

TOURANGEAU, BERNADETTE, religious organization administrator. Dir. religious edn. Roman Cath. Ch. in Can. Office: 90 Parent Ave, Ottawa, ON Canada KIN 7B1*

TOURTILLOTT, ELEANOR ALICE, nurse, educational consultant; b. North Hampton, N.H., Mar. 28, 1909; d. Herbert Shaw and Sarah (Fife) T. Diploma Melrose Hosp. Sch. Nursing, Melrose, Mass., 1930; BS, Columbia U., 1948, MA, 1949; edn. specialist Wayne State U., 1962. RN. Gen. pvt. duty nurse, Melrose, Mass., 1930-35; obstet. supr. Samaritan Hosp., Troy, N.Y., 1935-36, Meml. Hosp., Niagara Falls, N.Y., 1937-38, Lawrence Meml. Hosp., New London, Conn., 1939-42, New Eng. Hosp. for Women and Children, Boston, 1942-43; dir. H. W. Smith Sch. Practical Nursing, Syracuse, N.Y., 1949-53; founder, dir. assoc. degree nursing program Henry

Ford Community Coll., Dearborn, Mich., 1953-74; dir. pioneering use of learning techs. via mixed media USPHS, 1966-71; prin. cons., initial coord. Wayne State U. Coll. Nursing, Detroit, 1975-78; cons. curriculum design, modular devel., instructional media Tourtillott Cons., Inc., Dearborn, Mich., 1974—; condr. numerous workshops on curriculum design, instructional media at various colls., 1966—; mem. Mich. Bd. Nursing, 1966-73, chmn., 1970-72, mem. rev. com. for constrn. nurse tng. facilities, div. nursing USPHS, 1967-70, mem. nat. adv. coun. on nurse tng., Dept. Health Edn. and Welfare, 1972-76. Author: Commitment-A Lost Characteristic, 1982; contbg. co-author: Patient Assessment-History and Physical Examination, 1975-78; contbr. chpts., articles, speeches to profl. publs. Served to capt. Nurse Corps, U.S. Army, 1943-47; ETO. Recipient Disting. Alumnae award Tchrs. Coll. Columbia U., 1974, Spl. tribute 77th Legislature Mich., 1974, Disting. Alumnae award Wayne State U., 1975, Disting. Service award Henry Ford Community Coll., 1982; established and endowed Eleanor Tourtillott Outstanding Student Nurse of Yr. award at Henry Ford C.C., 1993. Mem. DAR, ANA, Nat. League Nursing (chmn. steering com. dept. assoc. degree programs 1965-67, bd. dirs. 1965-67, 71-73, mem. assembly constituent leagues 1971-73, council assoc. degree programs citation 1974, Mildred Montag Excellence in Leadership award coun. assoc. degree programs 1994), Mich. League for Nursing (pres. 1969-71), Mich. Acad. Sci., Arts and Letters, Am. Legion, Tchrs. Coll. Alumnae Assn., Wayne State U. Alumnae Assn., Phi Lambda Theta, Kappa Delta Pi.

TOUSSAINT, THERESA MARIE, cable company sales official; b. Washington, Dec. 22, 1964; d. Raymond William Toussaint and Judith K. (Bragg) Horrocks; 1 child, Shannon Marie. Student, Berea Coll., 1984. Saleswoman, booking agt. Omni Entertainment, Orlando, Fla., 1987-92; comml. and corp. saleswoman Media Gen. Cable, Chantilly, Va., 1992—. Mem. NAFE, Women in Telecom., Cable TV and Mktg. Assn. (sec. to pres. Balt.-Washington chpt.), Women in Arts, Washington Performing Arts. Republican. Methodist.

TOUSSIENG, YOLANDA, make-up artist. television work includes: (movies) Fallen Angel, 1981, Blue de Ville, 1986, (series) Pee-wee's Playhouse, 1986, (mini-series) North and South, Book II, 1986; films include: Blue City, 1986, No Man's Land, 1987, Beetlejuice, 1988, Gross Anatomy, 1989, Three Fugitives, 1989, Farewell to the King, 1989, Edward Scissorhands, 1990, Flatliners, 1990, Everybody Wins, 1990, Hoffa, 1992, Batman Returns, 1992, Mrs. Doubtfire, 1993, Rising Sun, 1993, Ed Wood, 1994 (Acad. award for Best Make-up 1994), Being Human, 1994, Junior, 1994. Office: IATSE Local 706 11519 Chandler Blvd North Hollywood CA 91601-2618*

TOVAR, CAROLE L., real estate management administrator; b. Toppenish, Wash., May 19, 1940; d. Harold Max and Gertrude Louisa (Spicer) Smith; m. Duane E. Clark, Aug. 1959 (div. 1963); 1 child, David Allen; m. Vance William Gribble, May 19, 1966 (div. 1989), m. Conrad T. Tovar, June 25, 1992. Student, Seattle Pacific Coll. Cert. profl. exec.; cert. profl. of occupancy. With B.F. Shearer, Seattle, 1959-60, Standard Oil, Seattle, 1960-62, Seattle Platen Co., 1962-70; ptnr. West Coast Platen, Los Angeles, 1970-87, Waldorf Towers Apts., Seattle, 1970—, Cascade Golf Course, North Bend, Wash., 1970-88; co-owner Pacific Wholesale Office Equipment, Seattle and L.A., 1972-87; owner Pacific Wholesale Office Equip., Seattle, L.A. and San Pablo, Calif., 1988-92, Pac Electronic Service Ctr., Commerce and San Pablo, Calif., 1988-90, Waldorf Mgmt. Co. dba Tovar Mgmt. Co., 1988—; Tovar Properties, 1993—. Mem. Nat. Ctr. Housing Mgmt. (cert. occupancy specialist), Assisted Housing Mgmt. Assn. (nat. cert., Wash. bd. dirs. 1995-96). Methodist. Office: 706 Pike St Seattle WA 98101-2301

TOVES, JO ANN VILLAMOR, nursing supervisor; b. Tamuning, Guam, May 14, 1955; d. James Gazer and Rosario Villamor; m. Pedro G. Toves, Feb. 8, 1975; children: Peter Justin, Paul Jay Henri, Francisco James. ASN, U. Guam, Mangilao, 1976, BSN magna cum laude, 1991. RN; cert. emergency nurse, cmty. health nurse, BLS, ACLS, neonatal resuscitation program, Pediatric Advanced Life Support, Trauma Nursing Core Course. Nurse Guam Meml. Hosp., Tamuning, 1976-77, LPN, 1977-78, emergency nurse, 1979-86, 92; cmty. health nurse Dept. Pub. Health, Mangilao, 1986-89, emergency nurse supr., 1993-95; clin. assoc. preceptorship program U. Guam, 1996. Mem. Father Duenas Booster Club, Mangilao, 1994, GNA Immunization Campaign, 1994. Regents scholar U. Guam, Mangilao, 1990. Mem. Am./Guam Nurses Assn., Emergency Nurses Assn. Roman Catholic. Home: 128 Etton Ln Sinajana GU 96926-4207

TOWER, RONI BETH, psychologist; b. Akron, Ohio, Dec. 11, 1943; d. Arnold Edward Weinstein and Elva Hermoine (Gross) MacRae; children: Jennifer, Daniel. BA, Barnard Coll., N.Y.C., 1964; MS, Yale U., 1977, M in Philosphy, 1979, PhD, 1980. Lic. in clin. psychology, Conn., Maine; diplomate Clin. Psychology Am. Bd. Profl. Psychology. Psychologist Silver Hill Found., New Canaan, Conn., 1979-81; pvt. practice Westport, Conn., 1981—; rsch. affiliate dept. epidemiology Yale U., New Haven, 1995—; lectr. in psychology Yale U., New Haven, 1981-89, Am. Bd. Profl. Psychology seminar, Washington, 1990; cons. in field. Cons. editor Jour. of Imagination Cognition and Personality, 1983—; contbr. numerous articles to profl. jours. Active Yale Alumni Fund Bd. Recipient Traineeship award USPHS, 1979-80; postdoctoral fellow Yale Sch. Epidemiology and Pub. Health, 1992-95. Mem. LWV, Am. Assn. for Study of Mental Imagery (pres. 1988-89, conf. organizer New Haven 1988), Am. Psychol. Assn., Am. Psychol. Soc., Conn. Psychol. Assn., Sigma Xi. Office: Yale Univ Dept Epidemiology 60 College St New Haven CT 06510-3210

TOWER, SUE WARNCKE, artist; b. Seattle, Mar. 25, 1940; d. Edgar Dean and Ione Althea (Smith) T.; m. Donald Frank Speyer, Dec. 31, 1958 (div. June 1968); children: Stacy, Monte. BFA, Pacific N.W. Coll. Art, 1982. vis. artist So. Oreg. State Coll., 1996; performing artist (slide presentation) Oreg. Arts Commn. Arts-in-Edn. Program, Salem region, 1996-98; featured artist Oreg. Symphony's Composer Program Cover Art Project, 1996. One woman exhibits include Jacobs Gallery Hult Ctr. Performing Arts, Eugene, Oreg., 1993, Littman Gallery, Portland (Oreg.) State U., 1994, BICC Libr., Oreg. Health Scis. U., 1994, City of Las Vegas Reed Whipple Cultural Ctr., 1996; group exhibits inlcude Bellvue Art Mus., 1992, Galerie Bratri Capku and The Okresni Mus., Prague and Jicin, Czech Republic, 1995, State Capital, Salem, Oreg., 1995. Fundraiser, donor Blackfish Gallery, Pacific N.W. Coll. Art, 1994; donor Cascade AIDS Project Benefit Art Auction, 1996.

TOWERS, MARSHA CAROL, commercial attache; b. N.Y.C., Nov. 4, 1945; d. Abner A. Towers and Marica (Cok) Miller; m. William Baer Endictor, Dec. 27, 1975 (div.). AB, Randolph-Macon Women's Coll., 1967; diplome superior, Sorbonne U., Paris, 1971; MBA, Ga. State U., 1978. Exec. trainee Macy's Dept. Store, Atlanta, 1967-70; clk. Orgn. for Econ. Coop. and Devel., Paris, 1971; sales rep. World Airways, Atlanta, 1972-75; dist. mgr. sales Overseas Nat. Airways, Atlanta, 1975, The Davis Agy., Atlanta, 1976; comml. attache Govt. of Quebec (Can.), Atlanta, 1979-96; ret., 1996. Active Paul Coverdell for Senator campaign, Atlanta, 1968-70. Mem. Can.-Am. Soc. (bd. dirs.), Atlanta Women in Internat. Trade (pres. 1992-93), Atlanta Women's Network, World Trade Club Atlanta (sec. bd. dirs. 1991-92), Randolpha-Macon Women's Coll. Alumni Assn. (Atlanta chpt.). Episcopalian.

TOWNE, PAULA RYSEWYK, artist; b. Rochester, N.Y., July 18, 1948; d. Charles John and Helen Kathrine (Johnson) Rysewyk; m. Jack Wolak, June 29, 1969 (div.); children: Jessie Wolak, Mason Wolak; m. Greg Langevin, June 18, 1982 (div.); children: Clinton Langevin, Daniel Langevin. AA, Mohawk Valley C.C., 1968. One-woman show: Frederick Remington Mus., Odgenburg, N.Y., 1981; various group shows; cartoonist: The Fedwells, Gouverneur Tribune Press, 1996—; author: Collecting with Esther and Smiley, 1994. Home and Office: Trinkets Art Gallery Studio & Printing Shop 26 Barnes St Gouverneur NY 13642

TOWNE, SARAH PATTON, physician; b. Fountain Hill, Pa., Aug. 28, 1953; d. William Frank and Arline Rose (Patton) T. Degree in Nursing, Geisinger Med. Ctr., Danville, Pa., 1973; BS magna cum laude, Kutztown U. Pa., 1988; DO, Phila. Coll. Osteo. Medicine, Phila., 1992; MSc in Family Practice, Ohila. Coll. Osteo. Medicine, 1995. Diplomate Nat. Bd. Osteo. Med. Examiners. Psychiatric nurse Allentown (Pa.) State Hosp., 1973-76, N.W. Inst. Psychiatry, Ft. Washington, Pa., 1976-78; RN, psychotherapist Boulder (Colo.) County Mental Health Ctr., 1979-85; intern Phila. Coll. Osteo. Medicine, 1992-93, resident in family practice, 1993-95; physician Troup (Tex.) Family Practice, 1995—; physician Harleysville (Pa.) Med. Assn., 1993-95. Bd. dirs. Boulder County Rape Crisis Team, 1979-81. Mem. Am. Osteo Assn., Am. Coll. Family Practitioners, Am. Coll. Osteo. Family Practitioners (bd. cert.), Pa. Osteo. Med. Assn., Pa. Osteo. Gen. Practitioners Soc., Tex. Med. Assn. Home: 1901 S Chilton St Tyler TX 75701 Office: Troup Family Practice 201 S Railroad St Troup TX 75789

TOWNER, MARGARET ELLEN, retired minister; b. Columbia, Mo., Mar. 19, 1925; d. Milton Carsley and Dorothy Marie (Schloeman) T. BA, Carleton Coll., 1948; MDiv, Union/Auburn Theol. Sem., 1954; MA in Guidance and Counseling, Western Mich. U., 1967; DDiv (hon.), Carroll Coll., 1989. Ordained to ministry, Presbyn. Ch., 1956. Dir. Christian edn. Takoma Park (Md.) Presbyn. Ch., 1954-55; min. of edn. 1st Presbyn. Ch., Allentown, Pa., 1955-58; assoc. pastor 1st Presbyn. Ch., Kalamazoo, Mich., 1958-69, Northminster Presbyn. Ch., Indpls., 1970-72; exec. dir. Kalamazoo YWCA, 1969-70; co-pastor Kettle Moraine Parish, Waukesha County, Wis., 1973-90; ret., 1990; mem. Christian edn. and youth coms. Washington City, Lehigh, Western and So. Mich. Presbyteries; chair synod sch. com. Synod of Mich.; mem. nominating com. Whitewater Presbytery, Ind.; mem. adv. com. on discipleship and worship Gen. Assembly Mission Coun., commr., 1965-81, vice moderator, mem. spl. com. to study nature of the ch. and practice of governance; chair Synod of Lakes and Prairies Comprehensive Rev. Com.; mem. coun. advisors Dubuque Theol. Sem. Contbr. articles, photographs to profl. publs. Pres. Timberlakes Homeowners Assn., Sarasota, 1992-95, Lakes Maintenance Bd., Sarasota, 1994-96; chair bd. trustees Camp Brainerd, Pa., 1955-56; mem. Sch. of Faith Com. and Faculty Greater Washington Coun. of Chs.; dean, dir. Coun. of Chs. Leadership Schs., Kalamazoo, mem. radio-TV, C.E. and youth coms., pub. sch. com.; mem. cmty. com. UNICEF; bd. dirs. Planned Parenthood; mem. inter-agy. exec. com. HEW, Kalamazoo; mem. Japan Internat. Christian U. Indpls. Com.; chair, vol. chaplain emergency rm. Waukesha Meml. Hosp., Meml. Hosp. of Oconomowoc, Wis. Recipient Disting. Alumnus award Carleton Coll., 1983. Mem. PEO (guard, historian 1972—), Nat. Assn. Presbyn. Clergywomen. Home and Office: 4580 Trails Dr Sarasota FL 34232-3461

TOWNSEND, ALAIR ANE, municipal official; b. Rochester, N.Y., Feb. 15, 1942; d. Harold Eugene and Dorothy (Sharpe) T.; m. Robert Harris, Dec. 31, 1970 (div. 1994). BS, Elmira Coll., 1962; MS, U. Wis., 1964; postgrad. Columbia U., 1970-71. Assoc. dir. budget priorities Com. on Budget, U.S. Ho. of Reps., Washington, 1975-79; dep. asst. sec. for budget HEW, Washington, 1979-80, asst. sec. for mgmt. and budget, 1980-81; dir. N.Y.C. Office Mgmt. and Budget, 1981-85; dep. mayor for fin. and econ. devel. City of N.Y., 1985-89; pub. Crain's N.Y. Bus., N.Y.C., 1989—; former vice chmn., trustee Elmira Coll.; former mem. Coun. on Fgn. Rels.; bd. govs. Am. Stock Exchange; chmn. Am. Woman's Econ. Devel. Corp.; bd. dir. Fay's Inc.; former chmn. N.Y.C. Sports Commn.; bd. dirs. Lincoln Ctr. Mem. Women's Forum, Fin. Women's Assn. N.Y., Advt. Women N.Y., N.Y.C. Partnership, N.Y. State Bus. Coun. (vice chmn.), N.Y. C. of C. and Industry (bd. dirs.). Office: Crain's NY Bus 220 E 42nd St New York NY 10017-5806

TOWNSEND, BARBARA LOUISE, reading specialist, elementary school educator; b. Elkhart Lake, Wis., Aug. 21, 1956; d. Ronald Ernst and Valeria Louise (Horneck) Mauk; m. Thomas Charles Townsend, Oct. 6, 1979; children: Evan Thomas, Eric Louis. BSE in Elem. Edn., U. Wis., Whitewater, 1978, MSE in Reading, 1983. Transp. coord., driver for disabled U. Wis., Whitewater, 1976-78; libr. Traver Grade Sch., Lake Geneva, Wis., 1978-90, tchr. grades 1 and 2, 1978-90; reading specialist Elkhorn (Wis.) Area Sch. Dist., 1990—; mem. strategic planning com. Elkhorn Area Sch. Dist., 1994, mem. strategic plan action team, 1994-95. Coun. mem., Sunday Sch. tchr., choir 1st Congl. United Ch. of Christ, Elkhorn, 1978—; leader CHAMPS, West Side Sch., Elkhorn, 1994—. Named Outstanding Leader in Edn. AAUW, Lake Geneva br., 1992. Mem. Internat. Reading Assn., Wis. State Reading Assn., So. Lakes Reading Coun. Home: 1309 Robincrest Ln Elkhorn WI 53121-9483 Office: West Side Elem Sch 222 Sunset Dr Elkhorn WI 53121-1220

TOWNSEND, IRENE FOGLEMAN, accountant, tax specialist; b. Birmingham, Ala., May 29, 1932; d. James Woods and Virginia (Martin) Fogleman; m. Kenneth Ross Townsend, Mar. 18, 1951; children: Marietta Irene, Martha Shapard, Kenneth Ross Jr., Elizabeth Buchanan. BSBA, East Carolina U., 1980. CPA, N.C., Va. Acct. Norwood P. Whitehurst & Assocs., Greenville, N.C., 1981-86; asst. v.p. Tenet Healthcare Corp., Vienna, Va., 1986—. Fellow AICPA, N.C. Assn. CPAs, D.C. Inst. CPAs, Va. Soc. CPAs; mem. DAR, N.C. Soc. Daus. of Colonial Wars, Colonial Dames 17th Century. Democrat. Episcopalian (lay reader, chalice bearer). Home: 2521 Paxton St Lakeridge VA 22192-3414 Office: Tenet Healthcare Corp Ste 333 501 Church St NE Vienna VA 22180-4734

TOWNSEND, JANE KALTENBACH, zoologist, educator; b. Chgo., Dec. 21, 1922; B.S., Beloit Coll., 1944; M.A., U. Wis., 1946; Ph.D., U. Iowa, 1950; m. 1966. Asst. in zoology U. Wis., 1944-47; asst., instr. U. Iowa, 1948-50; asst., project assoc. in pathology U. Wis., 1950-53; Am. Cancer Soc. research fellow Wenner-Grens Inst., Stockholm, 1953-56; asst. prof. zoology Northwestern U., 1956-58; asst. prof. to assoc. prof. zoology Mt. Holyoke Coll., South Hadley, Mass., 1958-70, prof., 1970-93, chmn. biol. scis., 1980-86, prof. emeritus, 1993—. Fellow AAAS (sec. sect. biol. sci. 1974-78); mem. Am. Assn. Anatomists, Am. Inst. Biol. Scis., Am. Soc. Zoologists, Soc. Experimental Biology and Medicine, Soc. Devel. Biology, Corp. of Marine Biol. Lab., Sigma Xi, Phi Beta Kappa. Office: Mount Holyoke Coll Dept Biology South Hadley MA 01075

TOWNSEND, KATHLEEN KENNEDY, state official; m. David Townsend; children: Meaghan, Maeve, Kate, Kerry. BA cum laude, Harvard U., 1974; JD, U. N.Mex., 1978. Former dep. asst. atty. gen. U.S. Dept. Justice, Washington; lt. gov. State of Md., 1994—; tchr. U. Md., Balt. County, Essex. C.C., Dundalk C.C., U. Pa.; past exec. dir. Md. Student Svcs. Alliance; chair so. region Nat. Conf. Lt. Govs., chair oversight com. Johns Hopkins U., Peobody Inst.; expert adv. bd. Export-Import Bank U.S. Editor U. N.Mex. Law Rev. Founder Robert F. Kennedy Human Rights award. Recipient 4 hon. degrees. Office: Lt Gov State House 100 State Cir Annapolis MD 21401-1925

TOWNSEND, LANDA, environmental artist; b. Portsmouth, Va., Feb. 20, 1958; d. Joseph and Sally Mae (Benson) T.; m. Joe Kin Wing Ng, May 2, 1992. Student, U. Maine, 1976-78; MFA, San Francisco Art Inst., 1985; BFA, Syracuse U., 1983. Tchg. assoc. San Francisco Art Inst., 1984-85, vis. faculty mem., 1995; molecular biologist IMBB/U. Calif., San Francisco, 1985-87, Triton Bioscis., Alameda, Calif., 1987-89; vis. vaculty mem. Mendocino (Calif.) Art Ctr., 1991; environ. artist Capp Street Project, San Francisco, 1992-93; environ. restoration artist Dublin (Calif.) Fine Art Commn., 1994—; artist-in-residence Kohler (Wis.) Arts/Industry, 1990, The Lab, San Francisco, 1994, Sika Ctr. for Art and Ecology, Otis, Oreg., 1996; Djerassi artist in residence, Woodside, Calif., 1996. Artist installations Treo Grafte: Sculpting in Time, 1992-93, Darwin's Bassoon, 1994, The Rose, 1996. Environ. project grantee Capp Street Projpect, 1992-93, Lef Found. grantee, 1993; regional fellow Western States Art Fedn./NEA, 1996. Mem. Coll. Art Assn. (travel grantee 1995, panel mem. ann. conf. 1995). Home: 4104 24th St # 431 San Francisco CA 94114

TOWNSEND, LINDA LADD, mental health nurse; b. Louisville, Apr. 26, 1948; d. Samuel Clyde and Mary Elizabeth (Denton) Ladd; m. Stanley Allen Oliver, June 7, 1970 (div. 1978); 1 child, Aaron; m. Warren Terry Townsend Jr., Jan. 1, 1979; children: Mark, Amy, Sarah. Student, Catherine Spalding Coll., 1966-67; BSN, Murray State U., 1970; MS in Psychiat./Mental Health Nursing, Tex. Woman's U., 1976. RN, Tex., Ky.; lic. advanced nurse practitioner, profl. counselor, marriage and family therapist, Tex.; cert. group psychotherapist. Charge nurse med. and pediatric units Murray (Ky.)-Calloway County Hosp., 1970-71; team leader surg./renal transplant unit VA Hosp., Nashville, 1971-73; team leader, charge nurse gen. med.-surg. unit Providence Hosp., Waco, Tex., 1973-74; outpatient therapist Mental Hygiene Clinic, Ft. Hood, Tex., 1975-76; outpatient nurse therapist Ctrl. Counties Ctr. for Mental Health/Mental Retardation, Copperas Cove & Lampasas, Tex., 1977-80; psychiat. nurse clin. specialist, marriage/family therapist Profl. Counseling Svc., Copperas Cove, 1979—; cons. Metroplex Hosp. and Pavilion, Killeen, Tex., 1980—. Founding mem. Family Outreach of Coryell County, Copperas Cove, 1986 , also past pres and past sec.; founding mem. Partnership for a Drug and Violence-Free Copperas Cove; vol. music therapist Windcrest Nursing Ctr.; advocate Tex. Peer Assistance Program for Nurses; active Walk to Emmaus, 1993. Recipient Mary M. Roberts Writing award Am. Jour. of Nursing, 1970; named Mem. of Yr.-Vol., Family Outreach of Coryell County. Mem. ANA (cert. clin. specialist in adult psychiat. and mental health nursing, cert. clin. specialist in child and adolescent psychiat. and mental health nursing), AAUW (v.p. for membership, past bd. dirs., sec.-treas.), Tex. Nurses Assn., Am. Group Psychotherapy Assn. (cert.), Learning Disabilities Assn., Inst. for Humanities at Salado, Sigma Theta Tau. Democrat. Methodist. Home: RR 1 Box 253-E Kempner TX 76539-9502 Office: Profl Counseling Svc 806 E Avenue D Ste F Copperas Cove TX 76522-2231

TOWNSEND, LUCY FORSYTH, historian, educator; b. Pikeville, Ky., Sept. 16, 1944; d. Frank J. and Lucy Dolores (Webber) Forsyth; m. James Arthur Townsend, Jan. 1, 1972. BA, Mich. State U., 1966; MA, Memphis State U., 1970, Fuller Theol. Sem., Pasadena, Calif., 1979; PhD, Loyola U., Chgo., 1985. Tchr. McKenzie (Tenn.) Jr. H.S., 1967-68; adj. prof. Crighton Coll., Memphis, Tenn., 1969-74; tchr. (part time) Evangelical Christian Sch., Memphis, 1970-73; tchr. Village Christian Sch., Sun Valley, Calif., 1975-77; dir. children's Christian edn. La Crescenta (Calif.) Presbyn. Ch., 1977-79; adj. prof. Azusa (Calif.) Pacific U., 1978-79; adj. instr. Elgin (Ill.) C.C., 1980-84; asst. prof. history of edn. No. Ill. U., De Kalb, 1987-93, assoc. prof., 1993—; archivist Blackwell History of Edn. Rsch. Collection, No. Ill. U., DeKalb, 1994-96, curator, 1996—; free lance writer, cons., editor David C. Cook Publ. Co., Elgin, 1979-86. Author: (biography) The Best Helpers of One Another, 1988; (children's book) Learning About Hidden Treasures, 1987; co-author: (book) Creative Dramatics for Young Children, 1986; co-editor: A Meere Scholler: Cross-Cultural Perspectives on our Educational Heritage, 1996; editor Vitae Scholasticae, 1987-88. Recipient Hon. Mention Children's Poem, Evangelical Press Assn., 1987. Mem. Internat. Soc. for Ednl. Biography (pres. 1994-95), Midwest History of Edn. Soc. (v.p. 1994-95, pres. 1995-96), Am. Ednl. Studies Assn., Am. Ednl. Rsch. Assn., History of Edn. Soc., Thresholds in Edn. Found. (mem. exec. bd. 1992—), Coun. Learned Socs. Edn. (bd. examiners Nat. Coun. Accreditation Tchr. Edn. 1995—). Office: No Ill University LEPS Dept De Kalb IL 60115

TOWNSEND, MARILYN MORAN, video production company executive; b. Seminole, Okla., Sept. 12, 1954; d. Melvin R. and Jasmine L. (Birchell) Moran; m. Bill Dean Townsend, July 31, 1976; children—Allison, Julie. B.A., Purdue U., 1976. Announcer Sta. KWSH, Seminole, Okla., 1973; news/weather anchorwoman Sta. WLFI TV, West Lafayette, Ind., 1973-76, Sta. WBBH, Ft. Myers, Fla., 1976-77, Sta. WKJG-TV Ft. Wayne, Ind., 1977-81; owner, mgr. Custom Video Corp., Ft. Wayne, 1981—; dir. Pvt. Industry Council Ft. Wayne, 1983-87, vice chmn., 1986; chmn. Small Bus. Council, Ft. Wayne, 1983-87; TV producer, series Heartbeat, 1982-84. Chmn. 1990 fund drive Ft. Wayne Fine Arts Found., 1990; active Parkview Hospice, 1978-80; chmn. United Way of Allen County, 1994-95, co-chmn. Human Svcs. Panel on Youth and Violence, 1994—. Recipient 1st place award for news documentary AP, Ind., 1979, for med. documentary Ind. Med. Assn., 1978-79, Ind. Women Entrepreneur of the Yr. award Inc. Mag. and Ernest and Young, 1988, Ind. Small Bus. Owner of the Yr. award Small Bus. Assn., 198, Bus. Women of the Yr. award Foellinger Found, 1990; Named Ind. Women Bus. Owners Advocate of Yr., SBA, 1985. Mem. Women in Communications (past pres.; numerous awards), Women Bus. Owners Assn. (founding mem.), Nat. Assn. Female Execs., Ft. Wayne C. of C. (dir. 1983—), Ind. C. of C. (vice chair 1994-95, chmn. bd. 1995-96). Home: 5131 Binford Ln Fort Wayne IN 46804-6503 Office: Custom Video Corp 811 Lawrence Dr Fort Wayne IN 46804-1193

TOWNSEND, SUSAN ELAINE, social service institute administrator, hostage survival consultant; b. Phila., Sept. 5, 1946; d. William Harrison and Eleanor Irene (Fox) Rogers; m. John Holt Townsend, May 1, 1976. BS in Secondary Edn., West Chester State U., 1968; MBA, Nat. U., 1978; PhD in Human Behavior, La Jolla U., 1984. Biology tchr. Methacton Sch. Dist., Fairview Village, Pa., 1968-70; bus. mgr., analyst profl. La Jolla Research Corp., San Diego, 1977-79; pastoral asst. Christ Ctr. Bible Therapy, San Diego, 1980-82, also bd. dirs.; v.p., pub. relations World Outreach Ctr. of Faith, San Diego, 1981-82, also bd. dirs.; owner, pres., cons. Townsend Research Inst., San Diego, 1983-89; teaching assoc. La Jolla U. Continuing Edn., 1985-86, adminstr., assoc. registrar, adj. faculty, 1990. Author: Hostage Survival-Resisting the Dynamics of Captivity, 1983; contbr. articles to profl. jours. Instr. USN Advanced Survival Evasion Resistance Escape Sch., 1986-89; security officer Shield Security, San Diego, 1991-92; bd. dirs. Christ Fellowship Ch. of San Diego, 1987-96, music dir., 1992—; religious vol. Met. Correctional Ctr., San Diego, 1983-89, San Diego County Jail Ministries, 1978—, scheduling coord., 1993—. Comdr. USN, 1970-76, USNR, 1976-93. Mem. Naval Res. Assn. (life), Res. Officers Assn. (outstanding Jr. Officer of Yr. Calif. chpt. 1982), Navy League U.S. (life), West Chester U. ALumni Assn., Nat. U. Alumni Assn. (life), La Jolla U. Alumni Assn., Gen. Fedn. Women;s Clubs (pres. Peninsula Woman's Club 1983-85, pres. Peninsula Woman's Club 1994-96, pres. Parliamentary Law Club 1984-86, 96—, res. sec. Past Pres.' Assn. 1994-96), Calif. Fedn. Women's Clubs (v.p.-at-large San Diego dist. 25 1982-84, rec. sec. 1994-96, 1st v.p./dean of chmn. 1996—).

TOWNSEND, TERRY, publishing executive; b. Camden, N.J., Dec. 14, 1920; d. Anthony and Rose DeMarco; BA, Duke U., 1942; LHD (hon.) Dowling Coll., 1991; m. Paul Brorstrom Townsend, Dec. 8, 1961; 1 son, Kim. Pub. rels. dir. North Shore Univ. Hosp., Manhasset, N.Y., 1955-68; pres. Theatre Soc. L.I., 1968-70; pres. Townsend Comm. Bur., Ronkonkoma, N.Y., 1970—, L.I. Communicating Service, Ronkonkoma, 1977—; columnist, writer L.I./Bus., Ronkonkoma, 1970-75; pub. L.I. Bus. News, 1978—; v.p. Parr Meadows Racetrack, Yaphank, N.Y., 1977. Assoc. trustee North Shore U. Hosp., 1968—; bd. govs. Adelphi U. Friends Fin. Edn., 1978-85; chmn. ann. archtl. awards competition N.Y. Inst. Tech., 1970-83; trustee Dowling Coll., 1984-96, L.I. Fine Arts Mus., 1984-85; pub. broadcasting Sta. WLIW TV, Garden City, L.I., N.Y., 1990-93; bd. dirs. Family Svc. Assn. Nassau County, 1982-92; dinner chmn. L.I. 400 Ball, 1987; trustee Mus. at Stony Brook, 1994—. Recipient Media award 110 Center Bus. and Profl. Women, 1977, Enterprise award Friends of Fin. Edn., 1981, L.I. Loves Bus. Showcase Salute, 1982, Community Svc. award N.Y. Diabetes Assn., 1983, Disting. Long Islander in Communications award L.I. United Epilepsy Assn., 1984, Spl. award Dowling Coll. Spring Tribute, 1989, Disting. Svc. award Episcopal Health Svcs., 1989, Disting. Citizen award Dowling Coll., 1991, Gilbert Tilles award Nat. Assn. Fundraising Execs., 1994; named First Lady of L.I., L.I. Public Relations Assn., 1973, L.I. Woman of Yr. L.I. Assn. Action Com., 1989. Office: LI Bus News 2150 Smithtown Ave Ronkonkoma NY 11779-7348

TOWNSEND-ANDERSON, DIANE, lawyer, arbitrator, mediator; b. Chgo.; d. Robert and Betty (Johnson) Townsend; m. Richard Elias Townsend-Anderson; 1 child, Minu Townsend-Anderson. BA, U. Minn., MBA; JD, Hamline U. Cert. arbitrator, mediator. Sales Xerox Corp., Mpls. and Phila., 1970-73; owner Val-Pak Mktg., Mpls., 1973-79; dist. atty. Buffalo and Pierce County Atty., Wis., 1979-85; ptnr. Townsend-Anderson, PA, Faribault, Mn., 1985—; arbitrator, mediator Am. Arbitration and Mediation Svcs., Mpls., 1990—; prof. Mankato (Minn.) State U., 1994-95; appointed adminstrv. law judge, Minn., 1991; diplomat Nat. Inst. Trial Attys. Mem. Minn. Women's Polit. Caucus; bd. dirs, chair allocations United Way, Faribault, Minn.; appointed Minn. Export Finance Auth.; mem. St. Lucas Cmty. Ch. Recipient Cert. Achievement World Trade Ctr. Dept. Justice. Mem. Minn. Trial Lawyers Assn. (Women Lawyers), Minn. State Bar Assn. (chmn. conflict mgmt., dispute resolution sect.). Office: Townsend-Anderson PA 625 NW 3rd Ave Faribault MN 55021

TOWNSEND-BUTTERWORTH, DIANA BARNARD, educational consultant, author; b. Albany, N.Y., Dec. 12; d. Barnard and Marjorie (Bradley) Townsend; m. J. Warner Butterworth, Jan. 23, 1969; children: James, Diana. AB, Harvard-Radcliffe Coll., 1960; MA, Tchrs. Coll., Columbia U., 1971. Tchr. St. Bernard's Sch., N.Y.C., 1963-78, head of lower sch. English, 1965-71, head of jr. sch., 1971-78; assoc. dir. Early Care Ctr., N.Y.C., 1984-87; acad. advisor Columbia Coll., N.Y.C., 1987-88; ednl. cons., lectr. N.Y.C., 1988—; dir. parent involvement initiative Dept. Continuing Profl. Edn.,

Tchrs. Coll., Columbia U., 1996, chmn. devel. com. alumni coun. Tchrs. Coll., 1994—; chmn. sub-com. Harvard schs. com. Harvard Coll., Cambridge, Mass., 1975—. Author: Preschool and Your Child: What You Should Know, 1995, Your Child's First School, 1992 (Parent's Choice award 1992), (book chpt.) Handbook of Clinical Assessment of Children and Adolescents; contbr. articles to ednl. publs. and jours. Mem. women's health symposium steering com. N.Y. Hosp., N.Y.C., 1988—. Mem. Assn. Lower Sch. Heads (co-founder 1975), Alumni Coun. Tchrs. Coll. (com. chair 1993-95), Harvard Faculty Club. Home: 1170 5th Ave New York NY 10029-6527

TOY, JANET, artist; b. Polo, Ill., June 3, 1926; d. David Alfred and Ellen May (Cockerton) Stenmark; m. William James Lovett, Oct. 12, 1948 (div. 1953); 1 child, Nona Linnea Lovett Stone; m. Bernard Toy, Mar. 17, 1962. Student, Sch. Art Inst. Chgo., Art Students League N.Y., Bklyn. Mus. Art Sch., Santa Ana C.C. Artist-designer Ilse Von Ehrn Christmas Cards, Pittstown, N.J., 1951; comml. artist Le Huray Lithographers, N.Y.C., 1953-56, Package Design, Inc., N.Y.C., 1957-60; package designer Irv Koons Assocs. Inc., N.Y.C., 1960-72; comml. artist Santa Fe Internat. Inc., Orange, Calif., 1974-82, Pix Slide Prodn., Santa Ana, Calif., 1982; artist-designer Antique Glass Works, Inc., Santa Ana, 1982-83; comml. artist Martin Graphics, Fullerton, Calif., 1983-84, Cox Hobbies, Corona, Calif., 1989-92; mem. Orange County Ctr. for Contemporary Art, Santa Ana, 1983-87, Gallery 318, L.A., 1985-88, Bowers Mus. Galleria Co-op Gallery, Santa Ana, 1985-88, Pahrump (Nev.) Visual and Performing Arts Coun., 1994-96. Ceramic artist, sculptor, exhibiting in solo and group shows. Recipient numerous awards for ceramic sculptures. Christian.

TOY, LINDA ARATA, financial analyst, accountant; b. Passaic, N.J., June 1, 1954; d. John and Rosalie (Reina) Arata; m. Thomas Stephen Toy, Sept. 1981 (dec. May 1989). BS in Acctg., Bklyn. Coll., 1976; MBA in Fin., Pace U., 1987. Sr. acct. Macmillan Pub., N.Y.C., 1976-81, Polygram Records, N.Y.C., 1981-82; fin. analyst Holt, Reinhold, Winston, N.Y.C., 1982-83; sr. fin. analyst CBS, Inc., N.Y.C., 1983-88; mgr. fin. planning Reed Reference Pub., 1988—. Mem. NAFE.

TOY, PEARL TAK-CHU YAU, transfusion medicine physician; b. Hong Kong, July 31, 1947; came to U.S., 1965; d. Tse-Wah Yau and Grace Liang; m. Larry Toy, Dec. 12, 1970; 1 child, Jennifer. BA, Smith Coll., 1969; MD, Stanford U., 1973. From asst. prof. to assoc. prof. dept. lab. medicine U. Calif. Sch. Medicine, San Francisco, 1980-91, prof. dept. lab. medicine, 1991—; chief blood bank and donor ctr. Moffitt-Long Hosp., U. Calif., San Francisco, 1991—; chair expert panel on autologous transfusion NIH, Bethesda, Md., 1988-94, chair rsch. tng. rev. com., 1992. Contbr. articles to profl. jours., chpts. to books. Recipient numerous grants NIH, 1983—. Mem. Phi Beta Kappa, Sigma Xi, Alpha Omega Alpha.

TRABULSI, JUDY, advertising and marketing executive; b. Houston; d. Richard Joseph and Genevieve (Jamail) T. BS in Comm., U. Tex., 1971. Exec. v.p., media dir. Gurasich, Spence, Darilek & McClure, Austin, Tex., 1971—. Mem. nat. adv. coun. SBA, Washington, 1994-96; adv. coun. U. Tex. Comm. Sch., Austin, 1996—; adv. mem. 21st Century Dems., 1996. Office: Gurasich Spence Darilek & McClure 1250 S Capital Of Texas Hwy Ste 304 Austin TX 78746-6443

TRACEY, MARGARET, dancer; b. Pueblo, Colo.. Student, Sch. Am. Ballet, 1982. With corps de ballet N.Y.C. Ballet, 1986-88, soloist, 1989-91, prin., 1991. Featured in ballets (Balanchine) Ivesiana, Tarantella, The Nutcracker, Symphony in C, Jewels, Square Dance, Tschaikovsky Pas de Deux, Tschaikovsky Suite No. 3, Vienna Waltzes, Apollo, Ballo Della Regina, Divertimento No. 15, Donizetti Variations, Harlequinade, A Midsummer Night's Dream, Sonatine, La Source, Stars and Stripes, Symphony in Three Movements, Valse Fantaisie, Western Symphony, Who Cares?, (Robbins) Afternoon of a Faun, The Four Seasons, The Goldberg Variations, (Martins) Les Petits Riens, Mozart Serenade, Fearful Symmetries, Zakouski, Sleeping Beauty, (Anderson) Baroque Variations; also appeared in N.Y.C. Ballet's Blanchine Celebration, 1993; toured in Europe, Asia. Recipient U.S.A. award Princess Grace Found., 1985-86; scholar Atlantic Richfield Found., 1982-85. Office: NYC Ballet NY State Theater Lincoln Ctr Plaza New York NY 10023

TRACHTENBERG, JUDITH, lawyer, educator; b. Newark, May 21, 1949; d. Bertram and Estelle (Meyers) T. Diplôme, McGill U., Montreal, Que., Can., 1970; BA in Math. and French, Rutgers U., 1971; MAT in French, Ind. U., 1973, JD, 1978. Bar: Ind. 1978, N.J. 1985, Pa., 1985. Various tchg. positions, 1973-76; assoc. Montgomery, Elsner & Pardiede, Seymour, Ind., 1978-80; pvt. practice Columbus, Ind., 1980-82; mng. atty. Women's Legal Clinic, South Bend, Ind., 1982-84; v.p. Ctr. for Non-Profit Corps., Princeton, N.J., 1985-91; instr. Fairleigh Dickinson U. and Seton Hall U., Madison and South Orange, N.J., 1990—; pvt. practice Roosevelt, N.J., 1991—; cons. Ctr. for Non-Profit Corps., Princeton, 1992—. Editor: (book chpt.) Bender's Federal Tax Service, 1992; mem. editl. bd. Non-Profit Sector Resource Institute, 1994—. Mem. charter class Leadership N.J., New Brunswick, 1986-87; sec., trustee Roosevelt Arts Project, 1988—; chair, trustee Mercer St. Friends Ctr., Trenton, N.J., 1991—; mem. numerous charitable orgns. Recipient Equal Justice medal Legal Svcs. of N.J., 1995. Office: PO Box 132 27 N Rochdale Ave Roosevelt NJ 08555

TRACHY, DEBRA A., managed healthcare consultant; b. Holyoke, Mass., Dec. 31, 1953; d. Richard H. and Julia J. (Scholl) T.; m. Sunil Ahuja, June 22, 1991. BBA, U. Mass., 1976; MPH, U. Calif., Berkeley, 1980; postgrad., Stanford U., 1984-85. Asst. to exec. dir. U. Mass. Health Ctr., Amherst, 1976-77, sys./health records mgr., 1977-78; benefit cost/fin. analyst Kaiser Found. Health Plan, Oakland, Calif., 1979-81; asst. adminstr. Kaiser Found. Hosp., Richmond and Hayward, Calif., 1981-83; health ctrs. adminstr. Kaiser Found. Health Plan, Hartford, Conn., 1983-86; v.p., exec. dir. Travelers Health Network, Pitts., 1986-87; dir. outpatient care network development HealthCare Compare Corp., Downers Grove, Ill., 1991-93; COO Health Empowerment, Inc., Scottsdale, Ariz., 1995—; pres. Trachy Healthcare Mgmt. Co., Scottsdale, 1987—; guest panelist Health Care Reform, FYI Pitts., Fox TV, 1994; guest spkr. Behavioral Health Soc., Pitts., 1994, Health Exec. Forum, 1994, Mgmt. Profls. in Health Care, 1991, Greater Pitts. Commn. on Women, 1990, Hosp. Coun. of Western Pa., Wexford, 1990, Marion Merrell Dow, Kansas City, Mo., 1990, Pa. Assn. HMOs, Phila., 1990; guest lectr. Carnegie Mellon U., 1987, 89, Comty. Coll. Allegheny County, 1989, U. Hartford, 1986, Yale U. Sch. Pub. Health, 1986, U. Mass. Sch. Pub. Health, 1985; preceptor Yale U., U. Calif., Berkeley, Mt. Holyoke Coll., U. Pitts. Author: Managed Care in Western Pennsylvania: Trends, Forecasts, Strategies, 1990; health care guest writer: The Pitts. Bus. Times, 1986-91, 93-94. V.p. bd. dirs. East Hartford C. of C., 1985-86, Women's Leadership Assembly, Pitts., 1993-95; treas. bd. dirs. Exec. Women's Coun., Pitts., 1990-91; mem. bd. dirs., com. chair Pitts., Action Against Rape, Pitts., 1994; mem. bd. dirs. Pa. Assn. of HMOs, Harrisburg, 1986-87. Mem. Soc. for Healthcare Planning & Mktg. Democrat. Home: 9288 E Hillery Way Scottsdale AZ 85260 Office: Health Empowerment Inc 4300 N Miller Rd Ste 217 Scottsdale AZ 85251

TRACI, KATHLEEN FRANCES, librarian; b. Chgo., Jan. 13, 1943; d. William Henry and Mary Teresa (O'Connor) Kammien; m. Paul A. Traci, Nov. 25, 1965; children: Sean, Meg, Beth, Patricia. MLS, U. Wis., 1975; EdS, Butler U., 1991; postgrad., Ind. U., 1991—. Libr. media specialist Waukesha (Wis.) Elem. Sch., 1976-84, Butler Middle Sch., Waukesha, 1984-86; libr. Marian Coll., Indpls., 1987-88; libr. media specialist Noblesville (Ind.) Middle Sch., 1990-91, Decatur Ctrl. High Sch., Indpls., 1991—. Pres. Friends of Hussey-Mayfield Libr., Zionsville, Ind. Mem. Assn. Ind. Media Educators, ASCD, Ind. U. Sch. Adminstrs. Assn. Home: 155 Raintree Dr Zionsville IN 46077-2012 Office: Decatur Cen H S 5251 Kentucky Ave Indianapolis IN 46221-3616

TRACY, BARBARA MARIE, lawyer; b. Mpls., Oct. 13, 1945; d. Thomas A. and Ruth C. (Roby) T. BA, U. Minn., 1971; JD, U. Okla., 1980. Bar: Okla. 1980, U.S. Dist. Ct. (we. dist.) Okla. 1980, U.S. Dist. Ct. (no. dist.) Tex. 1991, U.S. Supreme Ct. 1988, U.S. Dist. Ct. (ea. dist.) Tex. 1995. Assoc. Pierce, Couch, Hendrickson, Johnston & Baysinger, Oklahoma City, 1980-82; ptnr. Rizley & Tracy, Sayre, Okla., 1982-84; pvt. practice Oklahoma City, 1984-90; gen. atty. U.S. Army Corps Engrs., Ft. Worth, 1991—. Mem. citizens adv. bd. O'Donoghue Rehab. Inst., Oklahoma City. Mem. ABA, Okla. Bar Assn., Fed. Bar Assn., Internat. Tng. in Commn. (pres. Ace Club chpt.). Democrat. Roman Catholic. Office: 819 Taylor St Fort Worth TX 76102-6114

TRACY, JANET RUTH, legal educator, librarian; b. Denison, Iowa, July 16, 1941; d. L. M. and Grace (Harvey) T.; m. Rodd Mc Cormick Reynolds, Feb. 15, 1975 (dec. June 1993); children: Alexander, Lee. BA, U. Oreg., 1963; ML, U. Wash., 1964; JD, Harvard U., 1969. Bar: N.Y. 1970. Reference libr. Harvard Coll. Librs., Cambridge, Mass., 1964-66; assoc. Kelley Drye & Warren, N.Y.C., 1969-71; dir. data base design Mead Data Ctrl., Inc., N.Y.C., 1971-75; dir. rsch. Mvpl. Employees Legal Svc. Fund, N.Y.C., 1975-76; from asst. to assoc. prof. N.Y. Law Sch., N.Y.C., 1976-82; asst. libr. dir. Law Libr. Columbia U., N.Y.C., 1982-86; prof., law libr. dir. Fordham U., N.Y.C., 1986—; chmn. Conf. Law Librs. Jesuit Univs., 1988-89. Co-author: Professional Staffing and Job Security in Academic Law Libraries, 1989. Recipient Catalog Automation award Winston Found., 1990, 91, 92. Home: 285 Riverside Dr New York NY 10025-5276 Office: Fordham U Sch of Law 140 W 62nd St New York NY 10023-7407

TRACY, JEAN KENNEDY, psychotherapist, consultant; b. Salt Lake City, Feb. 5, 1936; d. Emmanuel George Laefas and Adelia Louise Kennedy; m. Gerald Albert Tracy: children: Melody Susan, Holly Ann, David Sean. BA, U. Colo., 1969; MSW, Denver U., 1971; PhD, Union Inst., 1978. Lic. clin. social worker. Psychiat. social worker Togus (Maine) VA Hosp., 1971-72; dir. br. office Mid Coast Mental Health Ctr., Rockland, Maine, 1972-75, outpatient clinician, 1972-77, dir. day hosp., 1974-77, dir. rape crisis, 1974-79; pvt. practice Rockland, Maine, 1977—; Cons. Maine State Prison, Thomaston, 1972-75, Sch. Adminstrv. Dist. 5, Rockland, 1973-74, Skyward, Rockland, 1978-85, Policy Rsch. Inst., Silver Springs, Md., 1995—; presenter NCA conf. Co-author: Alcohol and Drugs Are Women's Issues, 1991. Incorporator Penobscot Bay Hosp., Rockland, 1993—; bd. dirs. Waldo/Knox AIDS Coalition, Maine, 1995—. Mem. AAUW, NASW, Am. Group Psychotherapy Assn., Assn. Humanistic Psychiatry, Am. Orthopsychiat. Assn., Internat. Soc. Traumatic Stress Studies, Maine Soc. Clin. Social Work. Home: 1121 Oyster River Rd Warren ME 04864 Office: Wise Assoc 93 Park St Rockland ME 04841

TRACY, LOIS BARTLETT, painter; b. Jackson, Mich., Dec. 9, 1901; d. James Elwood and Nellie (Allen) Bartlett; m. Donald Lockwood Walker, Sept. 20, 1923 (div. Sept. 1931); 1 child, Donald Lockwood Walker; m. Harry Herbert Tracy, Sept. 21, 1931; 1 child, Nathan Bartlett. BA, Rollins Coll., 1929; MA, Mich. State, 1958. Head of art dept. Southeastern Community Coll. U. Ky., Edison Jr. Coll., Fla. One-woman shows include Studio Guild, N.Y.C., 1939-41, 41-43, Norlyst Gallery, N.Y.C., 1945-47, Charles E. Smith Gallery, Boston, 1949, Center St. Gallery, Boston, Burliuk Gallery, N.Y.C., 1952, Gallerie Internationale, N.Y.C., 1963, Fine Arts Mus., Greenville, S.C., Morse Mus. Art, Winter Park, Fla., Mus. Art, Clearwater, Fla., Wustun Mus., Racine, Wis., Fitchburg Art Mus., Mass., Gibbs Gallery, Charleston, S.C., Boise Art Mus., Idaho, Columbia Mus. Art, S.C., Worcester Art Ctr., Appleton, Wis., San Francisco Mus. Art, Syracuse Mus., Asheville Art Mus., N.C., Stork Gallery, Lynchburg, Va., Maryhill Mus. Fine Arts, Washington; represented in permanent collections Cornelle Mus. Art, Winter Park, Fla., 1994, Met. Mus. Art, N.Y.C., 1994, NAOAL Mus., Washington; represented in numerous pub. and pvt. collections; author: (books) Paintings, Principles and Practices, 1967, Adventuring in Art, 1989. State bd. mem LWV, Laconia, N.H.; active Dem. Nat. Com. Named Tchr. of Yr. Edison Coll., Ft. Myers, Fla.; recipient Award of Merit State of Fla, 1935, Most Creative Work of Art award Currier Mus., N.H., Gaisman Award Nat. Assn. Women Artists, Arvida award, Sarasota Art Assn., Watercolor prize Southeastern Annual High Mus., Atlanta, Norfolk Mus. Art., Pen & Brush, N.Y., Nat. Assn. Women Artists, Nat. Acad. Gallery, Sarasota Art Assn. Mem. LWV, Nat. Assn. Women Artists, Am. Assn. Univ. Women, Nat. League of Am. Pen Women, Fla. Artists Group, Artists Equity, Art Assn., Internat. Platform Assn. Democrat. Home: 580 Artist Ave Englewood FL 34223-2734

TRAGESER, RUTH BRICK, secondary school educator, education educator; b. Belgrade, Minn., Feb. 22, 1942; d. Othmar Adam and Eleanor Mary (Lenz) Brick; single; children: Thomas, Susan. BS in English and Bus. Edn., St. Cloud State U., 1963; MA in Edn., St. Mary's U., 1995. Tchr. English Kimball (Minn.) Pub. Schs., 1963-64; tchr. comms. Willmar (Minn.) Pub. Schs., 1964—; tchr., trainer on gender equity S.W., West Ctrl. Ednl. Svc. Unit, Marshall, Minn., 1994—; adj. instr. St. Mary's U., Mpls., 1996—; mem. evaln. team Minn. Bd. Tchg., 1994—. Assoc. chair kandiyohi Dem. Farmer Labor Party, Willmar, Minn., 1992-93. Mem. AAUW (legal advocacy fund state liaison 1992-94), Barn Theatre Play Readers (reader 1993—), N. Ctrl. Assn. (mem. evaln. team 1994—), Minn. Fedn. Tchrs. (chair human rights commn. 1993—). Mem. Democratic Farm Labor Party. Roman Catholic. Office: Willmar Sr H S 2701 30th Ave NE Willmar MN 56201

TRAHAN, MARIA G., high school counselor; b. Bay City, Mich., June 11, 1947; d. Harry E. and Grace E. (McManmon) T. BA, Marygrove Coll.; MA, U. Mich.; EdS, Wayne State U. Lic. counselor, Mich. Tchr. Buena Vista Schs., Saginaw, Mich., Mt. Clemens (Mich.) Schs.; counselor Van Hoosen Jr. H.S., Rochester, Mich., Adams H.S., Rochester; chair guidance and counseling review Adams H.S., 1985-87, 95—, mem. bus. partnership com., 1994-96. Mem. AAUW, Mich. Edn. Assn., Mich. Counseling Assn., Rochester Edn. Assn., Oakland Counseling Assn. (pres. 1979). Office: Adams HS 3200 W Tienken Rochester Hills MI 48306

TRAIL, MARGARET ANN, employee benefits company executive; b. Bryan, Tex., July 17, 1941; d. Louis Milton and Margaret (Stromberg) Thompson; m. Robert A. Rosemier, Aug. 25, 1962 (div. Feb. 1973); 1 child: Gretchen Elisabeth; m. Newt Shands Trail, Dec. 4, 1989. BS in Nursing, U. Iowa, 1963; MS, No. Ill. U., 1971. Instr. Cooley Dickinson Hosp., Northampton, Mass., 1964-65; dir. nursing De Kalb (Ill.) Pub. Hosp., Kishwaukee Community Hosp., 1972-76, Terre Haute (Ind.) Regional Hosp., 1976-78; from mgr. clin. systems to dir. spl. projects Hosp. Corp. Am., Nashville, 1978-86; from dir. med. mgmt. to v.p. Equicor, Nashville, 1986-90; divsn. v.p. The Travelers Ins. Co., Hartford, Conn., 1990-93; sr. mgr. health svcs. quality mgmt. Aetna US Healthcare, Hartford, 1993—. Mem. LWV (pres. DeKalb chpt. 1970-72), Nat. League Nursing, Am. Assn. Health Plans, Nat. Assn. Healthcare Quality (cert.). Office: Aetna 151 Farmington Ave Hartford CT 06156-0001

TRAIL, MOLLY LOU PIERCE, elementary education educator; b. Terrell, Tex., June 10, 1943; d. Willie Clyde and Nancy Elizabeth (Carden) Pierce; m. Robert Justin Trail, Jan. 25, 1964; children: Teresa Elizabeth Trail Parkey, Justin Neil. BS in Elem. Edn., East Tex. State U., 1968, MEd, 1987. 6th grade tchr. Ed Hodges Elem. Sch., Mesquite, Tex., 1968-75; 5th grade tchr. Tisinger Elem. Sch., Mesquite, 1975-77; 4th grade tchr. Rowlett (Tex.) Elem. Sch., 1981-95; reading recovery tchr. Spring Creek Elem. Sch., 1995-96; tchr. 1-5 Garland (Tex.) Summer Sch., 1989; tchr. Camp Garland Ind. Sch. Dist., 1990. Active Mesquite Symphony Guild, 1994—. Mem. AAUW, ASCD, Tex. State Tchrs. Assn., ATPE, Garland Assn. Tex. Profl. Educators. Methodist. Office: 1510 Spring Creek Dr Garland TX 75040-8533

TRAINA, PATRICIA ANNE, editor; b. Queens, N.Y., Apr. 20, 1968; d. Alfred James and Myrna Lee T. BA, Rutgers U., 1990; MA, Fairleigh Dickinson U., 1994. Creative svcs. coord. Reed Reference Publ., New Providence, N.J., 1990-94; project mgr. Suburban Propane, N.J., 1994—; freelance sports writer Giants Extra, Green Brook, N.J., 1994-95; editor, publisher, founder Giants News Subscription Svcs., Port Reading, N.J., 1994—. Mem. NAFE, North Jersey Assn. Female Execs., Profl. Football Writers Assn. Am. Republican. Roman Catholic. Office: Giants News Subscription Svcs PO Box 46 Port Reading NJ 07064

TRANSOU, LYNDA LEW, advertising art administrator; b. Atlanta, Dec. 11, 1949; d. Lewis Cole Transou and Ann Lynette (Taylor) Putnam; m. Lue Gregg Loso, Oct. 25, 1991. B.F.A. cum laude, U. Tex.-Austin, 1971. Art dir., The Pitluk Group, San Antonio, 1971, Campbell, McQuien & Lawson, Dallas, 1973-74, Bozell & Jacobs, Dallas, 1974-75; art dir., ptnr. The Assocs., Dallas, 1975-77; art dir. Belo Broadcasting, Dallas, 1977-80; creative dir., v.p. Allday & Assocs., Dallas, 1980-85; owner Lynda Transou Advt. & Design, 1986—. Recipient Merit award N.Y. Art Dirs. Show, 1980; Gold award Dallas Ad League, 1980, Silver award, 1980, Bronze award, 1981, 82, 2 Merit awards Houston Art Dirs. Club, 1978-86; Merit award Broadcast Designers Assn., 1980, 82; Merit awards Dallas Ad League, 1978, 87; Silver award Houston Art Dirs. Show; Gold award Tex. Pub. Relations Assn., 1982, 85; Gold award N.Y. One Show, 1982, Creativity award Art Direction mag., 1986, Print award Regional Design Annual, 1988, Telly Finalist, 1987. Mem. Am. Inst. Graphic Arts, Dallas Soc. Visual Communications (Bronze award 1980, Merit awards, 1978-86), Delta Gamma (historian 1969-70).

TRANTHAM, EMILY, association administrator; b. Nashville; d. Jack Lawrence and Bernita (Weinstein) Laribe; m. Richard Franklin Trantham, Feb. 20, 1963. BA, U. Tex., 1970, MA, 1972. Dir. svcs. to mil. families and vets. ARC, Ft. Worth, 1972-76; adminstrv. mgr. Houston Gen. Ins. Co., Ft. Worth, 1976-80; exec. dir. NCCJ, Ft. Worth, 1980—. Dir. Martin Luther King Bd., Ft. Worth, 1985-89, 95—, Tarrant County Youth Collaboration, Ft. Worth, 1985—; mem. Forum Ft. Worth, 1985—; com. mem. Tex. Conf. Chs., Austin, 1995—. Recipient Pride in Tarrant County award Ft. Worth Star-Telegram, 1989, Adopt-A-Sch. award, 1992, Models of Unity award Spiritual Assembly of Baha'is, 1994. Mem. Nat. Soc. Fundraising Execs. (cert.). Home: 903 Mission Dr Southlake TX 76092 Office: NCCJ 500 W Seventh St # 1707 Fort Worth TX 76102

TRAUDT, MARY B., elementary education educator; b. Chgo., Jan. 1, 1930; d. Lloyd Andrews Haldeman and Adele Eleanor (MacKinnon) Haldeman-Oliver; m. Eugene Peter Traudt, Dec. 6, 1952 (dec.); 1 child, Victoria Jean. BS, Cen. Mich. U., 1951; MA, Roosevelt U., 1978; postgrad., U. Ill., 1982. Asst. editor Commerce Clearing House, Chgo., 1951-53; tchr. Cleve. Elem. Sch., 1954-56, Chgo. Sch. System, 1956-57, Community Consolidated # 54, Hoffman Estates, Ill., 1957-64, Avoca Elem. Sch., Wilmette, Ill., 1964—; ret., 1995. Recipient Computer award Apple Computer Co. Mem. Avoca Edn. Assn. (v.p. 1986-91), Alpha Psi Omega. Presbyterian. Home: 107 Lincoln St Glenview IL 60025-4916 Office: Avoca Elem Sch 235 Beech Dr Glenview IL 60025-3274

TRAUGER, ALETA ARTHUR, judge. BA in English magna cum laude, Cornell Coll., Iowa, 1968; MAT, Vanderbilt U., 1972, JD, 1976. Tchr. Tenn., Eng., 1970-73; assoc., law clk. Barrett, Brandt & Barrett, P.C., Nashville, 1974-77; asst. U.S. atty., first asst., chief of criminal divsn. No. Dist. Ill. and Mid. Dist. Tenn., 1977-82; assoc. Hollins, Wagster & Yarbrough, P.C., Nashville, 1983-84; legal counsel Coll. of Charleston, S.C., 1984-85; ptnr. Wyatt, Tarrant, Combs, Gilbert & Milom, Nashville, 1985-91; judge Tenn. Ct. of the Judiciary, 1987-93; chief of staff Mayor's Office, Nashville, 1991-92; bankruptcy judge U.S. Bankruptcy Ct. (mid. dist.) Tenn., Nashville, 1993—; mem. hearing panel bd. profl. responsibility Tenn. Supreme Ct., 1983-84, mem. adv. com. on rules of civil and appellate procedure, 1989—; lectr. Vanderbilt U. Sch. Law, 1986-88, mem. alumni bd., 1989-92; master of bench Harry Phillips Am. Inn of Ct., 1990-94; mem. Internat. Women's Forum, 1993—, v.p. Tenn. chpt., 1996—; mem. Nat. Conf. Bankruptcy Judges, 1994—, chmn. ethics com., 1994—. Bd. dirs. Nashville Inst. for Arts, 1992—, Miriam's Promise (adoption agy.), 1995—; bd. dirs. Renewal House, 1996—. Fellow Am. Bar Found., Tenn. Bar Found., Nashville Bar Found.; mem. ABA (vice chmn. com. on bankrupcty judges jud. adminstrn. divsn), FBA (v.p. 1983-84, 85-86), Nashville Bar Assn. (bd. dirs. 1984, 89-91), Tenn. Lawyers Assn. for Women (bd. dirs. 1983-84, 86-88, v.p. 1988-89, pres. 1989-90), Nat. Assn. Women Judges. Office: Customs House 701 Broadway Fl 2 Nashville TN 37203-3944

TRAUGOTT, ELIZABETH CLOSS, linguistics educator and researcher; b. Bristol, Eng., Apr. 9, 1939; d. August and Hannah M.M. (Priebsch) Closs; m. John L. Traugott, Sept. 26, 1967; 1 dau., Isabel. BA in English, Oxford U., Eng., 1960; PhD in English lang., U. Calif., Berkeley, 1964. Asst. prof. English U. Calif., Berkeley, 1964-70; lectr. U. East Africa, Tanzania, 1965-66, U. York, Eng., 1966-67; lectr., then assoc. prof. linguistics and English Stanford U., Calif., 1970-77, prof., 1977—, chmn. linguistics dept., 1980-85; vice provost, dean grad. studies Stanford U., 1985-91, mem. grad. record examinations bd., 1989-93, mem. test of English as a fgn. lang. bd., 1989-91, chmn. test of English as a fgn. lang. bd., 1991-92; mem. higher edn. funding coun. Eng. Assessment Panel, 1996. Author: A History of English Syntax, 1972, (with Mary Pratt) Linguistics for Students of Literature, 1980, (with Paul Hopper) Grammaticalization, 1993; editor: (with ter Meulen, Reilly, Ferguson) On Conditionals, 1986, (with Heine) Approaches to Grammaticalization, 2 vols., 1991; contbr. numerous articles to profl. jours. Am. Coun. Learned Socs. fellow, 1975-76, Guggenheim fellow, 1983-84, Ctr. Advanced Study of Behavioral Scis. fellow, 1983-84. Mem. MLA, AAUP, AAUW, Linguistics Soc. Am. (pres. 1987, sec.-treas. 1994—), Internat. Soc. Hist. Linguistic (pres. 1979-81). Office: Stanford Univ Dept Linguistics Bldg 460 Stanford CA 94305-2150

TRAUTMANN, PATRICIA ANN, communications educator, storyteller; b. Hot Springs, S.D., Jan. 6, 1932; d.. Forest Houston and Clara Ruth (Allen) Doling; m. Robert D. Trautmann, Aug. 11, 1954; children: Kurt, Elaine, Sarah, Cynthia, Gretchen. BA, Jamestown Coll., 1954; MA, U. Northern Colo., 1962; PhD, Vanderbilt U., 1984; postgrad., Ga. Southern U., 1992-93. Tchr. various schs., Colo., N.D., Mich., 1954-67; part-time instr. English Kans. State Coll., Pittsburg, 1967-70; part-time instr. English, children's lit. Baldwin-Wallace Coll., Berea, Parma, Ohio, 1970-73; part-time instr. children's lit., reading, lang. arts U. Tenn., Nashville, 1973-78; English instr. Valdosta (Ga.) H.S., 1978-82; assoc. prof. English, Speech, Langs.; asst. dir. programs Ga. Mil. Coll., Milledgeville, 1982-86; assoc. prof. English, art, humanities, langs. South Ga. Coll., Douglas, 1986-94; assoc. prof. English, comm. skills Isothermal C.C., Spindale, N.C., 1995—; cons. for reading, children's books in schs. and other instns., Kans., Ohio, Tenn., Ga., N.C., 1964—. Storyteller, spkr., internat. lore, poetry, children's lit., world mythology, 1967—. Recipient Humanities award South Ga. Coll., 1993. Mem. AAUW, Music Club. Democrat. Home: 611 N Washington St Rutherfordton NC 28139 Office: Isothermal Cmty Coll Spindale NC 28139

TRAVER, MICHELE LEE, school counselor; b. Albany, N.Y., Sept. 13, 1969; d. William F. and Karen M. (Englert) T. BA, U. Albany, 1991; MSEd, Coll. Saint Rose, 1993. Cert. sch. counselor, N.Y. Sch. counselor-intern Troy (N.Y.) City Schs., 1993, Shenendehowa Ctrl. Sch. Dist., Clifton Park, N.Y., 1993; sch. counselor Brasher Falls (N.Y.) Ctrl. Sch. Dist., 1995-96; head coach jr. varsity girls basketball Brasher Falls Ctrl. Sch. Dist., 1994-95, head coach modified basketball, 1993-94, Amateur Athletic Union, Albany, 1993; asst. coach girls varsity basketball Shenendehowa Ctrl. Sch. Dist., 1992-93. Mem. ACA, Am. Sch. Counseling Assn., No. Zone Sch. Counselor Assn. Methodist.

TRAVERS, CAROL, mathematics educator; b. Oil City, Pa., July 10, 1941; d. Philip Patrick and Frances Mary (McNamara) Healy; divorced; children: William, Joseph, Bruce, Rose. BS in Elem. Edn., State U. Pa., 1962; MS in Elem. Edn., SUNY, Brockport, 1977. Tchr. elem. sch. Lincoln-Garfield Sch., New Castle, Pa., 1962-64; tchr. Mohawk Area Schs., Mt. Jackson, Pa., 1964-65; tchr. nursery sch. Learn 'N' Play Sch., Middleport, N.Y., 1970-77; tchr. remedial reading Royalton-Hartland, Middleport, N.Y., 1977-80; tchr. remedial reading, remedial math Middleport Elem. Sch., 1980—; co-chair bldg. team Sch. Bldg. Team, Middleport, 1989-91, 94-95; mem. computer coun. Roy-Hart Dist., Middleport, 1981—, chmn. prof. coun.; rep. Math. Standards Support Group, Lockport, N.Y., 1990—. Co-author/editor:)booklet) Child Study Team, 1989. Mem. Nat. Coun. Math. Tchrs., N.Y. State Maths. Tchrs., Assn. Compensatory Educators, PTA. Democrat. Roman Catholic. Office: Middleport Elem Sch State St Middleport NY 14105

TRAVIS, LAURA ROSE, elementary education educator; b. Waynesburg, Pa., Jan. 23, 1944; d. Isaac Jesse and Violet Rae (Hixenbaugh) Ammons; m. Bobby Dale Jones, July 20, 1963 (div. Aug. 1982); children: Bernard, Marvin, Tonya; m. Harold Dean Travis, June 21, 1990. BA in Edn., Glenville (W.Va.) State Coll., 1983; postgrad., W.Va. Grad. Coll., 1992-94. Tchr. Glade Elem. Sch., Cowen, W.Va., 1984-90; substitute tchr. Putnum County Sch. Bd., Winfield, W.Va., 1990-94; tchr. Rock Branch Elem. Sch., Nitro, W.Va., 1994—; coord. for sch. age East Nitro Christian Educare, 1991-94. Pres. Cowen Woman's Club, 1977-80; sec. Cowen Garden Club, 1978-81, chairperson for Sch. Improvement com., 1995—. Mem. Order Ea. Star, Kappa Delta Pi, Alpha Delta Kappa. Democrat.

TRAVIS, LUCINDA LOUISE, product designer, writer, editor; b. Holdrege, Nebr., June 28, 1948; d. Dale Edward Travis and Betty Louise (Watts) Travis McCreadie. Cultural diploma, U. Stranieri di Perugia, Italy, 1969, ITESM, Monterey, Mex., 1969, U. Granada, Spain, 1971; BA in Italian, UCLA, 1970; cultural diploma, U. Salamanca, Spain, 1971; BA in Spanish with high honors, Calif. State Coll., San Bernardino, 1972; MEd., U. Hawaii, 1975. Cert. secondary tchr., Calif. Producer, dir. promotions, programming Hawaii Pub. TV KHET, Honolulu, 1972-78; producer, writer Direcion Gen. Radio, TV y Cinemagrafia del Gobierno de Mex., Mexico City, 1978-80; dir. World's Children's Art Exhbn., L.A., 1983-89; coord. grant applications ind. filmmaker program Am. Film Inst., L.A., 1982-87; creative/pub. rels. specialist Ohio Art, Bryan, 1987-90; product designer Hama, Inc., Nokøbing Mors, Denmark, 1991—; editor Wee Deliver newsletter for Office of Literacy U.S. Postal Svc., Washington, 1991-93; instr. Payap Coll., Chiang Mai, Thailand, 1983, 84; designer, curator traveling mus. exhibit Gumby Exhibit, 1991-92; programming cons. Internat. Mass-Comm. Svc., Kvinesdal, Norway, 1984. Author: (poetry) Aire y Alma, 1971, Animation: A Resource Book, 1986; co-editor: Film/Television: Grants, Scholarships and Special Programs, 1985; patentee beading system for craft market. Speaker for various svc. and ednl. orgns.; Bible study tchr. Presbyn. and Bapt. Chs., Ontario, Calif., Bryan, Ohio, 1982-91; vol. missionary refugee work Am. Bapt. Chs., Thailand. Calif. Arts Coun. grantee, 1985. Mem. Alpha Gamma Delta.

TRAVIS, NANCY, actress; b. New York, NY, Sept. 21, 1961. BA, NYU. stage appearances include: Brighton Beach Memoirs (touring prodn.), It's Hard to Be a Jew, 1984, I'm Not Rappaport, 1986, The Signal Season of Dummy Hoy, 1987-88; television appearances include: High School Narc, 1985, Malice in Wonderland, 1985, Harem, 1986, I'll Be Home for Christmas, 1988, Almost Perfect, 1995—, (voice) Duckman, 1994; films include: Three Men and a Baby, 1987, Eight Men Out, 1988, Married to the Mob, 1988, Air America, 1990, Internal Affairs, 1990, Loose Cannons, 1990, Three Men and a Little Lady, 1990, Passed Away, 1992, Chaplin, 1992, The Vanishing, 1993, So I Married an Ax Murderer, 1993, Greedy, 1994, Fluke, 1995, Destiny Turns On the Radio, 1995, Lieberman in Love, 1995, Bogus, 1996. Office: CAA 9830 Wilshire Blvd Beverly Hills CA 90210*

TRAVIS, SUSAN FRANCES, pediatrician, educator; b. Bklyn., Dec. 10, 1940; d. Abraham and Mina (Bebrowsky) T.; widowed; children: Andrew Grossman, Sandra Grossman. AB, Syracuse U., 1961; MD, NYU, 1965. Diplomate Am. Bd. Pediatrics, Am. Bd. Pediatric Hematology/Oncology. Teaching asst., resident, fellow in pediatrics NYU, Bellevue Med. Ctr., N.Y.C., 1965-69; teaching asst., fellow in hematology U. Pa./Children's Hosp., Phila., 1969-71; instr. pediatrics, assoc. hematology Children's Hosp. Phila., 1971-72; asst. prof. pediatrics Thomas Jefferson U., Cardeza Found., Phila., 1973-79, assoc. prof., 1979-85, dir. pediatric hematology, 1973-85; assoc. prof. U. Medicine and Dentistry N.J.-Robert Wood Johnson Med. Sch., Camden, 1985—; cons. Our Lady of Lourdes Hosp., Camden, 1975-91, 94—, West Jersey Health System, Camden, 1993—; coord. clin. svcs. divsn. pediatric hematology/oncology Cooper Hosp./Univ. Med. Ctr., Camden, 1985—, dir. So. N.J. Regional Sickle Cell Ctr. Children, 1990—, dir. Regional Comprehensive Hemophilia Care & Treatment Ctr., 1992—; mem. sickle cell adv. com., spl. child health svcs., N.J. Dept. Health, chair patient care subcom. Contbr. articles to profl. jours. Recipient Physician's Recognition award AMA, 1992—. Fellow Am. Acad. Pediatrics; mem. Am. Soc. Pediatric Hematology/Oncology, Am. Soc. Hematology, Hemophilia Assn. N.J. (mem. med. adv. bd.), Phi Beta Kappa, Alpha Epsilon Delta, Phi Sigma Phi. Office: Cooper Hosp/Univ Med Ctr 3 Cooper Plz Rm 309 Camden NJ 08103-1438

TRAXLER, EVA MARIA, marketing administrator; b. Phorzheim, Germany, June 1, 1955; d. Wayne Delmar and Ruth Lydia (Mischak) Frasure; m. Richard John Traxler, Mar. 25, 1986. BS, U. Minn., 1980; MBA, U. St. Thomas, 1987. Ops. control planner Gen. Mills, Mpls., 1981; asst. prodn. planner Pillsbury, Mpls., 1982-87, planning specialist, 1987-88; new products planner Land O'Lakes, Mpls., 1988-89, mktg. asst., 1989-90; sr. product mgr., mgr. mdse. svcs. Anchor Hocking Plastics, St. Paul, 1990-94, product mgr. USA direct, 1994; mktg. mgr. Jostens, Mpls., 1995-96; brand mgr. Metacom, 1996—. Big sister Big Bros./Big Sisters, St. Paul, 1982-89, bd. mem., 1986-92.

TRAYLOR, ANGELIKA, stained glass artist; b. Munich, Bavaria, Germany, Aug. 24, 1942; Came to U.S., 1959; d. Walther Artur Ferdinand and Berta Kreszentia (Boeck) Klau; m. Lindsay Montgomery Donaldson, June 10, 1959 (div. 1970); 1 child, Cameron Maria Greta; m. Samuel William Traylor III, June 12, 1970. Student, Pvt. Handelsschule Morawetz Jr. Coll., Munich, 1958. Freelance artist, 1980—. Works featured in profl. jours. including the Daylily Jour., 1987, Design Jour., South Korea, 1989, The Traveler's Guide to American Crafts, 1990, Florida Mag., 1991, Florida Today, 1993, Melbourne Times, 1994, The Orbiter, 1996, The Glass Collector's Digest, 1996. Recipient Fragile Art award Glass Art mag., 1982, 1st Yr. Exhibitor award Stained Glass Assn. Am., 1984, 2d pl. Non-figurative Composition award Vitraux des USA, 1985, Best of Show Stained Glass Assn. Am., 1989, 3d pl., 1989, Merit award George Plimpton All-Star Space Coast Art Open, 1994; named Hist. Woman of Brevard, Brevard Cultural Alliance, 1991, one of 200 Best Am. Craftsmen Early Am. Life mag., 1994, 95. Home and Office: 100 Poinciana Dr Melbourne FL 32937

TREACY, SANDRA JOANNE PRATT, art educator, artist; b. New Haven, Aug. 5, 1934; d. Willis Hadley Jr. and Gladys May (Gell) P.; m. Gillette van Nuyse, Aug. 27, 1955; 1 child, Jonathan Todd. BFA, R.I. Sch. Design, 1956; student, William Paterson Coll., 1973-74. Cert. elem. and secondary tchr., N.J. Tchr. art and music Pkwy. Christian Ch., Ft. Lauderdale, Fla., 1964-66; developer Pequannock Twp. Bd. of Edn., Pompton Plains, N.J., 1970-72, tchr. art, 1972-76; vol. art tchr. Person County Bd. of Edn., Roxboro, N.C., 1978-80, tchr. art, 1980-91; tchr. art So. Jr. High Sch., Roxboro, 1989-91, Woodland Elem. Sch., Roxboro, 1989-93; tchr. Helena Elem. Sch., Timberlake, N.C., 1991-93; tchr. elem. art Bethel Hill Sch., Roxboro, 1974-79, vol. art tchr., 1979-80; tchr. basic art, vol. all elem. schs. Person County, Roxboro, 1977-80; tchr. arts and crafts, summers 1981-882; tchr. art home sch. So. Mid. Sch., 1993—, Person H.S., 1993-94. Artist, illustrator. Mem. Roxboro EMTs, 1979-81; bd. dirs. Person County Arts Coun., 1980--81, 93-95, pres., 1981-82; piano and organ choir accompanist Concord United Meth. Ch., 1981—; leader Morgan Trotters, 1992-94, asst. dir., 1993-96, bd. dirs.; mem. Roxboro Cmty. Choir, 1994—; coach, horseback riding for handicapped. Mem. NEA, Nat. Mus. of Women in the Arts (continuing charter), Smithsonian Assocs., N.C. Assn. Arts Edn., N.C. Assn. Educators, N.C. Art Soc. Mus. of Art, Internat. Platform Assn., Womans Club (tchr. Pompton Plains chpt. 1974-79), Person County Saddle Club (rec. sec. 1981-84), Puddingston Pony Club (dist. sec. 1974-75), Roxboro Garden Club (continuing, commr. 1980-82, pres. 1982-84, 87—, sec. 1993-94, v.p. 1993-95, pres. 1995—), Roxboro Woman's Club (arts dept.). Republican. Home: 1345 Kelly Brewer Rd Leasburg NC 27291-9720

TREADWAY-DILLMON, LINDA LEE, athletic trainer, actress; b. Woodbury, N.J., June 4, 1950; d. Leo Elmer and Ona Lee (Wyckoff) Treadway; m. Randall Kenneth Dillmon, June 19, 1982. BS in Health, Phys. Edn. & Recreation, West Chester State Coll., 1972, MS in Health and Phys. Edn., 1975; postgrad., Ctrl. Mich. U., 1978; Police Officer Stds. Tng. cert. complaint dispatcher, Goldenwest Coll., 1982. Cert. in safety edn. West Chester State Coll.; cert. EMT, Am. Acad. Orthopaedic Surgeons. Grad. asst., instr., asst. athletic trainer West Chester (Pa.) State Coll., 1972-76; asst. prof., program dir., asst. athletic trainer Ctrl. Mich. U., Mt. Pleasant, 1976-80; police dispatcher City of Westminster, Calif., 1980-89; oncology unit sec. Children's Hosp. Orange County, Orange, Calif., 1989-96. Stuntwoman, actress United Stunt Artists, SAG, L.A., 1982—; dancer Disneyland, Anaheim, Calif., 1988—; contbr. articles to profl. jours. Athletic trainer U.S. Olympic Women's Track and Field Trials, Frederick, Md., 1972, AAU Jr. World Wrestling Championships, Mt. Pleasant, Mich., 1977, Mich. Spl. Olympics, Mt. Pleasant, 1977, 78, 79. Named Outstanding Phys. Educator, Delta Psi Kappa, Ctrl. Mich. U., 1980, Outstanding Young Woman of Am., 1984; named to Disneyland Entertainment Hall of Fame, 1995. Mem. SAG, Nat. Athletic Trainers Assn. (cert., women and athletic tng. ad hoc com. 1974-75, placement com. 1974-79, program dirs. coun. 1976-80, ethics com. 1977-80, visitation team 1978-80), U.S. Field Hockey Assn. (player), Pacific S.W. Field Hockey Assn. (player, Nat. Champion 1980, 81, 82), L.A. Field Hockey Assn. (player), Swing Shift Dance Team (dancer). Presbyterian. Home: 15400 Belgrade St Apt 152 Westminster CA 92683-6962

TREANOR, HELEN JUNE, nursing administrator, geriatrics professional; b. Battle Creek, Mich., Dec. 22, 1931; d. Antoine Joseph and Helen June (Jevnem) Hudon; m. Richard Clifford Treanor, Aug. 8, 1953; children: Kathleen, Theresa, Peggy, Michael, John, Sharon, Thomas. Diploma, U. Ill./Cook Co. Sch. Nursing, 1953; BS, Barat Coll., 1986; MBA, Lake Forest Grad. Sch., 1990. RN, CNA, Ill.; cert. nursing home adminstr., Ill., 1992. Staff nurse McNeal Meml. Hosp., Berwyn, Ill., 1953-55, Lake Forest (Ill.) Hosp., 1977-79; staff nurse, head nurse Good Shepherd Hosp., Barrington, Ill., 1979-87; pres., CEO N.W. Suburban Microfilm, Inc., Arlington Heights, Ill., 1987-91; dir. nursing and aux. svcs. Libertyville (Ill.) Manor Rehab. and Healthcare Ctr., 1991—; adv. bd. Lake County Vocat. Sch., Grayslake, Ill., 1992—. Pres. Friends of the Ela Area Libr., Lake Zurich, 1976-77, St. Frances de Sales Women's Orgn., Lake Zurich, Ill., 1970's. Mem. Nat. Assn. Dirs. Nursing Adminstrn. Home: 21539 W Boschome Dr Kildeer IL 60047 Office: Libertyville Manor Rehab and Healthcare Ctr 610 Peterson Rd Libertyville IL 60048

TREAS, JUDITH KAY, sociology educator; b. Phoenix, Jan. 2, 1947; d. John Joseph and Hope Catherine (Thomas) Jennings; m. Benjamin C. Treas II, May 14, 1969; children: Stella, Evan. BA, Pitzer Coll., Claremont, Calif., 1969; MA, UCLA, 1972, PhD, 1976. Instr. U. So. Calif., L.A., 1974-75, asst. prof., 1975-81, assoc. prof., 1981-87, dept. chair, 1984-89, prof., 1987-89; prof. U. Calif., Irvine, 1989, dept. chair, 1989-94; bd. overseers Gen. Social Survey, 1986-88; cons. social sci. and population study sect. NIH, 1989-92. Contbr. articles to profl. jours. Trustee Pitzer Coll., 1977-79. Recipient Rsch. award NSF, 1978-81, 84-91, NIH, 1979-81; Univ. scholar U. So. Calif., 1982-83. Fellow Gerontological Assn. Am.; mem. Golden Key (hon.), Am. Sociol. Assn., Population Assn. Am. Office: U Calif-Irvine Dept Sociology Irvine CA 92697

TREAT, JESSICA THAYER, English educator, writer; b. Moncton, N.B., Can., Aug. 18, 1958; d. Robert Sherman and Mary Lou (Strassburger) T.; m. Henrik Sigurd Haaland; 1 child, Kai Thayer Haaland. BA, Evergreen State Coll., 1981; MFA, CUNY, 1989. Tech. translator Brockman y Schuh, S.A., Mexico City, 1984-86, Bancomer, S.N.C., N.Y.C., 1986-87; English tchr. Bklyn. Coll., 1987-92, Northwestern Conn. Cmty. Tech. Coll., Winsted, 1992—. Author: A Robber in the House, 1993, Dominion Review, 1996 (fiction award 1996); contbr. short stories Ms. Mag., 1993. Mem. Conn. Coalition English Tchrs., Assoc. Writing Programs. Democrat. Office: Northwestern Conn Cmty Tech Coll Park Pl E Winsted CT 06098

TREAT, SHARON ANGLIN, state legislator; b. Brattleboro, Vt., Jan. 30, 1956; d. Robert Sherman and Mary Lou (Strassburger) T. AB, Princeton U., 1978; JD cum laude, Georgetown U., 1982. Bar: Maine, N.J. Asst. dep. pub. adv. N.J. Dept. of the Pub. Adv., Trenton, 1982-85; assoc. atty. Ball, Livingston & Tykulsker, Newark, 1985-86; staff atty. Natural Resources Coun. Maine, Augusta, 1986-90; state rep. Maine State Legis., Augusta, 1991—; pvt. practice Gardiner, Maine, 1991—; leader Ctr. for Policy Alternatives, Washington, 1992—; house chair Human Resources Com., 1993-94, Judiciary Com., 1995-96. Bd. dirs. N.J. Environ. Lobby, Trenton, 1984-86, Maine People's Resource Ctr., Augusta, 1991—, N.E. Citizen Action Resource Ctr., Hartford, Conn., 1992—, Maine Assn. Conservation Commns., 1994—; co-founder, dir. Alliance, Portland, Maine, 1987; trustee Class of 1978 Found., White Plains, N.Y., 1988—; mem. adv. bd. Augusta Area Rape Crisis Ctr., 1992—; mem. adv. coun. Divsn. of Deafness, 1994—; mem. Natural Resources Coun. Maine, Maine Women's Lobby. Mem. Gardiner Libr. Assn., Rotary. Democrat. Office: PO Box 12 Gardiner ME 04345 also: Maine Ho of Reps State House Augusta ME 04333-0002

TREFTS, JOAN LANDENBERGER, principal, educator; b. Pitts., Jan. 31, 1930; d. William Henry III and Eleanore (Campbell) Landenberger; m. Albert Sharpe Trefts Sr., June 20, 1952; children: Dorothy, Albert Jr., William, Deborah, Elizabeth. AB, Western Coll. for Women, 1952; M., John Carroll U., 1982, John Carroll U., 1984. Cert. home economist, cert. prin., N.Y., Ohio, supr., biol. sci., econs., home econs., vocat. edn., pre-kindergarten edn. Summer sch. prin. John Adams High Sch., Cleve., 1972—; cons. Cleve. Partnership Program. Named Tchr. of Yr., Cleve., 1994. Mem. Colonial Dames Am. (pres. chpt., nat. officer ct. honor), Daus. Am. Colonists (state officer), Daus. XVIII Century (state pres.), DAR, Am. Home Econ. Assn., Ohio Vocat. Assn. (bd. dirs.), Am. Vocat. Assn. (nat. com). Republican. Presbyterian. Home: 20101 Malvern Rd Shaker Heights OH 44122

TREGO, NANCY REMINE, community health fund raiser; b. Richmond, Va., Feb. 18, 1948; d. James Andrew and Miriam Franklin (Bruce) ReM.; m. Geoffrey Garrett Trego, Sept. 26, 1982 (div. 1995); children: James Neal, Garrett Douglas. BA in Govt., William and Mary, 1970. With U.S. Dept. Labor, Washington, 1970-73; with Nat. Assn. Counties, Washington, 1973-82, dep. assoc. dir., 1978-82; freelance writer, 1993; policy analyst Nat. Commn. Employment Policy, Washington, 1983-85, congl. liaison, 1985-87; grants mgr., dir. fund devel. & fin. Bon Secours-St. Mary's Health Care Found., Richmond, 1994—; mem. Capital Area Pvt. Industry Coun., Richmond, 1994—; Project Immunize Va., 1995—. Editor, author Co. Manpower Report, 1973-82; editor: CETA Works, CETA Works for Business; contbr. articles to newspapers. Mem. Sch. Health Adv. Com. Henrico County, 1996, Healthy Families Task Force, Henrico County, 1995-96. Mem. Va. PTA (life). Office: Bon Secours-St Mary's Health Care Found 5008 Monument Ave Richmond VA 23230

TREICHEL, JEANIE NIERI, computer company executive; b. South San Francisco, May 23, 1931; d. Robert Tancredi and Lena Marie (Borelli) Nieri; m. Georg Treichel, Mar. 14, 1955; children: Carl Stanford, Tiffany (dec.), Todd (dec.), Jennifer (dec.), David (dec.). BA, San Jose State U., 1952, MA, 1955; MBA, Golden Gate U., 1983. Tchr. San Mateo (Calif.) City Sch. Dist., 1952-55; research assoc. The Conservation Found., Africa, 1956-58; from research sec. to systems doc., administrn. Xerox Palo Alto (Calif.) Research Cnt., 1974-82; asst. treas. Sutherland, Sproull & Assoc., Menlo Park, Calif., 1982-90; mgr. lab. ops. & pubs. Sun Microsys. Labs., Mountainview, Calif., 1990—. Mem. Assn. Computing Machinery, Alpine Hills Tennis Club, Sequoia Yacht Club. Republican. Roman Catholic. Office: Sun Microsystems Labs 2550 Garcia Ave Mountain View CA 94043-1109

TREJOS, CHARLOTTE MARIE, humanities educator, consultant; b. Trout Lake, Mich., July 5, 1920; d. Charles Floyd and Lula May (Force) Draper; m. J. Mario Trejos, Jan. 8, 1961; 1 child, J. Mario Jr. Tchg. credentials, State of Calif., 1989; MA (hon.), Hawthorne Coll., 1975; DD (hon.), Min. Salvation Ch., 1986. Tchr. English El Colegio Anglo-Am., Cochabamba, Bolivia, 1965-66; tchr. Hawthorne (Calif.) Christian Sch., 1966-75; owner Trejos Literary Cons., Carson, Calif., 1976—. Author: My Carson, Your Carson, 1987, Variegated Verse, 1973, Yesterday Was Sunday, 1994; contbg. editor Health Care Horizons, 1979-89; contbr. articles to profl. jours. Voter registerer Democrats, Carson, 1975—. With U.S. Army, 1942-43. Named Poet of Yr. Nat. Poetry Pub. Assn., 1974; recipient Cert. of Merit Dictionary of Internat. Biography, 1974, Medal of Honor Am. Biog. Inst., 1987, Golden Poet award World of Poetry, 1993. Mem. Soc. Ibero-Am. Escritores de Los Estados Unidos Am. (pres. 1985—, Cert. Recognition 1986), Profl. Writers L.A. Chpt. Home and Office: 18235 Avalon Blvd Carson CA 90746-1802

TRELKA, JANICE MARGARET NACE, secondary education educator; b. Cleve., Nov. 9, 1944; d. Allen Samuel and Ethel (Pinhard) Nace; m. Martin Frank Trelka, June 24, 1978. Student, Merrill-Palmer Inst., Detroit, 1965; BE, Ashland Coll., 1966, health tchr. cert., 1985; MEd, Cleve. State U., 1976. Supr. indsl. cafeteria Republic Steel, Cleve., 1967-68; bank teller Cen. Nat. Bank, Cleve., 1968-69; tchr. home econs. Lorain (Ohio) City Schs., 1969—; speaker Cleve. Ctr. for Econ. Edn., 1975, Ohio Home Econs. Conf., 1984, 86, 88, 89, 93, Ohio Edn. Assn., 1985; mem. impact home econs. curriculum guide task force State Dept. Edn., Columbus, Ohio, 1977, mem. mid. sch. resource guide devel., 1988. Tchr. Sunday sch., Cleve., 1967-74; treas. PTA Hawthorne-Boone Sch., Lorain, 1971-74; mem. state bd. Women's Commn., Columbus, 1978-86; mem. bd. Christian edn., Lorain, 1982-88; mem. Sexually Transmitted Disease Task Force, Lorain, 1989-92, Vocat. Task Force, Lorain, 1990-93; mem. choir. State Recognition for Martha Holden Jennings Grant Implementation, 1984; recipient Curriculum Writing Contest 3d Pl. award Ohio Coun. on Econ. Edn., 1984, 1st Pl. award, 1985, Nat. Cert. of Merit award Joint Coun. on Econ. Edn., 1986. Mem. NEA, Am. Vocat. Assn., Am. Home Econs. Assn. (cert.), Ohio Edn. Assn., Ohio Vocat. Assn., Ohio Home Econs. Assn., Lorain Edn. Assn., Lorain County Home Econs. Assn. Home: 2611 Denver Ave Lorain OH 44055-1457 Office: Lorain Mid Sch 602 Washington Ave Lorain OH 44052

TREMBATH, MARJORIE FAYE, elementary school educator; b. Fosston, Minn., July 4, 1949; d. Alvin G. and Margith E. (Hagen) Modin; m. Glen H. Trembath, June 9, 1973; children: Eric, Corey. BS, Bemidji State Coll., 1971; MA, U. St. Thomas, St. Paul, 1995. Tchr. 3rd grade Warren (Minn.) Pub. Sch., 1971-77; tchr. 2nd grade East Grand Forks (Minn.) Pub. Sch., 1977-81, tchr. 1st grade, 1981-84, tchr. 2nd grade, 1984—. Mem. libr. bd. Our Saviors Luth. Ch., East Grand Forks, 1975-88, confirmation instr., 1988-93. Mem. North Star Reading Coun. Democrat. Lutheran. Home: 29 Garden Ct NW East Grand Forks MN 56721-1237

TREMBLY, CRISTY, television executive; b. Oakland, Md., July 11, 1958; d. Charles Dee and Mary Louise (Cassidy) T. BA in Russian, German and Linguistics cum laude, W.Va. U., 1978, BS in Journalism, 1978, MS in Broadcast Journalism, 1979; advanced cert. travel, West L.A. Coll., 1982; advanced cert. recording engring., Soundmaster Schs., North Hollywood, Calif., 1985. Videotape engr. Sta. WWVU-TV, Morgantown, W.Va., 1976-80; announcer, engr. Sta. WVVW Radio, Grafton, W.Va., 1979; tech. dir., videotape supr. Sta. KMEX-TV, L.A., 1980-85; broadcast supr. Sta. KADY-TV, Oxnard, Calif., 1988-89; news tech. dir. Sta. KVEA-TV, Glendale, Calif., 1985-89; asst. editor, videotape technician CBS TV Network, Hollywood, Calif., 1989-90; videotape supr. Sta. KCBS-TV, Hollywood, 1990-91, mgr. electronic news gathering ops., 1991-92; studio mgr., engr.-in-charge CBS TV Network, Hollywood, 1992—; radio operator KJ6BX Malibu Disaster Comm., 1987—. Producer (TV show) The Mountain Scene, 1976-78. Sr. orgn. pres. Children of the Am. Revolution, Malibu, Calif., 1992—; chmn. adminstrv. coun. Malibu United Meth. Ch., 1994—; sec., mem. adv. com. Tamassee (S.C.) Sch., 1992—; vol. Ch. Coun., L.A. Riot Rebldg., Homeless shelter work, VA Hosps., Mus. docent; sponsor 3 overseas foster children. Recipient Outstanding Young Woman of Am., 1988, Asst. editor Emmy award Young and the Restless, 1989-90, Golden Mike award Radio/TV News assn., 1991, 92. Mem. DAR (state chair jr. membership 1987-88, state chair scholarships 1992-94, state chmn. jr. contest 1994-96, others, Malibu chpt. regent 1991, state chair motion pictures radio and TV Calif. 1988-90, Mex. 1990—, Nat. Outstanding Jr. 1993, nat. vice-chair broadcast media 1995—), Am. Women in Radio and TV (so. Calif. bd. 1984-85, 93-95, pres.-elect 1995-96, pres. 1996—), Soc. Profl. Journalists, Women in Comms., Travelers Century Club (program chair 1987—), Acad. TV Arts and Scis. (exec. com. electronic prodn. 1992—, nat. awards com. 1994—), Soc. Broadcast Engrs., Mensa (life), SMPTE, Beta Sigma Phi. Democrat. Methodist. Home: 2901 Searidge St Malibu CA 90265-2969 Office: CBS TV City 7800 Beverly Blvd Los Angeles CA 90036-2165

TREMONTE SPIGONARDO, ADA MARY, interior architect; b. Phila., Jan. 15, 1959; d. John Robert and Anne Rita (Di Carlo) Tremonte; m. Giuliano Spigonardo, Sept. 17, 1983; children: Ariella, Gianna, Vincenzo. BS, Drexel U., 1980. Design asst. Daroff Design Inc., Phila., 1978-80; project mgr. Curtis, Cox, Kennerly, Phila., 1980-85; project dir. The Design Partnership, Phila., 1985-87; assoc. Space Design, Phila., 1985-87; founding ptnr. AI-FIVE inc., Phila., 1987—; tchr. Architecture in Schs. program Phila. Pub. Schs., 1984-89. Active Unite of United Way, Darby, Pa., 1991. Mem. Found. for Architecture, Omicron Nu. Republican. Roman Catholic. Office: AI-FIVE Inc 1712 Walnut St # 2 Philadelphia PA 19103-6101

TREMPE, SUSAN CAROL, protective services official; b. Grosse Point, Mich., Nov. 7, 1951; d. William Augustus and Helen Louis (Murray) T.; 1 child, Susan Ann. AA, Chgo. City Coll., 1994. Cert. Law Enforcement, Chgo., 1986. Security agent Marshall Field, Skokie, Ill., 1975-77, asst. security mgr., 1977-83; security mgr. Marshall Field, Evanston, Ill., 1983-86; police officer Chgo. Police Dept., 1986—. Mem. Fraternal Order of Police, Ill. Women in Law Enforcement, Ill. Police Assn. Episcopalian. Office: City of Chgo Police Dept 1121 S State St Chicago IL 60601

TRENERY, MARY ELLEN, librarian; b. Conran, Mo., Jan. 10, 1939; d. John Herman and Stella Cecelia (Durbin) Hulshof; m. Frank E. Trenery, June 10, 1967. BA in Classics, Coll. New Rochelle, 1962; MALS, Rosary Coll., River Forest, Ill., 1966; postgrad., Fla. Atlantic U., Boca Raton, 1986-89. Tchr. grades 6, 8 Archdiocesan Sch. System, St. Louis, 1962-64; serials and acquisition libr. U. Ill., Chgo., 1966-69; acquisitions, circulation and cataloging libr. Rosary Coll., River Forest, Ill., 1964-66, 70-72; libr. media specialist St. Coleman Cath. Sch., Pompano Beach, Fla., 1973-94; coord. for self study St. Coleman Schs., 1982, 83, 89, 90; cons. Pompano Beach City Libr. Author: Policies and Procedures for School Libraries, 1976, UICC Call Number (founding editor), 1967-68, NIUCLA Newsletter (editor 1969-72). Fed. Funding liaison with Broward County Sch. Bd., 1974-94. Mem. Ill. Libr. Assn. (rsch. and tech. svcs. div. chair 1967-69), Cath. Libr. Assn. (No. Ill. unit chair, sec. 1969-72).

TRENT, JOYCE MILLER, librarian; b. Dayton, Ohio, Dec. 7, 1946; d. Fielding Leo and Joyce (Henry) Miller; m. Robert Cody Trent, Mar. 17, 1973; children—Michael Frederick Cody, Paul Templeton, Mark Fielding. B.A., Stephen F. Austin State U., 1969; M.L.S., U. Tex., Austin, 1975. Pub. service librarian Deer Park Pub. Library, Tex., 1969-73; system interlibrary loan librarian San Antonio Pub. Library, 1975-76; dir. system, county librarian Atascosa County Library System, Jourdanton, Tex., 1976-81; library dir. Leon Valley (Tex.) Pub. Library, 1981—. Biweekly columnist N.W. Leader, 1981—. Pres. parish council St. Brigid's Ch., San Antonio, 1980-81; del. Met. Congl. Alliance, San Antonio, 1982—; mem. civic affairs com. Tex. Sesquicentennial Com., Leon Valley, 1984—. Mem. ALA, Tex. Library Assn. (treas. dist. 10, vice chair-elect, then chair), Leon Valley Bus. and Profl. Assn., San Antonio Geneal. Hist. Soc. (sec. 1977-78). Democrat. Roman Catholic. Home: 5903 Forest Rim St San Antonio TX 78240-3218 Office: Leon Valley Pub Library 6425 Evers Rd San Antonio TX 78238-1453

TRENTHAM, EDWINA ANN, poet, English language educator; b. Hamilton, Bermuda, Dec. 9, 1940; came to U.S., 1959; d. Everard Noel Rye Trentham and Mary Winifride (Dobbin) Payne; m. Brian Berkeley Burland, July 7, 1962 (div. June 1975); 1 child, Benjamin De Lisle Burland. BA in English magna cum laude, Wesleyan U., 1980; MFA in Poetry, U. Mass., 1983. Assoc. prof. Asnuntuck Comty. Tech. Coll., Enfield, Conn., 1986—; adj. instr. Middlesex (Conn.) C.C., 1983-84, U. Hartford, West Hartford, Conn., 1984-86; vis. instr. continuing edn. Conn. Coll., New London, 1986-89; vis. instr. grad. liberal studies program Wesleyan U., Middletown, Conn., 1989—; group facilitator Southeastern Conn. Libr. Assn., 1987-90; presenter So. Conn. State U. Women's Studies Conf., 1991, 93, 29th Ann. N.E. Regional Conf. on English in 2-Yr. Colls., 1995; faculty rep. acad. affairs coun. Asnuntuck Comty. Tech. Coll., 1987-92, co-chair instrnl. excellence com., 1991—; poetry readings include Albertus Magnus Coll., New Haven, Ctr. for Creative Youth, Wesleyan U., Middletown, Hopkins Sch., New Haven, Verso Books, N.Y.C. Feature writer New Haven Advocate, 1978; actor, playwright New Haven St. and Children's Theatre, 1974-75; contbr. poetry to revs. and anthologies including The South Fla. Poetry Rev., The Poetry Miscellany, New Va. Rev., Harvard Mag., The Denny Poems, The Bridge, The Bermudian Mag., The Am. Voice, 1995-1996 Anthology of Mag. Verse and Poetry Year Book. Counselor New Haven Rape Crisis Ctr., 1973-75. Winner Gloucester County Coll. Poetry Contest, 1993, Embers 7th Poetry Competition, 1984, Billee Murray Denny Nat. Poetry Contest, 1983, 84, Chester H. Jones Nat. Poetry Competition, 1982, 90, 94; recipient N.Y. Poetry Forum prize, 1980; Yaddo fellow, summer 1989. Mem. Yeats Soc., Phi Beta Kappa. Home: 364 Central Ave New Haven CT 06515 Office: Asnuntuck Comty Tech Coll 170 Elm St Enfield CT 06082

TREPPLER, IRENE ESTHER, state senator; b. St. Louis County, Mo., Oct. 13, 1926; d. Martin H. and Julia C. (Bender) Hagemann; student

Meramec Community Coll., 1972; m. Walter J. Treppler, Aug. 18, 1950; children: John M., Steven A., Diane V. Anderson, Walter W. Payroll chief USAF Aero. Chart Plant, 1943-51; enumerator U.S. Census Bur., St. Louis, 1960, crew leader, 1970; mem. Mo. Ho. of Reps., Jefferson City, 1972-84; mem. Mo. Senate, Jefferson City, 1985—; chmn. Minority Caucus, 1991-92. ActiveGravois Twp. Rep. Club, Concord Twp. Rep. Club; alt. del. Rep. Nat. Conv., 1976, 84. Recipient Spirit Enterprise award Mo. C. of C., 1992, Appreciation award Mo. State Med. Assn., Nat. Otto Nuttli Earthquake Hazard Mitigation award, 1993, Disting. Legislator award Cmty. Colls. Mo., 1995; named Concord Twp. Rep. of Yr., 1992. Mem. Nat. Order Women Legislators (rec. sec. 1981-82, pres. 1985), Nat. Fedn. Rep. Women. Mem. Evangelical Ch. Office: Mo State Senate Rm 433 Jefferson City MO 65101

TRESCOTT, SARA LOU, water resources engineer; b. Frederick, Md., Nov. 17, 1954; d. Norton James and Mabel Elizabeth (Hall) T.; m. R. Jeffrey Franklin, Oct. 8, 1983. AA, Catonsville C.C., Balt., 1974; BA in Biol. Sci., U. Md., Balt., 1980. Sanitarian Md. Dept. Health & Mental Hygiene, Greenbelt, 1982; indsl. hygienist Md. Dept. Licensing & Regualtion, Balt., 1982-85; from water resources engr. to chief dredging div. Md. Dept. Natural Resources, Annapolis, 1985-92; chief navigation div. Md. Dept. Natural Resources, Stevensville, 1992-96, chief ops. & maintenance, 1996—; chair adv. bd. EEO, Annapolis, 1990-92; tech. com. Nat. Mgmt. Info. Systems, Balt., 1983. Contbr. articles to profl. jours. Mem. ASCE, County Engrs. Assn. Md. Democrat. Home: PO Box 22 Woodbine MD 21797-0022 Office: DNR Navigation Divsn 305 Marine Academy Dr Stevensville MD 21666-2859

TRESMONTAN-STITT, OLYMPIA DAVIS, clinical counselor, psychotherapy educator, consultant; b. Boston, Nov. 27, 1925; d. Peter Konstantin and Mary (Hazimanolis) Davis; B.S., Simmons Coll., 1946; M.A., Wayne State U., 1960; Ph.D. (Schaefer Found. grantee), U. Calif., Berkeley, 1971; m. Dion Marc Tresmontan, Sept. 15, 1957 (dec. Mar. 1961); m. 2d, Robert Baker Stitt, Mar. 21, 1974. Lic. clin. counselor. Child welfare worker San Francisco Dept. Social Service, 1964-66; sensitivity tng. NSF Sci. Curriculum Improvement Study, U. Calif., Berkeley, 1967-68; individual practice psychol. counseling, San Francisco, 1971-92, individual practice clin. counselor, Morrill, Maine, 1995—; dir. Studio Ten Services, San Francisco, Promise for Children, San Francisco, 1981-88; tchr. U. Calif. extension at San Francisco, 1971-72, Chapman Coll. Grad. Program in Counseling, Travis AFB, 1971-74; clin. cons. Childworth Learning Ctr., San Francisco, 1976-80; cons. project rape response Queen's Bench Found., San Francisco, 1977; adjunct instr. Unity Coll., Maine, 1992; adv. bd. Childrens' Multicultural Mus., San Francisco, 1988-92. Active Women's Heritage Mus., Palo Alto, Calif., 1991-92, Friends of Belfast (Maine) Free Libr., 1993—, Friends of the San Francisco Pub. Libr., 1971-92, 95—; bd. dirs. Childworth Learning Center, 1976-80. Mem. Am. Psychol. Assn., Am. Orthopsychiat. Assn., Calif. Assn. Marriage, Family and Child Therapists. Author: (with J. Morris) The Evaluation of A Compensatory Education Program, 1967; (Karplus edit.) What is Curriculum Evaluation, Six Answers, 1968. Home: RR 1 Box 632 Morrill ME 04952-9709

TRETTIS, LYDIA A., advertising executive; b. New Haven, Apr. 22, 1961; d. Donald Robert and Jane Frances (Mulvey) T. BA, U. Mass., 1983. Media assoc. Advt. Agy. Assocs., Newton, Mass.; chartist Fidelity Investments, Boston; rsch. dir., reporter The Bus. Jour. Charlotte, N.C.; pub. rels. mgr. Sci. Faction Corp., N.Y.C.; account exec. HWH Pub. Rels., N.Y.C.; dir. new media Connors Comm., N.Y.C. Mem. N.Y. New Media Assn. Office: Connors Comm 3 W 21st St New York NY 10010

TREVINO-COE, MERCEDES JOY, artist, art educator; b. Mexico City, Jan. 30, 1955; d. Manuel Treviño and Leora Ann Murphy; children: Brittany, Mercedes. BAA, U. Fla., 1979. Admissions dir. Ringling Sch. Art & Design, Sarasota, Fla., 1980-84; founder, dir. Thee Coffeehouse Art & Music, Sarasota, Fla., 1980-85; pres. Art Svcs., Sarasota, Fla., 1980—; v.p. pub. rels. mktg. Sta. WWZZ, Fla., 1985-89; assoc. dir., dir. pub. rels. Girls Inc., Sarasota, 1990-93; instr. Family's Creative Workshops Art & Healing Sch., Sarasota, Mercedes Trevino Sch. of Art and Alternative Healing, Sarasota; cons. dir. Differently Abled Persons, Sarasota, 1994—; art judge Sarasota Centennial Youth Art Exhibits, 1990, Fla. State Fair Authority, Tampa. Editor, artist: The Arts Guide, 1987; editor Featherweight, 1996. Active Amnesty Internat., N.Y.C., 1980—, Women's Internat. League Peace and Freedom; charter mem. Adv. Commn. Status of Women, Sarasota; bd. dirs. Mental Health Assn., Sarasota, 1988-92; chairperson, bd. dirs. Women's Resource Ctr., Sarasota, 1980—. Named One of 25 Leading Women Execs. in Southwest Fla., AT&T & Fla. Bus. Jour., 1985. Democrat. Home: 6715 Ave D Sarasota FL 34231

TREVOR, LESLIE JEAN, special education educator; b. Texas City, Tex., Mar. 22, 1957; d. William Giles and Betty Jo (Langhammer) Hill; m. Stephen Lynn Trevor, June 11, 1988. BS in Elem. Edn., U. Tex., 1979. Tchr. reading Wiederstein Elem. Sch., Cibolo, Tex., 1979-82; tchr. compensatory Olympia Elem. Sch., Universal City, Tex., 1992—. Mem. Jr. League San Antonio, 1994—. Mem. Assn. Tex. Profl. Educators, U. Tex. Austin Alumni Assn. (life), No. Hills Country Club, Gamma Phi Beta (pres. 1979-80), Gamma Phi. Republican. Lutheran. Home: 16650 Huebner Rd Apt 1012 San Antonio TX 78248 Office: Olympia Elem Sch 8439 Athenian Universal City TX 78148

TREXLER, SUZANNE FRANCES, geriatrics nurse; b. Harrisburg, Pa., Feb. 8, 1963; d. Walter Richard and Catherine Frances (Mourawski) Markham; m. Barry Kenneth Trexler, Nov. 9, 1991; children: William Chester, Brittany Nancy, Katye Iona. LPN, Harrisburg Stelton Highs, Sch. Practical Nursing, 1984; ADN, Harrisburg (Pa.) Area C.C., 1984; BA in Long Term Care Adminstrn., St. Joseph Coll., 1994, postgrad., 1994—; BSN, York (Pa.) Coll., 1996. Nurse ICU and critical care unit Meml. Hosp., York, Pa., 1987-88; staff nurse emergency dept. Polyclinic Med. Ctr., Harrisburg, 1988-91; assoc. prof. Nat. Edn. Ctr.-Jr. Coll., Harrisburg, 1991; dir. nursing Camp Hill (Pa.) Care Ctr., 1991-92; resident assessment supr. Susquehanna Ctr., Harrisburg, 1992-94; dir. nursing Susquehanna Luth. Village, Millersburg, Pa., 1994-95; asst. adminstr. Dauphin Manor, Harrisburg, 1995—; ACLS, CPR instr. Am. Heart Assn., Harrisburg, 1989—; BCLS, CPR instr. ARC, Harrisburg, 1992—; RN, paramedic Lebanon (Pa.) County First Aide and Safety Patrol, 1992—. Sec. Little People PTA, Harrisburg, 1991-92; pres. Student Human Resource Mgmt. Club, York (Pa.) Coll., 1992—. Recipient Nurse of Hope award Am. Cancer Soc., Dauphin County, Harrisburg, 1983-84. Mem. AACN, Pa. Nurses Assn., Pa. Dir. Nursing Assn. for Long Term Care, PANPHA (advocate). Roman Catholic. Office: Dauphen Manor Paxton St Harrisburg PA 17111

TREYBIG, EDWINA HALL, sales executive; b. Ft. Worth, Dec. 12, 1949; d. George Edward and Lillian Wanita (Herring) Hall; m. Jerry Kenneth Treybig, Sept. 20, 1980; children: Allison Lindsey, Gifford Carl, Brick Edward. BS in Home Econs., Tex. Tech U., 1972. Office mgr. Am. Internat. Rent-A-Car, Dallas, 1973, gen. mgr., 1973-74; sales rep. Martinez Mud Co., Denver, 1977-80, Am. Mud Co., Denver, 1980-83, Robinson Construction Co., Denver, 1983-87, Dig-It, Inc., N.Y.C., 1987-88; sales rep., corp. sec. Treybig Enterprises, Littleton, Colo., 1984—. Organizer Mile High Golf Tournament, Denver, 1980-84; mem. subcom. Colo. Devel. Disabilities Planning coun., Denver, 1989-90; mem. Coalition to Insure the Uninsurable, Denver, 1989-90. Mem. Soc. Petroleum Engrs. (organizer golf tournament), Internat. Assn. Drilling Contractors, Ind. Producers Assn. Mountain States, Assn. Retarded Citizens, Denver Petroleum Club (organizer golf tournament), Alpha Chi Omega (social chmn. 1970-72). Republican. Mem. Ch. of Christ. Home and Office: 7397 S Fillmore Cir Littleton CO 80122-1942

TRIBBLE, KAREN LYNN, music and gifted education educator; b. Erie, Pa., Feb. 17, 1965; d. Charles Alan and Nancy Louise (Sands) T. BS in Music Edn., Indiana U. of Pa., 1987. Oboist Erie Chamber Orch., 1987-90; instr. Mercyhurst Coll., Erie, 1990-92; music tchr. Fairview (Pa.) Sch. Dist., 1987—; visual ensemble technician Railmen Drum and Bugle Corps, Omaha, 1994—, Edinboro U. of Pa. Winter Colorguard, 1995—, Slippery Rock U. of Pa. Marching Band, 1995—, Cochranton (Pa.) H.S. Marching Band, 1986-87, Seneca H.S. Marching Band, Wattsburg, Pa., 1989-92; asst. dir. Lake Erie Regiment Drum and Bugle Corps, Erie, 1995-96. Vol. bd. dirs. Lake Erie Fanfare, Inc., Erie, 1990—. Mem. Delta Omicron (v.p. 1985-86). Lutheran. Home: 4167 W Ridge Rd Apt 2 Erie PA 16506-1751 Office: Fairview Sch Dist 7460 Mccray Rd Fairview PA 16415-2401

TRICHEL, MARY LYDIA, middle school educator; b. Rosenberg, Tex., Feb. 2, 1957; d. Henry John and Henrietta (Jurek) Pavlicek; m. Keith Trichel, Aug. 8, 1981; children: Daniel, Nicholas. BS cum laude, Tex. A & M U., 1980. Cert. tchr., Tex. Social studies tchr. grades 6, 7 and 8 St. Francis de Sales, Houston, 1980-81; English tchr. grades 7 and 8 Dean Morgan Jr. High, Casper, Wyo., 1983-86; English and journalism tchr. grades 9 and 11 Tecumseh (Okla.) High Sch., 1987; English tchr. grade 6 Christa McAuliffe Middle Sch., Houston, 1988-92; tchr. Tex. history grade 7, journalism grade 8 Lake Olympia Middle Sch., Missouri City, Tex., 1991-92; tchr. social studies 6th grade Lake Olympia Mid. Sch. Ft. Bend Ind. Sch. Dist., 1993—. Recipient teaching awards. Mem. Nat. Coun. Tchrs. English, Nat. Coun. Tchrs. Social Studies, Am. Fedn. Tchrs. Home: 3707 Pin Oak Ct Missouri City TX 77459-7018

TRICK, ANN LOUISE, accountant; b. Jefferson Parish, La.; d. Claybourne and Avis Margaret (Middleton) Waldrop; m. Joseph Michael Trick, Dec. 28, 1982 (div.); children: Philip Michael, Justin Anthony, Kristen Alicia. BA, Tex. Tech. U., 1979; M of Profl. Acctg., U. Tex., Arlington, 1992. CPA, Tex. Acct. exec., office mgr. DBG & H, Dallas, 1979-80; bus. mgr. Creative Microsystems, Inc., Dayton, Ohio, 1980-81; office mgr. Sinclair & Rush, Inc., Arlington, 1981-83, Norand Corp., Arlington, 1983-84; acct. Price Waterhouse, Ft. Worth, 1992-95; sr. acct. Millers Group, Ft. Worth, 1995—, sr. fin. analyst, 1995—. SERVA vol. Arlington Ind. Sch. Dist., 1990-91; den leader Cub Scout Pack 389, Arlington, 1992-93; mem. bd. fin. All Saints Luth. Ch. Recipient Scholarship Cert. of Merit, Inst. Cert. Mgmt. Accts., 1991; scholar Am. Women's Soc. CPAs, 1991, Mid Cities Assn. CPAs, 1991. Mem. Am. Soc. Women Accts., Tex. Soc. CPAs, Inst. Mgmt. Accts. (assoc. dir. acad. rels. 1991-92, dir. acad. rels. 1992-93), Beta Alpha Psi, Beta Gamma Sigma. Office: Millers Group PO Box 2269 Fort Worth TX 76113-2269

TRIEDMAN-SCHARFF, KAREN, design educator, consultant; b. N.Y.C., Dec. 15, 1957. AB in Am. Civilization, Brown U., 1975; MA in Arts, SUNY, Albany, 1982; MFA in Painting, U. Chgo., 1984. Tchg. asst., instr. drawing SUNY, 1980-82; instr. visual merchandising C.C. of R.I., Warwick, 1990-91; instr. visual merchandising, design, color theory RISD, Providence, 1988—; cons. on exhibit design, visual merchandising and color/. Contbr. articles to profl. jours. Treas. Miriam Hosp. Women's Assn., Providence, 1986-89; chmn. design com. The Tomorrow Fund at Hashbro Children's Hosp., Providence, 1996; mem. edn. com. Gordon Sch., East Providence, R.I., 1995-96. Grantee U. Chgo., 1982-84. Mem. Coll. Art Assn. Office: RDC PO Box 40303 Providence RI 02940-0303

TRIFOLI-CUNNIFF, LAURA CATHERINE, psychologist, consultant; b. L.I., N.Y., June 8, 1958; d. Peter Nicholas and Susan Maria (Graziano) T.; m. John Kevin Cunniff, June 6, 1992; 1 child, James Peter. BA, Hofstra U., Uniondale, N.Y., 1980, MA, 1982, PhD, 1986. Founder, prin. Quality Cons., West Islip, N.Y., 1980-87; sr. tng. officer Norstar Bank, Garden City, N.Y., 1985-87; asst. v.p. mgmt. devel. First Boston Corp., N.Y.C., 1986-90; mgr. exec. devel. Merrill Lynch, N.Y.C., 1990-91; pres. The Exec. Process, 1991—; cons. Am. Mgmt. Assn., N.Y.C., 1981-83, AT&T, Basking Ridge, N.H., 1982-83, The First Boston Corp., 1991—, Goldman Sachs, 1991—, Merrill Lynch & Co., 1991—, Union Bank of Switzerland, 1991—, Sanford C. Bernstein & Co., 1992—, Alexander & Alexander, 1993—, S.G. Warburg, 1994; instr. dept. psychology Hofstra U., 1983-85. Author: Vietnam Veterans: Post Traumatic Stress and its Effects, 1986; contbr. articles to profl. publs. Shift coord. Islip Hotline, 1976-78; eucharistic min. Hofstra U. Cath. Soc., 1980-85, Good Samaritan Hosp., West Islip, N.Y., 1988—. Scholar, Hofstra U., 1978-81, fellow, 1980, 81. Mem. Am. Psychol. Assn., Am. Soc. Tng. and Devel., Nat. Psychol. Honor Soc., Internat. Platform Soc. Roman Catholic. Office: 2906 Bree Hill Rd Oakton VA 22124-1212

TRIFONIDIS, BEVERLY ANN, lecturer, opera company manager, accountant; b. Dallas, Dec. 19, 1947; d. Philo McGill and Mary Elizabeth (Sikes) Burney; m. Paul Douglas Spikes, June, 1968 (div. 1976); m. Chris Trifonidis, August 1979 (div. 1986); 1 child, Alexandra. BBA, U. Tex., 1971, M in Profl. Acctg., 1976. CPA, Tex. Mgmt. trainee J.C. Penney Co., Austin, Tex., 1971-72; acctg. clk. SW Ednl. Devel. Lab., Austin, 1972-73; editorial asst. Jour. of Mktg., Austin, 1974-76; staff auditor Hurdman & Cranstoun, CPA's, San Francisco, 1976; instr. acctg. U. Tex., San Antonio, 1976-77; lectr. U. Tex., Austin, 1991; lectr. acctg. Simon Fraser U., Burnaby, B.C., Can., 1978-79, 81-84; gen. mgr. Vancouver (Can.) Opera, 1984-91; Bd. dirs. B.C. Devel. Corp., Banff Sch. Advanced Mgmt. Bd. dirs. United Way, 1988; mem. spl. coun. Com. on Arts, Vancouver, 1987; exec. bd. Vancouver Cultural Alliance, 1987. Mem. AICPA, Tex. Soc. CPAs. Presbyterian. Office: care Vancouver Arts Stabiltn Team, 1040 Burrard St Ste 200, Vancouver, BC Canada V6Z 2R9

TRIGERE, PAULINE, fashion designer; b. Paris, Nov. 4, 1912; came to U.S., 1937, naturalized, 1942; d. Alexandre and Cecile (Coriene) Trigere; children: Jean-Pierre, Philippe Radley. Student, Victor Hugo Coll., Paris. Began career at Martial et Armand, Paris, 1937, became asst. designer at Hattie Carnegie, N.Y.C.; started House of Trigere, N.Y.C., 1942. Recipient Coty Am. Fashion Critics award, 1994, Return award, 1951, Neiman-Marcus award, 1950, Cotton award Nat. Cotton Coun., 1959, award Filene's, 1959, Coty Hall of Fame award, 1959, Silver medal City of Paris, 1972, medal of Vermeil City of Paris, 1982, Lifetime Achievement award, 1992, Nat. Arts Club award, 1993, Coun. of Fashion Designers Lifetime Achievement award Lincoln Ctr., 1994; celebrated 50 yrs. in the bus. at Fashion Inst. Tech., 1992. Office: Trigere Inc 498 7th Ave New York NY 10018-6701

TRIGOBOFF, SYBELLE, artist, art educator, lecturer; b. Brooklyn, N.Y., Feb. 20, 1932; d. Sol and Esther Devorah (Novack) Rosenberg; m. Harold Trigoboff; children: Norman Jed, Sharon Malva, Hinda Leah. Curator, artist Amontri Gallery, N. Bellmore, N.Y., 1964-66; lectr., critique Greenbriar Art Workshops, N. Bellmore, N.Y., 1970—, Drawing From Life Model Workshops, N. Bellmore, N.Y., 1975—; vis. lectr. art assns., pub. librs., colls., L. I., N.Y., 1970—, B.O.C.E.S. Cultural Arts Ctr., Syosset, N.Y., 1990-91; mem. art adv. com. N. Bellmore Pub. Libr., 1972-77; owner, cons. Atrigart, L.I., N.Y., 1980—. Designer, artist 18 ft. menorah commd. by Nat. Com. for Furtherance of Jewish Edn., Nassau County, 1984; contbg. artist (on-line video, internet gallery installation) World's Women, 1995-96. Pres. LWV, Town of Hempstead, N.Y., 1965-67; adv., L.I. rep., Bais Chana Women Internat., 1994—. Home and Studio: 1272 Greenbriar Ln North Bellmore NY 11710

TRILLING, SHARON NAOMI, gifted and talented education educator; b. Chgo., Oct. 19, 1940; d. Solomon H. and Jessie (Pickman) Glassman; m. Joel Alan Trilling, Jan. 6, 1968; children: Jody Lynne, Amy Rebecca. BA, Roosevelt U., 1961; MEd, Leslie Coll., 1991. Tchr. cert. Ill., Colo. Tchr. Chgo. Bd. Edn., 1961-70, Solomon Schechter Sch., Northbrook, Ill., 1982-89; tchr., cons. ESL Ctrl. Agy. for Jewish Edn., Denver, 1989-95; prin. B'nai Havurah Religious Sch., Denver, 1992—; gifted and talented resource tchr. Littleton (Colo.) Pub. Schs., 1995—; cons., tchr. trainer, Denver, 1991—. Wexner fellow Jewish Edn. Svc. N.Am., Brandies U., Waltham, Mass., 1994, 95. Mem. Colo. TESOL (tchr. of yr. Rocky Mtn. region 1992), Coalition for Advancement in Jewish Edn. Office: Goddard Mid Sch 3800 W Berry Ave Littleton CO 80123

TRIMARCHI, RUTH ELLEN, educator, researcher, community activist; b. Adams, Mass., Jan. 9, 1954; d. Anthony Rocco and Millicent June (Brimmer) T.; m. David Wayne Miller, Sept. 17, 1981; children: Eliot, Jacob. BA in Biology, Vassar Coll., 1978; MEd, U. Mass., 1993. Cert. tchr., Mass. Rsch. asst. U. Ghent (Belgium), 1978-79, Harvard U., Cambridge, Mass., 1980-81; tchr. sci. Amherst (Mass.) Regional H.S., 1994—. Bd. dirs. LWV, Amherst, Mass., 1991-93; mem. adv. com. Children's Svcs. Dept., Amherst, 1990-93; fund raiser Abortion Rights Fund of Western Mass., Amherst, 1989—. Mem. Phi Delta Kappa. Office: Amherst Regional HS 22 Matoon St Amherst MA 01002-2139

TRIMBLE, GARNET O'CULL, elementary music educator; b. Maysville, Ky., Aug. 18, 1945; d. George and Grace (Thomas) O'Cull; m. Shelby C. Trimble; children: Shelby Scott, Bryant Keith. B of Music Edn., Morehead State U., 1970, MEd, 1974. Tchr. grade 5 May's Lick (Ky.) Elem. Sch., 1965-66; tchr. vocal music K-8 and h.s. chorus Ripley (Ohio)-Union-Lewis Schs., 1966-93; tchr. elem. vocal music Ripley Elem. Sch., 1993—; dist. XVI rep. for Ohio, Music in Our Schs. Month, Nat. Educators Nat. Conf., 1966—; mem. Best Effort Superior Team, Ripley Schs., 1993-94. Contbr. to mus. publs. and profl. jours. Leader 4-H Club, Orangeburg, Ky., 1990-94; past mem. Mason-Maysville Arts Commn., 1991-93; chmn. Cmty. Resource Night. Mem. NEA, Ohio Music Educators, Ripley-Union-Lewis Huntington Edn. Assn. (bldg. rep. 1993, 94, v.p. 1995), Orangeburg Lioness Club (sec., past pres. 1993—). Republican. Home: 7421 Mount Carmel Rd Maysville KY 41056-9496 Office: 500 S 2nd St Ripley OH 45167-1306

TRINKUS, LAIMA MARY, special education educator; b. Chgo., Mar. 6, 1950; d. Steven and Antonia (Ambrasas) Trinkus. BS in Sociology, Daemen Coll., Buffalo, 1974; MS in Behavioral Sci. Spl. Edn., SUNY, Buffalo, 1987. Cert. spl. edn. tchr., N.Y. Tchr. aide Cantalician Ctr. for Learning, Buffalo, 1975-78, tchr. spl. edn., 1978-85; tchr. spl. edn. Erie I Bd. Coop. Edn. Svcs., Lancaster, N.Y., 1985—. Vol. Spl. Olympics, Buffalo, 1976—. Home: 9821 Greiner Rd Clarence NY 14031

TRIPLETT, ARLENE ANN, travel company executive; b. Portland, Oreg., Jan. 21, 1942; d. Vincent Michael and Lorraine Catherine (Starr) Jakovich; m. William Karrol Triplett, Jan. 27, 1962; children: Stephen Michael, Patricia Ann. B.A. in Bus. Adminstrn., U. Calif., Berkeley, 1963. Budgets and reports analyst Cutter Labs., Berkeley, 1963-66; controller Citizens for Reagan, 1975-76; dir. adminstrn. Republican. Nat. Com., 1977-80; asst. sec. Dept. Commerce, Washington, 1981-83; assoc. dir. mgmt. Office Mgmt. and Budget, Exec. Office of Pres., Washington, 1983-85; prin. assoc. McManis Assocs., Inc., 1985-87, v.p., 1987-89, sr. v.p., 1989-93; v.p. Am. Tours Internat., Inc., L.A., 1993—, exec. v.p., 1994—. Roman Catholic. Office: Am Tours Internat Inc 6053 W Century Blvd Los Angeles CA 90045-5323

TRIPLETT, LOREN O., religious organization administrator; b. San Jose, Calif., July 5, 1926; m. Mildred Triplett; children: Donald, Debora, Marcus, Timothy. Grad., Bethany Bible Coll., 1946; student, Ctrl. Bible Coll., Evangel Coll., Dade Jr. Coll. Ordained min. Assemblies of God, 1950. Pastor various orgns., Oreg. and Nebr., 1947-54; missionary Life Pubs., Nicaragua, 1954-73; field dir. Divsn. Fgn. Missions, Springfield, Mo., 1973-89; exec. dir. Divsn. Fgn. Ministries, Springfield, Mo., 1990—. Contbr. articles to profl. jours. Office: Assemblies of God 1445 N Boonville Ave Springfield MO 65802-1894

TRIPP, KAREN BRYANT, lawyer; b. Rocky Mount, N.C., Sept. 2, 1955; d. Bryant and Katherine Rebecca (Watkins) Tripp; m. Robert Mark Burleson, June 25, 1977 (div. 1996). BA, U. N.C., 1976; JD, U. Ala., 1981. Bar: Tex. 1981, U.S. Dist. Ct. (so. dist.) Tex. 1982, U.S. Dist. Ct. (ea. dist.) Tex. 1991, U.S. Ct. Appeals (fed. cir.) 1983, U.S. Supreme Ct. 1994. Law clk. Tucker, Gray & Espy, Tuscaloosa, Ala., 1978-81, to presiding justice Ala. Supreme Ct., Montgomery, summer 1980; atty. Exxon Prodn. Rsch. Co., Houston, 1981-86, coord. tech. transfer, 1986-87; assoc. Arnold, White and Durkee, Attys. at Law, Houston, 1988-93, shareholder, 1994—; pres. Blake Barnett & Co., 1996—. Editor: Intellectual Property Law Review, 1995, 96; contbr. articles to profl. jours. Recipient Am. Jurisprudence award U. Ala., 1980, Dean's award, 1981. Mem. ABA (intellectual property law section, ethics com. 1992-95), Houston Bar Assn. (interprofl. rels. com. 1988-90), Houston Intellectual Property Lawyers Assn. (mem. outstanding inventor com. 1982-84, chmn. 1994-95, chmn. student edn. com. 1986, sec. 1987-88, chmn. awards com. 1988-89, chmn. program com. 1988-91, 95-96, treas. 1991-92, bd. dirs. 1992-94, nominations com. 1993, 96), Tex. Bar Assn. (antitrust law com. 1984-85, chmn. Internat. Law com. of Intellectual Property Law Sect. 1987-88, internat. transfer tech. com. 1983-84), Am. Intellectual Property Lawyers Assn. (mem. patent law com. 1995), Women in Tech. (founder), Phi Alpha Delta (clk. 1980). Democrat. Episcopalian. Office: Arnold White & Durkee PO Box 4433 Houston TX 77210-4433

TRIPP, MARIAN BARLOW LOOFE, public relations company executive; b. Lodge Pole, Nebr., July 26; d. Lewis Rockwell and Cora Dee (Davis) Barlow; m. James Edward Tripp, Feb. 9, 1957; children: Brendan Michael, Kevin Mark. BS, Iowa State U., 1944. Writer Dairy Record, St. Paul, 1944-45; head, product promotion div., pub. rels. dept. Swift & Co., Chgo., 1945-55; mgmt. supr., v.p. pub. rels. J. Walter Thompson Co., N.Y.C. and Chgo., 1956-74; v.p. consumer affairs, Chgo., 1974-76; pres. Marian Tripp Communications Inc., Chgo., 1976-94. Mem. Pub. Rels. Soc. Am., Am. Inst. Wine and Food, Les Dames d'Escoffier, Chgo. Network, Fortnightly Club, Confriere de la Chaine des Rotisseriers (officer Chgo. chpt.) Episcopalian. Office: 100 E Bellevue Pl Chicago IL 60611-1157

TRIPP, RUTH ENDERS, actress, writer; b. Hackensack, N.J., May 10, 1920; d. Howard Crosby and Ada Beatrice (Jursch) Enders; m. Paul Tripp, Aug. 8, 1943; children: Suzanne Tripp Jurmain, David Enders. Student, John Drew Theatre Sch., 1935-37, Thorndike Drama Sch., 1938. speech tchr. of retarded children, N.Y.C., 1941-62; tchr. Am. Acad. Dramatic Art, N.Y.C., 1958-61; pres. Fantasy Music Pub., N.Y.C., 1955-65. Broadway debut in The American Way, 1939, appeared in Twelfth Night, 1951; one woman nat. tours, 1940-46; TV appearances include Mr. I Magination, 1949-53 (Look award 1951), On the Carousel, 1954-60 (Ohio State and Emmy awards 1955), Birthday House, 1963-69, Verdict is Yours, 1960-63, numerous others; film appearances include The Christmas That Almost Wasn't, 1966; writer N.Y. Daily News, 1943-46, (theater) Sackful of Dreams, 1974. Mem. SAG, AFTRA, Acad. TV Arts and Scis., Actors Equity. Office: Silverstone & Rosenthal 230 Park Ave New York NY 10169-0005

TRIPPET, SUSAN ELAINE, nursing educator; b. Princeton, Ind., Nov. 3, 1946; d. Charles Kightly and Isabel (Key) T. AA, Ind. U., Indpls., 1971, MS in Nursing, 1983; DS in Nursing, U. Ala., Birmingham, 1988. Lectr. Ind. U., Indpls., 1976-83, asst. prof., 1983-84; CNS perinatal div. U. Hosps., Birmingham, 1984-85; assoc. prof. U. So. Miss., Hattiesurg, 1988-94; pres. D.J.S. Resources P.A., 1995—; pres. D.J.S. Resources P.A.; various presentations on older women, relationship issues, mothers & daughters, and therapeutic use of music. Mem. Am. Nursing Assn., So. Nursing Rsch. Soc., Internat. Coun. Women's Health Issues, Sigma Theta Tau, Sigma Tau Delta.

TRIPPLEHORN, JEANNE, actress; b. Tulsa, Okla., 1963; d. Tommy and Suzanne (Ferguson) T. Student, Juilliard Sch. Appeared in (theatre off-Broadway) The Big Funk, 1990, 'Tis Pity She's A Whore, 1992; (film) Basic Instinct, 1991, The Firm, 1993, The Night We Never Met, 1993, Reality Bites, 1994, Waterworld, 1995, 'Til There Was You, 1996. *

TRIPTOW, SUSAN GAIL, corporate lawyer; b. Peoria, Ill., Oct. 21, 1958; d. Howard H. and Sharon L. Kleine. BS, U. Ill., 1980; MBA, Washington U., 1994, JD, 1994. Bar: Mo., 1994. Quality control supr. John Morrell & Co., Chgo., 1981-84; product devel. Celestial Seasonings, Boulder, Colo., 1984-88; bus. mkt. analyst Coors Biotech., Westminster, Colo., 1988; corp. counsel Purina Mills, Inc., St. Louis, Mo., 1991—. Mem. ABA (Land Use Law award 1994), Bar Assn. Met. St. Louis, Am. Corp. Counsel Assn. Office: Purina Mills Inc PO Box 66812 Saint Louis MO 63166-6812

TROISPOUX, CHRISTIANNE VALERIE ANN, psychologist; b. Pasadena, Calif., June 10, 1968; d. Claude and Georgette (Guestault) T. BA in Psychology, Mt. St. Mary's Coll., 1990; MA in Psychology, Calif. State U, Northridge, 1993. Cert. sch. psychologist. Ednl. therapist Hillside Devel. Learning Ctr., La Canada, Calif., 1990-93; sch. psychologist L.A. Unified Sch. Dist., 1993—. Mem. Calif. Assn. Sch. Psychologists, NOW. Democrat. Roman Catholic. Office: LAUSD Spl Edn 450 N Grand Ave Los Angeles CA 90012

TROJAK, MAUREEN ANN, library media specialist; b. Phillips, Wis., Jan. 10, 1958; d. Edward Vincent and Therese Anne (DuMonte) T. BS, U. Wis., Superior, 1980; MEd in Profl. Devel., U. Wis., Eau Claire, 1994. Substitute tchr. Sch. Dist. of Phillips, Wis., 1980-86; libr. aide Phillips Middle Sch., 1985-86, libr. media specialist, 1986-88; libr. media specialist Phillips Elem., Kennan Elem. and Catawba Middle Schs., 1988—; girls volleyball, basketball and track coach Sch. Dist. of Phillips, 1980—, staff devel. com. mem., sec., 1990-94, dist. libr. com., 1988—, dist. computer com., 1991—, primary computer person, 1992—; RIF program coord. Kennan Elem. and Catawba Mid. Sch., 1988—; accelerated reader program coord. Phillips Elem., Kennan Elem. and Catawba Mid. Schs., 1993—. Mem. Wis. Bowhunters Assn. (life, Gold Pin Diamond 1993-95), Women's Softball Leagues, Price County Hist. Soc. (life), Ladies VFW Aux. 5778 (life, jr. v.p. 1996, banner bearer 1990—, comty. chmn. 1990-92, safety chmn. 1993—). Roman Catholic. Home: N11361 County Road F Phillips WI 54555-7115 Office: Sch Dist of Phillips PO Box 70 Phillips WI 54555-0070

TROMBETTA, ANNAMARIE, artist; b. Bklyn., Aug. 5, 1963; d. Philip and Maryann (Lepere) T. Student, Bklyn. Mus. Sch. Fine Arts, 1980-83, Parsons Sch. Design, N.Y.C., 1983-86, Nat. Acad. Sch. Fine Artts, N.Y.C., 1989-93; cert., N.Y. Acad. Art, N.Y.C., 1986-89. One-woman show Liederkrantz Club, N.Y.C., 1993; exhibited in group shows Bklyn. Mus., 1983, Parsons Sch. Design Art Gallery, 1985, Salmagundi Club, 1988, 92, 93. 94, 95, 96, NAD, 1990, 93, Columbia U., 1990, Lincoln Ctr., N.Y.C., 1991, 92, Union League Club, N.Y.C., 1991, Atlantic Gallery, N.Y.C., 1993, 95, First Street Gallery, N.Y.C., 1994, Nat. Arts Club, N.Y.C., 1994, also others; represented in pvt. collections. One-woman show Liederkrantz Club, N.Y.C., 1993; exhibited in group shows Bklyn. Mus., 1983, Parsons Sch. Design Art Gallery, 1985, Salamagundi Club, N.Y.C., 1988, 92, 93, 94, 95, 96, NAD, 1990, 93, Columbia U., 1990, Lincoln Ctr., 1991, 92, Union League Club, NY.C., 1991, Atlantic Gallery, N.Y.C., 1993, 95, First Street Gallery, N.Y.C., 1994, Nat. Arts Club, N.Y.C., 1994, also others; represented in pvt. collections, murar executed S.I. Ctr., 1981. Recipient prize for pastel NAD, 1989, painting award, 1990; Philip Isenberg Meml. award, 1991, Frank Dumond Meml. award, 1991, John and Anna Lee Stacey award, 1992, Valerie Delacorte Scholarship award, 1992, Philip Isenberg award, 1992, Arthur and Melville Philips award, 1993, Frank Duveneck Meml. award, 1994, Julius Allen award, 1996, Jacqueline Fowler award, 1996; scholar 1983-93. Mem. William Butler Yeats Soc. N.Y. (bd. dirs. 1991—, scholarship to W.B. Yeats Summer Sch., Sligo, Ireland 1990), Salmagundi Art Club N.Y. (com. 1996), Theosophical Soc., Painting Group in Soho. Home: 175 E 96th St Apt 14P New York NY 10128 Office: NAD Mus 1083 Fifth Ave New York NY 10128

TROMBLEY, DEBORAH PELKEY, crossword puzzle constructor; b. Plattsburgh, N.Y., May 12, 1950; d. Euclid Francis and Mary Dorothy (Rondeau) Pelkey; m. Edward John Trombley; 1 child, Jay Jessica. BA in English, SUNY, Plattsburgh, 1973, postgrad., 1985-87. Tchr. Adirondack Correctional, Treatment and Evaluation Ctr., Dannemora, N.Y., 1973-75; crossword puzzle constructor N.Y. Times, Simon & Schuster, Dell Champion, Penny Press, Games Mag., 1986—. Pres.-elect bd. dirs. Planned Parenthood, Plattsburgh, 1979; mem. exec. com. Rape Resources, Plattsburgh, 1977-79, Women, Inc., Plattsburgh, 1977-79; vol. United Way, Plattsburgh, 1978-79. Mem. Coll. Found./SUNY Plattsburgh, Kappa Delta Pi. Democrat.

TRONVOLD, LINDA JEAN, occupational therapist; b. Yankton, S.D., Dec. 8, 1950; m. Marvis D. Tronvold, July 7, 1976; children: Marcie, Tami, Kristi, Bradley, Cindy. Student, Mt. Marty Coll., 1989; AS, Kirkwood Community Coll., Cedar Rapids, Iowa, 1989; BS, Creighton U., 1991. Registered occupl. therapist, S.D., Neb., Iowa. Psychiatric aide S.D. Human Svcs. Ctr., Yankton, 1969-74, mental health technician, 1974-85, occpul. therapist asst., 1985-89, occupl. therapist, 1991-92; mem. edn. svc. unit Human Svcs. Ctr., Yankton, 1991-93; asst. program dir. occupl. therapy Western Iowa Tech. C.C., Sioux City, Iowa, 1993—; registered occupl. therapist Nova Care, Inc., 1993—; guest speaker Creighton U., Omaha, U. S.D., Vermillion; mem. student staff Upward Bound, Omaha, 1989-91,. Scout leader Boy Scouts Am., Hartington, Nebr., 1977-80, Girl Scouts USA, Yankton, 1986-89; Sunday sch. tchr. United Ch. of Christ, Yankton, 1984-88; mem. spl. populations staff YWCA, Cedar Rapids, Iowa, 1987-88. Mem. Am. Occupl. Therapy Assn., S.D. Occupl. Therapy Assn., Nebr. Occupl. Therapy Assn., Iowa Occupl. Therapy Assn., Creighton U. Student Occupl. Therapy Assn., VFW Aux., Sq. Dance Club (pres. 1979-81, 96, v.p. 1995-96), Alpha Tri Ota Club. Home: 705 Broadway St Yankton SD 57078-3923 Office: Western Iowa Tech CC 4647 Stone Blvd Sioux City IA 51102

TROPP, NHUMEY, artist, self-defense specialist; b. Newark, Feb. 24, 1952; d. Leon and Edna (Kroll) T. BA, U. Calif., Berkeley, 1977, MPH, 1979; PA, U. Wash., 1981. 5th Dan Black Belt, Internat. Tae Kwan Do Fedn., 1990, Black Belt N.W. Hwa Rang Do Assn., 1995; cert. NCCPA. Owner, chief instr. Traditional Tae Kwon Do & Hwa Rang Do, Seattle, 1984—, Tropp Systems: Strategies for Personal Safety, 1994—; physician asst. Group Health Cooperative, Wash., 1983—, Inter Island Med. Ctr., Friday Harbor, Wash., 1981-83; bd. dirs. PAWMA. Mem. Pacific Assn. Women Martial Artists, Nat. Women's Martial Arts Fedn., Am. Acad. Physician Assts., Wash. Acad. Physician Assts., Wash. State Med. Assn. Office: Tropp Systems TRAD TKO & HRD Strategies Personal Safety 8005 Greenwood Ave N Seattle WA 98103

TROTT, KAREN, actor; b. Lawrence, Mass.; d. Kenneth Francis and Eugenie Jeannette (Vaillancourt) T.; m. Peter Ragnar Herdrich, Oct. 2, 1993. BA, U. Vt., 1976. Playwright, performer one person show The Springhill Singing Disaster, 1995; played Maura in Return of the Secaucus 7, 1980; appeared on Broadway in Strider, 1979, Barnum, 1980; role of Anna Akhmatova in The Beautiful Lady, Mark Taper Forum, 1985; played in TV series City Kids, 1993, others. Recipient Helen Hayes award nomination, 1985, Drama Desk award nomination, 1996. Home: 446 W 47th St Apt 2D New York NY 10036-2379

TROTTER, GLORIA GILLENWATER, editor, publisher; b. Bristol, Tenn., Sept. 3, 1944; d. Wilfred Kelso and Minnie Lou (Davis) Gillenwater; m. Donald Wayne Trotter, Dec. 26, 1964; 1 child, Gregory Scott. BS in Journalism, Memphis State U., 1974. News dir. WOPI Radio, Bristol, Tenn., 1966; pub. info. officer Memphis State U., 1974-77, Randolph Tech. Coll., Asheboro, N.C., 1979-83; editor, publisher Countywide News, Inc., Tecumseh, Okla., 1983—; bd. dirs. Freedom Info. Okla., pres.-elect. Mem., sec. Friends of Libr.; com. mem. Frontier Days, 1983—, chmn., 1993; voter registrar County Election Bd., Pottawatomie County, Okla., 1984-95; bd. dirs., past pres. Ctrl. Okla. Juvenile Ctr., Tecumseh, 1994—. Mem. Okla. Press Assn. (newspaper contest com. 1983—), Tecumseh Bus. Profl. Women (pres. 1989-90, 93-94), Tecumseh Hist. Soc., LWV (1st v.p. 1995—). Methodist. Home: 412 S 9th St Tecumseh OK 74873 Office: Countywide News Inc 101 N Broadway Tecumseh OK 74873

TROTTER, GWENDOLYN DIANE NELSON, choral and vocal educator; b. Little Rock, Nov. 13, 1950; d. Milton Donaghey and Dora Elizabeth (Gillespie) N. BBA, U. Ark., 1972; MBA, Calif. State U., Dominguez Hills, 1979, postgrad. in voice/piano, 1980-81; postgrad. in acctg., UCLA, 1973-84. Adminstrv. asst. Ark. Plan, Inc., Little Rock, 1969-73; acct. Hughes Aircraft Co., L.A., 1973-80, ops. auditor, 1986-90, property mgmt. specialist, 1990-93; dir. music dept. Baldwin Hills Baptist Ch., L.A., 1979-94; choral, vocal instr. Crossroads Acad. Arts and Sci., 1994—; with By Faith Cons. & Pub., Inglewood, Calif.; auditor Baldwin Hills Baptist Ch., 1983—; cons. Air Force Procurement, Contractor Ops. Revs., L.A., 1984-88, LAUSO Saturday Fine Arts Conservatory, 1995—. Author music: (Christian mus. drama) Wings Like Eagles, 1988, mus. dir., L.A., 1988-89; playwright: Dissin' Your Body, 1993. Founder, exec. dir. Christian Action Now Is Good Econs., a visual and performing arts orgn. for at-risk youth, 1993; founder, pres. By Faith Cons. and Publishing, 1993; exec. dir. Change, performing arts orgn. for at-risk youth. Mem. Am. Choral Dirs. Assn., Heritage Music Found., Nat. Property Mgmt. Assn. (cert. profl. property specialist, invited speaker seminars and workshops), Mu Phi Epsilon, Alpha Kappa Alpha (grad. advisor 1978-79, del. 1980-81). Home: 227 E Plymouth St Inglewood CA 90302-2315

TROUILLE, MARY SEIDMAN, foreign language educator; b. Chgo., Feb. 23, 1951; d. Nathaniel and Virginia (Crosley) Seidman; m. Guy Andre Nodot, Apr. 5, 1971 (div. Sept. 1977); 1 child, Jennifer Lynn; m. Bruno Jean-Louis Trouille, Apr. 15, 1978; children: David Alexander, Laura Elizabeth. BA in French, Loyola U., 1972; MA in French, Northwestern U., 1974, PhD in French, 1988. Editor Scott, Foresman Publs., Glenview, Ill., 1976-83; grad. teaching asst. Northwestern U., Evanston, Ill., 1983-88, lectr. French, 1988-89; lectr. humanities & French U. Chgo., 1990-93; asst. prof. French Ill. State U., Normal, 1993-96, assoc. prof. French, 1996—; presenter in field. Author: The Writing of Melancholu: Modes of Opposition in Early French Modernism, 1987, Studies of Voltaire and rhe Eighteenth Century, 1994, Romantic Review, 1994, Eighteenth-Century Studies, 1991, Eighteenth-Century Life, 1989, La Femme Mal Mariée, 1996, Romance Notes, 1996; contbr. articles to profl. jours., chpts. to books. Travel grantee Am. Coun. LEarned Socs., 1995; Sch. Criticism & Theory fellow, 1985, Internat. Summer Inst. Semiotic and Structural Studies fellow, 1986. Mem. Am. Assn. Tchrs. French, Am. Soc. Eighteenth-Century Studies (co-chair women's caucus 1995—)), Midwestern Am. Soc. Eighteenth-Century Studies, Modern Lang. Assn., Internat. Soc. Eighteenth-Century Studies. Office: Ill State U Dept Fgn Langs Campus Box 4300 Normal IL 61790

TROUT, LINDA COPPLE, judge; b. Tokyo, Sept. 1, 1951. BA, U. Idaho, 1973, JD, 1977. Bar: Idaho 1977. Judge magistrate divsn. Idaho Dist. Ct. (2d jud. divsn.), 1983-90; dist. judge Idaho Dist. Ct. (2d jud. divsn.), Lewiston, 1991-92; acting trial ct. adminstr. Idaho Dist. Ct. (2d jud. divsn.), 1987-91; justice Idaho Supreme Ct., 1992—; instr. coll. law U. Idaho, 1983, 88. Mem. Idaho State Bar Assn., Clearwater Bar Assn. (pres. 1980-81).

TROUTWINE-BRAUN, CHARLOTTE TEMPERLEY, psychologist, educator, writer; b. Newton, Mass., Nov. 27, 1906; d. Joseph and Libbie (Kempton) Temperley; m. Arklay S. Richards, Nov. 28, 1928 (div. 1942); children: Whitman Albin, Lincoln Kempton, Sylvia Caroline; m. Harry Troutwine, May 3, 1945 (div. 1954); m. Charles E. McCrum, 1961 (div. 1965); m. Lester Lewis Walsh, Feb. 16, 1968 (div. Feb. 1972); m. George Braun, Feb. 6, 1975 (dec. Oct. 1975). BS, Simmons Coll., 1927; postgrad. Boston U., 1947-49; MA, Northeastern U., 1966; BES, Internat. Ch. Ageless Wisdom, 1981. Pvt. sec. pres. Hygrade Sylvania Electric Corp. Salem, Mass., 1927-28; pvt. and dept. exec. sec. Dr. Stanley Cobb, Bullard prof. neuropathology Harvard U. Med. Sch., 1928-31; part-time caseworker Friends of Framingham Reformatory, 1928-31, others, 1931-51; organizer, exec. dir. Postgrad. Med. Inst. under Mass. Med. Soc., Boston, 1951-57; mgr. Postgrad. Information Services, Lederle Labs. div. Am. Cyanamid Co., Pearl River, N.Y., 1957-61; exec. dir. postgrad. med. edn., Hahnemann Med. Coll. and Hosp. also exec. dir. Mary Bailey Inst. Cardiovascular Research, 1961; counselor, tchr. psychology Holliston High Sch., 1965-66. Counselor Falmouth (Mass.) High Sch., 1966-74; psychotherapist Hallgarth Clinic, 1974-75. Speaker for Am. Epilepsy League. Mem. Mass. Tchrs. Assn. (life), Spiritual Frontiers Assn. (life), N.E.A. (life), Nat. Ret. Tchrs. Assn. (life), Nat. Assn. Sch. Counselors (charter, life), Assn. Research Enlightenment, Soc. Mayflower Descs. (life), Simmons Coll. Alumnae Assn., AAUW, Med. Soc. Execs. Assn. (emeritus), Am. Soc. Psychical Research, States Med. Postgrad. Assn. (past sec.), Mass. Psychol. Assn. (life), Spiritual Frontiers Fellowship (life), World Fedn. Healers (healer mem.), Mass. Healers Assn. Author: Practicing the Silence, 1978, 5th edit., 1992, Open Windows, 1994; contbr. numerous articles in med., spiritual and psychol. fields. Mem. Soc. of Friends. Home: 83 Falmouth Ct Bedford MA 01730-2912

TROVATO-CANTORI, LORRAINE MARIA, art educator; b. Bklyn., Aug. 19, 1965; d. Joseph Charles and Frances Grace (Palma) Trovato; m. Chris D. Cantori, Sept. 20, 1992; 1 child, Ceasar-Augustus. BFA, Sch. Visual Arts, N.Y.C., 1987; MFA, Lehman Coll., 1992. Cert. tchr. fine art, N.Y. Art educator N.Y.C. Dept. Parks and Recreation, 1985-87, P.S. 33 N.Y.C. Bd. Edn., 1988-91, Middle Sch. 45 N.Y.C. Bd. Edn., 1991—; art edn. cons. Bronx (N.Y.) Coun. on Arts, 1991—; mus. educator N.Y.C. Bd. Edn./Met. Mus. Art, 1991—. Executed mural at P.S. 33, M.S. 45, 1991-96. Grantee Bronx Coun. on Arts, 1991, N.Y.C. Dept. Edn., 1992. Mem. Forum Italian Am. Educators. Roman Catholic. Office: Middle Sch 45 2502 Lorillard Pl Bronx NY 10458

TROW, JO ANNE JOHNSON, retired university official; b. Youngstown, Ohio, Feb. 10, 1931; d. Raymond Leonard Johnson and Mary Belle Beede; m. Clifford W. Trow, Oct. 10, 1969. BA, Denison U., 1953; MA, Ind. U., 1956; PhD, Mich. State U., 1965. Case worker Office Pub. Assistance, Cleve., 1953-54; asst. dean women Denison U., Granville, Ohio, 1956-59, Wash. State U., Pullman, 1959-63; asst. dir. resident program Mich. State U., East Lansing, 1964; dean women Oreg. State U., Corvallis, 1965-69, assoc. dean students, 1969-83, v.p. student affairs, 1983-95, program dir., 1983-95; presenter, speaker in field. Contbr. articles to profl. jours. Bd. dirs. Benton County Mental Health Assn., 1975-79, United Way Benton County, 1977—, United Way Oreg., 1977-80; mem. adv. bd. Old Mill Sch., 1979-95, chmn., 1983, 94-95; mem. Oreg. Cmty. Corrections Adv. Bd., 1988-95; moderator 1st Congl. Ch., 1977, trustee, 1979-83, 91-95; mem. Oreg. Gov.'s Com. on Status of Women, 1972-78, vice chmn., 1976-77; mem. fund campaign Good Samaritan Hosp. Found. Cancer Care Ctr., 1982-83. Recipient Corvallis Woman of Achievement award, 1974, Boss of Yr. award Oreg. State U. Office Personnel Assn., 1979, White Rose award March of Dimes, 1987, Elizabeth A Greenleaf Disting. Alumna award Ind. U., 1987, Scott Goodnight award, 1989, Disting. Alumni Citation, Denison U., 1993, Coun. Woman of Distinction award Oreg. State U. Meml. Union Program, 1993. Mem. Nat. Assn. Women Deans, Adminstrs. and Counselors (pres. 1981-82), Am. Coll. Personnel Assn. (sec. 1969-70), Nat. Assn. Student Personnel Adminstrs., Am. Coun. on Edn., N.W. Assn. Schs. and Colls. (comn. on colls. 1989-95), Am. Assn. for Higher Edn., N.W. Coll. Personnel Assn. (life, pres. 1969-70), Assn. Oreg. Faculties, AAUW (state and local bd. dirs.), LWV (bd. dirs., v.p. Corvallis 1966-69, 79-80), Corvallis Area C. of C. (bd. dirs. 1972-74, 78-80), Mortar Bd., Phi Delta Kappa, Phi Kappa Phi, Alpha Lambda Delta. Democrat.

TROXCLAIR, DEBRA ANN, gifted education educator; b. New Orleans, Jan. 29, 1953; d. Richard Joseph and Joyce Marie (Braud) Troxclair; divorced; 1 child, Christopher Richard Pinner. BA, U. New Orleans, 1976, MEd, 1989; postgrad., U. So. Miss., 1991—. Cert. edn. 4th grade tchr. Laurel Elem. Sch., New Orleans, 1977; 2d grade tchr. St. Frances Cabrini Elem., New Orleans, 1977-80; 1st grade tchr. St. Joseph Sch., Gretna, La., 1982-83; kindergarden tchr. Lake Castle Pvt. Sch., New Orleans, 1983-84; libr. St. Frances Cabrini, New Orleans, 1984-85; 3d grade tchr. Abney Elem. Sch., Slidell, La., 1985-89; gifted resource tchr. Little Oak Elem., Slidell, 1989—; instr. Delgado C.C., Slidell, 1991-94; cons. St. Tammany Parish Schs., Slidell, 1988-89, 90-91; presenter La. State Dept. Edn. Superconference, 1993, La. Assn. Gifted Students, 1993, Archdiocese of New Orleans Early Childhood Assn., 1996, U. So. Miss. Parenting Gifted Children Conf., 1995. Elder Northminster Presbyn. Ch., Pearl River, La. Recipient Disting. Teaching awrd Northwestern State U., 1996; Grad. Student scholar U. So. Miss., 1995-96; La. Assn. for Gifted and Talented grantee, 1996. Mem. AAUW (newsletter editor Slidell br. 1985-86), CEC, Nat. Assn. for Gifted Children (conv. presenter 1993), Miss. Assn. for Gifted Children, Northshore Reading Coun., La. Assn. Gifted and Talented Students (grantee 1995-96), Phi Delta Kappa (pres. St. Tammany Parish 1991). Presbyterian. Office: Little Oak Elem 59241 Rebel Dr Slidell LA 70461-3713

TROXELL, BONITA KLINE, school system administrator; b. Reading, Pa., Oct. 2, 1949. BA in English, Messiah Coll., 1971; MEd, cert. reading specialist, Kutztown U., 1976. 9-12th grade English tchr. No. York Area Sch. Dist., Dillsburg, Pa., 1971-73; asst. dir. area health edn. sys. Geisinger Med. Ctr., Danville, Pa., 1974-75; reading specialist Shikellamy Sch. Dist., Sunbury, Pa., 1975-80; reading. cons. Union/Snyder County Probation Office, Lewisburg, Pa., 1982-84; dir. tchr. intern program Susquehanna U., Selinsgrove, Pa., 1984-90, dir. tchr. intern program and instrn. edn. dept., 1990-93; dir. pupil svcs., curriculum and instrn. Selinsgrove Area Sch. Dist., 1993—; mem. Lead Tchr. Adv. Com., Lewisburg, 1990—; coord. N.E. Regional Ctr. for Drug Free Schs., Sayville, N.Y., 1990—. Bd. dirs. Priestley-Forsyth Meml. Libr., Northumberland, Pa., 1982-88; libr. Emmanual Bible Fellowship Ch., Sunbury, 1986—; mem. sch. and PTA coms. Shikellamy Sch. Dist., 1986—. Degenstein Found. edn. grantee, 1991, grantee N.E. Regional Ctr. for Drug Free Schs., 1992. Mem. ASCD, Internat. Reading Assn., Keystone Reading Assn., Susquehanna Valley Reading Coun., Am. Ednl. Rsch., Pa. Assn. Coll. and Tchr. Educators, Assn. Tchr. Educators, Kappa Delta Pi. Office: Selinsgrove Area Sch Dist 401 18th St Selinsgrove PA 17870-1153

TROXELL, LUCY DAVIS, consulting firm executive; b. Cambridge, Mass., Apr. 25, 1932; d. Ellsworth and Mildred (Enneking) Davis; m. Charles DeGroat Bader, June 13, 1952 (div. Aug. 1974); children: Christie P. Walker, Mary Ellsworth Bader, Charles D. Bader Jr., Davis Bradford Bader; m. Victor Daniel Shirer Troxell, Aug. 1974. BA, Smith Coll., Northampton, Mass., 1952. Cert. paralegal, employee benefit specialist, assoc. in risk mgmt. Paralegal O'Melveny & Myers, L.A., 1976-77; account exec. Olanie Hurst & Hemrich, L.A., 1977-78; asst. to trustee Oxford Ins. Mgmt., L.A., 1978-80; dir. corp. svcs., asst. corp. sec. Consolidated Elec. Distbrs., Inc., Westlake Village, Calif., 1980-93; pres. MONMAK LDT, Westlake Village, 1993—. Sustaining mem., bd. dirs. Jr. League, Hartford, Conn., L.A., 1952—; clk. St. Mathew's Parish Vestry, Pacific Palisades, Calif., 1988, sr. warden, 1989-90; bd. dirs. Smith Coll. Club, Hartford, L.A., 1952—, Nat. Charity League, L.A., 1964-68; lic. lay eucharistic minister Episcopal Ch. Sophia Smith scholar. Fellow Internat. Soc. Cert. Employee Benefit Specialists (charter mem., bd. dirs., sec., treas. 1988-89, pres. 1989-90, edn. chmn. 1986-88 L.A. chpt.), Risk and Ins. Mgmt. Soc. (program chmn. L.A. chpt. 1985-86), Theatre Palisades (bd. dirs. 1960-74). Republican. Home: 450 Puerto Del Mar Pacific Palisades CA 90272-4233 Office: MONMAK LDT 31220 La Baya Dr # 319 Westlake Village CA 91362-4008

TRUCKSIS, THERESA A., library director; b. Hubbard, Ohio, Sept. 1, 1924; d. Peter and Carmella (DiSilverio) Pagliasotti; m. Robert C. Trucksis, May 29, 1948 (dec. May 1980); children: M. Laura, Anne, Michele, Patricia, David, Robert, Claire, Peter; m. Philip P. Hickey, Oct. 19, 1985 (dec. May 1993). BS in Edn., Youngstown Coll., 1945; postgrad., Youngstown State U., 1968-71; MLS, Kent State U., 1972. Psychometrist Youngstown (Ohio) Coll., 1946-49; instr. ltd. svc. Youngstown State U., 1968-71; libr. Pub. Libr. Youngstown & Mahoning County, Youngstown, 1972-73, asst. dept. head, 1973-74, asst. dir., 1985-89, dir., 1989—; dir. NOLA Regional Libr. System, Youngstown, 1974-85. Contbr. articles to profl. jours. Mem. bd. Hubbard Sch. Dist., 1980-85. Mem. ALA, Ohio Libr. Assn. (bd. dirs. 1979-81), Pub. Libr. Assn. Office: Pub Libr Youngstown & Mahoning County 305 Wick Ave Youngstown OH 44503-1003

TRUE, JEAN DURLAND, entrepreneur, oil company executive; b. Olney, Ill., Nov. 27, 1915; d. Clyde Earl and Harriet Louise (Brayton) Durland; m. Henry Alfonso True, Jr., Mar. 20, 1938; children: Tamma Jean (Mrs. Donald G. Hatten), Henry Alfonso III, Diemer Durland, David Lanmon. Student, Mont. State U., 1935-36. Ptnr. True Drilling Co., Casper, Wyo., 1951—, True Oil Co., Casper, 1951-94, Eighty-Eight Oil Co., 1955-94, True Geothermal Energy Co., 1980—, True Ranches, 1981-94; officer, dir. White Stallion Ranch, Inc., Tucson, Smokey Oil Co., Casper. Mem. steering com. YMCA, Casper, 1954-55, bd. dirs., 1956-58; mem. bd. dirs. Gottsche Rehab. Ctr., Thermopolis, Wyo., 1966-93, mem. exec. bd. 1966-93, v.p., 1973-90; mem. adv. bd. for adult edn. U. Wyo., 1966-68; mem. Ft. Casper Commn., Casper, 1973-79; bd. dirs. Mus. of Rockies, Bozeman, Mont., 1983-87, bd. dirs. Nicolaysen Art Mus., 1988-93; mem. Nat. Fedn. Rep. Women's Clubs; del. Rep. nat. conv., 1972; trustee Trooper Found., 1995—. Mem. Rocky Mountain Oil and Gas Assn., Casper Area C. of C., Alpha Gamma Delta, Casper Country Club, Petroleum Club (Casper). Episcopalian. Office: Rivercross Rd PO Box 2360 Casper WY 82602-2360

TRUGLIA, CHRISTEL, state legislator; m. Anthony D. Truglia (dec.); 3 children. Student, Darien (Conn.) H.S. Mem. Conn. Ho. of Reps., 1973-84, 88—, Conn. Senate, 1984-87; mem. appropriations, human svcs., substance abuse prevention coms, L.I. task force, children at risk task force and gray haired caucus; mem. Dem. Leadership Coun., 1991—, Nat. Order of Women Legislators, 1991—, Lower Fairfield County Conf./Exhbn. Authority, 1992—, Com. on Edn. Excellence, 1992—. Vice chmn. Stamford (Conn.) Dem. City Com., 1976-78; bd. dirs. Com. on Tng. and Employment, 1990—; mem. exec. com. Lower Fairfield County Action Against Chem. Dependency, 1991—; active Coun. on Probate Jud. Conduct, 1976-88, Stamford Com. on Aging, 1978-88, Child Care Ctr. of Stamford, Family Re-entry, Inc., 1990—, Aide for Retarded Inc. Aux. Recipient Hannah G. Solomon Cmty. Svc. award Nat. Coun. Jewish Women, 1987, Spl. award Family Re-entry, 1990, Friend of Edn. award Conn. Coun. for Am. Pvt. Edn., 1991, Adv. Leadership award, 1991, Appreciation cert. Conn. Acad. Physicians Assts., 1991, Cmty. Svc. award Conn. Chs. and Synagogues, 1991, Law Day Liberty Bell award Stamford-Norwalk Regional Bar Assn., 1992, United Srs. in Action award Conn. Gen. Assembly, 1992, Child Adv. Legis. Leadership award Conn. Coalition for Children, 1992, Spl. Recognition award Coalition of 100 Black Women of Lower Fairfield County, 1992, Bd. dirs. Jewish Home for Elderly, 1992; named Child Adv. Legislator, State Coalition for Children and State Commn. on Children, 1990, Legis. Advisor of Yr., Conn. Youth Svcs. Assn., 1990. Mem. Rippowan Bus. and Profl. Women's Club (Woman of Yr. 1991). Democrat. Home: 7 Gypsy Moth Lndg Stamford CT 06902-7725 Office: Conn Ho of Reps State Capitol Hartford CT 06106-1591*

TRUITT, BARBARA ANN, nurse; b. Aug. 19, 1959. RN, Albert Einstein Med Ctr., Phila., 1979. RN, Pa., N.J., Del.; cert. IV nurse. Relief charge nurse ICU/CCU Warminster Gen. Hosp.; cardiac rehab. nurse Warminster, Pa.; chief clin. coord., critical care ProNurses Inc., Horsham, Pa.; dir. profl. svcs. Healthcare Profls. Inc., Montgomeryville, Pa., 1991-92; clin. br. dir. TeamCare, Inc., Huntington Valley, Pa., 1992-93; dir. clin. case mgmt. Critical Care Am., Norristown, Pa., 1993-94; nurse mgr. Coram, Malvern, Pa., 1994-95; area ops. mgr. Cardiac Solutions, Ft. Washington, Pa., 1995—; lectr. in field; instr. cardiac care course. Mem. Intravenous Nurses Soc.

TRUITT, CHARLOTTE FRANCES, clergywoman; b. Newark, Feb. 8, 1922; d. Frank Wilson and Charlotte (Hook) T.; m. Robert Kennedy Carter, Mar. 17, 1946 (div. 1972); children: Mary Elizabeth Carter O'Brien, Robert Truitt Carter; m. Robert Harold Bonthius Sr., Apr. 29, 1977. Student, Ohio State U., 1941-46; MA in Christian Edn., Meth. Theol. Sch., Delaware, Ohio, 1976, MDiv, 1977. Ordained to ministry United Ch. of Christ, 1979. Asst. dir. youth program YWCA, Columbus, Ohio, 1965-68, dir. youth program, 1968-70, dir. family life and racial justice programs, 1970-72; mission coord. and youth minister First Cmty. Ch., Columbus, 1972-75; min. Christian edn. Broad St. United Meth. Ch., Columbus, 1975-76; cons., trainer Action Tng. Network, Ohio and Maine, 1976-90; pres. bd. Family Life and Sex Edn. Coun., Columbus, 1971-72; bd. dirs. Ohio Coun. Chs., Columbus, 1973-74; del. United Ch. of Christ, Nicaragua, 1983, and co-founder Nat. Witness for Peace, 1983. Contbr. articles to religious jours. and publs. Pres. bd. dirs. North Ctrl. Mental Health Ctr., Columbus, 1973-74; mem. Columbus Urban League Edn. Commn., 1965-67, Hancock Comprehensive Plan Commn., Hancock, Maine, 1990; chair scholarship bd. Thorsen Scholarship Fund, Hancock, 1988-89; bd. dirs., fin. chair The Next Step Domestic Violence Project, Ellsworth, Maine, 1993-94; bd. dirs. Witness for Peace, pres. chair, 1983-85, chair, 1994-95. Recipient Martin Luther King Jr. award NAACP, Portland, Maine, 1989, Disting. Svc. award The Next Step Domestic Violence Project, Ellsworth, 1994. Mem. AAUW, Hancock-Waldo Clergy Assn., Friends Taunton Bay, Natural Resources Coun. of Maine, Peace Action, Religious Coalition for Reproductive Choice, United Ch. of Christ Christians for Justice Action. Mem. United Ch. of Christ. Home and Office: RR 1 Box 422A Hancock ME 04640

TRUITT, SHIRLEY ANN BOWDLE, middle school educator; b. Cambridge, Md., July 14, 1933; d. Thomas Woodrow and Sarah Virginia (Corkran) Bowdle; m. Herman James Truitt, June 19, 1955; children: Jennie Ann Knapp, Thomas Lee, Sarah Jane. BS, Salisbury (Md.) State Coll., 1955, MEd, 1977. Cert. reading specialist, elem. tchr., Md., Del. Tchr. North Salisbury Elem. Sch., Salisbury, 1955-57, Selbyville (Del.) Elem. Sch., 1963-64, Whaleyville (Md.) Elem. Sch., 1965-67, Phillip C. Showell Sch., Selbyville, 1970-73; reading specialist Selbyville Mid. Sch., 1974-91; lang. arts and math. tchr. Sussex Ctrl. Mid. Sch., Millsboro, Del., 1991—; cooperating tchr. Wilmington Coll., 1996, adv. bd., 1995—. Sec. Worcester County Recreation and Parks Commn., 1972-84; pres. United Meth. Ch., Whaleyville; troop leader Girl Scouts U.S., Berlin, Md., 1968-73; mem. adv. com. Wilmington Coll. Named Tchr. of Yr., Indian River Sch. Dist., 1973, 94, recipient Supts. award, 1993. Mem. AAUW (pres. Salisbury 1988—), Nat. Assn. Secondary Sch. Prins., Del. State Reading Assn. (pres. 1980-81), Sussex Country Orgn. Reading (pres. 1977, 86), Alpha Delta Kappa (pres. 1986), Phi Delta Kappa (charter mem. eastern shore chpt.). Home: 11517 Dale Rd Whaleyville MD 21872-2026

TRUITT, SUZANNE, real estate broker; b. Lewes, Del., Aug. 20, 1943; d. James Shockley and Dorothy Virginia (Shockley) T. Student, U. Del., 1961-62; AA, Goldey Beacom Coll., 1964; grad., Realtors Inst., 1988. Cert. in real estate brokerage mgmt., real estate appraiser, residential specialist;. Notary public State of Del., Dover, 1976—; property and casualty ins. agt. J. A. Montgomery Inc., Wilmington, 1984—; real estate broker C-21/Mann Moore Assocs., Inc., Rehoboth Beach, Del., 1988—; mktg. mgr. Long Neck Village, Millsboro, Del., 1991; broker of record, mgr. Gull Point, Patterson Schwartz Real Estate, Millsboro, 1991-93; with C-21/Mann Moore Assocs., Inc., Rehoboth Beach, Del., 1993—, Atlantic Appraisal, Rehoboth Beach, 1993—. Mem. NAFE (life), Am. Soc. Notaries, Ins. Women Sussex County, Women's Coun. Realtors. Republican. Methodist. Home: 8 Sheffield Rd Rehoboth Beach DE 19971-1400 Office: C21 Mann Moore Assocs Inc Atlantic Appraisal 4343 Highway One Rehoboth Beach DE 19971-1147

TRUJILLO, SANDRA SUE, nurse; b. Circle, Mont., July 5, 1945; d. Theodore Ward and Ethel Marie (Wilhelm) Keeland; m. Michael Savoie, June 1966 (div. Jan. 1980); children: Nichola, Helena, Jodi, Kevin; m. George N. Trujillo, Mar. 1984 (dec. May 1994). ADN, Mont. State U., 1966; BSN, U. N.Mex., 1991; MSN, Tex. A&M U., 1996—. Staff psychiat. nurse Mont. State Hosp., Warm Springs, 1966-81; critical care staff nurse Betsy Johnson Hosp., Dunn, N.C., 1981-82, Calais (Maine) Regional Hosp., 1982-83, Rumford (Maine) Cmty. Hosp., 1983-84, Albemarle Hosp., Elizabeth City, N.C., 1984-86; charge nurse, nurse mgr. St. Vincent Hosp., Sante Fe, 1986-91; nurse mgr. McAllen (Tex.) Med. Ctr., 1991-93; head nurse Scott & White Hosp., Temple, Tex., 1993—. Mem. Oncology Nurse Soc., Sigma Theta Tau. Home: PO Box 5255 Temple TX 76505-5255 Office: Scott & White Meml Hosp 2401 S 31st Temple TX 76505

TRULY, DIANE ELIZABETH, tax board administrator; b. Omaha, Aug. 15, 1943; d. Joseph and Elizabeth Ann (Lyle) Robbie; m. Reginald Wesley Vinson, Sept. 14, 1963 (div. Dec. 1971); 1 child, Laura Elizabeth; m. William Arthur Truly, Oct. 20, 1972 (div. June 1982); 1 child, Mara Yvonne. BA, Calif. State U., L.A., 1968; postgrad., Calif. State U., Sacramento, 1978-81. Planning cons. Franchise Tax Bd., Sacramento, 1982-83, mgr./legis. analysis and devel., 1983-84; dist. mgr. Franchise Tax Bd., San Jose, Calif., 1984-87, San Francisco, 1987-89; area adminstr. Franchise Tax Bd., L.A., 1989-92; dist. office bur. dir. Franchise Tax Bd., Sacramento, 1992-95; v.p., bd. dirs. Nelson Labs., Sioux Falls, S.D. Bd. dirs. Women Escaping a Violent Environ., Sacramento, 1993—, Nat. Coun. on Alcoholism and Drug Dependence, Sacramento chpt., 1994—. Democrat. Home: 925 Piedmont Dr Sacramento CA 95822

TRUMAN, MARGARET, author; b. Independence, Mo., Feb. 17, 1924; d. Harry S. (32nd Pres. U.S.) and Bess (Wallace) T.; m. E. Clifton Daniel Jr., Apr. 21, 1956; children: Clifton T., William, Harrison, Thomas. LHD, Wake Forest U., 1972; HHD, Rockhurst Coll., 1976. Concert singer, 1947-54, actess, broadcaster, author, 1954—; author: Souvenir, 1956, White House Pets, 1969, Harry S. Truman, 1973, Women of Courage, 1976, Murder in the White House, 1980, Murder on Capitol Hill, 1981, Letters from Father, 1981, Murder in the Supreme Ct., 1982, Murder in the Smithsonian, 1983, Murder on Embassy Row, 1985, Murder at the FBI, 1985, Muder in Georgetown, 1986, Bess W. Truman, 1986, Murder in the CIA, 1987, Muder at the Kennedy Center, 1989, Murder in the National Cathedral, 1990, Murder at the Pentagon, 1992, Murder on the Potomac, 1994, First Ladies, 1995; editor: Where the Buck Stops: The Personal and Private Writings of Harry S. Truman, 1989. Trustee and v.p. Harry S. Truman Inst.; sec. bd. trustees Harry S. Truman Found.

TRUMBLEY, BETTY JO, purchasing executive; b. Haleyville, Ala., Mar. 15, 1933; d. William Emmett and Mona Pauline (Wilson) Brown; Harvey Earl Trumbley, Sept. 28, 1957 (div. 1976); 1 child, Hellen Lucia. Grad. h.s., West Haven, Conn. Prodn. mgr. methods engr. Vanguard Systems, Stamford, Conn., 1975-78; printed cir. design mgr. Data Svc. Co., Stamford, 1978-79; acctg. technician Mil. Dept., Hartford, 1979-82; prodn. and purchasing mgr. Digital Diagnostic Corp., Hamden, Conn., 1982—. With WAC U.S. Army, 1952-54, USAR, 1954-58, Conn. Army N.G., 1975-93. Mem. NRA, NAFE, AMVETS, Am. Legion, Non-Commissioned Officers Club. Mem. Ch. of Christ. Home: 48 Wade St West Haven CT 06516 Office: Digital Diagnostic Corp 1020 Sherman Ave Hamden CT 06514

TRUMP, ROSEMARY, labor union executive; b. Smithfield, Pa., Aug. 23, 1944; d. Ralph Bryan and Mary Almeda (Elsey) Hugh; m. Thomas Reed Trump, June 10, 1967 (div. 1988). BA, Am. U., 1966. Social worker Commonwealth of Mass., Boston, 1967-69; labor organizer Svc. Employees, Washington, 1969-73; pres. Internat. Union SEIU Local 585, Pitts., 1973—; internat. v.p. SEIU, Washington, 1980—; sec.-treas. SEIU Joint Coun. 45, Harrisburg, Pa., 1974—; v.p. SEIU Ea. Conf., N.Y.C., 1974—; bd. dirs. AFL-CIO Food and Svc. Trade Dept., Washington, 1981—/. Del. Dem. Nat. Conv., San Francisco, 1984, Atlanta, 1988, N.Y.C., 1992, Chgo., 1996; mem. Com. to Prepare Allegheny County for 21st Century Commn., Pitts., 1995; active NOW. Named Woman of Yr. in Labor, Vectors, 1987. Mem. Coalition for Labor Union Women, Pa. Labor History Soc. Home: 5001 Nottingham Cir Murrysville PA 15668 Office: SEIU Local 585 237 6th St Pittsburgh PA 15238

TRUSKOSKI, ELAINE BARBARA, executive secretary; b. Torrington, Conn., July 19, 1947; d. Edward John and Wanda Mary (Tokarz) Drenzyk; m. Mark Lucian Truskoski, June 6, 1970; children: Ryan Thomas, Jason Todd. Student, Cambridge Sch. Bus./Broadcast, Boston. Prodn. asst. ESPN, Bristol, Conn., 1981, exec. sec., 1982-87, 1993—. Active Coalition to Stop Gun Violence, Washington, 1992. Named to 20 Great Am. Women, McCall's Mag., 1993. Mem. Conn. NOW (Alice-Paul award 1992), Nat. NOW. Roman Catholic. Home: 205 Wildcat Hill Rd Harwinton CT 06791-2509 Office: ESPN 935 Middle St Bristol CT 06010-1000

TRUTA, MARIANNE PATRICIA, oral and maxillofacial surgeon, educator, author; b. N.Y.C., Apr. 28, 1951; d. John J. and Helen Patricia (Donnelly) T.; m. William Christopher Donlon, May 28, 1983; 1 child Sean Liam Riobard Donlon. BS, St. John's U., 1974; DMD, SUNY, Stonybrook, 1977. Intern The Mt. Sinai Med. Ctr., N.Y.C., 1977-78, resident, 1978-80, chief resident, 1980-81; asst. prof. U. of the Pacific, San Francisco, 1983-85, clin. asst. prof., 1985-94; asst. dir. Facial Pain Rsch. Ctr., San Francisco, 1986-92; pvt. practice oral and maxillofacial surgery Peninsula Maxillofacial Surgery, South San Francisco, Calif., 1985—, Burlingame, Calif., 1988—, Redwood City, Calif., 1990-95, San Carlos, Calif., 1995—. Contbr. articles to profl. jours., chpts. to textbooks. Mem. Am. Assn. Oral Maxillofacial Surgeons, Am. Dental Soc. Anesthesiology, Am. Soc. Cosmetic Surgery, Am. Assn. Women Dentists, Western Soc. Oral Maxillofacial Surgeons, No. Calif. Soc. Oral Maxillofacial Surgeons, San Mateo County Dental Soc. (bd. dirs. 1995). Office: Peninsula Maxillofacial Surgery 1860 El Camino Real Ste 300 Burlingame CA 94010-3114

TSAI, MAVIS, clinical psychologist; b. Kowloon, Hong Kong, Sept. 30, 1954; came to U.S. 1966; d. Edwin Fang-Chin and Emily (Tseng) Tsai; m. Robert Joseph Kohlenberg, June 22, 1980; 1 child, Jeremy Tsai Kohlenberg. BA magna cum laude, UCLA, 1976; PhD, U. Wash., 1982. Undergrad. teaching asst. UCLA, 1975-76; teaching asst., predoctoral instr. U. Wash., Seattle, 1977-79; predoctoral lectr., psychology fellow Langley Parker Psychiat. Inst., San Francisco, 1980-81; predoctoral lectr. U. Wash., Seattle, 1981-82, ext. lectr., 1982-88; clin. psychologist in pvt. practice Seattle, 1982—; clin. supr. grad. students U. Wash., Seattle, 1989—. Coauthor: Functional Analytic Psychotherapy, 1991; contbr. articles to profl. jours. Bd. dirs. Asian Counseling and Referral Svc., Seattle, 1984-85, Gifted Women's Conf., U. Wash., 1986-87. Calif. State scholar, 1972-76; recipient APA Minority fellowship, 1977-82, Danforth fellowship honorable mention, 1977. Mem. APA, Wash. Psychol. Assn., Asian Am. Psychol. Assn., Phi Beta Kappa. Office: 3245 Fairview Ave E Ste 303 Seattle WA 98102-3053

TSAMIS, DONNA ROBIN, lawyer; b. Yonkers, N.Y., Sept. 26, 1957; d. Donald Charles and Lenore Angela (Boccia) Lanza; m. Vasili Tsamis, June 18, 1983; children: Niki Alexandra, Victoria Angela. BA summa cum laude, Fordham U., 1979, JD, 1982. Bar: N.Y. 1983, U.S. Dist. Ct. (so. and ea. dist.) N.Y., U.S. Supreme Ct. 1993. Assoc. Jackson, Lewis, Schnitzler & Krupman, N.Y.C., 1982-86, White Plains, N.Y., 1986-89; ptnr. Jackson, Lewis, Schnitzler & Krupman, 1990—. Vice chmn. ann. luncheon com. Girl Scouts U.S.A., Westchester, 1989-92. Mem. Westchester Women's Bar Assn. (chmn. Forum on Alternative Work Schedules for Atty. 1989, bd. dirs. 1990, 92, chmn. lawyering parenting com. 1989-91), Westchester Assn. Women Bus. Owners, Columbian Lawyers Assn. (bd. dirs. 1990-94). Office: Jackson Lewis Schnitzler & Krupman 1 N Broadway # 1502 White Plains NY 10601-2310

TSCHUMY, FREDA COFFING, artist, educator; b. Danville, Ill., Mar. 18, 1939; d. Frederick Winfield and Minnie Isabelle (Buck) Coffing; m. William Edward Tschumy, Jr., June 17, 1967; 1 child, William Coffing. BA, Vassar Coll., 1961; postgrad., Art Students' League N.Y., 1961-63, Accademia di Belli Arti, Rome, 1963; MFA, U. Miami, 1990. Instr. art Miami (Fla.) Fine Arts Conservatory, 1968; instr. ceramics Grove House, Coconut Grove, Fla., summer 1970; instr. sculpture Upstairs Gallery, Miami Beach, 1971, Continuum Gallery, Miami Beach, 1972-73; instr. painting Barry Coll., Miami, fall 1974; instr. sculpture Met. Mus. Sch., Coral Gables, Fla., 1980-89, Bass Mus. Sch., Miami Beach, 1989-92; teaching asst. U. Miami, Coral Gables, 1988-90, lectr. sculpture, pres., 1991—; pres. founding mem. Continuum Gallery, Miami Beach, 1971-75, treas. 1975-83; treas. The Gallery at Mayfair, Coconut Grove, 1982-83, pres., 1983-84; artist in residence Hawaii Sch. for Girls, Honolulu, 1987; founding dir. Foundry Guild, U. Miami, Coral Gables, 1993—. Prin. works include sculptures at Dade Metrorail Univ. Sta., Melbourne (Fla.) Libr.; traveling exhbn. various colls., Miami. Mem. Tropical Audubon Soc., Miami, 1975—, Fla. Conservation Found., 1978—, Fla. Pub. Interest Rsch. Group, 1986—, Fla. Abortion Rights Action League, 1985—. Recipient Excellence award, Sculptors Fla. 1972, Fine Art Achievement award Binney & Smith, 1990; grantee Posey Found., 1989. Mem. Am. Foundryman's Soc., Womens Caucus Art (1st v.p. local chpt. 1981-86, bd. dirs. 1980-91, nat. bd. dirs. 1982-85), Internat. Sculpture Ctr. Studio: 3610 Bayview Rd Miami FL 33133-6503

TSE, MAN-CHUN MARINA, special education educator; b. Kai-Ping, China, Dec. 14, 1948; came to U.S., 1972; d. Sun-Poo and Su-ling Cheung. BA in English, U. Chinese Culture, Taipei, Taiwan, 1970; MS in Spl. Edn., U. So. Calif., 1974. Cert. tchr., spl. edn. tchr., Calif. Rsch. asst. lit. U. Chinese Culture, 1970-72; English tchr. Tang-Suede Mid. Sch., Taiwan, 1970-72; instr. Willing Workers, Adult Handicapped Program L.A. Sch. Dist., 1976-77; instr. ESL Evans Adult Sch., L.A., 1977-82; instr. ESL, polit. sci. Lincoln Adult Sch., L.A., 1986-94; spl. edn. tchr. Duarte (Calif.) Unified Sch. Dist., 1977—; commr., program co-chair Calif. Spl. Edn. Adv. Commn., Sacramento, 1974—; coun. mem. L.A. County Children Planning Coun., 1995—; com. mem. L.A. County Sci. & Engring. Fair Com., 1993—; bd. dirs. Asian Youth Ctr., Rosemead, Calif., 1992—; mem. Calif. State Bd. Edn., 1996—. Appeared on numerous TV and radio programs. Bd. pres. Bruggemeyer Libr., Monterey Park, Calif., 1993—; pres. L.A. County Coun. Reps., 1994—; com. mem. United Way Diversity Com., Acadia, Calif., 1995—, Calif. Statewide Focus Group Diversity, Sacramento, 1995—; chair Chinese Am. Edn. Assn., 1993—; co-chair, co-founder Multi-Cultural Cmty. Assn., 1992—; bd. dirs. Rosemead-Taipei Sister City, 1993—, San Gabriel Valley Charity Night Com., 1992—; vol. chair L.A. County/Taipei County Friendship Com., 1996—. Recipient Recognition cert. Duarte Edn. Found., 1990, cert. Valley View Sch., 1991, award State Calif., 1991, Appreciation award City Rosemead, 1992, Commendation cert. Alhambra Sch. Dist., 1992-93, Edn. award Asian Youth Ctr., 1992, 1992, Commendation cert. City L.A., 1992, commendation County L.A., 1992, award U.S. Congress, 1993, Recognition cert. Calif. Legis. Assembly, 1993, Proclamation City Alhambra, 1993, Chinese Am. PTA award, 1993, John Anson Ford award L.A. County Human Rels. Com., 1993, Appreciation cert. Chinese Consolidated Benevolent Assn., 1994, Recognition cert. Calif. State Senate, 1994, Appreciation cert. City Monterey Park, 1995, numerous others. Mem. Calif. Tchr. Assn., Chinese Edn. Assn. Office: Duarte Unified Sch Dist 1620 Huntington Dr Duarte CA 91010

TSOUNIS, ROSE DINA, financial analyst, consultant; b. Athens, Greece, Nov. 11, 1966; arrived in U.S., 1969; d. Nickolas and Hariklea Tsounis; m. Angelo Christides; div. Apr. 1993. BS, Fairleigh Dickinson U., 1988, MBA, 1991. Financial analyst Bankers Trust, Jersey City, N.J., 1988-1990; financial analyst Automatic Data Processing, Roseland, N.J., 1990-93, sr. financial analyst, 1993—; cons. RDT, Livingston, N.J., 1990—. Mem. NAFE. Home: 32 Glendale Ave Livingston NJ 07039 Office: ADP 1 ADP Blvd MS 335 Roseland NJ 07068

TSUCHIYA, AKIKO, Spanish educator; b. Tokyo, Jan. 9, 1959; came to U.S., 1969; d. Mizuki and Kazuko (Seki) T.; m. Jonathan Mayhew, Aug. 24, 1960; 1 child, Julia E. Tsuchiya-Mayhew. BA, Cornell U., 1981, PhD, 1988; MA, Stanford U., 1983. Asst. prof. Spanish Purdue U., West Lafayette, Ind., 1987-92; asst. prof. Spanish Washington U., St. Louis, 1992-95, assoc. prof. Spanish, 1995—. Author: Images of the Sign: Semiotic Consciousness in the Novels of Benito Pérez Galdós, 1990; mem. editl. bd. Revista de Estudios Hispánicos, St. Louis, 1992—, book rev. editor, 1995—; mem. editl. bd. Jour. of Interdisciplinary Lit. Studies, 1993—; specialist reader Pubs. of MLA, Anales Galdosianos; contbr. articles to profl. publs. NEH fellow, 1994-95; NEH grantee, 1990. Mem. MLA, Midwest MLA, Asociación Internacional de Galdosistas, Feministas Unidas, Phi Beta Kappa. Office: Washington U Dept Romance Langs Box 1077 Saint Louis MO 63130

TSUI, MAY, construction company executive; b. Taipei, Taiwan, June 23, 1954; came to U.S., 1967; d. Robert and Lilian (ong) T.; divorced; 1 child, Danielle. BS, SUNY, Buffalo, 1976; MS, NYU, 1992. Engr. Pacific Gas & Electric Co., San Francisco; acct. Lubbock Fine & Co., London; with Turner Steiner Internat., N.Y.C., 1989—; cost engr. for internat. bus. devel. Office: Turner Steiner Internat 375 Hudson St New York NY 10014

TSUI, SOO HING, educational research consultant; b. Hong Kong, Aug. 2, 1959; came to U.S., 1985; d. Sik Tin and Yuk Kam (Cheung) T. BSW cum laude, Nat. Taiwan U., 1983; MSW cum laude, Columbua U., 1987, postgrad., 1992—. Cert. social worker, N.Y. Dir. cmty. handicapped ctr. Taipei, Taiwan, 1983-85; dir. youth recreational program N.Y., 1986; social work dept. supr. St. Margaret's House, N.Y.C., 1987-89; chief bilingual sch. social work N.Y.C. Bd. Edn., 1990—, rsch. cons., 1993—; chief rsch. cons. N.Y.C. Dept. Transp., 1993-96. Bilingual social worker Nat. Assn. Asian/Am. Edn., 1989—; union social work regional rep. N.Y.C. Bd. Edn., 1990-93, citywide bilingual social work rep., 1991-93, citywide social work budget allocation comms. rep., 1992-93; mem. conf. planning com. bd. Amb. For Christ, Boston, 1991-93; coord. doctoral colloquial com. bd., 1991-93, Scholarship Coun. Social Work Edn., Columbia U., N.Y.C., 1992-94; mem. planning com. social work bd. Asian Am. Comms., N.Y.C., 1991-95. Recipient Nat. Acad. award, 1979-83; Nat. Acad. scholar, 1987-88; Nat. Rsch. fellow Sch. Coun. on Social Work Edn., 1992-94. Home: 507 W 113th St Apt 22 New York NY 10025-8070

TSUNG, CHRISTINE CHAI-YI, financial executive, treasuruer; b. Nanking, China, Mar. 23, 1948; came to U.S., 1970; d. Chi-Huang Tsung and Siao-Tuan Huang; m. Icheng Wu, Aug. 14, 1971 (div. Dec. 1989); m. Jerome Chen, Aug. 10, 1990; children: Jonathan, Julia. BBA, Nat. Taiwan U., Taipei, 1970; postgrad., Washington U., St. Louis, 1970-71; MBA, U. Mo., 1973. Acct. Capital Land Co., St. Louis, 1972-74; chief acct. Servis Equipment Co., Inc., Dallas, 1974-75; acctg. supr. Calif. Microwave, Sunnyale, 1975-76; budget and sales mgr. Columbia Pictures TV Internat., Burbank, Calif., 1976-77; acctg. mgr. Husquarna, San Diego, 1977-82; sr. acct. City of Poway, Calif., 1982-88, fin. mgr., 1988-95; pres., treas. Jade Poly Investment, San Diego, 1989—; cons. assoc. Metro Properties, San Diego, 1989—. Tchr. San Diego North County Chinese Sch., 1985-86; v.p. San Diego Chinese Culture Assn., 1982-86, bd. dirs., 1988-90, 93-94. Mem. Govt. Fin. Officers Assn. (Cert. of Achievement 1988-94), Calif. Soc. Mcpl. Fin. Officers (standing com. membership devel., Cert. of Award 1988-94), Mcpl. Treas. Assn. U.S. and Can., Taiwanese C. of C. of N.Am. (bd. dirs. 1994-95). Home: 18766 Aceituno St San Diego CA 92128-1564 Office: Jade Poly Investments PO Box 302 Poway CA 92074-0302

TUAN, DEBBIE FU-TAI, chemistry educator; b. Kiangsu, China, Feb. 2, 1930; came to U.S., 1958; d. Shiau-gien and Chen (Lee) T.; m. John W. Reed, Aug. 15, 1987. BS in Chemistry, Nat. Taiwan U., Taipei, 1954, MS in Chemistry, 1958; MS in Chemistry, Yale U., 1960, PhD in Chemistry, 1961. Rsch. fellow Yale U., New Haven, 1961-64; rsch. assoc. U. Wis., Madison, 1964-65; asst. prof. Kent (Ohio) State U., 1965-70, assoc. prof., 1970-73, prof., 1973—; rsch. fellow Harvard U., Cambridge, 1969-70; vis. scientist SRI Internat., Menlo Park, Calif., 1981; rsch. assoc. Cornell U., Ithica, N.Y., 1983; vis. prof. Yeshiva U., N.Y.C., 1966, Academia Sinica of China, Nat. Taiwan U. and Nat. Tsing-Hwa U., summer 1967, Ohio State U., 1993, 95. Contbr. articles to profl. jours. Recipient NSF Career Advanced award, 1994—; U. Grad. fellow Nat. Taiwan U., 1955-58, F.W. Heyl-Anon F fellow Yale U., 1960-61, U. Faculty Rsch. fellow Kent State U., 1966, 68, 71, 85; Pres. Chiang's scholar Chinese Women Assn., 1954, 58, Grad. scholar in humanity and scis. China Found., 1955. Mem. Am. Chem. Soc., Am. Phys. Soc., Sigma Xi. Office: Kent State U Chemistry Dept Williams Hall Kent OH 44242

TUBBS, JOAN ROSE, accountant; b. Brownwood, Tex., May 25, 1943; d. Carl Russell and Alva Mae (Rose) Stanley; m. Thomas Milton Cole, June 1, 1963 (div. Feb. 1965); 1 child, Stanley Milton; m. James Arthur Tubbs, Mar. 22, 1979. Student, Howard Payne U., 1974-82, BBA cum laude, 1992; student, U. Tex. Permian Basin, Odessa, 1985-92. CPA. Sec., bookkeeper J.W. Fisher, P.A., Brownwood, 1962-68; cashier, bookkeeper Weakley-Watson Hardware, Brownwood, 1968-76; acct.'s asst. Leanco Corp., Brownwood, 1976-81; accounts payable clk. FMC Corp., Brownwood, 1981-82; chief acct. asst. Williamson Petroleum, Midland, Tex., 1982-84; full-charge bookkeeper Baytech, Inc., Midland, 1984-86; staff acct. EnClean, Inc., Odessa, 1986-93; controller Permian Petroleum Corp., Midland, Tex., 1994-96; dir. fin. Planned Parenthood of West Tex., Inc., 1996—. Scholar Petroleum Accts. Soc., 1990. Mem. U. Tex. Permian Basin Acctg. ASsn., Am. Bus. Women's Assn. (pres. 1982, Bluebonnet award 1981). Home: 6747 N Dixie Blvd Odessa TX 79762-2928 Office: Planned Parenthood of West Tex Inc 910-B South Grant Odessa TX 79761-4133

TUBESING, SANDY E., kindergarten educator; b. Cin., Jan. 6, 1950; d. Clyde Emmerson and Esther Louise (Coy) Small; m. Robert G. Tubesing, May 21, 1983; 1 child, Travis Robert. BEd, Georgetown Coll., 1972, MEd, 1974; postgrad., No. Ky. U., 1980-83. Cert. elem. tchr., Ky. 1st grade tchr. Grant County Schs., Williamstown, Ky., 1972-74, title I tchr., 1978-80, kindergarten tchr., 1980—; substitute tchr. Mil. Sch., Upper Heyford, Eng., 1974-76; program dir. U. N.D., Grand Forks, 1976-78; mem. Tchrs. Applying Whole Lang., Cin., 1982-84. Prodr., dir. videos: Math-Calendar, 1992, Parents/First Teachers, 1992. Rep. Grant County Edn. Assn., Williamstown, 1983. Recipient Ashland Oil Tchr. Achievement award, 1996; named Educator of Yr. Grant County C. of C., 1992. Mem. Ky., Assn. for Children Under Six. Democrat. Lutheran. Home: 250 Turner Dr Crittenden KY 41030-8942

TUCCERI, CLIVE KNOWLES, science writer and educator, consultant; b. Bryn Mawr, Pa., Apr. 20, 1953; d. William Henry and Clive Ellis (Knowles) Hulick; m. Eugene Angelo Tucceri, Sept. 1, 1984 (div. Nov. 1991); 1 child, Clive Edna. BA in Geology, Williams Coll., 1975; MS in Coastal Geology, Boston Coll., 1982. Head sci. dept. Stuart Hall Sch., Staunton, Va., 1975-77; mem. sci. faculty William Penn Charter Sch., Phila., 1977-79, Tower Sch., Marblehead, Mass., 1982-86, Bentley Coll., Waltham, Mass., 1986-88; adminstrv. dir., co-founder Stout Aquatic Libr. Nat. Marine and Aquatic Edn. Resource Ctr., Wakefield, R.I., 1982-89; mem. sci. faculty Mabelle B. Avery Sch., Somers, Conn., 1989-90; mem. faculty, head sci. dept. MacDuffie Sch., Springfield, Mass., 1992-93; mem. sci. faculty East Hampton (Conn.) Middle Sch., 1993—, sci. team leader, 1994-95, sci. chairperson grades K-12, 1995—; cons. Longmeadow (Mass.) Pub. Schs., 1989-94, Addison-Wesley Pub. Co., Menlo Prk, Calif., 1986—; cons., freelance writer Prentice-Hall Inc., Needham, Mass., 1991. Bd. dirs. People against Rape, Staunton, 1976-77. Mem. AAUW (bd. dirs., br. pres.-elect 1975-77, v.p. 1985-86, sec. 1986-87), NSTA, Nat. Marine Edn. Assn. (sec. 1986-87, chpt. rep. 1987-89), Mass. Marine Educators (pres. 1987-89, bd. dirs. 1983-91, editor Flotsam and Jetsam MA Marine Educators newsletter 1991—), Cousteau Soc., Oceanic Soc., Woods Hole Oceanographic Found., Mass. Environ. Edn. Soc. (bd. dirs. 1985-88), Sigma Xi. Episcopalian. Home: 12 Birchwood Dr East Hampton CT 06424-1312

TUCCI, ROSE, human resources executive; b. Gloversville, N.Y., Feb. 17, 1954; d. Lorenzo and Ida (Caputo) T. BA, U. N.C., Charlotte, 1979, Fla. Atlantic U., 1984; MS, Fla. Internat. U., 1992. Cert. tchr., 1984. Tchr. Dade and Broward County, Miami and Ft. Lauderdale, Fla., 1982-86; admissions officer Fla. Atlantic U., Boca Raton, 1987-89; employee rels. specialist S.E. Bank, Miami, 1989-90; dir. human resources Pan Am. Ocean Resort, Miami, 1990-93, Eden Roc Resort, Miami, 1994-95; pres. The Human Factor, Hollywood, Fla., 1992—; prof. music bus. Miami (Fla.) Dade C.C., 1996—. Mem. ASTD (external rels. chair 1992, 93, 94), Fla. Music Network (founder, pres. 1994—). Office: Creative Alliance of Fla 251 W Prospect Rd Fort Lauderdale FL 33309

TUCHOLKE, CHRISTEL-ANTHONY, artist, educator; b. Leczyca, Poland, Mar. 2, 1941; arrived in U.S., 1952; d. Alfred and Eleonore Marie (Mundt) T.; m. Anthony C. Stoeveken, June 9, 1967; children: Jennifer, Joshua. BS in Art Edn., U. Wis., Milw., 1964, MS in Fine Arts Drawing and Painting, 1965. Grad. tchg. asst. U. Wis., Milw., 1964-65; art instr. Milw. Pub. Schs., 1965-66; univ. instr. Western Carolina U., Cullowhee, N.C., 1966-67; print curator Tamarind Lithography WK, L.A., 1968; artist, 1970—; vis. artist, designer Artists Ltd. Edits., Kohler (Wis.) Co., 1989. Exhibited in more than 70 juried shows and invitational exhbns. and galleries, 1970—; commns. include Wis. Arts Bd., 1985, Miller Brewing Co., 1982, Northwestern Mut. Life, 1979. Mem. Profl. Dimensions (hon. mem.). Home: 8535 W Mequon Rd Mequon WI 53097

TUCK, CAROLYN WEAVER, middle school educator; b. Petersburg, Va., Nov. 18, 1947; d. Fred William Weaver and Virginia Evelyn (Fick) Lang; m. Michael Lewis Jones, Dec. 27, 1969 (div. 1991); children: Kristen Michelle Jones, Kara Denise Jones; m. Richard Harper Tuck, July 30, 1994. BS, Radford U., 1970, MS, 1971; adminstrv. cert., William and Mary Coll., 1991, George Washington U., 1991. Cert. secondary sch. prin., English and history tchr., Va. English tchr. Galax (Va.) City Schs., 1971-72, Waynesville (N.C.) Schs., 1973-75; circulation libr. Western Carolina U., Cullowhee, N.C., 1972-73; English and history tchr. Poquoson (Va.) City Schs., 1975-81, 85—; acting asst. prin. Poquoson (Va.) Mid. Schs., 1989; rep. to state MS conf. Va. Bd. Edn., Poquoson, 1991. Writer advanced social studies/English curriculum. Solicitor Am. Cancer Soc., Poquoson, 1992—, Mother's March of Dimes, 1996—; bible sch. tchr. Tabernacle Meth. Ch., Poquoson, 1994—. Mem. NEA, Va. Edn. Assn., Poquoson Edn. Assn., Nat. Mid. Sch. Assn., Pi Gamma Mu, Sigma Tau Delta. Office: Poquoson Mid Sch 985 Poquoson Ave Poquoson VA 23662

TUCK, TERRY MOSS, nurse practitioner; b. Hornell, N.Y., Sept. 15, 1956; d. Harold Robert and Elizabeth Marguerite (Ahearn) Moss; m. Michael Ray Tuck, Sept. 6; 1 child, Megan Elizabeth. AAS, Alfred State Coll., 1976; BS, Med. Coll. Va., 1980, MS, 1987. Staff RN St. Joseph's Hosp., Elmira, N.Y., 1976-77, Chesterfield County Nursing Home, Chester, Va., 1977-78; from staff RN to asst. prof. Southside Regional Med. Ctr., Petersburg, Va., 1978-95; nurse practitioner Allied Signal, Inc., Hopewell, Va., 1996—; pub. health nurse Richmond County Health Dept., Va., 1980; nurse cons. Health Mgmt. Corp., Richmond, 1995—. Chair sch. coun. Falling Creek Elem. Sch., Richmond, 1994-96. Mem. Am. Nurses Assn., Va. Nurses Assn., Va. Coun. Nurse Practitioners, Sigma Theta Tau, Sigma Tau Epsilon. Home: 3403 Oregon Oak Dr Richmond VA 23234 Office: Allied Signal Inc Regional Med Ctr PO Box 831 Hopewell VA 23386

TUCKER, ANNETTE BAUER, paleontologist; b. Phila., Aug. 29, 1942; d. Edward Ewing and Margaret (McConnell) Bauer; m. John Michael Tucker, Apr. 24, 1965; children: John Michael Jr., Jennifer Michelle, Jannette Mari. BS in Geology, Kent State U., 1985, MS in Geology, 1988, PhD in Geology, 1995. Rsch. asst. Kent (Ohio) State U., 1986-87, teaching fellow, 1988-92, temporary asst. prof., 1994—; summer intern Amoco Oil Co., Houston, 1988. Contbr. articles to profl. jours. Sec. Oaks of Aurora (Ohio) Assn., 1994-95. Amoco Found. Masters fellow Kent State U., 1987-88, Univ. fellow Kent State U., 1992, William B. Smith fellow Kent State U., 1994. Mem. Biol. Soc. Wash., Paleontol. Soc., Crustacean Soc., Sigma Xi (assoc.), Sigma Gamma Epsilon (pres. 1985-86). Home: 143 Royal Oak Dr Aurora OH 44202-8225 Office: Kent State U Dept Geology Kent OH 44242

TUCKER, BEVERLY SOWERS, information specialist; b. Trenton, N.J., Dec. 1, 1936; d. Eldon Jones and Verbeda Eleanor (Roberts) Sowers; m. Harvey Richard Tucker, Dec. 27, 1958 (div. Nov. 1983); children: Randall Richard, Brian Alan. BS in Chemistry with distinction, Purdue U., 1958;

MS in Geology, No. Ill. U., 1985; MA in Library and Info. Sci., Rosary Coll., 1989. Asst. rsch. librarian CPC Internat., Argo, Ill., 1958-62; chem. patent searcher Chgo., 1962-66; info. specialist C. Berger & Co., Wheaton, Ill., 1986, Amoco Corp., Naperville, Ill., 1987—; faculty Coll. Du Page, Glen Ellyn, Ill., 1989—. Mem. Spl. Libraries Assn., Ill. Fedn. Women's Club (treas. 5th dist. 1979-81, Outstanding Jr. Clubwoman award 1979-80), Garden Club Council Wheaton (pres. 1981-82), Wheaton Jr. Woman's Club (pres. 1977-78, Single Parent scholar 1984), Gardens Etc. Club (pres. 1978-79), Alpha Lambda Delta, Delta Rho Kappa, Theta Sigma Phi, Alpha Chi Omega (grantee 1985). Republican. Presbyterian. Home: 1507 Paula Ave Wheaton IL 60187-6135 Office: Amoco Corp PO Box 3083 Warrenville Rd and Mill St Naperville IL 60566

TUCKER, FRANCES LAUGHRIDGE, civic worker; b. Anderson, S.C., Dec. 4, 1916; d. John Franklin and Sallie V. (Cowart) Laughridge; m. Russell Hatch Tucker, Aug. 30, 1946 (dec. Aug. 1977); children—Russell Hatch, Pamela Tucker (dec.). Student U. Conn., 1970, Sacred Heart U., Fairfield, Conn., 1977, 79, Fairfield U., 1978, U. S.C., 1984. Sec. to atty., Asheville, N.C., 1935-37; sec. to gen. mgr. Ga. Talc Mining & Mfg., Asheville, 1937-42; sec. engring. dept. E.I. duPont de Nemours, Wilmington, Del., 1942-46. Chmn. radio com. D.C. chpt. ARC, 1947-48, bd. dirs., chmn. pub. rels. Westport-Weston Ct. chpt., 1968-73, mem. adv. coun. ARC Ct. Divsn., 1973-80, chmn. pub. rels., Hilton Head Island, S.C., 1981-84, 89-92, chmn. pub. rels. bloodmobile, Hilton Head Island, 1984-89; bd. dirs., mem. pub. relations com. United Fund, Westport-Weston, Conn., 1968-69, bd. dirs. Beaufort County chpt. ARC, 1982-87, 89-92; mem. media communications St. Luke's Episcopal Ch., Hilton Head Island, 1980-94, office vol., 1995—; with Hilton Head Hosp. Aux., 1984-89. Mem. Sea Pines Country Club. Home: 13 Willow Oak Rd Hilton Head Island SC 29928-5926

TUCKER, SHIRLEY LOIS COTTER, botany educator, researcher; b. St. Paul, Apr. 4, 1927; d. Ralph U. and Myra C. (Knutson) Cotter; m. Kenneth W. Tucker, Aug. 22, 1953. BA, U. Minn., 1949, MS, 1951; PhD, U. Calif., Davis, 1956. Asst. prof. botany La. State U., Baton Rouge, 1967-71, assoc. prof., 1971-76, prof., 1976-82, Boyd prof., 1982-95, prof. emerita, 1995—; adj. prof. dept. biology U. Calif., Santa Barbara, 1995—. Co-editor: Aspects of Floral Development, 1988, Advances in Legume Systematics, Vol. 6, 1994; Contbr. more than 90 articles on plant devel. to profl. jours. Fellow Linnean Soc., London, 1975—; Fulbright fellow Eng., 1952-53. Mem. Bot. Soc. Am. (v.p. 1979, program chmn. 1975-78, pres.-elect 1986-87, pres. 1987-88, Merit award 1989), Am. Bryological and Lichenological Soc., Brit. Lichenological Soc., Am. Inst. Biol. Scis., Am. Soc. Plant Taxonomists (pres.-elect 1994-95, pres. 1995-96), Phi Beta Kappa, Sigma Xi. Home: 3987 Primavera Rd Santa Barbara CA 93110 Office: Univ Calif Dept Biology EEMB U Calif Santa Barbara CA 93106

TUCKER, TANYA DENISE, singer; b. Seminole, Tex., Oct. 10, 1958; d. Beau and Juanita Tucker; children: Presley, Beau Grayson. Regular on Lew King Show; rec. artist formerly with Columbia Records, MCA Records, Capital Records; albums include Tear Me Apart, Chagnes, Delta Dawn, Dreamlovers, Here's Some Love, TNT, Girls Like Me, Greatest Hits, 1989, Greatest Hits (1972-75), Greatest Hits Encore, 1990, Greatest Country Hits, 1991, Greatest Hits 1990-92, 1993, Love Me Like You Use To, 1987, Strong Enough to Bend, 1988, Tanya Tucker Live, Tennesee Woman, 1990, What Do I Do With Me, 1991, (with Delbert McClinton) Can't Run From Youself, 1992, Soon, 1993, Fire to Fire, 1994, TV appearances include A Country Christmas, 1979, The Georgia Peaches, 1980; actress: (mini-series) The Rebels, 1979, (film) Jeremiah Johnson, 1968. Recipient: Country Music Assn. award, 1991, female vocalist of the year; 2 Grammy nominations, 1994. Office: Tanya Tucker Inc 5200 Maryland Way Ste 202 Brentwood TN 37027

TUCKER-KETO, CLAUDIA A., academic administrator; b. Phila., Jan. 24, 1948; d. Arthur and Erma (Miller) Tucker; children: Victor Lefa, James Lefanyana (twins). BA, Temple U., 1982. With adminstrv. office Pa. Supreme Ct., Phila.; coll. adminstr., family resource specialist Camden County Coll., Blackwood, N.J.; coord. women's programs Camden County Dept. Health and Human Svcs., Camden, N.J. mem. ethics com. Dist. IV Supreme Ct., 1993-95. Legis. chairwoman N.J. Fed. Dem. Women, Trenton, N.J.; mem. planning com. U.S. Dept. Labor Women's Bur. Region II, N.Y.; commr. N.J. Martin Luther King Jr. Organization, Trenton; bd. dir. N.J. Women's Summit, Sicklerville, N.J.; chairwomen Camden County Commn. on Women, N.J. Recipient Women in Bus. award Nat. Hookup of Black Women, 1992, Outstanding Svc. to Women award African Am. Women's Network, 1994. Mem. AAUW. Baptist. Home: 133-4 Kirkbride Rd Voorhees NJ 08043

TUDMAN, CATHI GRAVES, elementary education educator, music director; b. Fresno, Calif., June 24, 1953; d. Robert Eugene and Bettyelou (Seagraves) Graves; divorced; children: Colleen Melissa, Andrew James. BA in Music cum laude, Calif. State U., Fresno, 1978, MA in Communication, 1991. Gen. elem., English, music and gen. sci. teaching credentials, Calif. Founder, coord. Lake Sequoia Symphonic Music Camp, Miramonte, Calif., 1985—; asst. lectr. communications speech dept. Calif. State U., 1988-91, instr. reading ednl. opportunity program summer bridge, 1990, instr. writing ednl. opportunity program summer bridge, 1991, coach, judge Peach Blossom Festival, 1988-91; band dir. Yosemite Mid. Sch., 1991-96, Mayfair Elem. Sch., 1991—, Hidalgo Elem. Sch., 1991-92, 94-96, Balderas Elem., 1992-93, Turner Elem., 1993-96, Burroughs Annex Elem. Sch., 1993-95; instr. comms. dynamics Phillips Coll., Fresno, 1989-90; rsch. assoc. Renshaw Assocs., Fresno, 1989-91; flutist, piccoloist Fresno Philharm. Orch., 1981—, libr., 1985, pers. mgr., 1984-85; flute clinician Selmer Corp., Ind., 1988-93; festivals chmn. cen. sect. Calif. Music Educators, 1972-82, publicity chmn., 1992-93; pvt. tutor in math., music and social studies; chmn. Fresno Unified Showcase Mid. Sch. Massed Band, 1993. Flute clinician Fresno County Schs., 1980—; founder San Joaquin Valley Instrument Fund, 1984; bd. dirs. Community Concert Series, Fresno County, 1986-88; liaison com. bd. dirs. Fresno Philharm. Orch., 1992-94; asst. chair FMCMEA Hon. Band, 1992-93; bd. dirs. Cen. Valley YMCA, 1994-95; music chair Fresno Met. Mus., 1996—. Rsch. grantee Calif. State U., 1991; recipient Outstanding Teaching award Internat. Communication Assn., 1991. Mem. Western States Communication Assn., Fresno-Madera Music Educators Assn., Fresno Tchrs. Assn., Calif. Tchrs. Assn., Fresno Mus. Club (social chmn. 1992-95, Calif. Music Educators (festival chmn. cen. sect. 1972-82), Calif. State U.-Fresno Alumnae Assn. (sec. 1982-83, nat. friendship chmn. 1979-81), Blue Key, Phi Kappa Phi, Mu Phi Epsilon (pres., v.p. Phi Chi chpt.). Home: 5467 E Saginaw Way Fresno CA 93727-7536 Office: Yosemite Mid Sch 1292 N 9th St Fresno CA 93703-4229

TUDRYN, JOYCE MARIE, professional society administrator; b. Holyoke, Mass., July 27, 1959; d. Edward William and Frances Katherine (Bajor) T.; m. William Wallace Friberger III, Sept. 18, 1982; 1 child, Kristen. BS in Comm., Syracuse U., 1981. Asst. editor Nat. Assn. Broadcasters, Washington, 1981-83; dir. programs Internat. Radio and TV Soc. Found., N.Y.C., 1983-87; assoc. exec. dir. Internat. Radio and TV Soc., N.Y.C., 1988-94, exec. dir., 1994—; spkr. in field; nat. adv. bd. Alpha Epsilon Rho Broadcasting Soc., 1988-91, 93-94, hon. trustee, 1994—; v.p. Corp. for Ednl. Radio and TV, 1988-94. Editor-in-chief IRTS News, 1983—; columnist TV Facts, Figures and Film mag., 1983-88. Recipient Mass. Kodak Photography award, 1977; S.I. Newhouse scholar Syracuse U., 1980-81. Mem. N.Y. Media Roundtable, Gamma Phi Beta. Home: 602 Bennington Dr Union NJ 07083-9104 Office: Internat Radio and TV Soc Found Ste 1714 420 Lexington Ave New York NY 10170-1799

TUFT, MARY ANN, executive search firm executive; b. Easton, Pa., Oct. 11, 1934; d. Ben and Elizabeth (Reibman) T. BS, West Chester (Pa.) State Coll., 1956; MA, Lehigh U., 1960. Cert. assn. exec. Nat. trainer Girl Scouts U.S.A., N.Y.C., 1965-68; cons. Nat. League for Nursing, N.Y.C., 1968-69; exec. dir. Nat. Student Nurses Assn., N.Y.C., 1970-85; mem. Commn. on Dietetic Registration, Am. Dietetic Assn., 1981-85; pres. Specialized Cons. Ltd., 1983-85; exec. dir. Radiol. Soc. N.Am., Oak Brook, Ill., 1985-88; pres. Tuft & Assocs., Inc., 1989—. Bd. dirs. Nurses House, Inc., 1981-85; bd. dirs. Chgo. Sinai Cong., 1987-91, v.p., 1988. Mary Ann Tuft Scholarship Fund named in her honor Found. Nat. Student Nurses Assn.; Kepner-Tregoe scholar, 1966. Mem. ALA (pub. mem. com. on accreditation 1993-95), Am. Soc. AAssn. Execs. (bd. dirs. 1980-83, trustee for cert. 1980-83, vice chmn. 1983-84), N.Y. Soc. Assn. Execs. (pres. 1978-79, bd. dirs. 1975-78, 1st Outstanding Exec. award 1982), Continuing Care Accreditation Assn. (bd. dirs. 1983-85), Specialized Cons. in Nursing (faculty).

TUFTE, VIRGINIA JAMES, humanities educator, writer; b. Meadow Grove, Nebr.; d. Micah Dickerson and Sarah Elizabeth (Bartee) James; m. Edward E. Tufte; 1 child, Edward Rolf. BA, U. Nebr., 1944; PhD, UCLA, 1964. Prof. English Renaissance lit. U. So. Calif., L.A., 1964-89, disting. prof. of English emerita, 1993—; cons. Milton Studies and other jours., MLA, Ednl. Testing Svc., NEH. Co-author: Remembered Lives, 1992; co-editor: Changing Images of the Family, 1979; contbr. articles to profl. jours.; author: The Poetry of Marriage, 1970, Grammar as Style, 1971; co-author: Exercises in Creativity, 1971; author, prodr. (video) Reaching for Paradise: The Life and Art of Carlotta Petrina, 1994; editor: High Wedlock Then Be Honoured, 1970. Fellow William Andrew Clark Libr., L.A., 1963-64. Mem. MLA, AAUP, Renaissance Soc. Am., Renaissance Conf. So. Calif., Nat. Mus. Women in Arts, Phi Beta Kappa.

TUFTON, JANIE LEE (JANE TUFTON), dental hygienist, animal rights lobbyist, activist; b. Allentown, Pa., Jan. 6, 1949; d. Robert Harry and Jean Lorraine (Seng) T. BS in Edn., Indiana U. Pa., 1979; postgrad. in English, 1979-82. Registered dental hygienist, Pa., N.J., Calif.; cert. tchr., Pa. Dental hygientist pvt. dental practices, Pa., N.J., Calif., 1976-90. Author bd. game for dental health edn., 1974. Lobbyist, activist for animal rights; bd. dirs. and pub. rels. Lehigh Valley Animal Rights Coalition, 1984-93; active civil rights movement, cultural events, literacy programs, detoxification units for drug and alcohol abuse, venereal disease clinics, practical-life workshops for the cognitively impaired, suicide hotlines, YWCA, Girl Scouts U.S. Recipient recognition Pa. Dental Hygienists Assn., 1974; named Internat. Woman of Yr., Internat. Biog. Ctr., 1992-93, Internat. Profl. and Bus. Women's Hall of Fame, Am. Biog. Inst., Inc., 1994, Woman of Yr., Am. Biographical Inst., Inc., 1994. Mem. Am. Anit-Vivisect. Soc., Nat. Humane Edn. Soc., The Fund for Animals, The Humane Soc. of the U.S., Nat. Alliance for Animals, Internat. Soc. for Animal Rights, Physicians Com. for Responsible Medicine, Culture and Animals Found., Animal Legal Def. Fund, People for the Ethical Treatment of Animals, Farm Animal Reform Movement, Farm Sanctuary, Com. to Abolish Sport Hunting, Animal Rights Mobilization, In Def. of Animals, United Animal nations, Internat. Platform Assn., Internat. Network for Religion and Animals. Home: 2102 S Lehigh Ave Whitehall PA 18052-5532

TUGGLE, SHARON BUSH, retired language educator; b. Evansville, Ind., July 19, 1936; d. Leslie St. Clair and Roberta Catherine (Anders) Bush; m. Dennis Moore Tuggle, Aug. 14, 1971. AB in English, Ind. U., 1958, MAT in English, 1961. Tchr. Evansville (Ind.) Sch. Corp., 1958-60, North Ctrl. H.S., Indpls., 1961-64, New Trier H.S., Winnetka, Ill., 1964-71, Evansville Sch. Corp., 1971-95; ret., 1995. Bd. dirs. Philharm. Guild; mem. Reits Hist. Home Guild. Mem. AARP, NEA, Nat. Coun. Tchrs. English, Ind. Coun. Tchrs. English, Evansville Tchrs. Assn., Hawthorne Soc., Delta Kappa Gamma. Home: 319 Christ Evansville IN 47711

TULEY, KAREN ANN BUEDEL, volunteer, accountant; b. Evansville, Ind., July 27, 1960; d. Jerry Lewis and Betty Lee (Freudenberger) Buedel; m. Daniel J. Tuley, Dec. 19, 1981; children: Heath Andrew, Aaron Fielder. BS, U. So. Ind., Evansville, 1983. Sr. adminstrv. asst. 1980 Census Bur., Evansville, 1980; mgr. Roberts Stadium Parking, Evansville, 1980-81; groundskeeper Burdette Park, Evansville, summer 1981; asst., receptionist Dr. Steven Buedel, DDS, Evansville, 1982-84; bookkeeper Regor J Oil Co., Evansville, 1983-84; staff acct. Rutherford & Wright, Evansville, 1984-87; acct. Welborn Bapt. Hosp., Evansville, 1987-94; vol. Christ the King Sch., Evansville, 1994—. Treas. Christ the King PTA, 1995-96. Roman Catholic. Home: 531 S Alvord Blvd Evansville IN 47714

TULL, BARBARA MITCHELL, speech educator; b. Wooster, Ohio, Nov. 7, 1932; d. William Frederick and Margaret Christy (Robbins) Mitchell; m. David Emerson Tull, Aug. 27, 1955; children: Craig, Stephen, Christy, James, Anne. BS, Miami U., Oxford, Ohio, 1954; MA, Western Mich. U., 1955; PhD, Ohio Stat U., 1973. Cert. Tchr., Ohio, lic., cert. Clin. Competence Speech-Lang. Pathology. Asst. to deans Miami U., Oxford, Ohio, 1954; speech clin. Cmty. Speech and Hearing Ctr., Enid, Ok, 1995-62; asst. prof. Ohio Wesleyan U., Delaware, Ohio, 1962-74; lang. speech devel. Ohio Dept. Mental Retardation and Devel. Disabilities, Columbus, Ohio, 1974-81; supr. Morrow County Bd. of Mental Retardation and Devel. Disabilities, Mt. Gilead, Ohio, 1981-86; soc. svcs. cons. Delaware, 1986-89; dir. Home Share Ohio Dept. of Aging, Delaware, 1990-93. Author: 150 Years of Excellence, A Pictorial View of Ohio Wesleyan University, 1992; editor: Affectionately Rachel, Letters From India, 1860-1884, 1993. Chair Del. (Ohio) Met. Housing Authority, 1989—. Presbyterian. Home: 283 N Franklin St Delaware OH 43015

TULL, TANYA, social scientist; b. San Francisco, Mar. 22, 1943; d. Samuel Adams and Clare Sara (Weitzman) Cherry; widowed; children: Daniel, Deborah, Rebecca. BA, Scripps Coll. for Women, 1964; tchg. credential, UCLA, 1971; D Social Sci. (hon.), Whittier Coll., 1992. Founder, exec. dir. Para Los Niños, L.A., 1980-86, Beyond Shelter, L.A., 1988—; co-founder, co-dir. L.A. Family Housing Corp., L.A., 1983-88; founder, acting exec. dir. A Cmty. of Friends, L.A., 1988-90; cons. in field., 1986—. Recipient Jefferson award Nat. Inst. Pub. Svc., 1982, Pub. Affairs award Coro Found., 1983, Ethics in Action award Ethical Culture Soc., 1984, Disting. Alumna award Scripps Coll. for Women, 1986, Ralph Bunche Peace award UN Orgn., 1987, Founder's award NAFE, 1988, Woman of Yr. award Robinson's, 1993, Nonprofit Sector award Nat. Alliance to End Homelessness, 1996, Citizen Activist award Gleitsman Found., 1996; named one of A Hundred Heroes of Our Time, Newsweek mag., 1986, one of 26 leaders Visions for Future of Met. L.A., L.A. Mega-Cities Project, 1995. Democrat. Jewish. Home: 227 S Windsor Blvd Los Angeles CA 90004 Office: Beyond Shelter 3255 Wilshire Blvd # 902 Los Angeles CA 90010

TULL, TARA S., academic program director; b. Columbus, Ohio, Mar. 29, 1961; d. Jack Phillip and Kathryn Muriel (Wolter) T. BA in Women's Studies with distinction, U. Colo., 1985; MS in Women's Studies, Mankato State U., 1990; postgrad., Ctr. Dispute Resolution, 1990, Acad. Mgmt. Inst., 1991-92, Bryn Mawr Summer Inst., 1993. Grad. asst. Mankato (Minn.) State U., 1987-88, grad. rep. women's studies program bd., 1987-89, instr., 1988-89; coord. women's svcs. Met. State Coll. Denver, 1990—; mem. coord. com. Internat. Women's Week, Boulder, Colo., 1985-86; founding mem. Equal Protection Coalition, Boulder, 1986-87; night mgr. Echo House, Boulder, 1989-90; office mgr. Attention Homes, Boulder, 1989-90; campus liaison Colo. Com. Women's History, Coalition for '93, 1992-93; cons. Women's Ctr. Task Force, U. No. Colo., 1993; cons. affirmative action adv. coun. Met. State Coll. Denver, 1994; mem. numerous univ. coms., 1990—; presenter, cons. in field. Editor: Colorado Women: A Plan for Action, 1994; author: (with others) Women's Studies: Thinking Women, 1993. Treas. Colo. Women's Agenda, 1992-94, chair bd. recruitment, 1994-95, mem. activist summit com., 1996. Recipient Natural Helper award Metro Connections, 1991-93; named Woman of Yr., Downtown Denver Bus. and Profl. Women, 1996. Mem. AAUW, Nat. Women's Studies Assn., Nat. Women of Color Resource Ctr., Nat. Assn. Women in Edn., Nat. Assn. Women's Ctrs., Nat. Abortion and Reproductive Rights Action League, Colo. Network of Women's Resources, Women's Lobby of Colo., Colo. Wyo. Assn. Women in Edn. (chair Denver Connections and Conf. Coord. Com. 1991-93, v.p. conf. coord. com. 1993-94, pres. elect 1994-95, pres. 1995-96). Office: Met State Coll Box 36 PO Box 173362 Denver CO 80217

TULL, THERESA ANNE, ambassador; b. Runnemede, N.J., Oct. 2, 1936; d. John James and Anna Cecelia (Paull) T. B.A., U. Md., 1972; M.A., U. Mich., 1973; postgrad., Nat. War Coll., Washington, 1980. Fgn. svc. officer Dept. State, Washington, 1963, Brussels, 1965-67, Saigon, 1968-70; dep. prin. officer Am. Consulate General, Danang, Vietnam, 1973-75; prin. officer Cebu, Philippines, 1977-79; dir. office human rights, 1980-83; charge d'affaires Am. Embassy, Vientiane, Laos, 1983-86; Dept. State Senior Seminar, 1986-87; ambassador to Guyana, 1987-90; diplomat-in-residence Lincoln U., Pa., 1990-91; dir. office regional affairs, bur. East Asian & Pacific affairs Dept. State, Washington, 1991-93; amb. to Brunei Bandar Seri Begawan, 1993—. Recipient Civilian Service award Dept. of State, 1970, Superior Honor award, 1977. Mem. Am. Fgn. Svc. Assn. Home: care Waldis 416 N Washington Ave Moorestown NJ 08057-2411 Office: Am Embassy Box B APO AP 96440 also: Am Embassy, Bandar Seri Begawan, Brunei Darussalam

TULLEY, MONICA ELAINE, marketing professional; b. Jacksonville, Fla., Feb. 12, 1953; d. Douglas Campbell and Lucy (Balestrini) T. BA, U. North Fla., 1976; MBA, U. Calif., Irvine, 1991. Mktg. exec. Am. Hosp. Supply, Cin., 1977-79; mgr. nat. account programs Gen. Electric Med. Systems, Milw., 1979-85; mgr. mktg. svcs. Internat. Imaging, Chgo., 1985-88; mgr. strategic mktg. Toshiba Am. Med. Systems, Tustin, Calif., 1988-91; mgr. CT Products Picker Internat., Cleve., 1993—. Office: 595 Miner Rd Carmel IN 46033

TUMPSON, JOAN BERNA, lawyer. BA with highest distinction, Northwestern U., 1969; JD, Yale U., 1973. Bar: N.Y. 1974, U.S. Dist. Ct. (so. and ea. dists.) N.Y. 1974, U.S. Ct. Appeals (2d cir.) 1975, U.S. Dist. Ct. (no. dist.) Ohio 1977,. U.S. Supreme Ct., 1977, Ohio 1980, Fla. 1980, U.S. Dist. Ct. (so. dist.) Fla. 1981. Gen. assignment reporter, rewriteman AP, N.Y. Bur., A.P. Stringer, Yale U., 1970-72; assoc. Debevoise Plimpton Lyons & Gates (now Debevoise & Plimpton), N.Y.C., 1973-77; staff atty., lectr. law Cleve. Marshall Law Sch., Cleve. State U., 1977-78; vis. asst. prof. law Case Western Res. U., Cleve., 1978-79; assoc. Sage Gray Todd & Sims, Miami, Fla., 1980-82; ptnr. Tumpson & Astbury, Miami, 1982-92, Tumpson & Charchat, Miami, 1993—. Class of 73 sec. Yale Law Sch.; bd. dirs. Greater Miami Jewish Fedn. Cable TV, Inc., 1988-92, long term planning com.; trustee Dade County Art in Pub. Places Trust, 1989-93; host south Fla. talk show One to One Sta. WAXY-AM, 1994—. Mem. Fla. Bar, Yale Club. Office: Tumpson & Charchat 848 Brickell Ave Ste 400 Miami FL 33129

TUMY, KELLY EILEEN, English teacher; b. Tulsa, Dec. 4, 1967; d. Robert William Jr. and Suzanne (Rosen) T. BS Edn., Tex. Tech. U., 1991. Cert. tchr., Tex. Tchr. English North Shore High Sch., Houston, 1991—, lead tchr. English II, 1992—; mem. Campus Acad. Adv. Coun., Houston, 1994-95, North Shore H.S., 1994-96; del. Dist. Acad. Adv. Bd., Galena Park Ind. Sch. Dist., 1994-95. Author: (resource/curriculum) TAAS Notebook, 1993, (curriculum) Literary Genres/Practical Write, 1994. Mem. Nat. Coun. Tchrs. of English, Tex. Coun. Tchrs. of English. Baptist. Office: North Shore High Sch 13501 Hollypark Dr Houston TX 77015-2902

TUNISON, ELIZABETH LAMB, education educator; b. Portadown, Northern Ireland, Jan. 7, 1922; came to U.S., 1923; d. Richard Ernest and Ruby (Hill) Lamb; m. Ralph W. Tunison, Jan. 24, 1947 (dec. Apr. 1984); children: Eric Arthur, Christine Wait, Dana Paul. BA, Whittier Coll., 1943, MEd, 1963. Tchr. East Whittier (Calif.) Schs., 1943-59; tchr. T.V. Stas. TV Channels 13 and 28, So. Calif. Counties, 1960-75; dir. curriculum Bassett (Calif.) Schs., 1962-65; elem. sch. prin. Rowland Unified Schs., Rowland Heights, Calif., 1965-68; assoc. prof. edn. Calif. State Poly. U., Pomona, 1968-71; prof. Whittier Coll., 1968-88, prof. emerita, 1988—. Bd. dirs. Presbyn. Intercommunity Hosp. Found. Recipient Whittier Coll. Alumni Achievement award 1975; Helen Hefernan scholar 1963. Mem. AAUP, Assn. Calif. Sch. Adminstrs. (state bd., chmn. higher edn. com. 1983-86, region pres. 1981-83, Wilson Grace award 1983), PEO (pres. 1990-92), Assistance League of Whittier (v.p. 1994—), Delta Kappa Gamma. Home: 5636 Ben Alder Ave Whittier CA 90601-2111

TUNLEY, NAOMI LOUISE, retired nurse administrator; b. Henryretta, Okla., Jan. 10, 1936; d. Alexander and Ludia Bell (Franklin) T. BSN, Dillard U., 1958; MA, U. Mo., Kansas City, 1974. RN, Okla. Staff nurse, assoc. chief nursing svc. Oklahoma City VA Med. Ctr., 1958-65; instr. Iowa Luth. Hosp. Sch. Nursing, Des Moines, 1965-66; charge nurse emergency rm. Mercy Hosp., Iowa City, Iowa, 1966-67; charge nurse, assoc. chief nursing svc. Kansas City (Mo.) VA Med. Ctr., 1967-76, charge nurse neurol. unit, 1976-79, nurse mgr. orthopedic unit, 1979-80, nurse mgr. substance abuse unit, 1980-94; ret., 1994; equal employment opportunity counselor Kansas City (Mo.) VA Med. Ctr., 1976-86; trustee Nat. Coun. Alcohol and Other Drugs, Kansas City, 1986-90. Vol. Am. Cancer Soc., Kansas City, 1971-79, March of Dimes, Kansas City, 1971-79; big sister Big Bros.-Sisters Am., Kansas City, 1974-84. Mem. ARC, Sigma Theta Tau. Home: 3120 Poplar Ave Kansas City MO 64128-1803

TUNNELL, CLIDA DIANE, air transportation specialist; b. Durham, N.C., Nov. 20, 1946; d. Kermit Wilbur and Roberta (Brantley) T. BS cum laude, Atlantic Christian Coll., 1968; pvt. pilot rating, instr. rating, Air Care, Inc., 1971, 83. Cert. tchr. Tchr. Colegio Karl C. Parrish, Barranquilla, Colombia, 1968-69, Nash County Schs., Nashville, N.C., 1969-86; ground sch. instr. Nash Tech. Coll., Nashville, 1984-85; specialist Am. Airlines, Dallas-Ft. Worth Airport, Tex., 1987—, A300 lead developer in flight tng. program devel., 1988-89, with flight ops. procedures flight ops. tech., 1990—, F100-fleet specialist flight ops. tech., 1992—; ednl. cons., Euless, Tex., 1989—; profl. artist. State Tchrs. Scholar N.C., 1964-68, Bus. and Profl. Women Scholar, 1980-81. Mem. 99, Internat. Orgn. Women Pilots (various offices), AMR Mgmt. Club. Home: PO Box 234 Euless TX 76039-0234

TUNTLAND, MARY KATHLEEN, principal; b. Sioux Falls, S.D., Mar. 4, 1948; d. John J. and Shirley W. (Kleinsasser) Fox; m. Paul S. Tuntland, Aug. 7, 1970; children: Dereck, Jacqueline, Brock. BS in Elem. and Spl. Edn., No. State U., Aberdeen, S.D., 1970; MA in Ednl. Adminstrn., U. S.D., 1983. Elem. tchr. Lennox (S.D.) Sch. Dist. 4-1, 1970-74; spl. edn. tchr. Alcester (S.D.) Sch. Dist., 1975-77; ednl. cons. Area Schs., S.D., 1974-81; H.S. resource tchr. Lennox H.S., 1981-85; coord. gifted edn. program Lennox Area Schs., 1985-89; elem. prin. Elkton (S.D.) Sch. Dist., 1989—; bd. dirs. S.D. Odyssey of the Mind, Pierre, 1993—. Bd. dirs. Elkton Cmty. Libr., 1989—; pres. Elkton FHA Alumni and Friends. Grantee S.D. Dept. Elem. and Secondary Edn., Pierre, 1987, S.D. Sect. Spl. Edn., Pierre, 1989, S.D. Dept. Edn. & Cultural Affairs, 1993, S.D. Arts Coun., Elkton Cmty. Libr., 1993, N.E. Ednl. Svcs. Coop., 1994. Mem. ASCD, Internat. Reading Assn., S.D. Assn. Elem. Sch. Prins., Sch. Adminstrs. S.D., Dakota Valley Elem. Prins. (chmn. 1992—), S.D. Women in Adminstrn., S.D. Talented and Gifted Assn. (bd. dirs. 1986-88), Elkton Cmty. and Bus. Club. Office: Elkton Sch Dist 5-3 508 Buffalo Elkton SD 57026-0190

TURCOT, MARGUERITE HOGAN, innkeeper, medical researcher; b. White Plains, N.Y., May 19, 1934; d. Joseph William (dec.) and Marguerite Alice (dec.) Barrett) Hogan; children: Michael J., Susan A. Turcot, William R. Student, Syracuse U., 1951-54; BS in Nursing, U. Bridgeport, 1968. RN, Conn., N.C. Staff nurse Park City Hosp., Bridgeport, Conn., 1968-69, Meml. Mission Hosp., Asheville, N.C., 1969-70; instr. St. Joseph's Hosp., Asheville, 1970-71; oper. rm. nurse St. Joseph's Hosp., 1973-77, charge nurse urology-cystoscopy, 1977-85; tchr. Asheville-Buncombe Tech. Coll., Asheville, 1971-72, Buncombe County Child Devel., Asheville, 1972-73; researcher VA Med. Ctr., Asheville, 1988—; owner Reed House Bed & Breakfast, Asheville, 1985; bd. dirs. RiverLink. Charter mem. French Broad River Planning Com., Asheville, 1987—, Biltmore Village Hist. Mus.; mem. Asheville Bicentennial Commn., 1990-93. Recipient Griffin award, 1994, Friend of the River award Land of Sky Regional Coun., 1995; faculty scholar Syracuse U., 1951-54, U. Bridgeport, 1967-68, Sondley award Hist. Resources Commn. Asheville and Buncombe County, 1996. Mem. Am. Urology Assn. (presenter VA urology workshop Asheville chpt. 1981, nat. meeting allied), Am. Bd. Urologic Allied Health Profls., Nat. Trust for Hist. Preservation, Preservation Found. N.C., Blue Ridge Pkwy. Assn., Preservation Soc. Asheville and Buncombe County (bd. dirs., past pres.), Asheville Newcomers Club (founder, 1st pres.), Earthwatch, Friends of Blue Ridge Pkwy. Inc. Republican. Roman Catholic. Home: 119 Dodge St Asheville NC 28803-2731 Office: VA Med Ctr Tunnel Rd Asheville NC 28805-1233

TURCOTTE, MARGARET JANE, retired nurse; b. Stow, Ohio, May 17, 1927; d. Edward Carlton and Florence Margaret (Hanson) McCauley; R.N., St. Thomas Hosp., Akron, Ohio, 1949; m. Rene George Joseph, Nov. 24, 1961 (div. June 1967); 1 son, Michael Lawrence. Mem. nursing staff St. Thomas Hosp., 1949-50; pvt. duty nurse, 1950-57; polio nurse Akron's Children Hosp., 1953-54; mem. nursing staff Robinson Meml. Hosp., Ravenna, Ohio, 1958-67, head central service, 1963-67; supr. central service Brentwood Hosp., Warrensville Heights, Ohio, 1967-93; emergency med. technician. Mem. aux. Robinson Meml. Hosp., also hosp. vol.; active RSVP. Mem. St. Thomas Hosp. Alumni Assn. Democrat. Roman Catholic. Home: 6037 Highview St Lot 14-F Ravenna OH 44266

TURCZYN-TOLES, DOREEN MARIE, pharmaceutical consultant; b. Chelsea, Mass., Aug. 5, 1958; d. Francis Henry and Rosalie (Lomba) Turczyn; m. Ronald Eugene Toles, Oct. 19, 1986. BA cum laude, Boston U., 1981; MA, U. Chgo., 1984. Programming subcontr. Abbott Labs., Abbott Park, Ill., 1983-84; programmer, analyst Nat. Opinion Research Ctr., Chgo., 1984-88; statis. computing analyst G.D. Searle & Co., Skokie, Ill., 1988-90; supr. Parke-Davis Pharms., Ann Arbor, Mich., 1990-92; mgr. applications programming Univax Biologics, Inc., Rockville, Md., 1993-95; asst. project dir. Apache Med. Sys., Inc., McLean, Va., 1995-96; sr. systems analyst Westat, Inc., Rockville, Md., 1996—. Mem. Nat. Assn. Female Execs., NOW. Democrat. Roman Catholic.

TURECK, ROSALYN, concert performer, author, editor, educator; b. Chgo., Dec. 14, 1914; d. Samuel and Mary (Lipson) T.; (w. 1964). Piano studies with Sophia Brilliant-Liven, Chgo., 1925-29; with Jan Chiapusso, 1929-31; harpsichord studies with Gavin Williamson, Chgo., 1931-32; piano studies with Olga Samaroff, N.Y.C., 1931-35; BA cum laude, The Juilliard Sch. Music, 1935; MusD (hon.), Colby Coll., 1964, Roosevelt U., 1968, Wilson Coll., 1968, Oxford U., Eng., 1977, Music and Arts Inst., San Francisco, 1987. Mem. faculty Phila. Conservatory Music, 1935-42, Mannes Sch., N.Y.C., 1940-44, Juilliard Sch. Music, N.Y.C., 1943-55, Columbia U., N.Y.C., 1953-55; prof. music, lectr.; regents prof. U. Calif., San Diego, 1966, prof. music, 1966-74; vis. prof. Washington U., St. Louis, 1963-64, U. Md., 1981-85, Yale U., 1991-93; vis. fellow St. Hilda's Coll., Oxford (Eng.) U., 1974, hon. life fellow, 1974—; vis. fellow Wolfson Coll., Oxford, 1975—; lectr. numerous ednl. instns., U.S., Eng., Spain, Denmark, Holland, Can., Israel, Brazil, Argentina, Chile; lectr. Royal Inst. Great Britain, 1993, Boston U., 1993, 94, Smithsonian Instn., 1994, Rockefeller U., 1994, U. Calif., Santa Barbara, 1995, Hebrew U., Israel, Royal Inst. Gt. Britain, London, U. Southampton, Oxford U., 1993; 10th Internat. Congress Logic, Methodology and Philosophy Sci., 1995; founder Composers of Today, 1949-53; soc. for performance internat. contemporary music, founder, dir. Tureck Bach Players, London, 1957, N.Y.C., 1981; founder, dir. Internat. Bach Soc., Inst. for Bach Studies, 1968 ; founder, dir. Tureck Bach Inst., Inc., 1981, Symposia 1968-86, Tureck Bach Rsch. Found., Oxford, U.K., 1994; First Ann. Symposium, Structure: Principles and Applications in the Sciences and Music, 1995. Debut solo recital, Chgo., 1924; soloist Ravinia Park, Chgo., 1926, 2 all-Bachrecitals, Chgo., 1930; N.Y.C. debut Carnegie Hall with Phila. Orch., 1936; series 6 all-Bach recitals, Town Hall, N.Y.C., 1937, ann. series 3 all-Bach recitals, N.Y.C., 1944-54, 59—, ann. U.S.-Can. tours, 1937—; European debut Copenhagen, 1947; extensive ann. European tours; continuing ann. concert tours, recitals, master classes in Spain, Italy, Russia, Eng., Germany, U.S., 1995; world tours in Far East, India, Australia, Europe, 1971, S.Am., 1986, 87, 88, 89, 91, 92, Europe, Israel, Turkey, Spain, 1986-90, Argentina, Chile, 1989, 90, 91, 92, Casals Festival, 1991; N.Y.C. series Met. Mus. Art and Carnegie Hall, 1969—; numerous solo recitals including N.Y.C., 1992, Mostly Mozart Festival, Lincoln Ctr., N.Y.C. , 1994; appeared with leading orchs. U.S., Can., Europe, South Africa, S.Am., Israeli; condr., soloist Collegium Musicum, Copenhagen, 1957, London Philharm. Orch., 1959—, N.Y. Philharm., 1960, Tureck Bach Players, London, 1960-72, San Antonio Symphony, Okla. Symphony, 1962, Scottis Nat. Symphony, Edinburg, Glasgow, 1963, Israel Philharm., Tel Aviv, Haifa and Kol Israel orchs., 1963, Glyndebourne Internat. Bach Soc. Orch., N.Y.C., 1967—, Kans. City Philharm., 1968, Washington Nat. Symphony, 1970, Madrid Chamber Orch., 1970, Israel Festival, Internat. Bach Soc. Orchs., 1967, 69, 70, Carnegie Hall, N.Y., 1975-86, St. Louis Symphony Orch., 1981; Bach festivals cities, Eng., Ireland, Spain, 1959—, Carnegie Hall Ann. Series, N.Y.C., 1975—; TV series Well-Tempered Clavier, Book I, Granada TV, Eng., 1961; BBC series Well-Tempered Clavier, Books 1 and 2, 1976; numerous TV appearances, U.S., 1961—, including Wm. F. Buckley's Firing Line, 1970, 85, 87, 89, Today Show, Camera Three, Bach recitals on piano, harpsichord, clavichord, antique and electronic instruments, 1963—; video concert Teatro Colon, Buenos Aires, 1992; recs. for HMV, Odeon, Decca, Columbia Masterworks., Everest, Allegro, Sony, Video Artists Internat., 1993—, R. Tureck Plays Bach, Goldberg Variations, Great Solo Works Vol. 1 and 2, Live at the Teatro Colon, The R. Tureck Collection, vol. 1 The Young Firebrand, vol. 2 The Young Visionary, Tribute to a Keyboard Legend; author: Introduction to the Performance of Bach, 3 vols., 1960, Authenticity, 1994, J.S. Bach and Number, Symmetries and Other Relationships, Music and Mathematics, 1995, contbr. articles to various mags.; editor Bach-Sarabande, C minor, 1960, Tureck Bach Urtext Series: Italian Concerto, 1983, 2d edit., 1991, Lute Suite, E minor, 1984, C minor, 1985, Schirmer Music, Inc., Carl Fischer Paginini-Tureck: Moto Perpetuo, A. Scarlatti: Air and Gavotte; films: Fantasy and Fugue: Rosalyn Tureck Plays Bach, 1972, Rosalyn Tureck plays on Harpsichord and Organ, 1977, Joy of Bach, 1978, Camera 3: Bach on the Frontier of the Future, CBS film, Ephesus, Turkey, 1985. Decorated Officers Cross of the Order of Merit, Fed. Republic Germany, 1979; recipient 1st prize Greater Chgo. Piano Playing Tournament, 1928, 1st Town Hall Endowment award, 1937, Phi Beta award, 1946; named Schubert Meml. Contest winner, 1935, Nat. Fedn. Music Clubs Competition winner, 1935, Musician of Yr., Music Tchrs. Nat. Assn., 1987; NEH grantee. Fellow Guildhall Sch. Music and Drama (hon.); mem. Royal Mus. Assn. London, Am. Musicological Soc., Inc. Soc. Musicians (London), Royal Philharmonic Soc. London, Sebastian Bach de Belgique (hon.), Am. Bach Soc., Oxford Soc. Clubs: Century (N.Y.C., Oxford and Cambridge, London), Bohemians (N.Y.C.) (hon.). Office: care Christa Phelps, Lies Askonas Ltd 6 Henrietta St, London WC2 EALA, England also: Tureck Bach Rsch Found, Windrush House Davenant Rd, Oxford OX2 8BX, England

TUREK, SONIA FAY, journalist; b. N.Y.C., Aug. 2, 1949; d. Louis and Julia (Liebson) T.; m. Gilbert Curtis, June 18, 1995. BA in English, CCNY, 1970; MSLS, Drexel U., 1972; MS in Journalism, Boston U., 1979. Children's libr. Wissahickon Valley Pub. Libr., Ambler, Pa., 1973; supr. children's svcs. Somerville Pub. Libr., 1973-78; stringer The Watertown (Mass.) Sun, 1979, The Bedford (Mass.) Minuteman, 1979; reporter The Middlesex News, Framingham, Mass., 1979-82, county bur. chief, 1982-83; reporter The Boston Herald, 1983, asst. city editor, city editor, 1985-86, asst. mng. editor features, 1986-89, asst. mng. editor Sunday, 1989-93, dep. mng. editor, arts and features, 1993—; tchr. Cambridge (Mass.) Ctr. for Adult Edn., 1982, 83; adj. prof. Boston U., 1986; travel writer The Boston Herald, 1984-88, wine columnist, 1984—. Office: The Boston Herald One Herald Sq Boston MA 02106

TUREL, JOAN MARIE, religious program director; b. Kingston, Pa.; d. John Alexander and Anna (Kornova) T. MusB, Marywood Coll., 1964; MA, NYU, 1970, Notre Dame U., 1994. Cert. in music edn., Pa., N.Y. Chairperson music dept. St. Patrick's H.S., Scranton, Pa., 1967-69; music cons. Immaculata, St. Alphonsus, St. Stephen's High Schs., N.Y.C., 1969-72; chairperson music dept. Bishop Hoban High Sch., Wilkes-Barre, Pa., 1971-76; choral dir. Kings Coll., Wilkes-Barre, 1978-86; dir. music St. Aloysius Parish, Wilkes-Barre, 1983—; dir. worship Roman Cath. Diocese Scranton, Pa., 1986—; guest condr. Pa. Music Educators Assn., 1978, Nat. Shrine Immaculate Conception, Washington, 1982, Disneyworld, Orlando, Fla., 1983, 84. Editor: (jour.) The Assembly Celebrates, 1987—. State rep. Pa. Music Educators Assn., 1977; founder/condr. Annual Children's Charities Concerts, Wilkes-Barre, 1981-86; mem. Pastoral Formation Inst. Bd., 1988—; mem. Permanent Dioconate Bd., 1992—. Recipient Senatorial commendation Pa. Legis., 1973. Mem. Nat. Assn. Pastoral Musicians (program dir. 1986—, dir. music divsn. 1988—, chairperson nat. convention, 1987), Fedn. Diocesan Liturgial Com. (nat. bd. dirs., 1991—, chairperson ministry com. 1996—), Scranton Commn. on Ecumenism, N.Am. Forum (chairperson two nat. institutes 1989, 91), Pastoral Formation Inst. Bd. Roman Catholic. Office: Diocese of Scranton 300 Wyoming Ave Scranton PA 18503

TURETSKY, JUDITH, librarian, researcher; b. Bklyn., Jan. 19, 1944; d. Samuel and Ruth (Moskowitz) Turetsky. BS, Boston U., 1965; MS, Long Island U., 1969. Tchr. Trumbull (Conn.) Bd. Edn., 1965-66; libr. Darien (Conn.) Bd. Edn., 1968-69, Albert Einstein Coll., Bronx, 1969-74; researcher Koskoff, Koskoff & Bieder, Bridgeport, Conn., 1977-86. Author:(book and micro film), The History and Development of the D. Samuel Gottesman Library of Albert Eistein College of Medicine. Mem. Med. Libr. Assn. Democrat. Home and Office: 62 Gate Ridge Rd Fairfield CT 06432-1164

TURK, RUTH, writer; b. 1917. MA in Edn. Eng. tchr. N.Y. Sch. Sys.; writer, lectr. Author: You're Getting Older, So What?, 1976, More Than Friends, 1980, Hillary for President, 1989, They Reached for the Stars!, 1992, "15" Is the Pits, 1993, The Second Flowering, 1993, Lillian Hellman: Rebel Playwright, 1995, Noises in the Night, 1996, Edith Wharton: Beyond the Age of Innocence, 1996, Ray Charles: Genius of Soul, 1996, Rosalynn Carter: Steel Magnolia, 1996; contbr. poetry, short stories, articles to popular publs.; columnist. Mem. Soc. Children's Book Writers and Illustrators, Fla. Freelance Writers Assn. Home: 7320 Pine Park Dr N Lake Worth FL 33467*

TURKOT, DOROTHY REGESTER FELTON, writer, illustrator; b. Knoxville, Jan. 31, 1927; d. John William and Dorothy Ester (Regester) Felton; divorced; children: Lynda Anne, Karl Wayne, Terry Nolan, Paul Allison. Student, Chgo. Inst. Fine Arts, 1945. Art tchr. Haddonfield (N.J.) Friends, 1962-86; builder Progress Photos, Haddonfield, 1972; model, actress Phila. and N.Y.C., 1985—. Author, illustrator: (children's books) Mother Cat, 1989, Greta Goose, 1990, (cookbook) Star-lit Kitchens, 1996; designer toy Study Buddy, 1995; paintings exhibited in shows in N.J., Pa. (awards); solo shows include Beach Haven Yacht Club, 1984, High Bar Harbor Yacht Club, 1985; group shows include Phila. Bank, 1986-96, Pine Shore Art Assn., Manahawkin, N.J., 1988-96, Old New Castle, Del., 1991—; appeared in various stage prodns., including Arsenic and Old Lace, Fort Carats, Dear Me, The Sky is Falling, Second Time Around, The Man, The Children's Hour, Guys 'N Dolls, also various indsl. films and commls. Recipient award Nat. Libr. of Poetry, 1994. Mem. Long Beach Island Hist. Assn., Ship Bottom Civic Assn., N.Y. Theater Guild, Friends of Surf-light Theater. Home: 353 W 12th St Ship Bottom NJ 08008

TURLINGTON, PATRICIA RENFREW, artist, educator; b. Washington, Sept. 14, 1939; d. Henry Wilson and Anne Ruth (Bright) Renfrew; m. William Troy Turlington III, June 3, 1963 (div. Oct. 1971); children: William Troy IV, David Yelverton; m. William Archie Dees, Jr., June 4, 1994. Student, Meredith Coll., 1957, Washburn U., 1965-66, N.C. State UY., 1969-72. Comml. artist Adlers Inc. & McJoseph's, Raleigh, N.C., 1959-62; exec. dir. Goldsboro (N.C.) Art Ctr., 1973-78; elem. art tchr. Wayne Country Day Sch., Goldsboro, 1979-86; art prof. Wayne C.C., Goldsboro, 1986—; artist-in-residence Edward Laredo Inst. of the Humanities, Cochabamba, Bolivia, summer 1988; vis. artist Va. Western C.C., Roanoke, Va., 1986, Wake Forest U., Winston Salem, 1987, Catawba Valley C.C., Hickory, N.C., 1989, Salem Coll., Winston Salem, N.C., 1992. Works represented in permanent colections Blue Cross-Blue Shield, Durham, N.C., Duke Med. Ctr., Mint Mus., Charlotte, U. N.C., Chapel Hill, Wachovia Bank and Trust Co., Winston-Salem; corp. and pub. brick sculpture commissions Brick Assn. N.C., Greensboro, Cohn Enterprises, Lenoir, N.C., Cordova Elem. Sch., Rockingham, N.C., Wilkes C.C., Wilkesboro, N.C., Hocker Bros. Brick and Tile Co., Inc., Green Bay, Wis., Kincaid Brick Co., Tampa, Fla., Koontz Masonry, Lexington, N.C., McDonald's Restaurants, Knoxville, Tenn., Jonesville, N.C., Cary, N.C., Gastonia, N.C., Knightdale, N.C., Fayetteville, N.C, N.Y.C. Transit Authority, N.Y.C., North Dr. Elem. Sch., Goldsboro, N.C., Rowan Meml. Hosp., Salisbury, N.C. Atlantic Ctr. for the Arts fellow, New Smyrna Beach, Fla., 1986; Pntrs. of the Ams. grantee, U.S. Info. Agy., Washington, 1988. Home: 709 Park Ave Goldsboro NC 27530 Office: Turlington Brickworks PO Drawer 8 Goldsboro NC 27533

TURLO, MARGARET MARY, language educator; b. St. Cloud, Minn., July 11, 1934; d. Charles Joseph and Margaret Cecile (Brennan) Lauermann; m. John B. Turlo, Dec. 26, 1959; children: Mary Helen Turlo Fleer, Laura Brennan Turlo Roberts. BS, St. Cloud State U., 1956; MA, U. Mich., 1962; PhD, U. Calif., Riverside, 1991. Minn., Mich. life tchg. credential; Calif. secondary life tchg. credential. Lang. instr. Clarenceville Schs., Livonia, Mich., 1956-58; lang. instr. Farmington (Mich.) Schs., 1958-63, Coll. of the Desert, Palm Desert, Calif., 1975, 90, Palm Springs (Calif.) Unified Schs., 1963—; editor S.W. Conf. on Lang. Tchg., Phoenix, 1992—, Calif. Lang. Tchrs. Assn., San Diego, 1975-77. Pres. Palm Springs AAUW, 1978-80; S.E. dist. dir. AAUW, 1976-78; pres. Delta Kappa Gamma Palm Springs, 1982-84; v.p. World Affairs, Palm Springs, 1992-95. Recipient NEH fellowship Tufts U., 1985, Rockefeller Endowment fellowship Middlebury Coll., 1986, Chgo. State scholarship Delta Kappa Gamma, 1986, Internat. scholarship Delta Kappa Gamma, 1987. Mem. Am. Coun. Tchg. Fgn. Langs., Cmty. Concerts (pres. 1978-80), Nat. Charity League (v.p. 1977), Sweet Adelines (pub. rels. 1995-96), Desert Handbells Ensemble, Inland Empire Fgn. Lang. Assn. Roman Catholic. Home: 251 Lilliana Dr Palm Springs CA 92264-8916 Office: Palm Springs High School 2248 E Ramon Rd Palm Springs CA 92262

TURNBULL, MARGARET COOMBS, librarian; b. Manitowoc, Wis., June 28, 1953; d. Leonard Alden and Margaret Mary (Carlton) C.; m. Bruce Robert Turnbull, June 16, 1984; 1 child, Andrew Stuart. BA, U. Wis., 1975; M Libr. Info. Svcs., U. Tex., 1981; postgrad., W.Va. Inst. Grad. Coll., 1993, Concord Coll., 1995—. Libr. asst. Austin (Tex.) C.C., 1976-81, Tex. State Libr., Austin, 1981-82; staff libr. W.Va. Grad. Coll., Beckley, 1982-83; instr. libr. sci. Concord Coll., Athens, W.Va., 1983-86; adj. asst. prof. social scis. Concord Coll., Athens, 1989-93, reference libr., 1994-96; staff libr., archivist Bluefield (W.Va.) State Coll., 1996—. Treas. Mercer County Peace Coalition, Athens, 1986-88; sec. Bluefield Dist. United Meth. Women, 1990-94, treas., 1995—; sec.-treas. Citizens Against the High Voltage Power Line, Athens, 1991—. Home: PO Box 222 Athens WV 24712 Office: Bluefield State Coll Libr Bluefield WV 24701

TURNBULL, MARY REGINA, secondary education educator; b. Phila., Aug. 27, 1935; d. Thomas Lawrence and Mary Catherine (Shaughnessy) T. BA in Humanities, Villanova U., 1965; MA in Theology/Adolescent Psychology, LaSalle U., Phila., 1969. Cert. tchr., Pa. Tchr. elem. sch., suburban Phila., 1953-64, secondary sch., Warminster, Pa., 1964-69; supr. State Farm Ins., Springfield, Pa., 1969-73; optometric asst. Dr. Ellis S. Edelman, Newtowne Square, Pa., 1973-76; tchr. vocat. h.s., Phila., 1976-80, secondary sch., Drexel Hill, Pa., 1980—. Roman Catholic. Home: 2024 Rose Ln Broomall PA 19008 Office: Msgr Bonner HS 263 Lansdowne Ave Drexel Hill PA 19026

TURNBULL, MIRIAM DOROTHY, social worker; b. Waterloo, Iowa, June 20, 1920; d. Joseph and Bessie (Abelson) Lederman; m. James Gordon Turnbull, Aug. 27, 1945; children: Toni Jane, Thomas Roger, George Robert. BA, U. No. Iowa, 1942; MSW, U. Iowa, 1971. Tchr. Martelle (Iowa) Sch., 1942-43; fingerprint expert FBI, Washington, 1943-44; social worker Cook County Pub. Aid, Chgo., 1944-45; pub. welfare worker Johnson County, Iowa City, 1945-47, Story County, Ames, Iowa, 1947-48; pub. welfare worker, probation officer Black Hawk County, Waterloo, Iowa, 1963-69; social worker Polk County, Des Moines, 1971-88; supr. Black Hawk County Bd. Supervision, Waterloo, 1993—. Grantee U.S. Dept. Human Svcs., 1973. Mem. NASW (Waterloo br., cert.). Democrat. Home: 126 Barnett Dr Cedar Falls IA 50613 Office: Black Hawk County Bd Supr 315 5th St Waterloo IA 50701

TURNBULL, TERRI DURRETT, county and non-profit organization consultant; b. Marietta, Ga., May 22, 1957; d. Thomas Richard and Margaret (Mann) Durrett; m. Ian Richards, Oct. 23, 1973 (div. Nov. 1977); m. Dan Lancaster, June 22, 1989 (div. Nov. 1990); children: Angie Louise, Shannon Leigh, Matthew D.; m. Paul Douglas Turnbull, Feb. 14, 1991. Student, Kennesaw Coll., Marietta, Ga., 1989, West Ga. Coll., Carrollton, 1989. Adv. Protection & Advocacy, Rome, Ga., 1987-89; program mgr. Cobb County Cmty. Devel., Marietta, 1989—; law clk. U.S. SBA, Atlanta, 1984-85; entrepreneur, cons. Cobb Exec. Support Svcs., Rome and Marietta, Ga., 1985—. Contbr. articles to profl. jours. Mem. publicity and fundraising com. Cobb County Habitat for Humanity, Cobb St. Ministry Homeless Shelters, Cobb County Heritage Coun.; mem. Gov.'s Policy and Adv. Com. on Weatherization, DOE/HUD Initiative Com. Recipient Certs., Gov.'s Office of Energy Resources. Home: 328 Mt Carmel Church Rd Temple GA 30179 Office: Cobb Exec Support Svcs Ste 270 3180 Bankhead Hwy Lithia Springs GA 30057

TURNBULL, VERNONA HARMSEN, retired residence counselor, education educator; b. Teeds Grove, Iowa, Dec. 6, 1916; d. Henry Ferdinand and Ida Amelia (Dohrmann) Harmsen; m. Alexander Turnbull, Oct. 12, 1961. BA, Cornell Coll., Mt. Vernon, Iowa, 1939; MEd, U. Colo., Boulder, 1947, profl. cert. edn., 1955. Cert. secondary and h.s. tchr. Tchr. English, Latin and phys. edn. Winslow (Ill.) H.S., 1939-45; dir. women's activities, instr. Trinidad (Colo.) State Jr. Coll., 1947-53; counselor women, assoc. prof. edn. Western State Coll., Gunnison, Colo., 1953-54; instr., residence counselor Stephens Coll., Columbia, Mo., 1955-61. Active Salvation Army Aux. Mem. AAUW, Am. Assn. Ret. Persons (corr. sec. 1986-87), Kena Kampers Camping Club.

TURNDORF, JAMIE, clinical psychologist; b. Boston, July 12, 1958; d. Gary Owen and Sharon (Sandow) T.; m. Emile Jean Pin, Jan. 2, 1988. AB in Am. Culture, Vassar Coll., 1980; MSW, Adelphi U., 1983; PhD, Calif. Coast U., 1994. Lic. social worker, N.Y. Pvt. practice psychology N.Y.C. and Millbrook, N.Y., 1981—; lead creative movement and psychodrama program Lincoln Farms Work Camp, Roscoe, N.Y., 1976; with Astor Child Guidance Clinic, Poughkeepsie, N.Y., 1982-83; leader various pgroups Braig House Hosp., Beacon, N.Y., 1982-87, developer, dir.eating disorders program, 1984-86; founder, dir. INC.TIMACY, 1990—, J.T. Developers, Inc., Poughkeepsie, 1983-91; dir. Hudson Valley br. Ctr. for Advancement Group Studies, Ctr. for Emotional Comm., Millbrook, 1990—. Author: (with Emile Jean Pin) The Pleasure of Your Company: A Socio-Psychological Analysis of Modern Sociability, 1985; columnist Dr. Love various newspapers; relationship advice on world wide webb; host Ask Dr. Love, Sta. WEVD, N.Y.C., 1992; creator, inventor LoveQuest: The Game of Finding Mr. Right, 1990 (one of best new games award Fun and Games mag. 1991). Mem. NASW, N.Y. State Soc. Clin. Social Work Psychotherapists. Home and Office: PO Box 475 Millbrook NY 12545-0475

TURNER, (GENEVA) ANNE, nursing educator; b. Parris Island, S.C., Oct. 28, 1945; d. Frank Rex and Geneva Estella (Phillips) Hoffman; m. Raymond Daniel Turner Jr., Aug. 26, 1967; 4 children. Nursing diploma, Samuel Merritt, Oakland, Calif., 1966; BS in Natural Sci., Bapt. Coll., Charleston, S.C., 1985; MEd, Charleston So. Coll., 1989. RN, Fla., Calif., Ga.; cert. secondary tchr., S.C. Nurse Samuel Merritt, Oakland, 1966-67, Emory U., Atlanta, 1967-68, Fla. Hosp., Orlando, 1979-81; tchr. Stratford H.S. Berkeley County Schs., Goose Creek, S.C., 1986—; mem. strategic planning action team Berkeley County Schs., 1994-95. Mem. ASCD, Am. Bus. Women's Assn., Nat. Sci. Tchrs. Assn., Low Country Gem & Mineral. Southern Baptist.

TURNER, BERNICE HILBURN, recording industry executive; b. Black Rock, Ark., Jan. 13, 1937; d. Floyd W. and Clementime (Higgins) Hilburn; m. Doyle Turner, Feb. 28, 1957 (div. Jan. 1980); children: Johnny, P.J., Danny, Jill, Robby. PhD in Applied Psychology, 1974. Musician Hank Williams Sr., Nashville and Montgomery, Ala., 1950-52, 1952-76; owner Onyx Recording Studio, Memphis, 1985—, Turner Limousine Svc., Memphis, 1988—. Named Pioneer in Country Music, United Music Heritage of Tenn., 1989. Mem. Unity Ch. Home: 1646 Bonnie Dr Memphis TN 38116-5732

TURNER, BONESE COLLINS, artist, educator; b. Abilene, Kans.; d. Paul Edwin and Ruby (Seybold) Collins; m. Glenn E. Turner; 1 child, Craig Collins. BS in Edn., U. Idaho, MEd; MA, Calif. State U., Northridge, 1974. Instr. art L.A. Pierce Coll., Woodland Hills, Calif., 1964—; prof. art Calif. State U., Northridge, 1986-87; art instr. L.A. Valley Coll., Van Nuys, 1987-89, Moorpark (Calif.) Coll., 1988—, Arrowmont Coll. Arts & Crafts, Gatlinburg, Tenn., 1995-96; advisor Coll. Art and Arch. U. Idaho, 1988—; juror for numerous art exhbns. including Nat. Watercolor Soc., 1980, 91, San Diego Art Inst., Brand Nat. Watermedia Exhbn., 1980, 96-97, prin. gallery Orlando Gallery, Sherman Oaks, Calif. Prin. works exhibited in The White House, 1984, 85, Smithsonian Inst., 1984, 85, Olympic Arts Festival, L.A., 1984, Royal Birmingham Soc. of Artists Gallery, Birmingham, Eng., 1996; one-woman shows include Angel's Gate Gallery, San Pedro, Calif., 1989, Art Store Gallery, Studio City, Calif., 1988, L.A. Pierce Coll. Gallery, 1988, Brand Art Gallery, Glendale, Calif., 1988, 93, Coos (Oreg.) Art Mus., 1988, U. Nev., 1987, Orlando Gallery, Sherman Oaks, Calif., 1993, others; prin. works represented in pub. collections including Smithsonian Inst., Hartung Performing Arts Ctr., Moscow, Idaho, Home Savs. and Loan, San Bernardino Sun Telegram Newspapers, Oreg. Coun. for the Arts, Newport, Nebr. Pub. Librs., Lincoln (Nebr.) Indsl. Tile Corp. Recipient awards Springfield (Mo.) Art Mus., 1989, Butler Art Inst., 1989. Mem. Nat. Mortar Bd. Soc., Nat. Watercolor Soc. (life, past pres., Purchase prize 1979), Watercolor U.S.A. Honor Soc. (award), Watercolor West.

TURNER, CATHY, Olympic athlete; b. Apr. 10, 1962. BS in Computer Sys., No. Mich. U., 1991. Gold medal 500 meter short-track speedskating Albertville Olympic Games, 1992, also silver medal 3000 meters relay, 1992; Star made in Am. tour Ice Capades, 1992-93; Gold medalist 500 meter speedskating Winter Olympics, Lillehammer, Norway, 1994, Bronze medalist 3000 meter relay, 1994; owner, pres. Cathy Turner's Empire Fitness; motivational spkr. Profl. singer, songwriter, actress. Address: US Olympic Committee 1750 E Boulder St Colorado Springs CO 80909-5724

TURNER, CRISTINA BENITEZ, advertisting professional; b. Easton, Md., July 20, 1946; d. Rafael Celestino Benitez and Nancy Shannon Critchlow; divorced; 1 child, Todd Turner. BA, Furman U., 1971, MA, 1972. Spanish tchr. Greenville (S.C.) County Schs., 1971-80; account exec. Multimedia Comms., Greenville, 1980-85; account supr. Atwood Internat., N.Y.C., 1987-89; cons. Gannett Pub., N.Y.C., 1989; v.p., account svc. Grey Advt., N.Y.C., 1989-95; sr. v.p., Hispanic mktg. dir. Draft Direct Worldwide, Chgo., 1995—. Tutor Greenville Literacy Program, 1980-85; vol. St. Mary's Soup Kitchen, N.Y.C., 1990-95; mem. inaugural opening com. Chgo. Mus. Contemporary Art. Mem. Direct Mktg. Assn., Directo (operating com.), Women in Direct Mktg. (program com.), Hispanic Alliance for Career Enhancement, Chgo. Coun. on Fgn. Rels., Latin Am. C. of C. Office: Draft Direct Worldwide 142 E Ontario Chicago IL 60611-2818

TURNER, DENISE DUNN, writer; b. Cairo, Ill., Aug. 2, 1947; d. Robert James and Helen Grace (Dunn) Watkins; m. Revis Eugene Turner, Dec. 22, 1967; children: Rebecca Jill, Stephen Robert. Buyer Stewart's Dept. Store, Louisville, 1970-73; freelance writer Middletown, Ohio, 1976-88; newspaper reporter Middletown Jour., 1987-88; corr. Times-News, Twin Falls, Idaho, 1988-89; editor spl. sects. Times-News, Twin Falls, 1899-91; asst. features editor Times-News, Twin Falls, Idaho, 1991—; lectr. in field. Author: Home Sweet Fishbowl, 1982, Scuff Marks on the Ceiling, 1986; co-author: (book series) Guideposts, 1985; contbr. articles to mags. Chmn. publicity Charity Ball, Middletown, 1985; leader discussion Middletown Area Sr. Citizens, 1984-88; mem. women's com. Southern Baptist Theol. Seminary, Louisville. Recipient Recognition cert. Middletown C. of C., 1986, Assoc. Press award, 1994, Soc. of Profl. Journalists awards, 1995, 96. Mem. So. Ill. U. Alumni Found., Twin Falls Lions Club, Idaho Press Club, Phi Kappa Phi. Baptist. Home: 1880 Falls Ave E Twin Falls ID 83301-4224 Office: Times-News PO Box 548 Twin Falls ID 83303-0548

TURNER, ELIZABETH ADAMS NOBLE (BETTY TURNER), healthcare executive, former mayor; b. Yonkers, N.Y., May 18, 1931; d. James Kendrick and Orrel (Baldwin) Noble; m. Jack Rice Turner, July 11, 1953; children: Jay Kendrick, Randall Ray. BA, Vassar Coll., 1953; MA, Tex. A&I U., 1964. Ednl. cons. Noble & Noble Pub. Co., N.Y.C., 1956-67; psychometrist Corpus Christi Guidance Ctr., 1967-70; psychologist Corpus Christi State Sch., 1970-72, dir. programs, asst. supt., 1972, dir. devel. and vol. svc., 1972-76, dir. rsch. and tng., 1977-79, psychologist Tex. Mental Health and Mental Retardation, 1970-79; pres. Turner Co., 1979—; program cons. Tex. Dept. Mental Health and Mental Retardation, 1979-85; mayor pro tem. Corpus Christi, 1981-85, mayor, 1987-91; CEO, pres. Corpus Christi C. of C., 1991-94; v.p. bus. and govt. rels. ctrl. and south Tex. divsns. Columbia Healthcare Corp., 1994—. Dir. alumni Corpus Christi State U., 1976-77; coord. vols. Summer Head Start Program, Corpus Christi, 1967; chmn. spl. gifts coml United Way, Corpus Christi, 1970; mem. Corpus Christi City Coun., 1979-91; family founded Barnes and Noble, N.Y.C.; with Leadership Corpus Christi II; founder Com. of 100 and Goals for Corpus Christi; pres. USO; bd. dirs. Coastal Bends Coun. Govts., Corpus Christi Mus., Harbor Playhouse, Communities in Schs., Del Mar Coll. Found., Pres.' Coun., Food Bank, Salvation Army, Jr. League; bd. govs. Southside Community Hosp., 1987-93, Gulfway Nat. Bank, 1985-92, Bayview Hosp., 1992—, strategic planning com. Meml. Hosp., 1992, Tex. Capital Network Bd., 1992—, Humana Hosp., Rehab. Hosp. South Tex., Admiral Tex. Navy; apptd. Gov.'s Commn. for Women, 1984-85, Leadership Tex. Class I; founder Goals for Corpus Christi, Bay Area Sports Assn., Assn. Coastal

Bend Mayor's Alliance; founder Mayor's Commn. on the Disabled, Mayor's Task Force on the Homeless; active Port Aransas Cmty. Ch. Recipient Love award YWCA, 1970, Y's Women and Men in Careers award, 1988, Commander's Award for Pub. Svc. U.S. Army, Scroll of Honor award Navy League, award Tex. Hwy. Dept., Road Hand award Tex. Hwy. Commn., 1989; named Corpus Christi Newsmaker of Yr., 1987. Mem. Tex. Psychol. Assn. (pres., mem. exec. bd.), Psychol. Assn. (pres., founder), Tex. Mcpl. League (bd. dir.), Corpus Christi C. of C. (pres., CEO), Jr. League Corpus Christi, Tex. Bookman's Assn., Tex. Assn. Realtors, Kappa Kappa Gamma, Corpus Christi Town Club, Corpus Christi Yacht Club, Jr. Cotillion Club. Home: 4600 Ocean Dr Apt 801 Corpus Christi TX 78412-2543

TURNER, ESTHER NEGLEY, nursing administrator; b. Marinette, Wis., Sept. 4, 1938; d. Carl Leslie and Hanna (Kuhn) Negley; m. Charles M. Parker, Mar. 1, 1957 (div. June 1987); children: Cheri, Brad, Andrea; m. David William Turner, Aug. 3, 1995. BSN, St. Olaf Coll., 1975; MS, L.I. U., 1983. Tchr. Brandywine Sch. Nursing, Cain, Pa., 1985-88; nursing adminstr. VA Med. Ctr., Coatesville, Pa., 1988-89, South Oaks Psychiat. Hosp., Amityville, N.Y., 1989-90, Athens (Ohio) Mental Health Ctr., 1990-91, VA Med. Ctr., Knoxville, Iowa, 1993—; clin. specialist Nationwide Healthcare, Columbus, Ohio, 1991-92. Author: Hypnosis Questions and Answers, 1986, Family Therapy, 1988; contbr. articles to profl. jours. Group facilitator League Against Child Abuse, Columbus, 1989, Knoxville, 1993; vol., bd. dirs. Cancer Soc., Knoxville, 1993. Mem. AAUW, Iowa Nursing Assn., Iowa Psychiat. Nurse Assn., Sigma Theta Tau. Home: 409 W Main St Richland IA 52585 Office: VA Med Ctr 1515 Pleasant St Knoxville IA 50138

TURNER, FLORENCE FRANCES, ceramist; b. Detroit, Mar. 9, 1926; d. Paul Pokrywka and Catherine Gagal; m. Dwight Robert Turner, Oct. 23, 1948; children: Thomas Michael, Nancy Louise, Richard Scott, Garry Robert. Student, Oakland C.C., Royal Oak, Mich., 1975-85, U. Ariz., Yuma, 1985, U. Las Vegas, 1989—. Pres., founder Nev. Clay Guild, Henderson, 1990-94, mem. adv. bd., 1994—; workshop leader Greenfield Village, Dearborn, Mich., 1977-78, Plymouth (Mich.) Hist. Soc., 1979, Las Vegas Sch. System, 1989-90, Detroit Met. area, 1977-85. Bd. dirs. Las Vegas Art Mus., 1987-91; corr. sec. So. Nev. Creative Art Ctr., Las Vegas, 1990-94. Mem. So. Nev. Rock Art Enthusiasts, Las Vegas Gem Club, Nev. Camera Club, Golden Key, Phi Kappa Phi. Office: Nev Clay Guild PO Box 50004 Henderson NV 89016-0004

TURNER, HAZEL M., educator; b. Birmingham, Ala., Mar. 1, 1926; d. Will and Georgia Ann (Beard) McCarter; m. Victor Caesar Turner Jr., Nov. 28, 1957; children: Victor C. III, Michael David. BS in Elem. Edn., Tuskegee U., 1950; MA in Guidance and Counseling, NYU, 1952, EdD in Student Pers. Adminstrn., 1960. Dean of women Alcorn Coll., Lorman, Miss., 1950-53; dir. student svcs. Tuskegee (Ala.) U., 1955-58; dir. youth programs Lansing (Mich.) YWCA, 1960-61; dir. spl. edn. Lansing Pub. Schs., 1961-66; dir. student pers. svcs. Ann Arbor (Mich.) Pub. Schs., 1966-85; vis. lectr. Ea. Mich. U., Ypsilanti, 1985—; mem. from Mich. State Dept. Pub. Instrn. to seminar Harvard U., 1968. Co-chair fundraising Ann Arbor Cmty. Ctr., 1972-74; vol. United Way, Lansing and Ann Arbor, 1970-74; mem. divsnl. bd. Catherine McAuley Health Ctr., Mission Health, Ann Arbor, 1980-85; chair Ret. Sr. Vol. Program, Ann Arbor, 1988—, mem. adv. com. 1993-95; co-chair pers. com. Housing Bur. for Srs., 1990-94. Named Outstanding Female Educator, Delta Kappa Gamma, 1978; recipient Founder's Day award NYU, 1971. Mem. AAUW, Mich. Assn. Tchr. Educators, the Links, Inc. (v.p., pres. 1985-87, rep. to UN Decade of Women Conf., Nairobi, Kenya 1985), Alpha Kappa Alpha. Home: 1219 Ardmoor Ave Ann Arbor MI 48103

TURNER, JACQUELINE YVONNE, geriatric therapist; b. Waynesboro, Miss., Nov. 16, 1967. BS, Livingston U., 1991; MS, Miss. State U., Meridian, 1993. Specialist in group counseling Meridian, 1993—. Mem. ACA, Miss. Counseling Assn. Methodist. Home: 310 53d Ave Apt B Meridian MS 39307

TURNER, JANE ANN, federal agent; b. Rapid City, S.D., Aug. 26, 1951; d. John Owen and Wilma Veona (Thompson) T.; 1 child, Victoria Thompson. BA, Carroll Coll., 1973; student forensic psychology, John Jay Sch. Criminal Justice, N.Y.C., 1985-87. Spl. agt. FBI, Seattle and N.Y.C., 1978-87; sr. resident spl. agt. FBI, Minot, N.D., 1987—; spkr., instr. FBI, Seattle, N.Y.C. and Minot, 1978—, Psychol. Profiler, 1983—. Mem. Minot Commn. on the Status of Women, 1991-93. Mem. Gen. Fedn. Women's Clubs (v.p. 1992-93), Women in Law Enforcement, N.D. Peace Officer Assn., Optimist Club. Office: FBI PO Box 968 Fed Bldg Minot ND 58701

TURNER, JANET SULLIVAN, painter; b. Gardiner, Maine, Nov. 15, 1935; d. Clayton Jefferson and Frances (Leighton) Sullivan; m. Terry Turner, Oct. 6, 1956; children: Lisa Turner Reid, Michael Ross, Jonathan Brett. BA cum laude, Mich. State U., 1956; student, Haystack Mountain Sch. rep. Am. Women in Art, UN World Conf. on Women, Nairobi, Kenya, 1995. One-artist shows include San Diego Art Inst., 1971, Villanova (Pa.) U. Gallery, 1982, Pa. State U. Gallery, Middletown, 1985, Temple U. Gallery, 1986, Widener U. Art Mus., Chester, Pa., 1987, 94, Rosemont Coll., Pa., 1995; group shows include Del. Art Mus., Wilmington, 1978, Woodmere Art Mus., Phila., 1980, Port of History Mus., Phila., 1984, Allentown Art Mus., 1984, Trenton (N.J.) City Mus. Ellarslie Open VIII, 1989, Ammo Gallery, Bklyn., 1989, Pa. State Mus., Harrisburg, 1990-94, Galeria Mesa, Ariz., 1991, Del. Ctr. for Contemporary Arts, Wilmington, 1992, Holter Mus., Helena, Mont., 1992, S.w. Tex. State U., San Marcos, 1993, Fla. State U. Mus., Tallahassee, 1993, Newark Mus., 1993, U. Del., 1994, 1st St. Gallery, N.Y.C., 1994, Noyes Mus., N.J., 1995, Sande Webster Gallery, Phila. 1995, 96; represented in permanent collections Nat. Mus. Women in Arts, Washington, Mich. State U., East Lansing, ARA Svcs. Inc., Phila., Blue Cross/ Blue Shield, Phila., am. Nat. Bank and Trust co., Rockford, Ill., Burroughs Corp., Lisle, Ill., State Mus. Pa., Harrisburg, Bryn Mawr (Pa.) Coll., Rosemont Coll., Villanova (Pa.) Coll.; contbg. writer and art critic Art Matters, Phila., 1987. Bd. dirs. Rittenhouse Sq. Fine Arts Ann., Phila., 1984-86. Recipient 2d pl. award San Diego Art Inst. 19th Ann. Exhbn., 1971, award of merit Pavilion Gallery, Mt. Holly, N.J., 1991, 3d pl. Katonah Mus. of Art, N.Y., 1992, purchase award State Mus. of Pa., Harrisburg, 1992. Mem. Artists Equity (bd. dirs. 1985-86, 1st v.p. Phila. 1986-87, newsletter editor 1985-86, pres. 1987-88), Phila. Watercolor Club, Delta Phi Delta. Republican. Roman Catholic. Home and Studio: 88 Cambridge Dr Glen Mills PA 19342-1545

TURNER, JANINE, actress; b. Lincoln, Nebr., Dec. 6, 1963; d. Janice Gaunt. Appearences include (TV) Behind the Screen, 1981-82, General Hospital, 1982-83, Northern Exposure, 1990-95 (Hollywood Fgn. Press Assn. award 1992, Emmy award nominee 1993), (films) Young Doctors in Love, 1982, Knights of the City, 1985, Tai-Pan, 1986, Monkey Shines: An Experiment in Fear, 1988, Steel Magnolias, 1988, The Ambulance, 1990, Cliffhanger, 1993. Office: CAA 9830 Wilshire Blvd Beverly Hills CA 90212-1804*

TURNER, JILL LESLIE, sales executive; b. Santa Ana, Calif., Aug. 8, 1959; d. Russell Wesley and Virginia Lee (Andrews) Cuthbert; m. Robert Eugene Turner, Aug. 21, 1982 (div. 1994). BS in Mktg. Mgmt., Va. Poly. Inst., 1981. With sales dept. Diamond Shamrock Corp., Irving, Tex., 1981-83; with sales dept. Health Care Mktg. Svcs., Los Altos, Calif., 1984-90, sr. sales cons., 1990-94, sales cons., coach, 1994—. Mem. Midwest Healthcare Mktg. Assn., Med. Mktg. Assn. Office: Health Care Mktg Svcs 95 1st St Ste 200 Los Altos CA 94022

TURNER, JUDY A., elementary school educator; b. Trinidad, Colo., Feb. 11, 1948; d. Rudolph R. and Lillian Barbara (Gernazio) Icabone; m. George Edward Turner, Jan. 25, 1968; children: Chris, Brian. AA in Edn., Trinidad State Jr. Coll., 1969; BA in Elem. Edn., Adam State Coll., 1974; MA in Elem. Sch. Adminstrn., U. No. Colo., 1983. Tchr. asst. Trinidad Sch. Dist., 1969-71, Vista (Colo.) Sch. Dist., 1971-73; kindergarten, 1st, 3d and 4th grade tchr. Jefferson County Sch. Dist., Arvada, Colo., 1974-84; elem. tchr. Jefferson County Sch. Dist., Arvada, 1976-85; 6th grade tchr. Jefferson County Sch. Dist., Conifer, Colo., 1984-88; elem. tchr. Jefferson County Sch. Dist., Lakewood, Colo., 1988—, curriculum evaluator, 1987; tchr., parent partnership coord. Jefferson County Sch. Dist., Golden, Colo., 1983-85, law-related edn. curriculum writer, 1995; outdoor edn. lab. sch. cadre Jefferson County Outdoor Lab Schs., Golden, 1988—. Co-author: Library Books in the Classroom, 1984; contbr. articles to profl. jours. Treas. Homeowners Assn., 1986-88, tech. com., 1990-96. Mem. Jefferson County Tchrs. Assn. (instrn. and profl. devel. 1982-88, chair legis. liaison 1988-96), Phi Delta Kappa (historian 1994-96).

TURNER, KATHLEEN, actress; b. Springfield, Mo., June 19, 1954; m. Jay Weiss, 1984; 1 child, Rachel Ann. Student, Cen. Sch. of Speech and Drama, London, Southwest Mo. State U.; BFA, U. Md. various theater roles, Broadway debut: Gemini, 1978, Cat on a Hot Tin Roof, 1990, Indiscretions, 1995; appeared in TV series The Doctors, 1977; films include Body Heat, 1981, A Breed Apart, 1982, The Man With Two Brains, 1983, Crimes of Passion, 1984, Romancing the Stone, 1984, Prizzi's Honor (Golden Globe award for best actress), 1985, The Jewel of the Nile, 1985, Peggy Sue Got Married, (D.W. Griffith award for best actress, Oscar nomination for best actress) 1986, Julia and Julia, 1988, Switching Channels, 1988, Who Framed Roger Rabbit, 1988, Accidental Tourist, 1988, The War of the Roses, 1989. V.I. Warshawski, 1991, Undercover Blues, 1993, House of Cards, 1993, Serial Mom, 1994, Naked in New York, 1994; dir. (Showtime Cable movie) Leslie's Folly, 1994; also performed in radio shows with the BBC, 1992, 93. Office: ICM 8942 Wilshire Blvd Beverly Hills CA 90211*

TURNER, LESLIE MARIE, federal official; b. Neptune, N.J., Oct. 2, 1957. BS, NYU, 1980; JD, Georgetown U., 1985. Law clk. Cole, Raywid & Braverman, Washington, 1984-85; jud. clk. to Hon. William C. Pryor U.S. Ct. Appeals (D.C. cir.), Washington, 1985-86; assoc. Akin, Gump, Strauss, Hauer & Feld, L.L.P., Washington, 1986-93; asst. sec. for territorial and internat. affairs Dept. Interior, Washington, 1993—. Office: Dept Interior Territorial & Internat Affairs 1849 C St NW Washington DC 20240-0001*

TURNER, LISA HILL, county official; b. Rexburg, Idaho, Sept. 11, 1959; d. Dale A. and Betty Jean (Owens) Hill; m. Rick I. Turner, June 10, 1979; 1 child, Keith D. Staff mem. Fremont County Herald-Chronicle, St. Anthony, Idaho, 1977-93, editor, 1985-93; chief dep. treas. Fremont County, St. Anthony, Idaho, 1994-95, roll clk., security officer, systems operator, 1995—. Dir. Foster Grandparents, Fremont Gen. Hosp. Found., St. Anthony, Idaho. Named Most Respected Citizen, Free Fisherman's Breakfast, 1991, Hon. Chef, 1987; recipient Cert. of Appreciation, Idaho Gov. Cecil Andrus, 1990. Mem. So. Fremont C. of C. (sec. 1985-88, dir. 1986-89). Mem. LDS Ch.

TURNER, LISA JOYCE, paint manufacturing company executive; b. Galveston, Tex., June 1, 1959; d. Carlton and Dorothy Lee (McPeters) Pappas Kelly; m. E.D. Turner; 1 child, Alexander Carlton. Student N. Tex. State U., 1977, Richland Coll., 1978, U. Ark.-Little Rock, 1980, IBM Continuing Edn., 1981-82. Mktg. asst. Membership Services, Irving, Tex., 1978, tech. support asst., 1980; programmer, analyst Mail Mktg. Services, Little Rock, 1980-82; bus. broker VR Bus. Brokers, Longview, Tex., 1982-85; mgr., v.p. Creative Coatings Inc., Kilgore, Tex., 1985—, also bd. dirs. Mem. Mothers Against Drunk Drivers, Longview, Tex., 1985-86, v.p. Gregg County chpt.; sec. East Tex. Area Parkinsonism Soc., 1987—. Mem. Data Processing Mgrs. Assn., Nat. Assn. Sundry Distbrs. (adv. bd.). Baptist. Avocations: skiing, traveling. Home: 3715 Ben Hogan Dr Longview TX 75605-1623 Office: Creative Coatings Inc 428 N Longview St Kilgore TX 75662-5810

TURNER, LISA PHILLIPS, human resources executive; b. Waltham, Mass., Apr. 10, 1951; d. James Sinclair and Virginia (Heathcote) T. BA in Edn. and Philosophy magna cum laude, Washington Coll., Chestertown, Md., 1974; AS in Electronics Tech., AA in Engring., Palm Beach Jr. Coll., 1982; MBA, Nova U., 1986, DSc, 1989; PhD, Kennedy Western U., 1990. Cert. pers. adminstr., quality engr., human resource profl.; lic. USCG capt.; lic. pvt. pilot FAA. Founder, pres. Turner's Bicycle Svc., Inc., Delray Beach, Fla., 1975-80; electronics engr., quality engr. Audio Engring. and Video Arts, Boca Raton, 1980-81; tech. writing instr. Palm Beach Jr. Coll., Lake Worth, Fla., 1981-82; adminstr. tng. and devel. Mitel Inc., Boca Raton, 1982-88; mgr. communications and employee rels. Modular Computer Systems, Inc., Ft. Lauderdale, Fla., 1988-89; U.S. mktg. project mgr. Mitel, Inc., Boca Raton, Fla., 1990-91; v.p. human resources Connectronics, Inc., Ft. Lauderdale, Fla., 1991-93; mgr. human resources Sensormatic Electronics Corp., Boca Raton, Fla., 1993—. With USCG Aux. Mem. ASTD, Am. Soc. for Pers. Adminstrn., Internat. Assn. Quality Cirs., Am. Soc. Quality Control, Fla. Employment Mgmt. Assn., Am. Acad. Mgmt., Employment Assn. Fla., Am. Capts. Assn., Citizens Police Acad., Aircraft Owners and Pilot's Assn., Exptl. Aircraft Assn., Fla. Aero. Club. Home: 1358 Farifax Cir E Lantana FL 33462-7412 Office: Sensormatic Electronics Corp 6600 Congress Ave Boca Raton FL 33487-1213

TURNER, LULA MAE MANSUR, retail executive; b. Denver, Feb. 12, 1917; d. Daniel Isaiah and Elizabeth Wilhelmina (Bellin) Mansur; m. Gordon Eugene Turner, June 12, 1938; 1 child, Daniel Gordon. Grad. high sch., Creston, Iowa. With steongraphic and acctg. dept. Iowa So. Utilities, Creston, 1935-38; sales and acctg. Kunath's, Creston, 1944; stenographic clk. Union County Draft Office, Creston, 1941-44; asst. mgr. Turner Appliance & Gifts, Creston, 1945—. Mem. DAR (regent 1954-56, state conv. chmn. 1974-76), Creston Womens Club (pres. 1945-46), Creston C. of C. (chmn. women's bur. 1966-67). Republican. Christian Scientist. Office: Turner Appliances & Gifts 200 N Elm St Creston IA 50801-2304

TURNER, LYNDA LOIS, secondary educator, English; b. Corbin, Ky., Apr. 29, 1949; d. William Amos and Frances B. (Marshall) T. BA, Berea Coll., 1971; MA, U. Ky., 1973, MSLS, 1990; postgrad., Western Ky. U., 1993. Cert. tchr., Ky. Instr. German U. Ky., Lexington, 1971-73; actress, singer Wilderness Road, Berea, Ky., 1973-78; instr. German, English, theatre, libr. Frederick Fraize H.S., Cloverport, Ky., 1975—. Author: (poetry) Persona, 1990. Mem. ACLU, Louisville, 1990—. Grantee NEA, 1983, 90. Mem. ALA, NEA, AAUW, Am. Assn. Tchrs. German, Ky. Edn. Assn. Democrat. Baptist. Home: 111 Oak St Cloverport KY 40111

TURNER, MARGERY AUSTIN, government agency administrator; b. Ithaca, N.Y., July 10, 1955; d. William Weaver and Elizabeth Jane (Hallstrum) Austin; m. James Charles Turner, Aug. 26, 1979; children: James Austin, Benjamin Phillip. BA, Cornell U., 1977; M Urban Planning, George Washington U., 1984. Rschr. Urban Inst., Washington, 1977-88, dir. housing rsch., 1988-93; dep. asst. sec. for rsch. U.S. Dept. HUD, Washington, 1993—. Author: Housing Market Impacts of Rent Control, 1990; co-author: Urban Housing in the 1980's, 1985, Future U.S. Housing Policy, 1987, Opportunities Denied, Opportunities Diminished, 1991, Housing Markets and Residential Mobility, 1993. Mem., coach Boys and Girls Club, Camp Springs, Md., 1990—. Mem. Lambda Alpha.

TURNER, MARTA DAWN, youth program specialist; b. Morgantown, W.V., Oct. 7, 1954; d. Trubie Lemard and Dorothy Genevieve (Helmick) T.; m. David Michael Dunning, Mar. 1, 1980. Student, Royal Acad. Dramatic Art, London, 1975; BA with honors, Chatham Coll., 1976; grad. cert. in arts adminstrn., Adelphi U., 1982; MA Devel. Drama, Hunter Coll., 1988. Cert. video prodn. specialist. Asst. dir. Riverside Communications, N.Y.C., 1985-88; dir. drama, video youth environ. group Water Proof, Cornell Coop. Extension, 1989-91; playwright, dir. Awareness Players, The Disabled Theatre of Maine, 1993-95. Exec. prodr. video projects including Hispanic City Sounds, Time for Peace, Home, Home in Inwood, 1985—; asst. dir., dir. video series Riverside at Worship, 1985-88. Bd. dirs. Trinity Presbyn. Ch., N.Y.C., 1980-90, Am. Diabetes Assn., 1986-87. Home and Office: 818 Ohio St Apt 90 Bangor ME 04401-3100

TURNER, MARY ALICE, elementary school educator; b. Birmingham, Ala., Aug. 8, 1946; d. Henry and Elzona (Griffin) Johnson; m. Raymond Carver Turner, July 6, 1968; 1 child, Taunya Nicole. BS in Edn., Ala. A&M U., 1968, MEd, 1992. Cert. tchr. home econs. edn., elem. edn., early childhood edn. Elem. tchr. Huntsville (Ala.) City Schs., 1969—. Mem. Parent/Sch./Tchr. adv. bd. Ridgecrest Elem. Sch., Huntsville, 1978; tchr. rep. PTA, Rolling Hills Elem. Sch., Huntsville, 1988-93. Recipient Award for Dedicated Svc. Rolling Hills PTA, 1988. Mem. ASCD, NEA, Ala. Edn. Assn., Huntsville Edn. Assn. (sch. rep. 1969-96, mem. budget com., rule and regulations com. review), Ala. Reading Assn., Alpha Kappa Alpha. Democrat. Baptist. Home: 6508 Mercator Dr NW Huntsville AL 35810-1361 Office: Rolling Hills Elem Sch 2901 Hilltop Ter NW Huntsville AL 35810-1862

TURNER, MARY JANE, educational administrator; b. Colorado Springs, Colo., June 1, 1923; d. David Edward and Ina Mabel (Campbell) Nickelson; m. Harold Adair Turner, Feb. 15, 1945 (dec.); children: Mary Ann, Harold Adair III. BA in Polit. Sci., U. Colo., 1947, MPA in Pub. Adminstrn., 1968, PhD in Polit. Sci., 1978. Secondary tchr. Canon City (Colo.) Sch. Dist., 1950-53; tchr. assoc. in polit. sci. U. Colo., Denver, 1968-70, Boulder, 1970-71; rsch. asst. Social Sci. Edn. Consortium, Boulder, 1971, staff assoc., 1972-77; dir. Colo. Legal Edn. Program, Boulder, 1977-84; assoc. dir. Ctr. for Civic Edn., Calabasas, Calif., 1984-88; dir. Close Up Found., Alexandria, Va., 1988-92; sr. edn. advisor Close Up Found., Arlington, Va., 1992—. Author: Political Science in the New Social Studies, 1972; co-author: American Government: Principles and Practices, 1983, 4th edit., 1996; Civics: Citizens in Action, 1986, 2d edit., 1990, U.S. Government Resource Book, 1989; contbg. author: Internat. Ency. Dictionary of Edn. Mem. Nat. Coun. for Social Studies (chair nominations 1983-84, chair bicentennial com. 1986), Social Sci. Edn. Consortium (pres. 1986-87, bd. dirs. 1984-87), Pi Lambda Theta, Pi Sigma Alpha. Democrat. Presbyterian. Office: Close Up Found 44 Canal Center Plz Alexandria VA 22314-1592

TURNER, MEGAN WHALEN, author; b. Fort Sill, Okla., Nov. 21, 1965; d. Donald Peyton and Nora Courtenay (Green) Whalen; m. Mark Bernard Turner, June 20, 1987; children: John Whalen, Donald Peyton. BA in English Lang. and Lit. with hons., U. Chgo., 1987. Buyer of children's books Harper Court Bookstore, Chgo., 1988-89, Bick's Books, Washington, 1991-92. Author: (books) Instead of Three Wishes, 1995, The Thief. Mem. Authors' Guild.

TURNER, MILDRED EDITH, day care owner; b. Winnebago, Wis., Jan. 11, 1926; d. Jewett Candfield and Angeline Mary (Long) T. BS, State Tchrs. Coll., 1949; MS of Edn., U. Wis., Milw., 1962; postgrad., U. Wis., Oshkosh, 1965-70. Cert. tchr., Wis. Tchr. Winnebago County, Omro, Wis., 1945-47, Plymouth (Wis.) Pub. Schs., 1949-51, Ripon (Wis.) Pub. Schs., 1951-53, Omro Pub. Schs., 1953-88; instr. U. Wis., Oshkosh, 1971, supervising tchr. of student tchrs., 1970-91; owner, operator Wee Care Children's Ctr., Omro, 1974—. Contbr. articles to newspapers, profl. publs., children's books. Acolyte coord. Algoma Blvd. United Meth. Ch.; supt. Sunday sch., pianist, choir dir., ch. music dir. Eureka/Waukau United Meth. Ch.; sub-dist. children's dir. Watertown sub-dist. United Meth. Ch. Mem. Ret. Tchrs. Assn. Winnebago County, Ret. Tchrs. Assn. Omro, Fox Valley Assn. for Edn. of Young Children, Word and Pen Christian Writers (sec.-treas.), Alumni Assn. U. Wis. Oshkosh), Alumni Assn. Omro (treas.), Odd Fellows (past noble grand Rebekah lodge), Omro Study Club (past pres.). Home and Office: 305 E Scott St Omro WI 54963-1707

TURNER, PEGGY ANN, graphic designer, visual artist; b. Memphis, Jan. 17, 1951; d. James Patrick and Margaret Helen (Brastock) T. BFA, U. Tenn., 1974, MFA summa cum laude, 1992. Art dir. Turner Design, Knoxville, 1972-84; designer, illustrator Creative Displays, Knoxville, 1974-75; designer alumni affairs U. Tenn., Knoxville, 1975-81; sr. art dir. Whittle Comm., Knoxville, 1982-85; creative dir. Sullivan-St. Clair Advt., Mobile, Ala., 1985-89; grad. teaching asst. dept. art U. Tenn., Knoxville, 1989-91; prof. graphic design Savannah (Ga.) Coll. Art and Design, 1991-92; asst. prof. graphic design Va. Polytechnic Inst. and State U., 1992-96, Nicholls State U., Thibodaux, La., 1996—. One-woman shows include S. Morris Gallery, Savannah, 1992, Ewing Gallery, Knoxville, 1993, 94, Armory Art Gallery, Va. Poly. Inst. and State U., 1993, Gallery 303, Ga. So. U., 1994, Littman-White Gallery, Portland, Oreg., 1995; group shows include Women's Art Works III, Rochester, N.Y. (jury prize), Nat. Expos II, Chgo., 1993, Current Works '93, Kansas City, Mo., U. West Fla., 1994, Paper Stars, San Francisco, 1994, Nat. Exposures, Winston-Salem, N.C. Recipient nat. citation Coun. for Advancement Edn., 1981, award Warren Paper Co., 1984; Fred M. Roddy scholar, 1970, Blinn scholar for fgn. study, 1991; grantee Va. Poly. Inst. and State U., 1992, 93, Women's Rsch. Inst., 1993, 95. Mem. Am. Advt. Fedn., Coll. Art Assn., Alpha Lambda Delta. Democrat. Episcopalian. Home: 301 E 7th St Thibodaux LA 70301 Office: Nicholls State U Art Dept PO 2701 Thibodaux LA 70301

TURO, JOANN K., psychoanalyst, psychotherapist, consultant; b. Westerly, R.I., Feb. 13, 1938; d. Angelo and Anna Josephine (Drew) T. BS in Biology and Chemistry, U. R.I., 1959; MA in Human Rels. and Psychology, Ohio U., 1964; postgrad., NYU, 1966-71, N.Y. Freudian Inst., N.Y.C., 1977-85, Mental Health Inst., N.Y.C., 1977-80. Rsch. asst. biochemistry studies on schizophrenia Harvard U. Med. Sch., Boston, 1959-60; indsl. psychology asst. studies on managerial success N.Y. Telephone Co., N.Y.C., 1964-66; staff psychologist Testing and Advisement Ctr. NYU, 1966-70; psychology intern Kings County Hosp., Bklyn., 1970-71; staff psychologist M.D.C. Psychol. Svcs., N.Y.C., 1971-72; clin. dir. Greenwich House Substance Abuse Clinic, N.Y.C., 1973-76; cons. psychotherapist Mental Health Consultation Ctr., N.Y.C., 1977-82; pvt. practice psychoanlysis and psychotherapy N.Y.C., 1981—; mental health cons. Bklyn. Ctr. for Psychotherapy, 1976-78; with Psychoanaltyic Consultation Svcs., 1994—; presenter in field. Mem. Itnernat. Psychoanalytic Assn. (cert., presenter fall meeting 1995), Soc. for Personality Assessment (cert.), N.Y. Freudian Soc. (cert., co-chmn. grad. com. 1985-86, mem. continuing edn. com. 1986—, pub. rels. com. 1992-93, psychoanalytic consult svc. 1994—, tng. and supr. psychoanalyst 1995), N.Y. Coun. Psychoanalytic Psychotherapists (cert.), Met. Assn. for Coll. Mental Health Practitoners (cert.). Office: 175 W 12th St Apt 9H New York NY 10011-8221

TUROCK, BETTY JANE, library and information science educator, educational association administrator; b. Scranton, Pa., June 12; d. David and Ruth Carolyn (Sweetser) Argust; BA magna cum laude (Charles Weston scholar), Syracuse U., 1955; postgrad. (scholar) U. Pa., 1956; MLS, Rutgers U., 1970, PhD, 1981; m. Frank M. Turock, June 16, 1956; children: David L., B. Drew. Library and materials coordinator Holmdel (N.J.) Public Schs., 1963-65; story-teller Wheaton (Ill.) Public Library, 1965-67; ednl. media specialist Alhambra Public Sch., Phoenix, 1967-70; br. librarian, area librarian, head extension service Forsyth County Public Library System, Winston-Salem, N.C., 1970-73; asst. dir. Montclair (N.J.) Public Library, 1973-75, dir., 1975-77; asst. dir. Monroe County Library System, Rochester, N.Y., 1978-81; asst. prof. Rutgers U. Grad. Sch. Communications, Info. and Library Studies, 1981-87, assoc. prof. 1987-93, prof. 1994—, dept. chair, 1989-95, dir. MLS program, 1990-95; vis. prof. Rutgers U. Grad. Sch. Library and Info. Studies, 1980-81; adviser U.S. Dept. Edn. Office of Libr. Programs, 1988-89. Trustee, Raritan Twp. (N.J.) Public Library, 1961-62, Keystone Coll., 1991—, Freedom to Read Found., 1994—, Libs. for the Future, 1994—, Fund for Am.'s Libs., 1995; mem. Bd. Edn. Raritan Twp., 1962-66; mem. Title VII Adv. Bd., Montclair Public Schs., 1975-77; ALA coord. Task Force on Women, 1978-80, mem. action coun.; treas. Social Responsibilities Round Table, 1978-82. Recipient N.J. Libr. Leadership award, 1994; named Woman of Yr., Raritan-Holmdel Woman's Club, 1975. Mem. AAUP, Am. Soc. Info. Sci., Assn. Libr. and Info. Sci. Edn., Am. Libr. Assn. (pres. 1995—, pres.-elect 1994-95, exec. bd. 1991—, coun. 1988—), Rutgers U. Grad. Sch. Library and Info. Studies Alumni Assn. (pres. 1977-78, Disting. Alumni award 1994), Phi Theta Kappa, Psi Chi, Beta Phi Mu, Pi Beta Phi. Unitarian. Author: Serving Older Adults, 1983, Creating a Financial Plan, 1992; editor: The Bottom Line, 1984—; contbr. articles to profl. jours. Home: 39 Highwood Rd Somerset NJ 08873-1834 Office: Rutgers U 4 Huntington St New Brunswick NJ 08901-1071

TUROCK, JANE PARSICK, nutritionist; b. Peckville, Pa., Apr. 15, 1947; d. Paul Charles and Elizabeth Dorothy (Mistysyn) Parsick; m. Michael John, July 12, 1968; children: Eric Matthew, Nathan Andrew, J. Seth, Melanie Kay. BS, Marywood Coll., Scranton, 1969; MS, Marywood Coll., 1982. Registered dietitian; cert. nutrition specialist. Registered dietitian Jane P. Turock, Scranton, Pa., 1985—; founder and chief dietitian Gastric Bubble, Scranton, Pa., 1986—; prof. Penn State Coll., Scranton, Pa., 1987—; dietitian & presenter WNEP TV Healthwatch, Avoca, Pa., 1988—; dir. & chief dietitian Vascular Inst. of Northeast Pa., Pa., 1989—; owner, mgr. Nutrition...Plus/Fitness Unlimited, Scranton, Pa., 1991—; cons. Home Health Care Assn., Clarks Summit, 1985—; dietitian Clarks Summit, 1985—;

founder Nat. Nutrition Month Bakeoff; dir. Camp Jane. Treas. Lackawanna County Med. Soc. Aux., 1974-76, pres., 1979-80, bd. dirs., 1980-81; allocations com. United Way Lackawanna County, 1990—; mem. bd. dirs. Lupus Found., 1995, St. Francis of Assissi Kitchen, 1995. Mem. Am. Dietic Assn., Northeast Dist. Pa. Dietic Diet Therapy, Consulting Nutritionists in Pvt. Practice, Am. Diabetic Assn., Northeast Womens Network, Allied Wedding Firm. Republican. Roman Catholic. Office: Nutrition Plus Fitness Unltd 815 Smith St Scranton PA 18504-3150 also: Abington Family Svcs 211 N State St Clarks Summit PA 18411-1087 also: Lady Jane Inc dba The Ski Habit Elk Mountain PA 18470

TURPIN, JENNIFER ELLEN, sociology educator; b. San Antonio, Aug. 8, 1961; d. William Francis and Solveig Astrid (Skramstad) T.; m. Robert Alan Elias, June 3, 1993; 1 child, Madeleine Rachel Elias. BA in Psychology magna cum laude, U. Tex., 1983, MA in Sociology, 1986, PhD in Sociology, 1991. Instr. sociology Chapman Coll., Long Beach Naval Sta., Calif., 1990; lectr. sociology Calif. State U., Long Beach, 1990-91; coord. women's studies program U. San Francisco, 1991—, asst. prof. sociology, 1991-95, assoc. prof., chair dept. sociology, 1995—; mem. assoc. faculty European Univ. Ctr. for Peace Studies, UNESCO, Schlaining, Austria, 1992—; host USF Today, KUSF Radio, 1993-94; manuscript reviewer Lexington Books; presenter in field. Author: Reinventing the Soviet Self: Media and Social Change in the Former Soviet Union, 1995; co-editor: (with Lester Kurtz) The Web of Violence: From Interpersonel to Global, 1996, (with Lois Ann Lorentzen) The Gendered New World Order, 1996; author, co-editor: (with Robert Elias) Rethinking Peace, 1994; sr. editor Peace Review, 1991—; contbr. articles to profl. jours., chpts. to books. Counselor, pub. spkr. Austin Rape Crisis Ctr., 1983-88, co-chair Peace Edn. Ctr., Austin, 1986-88; adv. Tex.-Soviet Exchange Coun., 1988. Westlake scholar, 1979, U. Tex. scholar, 1982, Karl M. Dallenbach scholar, 1981, 82; grantee Samuel Rubin Found., 1986, U. Tex., 1987, 88, U. San Francisco, 1991-92, 92-93, MacArthur Found., 1992, Interfaith Hunger Appeal, 1993-94; recipient Outstanding Cmty. Svc. award, Austin, 1981. Mem. Am. Sociol. Assn. (chair-elect 1996—, mem. sect. sociology of peace and war 1989-90, assoc. editor peace and war sect. 1989-90, mem. com. peace and war sect. 1991-92, chair mem. com. peace and war sect. 1992-94, mem. social psychology com., mem. sex and gender com., Elise Boulding student paper award com. 1989-90), Internat. Peace Rsch. Assn., Am. Assn. Advancement Slavic Studies, Am. Soc. Criminologists (mem. nominating com. 1988), Network of East-West Women (com. 1992—), Peace Studies Assn. (coun. officer sect. peace and war 1992-93, conf. chair 1994), Psi Chi, Alpha Kappa Delta, Phi Kappa Phi. Office: U San Francisco Dept Sociology 2130 Fulton St San Francisco CA 94117-1080

TURYN, NOREEN A., television news anchor, reporter; b. St. Louis, July 19, 1962; d. Victor and Eileen Dorothy (Simpson) T. BS in Broadcast Journalism, U. Md., 1984. Rschr./investigator WJLA-TV, Washington, 1984-85; news stringer WAMT/WAJX Radio, Titusville, Fla., 1985-86; prodr./technician Balt. Radio Reading Svc., 1986-88; assignment editor WMAR-TV, Balt., 1988-90; reporter/anchor WSET-TV, Lynchburg, Va., 1990—. Mem. com. Woman's Resource Ctr., Lynchburg, 1994-95; bd. dirs. Big Bros./Big Sisters, Lynchburg, 1996—; mem. pub. rels. com. ARC, Lynchburg, 1995. Mem. Delta Delta Delta. Office: WSET-TV 2320 Langhorne Rd Lynchburg VA 24501

TUTT, NANCY JEAN, physical therapist; b. Washington, July 4; d. Lewis Jackson and Louise Monroe (Abbott) T. BS, U. Ky., 1947; MA, Columbia U., 1951, Cert. in Phys. Therapy, 1952. Staff Columbia-Presbyn. Med. Ctr., N.Y.C., 1952-54, 56-57; sr. phys. therapist St. Vincent's Hosp., N.Y.C., 1957-60; staff Hans Kraus, M.D., N.Y.C., 1955-56; pvt. practice N.Y.C., 1955-63; phys. therapist James Ewing Hosp., N.Y.C., 1962-63; sr. phys. therapist Inst. Phys Rehab., N.Y.C., 1963-66, Mt. Sinai Hosp./Elmhurst City Hosp., N.Y., 1966-68; asst. dir. phys. rehab. U. N.C. at Dix Hosp., Raleigh, 1968-70, Medictr., Raleigh, 1970-71; pres. Therapeutic Home Care Assocs., Inc., Raleigh, 1970-72, Tammy Lynn Ctr., Raleigh, 1971-72; with Rex Hosp. Wellness Ctr., Raleigh, 1991—. Vol. VA Hosp., Durham, N.C., 1980-82, Rex Hosp., Raleigh, 1983-84, Duke Inst. for Learning in Retirement, Durham, 1985—. With WAC, 1943-45. Named Ky. Col.; March of Dimes scholar, 1951-52. Mem. AAUW, DAV, Am. Soc. on Aging, Am. Phys. Therapy Assn., Rex Hosp. Wellness Ctr. Home: PO Box 51536 Durham NC 27717-1536

TUTTLE, EMILY ANNE, former county commissioner; b. Mpls., May 3, 1929; d. Frank A. R. and Emily Marie (Dunn) Mayer; m. Loring Mitchell Staples Jr., Sept. 10, 1954 (dec. June 1988); children: Mary, Thomas, Gregory, Kathryn; m. Gedney Tuttle, Jan. 14, 1995. BA, U. Minn., Mpls., 1950; MPA, Harvard U., Cambridge, 1982. Senator Minn. Senate, St. Paul, 1977-80; dir. cmty. rels. Spring Hill Conf. Ctr., Wayzata, Minn., 1983-88; county commr. Hennepin County, Mpls., 1992-94. Mem. bd. dirs. U. Minn. Found., Mpls., 1986—, Minn. Found., St. Paul, 1988—, Minn. Internat. Ctr., Mpls., 1990—, Tyrone Guthrie Theater, Mpls., 1995—; pres. Minn. Internat. Ctr., Mpls., 1996—. Recipient fellow Bush Found., 1982. Mem. Minn. Women's Forum, Minn. Women's Econ. Roundtable (founder). Democrat.

TUTTLE, LAURA SHIVE, healthcare educator, administrator; b. Morristown, N.J., Nov. 19, 1962; d. Richard Byron and Patricia (Butler) Shive; m. Richard Lawrence Tuttle, Dec. 15, 1984; 1 child, Marissa Lynn. BSN, Skidmore Coll., 1984; postgrad., Northeastern U., 1992—. RN. Pub. health nurse Navy Relief Vis. Nurse, San Diego, 1985-86; home health nurse Trend Home Health, San Diego, 1986-87, Scripps Home Health Care, San Diego, 1987, Community Health and Counseling Svcs., Bangor, Maine, 1988-89; clin. svcs. coord. Bangor Dist. Nursing Assn., 1989-91; clin. supr. Spl. Care Home Health Svcs., Woburn, Mass., 1991; br. dir. Spl. Care Home Health Svcs., Quincy, Mass., 1991-92; founder, pres. Career Visions, Inc., Brockton, Mass., 1992—; nursing instr. Eastern Maine Tech. Coll., Bangor, 1988-89; pub. speaker Maine Vets. Homes, Augusta, 1991, Bangor Dist. Nursing Assn., 1990-91. Co-author: Clinical Care of the Geriatric Patient, 1991. Mem. NAFE, Prof. Ski Instrs. Assn. (cert. 1982). Republican.

TUTTLE, LISA MCGAUGHEY, artist, curator; b. Little Rock, Sept. 25, 1951; d. Carroll Bradford and Louisa Brown (Beale) McGaughey; m. Robert Louis Tuttle, May 1, 1982. Student, U. N.C., Charlotte, 1970; BA in Humanities and Painting, New Coll., 1974; postgrad., Atlanta Coll. Art, 1980-81, Ga. State U., 1983-86. Assoc. curator Nexus Contemporary Art Ctr., Atlanta, 1983-85, gallery dir., 1985-86; gallery dir. Atlanta Coll. Art, 1986-93; visual arts dir. Arts Festival Atlanta, 1993—, co-artistic dir., 1995—; adj. faculty mem. Atlanta Coll. Art, 1990-94; chair programming arts adv. com. Brenau Coll., Gainesville, Ga., 1994—; juror student exhbn. U. Tenn., Knoxville, 1994, Riverview Arts Festival, Greenville, S.C., 1992, Montgomery (Ala.) Arts Guild, 1988. Solo exhbits include Albany (Ga.) Mus. Art, 1989, Sandler Hudson Gallery, Atlanta, 1994. Panelist airport art program Bur. Cultural Affairs, Atlanta, 1995, Ga. Coun. Arts, 1992-93, visual artists fellowships Ill. State Arts Coun., 1989; pub. art com. mem. Fulton County Arts Coun., 1993-95. Grantee Art Matters, Inc., 1994; So. Arts Fedn. Sculpture fellow, 1991, Photography fellow, 1995. Mem. Individual Visual Artist Coalition. Home: 1088 Amsterdam Ave NE Atlanta GA 30306-3543 Office: Arts Festival Atlanta 999 Peachtree St NE Ste 140 Atlanta GA 30309

TUTTLE, MARTHA BENEDICT, artist; b. Cin., Feb. 4, 1916; d. Harris Miller and Florence Stevens (McCrea) Benedict; m. Richard Salway Tuttle, June 3, 1939; children: Richard, Jr., McCrea Benedict (dec.), Martha (dec.), Elisabeth Hall. Grad. high sch., Cin.; student, Art Acad. Cin., 1934-38. V.p. Barg Bottling Co., Inc., Cin., 1948-80. One-woman shows include KKAE Gallery, 1963, Univ. Club, 1967, Miller Gallery, 1971, St. Clements, N.Y., 1973, Livingston Lodge, 1974, Holly Hill Antiques, 1979, Peterson Gallery, 1983, Art Acad. Cin., 1984, Closson Gallery, 1986, Camargo Gallery, 1992; represented in permanent collection Cin. Art Mus. Tchr. Sunday sch. Grace Episcopal Ch. and Indian Hill Ch., Cin., 1953-75; shareholder Cin. Art Mus.; founder partnership to save the William and Phebe Betts House; donor with partnership to The Nat. Soc. Colonial Dames of Am. the William and Phebe Betts House for establishing a Rsch. Ctr. Mem. Soc. Colonial Dames Am. (bd. dirs. 1976-89), Camargo Club, Univ. Club. Republican. Home: 5825 Drewry Farm Ln Cincinnati OH 45243-3441

TUTTLE, TONI BRODAX, swimming pool company executive; b. Bklyn., July 19, 1952; d. Abraham Paul and Marilyn (Monte) Brodax; m. Roy Lee, May 21, 1978; 1 child, Sean Monte. student Lesley Coll., 1972; B.A. in Journalism, U. R.I., 1974. Reporter Mexico City Daily News, 1972; free-lance photographer, writer N.Y. Yankees, Comm. Group, Ft. Lauderdale, Fla., 1974-78; editl. asst. Boating Mag., N.Y.C., 1974-76; pub. rels. cons. B. Altmans Dept. Store, N.Y.C., 1975-76; dir. pub. rels. Windjammer Barefoot Cruises, Miami, Fla., 1976-78; acct. exec. Art Jacobson Advt., Miami, 1978-79; v.p. Tuttle's Pool Co., Inc., Miami, 1979—. Mem. Dramatists Guild, Inc. Jewish. Home: 6740 SW 94th St Miami FL 33156-1735

TUTTLE, VIOLET MYREL, elementary school educator; b. Grassy Meadows, W.Va., Aug. 28, 1938; d. Alva Huston and Ila Myrel (Bowles) Fitzwater; m. Donald Silas Tuttle, Sept. 16, 1956; children: Donna Hope McCase, Donald Marion. AS, W.Va. State Coll., 1973, BS, 1975; postgrad., W.Va. U., 1985-92, MEd, 1983. Cert. elem. and secondary sch. tchr., W.Va. Tchr. aide Mary Ingles Sch. Kanawha County Schs., Tad, W.Va., 1969-75; tchr. Chelyan (W.Va.) Sch. Kanawha County Schs., 1975-86, tchr. Belle (W.Va.) Sch., 1986-94, v.p. PTA, 1991-92, computer specialist, 1987-93; tchr. evaluation com. Elk Elem. Ctr., Charleston, 1994—; tchr. evaluation com. Elk Elem. ctr., Charleston, 1994—, faculty senate treas., 1995—. Mem. Christian edn. bd. dirs. Judson Bapt. Ch., 1986-87, vacation Bible sch. dir., 1986-88; mem. Kanawha County Rep. exec. bd., 1995—; treas. Faculty Senate. Mem. Belle Women's Club (historian 1994—), Alpha Delta Kappa (v.p. Theta chpt. 1990-91, pres. 1992-94, corr. sec. 1994-96, Kanawha dist. coun. v.p. 1994—), Kanawha Coun. Tchrs. Math. Home: 786 Campbells Creek Dr Charleston WV 25306-6735 Office: Elk Elem Ctr 3320 Pennsylvania Ave Charleston WV 25302-4632

TVELIA, CAROL ANN, elementary school educator; b. Flushing, N.Y., Aug. 21, 1947; d. Calogero Frank and Mary Elizabeth (D'Alessio) Vitanza; m. Richard Anthony Tvelia, July 12, 1969 (div. Mar. 1984); children: Tracy Ann, Richard A. Jr.; m. Theodore William Polson, Aug. 22, 1986 (div. Aug. 1994). BA in Elem. Edn., Queens Coll., 1969; MA, SUNY, Stony Brook, 1974; cert. in advanced study supervision, Hofstra U., 1993. Cert. tchr., N.Y. Elem. tchr. Bayshore (N.Y.) Ctrl. Sch. Dist., 1969, Mid. Country Ctrl. Sch. Dist., Centereach, N.Y., 1969-70, Longwood Ctrl. Sch. Dist., Middle Island, N.Y., 1976—; house capt. Longwood Mid. Sch., Middle Island, N.Y., 1992—; sci. mentor K-8 N.Y. State Dept. Edn., Albany, 1991—, N.Y. Sci. and Tech. Project resource agt., 1993—. Author (newsletter) Nat. Mid. Level Sci. Level Line, 1992-93. Mem. ASCD, NSTA, N.Y. Sci. Tchrs. Assn. (Mid. Level Sci. Tchr. award 1991), Nat. Sci. Suprs. Assn., N.Y. State Sci. Suprs. Assn. (exec. bd. mem.), Nat. Soc. Studies Assn., N.Y. State Social Studies Assn., Suffolk County Social Studies Assn., Suffolk County Sci. Tchrs. Assn. Democrat. Home: 25 Stephani Ave East Patchogue NY 11772 Office: Longwood Mid Sch 41 Middle Island Yaphank Rd Middle Island NY 11953

TWEDDLE, JENNIFER LYNNE, mental health counselor; b. Toronto, Ont., July 15, 1963; d. Allan Stanley Tweddle and Beth Margaret (Gerry) Smith. Student, U. London, 1983; BA, Calif. State U., Hayward, 1986; MA, Gallaudet U., 1988. Lifeguard Sierra Madre (Calif.) Aquatic Program, 1979-85, instr. water safety, 1980-85, asst. mgr., 1982-85, dir. adapted aquatics, 1984-86; info. asst. Nat. Info. Ctr. on Deafness, Washington, 1986-87; rsch. asst. Gallaudet Rsch. Inst., Washington, 1987; mental health counselor Phoenix Day Sch. for Deaf, 1988-93; counselor Calif. Sch. for Deaf, Riverside, 1993—; speaker, guest Minn. Found. for Better Speech and Hearing, Mpls., 1988; speaker Breakout Conf., Washington, 1992, Calif. Edn. Conf., Sacramento, 1994; conf. coord. Drug Free Schs. Ariz. State U., 1993. Mem. ACD, Am. Sch. Counselor Assn. (speaker 1990), Kappa Delta Pi (speaker, guest 1987). Episcopalian. Office: Calif Sch for Deaf 3044 Horace St Riverside CA 92506-4420

TWEDDLE, LAURA ANN, substance abuse counselor; b. Grosse Pointe Farms, Mich., Jan. 20, 1969; d. Michael Edmond and Christine Ann (Beck) T. BA in Psychology, Mich. State U., 1991; MA in Counseling, Oakland U., 1993. Lic. profl. counselor, Mich. Therapist Bi-County Outpatient Counseling Ctr., Warren, Mich., 1994—; counselor Salvation Army Harbor Light, Clinton Twp., Mich., 1994—; counselor Counterpoint Runaway Shelter, Inkster, Mich., 1993-94. Mem. ACA, Mich. Counseling Assn., Mich. Mental Health Counselors Assn.

TWEEDT, ANNE ELIZABETH, legislative policy analyst; b. Hartford, Conn., May 29, 1966; d. William Patrick and Irene Fallon (Kelley) Murray; m. Darin Edward Tweedt, Sept. 11, 1993; children: Madeleine Clare, Samuel Edward. BA, Conn. State U., 1988; JD, Willamette U. Coll. Law, 1993. Bar: Oreg. 1993. Legis. asst. to Spkr. of Ho. Conn. Gen. Assembly, Hartford, 1987-89, fin. com. clk., 1989-90; atty. pvt. practice, Salem, Oreg., 1993-95; health and human svcs. policy analyst Legis. Policy and Rsch., Salem, Oreg., 1995—. Roman Catholic. Office: Policy and Rsch Office State Capitol Salem OR 97310

TWINING, HENRIETTA STOVER, retired English language educator; b. Pawnee, Okla., Feb. 25, 1931; d. Leonard E. and Olga (Wolf) Stover; children: Patricia T. Rioux, Donald E. BS in Edn. summa cum laude, Ctrl. State U. (now called U. Ctrl. Okla.), Edmond, Okla., 1962, M in Teaching cum laude, 1967; postgrad., Old Dominion U., 1970, Ala. A&M U., 1980-82. Cert. elem. sch. tchr., secondary sch. tchr., post secondary, Ala. Secondary tchr. Huntsville (Ala.) City Pub. Schs.; elem. and secondary tchr. Okla. City Pub. Schs., Okla.; prof. English Ala. A&M U., Huntsville, 1969-93; also chmn. textbook selection com. Ala. A&M U., Normal, Ala., 1981-93; ret., 1993; chair, co-chair sessions Conf. Coll. Composition & Comm. Internat. Orgn., 1988-93; co-chair Nat. Coun. Accreditation of Tchr. Edn., Ala. A&M U., 1988-89; chair editorial com. instl. self-study reaffirmation accreditation So. Assn. Colls. & Schs., Ala. A&M U., 1992-93. Author: Instructor's Quiz Book to accompany Prentice Hall Reader, 2d edit.; mem. editorial adv. bd. Collegiate Press, 1988-92; textbook reviewer Prentice Hall, Harcourt Brace, Collegiate Press, Allyn & Bacon, Wadsworth, et al., 1982-92. Sr. staff mem. Cmty. Action Agy. of Huntsville-Madison/Limestone Counties, Inc., 1978-92. Named Most Outststanding Female Instr., Ala. A&M U. Student Govt. Assn., 1979-80; recipient Recognitions for Cmty. Svc. Mem. NEA, MLA, Ala. Edn. Assn., Nat. Coun. Tchrs. English, Ala. Coun. Tchrs. English, Assn. Coll. English Tchrs. Ala., Ctrl. State U-U. Ctrl. Okla. Alumni Assn. (life), Alpha Chi, Kappa Delta Pi. Home: 2524 Leeshire Rd Tucker GA 30084-3026

TWOMEY, MARY REGINA, women's rights activist, writer; b. Trenton, N.J., Oct. 11, 1941; d. Anthony James and Mary Beatrice (Burns) Moran; div.; children: Moira Twomey Sandiford, Willliam III, Kathleen Twomey Westgate. Student, U. N.H., 1984; degree, McIntosh Coll., Dover, N.H., 1996. Engrs.' asst. U.S. Govt., Burlington, Mass., 1961-62; ptnr. nursing home bus. various orgns., Mass., 1969—; tchr. Sacred Heart Sch., Amesbury, Mass., 1974-75; sports writer Rockingham County Newspapers, Hampton, N.H., 1986-88; exec. planning com. Women in Sports Conf., New Agenda/Northeast, 1987—; runner NOW/NAGWS Run for Equality, Washington to Phila., 1986. Del. N.H. Dem. Convs., 1988, 90, 92; cand. for N.H. State Legis., 1990; del. Dem. Nat. Convs., 1986; mem. Lobbyist Epilepsy Found. Am., Landover, Md., 1970—; chair N.H. Nat. Girls and Women in Sports Day, 1990-96. Inducted into New Agenda/Northeast Sports Hall of Fame, 1990. Mem. AAUW, NOW (past state and local v.p. N.H. pres., local publicity chmn., 1st Women in N.H. (founding mem.), N.H. Women's Lobby, Women's Sports Found. (lobbyist, N.H. chmn. Nat. Women's Sports Day 1989, 90), Assn. for Women in Sports Media, N.H. Common Cause, Paralegal Assn. N.H., Paralegal Assn. of McIntosh Coll., N.H. Commn. of Sports Equity for Women. Democrat. Roman Catholic. Home: 7 Hedman Ave Hampton NH 03842-4022

TWYMAN, DEBORAH ANNE, secondary education educator; b. Kansas City, Mo., Nov. 30, 1957; d. Thomas Christian and Millicent Birchal (Sommerset) T.; m. Sterling Craig Whitney, Jan. 1, 1990; children: Matthew, Virginia. BA, Drury Coll., 1980; MAT, Webster U., 1989. Coord. drama Independence (Mo.) Parks & Recreation, 1976-80; tchr. mid. sch. speech & drama North Kansas City (Mo.) Pub. Schs., 1980-85, tchr. high sch. speech & drama, 1985-88, tchr. high sch. social studies, 1988—, coord. cmty. svc., 1991—, coord. dist. cmty. svc., 1994—; mem. dist. profl. devel. com., 1993—; presenter and speaker in field. Del. Dem. Nat. Conv., N.Y.C., 1992; com. mem. Clay County Dem. Ctrl. Com., 1992-94; mem. UMKC tchr. adv. bd., 1995—, Mo. reg. profl. devel. bd., 1995—; del. State Dem. Conv., 1992, 96. Grantee Nat. Starch Co., 1992, Learn & Serve Am. Corp., 1994; named Tchr. of Distinction, 1992. Mem. NEA (mem. resolutions com. 1992-93, nat. del. 1983, 84, 85, 91, 92, 93, 94, metro pres. 1984, 85), Nat. Coun. Social Studies, Mo. Edn. Assn. (state del. 1980-95), Mo. Coun. Social Studies, North Kansas City Edn. Assn. Episcopalian. Office: North Kansas City High Sch 620 E 23rd Ave North Kansas City MO 64116

TYAU, GAYLORE CHOY YEN, business educator; b. Honolulu, May 13, 1934; d. Moses M.F. and Bessie (Amana) T. BS, U. Calif., Berkeley, 1956, MBA, 1959; student, San Francisco State U., 1956-58. Cert. bus. tchr., instr., C.C. supervision credential, Calif. Tchr. bus. Richmond (Calif.) Union High Sch., 1959-64, Westmoor High Sch., Daly City, Calif., 1964-89; instr. bus. City Coll. San Francisco, 1978-87, 88—; office mgr. P.F. Freytag Assocs., San Francisco, 1978-86. Coordinator Pacific Telephone Co.'s Adopt-a-Sch. Program, Colma, Calif, 1987. Grantee Bechtel Corp., 1983. Mem. Nat. Bus. Edn. Assn., Calif. Bus. Assn. (chairperson program com. 1979, mem. program com. 1981-82, Pacific Bell contract edn. grantee 1989), Calif. Bus. Educatos Assn. (co-chair exec. bd. Bay sect. 1994—), Am. Vocat. Assn., ASCD, Western Bus. Edn. Assn., Internat. Soc. for Bus. Edn., City Coll. Faculty Assn., Jefferson Union High Sch. Dist. Tchrs. Assn., Commonwealth Club of Calif., Beta Phi Gamma. Republican. Episcopalian. Home: 4050 17th St # 1 San Francisco CA 94114-1903

TYERS, KATHY, writer, musician; b. Long Beach, Calif., July 21, 1952; d. H. Chester and Barbara Louise Moore; m. Mark J. Tyers, June 1, 1974; 1 child, Matthew Benjamin. BS, Mont. State Univ., 1974. Cert. elem. edn. tchr. Immunobiology technician Mont. State U., Bozeman, 1974-76; primary grades tchr. Christian Ctr. Sch., Bozeman, 1977-80; freelance writer, 1983—; pvt. flute instr., 1969—; flutist, Bozeman Symphony Orch., 1970-77; folk musician, 1972—. Author: Firebird, 1987, Fusion Fire, 1988, Crystal Witness, 1989, Shivering World, 1991, Exploring the Northern Rockes, 1991, Star Wars: The Truce at Bakura, 1994, One Mind's Eye, 1996. Bd. dirs. Friends of KUSM Pub. TV, 1991. Mem. Sci. Fiction and Fantasy Writers Am., Soc. children's Book Writers and Illustrators (newsletter editor Big Sky chpt. 1991-92), Nat. Space Soc., Mont. Authors Coalition. *

TYLER, ANNE (MRS. TAGHI M. MODARRESSI), author; b. Mpls., Oct. 25, 1941; d. Lloyd Parry and Phyllis (Mahon) T.; m. Taghi M. Modarressi, May 3, 1963; children: Tezh, Mitra. B.A., Duke U., 1961; postgrad., Columbia U., 1962. Author: If Morning Ever Comes, 1964, The Tin Can Tree, 1965, A Slipping-Down Life, 1970, The Clock Winder, 1972, Celestial Navigation, 1974, Searching for Caleb, 1976, Earthly Possessions, 1977, Morgan's Passing, 1980, Dinner at the Homesick Restaurant, 1982, The Accidental Tourist, 1985, Breathing Lessons, 1988 (Pulitzer Prize for fiction 1989), Saint Maybe, 1991, (juvenile) Tumble Tower, 1993, Ladder of Years, 1995; contbr. short stories to nat. mags. Home: 222 Tunbridge Rd Baltimore MD 21212-3422

TYLER, CECILIA K., army officer; b. McCall, Idaho, May 18, 1956; d. Cecil Edward and Ruby Ilene (Wine) Oatney; m. Nelvin Eugene (Gene) Tyler Jr., Dec. 24, 1991. BBA in Acctg., Idaho State U., 1978; MS in Econs. and Ops. Research, Colo. Sch. Mines, 1987. Commd. 2d lt. U.S. Army, 1978, advanced through grades to lt. col., 1995; platoon leader A, B and C Cos. 8th Signal Battalion U.S. Army, Bad Kreuznach, Fed. Republic of Germany, 1978-81, logistics officer, 1981; promoted to capt., 1982; div. radio officer 142d Signal Battalion U.S. Army, Ft. Hood, Tex., 1982-83, comdr. C Co. 142d Signal Battalion, 1983-85, asst. ops. officer, 1985; chief market analysis 6th Recruiting Brigade U.S. Army, Ft. Baker, Calif., 1987-89; with command and gen. staff coll. U.S. Army, Leavenworth, Kans., 1989-90; promoted to maj., 1990; chief strategic systems plans br. 5th Signal Command U.S. Army, Fed. Republc of Germany, 1990-91, chief plans & programs div., 1991; exec. officer 509th Signal Battalion U.S. Army, Italy, 1991-92; exec. officer office dep. chief staff, info. mgmt. U.S. Army, Germany, 1992-94; promoted to lt. col. U.S. Army, 1995; dep. brigade comdr. 2d Sig BDE, Germany, 1995-96; commdr. 504th Signal Battalion, Fort Huachuca, Ariz., 1996—. Pres. 4-H Club, Valley County, Idaho, 1973-74. Mem. Armed Forces Communication-Electronics Assn., Assn. U.S. Army. Home: PO Box 92 Donnelly ID 83615-0092 Office: HHD 2D Sig PO Box 12541 Fort Huachuca AZ 85670-2541

TYLER, GAIL FAIN (WINONA), music educator; b. Raleigh, N.C., Jan. 26, 1953; d. William Baker and Ruby Christine (Powell) Fain; m. Richard Jerome Tyler Jr., July 9, 1983; children: Winona Fain, Rukaiyah Jasmine. BS in Pub. Sch. Music, Va. State U., 1974, MS in Music Edn., 1976; MA in Edn. and Human Devel., George Washington U., 1981. Advanced profl. cert. pub. sch. music, human devel. Instrumental, gen. music specialist St. Mary's County Pub. Schs., Leonardtown, Md., 1976—; comer facilitator; creator all-county elem. honor band program, 1978. Parliamentarian Apple Grove PTA, Ft. Washington, 1993. Mem. NEA, NAFE, ASCD, Md. State Tchr.'s Assn., Edn. Assn. for St. Mary's County, Prince George's Talented and Gifted Assn., Alpha Kappa Alpha. Presbyterian. Home: 3335 Huntley Square Dr # A-2 Temple Hills MD 20748-6219

TYLER, GAIL MADELEINE, nurse; b. Dhahran, Saudi Arabia, Nov. 21, 1953 (parents Am. citizens); d. Louis Rogers and Nona Jean (Henderson) Tyler; m. Alan J. Moore, Sept. 29, 1990; 1 child, Sean James. AS, Front Range C.C., Westminster, Colo., 1979; BS in Nursing, U. Wyo., 1989. RN. Ward sec. Valley View Hosp., Thornton, Colo., 1975-79; nurse Scott and White Hosp., Temple, Tex., 1979-83, Meml. Hosp. Laramie County, Cheyenne, Wyo., 1983-89; dir. DePaul Home Health, 1989-91; field staff nurse Poudre Valley Hosp. Home Care, 1991—. Avocations: collecting internat. dolls, sewing, reading, travel.

TYLER, KATHRYN RUTH, business execuitve; b. N.Y.C., Nov. 5, 1964; d. Charles Raymond and Ruth Crandon (Nash) Tyler. Diploma, Winston Churchill H.S., Potomac, Md., 1982. Treas., sec. Tyler Bus. Svcs., Washington, 1982—; v.p. Tyler Bus. Svcs., 1996—; pres. Tyler Bus. Svcs., Inc., Washington, 1996—; editor Kenwood Golf & Country Club, Bethesda, Md., 1988-94; pres. Bon Vivant Inc., Bethesda, Md., 1994—, Divot Inc., Bethesda, Md., 1993-96. Vol. Charles E.Kettler Children's Hosp., Washington, 1993. Mem. Kenwood Golf & Country Club. Home: Divot Inc 5301 Westbard Cir #341 Bethesda MD 20816 Office: Tyler Bus Svcs Inc 2121 Wisconsin Ave NW Washington DC 20007 also: Bon Vivant Inc Ste 108 Box 269 5110 Ridgefield Rd Bethesda MD 20816

TYLER, PAYNE BOUKNIGHT, museum executive; b. Johnston, S.C., Mar. 11, 1933; d. William Miller and Frances Payne (Turner) B.; m. Harrison Ruffin Tyler, July 17, 1958; children, Harrison Ruffin Tyler Jr., Julia Gardiner Tyler Samaniego, William Bouknight. BA, U. S.C., 1955; postgrad., N.Y. Sch. Interior Design, 1956. Pres. Historic Sherwood Forest Corp., Charles City, Va., 1975—. Author: James River Plantations Cookbook, 1983, Virginia Presidents Cookbook, 1989. active Colonial Dames Am., Richmond, 1959, Jr. League Richmond, Va., 1959—; Jr. League vol. Valentine Mus. Docent, Richmond, Va., 1959-60, Va. Hist. Landmark, Richmond, 1960-61; bd. mem. Hist. Richmond (Va.) Found., 1960-61; pres. Hist. Richmond (Va.) Found., 1960-61; regional worker Rep. Party, Charles City, 1989—; sec. Planning Commn., Charles City, 1990—; coun. Va. Mus. Fine Arts; others. Mem. Deep Run Hunt Club (Richmond), Princess Anne Hunt Club (Charles City), Santa Fe Hounds (Rancho Santa Fe), Rancho Sante Fe (Calif.) Polo Club, Piedmont Womens Polo Club (Charlottesville, Va.), U.S. Polo Assn., County Club Va. (Richmond), Richmond Cotillion and Va. Creepers (Richmond), Garden Club Am. (Richmond), Jr. League Richmond. Episcopalian. Home: PO Drawer 8 Sherwood Forest Plantation Charles City VA 23030 Office: Historic Sherwood Forest Corp Sherwood Forest Plantation Charles City VA 23030

TYLER, PRISCILLA, retired English language and education educator; b. Cleve., Oct. 23, 1908; d. Ralph Sargent and Alice Lorraine (Campbell) T. BA in Latin and Greek, Radcliffe Coll., 1932; MA in Edn., Case Western Res. U., 1934, PhD in English, 1953; LLD (hon.), Carleton U., Ottawa, Ont., Can., 1993. Parole officer, case worker Cleve. Sch. for Girls, 1934-35; tchr. English, Latin and French Cleveland Heights (Ohio) Pub. Schs., 1935-45; instr. to asst. prof. English Flora Stone Mather Coll., Cleve., 1945-59; asst. dean Flora Stone Mather Coll. Western Reserve U., Cleve., 1957-59;

asst. prof. edn., head dept. English Sch. of Edn. Harvard U., Cambridge, Mass., 1959-63; assoc. prof. English, U. Ill., Champaign-Urbana, 1963-67, dir. freshman rhetoric, 1966-67; prof. English and edn. U. Mo., Kansas City, 1967-78, prof. emeritus, 1978—; instr. N.S. (Can.) Dept. Edn., Halifax, summers 1972-73; condr. numerous seminars; former lectr. U. Calif., Berkeley, U. Chgo., Purdue U., U. Mo., Columbia, U. Nebr., Emory U., Fresno State U., Calif. State U., Hayward, San Jose State Coll., Mills Coll., Ala., Tift Coll., Ga., Va. Poly. Inst. and Midwestern U., Tex. Editor: Harpers Modern Classics, 19 vols., 1963, Writers the Other Side of the Horizon, 1964, (with Maree Brooks) Inupiat Paitot, 1974; co-author introduction and co-editor: (with Maree Brooks) Sevukakmet, Ways of Life on St. Lawrence Island (Helen Slwooko Carius), 1979, The Epic of Qayaq, 1995 (Lela Kiana), World Literature Written in English, 1965-69; interviewed authors, Jan Carew, Guyana, George Lamming, Barbados, Christopher Okigbo, Nigeria, Wilson Harris, Derek Wolcott, St. Lucia, Andrew Salkey, Jamaica, Chinua Achebe; also articles. Mem. Ohio Gov.'s Com. on Employment of Physically Handicapped, 1957; mem. Friends of Art of Carleton U., Nelson Atkins Mus. Art, Kansas City, Ottawa (Kans.) Art Gallery, Friends of Libr., Ottawa. Recipient Outstanding Achievement and Contbns. in Field of Edn. award Western Res. U., 1962, Disting. Alumna award Laurel Sch., Cleve., 1994; Priscilla Tyler Endowment Fund named in her honor Case Western Res. U., 1980. Mem. MLA, NEA, Archaeol. Inst. Am., Nat. Coun. Tchrs. English (v.p. 1963, mem. com. on history of the profession 1965-68, Commn. on Composition 1968-71, trustee Rsch. Found. 1970-78, Disting. Svc. award 1978), Conf. on Coll. Composition and Comm. (pres. 1963), Arctic Inst. N.Am., Inuit Art Found., Franklin County Hist. Assn., Calif. Assn. Tchrs. English (hon.. Curriculum Commn. Ctrl. Calif.), Delta Kappa Gamma (pres. Upsilon chpt. 1950-52). Democrat. Presbyterian. Home: 4213 Kentucky Ter Ottawa KS 66067-8715

TYNER, BESSIE HUBBARD, mechanical engineer, mathematician; b. Fayetteville, N.C., Sept. 23, 1961; d. Kenneth Brigman and Ellen Merle H.; m. Kenneth Blake Tyner. BSME, N.C. State U., 1983, MME, 1985, BS in Applied Math., 1989, M in Pub. Admin., 1993. Registered profl. engr., N.C. Mech. engr. N.C. State Univ., Raleigh, 1985-94, asst. phys. plant dir. for design svcs., 1994-95; supr. capital improvement svcs. N.C. State U., Raleigh, 1995—; spl. engr. cons. United Daughters of Confederacy, Raleigh, 1989—; mem. faculty Indsl. Ventilation Conf., N.C. State U. Author: Marriage and Death Notices, 1991, (with others) NCSU Guidelines for Construction, 1988, 91. Editor Cumberland County Geneal. Soc., Fayetteville, 1991-93. Recipient Disting. Svc. award N.C. State U., 1994. Mem. DAR (sec. 1991—), ASHRAE, NSPE, ASME (chpt. historian 1987-88), N.C. Soc. Engrs. (Order of Engr. 1987), Order of Crown of Charlemagne, Jamestowne Soc., Nat. Soc. Daus. Colonial Wars, Nat. Soc. Daus. Founders and Patriots Am., Nat. Soc. Descs. Colonial Clerty, N.C. State U. Pipes and Drums, Tau Beta Pi, Pi Alpha Alpha. Republican. Home: 116 E Ransom St Fuquay Varina NC 27526-2426 Office: NC State U Phys Plant Campus Box 7219 Raleigh NC 27695

TYNES, PAMELA ANNE, federal magistrate; b. Natchitoches, La., Dec. 3, 1958; d. Robert Jerrell and Carol Ann (Murphy) T.; m. Joseph Henderson Hidalgo, Aug. 6, 1988. BA, Northwestern State U., Natchitoches, 1978; JD, La. State U., 1983. Bar: La. 1985, U.S. Dist. Ct. (ea., we. and mid. dists.) La. 1985, U.S. Ct. Appeals (5th cir.) 1988. Law clk. U.S. Dist. Ct. (we. dist.) La., Opelousas, 1983-85; assoc. Hunter & Plattsmier, Morgan City, La., 1985-86, Paul Guilliot, Lafayette, La., 1987-91; pvt. practice Lafayette, 1988-91; U.S. magistrate, judge U.S. Dist. Ct. (we. dist.) La., Lafayette, 1991—. Mem. Nat. Assn. Women Judges, Am. Inns of Ct., La. Bar Found., La. Bar Assn., Lafayette Parish Bar Assn., Acadiana Assn. Women Attys. Republican. Office: US District Court 705 Jefferson St St 178 Lafayette LA 70501-7059

TYNES, SUSAN FOURNET, counselor, educator; b. Lafayette, La.; d. J. Briant and Patricia T. Fournet; m. L. Lee Tynes, 1984. BS, U. Southwestern La., Lafayette, 1982, MS, 1983; PhD, U. New Orleans, 1993. Lic. profl. counselor; cert. disability mgmt. specialists. Acad. advisor, counselor U. Southwestern La., Lafayette, 1984; rehab. cons. Rehab. Providers, Baton Rouge, La., 1984-85; rehab. counselor Cmty. Re-Entry Svcs., Lynn, Mass., 1986-89; grad./rsch. asst. U. New Orleans, 1989-93, vis. asst. prof., 1993-94; pvt. practice profl. counselor New Orleans, 1993—; adj. asst. prof. U. New Orleans, 1994-95, vis. asst. prof., dir. grad. gerontology program, 1995—; clin. asst. prof. Tulane U. Sch. Medicine, New Orleans, 1995-96; adj. asst. prof., 1996—. Vol. spkr. Daus. of Charity, Neighborhood Health Partnership, New Orleans, 1995. Recipient Disting. Dissertation award Phi Delta Kappa Coll. Edn., U. New Orleans, 1994. Fellow Chi Sigma Iota (chpt. pres. 1990-91, nationally elected sec. 1992-94, chpt. faculty advisor 1993-94, coord. La. state chpt. 1994-95, Outstanding Mem. 1992); mem. ACA, AAUP, Assn. Adult Devel. and Aging, La. Counseling Assn., La. Assn. Counseling Edn. and Supervision. Office: U New Orleans New Orleans LA 70148

TYNG, ANNE GRISWOLD, architect; b. Kuling, Kiangsi, China, July 14, 1920; d. Walworth and Ethel Atkinson (Arens) T. (parents Am. citizens); 1 child, Alexandra Stevens. AB, Radcliffe Coll., 1942; M of Architecture, Harvard U., 1944; PhD, U. Pa., 1975. Assoc. Stonorov & Kahn, Architects, 1945-47; assoc. Louis I. Kahn Architect, 1947-73; pvt. practice architecture Phila., 1973—; adj. assoc. prof. architecture U. Pa. Grad. Sch. Fine Arts, 1968—; assoc. cons. architect Phila. Planning Commn. and Phila. Redevel. Plan, 1954; vis. disting. prof. Pratt Inst., 1979-81, vis. critic architecture, 1969; vis. critic architecture Rensselaer Poly. Inst., 1969, 78, Carnegie Mellon U., 1970, Drexel U., 1972-73, Cooper Union, 1974-75, U. Tex., Austin, 1976; lectr. Archtl. Assn., London, Xian U., China, Bath U., Eng., Mexico City, Hong Kong U., 1989, Baltic Summer Sch., Architecture and Planning, Tallinn, Estonia, Parnu, Estonia, 1993; panel spkr. Nat. Conv. Am. Inst. Architects, N.Y.C., 1988, also numerous univs., throughout U.S. and Can.; asst. leader People to People Archtl. del. to China, 1983; vis. artist Am. Acad., Rome, 1995. Subject of films Anne G. Tyng at Parsons Sch. of Design, 1972, Anne G. Tyng at U. of Minn., 1974, Connecting, 1976, Forming the Future, 1977; work included in Smithsonian Travelling Exhbn., 1979-81, 82, Louis I. Kahn: In the Realm of Architecture, 1990-94; contbr. articles to profl. publs.; prin. works include Walworth Tyng Farmhouse (Hon. mention award Phila. chpt. AIA 1953); builder (with G. Yanchenko) Probability Pyramid. Fellow Graham Found. for Advanced Study in Fine Arts, 1965, 79-81. Fellow AIA (Brunner grantee N.Y. chpt. 1964, 83, dir., mem. exec. bd. dirs. Phila. chpt. 1976-78, John Harbeson Disting. Svc. award Phila. chpt. 1991); mem. Nat. Acad. Design (nat. academician), C.G. Jung Ctr. Phila. (planning com. 1979—), Form Forum (co-founder, planning com. 1978—). Democrat. Episcopalian. Home: 2511 Waverly St Philadelphia PA 19146-1049 Office: Univ Pa Dept Architecture Grad Sch Fine Arts Philadelphia PA 19107

TYRRELL, BRENDA LAURENE, administrator; b. Washington, June 9, 1958; d. James Ralph Case and Roberta Mavis (Doucette) Nelson; m. Ronald Phillip Tyrrell, Oct. 7, 1978; children: Stacey Laurene, Ryan Phillip. Student, Prince Georges C.C., 1990; AA in Early Childhood Edn., Charles County C.C., 1994. Mktg. specialist Potomac Elec. Power Co., 1978-88; dir. Prime Time Children's Ctr., Owings, Md., 1988—. Pres. North Chesapeake Beach Bus. & Profl. Assn., 1994-95; coord. Calvert County Dirs. NEtwork, 1990—; mem. County Musicians Assn., Upper Marlborough, Md., 1984—. Mem. So. Md. Child Care Assn. (award 1994), So. Md. Assn. Edn. Young Children (pres.), Rotary, Kiwanis. Home: 1158 Amber Way Owings MD 20736-3500 Office: Prime Time Childrens Ctr 8816 Donalds Way Owings MD 20736

TYRRELL, L. CATHERINE, artist, educator; b. Holly Springs, Miss., May 3, 1920; d. Calvin Mason and Dora Hildred (Stone) Clayton; m. Robert L.F. Tyrrell, Jan. 13, 1951. Student, N.Y. State Tchrs. Coll., Plattsburgh, 1954, U. Pitts., 195533; student numerous art classes. Former tchr. oil painting techniques Schuler Sch. Fine Arts, Balt. Represented by Burien (Wash.) Arts Gallery, White Dove Gallery, Lakewood, Wash., also other Puget Sound galleries and Hawaii. Active environ. preservation. Recipient various awards for art. Mem. Haawaii Watercolor Soc., Puget Sound Sumi Artists Assn. Home and Studio: 7408 71st Avenue Ct SW Lakewood WA 98498-6396

TYRRELL, MARY MARGARET, community health educator; b. Superior, Wis., Apr. 1, 1943; d. Frank J. and Elsie Mary (Erbeck) O'Brien; m. Joseph Mark Tyrrell, Aug. 16, 1969 (div. Jan. 1975); children: Corey, Megan. BSN, Coll. of St. Scholastica, 1965; M of Pub. Health, U. Minn., 1979. RN, Minn. Patient edn. coord. Internat. Diabetes Ctr., Mpls., 1969; edn. intern Minn. Comprehensive Epilepsy Program, Mpls., 1978-79; dir. aging edn. A.H. Wilder Found., St. Paul, 1979-81; supr. St. John's Hosp. Home Care, St. Paul, 1981; cmty. health nurse coord. VA Med. Ctr., St. Cloud, Minn., 1982-88; asst. dir. Minn. Bd. of Nursing, St. Paul, 1988-92; study coord. Mpls. Med. Rsch. Fedn., Mpls., 1992-95; pres. Memoirs Inc., St. Paul, 1994—. Contbr. articles to profl. publs. Mem. Stearns County Health Adv. Bd., St. Cloud, 1983-89, chair, 1984-87; mem. Minn. West Ctrl. Adv. Bd., St. Cloud, 1983-86, chair 1984-87; mem. Eartwatch-Indonesian Health Care, Jakarta, Indonesia, 1992. Lt. USN, 1963-68. Named Outstanding Alumna award Coll. of St. Scholastica, 1990. Mem. Minn. Gerontol. Soc. (treas. 1991-93), Minn. Elders Coalition (exec. com. 1992-96), Am. Pub. Health Assn., Am. Gerontol. Soc., Sigma Theta Tau (com. chair 1991). Home and Office: 1669 Ford Pkwy Saint Paul MN 55116

TYRRELL, TAMARA JOAN, public affairs executive; b. St. Louis, Dec. 24, 1968; d. Charles Louis and Ann Wilken T. BA in Polit. Sci., Principia Coll., 1992. Press. asst. Clinton-Gore Campaign, Denver, 1992; mgr. Am. Trucking Assn., Alexandria, Va., 1993-94; mgr. pub. affairs Club Mgrs. Assn. Am., Alexandria, Va., 1994—. Co-author: Heartland Ethics, 1992. Donator Carpenter's Shelter, Alexandria, 1994-96, Prevention of Blindness Thriftshop, Alexandria, 1995-96. Recipient Cert. of Appreciation for Editl. Excellence, Unltd. Ideas for Editors, 1995. Mem. Am. Soc. Assn. Execs., Pub. Rels. Soc. Am. Office: Club Mgrs Assn Am 1733 King St Alexandria VA 22314

TYSON, CHARLOTTE ROSE, storage systems development manager; b. San Mateo, Calif., Aug. 14, 1954; d. Herbert Parry and Rose (Goldner) T.; m. Edward Philip Sejud, Aug. 11, 1979; children: Laura Rose, Elizabeth Ann. AA in Physics, DeAnza Coll., 1974; BS in Elec. Engring., U. Calif.-Berkeley, 1976; MS in Computer Info. Systems, U. Denver, 1992. Engr. IBM, Boulder, Colo., 1976-82, project engr. mgr., 1982-84, devel. engr. mgr., 1984-91, staff to lab. dir., 1986-87, 3820 program mgr., 1987-89, project office mgr. 3825, 1988-89, mgr. svc. process support, 1990-92, mgr. software mfg. ops., 1992-93; systems devel. and program mgr. Storage Tek, Louisville, Colo., 1993—, mgr. software solutions integrated svcs., 1996—. Leader Mountain Prairie Coun. Girl Scouts U.S., 1992-94; fund raiser Longmont Symphony Guild, 1994; team mgr., treas. girls competitive soccer St. Vrain Express, 1995-96. Mem. Soc. Women Engrs. (sr. life), IEEE (Debt of Gratitude award 1981, 82, 83, chmn. Denver sect. 1982-83), Electromagnetic Compatability Soc. (chmn. Boulder chpt. 1979-91, registration chmn. EMC internat. symposium 1981, bd. dirs. 1985-90, awards and membership chmn. 1986-90). Office: Storage Tek 2270 S 88th St Louisville CO 80028-0001

TYSON, CICELY, actress; b. N.Y.C., Dec. 19, 1933; d. William and Theodosia Tyson; m. Miles Davis, 1981 (div.). Student, N.Y. U., Actors Studio; hon. doctorates, Atlanta U., Loyola U., Lincoln U. Former sec., model; co-founder Dance Theatre of Harlem; bd. dirs. Urban Gateways. Stage appearances include: The Blacks, 1961-63, off-Broadway, Moon on a Rainbow Shawl, 1962-63, Tiger, Tiger, Burning Bright, Broadway; films include: Twelve Angry Men, 1957, Odds Against Tomorrow, 1959, The Last Angry Man, 1959, A Man Called Adam, 1966, The Comedians, 1967, The Heart is a Lonely Hunter, 1968, Sounder, 1972 (Best Actress, Atlanta Film Festival, Nat. Soc. Film Critics, Acad. award nominee, Best Actress, Emmy award, Best Actress in a spl., 1973), The Blue Bird, 1976, The River Niger, 1976, A Hero Ain't Nothin' but a Sandwich, 1978, The Concorde-Airport 79, 1979, Bustin' Loose, 1981, Fried Green Tomatoes, 1991, Jefferson in Paris, 1995; TV appearances include: (series) East Side, West Side, 1963, Sweet Justice, 1994-95, Road to Galveston, 1996; (films) Marriage: Year One, 1971, The Autobiography of Miss Jane Pittman, 1974, Just an Old Sweet Song, 1976, Wilma, 1977, Roots, 1977, A Woman Called Moses, 1978, King, 1978, The Marva Collins Story, 1981, Benny's Place, 1982, Playing With Fire, 1985, Samaritan: The Mitch Snyder Story, 1986, Acceptable Risks, 1986, Intimate Encounters, 1986, The Women of Brewster Place, 1989, Heat Wave, 1990, Winner Takes All, 1990, The Kid Who Loved Christmas, 1990, When No One Would Listen, 1992, Duplicates, 1993, House of Secrets, 1993, Oldest Living Confederate Widow Tells All, 1994 (Emmy Awd., Best Supporting Actress - Miniseries); other appearances include: Wednesday Night Out, 1972, Marlo Thomas and Friends in Free to Be...You and Me, 1974, CBS: On the Air, 1978, Liberty Weekend, 1986, The Blessings of Liberty, 1987, Without Borders, 1989, Visions of Freedom: A Time Television Special, 1990, Clippers, 1991, A Century of Women, 1994. Trustee Human Family Inst.; trustee Am. Film Inst. Recipient Vernon Price award, 1962; also awards NAACP Nat. Council Negro Women; Capitol Press award. Address: care CAA 9830 Wilshire Blvd Beverly Hills CA 90212-1804*

TYSON, CYNTHIA HALDENBY, academic administrator; b. Scunthorpe, Lincolnshire, Eng., July 2, 1937; came to U.S., 1959; d. Frederick and Florence Edna (Stacey) Haldenby; children: Marcus James, Alexandra Elizabeth. BA, U. Leeds, Eng., 1958, MA, 1959, PhD, 1971. Lectr. Brit. Council, Leeds, 1959; faculty U. Tenn., Knoxville, 1959-60, Seton Hall U., South Orange, N.J., 1963-69; faculty, v.p. Queens Coll., Charlotte, N.C., 1969-85; pres. Mary Baldwin Coll., Staunton, Va., 1985—; bd. dirs. Am. Coun. on Edn./Commn. on Higher Edn. and Adult Learning, Washington, 1981-85. Contbr. articles to profl. jours. Mem. Va. Internat. Trade Commn., Richmond, 1987; bd. dirs. Am. Frontier Culture Mus., Va., United Way, Staunton, 1986—; mem. Va. Lottery Bd.; trustee Woodrow Wilson Birthplace Found., Staunton, 1985—; ruling elder Presbyn. Ch.; mem. gov's. adv. coun. on self determination & federalism, 1995—. Fulbright scholar, 1959; Ford Found. grantee Harvard U., 1981; Shell Oil scholar Harvard U., 1982. Fellow Soc. for Values in Higher Edn.; mem. Operation Enterprise Coun. of Am. Mgmt. Assn., So. Assn. Colls. for Women (pres. 1980-81). Republican. Office: Mary Baldwin Coll Office of the President Staunton VA 24401

TYSON, HELEN FLYNN, civic leader; b. Wilmington, N.C.; d. Walter Thomas and Fannie Elizabeth (Smith) Flynn; Student Guilford Coll., Am. U., Washington; m. James Franklin Tyson, Dec. 25, 1940 (dec.). U.S. Civil Svc. auditor, Disbursing Office, AUS, Ft. Bragg, N.C., 1935-46, chief clerical asst. Disbursing Office, Pope AFB, N.C., 1946-49, asst. budget and acctg. officer, 1949-55, supervisory budget officer hdqrs. Mil. Transport Command, USAF, 1955-57, budget analyst Hdqrs. USAF, Washington, 1957-74, ret. Active Arlington Com. 100, Ft. Belvoir, Salvation Army Women's Aux., Inter-Svc. Club Coun. of Arlington. Recipient awards U.S. Treasury, 1945, 46, U.S. State Dept., 1970, Good Neighbor award Ft. Belvoir Civilian-Mil. Adv. Coun., 1978; awards U.S. First Army, 1973, ARC, 1977; named Arlington Woman of Yr., 1975; recipient Cert. of Recognition, 1981, Vol. Activists award Greater Washington Met. Area, 1981. Mem. NAFE, Nat. Fedn. Bus. and Profl. Women's Clubs, Am. Assn. Ret. Fed. Employees (hon.), Am. Soc. Mil. Comptrs. (hon., Outstanding Mem. award Washington chpt. 1988), Am. Inst. Parliamentarians, Guilford Coll. Alumni Assn., N.C. Soc. Washington, Altrusa Internat. Home: 4900 N Old Dominion Dr Arlington VA 22207-2834

TYSON, LAURA D'ANDREA, economist, government adviser, educator; b. Bayonne, N.J., June 28, 1947; m. Erik Tarloff; 1 child, Elliot. BA, Smith Coll., 1969; Ph.D., Mass. Inst. Tech., 1974. Prof. econ. and bus. adm. U. Calif., Berkeley, 1978—; chmn. Pres.'s Coun. Econ. Advisors, Washington, 1993-95; nat. econ. advisor to Pres. U.S. Nat. Econ. Coun., Washington, 1995—; dir. Inst. of Internat. Studies and Research, Univ. of Calif., Berkeley Roundtable on the Internat. Economics, Univ. of Calif.; visiting scholar Inst. for Internat. Economics; Subcom. on a global Economic Strategy for the U.S.. Editor: (with John Zysman) American Industry in International Competition, 1983, (with Ellen Comisso) Power, Purpose and Collective Choice: Economic Strategy in Socialist States, 1986, (with William Dickens and John Zysman) The Dynamics of Trade, 1988, (with Chalmers Johnson and John Zysman) Politics and Productivity: The Real Story of How Japan Works, 1989, Who's Bashing Whom? Trade Conflict in High Technology Industries, 1992. Office: Nat Econ Coun 2d Fl West Wing The White House Washington DC 20500

TYSON, LUCILLE A., administrator. AS, Middlesex County Coll.; BA, Wheaton Coll.; MSW, Rutgers U. Cert. gerontol. nurse. Dir. N.J. Parkinson Info. & Referral Ctr. Robert Wood Johnson U. Hosp., New Brunswick, N.J.; human svcs. planner Middlesex County Dept. Human Svcs., New Brunswick; dir., right ro know regulations Roosevelt Hosp., Edison, N.J.; dir., quality assurance Cen. N.J. Jewish Home for Aged, Somerset, N.J. Mem. Piscataway (N.J.) Twp. Coun., 1990—; mem. rev./appeals com. Middlesex County Dept. Human Svcs., 1992—; bd. dirs. Metlar Ho. Found.; mcpl. dir. Piscataway Rep. Orgn., 1995—; county committeewoman Middlesex County Rep. Orgn., 1995—. Mem. ANA, NASW, N.J. Nurses Assn., Assn. Quality Assurance Profls. N.J., Geriatric Inst. N.J.

TYTLER, LINDA JEAN, communications and public affairs executive; b. Rochester, N.Y., Aug. 31, 1947; d. Frederick Easton and Marian Elizabeth (Allen) T.; m. George Stephen Dragnich, May 2, 1970 (div. July 1976); m. James Douglas Fisher, Oct. 7, 1994. AS, So. Sem., Buena Vista, Va., 1967; student U. Va., 1973; student in pub. adminstrn. U. N. Mex., 1981-82. Spl. asst. to Congressman John Buchanan, Washington, 1971-75; legis. analyst U.S. Senator Robert Griffin, Washington, 1975-77; ops. supr. Pres. Ford Com., Washington, 1976; office mgr. U.S. Senator Pete Domenici Re-election, Albuquerque, 1977; pub. info. officer S.W. Community Health Service, Albuquerque, 1978-83; cons. pub. relations and mktg., Albuquerque, 1983-84; account exec. Rick Johnson & Co., Inc., Albuquerque, 1983-84; dir. mktg. and communications St. Joseph Healthcare Corp., 1984-88; mktg. and bus. devel. cons., 1987-90; mgr. communications and pub. affairs Def. Avionics Systems div., Honeywell Inc., 1990—; sgt. N.Mex. Mounted Patrol, 1993—; mem. N.Mex. Ho. of Reps., Santa Fe, 1983-95, ret. 1995, vice chmn. appropriations and fin. com., 1985-86, interim com. on children and youth, 1985-86, mem. consumer and pub. affairs com., transp. com., 1992-95; chmn. Rep. Caucus, 1985-88; chmn. legis. campaign com. Rep. Com.; del. to Republic of China, Am. Council of Young Polit. Leaders, 1988. Bd. dirs. N. Mex. chpt. ARC, Albuquerque, 1984. Recipient award N.Mex. Advt. Fedn., Albuquerque, 1981, 82, 85, 86, 87. Mem. Am. Soc. Hosp. Pub. Rels. (cert.), Nat. Advt. Fedn., Soc. Hosp. Planning and Mktg., Am. Mktg. Assn., N.Mex. Assn. Commerce and Industry (bd. dirs.), Republican. Baptist.

TYUNAITIS, PATRICIA ANN, elementary school educator; b. Kenosha, Wis., Feb. 15, 1942; d. John Anton and Antoinette (Tunkieicz) T. BS, Alverno U., 1966; MAT, Webster U., 1982; postgrad., Walden U., 1994—. Cert. elem., secondary tchr., Wis. Tchr. St. John the Bapt. Sch., Johnsburg, Wis., 1964-67, St. Matthew's Sch., Campbellsport, Wis., 1967-68, St. Monica's Sch., Whitefish Bay, Wis., 1968-71; math. tchr. New Holstein (Wis.) Elem. Sch., 1971—, mem. sch. restructuring com., 1994; adj. prof. Silver Lake Coll., Manitowoc, Wic., 1993—, Marian Coll., Fond du Lac, Wis., 1993—. Mem. performance assessment tng. team Dept. Pub. Instrn., Madison, Wis., 1992—. Recipient Herb Kohl award for excellence in teaching State of Wis., 1991, nomination Pres. award for excellence in tchg. math. Mem. ASCD, Nat. Coun. Tchrs. Math., Math. Assn. Am., Nat. Assn. Tchrs. Am., New Holstein Edn. Assn., Wis. Math. Coun., Optimist Club (coord. local forensic contest 1991—, sch. coach Odyssey of the Mind 1986—, sch. coord. Odyssey of the Mind 1992, regional dir. Stevens Point chpt. 1992—). Home: N 10335 Hwy 151 Malone WI 53049 Office: New Holstein Elem Sch 2226 Park Ave New Holstein WI 53061-1008

UCHIZONO, DONNA NAOMI, choreographer, dance teacher; b. Tokyo, Dec. 5, 1955; d. Roy Saburo and Agnes Hiroko (Tsunoda) Uchizono. BA, Calif. State U., Long Beach, 1983. Artistic dir., choreographer Donna Uchizono Co., N.Y.C., 1988—; co-curator Bread to the Bone, N.Y.C., 1989-92; chair Artist Adv. Bd./Danspace, Project New York, N.Y.C., 1990-95; vis. prof. U. Minn., Mpls., 1993; vis. artist, tchr. Wesleyan Coll., Middletown, Conn., 1994, Sarah Lawrence Coll., N.Y.C., 1996. Choreographer (dance): The Wayne Brothers, 1991, A Sage Passage, 1993, Drinking Ivy, 1994, Quietly Goes a Giant Jane, 1995. Choreography fellow NEA, 1993, 94, N.Y. Found. Arts, 1996; recipient Jerome Found. grant 1995-96. Home and Studio: Donna Uchizono Co 241 E 7th St # 6B New York NY 10009

UEHLING, BARBARA STANER, educational administrator; b. Wichita, Kans., June 12, 1932; d. Roy W. and Mary Elizabeth (Hilt) Staner; children: Jeffrey Steven, David Edward. B.A., U. Wichita, 1954; M.A., Northwestern U., 1956, Ph.D., 1958; hon. degree, Drury Coll., 1978; LLD (hon.), Ohio State U., 1980. Mem. psychology faculty Oglethorpe U., Atlanta, 1959-64, Emory U., Atlanta, 1966-69; adj. prof. U. R.I., Kingston, 1970-72; dean Roger Williams Coll., Bristol, R.I., 1972-74; dean arts scis. Ill. State U., Normal, 1974-76; provost U. Okla., Norman, 1976-78; chancellor U. Mo.-Columbia, 1978-86, U. Calif., Santa Barbara, 1987-94; sr. vis. fellow Am. Council Edn., 1987; exec. dir. bus./higher edn. forum, 1994-95; mem. Pacific Rim Pub. U. Pres. Conf., 1990-92; exec. dir. Bus. and Higher Edn. Forum, Washington, 1995—; cons. North Ctr. Accreditation Assn., 1974-86; mem. nat. educator adv. com. to Compt. Gen. of U.S., 1978-79; mem. Commn. on Mil.-Higher Edn. Rels., 1978-79, Am.Coun. on Edn., bd. dirs. 1979-83, treas., 1982-83, mem. Bus.-Higher Edn. Forum, 1980-94, exec. com. 1991-94; Commn. on Internat. Edn., 1992-94, vice chair 1993; bd. dirs. Coun. of Postsecondary Edn., 1986-87, 90-93, Meredith Corp., 1980—; mem. Transatlantic Dialogue, PEW Found., 1991-93. Author: Women in Academe: Steps to Greater Equality, 1979; editorial bd. Jour. Higher Edn. Mgmt., 1986—; contbr. articles to profl. jours. Bd. dirs., chmn. Nat. Ctr. Higher Edn. Mgmt. Sys., 1977-80; trustee Carnegie Found. for Advancement of Teaching, 1980-86, Santa Barbara Med. Found. Clinic, 1989-94; bd. dirs. Resources for the Futrue, 1985-94; mem. select com. on athletics NCAA, 1983-84, also mem. presdl. commn.; mem. Nat. Coun. on Edn. Rsch., 1980-82. Social Sci. Research Council fellow, 1954-55; NSF fellow, 1956-57; NIMH postdoctoral research fellow, 1964-67; named one of 100 Young Leaders of Acad. Change Mag. and ACE, 1978; recipient Alumni Achievement award Wichita State U., 1978, Alumnae award Northwestern U., 1985, Excellence in Edn. award Pi Lambda Theta, 1989. Mem. Am. Assn. Higher Edn. (bd. dirs. 1974-77, pres. 1977-78), Western Coll. Assn. (pres.-elect 1988-89,k pres. 1990-92), Golden Key, Sigma Xi. Office: Bus-Higher Edn Forum One Dupont Cir Ste 250 Washington DC 20036*

UENO, TAKEMI, lawyer; b. Bklyn., June 8, 1966; d. Hiromi and Ryuko (Kobayashi) U. AB magna cum laude, Harvard & Radcliffe Colls., 1987; MA with distinction, London Sch. of Econs., 1988; MPhil, Columbia U., 1990; JD cum laude, Harvard U., 1993. Bar: N.Y. 1994, D.C. 1996. Assoc. Winthrop, Stimson, Putnam & Roberts, N.Y.C., 1993—. Mem. Assn. of Bar of City of N.Y. (mem. com. on internat. human rights, 1995—, com. on fgn. and comparative law 1994-95). Democrat. Office: Winthrop Stimson Putnam & Roberts One Battery Pk Plz New York NY 10004

UGGAMS, LESLIE, entertainer; b. N.Y.C., May 25, 1943; d. Harolde Coyden and Juanita Ernestine (Smith) U.; m. Grahame John Kelvin-Pratt, Oct. 16, 1965; children: Danielle Nicole Pratt, Jason Harolde John Kelvin-Pratt. Student, Juillard Sch. Music, 1961-63; degree (hon.), Jarvis Coll., Tyler, Tex., Wilberforce (Ohio) U. Appeared on TV show Beulah, 1949; featured on Sing Along with Mitch, 1961-64; starred in Broadway play Hallelujah Baby, 1967 (Tony award 1968), Her First Roman Broadway Musical, 1968; star of weekly TV variety show The Leslie Uggams Show, 1969; appearances in nightclubs, top TV mus. variety shows; appeared in film Two Weeks in Another Town, Black Girl, 1962, Skyjacked, 1972, Poor Pretty Eddie, 1973, (ABC-TV film) Roots, 1977 (Critics Choice award as best supporting actress 1977), (TV) Sizzle, 1981, Harlem, 1993; star Broadway musicals Blues in the Night, 1982, Jerry's Girls, 1985, Anything Goes, 1987; star in TV mini-series Backstairs at the White House, 1979; co-host Fantasy TV, 1982-83 (Emmy award 1983); author: The Leslie Uggams Beauty Book, 1966. Founding mem. BRAVO chpt. City of Hope, Los Angeles, 1969, treas. 1969-79. Chosen best singer on TV, 1962, 63; recipient Drama Critics award Newspaper and TV critics, 1968, Tony award 1968, Emmy award 1983. Mem. AFTRA, Nat. Acad. Recording Arts and Scis., Screen Actors Guild, Actors' Equity Assn. Democrat. Presbyterian. Office: William Morris Agy care Ken Dicamillo 1325 Avenue of Americas New York NY 10019*

UHLENBECK, KAREN KESKULLA, mathematician, educator; b. Cleve., Aug. 24, 1942; d. Arnold Edward and Carolyn Elizabeth (Windeler) Keskulla; m. Olke Cornelis, June 12, 1965 (div.). BS in Math., U. Mich., 1964; PhD in Math., Brandeis U., 1968. Instr. math. MIT, Cambridge, 1968-69;

lectr. U. Calif., Berkeley, 1969-71; asst. prof., then assoc. prof. U. Ill., Urbana, 1971-76; assoc. prof., then prof. U. Ill., Chgo., 1977-83; prof. U. Chgo., 1983-88; Sid W. Richardson Found. Regents' Chair in Math. U. Tex., 1988—; spkr. plenary address Internat. Conress Maths., 1990; mem. com. women on sci. and engring. NRC, 1992-94; mem. steering com., dir. mentoring program for women Inst. for Advanced Study/Park City Math. Inst. Author: Instantons and Four Manifolds, 1984. Contbr. articles to profl. jours. Recipient Commonwealth award for Sci. and Invention, PNC Bank, 1995; NSF grad. fellow, 1964-68, Sloan Found. fellow, 1974-76, MacArthur Found. fellow, 1983-88. Mem. AAAS, NAS, Alumni Assn. U. Mich. (Alumnae of Yr. 1984), Am. Math. Soc., Assn. Women in Math., Phi Beta Kappa. Office: U Tex Dept Math Austin TX 78712

UILKEMA, GAYLE BURNS, mayor, councilwoman, business educator; b. Detroit, Sept. 2, 1938; d. Joseph A. and Pearl (Rasmussen) Burns; children: Lynn, Sharon. BS in Edn., U. Mich., 1959; MPA, Calif. State U., Hayward, 1987. Instr. bus. edn. and mgmt. subjects Heald Coll., Oakland, Calif., 1961-62; tchr. bus. edn. dept. Oakland High Sch., 1962-66; lectr. Calif. State U. Grad. Sch. Pub. Adminstrn., Hayward; mem. coun. City of Lafayette, 1978—, mayor, 1981-84, 90-91, 94-95; lectr. in field; cons. U. Calif. Ext., Berkeley; adj. prof. John F. Kennedy U. Sch. of Mgmt., Walnut Creek, Calif., 1989—; v.p. Dimensional Resources, Inc., Telecomms. Cons. Mem. Contra Costa Local Agy. Formation Commn., 1986—, commr., former chair, 1986, 95; mem. exec. bd. dirs. state bd. Calif. Assn. Local Agy. Formation Commn.; Lafayette dir., former chair, bd. dirs. Cen. Contra Costa Transit Authority, 1980—, chmn. fin. com., 1981-85, 94, chmn. ops. and scheduling, 1986, dir. ops. and scheduling com., 1987, chmn., 1989, bd. dirs., 1990—. Recipient award Met. Transp. Commn. Bay Area, 1981, Am. Leadership award Nat. Assn. Towns and Twps., Washington, 1996. Mem. AAUW (bd. dirs. 1971-78, pres. 1972-73, state bd. dirs. 1974-76, nat. rep. 1977-78, Disting. Woman award 1978), Soroptimists Internat. Republican. Roman Catholic. Home: 670 Sky Hy Cir Lafayette CA 94549-5228 Office: City of Lafayette PO Box 1968 Lafayette CA 94549-1968

UKPONMWAN, LUCY, elementary education educator; b. Dec. 27, 1958; d. Clement and Babine Kubeyinje; m. Osahon Ukponmwan, Dec. 27, 1980; children: Isiuwa, Wadi, Osato. BA, U. Ife, Nigeria, 1981; MPA, Suffolk U., 1985. Tchr. EDO Coll., Benin, Nigeria, 1981-82; substitute tchr. Yonkers (N.Y.) Bd. Edn., 1985-89; tchr. sixth grade N.Y.C. Bd. Edn., 1990—. Vol. Bronx Mcpl. Hosp., 1989. Mem. ASCD. Office: CES 64X 1425 Walton Ave Bronx NY 10452

ULBRICH, HOLLEY ROBERTA HEWITT, economics educator; b. Torrington, Conn., June 30, 1941; d. Theodore Alden and Dorothy Mary (Stewart) Hewitt; m. Carlton Wilbur Ulbrich, June 30, 1962; children: Christine Anne, Carla Kay, Katrina Dorothy. BA in Econs., U. Conn., 1963, MA in Econs., 1964, PhD in Econs., 1968. Instr. econs. Clemson (S.C.) U., 1967-69, asst. prof. econs., 1969-74, assoc. prof. econs., 1974-78, prof. econs., 1978-87, Alumni prof. econs., 1987—; pres. faculty senate Clemson U., 1983-84, sr. fellow Strom Thurmond Inst., Clemson U., 1983—; sr. policy analyst U.S. Adv. Commn. Intergovtl. Rels., Washington, 1984-85; cons. World Bank, Washington, 1990-94; cons. US Agy. Internat. Devel., Washington, 1991. Author: (with others) Priciples of Economics, 3rd edit., 1986, 4th edit., 1989, 5th edit., 1992, 6th edit., 1995, Introduction to Economics Principles, 1988, Essentials of Economics, 2nd edit., 1995. Pres. ch. coun. U. Luth. Ch., Clemson, 1981-84; bd. dirs. Unitarian Universalist Fellowship of Clemson, 1991-93, 95—, program chair, 1991-94. Recipient Leary award for Excellence in Pvt. Enterprise Edn., Freedom Found., 1980. Mem. LWV (pres. 1974-76, 90-92, v.p. programs S.C. chpt. 1992-95), Nat. Tax Assn., Clemson Homeowners Assn. (bd. dirs. 1996—). Democrat. Unitarian. Home: 106 Highland Dr Clemson SC 29631 Office: Clemson U Strom Thurmond Inst Clemson SC 29634

ULERY, SHARI LEE, lawyer; b. Marshalltown, Iowa, July 13, 1953; d. Kenneth Eugene and Edith Viola (Harding) U.; m. Steven Bernard Nelson (div. 1987); children: Benjamin, Christopher. BS, Iowa State U., 1975; JD, Drake U., 1980. Bar: Iowa 1980, Colo. 1981. Staff atty. Geico Fin. Svcs., Denver, 1985-87, asst. gen. counsel, 1987-89, v.p., gen. counsel, 1989—. Mem. Am. Assn. Corp. Counsel, Colo. Bar Assn., Colo. Womens Bar Assn. Office: Geico Fin Svcs Inc 10403 W Colfax Ave Lakewood CO 80215-3801

ULJON, LINDA JANE, computer project manager; b. St. Marys, Pa., July 20, 1951; d. Gabriel Joseph and Mary Elizabeth (Kordon) U.; m. Gordon Alan McKay, May 11, 1977; children: Gabrielle Alexandria, Alisa Michelle. BS in Maths., Carnegie-Mellon U., 1973; postgrad., UCLA, 1975-76. Project mgr. GeoControl Sys., Inc., Houston, 1982-83; gen. engr., scientific program analyst Ford Aerospace and Comm. Corp., Houston, 1983-89; project mgr. NASA/Johnson Space Ctr., Houston, 1989-94, office chief Telecomms. Sys. Office, 1994-96, dep. dir. control ctr. sys. divsn., 1995-96, mgr. portable computer sys., 1996—. Recipient Al Gore's Hammer award for Efficiency in Govt., 1994. Office: DA NASA Johnson Space Ctr 2101 NASA Rd Houston TX 77058

ULLMAN, GAIL BARBARA, counselor; b. Newark, May 16, 1942; d. Aaron and Sylvia (Blumenthal) Hirschorn; m. Neil R. Ullman, Aug. 31, 1963; children: Jay, Jonathan. BA in Psychology, Rutgers U., Newark, 1964; MA in Counseling, Montclair State Coll., 1980. Nat. cert. counselor. Spl. edn. tchr. various sch. dists., N.J., 1964-79; program cons., behavior counselor N.J. Divsn. Developmental Disabilities, Springfield, 1980-87; surp. counseling and psychol. svcs., counselor Morris-Union Jointure Commn. Sch. Dist., New Providence, N.J., 1987—; presenter workshops and confs., 1989—. Mem. ACLU, Am. Counseling Assn., League Women Voters (pres., sec., bd. dirs.), Coun. Exceptional Children. Office: Morris-Union Jointure Commn 340 Central Ave New Providence NJ 07974

ULLMAN, NELLY SZABO, statistician, educator; b. Vienna, Austria, Aug. 11, 1925; came to U.S., 1939; d. Viktor and Elizabeth (Rosenberg) Szabo; m. Robert Ullman, Mar. 20, 1947 (dec.); children: Buddy, William John, Martha Ann, Daniel Howard. BA, Hunter Coll., 1945; MA, Columbia U., 1948; PhD, U. Mich., 1969. Rsch. assoc. MIT Radiation Lab, Cambridge, Mass., 1945; instr. Polytechnic Inst. of Bklyn., 1945-63; asst. prof. to prof. Ea. Mich. U., Ypsilanti, 1963—. Author: Study Guide To Actuarial Exam, 1978; contbr. articles to profl. jours. Mem. Am. Math. Assn., Am. Stat. Assn., Biometric Soc., Am. Assn. Univ. Profs. Office: Ea Mich Univ Dept Math Ypsilanti MI 48197

ULLMAN, TRACEY, actress, singer; b. Slough, Eng., Dec. 30, 1959; m. Allan McKeown, 1984; children: Mabel Ellen, John Albert Victor. Student, Itaia Conti Stage Sch., London. Appeared in plays Gigi, Elvis, Grease, The Rocky Horror Show, Four in a Million, 1981 (London Theatre Critics award), The Taming of the Shrew, 1990, The Big Love, (one-woman stage show) 1991; films include The Young Visitors, 1984, Give My Regards to Broad Street, 1984, Plenty, 1985, Jumpin' Jack Flash, 1986, I Love You To Death, 1990, Household Saints, 1993, I'll Do Anything, 1994, Bullets over Broadway, 1994, Ready to Wear (Prêt-à-Porter), 1994, Everybody Says I Love You, 1996; Brit. TV shows include Three of a Kind, A Kick Up the Eighties, Girls on Top; actress TV series: The Tracey Ullman Show, from 1987-90 (Emmy award Best Performance, Outstanding Writing, 1990, Golden Globe award Best Actress, 1987), Tracey Takes On, 1996; album You Broke My Heart in Seventeen Places (Gold album). Recipient Brit. Acad. award, 1983, Am. Comedy award, 1988, 90, 91, Emmy award for Best Performance in a Variety/Music Series for "Tracey Ullman Takes on New York", 1994. *

ULLRICH, LINDA J., medical technologist; b. Rockford, Ill., May 10, 1944; d. Glenn H. and R. Catherine (Mathews) Person; m. John R. Brody, June 11, 1966 (div. July 1978); children: Kevin R. Brody, Keith A. Brody; m. Sterling O. Ullrich Sr., Mar. 10, 1979; stepchildren: Sterling O. Jr., Eugene, Lee Anna, Michelle. BA, Thiel Coll., 1966; MPA, Kent State U., 1993, postgrad., 1996—. Cert. med. tech., specialist in hematology. Staff med. tech. Sharon (Pa.) Gen. Hosp., 1966-76; supervisor hematology, coagulation, urinalysis sects. Sharon Regional Health Sys. (formerly Sharon Gen. Hosp.), 1976-96, lab. mgr., 1996—; edn. coord. Beaver County C.C., Pa., 1976-80; tech. supr. lab. Cancer Care Ctr., Hermitage, Pa., 1993—; adj. prof. Thiel Coll., Greenville, Pa., 1994-95; com. mem. Sharon Regional Health Sys., 1990—. Merit badge counselor, com. mem. Troop 67 Boy Scouts Am., Newton Falls, Ohio, 1982-95. Lutheran. Home: 1577 Wilson Ave Newton Falls OH 44444 Office: Sharon Regional Health Sys 740 E State St Sharon PA 16146

ULLRICH, ROXIE ANN, special education educator; b. Ft. Dodge, Iowa, Nov. 10, 1951; d. Rocco William and Mary Veronica (Casady) Jackowell; m. Thomas Earl Ullrich, Aug. 10, 1974; children: Holly Ann, Anthony Joseph. BA, Creighton U., 1973; MA in Teaching, Morningside Coll., 1991. Cert. tchr., Iowa. Tchr. Corpus Christi Sch., Ft. Dodge, Iowa, 1973-74, Westwood Community Schs., Sloan, Iowa, 1974-80, Sioux City Community Schs., 1987—. Cert. judge Iowa High Sch. Speech Assn., Des Moines, 1975—. Mem. Am. Paint Horse Assn., Am. Quarter Horse Assn., Sioux City Hist. Assn., M.I. Hummel Club, Phi Delta Kappa. Home: 819 Brown St Sloan IA 51055

ULMER, FRANCES ANN, state official; b. Madison, Wis., Feb. 1, 1947; m. Bill Council; children: Amy, Louis. BA in Econs. and Polit. Sci., U. Wis.; JD with honors, Wis. Sch. Law. Polit. advisor Gov. Jay Hammond, Alaska, 1973-83; former mayor City of Juneau, Alaska; mem. 4 terms, minority leader Alaska Ho. Reps.; lt. gov. State of Alaska, 1995—. Home: 1700 Angus Way Juneau AK 99801-1411 Office: State Capitol PO Box 110015 Juneau AK 99811

ULRICH, GERTRUDE ANNA, retired nurse; b. Steinauer, Nebr., Oct. 19, 1922; d. Fred, Jr. and Matilda (Rinne) U.; RN, Lincoln (Nebr.) Gen. Hosp., 1960; postgrad. Wesleyan U., Lincoln, 1960-61, B.S. in Natural Scis., 1972; postgrad. U. Nebr., 1967-68, Omaha U., 1966. Instr. Lincoln (Nebr.) Gen. Hosp. Sch. Nursing, 1960-61, 66-67; staff nurse Lincoln Gen. Hosp., 1961-62, 68-71; missionary nurse to Turkey, United Ch. Bd. World Ministries, N.Y.C., 1963-64; camp nurse Girl Scouts U.S.A., Nebraska City, Nebr., summer 1964; staff nurse Homestead Nursing Home, 1964-66; nursing supr. Tabitha Home, Lincoln, 1972-80, med. record supr., 1975-80; evening nursing supr. Homestead Nursing Home, Lincoln, 1980-87. Lincoln Found. ednl. grantee, 1971; named Nurse of Week, Sta. KFOR, 1973, 76. Mem. Reformed Ch. Am. Home: 410 S 41st St Lincoln NE 68510-3601

ULRICH, GLADYS MARJORIE, printing company executive; b. Chgo., Dec. 18, 1932; d. Harry Pikal and Rose Barbara (Vojta) Albert; m. William John Ulrich, Dec. 4, 1954; children: Valerie Lynn, Mark Robert, Laura Ann. Student, Gregg Coll., 1950-52. Owner, CEO Insty-Prints, Arlington Heights, Ill., 1978—; pres., owner Insty-Prints, Elk Grove Village, Ill., 1986—; mem. pres. coun. Insty-Prints, Mpls., 1987-90, nat. adv. governing com., 1987—. Organizer blood drive ARC/Cancer Soc., Elk Grove Village, 1970. Mem. Women's Resource Assn. (pres. 1988-89), Bus. & Profl. Women Assn. Republican. Office: Insty-Prints 2355 E Oakton St Arlington Heights IL 60005-4817

ULRICH, LAUREL THATCHER, historian, educator; b. Sugar City, Idaho, July 11, 1938; d. John Kenneth and Alice (Siddoway) Thatcher; m. Gael Dennis Ulrich, Sept. 22, 1958; children: Karl, Melinda, Nathan, Thatcher, Amy. BA in English, U. Utah, 1960; MA in English, Simmons Coll., 1971; PhD in History, U. N.H., 1980. Asst. prof. humanities U. N.H., Durham, 1980-84, asst. prof. history, 1985-88, assoc. prof. history, 1988-91, prof. history, 1991-95; prof. history and women's studies Harvard U., Cambridge, Mass., 1995—; audiocourse cons. Annenberg Found.; cons., participating humanist numerous exhibits, pub. programs, other projects; project humanist Warner (N.H.) Women's Oral History Project; bd. editors William & Mary Quar., 1989-91, Winterthur Portfolio, 1991—. Author: Good Wives: Image and Reality in the Lives of Women in Northern New England, 1650-1750, 1982, A Midwife's Tale: The Life of Martha Ballard Based on Her Diary, 1785-1812, 1990 (Pulitzer Prize for history 1991); contbr. articles, abstracts, essays and revs. to profl. publs. Coun. mem. Inst. Early Am. History and Culture, 1989-91; trustee Strawberry Banke Mus., 1987-93. John Simon Guggenheim fellow, 1991-92, NEH fellow, 1982, 84-85; women's studies rsch. grantee Woodrow Wilson Fellowship Found., 1979; co-recipient Best Book award Berkshire Conf. Women's Historians, 1990; recipient Best Book award Soc. for History of Early Republic, 1990, John S. Dunning prize and Joan Kelly Meml. prize Am. Hist. Assn., 1990, Bancroft Prize for Am. History, 1991. Mem. Orgn. Am. Historians (nominating com. 1992—, ABC-Clio award com. 1989), Am. Hist. Assn. (rsch. coun. 1993-96). Office: Harvard U Dept History Robinson Hall Cambridge MA 02138

ULTES, ELIZABETH CUMMINGS BRUCE, artist, retired art historian and librarian; b. Urbana, Ohio, Mar. 27, 1909; d. William Mansfield and Helen Finnette (Cummings) B.; m. William Ultes, Jr., May 2, 1934 (dec. Oct. 1973); 1 child, Elizabeth Cummings Ultes Hoffman. BA in Econs., Hollins Coll., 1930; BFA in History of Art, Wittenberg U., 1979; student painting, Positano, Italy, 1960, San Miguel Allende, Mex., 1980. Instr. art history continuing edn. dept. Wittenberg U., Springfield, Ohio, 1959-80; warder, art libr. Springfield Pub. Libr., 1959-70; ret., 1970; former writer art critiques Springfield Daily News-Sun. Exhibited in 2 one-woman shows, Springfield, group shows in Dayton Art Mus., Springfield Fair, Springfield Mus.; 3 paintings in permanent collection Clark County Hist. Mus. Recipient 1st, 2d and 3d prizes for paintings. Home: 5155 N High St Columbus OH 43214

ULVESTAD, ANNE ELIZABETH, art director; b. Yonkers, N.Y., Oct. 19, 1953; d. William George and Rita Agnes (Schug) Bachop; m. Odd Inge Ulvestad, July 1, 1982; 1 child, Kjersti Anita. BS, RN, Hunter/Bellevue Sch. Nursing, N.Y.C., 1974; postgrad., Unification Theol. Sem., Barrytown, N.Y., 1979-80. Missionary Unification Ch., N.Y.C., 1974-79; comms. dir. Assn. for Edn. and Devel., Kenya, 1980-82; high sch. art tchr. Muslim High Sch., The Gambia, 1982-84; dir. The Heart-Parent Scholarship Found., Banjul, The Gambia, 1982-84; graphic designer Trinity Corp., N.Y.C., 1985; sect. designer The World & I Mag., Washington, 1986-91, art dir., 1991—; founder Graphics for the World, Washington, 1993—. Founding mem. Unification Ednl. Found., Landover Hills, Md., 1990; sec. PTA New Hope Acad., Landover Hills, 1990-92. Recipient Cert. of Distinction for design Creativity '92, 1992, Cert. of Distinction for illustration Creativity '92, 1992, Annual Exhbn. award Illustrator's Club, 1993, 94. Mem. Am. Inst. Graphic Arts, Nat. Assn. Desk Top Pubs., Nat. Trust Hist. Preservation, Women's Fedn. for World Peace, Nat. Parks and Conservation Assn. Christian Appalachian Project. Office: The World and I Mag 3600 New York Ave NE Washington DC 20002

UMAN, SARAH DUNGEY, editor; b. Dayton, Ohio, July 22, 1942; d. Arthur Bertram and Lucretia M. (Nash) Dungey; child from previous marriage: Michael Uman; m. Marshall B. Allen; 1 child, Sebastian. Student, New Sch. for Social Rsch., 1962-64. Editorial assoc., publicity dir. Grove Press, Inc., N.Y.C., 1970-79; sr. editor Playboy Paperbacks, N.Y.C., 1979-81, Berkley Pub., N.Y.C., 1982-85; exec. editor Consumer Reports Books, Yonkers, N.Y., 1985-94, Rights Unltd., N.Y.C., 1994-96.

UMBDENSTOCK, JUDY JEAN, physical education educator, real estate agent, farmer, entrepreneur; b. Aurora, Ill., Feb. 12, 1952; d. Alfred Aloyuisious and Mary Emma (Orha) U. AA, Elgin (Ill.) Community Coll., 1972, AS, 1973; BA, Aurora U., 1977; grad., Robert Allens Wealth Tng. 2000, 1991; grad. real estate course, Profl. Edn. Inst., 1991. Cert. phys. edn. tchr., secondary edn. tchr.; lic. real estate salesperson, Ill. Tchr. phys. edn., varsity head coach volleyball and track St. Laurence Sch., Elgin, 1970-75; asst. coach varsity basketball East Aurora High Sch., 1976-77; jr. varsity coach softball St. Charles (Ill.) High Sch., 1978-79, phys. edn. tchr., 1978-79; head coach volleyball/basketball, tchr. algebra and geometry Canton Jr. H.S., Streamwood, Ill., 1979-82; varsity coach volleyball and softball Elgin High Sch., 1982-85, phys. edn. tchr., 1982-86, jr. varsity basketball coach, 1983-84; tchr. elem. phys. edn. Sch. Dist. U-46 Heritage Elem. Sch., Streamwood, 1986—, Parkwood Elem. Sch., Hanover Park, Ill., 1986—; substitute tchr. Elgin, St. Charles and Burlington (Ill.) H.S., 1977-78; Ill. H.S. rated sports referee Elgin and St. Charles Area H.S., 1970-85; cons. Draft and Carriage Horse Assn., Kane County, 1981—; owner Umbdenstock Country Feed & Seed Store, Elgin, 1988-94; owner/ptnr. Jud Enterprises, 1992—; real estate agent Century 21 New Heritage Inc., 1994—. Leader, youth counselor 4-H (farming and animal husbandry), Northern Ill. area, 1970—; campaign supporter state and local Reps. for re-election, Kane county, 1974-86. Served with U.S. Army, 1976-77, with USNR, 1981-87. Scholar Elgin Panhellenic Soc., 1972. Mem. NEA, NAFE, Ill. Edn. Assn., Nat. Farmers Orgn. (pub. relations 1967-80), Airplane Owners and Pilots Assn., Am. Assn. Health, Phys. Edn. and Recreation, Elgin Tchrs. Assn., South Elgin Bus. Assn., Elgin Assn. Realtors, Nat. Wildlife Assn., Nat. Audubon Soc., Disabled Am. Vet. Comdr. Club, People for the Ethnic Treatment Animals, Ill. Coaches Orgn., Am. Draft Horse Assn., Kane County Tchrs. Credit Union, Kane County Farm Bureau. Clubs: Barrington (Ill.) Carriage, 99's Women's Pilot Assn. Home: 8n129 Umbdenstock Rd Elgin IL 60123-8828 Office: Sch Dist U-46 E Chicago St Elgin IL 60120-5522 also: Century 21 New Heritage Inc 41 N McLean Blvd Elgin IL 60123

UMBERG, LORI ANN, designer; b. Cin., Apr. 6, 1964. Student, Atlanta Coll. Art, 1985-88. Graphic artist Ameripress Graphics, Marietta, Ga., 1989-91; electronic pre-press syss. operator Mead Packaging, Atlanta, 1991-95; prodn. mgr. Compack Design Assocs., Atlanta, 1995—; freelance artist Atlanta, 1985—. Mem. NOW, GLPCI, HRCF. Democrat. Roman Catholic. Home: 218 Derrydown Way Decatur GA 30030

UNDERHILL, KATHRYN MARIE, art educator; b. Lincoln, Nebr., Dec. 7, 1949; d. Lloyd A. and Ruth N. (Ollendorf) Engstrom; children: Dixie, Anne, Abigail. BA, Midland Luth. Coll., 1972; postgrad., Wichita State U., 1985-87; MEd, U. Nebr. Lincoln, 1993. Cert. tchr. art K-12, English 7-12, elem. edn. K-8. Tchr. art Wichita (Kans.) Pub. Schs., 1972-75; dir. social svc. and activity Terrace Gardens Retirement Ctr., Wichita, 1977-80; grad. asst. U. Nebr. Lincoln, 1991-93; tchr. mid. level Lincoln Pub. Schs., 1994—; instr. Pvt. Pilot Ground Sch., Wichita, 1974-75; vol. Food Net, Lincoln, 1989—; tchr. arts and crafts Parks and Recreation Cmty. Svcs., Lincoln, 1972—; tchr. Arts are Basic, 1995; spkr. in field. 4-H leader Lancaster County, 1993—. Recipient Muriel Green award NAS, 1991. Mem. NEA, Kans. Arts Coun., Nebr. Arts Coun., Nebr. Arts Edn. Assn. Home: 2755 S 36th St Lincoln NE 68506

UNDERWOOD, BARBARA ANN, mathematician, educator; b. Dayton, Ohio, Dec. 3, 1952; d. Gene Marklyn and Joan Patricia (Saaf) Sears; m. James Claude Underwood, July 18, 1975; children: Anna Marie, Blake. BS in Math. Edn., Presbyn. Coll., 1975. Cert. tchr. secondary. Tchr. math. Bell St. Mid. Sch., Clinton, S.C., 1975-86; tchr. algebra Clinton H.S., 1986—. Mem. Alpha Delta Kappa. Baptist. Home: Rt 3 Box 2065 Clinton SC 29325

UNDERWOOD, BRENDA S., microbiologist, grants administrator; b. Oak Ridge, Tenn., Mar. 19, 1948; d. William Henry Hensley and Maudell (Walker) Townsend; m. Thomas L. Janiszewski, Feb. 14, 1984; 1 child, Thomas Zachary Janiszewski. BS, U. Tenn., 1970; MS, Hood Coll., 1980; MBA, Mt. St. Mary's Coll., 1993. Scientist I chem. carcinogenesis Frederick (Md.) Cancer Rsch. Ctr., 1977-84; microbiologist NCI/NIH, Bethesda, Md., 1984-86; sci. tech. writer Engring. and Econs. Rsch., Germantown, Md., 1987-88; spl. asst. to dir., program dir. grants div. Cancer Biology Diagnosis Ctrs., NCI/NIH, Bethesda, 1988-91; indexer, div. extramural activities Rsch. Analysis and Evaluation br. NCI/NIH, Bethesda, 1991—. Vol. Riding for the Handicapped, Frederick, 1990-96; mem., recreational sec. Capital Hill Equestrian Soc., Washington, 1988. Mem. AAAS, Am. Soc. for Microbiology, Am. Assn. for Cancer Rsch., Women in Cancer Rsch., Federally Employed Women. Office: NCI-NIH RAEB Divsn Extramural Activ Bethesda MD 20892

UNDERWOOD, CAROLE ANN, English and Spanish language educator; b. Toledo, Ohio, May 9, 1943; d. Alton Ellsworth and Ruth Lillian (Hoefflin) Bahnsen; m. Winston Dale Underwood, Sept. 7, 1963; children: David, Shawna. BA in edn., Heidelberg Coll., 1966. Tchr. Lakota Local Schs., Sandusky County, Ohio, 1965-68, Bettsville (Ohio) Local Schs., 1970—. Author: Walden North, 1980. Mem. The Hemingway Soc., The Mich. Hemingway Soc.(bd. dirs. 1995—). Republican. Lutheran. Home: 1227 Van Buren St #47 Fostoria OH 44830 Office: Bettsville H S PO Box 6 Bettsville OH 44815

UNDERWOOD, JOANNA DEHAVEN, environmental research and education organizations president; b. N.Y.C., May 25, 1940; d. Louis Ivan and Helen (Guiterman) U.; m. Saul Lambert, July 31, 1982; stepchildren: Jonathan Whitty, Katherine Aviva. BA, Bryn Mawr Coll., 1962; Diplome d'etudes de Civilisation francaise with honors, Sorbonne U., Paris, 1965. Audio-visual dir. Planned Parenthood World Population, N.Y.C., 1968-70; co-dir. Council on Econ. Priorities, N.Y.C., 1970-73; founder, pres. INFORM, Inc., N.Y.C., 1973—; bd. dirs. N.Y. State Energy R&D Authority, Albany, Hampshire Rsch. Inst., Clean Sites, Rocky Mtn. Inst., Keystone Ctr.; mem. Dow Environ. Adv. Coun., 1992-96; awards com. Pres.'s Coun. on Environ. Quality, 1991; mem. eco-efficiency task force Pres.'s Coun. on Sustainable Devel., 1995. Author (with others) Voices from the Environmental Movement: Perspectives for a New Era, 1991; co-author: Paper Profits, 1971; editor: The Price of Power, 1972; contbr. articles to profl. jours. Circle of dirs. Planned Parenthood of N.Y.C. Recipient U.S. EPA Environ. Achievement award, 1987, 92. Home: 138 E 13th St New York NY 10003-5306 Office: Inform Inc 120 Wall St Fl 16 New York NY 10005-3904

UNDERWOOD, MARTHA JANE MENKE, artist, educator; b. Quincy, Ill., Nov. 28, 1934; d. Francis Norman Menke and Ruth Rosemary (Wells) Zoller; divorced; children: Leslie, Stephen. BA, Scripps Coll., 1956; MFA, Otis Art Inst., 1958. Cert. adult edn. and post secondary tchr. Designer staineglass windows Wallis-Wiley Studio, Pasadena, Calif., 1959-60; mural asst., designer Millard Sheets Murals, Inc., Claremont, Calif., 1960-68; art instr. adult edn. Monrovia, Pomona and Claremont Sch. Dists., Calif., 1967-69; prof. art Chaffey C.C., Alta Loma, Calif., 1970—; free lance illustrator Claremont, 1975—, watercolorist, 1970—; lectr. and demonstrator in field. Contbr. photographs to: How to Create Your Own Designs, 1968, Weaving Without Loom, 1969; illustrator: Opening a Can of Words, 1994, coloring books about baseball team mascots, 1995, 96; contbr. illustrations to Wayfarers Jour. Co-chmn. Recording for the Blind annual fundraiser, Upland, Calif., 1995, 96. Recipient Strathmore award, 1985, Grumbacher award, 1990, 92, 95; Faculty Initiated Projects Program grantee, 1991-92. Mem. Associated Artists, Soc. Children's Book Writers and Illustrators. Office: Chaffey Coll 5885 Haven Ave Alta Loma CA 91737-3002

UNGACTA, MALISSA SUMAGAYSAY, software engineer; b. Agana, Guam, July 3, 1967; d. Renerio Ong and Irene Acfalle (Salas) S. BS in Info. Sci., U. Hawaii, 1989; MS in Info. Tech. Mgmt., Johns Hopkins U., 1992. Cert. power builder developer assoc. Programmer, analyst Facilities Mgmt. Office, Honolulu, 1987-89, Data House Inc., Honolulu, 1989-90, ANSTEC Inc., Fairfax, Md., 1990-93; software specialist, project leader HJ Ford Assocs. Inc., Crystal City, Va., 1993-94; software cons. McDonnell Douglas Tech. Svcs., 1994—. Mem. NAFE. Home: PO Box 1546 Agana GU 96910-1546 Office: McDonnell Douglas 1807 Park 270 Ste 500 Saint Louis MO 63146-4021 also: 4554 Laclede Ave Apt 107 Saint Louis MO 63108-2145

UNGAR, MANYA SHAYON, volunteer, education consultant; b. N.Y.C., May 30, 1928; d. Samuel and Ethel M. (Liese) Shayon; m. Harry Fireman Ungar, June 25, 1950; children: Paul Benedict, Michael Shayon. BA, Mills Coll., 1950. Actress TV and radio NBC, CBS, N.Y.C., 1950-58; founder chpt. AFS, Scotch Plains-Fanwood, N.J., 1963; vol. project dir. handicapped cub scouts Boy Scouts Am., Plainfield, N.J., 1958-61; founder, co-dir. Summer Theater Workshop, Scotch Plains, 1967-78; legis. v.p. N.J. State PTA, 1977-79, pres., 1979-81; legis. v.p. Nat. PTA, Chgo., 1981-85, 1st v.p., 1985-87, pres., 1987-89; Mem. arts edn. adv. panel Nat. Endowment Arts, Washington, 1988-91, panel Nat. Inst. Work and Learning, 1988-91; adv. coun. Nat. Panel Drug Free Schs., Washington, 1989-91, edn. adv. bd. NBC, 1988-92, PBS, 1988-91, Scholastic, Inc., 1990-94; bd. dirs. Math. Sci. Edn. Bd., 1988-92. Trustee N.J. Children's Specialized Hosp., 1990—, N.J. Pub. Edn. Inst., 1987—; mem. adv. coun. Natural Resources Def. Coun., Mothers and Others, 1990—; mem. geography assessment adv. coun. Nat. Assessment Edn. Progress, 1991-92, mem. nat. oversite commn. on geog. stds., 1992-94; mem. N.J. Basic Skills Coun., 1990-94; chmn. N.J. Math. Coalition, 1994—; mem. accreditation com. APA, 1992—; mem. tchr. programs adv. panel Ednl. Testing Svc,. 1990-94; mem. external rev. com. Ctr. Disease Control Preventing Risk Behaviors in Adolescents, 1993; voters svc. dir. N.J. LWV, 1995-96; bd. dirs. Washington Rock Girl Scout Coun., 1995—. Manya Shayon Ungar Scholarship and Auditorium named in her honor, 1989; named Outstanding Citizen N.J. Jaycees, 1979, Scotch Plains Twp., 1989, 92,

State of N.J., 1987, Bd. of Freeholders, 1987; named life mem. nat. PTA, 45 state PTAs. Mem. LWV (chmn. voters svc. Westfield area 1991-95). Home: 10 Brandywine Ct Scotch Plains NJ 07076-2550

UNGAR, ROSELVA MAY, primary and elementary educator; b. Detroit, Oct. 31, 1926; d. John and Elva (Mutchler) Rushton; m. Kenneth Sawyer Goodman, Dec. 26, 1946 (div. 1950); m. Fred Ungar, June 22, 1952 (div. 1977); children: Daniel Brian, Carol Leslie, Lisa Maya. Student, U. Mich., 1946-48; BA, UCLA; postgrad., Pacific Oaks Coll. Recreation dir. Detroit City Parks and Recreation, 1946-50; recreation dir. L.A. Unified Sch. Dist., 1950-52, tchr., 1953-84; mentor tchr. elem. edn. L.A. Unified Sch. Dist., L.A., 1988-94; tchr. head start Found. Early Childhood Edn., L.A., 1965-73; staff organizer Early Childhood Fedn. Local 1475 AFT, L.A., 1973-79; staff rep. Calif. Fedn. Tchrs., L.A. contbr. articles to profl. jours. Com. mem. Gov's Adv. Com. Child Care, L.A., 1980-93; mem. Nat. Parks and Conservation Assn., Washington, 1988—, Sierra Club, 1978—; vol. So. Calif. Libr. Social Studies, L.A., 1989—; charter mem. Mus. Am. Indian Smithsonian Inst., 1994—; Nat. Ctr. Early Childhood Workforce Children's Def. Fund, Southwest Mus., Ctr. Sci in Pub. Interest, Internat. League for Peace and Freedom, ACLU, So. Poverty Law Ctr., Meiklejohn Civil Liberties Inst. Mem. Calif. Assn. Bilingual Edn., So. Calif. Assn. Edn. Young Children, Early Childhood Fedn. (pres. emeritus 1979—), United Tchrs. L.A. (chpt. chair 1984—, east area dir. and UTLA bd. dirs. 1996—), Coalition Labor Union Women (bd. mem. 1980-86). Home: 3131 Hamilton Way Los Angeles CA 90026-2107 Office: Glen Alta Sch LA Unified Sch Dist 3410 Sierra St Los Angeles CA 90031

UNGAR-KNOWLES, GENEVIEVE OPHELIA, civic volunteer, retired accountant; b. Arnold, Md., Mar. 5, 1941; d. Roger and Lillian Virgina (Day) Watts; m. Malachi Knowles, Jun. 25, 1967 (div. 1983); m. Otto Ungar, Nov. 28, 1993. BS in Bus. Adminstrn., Morgan State Univ., 1965. Tchr. D.C. Pub. Schs., Washington; program coord. recreation asst. D.C. Dept. Recreation, Washington; sec. Defense Logistics Agency, San Diego, Calif.; program aide HUD, Chgo.; sec. production rep. asst. HUD, L.A., Washington; accounting asst. Gen. Svcs. Adminstrn., Washington, 1990-94; ret., 1994. Active mem. Balt. Streetcar Mus., Nat. Railway Hist. Soc., Nat. Mus. Women in the Arts, World Affairs Coun. of Washington D.C., Nat. Fed. for the Blind, Nat. Rainbow Coalition, Am. Youth Hostels, All Souls Unitarian Ch. (Wayfarers Club), Arthritis Found. (D.C. Chpt.), Nat. Multiple Sclerosis Soc., Women's Fed. for World Peace, Rails to Trails Conservancy and many more. Mem. NOW, NAFE, AAUW, Older Women's League, Nat. Coun. Negro Women, Nat. Women's Political Caucus, Internat. Planned Parenthood Federation, Nat. Assn. Ret. Fed. Employees (life mem.), Nat. Assn. Housing and Redevelopment Officials, World Jewish Congress, League of Women Voters, Blacks in Govt. (life mem.), B'Nai B'Rith Found. of U.S., The English Speaking Union, U N Assn. of USA, Nat. Assn for the Edn. Young Children, Nat. Recreation and Park Assn., Nat. Trust for Historical Preservation, Am. Assn. Ret. Fed. Employees, Nat. Assn. Black Procurement Profls. (life mem.), Nat. Assn. Negro Bus. and Profl. Women's Club, Morgan State U. Alumni Assn. (life mem.). Home: PO Box 3564 Washington DC 20007

UNGARO, SUSAN KELLIHER, magazine editor. Editor-in-chief Family Circle mag., N.Y.C. Office: Family Circle 110 5th Ave New York NY 10011-5601*

UNGARO-BENAGES, URSULA MANCUSI, federal judge; b. Miami Beach, Fla., Jan. 29, 1951; d. Ludivico Mancusi-Ungaro and Ursula Berliner; m. Michael A. Benages, Mar., 1988. Student, Smith Coll., 1968-70; BA in English Lit., U. Miami, 1973; JD, U. Fla., 1975. Bar: Fla. 1975. Assoc. Frates, Floyd, Pearson et al, Miami, 1976-78, Blackwell, Walker, Gray et al, Miami, 1978-80, Finley, Kumble, Heine et al, Miami, 1980-85, Sparber, Shevin, Shapo et al, Miami, 1985-87; cir. judge State of Fla., Miami, 1987-92; U.S. dist. judge Miami, 1992—; mem. Fla. Supreme Ct. Race & Ethnic & Racial Bias Study Commn., Fla., 1989-92, St. Thomas U. Inns of Ct., Miami, 1991-92. Bd. dirs. United Family & Children's Svcs., Miami, 1981-82; mem. City of Miami Task Force, 1991-92. Mem. ABA, Fed. Judges Assn., Fla. Assn. Women Lawyers, Dade County Bar Assn., Eugene Spellman Inns of Ct. U. Miami. Office: US Dist Ct 300 NE 1st Ave Ste 243 Miami FL 33132-2135

UNGEMAH, MARIE SIANO, artist, educator; b. Irvington, N.J., Feb. 8, 1947; d. Alfred Rocco and Colette Carmel (DeVenzia) Siano; m. Donald Wayne Ungemah, Oct. 26, 1968; children: David Wayne, Joseph Michael. BA, Kean Coll., 1968. Cert. tchr., N.J. Art tchr. Clifton (N.J.) Pub. Schs., 1968-69; social worker Atlantic County Welfare Bd., Atlantic City, N.J., 1971-73; art instr. Foothills Recreation Dist., Jefferson County, Colo., 1980-83; freelance artist, 1982—; art instr. Arapahoe C.C., Littleton, Colo., 1992—; freelance workshop instr., Littleton, 1983—; custom framer, Littleton, 1986-91. Exhibited in group shows at Foothills Art Ctr. Nat. Art Competition, 1989, Depot Art Ctr., Littleton, 1990 (1st pl. award), Colo. Bus. for Arts, Denver, 1992 (1st pl. award). Mem. Littleton Fine Arts Com., 1986-87; judge Colo. H.S. Speech Assn., 1991-95; mem. Northfield (N.J.) Planning Bd., 1976-77. Democrat. Roman Catholic.

UNGER, BARBARA, poet, educator; b. N.Y.C., Oct. 2, 1932; d. David and Florence (Schuchalter) Frankel; m. Bernard Unger, 1954 (div. 1976); m. Theodore Sakano, 1987. B.A., CCNY, 1955, M.A., 1957; advanced cert. NYU, 1970; children: Deborah, Suzanne. Grad. asst. Yeshiva U., 1962-63; edn. editor County Citizen, Rockland County, N.Y., 1960-63; tchr. English, N.Y.C. Pub. Schs., 1955-58, Nyack (N.Y.) High Sch., 1963-67; guidance counselor Ardsley (N.Y.) High Sch., 1967-69; prof. English, Rockland Community Coll., Suffern, N.Y., 1969—; poetry fellow Squaw Valley Community of Writers, 1980; writer-in-residence Rockland Ctr. for Arts, 1986. Author: (poetry) Basement, 1975, Learning to Fox Trot, 1989, The Man Who Burned Money, 1980, Inside the Wind, 1986, Blue Depression Glass in Troika One, 1991; (fiction) Dying for Uncle Ray, 1990; contbr. poetry to over 50 lit. mags., including: Kans. Quar., Carolina Quar., Beloit Poetry Jour., Minn. Rev., Poet and Critic, The Nation, Poetry Now, Invisible City, Thirteenth Moon, So. Poetry Rev., Mass. Rev., Nebr. Rev., Wis. Rev., So. Humanities Rev., Denver Quarterly, Mississippi Valley REv., The G.W. Rev. Wordsmith; contbr. to Anthology Mag. Verse, Yearbook Am. Poetry, 1984, 89; contbr. poetry (anthologies) Two Worlds Walking, Life on the Line, Looking for Home, 80 on the Eighties, Disenchantments, Women and Work, If I Had a Hammer, Sexual Harassment: Women Speak Out; contbr. fiction to True to Life Adventure Stories, Midstream, Esprit, Beloit Fiction Jour., Am. Fiction '89 and numerous others; poetry reading in colls. and libraries throught N.Y. and elsewhere; critical reviewer Contact II. Ragdale Found. fellow, 1985, 86, 89, SUNY Creative Writing fellow, 1981-82, Edna St. Vincent Millay Colony fellow, 1984, Djerassi Found. fellow, 1991, Hambidge Ctr. for Creative Arts and Scis. fellow, 1988; NEH grantee, 1975. Recipient Goodman Poetry award, 1989, Anna Davidson Rosenberg award Judah Magnes Mus., 1989, Roberts Writing award, 1990, New Letters Literary awards, 1990; finalist Am. Fiction Competition, 1989, W.Va. Writing Competition, 1982, John Williams Narrative Poetry Competition, 1992; honorable mention Chester Jones Nat. Poetry Contest. Mem. Poets and Writers, Poetry Soc. Am., Writers' Community. Office: Rockland Community Coll 145 College Rd Suffern NY 10901-3611

UNGER, FRANCINE ANDREA, dentist; b. Huntsville, Ala., May 13, 1961; d. Raymond and Rita (Steinberg) U. BA, Vanderbilt U., 1982; DDS, U. Md., Balt., 1987. Assoc. Dr. Stephen Fred, Bethesda, Md., 1987, Dr. Daniel Hack, Washington, 1987, Dr. Beverly Dunn, Bethesda, 1988; dentist Montrose Dental Assocs., 1992; pvt. practice Gaithersburg, Md, 1994, Brite Dental Group, Potomac, Md., 1996—. Mem. ADA, NOW, Md. State Dental Assn. (recent grad. com.), So. Md. Dental Soc., Acad. Gen. Dentistry, Rockville Jr. C. of C. (Jaycee of the Month and Project of the Yr., chairperson "Just Say No to Drugs" poster contest, dir. cmty. devel.), So. Md. Acad. Gen. dentistry (pres.), Sierra Club, Gorgas Odontol. Honor Soc., Alpha Chi Sigma, Delta Phi Sigma. Democrat. Jewish. Home: 9300 Bells Mill Rd Potomac MD 20854

UNGER, KATHARINE ANN, educational administrator, consultant; b. Salem, Ohio, Apr. 7, 1951; d. Richard John and Nancy Jane (Roose) U. MusB, SUNY, Potsdam, 1973, postgrad., 1974-85; MEd, St. Lawrence U., 1989. Cert. K-12 music tchr., sch. adminstr. supr., dist. dist. adminstr., N.Y.; cert. prin., Md. Tchr. vocal and instrumental music Thousand Islands Consol. Sch. Dist., Dlaayaton, N.Y., 1973-90, dir. music edn., 1985-90; asst. prin. Webatuck H.S., N.E. Ctrl. Sch. Dist., Amenia, N.Y., 1990-94, acting prin., 1994; supr. The Alternative Sch., Ulster County Bd. Coop. Ednl. Svcs., Port Ewen, N.Y., 1994-95; prin. Easton (Md.) H.S., Talbot County Pub. Schs., 1995—; pres. Quantum Learning, Inc., Pelham, N.Y., 1995—. Composer Flute Meditations, 1989—. Mem. Phi Delta Kappa. Buddhist.

UNGER, LAURA S., lawyer; b. N.Y.C., Jan. 8, 1961; d. Raymond and Susan Marie (Vopata) Simone; m. Peter Van Buren Unger, June 29, 1991. BA in Rhetoric, U. Calif., Berkeley, 1983; JD, N.Y. Law Sch., 1987. Bar: Conn. 1987, N.Y. 1988. Staff atty. divsn. enforcement SEC, 1988-90; legis. counsel to Sen. Alfonse M. D'Amato, 1990-91; minority counsel Senate com. banking, housing and urban affairs, 1991-95, counsel, 1995—. Recipient Performance award SEC, N.Y., 1988, D.C., 1989. Mem. ABA (subcom. on civil litigation and SEC enforcement matters and subcom. on SEC adminstrn., budget and legislation of the ABA bus. law sect. com. on federal regulation of securities), Fed. Bar Assn., Jr. League Washington, Decade Soc., Women in Housing and Fin. Roman Catholic. Office: Banking Housing & Urban Affairs 534 Sen Dirksen Office Bldg Washington DC 20510

UNGER, MARIANNE LOUISE, computer graphics artist, consultant; b. Reading, Pa., June 8, 1957; d. Paul Richard and Virginia Ruth (Moyer) U. BS in Art Edn., Kutztown U., 1982. Art tchr. 7 local sch. dists., Reading, 1982-83; sec. Berks Cable, Reading, 1983-84, project asst. new bus. devel., 1984-85; art educator Reading Area Community Coll., 1983-87; pres. Unger Computer Graphics, Reading, 1985—; cons. in field, video and multi-image producer, dir., animator; dir. Christian Edn. Zion's UCC, Pottstown, Pa., 1991-95; instr. ballroom dancing. Grantee NET Ben Franklin Advanced Tech. Ctr., 1986-87. Mem. U.S. Amateur Ballroom Dancing Assn. Office: 38 Aldine Ave Reading PA 19606-1002

UNGER, SHARON LOUISE (SHERRY LANE), artist; b. Chgo., Nov. 9, 1942; d. Arthur Eugene Unger and La Rayne (De Baun) Birk; m. Stuart Lanoff, Dec. 30, 1962 (div. Oct. 1965); 1 child, Lawrence. BFA, Hunter Coll., 1977. Caricaturist Star mag., N.Y.C., 1983-86; dir., curator Westbeth Gallery, N.Y.C., 1983-85. One-woman shows Westbeth Gallery, N.Y.C., 1983, Ward-Nasse Gallery, N.Y.C., 1987, 88; exhibited in group shows Westbeth Gallery, 1974-92, Micro V-Now Gallery, N.Y.C., 1986, Ward-Nasse Gallery, 1988, 89, Salmagundi Club, N.Y.C., 1988, Phase III Gallery, Tulsa, 1990, Sherry Lane Gallery, N.Y.C., 1992; contbr. to Contemporary Graphic Artists, Ency. Living Artists, Erotic Art by Living Artists. Mem. Salmagundi Club (entertainment com. 1987-89, chmn. entertainment co. 1991-94, Ward-Nasse Gallery, Graphic Artists Guild, N.Y. Artists Equity Assn., Found. for Cmty. Artists, Caricaturists Collective Bur., Internat. Spl. Events Soc., Greenwich Village C. of C., Nat. Caricaturists Network (founder N.Y. chpt. 1993), Internat. Spl. Events Soc., Internat. Soc. Meeting Planners. Democrat. Home and Studio: 155 Bank St New York NY 10014

UNTERBERGER, BETTY MILLER, history educator, writer; b. Glasgow, Scotland, Dec. 27, 1923; d. Joseph C. and Leah Miller; m. Robert Ruppe, July 29, 1944; children: Glen, Gail, Gregg. B.A., Syracuse U., N.Y., 1943; M.A., Harvard U., 1946; Ph.D., Duke U., 1950. Asst. prof. E. Carolina U., Greenville, 1948-50; assoc. prof., dir. liberal arts ctr. Whittier Coll., Calif., 1954-61; assoc. prof. Calif. State U.-Fullerton, 1961-65, prof., chmn. grad. studies, 1965-68; prof. Tex. A&M U., College Station, 1968—; vis. prof. U. Hawaii, Honolulu, summer 1967, Peking U., Beijing, 1988; vis. disting. prof. U. Calif., Irvine, 1987—, Patricia and Bookman Peters prof. history, 1991—; vis. prof. Charles U., Prague, Czechoslovakia, summer 1992; mem. adv. com. fgn. rels. U.S. Dept. State, 1977-81, chair, 1981; mem. hist. adv. com. U.S. Dept. Army, 1980-82, USN, 1991—; mem. Nat. Hist. Publs. and Records Commn., 1980-84. Author: America's Siberian Expedition 1918-1920: A Study of National Policy, 1956, 69 (Pacific Coast award Am. Hist. Assn. 1956); editor: American Intervention in the Russian Civil War, 1969, Intervention Against Communism: Did the U.S. Try to Overthrow the Soviet Government, 1918-20, 1986, The United States, Revolutionary Russia and the Rise of Czechoslovakia, 1989; contbr.: Woodrow Wilson and Revolutionary World, 1982; editorial adv. bd.: The Papers of Woodrow Wilson, Princeton U., 1982-92; bd. editors: Diplomatic History, 1981-84, Red River Valley Hist. Rev., 1975-84. Trustee Am. Inst. Pakistan Studies, Villanova U., Pa., 1981—, sec., 1989-92; mem. League of Women Voters. Woodrow Wilson Found. fellow, 1979; recipient Disting. Univ. Tchr. award State of Calif. Legislature, 1966. Mem. LWV, NOW, AAUW, Am. Hist. Assn. (chair 1982-83, nominating com. 1980-83), Orgn. Am. Historians (govt. relations com.), Soc. Historians of Am. Fgn. Relations (exec. council 1978-81, 86-89, govt. relations com. 1982-84, v.p. 1985, pres. 1986, co-winner Myrna F. Bernath prize 1991), Am. Soc. for Advancement Slavic Studies, Coordinating Com. on Women in Hist. Profession, Rocky Mountain Assn. Slavic Studies (program chair 1973, v.p. 1973-74), So. Hist. Assn., Asian Studies Assn., Assn. Third World Studies, Czechoslovak Soc. Arts and Scis., Czechoslovak History Conf., Women's Fgn. Policy Coun., Beyond War, Peace History Soc., Sierra Club, Phi Beta Kappa, Phi Beta Delta. Office: Tex A&M U College Station TX 77843

UNTERBURGER, AMY L., editor; b. Detroit, 1957; d. George W. and Mary L. (Wilkerson) U.; m. David E. Salamie, Oct. 14, 1989. BA in Polit. Sci., Olivet (Mich.) Coll., 1979. Editl. asst. Gale Rsch., Detroit, 1983-84, asst. editor, 1984-86, sr. asst. editor, 1986-87, assoc. editor, 1987-88, editor, 1988-94; ptnr. InfoWorks Devel. Group, Parker, Colo., 1995—. Editor: Who's Who in Technology, 6th edit., 1989, Who's Who among Hispanic Americans, 1st edit., 1991, 2nd edit., 1992, 3rd edit., 1994, Who's Who among Asian Americans, Actors and Actresses vol. International Dictionary of Film and Filmakers, 3rd edit., 1996. Mem. Douglas County Extension Svc. (master gardener 1995—). Office: Infoworks Devel Group 8046 E Tempest Ridge Way Parker CO 80134

UNWIN, CYNTHIA GIRARD, secondary education educator; b. Littleton, Colo., May 3, 1964; d. Larry J. and Judith S. (Smiley) Girard; m. Brian K. Unwin, Aug. 10, 1985; children: Kelly Marie, Emily Elizabeth. BA Psychology, U. Colo., 1985; MEd, Auburn U., 1989, PhD, 1993. Cert. tchr., Ga. Classroom tchr. Holy Cross Sch., Garrett Park, Md., 1986-88; grad. tchg. asst. Auburn (Ala.) U., 1988-93, instr., 1994; instr. Columbus (Ga.) Coll., 1992-94; chpt. I tchr. Harlem (Ga.) Mid. Sch., 1994—. Youth ministry vol. Holy Cross Ch., Garrett Park, 1986-88, St. Anne Ch., Columbus, 1988-94. Mem. Internat. Reading Assn. (coun. pres. 1992-94), Nat. Coun. Tchrs. English, Assembly on Lit. for Adolescents/NCTE, Phi Delta Kappa (Outstanding Dissertation award Auburn chpt. 1994), Phi Beta Kappa. Roman Catholic. Home: 4121 Saddlehorn Dr Evans GA 30809-8543

UPBIN, SHARI, theatrical producer, director, agent, educator; b. N.Y.C.; children: Edward, Elyse, Danielle. Master tap instr. Talent mgr. Goldstar Talent Mgmt., Inc., N.Y.C., 1989-91; guest tchr. Total Theatre Lab., N.Y.C.; faculty Nat. Shakespeare Conservatory, N.Y. Asst. dir. 1st Black-Hispanic Shakespeare prodn. Julius Caesar, Coriolanus at Pub. Theatre, N.Y., 1979; dir., choreographer Matter of Opinion, Players Theatre, N.Y., 1980, Side by Side, Sondheim Forum Theatre, N.J., 1981 (Nominated Best Dir. of Season N.J. Theatre Critics); producer, dir. Vincent, The Passions of Van Gogh, N.Y., 1981; producer Bojangles, The Life of Bill Robinson, Broadway, 1984, Captain America, nat. Am. tour, Virtual Theatre, 1996; dir. Fiddler on the Roof, Cabaret, Life with Father, Roar of the Grease Paint, regional theatre, 1979-82; co-producer One Mo' Time, Village Gate, N.Y., nat. and internat. tour.; producer/dir. off-Broadway musical Flypaper, 1991-92, Women on Their Own, Things My Mother Never Told Me, Theatre East, N.Y., Virtual Theatre, N.Y. Founded Queens Playhouse, N.Y., Children's Theatre, Flushing, N.Y.; mem. Willy Mays' Found. Drug Abused Children. Recipient Jaycees Service award Jr. Miss Pageants Franklin Twp., N.J., 1976. Mem. League Profl. Theatre Women (pres.), Soc. Stage Dirs. and Choreographers, Actors Equity Assn., Villagers Barn Theatre (1st woman pres.), N.Y. Womens Agenda (bd. dirs.). Address: The Bristol 300 E 56th St New York NY 10022

UPDEGRAFF SPLETH, ANN L., church executive, pastor; b. Newark, Ohio, Sept. 15, 1949; d. John C. and Lela V. (Mervine) Updegraff; m. Randall Alan Spleth; children: Andrew Alan, Claire Campbell. BA, Transylvania Coll., 1971; MDiv, Vanderbilt U., 1974; DMin, Claremont Sch. Theology, 1985. Ordained min. Christian Ch. (Disciples of Christ), 1973. Assoc. min. First Christian Ch., New Castle, Ind., 1974-75, Sacramento, 1975-78; sr. assoc. regional min. Pacific S.W. region Christian Ch., L.A., 1978-85; exec. v.p. Divsn. Homeland Ministries, Indpls., 1985-89, pres., 1990—. Author: Youth Ministry Manual, 1980; co-author: Congregation: Sign of Hope, 1989, Worship and Spiritual Life, 1992; editor Vanguard, 1990—; contbr. articles to profl. jours. Founding mem. Profl. Women's Forum, L.A., 1978-85. Mem. Ind. Soc. of Washington. Democrat. Home: 8961 Sawmill Ct Indianapolis IN 46236-9171 Office: United Christian Missionary Society 130 E Washington St Indianapolis IN 46204-3615

UPRIGHT, DIANE WARNER, art dealer; b. Cleve.; d. Rodney Upright and Shirley (Warner) Lavine. Student, Wellesley Coll., 1965-67; BA, U. Pitts., 1969; MA, U. Mich., 1973, PhD, 1976. Asst. prof. U. Va., Charlottesville, 1976-78; assoc. prof. Harvard U., Cambridge, Mass., 1978-83; sr. curator Ft. Worth Art Mus., 1984-86; dir. Jan Krugier Gallery, N.Y.C., 1986-90; sr. v.p., head contemporary art dept. Christie's, N.Y.C., 1990-95; pres. Diane Upright Fine Arts, N.Y.C., 1995—; trustee Aldrich Mus. Contemporary Art, Ridgefield, Conn. Author: Morris Louis: The Complete Paintings, 1979, Ellsworth Kelly: Works on Paper, 1987, various exhbn. catalogues; contbr. articles to art jours. Mem. Art Table, Inc. Office: Diane Upright Fine Arts 20 East 68th St New York NY 10021

UPSHUR, CAROLE CHRISTOFK, psychologist, educator; b. Des Moines, Oct. 18, 1948; d. Robert Richard and Margaret (Davis) Christofk; 1 child, Emily. AB, U. So. Calif., 1969; EdM, Harvard U., 1970, EdD (NIMH fellow), 1975. Lic. psychologist, Mass. Planner, Mass. Com. on Criminal Justice, Boston, 1970-73; licensing specialist, planner, policy specialist Mass. Office for Children, Boston, 1973-76; asst. prof. Coll. Public and Cmty. Svc., U. Mass., Boston, 1976-81, assoc. prof., 1982-93, prof., 1993—, chmn. Ctr. for Cmty. Planning, 1979-81, 84-86, 1995-96, sr. rsch. fellow Maurice Gaston Inst. Latino Pub. Policy, 1993—, Ctr. Social Devel. & Edn., 1991—, sr. rsch. fellow Gerontology Inst., 1996—, dir. PhD in Pub. Policy program, 1995—; cons. to govt. and cmty. agys. on mental health and social svc. policy and mgmt., 1970—; cons. Harvard Family Rsch. Project, 1983-93; assoc. in pediatrics, sr. rsch. assoc. U. Mass. Med. Sch., 1983-94; adj. prof. Heller Sch. Social Welfare, Brandeis U., 1985—. Commr. Brookline Human Rels.-Youth Resources Commn., 1988-91, Gov's. Commn. on Facility Consolidation, 1991-92, Mass. Healthcare Adv. Com., 1993—. Fellow Mass. Psychol. Assn.; mem. APA, Am. Assn. on Mental Retardation (cons. editor Mental Retardation, Amer. Jour. on Mental Retardation 1981—, AJMR Monographs. Office: PhD Program in Public Policy U Mass Boston MA 02125

UPTEGROVE, JANICE, elementary school educator; b. Kansas City, Mo., Oct. 2, 1953; d. Roy W. and Betty Lee (Diamond) Watkins; m. Jack L. Uptegrove, July 14, 1973; children: Jeremy L., Kyle C., Andrew S. BA in Edn. with honors, U. Mo., Kansas City, 1991. Cert. tchr. elem. edn. Substitute tchr. North Kansas City (Mo.) Sch. Dist., 1989-91; tchr. Ctrs. for the Scientifically Curious, Kansas City, Mo., 1990-91; tchr. 4th grade Smithville (Mo.) Elem. Sch., 1991—. Youth sponsor Northland Cathedral, Kansas City, 1984—. Esther Teague scholar, 1990-91. Mem. Cmty. Tchrs. Assn., Mo. State Tchrs. Assn., No. Mo. Reading Coun. Republican. Assemblies of God. Home: 2106 NE 74th Ter Gladstone MO 64118-2320 Office: Smithville Elementary Sch 600 Maple Ave Smithville MO 64089-8257

UPTON, CLAUDETTE DIANA REED, editor, writer; b. Asheville, N.C., May 17, 1948; d. Haldee Lee and Helen (Tarasov) Reed; m. Philip Paine Upton, Jan. 3, 1977 (dec. Apr. 1984); stepchildren: Carl Donjek, Lowell Richard; m. Martin Andrew Keeley, Sept. 8, 1986. BA in English, Duke U., 1970. Social worker Anchorage Cmty. Hosp., 1971-73; abortion counselor Alaska Clinic, Anchorage, 1973-75; adminstrv. asst., editor Arctic Inst. N.Am., Anchorage, 1976-78; editor Arctic Inst. N.Am., Calgary, Alberta, Can., 1978-85; freelance editor Point Roberts, Wash. and Vancouver, B.C., 1986-93; mng. editor B.C. Med. Jour. B.C. Med. Assn., Vancouver, 1993—; contbg. editor Recovery Ins. Corp. B.C., Vancouver, 1991—; guest instr. in field. Editor: Physician's Guide to Therapeutic Massage, 1989, Lionheart: Matthew's Story, 1990; co-editor: Unveiling the Arctic, 1985, Choices Today, Options Tomorrow: Seniors' Housing in the 90's, 1990; writer, editor (pamphlet) Steroids, 1994 (Apex award 1995). Dir. Alberta (Can.) Status of Women Action Com., 1978-84, Point Roberts Registered Voters Assn., 1988-94; mem. Elected Wash. Women, Point Roberts, 1990-92; coord. Point Roberts Heron Preservation Com., 1988-96; commr. Point Roberts Water Dist. No. 4, 1990-95; Alberta rep. Women Shaping a Conserver Soc., Can., 1981-82. Mem. Coun. Biology Editors, Editors' Assn. Can. (chair Western Can. br. 1992-93, editor nat. newsletter 1994-96, nat. v.p. 1996), Bd. Editors in Life Scis., Am. Med. Writers Assn. Democrat. Home: PO Box 1421 610 S Beach Rd Point Roberts WA 98281 Office: BC Med Assn, 1665 W Broadway, Vancouver, BC Canada V6J 5A4

URANO, SUSAN COLE, arts administrator; b. New Castle, Pa., May 11, 1954; d. A. Wayne and Marjorie Jane (Logan) Cole; m. David Carl Urano, Jul. 20, 1991; children: Hannah Muir, Grace Cole. BFA, Kent State U., 1976; MA, Ohio State U., 1982. Exec. dir. Lima (Ohio) Art Assn., 1983-87, Arts Coun. of Roanoke, Va., 1987-91; project dir. Alliance of Ohio Cmty., 1991-92; exec. dir. Dairy Barn Southeastern Ohio Cultural Arts Ctr., Athens, 1993—; cp-pres. Cmty. Arts Assn. of Va., 1988-90, pres. Athens Area Arts Alliance, Athens, Ohio, 1993-95, treas. Alliance of Ohio Cmty. Arts Agencies, 1993-95, mem. Ohio Dept. of Edn. Arts, 1994-95. Sec. Big Sister Big Brother/Big Sisters Orgn., Roanoke, 1984-91, 88-91, mem. Roanoke Va. Tech. Advisory Com., 1988-91, trustee Roanoke Valley Convention & Vistors Bur., 1988-91. Mem. Am. Assn. of Mus., Athens Rotary Club, Ohio Mus. Assn. Democrat. Presbyterian. Office: Dairy Barn 1000 Dairy Ln Athens OH 45701

URATO, BARBRA CASALE, entrepreneur; b. Newark, Oct. 10, 1941; d. Dominick Anthony and Concetta (Castrichini) Casale; m. John Joseph Urato, June 20, 1965; children: Concetta U. Graves, Gina E., Joseph D. Student, Seton Hall U., 1961-63. File clk. Martin Gelber Esquire, Newark, 1956-58; policy typist Aetna Casualty Ins., Newark, 1959-61; sec. to dean Seton Hall U., South Orange, N.J., 1961-63; paralegal sec. Judge Robert A. McKinley, Newark, 1963-65, Joseph Garrubbo, Esquire, Newark, 1965-66; office mgr. Valiant I.M.C., Hackensack, N.J., 1971-73; asst. pers. mgr. Degussa Inc., Teterboro, N.J., 1975-78; night mgr. The Ferryboat Restaurant, River Edge, N.J., 1976-78; mgr. Fratello's and Ventilini's, Hilton Head, S.C., 1978-80; day mgr. Ramada Inn Restaurant, Paramus, N.J., 1980-81; mgr. Gottlieb's Bakery, Hilton Head, 1982-83; asst. mgr. closing dept. Hilton Head Mortgage Co., 1983-84; owner, mgr. All Cleaning Svc., Hilton Head, 1984—; owner Hilton Head Investigations, 1990-93, Hilton Head Island, 1990-92; owner Aaction Investigators, 1992-94. Mem. NAFE, Profl. Women of Hilton Head, Assn. for Rsch. and Enlightenment, Rosicrucian Order. Roman Catholic. Office: PO Box 4953 Hilton Head Island SC 29938

URBAN, CATHLEEN ANDREA, graphic designer, software developer; b. Elizabeth, N.J., June 7, 1947; d. Emil Martin and Susan (Rahoche) Cupec; m. Walter Robert Urban, Nov. 5, 1966; children: Karen Louise, Kimberly Ann. Student, Rutgers U., 1965-66, 91-94; AS in Computer Info. Systems, Raritan Valley Community Coll., North Branch, N.J., 1990, AAS in Computer Programming, 1990. Office mgr. K-Mart Corp., Somerville, N.J., 1987-90; software developer Bell Communications Rsch., Piscataway, N.J., 1990-93, sys. tech. support cons., 1993-94; software developer Bell Comm. Rsch., Piscataway, 1994-96, software quality assurance tester, 1996—; graphic designer, owner CathiCards, Inc., Neshanic Station, N.J., 1995—. Leader Somerset County 4-H Program, Bridgewater, 1978-87. Mem. NAFE, AAUW, Nat. Space Soc., Internat. Platform Assn., Internat. Guild Candle Artisans, Golden Key Honor Soc., Mensa, Phi Theta Kappa. Roman Catholic. Home: 570 Amwell Rd Neshanic Station NJ 08853-3404 Office: Bell Comm Rsch 444 Hoes Ln Piscataway NJ 08854-4104

URBAN, EDITH BROWN, school system administrator; b. Terra Alta, W.Va., Dec. 22, 1941; d. Charles Earl and Louise E. (Rector) Brown; m. Thomas E. Urban, Aug. 8, 1964; children: Philip Scott, Beth Ellen. BA, W.Va. Wesleyan Coll., 1964; MEd, U. Pitts., 1977; MEd in Adminstrn., St. Bonaventure U., 1991. Cert. elem. tchr., reading specialist, ednl. adminstr.,

Pa. Elem. tchr. North Attleboro (Mass.) Schs., 1964-68; homebound instr. Hempfield Sch. Dist., Irwin, Pa., 1968-69; presch. tchr. Room to Grow Presch., Bradford, Pa., 1975-76; reading specialist Bradford Area Sch. Dist., 1977-91, title I dir., 1991—. Eucharist lay minister Ch. of the Ascension, Bradford, 1990—; bd. dirs. Bradford Landmark Soc., Bradford, 1985-90; pres Bradford chpt. LWV, 1973-77. Mem. Pa. Assn. Fed. Coords., Internat. Reading Assn., Nat. Coun. Tchrs. English, EM Tchrs. Applying Whole Lang., Zonta Internat. (bd. dirs.), Delta Kappa Gamma. Democrat. Episcopalian. Home: 34 Laurel Dr Bradford PA 16701-1511 Office: Bradford Area Sch Dist 50 Congress St Bradford PA 16701-2221

URBANSKI, MARIE OLESEN, American literature educator, writer; b. Pitts., Mar. 12, 1922; d. Charles William and Esther Booth (Mitchell) Olesen; m. Edmund Stefan Urbanski (div. 1965); children: Jane Urbanski Robbins, Wanda; m. Joseph Boyd Whittaker, 1996. BA, U. Tex., 1944; MA, Western Ill. U., 1964; PhD, U. Ky., 1973. From instr. to prof. U. Maine, Orono, 1971-94; ret., 1994. Author: Margaret Fuller's Woman in the Nineteenth Century, 1980; editor: Margaret Fuller: Visionary of the New Age, 1994; editor Thoreau Jour. Quar., 1976-88; book reviewer; mem. editl. bd. Thoreau Quar., 1982-87, Legacy, 1987-94. Democrat. Episcopalian. Home: RR 2 Box 311 Ararat VA 24053

URCH, DIANE SHERMAN, librarian; b. Woodbury, N.J., Nov. 17, 1936; d. Arthur T. and Elizabeth V. (Haines) Sherman; m. Juergen K. Schoeler, Mar. 20, 1959 (div. June 1975); children: Jodi L. Schoeler Hecht, Susan E. Schoeler Anderson, Ellen Nell Schoeler; m. Wesley V. Urch, Apr. 18, 1991. BA in History, U. Del., 1958; MA in Librarianship, U. Denver, 1970. Circulation and acquisitions libr. Emporia (Kans.) State U., 1970-79; acquisitions libr. U. Tex., El Paso, 1979-84; asst. dir. libr. U. Wis., Oshkosh, 1984—. Mem., mem. Oshkosh adv. bd. Children's Svcs. Soc. Wis., 1991—. Mem. ALA, AAUW (pres. Oshkosh br. 1985—), Wis. Libr. Assn. Office: U Wis Librs and Learning Resource 800 Algoma Blvd Oshkosh WI 54901

URDANG, ALEXANDRA, book publishing executive; b. N.Y.C., June 29, 1956; d. Laurence Urdang and Irena (Ehrlich) Urdang de Tour. BA in English Lit., U. Conn., 1977. Customer svc. and fulfillment mgr. Universe Books, N.Y.C., 1978-79, sales mgr., assoc. mktg. mgr., 1980-82; asst. v.p., dir. spl. sales Macmillan Pub. Co., N.Y.C., 1982-88; v.p. new markets Warner Books, Inc., N.Y.C., 1988—. Office: Warner Books Inc Time and Life Bldg 1271 Avenue Of The Americas New York NY 10020

UREEL, PATRICIA LOIS, retired manufacturing company executive; b. Detroit, Nov. 29, 1923; d. Peter Walter and Ethel Estelle (Stewart) Murphy; grad. Detroit Bus. Inst., 1941; student Wayne State U., 1942, U. Detroit, 1943, U. Miami, 1945-46; m. Joseph Ralph Ureel, Jan. 4, 1947; children—Mary Patricia, Ronald Joseph. Exec. sec. to chmn. bd. and pres. Detroit Ball Bearing Co. of Mich., 1965-67; exec. sec. to partner charge Mich. dist. Ernst & Ernst, Detroit, 1967-71, Clubs of Inverrary, Lauderhill, Fla., 1971-72, partner charge of group Coopers & Lybrand, Miami, Fla., 1972-74; corp. sec., personnel mgr. Sanford Industries, Inc. and 4 subsidiaries, Pompano Beach, Fla., 1974-81; corp. sec., asso. Asphalt Assos., Ft. Lauderdale, 1982-86. Named Sec. of Yr. for City of Detroit, 1966; cert. profl. sec. Mem. Nat. Secs. Assn., Women's Econ. Club Detroit, Moose, Zeta Tau Alpha Sorority (Gamma Alpha chpt). Republican. Roman Catholic. Home: 19737 Suncrest Dr West Linn OR 97068

URMAN, RHODA M., social worker, psychotherapist; b. Newark, N.J., Sept. 9, 1946; d. George M. and Jean (Schlein) U.; m. Cristos Gianakos, Nov. 21, 1982; 1 child, Maia. BA cum laude, U. Pa., 1964-68; MSW, Yeshiva U., 1992. Cert. social worker, N.Y. Staff therapist, intake interviewer 5th Ave. Ctr. for Counseling and Psychotherapy, N.Y.C., 1990—; pvt. practice psychotherapy N.Y.C., 1992—; analytic group therapy candidate Postgrad. Ctr. for Mental Health, N.Y.C., 1995—; psychoanalytic psychotherapy candidate, Greenwich Inst. for psychoanalytic studies, N.Y.C., 1990-94. Recipient scholarship Jewish Found. for the Edn. of Women, N.Y.C., 1991. Mem. NASW, N.Y. State Soc. for Clin. Social Work. Office: 156 Fifth Ave Ste 612 New York NY 10010

URMER, DIANE HEDDA, management firm executive, financial officer; b. Bklyn., Dec. 15, 1934; d. Leo and Helen Sarah (Perlman) Leverant; m. Albert Heinz Urmer, Sept. 2, 1952; children: Michelle, Cynthia, Carl. Student U. Tex., 1951-52, Washington U., St. Louis, 1962-63; BA in Psychology, Calif. State U.-Northridge, 1969. Asst. auditor Tex. State Bank, Austin, 1952-55; v.p., contr. Enki Corp., Sepulveda, Calif., 1966-70, also dir., 1987—; v.p., fin. Cambia Way Hosp., Walnut Creek, Calif., 1973-78; v.p., contr. Enki Health & Rsch. Sys., Inc., Reseda, Calif., 1978—, also dir. Contbr. articles to profl. jours. Pres. Northridge PTA, 1971; chmn. Northridge Citizens Adv. Council, 1972-73. Mem. Women in Mgmt. Club: Tex. Execs. Avocations: bowling, sailing, handcrafts, golf. Office: Enki Health and Rsch Systems Inc 21601 Devonshire St Chatsworth CA 91311-2946

URQUHART, SALLY ANN, environmental scientist, chemist; b. Omaha, June 8, 1946; d. Howard E. and Mary Josephine (Johnson) Lee; m. Henry O. Urquhart, July 31, 1968; children: Mary L. Urquhart Kelly, Andrew L. BS in Chemistry, U. Tex., Arlington, 1968; MS in Environ. Scis., U. Tex., Dallas, 1986. Registered environ. mgr.; lic. asbestos mgmt. planner, Tex.; Asbestos Hazard Emergency Response Act accredited inspector, mgmt. planner, project designer. Rsch. asst. U. Tex. Dallas, Richardson, 1980-82; high sch. sci. tchr. Allen (Tex.) Ind. Sch. Dist., 1983-87; hazardous materials specialist Dallas Area Rapid Transit, 1987-90, environ. compliance officer, 1990-94, environmental compliance coordination officer, 1994-95; pres. Comprehensive Environ. Svcs. Inc., Dallas, 1995—. Pres. Beacon Sunday Sch. Spring Valley United Meth. Ch., Dallas, 1987, adminstrv. bd. dirs., 1989, com. status and role of women, 1992. Scholar Richardson (Tex.) Br. AAUW, 1980. Mem. Am. Inst. Chemists, Am. Chem. Soc., Am. Soc. Safety Engrs., Am. Indsl. Hygiene Assn., Am. Conf. Govtl. Indsl. Hygienists (affiliate), Nat. Registry Environ. Profls., Soc. Tex. Environ. Profls. (sec.-treas. Dallas chpt. 1994, v.p. 1996), U. Tex.-Dallas Alumnae Assn. (com. 1992-94), Soc. of Environ. Mgmt. and Tech. Home: 310 Sallie Cir Richardson TX 75081-4229

URSO, JOSETTE MARIE, artist; b. Tampa, Fla., June 5, 1959; d. Rosario and Connie Ann (Wood) U. BFA, U. South Fla., 1980, MFA, 1983. Art tchr. New Sch. for Visual Arts, Tampa, 1984-85, Hillsborough Community Coll., Tampa, 1984-85, Union County Coll., Cranford, N.J., 1986-88, The Chautauqua (N.Y.) Sch. Art, 1985-90, 92d St. YMHA, N.Y.C., 1985-90; art instr. to pvt. students, N.Y.C., 1990-92. One-woman shows include Tampa Mus. Art, Fla., 1995, Ednl. Testing Svcs., Princeton, N.J., 1995, Galerie Industria, Wuppertal, Germany, 1995. Painting fellow Art Matters, Inc., N.Y.C., 1988, Divsn. Cultural Affairs, Tampa, 1986; art resident Va. Ctr. for Arts, Sweetbriar, 1990, Millary Colony for Arts, Austerlitz, N.Y., 1990, Camargo Found., Cassis, France, 1991, Oberpfalzer Kunstlerhaus, Schwandorf, Germany, 1993, Ucross Found., Clearmont, N.Y., 1995; recipient grant Mid Atlantic Arts Found., 1994.

URSPRUNG, DEBORAH LYNN, special education educator; b. Liberty, Tex., Sept. 10, 1952; d. Norman Arnold and Roberta Starr (Gay) U.; m. Ernest Fredrick Fritzsching, July 14, 1979 (div. Dec. 1982). Grad., Sam Houston State U., Huntsville, Tex., 1975. Cert. tchr., Tex. Elem. tchr., tchr. spl. edn. Aldine Ind. Sch. Dist., Houston, 1976-79; secondary tchr. spl. edn. Tarkington (Tex.) Ind. Sch. Dist., 1982-85, Vidor (Tex.) Ind. Sch. Dist., 1985-93; secondary tchr. spl. edn., dir., mem. attendance bd. Hull Daisetta (Tex.) Ind. Sch. Dist., 1994—. Mem. ASCD, AAUW, Tex. Assn. Classroom Tchrs., Archaeol. Inst. Am., Alpha Delta Kappa (sec. 1996—). Republican. Roman Catholic. Home: PO Box 725 Rye TX 77369-0725 Office: Hull Daisetta Ind Sch Dist PO Box 477 Daisetta TX 77533-0477

USELMANN, CATHERINE ROSE (KIT USELMANN), small business owner, network marketer, behavioral researcher, financial independence consultant; b. Madison, Wis., Sept. 17, 1960; d. Richard Lewis and Evelyn Mae (Parr) U. AA, Madison Area Tech. Coll., 1982; BA in Sociology, U. Wis., 1984, MA in Rsch. and Analysis, 1985; DD (hon.), Charter Ecumenical Ministries Internat., 1994. Pub. utility rate analyst Pub. Svc. Commn. Wis., Madison, 1986-89; rsch. mgr. Wis. Lottery, Madison, 1989-90; energy cons., tech. analyst II HBRS, Inc., Madison, 1990-91; sr. cons., project mgr. XENERGY, Inc., Burlington, Mass., 1991-93; pres. CRU Prodns., Madison, 1993—; exec. Nutrition For Life Internat., Houston, 1995—, Trudeau Mktg. Group, Chgo., 1995—; team coord. I-Team, Cyberspace, 1996—; exec. Leaders Club, Columbus, Ohio, 1995—; speaker Nat. Assn. Regulatory Utility Commrs., 1987-89; contbg. mem., speaker Assn. for Demand-Side Mgmt. Profls., 1991-93. Univ. rep. operating com. Mall/Concourse, Madison, 1982-84; lobbyist Inst. for Rsch. Poverty, Madison, 1984; activist, mem. People for Ethical Treatment Animals, Washington, 1989—. Mem. Fin. Independence Assn., U. Wis. Alumni Assn., Badger Quarter Horse Assn. (life). Lakota. Home and Office: 3753 Robin Hood Way Madison WI 53704-6243

USHENKO, AUDREY ANDREYEVNA, painter, art historian, educator; b. Princeton, July 28, 1945; d. Andrew Pavlevitch and Fay (Hampton) U.; m. S.M. Harcaj; 1 child, Emily. Student, Sch. of Art Inst., 1963-64; BA, Ind. U., 1965; MA, Northwestern U., Evanston, Ill., 1967, PhD, 1979. Instr. Valparaiso (Ind.) U., 1968-73, asst. prof., 1978-79; instr. Alan R. Hite Inst. U. Louisville, 1973-74; asst. prof. Northwestern U., Evanston, Ill., 1974-75; vis. faculty Columbia Coll., 1980-88; assoc. prof. Ind.-Purdue U., Ft. Wayne, Ind., 1988—. Gallery artist Gruen Gallery, Chgo., 1983—, Denise Bibro Gallery, N.Y.C., 1993—, Yvonne Rapp Gallery, Louisville, 1989—; artist oil paintings Bacchus & Ariadne III, 1987 (NAD Clark prize), Social Security, 1987 (Purchase prize 1989), Chgo. Art Expo, 1996, Marriage Project-Traveling Exhbn., 1996. Mem. AAUP (sec. local chpt. 1990—), NAD. Democrat. Orthodox. Home: 2519 East Dr Fort Wayne IN 46805-3612

USINGER, MARTHA PUTNAM, counselor, educator; b. Pitts., Dec. 10, 1912; d. Milo Boone and Christiana (Haberstroh) Putnam; m. Robert Leslie Usinger, June 24, 1938 (dec Oct. 1968); children: Roberta Christine (dec.), Richard Putnam. AB cum laude, U. Calif., Berkeley, 1934; postgrad., Oreg. State U., 1935, U. Ghana, 1970, Coll. Nairobi, 1970. Tchr. Oakland (Calif.) Pub. Schs., 1936-38; tchr. Berkeley (Calif.) Pub. Schs., 1954-57, dean West Campus, counselor, 1957-78; lectr., photographer in field. Author: Ration Books and Christmas Crackers, 1989. Mem. DAR, Berkeley Ret. Tchrs., U. Calif. Emeriti Assn., U. Calif. Alumnae Assn., Prytanean Alumnae Assn. (pres. 1952-54), Berkeley Cagera Club, Mortar Bd., Delta Kappa Gamma.

USRY, JANA PRIVETTE, special education educator; b. Richmond, Va., Oct. 23, 1943; d. Millard Due and Dorothy (Daneman) Privette; m. David Page Usry, Feb. 5, 1972 (dec. Sept. 1975); 1 stepchild, Stephanie Page Usry. BA in Psychology, Mary Washington Coll.; MEd in Spl. Edn., U. Va.; postgrad., Va. Commonwealth U., 1984. Cert. tchr. psychology, and spl. edn.; cert. spl. edn. supr., elem. and secondary prin., secondary sch. adminstr. and supr. Tchr. emotionally disturbed Va. Treatment Ctr. for Children, summer 1966; program cons. Va. Soc. for Prevention of Blindness, Inc., 1966-67; tchr. emotionally disturbed, intermediate and self-contained Henrico County Pub. Schs., 1967-70; tchr. emotionally disturbed and learning disabled The Learning Ctr., St. Joseph's Villa, 1971-73; ednl. cons., tchr. dept. pediatrics, adolescent unit Med. Coll. of Va., 1973-74; spl. edn. tchr. Albert Hill Mid. Sch./Richmond Pub. Schs., 1974-78, Thomas Jefferson High Sch./Richmond Pub. Schs., 1978-86, United Meth. Family Svcs., 1986-87, Monacan High Sch., Chesterfield County, 1987-88, Higland Springs High Sch./Henrico County Pub. Schs., 1988-93; tchr. Henrico Juvenile Detention Home, Richmond, Va., 1993-95; tchr., adminstrv. asst. Henrico H.S., Richmond, 1995—; organizer learning disabilities workshop Supt.'s Sch. for the Gifted, 1980; condr. workshops and state convs. for learning disabled youth Va. Assn. for Children with Learning Disabilities, 1980, 81; condr. in-svc. workshop fgn. lang. tchrs. City of Richmond, 1982-83; participant learning disabilities workshop Va. State Dept. of Spl. Edn., Lynchburg, 1983; condr. learning disabilities workshops Richmond Pub. Schs., spring 1983; mem. com. on permanent records for exceptional edn. Richmond Pub. Schs., 1984, sponsor cheerleaders, pep club, other extracurricular activities; mem. spl. edn. curriculum task force Learning Disabilities Sect. Henrico County Pub. Schs., 1989-90; mem. leadership team, faculty trainer Highland Springs High Sch. Moving Up Project, 1989-90, 90-91; guest speaker Found. for Dyslexia, 1991. Member Westhampton Jr. Woman's Club, Richmond, 1967-71, Women's Com. of Richmond Symphony, 1971-78, Va. Mus. of Fine Arts, Richmond, 1967-78, Richmond Symphony Chorus, 1991—. Mem. NEA, ASCD, Va. Edn. Assn., Learning Disability Assn. Va., Learning Disability Assn. Richmond, Henrico Edn. Assn., Orton Dyslexia Soc., Coun. for Exceptional Children (past treas. state unit devel. com., past del. assembly Nat. Conv.), Learning Disabilities Assn., Richmond Jazz Soc., U. Va. Alumni Assn., Mary Washington Coll. Alumni Assn. (class agt., past pres. Richmond chpt.), Mu Phi Epsilon, Phi Delta Kappa. Home: 1512 Confederate Ave Richmond VA 23227-4406

USSERY, CHARLOTTE W., counselor, political consultant; b. Rogersville, Tenn., June 8, 1950; d. J. C. and Lenora (Linesay) Wallen; children: Caroline, Jonathan. BS in Gen. Sci., East Tenn. State U., 1972, MA in Sociology, 1974; AA in Theology, Christ for the Nations, Dallas, 1980; MS in Comm. counseling, Ga. State U., 1991. Owner, counselor Life Mgmt. Resources, Duluth, Ga., 1992—; therapist Family Counseling Svcs., Inc., Decatur, Ga., 1993—; polit. cons. McNair for Gov., Atlanta, 1994. Chmn. women's steering com. 6th Congl. Dist., Marietta, Ga., 1993-94; organizer Congressman Newt Gingrich, Marietta, Ga., 1993-94; nat. brick fund chmn. Ga. Fedn. of Rep. Women, 1991 ; mem., vol. organizer Ga. Rep. Found., Atlanta, 1992—. Mem. ACA; Ga. Rep. Found. Home and office: 3854 Pine Needle Dr Duluth GA 30136

USSERY, JENNIE LIND, administrative assistant, secretary; b. Lancaster County, S.C., July 24, 1933; d. Ralph Thurston and Mary Elizabeth (Haile) U.; m. Harry Duffield III, Mar. 28, 1953 (div. 1969); children: Kelley M., May L. Duffield Thomas, Leigh E. Duffield McCay. Student, Va. Polytech. Inst., 1951-52. Gbroadcloth inspector Spings Mills, Kershaw, S.C., 1952-53; sec. to exec. dir. Va. Heart Assn., Richmond, 1953-58; legal sec. McGuire, Woods, Battle & Boothe, L.L.P., Richmond, 1971—, calligrapher, 1980—, sec. to chmn., 1984-92. Sec. Va. Fedn. Young Rep. Clubs, 1957, Sandston (Va.) Civic Assn., 1968; singer Richmond Civic Opera, 1973-77, Richmond Symphony Chorus, 1987-92; calligrapher St. Paul's Epsicopal Ch., Richmond, 1980—. Republican. Epscopalian.

UTAIN, MARSHA, marriage, family, and child counselor, author, lecturer; b. Phila., Oct. 16, 1947; d. Charles and Diana Green; m. Arthur Melville, May 28, 1978. BA in English, Beaver Coll., 1969; MS in Counseling, Calif. State U., Long Beach, 1979. Lic. marriage family child counselor, Calif.; cert. high sch. and jr. coll. tchg., Calif. Tchr. Neshaminy (Pa.) Sr. H.S., 1969-71, spl. project tchr. Sch. Without Walls, 1971-72; chair dept. English-Reading Garden Gate Alternative H.S., L.A., 1976-79; co-tchr., spl. clin. supr. Calif. State U., Long Beach, 1979-81, co-tchr. Sch. Nursing Continuing Edn., 1980-81; co-host mental health mag. KFOX Radio, L.A., 1987-89; pvt. practice Long Beach, 1980—; cons. Orange County Dept. Mental Health, Laguna, Calif., 1983, Long Beach Psychiat. Clinic for Children, 1985; lectr./trainer U.S. Jour. Tng., Inc., Deerfield Beach, Fla., 1989-91; presenter Calif. Consortium for Prevention of Child Abuse, 1992; clin. dir. So. Calif. Youth Offender Recovery Program, 1991—. Author: (pamphlet) Stepping Out of Chaos, 1989; co-author: The Healing Relationship, 1989; contbg. author: The Partnership Way, 1990. Charter mem. Orange County Task Force on Organized Abuse of Children, Costa Mesa, Calif., 1991-93. Mem. ACA (clin. mem.), Calif. Assn. Marriage Family Therapists (clin. mem.), Phi Kappa Phi, Phi Delta Kappa, Kappa Delta Pi, Phi Alpha Theta (past sec.). Office: 5520 E 2nd St Ste K Long Beach CA 90803-3957

UTLEY, NANCY, film company executive. Exec. v.p. mktg., media, and rsch. 20th Century Fox, Beverly Hills, Calif. Office: 20th Century Fox PO Box 900 Beverly Hills CA 90213-0900*

UZSOY, PATRICIA J., nursing educator and administrator; b. Corning, Ark.; m. Namik K. Diploma, Mo. Bapt. Hosp. Sch. Nursing, St. Louis, 1960; BSN, Washington U., St. Louis, 1962; MEd, Lynchburg Coll., 1977, EdS, 1981; MS in Nursing, U. Va., 1987. RN, Va. Dir. sch. nursing Lynchburg (Va.) Gen. Hosp., dir. Mem. ANA, NLN, Va. Nurses Assn. (Nurse of Yr. dist. III 1987).

UZZELL-BAGGETT, KARON LYNETTE, career officer; b. Goldsboro, N.C., Apr. 28, 1964; d. Jesse Lee and Ernestine Smith (Merriweathers) Uzzell; m. Ronald Walter Baggett, July 26, 1990; stepchildren: Christina, Brian, Adam. BS, U. N.C., 1986; postgrad., U. Md., 1993-96. Commd. 2d lt. USAF, 1986, advanced through grades to capt., 1990; exec. officer 6ACCS USAF, Langley AFB, Va., 1986-88; ops. tng. officer 7393MUNSS USAF, Murted AFD, Turkey, 1988-89; command and control officer 52FW USAF, Spangdahlem AB, Germany, 1989-92; SENEX mission dir. 89AW USAF, Andrews AFB, Md., 1992-95, dep. chief classified control Office Sec. Def., 1995—. Emergency med. technician Orange County Rescue Squad, Hillsborough, N.C., 1985-86; treas. Melwood PTA, Upper Marlboro, Md., 1994—; meml. vol. Women in Mil. Svc., Washington, 1993—; entitlements vol. Whitman Walker Clinic, Washington, 1993—. Mem. Women in Mil. Svc. for Am., So. Poverty Law Ctr. Democrat. Baptist. Home: 10704 Tyrone Dr Upper Marlboro MD 20772-4631

VADAS, MELINDA MARGARET, philosopher; b. Miami, Nov. 9, 1948; d. Alexander and Judith Amalia (Jakabfy) V. BA, Fla. Internat. U., 1977; PhD, U. Miami, 1982. Asst. prof. philosophy Winston-Salem (N.C.) State U., 1982-85; ind. scholar Oak Ridge, N.C., 1985—; vis. lectr. Guilford Coll., Greensboro, N.C., 1990-91. Contbr. articles to profl. jours. Home and Office: 8326 W Harrell Rd Oak Ridge NC 27310

VADUS, GLORIA A., document examiner; b. Forrestville, Pa.. Diploma, Cole Sch. Graphology, Calif., 1978; BA in Psychology Counseling, Columbia Pacific U., 1981, MA in Psychology, 1982; diploma handwriting expert, Edith Eisenberg, Bethesda, Md., 1991. Cert. Am. Acad. Graphology, Washington, 1978, tchr. Coun. Graphological Socs., 1980; ct. qualified document examiner; registered graphologist; cert. behavioral profiling and cert. questioned documents, diplomate Am. Bd. Forensic Examiners, 1993/94. Pres., owner Graphinc, Inc., 1976—; accredited instr. graphology Montgomery County Schs., Md., 1978; instr. Psychogram Centre, 1978-85; testifier superior and probate cts. Author numerous studies, papers, and environ. articles in field. Chmn. Letter of Hope for POW's; vol. Montgomery County, 1987-88. Recipient Gold Nib Analyst of Yr. award, 1982, Dancing Fan award Marine Tech. Soc., Japan, 1991, Spl. award U.S./Japan Marine Facilities Panel, 1978-94, Valuable Contbns. Japanese Panel UJNR/MFP, 1994; named Woman of Yr. ABI, 1990, 93-96, IBC, 1992-93, 95-96. Fellow Am. Bd. Forensic Examiners (Outstanding Contrbn. cert.); mem. Am. Handwriting Analysis Found. (cert., pres. 1982-84, chmn. rsch. com., adv. bd. 1981-86, chmn. nominations com. 1985-86, officiator 1986, mem. policy planning and ethics com. 1986-91, ethics chmn. 1989-91, chmn., past pres. adv. bd. 1989-91), Nat. Forensic Ctr., Nat. Assn. Document Examiners (ethics hearing bd. 1986, chmn. nominations com. 1987-88, elections chmn. 1988, parliamentarian 1988-92), Internat. Platform Assn., Soc. Francaise de Graphologie, Am. Handwriting Analysis Found., Nat. Writers Club, Meninnger Found., Soroptimist Internat. (v.p., nom. pres., internat. chmn.), Nat. Capital Jaguars Club Am. (judge 1976-86), Henry Hicks Gard en Club of the Westburys (v.p., judge, chmn. flower shows), Sierra Club. Home: 8500 Timber Hill Ln Potomac MD 20854-4237

VAETH, AGATHA MIN-CHUN FANG, quality assurance nurse, wellness consultant, home health nurse; b. Beijing, Feb. 19, 1935; d. Yung-Cheng and Wen-Pu (Cheng) Fang; m. Randy H. Vaeth, July 20, 1971; children: David Sun, Elizabeth Cheng, Philip Cheng. Diploma, Mary View Hosp. Sch. Nursing, Portsmouth, Va., 1959; student, Okla. State U., 1969-73; BS, St. Joseph's Coll., North Windham, Maine, 1986, postgrad., 1989—; postgrad., La. State U., 1986. Staff nurse, charge nurse Stillwater (Okla.) Mcpl. Hosp., 1969-74; clin. nurse USIHH Hosp., Pawnee, Okla., 1974-75, clin. nurse, relief supr. Gillis W. Long Hansen's Disease Ctr., Carville, La., 1975-91, supervisory clin. nurse, 1991—; wellness cons.; part-time home health nurse, 1993—. Translator video cassettes on Hansens Disease; illustrator herpetology lab manuel; art exhbns. at Barton Rouge Art & Artist Guild, 1976-77. Recipient Outstanding Performance award GWLHD, PHS, DHHS, 1991, 1993, High Quality Performance award, 1978, Dedicated Svc. to Clin. Br. award, 1981, Outstanding Nurses award Baton Rouge Dist. Nurses' Assn., 1994. Fellow Internat. Biog. Assn. (life); mem. ANA, AAUW, La. Nurses Assn. (nominating com. 1990-94), Baton Rouge Nurses Assn., Am. Coll. Health Execs. Home: 1274 Marilyn Dr Baton Rouge LA 70815-4928

VAGLIO, DIANE HELEN, educator; b. Middletown, Conn., Feb. 7, 1950; d. Thomas Henry and Mary Ann (Kachinski) O'Brien; m. Nicholas Philip Vaglio, Nov. 30, 1974; children: Peter, Scott. AB in political sci., Stonehill Coll., 1972; student, NYU, Spain, 1972; MEd, Rutgers U., 1991. Mgmt. trainee program, underwriter Hartford (Conn.) Ins. Group, 1972-75; sr. underwriter Chubb & Son., N.Y., 1975-77; tchr. Eng. Lang. Svc. Corp., Staten Island, N.Y., 1980-83; adj. instr. Wagner Coll., Staten Island, N.Y., 1983-87; mem. adj. staff Rutgers U., New Brunswick, N.J., 1988; E.S.L. tchr. Parsippany (N.J.) Troy Hills Sch. Dist., 1989—. Author: National Library of Poetry, 1993. Recipient Geraldine R. Dodge Found. rsch. grant, 1992, Parsippany Troy Hills Bd. Edn., 1994, 95, Gov.'s recognition award for teaching, 1995, A for Kids disseminator grant, 1996. Mem. Nat. Coun. Tchrs. Eng., N.J. Tchrs. Eng. Second Lang., Kappa Delta Pi. Roman Catholic. Home: 52 Mine Mount Rd Bernardsville NJ 07924 Office: Ctrl Mid Sch Rte 46 Parsippany NJ 07054 also: Northvail Sch 10 Eileen Ct Parsippany NJ 07054

VAGNIERES, DOROTHY LEE, artist; b. Chgo., Feb. 7, 1934; d. William August and Linnea (Nelson) Wandrey; m. Robert Charles Vagnieres, June 13, 1953 (div. June 1995); children: Robert Charles Jr., Krista Jan, Ross Jon, Pamela Su. BFA, Sch. of the Art Inst. Chgo., 1980, MFA, 1985. mem. grant writing com. ARC Women's Coop Gallery, Chgo., 1988-92; nat. affiliate mem. Soho20 Gallery, N.Y.C., 1992-93. Sculptor: Coil, 1989 in private collection, Wasaw, 1992 McNeal Meml. Hosp. Bridgeview, Ill. Recipient 2d place award Phoenix Gallery Group Show, N.Y.C., 1991, Best in Show, Wright Mus. of Art, Beloit, Wis., 1991, 1st Place award Schoharie Arts Coun., Cobleskill, N.Y., 1992. Mem. Chgo. Womens Caucus for Art, Internat. Sculpture Ctr. Home and Studio: 1725 W North Ave # 301 Chicago IL 60622

VAIA, CHERYL LYNN, consultant; b. Newark, Ohio, Sept. 13, 1955; d. James Lee V. and Barbara N. (Barber) Canter; m. Herbert S. Bresler, Aug. 1, 1982; children: Reuben, Marika. BA, Capital U., 1977; MS, Wright State U., 1980. Economist Dept. Energy, Columbus, Ohio, 1979-80; econ. analyst Energy & Environ. Analysis, Arlington, Va., 1980-83; analyst, sys. analyst, mgr., dir., v.p. Orkand Corp., Silver Spring, Md., 1983-93; dir. fed. sys. KCM Cons., Inc., Greenbelt, Md., 1993-94; ind. cons., 1994; prin. Vaia Cons., Bexley, Ohio, 1995—; instr. Capital U., Columbus, 1980. Pres. Crofton (Md.) Meadows Home Owners Assn., 1984-85, sec., 1983. Mem. APHA, Am. Statis. Assn., Am. Mgmt. Contractors Assn., Women in Technology. Democrat. Jewish. Home and Office: 2610 E Broad St Columbus OH 43209

VAIL, IRIS JENNINGS, civic worker; b. N.Y.C., July 2, 1928; d. Lawrence K. and Beatrice (Black) Jennings; grad. Miss Porters Sch., Farmington, Conn.; m. Thomas V.H. Vail, Sept. 15, 1951; children: Siri J., Thomas V.H. Jr., Lawrence J.W. Exec. com. Garden Club Cleve., 1962-93; mem. women's coun. Western Res. Hist. Soc., 1960—, Cleve. Mus. Art, 1953—; chmn. Childrens Garden Fair, 1966-75, Public Square Dinner, 1975; bd. dirs. Garden Center Greater Cleve., 1963-77; trustee Cleve. Zool. Soc., 1971—; mem. Ohio Arts Coun., 1974-76, pub. sq. com. Greater Cleve. Growth Assn., 1976-93, pub. sq. preservation and maintenance com. Cleve. Found., 1989-93, chmn. pub. sq. planting com., 1993. Recipient Amy Angell Collier Montague medal Garden Club Am., 1976, Ohio Gov.'s award, 1977. Chagrin Valley Hunt Club, Cypress Point Club, Kirtland Country Club, Colony Club, Women's City of Cleve. Club (Margaret A. Ireland award). Home: 14950 County Line Rd Chagrin Falls OH 44022

VAITUKAITIS, JUDITH LOUISE, medical research administrator; b. Hartford, Conn., Aug. 29, 1940; d. Albert George and Julia Joan (Vaznikaitis) V. BS, Tufts U., 1962; MD, Boston U., 1966. Investigator, med. officer reproductive rsch. Nat. Inst. Child Health and Human Devel., NIH, Bethesda, Md., 1971-74; assoc. dir. clin. rsch. Nat. Ctr. Rsch. Resources NIH, Bethesda, Md., 1986-91, dir. gen. clin. rsch. ctr., 1986-91, dep. dir. extramural rsch., 1991; acting dir. Nat. Ctr. Rsch. Resources NIH, Bethesda, 1991-92, dir., 1993—; from assoc. prof. to prof. medicine Sch. Medicine Boston U., 1974-86, assoc. prof. physiology, 1975-80, assoc. prof. ob-gyn., 1977-80, program. dir. gen. clin. rsch. ctr., 1977-86, prof. physiology, 1980-86; head sect. endocrinology and metabolism Boston City Hosp., 1974-86. Mem. editorial bd. Jour. Clin. Endocrin. and Metabolism, 1973-80, Proc. Soc. Exptl. Biol. and Medicine, 1978-87, Endocrine Rsch., 1984-88. Author: Clinical Reproductive Neuroendocrinology, 1982; contbr. articles to profl. jours. Recipient Disting. Alumna award Sch. Medicine, Boston U., 1983, Mallincrodt award for Inv. Rsch. Clin. Radiossay Soc., 1980. Mem. Am. Fedn. Clin. Rsch., Endocrine Soc., Am. Soc. Clin. Rsch., Soc. Exptl. Biology and Medicine, Assn. Am. Physicians. Office: Nat Ctr Rsch Resources NIH Bldg 12A Rm 4007 12 South Dr MSC 5662 Bethesda MD 20892-5662

VALCIC, SUSAN JOAN, lawyer; b. N.Y.C., Mar. 23, 1956; d. Joseph and Eve Manderville; m. Alexander C. Valcic, July 28, 1979. BA magna cum laude, Columbia U., 1983; JD, Cardozo Sch. Law, 1986. Assoc. attorney Bailey, Marshall & Hoeniger, N.Y.C., 1986-87, Zalkin, Rodin & Goodman, N.Y.C., 1987-89; pvt. practice N.Y.C., 1989—. Apptd. adminstrv. law judge, N.Y., 1990. Mem. Assn. Bar City N.Y., N.Y. County Lawyers Assn., N.Y. State Bar. Assn., Fed. Bar. Assn., Columbia Club, Phi Beta Kappa.

VALDES-DAPENA, MARIE AGNES, pediatric pathologist, educator; b. Pottsville, Pa., July 14, 1921; d. Edgar Daniel and Marie Agnes (Rettig) Brown; m. Antonio M. Valdes-Dapena, Apr. 6, 1945 (div. Oct. 1980); children: Victoria Maria Valdes-Dapena Dead, Deborah Anne Valdes-Dapena Malle, Maria Cristina, Andres Antonio, Antonio Edgardo, Carlos Roberto, Marcos Antonio, Ricardo Daniel, Carmen Patricia Valdés-Dapena Fater, Catalina Inez Valdés-Dapena Amram, Pedro Pablo. BS, Immaculata Coll., 1941; MD, Temple U., 1944. Diplomate: Am. Bd. Pathology (spl. qualification-pediatric pathology 1990). Intern Phila. Gen. Hosp., 1944-45, resident in pathology, 1945-49; asst. pathologist Fitzgerald Mercy Hosp., Darby, Pa., 1949-51; dir. labs. Woman's Med. Coll. Pa., Phila., 1951-55; instr. pathology Woman's Med. Coll. Pa., 1947-51, asst. prof., 1951-55, assoc. prof., 1955-59; assoc. pathologist St. Christopher's Hosp. for Children, Phila., 1959-76; dir. sect. pediatric pathology U. Miami (Fla.)-Jackson Meml. Hosp., 1976-81, pediatric pathologist, dir. div. edn. in pathology, 1981-93, co.-dir. edn. in pathology, 1993—; cons., lectr. U.S. Naval Hosp., Phila., 1972-76; instr. pathology Sch. Medicine U. Pa., 1945-49; instr. Sch. Medicine U. Pa. (Sch. Dentistry), 1947, Sch. Medicine U. Pa. (Grad. Sch. Medicine), 1948-55, vis. lectr., 1960-62; asst. prof. Temple U. Med. Sch., 1959-63, assoc. prof., 1963-67, prof. pathology and pediatrics, 1967-76; prof. pathology and pediatrics U., Miami, 1976-93, prof. emeritus pathology and pediatrics, 1993—; cons. pediatric pathology div. med. examiner Dept. Pub. Health Phila., 1967-70; mem. perinatal biology and infant mortality research and tng. com. Nat. Inst. Child Health and Human Devel., NIH, 1971-73; mem. sci. adv. bd. Armed Forces Inst. Pathology, 1976-82; assoc. med. examiner, Dade County, Fla., 1976—; chmn. med. bd. Nat. Sudden Infant Death Syndrome Found., 1961-81, 87-91, pres., 1984-87, chmn. bd., 1985-88; mem. med. and sci. adv. coun. The SIDS Alliance, 1990—. Contbr. articles to profl. jours. NIH grantee. Mem. U.S. and Can. Acad. Pathology, Coll. Physicians Phila., Internat. Assn. Pediatric Pathology, Soc. for Pediatric Pathology (pres. 1980-81), Alpha Omega Alpha. Roman Catholic. Home: 179 Morningside Dr Miami FL 33166-5240 Office: Dept Pathology U Miami Sch Medicine PO Box 016960 Miami FL 33101-6960

VALDESPINO, ANNE AURELIA, journalist; b. San Antonio, Tex., July 9, 1958; d. Jose Maria and Gloria V.; m. Paul David Hodgins. BM in Piano Performance, U. Tex., San Antonio, 1980; MA in Musicology, U. Mich., Ann Arbor, 1983; MA in Journalism, U. Mich., 1986. Intern L.A. Daily News, 1985, L.A. Times, 1985; staff writer The Orange County Register, Santa Ana, Calif., 1987-96; speaker, adjudicator So. Calif. Music Tchrs. Assn., 1992-95. Mem. Orange County Press Club (Humor Category award 1993, 96, Entertainment Category award 1993). Democrat. Office: Orange County Register 625 N Grand Ave Santa Ana CA 92701

VALDEZ, FRANCES VALDEZ, lawyer; b. San Antonio, Tex., Sept. 7, 1954; d. Juan Ortiz and Basilisa Flores Valdez; m. Joe Albert Gonzales, Sept. 26, 1981; children: Ana Lisa, Martin Esteban. BA, Yale U., 1977; JD, U. Tex., 1980. Bar: Tex. 1980, U.S. Dist. Ct. (no. dist.) Tex. 1981, U.S. Ct. Appeals (5th cir.) 1981, U.S. Ct. Appeals (10th cir.) 1981. Trial atty. office of the solicitor U.S. Dept. Labor, Dallas, 1980-84; briefing atty. no. dist. Tex. U.S. Bankruptcy Ct., Dallas, 1984-85; dir., shareholder, atty. Geary Glast & Middleton P.C., Dallas, 1985-92; regulatory/environ. atty. J.C. Penney Co. Inc., Plano, Tex., 1992—; mem. adv. panel The Bus. Forum, 1993-96; bd. dirs. MiEscuelita. Law vol. Cath. Charities, Dallas, 1992-95; mentor, spkr. Nike Club, Dallas, 1994—. Mem. Dallas Bar Assn. (spkr. com. mem. environ. sect. 1992—, internat. sec. 1991—), Mex.-Am. Bar Assn., Bankruptcy Bar Assn. (co-chair ct. liaison com., chair), Yale Club of Dallas, Hispanic C. of C. (planning com. chair, spkr. com. chair 1985—). Democrat. Roman Catholic. Home: 9109 Livenshire Dr Dallas TX 75238 Office: JC Penney Co Inc Legal Dept 6501 Legacy Dr Plano TX 75024-3698

VALDEZ, REMY GROMYKO, realtor, home nursing care company owner; b. Rosales, The Philippines, Mar. 15, 1929; came to U.S., 1948; d. Grigory Tuminez Gromyko and Temotia (Valdez) Manangan; m. Gregorio Tuvera Valdez, Jan. 5, 1948 (div. Feb. 1974); children: George, Raymond, Donna, David. Diploma in acctg., Far Eastern U., Manila, The Philippines, 1947; LPN, Nat. Inst. Practical Nursing, Chgo., 1950; cert. pharmacy apprentice, Augustana Hosp., Chgo., 1960. naturalized;. Owner, operator Remy O. Valdez Real Estate, Chgo., 1948—; unit sec. Grant Hosp., Chgo., 1957-59, Augustana Hosp., Chgo., 1959-62; acct. asst. Spiegel Corp., Desplaines, Ill., 1962-63; dietary asst. Ill. Masonic Hosp., Chgo., 1963-64; unit sec. St. Joseph Hosp., Chgo., 1964-77; cost analyst Uptown Nat. Bank, Chgo., 1977-82; acct. asst. Broadway Bank, Chgo., 1982-83; pres. Remedial Home Care, Inc., Chgo., 1983—; mgr. Remy O. Valdez, Inc., Chgo., 1948—; pres. David Norris Valdez Land Devel., Inc., Chgo., 1975—. Judge Bd. Election, Chgo., 1980; mem. Dem. Congl. Campaign Com., 1983—, U.S. Capitol Hist. Soc., 1983—, Dem. Nat. Com., 1992—, Dem. Senatorial Campaign Com., 1992—, Dems. 2000, 1992—, The John F. Kennedy Libr. Found., 1994—. Recipient Honor cert. Dem. Nat. Com., Washington, 1996. Home and Office: 6445 N Sacramento Ave Chicago IL 60645-4214

VALE, MARGO ROSE, physician; b. Balt., June 16, 1950; d. Henry and Pauline Esther (Koplow) Hausdorff; m. Michael Allen Vale, Aug. 22, 1971; children: Edward, Judith. BA magna cum laude, Brandeis U., 1971; MD, Albert Einstein Coll. Medicine, 1975. Diplomate Am. Bd. Dermatology. Resident in internal medicine and dermatology NYU, N.Y.C., 1975-79, Bellevue Hosp., N.Y.C., 1975-79, VA Hosp., N.Y.C., 1975-79; staff physician HIP Greater N.Y., Bay Shore, 1979-81; pvt. practice medicine Huntington, N.Y., 1981—; cons. in dermatology Huntington Hosp., 1981—, Gurwin Jewish Geriatric Ctr., Commack, N.Y., 1990—. Contbr. articles to profl. jours. Mem. Am. Acad. Dermatology, Med. Soc. State N.Y., Long Island Dermatology Soc., Suffolk County Med. Soc., Suffolk Dermatology Soc. (pres. 1990-92), Phi Beta Kappa. Office: 205 E Main St Huntington NY 11743-2923

VALENCIA, MELANIE LAINE, music educator; b. Oneonta, N.Y., Dec. 5, 1962; d. Jose Lardizabal and Marcell Jewell (Wiseman) V.; m. Frederick John Kelly, Mar. 18, 1990; children: Laine, Valencia, Kelly. Student, Ithaca Coll., 1981-85; BS in Music, Wells Coll., 1985; MFA, Carnegie Mellon U., 1988. Tchr. flute, staff mem. various music stores, Johnson City & N.Y.C., 1981—; cons. bookings and adminstrv. various non-profit agys., N.Y.C., 1988-94; flutist, founder Keeping Co. Ensemble, N.Y.C., 1989—; flutist, dir. Valencia Duo, N.Y.C. & Binghamton, 1993—; flutist, founder, dir. Contemporary Collaborative Ensemble, N.Y.C., 1993—; instr. toddler music class Vestal (N.Y.) Recreation Dept., 1995—; flutist Quintessence, Woodwind Quartet, Binghamton, 1995—; piccoloist So. Tier Concert Band, Binghamton, 1995—; instr. elementary band Windsor (N.Y.) Sch. Dist., 1996—. Mem. Nat. Flute Assn., N.Y. State United Tchrs., Broome County Music Educators Assn., Phi Beta Kappa. Home: 57 Chestnut St Windsor NY 13865 Office: Windsor Ctrl Sch Dist Palmer Elem Sch 215 Main St Windsor NY 13865

VALENSTEIN, SUZANNE GEBHART, art historian; b. Balt., July 17, 1928; d. Jerome J. and Lonnie Cooper Gebhart; m. Murray A. Valenstein, Mar. 31, 1951. With dept. Asian Art Met. Mus. Art, N.Y.C., 1965—; rsch. curator Asian Art. Author: Ming Porcelains: A Retrospective, 1970, A Handbook of Chinese Ceramics, 1975, rev. and enlarged, 1989, Highlights of Chinese Ceramics, 1975, (with others) Oriental Ceramics: The World's Great Collections: The Metropolitan Museum, 1977, rev., 1983, The Herzman Collection of Chinese Ceramics, 1992. Mem. Oriental Ceramic Soc. (London), Oriental Ceramic Soc. (Hong Kong). Office: Met Mus Art Dept Asian Art Fifth Ave at 82nd St New York NY 10028

VALENTE, BENITA (BENITA V. CHECCHIA), lyric soprano; b. Delano, Calif.; d. Lawrence Guiseppe and Severina Antonia (Masdonati) V.; m. Anthony Phillip Checchia, Nov. 21, 1959; 1 son, Peter. Grad., Curtis Inst. Music, 1960; studied with, Chester Hayden, Martial Singher, Lotte Lehmann, Margaret Harshaw. Met. Opera debut, 1973; leading roles in: Orfeo Rigoletto, Traviata, Idomeneo, Marriage of Figaro, Faust, La Boheme, Falstaff, Turandot, Magic Flute, Rinaldo, Pelléas et Mélissande, Cosi Fan Tutte, Louise, Suor Angelica, Gianni Schicchi, Die Fledermaus, Arabella; appeared throughout U.S. and Europe in operas and recitals, with symphonies and in world premier of Rorem's Peony (Childhood Miracle). Winner Met. Opera Council Audition 1960. Recs. for Columbia Records, Desmar Records, RCA, Pantheon. Mem. Phila. Cosmopolitan Club, Phila. Chamber Music Soc. (music adv.com.).

VALENTI, JOANN MYER, environmental and mass communications researcher, educator; b. Miami, Fla., Apr. 6, 1945; d. Isaac William and Myra Cecile (Chawluk) Myer; m. Henry Vincent Valenti, Jr., Aug. 24, 1976; children: John Henry, Sarita Jo. BS in Journalism, U. Fla., 1967, MA in Mass Communication, 1969; PhD in Natural Resources, U. Mich., 1983. With pub. rels. dept. ENJAY Chem. Co., N.Y.C., 1967-68, Corn Products Co. Internat., N.Y.C., 1968-69; dir. tourism Brevard County, Cocoa Beach, Fla., 1969-70; exec. dir. Fla. Defenders of Environ., 1970-73; teaching fellow U. Mich., Ann Arbor, 1973-76; dir. community rels. Tampa (Fla.) Gen. Hosp., 1977-79; prof. journalism and communications U. Tampa, 1980-87; prof. journalism and mass communication U. Fla., Gainesville, 1987-92; prof. communications Brigham Young U., Provo, Utah, 1992—. Contbr. numerous articles to profl. jours. and media publs., also chpts. to books; producer TV talk show and documentaries. Rackham fellow, 1975, Rockefeller Bros. Found. fellow, 1975-76. Fellow AAAS; mem. Pub. Rels. Soc. Am. (bd. dirs.), Assn. Educators in Journalism and Mass Comm., Soc. Environ Journalists, Women in Comm., Inc. Home: 1531 Dawn Dr Salt Lake City UT 84121-2819 Office: Brigham Young U Dept Communications HfAC # 509 Provo UT 84602-1026

VALENTINE, LYNNE CAROL, development researcher; b. Chgo., July 20, 1941; d. Carl Axel and Doris Lillian (Peterson) Anderson; m. David Matthew Valentine, May 25, 1973; 1 child, David. AB, Cornell Coll., 1963. Tchr. Milw. Sch. Sys., 1963-67, Glenview (Ill.) Sch. Sys., 1967-69; asst. editor Am. Field, Chgo., 1969-71; copy editor Avon Products Co., N.Y.C., 1971-73; v.p., bookkeeper Richmond (Va.) Ready-Mix Corp., 1981-83; devel. rsch. asst. U. Richmond, 1986—. Equipment dir. Robious Athletic Assn., Midlothian, Va., 1984-89. Mem. Assn. Profl. Researchers for Advancement (treas. 1995—). Republican. Presbyterian. Home: 100 Holdsworth Rd Williamsburg VA 23185 Office: Univ Richmond Maryland Hall Rm G 20C Richmond VA 23173

VALENTINE, NORAH ERIKA, program director, consultant; b. Buenos Aires, Argentina, May 30, 1942; came to U.S., 1968, permanent resident, 1976; d. Erich K. and Camila E. (Schmidt) Hornemann; m. James Valentine, Dec. 8, 1964 (div. June 1989); children: Charles Edward, Sylvia Esther. BS in Psychology, Atlantic Union Coll., 1994. Exec./bilingual sec. SDA Conf., Buenos Aires, Argentina, 1961-64; asst. to v.p. finance River Plate Coll., Entre Rios, Argentina, 1964-66; exec. sec. SDA Conf., Mendoza, Argentina, 1966-68; exec./bilingual sec. SDA Conf., New Hyde Park, N.Y., 1969-73; sec. modern lang. dept., asst. student fin. dept. Andrews U., Berrien Springs, Mich., 1973-76; collections mgr. Atlantic Union Coll., Lancaster, Mass., 1976-78; asst. dir. student accounts Atlantic Union Coll., 1978-81, payroll mgr., 1981-90, asst. dir. acad. records, 1990-96, dir. acad. records (registrar), 1996—. Mem. NAFE, NEACROA/AACRAO. Office: Atlantic Union Coll. PO Box 1000 South Lancaster MA 01561

VALENTINE, TARA E., preschool and special education educator, behavioral consultant; b. Chester, N.Y., Nov. 10, 1969. BA, N.C. State U., Raleigh, 1991; postgrad., Rutgers U. Presch. handicapped tchr. Allegro, Cedar Knolls, N.J., 1991-94, South Orange and Maplewood (N.J.) Sch. Dist., 1995-96; autism tchr. Douglass Devel. Ctr., New Brunswick, N.J., 1994-95; behavior cons., spl. educator for autistic children Andover, 1996—; in-home behavioral cons., parent trainer cons. Active U.S. Master Swimming, 1993—, N.Y.C. Marathon, 1995. Recipient 1st Place 1 Mile Swim award Seaside Heights (N.J.) Dept. Recreation, 1995. Mem. Coun. Exceptional Children, Autism Soc. Am. Home: 27 Deer Run Andover NJ 07821

VALENTINO, MARILYN JEAN, English language educator; b. Youngstown, Ohio, Oct. 28, 1951; d. Ralph A. and Beatrice A. (Capatosto) V.; m. Thomas N. Cizmar, Feb. 15, 1975. BA in English, Youngstown State U., 1973, MA in English, 1982; PhD in Rhetoric & Linguistics, Ind. (Pa.) U., 1992. Cert. in higher edn. adminstrn. Tchr. English Bacchus Marsh (Victoria, Australia) High Sch., 1975-77, Geoghegan Coll., Melbourne, Australia, 1977-79; asst. mgr. Silverdale Hotel, London, 1979-80; instr. English Youngstown (Ohio) State U., 1980-82; prof. Lorain County C.C., Elyria, Ohio, 1982—; interim dir. divsn. arts & humanities Lorain County C.C.; reviewer textbooks Harper, St. Martin's pubs., 1993-95; cons. East Ohio Gas Co., Cleve., 1992-95; bd. mem. Teaching English in the Two-Year Coll., 1995—. chair women in leadership Lorain County C.C., Elyria, 1988-95; scholastic challeng reader high sch. competitions, Elyria, 1993-95; vol. Habitat for Humanity, Oberlin, 1995. Recipient Tchr. Excellence award Nat. Inst. Staff and Orgnl. Devel., 1993, Women of Achievement Merit award Lorain County, 1994; Summer Study grantee NEH, 1995. Home: 86 Hickory Hollow Ct Amherst OH 44001 Office: Lorain County CC Elyria OH 44035

VALESKIE-HAMNER, GAIL YVONNE, information systems specialist; b. San Francisco, May 16, 1953; d. John Benjamin and Vera Caroline (Granstrand) Valeskie; m. David Bryan Hamner, May 21, 1983. Student, Music Conservatory, Valencia, Spain, 1973, U. Valencia, 1973; BA magna cum laude, Lone Mountain Coll., 1973, MA, 1976. Fgn. exchange broker trainee Fgn. Exchange Ltd., San Francisco, 1978-79; fgn. exchange remittance supr. Security Pacific Nat. Bank, San Francisco, 1979-81; exec. sec. Bank of Am., San Francisco, 1981-83, fgn. exchange ops. supr, 1983-84; word processing specialist Wolborg-Michelson, San Francisco, 1984-86; office mgr. U.S. Leasing Corp., San Francisco, 1986-88; cons. Valeskie Data/Word Processing, San Francisco, 1987-89, pres., 1989—. Soc. chmn., mem. mission edn. com. Luth. Women's Missionary League, Vallejo, Calif., 1986-94; vol. Luth. Braille Workers, Vallejo, 1987; organist Shepherd of Hills Luth. Ch., San Francisco, 1988—. Mem. NAFE, Profl. Assn. Secretarial Svcs. (pres. 1993—), Am. Guild Organists, Am. Choral Dirs. Assn.

VALETTE, REBECCA MARIANNE, Romance languages educator; b. N.Y.C., Dec. 21, 1938; d. Gerhard and Ruth Adelgunde (Bischoff) Loose; m. Jean-Paul Valette, Aug. 6, 1959; children: Jean-Michel, Nathalie, Pierre. BA, Mt. Holyoke Coll., 1959, LHD (hon.), 1974; PhD, U. Colo., 1963. Instr., examiner in French and German U. So. Fla., 1961-63; instr. NATO Def. Coll., Paris, 1963-64, Wellesley Coll., 1964-65; asst. prof. Romance Langs. Boston Coll., 1965-68, assoc., 1968-73, prof., 1973—; lectr., cons. fgn. lang. pedagogy; Fulbright sr. lectr., Germany, 1974; Am. Council on Edn. fellow in acad. adminstrn., 1976-77. Author: Modern Language Testing, 1967, rev. edit., 1977, French for Mastery, 1975, rev. edit., 1988, Contacts, 1976, rev. edit., 1993, C'est Comme Ça, 1978, rev. edit., 1986, Spanish for Mastery, 1980, rev. edit., 1989, 94, Album: Cuentos del Mundo Hispanico, 1984, rev. edit., 1992, French for Fluency, 1985, Situations, 1988, rev. edit., 1994, Discovering French, 1994, A votre tour, 1995; contbr. articles to fgn. lang. pedagogy and lit. publs. Decorated officer Palmes académiques (France). Mem. Modern Lang. Assn. (chmn. div. on teaching of lang. 1980-81), Am. Coun. on Teaching Fgn. Langs., Am. Assn. Tchrs. French (v.p. 1980-86, pres. 1992-94), Am. Assn. Tchrs. German, Phi Beta Kappa, Alpha Sigma Nu, Palmes Academiques. Home: 16 Mt Alvernia Rd Chestnut Hill MA 02167-1019 Office: Boston Coll Lyons 311 Chestnut Hill MA 02167

VALKENIER, ELIZABETH KRIDL, history educator, writer; b. Warsaw, Poland, Nov. 13, 1926; came to U.S., 1941; d. Manfred Edward and Halina (Meylert) Kridl; m. Robert Willem Valkenier, Dec. 7, 1951; 1 child, Lisa Kridl Valkenier Garcia. BA, Smith Coll., 1948; MA, Yale U., 1949; PhD, Columbia U., 1973. Rsch. assoc. Coun. on Fgn. Rels., N.Y.C., 1953-62; prof. Russian history Hunter Coll., CUNY, 1973-74; rsch. asst. European Inst., Columbia U., N.Y.C., 1962-72, asst. curator Russian archives, 1975-78, resident scholar Harriman Inst., 1981—, prof. polit. sci., 1982—; presenter internat. acad. confs., Iran, USSR, Russia, Poland, U.K., Germany, Italy, also others; lectr. USIA, India, Mex., Brazil, 1984, 85. Author: Russian Realist Art, State and Society, 1977, 2d edit., 1989, The Soviet Union and the Third World, 1983, 2d edit., 1985, Ilya Repin and the World of Russian Art, 1990; editor: The Wanderers. Masters of Russian Painting, 1991; also numerous articles on Soviet and Russian foreign policy and cultural history. Rsch. grantee Internat. Rsch. and Exchs. Bd., 1974-90, Nat. Coun. for Soviet and Eastern European Rsch., 1979-90, MacArthur Found., 1985-86. Mem. Am. Assn. for Advancement Slavic Studies, Mid-Atlantic Assn. Slavic Studies (pres. 1993-94), Polish Inst. Arts and Scis., Overseas Devel. Coun. Office: Columbia U Harriman Inst 420 W 118th St New York NY 10027

VALLA, TERESSA MARIE, artist, textile designer; b. Lynchburg, Va., Nov. 23, 1957; d. James J. and Mary Theresa (Hopkins) V. BS, U. Vt., 1979; student, Studio Art Sch. Aegean, Samos, Greece, 1987, Art Students League, 1986-89, Vt. Studio Ctr., 1991. vis. artist Carnegie Hall, N.Y.C., 1994; stage & prop designer Video-Pollack Meets Picasso, N.Y.C., 1993; freelance layout designer Ralph Lauren, N.Y.C., 1994; artist in residence Prague (Czeck Republic) Painters Workshop, 1994. Exhibitions include 80 Washington Square East Galleries, N.Y.C., 1990, Lincoln Ctr., N.Y.C., 1990, Glass Art Gallery, N.Y.C., 1991, Clocktower Gallery, N.Y.C., 1991, Home Contemporary Theater & Art, N.Y.C., 1991, Kampo Cultural Ctr., N.Y.C., 1991, Ape Gallery, N.Y.C., 1992, La Mama La Galleria, N.Y.C., 1992, Alleycat Gallery, N.Y.C., 1993, CBGB's 313 Gallery, N.Y.C., 1993, Tweed Gallery, 1993, Art Dirs. Club, N.Y.C., 1993, Gallery One Twenty Eight, N.Y.C., 1993, Westbeth Gallery, N.Y.C., 1993-94, Artist Space, N.Y.C., 1993, Tompkins Sq. Pk., N.Y.C., 1994-95, World Fin. Ctr., N.Y.C., 1994, Palacio Pombal, Lisbon, Portugal, 1994, 450 B'way Gallery, N.Y.C., 1995; permanent collections include Paterson (N.J.) Mus., Mid Hudson Arts & Sci. Ctr.; also pvt. collections. Vol. United Cerebral Palsy N.Y., 1980-81, Earth Day, N.Y.C., 1994-95. Recipient Ezra Jack Keats Meml. award, 1988-89; grantee Art Students League, 1987-88, E.D. Found., 1994. Mem. Women's Caucus Art, Orgn. Ind. Artists, Art Initiative. Home: 170 W 78th St #2B New York NY 10024

VALLAS POSNER, MARY, educator, researcher; b. Norwich, Conn., Sept. 19, 1927; d. John and Irene (Tsakiris) Vallas; married, Oct. 16, 1956; children: John Buck, Rebecca Posner, Bessina Posner Harrar. BA, Bennington Coll., 1966; MA, NYU, 1984, PhD, 1992. Cert. English tchr., Conn. English tchr. Waterford (Conn.) H.S., 1968-88; English adj. Three Rivers Cmty. Tech. Coll., Norwich, Conn., 1988—; presenter in field. Author poems. Fellowship Yale-Mellon Vis. Tchr., 1995-96, Bush Fellow, Yale U., 1995—, (assoc.) Morse Coll., Yale U., 1995—; scholarship Wesleyan Univ., 1976. Office: Three Rivers Cmty Tech Coll Mahan Dr Norwich CT 06360

VALLBONA, RIMA-GRETEL ROTHE, foreign language educator, writer; b. San Jose, Costa Rica, Mar. 15, 1931; d. Ferdinand Hermann and Emilia (Strassburger) Rothe; m. Carlos Vallbona, Dec. 26, 1956; children: Rima-Nuri, Carlos-Fernando, Maria-Teresa, Maria-Luisa. BA/BS, Colegio Superior de Senoritas, San Jose, 1948; diploma, U. Paris, 1953; diploma in Spanish Philology, U. Salamanca, Spain, 1954; MA, U. Costa Rica, 1962; D in Modern Langs., Middlebury Coll., 1981. Tchr. Liceo J.J. Vargas Calvo, Costa Rica, 1955-56; faculty U. St. Thomas, Houston, 1964-95, prof. Spanish, 1978-95, Cullen Found. prof. Spanish, 1989, head dept. Spanish, 1966-71, chmn. dept. modern fgn. lang., 1978-80, prof. emeritus, 1995—; vis. prof. U. Houston, 1975-76, Rice U., 1980-83, U. St. Thomas, Argentina, 1972, vis. prof. U. St. Thomas Merida program, 1987-95; vis. prof. Rice U. program in Spain, 1974. Author: Noche en Vela, 1968, Yolanda Oreamuno, 1972, La Obra en Prosa de Eunice Odio, 1981, Baraja de Soledades, Las Sombras que Perseguimos, 1983, Polvo del Camino, 1972, La Salamandra Rosada, 1979, Mujeres y Agonias, 1982, Cosecha de Pecadores, 1988, El arcangel del perdon, 1990, Mundo, demonio y mujer, 1991, Los infiernos de la mujer y algo mas, 1992, Vida i sucesos de la Monja Alférez, critical edition, 1992, Flowering Inferno-Tales of Sinking Hearts, 1994; mem. editorial bd. Letras Femeninas, Alba de America, U.S.; co-dir. Foro Literario, Uruguay, 1987-89; contbg. editor The Americas Review, 1989—; contbr. numerous articles and short stories to lit. mags. Mem. scholarship com. Inst. Hispanic Culture, 1978-79, 88, 91, chmn., 1979, bd. dirs., 1974-76, 88-89, 91-92, chmn. cultural activities, 1979, 80, 85, 88-89; bd. dirs. Houston Pub. Libr., 1984-86; bd. dirs. Cultural Arts Coun. of Houston, 1991-92. Recipient Aquileo J. Echeverria Novel prize, 1968, Agripina Montes del Valle Novel prize, 1978, Jorge Luis Borges Short Story prize, Argentina, 1977, Lit. award S.W. Conf. Latin Am. Studies, 1982; Constantin Found. grantee for rsch. U. St. Thomas, 1981; Ancora Lit. award, Costa Rica, 1984, Civil Merit award King Juan Carlos I of Spain, 1989. Mem. MLA, Am. Assn. Tchrs. Spanish and Portuguese, Houston Area Tchrs. of Fgn. Langs., South Cen. MLA, S.W. conf. Orgn. Latin Am. Studies, Latin Am. Studies Assn., Inst. Internat. de Lit. Iberoam., Latin Am. Writers Assn. of Costa Rica, Inst. Hispanic Culture of Houston, Casa Argentina de Houston, Inst. Lit. y Cultural Hispanico, Phi Sigma Iota, Sigma Delta Pi (hon.), Nat. Writers Assn. Roman Catholic. Home: 3706 Lake St Houston TX 77098-5522

VALLBONA-RAYNER, MARISA, public relations counselor; b. Houston, Tex., Jan. 2, 1964; d. Carlos and Rima (Rothe) Vallbona; m. Don R. Rayner Jr., July 12, 1986; children: Donald R. Rayner III, Timothy Carlos Rayner. Student, U. Colo., U. de Dijon, France; BS in Journalism, U. Tex. Account exec. Jae Stefan & Assocs., Austin, Tex., 1987-88; media rels. asst. America's Cup XXVII, 1988; sr. account exec. pub. rels. Berkman & Daniels, 1988-90; prin. Rayner & Vallbona Inc. Advt. & Pub. Rels., San Diego, 1990—. Editor: Flowering Inferno, 1994, Soldiers Cry By Night, 1994, Assumed Name, 1994, People on the Prowl, 1995; contbr. articles to profl. jours. Pub. rels. chair, bd. dirs. Women of St. James Episc. Ch., 1994, 1st v.p., 1995; mem. pub. affairs disaster task force ARC, 1993—; pub. rels. chair Sunkist Am. Cancer Soc. Cup Regatta, 1989; mem. elections mktg. task force City of San Diego, 1989. Mem. Pub. Rels Soc. Am. (accredited, San Diego chpt. chair accreditation com. 1994, dir.-at-large 1995, bd. dirs. 1996—), Am. Soc. Health Care Mktg. and Pub. Rels., Health Care Communicators San Diego (v.p., bd. dirs. 1994, sec. 1993, numerous awards), Pub. Rels. Club San Diego (exec. bd. dirs. 1991-92, various awards), Jr. League San Diego. Office: Rayner & Vallbona Inc 6961 Petit St San Diego CA 92111-3303

VALLE, ALICE WARREN, psychiatrist, educator; b. Refugio, Tex., May 21, 1944; d. Guy Emerson and Mabyl E. (Walker) Warren; m. Calixto C. Valle III, Apr. 13, 1968 (div. 1996); 1 child, Alissa Clair. Degree, U. Tex., 1966, U. Colo., 1970. Diplomate Am. Bd. Neurology and Psychiatry. Dir. Beaverbrook Child Guidance, Waltham, Mass., 1977-80; clin. instr. Harvard Med. Sch., Boston, 1985—; cons. psychiatrist Andover Newton Theol. Sch., Newton, Mass., 1985-95, Episcopal Diocese Mass., Boston, 1985—; staff psychiatrist Westwood (Mass.) Lodge Hosp., 1990-92; consulting child psychiatrist Boston Cmty. Svcs., 1992—. Deacon First Bapt. Ch., Newton, 1993-96, bd. trustees, 1996—. Mem. Am. Med. Women's Assn., Assn. Women Psychiatrists, New England Coun. Child and Adolescent Psychiatry (bd. dirs. 1992-94). Office: 63 Nathan Rd Newton Center MA 02159

VALLEE, JUDITH DELANEY, environmentalist, fundraiser; b. N.Y.C., Mar. 14, 1948; d. Victor and Sally Hammer; m. John Delaney, Apr. 9, 1974 (div. 1978); m. Henry Richard Vallee, May 15, 1987. BA, CUNY, 1976. Exec. dir. Save the Manatee Club, Maitland, Fla., 1985—; apptd. U.S. Manatee Recovery Plan Team, Jacksonville, Fla., 1988—, Fla. Manatee Tech. Adv. Coun., Tallahassee, 1989—, Save the Manatee Com., Orlando, Fla., 1985-92, World Conservation Union/Sirenia Specialist Group, Switzerland, 1996; advisor Save the Wildlife Inc., Chuluota, Fla., 1992-93; bd. dirs. Environ. Fund for Fla. Lobbyist Save the Manatee Club, 1989; vol. Broward County Audubon Soc., Ft. Lauderdale, 1983, 84, Wild Bird Care Ctr., Ft. Lauderdale, 1984. Recipient Refuge Support award Chassahowitzka Nat. Wildlife Refuge, 1989. Mem. Fla. Coalition for Peace and Justice, People for Ethical Treatment of Animals, Friends of the Wekiva River. Democrat.

Office: Save the Manatee Club Inc 500 N Maitland Ave Maitland FL 32751-4482

VALLEE, MARIE LYDIA, library media specialist; b. St. Charles, Mo., Aug. 15, 1948; d. Leroy William and Lillian Irene (Pollien) Strack; m. James L. Vallee, Aug. 2, 1969; children: David, Ken. BS in Edn., U. Mo., 1969; MLS, Kans. State Tchrs. Coll., 1973. Cert. K-12 sch. libr., Mo. Libr. Blue Springs (Mo.) Jr.-Sr. H.S., 1969-70; libr. Harrisonville (Mo.) Sr. H.S., 1970-94, libr. media specialist, 1994—; mem. Harrisonville Cass R-IX Schs. Long-Range Planning Core Team, 1994-95. V.p. Harrisonville Cmty. Tchrs. Assn., 1974-75, pres., 1975-76. Named Educator of Yr., Harrisonville C. of C., 1991. Mem. NEA, Mo. Edn. Assn., Harrisonville Edn. Assn., Mo. Assn. Sch. Librs., Beta Sigma Phi (Girl of Yr. award). Home: 105 S Price Ave Harrisonville MO 64701-2011 Office: Harrisonville Sr HS 1504 E Elm St Harrisonville MO 64701-2022

VALLERY, JANET ALANE, industrial hygienist; b. Lincoln, Nebr., Apr. 4, 1948; d. Gerald William and Lois Florence (Robertson) V.; BS, U. Nebr., Lincoln, 1970; diploma Bryan Meml. Sch. Med. Tech., Lincoln, 1971. Med. technologist Lincoln Gen. Hosp., 1971-72; congressional sec., 1973; lab. scientist Nebr. Dept. Health, 1973-79; sr. indsl. hygienist Nebr. Dept. Labor, 1979-85; indsl. hygienist U.S. Dept. Labor OSHA, 1985-89; indsl. hygienist VA Med. Ctr., Omaha, Nebr., 1989—. Mem. Am. Conf. Govt. Indsl. Hygienists, Am. Soc. Clin. Pathologists (assoc.), Arabian Horse Assn. Nebr., Nebr. Dressage Assn., Am. Indsl. Hygiene Assn., Am. Legion Aux. Republican. Methodist. Home: 4900 S 30th St Lincoln NE 68516-1603 Office: VA Med Ctr 4101 Woolworth Ave Omaha NE 68105-1850

VALLONE-BRAUN, VIRGINIA LEE, management consultant; b. Pasadena, Calif., Mar. 23, 1956; d. Jack H. and Betty J. (Garbutt) Brown; children: Kendra, Kelly; m. Gerry C. Braun, Sept. 23, 1995; children: Paul, Brittany. AA, Long Beach City Coll., 1982; BA, Azusa Pacific U., 1986, BS, 1995, MS, 1996. Real estate broker Bumpstead Realty, La Verne, Calif., Messang Realty, Covina, Calif., 1975-83; sr. sales exec., corp. trainer Remedy Employment Svc., San Juan Capistrano, Calif., 1983-89; br. mgr. Talent Tree, Upland, Calif., 1989-91; area mgr. Apple One Employment Svcs., Glendale, Calif., 1990-92; v.p. client svcs. Exec. Horizons, Newport Beach, Calif., 1992-93; sr. v.p., mng. prin. Right Assocs., Pasadena, Calif., 1994—. Mem. hospitality com. San Gabriel Valley Rep. Women, 1995. Mem. Pasadena C. of C. (mem. econ. com. 1994-95), Univ. Club of Pasadena (corp. mem. rep. 1995). Presbyterian. Office: Right Mgmt Cons 2 N Lake Ste 1030 Pasadena CA 91101

VALVO, BARBARA-ANN, lawyer, surgeon; b. Elizabeth, N.J., June 7, 1949; d. Robert Richad and Vera (Kovach) V. BA in Biology, Hofsta U., 1971; MD, Pa. State U., 1975; JD, Loyola Sch. Law, 1993. Diplomate Am. Bd. Surgery; Bar: La. 1993. Surg. intern Nassau County Med. Ctr., East Meadow, N.Y., 1975-76; resident gen. surgery Allentown-Sacred Heart Med. Ctr., Allentown, Pa., 1976-80; asst. chief surgery USPHS, New Orleans, 1980-81; pvt. practice gen. surgery New Orleans, 1981-89, pvt. practice law, 1995—. Upjohn scholar, 1975. Fellow ACS; mem. ABA, FBA, La. Bar Assn., La. Trial Lawyers Assn. Republican. Home and Office: PO Box 640217 Kenner LA 70064-0217

VALYO, JUDY ANN, dean; b. N.Y.C., Mar. 25, 1945; d. John Andrew and Josephine Theresa (Hricko) V. BA, Molloy Coll. for Women, 1967; MA, NYU, 1969; EdD, Columbia U., 1985. Cert. secondary edn. educator, social studies, N.Y. state. Residence hall dir. Hofstra U., Hempstead, N.Y., 1969-71, area coord., 1971-72; asst. dir. student activities Ramapo Coll., Mahwah, N.J., 1972-74, dir. student activities, 1974-76; dir. student activities Rockland C.C., Suffern, N.Y., 1976-81; assoc. dean students N.J. Inst. Tech., Newark, 1981-87, 88-89, acting dean of students, 1987-88, 89-90, dean freshman studies, 1990—; peer reviewer NSF, Washington, 1991, 93. Literacy vol. LVA-Englewood (N.J.) Pub. Libr., 1988-93; bd. dirs. YWCA of Hackensack, 1989-90. Grantee NSF, 1991-92, 92-94, 94-97. Mem. Bus. & Profl. Women (v.p. 1983-84, 94-95, pres. 1995—), Am. Soc. Engring. Edn., Am. Assn. Higher Edn., Women Engrs. Program Advocates Network. Office: NJ Inst Tech University Heights Newark NJ 07102

VAMVAKETIS, CAROLE, health services administrator; b. Bklyn., Mar. 1, 1943; d. William and Helen (Calacanis) Vamvaketis; 1 child, William. AA, Packer Collegiate Inst., Bklyn., 1962; BS, Columbia U., 1964; MA, Columbia Tchrs. Coll., 1969; AAS in Nursing, Rockland C.C., Suffern, N.Y., 1981; BSN, Dominican Coll., 1991. Tchr. elem. sch. A. Fantis Parochial Sch., 1964-67; tchr. Adelphi Acad., 1967-72, girls dean, 1968-72; nurse Nyack (N.Y.) Hosp., 1981-91; nurse mgr. Kings Harbor Care Ctr., 1991-93; assoc. dir. nursing Port Chester Nursing Home, 1993-94; CQI/edn. coord. Highbridge Woodycrest Ctr., 1994-95; profl. svcs. cons. Multicare Cos., Inc., Nanuet, N.Y., 1995—, personal svcs. cons., 1995-96, divsn. dir. clin. svcs., 1996—; asst. dir. of nursing, dir. staff devel. Beth Abraham Health Svcs., Bronx, N.Y., 1996—. Home: 102 Poplar St Nanuet NY 10954-2007

VAN ALLEN, BONNIE DOROTHY, sculptor, fishing boat captain; b. Washington, N.J., Oct. 21, 1939; d. Robert J. and Dorothy L. (Henry) Schilp; m. Pieter J. Van Allen, July 21, 1939 (dec. Sept. 1981); children: Sara Bertucchio, Amy Rockeller Rose, Ivey; m. Theodore Harless, May 8, 1983; children: Charles, David (dec.). BA, U. South Fla., 1981, BFA, 1984. Sculptor Van Allen Studios, N.Y.C. and Homosassa, Fla., 1981-95; capt. fishing boat Van Allen Fish, Homosassa, 1995—; lectr. on women in arts, 1985—. Exhibited in numerous mus., galleries, alternative spaces; sculptures commd. for comml. and pvt. individuals. Bd. dirs. Sun Coast Seabird Sanctuary, Indian Rocks, Fla., 1972—. Grantee Gottlieb Found., 1993, Krause Pub., 1993, Art in Gen. Panel, 1993.

VAN ALLEN, KATRINA FRANCES, painter; b. Phoenix, Ariz., Feb. 18, 1933; d. Benjamin Cecile Sherrill and Magdalen Mary (Thomas) Adams; m. Ray C. Bennett II, Dec. 31, 1950 (div. 1955); m. William Allen Van Allen, Mar. 15, 1963 (dec. Mar. 1971); m. Donovan Wyatt Jacobs, Apr. 22, 1972; children: Ray Crawford Bennett III, Sherri Lou Bennett Maraney. Student, Stanford U., 1950, 51, 52, Torrance C.C., 1962, 63; MA, U. Tabriz, Iran, 1978; studied with Martin Lubner, Jerold Burchman, John Lepper, L.A.; student, Otis Art Inst., Immaculate Heart Coll.; studied with Russa Graeme. Office mgr. H.P. Adams Constrn. Co., Yuma, Ariz., 1952-59; nurse Moss-Hathaway Med. Clin., Torrance, Calif., 1962-63; interviewer for various assns. N.Y.C., 1964-70; studied with the late Russa Graeme. Solo shows include: Zella 9 Gallery, London, 1972, Hambleton Gallery, Maiden Newton, Eng., 1974, Intercontinental Gallery, Teheran, Iran, 1976, USIA Gallery, Teheran, 1977, 78, Coos Art Mus., Coos Bay, Oreg., 1993; exhibited in group shows at La Cienega Gallery, L.A., 1970, 80, 81, 82, Design Ctr. Gallery, Tucson, 1985, Coos Art Mus., 1992, 93, 94, 95, 96; represented in permanent collections at Bankers Trust Bd. Rm., London, Mfrs. Hanover Bank, London, U. Iowa Med. Sch., Iowa City, Bank of Am., Leonard E. Blakesley Internat. Law Offices, Marina del Rey, Calif., and numerous pvt. collections. Bd. dirs. Inst. for Cancer and Leukemia Rsch., 1966-67, 68. Recipient Five City Tour and Honorarium, Iran Am. Soc., 1977, Most Improved player Ladies Golf Assn., 1995. Mem. Nat. Women in the Arts, L.A. Art Assn., Coos Bay Art Assn., Coos Bay Power Squadron, Lower Umpqu Flycasters. Home and Studio: 3693 Cape Arago Coos Bay OR 97420-9604

VAN ALSTYNE, JUDITH STURGES, English language educator, writer; b. Columbus, Ohio, June 9, 1934; d. Rexford Leland and Wilma Irene (Styan) Van A.; m. Dan C. Duckham (div. 1964); children: Kenton Leland, Jeffrey Clarke. BA, Miami U., Oxford, Ohio, 1956; MEd, Fla. Atlantic U., 1967. Sr. prof. Broward C.C., Ft. Lauderdale, Fla., 1967-88; ret., 1988; spl. asst. for women's affairs Broward C.C., 1972-88, dir. cmty. svcs., 1973-74, dir. cultural affairs, 1974-75; spkr., cons. Malaysian Coll., 1984; ednl. travel group tour guide, 1992—; v.p., ptnr. Downtown Travel Ctr., Ft. Lauderdale, Fla., 1993—. Author: Write It Right, 1980, Professional and Technical Writing Strategies, 3d edit., 1992; freelance writer travel articles; contbr. articles and poetry to profl. jours. Bd. dirs. Broward C.C. Found., Inc., 1973-89, Broward Friends of the Libr., 1994—, Broward Friends of Miami City Ballet, 1994—; active Sister Cities/People to People, Ft. Lauderdale, 1988—; docent Ft. Lauderdale Mus. Art, 1988—; officer Friends of Mus., Ft. Lauderdale, 1992—. Recipient award of achievement Soc. for Tech. Comm., 1986, award of distinction Fla. Soc. for Tech. Comm., 1986. Mem. English-Speaking Union (bd. dirs. 1984-89). Democrat. Episcopalian. Home: 1688 S Ocean Ln # 265 Fort Lauderdale FL 33316-3346

VAN ALTENA, ALICIA MORA, language educator; b. San Juan, Argentina, May 31, 1945; came to U.S., 1986; d. Francisco and Pilar (Garcia) Mora; m. William Foster van Altena, June 2, 1986. MA in Edn., Nat. U., San Juan, 1978. Prof. 2d lang. state colls. and high schs., San Juan, 1971-80; asst. prof. State U., San Juan, 1981-86; teaching asst. So. Conn. State U., New Haven, 1987-88; lectr. Yale U., New Haven, 1987-91, dir .beginners, 1992-94, lang. coord., 1993-94, sr. lectr., 1993—; bd. dirs. Fedn. of Tchrs. of English, Argentina, 1983-86. Mem. MLA. Roman Catholic. Home: 105 Swarthmore St Hamden CT 06517 Office: Yale U Yale Spanish Dept 82-90 Wall St New Haven CT 06520

VANALTENBURG, BETTY MARIE, lumber company executive; b. Tulsa, Dec. 27, 1963; d. Floyd Albert and Charolette Virginia (Quinton) V. BA in Comm., U. Tulsa, 1986. Adminstrv. supr. All Wood Products Co., Tulsa, 1986—. Bd. mem. Tulsa Oklahomans for Human Rights, 1987-89, interim pres., 1989; mem. host com. Names Project, 1990, 93, 95, co-chair ctrl. region logistics, Washington, 1996; bd. mem. Follies Revue, Inc., Tulsa, 1993—, v.p., 1994—. Mem. Order of Eastern Star (worthy matron Tulsa chpt. # 133 1995-96), Daughters of The Nile Zibiah Temple #102 (Princess Tirzah 1995-96, Princess Royal 1996—). Republican. Presbyterian.

VAN AMBURGH, (BRENDA) ELIZABETH, elementary and gifted education educator; b. Dallas, July 22, 1963; d. Sam Wheeler Jr. and Brenda B. (Brock) Folsom; m. Michael Betts Van Amburgh, Dec. 19, 1987; children: Rachel, Hannah. BA in English, U. Tex., Arlington, 1985, BA in Elem. Edn., 1985; MEd, Tex. Woman's U., 1990. Cert. in reading, early childhood edn., gifted edn., supervision and adminstrn., Tex. Tchr. kindergarten -4th grade Highlands Elem. Sch., Cedar Hill, Tex., 1985—; presenter in field. Author: TAAS Tutor in Reading, 1990, Have the HOTS for Reading!, 1991, TAAS Analogies, 1993. Mem. ASCD, Internat. Reading Assn., Tex. Assn. for Improvement of Reading, Phi Kappa Phi. Methodist. Home: 308 Breseman St Cedar Hill TX 75104-5008 Office: Highlands Elem Sch 131 Sims Dr Cedar Hill TX 75104

VAN ANTWERPEN, REGINA LANE, underwriter, insurance company executive; b. Milw., Aug. 16, 1939; d. Joseph F. Gagliano and Sophia B. (Johannik) Wolfe; widowed; children: Thomas II, Victoria. Student, U. Wis., Milw., 1954-57. Office mgr. Gardner Bender Inc., Milw., 1972-80; mfg. rep. Rosenbloom & Co., Chgo., 1980-81; spl. agt. Northwestern Mut. Life Equities Inc., Milw., 1981-88, registered rep., 1985-88; account rep. Fin. Instn. Mktg. Co., Milw., 1988-93; investment specialist Fimco Securities Group, Inc., Milw., 1993—; pres. Anvers Ltd., 1990—, 1990—. Author: (poetry) One More Time Its Christmas, 1978, True Friendship, 1979, Beautiful Brown Eyes, 1990 (award 1992). Mgr. Sch. Bd. Elections, Fox Point, 1969; v.p. Suburban Rep. Women's CLub, Milw., 1968-72; vol. tchr. St. Eugene Sch., Milw., 1968-72. Mem. AAUW, Milw. Life Underwriters, Women's Life Underwriters (v.p. 1982-83), Legis. Orgn. Life Underwriters, Nat. Assn. Securities Dealers (lic.), Investment Club (sec. 1989-90, pres. 1990—). Republican. Roman Catholic. Office: Fin Instn Mktg Co 111 E Kilbourn Ave Ste 1850 Milwaukee WI 53202-6611

VAN ARK, JOAN, actress; d. Carroll and Dorothy Jean (Hemenway) Van A.; m. John Marshall, Feb. 1, 1966; 1 child, Vanessa Jeanne. Student, Yale Sch. Drama. Appeared at Tyrone Guthrie Theatre, Washington Arena Stage, in London, on Broadway; performances include: (stage) Barefoot in the Park, 1965, School for Wives, 1971, Rules of the Game, 1974, Cyrano de Bergerac, Ring Round the Moon, A Little Night Music, 1994, Three Tall Women, 1995; (TV series) Temperatures Rising, 1972-73, We've Got Each Other, 1977-78, Dallas, 1978-81, Knots Landing, 1979-92 (also dir. episodes Letting Go, Hints and Evasions); (TV movies) The Judge and Jake Wyler, 1972, Big Rose, 1974, Shell Game, 1975, The Last Dinosaur, 1977, Red Flag, 1981, Shakedown on the Sunset Strip, 1988, My First Love, 1989, Murder at the PTA, 1990, To Cast a Shadow, 1990, Always Remember I Love You, 1990, Grand Central Murders, 1992, Tainted Blood, 1992, Someone's Watching, 1993, When the Darkman Calls, 1994; (TV miniseries) Testimony of Two Men, 1978; dir., star ABC-TV Afterschool Spl. Boys Will Be Boys, 1993. Recipient Theatre World award, 1970-71, L.A. Drama Critics Circle award, 1973, Outstanding Actress award Soap Opera Digest, 1986, 89. Mem. AFTRA, SAG, Actors Equity Assn., San Fernando Valley Track Club. Address: care William Morris Agy Inc 151 S El Camino Dr Beverly Hills CA 90212-2704 also: 1325 Avenue Of The Americas New York NY 10019-4702*

VANARNHEM, SYLVIA, elementary education educator; b. Atlanta, Oct. 18, 1949; d. Arthur J. and Eva L. (Sadowsky) Frey; m. John Charles VanArnhem, Sept. 4, 1971; children: Chad Matthew, Jay Bradley. BS in Edn., Bowling Green State U., 1971; MA in Edn., Cleve. State U., 1991. Tchr. elem. sch. Montgomery County Schs., Blacksburg, Va., 1972-79, Willoughby (Ohio) - Eastlake Schs., 1984—; leader student coun. Royalview Elem. Sch., Willowick, Ohio, 1987—, conflict mediation, 1988—, chair 4th grade, 1992—. Treas. Willowick Baseball League, 1986-92, coach, 1982-92. Named TV 8 Tchr. of Week, 1995; W-E Schs. Sci. grantee, 1989. Mem. NEA, Ohio Edn. Assn., Willoughby-Eastlake Tchrs. Assn. Republican. Lutheran. Home: 8470 Mansion Blvd Mentor OH 44060-4142 Office: Royalview Elem Sch 31500 Royalview Dr Willowick OH 44095-4256

VANARSDALE, DIANA CORT, social worker; b. N.Y.C., Oct. 27, 1934; d. Arthur and Augusta Deutsch; B.S., N.Y.U., 1955; M.S.W., Columbia U., 1957; m. Leonard Van Arsdale, Sept. 17, 1978; children by previous marriage—Hayley, Daniel. Clinician, Payne Whitney Clinic, N.Y. Hosp., N.Y.C., 1957-59, psychiat. clinic Jewish Bd. Guardians, N.Y.C., 1959-61; founder, pres. Big Six Towers Nursery Sch., N.Y.C., 1962-67; dir. intake and social service L.I. Consultation Center, Forest Hills, N.Y., 1966-84, clin. dir., coordinator clin. services, 1984-86; supr., faculty mem. L.I. Inst. Mental Health, 1973-86; cons. in social work Bergen Ctr. for Child Devel., 1981-87; dir. Seniors Option Service, Allendale, N.J., 1980-90. Author: Transitions A Woman's Guide to Successful Retirement, 1991. Mem. Nat. Assn. Social Workers, N.Y. Soc. Clin. Social Workers. Home: 47-30 61st St Woodside NY 11377-5763

VAN ARSDALE, STEPHANIE KAY LORENZ, cardiovascular clinical specialist, nursing educator, researcher; b. Butte, Mont., June 20, 1952; d. Hubert Nelson and Pauline Anna (Tebo) Lorenz; m. Roy Burbank Van Arsdale, June 18, 1978; children: Christopher, Erica. Diploma, St. Johns McNamara, Sch. Nursing, 1975; BSN cum laude, U. Utah, 1978, MSN, 1979; EdD, U. Ark., 1993. RN, Ark.; cert. ACLS instr., Am. Heart Assn.; cert. BLS instr.-trainer, Am. Heart Assn. Staff nurse cardiovascular surg. ICU Presbyn. Hosp. Ctr., Albuquerque, 1975-76; staff nurse surg. ICU and CCU U. Utah Med. Ctr., Salt Lake City, 1976-78; clin. specialist residency LDS Hosp., Salt Lake City, 1979; asst. prof. dept. Baccalaureate Nursing Ea. Ky. U., Richmond, 1980-84; staff nurse critical care unit Pattie A. Clay Hosp., Richmond, 1981-83; med. clinician Washington Regional Med. Ctr., Fayetteville, Ark., 1985; cardiovascular clin. specialist VA Med. Ctr., Fayetteville, 1985-93; assoc. prof. U. Memphis, 1993-96; asst. prof. U. Ark. for Med. Scis., Little Rock, 1996—; CPR instr. in cmty., Fayetteville and Richmond, 1980-93; mem. adj. faculty div. nursing Northeastern State U., Tahlequah, Okla., 1986-93, U. Ark., Fayetteville, 1989-93; mem. adj. clin. faculty U. Ark. for Med. Scis. Coll. Nursing, Little Rock, 1988-93; charter mem., spkr. N.W. Ark. Critical Care Consortium Area Health Edn. Ctr., Fayetteville, 1989-93; presenter in field. Contbr. articles to profl. jours. Coord., vol. Home Meals Delivery Program, Richmond, Ky., 1981-84; adminstrv. bd., Sunday sch. tchr., sec. adult forum Ctrl. United Meth. Ch., Fayetteville, 1986-87; troop leader Girl Scouts Am. NOARK Coun., Fayetteville, 1987-90; sound sys. operator Christ United Meth. Ch., 1993—. Recipient Nurse of Yr. award for excellence in nursing practice Dist. 9, Ark. State Nurses Assn., 1987; grantee Ctrl. U.S. Earthquake Consortium, 1993, U.S. Geologic Survey, 1994, Miss. Emergency Mgmt. Agy., 1996. Mem. ANA (v.p. Dist. 9 1985-86, pres. 1987-88, mem. image com. 1990-93, chmn. program com. 1986-87, state 2d v.p. 1988-90, clin. nurse specialist coun. 1991—), AACN (CCRN; bd. dirs., chpt. sec. program com. 1994—), Nat. League for Nursing (mem. nominating com. Ky. 1984-85), Sigma Theta Tau. Methodist. Home: 8872 Farmoor Rd Germantown TN 38139-6517 Office: U Ark for Med Scis Coll Nursing Slot 529 4301 W Markham St Little Rock AR 72205-7199

VAN ARSDEL, MARY MARGARET, actress, voice educator; b. Seattle, Sept. 5, 1953; d. Paul Parr and Rosemary (Thorstenson) Van A. BA magna cum laude, Bowdoin Coll., Brunswick, Maine, 1975; AA, Am. Acad. Dramatic Arts, N.Y.C., 1977. Asst. mng. dir. Theatre West, Inc., L.A., 1988-94, mng. dir., 1994-96; pvt. voice and speech tchr. L.A., 1996—; asst. head coach BC Cons., L.A., 1995—; mng. dir. emeritus Theatre West, 1993—. Actress: (play) Survival of the Heart, 1990, (film) In the Line of Fire, 1994, (TV) L.A. Law, 1994, (TV pilot) Heart Attack and Vine, 1996. Recipient Outstanding Performance award Dramalogue, L.A., 1990, 92, 93. Mem. AFTRA, Actor's Equity Assn., Screen Actors Guild, Women's Referral Svc., Pacific Resident Theatre Ensemble. Office: PO Box 361133 Los Angeles CA 90036

VANARSDEL, ROSEMARY THORSTENSON, English studies educator; b. Seattle, Sept. 1, 1926; d. Odin and Helen Catherine (McGregor) Thorstenson; m. Paul P. VanArsdel Jr., July 7, 1950 (dec. Jan. 1994); children: Mary M., Andrew P. BA, U. Wash., 1947, MA, 1948; PhD, Columbia U., 1961. Grad. tchg. asst. Columbia U., N.Y.C., 1948-50; acting instr. U. Wash., Seattle, 1961-63; asst. prof. U. Puget Sound, Tacoma, Wash., 1967-69; assoc. prof. U. Puget Sound, Tacoma, 1970-77, prof. English, 1977-87, disting. prof. emeritus, 1987—, dir. Writing Inst., 1976-86, dir. semester abroad, 1977, dir. Legal English program Sch. Law, 1973-77; vis. prof. Gonzaga U., Pacific Luth. U., Whitman Coll., Willamette U., 1977. Author: Victorian Periodicals: A Guide to Research, Vol. I, 1978, Vol. II, 1989, George Eliot: A Centenary Tribune, 1982, Victorian Periodicals and Victorian Society, 1994, Periodicals of Queen Victoria's Empire, An Exploration, 1996; mem. editl. bd. Wellesley Index for Victorian Periodicals, 1968-89; contbr. articles to profl. jours. Recipient Doris Bronson Morrill award Kappa Kappa Gamma, 1982, Disting. Alumnae award Broadway H.S., Seattle, 1991. Mem. MLA, Royal Soc. Lit., Oxford Bibliog. Soc., Nat. Coun. Tchrs. English (Achievement awards, dir. 1974-77), Rsch. Soc. for Victorian Periodicals (pres. 1981-83). Home: 4702 NE 39th St Seattle WA 98105-5205

VANAUKER, LANA LEE, recreational therapist, educator; b. Youngstown, Ohio, Sept. 19, 1949; d. William Marshall and Joanne Norma (Kimmel) Speece; m. Dwight Edward VanAuker, Mar. 16, 1969 (div. 1976); 1 child, Heidi. BS in Edn. cum laude, Kent (Ohio) State U., 1974; MS in Edn., Youngstown (Ohio) U., 1989. Cert. tchr., Ohio; nat. cert. activity cons. Phys. edn. instr. St. Joseph Sch., Campbell, Ohio, 1973-75; program dir. YWCA, Youngstown, 1975-85; exercise technician Youngstown State U., 1985-86; health educator Park Vista Retirement Ctr., Youngstown, 1986-87; sch. tchr. Salem (Ohio) City Sch., 1987-88; recreational therapist Trumbull Meml. Hosp., Warren, Ohio, 1988—; activity cons. Mahoning/Trumbull Nursing Homes, Warren, 1990-92; adv. bd. rep. Ohio State Bur. Health Promotion Phys. Fitness, 1996—; mem. adv. bd. Ohio State Executive Physical Fitness Dept. Health, 1996. Producer chair exercise sr. video Excercise is the Fountain of Youth, 1993; photographer, choreographer. Vol. Am. Cancer Soc., 1980—, Am. Heart Assn., 1986—, Dance for Heart, 1980-86; mem. State of Ohio Phys. Fitness Adv. Bd., 1996. Youngstown State U. scholar, 1986-89. Mem. AAHPERD, Youngstown Camera Club (social chair 1989-90, pres. 1993-95), Resident Activity Profl. Assn. (pres. 1994, 95, 96), Pa. Activity Profl. Assn., Kappa Delta Pi. Democrat. Presbyterian. Home: 385 N Broad St Canfield OH 44406-1256 Office: Trumbull Meml Hosp 1350 E Market St Warren OH 44483-6608

VAN BARON, JUDITH E., college administrator; b. Mankato, Minn., Dec. 2, 1942; d. William Henry and Grace Eloise (Gerth) Appel; m. Clayton Junior Gorder, Dec. 22, 1962 (div. 1973); 1 child, Erika Gorder; m. Thomas William McCabe, Nov. 10, 1978. AA, Waldorf Coll., 1962; BA, Luther Coll., 1963; MA, U. Iowa, 1969, PhD, 1973. Tchr. San Jose (Calif.) State U., 1976-77; exec. dir. Monmouth Mus., Lincroft, N.J., 1977-79; tchr. U.S. Mil. Acad. Prep. Sch., Ft. Monmouth, N.J., 1983-90; dir. Stefanotti Gallery, N.Y.C., 1979-82; v.p. acad. affairs Savannah (Ga.) Coll. Art and Design, 1992-96, v.p. external affairs, 1996—; Pres. N.Y. Art Critics Circle, N.Y.C., 1979-83; vis. com. Met. Mus. Art, N.Y.C., 1974-76; bicentennial adv. com. to Borough Pres. Robert Abrams, 1975-76. Exec. dir., curator Bronx (N.Y.) Mus. Arts, 1974-76; pres. Middletown (N.J.) Preservation Adv. Commn., 1982-83. Kress Found. fellow, 1971. Mem. AAUW, Nat. Coun. Art Adminstrs., Assn. Collegiate Schs. Arch., Coll. Art Assn., Nat. Assn. Women in Edn.

VAN BEVER, M. ANN, lawyer; b. Dayton, Ohio, Aug. 26, 1948; d. William Harry and Marjorie Leah (Swarts) H.; m. James Rives-Jones, Aug. 7, 1970 (div. 1977); 1 child, James R. Jones II; m. Peter J. van Bever, May 2, 1979; children: Eleanor, Claire. BM, So. Meth. U., 1970, MM, 1978; JD, Marquette U., 1983. Bar: Wis. 1983 Fla. 1984, Tex. 185, Calif. 1992, Oreg. 1994. Assoc. Paul, Landy, Beiley & Harper, Miami, 1983-85, Haynes and Boone, Dallas, 1985-91, Pulliam & Assocs., Newport Beach, Calif., 1992-93, Preston, Gates & Ellis, Portland, Oreg., 1994—; judicial intern to Wis. Supreme Ct. Judge, Marquette Law Sch., Milw., 1982-83; spkr. Tex. State Bar, 1989. Contbr. articles to profl. jours., chpt. to book. 1987—. Bd. dirs., sec. Miami (Fla.) Bach Soc., 1983-85; bd. dirs. Dallas Chamber Orch., 1989-91; vol. oboist First Presbyn. Ch., Portland, Oreg., 1993—, music com., 1994—. Mem. ABA (bankruptcy sect. 1985-91, 1995—), Am. Bankruptcy Inst. (task force on preferences, 1994—, unsecured trade creditors com. 1994—), Oregon State Bar (debtor-creditor sect. 1993—, speaker, 1994-95). Democrat. Presbyterian. Office: Preston Gates & Ellis 111 SW Fifth Ave Ste 3200 Portland OR 97204

VAN BLARICUM, AMY JOAN, perioperative nurse; b. Englewood, N.J., Sept. 23, 1963; d. Julius Herbert Jr. and Mildred Doris Van Blaricum. BSN, Widener U., Chester, Pa., 1987. RN, Pa.; cert. in chemotherapy adminstrn., venipuncture, 1987. Nurse med.-surg. unit Mercy Cath. Med. Ctr., Darby, Pa., 1987, nurse oncology unit, 1988, nurse operating room, 1989. Mem. Assn. Oper. Rm. Nurses (cert. oper. rm. nurse, 1992).

VAN BOGAERT, CYNTHIA A., lawyer. BS in Math., U. Wis., 1980, JD, 1982; postgrad., U. Chgo., 1990-93. Bar: Ill. 1985. Atty. U.S. Steel Corp., Pitts. and Dallas, Peoples Gas, Chgo., Inland Steel Industries, Inc., Chgo., Adminstrv. Mgmt. Group, Arlington Heights, Ill., 1994-96, Boardman, Suhr, Curry & Field, Madison, Wis., 1996—. Mem. WEB, Chgo. Bar Assn.

VAN BOOVEN, JUDY LEE, data processing manager; b. Kansas City, Mo., Oct. 26, 1952; d. Gene Warren and Jane Lewis (Wallace) Pulley; m. Cecil Carlin Van Booven, Aug. 19, 1972; children: Walter Matthew, Leia Christine, Kelly Diane, Matthew Carlin. Student, Cen. Mo. State U., Warrensburg, 1970-72; AAS, Penn Valley Community Coll., Kansas City, Mo., 1981; BS, William Jewell Coll., 1988. Bookkeeper Century Mills, Wilmington, N.C., 1972-73; acctg. clk. Forest Siding, North Kansas City, Mo., 1974-75, computer operator, 1975-77, programmer/ops. mgr., 1977-80; programmer/analyst Western Water Mgmt., Inc., North Kansas City, Mo., 1980-88, data processing mgr., 1989-94, mgr. info. and adminstrv. svcs., 1995—; freelance programmer Modern Window Co., North Kansas City, 1978-80, Forest Lumber, Oklahoma City, 1975-80, Kay-Dee Systems, North Kansas City, 1980-82; systems cons. Forest Siding, 1980-82. Author 1st place essay, North Kansas City Centennial, 1988. Founder, chmn. Children's Book Drive, Kansas City, 1983—; mem. parent adv. com. Gracemor Accelerated Sch., Kansas City, 1988-89, bd. dirs. PTA, 1989—, co-chmn. newsletter, 1989-91, 1st v.p., 1991-92, treas., 1992-93, sec., 1993—; asst. soccer coach Sherwood Soccer Club, GU10, 1991—, soccer coach GU8, 1991-93. Recipient scholarship Bus. and Profl. Women's Assn., 1970, Bd. Regents, Mo., 1970; Mgr. of Yr. award Western Water Mgmt., 1992. Mem. ABWA (treas. 1983-84, sec. 1985-87, named Woman of the Yr. 1986), NAFE, Phi Theta Kappa. Baptist. Home: 5143 N Richmond Ave Kansas City MO 64119-4063 Office: Western Water Mgmt Inc 1345 Taney St Kansas City MO 64116-4414

VAN BUREN, ABIGAIL (PAULINE FRIEDMAN PHILLIPS), columnist, author, writer, lecturer; b. Sioux City, Iowa, July 4, 1918; d. Abraham and Rebecca (Rushall) Friedman; m. Morton Phillips, July 2, 1939; children: Edward Jay, Jeanne. Student, Morningside Coll., Sioux City, 1936-39; Litt.D. (hon.), Morningside Coll., 1965; L.H.D. (hon.), U. Jacksonville, Fla., 1984. Vol. worker for causes of better mental health Nat. Found. Infantile Paralysis; tng. Gray Ladies, ARC, 1939-56; pres. Minn.-Wis. council B'nai B'rith Aux., 1945-49; columnist Dear Abby San Francisco Chronicle, 1956, McNaught Syndicate, 1956-74, Chgo. Tribune Syndicate, 1974-80, Universal Press Syndicate, 1980—; syndicated U.S., Brazil, Mex., Japan, Philippines, Fed. Republic Germany, India, Holland, Denmark, Can., Korea, Thailand, Italy, Hong Kong, Taiwan, Ireland, Saudi Arabia, Greece, France, Dominican Republic, P.R., Costa Rica, U.S. Virgin Islands, Bermuda, Guam; host radio program The Dear Abby Show, CBS, 1963-75; life-time cons. Group for Advancement Psychiatry, 1985—. Author: Dear Abby, 1957 (also translated into Japanese, Dutch, German, Spanish, Danish, Italian, Finnish), Dear Teen Ager, 1959, Dear Abby on Marriage, 1962, The Best of Dear Abby, 1981, reissued, 1989, Dear Abby on Planning Your Wedding, 1988, Where Were You When President Kennedy Was Shot?: Memories and Tributes to a Slain President as Told to Dear Abby, 1993. Mem. nat. adv. council on aging NIH, HEW, 1978-81; hon. chairwoman 1st Nat. Women's Conf. on Cancer, Am. Cancer Soc., Los Angeles, 1979; mem. public adv. council Center for Study Multiple Gestation, 1981; trustee, mem. adv. bd. Westside Community for Ind. Living, 1981; bd. dirs. Guthrie Theatre, Mpls., 1970-74; charter mem. Franz Alexander Research Found., Los Angeles; charter trustee Armand Hammer United World Coll. of Am. West; bd. dirs. Am. Fedn. for Aging Research Inc.; mem. nat. bd. Goodwill Industries, 1968-75; nat. chmn. Crippled Children Soc., 1962; founding mem. The Amazing Blue Ribbon 400; hon. chmn. Easter Seal campaign Nat. Soc. Crippled Children and Adults, Washington, 1963; del. to Democratic Nat. Conf. from Calif., 1964; Calif. del. White House Conf. on Children and Youth, 1974; non. life mem. Concern for Dying-Am. Ednl. Council; mem. White House Conf. on Physically Handicapped, 1976, NIH, 1976; mem. adv. council Suicide Prevention Ctr., Los Angeles, 1977; mem. com. on aging HHS, 1977-82; council sponsor Assn. Vol. Sterilization, 1981; mem. Women's Trusteeship, 1980; sponsor Mayo Found., Rochester, 1982; bd. dirs. Lupus Found. Am., 1983; mem. adv. com. Ams. for Substance Abuse Prevention, 1984; participant XIII Internat. Congress Gerontology, N.Y.C., 1985; mem. adv. bd. Young Writer's Contest Found., 1985; bd. dirs. Am. Found. for AIDS Research, 1985—; mem. adv. bd. Nat. Council for Children's Rights, Washington, 1988; mem. adv. bd. San Diego Hospice, 1990; mem. adv. bd. Rhonda Fleming Mann Clinic for Women's Comprehensive Care, 1991; mem. Scripps Rsch. Coun. Recipient Times Mother of Yr. award, Los Angeles, 1958; Golden Kidney award, Los Angeles, 1960; Sarah Coventry award, Miami, 1961; Woman of Yr. award Internat. Rotary Club, Rome, 1965; award NCCJ, St. Louis, 1968; award for disting. service to sightless Internat. Lions Club, Dallas, 1972; Disting. Service award Suicide Prevention Center, San Mateo, Calif., 1975; Good Samaritan award Salvation Army, San Francisco, 1970; Margaret Sanger award Nat. Planned Parenthood, 1974; award for outstanding services in mental health So. Psychiat. Assn., 1974; Robert T. Morse writer's award Am. Psychiat. Assn., 1977; Tex. Gov.'s award in recognition of exceptional service to youth of Am. for Ops. Peace of Mind, 1979; Humanitarian award Gay Acad. Union, Los Angeles, 1979, Braille Inst. So. Calif., 1981, Gay and Lesbian Community Services Ctr., 1984; pub. Awardness trophy for Living Will, Soc. for Right to Die, 1983; citation of commendation Simon Weisenthal Found., 1984; Internat. Image in Media award Gay Fathers Coalition, 1985; 1st ann. Woman of Yr. Humanitarian award Rainbow Guild of Amy Karen Children's Cancer Clinic, Cedars-Sinai Med. Ctr., Los Angeles, 1985; Pub. Service award Nat. Kidney Found., 1985, John Rock award Ctr. Population Options, 1986, Serve Am. award Ladies Auxiliary to the VFW, 1986, Genesis award Fund for Animals, 1986, Disting. Service award Inst. Studies Destructive Behavior and Suicide Prevention Ctr., 1986, Citizen of Yr. award Beverly Hills, Calif. C. of C., 1988, Humanitarian award Nat. Council on Alcoholism, 1988, Helen B. Taussig medal Internat. Socs. for the Right to Die with Dignity, 1988, Media award So. Psychiat. Soc., 1988; named Hon. Dir. Found. for Craniofacial Deformities, 1988; Disting. Achievement award Nat. Assn. to Advance Fat Acceptance, 1988, Hand to Hand award Episc. Charities San Francisco, 1989; Nat. Media award for print Nat. Down Syndrome Congress, 1991; Sec.'s award for excellence in communication HHS, 1992; Dove award Assn. Retarded Citizens, 1992. Mem. Women in Communications (hon.), Am. Coll. Psychiatrists (hon. life mem.), Nat. Council Jewish Women (hon. life mem.), Newspapers Features Council, Soc. Profl. Journalists, Nat. Orgn. Women, "Women For", Nat. Com. Preserve Social Security and Medicare, Korean War Vets. Assn. (hon.), Sigma Delta Chi. Office: Phillips-Van Buren Inc Ste 2710 1900 Avenue of the Stars Los Angeles CA 90067

VANBUREN, DENISE DORING, media relations executive; b. Troy, N.Y., May 15, 1961; d. James L. and Eunice A. (Myers) Doring; m. Steven Paul VanBuren, Apr. 1, 1989; children: Schuyler Paul, Troy James Doring, Brett Steven VanBuren. BA in Mass Comm. magna cum laude, St. Bonaventure U., 1983; postgrad., Mount St. Mary Coll. Reporter, news anchor Sta. WGNY-AM-FM, Newburgh, N.Y., 1984; news dir., anchor NewsCtr. 6, Dutchess County, N.Y., 1985-90; dir. media rels. Ctrl. Hudson Gas & Electric, Poughkeepsie, 1993—; bd. dirs. Gateway Industries, Beacon, N.Y. City councilwoman City of Beacon, 1992-93; pres. Beacon Hist. Soc., 1989-94. Recipient Salute to Women in Bus. & Industry award D.C. YWCA, 1990. Mem. Nat. Soc. DAR (Melzingah chpt., vice-regent 1990—). Republican. Roman Catholic. Home: 37 Deerfield Pl Beacon NY 12508-1514 Office: Ctrl Hudson Gas & Electric Corp 284 South Ave Poughkeepsie NY 12601-4838

VAN BUREN, M. KATHERINE, business analyst; b. Tachikawa, Tokyo, Japan, Oct. 19, 1966; arrived in U.S., 1968; d. James Charles and Mary Ann (Brown) Messinger; m. Robert George Van Buren, Sept. 24, 1994. BA in Psychology, St. John Fisher Coll., Rochester, N.Y., 1988; MSW, SUNY, Albany, 1990, MPA, 1994. Adj. instr. SUNY, Albany, 1992-93; sr. adminstrv. analyst N.Y. State Dept. Civil Svc., Albany, 1994-96; sr. bus. analyst Key Svcs. Corp., Albany, 1996—; grad. intern SUNY, Albany, 1989-94, dept. summer coord., 1993; with Americorp Program, Albany, 1995. Youth min., catechist, St. Mary's Ch., Crescent, N.Y., 1994—, Ch. of Christ the King, Guilderland, N.Y., 1992-94; active Ptnrs. in Learning, Phillip Schuylerl Elem. Sch., Albany, 1993-94. Mem. ASPA, NASW, Coll. Student Pers. Assn., Interdepartmental Com. on Electronic Data Processing, N.Y. State Forum for Info. Mgmt. Republican. Roman Catholic. Home: 37 Tekakwitha Ct Clifton Park NY 12065 Office: Key Svcs Corp 22 Corporate Woods Albany NY 12211

VAN BUREN, MARY LOU, retired religious organization administrator; b. Toledo, Feb. 1, 1929; d. Martin Clyde and Norma Adella (Speers) Van B. BA, DePauw U., 1951; MA in Religious Edn., Union Theol. Sem., Tchrs. Coll. Columbia U., 1952. Dir. Christian edn. Met. Meml. Meth. Ch., Washington, 1952-54, Bexley United Meth. Ch., Columbus, Ohio, 1954-68; exec. sec. women's divsn. Bd. Global Ministries United Meth. Ch., N.Y.C., 1968-89; program devel. Bd. Global Ministries, United Meth. Ch., N.Y.C., 1968-76; spiritual and theol. concerns, 1976-89; nat. chairperson Meth. Dirs. Christian Edn., 1963-65; mem. alumni coun. Union Theol. Sem., N.Y.C., 1969-72; bd. dirs. Scarritt-Bennett Laity Ctr., Nashville, 1988—. Author: (booklet) Retreats, An Introductory Manual, 1976, (with others) Spirituality in Ecumenical Perspective, 1993; contbr. articles to Response Mag. Recipient Alumna tribute Union Theol. Sem., 1992, Centennial Laity award in spiritual formation Scarritt-Bennett Ctr., 1992. Mem. Christian Educators Fellowship, Ecumenical Inst. Spirituality. Democrat. Home: 4831 Buck Hill Rd N Trumansburg NY 14886

VAN BUREN, PHYLLIS EILEEN, Spanish and Helger German language educator; b. Montevideo, Minn., June 4, 1947; d. Helge Thorfin and Alice Lillian (Johnsrud) Goulson; m. Barry Redmond Van Buren, Apr. 4, 1970; children: Priscila Victoria Princesa, Barry Redmond Barón. Student, Escuela de Bellas Artes, Guadalajara, Mex., 1968; BS, St. Cloud (Minn.) State U., 1969, MS, 1976; postgrad., Goethe Inst., Mannheim, West Germany, 1984, U. Costa Rica, 1989; PhD, The Union Inst., Cin., 1992. Instr. in Spanish Red Wing (Minn.) Pub. Schs., 1969-70; instr. in Spanish and German St. Cloud Pub. Schs., 1970-80; prof. foreign lang. edn., German and Spanish St. Cloud State U., 1975, 79—; advanced placement reader Ednl. Testing Svcs., Princeton, N.J., 1987—; translator in field; mem. Cen. State Adv. Bd. Contbr. articles to El Noticiero, Minn. Lang. Rev., Hispania; textbook reviewer. Coord. children's programs St. Cloud, 1970—; vol. ELS instr. St. Cloud Community, 1973—; reviewer St. Cloud Pub. Schs., 1985-89. Dept. Def. fellow, 1969, Goethe Inst. fellow, 1983; grantee N.W. Area Found., 1985-86, Bush Found., 1986, Fund for the Improvement of Post-secondary Edn./NEH, 1993—. Mem. AAUW (exec. bd. 1988-92, grantee Minn. Internat. AR 1992), ASCD, MLA, Am. Assn. Tchrs. Spanish and Portuguese, Am. Assn. Tchrs. German, Am. Coun. Tchg. Fgn. Langs. (tester 1989—), Minn. Coun. Tchg. Fgn. Langs. (exec. bd.), Phi Kappa Phi (pres.-elect 1991-92, pres. 1992-93), Sigma Delta Pi, Delta Kappa Gamma, Delta Phi Alpha. Republican. Lutheran. Home: 3001 County Rd # 146 Clearwater MN 55320-1405 Office: St Cloud State U 720 4th Ave S Saint Cloud MN 56301-4442

VANBURKALOW, ANASTASIA, retired geography educator; b. Buchanan, N.Y., Mar. 16, 1911; d. James Turley and Mabel Ritchie (Ramsay) VanB. BA, Hunter Coll., 1931; MA, Columbia U., 1933, PhD, 1944. Rsch. asst. in geomorphology Columbia U., N.Y.C., 1934-37; from tutor to prof. geography Hunter Coll. CUNY, 1938-45, 48-75; rsch. and editorial asst. Am. Geog. Soc., N.Y.C., 1945-48; prof. Hunter Coll. CUNY, 1961-75, prof. emeritus Hunter Coll., 1975—; cons. geologist E.I. DuPont deNemours & Co., Wilmington, Del., 1945-59. Editor: Megalopolis (Jean Gottman), 1961, Geol. Edn., 1954-56; contbg. editor Geog. Rev., 1949-72; contbr. articles to profl. jours.; composer hymns. Bd. dirs. United Meth. City Soc., N.Y.C., 1972—, Bethany Deaconess Soc., 1982—, N.Y. Deaconess Assn., 1984—, Five Points Mission, N.Y.C., 1979-89; trustee John Street United Meth. Ch., N.Y.C., 1972-84. Kemp fellow, 1937-38. Fellow AAAS, N.Y. Acad. Scis. (sec. geology sect. 1957-58), Geol. Soc. Am., Hymn Soc. of Am. (recording sec. 1974-80); mem. Assn. Am. Geographers, Am. Geophys. Union, Am. Guild Organists, Soc. Woman Geographers (mem. exec. com. 1978-80, 83-85), Phi Beta Kappa, Sigma Xi. Home: 160 E 95th St New York NY 10128-2511

VAN BUSKIRK, JILL, medical librarian; b. Detroit, Mar. 9, 1951; d. Lloyd H. and Ellamae Christian Van B.; m. Robert Skonieczny, June 12, 1983 (div. 1987). BS in English, Ea. Mich. U., 1974; MA in Library Science, U. Mich., 1982. Med. libr. St. Joseph Mercy Hosp., Mt. Clemens, Mich., 1983, Detroit Meml. Hosp., 1983; asst. libr. Henry Ford Hosp., Detroit, 1983-85; dir. med. libr. Mt. Carmel Mercy Hosp., Detroit, 1985-91; dir. libr. audiovisual svcs. Grace Hosp., Detroit, 1991—. Mem. Med. Libr. Assn., DMC Libr. and Info. Svcs. Network Librs., Mich. Health Scis. Librs. Assn., Met. Detroit Med. Librs. Assn., Spl. Libr. Assn. Home: La Chaumiere #7 1287 US 131 S Petoskey MI 49770 Office: No Mich Hosp Health Scis Libr 416 Connable Ave Petoskey MI 49770

VAN CALCAR, PAMELA MARGARETHA, chemistry researcher; b. Salem, Oreg., Nov. 19, 1969; d. John Cornelius and Verna Mae (Hudson) Van C. BS, Willamette U., 1992; postgrad., U. Calif., Davis, 1992—. Model Cinderella Models Agy., Salem, 1985-90. Poll worker Yolo County, Calif., 1995. Borge fellow U. Calif., 1992. Mem. Am. Chem. Soc., NOW. Democrat.

VAN CAMPEN, DYANA EMMA, photographer; b. Bronx, N.Y., July 4, 1961; d. Lambert Adrian Van Campen and Gloria Cecilia Cimo; m. Robert William Cramer, June 11, 1994; 1 child, Max Philip Van Campen-Cramer. Student, Parsons Sch. of Design, 1981-82; AAS in Comm. with honors, Rockland C.C., Suffern, N.Y., 1983; BFA in Graphic Design/Photography with honors, Pratt Inst., Bklyn., 1985. With dept. sales/pers. Sears Roebuck, Nanuet, N.Y., 1976-82; first asst. Sheldon Secunda Photography, N.Y.C., 1986-87; studio mgr. Jerry Abramowitz Photography, N.Y.C., 1987-89; primary photojournalist O Mag., Amsterdam, The Netherlands, 1989-90; freelance photographer New City, N.Y., 1990—; adj. instr. Rockland C.C., Suffern, 1986-87; photographer Uniphoto, Washington, 1995—. One woman shows include Rockland C.C., 1986, Caffeine Jones, New City, N.Y., 1995; exhibited in group shows at Bklyn. Mus., 1988, UN 4th World Conf. on Women, Beijing, 1995 (1st and 3rd Place awards Am. divsn., 2nd Place award European divsn.), Alan Sheppard Gallery, Piermont, N.Y., 1995, The Visual Club, N.Y.C., 1996. Keynote spkr. People for the Ethical Treatment of Animals, 1995; contbg. photographer Westchester People's Action Coalition, Peekskill, N.Y., 1996. St. Regis Paper Co. scholar, 1983; recipient 1st and 3rd Place awards Paul Keating Photography Competition, N.Y., 1984. Studio: 462 S Mountain Rd New City NY 10956

VAN CASPEL, VENITA WALKER, retired financial planner; b. Sweetwater, Okla.; d. Leonard Rankin and Ella Belle (Jarnagin) Walker; m. Lyttleton T. Harris IV, Dec. 26, 1987. Student, Duke, 1944-46; B.A., U. Colo., 1948, postgrad., 1949-51; postgrad., N.Y. Inst. Fin., 1962. CFP. Stockbroker Rauscher Pierce & Co., Houston, 1962-65, A.G. Edwards & Sons, Houston, 1965-68; founder, pres., owner Van Caspel & Co., Inc., Houston, 1968—, Van Caspel Wealth Mgmt.; owner, mgr. Van Caspel Planning Service, Van Caspel Advt. Agy.; sr. v.p. investments Raymond James and Assocs., 1987-95; ret., 1995; owner Diamond V Ranch; moderator PBS TV show The Money Makers and Profiles of Success, 1980; 1st women mem. Pacific Stock Exchange. Author: Money Dynamics, 1978, Money Dynamics of the 1980's, 1980, The Power of Money Dynamics, Money Dynamics for the 1990's, 1988; editor: Money Dynamics Letter. Bd. dirs. Horatio Alger Assn., Robert Schuller Ministries. Recipient Matrix award Theta Sigma Phi, 1969, Horatio Alger award for Disting. Americans, 1982, Disting. Woman's medal, Northwood Univ., 1988, Georgia Norlin award U. Colo. Alumni Assn., 1987. Mem. Internat. Assn. Fin. Planners, Inst. Cert. Fin. Planners, Phi Gamma Mu, Phi Beta Kappa. Methodist. Home: 4 Saddlewood Estates Dr Houston TX 77024 Office: 6524 San Felipe Rd Ste 102 Houston TX 77057

VANCE, BETH KUNTZ, lawyer, staff counsel; b. July 29, 1953; d. Donald C. and Karin Kuntz; m. B. Wayne Vance. AA, BA, U. Fla., 1975, JD, 1978. Bar: Fla., 1979, D.C., 1986; U.S. Supreme Ct., 1986. Asst. counsel Ho. Com. on Ways and Means, Washington, 1978-84, staff dir. sub-com. on oversight, 1985-94, minority staff counsel, 1995—. Mem. Delta Delta Delta, Fla. Blue Key, Omicron Delta Kappa. Office: House Com on Ways & Means 1106 Longworth House Office Washington DC 20515

VANCE, CYNTHIA ELAINE, accountant; b. Moorefield, W.Va., Nov. 15, 1965; d. Calvin Jack E. and Hazel P. (Funkhouser) Hose; m. Clifton W. Vance, May 21, 1988. BS in Acctg. and Econs., Shepherd Coll., 1988; MBA, Shenandoah U., 1995. CPA, Va. Staff acct. Yount, Hyde & Barbour, PC, Winchester, Va., 1988-90; comptr. Shenandoah U., Winchester, 1990—. Ella May Turner scholar, Elizabeth Wilson scholar, Supertane scholar, 1984-88, McMurran scholar, 1987. Mem. Nat. Assn. Coll. and Univ. Bus. Officers, Inst. Mgmt. Accts., Va. Soc. CPAs. Home: 41 Cardinal Dr Bunker Hill WV 25413

VANCE, CYNTHIA LYNN, psychology educator; b. Norwalk, Calif., Mar. 31, 1960; d. Dennis Keith and Donna Kay (Harryman) V. BS, U. Oreg., 1982; MS, U. Wis., Milw., 1987, PhD, 1991. Teaching asst. U. Wis., Milw., 1983-89; computer graphics mgr. Montgomery Media, Inc., Milw., 1987-92; asst. prof. Cardinal Stritch Coll., Milw., 1992-93, Piedmont Coll., Demorest, Ga., 1993—. Contbr. articles to profl. jours. Vol. Dunwoody (Ga.)-DeKalb Kiwanis Club, 1993—. Mem. AAUP, APA, Assn. Women in Psychology, S.E. Psychol. Assn., Am. Psychol. Soc., Am. Assn. Higher Edn. Office: Piedmont Coll PO Box 10 Demorest GA 30535-0010

VANCE, KATHERINE MCCORMICK, lawyer; b. Missoula, Mont., Nov. 30, 1953; d. John Thomas and Camilla Fox (McCormick) V.; m. Gordon Bruce Sewell, May 1, 1982; children: Grant Clement, Emily Anne. BA in Govt., St. Lawrence U., 1976; JD, U. Tulsa, 1979. Bar: Okla., 1979. Pvt. practice Tulsa, 1979-84; estate adminstr. U.S. Bankruptcy Ct., Ea. Dist. Okla., Okmulgee, 1984-87; asst. U.S. trustee U.S. Dept. Justice, Tulsa, 1987—. Mem. Okla. Bar Assn. (bd. dirs. bankruptcy sect. 1991—, Outstanding Dir. young lawyers divsn. 1989). Democrat. Episcopalian. Office: Office of US Trustee 114 S Boulder Rm 225 Tulsa OK 74103

VANCE, PATSY MORRIS, elementary school educator; b. Suffolk, Va., Nov. 14, 1951; d. Robert Graham and Mary Eure (Lilley) Morris; m. Donald Bernard Vance, Dec. 29, 1981; children: Donald Alexander, Nicholas Christian. BS in Home Econs., U. N.C., Greensboro, 1973, MS in Home Econs., 1978. Cert. tchr. K-3, secondary home econs., vocat. child care. Tchr. kindergarten Moore County Schs., Carthage, N.C., 1974; tchr. day care Mecklenburg County, Charlotte, N.C., 1974-76; tchg. grad. asst. U. N.C., Greensboro, 1977-78; instr. individual and family studies Kent (Ohio) State U., 1978-81; tchr. h.s. vocat. edn. Euclid (Ohio) City Schs., 1982-85, tchr. primary, 1985—. Named Martha Holden Jennings Found. scholar, 1993-94; recipient Golden Apple Achiever award Ashland Oil, 1993, Ohio Elem. Computer Contest winner WVIZ, 1993. Mem. NEA, PTA, Internat. Reading Assn., Ohio Edn. Assn., Euclid Tchrs. Assn., Ravenna Heritage Assn. Methodist. Office: Euclid City Schs 1455 E 260th St Euclid OH 44132

VANCE, PHOEBE AVALON, educator; b. Chattanooga, Tenn., May 27, 1949; d. Thomas Byrd and Ava Lee (McCullough) V. BS, U. Tenn., 1973, MS, 1974, EdD, 1978. Lic. profl. counselor, Tenn.; nat. cert. counselor; cert. cognitive-behavioral therapist, level 1 trained in eye movement desensitization and reprocessing. Securities broker Henderson, Few & Co., Knoxville, Tenn., 1978; owner, oper. Vance Furniture Co., Jasper, Tenn., 1980-88; mem. grad. faculty, asst. prof. U. Tenn., Chattanooga, 1989—; mem. career adv. bd. Stephens Coll., Columbia, Mo., 1993—; mem. srs. adv. bd. Chattanooga State Tech. C.C., 1992-94; spkr., presenter in field. Mem. AAUP, ACA, Tenn. Counseling Assn., Tenn. Assn. Marriage and Family Counselors (charter), Tenn. Assn. Counselor Edn. and Supervision (sec. 1993-95), Internat. Assn. Marriage and Family Therapists, Tenn. Mental Health Counselors Assn. Home: 6755 Hickory Brook Rd Chattanooga TN 37421-1773 Office: U Tenn Chattanooga 615 McCallie Ave Chattanooga TN 37403

VANCE, SARAH S., federal judge; b. 1950. BA, La. State Univ., 1971; JD, Tulane Univ., 1978. With Stone, Pigman, Walther, Wittmann & Hutchinson, New Orleans, 1978-94; dist. judge U.S. Dist. Ct. (La. ea. dist.), 5th cir., New Orleans, 1994—. Recipient Phi Beta Kappa Faculty Group award. Mem. ABA, Am. Law Inst., Fed. Judges Assn., Nat. Assn. Women Judges, La. State Bar Assn., Fed. Bar Assn., New Orleans Bar Assn., Bar Assn. of the Fed. Fifth Circuit, Order of Coif. Address: US Courthouse 500 Camp St Rm C-255 New Orleans LA 70130-3313

VANCE, ZINNA BARTH, artist, writer; b. Phila., Sept. 28, 1917; d. Carl Paul Rudolph Barth and Dorothy Ellice (Wilson) Hart; m. Nathan E. Curry (div. 1959); m. Samuel Therrel Vance, Dec. 2, 1960; children: Barry, Scott Hart. BS in Edn. summa cum laude, Southwestern U., Georgetown, Tex., 1965; MA in Communications, U. Tex., 1969. Cert. in teaching langs., Tex. Freelance writer various publs., 1946-56; assoc. editor, newspaper Canacao Clipper, Philippines, 1956-58; dir. Region One Tex. Fine Arts Assn., Austin, 1962-63; curricular cons. U. Tex. Curricular Conf., 1966; sec. Tex. Fgn. Langs. Assn., 1967; publicity dir. Burnet (Tex.) Creative Arts, 1983—; freelance portrait artist, Liberty Hill, Tex.; owner Gallery Zinna Portrait Studio, Liberty Hill, Tex., 1978—; artist registry Hill Country Arts Found., Ingram, Tex., 1984—; art columnist two newspapers Burnet, 1983—. Contbr. numerous articles to profl. jours.; exhibited in pvt. and corp. collections; illustrator children's books; numerous one-woman shows. Active Hill Country Arts Found., 1978—, Burnet Creative Arts, 1980—, Hill Country Council of Arts, 1986—. Named one of Tex. Emerging Artists, Hill Country Arts Found., 1985; featured as Cover Story Philippines Internat. mag., 1957, featured in book Artists of Texas, 1989, 94. Mem. Nat. Mus. Women in Arts (charter mem.), Nat. Portrait Inst., Alpha Chi, Phi Kappa Phi. Republican. Episcopalian. Home: 937CR323 Liberty Hill TX 78642-9501

VANCE-HUNT, FLORENCE (F. V. HUNT), former state official; b. Cleve.; d. Harold Alexander and Mathilda Emile (Vance) Hunt. BA in Sociology, St. Xavier Coll., Chgo., 1945; postgrad., U. Chgo., 1943, NYU, 1952-53. With Pharm. Advt. Assocs., N.Y.C., 1957; pharm. copywriter Wm. Douglas McAdams, 1958-59; dir. sta. promotion, pub. mcpl. broadcasting WNYC Radio & TV, N.Y.C., 1960-62; with N.Y.C. Commn. Human Rights, 1962-66; dir. communications N.Y. State Dept. Mental Hygiene, 1970-72; pub. rels. staff N.Y.C. Health Svc. Adminstrn., 1973-74; dir. pub. info. N.Y.C. Employment Tng. Planning Coun., 1976-83; developer spl. prog. initiatives N.Y. State Ct. System, N.Y.C., 1984-92; cons. C.A.P.S., N.Y.C., 1983-84; playwright-in-residence Northeastern U., Boston, 1973-75. Prodr. 12 plays off-off Broadway; prodr. (one act plays) Dough, 1992, Andrgyny, 1992 (full length plays) Bird in Flight, Some Family Values; one woman sculpture show Chgo. Art Inst., 1947, New Sch., N.Y.C., 1952; group shows include Guggenheim Mus., 1951-52; represented Lincoln Ctr. Play Collection, Heritage Collection, U. Wyo., O'Neill's Am. Playwrights series, 2 vols., Anthology Women in Am. Theatre, 2 vols.; reviews of plays in N.Y. Times, Village Voice, Time Mag., Herald Tribune, Boston, Playboy Mag., Daily News, Show Biz. Recipient Brotherhood award, Nat. Assn. Christians and Jews, 1962-65; Guggenheim grantee, 1951; Va. Ctr. for Arts fellow, Edward MacDowgal Colony fellow. Mem. Dramatist Guild, PEN Am., Authors League of Am. Democrat. Episcopalian.

VANCE SIEBRASSE, KATHY ANN, newspaper publishing executive; b. Kansas City, Kans., Oct. 28, 1954; d. Donald Herbert Vance and Barbara June (Boris) Vance-Young; m. Charles Richard Siebrasse, Mar. 8, 1980; 1 stepson, Michael; 1 child, Bradley. BS in Journalism, No. Ill. U., 1976. Reporter Des Plaines (Ill.) Suburban Times and Park Ridge Herald, 1974-75, DeKalb (Ill.) Daily Chronicle, 1976-78; stringer Rockford (Ill.) Register Star, 1978; editor The MidWeek Newspaper, DeKalb, 1978-81, owner and pub., 1982—. Active No. Ill. U. Found., 1992—, mem. exec. bd., 1994—, chair bus. and industry for No. Ill. U. campaign, 1993-94; pres. DeKalb Athletic Barb Boosters, 1995—; chair Kishwaukee Hosp. Health Coun., 1984-92, DeKalb County Partnership for a Substance Abuse Free Environment, 1990—; bd. dirs. DeKalb Edn. Found., sec., 1987-89, pres., 1989-93, active, 1987-94; sponsor Big Bros./Big Sisters Bowl-a-Thon. Recipient Comty. Svc. award Nat. Assn. of Advt. Pubs., 1980, Athena award Oldsmobile, DeKalb C. of C., 1990, Bus. of Yr., 1994. Mem. Ill. Press Assn., No. Ill. Newspaper Assn., Ind. Free Papers Am. (Cmty. Svc. award 1992-93), Free Papers Am., DeKalb County Farm Bur., DeKalb and Sycamore C. of C. (editor Sycamore newsletter 1994-96, mem. DeKalb Athena award com., bd. dirs., v.p. DeKalb 1996). Office: The MidWeek Newspaper 121 Industrial Dr De Kalb IL 60115-3931

VAN CLEEF, LISA BERNADETTE, software company executive, educator, consultant; b. Honolulu, Nov. 18, 1958; d. Ronald James and Mildred (Ortega) Van C.; m. Mark D. Quintana, Aug. 27, 1994. BA in Am. Lit., San Diego State U., 1981. Dir. creative svcs. Dolby Labs., San Francisco, 1984-89; dir. publicity and advt. Lucas Arts Entertainment, San Rafael, Calif., 1989-93; co-founder, v.p. comm. Big Top Prodns., San Francisco, 1994—; charter instr. multimedia studies dept. San Francisco State U., 1993—; comm. cons. Sony Picture Imageworks, Culver City, Calif., 1995, LucasFilm, San Rafael, Calif., 1996—; career cons. for young women and mktg. cons., San Francisco, 1994—. Nursery vol. Strybing Arboretum, San Francisco, 1995. Mem. NOW (media svcs. com. San Francisco 1988-94).

VAN CURA, JOYCE BENNETT, librarian; b. Madison, Wis., Mar. 25, 1944; d. Ralph Eugene and Florence Marie (Cramer) Bennett; m. E. Jay Van Cura, July 5, 1986. BA in Liberal Arts (scholar), Bradley U., 1966; MLS, U. Ill., 1971. Library asst. rsch. library Caterpillar Tractor Co., Peoria, Ill., 1966-67; reference librarian, instr. library tech. Ill. Central Coll., East Peoria, 1967-73; asst. prof. Sangamon State U. (U. Ill.-Springfield), Springfield, Ill., 1973-80, assoc. prof., 1980-86; head library ref. and info. svcs. dept. Ill. Inst. Tech., 1987-90; dir. Learning Resources Ctr. Morton Coll., 1990—; mem. leaders program Nat. Inst. for Leadership Devel., 1995; convenor Coun. II, Ill. Clearinghouse for Acad. Library Instrn., 1978; presentor 7th Ann. Conf. Acad. Library Instrn., 1977, Nat. Women's Studies Assn., 1983, others; participant Gt. Lakes Women's Studies Summer Inst., 1981, Nat. Inst. Leadership Devel. seminar, 1995. Dem. precinct Committeewoman, 1982-85. Pres., Springfield chpt. NOW, 1978-79. Ill. state scholar, 1962-66; recipient Am. Legion citizenship award, 1962; cert. of recognition Ill. Bicentennial Commn., 1974; invited Susan B. Anthony luncheon, 1978, 79, vice-moderator Fourth Presbyn. Women, 1989-90; elder Riverside (Ill.) Presbyn. Ch., 1992—; mem. adv. bd. Suburban Libr. System, 1992-94, Nat. Commn. Learning Resources; v.p. membership Riverside chpt. Lyric Opera Chgo., 1994-96; active Riverside (Ill.) Arts Ctr. Mem. ALA, Assn. Coll. and Rsch. Librs., Libr. Adminstrn. and Mgmt. Assn. (mem. reference and adult svcs. divsn.), Libr. Info. and Tech. Assn., Nat. Assn. Women in C.C., Ill. Library Assn. (presentor 1984) Ill. Assn. Coll. and Rsch. Libraries (bibliog. instrn. com.), Spl. Libraries Assn., No. Ill. Learning Resources Consortium Bd., Am. Mgmt. Assn., Women in Mgmt., AAUW (chmn. standing com. on women Springfield br., mem. com. on women Ill. state divsn., bd. dirs. Riverside br., 1992-94), Nat. Women's Studies Assn. (presentor 1983, 84, 85), No. Ill. Learning Resources Coop. (del. 1990—), Springfield Art Assn.,

Nat. Trust Historic Preservation, Beta Phi Mu. Reviewer Libr. Jour., Am. Reference Books Ann. Contbr. article in field to publ. Home: 181 Scottswood Rd Riverside IL 60546-2221 Office: Morton Coll Learning Resources Ctr 3801 S Central Ave Chicago IL 60650-4306

VANDEGRIFT DAVALA, L(ISA), artist; b. Norristown, Pa., June 29, 1952; m. Justin Knecht; 1 child, Gabriel. Student, Aegean Sch. of Fine Arts, Paros, Cyclades, Greece, 1972, Ecole de Mime Potash, Montpellier, France, 1973; BFA in Painting, Tyler Sch. of Art of Temple U., 1975. lectr. in field. One-woman shows include Cork (Ireland) Arts Soc. Gallery, Philip and Muriel Berman Mus. Art at Ursinus Coll., Collegeville, Pa., 1991-92, Frank Martin Gallery, Muhlenberg Coll., Allentown, Pa., 1993-94, Art On View Studios, Phila., 1995; exhibited in group shows at Gimpel Fils, London, 1984, 91, Ducal Palace, Am. Ambassador, Leningrad, 1984-87, Guinness Hop Store, Dublin, Ireland, 1986, Irish Visual Arts Found., Project Arts Ctr., Dublin, 1987, Crawford Mcpl. Art Gallery, Cork, 1987, Bank of Ireland, Dublin, 1988, Royal Hibernian Acad., Dublin, 1989, Schacht Fine Arts Ctr., Troy, N.Y., 1990, 92, Hist. Landmarks, Phila., 1993, Kamin Gallery, Van Pelt Libr., U. Pa., Phila., 1993, Phila. Art Alliance, 1996, Philip and Muriel Berman Mus. Art at Ursinus, Coll., 1996; represented in permanent collections Nat. Libr. Ireland, Dublin, Philip and Muriel Berman Mus. Art, Corp. Ins. Conss., King of Prussia; represented in pvt. collections in Eng., Greece, Ireland, Malaysia, Spain, U.S.A. Recipient award for Outstanding Contbn. to Architecture and Design, Young Environmentalists of Ireland, 1984, First prize Fenderesky Art Gallery, Belfast, 1987, Adolph & Esther Gottlieb Found., 1991. Mem. Internat. Assn. Artists UNESCO, Coll. Art Assn.

VANDEL, DIANA GEIS, management consultant; b. San Antonio, Apr. 2, 1947; d. John George and Elma Ruth (Triplett) Geis; m. Jerry Dean Vandel, Apr. 17, 1976; 1 child, Jeremy Kyle. MusB, U. Tex., 1969. Cert. tchr., Tex.; lic. nursing home adminstr., Tex. Tchr. music Zilker Elem. Pub. Sch., Austin, Tex., 1969-70, Isely Sch., Austin, 1986; asst. adminstr. Hillside Manor Nursing Home, Inc., San Antonio, 1970-76, cons. to nursing homes, 1976-78, asst. adminstr., 1978-79, cons. adminstr., 1979-91, adminstr., 1988; mgmt. cons. Promoting Excellence Consultation, Austin, 1991-95, Winning Solutions, Austin, 1995—; owner, facilitator creative music and relaxation in motion classes, workshops and retreats, San Antonio, 1982-84; fine arts facilitator Cedar Creek Elem. Sch., Austin, 1988-91; seminar leader Movement Spiritual Inner Awareness, Austin, 1986—, min., 1989—. Austin rep. Peace Theol. Sem., L.A., 1988-93; mem. exec. bd. Cedar Creek Booster Club, 1989-91. Mem. ASTD, NAFE, Inst. Individual and World Peace, Nat. Spkrs. Assn.-Heart of Tex., Austin Internat. Soc. for Performance Improvement, S.W. Facilitators' Network. Home: 916 Terrace Mountain Dr Austin TX 78746-2732 Office: Winning Solutions 916 Calithea Austin TX 78746-2732

VANDELL, DEBORAH LOWE, educational psychology educator; b. Bryan, Tex., June 5, 1949; d. Charles Ray and Janice (Durrett) Lowe; m. Kerry Dean Vandell, May 16, 1970; children: Colin Buckner, Ashley Elizabeth. AB, Rice U., 1971; EdM, Harvard U., 1972; PhD, Boston U., 1977. Tchr. Walpole (Mass.) Pub. Schs., 1972-73; rschr. Ralph Nader Congress Project, Washington, 1972; asst. prof. U. Tex., Dallas, 1976-81, assoc. prof., 1981-89; prof. ednl. psychology U. Wis., Madison, 1989—; vis. scholar MacArthur Rsch. Network, Cambridge, Mass., 1985-86, U. Calif., Berkeley, 1988-89; mem. steering com. NICHD Study of Early Child Care. Assoc. editor Child Devel., 1993-95; mem. editl. bd. Child Devel., 1980-93, Jour. Family Issues, 1983-89, Devel. Psychology, 1989-93; co-author books; contbr. articles to profl. jours. Bd. dirs. Infant Mental Helath Assn., 1988-89; bd. dirs. Cmty. Coord. Child Care, Madison, Wis., chair, 1991-93; mem. Day Care Adv. Bd., State of Wis.; mem. altar guild and vestry St. Andrew's Ch., 1992-95. Named Outstanding Young Scholar, Found. for Child Devel., 1982. Mem. Am. Psychol. Assn. (exec. com. div. 7 1985-88), Southwestern Soc. Rsch. in Human Devel. (pres. 1988-90), Am. Psychol. Soc., Soc. for Rsch. in Child Devel., Phi Beta Kappa. Episcopalian. Office: U Wis Dept Ednl Psychology 1025 W Johnson St Madison WI 53706-1706

VAN DEMARK, RUTH ELAINE, lawyer; b. Santa Fe, N. Mex., May 16, 1944; d. Robert Eugene and Bertha Marie (Thompson) Van D.; m. Leland Wilkinson, June 23, 1967; children: Anne Marie, Caroline Cook. AB, Vassar Coll., 1966; MTS, Harvard U., 1969; JD with honors, U. Conn., 1976. Bar: Conn. 1976, U.S. Dist. Ct. Conn. 1976, Ill. 1977, U.S. Dist. Ct. (no. dist.) Ill. 1977, U.S. Supreme Ct. 1983, U.S. Ct. Appeals (7th cir.) 1984. Instr. legal research and writing Loyola U. Sch. Law, Chgo., 1976-79; assoc. Wildman, Harrold, Allen & Dixon, Chgo., 1977-84, ptnr., 1985-94; prin. Law Offices of Ruth E. Van Demark, Chgo., 1995—; bd. dirs., sec. Systat, Inc., Evanston, Ill., 1984-94; mem. Ill. Supreme Ct. Rules com., 1996—. Assoc. editor Conn. Law Rev., 1975-76. Mem. adv. bd. Horizon Hospice, Chgo., 1978—; del.-at-large White House Conf. on Families, Los Angeles, 1980; mem. adv. bd. YWCA Battered Women's Shelter, Evanston, Ill., 1982-86; mem. alumni coun. Harvard Divinity Sch., 1988-91; vol. atty. Pro Bono Advocates, Chgo., 1982-92, bd. dirs. 1993—, chair devel. com., 1993; bd. dirs. Friends of Pro Bono Advocates Orgn., 1987-89, New Voice Prodns., 1984-86, Byrne Piven Theater Workshop, 1987-90; founder, bd. dirs. Friends of Battered Women and their Children, 1986-87; chair 175th Reunion Fund Harvard U. Div. Sch., 1992. Mem. ABA, Ill. Bar Assn., Conn. Bar Assn., Chgo. Bar Assn., Appellate Lawyers Assn. Ill. (bd. dirs. 1985-87, treas. 1989-90, sec. 1990-91, v.p. 1991-92, pres. 1992-93), Women's Bar Assn. Ill., Jr. League Evanston (chair State Pub. Affairs Com. 1987-88, Vol. of Yr. 1983-84). Clubs: Chgo. Vassar (pres. 1979-81), Cosmopolitan (N.Y.C.). Home: 1127 Asbury Ave Evanston IL 60202-1136

VAN DEN AKKER, KOOS, fashion designer; b. The Hague, Netherlands, Mar. 16, 1939; came to U.S., 1968, naturalized, 1982; Student, Royal Acad. Arts, The Hague, 1956-58, Ecole Guerre Lavigne, Paris, 1961. Apprentice designer Christian Dior Fashion House, Paris, 1963-65; freelance designer, est. custom fashion boutique The Hague, 1965-68; designer Eve Stillman lingerie co., N.Y.C., 1969-70; freelance designer, est. boutique, 1971—, freelance designer, est. showroom, 1978—. Works include: collaged fur coat range, Ben Kahn Furs, 1981—, handbag range, Meyers Manufacturing, 1986-88; couture lingerie collections, La Lingerie stores, 1987—; collaged upholstery furniture ranges James II Galleries, 1988—. Recipient Gold Coast award, 1978, Tommy award Am. Painted Fabrics Coun., 1982. Office: 215 W 10th St New York NY 10014-3203*

VANDEN HEUVEL, KATRINA, magazine editor; b. N.Y.C., Oct. 7, 1959; d. William Jacobus and Jean Babette (Stein) Vanden H.; m. Stephen F. Cohen, Dec. 4, 1988; 1 child, Nicola Anna. BA summa cum laude in Politics, Princeton U., 1982. Prodn. assoc. ABC Closeup Documentaries, 1982-83; asst. editor The Nation, N.Y.C., 1984-89, editor-at-large, 1989-93, acting editor-in-chief, 1994-95, editor-in-chief, 1995—; vis. journalist Moscow News, 1989; Moscow coord. Conf. Investigative Journalism After the Cold War, 1992; co-founder, co-editor Vyi i Myi, 1990—. Editor: The Nation, 1865-1990: Selections from the Independent Magazine of Politics and Culture, 1990; co-editor: Voices of Glasnost: Interviews with Gorbachev's Reformers, 1989; contbr. articles to newspapers. Recipient Maggie award Planned Parenthood Fedn. Am., 1994. Mem. Correctional Assn. N.Y. (dir.), Coun. Fgn. Rels., Inst. Policy Studies (trustee), Network of East-West Women (bd. advisors), Franklin and Eleanor Roosevelt Inst. (trustee), Moscow Ctr. for Gender Studies (mem. adv. com.), MSNBC (contbr.). Office: The Nation 72 Fifth Ave New York NY 10011

VAN DE PUTTE, LETICIA, pharmacist, state official; b. Tacoma, Dec. 6, 1954; d. Daniel and Isabel (Aguilar) San Miguel; m. Henry P. Van de Putte, Jr., Oct. 223, 1977; children: Nichole, Vanessa, Henry, Gregory, Isabella, Paul. Student, St. Mary's U., San Antonio, 1973-74, U. Houston, 1975, 76-77, U. Tex., 1979; cert. JFK sch. exec. program, Harvard U., 1993. Registered pharmacist, Tex. Supr. MHMR T. L. Vordenbaument and Assocs., San Antonio, 1971-82; pharmacist in charge Botica Guadalupana, San Antonio, 1982-85; owner Loma Park Pharmacy, San Antonio, 1985-95; panelist Eil Lilly & Co. Pham. Adv. Panel, 1989—. Mem. St. Joseph's Cath. Ch., 1977—; mem. YWCA, 1983—, bd. dirs., 1983-86; appointee City Coun. Commn. on Status of Women, San Antonio, 1985; sec. Mex.-Am. Legis. Caucus; mem. Tex. Ho. of Reps. Labor and Employment Commn., 1991-92, Human Svcs. Commn., 1991-94, Internat. Cultural Rels., 1993-94, Econ. Devel. Commn. and Juvenile Justice and Family Issues Commn., 1995—; mem. Alamo Area Coun. Govts., 1992—; chair Interagy. Child Abuse Network Com. Recipient Mother and Leader award LULAC, 1992, Mujeres Project award Mex.-Am. Unity Coun., 1992; Kellogg fellow Harvard/JFK Exec. Elected Ofcls. program, 1993; named Young Career Woman of Yr., Mex.-Am. Profl. Women's Club, 1983, Outstanding Women in Politics, San Antonio Express News, 1992, Tex. Assn. Regional Coun. award, 1995, Tex. Med. Assn. Medicine Best award, 1995. Mem. Market Sq. Assn. (sec. 1985-86), Tex. Pharm. Assn. (coun. mem. 1987-90, Pharmacist of Yr. 1996), Bexar County Pharm. Assn., Nat. Assn. Retail Druggists, Women of the Moose. Democrat. Office: 3718 Blanco Rd Ste 2 San Antonio TX 78212-1308

VANDERBEKE, PATRICIA K., architect; b. Detroit, Apr. 3, 1963; d. B. H. and Dolores I. VanderBeke. BS in Architecture, U. Mich., 1985, MArch, 1987. Registered architect, Ill. Archtl. intern Hobbs & Black, Assocs., Ann Arbor, Mich., 1984-86, Fry Assocs., Ann Arbor, 1988; architect Decker & Kemp Architecture/Urban Design, Chgo., 1989-92; prin., founder P. K. VanderBeke, Architect, Chgo., 1992—. Contbr. photographs and articles to Inland Architect mag.; contbr. photographs to AIA calendar. Chair recycling com. Lake Point Tower Condo. Assn., Chgo., 1990T, chair. ops. com., 1993. George S. Booth travelling fellow, 1992. Mem. AIA (1st place photog. contest award 1992, hon. mention 1994), Chgo. Archtl. Club. Office: P K VanderBeke Architect 505 N Lake Shore Dr Apt 808 Chicago IL 60611-3402

VANDERBOSCH, JANE MARIA, writer, activist; b. N.Y., Aug. 2, 1944; d. Joseph William and Catherine Theresa (Bykowska) V. Student, St. Joseph's Coll. for Women, Bklyn., 1962-65; BA in English, Cabrini Coll., 1967; MA in English, Monmouth Coll., 1970; PhD in Women's Studies, U. Iowa, 1980. Assoc. dean. Hartwick Coll., Oneonta, N.Y., 1970-71; social worker Dept. Pub. Welfare, Phila., 1971-73; rsch. asst. U. Iowa, Iowa City, 1974-78, teaching assoc., 1979-80; rsch. assoc. U. Wis., Madison, 1981-83; state dir. Wis. NOW, Madison, 1984-88; co-dir. Wis. Women's Network, Madison, 1989; exec. dir. The United: Madison's Gay, Lesbian, Bisexual and Transgender Agy. for Social Change, 1991-95; freelance writer lesbian issues, Madison, 1980—. Contbr. articles to books and poems to mags. Author articles to books. Home: 2814 Lakeland # 3 Madison WI 53704

VANDERGRAFF, DONNA JEAN, dietitian; b. Milw., Oct. 24, 1956; d. Wayne Eugene and Geraldine Louise (Brever) Zabler; m. Jess Lee Vandergraff, Oct. 11, 1980; children: Daniel Joseph, Joshua David. BS in Dietetics with distinction, Purdue U., 1978, MS in Nutrition, 1990. Registered dietitian. Clin. dietitian Logansport (Ind.) State Hosp., 1979-81, Ind. Vets.' Home, Lafayette, Ind., 1981-84; pvt. practice dietitian West Lafayette, Ind., 1984-90; rsch. asst. foods and nutrition Purdue U., West Lafayette, 1988-90, ext. foods and nutrition asst., 1990-93; acting coord. Expanded Food and Nutrition Edn. Program Purdue U.Food and Nutrition Edn. Program, West Lafayette, 1993-94, coord. Expanded Food and Nutrition Edn. Program, 1994—; cons. dietitian Woodland Manor Nursing Ctr., Attica, Ind., 1985-88; presenter in field. Author: (brochures) Food, Dietary Fiber and You, 1989, Diabetes, Food and You, 1990; co-author: Have a Healthy Baby, 1991, Money Management, 1993. Mem. com. bd. western region Am. Heart Assn., Lafayette, 1985-88; youth advisor Covenant Presbyn. Ch., West Lafayette, 1980-89; active Interagy. Coun. Community Health Edn., Lafayette, 1984-88; mem. Concerned Women for Am., 1985—; pub. rels. com. Greater Lafayette and Tippecanoe County Interagy. Coun. for Community Health Edn., 1984-85, mem. health at worksite com., 1985; weight reduction group leader West Lafayette Parks and Recreation Dept., 1985, YWCA, 1985. Named Outstanding Young Woman of Am., 1984, 86; Lute Troutt fellow Ind. Dietetic Assn., 1989; recipient Mary Hebenstreit Meml. award Ind. Dietetic Assn., 1988; named Recognized Young Dietitian of Yr., Ind. Dietetic Assn., 1987, Epsilon Sigma Phi team award 1996. Mem. APHA, Nat. Perinatal Assn., Am. Dietetic Assn., Soc. for Nutrition Edn., Ind. Dietetic Assn. (chmn. coun. on practice 1987, nominating chmn. 1987-88, continuing edn. chmn. 1988-91, sec. 1991-93), Western Ind. Dist. Dietetic Assn. (co-chmn. cmty. dietetics, chmn. pub. rels., pres. 1983-84, spkrs. bur. chmn. 1985-87, cmty. dietetics chmn. 1987-92, career guidance 1994—), Healthy Mothers, Health Babies Coalition (bd. dirs., breastfeeding task force), Purdue Alumni Assn., Gamma Phi Beta, Gamma Sigma Delta, Kappa Omicron Nu. Republican. Presbyterian. Home: 854 N Salisbury St West Lafayette IN 47906-2764 Office: Purdue Univ Dept Foods and Nutrition 1264 Stone Hall West Lafayette IN 47907-1264

VANDERGRIFF, CHRISTINA RAI, controller; b. Prineville, Oreg., Nov. 13, 1964; d. Marvin Ronald and Virginia Lucille (Warren) Craig; m. Kenneth Wayne Vandergriff, Aug. 23, 1987. Cert. legal adminstrn. with honors, Trend Coll., Eugene, Oreg., 1989; BA in Acctg., Morrison Coll., Reno, Nev., 1996; Assoc. Bus. Adminstrn. in Bus. Mgmt., B of Bus. Adminstr. in Acctg. Shipper, asst. loan processor Centennial Mortgage Co., Inc., Eugene, 1989-90; asst. acct. Kimwood Corp., Cottage Grove, Oreg., 1990-91; sec., asst. Bill Vollendorff Appraisal, Walla Walla, Wash., 1991-92; inventory supr., purchaser Sierra Office Concepts/Nev. Copy Systems, Reno, 1992-95, mem. employee adv. com., 1993-94; with Tahoe Office Sys. Nev. Copy Sys., Tahoe City, Calif., 1995-96; asst. adminstrn., asst. contr. Interstate Safety and Supply, Inc., Sparks, Nev., 1996—. Active Adopt-A-Sch. Program, Reno, 1992;-co-sponsor Nev. Women's Fund, Reno, 1993. Democrat. Baptist. Office: Interstate Safety and Supply 901 Meredith Way Sparks NV 89431

VANDERGRIFF, SUSAN ELLEN, special education educator; b. Bklyn., June 10, 1951; d. Rudolph and Estelle (Gruber) Schiffman; m. John Oliver Vandergriff, Apr. 2, 1977; children: Remington Wyatt; stepchildren: Debbie, Denita, John, Jim. AA, Kingsboro C.C., Bklyn., 1971; BA in Psychology, CUNY, 1974; MEd, U. Ariz., 1981. Cert. tchr. Ariz., Mo. Presch. tchr. Children's Learning Ctr., Bklyn., 1974-75; remedial math. tchr. Laquey (Mo.) Elem. Sch., 1977-80; spl. edn. tchr. Tucson United Sch. Dist., 1982—. Mem. NEA, Coun. for Exceptional Children, Tucson Area Reading Coun., Learning Disability Assn. Office: Naylor Mid Sch 1701 S Columbus Blvd Tucson AZ 85711-5617

VAN DER HAER, PAULINE, real estate developer; b. Liverpool, England, Feb. 5, 1960; came to U.S., 1979; d. Gerald Van der H. and Margaret (Harry) Williams; m. Stan T. Foster, July 7, 1979 (div. Dec. 1986). Student, Childwall Hall Coll., 1976-79. Store mgr. U.S. Splty. Retailing Corp., Florence, Ky., 1982-84; regional salon mgr. Samoken Head, Inc., Dayton, Ohio, 1984-85; sales assoc. Levitz Furniture Corp., Cin., 1986-90; v.p. The Braddock Group, Inc., Cin., 1990—; ptnr. Dorian Devel., Cin., 1990—; cmty. adv. coun. Soc. Nat. Bank, Cin., 1996—; bd. dirs. Archtl. Found., Cin. Pres. Mt. Auburn Cmty. Coun., Cin., 1992-96; chair Neighborhood Advocacy Group, Cin., 1992—; mdm. Hamilton County Cmty. Corrections Adv. Partnership, Cin., 1994-96; bd. dirs. Invest in Neighborhoods, Cin., 1994—, Downtown Cin., Inc., 1995—. Recipient Cert. of Achievement Cin. Art Mus., 1994. Mem. Nat. Womens Polit. Caucus, Internat. Platform Assn., Urban Land Inst., Over the Rhine C. of C., Lincoln-Douglas Rep. Club. Office: Dorian Devel 2065 Francis Ln Cincinnati OH 45206

VANDERHEYDEN, MIRNA-MAR, resort management and services executive; b. Freeport, Ill., Oct. 8, 1932; d. Orville Ray and Frances Elmira (Miller) Van Brocklin; m. Roger Eugene Vanderheyden, Dec. 23, 1950 (div. 1983); children: Romayne Lee, Adana Dawn, Grayling Dwayne, Willow B., Tiffany LaMarr. Cert., Brown's Bus. Coll., Freeport, Ill., 1949; BA, Milliken U., 1953. Paralegal various locations, 1953-93; pres. Carlin Bay Corp., Coeur d'Alene, Idaho, 1981—. Lobbyist PTA, Springfield, Ill., 1972. Home and Office: 609 W Apple Dr Delta CO 81416-3062

VANDERHOOF, ANGELA ZEGARELLI, social services organization administrator; b. Utica, N.Y., Sept. 27, 1935; d. Vincent and Josephine (Arcuri) Zegarelli; m. Thomas Edmond VanDerhoof, Apr. 11, 1959; children: Thomas Scott, Rebecca Anne, Heidi Kathleen. BS, Alfred (N.Y.) U., 1957. Tchr. Utica (N.Y.) City Schs., 1957-67; exec. dir. Epilepsy Found., Utica, 1975-79, ARC of Oneida County, Utica, 1979—; bd. mem. Aging Mental Retardation/Developmental Disabilities Found., Utica, Oneida County Office for Aging, Sr. Svcs. of Utica, State Aging Adv. Coun., Albany, N.Y. Mem. Cmty. Svcs. Bd., Utica; mem. bd. Utica United Way, 1995. Recipient Athena award, Utica C. of C., 1993; named Woman of Yr., Beta Sigma Phi, 1977-78, Human Svcs. Woman of Yr., YWCA, 1992, Woman of Merit, Human Svcs. Mohawk Valley Women's History Project, 1988. Mem. Utica Rotary (chair sr. citizens com. 1995-96). Office: The ARC of Oneida County 14 Arnold Ave Utica NY 13502

VANDER HORST, KATHLEEN PURCELL, nonprofit association administrator; b. Glen Rock, N.J., Jan. 15, 1945; d. Thomas Ralph and Elizabeth Jeanne (Burnett) Purcell; m. John Vander Horst Jr., Feb. 12, 1972 (div. Oct. 1993). Dir. devel. svcs. Johns Hopkins U., Balt., 1968-71; dir. devel. Union of Colls. of Art, Kansas City, Mo., 1971-72; dir. pub. rels. Md. Ballet and Ctr. Stage, Balt., 1973-76; dir. program devel. Joint Ctr. for Polit. and Econ. Studies, Washington, 1976-90, v.p. for program devel., 1990—. Dir., chmn. fin. com. Roland Park Community Found., Balt., 1990—. Office: Joint Ctr for Polit & Econ 1090 Vermont Ave NW Washington DC 20005-4905

VANDERKOLK, MARY DEDECKER, nursing educator; b. Highland Park, Mich., Feb. 7, 1951; d. Frank Joseph and Jean Marie (Halmich) DeDecker; m. Michael Homer VanderKolk, June 18, 1977; children: Lauren, Christopher, Nicole, Allison. BS in Psychology, Mich. State U., 1972, BSN, 1975; MSN, Wayne State U., 1980, postgrad., 1989—; MBA, Lake Superior State U., 1993. Nurse externe E.W. Sparrow Hosp., Lansing, Mich., 1974-75, charge nurse gen. surgery unit, 1975-76, staff nurse ICU, 1976-77; staff nurse SICU Catherine McCauley Health Ctr., Ann Arbor, Mich., 1977-81, summer 1982; asst. prof. Ea. Mich. U., Ypsilanti, 1981-84; mem. contingency staff ICU Munson Med. Ctr., Traverse City, Mich., 1984-85; lead instr. advanced med./surg. nursing Northwestern Mich. Coll., Traverse City, 1985-87, dept. head nursing, 1987—; nurse expert witness Robison, Curphey & O'Connell, Toledo, 1989-94; mem. adj. fcculty MSN program Grand Valley State U., Grand Rapids, Mich., 1991; com. mem. devel. coun. Munson Med. Ctr., 1992-93; sec./treas. Rural Emergency Med. Edn. Consortium, Traverse City, 1993-95, bd. dirs., 1993—. Co-author: Adoption Without Fear, 1989; co-author, co-prodr. (video) Tracheostomy Care and Suctioning Techniques, 1984. Coord. health edn. team Immaculate Conception Ch., Traverse City, 1994-95, mem. adv. com. health ministry, 1994—. Recipient Excellence in Teaching award Nat. Inst. Staff & Orgnl. Devel., 1993. Mem. ANA, Nat. League Nursing, Mich. Nurses Assn. (mem. cabinet adminstrn. and edn., rep. at large bd. dirs. 1987-89, 89-91, rec. sec. 1988-89), Mich. Coun. Nursing Edn. Adminstrs. (corr. sec. bd. dirs. 1988-89, 89-90, v.p./pres. elect 1990-91, pres. 1991-92, immediate past pres. 1992-93), Mich. League Nursing (dir. area V 1994-96), County Med. Soc. Aux., Sigma Theta Tau. Office: Northwestern Mich Coll 1701 E Front St Traverse City MI 49686

VANDERLIP, ELIN BREKKE, philanthropic executive; b. Oslo, Norway, June 7, 1919; came to the U.S., 1934; m. Kelvin Cox, Nov., 1946 (dec. 1956); children: Kelvin Jr., Narcissa, Henrik and Katrina (twins). With Norwegian Embassy, Washington, Norwegian Fgn. Ministry, London, 1941-44, Red Cross, Calcutta, India; pres. Friends of French Art, Portuguese Bend, Calif.; sponsor of charity art conservation fundraising events Friends of French Art; tour leader Ile de France, Anjou, Bordelais, Provence-Cote d'Azur, Alsace, Dordogne, Lyonnais-Isere, Brittany, Burgundy, Normandy, Languedoc, Loire, Gascony, Le Nord, Charente and Champagne Eure et Loire, 1978-96. Decorated Comdr. Order of Arts and Letters (France). Home and Office: Villa Narcissa 100 Vanderlip Dr Rancho Palos Verdes CA 90275

VANDERLOOP, MARY KATHRYN, mental health therpist, coordinator; b. Mpls., May 16, 1965; d. George Anthony and Kathleen Mary (Driscoll) VanderLoop. BS in Vocat. Rehab., U. Wis. Stout, Menominee, Wis., 1987; MA in Counseling Psychology, St. Mary's U., Mpls., 1995. Resident supr. Homeword Bound, Inc., Bklyn. Park, Minn., 1984-91; comty. integration specialist Rise Inc, Coon Rapids, Minn., 1990-92; program coord. Mt. Olivet Rolling Acres, Excelsior, Minn., 1992—; mental health therapist The Village Family Svc. Ctr., Elk River, Minn., 1996—; personal care worker At Home Ltd., Mpls., 1996. Activist The Take Back the Night Annual March, 1990—, Marches for Equality, 1993, 95; vol. counselor Sexual Violence Ctr., Mpls., 1992-95. Mem. NOW, Minn. Women Psychologists.

VANDERPOOL, NANCY MARSTON, university dean; b. Portland, Oreg., Mar. 9, 1936; d. Karl M. and Margaret (Sherrell) Marston; m. Richard C. Vanderpool, Dec. 27, 1959; children: Franklin Karl, Ann Margaret. BA in English Lit., U. Oreg., 1958; MA in Student Pers., Syracuse U., 1960; PhD in Coll. Student Pers. Adminstrn., Oreg. State U., 1987. City recreation dir. City of Arlington, Oreg., summer 1959; residence hall counselor, house head resident Syracuse U., 1958-60; asst. dean women Pa. State U., State College, 1960-65; assoc. dean students No. Mont. Coll., Havre, 1967-69, dir. No. Mont. Coll. Found., 1977-79, exec. asst. to pres., 1977-79; edn. resource leader Van Orsdel United Meth. Ch., Havre, 1973-77; asst. dean students Oreg. State U., Corvallis, 1979-96, acting dean of students, 1996—; bd. chair North Mont. Shared Svcs. Project, Northern HiLine, 1976-78; cons. in field; coord. Mont. rural edn. grants N.W. Area Found., No. Mont., 1978-79. Contbr. to book: Guide to Guidance: Annotated Bibliography, 1960; contbr. articles to profl. jours. Chmn. long range planning bd. higher edn. ministry Meth. and Presbyn. chs., Oreg., Idaho, 1988-91; chmn. united campus ministry bd. Oreg. State U., 1982-84, 87-89; trustee Sch. Dist. 16, Havre, 1974-78; v.p. Human Resources Devel. Coun., Havre, 1974-75; pres., bd. dirs. Montessori Learning Ctr., Havre, 1970-73. Recipient Excellence in Svc. award Student Affairs, Oreg. State U., 1992, Woman of Achievement award Women's Ctr., 1987. Mem. Nat. Assn. Student Pers. Adminstrs., Am. Coll. Pers. Assn. (chair commn. XVII 1990-91, commn. rep., core coun. mem. svcs. and interests, 1995—, conv. program com. 1994—), Alpha Kappa Delta, Pi Lambda Theta. Office: Oreg State U Adminstrv Svc A200 Corvallis OR 97331-2133

VANDERSYPEN, RITA DEBONA, guidance counselor; b. Alexandria, La., Sept. 13, 1953; d. Sam S. and Myrtle (Genova) DeBona; m. Robert Louis Vandersypen, Aug. 17, 1974; children: Regina Marie, Ryan Matthew. BA summa cum laude, La. Coll., 1975; MEd, La. State U., 1980, postgrad., 1982; EdS, Northwestern State U., Natchitoches, La., 1993. Eligibility worker Rapides Parish Office Family Svcs., Alexandria, 1975-78; welfare social worker Rapides Parish Foster Care Svcs., Alexandria, 1978-79; tchr. A. Wettermark High Sch., Boyce, La., 1979-84; tchr. English English Alexandria Sr. High Sch., 1984-92, guidance counselor, 1992—. Contbr. to handbook and curriculum guide. Sponsor Future Voters Am. Club, 1984-89, 4-H Club, 1988—. Mem. AAUW, Rapides Parish Guidance Counselors Assn., Rapides Fedn. Tchrs., La. Sch. Counselor Assn., Rapides Livestock Club, Belguam-Am. Club, Am. Quarter Horse Assn., Phi Kappa Phi, Kappa Delta Pi. Roman Catholic. Office: Peabody Magnet High Sch 2727 Jones Ave Alexandria LA 71302-5619

VANDER VEER, SUZANNE, aupair business executive; b. Phila., Sept. 21, 1936; d. Joseph Bedford Vander Veer and Ethel K. Short; m. James Robb Ledwith, Nov. 29, 1958 (div. Sept. 1978); children: Cheryl Day, James Robb Jr., Scott Wiley; m. Herbert Keyser Zearfoss, Nov. 14, 1992. AA, Colby Sawyer Coll., 1957; postgrad., State U. Iowa, 1957-58. Tchr. Booth Sch., Bryn Mawr, Pa., 1958; profl. tour guide Cities of Phila., N.Y.C. and Washington, D.C., 1976-89; regional dir. Transdesigns, Woodstock, Ga., 1979-87; area rep. Welcome Wagon Internat., Tenn., 1987-93; mem. local bd. Welcome Wagon Internat., 1987-93; condo. complex mgr. St. Davids, Pa., 1990-93; area dir. E.F. Aupair, Cambridge, Mass., 1993—; art cons., 1979—. Chair host family program Internat. House of Phila., 1966-74; mem. women's com. Pa. Hosp., 1966-71; mem. com. Phila. Antique Show, 1995—; docent Phila. Mus. of Art, 1974-80; bd. dirs. Plays for Living, Phila., 1966-84. Mem. PEO (guard chaplin), Jr. League of Phila. (bd. dirs., sustainer chair 1993-95, Pres.' Cup 1995, sustainer bd. 1985—), Merion Cricket Club. Home: 532 Candace Ln Villanova PA 19085

VANDERWALKER, DIANE MARY, materials scientist; b. Springfield, Mass., Nov. 1, 1955. BS, Boston Coll., 1977; PhD, MIT, 1981. NATO fellow U. Oxford, Eng., 1981-82; asst. prof. SUNY, Stony Brook, 1983-85; materials rsch. engr. Army Rsch. Lab. (formerly U.S. Army Materials Tech. Lab.), Watertown, Mass., 1986-94; cons. IBM, Yorktown Heights, N.Y. Contbr. articles to profl. publs. Mem. N.Y. Acad. Scis. Roman Catholic.

VANDERWERF, MARY ANN, elementary school educator, consultant; b. Buffalo, N.Y., Aug. 18, 1938; d. Richard and Petronella Gertruida (Hell) V.; m. Malcolm Donald Brutman, Apr. 30, 1989; 1 child, Susan Still. BS in Edn., SUNY, Buffalo, 1970, MA in English, 1971, PhD in Rsch. and Evaluation in Edn., 1981. Cert. tchr., N.Y. Legal sec. Hetzelt & Watson, Buffalo,

1957-64; exec. sec. Bell Aerospace Corp., Wheatfield, N.Y., 1964-69; tchr. Amherst (N.Y.) Ctrl. Schs., 1972-94; instr. SUNY, Buffalo, 1979, 85-86, children's lit. cons., 1980-92; pres., cons., facilitator The Synergy Advantage, Inc., Amherst, 1994—; collaborator U.S. Space and Rocket Ctr./U.S. Space Acad., Huntsville, Ala., 1995—; presenter Williamsville Ctrl. Schs., Internat. Reading Assn., Ireland, 1982, Anaheim, Calif., 1983, New Orleans, 1985, 89, Toronto, Ont., Can., 1988, N.Y. State English Coun., Amherst, 1984, St. Bonaventure U., 1984, Amherst Ctrl. Sch. Dist., 1986, 92, 94, Creative Problem Solving Inst., Buffalo, 1986—, Early Childhood Edn. Conf., 1988, Early Childhood Edn. Coun. Western N.Y., Buffalo, 1990, U. Nev., Las Vegas, 1991; book reviewer Harper Collins Children's Books, 1991. Author: (with others) Science and Technology in Fact and Fiction/Children's, 1989, Science and Technology in Fact and Fiction: Young Adult, 1990, Teacher to Teacher: Strategies for the Elementary Classroom, 1993; contbr. articles to profl. jours. Advisor child life dept. Children's Hosp., Buffalo, 1984-85. Mem. Am. Fedn. Tchrs., Internat. Reading Assn. (cons. Niagara Frontier Reading Coun.), Creative Edn. Found., N.Y. State Coun. Tchrs. English (presenter), Children's Lit. Assn., Hans Christian Andersen Soc., Pi Lambda Theta (Alpha Nu chpt.). Home: 1860 N Forest Rd Williamsville NY 14221-1321 Office: The Synergy Advantage Inc 2495 Kensington Ave Amherst NY 14226-4929

VANDE STREEK, PENNY ROBILLARD, nuclear medicine physician, researcher, educator; b. Highland Park, Mich., May 23, 1953; d. Richard Charles Robillard and E. Louise (Gee) Armstrong; m. Harley Eugene Vande Streek, Oct. 22, 1977; children: Gregory, Elizabeth. BA, Spring Arbor Coll., 1977; DO, Univ. Osteo. Med./Health Scis., Des Moines, 1983. Diplomate Am. Bd. Internal Medicine, Am. Bd. Nuclear Medicine. Rsch. asst. Parke-Davis & Co., Detroit, 1977-79; anatomy and microbiology lab. asst. U. Osteo. Medicine, Des Moines, 1980-81; intern in family practice Scott AFB (Ill.) Med. Ctr., 1983-84; chief internal medicine Williams Hosp., Williams AFB, Ariz., 1987-88; resident in internal medicine Wilford Hall USAF Med. Ctr., San Antonio, 1984-87, nuc. medicine fellow, 1988-90, mem. staff nuc. medicine, 1990-91, chief positron emission tomography imaging svc., 1991-93; staff nuc. medicine physician Sutter-Roseville Med. Ctr., 1993—; asst. prof. radiology U. Calif., Davis, 1995—; asst. prof. radiology U. Tex. Health Sci. Ctr., San Antonio, 1991—; rsch. fellow Uniformed Svcs. U. Health Scis., Bethesda, Md., 1985-87; instr. Incarnate Word Coll., 1992, mem. adv. coun. nuc. medicine tech. program, 1991-93; guest lectr. various hosps. Author: Shoulder Imaging, 1995; contbr. chpts. to books. Participant City Disaster Preparedness, Des Moines, 1980, Phoenix, 1988. Maj. USAF, 1979-93, Operation Desert Storm. Decorated Meritorious Achievement medal; recipient Young Leader award Spring Arbor (Mich.) Coll., 1992; Mallinckrodt grantee, Cin., 1991. Fellow Am. Coll. Nuc. Physicians; mem. Soc. Nuc. Medicine, Soc. Air Force Physicians, Assn. Mil. Osteo. Physicians and Surgeons, Sierra Valley Nuc. Medicine Assn. (pres.), Greater Sacramento Osteo. Physicians, Placer Nev. Med. Soc., Sigma Sigma Phi. Office: PO Box 1328 Rocklin CA 95677-7328

VANDEVENDER, BARBARA JEWELL, elementary education educator, farmer; b. Trenton, Mo., Dec. 4, 1929; d. Raleigh Leon and Rose Rea (Dryer) S.; m. Delbert Lyle Vandevender, Aug. 15, 1948; children: Lyle Gail, James R. BS, N.E. Mo. State U., 1971, MA, 1973. Elem. tchr. Williams Sch., Spickard, Mo., 1948-49; reading specialist Spikard R-2 Sch., 1971-74, Princeton (Mo.) R-5 Sch., 1974-89; mem. ad hoc com. State Dept. Edn., Jefferson City, Mo., 1994-95; speaker in field. Pres. Spickard PTA, 1963-64, Women's Ext. Club, Galt, Mo.; foster mother Family Svcs., Trenton, Mi., 1972-79; mem. ad hoc com. State Dept. of Edn., Jefferson City, Mo., 1994-95. Pres. Spickard PTA, 1963-64, Women's Ext. Club, Galt, Mo.; foster mother Family Svcs., Trenton, Mo., 1972-79; mem. ad hoc com. State Dept. Edn., Jefferson City, Mo., 1994-95. Recipient Mo. State Conservation award Goodyear Tire Co., Akron, Ohio, 1972, Balanced Farming award Gulf Oil Co., N.Y.C., 1972, Mo. State Farming award Kansas City C. of C., 1974, FHA State Farming award, Jefferson City, Mo., 1974, Outstanding Leadership Mo. U., Columbia, 1976, Ednl. Leadership award MSTA, Columbia, 1984, Outstanding Contbn. to Internat. Reading Assn., Newark, Del., 1988. Mem. Internat. Reading Assn. (pres. North Ctrl. coun. 1985-86). Republican. Baptist.

VAN DE WORKEEN, PRISCILLA TOWNSEND, small business owner and executive; b. Denver, July 9, 1946; d. Reginald and Ruth (Poor) Townsend; m. Melvin Charles Van de Workeen, Oct. 27, 1973. BA in Chinese History, Wheaton Coll., Norton, Mass., 1968; postgrad., Cornell U., 1965. Asst. dir. Nat. Info. Bur., N.Y.C., 1969-73; dep. dir. Harkness Fellowships, N.Y.C. and London, 1973-83; owner, mgr. Vernalwood Enterprises, Splty. and Custom Crafts, Dudley, Mass., 1984-93; co-owner, mgr. Vernalwood Bed & Breakfast, Dudley, 1989-93, Folkstone Bed & Breakfast Reservation Svc., Dudley, 1989-94; co-founder, chairperson Vernalwood Conceptual Enhancements, Dudley, 1991-95. Tchr. quilting and needlework Chester Corbin Libr., Webster, Mass.; bd. dirs. Hubbard Regional Hosp. Guild, Webster, 1986-91, Internat. Ctr., Worcester, Mass., 1989-90; chair bd. trustees Pearle L. Crawford Libr., Town of Dudley, 1993—; coord. Nat. Coun. Internat. Visitors, Washington, 1989-90; founder, chmn. The Concordia Found., Dudley, 1992—. Mem. Webster Dudley Garden Club (bd. dirs.), The Tuesday Club (pres. 1994-95). Democrat. Home and Office: Vernalwood Darling Rd Dudley MA 01571

VANDIVER, BETTY JEAN, protective services professional; b. Harrodsburg, Ky., Sept. 27, 1950; d. Cecil Raymond and Ruby Marie (Hawkins) VanD. AA, Ea. Ky. U., 1971, BS, 1993—. Juvenile counselor, juvenile correctional officer Cabinet for Human Resources, Waddy, Ky., 1981-91; dir. admissions, adminstrv. asst. dept. mental health Ky. Correctional Psychiat. Ctr., LaGrange, Ky., 1991-94; ct. designated worker Cabinet of Justice-53rd Jud. Dist., various cities, Ky., 1994—; living instr. Best House Group; bd. mem. Local Interagy. Coun., Shelbyville, Ky., Youth Adv. Coun., Shelbyville, Taylorsville, Drug and Alcohol Adv. Coun., Shelbyville.Private Childcare, Christian Children's Homes of Kentucky. Mem. NAFE, NRA, Ea. Star (Hamilton chpt. 293). Address: PO Box 205 Lawrenceburg KY 40342 Home: 1012 Indian Trail Lawrenceburg KY 40342 Office: Cabinet for Justice 510 Washington St Shelbyville KY 40065

VANDIVER, PAMELA BOWREN, research scientist; b. Santa Monica, Calif., Jan. 12, 1946; d. Roy King and Patricia (Woolard) Evans; m. J. Kim Vandiver, Aug., 1968 (div. 1984); 1 child, Amy. BA in Humanities and Asian Studies, Scripps Coll., 1967; postgrad., U. Calif., Berkeley, 1968; MA in Art, Pacific Luth. U., 1971; MS in Ceramic Sci., MIT, 1983, PhD in Materials Sci. and Near Eastern Archeology, 1985. Instr. in glass and ceramics Mass. Coll. of Art, Boston, 1972; lectr. MIT, Cambridge, 1973-78, rsch. assoc., 1978-85; rsch. phys. scientist Conservation Analytical Lab., Washington, 1985-89; sr. scientist in ceramics C.A.L. Smithsonian Instn., Washington, 1989—; instr. semester-at-sea U. Pitts., spring 1995; bd. dirs. Rolatape Corp., Spokane, Wash.; guest rschr. Nat. Inst. Stds. and Tech., Gaithersburg, Md., 1989-91. Co-author: Ceramic Masterpieces, 1986; co-editor: Materials Issues in Art and Archaeology, 1988, 4th edit., 1995; bd. editors Archeomaterials, 1986-93; contbr. numerous articles to profl. jours. Sponsor mentorship program Thomas Jefferson H.S. of Sci. and Tech., Alexandria, 1992. Recipient Disting. Alumna Achievement award Scripps Coll., 1993. Mem. AAAS, Am. Inst. Archeology, Soc. Am. Archeology, Internat. Inst. of Conservation, Soc. for History of Tech., Am. Ceramics Soc. (ancient ceramics com. 1978—), Materials Rsch. Soc. (guest editor bull. 1992), Am. Chem. Soc., Cosmos Club, Sigma Xi. Office: Smithsonian Inst Conservation Analytical Lab Washington DC 20560

VAN DORP, AGATHE HENRIETTE, occupational therapist; b. Buurmalsen, The Netherlands, Jan. 8, 1961; came to U.S., 1988; d. Johan Henrik and Neeltje (van Iterson) van D.; m. David Leonard Giancoli, Apr. 25, 1995. BS, Occupl. Therapy Coll., Weesp, The Netherlands, 1984. Asst. tchr., occupl. therapist Presch. De Rutpol, Geldermalsen, The Netherlands, 1984; occupl. therapist Rehab. Ctr., Huizen, The Netherlands, 1985-88, Baptist Hosp., Nashville, 1989-90, High Hopes Inc., Nashville, 1990—; cons. pub. sch. sys. and regional behavior intervention programs, Columbia, Smithville, Pulaski and Nashville, Tenn., 1991—. Author: Preparing for Writing in Children with Sensory Integration Disorders, 1984. Recipient Unsung Hero award Coun. of Cmty. Svcs., Nashville, 1995. Office: High Hopes Inc PO Box 150932 3511 Belmont Blvd Nashville TN 37215

VAN DOVER, KAREN, middle and elementary school educator, curriculum consultant, language arts specialist; b. Astoria, N.Y.; d. Frederick A. and Frances L. (Thomas) Van D. BA, CUNY; MALS, SUNY, Stony Brook; postgrad., St. John's U., Jamaica, N.Y., 1992. Cert. permanent N-6 tchr., art tchr. K-12, sch. adminstr., supr., N.Y. Tchr., sch. dist. adminstr. St. James (N.Y.) Elem. Sch.; tchr. Nesaquake Intermediate Sch., St. James, lead tchr. English, 1984-92; lead tchr. English Smithtown Mid Sch., St. James, 1992-93, curriculum specialist, 1993—; leader staff devel. and curriculum devel. workshops Smithtown Sch. Dist., 1984—, mem. supt.'s adv. com. for gifted and talented, mem. supt. adv. com. for lang. arts assessment, mem. textbook selection coms. site-based mgmt. team, 1994—; mem. master tchr. bd. Prentice Hall, Englewood Cliffs, N.J., 1990—. Contbg. author: Prentice Hall Literature Copper, 1991, 94. Corr. sec. Yaphank Taxpayers and Civic Assn., 1984-86, Nesaquake Sch. PTA, 1990-91, mem., 1977-92; mem. Smithtown Mid. Sch. PTA, 1992—. Mem. ASCD, Am. Ednl. Rsch. Assn., Nat. Assn. Secondary Sch. Prins., Nat. Coun. Tchrs. English, Internat. Reading Assn., Nat. Middle Schs. Assn., N.Y. State English Coun., Nat. Assn. of Elem. Sch. Prins., Phi Delta Kappa. Home: 8 Penn Commons Yaphank NY 11980-2025 Office: Smithtown Middle Sch 10 School St Saint James NY 11780-1833

VAN DUSEN, DONNA BAYNE, educator, communication consultant, researcher; b. Phila., Apr. 21, 1949; d. John Culbertson and Evelyn Gertrude (Godfrey) Bayne; m. David William Van Dusen, Nov. 30, 1968 (div. Dec. 1989); children: Heather, James. BA, Temple U., 1984, MA, 1986, PhD, 1993. Instr. Kutztown (Pa.) U., 1986-87, Ursinus Coll., Collegeville, Pa., 1987-96; cons., rschr. Comm. Rsch. Assoc., Valley Forge, Pa., 1993—; asst. prof. Beaver Coll., Glenside, Pa., 1995—; rschr. Fox Chase Cancer Ctr., Phila., 1985-86; adj. faculty Temple U. Law Sch., 1994—, LaSalle U., 1994-96, Wharton Sch., U. Pa., 1994-95. Mem. NOW, AAUP, Speech Comm. Assn., Ea. Comm. Assn. Home: 15 Shirley Rd Narberth PA 19072-2015

VAN DUYN, MONA JANE, poet; b. Waterloo, Iowa, May 9, 1921; d. Earl George and Lora G. (Kramer) Van D.; m. Jarvis A. Thurston, Aug. 31, 1943. B.A., U. No. Iowa, 1942; M.A., U. Iowa, 1943; D.Litt. (hon.), Washington U., St. Louis, 1971, Cornell Coll., Iowa, 1972, U. No. Iowa, 1991, U. of the South, Sewanee, Tenn., 1993, George Wash. U., 1993; LHD, Georgetown U., 1993. Instr. in English U. Iowa, Iowa City, 1943-46; instr. in English U. Louisville, 1946-50; lectr. English Univ. Coll., Washington U., 1950-67; poetry editor, co-pub. Perspective, A Quar. of Lit., 1947-67; lectr. Salzburg (Austria) Seminar Am. Studies, 1973; adj. prof. poetry workshop Washington U., Spring 1983; vis. Hurst prof., 1987; poet-in-residence Sewanee Writers Conf., 1990, Breadloaf Writing Conf., Mass., 1974. Author: Valentines to the Wide World, 1959, A Time of Bees, 1964, To See, To Take, 1970, Bedtime Stories, 1972, Merciful Disguises, 1973, Letters from a Father and Other Poems, 1983, Near Changes, 1990 (Pulitzer Prize for poetry 1991), Firefall, 1993, If It Be Not I, 1993. Recipient Eunice Tietjens award, 1956, Helen Bullis prize, 1964, 76, Harriet Monroe award, 1968, Hart Crane Meml. award, 1968, Borestone Mountains 1st prize, 1968, Bollingen prize, 1970, Nat. Book award, 1971, Sandburg prize Cornell Coll., 1982, Shelley Meml. prize Poetry Soc. Am., 1987, Lilly prize for poetry, 1989, Mo. Arts award, 1990, Golden Plate award Am. Acad. Achievement, 1992, Arts and Edn. Coun. St. Louis award, 1994; named U.S. Poet Laureate, 1992-93; grantee Nat. Coun. Arts, 1967, NEA, 1985; Guggenheim fellow, 1972. Fellow Acad. Am. Poets (chancellor 1985); mem. NAAS, Nat. Acad. Arts and Letters (Loines prize 1976).

VAN DYCK, WENDY, dancer; b. Tokyo. Student, San Francisco Ballet Sch. With San Francisco Ballet, 1979—, prin. dancer, 1987—. Performances include Forgotten Land, The Sons of Horus, The Wanderer Fantasy, Romeo and Juliet, The Sleeping Beauty, Swan Lake, Concerto in d: Poulenc, Handel-a Celebration, Menuetto, Intimate Voices, Hamlet and Ophelia pas de deux, Connotations, Sunset, Rodin, In the Night, The Dream: pas de deux, La Sylphide, Beauty and the Beast, Variations de Ballet, Nutcracker, The Comfort Zone, Dreams of Harmony, Rodeo, Duo Concertant, Who Cares; performed at Reykjavik Arts Festival, Iceland, 1990, The 88th Conf. of the Internat. Olympic Com., L.A., 1984, with Kozlov and Co. Concord Pavilion; guest artist performing role Swan Lake (Act II), San Antonio Ballet, 1985, Giselle, Shreveport Met. Ballet, 1994; featured in the TV broadcast of Suite by Smuin. Office: San Francisco Ballet 455 Franklin St San Francisco CA 94102-4438

VAN DYKE, ELIZABETH MARIE, actress, director, educator; b. Oakland, May 7; d. Rudolph Vincent and Merrill (Reece) Van D. MFA, NYU, 1975. Roy Acuff chair of Excellence Austin Peay State U., Clarksville, Tenn., 1996—; advisor Zora Neale Hurston Festival, Orlando, Fla., 1992—; bd. mem. New Fed. Theatre, N.Y.C., 1995—. Appeared in plays Checkmates, The Piano Lesson, Antigone, Zora Neale Hurston, (TV) Law and Order, New York Undercover, L.A. Law; author: (one woman show) Love To All, Lorraine, 1985. Recipient Ace award Cable TV, 1985, Gold award Houston Film Festival, 1986, AUDELCO award for best actress Audience Devel. Com. Home: 243 E 83rd St New York NY 10028

VAN DYKE, WENDY JOHANNA, artist; b. Moline, Ill., July 22, 1955; d. Kreger D. and Sara K. (Weeks) Emry; m. Mikel P. Van Dyke, Feb. 11, 1978; children: Benjamin, Jonathan. BS in Bus. Adminstrn with highest honors, U. Ill., 1977. Mgr. Stringer Art Factory and Gallery, Davenport, IA, 1977-78, Warren L. Langwith, Inc., Davenport, IA, 1977-78; v. chmn. visual arts com. Quad Cities Arts Coun., Rock Island, Ill., 1979-80. Exhibited in group shows at Davenport Mus. of Art, 1977, 84, 88, 95, Muscatine (Iowa) Art Ctr., 1980, 83, 88, 90, Blanden Mem. Art Gallery, Ft. Dodge, Iowa, 1980, Graceland Coll., Lamoni, Iowa, 1980, Waterloo (Iowa) Mcpl. Art Galleries, 1980, Carrol (Iowa) Arts Coun., 1981, Clinton (Iowa) C.C., 1981, Algona (Iowa) H.S., 1981, Art Guild of Burlington, Iowa, 1981, Woodbine Comm. Schs., Iowa, 1981, Cen. Coll., Pella, Iowa, 1981, Augustana Coll. Art Gallery, Rock Island, Ill., 1996. Mem. fine arts com. Buchanan Sch. PTA, Davenport, 1983-92; mem. arts adv. com. Davenport Cmty. Schs., 1986-89; active Devel. of State of Iowa Art Curriculum, Des Moines, 1991-92; bd. dirs. Quad Cities Arts Coun., Rock Island, Ill., 1979-80. Mem. Quad City Arts, Art Inst. Chgo. (nat. assoc.), U. Ill. Alumni Assn. (life), Phi Kappa Phi, Beta Gamma Sigma, Phi Gamma Nu. Home: 2517 W 43rd St Davenport IA 52806

VAN DYKEN, AMY, swimmer, Olympic athlete; b. Feb. 15, 1973. Swimmer U.S. Nat. Resident Team, Colorado Springs, Colo., 1994, U.S. Olympic Team, Atlanta, Ga., 1996. Named Female NCAA Swimmer of the Year, 1994, Am. Record Holder 50 meter and 50 meter freestyle; recipient Bronze medal World Championships, 1994, Triple Gold medals Pan Am. Games, 1995, Silver medal Pan Am. Games, 1995, Gold medals: 50 meter freestyle, 100 meter butterfly, 4x100 meter freestyle relay, 4x100 meter relay Olympic Games, Atlanta, 1996. Office: US Swimming Inc 1 Olympic Plaza Colorado Springs CO 80909*

VAN DYNE, MICHELE MILEY, information engineer; b. Harrisburg, Pa., Sept. 8, 1959; d. Joseph Lawrence Miley and Tina Theresa (Dudash) Smollack; m. David Franklin Buck, Aug. 8, 1981 (div. July 1984); m. David George Van Dyne, Sept. 9, 1989. BA in Psychology, U. Mont., 1981, MS in Computer Sci., 1985; postgrad., U. Kans., 1992—. Div. sr. tech. programmer, analyst Allied-Signal Aerospace, Kansas City, Mo., 1985-89; knowledge engr. United Data Svcs., Inc., United Telecom, Overland Park, Kans., 1989-90; pres. IntelliDyne, Inc., Kansas City, Mo., 1990—; cons. Comprehensive Devel. Ctr., Missoula, Mont., 1984; speaker Sigart, Kansas City, 1988; chmn. Expert-Systems-Kans. and Mo. (ESKaMo), 1990-92. Vol. Planned Parenthood Greater Kansas City, 1986. United Bldg. Ctrs. scholar, 1976. Mem. IEEE Computer Soc., Am. Assn. for Artificial Intelligence, Internat. Neural Network Soc., Instrnl. Tech. Network (steering com. 1990-92), Women in Tech. Network (steering com. 1990-91, chmn. pub. rels. com. 1991-92), Alpha Lambda Delta. Democrat. Episcopalian. Home and Office: 6040 Wornall Rd Kansas City MO 64113-1418

VANE, DENA, magazine editor-in-chief. Editor-in-chief First for Women, Englewood Cliffs, N.J. Office: First for Women Bauer Pub Co 270 Sylvan Ave Englewood NJ 07632*

VAN EKEREN, YBI, artist; b. Zwolle, Overysel, The Netherlands, Aug. 2, 1927; arrived in Can., 1951; came to U.S., 1960; AA, Riverside City Coll., 1968; BA, Fullerton State U., 1977. Exhibited in group shows at Riverside (Calif.) Art Mus., 1969 (1st award for graphics, 3rd award for sculpture), Arlington (Calif.) Art Guild, 1970 (2nd Place award for graphics), Nat. Orange Show, San Bernardino, 1994 (2nd Place award), Calif. Mid-State Fair, Paso Robles, 1996 (2nd Place award). Mem. Cayucos Art Assn., Morro Bay Art Assn., San Luis Obispo Art Assn., Nat. Mus. of Women in the Arts. Office: Studio Art Gallery 731 Santa Ysabel Los Osos CA 93402

VAN ENGELEN, DEBRA LYNN, chemistry educator; b. Burley, Idaho, Dec. 31, 1952; d. W. Dean and Eyvonne (Campbell) Van Engelen; m. John L. Crawford, Dec. 19, 1987; 1 child, Aaron C. Coghlan. BA, Washington U., 1974; PhD, Oreg. State U., 1987. Grad. fellow Oreg. State U., Corvallis, 1982-86; asst. prof. U. N.C., Asheville, 1986-92, assoc. prof. chemistry, 1992—, dir. women's studies, 1994—; vis. prof. Emory U., Atlanta, summer 1992. Contbr. articles to profl. jours. NSF rsch. awardee, 1992, 93-96; grantee N.C. Bd. Sci. Tech., 1988-89, Blue Ridge Health Ctr., 1989. Mem. Am. Chem. Soc. (sec.-treas. 1991, chpt. chair 1993, fin. co-chair regional meeting 1996), Coun. on Undergrad. Rsch., Sigma Xi, Phi Kappa Phi, Phi Lambda Upsilon. Office: Univ of NC Dept Chemistry Asheville NC 28804

VAN ERT, HEIDI, gifted education educator, artist, art therapist; b. Honolulu, Jan. 4, 1955; d. Willard Lee and Gretchen (Schubert) Van E.; m. Thomas Patrick Casey, July 29, 1978 (div.); 1 child, Christopher Michael. BA in Humanities for Elem. Tchrs., Colo. Coll., 1976; MS in Spl. Edn., U. Utah, 1987, PhD in Gifted Edn., 1993, MA in Art Therapy, 1994. Cert. tchr. with gifted endorsement, Utah. Instr. and coach skiing Snowbird Learn-To-Race Program, Salt Lake City, 1971-73; assoc. jr. high sch. ministries 1st Presbyn. Ch., Colorado Springs, Colo., 1977-78; elem. tchr. Lincoln Consol. Schs., Ypsilanti, Mich., 1979-81, Willow Canyon Elem. Sch., Sandy, Utah, 1981-83, Rowland Hall-St. Mark's Sch., Salt Lake City, 1983-88; clin. instr. spl. edn. U. Utah, Salt Lake City, 1987-94; tchr. gifted and talented Peruvian Park Elem. Sch., Sandy, 1994—; art therapist, Salt Lake City, 1994—; counselor Essex Sch. for Gifted, Columbus, Ohio, 1985; team mem. rural staff devel.Ea. Utah region Utah Office Edn., 1989-91; edn., devel. and creativity cons. Black Bottoms, Salt Lake City, 1994; coord. Youth Acad. Excellence, U. Utah, 1996; presenter in field; mem. planning com. Regional Art Therapy Conf., Salt Lake City, 1991-92. Contbr. articles to profl. pubis.; one-woman show Petersen Art Ctr., 1995. Vol. with Navajo and Winnebago tribes 1st Presbyn. Ch., 1974, 76; trustee Realms of Inquiry Sch., Salt Lake City, 1991-92; hospice vol. Salt Lake Cmty. Nursing Svcs., 1993—. Named Tchr. of Month, Sandy C. of C., 1996; Steffensen-Cannon scholar U. Utah, 1990-92, leadership tng. grantee, 1992-93, rsch. fellow, 1992-93. Mem. Nat. Assn. Gifted Children, Am. Art Therapy Assn. (profl. art therapist), Utah Assn. Gifted Children, Rocky Mountain Art Therapy Assn., Mensa. Home: 1470 E Gilmer Dr Salt Lake City UT 84105 Office: Peruvian Park Elem Sch 1545 East 8425 South Sandy UT 84093

VAN ETTEN, EDYTHE AUGUSTA, retired occupational health nurse; b. Arthur, N.D., Oct. 13, 1921; d. Lacy Edward and Emma Erna (Mundt) Roach; m. Robert Scott Van Etten, Feb. 12, 1944; children: Ronald, Cynthia Czernysz, Martin, Roger, Randall, Janet K. Diploma, Mt. Sinai Hosp. Sch. Nursing, Chgo., 1945; AS, Waubonsee Community Coll., Sugar Grove, Ill., 1978; BSN, No. Ill. U., 1981. Cert. occupational health nurse; RN, Ill. Occupation health nurse Barber-Greene Co., Aurora, Ill., 1965-82; occupational health relief nurse No. Ill. Gas Co., Naperville, Ill., 1983-85; supr. or staff nurse Michealsen Health Ctr., Batavia, Ill., 1982-93; occupational health relief nurse The Dial Corp., Montgomery, Ill., 1982-94; occupational health nurse cons. AT&T Svc. Ctr., West Chicago, Ill., 1988-94. Mem. adminstrv. bd. Ch. of the Good Shepherd Meth., Oswego, Ill., 1988-94; active Fox Bend Ladies Golf League, United Meth. Women; mem. Lyric Opera of Chgo. Mem. Suburban Chgo. Assn. Occupational Health Nurses, Dist. 2 Ill. Nurses Assn. (del. state conv. 1985, Award for Excellence in Nursing Practice 1993), Sr. Svcs. Assn. Inc. (adv. 1983-87, Humanitarian award 1985), Oswegoland Women's Civic Club (bd. dirs. 1985—). Republican. Home: 427 S Madison St PO Box 1 Oswego IL 60543

VANGELLOW, DEBORAH SOPHIA, sports educator, administrator; b. Rochester, N.Y., Dec. 20, 1962; d. George and Catherine Sophia (Sarantis) V. BA, U. No. Iowa, 1986; MS, Miami (Ohio) U., 1988. Spl. events asst. U. No. Iowa, Cedar Falls, 1981-86, asst. track/field coach, 1985-86, advisor student athletic bd., 1989-92, mem. core com student athlete assistance program, 1989-92, head coach women's golf, 1991-92; grad. intern Office Recreational Sports, Miami U., Oxford, Ohio, 1986-88; program coord. Japanese "Superlady" Project Kathy Whitworth Golf Acad., West Columbia, Tex., 1992-94; teaching asst. Columbia Lakes Sch. of Golf, West Columbia, 1992-94; golf projects coord. Heritage of Golf Corp., Houston, 1994-96; golf sch. coord., instr. Heritage Sch. of Golf, Houston, 1994-96; LPGA teaching profl. Cullen & Co. Golf Instrn., 1996—; instr. wellness program U. No. Iowa, 1983-86, coord. residence hall, 1989-92, instr. health and phys. edn., 1990-92; instr. health and phys. edn. K-12, No. U. High Sch., Cedar Falls, 1986, asst. softball coach, 1987; adj. instr. dept. ednl. leadership Miami U., 1986-89, coord. summer conf. halls, 1988, freshman acad. advisor, residence hall dir., 1988-89; asst. dir. Golf Digest Jr. Instrnl. Schs., Hueston Woods, Ohio, summers 1988-92; activity dir. Columbia Lakes Jr. Sch. of Golf, West Columbia, summers 1991-92. Active Annunciation Greek Orthodox Cathedral, 1993—, Big Brothers/Big Sisters Northeast Iowa, 1990-92; vol. Spl. Olympics, 1982-86; instr. first aid and CPR, ARC, 1989-92, mem., 1989—; instr. cancer prevention program Am. Cancer Soc., 1990-92, bd. dirs., 1991-92. Recipient Mabel M. Wright Meml. Scholarship award, 1985-86; named one of Outstanding Young Women of Am., 1988, Top Flite Golfwoman of Yr., 1995; named coach golf team traveling to Holland, Internat. Sport for Understanding Program, 1996, Favorite Golf Instr., Golf for Women Mag., 1996. Mem. AAUW, LPGA, NAFE, Womensport International, Am. Coll. Pers. Assn., U.S. Golf Assn., Nat. Assn. Golf Educators, Nat. Strength and Conditioning Assn., Women's Sports Found., No. Iowa Alumni Assn., U. No. Iowa Athletic Club, Omicron Delta Kappa, Alpha Chi Omega. Home and Office: 4144 Greystone Way # 707 Sugar Land TX 77479

VAN GOETHEM, NANCY ANN, painter, educator; b. Detroit, June 27, 1950; d. Walter and Margaret E. (Cook) Van G.; m. Lawrence M. Joseph, Apr. 10, 1976. BFA, Pratt Inst., Bklyn., 1983. Artist Detroit Free Press, Detroit, 1972-81; ind. artist, 1983-92; instr. Parsons Sch. of Design, N.Y.C., 1992—. Artist in various jours. including Ontario Review, fall 1995, The Male Body U. Mich., 1994, Poetry East, fall 1993; exhbn.: History of Women in Am. Schlesinger Libr., 1994-95. Mem. Women's Caucus for Art, Coll. Art Assn. Home: 355 South End Ave #33 N New York NY 10280

VAN HOLLEN, CECILIA COALE, anthropologist; b. Washington, D.C., Dec. 18, 1964; d. Christopher and Edith Eliza (Farnsworth) Van H.; m. Jeffrey Pepper Rodgers, Aug. 17, 1991; 1 child, Lila Van Hollen Rodgers. BA in Anthropology and Religious Studies, Brown U., 1987; MA in Anthropology, U. Pa., 1992; postgrad., U. Calif., Berkeley, 1994—. Asst. organizer Bay Area Pueblo-to-People, San Francisco, 1987-88; program asst. The Asia Found., San Francisco, 1988-89; writing fellow U. Pa., Philadelphia, 1991; tchg. asst. U. Calif., Berkeley, 1996—. Fellow fgn. langs. and area studies U.S. Dept. Edn., 1989-94, Fulbright-Hays Doctoral Dissertation Rsch. Abroad, India, 1995. Mem. Am. Anthropol. Assn., Assn. Asian Studies, Coun. on Anthropology and Reprodn., Soc. for Med. Anthropol. Phi Beta Kappa. Home: 50 Elizabeth Way San Rafael CA 94901 Office: Dept Anthropology Univ Calif Berkeley CA 94720

VAN HOOSIER, JUDY ANN, elementary education educator; b. Huntingburg, Ind.; d. Victor John and Jean M. (Lichlyter) Fleck; m. Gary Wayne Van Hoosier, Oct. 21, 1967; children: Matthew, Michael. BS in Elem. Edn., St. Benedict Coll., 1967; MA in Elem. Edn., U. Evansville, 1978. Tchr. 3d grade Holy Redeemer Sch., Evansville, Ind., 1967-68; tchr. 2d grade Good Shepherd Sch., Evansville, 1969-71, 75—. Mem. textbook adoption com. Evansville Diocesan Schs., 1983-84, 88-89; mem. liturgy commn. St. Clement Ch., Boonville, Ind., 1994-96, edn. com., 1980-83; mem. VFW Aux., 1973-96. Mem. Internat. Reading Assn., Ind. State Reading Assn., Nat. Cath. Ednl. Assn., Evansville Area Reading Coun. (membership chmn. 1991-93, v.p. 1995-96, pres.-elect 1996—, reading tchr. of yr. 1991, bd. dirs. 1985-87, 94—, bldg. rep. 1981-96, outstanding educator award 1995), Delta Kappa Gamma (sec. 1994-96, 2d v.p. 1996—). Roman Catholic. Office: Good Shepherd Sch 2301 N Stockwell Rd Evansville IN 47715-1849

VAN HORN, LECIA JOSEPH, newswriter; b. L.A., Jan. 19, 1963; d. McKinley Joe and Opal Geneva (Ivie) Joseph; m. Philip Dale Van Horn, Apr. 19, 1986; children: Kari Christine, Brandon Joseph. BA in Journalism, U. Southern Calif., 1984. News reporter Sta. KSCR Radio, L.A., 1983; consumer news researcher Sta. KCBS-TV, L.A., 1983, Sta. KABC-TV, L.A., 1983-84; newswriter Headline News, Atlanta, 1984-85; editorial asst., newswriter, field producer Sta. KNBC-TV, Burbank, Calif., 1985-86; newswriter, assoc. producer Sta. WYFF-TV, Greenville, S.C., 1986; freelance newswriter, assoc. producer Sta. WSB-TV, Atlanta, 1987-88; newswriter CNN, Atlanta, 1987-94; freelance newswriter, assoc. producer Sta. KSTP-TV, St. Paul, 1995-96; freelance newswriter Sta. KABC-TV, L.A., 1996—. Author: Thoughts and Inspirational Sayings, 1985; contbr. poetry and articles to newspapers. Mem. U. So. Calif. Alumni. Mem. Science of Mind.

VAN HOUTEN, ELIZABETH ANN, corporate communications executive; b. Washington, Feb. 22, 1945; d. Raymond R. and Marian Edna (Hovemann) Van H. BA, Mary Washington Coll., 1966. Analyst U.S. Gov., Washington, 1966-68; dep. chief of publs. Found. for Coop. Housing, Washington, 1968-72; editor Nat. League of Savs. Inst., Washington, 1972-76; dir. pub. relations Fed. Nat. Mortgage Assn., Washington, 1976-83; v.p. communications & investor relations Sallie Mae (Student Loan Mktg. Assn.), Washington, 1983-93; v.p. corp. and investor rels. Sallie Mae, Washington, 1993-95; ret., 1995. Apptd. by city coun. to Master Plan Task Force, Alexandria, Va., 1987-92; chmn. emeritus Liz Lerman Dance Exch.; mem. campaign com. for Del Pepper, Alexandria, 1987; bd. dirs. Watergate of Alexandria, 1984-89, pres., 1988-89, Washington Studio Sch., 1995—. Mem. Nat. Assn. Real Estate Editors (bd. dirs. 1980-82).

VAN HOWE, ANNETTE EVELYN, retired real estate agent; b. Chgo., Feb. 16, 1921; d. Frank and Susan (Linstra) Van Howe; m. Edward L. Nezelek, Apr. 3, 1961. BA in History magna cum laude, Hofstra U., 1952; MA in Am. History, SUNY-Binghamton, 1966. Editorial asst. Salute Mag., N.Y.C., 1946-48; assoc. editor Med. Econs., Oradell, N.J., 1952-56; nat. mag. publicist Nat. Mental Health Assn., N.Y.C., 1956-60; exec. dir. Diabetes Assn. So. Calif., L.A., 1960-61; corp. sec., v.p., editor, pub. rels. dir. Edward L. Nezelek, Inc., Johnson City, N.Y., 1961-82; realtor, broker, Ft. Lauderdale, 1980-96, ret., 1996; mgr. condominium, Fort Lauderdale, Fla., 1982-83; dir. Sky Harbour East Condo, 1983-88; substitute tchr. high schs., Binghamton, N.Y., 1961-63. Editor newsletters Mental Health Assn., 1965-68, Unitarian-Universalist Ch. Weekly Newsletter, 1967-71. Bd. dirs. Broome County Mental Health Assn., 1961-65, Fine Arts Soc., Roberson Ctr. for Arts and Scis., 1968-70, Found. Wilson Meml. Hosp., Johnson City, 1972-81, White-Willis Theatre, 1988—, Found. SUNY, Binghamton, mem., 1991-95; mem. Fla. Women's Alliance, 1989—; v.p. Fla. Women's Polit. Caucus, 1989-92; chair Women's History Coalition, Broward County, 1986—; pres. Fla. Women's Consortium, 1989-92; trustee Broome C.C., 1973-78; v.p. Broward County Commn. on Status of Women, 1982-93; bd. dirs. Ft. Lauderdale Women's Coun. of Realtors, 1986-88, Broward Arts Guild, 1986; grad. Leadership Broward Class III, 1985, Leadership Am., 1988; trustee Unitarian-Universalist Ch. of Ft. Lauderdale, 1982-89; mem. adv. bd. Planned Parenthood, 1991-93; pres. Broward Alliance of Planned Parenthood, 1993-94; sec. Nat. Women's Conf. Com., 1994-96; bd. dirs. Nat. Women's Party, 1987-93. Named Feminist of Yr., Broward County, 1987; Women's Hall of Fame, Broward County, 1992, Feminist Heroine Nat. Am. Humanist Assn., 1996. Mem. AAUW (legis. chair Fla. divsn. 1986-87, chair women's issues 1989-94, v.p. Ft. Lauderdale br. 1993—), NAFE, Am. Med. Writers Assn., LWV (bd. dir. Broome County 1969-70), Alumni Assn. SUNY Binghamton (bd. dir. 1970-73), Fla. Bar Assn. (grievance com. 1991-94), Am. Acad. Polit. and Social Sci. Broward Women's Alliance, Broward County Voice for Choice (pres. 1995—), Am. Heritage Soc., Nature Conservancy, Nat. Hist. Soc., Symphony Soc., Pacers, Zonta, Alpha Theta Beta, Phi Alpha Theta, Phi Gamma Mu, Binghamton Garden Club, Binghamton Monday Afternoon Club, Acacia Garden Club (pres.), 110 Tower Club, Tower Forum Club (bd. dirs. 1989—), Downtown Coun., Ft. Lauderdale Woman's Club. Home: 2100 S Ocean Dr Fort Lauderdale FL 33316-3806

VAN KARNES, KATHLEEN WALKER, realtor; b. Providence, June 17, 1944; d. Robert Edward Walker and Mary Antoinette (Brouillard) Holl; m. Eugene Sergei Tolegian, Dec. 3, 1966 (div. 1987); children: Elisabeth Ani, Aram Eugene; m. Karl Robert Van Karnes, Mar. 31, 1990. Student, East L.A. Coll., 1970-71, Pan Am. Coll., 1962-63. Sec. 3M Co., Los Angeles, 1963-68; office adminstr. Imperial Clin. Lab., Inc., Lynwood, Calif., 1978-80, v.p., chief fin. officer, 1980-87; realtor Bliss Keeler, Inc., San Marino, Calif., 1986-90, Fred Sands Realtors, San Marino, 1990—. Co-chmn. program Los Angeles chpt. Foothill affiliate Am. Diabetes Assn., 1987. Mem. White Ho. Confederacy Mus. (founding), Nat. Assn. Realtors, Calif. Assn. Realtors, Braille Aux. Pasadena (pres. 1991-93). Republican. Presbyterian. Office: Fred Sands Realtors 2101 Huntington Dr San Marino CA 91108-2643

VAN KEUREN, KORINNE SUZANNE, pediatrics and orthopedics nurse; b. Fairfield, Calif., Mar. 31, 1963; d. Lawrin Wood and Janet Elizabeth (Yost) Van K. Student, Crouse Irving Meml. Sch., Syracuse, N.Y., 1985; BSN, SUNY, Buffalo, 1990; MSN, Northeastern U., 1991. Cert. orthopedic nurse clinician, ACLS, BLS Am. Heart Assn., PALS. Staff nurse ICU and OHU St. Joseph Hosp., Syracuse, 1986-88; med. rep. Gerber Products, Inc., Fremont, Mich., 1987-88; staff nurse NICU Children's Hosp. Buffalo, 1988-90, billing coord., 1989-90; staff relief nurse critical care Am. Nursing Resources, Buffalo, 1988-90; grad. asst. SUNY, Buffalo, 1990; rsch. asst. Northeastern U., Boston, 1991; homecare nurse Kimberly Quality Care, Boston, 1991; with Orthopedic/Ctr. for Health and Fitness, NP, Worcester, 1991-92; PNP U. Mass. Med. Ctr., Worcester, 1992—; nurse practitioner orthopedics West Roxbury (Mass.) VA Med. Ctr., Boston, 1992-94, New Eng. Bapt. Hosp., Boston, 1994-95; pain mgmt. pediatric nurse practitioner Children's Hosp., Boston, 1995—; primary rschr. in field. Mem. ANA (PNP), AACN, Nat. Assn. Orthopedics Nurses, Nurse Assocs. and Pediatric Nurse Practitioners (Ea. Mass. chpt. 1991—), Am. Acad. Nurse Practitioners, Sigma Theta Tau (Gamma Epsilon chpt. 1991—). Home: 349 Warren St Waltham MA 02154 Office: Childrens Hosp Pain Treatment Svc 300 Longwood Ave Boston MA 02115

VAN KILSDONK, CECELIA ANN, retired nursing administrator, volunteer; b. Beaver Dam, Wis., Sept. 28, 1930; d. Walter and Pauline (Yagodzinski) Klapinski; (div.); children: Dan, Greg, Paula, Steve. Diploma, Mercy Hosp. Sch. Nursing, 1951; BS, Coll. of St. Frances, Peoria, Ill., 1983. Clin. nurse Divsn. of Ambulatory Care, Phoenix, 1965-70, clin. charge nurse, 1970-82, regional nursing supr., 1982-87, nurse adminstr., 1987-92; mgr. nursing svc. Maricopa County Health Dept. Svcs., Phoenix. Mem. Continuing Edn. review Com., 1989—; vol. Primary Care Ctr.; disaster nurse ARC. Mem. ANA, Ariz. Nurse's Assn., Nat. League for Nursing, Phi Theta Kappa. Home: 2502 E Minnezona Ave Phoenix AZ 85016-4927

VANLEEUWEN, LIZ SUSAN (ELIZABETH VANLEEUWEN), state legislator, farmer; b. Lakeview, Oreg., Nov. 5, 1925; d. Charles Arthur and Mary Delphia (Hartzog) Nelson; B.S., Oreg. State U., 1947; m. George VanLeeuwen, June 15, 1947; children—Charles, Mary, James, Timothy. Secondary sch. and adult tchr., 1947-70; news reporter, feature writer The Times, Brownsville, Oreg., 1949—; co-mgr. VanLeeuwen Farm, Halsey, Oreg.; mem. Oreg. Ho. of Reps., 1981—; mem. Western States Forestry Legis. Task Force, Pacific Northwest Econ. Region; weekly radio commentator, 1973-81. Mem. E.R. Jackman Found., PTA, sch. adv. com.; precinct committeewoman; founder, Ct. Apptd. Spl. Advocates (CASA) Linn County Ct.; mem. regional strategies bd. Linn County Commn. on Children and Families. Recipient Outstanding Service award Oreg. Farm Bur., 1975, Oreg. Farm Family of Yr. award, 1983; Chevron Agrl. Spokesman of Yr. award, 1975. Mem. Oreg. Women for Agr. (pres.), Oreg. Women for Timber, Linn-Benton Women for Agr. (pres.), Linn County Farm Bur., Am. Legion (aux.), Linn County Econ. Devel. Com., Grange, Am. Agri-Women. Republican. Office: H-291 Capitol Bldg Salem OR 97310

VAN MATRE, JOYCE DIANNE, rehabilitation nurse; b. Bklyn., June 1, 1943; d. Gerard Thibault and Helene Clara (Wright) Hair; m. Richard Givens Van Matre, Aug. 27, 1965; children: Kimberly, Karyn, Richard. Diploma in Nursing, Gordon Keller Sch. Nursing, 1964; BS in Health Arts, Coll. of St. Francis, 1990. Cert. disability mgmt. specialist; Fla. rehab. svc. provider; cert. case mgr. Case supr. rehab. Vocat. Placement Svcs., Tampa, Fla., 1980-81; RN mgr. Always Care Nursing Svc., Tampa, 1981-82; staff nurse Vis. Nurse's Assn., Tampa, 1983-84; rehab. coord. Underwriter's Adjusting Co., Tampa, 1984-85; pres. of corp., case mgr., supr., bus. owner Ind. Group Consultants, Inc., Brandon, Fla., 1985-90; case mgr. Sullivan Health & Rehab. Mgmt., Inc., St. Petersburg, Fla., 1991-92; rehab. nurse Liberty Mut. Ins. Co., Tampa, 1992—. Recipient Disting. Acad. Achievement award Coll. of St. Francis, 1991. Mem. Assn. Rehab. Nurses, West Coast Regional Case Mgr. Assn. Office: Liberty Mut Ins Co 3350 Buschwood Park Dr Tampa FL 33618-4314

VANMETER, VANDELIA L., library director; b. Seibert, Colo., July 17, 1934; d. G.W. and A. Pearl Klockenteger; m. Victor M. VanMeter, Jan. 21, 1954; children: Allison C., Kristopher C. BA, Kansas Wesleyan U., 1957; MLS, Emporia State U., 1970; PhD, Tex. Woman's U., 1986. Cert. libr. media specialist. Tchr. Ottawa County Rural Sch., Kans., 1954-55; social scis. tchr. McClave (Colo.) High Sch., 1957-58, Ellsworth (Kans.) Jr. High Sch., 1959-68; libr., media specialist Ellsworth (Kans.) High Sch., 1968-84; asst. prof. libr. sci. U. So. Miss., Hattiesburg, 1986-90; chair dept. libr./info. sci. Spalding U., Louisville, 1990-96, libr. dir., 1991—; cons. to sch., pub. and spl. librs., Kans., Miss., Ky., 1970—; mem. Ky. NCATE Bd. Examiners. Author: American History for Children and Young Adults, 1990, World History for Children and Young Adults, 1992; editor: Mississippi Library Media Specialist Staff Development Modules, 1988, Library Lane Newsletter, 1991—; contbr. chpts. to books; contbr. articles to profl. jours. Active City Coun., Ellsworth, Kans., 1975-79, Park Bd., Ellsworth, 1975-79; bd. dirs. Robbins Meml. Libr., 1977-79. Grantee Kans. Demonstration Sch. Libr., 1970-72, Miss. Power Found., 1989; named Women of Yr. Bus. and Profl. Women of Ellsworth, Kans., 1976. Mem. ALA, Am. Assn. Sch. Librs., Nat. Assn. State Ednl. Media Profls., Assn. Coll. & Rsch. Librs., Ky. Libr. Assn., Ky. Sch. Media Assn., Ky. Assn. Tchr. Educators, Assn. for Libr. and Info. Sci. Educators. Office: Spalding U Libr 851 S 4th St Louisville KY 40203-2115

VAN NESS, PATRICIA CATHELINE, composer, violinist; b. Seattle, June 25, 1951; d. C. Charles and Marjorie Mae (Dexter) Van N.; m. Adam Sherman, June 26, 1983. Student in music, Wheaton (Ill.) Coll., 1969-70; student, Gordon Coll., 1972. Composer: ballet score for Beth Soll, 1985, 87, 94, for Monica Levy, 1988, for Boston Ballet, 1988, 90, for Charleston Ballet Theatre, 1994; text and music for voices and early instruments with text translated into Latin for Evensong, 1991, Five Meditations, 1993, Cor Mei Cordis, 1994, Arcanae, 1995, Ego sum Custos Angels, 1995, Tu Risa, 1996, The Nine Orders of the Angels, 1996; various scores, 1985, 86, 87, 88; rec. violinist A&M Records, Private Lightning, 1996, Telarc Internat. Arcanae and Ego sum Custos Angela, 1996; composer-in-residence First Church in Cambridge (Mass.), Congregational, 1996—. Grantee Mass. Cultural Coun., 1993, 96, New Eng. Biolabs. Founds., 1989, Mass. Arts Lottery Coun., 1988; recipient Spl. Recognition award Barlow Internat. Composition for Evensong, 1993. Mem. ASCAP (Spl. award 1996), Chamber Music America, Am. Music Ctr., Alliance of Women in Music.

VAN NESS, PATRICIA WOOD, religious studies educator, consultant; b. Peterborough, N.H., Sept. 12, 1925; d. Leslie Townsend and Bernice E. (Coburn) Wood; m. John Hasbrouck Van Ness, June 13, 1953; children: Peter Wood, Stephen Hasbrouck, Timothy Coburn. BA, U. Wash., 1947; MA, Inst. Transpersonal Psychology, Palo Alto, Calif., 1993. Leader various workshops and retreats, 1979—; records mgr. dept. pub. rels. Standard Oil Co., N.Y.C., 1948-50, sec. pub. rels. dept., 1951; sec. law dept. Johnson & Johnson, New Brunswick, N.J., 1953-54; reporter Hudson Valley Newspapers, Highland, N.Y., 1972-74; acting assoc. dir. office of pub. rels. SUNY, New Paltz, 1974; ednl. cons. Ulster County Assn. for Mental Health, Kingston, N.Y., 1973-76; coord. pub. rels., adminstrv. asst. Calif. Inst. Transpersonal Psychology, Menlo Park, 1981-83; adminstrv. asst. Ctr. for Cont. Edn. Calif. Economy, Palo Alto, 1983-84; profl. rep. pvt. practice Palo Alto, 1984; adminstrv. asst. Inventory Transfer Systems Inc., Palo Alto, 1984-85; ednl. cons. Bedford (N.H.) Presbyn. Ch., 1986-88; ednl. cons. Meth. ch., New Paltz, N.Y., 1976-78, White Plains (N.Y.) Presbyn. Ch., 1978-81. Assoc. editor: The Bible Workbench, 1993—; author: Transforming Bible Study with Children, 1991; contbr. numerous articles to profl. jours. Mem. Assn. Presbyn. Ch. Educators. Democrat. Home: 11 Jaquith Rd Jaffrey NH 03452

VAN NIMAN, CYNTHIA MARIE, family physician, artist; b. Cin., Feb. 5, 1958; d. Kempton Charles and Colette Catherine (Ast) Van N.; m. Daniel John Wissel, July 27, 1980 (div. Oct. 1985); children: Catherine Marie, Stephanie Ann; m. David Alan Hart, May 20, 1995; 1 stepchild, Kyle Michael Hart; 1 child, Patrick Matthew. Diploma in German studies, U. Vienna, Ströbl, Austria, 1978; BA summa cum laude, Edgecliff Coll., Cin., 1980; MA in Art Therapy, Wright State U., 1983, MD, 1991. Diplomate Am. Bd. Med. Examiners, Am. Bd. Family Practice; cert. ACLS, PALS, ATR, neonatal resuscitation. Reservationist Gogo Tours, Cin., 1975-81; primary tchr. German, St. Agnes Sch., Cin., 1977-78; asst. counselor Living Arrangements for Developmentally Disabled, Cin., 1977-78; art therapist U. Cin. Med. Ctr., 1983-87, Millcreek Psychiat. Ctr. for Children, Cin., 1987; resident in family practice St. Elizabeth Med. Ctr., Dayton, Ohio, 1991-94, mem. staff, 1994-95; pvt. practice Beavercreek, Ohio, 1995—; pvt. practice Ohio Valley Family Physicians, Hillsboro, Ohio, Sabina, Ohio, 1994-95; keynote speaker Assn. for Edn. Young Children, Cin., 1987. One-woman show Emery Art Gallery, Cin., 1980. Judge Montgomery County Sci. Fair, 1988. Acad. presdl. and German studies scholar, 1976, activity scholar Edgecliff Coll., 1978, grad. scholar Wright State U., 1982, Cornaro scholar, 1990. Mem. Am. Acad. Family Practice, Ohio Med. Assn., Greene County Med. Soc., Chi Sigma Iota, Kappa Gamma Pi, Psi Chi. Roman Catholic. Office: Forest View Family Practice 1911 N Fairfield Rd Dayton OH 45432-2754

VAN NORTWICK, BARBARA LOUISE, librarian, social science educator; b. Johnson City, N.Y., Jan. 3, 1940; d. Joseph John and Mary Louise (Hamzik) Goodwin; m. David Harry Van Nortwick, Nov. 17, 1962; children: Kimberly Lynn, Craig Michael. BA, Harpur Coll., 1961; MLS, State U. N.Y. at Albany, 1976; DA Info./Libr. Adminstrn. (U.S. Govt. Title II B fellow in libr. adminstrn.), Simmons Coll., Boston, 1986. Coord. ednl. facilities Maine-Endwell H.S., Endwell, N.Y., 1961-64; tchr. English, Guilderland H.S. (N.Y.), 1965-66; audiovisual libr. So. Colonie (N.Y.) H.S., 1974-76; head libr. Westfield (Mass.) H.S., 1976-78, Columbia H.S., East Greenbush, N.Y., 1978-79; libr. dir. N.Y. State Nurses Assn., 1979-84; dir. Com. Aging and Subcom. librs. N.Y. State Senate, 1983-84, dir. Select Com. Interstate Coop., 1985-89; adj. faculty Sch. Info. & Pub. Policy U. Albany, 1983-84, Coll. St. Rose, 1995—; assoc. prof. govt. documents and social scis. Skidmore Coll., Saratoga Springs, N.Y., 1989-94; libr. dir. New Lebanon (N.Y.) Jr./Sr. H.S., 1994-96; libr. faculty Hudson Valley C.C.; del. Mass. Gov.'s Conf. Librs. and Info. Svcs., 1978-79; trustee Capital Dist. Libr. Coun., 1990-95; cons. HEW grant on self-directed continuing edn. for nurses; adj. prof. Sch. Libr. and Info. Sci., SUNY-Albany, 1983-84; adj. libr. faculty Coll. St. Rose, Albany, 1995—; mem. editl. bd. Coll. and Undergrad. Librs. Jour., 1992-94. Mem. ALA, N.Y. Libr. Assn., Med. Libr. Assn. Methodist. Home: 274 Irish Hill Rd Nassau NY 12123-9723 Office: New Lebanon HS New Lebanon NY 12125

VAN NOSTRAND, CATHARINE MARIE HERR, human resources development executive, writer; b. Dubuque, Iowa, June 17, 1937; d. King George and Julia Marie (Hansen) Herr; m. David Michael Van Nostrand, July 16, 1960; children: Laura Susan Van Nostrand Caviani, Catharine Louise, Maren Thyra. Student, Grinnell (Iowa) Coll., 1955-57; BA in Music Edn., U. Iowa, 1959; MA in Human Devel., St. Mary's U. of Minn., Winona, 1989. Music specialist Bound Brook, N.J. and Brookline, Mass., 1959-62; coord. music and worship First United Meth. Ch., St. Cloud, Minn., 1970-75; founder, prin. cons. Catharine Van Nostrand & Assocs., St. Cloud, 1975—; guest lectr., author-in-residence nat. colls. and univs., regional, statewide, nat. and internat. acad. symposia, 1975—; tng. and devel. cons. numerous bus., govt., health and ednl. orgns.; keynote spkr. and workshop facilitator regional and nat. confs. and convs., 1987—; cons./featured spkr. on Equal Opportunity for European Union countries, 1995. Author: Gender-Responsible Leadership: Detecting Bias, Implementing Interventions, 1993; contbr. articles to profl. jours. Capt. prof. div. fundraising for area family YMCA, St. Cloud, 1975; founding bd. dirs. St. Cloud Civic Orch.; vol. radio interviewer Minn. Pub. Radio and WJON Radio, Collegeville/St. Cloud, 1976-77. Mem. AAUW, Forum Exec. Women, Nat. Spkrs. Assn., Minn. Spkrs. Assn., St. Cloud Area C. of C. Democrat. Methodist. Home: 36854 Winnebago Rd Saint Cloud MN 56303-9657 Office: 14 7th Ave N Saint Cloud MN 56303-4766

VAN NOY, CHRISTINE ANN, executive assistant; b. Oakland, CA, Mar. 25, 1948; d. Julio Ceaser and Bernice Thelma (Rose) Lucchesi; m. David Craik Van Noy, July 10, 1971; children: James Allan, Joseph Julio. Student, U. Calif., Berkeley, 1971-73, U. Phoenix, 1994—. Exec. sec. Kaiser Permanente Med. Care Program, Oakland, 1966-76; owner Secret Closet Boutique, Moraga, Calif., 1972-82; owner, operator The Wordshop, Moraga, 1976-86; owner, cons. Van Noy & Assocs., Moraga, 1979—; exec. sec. to sr. v.p., regional mgr. Kaiser Permanente Med. Care Program, 1986-88, chmn., CEO, 1988—; instr. U. Calif., Santa Cruz, 1983-84, Diablo Valley Coll., Concord, Calif., 1984; cons. Nat. Alliance Homebased Businesswomen, San Francisco, 1981-84. Author: Homebased Business Guide, 1982, (with others) Women Working Home, 1982. Mem. bd. Joaquis Moraga Sch. Dist., 1983-84, Calif. Federated Jr. Women's Clubs, 1972-77; bd. dirs. Orinda/Moraga Recreational Swimming Assn., 1984-85, St. Mark's United Methodist Ch., Moraga, 1983-84; pres. bd. Protect Our Nation's Youth Baseball Assn., 1987-90; dir. Ctr. for Living Skills, 1990—. Mem. Women Health Care Execs. Democrat. Roman Catholic. Home: 181 Paseo Del Rio Moraga CA 94556-1641 Office: Kaiser Permanente Med Program 1 Kaiser Plz Oakland CA 94612-3610

VAN PATTEN, JOYCE BENIGNIA, actress; b. Bklyn.; d. Richard Byron and Josephine (Acerno) Van P.; divorced; children: T. Casey King, Talia Balsam. Appeared in Broadway plays including Loves Old Sweet Song, 1941, Tomorrow the World, 1943, The Perfect Marriage, 1944, Wind is Ninety, 1945, Desk Set, 1956, Hole in the Head, 1957, Same Time Next Year, 1975, Murder at the Howard Johnson, 1978, The Supporting Cast, Rumors, Brighton Beach Memoirs, I Ought To Be In Pictures, Jake's Women (with daughter Talia Balsam), 1992, L.A. prodn., 1993, (off Broadway plays) Ivanov, The Seagull, All My Sons, A Fair Country; (films) Trust Me, Monkey Shines, St. Elmo's Fire, Falcon and the Snowman, Billy Galvin, Mame, Blind Date, Infinity (TV shows) The Haunted, Sirens, Under The Influence, Malice In Wonderland, First Lady of the World; (TV movie) Breathing Lessons, Jake's Women, Granpa's Funeral; (TV series) Unhappily Ever After; (short) Patricia Nixon Flying; writer (play) Donuts, (screenplay) Would You Show Us Your Legs Please?. Co-founder The Workshop Theatre West; fund raiser AIDS Project L.A., West Hollywood, 1989, 90. Mem. Am. Film Inst.

VAN PATTEN, MURIEL MAY, educational consultant; b. Quincy, Mich., Apr. 27, 1932; d. Lloyd Delmar and Edwina Weaver (Parsons) Van P. BS, Ea. Mich. U., 1954, MA, 1962; postgrad., Wayne State U., 1967. Art tchr. Fenton (Mich.) Pub. Schs., 1954-56; arts and crafts instr. Chgo. Park Dist., 1955-56; tchr. Wayne (Mich.) Cmty. Sch. Dist., 1956-60, dir. art, 1960-65, elem. sch. prin., 1965-74, learning cons., 1974-75; accountability liaison specialist Mich. State Dept. Edn., Lansing, 1975-77, supr. instrnl. specialist program, 1977-79, dir. sch. program svcs., 1979-84; cons. Detroit Pub. Schs., 1988-89, Kent County Intermediate Sch. Dist., Lansing, 1989-90; cons. in field, 1985—; dir. secondary edn., coord. student tchrs. Ea. Mich. U., 1962; vis. guest lectr. edn., art depts. Editor, author: (policy book) Michigan Core Curriculum, 1989-90; contbr. chpt. to book. Sch. liaison Soc. for Entertainment and Arts Devel., Charlotte County, Fla., 1987-88; v.p. Friends of Music, Charlotte County, 1987-88; grants co-chair Arts Coun., Charlotte County, 1988-89; local govt. chair LWV, Charlotte County, 1989. Mem. NEA, Nat. Art Edn. Assn., Mich. Art Edn. Assn., MIch. Dirs. Pub. Sch. Art Edn. (chmn. 1966-67), Mich. Assn. Supervision and Curriculum Devel., Mich. Assn. Elem. Prins., Coun. for Dem. and Secular Humanism, Inst. for Ojectivist Studies, Cato Inst., Phi Delta Kappa, Sigma Nu Phi (v.p. 1954), Soroptimist Fedn. Am., Soroptimist of Wayne (rec. sec. 1967). Home: 533 Skylark Ln Port Charlotte FL 33952

VAN PELT, FRANCES EVELYN, management consultant; b. Oregon, Ill., Aug. 25, 1937; d. Henry Benjamin and Bessie May (Himes) Ulferts; m. R. Richard Van Pelt, Oct. 28, 1953; children: R. Richard Jr., Robin F. Van Pelt Dobbs, Raymond Scott, Ronda Jean. Student, Waubonsee Coll., Sugar Grove, Ill., 1971-75. Adminstrv. asst. Sears, Roebuck & Co., Aurora, Ill., 1960-73; owner, mgr., pres. Outdoor World, Inc., Aurora, 1973-87; 20 group dir. Spader Mgmt. Groups, Inc., Sioux Falls, S.D., 1988—; bd. dirs. RV Consumer Care Commn., Fairfax, Va., 1985-88. Contbr. articles to profl. jours. Bd. dirs. Breaking Free, Aurora, 1988-90; cellist Fox Valley Symphony, Aurora, 1961-81. Mem. Aurora C. of C. Recrational Vehicle Dealers Assn. (bd. dirs. 1978-79, exec. bd. 1980-82, pres. 1983, chmn. bd. dirs. 1984), Ill. RV Dealers Assn. (pres., bd. dirs. 1978-79, exec. bd. 1980-82, pres. 1983, chmn. bd. dirs. 1984). Republican. Roman Catholic. Home: 1273 Colorado Ave Aurora IL 60506-2044 Office: PO Box M Sioux Falls SD 57101-1937

VAN PELT, JANET RUTH, insurance executive; b. Baltimore, Md., Jan. 28, 1948; d. John Francis and Helen Janet V. BA, Fla. State U., 1969, MA, 1972. Instr. Wayne State U., Detroit, Mich., 1971-72; promotion asst. Actors Theatre of Louisville, Ky., 1972-73; lecturer Towson State U., Towson, Md., 1973-75; workers' compensation Harry T. Campbell Sons' Co., Towson, 1973-74, claims representative Atlantic Mutual Companies, Hunt Vly., Md., 1974-78; claims supr. Atlantic Mut. Cos., N.Y., 1978-79; home office claims examiner Atlantic Mutual Co., N.Y., 1979-88; supr. home office excess claims Am. Home Assurance Co., East Orange, N.J., 1988, sr. supr. home office excess claims, 1989-90; claims mgr. GRE Ins. Group, Princeton, N.J., 1990-92, Elliston, Inc., New Hope, Pa., 1992—. Mem. Assn. of Research and Enlightment, Holistic Health Assn. Democratic. Episcopalian. Office: Elliston Inc Buckingham House 9 Reeder Rd New Hope PA 18938-1015

VANPOOL, CYNTHIA PAULA, special education educator, special services consultant; b. San Antonio, Dec. 8, 1946; d. Walter Foye and Pauline (Karger) Phillips; m. Darrell William Vanpool, Feb. 3, 1968; children: George Karger, William Davies. AB in English, Drury Coll., 1968; MS in Spl. Edn. Tchg., Pittsburg (Kans.) State U., 1987. Cert. tchr., Kans., Mo., Okla.; cert. instr. in Quest Skills for Adolescents. Tchr. lang. arts and journalism Miami (Okla.) Pub. Schs., 1968-69; dir. Christian edn./outreach ministries First Assembly of God, Miami, 1981-83; substitute tchr. Miami Pub. Sch. Dist., 1983-85, learning disabilities specialist, journalism sponsor/advisor, 1985-93, spl. svcs. cons., 1993—; chair spl. edn. dept. Will Rogers Jr. H.S./Mid. Sch., Miami, 1988-94, nat. jr. honor soc. advisor, 1993-94; homebound instr.; cooperating educator for student tchr. supervision, supr. resident tchr.; cons., tutor, presenter in field. Recipient Cert. of Appreciation, Miami Evening Lions Club, 1987, Disting. Svc. award Okla. Lions Clubs, 1988, Internat. Presdl. Cert. of Appreciation for Humanitarian Svc., Lions Internat., 1988; Miami Pub. Sch. Enrichment Found. grantee, 1995. Mem. Coun. for Exceptional Children, Divsn. for Learning Disabilities, Coun. for Children with Learning Disabilities, Phi Kappa Phi. Mem. Assembly of God. Ch. Home: Rt 2 Box 19 Miami OK 74354 Office: Miami Pub Schs 20th and B St NE Miami OK 74354

VAN RAALTE, BARBARA G., realtor; b. Rochester, N.Y., Apr. 11, 1932; d. Maurice Harry and Estelle Belle (Breman) Goldman; m. John Allen Van Raalte, Sept. 5, 1954 (div. July 1974); children: John Allen Jr., Peter Baird, Thomas Douglas, Andrea Lynn. BA in Econs. and Polit. Sci., Wellesley Coll., 1954; postgrad., Harvard Grad. Sch. Design, 1993, 95. Cert. buyer rep., N.C. Dir. devel. Stowe (Vt.) Sch., 1975-77; assoc. dir. devel. NYU Med. Ctr., The Rusk Inst. (formerly known as Inst. Rehab. Medicine), N.Y.C., 1977-80; dir. devel. Planned Parenthood of Vt., Burlington, 1980-83; realtor, sr. assoc. Foulsham Farms Real Estate, South Burlington, 1983-95, Trombley Real Estate, Burlington, 1995—. Bd. dirs., treas. Hist. Soc., Stowe, 1974-75; bd. dirs. emeritus Katonah (N.Y.) Mus. Art, 1980—; mem. Nat. Spkrs. Bur., United Jewish Appeal, 1982-84. Mem. Nat. Assn. Realtors, Vt. Assn. Realtors, Hadassah (bd. dirs. Mid. East affairs 1996). Jewish. Home: 5 Southwind Dr Burlington VT 05401 Office: Trombley Real Estate 23 Pine St Burlington VT 05401

VANRAVENSWAAY, MARTI, county commissioner; b. Abilene, Tex., May 9, 1946; d. Robert Reginald and Mary Lynn (Brown) Miller; m. Richard Bruce VanRavenswaay, Dec. 10, 1968; children: Robert Lyn, Scott Jeffrey. BA in Applied Bus., Dallas Baptist U., 1995. Pub. rels. office adminstr. Britt Phillips Co., Arlington, Tex., 1984-85; broker assoc. Century 21 Sutherland, Arlington, 1985-89; ptnr. Visions in Action, Arlington, 1989—; county commr. Tarrant County, Fort Worth, Tex., 1991—; mem. Tex. Civil Justice League, Austin, 1988—; pres. Tarrant County Indsl. Devel. Bd., Fort Worth, 1991—; mem. bd. dirs. Arlington C. of C., 1991—, Tarrant County Assn. of Mediators, Fort Worth, 1995—. Mem. Arlington Rep. Women, 1991—, Spinks Airport Bd., Fort Worth, 1992—; hon. bd. mem. Alliance For Children, Arlington, 1994—; mem. bd. dirs. Arlington C. of C., 1991—. Recipient Woman of the Yr. award Citizens Jour., 1984, Woman of Achievement award Zonta Internat., 1988, Friend of Edn. award Phi Delta Kappa, 1991, Outstanding Woman of the Yr. award Bus. & Profl. Women, 1993. Mem. Arlington Youth and Families (bd. dirs.), Dental Health for Arlington (adv. bd.), Tarrant Challenge (bd. dirs.), Tarrant County Citizen's Crime Awareness Network, AIDS Outreach Ctr. (bd. dirs.), Women's Shelter Aux. Republican. Baptist. Home: 5710 Overridge Ct Arlington TX 76017 Office: Tarrant County 724 E Border St Ste 103 Arlington TX 76010

VAN REENEN, JANE SMITH, speech and language pathologist; b. Baton Rouge, Sept. 16, 1949; d. William Robert and Mary Jane (Laidlaw) Smith; m. Dirk Andries van Reenen, Mar. 3, 1973; children: Andrea Lee, Erika Lynn. BS in Speech Pathology, La. State U., 1971; MEd in Speech Pathology, Ga. State U., 1984. Cert. clin. competence Am. Speech-Lang.-Hearing Assn.; lic. Ga.; cert. tchr. Ga. Speech-lang. pathologist Livingston Parish Schs., La., 1971-73, Gwinnett County (Ga.) Schs., 1973-75, 95—; pvt. practice speech-lang. pathology Norcross, Ga., 1975—; speech-lang. pathologist Nova Care, Atlanta, 1979—, Gwinnett County Schs., 1994—; grad. asst. Ga. State U., Atlanta, 1983-84, substitute clin. supr., 1988-90, interim clinic coord., 1991; speech-lang. pathologist Americana Nursing Home, Decatur, 1984; chairperson Atlanta (Ga.) Orofacial Myology Study Group, 1987-89; adv. com. Comm. Disorders Program, Atlanta, 1990-94; mem. Ga. Supervision Network, 1991—; mem. Cognitive Remediation Interest Group, Atlanta, 1993—. Mng. editor: Internat. Jour. Orofacial Myology, 1989-91; contbr. articles to profl. jours. Ruling elder Northminster Presbyn. Ch., Roswell, Ga., 1981; mem. local sch. adv. com. Pinckneyville Middle Sch., Norcross, 1987-92, co-founder sch. based drug/alchol abuse prevention program, 1988; v.p. Parent Tchr. Student Assn. Norcross High Sch., 1990-91; pres. River Valley Estates Homeowners Assn., Norcross, 1991; local sch. adv. com. Norcross High Sch., 1993—, AIDS rep. PTSA, 1993-96, drug/alcohol abuse rep., 1993-96, care team, 1993—. Recipient Positive Parenting awards Ga. State Supt. of Schs., Atlanta, 1987-88, 88-89; named Outstanding Sch. Vol., Gwinnet County Bd. Edn., Lawrenceville, Ga., 1989-90. Mem. Am. Speech-Lang.-Hearing Assn. (congl. action contact com. 1991—), Ga. Speech-Lang.-Hearing Assn. (honors and ethics com. 1989-91), Internat. Assn. Orofacial Myology (mng. editor 1989-91). Republican. Home and Office: 3992 Gunnin Rd Norcross GA 30092-1953

VAN RENNES, PAMELA ANN, school counselor; b. Brookline, Mass., Mar. 14; d. Albert Bernhardi and Mabel Jeannette (Chittenden) Van R. BA in German & Tchg., Franklin Coll., 1972; MS in German & Edn., Purdue U., 1977, English cert., 1981, counseling cert., 1993. German tchr. Sch. City of Hammond (Ind.), 1973-93, fgn. lang. coord., 1980-81, couselor, 1993—, crisis team coord., 1993—. Mem. ACA, Am. Sch. Counseling Assn., Ind. Counseling Assn., Phi Delta Kappa. Office: Sch City Hammond Scott Mid Sch 3635 173rd St Hammond IN 46323

VAN RY, GINGER LEE, school psychologist; b. Alexandria, Va., June 26, 1953; d. Ray Ellsworth Hensley and Bernice Anne (Weidel) Wolter; m. Willem Hendrik Van Ry, Aug 23, 1986; 1 child, Anika Claire. AA, U. Nev., Las Vegas, 1973; BA, U. Wash., 1983, MEd, 1985. Psychometrist The Mason Clinic, Seattle, 1980-84, supr., psychology lab., 1984-86; sch. psychologist Everett (Wash.) Sch. Dist., 1986—; mem. profl. ednl. adv. bd. U. Wash. Sch. Psychology, Seattle, 1995-98. Author: (with others) Wash. State Assn. of Sch. Psychologists Best Practice Handbook, 1993. Co-pres. Lake Cavanaugh Hghts. Assn., Seattle, 1994-95, chmn. long-range planning com., 1995—. Mem. AAUW, NEA, Nat. Assn. Sch. Psychologists (cert. sch. psychologist), Wash. State Assn. Sch. Psychologists (chair profl. devel. com. 1995—), Wash. State Edn. Assn., U. Wash. Alumni Assn. Democrat. Office: The Everett Sch Dist 4730 Colby Ave PO Box 2098 Everett WA 98203

VAN RYNBACH, ANGELA, association administrator; b. Amsterdam, Sept. 5, 1948; came to U.S., 1951; d. Jan Daniel and Georgette Y. Van Rynbach. BA, NYU, 1969, MA, 1971. Program mgr. UN, N.Y.C., 1974-81; program officer World Food Program, Rome, 1981-85; adviser World Food Program, Dhaka, Bangladesh, 1989-91; dep. country dir. World Food Program, New Delhi, 1993—; country dir. Save the Children, Dhaka, 1989-91; women/child program dir. Save the Children, Westport, Conn., 1991-93. V.p. Rotary, New Delhi, 1994-96. Mem. Assn. Women Devel. Democrat. Home: PO Box 1573 Shelter Island NY 11964-1573 Office: World Food Program, 53 Jor Bagh, New Delhi 110003, India

VANSANT, JOANNE FRANCES, academic administrator; b. Morehead, Ky., Dec. 29, 1924; d. Lewis L. and Dorothy (Greene) VanS. BA, Denison U., Granville, Ohio; MA, The Ohio State U.; postgrad., U. Colo. and The Ohio State U.; LLD (hon.), Albright Coll., 1975. Tchr., health and phys. edn. Mayfield, Kentucky High Sch., 1946-48; instr. Denison U., Granville, Ohio, 1948; instr. women's phys. edn. Otterbein Coll., Westerville, Ohio, 1948-52, assoc. prof., 1955-62, dept. chmn., 1950-62, chmn. div. profl. studies, 1961-65, dean of women, 1952-60, 62-64, dean of students, 1964-93, v.p. student affairs, 1968-93; v.p., dean student affairs emeritus, 1993—, cons. Instnl. Advancement, 1993—. Co-pres. Directions for Youth, 1983-84, pres., 1984-85; bd. dirs. North Area Mental Health; trustee Westerville Civic Symphony at Otterbein Coll., 1983-88; active numerous other community orgns.; ordained elder Presbyn. Ch., 1967. Named to hon. Order of Ky. Cols., 1957; recipient Focus on Youth award Columbus Dispath, 1983, Vol. of the Yr. award North Area Mental Health Svcs., 1982, citation Denison U., 1996. Mem. Am. Assn. Counseling and Devel., Ohio Personnel and Guidance Assn., Ohio Assn. Women Deans, Adminstrs., Counselors (treas., exec. bd. 1972-73), Nat. Assn. Student Personnel Adminstrs., Ohio Coll. Personnel Assn., Mortar Bd. (hon.), Zonta Internat. (pres. Columbus, Ohio club 1984-85, dist. gov. 1988-90), Vocal Arts Resource Network (chair bd. dirs. 1994-96), Cap and Dagger Club, Torch and Key Hon., Order Omega, Alpha Lambda Delta, Theta Alpha Phi, others. Home: 9100 Oakwood Pt Westerville OH 43082-9643 Office: Otterbein Coll Instnl Advancement Westerville OH 43081

VAN SCODER, LINDA I., respiratory therapy program director; b. Defiance, Ohio, Mar. 20, 1953; d. Robert Allen Van Scoder and Esther Irene (Miller) Blair. BS in Respiratory Therapy, U. Cin., 1975; MS in Allied Health Edn., Ind. U., 1979, EdD in Adult Edn., 1985. Registered respiratory therapist. Respiratory crit. care supr. Meth. Hosp., Indpls., 1975-76, chief of pediatric respiratory therapy, 1976-78, dir. clin. edn., 1978-79; dir. clin. edn. Butler Univ./Meth. Hosp., Indpls., 1979-85; asst. prof. gen. studies DePauw U., Greencastle, Ind., 1989-92; program dir. Ball State U./Meth. Hosp., Indpls., 1985—; adj. prof. Ball State U., 1985—. Co-author: Advanced Emergency Care for Paramedic Practice, 1992, (proceedings) Delineating the Education Direction for the Future, 1992, Year 2001: An Action Agenda, 1993; editor: Respiratory Care Edn. Ann., 1994—. Pub. health educator DePauw U., Puno, Peru, 1986, coord. health worker tng., Mactan, Philippines, 1987, Bo, Sierra Leone, 1989, Las Matas de Farfan, Dominican Rep., 1991. Mem. Am. Assn. Respiratory Care (Educator of Yr. 1993, editl. bd. 1992-94, cons. to com. on accreditation 1993), Ind. Soc. Respiratory Care (v.p. 1979), Ind. Allied Health Assn. (bd. dirs. 1990-91), Ind. Thoracic Soc., Respiratory Care Accreditation Bd. (rep., pres.-elect 1995, pres. 1996). Home: 1644 Marborough Ln Indianapolis IN 46260-5233

VANSELL, SHARON LEE, nursing administrator, nursing educator, researcher, obstetrical and psychiatric clinical nurse; b. Indpls., Feb. 7, 1944; d. Leo Roland and Mimadel (Klipsch) VanSell; m. Thomas Wayne Davidson, Apr. 10, 1967 (div. Nov. 1978); 1 child, Daniel Zane; m. Glenn William Meintz, Mar. 17, 1982 (div. Mar. 1995). BSN, Murray State U., 1968; MEd in Health Edn., Memphis State U., 1971; MS in Nursing Adminstrn., U. Colo., 1985; EdD in Guidance Counseling, U. Denver, 1986. Sr. rsch. assoc. Planning and Human Systems, Inc., Washington, 1975-77; ob-gyn coord. Meml. Hosp., Colorado Springs, Colo., 1978-79; indsl. nurse Ramport Industries, Colorado Springs, 1979-80; psychiat. nurse N.E.E.D. Jr./Sr. High Sch., Colorado Springs, 1980-84; dir. rsch. Ireland Corp., Englewood, Colo., 1984; staff nurse perinatal float pool Univ. Hosp., Denver, 1985; dir. reproductive and pediatric nursing, asst. dir. patient care svcs. U. Calif. Med. Ctr., San Diego, 1986-90; relief charge nurse Charter Hosp., Las Vegas, 1990-94; assoc. prof. U. Nev., Las Vegas, 1990—; relief charge nurse Manti Vista Hosp., 1994-95; maternal child nurse Sunrise Med. Ctr., 1995—; nursing cons. Comprehensive Health Care Devel., Inc., Fairfax, 1974—, Bur. Quality Assurance and Profl. Svcs. Revises Orgn., DHEW, Rockville, Md., 1972-75; pres., ceo C.P.E., Colorado Springs, 1977-80; founder NURMETRICS and computational nursing, 1990—; pres. Omega Techs., Inc., Las Vegas, 1995—. Editor: PSRO: Utilization and Adult, 1976, Alcoholism and Health, 1980; sr. author: Nursing Care Evaluation: Concurrent and Retrospective, 1977, Obstetrical Nursing, 1980; co-author: PSRR: The Promise Perspective, 1981; mem. editl. bd. RN, Family and Cmty. Health Jour.; contbr. articles to profl. jours. 1dst lt. U.S. Army Nurse Corps, 1966-69. U. Colo. Gannett scholar for excellence in nursing, 1985-86; recipient March of Dimes So. Nev. Nurse of the Yr. award in Edn., 1992, Disting. Women of Nev. award, 1995, Future Vision Sci. award, 1995. Mem. Nev. Nurses Assn., Western Inst. Nursing (nominating com. 1988-90), Phi Kappa Delta, Sigma Theta Tau. Home: 3678 Crest View Dr Las Vegas NV 89120-1202 Office: U Nev BHS 435 4505 S Maryland Pky Las Vegas NV 89154

VAN SOLKEMA-WAITZ, TERESE ELLEN, special education educator, consultant; b. West Palm Beach, Fla., Jan. 9, 1956; d. Richard Andrew Van Solkema and Deborah Bradshaw (Crockett) Stupey; m. John William Waitz, Oct. 4, 1986; children: Sarah Lindsay, Rebecca Elizabeth. BS, Fitchburg State Coll., 1979. Cert. tchr., spl. edn. tchr., Mass. Spl. edn. vision specialist Waltham (Mass.) Pub. Schs., 1979-80; tchr. head-injured, multi-impaired students Perkins Sch. for Blind, Watertown, Mass., 1979-83; spl. educator head-injury program Moss Rehab. Hosp., Phila., 1984-86; ind. cons., head injury home and community specialist Bensalem, Pa., 1986—; case mgr. Commonwealth of Pa. Head Injury Program, Harrisburg, 1989-96; presenter at profl. confs.; workshop leader; legal expert for Phila. law firms, 1986-87, 88. Mem. Coun. Exceptional Children, Nat. Head Injury Found., Pa. Head Injury Found., N.J. Head Injury Found., Pa. Assn. Rehab. Facilities (mem. head injury study tech. group). Mem. Soc. of Friends.

VANSTROM, MARILYN JUNE, retired elementary education educator; b. Mpls., June 10, 1924; d. Harry Clifford and Myrtle Agnes (Hagland) Christensen; m. Reginald Earl Vanstrom, Mar. 20, 1948; children: Gary Alan, Kathryn June Vanstrom Marinello. AA, U. Minn., 1943, BS, 1946. Cert. elem. tchr., N.Y., Ill. Tchr. Pub. Sch., St. Louis Park, Minn., 1946-47, Deephaven, Minn., 1947-50, Chicago Heights, Ill., 1950-52, Steger, Ill., 1964; substitute tchr. Pub. Sch., Dobbs Ferry, N.Y., 1965-72, Yonkers, N.Y., 1965-92. Mem. Ch. Women, Christ Meml. Luth. Ch. Mem. AAUW (life, pres. 1988-90, Ednl. Found. award 1990, Morning Book Club, Evening Book Club Met. West br.), Yonkers Fedn. Tchrs. Democrat. Home: 12300 Marion Ln W Apt 2105 Minnetonka MN 55305-1317

VANTAGGI, ZOLA MURIEL, musician; b. Hesper, Iowa, July 8, 1925; d. Ralph Leslie and Otilla Theodora (Ramlo) Fawcett; m. Reno Vantaggi, June 18, 1960. BA, Luther Coll., Decorah, Iowa, 1947; cert. in teaching, Sherwood Mus. Sch., Chgo., 1953. Tchr. Pub. sch., Lakefield, Minn., 1947-51, Chatfield, Minn., 1951-55; mgr. music store DeBellis Co., Riverside, Calif., 1955-56; tchr. Pub. Sch., Bloomington, Minn., 1956-60, Rochester, Minn., 1960-64; organist Gloria Dei Luth. Ch., Rochester, Minn., 1961—; therapist State Hosp., Rochester, 1966-67; pres. Gloria Dei Welca, Rochester, 1968-69, 89-90. AAUW grantee, 1993. Mem. AAUW, Am. Guild Organists (mem.-at-large, bd. dirs. 1990-95), Symphony Guild (pres. 1972-73). Home: Box 21 Byron MN 55920

VAN TREASE, SANDRA ANN, insurance company executive; b. St. Louis, Dec. 11, 1960; m. Virgil Van Trease; children: Shawna, Erin. BSBA, U. Mo., St. Louis, 1982; MBA, Washington U., St. Louis, 1992. CPA, Mo.; cert. mgmt. acct., Mo. Sr. mgr. audit divsn. Price Waterhouse, St. Louis, 1982-94; v.p. fin. rep. and investor rels. Alliance Blue Cross/Blue Shield, St. Louis, 1994-95, sr. v.p., CFO,, 1995—. Author practice cases, 1988, 90. Treas. Art-St. Louis, 1992-94, St. Louis County Fair and Air Show, 1993-94; chmn. adminstrn. Fair St. Louis, 1994-96. Mem. AICPA, Fin. Execs. Inst., Inst. Mgmt. Accts., Mo. Soc. CPA's. Office: Alliance Blue Cross/Blue Shield 1831 Chestnut St Saint Louis MO 63103

VAN TUYL, KATHRYN URSULA LEACH, retired secondary educator; b. New Bethlehem, Pa., Jan. 10, 1909; d. Alonzo and Catherine (Hoelzel) Leach; m. George Henry Van Tuyl Jr., Aug. 10, 1933; children: George Henry III, John Steelman. BA, Bucknell U., 1930; postgrad., Columbia U., 1932. Permanent teaching cert. Tchr. Summerville (Pa.) High Sch., 1930-33; part time teaching various high schs., Pa., N.Y., 1946-55; part time substitute tchr. various high schs., Garden City, N.Y., 1955-65; real estate sales person Garden City (N.Y.) Realty, 1965-72; high sch. drama coach, newspaper coach, Pa., N.Y.; founder English in Action fgn. student group Adelphi U., Garden City. Sunday sch. tchr. McKeesport, Pa., Garden City, 1940-80. Recipient scholarship Bucknell U., Lewisburg, Pa., 1926. Mem. AAUW (various positions), PEO. Republican. Methodist. Home: 459 Sandhill Rd Apt 656 Hershey PA 17033-2035

VAN UMMERSEN, CLAIRE A(NN), academic administrator, biologist, educator; b. Chelsea, Mass., July 28, 1935; d. George and Catherine (Courtovich); m. Frank Van Ummersen, June 7, 1958; children: Lynn, Scott. BS, Tufts U., 1957, MS, 1960, PhD, 1963; DSc (hon.), U. Mass., 1988, U. Maine, 1991. Rsch. asst. Tufts U., 1957-60, 60-67, grad. asst. in embryology, 1962, postdoctoral teaching asst., 1963-66, lectr. in biology, 1967-68; asst. prof. biology U. Mass., Boston, 1968-74; assoc. prof. U. Mass., 1974-86, assoc. dean acad. affairs, 1975-76, assoc. vice chancellor acad. affairs, 1976-78, chancellor, 1978-79, dir. Environ. Sci. Ctr., 1980-82; assoc. vice chancellor acad. affairs Mass. Bd. Regents for Higher Edn., 1982-85, vice chancellor for mgmt. systems and telecommunications, 1985-86; chancellor Univ. System N.H., Durham, 1986-92; sr. fellow New Eng. Bd. Higher Edn., 1992-93; sr. fellow New Eng. Resource Ctr. Higher Edn. U. Mass., 1992-93; pres. Cleve. (Ohio) State U., 1993—; cons. Mass. Bd. Regents, 1981-82, AGB, 1992—, Kuwait U., 1992-93; asst. Lancaster Course in Ophthalmology, Mass. Eye. and Ear Infirmary, 1962-69, lectr., 1970-93, also coord.; reviewer HEW; mem. rsch. team which established safety stds. for exposure to microwave radiation, 1958-65; participant Leadership Am. program, 1992-93. Mem. N.H. Ct. Systems Rev. Task Force, 1989-90; mem. New Eng. Bd. Higher Edn., 1986-92, mem. exec. com., 1989-92, N.H. adv. coun., 1990-92; chair Rhodes Scholarship Selection Com., 1986-91; bd. dirs. N.H. Bus. and Industry Assn., 1987-90, 90-93; governing bd. N.H. Math. Coalition, 1991-92; exec. com. 21st Century Learning Community, 1992-93; state panelist N.H. Women in Higher Edn., 1986-93; bd. dirs. Urban League Greater Cleve., 1993—, mem. strategic planning com., chair edn. com., 1996—; bd. dirs. Great Lakes Sci. & Tech. Mus., 1993—, Sci. & Tech. Coun. Cleve. Tomorrow, Ohio Aerospace Inst., 1993—, Northeast Ohio Coun. Higher Edn., 1993—; mem. Leadership Am. Class '93, Leadership Cleve. Class '95. Recipient Disting. Svc. medal U. Mass., 1979, Am. Cancer Soc. grantee Tufts U., 1960. Mem. Am. Coun. on Edn. (com. on self-regulation 1987-91), State Higher Exec. Officers (fed. rels. com., cost accountability task force, exec. com. 1990-92), ACE (comm. leadership devel.), Nat. Assn. Sys. Heads (exec. com. 1990-92), Nat. Ctr. for Edn. Stats. (network adv. com. 1989-92, chair accreditation teams 1988—), New Eng. Assn. Schs. and Colls. (commn. on higher edn. 1990-93), North Ctrl. Assn. Schs. and Colls. (evaluator 1993, 95, 96), Soc. Devel. Biology, Greater Cleve. Round Table (bd. dirs. 1993—), Cleve. Playhouse (trustee 1994—), United Way (bd. dirs. 1995—), Nat. Assn. State Univs. and Land Grant Colls. (exec. com. on urban agenda, state rep. AASCU), Phi Beta Kappa, Sigma Xi. Office: Cleve State Univ Rhodes Tower Euclid Ave at E 24th St Cleveland OH 44115

VAN WHY, REBECCA RIVERA, retired guidance counselor; b. Casa Blanca, N.Mex., Sept. 14, 1932; d. Charles and Doris (Thompson) Rivera; m. Raymond Richard Van Why, Aug. 27, 1955; children: Raymond R., Ronald R., Randall R. BS, U. N.Mex., 1959. Tchr. Bur. of Indian Affairs, Albuquerque, 1960-62, guidance counselor, 1969-94, tchr., supr., 1973-74, acting dir. student life, 1987, ret., 1994; head tchr. Laguna (N.Mex.) Headstart OEO, 1967-69, acting dir., 1969. Appt. N.Mex. Youth Conservation Corps Commn., 1992-96. Recipient Cert. of Recognition, Sec. of Interior, 1975, Cert. of Appreciation, State of N.Mex., 1986, N.Mex. Commn. on the Status of Women, 1993; named honoree Internat. Women's Day, U. N.Mex., 1987. Republican. Home: 14417 Central Ave NW Albuquerque NM 87121-7756

VAN WICKLIN, BARBARA LEE, curriculum coordinator; b. Spokane, Wash., Sept. 10, 1945; d. John Mueller and Dorothy Irene (Gorish) Johansen; m. John Floyd Van Wicklin, June 15, 1968; children: Robert Wayne, John Floyd II, Lynlee Ann. BS in English, Taylor U., 1967; MS in Englsih, Alfred U., 1968; student, Brockport State U., 1994—. Tchr. English Teaneck (N.J.) High Sch., 1967-70; tchr. nursery Playgarten, Valley Cottage, N.Y., 1976-78; tchr. gifted edn. Allegany-Cattaraugus Boces, Olean, N.Y., 1984-87; tchr. gifted edn. Fillmore (N.Y.) Sch. Dist., 1988-94, curriculum staff specialist, 1994-95; program mgr. Instructional Tech. BOCES, 1995—. Author: (with others) Nita-Resource of Creative and Inventive Activities, 1994. Co-dir. Royal Family Kids Kamp, Houghton, N.Y., 1994; mem. commn. edn. bd. Congressman Amory Houghton's, N.Y.C., 1992—; bd. dirs. Adv. Gifted and Talented Edn., N.Y.C., 1989—. Recipient Nat. Teaching award NEA Design Tech., 1994. Mem. ASCD, NSF, Nat. Invertive Thinking Assn., Nat. Staff Devel., Allegany Arts Assn. (v.p. 1992), Roundtable (commr. patents and trademarks 1987—). Republican. Home: 38 Park Dr Houghton NY 14744 Office: Bd Coop Edn Svcs 1825 Windfall Rd Olean NY 14760-9303

VAN WIJK, MAIKE HEDWIG GISELA, reporter; b. Vinkeveen, The Netherlands, Aug. 22, 1973; came to the U.S., 1990; d. Pieter Deventer and Birgitt (Gosse) van W. BA in Journalism cum laude, U. Houston, 1996. Clk. Little Prof. Bookcenter, Kingwood, Tex., 1995; reporter The Daily Cougar, Houston, 1995; intern reporter The Baytown (Tex.) Sun, 1996. Vol. newsletter coord. Forest Cove Bapt. Ch., Kingwood, 1992-94, middle sch. youth leader, 1992-94, 95-96. Scholar Press Club Houston, 1995-96. Mem. Soc. Profl. Journalists, Women in Comm., Golden Key. Home: 2115 Crystal River Dr Kingwood TX 77345

VAN ZANTE, SHIRLEY M(AE), magazine editor; b. Elma, Iowa; d. Vernon E. and Georgene (Woodmansee) Borland; m. Dirk C. Van Zante. AA, Grandview Coll., 1950; BA, Drake U., 1952. Assoc. editor Mchts. Trade Jour., Des Moines, 1952-55; copywriter Meredith Pub. Co., Des Moines, 1955-60, book editor, 1960-67; home furnishings editor Better Homes and Gardens Spl. Interest Publs., Meredith Corp., 1967-74; home furnishing and design editor Better Homes and Gardens mag., 1974-89; writer, editl. cons., 1989—. Named Advt. Woman of Yr. in Des Moines, 1961; recipient Dorothy Dawe award, 1971, 73, 75, 76, 77, Dallas Market Ctr. award, 1983, So. Furniture Market Writer's award, 1984. Mem. Am. Soc. Interior Designers (press affiliate), Alpha Xi Delta. Address: 1905 74th St Des Moines IA 50322-5701

VARADI, KATHLEEN FRANCES, obstetrician and gynecologist; b. Buffalo, Sept. 25, 1950; d. Louis Ernest and Marie Frances (Lenahen) V.; m. Charles Edward Terrio, Aug. 20, 1972 (div. Oct. 1980). BA, Merrimack Coll., 1972; MEd, Framingham (Mass.) State Coll., 1979; MD, U. Vt., 1983. Diplomate Am. Bd. Ob-Ghyn. Am. Bd. Gynlaparoscopy. Intern internal medicine U. Conn., Farmington, 1983-84; resident obstetrics and gynecology Danbury (Conn.) Hosp. Yale New Haven Affiliate, 1984-88; pvt. practice Baylor Richardson Hosp., Tex., 1988-94; ob-gyn. Med. Ctr. Plano, Tex., 1994—; mem. credentialing com. Baylor Richardsons Hosp., 1993-94. Fellow Am. Coll. Ob-Gyn.; mem. AMA, Am. Assn. Gyn. Laparascopists, Am. Soc. of Reproductive Medicine, Am. Urogynecology Soc., Gynecology Laser Soc., Rotary. Roman Catholic. Home: 4012 Pecan Orchard Dr Parker TX 75002 Office: North Tex Ob-Gyn 3709 W 15th St Plano TX 75075

VARALLO, DEBORAH GARR, marketing executive; b. Nashville, Feb. 14, 1952; d. August Anthony and Kathleen Marie (Baltz) Garr; m. James Edward Varallo, May 6, 1978. BS in Secondary Edn., Baylor U., 1976. With pub. relations dept. Hermitage (Tenn.) Landing, 1976-77; salesperson Elm Hill Meats, Nashville, 1977-78; asst. dir. ARC, Nashville, 1978-81; sales mgr. Varallo Foods, Inc., Nashville, 1981-85; salesperson Mid. Tenn. Equipment, Nashville, 1985-86, Garr Equipment Co., Mt. Juliet, Tenn., 1986-89, Scott Bolt & Screw, Nashville, 1989-90; owner, pres. Varallo & Assocs., Nashville, 1990—. Mem. adv com. Hemophilia Adv. Bd. Tenn. Health and Environment, 1986-90; chmn. Mid-Cumberland chpt. Hemophilia Found., 1986-88, treas., 1989-90; chairperson fund raiser, 1988; co-chair, Bus. Expo, 1988, bd. dirs. 1989-91, mem. chairperson 1989; rep. Metro Airport Wilson County, 1988; bd. dirs. Combined Health Appeal, 1988-90; bd. dirs. Cumberland Valley Girl Scouts Coun., 1993—, nomination chair, 1994, 95-96, Cookie Sculpture chair, 1993; speechcraft dir., mem. blood recruitment bd. for Tenn. ARC, blood svcs. bd. dirs., 1995-97, vice chair 1994—, chair blood recruitment com., Clara Barton charter mem., mem. blood svcs. task force, 1994, task force on roles and responsibilities and strategic planning, 1996; bd. dirs., publicity chair Our Kids, 1991—; mem. Nashville region membership recruitment Music City C. of C., 1991—; active First Tuesday Rep. Group, 1992—, 1st v.p., 1992-93, v.p. publicity, 1993-94, Women in the Nineties, 1993, 94, Leadership Nashville, 1993-94, co-chair, 1994-95; mem. Wilson County # 911 Bd., 1994-96; publicity chair Habitat for Humanity, 1995; bd. dirs. Nat. Conf. Christians and Jews, 1995-98; mem. recruitment com. YWCA, 1996. Recipient Outstanding Vol. award Mid-Cumberland Chpt. Hemophilia Found., 1985, Vols. award Metro Council Dirs. Nashville, 1987, Nat. Outstanding Leadership award Hemophilia Found., 1987, Humanitarian award Jan Van Eys 1988, Finalist award Athena, 1991; named to Davidson County Women of Yr., 1991. Mem. NAFE, Nat. Assn. Profl. Saleswomen (adv. bd. 1986-89, v.p. Nashville chpt. 1986-87, pres. 1987-89, chair nat. com. for membership retention 1987—, chair nat. task com. 1988, nat. publicity chairperson 1989-90, Pres.'s Cup 1989), Nashville Assn. Mfrs. Reps. (pres. 1979-81), Assn. Builders and Contractors (program dir. Tenn. chpt. 1986-87, membership com.), Am. Rental Assn., Wilson County Home Builders Assn. (membership com. 1988, bd. dirs. 1994—), Mt. Juliet West Wilson C. of C. (co-chairperson Mt. Juliet Expo '88, bd. dirs. 1988—, membership chairperson 1989, coun. dir. econ. devel. 1990, joint econ. and devel. bd. 1991—), Nashville C. of C. (mem. task force 1993, chair bus. Expo Promotions 1994, Vol. of Yr. award 1994, bd. govs. 1995-98, vice-chair comm. 1996-97, exec. bd. 1996-97, small bus. action coun. chair 1996, comm. com. 1996-97, spl. events com. 1996—), Nashville Assn. Profl. Saleswomen Toastmasters (v.p. 1988, Competent Toastmaster Designation 1990, dist. sec. sec. 1990-91), Brentwood Early Risers Toastmasters (v.p. publicity 1993), Nashville Women's Breakfast Club (sec. 1993-94). Club: Toastmasters (Nashville) (charter, pres. 1986-87). Home: 425 Beacon Hill Dr Mount Juliet TN 37122-2084

VARANO, DIANE, science educator, staff developer, consultant; b. Bklyn., Mar. 8, 1954; d. Frank Joseph and Marie Rose (Scandariato) Palmeri; children: Michael Louis, Brian Anthony. AAS in Early Childhood Edn., Kingsborough C.C., 1990; BA in Early Childhood Edn. summa cum laude, Bklyn. Coll., 1992; MA in Sci. Edn./Elem. Edn., NYU, 1995. Trainer Chem. Bank, N.Y.C., 1971-72, adminstrv. asst., 1972-77; tchr. trainer The Bklyn. Plan NSF, Bklyn., 1992; staff developer Summer Sci. Inst. LaGuardia Coll., Queens, N.Y., 1992; staff developer, cons. Ctr. for Ednl. Change, Bklyn., 1992—; tchr. after sch. sci. program Ctr. for the Urban Environ., Bklyn., 1993—; tchr. discovery program Pub. Sch. 261, Bklyn., 1992—, coord. Discovery Program, 1994—; sr. workshop facilitator, creator Children's Sci. Materials Workshop, Bklyn. Coll., 1991—; staff developer, educator Early Childhood Ctr., N.Y.C., 1991; v.p. bd. dirs. Muriel Langsam Sch., Bklyn., 1988-90; bd. dirs. sch. based mgmt. Pub. Sch. 261; co-dir./author NESCAUM Project "Air Currents", adj. prof. constructivist sci. methodology Bklyn. Coll., 1996; presenter in field. Curriculum writer constructivist sci./ESL, NSF, 1994-95, constructivist sci./interdisciplinary approach Children's Sci. Materials Workshop, 1991—. Recipient Ellie Zimmerling prize for excellence in elem. edn. Bklyn. Coll., 1992, Jay F. Greene Meml. scholarship for achievement Bklyn. Coll., 1991, Pres.'s award for disting. scholarship Kingsborough C.C., 1990, Early Childhood Edn. Program award Kingsborough C.C., 1990. Mem. Elem. Sch. Sci. Assn. (exec. bd. dirs. 1991—), Educators for Social Responsibility, Nat. Sci. Tchrs. Assn., Kappa Delta Pi, Phi Theta Kappa. Office: PS 261 314 Pacific St Brooklyn NY 11201

VARE, ETHLIE ANN, journalist; b. Montreal, Que., Can., Mar. 8, 1953; came to U.S., 1954; d. Ben Zion Herman and Shirley (Marder) Riley; 1 child, Russell Alexander. BA in World Lit., U. Calif., Santa Barbara, 1972. Columnist United Media, N.Y.C., 1979-91; chief West Coast bur. Syndicated

Internat. Network, London, 1993-96; pres. L.A. Women in Music, 1987-89. Author: Adventurous Spirit, 1992 (Pub. Libr. award 1992); co-author: Mothers of Invention, 1988 (Am. Libr. award 1988); editor: (book) Legend: Frank Sinatra and the American Dream, 1995; exec. editor: Rock Mag., 1984-87. Recipient Maggie award for best editl. content Western Mag. Pubs. Assn., 1986. Mem. ACLU, AAUW, Women in Film, Amnesty Internat. Democrat. Jewish.

VARELLAS, SANDRA MOTTE, judge; b. Anderson, S.C., Oct. 17, 1946; d. James E. and Helen Lucille (Gilliam) Motte; m. James John Varellas, July 3, 1971; children: James John III, David Todd. BA, Winthrop Coll., 1968; MA, U. Ky., 1970, JD, 1975. Bar: Ky. 1975, Fla. 1976, U.S. Dist. Ct. (ea. dist.) Ky. 1975, U.S. Ct. Appeals (6th cir.) 1976, U.S. Supreme Ct. 1978. Instr. Midway Coll., Ky., 1970-72; adj. prof. U. Ky. Coll. Law, Lexington, 1976-78; instr. dept. bus. adminstrn. U. Ky., Lexington, 1976-78; atty. Varellas, Pratt & Cooley, Lexington, 1975-93; atty. Varellas & Pratt, Lexington, 1993—; Fayette County judge exec., Ky., 1980—; hearing officer Ky. Natural Resources and Environ. Protection Cabinet, Frankfort, 1984-88. Committeewoman Ky. Young Dems., Frankfort, 1977-80; pres. Fayette County Young Dems., Lexington, 1977; bd. dirs. Ky. Dem. Women's Club, Frankfort, 1980-84; grad. Leadership Lexington, 1981; chairwoman Profl. Women's Forum, Lexington, Ky., 1985-86, bd. dirs., 1984-87, Aequum award com, 1989-92; mem. devel. coun. Midway Coll., 1990-92; co-chair Gift Club Com., 1992. Named Outstanding Young Dem. Woman, Ky. Young Dems., Frankfort, 1977, Outstanding Former Young Dem., Ky. Young Dems., 1983. Mem. Ky. Bar Assn. (treas. young lawyers div. 1978-79, long range planning com., 1988-89), Fla. Bar, Fayette County Bar Assn. (treas. 1977-78, bd. govs. 1978-80), LWV (nominating com 1984-85), Greater Lexington C. of C. (legis. affairs com. 1994-95, bd. dirs. coun. smaller enterprises 1992-95). Club: The Lexington Forum (bd. dirs. 1996—), Lexington Philharm. Guild (bd. dirs. 1979-81, 86—), Nat. Assn. Women Bus. Owners (chmn. community liaison/govtl. affairs com. 1992-93), Lexington Network (bd. dirs. and sec. 1994—). Office: Varellas & Pratt 167 W Main St Lexington KY 40507-1713

VARGAS, PATTIE LEE, author, editor; b. Spencer, S.D., Feb. 4, 1941; d. Gilbert Helmuth and Carol Maxine (Winans) Bohlman; m. Richard D. Gulling Sr., July 17, 1960 (div. 1977); children: Richard D. Jr., David M., Toni C.; m. Allen H. Vargas, May 9, 1979 (dec. 1993). BS in Secondary Edn. cum laude, Miami U., 1969; MA in English, U. Dayton, 1972. Tchr. Kettering (Ohio) City Schs., 1972-83; editor Gurney's Gardening News, Yankton, S.D., 1984-88; dir. pub. relations Gurney Seed and Nursery Co., Yankton, 1985-89; creative supr. catalogs Dakota Advt. div. Gurney Seed and Nursery Co., Yankton, 1986-89; v.p. A.H. Vargas Assocs., Vermillion, S.D., 1987-93; editl. project mgr. Mazer Corp., Dayton, Ohio, 1993—; v.p. A.H. Vargas Assocs. Mktg. and Comm. Cons., Vermillion, S.D., 1987-93; pub. rels. cons. Cath. Conf. of Ohio, Columbus, 1975-76. Author: Country Wines, 1991, Stay Well Without Going Broke, 1993, Cordially Yours, 1996; writer (movie): Planning Cath. Schs. Week, 1975, (multi-media show) Tribute to the Bicentennial, 1976. Mem. Miamisburg (Ohio) Sch. Bond Steering Com., 1980. Mem. Nat. Fedn. of Press Women (recipient Editorial Writing award, 1986, 87, 88), S.D. Press Women (recipient Sweepstakes award 1987, 1988, Catalog award 1988), Nat. Garden Writing Assn.

VARMA, ASHA, civilian military administrator, researcher; b. Bareilly, India, Mar. 19, 1942; came to U.S., 1966; d. Gulzari Mall and Javitri Devi Varma; m. Vinod Shanker Agarwala, Feb. 14, 1967; children: Veena V., Vinay. BSc, Agra U., Bareilly, 1958, MSc, 1960; PhD, Banaras Hindu U., Varanasi, India, 1963; exec. mgmt. diploma, Office Pers. Mgmt., 1988. Rsch. fellow Banaras Hindu U., 1960-64, Nat. Rsch. Lab, Poona, India, 1964-66; asst. dir. Forensic Sci. Lab., Sagar, India, 1966-68; sci. officer Coun. Sci. and Indsl. Rsch., Kanpur, 1969-70; rsch. assoc. U. Conn., Storrs, 1966-67, 73-76; rsch. scientist U. Pa., Phila., 1977-82; rsch. chemist Naval Air Devel. Ctr., Warminster, Pa., 1983-88, dep. dir., 1988-92; acting dir. Office Sci. and Tech., Naval Air Warfare Ctr., Warminster, 1992, sci. mgr. office sci. and tech., 1992—; chmn. Navy R & D Info. Exch. Conf., 1990-94. Author: Handbook of Atomic Absorption Spectroscopy, Vols. I and II, 1984, Handbook of Furnace Atomic Absorption, 1990, Handbook of Inductively Coupled Plasma Spectroscopy, 1991; editor CRC Press Inc., 1982-91; contbr. over 80 articles to profl. jours. Past mem. Indo-U.S. Orgn., Phila.; commr. Nat. Cert. Commn., A.I.C., 1991—; vol. judge sci. fairs at local schs. Recipient Performance awards, 1977-95, Appreciation award Office Pers. Mgmt., 1988, EEO award, 1994; Govt. of India scholar, 1954-66, fellow, 1963-76. Fellow Am. Inst. Chemists; mem. AAAS, Am. Chem. Soc., Navy Civilian Mgrs. Assn. (v.p 1991-93, pres. 1994-96, bd. dirs. 1995—), Federally Employed Women (pres. Buxmont chpt. 1986-87, chairperson fed. women's program com. 1988-89), Internat. Union of Pure and Applied Chemistry, Coblentz Soc., Am. Mus. Natural History, Nat. Wildlife Fedn., Internat. Wildlife Fedn., Women in Sci. Engring. Home: 1006 Marian Rd Warminster PA 18974-2728 Office: Office Sci & Tech Naval Air Warfare Ctr Aircraft Divsn Bldg 2187 Patuxent River MD 20670

VARNER, CHARLEEN LAVERNE MCCLANAHAN (MRS. ROBERT B. VARNER), nutritionist, educator, administrator, dietitian; b. Alba, Mo., Aug. 28, 1931; d. Roy Calvin and Lela Ruhama (Smith) McClanahan; student Joplin (Mo.) Jr. Coll., 1949-51; BS in Edn., Kans. State Coll. Pittsburg, 1953; MS, U. Ark., 1958; PhD, Tex. Woman's U. 1966; postgrad. Mich. State U., summer, 1955, U. Mo., summer 1962; m. Robert Bernard Varner, July 4, 1953. Apprentice county home agt. U. Mo., summer 1952; tchr. Ferry Pass Sch., Escambia County, Fla., 1953-54; tchr. biology, home econs. Joplin Sr. H.S., 1954-59; instr. home econs. Kans. State Coll., Pittsburg, 1959-63; lectr. foods, nutrition Coll. Household Arts and Scis., Tex. Woman's U., 1963-64, rsch. asst. NASA grant, 1964-66; assoc. prof. home econs. Central Mo. State U., Warrensburg, 1966-70, adviser to Colhecon, 1966-70, adviser to Alpha Sigma Alpha, 1967-70, 72, mem. bd. advisers Honors Group, 1967-70; prof., head dept. home econs. Kans. State Tchrs. Coll., Emporia, 1970-73; prof., chmn. dept. home econs. Benedictine Coll., Atchison, Kans., 1973-74; prof., chmn. dept. home econs. Baker U., Baldwin City, Kans., 1974-75; owner, operator Diet-Con Dietary Cons. Enterprises, cons. dietitian, 1973—, Home-Con Cons. Enterprises. Mem. Joplin Little Theater, 1956-60. Mem. NEA, Mo., Kans. state tchrs. assns., AAUW, Am., Mo., Kans. dietetics assns., Am., Mo., Kans. home econs. assns., Mo. Acad. Scis., AAUP, U. Ark. Alumni Assn., Alumni Assn. Kans. State Coll. of Pittsburg, Am. Vocat. Assn., Assn. Edn. Young Children, Sigma Xi, Beta Sigma Phi, Beta Beta Beta, Alpha Sigma Alpha, Delta Kappa Gamma, Kappa Kappa Iota, Phi Upsilon Omicron, Theta Alpha Pi, Kappa Phi. Methodist (organist). Home: PO Box 1009 Topeka KS 66601

VARNER, JOYCE EHRHARDT, librarian; b. Quincy, Ill., Sept. 13, 1938; d. Wilbur John and Florence Elizabeth (Mast) Ehrhardt; m. Donald Giles Varner, Sept. 12, 1959; children: Amy, Janice, Christian, Matthew, Nadine. BA, Northeastern Okla. State U., 1980; MLS, U. Okla., 1984. Lab. analyst Gardner Denver Co., Quincy, 1956-60; sales rep. Morrisonville, Ill., 1963-69; libr. clk. U. Ill., Urbana, 1973-75; libr. tech. asst. Northeastern Okla. State U., Tahlequah, 1976-86; asst. reference libr. Muskogee (Okla.) Pub. Libr., 1986-90; libr. Jess Dunn Correctional Ctr., Taft, Okla., 1990—. Editor Indian Nations Audubon Nature Notes, 1977-81, 96—; contbr. articles to newspaper. Vol. Lake-Wood coun. Girl Scouts U.S.A., 1975—, bd. dirs. 1992—, pres., 1995-96; sec.-treas. Cherokee County Rural Water Dist. 7, 1987—; edn. chmn. Indian Nations chpt. Nat. Audubon Soc., 1989—. Recipient Thanks Badge, Lake-Wood coun. Girl Scouts U.S.A., 1990. Mem. ALA, AAUW, Okla. Libr. Assn. (nominating com. 1989), Okla. Acad. Sci., Okla. Ornithol. Soc. (chmn. libr. com. 1978-88, Award of Merit 1990, pres.-elect 1994, pres. 1995-96), Am. Correctional Assn., Okla. Correctional Assn., Alpha Chi, Beta Beta Beta, Phi Delta Kappa (Found. rep. 1984-86, historian 1992—). Home: RR 1 Box 1 Welling OK 74471-9701 Office: Jess Dunn Correctional Ctr Leisure Libr PO Box 316 Taft OK 74463-0316

VARNON, SUZANNE, speech language pathologist; b. Dallas, Nov. 23, 1948; d. Howard A. and Mable Anne (Jacobsen) Muhm; m. Charles D. Varnon, Nov. 13, 1971; 1 child, Justin C. BA, Baylor U., 1970; deaf edn. cert., Tex. Woman's U., 1974; postgrad., East Tex. State U., 1991-95, East Tex. State U., 1991—. Cert. speech lang. pathologist, diagnotician, spl. edn. Speech lang. pathologist Richardson (Tex.) Ind. Sch. Dist., 1970-78; tchr. mother's day out Park Cities Bapt. Ch., Dallas, 1979-81; pvt. practice speech lang. pathologist Dallas, 1979-81; speech lang. pathologist Garland (Tex.) Ind. Sch. Dist., 1981—; supr. clin. fellowship year Garland (Tex.) Ind. Sch. Dist., 1982—; medicaid supr. non-Am. Speech Hearing Clin. Cert. Speech Therapists. Dir. vacation bible sch. Lake Highlands Bapt. Ch., Dallas, summer 1979—; sec.-treas. woman's missionary union, 1980-92; life mem. PTA, 1995—. Lic. speech lang. pathology, Tex. Mem. Am. Speech Hearing Assn. (cert. clin. competence), Tex. Speech Hearing Assn., North Dallas Speech and Hearing Assn., Kappa Kappa Gamma, Phi Delta Kappa. Republican. Baptist. Home: 10407 Chesterton Dr Dallas TX 75238-2205 Office: Garland Ind Sch Dist Toler Elem 3520 Guthrie Rd Garland TX 75043-6220

VARRICHIO, JEANNETTE MARIE, artist; b. N.Y.C., July 22, 1954; d. Henry Jules and Jeanne Marie (Guillou) Liévre; m. Lawrence Varrichio, Oct. 26, 1974; children: Jeannea Marie, James Lawrence, Nicholas James. Grad. H.S., Astoria, N.Y. Pvt. practice art tchr. Massapequa Park, N.Y., 1992—. Mem. Ind. Art Soc. Roman Catholic. Home and Office: 118 Wilson St Massapequa Park NY 11762

VARRO, BARBARA JOAN, editor; b. East Chicago, Ind., Jan. 25, 1938; d. Alexander R. and Lottie R. (Bess) V. B.A., Duquesne U., 1959. Feature reporter, asst. fashion editor Chgo. Sun-Times, 1959-64, fashion editor, 1964-76, feature writer, 1976-84; v.p. pub. rels. Daniel J. Edelman Inc., Chgo., 1984-85; v.p. PRB/Needham Porter Novelli, Chgo., 1985-86; editor Am. Hosp. Assn. News, Chgo., 1987-94; asst. editor spl. sects. Chgo. Tribune, 1995—. Recipient awards for feature writing Ill. AP, 1978, 79, 80. Office: Chgo Tribune 435 N Michigan Ave Chicago IL 60611-4001

VARTANIAN, ISABEL SYLVIA, dietitian; b. Duquesne, Pa.; d. Apel and Mary (Kasparian) V. BS, U. Ala., 1957; MS, Columbia U., 1962. Registered dietitian. Dietetic intern N.Y. Hosp./Cornell Med. Ctr., N.Y.C., 1957-58; therapeutic dietitian Vets. Affairs Med. Ctr., Bronx, N.Y., 1958-60, adminstrv. dietitian, 1960-62, nutrition clinic dietitian, 1962-63; rsch. and nutrition clinic dietitian Vets. Affairs Med. Ctr., Coral Gables, Fla., 1963; nutrition clinic dietitian Vets. Affairs Med. Ctr., Richmond, Va., 1963-66, chief nutritional therapy edn. and rsch sect., 1966-83, nutrition support dietitian, 1983—. Bd. dirs. Richmond Cmty. Action Program, 1978-83; adv. com. Social Svcs., Hopewell, Va., 1991—. Recipient Outstanding awards Vets. Affairs Med. Ctr., Superior Performance awards, Outstanding award. Mem. Richmond Dietetic Assn. (chairwoman diet therapy sect. 1966-67, pres.-elect 1967-68, pres. 1968-70, chairwoman Dial-A-Dietitian 1972-74, chairwoman pub. rels. 1973-74, 78-81, chairwoman Divsn. Cmty. Dietetics 1983-85, chairwoman program planning com. 1985), Va. Dietetic Assn. (chairwoman career guidance com. 1963-65, ednl. exhibits 1967, Dial-A-Dietitian 1972-74, pub. rels. 1982-84, visibility campaign 1984, exhibit com. 1984, program planning com. 1988, divsn. cmty. dietetic 1989-91), Va. Soc. Parenteral and Enteral Nutrition (chairwoman program planning com. 1988-89, membership com. 1990), Am. Dietetic Assn. (life, membership com.), Nat. Kidney Found. (renal nutrition sect.), Am. Soc. Parenteral and Enteral Nutrition. Home: 2005 Jackson St Hopewell VA 23860-3633 Office: VA Med Ctr 1201 Broad Rock Blvd Richmond VA 23249-0001

VARY, EVA MAROS, chemical company executive; b. Kecskemet, Hungary, Apr. 13, 1933; came to U.S., 1958; d. Anthony and Kathleen (Czencz) Maros; m. Eugen Szent-Vary, June 13, 1956 (div. 1958); 1 child, Susan Marie. Chem. engring. diploma, Tech. U. Budapest (Hungary), 1956; PhD in Phys. Chemistry, UCLA, 1966. Chem. engring. area supr. Ujpesti Textile Plant, Budapest, 1956-57; chemist geology dept. UCLA, 1958-65; rsch. chemist, staff chemist Fabrics and Finishes Dept. Dupont, Phila., 1966-71, rsch. supr., 1971-79; tech. area supt. Fabrics and Finishes Dept. Dupont, Parlin, N.J., 1979-80; asst. plant mgr. Fabrics and Finishes Dept. Dupont, Parlin, Toledo, 1980-85; product supt. mng. Tedlar plant Dupont Fabricated Products, Buffalo, 1985-87; environ. cons. Dupont Fabricated Products, Wilmington, Del., 1987-90; dir. product safety, regulatory affairs pigments div. Ciba-Geigy Corp., Newport, Del., 1990—. Inventor, patentee release coatings. Com. chair Zonta Internat., Toledo, 1984, Buffalo, 1987. Mem. Am. Chem. Soc. Roman Catholic. Home: 1100 Lovering Ave Apt 1508 Wilmington DE 19806-3288 Office: Ciba Geigy Corp Pigments Div 315 Water St Newport DE 19804-2410

VASILIADES, MARY CHRIST, writer, playwright; b. Lakewood, N.J., Sept. 5, 1930; d. Christ and Soultana Vasiliades. B of Journalism, U. Mo., 1953. Asst. editor McFadden Pubs., N.Y.C., 1958-60; editor Dauntless Books, N.Y.C., 1960-63, Universal Pub. Co., N.Y.C., 1963; account exec., writer Theodore Sills Pub. Rels., N.Y.C., 1964-68; writer, pub. rels. United Negro Coll. Fund, N.Y.C., 1968, Roosevelt Hosp., N.Y.C., 1968-72; dir. pub. rels. Beekman Downtown Hosp., N.Y.C., 1972-76; dir. fund raising pub. rels. Albert Einstein Coll. Medicine, N.Y.C., 1978-83; sr. writer Anti-Defamation League, N.Y.C., 1983-95. Author: (plays) Hidden Agenda, 1988, Graduation Party, 1990, Last Dance, 1995, (novel) Renegade Women, 1996. Bd. dirs. Publicity Club N.Y., 1970-72. Mem. NOW (bd. dirs. N.Y. chpt. 1973-75), Dramatist Guild. Home: 161 W 16th St Apt 15I New York NY 10011

VASLEF, IRENE, historian, librarian; b. Budapest, Hungary, Mar. 23, 1934; came to U.S., 1956, naturalized, 1960; d. Imre and Ilona (Selyebi-Kovats) Szabo; m. Nicholas P. Vaslef, Sept. 22, 1956; children—Suzanne, Steven. B.A., San Jose (Calif.) State U., 1960; M.S., Simmons Grad. Sch. Library Sci., Boston, 1963; postgrad., Columbia U., 1968, U. Colo., 1961-62, U. Munich, 1967-68; Ph.D., Catholic U. Am., 1984. Librarian Cambridge, Mass., 1962-64; librarian Colorado Springs (Colo.) Sch. System, 1964-67; head catalog librarian Colo. Coll., Colorado Springs, 1968-72; librarian Dumbarton Oaks Rsch. Libr., Trustees for Harvard U., 1972—. Editor/compiler Am. Byzantine Bibliography in Byzantine studies/Etudes Byzantines, 1979—, Classica et Mediaevalia, 1986, Leyden: Brill, 1986; contbr. articles to profl. jours. Mem. Spl. Libraries Assn., Art Libraries Assn. N.Am., Phi Gamma Mu. Home: 4131 N River St Mc Lean VA 22101-2512 Office: Harvard U Dumbarton Oaks Rsch Libr 1703 32nd St NW Washington DC 20007-2934

VASQUEZ, KRISTI LYNN, accountant; b. Seattle, Jan. 13, 1970; d. John D. and Terese M. (Gabriel) Hughes; m. Reynaldo Rene Vasquez, Oct. 2, 1993. BA in Acctg., Western Wash. U., Bellingham, 1992. CPA, CMA. Acctg. intern Columbia Colstor, Inc., Moses Lake, Wash., summer 1991, 92; cost acct. Lone Star N.W., Inc., Seattle, 1993-94, supr. tax and treasury, 1994-96; acct. Applied Precision, Inc., Issaquah, Wash., 1996—; vol. IRS-Volunteer Income Tax Assistance Program, Bellingham, 1992. Mem. Inst. Mgmt. Accts., Wash. Soc. CPAs (scholarship 1991), Am. Payroll Assn. Roman Catholic. Home: 555 Bremerton Ave NE # E202 Renton WA 98059 Office: Applied Precision Inc 1040 12th Ave NW Issaquah WA 98027-8929

VASS, JOAN, fashion designer; b. N.Y.C., May 19, 1925; d. Max S. and Rose L.; children by previous marriage: Richard, Sara, Jason. Student Vassar Coll., 1941; BA, U. Wis., 1946. Pres., Joan Vass Inc., N.Y.C., 1977—, Vass-Ludacer, N.Y.C., 1993—. Recipient Prix de Cachet, Prince Machiabelli, 1980, Coty award, 1979, Disting. Woman in Fashion award Smithsonian Instn., 1980. Office: Joan Vass Inc 117 E 29th St New York NY 10016-8022 also: 485 7th Ave Ste 510 New York NY 10018-6804

VASSILOPOULOU-SELLIN, RENA, medical educator; b. Dec. 29, 1949. MD, Albert Einstein Coll. Medicine, 1974. Resident Montefiore Hosp., Bronx, 1974-77; fellow Northwestern U., Chgo., 1977-80; prof. Univ. Tex., Houston, 1980—. Fellow ACP, Am. Assn. Clin. Endocrinol.; mem. AAAS, AMA, Am. Soc. Bone and Mineral Rsch., Am. Diabetes Assn., Am. Soc. Clin. Oncology, Endo Soc. Office: Anderson Cancer Ctr 1515 Holcombe Blvd # 15 Houston TX 77030-4009

VAUCLAIR, MARGUERITE RENÉE, public relations and sales promotion executive; b. Englewood, N.J., Jan. 26, 1945; d. Maurice Joseph and Yvonne Jeanne (Reynaud) V.; m. William Augustus Peeples II, (div. 1986). BS in Journalism, Bowling Green State U., 1967. Asst. promotion mgr. Internat. Herald Tribune, Paris, 1967-70; Europe promotion mgr. Vision-The European Bus. Mag., London, 1971; dir. programs and promotion Am. C. of C. in France, Paris, 1973-76; promotion and rsch. mgr. Johnston Internat. Pubs., N.Y.C., 1977-80; prin. Marguerite Vauclair Promotion-Pub. Rels.-Advt., 1981—; promotion mgr. L.A. Times Syndicate, 1985-88; advt. promotions and spl. sects. mgr. Soundings Publs. Inc., Essex, Conn., 1990. Collaborator on books, author: (guide) Guest Houses, Bed-and-Breakfasts, Inns and Hotels in Newport, R.I., 1982; contbr. travel articles and photographs to mags. and newspapers. Mem. Pub. Rels. Soc. Am. (Prisms awards com. L.A. 1988), Overseas Press Club Am., Women in Comm. (bd. dirs. L.A. 1987-89), French-Am. C. of C. in U.S., Inc. (publs. com. 1993—), World Trade Coun. of Westchester, Advt. Club of Westchester (bd. dirs. 1994—), Fairfield County Pub. Rels. Assn., Conn. Press Club, Kappa Delta (bd. dirs. UCLA chpt. 1986-88, U. Conn. 1990-91). Office: 131 Purchase St Rye NY 10580-2139

VAUGHAN, AUDREY JUDD, paralegal, musician; b. Washington, May 8, 1936; d. Deane Brewster and Elizabeth (Melamed) Judd; m. Arthur Harris Vaughan Jr., Feb. 7, 1959 (div. June 1976); 1 child, Erik Brewster. BA, Cornell U., 1958; postgrad., Eastman Sch. Music, 1959-62; cert. in paralegal studies, UCLA, 1977. Tchr. music Rochester (N.Y.) Sch. Sys., 1961-64, Gooden Sch., Sierra Madre, Calif., 1975-78; paralegal Nossaman, Kruger & Marsh, L.A., 1978-80, Latham Watkins, L.A., 1980-84, Burns Ammirato, Pasadena, Calif., 1984—; dir. Los Grillos, medieval and renaissance music performing group, Pasadena, 1965—. Organizer studies and presentations, bd. dirs., spkr. LWV, Pasadena, 1965-73. Mem. L.A. Paralegal Assn. (com. for paralegal edn., spkr. 1985—). Home: 2034 Glenview Ter Altadena CA 91001

VAUGHAN, BERNIECE MILLER, school system administrator, writer; b. Parkville, Mo., Jan. 24, 1913; d. Clarence Absalom and Elsa Alba (Duley) M.; m. George Lowell Vaughan, Aug. 12, 1935 (dec. 1980); children: Elsa Rae Pearce, Rosemary Anderson. BA with honors, Park Coll., Parkville, Mo., 1934; MA, U. of the Pacific, 1960. Tchr. various elem. schs., Platte County, Mo., 1935-39, Lodi (Calif.) elem. schs., 1948-60; tchr., adminstr. Lodi Elem. Sch. Dist., 1960-78; ret. Contbr. articles to various mags. Pres. Lodi Tchrs. Assn., 1960-65; sec. Calif. Tchrs. Assn., 1962-63. Recipient Citations of Excellence Lodi Schs., San Joaquin County, State of Calif. Mem. DAR, Calif. Ret. Tchrs., San Joaquin Geneology Club, Tokay Antique Club (pres. 1982-83, sec. 1983-84). Democrat. Methodist. Home: 2044 Kenway Court Lodi CA 95242

VAUGHAN, FRANCES ANN, educational consultant; b. Marshall, Tex., Dec. 1, 1947; d. James David and Doris Maxine (Clinkscales) Hooton; m. Charles Michael Vaughan, Aug. 1, 1971; children: Brandon Michael Vaughan, Courtney Allison Vaughan. BS in Edn., U. North Tex., 1970, postgrad., 1970-72. Cert. elem. tchr., Tex., Mo. Tchr. Dallas Ind. Sch. Dist., 1970-73; tchr. Greenhill Sch., Dallas, 1973-75, Lakehill Sch., Dallas, 1975-77; ednl. cons. Addison-Wesley Pub. Co., Menlo Park, Calif., 1986—. Mem. ASCD, Nat. Coun. Tchrs. Math. Home and Office: 306 Broadway St Lamar MO 64759-1044

VAUGHAN, LINDA, publishing executive. Pub. Soap Opera Digest, N.Y.C. *

VAUGHAN, MARGARET EVELYN, psychologist, consultant; b. Mpls., Nov. 9, 1948; d. Robert Bergh and Evelyn (Glockner) Cedergren; m. William Vaughan Jr., July 30, 1981. BA, St. Cloud (Minn.) State U., 1972; MA, Western Mich. U., 1977, PhD, 1980. Lic. psychologist, Mass. Asst. prof. psychology Kalamazoo (Mich.) Coll., 1979-81; postdoctoral fellow Harvard U., Cambridge, Mass., 1981-82, rsch. assoc., 1982-83, rsch. assoc. Sch. of Bus., 1983-84; asst. prof. psychology Salem (Mass.) State Coll., 1984-88, assoc. prof. psychology, 1988-93, prof., 1994—; cons. Shore Ednl. Collaborative, Medford, Mass., 1984—; bd. dirs. B.F. Skinner Found., Cambridge. Author: (with B.F. Skinner) Enjoy Old Age, 1983; editor-elect The Behavior Analyst Jour., 1991-93, editor, 1993—. Mem. APA, Assn. for Behavior Analysis, Phi Kappa Phi, Psi Chi, Alpha Lambda Delta. Office: Salem State Coll Dept Psychology Salem MA 01970

VAUGHAN, MARTHA, biochemist; b. Dodgeville, Wis., Aug. 4, 1926; d. John Anthony and Luciel (Ellingen) V.; m. Jack Orloff, Aug. 4, 1951 (dec. Dec. 1988); children: Jonathan Michael, David Geoffrey, Gregory Joshua. Ph.B., U. Chgo., 1944; M.D., Yale U., 1949. Intern New Haven Hosp., Conn., 1950-51; research fellow U. Pa., Phila., 1951-52; research fellow Nat. Heart Inst., Bethesda, Md., 1952-54, mem. research staff, 1954-68; head metabolism sect. Nat. Heart and Lung Inst., Bethesda, 1968-74; acting chief molecular disease br. Nat. Heart, Lung and Blood Inst., Bethesda, 1974-76, chief cell metabolism lab., 1974-94; dep. chief pulmonary and critical care medicine br. Nat. Heart, Lung, and Blood Inst., Bethesda, 1994—; mem. metabolism study sect. NIH, 1965-68; mem. bd. sci. counselors Nat. Inst. Alcohol Abuse and Alcoholism, 1988-91. Mem. editl. bd. Jour. Biol. Chemistry, 1971-76, 80-83, 88-90, assoc. editor, 1992—; editl. adv. bd. Molecular Pharmacology, 1972-80, Biochemistry, 1989-94; editor: Biochemistry and Biophysics Rsch. Comms., 1990-91; contbr. articles to profl. jours., chpts. to books. Bd. dirs. Found. Advanced Edn. in Scis., Inc., Bethesda, 1979-92, exec. com., 1980-92, treas., 1984-86, v.p., 1986-88, pres., 1988-90; mem. Yale U. Coun. com. med. affairs, New Haven, 1974-80. Recipient Meritorious Svc. medal HEW, 1974, Disting. Svc. medal NEW, 1979, Commd. Officer award USPHS, 1982, Superior Svc. award USPHS, 1993. Mem. NAS, Am. Acad. Arts and Scis., Am. Soc. Biol. Chemists (chmn. pub. com. 1984-86), Assn. Am. Physicians, Am. Soc. Clin. Investigation. Home: 11608 W Hill Dr Rockville MD 20852-3751 Office: Nat Heart Lung & Blood Inst NIH Bldg 10 Rm 5N-307 Bethesda MD 20892

VAUGHAN, STEPHANIE RUTH, water aerobics business owner, consultant; b. Winchester, Va., Feb. 27, 1956; d. Robert Hall Sr. and Peggy (Owen) Hahn; m. Ward Pierman Vaughan, Nov. 29, 1980; children: Carol Owen, Eva Virginia, Robert Alexander. BS in Biology, Shenandoah U., 1983, MBA, 1985. Sales rep., cashier Best Products, Roanoke, Va., 1977-78; dir. Peg-Ell Sch. Modeling, Winchester, 1978-79; mgr. purchasing and metal fabrication materials Fabritek Co., Inc., Winchester, 1979-84, sec. bd. dirs., 1980—; CEO, owner Splash Internat., Winchester, 1991—, internat. mktg. dir. original cabinet; tennis instr. Camp Camelot, Wilmington, N.C., summer 1978; cons. Fabritek Co., Inc., 1993-95; membership dir. Stonebrook Swim and Racquet Club, Winchester, 1992-93, corp. fitness dir., 1993; instr. Workout in Water class Crooked Run Fitness and racquet Club, Front Royal, Va., 1992—, Winchester Parks and Recreation Dept., 1991-92; instr., designer Children's Water Fitness Classes Winchester County Club, Va., 1993, Stonebrook Country Club, 1994; keynote spkr. Women's Fiar, 1996. Author: Water Exercises for Physicians, Physical Therapists and Water Fitness Instructors, 1994 (award); contbr. articles to profl. jours.; internat. aquatic exercise and therapy presenter. Steering com. mem. Habitat for Humanity, 1995; bd. dirs. Winchester Fred County. Patentee for water fitness product. Mem. AAHPERD, NAFE, AAUW, AMA, Am. Coll. Sports Medicine, Va. Assn. Health, Phys. Recreation and Dance (conf. presenter, chair aquatic coun. 1994-95, v.p. recreation coun. 1996—), Va. Recreation and Parks Soc. (conf. presenter), U.S. Water Fitness Assn. (adv. bd., chair tech. com. 1993—, mem. nat. tech. com. 1992—, C. Carson Conrad Top Water Fitness Leader for Va. award 1993, Deep Water Running Champion 1993, BEMA Nat. Water Fitness Champion 1993, cert. pool coord., cert. instr., nat. conf. aquatic fashion show dir. 1992, 93, 94, conf. presenter, leader 1st Nat. Aquatic Summit, Washington, Team Water Aerobics aquatic champion 1994, June Andrus Entrepreneur of Yr. award 1995, Champion Deep Water Instr. 1995), United Daus. of Confederacy, Aquatic Exercise Assn. (conf. presenter, regional rep. 1994-96), U.S. Synchronized Swimming, Shenandoah U. Alumni Assn. (bd. dirs.), Aquatic Alliance Internat. (internat. mktg. dir. 1996—), Aquatic Edn. Assn. Home: 115 Old Forest Cir Winchester VA 22602

VAUGHAN, SUSAN GINETTE, library director; b. Cortland, N.Y., July 4, 1946; d. Frederick George Adams and D. Virginia (Newell) Underwood; m. Jeffrey Howard Brainerd, Dec. 21, 1968 (div. May, 1982); children: Aaron Oliver, Nathan James; m. Ted Wayne Vaughan, July 26, 1987. AA., Cayuga C.C., Auburn, N.Y., 1982; BA, Syracuse U., 1983, MLS, 1984. Asst. libr. Isothermal C.C., Spindale, N.C., 1985-87; libr. dir. Isothermal C.C., Spindale, 1987—. Editor, researcher (local history handbook) Moravia's Early Days, 1984. Regional dir. Gov.'s Conf. on Librs. and Info. Svcs., N.C., 1990-91; campaign coord. United Way, Isothermal C.C., 1993. Named hon. mem. Phi Theta Kappa. Mem. ALA, Nature Conservancy, N.C. C.C. Learning Resources Assn. (dist. vice dir. 1986-87, dist. dir. 1987-88, parliamentarian 1988-89). Methodist. Office: Isothermal CC PO Box 804 Spindale NC 28160

VAUGHAN KROEKER, NADINE, psychologist; b. Tampa, Fla., Aug. 30, 1947; d. Joseph Marcus and Velna Pearl (Jones) Williams; m. E.L. Vaughan III, 1966 (div. Aug. 1976); children: E.L. Vaughan, Heather Vaughan Oyarzun; m. Dennis Wayne Kroeker, Apr. 9, 1982 (div. Jan. 1994); 1 child, Melanie Sage. BA in Criminal Justice, U. South Fla., 1974, MA with honors in Rehab. Counseling, 1975; PhD in Psychology, Saybrook Inst., 1990. Lic. clin. psychologist, Calif., Wash. Co-founder Women's Resource Ctr., Tampa, Fla., 1973—; exec. dir. Vocare Found., Oakland, Calif., 1976-78; cmty. and organizational devel. specialist STate of Calif., Berkeley, Sacramento, 1978-82; cons., trainer N. Vaughan Kroeker, PhD, 1982—, APA Hope Program, 1994—; mem. adj. faculty psychology Peninsula Coll. Mem. APA, Divsns. Health Psychology and Humanistic Psychology. Democrat.

VAUGHN, ALFREDA DIANNE, editor; b. Chgo., May 23, 1962; d. Alfred Edward Jr. and Johnnie Q. (Edwards) V.; 1 child, Taylor A. Northern. BA, Loyola U., Chgo., 1985. Editorial asst. Putman Publ., Chgo., 1982-88, asst. editor, 1986-88; editor Talcott Comm., Chgo., 1989-92, exec. editor, editorial dir., 1991-94; editor Shore-Varrone Inc., Atlanta, 1995—. Vol. Juvenile Diabetes Assn., Chgo., 1993—. Mem. Truck Cap & Accessory Assn., Automotive Parts and Accessories Assn. (mktg. and comm. com. 1995—), Bottomless Closet.

VAUGHN, MARY ANN, accountant; b. Kingfisher, Okla., Mar. 2, 1963; d. Joseph Charles and Charlotte Marie (Stafford) Coughlan; m. Steven Dale Vaughn, Oct. 21, 1980; children: Leah, Stormy. BS, U. Ctrl. Okla., 1988. CPA, Okla. Staff acct. BDO Seidman, Oklahoma City, 1988; staff acct. Grant Thornton LLP, Oklahoma City, 1988-91, sr. acct., 1991-93, supr., 1993-95, tax mgr., 1995—. Co-founder Westborough Neighborhood Assn., Inc., Edmond, Okla., 1992-93, treas., 1993-95, pres., 1995-96, block capt. chair, 1996—. Mem. AICPA, Inst. Mgmt. Accts. (v.p. mktg. 1992-93, v.p. adminstrn. and fin. 1993-94, chpt. pres. 1994-95, nat. bd. dirs. 1996—), Okla. Soc. CPAs. Roman Catholic. Office: Grant Thornton LLP 1 Leadership Sq Ste 1200 Oklahoma City OK 73102

VAUGHN, VICKI LYNN, education educator; b. New Castle, Ind., Nov. 10, 1947; d. Robert Allen and Geneva Aileen (Bishop) Fulton; m. Virgil Encil Vaughn, Jr., Aug. 26, 1967; children: Joshua Allen, Jordan Tanner. BS, Ball State U., Muncie, Ind., 1969, MA, 1973; PhD, Purdue U., 1991. Elem. tchr. New Castle (Ind.) Cmty. Sch. Corp., 1969-86; gifted/talented tchr. Marion (Ind.) Cmty. Sch. Corp., 1986-88, Lafayette (Ind.) Sch. Corp., 1988-93; prin./dept. chair/asst. prof. Ball State U., Muncie, 1993—; lectr. grad. courses Purdue U., West Lafayette, Ind., 1991—; assoc. Ctr. for Gifted Studies and Talent Devel., Muncie, 1993—, Ctr. for Creative Learning, Sarasota, Fla., 1994—; cons. Ind. schs., 1993—. Co-editor Nat. Assn. Labs. Schs. Jour.; reviewer articles Jour. Secondary Gifted Edn., Tchr. Educator, others; contbr. articles to profl. jours. Ind. Dept. Edn. learning grantee, 1993, 4Rs grantee, 1994. Mem. ASCD (assoc.), Nat. Assn. for Gifted Children, Nat. Assn. for Lab. Schs., Ind. Assn. for Gifted (rsch. com. 1988—), Phi Delta Kappa, Phi Kappa Phi. Home: 1004 N Meadow Ln Muncie IN 47304-6714 Office: Burris Laboratory Sch 2000 W University Ave Muncie IN 47306-1022

VAUGHT, TIFFANIE ANN, mathematician, educator; b. Lexington, Ky., July 28, 1968; d. Hugh Cycle and Peggy Ann (Honaker) Runner; m. Thomas Edgar Vaught, Aug. 18, 1990. BA in Math., We. Ky. U., 1990. Cert. tchr. Tchr. math., sci. Madison Acad., Huntsville, Ala., 1991-92; tchr. math. Lee H.S., Huntsville, 1992—. Judge Am. Jr. Miss Contest, North Ala. Mem. Nat. Coun. Tchrs. Math., Pi Phi Epsilon. Home: 8801 W Belleview Ave #E107 Littleton CO 80123

VAUGHT, WILMA L., foundation executive, retired air force officer; b. Pontiac, Mich., Mar. 15, 1930; d. Willard L. and Margaret J. (Pierce) V. BS, U. Ill., 1952; MBA, U. Ala., 1968; postgrad., Indsl. Coll. Armed Forces, 1972-73; D Pub. Affairs (hon.), Columbia Coll., 1992. Cert. cost acct. Commd. 2d lt. USAF, 1957, advanced through grades to brig. gen., 1980; chief data services div. 306th Combat Support Group USAF, McCoy AFB, Fla., 1963-67; mgmt. analyst Office Dep. Chief of Staff, comptroller Mil. Assistance Command USAF, Saigon, Vietnam, 1968-69; chief advanced logistics systems plans and mgmt. group Air Force Logistics Command USAF, Wright-Patterson AFB, Ohio, 1969-72; chief cost factors br., chief security assistance br. USAF, Washington, 1973-75, Directorate Mgmt. Analysis, Office of Comptroller, 1973-75; dir. program and budget Office Dep. Chief of Staff, comptroller Hdqrs. Air Force Systems Command USAF, Andrews AFB, Md., 1980-82; comdr. U.S. Mil. Entrance Processing Command USAF, North Chicago, Ill., 1982-85; ret. USAF, 1985; pres. Women in Mil. Svc. Meml. Found., Arlington, Va., 1987—; pres. bd. dirs. Pentagon Fed. Credit Union, 1975-82; bd. regents Inst. Cost Analysis, 1979-83; Air Force sr. mil. rep. Def. Adv. Com. on Women in Services, 1982-85; chmn. Com. on Women in Armed Forces, NATO, Brussels, 1984-85. Bd. dirs. Air Force Retired Officer Community, 1986-90; mem. adv. bd. Jane Addams Conf.; mem. bd. trustees The Teller Found. Decorated Bronze Star medal, Def. Disting. Service medal, U.S. Air Force Disting. Service medal; recipient Ill. Achievement award U. Ill., 1983. Mem. Internat. Women's Forum. Methodist. Home: 6658 Van Winkle Dr Falls Church VA 22044-1010 Office: Women in Mil Svc Meml Found 5510 Columbia Pike Ste 302 Arlington VA 22204-3123

VAUX, DORA LOUISE, sperm bank official, consultant; b. White Pine, Mont., Aug. 8, 1922; d. Martin Tinus and Edna Ruth (Pyatt) Palmlund; m. Robert Glenn Vaux, Oct. 25, 1941; children: Jacqueline, Cheryl, Richard, Jeanette. Grad. high sch., Bothell, Wash. Photographer Busco-Nestor Studios, San Diego, 1961-68; owner, mgr. Vaux Floors & Interiors, San Diego, 1968-82; cons., mgr. Repository for Germinal Choice, Escondido, Calif., 1983-91; adminstr. Found. for the Continuity of Mankind, Spokane, 1991—. Republican. Home: 2727 S Skipworth Rd Spokane WA 99206 Office: Found Continuity of Mankind 1209 W 1st Ave Spokane WA 99204-0601

VAZIRANI-FALES, HEEA, legislative staff member, lawyer; b. Calcutta, India, Apr. 1, 1938; d. Sunder J. Vazirani; m. John Fales Jr., 1978; children: Deepika, Reetika, Ashish, Monika, Jyotika, Denise. AB, Guilford Coll., 1959; JD, Howard U., 1979. Legis. dir. Montgomery County Del, Gen. Assembly of Md., 1981-87; legis. counsel to Congresswoman Constance A. Morella, U.S. Ho. of Reps., Washington, 1987-94, counsel subcom. on postal svc. com. govt. reform-oversight, 1995—. Mem. Phi Delta Phi. Presbyterian. Office: Subcom on Postal Svc B349C Rayburn House Off Bldg Washington DC 20515

VAZIRI, FAKHRI FAY, financial consultant, insurance broker; b. Teheran, Iran, July 4, 1929; came to U.S., 1947; d. Abass and Hamiyat (Monif) V.; divorced; 1 child, Kew. BA in Drama, Hofstra U., 1953; MA in Dramatic Art, Columbia U., 1955. Actress Bombay Film Co., 1942-47; film reporter by correspondence Iranian Dept. Info. and Radio, 1947-50; radio MC Voice of Am., N.Y.C., 1952-54; scriptwriter, announcer featured as "Star of the East" Voice of Am., Washington, 1954-61; agent Reserve Life Ins. Co., Dallas, 1962-81; fin. cons., ins. broker Vaziri Ins. Agy., Bethesda, Md., 1982—. Actress in numerous Persian films, including Shirin-Farhad, one of first Persian films made. Fellow Life Underwriters Tng. Coun.; named Woman of the Yr. Reserve Life Ins. Co., 1966, named to All-Star Honor Roll issue of Insurance mag., 1967; one of few women to be named a charter member for Nat. Sales Achievement award, Nat. Assn. Life Underwriters, 1966; named Agent of Yr. Atlantic Terr. Pruduential Ins. Co. Am., 1980; recipient Human Rights award UN Assn., 1990; numerous other awards from ins. industry, also subject of articles for industry publs. Mem. NOW, Women Leaders Roundtable of Nat. Assn. Life Underwriters, D.C. Life Underwriters Assn., Bus. and Profl. Women's Assn. (pres. Washington chpt. 1987, Woman of the Yr. 1987), Muslim Women Assn. Washington (co-founder, chairwoman postgrad. scholarship for Muslim girls 1985). Office: 5317 Sangamore Rd Bethesda MD 20816-2323

VAZQUEZ, MARTHA ALICIA, judge; b. Santa Barbara, Calif., Feb. 21, 1953; d. Remigio and Consuelo (Mendez) V.; m. Frank Mathew, Aug. 7, 1976; children: Cristina Vazquez Matthew, Nicholas Vazquez Matthew, Nathan Vazquez Matthew. BA in Govt., U. Notre Dame, 1975, JD, 1978. Bar: N.Mex. 1979, U.S. Dist. Ct. (we. dist.) N.Mex. 1979. Atty. Pub. Defender's Office, Santa Fe, 1979-81; ptnr. Jones, Snead, Wertheim, Rodriguez & Wentworth, Santa Fe, 1981-93; judge U.S. District Ct., 10th Circuit, Santa Fe, 1993—. Chmn. City Santa Fe Grievance Bd. Mem. N.Mex. Bar Assn. (fee arbitration com., chmn. trial practice sect. 1984-85, mem. task force on minority involvement in bar activities), Santa Fe Bar Assn. (jud. liasion com.), Nat. Assn. Criminal Def. Lawyers, Assn. Trial Lawyers Am., N.Mex. Trial Lawyers Assn. Democrat. Roman Catholic. Office: US Courthouse PO Box 2710 Santa Fe NM 87504-2710*

VCHULEK, B. DIANE, psychotherapist; b. El Paso, Tex., Nov. 30, 1953; d. Edward M. and Mary A. (Mozingo) Elliott; m. James Stuart Vchulek, Nov. 22, 1971; 1 child, James Stuart II. AA, Ctrl. Tex. Coll., 1983; BBA, Cameron U., 1989; MS, Troy State U., 1991; postgrad., U. West Fla., 1993. Lic. mental health counselor, Fla.; nat. bd. cert. clin. hypnotherapist. Region coord., preventive consultant Okla. Alliance Against Drugs/Comanche County Meml. Hosp., Lawton, Okla., 1988-90; prevention coord., therapist Avalon Ctr., Inc., Milton, Fla., 1990-91; clin. counselor, lic. mental health counselor West Fla. Cmty. Care, Milton, 1991-94; program coord., therapist Charter-Medfield Hosp., Largo, Fla., 1994-95; clin. coord., therapist Care Group, Inc.- Women's Inst. for Incorporation Therapy, Coral Springs, Fla., 1995; pvt. practice A Counseling Ctr., Cocoa, Fla., 1995—; v.p. clin. ops. Inner Values, Inc., Melbourne Beach, Fla., 1995—. Mem. ACA, Am. Psychol. Assn., Am. Mental Health Counselors Assn., Internat. Assn. Marriage and Family Counselors, Menninger Soc. Home: 810 Pine Valley Ct Rockledge FL 32955 Office: A Counseling Ctr 956 N Cocoa Blvd Ste 1125 Cocoa FL 32922

VEACH, LAURA JANE, counselor, educator, consultant; b. Winston-Salem, N.C., Sept. 24, 1955; d. Marvin H. and Betty (Lyon) V.; m. Michael Lee Boies, Aug. 2, 1975 (div. Oct. 1982); m. George David Harrelson Jr., Dec. 31, 1994. BA, Wake Forest U., 1979, MA in Edn., 1982; PhD in Counselor Edn., U. New Orleans, 1996. Nat. cert. counselor; cert. clin. supr., substance abuse counselor. Mental health worker Charter Hosp. Winston-Salem, 1981-84; sch. counselor Mendenhall Middle Sch., Greensboro, N.C., 1984; substance abuse counselor Alcohol Edn. Ctr., High Point, N.C., 1984-87; program adminstr. Genesis Charter Hosp. Winston-Salem, 1987-88; clin. dir. Medicorp Recovery Network, Winston-Salem, 1988-93; freelance clin. cons. New Orleans, 1993—; pvt. practice Williams Clinic, Winston-Salem, 1996—; vis. instr. Wake Forest U., Winston-Salem, 1989; part-time instr. Guildford Tech. C.C., Jamestown, N.C., 1987-89; faculty N.C. Sch. Alcohol & Drug Studies, Wilmington, 1993, 94, 95. Mem. Forsyth County Task Force on Women, Winston-Salem, 1990, 91; coalition mem. Winston-Salem/FC Coalition on Drugs, 1991. Wake Forest U. Grad. Sch. scholar, 1980, 81. Mem. Am. Counseling Assn., So. Assn. Counselor Edn. and Supervision, Chi Sigma Iota (Alpha Eta chpt., sec. 1995-96), Sports Car Club Assn. Am., Internat. Motor Sports Assn., Phi Delta Kappa, Lambda Alpha, Eta Sigma Pi. Democrat. Home: 4151 Glenn Hi Rd Winston Salem NC 27107

VEACH, MYRTLE R., retired religious education educator, consultant; b. El Dorado, Ark., Nov. 19, 1936; d. Harry and Eva Ray (Squyres) V. BA, U. Corpus Christi, Tex., 1959; MA in Religious Edn., Southwestern Baptist Theological Seminary, Fort Worth, Tex., 1964. Youth edn. dir. Meml. Baptist Ch., Tulsa, Okla., 1964-67, 1st Baptist Ch., Garland, Tex., 1967-69; cons. youth/gen. Baptist Sunday Sch. Bd., Nashville, 1969-77, youth mgr., 1977-94; pres., cons. Veach Youth Ministry, Brentwood, Tenn., 1994—. Author: (book) Youth Sunday Schoolwork, 1982, Basic Youth Sunday Schoolwork, 1987, Breakthrough: Youth Sunday Schoolwork, 1991. Baptist. Home: 201 Flowerwood Ct Brentwood TN 37027

VEACO, KRISTINA, lawyer; b. Sacramento, Calif., Mar. 4, 1948; d. Robert Glenn and Lelia (McCain) V. BA, U. Calif., Davis, 1978; JD, Hastings Coll. of the Law, 1981. Legal adv. to commr. William T. Bagley Calif. Public Utilities Commn., San Francisco, Calif., 1981-86; sr. counsel Pacific Telesis Group, San Francisco, Calif., 1986-94; sr. counsel corp. and securities and pol. law Air Touch Comms., San Francisco, 1994—. Mem. ABA, Calif. Women Lawyers, San Francisco Bar Assn., Am. Soc. Corp. Secs., Phi Beta Kappa. Democrat. Episcopalian. Office: Air Touch Coms 1 California St Rm 2108 San Francisco CA 94111-5401

VEATCH, JEAN LOUISE CORTY, telemetry nurse; b. Farmer City, Ill., June 4, 1932; d. Eugene Louis and Mary Violette (Mounce) Corty; m. July 23, 1955 (div.); children: Irvin, Ronald, Steven, Julie, James, Jeffery. Diploma, Holy Cross Cen. Sch. Nursing, 1954; BS, Coll. St. Francis, 1984; student, Valparaiso U. Cert. ACLS, coronary, critical care trained IMCU, obstetrics. Obstetrics nurse Holy Family Hosp., LaPorte, Ind., 1954-64; office nurse Dr. McDonald, Gulfport, Miss.; office nurse Dr. Jack Cartwright, LaPorte, Ind., med./telemetry unit nurse, 1977-96; staff nurse level III LaPorte Hosp., 1987-96, charge nurse, preceptor, 1988—. Mem. Am. Heart Assn., 1979-96; mem. Square Dance Club (B&B of Valparaiso, Ind.); organizer yearly square dance Toys for Tots, 1981-89; den mother Cub Scouts, Valparaiso. Mem. Am. Assn. Diabetic Educators. Home: 4409 Campbell St Valparaiso IN 46383-1303

VEATCH, SHEILA WILLIAMSON, counselor; b. Fitchburg, Mass., Jan. 10, 1950; d. William Robert Barse Jr. and Joan Jesse (Tothill) Williamson; stepfather George P. Williamson; m. Michael Alan Veatch, July 3, 1993; children: Michael and Katie Pitts. BSEd, U. Ga., 1971; MEd in Counseling, West Ga. Coll., 1991, EdS in Counseling, 1992. Nat. bd. cert. counselor; lic. profl. counselor. Tchr. Cobb County Schs., Marietta, Ga., 1971-73, 86-91, counselor, 1991—; pvt. practice, 1996—; instr. Cobb Staff Devel., Marietta, 1992-93; workshop leader Kennesaw (Ga.) Student Educators, 1993; presenter Cobb Mega Conf., 1992. Co-author: Manners Mania, 1993 (rsch. grantee 1992). Rsch. grantee social skills program Cobb County, 1991-92, 92-93, anger/aggression reduction, 1993-94, parenting edn., 1994-95. Mem. ACA, Ga. Sch. Counselors Assn. (presenter), Am. Sch. Counseling Assn., Cobb Sch. Counselor Assn. (v.p. 1995-96, pres. 1996—), Atlanta Adlerian Soc., PTA (hon., life State of Ga. 1992). Home: 3146 Due West Ct Dallas GA 30132-7300 Office: Cobb County Sch Sys Glover St Marietta GA 30060

VEAZEY, DORIS ANNE, field office administrator; b. Dawson Spring, Ky., Feb. 16, 1935; d. Bradley Basil and Lucy Mable (Hamby) Sisk; m. Herman Veazey Jr., Aug. 15, 1964 (dec. Sept. 1987); 1 child, Vickie Dianne Veazey Kicinski. Murray State U., 1952-54. Unemployment ins. examiner Dept. for Employment Svcs., Madisonville, Ky., 1954-73, unemployment ins. supr., 1973-85, field office mgr., 1985-95; bd. dirs., adv. bd. region II Vocat. Tech. Schs., Madisonville, 1988-92. Mem. Mayor's Work Force Devel. Com., 1993—, Ky. Indsl. Devel. Com., 1992—; dept. dir. Adult III Sunday Sch., 1994—, ch. choir, 1990—. Mem. Internat. Platform Assn., Internat. Assn. of Pers. in Employment Svcs., Southeastern Employment and Tng. Assn., Tenure, Order of Ky. Cols., Greater Madisonville C. of C. (dir. leadership 1988-93). Baptist. Office: Dept Employment Svcs 56 Federal St # 1226 Madisonville KY 42431-2043

VEDUS, KAREN LYNN, psychotherapist; b. Bklyn., Nov. 9, 1954; d. Philip and Sandra June (Risman) V.; m. Richard Manning Woolley, June 4, 1995. BFA, Pratt Inst., Bklyn., 1976; MA in Art Therapy, George Washington U., Washington D.C., 1982; EdS in Marriage and Family, Seton Hall U., South Orange, N.J., 1990. Lic. marriage and family therapist. Clinician Wayne (N.J.) Gen. Hosp., 1987-95; self employed Somerville, N.J., 1995—. Mem. Am. Assn. Marriage and Family Therapists (clin. mem.). Office: 73 West End Ave Somerville NJ 08876

VEGA, JANINE POMMY, poet, educator; b. Jersey City, Feb. 5, 1942. ESL tchr. Am. Ctr., Bogotá, Columbia, 1971-73; poet, tchr. Poets in Schs., N.Y.C., 1975-95, Alt. Lit. Programs in Schs., Albany, N.Y., 1992-96, Tchrs. & Writers, N.Y.C., 1995-96; mem. adv. bd. Willow Mixed Media, Glenford, N.Y., 1988-91; dir. Incisions/Arts. Author: (poetry) Journal of a Hermit, 1979, The Bard Owl, 1980, Drunk on a Glacier Talking to Flies, 1988; (travel) Threading the Maze, 1992. Mem. Save Overlook, Woodstock, N.Y., 1989. Orgnl. grantee N.Y. State Coun. Arts, 1978-96. Mem. PEN (prison writing com. 1992-96), Poets & Writers, Catskill 3500 Club. Democrat. Home: Box 162 Bearsville NY 12409

VEGA, MARYLOIS PURDY, journalist; b. Chgo., Nov. 4, 1914; d. William Thomas and Mary Helene (Buggy) Purdy; m. Carlos Juan Vega, Sept. 4, 1965. B.A., U. Wis., Madison, 1935. With Time mag., N.Y.C., 1942-84; chief Letters to the Editor, 1951-67, chief editl. rsch., 1967-76, assoc. editor, 1976-84. Roman Catholic. Club: Overseas Press. Home: 140 West End Ave New York NY 10023-6131 also: PO Box 266 Gardiner NY 12525

VEIT, CLAIRICE GENE TIPTON, measurement psychologist; b. Monterey Park, Calif., Feb. 20, 1939; d. Albert Vern and Gene (Bunning) Tipton; children: Steven, Barbara, Laurette, Catherine. BA, UCLA, 1969, MA, 1970, PhD, 1974. Asst. prof. psychology Calif. State U., L.A., 1975-77, assoc. prof. psychology, 1977-80; rsch. psychologist The Rand Corp., Santa Monica, Calif., 1977—; rsch. cons. NATO Tech. Ctr., The Hague, The Netherlands, 1980-81; faculty Rand Grad Sch., Santa Monica, 1993—. Developer subjective transfer function (STF) method to complex sys. analysis. Mem. LWV, NOW, Mil. Ops. Rsch. Soc. Am., Inst. Mgmt. Sci., Soc. Med. Decision-Making, Soc. for Judgement and Decision-Making, L.A. World Affairs Coun., L.A. Opera League. Office: The Rand Corp 1700 Main St Santa Monica CA 90401-3208

VEITH, MARY ROTH, assistant dean; b. Middletown, Conn., Feb. 7, 1931; d. John Stephen and Margaret (Healey) Roth; children: Richard, Frank, Margaret, Katherine. BS, U. Conn., 1952; MBA, Iona Coll., 1975. Registered dietitian. Asst. head dietitian St. Francis Hosp., Hartford, Conn., 1954-55; dietitian Quality Control Lab A&P Corp., N.Y.C., 1955-56; head dietitian Cabrini Hosp., N.Y.C., 1956; homemaker, 1957-75; instr. mgmt. Coll. New Rochelle, N.Y., 1975; instr. mktg. Iona Coll., New Rochelle, N.Y., 1975-78, asst. prof., 1979—; asst. dean Hagan Sch. of Bus., Iona Coll., New Rochelle, N.Y., 1985—; treas. Advt. Club Westchester, N.Y. Mem. Am. Dietetic Assn., N.Y. Dietetic Assn., Am. Mktg. Assn., World Trade Club (Westchester). Office: Hagan Sch Business Iona College 715 North Ave New Rochelle NY 10801-1830

VEJSICKY, CATHLEEN LYNN, management executive, educator; b. Columbus, Ohio, June 25, 1958; d. Eugene Joseph and Jane Ann (Thomas) V. BS, U. So. Calif., L.A., 1981, MBA, 1987, postgrad. Cert. tchr., bus. mgmt. and mktg. tchr., C.C. tchr., Calif., CLAD cert. Sr. product mgr. Dataproducts Corp., Woodland Hills, Calif., 1980-86; product mktg. mgr. Light Signatures, Century City, Calif., 1987-88; mgr., mgmt. cons. KPMG Peat Marwick, L.A., 1988-92; v.p. Stranberg & Assocs., Newport Beach, Calif., 1993—; substitute tchr. Long Beach (Calif.) Unified Sch. Dist., 1993-95; tchr. Anaheim (Calif.) City Sch. Dist., 1994—; guest mktg. lectr. U. So. Calif., 1986—; developer, leader U. So. Calif. Western Europe's Grad. Bus. Exch. Program, 1987. Polit. campaign vol., Long Beach, Calif., 1989—; mem. Patrick Henry Leadership Team, Anaheim Unified Sch. Dist. Ins. Com., P.Q.R. sci. Team; leader Anaheim Math. Republican. Presbyterian. Home: 6016 Bixby Village Dr Long Beach CA 90803

VELAZQUEZ, ANABEL, sales executive; b. Havana, Cuba, July 26, 1958; came to U.S, 1966; d. Joel Velazquez and Elsa (Miranda) V.; m. Richard P. DiBacco; children: Alexandra Chloe, Richard Philip. BS in Nursing, Fla. Internat. U., 1987; AS, So. Coll., Collegedale, Tenn., 1979. RN, Fla.; CRRN, CEN; cert. ins. rehab. specialist; cert. case mgr. Staff nurse Hialeah (Fla.) Hosp., 1980-85; home care supr. Med. Pers. Pool, Miami, 1985-88; regional mgr. Peninsular Rehab. Assocs., Winter Park, Fla., 1988-89; med. sales specialist Bristol Myers-Squibb, Evansville, Ind., 1989-91; clin. sales specialist, sr. hosp. sales rep. Fujisawa Pharm. Co., Ill., 1990-92; pres. Workers Rehab. Inc., Winter Park, Fla., 1993—. Recipient award Am. Legion. Mem. Coun. on Future of Nurses, Assn. Rehab. Nurses, Case Mgr. Soc. Assn. Home: 229 Crooked Stick Ct Orlando FL 32828-8831 Office: Workers Rehab Inc PO Box 2464 Goldenrod FL 32733-2464

VELAZQUEZ, NYDIA M., congresswoman; b. Yabucoa, P.R.. Grad., U. P.R.; MA, NYU, 1976. Mem. 103rd-104th Congress from 12th N.Y. dist., Washington, D.C., 1992—. Office: US Ho of Reps 132 Cannon Bldg Washington DC 20515-3212

VÉLEZ, EILEEN MCLELLAN DE, social worker; b. Boston, Apr. 26, 1955; d. Robert Francis and Mary Joan (McNulty) McLellan; m. Luis Arnaldo Vélez-Cortés. Bachelor in Journalism, Suffolk U., 1977; BS in Journalism. Cert. in cultural understanding in child welfare, substance abuse and family violence. Eligibility worker Dept. Pub. Welfare, Quincy, Mass., 1977-78; adminstrv. asst. Dept. Pub. Welfare, Quincy, 1978-80; sr. interviewer Div. Employment Security, Boston, 1980; social work tech. Dept. Social Services, Quincy, 1980-81, social worker III, 1981—, supr. B of Social Work student interns, 1990-94; hotline counselor Survival Crisis Lines, Quincy, 1978-80. Vol. spl. events, cmty. outreach coord. for fundraising AIDS Action Com., Boston, 1988—, asst. dir. of acquisitions Acad. Awards Night Fundraiser, 1992; mem. com. women's concerns, eucharistic minister Dignity-Boston, exec. bd., sec., 1993-95, mem.-at-large, 1995-96; active Greater Boston Bus. Coun., 1992-94, 500 Club-AIDS Walk for Life, 1991-96, Greenpeace, 1994-95; mem. Human Rights Campaign, 1996, Call to Action, Catholics Speak Out, 1995—; union stewart SEIU Local 509, 1990—. Named Social Worker of Yr., Mass. Foster Parent Assn., 1989. Mem. NOW, Parents and Friends Lesbians and Gays, Dignity-Boston, Suffolk U. Alumni Ambs., Gamma Sigma Sigma. Democrat. Roman Catholic. Home: 1153 Hyde Park Ave Hyde Park MA 02136-2808 Office: Dept Social Svcs 541 Main St Weymouth MA 02190-1845

VELICER, JANET SCHAFBUCH, elementary school educator; b. Cedar Rapids, Iowa, Aug. 27, 1941; d. Allan J. and Geraldine Frances (Stuart) Schafbuch; m. Leland Frank Velicer, Aug. 17, 1963; children: Mark Allan, Gregory Jon, Daniel James. BS, Iowa State U., 1963, MS, 1966; cert. Elem. Edn., Mich. State U., 1976. Tchr. chemistry Prendergast High Sch., Upper Darby, Pa., 1964-65; tchr. home econs. Cardinal O'Hara High Sch., Springfield, Pa., 1965-66; substitute tchr. Pa., Mich., 1967-76; elem. tchr. Winans Elem. Sch., Waverly, Mich., 1976-78, Wardcliff Elem. Sch., Okemos, Mich., 1978-94; tchr. gifted and talented alternative program grades 4 and 5 Hiawatha Elem. Sch., Okemos, 1994-95; tchr. grade 4 Wardcliff Elem. Sch., 1995—; computer coord., Great Books coord.; dist. com. mem. math, computer, substance abuse, cable TV, evaluation revision Okemos Pub. Schs., Instructional Coun. Author: (video) Wardcliff School Documentary, 1982, The Integrated Arts Program of the Okemos Elementary Schools, 1983. Citizens adv. com. to develop a five-yr. plan, 1982-83, Bldg. utilization adv. com., 1983-84, Community use of schs. adv. com., 1984-85, Strategic planning steering com., 1989-90, Taking our schs. into tomorrow com., 1990-91, Bonding election steering com., 1991; chmn. wellness com. Okemos Pub. Schs., 1993-95. Recipient Classrooms of Tomorrow Tchr. award Mich. Dept. Edn., 1990. Mem. NEA, NAFE, Mich. Edn. Assn., Inst. Noetic Scis., Okemos Edn. Assn., Phi Kappa Phi, Mich. Coun. Tchrs. Math., Omicron Nu, Iota Sigma Pi. Democrat. Home: 2678 Blue Haven Ct East Lansing MI 48823-3804 Office: Okemos Pub Schs 4406 Okemos Rd Okemos MI 48864-2553

VELIE, JEANNE ELIZABETH, financial manager, accounting; b. Winona, Minn., Dec. 14, 1949; d. Raymond J. and Margaret A. (Forseth) Mortinger; m. Dennis R. Velie, Sept. 19, 1970; children: Victoria, Daniel. BA in Bus. Mgmt., Alverno Coll., 1984; MPA, U. Wis., Oshkosh, 1995. Acct. II Fond du Lac (Wis.) County Fin., 1985-88; bus. mgr. DSS Fond du Lac (Wis.) Co., 1988-93; fiscal svcs., sys. mgr. Dept. Social Svcs., Comm. Pgrms. Health Care Ctr./Fond du Lac (Wis.) Co., 1993—. Vice chair Fond du Lac Housing Authority, 1992-94, bd. dirs., 1990-94. Recipient Plaque Fond du Lac Housing Authority, 1994. Mem. Wis. Human Svcs. Fin. Mgrs., Assn. Govt. Accts. Office: Fond du Lac County 87 Vincent St Fond Du Lac WI 54935

VELLA, SANDRA RACHAEL, principal; b. Springfield, Mass., Jan. 19, 1946; d. Joseph James and Josephine Anna (DiMonaco) V. BA, Coll. of Our Lady Of Elms, 1967; MA, Westfield State Coll., 1974, postgrad., 1975. Cert. elem. sch. tchr., prin. Tchr. elem. sch. Samuel Bowles Sch., Springfield, Mass., 1967-86, prin. elem. sch., 1986—. Historian Italian Cultural Ctr., 1988—; bd. dirs. Springfield Preservation Trust, 1988-94; coord. Com. Dimonaco for Mayor, Springfield, 1989-90; co-author drug program Healthy Me Gov. Alliance vs. Drug, 1992-94; bd. dirs. Forest Park Civic Assn., 1990-92; bd. dirs. New Eng. Puppetry Theatre, 1984-92; numerous ednl. and altruistic civic sub. coms. Recipient Serviam award Italian Cultural Ctr.

Western Mass., 1992, Mass. Gov.'s Alliance vs. Drugs award, 1988-90. Mem. Springfield Elem. Prins. Assn., Alpha Delta Kappa (Kappa pres. 1991-94, state chaplain 1994-96). Democrat. Roman Catholic. Home: 99 Appleton St Springfield MA 01108-2945 Office: Samuel Bowles Sch 24 Bowles Park Springfield MA 01104-1510

VELLENGA, KATHLEEN OSBORNE, former state legislator; b. Alliance, Nebr., Aug. 5, 1938; d. Howard Benson and Marjorie (Menke) Osborne; m. James Alan Vellenga, Aug. 9, 1959; children: Thomas, Charlotte Vellenga Landreau, Carolyn. BA, Macalester Coll., 1959. Tchr. St. Paul Pub. Schs., 1959-60, Children's Ctr. Montessori, St. Paul, 1973-74, Children's House Montessori, St. Paul, 1974-79; mem. Minn. Ho. of Reps., St. Paul, 1980-94, mem. tax. com. and rules com., 1991—, chmn. St. Paul del., 1985-89, chmn. criminal justice div., 1989-90, chmn. crime and family law div., 1987-88, mem. Dem. steering com., 1987-94; chmn. judiciary Minn. Ho. of Reps., 1991, 92, chmn. edn. fin., 1992-93, 93-94; mem. St. Paul Family Svcs. Bd., 1994-95; exec. dir. St. Paul/Ramsey County Children's Initiative, 1994—. Chmn. Healthstart, St. Paul, 1987-91; mem. Children, Youth and Families Consortium, 1995—, Macalester Coll. Bd. Alumni, 1995-96, Minn. Higher Edn. Svcs. Coun., 1995-96. Mem. LWV (v.p. St. Paul chpt. 1979), Minn. Women Elected Ofcls. (vice chair 1994). Democrat. Presbyterian. Office: A H Wilder 919 Lafond Ave Saint Paul MN 55104-2108

VELO, KATHLEEN LOUISE, photographic educator; b. Chgo., Oct. 5, 1950; d. Frank and Evelyn (Price) V.; m. Gerald Elias, Oct. 3, 1980 (div. Oct. 1992); children: Amber Rachel, Max Elliot. BA in Psychology, Ariz. State U., 1975; BFA in Sculpture, U. Wis., Milw., 1979; MA in Art Edn., U. Ariz., 1992. Photography, Art and Ariz. C.C. certs. Freelance photographer Tucson, 1982-90; program coord. Artworks Studio, U. Ariz., Tucson, 1989-90; photography instr. Sunnyside Unified Sch. Dist., Tucson, 1989-90; art edn. instr. U. Ariz., Tucson, 1989-91; photography instr. Pima C.C., Tucson, 1992-93, Tucson (Ariz.) Unified Sch. Dist., 1990—; vol. trainer Art program Lineweaver Elem. Sch., Tucson Unified Sch. Dist., 1988-94. Author: Teaching Photography Without the Expense, 1995. Mem. Photographic Imaging Edn. Assn., Group for Photographic Intentions, Ariz. Women's Caucus Art. Home: 5627 E Linden Tucson AZ 85712

VENABLE, SHARON FRANCES, chamber of commerce executive; b. Dallas, Oct. 4, 1942; d. James Moore and Billie Frances (Burns) Harwell; m. Charles C. VEnable, Jr., June 4, 1961; children: James Lynn, Erin Michelle. BBA, Dallas Bapt. U., 1982; MLA, So. Meth. U., 1989. With Southwestern Bell Telephone, Dallas, 1968-72, staff mgr. tng., 1972-76, area mgr. tng., 1976-84, area mgr. cmty. rels., 1984-91; dir. edn. and leadership devel. Greater Dallas Chamber, 1991-94, v.p. women's bus. issues, 1994—; mem. adv. bd. Women's Enterprise Mag., Dallas, 1995—; mem. adv. bd. work/family partnership U. North Tex., Denton and Dallas, 1995—; bd. dirs., founding mem. North Tex. Women's Bus. Devel. Coun., Dallas, 1994—. Bd. dirs. Tex. Woman's Univ. Found., Denton, 1995—, YWCA Women's Resource Ctr., Dallas, 1994—; pres. Dallas County Adult Literacy Coun., Dallas, 1994—; vol. chair World Cup Dallas '94, 1993-94; mem. steering com. Literacy Task Force, Dallas Citizens Coun., 1994—. Recipient various awards. Mem. Am. C. of C. Execs. Office: Greater Dallas Chamber 1201 Elm St Ste 2000 Dallas TX 75270

VENDLER, HELEN HENNESSY, literature educator, poetry critic; b. Boston, Mass., Apr. 30, 1933; d. George and Helen (Conway) Hennessy; 1 son, David. A.B., Emmanuel Coll., 1954; Ph.D., Harvard U., 1960; Ph.D. (hon.), U. Oslo; D.Litt. (hon.), Smith Coll., Kenyon Coll., U. Hartford, Union Coll.; Fitchburg State U.; D.Litt. (hon.), Columbia U., George Washington U., Marlboro Coll., St. Louis; DHL (hon.), Dartmouth Coll., U. Mass., Bates Coll., U. Toronto, Ont., Can., Trinity Coll., Dublin, Ireland, Fitchburg State U.; George Washington U. Instr. Cornell U., Ithaca, N.Y., 1960-63; lectr. Swarthmore (Pa.) Coll. and Haverford (Pa.) Coll., 1963-64; asst. prof. Smith Coll., Northampton, Mass., 1964-66; assoc. prof. Boston U., 1966-68, prof., 1968-85; Fulbright lectr. U. Bordeaux, France, 1968-69; vis. prof. Harvard U., 1981-85, Kenan prof., 1985—, Porter U. prof., 1990—, assoc. acad. dean, 1987-92, sr. fellow Harvard Soc. Fellows, 1981-93; poetry critic New Yorker, 1978—; mem. ednl. adv. bd. Guggenheim Found., 1991—, Pulitzer Prize Bd., 1991—. Author: Yeats's Vision and the Later Plays, 1963, On Extended Wings: Wallace Stevens' Longer Poems, 1969, The Poetry of George Herbert, 1975, Part of Nature, Part of Us, 1980, The Odes of John Keats, 1983, Wallace Stevens: Words Chosen Out of Desire, 1984; editor: Harvard Book of Contemporary American Poetry, 1985, Voices and Visions: The Poet in America, 1987, The Music of What Happens, 1988, Soul Says, 1995, The Given and the Made, 1995, The Breaking of Style, 1995, Poems, Poets, Poetry, 1995. Bd. dirs. Nat. Humanities Ctr., 1989-93. Recipient Lowell prize, 1969, Explicator prize, 1969, award Nat. Inst. Arts and Letters, 1975, Radcliffe Grad. Soc. medal, 1978, Nat. Book Critics award, 1980, Keats-Shelley Assn. award, 1994, Truman Capote award, 1996; Fulbright fellow, 1954, AAUW fellow, 1959, Guggenheim fellow, 1971-72, Am. Coun. Learned Socs. fellow, 1971-72, NEH fellow, 1980, 85, 94, Overseas fellow Churchill Coll., Cambridge, 1980, Charles Stewart Parnell fellow Magdalene Coll., Cambridge, 1996, hon. fellow, 1996—. Mem. MLA (exec. coun. 1972-75, pres. 1980), AAAL, English Inst. (trustee 1977-85), Am. Acad. Arts and Scis. (v.p. 1992-95), Norwegian Acad. Letters and Sci., Am. Philos. Soc., Phi Beta Kappa. Home: 54 Trowbridge St # 2 Cambridge MA 02138-4113 Office: Harvard U Dept English 8 Prescott St Cambridge MA 02138-3929

VENERABLE, SHIRLEY MARIE, gifted education educator; b. Washington, Nov. 12, 1931; d. John Henry and Jessie Josephine (Young) Washington; m. Wendell Grant Venerable, Feb. 15, 1959; children: Angela Elizabeth Maria Venerable-Joyner, Wendell Mark. PhB, Northwestern U., 1963; MA, Roosevelt U., 1976, postgrad., 1985. Cert. in diagnostic and prescriptive reading, gifted edn., finger math., fine arts, Ill. Tchr. Lewis Champlin Sch., 1963-74, John Hay Acad., Chgo., 1975-87, Leslie Lewis Elem. Sch., Chgo., 1988—; sponsor Reading Marathon Club, Chgo., 1991—; co-creator Project SMART (Stimulating Math. and Reading Techniques) John Hay Acad., Chgo., 1987-90, curriculum coord., 1985-87; creative dance student, tchr. Kathryn Duham Sch., N.Y.C., 1955-56; creative dance tchr. Doris Patterson Dance Sch., Washington, 1953-55; recorder evening divsn. Northwestern U., Chgo., 1956-62; exch. student tchr. Conservatory Dance Movements, Chgo., 1958-59; art cons. Chgo. Pub. Sch., 1967. Author primary activities Let's Act and Chat, 1991-94, Teaching Black History Through Classroom Tours, 1989-90. Solicitor, vol. United Negro Coll. Fund, Chgo., 1994; sponsor 21st Ward Reading Assn., Chgo., 1991-94; mem. St. Giles Coun. Cath. Women, 1985-96. Recipient Meritorious award United Negro Coll. Fund, 1990, 94, Recognition award Alderman Percy Giles, Chgo., 1993. Mem. ASCD (assoc., Recognition of Svcs. award 1989), Internat. Reading Assn., Eta Zi Sigma, Sigma Gamma Rho (Delta Sigma grad. chpt. 1963-93, Sigma chpt. 1992, Xi grad. chpt.), Phi Delta Kappa. Roman Catholic. Home: 1108 N Euclid Ave Oak Park IL 60302-1219

VENEZIA, JOYCE ANN, journalist; b. Englewood, N.J., Sept. 26, 1960; d. Rocco Peter and Maria L. (Matera) V.; m. Sherwin Alan Suss, Mar. 3, 1990; children: Rebecca Rose, Emily Elise. BA in Journalism and Am. Studies, Pa. State U., 1982. News. clk. Asbury Pk. (N.J.) Press, 1982; copy editor Montgomery County Record, Jenkintown, Pa., 1982-83; newswoman AP, Augusta, Maine and Hartford, Conn., 1983-85; corr. AP, Evansville, Ind., 1985-86, Atlantic City, 1986-89; reporter The Star-Ledger, Newark, 1989-95; freelance writer, 1995—. Roman Catholic. Home and Office: 438 Overbrook Rd Ridgewood NJ 07450-3417

VENIS, LINDA DIANE, academic administrator, educator; b. Pasadena, Calif., Nov. 15, 1948; d. Ashton Harwood Venis and Grace (Bullock) Miller; m. Gary Arther Berg, Mar. 9, 1991; 1 child, Laura Grace Berg. BA magna cum laude, UCLA, 1970, PhD, 1978. Lectr. English UCLA, 1982-85, adj. asst. prof. Dept. English, 1987-90; lectr. Sch. Fine Arts U. So. Calif., L.A., 1985—; assoc. dir. studies UCLA/London & Cambridge Programs UCLA Extension, 1986-91, head writers program, 1985—, dir. dept. arts, 1992—. Contbr. articles to profl. jours. Recipient Profl. Contbrns. to Continuing Edn. award Continuing Edn. Assn., UCLA Disting. Tchg. award, 1985. Mem. PEN USA/West (bd. dirs. 1993—, adv. bd. 1992-93), Women in Film, Assn. Acad. Women. Office: UCLA Extension The Arts 10995 Le Conte Ave Los Angeles CA 90024

VENNUM, JOAN FAY, artist; b. Long Branch, N.J., July 12, 1929; d. John Bourke and Edna Frances (Fay) V.; m. Ted Naomikurahara, 1954; children: Mie, Thomas, Leon. BFA, Washington U., 1951; MFA, U. Ill., 1953. Artist: solo exhbitions include: Columbia Univ., N.Y.C., 1984 (paintings), Konstmuseet Galleri Astley, Uttersberg, Sweden, 1991 (graphics), Gallieret, Eskilstuna, Sweden, 1992 (etchings), Lilla Galleri, Umeå, Sweden; group exhibitions include Westbeth, N.Y.C., Split Light Paintings and Projections, 1980, Fairleigh Dickenson U., Watercolor, 1981, Oil and Steel Gallery, N.Y.C., 1983, Light paintings and projections, City Gallery, N.Y.C., 1984 (prints), Galleri Astley, Uttersberg, Sweden, prints, drawings, watercolors, 1985, selected graphics, 1987, Grafiska Sallskapet, Stockholm, Selected Graphics, 1988, Maryland Inst., Balt., 1992, Anita Shopolsky Gallery, N.Y.C., Galleri Astley, Seattle, 1992, 93, (paintings and prints), Printmaking Workshop Gallery, N.Y.C., 1994 and others; co-producer: (with Susan Brockman and Sally Gross) (film) Lee's Ferry, 1982. Studio: 78 Greene St New York NY 10012

VENTIMIGLIA, KATHARINE JANE GARVER, education educator; b. Muncie, Ind., Sept. 1, 1949; d. Edwin Gilmore and Sybil Marie (Daughtry) Garver; m. Joseph John Ventimiglia, June 17, 1972; children: Joseph Marc, Robert Edwin, Jeffrey Peter, Matthew Patrick. BA in Edn., NE La. U., 1971; MEd, Dowling Coll., 1991; postgrd., Hofstra U. Cert. nursery and elem. tchr., Ill., N.Y. Tchr. Archdiocese of Chgo., 1971-72, Diocese of Bklyn., 1972-74; adj. asst. prof. coll. reading Suffolk Community Coll., Selden, N.Y., 1986-91, prof. reading, 1991—; asst. to dir. program learning disabled Dowling Coll., Oakdale, N.Y., 1991—; reading/writing specialist student support svcs. Dowling Coll., Oakdale, 1993—, adj. lectr. edn., 1994—; pvt. practicereading clinic; reading/learning disabilities specialist Dowling Coll., Oakdale, 1989—. Author: (with others) Successful Strategies for Learning Disabled College Students: Reading, Writing and Reasoning, 1991. Treas. Sagamore Jr. High Sch. PTA, Holtsville, N.Y., 1987-88, bd. dirs. 1986-89; treas. Gatelot Ave. PTA, Lake Ronkonkoma, N.Y., 1983-92, mem. exec. bd. 1979-92, project coord. Reading Is Fundamental, 1989-92. Mem. AAUW, DAR, Internat. Reading Assn., Orton Dyslexia Soc., Kappa Delta Pi, Alpha Upsilon Alpha. Office: Dowling Coll Student Support Svcs Fortunoff Hall Rm 007 Oakdale NY 11769 also: Suffolk Community Coll Sagtikos Bldg Crooked Hill Rd Rm 201 Brentwood NY 11717-1005

VEON, DOROTHY HELENE, educational consultant; b. Oxford, Nebr., May 31, 1924; d. John B. and Ella (Robertson) V. BSc, U. Nebr., 1945; MA, George Washington U., 1949; EdD, Columbia U., 1957; M. Med. Sci., Tulane U., 1969. Asst. prof. edn. George Washington U., Washington, 1945-50; prof. edn. Pa. State U., University Park, 1950-66; asst. dir. Sch. of Nursing Thomas Jefferson U., Phila., 1966-68; vis. prof. Ariz. State U., 1959-60, Drexel U., Phila., 1973-74, Temple U., Phila., 1974-75, U. Vt., 1966; Bradley U., 1962, U. Oreg., 1964; ednl. and bus. cons. Phila., 1988—; prof., dir. div. econs. and bus. adminstrn. C.C. Phila., 1970-88, NIH Schs., 1968-69. Editor Am. Bus. Edn. U.S. del. to World Congress of Women, Moscow, 1987; organizer, spkr. UN Decade for Women Conf., Nairobi, Kenya, 1985, UN Fourth World Conf. for Women, Beijing, 1995; NGO Forum for Women, Huairou, China, 1995; keynote spkr. Wilton Park Conf. NATO, West Sussex, Eng., 1994; mem. confs. Internat. Fedn. Univ. Women, Mexico City, 1965, Karlsruhe, Germany, 1968, Phila., 1971, Tokyo and Kyoto, 1974, Stirling, Scotland, 1977, Vancouver, B.C., Can., 1980, Groningen, The Netherlands, 1983, Christchurch, N.Z., 1986, Helsinki, 1989, Stanford U., 1992, Yokohama, Japan, 1995; seminar spkr. Trinity Coll., Dublin, Oxford U.,; bd. dirs. Virginia Gildersleeve Internat. Fund for Univ. Women, 1982-92; mem. Workers in Comm. Recipient Internat. Disting. Svc. award Status of Women, 1986; Radcliffe Rsch. scholar, 1988-90; named Internat. Woman of Yr., Internat. Biog. Ctr., Cambridge, Eng., 1993-94. Mem. NAFE, AAUW (nat. grantee 1968, 84, 93, v.p. Pa. divsn. 1964-66, Disting. award 1985, pres. Phila. br. 1983-85, Nat. 50 Yr. honoree 1992), Am. Acad. Nat. Scis., Am. Mgmt. Assn., Am. Mktg. Assn., Am. Bus. Comm. Assn. (v.p. 1962-65, nat. fellow 1970), Internat. Soc. Bus. Edn. (pres. 1958-60), Am. Econ. Assn., Am. Acctg. Assn., Am. Assn. Nat. Scis., World Affairs Coun. Phila., Fgn. Policy Rsch. Inst., Phila. Mus. Art, Nat. Space Soc., Pa. Acad. Fine Art, Mt. Vernon Soc. George Washington U. (hon.), Emerald Soc. (hon.), Nat. Mus. for Women Rights, Women in the Arts (Washington), Women in Comms., Inc., Kappa Delta (province pres. 1948-50, 62-64, 70-72, 50 Yr. honoree), Phi Delta Gamma, Pi Omega Pi, Delta Pi Epsilon (nat. pres. 1960-62, Nat. Rsch. award 1949), Pi Lambda Theta (nat. treas. 1960-64). Republican. Episcopalian. Home: 1700 Benjamin Franklin Pky Philadelphia PA 19103-1210

VERANI, PATRICIA LEWIS, sculptor; b. L.I., N.Y., Jan. 2, 1927; d. Tracy Hammond Lewis and Esther Tufts Latting; m. Osvaldo Verani, Apr. 24, 1950; children: Michela E., Margherita, Daniela E., Giovanni M. Diploma with honors, Boston Mus. Sch. Fine Arts, 1948. Co-owner Verani's Restaurant, Manchester, N.H., 1955-65; sec. Verani Real Estate Londonderry, N.H., 1965-77; technician H&O Dental, Manchester, 1977-78; freelance sculptor Londonderry, 1978—; commd. U.S. Capitol Hist. Soc. for Bill of Rights, 1991. Sculptor (8 ft. bronze statue) Fighting Black Bear of U. Maine, 1979; sculptor, designer U.S. Commemmorative Silver Dollar, 1987, Olympic U.S. Commemmorative Silver Dollar, 1988; designer The Flagbearer Olympic Coin, 1996. Treas. Londonderry PTA, 1961-65; vol. artist Londonderry Host. Soc., 1979, 94, 95; vol. Save Outdoor Sculpture, N.H., 1994; advisor Londonderry Commons Com., 1995—. Mrs. David Hunt Traveling scholar Boston Mus. Sch., 1948, Mrs. Louis Bennet Bas Relief prize nat. Sculpture Soc., 1989. Mem. Am. Numismatic Assn. (Gold medal 1995), New Eng. Sculptors Assn. (chartered), Copley Soc. Boston, Nat. Sculpure Soc., N.H. Art Assn., Pen & Brush. Home and Office: 474 Mammoth Rd Londonderry NH 03053-2370

VERBIEST, SARAH ZUBER, public health social worker; b. Coldwater, Mich., Nov. 21, 1966; d. David Howard and Patricia May (Tatko) Zuber; m. Dirk Verbiest, Dec. 31, 1993. Student, U. Rouen, France, 1987-88; BA, St. Lawrence U., 1989; postgrad. in Health Care, Boston U., 1993; MSW, MPH, U. N.C., 1995. Program asst. The Asia Found., Bangladesh, 1991-92; coord. project team HIV/AIDS telephone support group U. N.C. Sch. of Social Work, Chapel Hill, 1993-94; asst. coord. USAID evaluation project at Carolina Population Ctr., Chapel Hill, 1994-95; intern in policy dept. Internat. Projects Assistance Services, 1995, cons. for comm. dept., project mgr. child homicide study, 1995-96; project evaluator Substance Abuse Free Families and Environment, Durham, 1996—; instr. Internat. Culture and News Co., Japan, 1989-91; asst. coord. Bangladesh Nat. Family Life Edn. Exec. Com., 1992, cons. CARE, Bangladesh, 1992; case mgt. intern pediatric patients U. N.C. Sickle Cell Program, 1993-94; cons. JHPIEGO. Contbr. articles to profl. jours. Mem. NOW, Am. Pub. Health Assn., Nat. Assn. Social Workers (legis. focus group), UN Assn. (W. Triangle Park chpt bd. dirs.), N.C. Assn. Pub. Health Social Workers, Internat. Social Workers Exchange Program, N.C. Equity, Unitarian Universalist Fellowship, The Common Sense Found. Democrat. Home: 3428 Sandy Creek Dr Durham NC 27705

VERBOCKEL ROGERS, JOLENE MARY, auditor; b. Kaukauna, Wis., Nov. 17, 1964; d. Ralph and Elizabeth Louise (Sippel) Verbockel; m. Steven James Rogers, June 12, 1985; children: Tanner David, Thatcher Andrew. BBA, U. Wis., Oshkosh, 1990. CPA, Ill.; cert. mgmt. acct. Auditor, coord. ADP, Office Insp. Gen., U.S. Dept. Transp., Chgo., 1990—. Mem. Inst. Mgmt. Acct. (cert.), Assn. Govt. Accts. (meetings dir. 1996-97). Office: US Dept Transp OIG 111 N Canal St Ste 677 Chicago IL 60606

VERDERMAN, PATRICIA GREEK, lawyer; b. Wilmington, Del., 1951. BA, Ohio Wesleyan U., 1973; JD, So. Meth. U., 1976. Bar: Tex. 1976. Ptnr. Andrews & Kurth, LLP, Houston. Contbr. articles to law rev. Mem. State Bar Tex., ABA, Delta Theta Phi. Office: Andrews & Kurth LLP 600 Travis Ste 4200 Houston TX 77002*

VERDILL, ELAINE DENISE, artisan; b. Bellefontaine, Ohio, Nov. 5, 1955; d. Margaret (Miller) V. BS, Bowling Green State U., 1978. Coord. info. svcs. JILA, U. Colo., Boulder, 1990-96, budget analyst, 1996—. Mem. Hand-Weavers' Guild of Boulder. Office: JILA U Colo CB 440 Boulder CO 80309

VERDOLINI-SHEATS, SUSAN, sales and marketing company executive; b. Charleston, W.Va., Nov. 27, 1956; d. Vincent James and Sara Jane (Kier) Verdolini; m. James Francis Sheats III, Apr. 22, 1989; children: James Michael, Steven Zachary. BA, Coll. of Charleston, S.C., 1984. Lic. realtor, S.C. Realtor Century 21, Mt. Pleasant, S.C., 1977-80; mgr., corp. asst. No Name Cafe, Charleston, S.C., 1980-84; dir. sales and mktg. Planters Inn, Charleston, 1984-88; mktg. cons., Charleston, 1988-89; sales mgr. Omni Hotel Corp., Washington, 1989-90; pres. So. Exposures, Inc., Arlington, Va., 1990—. Mem. PROST, CTO, Skal Club, Nat. Honor Soc., Psi Chi, Phi Kappa Phi. Office: So Exposures Inc 1007 S 26th Rd Arlington VA 22202

VERDON, JANE KATHRYN, lawyer; b. Manchester, N.C., 1943. BA, Newton Coll., 1964; JD, U. San Diego, 1991. Bar: N.C. 1992. Legal intern San Diego City Atty. - Criminal Divsn., 1991; law clk. criminal def. Cheshire, Parker, Hughes and Manning, Raleigh, N.C., 1991-92; pvt. practice Raleigh, 1992—; creative dir., corp. v.p., ptnr. Internat. Creative Sys.; account exec., publicity dir., TV spokesperson H. Richard Silver, Inc.; fashion, beauty editor, spokesperson for major consumer mags., newspapers, TV; advt. and promotion in all areas of health, beauty and fashion. Assoc. fashion editor, assoc. managing editor Seventeen Mag.; fashion dir. Woman's World Mag.; contbg. editor, writer for newspapers and consumer mags.; designer newspaper, radio and TV features, brochures, scripts, promotional programs, mediation, negotiations; TV and comml. appearances. Mem. AFTRA, ABA, ATLA, N.C. Bar Assn., N.C. Trial Lawyers Assn., N.J. Foster Parents' Assn., Lawyers' Club, Phi Alpha Delta. Office: 7413 Six Forks Rd #151 Raleigh NC 27615-6164

VERED, RUTH, art gallery director; b. Tel Aviv, Sept. 26, 1940; d. Abraham and Helen (Psisuska) Rosenblum; children: Sharon, Oren. BA in Art Hisotry with honors, Bezalel U., Jerusalem, 1964. Freelance art cons., Israel and N.Y.C., 1965-75; dir. Vered Gallery, East Hampton, N.Y., 1977—. Sgt. paratroops Israeli Army, 1958-60. Home: 891 Park Ave New York NY 10021-0326 Office: Vered Gallery East Hampton NY 11937

VERGAMINI, JUDITH SHARON ENGEL, counselor, educator; b. Milw., May 21, 1941; d. Max E. and Rose (Ladish) Engel; m. Jerome Carl Vergamini, May 1, 1965; children: Michael David, Beth Allison, Daniel Carl. BS, U. Wis., 1963, postgrad., 1964, 66-76; MS, U. Oreg., 1978, postgrad., 1980—. Nat. cert. counselor; lic. profl. counsellor, tchr., sch. counselor, marriage and family therapist. Elem. tchr. Crestwood Elem. Sch., Northbrook, Ill., 1963-64, Odana Elem. Sch., Madison, Wis., 1964-65, Fitzmorris Elem. Sch., Arvada, Colo., 1965-66; tchr. Headstart, Madison, Wis., 1966; coord., founder parent vols. program Alternate Sch., Eugene, Oreg., 1976-77; pvt. practice counselor Eugene, 1978—; instr. Lane C.C., Eugene, Oreg., 1978—; lectr. Addictions Treatment Hosp. Program, 1989-92; mental health specialist Headstart of Lane County, Oreg., 1993-94; resource counselor Newman Ctr. U. Oreg., Eugene, 1979—, adj. prof., 1994—; presenter in field. Recipient Appreciation award Eugene Edn. Assn., 1980, Svc. to Edn. award, Oreg. Edn. Assn., 1980, Dedication and Performance award Nat. Disting. Svc. Registry, 1990, Outstanding Merit award Nat. Bd. Cert. Counselors, 1991. Fellow Am. Orthopsychiatric Assn.; mem. AACD, Am. Assn. for Marriage and Family Therapy (clin.), Am. Mental Health Counselors Assn., Oreg. Counseling Assn. Home: 1047 Brookside Dr Eugene OR 97405-4913 Office: 1508 Oak St Eugene OR 97401-4042

VERGANO, LYNN (MARILYNN BETTE VERGANO), artist; b. N.Y.C., Nov. 14; d. George and Sis Anagnostis (Helaine Haas); children: Scott, Stephen, Sandy, Sefton. Student, Pratt Inst., 1959-60; BA, NYU, Heights, 1963; MA, NYU, 1964. Lectr. art Morris County Coll., 1982; lectr. UN Pan Pacific and S.E. Asia Women's Assn., N.Y. chpt., 1996; lectr. in field; judge, art juror. Author/illustrator: (book) Paintings, 1980; one-woman shows include Papermill Playhouse, N.J., 1976, 79, 83, Fairleigh Dickinson U., N.J., 1977, Drew U., N.J., 1977, Rutgers U., N.J., 1978, 79, Hong Kong Arts Ctr., 1980, Am. Univ. Alumni, Bangkok, Thailand, 1980, Caldwell Coll., N.J., 1980, União Cultural Brasil-Estados Unidos, São Paulo, Brazil, 1982, Galleria Fenice, Venice, Italy, 1985, St. Sophia Mus., Istanbul, Turkey, 1988, Nat. Arts Club, N.Y.C., 1989, Centreplace, Hamilton, New Zealand, 1990; exhibited in group shows Monmouth Mus., Lincroft, N.J., 1976, 77, 82, Morris Mus., Morristown, N.J., 1977, 78, N.J. State Capital Mus., Trenton, 1979, Macculloch Hall Hist. Mus., N.J., Morristown, 1984, 87, 89, 92, 96, Nat. Audubon Artists, N.Y.C., 1981, Salmagundi Club, N.Y.C., 1981, World Trade Ctr., N.Y., 1981, Nat. Arts Club, N.Y.C., 1981-96, Bergen Mus., Paramus, N.J., 1983, Lincoln Ctr., N.Y.C., 1987, Bklyn. Botanic Gardens, N.Y., 1987, many others. Pres., chpt. charter mem., 1969-70, hon. mem. Welcome Wagon Club, Randolph, N.J., 1969—. Recipient UN 25th Anniversary Creative Writing award, 1970, John H. Miller award Morris County Coll., 1979, Grumbacher gold medallion, 1984, Torch award NYU, 1993. Mem. AAUW, Am. Watercolor Soc. (assoc.), UN Pan Pacific and S.E. Asia Women's Assn. Internat. (hon.), Am. Watercolor Soc. (assoc.), Nat. Arts Club (exhibiting), Nat. Soc. Arts and Letters (exec. bd. N.J. chpt. 1979—), Federated Art Assns. N.J. (trsutee 1982—, pres., chmn. bd. dirs. 1982-88, Heritage plaque 1989), Morris County Art Assn., Dover Art Assn. (hon.), Millburn-Short Hills Arts Ctr. Home: 80 Old Stonehouse Rd Bedminster NJ 07921 also: 229 Van Cortlandt Pk Ave Yonkers NY 10705-1520

VERGE, ANNE WILDER, program administrator, police officer; b. Detroit, Apr. 23, 1951; d. Donald Le Roy and Elizabeth (Wilder) Weismann; m. Richard Wallace Verge, Aug. 19, 1972 (div. May 1985); children: Natalie Wilder Verge, Jacob Wallace Verge. BA, Middlebury (Vt.) Coll., 1971; attended, Boston U. Sch. Law, 1976-77. Cert. police officer, N.H. Spl. asst. to pres. Boston U., 1974-78; police officer, selectman Town of South Hampton, N.H., 1978-86; patrolman, sgt. of police U. N.H., Durham, 1984-87; asst. to pres. Boston U., 1987-88, patrolman, capt. of police, 1988-89, dep. chief of police, 1989-91, asst. v.p., 1991-93, assoc. v.p. for enrollment, 1993-95, v.p. for enrollment, 1995—. Office: Boston U 881 Commonwealth Ave Boston MA 02215

VERHESEN, ANNA MARIA HUBERTINA, counselor; b. Heerenveen, Friesland, Netherland, Dec. 6, 1932; came to U.S., 1968; d. Hendrikus H. and Henrika C. (Kluessjen) V. BS, Mercy Coll. of Detroit, 1981; MA, Sienna Height, Adrian, Mich., 1992. Childcare worker Schiedam, Netherland, 1952-54; social worker Rotterdam Halfweg, Netherland, 1954-59; childcare worker Mt. St. Ann's Home, Worcester and Lawrence, Mass., 1968-70; chem. dependency social worker St. Vincent Med. Ctr., Toledo, Ohio, 1970-75; social worker St. Joseph Hosp., Nashua, N.H., 1975-78; vocation dir. Grey Nuns, Lexington, Mass., 1978-79; coord. community svcs. St. Vincents Med. Ctr., Toledo, 1981-91; pvt. practice clin. therapist Sylvania, Ohio, 1992—; alcohol/drug addiction/mental health counselor for ex-prisoners; founder St. Vincent Med. Ctr. Alcoholism Detox and Rehab. Unit, Toledo, 1970-75. Co-founder Transitional Residences for the Homeless, Toledo, 1981-90, Ohio Coalition for the Homeless, Columbus, 1982-89; co-founder of a home for persons with AIDS; co-chair City of Toledo Housing Policy, 1985-90; coord. Housing Now, Toledo, 1988-90. Recipient Woman of Achievement award Women in Communication, Toledo, 1986, Spirit of '87 award N.W. Ordinance and U.S. Constn. Bicentennial Commn., Toledo, 1987, Gov.'s Spl. Recognition award, 1988, Man for Others award St. John's High Sch., 1991; named Woman of Toledo, St. Vincent Med. Ctr. Aux., 1988, Ohio Ho. of Reps., 1987; featured in various mags. Roman Catholic. Home: 219 Page St Toledo OH 43620-1430 Office: Elliott and Assocs Inc 5600 Monroe St Sylvania OH 43560-2701

VERHOEK, SUSAN ELIZABETH, botany educator; b. Columbus, Ohio, 1942; m. S.E. Williams; 1 child. Student, Carleton Coll., 1960-62; BA, Ohio Wesleyan U., 1964; MA, Ind. U., 1966; PhD, Cornell U., 1975. Herbarium supr. Mo. Bot. Garden, St. Louis, 1966-70; asst. prof. Lebanon Valley Coll., Annville, Pa., 1974-82, assoc. prof., 1982-85, prof., 1985—; vis. researcher Cornell U., Ithaca, N.Y., 1982-83; content cons. Merrill Pub. Co., 1987-89; vis. profl. Chgo. Bot. Garden, 1991. Author: How to Know the Spring Flowers, 1982; contbr. articles to profl. jours., newspapers, and bulls. Trustee Lebanon Valley Coll., Annville, 1979-82, 84-90, 92—; dir. Lebanon Valley Coll. Arboretum, 1996—. Mem. Soc. for Econ. Botany (pres. 1985-86), Bot. Soc. Am., Am. Soc. Plant Taxonomists, Am. Assn. Bot. Gardens and Arboreta. Office: Lebanon Valley Coll Dept Botany Annville PA 17003-0501

VERLICH, JEAN ELAINE, writer, public relations consultant; b. McKeesport, Pa., July 5, 1950; d. Matthew Louis and Irene (Tomko) V.; m.

S(tanley) Wayne Wright, Sept. 29, 1979 (div. June 1988). Student, Bucknell U., 1968-69; BA, U. Pitts., 1971. Press sec. Com. to Re-elect President, S.W. Pa., 1972; adminstrv. asst. Pa. Rep. James B. Kelly III, 1972-73; reporter Beaver (Pa.) County Times, 1973-74; proofreader Ketchum, MacLeod & Grove, Pitts., 1975-76; community rels. specialist, PPG Industries, Pitts., 1976-77, editor PPG News, 1977-79, sr. staff writer, 1979-84, comm. coord., 1984-85; pub. rels. assoc. Glass Group, 1986-87; mgr. pub. rels. Glass Group PPG Industries, 1987-92; account mgr. Maddigan Comm., Pitts., 1992-93; owner JV Comm., Pitts., 1993—. Mem. Internat. Assn. Bus. Communicators (bd. dir. Pitts. chpt. 1981, v.p. pub. rels. Pitts. chpt. 1982, v.p. programs Pitts. chpt. 1985, pres. Pitts. chpt. 1986), Travelers Aid Soc. Pitts. (bd. dirs. 1992-95, v.p. 1994-95), Phi Beta Kappa, Delta Zeta. Office: JV Comm 3 Gateway Ctr Ste 1526 Pittsburgh PA 15222

VERMEER, MAUREEN DOROTHY, sales executive; b. Bronxville, N.Y., Mar. 21, 1945; d. Albert Casey and Helen (Valentine Casey) Vermeer; m. John R. Fassnacht, Feb. 11, 1966 (div. 1975); m. George M. Dallas Peltz IV, Oct. 26, 1985. Grad., NYU Real Estate Inst., 1976. Lic. real estate broker, notary pub., N.Y. With Douglas Elliman, N.Y.C., 1965-74, mgmt. supr., 1974-78, v.p., 1978-83; real estate broker Rachmani Corp., N.Y.C., 1983-84; v.p. sales and mktg. Carol Mgmt. Corp., N.Y.C., 1984-90; v.p. mktg. The Sunshine Group, N.Y.C., 1990; v.p., sec., bd. dirs. H.J. Kalikow & Co., N.Y.C., 1991—; mem. Real Estate Bd. N.Y.; speaker in field. Mem. Real Estate Bd. N.Y. (bd. dirs., residential mgmt. com.), Assn. Real Estate Women (sec., bd. dirs.). Republican. Presbyterian. Home: 111 Broadway Norwood NJ 07648 Office: H J Kalikow & Co 101 Park Ave New York NY 10178

VERMEULE, EMILY TOWNSEND (MRS. CORNELIUS C. VERMEULE, III), classicist, educator; b. N.Y.C., Aug. 11, 1928; d. Clinton Blake and Eleanor (Meneely) Townsend; m. Cornelius C. Vermeule III, Feb. 2, 1957; children: Emily Dickinson Blake, Cornelius Adrian Comstock. AB, Bryn Mawr Coll., 1950; student, Am. Sch. Classical Studies, Athens, 1950-51, St. Anne's Coll., Oxford U., 1953; MA, Harvard, 1954; PhD, Bryn Mawr Coll., 1956; DLitt, Douglass Coll.; D. Litt., Rutgers U., 1968, Tufts U., 1980, U. Pitts., 1983, Bates Coll., 1983, U. Miami, Oxford, Ohio, 1986; LL.D., Regis Coll., 1971; D. Fine Arts, U. Mass, Amherst, 1971; D.Litt., Smith Coll., 1972, Wheaton Coll., 1973, Trinity Coll., 1974; LHD, Emmanuel Coll., 1980, Princeton U., 1989, Bard Coll., 1994. Instr. Greek lang. Bryn Mawr Coll., 1956-57; instr. Wellesley (Mass.) Coll., 1957-58, prof. art and Greek, 1965-70, chmn. dept. art, 1966-67; asst. prof. classics Boston U., 1958-61, assoc. prof. classics, 1961-65; fellow for research Boston Mus. Fine Arts, 1965—; James C. Loeb vis. prof. classical philology Harvard, 1969; dir. univ. Cyprus expdn. Harvard U., 1971—, Samuel and Doris Zemurray Stone-Radcliffe prof., 1970-94; prof. emerita and Sather prof. U. Calif., Berkeley, 1975; Geddes-Harrower prof. Greek art and archaeology U. Aberdeen, 1980-81; Bernhard vis. prof. Williams Coll., 1986; excavations in Greece, Turkey, Libya, Cyprus. Author: Euripides v. Electra, 1959, Greece in the Bronze Age, 1964, The Trojan War in Greek Art, 1964, Götterkult, 1974, Toumba tou Skourou, The Mound of Darkness, 1975, Death in Early Greek Art and Poetry, Mycenaean Pictorial Vase-Painting (with U. Karageorghis), 1982, Toumba tou Skourou, A Bronze Age Potters' Quarter on Morphou Bay in Cyprus (with F.Z. Wolsky), 1990; contbr. articles to scholarly publs. Judge Nat. Book Award, 1977; bd. dirs. Humanities Rsch. Inst., U. Calif., 1988-91, bd. govs., 1988-90; trustee Isabella Stewart Gardner Mus., 1988-96. Recipient Gold medal for disting. achievement Radcliffe Coll. Grad. Soc., 1968; Guggenheim fellow, 1964-65. Fellow Soc. Antiquaries, Brit. Acad. (corr.), German Archaeol. Inst. (corr.); mem. AAAS, Am. Inst. Archaeology, Am. Philos. Soc. (v.p. 1978-81), Am. Philol. Assn. (Charles J. Goodwin award 1980, pres. 1995), Smithsonian Coun. (bd. scholars 1983-89), Hellenic Soc.

VERMYLEN, DEBRA MAE SINGLETON, sales executive; b. Tulsa, May 7, 1955; d. George Monroe and Jacqueline Romaine (Redman-Williams) Singleton; m. Patrick Roger Guy Vermylen, July 21, 1984; children: Nathan Christopher, Nicholas Patrick. AA, Erie Community Coll., Williamsville, N.Y., 1976; BS, SUNY, Buffalo, 1978. Sales rep. Kraft Inc., Columbia, Md., 1979-80, key sales rep., 1980-81, account mgr., 1981-82, sales supr. for Balt., 1982-84, sales supr. for Washington, 1984, supr. mil. sales, 1984-89; unit mgr. Kraft Gen. Foods, Columbia, 1989-90, sales mgr. ops., 1990-91; sales mgr. Kraft Gen. Foods, Houston, San Antonio, Rio Grande Valley, Austin, 1991-96, Fleming, Tom Thumb & Randalls, Humble, Tex., 1996—. Coord. Children's Time Presch., Columbia, 1990; aide The Learning Tree Sch., Humble, Tex., 1994-95. Republican. Baptist. Home and Office: 6007 Matt Rd Humble TX 77346

VERNER, LINDA HOGAN, manager cardiac surgery operating room; b. Washington, Aug. 24, 1945; d. Inman Curry and Julia Belk (Spratt) Hogan; m. David Howard Verner, Mar. 14, 1971 (div. Sept. 1976); children: Heather, Stacy. ASN, Ga. Southwestern Coll., 1966. RN, Ga. Staff nurse med. surg. unit St. Joseph's Hosp., Augusta, Ga., 1966-68; staff nurse operating room St. Joseph's Hosp., Atlanta, 1968-71, charge nurse neurosurgery, 1971-75, staff nurse cardiac surgery, 1976-79, mgr. cardiac surgery, 1979—; cons. Kimberly Clark Corp., Atlanta, 1992—, Goodroe and Assocs., Atlanta, 1994—. Producer (film) Introduction to the Cardiovascular Operating Room, Kimberly Clark, Atlanta, 1992; lectr. to hosps. and health oriented orgns. on cardiovascular operating procedures, 1984—. Coord. donations of supplies to third world countries St. Joseph's Hosp., Atlanta, 1988—, donations to Transplant Olympic Games, L.A., 1992; mem. cardiac surgery team to Hosp. Militar, San Salvador, El Salvador, 1995. Mem. AORN (tellers com. 1978—, chmn. 1981, bd. dirs. 1980, del. nat. congress 1979, 80), Cardiovascular Specialty Group AORN. Office: St Joseph's Hosp of Atlanta 5665 Peachtree Dunwoody Rd Atlanta GA 30342

VERNERDER, GLORIA JEAN, retired librarian; b. Ft. Wayne, Ind., June 2, 1930; d. John Otto and Vergie W. (Geiger) Krieg; m. Carl Penrod Vernerder, Dec. 25, 1952 (dec. Sept. 1984); children: Carla Jeanne Vernerder Kelly, Nina Marie Vernerder Anderson. Grad., Midway (Ky.) Coll.; student, Ind. U., Ft. Wayne, U. Ky. Br. libr. Pub. Libr. of Ft. Wayne and Allen County, 1950-52; children's libr. La Grange (Ill.) Pub. Libr., 1952-59; children's libr. Hinsdale (Ill.) Pub. Libr., 1961-68, head of youth svcs., 1969-95. Editor: Sunlight and Shadows, 1983, 87, 90, 92; contbr. articles to profl. jours. Adminstrv. bd. First United Meth. Ch., LaGrange, 1986-88, Stephen Ministry, 1986—. Mem. ALA, Ill. Library Assn., Library Adminstrs. Conf. of No. Ill. (treas. 1969). Republican. Methodist. Home: 732 7th Ave La Grange IL 60525-6706

VERNET, MICHELLE MARIE, jeweler, sculptor; b. Monongahala, Pa., Oct. 5, 1970; d. Fred George and Agnes Elaine (Nole) V. BA, Calif. U. Pa., 1992; MFA, Edinboro U. Pa., 1995. Mus. attendant Ft. LeBeouf Mus., Edinboro, 1994-95; jeweler Fine Jewelry Outlet, Castle Shannon, Pa., 1995—. Recipient scholarship Touchstone Ctr. for Arts, Pa., 1995; Presidential scholar Calif. U. Pa., 1991-92. Mem. Soc. N.Am. Goldsmiths.

VERNEY, JUDITH LA BAIE, health program administrator; b. Buffalo, Mar. 23, 1937; d. Arthur W. and Mary B. (Grant) La Baie; m. George R. Verney, Dec. 27, 1958; children: Michael, Timothy, Christopher. BSN, Russell Sage Coll., 1958; MS, Rutgers State U., Newark, 1977. Cert. clin. specialist, cmty. health nurse; cert. pub. mgr. State coord. provider svcs. Healthstart N.J. State Dept. Health, Trenton; dir. HealthStart, Trenton; coord. preventive and primary care svcs. N.J. State Dept. Health, 1993—; clin. instr. grad. nursing program Rutgers U.; clin. preceptor Grad. Nurse Program, Kean Coll. Mem. ANA, N.J. Pub. Health Assn., N.J. State Nurses Assn. (Cmty. Health Nurse of Yr. award 1986), Nat. Soc. Cert. Pub. Mgrs., N.J. Assn. Pub. Health Nurse Adminstrs., N.J. Nat. Svc. Corp. Commn.

VERNON, TAMMY MICHELLE, tobacco company specialist; b. Nashville, Dec. 19, 1963; d. Phillip Elliott Vernon and Joyce Ann (Monroe) Wilkerson. BA in Telecomms., Ky. Wesleyan Coll., 1986. Lic. real estate agt., Fla. Telemarketing mgr. Vistana Resort, inc., Lake Buena Vista, Fla., 1986-91; residential real estate agt. Jagoe Homes, Owensboro, Ky., 1991-92; mortgage cons. Lincoln Svc. Corp., Owensboro, 1992-93; sales rep. Mr. Tuxedo, Owensboro, 1993; sensory analyst Pinkerton Tobacco Co., Owensboro, 1993—. Bd. dirs. West End Day Care Inc., Owensboro, 1995—. Mem. ASTM, AAUW (local v.p. 1996—), NOW (local pres. 1991—), Ky. Women's Advocates (bd. dirs. 1995—). Baptist. Home: 201 Keystone Ct # 4 Owensboro KY 42301 Office: Pinkerton Tobacco Co 1121 Industrial Dr Owensboro KY 42301

VERONA, MONICA J., concert pianist, educator; b. Milw., July 2, 1956; d. Emanuel A. and Winifred M. V. BA in Italian and Art History, U. Wis., Milw., 1982; MusM, Manhattan Sch. Music, 1984; Performer's Cert. Degree, No. Ill. U., 1987; doctoral student, Manhattan Sch. Music, 1985-92. Teaching asst. piano and chamber music No. Ill. U., DeKalb, 1984-85; piano faculty The Fleming Sch., N.Y.C., 1987-90, The Calhoun Sch., N.Y.C., 1989—, Bklyn. Coll. Preparatory Ctr. for the Performing Arts, 1992—; sub. tchr. in solo and duo piano lit. Manhattan Sch. of Music Preparatory Divsn., 1987. Author: J.S. Bach's Chromatic Fantasy and Fuque: A Study of Virtuoso Keyboard Forms From the 16th to 18th Centuries, 1995; solo performance include: Met. Mus. Art, Salzburg Festival, Ravinia Festival, U.S. Dept. Interior/Am. Landmarks Festival, New Rochelle Pub. Libr. Series, Manhattan Sch. Music, Bklyn. Coll., No. Ill. U., PBS TV Milw., U. Wis., Goeth Inst. Milw., Park Ave. Christian Ch. Recital Series, N.Y.C., St. Paul's Recital Series, Nyack N.Y., Milw. Cath. Symphony Orchestra; chamber music performances include: Manhattan Sch. Music, No. Ill. U., Goeth Inst., and others; participant numerous music festivals. Recipient numerous sholarships, 1975-87, first prize Nat. Fedn. Music Clubs Competition, 1976, third prize Mu Phi Epsilon Scholarship Competition, 1977, first prize Ida Schroeder Found. Scholarship Competition, 1978. Roman Catholic. Home and Office: 45 Tiemann Pl 5M New York NY 10027

VERSCHOYLE, JULIA ANN, advocate, artist; b. San Antonio, July 17, 1954; d. Hubert Henry and Katherine Leota (Largent) V.; m. Herbert E. Jordan, Dec. 29, 1973; 3 children. Student, S.W. Tex. State U., 1972-73, 89. tchr. Carnegie Arts Ctr., Leavenworth, Kans., spring 1993, summer and fall, 1994; contractor as advocate, resource contact exceptional family mem. program (EFMP) Army Community Svcs. (ACS), 1993—; speaker Acad. Allergy and Immunology, Kansas City, Kans., 1994; various positions retail sales. Exhibited in San Antonio Area Art Shows, 1989, Kuntslerbund Cafe Art Guild Annual Show, Stuttgart, Germany, 1992, Gallery 93, Kansas City, Kans., 1993, Women Vision Art Show, Kansas City, Mo., 1993, Carnegie Arts Ctr., Leavenworth, 1990, 1995 Theme Show Muse Gallery, Kansas City, Corpus Christi Ctr. for the Arts, Demensions Art Show, 1995-96, Rockport Ctr. for the Arts, 1995-96, Rockport Tex. Vol. receptionist, newsletter editor/illustrator ACS, Ft. Bliss, Tex., 1981-83, parent rep. EFMP, Ft. Ord, Calif., 1983-84, Leavenworth 1992—; vol. Cystic Fibrosis Found., Tuscaloosa, Ala., 1984; coord. asthma support group, vol. EFMP office Brooke Army Med. Ctr., San Antonio, 1984-90; vol. parent speaker asthma seminars Am. Lung Assn., San Antoinio, 1984-90; den leader, treas., com. chmn. Boy Scouts Am., San Antonio, 1984-90, com. vol., Stuttgart, 1990-92; mayor U.S. mil. housing areas during Desert Storm, Stuttgart, 1990-92; facilitator med. care com. DA Family Symposium, Stuttgart, 1990-92; mem. DOD Families and Schs. Together, Stuttgart, 1990-92; bd. dirs. Army Cmty. Svcs., 6th Area Support Group, Robinson Barracks, Stuttgart, 1990-92; vol. Asthma & Allergy Found., Leavenworth, 1992-95; coord. Leavenworth Asthma Network, 1992—; mem. parents adv. coun. Leavenworth Special Edn. Coop., 1992-94; del. as advisor for handicapped Pioneers of Change handicapped, 1993, mem. pioneers of change state of Kansas; parent advocate Children with Spl. Needs, Leavenworth, 1993-94; com. mem. Levenworth County Spl. Edn. Coop. Transition Coun.; mem. Leavenworth Area Coordinating Coun. Early Childhood Devel.; vol. early childhood devel. program compliance reviews State of Kans. Recipient VII Corps Desert Shield/Storm Vol. award U.S. Army, 1992, Gahagen Svc. award.

VERSIC, LINDA JOAN, nurse educator, research company executive; b. Grove City, Pa., Aug. 27, 1944; d. Robert and Kathryn I. (Fagird) Davies; m. Ronald James Versic, June 11, 1966; children: Kathryn Clara, Paul Joseph. RN, Johns Hopkins Sch. of Nursing, 1965; BS in Health Edn., Ctrl. State U., 1980. Asst. head nurse Johns Hopkins Hosp., Balt., 1965-67; staff Nurse Registry Miami Valley Hosp., Dayton, Ohio, 1973-90; instr. Miami Jacobs Jr. Coll. Bus., Dayton, 1977-79; pres. Ronald T. Dodge Co., Dayton, 1979-86, chmn. bd., 1987—; chmn. bd. dirs. A-1 Travel, Inc. instr. Warren County (Ohio) Career Ctr., 1980-84, coord. diversified health occupations, 1984—. Coord. youth activities, mem. steering com. Queen of Apostles Cmty. Recipient Excellence in Tchg. award, 1992, award for Project Excellence, 1992. Active Miami Valley Mil. Affairs Assn., Glen Helen, Friends of Dayton Ballet, Dayton Art Inst., Cin. Art Mus. Mem. Ohio Vocat. Assn., Am. Vocat. Assn., Vocat. Indsl. Clubs Am. (chpt. advisor 1982—). Roman Catholic. Club: Johns Hopkins, Yugoslav of Greater Dayton. Home: 1601 Shafor Blvd Dayton OH 45419-3103 Office: Ronald T Dodge Co PO Box 630 Dayton OH 45459-0630

VER STEEG, DONNA LORRAINE FRANK, nurse, sociologist, educator; b. Minot, N.D., Sept. 23, 1929; d. John Jonas and Pearl H. (Denlinger) Frank; m. Richard W. Ver Steeg, Nov. 22, 1950; children: Juliana, Anne, Richard B. BSN, Stanford, 1951; MSN, U. Calif., San Francisco, 1967; MA in Sociology, UCLA, 1969, PhD in Sociology, 1973. Clin. instr. U. N.D. Sch. Nursing, 1962-63; USPHS nurse rsch. fellow UCLA, 1969-72; spl. cons., adv. com. on physicians' assts. and nurse practitioner programs Calif. State Bd. Med. Examiners, 1972-73; asst. prof. UCLA Sch. Nursing, 1973-79, assoc. prof., 1979-94, asst. dean, 1981-83, chmn. primary ambulatory care, 1976-87, assoc. dean, 1983-86, prof. emeritus (recalled 1994-96), chair primary care, 1994-96; co-prin. investigator PRIMEX Project, Family Nurse Practitioners, UCLA Extension, 1974-76; assoc. cons. Calif. Postsecondary Edn. Commn., 1975-76; spl. cons. Calif. Dept. Consumer Affairs, 1978; accredited visitor Western Assn. Schs. and Colls., 1985; mem. Calif. State Legis. Health Policy Forum, 1980-81; mem. nurse practitioner adv. com. Calif. Bd. RNs, 1995—. Contbr. chpts. to profl. books. Recipient Leadership award Calif. Area Health Edn. Ctr. System, 1989, Commendation award Calif. State Assembly, 1994; named Outstanding Faculty Mem. UCLA Sch. Nursing, 1982. Fellow Am. Acad. Nursing; mem. AAAS, ANA (interim chair Calif. 1995-96, pres. Calif. 1979-81), Am. Soc. Law and Medicine, Nat. League Nursing, Calif. League Nursing, N.Am. Nursing Diagnosis Assn., Am. Assn. History Nursing, Assn. Health Svcs. Rsch., Stanford Nurses Club, Sigma Theta Tau (Gamma Tau chpt. Leadership award 1994), Sigma Xi. Home: 708 Swarthmore Ave Pacific Palisades CA 90272-4353 Office: UCLA Sch Nursing 700 Tiverton Ave Box 956919 Los Angeles CA 90095

VERSTEGEN, DEBORAH A., education educator; b. Neenah, Wis., Oct. 27, 1946; d. Gerald C. and Margaret A. (Lamers) V. BA, Loretto Heights Coll., 1969; EdM, U. Rochester, 1972; MS, U. Wis., 1981, PhD, 1983. Adminstr. Iditarod Area Sch. Dist., McGrath, Alaska, 1976-79; rsch. asst. Wis. Ctr. for Edn. Rsch., 1981-84; dir. asst. prof. mid-mgmt. program U. Tex., Austin, 1984-86; asst. prof. U. Va., Charlottesville, 1986-91, assoc. prof., 1992—; rsch. assoc. Oxford U., Eng., 1991; adv. bd. U.S. Dept. Edn., 1989-92. Author over 100 books, reports, chpts., articles and revs., latest being The Impacts of Litigation and Legislation on Public School Finance, 1990, Spheres of Justice in Education, 1991; editor Jour. Edn. Fin., 1990-93, editor edn. policy, 1993—. Treas. LWV, 1986, mem. state board, Va., 1995—. Mem. AAUP, Am. Ednl. Fin. Assn. (bd. dirs., disting. svc. award 1989), Am. Ednl. Rsch. Assn., Univ. Coun. on Ednl. Adminstrn. (disting svc. award 1991, adv. bd. fin. ctr.), Phi Delta Kappa, Phi Kappa Phi. Home: 2030 Lambs Rd Charlottesville VA 22901-8978 Office: U Va Curry Sch Edn Ruffner Hall 405 Emmet St S Charlottesville VA 22903-2424

VERTS, LITA JEANNE, university administrator; b. Jonesboro, Ark., Apr. 13, 1935; d. William Gus and Lolita Josephine (Peeler) Nash; m. B. J. Verts, Aug. 29, 1954 (div. 1975); 1 child, William Trigg. BA, Oreg. State U., 1973; MA in Lingustics, U. Oreg., 1974; postgrad., U. Hawaii, 1977. Librarian Forest Research Lab., Corvallis, Oreg., 1966-69; instr. English Lang. Inst., Corvallis, 1974-80; dir. spl. svcs. Oreg. State U., Corvallis, 1980—, faculty senator, 1988-96. Editor ann. book: Trio Achievers, 1986, 87, 88; contbr. articles to profl. jours. Precinct com. Rep. Party, Corvallis, 1977-80; adminstrv. bd. 1st United Meth. Ch., Corvallis, 1987-89, mem. fin. com., 1987-93, tchr. Bible, 1978—; bd. dirs. Westminster Ho., United Campus Ministries, 1994-95; adv. coun. Disabilities Svc., Linn, Benton, Lincoln Counties, 1990—, vice-chmn., 1992-93, chmn. 1993-94. Mem. N.W. Assn. Spl. Programs (pres. 1985-86), Nat. Coun. Ednl. Opportunities Assn. (bd. dirs. 1984-87), Nat. Gardening Assn., Alpha Phi (mem. corp. bd. Beta Upsilon chpt. 1990-96). Republican. Methodist. Home: 530 SE Mayberry Ave Corvallis OR 97333-1866 Office: Spl Svcs Project Waldo 337 OSU Corvallis OR 97331

VERVERS, BEVERLY JOAN, cooperative education administrator; b. Paterson, N.J., June 13, 1953; d. Charles John and Helen V. BA, Ramapo Coll., Mahwah, N.J., 1975; MA, Montclair State Coll., Upper Montclair, N.J., 1990. Nat. cert. counselor, registered profl. counselor, N.J. Program asst. Planned Parenthood, Boonton/Morristown, N.J., 1974-78; employment interviewer N.J. State Employment Svc., Passaic, 1977-83; employment placement specialist Bergen Cmty. Coll., Paramus, N.J., 1983-85; asst. dir. coop. edn. Montclair State U., Upper Montclair, 1985—. Mem. Am. Counseling Assn., N.J. Coll. Pers. Assn., N.J. Counseling Assn., Coop. Edn. Assn. Office: Office of Coop Edn Montclair State U Montclair NJ 07043

VERVILLE, ELIZABETH GIAVANI, federal official; b. N.Y.C., July 13, 1940; d. Joseph and Gertrude (Levy) Giavani. BA, Duke U., 1961; LLB, Columbia U., 1964. Bar: Mass. 1965, U.S. Supreme Ct. 1970, D.C. 1980. Assoc. Snow Motley & Holt, successor Gaston Snow & Ely Bartlett, Boston, 1965-67; asst. atty. gen. Commonwealth of Mass., Boston, 1967-69; atty. advisor for African affairs U.S. Dept. State, Washington, 1979-72, asst. legal adviser for East Asian and Pacific affairs, 1972-80, dep. legal adviser, 1980-89; dep. asst. sec. state Bur. Politico-Mil. Affairs Bur. Politico-Mil. Affairs, Washington, 1989-92; sr. coord. Bur. Politico-Mil. Affairs, 1992-95; dir. for global and multilateral affairs Nat. Security Coun., Washington, 1995—. Recipient presdl. rank of meritorious exec., 1985, 90, presdl. rank disting. exec., 1988. Mem. Am. Soc. Internat. Law, Coun. on Fgn. Rels. Home: 3012 Dumbarton Ave NW Washington DC 20007-3305 Office: Nat Security Coun The White House Washington DC 20504

VERWERS, JODY ANN, secondary school mathematics educator; b. Anchorage, Alaska, Apr. 12, 1953; d. Victor Joseph Jr. and Shirley Josephine (Guarino) Frioux; m. Robert Andrew Verwers II, Dec. 29, 1979; children: Robert Andrew III, Michelle Elizabeth. BS in Math. Edn., U. Southwestern La., 1975. Cert. secondary math. tchr., La., Tex. Math. tchr. Corpus Christi (Tex.) Ind. Sch. Dist., 1975-82, head math. dept. Hamlin Jr. High Sch., 1980-82; math. tchr. Lafayette (La.) Parish Sch. Bd., 1982-85, Pasadena (Tex.) Ind. Sch. Dist., 1985-90, Clear Creek Ind. Sch. Dist., League City, Tex., 1990—. Mem. writing com. Advanced Mathematics 7th and 8th Grade Handbooks, 1981, Geometry and Honors Geometry Curriculum Guide, 1991. Mem. Nat. Coun. Tchrs. Math., Tex. Coun. Tchrs. Math., San Jacinto Coun. Tchrs. Math. Roman Catholic. Home: 706 Lochnell Dr Houston TX 77062-2609 Office: Clear Lake HS 2929 Bay Area Blvd Houston TX 77058

VERZAR, CHRISTINE BEATRICE, art historian, educator; b. Basel, Switzerland, Sept. 5, 1940; came to U.S., 1966; d. Fritz and Edith Jean (McDougall) V.; m. George Bornstein, Dec. 21, 1967 (div.); 1 child, Benjamin Jay; m. Daniel N. Fader, Oct. 15, 1988. Cert., U. Geneva, 1960; PhD, Basel U., Switzerland, 1966. Asst. prof. history of art Boston U., 1966-69; lectr. Princeton (N.J.) U., 1969-70; asst. prof. U. Mich., Ann Arbor, 1973-84, assoc. dir. Medieval and Renaissance Collegium, 1975-76; assoc. prof., chmn. Ohio State U., Columbus, 1984-89, prof., chair, 1989-95; prof., 1995—; chairperson The Ohio State U. Dept. History of Art, Columbus, 1984-95. Author: Portals and Politics in the Early Italian City-State, 1988, The Meeting of Two Worlds, 1981, Die Romanischen Skulpturen der Abtei Sagra di San Michele, 1968. Mem. Coll. Art Assn., Internat. Ctr. for Medieval Art (bd. dirs. 1985-88, 94—), Medieval Acad. Am. Office: The Ohio State U Dept Art History Columbus OH 43210

VESSUP, JOLENE ADRIEL, pastoral counselor; b. Lynwood, Calif., Oct. 26, 1951; d. Johannes Baltezar and Ellene Ernestine (Cravens) Vessup. BA, U. So. Calif., 1973. Choir dir., singer, sales girl Bethel Apostolic Faith Ch., San Bernardino, Calif., 1961-69; Sunday sch. tchr., cook Bethel Apostolic Faith Ch., San Bernardino, 1962-69, reading tutor, 1977-78; speech tutor, rsch. asst., pub. rels. spkr. U. So. Calif. and Pacific H.S., L.A. & San Bernardino, 1969-73; peer counselor Postgrad. Rehab. Ctr., N.Y.C., 1974-95; early childhood devel. vol. Calif. State U., L.A., 1975-79; spl. edn. tchr.'s asst. San Bernardino Unified Sch. Dist., 1979-80; unlicensed missionary Greater Refuge Temple Ch., N.Y.C., 1996—. Mem. AAUW, Nat. Geog. Soc., Wildlife Conservation Soc., Smithsonian Instn. Press, Stuttering Found. Am. Home: JAF PO Box 7679 New York NY 10116-4632

VEST, GAYLE SOUTHWORTH, obstetrician and gynecologist; b. Duluth, Minn., Apr. 7, 1948; d. Russell Eugene and Brandon (Young) Southworth; m. Steven Lee Vest, Nov. 27, 1971; 1 child, Matthew Steven. BS, U. Mich., 1970. Diplomate Am. Bd. Ob-Gyn. Intern in ob-gyn. Milw. County Gen. Hosp., 1974-75, So. Ill. U. Sch. Medicine, 1975-78; pvt. practice Chapel Hill (N.C.) Ob-Gyn., 1978-80; asst. attending physician dept. ob-gyn. U. N.C. Sch. Medicine, Chapel Hill, 1978-80; clin. assoc. dept. ob-gyn. Duke U. Med. Ctr., Durham, N.C., 1978-80; pvt. practice Big Stone Gap (Va.) Clinic, 1980-88, Norwise Ob-Gyn. Assocs., Norton, Va., 1988—. Fellow Am. Coll. Obstetricians and Gynegologists; mem. Am. Soc. Reproductive Medicine, Va. Ob-Gyn. Soc., Va. Perinatal Assn., Med. Soc. Va., Wise County Med. Soc. Office: Norwise Ob-Gyn Assocs Med Arts Bldg 3 102 15th St NW Norton VA 24273-1618

VEST, ROSEMARIE LYNN TORRES, secondary school educator; b. Pueblo, Colo., Jan. 16, 1958; d. Onesimo Bernabe and Maria Bersabe (Lucero) Torres; m. Donald R. Vest, May 1, 1982. BA, U. So. Colo., 1979, BS, 1991; cert. travel agt., Travel Trade Sch., Pueblo, 1986. Cert. secondary tchr., Colo.; cert. travel agt., Colo. Tutor U. So. Colo., Pueblo, 1977-79; sales rep. Intermountain Prodns., Colorado Springs, Colo., 1979-80; tutor, Pueblo, 1980-82, 84-85; travel agt. So. Colo. Travel, Pueblo, 1986-88; children's program facilitator El Mesias Family Support Program, Pueblo, 1987-88; substitute tchr. social studies Sch. Dist. 60, Pueblo, 1990—, Freed Mid. Sch., Pueblo, 1991, 92; Chpt. 1 Summer Reading Program, 1992, 93, 94, 95, chpt. 1 reading program, 1991, 92, 93, 94, 95, 96; instr. Travel and Tourism Dept. Pueblo C.C., 1994-95. Tchr. Sunday sch., chairperson adminstrv. bd. cert. lay spkr., lay rep. to ann. conf. Ch. Evangelism, co-chmn. Trinity United Meth. Ch., Pueblo, 1989-94, parish coun. rep. to Trinity/Bethel Coop. Parish; sponsor United Meth. Youth United Meth. Ch.; tchr. Sunday Sch., co-coord. vacation Bible sch., pastoral asst., edn. chairperson, 1994—, cert. lay spkr., ministerial program asst., lay leader Bethel United Meth. Ch., 1994—; craft facilitator Integrated Health Svcs., Pueblo, 1991—; spiritual devotions/worship leader Pueblo Manor Nursing Home, 1993—; vol. resident svcs. Pueblo County Bd. for Developmental Disabilities, 1989—; mem. conf. leadership team, parliamentarian Rocky Mountain Conf. United Meth. Ch., 1995; ministerial candidate United Meth. Ch.; conf. rep. Rocky Mountain Conf. Coun. on Fin. and Adminstrn., 1996. Recipient Excellence in Tchg. award Freed Mid. Sch., 1992, Vol. of Yr. award IHS of Pueblo, 1995. Mem. Assn. Am. Geographers, Nat. Oceanog. Soc., Nat. Geog. Soc. Democrat. Home: 1106 Berkley Ave Apt 1 Pueblo CO 81004-2802

VESTAL, THELMA SHAW, history educator; b. Spring Hill, Tenn., Apr. 19, 1946; d. Ester Lena McKissack; m. Danny Vestal, June 28, 1976; children: Danny La'Brian, Felecia De'Lece. BS, Tenn. State U., 1969, MS, 1972. Sec. Tenn. State U., Nashville, 1969-72, counselor, 1972-76; substitute tchr. Metro Pub. Schs., Nashville, 1977-85; U.S. history tchr. Dupont-Tyler Mid. Sch., Hermitage, Tenn., 1985—; Mem. Operation C.A.N., Nashville, 1985—. Active ARC, Nashville, 1988—. Named Educator of Yr., Nashville Mid. Sch. Assn., 1992-93; recipient Outstanding Christian award Schrader Lane Ch. of Christ, Nashville, 1989-90. Mem. Nat. Geographic Soc., Metro Nashville Coun. for Social Studies, Tenn. Edn. Assn., NEA, Nat. Coun. for Social Studies. Democrat. Ch. of Christ.

VETTER, LEAH BLOCK, educational administrator; b. N.Y.C., Dec. 19, 1934; d. Sam and Madlyn (Singer) Block; m. Henri Georges Vetter, Aug. 5, 1956; children: Rachel Vetter Huang, Yves-Alain. BSc in Edn. and History, SUNY, Albany, 1978; MEd in Sch. Adminstrn., Boston State Coll., 1981; M.Theol. Studies, Weston Sch. Theology, 1990. Cert. secondary, h.s., jr. h.s. supt., prin., elem. prin., gen. supr., elem. tchr., secondary history tchr. Tchr. history Edmonton (Alta.) Acad., 1958-60, Hyde Park H.S., Chgo., 1960-62; founder Ancona Montessori Sch., Chgo., 1962-64; supr. student tchrs. Simmons Coll., Boston, 1969-72; prin. New Eng. Hebrew Acad., Brookline, Mass., 1972-83; coord. off-campus programs Lesley Coll., Cambridge, Mass., 1983-86, lectr. edn., 1985-86; state coord. tchr. preparation/program approval Mass. Dept. Edn., 1986-92; dir. Mass. Acad. Math. and Sci.,

Worcester (Mass.) Poly. Inst., 1992—; prin. investigator Algebridge Summer, 1993, 94; mem. project adv. bd., tech. groups A computer curriculum for math tchr. enhancement BBN Sys. and Technologies, Cambridge, Mass., 1988-91, mem. project adv. bd. empowering tchrs.: math inquiry through tech., 1992-93; adv. bd. MESTEP, U. Mass., Amherst, 1993; mem. oversight com. comprehensive conceptual curriculum for physics U. Dallas, 1994; lectr. and panel mem. in field; guest lectr. Medieval Religious Lit. Northeastern U., 1992; lectr. edn. U. Mass., Boston, 1979-80;. Fulbright Summer Seminar grantee, Israel. Home: 30 Woodcliffe Rd Lexington MA 02173-7834 Office: Mass Acad Math and Sci 100 Institute Rd Worcester MA 01609-2247

VEYVODA, ALICE LORRAINE, chemistry educator; b. N.Y.C., Sept. 3, 1942; d. Joseph Francis and Alice Genevieve (Martin) V.; m. Gary Louis Annar, June 8, 1963 (div. Apr. 1974); children: Lorraine Elizabeth Annar, Susan Alice Annar. BS in Chemistry, Coll. of Mt. St. Vincent, 1963; MS in Sci. Edn., Hofstra U., 1973; MA in Liberal Studies, SUNY, Stony Brook, 1979. Tchr., secondary sci. Huntington (N.Y.) Cen. Sch. Dist., 1973-75, Bellmore-Merrick Cen. Sch. Dist., Bellmore, N.Y., 1975-76, Half Hallow Hills Cen. Sch. Dist., Dix Hills, N.Y., 1976—. Fellow Woodrow Wilson Found., 1993, U.S. Dept. Energy Tchr. Resource, 1994, Los Alamos (N.Mex.) Nat. Lab. Fellow Sci. Tchrs. Assn. of N.Y. (svc. award 1981, conf. award 1983, newsletter editor 1993—, v.p. 1988-89, pres. 1989-90); mem. Suffolk County Sci. Tchrs. Assn. (pres. 1978-79, 92-94). Home: 17 Tall Tree Ln Smithtown NY 11787 Office: Half Hollow Hills HS W 375 Wolf Hill Rd Dix Hills NY 11746

VEZINA, VICKY LYNNE, middle school educator; b. Cheyenne, Wyo., June 3, 1950; d. Charles James and Wanda Louise (Byers) Seidl; m. Gary Edward Vezina, June 30, 1968; children: Jeffrey James, Michelle Annette. AS in Elem. Edn., Parkland Jr. Coll., Champaign, Ill., 1989; BS in Edn., Ea. Ill. U., 1991. Cert. tchr. K-9 in social sci. arts, gen. sci., social sci. Food demonstrator Beatrice Foods, Cheyenne, 1967; chambermaid Home Ranch Motel, Cheyenne, 1968; dog bather/groomer Shellhart's Boarding Kennels & Grooming, Cheyenne, 1968-69; parent vol. Bement (Ill.) Grad Sch., 1985-87; substitute tchr. Bement, Monticello and Cerro Gordo (Ill.) Pub. Schs., 1991—; home bound tutor Bement H.S., 1992, 93; truancy tutor Bement Grade Sch., 1993, 94; presch. tester Bement Sch. Dist., 1986-87. Chmn. membership com. Bement PTA, 1986-87; tchr. Sunday sch./Bible sch. Christian Ch., Bement, 1973-79; vol. Bement Sch. Dist. #5, 1985-87. Named Vol. of the Yr., Bement Sch. Dist. #5, 1987. Mem. VFW Aux., Ill. Coun. Tchrs. Math., Kappa Delta Pi, Alpha Sigma Lambda, Alpha Omega. Democrat. Presbyterian. Home: 432 W Shumway St Bement IL 61813-1342

VICENZI, ANGELA ELIZABETH, nursing educator; b. N.Y.C., Aug. 19, 1938; d. Peter Christiaan and Angeline Elizabeth (Rudtke) Richard; m. Richard Emil Vicenzi, Nov. 11, 1961; children: Richard Martin, Paul Andrew, Stephen Mark, Douglas Emil. Diploma, St. Vincent's Hosp. Sch. Nursing, N.Y.C., 1959; BSN, Western Conn. State U., 1977; MEd in Cmty. Health Nursing, Columbia U., 1980, EdD in Health Edn., 1984. Pub. health nurse City of N.Y., 1960-61; pediat. staff nurse Norwalk (Conn.) Hosp., 1970-73; profl. nurse traineeship Columbia U. Tchrs. Coll., N.Y.C., 1978-80; clin. instr. Norwalk C.C., 1977-78; asst. prof. Sacred Heart U., Fairfield, Conn., 1980-83; from. asst. prof. to assoc. prof. So. Conn. State U., New Haven, 1985-95, prof., 1995—; cons. Corp. Health Cons., Norwalk, 1980-90; pres. faculty senate So. Conn. State U., 1991-94. Editor, pub. Complexity & Chaos in Nursing Jour., 1994-96; contbr. articles to profl. jours. Mem. St. Jerome Parish Coun., Norwalk, 1995. Grantee Conn. State U., 1994-95, Profl. Nurse Traineeship grantee Health and Human Svcs., 1991-94. Mem. AAUP (treas. 1995—), Assn. Comty. Health Nursing Educators (program chair 1995), Mu Beta, Sigma Theta Tau (pres. 1992-94). Office: So Conn State U Dept Nursing 501 Crescent St New Haven CT 06515

VICK, FRANCES BRANNEN, publishing executive; b. Trinity, Tex., Aug. 14, 1935; d. Carl Andrew and Bess (courtney) B.; m. Ross William Vick Jr., June 23, 1956; children: Karen Lynn, Ross William III, Patrick Brannen. BA, U. Tex., 1958; MA, Stephen F. Austin State U., 1968. Teaching fellow Stephen F. Austin State U., Nacogdoches, Tex., 1966-68, lectr., 1968-69; lectr. Angelina Coll., Lufkin, Tex., 1969-71, Baylor U., Waco, Tex., 1974-75, 77-78; vice prin. Vanguard Sch., Waco, 1975-77; pres. E-Heart Press, Inc., Dallas, 1979—; co-dir. UNT Press U. North Tex., Denton, 1987-89, dir., 1989—. Publisher 120 books; editor 40 books. Leadership coun. Ann Richards Com., Austin, 1990-94; amb. Inst. Texan Cultures, mem. Tex. Commn. on Arts, Lit., 1991. Mem. AAUW, Book Pubs. Tex. (v.p. 1990-96, pres. 1996), Tex. Folklore Soc. (councillor 1991-93), Tex. Humanities Resource Ctr. (bd. dirs. 1990-91), Conf. Coll. Tchrs. English, Western Lit. Assn., Western Writers Am., Philos. Soc. Tex., Pen Ctr. U.S.A. West, Tex. State Hist. Assn. (life), East Tex. Hist. Assn. (life), Western Writers Am., Western Lit. Assn., Soc. Scholarly Pub., Women in Scholarly Pub., Rocky Mountain Book Pubs. Assn., Leadership Tex., Leadership Am., Tex. Humanities Alliance, UNT League Profl. Women. Democrat. Episcopalian. Home: 3700 Mockingbird Ln Dallas TX 75205-2125 Office: U North Tex PO Box 13856 Denton TX 76203-6856

VICK, SUSAN, playwright, educator; b. Raleigh, N.C., Nov. 4, 1945; d. Thomas B. Jr. and Merle (Hayes) V. MFA, Southern Meth. U., 1969; PhD, U. Ill., 1979. Prof. drama/theatre Worcester (Mass.) Poly. Inst., 1981—, dir. theatre programs; dir. theatre tech., playwright Excuse Me For Living Prodns., Cambridge, Mass., 1989—, Festival Fringe, Edinburgh, 1989—; playwright Ensemble Studio Theatre, Glasgow, N.Y.C., 1981-83; founder WPI Ann. New Voices Festival of Original Plays, 1982. Editor: (2 vols.) Playwrights Press, Amherst, 1988—; playwright plays including When I Was Your Age, 1982, Ord-Way Ames-Gay, 1982, Investments, 1985, Half Naked, 1989, Quandary, 1983, Meat Selection, 1984, Give My Love to Everyone But, 1989; appeared in plays including Rip Van Winkle, 1979, Why I Live at The P.O., 1982, The Play Group, 1984-85, Present Stage, 1985, Sister Mary Ignatius Explain It All, 1986, Wipeout, 1988, Bogus Joan, 1992, 93; dir. play Give My Love to Everyone But, 1990 (Edinburgh Festival); theatre editor: Sojourner The Women's Forum, 1995—; dramaturg, script cons. Clyde Unity Theatre, Glasgow, Scotland, 1992—. Dir., Women's Community Theatre, Amherst, 1981-84, Upstart, Wis., 1994. Faculty fellow U. Ill., 1976-77. Mem. Drama League, Dramatists Guild (assoc.), Soc. Stage Dirs. and Choreographers (assoc.), Alpha Psi Omega (Svc. to Students award 1996). Office: Worcester Poly Tech Inst 100 Institute Rd Worcester MA 01609-2247

VICKERS, MONTEZ MOSER, public relations executive; b. North Miami, Fla., Oct. 12, 1953; d. William Thomas and Merrill Catherine (Small) Moser; m. Lewie Marks Vickers, Jan. 17, 1987. BA in Communications magna cum laude, U. Ala., 1981; MS in Founds. of Edn., Troy State U., Dothan, Ala., 1996. Admissions clk. Bapt. Med. Ctr.-Montclair, Birmingham, Ala., 1971-72; bus. mgmt. technician U.S. Small Bus. Adminstrn., Birmingham, 1972-79; intern Totalcom, Inc., Tuscaloosa, Ala., 1980-81; writer Birmingham (Ala.) Mag., 1981-82; dir. pub. relations, copywriter Gillis, Townsend and Riley Adv., Birmingham, 1982-83; free-lance copywriter Birmingham, 1983-85; adminstrv. sec. U. Ala., Birmingham, 1983-85; dir. pub. relations Enterprise (Ala.) State Jr. Coll., 1985—; co-owner Rocky Ridge Ranch Enterprises. Contbr. numerous articles to various mags., 1981-85. Bd. dirs. Nat. Spring Chicken Festival, Enterprise, 1986; libr. Elbethel Bapt. Ch. Mem. MLA, Nat. Coun. Tchrs. English, Hunter-Jumper Assn. Ala. (3 state championships 1983), Am. Bus. Women's Assn. (enterprise chpt. sec. 1987, Woman of Yr. award 1988), Ala. Edn. Assn., Ala. Coll. Sys. Assn., Ala. Coll. Pub. Rels. Assn. Baptist. Office: 600 Pla Dr Enterprise AL 36330

VICTOR, LORRAINE CAROL, critical care nurse; b. Duluth, Minn., June 14, 1953; d. George E. and Phyllis M. (Pierce) Drimel; m. Robert G. Victor. BA in Nursing, Coll. St. Scholastica, 1975; MS in Nursing, U. Minn., 1984. Cert. regional trainer for neonatal resuscitation program. Staff nurse St. Mary's Hosp., Rochester, Minn., 1975-79, 80-81, U. Wis. Hosp., Madison, 1979-80, U. Minn. Hosps., Mpls., 1981-84, 85-86; clin. instr. neonatal ICU, Children's Hosp. Inc., St. Paul, 1984-86; clin. nurse specialist neonatal ICU, Orlando (Fla.) Regional Med. Ctr., 1986-88, Children's Hosp. St. Paul, 1988—. Mem. AACN (Critical Care Nurse of Yr. award Greater Twin Cities chpt. 1992, cert. neonatal intensive care nursing), Nat. Cert. Corp. (cert. in neonatal intensive care nursing), Nat. Assn. Neonatal Nurses, Sigma Theta Tau. Office: Children's Health Care St Paul Birth Ctr 345 N Smith Ave Saint Paul MN 55102-2392

VIDA, VIRGINIA ELEANOR, ethics commission administrator, author; b. Chgo., May 26, 1939; d. Paul and Eleanor Mabel (Osman) V. BA in English, U. Ill., 1961; MA in English Linguistics, NYU, 1966. Tchr. English, 1961-65, editor children's textbooks, 1966-75; media dir. Nat. Gay Task Force, N.Y.C., 1975-80; dep. dir., lobbyist N.Y.C. Commn. on Status of Women, N.Y.C., 1980-91; assoc. dir. Santa Clara County Bar Assn., San Jose, Calif., 1992-93; dir. Office of Sexual Harassment Issues N.Y. State Divsn. Human Rights, Bklyn., 1993-95; investigator, auditor San Francisco Ethics Commn., 1995—. Author, editor: (anthology/resource book) Our Right to Love: A Lesbian Resource Book, 1978 (Gay Book award Nat. Libr. Assn. 1978), rev. edit. The New Our Right to Love: A Lesbian Resource Book, 1996; editor: Legislative Achievements for Women in New York State: A 20-Year Retrospective, 1985. Bd. dirs. N.Y. Civil Liberties Union, N.Y.C., 1977-79, Parents and Friends of Gays, N.Y.C., 1976-77; mem. Chancellor's Task Force on Sex Equality, N.Y.C., 1980-91, 93-95; mem. Mayor's Police Adv. Coun. on Lesbian and Gay Issues, N.Y.C., 1985-90. Recipient Women's History Month award Office of the Mayor, N.Y.C., 1991; named to Acad. of Women Achievers, YWCA of City of N.Y. Mem. NOW, Nat. Women's Polit. Caucus, Oakland Soc. Prevention Cruelty of Animals. Democrat. Methodist. Home: # 3 1124 Hollywood Ave Oakland CA 94602 Office: S F Ethics Commn Rm 701 1390 Market St San Francisco CA 94102

VIDAL, MAUREEN ERIS, English educator; b. Bklyn., Mar. 18, 1956; d. Louis and Lillian (Kaplan) Hendelman; m. Juan Vidal, June 25, 1974 (div. Sept. 1981); m. Guillermo Eduardo Uriarte, Dec. 22, 1986. BA, Bklyn. Coll., 1976, MS, 1981. English tchr. N.Y.C. Bd. Edn., 1976—. Mem. N.Y.C. Assn. Tchrs. English (exec. bd., v.p. 1990—, writing contest chair 1991—), Heights Players Theater Co. (arranger theatrical performance for residents of homeless shelters 1986—, exec. bd., sec. 1993—), Delta Psi Omega. Home: 3380 Nostrand Ave Brooklyn NY 11229 Office: I S 318 101 Walton St Brooklyn NY 11206

VIDERMAN, LINDA JEAN, paralegal, corporate executive; b. Follansbee, W.Va., Dec. 4, 1957; d. Charles Richard and Louise Edith (LeBoeuf) Roberts; m. David Gerald Viderman Jr., Mar. 15, 1974; children: Jessica Renae, April Mae, Melinda Dawn. AS, W.Va. No. Community Coll., 1983; Cert. income tax prep., H&R Block, Steubenville, Ohio, 1986. Cert. surg. tech.; cert. fin. counselor; lic. ins. agt. Food prep. pers. Bonanza Steak House, Weirton, W.Va., 1981-83; ward clk., food svcs. Weirton Med. Ctr., 1982-84; sec., treas. Mountaineer Security Systems, Inc., Wheeling, W.Va., 1983-86; owner, operator The Button Booth, Colliers, W.Va., 1985—; paralegal, adminstr. Atty. Dominic J. Potts, Steubenville, Ohio, 1987-92; gen. ptnr., executrix Panhandle Homes, Wellsburg, W.Va., 1988—; ins. agt. Milico, Mass. Indemnity, 1991-92, L&L Ins. Svcs., 1992-94; paralegal Atty. Fred Risovich II, Weirton, 1991-93; sec. The Hon. Fred Risovich II, Wheeling, 1993; paralegal atty. Christopher J. Paull, Wellsburg, W.Va., 1993—; owner Wellsburg Office Supply, 1993-94; notary pub., 1991—. Contbr. articles numerous jours.; author numerous poems. Chmn. safety com. Colliers (W.Va.) Primary PTA, 1985-87; mem., sec. LaLeche League, Steubenville, Ohio, 1978-80; vol. counselor W.Va. U. Fin. Counseling Svc., 1990—; IRS vol. Vol. Income Tax Assistance Program, 1991—. Mem. W.Va. Writers Assn., Legal Assts. of W.Va., Inc., Am. Affiliate of Nat. Assn. Legal Assts., W.Va. Trial Lawyers Assn., Wellsburg Art Assn., Phi Theta Kappa. Jehovah's Witness. Home: 137R St Johns Rd Colliers WV 26035 Office: Panhandle Homes 3027 Pleasant Ave Wellsburg WV 26070-1138

VIDRO, JILL RENEE SNYDER, financial specialist, accountant; b. Grand Rapids, Mich., Feb. 2, 1961; d. Clare Dean and Darlene Joyce (Ludlow) Snyder; m. Lawrence Edward Didur, June 7, 1986 (div. 1994), m. Charles Frank Vidro, Mar. ll, 1996. AA, Grand Rapids (Mich.) Jr. Coll., 1981; BS in Acctg., Ferris State U., 1983. Fin. acct. Smiths Ind. Aerospace & Defense Sys. Inc., Grand Rapids, Mich., 1995—; acctg. analyst Gen. Dynamics Services Co., Sterling Heights, Mich., 1985-86, fin. analyst, 1986-87, sr. fin. analyst, 1987-88; acctg. specialist Gen. Dynamics Services Co., St. Louis, 1988-89, sr. acctg. specialist, 1989-90, sr. fin. specialist, 1990-92; fin. cons. Union, Mo., 1992-94, Comstock Park, Mich., 1994-95. Mem. Inst. Mgmt. Accts.

VIEIRA, ELAINE PLUMMER, health services coordinator; b. Franklin, NH, Mar. 30, 1951; d. Walter M. and Lorraine I. (Verrier) Plummer; m. John P. Vieira; 3 children. RN diploma, Peter Bent Brigham Hosp., 1973; student, U. N.H. RN, cardiac care, ALS; cert. nursing mgmt. 1989. Charge nurse psychiat., elderly Columbus Nursing Home, Boston, 1975-76; charge nurse CCU CoHage Hosp., Woodsville, N.H., 1977-78; staff nurse Pemi Baker Home Health Agy., Plymouth, N.H., 1979-86; clin. svcs. coord., hospice coord. Pemi Baker Home Health, Plymouth, N.H., 1987—; sch. nurse Warren Village Grade Sch., Warren, N.H., 1984-86; supr. complex Grafton County Nursing Home and Jail, North Haverhill, N.H., 1986-87; vol. ostomy support Pemi Baker Home Health, Plymouth, N.H., 1994—; bd. dirs. Plymouth (N.H.) Regional Clinic; vol. Pemi Baker Hospice, Plymouth, N.H., 1990—; spkr. in field. Singer Pemi Choral Soc., 1990—; appeared in N.H. Music Festival, 1991—. Mem. ad hoc com. Youth at Risk, Plymouth, N.H., 1989-93; mem. com. Cmty. Health Alliance, Plymouth, N.H., 1991, 92; mem. subcom. Homophobia/Youth, Plymouth, N.H., 1989-94; judge Odyssey of the Mind N.H. program, 1993—; mem. com. Fin. Empowerment for Women AARP, Plymouth, N.H., 1995-96. Mem. Hospice Nurses Assn., N.H. Multiple Sclerosis Soc. (facilitator 1988—, PAC 1989), N.H. Homecare Assn. (clin. dir. com. 1988—, membership affairs com. 1989). Democrat. Office: Pemi Baker Home Health Agy 258 Highland St Ste 14 Plymouth NH 03264

VIEIRA, NANCY ELIZABETH, biologist, researcher; b. New Bedford, Mass., Nov. 1, 1951; d. Francisco and Silvina Costa (Frias) V. BS, U. Md., 1973, MS, 1975. Physiologist Nat. Inst. Child Health & Human Devel., Bethesda, Md., 1976-77, biologist, 1977—. Co-author: Kinetic Models of Trace Elements and Mineral Metabolism, 1995; contbr. articles to profl. jours. Elem. sch. team leader, participating vol. tchr. NIH, Bethesda, 1994—; mem. equal employment opportunity adv. com. Nat. Inst. Child Health & Human Devel., 1993—; mem. Rebounders, College Park, Md., 1987—. Mem. AAAS, Am. Inst. Nutrition, Am. Chem. Soc., Am. Soc. Mass Spectrometry. Office: NIH NICHD LTPB 10 Center Dr Bldg 10 Rm 6 C208 Bethesda MD 20892

VIEIRA-SUAREZ, LAURA M., educational administrator, consultant; b. Mt. Kisco, N.Y., Oct. 9, 1957; d. Albert Perry and Laura Marie Vieira; m. Ricardo Suarez, Oct. 17; children: Mark, Joseph, Alex. Ernesto, Robert, Raul. AAS in Early Childhood Edn., SUNY, Farmingdale, 1978; BS in Elem. Edn., Oneonta Coll., 1980; MS in Spl. Edn., Fordham U., 1986, PhD in Sch. Adminstrn., 1991. Cert. tchr. elem. edn., spl. edn., early childhood edn., sch. administration and supervision, school district administrator, N.Y. Counselor spl. edn. Green Chimneys Childrens Svcs., Brewster, N.Y., 1980-83; spl. edn. tchr. Green Chimneys Childrens Svcs., Brewster, 1983-85, master tchr. spl. edn., 1985-90, edn. clin. coord., 1990-92, asst. prin., 1992-94, dir. student svcs., 1994-95, dir. edn., 1995—; dir. utilizing talents with plants and animals Putnam Assn. for Retarded Citizens, (part time), 1985-90; cons. N.Y. Foster Care, Adoption Agys., 1986—, parent advocate, 1986—; ednl. conf. presenter, various, 1990—; mem. com. on spl. edn., chairperson Green Chimneys Childrens Svcs., Brewster, 1992—; adj. faculty So. Conn. State U., New Haven, 1993—; sight based mgmt. cons. Mem. Mt. Kisco (N.Y.) Fire Dept. Fife and Drum Corps, 1967—, com. mem., 1985—; vol. Spl. Olympics, 1985—, Green Chimneys Sch., Brewster, 1989—; com. mem. Boy Scouts Am., Fishkill, N.Y., 1988—. Recipient Ednl. Svcs. Excellence award ITT, 1980-81, BSA award Boys Scout of Am., Mt. Kisco Drum Corp. Svc. award Mt. Kisco Fire Dept., cert. Appreciation KC, 1992. Mem. N.E. Coalition for Exec. Leaders, Phi Delta Kappa. Roman Catholic. Home: 29 Moccasin View Rd Fishkill NY 12524 Office: Green Chimneys Childrens Svcs Caller Bx719 Putnam Lake Rd Brewster NY 10509

VIENNA, CAROLYN FRANCES, claims consultant; b. Balt., Aug. 1, 1954; d. Daniel Charles and Dorothy Mary (Demski) Haas; m. Frank Joseph Vienna, Jan. 31, 1983. Grad. high sch., Balt., 1972. Sec. Fidelity & Deposit Co. Md., Balt., 1972-80, adminstrv. asst., 1980-90, adminstrv. mgr., 1990—. Democrat. Roman Catholic. Office: Fidelity & Deposit Co Md 300 Saint Paul Pl Baltimore MD 21202

VIETMEIER, JODI LYNN, rehabilitation counselor; b. Billings, Mont., May 15, 1960; d. Dale LaVerne and Marge Ann (Thompson) V.; divorced; children: Jesse Dean Dahlin, Tenille Lynn Dahlin. B of Human Svcs., Eastern Mont. Coll., Billings, 1991, M in Rehab. Counseling, 1993. Coord. R.E.M. Mont. Inc., Billings, 1994—; founding mother Victim Svcs./Crisis Intervention Team, Billings, 1993-96. Mem. Billings Rape Task Force, 1990-96, Yellowstone Family Violence Task Force, 1995-96; bd. dirs. Mont. State Coalition Against Domestic Violence, 1992-96; mem. Cmty. Crime Prevention Coun., 1996; mem. Police Adv. Bd., 1993-96; active in other human rights and civil rights orgns. Democrat. Pentecostal. Home: 319 Mervin St Billings MT 59102

VIGEN, KATHRYN L. VOSS, nursing administrator, educator; b. Lakefield, Minn., Sept. 24, 1934; d. Edward Stanley and Bertha C. (Richter) Voss; m. David C. Vigen, June 23, 1956 (div. 1977); children: Eric. E., Amy Vigen Hemstad, Aana Marie. BS in Nursing magna cum laude, St. Olaf Coll., 1956; MEd, S.D. State U., 1975; MS, Rush U., 1980; PhD, U. Minn., 1987. RN. Staff nurse various hosps., Mpls, Boston, Chgo., 1956-68; nursing instr. S.E.A. Sch. Practical Nursing, Sioux Falls, S.D., 1969-74; statewide coord. upward mobility in nursing Augustana Coll., Sioux Falls, S.D., 1974-78; cons./researcher S.D. Commn. Higher Edn., 1974-79; gov. appointed bd. mem. S.D. Bd. Nursing, 1975-79; RN upward mobility project dir., chair/dir. div. of nursing Huron Coll. S.D. State U., 1978-79, mobility project dir., 1980-84; head dept. nursing, assoc. prof. Luther Coll., Decorah, Iowa, 1984-94; prof. nursing Graceland Coll., Independence, Mo., 1994—; cons. in field; developer outreach MSN programs Graceland Coll.; governing bd. mem. Midwest Alliance in Nursing, 1984-92; founder Soc. for Advancement of Nursing, Malta, 1992; developer Health Care in the Mediterranean Study Abroad Program, Greece and Malta, 1994, 96; developer summer internship for Maltese nursing students Mayo Med. Ctr. and Luther Coll.; presenter on internat. collaboration with Malta for nursing leadership 2d Internat. Acad. Congress on Nursing, Kansas City, 1996. Author: Role of a Dean in a Private Liberal Arts College, 1992; devel. and initiated 3 nursing programs in S.D., 1974-84 (named Women of Yr., 1982). Lobbyist Nursing Schs. in S.D., 1974-79; task force mem. Sen. Tom Harkin's Nurse's Adv. Com., 1986-94. Fellow to rep. U.S.A. ANA cand. in internat. coun. nursing 3M, St. Paul, 1978; recipient Leadership award Bush Found., St. Paul, 1979; tenure Luther Coll., 1986; Faculty fellow Minn. Area Geriatric Edn. Ctr. U. Minn., 1990-91; recipient Fulbright award Malta Coun. Internat. Exch. of Scholars, Washington, 1992—. Mem. AAUW, ANA, Am. Assn. Colls. Nursing (exec. devel. subcom. 1990—), Internat. Assn. Human Caring, Iowa Nurse's Assn. (bd. dirs. 1989-92, mem. nursing edn. com. 1989—, co-pres. 1989—), Midwest Alliance in Nursing (gov. bd. rep. Iowa 1989-92, chair membership com. 1989-92, S.D. gov. bd. rep. 1984-86, Rozella Schlotfeldt Leadership award 1993), Iowa Acad. Sci., Iowa Assn. Colls. Nursing Soc., Gerontol. Soc. Am., Rotary, Sigma Theta Tau. Democrat. Lutheran. Home: 4316 Northern Ave Apt 2633 Kansas City MO 64133-7249 Office: Graceland Coll Divsn Nursing 221 W Lexington Ave Independence MO 64050-3707

VIGIL, PAMELA EVELYN, interior designer; b. Fayetteville, Ark., Aug. 30, 1946; d. Thomas E. Duke and Evelyn. W. (Williamson) Cash; m. Terry W. Cole, Nov. 1963 (div.); 1 child, David W.; m. James B. Vigil, July 11, 1975. Grad., Am. Sch., 1964. Sales cons. RB Furniture, Scottsdale, Ariz., 1980-83; interior designer Vigil Interiors, Phoenix, Ariz., 1983-86; asst. designer Interdesign, Scottsdale, 1986-94; reservation sales agt. America West Airlines, Phoenix, 1992-95; adminstrv. asst. Michael Houtchens Interiors, Scottsdale, 1993-95, Lees Custom Homes, Scottsdale, 1995—. Mem. Internat. Interior Design Assn. (assoc., telephone com.). Democrat.

VIKEN, LINDA LEA MARGARET, lawyer; b. Sioux Falls, S.D., Oct. 27, 1945; d. Carl Thomas and Eleanor Bertha (Zehnpfennig) Crampton; m. Jerry Lee Miller, June 10, 1967 (div. 1975); m. Jeffrey Lynn Viken, Feb. 2, 1980. BS in Bus. Edn., U. S.D., 1967, JD in Law, 1977. Bar: S.D. 1978, U.S. Dist. Ct. S.D. 1978, U.S. Ct. Appeals (8th cir.) 1981. Tchr. Yankton (S.D.) High Sch., 1967-69, Edison Jr. High Sch., Sioux Falls, 1969-75; pvt. practice law Sioux Falls, 1978; ptnr. Finch, Viken, Viken, & Pechota, Rapid City, S.D., 1978-92, Viken, Viken, Pechota, Leach & Dewell, Rapid City, 1992—; part-time instr. Nat. Coll., Rapid City, 1978-80; magistrate judge Seventh Jud. Cir., Rapid City, 1983-84; chair S.D. Commn. on Child Support, 1985, 88; mem. S.D. Bd. of Bar Examiners, 1987-88. Contbr. articles to profl. jours. State rep. S.D. Legislature Minnehaha County, 1973-76, Pennington County, 1988-92; state party vice chair S.D. Dem. party, 1978-80, 92-94; chair Pennington County Dem. Party, Rapid City, 1985-87. Named Woman Atty. of Yr. Law Sch. Women, 1987. Fellow Am. Acad. Matrimonial Lawyers; mem. ABA, S.D. Bar, S.D. Trial Lawyers Assn. Democrat. Roman Catholic. Home: 4760 Trout Ct Rapid City SD 57702-4751 Office: Viken Viken Pechota Leach and Dewell 1617 Sheridan Lake Rd Rapid City SD 57702-3423

VILA, ADIS MARIA, corporate executive, former government official, lawyer; b. Cuba, Aug. 1, 1953; came to U.S., 1962; d. Calixto Vila and Adis C. Fernandez. BA with distinction, Rollins Coll., 1974; JD with honors, U. Fla., 1978; LLM with high honors, Institut Universitaire de Hautes Estudes Internationales, Geneva, 1981. Bar: Fla. 1979, D.C. 1984. Assoc. Paul & Thomson, 1979-82; White House fellow Office Pub. Liaison, Washington, 1982-83; spl. asst. to sec. state for inter-Am. affairs Dept. State, Washington, 1983-86; dir. Office of Mex. and Caribbean Basin, Dept. Commerce, Washington, 1986-87; sec. Dept. Adminstrn., State of Fla., 1987-89; asst. sec. for adminstrn. USDA, Washington, 1989-91; vis. asst., prof. Fla. Internat. U., 1993-94; vis. fellow Nat. Def. U., Washington, 1992-93; v.p. internat. devel. The Vigoro Corp., Chgo., 1994—; trustee So. Ctr. for Internat. Studies, 1987—. Bd. dirs. Rollings Coll. Alumni Coun., Winter Park, Fla., 1979—. Named one of 100 Most Influential Hispanics, 1988, Paul Harris fellow Rotary Internat., 1983, U.S.-Japan Leadership fellow, 1991-92, Eisenhower Exch. fellow, Beca Fiore, Argentina, 1992. Mem. Dade County Bar Assn. (bd. dirs. young and lawyers sect. 1979-87), Coun. Fgn. Rels (term mem. 1987-92), Am. Coun. Young Polit. Leaders (bd. dirs. 1984—), Women Execs. in State Govt. (bd. dirs. 1987—). Republican. Roman Catholic.

VILARDEBO, ANGIE MARIE, management consultant, parochial school educator; b. Tampa, Fla., July 15, 1938; d. Vincent and Antonina (Fazio) Noto; m. Charles Kenneth Vilardebo, June 26, 1960; children: Charles, Kenneth, Michele, Melanie. BA, Notre Dame Md., 1960; postgrad., Rollins Coll., 1980. Cert. tchr., Fla. Tchr. Sea Park Elem. Sch., Satellite Beach, Fla., 1960-61; office mgr. Computer Systems Enterprises, Satellite Beach, 1973-76; artist Satellite Beach, 1976-79; employment counselor Career Cons., Melbourne, Fla., 1979-80; tchr. Our Lady of Lourdes Parochial Sch., Melbourne, 1980-89; pres. Consol. Ventures, Inc., Satellite Beach, 1989—, Versatile Suppliers, Inc., Satellite Beach, 1989—; prin. search com. Diocese of Orlando, Fla., 1989-90. Patentee personal grading machine. V.p. Jaycees, Satellite Beach, 1976-77, pres., 1977-78. Recipient 1st Place Art award Fla. Fedn. Woman's Clubs, 1978, 2nd Place Art award, 1979, Honorable Mention, 1980. Mem. Satellite Beach Woman's Club, Paper Chaser's Investment Club, Brevard Arts Ctr. & Mus., Space Coast Art League (social chmn. 1987—). Roman Catholic. Home: 606 Barcelona Ct Melbourne FL 32937

VILIM, NANCY CATHERINE, advertising agency executive; b. Quincy, Mass., Jan. 15, 1952; d. John Robert and Rosemary (Malpede) V.; m. Geoffrey S. Horner, Feb. 16, 1992; children: Matthew Edward Cajda, Megan Catherine Cajda, Margaret Horner. Student, Miami U., Oxford, Ohio, 1970-72. Media asst. Draper Daniels, Inc., Chgo., 1972-74; asst. buyer Campbell Mithun, Chgo., 1974-75; buyer Tatham, Laird & Kudner, Chgo., 1975-77; media buyer Adcom, Inc. div. Quaker Oats Corp., Chgo., 1977-79; media supr. G.M. Feldman, Chgo., 1979-81; v.p. media dir. Media Mgmt., 1981-83; v.p. broadcast dir. Bozell, Jacobs, Kenyon & Eckhardt, Chgo., 1983-88; v.p., media mgr. McCann-Erickson, Inc., 1989—; judge 27th Internat. Broadcast Awards, Chgo., 1987. Co-pres. Immaculate Conception Religious Edn. Parents Club, 1995-96. Recipient Media All Star awards Sound Mgmt. Mag., N.Y.C., 1987. Mem. Broadcast Advt. Club Chgo., Mus. Broadcast Communications, NAFE. Office: McCann-Erickson Inc 625 N Michigan Ave Chicago IL 60611-3110

VILLACCI, IRENE V., lawyer; b. Queens, N.Y., July 30, 1964; d. Fred and Agnes (Iovino) V. BA, Molloy Coll., 1986; JD, Hofstra U. Sch. of Law, 1989. Bar: N.Y. 1990. Law clk. Douglas Null, P.C., Westbury, N.Y., 1987-

88; law clk. Mulry & Kirtland, Esqs., Port Washington, N.Y., 1988-89, assoc. atty., 1989-92; assoc. atty. Feldman, Kramer & Roberts, PC, Hauppauge, N.Y., 1992—; vol. lawyer Nassau-Suffolk Law Svcs., Mineola, N.Y., 1990—. Chairperson Ethics Bd., Inc. Village of Lynbrook, 1994—, mem., 1991—; pres. alumni bd. Molloy Coll. Alumni Assn., Rockville Centre, N.Y., 1995—, officer alumni bd., 1987—. Recipient Frank E. Gray award Phi Alpha Delta Law Fraternity, 1988-89, Veritas medal Pres. of Molloy Coll., 1993. Mem. Nat. Acad. Elder Law Attys., N.Y. State Bar Assn., Nassau County Women's Bar Assn. (co-chairperson Take Your Daughters to Work Day 1996), Nassau County Bar Assn., Cath. Lawyers Guild. Office: Feldman Kramer and Roberts 330 Motor Pkwy Ste 203 Hauppauge NY 11788

VILLAGONZALO, AMPARO DE LA CERNA, management analyst; b. Cebu, Philippines, Oct. 30, 1939; came to U.S.A., 1970; d. Ignacio Carangue and Josefa (De La Cerna) V.; adopted children: Victor, Emerald. AA, U. Visayas, 1956, LLB magna cum laude, 1960; postgrad., U. Philippines, 1966-67. Bar: Philippines, 1961. Atty. Villagonzalo Law Offices, Cebu City, Philippines, 1960-62; mgmt. analyst Presdl. Com. on Adminstrn. Performance Efficiency, Manila, Philippines, 1962-65; mgmt. analyst II Commn. on Elections, Manila, Philippines, 1965-70; spl. correspondent Bankers Life Ins. Co., Chgo., 1970-74; from transit mgmt. analyst to assoc. mgmt. analyst N.Y.C. Transit Authority, 1974-80, mgr., materials mgmt. dept., 1980—. Scholar U. Visayas, 1954-60, U. Philippines, 1966-67. Roman Catholic. Home: 15811 86th St Jamaica NY 11414-3002

VILLA-KOMAROFF, LYDIA, molecular biologist, educator, university official; b. Las Vegas, N.Mex., Aug. 7, 1947; d. John Dias and Drucilla (Jaramillo) V.; m. Anthony Leader Komaroff, June 18, 1970. BA, Goucher Coll., 1970; PhD, MIT, 1975; DSc (hon.), St. Thomas U., 1996. Rsch. fellow Harvard U., Cambridge, 1975-78; asst. prof. dept. microbiology U. Mass. Med. Ctr., Worcester, 1978-81, assoc. prof. dept. molecular genetics micro, 1982-85; assoc. prof. dept. neurology Harvard Med. Sch., Boston, 1986-95; sr. rsch. assoc. neurology Children's Hosp., Boston, 1985-95, assoc. dir. mental retardation rsch. ctr., 1987-94; assoc. v.p. rsch. adminstrn., prof. dept. neurology Northwestern U., Evanston, Ill., 1996—; mem. mammalian genetics study sect. NIH, 1982-84, mem. reviewers rsch., 1989, mem. neurol. disorders program project rev. com., 1989-94. Contbr. articles and abstracts to profl. jours.; patentee in field. Recipient Hispanic Engr. Nat. Achievement award, 1992; Helen Hay Whitney Found. fellow, 1975-78; NIH grantee, 1978-85, 89-96. Mem. Am. Soc. Microbiology, Assn. for Women in Sci., Soc. for Neurosci., Am. Coll. Cell Biology, Soc. for Advancement Chicanos and Native Ams. in Sci. (founding, bd. dirs. 1987-93, v.p. 1990-93). Office: Northwestern U 633 Clark St Evanston IL 60208-1111

VILLALON, DALISAY MANUEL, nurse, real estate broker; b. Angat, Bulacan, Philippines, Apr. 27, 1941; came to U.S., 1967; d. Federico Manuel and Librada (Garcia) Manuel; divorced; children: Ricky, May, Liberty, Derrick, Dolly Rose. BS in Nursing, Manila Cen. U., 1961; postgrad. in nursing, U. Ill., Chgo., 1972-74. RN, Ill. Instr. nursing Cen. Luzon Sch. Nursing, Philippines, 1966-67; staff nurse St. Alexis Hosp., Cleve., 1968-70, Augustana Hosp., Chgo., 1972-74; nurse mgr. Holy Child Med. Clinic, Chgo., 1976-80; nurse auditor 1st Health Care, Rosemont, Ill., 1982-83; dir. nurses North Shore Terr., Waukegan, Ill., 1983-90, Carlton House, 1991-94. Columnist Philippine News. Bd. dirs. Filipino Am. Coun., Chgo., 1978-80, v.p., 1980-82; bd. dirs. Asian Human Svcs., Chgo.; pres. Am.-Filipino Profl. Civic Alliance, Chgo., 1984-90, Philipino-Am. United for Svc.-Oriental Objective, 1991—; chmn. Philippine Week Com., 1979; past v.p. Filipino Ams. Concerned for Elderly; trustee Rizal-MacArthur Found.; past v.p. Filipino Svc. League, 1989-91; past exec. v.p. Asian Festival, Inc.; past chmn. various civic coms.; mem. Asian-Am. Adv. Coun. Mayor Daley, 1989-97. Recipient Cert. Appreciation Rizal-MacArthur Found., 1977, Most Outstanding Filipino in Midwest award Cavite Assn. Am., 1980, Outstanding Community Svc. Appreciation award Filipino Am. Coun., 1981, 89, NGHIA Sinh Internat., Inc., 1989, Outstanding Svc. award Asian-Am. Coaliton, 1989, Outstanding Contrn. award Dirs. Nursing and Adminstrs. Conf., 1988; named to Filipino Hall of Fame for comty. svc., 1996 Phil Reports TV. Mem. Ill. Nurses Assn. (bd. dirs., dist. senator 1989-91, human rights and ethics commn. 1990-91), Philippine Med. Assn. Aux. (pres. 1980, Outstanding Leadership award 19891), Chgo. Med. Soc. Aux. (v.p. 1980), Chgo. Philippine Lioness Club (pres. 1983-84, Outstanding Svc. award 1985), Filipino Woman's Club Chgo. (Outstanding Woman in Leadership 1992, Chgo. Filipino Hall of Fame award), Filipino Am. Polit. Assn. Democrat. Roman Catholic. Office: Vitas Health Care Corp Vitas Innovative Care 5215 Old Orchard Rd Skokie IL 60077

VILLA-MCDOWELL, THERESA, lawyer; b. Torrance, Calif., Dec. 20, 1949; d. Jose Rodriguez and Esperanza (Flores) Villa; m. Michael Lynn McDowell, apr. 12, 1969; 1 child, Bartholomew J. Villa-McDowell. AA, El Camino Coll., 1973; BA, Calif. State U., Long Beach, 1975; JD, U. So. Calif., 1991. Bar: Calif., 1991, U.S. Dist. Ct. (ctrl. dist.) Calif., U.S. Ct. Appeals (9th cir.). Asst. pub. rels. mgr. Knott's Berry Farm, Buena Park, Calif., 1976-79; dir. pub. rels. Buena Park Conv. and Visitor's Bur., 1979-81; editor Calif. Travel Report, Beverly Hills, Calif., 1981-82; dir. pub. rels. Long Beach Area Conv. and Visitor's Coun., Long Beach, Calif., 1982-88; clk. Manulkin, Glaser & Bennett, Fountain Valley, Calif., 1989 summer, Williams, Woolley, Cogswell, Nagazawa & Russell, Long Beach, Calif., 1990 summer; U. S.C. Irmas fellow Legal Aid Found., Long Beach, 1991-92; law clk. Hon. Linda Hodge McLaughlin U.S. Ctrl. Ct., Santa Ana, Calif., 1992-93; gen. counsel Queen Mary, Long Beach, Calif., 1993-94; staff atty. Legal Aid Found., Long Beach, 1994—; bd. dirs. Women in Comm., Long Beach and Orange County chpts., 1977-83; chmn. mktg. com. Long Beach C. of C.; treas. Western States chpt. Travel Writers of Am., 1986-88; ABA law student divsn. liason, standing com. on legal aid and indigent defense, 1990-91; clk. U. S.C. Post-conviction Justice Project, 1991; mem. planning com. U. S.C. Law Ctr. Symposium on Changing Legal Concepts of Motherhood, 1991; extern for Hon. David Kenyon U.S. Ctrl. Dist. Ct., 1991. Contbg. writer U. S.C. Law Street Jour., U. S.C. Rev. of Law and Women's Studies, 1993. Bd. dirs. and recording sec. Long Beach YWCA, WomenShelter, 1992; mem. adminstrv. com., Anaheim Street Festival, 1994; adv. bd. mem. Arts of Apsara, 1996; cmty. adv. bd. mem. Long Beach Youth Ctrs., Inc., 1996; bd. trustees Young Horizons, Inc, Long Beach, 1996. Recipient Cmty. Affairs award, Cambodian Bus. Assn., 1994. Office: Legal Aid Found 110 Pine Ave Ste 420 Long Beach CA 90802

VILLANUEVA, LIBRADA GERONCA, principal, consultant; b. Guinpana-an, Isabela, The Philippines, Oct. 26, 1939; came to U.S., 1981; d. Pedro Patino and Carmen Saravia Escosia Geronca; m. Norberto E. Villanueva, Aug. 26, 1961; 3 adopted children. BS in Edn., U. Negros Occidental-Recoletos, Bacolod City, The Philippines, 1965; MA in Edn., Uno-Recoletos, Bacolod City, The Philippines, 1968. With curriculum lab., ednl. leadership colloquia, nat. honors coun., internat. edn., fin. aid office, mid. coll. h.s. L.A. Cmty. Coll. Dist., 1984-92; prin. Ma-ao Elem. Sch., Bago City, The Philippines; pres. Bago Tchrs. Cooperative Credit Union, 1965-82; mem. grants writing seminar curriculum lab. L.A. Cmty. Coll. Dist., 1984-91. Jr. exec. tng. course commr., commr. wood badge course, trainer nat. trainers' course, del. First Asia-Pacific Jamboree, 1968 Boy Scouts of Philippines; mem. Kahirup Internat., L.A., 1981—, Negrenses Am., Inc., 1987—, United Ilonggo, Inc., L.A., 1990—; rector Cursillo Christiandad, Bago City, 1965-68; action officer clothing and cottage industry Ministry Human Settlements, Bago City, 1968-82. Mem. VFW (ladies aux.), Bago City Sch. Adminstrs. Assn., Tchrs. Coll. Student Coun. (pres.), Sons & Daus. Defenders Bataan & Corregidor, Builder Lions Club, Lions Club Internat. Democrat. Roman Catholic. Address: 211 N Coronado St Los Angeles CA 90026

VILLAREAL, BOBBIE RAE, lawyer; b. El Paso, Tex., Dec. 29, 1965; d. Joe Wiley and Irma Margaret (Ramirez) Yowell; m. Andres Villareal, June 5, 1993. BBA in Mktg., Baylor U., 1987, JD, 1990. Bar: Tex. Asst. dist. atty. Tarrant County Dist. Atty.'s Office, Fort Worth, 1991—. Vol. Fort Worth Ind. Sch.-Adopt A Sch, 1993, vol. CANN Child Ctr., Fort Worth, 1993. Mem. Tarrant County Bar Assn. Republican. Home: 2924 W Royal Ln #3095 Irving TX 75063

VILLECCO, JUDY DIANA, substance abuse, mental health counselor, director; b. Knoxville, Tenn., Jan. 19, 1948; d. William Arthur and Louise (Reagan) Chamberlain; m. Tucker, June 10, 1965 (div. 1974); children: Linda Louise (Tucker) Smith, Constance Christine; m. Roger Anthony Villecco, May 3, 1979. BA in Psychology, U. West Fla., 1988, MA in Psychology, 1992. Lic. mental health counselor, Fla.; cert. addiction profl., Fla.; internat. cert. alcohol and drug counselor. Counselor Gulf Coast Hosp., Ft. Walton Beach, Fla., 1986-87; peer counselor U. West Fla., Ft. Walton Beach, 1987-89; family and prevention counselor Okaloosa Guidance Clinic, Ft. Walton Beach, 1988-89; family svc. dir. Anon Anew of Tampa (Fla.), Inc., 1989-91; dir. Renew Counseling Ctr., Ft. Walton Beach, 1990-92; substance abuse dept. dir. Avalon Ctr., Milton, Fla., 1992-93; adult coord. Partial & Rivendell, Ft. Walton Beach, 1994-95; pvt. practice Emerald Coast Psychiat. Care, P.A., Fort Walton Beach, 1994-95, Associated Psychotherapists, Ft. Walton Beach, 1995—; internat. substance abuse counselor, dir. and presenter in field. Author: Co-dependency Treatment Manual, 1992; creator Effective Treatment for Codependants, 1992. Named Outstanding Mental Health Profl. of Yr. Mental Health Assn., 1994. Mem. Internat. Assn. for Offender Counselors, Fla. Alcohol, Drug, Substance Abuse Assn. (bd. dirs., regional rep., Regional Profl. of Yr. 1992-93, 95—), Am. Counseling Assn. (alt. rep.), Internat. Assn. for Marriage and Family Counseling, Phi Theta Kappa, Alpha Phi Sigma. Office: 348 Miracle Strip Pky Ste 38 Fort Walton Beach FL 32548

VILLEMAIRE, DIANE DAVIS, biologist, educator; b. Burlington, Vt., Nov. 21, 1946; d. Ellsworth Quinlan and Elizabeth Charlotte (Galvin) Davis; m. Bernard Philip Villemaire, Aug. 16, 1969; 1 child, Emily Jane. BS, U. Vt., 1968, MA, 1994; postgrad., McGill, 1995—. Cert. tchr. Vt. Rsch. asst. U. Vt., Burlington, 1965-68; tchr. Burlington H.S., 1968-71, Harwood Union H.S., Moretown, Vt., 1971-95; curriculum chair Harwood Union H.S., Moretown, 1993-95; cons. Vt. Inst. of Math Sci and Tech., 1995—. Recipient Am. Biology Tchrs. Assn., 1978. Mem. Am. Biology Tchrs. Assn., Am. Assn. U. Women, Soc. for Advancement of Am Philosophy. Office: Harwood Union H S RR1 Box 790 Moretown VT 05660

VILLOCH, KELLY CARNEY, art director; b. Kyoto, Japan, July 22, 1950; d. William Riley and stepdaughter Hazel Fowler Carney; m. Joe D. Villoch, Aug. 9, 1969; children: Jonathan Christopher, Jennifer. A in Fine Arts, Dade C.C., Miami, Fla., 1971; student, Metro Fine Arts, 1973-74, Fla. Internat. U., 1985-88. Design asst. Lanvin, Miami, 1971—, Fieldcrest, Miami, 1974-77; art dir. Advercolor, Miami, 1977-78; art dir. copywriter ABC, Miami, 1978-89; writer Armed Forces Radio & TV Network; multimedia dir. ADVITEC, 1989-91; art dir. writer Miami Write, 1979—; owner Beach Point Prodns., 1992—; lectr. Miami Dade C.C., cons. Studio Masters, North Miami, 1979-89. Prin. works include mixed media, 1974 (Best of Show 1974), pen and ink drawing, 1988 (Best Poster 1988); writer, dir., editor, prodr. (video film): Bif, 1988, Drink + Drive = Die, 1994; writer, dir., prodr. (pub. svc. announcement) Reading is the Real Adventure, 1990; film editor Talent Times Mag.; author: Winds of Freedom, 1994; art dir., exec. com. Miami Hispanic Media Conf., 1992, 93, 94; editor-in-chief, film editor: In Grove Miami Mag., 1994-96; webmaster, web content provider, website design cons., writer, graphic artist Guru Comms., 1996; editor-in-chief In Grove Miami Mag., 1994-96; web content provider WEBCOM; webmaster Guru Comm., 1996; web site designer, multimedia dir. State of Fla. grantee LimeLite Studios, Inc., 1990, William Douglas Pawley Found. grantee, Frances Wolfson scholar, Cultural Consortium grantee, 1993. Mem. Am. Film Inst., Phi Beta Kappa.

VINCENT, RABIAH, gallery director; b. Norfolk, Va., Dec. 24; d. George Ernest and Geraldine (Maples) Smith. Student, Tidewater C.C., 1974; MA in Native Am. Studies, SUNY, Buffalo, 1996. Tchr. art Virginia Beach (Va.) Art Ctr., 1977-78; prodn. asst. Record Plant Recording Studio, N.Y.C., 1978-82, Live Oak Sound Recording Studio, Norfolk, Va., 1982-84; v.p. Musicians Referral Svc., Norfolk, Va., 1984-85; program dir., air personality Sta. WVAB AM Radio, Virginia Beach, 1985-86; air personality Sta. WNUZ FM Radio, Virginia Beach, 1986-87; promotions-mktg. dir. Virginia Beach Omni Plaza Hotel, 1987-88; dir., founder The Working Gallery, Virginia Beach, 1988-90; dir. contemporary art Auslew Gallery, Virginia Beach, 1991—; lectr., dir. pub. rels. and mktg. Virginia Beach Ctr. for the Arts; lectr. Norfolk State U., dir. pub. rels./mktg. 1991 Fall Gala; coord. art exhibitions World Trade Ctr. Cen. Fidelity Bank, Norfolk, Mcpl. Ctr. Gallery Mayors Office, Virginia Beach, Va.; curator, 1992, curator Charles Taylor Art Ctr., Hampton, 1991-92; Native Am. history & art instr. Cape Henry Collegiate Sch., 1993—. Artist (water color painting) Thirty Pieces of Silver, 1988, (mixed media paintings) Dawn's Early Light, 1989, The Calling, 1989, Poppies, 1989; one woman exhibit Of Cats and Men, World Trade Ctr., Norfolk, 1992; Native Am. storyteller Cox Cable. Commr. Virginia Beach Adv. Commn., 1990—; mem. liaison com. resort area adv. commn. City of Virginia Beach Spl. Events, 1990—; vol. tchr. severely, profoundly and multi handicapped art Virginia Beach Ctr. for the Arts, 1990—, tchr. drawing, 1991—; vol. tchr. severely and profoundly retarded Princess Ann High Sch., 1990—; active Nat. Am. Indian Movement, 1992—. Grantee Virginia Commn. for the Arts, 1978; recipient Hon. Mention award WHRO Juried Art Exhibition, 1992. Mem. Virginia Beach Ctr. for the Arts, Nat. Artists Equity (Washington), Art and Co., Artists Svcs. Network, Richmond Slide Registry, Tidewater Artists Assn. (bd. dirs.), Working Gallery Artist Assn. (bd. dirs. 1989—). Home: 302 55th St Virginia Beach VA 23451-2214

VINCENT, SUZANNE, artist, educator; b. Boston, Mar. 30, 1962; d. Galen Stuart and Carol (Hersey) V.; m. Jerome Jordan Higgins, May 30, 1983 (div. Feb. 1989); m. Michael Robert Dinallo, Mar. 16, 1991. Diploma, Sch. of Mus. of Fine Arts, Boston, 1984, cert., 1985. Instr. Sch. of Mus. of Fine Arts, 1989-90, 91-93. One-woman shows include Stux Gallery, Boston, 1986, 88, Gallery NAGA, Boston, 1990, 93, 96; exhibited in group shows at Sch. Mus. Fine Arts, Boston, 1985, Stux Gallery, 1985-87, New Haven Creative Arts Workshop, 1987, Brockton (Mass.) Art Mus., 1987, Marvis Gallery, Westfield (Mass.) State Coll., 1987, Dodge Gallery and Richards Gallery, Northeastern U., Boston, 1988-89, Fitchburg (Mass.) Art Mus., 1989, 93, N.A.M.E. Gallery, Chgo., 1990, Art Inst. Boston, 1990, Fuller Mus. Art, Brockton, 1990, Rose Art Mus., Brandeis U., Waltham, Mass., 1990, Gallery NAGA, 1992. Traveling scholar Sch. of Mus. of Fine Arts, 1985, 94.

VINDENI, BRIGITTE HANNELORE, real estate associate; b. Duisburg, Germany, Aug. 23, 1954; came to U.S., 1957; d. Otto and Sophie (Weber) Preuss; m. Kenneth D. Vindeni, Sept. 12, 1982. BA, William Paterson Coll., 1980; postgrad., Fairleigh Dickinson U. Cert. real estate assoc., N.J., N.Y. Mgr. sales promotion Warner Lambert Co., Morris Plains, N.J., 1982-95; real estate assoc. Weichert Realtors, West Milford, N.J., 1005—; v.p. Lakeland Chiropractic Ctr., Wanaque, N.J. Office: Weichert Realtors 1433 Union Valley Rd West Milford NJ 07480

VINING, KIMBERLY TUCKER, educational materials representative, consultant; b. Hayti, Mo., Mar. 12, 1965; d. James Edward and Julia Ann (Barnett) Adkisson; m. David Scott Vining, Sept. 4, 1993. BS in English Edn., Remedial Reading, U. So. Miss., Hattiesburg, 1987. Tchr. 9th, 10th grades Lauderdale County Sch., Meridian, Miss., 1987-89, Chpt. I tchr., 1988-89; tchr. 9th grade Santa Rosa County, Gulf Breeze, Fla., 1989-90; edn. pub. Nystrom, Inc., Chgo., 1990-92, SRA McGraw Hill, Inc., Atlanta, 1992—; cons. Nystrom, Inc., Miss., Ala., 1990-92, SRA McGraw Hill, Miss., Ala., Ga., 1992-94. Named Tchr. of Yr., Meridian, Miss., 1988. Mem. ASCD, Nat. Coun. Tchrs. Math., Nat. Coun. Tchrs. English, Nat. Assn. Edn. of Young Children, Internat. Reading Assn. Baptist. Home: 6850 Payton Rd Cumming GA 30131 Office: SRA McGraw Hill 8939 Western Way Jacksonville FL 32256

VINOKUR-KAPLAN, DIANE RUTH, research scientist, educator; b. Milw., Nov. 30, 1947; d. Fred S. Kaplan and Hedy Malki; m. Amiram David Vinokur, Dec. 27, 1970; children: Nessa, Ariel S. BA in Sociology cum laude, Oberlin Coll., 1970; MSW, U. Mich., 1972, MA in Sociology, 1973, PhD, 1975. Rsch. coord. Nat. Child Welfare Tng. Ctr., Ann Arbor, Mich., 1980-82; dir. office of rsch. svcs., asst. rsch. scientist, Sch. Social Work U. Mich., Ann Arbor, 1984-86, asst. dean for rsch., Sch. Social Work, 1980-82, asst. prof., 1990-96, assoc. prof., 1996—. Contbr. numerous articles to profl. jours. Office: U Mich Sch Social Work 1065 Frieze Bldg Ann Arbor MI 48109-1285

VINSON, LEILA TERRY WALKER, retired gerontological social worker; b. Lynchburg, Va., July 28, 1928; d. William Terry and Ada Allen (Moore) Walker; m. Hughes Nelson Vinson, Aug. 11, 1951; children: Hughes Nelson, William Terry. Student, Agnes Scott Coll., 1946-48; BA, U. Ala., Tuscaloosa, 1950; postgrad., U. Ala., Birmingham, 1980-81, U. Va., 1950-51. Cert. gerontol. social worker, Ala. Tchr. English and Latin Marion County Bd. Edn., Hamilton, Ala., 1952-59; social worker I Marion County Dept. Pensions and Security, 1963-72, gerontol. social worker II, 1972-85; ret., 1985. Bd. dirs. Marion County Dept. Human Resources, 1985—; speaker on gen. subjects. Recipient Ala. Woman Committed to Excellence award Tuscaloosa coun. Girl Scouts U.S., 1987; named Mrs. Marion County, PTA, Gwin, Ala., 1969, Woman of Yr. Town of Hamilton, 1980, New Retiree of Yr. Ala. Ret. State Employees Assn., 1988, Woman of Yr. BPW, 1985; Gessener Harrison fellow U. Va., 1950-51. Mem. AAUW, DAR (flag chmn. Bedford chpt. 1988-90), UDC, Bus. and Profl. Women's Club (dist. dir. 1984-86, Outstanding Dir. award 1986), Ala. Fedn. Women's Club. Home: PO Box 1112 Hamilton AL 35570-1112 also: Military Rd Hamilton AL 35570

VINSONHALER, CHRIS, storyteller, musician, consultant; b. Ocala, Fla., Nov. 30, 1956; d. Henry and Dorothy (Hambrick) Martin; m. John S. Weldon, June 14, 1980 (div. 1989); children: Anna Margaret Vinsonhaler Weldon, Morgan Elaine Vinsonhaler Weldon. BS in English, U. Ga., Athens, 1978; MA in English, U. N.C., Chapel Hill, 1983; MLS, U. So. Miss., Hattiesburg, 1990. Cert. tchr. Miss. Reporter The Miss. Press, Pascagoula, 1987-88; reporter The Sun Herald, Ocean Springs, Miss., 1988-90, bur. chief Jackson County, 1989-90; columnist The Clarion Ledger, Jackson, Miss., 1991-94; librarian Westminster Acad., Gulfport, Miss., 1991-93; assoc. Marian Wingo & Assocs., Ocean Springs, 1991—; organizer, dir. Great Oaks Storytelling Festival, Ocean Springs, Friends of Folk, Camp Inspire. Performer (cassette tape) Wild & Crazy, 1993, Drench MY Soul, 1993, How To Survive School, 1996, Rain!, 1996. Mem. AAUW, Nat. Storytelling Assn. Democrat. Home: 1017 La Fontaine Ocean Springs MS 39564

VIOLAND-SANCHEZ, EMMA N., school administrator, educator; b. Cochabamba, Bolivia, Nov. 5, 1944; came to U.S., 1961; d. Adalberto Violand and Emma Sanchez; children: James, Julia. BS, Radford U., 1966, MS, 1968; EdD, George Washington U., 1987. Postgrad. profl. lic. Tchr., counselor Am. Coop. Sch., La Paz, Bolivia, 1963, 71-76; instr. Ariz. Western Coll., Yuma, 1967-68; tchr., counselor St. Andrews Sch., La Paz, 1968-71; rschr. Instituto Boliviano Estudio Accion Social, La Paz, 1968-71; bilingual resource specialist Arlington (Va.) Pub. Schs., 1976-78, secondary project coord. Title VII, 1978-80, supr. ESOL, 1980—; adj. prof. U. Catolica, La Paz, 1974-75, George Mason U., Fairfax, Va., 1986-94, George Washington U., Washington, 1988—; cons. sch. dists., univs., Ministry of Edn. in Bolivia, 1976—. Author: Vocational and Professional Handbook for Bolivia, 1971, Learning Styles in the ESL/EFL Classroom, 1995, (monographs) Ministry of Education, 1988, National Clearinghouse for Bilingual Education, 1990, 91. Founder, pres. coun. 4606 LULAC, Arlington, 1987-96; founder chair Immigration Rights Task Force, Arlington, 1989-92; bd. trustees United Way Nat. Capital Area, Washington, 1989-94; exec. bd. Com. of 100, Arlington, 1994-95. Named one of Notable Women of Arlington, Arlington County, 1993; recipient Outstanding Dissertation award Nat. Assn. Bilingual Edn., 1988; Am. fellow AAUW, 1986-87; Fulbright Sr. scholar, 1995-96. Mem. ASCD, TESOL (rsch. bd. 1979—). Office: Arlington Pub Schs 1426 N Quincy St Arlington VA 22207

VIOLENUS, AGNES A., retired school system administrator; b. N.Y.C., May 17, 1931; d. Antonio and Constance Violenus. BA, Hunter Coll., 1952; MA, Columbia U., 1958; EdD, Nova U., 1990. Tchr. N.Y. State Day Care, N.Y.C., 1952-53, N.Y.C. Bd. Edn., 1953-66; asst. prin. N.Y.C. Elem. and Jr. High Sch., 1966-91; adj. instr. computer dept. continuing edn. divsn. York Coll., N.Y.C., 1985-88; adj. instr. tchr. mentor program grad. edn. divsn. CCNY, 1990-91; reviewer ednl. and instrnl. films; judge news and documentary Emmy awards NATAS, 1995. Co-author: LOGO: K-12, 1980; contbr. articles to profl. jours. Mem. mid-Manhattan br. NAACP, mem. com. on Afro-Am. acad., cultural, and tech. olympics; life mem. Girl Scouts U.S., N.Y.C.; bd. visitors Manhattan Psychiat. Ctr., 1995; vol. advisor math., sci., computers Workshop Ctr., CCNY, 1995. Recipient Dedicated Svc. award Coun. Suprs. and Adminstrs., Appreciation award Aerospace Edn. Assn., 1985, Significant Contbn. award Am. Soc. for Aerospace Edn., 1985. Mem. ASCE, Am. Ednl. Rsch. Assn., Assn. for Advancement of Computing in Edn., Assn. for Computers in Math. and Sci. Tchg., Soc. for Info., Tech., and Tchr. Edn., Assn. for Women in Sci., N.Y. Acad. Scis. (scientists in schs. program 1995), Nat. Assn. Negro Bus. and Profl. Women's Clubs (scholarship com. 1989—, family math. com. 1995, rec. sec. 1994-96), Nat. Black Child Devel. Inst. (bd. dirs. 1991—, sci. exhibit com. 1995, pub. policy com. 1991—, Bridge Bldr.'s award 1995), Pub. Edn. Assn. (mem. good schs. exch. com. 1990), Schomburg Ctr. Rsch. in Black Culture (bd. trustee, co-chair corp. task force on African-Am. in math., sci., and tech. 1992—, pres. 1995), Doctorate Assn. N.Y. Educators, N.Y. Alliance Black Sch. Educators, Hunter Coll. Alumni Assn. (bd. dirs. 1993—, rec. sec. 1996—), Bank St. Alumni Coun. Greater N.Y. (asst. sect. 1991—), Wistarians Alumni Hunter Coll. (exec. com. 1990—, pres. 1990-94). Democrat. Roman Catholic. Office: Farley Bldg PO Box 699 New York NY 10116

VIOLETTE, DIANE MARIE, small business owner, consultant, editor; b. Pontiac, Mich., Apr. 19, 1958; d. Bernard Desmond and Mary Virginia (Bartosh) V.; m. Glenn Martin Payette, Apr. 18, 1987. BA in Journalism, Mich. State U., 1980; cert. in govt. contracts and mgmt., UCLA, 1987; MBA summa cum laude, Calif. State U., Northridge, 1991. Contract adminstr. Def. Contract Adminstrn. Services Mgmt. Area, Van Nuys, Calif., 1980-84, adminstrv. contract officer, 1984-87; pres. govt. contracting Diane Violette & Assocs., 1987—. Contbr. articles to profl. jours. Mem. Nat. Contract Mgmt. Assn.

VIORST, JUDITH STAHL, author; b. Newark, Feb. 2, 1931; d. Martin Leonard and Ruth June (Ehrenkranz) Stahl; m. Milton Viorst, Jan. 30, 1960; children: Anthony Jacob, Nicholas Nathan, Alexander Noah. BA, Rutgers U., 1952; grad., Washington Psychoanalytic Inst., 1981. Author: (children's books) Sunday Morning, 1968, I'll Fix Anthony, 1969, Try It Again Sam, 1970, The Tenth Good Thing About Barney, 1971 (Silver Pencil award 1973), Alexander and the Terrible Horrible No Good Very Bad Day, 1972, My Mama Says There Aren't Any Zombies, Ghosts, Vampires, Creatures, Demons, Monsters, Fiends, Goblins or Things, 1973, Rosie and Michael, 1974, Alexander, Who Used to Be Rich Last Sunday, 1978, The Good-Bye Book, 1988, Earrings!, 1990, The Alphabet from Z to A (with Much Confusion on the Way, 1994, Alexander, Who's Not (Do You Hear Me? I Mean It!) Going to Move, 1995; (poetry) The Village Square, 1965-66, It's Hard to Be Hip Over Thirty and Other Tragedies of Married Life, 1968, People and Other Aggravations, 1971, How Did I Get to Be Forty and Other Atrocities, 1976, If I Were in Charge of the World and Other Worries, 1981, When Did I Stop Being Twenty and Other Injustices, 1987, Forever Fifty and Other Negotiations, 1989, Sad Underwear and Other Complications, 1995; (with Milton Viorst) The Washington Underground Gourmet, 1970, Yes Married, 1972, A Visit From St. Nicholas (To a Liberated Household), 1977, Love and Guild and the Meaning of Life, Etc., 1979, Necessary Losses, 1986, Murdering Mr. Monti, 1994; columnist Redbook mag. (Penney-Mo. award 1974, Am. Acad. Pediatrics award 1977, AAUW 1980). Jewish. Home: 3432 Ashley Ter NW Washington DC 20008-3238

VIRES, JUDY DOAN, early childhood educator; b. London, Mar. 3, 1954; d. Chester Lee and Shirley Mae (Smith) Doan; m. Charles Edward Vires, June 2, 1973; children: Jordan Ross, Dylan Case. BS, West Ga. Coll., 1996. Dir. Great Atlanta Christian Sch., Peachtree City, Ga., 1987-92; tchr. 1st gr. Arlington Christian Sch., 1996; test adminstr. Arlington Christian Sch., Fairburn, Ga., 1992-96. Vol. vision screener Prevent Blindness Ga., Atlanta, 1994-96. Mem. Student Profl. Assn. Ga. Educators. Home: 748 Bridlepath Ln Peachtree City GA 30269

VIRGO, MURIEL AGNES, swimming school owner; b. Liverpool, Cheshire, Eng., Apr. 3, 1924; d. Harold Thornhill and Susan Ann (Duff) Franks; m. John Virgo, Aug. 13, 1942; children: John Michael, Angela Victoria, Barbara Ann, Collin Anthony, Donna Marie. Grad. parochial schs. Co-owner Virgo Swim Sch., Garden Grove, Calif., 1967—. Mem. Ancient Mystical Order Rosae Crucis, Traditional Martinist Order. Republican. Roman Catholic. Home: 12751 Crestwood Cir Garden Grove CA

92641-5250 Office: Virgo Swim Sch 12851 Brookhurst Way Garden Grove CA 92641-5205

VISCELLI, THERESE RAUTH, materials management consultant; b. Bitburg, Fed. Republic Germany, Nov. 18, 1955; d. David William and Joyce (Kelly) Rauth; m. Eugene R. Viscelli, Feb. 4, 1978; children: Christopher, Kathryn, Matthew. BS, Ga. Inst. Tech., 1977; postgrad., So. Tech. Inst., 1977-78, Ga. State U., 1982-83. Mktg. engr. Hughes Aircraft Corp., Carlsbad, Calif., 1978-79; indsl. engr. Kearfott-Singer, San Marcos, Calif., 1979-80; product analyst Control Data Corp., Atlanta, 1981-84; dir. R&D Am. Software, Inc., Atlanta, 1984-92; acct. mgr. The Coca-Cola Co., 1992-93; dir. info. sys. Mizuno, USA, Norcross, Ga., 1993—. Mem. Am. Prodn. and Inventory Control Soc. (program chmn. 1982-83, v.p. 1983-84). Republican. Roman Catholic.

VISOCKI, NANCY GAYLE, data processing consultant; b. Dumont, N.J., May 13, 1952; d. Thomas and Gloria (Valle) V. BA in Maths., Manhattanville Coll., 1974; MS in Ops. Rsch. and Stats., Rensselaer Poly. Inst., 1977. Rsch. asst. Coll. Physicians and Surgeons Columbia U., N.Y.C., 1974-75; programmer analyst R. Shriver Assocs., Parsippany, N.J., 1977-79; sr. tech. rep. GE Info. Svcs. Co., East Orange, N.J., 1979-81; mgr. project office GE Info. Svcs. Co., Morristown, N.J., 1981-83, tech. dir., 1983-87, tech. mgr., 1988-89; area mgr. system devel. and consulting GE Info. Svcs. Co., Parsippany, 1989-92; area tech. mgr. system devel. and cons., Fin. Info. Systems GE Info. Svcs. Co., Parsippany, N.J., 1992-93, sr. cons. electronic commerce info. svcs., 1993—. Active Western Hills Christian Ch., Tranquility, N.J., 1986—; vol. Women's Ctr., Hackettstown, N.J., 1989-93; class fundraising and gift chmn. Rensselaer Poly. Inst., 1991-95; vol. Elfun Soc. Manhattanville Coll. grantee, Purchase, N.Y., 1970-71; tuition fellow Rensselaer Poly. Inst., Troy, N.Y., 1975-77. Mem. NAFE, Women of Accomplishment. Home: 140 E Linden Ave Dumont NJ 07628-1916 Office: GE Info Svcs Co Ste 302 20 Waterview Blvd Parsippany NJ 07054-1219

VISSER, VALYA ELIZABETH, physician; b. Chgo., Oct. 2, 1947; d. Roy Warren and Tania Eugenia (Morozoff) Nelson; children: Kira Elizabeth Visser, Michael Philip Visser. BS, Iowa State U., 1968; MD, U. Iowa, 1973. Diplomate Am. Bd. Pediatrics, Sub-Bd. Neonatal-Perinatal Medicine. Resident pediatrics U. Iowa Hosps. and Clinics, Iowa City, 1976; fellow neonatology Children's Mercy Hosp., Kansas City, 1978; asst. prof. pediatrics U. Kans. Sch. Medicine, Kansas City, 1978-81; staff pediatrician U.S. Army Med. Corps., Ft. Bragg, N.C., 1981-83; attending neonatologist Carolinas Med. Ctr., Charlotte, 1983—; acting chair dept. pediatrics Carolinas Med. Ctr., Charlotte, 1991-94; conf. chair Extracorporeal Life Support Orgn., Ann Arbor, Mich., 1993-95. Major Med. Corps., 1981-83. Fellow Am. Acad. Pediatrics; mem. Soc. for Critical Care Medicine. Mem. Unitarian-Universalist Ch. Office: Carolinas Med Ctr Dept Pediatrics PO Box 32861 Charlotte NC 28232-2861

VITALE, CONCETTA, college administrator, nurse; b. New Kensington, Pa., May 21; m. Joseph Lewis Hlafcsak, Mar. 19, 1983; children: Susan, Judith. BS, U. Pitts., 1973, MS, 1975, PhD, 1995. Various clin. and teaching positions, 1960-95; dean instrn. C.C. Allegheny County, Pitts., 1995—.

VITALE, FRANCIS M., preschool director; b. Bronx, N.Y., Dec. 26, 1937; d. Peter Robert and Vitina (Incandella) DiPaola; m. Anthony Joseph Vitale, Apr. 26, 1970; children: Stephanie Maria, Jeffrey Anthony. BA, Coll. of New Rochelle, 1991. Founder, dir. The Caring Place, Inc., New Rochelle, N.Y. Mem. Westchester Assn. for Edn. of Young Children, Child Care Coun. Westchester, New Rochelle C. of C. Home: 36 Robins Rd New Rochelle NY 10801-1115

VITEK, VICTORIA LYNN, speech-language pathologist; b. St. Louis, Aug. 27, 1967; d. Ronald Vernon Vincent and Carol Marie (McCoy) Anderson; m. Scott Allen Vitek, Nov. 24, 1990. BS in Speech/Lang. Pathology, Ctrl. Mo. State U., Warrensburg, 1989, MS in Speech/Lang. Pathology, 1990. Speech./lang. pathologist Kansas City (Kans.) Pub. Schs., 1990—. Lutheran. Home: 113 Lakeland Dr Smithville MO 64089-8878

VITENSE, LAURI JO, county official, auditor; b. Cedar Rapids, Iowa, May 26, 1962; d. Eldon Lee and Barbara Kay (Eves) Werling; m. Raymond Henry Vitense, Oct. 24, 1981 (div. July 1994); children: Jake Henry, Kelsey Jo. AA in Liberal Arts, Kirkwood C.C., Cedar Rapids, 1994; student, Coe Coll., 1995—. Dep. auditor Cedar County, Tipton, Iowa, 1981—. Av. Cedar County scholar Kirkwood C.C., 1992-93, Crawford scholar Coe Coll., 1995, 96, scholar Carver Found., 1995, 96. Mem. Tipton Jaycees, Women of Moose, Alpha Sigma Lambda. Home: 323 W 3d St Tipton IA 52772

VITETTA, ELLEN SHAPIRO, microbiologist educator, immunologist. BA, Conn. Coll.; MS, NYU, 1966, PhD, MD, 1968. Prof. microbiology Southwestern Med. Sch., U. Tex., Dallas, 1976—; dir. Cancer Immunobiology Ctr., U. Tex., Dallas, 1988—; Sheryle Simmons Patigian Disting. chair in cancer immunobiology Southwestern Med. Sch., U. Tex., Dallas, 1989—; bd. sci. coun. NCI Cancer Treatment Bd., 1993; sci. adv. bd. Howard Hughes Med. Inst., 1992—; Kettering selection com. GM Cancer Rsch. Foun., 1987-88; task force NIAID in Immunology, 1989-90; mem. sci. bd. Ludwig Inst., 1983—. Mem. editl. bd.: Advances in Host Defense Mechanisms, 1983—, Annual Review of Immunology, 1991—, Bioconjugate Chemistry, 1989-93, Cellular Immunology, 1984-93, Current Opinions in Immunology, 1992—, FASEB Journal, 1987—, Internat. Jour. of Oncology, 1992—, Internat. Soc. Immunopharmacology, 1989—, Jour. of Immunology, 1975-78, Molecular Immunology, 1978-93; assoc. editor Cancer Research, 1986—; Immunochemistry sect. editor: Jour. of Immunology, 1978-82; co-editor in chief: Therapeutic Immunology, 1992—. Recipient Women's Excellence in Sci. award Fedn. Am. Soc. Exptl. Biology, 1991, Taittinger Breast Cancer Rsch. award Komen Found., 1983, Pierce Immunotoxin award, 1988, NIH Merit award, 1987—, U. Tex. Southwestern Med. Sch. Faculty Teaching awards 1989, 91, 92, 93, 94, FASED Excellence in Sci. award, 1991, Abbot Clinical Immunology award Am. Soc. Microbiologists, 1992, Past State Pres. award Tex. Fed. Bus. Profl. Women's Club, 1993. Richard and Hinda Rosenthal Found. award Am. Assn. Cancer Rsch 1995. Mem. Am. Assn. Immunologists (pres. 1993—), Nat. Acad. Scis. (Rosenthal award AACR 1995). Office: Univ of Texas Southwestern Medical Ctr Cancer Ctr 6000 Harry Hines Blvd Dallas TX 75235-5303

VITILLO, LISA ANNE, writer, researcher; b. Albany, N.Y., Apr. 9, 1970; d. Raphael Anthony and Marie Frances (Stagnitta) V. BS in Fine Art, Coll. of St. Rose, 1992; MA in English, SUNY, Albany, 1995. student youth mentor Albany/Colonie Regional C. of C. and Albany Sch. Humanities, 1995. Prodr., dir. video documentary N.Y.S. Capitol-West Lintel Crack, 1995; author, performer play: Quicksand, 1995; contbr. novel to The Little Mag. CD ROM. Mem. youth edn. adv. team St. Thomas Ch., Delmar, N.Y., 1995—, weekday and Sunday lector, 1995—; vol. March of Dimes, Albany, 1996, Multiple Sclerosis Soc., Albany, 1986-93. All Am. scholar, 1988-92. Mem. Delta Epsilon Sigma (exec. com., hospitality dir. 1995-96), Sigma Tau Delta. Republican. Roman Catholic.

VITOROVIC, NADEZDA, artist, poet; b. Priboj na Limu, Serbia, Yugoslavia, Oct. 18, 1935; Came to the U.S., 1980; d. Mile and Mileva (Urosevic) V.; m. Nathan Silberberg, Mar. 12, 1986. Degree Arts Acad., Belgrade U., Yugoslavia, 1963. Solo exhbns. include Mus. Collection of Rovinj, Croacia, 1965-90, Haus der Heimat, Iserlohn, Germany, 1966, Gallery of the Haus of Youth, Belgrade, 1969, DKVM-Gallery, Belgrade, 1970, DKRC, Novi Sad, 1971, Gallery of the Graphical Collective, 1972, Contemporary Gallery of the Ecka, Zrenjanin, Yugoslavia, 1974, Gallery DJNA, Beograd, Yugoslavia, 1975, Small Hall of the Cultural Ctr., Novi Sad, 1976, Gallery of the Cultural Ctr. of Belgrade, 1978, The BAAK Gallery, Boston, 1980, Cultural Informative Ctr. of Yugoslavia, N.Y.C., 1981, Guild Gallery, N.Y.C., 1982, Nathan Silberberg Gallery, N.Y.C., 1983, 85, 88, 89, Miromesnil Fine Art Gallery, Paris, 1990, Mus. Collection, Rovinj, Croatia, 1990, Galerie A & L Fine Art, Monchengladbach, Germany, 1991, SKC-Srecna Galerija, Beograd, 1995; collective exhbns. include The Artist Collony, Rovinj, 1965-90, ULUS exhibicione, Belgrado, 1967-95, October Salon, Belgrado, 1972-91, Ecka XVIII Exhibicione, Zrenjanin, 1973, Yugoslavia, Artehpo, N.Y., 1981, 82; author: The Creation of a Painting, Poetics, 1981, Another Stratum on the Painting in my Fine Art Creation and Meditation, 1995, (collection of poems) Discovery, 1989, The New World, Hunting, 1994. Home: 301 E 63d St New York NY 10021

VITTADINI, ADRIENNE, fashion designer; b. Gyor, Hungary; came to U.S., 1957; d. Alexander and Aranka (Langhiel) Toth; m. Gian Luigi Maria Vittadini, 1972; 1 stepchild, Emanuele. Ed., Moore Coll. Art, Phila. Designer Rosanna-Warneco, N.Y.C., 1970-76; v.p. for design Kimberly Knitwear-Gen. Mills, N.Y.C., 1976-78; chmn. bd. Adrienne Vittadini Inc., N.Y.C., 1979—. Recipient Design award Retail Fashion Authorities Am., 1979, Outstanding Phila. Fashion Designer award Council for Labor and Industry, Phila., 1984, Coty Am. Fashion Critics award, 1984. Office: Adrienne Vittadini Inc 575 7th Ave Fl 29 New York NY 10018-1805

VITTETOE, MARIE CLARE, retired medical technology educator; b. Keota, Iowa, May 19, 1927; d. Edward Daniel and Marcella Matilda Vittetoe. BS, Marycrest Coll., 1950; MS, W.Va. U., 1971, EdD, 1973. Staff technician St. Joseph Hosp., Ottumwa, Iowa, 1950-70; instr. Ottumwa Hosp. Sch. Med. Tech., 1957-70, St. Joseph Hosp. Sch. Nursing, Ottumwa, 1950-70; asst. prof. U. Ill., Champaign-Urbana, 1973-78; prof. clin. lab. scis. U. Ky., Lexington, 1978-94. Contbr. articles to profl. jours. Recipient Kingston award for Creative Teaching; Recognition award for svc. to edn. Commonwealth of Ky. Coun. on Higher Edn.; named Ky. Col. Mem. Am. Soc. for Med. Tech. (chmn. 1986-89, Profl. Achievement award 1991, Ky. Mem. of Yr. award 1994), Am. Soc. Clin. Lab. Scis., Am. Soc. Clin. Pathologists (assoc.), Alpha Mu Tau, Phi Delta Kappa, Alpha Eta.

VITUNAC, ANN E., judge; b. 1949. BS, Univ. of Fla., 1970; JD, Stetson Coll. of Law, 1972. Chief trial atty. Fla. State Attorney's Office, West Palm Beach, 1973-85; magistrate judge U.S. Dist. Ct. (Fla. so. dist.), 11th circuit, West Palm Beach, 1985—. Recipient Moot Court award Stetson Coll. of Law, 1972, Robert Sykes award Stetson Coll. of Law, 1973. Mem. Phi Delta Phi Legal Frat., Palm Beach County Bar Assn. Office: US Courthouse 701 Clematis St Rm 423 West Palm Beach FL 33401-5112

VIVIAN, LINDA BRADT, sales and public relations executive; b. Elmira, N.Y., Nov. 22, 1945; d. Lorenz Claude and Muriel (Dolan) Bradt; m. Robert W. Vivian, Apr. 5, 1968 (div. Sept. 1977). Student, Andrews U., 1963-66. Adminstrv. asst. Star-Gazette, Elmira, 1966-68; editor Guide, staff writer Palm Springs (Calif.) Life mag., 1970-75; dir. sales and pub. rels. Palm Springs Aerial Tramway, 1975—; sec. Hospitality and Bus. Industry Coun. Palm Springs Desert Resorts, 1989-91, vice-chmn. 1991-94, chmn., 1994-95. Mem. Hotel Sales and Mktg. Assn. (allied nominating chmn. Palm Springs chpt. 1986-88), Am. Soc. Assn. Execs., Travel Industry Assn., Hospitality Industry and Bus. Coun. of Palm Springs Resorts (sec. 1989-91, vice-chmn. 1991-94, chmn. 1994-95), Nat. Tour Assn. (co-chair Team Calif. promotions com. 1993—), Calif. Travel Industry Assn., Palm Springs C. of C. (bd. dirs. 1984-85). Republican. Office: Palm Springs Aerial Tramway One Tramway Rd Palm Springs CA 92262

VIZYAK, LINDY L., elementary education educator; b. Pueblo, Colo., May 19, 1949; d. Charles Eugene and Edna Leatha (Pennington) Berry; m. Joe A. Vizyak, Dec. 20, 1969; 1 child, Sean Joseph. BS, U. So. Colo., 1971. Tchr. first grade Adam County Five Star Schs., Northglenn, Colo., 1978—; freelance cons. Westminster, Colo., 1994. Author: Student Portfolios: A Practical Guide to Evaluation K-6, 1993, Student Portfolios: A Practical Guide to Evaluation, 1995; contbr. articles to profl. jours. Mem. NEA, Colo. Edn. Assn., Colo. Coun. Tchrs. Math. (Math Tchr. of Yr. 1991), Colo. Coun. Internat. Reading Assn., Internat. Reading Assn., Univ. So. Colo. Alumni Assn., Dist. Twelve Educators Assn., Phi Delta Kappa. Democrat. Home: 4591 W 110th Cir Westminster CO 80030-2020 Office: Cotton Creek Elem 11100 Vrain St Westminster CO 80030-2042

VOCE, JOAN A. CIFONELLI, elementary school educator; b. Utica, N.Y., Mar. 22, 1936; d. Albert and Theresa (Buono) Cifonelli; m. Eugene R. Voce Sr., Aug. 16, 1958; children: Eugene R. Jr., Lisa Voce Stewart, Mark L., Daniel A. BS in Elem. Edn., Coll. St. Rose, Albany, N.Y., 1958; MS in Elem. Edn., SUNY, Cortland, 1981. 1st grade tchr. Utica (N.Y.) Pub. Schs., 1958-59, 61-62, 1964-67; tchr. 1st and 2nd grades Deerfield Elem. Sch., Utica, 1968-91. Active YWCA. Mem. AAUW (Mohawk valley br.), N.Y. State United Tchrs., Whitesboro Tchrs. Assn., Am. Italian Heritage Assn., Am. Assn. Ret. Persons, Utica Area Ret. Tchrs. Assn. (sec.), N.Y. State Ret. Tchrs. Assn., Coll. St. Rose Alumni Assn., Skenandoa Golf and Country Club, Alpha Delta Kappa (v.p. 1974-76, pres. 1976-78, corr. sec. 1972-74, rec. sec. 1986-88, 90-91), Ladies of St. Anne, St. Anne's Ch., Whitesboro, N.Y., Utica Symphony League, Mohawk Valley Performing Arts, Inc. Home: 18 Calais Dr Whitesboro NY 13492-2527

VOGAN, LINDA LOU, elementary school educator, coach; b. Meadville, Pa., Apr. 17, 1953; d. Hubert Elsworth and Shirley Julieann (Knierman) V. BS in Recreation and Sociology, Asbury Coll., 1976; cert. in tchg., Glassboro State Coll., 1985; MA, Rowan Coll. N.J., 1995. Cert. K-12, health and phys. edn. tchr., N.J. Juvenile probation officer Crawford County Juvenile Police Office, Meadville, Pa., 1976-81; health and phys. edn. tchr., track coach Bethel Christian Sch., Port Republic, N.J., 1981—, girls basketball coach, 1983—. Mem. prevention and treatment com., ct. rep. Crawford County Drug and Alcohol Assn., Meadville, 1978-81; Sunday sch. tchr. Weekstown (N.J.) Ch. Recipient scholarship Charlotte W. Newcombe Found., 1994. Mem. AAHPERD, Pa. Assn. Probation, Parole and Corrections, Nat. Assn. for Girls and Women in Sports. Republican. Home: 5627 Pleasant Mills Rd Egg Harbor City NJ 08215-4609 Office: Bethel Christian Sch PO Box 196 Geona Ave Port Republic NJ 08241

VOGEL, ANITA STEIBER, human resources specialist, educator; b. Bridgeport, Conn., Aug. 23, 1918; d. Theodore Emil and Mariadina (Cohen) Steiber; m. Rudolf Vogel, Dec. 21, 1940 (dec. June 1976); children: Margaret Vogel Sheldon, Juliet Marcia Vogel; m. Richard Alan Sklarsky, July 3, 1982. BA, Smith Coll., Northampton, Mass., 1939. Asst. editor Consumer Reports, N.Y.C., 1942; youth employment cons. Nat. Com. on Employment of Youth, N.Y.C., 1961-62; assoc. dir. youth devel. Cmty. Progress, Inc., New Haven, Conn., 1962-64; dir. dept. adult employment Mobilization for Youth, N.Y.C., 1964-70; project dir. Models for Upward Mobility of Human Svc. Paraprofessionals Nat. Com. on Employment of Youth, N.Y.C., 1970-72; assoc. prof. Human Svcs. Divsn. Fiorello H. LaGuardia Cmty. Coll., L.I., 1972-76; pres., CEO Vogel Sales Corp., Bridgeport, Conn., 1976-80; dir. Dept. Human Resources Devel. City of Bridgeport, Conn., 1981-82; vis. lectr., curriculum cons., Sch. Social Work U. Buffalo, N.Y., 1983-84; youth employment cons. Corp. for Public and Pvt. Ventures, Phila., 1978, Work in America Inst., Scarsdale, N.Y., 1979; work edn. cons. Youthwork, Inc., Washington D.C., 1981; mem. adv. bd. dirs. Bridgeport (Conn.) Public Edn. Fund, 1988—. pres. Citizens' Com. for the Study of Bridgeport Public Schs., 1949-54; commr. Bd. Edn., Bridgeport, 1954-72; sec. Conn. Assn. Bds. of Edn., Hartford, 1958; chair Bridgeport Conf. on Sch. Drop-Outs, 1961-67; mem. Commn. on Cmty. Rels. Jewish Ctr. for Cmty. Svcs., Bridgeport, 1991—; co-chair Cmty. Closet, Bridgeport, 1991—; mem. bd. dirs. Sch. Vol. Assn., Bridgeport, 1990—, chair recruitment, 1992-95; vol. tutor Bridgeport Pub. Schs., 1990—. Recipient Hannah G. Soloman award Bridgeport chpt. Nat. Coun. of Jewish Women, 1966, Vol. of the Yr. award Bridgeport chpt. Jewish Ctr. for Cmty. Svc., 1996. Mem. AAUW (chair book club 1995—). Jewish.

VOGEL, ELVIRA MYRTLE, volunteer; b. George, Iowa, Jan. 9, 1922; d. Chris Henry E. and Ella Marie (Dammann) Locker; m. Louis Dwayne Vogel, Apr. 2, 1949; children: Virginia Louise, Valorie Lee, Sue Ellyn. BA, Iowa State Tchrs. Coll., 1942; Cert. Mgmt. Tng., Harvard/Radcliffe U., 1943. Job analyst, supr. merit review programs Marshal Field & Co., Chgo., 1944-49; vol. Red Cross, United Way, sch., County Commn. Coll. Advs., 1974-96; substitute tchr. Manchester (Mich.) Pub. Schs., 1962-72; mem., trustee Bd. Edn. Washtenaw Intermediate Sch. Dist., Ann Arbor, Mich., 1958-89. Moderator Mich. Conf. United Ch. of Christ, Lansing, 1979; bd. dirs. Spaulding for Children, Chelsea, Mich., 1976-79; pres. Mich Coun. Chs., Lansing, 1979; v.p.Washtenaw County Dist. Extension, 1994-96. Recipient Cert. of Svc. Manchester Cmty. Fair Bd., 1977, Coll. Svc. award Washtenaw C.C., Ann Arbor, Mich., 1984, Svc. award Mich. Assn. Sch. Bds., Lansing, 1983, award of Merit, Washtenaw C.C., 1996; named A Valiant Woman, 1985. Mem. AAUW, Covenant Assn. (Mich. Conf. at large 1992-94), Assn. Women's Fellowship (Woman of Yr. 1984, chair spiritual life 1994-95), Ch. Women United. Republican. Mem. United Ch. of Christ. Home: 11437 Pleasant Lake Rd Manchester MI 48158

VOGEL, H. VICTORIA, psychotherapist, educator. BA, U. Md., 1968; MA, NYU, 1970, 1975; MEd, Columbia U., 1982, postgrad., 1982—; cert., Am. Projective Drawing Inst., 1983. Art Therapist Childville, Bklyn., 1962-64; tchr., Montgomery County (Md.) Jr. H.S., 1968-69; with H.S. div. N.Y.C. Bd. Edn., 1970—, guidance counselor, instructor, psychotherapist in pvt. practice; clinical counseling cons. psychodiagnosis and devel. studies, art/play therapy, The Modern School, 1984—; art/play therapist Hosp. Ctr. for Neuromuscular Disease and Devel. Disorders, 1987—; employment counselor-adminstr. N.Y. State Dept. Labor Concentrated Employment Program, 1971-72; intern psychotherapy and psychoanalysis psychiat. divsn. Cen. Islip Hosp., 1973-75; with Calif. Grad. Inst., L.A.; Columbia U. Tchrs. Coll., N.Y. intern psychol. counseling and rehab. N.J. Coll. Medicine, Newark, 1979. Mem. com. for spl. events NYU, 1989; participant clin. and artistic perspectives Am. Acad. Psychoanalysis Conf., 1990, participant clin. postmodernism and psychoanalysis, 1996; auxilary police officer N.Y. Police Dept. Precinct 19, N.Y.C., 1994—; chair bylaws com. Columbia U., 1995—. Mem. APA, AAAS, Am. Psychol. Soc., Am. Orthopsychiat. Assn., Am. Soc. Group Psychotherapy & Psychodrama (publs. com. 1984—), Am. Counseling Assn., Am. Acad. Experts Traumatic Stress, N.Y.C. Art Tchrs. Assn., Art/Play Therapy, Assn. Humanistic Psychology (exec. sec. 1981), Tchrs. Coll. Adminstrv. Women in Edn., Phi Delta Kappa (editor chpt. newsletter 1981-84, exec. sec. Columbia U. chpt. 1984—, chmn. nominating com. for chpt. officers 1986—, nominating com. 1991, pub. rels. exec. bd. dirs. 1991, rsch. rep. 1986—), Phi Delta Kappa (v.p. programs NYU chpt. 1994—). Author: The Never Ending Story of Alcohol, Drugs and Other Substance Abuse, 1992, Variant Sexual Behavior and the Aesthetic Modern Nudes, 1992, Psychological Science of School Behavior Intervention, 1993, Joycean Conceptual Modernism: Relationships and Deviant Sexuality, 1995, Electronic Evil Eyes, 1995.

VOGEL, MALVINA GRAFF, video and infosystems specialist; b. N.Y.C., May 5, 1932; d. Daniel Louis and Rose Miriam (Kanarick) Graff; m. Seymour Vogel, Jan. 27, 1952 (div.); children: Howard Ferris, Hal Steven, Scott Leslie, David Michael, Lisa Gayle. AB, Hunter Coll., 1952, postgrad., 1953. Cert. tchr., N.Y., N.J. Tchr. Norwood (N.J.) Pub. Schs., 1952-53, Farmingdale (N.Y.) Pub. Schs., 1953-55; researcher, writer Sy Vogel Realty, Commack, N.Y., 1965-67; writer-editor E.D.L.-McGraw Hill, N.Y.C., 1967-73; writer ednl. programs Ednl. Concepts, Inc., Babylon, N.Y., 1973-75, Instructional Concepts, Inc., New Hyde Park, N.Y., 1973-75; editor-in-chief Waldman-Playmore Pub. Co., N.Y.C., 1976-83; v.p. creative services Kid Stuff/GameTek, Inc., North Miami Beach, Fla., 1983-90; owner, pres. MVP Writing/Editing Prodns., Sunrise, Fla., 1990-94; v.p. creative svcs. Herbko Internat., Hallandale, Fla., 1995—. Author short stories, reading and social studies programs; adaptor lit. classics for children; editor over 200 books for children and adults, over 50 computer software and video cartridge programs for preschoolers, children, teens and adults, over 600 crossword puzzles. Pres. Old Bethpage Elem. Sch. PTA, 1967-71; founder, pres. women's aux. Plainview, N.Y. Little League, 1968; scholarship chair Plainview-Old Bethpage Scholarship Fund, 1972-73. Scholarship for children's writing, Hofstra U., 1975. Mem. Nat. Assn. Female Execs., Soc. Children's Book Writers, Women in Communications, Soc. Preservation of English Lang. and Lit. Home: 9225 NW 45th St Fort Lauderdale FL 33351-5247

VOGEL, MARY ELLEN VIRGINIA, psychologist, learning consultant; b. Rochester, N.Y., May 19, 1938; d. Richard D. and Grace Margaret (Taylert) Krasucki; m. Emil Thomas Vogel Sr., Nov. 19, 1960; children: Pamela Ann, Emil Thomas Jr., Tobias Alan. BS, SUNY, Plattsburgh, 1959; MA, Fairleigh Dickinson U., N.J., 1983; PhD, Fordham U., N.Y., 1991. Cert. learning disabilities tchr. cons., sch. psychologist, psychologist, N.J. Tchr. Irondequoit N.Y. Bd. of Edn., Rochester, 1959-61, Rochester Bd. Edn., 1962-63; tchr., counselor, psychologist Ramsey (N.J.) Bd. Edn., 1972—. Mem., chair Jr. Women's Club, Ramsey, Parish Coun. St. Paul's Ch.; den leader Boy Scouts of Am., leader Girl Scouts of Am. Named Tchr. of the Yr. Gov. Thomas Kean (N.J.), 1987. Mem. APA, AAUW, Nat. Assn. Sch. Psychologists, Kappa Delta Pi, Phi Delta Kappa, Psi Chi Nat. Honor Soc. Home: 105 Deer Trl Ramsey NJ 07446

VOGEL, SARAH, state agency administrator, lawyer; b. Bismarck, N.D., May 3, 1946; d. Robert and Elsa Marie (Mork) V.; 1 child, Andrew. BA, U. N.D., 1967; JD, NYU, 1970. Bar: N.Y. 1970, N.D. 1982. Commr. N.D. Agrl. Dept., Bismarck, N.D. Office: ND Agrl Dept 600 E Boulevard Ave Bismarck ND 58505-0020

VOGEL, SUSAN CAROL, nursing administrator; b. Hartford, Conn., Oct. 9, 1948; d. Morton B. and Esther (Riback) Worshoufsky. Diploma in nursing, Grace Hosp., New Haven, 1969; B in Healthcare Mgmt., U. La Verne, 1991, M in Health Adminstrn., 1994. RN, Calif.; cert. nephrology nurse, Nephrology Nurse Cert. Bd. Oper. rm. nurse New Britain (Conn.) Gen. Hosp., 1970-72; staff nurse oper. rm. Parkview Cmty. Hosp., Riverside, Calif., 1972-74; staff nurse dialysis, IV team Cedars-Sinai Med. Ctr., L.A., 1974-82; clin. nurse III dialysis UCLA, 1982-88; nurse mgr. inpatient dialysis UCLA Med. Ctr., 1988-93; adminstr. South Valley Regional Dialysis Ctr., Encino, Calif., 1993—; pres. Renal Replacement Therapies, Inc. Author: (with others) Review of Hemodialysis for Nurses and Dialysis Personnel, 1993, Vascular Access, Principles & Practices, 3rd edit., 1996. Mem. NAFE, Am. Orgn. Nurse Execs., Am. Nephrology Nurses Assn. (pres. L.A. chpt. 1990-92, nat. chairperson hemodialysis spl. interest group 1993-95), Nat. Kidney Found. Office: South Valley Regional Dialysis Ctr 17815 Ventura Blvd Ste 100 Encino CA 91316-3612

VOGELGESANG, SANDRA LOUISE, federal government official; b. Canton, Ohio, July 27, 1942; d. Glenn Wesley and Louise (Forry) Vogelgesang; m. Geoffrey Ernest Wolfe, July 4, 1982. BA, Cornell U., 1964; MA, Tufts U., 1965, MA in Law and Diplomacy, 1966, PhD, 1971. With Dept. State, Washington, 1975—, policy planner for sec. state and European Bur., 1975-80, dir. Econ Analysis Office, Orgn. Econ. Coop. and Devel., 1981-82, econ. minister U.S. Embassy, Ottawa, Can., 1982-86, dep. asst. sec. Internat. Orgn. Affairs Bur., 1986-89; dep. asst. adminstr. Office Internat. Activities Environ. Protection Agy., Washington, 1989-92; with Dept. State, Washington, 1992; sr. policy advisor Agy. for Internat. Devel., 1993; U.S. amb. to Nepal Dept. State, Washington, 1994—; bd. dirs. Edward R. Murrow Ctr. for Pub. Diplomacy, Fletcher Sch., Medford, Mass., 1978-81; bd. advisors Am.'s Soc., N.Y.C., 1986-89. Author: Long Dark Night of the Soul, The American Intellectual Left and the Vietnam War, 1974, American Dream-Global Nightmare: The Dilemma of U.S. Human Rights Policy, 1980. Recipient Meritorious Service awards, 1973, 74, 82, 83, 86, Disting. Honor award, 1976 Dept. State, Pres.' Disting. Service award, 1985. Mem. Council on Fgn. Relations. Office: US Embassy Kathmandu Dept of State Washington DC 20521-6190

VOGELZANG, JEANNE MARIE, professional association executive, attorney; b. Hammond, Ind., Apr. 15, 1950; d. Richard and Laura Ann (Vanderaa) Jabaay; m. Nicholas John Vogelzang, May 17, 1971; children: Nick, Adam, Tim. BA, Trinity Christian Coll., Palos Heights, Ill., 1972; MBA, U. Minn., 1981; JD, U. Chgo., 1987. Bar: Ill. 1987; CPA, Ill. Tchr. Timothy Christian H.S., Elmhurst, Ill., 1972-74; tchg. assoc. in fin. U. Minn., Mpls., 1980-81; fin. analyst Quaker Oats Co., Chgo., 1982-84; atty. Baker & McKenzie, Chgo., 1987-89, Jenner & Block, Chgo., 1989-91; pres., owner J.M. Vogelzang & Assocs., Western Springs, Ill., 1991—; exec. dir. Structural Engrs. Assn. Ill., Chgo., 1992—, Nat. Coun. of Structural Engrs. Assn., Chgo., 1996—. Mem. jud. code com. Christian Reformed Ch. N.Am., Grand Rapids, Mich., 1991—; bd. dirs. Austin Christian Law Ctr., Chgo., 1989-92, Barnabas Found., Palos Heights, 1989—; com. mem. Western Springs Planning Commn., 1991-95, village trustee, 1995—, chmn. fin. com.; mem. adv. bd. CDL DuPage Internat. Trade Ctr., Glen Ellyn, Ill., 1992-94; bd. dirs., mem. acad. affairs com., planning com., exec. com. sec. Trinity Christian Coll., 1992—. Mem. ABA, Am. Soc. Assn. Execs., Ill. State Bar Assn., Chgo. Bar Assn. Mem. Christian Reformed Ch. Home: 5108 Fair Elms Ave Western Springs IL 60558-1808 Office: 203 N Wabash Ave Ste 1000 Chicago IL 60601-2412

VOGET, JANE J., city official, lawyer; b. Montréal, Que., Can., Jan. 2, 1949; d. Frederick Wilhelm and Mary Kay (Mee) V.; m. Frederick Walton

Hyde, Oct. 9, 1988. BA in German and Anthropology, So. Ill. U., 1971, MS in Planning and Cmty. Devel., 1977; JD, Lewis and Clark Coll., 1990. Bar: Wash. 1991. Program mgr. Ill. Dept. Local Govt. Affairs, Springfield, 1975-78, U.S. Dept. Housing and Urban Devel., Washington, 1978; mem. staff The White House, Office Asst. to Pres. for Intergovtl. Affairs, Washington, 1979-80; exec. dir. Ctr. for Collaborative Problem Solving, San Francisco, 1981-83; hotel asst. mgr. Hyatt Regency Waikiki, Honolulu, 1983-85; housing project mgr. Multnomah County, Portland, Oreg., 1985-88; sr. project mgr. City of Seattle, 1989—; pvt. practice, Seattle, 1991—. Co-author govtl. publs. Mem. admissions com. United Way Bay Area, 1983; vol. lawyer West Seattle Legal Clinic, 1994-95; active Halau Hula 'O Napualani, Seattle, 1995. Mem. ABA (mem. affordable housing fin. com. 1991-96, forum housing & cmty. devel. law, probate and real property sect., state and local govt. sect.), Wash. State Bar Assn., King County Bar Assn. (mem. legis. com., govt. ops. subcom. 1995). Avocations: swimming, Hawaiian music and dance, animal rights advocate. Home: 5946 39th Ave SW Seattle WA 98136 Office: City of Seattle 618 Second Ave Seattle WA 98104

VOGRIN, LISA MARIETTE, elementary education educator; b. Hinsdale, Ill., Dec. 29, 1968; d. George Bernard and JoAnn (Jata) V. BS in Elem. Edn., East Tex. State U., Commerce, 1990, MEd in Reading, 1995. Cert. in elem. edn., Tex. Tchr. 4th grade St. Luke Cath. Sch., Irving, Tex., 1991-95; tchr. 8th grade reading, dept. reading chairperson Permenter Mid. Sch., Cedar Hill, Tex., 1995—. Mem. ASCD, Tex. Mid. Sch. Assn., Kappa Delta Pi (mem. campus decision making com. 1995—). Roman Catholic. Office: Permenter Mid Sch 421 W Parkerville Rd Cedar Hill TX 75104

VOGT-DOWNEY, MARILYN JUNE, secondary education educator, Sovietologist; b. Fairbury, Ill., June 29, 1943; d. Horace William and Viola Gertrude (Munz) Goembel; m. William Paul Vogt, Dec. 1963 (div. 1972); 1 child, Erika Lynn; m. John Nicholas Downey, Mar. 11, 1983. BA in Russian Lang., Ill. State Normal U., 1966; MA in L.Am. Studies, Ind. U., 1971. Translator of Russian, Pathfinder Press, N.Y.C., 1972-74; adminstrv. sec. Robin A. Wilson, N.Y.C., 1975-80; pipefitter 2d class Coastal Drydock & Repair Corp., Bklyn., 1980-81; mem. tech. staff Internat. Viewpoint, Paris, 1982; sec. Merrill Lynch Capital Markets, N.Y.C., 1982-85, Olympia & York Battery Park Co., N.Y.C., 1985-86; tchr. social studies City-As-Sch. H.S., N.Y.C., 1986—. Author, editor: The USSR 1987-1991: Marxist Perspectives, 1993; translator: Notebooks for the Grandchildren, 1995; contbr. translator: Leon Trotsky Writings, 1929-40, 1972-80; editl. com., journalist Bull. in Def. of Marxism, 1986-96. Coord. Moscow Trials Campaign Com., N.Y.C., 1988-90, U.S.-Soviet Workers Info. Com., N.Y.C., 1990-93; mem. coordinating com. U.S. Com. for Dem. Human Rights in Russia, N.Y.C., 1991-93; mem. Internat. Coord. Com. for Study of Leon Trotsky's Legacy, Russia and N.Y., 1994—. Mem. United Fedn. Tchrs. (chpt. exec. com. 1995—).

VOIGHT, MARGARET SCHNEIDER, retired newspaper editor; b. N.Y.C., Apr. 10, 1928; d. Harold D. Schneider and Margaret Grant; m. Leonard Mark Voight, May 10, 1953 (dec. June 1989); children: Paul R., Mark G. BA, Barnard Coll., 1949. Pub. rels. writer various not-for-profit assns., N.Y.C., 1949-53; women's editor Caracas Daily Jour., Venezuela, 1958-59; reporter, editor White Plains (N.Y.) Reporter Dispatch, 1964-73; news editor Mt. Vernon (N.Y.) Daily Argus, 1973-78; mng. editor Bronxville (N.Y.) Review Press-Reporter, 1978-90; adj. prof. journalism Pace U., White Plains, 1975-80. Trustee, sec. Boothbay Region Hist. Soc., 1993—; trustee, newsletter editor Boothbay Region Land Trust, 1994—. Mem. Maine Media Women, Maine Writers Alliance, Boothbay Region Writers Group. Home: Murray Hill Rd PO Box 391 East Boothbay ME 04544

VOIGT, CYNTHIA, author; b. Boston, Feb. 25, 1942; d. Frederick C. and Elise (Keeney) Irving; married, 1964 (div. 1972); m. Walter Voigt, Aug. 30, 1974; children: Jessica, Peter. BA, Smith Coll., 1963. High sch. tchr. English Glen Burnie, Md., 1965-67; tchr. English Key Sch., Annapolis, Md., 1968-69, dept. chmn., 1971-79, tchr., dept. chmn., 1981-88. Author: Homecoming, 1981, Tell Me If the Lovers Are Losers, 1982, Dicey's Song, 1982 (John Newbery medal 1983), The Callender Papers, 1983 (Edgar award 1984), A Solitary Blue, 1983, Building Blocks, 1984, Jackeroo, 1985, The Runner, 1985 (Silver Pencil award 1988, Deutscher Jugend Literator Preis 1989, ALAN award 1989), Come a Stranger, 1986, Izzy, Willy Nilly, 1986 (Calif. Young Reader's award 1990), Stories About Rosie, 1986, Sons From Afar, 1987, Tree by Leaf, 1988, Seventeen Against the Dealer, 1989, On Fortune's Wheel, 1990, The Vandemark Mummy, 1991, Orfe, 1992, Glass Mountain, 1991, David and Jonathan, 1992, The Wings of a Falcon, 1993, When She Hollers, 1994. *

VOLID, RUTH, art gallery owner; b. Chgo.; d. Ben and Ida (Saykowitch) Volid; ed. Art Inst. Chgo., U. Chgo., Chouinard Art Sch., Otis Art Inst., Am. Acad. Art; 2 daus. Art tchr., Chgo., 1950-52; owner, designer Fashion Hat Bus., 1945-47; interior designer, graphic designer, copy chief Meyer Both Co., 1939-45; owner, designer Dude Ranch, 1947-50; creative dir. King Korn Stamp Co., Chgo., 1962-70; public relations staff Merchandising Group, N.Y.C., 1970-72; owner Ruth Volid Gallery, Ltd., Chgo., 1970-91; art cons. major collections, 1991—; judge art shows; speaker in field. Mem. U.S. affiliated bd. Mus. Contemporary Art, 1976; mem. exec. bd. Sinfonia Orch. Chgo. Mem. Archives Am. Art, Am. Soc. Interior Designers Industry Found. Bd., Soc. Archtl. Historians, North Shore Art League, Arts Club Chgo. Club: President's. Author: The Designer; Investor Collector; Executive 40; contbr. Crain's Chgo. Bus., Great Poems of the Western World, vol. II.

VOLK, KRISTIN, advertising agency executive; b. Phila., Feb. 26, 1953; d. Richard H. and Doris (Colasanti) V. BS in Biology, Tufts U., 1976; MPH, Boston U. Sch. Med., 1981. Rsch. technician Beth Israel Hosp., Boston, 1976; rsch. asst. Dana-Farber Cancer Inst., Boston, 1976-78; sr. rsch. asst. Beth Israel Hosp., Boston, 1978-81; rsch. supr. Schneider Parker Jakuc Advt., Boston, 1981-86; v.p., assoc. rsch. dir. HBM/Creamer, Boston, 1986-88, Della Femina McNamee, Boston, 1988-90; v.p., dir. rsch. Lawner Reingold Britton & Ptnrs., Boston, 1990-93; sr. v.p., dir. consumer insight group Arnold Fortuna Lawner & Cabot, Boston, 1993-95; exec. v.p., dir. consumer insight group Arnold Comm., Inc., Boston, 1995—; guest lectr. colls. and univs., Boston. Contbr. articles to profl. jours. Mem. Ad Club Boston. Office: Arnold Comm Inc 101 Arch St Boston MA 02110

VOLK, THERESA JEAN, accountant; b. Quincy, Ill., Nov. 6, 1973; d. Ronald Lee and Mechtild Maria (Karg) Kosin; m. Steven Henry Volk, Sept. 16, 1995. BS in Acctg. with honors, Quincy U., 1994. CPA, Ill. Staff acct. Moorman Mfg. Co., Quincy, 1993-95; payroll acct. J. McDaniel, Inc., Newton, Ill., 1995—. Mem. Am. Bus. Women's Assn. Home: 2682 N 500th St Newton IL 62448 Office: J McDaniel Inc PO Box 126 Newton IL 62448

VOLKMANN, FRANCES COOPER, psychologist, educator; b. Harlingen, Tex., May 4, 1935; d. Edward O. and Elizabeth (Bass) C.; m. John Volkmann, Nov. 1, 1958 (dec.); children: Stephen Edward, Thomas Frederick. A.B. magna cum laude, Mt. Holyoke Coll., 1957; M.A., Brown U., 1959, Ph.D., 1961; DSci., Mt. Holyoke Coll., 1987. Research assoc. Mt. Holyoke Coll., South Hadley, Mass., 1964-65; lectr. U. Mass., Amherst, 1964-65, Smith Coll., Northampton, Mass., 1966-67; asst. prof. Smith Coll., 1967-72, assoc. prof., 1972-78, prof. psychology, 1978—, dean faculty, 1983-88, Harold E. Israel and Elsa M. Siipola prof. psychology, 1988—, acting pres., 1991; vis. assoc. prof. Brown U., Providence, 1974, vis. prof., 1978-82; vis. scholar U. Wash., Seattle, summer 1977. Contbr. articles to profl. jours. Trustee Chatham Coll., 1987—. USPHS fellow, 1961-62; NSF grantee, 1974-78; Nat. Eye Inst. grantee, 1978-82. Fellow APA, AAAS, Optical Soc. Am.; mem. Ea. Psychol. Assn., Soc. Neurosci. Psychonomic Soc., Assn. Rsch. in Vision and Ophthalmology, New Eng. Assn. Schs. and Colls. (vice chair commn. instns. higher edn. 1991-93, chair 1993-95). Home: 40 Arlington St Northampton MA 01060-2003 Office: Smith Coll Northampton MA 01063

VOLPE, EILEEN RAE, special education educator; b. Fort Morgan, Colo., Aug. 23, 1942; d. Earl Lester and Ellen Ada (Hearting) Moore; m. David P. Volpe, July 28, 1965 (div. 1980); children: David P. Jr., Christina Marie. BA, U. No. Colo., 1964, MA, 1978. Cert. fine art tchr., learning handicapped specialist, resource specialist. 5th grade tchr. Meml. Elem. Sch., Milford, Mass., 1967-68; fine arts jr./sr. high tchr. Nipmuc Regional Jr. Sr. H.S., Mendon, Mass., 1968-69; spl. edn. tchr. Saugus (Calif.) High Sch., 1979—; publicity dir. Sacred Heart Ch. Sch., Milford, Mass., 1974-75, float coord. bicentennial parade, 1975. Author: (poetry) Seasons to Come, 1994. Mem. Calif. Tchr. Assn., Coun. for Exceptional Children, DAR, Phi Delta Kappa, Kappa Delta Pi. Republican. Office: Saugus High Sch 219000 W Centurion Way Santa Clarita CA 91350

VOLPE, ELLEN MARIE, middle school educator; b. Bronx, N.Y., Aug. 2, 1949; d. George Thomas and Mary (Popadinecz) Soloweyko; m. Ronald Edward Volpe, May 22, 1971; children: Keith, Daniel, Christopher, Stephanie. BBA, Pace U., 1971; MA in Teaching, Sacred Heart U., 1986. Tchr. Conn. Bus. Inst., Stratford, 1979-80, Katherine Gibbs Sch., Norwalk, Conn., 1980-89; adj. instr. So. Cen. Community Coll., New Haven, 1986-87, Salt Lake C. C., Phillips Jr. Coll., Salt Lake City, 1992-93; instr. Bryman Sch., Salt Lake City, 1990-92; tchr. Indian Hills Mid. Sch., Sandy, Utah, 1993—; mem. reaccreditation and tech. coms. Indian Hills Mid. Sch.; mem. curriculum rev. com. Katharine Gibbs Sch., 1989-90. Mem. ASCD, NEA, Am. Vocat. Assn., Nat. Bus. Edn. Assn., Western Bus. Edn. Assn. Home: 8390 Sublette Cir Sandy UT 84093-1164

VOLPE, MARIA R., conflict resolution educator; b. Peekskill, N.Y., Aug. 5, 1948; d. Mariano and Osilde (Tangredi) V. BA, SUNY, Plattsburgh, 1970; MA, NYU, 1975, PhD, 1981. Prof. sociology, dir. dispute resolution program John Jay Coll. Criminal Justice, CUNY, N.Y.C., 1981—, convenor dispute resolution consortium, 1992—; bd. editors Jour. of Contemporary Criminal Justice, 1988—; mem. editorial bd. Mediation Quarterly, 1989—; mem. internat. adv. bd. Negotiation Jour., 1995—; adv. com. N.Y. State atty. gen.'s program for young negotiators, 1996—; bd. dirs. N.Y. State forum on conflict and consensus. Co-editor: Conflict Processing, 1992; contbr. articles to profl. jours. Recipient Peacemaker award Increase the Peace Vol. Corps Office of the Mayor, 1993; NIMH fellow NYU, 1970-72, William and Flora Hewlett Found. grantee, 1993-94. Mem. Internat. Soc. of Profls. in Dispute Resolution (pres. 1996—). Office: JJ Coll Criminal Justice CUNY 445 W 59th St New York NY 10019

VOLTZ, JEANNE APPLETON, author b. Collinsville, Ala.; d. James Lamar and Marie (Sewell) Appleton; m. Luther Manship Voltz, July 31, 1943 (dec. Aug. 1977); children: Luther Manship, Jeanne Marie; m. Frank B. MacKnight, Aug. 6, 1988 (div. Sept. 1994). AB, U. Montevallo, Ala., 1942. Corr., The Birmingham (Ala.) News, 1939-42; reporter The Press-Register, Mobile, Ala., 1942-45; reporter, feature writer The Miami Herald, 1947-53, food editor, 1953-60; food editor Los Angeles Times, 1960-73, Woman's Day, N.Y.C., 1973-84; free-lance writer, N.Y.C., 1984-88, Chapel Hill, N.C., 1988—; instr. wine and food in civilization UCLA, 1972-73; expert witness Senate Com. on Nutrition and Health, Ft. Lauderdale, Fla., 1980; adj. prof. Dept. Nutrition Hotel Mgmt. NYU, 1986—, Home Econs. Hotel Mgmt., 1987—; judge Hardee's Willow Creek Rib Cook-Off, Raleigh, N.C., 1993-96; Blue Ridge Barbecue and Rib Festival, Tryon, N.C., 1994-96. Author: The California Cookbook, 1970 (Tastemaker award 1970), The Los Angeles Times Natural Foods Cookbook, 1974, The Flavor of the South, 1976 (Tastemaker award 1976), An Apple A Day, 1983, Barbecued Ribs and Other Great Feeds, 1985 (Tastemaker award 1985), Community Suppers, 1987, Barbecued Ribs, Smoked Butts and Other Great Feeds, 1991; author: (with Burks Hamner) The L.A. Gourmet, 1971, (with Elayne Kleeman) How to Turn a Passion for Food into Profit, 1979, (with Caroline Stuart) The Florida Cookbook, 1993. Mem. N.C. Mus. Art, Raleigh. Recipient Vesta award Am. Meat Inst., 1962-72; Alumna of Yr. award U. Montevallo, 1981. Mem. Les Dames d'Escoffier (dir. 1976, pres. 1985-86, internat. pres. 1986-87), Inst. Food Technologists, Women in Communications, Soc. Women Geographers, Internat. Assn. Culinary Profls., The Authors' Guild N.Y., Am. Inst. Wine and Food (chairperson Piedmont chpt.), Culinary Historians N.Y., Phi Tau Sigma. Democrat. Methodist.

VOLTZ-MILLER, DEBRA, lawyer; b. Decatur, Ind., Oct. 16, 1954; d. Alfred C. Voltz and Linda A. (Burton) Fox; m. Philip Miller, Apr. 1, 1985; children: Kena King, Krishna Lundgard. B of Gen. Studies, Ind. U., South Bend, 1986; JD, Notre Dame U., 1989. Bar: Wash. 1990, Ind. 1990; cert. mediator, Ind. Mgr. Assocs. Corp. N.A., South Bend, 1985-94; lawyer Fred R. Hains & Assocs., South Bend, 1994—. Mem. com. United Way, St. Joseph County, Ind., 1993-95. Mem. Data Processing Mgmt. Assn. (program chair 1995-96). Office: Fred R Hains & Assocs 413 W Jefferson Blvd South Bend IN 46601

VOLZ, ANNABELLE WEKAR, learning disabilities educator, consultant; b. Niagara Falls, N.Y., May 24, 1926; d. Fred Wekar and Margaret Eleanor (McGillivray) Treadwell; m. William Mount Volz, May 9, 1958; children: Amy D., William M. Jr. BA, Seton Hill Coll., 1948; MS in Elem. Edn., N.Y. State Univ. Coll., 1956. Cert. learning disabilities cons. N.J. Lab. technician Moore Bus. Forms Inc., Niagara Falls, 1948-50, Niagara Falls Health Dept., 1950-53; tchr. Niagara Falls Bd. Edn., 1953-56, Am. Dependent Sch., Ashiya, Japan, 1956-58, Mehlville Bd. Edn., St. Louis County, Mo., 1968-70, U.S. Dependent Schs. European Theatre, Weisbaden, Fed. Republic of Germany, 1970-74; para-profl. Medford (N.J.) Bd. Edn., 1978-81; learning disabilities tchr., cons. Southampton Bd. Edn., Vincentown, N.J., 1981-91. Mem. Womens Fin. Info. Program, Burlington County, 1990-91. Mem. NEA, LWV (sec. 1994-96, mem. chair 1996—, voter's guide chair 1996), AAUW (scholar chmn. 1984, publicity chmn. 1991-92, treas. 1994—), Assn. Learning Cons., Seton Hill Alumnae Assn., Kappa Delta Pi. Home: 5080 Mountain View Rd Winston Salem NC 27104-5110

VOLZ, ELIZABETH LANGWORTHY, social worker, educator; b. Cambridge, Mass., Dec. 16, 1967; d. Christofer Volz and Jennifer E. (Langworthy) Hansen; m. Ira Dale Price, June 4, 1991; children: Alexander I. Volz-Price, Wesley D. Volz-Price, Ian I. Volz-Price. BA in Polit. Sci. and Women's Studies, Swarthmore Coll., 1990. Cert. social worker, N.J. Counselor Cherry Hill (N.J.) Women's Ctr., 1987-91, Northeast Women's Ctr., Phila., 1990-91; head counselor, pub. rels. Am. Women's Ctr., Voorhees, N.J., 1992-94; tchr. Glassboro (N.J.) Pub. Schs., 1994—; program coord. Glassboro People in Transition, 1995—; svcs. coord. Glassboro Housing Authority, 1995—. Mem. NOW (v.p. N.J. 1995—). Office: NOW 114 State St Trenton NJ 08608

VON BEHREN, RUTH LECHNER, adult day health care specialist, retired; b. Dubuque, Iowa, Apr. 10, 1933; d. Adolph J. and Elva M. (Federer) Lechner; m. Donald D. Von Behren, Dec. 16, 1952 (div. 1965); children: Debi, Jerry, LuAnn. BS, Ill. State U., 1965, MA, 1968; PhD, U. Calif., Davis, 1972. Tchr. Centennial Sch., El Paso, Ill., 1962-65; grad. asst. Ill. State U., Normal, 1967-68; assoc. in History U. Calif., 1968-71; rsch. asst. Calif. Health and Welfare Agy., Sacramento, 1972-74; asst. prof. Sacramento State U., 1970-71, 78-79; analyst Calif. Dept. Health Svcs., Sacramento, 1974-75, sect. chief adult day health care, 1975-80; project dir. State Health and Welfare Agy., Sacramento, 1980-82; adult day health care specialist On Lok Sr. Health Svcs., San Francisco, 1982-95; ret., 1995; cons. adult day health care various orgns. Author: Adult Day Care in America, 1986, Adult Day Care: A Program for the Functionally Impaired, 1989, (with others) Planning and Managing Adult Day Care, 1989; contbr. articles to profl. jours. Sec. Yolo County Hist. Soc., Woodland, Calif., 1976-80; dir. Yolo County Mus. Assocs., Woodland, 1980-82. Recipient Adult Day Health Care Tech. Assistance award Kaiser Found., 1983-86, Rural Adult Day Care Model award Sierra Found., 1988-89. Mem. Nat. Coun. on Aging, Inc., Nat. Inst. on Adult Day Care (chair 1988-90, Ruth Von Behren award for Outstanding Dedication to Growth and Devel. of Adult Day Care, Nat. Inst. on Adult Day Care, 1992), Phi Alpha Theta, Alpha Phi Gamma, Alpha Psi Omega, Kappa Delta Phi, Phi Kappa Phi. Home: 1813 Chapman Pl Davis CA 95616

VON BERGEN WESSELS, PENNIE LEA, state legislator; b. Sterling, Ill., Mar. 19, 1949; d. Donald LeRoy and Mary Lou (Hammerle) von Bergen; m. Michael J. Wessels, Aug. 23, 1969. AA, Sauk Valley Coll., 1969; BSEd in English and Theater, No. Ill. U., 1971; postgrad., So. Ill. U., 1972-73; JD magna cum laude, U. Ill., 1983. Bar: Ill., 1983; cert. tchr., Ill. English and theater tchr. various schs., Ill., 1971-80; pvt. practice law Morrison, Ill., 1984-85; mem. Whiteside County Bd., Morrison, 1984-88, Ill. Gen. Assembly, Springfield, 1993-95. Bd. dirs. Ill. Citizens Utility Bd., 1989-92, Equip for Equality, 1994—, Ill. Alliance for Arts Edn., 1994—; del. candidate Dem. Nat. Convention, 1980, 92. Named Outstanding Working Woman of Ill. Ill. Bus. and Profl. Women, 1988; recipient Mounders Pride award Mt. Morris Sch. Dist., 1993, Friend of Agr. award Farm Bus. Activator Com., 1994, Outstanding Freshman Legislator award Ill. Edn. Assn., 1994. Unitarian. Home: 1300 Sinnissippi Park Rd Sterling IL 61081-4127

VON BRANDENSTEIN, PATRIZIA, production designer. Prodn. designer films including Girlfriends, 1978, Heartland, 1979, Breaking Away, 1979, Ragtime, 1981 (Academy Award nomination best art direction 1981), Silkwood, 1983, Amadeus, 1984 (Academy Award best art direction 1984), Beat Street, 1984, A Chorus Line, 1985, The Money Pit, 1986, No Mercy, 1987, The Untouchables, 1987 (Academy Award nomination best art direction 1987), Betrayed, 1988, Working Girl, 1988, The Lemon Sisters, 1990, Postcards From the Edge, 1990, State of Grace, 1990, Billy Bathgate, 1992, Sneakers, 1992, Leap of Faith, 1993, Six Degrees of Separation, 1993, The Quick and the Dead, 1995, Just Cause, 1995; costume designer films including Between the Lines, 1977, Saturday Night Fever, 1977, A Little Sex, 1982. Address: 161 W 15th St Apt 7B New York NY 10011-6768 Office: care Lawrence Mirisch The Mirisch Agency 10100 Santa Monica Blvd Ste 700 Los Angeles CA 90067-4011

VON BURG, MARY M., advocate, social services administrator; b. Montezuma, Ind., Feb. 13, 1937; d. Jesse and Gertrude (Wilburn) Thomas.; m. Raymond E. Von Burg, Feb. 28, 1958; 1 child, Raymond E. BS in Secondary Edn., Ind. U., Indpls., 1980; MS in Counseling and Student Pers., Ind. U., 1984, postgrad., 1989—. Sec., treas. Brownsburg H.S., 1958-81; rsch. asst., faculty sec. Sch. Pub. & Environ. Affairs, Ind. U., Indpls., 1980-81; adminstrv. sec. dean's office Sch. Medicine, Ind. U., Indpls., 1981-85; counseling Marion County Prosecutor's Alternative Runaways Program, 1984-85; instr. Ind. U., Indpls., 1984-85, adminstrv. coord. cmty. child abuse project Sch. Medicine Dept. Pediats., 1985—; exec. sec. dept. pediatrics Sch. Medicine Ind. U., Indpls., 1985-88; project mgr. Regionalization Care for Abused Children, Indpls., 1988—; coord. adminstrn. Cmty. Child Abuse Project., 1985—, Liaison Child Abuse Forum, Indpls., 1988—; mem. com. Child Advocacy Ind. U. Hosp., Indpls., 1989—; delegation to Russia and Lithuania Citizen Amb. Program People to People Internat., 1994; pres. Domestic Violence Network, 1994-96. Contbr. numerous articles to profl. jours. Mem. violence awareness com. Wishard Meml. Hosp., 1995—; chair battered women's protocol com. Marion County, 1994—, statewide tng., 1994—, mem. prevention of child abuse and neglect through dental awareness coalition, 1994—; chair Marion County Ind. Hosp. Liaison Child Abuse, 1987—, Sch. Liaison Child Abuse Forum, 1992—; pres. Domestic Violence Network, 1994—. Mem. Child Welfare League Am., Nat. Assn. Counsel Children, Am. Assn. Protecting Children, Nat. Com. Prevention Child Abuse and Neglect (Ind. chpt.), Sigma Pi Alpha. Office: Ind U Comm Child Abuse Projects Dept Pediats 1001 W 10th St Myers Bldg D503 Indianapolis IN 46202-2897

VON DEBARDELEBEN, ANNA, psychologist, art therapist, intercultural communications consultant, educator; b. Birmingham, Ala., Sept. 21, 1947; d. James Duncan and Margaret (Mattison) Hunter; m. Louis Wilds McLeod, Nov. 6, 1979 (div. 1983); 1 child, Margaret Candler McLeod. Student, Inst. Tech. y de Estudios Superios de Monterrey, Mex., 1966, 69, U. Salzberg, Austria, 1967, N.Y.U. in Madrid, 1968; BA in Spanish and German, Ohio Wesleyan U., 1969; MA in Spanish Literature and Art History, Vanderbilt U., 1972; postgrad., Emory U., 1972-74, Ga. State U., 1979, U. Iberoamericano, Mex. City, 1985; D in Homeopath, Brit. Inst. Homeopathy; D in Naturopath, Clayton Coll. Naturopath/Am. Inst. Nutrition, 1994. Office sec., asst. mgr. fgn. langs. dept. Ga. State U., Atlanta, 1970; instr. Miles Coll., Birmingham, Ala., 1970; ESL instr. Adult Basic Edn. Fulton County Pub. Sch. Sys., Atlanta, 1972-73; catalog editor, devel. writer publ. svcs. Emory U., Atlanta, 1972-76, instr. cmty. ednl. svcs., 1975-94, dir. alumni rels., dir. Emory law sch. fund, 1981; instr. VA Med. Ctr., Atlanta, 1979—; pvt. practice as comms. cons., 1982—; instr., coord. Spanish lang. program Elem. Sch. Sys., Decatur, Ga., 1982-89; coord. for vols. DeKalb Counsel of Aging, Decatur, Ga., 1985-86; instr. Spellman Coll., Atlanta, 1987-89; dir. pub. rels. Art Festival of Atlanta, 1973, 74; dir. Spanish programs Atlanta Pub. Libr., 1977-79; founder Multiple Sclerosis Support Groups Ga. Bapt. Hosp., Atlanta, 1979, Facilitation Tuscaloosa MS Support Group, 1996—; instr. Neil Assocs., Inc., Atlanta, 1980; presenter in field; originator, dir. Internat. Ctr. for Cultural Arts & Edn., 1988; consulate Karla Jordan Internat., Inc., Atlanta, 1989-94; founder, instr. The Living Tree Ctr., Inc., Atlanta, 1990—; cons. Beauty for all Seasons, Inc., Atlanta, Weekenders Casual Wear, Inc., Atlanta and Tuscaloosa, Ala.; lectr. and instr. Ala. MS Soc., 1996—. Mem. editl. bd. Abstract newsletter, 1974-80, editor, 1976. Mem. AVANCE. Democrat. Methodist. Home and Office: 1248 38th Ave E Tuscaloosa AL 35404

VON DRACHENFELS, SUZANNE HAMILTON, writer; b. L.A., May 26, 1928; d. Augustus Adolphus and Floribel Hargett (Kelly) Hamilton; m. James True Luscombe, July 14, 1950 (div. 1969); children: James Hamilton, Kelly Ann Chisholm, Elizabeth Scott Buckingham, Patricia Jane Pecoulas; m. Louis Wood Robinson, Aug. 1972 (div. 1988); m. Alec Verner, Baron von Drachenfels, Aug. 14, 1990. BS, U. So. Calif., 1950. Tabletop cons., spkr. Fitz & Floyd, Dallas, 1983-90; contbg. editor Giftware News, Chgo., 1987-91. Vol., mem. bd. Jr. League Pasadena, 1958-83; docent Huntington Libr. & Art Gallery, Pasadena, 1962-68, L.A. County Mus. of Art, 1969-74; pres. Jr. League Sustainers, Pasadena, 1977. Republican. Episcopalian. Home: 149 Littlefield Rd Monterey CA 93940

VONEIDA, JANE DIANE, government official; b. Williamsport, Pa., Sept. 22, 1944; d. R. LeRoy and Emily Jane (Waltman) V. BA, Dickinson Coll., 1965; MA, Shippensburg U., 1970; MS, U. New Orleans, 1975. Planner Planning Commn., New Orleans, 1970-72; planning cons. New Orleans, 1972-76; dir. Community Devel. Commn., Gulfport, Miss., 1976-84, City of Rockford (Ill.) Community Devel. Dept., 1984—; cons. in field. Bd. dirs. Nat. Cmty. Devel. Assn., Washington, 1978—, YMCA, Rockford, 1987-96, First of Am. Cmty. Devel. Corp., Kalamazoo, Mich., 1991—, Conv. and Visitors Bur., Rockford, 1986-95, Children's Home and Aid Soc., Rockford, 1995—. John J. McCloy fellow Fed. Republic of Germany, 1985, Sr. Exec. Program fellow HUD, 1986. Office: City of Rockford 425 E State St Rockford IL 61104

VON EULER, MARY, lawyer, educator; b. New York, Apr. 9, 1930; d. Theodore Michael and Marion (Klein) Sanders; m. Leo Hans von Euler, Sept. 10, 1955; children: Barbara, Peter Michael. AB, Radcliffe Coll., 1952; MA, Columbia Teacher's Coll., 1956; JD, Cath. U. Am., 1975. Bar: D.C. 1976. Rsch. and editl. asst. Henry St. Settlement, N.Y.C., 1949-50; legis. sec. Office of U.S. Senator Hubert Humphrey, Washington, 1953-55; tchr. history and social studies Hamden (Conn.) Pub. Schs., 1956-58; tchr. history and govt. Montgomery County Pub. Schs., Rockville, Md., 1966-68; rsch. asst. Brookings Inst., Washington, 1969-72; legal intern Ctr. Nat. Policy Rev., Washington, 1974; staff atty. Legal Rsch. and Svcs. for Elderly, Washington, 1975-76; rsch. assoc. Nat. Inst. Edn., Washington, 1976-80; atty. advisor Office for Civil Rights U.S. Dept. Edn., Washington, 1980-92; cons. NEA, Washington, 1992-96; legal advisor Good Sports, Inc., Oakton, Va., 1994—. Author: Race Relations in America, 1996; co-author: A Citizen's Guide to School Desegregation Law, 1978; co-editor: The Catholic Community and the Integration of Public and Catholic Schools, 1979; contbr. articles to profl. jours. Bd. dirs. Suburban Md. Fair Housing, Montgomery County, Md., 1978-86, pres., 1982-83; vol. rsch. and writing Ams. for Dem. Action, Washington, 1992-96, Nat. Bd., 1995—. Mem. ABA (sects. individual rights and responsibilities). Home and Office: 5900 Ramsgate Rd Bethesda MD 20816-1128

VON FRAUNHOFER-KOSINSKI, KATHERINA, bank executive; b. N.Y.C.; m. Jerzy Kosinski, Feb. 15, 1987 (dec. May 3, 1991). Student, St. Joseph's Convent, London, Clark's Coll., London. Various positions Robert W. Orr & Assocs., N.Y.C., 1954-55; with traffic dept. Compton Advt., Inc., N.Y.C., 1956-63; acct. exec. J. Walter Thompson Co., N.Y.C., 1963-69; product mgr. Natural Wonder line Revlon Co., N.Y., 1969-71; pres. Scientia Factum, Inc., N.Y.C., 1971—; co-founder Polish Am. Resources Corp., N.Y.C., 1988—, pres., CEO, 1992—; founder, CEO, pres. Polish Am. Techs., L.P., N.Y.C., 1992—; chmn. bd. dirs. AmerBank, Warsaw, 1991—. Co-founder Westchester Sports Club. Home: 60 W 57th St New York NY 10019-3911

VON FURSTENBERG, BETSY, actress, writer; b. Neiheim Heusen, Germany, Aug. 16, 1931; d. Count Franz-Egon and Elizabeth (Johnson) von F.; m. Guy Vincent de la Maisoneuve (div.); 2 children.; m. John J. Reynolds, Mar. 26, 1984. Attended Miss Hewitt's Classes, N.Y. Tutoring Sch.; prepared for stage with Sanford Meisner at Neighborhood Playhouse. Made Broadway stage debut in Second Threshold, N.Y., 1951; appeared in Dear Barbarians, 1952, Oh Men Oh Women, 1954, The Chalk Garden, 1955, Child of Fortune, 1956, Nature's Way, 1957, Much Ado About Nothing, 1959, Mary Mary, 1965, Paisley Convertible, 1967, Avanti, 1968, The Gingerbread Lady, 1970 (toured 1971), Absurd Person Singular, 1976; off Broadway appearances include For Love or Money, 1951; toured in Petrified Forest, Jason and Second Man, 1952; appeared in Josephine, 1953; subsequently toured, 1955; What Every Woman Knows, 1955, The Making of Moo, 1958 (toured 1958), Say Darling, 1959, Wonderful Town, 1959, Season of Choice, 1959, Beyond Desire, 1967, Private Lives, 1968, Does Anyone Here Do the Peabody, 1976; appeared in Along Came a Spider, Theatre in the Park, N.Y.C., 1985; appeared in film Women Without Names, 1950; TV appearances include Robert Montgomery Show, Ed Sullivan Show, Alfred Hitchcock Presents, One Step Beyond, The Mike Wallace Show, Johnny Carson Show, Omnibus, Theatre of the Week, The Secret Storm, As the World Turns, Movie of the Week, Your Money or Your Wife, Another World; writer syndicated column More Than Beauty; contbr. articles to newspapers and mags. including N.Y. Times Sunday Arts and Leisure, Saturday Rev. of Literature, People, Good Housekeeping, Art News, Pan Am Travel; co-author: (novel) Mirror, Mirror, 1988. Office: care Don Buchwald 10 E 44th St New York NY 10017-3601

VON HAKE, MARGARET JOAN, librarian; b. Santa Monica, Calif., Oct. 27, 1933; d. Carl August and Inez Garnet (Johnson) von Hake;. BA, La Sierra U., 1955; MS in Library Sci., U. So. Calif., 1963. Tchr. Newbury Park (Calif.) Acad., 1955-60, librarian, 1957-60; librarian Columbia Union Coll., Takoma Park, Md., 1962-67, library dir., 1967—. Mem. ALA, Md. Libr. Assn., Congress of Acad. Libr. Dirs. of Md., Md. Ind. Coll.and Univ. Assn. Libr. Dirs. Roundtable, Assn. Seventh Day Adventist Librs. (newsletter editor 1982, 83, pres. 1989-90), Paul Hill Chorale, Sligo Federated Music Club (pres. 1988-89). Republican. Office: Columbia Union Coll 7600 Flower Ave Silver Spring MD 20912-7796

VON KELLENBACH, KATHARINA, religious studies educator; b. Stuttgart, Germany, May 18, 1960; d. Karl and Brigitte Von Kellenbach; m. Björn Krondorfer, May 18, 1991; children: Zadekia S., Tabitha I. Diploma in Evang. Theology, Georg August U., Göttingen, Germany, 1983; MA, Temple U., 1984, PhD, 1990. Asst. prof. St. Mary's (Md.) Coll. of Md., 1991—; vis. lectr. Lehigh U., Bethlehem, Pa., 1989, 90-91. Author: (book) Anti-Judaism in Feminist Religous Writings, 1994. Charlotte Newcombe fellow, Woodrow Wilson Found., Princeton, !989-90. Mem. Am. Acad. Religion, Soc. for Values in Higher Edn., European Soc. for Women in Theol. Rsch. Home: PO Box 302 Saint Marys City MD 20686 Office: St Marys Coll of Md Saint Marys City MD 20686

VON PRINCE, KILULU MAGDALENA, occupational therapist, sculptor; b. Bumbuli, Lushoto, Tanzania, Jan. 9, 1929; came to U.S., 1949; d. Tom Adalbert and Juliane (Martini) Von P. BA in Occupational Therapy, San Jose State U., 1958, MS in Occupational Therapy, 1972; EdD, U. So. Calif., 1980. Registered occupational therapist; cert. work evaluator, work adjustment specialist. Commd. 2d lt. U.S. Army, 1959, advanced through grades to lt. col.; staff asst. U.S. Army, Denver, 1959-62; hand rehab. asst., hand therapy Walter Reed Army Med. Ctr., 1962-65; hand rehab. asst. occupational therapist 97th Gen. Hosp., U.S. Army, Frankfurt, Fed. Republic Germany, 1965-68; occupational therapist Inst. Surg. Rsch. U.S. Army, Ft. Sam Houston, Tex., 1967-70; occupational therapy dir., cons. U.S. Army, Honolulu, 1972-75; adminstr. occupational therapy clinic, cons. LAMC U.S. Army, Presido, Calif., 1975; asst. evening coll. program San Jose (Calif.) C.C., 1976-77; postdoctoral fellow allied health adminstrn. SUNY, Buffalo, 1978, Commonwealth U., Richmond, Va., 1978-79; project dir. Ctr. of Design, Palo Alto, 1980; part-time staff project developing preretirement program older adults De Anza Coll., Cupertino, Calif., 1980-81; part-time instr. Stroke Activity Ctr. Cabrillo Coll., Santa Cruz, Calif., 1981; dir. occupl. therapy Presbyn. Med. Ctr., 1981-86; ptnr., mgr. retail store, 1986-89; dir. rehab. therapy Merrithew Meml. Hosp. Contra Costa Med. Ctr., Martinez, Calif., 1990-93; sculptor, 1993—; part-time activity program coord. Calif. Women's Detention Facility, Chowchilla, Calif., 1994—; researcher, presenter workshops and seminars in field. Co-author: Splinting of Burned Patients, 1974; producer videos: Elbow Splinting of the Burned Patient, 1970, Self-Instruction Unit: Principles of Elbow Splinting, 1971; contbr. articles to profl. jours. Decorated Legion of Merit; recipient Disting. Alumni Honors award San Jose State U., 1982; grad. scholar U.S. Surgeon Gen.; Kellogg Found. postdoctoral fellow, 1979. Mem. Am. Occupational Therapy Assn., Occupational Therapy Assn. Calif. (award of excellence 1986, v.p. 1981-84, state chair pers. 1981-84, state chair continuing edn. 1984-86, Lifetime Achievement award 1994), Am. Soc. Hand Therapists (hon., life). Home: 36141 Manon Ave Madera CA 93638-8613 Office: Calif Women's Detention Facility Chowchilla CA 93610-1501

VON RAFFLER-ENGEL, WALBURGA (WALBURGA ENGEL), linguist, lecturer, writer; b. Munich, Germany, Sept. 25, 1920; came to U.S., 1949, naturalized, 1955; d. Friedrich J. and Gertrud E. (Kiefer) von R.; m. A. Ferdinand Engel, June 2, 1957; children: Lea Maxine, Eric Robert von Raffler. DLitt, U. Turin, Italy, 1947; MS, Columbia U., 1951; PhD, Ind. U., 1953. Free-lance journalist, 1949-58; mem. faculty Bennett Coll., Greensboro, N.C., 1953-55, U. Charleston (formerly Morris Harvey Coll.), W.Va., 1955-57, Adelphi U., CUNY, 1957-58, NYU, 1958-59, U. Florence, Italy, 1959-60, Istituto Postuniversitario Organizzazione Aziendale, Turin, 1960-61, Bologna Center of Johns Hopkins U., 1964; assoc. prof. linguistics Vanderbilt U., Nashville, 1965-77, prof. linguistics, 1977-85, prof. emerita, sr. rsch. assoc. Inst. Pub. Policy Studies, 1985—; dir. linguistics program Vanderbilt U., 1978-86; chmn. com. on linguistics Nashville U. Ctr., 1974-79; Italian NSF prof. Psychol. Inst. U. Florence, Italy, 1986-87; prof. NATO Advanced Study Inst., Cortona, Italy, 1988; pres. Kinesics Internat., 1988—; vis. prof. linguistics Shanxi U., Peoples Republic China, 1985; vis. prof. U. Ottawa, Ont., Can., 1971-72, Lang. Scis. Inst., Internat. Christian U., Tokyo, 1976; grant evaluator NEH, NSF, Can. Coun.; manuscript reader Ind. U. Press, U. Ill. Press, Prentice-Hall; advisor Trinity U., Simon Frazer U.; pres. Kinesics Internat., 1988—; lectr. in field; dir. internat. seminar Cron-Cultural Comm., 1986-87. Author: Il prelinguaggio infantile, 1964, The Perception of Nonverbal Behavior in the Career Interview, 1983, The Perception of the Unborn Across the Cultures of the World, Japanese edit., 1993, English edit., 1994 (transl. into Chinese); co-author: Language Intervention Programs, 1960-74, 75; editor, co-editor 12 books; author films and videotape; contbr. over 300 articles to scholarly jours., over 200 to profl. and popular publs. in various countries. Grantee Am. Coun. Learned Socs., NSF, Can. Coun., Ford Found., Kenan Venture Fund, Japanese Ministry Edn., NATO, UNESCO, Finnish Acad., Meharry Med. Coll., Internat. Sociol. Assn., Internat. Coun. Linguists, Tex. A&M U., Vanderbilt U., others. Mem. AAUP, Internat. Linguistic Assn., Linguistic Soc. Am. (chmn. Golden Anniversary film com. 1974, emerita 1985—), Linguistic Assn. Can. and the U.S., Internat. Assn. for Applied Linguistics (com. on discourse analyses, sessions chmn. 1978), Lang. Origins Soc. (exec. com. 1985—, chmn. internat. congress, 1987), Internat. Sociol. Assn. (rsch. com. for sociolinguistics, session co-chmn. internat. conf. 1983, session chmn. profl. conf. 1983), Internat. Assn. for Study of Child Lang. (v.p. 1975-78, chmn. internat. conf. 1972), Inst. for Nonverbal Communication Research (workshop leader 1981), Southeastern Conf. on Linguistics, 1980— (hon. mem. 1985—), Semiotic Soc. Am. (organizing com. Internat. Semiotics Inst. 1981), Sietar Internat., Nat. Assn. Scholars. Home and Office: 116 Brighton Close Nashville TN 37205-2501

VON RYDINGSVARD, URSULA KAROLISZYN, sculptor; b. Deensen, Germany, July 26, 1942; cmae to U.S., 1950; d. Ignacy and Konegunda (Sternal) Karoliszyn; m. Pual Greengard. BA, MA, U. Miami, Coral Gables, Fla., 1965; postgrad., U. Calif., Berkeley, 1969-70; MFA, Columbia U., 1975; PhD (hon.), Md. Inst. Art, 1991. Instr. Sch. Visual Arts, N.Y.C., 1981-82; asst. prof. Pratt Inst., Bklyn., 1978-82, Fordham U., Bronx, N.Y., 1980-82; assoc. prof. Yale U., New Haven, 1982-86; prof. grad. divsn. Sch. Visual Arts, N.Y.C., 1986—. One-woman shows include Rosa Esman Gallery, 1981, 82, Studio Bassanese, Trieste, 1985, Laumeier Sculpture Gallery, St. Louis, 1988, Capp St. Project San Francisco, 1990, Lorence-Monk Gallery, N.Y.C., 1990-91, Zamek Ujazdowski Contemporary Art Ctr., Warsaw, Poland, 1992, Storm King Art Ctr., Mountainville, N.Y., 1992-94, Galerie Lelong, N.Y.C., 1994, Mus. Art R.I. Sch. Design, Providence, 1996; exhibited in group shows at Lowe Art Mus., Coral Gables, Fla., 1975, Aldrich Mus. Contemporary Art, Ridgefield, Conn., 1976, 55 Mercer Gallery, N.Y.C., 1983, Pratt Inst., Bklyn., 1985, Contemporary Arts Ctr., Cin., 1987, Krygier/Landau Contemporary Art Gallery, Santa Monica, Calif., 1989, Damon Brandt Gallery, N.Y.C., 1989, Met. Mus. Art, N.Y.C., 1989-93, Whitney Mus. Contemporary Art, 1990, Cultural Ctr., Chgo., 1991, Ctrl. Bur. Art Exhbns., Warsaw and Krakow, Poland, 1991, The Cultural Space/Exit Art, N.Y.C., 1992, Galerie Lelong, N.Y.C., 1993, Denver Art Mus. and Columbus Art Mus., 1994—, others; outdoor exhbns include Pelham Bay Park, Bronx, N.Y., 1978, Neuberger Mus., Purchase, N.Y., 1979, Artpark, Lewiston, N.Y., 1979, Laumeier Sculpture Park, St. Louis, 1989-94, Walker Art Ctr., Mpls., 1990-93, Oliver Ranch, Geyserville, Calif., Storm King Art Ctr., Mountainville, N.Y., 1992-93; contbr. articles to profl. jours. Fulbright Hays travel grantee, 1975; grantee N.Y. State Coun. Arts, Am. the Beautiful Fund, Nat. Endowment for Arts, Creative Artists Program Svc.; Griswald traveling grantee Yale U., 1985; Guggenheim fellow, 1983-84; Nat. Endowment for Arts individual artists grantee, 1986-87; recipient Alfred Turzykowski Found. Fine Arts award, 1996. Studio: 429 S 5th St Brooklyn NY 11211-7425

VON SCHWARZ, CAROLYN M. GEIGER, psychotherapist, educator; b. Greenville, Mich., May 16, 1949; d. Raymond Lavern and Bernice Clara (Schoenborn) Geiger; m. Jeffrey George von Schwarz, Apr. 25, 1970 (div. Sept. 1979); children: Sean Raymond, Laura Elizabeth. BA, Wayne State U., 1988, MEd, 1992. Lic. profl. counselor. Counselor Edn. Tng. Rsch. Found., 1986-89; dir., therapist von Schwarz Assocs., Grosse Pointe Farms, Mich., 1989—; spkr. in field. COO Grateful Home, Homeless Shelter, Treatment Shelter, Detroit, 1991-93; vol. Sacred Heart Ctr., Detroit, 1978—, SAC2, Grosse Pointe Farms, 1985—; cons. Treehouse Players, Grosse Pointe Woods. Mem. Psi Chi. Republican. Roman Catholic.

VON STAR, BRENDA LEE, primary care family nurse practitioner; b. Lakeview, Oreg., Feb. 5, 1948; d. Leslie Darrell and May Mabel (Hirsch) Denstedt; m. Jimmie E. Muro, Aug. 20, 1977 (div. Nov. 1990); children: Michael, Christine. AS, Lane C.C., Eugene, Oreg., 1972; BSN, Met. State U., Denver, 1978. Cert. FNP; ACLS. Staff nurse med. unit Presbyn. Intercmty. Hosp., Kalmath Falls, Oreg., 1972-73; surg. ICU nurse St. Luke's Hosp., Denver, 1973-76; burn unit nurse U. Colo. Health Sci. Ctr., Denver, 1976-80; family pediatric nurse practitioner Tri-County Health Dept., Denver, 1980-85; pvt. collaborative practice Luth. Family Practice, Arvada, Colo., 1985-90; clin. dir. rsch. Family Futures Project, Denver, 1990-91; pvt. practice FNP Arbor Family Medicine, Thornton, Colo., 1991-95. With USN, 1967-70. Mem. Am. Acad. Nurse Practitioners, Colo. Nurses Assn. Unity Ch. Office: Family Medicine 1022 Depot Hill Broomfield CO 80027

VON TAAFFE-ROSSMANN, COSIMA T., physician, writer, inventor; b. Kuklov, Slovakia, Czechoslovakia, Nov. 21, 1944; came to U.S., 1988; d. Theophil and Marianna Hajossy; m. Charles Boris Rossmann, Oct. 19, 1979; children: Nathalie Nissa Cora, Nadine Nicole. MD, Purkyne U., Brno, Czechoslovakia, 1967. Intern Valtice (Czechoslovakia) Gen. Hosp., 1967-68, resident ob-gyn, 1968-69; med. researcher Kidney Disease Inst., Albany, N.Y., 1970-71; resident internal medicine Valtice Gen. Hosp., 1972-73; gen. practice Nat. Health System, Czechoslovakia, 1973-74; pvt. practice West Germany, 1974-80; med. officer Baragwanath Hosp., Johannesburg, South Africa, 1984-85, Edendale Hosp., Pietermaritzburg, South Africa, 1985-86; pvt. practice Huntingburg, Ind., 1988-90, Valdosta, Ga., 1990—; med. researcher, 1966—. Contbr. articles on medicine to profl. jours.; inventor, patentee in field. Office: 2301 N Ashley St Valdosta GA 31602-2620

VONTUR, RUTH POTH, elementary physical education educator; b. Beeville, Tex., Sept. 10, 1944; d. Robert Bennal and Ruth (Matejek) Poth; m. Robert F. Vontur, Aug. 8, 1964; children: Catherine Anne, Craig Robert, Cynthia Anne. BS in Edn., Southwest Tex. State U., 1966. Cert. health and phys. edn. tchr., biology tchr. Tex. Teachng asst. Blessed Sacrament Confraternity Christian Doctrine, Poth, Tex., 1958-64; phys. edn. tchr. Judson Ind. Sch. Dist., Converse, Tex., 1966-68; substitute tchr. St. Monica's Confraternity Christian Doctrine, Converse, 1971—; substitute tchr. Judson Ind. Sch. Dist., Converse, 1972-75, 80, phys. edn. tchr., 1966-68, 81—; county adv. bd. Am. Heart Assn., San Antonio, Tex., 1985-88, jump rope for heart coord., 1984—, heart ptnr., 1992—. Pres. St. Monica's Coun. Cath. Women, Converse, 1975; sponsor Young Astronauts, 1993—. Mem. NEA, AAHPERD, Alamo Area Tex. Assn. Health, Phys. Edn., Recreation and Dance, Tex. Assn. Health, Phys. Edn., Recreation and Dance, Judson Tchrs. Assn. (exec. dir. 1993-95), Tex. State Tchrs. Assn., Judson Athletic Booster Club. Roman Catholic. Home: 105 Norris Dr W Converse TX 78109-1905 Office: Judson Ind Sch Dist Converse Elem Sch 102 School St Converse TX 78109-1320

VON ZWECK, DINA, writer, painter; b. N.Y.C., Oct. 16, 1933; d. Baron Rudolph Zweck von und zu Zweckenburg and Adele Veit. Dir. pub. CBS Inc., N.Y.C., 1972-85; cons. CBS Inc., N.Y.C., 1985-86; writing tchr., N.Y.C., 1987—; book prodr. Better Homes & Gardens Book Clubs, 1985-94. Author: (fiction) The Beekeeper, Wheel of Fire, Dominga; (non-fiction) How to Organize Everything, Teen Diets for Girls, Grammar for Grown-Ups, How to Prepare Your Will, Family Recordkeeping, A Little Book of Christmas, A Perfect Mirror: Journalwriting, A Holiday Treasury, Venus Unbound; (children's books) I Am Dreaming, Make Zoup, Imagine That, All About Me at School, Questions, Questions, Questions, My Birthday Book, My First Calendar, What Does It Mean?, Creative Writing for Kids; (poetry) Gifts, Electric Karma, Out of My Head, Series, After Santa Fe, Sam Shepard's Dog, Halloween & Other Poems; (screenplays) Death & Diamonds, Danger Zone, Justice; co-author: American Victorian. Grantee Mass. Coun. Arts, 1984, Altos de Chavon, Dominican Republic, 1990. Mem. PEN, Poets & Writers, Artist Equity.

VOORHEES, S. JANE, artist; b. Bartlesville, Okla., Feb. 27, 1942; d. Jack and Ora Lee (Pinner) Lutton; m. Vernon W. Voorhees II, June 6, 1964; children: Sarah Elizabeth, Katherine Anne. BFA, U. Kans., 1964; MA, U. Mo., Kansas City, 1995. Artist, designer Hallmark Cards, Kansas City, Mo., 1965-72; staff mem. continuing edn. Kansas City Art Inst. Exhibited in solo show at Ctrl. Exch., Kansas City, Mo., 1994, in two-person show at U. Mo. Kansas City Gallery of Art, 1995; group shows include Johnson County C.C. Art Gallery, 1994, U. Wis. Parkside, 1996, Erector Sq. Gallery, New Haven, 1996; permanent collections include Hallmark Cards, Kansas City, Mo., Twentieth Century Investments, Kansas City, Sprint, Indpls., Fed. Res. Bank, St. Louis. Active Jr. League of Johnson and Wyandohe Counties, 1971—. Recipient James Lamar and Clara Wislow Sandusky Meml. award U. Mo.-Kansas City, 1995. Mem. Hand Print Press, Kansas City Art Coaliton, Soc. of Fellows/Netlson Atkins Mus., U. Mo. Kansas City Gallery of Art.

VOORHESS, MARY LOUISE, pediatric endocrinologist; b. Livingston Manor, N.Y., June 2, 1926; d. Harry William and Helen Grace (Schwartz) V. BA in Zoology, U. Tex., 1952; MD, Baylor Coll., Houston, 1956. Diplomate Am. Bd. Pediatrics and Pediatric Endocrinology. Rotating intern Albany (N.Y.) Med. Ctr., 1956-57, asst. resident pediatrics, 1957-58, chief resident pediatrics, 1958-59; rsch. fellow pediatric endocrinology and genetics SUNY Health Sci. Ctr., Syracuse, 1959-61, asst. prof. pediatrics, 1961-65, assoc. prof. pediatrics, 1965-70, prof. pediatrics, 1970-76; prof. pediatrics SUNY Sch. Medicine and Biomed. Scis., Buffalo, 1976-91, prof. pediatrics emeritus, 1991—; co-chief div. endocrinology Children's Hosp. Buffalo, 1976-91; ad hoc reviewer Jour. Pediatrics, Pediatrics, Am. Jour. Diseases Children, other. Contbr. sci. articles to profl. jours., chpts. to books. Mem. adv. bd. Interim Healthcare inc., 1991—; mem. devel. coun. Children's Hosp. Buffalo Found., 1991—; med. dir. Children's Growth Found., Buffalo, 1976—; cmty. advisor Assn. for Rsch. Childhood Cancer, Buffalo, 1990—. Recipient rsch. career devel. award Nat. Caneer Inst., 1961-71, Dean's award SUNY Sch. Medicine and Biomed. Scis., 1991. Fellow Am. Acad. Pediatrics, AAAS; mem. Soc. Pediatric Rsch., Am. Pediatric Soc., Endocrine Soc., Lawson Wilkins Pediatric Endocrine Soc., Buffalo Pediatric Soc., Zonta Internat., Phi Beta Kappa, Alpha Omega Alpha. Presbyterian. Home: 325 Lincoln Pky Buffalo NY 14216-3120 Office: Children Hosp 219 Bryant St Buffalo NY 14222-2006

VORE, MARY EDITH, pharmacology educator, researcher; b. Guatemala City, Guatemala, June 27, 1947; came to U.S., 1962; d. Charles Schrater and Sammye (Smith) V.; m. Edgar Tadasu Iwamoto, Dec. 27, 1976; children: Kenneth Edgar, Daniel Vore. BA, Asbury Coll., Wilmore, Ky., 1968; PhD, Vanderbilt U., Nashville, Tenn., 1972. Postdoctoral fellow Hoffman-LaRoche, Nutley, N.J., 1972-74; asst. prof. U. Calif., San Francisco, 1974-78; asst. prof. pharmacology U. Ky., Lexington, 1978-81, assoc. prof., 1981-86, prof., 1986—, vice chmn. dept., 1983-94, dir. grad. ctr. for toxicology, 1994—; cons. NIH, Bethesda, Md., 1983-87. Contbr. numerous articles to profl. jours., chpts. to books. Mem. Nat. Adv. Environ. Health Scis. Coun., 1991-94. USPHS grantee, 1979—. Mem. Soc. Toxicology, Am. Assn. Study of Liver Disease, Am. Soc. Pharmacology and Exptl. Therapeutics (sec., treas. 1986-89). Office: U Ky Coll Medicine 800 Rose St Lexington KY 40536-0001

VOROUS, MARGARET ESTELLE, primary and secondary school educator; b. Charles Town, W.Va., Feb. 14, 1947; d. Benjamin Welton and Helen Virginia (Owens) Vorous. AA in Pre-Edn. (Laureate Scholar), Potomac State Coll., W.Va. U., 1967; BS in Elem. Edn., James Madison U., 1970, MS in Edn., 1975, postgrad., spring 1978, fall 1979, summer 1979, 81; postgrad. U. Va., summers 1977, 78, fall 1978, 89, 91, James Madison U., fall 1981-82, summer 1979, 81-82; MEd in Media Svcs., East Tenn. State U., 1988, 89. Cert. library sci., cert. adminstrn./supervisory. Tchr. 3d-4th grade Highview Sch., Frederick County, Va., 1968-69, 3d grade Kernstown Elem. Sch., Frederick County, 1970-71, E. Wilson Morrison Elem. Sch., Front Royal, Va., 1971-72, Stonewall Elem. Sch., Frederick County, 1972-78; tchr. 4th grade South Jefferson Elem. Sch., Jefferson County (W.Va.) Schs., 1978-79, Emergency Sch. Aid Act reading tchr./reading specialist, 1980-82, reading tchr./specialist Page Jackson Solar Elem. Sch., 1983-87; adult basic edn. tchr. Dowell J. Howard Vocat. Ctr., Winchester, Va., 1984-87, G.E.D. tchr., coordinator, 1985-87; libr., media specialist Powell Valley Middle Sch., 1988-91; ABE/GED/ESL tchr. for JOBS program Berkeley County Schs., 1992-94; libr., media specialist Northwestern Elem., 1994-95, first grade tchr., 1995—; tchr. 4th grade Ranson (W.Va.) Elem. Sch., 1979; reading tutor; reading tutor, trainer Laubach Literacy Internat., 1989; art rep. Creative Arts Festival at Kernstown, 1971, Stonewall elem. schs., 1973-77; mem. cultural task force Frederick County Sch., 1974-75, music task force, 1973-74, textbook adoption com. for reading, writing, 1976-77. Founder, editor: The Reading Gazette, The Reading Tribune, Emergency Sch. Aid Act Reading Program, South Jefferson Elem. Sch., 1980-81, Shepherdstown Elem. Sch., 1981-82; creator numerous reading games, activities. Vol. fundraiser Am. Cancer Soc., Frederick County, Va., 1981; vol. blood donor Am. Red Cross, 1978—; mem. Frederick County Polit. Action Com., Jefferson County Polit. Action Com.; del. 103-109th Ann. Diocesan Convs., Episc. Ch., registrar of vestry Grace Episc. Ch., Middleway, W.Va., 1980-87, lic. lay reader, 1980-90, lic. chalice bearer, 1983-90; lic. lay reader, lay eucharistic min. St. Pauls's Episc. Ch.-on-the-Hill, Winchester, Va., 1996—; committeeperson Lebanon Dems., 1988-89; commd. mem. Order of Jerusalem, 1985—; VEMA leadership participant, 1989-91, 95; facilitator VEMA Conf., 1994; participant Seven Habits program Covey Leadership Ctr., 1993; Recipient various awards, including being named Miss Alpine Princess, award for Excellence in Adult Basic Edn. Dept. Edn., Charleston, W.Va., 1994, RIF Site Coord. for Honorable mention, 1995, Asst Coord. Pritt for Gov. Campaign (DEM), 1995-96, RIF Nat. Poster contest Storyteller for Chpt. I workshop and Ctrl. Elementary, 1994-96, Sigma Phi Omega, 1967. Mem. Internat. Reading Assn., NEA, Va. Reading Assn., Shenandoah Valley Reading Council, Assn. Supervision and Curriculum Devel., W.Va. Edn. Assn., NEA. Jefferson County Edn. Assn. (faculty rep.), Fauquier County Edn. Assn., Va. Edn. Assn., W.Va. Adult Edn. Assn., Va. Ednl. Media Assn., South Jefferson PTA, Potomac State Coll. Alumni Assn., James Madison U. Alumni Assn., Frederick County Dem. Women, Kappa Delta Pi, Phi Delta Kappa, Phi Kappa Phi.

VORTMAN, SHEILA M., electric power industry executive. Sr. v.p. corp. and regulatory affairs Puget Sound Power & Light Co., Bellevue, Wash. Office: Puget Sound Power & Light Co 411 108th Ave NE Bellevue WA 98004-5515*

VOS, THERESA CARMELLA, nurse; b. Kenosha, Wis., Apr. 12, 1950; d. Joseph A. and Mafalda M. (Bambino) Corradini; m. Ronald B. Vos, June 16, 1973; children: Christopher, Brian, Mark. Diploma, St. Lukes Sch. Nursing, 1971. CGRN. Intensive care nurse Kenosha (Wis.) Meml. Hosp., 1971-73; cardiac care nurse St. Luke's, Racine, Wis., 1973-74; nurse mgr. gastrointestinal unit St. Lukes Hosp., 1974-75, coord. edn. & equipment digestive disease ctr., 1984-93; coord. endscopy nurse Gastroenterology Cons., Ltd., Milw., 1993—; pancreatic biliary edn. coord. St. Lukes Med. Ctr., Milw., 1994—; faculty Orgns. of Soc. Gastroenterology nurses and assoc., 1992-96; course co-dir. and Faculty Advanced Therapeutic Endoscopic Retrograde Cholangiopancreatography for Nurses & Assocs., Milw., 1994-96; lectr. and fac. Multi-Regional and Nat. Level; course coord. internat. therapeutic Endoscopic Retrograde Cholangiopancreatography course for physician, 1996. Co-author of teaching module for Endoscopic Retrograde Cholangiopancreatography Nat. Soc. Gastroenterology Nurses and Assocs. Cert. Bd., 1995. Mem. Nat. Soc. Gastroenterology Nurses & Assocs. (mem. Wis. chpt.), Internat. Soc. Gastroenterology Nurses & Assocs., Soc. Gastroenterology Nurses Assocs.-Endoscopic Retrograde Cholangiopancreatography Spec. Interest Group (chair), Nat. Soc. Gastroentorology Nurses and Assocs. (consumer rels. com.). Office: Gastroenterology Cons Ltd 2901 W KK River Pkwy Milwaukee WI 53215 also: St Luke's Med Ctr 2900 W Oklahoma Ave Milwaukee WI 53215

VOSBURGH, VICTORIA LYNN, rehabilitation services executive; b. Putnam, Conn., Aug. 7, 1965; d. Douglas Warren Vosburgh and Margaret Jean (Grenier) Baggetta; m. Michael R. DeNardis, Aug. 7, 1988. Paralegal diploma, Westchester Sch., 1985. Adminstrv. asst. Hospitality House T.C., Inc., Albany, N.Y., 1985-87; exec. adminstr. Hospitality House T.C., Inc., Albany, 1987-91; human immunodeficiency virus issues coord. Hospitality House T.C., Inc., Albany, N.Y., 1989-91, dir. adminstrn., 1991—. Mem. North Shore Animal League, Divers Alert Network. Home: 203 Blue Barns Rd Burnt Hills NY 12027-9527 Office: Hospitality House TC Inc 271 Central Ave Albany NY 12206-2611

VOSKA, KATHRYN CAPLES, consultant, facilitator; b. Berkeley, Cal., Dec. 26, 1942; d. Donald Buxton and Ellen Marion (Smith) Caples; m. David Karl Nehrling, Aug. 15, 1964 (div. Nov. 1980); children: Sandra E. Nehrling-Swift, Barbara M. Nehrling, Melissa A. Nehrling-Holmgren; m. James Edward Voska, Aug. 31, 1985. BS, Northwestern U., 1964; MS, Nat.-Louis U., 1989. Cert. teacher, Ill. Tchr. Pub. Schs., Northbrook and Evanston, Ill., 1964-65; acting phys. dir. YWCA, Evanston, Ill., 1975; quality control technician Baxter Travenol, Morton Grove, Ill., 1978-80; sr. quality assurance analyst Hollister Inc., Libertyville, Ill., 1980-85; info. ctr. trainer, tech. training mgr. Rand McNally, Skokie, Ill., 1985-92; cons., facilitator Capka & Assocs., Skokie and Kansas City, 1992—; dir. edn. Nat. Office Machine Dealers, 1992-94; career mgmt. cons. Right Assocs., 1994—; pvt. practice estate conservator; bd. dirs. Coro/Kansas City, 1996—. Telephone worker Contact Chgo. Crisis Hotline, 1989-90; CPR instr. trainer Amer. Heart Assn., Chgo., 1977-89; aquatic dir. YMCA, Evanston, Ill., 1969-80; rep. Alumnae Panhellenic Coun., Evanston, 1969-75; grad. Leadership Overland Park, 1996. Mem. ASTD, Soc. Human Resource Mgmt., Midwest Soc. Profl. Cons., Assn. for Mgmt. Orgn. Design, Assn. Suprs. Curriculum and Devel., Chicago Orgn. of Data Processing Educators, Chicago Computer Soc., Info. Ctr. Exch. of Chgo., Assn. Quality and Participation, Am. Soc. for Quality Control (teller N.E. Ill. section 1982-84), Internat. Soc. for Performance Improvement, The Learning Resource Network. Presbyterian. Home: 1001 E 118th Ter Kansas City MO 64131-3828 Office: Right Assocs 7300 W 110th Overland Park KS 66210

VOSS, ALI ANNELIES, history of art educator, antique dealer; b. Hamburg, Germany, July 24, 1917; Came to the U.S., 1948; d. Hans Joachim Meisterknecht-Von Brussel and Paula Dorothea Lisette (Rothenburg) Meisterkuecht; m. Thomas A. Beasley, Jan. 17, 1948 (div. Jan. 1968); m. Edgar O. Voss (dec.). Attended, Art Inst., Hamburg, U. Hamburg, Stockholm U.; PhD, Heidelberg (Germany) U., 1945, Cert. tchr., 1948. Tchr. Monterey (Calif.) Peninsula Coll.; part-owner Antiques Internat., La Jolla, Calif.; owner Antiques Internat., Moss Landing, Calif.; asst. prof. Heidelberg U., 1961-63. Mem. AAUW (life). Democrat. Home: 111

17th St Pacific Grove CA 93950 Office: Antiques Internat/Showrooms 111 17th St Pacific Grove CA 93950

VOSS, KATHERINE EVELYN, international management consultant; b. Cleve., Sept. 2, 1957; d. Wendell Grant and Ann Terry (Miller) Voss; m. James Everett Mathias, Oct. 6, 1984 (div. Dec. 1988). BS, Bowling Green State U., 1979, MBA, 1981. Sci. systems analyst Eli Lilly & Co., Indpls., 1981-83, systems tng. cons., 1983-84; customer liaison mgr. Ind. U., Bloomington, 1985; prodn. ops. mgr. Ind. U., Indpls., 1985-86; prin. systems cons. Wang Labs., Inc., Carmel, Ind., 1986-93; mgmt. cons. AMT-Sybex (I) Ltd., Dublin, 1994—; cons. Ind. Univ., Bloomington, 1984-85, Allied Irish Bank, Dublin, Ireland, 1990-91. Contbr. (book) Introduction to Business, 1980, Introduction to Accounting, 1981, Computers and Data Processing, 1981. Presidental advisor Jr. Achievement, Indpls., 1982-83; pres. PEO Chpt. AM, Indpls., 1987-89, Irish rep., 1995—. Mem. Assn. for Image and Info. Mgmt., Irish Computer Soc., Beta Beta Beta. Republican. Presbyterian. Home: Hill Cottage, Brennanstown Rd Cabinteely, Dublin 18, Ireland Office: AMT-Sybex (I) Ltd, Elm House, Leopardstown Office Park, Foxrock Dublin 18, Ireland

VOSTAD, NANCY JANE, accountant; b. Greenway, S.D., Sept. 24, 1938; d. Adam E. Joachim and Mildred (Wittmayer) Beck; children: Evan, Eric, Renee. BS, Northern State U., 1987. CPA, S.D. Tax mgr. Eide Helmeke & Co., Aberdeen, S.D., 1962-89; acct. Nancy J. Vostad, CPA, Aberdeen, S.D., 1989-92, 94—; ptnr. Medinger & Vostad, CPAs, Aberdeen, S.D., 1992-94. Founding mother Resource Ctr. Women, Aberdeen, 1975. Vol. of Yr. S.D. Gov., 1986. Mem. Am. Inst. CPAs, S.D. CPA Soc., Resource Ctr. Women (treas. 1980, pres. 1981), Aberdeen Area AAUW. Home: 220 S Park St Aberdeen SD 57401 Office: Nancy J Vostad CPA 121 3d Ave SW Aberdeen SD 57401

VOTH, DONNA LEE, physical education educator, coach; b. Kalispell, Mont., July 3, 1953; d. Vernon Paul and Mildred Louise (West) V. BA in Missions, Crown Coll., St. Bonifacius, Minn., 1975; BS in Phys. Edn., U. Minn., 1978; MA in Instrnl. Leadership, U. Ala., Tuscaloosa, 1987. Instr., coach St. Paul Bible Coll., Crown Coll., St. Bonifacius, 1975-79; tchr., coach Alliance Acad., Quito, Ecuador, 1979-87, Faith Christian Sch., Sterling, Va., 1987-90; asst. prof., assoc. coach Simpson Coll., Redding, Calif., 1990—. Office: Simpson Coll 2211 College View Dr Redding CA 96003-8601

VOYTKO, MARY LOU, neuroscientist; b. Cleve., May 22, 1957; d. Thomas Lee and Rita Ann (Pekarcik) V.; m. Joseph R. Tobin, Sept. 21, 1985. BS, Baldwin-Wallace Coll., 1979; PhD, SUNY, Syracuse, 1985. Postdoctoral fellow SUNY, Syracuse, 1985-87; from postdoctoral fellow to instr. Johns Hopkins Sch. Medicine, Balt., 1987-93; asst. prof. Bowman Gray Sch. Medicine, Winston-Salem, N.C., 1993—. Mem. Internat. Primatologic Soc., Internat. Brain Rsch. Orgn., Found. Biomed. Rsch., Soc. for Neurosci. (councilor Western N.C. chpt. 1994—). Office: Bowman Gray Sch Medicine Dept Comparative Medicine Med Ctr Blvd Winston Salem NC 27157-1040

VRATIL, KATHRYN HOEFER, federal judge; b. Manhattan, Kans., Apr. 21, 1949; d. John J. and Kathryn Ruth (Fryer) Hoefer; children: Alison K., John A., Ashley A. BA, U. Kans., 1971, JD, 1975; postgrad., Exeter U., 1971-72. Bar: Kans. 1975, Mo. 1978, U.S. Dist. Ct. Kans. 1975, U.S. Dist. Ct. (we. dist.) Mo. 1978, U.S. Dist. Ct. (ea. dist.) Mo. 1985, U.S. Ct. Appeals (8th cir.) 1978, U.S. Ct. Appeals (10th cir.) 1980, U.S. Ct. Appeals (11th dist.) 1983, U.S. Supreme Ct., 1995. Law clk. U.S. Dist. Ct., Kansas City, Kans., 1975-78; assoc. Lathrop Koontz & Norquist, Kansas City, Mo., 1978-83; ptnr. Lathrop & Norquist, Kansas City, 1984-92; judge City of Prairie Village, Kans., 1991-92; bd. dirs. Kans. Legal Svcs. Bd. editors Kans. Law Rev., 1974-75, Jour. Kans. Bar Assn., 1992—. Mem. Kansas City Tomorrow (XIV); bd. trustees, shepherd-deacon Village Presbyn. Ch.; nat. adv. bd. U. Kans. Ctr. for Environ. Edn. and Tng., 1993-95. Fellow Kans. Bar Foun., Am. Bar Found.; mem. ABA, Am. Judicature Soc., Nat. Assn. Judges, Fed. Judges Assn., Kans. Bar Assn., Mo. Bar Assn., Kansas City Met. Area Bar Assn., Wyandotte County Bar Assn., Johnson Coutny Bar Assn., Assn. Women Lawyers, Lawyers Assn. Kansas City, Supreme Ct. Hist. Soc., Kans. State Hist. Soc., U. Kans. Law Soc. (bd. govs. 1978-81), Kans. U. Alumni Assn. (mem. devel. com. 1985—, mem. Kansas City chpt. alumni bd. 1990-92, nat. bd. dirs. 1991—, bd. govs. Adams alumni ctr. 1992—, pres. 1985-86, membership chair 1983-84, mem. learned club 1992ú, mem. chancellor's club 1993—, mem. Williams ednl. fund 1993—, mem. Jayhawks for higher edn. 1993—), Homestead Country Club Prairie Village (pres.), Sons and Daus of Kans. (life), Rotary, Jr. League Wyandotte and Johnson Counties, Kans. State Hist. Soc., Order of Coif, Kans. Inn of Ct. (master 1993—), Overland Park Rotary, Univ. Club, Phi Kappa Phi. Republican. Presbyterian. Office: US Courthouse 511 500 State Ave Kansas City KS 66101-2403

VUCANOVICH, BARBARA FARRELL, congresswoman; b. Fort Dix, N.J., June 22, 1921; d. Thomas F. and Ynez (White) Farrell; m. Ken Dillon, Mar. 8, 1950 (div. 1964); children: Patty Dillon Cafferata, Mike, Ken, Tom, Susan Dillon Stoddard; m. George Vucanovich, June 19, 1965. Student, Manhattanville Coll. of Sacred Heart, 1938-39. Owner, operator Welcome Aboard Travel, Reno, 1968-74; Nev. rep. for Senator Paul Laxalt, 1974-82; mem. 98th-104th Congresses from 2d Nev. dist., 1983—; chmn. appropriations subcom. on military construction. Pres. Nev. Fedn. Republican Women, Reno, 1955-56; former pres. St. Mary's Hosp. Guild, Lawyer's Wives. Roman Catholic. Club: Hidden Valley Country (Reno). Office: US Ho of Reps 2202 Rayburn Washington DC 20515*

VUCKOVICH, CAROL YETSO (MRS. MICHAEL VUCKOVICH), librarian; b. East Liverpool, Ohio, Sept. 23, 1940; d. Stephen A. and Louise (Sever) Yetso; m. Michael Vuckovich, Sept. 24, 1970. BS, Geneva Coll., 1966; MLS, U. Pitts., 1968. Computation analyst Crucible Steel div. Colt Industries, Midland, Pa., 1958-62; library dir. Community Coll. Beaver County, Monaca, Pa., 1968—, instr. human anatomy and physiology, 1970—. Mem. Am. Library Assn., Pa. Library Assn., Spl. Libraries Assn., Am. Inst. Biol. Scis., Am. Anti-Vivisection Soc., Nat. Wildlife Fedn., Coll. and Research Libraries. Home: 21 Elm St Midland PA 15059-1615

VUICK, SARA ELLEN, non-profit organization administrator; b. Dayton, Ohio, Aug. 28, 1969; d. Merrill Quentin Games and Diana F. (Fryman) Jackson; m. Stephen Micheal Vuick, May 21, 1994. BA, U. Pitts., 1991. Promotion and mktg. asst. U. Pitts. Press, 1991-92, advt. and pub. rels. coord., 1992-93; comms. specialist Am. Heart Assn., Pitts., 1993—. Mem. adv. bd. Competitive Employment Opportunity, Pitts., 1996—. Mem. Women in Comms., Pitts. Cares, Press Club of Western Pa. Republican. Office: Am Heart Assn 10 Duff Rd Ste 304 Pittsburgh PA 15235

VUILLEMOT, JOANNE ELAINE, art educator, artist; b. Flint, Mich., Mar. 11, 1936; d. Russell Herman and Selena Mary (McLeod) V.; m. Lawrence Elson Winchell (dec. 1970). BFA, U. Ariz., 1972, MFA, 1975. Instr. Pima C.C., Tucson, 1975; prof. art C.C. of So. Nev., North Las Vegas, 1976—, chmn. faculty senate, 1996—. Artist, metalsmith showing work in numerous exhbns., including Nev. Inst. for Contemporary Art, Las Vegas, 1996, Rio Suite Hotel and Casino, Las Vegas, 1996, also in Ariz. and Mo. Recipient Individual Artist grant Nev. State Coun. on Arts, 1982, Honorable Mention award Cottey/PEO Nat. Art Exhbn., Nevada, Mo., 1991, Juror's award Biennial Nev. Artist Competition, 1992. Mem. Nev. Faculty Alliance (pres. 1994-96), PEO (pres. 1988-90, corr. sec. 1993-95, chaplain 1995-96).

VULGAMORE, ALLISON, performing arts administrator. BMus, Oberlin Coll. Former gen. mgr., artistic adminstr., mgr. ops. Nat. Symphony Orch., Washington; former gen. mgr. N.Y. Philharm. Orch., N.Y.C.; pres. Atlanta Symphony Orch., 1993—; bd. dirs. Oberlin Coll.; mem. arts challenge panel in music NEH. Bd. dirs. Midtown Alliance; active Vision 2000 Econ. Devel. Collaborative. Am. Symphony Orch. League fellow, 1980. Mem. Atlanta Rotary. Office: Atlanta Symphony Orchestra Robert W Woodruff Arts Ctr 1293 Peachtree St NE Ste 300 Atlanta GA 30309-3527

VULTAGGIO, LAURA MARIE, editor; b. Detroit, Mar. 7, 1969; d. Joseph Roy and Maria Assunta (Serra) V. BA, Oakland Univ., 1991. Acad. asst. Wayne State Univ., Sterling Heights, Mich., 1988-92; freelancer Ameritech Publ., Inc., Troy, Mich., 1991; editorial intern Volkswagon of Am., Inc., Auburn Hills, Mich., 1991; editor, training asst. The WW Group, Inc., Farmington Hills, Mich., 1992-94; comm. specialist Geometric Results, Inc., Southfield, Mich., 1994—. Vol. Nat. Dem. Party, Mt. Clemens, Mich., 1992. Mem. Internat. Assn. Bus. Communicators. Democrat. Roman Catholic. Office: Geometric Results Inc Ste 400 28333 Telegraph Rd Southfield MI 48034

WAAGE, ELAINE, community health nurse; b. Bklyn., Feb. 22, 1956; d. John and Josephine (Parcarelli) Diaz; m. Jeffrey Jay Waage, Aug. 29, 1976 (div. Aug. 1984); 1 child, John. BS in Nursing, Adelphi U., 1987. RN, N.Y.; cert. BLS, in peripherally inserted catheter. Staff nurse St. Joseph's Hosp.-Cath. Med. Ctr., Flushing, N.Y., 1987-88; vis. nurse, staff Healthforce Inc., Hempstead, N.Y., 1988-90; staff nurse surg. step down South Nassau Cmty. Hosp., Oceanside, N.Y., 1990-94; vis. nurse, on call supr. T.P.N. Svcs. Inc., Jericho, N.Y., 1990-94; IV therapy instr. All County Care, Ronkonkoma, N.Y., 1994; med. care rep., case mgr. catastrophic rehab. unit N.Y. State Ins. Fund, Hempstead, 1994—. Catechist tchr. St. Thomas the Apostle, West Hempstead, N.Y., 1984-88, St. Anne's, Garden City, N.Y., 1988-89. Mem. ANCC (cert. med.- surg. nurse), ANA, Nat. League Nursing, Nat. Assn. Vascular Access Network, Homehealth Care Nurses Assn., N.Y. State Nurses Assn. Republican. Roman Catholic. Home: 686 Pineneck Rd Seaford NY 11783-1220

WAAGNER, SHARON FLANNERY, library media specialist; b. Teaneck, N.J., Nov. 4, 1941; d. Frederick Worth Sr. and Virginia Mae (Rhode) Flannery; m. Louis Leonard Jr., Sept. 7, 1963; children: Gregory Louis, Susan Lynne Waagner Diaferio. BS in Edn., Empire State Coll., 1990; MLS, SUNY, Albany, 1992. Customer svc. rep. N.J. Bell, Ridgewood, N.J., 1961-64; bookkeeper The Times Press, Rutherford, N.J., 1967-79; libr. media specialist Long Lake (N.Y.) Ctrl. Sch., 1990—; new corrs. The Post Star, Glen Falls, N.Y., 1980-88, Hamilton County News, 1980-88, Tupper Lake Free Press, 1980-88. Mem. EMT Long Lake Resque Squad, 1980-93; past pres. Wood-Ridge PTA, 1977-79; dir. Hamilton County Red Cross, Speculator, N.Y., 1985; treas. Long Lake Fire Dept., 1980-82; mem. Long Lake Cmty. Choir, 1980—. Trustee Wood-Ridge Pub. Libr., 1975-79, So. Adk. Libr. System, Saratoga Springs, N.Y., 1985-90, Friends of Long Lake Libr., 1992—; adv. bd. F-E-H Sch. Libr. Systems, Malone, N.Y., 1992—; class advisor Long Lake Ctrl. Class of 1999; children's program coord. Long Lake Libr. Mem. N.Y. State Libr. Assn., Long Lake Ctrl. Sch. Tech. Com., Adirondack Mus. Republican. Roman Catholic. Home: PO Box 155 Newcomb Rd Long Lake NY 12847 Office: Long Lake Central Sch School St PO Box 217 Long Lake NY 12847

WACHA, DONNA MARIE, mathematics educator; b. Teaneck, N.J., Feb. 10, 1951; d. Donald and Claire Marie (Jarvie) W. BS, Trenton State Coll., 1973; MA, Georgian Court Coll., 1983. Cert. math. tchr., N.J., elem. tchr., N.J., supr., prin. Math. tchr. Point Pleasant (N.J.) High Sch. Point Pleasant Bd. Edn., 1977—; instrnl. cons. Am. Inst. Banking, Mid Jersey chpt. Recipient summer internship N.J. Bus.-Industry-Sci. Edn. Consortium, 1992. Mem. Nat. Coun. Math. Tchrs., Assn. Math. Tchrs. N.J., Ocean County Edn. Assn., Point Pleasant Edn. Assn., N.J. Edn. Assn. Home: 1034 Tammy Ct Brick NJ 08724 Office: Point Pleasant High Sch Laura Herbert Dr Point Pleasant NJ 08742

WACHNER, LINDA JOY, apparel marketing and manufacturing executive; b. N.Y.C., Feb. 3, 1946; d. Herman and Shirley W.; m. Seymour Applebaum, Dec. 21, 1973 (dec., 1983). BS in Econs. and Bus., U. Buffalo, 1966. Buyer Foley's Federated Dept. Store, Houston, 1968-69; sr. buyer R.H. Macy's, N.Y.C., 1969-74; v.p. Warner divsn. Warnaco, Bridgeport, Conn., 1974-77; v.p. corp. mktg. Caron Internat., N.Y.C., 1977-79; chief exec. officer U.S. divsn. Max Factor & Co., Hollywood, Calif., 1979-82, pres., chief exec. officer, 1982-83; pres., chief exec. officer Max Factor & Co. Worldwide, 1983-84; mng. dir. Adler & Shaykin, N.Y.C., 1985-86; pres., CEO, chmn. Warnaco Inc., N.Y.C., 1986—; chmn., CEO Authentic Fitness Corp., 1991—; bd. dirs. The Travellers, Inc. Presdl. appointee Adv. Com. for Trade, Policy, Negotiations; trustee U. Buffalo Found., Carnegie Hall, Aspen Inst., Thirteen/WNET; bd. overseers Meml. Sloan-Kettering Cancer Ctr. Recipient Silver Achievement award L.A. YWCA; named Outstanding Woman in Bus. Women's Equity Action League, 1980, Woman of Yr., MS. Mag., 1986, one of the Yr.'s Most Fascinating Bus. People, Fortune Mag., 1986, one of 10 Most Powerful Women in Corp. Am., Savvy Woman Mag., 1989, 90, Am.'s Most Successful Bus. Woman, Fortune Mag., 1992, Queen of Cash Flow, Chief Exec. Mag., 1994. Mem. Am. Mgmt. Assn., Am. Apparel Mktg. Assn. (bd. dirs.), Bus. Roundtable, Coun. on Fgn. Rels. Republican. Jewish. Office: Warnaco Inc/Authentic Fitness Corp 90 Park Ave New York NY 10016

WACHSTEIN, JOAN MARTHA, dental hygienist; b. Phila., Nov. 12, 1941; d. Milton and Mabel Louise (Friedman) Hertzfeld; m. Mortimer Berwyn Wachstein, July 14, 1962 (dec. 1989); children: Lisa Beth, Esther Lynn. RDH, Temple U., Phila., 1961. Registered dental hygienist; cert. gerontology referral Union Am. Hebrew Congregations and Hebrew Union Coll. Jewish Inst. Religion. Dental hygienist Dr. M.B. Wachstein, Newark, Del., 1970-89; campaign mgr. Milton and Hattie Kutz Home for Capital Campaign, 1995. Mem. allocations panel & mem. planning coms. United Way, Wilmington, Del., 1986-92, bd. dirs., 1994—, allocations panel chair, 1994—, mem. strategic planning com., ethics com., 1994-95, chair spl. gifts divsn. United Way campaign, 1996; bd. dirs. Jewish Family Svcs., del., 1983—, rec. sec., 1984-86, 88-91, pres., 1992-94, treas. 1989-91, Milton and Hattie Kutz Home, Inc., 1987—, v.p., 1988-96, treas., 1994-96; bd. mem. Associated Jewish Family and Childrens Agys., 1995—; pres. Aux. Milton and Hattie Kutz Home, Inc., 1985-87; bd. dirs. Jewish Fedn. Del., 1983-89, 91-92, 94—, mem. exec. com., 1992-93, mem. Jewish Cmty. endowment com., Mid-Atlantic coun. Union Am. Hebrew Congregations, 1981—, vice chair biennial program com., 1990-92, chair 1992-94, bd. dirs., 1994—, v.p. 1992—, bd. trustees Union of Am. Hebrew Congregations, 1994—, mem. com. on Jewish family, mem. commn. on religious living, mem. outreach commn. exec. com., vice chair com. on older adults, 1996—; mem. Women of Reform Judaism, Fedn. Temple Sisterhoods, 1975—, v.p. 1987-89, 89-91, 91-93, mem. at large bd. dirs., 1993—; pres. Beth Emeth Sisterhood, 1968-70; mem. jr. bd. Med. Ctr. Del., Inc.; apptd. commn adult entertainment establishments, State of Del., 1993—; mem. N.Am. bd. World Union Progressive Judaism; chair Women for Carper com. for Gov. State of Del., 1993-96. Recipient Community Builder award NCCJ, 1985, Keva cert. Ctrl. Conf. Am. Rabbis and Nat. Assn. Temple Educators. Mem. Nat. Coun. Jewish Women, Orgn. for Rehab. and Tng., Temple U. Dental Hygiene Alumni Assn., B'nai B'rith, Hadassah. Jewish. Home: 3331 Silverside Rd Wilmington DE 19810-3306

WACKER, KAREN LOUISE, special education educator; b. Mobile, Ala., Aug. 6, 1960; d. Charles Frederick Jr. and Mary Louise (Pond) W. BS, U. Ala., 1982; MS, U. South Ala., 1988. Behavior disorders tchr. Houston County Schs., Dothan, Ala., 1983-84, John F. Kennedy H.S., Tamuning, Guam, 1984-85, Mobile (Ala.) County Schs., 1985-86; behavior disorders/learning disabilities tchr. Baldwin County Schs., Bay Minette, Ala., 1986-93; interrelated resource/behavior disorders tchr. Cobb County Schs., Atlanta, 1993—; dept. chmn. John F. Kennedy High, Tamuning, 1984-85; cheerleader sponsor Gulf Shores (Ala.) Middle Sch., 1987-89; extended day program coord. Bay Minette (Ala.) Elem., 1990-93. Vol. 1996 Centennial Olympic Games, Atlanta. Named Outstanding Young Women of Am., 1986. Mem. Ala. Alumni Assn., Baldwin County Jr. Women's Club, Cath. H.S. Alumni, Order Polka Dots (sec. 1990-92), Phi Eta Sigma, Kappa Delta Pi, Phi Kappa Delta, Alpha Lambda Delta. Roman Catholic. Home: 1185 Collier Rd NW Apt 14E Atlanta GA 30318-8220

WACKER-BERTRAM, DEBORAH, secondary Spanish and special education educator; b. San Diego, Dec. 22, 1945; d. Robert Eugene and Marion Llewella (Bancroft) Wacker; m. William E. Calvert, Dec. 22, 1966 (div. Aug. 1984); 1 child, William E. Calvert II; m. John Steven Bertram, Mar. 8, 1985. BA, Belhaven Coll., Jackson, Miss., 1967. Cert. tchr., Miss., Tex. Mid. sch. spl. edn. tchr. Killeen (Tex.) Ind. Sch. Dist., 1982-85; elem. sch. spl. edn. tchr., tchr. ESL, Mansfield (Tex.) Ind. Sch. Dist., 1985-86; jr. high sch. spl. edn. tchr., head dept. Arlington (Tex.) Ind. Sch. Dist., 1986-90; jr. high sch. spl. edn. tchr. Conroe (Tex.) Ind. Sch. Dist., 1990-92, high sch. spl. edn. tchr., 1992-93, tchr. Spanish., 1993—, com. mem. supt.'s tchr. adv. bd., 1991-92, com. mem. prin.'s site-based mgmt. adv. team, 1991-92, mem. health benefits com., 1991-94, mem. benefits com., 1995-96. Soprano Montgomery County Choral Soc., Conroe, 1991-94, sect. leader, 1995-96; mem. Campus Site-Based Decision Making Team, 1996—; mem. Arlington Choral Soc., 1986-89; sponsor Tex. Future Tchrs. Am., 1995—. Mem. AAUW, NEA, Tex. Fgn. Lang. Assn., Tex. State Tchrs. Assn. (1st presx. 1991, mem. spl. edn. caucus), Conroe Edn. Assn. (pres.-elect 1990-92, 95—, exec. com. 1994—), Am. Coun. Tchrs. Fgn. Lang., Internat. Club. (sponsor). Republican. Methodist. Home: 1414 Pine Gap Dr Houston TX 77090-2128 Office: Oak Ridge HS Oak Ridge School Rd Conroe TX 77385

WADDINGTON, BETTE HOPE (ELISABETH CROWDER), violinist, educator; b. San Francisco, July 27, 1921; d. John and Marguerite (Crowder) Waddington; BA in Music, U. Calif. at Berkeley, 1945, postgrad.; postgrad. (scholarship) Juilliard Sch. Music, 1950, San Jose State Coll., 1955; MA in Music and Art, San Francisco U., 1953; violin student of Joseph Fuchs, Melvin Ritter, Frank Gittelson, Felix Khuner, Daniel Bonsack, D.C. Dounis, Naoum Blinder, Eddy Brown. Cert. tchr. music and art K-12 and jr. coll., Calif., libr. elem., secondary and jr. coll., Calif. Violinist Erie (Pa.) Symphony, 1950-51, Dallas Symphony, 1957-58, St. Louis Symphony, 1958-95. Cert. gen. elem. and secondary tchr., Calif.; life cert. music and art for jr. coll.; cert. in librarianship from elem. sch. to jr. coll., Calif. Toured alone and with St. Louis Symphony U.S., Can., Middle East, Japan, China, England, Korea, Europe, Africa; concert master Peninsula Symphony, Redwood City and San Mateo, Calif., Grove Music Soc., N.Y.C.; violinist St. Louis Symphony, 1958-95, violinist emeritus, 1995—; numerous recordings St. Louis Symphony, 1958—. Mem. Am. String Tchrs. Assn., Am. Musicians Union (St. Louis and San Francisco chpts. life), U. Calif. Alumnae Assn. (Berkeley, life), San Francisco State U. Alumni Assn. (life), Am. String Tchrs. Assn., San Jose State U. Alumni Assn. (life), Sierra Club (life), Alpha Beta Alpha. Avocations: travel, art and archeology history, drawing, painting. Office: St Louis Symphony Orch care Powell Symphony Hall 718 N Grand Blvd Saint Louis MO 63103-1011

WADDY, WILLANNA RUTH, artist; b. Lincoln, Nebr., Jan. 7, 1909; d. John Moses Gilliam and Willie Anna Choran; m. William Henry Waddy; 1 child, Marianna. Student, U. Minn., 1922; DFA (hon.), U. N.Y., 1987. Domestic worker Mpls., 1922-29; clk. U.S. Postal Svc., Chgo., 1929-30; med. clk. Chgo. Gen. Hosp., 1930; admissions worker L.A. County Hosp., L.A., 1936; riveter McDonald Douglas Aircraft, L.A., 1942; founder Art West Inc., L.A., 1963. Mem. ACLU. Home: 1240 Fillmore St #410 San Francisco CA 94115

WADE, BRENDA LYNN, chef; b. Shelby, Mich., Oct. 19, 1962; d. John and Marcella Wade. Student, Grand Rapid Jr. Coll. Chef C. A. Muer Corp., Detroit, 1981—. C.A. Muer Corp. scholar, James Beard Found. scholar. Mem. Round Table FOr Women in Food Service. Home: 404 SE 6th Ave Deerfield Beach FL 33441 Office: C A Muer Corp 1755 SE 3d Ct Deerfield Beach FL 33441

WADLEY, SUSAN SNOW, anthropologist; b. Balt., Nov. 18, 1943; d. Chester Page and Ellen Snow (Foster) W.; m. Bruce Woods Derr, Dec. 28, 1971 (div. July 1989); children: Shona Snow, Laura Woods; m. Richard Olanoff, July 4, 1992. BA, Carleton Coll., Northfield, 1965; MA, U. Chgo., 1967, PhD, 1973. Instr. Syracuse U., 1970-73, asst. prof., 1973-76, dir. fgn. and comparative studies program, 1978-83, prof., 1982, dir. So. Asia Ctr., 1985—, Ford-Maxwell prof. South Asian Studies, 1996—, chair anthropology dept., 1990-95; trustee Am. Inst. Indian Studies, Chgo., 1984—, exec. com., 1991-94; mem. joint com. South Asia Social Sci. Rsch. Coun., 1982-89. Author: Shakti: Power in the Conceptual Struture of Krimpur Women, 1975, Women in India: Two Perspectives, 1978, revised, 1989, 95, Struggling with Destiny in Karimpur, 1925-84, 1994; editor: Power of Tamil Women, 1980, Oral Epics in India, 1989, Media and the Transformation of Religion in South Asia, 1995. Pres. Edward Smith Parent Tchr. Orgn., Syracuse, 1988-89. Grantee NSF, 1967-69, U.S. Dept. Edn., 1983-84, Smithsonian Instn., 1983-84, Am. Inst. Indian Studies, 1989, Social Scis. Rsch. Coun., 1989, NEH, 1995. Mem. Am. Anthropological Soc., Am. Folklore Soc., Soc. for Ethnomusicology, Assn. for Asian Studies. Home: 302 Carlton Dr Syracuse NY 13214-1906 Office: Syracuse U Maxwell Sch Syracuse NY 13244

WADLOW, JOAN KRUEGER, academic administrator; b. LeMars, Iowa, Aug. 21, 1932; d. R. John and Norma I. (IhLe) Krueger; m. Richard R. Wadlow, July 27, 1958; children: Dawn, Kit. B.A., U. Nebr., Lincoln, 1953; M.A. (Seacrest Journalism fellow 1953-54), Fletcher Sch. Law and Diplomacy, 1956; Ph.D. (Rotary fellow 1956-57), U. Nebr., Lincoln, 1963; cert., Grad. Inst. Internat. Studies, Geneva, 1957. Mem. faculty U. Nebr., Lincoln, 1966-79; prof. polit. scis. U. Nebr., 1964-79, assoc. dean Coll. Arts and Scis., 1972-79; prof. polit. scis., dean Coll. Arts and Scis., U. Wyo., Laramie, 1979-84, v.p. acad. affairs, 1984-86; prof. polit. sci., provost U. Okla., Norman, 1986-91; chancellor U. Alaska, Fairbanks, 1991—; cons. on fed. grants; bd. dirs. Key Bank Alaska; mem. Commn. Colls. N.W. Assn. Author articles in field. Bd. dirs. Nat. Merit Scholarship Corp., Lincoln United Way, 1976-77, Bryan Hosp., Lincoln, 1978-79, Washington Ctr., 1986—, Key Bank of Alaska; v.p., exec. commr. North Cen. Assn., pres., 1991; pres. adv. bd. Lincoln YWCA, 1970-71; mem. def. adv. com. Women in the Svcs., 1987-89; mem. community adv. bd. Alaska Airlines. Recipient Mortar Board Teaching award, 1976, Disting. Teaching award U. Nebr., Lincoln, 1979; fellow Conf. Coop. Man, Lund, Sweden, 1956. Mem. Internat. Studies Assn. (co-editor Internat. Studies Notes 1978-91), Nat. Assn. State Univs. and Land-Grant Colls. (exec. com. coun. acad. affairs 1989-91), Western Assn. Africanists (pres. 1980-82), Assn. Western Univs. (pres.-elect 1993—), Coun. Colls. Arts and Scis. (pres. 1983-84), Greater Fairbanks C. of C., Gamma Phi Beta. Republican. Congregationalist. Office: U Alaska Fairbanks Singers Hall Ste 320 Fairbanks AK 99775

WADSWORTH, JACQUELINE DORÈT, real estate developer, private investor; b. San Diego, June 15, 1928; d. Benjamin H. Dilley and Georgia E. (Elliott) Dilley Waters; m. Charles Desmond Wadsworth Jr., June 16, 1954 (dec. 1963); 1 child, Georgia Duncan Wadsworth Barber. BS, U. Oreg., 1946-50; MA, San Diego State U., 1950-52. Cert. tchr. Calif., Oreg. Dir. Jr. Red Cross, San Diego County chpt. ARC, 1952-59; asst. dir. leadership ctrs. for 8 western states ARC, Calif., 1954-59; pvt. investor, comml. real estate and property devel., 1974—; interior designer J. Wadsworth Interiors, La Jolla, Calif., 1990—. Vol. chairperson nat. conv. ARC, San Diego, 1966; vol., fundraiser San Diego Symphony Orch. Orgn., 1974-83; mem. Gold Ribbon Patron com. San Diego Symphony, 1995—; friends mem., vol. San Diego Mus. Art, 1958—, Asian Arts Com., 1996—; mem. Scripps Found. for Medicine and Sci., 1990—; life mem., bd. programs Mercy Hosp. Aux., 1965—; life mem., chairperson, bd. dirs. Social Svc. Aux., 1968—. Recipient Svc. awards Mercy Hosp. Aux., 1967-70. Mem. Caridad Internat., Globe Gilders Theatre Aux. (activity chairperson 1966-85), San Diego Zool. Soc. (curator 1976—), Country Friends Charities La Jolla Group, Mus. Contemporary Art San Diego. Republican.

WAECHTER, ELEANOR, not for profit corporation administrator; b. Yonkers, N.Y., Sept. 3, 1939; d. John Knox and Eleanor Wilfong (Horwood) Morrison; m. Robert Louis Waechter, Mar. 21, 1964; children: Elizabeth Anne, Robert Louis Jr. BS, SUNY, New Paltz, 1961, postgrad., 1963. Cert. tchr., N.Y. Tchr. English Yonkers Pub. Sch. System, 1961-65; dir. camp Taconic Girl Scout Coun., Inc., Katonah, N.Y., 1973-78, field exec., 1975-77, mgr. field svc., 1977-79; asst. exec. dir. Girl Scouts Westchester-Putnam, Inc, Valhalla, N.Y., 1979-82; exec. dir. Girl Scouts Westchester-Putnam, Inc, Pleasantville, N.Y., 1982—; mem. N.Y. Girl Scout Legis. Network, Albany, 1985—, mem. 1st cert. Girl Scout Exec. Dir. Group, 1995. Instr. ARC, Westchester, White Plains, N.Y., 1975-82; campaign vol. United Way of Westchester, White Plains, 1982—; bd. dirs. Vol. Svc. Bur., Westchester, 1989-94, Westchester Coalition, 1990-93. Mem. Westchester County Assn., Alpha Delta Kappa. Presbyterian. Office: Girl Scouts of Westchester-Putnam Inc 2 Great Oak Ln Pleasantville NY 10570-2110

WAGEMAN, VIRGINIA FARLEY, editor; b. Jersey City, N.J., Feb. 18, 1941; d. James Christopher and Charlotte Carter (Stebbins) Farley; m. Steven Lipson, Dec. 26, 1962 (div. 1964); 1 child, Melissa; m. James Carter Wageman, Apr. 22, 1968; children: Robinson Michael, Sarah Carter. BA, Bard Coll., 1964. Book editor, prodn. asst. AICPA, N.Y.C., 1964-67; prodn. mgr. U. Hawaii Press, 1967-68; asst. dir. office univ. rels. U. Md., Balt.,

1968-70; dir. publs. art mus. Princeton U., 1971-81; writer, editor Hirshhorn Mus. and Sculpture Garden, Washington, 1982-86; freelance editor, 1986—; sr. editor Hudson Hills (N.Y.) Press, 1988-89; mgr. publs. Coll. Art Assn., N.Y.C., 1989—. Recipient Smithsonian Commendation for Exceptional Svc. Mem. Art Table, Assn. Freelance Art Editors (pres. 1984-86), Princeton Rsch. Forum. Home: 360 Ridgeview Rd Princeton NJ 08540-7667 Office: Coll Art Assn 275 7th Ave New York NY 10001-6708

WAGERER, DONNA LYNN, real estate company official; b. Chgo., Oct. 15, 1959; d. James Robert and Faith Josephine (Jackson) Michalak; m. Thomas Peter Wagener, Sept. 26, 1987; 1 child, Trevor Michael. BS in Fin., U. Ill., Chgo., 1985. Sales mgr., advt. mgr. Menconi Co., Chgo., 1979-81; asst. v.p. constrn. Jupiter Realty Corp., Chgo., 1985—; cons. Captive Audience, Chgo., 1988—. Mem. AAUW, NAFE. Home: 1911 N Mohawk St Unit A Chicago IL 60614-5219 Office: Jupiter Realty Corp 919 N Michigan Ave Chicago IL 60611

WAGER, DEBORAH MILLER, researcher, consultant; b. Phila., Sept. 5, 1938; d. Albert S. and Pauline (Goldberg) Miller; m. Robert J. Wager, July 3, 1966; 1 child, James M. BA, Skidmore Coll., 1960; MAT, Columbia U., 1963. Editor Toy Quality and Safety Report, Washington, 1972-88; cons. Wager Rsch., Washington, 1989—; devel. rschr. Sidwell Friends Sch., Washington, 1988-89, 92-93; trustee Sheridan Sch., Washington, 1978-84. Author: Good Toys, 1986. Mem. Assn. Profl. Rschrs. Advancement. Office: Wager Rsch Consulting 4545 29th St NW Washington DC 20008-2144

WAGER, PAULA JEAN, artist; b. Lansing, Mich., Dec. 19, 1929; d. Mervin Elihu and Cora Della (Raymer) Fowler; m. William Douglas Wager, May 4, 1952; children: Pamela Ann, Scott Alan. Student, Mich. State U., 1949-52. Music tchr. Toledo, Ohio, 1968-72, Union Lake, Mich., 1972-76; tchr. art, artist Paula Wager's Art Studio, Commerce Twp., Mich., 1984—; hostess Artistic Touch with Paula, Cable Comcast channel 44, Waterford, Mich., 1991-94, 96—, TCI West Oakland, Walled Lake, Mich., Channel 10, 1991-94. Exhibited in group shows including Village Art Supplies, 1982-88, Pontiac Oakland Soc. Artists, 1983—, Pontiac Galleria, 1983, Oakland C.C., Commerce Twp., 1985, Red Piano Gallery, Hilton Head, S.C., 1985-89, Mich. State U., East Lansing, 1986, Silver Pencil Gallery, Pontiac, 1987-89, Wooden Sleight, Vestaburg, Mich., 1988-93, Art Pad, Keego Harbor, Mich., 1990-93, Local Color Gallery, Union Pier, Mich., 1992-94, Mich. Assn. Artists, Southfield Civ. Ctr. Mich. 1995; solo exhbns. include Waterford Pub. Lib., 1996, Swann Gallery, Detroit, 1995—, Millers Artist Supplies, Ferndale, Mich., 1996, Waterford Twp. Hall, 1996; represented in pvt. collections. Recipient Outstanding Achievement award in instructional programming Comcast Cable TV, Waterford, 1992, 1st place, Waterford Friends of the Arts Art Show, 1988, Pontiac Oakland Soc. Artists Cmty. Rm., 1990, Am. Biog. Inst. Woman of Yr. Commemorative medal, 1995; Waterford Cable Commn. grantee, 1991, 93, Charter Twp. of Waterford grantee, 1991-94. Mem. Nat. Assn. Female Exec. Pontiac Oakland Soc. Artists, Waterford Friends of the Arts, Mich. Watercolor Soc., Birmingham Bloomfield Art Assn., Colored Pencil Soc. Am., Colored Pencil Soc. Detroit, Village Fine Arts Assn., Paint Creek Ctr. for the Arts. Home and Studio: 3316 Greenlawn Ave Commerce Township MI 48382-4629

WAGGETT, JEAN MCMONIGLE, lawyer, corporate; b. Kansas City, Mo., May 20, 1941; d. Vivian Whitley and Ruth McMonigle. BS, U. Mo., 1963; JD, U. Mich., 1975. Bar: Conn. 1977. Atty. Health, Edn. and Welfare, Washington, 1975-77; counsel, v.p. Aetna Life & Casualty, Hartford, Conn., 1977—; gen. counsel, sr. v.p. Aetna Internat., Inc., Hartford, Conn., 1987-93, v.p. and corp. sec., 1993-95; v.p. N. Am. Strate, 1995; gen. counsel, corp. sec. Terra Nova Bermuda Holdings, Hamilton, 1996—. Mem. ABA, Internat. Bar Assn., Am. Corp. Counsel Assn., Am. Soc. Corp. Sec. Home: Helms a Lee, Glencoe Village, Paget Bermuda Office: Terra Nova, 12 Par La Ville Rd, Hamilton HM08, Bermuda

WAGGONER, RENEÉ, medical and surgical nurse; b. Dayton, Ohio, Oct. 19, 1955; d. Norman and Ethel (Sinclair) Fountain; m. Ronnie Davis Waggoner, June 12, 1976; children: Danielle Nicole, Ronesha Darlese. Assoc. Liberal Arts, Sinclair Coll., Dayton, Ohio, 1982; B Social Work, U. Dayton, 1984; Assoc. Nursing, Clark State Coll., Springfield, Ohio, 1989; B Nursing, Miami U., Oxford, Ohio, 1994; postgrad., Wright State U., 1994—. Cert. BLS, ACLS Am. Heart Assn. Primary nurse I oncology Miami Valley Hosp., Dayton, 1989-90; staff nurse med.-surg. Dept. Vets. Affairs, Dayton, 1990, Grandview Hosp., Dayton, 1990-91, Dept. Vets. Affairs, Dayton, 1992—; hospice home care nurse Hospice Home Health, 1996; staff nurse neurology Good Samaritan Hosp., 1996; vol. Heartfest Dept. Vets. Affairs, Dayton, 1994, mem. black affairs com. Mem. Nat. Black Women's Health Project, Atlanta, 1994; trained vol. Scan Stop Child Abuse and Neglect. Mem. NAACP, Transcultura Nursing Soc., Miami U. Honor Soc. (founder 1995). Democrat. Methodist. Home: 5021 Laguna Rd Trotwood OH 45426-3864

WAGLE, SUSAN, state legislator, small business owner; b. Allentown, Pa., Sept. 27, 1953; m. John Thomas Wagle, Apr. 3, 1980; children: Julia Marie, Andrea Elizabeth, John Timothy, Paul Thomas. BA in Elem. Edn. cum laude, Wichita State U., 1979, post grad., 1979 82. Tchr. Chisholm Trail Elem., Kans., 1979-80; tchr. emotionally disturbed, special edn. Price Elem., Kans., 1980-82; real estate investor Kans., 1980—; prin. Wichita Bus. Inc., Kans., 1983—; mem. Kansas Ho. Reps., 1990, 92, 94—, speaker pro tem, 1994—. Mem. Am. Legis. Exchange Coun. (Outstanding Legis. of the Yr. 1994), Farm Bur., Nat. Fedn. Ind. Bus., Nat. Restaurant Assn., Wichita Ind. Bus. Assn. Home: 14 N Sandalwood St Wichita KS 67230-6612 Office: Kans Ho of Reps Rm 330 N State Capitol Topeka KS 66612-1504

WAGNER, ANNICE MCBRYDE, judge. BA, Wayne State U., law degree. With Houston and Gardner; gen. counsel Nat. Capital Housing Authority; people's counsel D.C.; assoc. judge Superior Court D.C., 1977-90; assoc. judge D.C. Ct. Appeals, 1990—, now chief judge; mem. teaching team, trial advocacy workshop Harvard U. Office: Dist of Columbia Ct 500 Indiana Ave NW Rm 6000 Washington DC 20001-2131*

WAGNER, AUDREY ANN, child care provider; b. Moulton, Tex., June 12, 1949; d. Dannis Shelton and Eleanor Mary (Butschek) W.; m. William Martin Hanson, Jan. 16, 19 ; children: Sven Wagner Hanson, Kell Hanson Wagner. BA, Southwest Tex. State U., 1971. Child care provider Billings, Mont., 1981-96. Vol. Garfield Elem. Sch., Billings, 1988—, Global Village, Billings, 1991—, Friday Night Open Gym, Billings, 1995—, Riverside Middle Sch., 1995—; mem. state bd. Mont. Women's Lobby, 1994—; v.p. Friends of the Libr., Billings, 191—; v.p. PTA Garfield Elem. Sch., 1994—. Mem. NOW (ea. v.p. Mont. chpt., 1993—). Democrat. Roman Catholic. Home: 320 S 35th St Billings MT 59101

WAGNER, CAROLYN A(NN), adult and gerontological nurse practitioner; b. Harrisburg, Pa., Nov. 9, 1944; d. Robert E. and Thelma (Eshenour) Sheaffer; m. William F. Wagner, Aug. 10, 1963; children: William J., Elizabeth M. Diploma, Reading Hosp. Sch. Nursing, West Reading, Pa., 1967; AS, No. Va. C.C., Manassas, 1982; BSN, George Mason U., 1991, MSN, 1993. RN, Pa., Va., W.Va.; cert. adult nurse practitioner; cert. BLS; cert. gerontol. nurse practitioner; cert. ACLS. Staff nurse Cmty. Nursing Svc. of Delaware County, Lansdowne, Pa., 1970-73; insvc. dir., asst. dir. nurses Manassas Manor, 1973-79; staff nurse Fairfax (Va.) Nursing Ctr., 1975-77, 86-87, nursing supr., 1977-78, dir. ctrl. supply/insvc.dir., 1978-79, dir. purchasing, dir. ctrl. supply, 1979-86; patient care coord. Commonwealth Care Ctr., Fairfax, 1987-93; adult nurse practitioner Valley Health Sys., Winchester, Va., 1993—; adj. faculty Shenandoah U., Winchester, Va., 1995—; affiliate faculty George Mason U., Fairfax, Va., 1996—; clin. prof. U. Va., 1996—; mem. Gov.'s Conf. on Aging, Richmond, Va., 1993; chair adv. bd. Health Depot, Winchester, 1993—. Mem. Parish Nurse Caring Com., Winchester, 1993-96, N.W. Va. Parish Nurse Coalition, 1996—. Mem. No. Va. Coun. Nurse Practitioners, Va. Coalition for the Aging, Va. Nurses Assn. (v.p. dist. 12 1996-97), ANA. Roman Catholic. Home: 116 Bell Haven Circle Stephens City VA 22655-9802 Office: Health Depot Valley Health Sys 333 W Cork St Winchester VA 22601-3862

WAGNER, CHARLENE BROOK, middle school educator, consultant; b. L.A.; d. Edward J. and Eva (Anderson) Brook; m. Gordon Boswell Jr. (div.); children: Gordon, Brook, John. BS, Tex. Christian U., 1952; MEd, Sam Houston U., 1973; postgrad., U. Tex., Austin, 1975, Tex. A&M U., 1977. Sci. educator Spring Branch Ind. Sch. Dist., Houston, 1970—; cons. Scott Foresman Pub. Co., 1982-83; owner Sci. Instrnl. Sys. Co., 1988—; rep. World Class Network. Mem. Houston Opera Guild, Houston Symphony League, 1992, Mus. Fine Arts, Mus. of Art of Am. West, Houston, 1989, Women's Christian Home, Houston, 1991; social chmn. Encore, 1988; mem. Magic Circle Rep. Women's Club. Mem. NEA, NAFE, AAUW, Tex. State Tchrs. Assn., Spring Branch Edn. Assn., Internat. Platform Assn., Wellington Soc. for Arts (Houston chpt.), Shepherd Soc., Watercolor Arts Soc., Art League Houston, Clan Anderson Soc., Heather and Thistle Soc., Houston Highland Games Assn. Episcopalian. Home: B54 2670 Marilee Ln Houston TX 77057-4264 Office: Spring Oaks Mid Sch 2150 Shadowdale Dr Houston TX 77043-2608

WAGNER, CYNTHIA GAIL, editor, writer; b. Bethesda, Md., Oct. 3, 1956; d. Robert Cheney and Marjory Jane (Kletzing) W. BA in English, Grinnell Coll., 1978; MA in Comms., Syracuse U., 1981. Editorial asst. The Futurist/World Future Soc., Bethesda, Md., 1981-82, staff editor, 1982-85, asst. editor, 1985-91, sr. editor, 1991-92, mng. editor, 1992—. Author: (plays) Discriminating Dining, 1993, Limited Engagement, 1993; columnist 3-2-1 Contact, 1994; contbr. Encyclopedia of the Future, 1995. Mem. Theatre Comm. Group, Soc. Profl. Journalists. Office: The Futurist World Future Soc 7910 Woodmont Ave Ste 450 Bethesda MD 20814-3015

WAGNER, CYNTHIA KAYE, business administration educator, consultant; b. Lincoln, Nebr., Jan. 29, 1957; d. Richard and Gloria Jean (Larsen) W. BS in Agronomy with honors, Ohio State U., 1979, MS in Agronomy, 1980; PhD in Bus. Adminstrn., U. Pa., 1986. Rsch. assoc. Physiology Lab., Ohio State U., Columbus, 1977-80; rsch. scientist Battelle Columbus Labs., 1980-82; rsch. asst. Mgmt. and Behavioral Sci. Ctr., Wharton Sch., U. Pa., Phila., 1983-85; cons. UN Devel. Program, N.Y.C., 1985-86; bus. mgr. Pioneer Hi-Bred Internat., Des Moines, 1987-90; from asst. prof. to assoc. prof. bus. adminstrn. U. Pacific, Stockton, Calif., 1990—. Contbr. articles on mgmt. of tech. to profl. jours. Dean's fellow Wharton Sch., U. Pa., 1983-84. Mem. AAAS. Office: U Pacific Sch Bus-Pub Admin 3601 Pacific Cir Stockton CA 95211-0110

WAGNER, DOROTHY MARIE, retired creative designer, artist; b. Chgo., Jan. 12, 1926; d. William Christopher and Margaret Frances (Rowell) W. Student, Kalamazoo Coll., 1943-45; BS, Western Mich. U., 1947; BFA, Art Ctr. Coll. Design, L.A., 1962. Dir. electroencephalography lab. Bronson Hosp., Kalamazoo, 1945-51; dir. EEG lab. Terr. Hosp., Kaneohe, Hawaii, 1951-55, UCLA Med. Ctr., 1955-60; sr. creative designer GM Tech. Ctr. Styling, Warren, Mich., 1962-82; cons. in EEG, Army Hosp., Honolulu, 1950-55; dir. sales and rental gallery Pt. Huron (Mich.) Mus., 1989-93, art and painting instr., 1992-96. Recipient Best of Show award Ea. Mich. Internat. Art Show, 1992, 1st pl. award, 1988, 89, 94. Mem. Blue Water Art Assn. (pres. 1990-96), Orion Art Ctr. Episcopalian. Home: 14841 Pine Knoll Ln Capac MI 48014

WAGNER, FLORENCE ZELEZNIK, telecommunications executive; b. McKeesport, Pa., Sept. 23, 1926; d. George and Sophia (Petros) Zeleznik; BA magna cum laude, U. Pitts., 1977, MPA, 1981; m. Francis Xavier Wagner, June 18, 1946; children: Deborah Elaine Wagner Franke, Rebecca Susan Wagner Schroettinger, Melissa Catherine Wagner Good, Francis Xavier, Robert Francis. Sec. to pres. Tube City Iron & Metal Co., Glassport, Pa., 1944-50; cons. Raw Materials, Inc., Pitts., 1955; gen. mgr. Carson Compressed Steel Products, Pitts., 1967-69; ptnr. Universal Steel Products, Pitts., 1970-71; gen. mgr. Josh Steel Co., Braddock, Pa., 1971-78; owner Wagner's Candy Box, Mt. Lebanon, Pa., 1979-80; borough sec./treas. Borough of Pennsbury Village, Allegheny County, Pa., 1980-88; ptnr. Telecommunications of Am., Burgettstown, Pa., 1984-86; trustee Profit-Sharing trust, Pension trust Josh Steel Co., 1986—, Consol, Inc., Upper St. Clair, Pa., 1989—; mem. Foster Parents, Jefferson Twp. Planning Commn., Washington County, Pa.; mem. sch. bd. St. Bernard Cath. Elem. Sch., Mt. Lebanon, Pa., sec., 1995—. Mem. AAUW, Pitts. Symphony Soc., Pitts. Ballet Theater Guild. Mem. Soc. Pub. Adminstrn. (founder U. Pitts. br.), Acad. Polit. Sci., U.S. Strategic Inst., Southwestern Pa. Sec. Assn., Alpha Sigma Lambda (past treas., sec., pres.). Republican. Home: 1611 Upper Saint Clair Dr Pittsburgh PA 15241

WAGNER, JANICE MARY, occupational therapist; b. Cleve., Jan. 18, 1960; d. George V. and Judy F. (Feliciano) W.; m. Chris James Cherrie, Aug. 12, 1995. BS, Ohio State U., 1986. Registered and lic. occupational therapist. Sr. occupational therapist St. John & Westshore Hosp., Westlake, Ohio, 1986-94; occupational therapist Phoenix-Hudson Corp., Cleve., 1995—. Mem. N.E. Ohio Hand Study Group, Phi Theta Epsilon. Unitarian.

WAGNER, JEANETTE SARKISIAN, cosmetics company executive; m. Paul A. Wagner. BS cum laude, Northwestern U.; MBA, Harvard U. Former editor-in-chief internat. editions, dir. new ventures Hearst Corp.; former editor Saturday Evening Post; with Estee Lauder Cos., 1975—, from v.p., dir. mktg. internat. divsn. to sr. v.p. Estee Lauder and Prescriptives Internat., past corp. sr. v.p., now pres. Estee Lauder Internat., Inc.; chmn. bd. dirs. Fragrance Found.; bd. dirs. White House Adv. Com. on Trade Policy Negotiations; bd. dirs., mem. audit and compensation coms. Am. Greetings.; bd. dirs., audit and nominating coms. Stride Rite Corp.; bd. dirs. Bus. Coun. for Internat. Understanding. Bd. dirs. Breastcancer Rsch. Found. Recipient Director's Choice award Nat. Women's Econ. Alliance Form, 1995, Achiever award CEW, 1996. Mem. Fashion Group Internat. (past pres. and chmn.), Cosmetic Exec. Women, Econ. Club, Harvard Bus. Sch. Club Greater N.Y. (past v.p., honor roll), Harvard Bus. Sch. Network Women Alumni, Womens Forum N.Y. (bd. dirs., exec. com.), Northwestern Coun. 100, Com. 200 (bd. dirs., chair long range planning), Asia Soc., China Inst., Japan Soc., Korean Soc., Fgn. Policy Assn., Women's Econ. Roundtable, Northwestern Univ. Alumni Assn. (alumni medal, 1995). Office: Estee Lauder Inc 767 Fifth Ave New York NY 10153

WAGNER, JUDI, artist, art educator, writer; b. Phila., Nov. 10, 1936; d. George P. and Vera W. (Wicks) Slockbower; children: Karen Jane Tonjes, Konrad Norbert. Student, Brarcliff Coll., 1954-56; AA, Bucks (Pa.) C.C., 1978; BFA, Parsons Sch. Design, 1980, MS, 1983. asst. John Pike studio, Woodstock, N.Y., 1969-79; art tchr., 1980-84; art staff, admintr. Parsons Sch. Design, Paris and Italy. Co-author: The Watercolor Fix It Book, 1991, Painting with the White of the Paper, 1994; numerous one woman exhbns. and group exhbns. including Dearborn Gallery, Portland, 1995, Watercolor Art Soc., Houston, 1996, Soc. Watercolor Artists, Ft. Worth, 1996, New England Watercolor Soc., Boston, 1996, Watercolor Soc. of Ala., Birmingham, 1996. Recipient Louis Sealy award Salgamundi Club, 1984, The Holbein award Montana Watercolor Soc., 1994, Patrons of Arts award, Tex. Watercolor Soc., Honorable Mention award finalist Inaugural Arts Botanica, 1994. Mem. Fla. Watercolor Soc., Me. Art Gallery, Boothbay Region Art Found. Home and Studio: 1563 Canterbury Ln Fernandina Beach FL 32034 also: HC 65 Box 834 Ocean Point Rd East Boothbay ME 04544

WAGNER, JUDITH BUCK, investment firm executive; b. Altoona, Pa. Sept. 25, 1943; d. Harry Bud and Mary Elizabeth (Rhodes) B.; m. Joseph E. Wagner, Mar. 15, 1980; 1 child, Elizabeth. BA in History, U. Wash., 1965; grad. N.Y. Inst. Fin., 1968. Registered Am. Stock Exch., N.Y. Stock Exch., investment advisor. Security analyst Morgan, Olmstead, Kennedy & Gardner, L.A., 1968-71; security analyst Boettcher & Co., Denver, 1972-75; pres. Wagner Investment Mgmt., Denver, 1975—; chmn., bd. dirs. The Women's Bank, N.A., Denver, 1977-94, organizational group pres., 1975-77; chmn. Equitable Bankshares Colo., Inc., Denver, 1980-94; bd. dirs. Equitable Bank of Littleton, 1983-88, pres., 1985; bd. dirs. Colo. Growth Capital, 1979-82; lectr. Denver U., Metro State, 1975-80. Author: Woman and Money series Colo. Woman Mag., 1976; moderator 'Catch 2' Sta. KWGN-TV, 1978-79. Pres. Big Sisters Colo., Denver, 1977-82, bd. dirs., 1973-83; bd. fellows U. Denver, 1985-90; bd. dirs. Red Cross, 1980, Assn. Children's Hosps., 1985, Colo. Health Facilities Authority, 1978-84, Jr. League Community Adv. Com., 1979-92, Brother's Redevel., Inc., 1979-80; mem. agy. rels. com. Mile High United Way, 1978-81, chmn. United Way Venture Grant com., 1980-81; bd. dirs. Downtown Denver Inc., 1988-95; bd. dirs., v.p., treas. The Women's Found. Colo., 1987-91; treas., trustee, v.p., Graland Country Day Sch., 1990—, pres. 1994—; trustee Denver Rotary Found., 1990-95; trustee Hunt Alternatives Fund, 1992—. Recipient Making It award Cosmopolitan Mag., 1977, Women on the Go award, Savvy mag., 1983, Minouri Yasoui award, 1986, Salute Spl. Honoree award, Big Sisters, 1987; named one of the Outstanding Young Women in Am., 1979; recipient Woman Who Makes A Difference award Internat. Women's Forum, 1987. Fellow Assn. Investment Mgmt. and Rsch.; mem. Women's Forum of Colo. (pres. 1979), Women's Found. Colo., Inc. (bd. dirs. 1986-91), Denver Soc. Security Analysts (bd. dirs. 1976-83, v.p. 1980-81, pres. 1981-82), Colo. Investment Advisors Assn., Rotary (treas. Denver chpt. found., pres. 1993-94), Leadership Denver (Outstanding Alumna award 1987), Pi Beta Phi (pres. U. Wash. chpt. 1964-65). Office: Wagner Investment Mgmt Inc 3200 Cherry Creek S Dr Ste 240 Denver CO 80209

WAGNER, LINDA BYRD, counselor; b. Erie, Pa.; d. Alfred Thomas and Jeannette Louise (Dunham) Mitchell; children: Eric Thomas, Ryan Douglas; m. David Jeffrey Wagner, Jan. 20, 1984. BS, Alderson-Broaddus Coll., 1970; MEd, S.D. State U., 1974. Dental asst. Office of David McChesney, DDS, Erie, 1982-84; drug and alcohol prevention specialist Greater Erie Cmty. Action Com., 1984-88; coord. Drug Free Schs. program pupil svcs. Northwest Tri-County Intermediate Unit # 5 Sch. Dist., Erie, 1989-90; intervention counselor Harbor Creek (Pa.) Sch. Dist., 1988—, coord. student assistance program, 1988—, coord. drug free/safe schs. program, 1988—, chair adv. coun., 1988—, mem. county student assistance program consortium, 1991—. Mem. NEA, Erie County Counselors Assn., Pa. State Edn. Assn., Harbor Creek Edn. Assn. Episcopalian. Home: 5667 Gardner Dr Erie PA 16509-3056

WAGNER, MARY KATHRYN, sociology educator, former state legislator; b. Madison, S.D., June 19, 1932; d. Irving Macaulay and Mary Browning (Wines) Mumford; m. Robert Todd Wagner, June 23, 1954; children: Christopher John, Andrea Browning. BA, U. S.D., 1954; MEd, S.D. State U., 1974, PhD, 1978. Sec. R.A. Burleigh & Assocs., Evanston, Ill., 1954-57; dir. resource ctr. Watertown (S.D.) Sr. High Sch., 1969-71, Brookings (S.D.) High Sch., 1971-74; asst. dir. S.D. Com. on the Humanities, Brookings, 1976-90; asst. prof. rural sociology S.D. State U., 1990—; mem. S.D. Ho. of Reps., 1981-88, S.D. Senate, 1988-92. Mem., pres. Brookings Sch. Bd., 1975-81; chair fund dr. Brookings United Way, 1985; bd. dirs. Brookings Chamber music Soc., 1981—, Advance and Career Learning Ctr. Named Woman of Yr., Bus. and Profl. Women, 1981, Legislator Conservationist of Yr., Nat. and S.D. Wildlife Fedn., 1988. Mem. Population Assn. Am., Midwest Sociol. Soc., Rural Sociol. Soc., Brookings C. of C. (mem. indsl. devel. com. 1988—), PEO, Rotary. Republican. Episcopalian. Home: 929 Harvey Dunn St Brookings SD 57006-1347

WAGNER, MARY MARGARET, library and information science educator; b. Mpls., Feb. 4, 1946; d. Harvey F.J. and Yvonne M. (Brettner) W.; m. William Moore, June 16, 1988; children: Lebohang Y.C., Nora M. BA, Coll. St. Catherine, St. Paul, 1969; MLS, U. Wash., 1973. Asst. libr. St. Margarets Acad., Mpls., 1969-70; libr. Derham Hall High Sch., St. Paul, 1970-71; youth worker The Bridge for Runaways, Mpls., 1971-72; libr. Guthrie Theater Reference and Rsch. Libr., Mpls., 1973-75; asst. br. libr. St. Paul Pub. Libr., 1975; assoc. prof. dept. info. mgmt. Coll. St. Catherine, St. Paul, 1975—; del. Minn. Gov.'s Pre-White House Conf. on Librs. and Info. Svcs., 1990; mem. Minn. Pre-White House Program Com., 1989-90, Continuing Libr. Info. and Media Edn. Com. Minn. Dept. Edn., Libr. Devel. and Svcs., 1980-83, 87—; mem. cmty. faculty Met. State U., St. Paul, 1980—; mem. core revision com. Coll. St. Catherine, 1992-93, faculty budget adv. com., 1992-95, faculty pers. com., 1989-92, acad. computing com. 1991-96; chair curriculum subcom. Minn. Vol. Cert. Com., 1993—. Contbr. articles to profl. jours. Bd. dirs. Christian Sharing Fund, 1976-80, chair, 1977-78. Grantee: U.S. Embassy, Maseru, Lesotho, Africa, Brit. Consulate, Maseru, various founds.; Upper Midwest Assn. for Intercultural Edn. travel grantee Assoc. Colls. Twin Cities. Mem ALA (libr. book fellows program 1990 91), Am. Soc. Info. Sci., Am. Soc. Indexers, Spl. Libr. Assn., Minn. Libr. Assn. (pres. 1981-82, chair continuing edn. com. 1987-90, steering com. Readers Adv. Roundtable, 1989-91), Minn. Ednl. Media Orgn., Twin Cities Women in Computing. Office: Coll St Catherine Dept Info Mgmt 2004 Randolph Ave Saint Paul MN 55105-1750

WAGNER, MEREDITH, broadcast executive. BA in English, Skidmore Coll. Rsch. coord. pub. rels. dept. ABC-TV, 1980; publicist WCBS-TV; sr. publicist CBS TV; mgr. pub. affairs Lifetime Television, N.Y.C., 1987, dir., 1988, v.p. pub. affairs, 1989-92, sr. v.p. pub. affairs, 1992—. Bd. dirs. Women's Project & Prodns.; bd. trustees Women in Table & Telecomms. Mem. Nat. Cable TV Assn. (bd. dirs. pub. affairs com.), Cable TV Pub. Affairs Assn. (past-pres.). Office: Lifetime Tel 16th and 17th Fls 309 W 49th St New York NY 10019-7316

WAGNER, MURIEL GINSBERG, nutrition therapist; b. N.Y.C., Apr. 6, 1926; d. Irving A. and Anna Ginsberg; divorced; 1 child, Emily Lucinda Faith. BA, Wayne State U., 1948, MS, 1951; PhD, U. Mich., 1982. Registered dietitian. Nutritionist Merrill-Palmer Inst., Detroit, 1951-74; pvt. practice, nutritional therapist Southfield, Mich., 1976—; cons. select com. on nutrition U.S. Senate, 1973-74, Ford Motor Co., Dearborn, Mich., 1975-78, Detroit Dept. Consumer Affairs, 1979—; adj. faculty mem. Wayne State U., Detroit, 1970-80, U. Mich., Dearborn, 1974-79. Author: (cookbook) Tun...ahhh, 1993; contbr. articles to profl. publs. Vol. Am. Heart Assn. of Mich.; also various local and nat. govtl. groups. Recipient Outstanding Cmty. Svc. award Am. Heart Assn., 1990; named Outstanding Profl., Mich. Dietetic Assn., 1974. Fellow Am. Dietetic Assn. (organizer Dial-A-Dietitian); mem. Soc. Nutrition Edn., Am. Diabetes Assn. Office: 4400 Town Ctr Ste 275 Southfield MI 48075

WAGNER, NANCY HUGHES, secondary school educator, state legislator; b. Raleigh, N.C., Sept. 27, 1943; d. Eugene Anderson and Miriam St. Clair (Morgan) Hughes; m. Clarence Cobaugh Wagner II, Sept. 12, 1970; children: Morgan Anderson, Cobaugh Wagner III. BA, Salem Coll., Winston-Salem, N.C., 1965; MS, Wilmington (Del.) Coll., 1989. Tchr. Milford (Del.) Sch. Dist., 1965-66, Capital Sch. Dist., Dover, Del., 1966-70, 89—; job specialist Jobs for Del. Grads., Dover, 1987-89; rep. Del. Ho. of Reps., Dover, 1992—. Mem. parents bd. U. Del., Newark, 1991-93; bd. visitors Del. State U., Dover, 1995—; bd. dirs. Modern Maturity Ctr., Dover, 1995—, 801 House Aid in Dover, 1995—, Because We Care, Dover, 1995—; mem. Kent County Parks and Recreation Commn., Dover, 1990-92; pres. South Run Crossing Civic Assn., Springfield, Va., 1982-85, PTA Dover H.S., 1987-89; mem. Rep. State Com., Kent County Rep. Women's Club. Mem. AAUW, C. of C., Nat. Coun. State Legislators, Coun. of State Govts., Capital Edn. Assn., Del. Edn. Assn., Delta Kappa Gamma Soc. Internat. Republican. Presbyterian. Home: 283 Troon Rd Dover DE 19904 Office: House of Representatives Legislative Hall Dover DE 19901

WAGNER, PATRICIA HAMM, lawyer; b. Gastonia, N.C., Feb. 1, 1936; d. Luther Boyd and Mildred Ruth (Wheeler) Hamm; married; children: David Marion, Michael Marion, Laura Marion. AB summa cum laude, Wittenberg U., 1958; JD with distinction, Duke U., 1974. Bar: N.C. 1974, Wash. 1984. Asst. univ. counsel Duke U., Durham, N.C., 1974-75, assoc. univ. counsel health affairs, 1977-80; atty. N.C. Meml. Hosp., 1975-77; assoc. N.C. Atty. Gen. Office, 1975-77; assoc. Powe, Porter & Alphin, Durham, 1980-81, prin., 1981-83; assoc. Williams, Kastner & Gibbs, 1984-86, Wickwire, Goldmark & Schorr, 1986-88; spl. counsel Heller, Ehrman, White & McAuliffe, 1988-90, ptnr., 1990—; arbitrator Am. Arbitration Assn., 1978—; arbitrator, pro tem judge King County Superior Ct., 1986—; tchr. in field. Mem. bd. vis. Law Sch. Duke U., 1992—; bd. dirs. Seattle Edn. Ctr., 1990-91, Metroctr. YMCA, 1991-94, Cmty. Psychiat. Clinic, Seattle, 1984-86; bd. dirs., sec.-treas. N.C. Found. Alternative Health Programs, Inc., 1982-84; bd. dirs., sec.-treas. N.C. Ctr. Pub. Policy Rsch., 1976-83, vice-chmn., 1977-80; mem. task force on commitment law N.C. Dept. Human Resources, 1978; active Def. Rsch. Inst. 1982-84; bd. dirs. Law Fund, 1992—, v.p., 1993—. Fellow Am. Bar Found.; mem. ABA (mem. ho. dels. Seattle-King County Bar Assn. 1991-94, mem. litigation sect.), Am. Soc. Hosp. Attys., Wash. State Bar Assn. (mem. domestic rels. task force 1991-93), Seattle-King Bar Assn. (mem. bd. trustees 1990-93, sec. bd. 1989-90, chair judiciary and cts. com. 1987-89, mem. King County Superior Ct. delay reduction task force 1987-89, mem. gender bias com. 1990-94, chair 1990-91), Wash. Def. Trial Lawyers (chmn. ct. rules and procedures com. 1987, co-editor newsletter 1985-86), Wash. State Soc. Hosp. Attys., Wash. Women Lawyers (treas. 1986, 87). Office: Heller Ehrman White & McAuliffe 6100 Columbia Ctr 701 5th Ave Seattle WA 98104-7016

WAGNER, ROBYN L., retail services company executive; b. Bethlehem, Pa., Aug. 6, 1969; d. Robert C. and Marilyn C. (Chanitz) W. BA, Moravian Coll., 1991; postgrad., Widener U. Sch. Law, 1994-95. Mktg. coord. Budget Car & Truck Rental, Allentown, Pa., 1990-93; sales mgr. This End Up Furniture, Co., Media, Pa., 1993—. Vol. Keystone State Games, Bethleham, Pa., 1991, Adult Literacy Ctr., Bethlehem, 1996. Mem. NAFE, AAUW. Office: This End Up Furniture Granite Run Mall 1067 W Baltimore Pike Media PA 19063

WAGNER, SANDRA LYNN, accountant, writer; b. Hillsdale, Mich., June 11, 1948; d. Noyle Throne and Donna Narice (Fry) McClellan; m. Donald Keith Brown, June 21, 1969 (div. Jan. 1980); children: Ginny Crawford, Angela Brown, Kevin Brown; m. Phillip Paul Wagner, Aug. 22, 1991. BA magna cum laude, Spring Arbor (Mich.) Coll., 1971; BS magna cum laude, Eastern Mich. U., 1983. Tchr. Hillsdale Pub. Schs., 1971-72; dir. Karen Jenkins Presch., Hillsdale, 1978-80; owner Brown Acctg., Jackson, Mich., 1980-89; contr. Metallist, Inc., Hillsdale, 1989-92; asst. contr. Isaac Corp., Maumee, Ohio, 1992—; cons. Jackson Pub. Schs., 1983-86; dir. Jackson Recycling, 1985-87, Up the Down Staircase, Jackson, 1986-88; speaker in field. Contbr. articles to profl. jours. Founder Jackson City Latchkey Program, 1983; co-founder Jackson chmn. Amnesty Internat., 1988; precinct leader Dem. Party, Jackson, 1987-88; Midwest dir. Christians for Urgent Action in El Salvador, 1984-86; publicity dir. Prison Fellowship, Jackson, 1982-85. Mem. Nat. Assn. Accts., Nat. Soc. Tax Practitioners, Ohio Assn. Ind. Accts. (charter). Home: 433 S Walnut St Bryan OH 43506

WAGNER, SUSAN JANE, sales and marketing consulting company executive; b. Englewood, N.J., Aug. 11; d. Jules A. and Florence I. (Froeba) W.; m. Mark E. McKenna, May 4, 1984. MusB with honors, Syracuse U., 1974; MPA with honors, Fairleigh Dickinson U., 1983. Dir. music, theater dependant sch. U.S. Dept. Def., Fed. Republic Germany, 1976-82; grad. asst. Fairleigh Dickinson U., Rutherford, N.J., 1982-83; account exec. Katz Radio/Katz Communications, Inc., N.Y.C., 1983-85; account mgr. network Katz Radio Group, N.Y.C., 1985-87, v.p., dir. mktg., 1987-90, sr. v.p. dir.mktg., 1990-91; v.p. corp. mktg. Katz Comm., Inc., N.Y.C., 1992-93; owner Exec. Dynamics Inc., Mahwah, N.J., 1993—. Mem. Am. Women in Radio and TV, Electronic Media Mktg. Assn., Am. Mktg. Assn., Promotion Mktg. Assn. Am., Broadcast Promotion Mktg. Execs., Sigma Alpha Iota, Gamma Phi Beta. Office: Exec Dynamics 2 James Brite Cir Mahwah NJ 07430-2527

WAGNER, TERESA ANN, handwriting analyst; b. Spokane, Wash., Jan. 5, 1954; d. Alexander Lazarus and Pauline Joyce (Hodgson) Birch; m. Robert Earl Hurt, Aug. 11, 1973 (div. Jan. 1986); 1 child, Melinda Eslie Ann; m. Gary William Wagner, Aug. 25, 1996. AAS in Paralegal Studies, Spokane C.C., 1995. Cert. in behavioral profiling and forensic document exams., Am. Bd. Forensic Examiners, 1993; cert. in document exam., Nat. Assn. Document Examiners, 1995. Owner Profl. Handwriting Analysis, Spokane, 1986—; instr. Spokane Falls C.C., 1989-92, 92-94. Mem. Am. Handwriting Analysis Found. (cert., com. mem.), Coun. Graphological Soc., Nat. Assn. Document Examiners (treas., cert. document examiner), Nat. Questioned Document Assn. Office: Profl Handwriting Analysis 10 N Post St Ste 550 Spokane WA 99201-0705

WAGNER, TERESA LEE, training and organization consultant; b. Reading, Pa., Jan. 24, 1954; d. Fred LeRoy and Emily (Wiest) W. BA in Psychology magna cum laude, Alvernia Coll., 1977; postgrad., U. Nottingham, Eng., 1978; MS in Counseling and Human Rels., Villanova U., 1981; postgrad., Columbia U., 1985-86. Trainer Juvenile Justice Ctr. Nat. Tng. Inst., Phila., 1977-80; sr. indsl. rels. rep. missile and surface radar RCA, Moorestown, N.J., 1980-81; mgr. orgnl. devel. govt. systems divsn. RCA, Cherry Hill, N.J., 1981-84; mgr. orgn. planning and devel. RCA Global Comms., Inc., N.Y.C., 1984-88; pres. T. L. Wagner Assocs., Monterey, Calif., 1988—; bd. dirs. Intersea Rsch. Author: (tng. manuals) Recovering from Grief, 1990, Managing Job Loss, 1991, Grief Support Skills, 1993, (self-assessment instrument) Grief Support Skills Assessment Profile, 1990. Docent Point Lobos State Res., Carmel, Calif., 1990—; mem. beach and seal watch, Am. Cetacean Soc., Monterey, 1990—; bd. dirs. Friends of Monterey County Wildlife, 1993—, Horse Power Internat., Monterey, 1990—, Assisi Animal Inst., 1994—. Mem. ASTD, Orgn. Devel. Network, Assn. for Death Edn. and Counseling. Home and Office: T L Wagner Assocs PO Box 522 Monterey CA 93942-0522

WAGNER-WESTBROOK, BONNIE JOAN, management professional; b. Watertown, N.Y., July 18, 1953; d. Elmer Ethan and Joan Eleanor (Niedermeier) Wagner; m. John Drewry Westbrook Jr., Aug. 21, 1982. BS, SUNY, Geneseo, 1975, MS, 1981; EdD, Rutgers U., 1989. Tchr. elem. Rochester (N.Y.) Sch. for the Deaf, 1975-80; instr. adult basic edn. Rochester City Sch. Dist., 1981-82; profl. interpreter Nat. Tech. Inst. for the Deaf, Rochester, 1981-83; instr., interpreter Henrietta (N.Y.) Cen. Sch. Dist., 1983-84; intern Middlesex County Vocat. Tech. Schs., New Brunwsick, N.J., 1985; cons. on urban initiative for N.J. Dept. Edn. Rutgers U., New Brunwsick, N.J., 1985-86, program specialist, 1987-88, rsch. assoc. for N.J. Commn. on Employment and Tng., 1988-89, also senator Grad. Sch. Edn., 1985-87; adminstr. Pub. Svc. Electric and Gas Co., Newark, 1990-91; program dir. Rutgers U., New Brunswick, N.J., 1991—; cons. Blueprint Project, Hudson County C.C., 1992-93, Pub. Svc. Electric & Gas Co., Newark, 1986-89. Vol. Rochester Sch. for the Deaf, 1977; mem. Rochester Oratorio Soc., 1978-81, SUNY Geneseo Chamber Singers, 1971-75. Rutgers U. scholar, 1986; Rutgers U. fellow, 1987. Mem. ASTD, Am. Ednl. Rsch. Assn., Am. Coun. on Edn. of Deaf, Am. Vocat. Assn., Am. Mgmt. Assn., Nat. Registry Interpreters for Deaf, Rochester Amateur Radio Assn., Rutgers Univ. Alumni Assn., Omicron Tau Theta. Republican. Home: 327 Becker St Highland Park NJ 08904-2522 Office: Rutgers U Sch Mgmt & Labor Rels Ctr Mgmt Devel PO Box 5062 New Brunswick NJ 08903-5062

WAGNON, JOAN, former state legislator, association executive; b. Texarkana, Ark., Oct. 17, 1940; d. Jack and Louise (lucas) D.; m. William O. Wagnon Jr., June 4, 1964; children: Jack, William O. III. BA in Biology, Hendrix Coll., Conway, Ark., 1962; MEd in Guidance and Counseling, U. Mo., 1968. Sr. research technician U. Ark. Med. Sch., Little Rock, 1962-64; sr. research asst. U. Ark. Med. Sch., Columbia, Mo., 1964-68; tchr. No. Hills Jr. High Sch., Topeka, 1968-69, J.S. Kendall Sch., Boston, 1970-71; counselor Neighborhood Youth Corps, Topeka, 1973-74; exec. dir. Topeka YWCA, 1977-93; mem. Kans. Legislature, 1983-94. Mem. Health Planning Rev. Commn., Topeka, 1984-85. Recipient Service to Edn. award, Topeka NEA, 1979, Outstanding Achievement award, Kans. Home Econs. Assn., 1985; named Woman of Yr. Mayors Council Status of Women, 1983; named one of Top Ten Legislators Kans. Mag., Wichita, 1986. Mem. Topeka Assn. Human Svc. Execs. (pres. 1981-83), Topekans for Ednl. Involvement (pres. 1979-82), Women's Polit. Caucus (state chair). Democrat. Methodist. Lodge: Rotary. Home: 1606 SW Boswell Ave Topeka KS 66604-2729 Office: Kans Families for Kids 2209 SW 29th St Topeka KS 66611-1908

WAINESS, MARCIA WATSON, legal management consultant; b. Bklyn., Dec. 17, 1949; d. Stanley and Seena (Klein) Watson; m. Steven Richard Wainess, Aug. 7, 1975. Student, UCLA, 1967-71, 80-81, Grad. Sch. Mgmt. Exec. Program, 1987-88, grad. Grad. Sch. Mgmt. Exec. Program, 1988. Office mgr., paralegal Lewis, Marenstein & Kadar, L.A., 1977-81; office mgr. Rosenfeld, Meyer & Susman, Beverly Hills, Calif., 1981-83; adminstr. Rudin, Richman & Appel, Beverly Hills, 1983; dir. adminstrn. Kadison, Pfaelzer, L.A., 1983-87; exec. dir. Richards, Watson and Gershon, L.A., 1987-93; legal mgmt. cons. Wainess & Co., Beverly Hills, 1993—; faculty mem. UCLA Legal Mgmt. & Adminstrn. Program, 1983, U. So. Calif. Paralegal Program, L.A., 1985; mem. adv. bd. atty. asst. tng. program, UCLA, 1984-88. Mem. ABA (chair Displaywrite Users Group 1986, legal tech. adv. coun. litig. support working group 1986-87), L.A. County Bar Assn., San Fernando Valley Bar Assn., Profl. Liability Underwriting Soc., Assn. Legal Adminstrs. (bd. dirs. 1990-92, asst. regional v.p. Calif. 1987-88, regional v.p. 1988-89, pres. Beverly Hills chpt. 1985-86, membership chair 1984-85, chair new adminstrn. sect. 1982-84, mktg. mgmt. sect. com. 1989-90, internat. conf. com.), Beverly Hills Bar Assn., Internat. Platform Assn., Cons. Roundtable of So. Calif. Office: 415 N Camden Dr Beverly Hills CA 90210

WAINWRIGHT, CYNTHIA CRAWFORD, banker; b. N.Y.C., July 5, 1945; d. Townsend Wainwright and Rosalie deForest (Crosby) Gevers; m. Stephen Berger, Sept. 24, 1977; children: Robin Wainwright Berger, Diana Wainwright Berger. MBA, Columbia Bus. Sch., 1984. Sec., adminstrv. asst. Time-Life Broadcast, N.Y.C., 1965-68; adminstrv. asst. Downe Comms., N.Y.C., 1968-69, Office of the Mayor, N.Y.C., 1969-71; program mgr. Dept. of Correction, N.Y.C., 1972-73, dir. adminstrn., 1973-75, dep. commr., 1978-79; dir. of spl. projects N.Y. State Dept. Correctional Svcs., Albany, 1975-76; asst. dir. Offender-Based Transaction Svcs./Divsn. Criminal Justice, Albany, 1976-77; various positions Chem. Bank, N.Y.C., 1979-96; dir. corp. soc. resp. Chase Bank, N.Y.C., 1996—. Chmn. adv. comms. N.Y. State Office of Parks, N.Y.C., 1986-95; bd. dirs., chmn. Hist. House Trust of N.Y.C., 1989—; bd. dirs., past pres. The Bridge, Inc., N.Y.C., 1984—; trustee, past pres. Preservation League of N.Y. State, Albany, 1984—; trustee The Chapin Sch., Ltd., N.Y.C., 1989—. Named Woman of the Yr. East Manhattan C. of C., 1984; recipient Mental Health award The Bridge, Inc., N.Y.C., 1992, award for acad. excellence Columbia Bus. Sch., N.Y.C., 1983. Office: Chem Bank 600 Fifth Ave Fl 3 New York NY 10020-2302

WAISANEN, CHRISTINE M., lawyer, writer; b. Hancock, Mich., May 27, 1949; d. Frederick B. and Helen M. (Hill) W.; m. Robert John Katzenstein, Apr. 21, 1979; children: Jeffrey Hunt, Erick Hill. BA with honors, U. Mich., 1971; JD, U. Denver, 1975. Bar: Colo. 1975, D.C. 1978. Labor rels. atty. U.S. C. of C., Washington, 1976-79; govt. rels. specialist ICI Americas, Inc., Wilmington, Del., 1979-87; dir. cultural affairs City of Wilmington, 1987; founder, chief writer Hill, Katzenstein & Waisanen, 1988—. Chmn. Delaware State Coastal Zone Indsl. Control Bd., 1993—. Mem. Fed. Bar Assn., Jr. League of Wilmington (v.p. 1985-86), Women's Rep. Club of Wilmington (bd. dirs. 1988-93). Republican. Presbyterian. Home: 1609 Mt Salem Ln Wilmington DE 19806-1134

WAIT, CAROL GRACE COX, organization administrator; b. L.A., Dec. 20, 1942; d. Earl George Atkinson Sr. and Virginia Rose (Clanton) Boggs; m. David L. Edwards (div. 1974); children: Nicole Rose Smith, Alexandra Edwards; m. Gary G. Cox, Jan. 25, 1975 (div. 1982); m. Robert Atwood Wait, July 4, 1991. AA in Pre Law, Cerritos Coll., 1966; AB in History, Whittier Coll., 1969. Probation counselor Los Angeles County Probation Dept., Downey, Calif., 1967-69; corp. sec., mgr. Dennis and Dennis Personnel, Santa Ana, Calif., 1969-71; owner, pres. Cox Edwards & Assocs., Santa Ana, 1971-73; adminstrv. services officer County of Santa Cruz (Calif.), 1973-74; cons. State of Calif., Sacramento, 1974-75; project dir. Nat. Assn. Counties, Washington, 1975-77; legis. dir. U.S. Senate Com. on the Budget, Washington, 1977-81; pres. Com. for a Responsible Budget, Washington, 1981—, Carol Cox & Assocs., Washington, 1984—; bd. dirs. Cigna Corp.; cons. to bus. and other orgns. on the fed. budget, the budget process and other econ. issues; writer and speaker on the budget and budget process. Am. participant USIS/Brazilian Senate Symposium on Budget Process, Brazilia, Brazil, 1985—, Ampart speaker on 1990 budget agreement France, Ger., 1990. Named one of 150 Who Make a Difference Nat. Jour., 1986; recipient Nat. Disting. Svc. award Am. Assn. Budget and Program Analysis. Mem. Washington Women's Forum, Internat. Women's Forum (pres.). Republican. Episcopalian. Office: Com Responsible Fed Budget 10648 Old Valley Pike Mount Jackson VA 22842

WAITE, ELLEN JANE, vice presidentof academic services; b. Oshkosh, Wis., Feb. 17, 1951; d. Earl Vincent and Margaret (Luft) W.; m. Thomas H. Dollar, Aug. 19, 1977 (div. July 1984); m. Kent Hendrickson, Mar. 26, 1994 (div. Dec. 1995). BA, U. Wis., Oshkosh, 1973; MLS, U. Wis., Milw., 1977. Head of cataloging Marquette U., Milw., 1977-82; head catalog librarian U. Ariz., Tucson, 1983-85; assoc. dir. libraries Loyola U., Chgo., 1985-86, acting dir. libraries, 1986-87, dir. libraries, 1987-94, v.p. acad. svcs., 1994—; cons. Loyola U., Chgo., 1984, Boston Coll., 1986, U. San Francisco, 1989; bd. trustees Online Computer Lib. Ctr., Dublin, Ohio, 1994—. Contbg. author: Research Libraries and Their Implementation of AACR2, 1985; author: (with others) Women in LC's Terms: A Thesaurus of Subject Headings Related to Women, 1988. Mem. ALA. Office: Loyola U 25 E Pearson St Chicago IL 60611-2001

WAITE, HELEN ELEANOR, funeral director; b. Richmond, Va., Aug. 7, 1947; d. Julia F. (Braxton) Candia; m. Malcolm L. Waite, July 24, 1982. AB, Va. State U., 1968, MA, 1977; degree in funeral svc., Northampton C.C., Bethlehem, Pa., 1994. Cert. tchr., Pa., N.J. Tchr. Westmoreland County Schs., Montross, Va.; tchr. English Rittenhouse Acad., Phila.; funeral dir. T.W. Waite Funeral Home, Phila. Mem. Nat. Coun. Tchrs. English, Pa. Coun. Tchrs. English, Nat. Funeral Dirrs. Assn., Pa. Funeral Dirs. Assn. Home: 820 N 65th St Philadelphia PA 19151-3303

WAITES, CANDY YAGHJIAN, former state official; b. N.Y.C., Feb. 21, 1943; d. Edmund Kirken and Dorothy Joanne (Candy) Yaghjian; children: Jennifer Lisa, Robin Shelley. B.A., Wheaton Coll., Mass., 1965. Elected county councilwoman Richland County, S.C., 1976-88, mem. S.C. Ho., 1988-94; dir. external programs The Leadership Inst., Columbia Coll., 1993—; vice chmn. Adv. Commn. on Intergovtl. Relations, S.C., 1977-87; bd. dirs. Interagy. Council on Pub. Transp., S.C., 1977-85, Central Midlands Regional Planning Council, Columbia, S.C., 1977-84; dir. Wachovia Bank. Vice pres. bd. dirs. United Way of Midlands, 1977-89; trustee Columbia Mus. Art, 1982-88; bd. dirs. Rape Crisis Network, 1984-87; chmn. County Coun. Coalition; mem. C. of C. Leadership Forum, S.C. Fedn. of the Blind; mem. adv. bd. U. S.C. Hunanities and Social Scis. Coll., Family Shelter, Nurturing Ctr.; pres Trinity Housing Corp.; found. bd. Richland Meml. Hosp., 1995. Named Outstanding Young Career Woman, Columbia YWCA, 1980, YWCA Hall of Fame, 1993, Outstanding Young Woman of Yr., Columbia Jaycees, 1975, Pub. Citizen of Yr. Nat. Assn. Social Workers, hon. mem. Mortar Bd. Soc., 1994; recipient Ann. Legis. award Common Cause S.C., 1990, 91, Legis. Yr. award by S.C. Assn. Counties, 1992. Mem. S.C. Women in Govt. (vice chmn. 1984-86), S.C. Assn. Counties (bd. dirs. 1982-88 , Pres's award 1983), Network Female Execs., LWV (pres. 1973-76), Omicron Delta Kappa. Democrat. Episcopalian. Club: Univ. Assocs. (Columbia). Avocations: exercising, drawing, gardening, walking. Home: 3419 Duncan St Columbia SC 29205-2705 Office: Columbia Coll Leadership Inst 1301 Cola Coll Dr Columbia SC 29203

WAITKEVICZ, H(ELEN) JOAN, physician, internal medicine; b. N.Y.C., Dec. 18, 1946; d. Peter J. and Helen I. (Zakiewicz) W. BA, Goucher Coll., 1966; MD, Tufts U., 1970. Diplomate Am. Bd. Internal Medicine. Intern medicine and pediatrics Rochester (N.Y.) Gen. Hosp., 1970-71; residency internal medicine Lincoln Hops., Bronx, N.Y., 1971-74; attending physician Lincoln Hosp., Bronx, N.Y., 1975-76, chief geriat. clinic, 1977-81; asst. attending physician montefiore Hosp., Bronx, 1977-81, N.Y. Downtown Hosp., N.Y.C., 1981—. Vol. physician People's Health Ctr., Bronx, 1974-81, St. Mark's Women's Health ollective, N.Y.C., 1973-95. Mem. ACP, Am. Med. Women's Assn., Gay and Lesbian Med. Assn. Democrat. Office: 13 E 15th St New York NY 10003

WAITZKIN, STELLA, artist. Student, Alfred U., NYU, Columbia U. One-woman shows at Iris Clert, Paris, 1973, Yale U. Art Gallery, New Haven, 1974, James Yu Gallery, N.Y., 1974, 75, 77, Lowenstein Libr., Fordham U., N.Y., 1975, Donnell Libr., N.Y., 1976, E.P. Gurewitsch, N.Y., 1977, Everson Mus. of Art, Syracuse, N.Y., 1983, Creiger Sesen Gallery, Boston, 1984, Galerie Caroline Corre, Paris, 1989, Gay Head Gallery, Martha's Vineyard, Mass., 1990; exhibited in numerous group shows, including Franklin Furnace, N.Y.C., 1981, La Bibliotheque Publique de Ctr. Nat. D'Art et Culture Georges Pompideau, Paris, 1982, N.Y. Pub. Libr., 1984, Cleve. Mus. Art, 1984, Mus. Nat. Modern Art, Paris, 1985, Robeson Ctr. Gallery, Rutgers U., Newark, 1985, 87, Met. Mus. Art, N.Y.C., 1985, Bibliotheque Discotheque Faidherde, Paris, 1985, Jewish Mus., N.Y.C., 1986, Caroline Corre Gallery, Paris, 1987, Anita Shapolsky Gallery, N.Y.C., 1987, 89, 90, 94, Witkin Gallery, N.Y.C., 1987, Sweetbriar (Va.) Coll., 1987, Queens Mus., N.Y.C., 1987, Patricia Carrega Gallery, Washington, 1988, Ft. Wayne (Ind.) Mus. Art, 1988, Fox, Ley, Leech, Carrega Gallery, Washington, 1989, Fonds Regional D'Art Contemporien Normandie, Rouen, France, 1989, N.J. State Mus., Trenton, 1989, 93, Bibliotheek de wolfenbuttel, Germany, 1989, Hotel del La Region, Roune, 1989, Mediatheque D'Elbeuf, France, 1989, Barbara Fendrick Gallery, N.Y., 1990, Peter M. David Gallery, Mpls., 1990, Book Arts Ctr., N.Y., 1990, Le Chateau de Vascoeuil, France, 1990, Ctr. Culturel "La Nacelle" a Auberginville, France, 1991, Bi-Nat. Ctr., Bogota, Colombia, 1992, numerous others. Home: PO Box 234 Chilmark MA 02535-0234

WAKE, MADELINE MUSANTE, nursing educator. Diploma, St. Francis Hosp. Sch. Nursing, 1963; BS in Nursing, Marquette U., 1968, MS in Nursing, 1971; PhD, U. Wis., Milw., 1986. Clin. nurse specialist St. Mary's Hosp., Milw., 1971-74, asst. dir. nursing, 1974-77; dir. continuing nursing edn. Marquette U., Milw., 1977-92, asst. prof., 1977-90, assoc. prof., 1991—, dean Coll. Nursing, 1993—. Chmn. bd. dirs. Trinity Meml. Hosp., Cudahy, Wis., 1991-96. Recipient Profl. Svc. award Am. Diabetes Assn.-Wis. affiliate, 1978, Excellence in Nursing Edn. award Wis. Nurses Assn., 1989; named Disting. Lectr. Sigma Theta Tau Internat., 1991. Fellow Am. Acad. Nursing; mem. ANA, AACN, Am. Orgn. Nurse Execs. Office: Marquette Univ Sch Nursing Milwaukee WI 53201-1881

WAKE, MARVALEE HENDRICKS, biology educator; b. Orange, Calif., July 31, 1939; d. Marvin Carlton and Velvalee (Borter) H.; m. David B. Wake, June 23, 1962; 1 child, Thomas A. BA, U. So. Calif., 1961, MS, 1964, PhD, 1968. Teaching asst./instr. U. Ill., Chgo., 1964-68, asst. prof., 1968-69; lectr. U. Calif., Berkeley, 1969-73, asst. prof., 1973-76, assoc. prof., 1976-80, prof. zoology, 1980-89, chmn. dept. zoology, 1985-89, chmn. dept. integrative biology, 1989-91, assoc. dean Coll. Letters and Sci., 1975-78, prof. integrative biology, 1989—; mem. NAS/NRC Bd. on Sustainable Devel., 1995—. Editor, co-author: Hyman's Comparative Vertebrate Anatomy, 1979; co-author: Biology, 1978; contbr. articles to profl. jours. NSF grantee, 1978—; Guggenheim fellow, 1988-89. Fellow AAAS, Calif. Acad. Sci. (trustee 1992—); mem. Am. Soc. Ichthyologists and Herpetologists (pres. 1984, bd. govs. 1978—), Internat. Union Biol. Scis. (U.S. nat. com. 1986-95, chair 1992-95; sec.-gen. 1994—), World Congress of Herpetology (sec.-gen. 1994—). Home: 999 Middlefield Rd Berkeley CA 94708-1509 Office: U Calif Dept Integrative Biology Berkeley CA 94720

WAKEFIELD, JANET RUTH, clinical psychologist; b. Derby, Conn., Nov. 29, 1926; d. George Alexander and Ruth Anna (Hall) W.; m. Donald Gabriel Forgays, Dec. 18, 1948 (div. July 1979); children: Janice Anne, Gabrielle, Ian Wakefield, Donal Hall. BA, Conn. Coll. for Women, New London, 1948; MEd, U. Vt., 1967, PhD, 1979. Lic. psychologist, Vt.; cert. psychologist, N.H. Rsch. asst. dept. psychology McGill U., Montreal, Can., 1949-50, Western Mich. U., Kalamazoo, 1950-51, Cornell U., Ithaca, N.Y., 1953-54; asst. survey dir. dept. interdisciplinary studies Rutgers U., New Brunswick, N.J., 1954-56; psychol. counselor U. Vt., Burlington, 1966-78, rschr. dept. psychiatry, 1979-80; psychologist Psychol. Assoc. Vt., Burlington, 1979-81; chief psychologist No. N.H. Mental Health & Devel. Svcs., Littleton, 1981-94; rschr., cons. Weiss Assoc., Montpelier, Vt., 1979; Country Village Health Care Ctr., Lancaster, N.H., 1988-94. Vice chmn. bd. trustees Sugar Hill (N.H.) Cemetery, 1996—; sec. Sugar Hill Improvement Assn., 1984—; mem. publicity com. White Mt. Garden Club, Sugar Hill, 1989—; mem. Sugar Hill Conservation Commn., 1995—, Sugar Hill Zoning Bd. of Adjustment, 1993—, North Country Chorus. Nat. Found. for Infantile Paralysis grantee, 1954. Mem. APA, N.H. Psychol. Orgn. (ethics com. 1981-94), Profile Club, Inc., North Country Psychologists Jour. Club (founder). Home and Office: Main St Sugar Hill NH 03585

WAKEFIELD, M. J., religious organization administrator. Home and Office: PO Box 1643 Oroville WA 98844-1643*

WAKEMAN, OLIVIA VAN HORN, marketing professional; b. Starkville, Miss.; d. Thomas Oliver and Mary Jeanne (Walker) W. BA in Mgmt., Eckerd Coll., St. Petersburg, Fla., 1980; MIM in Mktg./Advt., Am. Grad. Sch. Internat. Mgmt., 1982. Bus. analyst Dun & Bradstreet, Tampa, Fla., 1980; mgmt. cons. Cardinal Mgmt. Assocs., L.A., 1982-83; asst. account exec. McCann-Erickson, N.Y.C., 1984-86; account exec. Hearst Mag., N.Y.C., 1986-87, Ribaudo & Schaefer, N.Y.C., 1987-88; dir. pub. affairs/bus. soc. and ethics program Carnegie Coun. on Ethics and Internat. Affairs, N.Y.C., 1989-93; mgr. client svcs. Burson-Marsteller, Inc., 1994—; adult edn. mktg. prof. Touro Coll., N.Y.C., 1989; mktg. comm. cons. Hoffmann-La Roche, Inc., McGraw-Hill Inc., Daniel J. Edelman, Inc., Dilenschneider Group, Stingray Ptnrs., N.Y.C., 1993-94. Reading vol. Vol. Svcs. for Children, N.Y.C., 1991-93. Episcopalian.

WAKSLER, RACHELLE, theoretical linguist, educator; b. Yonkers, N.Y., Sept. 4, 1956; d. Morton and Barbara Lee (Pitasky) W. BA magna cum laude, Cornell U., 1978; PhD in Linguistics, Harvard U., 1990. Postdoctoral fellow U. Cambridge, Cambridge, Eng., 1988-90; chair linguistics program San Francisco State U., 1990—, asst. prof., 1990-94, assoc. prof., 1994—; vis. rschr. Max Planck Inst., Nijmegen, The Netherlands, 1989, 92; vis. rschr. U. Birmingham, Eng., 1994, 1996. Contbr. articles to profl. jours. Grantee U. Cambridge, 1989, Chancellor grantee Conf. Excellence Coll. Tchg., 1994. Mem. Linguistic Soc. Am., Internat. Linguistic Assn., Phi Beta Kappa. Office: San Francisco State U Humanities-Linguistics Program 1600 Holloway Ave San Francisco CA 94132

WALASH, EILEEN ROBIN (LEE), theater promotions and public relations specialist; b. Bklyn., Jan. 30, 1964; d. Myron and Marilyn Estelle (Rosner) W. BA, Miami U., Oxford, Ohio, 1986. Asst. editor Gralla Publs., N.Y.C., 1986-88; market editor Women's Wear Daily, N.Y.C., 1988-89; account supr. The Rowland Co., N.Y.C., 1989-92; pub. rels. and promotions cons., freelance writer N.Y.C., 1992-94; ind. promotions mgr. Radio City Music Hall, N.Y.C., 1994-95, promotions mgr., 1995—. Vol. N.Y. Cares, N.Y.C., 1993—, Gay Men's Health Crisis, 1995—. Mem. Pub. Rels. Soc. Am., N.Y. Alumni Assn. Miami U. (steering com.). Democrat.

WALCHER, JENNIFER LYNNE, city official; b. Denver, Feb. 8, 1956; d. Donald Robert and Winifred Edmunde (O'Dell) W. AS in Adminstrn. of Justice, Arapahoe C.C., Littleton, Colo., 1984; BS in Criminal Justice, Columbia Coll., Aurora, Colo. and Columbia, Mo., 1986; AS in Occupl. Safety, Trinidad State Jr. Coll., 1994. Cert. water distbn. sys. technician, Colo. Security patrolman Mission Viejo, Highlands Ranch, Colo., 1983-84; security officer Denver Water Dept., 1985-87, water serviceman I, 1987-88, safety and loss control specialist, 1988—. Contbr. articles to profl. publs. Instr. CPR and first aid Colo. Safety Assn., Denver, 1988—; instr. defensive driving Nat. Safety Coun., 1988—. With USN, 1974-81. Mem. Am. Soc. Safety Engrs., Phi Theta Kappa. Lutheran. Home: 2720 S Newland St Denver CO 80227-3519 Office: Denver Water Dept 1600 W 12th Ave Denver CO 80254

WALCK, PATRICIA NELSON, nursing educator, consultant; b. Hershey, Pa., June 15, 1947; d. James David and Agnes Bridget (Doyle) Nelson; m. Stanley Anthony Skowronek, June 22, 1968 (div. May, 1976); children: Katrina Lorraine, Alena Kathleen; m. Donald Leroy Walck, Apr. 27, 1984; 1 child, Erica Dawn. BSN cum laude, Catholic U., Washington, 1969; MS in Health Svcs. Adminstrn. with hons., Coll. of St. Francis, Joliet, Ill., 1990. RN. Staff nurse pediat. D.C. Gen. Hosp., Washington, 1969-70; float nurse Hartford (Conn.) Hosp., 1970-72, staff nurse, charge nurse intensive care, 1972-74; staff and charge nurse telemetry St. Francis Hosp., Hartford, 1975-76; staff nurse ICU Carlisle (Pa.) Hosp., 1979, head nurse ICU, critical care nurse, 1979-87; nurse educator Comty. Gen. Osteopathic Hosp., Harrisburg, Pa., 1987-89; cons. (assoc.) Fairfield (Pa.) Cons. Assocs., 1991—; cons. BDM Internat. for USAF, San Antonio, Frederic Med., McLean, Va., 1991-95; adj. faculty Harrisburg Area C.C., 1992—; clin. reviewer for acquisitions editor Med. Econs. Books Pub., 1985. Mem. pastoral coun. St. Francis Xavier Cath. Ch., Gettysburg, Pa., 1987—, consultations coord. Diocese of Harrisburg, Pa., 1990—; workshop presenter Adams County SPOC, Gettysburg, 1992—. Named Subcontractor of Yr. BDM, Internat., McLean, Va., 1991. Mem. AACN (vol. participatory sampling, VIP 1992-93). Home: 58 Marie Ln PO Box 246 Biglerville PA 17307 Office: Fairfield Cons Assocs 2 Snow Trl Fairfield PA 17320-8513

WALCZAK, ANN MARIE, elementary education educator; b. Fernandina Beach, Fla., May 10, 1947; d. Francis L. and Marie (Halter) Artelli; m. Stanley A. Walczak, Aug. 17, 1969; children: Sandra Ann, Christopher, Brian, Heather Marie. BA in Early Childhood Edn., William Paterson Coll.,

1969, MA in Reading/Lang. Arts, 1975; postgrad., Seaton Hall U., 1991—. Cert. elem. tchr., prin./supr., N.J.; cert. libr. Elem. tchr. Ridgewood (N.J.) Bd. Edn., 1969—; dist. coord. Writing to Read, Ridgewood Bd. Edn., 1985-90, spl. programs coord. Instrnl. Svcs., 1986-92, coord. Saturady Programs in Problem Solving, 1986-92, acting dir. curriculum and instrn., 1990-91, intern prin., 1992-93, acting dir. Infant-Toddler Ctr., 1993; IBM Writing to Read tchr. trainer IBM/Ridgewood Pub. Schs., 1986-90; tchr. trainer Mainland Inst., Pa., 1980; cons., adv. bd. Mini-Round Table Consortium, N.J., 1990-92. Curator Travell Children's Mus., 1993; author, editor: Analogy Masters, 1986; author, editor Connections mag., 1989; editor (brochure) Martin Luther King, Jr., 1989. Chairperson scholarship com. Marching Band, Ridgewood, 1995; Cornerstone dir. Holy Trinity Ch., Hackensack, N.J., 1994; parent vol. Girl Scouts Am., Ridgewood, 1990; fundraising New Players, Ridgewood, 1995—. Recipient grant Pub. Edn. Found., 1993. Mem. NEA, ASCD, N.J. Tchrs. Assn., Bergen County Tchrs. Assn., Early Childhood Edn. Assn., Reading Tchrs. Assn., Nat. Coun. Tchrs. Math., Phi Lamba Theta. Roman Catholic. Home: 142 Buckingham Dr Hackensack NJ 07601 Office: Ridgewood Pub Schs 49 Cottage Pl Ridgewood NJ 07450

WALCZAK, JOANNE CAROL, accountant; b. Buffalo, Feb. 8, 1959; d. Joseph Charles and Carol Dolores (Nicklas) Moorhouse; m. John T. Walczak, Aug. 2, 1980; 1 child, Bryan. BS in Acctg., SUNY, Geneseo, 1986; MBA in Fin. and Corp. Acctg., U. Rochester, 1991. CPA, N.Y. Staff acct. Genesee C.C., Batavia, N.Y., 1986-87; sr. acct. Strong Meml. Hosp., Rochester, N.Y., 1987-88; ptnr. J&L Assocs., Batavia, 1988-93, Landers & Walczak, Batavia, 1993—; adj. faculty Genesee C.C., 1988—. Bd. dirs. YWCA Genesee County, Inc., Batavia, 1989-90; mem. bus. devel. com. Genesee County C. of C., 1992—; v.p. Zonta Club of Batavia-Genesee, 1994-95, pres. 1996-97. Mem. N.Y. State Soc. CPAs. Roman Catholic. Home: 16 Linwood Ave Batavia NY 14020-3714 Office: Landers & Walczak 12 Center St Batavia NY 14020-3204

WALD, BARBARA ANN, software consultant, retired; b. Council Bluffs, Iowa, Mar. 9, 1935; d. Leon Shevah and Mildred Meyerson Frankel; m. Martin Wald, Aug. 3, 1958; children: Leah Wald Zollman, Marcie Sue, Adam David. AB, U. Chgo., 1957. Advt. copywriter Brandeis Dept. Store, Omaha, 1953; tchr. White Plains (N.Y.) Pub. Sch. System, 1957-58, West Allyce (Wis.) Pub. Sch. System, 1958-59, Akiba Jewish Day Sch., Chgo., 1961-64; writing tchr. Drexel U., Phila., 1971-72; owner, cons. Software Supporters, Merion, Pa., 1983-89. Author: Achieving Patient Power: One Family Masters the Medical Maze, 1992; contbr. articles to profl. pubs. Com. chmn. Religious Sch. Main Line Reform Temple, Wynnewood, Pa., 1974-77; active patroller Lower Merion Cmty. Watch, Ardmore, Pa., 1978-87; del. Fedn. Civic Assn., Lower Merion, 1984-91; v.p. Merion Civic Assn., 1981-84; bd. dirs. Smart Family Found., Inc., 1991-94, Auerbach Ctrl. Agy. for Jewish Edn., 1995-96. Mem. Ind. Computer Cons., Main Line Women's Bus. Network (charter), Home Based Bus. Profls. (pres. 1987-88), Nat. Better Bus. Bur. (arbitrator 1988-90).

WALD, FRANCINE JOY WEINTRAUB (MRS. BERNARD J. WALD), physicist, academic administrator; b. Bklyn., Jan. 13, 1938; d. Irving and Minnie (Reisig) Weintraub; student Bklyn. Coll., 1955-57; BEE, CCNY, 1960; MS, Poly. Inst. Bklyn., 1962, PhD, 1969; m. Bernard J. Wald, Feb. 2, 1964; children: David Evan, Kevin Mitchell. Engr., Remington Rand Univac div. Sperry Rand Corp., Phila., 1960; instr. Poly. Inst. Bklyn., 1962-64, adj. research asso., 1969-70; lectr. N.Y. C.C., Bklyn., 1969, 70; instr. sci. Friends Sem., N.Y.C., 1975-76, chmn. dept. sci., 1976-94; instr. sci., chmn. dept. sci. Nightingale-Bamford Sch., N.Y.C., 1994—. NDEA fellow, 1962-64. Mem. Am. Phys. Soc., Am. Assn. Physics Tchrs., Assn. Tchrs. in Ind. Schs., N.Y. Acad. Scis., Nat. Sci. Tchrs. Assn., AAAS, Sigma Xi, Tau Beta Pi, Eta Kappa Nu.

WALD, MARY S., risk management and personal finance educator; b. Baker, Oreg., June 17, 1943; d. Paul H. and Mary Elsie (Bartshe) Stoner; m. Lance Albert Wald, June 22, 1968. BA in English, Coll. of Idaho, Caldwell, 1966; MBA in Fin., Temple U., 1984. Tchr. Salt Lake City Bd. Edn., 1967-74; office mgr. Montgomery County Homemaker-Home Health Aide Svc., Inc., Blue Bell, Pa., 1975-82; adj. instr. risk mgmt. and personal fin. Temple U., Phila., 1984—; advisor Ambler Banking and Fin. Club. Co-author: Controlling Your Money, Step By Step, 1987. Named Outstanding Tchr. of Yr., Salt Lake City Bd. Edn., 1973-74. Mem. Am. Risk and Ins. Assn., Gamma Iota Sigma, Golden Key Nat. Honor Soc. (hon. mem.). Republican. Office: Temple U Ambler Campus 580 Meetinghouse Rd Ambler PA 19002-3923

WALD, PATRICIA MCGOWAN, federal judge; b. Torrington, Conn., Sept. 16, 1928; d. Joseph F. and Margaret (O'Keefe) McGowan; m. Robert L. Wald, June 22, 1952; children—Sarah, Douglas, Johanna, Frederica, Thomas. BA, Conn. Coll., 1948; LLB, Yale U., 1951; HHD (hon.), Mt. Vernon Jr. Coll., 1980; LLD (hon.), George Washington Law Sch., 1983, CUNY, 1984, Notre Dame U., John Jay Sch. Criminal Justice, Mt. Holyoke Coll., 1985, Georgetown U., 1987, Villanova U. Law Sch., Amherst Coll., N.Y. Law Sch., 1988, Colgate U., 1989, Hofstra Law Sch., 1991, New Eng. Coll., 1991, Hoffstra U., 1991, Vermont Law Sch., 1995. Bar: D.C. 1952. Clk. to judge Jerome Frank U.S. Ct. Appeals, 1951-52; asso. firm Arnold, Fortas & Porter, Washington, 1952-53; mem. D.C. Crime Commn., 1964-65; atty. Office of Criminal Justice, 1967-68, Neighborhood Legal Svc., Washington, 1968-70; co-dir. Ford Found. Project on Drug Abuse, 1970, Ctr. for Law and Social Policy, 1971-72, Mental Health Law Project, 1972-77; asst. atty. gen. for legis. affairs U.S. Dept. Justice, Washington, 1977-79; judge U.S. Ct. Appeals (D.C. cir.), 1979—, chief judge, 1986-91. Author: Law and Poverty, 1965; co-author: Bail in the United States, 1964, Dealing with Drug Abuse, 1973; contbr. articles on legal topics. Trustee Ford Found., 1972-77, Phillips Exeter Acad., 1975-77, Agnes Meyer Found., 1976-77, Conn. Coll., 1976-77; mem. Carnegie Council on Children, 1972-77. Mem. ABA (exec. bd. 1994—, bd. editors ABA Jour. 1978-86), Am. Law Inst. (coun. 1979—, exec. com. 1985—, 2d v.p. 1988-93, 1st v.p. 1993—), Inst. Medicine, Am. Acad. Arts and Scis., Phi Beta Kappa. Office: US Ct Appeals US Courthouse 3rd & Constitution Ave NW Washington DC 20001

WALD, SYLVIA, artist; b. Phila., Oct. 30, 1915. Ed., Moore Inst. Art, Sci. and Industry. One-woman shows include U. Louisville, 1945, 49, Kent State Coll., 1945, Nat. Serigraph Soc., 1946, Grand Central Moderns, N.Y.C., 1957, Devorah Sherman Gallery, Chgo., 1960, New Sch., 1967, Book Gallery, White Plains, N.Y., 1968, Benson Gallery, Bridgehampton, L.I., 1977, Knoll Internat., Munich, Germany, 1979, Amerika Havs, Munich, 1979, Aaron Berman Gallery, N.Y.C., 1981, Hirschltadler Gallery, 1994, New Britain (Conn.) Mus., 1994, Dongah Art Gallery, Seoul, Korea, 1995, Hanlim Art Gallery, Daejun, 1995-96, Kwanju City art Mus, Pusanm Korea; group shows include Nat. Sculpture Soc., 1940, Sculpture Internat., Phila., 1940, Chgo. Art Inst., 1941, Bklyn. Mus., 1975, Library of Congress, 1943, 52, 58, Smithsonian Instn., 1954, Internat. Print Exhbn., Salzburg and Vienna, 1952, 2d Sao Paulo Biennial, 1953, N.Y. Cultural Center, 1973, Mus. Modern Art, N.Y.C., 1975, Benson Gallery, Bridgehampton, L.I., 1982, Dumon-Landis Gallery, New Brunswick, N.J., 1982-83, Suzuki Gallery, N.Y.C., 1982, Sid Deutch Gallery, N.Y.C., 1983, Aaron Berman Gallery, N.Y.C., 1983, Full House Gallery, Kingston, N.J., 1984, Worcester Mus., 1991, Boston Mus. Fine Arts, 1991, Hirschl & Adler Gallery, N.Y.C., 1993, others; represented in permanent collections Aetna Oil Co., Am. Assn. U. Women, Ball State Tchrs. Coll., Bibliotheque Nationale, Paris, Bklyn. Mus., Howard U., State U. Iowa, Library of Congress, U. Louisville, Nat. Gallery, Mus. Modern Art, Phila. Mus., N.C. Mus., Rose Mus. Art at Brandeis U., Whitney Mus., N.Y.C., Finch Coll. Mus., N.Y.C., U. Nebr., Ohio U., U. Okla., Princeton, Victoria and Albert Mus., Walker Gallery, Worcester (Mass.) Art Mus., Guggenheim Mus., N.Y.C., Grunewald Mus., U.Calif. Los Angeles, Rutgers Mus., N.J., Aschenbach Collection Mus., San Francisco, Grunewald Coll. Mus. UCLA; Contbr. to profl. publs. Address: 417 Lafayette St New York NY 10003-7005

WALDBAUM, JANE COHN, art history educator; b. N.Y.C., Jan. 28, 1940; d. Max Arthur and Sarah (Waldstein) Cohn. BA, Brandeis U., 1962; MA, Harvard U., 1964, PhD, 1968. Rsch. fellow in classical archaeology Harvard U., Cambridge, Mass., 1968-70, 72-73; asst. prof. U. Wis.-Milw., 1973-78, assoc. prof., 1978-84, prof. art history, 1984—, chmn. dept., 1982-85, 86-89, 91-92; Dorot rsch. prof. W.F. Albright Inst. Archaeol. Rsch., Jerusalem, 1990-91, trustee, 1996—, mem. governance com., 1996. Author: From Bronze to Iron, 1978; Metalwork from Sardis, 1983; author (with others), editor Sardis Report I, 1975; mem. editorial bd. Bull. Am. Schs. Oriental Rsch., 1994—; contbr. numerous articles to profl. jours. Bd. dirs. Milw. Soc. of Archaeol. Inst., 1973—, pres., 1983-85, 91-95. Woodrow Wilson Found. fellow, dissertation fellow, 1962-63, 65-66, NEH postdoctoral rsch., Jerusalem, 1989-90; grantee Am. Philos. Soc., 1972, NEH, summer 1975, U. Wis.-Milw. Found., 1983. Mem. Am. Schs. Oriental Research, Soc. for Archaeol. Sci., Archaeol. Inst. Am. (exec. com. 1975-77, chmn. com. on membership programs 1977-81, nominating com. 1984, chmn. com. on lecture program 1985-87, acad. trustee 1993—, com. profl. responsibilities 1993—, fellowships com. 1993—, gold medal com. 1993—, mem. Ancient Near East com. 1993—, chair 1996—), W.F. Albright Inst. Archaeol. Rsch. (trustee 1996—, mem. governance com. 1996—), Phi Beta Kappa. Office: U Wis Dept Art History PO Box 413 Milwaukee WI 53201-0413

WALDEN, BERDENA JOHNSON, elementary education educator; b. Pinkstaff, Ill., Oct. 6, 1945; d. Burl Logan and Mildred Lotha Mae (Clingman) Johnson; m. Walter Carter Walden, June 27, 1979 (div. Feb. 1985); children: Sylvia, Julia, Sysine. B in Elem. Edn., Oakland City (Ind.) U., 1986; MEd, Ind. Wesleyan U., Marion, 1994. Cert. tchr., Ind. Clk. typist/payroll clk. Golden Rule and Congl. Life Ins., Lawrenceville, Ind., 1963-72; elem. tchr. Harper Sch., Evansville (Ill.) Vanderburgh Sch. Corp., 1986—; Sec. Evansville Area Reading Coun., 1994; tchr. cons. GENI, Ind., 1995—; acad. coach for gifted and talented Odyssey of the Mind; workshop presenter. Vol. coord. campaign Fourth Ward Candidate, Evansville, 1995; vol. allocations panel United Way of Evansville; vol. fundraiser, patron mem. Evansville Philharmonic. Rotary grantee, 1995-96. Mem. AAUW, NAACP, Am. Legion, Hoosier Assn. Sci. Tchrs., Phi Delta Kappa (pres. chpt. 1996). Democrat. Baptist. Home: PO Box 15126 Evansville IN 47716-0126 Office: Harper Sch 21 S Alvord Blvd Evansville IN 47714

WALDEN, LINDA L., lawyer; b. Dallas, Aug. 16, 1951; d. Leslie LaFayette Jr. and Neva Irene (McBee) W.; m. David Lee Finney, June 9, 1984. BA, Tex. Women's U., 1972; JD, St. Mary's U., 1975. Asst. city atty. City of Amarillo, Tex., 1976-77; asst. dist. atty. 84th Jud. Dist., Borger, Tex., 1977-79; asst. atty. gen. Office Atty. Gen. Tex., Austin, 1979-84; litigation atty. Friedman & Ginsberg, Dallas, 1984-86, Bradford & Snyder, Dallas, 1986-88; corp. counsel Occidental Chem. Co., Dallas, 1988—. Home: 2209 Greenview Dr Carrollton TX 75010-4110 Office: Occidental Chem Corp 5005 Lyndon B Johnson Fwy Dallas TX 75244-6119

WALDEN, PAMELA LADD, airport engineer; b. Washington, May 13, 1960; d. Alan M. and Patricia C. (Carr) W.; m. Julius Augustus Phillips III. Student, Fla. Inst. Tech., 1982. Aircraft mainenance Teterboro (N.J.) Flight Acad., 1979-82; aircraft line svc. Piper Air, Long Beach, Calif., 1982-83, Aero Svcs., Teterboro, 1983-84; airport engr. Port Authority N.Y.-N.J., 1984-90, sr. airport engr., 1990—; spkr. in field. Contbr. articles to profl. jours. Mem. Nat. fire Protection Assn. (dir. aviation sect. 1990-93), Am. Assn. Airport Execs. (chair R&D snow symposium 1993—, tech. com. on security and aircraft rescue and fire fighting). Office: Port Authority NY-NJ One World Trade Ctr 65N New York NY 10048

WALDHAUSER, CATHY HOWARD, financial services executive; b. St. Paul, Oct. 18, 1949; d. Jack Roger and Lois (Johnson) Howard; m. Stanley Jay Waldhauser, Feb. 3, 1973. BA in Math. and Econs., Gustavus Adolphus Coll., 1971. Various actuarial positions IDS Life Ins. Co., Mpls., 1971-81; v.p. IDS Life Ins. Co., 1981-91; chief acctg. officer IDS Fin. Svcs., 1991-93; dir. Fin. Instns. Group, 1993—. Trustee Gustavus Adolphus Coll., 1993—, mem. alumni bd. dirs., 1984-90; active Golden Valley (Minn.) LWV, 1986-89; sec., treas. Calvary Luth. Ch., Golden Valley, 1988-89; allocations vol. United Way, Mpls., 1988-90; mem. family selection com. Habitat for Humanity, 1993—. Fellow Soc. Actuaries (product devel. sect. coun. and rsch. com. 1985-88, edn. and exam. com. 1980-81, 83, panelist, lectr. 1980, 87-90), Am. Acad. Actuaries, Minn. Life and Health Guarantee Assn. (bd. dirs. 1984-92), Life Office Mgmt. Assn. (mgmt. rsch. com. 1987-90), Twin Cities Actuarial Club.

WALDINGER SEFF, MARGARET, special elementary education educator; b. N.Y.C., June 12, 1949; d. Herbert Francis Waldinger and Michelle (Rubin) Cohen; children: Dylan Paul Seff, Courtney Sara Seff, Blake Adam Seff. BA, Hofstra U., 1971; postgrad., NYU, 1971-73; MA, Fairleigh Dickinson U., 1986. Cert. elem. sch. tchr., tchr. of handicapped, learning disability tchr. cons., N.J. Tchr. pub. schs., N.J., N.Y., 1984-88; learning specialist Manchester (Vt.) Elem. Sch., 1988—; adv., ednl. therapist, N.J., 1983-88.. Reading grantee Tuxedo Park Sch., 1986, Bennington Rutland Supervisory Union, 1992. Home: RR 1 Box 2291 Manchester Center VT 05255 Office: Manchester Elem Sch Memorial Dr Manchester Center VT 05255

WALDON, GRACE ROBERTA, insurance agent; b. Surry County, N.C., July 8, 1941; d. Brady Warren and Kathleen (Riggs) Felts; m. Jesse James Waldon Jr., May 17, 1958; children: James, Forrest. BS in Econs., U. N.C., 1981, postgrad., 1983-84. Registered rep. NML Investment Svcs., Inc. Real estate agt. Rob Ramby Real Estate, Abilene, Tex., 1982-84; asst. to v.p. Life Ins. Svcs., Charlotte, N.C., 1984-85; v.p. James R. Worrell Gen. Agy., N.W. Mut. Life,, Charlotte, 1985—; investment officer Robert W. Baird & Co. Inc. Officer Symphony Guild, Abilene, 1972, Internat. Mgmt. Coun., Charlotte, 1989; chmn. faculty wives La. Tech. Inst., Ruston, 1966. Named Outstanding Mem. St. Paul's Meth. Ch., 1973. Mem. CLU, Chartered Fin. Cons., Charlotte Sales and Mktg. Execs. Republican. Office: NW Mut Life 1900 Rexford Rd Ste 120 Charlotte NC 28211-3481

WALDOR, CATHY LYNN, lawyer; b. Newark, Aug. 14, 1952; d. Milton and Mona (McCloskey) W.; m. B. Vincent Carlesimo; stepchildren: Alexis, Christopher. BA, U. Md., 1974; JD, Seton Hall U., 1977. Bar: N.J. 1977, U.S. Dist. Ct. N.J. 1977, D.C. 1979, N.Y. 1989, U.S. Ct. Appeals (3rd cir.) 1989, U.S. Dist. Ct. (so. dist.) N.Y. 1991. Pub. defender Office of Pub. Defender, Newark, 1978-86; ptnr. Waldor, Carlesimo, Biancone, Montclair, N.J., 1986—. Dir. of access Women's Fund N.J., 1995—; mem. women's symposium Seton Hall Law Sch., Newark, 1996. Mem. Assn. Criminal Def. Lawyers (pres. 1996-97), N.J. State Bar Assn. Home: 30 Forest Ave Verona NJ 07044 Office: Waldor Carlesimo & Biancone 88 Park St Montclair NJ 07042

WALDRON, ANN W., writer; b. Birmingham, Dec. 14, 1924; d. Earl Watson and Elizabeth (Roberts) Wood; m. Martin Waldron (dec.); children: Peter, Thomas William, Martin III, Laura O'Brien. AB, U. Ala., 1945. Reporter Atlanta Constitution, 1945-47; reporter, columnist Tampa Tribune, Fla., 1957-60, St. Petersburg Times, Fla., 1960-65; book editor Houston Chronicle, 1970-75; editor Princeton (N.J.) U., 1978-89. Author: (books) The House on Pendleton Block, 1975, The Integration of Mary-Larkin Thornhill, 1975 (Notable Book of the ALA, Best Book of the Child Study Assn.), The Luckie Star, 1977, Scaredy Cat, 1978, The French Detection, 1979 (Notable Book for Social Studies, Children's Book Coun.), The Blueberry Collection, 1981, True or False? The Detection of Art Forgeries, 1983, Close Connections: Caroline Gordon and the Southern Renaissance, 1987 (Nonfiction award Ala. Libr. Assn.), Claude Monet, 1991, Francisco Goya, 1992, Hodding Carter: The Reconstruction of a Racist, 1993.

WALDROP, LINDA M., medical administrator; b. Jefferson County, Ala., Oct. 24, 1942; d. Luther Grady Jr. and Anna Katherine (Gray) McGill; m. Bennie Lee Waldrop Jr., Mar. 14, 1961; children: Tracy L., Terry L. AS, Jefferson State Jr. Coll., 1971; BSN, Samford U., 1985; MA, U. Ala., Birmingham, 1989. Head nurse open heart ICU Bapt. Med. Ctr.-Montclair, Birmingham, 1976-82, head nurse telemetry unit, 1985-87, head nurse med. unit, 1983-85, head nurse oncology unit, 1987-90, edn. coord.; internal auditor Bapt. Med. Ctr.-Montclair, 1991; dir. med.-surg. telemetry nursing Shelby Med. Ctr., Alabaster, Ala., 1991-96, dir. gastroenterol. svcs., 1993-95, nursing internal auditor, 1993—, dir. women's svcs., 1994-95, dir. edn., 1996—. Mem. ANA (cert. nursing adminstrn.), AACN, Oncology Nursing Soc., Nat. Mgmt. Assn., Ala. Orgn. Nurse Execs., Birmingham Regional Orgn. Nurse Execs.

WALENGA, JEANINE MARIE, medical educator, researcher; b. Evergreen Park, Ill., Nov. 21, 1955; d. Eugene Adam and Therese Marie (Podsiadlik) W. BS, U. Ill., Chgo., 1978; Diplome d'Etudes Approfondies, U. Paris VI, 1984, PhD, 1987; postgrad., Loyola U., Maywood, Ill., 1981-84. Cert. med. technologist. Med. technologist MacNeal Hosp., Berwyn, Ill., 1978-79; rsch. asst. Loyola U. Med. Ctr., Maywood, 1979-80, hemostasis rsch. lab. supr., 1980-87, co-dir. hemostasis rsch. lab., 1987—, asst. prof. thoracic/cardiovascular surgery/pathology, 1988-94, assoc. prof., 1994—; mem. Cardiovascular Inst., Loyola U., 1995—; cons. in field; lectr. in field; observer Nat. Com. for Clin. Lab. Stds., 1988—; del. US Pharmacopeia, 1990—. Contbr. articles to profl. jours. Named Alumnus of Yr., U. Ill., 1990; NHLBI rsch. grantee, 1989—; recipient Investigator Recognition award, 1993. Fellow Am. Coll. Angiology; mem. Internat. Inst. for Thrombotic Diseases (sec. 1989—), Am. Assn. Pathologists, Am. Soc. Hematology, Internat. Soc. Thrombosis and Hemostasis (sci. and standardization subcom. on heparin 1990-93), Am. Soc. Clin. Pathologists, Am. Heart Assn., Am. Soc. Med. Tech.

WALENTIK, CORINNE ANNE, pediatrician; b. Rockville Centre, N.Y., Nov. 24, 1949; d. Edward Robert and Evelyn Mary (Brinskele) Finno; m. David Stephen Walentik, June 24, 1972; children: Anne, Stephen, Kristine. AB with honors, St. Louis U., 1970, MD, 1974, MPH, 1992. Diplomate Am. Bd. Pediatrics, Am. Bd. Neonatal and Perinatal Medicine. Resident in pediatrics St. Louis U. Group Hosps., 1974-76, fellow in neonatalogy, 1976-78; neonatalogist St. Mary's Health Ctr., St. Louis, 1978-79; co-dir. neonatal unit St. Louis City Hosps., 1979-83, dir. neonatal unit, 1983-85; dir. neonatalogy St. Louis Regional Med. Ctr., 1985—; asst. prof. pediatrics St. Louis U., 1980-94, assoc. clin. prof., 1994—; supr. nursery follow up program Cardinal Glennon Children's Hosp., 1979—. Contbr. articles to profl. jours. Mem. adv. com. Mo. Perinatal Program., 1983-86. Fellow Am. Acad. Pediats.; mem. APHA, Mo. Pub. Health Assn. (pres. St. Louis chpt. 1995-96), Mo. Perinatal Assn. (pres. 1983), Nat. Perinatal Assn. (coun. 1984-87), Mo. State Med. Assn., St. Louis Met. Med. Soc. Roman Catholic. Home: 7234 Princeton Ave Saint Louis MO 63130-3027 Office: St Louis Regional Med Ctr 5535 Delmar Blvd Saint Louis MO 63112-3005

WALES, PATRICE, school system administrator; b. Washington, Sept. 9, 1935; d. Robert Corning and Bernadette Mary (Dyer) W. BA, Dunbarton Coll. of Holy Cross, 1957; MTS, Cath. U. Am., 1978; PhD, U. Md., 1993. Cert. tchr., supt., Md. Tchr. mid. sch. St. Marys, Laurel, Md., 1960-61; tchr. high sch. St. Vincent Pallotti High Sch., Laurel, Md., 1962-65; instr. nursing sch. St. Mary's Sch. Nursing, Huntington, W.Va., 1965-66; tchr. St. Vincent Pallotti High Sch., Laurel, 1967-76, adminstr., 1976—, chair sci. dept., 1962-80, dean students, 1976-87, sponsorship dir., 1988—; bd. dirs. St. Vincent Pallotti H.S., Laurel, 1988—; trustee St. Joseph's Hosp., Backhannon, W.Va., 1990—; dir. German Exch. Program, Laurel, Ahlen, Germany, 1976—. Senator Sisters Senate Archdiocese of Washington, 1993—. NSF grantee, 1967, 69, 71. Mem. ASCD, Nat. Cath. Edn. Assn. Roman Catholic. Home: 404 8th St Laurel MD 20707-4032 Office: St Vincent Pallotti High Sch 113 8th St Laurel MD 20707-4025

WALHOUT, JUSTINE SIMON, chemistry educator; b. Aberdeen, S.D., Dec. 11, 1930; d. Otto August and Mabel Ida (Tews) S.; m. Donald Walhout, Feb. 1, 1958; children: Mark, Timothy, Lynne, Peter. BS, Wheaton Coll., 1952; PhD, Northwestern U., 1956. Instr. Wright City Community Coll., Chgo., 1955-56; asst. prof. Rockford (Ill.) Coll., 1956-59, assoc. prof., 1959-66, 81-89, prof., 1989-96, prof. emeritus, 1996—, dept. chmn., 1987-95; cons. Pierce Chem. Co., Rockford, 1968-69; trustee Rockford (Ill.) Coll., 1987-91. Contbr. articles to profl. jours. Mem. Ill. Bd. Edn., 1974-81. Mem. AAUW (Ill. bd. mem. 1985-87), Am. Chem. Soc. (councilor 1993—), Rockford LWV (bd. dirs. 1983-85), Sigma Xi. Presbyterian. Home: 320 N Rockford Ave Rockford IL 61107-4547 Office: Rockford Coll 5050 E State St Rockford IL 61108-2311

WALISH, GERALYN ROSE, business consultant, analyst; b. Bryn Mawr, Pa., Jan. 9, 1956; d. George Martin and Carolyn Rose (O'Neill) W.; m. John Francis Aigeltinger, June 24, 1978 (div. 1983); m. Robert Kenneth Cole, June 25, 1989. BA in Orgnl. Mgmt., Eastern Coll., 1994. Systems mgr. Nat. Liberty Corp., Frazer, Pa., 1978-85; project mgr. Reliance Life Cos., Phila., 1985-86; cons. Fidelity Mut. Life Ins. Co., Radnor, Pa., 1986-89; sr. bus. analyst Aon, Trevose, Pa., 1989-93, sys. dir., 1993-95; v.p. Tenic, Inc., Hartford, Conn., 1995—. Chmn. Moonlighting Soc., Multiple Sclerosis Soc., Phila, 1986-88; mem. Super Cities Walk Adv. Com., Devel. Com., Multiple Sclerosis Soc., Phila., 1989; trustee Greater Del. Valley Multiple Sclerosis Soc., 1990—. Mem. Life Office Mgmt. Assn., Am. Bus. Women's Assn. (treas. Frazer, Pa. 1980-82). Home and Office: 632 Greenridge Rd Glenmoore PA 19343-9500

WALKER, ALICE MALSENIOR, author; b. Eatonton, Ga., Feb. 9, 1944; d. Willie Lee and Minnie (Grant) W.; m. Melvyn R. Leventhal, Mar. 17, 1967 (div. 1976); 1 dau., Rebecca Walker Leventhal. BA, Sarah Lawrence Coll., 1966; PhD (hon.), Russell Sage U., 1972; DHL (hon.), U. Mass., 1983. Co-founder, pub. Wild Trees Pr., Navarro, Calif., 1984-88; writer in residence, tchr. black studies Jackson State Coll., 1968-69, Tougaloo Coll., 1970-71; lectr. literature Wellesley Coll., 1972-73, U. Mass., Boston, 1972-73; disting. writer Afro-American studies dept. U. Calif., Berkeley, 1982; Fannie Hurst Prof. of Literature Brandeis U., Waltham, Mass., 1982; cons. Friends of the Children of Miss., 1967. Author: Once, 1968, The Third Life of Grange Copeland, 1970, Five Poems, 1972, Revolutionary Petunias and Other Poems, 1973 (Nat. Book award nomination 1973, Lillian Smith award So. Regional Coun. 1973), In Love and Trouble, 1973 (Richard and Hinda Rosenthal Found. award Am. Acad. and Inst. of Arts and Letters 1974) Langston Hughes: American Poet, 1973, Meridian, 1976, Goodnight, Willie Lee, I'll See You in the Morning, 1979, You Can't Keep a Good Woman Down, 1981, The Color Purple, 1982 (Nat. Book Critics Circle award nomination 1982, Pulitzer Prize for fiction 1983, Am. Book award 1983), In Search of Our Mothers' Gardens, 1983, Horses Make a Landscape Look More Beautiful, 1984, To Hell With Dying, 1988, Living By the Word: Selected Writings, 1973-1987, 1988, The Temple of My Familiar, 1989, Her Blue Body Everything We Know: Earthling Poems, 1965-1990, 1991, Finding the Green Stone, 1991, Possessing the Secret of Joy, 1992, (with Pratibha Parmar) Warrior Marks, 1993, (with others) Double Stitch: Black Women Write About Mothers & Daughters, 1993, Everyday Use, 1994; editor: I Love Myself When I'm Laughing... And Then Again When I'm Looking Mean and Impressive, 1979. Recipient first prize Am. Scholar essay contest, 1967, O. Henry award for "Kindred Spirits", 1986, Nora Astorga Leadership award, 1989, Fred Cody award for lifetime achievement Bay Area Book Reviewers Assn., 1990, Freedom to Write award PEN Ctr. USA West, 1990; Bread Loaf Writer's Conf. scholar, 1966; Merrill writing fellowship, 1967; McDowell Colony fellowship, 1967, 77-78; National Endowment for the Arts grantee, 1969, 77; Radcliffe Inst. fellowship, 1971-73; Guggenheim fellow, 1977-78. *

WALKER, ANNETTE, counseling administrator; b. Birmingham, Ala., Sept. 20, 1953; d. Jesse and Luegene (Wright) W. BS in Edn., Huntingdon Coll., 1976; MS in Adminstrn. and Supervision, Troy State U., 1977, 78, MS in Sch. Counseling, 1990, AA in Sch. Adminstrn., 1992; diploma, World Travel Sch., 1990; diploma in Cosmetology, John Patterson Coll., 1992; MEd in higher Edn. Adminstrn., Auburn (Ala.) U., 1995. Cert. tchr., adminstr., Ala.; lic. cosmetologist, Ala. Tchr. Montgomery (Ala.) Pub. Sch. System, 1976-89, sch. counselor, 1989—; gymnastics tchr. Cleveland Ave. YMCA, 1971-76; girls coach Montgomery Parks and Recreation, 1973-76; summer sch. sci. tchr. grades 7-9, 1977-88; chmn. dept. sci. Bellingrath Sch., 1987-90, courtesy com., 1987-88, sch. discipline com., 1977-84; recreation asst. Gunter AFB, Ala., 1981-83; calligraphy tchr. Gunter Youth Ctr., 1982; program dir. Maxwell AFB, Ala., 1983-89, vol. tchr. Internat. Officer Sch., 1985—, Ala. Goodwill Amb., 1985—, day camp dir., 1987, calligraphy tchr., 1988; trainer internat. law for sec. students, Ala., 1995—; leader of workshops in field; evening computer tchr. high sch. diploma program, 1995—; sales rep. Ala. World Travel, 1990—; behavior aid Brantwood Children's Home, 1996—; computer tchr. h.s. diploma program Montgomery County Sch., 1995—; behavior aide Brantwood Children's Home, 1995—; hotel auditor, 1995—. Mem. CAP; tchr. Sunday sch. Beulah Bapt. Ch., Montgomery; vol. zoo activities Tech. Scholarship Program for Ala. Tchrs. Computer Courses, Montgomery, Ala.; bd. dirs. Cleveland Ave. YMCA, 1976-80; sponsor Bell-Howe chpt. Young Astronauts, 1986-90, Pate Howe chpt. Young Astronauts, 1991-92; judge Montgomery County Children Festival Elem. Sci. Fair, 1988-90; bd. dirs. Troy State U. Drug Free Schs., 1992—; chmn. Maxwell AFB Red Cross-Youth, 1986-88; goodwill amb. sponsor to various families (award 1989, 95); State of Ala. rep. P.A.T.C.H.-Internat. Law Inst., 1995. Recipient Outstanding High Sch. Sci./Math. Tchr. award Sigma Xi, 1989, Most Outstanding Youth Coun. Leader award Maxwell AFB Youth Ctr., 1987, Outstanding Ala. Goodwill Amb. award, 1989, 95; named Tchr. of the Week, WCOV-TV, 1992, Ala. Tchr. in Space Program, summer 1989, Local Coord. Young Astronaut Program, 1988. Mem. NEA, Internat. Platform Assn., Nat. Sci. Tchrs. Assn., Ala. Sch. Counselors, Montgomery Sch. Counselors Assn., Montgomery County Ednl. Assn., Space Camp Amb., Huntingdon Alumni Assn. (sec.-treas.), Ala. Goodwill Amb., Montgomery Capital City Club, Young Astronauts, Ea. Star, Zeta Phi Beta, Chi Delta Phi, Kappa Pi. Home: 2501 Westwood Dr Montgomery AL 36108-4448 Office: Bellingrath Sch 3488 S Court St Montgomery AL 36104

WALKER, BARBARA ROSS, secondary education educator; b. Texarkana, Ark., Feb. 3, 1946; d. Ervie J. and Ella R. (Keel) Ross; m. Emory L. Walker, Oct. 10, 1969; children: Daphne, Brandon, Christel, Justin. BA, So. Ark. U., Magnolia, 1969; MS, East Tex. State U., Texarkana, 1983, MEd, 1985. Cert. secondary tchr. social studies, history and govt., Ark., tex. Registrar Texarkana (Tex.) Hist. Mus., 1977-78; tchr. Am. history and African-Am. history Texarkana (Ark.) Sch. Dist. 7, 1980—; mem. Texarkana Hist. Mus. Systems, 1993—. Asst. dir. music Lonoke Bapt. Ch. NEH grantee 1984, 85, 92, 93, 94, 95, 96. Mem. NAACP, NEA, Orgn. Am. Historians, Nat. Coun. for Social Studies, Ark. Coun. for Social Studies, Ark. Edn. Assn. (mem. state human rels. commn. 1984-87, ACT 963 history com. 1994), Texarkana Classroom Tchrs. Assn. (chmn. gov.'s com., dist. social studies team 1994), Ark. Hist. Assn. Democrat. Baptist. Home: 1207 Louisiana St Texarkana AR 75502-4665 Office: Ark Sr High Sch Texarkana AR 75502

WALKER, BERNICE BAKER, artist; b. Carbondale, Pa., Dec. 25, 1928; d. William Robert and Bernice Mary (Parry) Baker; m. Joseph Henry Walker, Sept. 13, 1952. Student, Richmond Profl. Inst., 1946-47; BFA, R.I. Sch. Design, 1952. Artist Highlights for Children, 1952-55, Studio K, Lancaster, Pa., 1959-64; tchr. Heintzelman Art Assn., Manaheim, Pa., 1975-86; owner The Design Corner, Lancaster, 1989—. Tchr. Lancaster County Art Assn., 1962-64, bd. dirs., 1990-92. Mem. Lancaster Spinners & Weavers, Lancaster County Art Assn., Mid Atlantic Weavers, Village Art Assn., Lancaster Camera Club. Office: The Design Corner 21 N Mulberry St Lancaster PA 17603

WALKER, BEULAH CRUMEDY-VARNADO, postal service administrator; b. Prentiss, Miss., Sept. 11, 1955; d. Leroy and Porah (Price) Crumedy; m. Frederick Eugene Varnado, Mar. 24, 1975 (div. 1977); children: Tanishia René Varnado; m. William Phillip Walker, Mar. 29, 1980; children: Danderia Philesa, William Phillip Jr. BS, Alcorn State U., 1975, MS, 1976. Instr. Utica Jr. Coll., 1977-79, East Columbia H.S., Columbia, Miss., 1979-80, Piney Woods (Miss.) Country Life Sch., 1980-83; city letter carrier U.S. Postal Svc., Jackson, Miss., 1983-86, training tech., 1986-87, driving instr., examiner, 1987-88, supr. customer svc., 1988—. Life mem. Girl Scouts, Miss., 1988; asst. cubmaster Boy Scouts, Miss., 1995. Mem. NAFE, NAACP (youth advisor), Nat. Alliance of Postal and Fed. Employees, Nat. Assn. Postal Suprs., Sigma Gamma Rho (life mem.). Democrat. Baptist. Home: 252 Old Enochs Rd Florence MS 39073-9032 Office: US Postal Svc 955 Westland Service Dr Jackson MS 39209-9998

WALKER, BOBBIE N., academic administrator; b. Ada, Okla., Feb. 25, 1938; d. E.E. Bob and Leila E. (Merritt) Nash; m. Jose Atanasio Hernandez, June 19, 1965 (dec. Nov. 1992); 1 child, Steven Joseph; 1 child from previous marriage, Daniel Marc Stewart; m. Owen Heywood Walker, July 20, 1995. BA in English and Spanish, U. Houston, 1970, MS in Edn., 1975; PhD, U. Tex., Austin, 1987. Secondary tchr. Ft. Bend Ind. Sch. Dist., Stafford, Tex., 1971-75, New Braunfels (Tex.) Ind. Sch. Dist., 1975-76, Lamar and Bowie Schs., San Marcos, Tex., 1976-78; adminstr., asst. dean Southwest Tex. State U., San Marcos, 1978-87; v.p. for student affairs Cameron U., Lawton, Okla., 1987-90, U. Tex., San Antonio, 1990—. Bd. dirs., YMCA, 1991—, Women's Chamber, San Antonio. Mem. Okla. Hills Rotary of San Antonio (v.p.), Women's C. of C. Republican. Home: 27 Legend Ln Houston TX 77024 Office: U Tex at San Antonio 6900 N Loop 1604 W San Antonio TX 78249-1130

WALKER, BRIGITTE MARIA, translator, linguistic consultant; b. Stolp, Germany, Sept. 20, 1934; came to U.S., 1957; d. Joseph Karl and Ursula Maria Margot Ehrler; m. John V. Kelley (div.); 1 child, John V. Jr.; m. Edward D. Walker, July 3, 1977. Grad., Erlangen Translator's Sch., Germany, 1956; grad. fgn. corres., Berlitz Sch., Germany, 1956. Bilingual sec., translator Spencer Patent Law Office, Washington, 1959-62; office mgr., translator I. William Millen, Millen and White, Patent Law, Washington, 1962-67; prin. Tech. Translating Bur., Washington, 1967-68, St. Petersburg Beach, Fla., 1968—; cons. for patent law offices, Washington, 1962—; ofcl. expert for ct. Paul M. Craig, Patent Atty., Rockford, Ill., 1981; cons. to sci. editor Merriam-Webster, Inc., Springfield, Mass., 1987—. Author: German-English/English-German Last-Resort Dictionary for Technical Translators, 1991, (poetry) The Other Side of the Mirror, 1992 (Poetry award Nat. League Am. Pen Women 1994); co-translator: The Many Faces of Research, 1980; holder of trademark in field. Evaluator fgn. textbooks Pinellas County Sch. Bd., St. Petersburg, 1987, German judge, 1988. Recipient Recoginition award Pinellas County Sch. Bd., 1988, Meritorious Pub. Svc. award City of St. Petersburg Beach, 1987, Poetry award Nat. League Am. Pen Women, 1994, Essay award, 1996. Mem. Mensa. Democrat. Lutheran. Home and Office: 7150 Sunset Way Apt 1007 Saint Petersburg FL 33706-3650

WALKER, CAROLYN PEYTON, English language educator; b. Charlottesville, Va., Sept. 15, 1942; d. Clay M. and Ruth Peyton. BA in Am. History and Lit., Sweet Briar Coll., 1965; cert. in French, Alliance Francaise, Paris, 1966; EdM, Tufts U., 1970; MA in English and Am. Lit., Stanford U., 1974, PhD in English Edn., Stanford U., 1977. Tchr. Elem. and jr. high schs. in Switzerland, 1967-69; tchr. elem. grades Boston Sch. System, 1966-67, 69-70; Newark (Calif.) Unified Sch. System, 1970-72; instr. div. humanities Canada Coll., Redwood City, Calif., 1973, 76-78; instr. Sch. Bus., U. San Francisco, 1973-74; evaluation cons. Inst. Profl. Devel., San Jose, Calif., 1975-76; asst. dir. Learning Assistance Ctr., Stanford U., Calif., 1972-77, dir., 1977-84, lectr. Sch. Edn., 1975-84, dept. English, 1977-84, supr. counselors, tutors and tchrs., 1972-84; assoc. prof. dept. English, San Jose State U., Calif., 1984-93; dir. English dept. Writing Ctr., 1986-93, Steinbeck Rsch. Ctr., 1986-87; mem. faculty U. Calif., Berkeley and Santa Cruz, 1995—; corp. trainer, 1993—; pres. Waverley Edn., Inc., Ednl. Cons., 1983-91, tchr. writing and Am. culture for fgn. profls., U. Calif. at Berkeley, 1995—, pvt. prac. corp. trng., 1983—; head cons. to pres. to evaluate coll.'s writing program, San Jose City Coll., 1985-87; cons. U. Tex., Dallas, 1984, Stanford U., 1984, 1977-78, CCNY, 1979, U. Wis., 1980, numerous testing programs; cons. to pres. San Diego State U., 1982, Ednl. Testing Svc., 1985-88, also to numerous univs. and colls.; condr. reading and writing workshops, 1972—; reviewer Random House Books, 1978—, Rsch. in the Teaching of English, 1983—, Course Tech., Inc., 1990—; cons. Basic Skills Task Force, U.S. Office Edn., 1977-79, Right to Read, Calif. State Dept. Edn., 1977-82, Program for Gifted and Talented, Fremont (Calif.) Unified Sch. Dist., 1981-82; bd. dirs. high tech. sci. ctr., San Jose, 1983-84; speaker numerous profl. confs. Author: (with Patricia Killen) Handbook for Teaching Assistants at Stanford University, 1977, Learning Center Courses for Faculty and Staff: Reading, Writing, and Time Management, 1981, How to Succeed as a New Teacher: A Handbook for Teaching Assistants, 1978, ESL Courses for Faculty & Staff: An Additional Opportunity to Serve the Campus Community, 1983, (with Karen Wilson) Tutor Handbook for the Writing Center at San Jose State University, 1989, (with others) Academic Tutoring at the Learning Assistance Center, 1980, Writing Conference Talk: Factors Associated with High and Low Rated Writing Conferences, 1987, Lifeline Mac: A Handbook for Instructors in the Macintosh Computer Classrooms, 1989, Communications with the Faculty: Vital Links for the Success of Writing Centers, 1991, Coming to America, 1993, Teacher Dominance in the Writing Conference, 1992, Instant Curriculum: Just Add Tutors and Students, 1993; contbr. chpts. to Black American Literature Forum, 1991; contbr. articles to profl. jours. Vol. fundraiser Peninsula Ctr. for the Blind, Palo Alto, Calif., 1982—, The Resource Ctr. for Women, Palo Alto, 1975-76. Recipient Award for Outstanding Contbns., U.S. HEW, 1979, award ASPIRE (federally funded program), 1985, two awards Student Affirmative Action, 1986, award Western Coll. Reading & Learning Assn., 1984; numerous other awards and grants. Mem. MLA, Coll. Reading & Learning Assn. (treas. 1982-84, bd. dirs. 1982-84), Nat. Coun. Tchrs. English, No. Calif. Coll. Reading Assn. (sec.-treas. 1976-78), Am. Assn. U. Profs., Jr. League Palo Alto (bd. dirs. 1977-78, 83-84). Home: 2350 Waverley St Palo Alto CA 94301-4143

WALKER, CAROLYN SMITH, college services administrator, counselor; b. Atlanta, May 9, 1946; d. George Taft and Lonnie Bell (Bates) Smith; 1 child from previous marriage, Gary Sherard Walker II. BA in Psychology, Clark Coll., Atlanta, 1970; MS in Counseling & Guidance, U. Nebr., Omaha, 1975. Lic. profl. counselor, Ga. Adult basic edn. instr. Atlanta Pub. Schs., 1970-71, adult basic edn. site coord., 1971; adult basic edn. instr. Omaha-Nebr. Tech. C.C., Omaha, 1971-74, dir. adult basic edn., 1974; guidance counselor Omaha Pub. Schs., 1974-76; recruitment counselor Minority Women Employment Program, Atlanta, 1976-77; career planning and employment preparation instr. Discovery Learning Inc., Job Tng. and Pntrship Act, Atlanta, 1985-86; dir. counseling and testing svcs. Atlanta Met. Coll., 1977—; test supr. Ednl. Testing Svc., Princeton, N.J., 1980—, Psychology Corp., San Antonio, 1991—, Law Sch. Admissions Test, Newtown, Pa., 1991—; cons. Commn. on Colls., So. Assn. Colls. and Schs., Atlanta, 1978—; jr. c.c. rep. Placement & Coop. Edn., Atlanta, 1987-90. Editor newsletters The Brief, 1984, 85, Guided Studies News, 1974; contbg. author: (manual) AJC Self-Study, 1981; author: (manual) Policies and Procedures for Coordinated Counseling, 1981, 2d edit., 1991, Women's Coalition for Habitat for Humanity in Atlanta, 1993-95. Pres. Atlanta Barristers Wives Inc., 1984, 85; mem. steering com. Atlanta Mayor's Masked Ball, 1987; mem. memberships sales com. Atlanta Arts Festival, 1986, Neighborhood Arts Ctr., 1986; state host Dem. Nat. Conv., Atlanta, 1988; mem. Heritage Valley Cmty. Neighborhood Assn., 1982—. Recipient Outstanding Svc. award Nat. Orientation Dirs. Assn., 1985, 86, Literacy Action, Inc., 1978, Atlanta Met. Coll., 1987, others. Mem. Ga. Coll. Personnel Assn., Ga. Mental Health Counselors Assn., Nat. Coun. Student Devel., Univ. System Counseling Dirs., 100 Women Internat. Inc. (charter mem.), Am. Assn. Community and Jr. Colls., The Links Inc., Ga. Assn. Women Deans, Counselors and Adminstrs., Ga. Coll. Conselors Assn. Democrat. Methodist. Home: 3511 Toll House Ln SW Atlanta GA 30331-2330 Office: Atlanta Metro Coll 1630 Stewart Ave SW Atlanta GA 30310-4448

WALKER, DEBRA JOANN, electrical engineer; b. Liberal, Kans., Aug. 27, 1968; m. Robert Walker. BSEE, U. Evansville, 1991. Cert. engr.-in-tng., Ind. Engr. Cinergy - Gibson Sta., Owensville, Ind., 1991-92; engr. PSI Energy - Gibson Sta., Owensville, Ind., 1992-94, staff engr., 1994—. Mem. Alpha Omicron Pi. Office: Cinergy - Gibson Sta Box 300 RR 1 Owensville IN 47665

WALKER, DEBRA MAY, marketing professional; b. Flint, Mich., May 11, 1956; d. Vern Luke and Rosemary (Deanhofer) W.; m. Stephen Robert Strong, Aug. 14, 1982; 1 child, Evan Walker Strong. BA in Advt., Mich. State U., 1978, MA in Advt., 1979. Sr. bus. analyst Goodyear Tire & Rubber Co., Akron, Ohio, 1979-81, mgr. advt. rsch., 1981-82, mgr. market planning systems, 1982-85; mktg. strategy mgr. Europe Goodyear Tire & Rubber Co., Brussels, 1985-89; mktg. strategy mgr. U.S. Goodyear Tire & Rubber Co., Akron, 1989-90, mktg. mgr. retail stores div., 1990-91, gen. mktg. mgr. retail, 1991-92; mktg. mgr. auto tires Goodyear Tire & Rubber Co., 1992-94; mgr. dealer sales San Leandro, Calif., 1994-95; dir. retail sys. Goodyear Tire & Rubber Co., Akron, 1995-96, v.p. retail systems, 1996—; speaker on mktg. distbn. and info. tech. topics. Contbr. articles to various publs. Mem. Am. Mgmt. Assn. Office: Goodyear Tire & Rubber Co 1144 E Market St Dept 704 Akron OH 44316

WALKER, ELIZABETH PRESCOTT, journalist; b. Detroit, Dec. 15, 1925; d. Joel Henry and Ruth Magdalen (Weber) Prescott; m. Richard Dilworth Walker, May 23, 1959; 1 child, Richard Dilworth. BA in English Lit., Western Coll. for Women, 1948. Cert. Nat. Book Critics Circle. Asst. editor bull. Sigma Gamma Assn., Detroit, 1955-60; reporter bull. Jr. League, Detroit, 1967-75; editor quarterly jour. Book Club Detroit, 1967-68; columnist The Hearing Eye AGBell Assn. Mich. Chpt., Detroit, 1985-89; book reviewer Biblio-chat The Alpena (Mich.) News, 1991—; book reviewer Biblio-file Grosse Pointe (Mich.) News, 1991—. Mem. Quota Internat. Iosco County (bd. dirs. 1995-97, Deaf Woman of the Yr. 1996), Sigma Gamma Assn. Republican. Episcopalian. Home: 3261 South US-23 Greenbush MI 48738

WALKER, ELJANA M. DU VALL, civic worker; b. France, Jan. 18, 1924; came to U.S., 1948; naturalized, 1954; student Med. Inst., U. Paris, 1942-47; m. John S. Walker, Jr., Dec. 31, 1947; children: John, Peter, Barbara. Pres., Loyola Sch. PTA, 1958-59; bd. dirs. Santa Claus shop, 1959-73; treas. Archdiocese Denver Catholic Women, 1962-64; rep. Cath. Parent-Tchr League, 1962-65; pres. Aux. Denver Gen. Hosp., 1966-69; precinct committeewoman Arapahoe County Republican Women's Com., 1973-74; mem. re-election com. Arapahoe County Rep. Party, 1973-78, Reagan election com., 1980; block worker Arapahoe County March of Dimes, Heart Assn., Hemophilia Drive, Muscular Dystrophy and Multiple Sclerosis Drive, 1978-81; cen. city asst. Guild Debutante Charities, Inc. Recipient Distinguished Service award Am.-by-choice, 1966; named to Honor Roll, ARC, 1971. Mem. Cherry Hills Symphony, Lyric Opera Guild, Alliance Franciase (life mem.), ARC, Civic Ballet Guild (life mem.), Needlework Guild Am. (v.p. 1980-82), Kidney Found. (life), Denver Art Mus., U. Denver Art and Conservation Assns. (chmn. 1980-82), U. Denver Women's Library Assn., Chancellors Soc, Passage Inc., Friends of the Fine Arts Found. (life), CHildren's Diabetes Found. (life). Roman Catholic. Clubs: Union (Chgo.); Denver Athletic, 26 (Denver); Welcome to Colo. Internat. Address: 2301 Green Oaks Dr Greenwood Village CO 80121

WALKER, ELLEN MARCIA, lawyer; b. N.Y.C., Sept. 30, 1955; d. Harold Lester and Norma (Levy) W.; 1 child, Paul Walker Schaffel. BA, Queens Coll., 1976; JD, Bklyn. Law Sch., 1979. Bar: N.Y. 1980. Assoc. Harvis & Zeichner, N.Y.C., 1979-80; v.p., gen. counsel Elk Assocs. Funding Corp., N.Y.C., 1980—, also bd. dirs.; v.p. GCG Assocs., Inc., N.Y.C., 1985—; ptnr. Granoff, Walker & Forlenza, N.Y.C., 1981—. Mem. ABA, N.Y. State Bar Assn., N.Y. County Bar Assn., Bar Assn. City N.Y., N.Y. County Women's Bar Assn. Office: Granoff Walker & Forlenza 747 3rd Ave New York NY 10017-2803

WALKER, ELVA MAE DAWSON, health consultant; b. Everett, Mass., June 29, 1914; d. Charles Edward and Mary Elizabeth (Livingston) Dawson; m. John J. Spillane Jr. R.N., Peter Bent Brigham Hosp., Boston, 1937; student Simmons Coll., 1935, U. Minn., 1945-48; m. Walter Willard Walker, Dec. 16, 1939 (div. 1969). Supr. nursery Wesson Maternity Hosp., Springfield, Mass., 1937-38; asst. supr. out-patient dept. Peter Bent Brigham Hosp., Boston, 1938-40; supr. surgery and out-patient dept. Univ. Hosps., Mpls., 1945. Chmn. Gov.'s Citizens Coun. on Aging, Minn., 1960-68, acting dir., 1962-66, Econ. Opportunity Com. Hennepin County, 1964-69; v.p., treas. Nat. Purity Soap & Chem. Co., 1968-69, pres., 1969-76, chmn. bd., 1976—, co. exec. officer, 1993—; cons. on aging to Minn. Dept. Pub. Welfare, 1962-67; mem. nat. adv. Coun. for Nurse Tng. Act, 1965-69, Com. Status on Women in Armed Svcs., 1967-70; dir. Nat. Coun. on the Aging, 1963-67, sec., 1965-67, 1986-88, chairperson, 1988-91; chmn. Minn. Bd. on Aging, 1982-91, Nat. Retiree Vol. Ctr., 1982-89; dir. Planning Agy. for Hosps. of Met. Mpls., 1963-67, United Hosp. Fund of Hennepin County, 1955-60, Nat. Coun. Social Work Edn., 1966-68; vice chmn. Hennepin County Gen. Hosp. Adv. Bd., 1965-68; sec. Hennepin County Health Coalition, 1973; chmn. bd. dirs. Am. Rehab. Found, 1962-68, vice chmn., 1968-70, chmn. Minn. Bd. On Aging, 1988-91, Sr. Resources, 1985-87, Older Persons Vision Coun., United Way, 1995—; pres. bd. trustees Northwestern Hosp., 1956-59, Children's Hosp. Mpls., 1961-65; dir. Twin Cities Internat. Program for Youth Leaders and Social Workers, Inc., 1965-67; mem. community adv. coun. United Cmty. Funds and Coun. Am., Inc., 1968, Nat. Assembly Social Policy and Devel., Inc., 1968-74, Minn. Action for Children Commn., 1989—, mem., 1991—; mem. priorities determination com. United Fund Mpls., 1971; vice chmn. govt. specifications com. Soap and Detergent Assn., 1972-76, vice-chmn. indsl. and instn. com., 1974-76, chmn., 1976-78, bd. dirs., 1974—; candidate for Congress, 3d Minn. Dist., 1966; trustee Macalester Coll., Archie D. and Bertha H. Walker Found.; chmn. St. Mary's Jr. Coll. Bd., 1970-74, 78-80, Older Persons vis. com. coun. United Way, 1996—; pres. U. Minn. Sch. Nursing Found., 1958-70; pres. Minn. Gerontological Soc., 1994-95; sec. Metro Area Agy. Aging Minn., 1995—. Mem. Am. Pub. Welfare Assn., Minn. Gerontol. Soc. (pres. 1994—), Mpls. Med. Research Found., Minn. League Nursing (pres. 1971-73), Jr. League Mpls. Democrat. Presbyterian. Home: 3655 Northome Rd Wayzata MN 55391-3020 Office: Nat Purity Soap & Chem Co 434 Lakeside Ave Minneapolis MN 55405-1529

WALKER, EVELYN, retired educational television executive; b. Birmingham, Ala.; d. Preston Lucas and Mattie (Williams) W.; AB, Huntingdon Coll., 1927; student Cornell U., 1927-28; MA, U. Ala., 1963; LHD, Huntingdon Coll., 1974. Speech instr. Phillips High Sch., Birmingham, 1930-34; head speech dept. Ramsay High Sch., Birmingham, 1934-52; chmn. radio and TV, Birmingham Pub. Schs., 1944-75, head instructional TV programming svcs., 1969-75; mem. summer faculty extension div. U. Va., 1965, 66, 67; former regional cons. ednl. TV broadcasting; Miss Ann, broadcaster children's daily radio program, Birmingham, 1946-57; prodr. Our Am. Heritage radio series, 1944-54; TV staff prodr. programs shown daily Ala. Pub. TV Network, 1954-75; past cons. Gov.'s Ednl. TV Legis. Study Com., 1953; nat. del. Asian-Am. Women Broadcasters Conf., 1966; former regional cons. Ednl. TV Broadcasting. Mem. emerita Nat. Def. Adv. Com. on Women in Svcs.; past TV-radio co-chmn. Gov.'s Adv. Bd. Safety Com.; past chmn. creative TV-radio writing competition Festival of Arts; past audio-visual chmn. Ala. Congress, also past mem. Birmingham coun. PTA; media chmn. Gov.'s Commn. on Yr. of the Child; bd. dirs. Women's Army Corps Mus., Fort MiClellen, 1960-93. Recipient Alumnae Achievement award Huntingdon Coll., 1958; Tops in Our Town award Birmingham News, 1957; Air Force Recruiting plaque, 1961; Spl. Bowl award for promoting arts through Ednl. TV. Birmingham Festival of Arts, 1962; citation 4th Army Corps., 1962; cert. of appreciation Ala. Multiple Sclerosis Soc., 1962; Freedoms Found. at Valley Forge Educator's medal award, 1963; Top TV award ARC, 1964; Ala. Woman of Achievement award, 1966; Bronze plaque Ala. Dist. Exch. Clubs, 1969; cert. of appreciation Birmingham Bd. Edn., 1975; Obelisk award Children's Theatre, 1976; 20-Yr. Svc. award Ala. Ednl. TV Commn.; key to city of Birmingham, 1966; named Woman of Yr., Birmingham, 1965; named Ala. Woman of Yr., Progressive Farmer mag., 1966; hon. col. Ala. Militia. Mem. Am. Assn. Ret. Persons, Ala. Assn. Ret. Tchrs., Huntingdon Coll. Alumnae Assn. (former internat. pres.), Former Am. Women in Radio and TV, Arlington Hist. Assn. (dir., pres. 1981-83), Magna Charta Dames (past state sec.-treas.), DAR (former pub. rels. com. Ala., TV chmn., state program chmn. 1979-85, state chmn. Seimes Microfilm com. 1985-88, state chmn. Motion Picture, Radio TV com. 1988-94, tricom. chmn. 1988-94), Colonial Dames 17th Century, U.S. Daus. 1812 (past state TV chmn.), Daus. Am. Colonists (past 2d v.p. local chpt., past state TV and radio chmn.), Ams. Royal Descent, Royal Order Garter, Plantagenets Soc. Am., Salvation Army Women's Aux., Symphony Aux., Humane Soc. Aux., Eagle Forum, Nat. League Am. Pen Women, Womens's Com. 100 for Birmingham (bd. dirs.), Royal Order Crown, Women in Communications (past local pres., nat. headliner 1965), Internat. Platform Assn., Birmingham-Jefferson Hist. Soc., Delta Delta Delta (mem. Golden Circle), Ladies Golf Assn., Birmingham Country Club, The Club. Methodist. Home: Mountain Brook 744 Euclid Ave Birmingham AL 35213-2538

WALKER, JANE MUZETTE BRICE, special education educator; b. Uvalde, Tex., Jan. 13, 1956; d. James Watkins Brice and Pauline (Mantzares) Montgomery; m. John Steven Walker, July 18, 1981; children: Kathleen Camille, Jessica Suzanne, Seth Brice. Student, S.W. Tex. Jr. Coll., Uvalde, 1974-75; BS, Tex. Tech. U., 1978. Cert. spl. edn. tchr., Tex. Multihandicapped spl. edn. tchr. Uvalde Consol. Sch. Dist., 1978-79; dir. programs Dale Evans Sheltered Children's Ctr., Uvalde, 1979-81; mentally retarded spl. edn. tchr. Brownsville (Tex.) Ind. Sch. Dist., 1981-83, gifted and talented tchr., 1986-90, emotionally handicapped spl. edn. tchr., 1990-93, dyslexia resource spl. edn. tchr., sch.-wide monitor, 1993—; migrant reading tchr. Los Fresnos (Tex.) Ind. Sch. Dist., 1983-84, multihandicapped spl. edn. tchr., 1984-86; vol. tchr. Mem. Episcopal Ch. of the Advent, Brownsville, Tex., Mary Martha's Guild, 1991—, Los Ebanos Neighborhood Assn., Brownsville, 1990—. Recipient Outstanding Sci. Tchr. of Tex. award Sci. Tchrs. Assn. Tex., 1993, Spl. Edn. Chair for Tchg. Excellence award Brownsville Rotary Club, 1992, 93, Founder's award Uvalde Spl. Olympic Com., 1988, Nat. Adn. award 1995 Nat. Arbor Day Awards. Mem. Sigma Kappa (pres. 1976-77). Home: 215 Sunset Dr Brownsville TX 78520-7313 Office: Filomen B Vela Mid Sch Paredes Line Rd Brownsville TX 78521

WALKER, JANICE CARDWELL, elementary school principal; b. Louisville, Apr. 28, 1952; d. Allen Lee and Mildred Louise (Beckwith) Cardwell; m. Earl W. Walker, May 20, 1972; 1 child, Bret A. BS in Elem. Edn., U. Louisville, 1974, MEd, 1976. Tchr. Dann C. Byck Elem. Sch., Louisville, 1974-77; instructional coord. Dann C. Byck Elem. Sch., 1977-81; intermediate tchr. Kenwood Elem. Sch., Louisville, 1981-86; tchr. remedial reading Carter Elem. Sch., Gutermuth Elem. Sch., Louisville, 1986-87; prin. Milburn T. Maupin Elem. Sch., Louisville, 1987-91, Ruth Dunn Elem. Sch., Louisville, 1991—. Co-author: Successful Urban Elementary Schools. Coord. neighborhood fund drive Am. Lung Assn., Floyds Knobs, Ind. Mem. Ky. Assn. Sch. Adminstrs., Jefferson County Assn. Sch. Adminstrs., Jefferson County Assn. Elem. Sch. Prins., Phi Delta Kappa. Democrat. Office: Ruth Dunn Elem Sch 2010 Rudy Ln Louisville KY 40207

WALKER, JANICE DIANNE, librarian; b. Talladega, Ala., Sept. 17, 1953; d. Jack Dixon and Flora May (Patterson) Cooper; m. Robert Dennis Walker, Oct. 1, 1976; children: Robert Anthony, Elizabeth Suzanne. BS in Edn., Emporia State U., 1975, MS, 1981, MLS, 1993. Tchr. Basehor (Kans.) Elem. Sch., 1978-91, libr., 1992—. Mem. PTA, Basehor, 1978—, Alpha Delta Kappa (recording, corresponding sec. 1996—). Mem. NEA, Kans. Assn. Sch. Librs., Alpha Delta Kappa (treas. 1992-94). Home: PO Box 138 Basehor KS 66007 Office: Basehor Elem Sch 15602 Leavenworth Rd Basehor KS 66007

WALKER, JESSYE WILMA DORMAN, educator; b. Orangeburg, S.C., Mar. 28, 1929; d. John Albert and Georgia Anna (Hammond) Dorman; m. John Lee Walker, Sept. 27, 1953; children: Derryll Shomarka, Marlon, Yvonne, Sia Ann. AB, Knoxville Coll., 1949; MS, Nova Southwestern U., 1985. Tchr. choral music, English Sims H.S., Union, S.C., 1949-50; tchr. music Douglas H.S., Lillie, La., 1950-51; tchr. choral music Booker T. Washington H.S., Columbia, S.C., 1952-54; tchr. music Voorhees Elem. Sch., Denmark, S.C., 1955-59; tchr. 4th grade Meanscourt Elem. Sch., Ft. Pierce, Fla., 1963-64, Garden City Elem. Sch., Ft. Pierce, Fla., 1964-66, Lawnwood Elem. Sch., Ft. Pierce, Fla., 1966-69; tchr. English, reading St. Lucie Mid. Sch., Ft. Pierce, Fla., 1970-80; tchr. choral music, English, reading Dan McCarty Mid. Sch., Ft. Pierce, Fla., 1980-95; retired, 1996; group sec. 4th grade St. Lucie County, 1964-66, chmn. 4th grade Lawnwood Elem. Sch., 1968-69. Treas. Club Utilitas/Teen Ctr., Ft. Pierce, 1993—; pub. rels. chmn. Martin Luther King Jr. Com., Ft. Pierce, 1995—; vol. ARC, St. Lucie County, 1991—. Mem. AAUW (v.p. 1995—), LVW (exec. bd. 1994—), African-Am. Exposition for Arts (exec. bd. 1990—), Alpha Kappa Alpha (pres. 1991-93). Episcopalian. Home: 2102 Valencia Ave Fort Pierce FL 34946

WALKER, LINDA LEE, lawyer; b. Phila., Jan. 24, 1954; d. M. Lorenzo and Romaine Yvonne (Smith) W.; m. Bruce McIntyre, Sept. 16, 1981; children: Jessica Marie, Nicole Yvonne. BA with honors, U. Pa., 1975; JD, Yale U., 1978. Bar: N.Y. 1979, U.S. Dist. Ct. (so. and ea. dists.) N.Y. 1982, U.S. Ct. Appeals (1st cir.) 1982. Asst. regional atty. U.S. Dept. Health & Human Svcs., N.Y.C., 1978-82; assoc. Shea & Gould, N.Y.C., 1982-85; v.p., sr. assoc. counsel Chase Manhattan Bank, N.A., N.Y.C., 1985-89; v.p., assoc. gen. counsel Citicorp Credit Svcs., N.Y.C., 1989—. Mem. ABA, Phi Beta Kappa. Office: Citicorp Credit Svcs Inc 1 Court Sq Long Island City NY 11120-0001

WALKER, LUCY MARGARET, arts administrator; b. Memphis, Sept. 20, 1927; d. Alfred Buster and Florida Thompson (Wade) Brown; children: Floyd Dennis, Lynne Yvonne. BS, Cen. State U., Wilberforce, Ohio, 1949. Clk.-typist Fed. Govt., Denver, 1950-54; tchr. Denver Pub. Schs., 1956-63; spl. projects dir. Camp Fire Girls, Dallas, 1963-67; job corp counselor YWCA, Denver, 1968-70; ch. adminstr. 1st Unitarian Ch., Denver, 1970-71; comty. rels. dir. Opportunities Industrialization Ctr., Denver, 1971-74; title

IX affirmative action officer U. Colo. Med. Ctr., Denver, 1974-75; program dir. Human Svcs., Inc., Denver, 1975-81; exec. dir., founder EDEN Theatrical Workshop, Inc., Denver, 1975—. Author: All Things Are Connected, 1988; playwright: (drama) Blood, Booze and Booty, 1978. Pres. Montbello Citizen's Com., Denver, 1974-75; precinct committeewoman Dem. Party, Denver, 1963-65; sec. Denver LWV, 1964-65. Recipient Mister Brown award Nat. Conf. African Am. Theatre, Inc., 1996, Coors Celebrates Women award Coors Brewing Co., 1984, Mountain award African Am. Leadership Inst., 1996; 1st pl. winner essay contest Colo. Centennial Bi-centennial Commn., 1976; named Bus. Woman of Yr. Iota Phi Lambda, 1994. Home: 2410 Franklin St Denver CO 80205 Office: EDEN Theatrical Workshop 1570 Gilpin St Denver CO 80218

WALKER, MARGARET SMITH, real estate company executive; b. Lancashire, Eng., Oct. 14, 1943; came to U.S., 1964; d. Arthur Edward and Doris Audrey (Dawson) Smith; m. James E. Walker, Feb. 6, 1992. Lic. real estate agt., Hawaii. Broker Lawson-Worrall Inc. (now Worrall-McCarter), Honolulu, 1974-81; pres. Maggie Parkes & Assocs., Inc., Honolulu, 1981—. Bd. dirs. Hawaii Combined Tng. Assn., Honolulu, 1985—; dist. commr. Lio Lii Pony Club, Honolulu, 1980; com. chmn. Hist. Hawaii Found., Honolulu, 1990. Mem. Am. Horse Shows Assn., Hawaii Horse Shows Assn., Outrigger Canoe Club. Episcopalian. Office: PO Box 25083 Honolulu HI 96825-0083

WALKER, MARGERY FAYE, alternative elementary/middle school educator; b. Mount Vernon, Wash., Jan. 22, 1947; d. Victor Worth and Erdice Gertrude Cain; children: Jacob Ali, Wren Marie. BA in Edn., U. Wash., 1970; MA in Psychology, Antioch U., 1989; postgrad. in Drama, North Seattle C.C., 1994-95. Cert. tchr., Wash. Alternative educator New Sch. for Children, Seattle, 1971, Alternative Sch. # 1, Seattle, 1971-79, 85—; family planning counselor Seattle King County Family Planning, 1971; alternative prin. Alternative Sch. # 1, 1977-79, site coun. mem., 1971-79, 85-94; alternative educator Orca Sch., Seattle, 1972-78; founder, dir. Whole Brain Learning, Seattle, 1985—. Prodr.: (TV show) Meet Your Local Artist, 1994; actress, playwright, dir., theatrical presentations, 1988—. Bd. dirs. Unity Ch. of Truth, Seattle, 1989. Office: Alternative Sch # 1 11530 12th Ave NE Seattle WA 98125-6310

WALKER, MARIA LATANYA, physician; b. Greenwood, S.C., July 3, 1957; d. Hervey Wesley Jr. and Leola Marian (Grant) W.; m. Albert L. Thompson, July 27, 1991; 1 child, Albert IV. BS in Chemistry, Furman U., 1978; MD, Harvard U., 1982. Intern Grady Meml. Hosp., Atlanta, 1983; physician pvt. practice, Atlanta, 1983—, Snapfinger Woods Family Practice Group, Atlanta, 1990—; resident in internal medicine Ga. Bapt. Hosp., Atlanta, 1995. Fellow Am. Coll. Phycisians; mem. AMA, Nat. Med. Assn. Republican. Methodist. Home: 5118 N Ivy Rd Atlanta GA 30342 Office: Snapfinger Woods Family Practice Group 5040 Snapfinger Woods Dr Decatur GA 30035

WALKER, MARIE FULLER, elementary education educator; d. Gladys Fuller; m. Frederick T. Walker; children: Frederick T. Jr., Nicole Marie. BA in History, U. Philippines, 1969; MEd, West Chester U., 1992. Cert. elem. tchr., Calif., Pa., N.C., Okla., Ala.; cert. elem. adminstr., prin., Pa. Tchr. ESL Royal Thai Army Sch. Nursing, Bangkok, Thailand, 1975; tchr. 2d grade Ruam Rudee Internat. Sch., Bangkok, Thailand, 1975-76; tchr. 3d grade St. Adelaide Sch., Highland, Calif., 1976-77; tchr. Midwest City (Okla.) Sch., 1980-82; tchr. 4th grade Rainbow Elem. Sch., Coatesville, Pa., 1989—. Administered vol. programs ARC, Ft. Bragg and Pope AFB, recruited and trained vols., official community spokesperson, nat. cons., Washington, vol. cons., 1984 (Vol. of Yr. award N.C., 1983, Achievements awards 1983, 84, 85, Clara Barton award 1984). Recipient N.C. Outstanding Vol. Adminstr./Coord., Gov., 1984, Gift of Time award Family Inst., 1992, Dir. Edn. Excellence award IST PDE, 1994; grantee Math, 1994, grantee Butterfly Garden, 1995, grantee Arts Spl. Edn., 1995, 96, grantee Arts in Edn., 1995, 96, grantee Math. Lab., 1996. Mem. NEA, NAESP, PTA, Pa. Assn. Elem. Sch. Prins., Phi Delta Kappa. Home: 17 Willow Pond Rd Malvern PA 19355-2888 Office: Rainbow Elem Sch 50 Country Club Rd Coatesville PA 19320-1813

WALKER, MARY L., lawyer; b. Dayton, Ohio, Dec. 1, 1948; d. William Willard and Lady D. Walker; 1 child, Winston Samuel. Student, U. Calif., Irvine, 1966-68; BA in Biology/Ecology, U. Calif., Berkeley, 1970; postgrad., UCLA, 1972-73; JD, Boston U., 1973. Bar: Calif. 1973, U.S. Supreme Ct. 1979. Atty. So. Pacific Co., San Francisco, 1973-76; from assoc. to ptnr. Richards, Watson, & Gershon, L.A., 1976-82; dep. asst. atty. gen. lands div. U.S. Dept. Justice, Washington, 1982-84; dep. solicitor U.S. Dept. Interior, Washington, 1984-85; asst. sec. for environment, safety and health U.S. Dept. Energy, Washington, 1985-88; spl. cons. to chmn. bd. Law Engring., Atlanta, 1988-89; v.p., West Coast and the Pacific Law Environ., Inc., San Francisco, 1989; ptnr., head environ. law dept. Richards, Watson & Gershon, San Francisco, 1989-91; ptnr. Luce, Forward, Hamilton & Scripps, San Diego, 1991-94; ptnr. and head San Diego Environ. Practice Group Brobeck, Phleger & Harrison, San Diego, 1994—; U.S. commr. InterAm. Tropical Tuna Commn., 1989-95. Bd. dirs. Endowment for Comty. Leadership, 1987—. Mem. Calif. Bar Assn., San Diego Bar Assn., San Diego BioCommerce Assn. (bd. dirs. 1991-96, pres. 1994), Profl. Women's Fellowship-San Diego (co-founder, pres. 1996—), World Affairs Coun., Renaissance Women. Republican.

WALKER, MELISSA A., historian, educator; b. Maryville, Tenn., Sept. 13, 1962; d. Guy E. and Rachel E. (Lewellyn) W. BA in History, Maryville Coll., 1985; MA in History, Providence Coll., 1993; PhD in History, Clark U., 1996. Office mgr. Maryville Coll., 1985-86, dir. alumni rels., 1986-87; assoc. dir. alumni rels. Bryant Coll., Smithfield, R.I., 1987-92, asst. dir. devel. rsch., 1992-96; asst. prof. history Converse Coll., Spartanburg, S.C., 1996—; adj. prof. C.C. of R.I., Providence, 1995, Bryant Coll., 1996; cons. Alumni Job Fair Consortium, Boston, 1992-94. Contbr. articles to profl. jours. Vol. United Way, Providence, 1988, 90, Maryville, 1986; mem. fundraising com. R.I. Women's Health Collective, Pawtucket, R.I., 1995-96. Recipient Outstanding Advisor award Bryant Coll., 1991, Don Sahli award Tenn. Edn. Assn., 1984; Rockefeller Archives Ctr. grantee, 1994. Mem. Am. Hist. Assn., Orgn. Am. Historians, So. Hist. Assn., Agrl. History Soc., New Eng. Devel. Rsch. Assn., Coun. for Advancement and Support of Edn. (conf. sub-chair, spkr. 1985-92). Office: Converse College 580 E Main St Spartanburg SC 29302

WALKER, MOIRA KAYE, sales executive; b. Riverside, Calif., Aug. 2, 1940; d. Frank Leroy and Arline Rufina (Roach) Porter; m. Timothy P. Walker, Aug. 30, 1958 (div. 1964); children: Brian A., Benjamin D., Blair K., Beth E. Student, Riverside City Coll., 1973. With Bank of Am., Riverside, 1965-68, Abitibi Corp., Cucamonga, Calif., 1968-70; with Lily div. Owens-Illinois, Riverside, 1970-73; salesperson Lily div. Owens-Illinois, Houston, 1973-77; salesperson Kent H. Landsberg div. Sunclipse, Montebello, Calif., 1977-83, sales mgr., 1983-85; v.p., sales mgr. Kent H. Landsberg div. Sunclipse, Riverside, 1985—. Mem. NAFE, Women in Paper (treas. 1978-84), Kent H. Landsberg President's Club (1st female to make club, 1994, 95. Lutheran. Office: Kent H Landsberg Div Sunclipse 1180 W Spring St Riverside CA 92507-1327

WALKER, OLENE S., lieutenant governor; b. Ogden, Utah, Nov. 15, 1930; d. Thomas Ole and Nina Hadley (Smith) W.; m. J. Myron Walker, 1957; children: Stephen Brett, David Walden, Bryan Jesse, Lori, Mylene, Nina, Thomas Myron. BA, Brigham Young U., 1954; MA, Stanford U., 1954; PhD, U. Utah, 1986. V.p. Country Crisp Foods; mem. Utah Ho. of Reps. Dist. 24; lt. gov. State of Utah, 1993—. Mem. Salt Lake Edn. Found. bd. dirs. 1983-90; dir. community econ. devel.; mem. Ballet West, Sch. Vol., United Way, Commn. on Youth, Girls Village, Salt Lake Conv. and Tourism Bd. Mormon. Office: Lieutenant Governor 203 State Capitol Building Salt Lake City UT 84114-1202

WALKER, PEGGY JEAN, social work agency administrator; b. Carbondale, Ill., Aug. 9, 1940; d. George William and Lola Almeda (Black) Robinson; children: Edith Nell and Keith Alan. BA, So. Ill. U., 1962, PhD, 1986; MSW, Washington U., St. Louis, 1967. Lic. clin. social worker. Caseworker, casework supr. Ill. Dept. Pub. Aid, 1964-71; child welfare adminstr. Ill. Dept. Children and Family Svc., 1971-75; mem. faculty social work program So. Ill. U., 1975-79; exec. dir. Western divsn. Children's Home Soc. of Fla., Pensacola, 1979—; appointed to Fla. State Coord. Coun. for Early Childhood Devel., 1994—; adj. adv. bd. dept. social work U. West Fla., 1982—; appt. by Fla. Dept. Edn. to task force Edn. for Children of the Homeless, 1989—, Dept. of Health and Rehab. Svcs. Dist. Task Force on Family Preservation and Support Svcs., 1985—, chmn. 1988, 89; dept. juvenile justice coun., 1994, chmn., 1996. Bd. dirs. United Way Escambia County, Fla., 1992—, co-chair chief judge task force for children, 1994—; mem. Leadership Fla., 1988—. Recipient Disting. Cmty. Svc. award United Way of Escambia County, 1995. Mem. NASW (cert.), Acad. Cert. Social Workers. Presbyterian. Home: 613 Silverthorn Rd Gulf Breeze FL 32561-4625 Office: 5375 N 9th Ave Pensacola FL 32504-8725

WALKER, ROBERTA SMYTH, school system administrator; b. Tacoma, June 18, 1943; d. Robert Middleton and Maxine (Hartl) Smyth; m. Ronald E. Walker, Apr. 1962 (div. Mar. 1965); 1 child, David M.; m. James R. Hawkins, July 19, 1985 (dec. Sept. 1991). BA, Evergreen State Coll., Olympia, Wash., 1982; MS, Seattle Pacific U., 1989. Pers. analyst Seattle Sch. Dist., 1977-83, dir. staff rels., 1983-86; exec. dir. employee rels. Renton (Wash.) Sch. Dist., 1986—; adj. faculty Seattle Pacific U., 1989—, Western Wash. U., 1995—. Vol. Crisis Clinic, Seattle, 1993—. Recipient Angel in Seattle award AT&T Wireless and Intiman Theatre, 1995. Mem. Wash. Assn. Sch. Adminstrs., Employee Rels. and Negotiations Network (pres. 1991-92), Sno-King Negotiators. Office: Renton Sch Dist 435 Main Ave S Renton WA 98055-2711

WALKER, SALLY BARBARA, retired glass company executive; b. Bellerose, N.Y., Nov. 21, 1921; d. Lambert Roger and Edith Demerest (Parkhouse) W. Diploma Cathedral Sch. St. Mary, 1939; AA, Finch Jr. Coll., 1941. Tchr. interior design Finch Coll., 1941-42; draftsman AT&T, 1942-43; with Steuben Glass Co., N.Y.C., 1943—, exec. v.p., 1959-62, exec. v.p. ops., 1962-78, exec. v.p. ops. and sales, 1978-83, exec. v.p., 1983-88, ret. 1988. Pres. 116 E. 66th St. Corp. Mem. Fifth Ave. Assn. Republican. Episcopalian. Clubs: Rockaway Hunting, Lawrence Beach, U.S. Lawn Tennis, Colony, English-Speaking Union. Home: 116 E 66th St New York NY 10021-6547

WALKER, SAMMIE LEE, retired elementary education educator; b. Elkhart, Tex., July 10, 1927; d. Samuel and Mary (Pigford) Nathaniel; m. R.L. Walker, Oct. 12, 1952 (dec. 1994); children: Winfred, Frederick, Mary, Pearlene, Gladys, Robert, Ethel. BS, Tex. Coll., 1951; MEd, Tex. So. U., 1979. Cert. tchr., home econs. educator, elem. educator. Seamstress Madonna Guild Factory, Houston, 1958-60; presch. tchr. Project Head Start, Houston, 1961-64; tchr. Houston Ind. Schs., 1964-86; tchr. Harris County Youth Authority, Clear Lake, Tex., 1985; costume maker CETA program Houston Ind. Sch. Dist., 1984. Tchr. Trinity Garden Ch. of Christ, 1956—; phys. fitness coord. Kashmere Garden Sr. Citizen Club, Houston, 1986-92; home care provider Tex. Home Health Care, Houston, 1988-93. Recipient Friendship award Houston Christian Inst., 1993. Mem. NEA. Home: 7911 Shotwell St Houston TX 77016-6548

WALKER, SAVANNAH T., executive assistant, legislative assistant; b. Lubbock, Tex., Nov. 23, 1930; d. John Hanford and Lenore Belle (Muecke) Tunnell; m. Julius Waring Walker, Jr., July 29, 1956; children: Savannah Waring, Lucile Lenore, George Julius Stewart. BA, Tex. Tech. U., 1951; student, Radcliffe Coll., 1951. Cert. secondary sch. tchr., Tex. Tchr., English and journalism Phillips (Tex.) Ind. Sch. Dist., 1951-52; asst. to congressman Mahon U.S. Congress, Washington, 1952-54, adminstrv., exec. asst., 1954-58, 63-66; legis. asst. to chmn. House Appropriations U.S. Ho. of Reps., Washington, 1973-78; exec. asst. to v.p. Nat. Assn. Mfrs., Washington, 1985-89; exec. asst. to pres. Ogilvy Adams & Rinehart, Washington, 1990—. Vol., fundraiser for charitable orgns., Chad and Eng., 1966-73; pres. Am. Women in London, 1971-72, Am. Women in Liberia, Monrovia, 1979-80. Mem. AAUW, PEO, Am. Women in the Arts Mus., Internat. Women's club (founder pres.) (Ouagadougou, Burkina, Faso), Delta Delta Delta. Home: 3801 Jenifer St NW Washington DC 20015 Office: Ogilvy Adams & Rinehart 1901 L St NW Ste 300 Washington DC 20036

WALKER, SHARON LOUISE, gifted education educator; b. St. Paul, Mar. 26, 1944; d. John Franklin and Catherine G. (Keiffer) Corkill; m. David Glenn Smith, June 11, 1964 (div. Feb. 1980); 1 child, Carina Ann Smith; m. William Laurens Walker III, Nov. 10, 1981. BS in Edn., U. Md., 1971; M in Adminstrn. and Supervision, U. Va., 1990. Cert. elem. sch. prin., K-12 tchr. of gifted, 1-7 classroom tchr., K-12 tchr. art, Va. Tchr. 3rd and 4th grades Seat Pleasant (Md.) Elem. Sch., 1971-75; tchr. 4th grade Venable Elem. Sch., Charlottesville, Va., 1975-79; tchr. 3rd and 4th grade gifted edn. Quest program Charlottesville City Schs., 1979—; coord. acad. summer sch. Summer Discovery grades kindergarten through 4 Charlottesville City Schs., 1988-94, mem. various curriculum, staff devel., award coms., 1990—; seminar leader summer enrichment program U. Va., Charlottesville, 1986-89. Mem., chairperson placement com. Jr. League, Charlottesville, 1977—; mem. edn. com. Bayly Art Mus., Charlottesville, 1984-89; bd. dirs., devel. chairperson Charlottesville Albemarle Youth Orch., 1991-93; bd. dirs., mem. program com. Madison Ho., U. Va., 1994—, bd. dirs., co-chair, 1996—. Mem. Charlottesville Edn. Assn., Phi Delta Kappa (U. Va. chpt.), Delta Kappa Gamma (v.p. 1993-95). Home: 1180 Old Garth Rd Charlottesville VA 22901-1916 Office: Quest Ctr 406 14th St NW Charlottesville VA 22903-2305

WALKER, WANDA GAIL, special education educator; b. Montgomery, Ala., June 7, 1946; d. Carter Warren Gamaliel and Ruth Jones (Carter) Walker. BS in Elem. Edn., Campbell U., 1968; MA in Christian Edn., Scarritt Coll., 1970; cert. in tchg. of learning disabled, Pembroke U., 1994. Cert. tchr. class A, N.C. Dir. Christian edn. United Meth. Ch., Roxboro, N.C., 1970-76; diaconal min. United Meth. Ch., Hamlet, N.C., 1976-77, Rockingham, N.C., 1977-85; head teller Montgomery Savs. and Loan, Rockingham, 1985-87; loan officer-credit R.W. Goodman Co., Rockingham, 1987-89; tchr. spl. edn. Richmond County Schs., Hamlet, 1989—; active Richmond County Reading Coun., Hamlet, 1989—. Bd. dirs. Sandhill Manor Group Home, Hamlet, 1977—; mem. Woman's Club Hamlet, 1989-94, treas., 1989-91, 1st v.p., 1992-94. Eisenhower grantee U. N.C., 1994; recipient Mission award United Meth. Women, N.C. Conf., 1990; named Best Working Mem., Women's Club Hamlet, 1991. Democrat. Home: 344 Raleigh St Hamlet NC 28345-2750 Office: Richmond County Schs Hamlet Ave Hamlet NC 28345

WALKER, WANDA MEDORA, retired elementary school educator, consultant; b. San Diego, Aug. 28, 1923; d. Bryant Hereford and Anna Genevieve (Barnes) Howard; m. Elmer Manfred Walker, Nov. 23, 1949 (dec. Aug. 1978); children: Kathleen May Stewart (dec.), Mary Ellen Quessenberry, Sydney Edward, Jessie Ann Meacham. BA, San Diego State U., 1947; MA, U. Wash., 1948; PhD, Calif. Western U., 1967. Cert. (life) spl. secondary music tchr., elem. tchr., sch. adminstr. Elem. tchr. Lakeside (Calif.) Elem. Dist., 1948-50, La Mesa (Calif.) Sch. Dist., 1951-53; elem. tchr. San Diego Schs. Dist., 1953-57, cons. gifted, 1957-59, vice prin., 1959-62, prin., 1962-88; rep. San Diego Schs. War Against Litter, 1971-76; pres. Assn. Calif. Sch. Adminstrs. Ret., 1992-94. Poet, composer. Recipient Am. Educators medal Freedoms Found. Valley Forge, 1973, Woman of Yr. award Pres. Coun. Women's Svc., Bus. & Profl. Clubs San Diego, 1980, Woman of Action award Soroptimists Internat. El Cajon, 1992. Mem. Am. Assn. Women (parliamentarian 1989—, Appreciation award 1992), Calif. Retired Tchrs., Assn. Calif. Sch. Adminstrs. (pres. 1978-79), Singing Hills Women's Golf, Sr. Resource Ctr. (adv. bd., chmn. 1991—). Home: 13208 Julian Ave Lakeside CA 92040-4312

WALKER, WENDY ALISON, writer, educator; b. N.Y.C., Jan. 25, 1951; d. Alexander and Hannah Lee (Eisner) W.; m. Thomas Sergeant La Farge, Nov. 26, 1982. AB cum laude, Harvard U., 1972; MA in Art and Edn., Columbia U., 1974. Tchr. art Profl. Children's Sch., N.Y.C., 1974-76; tchr. art and art history St. Hilda's and St. Hugh's Sch., N.Y.C., 1981-93; adj. asst. prof. writing program New Coll., Hofstra U., Hempstead, N.Y., 1995—, instr. fiction 23d Ann. Writers' Conf., 1995; resident Yaddo, Saratoga Springs, N.Y., 1994. Author: The Sea-Rabbit, or, The Artist of Life, 1988, The Secret Service, 1992, Stories Out of Omarie, 1995. Bd. dirs. Art Awareness, Lexington, N.Y., 1992—, visual arts cons., 1994-95. Recipient Gertrude Stein award in innovative Am. poetry Contemporary Arts Ednl. Project, L.A.,1995; fellow MacDowell Colony, Peterborough, N.H., 1993, NEH-Union Coll., Schenectady, 1993. Mem. PEN. Democrat. Home: 855 West End Ave Apt 6A New York NY 10025 Office: 130 Hofstra U New Coll Roosevelt Hall Hempstead NY 11550-1090

WALKER, WENDY K., state agency administrator; b. Alma, Mich., Oct. 28, 1965; d. Franklin D. and Bethel A. (Rose) W. BA, Grand Valley State Coll., 1987; MPA, Grand Valley State U., 1990. Rsch. assoc. Grand Rapids (Mich.) Pub. Mus., 1987-88; adminstrv. asst. YWCA, Grand Rapids, 1989-90; program asst. cmty. and econ. devel. Southwestern Mich. Commn., Benton Harbor, 1990-91, assoc. program mgr. cmty. and econ. devel., 1992-95, program mgr. planning and info., 1995—; reviewer Econ. Devel. Quar., Cleve., 1994—; planning com. Upjohn Inst. Bus. Outlook, Kalamazoo, Mich., 1991—. Mem. ASPA (nat. young profl. forum region VI rep., exec. bd.), Mich. Soc. Planning Officials, Mich. Rural Devel. Coun. Democrat. Office: Southwestern Mich Commn 185 E Main Ste 701 Benton Harbor MI 49022

WALKER, YVONNE DENISE, budget examiner; b. Warren, Ohio, Oct. 11, 1967. BA, Hiram (Ohio) Coll., 1990; MBA, SUNY, Albany. Sr. budget examiner N.Y. State Divsn. of Budget, Albany, 1990—. Bd. dirs. Camp Thatcher Opportunities, Albany, 1994—, Albany County Youth Burs., 1995—; chair N.Y. State Divsn. of Budget Affirmative Action Com., 1991—. Home: PO Box 7217 Albany NY 12224 Office: NY State Divsn of the Budget State Capitol Albany NY 12224

WALKER-LEWIS, ROSALIND GISELE, purchasing manager; b. Memphis, July 1, 1960; d. Joseph Louis and Georgia Ann (Whitaker) Walker; m. Rudolph Clifton Lewis, July 1985; children: Damon Walker, Desmond Lewis. BS in Indsl. Engring., U. Louisville, 1982. Quality control engr. GE, Utica, N.Y., 1984-87; advanced quality engr. GE, Utica, 1987-89, team mgr., 1989-90; vendor liaison mgr. Martin Marietta, Camden, N.J., 1990-92; commodity/liaison mgr. Martin Marietta, Camden, 1992-94; sourcing devel. programs mgr. Martin Marietta, Moorestown, N.J., 1994-96; site sourcing mgr. Lockheed Martin, Camden, 1996—; pres. bd. dirs. A Better Place Preparatory Sch. Inc., Lawnside, N.J., 1992—. Mem. Nat. Assn. Purchasing Mgmt., Toastmasters Internat. (competent toastmaster 1996). Baptist. Home: 31 Lakefield Dr Marlton NJ 08053

WALKER-SHIVERS, DAUPHINE, humanities educator; b. Marion, Ark.; d. Geoffrey and Myrtle Juanita Walker; m. James Shivers, Aug. 29, 1981 (dec. Apr. 1994). BA, Wayne State U., MA, 1967; PhD, U. Mich., 1980. Newspaper reporter Mich. Chronicle, Detroit, 1953-55; social worker Detroit Dept. Social Svcs., Detroit, 1955-56; tchr. Detroit Pub. Schs., 1956-60, U.S. Overseas Schs., France, 1960-64, Detroit Pub. Schs., 1964-70; prof. Wayne County C.C., Detroit, 1970-76, 81—, dept. chair humanities, speech, philosophy, 1976-81; pres., CEO Pub. Comm. & Concepts, Detroit, 1984-90. Editor: Detroit NAACP Reporter, 1984. Pres. Top Ladies of Distinction, Detroit, 1984-89, nat. historian, 1986-90; 1st v.p. Consortium Cmty. Orgns., 1995—; pub. local ch. newspapers, Detroit, 1983-88; mem. exec. bd. Fair Housing Ctr. Detroit, 1986—; fundraiser Detroit Inst. Arts, African Art Gallery, 1968-70. Named Top Solicitor Detroit NAACP, 1993, 93, 94; recipient Outstanding Svc. award Detroit NAACP, 1992, Sustained Superior Svc. award U.S. Overseas Schs., U.S. Army, France, 1964. Mem. AAUW, Met. Detroit Alliance Black Educators, Detroit Assn. Black Storytellers. Office: Wayne County CC 8551 Greenfield Detroit MI 48226

WALL, BARBARA WARTELLE, lawyer; b. New Orleans, Sept. 30, 1954; d. Richard Cole and Ruth Druhan (Power) W.; m. Christopher Read Wall, June 21, 1980; children: Christopher, Louisa. BA, U. Va., 1976, JD, 1979. Bar: N.Y. 1980, U.S. Dist. Ct. (so. and ea. dists.) N.Y. 1980. Assoc. Satterlee & Stephens, N.Y.C., 1979-85; asst. gen. counsel Gannett Co., Inc., Arlington, Va., 1985-90, sr. legal counsel, 1990-93, v.p., sr. legal counsel, 1993—. Mem. ABA (chair forum on comm. law), N.Y. State Bar Assn., Assn. of Bar of City of N.Y. Republican. Roman Catholic. Home: 5026 Tilden St NW Washington DC 20016-2334 Office: Gannett Co Inc 1100 Wilson Blvd Arlington VA 22209-2297

WALL, BETTY JANE, real estate consultant; b. Wichita Falls, Tex., Mar. 23, 1936; d. Albert Willis and Winnie Belle (Goodloe) Beard; m. Richard Lee Wall, Feb. 21, 1959; 1 child, Cynthia Lynn. BS, Vocat.Home Econs. Edn, U. Okla., 1958, MEd, Midwestern U., 1959. Lic. real estate salesperson, Tex. Tchr. San Diego County Schs., 1959-60, Long Beach (Calif.) City Schs., 1960-61, Norman (Okla.) Kindergarten Assn., 1961-65; real estate salesperson WestMark Realtors, Lubbock, Tex., 1983-85; now ind. real estate salesperson Lubbock; coll. adviser Nat. Panhellenic Conf., Tex., 1979-91; judge talent and beauty pageants, Tex. N.Mex., Okla., 1984—. Treas. Lubbock Symphony Guild, 1985-87, v.p. ways and means com., 1987-88, chmn. ball, 1990, pres. elect, 1993-94, pres., 1994-95; bd. dirs. Tex. Assn. of Symphony Orchs., 1994-95; pres., bd. dirs. Miss Lubbock Pageant, 1992—. Recipient Tex. Tech. U. Outstanding Greek Alumni award, 1994. Mem. Tex. Real Estate Assn., Jr. League Lubbock (treas. 1976-78, sustaining advisor fin. com. 1979-83, hdqrs. commn. advisor 1989-94), West Tex. Mus. Assn. (chmn. planetarium com., 1996, bd. dirs., women's coun.), Nat. Platform Assn., Women's C. of C., Lubbock Women's Club (bd. dirs. 1996—), Tex. Tech. U. Faculty Women's Club (v.p. & pres. 1967-69, Lubbock chpt. Achievement Rewards for Coll. Sci. bd. 1995—), Alpha Chi Omega (nat. coun., nat. panhellenic del. 1978-83, 88-90, nat. v.p. membership 1985-88, nat. v.p. collegians 1990-92, co-chmn. Performance Lubbock '96 1996). Republican. Methodist. Home and Office: 3610 63rd Dr Lubbock TX 79413-5308

WALL, DIANE EVE, political science educator; b. Detroit, Nov. 17, 1944; d. Albert George and Jean Carol (Young) Bradley. BA in History and Edn., Mich. State U., 1966, MA in History, 1969, MA in Polit. Sci., 1979, PhD in Polit. Sci., 1983. Cert. permanent secondary tchr., Mich. Secondary tchr. Corunna (Mich.) Pub. Schs., 1966-67, N.W. Pub. Schs., Rives Junction, Mich., 1967-73; lectr. Tidewater Community Coll., Chesapeake, Va., 1974-77; instr. Lansing (Mich.) Community Coll., 1981-83; prof. dept. polit. sci. Miss. State U., 1983—, undergrad. coord., 1993—; instr. Wayne State U., Detroit, fall 1980, Ctrl. Mich. U., Mt. Pleasant, spring 1982; pre-law advisor Miss. State U., 1990-93, chair, 1993—. Contbr. articles, revs. to profl. jours., chpt. to book. Evaluator Citizen's Task Force, Chesapeake, Va., 1977; panelist flag burning program Ednl. TV, Mississippi State, 1990. Recipient Paideia award Miss. State U. Coll. Arts and Scis., 1988, Miss. State U. Outstanding Woman Teaching Faculty award Pres.'s Commn. on Status of Women, 1994, Acad. Advising award Miss. State U., 1994, Outstanding Advisor award Nat. Acad. Advising Assn., 1995; Grad. Office fellow Mich. State U., 1980; Miss. State U. rsch. grantee, 1984. Mem. ASPA (exec. bd. Sect. for Women 1987-90, Miss. chpt. pres. 1992-93), LWV (Chesapeake charter pres. 1976-77), Miss. Polit. Sci. Assn. (exec. dir. 1991-93), Miss. State U. Soc. Scholars (pres. 1992-93), Miss. State U. Faculty Women's Assn. (v.p. 1985-86, pres. 1986-88, scholar 1987-89), Phi Kappa Phi (v.p. 1985-86, pres. 1986-88), Pi Sigma Alpha (Ann. Chpt. Activities award 1991). Democrat. Methodist. Office: Miss State U PO Drawer PC Mississippi State MS 39762

WALL, GLENNIE MURRAY, historic preservation professional; b. Roseburg, Oreg., Oct. 8, 1931; d. James Matheny and Emily Lenore (Aten) Corbin; m. Louis Samuel Wall, Jan. 3, 1975; 2 daus. BS, Portland (Oreg.) State U., 1965, postgrad., 1966; postgrad., U. Mo., Springfield, 1969, U. Mich., 1978, Practicing Law Inst., N.Y.C., 1980-82. Historian, Pipestone (Minn.) Nat. Monument Nat. Pk. Svc., 1966-68; historian, pk. supt. Herbert Hoover Hist. Site Nat. Pk. Svc., West Branch, Iowa, 1968-69; historian, landmark specialist western regional office Nat. Park Svc., San Francisco, 1969-72; div. chief Denver Svc. Ctr. Nat. Park Svc., 1974-83; mus. mgr. (maritime) Nat. Park Svc., San Francisco, 1983-89, cultural resources specialist, curator Presidio Project, 1989-90; prin. Hist. Preservation Planning, San Francisco, 1990—; instr., lectr. on preservation law and policy Nat. Pk. Svc., 1974-83; lectr. Nat. Trust for Hist. Preservation, washington, 1971-89; dir. Coun. Am. Maritime Mus., Phila., 1987-88, Nat. Maritime Mus. Assn., San Francisco, 1983-88; chair Equal Opportunity Com., Nat. Pk. Svc., Denver, 1979-81. Author, editor: Maritime Preservation, 1987, Agency Guidelines for Cultural resources Management, 1979-83; photographer: Pipes on the Plains, 1967; author, photographer numerous plans and studies. Treas. Colo. Corral of Westerners, Denver, 1974-76; mem. Com. for Green Foothills, San Mateo, Calif., 1984-88, Sta. KQED-TV, San Francisco, 1985—. Recipient spl. achievement awards Dept. Interior, 1969, 72, citation for excellence, 1976; Nat. Preservation award President's Adv.

Coun., Washington, 1988., 72; Hoover scholar, 1993. Mem. Am. Decorative Arts Forum, Am. Assn. Mus., Internat. Coun. Mus., Internat. Congress Maritime Mus., Am. Assn. for State and Local History, NOW. Office: PO Box 370634 Montara CA 94037-0634

WALL, HARRIET MARIE, psychology educator; b. St. Louis, Oct. 21, 1942; d. Solomon P. and Charlotte B. (Goldman) Shakofsky; m. Daniel Braunstein, Aug. 5, 1962 (div. Apr., 1978); 1 child, Laura Ruth; m. Vance George Marshall II, Sept. 26, 1988. BS, Purdue U., 1963; MS, San Diego State U., 1965; PhD, U. Rochester, 1971. Rsch. asst. U.S. Navy, San Diego, 1963-65, U. of Rochester (N.Y.) Med. Sch., 1965-66; asst. prof. Monroe C.C., Rochester, 1970-71; prof. psychology, dir. rsch., assoc. dean U. Mich., Flint, 1972—. Home: 1014 S Franklin Ave Flint MI 48503-2818 Office: U Mich Flint Coll Arts and Scis 410 C ROB Flint MI 48502-2186

WALL, JENNY-LYNN, music educator; b. St. Charles, Mo., Apr. 5, 1970; d. Everett Eugene and Irma Linda (Burger) W. BS, William Jewell Coll., 1992; postgrad., S.W. Bapt. U., 1994—. Cert. vocal music tchr. k-12, Mo. Substitute tchr. various local schs., Mo., 1992-93; tchr. music and at-risk Lincoln County RIV Intermediate Sch., Winfield, Mo., 1993—; piano tchr., pvt. practice, Elsberry, Mo., 1992—, part time accompanist, singer at local events, 1994—; created honors choir program for intermediate sch. students, initiated recorders study program. Mem. Music Educators Nat. Conf., Mo. Music Educators Assn. Office: RIV Intermed Sch 701 Elm Winfield MO 63389

WALL, JUDITH LINDLEY, data entry professional; b. Burley, Idaho, Oct. 18, 1943; d. Raymond Earl and Helen Margaret (Knettle) W. BA, U. Calif., Berkeley, 1964; MA, Calif. State U., Chico, 1976. Life tchg. credentials elem., secondary, jr. coll., Calif. Tchr. Enterprise Elem. Sch. Dist., Redding, Calif., 1968-79; computer terminal operator 1st Ch. of Christian Scientist, Boston, 1979-82; substitute tchr. Boise (Idaho) Ind. Sch. Dist., 1983-91; data entry professional State of Idaho, Boise, 1991—. Patentee structural object; contbr. articles to profl. publs. Mem. Ada County Rep. Women's Club, Boise, 1996; charter mem. Women in the Arts Mus., Washington, 1990s. Mem. AAUW (bd. dirs. 1990), U.S. Naval Inst., Edelweiss Club. Christian Scientist. Home: 2209 Brumback St Boise ID 83702

WALL, SONJA ELOISE, nurse administrator; b. Santa Cruz, Calif., Mar. 28, 1938; d. Ray Theothornton and Reva Mattie (Wingo) W.; m. Edward Gleason Holmes, Aug. 1959 (div. Jan. 1968); children: Deborah Lynn, Lance Edward; m. John Aspesi, Sept. 1969 (div. 1977); children: Sabrina Jean, Daniel John; m. Kenneth Talbot LaBoube, Nov. 1, 1978 (div. 1989); 1 child, Tiffany Amber. BA, San Jose Jr. Coll., 1959; BS, Madonna Coll., 1967; student, U. Mich., 1968-70; postgrad., Wayne State U., 1967-68. RN, Calif., Mich., Colo. Staff nurse Santa Clara Valley Med. Ctr., San Jose, Calif., 1959-67, U. Mich. Hosp., Ann Arbor, 1967-73, Porter and Swedish Med. Hosp., Denver, 1973-77, Laurel Grove Hosp., Castro Valley, Calif., 1977-79, Advent Hosp., Ukiah, Calif., 1984-86; motel owner LaBoube Enterprises, Fairfield, Point Arena, Willits, Calif., 1979—; staff nurse Northridge Hosp., L.A., 1986-87, Folsom State Prison, Calif., 1987; co-owner, mgr. nursing registry Around the Clock Nursing Svc., Ukiah, 1985—; critical care staff nurse Kaiser Permanente Hosp., Sacramento, 1986-89; nurse Snowline Hospice, Sacramento, 1989-92; carepoint home care and travel nurse Hosp. Staffing Svcs. Inc., Placerville, Calif., 1992-94, interim home health nurse, 1994-95; nurse Senders Home Health Care, 1996; owner Sunshire Manor Resdl. Care Home, Placerville, Calif., 1995—; owner Royal Plantation Petites Miniature Horse Farm. Contbr. articles to various publs. Leader Coloma 4-H, 1987-91; mem. mounted divsn. El Dorado County Search and Rescue, 1991-93; docent Calif. Marshall Gold Discovery State Hist. Park, Coloma, Calif. Mem. AACN, NAFE, Soc. Critical Care Medicine, Am. Heart Assn. (CPR trainer, recipient awards), Calif. Bd. RNs, Calif. Nursing Rev., Calif. Critical Care Nurses, Soc. Critical Care Nurses, Am. Motel Assn. (beautification and remodeling award 1985), Nat. Hospice Nurses Assn., Cmty. Residential Care Assn. Calif., Soroptimist Internat. Calif., Am. Miniature Horse Assn. (winner nat. grand championship 1981-82, 83, 85, 89), DAR (Jobs Daus. hon. mem.), Cameron Park Country Club. Republican. Episcopalian. Home and Office: Around the Clock Nursing Svc 2809 Easy St Placerville CA 95667-0559

WALLACE, ALICEANNE, civic worker; b. Chgo., Sept. 28, 1925; d. Alexander and Mary (Zurek) Zalac; m. Henry Clay Wallace, Jr., Apr. 10, 1948; children: Laura Lillian Wallace Bergin, Christine Claire Wallace Stockwell. Student, St. Teresa Coll., Winona, Minn., 1944-45, DePaul U., 1946-48, North Tex. State U., 1971, 72. City sec. City of Southlake, Tex., 1969-77; pres. AZW, Inc., real estate sales, Roanoke, Tex., 1977-84. Mem. Trinity Valley Mental Health-Mental Retardation, Ft. Worth, 1971-72; chmn. ways and means Tex. Silver-Haired Legis., Austin, 1986-90, parliamentarian, 1991-94; treas. TSHL Found., 1990-92, pres., 1992-96; sec., bd. dirs. Sr. Citizens Activities, Inc., Temple, Tex., 1989-90; sec. CTCOG Area Agy. on Aging, Citizens Adv. Comm. Bd., Belton, Tex., 1991; bd. dirs. Tex. Dept. on Aging, Austin, 1991—; congl. sr. intern U.S. Ho. of Reps., Washington, 1991; pres. Tri-County Tex. Dem. Women, 1990-94; congl. del. White House Conf. on Aging, 1995; elected State Dem. Exec. Com. Senatorial Dist. #24, 1994—. Mem. Am. Assn. Ret. Persons (legis. chmn. Temple chpt. 1990-94, regional coord. VOTE 1991-96, assoc. state coord. 1996—), Tex. Fedn. Women's Clubs (state legis. chmn. 1990-92, resolutions chmn. 1992-94, parliamentarian Capitol dist. 1990-92), North Ctrl. Tex. Secy. Assn. (pres. 19760, City Fedn. Women's Clubs (corr. sec. 1991-92, records custodian 1991—), Triangle Forum (pres. 1992-94), Daus. Republic Tex. (assoc.), Internat. Inst. Mcpl. Clks. (state cert.), Epsilon Eta Phi. Home: RR 2 Box 2585 Belton TX 76513-9611

WALLACE, ANNE COPE, poet, educator; b. Union Springs, Ala., Aug. 7, 1931; d. Robert E. Lee and Kathleen (Hollingsworth) Cope; m. Jack J. Longley, June 1959 (div.); children: James, Allison, Edward; m. Frank E. Wallace, Aug. 19, 1972. BA in English Lit., Auburn U., 1952; MA in Psychology, Kean Coll., 1989. Tutor high sch. English Madison, N.J., 1983-89; adj. prof. psychology Morris County Coll., Randolph, N.J., 1992; bus. writer The Writer, Madison, 1992-95; tchr. poetry workshops N.J. Elem. Schs., Morristown, Roseland, Maplewood, 1993-96; guest reader N.J. Composers Guild, 1994, Waterloo (N.J.) Nat. Poetry Festival, 1994; tchr. writing workshops Inst. Allende, San Miguel de Allende, Mex., 1996. Author: The Princess of Peachburg, 1995; contbr. poems to Footwork, The McGuffin, The Midland Rev. Vol. Dem. campaign, 1991-92; chair bd. pub. rels. ARC, Madison, 1986-96, disaster vol., 1992-96. Recipient Allen Ginsberg award Passaic County Coll., 1992. Mem. NOW, Internat. Women's Writers Guild, South Mountain Poets (pres. 1992), The Sierra Club, Phi Kappa Phi. Presbyterian. Home: 27 Norman Cir Madison NJ 07940

WALLACE, BETTY JEAN, elementary school educator, lay minister; b. Denison, Tex., Dec. 5, 1927; d. Claude Herman and Pearl Victoria (Freels) Moore; m. Billy Dean McKneely, Sept. 2, 1950 (div. Nov. 1964); children: Rebecca Lynn, Paul King, David Freels, John Walker, Philip Andrew McKneely. Student, Tulane U., 1947; BA, Baylor U., 1949; postgrad., U. Houston, 1949-50, 74, 81, Rocky Mountain Bible Inst., 1959, U. Colo., 1969-70, U. No. Colo., 1965, 68, 72, U. St. Thomas, 1992, Autonomous U. Guadalajara, summer 1993; MEd, Houston Bapt. U., 1985. Cert. life profl. elem., high sch., life profl. reading specialist, secondary field ESL tchr., Tex. Tchr. Galena Park (Tex.) Ind. Sch. Dist., 1949-50, 52-53, 72—, Corpus Christi (Tex.) Independent Sch. Dist., 1950-51, Denver Pub. Schs., 1953-54, 63-72. Author: The Holy Spirit Today, 1989, Our God of Infinite Variety, 1991, God Speaks in a Variety of Ways, 1991. Sunday sch. tchr. So. Bapt. Conv. chs., Tex., 1946-50, Denver, 1952-56; tchr. kindergarten Emmanuel Bapt. Ch., Denver, 1956-59, 60-63; missionary, Queretaro, Mex., 1977, 78; mem. Rep. Senatorial Inner Circle, Washington, 1989-91, Round Table for Ronald Reagan, Washington, 1989-90; helper Feed the Poor, Houston, 1983-85; active Suicide Prevention, Houston, 1973-76, Literacy, Houston, 1978-81; rep. NEA, Denver, 1966-72; mem. Retirement Com., Denver, 1970-72; bd. advisors Oliver North, 1994. Recipient Rep. Senatorial medal of freedom, 1994; grantee NSF, 1969-70. Mem. Tex. Classroom Tchrs. Assn. (officer rep., pres. Galena Park chpt. 1988-91), Delta Alpha Pi (pres. Waco chpt. 1948-49), Alpha Epsilon Delta. Republican. Home: 14831 Anoka Dr Channelview TX 77530-3201 Office: North Shore Elem Sch 14310 Duncannon Dr Houston TX 77015-2514

WALLACE, BETTY LOUISE DOLLAR, religious educator; b. Glenwood, Ark.; d. James Herbert and Ora Lee (Yarbrough) Dollar; m. Robert Stanley Wallace, Oct. 7, 1965; children: David, Debra, Sarah. Diploma, Moore's Career Coll., Sacramento, 1959, Liberty Bapt. Coll., Lynchburg, Va., 1980; DD, Am. Bible Inst., Kansas City, Mo., 1983; cert., Jerusalem Ctr. for Biblical Studies, 1984-85; freelance writer, speaker, Campbell, Calif., 1965-83; ministry assoc., educator, Seventh Presbyn. Ch., Cin., 1983—. Pres. beauty salons and products Campbell, Calif., 1960-65. Author: Prayers for Mother and Child, 1970, Children's Prayers, Praises and Pledges, 1976, God in My Kitchen, 1977, (with others) Faith and Heritage, 1976; TV producer, hostess Children's Church, Noblesville, Ind., 1979-81. Mem. adv. com. Granby (Colo.) Elem. Sch., 1975-77; mem. Walnut Hlls Block Watch, Cin., 1984—; hon. life mem. Program Agy. United Presbyn. Ch., 1987. Recipient Jerusalem Pilgrim award Minister of Tourism and Mayor of Jerusalem, Israel, 1983, Interdenominational Clergy Achievement award, Korea, 1988, Cin. Jewish Welfare Fund medal, 1990, Citation, Beyer Mus. Soc., 1992; established Mayor's Proclamation "Betty Wallace" Day, Cin., 1992. Mem. NAFE, LWV, Nat. League of Am. Pen Women, Inc., Nat. Story League, Poetry Soc. Colo., Ch. Women United, Christian Writers' League Am., Nat. League Am. Pen Women Inc., Beyer Mus. Soc., Assn. Presbyn. Ch. Educators, World Found. of Successful Women (charter life). Home: 2726 Cleinview Ave Cincinnati OH 45206-1813 Office: Seventh Presbyn Ch 1721 Madison Rd Cincinnati OH 45206-1864

WALLACE, BONNIE ANN, biochemistry and biophysics educator, researcher; b. Greenwich, Conn., Aug. 10, 1951; d. Arthur Victor and Maryjane Ann W. BS in Chemistry, Rensselaer Poly. Inst., 1973; PhD in Molecular Biophysics and Biochemistry, Yale U., 1977. Postdoctoral rsch. fellow Harvard U., Boston, 1977-78; asst. prof. dept. biochemistry and molecular biophysics Columbia U., N.Y.C., 1979-86, assoc. prof. 1986; prof. dept. chemistry, dir. Ctr. for Biophysics Rensselaer Poly. Inst., 1987-92; reader in crystallography U. London, 1991—; vis. scientist MRC Lab. Molecular Biology, Cambridge, Eng., 1978; Fogarty sr. fellow Birkbeck Coll., U. London, 1990. Assoc. editor Peptide and Protein Letters; contbr. numerous articles to profl. jours. and books. Jane Coffin Childs fellow, 1977-79; recipient Irma T. Hirschl award, 1980-84; Camille and Henry Dreyfus tchr.-scholar, 1986; named Hot Young Scientist Fortune Mag., 1990; Subject of Documentary Film: Hypertension Research for the Future, 1995. Fellow Royal Soc. Chemistry; mem. Aspen Ctr. for Physics Fellowship, 1986, Biophys. Soc. (nat. coun., Dayhoff award 1985), Am. Crystallographic Assn., Brit. Crystallographic Assn. (BSG award 1994), Biochem. Soc. Britain (coun. mem. peptides and proteins group), Sigma Xi, Phi Lambda Upsilon. Office: U London Birkbeck Coll, Dept Crystallography, London WC1E 7HX, England

WALLACE, CONSTANCE WOLYNIEC, photographer, marketing executive, artist, consultant b. N.Y.C., Jan. 17, 1954; d. Adolph B. and Marion (Jankowsky) W. BS cum laude in Bus. Adminstrn., Ithaca Coll., 1974; MBA, Babson Coll., 1978. Systems mktg. rep. Control Data Corp., Boston, 1974-78, sales trainer, Greenwich, Conn., 1978-80; dir. Strategic Projects, internat. market entry and devel. co., St. John, V.I., 1980-88; pres. The Clothing Studio Inc., Mongoose Jct., St. John, 1984—; gen. mgr. Maine Photographic Resource, 1992; advtg. dir., staff photographer Tradewinds Newspaper, St. John USVI, 1995-96; photography shown at Caribbean Perspectives Gallery, Cruz Bay, VI; photography represented by Island Fancy Gallery, St. John, V.I. Photographic exhibitions include Maine Photo Workshop, Rockport, Maine, 1992, Chase Manhattan Bank, St. John, V.I., 1992, 93, 96, Island Fancy Gallery, St. John, 1993, 94, 95; photographer: (booklets) The Day After, St. John, 1995, St. John's Favorite Florals, 1996. Bd. dirs. St. John Community Found., chmn. mktg. and pub. rels. com.; govs. Tourism Policy Coun. Named Artist of Month St. John Sch. Arts, 1992, 93, 96. Mem. Mongoose Junction Mcht. Assn. (co-chmn. advtg. com. 1996), Mensa. Lutheran. Home: PO Box 8301 Cruz Bay VI 00831-8301 Office: Strategic Projects PO Box 8301 Cruz Bay VI 00831-8301 also: PO Box 396 Camden ME 04843-0396

WALLACE, DOROTHY ALENE, special education administrator; b. Wright County, Mo., Sept. 11, 1942; d. Stephen Foster and Lois Alene (Breman) Dudley; widowed; children: Michael Dean Huckaby, David Lee. BS in Edn., Drury Coll., 1975, MS in Edn., 1978; Specialist in Ednl. Adminstrn., Southwest Mo. State U., 1988. Cert. tchr. and adminstr., Mo. Tchr. 3rd grade Mansfield (Mo.) R-IV Schs., 1975-78, tchr. 1st grade, 1978-85, tchr. learning disabled, 1985-89, adminstr. spl. edn., 1989-92, adminstr. spl. svcs., 1992—; active sch. coms. on curriculum and nutrition Mansfield R-IV Schs., mem. sch./cmty. adv. coun., 1992—. Mem. Am. Salers Assn., Mo. State Tchrs. Assn., Mo. Coun. Adminstrs. of Spl. Edn., Coun. for Exceptional Children, Coun. Adminstrs. of Spl. Edn., Local Adminstrs. of Spl. Edn., Cmty. Tchrs. Assn. Home: 3489 Jerico Rd Seymour MO 65746

WALLACE, GLADYS BALDWIN, librarian; b. Macon, Ga., June 5, 1923; d. Carter Shepherd and Dorothy (Richard) Baldwin; m. Hugh Loring Wallace, Jr., Oct. 14, 1941 (div. Sept. 1968); children: Dorothy, Hugh Loring III. BS in Edn., Oglethorpe U., 1961; MLS, Emory U., 1966; EdS, Ga. State U., 1980. Libr. pub. elem. schs., Atlanta, 1956-66; libr. Northside High Sch., Atlanta, 1966-87, Episc. Cathedral St. Philip. Author: The Time of My Life, 1994. Mem. High Mus. Art, Madison-Morgan Cultural Ctr. Ga. Dept. Edn. grantee, 1950, NDEA grantee, 1963, 65. Mem. AAUW, Atlanta Bonsai Soc., Inc., Nat. Audubon Soc., The Cousteau Soc., Atlanta Bot. Garden, Am. Assn. Ret. Persons, Ga. Conservancy, Ga. Geneal. Soc., Oglethorpe U. Nat. Alumni Assn., Emory U. Alumni Assn., Ga. State U. Alumni Assn., Atlanta Hist. Soc., Ga. Trust for Historic Preservation, Piedmont Health and Fitness Club. Home: NC 6 136 Peachtree Memorial Dr NW Atlanta GA 30309-1030

WALLACE, HELEN MARGARET, physician, educator; b. Hoosick Falls, N.Y., Feb. 18, 1913; d. Jonas and Ray (Schweizer) W. AB, Wellesley Coll., 1933; MD, Columbia U., 1937; MPH cum laude, Harvard U., 1943. Diplomate Am. Bd. Pediatrics, Am. Bd. Preventive Medicine. Intern Bellevue Hosp., N.Y.C., 1938-40; child hygiene physician Conn. Health Dept., 1941-42; successively jr. health officer, health officer, chief maternity and new born div., dir. bur. for handicapped children N.Y.C. Health Dept., 1943-55; prof., dir. dept. pub. health N.Y. Med. Coll., 1955-56; prof. maternal and child health U. Minn. Sch. Pub. Health, 1956-59; chief profl. tng. U.S. Children's Bur., 1959-60, chief child health studies, 1961-62; prof. maternal and child health U. Calif. Sch. Pub. Health, Berkeley, 1962-80; prof., head divsn. maternal and child health Sch. Pub. Health San Diego State U., 1980—; Univ. Research lectr. San Diego State U., 1985—; cons. WHO numerous locations, including Uganda, The Philippines, Turkey, India, Geneva, Iran, Burma, Sri Lanka, East Africa, Australia, Indonesia, China, Taiwan, 1961—, traveling fellow, 1989—; cons. Hahnemann U., Phila., 1993, Ford Found., Colombia, 1971; UN cons. to Health Bur., Beijing, China, 1987; fellow Aiiku Inst. on Maternal and Child Health, Tokyo, and NIH Inst. Child Health and Human Devel., 1994; dir. Family Planning Project, Zimbabwe, 1984-87. Author, editor 10 textbooks; contbr. 325 articles to profl. jours. Mem. coun. on Disabled Children to Media, 1991; dir. San Diego County Infant Mortality Study, 1989—, San Diego Study of Prenatal Care, 1991. Recipient Alumnae Achievement award Wellesley Coll., 1982, U. Minn. award, 1985; Ford Found. study grantee, 1986, 87, 88; fellow World Rehab. Fund, India, 1991-92, Fulbright Found., 1992—, NIH Inst. Child Health and Human Devel., 1994, Aiiku Inst. of Maternal-Child Health, Tokyo, 1994. Fellow APHA (officer sect., Martha May Eliot award 1978), Am. Acad. Pediatrics (Job Smith award 1980, award 1989); mem. AMA, Assn. Tchrs. Maternal and Child Health, Am. Acad. Cerebral Palsy, Ambulatory Pediatric Assn., Am. Sch. Preventive Medicine. Home: 850 State St San Diego CA 92101-6046

WALLACE, HELEN MARIE, secondary school educator, coach; b. Chgo., Mar. 4, 1939; d. James and Birdie (Burdett) W. BS in Health and Phys. Edn., George Williams Coll., 1963, MS in Counseling Psychology, 1973, MS in Adminstrn., 1973. Cert. tchr. and adminstr., Ill. Girls and boys track, volleyball, and swimming coach Chgo. Pub. H.S.; adminstrv. asst. Chgo. Commn. on Urban Opportunity, summers 1965-68; phys. instr. Chgo. Park Dist., 1958-64; phys. edn. tchr. Chgo. Pub. Sch. Sys., 1963—, athletic dir. Harrison H.S., 1967-87, phys. edn. tchr. Lincoln Park H.S., 1987—, mem. citywide objectives for phys. edn. com., 1993-94, mem. health edn. curriculum com., 1992-94, mem. co-chair girls track com., 1983—; phys. edn. tchr., dept. chair Lincoln Park H.S.; mem. state track com. Ill. H.S.; co-author health edn. curriculum Chgo. Pub. H.S.'s; cons. for devel. of health and phys. edn. programs, adminstrv. guidelines, inter-intra-mural sport programs. Jr. ch. organist, celestial choir dir., organist dir. and orgnaist for women's chorus Original Providence Bapt. Ch.; soprano soloist numerous functions. Mem. AAHPERD, Am. Choral Dirs. Assn., Gospel Music Workshop Am. Office: Lincoln Park HS 2001 N Orchard St Chicago IL 60614-4415

WALLACE, JANE HOUSE, geologist; b. Ft. Worth, Aug. 12, 1926; d. Fred Leroy and Helen Gould (Kixmiller) Wallace; A.B., Smith Coll., 1947, M.A., 1949; postgrad. Bryn Mawr Coll., 1949-52. Geologist, U.S. Geol. Survey, 1952—, chief Pub. Inquiries Offices, Washington, 1964-72, spl. asst. to dir., 1974—, dep. bur. ethics counselor, 1975—, Washington liaison Office of Dir., 1978—. Recipient Meritorious Service award Dept. Interior, 1971, Disting. Svc. award, 1976, Sec.'s Commendation, 1988, Smith Coll. medal, 1992. Fellow Geol. Socs. Am., Washington (treas. 1963-67); mem. Sigma Xi (asso.). Home: 3003 Van Ness St NW Washington DC 20008-4701 Office: Interior Bldg 19th and C Sts NW Washington DC 20240 also: US Geol Survey 103 National Ctr Reston VA 22092

WALLACE, JANE YOUNG (MRS. DONALD H. WALLACE), editor; b. Geneseo, Ill., Feb. 17, 1933; d. Worling R. and Margaret C. (McBroom) Young; m. Donald H. Wallace, Aug. 24, 1959; children: Robert, Julia. BS in Journalism, Northwestern U., 1955, MS in Journalism, 1956; LittD (hon.), Johnson and Wales U., 1990. Diplomate Nat. Restaurant Assn. Edn. Found., 1991. Editor house organ Libby McNeill & Libby, Chgo., 1956-58; prodn. editor Instns. Mag., Chgo., 1958-61; food editor Instns. Mag., 1961-65, mng. editor, 1965-68, editor-in-chief, 1968-85; editor Restaurants and Instns., 1970-85, editorial dir., 1985-89, assoc. pub., 1985-89, pub., 1989-94; pub. R & I Market Pl., 1989-94, v.p., editor/pub. emeritus, 1994—; editorial dir. Hotels and Restaurants Internat. Mag., 1971-89; v.p., editor/pub. emeritus Restaurants and Instns., 1994—; editorial dir. Foodservice Equipment Specialist Mag., 1975-89; v.p. Cahners Pub. Co. (Reed USA), 1982; mem. editorial quality audit bd. Reed USA, 1993—; cons. Nat. Restaurant Assn., dir., 1977-82; cons. Nat. Inst. for Food Svc. Industry; vis. lectr. Fla. Internat. U., 1980. Editor: The Professional Chef, 1962, The Professional Chef's Book of Buffets, 1965, Culinary Olympics Cookbook, 1980, 3d edit., 1988, Academy of American Culinary Foundation Cookbook, 1985, American Dietetic Associaton Foundation Cookbook, 1986; contbr. restaurant chpt. World Book Ency., 1975, 94, Food Service Trends, American Quantity Cooking, 1976. Mem. com. investigation vocat. needs for food svc. tng. U.S. Dept. Edn., 1969; mem. Inst. Food Editors' Conf., 1959-88, pres., 1967; mem. hospitality industry edn. adv. bd. Ill. Dept. Edn., 1976, mem. adv. bd. Ill. sch. foodsvc., 1978; mem. corp. adv. bd. Am. Dietetic Assn. Found., 1981-92, bd. dirs., 1996—; trustee Presbyn. Ch., Barrington, Ill., 1983-85; bd. trustees Culinary Inst. Am., 1987—. Recipient Jesse H. Neal award for best bus. press editorial, 1969, 70, 73, 76, 77, 79, 82, 87, Diplomate award Nat. Restaurant Assn. Edn. Found., 1991; named Outstanding Woman Northwood Inst., 1983. Fellow Soc. for Advancement Foodservice Rsch. (dir. 1975-77, sec. 1980); mem. Internat. Foodservice Mfrs. Assn. (Spark Plug award 1979), Nat. Assn. Foodservice Equipment Mfrs., Am. Bus. Press Assn. (chmn. editl. com. 1978), Am. Inst. Interior Designers (assoc.), Women in Comms. (v.p. Chgo. 1957-58), Ivy Soc. Restaurateurs of Distinction (co-founder 1970—), Am. Dietetic Assn. (hon., bd. dirs. 1996—), Roundtable for Women in Food Service (bd. dirs. 1980-84; Foodservice Woman of Yr. 1988, Lifetime Recognition award 1994), Les Dames d'Escoffier (charter mem.), Culinary Inst. of Am. (ambassador 1986, trustee 1987—), Brotherhood of Knights of Vine (Gentlelady award 1980, 81), Disting. Restaurateurs of N.Am. (Hall of Fame award 1994), Internat. Assn. Cooking Profls., Gamma Phi Beta, Kappa Tau Alpha. Home: 186 Signal Hill Rd Barrington IL 60010-1929 Office: Cahners Publishing PO Box 5080 1350 E Touhy Ave Des Plaines IL 60018-3303 *Died May 16, 1996.*

WALLACE, JEANNETTE OWENS, state legislator; b. Scottsdale, Ariz., Jan. 16, 1934; d. Albert and Velma (Whinery) Owens; m. Terry Charles Wallace Sr., May 21, 1955; children: Terry C. Jr., Randall J., Timothy A., Sheryl L., Janice M. BS, Ariz. State U., 1955. Mem. Los Alamos (N.Mex.) County Coun., 1981-82; cons. County of Los Alamos, 1983-84; chmn., vice chmn. Los Alamos County Coun., 1985-88; cons. County of Los Alamos, Los Alamos Schs., 1989-90; rep. N.Mex. State Legislature, 1991—; mem. appropriations and fin. govt. and urban affairs, N.Mex., 1991—, legis. fin. com., Indian affairs, radioactive and hazardous materials, co-chmn. Los Alamos County's dept. energy negotiating com., 1987-88; mem. legis. policy com. Mcpl. League, N.Mex., 1986-88. Bd. dirs. Tri-Area Econ. Devel., 1988-94, 96—, Crime Stoppers, Los Alamos, 1988-92, Los Alamos Citizens Against Substance Abuse, 1989-94; mem. N.Mex. First, Albuquerque, 1989-96; legis. chmn. LWV, 1990; mem. Los Alamos Rep. Women, pres., 1989-90. Mem. Los Alamos Bus. & Profl. Women (legis. chmn. 1990), Los Alamos C. of C., Mana del Norte, Kiwanis. Methodist. Home: 146 Monte Rey Dr S Los Alamos NM 87544-3826

WALLACE, JOAN SCOTT, psychologist, social worker, international consultant; b. Chgo., Nov. 8, 1930; d. William Edouard and Esther (Fulks) Scott; m. John Wallace, June 12, 1954 (div. Mar. 1976); children—Mark, Eric, Victor; m. Maurice A. Dawkins, Oct. 14, 1979. A.B., Bradley U., 1952; M.S.W., Columbia U., 1954; postgrad., U. Chgo., 1965; Ph.D., Northwestern U., 1973; H.H.D. (hon.), U. Md., 1979; L.H.D. (hon.), Bowie State Coll., 1981; LLD (hon.), Ala. A&M U., 1990. Lic. social psychologist, social worker. Asst. prof., then assoc. prof. U. Ill.-Chgo., 1967-73; assoc. dean, prof. Howard U., Washington, 1973-76; v.p.-programs Nat. Urban League, N.Y.C., 1975-76; v.p. adminstrn. Morgan State U., Balt., 1976-77; asst. sec. adminstrn. USDA, Washington, 1977-81, adminstr. Office Internat. Cooperation and Devel., 1981-89; rep. to Trinidad and Tobago Inter Am. Inst. for Cooperation in Agr., USDA, 1989; internat. cons. U.S. Partnerships Internat., Ft. Lauderdale, 1993—; speaker in field. Contbr. articles, chpts. to profl. publs. Chair Binat. Agrl. Research and Devel. Fund, 1987. Recipient Disting. Alumni award Bradley U., 1978, Meritorious award Delta Sigma Theta, 1978, award for leadership Lambda Kappa Mu, 1978, award for outstanding achievement and svc. to nation Capital Hill Kiwanis Club, 1978, Links Achievement award, 1979, Presdl. Rank for Meritorious Exec., 1980, NAFEO award, 1989, Community Svc. award Alpha Phi Alpha, 1987, Pres.' award for outstanding pub. svc. Fla. A&M U., 1990. Mem. APA, NASW, AAAS, Am. Consortium for Internat. Pub. Adminstrn. (exec. com., governing bd. 1987), Soc. Internat. Devel. (Washington chpt.), Sr. Exec. Assn., Soc. for Internat. Devel., White House Com. on Internat. Sci., Engring. and Tech., Internat. Sci. and Edn. Coun. (chmn. 1981-89), Am. Evaluation Assn., Consortium Internat. Higher Edn. (adv. com.), Caribbean Studies Soc., Caribbean Assn. of Agriculture Economists, Assn. Polit. Psychologists, Pi Gamma Mu. Presbyterian. Home: 6010 S Falls Circle Dr Fort Lauderdale FL 33319-6900 Office: Joan Wallace and Assocs 5557 W Oakland Park Blvd Fort Lauderdale FL 33313-1411 also: Ams for Democracy in Africa 11921 Freedom Dr # 505 Reston VA 22090

WALLACE, JOYCE IRENE MALAKOFF, internist; b. Phila., Nov. 25, 1940; d. Samuel Leonard and Henrietta (Hameroff) Malakoff; A.B., Queens Coll., City U. N.Y., 1961; postgrad. Columbia U., 1962-64; M.D, State U. N.Y., 1968; m. Lance Arthur Wallace, Aug. 30, 1964 (div. 1974); 1 dau., Julia Ruth; m. Arthur H. Kahn, Oct. 7, 1979 (div. 1986); 1 son, Aryeh N. Kahn. Intern, St. Vincent's Hosp. Med. Center, N.Y.C., 1968-70; resident Manhattan VA Hosp., N.Y.C. and Nassau County Med. Center, East Meadow, N.Y., 1972-73; practice medicine, N.Y.C., 1970-71, North Conway, N.H., 1974-75; practice medicine specializing in internal medicine, N.Y.C., 1976—; mem. attending staff Nassau County Med. Center, 1974, St. Vincent's Hosp. and Med. Center, N.Y.C., 1977—; asst. prof. medicine Mt. Sinai Med. Sch., N.Y.C.; pres. Found. for Research on Sexually Transmitted Diseases, Inc., 1986-89, exec. and med. dir., 1989—. Diplomate Am. Bd. Internal Medicine. Fellow ACP, N.Y. Acad. Medicine; mem. Am. Med. Women's Assn., N.Y. County, N.Y. State med. socs. Office: 369 8th Ave New York NY 10001-4852

WALLACE, JULIA DIANE, newspaper editor; b. Davenport, Iowa, Dec. 3, 1956; d. Franklin Sherwood and Eleanor Ruth (Pope) W.; m. Doniver Dean Campbell, Aug. 23, 1986; children: Emmaline Livingston Campbell, Eden Jennifer Campbell. BS in Journalism, Northwestern U., 1978. Reporter Norfolk (Va.) Ledger-Star, 1978-80, Dallas Times Herald, 1980-82; reporter, editor News sect. USA Today, Arlington, Va., 1982-89, mng. editor spl. projects, 1989-92; mng. editor Chgo. Sun-Times, 1992—. Mem. Am. Soc. Newspaper Editors. Office: Chgo Sun-Times 401 N Wabash Ave Chicago IL 60611-3532

WALLACE, MARGARET ELLEN, artist, art gallery owner; b. Cleve., Feb. 14, 1953; d. George Maslin and Grace Marie (Emanuel) Gilkeson; m. Kenneth Kerry Wallace, June 12, 1975 (div. Jan. 1994); 1 child, Patrick Marlowe. BFA, U. Houston, 1976; MFA, Sam Houston State U., 1980. Author: 1996 Womyn's Calendar, 1996; artist: (installation) Journey Toward the Goddess, 1995. Multidisciplinary grantee Dept. Arts and Cultural Affairs, 1994. Mem. Women's Caucus for Art (chpt. liaison, v.p.), San Antonio Women's Caucus for Art (pres. 1991-92). Democrat. Office: Wallace-Musket Gallery # 104G 1420 S Alamo San Antonio TX 78210

WALLACE, MARILYN JEAN, academic director; b. Oak Park, Ill., Feb. 11, 1950; d. Jay Emmons and Libbie (Novak) Phillips; m. David Stuart Wallace, Sept. 11, 1971; children: David, Douglas. BA, Principia Coll., 1972. Cert. music and edn. elem. and secondary grade levels. Music tchr. Granneman Elem., Hazelwood, Mo., 1972-73, Chicago Jr. Sch., Elgin, Ill., 1973-74, Sch. Dist. 30, Northbrook, Ill., 1974-77; 2nd grade tchr. Sch. Dist. 27, Northbrook, 1978-79; 5th grade tchr. Sch. Dist. 30, Northbrook, 1979-83, 2nd grade tchr., 1984-86; middle sch. social studies tchr. Creative Children's Acad., Mt. Prospect, Ill., 1991-92; acad. dean Creative Children's Acad., Mt. Prospect, 1992-93; acad. dir. Creative Children's Acad., Palatine, Ill., 1993—; mem. adv. bd. Joyful Parenting, Oconomowoc, Wis., 1994—, Understanding Our Gifted, Boulder, Colo., 1994—, Nat. Louis U., Evanston, Ill., 1995—; presenter in field. Named Educator of Yr., Phi Delta Kappa, Evanston, 1993. Mem. Nat. Assn. for Gifted Children, Ill. Assn. for Gifted Children. Home: 502 Brockway Palatine IL 60067 Office: Creative Childrens Acad 500 N Benton Palatine IL 60067

WALLACE, MARY ELAINE, opera director, author; m. Robert House. BFA cum laude, U. Nebr., Kearney, 1940; MusM, U. Ill., 1954; postgrad., Music Acad. West, Santa Barbara, Calif., 1955, Eastman Sch. Music, 1960, Fla. State U., 1962. Prof. voice, dir. opera La. Tech. U., Ruston, 1954-62, SUNY-Fredonia, 1962-69, So. Ill. U.-Carbondale, 1969-79; dir. Marjorie Lawrence Opera Theatre, Opera on Wheels; adminstrv. adviser Summer Playhouse, Carbondale; stage mgr. Chautauqua Opera Co., N.Y., 1963; asst. mus. dir., condr. Asolo Festival, Sarasota, Fla., 1961; music editor, critic The Chautauquan Daily; adjudicator Met. Opera auditions; exec. sec. Nat. Opera Assn., 1981-91. Co-author: Opera Scenes for Class and Stage, 1979, (with Robert Wallace) More Operas Scenes for Class and Stage, 1990, Upstage Downstage, 1992. Mem. Nat. Opera Assn. (pres. 1974, 75), Music Tchrs. Nat. Assn., Nat. Assn. Tchrs. Singing, AAUP, AAUW, Met. Opera Guild, Mortar Bd., Sigma Tau Delta, Pi Kappa Lambda, Phi Beta, Alpha Psi Omega, Delta Kappa Gamma. Address: 3106 Lakeside Dr Rockwall TX 75087-5319

WALLACE, MARY MONAHAN, elementary and secondary schools educator; b. Teaneck, N.J., Nov. 22, 1943; d. Thomas Gabriel and Louise Grace (Monaco) Monahan; m. James Anthony Wallace, Nov. 22, 1978; (dec. May, 1992); 1 child, Meg. BS, Fordham U., 1967; MA, 1971; postgrad. in Supervision, Montclair U., 1978; postgrad. in Edn., various colls. Cert. tchr. language arts, supr., N.Y. 1st and 4th grades tchr. Holy Rosary Sch., Harlem, N.Y., 1963-65; 7th grade tchr. Immaculate Conception Sch., Bronx, N.Y., 1965-66; 8th grade tchr. St. Finbar Sch., Bklyn., 1966-68, St. Patrick Mil. Acad., Harriman, N.Y., 1968-69; English tchr. St. Stephen H.S., Bklyn., N.Y., 1969-70, Holy Rosary Acad., Union City, N.J., 1970-71, Harriman (N.Y.) Coll., 1971-72, Montclair (N.J.) Coll., 1981-82; English tchr. elem. and secondary schs. Fairlawn (N.J.) Schs., 1972—; advisor Fair Lawn H.S. Yearbook, 1977-80, Nat. Lang. Arts Olympiad, Fair Lawn, 1987-89; mem. Mid. Sch. Task Force Fair Lawn Schs., 1991-93, dist. wide steering com. Edn. Recognition Day, Fair Lawn, 1992, 93, mem. steering com. Fair Lawn Mid. Schs., 1994—. Editor (newsletter) Concern, 1970-72; mem. editorial staff (newsletter) Flea Bytes, 1988, 89, 90. Participant Summer in the City U.S. Antipoverty Program, Staten Island, N.Y., 1965; pres. Bear Pond Improvement Assn., 1996—. Named Meml. Sch. Tchr. of Yr. N.J. Gov.'s Recognition Program, 1993. Mem. NEA, N.J. Edn. Assn., N.J. Middle Sch. Assn., Nat. Coun. Tchrs. of English, Fair Lawn Edn. Assn. (treas. 1990-93, pres. 1993—). Roman Catholic. Home: 20-18 Saddle River Rd Fair Lawn NJ 07410-5933 Office: Fair Lawn Edn. Assn. 3-13 4th St Fair Lawn NJ 07410

WALLACE, PEGGY MARIE, state commissioner; b. Barbourville, Ky., Jan. 3, 1950; d. Chester and Katherine (White) W. BS, Union Coll., 1971; MSSW, U. Louisville, 1977. Eligibility worker Dept. Econ. Security, State of Ky., Barbourville, 1972-74; social worker Dept. Social Svcs., Barbourville, 1974-76; social svcs. trainer, cons. Dept. Social Svcs., Frankfort, 1977-78, budget analyst, 1978-80, adminstrv. asst., 1980-81, adminstrv. supr., 1981, exec. asst., 1981-85, prin. asst., 1985-88, dep. commr., 1988-92, commr., 1992—; mem. Ky. Atty. Gen's. Task Force on Child Sexual Abuse, Ky. Child Labor Task Force, Ky. Multi-Disciplinary Commn. on Child Sexual Abuse, Ky. Crime Commn. (mem. juvenile justice adv. com.), Ky. Children's Justice Act Task Force, Ky. Family Resource and Youth Svcs. Ctr. Task Force, Ky. Child Care Policy Coun., Ky. Adv. Coun. on the Homeless, Ky. Early Intervention System Interagy. Coord. Coun., Ky. Gender Fairness Standing Com. (mem. subcom. on domestic violence), Ky. Birth Surveillance Adv. Com., Ky. Long Range Juvenile Detention Planning Com., Ky. State Interagy. Coun. for Children and Youth; chair Am. Pub. Welfare Assn's. Children, Families and Adult Svcs. Com. Mem. NASW (mem. bluegrass chpt.), Nat. Forum for Black Pub. Adminstrs. Baptist. Office: Social Svcs Dept 275 E Main St Frankfort KY 40601-2321

WALLACE, ROANNE, hosiery company executive; b. Greenwood, Miss., Dec. 18, 1949; d. Robert Carter and Lois Anne (Vick) W. BM, U. Tenn., 1971; MA, U. N.C., 1976; MBA, Wake Forest U., 1982. Exec. dir. Am. Bd. Clin. Chemistry, Winston-Salem, N.C., 1977-78; administrv. officer Winston-Salem/Forsyth County Office Emergency Mgmt., 1978-79, sr. asst. dir., 1979-82; with Sara Lee Hosiery, Winston-Salem, 1982—, mktg. dir., 1988—; product mgr. L'eggs Products, Inc., Winston-Salem, 1986-88. Mem. adv. coun. Winston-Salem/Forsyth County Office Emergency Mgmt.; bd. dirs. Piedmont Opera Theatre, Inc. Miss U. Tenn., 1970. Home: 803 Devon Ct Winston Salem NC 27104-1263 Office: L'Eggs Products Inc PO Box 2495 Winston Salem NC 27102-2495

WALLACE, SARAH ANNE, clothing company executive; b. Washington, May 20, 1967; d. Don and Daphne (Wickham) W. BA, Yale U., 1990; MBA, Columbia U., 1995. Exec. asst. to pres. The Donna Karan Co., N.Y.C., 1990-91, sales assoc. DKNY, 1991-92, account exec., 1992-93, dir. internat. planning and ops., 1995—. Home: 74 W 68th Apt 6F New York NY 10023 Office: The Donna Karan Co 550 7th Ave 14th Fl New York NY 10018

WALLACE, SHARON MARIE, pharmacist; b. Somerville, N.J., Mar. 3, 1956; d. George and Anne Marie (Mitchell) Sweet; m. James Michael Kammerer, Sept. 7, 1982 (div. July 1989); 1 child, Michael John Kammerer; m. Gary Everett Wallace, July 21, 1990; 1 child, Christopher Marc. BS, Rutgers U., 1979. Registered pharmacist, N.J., Pa., N.Y. Pharmacy technician, intern Somerset Med. Ctr., Somerville, N.J., 1974-80; staff pharmacist Newton (N.J.) Meml. Hosp., 1980-82, CVS Pharmacy, Binghamton, N.Y., 1982-86; pharmacy mgr. The Rx Place, Levittown, Pa., 1986-88; staff pharmacist Lower Bucks Hosp., Levittown, Pa., 1988-92, Rite-Aid Corp., Levittown, Pa., 1992—. Regional rep. Bread for the World, Sussex County, N.J., 1980-81. Mem. Amnesty Internat. Democrat. Presbyterian. Office: Rite-Aid Corp Levittown PA 19057

WALLACE-CARR, SUSAN REBECCA, art educator; b. Indpls., Dec. 24, 1960; d. James Clarence and Helen Louise (Smith) Wallace; m. Alvin Brian Carr, May 21, 1983; children: Alexander B., Chelsea Lee. BFA in Art Edn., Kent State U., 1983. Cert. tchr., N.C. Graphic artist Sign of Art, Clearwater, Fla., 1983-88; elem. tchr. art Wallace Elem. Sch., N.C., 1988-93; art tchr. Jacksonville HS, N.C., 1993-95, White Oak Elem. Sch., Cape Carteret, N.C., 1995—; tchg. asst. Cuyahoga Heights (Ohio) Summer Sch., 1980, 82; instr. sailing Cleve. Sailing Sch., 1981; camp counselor Art in Park, Brooklyn Heights, Ohio, 1982-84; tchr. art Fla. Gulf Coast Art Ctr., Belleair, 1985-88, Creative Tchg. Svcs., Seminole, Fla., 1987; resource rep. sch. improvement team Wallace Elem. Sch., 1982-83. Choreographer America: Our Cultural Tapestry, 1989; dir., videographer Rites of Passage, 1992-93. Worker Youth Conservation Corps, Wooster, Ohio, 1979; commodore Kent (Ohio) State Sailing Club, 1980-82; co-sponsor Board Sailors Unite, Fairport Harbor, Ohio, 1983-85. Grantee Duplin County Bd. Edn., 1989, Getty Ctr. for Arts, 1991, N.C. Ctr. for Advancement Tchg., 1992, 95, Very Spl. Arts grant Kennedy Ctr. Performing Arts; recipient Jones-Onslow Electric Membership "Bright Ideas grant", 1985, 86. Mem. Nat. Art Edn. Assn., N.C. Art Edn. Assn. (conf. presenter 1989, 90), Internat. Soc. for Edn. in Arts. Unitarian. Office: White Oak Elem Sch 555 McClean Blvd Cape Carteret NC 28584

WALLACE WILLIAMS, MELISSA JOI, software analyst; b. Decatur, Ala., Oct. 31, 1962; d. Walter Waymon and Joyce Ann (Waldrop) W.; m. James Linderman Williams, Mar. 12, 1994. BS, Jacksonville (Ala.) State, 1984; attended, U. Ala., Huntsville, 1995—. Software analyst Intergraph Corp., Huntsville, 1984-90, sr. software analyst, 1990—. Office: Intergraph Corp Huntsville AL 35894

WALLACH, AMEI MARIONE, journalist, art critic; b. N.Y.C., Sept. 21, 1941; d. Gert M.K. and Gerda (Lewenz) W.; m. William Edwards, 1989; student U. Chgo., 1959-61; B.S. in Comparative Lit., Columbia U., 1965. Editorial trainee McGraw Hill, Inc., N.Y.C., 1965, asso. editor cover stories and features Merchandising Week, 1966-68; reporter, reviewer UPI, 1968-69; editor Modern Living sect. Newsday, Garden City, N.Y., 1969-72, cultural affairs writer, 1972-83, chief art critic N.Y. Newsday, N.Y.C., 1984-95; arts essayist The MacNeil/Lehrer Newshour, 1987-95; lectr., seminar leader in field. Recipient Front Page award in columnist category Newswomen's Club of N.Y., 1970, 85, 94, Clarion award for article Andrew Wyeth, a Painter's World; Nat. Endowment Humanities profl. journalism fellow Stanford U., 1983-84; Newsday Publisher's award, 1986. Am. Women in Communication, 1977. Among initiators Newsday Part II, expanded modern living sect.; initiated interactive art coverage; contbr. to N.Y. Times, Vanity Fair, Vogue, Elle, Elle Decor, Archtl. Digest, MS Mag., German Esquire, Art in Am., Lears, Coll. Art Jour., L.A. Times, Art News, Antiques World, Portfolio, N.Y. Mag., Horizon, Conn. Mag. Author intro. to Tetrascroll (Buckminster Fuller), 1982, intro. to Universal Limited Art Editions, 1989, Ilya Kabakov: The Man Who Never Threw Anything Away, 1996. Mem. Art Table (v.p. 1985), Internat. Assn. Art Critics (bd. dirs. USA sect.). Home: 4 Horizon Rd Apt 1022 Fort Lee NJ 07024 Office: Newsday 780 3d Ave New York NY 10017

WALLACH, ANNE JACKSON See JACKSON, ANNE

WALLACH, BARBARA PRICE, classicist, educator; b. Roanoke, Va., Aug. 31, 1946; d. Benjamin Thomas and Geneva Mae (Bittinger) Price; m. Luitpold Wallach, Aug. 22, 1970 (dec. Nov. 1986). BA in Latin, Mary Washington Coll., 1968; MA in Classics, U. Ill., 1970, PhD in Classical Philology, 1974. Summer vis. lectr. U. Ill., Urbana, 1977; vis. asst. prof. U. Pitts., 1979-80; asst. prof. U. Mo., Columbia, 1980-85, assoc. prof., 1985—. Author: Lucretius and the Diatribe, 1976; contbr. articles to profl. jours. Mem. Am. Philol. Assn., Classical Assn. Middle West and South, Internat. Soc. for the History of Rhetoric, Soc. for Ancient Greek Philosophy, Vergilian Soc., Internat. Plutarch Soc., Phi Beta Kappa. Democrat. Office: U Mo Dept Classical Studies Columbia MO 65211

WALLACH, MAGDALENA FALKENBERG (CARLA WALLACH), writer; b. Brussels; d. Carl Albert and Renee Antoinette (Meunier) Falkenberg; m. Philip Charles Wallach, Mar. 5, 1950. Student, Columbia U., Hunter Coll., New Sch. for Social Rsch. Ptnr. Williams-Falkenberg Advt. Assocs., Inc., N.Y.C., 1951-55. Author: Reluctant Weekend Gardener, 1971, Interior Decorating with Plants, 1976, Gardening in the City, 1976, Garden in a Teacup, 1978; contbr. articles to N.Y. Times, Glamour, Working Woman, others. Former bd. dirs. ARC, N.Y.C.; active Bruce Mus., 1987—, chmn. spl. events 75th anniversary gala, nominating com., chmn. Renaissance Ball, mem., bd. dirs. also other fundraising activities; bd. dirs., v.p. Greenwich Adult Day Ctr. Mem. Nat. League Am. PEN Women (pres. Greenwich br. 1987-92), Authors Guild, Garden Writers Assn., English-Speaking Union (bd. dirs. Greenwich br.), Alliance Francaise, Nat. Inst. Social Scis. Roman Catholic. Home: 126 WestLyon Farm Dr Greenwich CT 06831

WALLACH, PATRICIA, mayor; b. Chgo.; m. Ed Wallach; 3 children. Grad., Pasadena City Coll. Mem. city coun. City of El Monte, Calif., 1990-92, mayor, 1992—; tchr.'s aide Mountain View Sch. Dist. Past trustee El Monte Union High Sch. Dist., L.A. County High Sch. for the Arts; chief amb. of goodwill Zamora, Michoacan, Mex., Marcq-en-Baroeul, France, Yung Kang, Hsiang, Republic of China, Minhang, Peoples Republic of China; mem. L.A. County Libr. Commn.; mem. air quality com. West San Gabriel Valley; chairperson of bd. Cmty. Redevel. Agy.; mem. bd. El Monte Cmty. Access TV Corp.; mem. PTA, Little League Assns.; mem. exec. bd. Foothill Transit. Mem. League of Calif. Cities, San Gabriel Valley Assn. of Cities, Independent Cities Assn., Bus. and Profl. Women, U.S./Mex. Sister Cities Assn., Sister Cities Internat. Office: 11333 Valley Blvd El Monte CA 91731-3210

WALLACH, WENDEE ESTHER, secondary school educator; b. N.Y.C., Dec. 29, 1948; d. Leonard Morris and Annette (Cohen) W.; divorced; 1 child, Nanette René. BS in Edn., SUNY, Cortland, 1970; MA in Teaching, N.Mex. State U., 1975. Cert. tchr., N.Mex. Tchr. phys. edn. Las Cruces (N.Mex.) Pub. Schs., 1970-96; mem. Shoemaker-Levy Observing Team, 1996—; intramural and athletic coord. White Sands Sch., 1970-93; instr. swimming N.Mex. State U. Weekend Coll., Las Cruces, 1986-96; dir., coord. learn to swim program ARC, Las Cruces, 1973-96; instr. phys. edn., coach volleyball and track, athletic coord. Sierra Mid. Sch., 1993-96. Instr. trainer water safety ARC, 1973—, CPR, 1974—; instr. life guard, trainer, health and safety specialist, 1988-96, instr., trainer standard first aid, 1991—; chair com. health and safety svcs. Don Ana County Red Cross. Named Water Safety Instr. of Yr. ARC, Las Cruces, 1986, 89, 25 Yr. Svc. award, 1992. Mem. AAHPERD, N.Mex. Alliance Health, Phys. Edn. Recreation and Dance (spkr. 1988, 92, 93, aquatic chmn. 1990-92), Nat. Intramural-Recreational Sports Assn., N.Mex. H.S. Athletic Dirs. Assn. Democrat. Jewish. Home and Office: 2500 E Wetstones Rd Vail AZ 85641

WALLACK-ROSELLI, RINA EVELYN, lawyer; b. Pitts.; d. Erwin Norman and Gloria A. (Schacher). AD in Nursing, Delta Coll., 1973; BS cum laude in Psychology, Eastern Mich. U., 1980; JD cum laude, Wayne State U., 1983. Registered nurse Mich.; bar: Calif. 1983. Psychiat. head nurse Ypsilanti (Mich.) State Hosp., 1973-77, instr., nursing educator, 1977-80; teaching asst. contracts Wayne State U., Detroit, 1981-83; legal asst. Wayne County Prosecutor's Office, 1982-83; atty. NLRB, L.A., 1983-86, dir. employee rels. legal svcs. Paramount Pictures Corp., L.A., 1986-89, v.p., 1989—. Contbr. articles to profl. jours. Instr. ARC, Mich., 1978-80. Recipient Am. Jurisprudence Book award, 1983. Mem. ABA, L.A. County Bar Assn., Am. Trial Lawyers Assn., Mich. Bar Assn., Calif. Bar Assn., Order of Coif. Avocations: shooting, movies, dancing, reading, photography.

WALLCRAFT, MARY JANE LOUISE, religious organization executive, songwriter, author; b. Deloraine, Man., Can., Nov. 2, 1933; d. Norman Zephaniah and Mary Jane (McKinney) Sexton; m. James Orval Wallcraft, Oct. 13, 1956; children: Angela Mae, Ronald Clarke. Assoc. in piano, Royal Conservatory Toronto, Brandon, Man., 1952; AA, Victor Valley Coll., 1973. Tchr. piano Souris, Man., 1963-67; church organist St. George's Anglican, Brandon, 1960-63, St. Lukes Anglican, Souris, Man., 1963-67, Victorville (Calif.) United Meth. Ch., 1970-74; tchr. piano Hines House of Music, Victorville, 1969-72; ch. sec. Fredericksburg (Va.) United Meth. Ch., 1977-79; med. transcriptionist Mary Washington Hosp., Fredericksburg, 1985-87, Shady Grove Adventist, Rockville, Md., 1987-89; founder, pres. Make Me a Blessing Ministries, Inc., Zellwood, Fla., 1992—. Author: Make Me a Blessing, 1991, Sing Your Way to Victory, "Reflections", 1994, A Modern Day Psalter, Shadows, Symbols, and Strategies, 1994; songwriter (albums) Make Me a Blassing, 1992, Grandkid's Praise, 1993, Grandma Jane's Unity Rap, 1993, A Word of Encouragement From Make Me A Blessing, Music from the Psalms, Vol. 1, 1995, vols. 2 and 3, 1996; completion of 5-yr. investigation of Benny Hinn; choir accompanist New Hope Presbyn. Ch., 1995, 96; recommenced ministry to Care Homes, 1996. Choir accompanist, alt. pianist New Hope Presbyn. Ch., Eustis, Fla., 1995—. Republican. Home and Office: 4162 Greenbluff Ct Zellwood FL 32798-9005

WALLEN, LINA HAMBALI, educator, consultant; b. Garut, West Java, Indonesia, Mar. 24, 1952; came to U.S., 1986; d. Mulyadi and Indra (Hudiyana) Hambali; m. Norman E. Wallen, Apr. 16, 1986. BA, IKIP, Bandung, Indonesia, 1975, DRA, 1984; PhD in Psychology, Columbia Pacific U., San Rafael, Calif., 1990; MA in Economics, San Francisco State U., 1993. Cert. tchr. Clk. PT Radio Frequency Communication, Bandung, 1972-74; adminstrv. mgr. CV Electronics Engring., Jakarta, Indonesia, 1974-76; exec. sec. PT Tanabe Abadi, Bandung, 1977-81; br. mgr. PT Ama Forta, Bandung, 1982-84; tchr. SMA Pembangunan, Bandung, 1976-83, Patuha Coll., Bandung, 1980-84.

WALLEN, MARTHA LOUISE, foreign language educator; b. Mpls., Aug. 13, 1946; d. Clarence Melvin and Myrthel Evangeline (Nelson) W. BA summa cum laude, St. Olaf Coll., 1968; MA, U. Wis., 1969, PhD, 1972; MA, Middlebury Coll., 1976. From asst. prof. to prof. fgn. lang., fgn. lang. coordinator U. Wis.-Stout, Menomonie, 1972—. Contbr. articles to profl. jours.; asst. editor: Annals of Tourism Research, 1976—. Faculty grantee U. Wis., 1984-85, 90-95. Mem. Internat. Arthurian Soc., Am. Assn. Tchrs. French, Phi Beta Kappa. Lutheran. Office: U Wis-Stout Dept of Fgn Lang Menomonie WI 54751

WALLENBORN, JANICE RAE, retired elementary education educator; b. Chgo., Jan. 22, 1938; d. Ramon Joseph and Anne Joan (Seaquist) W. BEd, Beloit Coll., 1960; MEd, The George Washington U., 1966; postgrad., George Mason U., 1987-88, U. Va., 1965-85; Degree in Theol. Edn., U. of South, 1989. Cert. tchr. Va. Tchr. Quantico (Va.) Marine Base, 1960-62; elem. tchr. Pearl Harbor Elem. Sch., Honolulu, 1962-64; elem. tchr. Quantico Dependents Sch. System, 1964-95, ret., 1995. Counselor Diet Ctr., Springfield, Va., 1979-89. Mem. NEA (life), Quantico Edn. Assn. (treas. 1968-72), Va. Edn. Assn., Pi Lambda Theta (life), Kappa Alpha Theta (treas. 1979-81, pres. North Va. chpt. 1981-85, alumni dist. pres. 1989-95). Republican. Episcopalian. Home: 8576 Gwynedd Way Springfield VA 22153-3422 also: PO Box 427 Cobbs Creek VA 23035

WALLER, MITZI DUNCAN, special education educator; b. Nathalie, Va., Dec. 22, 1955; d. Richard Edward Sr. and Barbara Gayle (Brown) Duncan; m. Ronnie Lee Waller, Mar. 3, 1979; children: Blair Marie, Blake Edward. BS in Therapeutic Recreation, Longwood Coll., 1979, MS in Edn., 1994. Edn. students with learning disabilities Halifax (Va.) County/South Boston City Pub. Schs., 1991—; chmn. sch. renewal com. Volens Elem., Nathalie, Va., 1994—. Sunday sch. pianist Mulberry Bapt. Ch., Nathalie, 1980-94, Sunday sch. tchr., 1980-95; pres. North Halifax Ladies' Aux., Nathalie, 1982-84; parent Lucky Leaf 4-H Club, Nathalie, 1990—. Mem. NEA, Va. Edn. Assn. Baptist. Home: 3098 Golden Leaf Rd Nathalie VA 24577 Office: Volens Elem Sch Rt 3 Box 157 Nathalie VA 24577

WALLER, PATRICIA FOSSUM, transportation executive, researcher, psychologist; b. Winnipeg, Man., Can., Oct. 12, 1932; d. Magnus Samuel and Diana Isabel (Briggs) Fossum; m. Marcus Bishop Waller, Feb. 27, 1957; children: Anna Estelle, Justin Magnus, Martha Wilkinson, Benjamin Earl. AB in Psychology cum laude, U. Miami, Coral Gables, 1953, MS in Psychology, 1955; PhD in Psychology, U. N.C., 1959. Lic. psychologist, N.C. Psychology intern VA Hosp., Salem, Va., 1956; psychology instr. Med. Sch. U. N.C., Chapel Hill, 1957; USPHS postdoctoral fellow R.B. Jackson Lab., Bar Harbor, Maine, 1958-60; psychologist VA Hosp., Brockton, Mass., 1961-62; psychology lectr. U. N.C., Chapel Hill, Greensboro, 1962-67; assoc. dir. driver studies Hwy. Safety Rsch. Ctr. U. N.C., Chapel Hill, 1967-89, dir. Injury Prevention Rsch. Ctr., 1987-89; dir. Transp. Rsch. Inst. U. Mich., Ann Arbor, 1989—; bd. dirs. Intelligent Transp. Soc. Am., Washington, 1991—, Traffic Safety Assn. Mich., Lansing, 1991—; bd. advisors Eno Transp. Found., Inc., Landsdowne, Va., 1994—; chair group 5 coun. Transp. Rsch. Bd. of NRC, Washington, 1992-95, chmn. Task Force Operator Regulations, 1974-76, mem. study com. devel. ranking rail safety R&D projects, 1980-82, chmn. group 3 coun. operation, safety and maintenance transp. facilities, 1980-83, mem. IVHS-IDEA tech. rev. panel, 1993—, chair workshop human factors rsch. in hwy. safety, 1992, chair ad hoc com. environ. activies, 1992, mem. task force on elderly drivers, 1990-93, mem. com. vehicle user characteristics, 1983-86, mem. com. planning and adminstrn. of transp. safety, 1986-92, mem. com. alcohol, other drugs and transp., 1986—, numerous other coms., mem. spl. coms. including Inst. Medicine Dana Award com., 1986-90, com. of 55MPH nat. maximum speed limit, 1983-84; mem. motor vehicle safety rsch. adv. com. Dept. Transp., Washington, 1991—; reviewer JAMA, Jour. Studies on Alcohol, Jour. of Gerontology, Am. Jour. Pub. Health; apptd. Pres. Coun. Spinal Cord Injury, 1981; apptd. advisor Nat. Hwy. Safety Adv. Com. to Sec. U.S. Dept. Transp., 1979-80, 80-83; author numerous reports on transp. to govtl. coms. and univs. Author: (with Paul G. Shinkman) Instructor's Manual for Mogan and King: Introduction to Psychology, 1971; author: (with others) Psychological Concepts in the Classroom, 1974, Drinking: Alcohol in American Society—Issues and Current Research, 1978, The American Handbook of Alcoholism, 1982, The Role of the Civil Engineer in Highway Safety, 1983, Aging and Public Health, 1985, Young Driver Accidents: In Search of Solutions, 1985, Alcohol, Accidents and Injuries, 1986, Transportation in an Aging Society: Improving the Mobility and Safety for Older Persons, 1988, Young Drivers Impaired by Alcohol and Drugs, 1988; mem. editorial bd. Jour. Safety Rsch., 1979—; assoc. guest editor Health Edn. Quar., 1989; assoc. editor Accident, Analysis, and Prevention, 1978-84, mem. editorial bd., 1976-87; contbr. articles to profl. jours. Grantee HHS, 1982, 92, 93, NIH; named Widmark laureate Internat. Coun. Alcohol, Drugs and Traffic Safety, 1995. Mem. AAAS, APA (Harold M. Hildreth award 1993), APHA (injury control and emergency health svcs. sect., Disting. Career award 1994, transp. rsch. bd., Roy W. Crum award for rsch. contbns. 1995), Assn. for the Advancement of Automotive Medicine (chmn. human factors sect. 1978-80, bd. dirs. 1979-82, pres. 1981-82), Coun. Univ. Transp. Ctrs. (exec. com. 1991—), Transp. Rsch. Bd., Ea. Psychol. Assn., Sigma Xi. Democrat. Office: U Mich Transp Rsch Inst 2901 Baxter Rd Ann Arbor MI 48109-2150

WALLER, WILMA RUTH, retired secondary school educator and librarian; b. Jacksonville, Tex., Nov. 15, 1921; d. William Wesley and Myrtle (Nesbitt) W. BA with honors, Tex. Woman's U., 1954, MA with honors, 1963, MLS with honors, 1976. Tchr. English Dell (Ark.) High Sch., 1953-54, Jefferson (Tex.) Ind. Schs., 1954-56, Tyler (Tex.) Ind. Schs., 1956-68; librarian Wise County Schs., Decatur, Tex., 1969-71, Thomas K. Gorman High Sch., Tyler, 1971-74, Sweetwater (Tex.) Ind. Sch. Dist., 1974-86; ret.; lectr., book reviewer for various clubs. Active in past as vol. for ARC, U. Tex. Health Ctr. Ford Found. fellow, 1959; recipient Delta Kappa Gamma Achievement award, 1992. Mem. AAUW (past chmn. book, critique, drama and contemporary interests groups), UDC, Smith County Ret. Sch. Pers., Bible Study Group, Delta Kappa Gamma. Republican. Baptist. Home: 1117 N Azalea Dr Tyler TX 75701-5206

WALLING, DEBRA ANN, recreational therapist; b. Red Bank, N.J., Jan. 22, 1965; d. Charles James and Patricia Ann (Keane) W. BA, Slippery Rock U., 1988; postgrad., Georgian Ct. Coll. Recreational therapist Bayshore Health Care Ctr., Holmdel, N.J., 1988, 89-90, 1994—; pharmacy/I.V. tech. Bayshore Cmty. Hosp., Holmdel, 1988-89; co-mgr. Lane Bryant, Limited Inc., Ocean, N.J., 1990-92, store sales mgr., 1992-94; mem. activities com. Bayshore Cmty. Health Svcs. Inc., 1995—. Mem. social ministry com. King of Kings Luth. Ch., Middletown, N.J., 1994—, fellowship com., 1994—. Home: 146 Main St Port Monmouth NJ 07758

WALLINGFORD, ANNE, writer, project developer; b. Chgo., June 29, 1949; d. Lester Arlyn and Roseanne (Jones) W. BS in Edn., Chgo. State U., 1975. Cert. elem. and mid. sch. tchr., Ill. Profl. dressmaker Annie's Original's, Chgo., 1968-72; instr., asst. prin., St. Bonaventure Sch., Chgo., 1972-81; instr., chairperson sci. dept. Our Lady of Lourdes Sch., Chgo., 1981-88; product designer, catalog mgr. FSC Ednl., Inc., Mansfield, Ohio, 1988-91; founder, dir. The Wordsmiths, Chgo., 1992—. Contbr. bus. profiles to profl. publs., 1990—. Active The Vol. Ctr., Mansfield, 1992-93, steering com. Wright Community Ctr., 1991; treas. Wolfram St. Block Club, Chgo., 1975-78. Recipient Gold award Adler Planetarium, Chgo., 1985. Mem.

Nat. Writers's Union, Chgo., Women in Pub. (Individual Excellence in Prodn., 1994, 95), Soc. Tech. Communicators, Profl. Freelance Assn. (founder, pres., 1991-92), Mensa. Office: 6155 N Moody Ave Chicago IL 60646-3806

WALLINGTON, PATRICIA MCDEVITT, computer company executive; b. Phila., July 29, 1940; d. James J. and Mary (Eschbach) McDevitt; m. William R. Wallington; 1 child, Colleen Xydis. BBA, U. Pa., 1975; MBA, Drexel U., 1978; postgrad. mgmt. devel., Harvard U., 1981. Project mgr. Fidelity Mut., Phila., 1965-72, Penn Mut. Ins. Co., Phila., 1972-77; mgr. info. systems Sun Info. Svcs., Phila., 1977-81; dir. info. systems Sun Exploration & Prodn. Co., Dallas, 1981-87; sr. v.p., chief info. officer Mass. Mut. Life Ins. Co., Springfield, 1987-89; corp. v.p., chief info. officer Xerox Corp., Rochester, N.Y., 1989—; mem. MBA adv. bd. Baylor U., Waco, Tex., 1986-88; bd. dirs. FINA, Inc., Middlesex Mut. P&C Co. Mem. adv. bd. Handicap Ctr.-HUP, Phila., 1978-80; v.p. fin. Girls Club Dallas, 1986-87. Mem. Soc. for Info. Mgmt. (treas. Dallas 1987, v.p. fin. 1990-91, pres.-elect 1991—). Office: Xerox Corp 800 Long Ridge Rd Stamford CT 06904

WALLISON, FRIEDA K., lawyer; b. N.Y.C., Jan. 15, 1943; d. Ruvin H. and Edith (Landes) Koslow; m. Peter J. Wallison, Nov. 24, 1966; children: Ethan S., Jeremy L., Rebecca K. AB, Smith Coll., 1963; LLB, Harvard U., 1966. Bar: N.Y. 1967, DC 1982. Assoc. Carter, Ledyard & Milburn, N.Y.C., 1966-75; spl. counsel, div. market regulation Securities & Exchange Commn., Washington, 1975; exec. dir., gen. counsel Mcpl. Securities Rulemaking Bd., Washington, 1975-78; ptnr. Rogers & Wells, N.Y.C. and Washington, 1978-83; ptnr. Jones, Day, Reavis & Pogue, N.Y.C., and Washington, 1983—; mem. Govtl. Acctg. Standards Adv. Council, Washington, 1984-90, Nat. Council on Pub. Works Improvement, Washington, 1985-88; mem. environ. fin. adv. bd. EPA. Fellow Am. Bar Found.; mem. Nat. Assn. Bond Lawyers, N.Y.C. Bar Assn. Contbr. articles to profl. jours. Office: Jones Day Reavis & Pogue 1450 G St NW Ste 600 Washington DC 20005-2088

WALLNER, AMANDA OBER, music educator; b. Corning, N.Y., Nov. 16, 1942; d. William Bertrand Ober and Louise (Higbie) Ober Jughulian; m. William Edward Wallner, June 27, 1964; children: Abbie, Christine. BS, Ithaca Coll., 1964; postgrad., Conn. Coll., 1988-89, U. Freiburg, Germany, 1972. Cert. tchr. Music educator Guilford (Conn.) Pub. Schs., 1978—; founder, dir. Checkerberry Theater Prodns., Guilford, Conn., 1981, 82,. Founder, pres. E. Lansing (Mich.) Com. for Children's TV, 1973-76, founder Citizen's United for Better Broadcasting, E. Lansing, 1973; vol. Dem. campaigns, Guilford, Conn., 1990-95, Put Guilford (Conn.) First, 1993-94; mem. adv. com. WGRS, WMNR Fie Arts Radio, 1996—. Recipient Resolution of Tribute, Diana award, citation LVW, 1996; Senate Concurrent Resolution, East Lansing, 1975, Gen. Assembly Official Citation, the Conn. House, 1995, Celebration of Excellence, Conn. State Bd. of Edn., Hartford, 1995, Katherine Dunham award, Conn. Edn. Assn., Human and Civil Rights Com., Hartford, 1995, selected Internat. Festival Arts & Ideas Youth Summit, New Haven, 1996; Hilda Maehling grant Nat. Found. Improvement of Edn., 1995. Mem. AAUW, Guilford Edn. Assn. (rep. 1992), Feminist Majority, Common Cause, Emily's List. Democrat. Methodist. Office: EC Adams Mid Sch 233 Church St Guilford CT 06437

WALLNER, MARY JANE, state legislator, director child care organization; b. St. Louis, Oct. 25, 1946; d. Arthur M. and Frances (Fulkerson) Bills; m. Nicholas Anthony Wallner, Mar. 10, 1967; children: Jenny, Jessy. BS in Child and Family, U. N.H., 1971; postgrad, Wheelock Coll., 1974-76. Child care worker Newmarket (N.H.) Day Care, 1967-69, dir., 1971-72; tchr. Exeter (N.J.) Head Start, 1969-70; dir. Merrimack Valley Day Care, Concord, N.H., 1973—; mem. N.H. Ho. of Reps., Concord, 1980—. VISTA vol. Jane Adams Hull House, Chgo., 1966; bd. dirs. N.H. Womens Lobby, Concord, 1991—, Meritorious Svc. award, 1988; bd. dirs. N.H. Task Force for the Prevention Child Abuse, Concord, 1985-91; trustee Trust Fund for the Prevention Child Abuse, Concord, 1987-91. Recipient Friend of Children award N.H. Group Home Assn., 1988, Commitment to Young Children award N.H. Assn. for the Edn. Young Children, 1989, Voice for Children award Child and Family Svcs., 1990. Mem. Zonta (sec. 1980—). Democrat. Office: Merrimack Valley Day Care Svcs 19 N Fruit St Concord NH 03301-2905 also: NH Ho of Reps State House Concord NH 03301*

WALLS, DEANNA KAY, special education educator; b. Dallas, June 23, 1966; d. Frank Austin and Glenda Mae (Bannister) Bumpus; m. William H. Walls Jr., July 31, 1993. BA, St. Mary's U., San Antonio, 1988; postgrad., S.W. Tex. State U., San Marcos, 1995. Cert. tchr. grades 1-8, cert. spl. edn. tchr. grades pre-kindergarten-12, Tex.; cert. ednl. diagnostician. Resource tchr. Harlandale Ind. Sch. Dist., San Antonio, 1989-90, self-contained tchr., 1990-92; tchr. of emotionally disturbed Schertz, Cibolo, Universal City (Tex.) Ind. Sch. Dist., 1992-95, Judson Ind. Sch. Dist., 1995—; mem. inclusion com. Schertz, , 1993-95, after sch. tutoring program, 1995-96. Mem. Assn. Tex. Profl. Educators, Am. Diabetes Assn. Office: Judson Ind Sch Dist Converse Elem 102 School St Converse TX 78109

WALLS, MARTHA ANN WILLIAMS (MRS. B. CARMAGE WALLS), newspaper executive; b. Gadsden, Ala., Apr. 21, 1927; d. Aubrey Joseph and Inez (Cooper) Williams; m. B. Carmage Walls, Jan. 2, 1954; children: Byrd Cooper, Lissa Walls Vahldiek. Student pub. schs., Gadsden. Pres., dir. Walls Newspapers, Inc., 1969-70; sec., treas., dir. Summer Camps, Inc., Guntersville, Ala., 1954-69; CEO, pres., dir. So. Newspapers, Inc., Houston, 1970—; v.p., dir. Scottsboro (Ala.) Newspapers, Angleton (Tex.) Times, Ft. Payne (Ala.) Newspapers, Inc.; sec.-treas., dir. Portales (N.M.) News Tribune Publ. Co., Quay County Sun Newspaper, Inc., Tucumcari, N.M.; v.p., dir. Bay City (Tex.) Newspapers, Inc.; bd. dirs. Liberal (Kans.) Newspapers, Inc., Monroe (Ga.) Newspapers, Inc., Moore Newspapers, Inc., Dumas, Tex., Jefferson Pilot Corp., Greensboro, N.C., Jefferson-Pilot Life Ins. Co., Jefferson Pilot Communications. Bd. dirs. Montgomery Acad., 1970-74. Mem. Soc. Profl. Journalists, The Houstonian. Episcopalian. Office: So Newspapers Inc 1050 Wilcrest Dr Houston TX 77042-1608

WALRATH, PATRICIA A., state legislator; b. Brainerd, Minn., Aug. 11, 1941; d. Joseph James and Pansy Patricia (Drake) McCarvill; m. Robert Eugene Walrath, Sept. 1, 1961; children: Karen, Susan, David, Julie. BS, Bemidji State U., 1962; MS, SUNY, Oswego, 1975. Cert. secondary math. tchr., N.Y., Mass. Programmer analyst Control Data Corp., Mpls., 1962-65; crewleader dept. commerce U.S. Census, Middlesex County, Mass., 1979-80; selectman Town of Stow, Mass., 1980-85; tchr. math. Hale Jr. High Sch., Stow, 1981-82; instr. math. Johnson & Wale Coll. Hanscom AFB, Bedford, Mass., 1983-84; test examiner Hanscom AFB, Bedford, 1983-84; state rep. 3d Middlesex dist. State of Mass., Boston, 1985—; mem. House Ways and Means com., 1987-92, 96—, joint coms. on local affairs, 1993-95, pub. svc., 1993-96, election law, 1985-86, 95-96, sci. and tech. com., 1995—, commerce and labor, 1996—, govt. rels., 1996—. Chmn. Mass. Indoor Air Pollution Commn., Boston, 1987-88; mem. Stow Dem. Com., 1988—; merit badge counselor Boy Scouts Am., Stow and Hudson, Mass., 1990—; bd. dirs. Hudson Arts Alliance, 1991—. Recipient Disting. Svc. award Auburn N.Y. Jaycees, 1976. Mem. LWV (pres. 1973-76, dir. fin. 1977-78), Am. Legis. Exch. Coun., Mass. Legislators' Assn., Mass. Dem. Leadership Coun. (v.p. 1991-92, co-chmn. 1993-94, treas. 1995-96), Mass. Women's Legis. Caucus (chair 1986). Roman Catholic. Home: 20 Middlemost Way Stow MA 01775-1363 Office: State Capital RM 275 Boston MA 02133

WALSH, DIANA CHAPMAN, academic administrator, social and behavioral sciences educator; b. Phila., July 30, 1944; d. Robert Francis and Gwen (Jenkins) Chapman; m. Christopher Thomas Walsh, June 18, 1966; 1 child, Allison Chapman Walsh. BA, Wellesley Coll., 1966; MS, Boston U. Sch. of Pub. Comm., 1971; PhD, Boston U., 1983; LHD (hon.), Boston U, 1994, Amer. Coll. of Greece, Athens, 1995. Mgr. spl. events Barnard Coll., N.Y.C., 1967-70; dir. info., edn. Planned Parenthood League, Newton, Mass., 1971-74; sr. program assoc. Dept Pub. Health, Boston, 1974-76; assoc. dir. Boston U. Health Policy Inst., 1985-90; prof. Sch. Pub. Health, Sch. Medicine, Boston U., 1987-90, prof., 1988-90, adj. prof. pub. health, 1990—; adj. prof. Harvard Sch. Pub. Health, 1993—; pres. Wellesley Coll., 1993—. Author: (book) Corporate Physicians, 1987; editor: Women, Work, and Health: Challenges to Corporate Policy, 1980, (book series) Industry and Health Care, 1977-80; contbr. articles to profl. jours. Bd. dirs. Planned Parenthood League of Mass., 1974-79, 1981-85, bd. of overseers 1993-94; trustee Occupational Physicians Scholarship Fund, 1987-94; trustee WGBH Educational Found., 1993—. Kellogg Nat. fellow, 1987-90. Mem. AAAS. Office: Wellesley Coll Office of the Pres Wellesley MA 02181

WALSH, DIANE, pianist; b. Washington, Aug. 16, 1950; d. William Donald and Estelle Louise (Stokes) W.; m. Henry Forbes, 1969 (div. 1979); m. Richard Pollak, 1982. MusB, Juilliard Sch. Music, 1971, MusM, Mannes Coll., 1982. Vis. assoc. prof. Hunter Coll. CCNY, 1991-92, Vassar College, 1992-93. N.Y.C. debut Young Concert Artists Series, 1974; founding mem. Mannes Trio, 1983-94; solo appearances include: Kennedy Ctr. for Performing Arts, Washington, 1976, Met. Mus., N.Y.C., 1976, Wigmore Hall, London, 1980, Merkin Concert Hall, 1989, Miller Theatre, 1994; with Mannes Trio: Lincoln Ctr.'s Alice Tully Hall, Library of Congress, 1987; appeared with maj. orchs. worldwide, including St. Louis Symphony, Indpls. Symphony, San Francisco Symphony, Bavarian Radio Symphony of Munich, Berlin Radio Symphony, Radio Symphony Frankfurt, Radio Symphony Stuttgart; has toured Europe, N.Am., S.Am., C.Am., former Soviet Union, Marlboro Festival, 1982, Bard Festival, 1990-95; recs. for Nonesuch Records, 1980, 82, Book-of-Month Records, 1985, Music and Arts, 1990, CRI, 1991, Koch, 1995, Biddulph Records, 1996; mem. piano and chamber music faculty Mannes Coll. Music, 1982-96. Recipient 3d prize Busoni Internat. Piano Competition, Italy, 1974, 2d prize Mozart Internat. Piano Competition, Salzburg, Austria, 1975, 1st prize Munich Internat. Piano Competition, 1975, Naumburg Chamber Music award, 1986; NEA grantee, 1981.

WALSH, EDWINA ESTELLE, computer educator; b. Yonkers, N.Y., June 3, 1935; d. Francis Paul and Estelle Casimira (Piekarski) W.; m. Kenneth Forrest Gatton, Dec. 10, 1934. BS in Edn., Fordham U., Bronx, N.Y., 1957; MA in English, Coll. St. Rose, Albany, N.Y., 1967. Cert. elem., secondary English teaching credential, Calif., N.Y. Elem. tchr. N.Y. Archdiocese, Yonkers, 1957-61; tchr. English Maria Regina H.S., Hartsdale, N.Y., 1962-66, Averill Park (N.Y.) H.S., 1967; tchr. elem. spl. edn. Obrien Sch., Albany, 1968; tchr. secondary English Dover Plains (N.Y.) Jr. H.S., 1969; tchr. spl. edn. Walker Jr. H.S., La Palma, Calif., 1970-87, tchr. computers, 1987-92; mentortchr. Anaheim Union H.S. Dist., 1986-87, chairperson com. for site based mgmt., 1991-92. Author: Schoolmarms Women in Americas Schools, 1995. Chairperson com. on sexism in textbooks Orange County NOW, 1972, pres., 1972. Mem. AAUW, Calif. Tchrs. Assn. (exec. dir. Anaheim chpt. 1991-92), Nat. Edn. Retired Tchrs., Writers Group Albany. Home: 344 Madison Ave Albany NY 12210-1712

WALSH, JEANNE See SINGER, JEANNE

WALSH, JOANNE ELIZABETH, educator, librarian; b. Chgo., Nov. 25, 1942; d. Joseph Frank and Elizabeth Margaret (Gretz) Fiali; m. John Kerwin Walsh, July 17, 1976; 1 child, Kevin Joseph. BA in English, Mundelein Coll., Chgo., 1965; MEd Ednl. Adminstrn. and Supervision, Loyola U., Chgo., 1969. Tchr. Chgo. Pub. Schs., 1965-83, prin., 1983-89; tchr. libr. Burbank (Ill.) Dist III, 1990-93; tchr. art Tate Sch. of Discovery, Knoxville, Tenn., 1994-95. Vol. Palos Community Hosp., Palos Park, Ill., 1990, Palos Heights Libr., 1993; Rainbow facilitator, 1992, 93; mem. St. John Neumann Cath. Ch. Recipent Tchr. of Yr. award McCord Sch., 1992-93. Mem. Chgo. Prins. Club, Aquin Guild, Knoxville Welcome Wagon Club, Knoxville Newcomers Club. Home: 12301 Butternut Cir Knoxville TN 37922-4682

WALSH, JULIA SANCHEZ, fashion designer; b. N.Y.C., June 9, 1967; d. James Kevin and Beatrice (Sanchez) W. BFA, Fashion Inst. Tech., 1989. Asst. designer Liz Claiborne, Inc., N.Y.C., 1987-90; assoc. designer Ellesse USA, N.Y.C., 1990-92; designer Club DeFrance, N.Y.C., 1992-93; free-lance designer pvt. practice, N.Y.C., 1993-94; designer Alfred Dunner, N.Y.C., 1994-96, Item-Eyes, N.Y.C., 1996—. Nominated Dallas Fashion award, 1993. Democrat. Roman Catholic.

WALSH, KATHLEEN, lawyer; b. Madison, Wis., Apr. 16, 1951; d. William Patrick and Joan Iris (Staedtler) W.; m. Stephen Michael Glynn, Mar. 17, 1981; stepchildren: Stephen Michael Jr., Theron Benson. BS, U. Wis., La Crosse, 1973; JD, U. Wis., Madison, 1984. Bar: Wis. 1984, U.S. Dist. Ct. (ea. and we. dists.) Wis. 1984. Investigator Office State Pub. Defender, Milw., 1977-80, adminstrv. asst., 1980-81; asst. city atty. City of Milw., 1984-85; project atty. Legal Aid Soc. Milw., Inc., 1985-92, 95—; adj. prof. Marquette U. Law Sch., Milw., 1986-92; bd. dirs. Ctr. for Pub. Representation, Madison, 1986-90; mem. faculty Supreme Ct. Wis., 1987-93, Milw. Young Lawyers Assn., 1985-92. Contbr. chpt. to book, articles to profl. publs. Coord., dir. Milw. Clinic Protection Coalition, 1992-95. Named Civil Libertarian of Yr., Wis. Civil Liberties Union, 1993. Mem. ACLU, NARAL, State Bar Wis. (bd. dirs. Individual rights and responsibilities sect. 1986—), Milw. Young Lawyers Assn. (Pro Bono Tng. Seminars), Milw. Bar Assn. (faculty 1985-92, Def. Lawyer of Yr. award 1991), NOW, Planned Parenthood Wiss. (Voice for Choice award 1993), Wis. Coalition Against Death Penalty, Nature Conservancy, World Wildlife Fund. Democrat. Home: 929 N Astor St Milwaukee WI 53202 Office: Legal Aid Soc Milw Inc 229 E Wisconsin Ave Milwaukee WI 53202

WALSH, MARIE LECLERC, nurse; b. Providence, Sept. 11, 1928; d. Walter Normand and Anna Mary (Ryan) Leclerc; m. John Breffni Walsh, June 18, 1955; children: George Breffni, John Leclerc, Darina Louise. Grad., Waterbury Hosp. Sch. Nursing, Conn., 1951; BS, Columbia U., 1954, MA, 1955. Team leader Hartford (Conn.) Hosp., 1951-53; pvt. duty nurse St. Luke's Hosp., N.Y.C., 1953-57; sch. nurse tchr. Agnes Russel Ctr., Tchrs. Coll. Columbia U., N.Y.C., 1955-56; clin. nursing instr. St. Luke's Hosp., N.Y.C., 1957-58; chmn. disaster nursing ARC Fairfax County, Va., 1975; course coord. occupational health nursing U. Va. Sch. Continuing Edn., Falls Church, 1975-77; mem. disaster steering com. No. Va. C.C., Annandale, 1976; adj. faculty U. Va. Sch. Continuing Edn., Falls Church, 1981; disaster svcs. nurse ARC, Wichita, Kans., 1985-90; disaster svcs. nurse Seattle-King County chpt. ARC, Seattle, 1990-96; rsch. and statis. analyst U. Va. Sch. Continuing Edn. Nursing, Falls Church, 1975; rsch. libr. Olive Garvey Ctr. for Improvement Human Functioning, Inc., Wichita, 1985. Sec. Dem. party, Cresskill, N.J., 1964-66; county committeewoman, Bergen County, N.J., 1965-66; pres., v.p., Internat. Staff Wives, NATO, Brussels, Belgium, 1978-80; election officer, supr. Election Bd., Wichita, 1987, 88. Mem. AAAS, AAUW, N.Y. Acad. Sci., Pi Lambda Theta, Sigma Theta Tau. Home: 8800 Prestwould Pl Mc Lean VA 22102

WALSH, MARY D. FLEMING, civic worker; b. Whitewright, Tex., Oct. 29, 1913; d. William Fleming and Anna Maud (Lewis) Fleming; B.A., So. Meth. U., 1934; LL.D. (hon.), Tex. Christian U., 1979; m. F. Howard Walsh, Mar. 13, 1937; children: Richard, Howard, D'Ann Walsh Bonnell, Maudi Walsh Roe, William Lloyd. Pres. Fleming Found.; v.p. Walsh Found.; partner Walsh Co.; charter mem. Lloyd Shaw Found., Colorado Springs; mem. Big Bros. Tarrant County; guarantor Fort Worth Arts Council, Scholar Cantorum, Fort Worth Opera, Fort Worth Ballet, Fort Worth Theater, Tex. Boys Choir; hon. mem. bd. dirs. Van Cliburn Internat. Piano Competition; co-founder Am. Field Service in Ft. Worth; mem. Tex. Commn. for Arts and Humanities, 1968-72, mem. adv. council, 1972-84; bd. dirs. Wm. Edrington Scott Theatre, 1977-83, Colorado Springs Day Nursery, Colorado Springs Symphony, Ft. Worth Symphony, 1974-81; hon. chmn. Opera Ball, 1975, Opera Guild Internat. Conf., 1976; co-presenter (with husband) through Walsh Found., Tex. Boys Choir and Dorothy Shaw Bell Choir ann. presentation of The Littlest Wiseman to City of Ft. Worth; granted with husband land and bldgs. to Tex. Boys Choir for permanent home, 1971, Walsh-Wurlitzer organ to Casa Manana, 1972. Sem. Recipient numerous awards, including Altrusa Civic award as 1st Lady of Ft. Worth, 1968; (with husband) Disting. Service award So. Bapt. Radio and Television Commn., 1972; Opera award Girl Scouts, 1977-79; award Streams and Valleys, 1976-80; named (with husband) Patron of Arts in Ft. Worth, 1970, 91, Edna Gladney Internat. Grandparents of 1972, (with husband) Sr. Citizens of Yr, 1985; Mary D. and Howard Walsh Meml. Organ dedicated by Bapt. Radio and TV Commn., 1967, tng. ctr. named for the Walshes, 1976; Mary D. and Howard Walsh Med. Bldg., Southwestern Bapt. Theol. Sem.; library at Tarrant County Jr. Coll. N.W. Campus dedicated to her and husband, 1978; Brotherhood citation Tarrant County chpt. NCCJ, 1978; Spl. Recognition award Ft. Worth Ballet Assn.; Royal Purple award Tex. Christian U., 1979; Friends of Tex. Boys Choir award, 1981; appreciation award Southwestern Bapt. Theol. Sem., 1981, B. H. Carroll Founders award, 1982, (with husband) Patrons of the Arts award, 1991; Outstanding Women of Fort Worth award City of Fort Worth, 1994, numerous other award for civic activities. Mem. Ft. Worth Boys Club, Ft. Worth Children's Hosp., Jewel Charity Ball, Ft. Worth Pan Hellenic (pres. 1940), Opera Guild, Fine Arts Found. Guild of Tex. Christian U., Girl's Service League (hon. life, hon. chmn. Fine Arts Guild Spring Ballet, 1985), AAUW, Goodwill Industries Aux., Child Study Center, Tarrant County Aux. of Edna Gladney Home, YWCA (life), Ft. Worth Art Assn., Ft. Worth Ballet Assn., Tex. Boys Choir Aux., Friends of Tex. Boys Choir, Round Table, Colorado Springs Fine Art Center, Am. Automobile Assn., Nat. Assn. Cowbelles, Ft. Worth Arts Council (hon. bd. mem.), Am. Guild Organists (hon., Ft. Worth chpt.), Rae Reimers Bible Study Class (pres. 1968), Tex. League Composers (hon. life), Children's Hosp. Woman's Bd. (hon. 1991), Chi Omega (pres. 1935-36, hon. chmn. 1986), others. Baptist. Clubs: The Woman's (Club Fidelite), Colorado Springs Country, Garden of Gods, Colonial Country, Ridglea Country, Shady Oaks Country, Chi Omega Mothers, Chi Omega Carousel, TCU Woman's. Home: 2425 Stadium Dr Fort Worth TX 76109-1055 also: 1801 Culebra Ave Colorado Springs CO 80907-7328

WALSH, PAMELA K., accountant; b. Cin., Mar. 24, 1963; d. Bruce George and Paula Louise (Buerkle) Kelley; m. John Timothy Walsh, Aug. 30, 1986; children: Bryan Kelley Walsh, (triplets) Austin Kelley Walsh, Conner Kelley Walsh, Sean Kelley Walsh. BA in Bus. Adminstrn., Coll. Mount St. Joseph, Cin., 1985. CPA, CMA. Acct. Gibson Greeting Cards, Cin., 1985-87, sr. acct., 1987-89, acctg. supervisor, 1989-90; acct. Procter & Gamble, Cin., 1990-95, sr. acct., 1995—; acct. recruiter Procter & Gamble, Cin., 1990—. 6th gr. facilitator Jr. Achievement, Cin., 1994, 95; vol. job fair Coll. Mount St. Joseph, Cin., 1995, vol. profl. panel, 1995. Mem. AICPA. Ohio Soc. CPAs, Inst. Mgmt. Accts. Office: Procter & Gamble 11310 Cornell Park Dr Cincinnati OH 45242

WALSH, SANDRA M., nursing educator, researcher; b. Winston-Salem, N.C., Mar. 18, 1938; d. Jesse Theron and Florence Frost (Alley) W.; m. W.M. Taylor Jr., Aug. 23, 1958 (div. Oct. 1979); children: William David Taylor, Carolyn Taylor Hale, Michael Walsh Taylor. BSN, Duke U., 1960; MA in Edn., Wake Forest U., 1973; MSN, East Carolina U., 1984; PhD, U. S.C., 1991. RN, N.C. Staff nurse Duke Hosp., Durham, N.C., 1960; instr. Forsyth Meml. Hosp., Winston-Salem, 1965-66, N.C. Bapt. Hosp. Sch. Nursing, Winston-Salem, 1968-72; asst. prof. U. N.C.-Greensboro Sch. Nursing, 1973-82; clin. coord., asst. prof. East Carolina U. Sch. Nursing, Greenville, N.C., 1984-88, from asst. prof. to assoc. prof., 1991-95; mem. faculty U. Miami Sch. Nursing, 1995—; bd. dirs. Greenville Mental Health Assn., 1984-88, N.C. Mental Health Assn., 1986-88. Author workbook; contbr. articles to profl. jours. Recipient several grants. Mem. N.C. Nurses Assn., Sigma Theta Tau. Democrat. Home: 540 Brickell Key Dr # 1723 Miami FL 33131 Office: U Miami Sch Nursing 5801 Red Rd Miami FL 33143

WALSH, SUSAN SIVITZ, municipal administrator; b. Cin., Sept. 8, 1956; d. Moses and Blessing (Schmidt) Sivitz; m. Gregory Edward Walsh, Apr. 28, 1979; 1 child, Carissa. BS, U. Cin., 1979. Income maintenance worker Hamilton County Welfare Dept., Cin., 1979-81; from housing specialist to dep. dir. Hamilton County Dept. Cmty. Devel., 1984—. Chair welcome com. Anderson H.S. PTA, Cin., 1994—. Mem. Ohio Conf. Cmty. Devel. (legis. com. 1993-95, policy com. 1994-95, chair membership com. 1995-96, sec. 1996—). Home: 305 Eight Mile Rd Cincinnati OH 45255 Office: Hamilton County Cmty Devel 138 E Court St Rm 507 Cincinnati OH 45202

WALTER, HELEN JOY, executive director, teacher; b. Bronx, May 22, 1938; d. David and Frieda (Halpern) Presby; m. Wolfgang Walter, Feb. 4, 1962; children: Cheryl, Rochelle, Laurie. BA, Yeshiva U., 1961; MEd, Northeastern U., Boston, 1979. Tchr. Maimonides Day Sch., Brookline, Mass., N.Y.C. Pub. Schs.; counselor Northeastern U.; exec. dir. Brookline C. of C., 1979—. Office: Brookline C of C 1330 Beacon St Brookline MA 02146-3202

WALTER, SHERYL LYNN, lawyer; b. Morris, Ill., July 18, 1956; d. C. Frank and Margaret (Juhl) W. BA in History cum laude, Grinnell (Iowa) Coll., 1978; JD cum laude, U. Minn., 1984. Bar: Minn. 1984, U.S. Dist. Ct. Minn. 1987, U.S. Ct. Appeals (8th cir.) 1987, D.C. 1989, U.S. Dist. Ct. D.C. 1989, U.S. Ct. Appeals (D.C. cir.) 1989. Law clk. to presiding judge 3d Jud. Dist. of Minn., Rochester, 1984-85; law clk. to Chief Judge Donald P. Lay U.S. Ct. Appeals (8th cir.), St. Paul, 1985-87; assoc. Mayer, Brown & Platt, Washington, 1987-89; gen. counsel Nat. Security Archive, Washington, 1989-94, Assn. Records Review Bd., 1994-95, Commn. Protecting and Reducing Govt. Secrecy, 1995—; cons. Amnesty Internat., Washington, 1988-89. Mem. ABA (vice chmn. adminstrv. law sect. govt. info. subcom. 1990—), D.C. Bar Assn. (steering com., adminstrv. law sect. 1990—), Am. Judicature Soc., Am. Soc. Access Profls. (bd. dirs. 1990-95, pres. 1996—), Brit.-Am. Security Info. Coun. (bd. dirs. 1994—), Lawyers Alliance for World Security (bd. dirs. 1994—). Office: SA-44 Rm 225 2201 C St NW Washington DC 20522

WALTER, TINA GRAY, planning and zoning administrator; b. Cambridge, Md., Apr. 3, 1960; d. Harvey Watson Sr. and Rose Ann (Spear) Gray; m. Laurence Joseph Walter Jr., Aug. 20, 1977; children: Melissa Dawn Walter, Laurence Joseph Walter III. Grad. h.s., Cambridge. Bookkeeper, cashier Personal Thrift Plan, Inc., Cambridge, 1978-80; quality control inspector Rob Roy, Inc., Cambridge, 1980-81; sec. Cambridge, Inc., 1981-83; sec. II Dept. Pub. Works, City of Cambridge, 1983-93, planning and zoning adminstr., 1993—; mem. County Sch. Redistricting Comm., Cambridge, 1996; advisor Planning and Zoning Commn., Cambridge, 1993—, Bd. of Zoning Appeals, Cambridge, 1993—, Archtl. Bd. of Rev., Cambridge, 1993—. Mem. Bldg. Ofcls. and Codes Adminstrs. Internat., Code Enforcement and Zoning Ofcls. Assn. Md. Democrat. Pentecostal. Office: City of Cambridge Dept Pub Works 705 Leonard Ln Cambridge MD 21613

WALTERS, BARBARA, television journalist; b. Sept. 25, 1931; d. Lou and Dena (Selett) W.; 1 child, Jacqueline. Grad., Sarah Lawrence Coll., 1953; LHD (hon.), Ohio State U., Marymount Coll., Tarrytown, N.Y., 1975, Wheaton Coll., 1983. Former writer-producer WNBC-TV; then with Stas. WPIX and CBS-TV; joined Today Show, 1961, regular panel mem., 1964-74, co-host, 1974-76; moderator syndicated program Not For Women Only, 1974-76; newscaster ABC Evening News (now ABC World News Tonight), 1976-78; host The Barbara Walters Spls., 1976—; co-host ABC TV news show 20/20, 1979—. Contbr. to ABC programs Issues and Answers. Author: How To Talk With Practically Anybody About Practically Anything, 1970; contbr. to Reader's Digest, Good Housekeeping, Family Weekly. Recipient award of yr. Nat. Assn. TV Program Execs., 1975, Emmy award Nat. Acad. TV Arts and Scis., 1975, Mass Media award Am. Jewish Com. Inst. Human Relations, 1975, Hubert H. Humphrey Freedom prize Anti-Defamation League-B'nai B'rith, 1978, Matrix award N.Y. Women in Communications, 1977, Barbara Walters' Coll. Scholarship in Broadcast Journalism established in her honor Ill. Broadcasters Assn., 1975, Pres.'s award Overseas Press Club, 1988, Lowell Thomas award Marist Coll., 1990, Lifetime Achievement award Internat. Women's Media Found., 1992; named to 100 Women Accomplishment Harper's Bazaar, 1967, 71, One of Am.'s 75 Most Important Women Ladies' Home Jour., 1970, One of 10 Women of Decade Ladies' Home Jour., 1979, One of Am.'s 100 Most Important Women Ladies' Home Jour., 1983, Woman of Year in Communications, 1974, Woman of Year Theta Sigma Phi, Broadcaster of Yr. Internat. Radio and TV Soc., 1975, One of 200 Leaders of Future Time Mag., 1974, One of Most Important Women of 1979 Roper Report, One of Women Most Admired by Am. People Gallup Poll, 1982, 84, to Hall of Fame Acad. TV Arts and Scis., 1990. Office: 20/20 147 Columbus Ave Fl 10 New York NY 10023-5900 also: Barwall Productions The Barbara Walters Specials 825 7th Ave Fl 3 New York NY 10019-6014*

WALTERS, BETTE JEAN, lawyer; b. Norristown, Pa., Sept. 5, 1946. BA, U. Pitts., 1967; JD, Temple U., 1970, LLM in Taxation, 1974. Bar: Pa. 1970, U.S. Dist. Ct. (ea. dist.) Pa. 1971. Law clk., assoc. William R. Cooper, Lansdale, Pa., 1969-72; spl. asst. to pub. defender Montgomery County (Pa.), 1973; pvt. practice North Wales, Pa., 1972-73; assoc. counsel Alco Standard Corp., Valley Forge, Pa., 1973-79, group counsel mfg., 1979-83; v.p., gen. counsel, sec. Alco Industries, Inc., Valley Forge, 1983—, also bd. dirs., 1983—. Mem. corp. sponsors com. Zool. Soc. of Phila. Mem. ABA, DAR, Pa. Bar Assn., Montgomery County Bar Assn., Am. Corp. Counsel Assn.,

Licensing Execs. Soc.. Republican. Office: Alco Industries Inc PO Box 937 Valley Forge PA 19482-0937

WALTERS, DORIS LAVONNE, pastoral counselor, counseling services facility administrator; b. Peachland, N.C., Feb. 24, 1931; d. H. Lloyd and Mary Lou (Helms) W. BA cum laude, Carson-Newman Coll., 1961; MRE, Southwestern Bapt. Theol. Sem., 1963; MA in Pastoral Counseling, Wake Forest U., 1982; DMIn in Pastoral Counseling, Southeastern Bapt. Theol. Sem., 1988. Min. of edn. and youth First Bapt. Ch., Orange, Tex., 1963-66; assoc. prof. Seinan Jo Gakuin Jr. Coll., Japan, 1968-72; dir. Fukuoka (Japan) Friendship House, 1972-88, pastoral counselor, chaplain, 1983-86; Tokyo lifeline referral counselor (in English) Hiroshima-South, Fukuoka, 1983-86; supr. Japanese and Am. staff Fukuoka Friendship House, 1972-86; with chaplaincy Med. Coll. Va., Richmond, 1976; resident chaplain N.C. Bapt. Hosp., Winston-Salem, 1981-82, counselor-in-tng. pastoral care dept., 1986-88; dir. missionary counseling and support svcs. Pastoral Care Found. N.C. Bapt. Hosp., Winston-Salem, 1989-93; dir. Missionary Family Counseling Svcs., Inc., Winston-Salem, 1993—; mem. Japan Bapt. Mission Exec. Com., Tokyo, 1973-76. Author: An Assessment of the Reentry Issues of the Children of Missionaries, 1991; translator: The Story of the Craft Dogs, 1983. J.M. Price scholar Southwestern Bapt. Theol. Sem., 1962; First Bapt. Ch. Blackwell grantee Southeastern Sem., 1986-88. Mem. Assn. for Clin. Pastoral Counselors (assoc.), Am. Assn. Pastoral Counselors (pastoral affiliate). Democrat. Home: 208 Oakwood Sq Winston Salem NC 27103-1914 Office: Missionary Family Counseling Svcs Inc 514 S Stratford Rd Winston Salem NC 27103-1823

WALTERS, JUDITH RICHMOND, neuropharmacologist; b. Concord, N.H., June 20, 1944; d. Samuel Smith and Hazel Albertina (Stewart) Richmond; m. James Wilson Walters, Aug. 23, 1969 (div. 1992); children: James Richmond, Gregory Stewart, Douglas Powers. BA, Mt. Holyoke Coll., 1966; PhD, Yale U., 1972. Postdoctoral fellow dept. psychiatry Yale U. Med. Sch., New Haven, rsch. assoc. dept. pharmacology, asst. prof. dept. psychiatry; unit chief neurophysiol. pharmacology sect. exptl. therapeutics br. Nat. Inst. Neurol. Disease and Stroke, Bethesda, Md., 1976-81, sect. chief physiol. neuropharmacology sect. exptl. therapeutics br.; mem. sci. adv. bd. Hereditary Disease Found., L.A., 1977-80, 82-86, Tourette Syndrome Assn., 1992—; mem. bd. sci. counselors Nat. Inst. on Alcohol Abuse and Alcoholism, 1992-95; mem. Inst. of Medicine Com. to Raise the Profile of Rsch. on Substance Abuse, 1995-96. Sect. editor Neuroscience.net, 1996—; contbr. more than 100 articles on neuropharmacology and neurophysiology to profl. jours. Recipient NIH Dir.'s award, 1994. Mem. Am. Soc. Pharmacology and Exptl. Therapeutics, Soc. for Neurosci. (mem. com. 1995-98). Home: 3615 Littledale Rd Kensington MD 20895-3435 Office: NIH Bldg 10 Rm 5C106 Bethesda MD 20892

WALTERS, KATHLEEN JANE, realtor, emergency telecommunication operator; b. Grand Island, Nebr., Apr. 19, 1947; d. Francis J. and Mary Jane (Thrasher) Albrecht; m. Richard Lee Walters, July 25, 1968; children: Sara Jane, Joshua Lee. BS in Edn., Ea. Mont. Coll., 1969. Lic. realtor Mont. State Bd. Realty Regulation. Aquatics/health club dir. Rocky Mountain Coll., Billings, 1977-93; owner Indsl. Lubricants Co., Billings, Mont., 1993-96; office mgr. Jan Barry Ct. Reporting, Billings, 1993—; realtor Century 21, Billings, 1993—; emergency telecomm. operator City of Billings, 1996—; tutor, Billings, 1992—. Guest columnist: (newspaper) Billings Gazette, 1984. Vice-chairperson Pks., Recreation, Pub. Lands Bd., Billings, 1984—; water safety chairperson ARC, Billings, 1980-88; com. mem. Habitat for Humanity, 1992—; commr. Local Govt. Rev. Com., Billings, 1994-96; membership com. ACLU, Billings, 1993; vestry mem. St. Stephen's Episcopal Ch., Billings, 1984-88; mem. Mont. Women's Lobby, Helena, 1990—. Mem. Mont. Arabian Horse Assn. (sec. 1992-93, editor periodical 1986, Dir.'s award 1990). Democrat. Home: 3104 Radcliff Dr Billings MT 59102 Office: City of Billings Comm Ctr 2305 8th Ave N Billings MT 59101

WALTERS, REBECCA RUSSELL YARBOROUGH, medical technologist; b. Lancaster, S.C., Mar. 9, 1951; d. William Peurifoy and Anna Beth (Cheatham) Yarborough; m. Thomas Edward Walters, Oct. 15, 1983; 1 child, Katherine Rebecca. BA, Winthrop Coll., 1972; postgrad. in med. tech., Bapt. Med. Ctr., Columbia, S.C., 1974; MA, Cen. Mich. U., 1978. Diplomate in Lab. Mgmt. ASCP. Teaching asst. in biology Winthrop Coll., Rock Hill, S.C., 1972-73; microbiology technologist Bapt. Med. Ctr., 1974-76, night shift supr., 1976-77, asst. adminstrv. dir., 1977—, tchr. Sch. Med. Tech., 1974—; article reviewer Med. Lab. Observer; mem. Nat. Cert. Agy. for Med. Lab. Personnel. Hycel, Inc. scholar, 1976, 77. Mem. Am. Soc. for Med. Tech. (scholar 1977), S.C. Soc. Med. Tech. (pres. 1979-80, scholar 1976), Am. Soc. Clin. Pathologists (assoc.), Clin. Lab. Mgmt. Assn., Beta Beta Beta, Alpha Mu Tau (scholar 1977). Republican. Presbyterian. Home: 155 Shawn Rd Chapin SC 29036-9215 Office: Bapt Med Ctr Taylor At Marion Columbia SC 29220

WALTERS, TERESA, musician, music educator; b. Lincoln, Nebr.; d. E.G. and Helen (Fritz) Hietbrink; m. Jeffrey L. Walters. BA in Music, U. Nebr., MA in Music, D. Mus. Arts, Johns Hopkins U. Prof. music, artist-in-residence, head music dept. Coll. St. Elizabeth, Morristown, N.J., 1986—. Rec. includes (inaugural vol. in series) The Abbé Liszt, 1995-96; composer: (cantata) The Kingdom, (cantata) One Man, Mass for Bell Choir; performances at Villa d'Este, Rome, Liszt Soc., Seville (Spain) Universal Exposition, Boston Conservatory, Carnegie Hall, N.Y., Wigmore Hall, London, Moscow Conservatory, Palais des Beaux-Arts, Brussels, Ecole Normale de Musique, Paris, Genva Conservatory, Am. Ch., Paris, YMCA, Jerusalem, (debut) Conservatorio Monteverdi, Italy, Chgo. Cultural Art Ctr. Internat. Grad. fellow, Paris, Kathryn Sisson Phillips Nat. fellow; study grantee Ladd Found., De Wolf Found., Franck Found., Miller Found., Rotary Internat.; recipient Vreeland Award for Music, Internat. Edn. award Rotary Found. Mem. Am. Liszt Soc., ASCAP, Mortar Bd., Sigma Alpha Iota, Alpha Lambda Delta, Phi Beta Kappa. Office: Coll St Elizabeth 2 Convent Rd Morristown NJ 07960

WALTHER, CELESTE ANN, public relations executive, museum professional; b. Indpls., Feb. 8, 1958; d. Howard Loring and Nancy Lou (Barnum) Hauser; m. Kevin Douglas Huddleston, July 31, 1976 (div. Aug. 1981); 1 child, Nathan Gabriel; m. James Kent Walther, May 16, 1992. BA in Bus. Adminstrn. cum laude, Milligan Coll., 1979. Outreach mktg. coord. Cumberland Sci. Mus., Nashville, 1990-91; mktg. dir. Cumberland Mus. Inc., Nashville, 1991-93; dir. mktg. Ft. Lauderdale (Fla.) Hist. Soc., 1993-94; pub. rels./membership coord. Mus. of Discovery and Sci., Ft. Lauderdale, 1994, pub. rels. mgr., 1994—; mktg. chair Inter-Mus. Coun., Nashville, 1992-93. Mem. Women in Comm. (liaison bus. conf. 1993-94, membership chair 1994-95, pres. 1996—), Am. Assn. Mus. (pub. rels. and mktg. com. 1992—), Fla. Assn. Mus. Home: 6880 NW 5 Ct Plantation FL 33317

WALTHER, ZERITA, paralegal; b. N.Y.C., Nov. 22, 1927; d. James Alexander and Sarah Rebecca (Esperance) Potter; m. George P. Walther II; children: Joseph, Leona. BS in Edn., Met. Inst., London, 1973; cert. in labor studies, Cornell U., 1979; paralegal cert., Manhattanville Coll., 1984. Tchr. OEO, L.I. City, N.Y., 1966-69, Washington Bus. Inst., N.Y.C., 1969-70; editorial asst., feature writer N.Y. Times, N.Y.C., 1973-85; corp. legal asst. Kim Taylor Profls., White Plains, N.Y., 1988-92; casting cons., 1962-63; bd. dirs., cons. Rockingchair Press News Svc., Elmsford, N.Y., 1978-93. Soprano Westfair Chamber Singers, Westchester, Fairfield Counties, 1991-94, White Plains Coalition Singers, 1993—, Our Lady of Mt. Carmel Adult Choir, Elmsford, 1989-94, St. Christopher's Adult Choir, Buchanan, 1994—. Sec. Women of Westchester, 1978-80; mem. Westchester Black Women's Polit. Caucus, 1989-91; coord. Elmsford chpt. Women in Self Help, 1982-84; mediator, vol. BBB, White Plains, 1983-85, Westchester Mediation Ctr., Yonkers, N.Y., 1988—; legis. asst. to 12th dist. Westchester County legislator, White Plains, 1984-92; cert. ombudsmon N.Y. State Office for the Aging, 1994—, VITA/TCE, AARP tax aide, Peekskill, 1995—. Lily Endowment Found. and Smithsonian Inst. scholar Sarah Lawrence Coll., summer 1979. Democrat. Roman Catholic.

WALTON, ALICE L., bank executive; b. Newport, Ark., Oct. 7, 1949; d. Sam and Helen (Robson) W. BBA, Trinity U., 1971; D. of Bus. Adminstrn. (hon.), S.W. Bapt. U., 1988. Investment analyst First Commerce Corp., New Orleans, 1972-75; dir., v.p. investments Walton Enterprises, Bentonville, Ark., 1975—; retail & investment broker E.F. Hutton Co., New Orleans, 1975-79; vice chair, investment dir. Walton Bank Group, Bentonville, Ark., 1982-88; pres., chair, CEO Llama Co./Llama Asset Mgmt. Co., Fayetteville, Ark., 1988—; dean's adv. coun. U. Ark. Coll. Bus. Adminstrn., Fayetteville, 1989-90; internat. judge Students in Free Enterprise, Springfield, Mo., 1990; bd. trustees The Asia Soc., N.Y.C., 1991. Chairperson N.W. Ark. Coun., Fayetteville, 1990—; bd. dirs. Pillar's Club-United Way, Easter Seals Soc.-Arkansas of Yr., Walton Arts Ctr. Coun., Fayetteville, Ark. Named Disting. Bus. Lectr. Cen. State U., Edmond, Okla., 1989. Office: Llama Company One McIlroy Pla Fayetteville AR 72701*

WALTON, AMANDA LORETTA, secondary school educator; b. Millen, Ga., Sept. 16, 1941; d. Willie (dec.) and Gussia (Wilson) Jones; m. Van L. Walton, July 3, 1966 (dec.); children: Myshiel Massa, Van Lawrence Walton Jr. AA in Liberal Arts, Manhatten Community Coll., 1975; BA in Polit. Sci., York Coll., 1980; M, City Coll. of N.Y., 1983, postgrad., 1985. Teacher asst. Pub. Sch. 200, Manhatten, 1970-73; aux. trainer Pub. Sch. 132, N.Y.C., 1974-81; tchr. Pub. Sch. 274, Bklyn., 1981—; ednl. cons., Queens, N.Y., 1981—; developer grant N.Y. Bd. Edn., 1989-90; adaptor grant N.Y. Bd. Edn., 1989-90 Calif. Books Across Am., 1991-92. Mem. legisl. adv. com., Albany, N.Y., 1981, Queens Village Bellrose Dems., Queens Village, 1983. Grantee Am. Heart Assn., Am. Cancer Soc., Cool Cats Don't Smoke, 1989-90, Nat. Diffusion Network, 1991-92. Mem. NAFE, Internat. Reading Assn., Manhattan Reading Coun. Democrat. Roman Catholic. Home: 22139 112th Ave Jamaica NY 11429-2510

WALTON, CAROLE LORRAINE, clinical social worker; b. Harrison, Ark., Oct. 20, 1949; d. Leo Woodrow Walton and Arlette Alegra (Cohen) Armstrong. BA, Lambuth Coll., Jackson, Tenn., 1971; MA, U. Chgo., 1974. Diplomate Clin. Social Work, Acad. Cert. Social Workers; bd. cert. diplomate; lic. clin. social worker. Social worker Community Mental Health, Flint, Mich., 1971-72; clin. social worker Community Mental Health, Westchester, Ill., 1974-76; dir. self-travel program Chgo. Assn. Retarded Citizens, 1973; coord. family svcs. Inner Harbors Psych. Hosp., Douglasville, Ga., 1976-83; sr. mental health clinician Northside Mental Health Ctr., Atlanta, 1983—. Mem. NASW, Ga. Soc. for Clin. Work (pres. 1981-82, pres. 1993-95). Office: Northside Mental Health Ctr 5825 Glenridge Dr NE Bldg 4 Atlanta GA 30328-5387

WALTON, CHERI ST. GERMAIN, artist, educator; b. Bangor, Maine, Jan. 4, 1945; d. Ross and Jeannette Nadine (Littlefield) St. Germain; m. Philip Alan Walton, Sept. 12, 1969 (div.); children: Carrie Elizabeth, Jesse Ross. BA in Modern Lang., U. Maine, 1967, postgrad., 1987—. Psychiat. social worker State of Maine, Bangor, 1969-71; needlepoint designer Needlepaint, Bangor, 1979—; photog. artist Baker Studio, Hampden, Maine, 1988-90, Foster Studio and Color Lab., Bangor, 1991-93; instr. art Old Town (Maine) H.S., 1988—; art instr. Bangor Art Soc., 1984-85, Bangor YWCA, 1986-87; courtrm. artist Channel 2 and Channel 7, Bangor, 1993—; freelance artist and tchr., workshop leader, 1982—; gallery dir. Bangor Art Soc., 1982-84, sec., 1984-86, pres., 1986-94. Exhibited paintings, prints, sculptures in numerous shows; represented in pvt. collections. Recipient Best of Show awards in numerous shows; recipient scholarships and faculty awards. Mem. Union Maine Visual Artists, Maine Women in the Arts, Intown Arts Ctr. (v.p. 1990—), Eastport Art Gallery. Democrat. Home: 91 Main St Bangor ME 04401 Office: Intown Arts Ctr 15 Central St Bangor ME 04401

WALTON, FLORENCE GOODSTEIN See GOODSTEIN-SHAPIRO, FLORENCE

WALTON, GLORIA JEAN, secretary; b. Mpls., July 7, 1942; d. Harvey William and Edna May (Akins) Nash; m. Louis Edward Walton, Aug. 23, 1964; children: Lisa, Louis Jr., Timothy, Teresa. AA, U. Minn., 1985, BS, 1991. Clerk typist St. Paul (Minn.) Urban League, 1959-62; with Norwest Bank, Mpls., 1962-65; clerk typist Munsingwear, Mpls., 1967-68; transcriber typist Hennepin County Dept. Ct. Svcs., Mpls., 1968-70; sec. Trinity Tabernacle Assembly of God, Mpls., 1970—; clerk typist Stivers Temporary Pers., Mpls., 1983-90. Recipient Bus. scholarship Pragmatela Sorority, 1960, recognition for faithful ministry of music Trinity Tabernacle, 1986. Mem. U. Minn. Alumni Assn. (life), Women's Ministries (pres. 1980-95). Home: 2206 Queen Ave N Minneapolis MN 55411

WALTON, JOCELYN COLEMAN, educational consultant; b. Boston, June 11, 1939; d. J. Riche and Estelle Rae (Mitchell) Coleman; m. Artie B. Williams, Aug. 16, 1963 (div. Mar. 1983); children: David, Kyle; m. Duncan Edward Walton, Aug. 6, 1983; stepchildren: Brian, Steven, Janet, Deborah. BS in Math., Morgan State U., 1961, MA in Math., 1966. Cert. tchr., supr. N.J., Md. Math. tchr. Douglass H.S., Balt., 1961-65, 66-68, Lawrence H.S., Lawrence Twp., N.J., 1972-73, Summit (N.J.) Jr. H.S., 1979-80; head dept. math. Dunbar H.S., Balt., 1968-72; tchr. methods of math. tchg. Morgan State U., Balt., 1969-70; math./sci. curriculum supr. Montgomery Twp. Pub. Schs., Skillman, N.J., 1973-75; dir. curriculum Madison (N.J.) Borough Pub. Schs., 1975-79; math. supr. Plainfield (N.J.) H.S., 1980-93; ret., 1993; cons. Roselle (N.J.) Pub. Schs., Jersey City Pub. Schs., Orange Pub. Schs., Plainfield Pub. Schs., Trenton (N.J.) Pub. Schs., Pittsgrove (N.J.) Pub. Schs., 1993-94, Houghton Mifflin Pub. Co., Boston, 1992. Author: Sprint Through Mathematics, 1986, Achieving Mathematical Standards, 1992 (Book 1, Book 2); contbg. author: Integrated Mathematics, 1993. Mem. Nat. Coun. Tchrs. Math., Assn. Math. Tchrs. N.J., N.J. Prin./Suprs. Assn., Delta Sigma Theta. Democrat. Baptist. Home: 915 Knollwood Ct Plainfield NJ 07062-2212

WALTON, KATHLEEN ENDRES, librarian; b. Columbus, Ohio, Mar. 24, 1961; d. Kenneth Raymond and Mary Margaret (Brown) Endres; m. Thomas Walton, Dec. 7, 1985; children: Tristan James, Arden Siobhan. BA, U. Md., 1982; MLS, Cath. U. Am., 1985. Head engrng./architecture/math libr. Cath. U. Am. Libr., Washington, 1985-87; libr. Congl. Quarterly Inc., Washington, 1987-90, head libr., 1991-92, libr. dir., 1992—. Mem. ALA, Am. Assn. Law Librs., D.C. Libr. Assn., Spl. Librs. Assn. Roman Catholic. Office: Congl Quarterly Inc 1414 22nd St NW Washington DC 20037-1003

WALTON, PAULA ANDERSON, language arts educator; b. Greenville, Ala., May 6, 1937; d. Paul and Lois Alene (Plaxco) Anderson; divorced; 1 child, Jennifer. BS, Auburn U., 1958. Tchr. Newport Richey (Fla.) Sch., 1958-59, Apopka (Fla.) Sch., 1960-61, Wellington (Mo.) High Sch., 1961-62, St. Joan of Arc, La Place, La., 1970—. Home: 526 Cedar St Apt 6 La Place LA 70068 Office: St Joan of Arc 412 Fir St La Place LA 70068-4310

WALTON, VALLI YVONNE, insurance consultant; b. Bronx, N.Y., May 24, 1950; d. William Jackson Sr. and Addie Ruby (Scott) Foy; m. Haywood Walton Sr., May 23, 1981. BA magna cum laude, Barrington Coll., 1971; postgrad., New Sch. for Social Rsch., 1975; cert. small bus. mgmt., NYU, 1976; MA in Liberal Studies, SUNY, Stony Brook, 1980; postgrad., Rutgers U., 1980; DDiv (hon.), London Inst. Applied Rsch., 1992. Approver group health benefits Metro. Life Ins. Co., Hauppauge, N.Y., 1971-73; account analyst, sales agt., publs. specialist group benefits dept. Equitable Life Assurance Soc. of the U.S., N.Y.C., 1973-76, litigations specialist, 1980-82; supr. major med. and death benefits Program Planners Ins. Cons., N.Y.C., 1976-77; group health and disability benefits specialist Operating Engrs. Local 825 Welfare Fund, Newark, N.J., 1982-91; sr. cons. group ins. N.Y. Life, N.Y.C., 1991-96, NYL Care Health Plans, Inc., N.Y.C., 1996—; litigation specialist, sr. supr., mgr., dir. legis. svcs. Mut. of N.Y., Purchase; assoc. mem. Practising Law Inst., N.Y.C., 1985—, dep. gov. Am. Biog. Inst., 1989, rsch. bd. advisors, 1989. Mem. Nat. Com. to Preserve Social Security and Medicare, Rep. Nat. Com., Washington, 1986—; dir. Bklyn. Dist. Children; dir. Christian edn. Durham A.M.E. Zion Ch., 1972. Mem. NAFE (cert. 1987), N.Y. Acad. Scis. (assoc.). Home: 1 Fordham Hill Oval Bronx NY 10468-8002

WALTZ, MARY ANNE, librarian; b. Charleroi, Pa., Aug. 28, 1951; d. Michael, Jr. and Margaret Louise (Shemasek) Luketich; m. Edward Carl Waltz, Apr. 28, 1973; children: Geoffrey Vankirk, Elissa Renate. BS in Edn. summa cum laude, Ind. U. of Pa., 1973; MSLS, Syracuse U., 1979. Geography/maps libr. Syracuse (N.Y.) U. Libr., 1979-91, head maps unit, 1987-91, social scis. coord., 1991-94, head, maps/govt. info. dept., 1991-94; asst. dir. for user svcs. Univ. Libr. SUNY, Albany, 1994—; cons. Parliamentary Libr., Russian Fedn., Moscow, 1992-95. Contbg. author: (book chpts.) Teaching the Online Catalog User, 1988, Guide to Reference Books 10th edit. (supplement), 1992, 11th edit., 1996; compiler chpts.: Guide to U.S. Map Resources, 1990, Geographic Cutters, 1989, Anglo-American Cataloging Rules, 1988. Cons. Jamesville-Dewitt Mid. Sch. social studies program, Dewitt, N.Y., 1988-89. Mem. ALA (chair map/geography roundtable 1988-89), Human Rels. Area Files (mem. exec. bd. 1993-94), N.Y. Libr. Assn., SUNY Library Assn., Beta Phi Mu, Kappa Delta Pi, Phi Alpha Theta. Office: SUNY Albany Univ Librs 1400 Washington Ave Albany NY 12222-0100

WALZER, JUDITH BORODOVKO, academic administrator, educator; b. N.Y.C., May 27, 1935; d. Isidore and Ida (Gins) Borodovko; m. Michael L. Walzer, June 17, 1956; children—Sarah, Rebecca. B.A., Brandeis U., 1958, M.A., 1960, Ph.D., 1967. Dir. office women's edn. Radcliffe Coll., Cambridge, Mass., 1974-77, assoc. dean., 1976-77; Allston Burr sr. tutor, asst. dean for co-edn. Harvard Coll., Cambridge, Mass., 1977-80; asst. to the pres. Princeton U., N.J., 1980-85; provost New Sch. for Social Research, N.Y.C., 1985—. Mem. alumni fund com. Brandeis U., Waltham, Mass., 1983—; mem. adv. com. Overseas Sch., Hebrew U. in Jerusalem, 1989—; bd. dirs. Woodrow Wilson Found., Princeton U., 1991—. Democrat. Jewish. Office: New Sch for Social Rsch 66 W 12th St New York NY 10011-8693

WAMBLES, LYNDA ENGLAND, educational sales consultant, retired; b. Nashville, Dec. 30, 1937; d. Henry Russell and Doris Olivia (Stuart) England; m. Byron Adolph Wambles, Sept. 3, 1965; 1 child, Teri Leigh Moore Wambles Taylor. Student, U. Tenn., 1964-65, 73-74, Washington U., St. Louis, 1984-86. Cert. profl. sec. Exec. sec. Gen. Truck Sales, Knoxville, Tenn., 1972-74; asst. to dean Coll. Law U. Tenn., Knoxville, 1974-76; office mgr. Washington U. Sch. Bus., St. Louis, 1977-78, registrar, dir. info. systems, 1978-83, asst. dean for faculty and adminstrn. services, 1983-86; cons. in field St. Louis, 1978-86, Overland Park, Kans., 1986—; acct. rep. Met. Life and Affiliated Cos., Shawnee Mission, Kans., 1992-94; retired, 1996; cons. in field St. Louis, 1978; lectr. divsn. continuing edn. Washington U., St. Louis, 1978-80. Author: (with others) Procedures Manual and Information for State Guaranty Associations, 1987. Active United Way of Greater Knoxville, 1973-74; leader lunch participant YWCA, St. Louis, 1981-83. Fellow Acad. Cert. Profl. Secs.; mem. Prof. Secs. Internat., Nat. Secs. Assn. (Sec. of the Yr. 1975). Republican. Presbyterian. Home and Office: 8425 W 113th St Shawnee Mission KS 66210-2437

WAMPLER, BARBARA BEDFORD, entrepreneur; b. New Bedford, Mass., July 23, 1932; d. William and Mary (Fitzpatrick) Bedford; m. John H. Wampler, Oct. 21, 1950; children: John H. Jr., William C., James B., Robert T. AS, Tunxis C.C., 1975; MEd, Cambridge Coll., 1996. Lic. real estate agt., Mass., 1986-95. Counselor Wampler Rehab. Counseling Svcs., Farmington, Conn., 1975-85; owner, mgr. Wampler Mktg., Farmington, 1980-84, Earth Campgrounds I and II, Otis, Mass., 1984—; pres., mgr. Earth Works (name now Earth Enterprises), Otis, Mass., 1984—; founder, pres. Advt. Matters, Otis, 1989-96; v.p. Mastery Books, Otis, 1989—; mem., clk. Zoning Bd. Appeals, Otis, Mass., 1988-92; notary pub., 1986—; aft. Primerica Fin. Svcs., 1992-94. Author: Do It Yourself Empowerment; creator Calendar Journal; contbr. articles to profl. jours. Dir. music First Congl. Ch., Otis, trustee, 1994-96; family counselor Berkshire Coun. Alcoholism and Addiction, 1994-96, Mediation Option/PLYS, 1994—. Faculty scholar U. Hartford, 1976. Mem. Acad. Family Mediators, Am. Assn. Christian Counselors, Bus. Mgrs. Assn., Kiwanis. Home and Office: Earth Enterprises 1856 S Main Rd Box 690 Otis MA 01253

WANAMAKER, ELLEN PONCE, tax specialist; b. Newark, June 27, 1956; d. Arthur Zachary and Charlotte Rhoda (Frisch) Ponce; m. William A. Wanamaker, Aug. 8, 1979; 1 child, Marlee Ann. AS in Dental Hygiene, Fairleigh Dickinson U., 1978, BS in Dental Hygiene, 1979; student, H&R Block tax tng. seminars, Wayne, N.J., 1984-90, William Paterson Coll., 1975-76 90—. Registered dental hygienist, N.J., dental hygiene specialist, N.J.; cert. dental asst. patient accounts mgr., inst. dental assisting; accredited tax perparer; accredited tax advisor; IRS licensure-enrolled agt. status. Dental hygienist, dental asst. Arthur Ponce, DDS, Bloomingdale, N.J., 1972-80; dental asst., dental hygienist various dentists, N.J., 1977-80; instr., dept. chmn. Berdan Inst., Totowa, N.J., 1980-83; prodn. coord., cons. performer These Days Prodns., Ltd., Pompton Lakes, N.J., 1981—; tax preparer H&R Block, Wayne, N.J., 1985-90; mgr. William Paterson Coll., Wayne, N.J., 1975-76, 90-91; pvt. practice tax advisor, tax preparer Bloomingdale, 1985—; pvt. instrn. dental assts. and dental hygienists, Ellen Wanamaker, Bloomingdale, 1981-83; instr. County Coll. of Morris, Randolph, N.J., 1979-80. Vol. dental asst. N.E. Regional Bd. Dental Licensing Exams., 1978-86, Head Start Program, 1979, Bloomingdale Saturday Sch. Bloomingdale Bd. of Health, 1981, Ann. Bloomingdale Health Fair, 1983-93. Recipient Gold cert. Music Educators Assn., 1967-69. Mem. NOW, Am. Speech and Hearing Assn., Am. Dental Hygiene Assn., Nat. Assn. Tax Practitioners, Nat. Soc. Pub. Accts., Nat. Assn. Dental Assts., N.J. Dental Assn., FDU Dental Hygiene Assn., FDU Alumni Assn., Phi Omega Epsilon. Office: William A Wanamaker DMD MS 14 Leary Ave Bloomingdale NJ 07403-1612

WAND, PATRICIA ANN, librarian; b. Portland, Oreg., Mar. 28, 1942; d. Ignatius Bernard and Alice Ruth (Suhr) W.; m. Francis Dean Silvernail, Dec. 20, 1966 (div. Jan. 19, 1986); children: Marjorie Lynn Silvernail, Kirk Dean Silvernail. BA, Seattle U., 1963; MAT, Antioch Grad. Sch., 1967; AMLS, U. Mich., 1972. Vol. Peace Corps, Colombia, S.Am., 1963-65; secondary tchr. Langley Jr. High Sch., Washington, 1965-66; asst. libr. Wittenberg U. Libr., Springfield, Ohio, 1967-69; secondary tchr. Caro (Mich.) High Sch., 1969-70; assoc. libr. Coll. of S.I. (N.Y.) Libr., 1972-77; head, access svcs. Columbia U. Librs., N.Y.C., 1977-82; asst. univ. libr. U. Oreg., Eugene, 1982-89; univ. libr. The Am. U., Washington, 1989—; cons. Bloomsburg (Pa.) U. Libr., 1990. Contbr. articles to profl. jours. Pres. West Cascade Returned Peace Corps Vols., Eugene, 1985-88; v.p. Friends of Colombia, Washington, 1990—; speaker on Peace Corps, 1965—, libr. and info. svcs., 1979—. Honors Program scholarship Seattle U., 1960-62, Peace Corps scholarship Antioch U., 1965-66; recipient Beyond War award, 1987, Fulbright Sr. Lectr. award Fulbright, 1989, Disting. Alumnus award Sch. of Info. and Libr. Studies, U. Mich., 1992. Mem. ALA, Assn. Coll. and Rsch. Librs. (chair budge and fin. bd. dirs. 1987-89, chair WHCLIS task force 1989-92), On-line Computer Librs. Ctr. (adv. com. on coll. and univ. librs. 1991-96), D.C. Libr. Assn. (bd. dirs. 1993—, pres. 1996—). Home: 4854 Bayard Blvd Bethesda MD 20816-1785 Office: Am Univ Libr 4400 Massachusetts Ave NW Washington DC 20016-8001

WANDEL, SHARON LEE, sculptor; b. Bemidji, Minn., Mar. 19, 1940; d. Roy J. and Bonnie (Englund) Opsahl; m. Thaddeus Ludwik Wandel, Oct. 17, 1970; children: Holly, Erika. BA, Gustavus Adolphus Coll., 1962; MSW, Columbia U., 1965; Cert. in Arts Mgmt., SUNY, Purchase, 1993. Caseworker Manhattan State Hosp., N.Y.C., 1963-64; caseworker/rschr. Cmty. Svc. Soc., N.Y.C., 1965-67; teaching asst. dept. medicine NYU Med. Ctr., N.Y.C., 1967-70. One-person shows at Silvermine Guild of Artists, New Canaan, Conn., 1993, Pen and Brush, N.Y.C., 1994, Clark Whitney Gallery, Lenox, Mass., 1994, James Cox Gallery, Woodstock, N.Y., 1996; group shows include Nat. Acad. Design, N.Y.C., 1988, 90, 92, 94, 95, Nat. Sculpture Soc., N.Y.C., 1989, 91, 93, 94, Palazzo Mediceo in Seravezza, Italy, 1994, Knickerbocker Artists, N.Y.C., 1989, 90, 92, Art of N.E. U.S.A., New Canaan, Conn., 1989, 92, Mus. of Hudson Highlands, Cornwall, N.Y., 1990, James Cox Gallery, 1992, 93, 95, N.Y. Soc. Women Artists, Cork Gallery at Lincoln Ctr., 1991, Broome St. Gallery, N.Y.C., 1991, 92, Warner Comm., 1989, Lever House, N.Y.C., 1993, 94, 96, Kohn Pederson Fox Gallery, N.Y.C., 1996, Patio Azul Gallery, Sedona, Ariz., 1995, Williamsville Sculpture Garden, 1995-96, Elaine Benson Gallery, Bridgehampton, 1996, Chapel St. Art Gallery, New Haven, U. Conn.; works in permanent collections at Art Students League, 1989, Westinghouse Corp. Collection, Pitts., 1990, Nat. Acad. Design, 1994; commns. include two 8' bronze figures for Ihilani Resort, Kapolei, Hawaii, 1993, 2 5" figures Silvermine Galleries, 1993. Mem. rsch. com. Arthritis Found., N.Y.C., 1968-69. Recipient N.Am. Sculpture Exhbn. 2d place, 1991, Three River Arts Festival (Carnegie Inst.) Purchase award, 1990, Hakone Open Air Mus. (Japan) 3d and 4th Rodin Grand Prize Exhbn. Excellent Maquettes, 1990, 92, Matrix Gallery 1st prize for sculpture, 1990, Ariel Gallery Internat. Competition Group Show award, 1989, Salmagundi Club McReynolds award, 1989, Barret Coleco award, 1988. Mem. Silvermine Guild of Artists (Solo Show award

1992), N.Y. Soc. Woman Artists (pres.), Knickerbocker Artists USA, The Pen and Brush (Meisner award 1990, Solo Show award 1993), Nat. Acad. Design (Cleo Hartwig award 1990), Nat. Sculpture Soc. (Meisner award 1994, Hexter award 1993, Spring award 1991, Meiselman award 1990), Audubon Artists (Chaim Gross Found. award 1993), Sculptures Guild. Home: 136 Old Post Rd N Croton-on-Hudson NY 10520 Studio: 168 Irving Ave Port Chester NY 10573

WANDER-PERNA, LUCY, film company executive. Sr. v.p. Sony Pictures Entertainment, Inc., Culver City, Calif. Office: Sony Pictures Entertainment, Inc. 10202 W Washington Blvd Culver City CA 90232*

WANDLING, MARILYN ELIZABETH BRANSON, artist, art educator; b. Alton, Ill., May 16, 1932; d. Ralph Marion and Mary Mildred (Branson) W.; children: Jeffrey, Douglas, Pamela. Student, Monticello Coll., Godfrey, Ill, 1950-51, U. Ill. U-C Sch. Fine Arts, 1951-53; BA in Art, Webster U., St. Louis, 1968; MA Edn. in Art Edn., Washington U., St. Louis, 1975. Cert. tchr. art Kindergarten-Grade 12, Mo. 4th grade tchr. Alton (Ill.) Pub. Schs., 1961-62; art. buuying dept. Gardner Advt. Co. Inc., St. Louis, 1962-63; art tchr. mid. sch. Lindbergh Sch. Dist., St. Louis, 1968-75; cons., designer V.P. Fair, Inc., St. Louis, 1982; adminstrv. asst. to headmaster, coll. counseling dept. John Burroughs Sch., St. Louis, 1979-82; dir. pub. rels. and advt. Dance St. Louis, 1983-85; freelance art and design St. Louis, 1970—; art tchr. mid. sch. St. Louis Pub. Schs., 1987-90, art tchr. Elem. Magnet Sch. for Visual & Performing Arts, 1990—; tchr. drawing and painting Summer Arts Inst., St. Louis Pub. Schs., 1992, graphic arts designer, cons. comty. affairs divsn., 1985—, sch. vol. divsn., 1990-92, Webster Groves (Mo.) Sch. Dist., 1989-90, Pub. Sch. Retirement Sys., St. Louis, 1991; implementer classroom multi-cultural art edn. projects, 1987—; summer participant Improving Visual Arts Edn., Getty Ctr. for Edn. in Arts, 1990; book illustrator-McGraw Hill Inter-Americana de Mexico, Mexico City, 1994-95. Designer Centennial Logo for St. Louis Pub. Schs. Sesquicentennial, 1988; painter, designer murals for Ctrl. Presbyn. Ch. Nursery, 1978-79, St. Nicholas Greek Orthodox Ch., 1980; designer two outdoor villages VP Fair, Arch Grounds, St. Louis, 1982. Recipient merit and honor awards Nat. Sch. Pub. Rels. Assn., 1990, 91, 92, 93, Mo. Sch. Pub. Rels. Assn., 1989-90, 91, 92, 93. Mem. Nat. Art Edn. Assn., St. Louis Art Mus., PEO Sisterhood, Nat. Soc. DAR, Chi Omega Alumnae. Office: Ames Visual & Performing Arts Center Admin Office 2900 Hadley St Saint Louis MO 63107-3911

WANG, JOSEPHINE L. FEN, physician; b. Taiwan, China, Jan 2, 1948; came to U.S., 1974; d. Pao-San and Ann-Nam (Chen) Chao; m. Chang-Yang Wang, Dec. 20, 1973; children: Edward, Eileen. MD, Nat. Taiwan U., Taipei, 1974. Diplomate Am. Bd. Pediatrics, Am. Bd. Allergy and Immunology. Intern Nat. Taiwan U. Hosp., 1973-74; resident U. Ill. Hosp., Chgo., 1974-76; fellow Northwestern U. Med. Ctr., Chgo., 1976-78, instr. pediatrics, 1978—; cons. Holy Cross Hosp., Chgo., 1978—, Meth. Hosp. Ind., 1979—, St. Anthony Hosp., 1985—, Christ Hosp., 1995—. Fellow Am. Coll. Allergy; mem. AMA, Am. Acad. Allergy. Office: 9012 Connecticut Dr Merrillville IN 46410-7170 also: 4901 W 79th St Burbank IL 60459-1501

WANG, VERA, fashion designer; b. 1950; d. Cheng Ching Wang; m. Arthur Becker; children: Cecilia, Josephine. Grad., Sarah Lawrence Coll., New York. Sr. fashion editor Vogue, N.Y.C.; design dir. Ralph Lauren Women's Wear, N.Y.C., 1987-89; prin. Vera Wang Bridal House Ltd., N.Y.C., 1990—. Office: Vera Wang Bridal House 225 W 39th St 10th Fl New York NY 10018*

WANZER, MARY KATHRYN, computer company executive, consultant; b. South Bend, Ind., Sept. 12, 1942; d. Cyril Joseph and Kathryn Alice (Dumke) Tlusty; m. Boyd Eugene Wanzer, May 30, 1964; children: Adam James, Christopher James. BS, Northland Coll., 1964; student, Am. U., Washington, 1972-75. Tchr. Montgomery Co. Md. Schs., Rockville, 1964-66; mathematician Johns Hopkins U., Silver Spring, Md., 1966-68; systems analyst ITT Fed. Elec. Corp., Kennedy Space Ctr., Fla., 1968-69; computer programmer Atlantic City (N.J.) Hosp., 1969-71; project leader Fairfax Hosp. Assn., Falls Church, Va., 1971-73; sr. systems analyst Xerox Corp., Leesburg, Va., 1973-76; software engr. E-Systems, Falls Church, Va., 1982-85; pres. Atlantic Office Svcs., Ltd., Bethany Beach, Del., 1988—; cons. Chespeake Utilities, Dover, Del., 1990, Intervet., Millsoboro, Del., 1990-92; MIS mgr. Thompson Pub. Group, Salisbury, Md., 1992-93; systems analyst Mountaire, Selbyville, Del., 1993-96, Peninsula Regional Med. Ctr., Salisbury, Md., 1996—. Leader LaLeche League, Annandale, Va., 1980-83; v.p. No. Va. Hockey Club, Fairfax County, Va., 1986-87. Roman Catholic. Home: 941 Lake View Dr Bethany Beach DE 19930-9675 Office: Atlantic Office Svcs Ltd 5 Starboard Ct # 1 Bethany Beach DE 19930-9679

WAPNIR, IRENE LEONOR, medical educator; b. Buenos Aires, Argentina, May 11, 1954; came to U.S., 1963; d. Raul Alberto and Elsa (Michalewicz) W.; m. Ralph Steven Greco, Feb. 23, 1991; children: Justin Michael, Eric Matthew, Ilana Rose. BA, Goucher Coll., Balt., 1975; MD, U. Autonoma Metropolitana, Mexico City, 1980. Diplomate Am. Bd. Surgery. Intern, resident N.Y. Med. Coll., Bronx, 1980-85; attending physician and asst. prof. surgery Lincoln Hosp.-N.Y. Med. Coll., 1985-87; asst. prof. surgery UMDNJ-Robert Wood Johnson Med. Sch., New Brunswick, 1988-95; chief divsn. comprehensive breast svcs. UMDNJ-Robert Wood Johnson Med. Sch., 1991-93, assoc. prof. clin. surgery, 1995—; adv. bd. Breast Cancer Resource, Princeton, N.J., Race for the Cure, Princeton. Contbr. articles to profl. jours. Recipient Breast Disease fellowship UMDNJ-Robert Wood Johnson Med. Sch., 1987-88, rsch. grant for breast cancer UMDNJ Found., 1992, grad. rsch. UMDNJ-Robert Wood Johnson Med. Sch., 1989. Office: Dept Surgery UMDNJ Robert Wood Johnson Med Sch 1 R W Johnson Pl New Brunswick NJ 08903

WARANIUS VASS, ROSALIE JEAN, artist, art educator; b. Fond du Lac, Wis., Dec. 10, 1938; d. John Stanley and Anna Francis (Jonaitis) Waranius; m. Kenneth James Vass, June 11, 1960; children: Kealie, Ross, Kenlyn, Jason. BA, Alverno Coll., 1960. Cert. art tchr., Ill. Art tchr. East Aurora (Ill.) H.S., 1979-83; dir. Doctor Scholl Art Gallery, Aurora, 1984-90; studio art tchr. Marmion Acad., Aurora, 1985-90. One-woman shows include Batavia (Ill.) Pub. Libr., 1987, The Holmstad, Ill., 1988, Bellarmine Coll., Ky., 1989, Aurora (Ill.) U., 1989, St. Charles (Ill.) Pub. Libr., 1989, Roberta Campbell Art Gallery, Ill., 1991, 95, Rolling Meadows (Ill.) Libr. Art Gallery, 1991, Alverno Coll. Art Gallery, Wis., 1991, Ill. Artisan Shop, 1992, Jesse Besser Mus., Mich., 1993, Beacon St. Gallery, Ill., 1995; exhibited in group shows including 17th Internat. Exhbn. Water Color Soc., Houston, 1994, NWS Signature Mem. Juried Exhbn., Norwalk, Calif., 1994, Aurora U., 1994, Invitational Batavia Artists, 1994, Women Artists : A Celebration, Youngstown, Ohio, 1994, No. Art Competition, Rhinelander, Wis., 1994, Watercolor Masters: Midwest Show, Lincolnwood, Ill., 1995, Norris Cultural Arts Ctr., St. Charles, 1989-96, others; represented in permanent collections at Art and Music Festival, Ill., Whirlpool Corp., Ill., Security Bank, Iowa, First Chgo. Bank, Glenwood Hosp., Ill., Jesse Besser Mus., Mich., Easter Seal, Ill., St. Francis Hosp., Ill., others. Mem. Nat. Watercolor Soc. (signature mem., life), Nat. Mus. Women in Arts, Chgo. Artists Coalition, Art Inst. Chgo. Home and Studio: O S 888 Wenmoth Rd Batavia IL 60510-9711

WARD, ALICE FAYE, elementary education educator; b. Swartz, La.. BS, Grambling (La.) U., 1973; postgrad., N.E. U., 1976-79. Tchr. Robinson Elem. Sch., Monroe, 1971-73, Poinciana Elem. Sch., Boynton Beach, Fla., 1973-76, Melaleuca Elem. Sch., West Palm Beach, Fla.; tchr., dir. after sch. program Melaleuca Elem. Sch., West Palm Beach. Dir. Just Say No Club, 1994-95, K-Kid Club, 1994-95, After Sch. Program, 1994. Named Tchr. of Week Palm Beach Post Newspaper, 1994. Mem. NEA, CTA. Democrat. Baptist. Office: Melaleuca Elem Sch 5759 W Gun Club Rd West Palm Beach FL 33415-2505

WARD, CHARLOTTE LOWREY, guidance counselor; b. Ft. Smith, Ark., May 17, 1942; d. Rudolph Cley and Clovis (Baggarly) Lowrey; m. James Carl Ward, Dec. 2, 1941; children: Sonya Yvette, Craig Alan, Cary Scott. BA in Edn., LA Tech. U., 1964; MEd, Northwestern State U., Natchitoches, La., 1980, postgrad., 1988. Libr. Pub. Libr., Ruston, La., 1964-65, Houston, Tex., 1965-66; sch. libr. Houston Ind. Dist., 1966-67; tchr. kindergarten Winn Parish Schs., Sikes, La., 1974-75; sch. libr. Atlanta (La.) H.S./Winn Parish Schs., 1979—; guidance counselor Winnfield (La.) Mid. - Winn Parish Sch., 1987—; profl. counselor, La., 1987—. Sunday sch. dir., grades five and six First Bapt. Ch., Winnfield, 1975—, dir. of girls in action missionary study, 1968-80, mem. budget com., 1992—, long-range com., 1985—. Named Woman of Yr., Winnfield Women's Club, 1980. Mem. La. Tech. Alumni, Northwestern State U. Alumni, La. Counselor's Assn., la. Sch. Counselors Assn., La. Assn. Marriages and Family Counselors, La. Mental health Counselors Assn., La. Educators Assn., NEA, Am. Counselors Assn., Nat. Peer Helpers Assn., Alpha Delta Kappa. Republican. Office: Winnfield Mid Sch PO Box 1140 Hwy 167N Winnfield LA 71483

WARD, DEBORAH SUZANNE, private school educator; b. Inglewood, Calif., Mar. 27, 1961; d. F. Willard and Z. Janelle (Hardgrave) Bloodworth; m. Donald Ray Ward Jr., Dec. 19, 1992. BA, Fresno Pacific Coll., 1988; MS, Nat. U., 1990. Cert. tchr., Calif. Elem. tchr. First Ch. Christian Ctr., Fresno, 1983-86, summer sch. dir., 1984-85; elem. tchr. Bapt. Mid-Missions, Brazil, S.Am., 1987-88, Sante Fe Christian Schs., Solana Beach, Calif., 1989—. Mem. ASCD. Office: Santa Fe Christian Schs 838 Academy Dr Solana Beach CA 92075-2034

WARD, ERICA ANNE, lawyer, educator; b. Okiyama, Japan, Oct. 20, 1950; d. Robert Edward and Constance Regina (Barnett) W.; m. Ralph Joseph Gerson, May 20, 1979; children: Stephanie Claire, Madeleine Ward Gerson. B.A., Stanford U., 1972; J.D., U. Mich., 1975. Bar: Calif. 1975, D.C. 1976, U.S. Ct. Appeals (5th and D.C. cirs.) 1977, Temporary Emergency Ct. Appeals 1983, Mich. 1989. Assoc. Wilmer, Cutler & Pickering, Washington, 1975-77; staff counsel U.S. Senate Ethics Com., Washington, 1977-78; exec. asst. gen. counsel Dept. Energy, Washington, 1978-79, counsellor to dep. sec., 1980; assoc. dir. energy and natural resources, domestic policy staff White House, Washington, 1980-81; of counsel Skadden, Arps, Slate, Meagher & Flom, Washington, 1981-87, ptnr., 1987—; adj. prof. law U. Mich., Ann Arbor, 1984-85. Editor Mich. Law Rev., 1975. Commr. Mackinac Island (Mich.) State Park Commn., 1989-95; mem. adv. bd. Ctr. Edn. of Women U. Mich., Ann Arbor, 1989—; bd. trustees Cranbrook Ednl. Cmty., 1993—; mem. visitors com. U. Mich. Law Sch. Recipient Outstanding Svc. medal Dept. Energy, 1981. Mem. ABA, Women's Bar Assn. D.C. Democrat. Jewish. Office: Skadden Arps Slate Meagher Flom 1440 New York Ave NW Washington DC 20005-2111

WARD, JEANNE LAWTON, family counselor, consultant; b. Bklyn., Mar. 23, 1945; d. James Joseph and Grace Frances (Brennan) Lawton; m. Robert L. Bucher, June 11, 1966 (div. Aug. 1977); children: Barbara Anne, Laura Jeanne; m. Charles F. Ward Jr., Aug. 19, 1983. BA in Edn., St. Catherine's Coll., St. Paul, 1966; MA in Counseling and Psychology, Coll. St. Thomas, St. Paul, 1970. Elem. tchr. Cooper Elem. Sch., 1966-69; spl. edn. resource tchr. Susie Tolbert 6th Grade Ctr., Jacksonville, Fla., 1976-78, sch. counselor, Arlington Heights Elem. Sch., Jacksonville, Fla., 1978-83; instr. Fla. C. C., Jacksonville, 1978-88; pvt. practice family counseling, Jacksonville, 1984-88; dir. tng. staff devel. City of Jacksonville, Fla., 1987-88; adj. prof. U. North Fla., 1990-92; dir. legis. affairs Mayors Office Jacksonville, Fla., 1992—. cons. mktg. tng. design and devel. Am. Transtech, Jacksonville, 1985-87; cons. child care Community Coll. Jacksonville, 1990-92; founder, dir. Divorce Ministry Diocese of St. Augustine, Jacksonville, 1979-83; Fla. del. White House Conf. on Families, 1980; regular panelist Sta. WJXT, Jacksonville, 1982—, editorial writer, 1990-92. Author curriculum. Bd. dirs., chmn. pers. com. Child Guidance Clinic, Jacksonville, 1977—; bd. dirs. Girls Club of Jacksonville, 1981-83; chairperson Mayors Commn. on Status of Women, Jacksonville, 1985-87; bd. dir. tng. and staff devel. City of Jacksonville, 1986-87; chmn. task force Corp. Child Care, 1985—, founding dir., 1985—; cons. Fla. Community Coll., 1988—; bd. dirs. YWCA, Jacksonville Symphony, Hope Haven, Family Care Connections, Inc., Nutcracker Ballet; chmn. bd. dirs. Child Guidance Ctr.; mem. Literacy Coalition, Coalition for a Drug Free Jacksonville, Leadership Jacksonville. Recipient Eve award Fla. Times Union, 1990, Woman of Achievement award Bus. and Profl. Women. Mem. AAUW, NAFE, ASTD, Nat. Coun. of Family Rels., Phi Delta Kappa, N.E. Fla. Soc. Parents of Visually Impaired Children Club (program chmn. 1985—). Democrat. Roman Catholic. Home: 3523 Park St Jacksonville FL 32205-7726 Office: Office of the Mayor 220 E Bay St Jacksonville FL 32202-3429

WARD, JEANNETTE POOLE, psychologist, educator; b. Honolulu, June 19, 1932; d. Russell Masterton and Bessie Naomi (Hammett) Poole; children: John Russell Ward, Lisa Joy Ward. BA, Birmingham (Ala.) So. Coll., 1963; PhD in Psychology, Vanderbilt U., 1969. NSF summer rsch. asst. U. Iowa, Iowa City, 1962; NSF summer rsch. asst. Vanderbilt U., Nashville, 1963, NASA fellow, 1963-66, NIH postdoctoral fellow, 1966-67; spl. rsch. fellow Duke U., Durham, N.C., 1970-71; asst. prof. psychology Memphis State U., 1967-72, assoc. prof. psychology, 1972-77, prof. psychology, 1977—. Editor: Current Research in Primate Laterality, 1990, Primate Laterality, 1992; mem. editl. bd. Jour. Comparative Psychology, 1988-95, Internat. Jour. of Comparative Psychology, 1995—; contbr. chpts. to books and articles to profl. jours. Fellow Am. Psychol. Soc.; mem. Psychonomic Soc., Animal Behavior Soc., Am. Psychol. Assn., Am. Primatology Soc., Southeastern Psychol. Assn., Soc. for Neuroscis., Internat. Soc. for Comparative Psychology (treas. 1989-90, pres.-elect 1996—), Sigma Xi (pres. Memphis State U. chpt. 1989-90, rsch. award 1985). Democrat. Office: Univ of Memphis Dept Psychology Memphis TN 38152

WARD, JO ALICE, computer consultant, educator; b. Ft. Worth, Aug. 14, 1939; d. Boyd Wheeler and Frances Elizabeth (Wheeler) Patton; m. John Oliver Ward, Mar. 19, 1960 (div. Feb. 1976); children: Russell Scott, Pamela Joan Ward Watson. BA in Math., North Tex. State U., 1961, MA in Math., 1965, postgrad., 1969-72. Instr. math. North Tex. State U., Denton, 1965-67, grad. asst., 1968-72; instr. math. Tarrant County Jr. Coll., Ft. Worth, 1967-68; math. tchr. Aldine Ind. Schs., Houston, 1973-76; math. instr. U. Houston Downtown, 1974-80; sys. analyst Conoco Inc, Houston, 1981-93; computer cons. Quality First Computer Svcs., Houston, 1994—. Vol. facilitator for family violence program Houston Area Women's Ctr., 1993-94; adminstrv. vol. Citizens for Animal Protection, 1993—; vol. Bering Cmty. Svc. Found., 1995—. Recipient Outstanding Adminstrv. Vol. award Citizens for Animal Protection, 1995. Home: 11943 Briar Forest Dr Houston TX 77077-4132

WARD, JOLENE SCARBOROUGH, school administrator; b. Moultrie, Ga., Aug. 8, 1949; d. Charles Ellis and Everlene (Chapman) Scarborough; m. Stanley Harding Ward, Jr., Aug. 24, 1968; children: Alisha Renee, Stanley Jared. BS, Ga. Southwestern Coll., Americus, 1972, MEd, 1989; EdS, Columbus (Ga.) Coll., 1993. Cert. tchr., Ga. Tchr. Marion County Bd. Edn., Buena Vista, Ga., 1972-90, asst. prin., 1990-95; prin., 1995—. Mem. Drug-Free Adv. Bd., Ellaville, Ga., 1992—, Am. Cancer Soc., Buena Vista, 1987—. Mem. ASCD, Profl. Assn. Ga. Educators (pres.), Ga. Assn. Elem. Sch. Prins., Delta Kappa Gamma. Democrat. Methodist. Home: PO Box 475 Buena Vista GA 31803-0475 Office: Marion County Elem Sch PO Box 16 Buena Vista GA 31803

WARD, JUDY KITCHEN, bank executive; b. Asheville, N.C., Jan. 19, 1940; d. Jesse Ernest and Mary Daisy (Pressley) Kitchen; m. Wayne Leigh; children: Robert Wayne, Shari Leigh, Rodney Victor; m. Jerry Ellsworth Ward; 1 child, Jerry E. Jr. Student, Thomas Nelson Community Coll., Hampton, Va., 1987. Bank teller 1st City Bank, Newport News, Va., 1977-82; adminstrv. asst. Va. Nat. Bank, Newport News, 1982-84; br. mgr. 1st Am. Bank Va., Newport News, 1984-91, asst. v.p., 1991—. Treas. Alternatives/Drug Abuse, Newport News and Hampton, 1986-88, bd. dirs., 1986—; cabinet mem. United Way, Newport News, 1988; mem. ways and means com. Dem. Orgn., 1987—; sec. Denbigh Little League, 1974-76; pres. local PTA, 1972-73, Block Mother's Prevention Against Child Abuse, 1967-69; bd. dirs. Dem. City Com., 1992. Recipient cert. United, 1984-88, Mar. of Dimes, 1982-88. Mem. Am. Inst. Banking (chief consul 1986, award 1987, v.p. 1990—, bd. dirs. 1991, chmn. child abuse 1992), Exch. Club (pres. James River chpt. 1990—). Episcopalian. Home: 193 Compton Pl Newport News VA 23606-1626 Office: 1st Am Bank Va 2901 Huntington Ave Newport News VA 23607-3917

WARD, JULIE MCDUFF, real estate marketing specialist; b. Birmingham, Ala., Mar. 26, 1946; d. Oliver Tabor and Julia Frances (Cooper) McDuff; m. David William Ward, Jan. 19, 1968; 1 child, Brian William. BS in Edn., U. Ala., 1968. Mgmt. trainee Bell Telephone Co., Birmingham, 1964-68; tchr. elem. edn. Huntsville (Ala.) City Schs., 1969-73; real estate agt. Frontier Better Homes and Gardens, Littleton, Colo., 1988—. Mem. pers. com. Ken Caryl Bapt. Ch., Littleton, 1992-95. Mem. Colo. Assn. Realtors (grad. realtor inst. designation), Jefferson County Assn. Realtors. Office: Frontier Better Homes 5944 S Kipling St Ste 100 Littleton CO 80127-2590

WARD, KATHERINE MARIE, school system administrator; b. Raton, N.Mex., Oct. 31, 1936; d. Robert Lee and Lucille (Gasperetti) Davis; m. Leonard Carlin Ward, Aug. 30, 1953; children: Kathy Ann, Ronnie, Tonia, Jess. BS, Ea. N.Mex. U., 1972, MEd, 1977; edn. specialist, U. N.Mex., 1981. Data reduction tech. phys. sci. lab. N.Mex. State U., Las Cruces, 1955-61; 3d and 4th grade tchr. Clayton Pub. Schs., Amistad, N.Mex., 1972-74; 4th grade tchr. Grants/Cibola County (N.Mex.) Schs., 1974-76, Title I reading tchr., 1976-77, Title I coord., 1977-82, Chpt. I coord., 1982-89, coord. Chpt. I and drug free sch. and cmtys., 1989-90, coord. Chpt. I, drug free, DARE and Title II, 1990-92, coord. Chpt. I, Title I, drug free and Title II, 1992-96, fed. program coord., 1996—. Leader Girl Scouts U.S., Las Cruces, 1966-67, 4-H, Grants, 1977-80; mem., sec. Fighting Back Robert Wood Johnson Found. Prevent Drug and Alcohol Use Grants, 1991-96. Recipient Adminstrn. award N.Mex. Study and Rsch. Coun., 1986, Chpt. I Exemplary award U.S. Dept. Edn., 1988, Merit award DARE program Grants Police Dept., 1991. Mem. N.Mex. Sch. Adminstrs., Internat. Reading Assn., Malpais Internat. Reading Assn. (pres. 1977-79, Literacy award 1979), N.Mex. Internat. Reading Assn. (Land of Enchantment Book award com. 1983-86). Home: PO Box 188 2100 Ann St Grants NM 87020 Office: Grants Cibola County Schs Grants NM 87020

WARD, KATHRYN ELIZABETH KUREK, home health nurse; b. Washington, Mar. 7, 1952; d. K.J. Kurek and Kathryn Gay (Corbin) Kurek Stewart; m. Paul G. Ward Jr.; children: Steven Paul, Brent Corbin. BSN, U. Va., 1987. RN, Va.; cert. community health nurse. Staff nurse Waynesboro Cmty. Hosp., 1973-75, 78-87, office nurse, 1975-77; staff nurse, case mgr. Community Home Health, Augusta Hosp. Corp., Waynesboro, Va., 1987-89, hosp. liaison, referral nurse, 1989-90, clin. coord./supr., 1990-95; dir. Augusta Home Care, 1995—. Vol. spkr. AID Support Group; bd. mem. Hospice. Mem. AAUW, Va. Assn. Home Care, Sigma Theta Tau. Roman Catholic. Home: 3159 Village Dr Waynesboro VA 22980 Office: Augusta Cmty Care 446 Commerce Rd Staunton VA 24401

WARD, LESLIE GILES, special education educator; b. Tuscaloosa, Ala., Sept. 9, 1966; d. Jerry Willard and Helen Corinne (Senna) Giles; m. Thomas Matthew Ward, May 23, 1992. BS, U. Ala., 1988, MA, 1992. Cert. tchr. spl. edn., Ala. Spl. edn. tchr. Hoover (Ala.) City Schs., 1991—; child study team mem. Hoover City Schs., 1991—, pvt. tutor, 1991—. Youth dir. St. Matthias' Episcopal Ch., Tuscaloosa, 1993—. Mem. Alpha Delta Kappa. Episcopalian. Home: 5767 Willow Lake Dr Hoover AL 35244

WARD, LINDA V., nursing administrator; b. Oxford, N.C., May 3, 1948; d. Caspair and Annie Louise (Hicks) Cooper; m. Alan C. Ward, May 4, 1968; children: Alan, Lenore. Diploma, Sharon Gen. Hosp. Sch. Nursing, 1981; BSN, Pa. State U., 1994. Cert. for insertion of peripheral indwelling cen. catheters; cert. neonatal resuscitation instr., neonatal intensive care nurse, Resolve Through Sharing bereavement counselor, clin. nurse III clin. ladder program; cert. pediat. life support instr. Gen. staff nurse med. (renal) fl. Western Res. Care System, Youngstown, Ohio, 1981-82, gen. staff nurse neonatal ICU, 1982-87, acting clin. nurse mgr., 1991, asst. clin. nurse mgr. neonatal ICU, 1987—. Mem. Nat. Assn. Neonatal Nurses, Ohio Nurses Assn., Youngstown Gen. Duty Nurses Assn., Pa. State Alumna Assn., Alpha Sigma Lambda. Democrat. Baptist. Office: Western Res Care Systems 500 Gypsy Ln Youngstown OH 44504-1315

WARD, LYNDA SUE SCOVILLE, special education educator, writer; b. Pampa, Tex., Jan. 5, 1945; d. Kenneth E. and Opal Myrle (Turner) Scoville; m. Bruce C. Ward, Oct. 1, 1976; children: J. Wade Bainum, Jennifer L. Bainum. BS in Edn., Emporia (Kans.) State U., 1967; MS in Edn., U. Kans., 1973; postgrad., Wichita (Kans.) State U. Cert. learning disabled, educable mentally handicapped, psychology, composition and lit., Kans., Tex. Tchr. educable mentally handicapped and learning disabled Shawnee Mission (Kans.) Pub. Schs., 1967-69; tchr. headstart program Hutchinson Pub. Schs., 1968; tchr. educable mentally handicapped Chanute High Sch., Iola, Kans., 1974-76; tchr. learning and behavior disabled Sedgwick County Area Spl. Edn. Svcs. Coop., Goddard, Kans., 1979-80; tchr. learning disabled coun. spl. edn. program Butler County Sch. Bd., El Dorado, Kans., 1986-87; tchr. learning disabled Wichita Pub. Schs., 1987-89; writer and researcher, Andover, Kans., 1989-91; legal adminstrv. asst., 1992-94; tchr. learning and behavior disabled So. Tex. Ind. Sch. Dist., Mercedes, 1995-96. Author: A Scoville Branch in America: A Genealogy and Story (1660-1990). Grantee U. Kans. Mem. AAUW, ASCD, DAR (Eunice Sterling chpt. registrar), Coun. for Exceptional Children, Psi Chi.

WARD, MARTHA GAIL JOINER, adult education educator; d. Wofford Johnston and Tommie Lee Joiner; m. James Edward Ward; 1 child, Jonathan Calder. Student, Brunswick (Ga.) Jr. Coll., 1971; BFA in Art Edn., Valdosta State Coll., 1974; MEd in Early Childhood Edn., Ga. So. Coll., 1985, postgrad., 1987. Reading instr. Madison County (Fla.) Sch. Bd., 1974-76; tchr. David Emanuel Acad., Stillmore, Ga., 1976-78, Candler County Bd. Edn., Metter, Ga., 1979-87; learning svcs. coord. The Job Network Ctr., Ga. So. U., Statesboro, 1987-90; adult edn. instr. Swainsboro Tech. Inst., 1990—. Reviewer series of math books: Math Matters for Adults, 1992. Recipient Most Innovative Program of the Yr. award State of Ga.'s Job Tng. Partnership Act 8% Grant, 1989. Mem. Ga. Adult Literacy Assn., Profl. Assn. Ga. Educators (state student group liaison, Candler County chpt. pres. 1986), Ga. Adult Edn. Assn., Inc., Kappa Delta Pi (chpt. pres. 1989-90), Delta Kappa Gamma Soc. Internat. (Beta Beta chpt.). Home: RR 2 Box 110 Metter GA 30439-9548 Office: Swainsboro Tech Inst 201 Kite Rd Swainsboro GA 30401-1852

WARD, MARTHA JANE, elementary education educator; b. Kingsport, Tenn., Feb. 19, 1943; d. Will Sharpe and Martha Emiline (Morrison) King; m. Lawrence Allen Ward, Aug. 25, 1963; children: Lawrence Allen Jr., Martha Jeannine Morris, Sarah Louise Stevens. BS, East Tenn. State U., 1963, MEd, 1985. Cert. elem. tchr., Tenn. 1st grade tchr. Sullivan County Schs., Kingsport, Tenn., 1976—. Mem. ASCD, Nat. Coun. Tchrs. English, Internat. Reading Assn., Delta Kappa Gamma. Methodist. Home: 886 Rock Springs Rd Kingsport TN 37664

WARD, SARAH M., lawyer; b. Elizabeth, N.J., 1957. AB, Princeton U., 1981; JD, Fordham U., 1987. Bar: N.Y. 1987. Ptnr. Skadden, Arps, Slate, Meagher & Flom, N.Y.C. Office: Skadden Arps Slate Meagher & Flom 919 3d Ave New York NY 10022*

WARD, SELA, actress; b. Meridian, Miss.; d. Granberry Holland and Annie Kate Ward. BA, U. Ala. Appearances include: (TV series) Emerald Point, N.A.S., 1983-84, Sisters, 1991— (Emmy award for Lead Actress in Drama Series 1994), (TV movies) Rainbow Drive, 1990, Double Jeopardy, 1993, Almost Golden: The Jessica Savitch Story, 1995, (films) Rustler's Rhapsody, 1985, Nothing in Common, 1986, Hello Again, 1987, The Fugitive, 1993. Office: Ste 469 289 S Robertson Blvd Beverly Hills CA 90211

WARD, SONYA YVETTE, hydrogeologist; b. Houston, Dec. 10, 1965; d. James Carl and Charlotte (Lowrey) W. BS, N.E. La. U., 1987; MS, Baylor U., 1989. Hydrogeologist, project mgr. Triegel & Assocs., Inc., Berwyn, Pa., 1990—; presenter Am. Water Resources Assn., 1994. Vol. Chester County Literacy Program, Exton, Pa., 1991—, Habitat for Humanity of Chester County, 1995—. Mem. Assn. Ground Water Scientists and Engrs. Baptist. Office: Triegel & Assocs Inc Ste 125 2570 Blvd of the Generals Norristown PA 19403

WARD, SUE ELLEANORE FRYER, social worker, state agency administrator; b. Albuquerque, Oct. 28, 1935; d. E. Reeseman and Florence Ione (Pierce) F.; m. Archibald Floyd Ward, Nov. 3, 1959; children: Beth Ione, Lucille Elleanore. BA, Coll. William and Mary, 1957; MSW, U. Utah, 1961; postgrad., Am. U., Beirut, McGill U., Montreal, Can. Cert. social worker; diplomate in clin. social work Am. Bd. Examiners in Clin. Social Work. Social worker, clin. social worker State Hosp. South, Blackfoot, Idaho, 1959-

61; social worker Children's Convalescent Hosp., Washington, 1961-62; caseworker Children's Home Soc. N.C., Greensboro, 1967-68; social worker Mental Health Study Ctr., NIMH, Adelphi, Md., 1968-70; therapist in pvt. practice Annapolis, Md., 1970-74, Clinton, Md., 1973-77; dir. Charles County Children's Aid Soc., La Plata, Md., 1977; project coord. Regional Direction Ctr. for Handicapped, Upper Marlboro, Md., 1980; dir. spl. projects Viacom Cablevision of Md., Rockville, 1981-82; dir. Prince George's County Dept. Aging, Hyattsville, Md., 1982-91, dir. dept. family svcs., 1991-95; dir. Md. Office on Aging, Balt., 1995—; mem. faculty and adv. bd. U. Md. Leisure and Aging, Therapeutic Recreation Mgmt. Sch., 1984-89; chmn. Elder Abuse and Neglect Project Oversight Com. Prince George's County; mem. Md. Gov.'s Task Force on Delivery Svcs. to Elderly, 1990. Contbr. articles to profl. jours. Mem., treas., chmn. bd. Hospice of Prince George's County, Md., 1983—; chmn. profl. adv. com. Prince George's Mental Health Assn., 1983-90; Dem. nominee from 4th Congl. dist., Md., 1978; bd. dirs. Md. Congress Parents and Tchrs., 1974-82; sec. Older Women's League, Prince George's County, 1988-90; pres. Women's Polit. Caucus, Prince George's County, 1986. Recipient Gladys Noon Spellman award for excellence in pub. svc., 1994; certs. for pub. svc. and awards. Mem. NASW, Acad. Cert. Social Workers, Nat. Assn. Area Agys. on Aging (bd. dirs., 2d v.p., pres. 1988-92), Md. Assn. Area Agys. on Aging (chmn. 1989-92), Md. Gerontological Assn. (mem. bd. 1995—). Home: 6109 Buckler Rd Clinton MD 20735-3417

WARD, SUSAN MARIE, cultural organization administrator; b. Detroit, Jan. 29, 1954; d. Richard Guerin and Helen Marie (Stone) W. BA in Art History, Wayne State U., 1983; MA in Decorative Arts, Parsons Sch. Design/Cooper-Hewitt Mus., 1985. Intern Met. Mus. Art, N.Y.C., 1985; asst. curator Biltmore Estate, Asheville, N.C., 1985-86, curator, 1987-92; exec. dir. Travellers Rest, Nashville, 1992-94; founder, dir. Heritage Comm., Brentwood, Tenn., 1994—; sec. Biltmore Village Hist. Mus., Asheville, 1989-91; adj. prof. O'More Coll. Design, Franklin, Tenn., 1995—; instr. Watkins Inst. of Design, Nashville. Author: The Gilded Age at Biltmore Estate, 1990. Vol. Big Bros. and Sisters, Asheville, 1988-92; com. mem. Bele Cher, Asheville, 1989; vol. cons. Jr. Achievement, 1994. Mem. Am. Assn. State and Local History (state membership chmn. 1989), N.C. Mus. Coun. (chmn. computers and museums com.), Southeast Museums Conf. (chmn. intern staff devel. com.), Asheville Mus. of Art (bd. dirs. 1991-92).

WARD, VENUS JOYCE, academic administrator; b. Eureka, Kans., June 8, 1947; d. Edward William and Mildred Louella (Nitsche) W. BS in Biology, Wichita State U., 1970, BS in Med. Tech., 1971; MS, SUNY, Buffalo, 1985; PhD in Ednl. Policy and Leadership, U. Kans., 1995. Cert. med. technologist. Med. technologist St. Joseph Med. Ctr., Wichita, 1971, VA Med. Ctr., Miami, Fla., 1971-73; med. technologist, clin. lab. dir., instr. Raleigh Fitkin Meml. Hosp., Manzini, Swaziland, 1973-83; teaching asst. SUNY, Buffalo, 1983-85; instr., edn. coord. dept. med. tech. U. Kans. Med. Ctr., Kansas City, 1985-91, asst. chair dept. med. tech., 1989-91, asst. prof., chair dept. med. tech., 1991—; accreditation site visitor Nat. Accrediting Agy. for Clin. Lab. Scis., Chgo., 1989, 93; BRIDGES grant reviewer NIH, Bethesda, Md., 1993; external examiner Swaziland Nursing Coun., 1981, 82. Contbr. articles to profl. jours. Missionary Internat. Ch. Nazarene, Kansas City, Mo., 1973-84; active Antioch Ch. Nazarene, Overland Park, Kans., 1985—, v.p. missions soc., 1989-91, 94—. Recipient Disting. Svc. award Westside Ch. of Nazarene, 1984; Baxter Healthcare Corp. scholar Am. Soc. for Clin. Lab. Sci., 1990. Mem. Am. Soc. for Clin. Lab. Sci. (del. 1987-90), Kans. Soc. for Clin. Lab. Sci. (dist. rep. 1986-88, bd. dirs. 1988-90, pres.-elect 1996-97), Greater Kansas City Educators Conf. for Clin. Lab. Sci. (sec. 1986-87, pres. 1989-90), Clin. Lab. Mgmt. Assn. Office: U Kans Med Ctr 3901 Rainbow Blvd Kansas City KS 66160-7608

WARDELL, GLORIA JEAN, executive secretary; b. Montgomery, Ala., Dec. 31, 1951; d. Sam William and Annie Mae (Johnson) W. BS in Bus. Edn., Ala. State U., 1974, MEd in Adminstrn. and Supervision, 1979. Exec. sec. State Ala. Supreme Judicial Ct., Montgomery, 1977-95, Adminstrv. Office of Judicial Cts., Montgomery, 1995—. Mem. Ala. Young Democrats, Montgomery, 1978; hon. mem. So. Christian Leadership Conf., Montgomery, 1993—; ch. clk., 1988-90. Mem. Ala. State Retirement Assn., Ala. State Employee Assn., Alpha Pi Chi. Democrat. Baptist. Home: 617 Community St Montgomery AL 36108 Office: Adminstrv Office of Judicial Cts 300 Dexter Ave Montgomery AL 36104-3741

WARDEN, KAREN BARBARA, special education educator; b. Camden, N.J., Jan. 19, 1949; d. Russell James Jr. and Harriet May (Tupper) W. BS, Vanderbilt U., 1971; student, N.J. Tchr.-Artist Inst., 1990-91, 93-94, Peters Valley, 1994. Cert. elem. edn., spl. edn., and art edn. tchr., N.J. Tchr. of handicapped Camden County Tng. Ctr., Cherry Hill, N.J., 1979, sch. art coord., 1992; tchr., facilitator cmty. awareness program, vol. cmty. tng. program Camden County Libr., Voorhees, N.J., 1987—, Cherry Hill, N.J., 1991—; tchr., facilitator integration of spl. students Magnolia (N.J.) Pub. Schs., 1990-92. Mem. Coun. Exceptional Children, N.J. Art Educators Assn., Ctr. Arts Co. N.J., Love Apple Quilters, South Jersey Spinners and Weavers (asst. pres. 1995—), Third Star Fiber Arts Guild, Garden Patch Quilters. Home: 216 Atlantic Ave SW Magnolia NJ 08049-1716

WARDEN, KAREN ELEANOR, biomedical engineer, researcher; b. Mpls., Aug. 12, 1959; d. Herbert Edgar and Audrey Eleanor (Flaten) W. BSME, W.Va. U., 1981; ME in Biomed. Engring., U. Va., 1986. Cert. engr. intern, W.Va. Engr. E.I. Du Pont de Nemours & Co. Inc., Orange, Tex., 1981-83; project engr. Johns Hopkins U. Sch. Medicine, Balt., 1986-90; rsch. and devel. engr. AcroMed Corp., Cleve., 1990-95. Contbr. articles to profl. jours. Mem. Balt. Women's Com., 1988-89, Fells Point Owners and Renters Assn., Balt., 1988-89, Cleve. Waterfront Coalition, 1990-94. Recipient award Blaustein Found., 1988, award Volvo, Inc., 1989. Mem. ASME, ASTM, DAR, AAUW, Am. Soc. Biomechanics, Internat. Soc. Biomechanics, Biomed. Engring. Soc., Orthopaedic Rsch. Soc., Cleve. Engring. Soc. Republican. Methodist.

WARDEN, PATRICIA STARRATT, writer, actress, composer; b. Boston, Nov. 7, 1943; d. Alfred Byron and Anna (Mazur) S.; m. David W. Warden, Dec. 20, 1995; AB, Smith Coll., 1965; grad. prep. dept. Peabody Conservatory Music, 1961. Teaching asst. Harvard U. Grad. Sch. Bus. Aminstrn., 1965-67; mng. dir. INS Assocs., Washington, 1967-68; adminstrv. asst. George Washington U. Hosp., 1970-71; legal asst. Morgan, Lewis & Bockius, Washington, 1971-72; profl. staff energy analyst Nat. Fuels and Energy Policy Study, U.S. Senate Interior Com., 1972-74; cons., exec. asst. energy resource devel. Fed. Energy Adminstrn., Washington, 1974-75; sr. cons. energy policy Atlantic Richfield Co., 1975-76; energy cons., Alaska, 1977-78; govt. affairs assoc. Sohio Alaska Petroleum Co., Anchorage, 1978-85; legal asst. Hughes, Thorsness, Gantz, Powell and Brudin, Anchorage, 1989-90; writer, media specialist corp. affairs Alyeska Pipeline Svc., Co., 1990-95; legal asst. Hughes Thorsness Powell Huddleston & Bauman LLC, 1996—, pres. Starratt Monarch Prodns., 1986—; Econ. Devel. Commn., Municipality of Anchorage, 1981; actress/asst. dir. Brattle St. Players, Boston, 1966-67, Washington Theater Club 1967-68, Gene Frankel, Broadway 1968-69; actress Aspen Resident Theater, Colo. 1985-86, Ranyevskya (The Cherry Orchard), Anchorage, 1994, Bonfila (SLAVS!), Frau Schmidt (The Sound of Music), Anchorage, 1995; writer and assoc. producer Then One Night I Hit Her, 1983; screenwriter, prodr., actress, composer/pianist A Call to Live, 1995; appeared Off-Broadway in To Be Young, Gifted and Black; performed as Mary in Tennessee, Blanche in A Streetcar Named Desire, Stephanie Dickinson in Cactus Flower, Angela in Papa's Wine, Elizabeth Procter in The Crucible, Candida in Candida, Zeuss in J.B., Martha in Who's Afraid of Virginia Woolf, Amy in Dinny and The Witches, as Columbina in Servant of Two Masters, as Singer in Death of Morris Biederman, as Joan in Joan of Lorraine, as Mado in Amadee, as Mrs. Rowlands in Before Breakfast, as the girl in Hello Out There, as Angela in Bedtime Story, as Hannah in Night of the Iguana, as Lavinia in Androcles and the Lion, as Catherine in Great Catherine, as Julie in Lilliom, as First Nurse in Death of Bessie Smith, as Laura in Tea and Sympathy, as Amelia Earheart in Chamber Music; appeared at Detroit Summer Theatre in Oklahoma, Guys and Dolls, Carousel, Brigadoon, Kiss Me Kate, Finnian's Rainbow; asst. to dir. Broadway plays A Cry Of Players, A Way Of Life, Off-Broadway play To Be Young, Gifted, and Black; screenwriter Challenge in Alaska, 1986, Martin Poll Films; asst. dir. Dustin Hoffman, 1974; contbr. articles on natural gas and Alaskan econ. and environ. to profl. jours. Bd. dirs. Anchorage Community Theatre, Alaska Assn. Legal Assts., 1996—; industry rep. Alaska Eskimo Whaling Commn.; mem. Alaska New Music Forum. Mem. Actors' Equity. Episcopalian. Avocations: skiing, horseback riding, biking, hiking. Home: 1054 W 20th Ave Apt 4 Anchorage AK 99503-1749

WARDEN, WALDIA ANN, archdiocese official; b. New Orleans, Jan. 15, 1933; d. Walter Emmer and Lydia Eugenie (LeBlanc) W.; B.S., St. Mary's Dominican Coll., 1961; M.S. in Dietetics, St. Louis U., 1964, JCL The Cath. U. of Am., 1988. Joined Dominican Sisters, Congregation of St. Mary, Roman Cath. Ch., 1953; tchr. elem. schs., 1954-62; instr. foods and nutrition Dominican Coll., New Orleans, 1964-66, chmn. home econs. dept., 1966-69, asst. dean students, 1969-75, chmn. dept. home econs., 1975-78, chmn. Coll. Planning Council, 1972-76; dir. Rosaryville Center, Ponchatoula, La., 1979-81; pres. St. Mary's Dominican Coll., New Orleans, 1983-86; defender of the Bond for Tribunal, Archdiocese of New Orleans, 1989—; pres. St. Mary's Dominican H.S., 1990-94; exec. sec. First Ct. Met. Tribunal, Archdiocese of New Orleans, 1994—. Trustee, St. Mary's Dominican Coll., 1973-79, 83-86, 90-93; bd. regents Our Lady of Holy Cross Coll., New Orleans, 1992—. Mem. La. Dietetic Assn. (editor jour. 1966-68), La. Leadership Conf. Women Religious, Am. Dietetic Assn., Am. Home Econs. Assn., Canon Law Soc. Am. Home: 2712 Whitney Pl #627 Metairie LA 70002 Office: Met Tribunal Archdiocese New Orleans 7887 Walmsley Ave New Orleans LA 70125

WARDER, CAROLYN DENISE, sales representative; b. Dallas, Feb. 28, 1953; d. Ralph Leon Trimble and Peggy Ruth Ward; m. John Moser Warder, Feb. 26, 1976 (div. Mar. 1985). BS, Tex. Woman's U., 1987. Owner Denison, Sherman, Tex., 1977-83; head real estate Skoglund Comm., Duluth, Minn., 1985-86; sales and ops. Holly Outdoor Advt., Fort Worth, 1987-89; sr. sales rep. Berol USA, Brentwood, Tenn., 1990-95; sales rep. KOH-I-NOOR/Grumbacher, Bloomsbury, N.J., 1995—. Democrat. Office: KOH-I-NOOR Grumbacher 100 North St PO Box 68 Bloomsbury NJ 08804

WARD-JACOBS, BARBARA CONNER, risk management professional, financial consultant; b. Plainview, Tex., Apr. 13, 1940; d. William Elbert and Sarah Pauline (Lovell) Conner; children: Dana Renyce, Lisa Suzaune; m. Jerry Jacobs. Student, U. Houston, 1979-82, BS, 1982. Office adminstr., cashier Interstate Securities, Odessa, Tex., 1964-65; dept. asst. supr. Ft. Bend Ind. Sch. Dist., Sugar Land, Tex., 1974-78; organ. cons. B.C. Ward Enterprises, Inc., Sugar Land, 1982-86; ins. sales, cons. Multi-Ins. Service Co., Houston, 1986-87; coordinator flexible benefits Tex. Assn. Sch. Bds., 1988-92; risk mgmt. cons., 1988-92; cons., pres. Leadership Unltd., Inc., 1991-94; pres. Risk Cons. Group, 1994; registered rep. InterSecurities, Inc. and Western Res. Life Co., 1995—. Host parent Am. Field Svc., Houston, 1980; elder First Presbyn. Ch., Sugar Land, 1982-85; community liaison Ft. Bend Assn. Retarded Citizens, 1984-87, fundraiser, 1985-87, Vol. of Yr., 1985; bd. dirs. Youth Opportunities Unltd., Richmond, Tex., 1985; co-founder For Women Only, Inc., 1992—; corp. devel. mem. Austin Habitat for Humanity, 1991—; vol. Spl. Olympics, 1990—. Recipient Service award Richmond State Sch., 1985-87. Mem. Tex. Investors Tng. Enterprises (sec. 1986-87), Houston Assn. Life Underwriters, PEO. Republican.

WARD-LONERGAN, JEANNENE MARIE, speech pathology professional, educator; b. Roseville, Calif., Dec. 7, 1962; d. Lyle Robert and Jeanne (Landry) Ward; m. George Patrick Lonergan, June 23, 1990. BS in Spl. Edn./Child Study, St. Joseph Coll., West Hartford, Conn., 1984; MS in Speech-Lang. Pathology, Boston U., 1989; PhD in Communication Sci., U. Conn., 1995. Cert. clin. competence, Am. Speech-Lang. Hearing Assn.; lic. speech-lang. pathologist, Ohio; cert. speech-lang. pathologist, Conn., Mass. Program coord., counselor, asst. dir. Camp Harkness Conn. Assn. for Retarded Citizens, Waterford, 1981-84; spl. edn. tchr. Killingly Pub. Schs., Danielson, Conn., 1984-85; spl. edn. tchr./curriculum devel. specialist Parish Hill H.S., Chaplin, Conn., 1985-86; rsch. asst. Dr. Janine Cairn U. Conn., Storrs, 1986; rsch. speech-lang. pathologist VA Med. Ctr., Boston, 1988-90; spl. edn. tchr./speech-lang. pathologist Newington (Conn.) Children's Hosp., 1990-91, 92; adj. faculty/lectr. Dept. Communication Scis. U. Conn., 1992, 93; instr./clin. supr. Bowling Green State U., Bowling Green, Ohio, 1994-96, asst. prof., 1996—; editl. cons. Jour. Speech-Hearing Disorders, 1990; book reviewer Doody Pub., Inc., 1996—. Contbr. articles to profl. jours. Sunday Sch. tchr. 1st Congl. Ch., Wyandotte, Mich., 1995—, sanctuary guild com., 1995—; citizen activist for environ. issues, 1995—. Recipient Dudley Allen Sargent Coll. Rsch. grant Boston U., 1988, doctoral fellowship, scholarship and assistantship Dept. Communication Scis., U. Conn., 1991-94. Mem. NOW, LWV (Grosse Ile nat. resources com. mem., treas. 1996), AAUW, Am. Speech-Lang. Hearing Assn., Mich. Speech-Lang. Hearing Assn., Ohio Speech and Hearing Assn., Conn. Speech-Lang. Hearing Assn., Nat. Student Speech-Lang. Hearing Assn., Coun. for Exceptional Children. Democrat. Congregationalist. Home: 17700 Parke Ln Grosse Ile MI 48138 Office: Dept Comm Disorders Bowling Green State U Bowling Green OH 43403

WARD-SHAW, SHEILA THERESA, nurse; b. N.Y.C., June 20, 1951; d. Arthur and Cynthia Melba (Mapp) Jenkins; m. Howard J. Ward, Nov. 1977 (div. 1981); m. Thomas N. Shaw, Sept. 1988; children: Tanyatta, Barbara, Thomas. Student, Rockland Community Coll., 1973, U. Nev., Las Vegas, 1984, San Jose State U., 1994-95; BSN, 1995. Charge nurse Hillcrest (N.Y.) Nursing Home, 1973-74; infirmary nurse St. Agatha's Home for Children, Nanuet, N.Y., 1974-75; temp. bldg. charge nurse Letchworth Village, Thiells, N.Y., 1976; charge nurse New Paltz (N.Y.) Nursing Home, 1977; non secure detention, foster bdg. parent St. Agatha's Home for Children, Nanuet, 1977-79; asst. nursing supr., inservice coord., infection control nurse So Nev. Mental Retardation, Las Vegas, 1979-84; psychiat. nurse II evening duty officer Harbor View Devel. Ctr., Valdez, Alaska, 1987-89; infection control, employee health nurse, unit coord. North Star Hosp., Anchorage, 1989-92; psychiat. nurse, infection control Oak Creek Hosp., San Jose, Calif., 1992-93, writer, producer OSHA precaution tng. staff video, 1993; psychiat. nurse Menlo Park divsn. VA Hosp., Palo Alto, 1992-95, psychiat. nurse Palo Alto divsn., 1995—. Campaign worker Nev. Gov. Bryan Dem. Candidate, Las Vegas, 1983-84, Pearson for County Comm. Race, Las Vegas, 1984; pres. Clark County Health Educators, 1983; mem. APIC., 1980-85. Mem. Nat. Assn. Black Nurses, South BAy Black Nurses Assn., San Jose State U. Students of African Descent Assn. (chmn. pub. affairs, newsletter editor 1995), Sant Jose State U. Coll. Applied Sci. and Art Friends and Alumni Sch. Nursing (editor newsletter 1995—), Sant Jose State U. Alumni Assn., Assn. for Practioners of Infection Control, Nat. Assn. Black Nurses., San Jose State U. Alumni Assn., San Jose State U. Sch. Nursing Alumni and Friends. Roman Catholic. Office: VA Hosp Palo Alto MPD 3801 Miranda Ave Palo Alto CA 94304-1207

WARE, DOROTHY B., mental health counselor, researcher; b. Cornwall, N.Y., Feb. 2, 1943; d. Ted A. and Virginia L. (MacNary) Bajgert; m. Auddy C. Ware, Mar. 15, 1962 (div. Apr. 1987); life ptnr. Joan Green; children: Virginia, Dorothy, Audra, Matthew. BA, Mo. So. State Coll., Joplin, 1993; MS, Pittsburg (Kans.) State U., 1995, EdS, 1996; postgrad., U. Ark. Lic. profl. counselor. Contbr. articles to profl. jours. Mem. ACA, Am. Assn. Marriage and Family Therapy, Chi Sigma Iota, Psi Chi. Home: 815 Olive St Carthage MO 64836-1922

WARE, PEARL CUNNINGHAM, health educator; b. Greensboro, N.C., Aug. 18, 1939; d. Cyprian Reginald and Ida (Williams) Cunningham. BA summa cum laude, N.C. Agrl. and Tech. Coll., 1959; MA, Columbia U., 1962. Cert. English and spl. edn. tchr., N.Y. Tchr. Raleigh (N.C.) Pub. Schs., 1959-61; office worker Tchrs.' Coll., Columbia U., N.Y.C., 1961-62; hosp. tchr. N.Y.C. Pub. Schs., 1962—. Candidate for N.Y. State Assembly, N.Y. State Right-to-Life Party, 1980, 82, candidate for N.Y. State Senate, 1984. Recipient plaque Boy Scouts Am., Bklyn., 1984, Honor cert. N.Y. Alliance Pub. Schs., 1987. Mem. Nat. Honor Soc. Secondary Schs., Alpha Kappa Mu, Sigma Rho Sigma, Kappa Delta Pi, Nat. Sorority Phi Delta Kappa (Theta chpt., recording sec. 1995-96). Home: 91 E 91st St Brooklyn NY 11212-1501 Office: Interfaith Hosp PS 403 Annex 1545 Atlantic Ave Brooklyn NY 11213-1122

WARE, PEGGY JENKINS, photographer, writer, artist, dancer; b. Santa Monica, Calif., Sept. 6, 1947; d. Stanley Lauder Mahony and Patricia Lou Chapman Covo; m. James Michael Jenkins, Feb. 5, 1966 (div. May 1982) 1 child, Cheryl Denise Jenkins; m. Wiley Neal Ware, Jan. 1, 1988. Dance student of Eugene Loring, U. Calif., Irvine, 1979; dance student Valentina Oumansky, Dramatic Dance Ensemble, North Hollywood, Calif., 1969-72; dance student, Jerry Bywaters Cochran, Dallas, 1972-75; photography student of James Baker, U. Tex., Dallas, Richardson, 1984-86; BA in English, U. Tex. at Dallas, Richardson, 1986, postgrad., 1987. Propr. Mahony/Jenkins & Assocs., Richardson, 1980-82; mng. editor, writer Happenings Mag., Dallas, 1983; prodn. supr. Publishing Concepts, Dallas, 1983-85; mem. book prodn. team David Marquis/Robin Sachs-Corp. for Edn., Dallas, 1990; freelance photographer and artist Dallas, 1984-95, Sedona, Ariz., 1995—; rsch. editor Prin. Fin. Securities, Dallas, 1994; dance rsch. interviewer Simon Semenoff, Ballet Russe, Sol Hurok, Impressario. Exhbns. include Allen St. Gallery, Dallas, 1985, Oak Cliff Art Festival, Dallas, 1991, 500 Inc. Artfest, Dallas, 1992, Sedona Art and Wine Festival, 1993, Good Dog/Bad Dog, Dallas, 1994, Internat. FotoFest, 1994, Lakewood Svc. League, Dallas, 1995, Bath House Cultural Ctr., 1995, Irvine (Calif.) Fine Arts Ctr., 1995-96, Select Art Gallery, Sedona, 1996; transcribing editor: I Am a Teacher, A Tribute to America's Teachers, 1990; photographer: Photo Essay of the Berlin Wall, 1988; contbr. articles and photos to mags. Exec. bd. Friends of Photography, Dallas Mus. Art, 1993-94; bd. dirs., trustee Dancers Unltd. Repertory Co., Dallas, 1990-91; contbr. photographer Lakewood Svc. League, Dallas, 1992; writer, video producer Women's Conf., Women's Caucus for Art, Dallas, 1986. Home: 62 Morning Sun Dr Sedona AZ 86336 Office: PO Box 1891 Sedona AZ 86339

WARG, PAULINE, artist, educator; b. Detroit, Mich., Oct. 15, 1951; d. Clifford Rudolf and Marguerite Evelyn (Kaiser) W.; m. Gary Dean Snider, Apr. 14, 1990. Student, Bowling Green State U., 1969-72, diploma, 1972-75; postgrad., U. So. Maine, 1992—. Cert. Spl. Needs Vocat. Instr. Maine. Owner, pres. Warg Designs Inc., Scarborough, Maine, 1975—; instr. The Jewelry Inst., Providence, R.I., 1983-87; resident instr. Lexington Arts & Crafts Ctr., Lexington, Mass., 1987; asst. mgr. cons. J.S. Ritter Jewelers Tool & Supply Co., Portland, Maine, 1991-92; instr. Maine Coll. of Art, Portland, 1992—; owner, dir. metalsmithing program Future Builders, Inc., Scarborough, Maine, 1992—; lectr. Paul Revere House Mus., Boston, 1981, juror League of N.H. Craftsmen, Concord, N.H., 1985-87, stds. com. juror League of N.H. Craftsman, Concord, 1985-87, exhbn. juror Boston Mus. Sch., Boston, 1992. Contbr. articles to profl. jours. Founding mem. Portsmouth Artisans, Portsmouth, N.H., 1975-77, founding owners, treas. Sail Loft Cmty. Arts Program, Portsmouth, 1977-79. Mem. Soc. Am. Silversmiths (artisan mem. 1992—), Maine Crafts Assn. Democratic. Office: Warg Designs Inc Pine Point Business Park 15 Holly St #106 Scarborough ME 04074

WARING, MARY LOUISE, social work administrator; b. Pitts., Feb. 15, 1928; d. Harold R. and Edith (McCallum) W. AB, Duke U., 1949; MSS, Smith Coll., 1951; PhD, Brandeis U., 1974. Lic. clin. social worker, Tenn. Sr. supervising social worker Judge Baker Guidance Ctr., Boston, 1955-65; dir. social svc. Cambridge (Mass.) Mental Health Ctr., 1965-70; assoc. prof. Sch. Social Work Fla. State U., Tallahassee, 1974-77; prof. Fordham U., N.Y.C., 1977-82; cons. Dept. Human Svc., N.J., 1983-84; cons., sr. staff mem. Family Counseling Svc. Bergen County, Hackensack, N.J., 1984-86; dir. Step One Employee Assistance Program Fortwood Ctr., Inc., Chattanooga, 1986—; mem. ethics com. Chattanooga Rehab. Hosp., 1995. Contbr. articles to profl. jours. Mem. Citizen Amb. Program Human Resource Mgmt. Delegation to Russia, 1993; active Nat. Trust for Hist. Preservation, Nature Conservancy, Hunter Mus. Am. Art, Chattanooga Symphony and Opera Assn., Friends of Hamilton County Bicentennial Libr. Recipient Career Tchr. award Nat. Inst. Alchohol and Alchohol Abuse, 1972-74; traineeship NIMH, 1949-51. Mem. NASW (charter), Acad. Cert. Social Workers, Nat. Mus. Women in Arts (charter), Smithsonian Assocs., Cmty. Svcs. Club Greater Chattanooga (pres. 1995, 96, v.p. 1994, 97). Office: Fortwood Ctr Inc 1028 E 3rd St Chattanooga TN 37403-2107

WARLICK, KARLA JAN, school counselor; b. Levelland, Tex., Aug. 6, 1949; d. Milton Jr. and Mary Tom (Bradford) Tankersley; m. Philip Owen Warlick, Aug. 24, 1968 (div. Oct. 1994); children: Allyson Wynn, Philip Owen II. BS, Tex. Women's U., 1970; MA, U. Tex., Odessa, 1991. Tchr. Richardson (Tex.) Ind. Sch. Dist., 1970-72; agt. Irene Smith Realtors, Austin, 1977-79; broker Bohannan Realtors, Midland, Tex., 1979-80; broker in pvt. practice Midland, 1980-92; tchr. Hillander Sch., Midland, 1980-81; assessment coord. Midland Coll., Midland, 1988-90; therapist, substance abuse supr. Dept. Family Svcs., Midland, 1990-91; counselor Midland Ind. Sch. Dist., Midland, 1991—; counselor in pvt. practice Midland, 1992—; counselor Grapevine-Colleyville (Tex.) Ind. Sch. Dist., 1995—; mem. gifted and talented com. Midland Ind. Sch. Dist., 1992—. Active Midland Symphony Guild; bd. dirs. Am. Heart Assn., Midland, 1982-85. Mem. Am. Counseling Assn., Tex. Counseling Assn., Permian Basin Counseling Assn. (mem. legis. com. 1992—), Zeta Tau Alpha. Methodist. Home: 365 Parkway Blvd Coppell TX 75019

WARMBROD, CATHARINE PHELPS, educational researcher, consultant; b. Lost Nation, Iowa, July 2, 1929; d. Paul Edward and Ruth Dorthea (Langhorst) Phelps; m. J. Robert Warmbrod, Jan. 30, 1965. BA, U. Iowa, 1952; MS, U. Ill., 1965, advanced cert. in edn., 1967. Head supr. student tchrs. in bus. edn. U. Ill., Urbana, 1966-67; chmn. office adminstrn. Columbus (Ohio) State Community Coll., 1970-77; rsch. specialist NCRVE Ohio State U., Columbus, 1977-88, rsch. specialist emeritus, 1988—; prin. Warmbrod Ednl. Svcs., Columbus, 1988—; bd. dirs. Nat. Assn. Industry/Edn. Cooperation, Buffalo, 1980-88. Author: Retraining and Upgrading Workers, 1983; contbr. to profl. publs.; editor: VocEd Insider for Tech. Edn., 1981. Bd. dirs. Ohio Women, Inc., Columbus, 1986-92, Friendship Village, Dublin, Columbus, 1990—. Mem. Am. Vocat. Assn. (policy com. 1980-83), Assn. Faculty and Profl. Women Ohio State U. (pres. 1984-85), Am. Assn. Cmty. Colls., Am. Tech. Edn. Assn., Delta Pi Epsilon. Presbyterian. Office: Warmbrod Ednl Svcs 3853 Surrey Hill Pl Columbus OH 43220-4778

WARNAT, WINIFRED IRENE, federal agency administrator; b. Grosse Point, Mich., Feb. 8, 1943; d. Rudolf Paul Walter and Frieda (Lupp) W. BA, Fla. Atlantic U., 1965, MEd, 1967; PhD, Am. U., 1971. Dept. mgr., exec. trainee Burdine's Dept. Store, Miami, Fla., 1965-69; asst. dean Grad. Sch. Arts and Sci., clin. prof. Coll. of Medicine, chair, prof. Sch. of Edn. Howard U., Washington, 1969-77; dir. Adult Learning Potential Inst., rsch. prof. Sch. of Edn. Am. U., 1977-81; dir. Nat. Ctr. Teaching and Learning Eastern Mich. U., 1981-84; tech., trade and indsl. edn. specialist Dept. of Edn., Washington, 1984-88, dir. divsn. vocat.- tech. edn. Office of Vocat. and Adult Edn., 1988—; coord. of internat. projects on vocat. edn. Orgn. Econ. Cooperation and Devel. and European Cmty., 1990—; spl. edn. tchr. Deerfield Beach Jr. High Sch., Fla.; vocat. rehab. counselor Broward County, Fla.; career guidance and placement counselor Gallaudet Coll., Washington; disting. lectr. Mich. Dept. of Edn., 1983, 84. Contbr. articles to profl. jours., chpts. to books. Commr. Montgomery County Commn. on Women, Md., 1974-76; U.S. del. World Congress on Vocat. Edn., Sydney, Australia, 1988; U.S. del., U.S. Dept. of Edn. rep. to Conf. on Tech. Change and Human Resources Devel.: the Svc. Sector, Orgn. Econ. Coop. and Devel., Utrecht, Netherlands, 1989, U.S. study coord. Project on The Changing Role of Vocat. and Tech. Edn. and Tng. Office: Office of Vocational & Adult Edn Dept of Edn 330 C St SW Rm 4315 Washington DC 20201-0001

WARNATH, MAXINE AMMER, organizational psychologist, mediator; b. N.Y.C., Dec. 3, 1928; d. Philip and Jeanette Ammer; m. Charles Frederick Warnath, Aug. 20, 1952; children: Stephen Charles, Cindy Ruth. BA, Bklyn. Coll., 1949; MA, Columbia U., 1951, EdD, 1982. Lic. psychologist, Oreg. Various profl. positions Hunter Coll., U. Minn., U. Nebr., U. Oreg., 1951-62; asst. prof. psychology Oreg. Coll. Edn., Monmouth, 1962-77; assoc. prof. psychology, chmn. dept. psychology and spl. edn. Western Oreg. St. Coll., Monmouth, 1978-83, prof. 1986—, dir. organizational psychology program 1983—; pres. Profl. Perspectives Internat., Salem, Oreg., 1987—; cons., dir. Orgn. R & D, Salem, Oreg., 1983-87, seminar leader Endeavors for Excellence program. Author: Power Dynamism, 1987. Mem. APA (com. pre-coll. psychology 1970-74), ASTD, N.Y. Acad. Sci., Oreg. Acad. Sci., Oreg. Psychol. Assn. (pres. 1980-81, pres.-elect 1979-80, legis. liaison 1977-78), Western Psychol. Assn. Office: Profl Perspectives Internat PO Box 2265 Salem OR 97308-2265

WARNER, AMI BETH, secondary school educator; b. Richlands, Va., Oct. 28, 1969; d. Buford R. and Doris Ann Davis. AS, S.W. Va. C.C., Richlands, 1989; B of Sci. and Arts, Radford U., 1991. Cert. tchr., Va. Tchr. Richlands H.S., Va., 1992—. Mem. Pi Gamma Mu, Phi Theta Kappa Alumni. Baptist. Home: Rt 1 Box 1016 Pounding Mill VA 24637 Office: Richlands HS Tornado Alley Richlands VA 24641

WARNER, HEIDI C., clinical research nurse; b. Thomasville, N.C., Nov. 7, 1962. BSN, N.C. U., Charlotte, 1985. RN, N.C.; cert. in audiometry. Clin. rsch. assoc. tng. The Blethen Group, Research Triangle Park, N.C.; clin. rsch. nurse Olsten-Kimberly Quality Care, Indpls.; clin. cons. Pathogenesis Corp., Seattle. Walter C. Teagle Found. nursing scholar, Exxon Co. USA. Mem. Nat. Assn. Female Execs., Phi Eta Sigma. Republican. Methodist.

WARNER, JANET CLAIRE, software design engineer; b. Portland, Oreg., May 2, 1964; d. W. J. and Wendelyn A. (Twombly) W. Student, Clackamas Community Coll., 1982-85; BS in Computer Sci., U. Portland, 1987, MSEE, 1992. Systems asst. U. Portland, 1986-87, programmer Applied Rsch. Ctr., 1987; software design engr. Photon Kinetics, Inc., Beaverton, Oreg., 1987-92; software engr. FLIR Sys., Inc., Portland, 1993; ind. software cons., 1993—. Mem. IEEE, Assn. Computing Machinery (chmn. U. Portland chpt. 1986-87), Soc. Women Engrs. (treas. Oreg. sect. 1988-89), U. Portland Alumni Assn. (Portland programming bd. 1993—), Portland Rose Soc., Eta Kappa Nu (treas. chpt. 1991-92).

WARNER, JUDITH (ANNE) HUSS, educator; b. Plainfield, N.J., June 15, 1936; d. Charles and Martha McMullen (Miller) Huss; m. Howard R. Warner, June 14, 1958; children: Barbara, Robert. BS in Elem. Edn., Russell Sage Coll., 1959. Elem. tchr. Pitts. Bd. Edn., 1959-60; home tchr. Napa (Calif.) Sch. Bd., 1974-77; substitute tchr. Allegheny Intermediate Unit, Pitts., 1977—. Leader Girl Scouts U.S.A., Pitts., 1966-70; vol. Children's Hosp., PItts., 1967-74, Jefferson Hosp., Pitts., 1977-88; pres., trustee Whitehall Libr., Pitts., 1984-92; pres., bd. dirs. Friends of Whitehall Libr., Pitts., 1969-94. Mem. AAUW, DAR. Republican. Methodist. Home: 4985 Wheaton Dr Pittsburgh PA 15236-2064

WARNER, LAURA GAIL, architect; b. Lawrence, Kans., Mar. 31, 1962; d. James Donald and Mary Lynn (Spencer) Warner; m. William Bradley Herrin, Oct. 5, 1995. BA in Arch., U. Calif., Berkeley, 1984. Registered architect, Calif. Project designer SGPA Architects & Planning, San Diego, 1985-89, Callison Partnership, San Diego, 1989-91; prin. Warner Architecture and Design, San Diego, 1991-93. Bd. dirs. Ocean Beach Planning Bd., 1993-95, Ocean Beach Cmty. Devel. Corp., 1993—, Ptnrs. for Livable Places; cons. pro-bono North Ocean Beach Improvement Group, 1994—. Mem. NOW (chpt. pres. 1992, v.p. 1993-95, bd. dirs. 1996, Dist. #1 bd. dirs. polit. action com. Calif. chpt. 1994—, Susan B. Anthony award 1995). Democrat. Office: Warner Architecture & Design 832 Fifth Ave Ste 6 San Diego CA 92101

WARNER, LAVERNE, education educator; b. Huntsville, Tex., Aug. 14, 1941; d. Clifton Partney and Velma Oneta (Steely) W. BS, Sam Houston State U., 1962, MEd, 1969; PhD, East Tex. State U., 1977. Cert. elem. sch. tchr., Tex. First grade tchr. Port Arthur (Tex.) Ind. Sch. Dist., 1962-64; kindergarten tchr. Burlington (Vt.) Community Schs., 1964-66; first grade tchr. Aldine Sch. Dist., Houston, 1967-68; music tchr. Crawfordsville (Ind.) Community Schs., 1968-71; prof. early childhood edn. Sam Houston State U., Huntsville, 1975—, chmn. faculty senate, 1988-89; chair faculty senate Sam Houston State U., 1990-91, chair-elect, 1989-90. Author: (with P. Berry) Tunes for Tots, 1982, (with K. Craycraft) Fun with Familiar Tunes, 1987, Language in Centers: Kids Communicating, 1991, Theme Escapades, 1992, What If...Themes, 1993; contbg. editor Good Apple, Inc., Carthage, Ill., 1986-88, 91-93; contbr. over 60 articles to profl. jours. Mem. Huntsville Leadership Inst., 1986-88, chmn. adv. bd. 1987-88, chmn. 1987-88; Community Child Care Assn., Huntsville, 1988-90. Recipient Sam Houston State U. Excellence in Teaching award, 1992, Tchr. Educator of Yr. award Tex. Assn. for Edn. Young Children, 1992. Mem. Tex. Assn. Coll. Tchrs. (life, past pres.), Nat. Assn. for Edn. Young Children (life), Tex. Elementary-Kindergarten Nursery Educators (state pres. 1982-84), Tex. Assn. for Edn. Young Children (v.p. 1988-89, newsletter editor, 1991-93, Teacher Educator of Yr. 1992, pres.-elect 1993—, pres. 1995), Huntsville Leadership Inst. Alumni Assn. (pres. 1988-89), Phi Delta Kappa (area 3H coord. 1986-92, Svc. Key 1987), Sam Houston Assn. for Edn. Young Children (charter, pres.-elect, 1991-92, pres. 1992-93), Sam Houston Univ. Women (pres. 1985-86), Huntsville High Sch. Ex-Students Assn. (charter, pres. 1989-91). Mem. Ch. of Christ. Office: Sam Houston State U Coll Edn and Applied Sci Huntsville TX 77341

WARNER, PATRICIA JOAN, psychotherapist; b. Greenville, N.C., Mar. 5, 1947; d. Joseph Ophir and Florence Genevieve (Jenkins) Teel; m. Richard Barr Cayton, May 21, 1971 (div. 1978); 1 child, Heather Jeanine; m. Michael Roy Warner, Jan. 9, 1987. BS in Elem. Edn., East Carolina U., 1968, MA in Guidance an Counseling, 1969. Lic. profl. counselor, Ga., Tenn.; nat. cert. counselor. Mental retardation counselor Pineland Mental Health, Jesup, Ga., 1983-85; mental health counselor Jesup, 1985-89; therapist, adolescence substance abuse Sci. Applications Internat., Nuernberg, Germany, 1989-92; adolescent therapist Harriett Cohn Ctr., Clarksville, Tenn., 1992—; chairperson Troubled Childrens Com., Baxley, Ga., 1988; presenter Am. Women's Activities in Germany, 1989. Recipient Letter of Commendation Comdr. U.S. Army Europe, 1991. Mem. Am. Counseling Assn., Erlangen Amateur Radio Soc. (sec. 1990-92), Clarksville Amateur Transmitting Soc., Assn. of Specialists in Group Work. Democrat. Home: 447 Winding Way Rd Clarksville TN 37043-5191 Office: Harriett Cohn Mental Health Ctr 511 8th St Clarksville TN 37040-3093

WARNER-SIEGEL, MARIETTA GERALDINE, artist; b. N.Y.C., Jan. 3, 1934; d. Bernard and Mae Loretta (Lope) Warner; m. Roy F. Siegel, Dec. 20, 1958; 1 child, David Warner. BS in Edn., NYU, 1955, MA, 1956, PhD, 1980; cert. d'etudes, École Nat. des Beaux Arts, Paris, 1964. Cert. tchr. art K-12, N.Y., tchr. art 7-12, N.Y., French and Spanish 7-12, N.Y. With N.Y.C. Pub. Schs., 1955-58, L.I. Pub. Schs., 1958-89; ret., 1989; asst prof. fine arts St. John's Univ., 1965-69; instr. fine arts Molloy Coll., Rockville Centre, N.Y., 1970, Coll. of New Rochelle, 1985; founder, exhbns. dir. Stage Gallery, Merrick, N.Y., 1996—; founder, dir. S.P.E.C.I.A.L. (planning, operating and leading H.S. and coll. art-study tours throughout Europe), 1971-75. One-woman shows include Carus Gallery, N.Y.C., 1962, Trenton State Coll. Phelps Hall Gallery, 1963, E.B. Crocker Mcpl. Art Mus., Sacramento, Calif., 1965, Musée d'Art Moderne de la Ville de Paris, 1965, South Nassau Universal Gallery, 1967, Max Hutchinson Gallery, Soho, 1972, Spectrum Gallery, Soho, N.Y.C., 1972, Village East Gallery, L.I., 1975, Razor Gallery, Soho, N.Y.C., 1975, 80, Hell's Kitchen Gallery, Provincetown, Mass., 1985, 91, 94, The Islip Art Mus., East Islip, N.Y., 1995, The Stage Gallery, L.I., 1995, Erector Sq. Gallery, New Haven, 1996, and numerous others; group shows include Musée de l'École des Beaux Arts, Paris, 1964 (first mention 1964), XVth Salon de la Jeune Peinture Musée d'Art Moderne, Paris, 1964, Butler Inst. Am. Art, Athens, Ohio, 1965, Ward Eggleston Galleries, N.Y.C., 1965 (first prize Emily Lowe painting competition 1965), John Gibson Gallery, 1970, Max Hutchinson Gallery, Soho, N.Y.C., 1972, Razor Gallery, Soho, N.Y.C., 1977, 79, Islip Art Mus., 1995, Erector Sq. Gallery, New Haven, Conn., 1996, Hopper House Art Ctr., Nyack, N.Y., 1996, and numerous others; represented in permanent collections at Yale U., Trenton State Coll., NYU; represent in nat. and internat. pvt. collections; executed murals Nassau Cmty. Temple, West Hempstead, N.Y., 1964, École des Beaux Arts, Paris; translator (from French) La Fresque, 1964; editor-in-chief Lines and Letters NYU, 1952-53, Education Violet Yearbooks NYU, 1954-55; founder, exhbns. dir. The Stage Gallery, Merrick, N.Y., 1996—. Pres. Worthwhile Holidays, Nassau County, N.Y., 1974-76. Recipient Emily Lowe Nat. award for painting Joe & Emily Lowe Found., 1965, First prize for painting, 1966, first prize sculpture Locust Valley Exhbn., 1962; full undergrad. scholarship for merit NYU, 1951-55, full grad. scholarship NYU, 1955-56. Mem. NEA, Internat. Fund for Animal Welfare, Kappa Delta Epsilon (sec. 1954-55), Pi Delta Kappa.

WARNOCK, BETTYE ANN, accountant; b. Madisonville, Tex., Apr. 25, 1936; d. Velma Verna and Carrie (Bledsoe) Jones; m. Charles Edwin Warnock, Dec. 9, 1971. BBA, Sul Ross State U., 1989, Sul Ross State U., 1989. Bus. mgr. GM Warnock Motor Co., Ft. Stockton, Tex., 1966-73, Warr Motors, Inc., Ft. Stockton, Tex., 1973-74; student adv. Midland Coll., Ft. Stockton, Tex., 1990-91; county auditor Pecos County, Ft. Stockton, Tex., 1991-93; property acct. Urban Retail Properties, Odessa, Tex., 1993—; bd. dirs. Ctr. for Big Bend Studies. Past chair Ft. Stockton (Tex.) Housing Bd., 1980-86, Mental Health-Mental Retardation adv. bd., Ft. Stockton, 1981-93, Viss. Devel. Bd., Ft. Stockton, 1981-83. Mem. Odessa (Tex.) Bus. and Profl. Women (treas. 1995-96), Daus. Republic Tex. (press. chpt.), United Daus. Confederacy (Permian Basin chpt.), Alpha Chi. Democrat. Methodist. Office: Permian Mall Urban Retail Properties 4101 E 42nd St Odessa TX 79762

WARREN, CHARMAINE PATRICIA, dancer, historian, journalist; b. Kingston, Jamaica, Mar. 22, 1961; came to U.S., 1972; d. Theophilus Anthony and Pearline Theresa (Goldson) Warren. BA in English, Montclair State Coll., 1984, BA in Theatre, 1988; MA in Dance Rsch., CCNY. dance history & theory tchr. Jamaica Sch. Dance, Kingston, 1988-90, Alvin Ailey Am. Dance Theater Found., 1990, Duke U., 1996—; tchr. Leake & Watts Children's Home, Inc., 1992, Exercise Studio, East Orange, N.J., 1982-83, YMCA, Montclair, 1984-86, Pineapple Dance Studios, 1984, CUNY, 1987-88, Howard U., 1994, George Washington U., 1994, Aris. State U., 1994, Sch. Modern Dance, 1994, Texas Tech U., 1995, U. Pa., 1996, U. Calif., Berkeley, 1996; Healthland, Syndey, Australia, 1985, Key Enzymes Studio, Stockholm, Sture Badet, Stockholm, 1991-93, Theatre Contemporain de la Dance, Paris, 1993, Festival Biennale de Dance, Lyon, France, Nat. Dance Theater Co. Jamaica, 1988—; lectr. in field; asst. dir. David Rousseve/REALITY, 1994-96; choreographer Festival Biennale de Danse Student Workshop, 1994, Theatre Contemporain de la Danse Student Workshop, 1993; choreographer, dir. Jamaica Sch. Dance, 1988—; dancer, choreographer grad. dance concerts CCNY, 1987-88; dance writer New Yorker, 1996—. Appeared on various TV and radio programs; dance reviewer, critic Amsterdam News, 1992—; arts & entertainment editor, writer Carib News, 1992; contbr. articles to profl. jours. and mags. including The New Yorker. Recipient Artistic Achievement award Ednl. Testing Svc., Minority Recognition award Black & Hispanic Alumni Com. Montclair State Coll; dance scholar Jennifer Muller/The Works, Montclair State Coll., Garden State Ballet/. Home: 347 Manhattan Ave Apt 5C New York NY 10026-2654

WARREN, CYNTHIA W. (CINDEE WARREN), food products executive; b. New Orleans. Pres., CEO Confectionately Yours, Inc., Marietta, Ga.; chair vendors exhibits Internat. Cake Exploration Soc. Convention, 1989. Office: Confectionately Yours Inc 105 Denmeade St Marietta GA 30060

WARREN, JENNIFER LEIGH, marketing professional; b. Greenville, Tex., Dec. 16, 1965. BBA in Finance, Marketing cum laude, U. Denver, 1988; MS in European Studies, London Sch. Economics, 1989; postgrad., Sotheby's, London, 1989-90. Law clk. Jack Kintzele, Esq., Denver, 1984-85, Paula Tyo Englander, Esq., Denver, 1985-87; rschr. Markman Co., London, Eng., 1989; v.p. product devel. Markman Internat., Dallas, 1992—; cons. London, Eng., 1991-92; lectr. mktg. dept. U. Tex., Arlington. Mem. Dallas Com. on Fgn. Rels. Mem. Dallas Coun. on World Affairs, Dallas Com. on Fgn. Rels., Delta Sigma Pi. Office: Markman Internat 14901 Quorum Dr Ste 900 Dallas TX 75240

WARREN, LESLEY ANN, actress; b. N.Y.C., Aug. 16, 1948. Studied ballet, N.Y.C.; studied acting, The Actors Studio, N.Y.C. TV appearances include Rodgers and Hammerstein's Cinderella, 1964, Fight for Jenny, 1986, 27 Wagons Full of Cotton, 1990, A Seduction in Travis County, 1991, In Sickness and in Health, 1991; Broadway debut in 110 in the Shade, 1963, Drat the Cat, 1964, Metamorphosis, Three Penny Opera; films include The Happiest Millionaire, 1967, Harry and Walter Go to New York, 1976, Victor/Victoria, 1982, Songwriter, Choose Me, Clue, Apology, 1986, Burglar, 1987, Cop, 1988, Baja Oklahoma, 1988, Worth Winning, 1989, Life Stinks, 1991, Pure Country, 1992, The Color of Night, 1994; TV mini-series include 79 Park Ave., 1977, Beulah Land, 1980, Pearl, Evergreen, 1985, Family of Spies, 1990; TV films include Seven in Darkness, 1969, Love Hate Love, 1971, Assignment Munich, 1972, The Daughters of Joshua Cabe, 1972, The Letters, 1973, The Legend of Valentino, 1975, Betrayal, 1978, Portrait of a Stripper, 1979, Beulah Land, 1980, Portrait of a Showgirl, 1982, A Flight for Jenny, 1986, Baja Oklahoma, 1988, Family of Spies, 1990, A Seduction in Travis County, 1991, In Sickness and Health, 1992, Willing to Kill: The Texas Cheerleader Story, 1992, Joseph, 1995, Murderous Intent, 1995; films include Bird of Prey, 1995. Office: care ICM 8942 Wilshire Blvd Beverly Hills CA 90211

WARREN, MAXINE WOOD, artist, art educator; b. Ponca City, Okla., Jan. 14, 1927; d. William Roy and Helen Enrica (Huffer) Wood; m. William Guy Warren, Jr., June 1, 1949; 1 child, Alison. BFA, Okla. State U., 1948, MS, 1971. Art tchr. McKinley Elem. Sch., Ponca City, 1950, 56-60; dir.-initiator Park Bldg. Contemporary Gallery Conoco, Inc., Ponca City, 1962-65; art tchr. Trout Elem., Ponca City, 1967-70; chmn. art dept. Ponca City Sr. H.S., 1971-86; studio artist paintings and monotypes Riverbluff Studio, Ponca City, 1986—; artist cons. Native Am. Found.-Chief Standing Bear, Ponca City, 1994—; mem. art faculty Arts Adventure, Ponca City, 1993, 94; bd. trustees Okla. Visual Artists Coalition, Oklahoma City, 1992—; chmn. visual arts Marland Estate Commn., Ponca City, 1976-79. Represented in permanent collections Okla. Contemporary Art Mus., Oklahoma City, 1969; Philbrook Art Mus., Tulsa (honorable mention 1948, 66, 68). Recipient 2d prize Internat. Am. Greetings, 5th prize Internat. Ford Times Mag., 1963, 2d prize Internat. Golden Press Book illustration, 1962. Mem. OEA, Nat. Mus. Women in Arts, Okla. Art Inst., Ind. Artists Okla., Zeta Tau Alpha. Republican. Home: RR 2 Box 227 Ponca City OK 74604

WARREN, PATRICIA NELL, publisher, writer; b. Helena, Mont., June 15, 1936; d. Conrad Kohrs and Nellie Bradford (Flinn) W. AA, Stephens Coll., Columbia, 1955; BA, Manhattanville Coll., Purchase, N.Y., 1957. Copy editor Reader's Digest, Pleasantville, N.Y., 1959-64, book editor-mag., 1964-72, book editor-Condensed Book Club, 1972-81; co-founder, ptnr. Wildcat Press, Beverly Hills, Calif., 1994—; co-editor, co-publisher YouthArts West, L.A., 1995—, Youth Arts East, 1995—. Author: (books) The Last Centennial, 1971, The Front Runner, 1974, The Fancy Dancer, 1976, The Beauty Queen, 1978, One is the Sun, 1991, Harlan's Race, 1994. Commr. Gay & Lesbian Ednl. Commn. L.A. Unified Sch. Dist., 1996. Recipient Walt Whitman Literature award Walt Whitman Award Com., 1978, Western Heritage award Nat. Cowboy Hall of Fame, 1982. Mem. ACLU, Author's Guild (com. on free speech 1995—). Office: Wildcat Press 8306 Wilshire Blvd Box 8306 Beverly Hills CA 90211

WARSHAUER, IRENE CONRAD, lawyer; b. N.Y.C., May 4, 1942; d. A. Alfred and Sylvia (Bober) Conrad; m. Alan M. Warshauer, Nov. 27, 1966; 1 dau., Susan L. B.A. with distinction, U. Mich., 1963; LL.B. cum laude, Columbia U., 1966. Bar: N.Y. 1966, U.S. Dist. Ct. (so. and ea. dists.) N.Y. 1969, U.S. Ct. Appeals (2d cir.) 1969, U.S. Supreme Ct. 1972, U.S. Dist. Ct. (no. dist.) N.Y. 1980. With First Jud. Dept., N.Y. State Mental Health Info. Service, 1966-68; assoc. Chadbourne Parke Whiteside & Wolff, 1968-75; mem. Anderson Kill & Olick & Oshinsky, P.C., N.Y.C., 1975—; lectr. Def. Research Inst., Aspen Inst. Humanistic Studies, ABA, Rocky Mountain Mineral Law Found., CPR Inst. Dispute Resolution, panelist Am. Arbitration Assn., 1973—; mediator U.S. Dist. Ct. So. Dist., N.Y. Contbr. articles, chpts. to profl. lit. Mem. Democratic County Com., 1968—. Named to Hon. Order Ky. Cols. Mem. Assn. of Bar of City of N.Y. (judiciary com. 1982-84), N.Y. State Bar Assn. (chairperson subcom. mentally disabled and community 1978-82), ABA. Avocations: gardening, cooking, birding. Office: Anderson Kill Olick & Oshinsky 1251 Avenue Of The Americas New York NY 10020-1104

WARSHAW, ROBERTA SUE, lawyer, financial specialist; b. Chgo., July 10, 1934; d. Charles and Frieda (Feldman) Weiner; m. Lawrence Warshaw, July 5, 1959 (div. June 1978); children: Nan R., Adam; m. Paul A. Heise, Apr. 2, 1994. Student, U. Ill., 1952-55; BFA, U. So. Calif., 1956; JD, Northwestern U., 1980. Bar: Ill. 1980. Atty., fin. specialist Housing Svcs. Ctr., Chgo., 1980-84, Chgo. Rehab. Network, 1985-91, 92-95; dir. housing State Treas., State of Ill., Chgo., 1991; sole practitioner, 1995—; legal worker Sch. of Law, Northwestern U. Legal Clinic, Chgo., 1977-80; real estate developer, mgr., marketer, Chgo., 1961-77; bd. dirs. Single Room Housing Assistance Corp. Co-author: (manual) The Cook County Scavenger Sale Program and The City of Chicago Reactivation Program, 1991, (booklet) Fix the Worst First, 1989; co-editor: The Caring Contract, Voices of American Leaders, 1996. Alderman 9th ward City of Evanston, Ill., 1985-93, mem. planning and devel., rules com., unified budget com., chair flood and pollution control com.; pres. Sister Cities Found.; mem. cmty. and econ. devel. policy Nat. League Cities, 1990-93; mem. Dem. Nat. Com.; bd. dirs. Dem. Ctrl. Com. Evanston, 1973—; elected committeeman Evanston Twp. Dem. Com., 1994—; del. Dem. Nat. Conv., 1996. Mem. ABA (affordable housing com.), Ill. State Bar Assn., Chgo. Bar Assn. (real estate coms.), Decalogue Soc. Lawyers, Chgo. Coun. Lawyers (housing com.). Home: 550 Sheridan Sq # 5G Evanston IL 60202-3169

WARWICK, DIONNE, singer; b. East Orange, N.J., Dec. 12, 1940; m. Bill Elliott (div. 1975); children: David, Damon. Ed., Hartt Coll. Music, Hartford, Conn. As teen-ager formed Gospelaires and Drinkard Singers, then sang background for rec. studio, 1966; debut, Philharmonic Hall, N.Y. Lincoln Center, 1966; appearances include London Palladium, Olympia, Paris, Lincoln Ctr. Performing Arts, N.Y.C.; records include Don't Make Me Over, 1962, Walk On By, Do You Know The Way to San José, What The World Needs Now, Message To Michael, I'll Never Fall In Love Again, I'll Never Love This Way Again, Deja Vu, Heartbreaker, That's What Friends are For; albums include Valley of the Dolls and Others, 1968, Promises, Promises, 1975, Dionne, 1979, Then Came You, Friends, 1986, Reservations for Two, 1987, Greatest Hits, 1990, Dionne Warwick Sings Cole Porter, 1990, Hidden Gems; The Best of Dionne Warwick, Vol. 2, 1992, (with Whitney Houston) Friends Can Be Lovers, 1993; TV appearance in Sisters in the Name of Love, HBO, 1986; screen debut Slaves, 1969, No Night, So Long, also, Hot! Live and Otherwise; co-host: TV show Solid Gold; host: TV show A Gift of Music, 1981; star: TV show Dionne Warwick Spl. Founder Dionne Warwick Scholarship Fund, 1968, charity group BRAVO (Blood Revolves Around Victorious Optimism), Warwick Found. to Help Fight AIDS; spokeswoman Am. Sudden Infant Death Syndrome; participant U.S.A for Africa; Am. Amb. of Health, 1987. Recipient Grammy awards, 1969, 70, 80; NAACP Key of Life award, 1990. Address: Arista Records Inc 6 W 57th St New York NY 10019-3913*

WASCO, MARY JO, art educator; b. Pitts., Aug. 24, 1943; d. John Lawrence and Pauline (Straka) McCartney; m. John Charles Wasco, Oct. 24, 1970; children: Michael John Wasco, David Charles Wasco. BS in Edn. cum laude, Pa. State U., 1965; postgrad., Indiana U. of Pa., 1970-73, Duquesne U., 1982-83. Cert. art tchr., grades K-12, Pa. Art tchr. Baldwin-Whitehall Schs., Pitts., 1965; art tchr. Detroit Pub. Schs., 1966-69, Peters Twp. Sch. Dist., McMurray, Pa., 1970—; staff devel. com. Peters Twp. Schs., 1992—. Calligrapher: (book) Blueberries, Barnacles and Licorice Shoestrings, 1982; exhibited in weaving show Warren Stone Mus., 1988. Mem., pres., treas., bd. dirs. McDonald (Pa.) Free Libr., 1983-90; treas. Environ. Neighbors, Bulger, Pa., 1988-92; pres. Peters Twp. Edn. Assn., 1990-93. Participant 1st Nat. Conf. on Art Edn. The Getty Ctr. for Edn. in the Arts, L.A., 1994. Mem. NEA, Nat. Art Edn. Assn., Washington County Edn. Assn. Democrat. Roman Catholic. Office: McMurray Elem Sch 626 McMurray Rd McMurray PA 15317

WASELIK, SALLY ANN, computer scientist; b. Morristown, N.J., June 22, 1962; d. Walter and Mary (Mellody) W. BS, Bloomsburg U., 1984. Specialist Virtual Telecomms. Network, East Brunswick, N.J., 1988-90, Federal Telecomms. Svcs. 2000, Somerset, N.J., 1990-91; sr. specialist Premium Billing Svc., Somerset, 1991-92, Bus. Sys. Architecture, Bridgewater, 1992-93, Global Billing Strategies, Bridgewater, 1993-95; mgr. Global Tech. Platforms, Bridgewater, 1995—, dist. mgr. local, wireless billing, 1996—. Home: 11 Forest Ave Bridgewater NJ 08807 Office: Bus Comms Svcs 55 Corporate Dr Bridgewater NJ 08807

WASHBURN, DOROTHY A., entrepreneur; b. Detroit, Oct. 28, 1934; d. Dajad and Mary (Pevrenkjian) Katchadoorian; m. Floyd Donald Washburn, June 23, 1956; children: Mary Susan, Dorothy Ann, Sherry Lynn, Tina Marie. Addressograph and graphotype instr. Burrough's Corp., Detroit, 1952-54; sec. to wire divsn. mgr. Mich. Oven Co., Detroit, 1954-58; exec. sec. to pres. Walch Metal Products, Detroit, 1961-62; sec. and treas. Record Distbrs. Corp., Detroit, 1963-65; fundraiser and trip coord. Edison High Sch., Huntington Beach, Calif., 1972-90; pres. Sunset Sales, Huntington Beach, 1977—. Editor: Annual Assembly Booklet of Ladies Society of the Armenian Church of North America Western Diocese, 1993-96. Campaign com. Gov. George Deukmejian, Doris Allen Campaign com.; chair band boosters Edison High Sch., 1975-77, chair choir boosters, 1988-90; vice chair parish coun. St. Mary Armenian Apostolic Ch., 1994, treas., social and entertainment com., 1993, advisor Ladies Soc., 1994—, advisor cultural com., 1993—, tchr. Sunday sch., 1992-96; corr. sec. Armenian ch. N.Am., Western Diocese, Ladies Ctrl. Coun., 1985—. Recipient Hon. Svc. award Calif. Congress of Parents, Tchrs. and Students, 1990. Armenian Orthodox.

WASHBURN, HARRIET CAROLINE, secondary education educator; b. Hallock, Minn., Mar. 15, 1920; d. John W. and Anna Melinda (Younggren) Swanson; m. Edward James Washburn, Jan. 22, 1971 (dec. 1993); children: Jacqueline Ann Batt, stepchild, Margaret; m. Ohls Batt. BA cum laude, Macalester Coll., 1941; MA in Pupil Personnel Svcs., San Jose State U., 1969. Tchr. Latin, English, phys. edn. Renville (Minn.) Pub. Sch., 1941-43; tchr. phys. edn. St. Cloud (Minn.) Jr. H. S., 1943-44, Fremont (Calif.) Unified Sch. Dist., 1958-69; recreation specialist City Recreation Dept., Lincoln, Nebr., 1946-50; dir. youth activities Trinity Meth. Ch., Lincoln, 1950-53; counselor Milpitas (Calif.) Unified Sch. Dist., 1969-75, head counselor, 1975-80; cons., trainer, speaker Stockton, Calif., 1980—; coord. bank acct. Bank of Stockton, 1989—; mem., presenter Internat. Tng., Anaheim, 1978—; cons. personal, profl. devel. Personal Dynamics, Inc., Mpls., 1980-87. Guest speaker Kiwanis, Lions, Candy Stripers, Ctrl. Meth. Ch., MCClellan AFB, and numerous others, 1980—, presenter Asian Am. Found., Stockton, 1995—. With USN, 1944-46. Recipient Sch. Counselor Svc. award Calif. Sch. Counselor Assn., Milpitas, 1980. Mem. AAUW, Beginners Luck Investment Club, Alliance for the Mentally Ill of S.J. County, Rep. Women's Club. Presbyterian. Office: Bank of Stockton 301 E Miner St Stockton CA 95201

WASHBURN, NAN, conductor. Music dir Camellia Symphony Orchestra, Sacramento, CA. Office: Camella Symphony Orch PO Box 19786 Sacramento CA 95819-0786*

WASHBUSH, KAREN J., marketing executive, foundation administrator; b. Dallas, Nov. 6, 1961; d. Charles E. and Jane C. (Coonen) W. BSBA, Bowling Green State U., 1984. Account exec., sr. account exec. Boy Scouts Am., Columbus, Ohio, 1985-92; agt., v.p. mktg. Edward L. Burgess & Assocs., Columbus, 1989—; mktg. dir. Corp. Fin. Assocs., Columbus, 1993; ddonor svcs. officer, advancement officer Columbus Found., 1993—. Mem. steering com. Women in Transition, Columbus, 1995—. Mem. Ctrl. Ohio Planning Giving Coun., Nat. Soc. Fundraising Execs., Worthington Estate Planning Coun. Home: 2059-E Park Run Dr Columbus OH 43220 Office: Columbus Found 1234 E Broad St Columbus OH 43205

WASHINGTON, BEVERLY JEAN, secondary education educator; b. Chgo., Aug. 26, 1948; d. Eugene and Helen Louise (Rogers) Leonard; divorced; children: Sherri, Terri. BA, Iowa Wesleyan Coll., 1970; MS, Chgo. State U., 1974. Cert. tchr., Ill. Tchr. Chgo. Pub. Schs., 1970—. Author: For Our People We Shall Spear, 1994. Mem. Nat. Coun. Tchrs. English, Ill. Assn. Tchrs. English.

WASHINGTON, LEANNA M., state legislator; b. Phila., July 28, 1945; children: William, Edward, Tracey. MA, Lincoln U., 1989. Committeewoman 50th Dem. Ward, Phila., 1980; dist. office mgr. Senator Joseph Rocks, Harrisburg, 1985-88; Pa. state rep. Dist. 200, 1994—; mem. aging and youth, health and human svc. and urban affairs coms., chmn. first class cities and counties subcom., 1990-93; mem. women's and substance abuse caucus Pa. House Reps., Phila., 1993—; mem. bd. dirs. Women in Transition, Phila., 1987-89, Gaudenzia Ea. Reg., Phila., 1994—, Agape Outreach, Phila., 1993—. Committeewoman 50th Dem. Ward, Phila., 1982. Recipient Senate Proclamation Senator Roxanne Jones. Democrat. Baptist. Office: Pa Ho of Reps State Capitol 307 South Office Bldg Harrisburg PA 17120

WASHINGTON, NANCY JANE HAYES, librarian; b. High Point, Dec. 31, 1936; d. Lester Eli and Annie Rose (Caldwell) Hayes; m. Charles D. Washington, Dec. 26, 1969 (div. June 1981). AA, Mars Hill Coll., 1957; BA, U. S.C., 1959; MA, U. West Fla., 1980; MLS, Fla. State U., 1982. Music tchr. private studio, Columbia, S.C., 1959-67; asst. dir. film libr. State Dept. Edn., Columbia, 1967-68; elem. sch. tchr. Richland County Schs., Columbia, 1969-71; serials cataloging and acquisitions asst. U. West Fla., Pensacola, 1972-83, serials acquisitions libr., reference libr., 1983-84; bibliographer humanities, arts and social scis. U. S.W. La., Lafayette, 1984-86; asst. dir. sys. libr. svcs. U. S.C., Columbia, 1986-94, dir. publs. divsn. librs. and info. sys., 1994—. Author: Univ. S.C. Regional Campuses Faculty Senate: It's First 25 Years, 1993; editor Ex Libris, 1994, 95; contbr. articles to profl. jours. Bd. dirs. Columbia Mus. Art, 1992-94. Mem. Am. Libr. Assn., S.E. Libr. Assn., S.C. Lib. Assn., Richland Kiwanis Club (sec.), Phi Kappa Phi, Beta Phi Mu. Episcopalian. Office: Thomas Cooper Libr Univ SC Greene St Columbia SC 29208

WASHINGTON, PATRICIA LANE, retired school counselor; b. Junction City, Kans., June 23, 1943; d. LeRoy and Rose Mary (Strong) Lane; children: Janet Rosemarie, Kelly Edward. BS in Elem. Edn., Lincoln U., 1965; postgrad., U. Kans., 1968, 69, 70; specialist in counseling, U. Mo., Kansas City, 1972, postgrad., 1990-93; MS in Learning Disabilities, Ctrl. Mo. State U., 1975; postgrad., Met. C.C., Kansas City, Mo., 1979, Nat. Coll., Kansas City, 1983, Ottawa U., 1984, Avilla Coll., 1993. Cert. elem. and secondary tchr., tchr. of bevavioral disordered, learning disabled, psychol. examiner, counselor, Mo. 1st grade tchr. Kansas City Sch. Dist., 1965-68, head start instr., 1966-69, sr. instr., 1968-75, K-6 grade resource tchr., 1975-77, ednl. resource tchr. with gifted and talented students, 1979, ednl. resource tchr. early identification screening program, 1980, mem. screening team, 1980-81; sr. H.S. learning disabilities instr. Kansas City Bd. Edn., 1981, mem. spl. edn. placement team., 1981-84, sch. psychol. examiner, 1984-88, placement advisor, psychol. examiner, 1988-89, learning disabilities high sch. instr., 1989-90, elem. guidance counselor, 1990-91, mid. sch. guidance counselor, 1991-92, high sch. guidance counselor, 1992-93, chpt. I counselor grades K-5, 1993-94, mid. sch. counselor, 1994-95; ret., 1995; exec. dir., owner Upper Pathways - The Wave of the Future, Kansas City, 1996—; dir., counselor Jackson County Ct., summer 1971; instr. Pioneer C.C., 1970-80, 80-81, 82; coord., instr. Second Bapt. Ch. Adminstr., 1983; spkr. in field. Pres. Host-Hostess ministry 2d Missionary Bapt. Ch. Mem. Am. Legion, Optimist Club. Democrat. Baptist. Home and Office: 9716 Elm Ave Kansas City MO 64134-2221

WASHINGTON, REBECCA NAN, assistant principal; b. Amherst, Tex., Jan. 21, 1950; d. James Earl and Betty (Hinson) Parish; m. Randy Paul Washington, June 12, 1970; children: Christopher Paul, Stacy Bea. BS in Edn., Tex. Tech. U., 1973; MEd, S.W. Tex. State U., 1994. Cert. ednl. adminstr., Tex. Tchr. Round Rock (Tex.) H.S., 1976-78; dir. Hyde Park Weekday Childcare, Austin, Tex., 1979-83, Stepping Stones Presch., Georgetown, Tex., 1985-89; tchr. Georgetown Jr. H.S., 1989-94; asst. prin. Purl Elem. Sch., Georgetown, 1994-96; prin. Williams Elem., Georgetown, 1996—; trainor Dimensions of Learning. Adv. bd. Bapt. Gen. Conv. of Tex. Weekday Early Edn. Divsn., Dallas, 1987-89. Named Outstanding Tchr., Am. Ent. Forum, Houston, 1991. Mem. ASCD, Tex. Hist. Assn. (Commendation 1993), Tex. Elem. Prins. and Suprs. Assn., Tex. Coun. for the Social Studies, Tex. Social Studies Suprs. Assn., Phi Delta Kappa.

WASHINGTON, SHELLEY LYNNE, dancer; b. Washington, Nov. 3, 1954; d. Edward Freeman and Geraldine (Butler) W. Student, Interlochen Arts Acad., 1969-72, Juilliard Acad., N.Y.C., 1972-74. Dancer Martha Graham, N.Y.C., 1974-75, Twyla Tharp Dance Found., N.Y.C., 1975—, Am. Ballet Theatre, N.Y.C., 1988-91; ballet mistress and artistic assoc. dir. for Twyla Tharp, including repertory for Boston Ballet, Hubbard St. Dance Co., Martha Graham Dance Co., Am. Ballet Theatre, The Royal Ballet, London. Dancer in film Hair, 1978; in Broadway show Singin in the Rain, 1985-86. Recipient Bessie Schonberg award for Outstanding Performing, 1987. Office: Twyla Tharp Dance Found Tharp Prodns 336 Central Park W New York NY 10025-7111

WASHINGTON, VALORA, foundation administrator; b. Columbus, Ohio, Dec. 16, 1953; d. Timothy Washington and Elizabeth (Jackson) Barbour; children: Omari, Kamilah. BA in Social Sci. with honors, Mich. State U., 1974; PhD, Ind. U., 1978; PhD (hon.), Bennett Coll., 1992. Assoc. instr. sch. edn. Ind. U., Bloomington, 1975-77; dir., cons. Urban League Ind., Indpls., 1977-78; substitute tchr. Indpl. Pub. Schs., 1978; dir. U. N.C., Chapel Hill, 1980-82; congrl. sci. fellow Soc. for Rsch. in Child Devel., Washington, 1981-82; prof. edn. U. N.C., Chapel Hill, 1978-83; asst. dean, assoc. prof. Howard U., Washington, 1983-86, Am. U., Washington, 1986-87; prof., v.p. Antioch Coll., Yellow Springs, Ohio, 1987-90; v.p. Kellogg Found., Battle Creek, Mich., 1990—; cons. Ford Found., N.Y.C., 1990; project evaluator Carnegie Corp., N.Y.C., 1989-90, Ohio Bd. Regents, Columbus, 1990—. Author: (with others) Creating New Linkages for the Adoption of Black Children, 1984, Project Head Start: Past, Present and Future Trends in the Context of Family Needs, 1987, Black Children and American Institutions: An Ecological Review and Resource Guide, 1988, Affirmative Rhetoric, Negative Action: The Status of Black and Hispanic Faculty in Higher Education, 1989; contbr. articles to profl. jours; contbr. chapters to numerous books. Recipient Capital U. award, 1990, award Springfield Alliance Black Educators, 1989; named one of Ten Outstanding Young Women Am., 1980, Outstanding Young Woman N.C., 1980, one of 100 Young Women of Promise Good Housekeeping Mag., 1985. Mem. Nat. Coun. Negro Women (chmn. 1982-83), Am. Assn. for Higher Edn. (sec. black caucus 1989), Soc. for Rsch. in Child Devel. (pres. black caucus 1987-89), Nat. Assn. for the Edn. of Young Children (sec. of bd. dir. 1990—), Phi Delta Kappa, Delta Kappa Gamma.

WASHINGTON, VIVIAN EDWARDS, social worker, former government official; b. Claremont, N.H., Oct. 26, 1914; d. Valdemar and Irene (Quashie) Edwards; m. George Luther Washington, Dec. 22, 1950; 1 child, Valdemar Luther. AB, Howard U., 1938, MA, 1946, MSW, 1956; LHD (hon.), U. Balt., 1993. Tchr., guidance counselor, sch. social worker, asst. prin., prin. Edgar Allan Poe Sch. Program for Pregnant Girls, Balt., 1966-73; cons. Office Adolescent Pregnancy Programs, HEW, Washington, 1978-80, program devel. specialist, 1980-81; exec. dir. Balt. Coun. on Adolescent Pregnancy, Parenting and Pregnancy Prevention Inc., 1982-86, cons., 1986—; cons. to adolescent parents. Author: I Am Somebody, I Am Me, 1986; contbr. articles to profl. jours. Bd. dirs. Nat. Alliance Concerned with Sch.-Age Parents, 1970-76, pres., 1970-72; YWCA, Balt., 1966-69, United Way Central Md., 1971-80; mem. bd. visitors U. Balt., 1978-80, U. Balt. Ednl. Found., 1980, 92-94, chair, 1992-94; adv. commn. on social services City of Balt., 1978-85, Govs. Coun. on Adolescent Pregnancy, 1986; chmn. Md. Gov.'s Commn. on Children and Youth, 1972-77, active 1987. Recipient Alumni award Howard U. Sch. Social Work, 1966, Clementine Peters award United Way, 1980, Sojourner Truth award Nat. Bus. and Profl. Women, 1979, Vashti Turley Murphy award Balt. chpt. Delta Sigma Theta, 1981, Balt.'s Best Blue and Silver award, 1983, Pvt. Sector Vol. Svc. award Pres. Reagan, 1984, United Way Community Svc. award, 1985, H. Mebane Turner Svc. award U. Balt. Alumni Assn., 1991, 94, Disting. Black Marylander award Towson State U., 1992, Cmty. Svc. award For Sisters Only, 1994, Learn and Earn Program Pioneer award Balt. City 4-H, 1993, Citizen Citation City of Balt., 1995; named to Balt. Women's Hall of Fame, 1989, Md.'s. Outstanding Ch. Woman Nat. Episc. Triennial, 1991; Paul Harris fellow Balt. Rotary, 1985. Mem. Am. Heritage Soc., Great Cir. Md. Living Legend, Nat. Assn. Social Work, LWV, Nat. Coun. Negro Women (life), Balt. Urban League (Equal Opportunity award 1987), Balt. Mus. Art, Delta Sigma Theta (nat. treas. 1958-63, Las Amigas Svc. award Balt. chpt. 1973), Pierians Club. Democrat. Episcopalian. Home: 3507 Ellamont Rd Baltimore MD 21215-7422

WASHINGTON, WILMA JEANNE, business executive; b. Magnolia, Miss., Oct. 14, 1949; d. Melvin and Wilma Magee; m. Michael Washington, Dec. 18, 1971 (div. 1978); children: Charisse, Jay. Student, Ind. U., 1973-80. Adminstrv. asst. Fred Harvey, Inc., Chgo., 1970-72; office mgr. Model Cities Agy., Gary, Ind., 1972-76; adminstrv. mgr. Med. Ctr. of Gary, 1976-81; events coord. Genesis Convention Ctr., Gary, 1981-83, exec. mgr., 1983-85; mgr. corp. devel. Dimensions Unltd., Inc., Chgo., 1985-87, v.p., 1987-92; owner Splty. Promotions, Gary, 1992—; booking agt. New Regal Theater, Chgo., 1995—. Mem. Miller Citizens Orgn., 1976—. Recipient appreciation cert. Northwest in Black Expo, 1985. Mem. NAFE, Gary C. of C. Baptist. Home & Office: 7741 Oak Ave Gary IN 46403-1364

WASILIK, JEANNE MARIE, artist; b. Washington, Mar. 10, 1954; d. John Huber and Ann Mary (Walsh) W. BA, U. Del., 1975. Graphic designer Profile Press, N.Y.C., 1976; freelance graphic designer N.Y.C., 1977-79; asst. dir. prints and photographs Marlborough Gallery, N.Y.C., 1979-81; gallery asst. Galleria L'Isola, Rome, 1982; freelance curatorial and adminstrv. asst. to artists N.Y.C., 1982-84; freelance English tchr. Rome, 1984-85; editor, curator, adminstr. Kent Gallery, N.Y.C., 1986-93; freelance writer, translator, curator N.Y.C., 1994-96. Editor, rschr., translator: Medardo Rosso, 1988; editor: Eugene Carrière, 1990; author: Maryan: Behold A Man and His Work, 1996. Tutor Robert Siegel Ctr., N.Y.C., 1989-95. Recipient 2d prize Chord and Discord Exhbn., Hudson River Mus., Yonkers, N.Y., 1991, award 6th Annual Small Works Competition, Amos Eno Gallery, N.Y.C., 1991. Home: 124 East 4th St New York NY 10003

WASIUK, KATHLEEN PAGE, secondary education educator; b. Princeton, N.J., Feb. 22, 1947; d. Warren Kempton amd Martha Jane (Lutz) Page; m. Joseph Steven Wasiuk, July 29, 1967; 1 child, Virginia Hope. BFA, U. Ariz., 1970; MA in Liberal Studies, Dartmouth Coll., 1988. Tchr. Tilton (N.H.) Sch., 1975-87; tchr. Northfield (Mass.) Mt. Hermon Sch., 1988—, chmn. history dept., 1990-94, dir. acad. resources, 1995—. Named Outstanding Young Career Woman, Bus. and Profl. Women's Club N.H., 1974. Mem. Elephant Rock Assn. (pres.). Congregationalist.

WASKO-FLOOD, SANDRA JEAN, artist, educator; b. N.Y.C., Mar. 12, 1943; d. Peter Edmund and Margaret Dalores (Kubek) Wasko; m. Michael Timothy Flood, June 28, 1969. BA, UCLA, 1965, postgrad., 1968-69; postgrad., Calif. State U., Northridge, summer 1968; student, Otis Art Inst., L.A., 1969, Marie Kaufman, Rio de Janeiro, 1970-72, Museo de Arte Moderno, Rio de Janeiro, 1970-73, Foothill Coll., Los Altos, Calif., 1973-74, Claremont (Calif.) Coll., 1975, U. Wis., Janesville, 1977, Beloit (Wis.) Coll., 1977-78, U. Wis., 1977-78; grad. etching student, Warrington Colescott. Instr. printmaking Washington Women's Arts Ctr., 1983; artist-in-residence U. Md., College Park, 1984; instr. printmaking Arlington (Va.) Arts Ctr., 1984-85; prof. St. Mary's (Md.) Coll., 1985; instr. printmaking Arlington County Lee Arts Ctr., 1989-95; workshop coord. cultural affairs div. Arlington County Parks, Recreation and Community Resources, 1989-96. One woman shows include Wisconsin Women in the Arts Gallery, Madison, 1977, Mbari Art, Washington, 1981, Miya Gallery, Washington, 1981, Slavin Gallery, Washington, 1982, Stuart Mott House, Washington, 1983, Washington Printmakers Gallery, 1986, 88, 91, St. Peter's Ch., N.Y.C., 1989, Montana Gallery, Alexandria, Va., 1991, Montpelier Cultural Arts Ctr., Laurel, Md., 1992, Gallery 10, Washington, 1994; mus. and internat. shows include Boston Printmakers: The 39th North Am. Print Exhbn., Framingham, Mass., Jan.-Mar., 1986, Internat. Graphic Arts Found. and Silvermine Guild Arts Ctr., New Canaan, Conn., Feb., 1988, prints: Washington, The Phillips Collection, Washington, Sept.-Oct., 1988, Contemporary Am. Graphics, Book Chamber Internat., Moscow, 1990, Gallery 10 Artists of Washington D.C. Vartai Gallery, Lithuania, 1994, Peninsula Fine Arts Ctr., Newport News, Va., 1995-96, and numerous others; juried shows include Washington Women's Arts Ctr.: Printmakers VII show, 1985, Washington Women's Arts Ctr., 1981, 82, Seventh Ann. Faber Birren Color Show Nat. Juried Open Exhibit, Stamford, Conn., 1987, Acad. of the Arts 25th Ann. Juried Exhbn., 1989, Fla. Printmakers Nat., 1994, S.W. Tex. State U., 1995, and numerous others; invitational shows include Office of the Mayor, Mini Art Gallery, Washington, "Glimpses: Women Printmakers", 1981, Pyramid Paperworks, Balt., 1984, Gallery 10 "Nightmare Show": Washington, D.C., 1987, The Intaglio Process, The Benedicta Art Ctr. Gallery, St. Joseph, Minn., 1988, Women's Caucus for Art, Washington Artists in Perspective, Westbeth Gallery, N.Y.C., 1990, 91, Wesley Theol. Sem., 1992, Balt. City Hall, N.Am. Print Alliance, 1993, The Five Elements Women's Caucus For Art. 1994, and numerous others; galleries: Slavin Gallery, Washington, D.C., 1981-83, Washington Printmakers Gallery, Washington, 1985-96, White Light Collaborative, Inc., N.Y.C., 1988-89, Montana Gallery, Alexandria, Va., 1989-91, Gallery 10, Washington, 1992—, and numerous others; collections include Nat. Mus. of Women in the Arts, Washington, Corcoran Gallery of Art, Washington, Museo de Arte Moderno, Buenos Aires, Cultural Found., USSR, Coll. Notre Dame, Balt. Pres. Washington Area Printmakers, Washington, D.C., 1985-86; pub. rels. dir. Washington Women's Arts Ctr., 1980; bd. dirs. Washington Women's Arts Ctr., 1981-82. Grantee Friends of the Torpedo Factory Art Ctr., Alexandria, Va., 1989, Va. Commn. on the Arts, 1994; recipient Award of Honorable Mention Nat. Gallery of Art, 1989. Mem. Nat. Print Orgn., Pyramic Atlantic, So. Graphics Coun., Women's Caucus for Art, Coalition Washington Artists, L.A. Printmaking Soc., Washington Ctr. for Photography, Md. Printmakers, Calif. Printmakers, Calif. Printmaking Soc., Am. Print Alliance, Corcoran Gallery/Washington Project for the Arts, Washington Sculpture Group. Home: 8106 Norwood Dr Alexandria VA 22309-1331 Studio: 57 N St NW Washington DC 20001-1254

WASKOW, JOYCE ANN, school administrator; b. Meriden, Iowa, Aug. 15, 1941; d. Clarence Emory and Lucille Dorothy (Horstman) Smith; m. James R. Waskow, July 6, 1963; children: Susan, Brent. BS, Iowa State U., 1963; MA, U. Mo., St. Louis, 1992. Cert. edn. specialist, Mo. Home econs./sci. tchr. Collins (Iowa) H.S., 1963-64; home economist Met. Sewer Dist., Omaha, Nebr., 1964-65; home econs. tchr. Westbrook Jr. H.S., Omaha, 1965-67; home economist The Merchandising Group, N.Y.C., 1970-76; home econs. tchr. Pattonville H.S., St. Louis, 1976-79, Maplewood-Richmond Hts. H.S., St. Louis, 1979-80, Webster Groves H.S., St. Louis, 1980-93; dir. Tchr.'s Acad. Network for Ednl. Devel., St. Louis, 1989-92; asst. prin. Lafayette H.S., St. Louis, 1993—; spkr./workshop leader Network for Edn. Devel., 1987—. Mem. ASCD, Nat. Assn. Secondary Sch. Prins., Am. Home Econs. Assn. (nominating com.), Suburban Home Econs. Assn. (pres. 1986-87), Nat. Assn. Vocat. Home Econs. Tchrs. (Disting. Svc. award 1989), Mo. Home Econs. Tchrs. Assn. (Tchr. of the Yr. 1987, nominating com. 1987-88). Office: Lafayette High School 17050 Clayton Rd Ballwin MO 63011-1792

WASS, HANNELORE LINA, educational psychology educator; b. Heidelberg, Germany, Sept. 12, 1926; came to U.S., 1957, naturalized, 1963; d. Hermann and Mina (Lasch) Kraft; m. Irvin R. Wass, Nov. 24, 1959 (dec.); 1 child, Brian C.; m. Harry H. Sisler, Apr. 13, 1978. B.A., Tchrs. Coll., Heidelberg, 1951; M.A., U. Mich., 1960, Ph.D., 1968. Tchr. W. Ger. Univ. Lab. Schs., 1958-60; mem. faculty U. Mich., Ann Arbor, 1958-60, U. Chgo. Lab. Sch., 1960-61, U. Mich., 1963-64, Eastern Mich. U., 1965-69; prof. ednl. psychology U. Fla., Gainesville, 1969-92; prof. emeritus, 1992—; faculty assoc. Ctr. for Gerontol. Studies U. Fla., Gainesville; cons., lectr. in thanatology. Author: The Professional Education of Teachers, 1974, Dying-Facing the Facts, 1979, 2d edit., 1988, 3d edit., 1995, Death Education: An Annotated Resource Guide, 1980, vol. 2, 1985, Helping Children Cope With Death, 1982, 2d edit., 1984, Childhood and Death, 1984; founding editor (jour.) Death Studies, 1977—; cons. editor: Ednl. Gerontology, 1977-92, (book series) Death Education, Aging and Health Care; contbr. approximately 200 articles to profl. jours. and chpts. in books. Mem. Am. Psychol. Assn., Gerontol. Soc., Internat. Work Group Dying, Death and Bereavement (bd. dirs.), Assn. Death Edn. and Counseling. Home: 6014 NW 54th Way Gainesville FL 32653-3265 Office: U Fla 346 Norman Hall Gainesville FL 32611-2053

WASSELL, IRENE MARTIN, food editor; b. Siloam Springs, Ark., Sept. 19, 1931; d. Leslie and Cora Etna (Jones) Martin; m. Bill J. Wassell, Mar. 29, 1953; children: Lisa Annette, Cynthia Lenore, Eric Lyndon. BA, U. Ark., 1978; MA, U. Ark., Little Rock, 1983. Woman's editor The Times of North Little Rock, 1978-80; staff features writer Ark. Gazette, Little Rock, 1980-90, food editor, 1990-91; food editor Ark. Dem.-Gazette, Little Rock, 1992—. Office: Ark Dem Gazette 121 E Capitol Ave Little Rock AR 72201-3819

WASSENICH, LINDA PILCHER, health policy analyst, fund raiser; b. Washington, Aug. 27, 1943; d. Mason Johnson and Vera Bell (Stephenson) Pilcher; m. Mark Wassenich, May 14, 1965; children: Paul Mason, David Mark. BA magna cum laude, Tex. Christian U., 1965; MSW, U. N.C., 1970. Licensed advanced practitioner, cert. social worker, Tex. Counselor family ct. Dallas County Juvenile Dept., Dallas, 1970-73, 75-76; dir. govt. rels. Vis. Nurse Assn., Dallas, 1980-84, exec. officer of hospice, 1984-85; exec. dir. Incest Recovery Assn., Dallas, 1985-86; assoc. exec. dir. Lone Star Coun. Camp Fire, Dallas, 1986-89; exec. v.p. Vis. Nurse Assn. Found., Dallas, 1989-91; dir. policy & resource devel. Vis. Nurse Assn. Tex., Dallas, 1992—. Contbr. articles to profl. pubs. Bd. dirs. Women's Coun. Dallas County, 1986-95, pres., 1992-93; chmn. Dallas County Welfare Adv. Bd., 1991-95; bd. dirs. United Way of Met. Dallas, 1992-94, Youth Impact Ctrs., Dallas, 1993-94; mem. adv. bd. Maternal Health and Family Planning Dallas, 1990-94; mem. Leadership Dallas, 1988-89. Recipient AAUW, Dallas, Laurel award, 1995. Mem. NASW (Tex. bd. dirs., nominating chmn. 1990-92, co-chmn. Dallas unit 1981-82, Social Worker of Yr. award 1988), LWV (bd. dirs. Dallas 1974-80, 95—, pres. 1995—), Acad. Cert. Social Workers, Nat. Soc. Fundraising Execs. (cert., bd. dirs. Dallas chpt. 1994—, v.p. governance 1995-96). Home: 6948 Kenwhite Dr Dallas TX 75231-5640 Office: 1440 W Mockingbird Ln Dallas TX 75247-4929

WASSERMAN, HELENE WALTMAN, art dealer, artist; b. Phila., Jan. 29, 1929; d. William T. and Bertha (Brener) Waltman; m. Richard M. Wasserman, June 23, 1950 (div. 1972); children: Ann Zelver, Ellen Rubinfield, Stephen; m. Mark C. Cooper, Jan. 22, 1988. BFA, U. Pa., 1951. Pvt. practice art dealer, 1972—; apptd. appraiser Supreme Ct., State of N.Y., 1978. One-woman shows at Philmont Gallery, Phila., 1964, Roko Gallery, N.Y., 1965; exhibited in group shows at Phila. Mus. Art, Pa. Acad. Fine Arts, Philbrook Mus., Tulsa, Woodmere Gallery, Roko Gallery, 1953-68. Active Nassau County Art Commn., 1968-72; trustee, Sculpture Ctr., N.Y.C., bd. dirs., 1991. Mem. Pvt. Art Dealers Assn., Cosmopolitan Club, Nature Conservancy.

WASSERMAN, MARLIE P(ARKER), publisher; b. Chgo., Feb. 14, 1947; d. Theodore E. and Faye (Beller) Parker; m. Mark Wasserman, Nov. 24, 1968; children—Aaron David, Danielle Elizabeth. B.A., Duke U., 1969; M.A., Old Dominion U., 1970. Editor, U. Chgo. Press, 1970-78; sr. editor Rutgers U. Press, New Brunswick, N.J., 1978-83, asst. dir. and editor-in-chief, 1983-87, assoc. dir., editor-in-chief, 1987-94; exec. editor social sciences Routledge, N.Y.C., 1994-95; dir. Rutgers U. Press, New Brunswick, 1995—. Office: Rutgers U Press Livingston Campus Rutgers U New Brunswick NJ 08903

WASSERMAN, MURIEL, artist, art educator; b. N.Y.C., May 27, 1935; d. Max Weintraub and Mollie (Baum); m. Stanley Eli Wasserman, May 22, 1955; children: Debra, David, Mark. BA, Queen's Coll., N.Y., 1976; MA, Pratt Inst., Bklyn., 1982; postgrad, Adelphi U., Bklyn. Mus. Art Sch., Five Town Music & Arts Found., N.Y., Newark (N.J.) Sch. of Art, Bklyn. Coll., N.Y.; studied with Phillip Guston, Rudolf Nakien, Richard Bove, Arthur Coppedge, Jack Rabinowitz. Fine art instr. Valley Stream Library, L.I., 1975-78; art instr. Valley Stream Adult Edn., L.I., 1978—, St. John's U., Queens, N.Y., 1980-94; docent Nassau Mus. Adminstrn., L.I., 1975-76, cataloger, 1976. Columnist: Sunstorm L.I. Art Periodical, 1983-84; one-woman shows include The Gallery at the Bryant Libr., Roslyn, N.Y.; exhibited in group shows at Long Beach (N.Y.) Mus. Art (numerous shows), Isis Gallery, Port Washington, N.Y., Five Town Music & Art Found. (numerous shows), Nat. Assn. Women Artists (numerous shows), Hechscher Mus., N.Y. (numerous shows), Sarah Lawrence Coll., Bronxville, N.Y., Ark. Arts & Sci. Ctr., Pine Bluff, Schenectady (N.Y.) Mus. & Planetarium, Candada Beach Hotel Gallery, P.R., Firehouse Gallery, Nassau C.C., N.Y., Pace U. Art Gallery, Pleasantville, N.Y., Mus. of the Southwest, Midland, Tex., N.Y. Acad. Sci., Christina Rose Gallery, N.Y.C., numerous others. Recipient Painting award Town of Hempstead, Am. Artist Mag. Mem. Nat. Assn. Women Artists (numerous awards), L.I. Craft Guild. Home: 70 Brentwood Ln Valley Stream NY 11581

WASSERMAN, SUSAN VALESKY, accountant; b. St. Petersburg, Fla., June 5, 1956; d. Charles B. Valesky and Jeanne I. (Schulz) Morgan; m. Fred Wasserman III, May 19, 1990; 1 child, Sara Elisabeth. BS in Merchandising, Fla. State U., 1978; BA in Acctg., U. South Fla., 1983; ChFC, Am. Coll., 1991. CPA, Fla.; ChFC, Fla. Mgmt. trainee Burdines Dept. Stores, Miami, Fla., 1978-79; store mgr. Levi Straus Inc., San Francisco, 1979; pvt. practice St. Petersburg, Fla., 1980—; internet practice, 1996—. Paintings shown at Longboat Key (Fla.) Art Ctr. Watercolor 10 Art Show, 1993, Fla. Suncoast Watercolor Soc. Aqueous Show, Sarasota, 1994. Mem. AICPA (personal fin. specialist), Am. Soc. CLUs and ChFCs (bd. dirs.), Fla. Inst. CPAs. Office: PO Box 406 Terra Ceia FL 34250

WASSERMAN, TINA BETH, assistant director career development, writer/media artist, film historian; b. Chgo.; d. Edward M. and Eileen M. (Kronberg) W. BA, U. Wis., 1980; MA, NYU, 1987; postgrad., Whitney Mus. Am. Art, N.Y.C., 1985-86, NYU, 1987—. Rsch. and tchg. asst. NYU, N.Y.C., 1985-89; asst. dir. career devel. Sch. Art Inst. Chgo., 1993—; vis. instr. Sch. Art Inst., Chgo., 1993, 96, Oakton C.C., Des Plaines, Ill., 1993, Columbia Coll., Chgo., 1993-95; paper presenter Internat. Exptl. Film Congress, Toronto, 1989; film juror student awards Acad. Motion Picture Arts, Chgo., 1993, Chgo. Internat. Film Festival, 1994, 95; art and film juror Ragdale Found., Lake Forest, Ill., 1996; art critic New Art Examiner, 1990—, Dialogue, 1992—, Art Muscle, 1993; mem. exhbn. com. N.A.M.E. Gallery, 1994—; bd. dirs. Exptl. Film Coalition, 1992-96. Filmmaker trilogy Notes from the Twentieth Century, 1985, 91, 95; film exhbn. includes London Film Festival, 1989, Chgo. Filmmakers, 1985, 92. Interviewer Holocaust testimonials Shoah Visual History Found., Chgo., 1995. Fellow Ragdale Found., 1987, Banff Ctr. for Arts, 1988, U Cross Found., 1992; travel grantee NYU, 1989, grantee Cmty. Film Workshop, 1994, Ctr. for New TV, 1994, Chgo. Dept. Cultural Affairs, 1995.

WASSERSTEIN, WENDY, playwright; b. Bklyn., Oct. 18, 1950; d. Morris and Lola W. BA, Mt. Holyoke Coll., 1971; MA, CCNY, 1973; MFA, Yale Drama Sch., 1976. Author: (plays) Any Woman Can't, 1973, Happy Birthday, Montpelier Pizz-zazz, 1974, (with Christopher Durang) When Dinah Shore Ruled the Earth, 1975, Uncommon Women and Others, 1975, Isn't It Romantic, 1981, Tender Offer, 1983, The Man in a Case, 1986, Miami, 1986, The Heidi Chronicles, 1988 (Pulitzer prize for drama 1989, Outer Critics Cir. award for best play 1989, N.Y. Drama Critics Cir. award 1989, Susan Smith Blackburn prize 1989), The Sisters Rosenzweig, 1991 (Outer Critics Cir. award 1993); (essays) Bachelor Girls, 1990; (screenplays) Uncommon Women and Others, 1978, The Sorrows of Gin, 1979, (with Durang) House of Husbands, Isn't It Romantic, The Heidi Chronicles; (children's book) Pamela's First Musical. Bd. dirs. Channel Thirteen MacDowell Colony, British Am. Arts. Assn. Am. Playwrights Project grantee, 1988, Brit.-Am. Arts Assn. grantee, Hale Matthews Found. award, Commissioning Program Phoenix Theater grantee, Guggenheim fellow, 1983. Mem. Coun. Dramatists Guild.

WASSON, BARBARA HICKAM, music educator; b. Spencer, Ind., Feb. 12, 1918. Student, DePauw U., 1937-38; BA, Vassar Coll., 1939; MusM, Chgo. Mus. Coll., 1944; postgrad., Ind. U., 1962-63. Founder, co-dir. Wasson Piano Studios, Dayton, 1946—; instr. Cedarville (Ohio) Coll., Dayton, 1970-72; adj. prof. Wright State U., Dayton, 1973-78; asst. prof. U. Cin., 1982-87. Mem. Ohio Music Tchrs. Assn. (pres. 1980-82), Dayton Music Club (pres. 1989-91), Mu Phi Epsilon (pres. Dayton alumnae chpt. 1986-88). Home: 5797 Paddington Rd Dayton OH 45459-1749

WATANABE, RUTH TAIKO, music historian, library science educator; b. Los Angeles, May 12, 1916; d. Kohei and Iwa (Watanabe) W. B.Mus., U. So. Calif., 1937, A.B., 1939, A.M., 1941, M.Mus., 1942; postgrad., Eastman Sch. Music, Rochester, N.Y., 1942-46, Columbia U., 1947; Ph.D., U. Rochester, 1952. Dir. Sibley Music Library Eastman Sch. of Music, Rochester, N.Y., 1947-84; prof. music bibliography Eastman Sch. of Music, 1978-85, historian, archivist, 1984—; adj. prof. Sch. Library Sci. State U. Coll. at Geneseo, 1975-83; coordinator adult edn. program Rochester Civic Music Assn., 1963-75; mem. adv. com. Hochstein Music Sch.; lectr. on music, book reviewer, 1966—; program annotater Rochester Philharmonic Orch., 1959—. Author: Introduction to Music Research, 1967, Madrigali-II Verso, 1978; editor: Scribners New Music Library, Vols. 2, 5, 8, 1973, Treasury of Four Hand Piano Music, 1979; contbr. articles to profl. jours., contbr. symphony orchs. of U.S., 1986, internat. music jours.; modern music librarianship, 1989; contbr. to Festschrift for Carleton Sprague Smith, 1989,

De Mösica Hispana et aliis, 1990. Mem. overseers vis. com. Baxter Sch. Library Sci., Case Western Res. U., 1979-85, Alderman Book Com., 1986-89. Mem. ALA, AAUW (Pa.-Del. fellowship. 1949-50, 1st v.p. Rochester 1964-65, mem. N.Y. state bd. 1965-66, mem. nat. com. on soc.'s reflection on arts 1967-69, nat. com. Am. fellowships awards 1969-74, br. pres. 1969-71, hon. co-chair Capital Fund Drive, 1986-88, Woman of Yr. award 1990), Internat. Assn. Music Librs. (2d v.p. commn. on conservatory libraries, commn. research librs.), Am. Musicol. Soc., Music Libr. Assn. (v.p. 1968-70, citation 1986, mem. editl. bd. 1967-95, pres. 1979-81), Music Libr. Assn./Internat. Assn. Music Librs. (joint com., 1986-87), Civic Music Assn. Rochester, Riemenscheider Bach Inst. (hon.), Hanson Inst. Am. Music (bd. mem. 1981—), Univ. Club, Century Club, Phi Beta Kappa (pres. Iota chpt. of N.Y. 1969-71), Phi Kappa Phi, Mu Phi Epsilon (gen. chmn. nat. conv. 1956, nat. librarian 1958-60, recipient citation 1977, Ora Ashley Lambke award 1989), Pi Kappa Lambda (sec. 1978—, treas. 1980—), Delta Phi Alpha, Epsilon Phi, Delta Kappa Gamma (parliamentarian 1986-88). Home: 111 East Ave Apt 610 Rochester NY 14604-2539 Office: Eastman Sch Music 26 Gibbs St Rochester NY 14604

WATERER, BONNIE CLAUSING, high school educator; b. Toledo, Sept. 25, 1940; d. Kermit Henry and Helen Ethel (Waggoner) Clausing; m. Louis P. Waterer, June 17, 1961; children: Ryan, Reid. BS in Home Econs. Edn., Ohio State U., 1962; MA in Home Econs. Edn., San Jose State U., 1966. Cert. family and consumer scis. Tchr. James Lick High Sch., San Jose, 1963-67, 1973-76; adult edn. instr. Met. Adult Edn. Program, San Jose, 1968-75; home econs. instr. Independence H. S., San Jose, 1976—, home econs. dept. chair, 1976-81; home econs. coord. East Side Union High Sch. Dist., San Jose, 1981—; child care occupations instr. Ctrl. County Occupl. Ctr., San Jose, 1989—; child devel. instr. Evergreen Valley Coll., San Jose, 1995. Mem. Nat. Assn. Family and Consumer Sci., Am. Vocat. Assn., Assn. Calif. Sch. Adminstrs., Calif. Assn. Family and Consumer Scis. (mem. articulation com., Tchr. of Yr. award 1994), Home Econs. Tchrs. Assn. Calif. (pres. 1989-91, Outstanding Tchr. award 1987), Omicron Nu, Delta Kappa Gamma, Phi Upsilon Omicron. Republican. Methodist. Home: 3836 Suncrest Ave San Jose CA 95132-3204 Office: Eastside Union High Sch Dist 830 N Capitol Ave San Jose CA 95133-1316

WATERHOUSE, MONA ELISABETH, artist; b. Grangesberg, Dalarna, Sweden, June 9, 1942; came to U.S., 1966; d. Rolf Folke and Gunborg Sofia (Skog) Johansson; m. John Fredric Waterhouse, Aug. 17, 1961; 1 child, Andrew John. Student, Coventry (Eng.) Coll. Art, 1961-63; BFA summa cum laude, U. Mass., 1975, MAT, 1978. Cert. art instr., Mass., Wis. Tchr. art Covington (Va.) High Sch., 1968-70; art and critic tchr. Clarke Sch. for Deaf, Northampton, Mass., 1976-78; tchr. art John F. Kennedy Jr. High Sch., Florence, Mass., 1978, Westfield (Mass.) State Coll., 1979; instr. art U. Mass., Amherst, 1978-81; tchr. art Hadley (Mass.) Elem. Schs., 1979-81; asst. adminstr. Appleton (Wis.) Gallery Arts, 1981-84; instr. art St. Thomas More Sch., Appleton, 1983-89; free-lance artist Peachtree City, Ga., 1989—; art cons. Dignity of Man Found., San Francisco, 1975-81; art judge various art events; artist-in-residence Ga. Coun. for the Arts, 1991—, Fulton County Sch. Arts Program, 1991—. One-person shows include Bergstrom-Mahler Mus., Neenah, Wis., 1996; exhbns. include Heter Gallery, U. Mass., Amherst, 1980, Hampshire Coll., Amherst, 1981, U. Wis., Oshkosh, 1984, Edna Carlsten Gallery U. Wis., Stevens Point, 1985, U. Wis., Menasha, 1985, Marquette Haggerty Mus., Milw., 1986, Dard Hunter Mus., Appleton, Wis., 1986, 87, The Arts Ctr., Iowa City, 1986, Neville Pub. Mus., Green Bay, Wis., 1986, 87, Milw. Inst. Art and Design, 1986, GEF Bldg., Madison, Wis., 1987, Edgewood Orchard Galleries, Fish Creek, Wis., 1987, No. Mich. U., Marquette, 1987, Fine Arts Gallery Ind. U., Bloomington, 1988, Wis. Women in the Arts, 1988-89 (travelling exhibit), Mindscape Gallery, Evanston, Ill., 1988, Milw. Art Mus., 1989, West Bend Gallery of Fine Arts, Wis., 1989, TAPPI's Internat. Paper Art Festival, Atlanta, 1990, Columbia Coll., Mo., 1991, Perspectives Gallery, Mpls., 1991, Arts Ctr., Athen, Ohio, 1991, Arts Ctr., Cartersville, Ga., 1992, Forum Gallery, Jamestown, N.Y., 1992, Hastings Seed Bldg., Atlanta, 1993, Univ. Milw. Art Gallery, 1993, Westbrook Gallery, Atlanta, 1993, Kvarnen, Sundborn, Sweden, 1995; publs. include Chgo. Art Rev., 1989, Fiber Arts Design Book 4, 1991, Book 5, 1995. Active Amnesty Interant., Save the Children. Individual Artist grantee Ga. Coun. for Arts and Fulton County Arts Coun., 1994, Hartsfield Internat. Airport Olympic Centennial Youth Art Project grantee, Atlanta, 1996. Mem. Nat. Art Edn. Assn., Internat. Assn. Paper Artists, Friends Dard Hunter Paper Mus. Democrat. Home and Office: 102 Delbank Pt Peachtree City GA 30269-1184

WATERMAN, DIANE CORRINE, artist, educator; b. Bklyn., Feb. 9, 1949; d. Beverly D. and Bernice Iona (Dowling) Waterman; children: Christopher, Tutankhamon, Joy, Derrick, Idiah, Kia. BA, Hunter Coll., 1984; postgrad., L.I. U., 1984-86. Cert. leisure profl., N.Y. Art instr./adminstr. Afro-Am. Experience, Hempstead, N.Y., 1968-73; art specialist/adminstr. MLK Youth Ctr., Westbury, N.Y., 1968-71; substance abuse counselor 5 Town Cmty. Ctr., Lawrence, N.Y., 1969-71; adminstr., counselor UJAMAA Acad., Hempstead, 1971-75; adminstr. asst. Inservice Learning Program Hunter Coll., 1981-84; unit mgr., youth divsn. counselor N.Y. State Divsn. for Youth, Bklyn., 1986-89; dean of women Claflin Coll., Orangeburg, S.C., 1989-90; dir. recreation and art therapy Dept. Homeless Svcs., N.Y.C., 1984-95; adj. prof. Touro Coll., Bklyn., 1995—; founder Renaissance Woman Cons., N.Y.C., 1984—; pres., founder Better Living Gen. Svc., N.Y.C., 1988—; designer Ethnic Wear, Empress Fashions, N.Y.C., 1993—; founder Artist in Focus, N.Y.C., 1991-94. Mem. PTA (pres. Bklyn. 1985), Citizens Com. N.Y.C., 1986, Dynamics of Leadership, Bklyn., 1995. Recipient Outstanding Cooperation award Dept. Homeless Svcs., 1994, Outstanding Svc. award N.Y.C. Tech. Coll., 1987, Cert. of Appreciation Edwin Gould Svcs. for Children, 1984. Mem. Lioness Club, Zeta Iota Phi (sec. 1968—). Democrat. Jewish. Home and Office: PO Box 466 Westbury NY 11590

WATERMAN, MIGNON REDFIELD, public relations executive, state legislator; b. Billings, Mont., Oct. 13, 1944; d. Zell Ashley and Mable Erma (Young) Redfield; m. Ronald Fredrick Waterman, Sept. 11, 1965; children: Briar, Kyle. Student, U. Mont., 1963-66. Lobbyist Mont. Assn. Chs., Helena, 1986-90; senator State of Mont., Helena, 1990—; with pub. rels. dept. Mont. Coun. Tchrs. Math., Helena, 1991—; mem. edn., pub. welfare and instns. sub-com. fin. and claims commn. Mont. Senate; chair interim com. on job tng. partnership act, 1991-92. Sch. trustee Helena (Mont.) Sch. Dist. 1, 1978-90; bd. dirs. Mont. Hunger Coalition, 1985—; pres. Mont. Sch. Bds. Assn., 1989-90; active Mont. Alliance for Mentally Ill (Mon Ami award 1991). Recipient Marvin Heintz award Mont. Sch. Bds. Assn., 1987, Friends of Edn. award Mont. Assn. Elem. and Middle Sch. Prins., 1989, Child Advocacy award Mont. PTA, 1991, award Mont. Alliance for Mentally Ill, 1991. Mem. Mont. Sch. Bds. Assn. (Marvin Heintz award 1988, pres.1989-90), Mont. Elem. Sch. Prins., Mont. Parent, Teacher, Student Assn. (child advocacy award 1991). Democrat. Methodist. Home and Office: 530 Hazelgreen Ct Helena MT 59601-5410 Office: Mt State Senate State Capitol Helena MT 59620

WATERS, BETTY LOU, newspaper reporter, writer; b. Texarkana, Tex., June 13, 1943; d. Chester Hinton and Una Erby (Walls) W. AA, Texarkana Jr. Coll., 1963; BA, East Tex. State U., 1965. Gen. assignment reporter Galveston County Pub. Co., Galveston and Texas City, 1965-68; news and feature writer Ind. and Daily Mail, Anderson, S.C., 1968-69; reporter Citizen-Times newspaper, Asheville, N.C., 1969-74; edn. and med. reporter News Star World Pub. Co., Monroe, La., 1974-79; reporter, writer Delta Democrat Times, Greenville, Miss., 1980-89; staff writer Tyler (Tex.) Morning Telegraph, 1990—. Recipient 1st place award for articles La. Press Women's Contest, 1978, 1st place for interview, 1979; news media award N.C. Easter Seal Soc., 1973; 3d place award for feature writing Miss. Press Assn., 1984, for gen. news, 1983, for investigative reporting, 1988, 1st place for best series of articles, 1990; hon. mentions Tex. AP, 1966. Mem. Sigma Delta Chi.

WATERS, CHERYL DIANE, accountant; b. Kalamazoo, Mich., May 24, 1966; d. Milton Oneal and Delores Roberta (Holloway) W. BA, U. Mich., Dearborn, 1989; postgrad., U. Phoenix, 1996—. Valuation specialist, Mich., 1993. Loan counselor Source One Mortgage, Farmington Hills, Mich., 1989-91; substitute tchr. Detroit Pub. Schs., 1991; Student Employee In Tng. program Mich. Dept. Transp., Lansing, 1993-94; lead worker, prin. clerk City of Lansing, 1994-96; accountant Holland Sys. Corp., Lansing, 1996—. Mem. Mich. Assn. CPAs, Inst. Mgmt. Accts., U. Mich. Alumni Assn., Delta Sigma Theta (asst. leader minerva circle 1990-91).

WATERS, CRYSTAL, vocalist, songwriter; b. Camden, NJ. BA, Howard U., 1985. With Parole Bd., Washington; represented by Mercury Records, 1989—. Songwriter, Basement Boys, 1987; albums include Surprise, 1991, Storyteller, 1994. Office: Mercury Records 825 8th Ave New York NY 10019 also: AM PM Entertainment Concepts Inc Vito Bruno 270 Lafayette St Ste 602 New York NY 10012*

WATERS, ELLEN MAUREEN, publishing executive, writer; b. Liberty, Ill., Aug. 19, 1938; d. Charles Francis and Virginia Elizabeth (Robinson) Linker; m. Gerald Louis Waters, Jan. 18, 1957 (div. 1990); children: Tamara, Gerri-Layne, Christina, Andrea. Student, Baker U., 1977-82, 88—; grad. Women's Leadership Inst., Avila Coll., 1990, grad. Women's Entrepreneur Program, 1990. Typesetter, reporter Baldwin (Kans.) Ledger, 1967-73; editor Wellsville (Kans.) Globe, 1973-74; asst. registrar Baker U., Baldwin City, 1975-77, registrar, 1977-82; mng. editor Mag. Design and Prodn., editor Pre mag. Southwind Pub. Co., Prairie Village, Kans., 1985-92; editor Signature mag., 1992-94; freelance writer, Baldwin City, 1974—, Overland Park, 1984—; owner, operator Mentor Editl. Svc., Overland Park; lectr., cons. on mentoring. Editor, publ. Mentor newsletter. Mentor, Women's Network for Entrepreneurial Tng., SBA. Mem. Internat. Mentoring Assn., Nat. Spkrs. Assn. (v.p. profl. devel. Kansas City chpt.). Office: PO Box 4382 Overland Park KS 66204-0382

WATERS, KAREN MARIE, journalist; b. Chgo., Jan. 9, 1968; d. Leon and Mary Ruth (Causey) W. BS in Comms., U. of Ill., Chgo., 1990; student, DePaul U., 1994—. Asst. comms. coord. dept. of ophthalmology U. of Ill., Chgo., 1988-89; staff assoc./intern Centel Corp., Chgo., 1989; assoc. producer Chgo. Cable Access Corp., 1991-92; editorial asst. Morningstar, Chgo., 1991-92; dir. coord. Pensions and Investments, Chgo., 1992-95; law clk. State's Atty.'s Officer, 1995; legal asst. Edelman & Combs, Chgo., 1995—; cons. print journalism Black Media Coalition, Chgo., 1991-93, Chgo. Assn. Black Journalists, Chgo., 1993—. Mem. Pres.'s Leadership Coun., 1989; vol. Community Law Project, Chgo., 1994—, Blind Svc. Assn., Chgo., 1993—; vol./asst. chair spl. Projects Starlight Found., Chgo., 1992-93; bd. dirs. Habitat for Humanity, Chgo., 1992—. Legal scholar DePaul Sch. Law, Chgo., 1994, DePaul scholar, 1994, Mayor's Leadership 2000 scholar, 1994. Mem. Chgo. Assn. Black Journalists, Black Media Coalition. Roman Catholic. Office: Edelman & Combs 135 S LaSalle Ste 2040 Chicago IL 10603

WATERS, KAREN VOLLAND, secondary education administrator; b. Washington, Nov. 26, 1944; d. Robert Joseph and Louise Edith (Prescott) Volland; m. Elzberry Waters, Jr., Aug. 5, 1971; children: Guy Prentiss, Janine Louise. BA, U. Md., College Park, 1967; MA, George Washington U., Washington, 1972; PhD, U. Md., College Park, 1993. Visiting lectr. Northern Va. C.C., Annandale, Va., 1972-86, U. Va., Falls Church, 1972-86, Charles County C.C., La Plata, Md., 1972-86, Marymount Coll. of Va., Arlington, 1972-86; instr. Marymount U., Arlington, 1986-88; asst. prof. Marymount U., 1988-94, assoc. prof., chair freshman composition program, 1994—; mem. Capital Area Womens Studies Leadership Group, Washington, 1995—. Author: Virginia Woolf, 1995, The Perfect Gentleman: Masculine Control in Victorian Mens Fiction, 1996; author: (with others) Masterpieces of Women's Literature, 1995; contbr. articles to profl. jours. Mem. Modern Language Assn., Emily Dickinson Soc., Virginia Woolf Soc., Nineteenth-Century Studies Assn., The Victorians Inst. Democrat. Lutheran. Office: Marymount U 2807 N Glebe Rd Arlington VA 22207

WATERS, MAXINE, congresswoman; b. St. Louis, Aug. 15, 1938; d. Remus and Velma (Moore) Carr; m. Sidney Williams, July 23, 1977; children: Edward, Karen. Grad. in sociology Calif. State U., L.A.; hon. doctorates, Spelman Coll., N.C. Agrl. & Tech. State U., Morgan State U. Former tchr. Head Start; mem. Calif. Assembly from dist. 48, 1976-91, Dem. caucus chair, 1984; mem. 102nd-104th Congresses from Dist. 35, Calif., 1991—; mem. Banking, Fin., Urban Affairs com., Ho. subcom. on banking, capitol subcom. on banking, employment and tng. subcom. on vets., veterans affairs com. Mem. Dem. Nat. Com., Dem. Congrl. Campaign com.; del. Dem. Nat. Conv., 1972, 76, 80, 84, 88, 92, mem. rules com. 1984; mem. Nat. Adv. Com. for Women, 1978—; bd. dirs. TransAfrica Found., Nat. Women's Polit. Caucus, Ctr. Nat. Policy, Clara Elizabeth Jackson Carter Found. Spellman Coll., Nat. Minority AIDS Project, Women for a Meaningful Summit, Nat. Coun. Negro Women, Black Women's Agenda; founder Black Women's Forum. Office: US Ho of Reps 330 Cannon HOB Washington DC 20515*

WATERSTON, ALISSE, anthropologist; b. Bronx, N.Y., Apr. 25, 1951; d. Michael and Louise Maude (Stone) W.; m. Howard Horowitz, July 3, 1991; children: Leah Gabrielle, Matthew Zuckerman. BA, NYU, 1973; MA, Columbia U., 1980; PhD, CUNY, N.Y.C., 1990. Permanent N.Y. state tchr. certification social studies grades 7-12 and nursery-grade 6. Instr. Pace Univ., White Plains, N.Y., 1981-85; needs-assessment rschr. Westchester County Youth Bur., White Plains, 1982-85; adj. asst. prof. SUNY, Purchase, 1991-92, Fordham U., Bronx, 1992-93; pres. Surveys Unlimited, Larchmont, N.Y., 1992—; rsch. assoc. HIV Ctr. at Columbia U., N.Y.C., 1994—; rsch. cons. Historic Hudson Valley, Tarrytown, N.Y., 1988-89; reviewer Am. Jour. Pub. Health, Washington, 1994—; vis. assoc. prof. grad. faculty New Sch. Social Rsch., N.Y.C, 1996-97. Author: Street Addicts in the Political Economy, 1993; contbr. articles to profl. jours. Pres., founding v.p. Tuckahoe (N.Y.) After Sch. Care, 1985-89. Univ. fellow CUNY Grad. Ctr., N.Y., 1982-85; Predoctoral rsch. fellow Nat. Devel. Rsch. Inst., N.Y., 1986-90; Postdoctoral rsch. fellow Nat. Devel. Rsch. Inst., N.Y., 1990-91, HIV Ctr. of Columbia U., N.Y., 1994-96. Fellow Soc. for Applied Anthropology; mem. APHA, Am. Anthropol. Assn. (co-chair family policy task force 1995—), Am. Ethnol. Assn., Am. Sociol. Assn., Soc. for the Anthropology of N.Am. Home: 8 Forest Pl New Rochelle NY 10804 Office: Surveys Unltd 1971 Palmer Ave Larchmont NY 10538

WATFORD, JAMIE DENISE (JAMIE DENISE JONES), mechanical engineer; b. Gadsden, Ala., Aug. 16, 1955; d. James A. and Jennie Ruth (Amberson) Jones; m. William Edward Reinecke, May 21, 1977 (div. Nov. 1981); 1 child, Jennifer Louise; m. Robert Michael Watford Jr., Aug. 14, 1982; 1 child, Robert James. Student, Jacksonville (Ala.) State U., 1975; BSME, U. Ala., 1977. With chem. div. PPG Industries, Lake Charles, La., 1976, summers 1977-79, mech. engr., 1979-80, design engr., mech., 1980-81, tech. asst. maintenance, 1981-85, design engr. mech., 1981-85; mech. engr. maintenance dept. Shawnee Fossil Plant TVA, West Paducah, Ky., 1986—. Seamstress Joan Crawford Sch. Dance, Paducah, 1990-91; pianist Music Makers Choir, Reidland Bapt. Ch., Paducah, 1990-95, asst. dir. adult handbell choir, 1990-94, dir. adult handbell choir, 1994—, dir. youth handbell choir, 1996—; asst. Webelos den leader Cub Scouts, 1993-95. Recipient one of Outstanding Young Women Am. award, 1979. Mem. TVA Engring. Assn., Capstone Engring. Soc., U. Ala. Nat. Alumni Assn., Pi Tau Sigma, Delta Gamma. Home: 1005 Tyree Rd Paducah KY 42003-9417 Office: TVA Shawnee Fossil Plant 7900 Metropolis Lake Rd West Paducah KY 42086

WATKINS, ANN CATHARINE, secondary education educator; b. Enid, Okla., May 31, 1946; d. Robert Hughes and Catharine Melvina (Turner) Tefft; children: Randall, Robert, Sandra, Brooke. BA in Bus., Okla. State U., 1968; MA in Edn., Northwestern Okla. State U., 1993. Tchr. h.s. Kremlin-Hillsdale Sch., Kremlin, Okla., 1978—, counselor, 1993—. Mem. Okla. Edn. Assn., NEA, Am. Counseling Assn., Am. Sch. Counselors Assn.

WATKINS, CAROL CHARLES, hotel, timeshare, apartments, shopping center executive, fundraiser; b. Walsenberg, Colo., Sept. 7, 1933; d. Iestyn Martin and Marion Lucretia (Lammè) Charles; m. James McKenzie Watkins, Sept. 11, 1954; children: Kathleen Watkins Leeger, Kristina Watkins McCubbins, James M. Jr., Karen Charisse Watkins Vafiadis. Student, U. Oreg., U. Wyo. Worked in display advt. San Dieguito Citizen newspaper, Visalia Times-Delta, 1966-68; co-owner Winners Circle Resorts Internat., Calif., 1968—; establisher chain pie shops including Mr. Pie Man, The Sugar Plum, 4 art galleries including Vintage Press, Christmas Carol's, Destiny Gallery, Grunion's Run. Contbr. articles to newspapers. Chairwoman J. F. Duffy Found. Benefit, Del Mar, Calif., 1984; chairperson, tournament dir. 5-yrs. Ann. Bacharach-Shoemaker Horsemen's Benevolent and Protective Assn., Celebrity Tennis Charity, Del Mar; founder Turn in a Pusher program, So. Calif.; creator, chairwoman Bruce Jenner Benefit for Free Arts Clinic for Battered and Abused Children; hon. dep. San Diego Sheriff's Dept.; fundraiser San Dieguito Boys and Girls Club, YMCA, Encinitas, Calif., Guide Dogs of the Desert, Canine Companions. Mem. Del Mar (Calif.) C. of C. (Woman of the Year 1981), Hon. Dep. Sheriff's Assn. (chmn. first annual fundraiser), A.A., Toastmasters, Laughmasters, Rotary Internat. (Paul Harris fellow), Kappa Kappa Gamma. Home: 2187 Opal Ridge Vista CA 92083 Office: Winners Circle Resorts Internat P O Box 99 Statford 58 Del Mar CA 92014

WATKINS, CATHY COLLINS, corporate purchasing agent; b. Memphis, Sept. 20, 1952; d. Amos Verlyn and Ruby Etoile (Mayo) Collins; m. Lewis McGill Watkins Jr., May 21, 1988. AA, Clarke Coll., 1972; BMus, William Carey Coll., 1974. Sales assoc., mgr. inventory and receiving Waldoff's Inc., Hattiesburg, Miss., 1974-80; buyer Forrest Gen. Hosp., Hattiesburg, 1980-81; asst. mgr. Ward's Fast Food of Laurel (Miss.), Inc., 1981-82; buyer, sole purchasing agent Eagle Distbrs., Hattiesburg, 1982-85; inventory coord., purchasing agent Miss. Music, Inc., Hattiesburg, 1985—. Photographer campus yearbook Carey Crusader, 1974; editor: (newsletter) Mississippi Bandmaster, 1988—. Mem. Nat. Assn. Music Merchants. Baptist. Home: 105 Elaine Cir Hattiesburg MS 39402-3305 Office: Miss Music Inc PO Box 1705 222 S Main Hattiesburg MS 39401

WATKINS, CHERYL DENISE, special education educator; b. Chgo., Dec. 15, 1963; d. Henry Eugene and Jean (Ingram) W. BS Edn. in Spl. Edn., Chgo. State U., 1987; MEd, U. Ill., 1992. Tchr. children with spl. needs Chgo. Bd. Edn., 1987—; cons. in field; adj. faculty Columbia Coll., Chgo., 1993, Nat. Louis U., Chgo. State U., Elmhurst Coll.; spkr. ednl. topics Chgo., St. Louis, Ill., Iowa, Fla., Md., Ala., Tex. Author: You Can Do Anything: A Story for Ryan, 1993, Living with Autism, 1995. Vol. workshops Cabrini Green Tutoring Program, Chgo. Recipient Golden Apple award Golden Apple Found., 1991, Disting. Alumni award Nat. Assn. for Equal Opportunity in Higher Edn./Chgo. State U., 1992, Kizzy award, 1992, Tchr. Achiever award Michael Jordan Found. Edn. Club, 1993, Swanegan Tchr. award Trinity United Ch. of Christ, 1996; named Outstanding Young Woman in Am., 1986. Mem. Nat. Bd. Profl. Teaching Standards (spl. needs com.), Kappa Delta Pi, Phi Delta Kappa, Delta Sigma Theta.

WATKINS, DIANE LUCILLE, biology educator; b. L.A., Apr. 13, 1958; d. Walter and Carolyn (Hankins) W.; 1 child, Kevin Tracey McGee. BS, Johnson C. Smith U., 1986; BS in Metaphysics, U. Metaphysics, 1996. Master hypnotist; Silva Stress Mgmt. instr. Tchr. L.A. Unified Sch. Dist., 1986—; master tchr. U. So. Calif., L.A., 1989-90, Teach Am., L.A., 1988-90, Nat. U., L.A., 1993-94. L.A. Ednl. Partnership grantee, 1989, Eisenhower grantee, 1994. Mem. Nat. Sci. Tchrs. Assn., Calif. Sci. Tchrs. Assn., Nat. Guild Hypnotists, Alpha Kappa Alpha. Office: LA Ctr Enriched Studies 5931 W 18th St Los Angeles CA 90035-4000

WATKINS, HORTENSE CATHERINE, middle school educator; b. St. Louis, Nov. 29, 1924; d. Isaiah S. and Katie M. (Phelps) W. BA, Harris-Stowe State Coll., St. Louis, 1946; MEd, U. Ill., 1953; postgrad. U. Chgo., InterAm. U., Saltillo, Coahuila, Mex.; postgrad., U. Seville, Spain, Webster U., St. Louis. Cert. life tchr., reading specialist, Mo. Coord. urban rural programs Carver-Dunbar Schs., St. Louis, 1975-76; adminstrv. asst. Shaw Visual Performing Arts Sch., St. Louis, 1978-82; team IV leader Woerner IGE, St. Louis, 1982-87; tchr., head lang. arts dept. Nottingham Mid. Sch., St. Louis, 1987-92; tutor fgn.-speaking religious, presenter, lectr. numerous workshops; curriculum advisor St. Louis Pub. Schs. Active numerous cmty. orgns.; bd. dirs. St. Louis Cathedral Sch., St. Louis Metro Singers, Concert Series of St. Louis Cathedral. Mem. ASCD, Nat. Coun. Tchrs. English, Mo. State Tchrs. Assn., Greater St. Louis Coun. Social Studies, Delta Sigma Theta (Golden life), Delta Kappa Gamma. Home: 5070A Enright Ave Saint Louis MO 63108-1008

WATKINS, JOAN MARIE, osteopath, occupational medicine physician; b. Anderson, Ind., Mar. 9, 1943; d. Curtis David and Dorothy Ruth (Beckett) W.; m. Stanley G. Nodvik, Dec. 25, 1969 (div. Apr. 1974). BS, West Liberty State Coll., 1965; Cert. of Grad. Phy. Therapy, Ohio State U., 1966; DO, Phila. Coll. Osteo., 1972; M of Health Professions Edn., U. Ill., Chgo., 1986; MPH, U. Ill., 1989. Diplomate Osteo. Nat. Bds., Am. Bd. Preventive Medicine. Emergency osteo. physician Cooper Med. Ctr., Camden, N.J., 1974-79, Shore Meml. Hosp., Somers Point, N.J., 1979-81, St. Francis Hosp., Blue Island, Ill., 1981-82; emergency osteo. physician Mercy Hosp. and Med. Ctr., Chgo., 1982-90, dir. emergency ctr., 1984-88; resident in occupational and preventive medicine U. Ill., 1988-90; corp. med. dir. occupl. health svc. Univ. Cmty. Hosp., Tampa, 1992—. Fellow Am. Coll. Occupl. and Environ. Medicine, Am. Co.. Preventive Medicine. Home: 4306 Harbor House Dr Tampa FL 33615-5408 Office: U Community Hosp Occupational Health Svcs 3100 E Fletcher Ave Tampa FL 33613-4613

WATKINS, LINDA THERESA, educational researcher; b. York, Pa., Sept. 29, 1947; d. Nathan Franklin and Madelyn Marie (Mandl) W.; m. Hugh Jerald Silverman, June 22, 1968 (div. Apr. 1983); children: Claire Christine Silverman, Hugh Christopher Silverman; m. Patrick Grim. BA, Muhlenberg Coll., 1968; MA, San Jose (Calif.) State Coll., 1970; PhD, Stanford (Calif.) U., 1977; cert., Hofstra U., 1991. Rsch. asst. prof. L.I. Rsch. Inst., Stony Brook, N.Y., 1977-79; asst. prof. NYU, 1979-85; rsch. assoc. Psychiatry dept. SUNY, Stony Brook, 1985-87; adminstr. for rsch., planning and grants mgmt. Bd. Coop. Ednl. Svcs. Eastern Suffolk, Patchogue, N.Y., 1987—; adj. lectr. SUNY Sch. Soc. Welfare, 1994; cons. Dowling Coll., Oakdale, N.Y., 1991, Tele-Niger Evaluation Project, Paris, 1972; survey cons. Redbook Mag., N.Y., 1987; interviewer Am. Inst. for Rsch., Kensington, Md., 1973. Contbr. articles to profl. jours. Rsch. grant Ronald McDonald Children's Charities, 1988, Am. Broadcasting Co., 1978, Dissertation rsch. grant Nat. Assn. of Broadcasters, 1974; NDEA fellowship, 1972. Mem. ASCD, Am. Psychol. Assn., Soc. for Rsch. in Child Devel., Am. Ednl. Rsch. Assn. Home: 99 Sweezey St Patchogue NY 11772-4160 Office: Bd Coop Ednl Svcs Suffolk 1 201 Sunrise Hwy Patchogue NY 11772

WATKINS, LOIS IRENE, English educator; b. Sterling, Nebr., Mar. 12, 1926; d. August Ralph and Magdalena Anna (Foss) Bargman; m. Morris Grant Watkins, Dec. 28, 1947 (dec. May 1996); children: Sharon Thomas, Stephen, Mark, Paul, Debra Walters, Joanna Hutchinson, David. Student, Concordia Tchrs. Coll., 1945-47; BA in Applied Linguistics, Calif. State U., Fullerton, 1976, MA in Applied Linguistics, 1978. 2d grade tchr. Canoga Park (Calif.) Luth. Sch., 1961-62; asst. prof. William Carey U., Pasadena, Calif., 1978-80; asst. to pres. All Nations Lit., Calif., Ind., Wash., 1972-92; dir. literature and literacy All Nations Lit., Colorado Springs, Colo., 1992-94, pres., bd. dirs., 1994—; missionary wife Luth. Ch.-Mo. Synod, Uyo, Nigeria, 1950-52, Ogojo, Nigeria, 1959-63. Author, sr. instr. manual and video series Bridge of Love, 1994; co-editor: All Nations English Dictionary, 1990. Mem. Rep. Nat. Com., Washington. Mem. Luth. Soc. for Missiology (bd. dirs. 1994-96). Home: 5475 Jennifer Ln Colorado Springs CO 80917

WATKINS, SHERRY LYNNE, elementary school educator; b. Bloomington, Ind., Oct. 13, 1944; d. Quentin Odell and Velma Ruth W. BSEd, Ind. U., 1966, MSEd, 1968. Tchr. 4th grade North Grove Elem. Sch., Ctr. Grove Sch. Dist., Greenwood, Ind., 1966-68; tchr. 4th and 6th grades John Strange Sch., Met. Dist. of Wash. Twp., Indpls., 1968-91; tchr. 4th grade Allisonville Sch. Met. Sch. Dist. of Wash. Twp., Indpls., 1991—. Mem. People for Ethical Treatment of Animals. Mem. NEA (nat. del. 1978—), ACLU, AAUW, Ind. Tchrs. Assn. (state del. 1966—), Washington Twp. Edn. Assn. (pres. 1986-89), World Confedn. Orgn. of Tchg. Profls. (del. Costa Rica 1990), Delta Kappa Gamma (chpt. pres. 1992-94, chmn. coord. coun. Indpls. area 1994-96), Alpha Omicron Pi. Office: Allisonville Sch 4920 E 79th St Indianapolis IN 46250-1615

WATKINS, TIONNE, singer; b. Des Moines, Apr. 26, 1970. Singer, mem. TLC, 1991—. Recipient Grammy for "CreepP, 1995. Office: LaFace Records One Capital City Plz 3350 Peachtree Rd Ste 1500 Atlanta GA 30326-1040*

WATRO, MARSHA MARILYN, secondary education educator; b. Paterson, N.J., Apr. 20, 1948; d. Frank C. and Helen J. (Tamer) Aleksa; m. John P. Watro, Aug. 14, 1971; 1 child, Ami L. BA, Trenton State Coll., 1971. Tchr. social studies Fisher Sch., Ewing, N.J., 1971—; chairperson multicultural diversity action com. Ewing Twp. Pub. Schs., Ewing, 1993—. Recipient N.J. Gov.'s Tchrs. Recognition award, 1991, A Plus for Kids award, 1990. Mem. NEA, N.J. Edn. Assn., Ewing Twp. Edn. Assn., Ewing Women's Club (pres. 1981-83). Roman Catholic. Home: 117 Ingleside Ave Pennington NJ 08534-3102 Office: Ewing Twp Bd Edn 1335 Lower Ferry Rd Ewing NJ 08618-1409

WATSON, ALICE JEWELL, retired company owner; b. Benton, Mo., Mar. 4, 1932; d. Benjamin F. and Della Jewell (Sadler) Vinyard; m. Richard D. Dobson, Dec. 1, 1950 (div. Apr. 1965); children: Richard D. Jr., Cynthia Dobson Tucker, Mitchell; m. S.M. Watson, July 1, 1965 (dec. June 1977). Student, Wichita State U. Owner Yogurt Works, Inc., Dayton, Ohio, 1977-80, A.J.'s Hi Spot, Miamisburg, Ohio, 1980-88; mgr. Cotton Mill Inc., Miamisburg, 1988-90. Co-chmn. Kennedy-Johnson Campaign, Wichita. Democrat. Home: 355 S Riverview Miamisburg OH 45342

WATSON, ARLENE J., secondary school educator; b. Moline, Ill., Nov. 7, 1938; d. Carl Hilding and Emily Antoinette (Ekstrom) Johnson; m. Robert G. Watson, Nov. 24, 1961; children: Jennifer, Amy. BA, Augustana Coll., 1960; MA, Purdue U., 1965. Tchg. asst. Purdue U., West Lafayette, Ind., 1960-61; English tchr. Branford (Conn.) Jr. H.S., 1962-64, Attica (Ind.) H.S., 1965-66, Morton East H.S., Cicero, Ill., 1976—. Mem. AAUW, Nat. Coun. Tchrs. English, Ill. Assn. Tchrs. English, Phi Beta Kappa. Office: Morton HS 2423 S Austin Blvd Cicero IL 60804

WATSON, BETTY, artist; b. Passaic, N.J., Feb. 19, 1928; d. Joseph Francis and Doris Lillian (Wilcox) Rean; m. Robert Watson; children: Winthrop, Caroline Watson Keens. Student, Phoenix Sch. of Design, N.Y.C., 1946, Pa. Acad. Fine Arts, 1947, Art Students League, N.Y.C., 1947, 48, 49-51; BA, Wellesley Coll., 1949; postgrad., NYU, 1950-51; MFA, U. N.C., 1965. Asst. in art Barnard Coll., N.Y.C., 1949-51; asst. to Ferdinand Roten, Art Dealer Balt., 1952; instr. art Calif. State U., Northridge, 1968-69. One person shows include U. N.C., Greensboro, 1962, Place Gallery, Provincetown, Mass., 1966, Newsweek Gallery, N.Y.C., 1966, Gallery Saint, Norfolk, Va., 1966, Elliott U. Ctr., 1972, Morehead Gallery, 1982, GAL Gallery, Greensboro, 1993; exhibited in group shows at Nat. Acad. Design, N.Y.C., Am. Gallery, N.Y.C., A.M. Sachs Gallery, N.Y.C., Beilin Gallery, N.Y.C., Waverly Gallery, N.Y.C., N.C. Mus. of Art, Raleigh, Montclair (N.J.) Arts Mus., South Eastern Ctr. Contemporary Art, Winston-Salem, N.C., Calif. State U., Northridge, Collector's Gallery at N.C. Mus. of Art, Raleigh, Weatherspoon Gallery, U. N.C., Greensboro, Corp. Art Directions, N.Y.C., 1951-95. Mem. Phi Beta Kappa. Home: 9 Fountain Manor Dr Apt D Greensboro NC 27405

WATSON, BEVERLY ANN, nurse; b. Springfield, Mass., Aug. 31, 1948; d. Paul Michael and Ann Theresa (Wheeler) Urekew; m. Kenneth A. Watson Jr., Dec. 17, 1977. Diploma in Nursing, Framingham Union Hosp., 1970. RN; cert. nursing supr., Ga. Staff nurse Hartford (Conn.) Hosp.; charge nurse Ridgeview Nursing Home, Springfield, Vespers Nursing Home, Wilkesboro, N.C.; asst. dir. nurses North Macon Health Care, Macon, Ga.; medical supr. Hospitality Care Ctr., Macon, Ga. Mem. ANA, Ga. Nurses Assn. Address: PO Box 13144 Macon GA 31208-3144

WATSON, CATHERINE ELAINE, journalist; b. Mpls., Feb. 9, 1944; d. Richard Edward and LaVonne (Slater) W.; m. Al Sicherman (div.); children: Joseph Sicherman, David Sicherman. B.A. in Journalism, U. Minn., 1967; M.A. in Teaching, Coll. of St. Thomas, 1971. Reporter Mpls. Star Tribune, 1966-72; editor Picture mag., 1972-78, Travel sect., 1978—; editor in chief Galena (Ill.) Gazette, 1990-91. Author: Travel Basics, 1984. Contbr. articles to newspapers and travel mags. Recipient Newspaper Mag. Picture Editor's award Pictures of Yr. Competition, 1974, 75, awards for writing and photography Soc. Am. Travel Writers, 1983-95, Photographer of Yr. award, 1990, Alumna of Notable Achievement award U. Minn. Coll. Liberal Arts, 1994; named Lowell Thomas Travel Journalist of Yr., 1990. Mem. Am. Newspaper Guild, Soc. Am. Travel Writers, Phi Beta Kappa, Kappa Tau Alpha, Alpha Omicron Pi. Office: 425 Portland Ave Minneapolis MN 55488-0001

WATSON, CHERYL S., cell and molecular biology educator; b. Evansville, Ind., Apr. 29, 1950; d. Casey Lee and Thelma Ruth (Meyer) W. BS, Purdue U., 1972, MS, 1974; PhD, Baylor Coll. Medicine, 1980; postgrad., Nat. Inst. Med. Rsch., London, 1980-82, Population Coun./Rockefeller, U., 1982-85. Instr. Purdue U., W. Lafayette, Ind., 1972-74; asst. prof. U. Tex. Med. Br., Galveston, 1985-93, assoc. prof., 1993—; manuscript reviewer and grant reviewer in field. Contbr. numerous articles to profl. jours.; contbg. author: Recent Progress in Hormone Research, 1986, Steroid Hormone Resistance, Mechanisms and Clinical Aspects, 1986, others; co-editor: (book intro.) Neuroendocrine Modulation of Central Nervous Function, 1988. Recipient award Assn. for Women in Sci., 1975, Nat. Student Rsch. Forum, 1977, 1978; NIH postdoctoral fellow NIH, London, 1980-82, Population Coun. postdoctoral fellow, N.Y., 1982-85; recipient numerous grants in field. Mem. AAAS, Am. Soc. Cell Biology, Endocrine Soc.

WATSON, DENISE SANDER, medical products sales executive; b. Bellville, Tex., July 19, 1960; d. Charles Morris and Corinne Olive (Bakke) S. Assoc., S.W. Tex. State U., 1981, BS in Allied Health Mgmt., 1982. Cardiodiagnostician Katy Community Hosp., Katy, Tex., 1982-84; staff cardiodiagnostician Sharpstown Gen. Hosp., Houston, 1984-85; cardiodiagnostician, noninvasive lab. supr. W. Houston Med. Ctr., Houston, 1985-86; with Pro-Tech Med. Assocs., Houston, 1985-86; clinical applications specialist Hewlett-Packard Co., Houston, 1986-87; field application specialist Acuson, Houston, 1987-92; dist. medical product sales rep. Acuson, St. Louis, 1992—. Named Field Application Specialist of Yr., Western Cardiology Region, 1990. Fellow Am. Registry Diagnostic Med. Sonographers, Am. Soc. Diagnostics Med. Sonographers, Am. Soc. Echocardiography, Soc. Vascular Tech.; mem. Ctrl. West End Assn., Bluebonnet Soc. Bellville, Alpha Delta Pi. Republican. Episcopalian. Office: Acuson 1899 Powers Ferry Rd Ste 100 Atlanta GA 30339-5653

WATSON, DIANE EDITH, state legislator; b. L.A., Nov. 12, 1933; d. William Allen Louis and Dorothy Elizabeth (O'Neal) Watson. A.A., L.A. City Coll., 1954, B.A., UCLA, 1956; M.S., Calif. State U., Los Angeles, PhD Claremont Grad. Sch., 1987. Tchr., sch. psychologist L.A. Unified Sch. Dist., 1960-69, 73-74; assoc. prof. Calif. State U., L.A., 1969-71; health occupations specialist Bur. Indsl. Edn., Calif. Dept. Edn., 1971-73; mem. L.A. Unified Sch. Bd., 1975-78; mem. Calif. Senate from dist. 26, 1978—, chairperson health and human svcs. com.; Legis. Black Caucus, mem. edn. com., budget and fiscal rev. com., criminal procedure com., housing and land use com.; del. Calif. Democratic Party; mem. exec. com. Nat. Conf. State Legislators. Author: Health Occupations Instructional Units-Secondary Schools, 1975; Planning Guide for Health Occupations, 1975; co-author; Introduction to Health Care, 1976. Del. Democratic Nat. Conv., 1980. Recipient Mary Church Terrell award, 1976, Brotherhood Crusade award, 1981, Black Woman of Achievement award NAACP Legal Def. Fund, 1988; named Alumnus of Yr., UCLA, 1980, 82. Mem. Calif. Assn. Sch. Psychologists, Los Angeles Urban League, Calif. Tchrs. Assn., Calif. Commn. on Status Women. Roman Catholic. Office: 4401 Crenshaw Blvd # 300 Los Angeles CA 90043-1200

WATSON, DOROTHY COLETTE, real estate broker; b. Boston, Oct. 26, 1938; d. Edward Vincent and Ethel May (Sanford) Walsh. Student, Regis Coll., 1957-59; BS, Harvard U., 1960; m. Gerald C. McDonald, May 23, 1959 (dec.); children: Gerald C., Deborah L. McDonald, Hermanson, Gregory Christopher (dec.); m. William G. Watson, May 29, 1993. Various secretarial positions, 1958-59. model, 1958-75; guidance counselor Newton High Sch., 1959-60; model, personal shopper Filene's, Chestnut Hill, Mass., 1974-78; designer program covers Boston Red Sox, 1974-76; TV facts girl for TV comml. T.V. Facts mag., 1974-75; real estate broker Channing Assocs., Inc., Wellesley, Mass., 1976-81, Boca Blossom Realty Co., Boca Raton, Fla., 1979-81, N.B. Taylor & Co., Inc., Sudbury, Mass., 1986—; fashion coord. Ava Botélle Fashions, Natick, Mass., 1988-90, mgr. Newton store, 1990-93. Roman Catholic. Home: 11 Saunders Rd Sudbury MA 01776-1282 Office: NB Taylor & Co Inc 356 Boston Post Rd Sudbury MA 01776-3007

WATSON, ELIZABETH MARION, protective services official; b. Phila., Aug. 25, 1949; d John Julian and Elizabeth Gertrude (Judge) Herrmann; m. Robert LLoyd Watson, June 18, 1976; children: Susan, Mark, David. BA in Psychology with honors, Tex. Tech. U., 1971. With Houston Police Dept., 1972-92, detective homicide, burglary and theft, 1976-81, lt. records div. northeast patrol div., 1981-84, capt. inspections div., auto theft div., 1984-87, dep. chief west patrol bur., 1987-90, police chief, 1990-92; with Austin, Tex. Police Dept., 1992—, police chief, 1992—; mem. editorial bd. S.W. Law Enforcement Inst., Richardson,Tex., 1990—. Mem. editorial bd. Am. Jour. Police, 1991—. mem. Internat. Assn. Chiefs of Police (mem. exec. com., mem. civil rights com.), Police Exec. Rsch. Form, Tex. Police Chiefs Assn. Roman Catholic. Office: Police Department PO Box 1088 Austin TX 78767-8865

WATSON, ELLEN I., academic administrator; b. Sioux City, Iowa, Jan. 14, 1948; d. Homer V. and Elsie (Bertelsen) W. AB, Wellesley Coll., 1970; MLS, U. Md., 1973. Cataloger Eisenhower Libr. Johns Hopkins U., Balt., 1970-74; appointments sec. to mayor City of Balt., 1974-75; libr. C.C. Balt., 1975-82, acting dir. librs., 1982-83; dir. learning resources ctr. Ark. Coll., Batesville, 1983-88; dir. Cullom-Davis Libr. Bradley U., Peoria, Ill., 1988-95, assoc. provost info. resources and tech., 1995—; adv. bd. Ill. Valley Libr. System, Pekin, 1989-95. Contbr. articles to profl. jours. and chpts. to books. Mem. ALA, Assn. Coll. and Rsch. Librs., Libr. Adminstrn. and Mgmt. Assn., Libr. and Info. Tech. Assn., Ill. Libr. Assn., Ill. Assn. Coll. and Rsch. Librs., Phi Kappa Phi. Office: Bradley Univ 106 Bradley Hall 1501 W Bradley Ave Peoria IL 61625

WATSON, EVELYN EGNER, radiation scientist; b. Corbin, Ky., Dec. 15, 1928; d. Edgar Mattison and Bertha Mae (Mayfield) Egner; m. Earl Greene Watson, Nov. 10, 1953; children: Nancy Eileen, Philip Allen. AA, Cumberland Coll., 1946; student, Lincoln Meml. U., 1947-48; BA, U. Ky., 1949; postgrad., U. Tenn., 1968. Math. and sci. tchr. Lynch (Ky.) High Sch., 1949-50; office mgr. Whitley County Sch. System, Williamsburg, Ky., 1950-53; sr. lab. tech. Radiation Internal Dose Ctr. Oak Ridge (Tenn.) Assoc. Univs., 1961-71, scientist, 1971-79, program mgr., 1979-89, program dir., 1989-94; lectr. in field; cons. USFDA, Rockville, Md., 1983-88. Assoc. editor Jour. Nuclear Medicine, 1981-86; editor newsletter Soc. Nuclear Medicine S.E. chpt., 1988—; co-author: MIRD Primer, 1988; contbr. articles to profl., chpts. to books. Bd. dirs. Youth Haven, Oak Ridge, Tenn., 1970-74, Clinch River Home Health, Clinton, Tenn., 1988-94. Recipient Excellence in Tech. Transfer award Fed. Lab. Consortium, 1985, Lifetime Scientific Achievement award Assn. Women in Sci., 1993. Mem. Soc. Nuclear Medicine (med. internal radiation dose com. 1980—, chmn. 1994—), Health Physics Soc. (Disting. Svc. award 1981, treas. 1976-77), European Assn. Nuclear Medicine, Nat. Coun. on Radiation Protection and Measurements (sci. com. 1986—), Sigma Xi. Mem. Ch. of Christ. Home: 104 New Bedford Ln Oak Ridge TN 37830-8289 Office: Oak Ridge Assoc Univs PO Box 117 Oak Ridge TN 37831-0117

WATSON, GAIL G., lawyer; b. N.Y.C., Aug. 6, 1947. BA, Boston U., 1968; JD, Bklyn. Law Sch., 1980. Bar: N.Y. 1981. Ptnr. Brown & Wood, N.Y.C. Office: Brown & Wood One World Trade Ctr New York NY 10048-0557*

WATSON, JANE WERNER, writer; b. Fond du Lac, Wis., July 11, 1915; d. Henry Charles and Elsa Elizabeth (Nast) W; m. Earnest C. Watson (dec. 1954). BA, U. Wis., 1936, DHL (hon.). Editor Western Printing & Pub. Co., Racine, Wis., 1938-42, N.Y.C., 1942-46, Beverly Hills, Calif., 1946-47, N.Y.C., 1947-54; freelance writer Pasadena, 1954-60, New Delhi, 1960-62, Santa Barbara, Calif., 1962—; part-time tchr. writing Santa Barbara City Coll. Adult Edn., 1963—. Author: Living Together in Tomorrow's World, The Case of the Semi Human Beans, The Case of the Vanishing Space Ship, World in Danger: Too Many People, The First Americans, Which is the Witch?, A Farm Story, A Woods Story, Walt Disney's Living Desert, Walt Disney's Vanishing Prairie, Alternate Energy Sources, Conservation of Energy, The Volga, (with David Todd) Rescue!, Canada: Giant Nation of the North, Egypt: Child of the Nile, Ethiopia: Mountain Kingdom, Finland: Champion of Independence, Greece: Land of Golden Light, India: Old Land, New Nation, Iran: Crossroads of Caravans, Mexico: Land of the Plumed Serpent, Nigeria: Republic of a Hundred Kings, Peru: Land Astride the Andes, Soviet Union: Land of Many Peoples, Thailand: Rice Bowl of Asia, Castles in Spain, India Celebrates, The Indus, Dance to a Happy Song, The Mysterious Gold and Purple Box, Parade of Soviet Holidays, Rama of the Golden Age, Tanya and the Geese, The Volga, The World of Science, 1958 (L.A. Times Woman of the Yr. for Literature 1959). Hon. bd. dirs. Planned Parenthood of Santa Barbara, 1994—. Mem. Santa Barbara Mus. of Art (hon. bd. dirs. 1995—), Channel City Club (bd. mem.), Little Town Club (former bd. dirs., sec. 1989-95). Democrat. Home: 2661 Tallant Rd # 850 Santa Barbara CA 93105

WATSON, JOYCE LESLIE, elementary educator; b. Riverside, N.J., May 31, 1950; d. Robert Eugene and Doris Virginia (Robinson) Stockton; m. Edward Donald Watson, Oct. 4, 1980; 1 child, Michelle Leslie. BS, Trenton State Coll., 1972, MEd, 1978. Cert. elem. tchr., N.J., Pa. Tchr. elem. Willingboro (N.J.) Sch. Dist., 1972-81, Pennsbury Sch. Dist., Fallsington, Pa., 1987—; tchr. gifted/talented Pennsbury Sch. Dist., Fallsington, 1987-88, 92—; elem. demonstration tchr. Pennsbury Sch. Dist., 1995—; coach Odyssey of Mind, Pennwood Mid Sch., Yardley, Pa., 1993-94; participant 8th Ann. Capital Area Space Orientation Program, Washington, 1996. Mem. NEA, ASCD, Coun. Exceptional Children, Talented and Gifted, Pa. Assn. for Gifted Edn., Pa. State Edn. Assn., Airplane Owners and Pilots Assn., Phi Delta Kappa. Home: 10 Shelley Ln Yardley PA 19067-7320 Office: Makefield Elem Sch Makefield Rd Yardley PA 19067

WATSON, KATHARINE JOHNSON, art museum director, art historian; b. Providence, Nov. 11, 1942; d. William Randolph and Katharine Johnson (Badger) W.; m. Paul Luther Nyhus, Dec. 17, 1983; stepchildren: Kristina Victoria, Karen Ida, Katharine Ellen. BA, Duke U., 1964; MA, U. Pa., 1967, PhD, 1973. Teaching asst. U. Pa., 1966-67; instr., curator exhbns. U. Pitts., 1969-70; curator of art before 1800 Allen Meml. Art Mus., Oberlin, Ohio, 1973-77; lectr. Oberlin Coll., 1973-77; dir. Peary-MacMillan Artic Mus. Bowdoin Coll., Brunswick, Maine, 1977-83, dir. Mus. of Art, 1977—; trustee Mus. Art of Ogunquit, 1977-89, Regional Art Conservation Lab., Williamstown, 1977-90, Surf Point Found., York, Maine; mem. Smithsonian Coun. Author: Pietro Tacca, 1983; author text for exhbn. catalogues; co-editor: Allen Meml. Art Mus. Bull, 1974-77; contbr. articles to profl. jours. Mem. profl. adv. com. Victoria Soc. Maine, 1988-93; mem. adv. coun. Archives of Am. Art, 1982-90. Kress Found. fellow, 1967-68, Chester Dale Fellow, 1970-71, Am. Coun. Learned Socs. fellow, 1977-78, Villa I Tatti fellow, 1977-78. Mem. Am. Assn. Art Mus. Dirs., Am. Assn. Museums, Coll. Art Assn. Office: Bowdoin Coll Mus Art Walker Art Bldg Brunswick ME 04011

WATSON, KAY, retired school system administrator; b. Rotan, Tex., Feb. 5, 1942; d. C.M. and Marie (Reeder) W. BA, Baylor U., 1964; MA, Colo. State Coll., 1968; MEd, Sul Ross State U., Alpine, Tex., 1982; EdD, Tex. Tech. U., 1988. Tchr. grade 6 Dallas Ind. Sch. Dist., Dallas, 1964-67, counselor J.L. Long Jr. H.S., 1968-70, tchr. grade 7, 1970-72; tchr. grade 5 Weatherford (Tex.) Ind. Sch. Dist., 1972-73; spl. edn. counselor Parker County Coop., Weatherford, 1973-74; spl. edn. counselor Monahans (Tex.)-Wickett-Pyote Ind. Sch. Dist., 1974-78, dir. spl. edn., 1978-85; supr. pre-sch. ctr. Ector County Ind. Sch. Dist., Odessa, Tex., 1985-86, prin. elem. Magnet Sch. at Travis, 1986-89, prin. LBJ Elem. Sch., 1989-90, assoc. dir. elem. edn., 1990-92, assoc. exec. dir., clusters I and II, 1992; asst. supt. Calhoun County Ind. Sch. Dist., Port Lavaca, Tex., 1992-96; vis. asst. prof. U. Tex. of the Permian Basin, Odessa, 1996—. Bd. dirs. Am. Cancer Soc., Odessa, 1991-92; mem. Odessa Symphony Guild, 1990-92, Port Lavaca Crisis Hotline Vol.; bd. dirs. United Way of Calhoun County, 1996. Mem. ASCD, Tex. Elem. Prins. and Suprs. Assn., Tex. Assn. Secondary Sch. Adminstrs., Tex. Assn. Sch. Adminstrs., Tex. Assn. Profl. Educators, Pilot Club Internat. (dir. 1991-92, 93-96), Rotary Club Internat. (dir. 1995-96), Delta Kappa Gamma Soc. Internat. Baptist. Home: 1204 S Eric Monahans TX 79756 Office: Univ of the Permain Basin #307 Sch Edn 4901 E University Odessa TX 79762-0001

WATSON, MARY ELLEN, ophthalmic technologist; b. San Jose, Calif., Oct. 29, 1931; d. Fred Sidney and Emma Grace (Capps) Doney; m. Joseph Garrett Watson, May 11, 1950; children: Ted Joseph, Tom Fred, Pamela Kay Watson. Cert. ophthalmic med. technologist and surg. asst. Ophthalmic technician Kent W. Christoferson, M.D., Eugene, 1965-80; ophthalmic technologist, surg. asst., adminstr. I. Howard Fine, M.D., Eugene, 1980—; course dir. Joint Commn. Allied Health Pers. in Ophthalmolgy, 1976—, lectr., mem. faculty, 1983—, skill evaluator and site coord., Eugene, 1988—; internat. instr. advanced surgical techniques. Contbr. articles to profl. jours. Recipient 5-Yr. Faculty award Joint Commn. for Allied Health Pers. in Ophthalmology, 1989. Mem. Allied Tech. Pers. in Ophthalmology, Internat. Women's Pilots Assn. Home: 2560 Chaucer Ct Eugene OR 97405-1217 Office: I Howard Fine MD 1550 Oak St Eugene OR 97401-7701

WATSON, MARY JO, special education educator; b. Candandaigua, N.Y., May 7, 1947; d. Joseph William and Mary (Treble) W. BS, Pembroke State U., 1970; postgrad., U. N.C., 1970, East Carolina U., 1977; MS, SUNY, Geneseo, 1983. Cert. tchr. phys. edn., N.C., tchr. phys. edn. and spl. edn., N.Y. Tchr. 3rd grade Scurlock Elem. Sch., Raeford, N.C., 1970-71; tchr. phys. edn., tennis coach, creative dance instr. E.E. Smith Sr. High Sch., Fayetteville, N.C., 1971-73; tchr. social studies and art for gifted students Reilly Rd. Elem. Sch., Fayetteville, 1973-74, specialist elem. phys. edn. resource, 1974-78; devel. specialist Craig Devel. Ctr., Sonyea, N.Y., summer 1981; tchr. spl. edn. Naples (N.Y.) Ctrl. Sch., 1984—; mem. com. special edn. membership, Naples (N.Y.) Ctrl. Sch., special olympic com.- Cumberland County, Reilly Rd. Elem. Sch., Fayetteville, Curriculum Com. E.E. Smith Sr. High Sch., Fayetteville. Author, publisher (jour.) Teaching Exceptional Children, 1982, Learning Disabilities Advocacy Newsletter, The Advocator, 1993. Fellow ASCD, Coun. for Exceptional Children (presenter nat. conf. 1980, 81, Conn. and N.Y. state conf. 1981), N.Y. State United Tchrs., Naples Tchrs. Assn. Home: PO Box 277 Honeoye NY 14471-0277 Office: Naples Ctrl Sch 136 N Main St Naples NY 14512-9201

WATSON, PATRICIA L., library director; b. Jan. 15, 1939; m. Jack Samuel Watson, 1960; children: Bradley, Amanda. BA, Univ. Tenn., 1961, MS in Libr. and Info. Sci., 1975. Cataloging asst. tech. svcs. dept. Knoxville Pub. Libr., 1961-65; adminstrv. asst. Knoxville-Knox County Pub. Libr., 1975-78, head West Knoxville br. libr., 1978-85; dir. Knox County Pub. Libr. System, 1985—. Bd. dirs. Tanasi Girl Scout Coun., 1981-86; treas. Univ. Tenn. Grad. Sch. Libr. and Info. Sci. Alumni Orgn., 1983-84; elder Farragut Presbyn. Ch. Mem. ALA, Tenn. Libr. Assn. (pres. 1992-93), East Tenn. Libr. Assn. (pres. 1988-89), Rotary Internat. Office: Knox County Pub Libr System 500 W Church Ave Knoxville TN 37902-2505

WATSON, PATTY JO, anthropology educator; b. Superior, Nebr., Apr. 26, 1932; d. Ralph Clifton and Elaine Elizabeth (Lance) Andersen; m. Richard Allan Watson, July 30, 1955; 1 child, Anna Melissa. M.A., U. Chgo., 1956, Ph.D. in Anthropology, 1959. Archaeologist-ethnographer Oriental Inst.-U. Chgo., 1959-60, research assoc., archaeologist, 1964-70; instr. anthropology U. So. Calif., Los Angeles, 1961, UCLA, 1961, L.A. State U., 1961; asst. prof. anthropology Washington U., St. Louis, 1969-70, assoc. prof., 1970-73, prof., 1973—, Edward Mallinckrodt disting. univ. prof., 1993—; mem. rev. panel NSF, Washington, 1974-76; fellow Ctr. Advanced Study in Behavioral Scis., Stanford, Calif., 1981-82, 91-92. Author: The Prehistory of Salts Cave, Kentucky, 1969, Archaeological Ethnography in Western Iran, 1979, (with others) Man and Nature, 1969, Explanation in Archaeology, 1971, Archaeological Explanation, 1984, Girikihaciyan, A Halafian Site in Southeastern Turkey; author, editor: Archaeology of the Mammoth Cave Area, 1974, Prehistoric Archaeology Along the Zagros Flanks, 1983; co-editor: The Origins of Agriculture, 1992, Of Caves and Shell Mounds, 1996. Grantee NSF, 1959-60, 68, 70, 72-74, 78-79, NEH, 1977-78, Nat. Geog. Soc., 1969-75. Fellow Am. Anthropol. Assn. (editor for archaeology 1973-77), AAAS (chair sect. H 1991-92); mem. NAS, Soc. Am. Archaeology (exec. com. 1974-76, 82-84, editor Am. Antiquity 1984-87, Fryxell medal 1990), Cave Rsch. Found., Assn. Paleorient (sci. bd.), Nat. Speleological Soc. (hon. life, editorial bd. bull. 1979—). Office: Washington U Dept Anthropol CB # 1114 Saint Louis MO 63130-4899

WATSON, PAULA D., library administrator; b. N.Y.C., Mar. 6, 1945; d. Joseph Francis and Anna Julia (Miksza) De Simone; m. William Douglas Watson, Aug. 23, 1969; children—Lucia, Elizabeth. A.B., Barnard Coll., 1965; M.A., Columbia U., 1966; M.S.L.S., Syracuse U., 1972. Reference librarian U. Ill., Urbana, 1972-77, city planning and landscape architecture librarian, 1977-79, head documents library, 1979-81; asst. dir. gen. services U. Ill. Library, Urbana, 1981—, acting dir. gen. svcs., 1988-93, dir. ctrl. pub. svcs., 1989-93, asst. univ. libr., 1993-95, dir. electronic info. svcs., 1995—. Contbr. articles to profl. jours. N.Y. State Regents fellow Columbia U., N.Y.C., 1965-66; Council on Library Resources profl. edn. and tng. for librarianship grantee, 1983. Mem. ALA (sec. univ. librs. sect. ALA-Assn. Coll. and Rsch. Librs. 1989-91, mem. libr. adminstrn. mgmt. sect. com. on comparative libr. orgn. 1988-89, mem. conf. planning com. optical disk interest group 1988), Ill. Library Assn. Home: 715 W Delaware Ave Urbana IL 61801-4806 Office: U Ill 246 A Library 1408 W Gregory Dr Urbana IL 61801-3607

WATSON, REBECCA WALLACE, school system administrator; b. Indpls., June 20, 1947; d. James Gillespie and Charlotte Ann (McCloud) Wallace; m. Harold Lawrence Watson, July 18, 1970; children: John McClain, Rebecca Hadley. BS, Barton Coll., 1969; MA in Edn., East Carolina U., 1992; EdD, N.C. State U., 1995, N.C. State U.; supr.'s cert., N.C. State U., 1995. Tchr. Raleigh City, Rocky Mount City and Wilson County Schs., N.C., 1970-82; mgr. Evergreen Meml. Gardens, Wilson, N.C., 1982-91; instr. N.C. State U., Raleigh, 1993—; program asst. Johnson County Schs., Zebulon, N.C., 1994—; asst. dir. Model Clin. Teaching Network, 1995. Contbr. book revs. to profl. publs. V.p. N.C. Cemetery Assn., Wilson, 1990-92; bd. dirs. Wilson Arts Coun.; deacon First Presbyn. Ch., Wilson. Named Outstanding Tchr. N.C. State U. Alumni Assn., 1994. Mem. AAUW, ASCD, Nat. Coun. Tchrs. English, Assn. Tchr. Educators, Phi Delta Kappa. Home: 510 Clyde Ave NW Wilson NC 27893-2334

WATSON, SANDRA LEA, school counselor, consultant; b. Austin, Tex., Jan. 22, 1950; d. K. Bert and Joy (Willhoite) Watson; m. Jack Sowers, May, 1979 (div. Nov. 1983); 1 child, Chris Sowers; m. Lew Browder, Dec. 29, 1972 (div. Feb. 1978); children: David, Jennifer. BS in Edn., U. Tex., 1972; M in Ednl. Psychology, 1982. Tchr. Austin (Tex.) Ind. Schs., 1972-82, counselor, 1982-84; counselor Amarillo (Tex.) Ind. Schs., 1984—; mem. Drug Free Schs. and Comty., Amarillo, 1989—. V.p. Randall H.S. Drill Team Booster Club, Amarillo, 1992-94. Mem. NEA, Tex. Assn. Counseling and Devel., Amarillo Guidance Assn., High Plains Counseling Assn. Office: Sam Houston Sch 815 S Independence St Amarillo TX 79106-6973

WATSON, SHARON GITIN, psychologist, executive; b. N.Y.C., Oct. 21, 1943; d. Louis Leonard and Miriam (Myers) Gitin; m. Eric Watson, Oct. 31, 1969; 1 child, Carrie Dunbar. B.A. cum laude, Cornell U., 1965; M.A., U. Ill., 1968, Ph.D., 1971. Psychologist City N.Y. Prison Mental Health, Riker's Island, 1973-74; psychologist Youth Services Ctr., Los Angeles County Dept. Pub. Social Services, Los Angeles, 1975-77, dir. clin. services, 1978, dir. Youth Services Ctr., 1978-80; exec. dir. Crittenton Ctr. for Young Women and Infants, Los Angeles, 1980-89, Assn. Children's Svcs. Agys. of So. Calif., L.A., 1989-92, L.A. County Children's Planning Coun., 1992—. Contbr. articles to profl. jours. Mem. Commn. for Children's Svcs. Family Preservation Policy Com., Mayor's Com. on Children, Youth and Families, L.A. Learning Ctrs. Design Team, Interagy. Coun. Child Abuse and Neglect Policy Com., L.A. Unified Sch. Dist. Bd. Edn.'s Com. on Student and Health and Human Svcs.; bd. dirs. L.A. Roundtable for Children, 1988-94, Adolescent Pregnancy Childwatch, 1985-89; trustee L.A. Ednl. Alliance for Restructuring Now; co-chmn. Los Angeles County Drug and Alcohol Abuse Task Force, 1990; mem. Cmty. Adv. Coun. Dept. Children's Svcs., 1989-90; mem. steering com. western region Child Welfare League Am., 1985-87. Mem. APA, Calif. Assn. Svcs. for Children (sec.-treas. 1983-84, pres. elect 1985-86, pres. 1986-87), Assn. Children's Svcs. Agys. So. Calif. (sec. 1981-83, pres. elect 1983-84, pres. 1984-85), Town Hall Calif., U.S. Figure Skating Assn. (bd. dirs., chair, membership com. 1996, sanctions and eligibility 1993-96), Pasadena Figure Skating Club (bd. dirs., pres. 1985-87, 89-90). Home: 4056 Camino Real Los Angeles CA 90065-3928 Office: LA County Children's Planning Coun 500 W Temple St Rm B-26 Los Angeles CA 90012-2713

WATTERS, KATHERINE DELORES, school counselor, secondary school educator; b. Jackson, Tenn., Mar. 1, 1952; d. James William and Minnie Katherine (Heath) Jones; m. Danny Bruce Watters; children: Joshua Wade, Jacob William. BS in Maths., Lambuth Coll., 1974; MS in Guidance and Personnel, Memphis State U., 1977; postgrad., Jackson State C.C., 1985, U. Tenn., 1986. Cert. tchr. and guidance counselor, Tenn., Fla. Classroom tchr. Beech Bluff (Tenn.) Jr. High/H.S., 1974-87; guidance counselor Taylor County H.S., Perry, Fla., 1987-91, Taylor County Mid. Sch., Perry, Fla., 1991—. Bd. dirs. Perry-Taylor County Boys & Girls Club, 1989—; youth leader First United Meth. Ch., 1991-94. Mem. NEA, Nat. Tchg. Assn., Fla. Tchg. Profession, Fla. Counseling Assn., Taylor County Edn. Assn., Suwannee River Counseling Assn. (pres. 1991, 94—). Home: Rte 4 Box 228 Perry FL 32347 Office: Taylor Co Middle Sch 601 E Lafayette Perry FL 32347

WATTERS, MARY TERESA, communications executive; b. Princeton, N.J., Aug. 12, 1954; d. Raymond L. and Ruth (Belcher) W.; m. Thomas Richard Whittington, Sept. 16, 1978 (div. 1993); children: Matthew A. Whittington, Samuel B. Whittington. BS, Concord Coll., 1976; MFA, Catholic U. Am., 1978. Wardrobe asst. Arena Stage, Washington, 1978; wardrobe mistress Folger Theatre Group, Washington, 1979-80; program asst. Nat. Exec. Search, Washington, 1980-82; chief writer The Resume Place, Washington, 1983-86; writer, editor J. Cooper & Assocs., Washington, 1987-88; dir. mktg. & promotion Blue Sky Puppet Theatre, Riverdale, Md., 1988-89; sr. writer Ullico Inc., Washington, 1989—. Author: (plays) Quilting Bee, 1977, The Rage, 1995, His Nightmare, 1995, If We Shadows Have Offended, 1996. Chair Citizens for Doyle Niemann, 1990; coord. Ams. for Harkin, 1992; chair bd. dirs. Christian Family Montessori Sch., Mt. Rainier, Md., 1985-87. Recipient Award of Excellence Life Communicators Assn., 1995. Mem. Women in Comm., Potomac Writer's Group. Democrat. Home: 4230 31st St Mount Rainier MD 20712 Office: Union Labor Life Ins Co 111 Massachusetts Ave NW Washington DC 20001

WATTERS, TERESA MARIE, health care administrator; b. Columbus, Ohio, Dec. 11, 1961; d. James Lilburn Banner and Eleanor Jane (Lewis) Smith; m. Jerome Wendell Watters, Sept. 9, 1989; 1 child, Ashley Lauren. BS, Howard U., 1984; M in Health Svc. Adminstrn., George Washington U., 1991. From adminstrv. asst. to exec. asst. for clin. ops. George Washington U. Med. Ctr., Washington, 1987-91; from exec. assoc. to dir. bus. ops. VITAS Healthcare Corp., Miami, Fla. and Ft. Worth, 1991-93; regional dir. bus. ops. VITAS Healthcare Corp., Dallas, Ft. Worth, 1993-95; branch dir. Olsten Kimberly Quality Care, Dallas, 1995—. Coord. D.C. CARE Health Directory, 1989. Adminstrv. vol. Dept. Health and Human Svcs., Washington, 1987. Mem. Am. Coll. Healthcare Execs. (assoc. 1991—), Nat. Assn. Healthcare Exec., Nat. Hospice Assn., Tex. Hospice Assn. Home: 717 Bear Run Dr Grapevine TX 76051

WATTERSON, JOYCE GRANDE, editor, publisher; b. Cleve., May 15, 1937; d. Anthony John Sr. and Helen Bernice (Kramer) Grande; m. Thomas Batchelor, Sept. 27, 1968; children: Sean Anthony, William Grande. BA, Notre Dame Ohio, 1960; Cert. Pratique, U. Paris, 1964; MA, Case Western Res., 1967. Cert. sales profl.; cert. tchr., Ohio. Tchr. Cleve. Bd. Edn., 1960-63, 64-65; asst. pers. dir. Cleve., Ohio Retail, 1965-66; tchr. Shaker Heights (Ohio) Bd. Edn., 1966-69, 71-72, 1983-85; lectr. Cleve. State U., 1987-88, Notre Dame Coll. Ohio, Cleve., 1990-91; adminstrv. dir. No. Ohio Acad. Pharmacy, Cleve., 1991-94; editor, pub. Concord Gazette GrandeLine Custom Comms., 1994—. Author, editor, pub.: Cascade Valley Soups, 1989, Cascade Valley Beans, 1992; editor/pub. Concord Gazette, 1994—. Advisor Alateens, Cleve., 1970-73; pres. Parents of U. Sch., Hunting Valley, Ohio, 1986-87; mem. adv. com. Painesville Adult Basic and Literacy Edn. Project, 1995—; mem. 50th anniversary com. Lake County Soil and Water Conservation Dist. Mem. Lake County Soil and Water Conservation Dist. (50th Ann. Com.), Le Cercle des Conferences Francaises of Cleve. (pres. 1986-88, life). Republican. Roman Catholic. Home: 7067 Cascade Rd Concord OH 44077-9509 Office: GrandeLine Custom Comm 7067 Cascade Rd Concord OH 44077-9509

WATTLETON, (ALYCE) FAYE, educational association administrator; b. St. Louis, July 8, 1943; d. George and Ozie (Garret) Wattleton; m. Franklin Gordon (div.); 1 child, Felicia. BS in Nursing, Ohio State U., 1964; MS in Maternal and Infant Health Care, Columbia U., 1967; LLD (hon.), Northeastern Univ. Law Sch., 1990; LHD (hon.), Long Island Univ., 1990, Univ. of Pa., 1990, Bard Coll., 1991; HHD (hon.), Oberlin Coll., 1991; LLD (hon.), Wesleyan Univ., 1991. Tchr. Miami Valley Hosp. Sch. Nursing, Dayton, Ohio, 1964-66; asst. dir. Montgomery County Combined Pub. Health Dist., Dayton, 1967-70; exec. dir. Planned Parenthood, Dayton, 1970-78; pres. Planned Parenthood Fedn. Am., Inc., N.Y.C., 1978-92; host syndicated TV show Tribune Entertainment, Chgo., 1992—. Author: How to Talk to Your Child About Sexuality, 1986. Bd. dirs. Kaiser Family Found., Calif. Wellness Found., WNET, Inst. for Internat. Edn., Quidel, Empire Blue Cross Blue Shield, Leslie Fay Cos. Recipient Claude Pepper Humanitarian award Internat. Platform Assn., 1990, Pioneer of Civil Rights and Human Rights award Nat. Conf. of Black Lawyers, 1990, Florina Lasker award N.Y. Civil Liberties Union Found., 1990, Whitney M. Young Jr. Service award Boy Scouts of Am., 1990, Ministry of Women award Unitarian Universalist Women's Fed., 1990, Spirit of Achievement award Albert Einstein Coll. of Med. Yeshiva Univ., 1991, 20th Anniversary Advocacy award Nat. Family Planning and Reproductive Health Assn., 1991, Women of Achievement award Women's Projects and Production, 1991, Margaret Sanger award, 1992, Jefferson Public Service award, 1992, Dean's Distinguished Service award Columbia Sch. of Public Health, 1992. Office: care Fischer-Ross Agy 211 E 49th St New York NY 10017*

WATTLEWORTH, ROBERTA ANN, family practice physician, nursing home director; b. Sioux City, Iowa, Dec. 26, 1955; d. Roland Joseph and Elizabeth Ann (Ahart) Eickholt; m. John Wade Wattleworth, Nov. 7, 1984; children: Adam, Ashley. BS, Morningside Coll., Sioux City, 1978; D of Osteopathy, Coll. Osteopathic Medicine and Surgery, Des Moines, 1981. Intern Richmond Heights (Ohio) Gen. Hosp., 1981-82, resident in anesthesiology, 1982-84; anesthesiologist Doctor's Gen. Hosp., Plantation, Fla., 1984-85; resident in family practice J.F. Kennedy Hosp., Stratford, N.J., 1985-87; educator family practice U. Osteopathic Medicine and Health Scis., Des Moines, 1987-89; family practitioner McFarland Clinic, P.C., Jewell, Iowa, 1989-94; med. dir. nursing home Bethany Manor, Story City, Iowa, 1990—, Jewell Vol. Fire and Rescue Squad, 1990—. Bd. dirs. Heartland Sr. Svcs., 1995—. Mem. Am. Osteopathic Assn., Am. Acad. Osteopathy, Am. Coll. Gen. Practitioners in Osteopathic Medicine and Surgery, Am. Med. Dirs. Assn., Am. Geriatric Assn., Am. Coll. Osteopathic Family Physicians (pres. Iowa chpt. 1995-96), Iowa Osteopathic Med. Assn. Lutheran. Office: 212 Lafayette Story City IA 50248

WATTS, BEVERLY L., civil rights executive; b. Nashville, Feb. 4, 1948; d. Willliam E. and Evelyn L. (Bender) Lindsley; 1 child, Lauren. BS, Tenn. State U., 1969; MS, So. Ill. U., 1973. Mgr., exec. sec. State of Ill. Minority and Female Bus. Enterprise Program, Chgo.; equal opportunity specialist U.S. Dept. of Health, Edn., and Welfare, Chgo.; reginal dir., civil rights/equal employment opportunity USDA, Chgo. Grad. Leadership Louisville, 1994, Leadership Ky., 1995, Duke U. Strategic Leadership for State Execs.; mem. long term planning commn. Ky. Health Policy Bd.; mem. Ohio Valley March of Dimes; mem. equal opportunity com. Ky. Coun. on Higher Edn., Louisville Met. Housing Coalition. Recipient Chgo. Forum Gavel award, BEEP Gold Seal award. Mem. Nat. Urban Affairs Coun., Ky. Women's Leadership Network, Chgo. Forum, Affirmative Action Assn., Chgo. Urban Affairs Coun. (pres.), Coalition 100 Black Women. Office: Ky Commn on Human Rights 322 W Broadway Fl 7 Louisville KY 40202-2106

WATTS, EMILY STIPES, English language educator; b. Urbana, Ill., Mar. 16, 1936; d. Royal Arthur and Virginia Louise (Schenck) Stipes; m. Robert Allan Watts, Aug. 30, 1958; children: Benjamin, Edward, Thomas. Student, Smith Coll., 1954-56; A.B., U. Ill., 1958, M.A. (Woodrow Wilson Nat. fellow), 1959, Ph.D., 1963. Instr. English U. Ill., Urbana, 1963-67, asst. prof., 1967-73, assoc. prof., 1973-77, prof., dir. grad. studies dept. English, 1977—; bd. dirs. U. Ill. Athletic Assn., chmn., 1981-83; mem. faculty adv. com. Ill. Bd. Higher Edn., 1984—, vice chmn., 1986-87, chmn., 1987-88. Author: Ernest Hemingway and The Arts, 1971, The Poetry of American Women from 1632 to 1945, 1977, The Businessman in American Literature, 1982; contbg. editor: English Women Writers from the Middle Ages to the Present, 1990; contbr. articles on Jonathan Edwards, Anne Bradstreet to lit. jours. John Simon Guggenheim Meml. Found. fellow, 1973-74. Mem. MLA, AAUP, Midwest MLA, Am. Inst. Archaeology, Authors Build, Ill. Hist. Soc., Phi Beta Kappa, Phi Kappa Phi. Presbyterian. Home: 1009 W University Ave Champaign IL 61821-3317 Office: U Ill 208 English Urbana IL 61801

WATTS, HELENA ROSELLE, military analyst; b. East Lynne, Mo., May 29, 1921; d. Elmer Wayne and Nellie Irene (Barrington) Long; m. Henry Millard Watts, June 14, 1940; children: Helena Roselle Watts Scott, Patricia Marie Watts Foble. B.A., Johns Hopkins U., 1952, postgrad., 1952-53. Assoc. engr., Westinghouse Corp., Balt., 1965-67; sr. analyst Merck, Sharp & Dohme, Westpoint, Pa., 1967-69; sr. engr. Bendix Radio div. Bendix Corp., Balt., 1970-72; sr. scientist Sci. Applications Internat. Corp., McLean, Va., 1975-84; mem. tech. staff The MITRE Corp., McLean, 1985-94, ret., 1994; adj. prof. Def. Intelligence Coll., Washington, 1984-85. Contbr. articles to tech. jours. Mem. IEEE, AAAS, AIAA, Nat. Mil. Intelligence Assn., U.S. Naval Inst., Navy League of U.S., Air Force Assn., Assn. Former Intelligence Officers, Assn. Old Crows, Mensa, N.Y. Acad. Sci. Republican. Roman Catholic. Avocations: photography, gardening, reading. Home: 4302 Roberts Ave Annandale VA 22003-3508

WATTS, JACKIE SUE, elementary education educator; b. Springfield, Mo., Mar. 12, 1959; d. William Russell and Phyllis June (Lowrey) Green; m. William Kent Watts, Mar. 22, 1981; children: Melinda Beth, Jennifer Lynn. BA, Coll. of the Ozarks, 1982. Cert. elem. edn. Tchr. lang. arts Dixon (Mo.) Mid. Sch., 1981-83; tchr. chpt. 1 math. Richards R-5, West Plains, Mo., 1983-84; primary tchr. West Plains R-7 Schs., 1984-87; primary tchr. Springfield R-12 Schs., 1987-95, tchr. kindergarten, 1995—; tech. coord. Wanda Gray Elem., Springfield, 1992—; cons. elem. computer lab. com. Springfield R-12, 1994—. Children's tchr. South Gate Bapt. Ch., Springfield, 1993—. Named Tchr. of Month, Springfield R-12 Schs., 1994. Mem. Internat. Reading Assn., Mo. State Tchrs. Assn., Springfield Edn. Assn. Office: Wanda Gray Elem Sch 2102 W Plainview Rd Springfield MO 65810

WATTS, JOAN, artist, innkeeper; b. N.Y.C., Nov. 14, 1938; d. Alan Wilson Watts and Eleanor (Everett) Gamer; m. John Sudlow, Aug. 17, 1957 (div. June, 1969); children: David, Elizabeth, Christopher; m. Timothy J. Tabernik, Nov. 8, 1969 (div. June, 1995); children: Laura, Joy. Student, Colo. Springs Fine Arts Ctr., 1954-56; pvt. studies in Sumi-e pottery, Kyoto, Japan, 1956-58; student, John Herron Art Inst., Indpls., 1959-60, Dayton (Ohio) Art Inst., 1968, Acad. of Art Coll., San Francisco, 1989. Adminstrv. asst., diet cons. Full Circle Programs, Bolinas, Calif., 1973-76; exec. dir. Terwilliger Nature Edn. Ctr., Corte Madera, Calif., 1984-88; dir. devel. and mktg. San Domenico Sch., San Anselmo, Calif., 1988-91; artist pvt. practice, San Rafael, Calif., 1991—; executor Estate of author/philosopher Alan W. Watts, Livingston, Mont., 1994—; owner, mgr. Blue Winged Olive Bed and Breakfast, Livington, 1995—. Works exhibited in one-woman show San Francisco Zen Ctr., 1994; group exhbns. include Nat. and Small Works Exhibit Schoharie Arts Coun., Cobleskill, N.Y., 1992, Calif. State Fair, Sacramento, 1992 (Merit award), Contemporary Artists of N.W., Boise State U., 1993, Affaire in the Gardens, Beverly Hills, Calif., 1993 (3rd pl.). Bd. dirs. Marin Ballet , San Rafael, Calif., 1981-85, Slide Ranch Outdoor Edn., Muir Beach, Calif., 1987-90; bd. dirs., co-founder Marin Environ. Alliance, Marin County, Calif., 1985-88. Mem. Livingston C. of C. Office: PO Box 1551 Livingston MT 59047

WATTS, ROLANDA, television talk show host; b. Winston-Salem, N.C.. Attended, Spelman Coll., Columbia Univ. Weekend anchor NBC TV; news anchor, reporter WABC-TV; sr. corr., weekend anchor Inside Edition; hostess Rolanda, 1994—. Emmy nominee. Office: Rolanda 411 E 75th St New York NY 10021*

WATTS, TERESSA ELAINE, sales engineer; b. Glens Falls, N.Y., Mar. 3, 1967; d. Thomas Burton and Carol Elaine (Flasser) Gries; m. Mark David Watts, Apr. 15, 1995. BSEE, Pa. State U., 1989. Sr. sales engr. Telecom. Techniques Corp., Germantown, Md., 1989—. Home: 3355 TCU Blvd Orlando FL 32817 Office: Telecom Techniques Corp 20410 Observation Dr Germantown MD 20876

WATTS, WENDY HAZEL, wine consultant; b. York, Pa., Oct. 9, 1952; d. Alphonso Irving and Daphne Jean (Gainsford) Watts; m. Frederic Joseph Bonnie, (div. 1986); m. Kenneth Scott Herron, Feb. 14, 1987 (div. Jan. 1992). BS, U. Cin., 1975. Store mgr. The Grapevine, Inc., Birmingham, Ala., 1978-81; sales rep. Supreme Beverage Co., Birmingham, 1981-84, Internat. Wines Co., Birmingham, 1984-90; nat. sales exec. Kermit Lynch Wine Mcht., Berkeley, Calif., 1990-91; on-premise mgr., fine wine mgr. Premier Beverage Co., Birmingham, 1991-94; key accounts mgr. Ala. Crown Distbg. Co., Birmingham, 1994-95; dir. of wine Western Supermarkets, 1995—, Western Mountain Brook, Ala., 1995—; instr. ednl. wine tasting classes, 1996—; spkr., instr. various groups, Birmingham; co-chmn. Sonoma Wine Tour of Birmingham, 1987-88, chmn., 1989-90; chmn. Wine Tour of France, Birmingham, 1988-89; mem. exec. com. Taste of the Nation, 1992—. Wine columnist Black and White, 1992—; wine radio show host, 1992—. Co-chmn. Multiple Sclerosis Wine Auction, 1992—, mem. exec. com., 1990—. Mem. Wine Educator's Soc., Tuesday Tasting Group. Democrat. Mem. United Ch. Christ.

WATTS PAILLIOTET, RUTH ANN, education educator; b. Long Beach, Calif., Oct. 10, 1955; d. James Henry and Ruth Adele (Weber) Peters; m. Paul Milo Pailliotet, Oct. 11, 1991. BA in English Edn., Coll. Santa Fe, 1991; MS in English Edn., Syracuse U., 1992, PhD in English Edn., 1995. Cert. English secondary, N.Y.; cert. English and social studies tchr., N.Mex. Supr., tech. dir. Snow Valley Ski Resort, Running Springs, Calif., 1979-89; columnist The Santa Fe (N.Mex.) Sun, 1990-91; grad. asst. Syracuse (N.Y.) U., 1991-92, doctoral fellow, 1992-95, instr., 1993-94; instr. SUNY, Oswego, 1994-95; asst. prof. Whitman Coll., Walla Walla, Wash., 1995—; writing cons. Syracuse (N.Y.) U., 1991—. Contbr. articles to profl. jours. Recipient Rsch. award Nat. Reading Conf., 1994. Mem. Am. Ednl. Rsch. Assn., Assn. Tchr. Educators, Nat. Reading Conf. (grad. award 1994), Nat. Coun. Tchrs. English, Internat. Visual Literacy Assn., Am. Mensa Ltd. (Levine award for ednl. essay 1992), Nat. Wildlife Fedn., Phi Delta Kappa. Office: Whitman Coll Edn 122 Maxey Hall Walla Walla WA 99362

WAUGAMAN, WYNNE RYSER, nurse anesthesia educator; b. Pitts., July 22, 1950; d. Howard Edward and Gladys Marie (Smith) Ryser; m. H. Byron Waugaman, Dec. 26, 1975 (div. 1983); m. Philip B. Hollander, Feb. 14, 1984 (div. Nov. 1990); children: Rachel Blythe Hollander, Sara Elizabeth Hollander; m. Leo David Strom, Nov. 16, 1981; children: Susan Katherine Strom, David Josef Strom. Diploma in nursing, Western Pa. Hosp. Sch. Nursing, 1971; cert. nurse anesthesia, Shadyside Hosp. Sch. Nurse Anesthesia, Pitts., 1978; BS in Edn., California U. Pa., 1975; MEd, U. Pitts., 1978, PhD, 1981; MSN, Case Western Reserve U., 1993. RN Pa., Ohio, Calif. Staff RN emergency rm. Western Pa. Hosp., Pitts., 1971-73, staff nurse anesthetist, 1974-76; dir. sch. nurse anesthesia Shadyside Hosp., Pitts., 1976-81; asst. prof. dir. nurse anesthesia divsn. Ohio State U., Columbus, 1981-88; prof., dir. nurse anesthesia program UCLA, 1988-96; assoc. prof., dir. nurse anesthesia program U. So. Calif., L.A., 1996—; chmn. Am. Assn. Nurse Anesthetists Found.,Park Ridge, Ill., 1996—; cons. Calif. Bd. Registered Nursing, L.A., 1992—. Author, editor: Principles & Practice of Nurse Anesthesia, 1988, 2d edit., 1992, Certification Review in Nurse Anesthesia, 1990; editor Nurse Anesthesia Jour., 1990-94; mem. editl. bd. Cost & Quality Jour., Am. Assn. Nurse Anesthetists Jour., Advanced Practice Nursing Quarterly. Treas. Hadassah Nurses Coun., L.A., 1994—; camp nurse Brandeis (Calif.) Bardin Inst., 1994—; dir. Temple Ner Maarav Youth Choir, L.A., 1990-93, Ner Maarav Signers, L.A., 1993-94. Recipient Disting. Alumni award Western Pa. Hosp. Sch. Nursing Alumni, 1988; HHS grantee, 1993-96. Mem. Am. Assn. Nurse Anesthetists (edn. com., resolutions com.), Calif. Assn. Nurse Anesthetists (past pres., dir. 1988—), Coun. Accreditation Nurse Anesthesia Edn. Programs (chair, reviewer 1984—), Sigma Theta Tau. Republican. Jewish. Home: 17842 Margate St Encino CA 91316-2223 Office: Dept Nursing Rm 222 1540 E Alcazar St Los Angeles CA 90033

WAVLE, ELIZABETH MARGARET, music educator, college official; b. Homer, N.Y., Jan. 18, 1957; d. John Andrew Jr. and Louise Hayford (Estey) W. BMus, SUNY, Potsdam, 1979; AM in Libr. Sci., U. Mich., 1980; MS in Edn., Elmira Coll., 1990. Sr. libr. asst. U. Mich., Ann Arbor, 1979-80; pub. svcs. libr. Elmira (N.Y.) Coll., 1980-84, instr. music, 1981—, head tech. svcs., 1984—, coord. women's studies, 1992, 96-97; mem. South Ctrl. Rsch. Libr. Coun. Interlibr. Loan Adv. Com., Ithaca, N.Y., 1991-93; mem. South Ctrl. Rsch. Libr. Coun. Regional Automation Com., Ithaca, 1994-95, resource sharing com., 1996—. Contbr. revs., essays to profl. publs. Mem. Ithaca Concert Band, 1st Unitarian Ch. of Ithaca. Mem. ALA. Democrat. Home: 700 Comfort Rd Spencer NY 14883-9622 Office: Elmira Coll PO Box 7023 Elmira NY 14901

WAX, NADINE VIRGINIA, retired banker; b. Van Horne, Iowa, Dec. 7, 1927; d. Laurel Lloyd and Viola Henrietta (Schrader) Bobzien; divorced; 1 child, Sharlyn K. Wax Munns. Student, U. Iowa, 1970-71; grad. Nat. Sch. Real Estate and Fin., Ohio State U., 1980-81. Jr. acct. McGladrey, Hansen, Dunn (now McGladrey-Pullen Co., CPAs), Cedar Rapids, Iowa, 1944-47; office mgr. Iowa Securities Co. (now Norwest Mortgage Co.), Cedar Rapids, 1954-55; asst. cashier Mchts. Nat. Bank, Cedar Rapids, 1956-75, asst. v.p., 1976-78, v.p., 1979-91; ret., 1991. Bd. dirs., v.p. Kirkwood C.C. Facilities Found., Cedar Rapids, 1970-96; bd. dirs., treas. Kirkwood C.C., 1984-91; trustee Indian Creek Nature Ctr., Cedar Rapids, 1974—, pres., 1980-81; vol. St. Luke's Hosp. Aux., Cedar Rapids, 1981-85; mem. Linn County Regional Planning Commn., 1982-92, Cedar Rapids-Marion Fine Arts Coun., 1994—; bd. suprs. Compensation Commn. for Condemnation, 1987-92; bd. dirs. Am. Heart Assn., Cedar Rapids, 1983-94; mem. Iowa Employment and Tng. Coun., Des Moines, 1982-83. Recipient Outstanding Woman award Cedar Rapids Tribute to Women and Industry, 1984. Mem. Fin. Women Internat. (state edn. chmn. 1982-83), Am. Inst. Banking (bd. dirs. 1968-70), Soc. Real Estate Appraisers (treas. 1978-80), Linn. County Bankers Assn. (pres. 1979-80), Cedar Rapids Bd. Realtors, Cedar Rapids C. of C. (bus.-edn. com. 1986-91), Cedar Rapids Country Club. Republican. Lutheran. Home: 147 Ashcombe SE Cedar Rapids IA 52403-1700

WAXBERG, EMILY S., educator; b. N.Y.C., Nov. 19, 1918; d. Samuel M. and Leonora Steinhardt; m. Ira L. Waxberg; children: Ronald, Drew, Kelton. BA in Art, Empire State U.; MS, C.W. Post; MA, PhD, Nova U. Lic. spl. edn. tchr., N.Y. Tchr. Bd. Edn., N.Y.; cons. Wartburg Day Health Care Ctr., Bklyn.; recreation therapist, supr. Pilgrim State Hosp., Brentwood, N.Y.; subs. tchr. BOCES, L.I.; past pres. Town of Oyster Bay (N.Y.) Arts Coun., Suburban Art League, L.I. Docent Nassau County Art Mus., Roslyn, N.Y., 1990—, Coe Mansion, Oyster Bay, 1990—; ombondsman United Presbyn. Home, Syosset, N.Y., 1996—. Grantee, N.Y. State, 1995. Mem. Nat. League Am. Pen Women, Art League Nassau County, L.I. Arts Coun., BACCA Ind. Art League. Home: 37 Fox Pl Hicksville NY 11801

WAXLER, BEVERLY JEAN, anesthesiologist, physician; b. Chgo., Apr. 11, 1949; d. Isadore and Ada Belle (Gross) Marcus; m. Richard Norman Waxler, Dec. 24, 1972; 1 child, Adam R. BS in Biology, No. Ill. U., 1971; MD, U. Ill., Chgo., 1975. Diplomate Am. Bd. Anesthesiology, Am. Bd. Pathology. Intern dept. pathology Northwestern U., Chgo., 1975-76, resident, 1976-79; instr. Rush Presbyn. St. Luke's Med. Ctr., Chgo., 1979-81; asst. prof. pathology Loyola U., Maywood, Ill., 1981-84; resident dept. anesthesiology Cook County Hosp., Chgo., 1984-87, attending anesthesiologist, 1987—; clin. asst. prof. U. Ill., Chgo., 1988-95, Rush Med. Coll., Chgo., 1996—. Contbr. papers to Tissue and Cell, British Jour. Exptl. Pathology, Biochem. Medicine, Calcified Tissue Internat., Jour. Lab. Clin. Med. Recipient B.B. Sankey Anesthesia Advancement award Internat. Anesthesia Rsch. Soc., 1989; Nat. Rsch. Svc. award fellow Nat. Cancer Inst., 1980; grantee Varlen Corp., 1982. Mem. AAAS, Internat. Anesthesia Rsch. Soc., Am. Soc. Anesthesiologists, Sigma Xi. Home: 7615 Church St Morton Grove IL 60053-1618 Office: Cook County Hosp Chicago IL 60612

WAY, BARBARA HAIGHT, dermatologist; b. Franklin, N.J., Dec. 27, 1941; d. Charles Padley and Alice Barbara (Haight) Shoemaker; m. Anthony Biden Way; children: Matthew Shoemaker Way, Sarah Shoemaker Way. AB in Music cum laude, Bryn Mawr Coll., 1962, postgrad., 1963-64; MD, U. Pa., 1968. Diplomate Am. Bd. Dermatology. Systems engr. IBM, Balt., 1962-63; mem. dean's staff Bryn Mawr (Pa.) Coll., 1963-64; med. intern U. Wis. Hosps., Madison, 1968-69, resident in dermatology, 1969-72; physician emergency rm. St. Francis Hosp., La Crosse, Wis., 1969-72, founder dept. of dermatology, 1972; asst. prof. dept. dermatology Tex. Tech U. Sch. Medicine, Lubbock, 1972-73, from asst. clin. to assoc. clin. prof., 1973-74, asst. prof., assoc. chair, 1974-76, assoc. prof., chair, 1976-81; assoc. clin. prof. Tex. Tech U. Health Scis. Ctr. (formerly Tex. Tech U. Sch. Medicine), Lubbock, 1981-92; clin. prof. Tex. Tech U. Health Scis. Ctr., Lubbock, 1995—; founder, dir. dermatology residency tng. program Tex. Tech U. Health Scis. Ctr. (formerly Tex. Tech U. Sch. Medicine), Lubbock, 1978-81; pvt. practice Lubbock, 1973-74, 81—; acting dir. Lubbock City Health Dept., 1982-83; active staff Meth. Hosp., Lubbock, subsection chief, 1992, 94; active staff St. Mary of Plains Hosp., Lubbock, mem. credentials com., 1990, 92, 94, 95, founding dir. phototherapy unit, 1990-91, 93, mem. exec. com., 1991, 93, chief dermatology sect., 1991, 93. Alumna admissions rep. Bryn Mawr Coll., 1972-75, 87-95; mem. selection com. outstanding physician Lubbock chpt. Am. Cancer Soc., 1991-94, chmn., 1991; bd. dirs. Tex. Tech U. Med. Found., 1987-89, Double T. Connection, 1988-90. Fellow Am. Acad. Dermatology (reviewer jour.); mem. AMA, Am. Soc. Dermatologic Surgery, Tex. Dermatol. Soc. (chmn. roster com. 1980), Tex. Med. Assn. (mem. sexually transmitted diseases com. 1986-90, mem. coun. pub. health 1990-92, vice councillor dist. III 1992—, chmn. reference com. fin. and orgnl. affairs ann. session 1992), Lubbock County-Garza County Med. Soc. (mem. various coms. 1980—, chmn. sch. and pub. health com. 1983, mem. bd. censors 1983-85, chair 1985, sec. 1986, v.p. 1987, liaison with Tex. Tech. U. Health Scis. Ctr. com. 1988-91, co-chmn. pub. rels. com. 1988-89, alt. Tex. Med. Assn. del. 1988-89, del. 1990-95, pres.-elect 1989, pres. 1990, chmn. ad hoc bylaws com. 1991-94, chmn. Hippocratic award 1991), Soc. Pediatric Dermatology, Women's Dermatologic Soc. (founding mem.). Office: 4102 24th St Ste 201 Lubbock TX 79410-1801

WAYMIRE, BONNIE GLADINE, nursing administrator; b. Williamsport, Ind., Dec. 16, 1954; d. Jackie Lee and Mary Lou (Jennings) W. LPN diploma, Danville Jr. Coll., 1978; diploma, Lakeview Sch. Nursing, 1986; BS in Bus. Mgmt., Ind. Inst. of Tech., 1996. RN, Ind., Ill., Tenn.; cert. vascular nurse, dir. nursing. Supr. evening shift Vermillion Manor, Danville, Ill., 1986; staff nurse, rsch. coord. VA Med. Ctr., Indpls., 1986-92; vis. nurse Vis. Nurse Svc., Indpls., 1992; charge nurse Eagle Valley Health Care, Indpls., 1992; DON Vinewood Health Care, Plainfield, Ind., 1992-93, Records Autumn Care, Franklin, Ind., 1993, Bloomfield (Ind.) Health Care, 1993-94, Shakamak Good Samaritan, Jasonville, Ind., 1994—. Co-author: Am. Jour. Vascular Surgery, 1992. Mem. Soc. Vascular Nursing (nursing standard and practice Acte com. 1988-92), Nat. Assn. Dirs. Nursing Adminstrn. in Long Term Care, VFW Aux., Women of the Moose (Acad. Friendship award 1992, Am. Legion Aux., Shakamak Women's Civic Club, Wednesday Rsch. Club. Roman Catholic. Home: 387 E Main St Bloomfield IN 47424-1458

WEAKLAND, ANNA WU, artist, art educator; b. Shanghai, China, May 1, 1924; came to the U.S., 1947; d. Tse-Chien and Kwei-Ying (Sze) Wu; m. John H. Weakland, Feb. 11, 1950; children: Alan Wade, Lewis Francis, Joan. BA, U. Shanghai, China, 1943; MA, Columbia U., 1948; postgrad., Stanford U., 1953-55. art instr. U. Calif., 1968, 72, 78, 82, 84, Stanford (Calif.) U., 1990; vis. art prof. Zhejiang Acad. Arts, Hangzhou, China, 1991. One-woman shows include De Young Mus., San Francisco, 1959, San Francisco Mus. Modern Art, 1961, Chathan Gallery, Hong Kong, 1963, Seattle Art Mus., 1964, Ashmolian Mus., Oxford, Eng., 1964, Sale Internat./Palacio De Bellas, Mexico City, 1966, Downtown Gallery, N.Y., 1967, Victoria (Can.) Art Mus., 1967, Heritage Gallery, L.A., 1971, Wells Fargo Bank Hdqs., San Francisco, 1973, Macy's, Palo Alto, 1976, I. Magnin, Palo Alto, 1981, Tresidor Union Gallery, Stanfor U., 1982, Palo Alto (Calif.) Med. Found., 1984, Stanford (Calif.) Mus. Art, 1988, Hewlett-Packard Co. Art Gallery, Palo Alto, 1989, Gump's Art Gallery, San Francisco, 1990, Marin County Civic Ctr., San Rafael, Calif., 1994; represented in permanent collections including Ashmolean Mus., Oxford, Eng., U. B.C., Vancouver,

Fukuoka (Japan) U., Stanford U., Seattle (Wash.) Art Mus., IBM Corp., others. Named Artist of the Yr., Friends of The Libr. award, Palo Alto, Calif., 1979, Artist of the Month, No. Calif. Home and Garden Mag., Redwood City, Calif., 1992. Mem. Am. Women Caucas for Art, Asian Am. Women Artists Assn. Home: 4245 Manuela Ct Palo Alto CA 94306-3731

WEAN, BLANCHE MCNEELY, accountant; b. Monroe County, Ind., Jan. 28, 1901; d. Homer Clark and Ruth Jane (Tutterrow) McNeely; m. Francis Willard Wean, June 16, 1926 (dec.); children: Jane, Doris, Ruth. BA, Ind. U., 1923, MA, 1932, postgrad., 1945-46. CPA, Ind. Tchr. Mt. Carroll (Ill.) High Sch., 1918-19, Bloomington (Ind.) High Sch., 1923-26, Jefferson High Sch., Lafayette, Ind., 1923-26; head bus. dept. Cen. Normal Coll., Danville, Ind., 1931-47; acct. Wean Acctg., Danville, 1947-80, Wean, Andrews & Co., Danville, 1980—. Author: Blanche Accented, 1996. Mem. Danville Pub. Libr. Bd., 1969-82, treas. Recipient John F. Jenner III Citizenship award, 1972. Mem. Nat. Assn. Pub. Accts., Ind. Pub. Accts. Assn. (pres. 1977-78, 89, Hall of Fame), Danville C. of C. (sec. 1950-75), Bus. and Profl. Womens Assn., Beta Gamma Sigma. Republican. Home and Office: PO Box 128 Danville IN 46122-0128

WEATHERBEE, ELLEN GENE ELLIOTT, botanist, educator; b. Lansing, Mich., Sept. 16, 1939; d. Eugene Bradley and Wilma Alcott (Gardner) Elliott; m. Lee Weatherbee, Aug. 18, 1958 (dec. 1996); children: Anne Susan, Brent Robert, Julie Patricia. BA in Edn., U. Mich., 1960, postgrad., 1972-77; MA in English Lit., Eastern Mich. U., 1962. Cert. tchr. Tchr. adult edn. Schoolcraft Coll., Livonia, Mich., 1983-85; tchr. adult edn. lifelong learning program U. Mich./Wayne State U., Ann Arbor and Detroit, 1973-84; tchr. adult edn. Leelanau Schs./Sleeping Bear Nat. Lakeshore, 1982-86; tchr., nature trip leader adult edn. program Matthaei Bot. Gardens, U. Mich., Ann Arbor, 1984—, dir., founder adult edn. program, 1984—; cons. botanist U. Mich., Ann Arbor, 1977—; cons. on plant and mushroom identification Mich. Hosps. Poison Control Ctr., 1978—; founder, dir. Weatherbee's Bot. Trips, 1990—; field worker for wetlands and threatened and endangered species Mich. Dept. Natural Resources and Army Corp of Engrs.; bot. cons. for wetlands permits, 1991—. Co-author: Edible Wild Plants, A Guide to Collecting and Cooking, 1982; mem. editorial bd. Mich. Botanist, 1978—; contbr. articles to profl. jours. Constable Dem. party,Ann Arbor Twp., Mich. Mem. Austrian Mountain Climbing Soc., British Canoe Union, Fedn. Ont. Naturalists, Great Lakes Sea Kayaking Club, Mich. Acad. Sci., Mich. Bot. Club, Nature Conservancy, N.Am. Mycological Assn., Pipsissewa Chamber Music Soc. Home: 11405 Patterson Lake Dr Pinckney MI 48169-9748 Office: U Mich Matthaei Bot Gardens 1800 N Dixboro Rd Ann Arbor MI 48105-9741

WEATHERBEE, KAREN D'ANNUNZIO, art educator; b. Trenton, N.J., Nov. 17, 1953; d. Terige and Pauline (Renshaw) D'Annunzio; m. Jason Weatherbee, Aug. 3, 1984. BA in Fine Arts, Montclair State U., 1975; MS in Reading/Lang. Arts, U. Pa., 1978, cert. advanced study, 1987. Cert. art tchr., N.J., English tchr., N.J., reading tchr., N.J., reading specialist, N.J. Reading specialist Hamilton Twp. Schs., Trenton/Hamilton Twp., N.J., 1978-79; reading specialist Ea. Regional H.S., Voorhees, N.J., 1979-90, reading specialist, tchr. English, 1990-91, instr. gifted and talented, 1991-93, art instr., 1993—; sys. operator cyperforum CompuServe Network, Columbus, Ohio, 1994—; forum mgr. art/desktop publishing N.J. Link network, Trenton, 1992-95. Artist: (book) Compuserve Graphics, 1992, (CD-Rom) Artist Sampler, 1992; artist, coord.: (on-line project/publ.) Virtual Cities, 1994; art/calligraphy contbr.: (book) The Chaucerian Handbook, 1993. History educator 1st Bn. of N.J. Vols., various hist. sites, 1986—. Mem. NEA, Nat. Art Edn. Assn., Virtual Reality Alliance of Students of Profls. Office: Ea Sr H S Voorhees NJ 08043

WEATHERFORD-BATMAN, MARY VIRGINIA, rehabilitation counselor, educator; b. St. Louis, Mar. 28; d. John Ely and Virginia Louise (Cox) Weatherford; m. Aug. 28, 1965 (div. Jan. 1976); 1 child, Christopher James Batman. Cert. med. technologist, Jackson Meml. Hosp., Miami, Fla., 1966; BS, Barry U., 1984, MBA, 1986, EdS, 1992; postgrad., Union Inst. Cert. rehab. counselor; cert. case mgr. Crossmatch technologist John Elliott Blood Bank, Miami, 1966-68; nurse D. E. Fortner MD, P.A. Gutlohn MD, Miami, 1969-75; allergy technologist Dadeland Allergy, Ear, Nose and Throat Assocs., Miami, 1975-78; tech. mgr. Morris Beck MD, Miami, 1978-86; sales rep. Glaxo, Inc., Research Triangle Park, N.C., 1987-88; med. ctr. specialist Wyeth Ayerst, Phila., 1988-90; hosp. rep. Allen & Hanburys, Div. Glaxo, Inc., Research Triangle Park, 1990; sales cons. Profl. Detailing Network, Princeton, N.J., 1991—; adj. prof. Union Inst., Miami, 1993—; chief psychology intern Miami Heart Inst., 1994-95; rehab. counselor Nat. Health and Rehab. Cons., Inc., Miami, 1991-94; therapist Ctrs. for Psychol. Growth, 1994; chief psychology intern Miami Heart Inst., 1994-95. Vocat. devel. vol. Jackson Meml. Hosp., U. Miami, 1991—; vol. Crippled Children's Soc., Miami, 1968-69, South Miami Hosp., 1959-63. Recipient award DAR, 1962; Tng. scholar NIH, 1962, Lucille Funk Keely Trust scholar, 1991, 92. Mem. ACA, APA, Assn. for Adult Devel. and Aging, Am. Rehab. Counseling Assn., Fla. Counseling Assn., Fla. Assn. for Adult Devel. and Aging (pres.), Fla. Soc. Med. Technologists, Barry U. Counseling Assn., Toastmasters Internat. Inc., Miami Parrot Club, Country Club of Coral Gables, Delta Epsilon Sigma. Methodist. Office: PO Box 141217 Coral Gables FL 33114-1196

WEATHERHOLTZ, DONNA BAKER, education educator; b. Savannah, Ga., Dec. 6, 1950; m. Ruben Earnest Weatherholtz III, Dec. 19, 1970; children: Kathern Kinnett, James Earnest. BS in Elem. Edn., Coll. Charleston, S.C., 1980; MEd in Adminstrn. and Supervision, U. Va., 1988; postgrad., Ohio State U., 1993—. Cert. elem. tchr. and prin., supt., Va. Tchr. Charleston County Pub. Schs., 1980-83; adminstr. law libr. U.S. Senate Jud. Com., Washington, 1983-84; spl. asst. Office Intergovtl. & Interagy. Affairs U.S. Dept. of Edn., Washington, 1984-86; asst. prin. Shenandoah County Pub. Schs., Woodstock, Va., 1986-89; grad. teaching asst. Ohio State U., Columbus, 1993-96; pres. Donna Weatherholtz & Assocs., Ednl. Cons., 1996—; bd. govs. S.C. Med. Malpractice Patient Compensation Fund, Columbia, S.C., 1976-83; edn. adv. bd. Shenandoah County Sch. Bd, 1990-92. Mem. nat. exec. com. S.C. Young Reps., Columbia, 1976. Named Outstanding Young Women of Am., 1976, Earl W. Anderson Leadership award, 1994, Campbell Meml. Scholarship Fund in Edn. Adminstrn., 1995, John A. Ramseyer Meml. fellowship, 1995. Mem. Am. Assn. Sch. Adminstrs., Nat. Assn. Elem. Sch. Prins., Nat. Assn. Gifted Children, Am. Ednl. Rsch. Assn., Assn. Faculty and Profl. Women, Univ. Coun. for Ednl. Adminstrn., Phi Delta Kappa. Office: 10185 Valentino Dr Oakton VA 22124

WEATHERS, MELBA ROSE, hospital administrator; b. Ladonia, Tex., Mar. 31, 1940; d. E. Carl and Rosa Lee (Evans) W. BSN, Holy Family Coll., 1974; BS, Tex. Woman's U., 1989. Staff/charge nurse maternal and child health St. Paul Med. Ctr., Dallas, 1974-87; rev. coord. Tex. Med. Found., Austin, 1989-95; utilization review mgmt. coord. Marshall (Tex.) Meml. Hosp., 1995—. Mem. Am. Health Info. Mgmt. Assn., VFW Ladies Aux. Roman Catholic. Home: 100 Stonecreek Dr #210 Marshall TX 75670-4580

WEATHERUP, WENDY GAINES, graphic designer, writer; b. Glendale, Calif., Oct. 20, 1952; d. William Hughes and Janet Ruth (Neptune) Gaines; m. Roy Garfield Weatherup, Sept. 10, 1977; children—Jennifer, Christine. B.A., U. So. Calif., 1974; Lic. ins. agt. Freelance graphic designer, desktop pub., Northridge, Calif. Mem. Nat. Assn. Female Execs., U. So. Calif. Alumni Assn., Alpha Gamma Delta. Republican. Methodist. Avocations: photography; travel; writing novels; computers. Home: 17260 Rayen St Northridge CA 91325-2919

WEAVER, ANN ROGERSON, art educator; b. Wilson, N.C., Oct. 22, 1948; d. James Emblic and Crecia (O'Neal) Rogerson; m. Johnny Douglas Weaver, July 7, 1983; children: Crecia, Jamie; stepchildren: John, Scott. BS in Art Edn., East Carolina U., 1971. Art tchr. Johnston County Schs., Smithfield, N.C., 1972-75, 85—; bookkeeper, receptionist, sec. John Hackney Ins./Hackney & Harris Realty, Wilson, 1976-80; owner, mgr. Ann's Sewing Rm., Wilson, 1980-85; sec. Johnston County Art Tchrs. Network, Smithfield, 1994-95, pres., 1996; organizer, facilitator student art auctions, Glendale-Kenly Elem. Sch., Micro-Pine Level Elem. Sch., N.C., 1992-95; mem. Johnston County Tchr. Advisory Coun., Smithfield, 1994—. Producer (video) Computers in the Art Room, 1994; designer Tobacco Farm Life Mus. logo, 1990, Kenly So. Heritage Festival logo, 1991. Bd. dirs. Johnston County Arts Coun., Smithfield, 1991, Johnston Meml. Hosp. Found., Smithfield, 1992—, Johnston Soil & Water Conservation Dist. Bd., Smithfield, 1989-94, Keep Johnston County Beautiful, Smithfield, 1989-94. Named Tchr. of Yr. Glendale-Kenly Elem., 1991-92; Johnston County Edn. Found. grantee, 1991-96; recipient Celebration award Johnston County Edn. Summit, 1990-96. Mem. Nat. Art Edn. Assn., N.C. Art Edn. Assn. (state conf. presenter 1991-95, apptd. Dist. III coord. Alumni N.C. Ctr. for Advancement of Tchrs. 1995, N.C. Elem. Art Educator of Yr. 1994, N.C. Entomol. Tchr. award 1995, East Carolina U. Disting. Educator award 1996), N.C. Real Estate Assn. (lic.), Kenly Area C. of C. Democrat. Baptist. Home: 235 Beulahtown Rd Kenly NC 27542-8686

WEAVER, BARBARA FRANCES, librarian; b. Boston, Aug. 29, 1927; d. Leo Francis and Nina Margaret (Durham) Weisse; m. George B. Weaver, June 6, 1951; 1 dau., Valerie S. Clark. B.A., Radcliffe Coll., 1949; M.L.S., U. R.I., 1968; Ed.M., Boston U., 1978. Head libr. Thompson (Conn.) Pub. Libr., 1961-69; dir. Conn. State Libr. Svc. Ctr., Willimantic, 1969-72; regional adminstr. Cen. Mass. Regional Libr. System, Worcester, 1972-78; asst. commr. of edn., state libr. State of N.J., Trenton, 1978-91; dir. R.I. Dept. State Libr. Svcs., Providence, 1991-96; chief info. officer State of R.I., 1996—; lectr. Simmons Coll., Boston, 1976-78. Mem. ALA, R.I. Libr. Assn., Chief Officers State Libr. Agys. Office: State Libr Svcs Dept 300 Richmond St Providence RI 02903-4222

WEAVER, BETH ANN, sales manager; b. Danville, Ill., Feb. 27, 1958; d. John Francis and Margaret Ann (Orr) Bjorback; m. Mark M. Weaver, Feb. 2, 1980; 1 child, Bailey Alexandra. BS, U. Mo., 1989. Paralegal Gray Plant Mooty Mooty, Mpls., 1986-87, Bryan Cave, St. Louis, 1987-90; sales mgr. Weekender Casual Wear, Chgo., 1993—. Com. chair Danville-Alamo Newcomers, Danville, 1994, chair programs and luncheons, 1995. Mem. AAUW, Women's Network Contra Costa County.

WEAVER, DONNA RAE, company executive; b. Chgo., Oct. 15, 1945; d. Albert Louis and Gloria Elaine (Graffis) Florence; m. Clifford L. Weaver, Aug. 20, 1966; 1 child, Megan Rae. BS in Edn., No. Ill. U., 1966, EdD, 1977; MEd, De Paul U., 1974. Tchr. H.L. Richards High Sch., Oak Lawn, Ill., 1966-71, Sawyer Coll. Bus., Evanston, Ill., 1971-72; asst. prof. Oakton Community Coll., Morton Grove, Ill., 1972-75; vis. prof. U. Ill., Chgo., 1977-78; dir. devel. Mallinckrodt Coll., Wilmette, Ill., 1978-80, dean, 1980-83; campus dir. Nat.-Louis U., Chgo., 1983-90, dean div. applied behavioral scis., 1985-89; dean Coll. Mgmt. and Bus., 1989-90; pres. The Oliver Group, Inc., Kenilworth, Ill., 1993—; mng. ptnr. Le Niccine, Tuscany, Italy; cons. Nancy Lovely and Assocs., Wilmette, 1981-84, North Ctrl. Assn., Chgo., 1982-90; ptnr. Le Miccine, Gaiole-in-Chianti, Italy. Contbr. articles to Am. Vocat. Jour., Ill. Bus. Edn. Assn. Monograph, Nat. Coll. Edn.'s ABS Rev., Nat. View. Mem. Ill. Quality of Work Life Coun., 1987-90, New Trier Twp. Health and Human Svcs. Adv. Bd., Winnetka, Ill., 1985-88; bd. dirs. Open Lands Project, 1985-87, Kenilworth (Ill.) Village House, 1986-87. Recipient Achievement award Women in Mgmt., 1981; Am. Bd. Master Educators charter disting. fellow, 1986. Mem. Nat. Bus. Edn. Assn., Delta Pi Epsilon (past pres.). Office: 505 N Lake Shore Dr Ste 4010 Chicago IL 60611-3408

WEAVER, ELIZABETH A, judge; b. New Orleans; d. Louis and Mary Weaver. BA, Newcomb Coll.; JD, Tulane U. Elem. tchr. Glen Lake Cmty. Sch., Maple City, Mich.; French tchr. Leelanau Sch., Glen Arbor, Mich.; pvt. practice Glen Arbor, Mich.; law clk. Civil Dist. Ct., New Orleans; atty. Coleman, Dutrey & Thomson, New Orleans; atty., title specialist Chevron Oil Co., New Orleans; probate and juvenile judge Leelanau County, Mich., 1975-86; judge U.S. Ct. of Appeals (3d cir.), Mich., 1987-94, Mich. Supreme Ct., Lansing, 1995—; rep. Mich. com. on juvenile justice Nat. Conv. State Adv. Groups on Juvenile Judtice for U.S. Office Juvenile Justice and Delinquency Prevention; treas. Children's Charter of Cts. of Mich. Chairperson Western Mich. U. Continuing Legal Adv. Bd.; mem. steering com. Grand Traverse/Leelanau Commn. on Youth; mem. Glen Arbor Twp. Zoning Bd.; mem. chamber arts north Leelanau County; mem. citizen's adv. coun. Arnell Engstrom Children's Ctr.; mem. cmty. adv. com. Pathfinder Sch. Treaty Law Demonstration Project; active Grand Traverse/Leelanau Mental Health Found. Named one of five Outstanding Young Women in Mich., Mich. Jaycees. Fellow Mich. State Bar Found.; mem. ABA, Mich. Bar Assn. (chair continuing legal edn. adv. bd., chair crime prevention ctr., chair juvenile law com.), Nat. Coun. Juvenile and Family Judges, La. Bar Assn., Grand Traverse County Bar Assn., Leelanau County Bar Assn., Antrim County Bar Assn., Delta Kappa Gamma (hon.). Office: 2nd Fl Law Bldg PO Box 30052 Lansing MI 48909*

WEAVER, JACQUELYN KUNKEL IVEY, artist, educator; b. Richmond, Ky., Mar. 14, 1931; d. Marion David and Margaret Tabitha (Brandenburg) Kunkel; m. George Thomas IveySr., 1951 (dec. 1989); children: George Thomas Ivey Jr., David Richard Ivey; m. Harrell Fuller Weaver, 1991. BFA, Wesleyan Coll., 1987. Owner J. K. Ivey Art, Macon, Ga., 1974-91, Ivey-Weaver Art Studio, Macon, 1991—. Exhibited in galleries including Mid. Ga. Art Assn. Gallery, Macon, 1980—, Attaway Cottage, Macon, 1990—, AAPL Salmungundi Club, N.Y.C., 1992, Frames and Art Gallery, Macon, 1995—, CLWAC Nat. Arts Club, N.Y.C., 1996. Bd. dirs., treas. Mid. Ga. Art Assn., Macon, 1981-84, 92, publicity chmn., 1988-89, nom. com., 1991. Mem. Nat. Mus. of Women in the Arts, Wesleyan Coll. Alumnae Assn., Mus. of Arts & Scis., Catherine Lorillard Wolf Art Club. Presbyterian. Office: Ivey-Weaver Art Studio 6183 Hwy 87 Macon GA 31210

WEAVER, JEANNE MOORE, retired history educator; b. Elba, Ala., July 9, 1927; d. Joseph Jackson and Mamie (Rushing) Moore; divorced; children: Claudia Smalley, Paul, Phoebe Stern, Noccalula M. Moon, Mary Croninger, Julia Weaver Bernstein. AA, Freed-Hardeman Coll., 1946; BA, George Peabody Coll., 1948; MA, Mid. Tenn. State U., 1962; PhD, Auburn U., 1988. Instr. Freed-Hardeman Coll., Henderson, Tenn., 1948-49, Jefferson State C.C., Birmingham, Ala., 1965-94; emeritus, 1994; chmn. faculty senate Jefferson State C.C., 1991-93; writer, lectr., reviewer in field. Mem. Ala. chpt. ACLU, 1985—, Common Cause, Washington, 1985—; vol. programs for homeless, including Bread and Roses Shelter, Birmingham, 1989, Firehouse Shelter, 1991-92, YWCA Kids Korner, 1996—; vol. Amnesty Internat., Birmingham, 1980—, Planned Parenthood, 1985—, Dem. Fundraising, Birmingham, 1980—. Mem. AAUW, So. Assn. Women Historians, So. Hist. Assn., Ala. Assn. Historians (exec. bd. 1989-91), Phi Alpha Theta. Unitarian. Home: 2409 5th St NW Birmingham AL 35215-2321

WEAVER, JOYCE R., hypnotherapist; b. Mineola, N.Y., Aug. 11, 1938; d. Samuel H. and Anne (Feinberg) Rosnel; m. Paul G. Weaver, June 5, 1960; children: Caryn L. Weaver Sutherland, Greg G. BA, SUNY, Albany, 1960, MA, 1965; MS, L.I. Univ., 1978; PhD, LaSalle U., 1995. Cert. secondary educator, N.Y.; advanced clin. hypnotherapy instr. Tchr. English Washingtonville (N.Y.) Pub. Schs., 1960-61, Valley Ctrl. Pub. Schs., Montgomery, N.Y., 1961-63; hotline coord. Town of Islip (N.Y.) Drug & Alcohol Counseling Ctr., 1973-78; sr. counselor Smithhaven Ministries Seabury Barn, Stony Brook, N.Y., 1979; adminstr. I Suffolk County Dept. Social Svcs., Hauppauge, N.Y., 1980-91; pvt. practice hypnotherapy Tranquility, East Islip, N.Y., 1991—; workshop leader Assn. for Past-Life Rsch. & Therapies, Riverside, Calif., 1995-96. Pres. Islip Dist. PTA, 1971-72; bd. dirs. Great South Bay YMCA, Bay Shore, N.Y., 1974-76; chaplain's asst. Southside Hosp., Bay Shore, 1977-80. Mem. AAUW, Nat. Guild Hypnotists (seminar spkr. 1995, trainer 1993-96), Nat. Bd. Hypnosis and Hypnotic Anesthesiology. Mem. Soc. of Friends. Office: Tranquility PO Box 14 East Islip NY 11730

WEAVER, JUDYTH O., educator; b. Detroit, Apr. 15, 1939; d. Samuel Shep and Pearl (Bernstein) Ofsowitz; m. Ben Weaver, May 25, 1970 (div. June 1973); children: Tara Austen, Gabriel David. PhD, Internat. Coll., Calif., 1979. Cert. Reichian therapist, Rosen Method practitioner, T'ai Chi Ch'uan tchr., Sensory Awareness leader. Prof. east/west psychology and somatics Calif. Inst. Integral Studies, San Francisco, 1980—; educator/counselor Somatic Reclaiming Mill Valley, Calif., 1976—; instr. T'ai Chi Ch'uan Naropa Inst., Colo., 1974-76, Hollyhock, B.C., Can., 1986—; sensory awareness instr. Japan Assn. for Humanistic Edn., Japan, 1988—; workshop leader Esalen Inst., Big Sur, Calif., 1970—, Hollyhock Farm, Cortes Island, B.C., Can., 1986—; adv. bd. Hollyhock Farm, Japan Assn. for Humanistic Edn. Tchr. Rosen Method Salus Internat. Health Inst., Moscow, 1993, 94, 96; leader lay meditation group, Mill Valley, 1982—; vol. clin. worker Healing Ctr. for Survivors of Polit. Torture, San Francisco, 1995—; bd. dirs. Tang Pulu Kaba Aye Monastery, Boulder Creek, Calif., 1985-90, Tibetan Nuns Project, San Geronimo, Calif., 1996—; v.p. Sensory Awareness Found., 1996—. Mem. Sensory Awareness Leaders Guild, Sensory Awareness Found. (v.p. 1996—), Rosen Method Profl. Assn. Home: 73 Montford Ave Mill Valley CA 94941

WEAVER, L. KAREN, reading specialist; b. Nyack, N.Y., Aug. 16, 1945; d. Roland Oswald and Louise (Castaldo) Lyle; m. Kenneth Allen Weaver, Apr. 27, 1968; children: Allison Nicole, Danielle Beth. BS Elem. Edn., SUNY, Brockport, 1967; MS Elem. Edn., SUNY, New Paltz, 1971; postgrad., Coll. New Rochell/L.I. Univ., 1981-92. Cert. tchr. reading, adminstr., N.Y. Tchr. grades 3 and 4 Ramapo Cen. Sch. Dist., Hillburn, N.Y., 1967-71; substitute tchr. North Rockland Cen. Sch. Dist., Garnerville, N.Y., 1971-81; reading tchr. Westwood (N.J.) Regional Sch. Dist., 1981-83; remedial reading specialist North Rockland Cen. Sch. Dist., Garnerville, N.Y., 1984—; sch. improvement planning team, West Haverstraw Elem. Sch., 1992—; adj. prof. CCNY, 1995. Sec. bd. trustees King's Daus. Pub. Libr., Haverstraw, N.Y., 1985—; vestry person Trinity Episcopal Ch., Garnerville, N.Y., 1978-80, ch. sch. supt., 1975-81. Mem. Internat. Reading Assn., N.Y. State Reading Coun., Rockland Reading Coun., N.Y. State United Tchrs., NEA, Assn. Sch. Dist. Adminstrs. Republican. Home: 3 Lyle Ter Garnerville NY 10923-1734 Office: West Haverstraw Elem Sch Blauvelt Ave West Haverstraw NY 10993

WEAVER, LOIS JEAN, physician, educator; b. Wheeling, W.Va., May 23, 1944; d. Lewis Everett and Ann (Novak) W. BA, Oberlin Coll., 1966; MD, U. Chgo., 1970. Pulmonary fellow Northwestern U., Evanston, Ill., 1975-77; trauma fellow U. Wash. Harborview Hosp., Seattle, 1977-79, research assoc., instr. medicine, 1979-81, clin. asst. prof. medicine, 1983—; clin. research fellow Virginia Mason Med. Research Ctr., Seattle, 1981-82; mem. med. staff Swedish Hosp., Seattle, 1984-92; pulmonary cons. Fred Hutchinson Cancer Research Inst., Seattle, 1984-86, regional med. advisor and med. cons., disability quality br. Social Security, Seattle, 1985—. Contbr. sci. articles to profl. jours. La Verne Noyes scholar U. Chgo., 1966; Parker B. Francis fellow Northwestern U., 1975. Mem. AMA, Am. Thoracic Soc., Wash. Lung Assn., Sigma Xi. Home: PO Box 2098 Kirkland WA 98083-2098 Office: 2201 6th Ave # 53 Seattle WA 98121-1836

WEAVER, MARGUERITE MCKINNIE (PEGGY WEAVER), plantation owner; b. Jackson, Tenn., June 7, 1925; d. Franklin Allen and Mary Alice (Caradine) McKinnie; children: Elizabeth Lynn, Thomas Jackson III, Franklin A. McKinnie. Student, U. Colo., 1943-45, Am. Acad. Dramatic Arts, 1945-46, S. Meisner's Profl. Classes, 1949, Oxford U., 1990, 91. Actress, 1946-52; mem. staff Mus. Modern Art, N.Y.C., 1949-50; woman's editor radio sta. WTJS-AM-FM, Jackson, Tenn., 1952-55; editor, radio/TV Jackson Sun Newspaper, 1952-55; columnist Bolivar (Tenn.) Bulletin-Times, 1986—; chmn. Ho. of Reps. of Old Line Dist., Hardeman County, Tenn., 1985-91, 94—. Founder Paris-Henry County (Tenn.) Arts Coun., 1965; pres. Assn. Preservation of Tenn. Antiquities, Hardeman County chpt., 1991-95; charter mem. adv. bd. Tenn. Arts Commn., Nashville, 1967-74, Tenn. Performing Arts Ctr., Nashville, 1972—; chmn. Tenn. Libr. Assn., Nashville, 1973-74; regional chmn. Opera Memphis, 1979-91; mem. nat. coun. Met. Opera, N.Y.C., 1980-92, Tenn. Bicentennial Com., Hardeman County, 1993—. Mem. DAR, Nat. Soc. Colonial Dames Am. (treas. Memphis chpt. 1996—), Am. Women i Radio and TV, Jackson Golf and Country, English Speaking Union (London chpt.), Summit (Memphis), Dilettantes (Memphis). Methodist.

WEAVER, MOLLIE LITTLE, lawyer; b. Alma, Ga., Mar. 11; d. Alfred Ross and Annis Mae (Bowles) Little; m. Jack Delano Nelson, Sept. 12, 1953 (div. May 1970); 1 dau., Cynthia Ann; m. 2d, Hobart Ayres Weaver, June 10, 1970; stepchildren: Hobart Jr., Mary Essa, Robert. BA in History, U. Richmond, 1978; JD, Wake Forest U., 1981. Bar; N.C. 1982, Fla. 1983; Cert. profl. sec.; cert. adminstrv. mgr. Supr., Western Electric Co., Richmond, Va., 1952-75; cons., owner Cert. Mgmt. Assocs., Richmond, 1975-76; sole practice, Ft. Lauderdale, Fla., 1982-86, Emerald Isle, N.C., 1986-89, Richmond, 1989—. Author: Secretary's Reference Manual, 1973. Mem. adv. coun. to Bus. and Office Edn., Greensboro, N.C., 1970-73, adv. com. to bus. edn. Va. Commonwealth U., Richmond, 1977. Recipient Key to City of Winston-Salem, N.C., 1963; Epps award for scholarship, 1978. Mem. ABA, N.C. Bar Assn., Fla. Bar Assn., Word Processing Assn. (v.p., founder Richmond 1973-75), Adminstrv. Mgmt. Soc. (com. chmn. Richmond, 1973-75), Phi Beta Kappa, Eta Sigma Phi, Phi Alpha Theta. Republican. Home: 12301 Renwick Pl Glen Allen VA 23060-6959

WEAVER, PAMELA ANN, hospitality research professional; b. Little Falls, N.Y., July 7, 1947; d. Floyd Aron Weaver and Norma May (Putnam) Hoyer; m. Ken Ward McCleary, Mar. 2, 1947; children: Brian Wilson, Blake McCleary, Ryan McCleary. AA, Fulton Montgomery Community Co, Amsterdam, NY, 1968; BA, SUNY, 1970; MA, U. S. Fla., 1973; PhD, Mich. State U., East Lansing, 1978. Mem. Mathematics Dept., Riviera Jr. High Sch., Miami, Fla., 1970-72; grad. asst. Office of Med., Edn. Research and Devel., Mich. State U., East Lansing, 1973-74, Dept. of Mktg., Mich. State U., East Lansing, 1974-75; instr. mktg. Mich. State U., East Lansing; asst. prof. mktg., hospitality svcs. adminstrn. Cen. Mich. State U., Mt. Pleasant, 1978-79, Cen. Mich. U., 1982-86; chair acad. senate Cen. Mich. U., Mt. Pleasant, 1985-86, prof. mktg., hospitality svcs. adminstrn., 1986-89; prof. Dept. Hospitality and Tourism Mgmt. Va. Poly. Inst. and State U., Blacksburg, 1989—. Contbr. articles to profl. jours. Recipient John Wiley and Sons award for Lifetime Achievent to Hospitality Industry, 1994. Mem. Coun. on Hotel, Restaurant and Instln. Edn., Acad. Mktg. Sci., So. Mktg. Assn. Office: Va Poly Inst and State U Wallace Hall Blacksburg VA 24061-0429

WEAVER, SARA LEE, sales executive; b. Jefferson City, Mo., Apr. 4, 1962; d. Thomas Henry and Majorie Gwendolyn (Jones) W. BJ, BA, BS, U. Mo., 1984; student, U. London, 1980, Université Laval, 1983. Sales asst. Katz Communications, Dallas, 1985-87, Chgo., 1987-88; media systems trainer Katz Communications, N.Y.C., 1988-90; sales exec. Katz Communications, Chgo., 1990-94, Sta. KGO-TV, San Francisco, 1994—. Bd. dirs. Art Span, San Francisco; mem. steering com. ARC, San Francisco. Mem. AAUW (v.p. membership San Francisco br.),Omicron Delta Kappa, Sigma Rho Sigma, Kappa Epsilon Alpha, Pi Beta Phi. Democrat. Presbyterian. Office: Sta KGO-TV 900 Front St San Francisco CA 94111

WEAVER, SHARON JOAN, fashion designer; b. Bethlehem, Pa., Feb. 28, 1951; d. Donald Edgar and Eleanor Lona (Flammer) W.; m. Stephen Henry Sage, May 1981 (div. July 1987); m. Andrew John Hollan Ward, Feb. 16, 1994. Student, Moore Coll. Art, Phila., 1969-71; cert. in Fashion Design, Parsons Sch. Design, N.Y.C., 1974. Designer Jonathan Logan, N.Y.C., 1973-75; stylist Huk-A-Poo, N.Y.C., 1976-77; designer Salant Corp., N.Y.C., 1977-78; head designer Regal Acc., N.Y.C., 1978-80; head merchandiser Tomboy of Calif., L.A., 1981-85; merchandiser, designer Back to Back, L.A., 1985-88; merchandiser, designer, sales Beverly Hills Knitting Mills, L.A., 1988-92, Knit Maven, N.Y.C., 1992-94, Rio, Inc., L.A., 1994—; cons. Jasper Bros., L.A., 1988-91, Hobie Sport, L.A., 1989-93, Avru Corp., Montreal, Can., 1990, U.S. Sweaters, N.Y.C., 1987-94. Scholar Am. Wool Bur., 1971-74. Mem. ACLU, Sierra Club Legal Def., Feminist Majority, Rainforest Action Network (lobbyist, activist, spokesperson). Office: 10153 1/2 Riverside Dr #405 Toluca Lake CA 91602

WEAVER, SIGOURNEY (SUSAN ALEXANDRA WEAVER), actress; b. N.Y.C., Oct. 8, 1949; d. Sylvester (Pat) Weaver and Elizabeth Inglish; m. James Simpson, 1984; 1 child, Charlotte. BA in English, Stanford U., 1971; MA in Drama, Yale U., 1974. First profl. theater appearance in The Constant Wife, 1974; other roles in Beyond Therapy, Hurlyburly, 1984, The Merchant of Venice, 1987; films include: Annie Hall, 1977, Alien, 1979, Eyewitness, 1981, The Year of Living Dangerously, 1982, Deal of the Century, 1983, Ghostbusters, 1984, Aliens, 1986 (Acad. award nomination for best actress), Half Moon Street, 1986, One Woman or Two, 1987, Working Girl, 1988, Gorillas in the Mist, 1988 (Golden Globe award 1989), Ghostbusters II, 1989, Alien 3, 1992, 1492: Conquest of Paradise, 1992,

Dave, 1993, Death and the Maiden, 1994, Jeffrey, 1995, Copycat, 1995, Snow White in the Black Forest, 1996, Ice Storm, 1996. Office: ICM 8942 Wilshire Blvd Beverly Hills CA 90211*

WEAVER, SUSAN LYNNE, elementary education educator, consultant; b. Denton, Tex., Apr. 1, 1951; d. Floyd Chester and Anita Newman (Stoddard) Parker; m. Gayle M. Weaver, Jul. 7, 1984; children: John Michael, Christi Michelle. EdD, East Tex. State U., 1992. Profl. cert. elem. edn. Elem. tchr. Mesquite (Tex.) I.S.D., 1983-91; asst. prof. East Tex. State U., Commerce, Tex., 1991—; cons. Mesquite Ind. Sch. Dist., Grand Prairie Ind. Sch. Dist., Jacksonville Ind. Sch. Dist., 1991—. Contbr. articles to profl. jours. Mem. ASCD, Nat. Coun. Tchrs. Eng., Assn. Tex. Profl. Edn., Kappa Delta Pi, Phi Delta Kappa. Home: Rte 4 Bos 223A Wills Point TX 75169 Office: East Tex State U 2600 Motley Mesquite TX 75150

WEAVER, VELATHER EDWARDS (VAL WEAVER), small business owner; d. Willie and Ethel Edwards; m. Ellerson Weaver; children: Frank Mattox Jr., Terence Mattox, Christopher Williams, Sharon, Shelley, Stephanie. Student, Sonoma State Coll., 1972, U. Calif., Berkeley, 1972; BA, Calif. State U., Hayward, 1973; MBA, St. Mary's Coll., Moraga, Calif., 1989. Coach, counselor Opportunities Industrialization Ctr., Oakland, Calif., 1967-69; tchr. Berkeley Headstart, 1969-70; instr., cons. external degree program Antioch Coll.-West, San Francisco, 1971-74; market analyst World Airways, Inc., Oakland, 1972-75, affirmative action adminstr., 1975-78; cons. A.C. Transit, Oakland, 1982; owner, mgr. Val's Designs and Profl. Svcs., Lafayette, Calif., 1980—; mgr. adminstrn., tng. supr. North Oakland Pharmacy, Inc., 1970—, also bd. dirs.; adv. bd. The Tribune, Oakland, 1982-88. Author RAPRO Self Mgmt. Program, 1985. Program coord., mem. publicity com. Lafayette Arts and Sci. Found., 1982-83; mem. admission bd. St. Mary's Coll. Grad. Sch. Bus., 1990; bd. dirs. Acalanes H.S., Lafayette, 1980-82, Lafayette Elem. Sch., 1975-80; mem. Lafayette Econ. Devel. Task Force, 1994-95; vice chmn. Lafayette Econ. Devel. Commn., 1995—. Mem. Calif. State Pharmacists Assn. Aux. (pres. Contra Costa Aux. 1980, pres. state aux. 1986-88, recognition award 1987), Calif. Pharmacists Polit. Action Com. (appreciation award 1988), Diablo Valley Bus. and Profl. Women (pub. rels. com. 1986-87, best local orgn. award 1987, author yearbook 1987), No. Calif. Med., Dental and Pharm. Assn. Aux. (bd. dirs., com. chair 1975—, pres. elect 1991, pres. 1991-93), Internat. Platform Assn., Links, Inc. Office: North Oakland Pharmacy Inc 5705 Market St Emeryville CA 94608-2811

WEAVER, VIRGINIA DOVE, museum executive; b. Westerly, R.I.; d. Ronald Cross and Elva Gertrude (Burdick) Dove; m. Water Albert Weaver, Jr. (div. Apr. 1982); children—Marshall Gueringer, Claudia Cross, Leila Jane. B.A., Tulane U., 1973; M.A., 1977. Dir. vols.Hermann Grima Hist. House, New Orleans, 1976-77; adminstrv. analyst City Chief Adminstrv. Office, New Orleans, 1977-83; dir. pub. rels. New Orleans Mus. Art, 1983-95, Vincent Mann Art Gallery, New Orleans, 1996—; chmn. publicity 15th Triennial Vol. Commns. Art Mus. Internat. Conf., New Orleans, 1994. Coeditor: Letters From Young Audiences, 1971; contbr. articles to profl. jours. Bd. dirs. New Orleans chpt. Young Audiences, Inc., 1968-77; co-chmn. New Orleans Symphony Book Fair, 1973-74; mem. city coun. investigative panel SPCA, New Orleans, 1981-82; nat. pub. rels. chmn. Nat. Soc. Daus. of Founders and Patriots Am., 1985-88, publicity chmn. Spirit of 76 chpt. DAR, 1988-90. Nat. Coun. Jewish Women grantee, 1977. Episcopalian. Bd. dirs. Symphony Womens Com., 1982-86; mem. steering com. Mayors Arts Task Force, New Orleans, 1978-79. Clubs: Orleans (fine arts com., current events com., hist. com. 1990-92, chair lecture com. 1996, chmn. Discovery Tours 1996—); Le Petit Salon (chmn. publicity for 150th anniversary 1988, co-chmn. programs 1989, 90-96, chmn. summer programs 1994), France-Amérique de la Louisiane, Inc. (bd. dirs. 1992-96, 1st v.p. 1996—), Vol. Commits. of Art Mus. (host. com. internat. triennial conf. 1994). Avocation: piano. Home: 7478 Hurst St New Orleans LA 70118-3641 Office: New Orleans Mus Art PO Box 19123 New Orleans LA 70179-0123

WEBB, BERNICE LARSON, writer, consultant, press owner, publisher; b. Ludell, Kans.; d. Carl Godfred and Ida Genevieve (Tongish) Larson; m. Ralph Raymond Schear, Aug. 9, 1942 (div. July 1956, dec. Aug., 1981); children: William Carl Schear, Rebecca Rae Schear Gentry; m. Robert MacHardy Webb, July 14, 1961 (dec. June 1983). BA, U. Kans., 1956, MA, 1957, PhD, 1961; postgrad., U. Aberdeen, Scotland, 1959-60. Cert. counseler Nat. Multiple Sclerosis Soc., peer counselor for cancer, ARC. Asst. instr. English U. Kans., Lawrence, 1958-59, 60-61; asst. prof. U. Southwestern La., Lafayette, 1961-67, assoc. prof., 1967-80, prof., 1980-87; owner, publisher Spider Press, 1991—; vis. assoc. prof. S.S. Universe Campus/World Campus Afloat, 1972; coord. Poetry in the Schs., Lafayette Parish, La., 1974; dir. grad. seminars NDEA Inst. Intellectual and Cultural History, Lafayette, summer 1966; poetry cons. Acadiana Arts Coun., 1976-87, Lafayette Parish Schs., 1976-87; bd. dirs. Deep South Writers Conf., 1978-87; acting dir. English reading-writing lab. U. Southwestern La., summers 1977, 78, 79, writing cons., 1987—; founder, coord. Webb's Writers, 1974—. Author: The Basketball Man, 1973, transl. to Japanese, 1981, new edit., 1994, Beware of Ostriches, 1978, Poetry on the Stage, 1979, Lady Doctor on a Homestead, 1987, Two Peach Baskets, 1991 (with J. Allan) Born to Be a Loser, 1993, Spider Web, 1993; contbr. poetry and articles to various publs.; book reviewer Jour. Am. Culture, Jour. Popular Culture, 1980-87; actress Little Theater, La., 1969-83, off-off Broadway, 1980. Vol. Mayor's Commn. on the Needs of Women, City of Lafayette, 1976-86; vol. La. Talent Bank of Women, 1978-86; judge of writing contests for schs., clubs, profl. socs., La. and U.S., 1961—; newsletter editor Bayou coun. Girl Scouts of Am., 1964-66; guest editor The New Laurel Rev., 1976. Mem. AAUW (bd. dirs. br. 1967-71, state editor 1967-71, grantee 1978-80, faculty rsch. grant U. Southwestern La. 1980-81, 85-86), Soc. for Values in Higher Edn. (Svc. award 1995), South Cen. Coll. English Assn. (pres. 1986-87), S.W. Br. Poetry (pres. 1988—), La. State Poetry Soc. (Disting. Lifetime mem., pres. 1978-79, 81-82, editor 1970-90), South Cen. MLA, Coll. English Assn. (life mem.), Am. Folklore Soc., Conf. on Christianity and Lit., Nat. Fedn. State Poetry Socs., Inc. (Queen of Poetry 1993), Phi Beta Kappa (regional pres. 1976-77, 83-84). Democrat. Roman Catholic. Home: 159 Whittington Dr Lafayette LA 70503-2741

WEBB, EMILY, retired plant morphologist; b. Charleston, S.C., Apr. 10, 1924; d. Malcolm Syfan and Emily Kirk (Moore) W.; m. John James Rosemond, Apr. 23, 1942 (div. 1953); 1 child, John Kirk; m. Julius Goldberg, Sept. 9, 1954; children: Michael, Judith. AB in Liberal Arts and Sci. with honors, U. Ill., Chgo., 1968, MS in Biol. Scis., 1972, PhD in Biol. Scis., 1985. Undergrad. fellow in bacteriology Med. Coll. S.C., Charleston, 1952-54; teaching asst. U. Ill., Chgo., 1969-72, 77-84, rsch. asst., 1977; teaching fellow W.Va. U., Morgantown, 1974, instr., 1974-75; rsch. in N.Am. bot. needlework art, 1986—. Author: Studies in Several North American Species of Ophioglossum, 1986; translator Nat. Transl. Ctr., Chgo., 1976; contbr. articles to profl. jours. James scholar U. Ill., 1968-69. Mem. DAR. Democrat. Episcopalian. Home and Office: 1356 Mandel Ave Westchester IL 60154-3433

WEBB, ERMA LEE, nurse educator; b. Hitchcock, Okla., Mar. 16, 1933; d. Edward B. and Annabelle G. (Schnell) Haffner; m. James M. Webb, Apr. 4, 1959; children: Scott, Sandee, Steve. BSN, Union Coll., 1957; MSN, Loma Linda (Calif.) U., 1976. Charge and staff nurse pediatrics and surg. units Porter Meml. Hosp., Denver, 1960-68; dir. LPN program Hialeah (Fla.) Hosp., 1969-72; asst. prof. Loma Linda U., 1972-76; assoc. prof. So. Coll. 7th Day Adventists, Orlando, Fla., 1976—, coord. BS program Fla. campuses, 1976—. Mem. Fla. Nurse's Assn., Fla. League Nursing, So. Regional Edn. Bd., Sigma Theta Tau. Home: 3233 Holiday Ave Apopka FL 32703-6635

WEBB, LYNDAL MILLER, principal; b. Deerfield, Fla., Feb. 14, 1933; d. Bowling Dickinson Miller and Cerece Monique (Walker) Miller-Mahoney; m. Thomas Lavelle Webb, Feb. 11, 1951; children: Fredonia W. Ray, Nancy W. Nevil, Gay W. Davis, Susan W. Elsinger. BS in Edn., Valdosta State Coll., 1965, EdM in Elem. Edn., 1968, EdM in Adminstrn. and Supervision, 1971, ednl. specialist, 1982. Cert. adminstrn. and supervision in edn. Resource tchr., classroom tchr. Pine Grove Lowndes County, Valdosta, Ga., 1965-71; asst. prin. Pine Grove Primary, Valdosta, 1971-80, Pine Grove Elem., Valdosta, 1980-83; prin. Hahira Elem. Sch., Valdosta, 1984—. Bd. dirs. Locoga Credit Union, Valdosta, 1979-93; dir. vacation bible sch. Bemiss United Meth. Ch., Valdosta, 1990-94. Mem. AAUW (v.p. 1986-88), NEA, Ga. Assn. Educators, Lowndes Assn. Educators (pres.), Ga. ASCD (bd. dirs. 1992-96), Internat. Reading Assn., Partnership 2000 (bd. dirs. 1994—), Phi Delta Kappa (pres.), Delta Kappa Gamma (pres. Sigma chpt. 1989-91). Republican. Methodist. Office: Hahira Elem Sch 350 Claudia Dr Hahira GA 31632

WEBB, LYNNE MCGOVERN, communication educator, consultant; b. Shamokin, Pa., Mar. 20, 1951; d. Charles Ralph and Ethel Elizabeth (Harris) McGovern; m. Ronald E. Webb, Sept. 28, 1978 (div. June 1981); m. Robert Blakely Moberly, Apr. 6, 1984; children: Laura Ellen, Richard Edward, Reed JeeMinSeo. BS, Pa. State U., 1972; MS, U. Oreg., 1975, PhD, 1980. Field rep. East Central Ill. Area Agy. on Aging, Campaign, Ill., 1972-74; grad. teaching asst. U. Oreg., Eugene, 1974-78; instr. Berea Coll., Berea, Ky., 1978-80; asst. prof. U. Fla., Gainesville, 1980-86, assoc. prof., 1986-90; vis. assoc. prof. U. Hawaii, Honolulu, 1990-91; assoc. prof. U. Memphis, 1991—; cons. Fla. Farm Bur., Gainesville, 1981, Clay County Electric Coop., Keystone Heights, Fla., 1987, Retirement Rsch. Found., Chgo., 1988. Mem. Fla. Speech Comm. Assn. (v.p. 1986-87), So. States Comm. Assn. (chair applied comm. divsn. 1989-90, chair gender studies divsn. 1992-93, chair membership 1993, v.p. 1994, pres. 1995), Speech Comm. Assn. (chair com. on comm. and aging 1982-83, legis. coun. 1989-92, chair applied comm. sect. 1994-95). Democrat. Methodist. Office: Univ Memphis 143 Theatre and Comm Arts Memphis TN 38152

WEBB, NANCY MCIVOR, sculptor; b. Concord, N.H., Dec. 27, 1926; d. Donald Guy and Violet (Locke) McIvor; m. Dwight Willson Webb, Sept. 27, 1947; children: Alexander, Patrick, Sophie. Student, Smith Coll., 1944-47. Art dir. Noonday Press, N.Y.C., 1955-59; One-woman shows include Cherry Stone Gallery, Wellfleet, Mass., 1974-77, Hunt Inst. Carnegie-Mellon Inst., Pitts., 1981, Mass. Hort. Soc., Boston, 1981; exhibited in group shows at Far Gallery, N.Y.C., 1973-79, De Cordova Mus., Lincoln, Mass., 1975, 79, Mus. of Sci., Boston, 1979-80, Washington Art Assn., 1989, Wiggin Gallery Boston Pub. Libr., 1992, Cape Mus. Fine Arts, Dennis, Mass., 1994; represented in permanent collections including Alewife Sta., Cambridge, Mass., Steamship Auth., Woods Hole, Mass., Port Auth., Charlestown, Mass., Charles Park, Cambridge; author, illustrator Aguk of Alaska, 1963, Makema of the Rain Forest, 1963. Office: 11 Miller St Studio 114 Somerville MA 02143

WEBB, PATRICIA DYAN W., speech and language pathologist, sign language educator; b. Anniston, Ala., July 16, 1948; d. Gary Gene and Jewell Frances (Billingsley) West; m. Thomas Elliott Webb, May 11, 1969; children: Amy Kristin, Michael Elliott. BA in Comm., Winthrop U., 1969, MS in Speech Pathology, 1974; MS in Speech Pathology, U. S.C., 1993, Specialist Cert., 1993. Cert. clin. competence-speech lang. pathologist; specialist in spl. edn. Speech/lang. pathologist York (S.C.) Sch. Dist. 1, 1974-76, St. Nicholas Speech and Hearing Ctr., Greenwood, S.C., 1980-81; speech pathologist Abbeville (S.C.) Sch. Dist. 60, 1981-88; speech/lang. pathologist Greenwood Sch. Dist. 51, Ware Shoals, S.C., 1988—; sign lang. instr. Piedmont Tech. Coll., Greenwood, S.C., 1990—; accents and dialects cons., Greenwood, 1993—; interpretor for deaf Self Meml. Hosp., Greenwood, 1990—; pres. bd. dirs. S.C. Ednl. Found., Columbia; owner/pres. Corp. Comm. Co-author Multi-age language and articulation screening test, 1986; author "How to Tame a Wild Accent" accent modification program; participant (video) Use of Cued Speech With Minimally Impaired Children", 1989. Fundraiser Greenwood County Women's Shelter, 1991—; past pres. Greenwood Bus. and Profl. Women. Mem. AAUW, Am. Speech and Hearing Assn., S.C. Speech and Hearing Assn., Upper Savannah Consortium of Speech-Lang. Pathologists (co-chair 1991-94), Phi Delta Kappa, Phi Kappa Phi. Home: 123 Fawnbrook Dr Greenwood SC 29646-7531 Office: Greenwood Sch Dist 51 42 Sparks Ave Ware Shoals SC 29692-1626

WEBB, RUTH CAMERON, retired educator; b. Honolulu, June 1, 1923; d. William Henry and Ruth Gray (Cameron) W. AB, Drew U., 1948, DHL, 1972; MA, Syracuse U., 1949; PhD, U. Ill., 1963. Nursery sch. cons. Swarthmore, Pa., 1953-55; with Jewish Vocat. Soc., Milw., 1963-66, Hamburg (Pa.) Hosp. Sch., 1966-87, Glenwood (Iowa) State Sch., 1989—. Author: Journey into Personhood, 1994. Home: 619 Park St Apt B104 Grinnell IA 50112-2269

WEBB, THEORA GRAVES, public relations executive; b. Norfolk, Va., July 21, 1941; d. Lemuel and Theora (Weaver) Graves. BA, Wilson Coll., 1962. Chmn. modern langs. dept. William Henry High Sch., Dover, Del., 1962-64; abstractor-indexer, Rockville, Md., 1966-67; owner RML Translations, Acton, Mass., 1969-70; asst. dir. communications and pub. relations, acting dir. publs. br., spl. asst. to dep. supt., cons.-expert, instr. adult edn. pub. schs. D.C., 1971-78; regional coordinator, cons. Nat. Energy Edn. Day, Cedar Rapids, Iowa, 1979; projects mgr. U.S. Com. for Energy Awareness, Washington, 1980-83; dir. office pub. affairs Internat. Trade Adminstrn., U.S. Dept. Commerce, Washington, 1983-86; pres. HSW Comm., 1986-92; dir. pub. affairs Duracell Internat., Bethel, Conn., 1992—; bd. dirs. U. Found. of Weskin Conn.; bd. advisors Ctr. for Corp. Cmty. Rels. Boston Coll., 1996—. Mem. energy and econ. devel. com. nat. NAACP, 1980-83, energy task force Nat. Conf. Black Mayors, 1982-83; adv. council vol. svcs. Dist. 7 Dept. Correctional Svcs., 1979-80; adv. bd. Linn County Jail Chaplaincy, 1979-80, Cedar Rapids YWCA, 1978-80; mem. bd. dirs. Wilson Coll., 1992-94; bd. dirs. Young Audiences of Conn., 1995—. Mem. Am. Assn. Blacks in Energy, Md. State Right to Read Task Force, Nat. Sch. Pub. Rels. Assn., Nat. Assn. Women's Bus. Owners. Coun. of 100, Nat. Press Club. Home: 2 Davis Ct Martinsville NJ 08836-2314 Office: Duracell Internat Inc Berkshire Corporate Park Bethel CT 06801

WEBER, ADELHEID LISA, former nurse, chemist; b. Cottbus, Germany, June 1, 1934; came to the U.S., 1958; d. Johannes Gustav Paul and Johanna Katinka (Askevold) Haertwig; m. Joseph Cotrell Weber (dec. 1986), Oct. 25, 1957; children: Robert Andreas, Miriam Lisa. RN, Stadtisches Hosp., Dortmund, Germany, 1956; BS in Distributive Sci., Am. U., 1983; MBA, U. Md., 1991. RN. Nurse Krankenhaus, Wuppertal, Germany, 1956-57; pvt. nurse Wellesley, Mass., 1969-74; lab. tech. Microbiol. Assocs., Bethesda, Md., 1979-84; switchboard operator Best Products Co., Bethesda, 1983-87; lab. tech. Uniformed Svcs. U. Health Scis., Bethesda, 1984-90; info. rsch. tech. Info. Rsch. Internat. Inc., Bethesda, 1987; chemist USDA, Beltsville, Md., 1990-93; ret., 1993. Vol. Sibley Meml. Hosp., Washington, 1991. Recipient Cert. award County of Montgomery, Md., 1988, Whitman Walker Clinic, 1987. Mem. NAFE, Soc. for Rsch. Adminstrs., Am. Chem. Soc., Nat. Assn. for Amputees, Soc. for Applied Spectroscopy, Nat. Trust for Historic Preservation, Hemlock Soc. Nat. Capital Area, Nat. Mus. for Women in Arts, Wash. Performing Arts Soc. Home: 23 Sunset Ln Osterville MA 02655-2035

WEBER, CAROL, art consultant; b. Anspach, Germany, Nov. 22, 1947; arrived in U.S., 1951; m. Mike Weber (dec. 1994); children: David, Paula. AAS, Fashion Inst. of Tech., 1966; BBS, Baruch Coll., 1976. Account exec. Graphic Workshop, N.Y.C., 1967-70; sales mgr. IFT Internat., N.Y.C., 1970-73; advt. dir. Beldoch Industries, N.Y.C., 1973-75; v.p. Boutique Sportswear Ltd., N.Y.C., 1975-90, pres., 1990-92; pres. Carol Weber Fine Art, N.Y.C., 1992—. Pres. PTA Park Ave. Synagogue Religious Sch., N.Y.C., 1989-90. Home and Office: 25 East 86th St New York NY 10028

WEBER, DARLENE MARIE, health educator; b. Tarentum, Pa., Nov. 17, 1939; d. Thomas J. and Agnes M. (Reiger) Hohman; m. David F. Weber, Aug. 17, 1963; children: JuliLynne, Mark David. BS, SUNY, Cortland, 1961; MS, Ind. U., 1963, D of Health and Safety, 1964. Cert. vision/hearing specialist, Ill., sanitation cert., Ill. Instr. SUNY, Buffalo, 1961-62; grad. asst. Ind. U., Bloomington, 1962-63, vis. lectr., 1963-64; tchr. Martinsville (Ind.) H.S., 1964-65; area dir. Ind. Heart Assn., Indpls., 1965-66; assoc. prof. Ill. State U., Bloomington, 1967-89; health coord. Heartland Head Start, Bloomington, 1989—; cons. health, mental health and nutrition Tech. Assistance Support Ctr. Ohio State U., Columbus, 1993—; peer reviewer region V Head Start, Chgo., 1985-96; USDA cons. Ill. Dept. Edn., Springfield, 1994-96. Title I grantee HHS, Fed. Govt., 1980-82. Mem. Ill. Pub. Health Assn. Home: 2115 E Taylor St Bloomington IL 61701-5725

WEBER, GLORIA RICHIE, minister, retired state representative; married; 4 children. BA, Washington U., St. Louis; MA, MDiv, Eden Theol. Sem., Webster Groves, Mo. Ordained to ministry Evang. Luth. Ch. Am., St. Louis, 1974;. Min. Am. Luth. Ch., St. Louis, 1974; family life educator Luth. Family & Children's Svcs. Mo.; state representative State of Mo., 1993-94; Mo. state organizer, dir. comm. Mainstream Voters C.A.R.E., 1995. Exec. dir. Older Women's League, 1990-95; Dem. candidate for Mo. State Senate, 1996. Recipient Woman of Achievement award St. Louis Globe-Dem., 1977, Unselfish Cmty. Svc. award St. Louis Sentinel Newspaper, 1985, Faith in Action award Luth. Svcs. St. Louis, 1994, Outstanding Woman award Coalition of St. Louis Labor Women, 1994; named Woman of Yr., Variety Club, 1978, Woman of Worth, Older Women's League, 1993. Democrat. Home and Office: 4910 Valley Crest Dr Saint Louis MO 63128-1829

WEBER, JANET M., nurse; b. Lansdale, Pa., Mar. 12, 1936; d. Russell H. and Naomi (dec.) Moyer W. Diploma in nursing, Washington County Hosp. Sch. Nursing, 1959; B.S. in Nursing, Grace Coll., 1960; M.Ed., Duquesne U., 1969. Staff nurse, supr. Murphy Med. Ctr., Warsaw, Ind., 1959-60; coll. nurse Grace Coll., Winona Lake, Ind., 1959-60; med. surg. nursing instr. Washington County Hosp. Sch. Nursing, Hagerstown, Md., 1961-64; pvt. duty nurse Washington County Hosp., Hagerstown, 1964; chmn. found. of nursing Presbyn. Univ. Hosp. Sch. Nursing, Pitts., 1964-72; curriculum coordinator Albert Einstein Med. Ctr. Sch. Nursing, Phila., 1972-73; assoc. dir. Albert Einstein Med. Ctr. Sch. Nursing, 1973-74, acting dir., 1974, dir., 1974-87; staff nurse ARC Penn-Jersey Blood Drive Donor Services, Phila., 1988-92, asst. nurse mgr., 1992—; nurse mgr. ARC Penn-Jersey Blood Drivce Donor Svcs., Phila., 1992—; cons. Md. Bd. Higher Edn., 1981-82. Author: The Faculty's Role in Policy Development, 1981, Assisting Students with Educational Deficiencies, 1975. Mem. Washington County Hosp. Nurses Alumni Assn. (pres. 1962-64), Grace Coll. Alumni Assn., Duquesne U. Alumni Assn. Republican. Home: 5640 Arbor St Philadelphia PA 19120-2502 Office: ARC Blood Donor Svcs 700 Spring Garden St Philadelphia PA 19123-3508

WEBER, LINDA JEANNE, special education educator; b. Youngstown, Ohio, Oct. 6, 1949; d. Sam and Gladys (Shulman) Saul; m. Richard Allen Weber, Dec. 20, 1970; children: Heath, Samantha. BS in Speech and Hearing Scis., Ohio U., 1971, MS in Audiology, 1972; PhD coursework, Kent State U., 1974-78; supr. cert. in spl. edn., Youngstown State U., 1986. Speech pathologist, audiologist Polk (Pa.) State Sch. and Hosp., 1972-74; instr. Kent (Ohio) State U., 1974-78; speech pathologist Ravenna (Ohio) Portage County Schs., 1978-79, Liberty Local Schs., Youngstown, 1979-89; audiologist in pvt. practice Youngstown, Niles, Ohio, 1983—; ednl. assessment coord. Northeast Ohio Spl. Edn. Regional Rsch. Ctr., Warren, 1989-91, early childhood coord., 1991—; audiologist Easter Seals, Youngstown, 1981-86, Trumbull County Bd. of Edn., Warren, 1985-87. Dir. nat. alumni bd. Ohio U., 1990-93; mem. trustee's acad. Ohio U., Athens, 1991—. Mem. Nat. Assn. for the Edn. of Young Children, Ohio U. Alumni Assn. (co-chair 1982—). Office: NE Ohio Spl Edn Regional Resource Ctr 409 Harmon Ave NW Warren OH 44483-4808

WEBER, MARY LINDA, preschool educator; b. Hermon, N.Y., May 21, 1947; d. Stanley Albert and Shirley Lucille (Holland) Morrill; m. John Weber, July 23, 1966 (div. Nov. 1980); children: James, Mark. AAS, Agrl. and Tech. Coll., Canton, N.Y., 1971; BA, SUNY, Potsdam, 1973; MA, U. South Fla., 1981. Cert. pre-sch., elem. and reading K-12 tchr., N.Y., Fla.;. Tchr. elem. Hermon-DeKalb Ctrl. Sch., DeKalb Junction, N.Y., 1974-76, Westside Elem. Sch., Spring Hill, Fla., 1976-77; tchr. kindergarten Spring Hill Elem. Sch., 1977-89; tchr. pre-kindergarten Deltona Elem. Sch., Spring Hill, 1989—. Author mini-grant Home-Sch. Partnerships, 1990, Multi-Cultural Ctr., 1992, Family Info. Ctr., 1993, Parent Partners in Literacy, 1996. Mem. NEA (Young Children sect.), Assn. Childhood Edn. Internat., Internat. Reading Assn., So. Early Childhood Assn., Fla. Reading Assn., Hernando County Reading Coun. Home: 4132 Redwing Dr Spring Hill FL 34606-2425 Office: Deltona Elem Sch 2055 Deltona Blvd Spring Hill FL 34606-3216

WEBER, NANCY WALKER, charitable trust administrator; b. Adrian, W.Va., Aug. 26, 1936; d. James Everett and Wanna Virginia (Alderman) Walker; m. J. Raymond Jacob, Jr., June 12, 1955 (div. 1967); children: Paul M., Sharon L.; m. George Harry Weber, Apr. 27, 1983 (dec. Mar. 1995). Student, Peabody Prep. Mus., 1946-53, Peabody Conservatory Mus., 1954-56. Asst. buyer cosmetics Hutzler's Dept. Store, Balt., 1967-69; exec. sec. to exec. v.p. Martin Marietta Corp., Bethesda, Md., 1969-75; asst. exec. to exec. dir. hosp. U. Utah, Salt Lake City, 1976-80; dir. program adminstrn. Lucille P. Markey Charitable Trust, Miami, Fla., 1983—. Pianist, organist Middle River Bapt. Ch., Balt., 1953-61. Named Mrs. Del. in Mrs. Del./Am. Pagent, 1966. Office: Lucille P Markey Charitable Trust 3250 Mary St Ste 405 Miami FL 33133-5232

WEBER, PATRICIA ANN, counselor; b. Lansing, Mich., Mar. 20, 1956; d. James John and Victoria S. (Voda) W. BS, Utah State U., 1978; MEd, U. Idaho, 1992. Spl. edn. tchr. Fremont County Sch. Dist., Ashton, Idaho, 1978-80; spl. edn. tchr. Challis (Idaho) Sch. Dist., 1981-92, sch. counselor, 1992—; chair guidance adv. com. Challis (Idaho) Sch. Dist., 1992—; EAP counselor Vocat. Resources, Inc., Challis, 1993-95. Bd. dirs. Challis Arts Coun., 1987-94; EMT Challis EMT's, 1984-88. Mem. ACA, Am. Sch. Counseling Assn., Idaho Counseling Assn., Idaho Sch. Counseling Assn. Home: PO Box 1164 Challis ID 83226 Office: Challis High Sch Box 304 Challis ID 83226

WEBER, ROBYN VICTORIA, environmental engineer; b. Landover, Md., June 7, 1965. BS in Petroleum Engring., U. Mo., Rolla, 1987; postgrad., U. Okla., 1995—. Ops. engr. Mobil Oil Corp., Ada, Countyline, Okla., 1988-92; project mgr., environ. engr. StanTech Environ. Svcs., Oklahoma City, Okla., 1992-94, Gulf-Pacific Environ. Engring., Oklahoma City, Okla., 1994-95; pres. Advantage Environ. Svcs., Oklahoma City, Okla., 1995—; reservoir mgmt. team leader Mobil Oil Corp., Countyline, 1990-92; presenter at confs. Vol. Second Chance Animal Sanctuary, 1991-92. Mem. ASTM, DAR, Soc. Petroleum Engrs., Okla. Soc. Environ. Profls., Nat. Groundwater Assn., Air and Waste Mgmt. Assn., Okla. Hazardous Materials Assn. Home: 11637 SW 4th Terr Yukon OK 73099 Office: Advantage Environ Svcs P O Box 890566 Oklahoma City OK 73189

WEBER, SUSAN LEE, marketing consultant; b. Honolulu, Nov. 30, 1948; d. Kenneth Charles and Valerie (June) W. BBA, San Jose (Calif.) State U., 1970; postgrad., U. Calif., Berkeley, 1972-73, Pepperdine U., 1977-78; Cert. in Mktg., Harvard U. Small bus. organizer VISTA, Roseville, N.C., 1970-72; cosmetics buyer USN Commissary Supply, Oakland, Calif., 1972-74; cosmetics product mgr. Shaklee Corp., San Francisco, 1974-76; mktg. mgr. Max Factor, Inc., Hollywood, Calif., 1976-81; v.p. electronic mktg. Bank of Am., San Francisco, 1981-83, v.p. bank card merchandising, 1983-85, v.p., upscale mktg., sales, 1985-88; pres. Mktg. Fundamentals, San Francisco, 1988—. Mem. Am. Mktg. Assn., Bank Mktg. Assn., Bay Area Women's Network, NAFE, Fin. Insts. Mktg. Assn. Republican. Presbyterian. Office: Mktg Fundamentals 977 E Stanley Blvd Ste 227 Livermore CA 94550-4009

WEBER-JAVERS, FLORENCE R., nurse; b. Milw., Mar. 29, 1953; d. Frank A. and E. Mae (Brown) Weber; m. Lawrence P. Wittig, Aug. 17, 1974 (div. Jan. 1983); children: Jodi, Drew; m. Russell L. Weber-Javers, Sept. 9, 1983; stepchildren: Andrea K. Javers Notaro, Jennifer L. Javers, John R. Javers. ADN, Milw. Area Tech. Coll., 1978; Diploma in Enterostomal Therapy Edn., Jewish Hosp./Washington U., St. Louis, 1980. RN. RN St. Michael Hosp., Milw., 1978-80; cert. orthopedic fitter Knneppel's, Milw., 1974-84; enterostomal therapy nurse Stein Med., Milw., 1984-86; home health enterostomal therapy Nurse Case Mgr., Las Vegas, 1986-88; enterostomal therapy nurse Home Care/Olsten Kimberly, Las Vegas, 1988—; nurse various home health agys., HMOs, and med. facilities, Las Vegas, 1988—; pressure reduction mattress sales cons., Pegasus, Fla., 1985; clin. trial cons. Convatec (Squibb), N.J., 1982-86, Hollister, Inc., Libertyville, Ill., 1982-84. Editor: Am. Ostomy Supply newsletter, 1985—. Vol. Am. Cancer Soc., 1980—. 1st lt. U.S. Army Nurse Corps Res., 1984-89. Recipient scholarship Am. Cancer Soc., Milw., 1980; named Comm. Nurse of the Yr., March of Dimes, Las Vegas, 1995. Mem. Wound, Ostomy and Continence Nurses Soc., United Ostomy Assn. of So. Nev. (advisor 1986—). Home: 8433 Honeywood Cir Las Vegas NV 89128

WEBRE, ELIZABETH CANCIENNE, education educator; b. Houma, La., Nov. 20, 1949; d. Philip John and Vivian Margaret Cancienne; m. Alfred Joseph Webre, Aug 20, 1983; 1 child, Nicholas. BA, Nicholls State U., 1971, MEd, 1975; EdD, N.E. La. U., 1979. Elem. tchr. Lafourche Parish, Thibodaux, La., 1971-76; grad. asst. N.E. La. U., Monroe, 1976-79; dir. presch. handicapped program Madison, Tensas, E. and W. Carroll Consortium, Tallulah, La., 1979-80; asst. prof. U. So. Miss., Hattiesburg, 1980-83; elem. tchr. Lafayette (La.) Parish, 1983-86; assoc. prof. U. Southwestern La., Lafayette, 1986—. Contbr. articles to profl. jours. Mem. La. Assn. Tchr. Educators (sec. 1993-94), Internat. Reading Assn., Nat. Coun. Tchrs. English, La. Reading Assn., Phi Delta Kappa. Office: Univ Southwestern La Box 42051 Lafayette LA 70504

WEBSTER, BARBARA SHEPPARD, art association administrator; b. Atlantic City, N.J., Apr. 25, 1936; d. Edward Francis and Rita Joan (Gargale) Sheppard; m. Russell Thomas Webster, Sept. 7, 1957 (dec. Sept. 1976); children: Russell Todd, Catherine Sheppard. BA, Douglass Coll., 1957; MEd, Rutgers U., 1965. Asst. field dir. Pub. Opinion Surveys, Princeton, N.J., 1957-60; tchr., counselor Bound Brook (N.J.) H.S., 1960-62; tchr., performer, choreographer divsn. continuing edn. Westport (Conn.) Pub. Summer Sch., Staples H.S., 1968-86; mng. dir. Levitt Pavilion for Performing Arts, Westport, Conn., 1983-85; exec. dir. Stamford (Conn.) Cmty. Arts Coun., 1985-87, Artspace, Inc., New Haven, Conn., 1987—; mentor Inner City Cultural Devel. Conn. Commn. Arts, Bridgeport, 1992-93, Hartford, 1993-94, New Haven, 1994—; participant Alliance N.Y. State Arts Couns., Greenwich, Conn., 1986, Yale Sch. Orgn. and Mgmt., 1987; founding dir. Media Arts Ctr., New Haven, 1991-95; founder Summer Arts for Youth-SAY!, 1994—. Choreographer opening ceremonies 28th gen. assembly Unitarian Universalists, New Haven, 1989. Mem. Arts and Bus. Roundtable, New Haven, 1995—, Arts! Artists! Athletes! Spl. Olympics World Games, New Haven, 1994-95; participant Vision Project Gtr. New Haven, 1994. Mem. AAUW (Norwalk-Westport (Conn.) chpt. 1994—, Bound Brook (N.J.) chpt. 1960-63), New Haven Rotary (chair Outstanding com. 1994-96, dir. 1996—). Mem. Unitarian Universalist Ch. Home: 13 Reimer Rd Westport CT 06880 Office: Artspace 70 Audubon St New Haven CT 06510

WEBSTER, COLLEEN MICHAEL, english language educator; b. Sunnyvale, Calif., Sept. 21, 1965; d. E. Patrick and Patricia Colleen (Medlar) W. BA in English, Coll. of Notre Dame of Md., 1987; MA in English, U. Del., 1989, ABD, 1992. Adj. faculty Coll. of Notre Dame, Balt., 1990-94, Harford C.C., Bel Air, Md., 1991-94; asst. prof. Harford C.C., Bel Air, 1994—; adj. faculty Goucher Coll., Balt., 1992-93, Towson State U., Balt., 1992-93; book club organizer/moderator Coll. of Notre Dame, Balt., 1994-95; book club moderator Pikesville C.C., 1994-95; poetry reading coord. Steppingstone Mus., Havre de Grace, Md., 1995—. Recipient Judson Jerome Poetry scholar Antioch Writer's Conf., 1995. Mem. Md. Jr. Coll. Women's LaCrosse League; lacross coach Harford C.C. Democrat. Office: Harford Cmty Coll 401 Thomas Run Rd Bel Air MD 21015

WEBSTER, LINDA JEAN, communication educator, media consultant; b. L.A., July 16, 1948; d. Stanley Stewart and Irene M. (Sabo) W. BS, So. Conn. State U., New Haven, 1981, MA, 1983; PhD, La. State U., Baton Rouge, 1987. CEO CBE Enterprises, Inc., Baton Rouge, 1984-89; rsch. fellow La. State U., Baton Rouge, 1983-87; instr. speech Southeastern La. U., Hammond, 1984-89, Hancock Coll., Santa Maria, Calif., 1989; curator of edn. Lompoc (Calif.) Mus., 1989; asst. prof. speech U. Ark., Monticello, 1990-95, assoc. prof. speech, 1995—, dir. honors program, 1995—; exec. dir. Drew County Hist. Mus., Monticello, 1992-95; media dir. Oasis Resources-Homeless Shelter, Warren, Ark., 1991—; bur. chief Pine Bluff (Ark.) Comml., 1992-94; media consulting WZXS-FM radio, Holly Ridge, N.C., 1995—. Contbr. chpts. to books and articles to jours. in field. Vol. media chair Oasis Transitional Shelter, Warren, 1991—, Boys/Girls Club, Monticello, 1992-93; campaign dir. Gloria Wright election, Monticello, 1995; campaign media dir. Ken Harper election-Dist. 82, 1996. Recipient Noel Ross Strader award Coll. Media Advisors, Inc., 1991, Coll. Tchr. of the Yr. award Ark. State Commn. Assn., 1993. Mem. Ark. Press Women (state pres. 1993-95, Communicator of Achievement award 1991), Ark. State Communication Assn. (nom. 1st v.p. 1996), So. State Communication Assn. (chair honors session 1995—), Internat. Communication Assn., Oral History Assn., Speech Communication Assn. (commn. chair 1993-96). Roman Catholic. Office: U Ark-Arts & Langs Monticello AR 71656

WEBSTER, SUSAN, lawyer; b. Hartford, Conn., Dec. 21, 1956. BA, Wesleyan U., 1977; JD, Fordham U., 1984. Bar: N.Y. 1985. Ptnr. Cravath, Swaine & Moore, N.Y.C. Mem. ABA, N.Y. State Bar Assn., Assn. of Bar of City of N.Y. Office: Cravath Swaine & Moore Worldwide Plz 825 Eighth Ave New York NY 10019*

WEBSTER, SYLVIA DOREEN, administrative assistant; b. Northampton, Mass., Aug. 5, 1961; d. Clyde Joseph Sanger Jr. and Clara Ann (Nugent) Shea. Assembler Citizen Security, Belchertown, Mass., 1985; adminstrv. asst. Northampton Plumbling Supply Co. Inc., 1986—; ind. distbr. HerbaLife Internat., L.A., 1992—. Mem. Easthampton Lions Internat. (bd. dirs., 3rd v.p.), Northampton Muscular Dystrophy Assn. (chairperson 1983-94). Home: PO Box 1091 Northampton MA 01061

WECHSLER, JESSICA See JOSELL, JESSICA

WECHSLER, MARY HEYRMAN, lawyer; b. Green Bay, Wis., Jan. 8, 1948; d. Donald Hubert and Helen (Polcyn) Heyrman; m. Roger Wechsler, Aug. 1971 (div. 1977); 1 child, Risa Heyrman; m. David Jay Sellinger, Aug. 15, 1981; 1 stepchild, Kirk Benjamin; 1 child, Michael Paul. Student, U. Chgo., 1966-67, 68-69; BA, U. Wash., 1971; JD cum laude, U. Puget Sound, 1979. Bar: Wash. 1979. Assoc. Law Offices Ann Johnson, Seattle, 1979-81; ptnr. Johnson, Wechsler, Thompson, Seattle, 1981-83, Mussehl, Rosenberg et al., Seattle, 1987-88; pvt. practice Seattle, 1984-87; ptnr. Wechsler, Besk, Erickson, Ross & Roubit, Seattle, 1988—; mem. Walsh Commn. on Jud. Selection, 1995-96; Supreme Ct. Commn. on Domestic Rels., 1996; chair edn. com. Access to Justice Bd., 1996; presenter in field. Author: Family Law in Washington, 1987, rev. edit., 1988, Marriage and Separation, Divorce and Your Rights, 1994; contbr. articles to legal publs. Mem. Wash. State Ethics Adv. Com., 1992-95; bd. dirs. Seattle LWV, 1991-92. Fellow Am. Acad. Matrimonial Lawyers (trustee Wash. state chpt. 1994, sec. Wash. state chpt. 1996, mem. Supreme Ct. domestic rels. com. 1996); mem. ABA (chmn. Wash. state 1987-88), Wash. State Bar Assn. (exec. com. family law sect. 1985-91, chair 1988-89, legis. com. 1991—, Outstanding Atty. of Yr. family law sect. 1988), Wash. Women Lawyers, King County Bar Assn. (legis. com. 1985—, vice chmn. 1990-91, chair family law sect. 1986-87, chair domestic violence com. 1986-87, trustee 1988-90, policy planning com. 1991-92, 2d v.p. 1992-93, 1st v.p. 1993-94, pres. 1994-95), Nat. Conf. of Bar Pres. (commn. com. 1994-95, long range planning com. 1996). Office: Wechsler Besk Erickson Ross & Roubik 701 5th Ave Seattle WA 98104-7016

WECHSLER, SUSAN LINDA, software design engineer; b. Burbank, Calif., Oct. 7, 1956; d. Robert Edward and Sharron Ilene Wechsler; m. Gary Daniel Grove, Aug. 24, 1975 (dec. Dec. 1980); m. Dane Bruce Rogers, Feb. 28, 1987; children: Shayna Marneen Rogers, Ayla Corinne Rogers. BA in Math., Calif. State U., Long Beach, 1979. R&D software engr. Hewlett-Packard Co., Corvallis, Oreg., 1980—; Presenter N.W. Software Quality Conf., 1984. Contbr. articles to profl. publs.; co-developer nine calculators and handheld computers; patentee in field; co-designer HP 200LX Palmtop PC/Organizer, 1994; writer software for laptop computers. Pres. Gifts for a Better World, Corvallis, Oreg., 1994, bd. dirs. 1990-1995. Democrat. Office: Hewlett-Packard 1000 NE Circle Blvd Corvallis OR 97330-4239

WECHTER, CLARI ANN, paint manufacturing company executive; b. Chgo., June 1, 1953; d. Norman Robert and Harriet Beverly (Golub) W.; m. Gordon Jay Siegel, Feb. 10, 1980; 1 child, Alix Jessica. BA, U. Ariz., 1975; BE, Loyola U., Chgo., 1977. Cert. tchr., Ill. Saleswoman, v.p. sales Federated Paint Mfg. Co., Chgo., 1979—. Republican. Jewish. Home: 25 E Cedar St Chicago IL 60611-1151 Office: Federated Paint Mfg Co 1882 S Normal Ave Chicago IL 60616-1013

WECK, KRISTIN WILLA, savings bank executive; b. Elgin, Ill., Nov. 5, 1959; d. John Francis and Florence Elaine (Ebel) W. BBA, Augustana Coll., Rock Island, Ill., 1981. Lic. real estate broker, Ill., life/health ins. producer; registered securities rep. (series 7 and series 24). Intern with investment banking group First Chgo. Bank, London, 1980; intern Prudential-Bache Co., Ft. Lauderdale, Fla., 1981; residential appraiser Fox Valley Appraisal Counselors, Ltd., West Dundee, Ill., 1982-84; asst. real estate loan officer First Nat. Bank, Barrington, Ill., 1982-84; savs. and loan field examiner III Office of Thrift Supervision, Chgo., 1984-90; mng. agt. Resolution Trust Corp., Elk Grove Village, Ill., 1990-91; sr. v.p., treas., bd. dirs. Cardunal Savs. Bank, West Dundee, Ill., 1991—. Vice pres. Brandywine Condo Assn., Crystal Lake, Ill., 1983; Project Bus. cons. Jr. Achievement, 1992—. Recipient Outstanding Achievement award Fed. Home Loan Bank Bd., 1985. Mem. Nat. Assn. Securities Dealers (registered rep., registered prin.). Republican. Lutheran. Home: PO Box 930 Dundee IL 60118-0930 Office: Cardunal Savs Bank FSB 704 W Main St # 97 Dundee IL 60118-2028

WEDDINGTON, ELIZABETH GARDNER (LIZ GARDNER), actress, editor; b. N.Y.C., Oct. 13, 1932; d. A. Adolph and Anne Mary (Gardner) Blank; m. George Lee Weddington, Jr., Oct. 23, 1965; 1 child, Georgiana Marie. Actress TV, radio, telephone, N.Y./Calif, 1957—; editor comml. scripts N.Y., 1969—; freelance writer N.Y. City Tribune, various other publs., N.Y., nat., 1984—. Columnist polit. commentary, 1984—; appeared in over 300 TV commls., also TV and radio voice-overs. Mem. County Com., Conservative Party, N.Y.C., 1988-90, 94-96, 17th Precinct Cmty. Coun., N.Y.C., 1974-96; rep. Yorkville Area Cath. Coun., N.Y.C., 1986-93. Recipient Mayor's Vol. Action Ctr. award, N.Y.C., 1981-82, Cert. Recognition N.Y.C. Dept. Police Dep. Commr. Community Affairs, 1981. Mem. Screen Actors Guild, Am. Fedn. Radio and TV artists, Nat. League Am. Pen Women, Internat. Platform assn., Nat. Soc. Children of Am. Revolution - Fraunces Tavern Soc. (sr. pres. 1985-89), N.Y. State Soc. Children Am. Revolution (sr. historian 1988-90, sr. 2d v.p. 1990-92), Nat. Soc. DAR (chmn. com. Mary Washington Colonial chpt., corr. sec. 1992-94), Nat. Soc. U.S. Daughters of 1812 (organizing pres. Pres. James Madison Chpt. 360 1988—), N.Y. State Soc. Daughters 1812, N.Y. State Soc. Dames of Ct. of Honor (pres. 1984-88), United Daughters of Confederacy (pres. N.Y. div. 1988-90, nat. chmn. revision of gen. bylaws com. 1989-91, McMath Scholarship gen. com. 1991-92, nat. chmn. gen. bylaws com. 1992-96), Daus. Colonial Wars (N.Y. State chpt.), Nat. Geneal. Soc., Colonial Dames of Am. (parent chpt. N.Y. claims com. 1993-96). Republican. Roman Catholic.

WEDGEWORTH, ANN, actress; b. Abilene, Tex., Jan. 21, 1935; m. Rip Torn (div.); 1 child, Danae; m. Ernest Martin; 1 child, Dianna. Attended, U. Tex.; B.A. in Drama, So. Methodist U. Broadway debut in Make A Million, 1958; other Broadway appearances Chapter Two (Tony award), Thieves, Blues for Mr. Charlie, The Last Analysis; off-Broadway appearances Line, Chapparal, The Crucible, Days and Nights of Beebee Fenstermaker, Ludlow Fair, The Honest to God Shnozzola, A Lie of the Mind; toured with nat. cos. of The Sign in Sidney Brustein's Window and Kennedy's Children; appeared: in TV series Three's Company, The Edge of Night, Another World, Somerset, Filthy Rich, Evening Shade; other TV appearances All That Glitters, The Defenders, Bronk, Evening Shade, Twilight Zone, Trapper John, M.D.; TV film The War Between the Tates, Bogey, Right to Kill, A Stranger Waits; movies Handle With Care (Nat. Soc. Film Critics award), Thieves, Bang the Drum Slowly, Scarecrow, Catamount Killing, Law and Disorder, One Summer Love, Dragon-Fly, Birch Intervals, Soggy Bottom, USA, No Small Affair, Sweet Dreams, Mens Club, A Tiger's Tale, Made in Heaven, Far North, Miss Firecracker, Green Card. Office: care Paradigm Talent Agy 10100 Santa Monica Blvd 25th Fl Los Angeles CA 90067

WEDGWOOD, RUTH, law educator; b. N.Y.C.; d. Morris P. and Anne (Williams) Glushien; m. Josiah Francis Wedgwood; May 29, 1982. BA magna cum laude, Harvard U., 1972; fellow, London Sch. Econs., 1972-73; JD, Yale U., 1976. Bar: D.C., N.Y. Law clk. to judge Henry Friendly U.S. Ct. Appeals (2d cir.), N.Y.C., 1976-77; law clk. to justice Harry Blackmun U.S. Supreme Ct., Washington, 1977-78; spl. asst. to asst. atty. gen. U.S. Dept. Justice, Washington, 1978-80; asst. U.S. atty. U.S. Dist. Ct. (so. dist.) N.Y., N.Y.C., 1980-86; prof. law Yale U., New Haven, 1986—, faculty fellow Inst. for Social and Policy Studies, 1989—, faculty fellow Berkeley Coll., 1989—, faculty mem. Yale Internat. Security program, 1992—; faculty Yale UN Studies program, 1992—; mem. Sec. of State's Adv. Com. Internat. Law, 1993—; dir. Coun. Fgn. Rels. study group on UN and Regional Peacekeeping and Conflict Resolution, 1993—; sr. fellow, dir. Coun. Fgn. Rels. Project on Internat. Orgns. and Law, 1994—. Exec. editor Yale Law Jour., 1975-76. Prin. rapporteur U.S. Atty. Gen.'s Guidelines on FBI Undercover Ops., Informant Use and Racketeering and Gen. Crime Investigations, 1980; bd. dirs. Lawyers Com. for Human Rights, N.Y.C., 1988-94. Recipient Israel Peres prize, 1976, Ford Found. rsch. grant; Rockefeller Found. fellowship. Mem. ABA, Am. Law Inst., Am. Soc. Internat. Law (exec. com. 1995—, chmn. N.Y. Ctr. 1994—), Internat. Law Assn. (v.p. 1994—, program chmn. Am. br. 1992, exec. coun. 1992-94), Assn. Am. Law Sch. (chmn. sect. internat. law 1995-96), Assn. Bar City N.Y. (arms control and internat. security affairs com., chmn. 1989-92, chmn. internat. affairs coun. 1992-95, exec. com. 1995—), Union Internationale des Avocats, U.S.A. (chpt. bd. govs. 1993—, rep. to UN 1995—), Coun. on Fgn. Rels., Elizabethan Club, Yale Club (N.Y.C.), Mchts. Club (N.Y.C.). Office: Yale U Sch Law PO Box 208215 New Haven CT 06520-8215 also: Coun on Fgn Rels 58 E 68th St New York NY 10021-5984

WEDL, LOIS CATHERINE, counselor, educator; b. Cold Spring, Minn., Mar. 5, 1931; d. John Michael and Marie Eva (Lill) W. BA, Coll. of St. Benedict, St. Joseph, Minn., 1966; MEd, Ohio U., 1982, PhD, 1986. Jr. high sch. tchr. Holy Angels Sch., St. Cloud, Minn., 1956-60, St. Mary's Schs., Long Prairie, Minn., 1960-64; tchr., adminstr. Colegio San Benito, Humacao, P.R., 1964-70, Colegio San Antonio, Humacao, 1970-74; prof. Coll. of St. Benedict, 1986—, St. Cloud State U., 1986-88; cons. gerontology Order of St. Benedict, 1949—, dir. Elderhostel program. Editor Dept. Edn. Newsletter, Sch. Applied Behavioral Scis. and Ednl. Leadership, Ohio U., 1981-84. Mem. athletic adv. com. Coll. of St. Benedict, 1989—. Recipient 2 Nat. Literary awards Am. Rehabilitating Counseling Assn., 1983-84; Bremer Found. gerontology grantee, 1988. Mem. Am. Assn. Adult Devel. and Aging (chairperson aging/religion com., chairperson awards com.), Chi Sigma Iota (internat. sect., chair awards com., Faculty Advisor of Yr. 1995, Nat. Lit. awards, Outstanding Leadership award 1995). Home and Office: 37 College Ave S Saint Joseph MN 56374-2001

WEED, PATRICIA ANN WHITE, secondary foreign language educator; b. Denver, Apr. 13, 1947; d. Aaron Everitt and Jane Elizabeth (Morris) White; m. John Potter Weed, May 26, 1968 (div.); 1 child, Matthew Aaron; m. Paul Ronald Hansen, Aug. 9, 1986. BA, Colo. Coll., 1969, M in Tchg., 1991; MPA, U. Colo., 1979. Camp counselor Sanborn Western Camps, Florissant, Colo., summer 1966; air control staff Western Aviation, Loveland, Colo., summer 1967; educator Colorado Springs (Colo.) Sch., 1969-70, Fort Carson (Colo.) Confinement Facility, 1972-78, West Jr. H.S., Colorado Springs, 1978-83, Coronado H.S., Colorado Springs, 1983—; sales staff Criterium Bike Shop, Colorado Springs, 1993-95; steering com. Renaissance Sch., Colorado Springs, 1995-96. Contbr. Cultural Perspectives in Education, 1986. Vol. coord. Colorado Springs Soup Kitchens, 1990-96. Danforth fellow Danforth Found., 1988. Mem. Phi Delta Kappa. Office: Coronado High Sch 1590 W Fillmore Colorado Springs CO 80904

WEEDEN, MARY ANN, organizational development consultant; b. Troy, N.Y., July 23, 1948; d. John James and Antionette Catherine Foley; m. Paul Joseph Weeden, Aug. 31, 1968; 1 child, Eric Paul. BSBA, Russell Sage Coll., 1978. Corp. rels .rep. Ariz. Pub. Svc., Phoenix, 1983-85, contract adminstr., 1985-88, sr. trainer mgmt. devel., internal cons., 1988-91; organizational devel. adminstr. Data Mgmt. div. Ariz. Dept. Adminstrn., Phoenix, 1991; quality circle leader and facilitator Ariz. Nuclear Power Project, Phoenix, 1988-91; cons., trainer Inroads of Phoenix, 1988-91. Editor The Signature, 1973. Candidates' forum coord. LWV, Albany, 1975-80; coord. Project S.H.A.R.E., Phoenix, 1984-85; exec. advisor Jr. Achievement, Phoenix, 1985-87, Bus. Leader Advisor award, 1986, 87; environ. issues coord. Maricopa County Platform, Phoenix, 1986. Recipient Community Action award Salvation Army, 1985. Mem. Am. Mgmt. Assn., Am. Bus. Women's Assn. (exec. bd. mem., edn. com. chmn. 1984-86), World Affairs Coun.

WEEDMAN, JUDITH ELVIRA, information science educator; b. Vallejo, Calif., Aug. 30, 1949; d. Gerald Exavior Weedman and Ruth Betty Cline Nuzum; m. Thomas Scott Mackie, Oct. 23, 1971 (div. Oct. 1980). BA, U. Colo., 1972; MLS, U. Oreg., 1976; PhD, U. Mich., 1989. Indexer U. Oreg., Eugene, 1973-75; sch. libr. media specialist Mt. Angel (Oreg.) and Salem (Oreg.) Pub. Schs., 1975-80; indexer, editor Univ. Microfilms Internat., Ann Arbor, Mich., 1980-87; rsch. assoc. J.H. Behler & Assocs., Ann Arbor, 1982-87; lectr. U. Mich., Ann Arbor, 1982-87; asst. prof. U. Calif., Berkeley, 1987-94; vis. asst. prof. Grad. Sch. Libr. Info. Sci. U. Ill., Champaign, 1993-95; assoc. prof. Sch. Libr. Info. Sci. San Jose State U., Fullerton, Calif., 1995—; cons. Indsl. Tech. Inst., Ann Arbor, 1986-87; mem. adv. bd. Youth at Risk Program, Oakland, Calif., 1990-92. Contbr. articles to profl. jours. Bd. dirs. Stepping Stones Growth Ctr. for the Developmentally Disabled, Oakland, 1992-93. Mem. ALA, Am. Soc. for Info. Sci., Am. Soc. Indexers, Internat. Network for Social Network Analysis, Assn. for Libr. and Info. Sci. Edn. Lutheran. Office: San Jose State U Sch Libr and Info Sci PO Box 4150 Fullerton CA 92634-4150

WEEKLEY, BARBARA LOUISE, secondary school educator; b. St. Louis, Dec. 24, 1952; d. Eugene Edward and Dorothy Marie (Heinrich) Mees; m. Walter Robert Weekley, Apr. 10, 1976. AB, Harris Tchr. Coll., 1974; MA in Tchg., Webster U., 1979. Cert. tchr., Mo. Sci. tchr. Pattonville Heights, Maryland Heights, Mo., 1974-82; biology tchr. Pattonville H.S., Maryland Heights, Mo., 1982—; staff devel. facilitator Lindberg H.S., St. Louis, 1992-93; sci. cons. Normandy Sch. Dist., St. Louis, 1993-94; presenter Nat. Biology Tchrs., 1994, NSTA, 1994, 95. Co-founder ZooTchrs., St. Louis, 1989—. Mem. NSTA, NEA, Nat. Biology Tchrs. Assn., Sci. Tchrs. Mo., Delta Kappa Gamma. Presbyterian. Office: Pattonville Sch Dist 11097 St Charles Rock Rd Saint Ann MO 63074

WEEKS, BRIGITTE, publishing executive; b. Whitchurch, Hants, Eng., Aug. 28, 1943; came to U.S., 1965; d. Jack and Margery May (Millett) W.; m. Edward A. Herscher, Sept. 6, 1969; children—Hilary, Charlotte, Daniel. Student, Univ. Coll. of North Wales, Bangor, 1962-65. Asst. editor Boston Mag., 1966-70; editor Kodansha Internat., Tokyo, 1969-72, Resources for the Future, 1973-74; asst. editor The Washington Post Book World, 1974-78, editor, 1978-88; sr. v.p., editor-in-chief Book-of-the-Month Club, N.Y.C., 1988-94; editor-in-chief Guideposts Books, N.Y.C., 1994—; pres. Nat. Book Critics Circle, 1984-86; bd. dirs. Nat. Book Found. Office: Guideposts Books 16 E 34th St New York NY 10016-4328

WEEKS, DONNA RITA, human rights administrative assistant, artist; b. Chgo., July 14, 1935; d. William Leroy and Rita Mary (Graham) Dubbs; m. Everette J. Weeks, Nov. 23, 1961 (div. Feb. 1983); children: David James, Joseph Everette, Mary Anne Weeks Collins. Exec. sec., Moser Bus. Sch., 1959; BA, U. Tenn., 1983; postgrad., Atlanta Inst. Art Therapy, 1983-85, Loyola U., New Orleans. Cert. paralegal, Tenn. Sec. Leo Burnett Advt. Agy., Chgo., 1959-61; sec. devel. dept. U. Tenn., Chattanooga, 1977-78, sec. art dept., 1978-83, sec. Engring. Sch., 1983-87; sec. Allied Arts, Chattanooga, 1987-90; adminstrv. asst. Chattanooga Human Rights/Human Rels. Commn., 1990-92, 93-94, interim dir., 1992—. One-woman show includes All Five Senses Used, 1989. Ballot chmn. Election Commn., Chattanooga, 1981-82; human rights activist Chattanooga Human Rights Commn., 1990-91; facilitator Creative Spirituality Classes, Chattanooga, 1989-91, Spl. Arts Festival Retarded, Chattanooga, 1984. Mem. Am. Bus. Women's Assn. (pres. 1985-86, bulletin chmn. 1989-90, sec. 1990-91, program chmn. 1991-92, scholarship chmn. 1992-94). Roman Catholic. Office: Chattanooga Human Rights Human Rels Commn 305 City Hall Anx Chattanooga TN 37402

WEEKS, MARIE COOK, health and physical education educator; b. High Point, N.C., Jan. 21, 1949; d. Paul Hue Cook and Beulah Edna (Smith) Townsend; m. Lewis Tirey Weeks, June 5, 1970; children: Gina, Corby. BS in Edn., Western Carolina U., 1971. Tchr. grades 6,7,8, math. science, health, physical edn. Ramseur (N.C.) Elem. Sch., 1971-91; tchr. grades 6,7,8, health and physical edn. Archdale-Trinity Middle Sch., Trinity, N.C., 1991—; coach girls softball and volleyball Randolph County Schs., Asheboro, N.C., 1971—; mentor tchr. Randolph County Schs., Asheboro, 1989—; student tchr. supr. Archdale Trinity Middle Sch. 1993—, head of health and phys. edn. dept., 1993—. Coach girls' softball Hillsville (N.C.) Civitan's Youth Softball League, 1984—. Named Ramseur Sch. Tchr. of Yr., Ramseur Faculty, 1983, 89, Outstanding Young Educator Asheboro/Randolph County, Asheboro Jaycees, 1989. Mem. NEA, N.C. AAHPERD, Nat. Fedn. Coaches, N.C. Assn. Educators. Baptist. Home: 3725 Lynn Oaks Dr Trinity NC 27370-9445 Office: Archdale-Trinity Mid Sch 5105 Archdale Rd Trinity NC 27370

WEEKS, MARTA JOAN, priest; b. Buenos Aires, May 24, 1930; came to U.S., 1932; d. Frederick Albert and Anne (Newman) Sutton; m. Lewis Austin Weeks, Aug. 17, 1951; children: Kermit Austin, Leslie Anne. BA in Polit. Sci., Stanford U., 1951; MDiv, Episcopal Theol. Sem. S.W., 1991. Ordained priest Episcopal Ch., 1992. Legal libr., sec. Mene Grande Oil Co., Caracas, Venezuela, 1948; English tchr. Centro-Venezolano Americano, Caracas, 1948; sec. Household Fin. Corp., Salt Lake City, 1951; legal sec. McKelvey & McKelvey Attys., Durango, Colo., 1952; sec., dir. Weeks Air Mus., Miami, Fla., 1985—; chaplain Jackson Meml. Hosp., 1992-93; priest-at-large Episcopal Diocese of S.E. Fla., until 1996; interim asst. St. James Episcopal Ch., Salt Lake City, 1994-95. Trustee Beloit (Wis.) Coll., 1980-82, U. Miami, 1983-88, 95—, Bishop Gray Inns, Lake Worth and Davenport, Fla., 1992—. Mem. Am. Soc. Order St. John of Jerusalem. Address: 7350 SW 162nd St Miami FL 33157-3820

WEEKS, SANDRA KENNEY, healthcare administrator; b. Akron, Ohio. BSN, Stockton State Coll.; MSN, Trenton State Coll., 1995. RN, N.J., cert. rehab. registered nurse Assn. Rehab. Nurses. Staff nurse Akron (Ohio) Childrens Hosp., William Beaumont Hosp., Royal Oak, Mich.; elected pub. official Twp. of Cranford (N.J.); rehab. nurse Kessler Inst. Rehab., West Orange, N.J.; supr. HIP/HMO Ambulatory Care Ctr., Medford, N.J.; rehab. nurse mgr. Lourdes Rehab. Ctr., Camden, N.J.; rschr. in nursing. Contbr. articles to profl. jours. Bd. dirs. United Way; trustee pub. libr.; mem. Twp. Com. Bd. Health. Mem. Am. Nurses Assn., N.J. Nurses Assn., Assn. Rehab. Nurses, Sigma Theta Tau. Home: 3 Dewberry Ct Medford NJ 08055-9159 Office: Lourdes Regional Rehab Ctr 1600 Haddon Ave Camden NJ 08103-3101

WEEMS, JO ELLEN, elementary school educator; b. Crawfordsville, Ind., June 9, 1957; d. Robert Thomas and Betty Jo (Patton) Sowers; m. Alan Dale Weems. BS magna cum laude, Ind. State U., 1978, MS, 1981. Tchr. 3d grade Huntington (Ind.) Cmty. Schs., 1979-80; head tchr./asst. dir. Early Learners Child Care, South Bend, Ind., 1980-81; kindergarten tchr. Clark-Pleasant Cmty. Sch. Corp., Whiteland, Ind., 1982—; trainer Primary Grades Health Curriculum, Indpls., 1986; presenter on early childhood social studies curriculum U. Indpls., 1991. Co-author: Creative Science for Young Children, 1988. Mem. Friends of the Libr., Franklin, Ind., 1989—; guardian ad litem Johnson County Cir. Ct., Franklin, 1988—; surrogate parent Spl. Svcs., Johnson County, Ind., 1994—; mem. Franklin Meml. Christian Ch., 1982—. Mem. Nat. Assn. for Edn. Young Children, Ind. Assn. for Edn. Young Children, Ind. Reading Assn., Johnson County Reading Coun. (v.p. 1989-90), Johnson County Garden Club, Mortar Bd.

WEERTMAN, JULIA RANDALL, materials science and engineering educator; b. Muskegon, Mich., Feb. 10, 1926. BS in Physics, Carnegie-Mellon U., 1946, MS in Physics, 1947, DSc in Physics, 1951. Physicist U.S. Naval Rsch. Lab., Washington, 1952-58; vis. asst. prof. dept. materials sci. and engring. Northwestern U., Evanston, Ill., 1972-73, assoc. prof., 1978-82, prof., 1982—, Walter P. Murphy prof., 1989, chmn. dept., 1987-92, asst. to dean grad. studies and rsch. Tech. Inst., 1973-76; mem. various NRC coms. and panels. Co-author: Elementary Dislocation Theory, 1964, 1992, also pub. in French, Japanese and Polish; contbr. numerous articles to profl. jours. Mem. Evanston Environ. Control Bd., 1972-79. Recipient Creativity award NSF, 1981, 86; Guggenheim Found. fellow, 1986-87. Fellow Am. Soc. Metals Internat., Minerals, Metals and Materials Soc.; mem. ASTM, NAE, Am. Phys. Soc., Materials Rsch. Soc., Soc. Women Engrs. (disting.

engring. educator award 1989, achievement award 1991). Home: 834 Lincoln St Evanston IL 60201-2405 Office: Northwestern U Dept Material Sci & Engring 2225 N Campus Dr Evanston IL 60208-3108

WEESE, CYNTHIA ROGERS, architect, educator; b. Des Moines, June 23, 1940; d. Gilbert Taylor and Catharine (Wingard) Rogers; m. Benjamin H. Weese, July 5, 1963; children: Daniel Peter, Catharine Mohr. B.S.A.S., Washington U., St. Louis, 1962; B.Arch., Washington U., 1965. Registered architect, Ill. Pvt. practice architecture Chgo., 1965-72, 74-77; draftsperson, designer Harry Weese & Assocs., Chgo., 1972-74; prin. Weese Langley Weese Ltd., Chgo., 1977—; design critic Ball State U., Muncie, Ind., Miami U., Oxford, Ohio, 1979, U. Wis.-Milw., 1980, U. Ill.-Chgo., 1981, 85, Iowa State U., Ames, 1982, Washington U., St. Louis, 1984, U. Ill., Champaign, 1987-92, Kans. State U., 1992; dean sch. architecture Washington U., St. Louis, 1993—. Bd. regents Am. Architecture Found., 1990-93. Recipient Alpha Rho Chi award Washington U., 1965, Met. Chgo. YWCA Outstanding Achievement award, 1990. Mem. AIA (bd. dirs. Chgo. chpt. 1980-83, v.p. 1983-85, 1st v.p. 1986-87, pres. 1987-88, regional dir. 1990-92, Disting. Bldg. awards 1977, 81-83, 86, 91, 95, Interior Architecture award 1981, 90, 92, nat. v.p. 1993), AIA/ACSA Coun. on Archtl. Rsch. (chair 1991-92), AIA Found. (pres. Chgo. chpt. 1988-89), Soc. Archtl. Historians (bd. dirs. 1992—), Chgo. Women Architecture, Chgo. Network, Nat. Inst. Archtl. Edn. (bd. dirs. 1988-90), Chgo. Archtl. Club (pres. 1988-89), Washington U. Sch. Architecture Alumni (nat. coun. 1988-93), Lambda Alpha. Democrat. Clubs: Arts, Chgo. Archtl. Office: Washington University Architecture DEpt. 1 Brookings Drive Saint Louis MO 63130

WEESNER, BETTY JEAN, editor; b. Danville, Ind., Jan. 22, 1926; d. Edward Jabin and Ruth Leah (Daugherty) W. BA, Ind. U., 1951. Sports writer The Rep., Danville, 1940-44, reporter and advt., 1951-69, editor, 1969—; Pres., treas. Hendricks County Rep., Inc., Danville, 1974—. Mem. Ind. Rep. Editorial Assn., Hoosier State Press Assn., Ind. U. Alumni Assn., Women's Press Club Ind., DAR, Am. Legion Aux. Republican. Mem. Christian Ch. Office: The Rep 6 E Main St Danville IN 46122-1818

WEGERT, MARY MAGDALENE HARDEL, special education director, consultant; b. Knox, Ind., Nov. 3, 1942; d. Adam Alford and Lucy (Fletcher) Hardel; m. Dennis Harold Wegert, Dec. 20, 1964. Student, Ball State U., 1960-61; BSE, Ark. State U., Jonesboro, 1964, MSE, 1967, postgrad., 1967-77; postgrad., U. S.W. La., 1972, U. Cen. Ark., 1977. Spl. edn. tchr. Knox (Ind.) Ctr. Washington Schs., 1964-65; 1st grade tchr. Jonesboro (Ark.) Pub. Schs., 1965-66; spl. edn. tchr. Dudley Sch. for Handicapped, Jonesboro, 1967-75; adult edn. tchr. Jonesboro Pub. Schs., 1970-75, spl. edn. tchr., 1975-77, spl. edn. dir., 1977—. Recipient Outstanding Alumnus award Coll. Spl. Edn. and Communicative Disorders Ark. State U., 1991. Mem. Ark. Assn. Edn. Adminstrs., Ark. Assn. Spl. Edn. Adminstrs. (various chairmanships 1977—), Ark. Assn. for Pub. Continuing and Adult Edn. (pres. 1971-72). Office: Jonesboro Pub Schs Dept Spl Edn 1307 Flint St Jonesboro AR 72401-3968

WEHLBURG, CATHERINE MARGARET, psychology educator; b. Gainesville, Fla., Aug. 1, 1965; d. Albert F.C. and Susan (Beckenbach) W. BS in Ednl. Psychology, U. Fla., 1987, MEd in Ednl. Psychology, 1988, PhD, 1991. Prof. psychology Stephens Coll., Columbia, Mo., 1990—; cons. in field. Treas Columbia Cmty Band, 1993—; mem. Jefferson City (Mo.) Symphony Orch., 1993—. Mem. Am. Psychol. Assn., Am. Ednl. Rsch. Assn. Office: Stephens Coll 1200 E Broadway Columbia MO 65201-4978

WEHRMAN, THERESA ANNE, school psychologist; b. Waconia, Minn., Mar. 15, 1961; d. Thomas Hubert and Phyllis Jean (Cooper) Logelin; m. Keith Allen Wehrman, June 27, 1987; children: Nathan Daniel, Emily Anne. BA in Psychology, Moorhead State U., 1983, MS in Sch. Psychology, 1986. Nat. cert. sch. psychologist; lic. sch. psychologist, Minn. Sch. psychologist Wil-Mac Multidist. Spl. Edn. Coop., Williston, N.D., 1985-90, Zumbro Edn. Dist., Byron, Minn., 1990—. Mem. Nat. Assn. Sch. Psychologists.

WEHRWEIN-HUNT, JERI LYNN, elementary education educator; b. New Richmond, Wis., Aug. 13, 1952; d. Harlan Fredric and Olive Angeline (Steis) Wehrwein; 1 child, Katie Lynn. BS in Elem. Edn., St. Cloud State U., 1973, BS in Spl. Edn., 1973; MEd, U. Minn., 1990. cert. elem. and spl. edn. tchr., Minn. Coord. social studies curriculum Minneapolis Pub. Schs., 1977-78, tchr., 1973—, asst. spl. edn. camp program coord., 1982, coord. and tchr. gifted program, 1984-86. Recipient recognition for outstanding environmental activities in the classroom, Minn. Atty. Gen., 1994. Mem. Am. Fedn. Tchrs., Minn. Fedn. Tchrs. Roman Catholic. Office: Jenny Lind Elem Sch 5025 Bryant Ave N Minneapolis MN 55430

WEIBEL, MARGUERITE CROWLEY, librarian, educator; b. N.Y.C., July 13, 1946; d. Michael Bernard and Nellie (O'Connell) Crowley; m. Stuart Little Weibel, Nov. 21, 1981; children: Mathias, Brendan. BA in Biology, Coll. of New Rochelle, 1968; MS Teaching in Elem. Edn., U. Chgo., 1969; MA in Adult Edn., Ohio State U., 1976; MLS, Kent State U., 1984. Elem. tchr. Boston Pub. Schs., 1969-70, 72-73; rsch. asst. dept. adult edn. Ohio State U., Columbus, 1975-76, ednl. coord. Right to Read program, 1977-80, libr., asst. prof., 1984—; instr. in basic English Ohio Inst. Tech., Columbus, 1975-76; instr. in basic writing Franklin U., Columbus, 1977; adult edn. instr. Columbus Literacy Coun., 1981; libr. literacy coord. Columbus Met. Libr., 1982-84; mem. adv. bd. State Libr. of Ohio, Columbus, 1989-92; mem. task force on adult new readers Ohio Libr. Assn., Columbus, 1981-83; cons., instr. Adult Basic Literacy program Ohio State U. Hosps., Columbus, 1992—; speaker in field. Author: The Library Literacy Connection, 1984, The Library as Literacy Classroom, 1992, Choosing and Using Books with Adult New Readers, 1996; contbr. articles to profl. publs. Mem. ALA, Am. Assn. Adult and Continuing Edn., Internat. Reading Assn., Ohio Libr. Coun. Home: 259 Richards Rd Columbus OH 43214-3737 Office: Prior Health Scis Libr 376 W 10th Ave Columbus OH 43210

WEICHLER, NANCY KAREN, pediatric nurse; b. Pitts., Feb. 19, 1959; d. John James and Ruth Catherine (Miller) Janosko; m. Kevin William Weichler, June 4, 1983; children: Kara Lenore, Karleigh Josephine. BSN, Villanova U., 1981; MSN, U. Pitts., 1987. RN, Pa. Nurse's aide Negley House, 1978; nurse technician Shadyside, 1980; nurse's aide United Presbyn. Nursing Home, Wilkinsburg, Pa., 1979; surg./transplant staff nurse Children's Hosp. Pitts., 1981-87, clin. nurse facilitator, 1987-89, amb., 1988, renal clin. nurse specialist, 1989-95; pediatric ICU staff nurse, educator Brandon (Fla.) Hosp., Fla., 1995—; adj. faculty nursing care children grad. program U. Pitts., 1988-95; lectr. nursing Carlow Coll., Pitts., 1989-90; researcher and presenter in field. Contbr. articles to profl. and med. jours. March of Dimes scholar, 1977; Disting. Nursing Alumni award Villanova U., 1994. Mem. Am. Nephrology Nurses Assn., Soc. Pediatric Nephrology Nurses, Hosp. Asn. Pa. (Achievement award 1988), Villanova Sch. Nursing Alumni Assn. (recruiter 1987-89), Sigma Theta Tau. Roman Catholic.

WEICKSEL, CHARLENE MARIE, principal; b. York, Pa., June 16, 1945; d. Edward A. and Mary Elizabeth (Hoffman) Debes; m. Stephen A. Weicksel, Aug. 27, 1967; children: Ann, Andrew. B Music Edn., Westminster Choir Coll., 1967; MEd, Trenton State Coll., 1986. Cert. tchr., prin., supr., N.J. Tchr. Hillsborough Twp. Bd. Edn., Neshanic, N.J., 1967-87, curriculum supr. fine and performing arts, 1987-93; prin. Triangle Rd. Elem. Sch., Hillsborough, N.J., 1993—. Bd. dirs. Lenape Swim Club, Skillman, N.J., 1990-93, Raritan Valley Chorus, Belle Mead, N.J., 1991-92. Mem. NEA, Nat. Art Educators Assn., Nat. Assn. Elem. Sch. Prins., Art Educators N.J., N.J. Edn. Assn., Jazz Educators, N.J. Prins. and Suprs. Assn. Democrat. Presbyterian. Home: 302 Sunset Rd Skillman NJ 08558-1628 Office: Hillsborough Twp Bd Edn 555 Amwell Rd Neshanic Station NJ 08853-3409

WEIDEMANN, CELIA JEAN, social scientist, international business and financial development consultant; b. Denver, Dec. 6, 1942; d. John Clement and Hazel (Van Tuyl) Kirlin; m. Wesley Clark Weidemann, July 1, 1972; 1 child, Stephanie Jean. BS, Iowa State U., 1964; MS, U. Wis.-Madison, 1970, PhD, 1973; postgrad. U. So. Calif., 1983. Advisor, UN Food & Agr. Orgn., Ibadan, Nigeria, 1973-77; ind. researcher, Asia and Near East, 1977-78; program coord., asst. prof., rsch. assoc. U. Wis., Madison, 1979-81; chief institutional and human resources U.S. Agy. for Internat. Devel., Washington, 1982-85, team leader, cons., Sumatra, Indonesia, 1984; dir. fed. econs. program Midwest Rsch. Inst., Washington, 1985-86; pres., CEO Weidemann Assocs., Arlington, Va., 1986—; cons. U.S. Congress, Aspen Inst., Ford Found., World Bank, Egypt, Nigeria, Gambia, Pakistan, Indonesia, AID, Thailand, Jamaica, Panama, Philippines, Sierra Leone, Kenya, Jordan, Poland, India, Egypt, Russia, Finnish Internat. Devel. Agy., Namibia, pvt. client, Estonia, Lativa, Russia, Japan, Internat. Ctr. Rsch. on Women, Zaire, UN Food and Agriculture Orgn., Ghana, Internat. Statis. Inst., The Netherlands, Global Exchange, 1986-87, Asian Devel. Bank, Mongolia, Nepal, Vietnam, Bangladesh, Indonesia, Philippines. Author: Planning Home Economics Curriculum for Social and Economic Development, Agricultural Extension for Women Farmers in Africa, 1990, Financial Services for Women, 1992, Egyptian Women and Microenterprise: The Invisible Entrepreneurs, 1992, Small Enterprise Development in Poland: Does Gender Matter?, 1994; contbr. chpts. to books and articles to profl. jours. Am. Home Econs. Assn. fellow, 1969-73 (recipient research grant Ford Found. 1987-89). Mem. Soc. Internat. Devel., Am. Sociol. Assn., U.S. Dirs. of Internat. Agrl. Programs, Assn. for Women in Devel. (pres. 1989, founder, bd. dirs.), Internat. Devel. Conf. (bd. dirs., exec. com.), Am. Home Econs. Assn. (Wis. internat. chmn. 1980-81), Internat. Fedn. Home Econs., Internat. Platform Assn., Pi Lambda Theta, Omicron Nu. Roman Catholic. Avocations: mountain trekking, piano/pipe organ, canoeing, photography, poetry. Home and Office: 2607 24th St N Arlington VA 22207-4908

WEIDEMANN, JULIA CLARK, principal, educator; b. Batavia, N.Y., May 21, 1937; d. Edward Thomas and Grace Eloise (Kenna) Clark; m. Rudolph John Weidemann, July 9, 1960 (dec.); 1 child, Michael John (dec.). BA in English, Daemen Coll., 1958; MS in Edn., SUNY, Buffalo, 1961, MEd in Reading Edn., 1973, postgrad, 1985-86. Cert. sch. adminstr., supr. Tchr Buffalo Pub. Schs., 1958-61, 66-67; remedial reading tchr. West Seneca (N.Y.) Cen. Sch. Dist., 1972-79, coord. chpt. I reading program, 1974-79, reading coord., 1980-87; prin. Parkdale Elem. Sch. East Aurora (N.Y.) Union Free Sch., 1987—; adj. prof. edn. Canisius Coll., Medaille Coll.; tchr. cons. Scott Foresman Lang. Arts Textbooks; chmn. elem. com. staff devel. West Seneca Ctrl. Sch., 1985-87; mem. adv. coun. Medaille Coll.; chmn. various confs.; lectr. in field. Author numerous poems. Mem. West Seneca Dist. Computer Adv. Com., 1980-87, East Aurora Hist. Soc., 1990—; mem. cmty. adv. coun. SUNY, Buffalo, 1994—, Women's Health Initiative, 1994—; Women's Action Coalition of Buffalo, 1994; pres. Roycroft Wordsmiths. Scholar Rosary Hill Coll., 1954, N.Y. State Regents, 1954; recipient Reading award Niagara Frontier Reading Coun., 1986. Mem. AAUW (life, pres. Buffalo br. 1994-95, exec. bd. dirs., named gift ednl. found., state bd. dirs. equity in edn. com. 1995—), Assn. Compensatory Edn. (pres. 1984-85, exec. bd. Region VI 1983-87, conf. chmn. Region VI 1985-87), Internat. Reading Assn. (acting chmn. 3d ea. regional reading conf. 1980), Niagara Frontier Reading Assn. (pres. 1979-80, fin. com. chmn., bd. dirs. 1973—), Daeman Coll. Alumni Assn. (bd. govs. 1987, chmn. alumni reunion weekend, chmn. sr. reception, Disting. Alumna 1989), Assn. Supervision and Devel., Assn. Tchr. Educators, Delta Kappa Gamma (pres., Ruth Fraser scholar 1986), Beta Zeta (pres.), Phi Delta Kappa (Buffalo-South chpt. 1989). Democrat. Roman Catholic. Home: 50 Boxwood Cir Hamburg NY 14075-4212 Office: Parkdale Elem Sch 80 Parkdale Ave East Aurora NY 14052-1615

WEIDENFELD, SHEILA RABB, television producer, author; b. Cambridge, Mass., Sept. 7, 1943; d. Maxwell M. and Ruth (Cryden) Rabb; BA, Brandeis U., 1965; m. Edward L. Weidenfeld, Aug. 11, 1968; children: Nicholas Rabb, Daniel Rabb. Assoc. producer Metromedia, Inc., WNEW-TV, N.Y.C., 1965-68; talent coord. That Show with Joan Rivers, NBC, N.Y.C., 1968-71; coord. NBC network game programs, N.Y.C., 1968-71; producer Metromedia, Inc., WTTG-TV, Washington, 1971-73; creator/producer Take It From Here, NBC (WRC-TV), Washington, 1973-74; press sec. to first lady Betty Ford and spl. asst. to Pres. Gerald R. Ford 1974-77; mem. Pres.'s Adv. Commn. on Historic Preservation, 1977-81; TV producer, moderator On the Record, NBC-TV, WRC-TV, Washington, 1978-79; pres. D.C. Prodns., Ltd., 1978; producer, host Your Personal Decorator, 1987; mem. sec. State's Adv. Commn. on Fgn. Service Inst., 1972-74; founding mem. Project Censured Panel of Judges, 1976—. Author: First Lady's Lady, 1979. Mem. U.S. Holocaust Meml. Council, 1987—; corporator, Dana Hall Sch., Wellesley, Mass; bd. dirs. Wolf Trap Found., Women's Campaign Fund, 1978-79; bd. dirs. D.C. Contemporary Dance Theatre, 1986-88, D.C. Rep. Cen. Com., 1984—, D.C. Preservation League, 1987-90; chmn. C&O Canal Nat. Hist. Park Commn, 1988—; bd. dirs. Am. Univ. Rome, 1988—. Recipient awards for outstanding achievement in the media AAUW, 1973, 74, Silver Screen award A Campaign to Remember for the U.S. Holocaust Meml. Coun., 1989, Bronze medal Internat. Film and Video Festival N.Y., 1990; named hon. consul gen. of Republic of San Marino to Washington; knighted by Order of St. Agatha, Republic of San Marino, 1986. Mem. NATAS (Emmy award 1972), Washington Press Club, Am. Newspaper Women's Club, Am. Women in Radio and TV, Cosmos Club, Consular Corps, Sigma Delta Chi. Home and Office: 3059 Q St NW Washington DC 20007-3081

WEIDENFELLER, GERALDINE CARNEY, speech and language pathologist; b. Kearny, N.J., Oct. 12, 1933; d. Joseph Gerald and Catherine Grace (Doyle) Carney; BS, Newark State U., 1954; postgrad. Northwestern U., summer 1956, U. Wis., summer 1960; MA, NYU, 1962; m. James Weidenfeller, Apr. 4, 1964; children: Anne, David. Lic speech/language pathologist, N.J. Speech pathologist Kearny (N.J.) Public Schs., 1954-61, North Brunswick (N.J.) Public Schs., 1961-65, Bridgewater (N.J.) Public Schs., 1969-72; speech therapist Somerset County Ednl. Commn., 1983-88; real estate agt., N.J., 1982-89; pvt. practice speech therapy, Somerville, N.J., 1980-92; speech therapist no. br. Midland Sch., 1989, No. Plainfield, N.J., 1989-90. V.p. Rosary Soc., Hillsborough, N.J., 1986—; Rep. county com. woman, 1989-96, chmn. scholarship com.; chmn. fedn. of Rep. women program com., Somerset, program chmn., scholarship chmn. 1991—; dancer Hillsborough Rockettes, 1994—; tudor Literacy Vol. of Am., 1993-96; storyteller Cath. Charities, 1992-93. Mem. Am. Speech and Hearing Assn., N.J. Speech and Hearing Assn. Roman Catholic. Club: Toastmasters (winner dist. humorous speech contest 1984, sec. 1985, advanced Toastmaster 1986). Home: 3 Banor Dr Somerville NJ 08876-4501

WEIDLER, PATRICIA ELLIN, secondary school educator; b. Schenectady, May 22, 1954; d. Sten-Eric Edward and Audrey Wilma Weidler; 1 child, Samuel Josiah. BS, Cornell U., 1976; MEd, U. Maine, 1991. Cert. K-12 health edn., Maine. Coord. Main-Line, Ithaca, N.Y., 1976; ednl. dir. Creekwood Youth Home, Ithaca, 1977; youth worker Ithaca Youth Bur., 1978-79; instr. Ctrl. Maine Tech. Coll., Auburn, 1988-90; tchr. coord. Northern Oxford Vocational Area Adult and Cmty. Edn. Program, Rumford, Maine, 1987-91; lead tchr. alternative edn. program NOVA Adult and Cmty. Edn. Program, Rumford, Maine, 1991-93; tchr. alternative edn. program Sch. Adminstrv. Dist. 43, Rumford, 1993—, chair dist. evaluation com., 1996—; curriculum cons. Maine External Credit Option, Augusta, 1990. Coord., treas., EMT, dispatcher Tri-Town Ambulance and Emergency Rescue Svc., West Paris, Maine, 1982—; pers. mem. critical incident stress debriefing team Tri County Emergency Med. Svc., Oxford, Franklin and Androscoggin Counties, 1987-91. Recipient Outstanding Svc. award Tri-Town Ambulance and Emergency Rescue Svc., 1988. Home: 105 Cushman Hill Rd Bryant Pond ME 04219-6207 Office: Mountain Valley Alternative 59 Congress St Rumford ME 04276-2014

WEIDMAN, ANNA KATHRYN, publishing company financial executive; b. Redwood City, Calif., July 6, 1962; d. Ronald Frank and Jane (Cotton) W.; m. Charles Shaw Robinson, Nov. 1, 1993. BA, U. Calif., Berkeley, 1984, MBA, 1992. Asst. to dir. U. Calif. Press, Berkeley, 1985-91, exhibits/sales mgr., 1991-93, CFO, 1993—; bd. dirs. Mercury House Pubs.; ind. cons., Berkeley, 1991-93; treas., bd. dirs. Assocs. of U. Calif. Press, Berkeley, 1992—. Mem. vestry, bd. dirs. St. Mark's Episcopal Ch., Berkeley, 1993-95. Democrat. Office: U Calif Press 2120 Berkeley Way Berkeley CA 94720

WEIGEL, BARBARA BROBACK, community activist; b. Orange, N.J., Nov. 26, 1935; m. Robert F. Weigel, June 3, 1961; children: Eric P., Dana E. BA in Art History, Wellesley Coll., 1957. With pub. rels. dept., exec. sec. NBC, N.Y.C., 1957-58; sec. to dir. pub. rels., compt. and curator Mus. Primitive Art, N.Y.C., 1958-62; teaching asst. libr. and spl. edn. Piscataway (N.J.) Bd. Edn., 1975-77; pvt. tutor spl. edn., reading, math., 1977; ind. sales rep. Avon, Piscataway, 1977-87. Polit. Cons. People for Whitman gabernatorial campaign, 1993, co-dir. New Market Residents Assn., 1986—; mem. Dist. Election Bd., Middlesex County, 1972-79; committeewoman Piscataway Rep. Orgn., 1986—, corr. sec., membership chair, 1988—; candidate Piscataway Twp. Coun., 1989, Piscataway Twp. Coun.-at-Large, 1992, N.J. State Assemby, 1991; mem. environ. adv. com. Congressman Jim Courter for Gov. campaign, 1989; vol. coord. Senator Dick Zimmer for Congress campaign, 1990; coord. Piscataway Rep. campaign, 1990, 94, campaign mgr. 17th dist. State Assembbly, 1993. Mem. AAUW (bd. dirs. Plainfield chpt., v.p. membership, chair pub. policy and legal advocacy, mem. scholarship com., Outstanding Young Woman of Am. award 1971), LWV, MADD, Women's Polit. Caucus (Leg. N.J. Rep. Task Force), Rep. Women of the90's (exec. bd.), Coun. for Citizens Against Gov. Waste, Registered Voters Organized to Limit Terms, Friends of Rutgers Ecol. Preserve, N.J. Wellesley Club.

WEIKSNER, SANDRA S., lawyer; b. D.C., Nov. 9, 1945; d. Donald B. and Dick (Cutter) Smiley; m. George B. Weiksner, Aug. 19, 1969; children: Michael, Nicholas. BA in Psychology, Stanford U., 1966, JD, 1969. Teaching fellow Stanford U., Calif., 1969-70; assoc. Cleary, Gottlieb, Steen & Hamilton, N.Y.C., 1970-77, ptnr., 1978—; vis. lectr. Yale Law Sch., 1991-92. Bd. dirs. N.Y. Law Sch. Fellow Am. Bar Found., Am. Coll. Trusts and Estates Counsel, Internat. Acad. Estate and Trust Law; mem. ABA, N.Y. State Bar Assn., Assn. Bar of City of N.Y., Conn. Bar Assn., N.Y. Women's Found. (dir.), N.Y. Law Sch. (dir.). Democrat. Unitarian. Home: 164 E 81st St New York NY 10028-1804 Office: Cleary Gottlieb Steen & Hamilton 1 Liberty Plz New York NY 10006-1404

WEIL, DEANNA LYNN, military officer, electrical engineer; b. St. Louis, Sept. 5, 1968; d. Darryll Joseph Weil and Christine Margaret (Emrie) Simino. BSEE, U. Mo., Rolla, 1991. Commd. 2d lt. USAF, 1991, advanced through grades to capt., 1991; devel. engr. Procter & Gamble, Cape Girardeau, Mo., 1991-92; elec. combat test dir. 16th Test Squadron, Eglin AFB, Fla., 1992-95; weapons devel. test engr. 39th Flight Test Squadron, Eglin AFB, 1995-96; in flight tng. Naval Air Sta., Pensacola, 1996—. Eucharistic min., lectr. St. Michael's Ch., Eglin AFB, 1995; vol. Meals on Wheels, Ft. Walton Beach, Fla., 1994-95; Give a Child a Christmas, Ft. Walton Beach, 1992-95; religious instr. Immaculate Conception Ch., Jackson, Mo., 1991. Mem. Air Force Assn. (young mems. recruiting officer), Assn. Old Crows, Co. Grade Officer's Coun. (exec. officer 1993-94). Republican. Roman Catholic. Home: 10413 Gulf Beach Hwy Pensacola FL 32507-9115

WEIL, NANCY HECHT, psychologist, educator; b. Chgo., Apr. 15, 1936; d. Theodore R. and Jenice (Abrams) Hecht; children: Lynda Jo, Edward S. Student Cornell U., 1954-57; MEd, Nat. Coll. Edn., Ill., 1974; PhD, Northwestern U., 1976; postgrad. Chgo. Inst. Psychoanalysis, 1972-74; attending staff Michael Reese Hosp., 1978—; clin. asst. prof. U. Chgo. Pritzker Sch. of Medicine, 1985-90; asst. prof. psychiatry Coll. Medicine, U. Ill. at Chgo., 1990; med. staff, clin. asst. prof. psychiatry U. Ill. Abraham Sch. Medicine, Chgo., 1990—; mental health cons., State of Ill., writer mental health prevention plan; vice-chair Ill. Mental Health Planning Bd., 1973-75; cons. Ill. Comprehensive Health/Planning Agency, 1974; bd. trustees Chgo Inst. for Psychoanalysis, 1973—, faculty continuing edn., 1976, 87; asst. prof. Northwestern U. Med. Sch., 1976-77, assoc. prof., 1977-79; lectr. U. Chgo. Pritzker Sch. Medicine, 1978-85; chmn. adv. council Ill. Dept. Mental Health 5-Yr. Plan, 1975-80. Bd. dirs. Chgo. Focus. Fellow Am. Orthospsychiat. Assn.; mem. Am. Psychol. Assn., Ill. Psychol. Assn., Nat. Health Register Assn., Chgo. Assn. Psychoanalytic Psychology, AAUP. Contbr. articles to profl. jours.; lectr. applied psychoanalysis. Home: 200 E Delaware Pl Apt 24 C Chicago IL 60611-1736 Office: 180 N Michigan Ave Chicago IL 60601-7401

WEIMER, JEAN ELAINE, nursing educator; b. Denver, June 8, 1932; d. John and Marquerite Christina (Friehauf) Jacoby; m. James David Weimer, Aug. 5, 1956; 1 dau., Lisa Marie. Diploma in nursing Children's Hosp. Sch. Nursing, Denver, 1953; BS in Nursing, U. Denver, 1954; MA, NYU, 1962. RN, Colo., S.D., N.Y., Ill. Staff nurse Children's Hosp., Denver, 1953-54, head nurse, 1954-56; dir. nursing edn. Yankton (S.D.) State Hosp., 1956-60; instr. Mt. Sinai Hosp. Sch. Nursing, N.Y.C., 1962-63, curriculum coord., 1964-67; asst. prof. nursing City Colls. Chgo., 1968-78, assoc. prof., 1978-85, prof., 1985—, Disting. prof., 1995-96, co-chmn. nursing dept. Truman Coll., 1984-93, chmn. 1993—; chmn. program com. RN Tutoring project, 1988-92. Deacon United Ch. of Christ, 1988-90. NIMH grantee, 1960-62. Mem. Am. Nurses Assn., Coun. Advanced Practioners Psychiat. Coun. of Dirs. of Assoc. Degree Nursing Programs, Nursing Truman Coll. Faculty Coun., City Coll. Faculty Coun., Kappa Delta Pi, Pi Lambda Theta. Home: 50 E Bellevue Pl Apt 904 Chicago IL 60611-1167 Office: Truman Coll 1145 W Wilson Ave # 184 Chicago IL 60640-5616

WEIMER, JOAN, English language educator; b. Cambridge, Mass., Mar. 12, 1936; d. David Levetan Shoolman and J. Florence Hurwitz; m. Ronald E. Myers, Nov. 3, 1956 (div. Jan. 1970); children: David, Mark, Leslie; m. David R. Weimer, Mar. 21, 1971. BA, Tufts U., 1957; PhD, Rutgers U., 1970. Prof. English Drew U., Madison, N.J., 1968—; leader workshops on writing spiritual memoirs, writing through improvisation, writing with imagined collaborator for colls., confs., and bookstores, 1994—. Author: Back Talk: Teaching Lost Selves to Speak, 1994; editor: Women Artists, Women Exiles: ...stories by Constance Fenimore Woolson, 1988; co-editor: (with David Weimer) Literature of America, 1973; co-author: (with Phyllis Paullette; play) Back Talk, 1996; contbr. chpts. to The Writer's Journal, 1996, Critical Essays on Constance Fenimore Woolson, 1992; contbr. articles to profl. publs. and mags. Mem. coord. com. N.J./Masaya Nicaragua Friendship Cities, Plainfield, N.J., 1985-88; co-founder Madison area chpt. Amnesty Internat., 1963. Recipient McGinnis award for nonfiction S.W. Rev., 1977. Office: Drew U Dept English Madison NJ 07940

WEINBERG, HELEN ARNSTEIN, American art and literature educator; b. Orange, N.J., June 17, 1927; d. Morris Jerome and Jeannette (Tepperman) Arnstein; m. Kenneth Gene Weinberg, Sept. 12, 1949; children: Janet Sue Weinberg Strassner, Hugh Benjamin, John Arnstein. BA in English Lit., Wellesley Coll., 1949; MA in English Lit., Western Res. U., 1953, PhD in English Lit., 1966. Teaching fellow Ohio State U., Columbus, 1949-51, Western Res. U., Cleve., 1953-57; instr. to prof. Cleve. (Ohio) Inst. Art, 1958—; standing officer Coll. English Assn. Ohio, 1987-90; vis. tchr. NYU, 1985, Sch. Visual Art's, 1981; lecture tours Israel, 1968, 70, 71. Author: The New Novel in America: The Kafkan Mode in Contemporary Fiction, 1970. Recipient fellowship in art history NEH, Columbia U., N.Y.C., 1977-78; Recipient Am. Culture grantee NEH/Vassar Coll., 1993. Mem. AAUP, Modern Lang. Assn., Coll. Art Assn. Democrat. Jewish. Home: 3015 Huntington Rd Shaker Hts OH 44120-2407 Office: Cleve Inst Art 11141 East Blvd Cleveland OH 44106-1710

WEINBERG, LORETTA, state legislator; b. N.Y.C., Feb. 6, 1935; d. Murray Issacs and Raya Hamilton; m. Irwin S. Weinberg, July 25, 1960; children: Daniel J., Francine S.; d. Murray Isaacs and Raya Hamilton; m. Irwin S. Weinberg, July 25, 1960; children: Daniel J. Francine S.. BA, UCLA, 1956. Former aide N.J. Assemblyman D. Bennett Mazur, Trenton; mem. N.J. Assembly, Trenton, 1992—. Vice chair N.J. State Dem. Com., Trenton; mem. Teaneck Coun., 1990-94. Recipient Legis. Leadership award No. N.J. Chiropractic Assn., 1992, Woman of Achievement award Bus. and Profl. Women's Club of East Bergen, 1993; named Citizen of Yr. N.J. Jewish War Vets. Mem. Nat. Coun. Jewish Women (life mem., Hannah G. Solomon award 1995, Disting. Achievement award Women's Commn.). Democrat. Jewish. Address: 545 Cedar Ln Teaneck NJ 07666-1740

WEINBERG, LOUISE, lawyer, educator, author; b. N.Y.C.; m. Steven Weinberg; 1 child, Elizabeth. AB summa cum laude, Cornell U.; JD, Harvard U., 1969, LLM, 1974. Bar: Mass. Sr. law clk. Hon. Chas. E. Wyzanski, Jr., Boston, 1971-72; assoc. in law Bingham, Dana & Gould, Boston, 1969-72; teaching fellow Harvard Law Sch., Boston, 1972-74; lectr. law Brandeis U., Waltham, Mass., 1974; assoc. prof. law Suffolk U., Boston, 1974-76, prof., 1977-80; vis. assoc. prof. law Stanford U., Palo Alto, Calif., 1976-77; vis. prof. law U. Tex., Austin, 1979; prof. law Sch. Law, U. Tex., Austin, 1980-84, Thompson prof., 1984-90, Andrews and Kurth prof. law, 1990-92; Fulbright and Jaworski regents rsch. prof. U. Tex., Austin, 1991-92,

Angus G. Wynne, Sr. prof. civil jurisprudence, 1992—, Fondren chair faculty excellence, 1995-96, Eugene R. Smith Centennial rsch. prof. law, 1993; vis. scholar Hebrew U., Jerusalem, 1989; Forum fellow World Econ. Forum, Davos, Switzerland, 1995—; lectr. in field. Author: Federal Courts: Judicial Federalsim and Judicial Power, 1994, and ann. supplements; co-author: Conflict of Laws, 1990; contbr. chpts. to books, articles to profl. jours. Bd. dirs. Ballet Austin, 1986-88, Austin Coun. on Fgn. Affairs, 1985—. Recipient Disting. Educator award Tex. Exes Assn., 1996. Mem. Am. Law Inst. (consultative com. complex litigation 1989-93, consultative com. enterprise liability 1990—), The Philos. Soc. Tex., Assn. Am. Law Schs. (chmn. com. on conflict laws 1991-93, exec. coun. 1989-90), Maritime Law Assn., Scribes, Phi Beta Kappa, Phi Kappa Phi. Office: U Tex Sch Law 727 E 26th St Austin TX 78705-3224

WEINBERG, SYDNEY STAHL, historian; b. N.Y.C., Oct. 2, 1938; d. David Leslie and Berenice (Jarvis) Stahl; B.A., Barnard Coll., 1960; M.A., Columbia U., 1964; Ph.D., 1969; divorced; children: Deborah Sara, Elisa Rachel; m. Gerald Tenenbaum, Mar. 23, 1996. Instr. history N.J. Inst. Tech., 1967-69, asst. prof., 1969-72; asso. prof. history Ramapo Coll. N.J., Mahwah, 1972-74, prof., 1974—; dir. Master of Arts Program in Liberal Studies, 1994—; dir. Garden State Immigration History Consortium, 1987-89. Nat. Endowment for Humanities fellow, 1977-78; sec./treas. Berkshire Conf. Women Historians, 1994—. Mem. Am. Hist. Assn., Orgn. Am. Historians, Am. Studies Assn., Jewish Studies Assn., Assn. of Graduate Liberal Studies Programs. Author: The World of Our Mothers: The Lives of Jewish Immigrant Women, 1988; contbr. articles to profl. jours. Home: 80 La Salle St Apt 19F New York NY 10027-4760 Office: Ramapo Coll MA Liberal Studies Program Office Mahwah NJ 07430

WEINBERG, WENDY LEE, video specialist, filmmaker; b. Chgo., Dec. 11, 1955; d. Michael and Joan Frances (Rusnak) W. BA, U. Mich., Ann Arbor, 1981; MFA, Temple U., Phila., 1991. Lectr. in film and video Temple U., Ursinus Coll., Phila., Collegeville, Pa., 1986-88, 92; video editor Videovation, Phila., 1988-89; field producer, 1987-89; ind. contractor Colonial Penn Group, 1986-92; adjunct asst. prof. Temple U., Drexel U., 1992-95; ind. film/video producer pvt. practice, 1986—; workshop coord. Phila. Ind. Film/Video Assn., 1994-95; editing instr. Scribe Video, 1994-95; sr. segment producer Classroom Closeup, Trenton, N.J., 1994—; festival com. mem. Phila. Festival of World Cinema, 1994—; cmty. visions facilitator Scribe Video, Phila., 1994—; spl. event com. mem. Women in Transition, Phila., 1995—; guest filmmaker Hot Springs Festival, U. Cinn., Arkansas, Ohio, 1992-93. Filmmaker: Beyond Imagining, 1991; prodr., editor: Classroom Close-up, New Jersey, 1995—. Mem. Art Emergency Coalition, Phila., 1990-92. Recipient Student Acad. award Acad. Motion Picture Arts and Scis., 1992, 3d Pl. award U. Film and Video Assn., 1993, 96, Acad. award nomination for short documentary Acad. Motion Picture Arts and Scis., 1993, Hon. Mention, Am. Film and Video Assn., 1992, CAPE award for best overall program Cable TV Network, 1996, All-Star Video award NEA Pub. Rels. Coun., 1996; Film Finishing Fund grantee Women in Film Found., L.A., 1991. Mem. Phila. Ind. Film/Video Assn., Assn. Ind. Video and Filmmakers, Women in Film, Univ. Film and Video Assn. Home: 41 E Mt Pleasant Ave Philadelphia PA 19119

WEINBERGER, ADRIENNE, artist; b. Washington, Apr. 28, 1948; d. Samuel Aaron and Marta (Barta) W.; m. Edward Herschel Egelman, Mar. 21, 1980; children: Serge Maurice, Liana Dora. BA, Goucher Coll., 1970; MEd, Johns Hopkins U., 1973; MA, Northwestern U., 1974; postgrad., Sch. of Mus. of Fine Arts, 1979-82. Lectr. Art Inst. Chgo., 1973-75; lectr., docent trainer Mus. of Fine Arts, Boston, 1978-82; mus. educator Yale Ctr. Brit. Art, Yale Art Gallery, New Haven, 1984-86; instr., coord. alumni coll. Albertus Magnus Coll., New Haven, 1987-89; instr. Mpls. C.C., 1989-94; propr. Studio 95, Edina, Minn., 1995—; panelist New England Regional Confs., Am. Assn. Muss., Mass., Conn., 1976-77; mem., workshop leader New Haven Green Found., New Haven 350 Com., 1987-88. Author, illustrator, pub.: New Haven Coloring Book, 1987, CulchaMan Visits New York City, 1988, CulchaMan Visits Washinton, D.C., 1988. Participant Edina Futures Forum, 1990; mem. adv. bd. gifted edn. svcs. Edina Pub. Schs., 1993—; del. chair, mem. nominating com. Dem. State Conv., St. Paul, 1994, del. chair, Rochester, 1996; sec. Dem.-Farmer Labor Party, Edina, Eden Prairie, 1990-94, chair, 1994-96; mem. Dem. State Cen. Com., 1994—. Recipient Juror's award Berkshire Mus., Pittsfield, Mass., 1981, New Haven Brush & Palette Club, 1985, Edina Art Ctr., 1991. Mem. Am. Soc. of Appraisers (cert.). Home: 6624 Brittany Rd Edina MN 55435 Office: Studio 95 7104 Ohms Ln Ste 201 Minneapolis MN 55439

WEINBERGER, DIANE LYNNE, image consultant; b. Chgo., Feb. 9, 1948; d. James Charles and Alice Valestin; married Oct. 9, 1976. BA in Drawing and Design, U. Mo. Sec./salesperson IBM, St. Louis, 1970-81; model St. Louis, 1981-82, artist, 1970—; ind. image cons. Color Me Beautiful, Rancho Palos Verdes, Calif., 1995—; motivational spkr. in field. Mem ABWA, New Neighbors of Palos Verdes Peninsula (major fundraising chmn., v.p. ways and means), Leads Club (past dir.), Greater St. Louis Artists (past pres. 1985-86).

WEINBERGER, GERALDINE, hospital official; b. N.Y.C., July 17, 1925, d. Jack Horowitz and Irene (Glass) Golub; m. Gerald Sanford Weinberger, June 24, 1951; children: Michael Laurence, Ellen Debra. BA in Biology, CUNY, 1947. Bacteriologist Goldwater Meml. Hosp., N.Y.C., 1947-50, Sydenham Hosp., N.Y.C., 1950-52, U.S. Vitamin Corp., Yonkers, N.Y., 1952-54; patient rep. Beth Abraham Hosp., Bronx, N.Y., 1977—; lectr. N.Y. Geriatric Edn. Ctr., Columbia U., Bronx, 1995-96. Pres. Ardsley (N.Y.) Cmty. Nursery Sch., 1964-65; membership chmn. PTA, Ardsley, 1968-69; fundraising chmn. United Jewish Appeal, Ardsley, 1970; vol. Ardsley Libr., 1975-77. Mem. APHA, Am. Hosp. Assn. Patient Representation, N.Y. State Soc. Patient Reps. Jewish. Office: Beth Abraham Hosp 612 Allerton Ave Bronx NY 10467

WEINER, ANNETTE BARBARA, university dean, anthropology educator; b. Philadelphia, Pa., Feb. 14, 1933; d. Archibald W. and Phyllis M. (Stein-Goldman) Cohen; m. Martin Weiner, 1953 (div. 1973); children: Linda Matisse, Jonathan Weiner; m. Robert Palter, 1979 (div. 1982); m. William E. Mitchell, 1987. B.A., U. Pa., 1968; Ph.D., Bryn Mawr Coll., 1974. Vis. asst. prof. Franklin and Marshall Coll., Lancaster, Pa., 1973-74; assoc. prof. Clare Hall, Cambridge, Eng., 1976; asst. prof. anthropology U. Tex., Austin, 1974-80, assoc. prof., 1980-81; prof., chmn. dept. anthropology NYU, N.Y.C., 1981-91; David B. Kriser prof. NYU, 1985—; dean Grad. Sch. Arts and Scis. NYU, N.Y.C., 1991—, dean Social Scis., 1993—; mem. adv. com. NRC, 1993—; bd. dirs. Social Sci. Rsch. Coun. Author: Women of Value: Men of Renown: New Perspectives in Trobriand Exchange, 1976, The Trobrianders of Papua New Guinea, 1989; editor (with J. Schneider) Cloth and Human Experience, 1989, (film, with D. Wason) The Trobriand Islanders of Papua New Guinea, Bilan du Film Ethnographique, Paris, 1991 (Grand Prix award), Inalienable Possessions: The Paradox of Keeping-While-Giving, 1992. Guggenheim fellow, 1980; grantee Wenner-Gren Found. Anthrop. Rsch., 1982, 85, 86, NEH, 1976, 85, Am. Council Learned Socs., 1976, NIMH, 1972-73. Fellow Am. Anthrop. Assn. (pres. 1991-93), Royal Anthrop. Inst. Gt. Britain and Ireland, Assn. Social Anthropology in Oceania, Soc. Cultural Anthropology (bd. dirs. 1985-87, pres. 1988-89), N.Y. Inst. of the Humanities; mem. Cibola Anthrop. Assn. (pres. 1977-79), Commn. Visual Anthropology, Nat. Rsch. Coun. (adv. com. 1993—), Social Sci. Rsch. Coun. (bd. dirs. 1993-95). Office: NYU Dean Grad Sch 6 Washington Sq N New York NY 10003-6635

WEINER, CLAIRE MURIEL, freelance writer; b. Bronx, N.Y., Dec. 18, 1951; d. David and Norma (Berry) W. BA, U. Miami, Coral Gables, Fla., 1973; MA, U. Md., 1980. Pub. rels. specialist Hialeah Recreation Div., Hialeah, Fla., 1974-77; freelance writer North Miami Beach, 1977-78, Germantown, Md., 1989—, Montgomery County, Md., 1981—; govt. affairs liaison for new ednl. data base co. being formed, Montgomery County, 1982—; acting comm. dir. Ednl. Info. Svcs., 1996—. Contbr. articles to local newspapers; contbr. travel articles to profl. jours, mags. Active membership com. newsletter Greater Miami Jewish Fedn., 1974-77; charter mem. Women for Today chpt. B'nai B'rith Women, Washington, 1985-89. Named Hon. Citizen of Historic Williamburg. Life fellow Am. Biog. Inst. Rsch. Assn., World Lit. Acad.; mem. NAFE, Pub. Rels. Soc. Am., Internat. Platform Assn., Nat. Trust for Hist. Preservation. Jewish. Home: 18828 Sky Blue Cir Germantown MD 20874-5398

WEINER, CLARE FRANCES, social worker, psychotherapist; b. Phila., Dec. 3, 1929; d. Jack and Jessie (Rosengarten) Weinbaum; m. George C. Wheeler, Jan. 21, 1978; children by previous marriage: Justin M., Kate J., Lucian J. BS, Temple U., 1951; MSW, U. Wis., 1967. Diplomate Am. Bd. Examiners in Clin. Social Work. Social worker Ohio Valley Mental Retardation Evaluation Unit, Athens, Ohio, 1968-69; social worker inpatient psychiat. svc. VA Hosp., Albany, N.Y., 1969-70; chief social worker Schenectady County Outpatient Mental Health Clinic, 1970-76; adult treatment team leader, supervising social worker Saratoga County Mental Health Ctr., N.Y., 1976-81; pvt. practice psychotherapy individuals, couples, families Schenectady, 1975—. Fellow N.Y. State Soc. for Clin. Social Workers (diplomate), Nat. Assn. Social Workers (diplomate); mem. Gestalt Inst. Cleve., Thursday Mus. Soc. Office: 29 Front St Schenectady NY 12305-1301

WEINER, KAREN COLBY (KAREN LYNN COLBY), psychologist, lawyer; b. Oak Park, Ill., Oct. 28, 1943; d. Leonard L. and Mildred Irene (Berman) Colby; m. J. Laevin Weiner, July 26, 1964; children: Joel Laevin, Doren Robin, Anthony Justin. BA, Mich. State U., East Lansing, 1964; JD, U. Detroit, 1977, MA, 1986, PhD, 1988. Bar: Mich. 1977, D.C. 1978. Speech therapist Oak Park Sch. Dist., 1965-68; law clk. justice G. Mennen Williams Mich. Supreme Ct., Lansing, 1977-79; assoc. Dickinson, Wright, Moon, Van Dusen & Freeman, Detroit, 1979-83; intern in psychology Detroit Psychiat. Inst., 1986-88; psychologist Northland Clinic, Southfield, Mich., 1987-88, Counseling Assocs., Southfield, 1988—; postdoctoral intern Wyandotte (Mich.) Hosp. and Health Ctr., 1988-90; dir. psychol. svcs., quality assurance coord. Counseling Assocs., Southfield, 1991—; hearing panelist Atty. Discipline Bd., Detroit, 1982-95; hearing referee Mich. Civil Rights Commn., Detroit, 1983-91. Contbr. articles to profl. jours. Mem. adv. bd. Mich. chpt. Anti-Defamation League, 1981-90. Mem. APA, Mich. Psychol. Assn. (mem. ethics com. 1992—, chmn. legis. com. 1993), Mich. Soc. for Psychoanalytic Psychology (pres. 1995-97, sec. 1991-92, treas. 1992—), Assn. for Advancement of Psychoanalysis (pres. 1995—), Women Lawyers Assn. Mich. (pres. 1981-82, pres. Found. 1982-83), Mich. Bar Assn. (chmn. spl. com. for expansion under represented groups in law 1980-83). Democrat. Jewish. Home: 1764 Alexander Dr Bloomfield Hills MI 48302-1201 Office: 29260 Franklin Rd Ste 115 Southfield MI 48034-1144

WEINER, MARIAN MURPHY, insurance executive, consultant; b. N.Y.C., Mar. 20, 1954; d. Stephen Patrick and Evelyn (McTiernan) Murphy; m. Joseph Longo, Feb. 15, 1975 (div. May 1977); m. Ira Elliott Weiner, Sept. 23, 1983; children: Joshua Stephen, Samantha Beth. BA, William Paterson Coll., 1984. CPCU, CIC. Bookkeeper RJT, Inc. trading as The Turner Group, Pine Brook, N.J., 1973-75; ins. broker RJT, Inc. T-A The Turner Group, Pine Brook, N.J., 1975-80, office mgr., 1980-82, exec. v.p., 1982—. Bd. dirs. Homeowners Assn., Vernon, N.J., 1989. Mem. Profl. Ins. Agts. Democrat. Roman Catholic. Home: 7 Curtis Dr Vernon NJ 07462 Office: The Turner Group 350 Main Rd Montville NJ 07045-9730

WEINER, NONA, artist, computer resource educator; b. Oakland, Calif., Dec. 9, 1946; d. Duncan Rawsel and Marian Lucille (McMillan) Gardner; m. Donald David Weiner, Feb. 10, 1965 (div. Aug. 1971); children: Donald David II, Jonathan Andrew. BA in Am. Studies, U. Miami, 1968; MA in Edn. Tech., San Francisco State U., 1995. EMT, Calif. With various film and TV prodn. cos., 1979-81; prodn. mgr. Anne Murray spl. Smith-Hemion Prodns., L.A., 1981; artist Pt. Arena, Calif., 1987—; computer resource tchr. Tehiyah Day Sch., El Cerrito, Calif., 1995—. Prin. works include clay sculpture, 1995 (1st Clay Art in the Redwoods). Disaster svc. caseworker ARC, San Francisco, 1994—, CPR/1st aid instr., 1991—. Donna Cuneo Meml. scholar, 1993. Mem. NEA, Am. Fedn. Tchrs., Internat. Soc. Tech. Edn., Gualala Arts, Amnesty Internat., Asian Art Mus., Nat. Mus. Am. Indian, NCECA.

WEINER, SANDRA JOAN, purchasing executive; b. N.Y.C., Oct. 27, 1951; d. Louis and Rose (Rosansky) Kornbluth; m. Gerald Weiner, Feb. 14, 1992. BA magna cum laude, Queens Coll., 1973; MA in Romance Langs., Princeton U., 1975. Instr. French lang. Princeton (N.J.) U., 1973-77; mgr. cargo tariffs Air France, N.Y.C., 1977-82; mgr. internat. pricing Emery Worldwide, Wilton, Conn., 1982-86, dir. pricing, 1986-89; pres. Riverview Traffic Group, Trumbull, Conn., 1989-90; mgr. strategic sourcing, program mgr. Pitney Bowes, Shelton, Conn., 1990-94; mgr. quality and adminstrn. Entex Info. Svcs., Rye Brook, N.Y., 1994-95; dir. purchasing Micro Warehouse Inc., Norwalk, Conn., 1995—; mem. adv. bd. Cargo Rate Services, Miami, Fla., 1984—. Bd. dirs. Literacy Vols. Greater Norwalk, 1987. Fullbright-Hayes scholar, 1973. Office: Micro Warehouse Inc 535 Connecticut Ave Norwalk CT 06854

WEINER, SANDRA SAMUEL, critical care nurse, nursing consultant; b. N.Y.C., Jan. 12, 1947; d. Herbert A. and Ruth (Wallerstein) Samuel; m. Neil D. Weiner, June 15, 1969 (div. June 1980); 1 child, Jaime Michelle. BS in Nursing, SUNY, Buffalo, 1968; cert. in critical care, Golden West Coll., 1982; postgrad. UCLA, U. West L.A. Sch. of Law, 1992. RN, Pa., Calif. Staff nurse N.Y. Hosp.-Cornell Med. Ctr., 1968-69; head nurse med.-surg. nursing Abington (Pa.) Hosp., 1969; assoc. prof. Sch. Nursing, U. Pa., Phila., 1970; instr. nursing Coll. of Med. Assts., Long Beach, Calif., 1971-72; surg. staff nurse Med. Ctr. of Tarzana, Calif., 1978-79, Cedar-Sinai Med. Ctr., L.A., 1979-81; supr. recovery room Beverly Hills Med. Ctr., L.A., 1981-92; Post Anesthesia Care Unit nurse Westside Hosp., 1992—; med. cons. RJA & Assocs., Beverly Hills, Calif., 1984-92; instr. CPR, L.A., 1986-95. Mem. women's aux. Ctr. Theater Group Vols., L.A., 1986—, Maple Ctr., Beverly Hills, 1987—. Mem. Am. Nursing Assn., Am. Soc. Post-Anesthesia Nursing, Am. Assn. Critical Care Nurses, Heart and Lung Assn., Post Anesthesia Nurses Assn., U.S. Ski Assn. Democrat. Jewish. Avocations: skiing, running, travel, theater, ballet. Home: 12633 Moorpark St Studio City CA 91604-4537

WEINER-HEUSCHKEL, SYDELL, theater educator; b. N.Y.C., Feb. 18, 1947; d. Milton A. and Janet (Kay) Horowitz; children: Jason, Emily; m. Rex Heuschkel, Sept. 3, 1992. BA, SUNY, Binghamton, 1968; MA, Calif. State U., L.A., 1974; PhD, NYU, 1986; postgrad. in acting, Yale U., 1968-70. Prof. theater arts, chmn. dept., dir. honors program Calif. State U. Dominguez Hills, Carson, 1984—; guest lectr. Calif. Inst. Arts, 1988. Appeared in play Vikings, Grove Shakespeare Festival, 1988; dir. Plaza Suite, Brea (Calif.) Civic Theatre, 1982, Gypsy, Carson Civic Light Opera, 1990, Same Time Next Year, Muckehthaler, 1987, Slow Dance on the Killing Ground, Alternative Repertory Theatre, 1989; co-author: School and Community Theatre Problems: A Handbook for Survival, 1978, (software) Public Speaking, 1991. Yale U. fellow, 1969; recipient Lyle Gibson Disting. Tchr. award, 1989. Mem. Screen Actors Guild, Am. Fedn. TV and Radio Artists, Calif. State U. Women's Coun. (treas. 1989-91), Phi Kappa Phi.

WEINFURTNER, CHERYL BRAJNER, fine artist; b. Nashville, Mar. 12, 1959; d. Virginia Rose (Francis) Grimm; m. Paul Hartnett Weinfurtner. Grad. high sch., Flatwoods, Ky.; student, Russell Area Vocat. Tech. Sch., 1977, Ashland State Vocat., 1979, Somerset Aero. Tech. Sch., 1984. Mech. draftsperson The Kroger Co., Cin., 1984-87; archtl. draftsperson Foxcraft Homebuilders, Cumberland, Md., 1987-90; draftsperson Bedford, Pa., 1990-92; fine artist, framer Short Gap, W.Va., 1992-94; graphic designer Cumberland, Md., 1994-95; fine artist Short Gap, W.Va., 1995—. One-woman shows include Ky. Highlands Mus., 1994-95, Bedford (Pa.) County Arts Ctr., 1994-95, WJJB Broadcast Gallery, 1993-94, Cumberland Creative Arts Ctr., 1993-96. Demonstrating artist The Art Dept. and Cumberland Heritage Days, 1994, 95, Hampshire County Heritage Days, Romney, W.Va., 1995-96, Allegany Area Art Alliance, Cumberland, 1993, Md. Theatre Arts Children's Arts Festival; selection com. Cumberland Summer Theatre, 1994-96, contract chairperson, 1994-96. Recipient First Pl. Mechanical Drafting Gold medal Ky. State Vocat. Indsl. Club of Am., 1977. Mem. Western Md. Watercolor Soc. (pres. 1992-95, 1st Place award 1993, 1st Place and Hon. Mention awards 1994), W.Va. Watercolor Soc., Allegany Area Arts Alliance (historian 1992-94, Hon. Mention award 1992, 3d Place award 1993), Somerset County Artist Assn. (Best of Show award 1993, 1sdt Place 1994), Bedford County Artist Assn., Allegany Area Arts Coun. Studio: Rt 2 Box 604 Ridgeley WV 26753-9676

WEINGART, JEANNE, public relations executive. Ptnr., adminstv. dir. Fin. Rels. Bd., Chgo. Office: Fin Rels Bd John Hancock Ctr 875 N Michigan Ave Chicago IL 60611-1801*

WEINHAGEN, SUSAN POUCH, emergency care nurse; b. Dallas, Jan. 17, 1954; d. Arnold Cornwall and Barbara Anne (Noakes) Pouch; m. Charles Winthrop Weinhagen, Apr. 23, 1977 (div. May 1985); children: Francine Melanie, Kurt Woodbury; m. Giles Milton Ellis, Apr. 14, 1989. Diploma in nursing, Jackson Meml. Hosp. Sch., 1977. RN, N.C., Wis.; cert. ACLS, basic trauma life support, mobil intensive care nurse, pediatric advanced life support. Nurse pvt. med. office, Ellensburg, Wash., 1977; staff nurse orthopedics floor St. Joseph Hosp., Madison, Wis., 1977-80; staff nurse emergency St. Joseph Hosp., Madison, 1980-83, Haywood County Hosp., Waynesville, N.C., 1983; staff nurse emergency care ctr. Meml. Mission Hosp., Asheville, N.C., 1983-86, charge nurse emergency care ctr., 1986-89, mgr. emergency care ctr., 1989-95; charge nurse, Emergency Care Ctr., 1995—; mem. nursing practice coun. Meml. Mission Hosp., Asheville, 1992-94, mem. nursing adminstrv. coun., 1994-95, charge nurse emergency care ctr., 1995—. Mem. Emergency Nurses Assn. Home: 8 Simpson Hollow Rd Asheville NC 28803-9003 Office: Meml Mission Hosp 509 Biltmore Ave Asheville NC 28801-4601

WEINHOLD, LINDA LILLIAN, psychologist, researcher; b. Reading, Pa., Nov. 9, 1948; d. Aaron Zerbe Weinhold and Nancy Louise (Spotts) Weikel; m. Jack Wayne Prisk, Jan. 21, 1967 (div. 1969). Lic. practical nurse, AVTS, 1970; BS, Penn State U., 1975; MS, C.W. Post Ctr., 1982; PhD, Fordham U., 1986. Lic. Practical nurse. Instr., asst. prof. Gettysburg (Pa.) Coll., 1985-86; post doc. fellow John Hopkins U., Balt., 1986-88; staff fellow NIH NIDA Addiction Rsch. Ctr., Balt., 1988-93; cons. NIH NIDA Medications Devel., Rockville, Md., 1993-94; soc. sci. program coord. Med. Ctr. NIDA Rsch., Washington, 1994-95; cons. The Clin. Cons. Group Antech, Inc., Balt., 1995. Various presentations. Mem. Am. Psychological Assn., Phi Kappa Phi, Sigma Xi. Democrat. Home: 210 Congressional Ln #104 Rockville MD 20852-1507 Office: Antech Inc Hopkins Bayview Rsch Campus Baltimore MD 21224

WEINKAUF, MARY LOUISE STANLEY, clergywoman; b. Eau Claire, Wis., Sept. 22, 1938; d. Joseph Michael and Marie Barbara (Holzinger) Stanley; m. Alan D. Weinkauf, Oct. 12, 1962; children: Stephen, Xanti. BA, Wis. State U., 1961; MA, U. Tenn., 1962, PhD, 1966; MDiv Luth. Sch. Theology, Chgo., 1993. Grad. asst., instr. U. Tenn., 1961-66; asst. prof. English, Adrian Coll., 1966-69; prof., head dept. English, Dakota Wesleyan U., Mitchell, S.D., 1969-89; instr. Columbia Coll., 1989-91; pastor Siloa Lutheran Ch., Ontonagon Faith, White Pine, Mich., Gowrie, Iowa. Mem. Mitchell Arts Council; bd. trustees, The Ednl. Found., 1986—; bd. dirs. Ontonagon County Habitat for Humanity, 1995—. Author: Hard-Boiled Heretic, 1994, Sermons in Science Fiction, 1994, Murder Most Poetic, 1996. Mem. Nat. Council Tchrs. English, S.D. Council Tchrs. English, Sci. Fiction Research Assn., Popular Culture Assn., Milton Soc., AAUW (div. pres. 1978-80), S.D. State Poetry Soc. (pres. 1982-83), Delta Kappa Gamma (pres. local chpt., mem. state bd. 1972-89 , state v.p. 1979-83, state pres. 1983-85), Sigma Tau Delta, Pi Kappa Delta, Phi Kappa Phi. Republican. Lutheran.

WEINRICH, GLORIA JOAN CASTORIA, retired elementary education educator; b. Bklyn., Dec. 12, 1930; d. Louis and Elsie (Doddato) Castoria; m. Robert L. Weinrich, Aug. 16, 1952 (dec. 1993); 1 child, Russell Louis. BA, Hofstra U., 1952, MS, 1962. Cert. tchr., N.Y. Tchr. Oceanside (N.Y.) Bd. Edn., 1952-53, Troy (N.Y.) Bd. Edn., 1953-56, Carle Place (N.Y.) Bd. Edn., 1956-60, 69-93; ret., 1993. Mem. nominating com. Western Garden City Property Owners, 1995, mem. bird sanctuary com., 1995. Mem. AAUW, N.Y. State Ret. Tchrs. Assn. (co-chairperson polit. action 1993-96), Carle Pl. Ret. Tchrs. Assn. (pres. 1993-95), Alpha Upsilon, Delta Kappa Gamma (pres. 1992-96). Roman Catholic. Home: 1 Hawthorne Rd Garden City NY 11530-1017

WEINSHIENK, ZITA LEESON, federal judge; b. St. Paul, Apr. 3, 1933; d. Louis and Ada (Dubov) Leeson; m. Hubert Troy Weinshienk, July 8, 1956 (dec. 1983); children: Edith Blair, Kay Anne, Darcy Jill; m. James N. Schaffner, Nov. 15, 1986. Student, U. Colo., 1952-53; BA magna cum laude, U. Ariz., 1955; JD cum laude, Harvard U., 1958; Fulbright grantee, U. Copenhagen, Denmark, 1959; LHD (hon.), Loretto Heights Coll., 1985; LLD (hon.), U. Denver, 1990. Bar: Colo. 1959. Probation counselor, legal adviser, referee Denver Juvenile Ct., 1959-64; judge Denver Mcpl. Ct., 1964-65, Denver County Ct., 1965-71, Denver Dist. Ct., 1972-79, U.S. Dist. Ct. Colo., Denver, 1979—. Precinct committeewoman Denver Democratic Com., 1963-64; bd. dirs. Crime Stoppers. Named one of 100 Women in Touch with Our Time Harper's Bazaar Mag., 1971, Woman of Yr., Denver Bus. and Profl. Women, 1969; recipient Women Helping Women award Soroptimist Internat. of Denver, 1983, Hanna G. Solomon award Nat. Coun. Jewish Women, Denver, 1986. Fellow Colo. Bar Found., Am. Bar Found.; mem. ABA, Denver Bar Assn., Colo. Bar Assn., Nat. Conf. Fed. Trial Judges (exec. com.), Dist. Judges' Assn. of 10th Cir. (past pres.), Colo. Women's Bar Assn., Fed. Judges Assn., Denver Crime Stoppers Inc. (bd.dirs.), Devner LWV, Women's Forum Colo., Harvard Law Sch. Assn., Phi Beta Kappa, Phi Kappa Phi, Order of Coif (hon. Colo. chpt.). Office: US Dist Ct US Courthouse Rm C-418 1929 Stout St Denver CO 80294-2900

WEINSTEIN, CHERYL ERMANN, physician, medical educator; b. Hartford, Conn., May 21, 1944; d. Fred H. and Trude (Lion) Ermann; m. Meredith Allen Weinstein, Dec. 21, 1968. BA, Mt. Holyoke Coll., South Hadley, Mass., 1966; MD, Johns Hopkins U. Sch. Medicine, Balt., 1972. Diplomate Am. Bd. Internal Medicine with added qualification in geriatric medic ne, Am. Coll. Physicians. Staff physician Cleve. Clinic Found., 1976—; clin. asst. prof. medicine Case Western Reserve Coll. Medicine, Cleve., 1977-96; clin. assoc. prof. medicine Pa. State U. Sch. Medicine, Hershey, 1991-96; asst. prof. medicine Ohio State U. Coll. Medicine, Columbus, 1993-96; vol. physician Free Med. Clinic, Cleve.. 1976-96. Contbr. chpt. to book. lectr. on health topics Women's Cmty. Found., 1975—; vice chair physician divsn. Jewish Cmty. Fedn., Cleve., 1993. Fellow ACP; mem. Am. Med. Women's Assn. (dir., com. chair), Am. Geriatric Soc., Am. Acad. on Physician and Patient, Women's Med. Soc. Cleve. (exec. bd. 1978-96). Jewish. Office: Cleve Clinic Found 9500 Euclid Ave Cleveland OH 44195

WEINSTEIN, DIANE GILBERT, federal judge, lawyer; b. Rochester, N.Y., June 14, 1947; d. Myron Birne and Doris Isabelle (Robie) Gilbert; m. Dwight Douglas Sypolt; children: Andrew, David. BA, Smith Coll., Northampton, Mass., 1969; postgrad., Stanford U., 1977-78, Georgetown U., 1978; JD, Boston U., 1979. Bar: D.C. 1979, Mass. 1979. Law clk. to judge D.C. Ct. Appeals, Washington, 1979-80; assoc. Peabody, Lambert & Meyers, Washington, 1980-83; asst. gen. counsel Office of Mgmt. and Budget, Washington, 1983-86; dep. gen. counsel U.S. Dept. Edn., Washington, 1986-88, acting gen. counsel, 1988-89; legal counselor to V.P. of U.S., White House; counsel Pres.'s Competitiveness Coun., Washington, 1989-90; judge U.S. Ct. Fed. Claims, Washington, 1990—. Recipient Young Lawyer's award Boston U. Law Sch., 1989. Mem. Fed. Am. Inn of Ct., Federalist Soc., Univ. Club. Republican. Home: 3927 Massachusetts Ave NW Washington DC 20016-5104

WEINSTEIN, EILEEN ANN, elementary education educator; b. Phila., Sept. 11, 1947; d. Bernard and Eleanor (Cohen) Cobert; m. Philip Weinstein, Aug. 16, 1970; children: Lawrence, Steven. BS in Edn. with honors, Temple U., 1969, MEd with honors, 1972. Cert. elem. tchr., psychology of reading, Pa. 1st grade tchr. Phila. Sch. Dist., 1969-70; 1st grade tchr. Neshaminy Sch. Dist., Langhorne, Pa., 1970-74, tchr. reading and 3d grade, 1985—; kindergarten tchr. Jewish Cmty. Ctr., Phila., 1981-85; mem. instrnl. support team Neshaminy Sch. Dist., 1987—, mem. student assistance team, 1992—. Active Dem. Nat. Com., 1992—. Recipient Teaching award Children with ADD, 1994-95. Mem. Internat. Reading Assn., Neshaminy Fedn. Tchrs. (union rep. 1986—), Women's Am. ORT (officer, bd. mem. 1973—), Hadassah (officer and bd. mem. 1969—). Jewish. Home: 83 Cypress Cir Richboro PA 18954-1653 Office: Neshaminy Sch Dist Oliver Heckman Sch Cherry St Langhorne PA 19047

WEINSTEIN, JOYCE, artist; b. N.Y.C., June 7, 1931; d. Sidney and Rose (Bier) W.; student CCNY, 1948-50, Art Students League, 1948-52; m. Stanley Boxer, Nov. 28, 1952. Exhibited in one-women shows: Perdalma

Gallery, N.Y.C., 1953-56, L.I. U., Bklyn., 1969, U. Calif.-Santa Cruz, 1969, T. Bortolazzo Gallery, Santa Barbara, Calif., 1972, Dorsky Gallery, N.Y.C., 1972, 74, Galerie Ariadne, N.Y.C., 1975, Gloria Cortella Gallery, N.Y.C., 1976, Meredith Long Contemporary Gallery, N.Y.C. 1978, 79, 88-90, Martin Gerard Gallery, Edmonton, Alta., Can., 1981, 82, 84, Galerie Wentzel, Cologne, W.Ger., 1982, Haber Theodore Gallery, N.Y.C., 1983, 85, Cologne, W.Ger., 1987, Gallery One, Toronto, Ont., Can., 1983, Paul Kuhn Gallery, Calgery, 1985, Eva Cohn Gallery, Highland Park, Chgo, Ill., 1985, Galerie Wentzell, Cologne, 1987, Meredith Long & Co., Houston, 1988, Alena Adlung Gallery, N.Y.C., 1989, Meredith Long & Co., Houston, 1990; group shows: Marlborough Gallery, N.Y.C., 1968, Bula Mus. Art, Calcutta, India, 1970, Phoenix Gallery, N.Y.C., 1988, 1988, Provident Nat. Bank, Phila., 1988, Alena Adlung Gallery, N.Y.C., 1989, 90, Edmonton Art Mus., 1989, Rose Fried Gallery, N.Y.C., 1970, Hudson River Mus., 1971, Dorsky Gallery, 1972, 94, Suffolk Mus., Stony Brook, N.Y., 1972, New York Cultural Center, 1973, Stamford (Conn.) Mus., 1973, Landmark Gallery, N.Y.C., 1974, Women's Interart Center, N.Y.C., 1974, 75, 78, New Sch. Social Research, N.Y.C., 1975, Bklyn. Mus., 1975, Galerie Areadne, N.Y.C., 1975, Edmonton Art Gallery Mus., Alta., Can., 1989, Mus. of Modern Art N.Y.C., 1980, The Queens Mus. N.Y., 1984, The Centre de Creacio Contemporania, Barcelona, Spain, 1987, Fairleigh Dickinson U., Hackensack, N.J., 1976, Gloria Cortella, Inc., 1976, Edmonton Art Gallery Mus., 1977, 77, 83, Northeastern U., Boston, 1977, Lehigh (Pa.) U., 1977, Meredith Long Contemporary Gallery, 1977, 78, 79, 80, Mus. Modern Art, N.Y.C., 1981, Galerie Wentzel, Cologne, W.Ger., 1981-85, Martin Gerard Gallery, Edmonton, 1981, Gallery One, Toronto, 1983, 84, Martin Girard Gallery, 1981-84, Haber Theodore Gallery, 1982-85, Queens Mus., N.Y.C., 1984, Jerald Melberg Gallery, Charlotte, N.C., 1984, Edmonton Art Gallery Mus., 1985, Richard Green Gallery, N.Y.C., Rosel Art Fair, Basel, Switzerland, 1986, Centre de Creacio, Barcelona, Spain, 1987, Meredith Long & Co. Gallery, Houston, 1988-90, Broome St. Gallery, N.Y.C., 1991, Andre Zarre Gallery, N.Y.C., 1990, Alena Adlung Gallery, N.Y.C., 1989-90, Cork Gallery, N.Y.C., 1990, Chgo. Internat. Art Expn., 1990, Queens Coll., N.Y.C., 1991, Miami Art Fair, 1993, Meredith Long & Co. Gallery, Houston, 1988, 89, 90, 93, Bklyn. Botanic Gardens, 1994, Flanders Contemporary Art Gallery, 1996; also numerous univs. and colls.; represented in permanent collections: Pa. Acad. Fine Arts, N.J. State Mus., Ciba-Geigy Corp., New Sch. Social Research, Bula Mus. Art, U. Calif., Mus. Modern Art, N.Y.C., McMullen Gallery, Edmonton, Ga., De Spisset Mus., U. Santa Clara, Edmonton Art Gallery Mus., Edmonton, The Hines Collection, Boston, others; represented by Hokin Gallery, Palm Beach and Miami, Fla., Galerie Wentzel, Cologne, W. Ger., Meredith Long and Co., Houston , Dorsky Gallery, N.Y.C., Gallery One, Toronto, Can., Smith Anderson Gallery, Palo Alto, Calif.; exec. coordinator Women in Arts Found., Inc., 1975-79, 81-82, coordinating bd., 1983-87. Recipient Lambert Fund award Pa. Acad. Fine Arts, 1955; Susan B. Anthony award NOW, 1983. Home and Studio: 46 Fox Hill Rd Ancramdale NY 12503-5311

WEINSTEIN, MARIE PASTORE, psychologist; b. N.Y.C., Oct. 3, 1940; d. Edward and Sarah (Mancuso) Pastore; children: Arielle Rebecca, Damon Alexander. BA in Polit. Sci. and Lit., Ind. U.; MS in Psychology, L.I. U.; PhD in Ednl. Psychology, CCNY, 1986. Cert. sch. psychologist; lic. psychologist, N.Y. Sch. psychologist evaluation unit Bd. Edn., N.Y.C., 1977-78; dir., adminstr. learning ctr. Guidance Ctr. Flatbush, Bklyn., 1978-82; clin. team coord./psychologist Lorge Upper and Lower Sch., N.Y.C., 1982-85; psychologist devel. disabilities ctr. Roosevelt Hosp., N.Y.C., 1985-87; chief psychologist Blueberry Treatment Ctrs., Bklyn., 1987-89; cons. psychologist Ctr. for Children & Families, St. Albans, N.Y., 1989—; cons. psychologist United Cerebral Palsy Hearst Presch., Bklyn., 1988-89, Charles Drew Day Ctr., Queens Village, N.Y., 1982-85, Warbasse Nursery Sch., Bklyn., 1981-85, YWCA Montessori Sch., 1993-94; adj. asst. prof. Baruch Coll. CUNY, 1989; pvt. practice, Bklyn.; rsch. cons. Children's TV Workshop, N.Y.C., 1979; clin. cons. Bedford Stuyvesant Mental Health Ctr., Bklyn., 1990, Youth Counseling League, N.Y.C., 1993; cons. dist. 2 N.Y.C. Bd. Edn., 1988; guest lectr. Met. Hosp. Dept. Psychiatry, N.Y.C., 1988, Dist. 3 Bd. Edn., 1993; edn. cons. Lit. Vols. N.Y., 1974-76. Contbg. author to children's ency., 1970. Bd. dirs. Artists in Search of. . . . Fellow Am. Orthopsychiat. Assn. (program com. 1990—); mem. APA, Internat. Congress on Child Abuse and Neglect, Manhattan Fedn. Child and Adolescent Svcs. Office: 26 Court St Ste 2112 Brooklyn NY 11242-0103

WEINSTEIN, RHONDA KRUGER, elementary mathematics educator, administrator; b. Boston, May 18, 1948; d. David Solomon and Henrietta Reina (Slocum) Kruger; m. Milton Charles Weinstein, June 14, 1970; children: Jeffrey William, Daniel Jay. AB, Mt. Holyoke Coll., 1970; MA, Suffolk U., 1973. Cert. supr./dir.; math. 7-12; elem. K-8; elem. prin.; supt., Mass. Tchr. grade 3 Brookline (Mass.) Pub. Schs., 1974-78, math. resource tchr. K-6, 1980-81, math. resource tchr. K-8, 1981-82, elem. curriculum coord. for math., 1982—; program evaluator Newton (Mass.) Pub. Schs., 1992-93; part-time instr. Suffolk U., Boston, 1976, 79; mem. math. adv. bd. Ency. Britannica, Chgo., 1993-95; cons. Mass. sch. sys. including Northborough/ Southborough, 1987-88, Sudbury, 1987, North Andover, 1993; spkr. profl. meetings Assn. Tchrs. Math. in New Eng., 1990, 94, 95, ASCD, Boston, 1988. Co-author: Calculator Activities, 1987; reviewer 2 books Arithmetic Teacher, 1991. Alumnae fund vol. Mt. Holyoke Coll., South Hadley, Mass., 1985-90; vol. Am. Heart Assn., Brookline, 1982-93; mem. PTO, Baker Sch., Brookline, 1983-95. Sarah Williston scholar Mt. Holyoke Coll., 1967; grantee Brookline Found., 1994, Tchrs. and Adminstrs. Tng. Fund, 1992, 96. Mem. Nat. Coun. Tchrs. Math. (nat. conv. com. chair 1995, speaker profl. meeting 1993), Nat. Coun. Suprs. of Math., Assn. Tchrs. of Math. in Mass., Boston Area Math. Specialists, Phi Beta Kappa. Home: 50 Princeton Rd Chestnut Hill MA 02167-3061 Office: Brookline Pub Schs 88 Harvard St Brookline MA 02146-6899

WEINSTEIN, RUTH ANN, language educator; b. Boston, July 23, 1940; d. Morris and Rose (Kramer) Sokolove; children: Samara, Rachel, Dina. BA, Boston U., 1962; EdM, Boston State U., 1963. ESL tchr. Boston Pub. Schs., 1986—. Home: 12 Hurd Rd Belmont MA 02178-3548

WEINSTEIN, SHARON SCHLEIN, public relations executive, educator; b. Newark, Apr. 15, 1942; d. Louis Charles and Ruth Margaret (Franzblau) Schlein; m. Elliott Henry Weinstein, May 7, 1978. BA, U. Pa., 1964; MA, New Sch. for Social Rsch., N.Y.C., 1985. Researcher London Daily Express, N.Y.C., 1965-69; reporter Forbes mag., N.Y.C., 1969-72; sr. editor Merrill Lynch, N.Y.C., 1972-74; pub. rels. officer Chase Manhattan Bank, N.Y.C., 1974-79; v.p. pub. rels. and advt. Blyth, Eastman, Dillion, N.Y.C., 1979-80; mgr. corp. communication Sanford C. Berstein & Co., N.Y.C., 1980-83; v.p. corp. affairs Nat. Westminster Bancorp, N.Y.C., 1983-95; dir. corp. comms. Nat. Securities Clearing Corp., N.Y.C., 1995—; adj. asst. prof. NYU, 1988—. Home: 161 W 15th St New York NY 10011-6720

WEINSTEIN, SUSAN IRENE, public relations specialist, writer; b. Phila., Aug. 9, 1951; d. Mayer Bernard and Millicent (Levin) W.; m. Carl P. Kanev, Dec. 11, 1993. BFA, Temple U., 1973; student Playwrights Workshop, U. Iowa, 1975. Sole propr. Susan Weinstein Pub. Rels., N.Y.C., 1988—. Mem. Dramatists Guild. Democrat. Office: Susan Weinstein Pub Rels 41 Union Sq W Rm 919 New York NY 10014

WEINSTOCK, GRACE EVANGELINE, librarian, retired educator; b. Currie, Minn., Dec. 16, 1904; d. Charles Clementine and Lydia Hannah (Halland) O'Neill; m. Joseph Marshall Weinstock, Sept. 1, 1945 (dec. July 1973). BA, Hamline U., 1925; AAS in Libr. Sci. Tech., Coll. Lake County, 1988. High sch. tchr. Latin, history, phys. edn. Bd. Edn., Grafton, N.D., 1925-27; high sch. tchr. Latin, history, phys. edn. Bd. Edn., Norwood, Minn., 1928-32; high sch. tchr. Latin, English, libr. Bd. Edn., Wells, Minn., 1932-38; interviewer I Minn. State Employment Svc., Redwood Falls, Minn., 1938-45; interviewer II U.S. Employment Svc., Mpls., 1938-45; substitute tchr. English and bus. depts. North Chicago (Ill.) High Sch. Dist. 123, 1956-72; contractual employment instr. typing U.S. Dept. Army 5th U.S. Army Edn. Ctr., Ft. Sheridan, Ill., 1959-71; mil. personnel clk. Dept. Def., USN, Great Lakes, Ill., 1972-86; part-time libr. Outboard Marine Corp., Waukegan, Ill., 1988-90; part-time clerical worker Highland Park (Ill.) Hosp., 1990-91. bd. dirs. Lake County Community Concert Org., Waukegan, 1990. Grantee Waukegan br. Ednl. Found., 1993. Mem. AAUW (program chmn. Waukegan br. 1960), Navy League U.S., Phi Theta Kappa, Alpha Kappa Delta, Pi Gamma Mu. Home: 450 Pine Ct Lake Bluff IL 60044-2433

WEINTZ, CAROLINE GILES, non-profit association consultant, travel writer; b. Columbia, Tenn., Dec. 8, 1952; d. Raymond Clark Jr. and Caroline Higdon (Wagstaff) Giles; m. Walter Louis Weintz; children: Alexander Harwood, Elizabeth Pettus. AB, Princeton U., 1974; postgrad. diploma, U. London, 1976. Dir. advt. and promotion E.P. Dutton Pubs., N.Y.C., 1977-86; advt. cons. Assn. Jr. Leagues Internat., N.Y.C., 1986-91, advt. mgr., 1992-94, dir. of systems, 1994—. Author: The Discount Guide for Travelers over 55, 4th edit., 1988. Vol. researcher St. Paul's Nat. Hist. Site and Bill of Rights Mus., Westchester, N.Y., 1986—; treas. Soc. Nat. Shrine of The Bill of Rights; mem. Jr. League, Pelham, N.Y. Mem. Authors Guild, Nat. Soc. Colonial Dames, Huguenot Soc. Am., Daus. Cin., Mensa. Episcopalian. Home: 806 Pines Bridge Rd Ossining NY 10562

WEINZIERL, ANN CATHERINE, accountant; b. Flint, Mich., June 14, 1957; d. Thomas William and Marianne Rose (Cupal) Charlton; m. Bruce Lee Weinzierl, Feb. 24, 1979; children: Robert William, Sarah, Amanda Elizabeth; 1 stepdaughter, Christine Marie. BBA in Acctg., U. Mich., 1982. Acctg. bus. mgr. Jim Kanary Chevrolet, Millington, Mich., 1978-80; contr. R.L. White Cons., Grand Bianc, Mich., 1982-83; sr. cost acct. Gen. Instrument, Hatboro, Pa., 1984-85; dir., investment banker Butcher & Co., Phila., 1985-89; contr. Kirtley-Cole Cons., Snohomish, Wash., 1990-93; exec. dir. Rosehill Cmty. Ctr., Mukilteo, Wash., 1993-95. Coun. mem. Everett Coun. Neighborhoods, 1992-94, Everett City Coun., 1994-95; exec. bd. mem. Puget Sound Regional Coun., Seattle, 1994-95; bd. dirs. Sno County Childrens Mus., 1995-96, Sno County Alliance Mentall Ill, 1993-96; candidate for U.S. Congress, 1996. Mem. LWV, Everett Navy League (bd. dirs. 1994—), Everett Woman's Book Club (1st v.p. 1991—), Everett C. of C. Democrat. Roman Catholic.

WEIR, CAROL SWAIN, theologian; b. Oakland, Calif., Dec. 15, 1924; d. Albert George Swain and Clara Martha Armes; m. Benjamin Martin Wier, Sept. 2, 1949; children: Christine, Susan, John, Ann (dec.). BS, U. Calif., Berkeley, 1946; MA, San Francisco Theol. Sem., 1970, Am. U. Beirut, Lebanon, 1976. RN, Calif. Pub. health nurse San Francisco City and County, 1946-48; missionary Presbyn. Ch. U.S.A., N.Y.C., 1953-85; asst. prof. Christian edn. Near East Sch. Theology, Beirut, 1971-85; prof. mission and evangelism San Francisco Theol. Sem., San Anselmo, Calif., 1986-94. Co-author: Hostage Gound, Hostage Free, 1996. Mem. Am. Soc. Missiology. Democrat. Home: 7 Orinda Vista Dr Oakland CA 94605

WEIR, DARLENE, elementary education educator; b. Mt. Carmel, Ill., Jan. 18, 1953; d. Benton Douglas and Norma Jean (McClane) Rayborn; m. Patrick Lee Weir, Jan. 6, 1973; children: Trinity Janeen, Destiny Ellen. AS, Wabash Valley Coll., 1973; BA, Oakland City Coll., 1988. Cert. elem. and secondary edn., Ill. Spl. reading and math. tchr. chpt. I Bellmont (Ill.) Sch. Dist. 348, 1989-90; 2d grade tchr. South Elem. Dist. 348, Mt. Carmel, 1990—; mem. curriculum adv. bd. Nat. Curriculum Com., 1990-92; presenter sci. workshop South Sch., 1992; mem. sci. assessment com. South Dist. 348, 1993-95. City commr. Town Bd., Keensburg, Ill., 1979-81; explorer scout leader Boy Scouts Am., Mt. Carmel, 1979-80; first aid instr. ARC, Mt. Carmel, 1980—; aux. pres. Little League, Mt. Carmel, 1988-90; pres. Families Against Drugs, Mt. Carmel, 1988-92; ladies class tchr. Ch. of Christ, 1994—. Mem. South Sch. Singers. Republican. Office: South Elem Sch 715 W 3rd St Mount Carmel IL 62863-1753

WEIR, SONJA ANN, artist; b. Hazleton, Pa., Oct. 12, 1934; d. Stephen and Anna (Prehatny) Tatusko; m. Richard Clayton Weir, Jan. 14, 1956; children: Robert, Carl, Donna, Lisa, Nancy. Student of Mary Ellen Silkotch, 1963-83; student, Art Students League, N.Y.C., 1985-87. Artist Knickerbocker Toy Co., Middlesex, N.J., 1980; represented by Agora Gallery, Soho, N.Y., 1996; guest speaker career day Bridgewater High Sch., 1993, 94. One-person shows include Johnson & Johnson, Piscataway, N.J., 1992, Somerset County Libr., Bridgewater, N.J., 1992-94, Manville (N.J.) Pub. Libr., 1994; group shows include Raritan Valley Art Assn., 1982-83 (Best in Show award), Ariel Gallery, N.Y.C., 1991, Am. Artists Profl. League, 1991, 94, Barren Art Ctr., Woodbridge, N.J., 1993, Raritan Valley Art Assn., 1995 (2d prize), Agora Gallery, Soho, N.Y., 1995-96; represented in permanent collections N.W.B. Bank of South Bound Brook, N.J. Mem. Am. Artist Profl. League (editor newsletter 1992-96), Nat. Mus. of Women in the Arts, Am. Artists Profl. League (v.p. N.J. chpt. 1988-91, pres. N.J. chpt. 1992-95, show chmn. 1989-91, publicity com. 1988-91), Raritan Valley Arts Assn. (pres. 1982-84), Nat. Miniature Assn. (assoc.), Miniature Art Soc. Fla., Miniature Art Soc. Mont. Home and Studio: 25 Madison St South Bound Brook NJ 08880-1244

WEIR, SUSAN PATRICIA, Montessori administrator, consultant; b. Abington, Pa., Sept. 7, 1946; d. Francis Joseph Sheridan and Dolores Ann (Dallmer) Sheridan-Lazar; m. Thomas Albert Weir III, July 11, 1970; children: Christina Anne, David Ian, Joseph Kyle, Shawn Thomas, Tevis Edward, Brock Kenneth. BS in Elem./Spl. Edn., West Chester (Pa.) State Coll., 1968; postgrad., Temple U., 1968-70, Beaver Coll., 1989—. Cert. elem., spl. edn., nursery sch. tchr., Pa. Spl. edn. tchr. Abington Sch. Dist., 1968-71; Montessori tchr., head of sch., asst. dir. AERCO tchr. tng. Phila., 1979-87; dir. child care svcs. West Jersey Health Sys., Camden, N.J., 1989-96; adminstr. Children's House of Bucks County, Fairless Hills, Pa., 1996—; mem. vis. evaluative teams Mid. States Am. Montessori Soc. accreditation, Phila., 1992—; bd. dirs., v.p., Child Abuse Prevention Effort, Phila., 1973—. Dir., tchr. pre-sch. Confraternity of Christian Doctrine-Presentation Blessed Virgin Mary Parish, Cheltenham, Pa., 1980—; den mother Cub Scout pack 321, Boy Scouts Am., Cheltenham, 1983—. Recipient Legion of Honor award Chapel of Four Chaplains, Phila., 1983, Cert. of Appreciation Atlantic Human Resources, Atlantic City, N.J., 1994. Mem. Nat. Assn. for the Edn. of Young Children (field advisor Child Devel. Assoc., Pa./N.J., 1993—), Am. Montessori Soc. Home: 342 Kerper St Philadelphia PA 19111-4611 Office: Childrens House of Bucks County 840 Trenton Rd Fairless Hills PA 19030-1132

WEIRAUCH, DRUCILLA CONNER, faculty director; b. Washington, June 16, 1950; d. Arthur John and Lois Marie (Waters) Conner; m. Douglas Allan Weirauch, Jr., Mar. 19, 1977; children: Matthew Tyson, Daniel Ross. BA in English, Sec. Teaching, Pa. State U., 1968-72, MEd in Adult Edn., 1995. English tchr. Susquenita H.S., Duncannon, Pa., 1972-74, Park Forest Jr. H.S., State College, Pa., 1974-77; staff asst. Denison U., Granville, Ohio, 1978-84; program specialist The Carnegie, Pitts., 1991-96; faculty coord., dir. CCAC/IUP Collaborative Elem. Program, Indiana Univ. Pa, Indiana, Pa., 1995—; prof. studies in edn. Indiana Univ. Pa., Indiana, Pa.; ESL cons. Owens-Corning Fiberglass, Granville, 1980-84; chair publicity bd. Discovery, Murrysville, Pa., 1988-91; founding mem. steering com. Pa. Adult and Continuing Edn. Rsch. Conf., Monroeville, Pa., 1994; Action Rsch. literacy trainer Pa. State U., 1995—. Mem. Am. Assn. for Adult and Cont. Edn., Pa. Assn. Adult and Cont. Edn., Pi Lambda Theta. Home: 3925 Laurel Oak Dr Murrysville PA 15668-8500 Office: Indiana Univ Pa 303 Davis Hall Indiana PA 15705

WEIS, JUDITH SHULMAN, biology educator; b. N.Y.C., May 29, 1941; d. Saul B. and Pearl (Cooper) Shulman; m. Peddrick Weis; children: Jennifer, Eric. BA, Cornell U., 1962; MS, NYU, 1964, PhD, 1967. Lectr. CUNY, 1964-67; asst. prof. Rutgers U., Newark, 1967-71, assoc. prof., 1971-76, prof., 1976—; Congl. sci. fellow U.S. Senate, Washington, 1983-84; mem. grant rev. panel NSF, Washington, 1976-82, program dir., 1988-90; mem. rev. panel EPA, 1984-92; vis. scientist EPA Lab., Gulf Breeze, Fla., 1992. Mem. marine bd. NAS, 1991—. Grantee NOAA, 1977—, N.J. EPA Rsch., 1978-79, 81-83, N.J. Marine Scis. Consortium Rsch., 1987—; NSF fellow, 1962-64. Mem. Am. Inst. for Biol. Scis. (bd. dirs. 1986-88, 89-91), Soc. Environ. Toxicology and Chemistry (bd. dirs. 1990-93), Estuarine Rsch. Fedn., Ecol. Soc. Am., NOW (pres. Essex County 1972), Sierra Club (bd. dirs. N.J. chpt. 1986-88). Office: Rutgers U Dept Biol Scis Newark NJ 07102

WEISBERG, LYNNE WILLING, psychiatrist, consultant; b. N.Y.C., Apr. 11, 1948; d. Stanley S. and Pearl R. Willing. BA, Barnard Coll., 1969; PhD, U. Mich., 1972; MD, SUNY, Downstate, 1978. Diplomate Am. Bd. Psychiatry and Neurology, Am. Bd. Adolescent Psychiatry. Intern NYU Med. Ctr., 1978-79; resident in adult psychiatry Mt. Sinai Hosp., N.Y.C., 1979-81; fellow in child psychiatry Columbia Med. Ctr., 1981-83; staff psychiatrist Fair Oaks Hosp., Summit, N.J., 1983-85, asst. dir. child and adolescent psychiatry, 1985-88, assoc. dir. child and adolescent psychiatry, 1988-92; dir. child and adolescent outpatient psychiat. svcs. Psychiat. Assocs. N.J. at Fair Oaks Hosp., Summit, 1992—; pvt. practice Morristown, N.J., 1992—; cons. Bonnie Brae Sch., Millington, N.J., 1984-92. Author: When Acting Out Isn't Acting, 1991. Horace Rackham Prize fellow, 1972. Mem. AMA, Med. Soc. N.J. Office: 20 Community Pl Morristown NJ 07960-7501

WEISBURGER, ELIZABETH KREISER, retired chemist, editor; b. Greenlane, Pa., Apr. 9, 1924; d. Raymond Samuel and Amy Elizabeth (Snavely) Kreiser; m. John H. Weisburger, Apr. 7, 1947 (div. May 1974); children: William Raymond, Diane Susan, Andrew John. BS, Lebanon Valley Coll., Annville, Pa., 1944, DSc (hon.), 1989; PhD, U. Cin., 1947, DSc (hon.), 1981. Rsch. assoc. U. Cin., 1947-49; col. USPHS, 1951-89; postdoctoral fellow Nat. Cancer Inst., Bethesda, Md., 1949-51, chemist, 1951-73, chief carcinogen metabolism and toxicology br., 1972-75, chief Lab. Carcinogen Metabolism, 1975-81, asst. dir. chem. carcinogenesis, 1981-89, ret.; cons. in field; lectr. Found. for Advanced Edn. in Scis., Bethesda, 1980-95; adj. prof. Am. U., Washington, 1982—. Asst. editor-in-chief Jour. Nat. Cancer Inst., 1971-87; mem. editl. adv. bd. Environ. Health Perspectives, 1993—; mem. editl. bd. Chem. Health and Safety, 1994—; contbr. articles to profl. jours. Trustee Lebanon Valley Coll., 1970—, pres. bd. trustees, 1985-89. Recipient Meritorious Svc. medal USPHS, 1973, Disting. Svc. medal, 1985; Hillebrand prize Chem. Soc. Washington, 1981. Fellow AAAS (nominating com. 1978-81); mem. Am. Chem. Soc. (Garvan medal 1981), Am. Assn. Cancer Research, Soc. Toxicology, Am. Soc. Biochem. and Molecular Biology, Royal Soc. Chemistry, Am. Conf. Govtl. Indsl. Hygienists (Herbert Stokinger award 1996), Grad. Women in Sci. (hon.), Iota Sigma Pi (hon.). Lutheran.

WEISENSEE, MARILYNN, art educator; b. N.Y.C., June 28, 1944; d. John G. and Dorothy Marie (Comoss) W. BS, SUNY, 1966; MS, Queens Coll., 1972; PhD, Pa. State U., 1980. Cert. tchr. grades K-12, N.Y. Tchr. art Midle Coutnry Sch. Dist., Centereach, N.Y., 1966-76; grad. tchg. asst. Pa. State U., University Park, 1976-80, office mgr., 1981-87; tchr. art Marlboro (N.Y.) Elem. Sch., 1987-88; asst. prof. SUNY, New Paltz, 1988-93, Winston-Salem (N.C.) State U., 1994—; mem. adv. bd. Diggs Gallery, Winston-Salem, N.C., 1995. Title III grantee Fed. Govt., 1995. Mem. ASCD, Nat. Art Educators Assn., N.C. Art Educators Assn. Office: Winston-Salem State U 601 Martin Luther King Jr Dr Winston Salem NC 27110

WEISHAAR, MARILYN HELEN, journalist, editor; b. Deadwood, S.D., July 24, 1942; d. Edward Herbert and Helen Katherine (Bloom) Hendrickson; m. Leland Arthur Weishaar, June 22, 1968 (dec. Aug. 1995); 1 child, Brenda Rae. BS in Journalism, S.D. State U., 1964. Reporter Aberdeen (S.D.) Am. News, 1964-75, copy editor spl. sects., 1975-82, focus editor, 1982-92, day content editor, 1992—. Mem. Aberdeen (S.D.) Cmty. Theatre. Lutheran. Home: 1511 S 6th St Aberdeen SD 57401 Office: Aberdeen Am News 124 S 2nd St Aberdeen SD 57401

WEISHAUS, SYLVIA, marriage and family therapist; b. Chgo., Oct. 17, 1920; d. Isaac and Rose (Movich) Silverstein; m. James Weishaus, Oct. 25, 1940; children: Marc, Kent. BA, U. Chgo., 1942; MA, U. So. Calif., 1972, postgrad., 1974-81, PhD, 1978. Cert. marriage, family and child therapy, Calif. Dir. consumer rels. Waste King Corp., L.A., 1947-68; teaching asst. U. So. Calif., L.A., 1970-73; pvt. practice L.A., 1972—; clin. dir. marriage program U. Judaism, L.A., 1977—; rsch. assoc. Pa. State U., University Park, 1982-84. Author: Making Marriage Work, 1996; contbr. articles to profl. jours. Workshop leader Allen Hancock Coll., Santa Maria, Calif., 1980's, Calif. State U., San Bernadino, 1980's, Riverside, 1980's, Glendale (Calif.) YWCA, 1980's. Mem. Am. Assn. for Marriage and Family Therapy, So. Calif. Assn. for Marriage and Family Therapy (pres. 1980-81), Nat. Coun. on Family Rels., Western Gerontol. Assn., Am. Sociol. Assn.

WEISMAN, AMY LUDWIG, public relations executive. Investment banker Smith Barney, N.Y.C.; v.p. Drexel, Burnham, Lambert, N.Y.C.; dir. IR programs Mallory Factor, Inc., N.Y.C., 1990-91; asst. v.p. Morgen-Walke Assocs., N.Y.C., 1992-93, v.p., group head, 1993-94, sr. v.p., 1994—. Office: Morgen-Walke Assocs 380 Lexington Ave Fl 50 New York NY 10168-0002*

WEISMAN, ELIZABETH HEIN, elementary education educator; b. Muskogee, Okla., Dec. 24, 1943; d. Leonel Henry and Alice Blanche (Jones) Hein; m. Henry G. Weisman, June 18, 1966 (div. 1978); children: Julie W. Roberts, Amy S. BS in Edn., U. Ga., 1965; MS in Math. Edn., Fla. State U., 1985. Tchr. grades 6-7 DeKalb County Schs., Atlanta, 1965-70; tchr. grades 6-8 Fairview Middle Sch., Tallahassee, Fla., 1980-93, Second Chance Sch., Tallahassee, 1993—; team leader Fairview Middle Sch., 1989-93, mem. sch. improvement team, 1987-93; mem. Alternative Edn. Inst., Leon County, Fla., 1988, 89, mem. tchr. edn. adv. com., 1993-95. Mem. Fla. Assn. Alternative Educators, Leon County Tchrs. Assn., Phi Kappa Phi, Kappa Delta Pi. Office: Second Chance Sch 2600 Plant St Tallahassee FL 32304-4402

WEISS, ANN, filmmaker, editor, writer, photographer, information specialist, educational association director, consultant, researcher; b. Modena, Italy, July 17, 1949; came to U.S., 1951, naturalized, 1959; d. Leo and Athalie Weiss; children: Julia Emily, Rebecca Lauren. BA magna cum laude in English Lit. and Edn., U. Rochester, 1971; MA in Info. Sci. summa cum laude, Drexel U., 1973; MA in Comm., U. Pa., 1994, postgrad. in Edn., Culture and Soc., 1994—. Editor, chief cons. monographs, articles, freelance photographer, 1974—; cataloguer Drexel U., Phila., 1971-73; libr. Akiba Lower Sch., Merion, Pa., 1973; head children's dept. Tredyffrin Pub. Libr., Strafford, Pa., 1973-79, co-head reference dept., 1979-87; cons. in edn. and librs. Gulf Arab States Edn. and Rsch. Ctr. UNESCO, 1977—, cons. Rabbi Zalman Schachter-Shalomi, P'nai or Fellowship, 1987-88; photojournalist in Ea. Europe, mainly Poland, Ukraine and Czechoslovakia, 1987—; mem. editl. bd. Studies of Shoah, 1991—; primary investigator Holocaust rsch. team U. Pa., Transcending Trauma: Psychological Mechanism of Survival, 1989—; exec. dir. Eyes From the Ashes, 1988—, curator, 1995—. Dir., exec. producer (video documentary and archive creation) oral history project Inst. Pa. Hosp. U. Pa., (video documentary) The Institute: An Intimate History, 1992; dir., producer, writer, narrator, photographer (video documentary) Eyes From The Ashes, Archival Photographs from Auschwitz, 1989-90; dir., producer, writer, narrator, photographer; author, lyricist (with Thaddeus Lorentz/musical), Zosia: An Immigrant's Story; chief editorial cons. Puppetry and the Art of Story Creation, 1981, Puppetry in Early Childhood Education, 1982, Puppetry, Language and the Special Child: Discovering Alternative Language, 1984, Humanizing the Enemy...and Ourselves, 1986, Imagination, 1987; one-person photographic shows in U.S., Europe, Israel; represented in permanent collections including Martyr's Meml. Mus./Yad Vashem, Simon Wiesenthal Ctr./Mus. Tolerance. Active So. Poverty Law Ctr., Common Cause, promoting dialogue and understanding between Jews and Arabs, Jews and Poles; active Coun. for Soviet Jews, Internat. Network Children Holocaust Survivors; photographer Bob Edgar's Campaign U.S. Senate, 1985-86, David Landau's Congl. Campaign, 1986; mem. 2d generation adv. coun. U.S. Holocaust Meml. Mus., 1995—. Mem. ACLU, NOW, SANE, Free Wallenberg Alliance, Physicians for Social Responsibility, Amnesty Internat., New Israel Fund, Sierra Club, Shefa Fund. Office: PO Box 1133 Bryn Mawr PA 19010-7133

WEISS, CORA, foundation administrator; b. N.Y.C., Oct. 2, 1934; d. Samuel and Vera (Dourmashkin) Rubin; m. Peter Weiss, June 17, 1956; children: Judith, Tamara, Daniel. BA, U. Wis., 1956; postgrad., Hunter Coll., 1956-58. Pres. Samuel Rubin Found., N.Y.C., 1978—. Author: Women's Peace Platform for the 21st Century; radio commentator WRVR-FM, 1974-78. Vol. N.Y.C. schs., 1958-68; exec. dir., bd. dirs. African-Am. Students Found., 1959-63; exec. dir. Friendshipment, 1975-78; nat. bd. dirs. Women Strike for Peace, 1961-73; nat. co-chair Nat. Mobilization to End War in Vietnam, Washington, 1969; co-chair, dir. Com. of Liaison with Famlies of Prisoners Detained in Vietnam, 1969-73; treas. Ghandi Soc. for Human Rights, 1960-67; vol. Ch. World Svc., 1978; bd. dirs. Peace Action, 1986—, internat. rep., 1988—, mem. exec. com., 1986-94; v.p. Internat. Peace Bur., Geneva, 1989—; election observer 1st Palestinian elections, 1996; del.

4th World Conf. on Women, Beijing, 1995; bd. dirs. Nat. Network Grantmakers, 1991-92, co-chair ann. nat. conf., 1992; bd. dirs., chair exec. com. Interlegal U.S.A., 1990—; bd. dirs. US-NIS Women's Consortium, 1993—, Christianity & Crisis, 1991-92, Peace Child Found., 1989, Downtown Cmty. TV, N.Y.C., 1987—; bd. dirs., exec. com. Women for Meaningful Summits, 1985-91, del. summit meeting of Pres. Reagan and Sec. Gorbachev, Geneva, 1995, del. to Moscow Women's Conf., 1987; trustee Hampshire Coll., Amherst, Mass., 1978-81, trustee emerita, 1991—; founder, dir. Riverside Ch. Disarmament Program, N.Y., 1978-88; del. to World Coun. Chs. to Nairobi conf. Decade for Women, 1985; mem. adv. bd. Alternative Security Coun., Inst. for Def. and Disarmament Studies, Pacem In Terris Inst., Manhattan Coll., Nat. Abortion Rights Action League, Com. on Common Security, UN Amendment Conf. on Nuclear Test Ban, 1991; juror Olive Br. Award, 1991; rep. NGO Conf. on Women, 1995. Recipient Joseph C. Wilson award Rochester Assn. for UN, 1995, Lifetime Achievement award Peace Action, 1992, "We the Peoples..." award for contbn. on world peace, 1995. Mem. Coun. on Fgn. Rels., Women in Internat. Security. Democrat. Jewish. Home: 5022 Waldo Ave Bronx NY 10471

WEISS, ELAINE LANDSBERG, community development management official; b. N.Y.C.; d. Louis and Sadie Blossum (Schoenfeld); divorced. BA in Philosophy and Polit. Sci., Bklyn. Coll., 1960; postgrad., NYU Law Sch., 1960-62; MA in Sociology, Hunter Coll., N.Y.C., 1969. Social investigator N.Y.C. Dept. Social Services, 1963-64; intern, fellow Eleanor Roosevelt Meml. Found., Nat. Assn. Intergroup Relations Ofcls., 1964-65; asst. dir. housing and asst. project dir. Operation Equality, Nat. Urban League, 1965-67; program assoc. housing div. ch. missions Am. Bapt. Home Mission Socs., 1967-70; pres. E.L. Weiss Assocs., 1970-76; exec. dir. Suffolk Community Devel. Corp., Coram, N.Y., 1976-89, E.L. Weiss Assocs., East Quoque, N.Y., 1990—, Grenadier Realty Corp., 1990-92; COO Morningside Heights Housing Corp., 1992-95; exec. dir. Fairmont Housing Corp. (N.J.) subsidiary YWCA Hudson County, 1995—; mem. citizens adv. com. N.Y.C. Dept. Housing Preservation and Devel.; exec. com. L.I. Community Devel. Orgn.; past 2d v.p. Suffolk Housing Task Force; chmn. Suffolk County Citizens Adv. Com., 1981-82. Recipient cert. of commendation L.I. Council Chs., 1981, Woman of Yr. award, 1994. Mem. Nat. Assn. Housing Ofcls., N.Y. State Assn. Housing and Redevel. Ofcls., Am. Contract Bridge League (life master). Home: PO Box 1532 East Quogue NY 11942-1333

WEISS, FAEDRA LAZAR, researcher; b. Chgo., Mar. 17, 1955; d. Howard Bernard and Frances Joyce (Gameril) Lazar; m. Lewis Jay Weiss, June 1, 1980; children: Alexandra Michelle, Marjorie Ellen, Dena Nathalia. AB, Brown U., 1976; MA in Hebrew Lit., Hebrew Union Coll., Cin., 1980. Ordained rabbi 1981. Editorial asst. Hebrew Union Coll. Press, Cin., 1984-88, asst. to publs. com., 1988-89; clergy counselor Koala Hosp., Indpls., 1989-90; rsch. asst. Girls Incorp., Indpls., 1990-93, rsch. assoc., 1993—. Author: (with others) Cost-Effectiveness in the Non-Profit Sector, 1993, Informal Science Learning, 1994, Religious Methods and Resources in Bioethics, 1994, Prevention and Parity, 1996. Mem. health profls. adv. com. March of Dimes, Cin.,1986-89, Indpls, 1989-91; coun., trainer, troop leader Hoosier Capitol coun. Girl Scouts U.S., Indpls., 1989—, bd. dirs., 1990-96; mem. Indpls. Bd. Rabbis, 1989—, Rabbis and Profls., Indpls, 1989—, Indpls Arts Chorale, 1989—. Mem. AAAS, Am. Acad. Religion (co-chair religion, ethics and health care 1991-94), Am. Ednl. Rsch. Assn., Ctrl. Con. Am. Rabbis. Jewish. Home: 7805 Mohawk Ln Indianapolis IN 46260-3339 Office: Girls Incorp Nat Resource Ctr 441 W Michigan St Indianapolis IN 46260

WEISS, GAIL ELLEN, legislative staff director; b. N.Y.C., Apr. 11, 1946; d. Joseph and Elaine (Klein) W.; m. John A. Kelly. BA, U. Md., 1967. Staff asst. U.S. Office Econ. Opportunity/Job Corps, Washington, 1967-69; legis. asst. Hon. William L. Clay, Mem. Congress, Washington, 1969-72; rsch. asst. Rt. Hon. Roy Hattersley, Mem. Parliament, London, 1972-73; legis. asst. various coms. U.S. Ho. of Reps., Washington, 1973-90, staff dir. Com. on P.O. and Civil Svc., 1991-94, Dem. staff dir. Com. on Econ. and Ednl. Opportunities, 1995—; mem. working group Pres.'s Task Force on Nat. Health Reform, 1993. Democrat. Jewish. Office: Com on Econ and Ednl Opp 2100 Rayburn Ho Office Bldg Washington DC 20515

WEISS, JOANNE MARION, writer; b. Wayne, N.J., Mar. 16, 1960; d. Henry Daniel and Florence Frances (Zaratkiewicz) W. BA, Bennington Coll., 1982; MA, U. Cambridge, Eng., 1988. Prodn. mgr. The Suburban News, N.J., 1982-83; gardener Artistic Landscaping, N.J., 1983; case mgr. Mid-Bergan Mental Health Ctr., N.J., 1985-86; founder Isis Farm Writers, 1995—. Author, dir.; (play) The Gift, 1987, 88. Translator Solidarity, Poland, 1983; co-leader Vols. for Peace, 1986; mem., worker Pregnancy Adv. Svc., Cambridge, 1991-92. Recipient scholarship Inst. for Brit. and Irish Studies, Trinity Coll., Dublin, 1985, Chancellor's medal for poetry U. Cambridge, Eng., 1988, grants for Edinburgh, Sir John Gielgud, 1988, grant Judith Wilson Fund, U. Cambridge, Eng., 1988. Mem. People for Ethical Treatment of Animals. Home: Isis Farm 265 River Rd Suncook NH 03275

WEISS, JUDITH MIRIAM, psychologist; b. Chgo., June 29, 1939; d. Louis and Annette (Frazin) Schmerling; m. Jon Howard Kaas, May 19, 1963 (div. Dec. 1984); children: Lisa Karen, Jon Michael; m. Stephen Fred Weiss, Dec. 22, 1988. AB in Liberal Arts, Northwestern U., 1961; PhD, Duke U., 1969. Lic. clin. psychologist, Tenn. Postdoctoral fellow U. Wis. Hosp., Madison, 1969-71; neuropsychologist Mental Health Assocs., Madison, 1971-72; asst. prof. George Peabody Coll., Nashville, 1972-77, Vanderbilt U., Nashville, 1972-77; neuropsychologist Comprehensive Clin. Svcs., Nashville, 1977—; advocate, cons. Tenn. Protection and Advocacy, Inc., Nashville, 1976—. Mem. CABLE, Nashville. Mem. APA, Tenn. Psychol. Assn., Internat. Neuropsychol. Assn., Nat. Acad. Neuropsychology, U.s.-China Peoples Friendship Assn., Tenn. Head Injury Assn., B.R.A.I.N., Tenn. Assn. for the Talented and Gifted, Tenn. Assn. Audiologists and Speech-Lang. Pathologists, Nashville Area Psychol. Assn., Coun. for Learning Disabilities, Assn. for Children with Learning Disabilities. Jewish. Home: 893 Stirrup Dr Nashville TN 37221-1918 Office: Comprehensive Clin Svcs 102 Woodmont Blvd Ste 215 Nashville TN 37205-2287

WEISS, LINDA WOLFF, health systems administrator; b. Albany, N.Y., Apr. 12, 1953; d. Charles Vincent and Hilda Bertha (Kitzman) Wolff; divorced; 1 child, Russell. AAS, Hudson Valley C.C., Troy, N.Y., 1973; BS, Empire State Coll., 1983; MS in Health Sys. Mgmt., Union Coll., 1987. Staff nuc. medicine technologist VA Med. Ctr., Albany, 1973-83, chief technologist nuc. medicine, 1983-84, asst. chief radiology/nuc. medicine svc., 1984-87, area mgr. emergency medicine preparedness office, 1987-94; area mgr. emergency medicine preparedness office U.S. Dept VA, Albany and Syracuse, N.Y., 1994-96; dir. managed care and planning Upstate N.Y. VA Network, Albany, 1996—; mem. N.Y. State Disaster Preparedness Commn., Albany; charter mem. human needs in disaster standing com., 1989-96, Albany County Local Emergency Preparedness Commn., 1987-96, N.Y. State Vol. Orgns. Active in Disaster, 1989; mem. adj. faculty, tutor Empire State Coll., Albany; investigator Northridge Earthquake Epidemiology Study, 1995-96. Contbg. editor Jour. Clin. Ultrasound, 1981-85, Med. Ultrasound, 1981-83; mem. editl. bd. EMPO News, 1992-96. W.K. Kellogg Found. Ptnrs. fellow in internat. leadership and devel., 1990-93; Leadership VA Class of 1996; recipient Dir.'s cert. Hurricane Andrews Response, 1992. Mem. Ptnrs. of the Am. (W.K. Kellogg Found. fellow 1990-93, chair emergency preparedness com. 1991—), Proctor's Theater, Barn Raisers. Lutheran. Office: Upstate NY VA Healthcare PO Box 8980 Albany NY 12208-0980

WEISS, MADELINE, artist; b. N.Y.C., July 5, 1926; d. Max and Esther (Reiter) Stern; m. Philip Weiss, Mar. 2, 1946; children: Mark Ira, Joseph. Studied with, Lillian Orlowsky and William, Freed (proteges of Hans Hofmann), N.Y.C. Founder, pres. Nat. Assn. Women Artists Fla. chpt. Contbr. to Who's Who in Am. Art, Kravis Ctr. for Performing Art, Palm Beach Jewish Times, Culture Mag., Images Mag., News/Sun-Sentinel (Palm Beach), 1995, Ice Mag., 1994, N.Y. Times, Art in America, Artspeak Mag., 1988, numerous others; works in pub. collections/commns. include Tustin Rehab. Ctr., Santa Ana, Calif., Good Samaritan Hosp., West Palm Beach, Fla., J.F.K. Med. Ctr., Edison, N.J., Gen. Instrument Corp., N.Y., Transamerica Devel. Corp., N.Y.C., The Palm Beach County Home, Matson, Driscoll and Damico, N.Y.C., The State of Fla., Cocoa; one-woman shows include: The Hodgell Gallery, Sarasota, Fla., 1995, Studio 412, West Palm Beach, 1994, Jewish Community Ctr., West Palm Beach, 1993, Riverside Comm. Ctr., Palm Beach Gardens, Fla., 1993, Northwood Inst., West Palm Beach, 1992—, Deanna Harris Gallery, Lake Worth, Fla., 1991, United Technologies, Palm Beach Gardens, 1990, Governors Club, 1989, others; group shows include Northwood Univ. Gallery, West Palm Beach, 1995—, Royal Palm Beach Cultural Ctr., 1995—, Norton Mus. of Art, West Palm Beach, 1994, numerous others; creator of Tubular Constrns. and Geometric Abstracts. Nominated to Fla. Artists Hall of Fame, 1995, Channel 20/Artist Scene, 1992, Channel 2/PBS, 1986. Home: 117 Lake Gloria Dr West Palm Beach FL 33411

WEISS, MAREDA RUTH, dean; b. Chgo., Sept. 23, 1941; d. William Arthur and Ruth Emily (Schauble) W. BBA, U. Wis., 1963. Acct., then supr. rsch. adminstrn./fin. U. Wis. System, Madison, 1964-69; specialist, asst. dean, now assoc. dean, dir. rsch. svcs. U. Wis., Madison, 1969—; univ. chair State Employees Combined Campaign, Madison, 1986. Treas. Wis. Cen. Ctr. Aux., Madison, 1971-73, 75-77, 79-81, Frineds of WHA-TV pub. tv, Madison, 1989-91; chair nominating com. U. Wis. Credit Union, 1982-88. Mem. Nat. Coun. Univ. Rsch. Adminstrs. (presenter workshops, sec.-treas. 1980-83, chair, vice-chair mid-Am. region 1989-91, Disting. Svc. award 1989), Univ. Ins. Assn. (bd. dirs. 1982—). Office: U Wis Grad Sch 500 Lincoln Dr Madison WI 53706-1314

WEISS, MARIA CRISTINA RODRIGUEZ, cardiovascular nurse; b. San Antonio, Dec. 4, 1949; d. Rodolfo and Gregoria (Gonzales) R.; m. Laurence Rosen, May 12, 1973 (div. Feb. 1980); m. Martin Weiss. Assoc. degree, San Antonio Coll., 1971; BS in Nursing, U. Tex., San Antonio, 1973, postgrad., 1977, 1980—. Lic. nurse, Tex., 1973. Charge nurse Bexar County Hosp., San Antonio, 1973-74; ground floor supr. Luth. Gen. Hosp., San Antonio, 1974; surg. intensive care nurse Audie Murphy Vets. Adminstrn. Hosp., San Antonio, 1974-77; office adminstr., cardiovascular nurse specialist Robert N. Schnitzler, M.D., San Antonio, 1977—; med. cons. papal visit City of San Antonio, 1987, Mayor's Task Force Earthquake Relief, 1985; freelance consulting office mgr., San Antonio, 1977—; freelance fundraiser cons., San Antonio, 1977—; cardiovascular nurse cons. St. Luke's Hosp., Met. Hosp., San Antonio Cmty. Hosp.; lectr. in field, 1979-82. Treas. Yolanda Vera for City Councilwoman, San Antonio, 1986; del. Michael Dukakis for Pres., Bexar County, Tex., 1988; fundraising, phone coord. Judge Roy Barrera for Atty. Gen., 1986; bd. dirs. Arthritis Found., 1982-85, Target 90, San Antonio, 1985-90, Cen. Bario Med. Clin., 1988; active San Antonio Drug Task Force, 1986-88, Health Profls. San Antonio Honoring Mayor Cisneros; steering com. mem. Am. Diabetes Assn., 1986; speakers bur. mem. Am. Heart Assn. Smoking Coalition, 1986, non-smoker coalition speakers bur., Am. Lung Assn., 1986; cmty. liaison St. Joseph's, St. Peter's Children's Homes, 1980-82; adv. bd. San Antonio Handicap Access, 1985; pub. rels. liason United San Antonio, 1982. Named Outstanding Young Woman Am., 1977; recipient Outstanding Accomplishments in Nursing by a Nursing Cons. in Edn. and Health Svcs., 1990. Mem. Am. Heart Assn. (bd. dirs., cardiovascular nursing task force 1977-84, cardiopulmonary resuscitation task force 1980-82, cmty. svc. task force 1980-82, legis. network 1984—, speakers bur. 1986-90, active numerous fundraisers, Outstanding Achievement award 1990), Am. Critical Care Nurses Assn., San Antonio 100, Spanish Honor Soc., Sigma Theta Tau (Nurse Image Maker award Delta Alpha chpt. 1984).

WEISS, MYRNA GRACE, business consultant; b. N.Y.C., June 22, 1939; d. Herman and Blanche (Stiftel) Ziegler; m. Arthur H. Weiss; children: Debra Anne Huddleston, Louise Esther. BA, Barnard Coll., 1958; MA, Hunter Coll., 1968; MPA, NYU, 1978; cert. in Mktg., U. Pa. Tchr. N.Y.C. and Vallejo, Calif., 1959-68; dir. admissions Columbia Prep. Sch., N.Y.C., 1969-72; dir. PREP counselling NYU, N.Y.C., 1973-74; dept. head Hewitt Sch., N.Y.C., 1974-79; mgr. Met. Ins. Co., N.Y.C., 1979-84; mktg. exec. Rothschild, Inc., N.Y.C., 1984-85; pres. First Mktg. Capital Group Ltd., N.Y.C., 1985—; mng. dir. Wrap Co. Internat. N.V., 1992—; advisor Lared Group, N.Y.C., 1987—; advisor Gov.'s Hwy. Safety Com., N.Y.C., 1985-88; pres. Fin. Women's Assn. N.Y., 1984-85. Bd. dirs. 92nd Y, N.Y.C., 1972-90, ARC, N.Y.C., 1989-96, asst. treas., 1993-96. Mem. Internat. Women's Forum (bd. dirs. 1990-92), Econ. Club N.Y., Women's Econ. Roundtable (bd. dirs. 1988-90). Office: 1st Mktg Capital Group Ltd 1056 Fifth Ave New York NY 10028-0112

WEISS, RENÉE KAROL, editor, writer, musician; b. Allentown, Pa., Sept. 11, 1923; d. Abraham S. and Elizabeth (Levitt) Karol; m. Theodore Weiss. BA, Bard Coll., 1951; student, Conn. Sch. Dance; studied violin with, Sascha Jacobinoff, Boris Koutzen, Emile Hauser, Ivan Galamian. Mem. Miami U. Symphony Orch., 1941, N.C. State Sympnony, 1942-45, Oxford U. Symphony, Opera Orchs., Eng., 1953-54, Woodstock String Quartet, 1956-60, Bard Coll. Chamber Ensemble, 1950-66, Hudson Valley Philharmonic, 1960-66, Hudson Valley String Quartet, 1965, Princeton Chamber Orch., 1980-93; orchestral, chamber, solo work, 1966—; mem. Theodore Weiss poetry writing workshops Princeton U., 1985, Hofstra Coll., 1985, modern poetry workshop Cooper Union, 1988; tchr. modern dance to children Bard Coll., Kindergarten Tivoli, N.Y. Pub. Sch., 1955-58. Author: (children's books) To Win A Race, 1966, A Paper Zoo, 1968 (best books for children N.Y. Times, Book World 1968, N.J. Author's award 1968, 70, 88), The Bird From the Sea, 1970, David Schubert: Works and Days, 1984; co-editor, mgr. Quar. Rev. Lit., 1945—; contbr. poems to various jours.; poetry readings (with Theodore Weiss) at various colls. in U.S. and abroad, including China. Office: Q R L Poetry Series 26 Haslet Ave Princeton NJ 08540-4914

WEISS, RITA S., transportation executive; b. Phila., May 24, 1935; d. Jack J. and Cecelia (Alper) Brown; m. Irvin J. Weiss, Oct. 29, 1955; children: Brett David, Judith Weiss Bohn. BS in Edn., Temple U., 1955; MA in Edn., U. Md., 1976. Cert. elem. tchr., Md. Tchr. Solis-Cohen Elem. Sch., Phila., Va., 1955-59, Geneva Nursery Sch., Rockville, Md., 1966-71; dir. Har Shalom Nursery Sch., Potomac, Md., 1971-78; ednl. cons. Am. Automobile Assn., Falls Church, Va., 1978-88; program analyst Nat. Hwy. Traffic Safety Adminstrn. U.S. Dept. Transp., Washington, 1988-93, divsn. chief Nat. Hwy. Traffic Safety Adminstrn. State and Cmty. Svcs., 1994—. Author numerous traffic safety publs. Dept. Transp. fellow, 1993-94; recipient Disting. Svc. to Safety award Nat. Safety Coun., 1994. Mem. NHTSA Profl. Women's Assn. (rec. sec., area rep.), Nat. Safety Coun. (bd. dirs., chmn. edn. resources div., chmn. community agys. sect.), Md. Community Assn. for Edn. Young Children (pres., newsletter editor, historian), Childhood Edn. Internat. (assoc.), U. Md. Alumni Assn., Women's Transp. Seminar. Office: US Dept Transp NHTSA State & Cmty Svcs NSC-20 400 7th St SW Washington DC 20590-0001

WEISS, SALLY ANN, nursing educator; b. Wilkes-Barre, Pa., May 5, 1950; d. Bernard S. and Eleanor F. (Friedman) Barton; m. R. Joel Weiss, June 11, 1972; children: Stefan Craig, Alyssa Danielle. BSN, Am. U., 1972; MSN, U. Miami, 1986. RN, Fla. Clin. nurse ICU Wilkes-Barre Gen. Hosp., 1972; pub. health nurse team leader Luzerne County Vis. Nurse Assn., Wilkes-Barre, 1972-73; pub. health nurse II, coord. Pa. State Health Dept., Wilkes-Barre, 1973-74; clin. instr. community health nursing, BSN program Coll. Misericordia, Dallas, Pa., 1974; recovery rm. charge nurse Ambulatory Surg. Facility, Hollywood, Fla., 1978-85; assoc. prof. med.-surg. nursing, ADN program Broward C.C., Ft. Lauderdale, 1981—; clin. nurse specialist Neurol. Cons., P.A., Hollywood, 1994—; nursing coord. project Headstart, Broward County Health Dept., Ft. Lauderdale, 1979-81; nursing cons. spl. projects Hollywood Meml. Hosp., 1987-90, developer standards of care and practice; mem. adj. faculty, instr. state bd. rev. course Med. Coll. Pa., Phila., 1990—; presenter in field. Mem. Art and Cultural Ctr., Hollywood, 1993—, Friends of Broward Ctr. Performing Arts, Ft. Lauderdale, 1994—. Mem. AACN, Am. Assn. Neuroscience Nurses, Sigma Theta Tau. Office: Broward Community Coll 7200 Pines Blvd Hollywood FL 33024-7225

WEISS, SHIRLEY F., urban and regional planner, economist, educator; b. N.Y.C., Feb. 26, 1921; d. Max and Vera (Hendel) Friedlander; m. Charles M. Weiss, June 7, 1942. BA, Rutgers U., 1942; postgrad., Johns Hopkins U., 1949-50; M in Regional Planning, U. N.C., 1958; PhD, Duke U., 1973. Assoc. research dir. Ctr. for Urban and Regional Studies U. N.C., Chapel Hill, 1957-91, lectr. in planning, 1958-62, assoc. prof., 1962-73, prof., 1973-91, prof. emeritus, 1991—; joint creator-sponsor Charles and Shirley Weiss Urban Livability Program, U. N.C., Chapel Hill, 1992—; research assoc. Inst. for Research in Social Sci., U. N.C., 1957-73; research prof. U. N.C., Chapel Hill, 1973-91, acting dir. women's studies program Coll. Arts and Scis., 1985, faculty marshal, 1988-91; mem. tech. com. Water Resources Rsch. Inst., 1976-79; mem. adv. com. on housing for 1980 census Dept. Commerce, 1976-81; cons. Urban Inst., Washington, 1977-80; mem. rev. panel Exptl. Housing Allowance Program, HUD, 1977-80; mem. adv. bd. on built environ. Nat. Acad. Scis.-NRC, 1981-83, mem. program coordinating com. fed. constrn. coun. of adv. bd. on built environ., 1982-83; mem. Planning Accreditation Bd., Site Visitation Pool, Am. Inst. Cert. Planners and Assn. Collegiate Schs. Planning, 1985—; mem. discipline screening com. Fulbright Scholar awards in Architecture and City Planning, Coun. for Internat. Exchange of Scholars, 1985-88. Author: The Central Business District in Transition: Methodological Approaches to CBD Analysis and Forecasting Future Space Requirements, 1957, New Town Development in the United States: Experiment in Private Entrepreneurship, 1973; co-author: A Probabilistic Model for Residential Growth, 1964, Residential Developer Decisions: A Focused View of the Urban Growth Process, 1966, New Communities U.S.A., 1976; co-author, co-editor: New Community Development: Planning Process, Implementation and Emerging Social Concerns, vols. 1, 2, 1971, City Centers in Transition, 1976, New Communities Research Series, 1976-77; mem. editl. bd.: Jour. Am. Inst. Planners, 1963-68, Rev. of Regional Studies, 1969-74, 82-92, Internat. Regional Sci. Rev., 1975-81. Trustee Friends of Libr., U. N.C., Chapel Hill, 1988-94, Santa Fe Chamber Music Festival, adv. coun., 1990-91, trustee, 1991—; bd. dirs. Triangle Opera Theatre, 1986-89, 91—. Recipient Cornelia Phillips Spencer Bell award in recognition of contbns. to life and success of U. N.C. at Chapel Hill, 1996, Disting. Alumni award in recognition of outstanding contbns. in field of city and regional planning Alumni Assn. Dept. City and Regional Planning, U. N.C. at Chapel Hill, 1996, Mary Turner Lane award Assn. Women Faculty, 1994; Adelaide M. Zagoren fellow Douglass Coll., Rutgers U., 1994. Fellow Urban Land Inst. (sr., exec. group, community devel. coun. 1978—); mem. Am. Inst. Planners (sec., treas. southeast chpt. 1957-59, v.p. 1960-61), Am. Inst. Cert. Planners, Am. Planning Assn., Am. Econ. Assn., So. Regional Sci. Assn. (pres. 1977-78), Regional Sci. Assn. (councillor 1971-74, v.p. 1976-77), Nat. Assn. Housing and Redevelopment Ofcls., Interamerican Planning Soc., Internat. Fedn. Housing and Planning, Town and Country Planning Assn., Internat. Urban Devel. Assn., Econ. History Assn., Am. Real Estate and Urban Econs. Assn. (regional membership chmn. 1976-82, 84-85, dir. 1977-80), AAUP (chpt. pres. 1976-77, pres. N.C. Conf. 1978-79, mem. nat. council 1983-86, William S. Tacey award Assembly of State Confs.), Douglass Soc., Order of Valkyries, Phi Beta Kappa. Home: 155 N Hamilton Rd Chapel Hill NC 27514-5628

WEISS, SUSETTE MARIE, technical consultant, specialist in imaging; b. New Orleans, June 14, 1957; d. Stanley and Dorothy Lee (Cambre) Weiss. AA in Photojournalism, No. La. U., Monroe, 1977; PhD in Religion, Universal Life Coll., Modesto, Calif., 1990. Cert. retinal angiographer, ophthalmic asst., CPR. Prodn. supr., lab. mgr. Colorpix Custom Photogs., Inc., New Orleans, 1978-84; ophthalmic photographer Ochsner Clinic, New Orleans, 1984-85; dir. ophthalmic photography Omni/Medivision, Metairie, La., 1986-87; audivisual meeting planner, technician and cons. New Orleans, 1988-89; tech. supr. Retina and Vitreous Assocs. of Ala., Mobile, 1989; dir .photography Dauphin West Eye, Ear, Nose and Throat Specialists, Mobile, 1989-91; tech. sales rep., tech. specialist Nikon, Inc., Melville, N.Y., 1992-95; contractual cons. Simply Susette, Inc., New Orleans, 1995—. Inventor stereo-imaging calibrator and quantitative stereopsis technique. Home and Office: 5905 Colbert St New Orleans LA 70124

WEISS, TERESA ANN, elementary school educator; b. Maryville, Tenn., Jan. 13, 1962; d. Edwin Michael and Barbara Lou (French) C.; m. Benjamin C. Weiss, Mar. 17, 1988. BA, Cedarville (Ohio) Coll., 1990; MEd, Wright State U., 1994. Kindergarten tchr. Dayton (Ohio) Christian Schs., 1990; 1st grade tchr. Kettering (Ohio) City Schs., 1990—. Mem. Reading Recovery Coun. of N.Am., South Whole Lang. Support Group, Kappa Delta Pi. Republican. Southern Baptist. Home: 9976 Ainsworth Ct Miamisburg OH 45342-4570 Office: Indian Riffle Elem 3090 Glengarry Dr Kettering OH 45420-1227

WEISS, WENDY ARLENE, anthropologist, educator; b. Glen Ridge, N.J.; d. Lawrence Harold and Joyce Francine (Cohen) Weiss; m. Stephen E.Shay, May 30, 1982; children: David Weiss Shay, Rachel Lucy Shay. BS, Hamilton-Kirkland Coll., Clinton, N.C., 1973; MA, Bryn Mawr Coll., 1977, PhD in Anthropology, 1985. Asst. prof. Wheaton Coll., Norton, Mass., 1987-95; editor Jour. Latin Am. Anthropology, 1994—; resident scholar in women's studies Brandeis U., Waltham, Mass., 1994—. Doherty predoctoral grantee Doherty Found./Princeton U., 1980; NSF postdoctoral rschr., 1985, NEH postdoctoral summer grantee, 1990. Mem. Soc. for Latin Am. Anthropology (bd. councillors 1994), New Eng. Coun. for Latin Am. Studies (exec. com. 1993-95). Jewish. Office: Jour Latin Am Anthropology Women's Studies Brandeis U Waltham MA 02254-9110

WEISS-CORNWELL, AMY, interior designer; b. Mpls., Dec. 8, 1950; d. August Carl and Margaret Amelia (Wittman) Weiss; m. Dan Cornwell, July 31, 1995; 1 child, Emma Elizabeth. AA in Home Econs., Cerritos Coll.; student, Long Beach State U., Santa Ana Jr. Coll. Asst. to interior designer Pati Pfahler Designs, Canoga Park, Calif., 1974-75; interior designer B.A. Interiors, Fullerton, Calif., 1976-78, Birns Cos., Rancho Mirage, Calif., 1978-79, Carole Eichen Interiors, Fullerton, 1981, Sears, Roebuck and Co., Alhambra, Calif., 1982-84; staff interior designer Assoc. Design Studios, Costa Mesa, Calif., 1979-81; sr. corp. designer, mgr. design studio Barratt Am., Irvine, Calif., 1984-88; owner Amy Weiss Designs, Coronado, Calif., 1988—; designer in residence San Diego Design Ctr., 1990-94. Mem. Am. Soc. Interior Designers (Globe-Guilders steering com. 1989-92, chmn. Christmas party, co-chmn. Christmas on Prado 1989, 89, designer for ASID showcase house 1992, 93), Bldg. Industry Assn. (sales and mktg. coun. awards com. 1993, mem. sales and mktg. coun. 1986-88, mem. home builders coun. 1994, 2d place M.A.M.E. award 1987, 1st place M.A.M.E. award 1986, 2d place S.A.M. award 1987), Building Industry Assn. Remodeler's Coun., Nat. Kitchen and Bath Assn., Coronado C. of C., Coronado Rotary; participant in Pacific Design Ctr. Designer on Call program, L.A.. Coronado Cays Yacht Club. Home and Office: Amy Weiss Designs 10 Admiralty Cross Coronado CA 92118

WEITZMAN, EILEEN, lawyer, artist, educator; b. Chgo., Feb. 28, 1951; d. Leonard and Estelle (Apfelbaum) W. BS, U. Ill., 1973, MSW, 1975; JD, U. Minn., 1984. Substitute tchr. N.Y.C. Pub. Schs., 1993—; tchr. Jamaica Arts Ctr., Queens, N.Y., 1994—; assoc. Sheila Dugan, Esq., N.Y.C., 1995—. One-woman shows include Jamaica (N.Y.) Arts Ctr., 1993, Kentler Gallery, Bklyn., 1995; 2-woman show 101 Wooster, N.Y.C., 1992. Grantee NEH, 1978, Artists Space, 1991. Home: 784 Manhattan Ave Apt 4L Brooklyn NY 11222 Office: 233 Broadway New York NY 10279

WELCH, ANNA LIVIA, public relations administrator; b. Youngstown, Ohio, May 26, 1971; d. Roy Mathew and Marcia Jean (Lanz) W. BA, Ohio State U., 1994. Editl. asst. WOSU AM-FM-TV, Columbus, Ohio, 1992-94; assoc. dir. pub. rels. Pa. Acad. Fine Arts, Phila., 1994—. Chairperson workplace campaign United Way, Phila., 1995; mem. com. Working Fund for Phila. Area Artists Living with HIV/AIDS, 1995—; mem. events com. Phila.-DC AIDS Ride, 1996.; buddy Action AIDS, Phila., 1995—, work group mem., 1994—. Democrat. Home: 1726 Pine St Apt 3R Philadelphia PA 19103

WELCH, CAROL MAE, lawyer; b. Rockford, Ill., Oct. 23, 1947; d. Leonard John and LaVerna Helen (Ang) Nyberg; m. Donald Peter Welch, Nov. 23, 1968 (dec. Sept. 1976). BA in Spanish, Wheaton Coll., 1968; JD, U. Denver, 1976. Bar: Colo. 1977, U.S. Dist. Ct. Colo. 1977, U.S. Ct. Appeals (10th cir.) 1977, U.S. Supreme Ct. 1981. Tchr. State Hosp., Dixon, Ill., 1969, Polo Cmty. Schs., Ill., 1969-70; registrar Sch. Nursing Hosp. of U. Pa., Phila., 1970; assoc. Hall & Evans, Denver, 1977-81, ptnr., 1981-92, spec. counsel, 1993-94; mem. Miller & Welch, L.L.C., Denver, 1995—. mem. Colo. Supreme Ct. Jury Inst., Denver, 1982—; vice chmn. com. on conduct U.S. Dist. Ct., Denver, 1982-83, chmn., 1983-84; lectr. in field. Pres. Family Tree, Inc. Named to Order St. Ives, U. Denver Coll. Law, 1977. Mem. ABA, Am. Coll. Trial Lawyers (state com.), Internat. Soc. Barristers, Internat. Assn. Def. Counsel, Am. Bd. Trial Advs. (treas. Colo. chpt. 1991-92, pres. 1992-93), Colo. Def. Lawyers Assn. (treas. 1982-83, v.p. 1983-84, pres. 1984-

85), Denver Bar Assn., Colo. Bar Assn. (mem. litigation sect. coun. 1987-90), Colo. Bar Found. (trustee 1992—, pres. 1995), Def. Rsch. Inst. (chmn. Colo. chpt. 1987-90, regional v.p. 1990-93, bd. dirs. 1993—), William E. Doyle Inn. Office: Miller & Welch LLC 730 17th St # 370 Denver CO 80202-3503

WELCH, JANE SARAH, lawyer; b. Rochester, Minn., May 18, 1951; d. John and Eleanore Welch; m. Daniel Schowengerdt, May 20, 1989. BA, Ripon Coll., 1973; JD, William Mitchell Coll. Law, 1982. Bar: Minn. 1982. Adminstr. EEO programs NW Airlines, Inc., Mpls., 1974-80; rsch. asst. William Mitchell Coll. Law, St. Paul, 1981-82; law clk. Minn. Atty. Gen./Dept. Revenue, St. Paul, summer 1981, U.S. Bankruptcy Ct., St. Paul, 1983-85; assoc. Rider, Bennett, Egan & Arundel, Mpls., 1985-89, ptnr., 1990—; adj. faculty U. Minn. Law Sch., 1989. Mem. Fed. Bar Assn. (bd. dirs., v.p., sec. 1983—), Nat. Assn. Women Bus. Owners, Minn. State Bar Assn. (bankruptcy sect. 1986—, treas. 1989-90, sec. 1990-91, vice chair 1991-92, chair 1992-93, CLE planning com. 1986-94), Hennpin County Bar Assn., Minn. Women Lawyers, Minn. 100. Office: Rider Bennett Egan Arundel 2000 Metropolitan Ctr Minneapolis MN 55402

WELCH, JEANIE MAXINE, librarian; b. L.A., Jan. 22, 1946; d. Howard Carlton and Roberta Jean (Dunsmuir) W. BA, U. Denver, 1967, MA, 1968; M of Internat. Mgmt., Am. Grad. Sch. Internat. Mgmt., 1981. Asst. libr. Am. Grad. Sch. Internat. Mgmt., Glendale, Ariz., 1968-83; reference libr. Lamar U., Beaumont, Tex., 1983-85, head reference, 1985-87; reference unit head U. N.C., Charlotte, 1988—. Author: The Spice Trade, 1994; contbr. articles to profl. jours. Chpt. pres. NOW, Beaumont, 1985-87, state sec., Tex., 1986; exec. bd. Ariz. State Libr. Assn., 1976-80. Rsch. grantee Tex. Libr. Assn., 1986; named Dun & Bradstreet Info. Svcs. Online Champion of Yr., 1996. Mem. ALA, N.C. Libr. Assn. Democrat. Methodist. Office: U NC Atkins Libr Charlotte NC 28223

WELCH, J(OAN) KATHLEEN, entrepreneur; b. Pensacola, Fla., Jan. 28, 1950; d. Leslie Peter and Frances Louise (Hughes) Morales. Salesperson with Arthur Murray Dance Studio, Colo., Fla., Pa. and N.J., 1970-81; sales rep. Warner-Lambert Co., Morris Plains, N.J., 1981-83; supr., mgr. Dance Club Internat., Chatham, N.J., 1983-90; dist. rep. Nat. Fedn. Ind. Bus., 1990-95; pres. I Am Consulting, 1993—; radio sales rep. Frees Media, 1995—; developed sales program adopted nationwide by Dance Club Internat.; judge Nat. Dance Coun. Am., 1977-90; dance coach, 1975-90; coached winners U.S. Ballroom Championships Hustle divsn., 1978, choreographer, 1971-90, competitor, 1972-81; condr. New Age lectrs., seminars and workshops, 1994—, Kofutu Touch Healing, 1994—, Reiki practitioner, 1995—, Kinesiology, 1995—, Regenesis Practitioner, 1996—. Co-prodr., promoter, talent scout for TV program: Astrology Today (formerly It's in the Stars), 1989-94; performed on nat. TV with leading personalities including George Raft, Donald O'Connor and Mike Douglas. Recipient awards Arthur Murray Studio, 1971-81, 1st place counselor award Arthur Murray All Star Tournament, 1977, 1st place Supr. award Dance Club Internat., 1st place Registrar award Dance Club Internat. in the Tournament of Champions, 1984; ranked No. 1 rep. in Profls. Corner, N.Y. div. Nat. Fedn. Ind. Bus., 1991, ranked No. 2 rep., 1992, named Internat. Woman of Yr., 1993. Mem. Imperial Soc. Tchrs. of Dancing (assoc. Ballroom br., Latin-Am. br.), Am. Dance Tchrs. Assn. Mem. Unity Ch. Home and Office: PO Box 1177 Elizabeth NJ 07207-1177

WELCH, KATHY JANE, information technology executive; b. San Antonio, Aug. 5, 1952; d. John Dee and Pauline Ann (Overstreet) W.; m. John Thomas Unger, Jan. 8, 1977. BAS in Computer Sci., So. Meth. U., 1974; MBA in Fin., U. Houston, 1978. Programmer, analyst Tex. Instruments, Houston, 1974-76, project leader, 1976-78, br. mgr., 1978-81; mgr. systems and programming Global Marine, Houston, 1981-84, mgr. office automation, 1984-85, mgr. user systems, 1985-88, dir. MIS, Advanced Tech. div. Browning-Ferris Industries, Houston, 1988-89, dir. Telecom. and Computer Svcs., 1989-93; v.p. info. tech. Talent Tree Svcs., Inc., Houston, 1993-96; info. tech. cons. Tech. Ptnrs., Inc., Houston, 1996—. Mem. Mensa, Beta Gamma Sigma. Office: Talent Tree Svcs Inc 9703 Richmond Ave Houston TX 77042-4620

WELCH, RAQUEL, actress; b. Chgo., Sept. 5, 1940; d. Arm and Josepha (Hall) Tejada; m. James Westley Welch, May 8, 1959 (div.); children: Damon, Tahnee; m. Patrick Curtis (div.); m. Andre Weinfeld, July 1980 (div.). Actress: (films) including Fantastic Voyage, 1966, One Million B.C, 1967, The Biggest Bundle of Them All, 1968, Fathom, 1967, The Queens, 1967, 100 Rifles, 1969, Magic Christian, 1970, Bedazzled, 1971, Fuzz, 1972, Bluebeard, 1972, Hannie Caulder, 1972, Kansas City Bomber, 1972, Myra Breckinridge, 1970, The Last of Sheila, 1973, The Three Musketeers, 1974 (Golden Globe award for best actress), The Wild Party, 1975, The Four Musketeers, 1975, Mother, Jugs and Speed, 1976, Crossed Swords, 1978, L'Animal, 1979, (TV movies) The Legend of Walks Far Woman, 1982, Right to Die, 1987, Scandal in a Small Town, 1988, Trouble in Paradise, 1989, Torch Song, 1993, Naked Gun 33 1/3, 1993, (Broadway debut) Woman of the Year, 1982; author: The Raquel Welch Total Beauty and Fitness Program, 1984. Address: Innovative Artists 1999 Ave of the Stars Ste 2850 Los Angeles CA 90067*

WELCH, R(OBERTA) SUE, publisher, editor; b. Lander, Wyo., Feb. 3, 1943; d. Robert Ernest and Georgi Earlene (Melson) Meyer; m. Pat H. Welch, June 24, 1972; children: Heather Marie, Holly Erin, Brian Patrick. BA, Lewis & Clark Coll., 1970. Pub., editor The Tchg. Home mag., Portland, Oreg., 1980—. Office: The Tchg Home PO Box 20219 Portland OR 97220-0219

WELCH, SUSAN ELISABETH, secondary education educator; b. Crossett, Ark., Oct. 16, 1944; d. Gordon Dean and Alma Louise (Seely) Hartrick; m. Jerry F. McDonald, June 1968 (div. Aug. 1982); children: Kevin W., Brian W.; m. John C. Welch, Feb. 1995. BA in Math., Hendrix Coll., 1964; postgrad., U. Mo., St. Louis, 1965-66, U. Ctrl. Ark., 1983-86. Cert. tchr. secondary and mid. sch. math. and physics, Ark. Cartographer Aero. Chart and Info. Ctr., St. Louis, 1964-65; bus. computer programmer McDonnell Douglas Automation Co., St. Louis, 1966-73; substitute tchr. Mehlville Sch. Dist., St. Louis, 1982-83; tchr. math., physics and computer sci. TriCounty H.S., Big Flat, Ark., 1984-92; tchr. math. and physics Timbo (Ark.) H.S., 1992—; writer Pubs. Resource Group, Austin, Tex., 1996—; tchr. coll. prep. enrichment program North Ark. Edn. Svc. Coop., Mountain View, 1992-95; tutor, sponsor jr. and sr. h.s. quiz bowls Timbo H.S., 1992—. Mem. bd. trustees Leslie (Ark.) United Meth. Ch., 1993-95, mem. choir. Mem. ASCD, Nat. Coun. Tchrs. of Math., Ark. Coun. Tchrs. of Math. Home: HCR 78 Box 526 Leslie AR 72645-8916 Office: Timbo HS PO Box 6 Timbo AR 72680

WELCOM, JUDITH, lawyer; b. N.Y.C., Mar. 9, 1953. AB, Bryn Mawr Coll., 1974; JD, Boston U., 1978. Bar: N.Y. 1979. Ptnr. Brown & Wood, N.Y.C. Office: Brown & Wood One World Trade Ctr New York NY 10048-0557*

WELDEN, ALICIA GALAZ-VIVAR, foreign language educator; b. Valparaiso, Chile, Dec. 4, 1937; came to U.S., 1976; d. Pedro and Juanita (Vivar) Galaz; m. Oliver Welden, May 2, 1973; children: Arnold, Jacqueline, Cinthya, Jonathan. Grad., U. Chile, Santiago, 1955; PhD, U. Ala., Tuscaloosa, 1980. Prof. U. Chile, 1966-76; lectr. Appalachian State U., N.C., 1982-89; asst. prof. U. Tenn., Martin, 1989—; dept. chair U. Chile, Antofagasta, 1966-68; founder, editor Tebaida Lit. Rev., Chile, 1968-70. Author: Antologia de Gongora, 1962, Jaula Gruesa, 1972, Oficio de Mudanza, 1987, Alta Marea, 1989, Senas Distantes, 1990. Regional pres. Pablo Neruda's Presidential Candidacy, Chile, 1969-70. Mem. MLA, Am. Coun. Tchrs. Fgn. Langs., Tenn. Philological Assn., Soc. Chilean Writers, Ctr. Poetical Hispanic Studies, Phi Kappa Phi. Roman Catholic. Office: Univ Tenn Modern Fgn Langs Martin TN 38238

WELDEN, MARY CLARE, nurse; b. Wichita, Kans., Mar. 4, 1943; d. Lee Henry and Betty Clare (Lansdowne) Pates; m. Francis Bernard Hacker, Apr. 18, 1964 (div. Apr. 1978); children: Stephen (dec.), Michael, William. Diploma in nursing, St. Joseph Sch. Nursing, 1964; BS in Healthcare Adminstrn., Okla. City U., 1996. Staff nurse, supr. Richardson (Tex.) Gen. Hosp., 1968-70; supr., obstetrics supr. Collin Meml. Hosp., McKinney, Tex., 1970-77; staff nurse, charge nurse Presbyn. Hosp., Dallas, 1977-81; staff nurse Integris Bapt. Med. Ctr., Oklahoma City, 1981-88, quality assurance nurse, 1988—. Mem. Compassionate Friends. Democrat. Roman Catholic. Home: 1752 Lionsgate Cir Bethany OK 73008-6167 Office: Bapt Med Ctr 3300 NW Expressway St Oklahoma City OK 73112-4999

WELDIN, DONNA JO, educational administrator, educator; b. Warren, Pa., Mar. 11, 1958; d. Theodore Edward and Shirley May (Hepler) Gustafson; m. John C. Weldin; 1 child, Alicia Jo. BS, Edinboro U., 1979; MA, Hood Coll., 1987; EdD, Va. Poly. Inst. and State U., 1994. Cert. tchr., elem. and mid. sch. prin., supr., Md. 2d and 4th grade tchr. Ft.-LeBoeuf Sch. Dist., Waterford, Pa., 1980-85; 1st and 2d grade tchr. Montgomery County Pub. Schs., Rockville, Md., 1985-88, elem. curriculum specialist, 1988-89, 90-91, ednl. specialist, 1989-90, elem. sch. asst. prin., 1991-93; elem. sch. prin. Montgomery County Pub. Schs., Rockville, 1993—, tchr. cons., trainer, 1987-92; adj. prof. Johns Hopkins U., Balt.; presenter at nat., state and county confs. on alternative assessment, portfolio assessment, differentiation and curricular integration. Contbr. articles to ednl. jours.; cons. local TV show. Mem. ASCD, Nat. Coun. Tchrs. English, Elem. Sch. Adminstr. Assn., Montgomery County Assn. Adminstrv. and Supervisory Pers., Internat. Reading Assn. (Outstanding Rsch. award State of Md. chpt. 1995), Gaithersburg C. of C. Home: 15509 Quince Valley Ter North Potomac MD 20878-4721

WELDON, VIRGINIA V., corporate executive, physician; b. Toronto, Sept. 8, 1935; came to U.S., 1937; d. John Edward and Carolyn Edith (Swift) Verral; children: Ann Stuart, Susan Shaeffer. A.B. cum laude, Smith Coll., 1957; M.D., SUNY-Buffalo, 1962; L.H.D. (hon.), Rush U., 1985. Diplomate Am. Bd. Pediatrics in pediatric endocrinology and metabolism. Intern Johns Hopkins Hosp., Balt., 1962-63, resident in pediatrics, 1963-64; fellow pediatric endocrinology Johns Hopkins U., Balt., 1964-67, instr. pediatrics, 1967-68; instr. pediatrics Washington U., St. Louis, 1968-69, asst. prof., 1969-73, assoc. prof. pediatrics, 1973-79, prof. pediatrics, 1979-89, v.p. Med. Ctr., 1980-89, dep. vice chancellor med. affairs, 1983-89; v.p. sci. affairs Monsanto Co., St. Louis, 1989, v.p. pub. policy, 1989-93, sr. v.p. pub. policy, 1993—; mem. gen. clin. rsch. ctrs. adv. com. NIH, Bethesda, Md., 1976-80, mem. rsch. resources adv. coun., 1980-84; bd. dirs. Gen. Am. Life Ins. Co., Security Equity Life Ins. Co., G.D. Searle & Co.; bd. dirs., advisor Monsanto Co., 1989—. Contbr. articles to sci. jours. Bd. trustees Calif. Inst. Tech., 1996—; commr. St. Louis Zool. Park, 1983-92; bd. dirs., vice chmn. St. Louis Symphony Orch.; bd. dirs. United Way Greater St. Louis, 1978-90, St. Louis Regional Health Care Corp., 1985-91; mem. risk assessment mgmt. commn. EPA, 1992—; mem. Pres.'s Com. of Advisors on Sci. and Tech., 1994—. Fellow AAAS, Am. Acad. Pediatrics; mem. Inst. Medicine, Assn. Am. Med. Colls. (del., chmn. coun. acad. socs. 1984-85, chmn. assembly 1985-86), Am. Pediatric Soc., Nat. Bd. Med. Examiners (bd. dirs. 1987-89), Endocrine Soc., Soc. Pediatric Rsch., St. Louis Med. Soc., Sigma Xi, Alpha Omega Alpha. Roman Catholic. Home: 242 Carlyle Lake Dr Saint Louis MO 63141-7544 Office: Monsanto Co DIA 800 N Lindbergh Blvd Saint Louis MO 63141-7843

WELLEN, SARAH, retired secondary education educator; b. Bklyn., Mar. 25, 1930; d. John and Frances (Patruno) Cifarelli; m. Richard Earl Wellen, Feb. 21, 1953; children: Tami, Nina, Jemma, Alex. BA, MA, Adelphi Coll., 1951, MA, 1952. Cert. elem. and secondary English tchr., N.Y. Elem. tchr. Meadowbrook Sch., East Meadow, N.Y., 1951-52, secondary tchr. English, 1952-57; tchr. English, Commonwealth Sch., P.R., 1958-59; ESL tchr. IBM, Yorktown, N.Y., 1980-86; freelance tutor ESL, 1974-92; ESL tchr. Ossining (N.Y.) Adult Edn., 1978-80; ESL adj. Manhattanville English Lang. Inst., Purchase, N.Y., 1984-86; lectr. Horace Greeley H.S., 1974-75. Contbr. articles on folk music and poems to various mags. and newspapers. Pres., sec. Stornowaye Assocs., Chappaqua, N.Y., 1970-72; bd. dirs. PTA, Chappaqua, 1974-75. Mem. AAUW (co-chmn. social issues forum 1995-96), TESOL (membership chair Westchester br. 1984-86), Italian Club (dir. 1995-96).

WELLER, JANET LOUISE, lawyer; b. Boston, Sept. 17, 1953; d. Thomas Huckle and Kathleen (Fahey) W.; m. John Lee Holloway; children: Kelly Brianna, Janine Fahey. BA, Harvard U., 1975; JD, U. Mich., 1978. Bar: D.C. 1978, U.S. Dist. Ct. D.C. 1978, U.S. Ct. Appeals (D.C. cir.) 1979. Assoc. Cleary, Gottlieb, Steen & Hamilton, Washington, 1978-86, ptnr., 1986—. Office: Cleary Gottlieb Steen 1752 N St NW Washington DC 20036-2806

WELLES, MELINDA FASSETT, artist, educator; b. Palo Alto, Calif., Jan. 4, 1943; d. George Edward and Barbara Helena (Todd) W. Student, San Francisco Inst. Art, 1959-60, U. Oreg., 1960-62; BA in Fine Arts, UCLA, 1964, MA in Spl. Edn., 1971, PhD in Ednl. Psychology, 1976; student fine arts and illustration Art Ctr. Coll. Design, 1977-80. Cert. ednl. psychologist, Calif. Asst. prof. Calif. State U., Northridge, 1979-82, Pepperdine U., L.A., 1979-82; assoc. prof. curriculum, teaching and spl. edn. U. So. Calif., L.A., 1980-89; prof. liberal studies Art Ctr. Coll. Design, 1978—; mem. acad. faculty Pasadena City Coll., 1973-79, Otis Coll. Art and Design, L.A., 1986—, UCLA Extension, 1980-84, Coll. Devel. Studies, L.A., 1978-87, El Camino C.C., Redondo Beach, Calif., 1982-86; cons. spl. edn.; pub. adminstrn. analyst UCLA Spl. Edn. Rsch. Program, 1973-76; exec. dir. Atwater Park Ctr. Disabled Children, L.A., 1976-78; coord. Pacific Oaks Coll. in svc. programs for L.A. Unified Schs., Pasadena, 1978-81; mem. Southwest Blue Book, Freedom's Found. at Valley Forge, The Mannequins, bd. dirs. Costume Coun. L.A. County Mus. of Art., Assistance League of So. Calif. Author: Calif. Dept. Edn. Tech. Reports, 1972-76; editor: Teaching Special Students in the Mainstream, 1981, Educating Special Learners, 1986, 88, Teaching Students with Learning Problems, 1988, Exceptional Children and Youth, 1989; group shows include: San Francisco Inst. Art, 1960, U. Hawaii, 1978, Barnsdall Gallery, L.A., 1979, 80; represented in various pvt. collections. HEW fellow, 1971-72; grantee Calif. Dept. Edn., 1975-76, Calif. Dept. Health, 1978. Mem. Am. Psych. Assn., Calif. Learning Disabilities Assn., Am. Council Learning Disabilities, Calif. Scholarship Fedn. (life), Alpha Chi Omega. Office: 700 Levering Ave Apt 1 Los Angeles CA 90024-2795

WELLHOUSEN, KARYN RHEA, education educator; b. Tulsa, Dec. 14, 1959; d. Jack Eugene and Kathryn (Wakeford) W.; m. Jeffrey D. Tunks; 1 child, Katy Jo Wellhousen. BS in Early Childhood Edn., U. South Ala., 1981, MEd in Early Childhood Edn., 1982; PhD in Early Childhood Edn., Fla. State U., 1988. Tchr. Mobile (Ala.) County Pub. Schs., 1981-86; asst. prof. U. Tex., Tyler, 1988-93, San Antonio, 1993-94; asst. prof. U. New Orleans, 1995—. Contbr. articles to profl. jours. Recipient rsch. scholarship U. Tex., 1992, U. New Orleans, 1995. Mem. Assn. for Childhood Edn. Internat., Nat. Assn. for the Edn. of Young Children, Tex. Assn. for the Edn. of Young Children, La. Assn. for the Edn. of Young Children, So. Early Childhood Assn. Democrat. Methodist. Office: U New Orleans Dept Curriculum and Instrn New Orleans LA 70148

WELLING, KATHRYN MARIE, editor; b. Ft. Wayne, Ind., Feb. 4, 1952; d. Arthur Russell Sr. and Genevieve (Disser) W.; m. Donald Robert Boyle, Oct. 21, 1978; children: Brian Joseph, Thomas Arthur. BS in Journalism, Northwestern U., 1974. Copy reader Dow Jones News Retrieval, N.Y.C., 1974-75; copy reader/reporter AP-Dow Jones, N.Y.C., 1975-76; copy editor Wall Street Jour., N.Y.C., 1976; reporter Barron's, N.Y.C., 1976-81, asst. to editor, 1981, mng. editor, 1982-92, assoc. editor, 1992—. Charter mem. Northwestern U. Coun. of One Hundred. Office: Barron's 200 Liberty St New York NY 10281-1003

WELLS, CAROLYN CRESSY, social work educator; b. Boston, July 26, 1943; d. Harris Shipman Wells and Marianne Elizabeth (Monroe) Glazier; m. Dale Reed Konle, Oct. 11, 1970 (div. Sept. 3, 1982); m. Dennis Alan Loefler, Sept. 29, 1990. BA, U. Calif., Berkeley, 1965; MSW, U. Wis., 1968, PhD, 1973. Cert. ind. clin. social worker, marriage and family therapist. Vol. VISTA, Espanola, N.Mex., 1965-66; social worker Project Six Cen. Wis. Colony, Madison, 1968, Milw. Dept. Pub. Welfare, 1969, Shorewood (Wis.) Manor Nursing Home, 1972; sch. social worker Jefferson (Wis.) County Spl. Edn., 1977-78; lectr. sociology and social work Marquette U., Milw., 1972-73, dir. social work program, 1973-90, 93—, assoc. prof. social work, 1981-94, prof. social work, 1994—; social work therapist Lighthouse Counseling Assocs., Racine, Wis., 1989-91, The Cambridge Group, 1991-92; Achievement Assocs., 1992-95; vis. lectr. social work U. Canterbury, Christchurch, N.Z., 1983. Author: Social Work Day to Day, 1982, rev. edit., 1988, Social Work Ethics Day to Day, 1986; co-author: The Social Work Experience, 1991, rev. edit., 1996. Mem. Wis. Coun. on Social Work Edn., pres., 1980-82, sec., 1985-87, mem. exec. com., 1993—. Mem. NASW, Am. Assn. Profl. Hypnotherapists, Coun. on Social Work Edn. (mem. publs. and media com. 1989-91, site visitor for accreditation 1987—), Acad. Cert. Social Workers, Assn. Baccalaureate Program Dirs. Democrat. Home: 4173 Sleeping Dragon Rd West Bend WI 53095-9296 Office: Marquette U Social Work Program 526 N 14th St Milwaukee WI 53233-2211

WELLS, CHRISTINE, foundation executive; b. Grayling, Mich., Aug. 6, 1948; d. Chester John and Mary W. BA, Mich. State U., 1970, MLIR, 1982; MLS, U. Mich., 1976. Head libr. Lansing State Jour., E. Lansing, Mich., 1973-82; mng. editor libr. svcs. USA TODAY, Washington, 1982-87; libr. dir. Gannett Co., Inc., Washington, 1985-87, chief staff, chmn. and CEO office, 1988-89; v.p. adminstrn. Gannett Found., Washington, 1989-90; v.p. internat. The Freedom Forum, Washington, 1991—; exec. dir. The Newseum, 1993-94; sr. v.p. The Freedom Forum, 1994—. Mem. bd. overseers Internat. Press Ctr. and Club, Moscow; mem. bd. visitors Coll. Sci., Mich. State U. Recipient Dising. Alumni award U. Mich., 1991. Mem. ALA, Spl. Librs. Assn. (Profl. award 1994). Office: The Freedom Forum 1101 Wilson Blvd Arlington VA 22209-2248

WELLS, CHRISTINE VALERIE, music educator; b. Flushing, N.Y., Sept. 25, 1948; d. Roland Clifford and Frances Marie (Da Ros) Stoehr; m. Jonathan Freda Wells, June 20, 1970 (dec. Nov. 1989); children: Jennifer Lee, Kevin Michael, Frederick Joseph. BMus cum laude, Bucknell U., 1970; MA, U. Md., 1974. Elem. vocal music tchr. Prince George's County Pub. Schs., Upper Marlboro, Md., 1970—; cantor, substitute organist Holy Trinity Cath. Ch., Glen Burnie, Md., 1980-81, St. Stanislaus Kostka Ch., Balt., 1983—; choir dir. Gregorian Singers, Glen Burnie, 1981-90; music dir. numerous plays Pasadena Theatre Co., Millersville, Md., 1981—; music dir. for plays Act II Dinner Theatre, Rosedale, Md., 1994-95, Timonium (Md.) Dinner Theatre, 1994-95. Active fundraising Leukemia Soc., Am. Heart Assn., Glen Burnie; cantor, organist, lector Good Shepherd Cath. Ch., Glen Burnie, 1982—. Mem. Nat. Mus. Women in the Arts (charter). Republican. Roman Catholic. Home: 303 Glenwood Ave Glen Burnie MD 21061 Office: Columbia Park Elem Sch 1901 Kent Village Dr Hyattsville MD 20785

WELLS, DEBORAH JANE, elementary education educator; b. Houston, Mo., Apr. 12, 1972; d. David Clark and Patty Jo Anne (Larson) W. BS in Elem. Edn., U. Mo., 1993. Cert. tchr. Mo. 1-8 grades, Kans. K-9th grades. Tchr. 6th grade Northwood R-4, Salem, Mo., 1993—; piano tchr. pvt. practice, Salem, Mo., 1981—. Author: (poem) A Question of Balance, 1993. Mem. Nat. Coun. Tchrs. of Math., Mo. State Tchrs. Assn., Mo. Coun. for Social Studies, Sci. Tchrs. of Mo., Mid-Mo. Reading Assn., Univ. Mo. Alumni Assn. Home: 809 N Jackson Salem MO 65560

WELLS, DELLA WAGER, lawyer; b. Watertown, N.Y., Jan. 23, 1960. BA magna cum laude, U. Ga., 1980; MA, U. Va., 1983; JD with distinction, Emory U., 1986. Bar: Ga. 1986. Ptnr. Alston & Bird, Atlanta. Author: George Woodruff: A Life of Quiet Achievement, The First Hundred Years: A Centennial History of King & Spalding. Mem. ABA, State Bar of Ga. (founder writing com. 1988-89, co-chair 1989-91), Nat. Assn. Bond Lawyers, Atlanta Bar Assn., Phi Beta Kappa, Phi Kappa Phi, Golden Key. Office: Alston & Bird 1 Atlantic Ctr 1201 W Peachtree St Atlanta GA 30309-3424*

WELLS, KAREN KAY, medical librarian; b. Petaluma, Calif., Jan. 9, 1956; d. Albert Lee and Miyoko (Kay) W.; m. John Edward Guth, Aug. 4, 1979 (div. 1986). BS with honors, U. Colo., 1977; MEd with honors, U. Ill., 1980, MS with honors, 1982. Cert. tchr., Colo., Ill. Grad. asst. grad. libr. U. Ill., Urbana, 1981-82; asst. prof. med. libr. svcs. sch. medicine Mercer U., Macon, Ga., 1982-83; libr., head Presbyn.-St. Luke's Med. Ctr., Presbyn.-Denver Hosp., 1983-84; libr., dept. head AMI-St. Luke's Hosp. Health Scis. Libr., Denver, 1984-88, instr., cons. dialog pharm. database, 1985-87; head libr. Manville Health, Safety and Environ. Libr., Denver, 1988-89; info. cons. Wells Info. Svc., Denver, 1989—; sr. rsch. analyst EG & G, Golden, Colo., 1990-94; sr. adminstrv. assessor, 1994—. Editor Infosource newsletter, 1983-88. Mem. ALA, Med. Libr. Assn., Colo. Coun. Med. Librs. (cons. med.-sci. databases 1984—), Denver Area Health Scis. Libr. Consortium, IBM PC XT Users Group, U. Colo. Alumni Assn., U. Ill. Alumni Assn., Beta Phi Mu, Kappa Delta Pi. Democrat. Presbyterian.

WELLS, KATHLEEN ANNE, social services administrator; b. Santa Monica, Calif., Apr. 6, 1951; d. Gordon Thomas and Mary Clare (Sharer) Gibbs; m. Dennis Franklin Wells, June 29, 1978; 1 child, Jennifer Stacey Wells Long. BA in Comm. Arts, U Ala., Huntsville, 1988. Materials mgmt. coord. Saginaw divsn. GM, Athens, Ala., 1976-82; purchasing coord. ConAgra, Inc., Decatur, Ala., 1982-85; customer end. cons. McCormack & Dodge, Huntsville, 1986-89; aide to mayor City of Madison, Ala., 1989-90; sr. info. designer D & B Software, Huntsville, 1990-91; asst. dir. Nat. Resource Ctr. on Child Sexual Abuse Nat. Children's Advocacy Ctr., Huntsville, 1991-94, project dir. nat. tng. program on effective treatment, 1992-94; exec. dir. HOPE Pl., Inc., Huntsville, 1995—, cons., 1994-95. Bd. dirs. HOPE Pl., 1984-89, 90-93, Ala. Coalition Against Domestic Violence, Montgomery, 1995—; co-chair Madison County Coalition Against Domestic Violence, 1994—; pres. Ala. Coalition Against Domestic Violence, 1996—; mem. Mayor's Homeless Commn., Huntsville, 1995—. Recipient award for outstanding svcs. to families Gov. of State of Ala., 1987, award for outstanding svc. and dedication to families U.S. Dept. of Justice, 1990. Mem. Am. Profl. Soc. on Abuse of Children, Nat. Coalition Against Domestic Violence, United Way Exec. Dir.'s Assn. Roman Catholic. Home: 95 Oakland Trace Madison AL 35758 Office: HOPE Pl Inc PO Box 687 Huntsville AL 35804

WELLS, LESLEY BROOKS, judge; b. Muskegon, Mich., Oct. 6, 1937; d. James Franklin and Inez Simpson W.; m. Arthur V.N. Brooks, June 20, 1959; (div.); children: Lauren Elizabeth, Caryn Alison, Anne Kristin, Thomas Eliot. BA, Chatham Coll., Pitts., 1959; JD cum laude, Cleve. State U., 1974; cert. Nat. Jud. Coll., Reno, 1983, 85, 87, 89. Bar: Ohio 1975, U.S. Dist. Ct. (no. dist.) Ohio 1975. Pvt. practice, Cleve., 1975; ptnr. Brooks & Moffet, Cleve., 1975-79; dir., atty. ABAR Litigation Ctr., Cleve., 1979-80; assoc. Schneider, Smeltz, Huston & Ranney, Cleve., 1980-83; judge Ct. of Common Pleas Cleve., 1983-94; judge, U.S. District Ct. (no. Ohio)6th Cir., Cleveland, 1994—; adj. prof. law and urban policy Cleve. State U., 1979-82. Editor, author: Litigation Manual, 1980. Past pres. Cleve. Legal Aid Soc.; legal chmn. Nat. Women's Polit. Caucus, 1981-82; chmn. Gov.'s Task Force on Family Violence, Ohio, 1983-87; mem. biomedical ethics com. Case Western Res. U. Med. Sch., 1985-94; master Inns of Ct., 1989—, Northwest Ordinance U.S. Constitution Commn., Ohio, 1986-88; trustee Miami U., 1988-92, Urban League of Clevel., 1989-90, Rosemary Ctr., 1986-92, Chatham Coll., 1989-94. Recipient Disting. Alumna award Chatham Coll., 1988, Superior Jud. award Supreme Ct. of Ohio, 1983; J. Irwin award Womenspace, Ohio, 1984, award Womens City Club, 1985, Alumni Civic Achievement award Cleve. State U., 1992, Golden Gavel award Ohio Judges Assn., 1994, Outstanding Alumi award Cleve. Marshall Law Alumni Assn., 1994, Greater Cleve. Achievement award YWCA, 1995. Mem. ABA, Ohio Bar Assn., Cleve. Bar Assn. (Merit Svc. award 1983), Cuyahoga County Bar Assn., Nat. Assn. Women Judges, Philosophy Club. Office: US Courthouse 201 Superior Ave E Ste 338 Cleveland OH 44114-1201

WELLS, LINDA ANN, editor-in-chief; b. N.Y.C., Aug. 9, 1958; d. H. Wayne and Jean (Burchell) W.; m. Charles King Thompson, Nov., 1993. BA in English, Trinity Coll., 1980. Edit. asst. Vogue Mag., N.Y.C., 1980-83, assoc. editor beauty, 1983-85; style reporter New York Times, N.Y.C., 1985, beauty editor, food editor, 1985-90; founding editor, editor-in-chief Allure Mag., N.Y.C., 1990—; speaker Am. Womens' Econ. Devel., N.Y., 1988-89. Contbr. numerous articles to N.Y. Times Mag., Allure Mag., 1985—. Chmn. N.Y. Shakespeare Festival, 1993, 94. Recipient Fragrance Found. award, 1991, Nat. Mag. Design award, 1994, Legal Def. and Edn. Fund Equal Opportunity award NOW, 1994. Mem. Am. Soc. Mag. Editors (bd. dirs. 1993—). Office: Allure Mag Condé Nast Publs 360 Madison Ave New York NY 10017-3136

WELLS, MARTHA JOHANNA, elementary education educator; b. Rock Springs, Wyo., Feb. 25, 1941; d. Harold Richard and Mae Amber Rose (Langmack) Frey; children: Timothy, Duane, Amber Jo Wells Sutter. BA, Wayne State, 1964. Cert. tchr. grades K-9. Kindergarten tchr. Cherokee (Iowa) Cmty. Schs., 1960-63, Harris-Lake Park (Iowa) Cmty. Schs., 1964-66, Norfolk (Nebr.) Cmty. Schs., 1966-68; sr. primary tchr. Emmetsburg (Iowa) Cmty. Schs., 1969-75, first grade tchr., 1975-82, kindergarten tchr., 1982-92, second grade tchr., 1992—; critical reader adv. bd. Perfection Form Co., Des Moines, 1985-86; team mem. for evaluation on Paulina (Iowa) Schs.-Dept. Edn., 1985; presenter in field. Vol. helper Party for John Glenn, Marcie Frevert's Home, Emmetsburg, 1983. Mem. Internat. Reading Assn., Iowa Reading Assn. (zone coord. 1983-93, dir. membership 1993—, hospitality chairperson regional conf. 1995—, Appreciation cert. 1983), Iowa State Edn. Assn. (team interviewer 1994), Emmetsburg Edn. Assn. (profl. rights and responsibilities com. 1992—), Palo Alto Clay Kossuth Reading Coun. (newspaper in edn. com. 1990-92), Meth. Women. Democrat. Home: 1603 8th St Emmetsburg IA 50536-1442

WELLS, PATSY MAY, special education educator; b. Sayre, Okla., Sept. 22, 1949; d. Wilburn Leon and Mary June (Cole) Brown; children from previous marriage: Patricia Michele Blakley McCurdy, Mandy Camille Blakley; m. Jeré Leverette Wells; children: Jeffrey Lynn, Jason Jeré, Jeremy Wayne, Joshua William. AA, Frank Phillips Jr. Coll., 1969; BEd, West Tex. State U., 1971, MEd, 1972. Profl. spl. edn. supr. Tchr. lang. arts and social studies 5th grade Whittier Elem. Sch., Amarillo, Tex., 1972-73; tchr. kindergarten Lawndale Elem. Sch., Amarillo, 1973-77; tchr. pre-sch. E.M.H./T.M.H. Amarillo State Ctr., 1978-80; tchr. early childhood handicapped North Heights Ctr., Amarillo, 1980-85; instr. E.M.H. Acad. Elem. Sch., Guymon, Okla., 1985-86; tchr. T.M.H./multihandicapped Edison Sch., Guymon, 1986-92, Cen. Jr. H.S., Guymon, 1992; interrelated instr. Heller Elem. Sch., Neodesha, Kans., 1993-94, Thayer (Kans.) Schs., 1994—; coach bowling, track and field Spl. Olympics, Guymon, 1986-92, area 17 coord., 1990-92; chmn. curriculum and assessment com. State Ctr., Amarillo, 1978-89. Gen. bd. dirs. Disciples of Christ, U.S. and Can., 1991-95. Named Sigma Phi Tchr. of Yr., 1991, Outstanding Spl. Educator of Okla., Coun. for Exceptional Children, 1988, Spl. Edn. Tchr. of Yr., Tex. County Assn. for Handicapped, 1987-88. Mem. NEA, ASCD, Kans. Edn. Assn., Tri County Edn. Assn. Democrat. Home: 217 W 3rd St Erie KS 66733-1318 Office: Erie HS 410 W 3d St Erie KS 66733

WELLS, SHARON A(NN), primary education educator; b. Johnson City, N.Y., Dec. 6, 1943; m. WIlliam John Wells, July 29, 1967; childrne: Mardu Maree, William Mykle Jocef. BS, SUNY, Oswego, 1965; spl. edn. cert., SUNY, Binghamton, 1982; MEd, McNeese U., 1971; EdD, Nova U., 1991. Cert. early and middle childhood tchr., adminstrn. and supervision, N.Y. Tchr. Union-Endicott (N.Y.) Schs., 1965-68, 72-81, prin., 1981-82, tchr., 1982—; tchr., specialist Westlake Elem. Sch., Lake Charles, La., 1969-71; adj. prof. Broome C.C., Binghamton, 1993—; cons., Endicott, 1986—; mem. adv. bd. Day Nursery Assn., Binghamton, 1993—. Contbr. articles to profl. jours.; author: Appleseed Day Care, 1985. Coord. Cmty. Action Fund, Endicott, 1985—. Mem. Binghamton Assn. Edn. Young Children, Binghamton Reading Assn., Woman's Aux. Legion, Pre-First and Developmentally Appropriate Edn. Home: 327 Skye Island Dr Endicott NY 13760-2763

WELLS-JOHNSON, VESTA LYNN, audio/video production and manufacturing executive; b. Rapid City, S.D., Sept. 28, 1950; d. Ervin Haefs and Helen Eliza (Nelson) Wells; m. Tim Johnson, Sept. 2, 1995; children: Jessica Feliz, Amanda Renee. Grad., Rapid City High Sch., 1968; student, U. S.D., 1992—. Profl. singer midwest U.S., 1973—; owner, mgr. Creative Communications Cos., Sioux Falls, S.D., 1977-93; owner Creative Cassette, Rapid City, 1993—; model, 1968—. Active PTA, Sioux Falls, 1984-92. Recipient Addy award, 1993-94; named Miss 16 of S.D. Sixteen Mag., 1966. Mem. S.D. Advt. Fedn., Sioux Falls C. of C. Home & Office: Creative Cassette 911 Explorer St Rapid City SD 57701-0524

WELNA, CECILIA, mathematics educator; b. New Britain, Conn., July 15; d. Joseph and Sophie (Roman) W. B.S., St. Joseph Coll., 1949; M.A., U. Conn., 1952, Ph.D., 1960. Instr. Mt. St. Joseph Acad., 1949-50; asst. instr. U. Conn., 1950-55; instr. U. Mass., Amherst, 1955-56; prof., chmn. dept. math. and physics U. Hartford, 1957-82, dean Coll. Edn., Nursing and Health Professions, 1982-91, prof. math., 1991—. Mem. Math. Assn. Am., Nat. Council Tchrs. Math., Assn. Tchrs. Math. Conn., Sigma Xi. Office: U Hartford Dana 295A Bloomfield Ave West Hartford CT 06117

WELSH, DEBORAH PERLMAN, psychology educator, clinical psychologist; b. Rochester, N.Y., Feb. 17, 1964; d. Matthew S. and Linda (Lesker) Perlman; m. Christopher John Edward Welsh, July 22, 1989; 1 child, Rachel. BS, Cornell U., 1986; MS, U. Mass., 1988, PhD, 1992. Lic. psychologist, Tenn. Postdoctoral fellow U. Mass., 1992-93; asst. prof. psychology U. Tenn., Knoxville, 1993—; manuscript reviewer, Jour. Adolescent Rsch., Jour. Early Adolescence, 1993—. Recipient J.H. Block Dissertation award, Henry Murray Rsch. Ctr. Radcliffe Coll., 1990; rsch. grantee NIMH, 1995-96. Mem. APA, Nat. Adolescent Health Promotion Network, Soc. Rsch. on Adolescence. Office: Univ Tenn Dept Psychology Austin Peay Bldg Knoxville TN 37996-0900

WELSH, DIANE M., judge. BA in Polit. Sci. magna cum laude, Villanova U., 1976, JD, 1979. Bar: Pa. 1979, U.S. Dist. Ct. (ea. dist.) Pa. 1981, U.S. Ct. Appeals (3rd cir.) 1984, U.S. Supreme Ct. 1985. Legal counsel Pa. Senate Judiciary Com., 1980-81; dep. dist. atty. Bucks County Dist. Atty.'s Office, Pa., 1981-84; ptnr. Gold-Bikin Welsh & Assocs., 1984-94; magistrate judge U.S. Dist. Ct. (ea. dist.) Pa., Phila., 1994—; spkr. in field. Contbr. articles to legal jours. Trustee Manor Jr. Coll., 1981-83, Norristown State Hosp., 1987-90. Mem. ABA, Fed. Bar Assn., Fed. Magistrate Judge Assn., Nat. Assn. Women Judges, Pa. Bar Assn., Montgomery County Bar Assn., Phila. Bar Assn., Brehon Law Soc. Office: US Courthouse 601 Market St Rm 4613 Philadelphia PA 19106-1510

WELSH, DOROTHY DELL, educator, author; b. Pryor, Okla., Feb. 13, 1935; d. Roland Fields and Martha Gladys (Sheppard) Butler; m. James Robert Welsh, June 26, 1965; children—Pamela Jeanne (dec.), James Michael, Julie Marie. B.A., U. Okla., 1957, M.A., 1964; postgrad. U. Tex.-Austin, 1983-84, Tex.-San Antonio, 1984. Newspaper reporter Pryor Jeffersonian (Okla.), 1955; tchr. English and journalism Classen High Sch., Oklahoma City, 1957-61, Henderson Jr. High Sch. (Nev.), 1961-62; dir. publs. Amarillo High Sch. (Tex.), 1962-64; tchr. English, Palmdale High Sch. (Calif.), 1964-65; tchr. English and journalism Desert High Sch., Edwards, Calif., 1965-66; lectr. English, San Antonio Coll., 1979-88; teaching assoc. U. Tex., San Antonio, 1986-91; reporter Swimming World mag., Sedona, Ariz., 1980—; lectr. journalism John Brown U., 1992. Author: Fact, Fiction and Poetic License, To Seattle for a Bone Marrow Transplant, The Butlers of Oklahoma. Editor The Cresent News, 1974-80, 83-86, The Swimmer's Ear, 1983-84, Off the Blocks, 1985-86; contbr. articles to profl. jours. Bd. dirs., publicity chmn. South Tex. Swimming Assn., Austin, 1982-84; info. com. Tex. Swimming Assn., San Antonio, 1983-84. Recipient Service award San Antonio Aquatic Club, 1983; Proficiency citation Superior work journalism Univ. Interscholastic League, Austin, 1964. Mem. MLA, MLA South Central chapter, Society Professional Journalists, Women in Communications, Inc., Journalism Educators Assn., U. Okla. Assn., Mayes County Hist. Soc., Nat. Council Tchrs. of English, Conf. Coll. Composition Commun. Gamma Phi Beta (svc. award 1977, Internat. Merit Roll 1986, pres. 1972-73, v.p. 1973-74). Baptist. Office: PO Box 122 Collinsville OK 74021

WELSH, MELINDA ANN, editor; b. L.A., Sept. 3, 1956; d. Martin G. and Patricia (Corkill) W.; m. Dave Webb, Apr. 3, 1982. BS, U. Calif., Davis, 1981. Journalist, 1982—; editor Sacramento News & Rev., 1989—; exec. editor 3 newspapers News & Rev., Sacramento, Chico, Reno, 1995—; bd. dirs. Inst. for Alternative Journalism, San Francisco; bd. dirs., v.p. Chico Cmty. Pub. Inc. Recipient 24 1st and 2d place awards Calif. Newspaper Pubs. Assn., 1990-95, award for newspaper excellence Nat. Newspaper Assn., 1993. Mem. Soc. for Profl. Journalists (award for excellence), First Amendment Coalition, Assn. of Alternative Newsweeklies. Democrat. Home: 914 Snyder Dr Davis CA 95616 Office: Sacramento News & Review 1015 20th St Sacramento CA 95814

WELSHIMER, GWEN R., state legislator, real estate broker, appraiser, tax consultant; b. Poughkeepsie, N.Y., Nov. 5, 1935; d. Freanor Ralph and Beulah M. (Reedy) Grant; m. Billy L. Blake (div. 1979); children: Donald E., Jerry A.; m. Robert E. Welshimer. Student, Kans. State U., 1953-54; cert., Jones Real Estate Coll., Colorado Springs, Colo., 1975. Cert. real estate appraiser, 1993. Exec. sec. Coll. Bd. Trustees, Bellevue, Wash., 1967-69; exec. sec. to chmn. bd. dirs. Garvey Industries, Wichita, Kans., 1969-73, adminstrv. asst. pers. and pub. affairs, 1969-73; copywriter Walter Drake & Sons, Colorado Springs, 1973-75; real estate agt. UTE Realty, Colorado Springs, 1975-76; newspaper pub., owner Black Forrest News, Colorado Springs, 1976-79; real estate broker, appraiser Gwen Welshimer Real Estate, Wichita, 1979—; coord. Epic Real Estate Sch., Wichita, 1988—; legislator Kans. Ho. of Reps., Topeka, 1990—; mem. taxation com., mem. banking and ins. com. Kans. Ho. or Reps., Topeka, 1991-96; minority leader local govt. and joint com. adminstrv. rules regulations Kans. Ho. of Reps., Topeka, 1994-96. Dem. precinct committeewomen, Wichita; bd. dirs. United Meth. Urban Ministries, Wichita, 1990—. Mem. NOW, Nat. Women's Polit. Caucus, Nat. Order Women Legislators (state dir. 1994-96), Nat. Conf. State Legislators (Kans. mem. Art and Tourism Ctr.). Democrat. Methodist. Home: 6103 Castle Dr Wichita KS 67218-3601 Office: Kans Ho of Reps State Capitol Topeka KS 66612

WELSOME, EILEEN, journalist; b. N.Y.C., Mar. 12, 1951; d. Richard H. and Jane M. (Garity) W.; m. James R. Martin, Aug. 3, 1983. BJ with honors, U. Tex., 1980. Reporter Beaumont (Tex.) Enterprise, 1980-82, San Antonio Light, 1982-83, San Antonio Express-News, 1983-86, Albuquerque Tribune, 1987-94. Recipient Clarion award, 1989, News Reporting award Nat. Headliners, 1989, John Hancock award, 1991, Mng. Editors Pub. Svc. award AP, 1991, 94, Roy Howard award 1994, James Aronson award, 1994, Gold Medal award Investigative Reporters and Editors, 1994, Sigma Delta Chi award, 1994, Investigative Reporting award Nat. Headliners, 1994, Selden Ring award, 1994, Heywood Broun award, 1994, George Polk award, 1994, Sidney Hillman Found. award, 1994, Pulitzer Prize for nat. reporting, 1994; John S. Knight fellow Stanford U., 1991-92.

WELTER, LINDA ALLAIRE, development executive; b. Bayonne, N.J., Aug. 11, 1949; d. Godfrey Adolf and Grace Elizabeth (Buss) W. BA in Philosophy and Polit. Sci., Drew U., 1971, postgrad., 1972-73; postgrad., Harvard U., 1985; MBA, Boston Coll., 1987. Development asst. Harvard U., Cambridge, Mass., 1980-83, development assoc., 1983-85, dir. class and area programs, 1985-86, sr. development officer, 1986-87; from capital campaign dir. to asst. v.p. for resources Wellesley (Mass.) Coll., 1987-93; v.p., gen. mgr. for development ops. ARC, Washington, 1993-94; dir. major gifts U. Calif., Berkeley, 1994—; instr. Stonehill Coll., Easton, Mass.; lectr. Northeastern U., Boston; cons. Vassar Coll.; fundraising cons. Dimock Comty. Health Ctr., Boston, 1992. Vol. co-chair fundraising Ruah; mem. capital campaign com. Fenway Cmty. Health Ctr.; vol. Nat. Network on Women as Philanthropists. Mem. Women in Development (bd. dirs., chair city svc. project), Coun. for Advancement and Support of Edn. (teaching faculty 1985—), Women in Philanthropy. Office: U Calif Univ Rels 2440 Bancroft Way Berkeley CA 94720

WELTMAN, EVELYN R., accountant; b. Chgo., Mar. 26, 1916; d. Benjamin M. and Anna (Miner) Shulman; m. Seymour Pollyea, June 1938 (wid. Nov. 1941); m. Paul L. Weltman, Sept. 25, 1943; children: Adele M., Burton D., Stewart M. BA, Northwestern U., Evanston, Ill., 1937. CPA. CPA H.R. Hurwitz & Co., Chgo., 1942-44, Weltman & Co., Chgo., 1946-89, Weltman, Katz, Mirell & Nechtow, Ltd., Chgo., 1989—. Treas., co-founder Cancer Prevention Ctr., Chgo., 1942; pres. Portes Cancer Prevention Ctr., Chgo., 1976-80; bd. dirs. Jewish Coun. of Urban Affairs, Chgo., Jewish Coun. of Urban Affairs, 1970—, Harpen Ct. Found., 1972—. Recipient Civic award City of Chgo., 1977, Hon. award Nat. Conf. of Christians and Jews, Chgo., 1977, Yr. of the Woman award Operation Push, Chgo., 1978. Office: Weltman Katz Mikell & Nechton Ltd 8 S Michigan Ave Chicago IL 60603

WELTON, ALICE GORDON (GUILFOY), artist; b. Balt., May 26, 1948; d. John Berryman and Helen (Gaddy) Guilfoy; m. James Frank Welton, Nov. 23, 1968; children: Jaime Alan, Eric Grahame. Student, No. Ill. U., 1966-67, Elgin C.C., 1976-79, 87-89; studied sculpture and pottery with Dale Raddatz and Michael Brown, 1972-74; studied watercolor with Alan Yau, 1981-83. Draftsperson Western Electric, Rolling Meadows, Ill., 1968-69; tech. illustrator Hallicrafters, Palatine, Ill., 1969-70; advt. mgr. ABC Records & Tapes, Elk Grove, 1970-71; performer, studio singer Chgo., 1972-76; fine artist Welton Fine Arts, Elgin, Ill., 1977—; instr. gifted art program U46 Sch. Dist. Coleman Sch., Elgin, 1982; presenter watercolor workshop U. Wis., Whitewater, 1982, Des Plaines (Ill.) Art Guild, 1987, handmade paper workshop Mary Bell Galleries, Chgo., 1989, Lincoln Coll., 1990; guest artist Artist to Artist, 1990. One-woman shows include Ill. Inst. Tech., Chgo., 1987, Mary Bell Galleries, Chgo., 1983, 84, 85, 86-87, 88, 89, 90, 92, 95, Judith Posner Gallery, Milw., 1989, 93, Mary Bell Galleries, 1995; exhibited in group shows at Mazur-Mazur Gallery, Deerfield, Ill., 1982, Mary Bell Galleries, 1983, 84, 86, 88, 93, 94, 95, 96, No. Ill. U. Swen Parson Gallery, DeKalb, 1986, Art Expo, N.Y.C., 1988, Katy Gingrass Galleries, Milw., 1993, Corp. Artworks, Schaumburg, Ill., 1993, 94; juried and nat. competitions House Gallery Mus., Oklahoma City, 1981, Westmoreland County Mus. Art, Greensburg, Pa., 1982, others; corp. collections include United Airlines, Arthur Young, Amoco, Prudential Ins. of Chgo., OCE USA, Chgo. Title and Trust, La Salle Internat. Group, Inc., Marshall Field and Co., Nat. Assn. Ind. Insurers; represented by Mary Bell Galleries, Chgo., Posner Fine Art, L.A., Corp. Art Works, Schaumburg, Kity Gingrass Gallery, Windsor Gallery, Dania, Fla. 2d degree Black Belt instr. Kwon's Taekwondo, Bloomingdale, Ill., 1992-93. Recipient Sparring Gold medal Wis. State Champion World Taekwondo Fedn., exec. sr. div. 1991, Forms Gold medal, Sparring Bronze medal Ill. State Champion, 1992, Forms Gold medal, Sparring Silver medal Nat. Champion World Taekwondo Fedn. Hampton (Va.) Coliseum, 1992. Mem. Am. Watercolor Soc. (assoc.), Midwest Watercolor Soc., Ill. Watercolor Soc., Ga. Watercolor Soc., Chgo. Artist Coalition.

WELTY, EUDORA, author; b. Jackson, Miss.; d. Christian Webb and Chestina (Andrews) W. Student, Miss. State Coll. for Women; B.A., U. Wis., 1929; postgrad., Columbia Sch. Advt., 1930-31. Author: A Curtain of Green, 1941, The Robber Bridegroom, 1942, The Wide Net, 1943, Delta Wedding, 1946, Music From Spain, 1948, Short Stories, 1949, The Golden Apples, 1949, The Ponder Heart, 1954 (William Dean Howells medal Am. Acad. Arts and Letters 1955), The Bride of the Innisfallen, 1955, Place in Fiction, 1957, The Shoe Bird, 1964, Thirteen Stories, 1965, A Sweet Devouring, 1969, Losing Battles, 1970 (Nat. Book award nomination 1971), One Time, One Place, 1971 (Christopher Book award 1972), The Optimist's Daughter, 1972 (Pulitzer prize in fiction 1973), The Eye of the Story, 1978, The Collected Stories of Eudora Welty, 1980 (Notable Book award ALA 1980, Am. Book award 1981), One Writer's Beginnings, 1985 (Am. Book award 1984, Nat. Book Critics Circle award nomination 1984), Eudora Welty Photographs, 1989, A Writer's Eye: Collected Book Reviews, 1994, Monuments to Interruption: Collected Book Reviews, 1994; editor: (with Ronald A. Sharp) The Norton Book of Friendship, 1991; contbr.: New Yorker. Recipient O. Henry award, 1942, 43, 68, Creative Arts medal for fiction Brandeis U., 1966, Nat. Inst. Arts and Letters Gold Medal, 1972, Nat. Medal for Lit., 1980, Presdl. Medal of Freedom, 1980, Commonwealth medal MLA, 1984, Nat. Medal of Arts, 1987; Lit. grantee Nat. Inst. Arts and Letters, 1944; Guggenheim fellow, 1942; Chevalier de l'Ordre des Arts et Lettres (France), 1987. Mem. Am. Acad. Arts and Letters. Home: 1119 Pinehurst Pl Jackson MS 39202-1812*

WEMPLE-KINDER, SUZANNE FONAY, history educator; b. Veszprém, Hungary, Aug. 1, 1927; came to U.S., 1949; d. Ernest Fonay and Magda (Mihalyfy) Széchényi; m. George Barr Wemple, June 17, 1956 (dec. Apr. 1988); children: Peter, Stephen, Carolyn; m. Gordon T. Kinder, May 26, 1990. Student, English Sisters, Budapest, Hungary, 1945; BA, U. Calif., Berkeley, 1953; MLS, Columbia U., 1955, PhD, 1967. Reference asst. Columbia U. Libr., N.Y.C., 1955-58, Stern Coll., N.Y.C., 1963-64, Tchr.'s Coll., N.Y.C., 1964-66; prof. Columbia U., Barnard Coll., N.Y.C., 1966-92, prof. emerita, 1992—. Author: Atto of Vercelli, Church, State and Society in the Tenth Century, 1979, Women in Frankish Society, Marriage and the Cloister, 1981 (Berkshire Book prize 1982); co-editor: Women in Medieval Society, 1983; contbr. essay to A History of Women Vol. II: Silences of the Middle Ages, 1992; contbr. articles to profl. jours., essays to books. Grantee Spivak-Summer Barnard Coll., 1970, 81, NEH, 1974-75, 81-86, Fulbright Found., 1982. Home: 1285 Gulf Shore Blvd N Naples FL 34102

WENC, CHARLENE CATHERINE, clinical counselor, speaker, educator, author; b. Chgo., Nov. 11, 1942; d. Ralph Raymond and Catherine Frances (Rabig) Wege; m. Stephen Henry Wenc, Jan. 30, 1965; children: Stephen, Matthew. BS, Alverno Coll., Milw., 1964; MEd, DePaul U., 1971. Lic. clin. counselor, Ill. Sch. counselor sch. dist., Oak Brook, Ill., Glen Ellyn, Ill.; sch. counselor Sch. Dist. 180, Burr Ridge, Ill.; profl. speaker CCW Enterprises, Burr Ridge; pvt. practice counseling, Burr Ridge; prof. Adler Sch. Profl. Psychology, Chgo.; presenter on cable TV, Ill.; drug prevention counselor Sch. Dist. 63, Burr Ridge. Author: Cooperation: Learning through Laughter, Parenting-Are We Having Fun Yet!. Mem. sch. bd. Sch. Dist. 180. Recipient Those Who Excell in Edn., State of Ill. Mem. ACA, Nat. Speakers Assn. Roman Catholic. Home and Office: 10 S 550 Glen Dr Burr Ridge IL 60521

WENDELBOE, FRANCINE, legislator; b. N.Y.C., Mar. 28, 1953; d. Jesse Ernest and Lucille (Grassi) Smith; m. Matthew Wendelboe, Oct. 26, 1976; children: Jonathan, Christopher. AA in Criminal Justice, U. No. Fla., 1975; graduate, Fla. Police Acad., 1975. Retail merchandiser Montgomery Wards, N.Y.C., 1977-78; self-employed real estate broker, 1980—; mem. N.H. Legislature, Concord, 1995—; owner Little Treasures Day Care, Ashland, N.H., 1985-90. Bd. dirs. State Fair, Plymouth, N.H., 1985-92, pres., 1992-93; local dir. Miss Am. Scholarship Program, N.H., 1985-94; religious class tchr. St. Agnes Ch., Ashland, 1990-96; mem. bldgs. com., nursing homes com. Belknap County Commr., Laconia, N.H., 1993-96. Mem. New Hampton Garden Club (pres. 1981-85, dist. dir. 1983-96). Republican. Roman Catholic. Home: Treasure Valley RF01 Ashland NH 03217 Office: PO Box Xb 244 New Hampton NH 03256

WENDELL, BARBARA TAYLOR, retired real estate agent; b. Ames, Iowa, Jan. 30, 1920; d. Harvey Nelson and Ruby (Britten) Taylor; m. Donald Thomas Davidson Sr., May 22, 1942 (dec. Oct. 1962); children: Donald Thomas Jr., John Taylor, Ann Elizabeth Davidson Costanzo; m. Connell S. Wendell, Oct. 10, 1992 (dec. Sept. 1995). BS in Home Econs. Sci., Iowa State U., 1943. Assoc. tchr. Ames (Iowa) Pub. Schs., 1970-73; retail mgr. Gen. Nutrition Ctr., Ames, 1974-77; sales assoc. Century 21 Real Estate, Ames, 1978-82, Friedrich Realty, Ames, 1982-89. Pres. Ames City PTA Coun., 1950; leader, advisor Boy Scouts Am., Ames, 1952-58; chmn. Campfire Leaders' Assn., Ames, 1959-61; sec. bd. dirs. Campfire Girls, Ames, 1964-66; property com. United Meth. Ch., Ames, 1964-67; vol. Para-Legal Svcs. for Elderly; active Octagon for the Arts, Brunier Gallery, Med. Ctr. Aux., Art Gallery Com. Mem. Nat. Home Econs. in Homemaking (chmn. fgn. student rels. com.), Internat. Orch. Assn., Iowa State U. Meml. Union (life), Iowa State U. Alumni Assn. (life), Ames Community Arts Coun. Republican. Home: 1110 Johnson St Ames IA 50010-4206

WENDELL, MARIE ELLEN, retired special education educator; b. West Frankfort, Ill., May 28, 1928; d. James Chris and Albina (Pavlaskas) Nickoloff; m. Donald George Wendell, Dec. 18, 1954 (dec. Oct. 1988); children: Donald II (dec.), Nancy Marie (dec.). BS in Edn., So. Ill. U., 1954; postgrad., U. Louisville, 1961. Tchr. elem. schs. Springfield, Ill., 1954-56; tchr. spl. edn. Allentown, Pa., 1956-58; counselor edn. N.J. Commn. for the Blind, Newark, 1959-60; tchr. educable handicapped grades 7-12 Louisville, 1961-88. Mem. NEA, Ky. Edn. Assn. Roman Catholic. Home: PO Box 91533 Louisville KY 40291-0533

WENDELN, DARLENE DORIS, English language educator; b. Indpls., July 18, 1956; d. Robert Edward and Doris Mae (Brabender) W. BS, U. Indpls., 1978; MS, Ind. U., 1986. Lic. tchr., Ind. Secondary English tchr., coach Centerville (Ind.)-Abington Sch. Corp., 1978—; coach girls' tennis regional and sectional championships. Mem. NEA, Nat. Coun. Tchrs. English, Ind. H.S. Tennis Coaches Assn., U.S. Tennis Assn. Lutheran. Office: Centerville High Sch Willow Grove Rd Centerville IN 47330

WENDER, DEBORAH ELIZABETH, policy consultant, social worker; b. Sacramento, June 30, 1954; d. Joseph Andrew Sr. and Caroline Elizabeth (Wulff) Wender; adopted children: Alexander Darius Andrew, Zodie Miriam Caroline. AA, American River Coll., Sacramento, 1974; BA, Calif. State U., Sacramento, 1980, MSW, 1988. Counselor coord. Sacramento Women's Ctr., 1980-81, rape crisis project dir., 1981-84; program coord. Rape Prevention Edn. Program, U. Calif., Davis, 1984-87; criminal justice specialist Calif. Office Criminal Justice Planning, Sacramento, 1988-89; assoc. health program advisor Office of AIDS Calif. Dept. Health Svcs., Sacramento, 1989-91, pub. health social work cons. maternal and child health, 1991-93, assoc. govtl. program analyst Medi-Cal Eligibility, 1993-95; social svcs. consultant III Child Welfare Svcs. Bur. Calif. Dept. Social Svcs., 1995—; contract social worker Family Connections Adoptions, 1995—. Bd. dirs. Child Sexual Abuse Treatment Ctr., Yolo County, Woodland, Calif., 1984-86, WomanKind Health Clinic, Sacramento, 1984-86; bd. dirs. Sacramento Women's Ctr., 1987-91, bd. pres. 1989-91. Democrat. Home: 8649 Glenroy Way Sacramento CA 95826-1743

WENDLAND, CLAIRE, nursing administrator, geriatrics nurse; b. Havre, Mont., July 5, 1952; d. Sam W. and W. Inez (Dent) Berge; m. John Wendland, Sept. 20, 1975; children: Erin Mariah, Jared Keefe. ADN, No. Mont. Coll., 1973, BSN, 1993. RN, Mont. Staff nurse II pediatric unit Mont. Deaconess Med. Ctr., Great Falls, 1973-75; supr. staff nurse Lutheran Home of the Good Shepherd, Havre, 1985-87, dir. insvc. edn., 1987-88, DON, 1989-94, adminstr., 1993-94; cmty. programs coord. No. Mont. Hosp., Havre, 1995—. Mem. Evang. Luth. Ch. Am. Mem. Mont. Dirs. Long Term Care, Mont. Health Care Assn., Mont. Gerentol. Soc., Nat. League Nursing.

WENDROW, SYLVIA DIANN, speech and language pathologist; b. Ann Arbor, Mich.; d. Barnaby Alex and Margaret (Myers) W. AB, U. Mich., 1959, MS, 1963. Speech pathologist Lenawee Intermediate Sch. Dist., Adrian, Mich., 1959—; critic tchr. U. Mich., Ann Arbor, Mich., 1966-69; guest lectr. Adrian Coll., 1984; speech cons. Adrian Community Nursery, 1969-70. Sec., bd. dirs., performer Lenawee Pops Orch., Adrian, 1970-74; bd. dirs. Lenawee Community Concert Assn., Adrian, 1969-78. Named Spl. Edn. Itinerant Tchr. of Yr., 1990. Mem. NEA, AAUW (pres. 1966-68, bd. dirs.), LWV (bd. dirs. Lenawee chpt. 1974-78), Am. Speech-Lang.-Hearing Assn. (Continuing Edn. award 1990, 92, 95), Lenawee Intermediate Edn. Assn., Mich. Speech-Lang.-Hearing Assn., Sigma Alpha Iota. Office: Lenawee Schs Spl Edn Ctr 2946 Sutton Rd Adrian MI 49221-8301

WENDT, CHRISTINE HOLLY, physician, researcher; b. Madison, Wis., Dec. 25, 1959; d. Earl S. and Ruth Sylvia (Wittwer) Johnson. BS summa cum laude, U. Minn., 1982, MD, 1986. Diplomate Am. Bd. Internal Medicine. Resident in internal medicine U. Minn., Mpls., 1986-89, chief resident in internal medicine, 1989-90, fellow in pulmonary and critical care, 1990-93, instr. pulmonary and critical care, 1993-94, asst. prof. medicine, 1994—. Recipient Fellowship award Am. Lung Assn., 1992-94, Cecil Watson award Minn. Soc. for Internal Medicine, 1993, Clin. Investigation Devel. award NIH, 1994—; Am. Heart Assn. grantee, 1996—. Mem. ACP, Am. Thoracic Soc., Am. Coll. Chest Physicians, Alpha Omega Alpha. Office: Univ Minn Box 276 UMHC 420 Delaware St SE Minneapolis MN 55455

WENDT, KRISTINE ADAMS, librarian; b. Beaver Dam, Wis., May 29, 1951; d. Howard Thomas and Dorothy H.M. (Bernhardt) Adams; m. Gene Richard Wendt, Oct. 29, 1977. BA in History/Broad Field Social Studies, Carroll Coll., 1973; MA in Libr. Sci., U. Wis., 1974. Cert. grade 1 pub. libr. Children's libr., asst. dir. Rhinelander (Wis.) Dist. Libr., 1974—. Columnist Rhinelander Daily News, 1976—. Vol. Sta. WXPR Pub. Radio, Rhinelander, 1989—; coord. Great Am. Libr. Worm Race, Rhinelander, 1989—; co-chair Children's Book Fest, Rhinelander, 1988—; adv. bd. Wis. State Hist. Soc. Office Sch. Svcs., 1995—, Coop. Children's Book Ctr., 1986-89, 92-95, chair adv. bd., 1994-95. Recipient Woman of Achievement award Rhinelander Bus. and Profl. Women, 1992, Exemplary Svc. in Promotion of Literacy award Internat. Reading Assn. and Headwaters Reading Coun., 1995. Mem. Antique Automobile Club Am., Wis. Libr. Assn. (nominations com. 1995-96, long range planning com. 1992-95, chair long range planning com. 1993, ad-hoc com. affiliations 1993, sec. 1989, intellectual freedom com. 1985-88, fed. legis. network 1993—, state legis. network 1987—, youth svcs. sect. 1975—, chair youth svcs. sect. 1982, named Libr. of Yr. 1993), Wis. Lincoln Fellowship, Horseless Carriage Club. United Methodist. Office: Rhinelander Dist Libr 106 N Stevens St Rhinelander WI 54501

WENDT, LINDA M., educational association administrator; b. Garmisch Partenkirchen, Germany; m. Martin J. Wendt; 1 child, Angelica. BS, Western Mich. U., 1967. Cert. fund raising exec., Va. Tchr. Mich. (Tex.) Pub. Schs., 1968-80; small bus. owner Battle Creek, Mich., 1980-85; supr. Allied Stores, Battle Creek, Mich., 1985-86; pres. Jr. Achievement, Battle Creek, Mich., 1986—; steering com. Ctr. for Workforce Excellence, Battle Creek, 1991—; edn. subcom. Econ. Devel. Forum, Battle Creek, 1991—; v.p. Volunteerism in Action, Battle Creek, 1988-91; chair Oper. GRAD Oversight, Battle Creek, 1995—. Com chair Cereal Fest, Battle Creek, 1986-91; campaign divsn. chair United Arts Coun., Battle Creek, 1990; campaign vol. United Way, Battle Creek, 1986—. U.S.-China Ednl. Inst. fellow, 1995. Mem. AAUW, Rotary (com chair 1993—), Battle Creek C. of C. Office: Jr Achievement S Ctrl Mich Four Riverwalk Ctr Ste B Battle Creek MI 49017

WENDT, MARILYNN SUZANN, elementary school educator, principal; b. Bay City, Mich., Oct. 6, 1939; d. Clarence Henry and Margaret Viola (Rugenstein) W. AA, Bay City Jr. Coll., 1959; BA, Ctrl. Mich. U., 1962, MA, 1964; EdD, Wayne State U., 1971. Cert. elem. adminstr., Mich. Tchr., teaching prin. Baxman Sch., Bay City, 1959-62; tchr., guidance counselor, dir. elem. edn. Essexville (Mich.)-Hampton Schs., 1962-66; tchr., dir. elem. edn., dir. curriculum rsch. Bloomfield Hills (Mich.) Schs., 1966-78; elem. prin., staff development trainer, learning improvement ctr. supr. Waterford (Mich.) Schs., 1978—; consortium facilitator Mich. Dept. Edn. Exptl. & Demonstration Ctr., Lansing, 1975-76; part time faculty mem. Wayne State U., Detroit, 1972-78. Co-author: Rational Basis for Planning School Accountability, 1976; contbr. articles to profl. jours. Trustee, v.p. Waterford Twp. Libr., 1990-95; trustee St. Mark's Bd. Edn., West Bloomfield, Mich., 1991-95. Recipient Outstanding Educator award U.S. Office of Edn.-Harold Howe II, 1968, Disting. Svc. award Bloomfield Hills Schs., 1980. Mem. ASCD, Nat. Coun. Tchrs. English, Internat. Reading Assn., Mich. Reading Assn. (Celebrate Literacy award 1989, Adminstr. of Yr. 1991), Mich. ASCD (editor newsletter, conf. planner), Oakland County Reading Assn., Oakland County State & Fed. Program Specialists, Delta Kappa Gamma (v.p. 1990-93, Woman of Distinction 1982).

WENDTLAND, MONA BOHLMANN, dietitian, consultant; b. Schulenburg, Tex., Mar. 30, 1930; d. Willy Frank and Leona A. (Bruns) Bohlmann; m. Charles William Ewing, Mar. 8, 1953 (div. Sept. 1975); children: Charles William Jr., Deborah Susan Ewing Richmond; m. William Wolters Wendtland, Jan. 12, 1991. BS in Home Econs., U. Tex., 1952, postgrad., 1952-57. Registered dietitian, Tex. Dietitian sch. lunch program Port Arthur (Tex.) Ind. Sch. Dist., 1952-53; elem. tchr. Portsmouth (Va.) Sch. Dist., 1953-54; dietitian, mgr. lunch room E.M. Scarbrough Dept. Store, Austin, Tex., 1955-57; asst. chief adminstrv. dietitian John Sealy HOsp., Galveston, Tex., 1957-59; chief therapeutic dietitian USPHS Hosp., Galveston, 1959-60, asst. chief dietitian, 1960-62; cons. dietitian Sinton (Tex.) Nursing Home, 1963-65; dietary cons. Deaton Hosp., Galena Park, Tex., 1966-68; dir. food svcs. Nat. Health Enterprises, Houston, 1975-76; dietary cons. to nursing homes and retirement ctrs. Drug Abuse Ctr., Houston, 1976—. Del. Internat. Congress Arts & Comm., 1993. Mem. Am. Dietetic Assn. (registered), Tex. Dietetic Assn., South Tex. Dietetic Assn. (chmn. cons. interest group 1978-79), U. Tex. Home Econs. Assn., Dietitians in Bus. and Industry (nat. rep. to mgmt. practices group 1980-83, treas. Houston chpt. 1980-81, pres. 1981-82, advisor 1983-84), Tex. Gerontol Nutritionists (sec. 1994-95), Tex. Cons. Dietitians in Healthcare Facilities, Tex. Nutrition Coun., Dietary Mgrs. Assn. (advisor Houston dist. 1979-92). Republican. Methodist. Home and Office: 5463 Jason St Houston TX 77096-1238

WENGER, SHARON LOUISE, pediatrics educator, researcher, cytogeneticist; b. Washington, Sept. 25, 1949; d. William Fred and Lois Helen (Compton) W.; m. George E. Fromlak Jr., Jan. 10, 1976; children: Nicholas Edward, Holly Louise, Andrea Lee. BA in Biology, Thiel Coll., 1971; MS in Human Genetics, U. Pitts., 1973, PhD in Human Genetics, 1976. Asst. prof. Sch. of Medicine U. Pitts., 1980-89, assoc. prof. Sch. of Medicine, 1989—. Contbr. articles to profl. jours. Mem. Am. Soc. Human Genetics, Midwest Soc. for Pediatric Rsch. Office: Children's Hosp Pitts 3705 5th Ave Pittsburgh PA 15213-2583

WENGER, VICKI, interior designer; b. Indpls., Aug. 30, 1928. Ed., U. Nebr., Internat. Inst. Interior Design, Parsons in Paris. Pres. Vicki Wenger Interiors, Bethesda, Md., 1963-71, Washington, 1982-95; pres. Beautiful Spaces Inc., Washington, 1982-95; chief designer Creative Design, Capitol Heights, Md., 1969-84; lectr. Nat. Assn. Home Builders, 1983-88; mem. programs com. D.C. Assn. Home Builders, 1983-88. Author-host: (patented TV interior design show) Beautiful Spaces 1984; producer, host (cable TV show) Design Edition, 1988—. Designer Gourmet Gala, March of Dimes, Washington, 1986-88; decorator showhouse Nat. Symphony Orch., Washington, 1983-94, 96, chmn. women's com., 1991-92; decorator showhouse Am. Cancer Soc., Washington, 1983, Alexandria Comty. YWCA, 1990. Mem. Am. Soc. Interior Designers (profl., nat. bd. dirs. 1973-75, nat. examining com. 1977-78, pres. Md. chpt. 1976, bd. dirs. Washington Metro chpt. 1989-91, pres. 1995-96, past pres. 1996-97, mem. pres.'s barrier free com. 1980), Nat. Trust Hist. Preservation, Smithsonian Instn. (sponsor), Nat. Press Club. Democrat. Presbyterian.

WENHAM, CHARLOTTE LOUISE, educational administrator; b. South Haven, Mich., May 27, 1946; d. Robert and Louise (Hurley) McConnell. BA in Speech, Mich. State U., 1968, MA in English, 1979; EdD in Ednl. Leadership, Western Mich. U., 1987. Cert. sch. adminstr., Mich. Tchr. St. Joseph (Mich.) Pub. Schs., 1968-78, coord., 1978-82, prin., 1982-91, dir. curriculum, 1985-93, asst. supt., 1993—. Chmn. Reps. Berrien County, St. Joseph, 1976-90; com. mem. 4th Congl. Dist. Com., Paw Paw, Mich., 1985-90, Reps. Mich., Lansing, 1989-90; pres. Planned Parenthood Southwestern Mich., Benton Harbor, 1989, 90, 91. Mem. ASCD, Mich. Assn. Mid. Sch. Educators, Berrien-Cass Prins. Assn., Phi Delta Kappa (com. mem. 1986—, rsch. chmn. 1986-88, chmn. personal growth Rho dhpt. 1982-84, pres. 1988-90). Office: St Joseph Pub Schs 2214 S State St Saint Joseph MI 49085-1910

WENIG, MARY MOERS, law educator; b. N.Y.C.; d. Robert and Celia Lewis (Kauffman) Moers; m. Jerome Wenig, Dec. 19, 1946; children: Margaret Moers Wenig Rubenstein, Michael M. Wenig. BA, Vassar Coll., 1946; JD, Columbia U., 1951. Bar: N.Y. 1952, U.S. Ct. Appeals (2d cir.) 1954, U.S. Dist. Ct. (so. dist.) N.Y. 1956, Conn. 1977. Assoc. Cahill, Gordon, Reindel & Ohl, N.Y.C., 1951-57; assoc. Greenbaum, Wolff & Ernst, N.Y.C., 1957-60, Skadden, Arps, Slate, Meagher & Flom, N.Y.C., 1960-71; asst. prof. sch. law St. John's U., N.Y.C., 1971-75, assoc. prof. sch. law, 1975-78; rsch. affiliate Yale Law Sch., New Haven, 1978-79; prof. sch. law U. Bridgeport, Conn., 1978-82, Charles A. Dana prof. law, 1982-92; prof. sch. law Quinnipiac Coll., Bridgeport, 1992-95, Hamden, 1995—; cons. The Merrill Anderson Co., Stratford, Conn., 1982—, Conn. Permanent Commn. on Status of Women, 1978-79; vis. prof. sch. law Pace U., White Plains, N.Y., 1979; bd. dirs. Tax Analysts/TAX NOTES, Fairfax, N.Y., 1980—; bd. dirs., pres. Conn. Women's Ednl. & Legal Fund, Inc., New Haven, 1973; commr. State of Conn. Permanent Commn. on Status of Women, 1985-91; mem. Conn. Gen. Assembly's Adv. Commn. to Study the Uniform Marital Property's Act., 1985-86; lectr. in field; bd. dirs. Tax Analysts. Editor: PLI Tax Handbooks, 1978-86; co-editor: Bittker, Fundamentals of Federal Income Taxation, 1983; co-author: (with Douthwaite) Unmarried Couples and the Law, 1979; contbr. tax, estate planning, trust and estates and marital property articles to profl. jours.; editorial adv. bd. Estate Planning for the Elderly & Disabled, 1987-90, Community Property Jour., 1986-88, Estate Planning, 1975—, Estates, Gifts & Trusts Jour., 1976—. Mem. probate com. Conn. Law Revision Commn., 1985—, com. to study the probate system Conn. Probate Assembly, 1988-91, task force on the legal rights of women in marriage NOW, 1987-91; 2nd cir. rep. Fedn. of Women Lawyers Jud. Screening Panel, 1979; bd. govs. Radcliffe Club N.Y., 1975-77; mem. 1st selectman's com. on taxation relief for the elderly Town of Westport, 1974-75; pres. bd. dirs. Conn. Women's Ednl. and Legal Fund, Inc., 1975-79, bd. dirs., 1973-79. Named Salute to Women honoree Outstanding Women of Conn., Greater Bridgeport YWCA, 1990, Women in Leadership honoree New Haven YWCA, 1979, honoree U. Bridgeport Sch. Law Women's Law Assn., 1990; Harlan Fiske Stone scholar Columbia U. Sch. Law, 1949; recipient Award for Equality United Nations Assn.-USA of Conn., 1987; Summer Stipend grantee NEH, 1984, rsch. grantee Conn. Bar Found., 1980. Fellow Am. Coll. Trust & Estate Counsel (bd. regents 1985-91); mem. ABA (advisor to NCCUSL 1980-84, sect. coun. mem. 1970-72), Internat. Acad. Estates & Trust Law (academician, exec. coun. mem. 1992-94), Conn. Bar Assn. (sects.' exec. coun., Disting. Svc. commendation 1977), Assn. Am. Law Schs., Assn. of Bar of City of N.Y., N.Y. State Bar Assn., Am. Law Inst. (hon.), Am. Coll. Tax Counsel (hon.). Democrat. Jewish. Home: 5 Lamplight Ln Westport CT 06880-6106 Office: Quinnipiac Coll School of Law 275 Mt Carmel Ave New Haven CT 06518-1947

WENTISCH, PENNY MARIE, pediatric nurse; b. Brookhaven, N.Y., Mar. 12, 1964; d. Roy James and Miriam May (Reisig) W. ADN, Suffolk (N.Y.) C.C., 1985; BSN, SUNY, Binghamton, 1988. RN, N.Y., N.C. Staff nurse Ctrl. Suffolk Hosp., Riverhead, N.Y., 1985-86; staff nurse Carolinas Med. Ctr., Charlotte, N.C., 1988-91, asst. nursemgr., 1991-94, staff nurse, 1994—; implementation analyst HBO & Co., Charlotte, 1994—. Mem. Habitat for Humanity, Cath. Singles of Charlotte (chmn. social events 1990). Home: 11313 Valerian Ct Charlotte NC 28213 Office: HBO & Co 10101 Claude Freeman Dr Charlotte NC 28262

WENTS, DORIS ROBERTA, psychologist; b. L.A., Aug. 26, 1944; d. John Henry and Julia (Cole) W. BA, UCLA, 1966; MA, San Francisco State U., 1968; postgrad., Calif. State U., L.A., 1989-90, Claremont (Calif.) Grad. Sch., 1990—. Lic. ednl. psychologist, credentialed sch. psychologist, Calif. Sch. psychologist Diagnostic Sch. for Neurologically Handicapped Children, L.A., 1969-86; pvt. practice Monterey Park, Calif., 1986—; instr. Calif. State U., L.A., 1977. Co-author: Southern California Ordinal Scales of Development, 1977. Mem. Western Psychol. Assn., L.A. World Affairs Coun., L.A. Conservancy, Zeta Tau Alpha (officer Santa Monica alumnae chpt. 1970—, Cert. of Merit 1979), Sigma Xi. Office: Claremont Grad Sch Dept Psychology Claremont CA 91711

WENTWORTH, MALINDA ANN NACHMAN, former small business owner, real estate broker; b. Greenville, S.C.; d. Mordecai and Frances (Brown) Nachman; m. William A. Wentworth, June 22, 1964; children: William Allen Jr., Linda Ann. BBA, U. Miami, 1960. Registered rep. brokerage, real estate broker. Personnel Mgrs. Asst. Jordan March, Miami, 1960-61; stock broker Barron & Co., Inc., Greenville, 1961-64; real estate agt. Par Realty, Inc., Conyers, Ga., 1969-72; real estate broker Par Realty, Inc., Conyers, 1972-83; owner/ops. Rockdale Cablevision, Conyers, 1979-83; real estate broker Coldwell Banker, Conyers, 1983-85; owner, operator Wentworth's Gym & Fitness Ctr., Conyers, 1981-90; real estate broker First Realty, Conyers, 1981-89; ptnr. and dir. Santa Barbara (Calif.) Cellular Systems, Inc., 1986-89; v.p. Santa Barbara Cellular Systems, Inc., Atlanta, 1986-87; investor, Cocoa Beach, Fla., 1990—. Producer and dir.: local sport events on cable to sta., 1979, '80, '81, '87. Founding dir., past pres. Porterdale PTO, 1972-79; mem. Nat. Cable TV Assn., 1979-83, pres. Unity Ch. of Rockdale, Conyers, 1984-85, dir., 1984-89. Named Lt. Col.--Aide-De-Camp, Gov. Staff, state of Ga., Gov. George Busbee, 1979, Appreciation Plaque award, Rockdale County High Sch. Football, 1987. Mem. Nat. Health & Strength Assn., Rockdale County Bd. of Realtors, Cellular Telephone Industry Assn., Rockdale County C. of C.

WENTZEL, KAREN LYNN, secondary education educator; b. Granite City, Ill., May 22, 1949; d. Mike J. and Virginia L. (Prewett) Firtos; m. Joseph A. Wentzel Jr., June 2, 1967 (div. 1989); 1 child, David J. AA, St. Louis Community Coll., 1988; BA summa cum laude, Fontbonne Coll., 1990; MEd, U. Mo., St. Louis, 1994. Cert. secondary tchr., Mo. Instr. writing Meramec Coll., St. Louis, 1990-91; tchr. Div. of Youth Svcs., St. Louis, 1991; tchr. lang. arts North Kirkwood Mid. Sch., St. Louis, 1991—. Features editor newspaper Fontbanner, 1990; mng. editor newsletter Hogan Highlights, 1991. Recipient Meramec's Exemplary Svc. award, 1991. Mem. Mo. Mid. Sch. Assn., Nat. Coun. Tchrs. English, Phi Theta Kappa, Sigma Tau Delta, Phi Delta Kappa, Chi Sigma Iota, Phi Kappa Phi. Home: 4908 Fite Dr Imperial MO 63052-1412 Office: North Kirkwood Mid Sch 11287 Manchester Rd Saint Louis MO 63122-1122

WENZEL, JOAN ELLEN, artist; b. N.Y.C., July 23, 1944; d. Irwin S. and Pearl (Silverman) Rever; m. Allen Jay Wenzel, June 12, 1966 (div. June 1987); 1 child, Kimberly Anne; m. Robert Harold Messing, July 23, 1987 (dec.). Student, Syracuse U., 1962-64; BS in Painting, NYU, 1966, MA in Painting, 1976; postgrad., Harvard U., 1967. One-woman shows include Helander Gallery, Palm Beach, Fla., 1985, 89, 95, Adamar Fine Art, Miami, 1993, Gallery Contemporena, Jacksonville, Fla., 1993, Alexander Brest Mus., Jacksonville, 1993, Albertson Peterson Gallery, Winter Park, Fla., 1992, Amerifest, Miami, 1991, Gallery Yves Arman, N.Y.C., 1982, Palm Beach County Court House, West Palm Beach, Fla., 1991, One Brickall Square, Miami, 1992, Lighthouse Gallery, Tequesta, Fla., 1995-96, Esperante Ctr., West Palm Beach, 1996; exhbns. include Aldrich Mus., Ridgefield, Conn., 1977, Queens Mus., N.Y.C., 1981. Democrat. Jewish. Home: 2275 Ibis Isle Rd W Palm Beach FL 33480-5307

WEPFER, JULIA M., psychologist; b. El Dorado, Ark., May 12, 1936; d. Joseph Gottlieb and Julia Witherspoon (Fletcher) W.; m. Harry Ames Metcalf, June 1, 1957 (div.); 1 child, Holly Kinyon. BS in Bus. Adminstrn., U. Ark., 1958, MA in Psychology, 1965; PsyD, Fla. Inst. Tech., 1980. Lic. psychologist, Ark. Market analyst Am. Investment Advisors, Little Rock, 1958; office mgr. to orthodontist Little Rock, 1958-60, office mgr. to psychiatrist, 1961-64; psycholog. examiner U. Ark. for Med. Scis. Dept. Psychiatry, Little Rock, 1966-67, tchg. asst., 1967-69, instr., 1969-75, asst. prof., 1975-85; pvt. practice Little Rock, 1985—; mem. Ark. Bd. Examiners in Psychology, Little Rock, 1973-78. Ark. coord. Deaf-Blind Project, Little Rock, 1971-72; mem. Regional AIDS Interfaith Network Care Team, Little Rock, 1992—; mem. commn. on ministry Episcopal Diocese of Ark., Little Rock, 1994—; vol. Stewpot Free Kitchen, Little Rock; v.p. bd. dirs. Columbia Land & Timber Co., Beauregard Parish, La. Fellow Ark. Psychol. Assn. (pres. 1982-83); mem. APA, Assn. for Study of Dreams, Chi Omega (Psi chpt.). Democrat. Home and Office: 13001 Ridgehaven Rd Little Rock AR 72211-2211

WERDEGAR, KATHRYN MICKLE, judge; b. San Francisco; d. Benjamin Christie and Kathryn Marie (Clark) Mickle; m. David Werdegar; children: Maurice Clark, Matthew Mickle. Student, Wellesley Coll., 1954-55; AB with honors, U. Calif., Berkeley, 1957; JD with distinction, George Washington U., 1962; JD, U. Calif., Berkeley, 1990. Bar: Calif. 1964, U.S. Dist. Ct. (no. dist.) Calif. 1964, U.S. Ct. Appeals (9th cir.) 1964, Calif. Supreme Ct. 1964. Legal asst. civil rights divsn. U.S. Dept. Justice, Washington, 1962-63; cons. Calif. Study Commn. on Mental Retardation, 1963-64; assoc. U. Calif. Ctr. for Study of Law and Soc., Berkeley, 1965-67; spl. cons. State Dept. Mental Hygiene, 1967-68; cons. Calif. Coll. Trial Judges, 1968-71; atty., head criminal divsn. Calif. Continuing Edn. of Bar, 1971-78; assoc. dean acad. and student affairs, assoc. prof. Sch. Law, U. San Francisco, 1978-81; sr. staff atty. Calif. 1st Dist. Ct. Appeal, 1981-85, Calif. Supreme Ct., 1985-91; assoc. justice Calif. 1st Dist. Ct. Appeal, 1991-94, Calif. Supreme Ct., San Francisco, 1994—. Author: Benchbook: Misdemeanor Procedure, 1971, Misdemeanor Procedure Benchbook, 1975, 83; contbr. California Continuing Education of the Bar books; editor: California Criminal Law Practice series, 1972, California Uninsured Motorist Practice, 1973, I California Civil Procedure Before Trial, 1977. Recipient Charles Glover award George Washington U., J. William Fulbright award for disting. pub. svc. George Washington U. Law Sch. Alumni Assn., award of excellence Calif. Alumni Assn., also 5 Am. Jurisprudence awards. Mem. Nat. Assn. Women Judges, Calif. Judges Assn., Nev./Calif. Women Judges Assn., Boalt Hall Alumni Assn. (bd. dirs.), Order of the Coif. Office: Calif Supreme Court South Tower 303 2nd St San Francisco CA 94107-1366

WERKMAN, ROSEMARIE ANNE, past public relations professional, civic worker; b. Washingtonville, N.Y., Apr. 21, 1926; d. Alexander and Michelina (Russo) Di Benedetto; m. Henry J. Werkman, June 29, 1947; children: Elizabeth, Kristine, Hendrik. Student, U. Miami, Fla. Billing clk. Stern's Dept. Store, N.Y.C., 1945; clk., typist Doubleday-Doran Book Pub., N.Y.C., 1945-46; receptionist Moser & Cotins Advt. Agy., Utica, N.Y., 1947-48, Washingtonville Sch., N.Y., 1960-75. Author: (biography/autobiography) Love, War and Remembrance, 1992; author short stories; poetry pub. in several anthologies. Mem. Dem. Com., Blooming Grove; bd. dirs. Blooming Grove Hist. Assn.; mem. com. Update: Blooming Grove Master Plan; mem. Orange County Coun. Disabled; bd. dirs. Rehab. Support Svcs. Named Poet of Merit, Am. Poetry Assn., 1989; recipient Notable Civic Contbns. award Blooming Grove/Washingtonville C. of C., 1996. Mem. Blooming Grove C. of C. (v.p.), Orange County Classic Choral Soc., Clearwater (Fla.) Chorus. Democrat. Roman Catholic.

WERMUTH, MARY LOUELLA, secondary education educator; b. Oakland County, Mich., May 2, 1943; d. Burt and Ila A. (Cole) W.; m. David J. Kohne, Dec. 28, 1975; 1 child, John B. BA, Oakland U., 1965, MA, 1969, 81. Tchr. Rochester Cmty. Schs., Rochester Hills, Mich., 1965-96; instr., counselor Internat. Acad., Bloomfield Hills, Mich., 1996—; farmer, 1964—; presenter various English confs., 1982, 84, 87; mem. bd. dirs. Mich. Future Problem Solving, 1992—; exchange tchr. New South Wales, Australia, 1996. Author: Images of Michigan, 1981, Michigan Centennial Farm History, 1986. Pres. Horizons Residential Ctrs., Inc., New Baltimore, Mich., 1984—. Recipient Disting. Alumni award Oakland U., 1976. Mem. NEA, Rochester Edn. Assn., Mich. Edn. Assn., Mich. Coun. Tchrs. English (coms. 1985, 87), Oakland U. Alumni Assn. (pres. 1971-73), Mich. Centennial Farm Assn. (bd. dirs. 1979—), Mich. Assn. Gifted Edn. (v.p. 1991-93), Oakland County Tchrs. English (coms. 1985-93), Internat. Acad. (faculty, chmn. English dept. 1996—). Office: Rochester Sch 180 S Livernois Rd Rochester MI 48307-1840

WERNER, ELIZABETH HELEN, librarian, Spanish language educator; b. Palo Alto, Calif., June 21, 1944; d. Fielding and Lucy Elizabeth (Hart) McDearmon; m. Michael Andrew Werner, Aug. 21, 1976. BA, Mills Coll., 1966; MA, Ind. U., 1968; MLS, U. Md., 1973. Instr. Spanish, Western Md. Coll., Westminster, 1968-72; libr., assoc. prof. Clearwater (Fla.) Christian Coll., 1975—; sec. Sunline Libr. users group Tampa Bay Libr. Consortium, Tampa, Fla., 1993-94. Contbr. book revs. to profl. jours. Com. mem. Upper Pinellas County Post Office Customers' Adv. Coun., Clearwater, 1992—. Mem. Fla. Libr. Assn., Assn. Christian Librs., Fla. Assn. Christian Librs. (pres. 1991-94), Friends of the Clearwater Libr., Am. Assn. Tchrs. Spanish and Portuguese. Office: Clearwater Christian Coll 3400 Gulf To Bay Blvd Clearwater FL 34619-4514

WERNER, GLORIA S., librarian; b. Seattle, Dec. 12, 1940; d. Irving L. and Eva H. Stolzoff; m. Newton Davis Werner, June 30, 1963; 1 son, Adam Davis. BA, Oberlin Coll., 1961; ML, U. Wash., 1962; postgrad. UCLA, 1962-63. Reference librarian UCLA Biomed Library, 1963-64, asst. head pub. services dept., 1964-66, head pub. services dept., head reference div., 1966-72, asst. biomed. librarian public services, 1972-77, asso. biomed. librarian, 1977-78, biomed. librarian, assoc. univ. librarian, dir. Pacific S.W. regional Med. Library Service, 1979-83; asst. dean library services UCLA Sch. Medicine, 1980-83; assoc. univ. librarian for tech. services, 1983-89, dir. libraries, acting univ. librarian, 1989-90, univ. librarian, 1990—; adj. lectr. UCLA Grad. Sch. Library and Info. Sci., 1977-83. Editor, Bull. Med. Library Assn., 1979-82, asso. editor, 1974-79; mem. editorial bd. Ann. Stats. Med. Sch. Libraries U.S. and Can., 1980-83; mem. accrediting commn. Western Assn. Schs. and Colls., N.W. Assn. Schs. and Colls. Mem. ALA, Assn. Rsch. Librs. (bd. dirs. 1993—, v.p./pres.-elect 1995-96). Office: UCLA Rsch Libr Libr Adminstrv Office 405 Hilgard Ave Los Angeles CA 90024-1301

WERNER, PATRICE (PATRICIA ANN WERNER), college president; b. Jersey City, May 31, 1937; d. Louis and Ella Blanche (Smith) W. BA in French, Caldwell Coll., 1966; MA in French, McGill U., 1970; PhD in French, NYU, 1976; postgrad. Inst. Ednl. Mgmt., Harvard U., 1991. Joined Dominican Sisters of Caldwell, 1954. Sch. tchr. Archdiocesan Sch. Systems, N.J., Ala., 1954-62; tchr. French, Latin Jersey City, Caldwell, N.J., 1962-72; instr. French Caldwell Coll., 1973-76; dir. continuing edn. Caldwell Coll., Caldwell, 1976-79, chair dept. fgn. langs., assoc. prof. French, 1979-85, acad. dean, prof. French, 1985-94; pres. Caldwell Coll., 1994—; cons. Dept. of Higher Edn. Grant Program, 1986; bd. trustees Caldwell Coll. Mem. NAICU (com. on financing higher edn.), Am. Assn. Higher Edn., Assn. Ind. Colls. and Univs. N.J., N.J. Presidents Coun. (new program rev. com.), Coun. of Ind. Colls. Office: Caldwell Coll 9 Ryerson Ave Caldwell NJ 07006-6195

WERNER, SYBILLE, orchestra conductor; b. Schwabach, Germany, Feb. 18, 1954; came to the U.S., 1972; d. Joachim and Erna (Bauer) W. BA magna cum laude, Calif. State U., 1975, MA, 1978. Asst. condr. Calif. State U., L.A., 1976-78; music dir., condr. Pro Solisti Chamber Orch., N.Y.C., 1980-82; asst. condr. Met. Y Orch., West Orange, N.J., 1982-84; music dir., condr. Manhattan Opera Assn., N.Y.C., 1985-88, Rockaway-Five-Towns Symphony, N.Y.C., 1988-90, Philharmonia Orch. N.Y., N.Y.C., 1988—; guest condr. Opera Amici, Manhattan, L.I. Opera Co., N.Y. Symphonic Arts Ensemble, Greenwich Village Orch., Fort Collins (Colo.) Symphony, Czestochowa State Philharmonic, Kalisz Symphony, Poland, Walbrzych Philharmonic, 1996, Plock Philharmonic, 1996, Torun Philharmonic, 1996, Bialystock Philharmonic, 1996, Koszalin Symphony, others. Zack Meml. scholar Calif. State U., 1973-75. Mem. Condrs. Guild. Home and Office: 77 Seaman Ave Apt 5 B New York NY 10034

WERNETTE, KAREN MARIE, veterinarian; b. Eaton Rapids, Mich., Apr. 24, 1954; d. Victor Joseph and Pauline R. (Strong) W.; m. David John Cushman, Apr. 9, 1988; children: Alex David Cushman, Kevin Andrew Cushman. BS in Zoology, U. Mich., 1975; BS in Animal Husbandry, Mich. State U., 1977, DVM, 1982. Assoc. vet. Animal Health Clinic & Hosp., Waukegan, Ill., 1982; emergency vet. A-Northshore Emergency Vet. Ctr., Northfield, Ill., 1983, 94-95; anesthesiology resident Ohio State U. Coll. Vet. Medicine, Columbus, 1983-84; assoc. vet. Noyes Animal Hosp., Barrington, Ill., 1995-96; asst. dir. AVMA, Schaumburg, Ill., 1996—. Bd. dirs. Nat. Mastitis Coun., Madison, Wis., 1992-95; mem. PTA. Named Outstanding Young Woman of Am., 1984. Mem. AVMA, Mich. Vet. Med. Assn., Chgo. Soc. Assn. Execs., Toastmaster's Club (pres. 1994-95, v.p. 1995-96). United Methodist. Home: 511 N Country Ridge Ct Lake Zurich IL 60047 Office: AVMA 1931 Meacham Rd Schaumburg IL 60173

WERNICK, SANDIE MARGOT, advertising and public relations executive; b. Tampa, Sept. 13, 1944; d. Nathan and Sylvia (Bienstock) Rothstein. BA in English, U. Fla., 1966. Tchr. English Miami Beach (Fla.) Sr. High Sch., 1967; adminstrv. asst. pub. rels. Bozell & Jacobs, Inc., N.Y.C., 1968-69; asst. to dir. pub. rels. Waldorf-Astoria, N.Y.C., 1969-70; dir. advt. and pub. rels. Hyatt on Union Square, San Francisco, 1974-82; pres. Wernick Mktg. Group, San Francisco, 1982—. Bd. mem. Nat. Kidney Assn., San Francisco, 1985-87; advisor Swords to Plowshares, San Francisco, 1988-89. Recipient Award of Merit, San Francisco Advt. and Cable Car Awards, 1979, Award of Excellence, San Francisco Art Dirs, 1978, awards Am. Hotel and Motel Assn., 1981, 82, awards of excellence San Francisco Publicity Club, 1990. Mem. Women in Comms. (bd. dirs. 1987-89), Am. Women in Radio and TV (bd. dirs. 1989-90), Pub. Rels. Soc. Am., San Francisco Publicity Club (pres. 1989), Variety Club, Profl. Bus. Women's Assn., Calif. Pacific Med. Ctr. (aux. 1988-95). Democrat. Jewish. Home: 1690 Broadway St San Francisco CA 94109-2419 Office: Wernick Marketing Group 444 Market St Ste 1125 San Francisco CA 94111-5328

WERPS, ANNE SPIGELMIRE, elementary education educator, writer; b. Balt., Mar. 14, 1951; d. James Sydney and Marcella (Dean) Spigelmire; m. Ben Werps; children: Nico, Martijn. BS in Edn., Towson State U., Md., 1979; MEd in Edn., 1985. Tchr. 5th, 6th grades Summit Park Elem. Sch., Balt., 1980-84; reading specialist Internat. Sch. Amsterdam, Netherlands, 1985-88; English as fgn. lang. tchr. Elseviers Lang. Inst., Rijswyk, Netherlands, 1988-89; tchr. 5th grade Edgemere Elem. Sch., Balt., 1989-92; reading specialist Dundalk Middle Sch., Balt., 1992-93, instrnl. facilitator, 1993-94, team leader, lang. arts tchr., 1993—; travel agt. employee Travel Agy Beuk, Noordwyk, The Netherlands, 1976-80. Contbr. articles to profl. jours. and newspapers. Mem. Internat. Reading Assn., Nat. Middle Sch. Assn. Democrat. Roman Catholic.

WERT, BARBARA J. YINGLING, special education educator; b. Hanover, Pa., May 18, 1953; d. Richard Bruce and Jacqueline Louise (Myers) Yingling; m. Barry Thomas Wert, Aug. 23, 1975; children: Jennifer Allison,

Jason Frederick. BS in Elem. Edn., Kutztown (Pa.) U., 1975; MS in Spl. Edn., Bloomsburg (Pa.) U., 1990. Cert. in elem. edn., spl. edn., Pa. Dir. children's program Coun. for United Ch. Ministries of Reading, Reading, Pa., 1975-76; instr. Berks County Vo-Tech., Oley Valley, Pa., 1976-77; asst. tchr. Ostrander Elem. Sch., Wallkill, N.Y., 1982-85; spl. needs surp., instrnl. support tchr., cons. Danville (Pa.) Child Devel. Ctr., 1986—; dir. Little Learners Pre-Sch., Northumberland, Pa., 1991-94, ednl. cons., 1991—; pvt. cons. Families with Spl. Needs, Northumberland, 1991—; adj. prof. spl. edn., 1995. Recipient Parent Profl. Partnership award 1993. Mem. ASCD, Coun. for Exceptional Children (exec. bd. dirs. divsn. early childhood 1991—, sec. 1991-93, newsletter editor, v.p. 1993-94, pres. 1995-96), Nat. Assn. for Edn. Young Children (v.p. Pa. divsn. for early childhood 1993—, tchr. edn. divsn., coun. for behavior disorders divsn., learning disabilities divsn.), Local Autism Support and Advocacy Group. Home: RR 1 Box 372-n Northumberland PA 17857-9717 Office: Danville Child Devel Ctr PO Box 183 Danville PA 17821-0183

WERT, RITA K., organization executive; m. Don H. Wert; children: Anthony Charles, Kelly Mae, Mary Christina, Joshua Henry. Student, Evang. Sch. Theology, Myerstown, Pa. Nat. YTC exec. dir. Nat. Women's Christian Temperance Union, Evanston, Ill, nat. v.p.; youth supt. World Women's Christian Temperance Union. Organizer, executor Pastor's Wifes' Retreats, Ea. Conf., Evang. Congl. Ch.; sr. choir dir., dir. children's choir local ch.; dir. Daily Vacation Bible Sch. 3 chs.; Sunday sch. tchr.; guest spkr. numerous chs. Office: Nat Woman's Christian Temperance Union 1730 Chicago Ave Evanston IL 60201

WERTHAN, LEAH ROSE, social worker, volunteer; b. Nashville, Tenn., May 9, 1908; d. Clarence and Daisy (Marx) Bernstein; m. Bernard Leonard Werthan; children: Bernard L. Jr., Joan, Morris II. BA, Wellesley Coll., 1929; postgrad. studies, Tenn. Sch. of Social Work, 1944. Founder Coun. Home for Convalescent Children, Nashville, 1947; mem. Gov.'s Com. on Children, Nashville, Tenn., 1947-49; officer Middle Tenn. Health Assn., Nashville, 1948-52; dir. Hearing and Speech Found., Nashville, 1950; del. Mid Century White House Conf. on Childen and Youth, Washington, 1950; exec. com. and founder Sr. Citizens, Inc., Washington, 1955—; founder White House Conf. on Aging. Vol. worker to help found the Dede Wallace Ctr., Sr. Citizens, Inc., Cumberland House for Emotionally Disturbed Children, Coun. Home for Convalescent Children and the Leah Rose Residence for Senior Citizens; bd. dirs. Park Ctr., Nashville Meml. Hosp. Found. Bd.; active for Bill Wilkerson Hearing and Speech Ctr., Green Hills Health Ctr., Family Shelter, SAGA and others; bd. trustees Wellesley Coll., 1970-76. Named Woman of Yr. Bus and Profl. Women's Assn. 1970, Philantrophist of Yr., Nat. Soc. Fund Raising Execs., 1990; recipient Jewel Fulton Tennessean award 1971, Nat. Mental Health Assn. Golden Key award 1984, Gov.'s Outstanding Tennessean award 1984, Eleanor Roosvelt Centennial award Israel Bond Com., 1984, Jack C. Massey Leadership award, 1988, Sr. Citizen's Crowning Achievement award, 1990; mem. YWCA Acad. for Women of Achievement, 1995. Mem. Wellesley Coll. Club, Nashville (pres. 1940-42). Jewish. Home: 6666 Brookmont Ter # 1204 Nashville TN 37205

WERTHEIM, SALLY HARRIS, academic administrator, dean, education educator; b. Cleve., Nov. 1, 1931; d. Arthur I. and Anne (Manheim) Harris; m. Stanley E. Wertheim, Aug. 6, 1950; children: Kathryn, Susan B., Carole J. BS, Flora Stone Mather Coll., 1953; MA, Case Western Res. U., 1967, PhD, 1970. Cert. elem. and secondary edn. tchr., Ohio. Social worker U. Hosps., Cleve., 1953-54; tchr. Fairmount Temple Religious Sch., Cleve., 1957-72; mem. faculty John Carroll U., Cleve., 1969—, prof., 1980—, dean grad. sch., rsch. coord., 1986-93, acad. v.p., 1993-94, 95; dean Grad. Sch., coord. faculty rsch. John Carroll U., Cleve., 1994—; cons. in field; cons. Jennings Found., Cleve.; chmn. sch. com. Cleve. Commn. on Higher Edn., 1987—. Contbr. articles to profl. jours. Sec. Cuyahoga County Mental Health Bd., Cleve., 1978-82; pres. Jewish Family Svc. Assn., Cleve., 1974-77, Montefiore Home for Aged, Cleve., 1987-90; bd. dirs. Mt. Sinai Med. Ctr., Cleve., 1984-93, Cleve. Edn. Fund, 1992-94; v.p. Jewish Cmty. Fedn., 1988-91, pres., 1994—, bd. trustees, 1992—; chairperson edn. com. Cleve. Found. Commn. on Poverty, 1988-93, Cleve. Cmty. Bldg. Initiative, 1993-95, United Way Svcs., 1994—. Named One of 100 Most Influential Women, Cleve. mag., 1983; recipient award Jewish Communty Fedn.; grantee Jennings Found., 1984-87, Cleve. and Gund Found., 1987-90, Lilly Found., 1988. Mem. Am. Assn. Colls. for Tchrs. Edn. (bd. dirs. 1982-85), Ohio Assn. Colls. for Tchrs. Edn. (pres. 1981-83), Coun. of Grad. Schs. Office: John Carroll U Grad Sch Cleveland OH 44118

WERTHEIMER, LINDA, broadcaster. Disting. grad., Wellesley Coll., 1965. Congl. corr. Nat. Pub. Radio, Washington, 1971-76, polit. corr., 1976-89, host All Things Considered newsmag., 1989—. Recipient Alfred I. duPond-Columbia U. spl. citation, 1978, Corp. Pub. Broadcasting award, 1988. Office: Nat Pub Radio All Things Considered 635 Massachusetts Ave NW Washington DC 20001-3752*

WERTS, JOSEPHINE STARR, artist; b. Osage, Iowa, Aug. 5, 1903; d. William Jessie and Edna Lavinia (Wheeland) Starr; m. Leo Robert Werts, June 15, 1929 (div. 1947); 1 child, Barbara Werts Blatt. BA in Phys. Edn., Iowa State Tchrs. Coll., 1926; postgrad., Art Inst. Chgo., 1945, 46, U. Chgo., 1945, 46; MA in Fine Arts, U. So. Calif., 1961. One-woman shows include Cambria (Calif.) Coast Gallery, Ten Directions Gallery, Baywood Park, Calif., San Luis Obispo (Calif.) Art Ctr.; group shows include San Luis Obispo Art Ctr., U. So. Calif., Oakland (Calif.) Art Mus., Pasadena (Calif.) Art Mus., M.H. de Young Meml. Mus., San Francisco, Richmond (Calif.) Art Mus., Otis Art Inst., L.A., Long Beach (Calif.) Mus. Art, La Jolla (Calif.) Art Ctr., Ten Directions Gallery, Baywood Park, Calif., 1994, Kings County Art Ctr., Hanford, Calif., 1995, Paso Robles (Calif.) Art Ctr., 1996; represented in permanent collections Va. Mus. Fine Arts, Richmond, U. So. Calif. Fisher Gallery, also pvt. collections. Recipient award Palos Verdes Community Arts Assn., 1954, 57. Mem. Nat. Watercolor Soc. (bd. dirs. 1965, corr. sec. 1965, D'Arches award 1969), Watercolor U.S.A. Honor Soc. (Jurors award 1990), Ctrl. Coast Printmakers Soc., San Luis Art Assn. Democrat. Home and Studio: 2050 Emmons Rd Cambria CA 93428-4510

WERTZ, ALTA HAPP, artist, educator; b. Kennewick, Wash., Feb. 19, 1921; d. Henry Lewis and Annie Elizabeth (Yates) Leckliter; student Bakersfield Jr. Coll., 1939-40; m. Richard Clarence Smith (div. 1961); children: Robin Smith McBride, Alan Montgomery, Shelley Elisabeth Smith Stoye; m. William Morris Happ, Jan. 19, 1967 (dec. 1980); m. Harvey William Wertz, Feb. 26, 1984 (dec. Dec. 1989). Instr. oil painting, adult edn. Palomar Coll., San Marcos, Calif., 1958-62; pvt. tchr., lectr. in field, 1962—. One-woman shows The Atheneaum, La Jolla, Calif., 1959, Jeane's Gallery, La Jolla, 1961, Palomar Coll., 1959-61, The Little Galleries, Escondido, Calif., 1964, La Pina Ltd., La Jolla, 1965, 66, 67, Gray's Gallery, Escondido, 1973, Carlsbad Oceanside Art League Gallery, 1973; exhibited in group shows San Diego Mus. Art, San Diego Art Inst., Riverside Mus. Art, San Bernardino Mus. Art, So. Calif. Expn., Del Mar, also various galleries represented in permanent collections; contbr. articles to profl. jours. Lectr. on psychology and symbology of color in music and art. Active Palomar Hosp. aux., 1957-59; pres. Showcase of Arts, Escondido, 1961-62; rep. to San Diego Coun. of Visual Arts, 1966-67; mem. Escondido Cultural Arts Com., 1972-73; chmn. Mission Valley (Calif.) Expn. Art, 1967; bd. dirs. Philos. Religious Free Libr., 1970-74, Pala Mission Indian Sch., 1965-72; vol. Bishop Morris Care Ctr., Portland, Oreg. Huntington Hartford Found. fellow, Pacific Palisades, Calif., 1964. Recipient numerous other awards. Mem. San Diego Art Inst., San Diego Art Guild of Fine Arts Soc., San Diego Watercolor Soc., Nat. League of Am. Pen Women (pres. 1974-76), Watercolor West, Oreg. Astrol. Assn. Home: 16348 SW Estuary Dr Apt 205 Beaverton OR 97006-7926

WERTZ, ELIZABETH MARIE, critical care nurse, administrator; b. Ft. Worth, July 31, 1956; d. William B. and Helen Anne (Stiffler) Hodgson; m. Patrick L. Wertz, May 7, 1983; children: Patrick F., Amanda Elizabeth, Ashley Marie. Diploma, St. Francis Gen. Hosp., Pitts., 1980; BSN, Carlow Coll., Pitts., 1993; postgrad. in Pub. Mgmt., Carnegie Mellon U., 1996. RN, Pa.; cert. CPR instr., ACLS instr., PALS instr., ENPC instr., PHTLS instr., PHTLS affiliate faculty, pre-hosp. RN, ACLS affiliate faculty. Med. sec., asst. Cardiovascular Assocs., Pitts., 1976-78; nurse in cardiovasc. ICU St. Francis Gen. Hosp., 1980-84, 91-93; flight nurse Allegheny Gen. Hosp. Life Flight, Pitts., 1986-88; paramedic coord. Allegheny Gen. Hosp., 1984-87; mgr. office of prehosp. care Allegheny Gen. Hosp., 1987-93, mgr. life support tng. ctr., 1993-95. Co-chair emergency med. svc. for children adv. com., nursing adv. com., mem. EMT-paramedic adv. com. Pa. Emergency Health Svcs. Coun., 1984; mem. Nat. Safe Kids Campaign; mem. profl. adv. bd. Epilepsy Found. We. Pa.; mem. aux. and various coms. Easter Seal Soc. Allegheny County; mem. Pa. Protection and Adv. Devel. Disabilities Coun.; mem. Valley Ambulance Assn. Recipient Mildred K. Fincke, RN, Emergency Nursing award Pa. Emergency Health Svcs. Coun., 1990. Mem. Nat. EMTs (chair nat. pre-hosp. trauma life support com., bd. dirs., bd. govs., Leadership award 1988), Emergency Nurses Assn. Home: 828 Wellington Dr Mars PA 16046-8028

WESCHLER, ANITA, sculptor, painter; b. N.Y.C.; d. J. Charles and Hulda Eva (Mayer) W.; married. del. U.S. Com. Internat. Assn. Art, Fine Arts Fedn., N.Y. Exhibited in group shows at Met. Mus. Art, Mus. Modern Art, Art Inst. Chgo., Phila. Mus. Internat., Am. Acad., Inst. Arts and Letters, Bklyn. Mus., Newark Mus., Hofstra Mus., U. Conn., Carnegie Inst. Internat., Whitney Mus. Annuals, Storm King Art Ctr., mus. and galleries throughout U.S.; represented in permanent collections U. Pa., Michael Wolfson Found., Miami, Fla., Met. Mus. Art, Syracuse U., Butler Art Inst., Whitney Mus., Norfolk Mus., Brandeis U., Middlebury Coll., Amherst Coll., Yale U., Wichita State Mus., SUNY-Binghamton, U. Iowa, N.Y. Design Ctr., La Salle U., Pa. Acad. Fine Arts, Insts. for Achievement of Human Potential in Pa., Italy, and Brazil, Art Students League; one-man shows include Birmingham (Ala.) Mus. Art, Main Libr., Winston-Salem, N.C., U. Wis., Milw., Miami Beach Art Ctr., Tel Fair Acad., Savannah, Ga., Columbia (S.C.) Mus., U. N.C.-Chapel Hill, Stover Mill Gallery, Erwinna, Pa., Suffolk Art Mus., Stony Brook, N.Y., Cast Iron Gallery, N.Y., 1994, Kyoto Japan, also 50 traveling and stationary shows in N.Y.C. and nationwide, 1993; exhibited in over 500 shows; creator plastic resins and fiberglass as sculpture medium (bonded bronze), synthetic glazes as painting medium; author: (poetry) Nightshade, A Sculptor's Summary. Recipient prizes Corcoran Gallery, San Francisco Mus., Am. Fedn. Arts Traveling Show, Montclair Art Mus.; fellow MacDowell Colony, Yaddo. Mem. Archtl. League Sculptors Guild (past bd. dirs., treas.), Nat. Assn. Women Artists, Nat. Mus. Women in the Arts, Artist Craftsmen N.Y., Fedn. Modern Painters and Sculptors. Address: 136 Waverly Pl New York NY 10014-6821

WESEN, LISA JUSTICE, management executive; b. Camden, N.J., Mar. 23, 1965; d. William F. and Joan E. (Bryson) Justice; m. Robert M. Wesen, Dec. 1, 1990. BA in Comms., Rowan Coll., 1987. Tng. coord. Micrognosis, Danbury, Conn., 1988-89; prin. adminstrv. assoc. Pathfinder, Inc., Cherry Hill, N.J., 1989-95; asst. gen. mgr. Internat. Project Mgmt. Acad. divsn. Pathfinder, Inc., Cherry Hill, 1995—. Contbr. articles to profl. publs. Mem. NAFE. Office: Pathfinder Inc Internat Project Mgmt Acad 11 Allison Dr Cherry Hill NJ 08034

WESOLOWSKI, WANDA E., radiologic technology educator, consultant; b. Phila., Jan. 14, 1939; d. Thaddeus Joseph and Maryanna (Luszczak) W. AS, Hahnemann U., Phila., 1974; BA, LaSalle U., Phila., 1980; MA Ed, Beaver Coll., Glenside, Pa., 1983. Lic. Am. Reg. of Radiologic Technologists. Staff radiographer Einstein Med. Ctr., Phila., 1958-64, angiography supr., 1964-74; prof. Cmty. Coll. of Phila., 1974—; cons. N.J. Bur. Environ. Protection, Trenton, 1979-82, St. Louis U. Catholic Hosp. Assn., 1978-84. Co-author: (book) Introduction to Radiologic Technology, 1982, 86; contbr. articles to profl. jours. Recipient Alumni Spl. Achievement award Thomas Jefferson U., 1981. Fellow Am. Soc. Radiologic Technologists (NEMA award 1973); mem. Alpha Eta Allied Health Honor Soc. Office: CC Phila 1700 Spring Garden St Philadelphia PA 19130

WESSEL, MARJORIE PARKER, educator; b. N.Y.C., Nov. 13, 1930; d. Joseph Henry and Margie (O'Neill) Parker; m. Louis Joseph Wessel, Jan. 4, 1958; children: Margie W. Scott, Joseph A., Ann Marie. BS, Fla. State U., 1952; MA, U. Miami, 1958, EdD, 1989. Cert. tchr., Fla.; cert. counselor. Tchr. Dade County Schs., Miami, 1952-58, dean girls, 1958-64; asst. prin. guidance Hialeah Jr. H.S., Miami, 1967-70, Hialeah-Miami Lakes H.S., 1970-75; asst. prin. adminstrn. Am. Sr. H.S., Miami, 1976-78; asst. prin. curriculum Miami Norland S.H., Miami, 1978—. Contbr. articles to profl. jours. Fla. govs. commn. on women's and girl's participation in athletics and extracurricular activities, 1991-93; mem. Dade County Curriculum Coun.; mem. Project Visit, Washington, many others. Recipient Woman of Yr. award 1995, Commn. Status of Women Unsung Heroine award City of Miami, 1995, Lumen Christi award Cath. Educators' Guild, 1982, Lifetime of Giving award Sports Soc.; named Miami Herald Outstanding Citizen, 1958. Mem. H.S. Activities Assn. (commr. of edn., bd. dirs.), So. Assn. Self-Study and Evaluations Supts. Task Force on Athletics, So. Assn. of Colls. and Univs. (mem. forty five evaluation teams), Nat. Assn. of Coll. Admission Counselors (com. chairperson 34 annual conf., chairperson local coll. fair). Home: 14201 NW 14th Dr Miami FL 33167 Office: Marland Sr High Sch 1050 NW 195th St Miami FL 33169

WESSER, YVONNE, artist; b. London, 1935; m. David R. Wesser (div.); children: Marius, Pavelle. BA in Religion, CUNY, 1991. One-woman shows include Main St. Gallery, Brewster, N.Y., 1975, Little Carnegie Art Gallery, N.Y.C., 1980, 34th St. Theatre Gallery, N.Y.C., 1980, Lida Gallery, N.Y.C., 1982, Gallery 84, N.Y.C., 1984, 85, Discovery Art Gallery, Glen Cove, N.Y., 1987, Plaza Gallery, City Hall Bldg., Binghampton, N.Y., 1987, Stehle-Rd. Gallery, Midland, Tex., 1987, Pleiades Gallery, N.Y.C., 1991; exhibited in group shows at Galeria Mesa, Ariz., 1988, Scoharie County Arts Coun., Cobbleskill, N.Y., Cen. Mo. State Univ. Art Ctr. Gallery, Warrensburg, 1989, Viridian Gallery, N.Y.C., 1990, Columbus (Ohio) Art Gallery, 1991, Jacob Javits Fed. Bldg., N.Y.C., 1991, Multi Media Gallery, N.Y.C., 1991, The Corner Gallery, N.Y.C., 1991, Broadway Mall Gallery, N.Y.C., 1991; represented in permanent collections including Barky Hosp., Saigon, Vietnam, Art Students League, N.Y.C., Nat. Art Mus. of Sport U. New Haven, West Haven, Conn.; commns. include for Barsky Hosp., John Disiere, Larry Freed. Mem. Whitney Mus., Mus. Modern Art, Burr Artists. Recipient Elmer Perkin award Mus. Modern Art, N.Y.C., 1986, Juror's Merit award Alexandria Mus., N.Y.C., 1986, 2d prize Mus. of Contemporary Art, L.A., 1989, 1st prize Whitney Mus., N.Y.C., 1987. Mem. Nat. Assn. Women's Pen League, Visual Individualists United, N.Y. Acad. Sci. Roman Catholic. Home: 12 E 86th St Apt 1631 New York NY 10028-0517

WESSLER, MARY HRAHA, marketing executive; b. Des Moines, Nov. 4, 1961; d. Francis M. and Shirley A. (Malone) Hraha; 1 child, Nick. BA in Mass Communications, Iowa State U., 1984; postgrad., U. Denver, 1990. Asst. mktg. dir. Des Moines Ballet Co.; asst. press sec. Governor State of Iowa, Des Moines; dir. mktg. Real Estate Mgmt. Corp., Scottsdale, Ariz., 1984-87; v.p. Great West Mgmt. and Realty, Ltd., Denver, 1987—; instr., spkr. for apt. assns., Multi-Housing World and IREM. Mem. Nat. Apt. Assn., Colo. Apt. Assn., Apt. Assn. of Metro Denver (sec., bd. dirs., Owner of Yr. 1992-93, 95, Woman of Yr. 1989-90), Met. Club. Home: 2685 S Dayton Way #187 Denver CO 80231

WESSLING, SUSAN A., sports editor; b. Boston, Jan. 7, 1963; d. Bernard William and Carmella Josephine (Visco) W. BA, Clark U., 1985. Resdl. instr. New Engl Resdl. Svcs., Holden, Mass., 1985-86; reporter Nashoba Publs., Ayer, Mass., 1986-87; editor-in-chief The Banner/Coulter Press, West Boylston, Mass., 1987-90; sports editor Daily Item/Coulter Press, Clinton, Mass., 1990—. Co-dir. Tribute Road Race, Clinton, Mass., 1990—. Mem. Nat. Newspaper Assn. (best sports column 1994), New Eng. Press Assn. (best sports column 1991).

WESSNER, DEBORAH MARIE, telecommunications executive, computer consultant; b. St. Louis, Aug. 15, 1950; d. John George and Mary Jane (Beetz) Eyerman; m. Brian Paul Wessner, Sept. 15, 1972; children: Krystin, David. BA in Math. and Chemistry, St. Louis U., 1972; M Computer Info. Sci., U. New Haven, 1980. Statistician Armstrong Rubber Co., New Haven, 1972-74; programmer analyst Sikorsky div. United Techs., Stratford, Conn., 1974-77; project engr. GE, Bridgeport, Conn., 1977-79; software mgr. GE, Arlington, Va., 1979-81; mgr. software ops. Satellite Bus. Systems, McLean, Va., 1981-83; v.p. ops. DAMA Telecommunications, Rockville, Md., 1983-87; dir. network ops. and adminstrn. Data Gen. Network Svcs., Rockville, 1987-91; dir. bus. ops. Sprint Internat., Reston, Va., 1991-92; v.p. network adminstrn. Citicorp, Washington, 1992-93; v.p. telecomm. product mgmt. Citicorp, Reston, Va., 1994-95, v.p. product mgmt., 1996—; assoc., cons. KDB Assocs., Columbia, Md., 1986—. Mem. Am. Bus. Women's Assn., NAFE. Office: Citicorp Reston VA 22091

WESSON, MARIANNE, law educator; b. Houston, Sept. 14, 1948; d. Lawrence M. and Julia Lorena (Moore) W.; m. David Mastbaum, Dec. 27, 1989; 1 child, Benjamin W. Cantrick. AB, Vassar Coll., 1970; JD, U. Tex., 1973. Bar: Tex. 1974, Colo. 1977, U.S. Ct. Appeals (5th cir.) 1976, U.S. Ct. Appeals (10th cir.) 1980. Law clk. to judge U.S. Dist. Ct. (ea. dist.) Tex., Tyler, 1973-75; asst. atty. gen. State of Tex., Austin, 1976; asst. U.S. atty. Office U.S. Atty., Denver, 1980-82; assoc. prof. U. Colo., Boulder., 1976-90, prof. law, 1990—; acting assoc. v.p. for acad. affairs U. Colo., Boulder, 1989-90, pres.'s teaching scholar, 1992—, interim dean, 1995-96; mem. test devel. com. multistate bar exam. Nat. Conf. Bar Examiners, 1978—; mem. com. on rules criminal procedure Colo. Supreme Ct., Denver, 1982-88, mem. grievance com., 1989—; mem. criminal justice act com. U.S. Dist. Ct. Colo., 1991-93; mem. bd. advisers Tex. Women's Law Jour., 1991—. Author: Crimes and Defenses in Colorado, 1989; editor-in-chief Am. Jour. Criminal Law, 1972-73; mem. bd. editors Frontiers: Jour. Women Studies, 1988-90; contbr. articles to legal and feminist jours. Samuel E. Zeigler Found. fellow, 1978-79; recipient Mary Lathrop award for outstanding woman lawyer Colo. Women's Bar Assn., 1996. Mem. ABA, APA, Am. Law Inst., Assn. Am. Law Schs. (chmn. sect. on law and psychiatry 1987). Democrat. Office: U Colo Sch Law PO Box 401 Boulder CO 80303

WEST, ANN LEE, nursing educator, trauma nurse coordinator; b. Terre Haute, Ind., Aug. 11, 1943; d. Paul Everette and Margaret Alice (Roush) Corbin; m. Donald J. West, Aug. 29, 1964; children: Lee Ann, Kevin, Brian, Christopher. Diploma in nursing, St. Vincent's Hosp., 1964; BS, St. Joseph's Coll., 1983; MSN, Med. Coll. Ohio, 1992. RN, Ohio; ACLS, Advanced Cardiac Life Support provider instr.; cert. pediatric advanced life support, emergency nurse, trauma nurse core curriculum, basic life support; emergency nursing pediatric course provider, instr. Staff nurse St. Vincent Med. Ctr., Toledo, Ohio, 1964-67; office nurse Dr. Richard Leahy, Tiffin, Ohio, 1976-77; project nurse, relief nurse Clinicas Migrantes Reg., Fremont, Ohio, 1977-79; head nurse emergency dept. Bellevue Hosp., 1979-81; relief charge nurse Fireland's Cmty. Hosp., Sandusky, Ohio, 1981-95; staff devel. educator Med. Coll. Hosps., Toledo, 1993-96; trauma nurse coord. Med. Coll. Hosps., 1995—; med. and nursing educator Firelands Cmty. Hosp., Sandusky, 1987-95; trauma prevention/outreach, patient educator Med. Coll. Hosp., Toledo, 1994-96; disting. lectr. Am. Acad. Allergy and Immunology, 1993. Author booklet for Am. Lung Assn.; contbr. articles to profl. jours. Mem. Am. Acad. Poison Ctr., Am. Lung Assn. (bd. dirs., sec., sch. edn. chair 1984-96), Seagate Emergency Nurse Assn. (pres. 1996), Rolls Royce Owner's Club, Lion's Club Internat. (v.p.). Roman Catholic. Home: 320 Douglas Dr Bellevue OH 44811-1305 Office: Med Coll Ohio 3000 Arlington Ave Toledo OH 43699-0008

WEST, ANNA, artist, photographer; b. Reading, Pa., Feb. 8, 1956; d. Henry James Ferner and Rebecca Louise (Supplee) Lundgren. Student, Reading-Muhlenburg, 1976, Sch. Visual Arts, N.Y.C., 1989-90. Mgr. K&L Photolab., N.Y.C., 1988-90; self-employed Bklyn., 1990—; cons. CCT Internat., N.Y.C., 1990—. Photo editor San Francisco Music mag., 1984, cover photo N.Y. mag., 1992; publ. art work N.Y. Times, 1991. Dir. Williamsburg Organized Walkway, Bklyn., 1990-92; bd. dirs. Transp. Alternatives, N.Y.C., 1991-93. Recipient Etching Art grant Manhattan Graphics, 1992. Mem. Bklyn. Waterfront Artist Coalition. Home and Office: 109 South 9 St Brooklyn NY 11211

WEST, BRENDA KAY, educational coordinator; b. South Charleston, W.Va., May 27, 1951; d. Elton Theo and Anna Marguerite (Gibson) Maddox; m. David Robert West, Nov. 17, 1973 (div. Jan. 1995); children: Lisa Ann, Christopher David. BS in Biol. and Gen. Sci., Alderson-Broaddus Coll., Philippi, W.Va., 1973; cert. in 4-8 math., W.Va. State Coll., 1981; MS in Biol. Sci., Marshall U., 1984. Tchr. sci. and math. Putnam County Bd. Edn., Winfield, W.Va., 1973-95; program coord. project Coordinated and Thematic Sci. W.Va. Dept. Edn., Charleston, 1995—; cons. W.Va. sci. curriculum framework tng. cadre W.Va. Dept. Edn., Charleston, 1992—; ednl. instrnl. specialist IBM, Charleston, 1994—; mem. blue ribbon com. Holt, Rinehart, Winston Pubs., Tex. Author: Symposium on Wetlands of the Unglaciated, 1982. Bd. dirs., sec. Great Teays Soccer Club, Scott Depot, W.Va., 1981-86. Grantee Greater Kanawha Valley Found., W.Va. Dept. Edn.; W.Va. nominee for Presdl. award for Excellence in Sci. Teaching, 1995. Mem. NSTA, W.Va. Sci. Tchrs. Assn. (conf. com. 1993-96), Putnam County Sci. Tchrs. (co-chmn. 1990-95), Ctrl. Region Math. and Sci. Consortia (sec., pres.-elect 1995), Alpha Delta Kappa. Republican. Home: 4743 Teays Valley Rd Scott Depot WV 25560-9695 Office: WVa Dept Edn Bldg 6 Rm 330 1900 Kanawha Blvd E Charleston WV 25305

WEST, CYNTHIA KAYE, marketing executive; b. Greenville, Pa., June 6, 1964; d. Thomas Weldon and Lynn Virginia W.; m. Eric William Heinrich Gildenhuys, Aug. 20, 1994. BA, U. Calif., Santa Barbara, 1986, MA, 1988. Acct. exec. Cox Enterprises, Santa Barbara, 1988-90; western sales mgr. Found. for Nat. Progress, San Francisco, 1990-91; northwest acct. mgr. M&T Publishing., San Mateo, Calif., 1991-93; dir. sales TestDrive Corp., Santa Clara, Calif., 1993-94; v.p. strategic alliances Audio Hwy., Cupertino, Calif., 1994—; cons. Pacific Genesys, Vancouver, B.C., Can., 1992-93. Co-founder Women for Change, 1989. Mem. Phi Beta Kappa, Alpha Lambda Delta. Office: Audio Hwy 20600 Mariani Ave Cupertino CA 95014

WEST, DOE, bioethicist, social justice activist; b. Tucson, July 14, 1951; d. George Oliver and Dorothy Marie (Watson) W.; m. Bruce Malcolm Gale, Feb. 1, 1980. AA, Dutchess Community Coll., 1975; BS, SUNY, New Paltz, 1977; BA, Logos Bible Coll., 1986, MDiv, 1993; MS, Boston U., 1980; PhD, Northeastern U., 1996. Dir. 504/compliance officer dept. health and hosps. City of Boston, 1979-81, commr. handicap affairs, 1981-84; pres. Myth Breakers, Inc., 1984—; writer, photographer; exec. dir. Social Action Ministries of Gtr. Boston, 1996—; lectr. Northeastern U., Mt. Ida Coll., 1982—; dir. chaplaincy svcs. Quincy (Mass.) Hosp., 1991-92; chief of staff State House Boston, 1992-94; project coord. task force on human subject rsch. Fernald State Sch., 1994. Home: PO Box 2006 Brookline MA 02146

WEST, DORCAS JOY, women's health nurse; b. Friend, Nebr., Apr. 4, 1940; d. Ernest Emerson and Ruth Louise (Stuemky) Horner; m. Paul N. West, Nov. 8, 1969; children: Dale E., Charles B., Natalie Joy. RN, Bryan Meml. Sch. Nursing, Lincoln, Nebr., 1963; BS, Nebr. Wesleyan U., 1964; cert., Spanish Lang. Inst., San José, Costa Rica, 1964, Domestic Violence Coun., N.Mex., 1985. RN, N.Mex., Nebr.; cert. domestic violence counselor, N.Mex. RN obstetrics Bryan Meml. Hosp., Lincoln, 1963-64; missionary nurse Bd. Global Ministries, United Meth. Ch., Mex., 1964-66, Malaysia, 1970-75; office and surg. RN G. William LeWorthy MD, Reconstructive and Plastic Surgery, Lincoln, 1966-69; RN obstetrics Evanston (Ill.) Hosp., 1970; dir. Home for Women & Children, Shiprock, N.Mex., 1978-86; cons. RN quality assurance Shiprock (N.Mex.) Cmty. Health Ctr., 1988; RN obstetrics Navajo Area Indian Health Svc., Shiprock, 1989—; cons. Home for Women and Children, Shiprock, 1986—. Patricipant Internat. Christian Youth Exch., N.Y.C., 1958, Germany, 1958-59, host, 1985; pres. United Meth. Women, 1971-73, dist. pres., 1973-74, sec., 1988-91, mem., 1970—; mem. Four Corners Native Am. Ministry, 1977—; mem. Camp Farthest Out, 1984—, sec., 1990—; mem. social concerns com. United Meth. Ch., Shiprock, 1984-91, Sunday sch. tchr., 1966-69, 74-95; mem., asst. scoutmaster Anasazi dist. Boy Scouts Am., Shiprock, 1985—; mem. Concerned Women for Am., Washington, 1987—, Walk to Emmaus, 1991—. Recipient cert. of appreciation Home for Women and Children, Shiprock, 1984, appreciation award, 1994; named Nursing Employee of Month, Indian Health Svc., USPHS, 1991. Mem. Women's Soc. Christian Svc. (life). Home: PO Box 400 Shiprock NM 87420-0400

WEST, EILEEN M., caseworker; b. Somerset, Pa.; d. Casimir M. and Beatrice T. Stanis; m. Richard E. West (div. 1981); children: Theodore, Cynthia, Michael. BA, Pa. State U., 1970. Cert. FACTS program leader, Pa. Caseworker Susquehanna County Bd. Assistance, Montrose, Pa., 1970-73, Cumberland County Children & Youth Agy., Carlisle, Pa., 1988-89, ChildLine, Harrisburg, Pa., 1989—; Pa. Dept. Pub. Welfare liaison to Pa. Coalition Against Rape, Harrisburg, 1993-95. Chief shop stewart Svc. Employees Internat. Union 668, 1991—, alt. mem. statewide grievance appeal com., 1992-93, chair, 1993—, mem. statewide mobilization com. 1992-93, chpt. mobilizer, 1992-93, mem. statewide budget and fin. com., 1993, chpt. treas., 1993, chpt. v.p., 1994, area contract mobilizer, 1995—, del. Ea. Regional Women's Conf., Boston, 1995; mem. Molly Pitcher Stitchers Embroiderers' Guild Am., 1993—, publicity chairperson Susquehanna chpt., 1992-94, mem. Wyoming Valley chpt. 1995—, program chairperson Susquehanna chpt. 1996—, pres., 1996—; mem. 146 Knights of Lithuania Coun., 1991, v.p., 1992, pres., 1993, ritual chair, 1994—; tchr. Polyclinic Needlework Show, Harrisburg, 1993, 95. Republican. Roman Catholic. Home: 410 Norman Rd Camp Hill PA 17011-6130 Office: Commonwealth of Pa DPW ChildLine PO Box 2675 Harrisburg PA 17105-2675

WEST, EULA KIRKPATRICK, retired elementary education educator; b. Fox, Okla., Oct. 16, 1930; d. William B. and Eva (Williams) Kirkpatrick; m. Billy G. West, June 6, 1948 (dec. Apr. 1977); children: William G., Carol Ann West Rushing. Student, Hills Bus. Coll., 1950; BS, U. Southern Miss., 1972. Sec. Social Security Adminstrn., Amarillo, Tex., 1952-61; tchr. Harrison County, Gulfport, Miss., 1968-70; tchr. Biloxi (Miss.) Pub. Sch., 1971-96, ret., 1996. Sunday sch. tchr., 1953—. Mem. Miss. Profl. Educators, Eastern Star, Delta Kappa Gamma (sec., treas. pres., fin. com., Women of Distinction 1993). Baptist. Home: 11471 Pine Dr Gulfport MS 39503

WEST, FRANCES LEE, doll artist, freelance writer; b. Groves, Tex., Jan. 31, 1934; d. Henry Brewer Crittenden and Nora Josephine Billiot Showalter; m. Ronald Bruce West, May 14, 1955; children: Berry Jo Carter, Melissa Alyce Nelson. Student, Craft Burs. Am., Houston, 1957. Owner Dälzenstuff, Flower Mound, Tex., 1992—. Staff writer Craft Entrepreneur, 1994—; contbr. articles to The Crafter's Network, 1994. Mem. The Crafter's Network, Artists' Breakfast Club. Democrat. Home: 3708 Spring Meadow Ln Flower Mound TX 75028

WEST, GINA MARIA, educator; b. Boulder, Colo., July 9, 1948; d. Lyle Russell and Carmen Maria (Monge) West; m. Richard Carl Kline, Sept. 22, 1967 (div. 1992); children: Russell, Matthew, Kevin. AAS, Aims Cmty. Coll., 1988; BA summa cum laude, U. No. Colo., 1994. Flight instr. Greeley, Colo., 1983-87; charter captain Imperial Aviation, Greeley, Colo., 1983-87; tchr., pilot Aims C.C., Greeley, 1987—; owner Quick Link, Inc., Loveland, Colo., 1995—; cons. Miami-Dade C. C., 1989, liaison to pub. elem. schs. Aims C. C., Greeley, 1994—. Democratic. Home: 2550 Frederick Dr Loveland CO 80537 Office: Aims C C Greeley CO 80631

WEST, LINDA TARPLEY, civilian military employee; b. Portage, Wis., Dec. 15, 1951; d. Philip Lewis and Doris Jeanette (Grossmann) Tarpley; m. William Allen West, Dec. 30, 1986; children: Colleen Catherine, Lindsey Michelle, Jonathan Allen. BS in Recreation, U. Wis., La Crosse, 1974; MS in Adminstrn., Ctrl. Mich. U., 1995. Recreation specialist, case worker ARC, Ft. Worth, San Antonio, Wichita Falls, Tex., 1970-74; recreation specialist U.S. Army Walter Reed Med. Ctr., Washington, 1979-80; recreation specialist, program analyst U.S. Army, The Netherlands & Germany, 1980-88; mgmt. analyst U.S. Army, Germany, 1988-90, U.S. Army Med. Commd., San Antonio, 1991-94, Defense Logistics Agy., Dayton, Ohio, 1994-96, USAF, Dayton, Ohio, 1996—. Mem. altar guild/Abiding Christ Luth. Ch., Fairborn, Ohio, 1995—. Recipiemt Meritorious Civilian Svc. award, San Antonio, 1993-94. Mem. Am. Soc. Mil. Controllers (Team Achievement award 1993), Sigma Iota Epsilon.

WEST, LORETTA MARIE, underwriter; b. N.Y.C., Feb. 2, 1950; d. James L. and Alice (Richardson) W. AB, Washington Coll., Chestertown, Md., 1972. CPCU; cert. profl. ins. woman. Disbursements cashier Middlesex Ins. Co., Concord, Mass., 1972-76, tech. asst., 1976-78, comml. lines underwriter, 1978-83; sr. comml. lines underwriter Sentry Ins. Co., Concord, 1983-86, large acct. underwriter, 1986-88, sr. large account underwriter, 1988-92; with Hoffman Ins. Svcs., Inc., Wellesley, Mass., 1992—. Mem. Framingham (Mass.) Rep. Town Com., 1988-92; sec. Mass. Fedn. Rep. Women, 1992-94; trustee Prescott Gardens Condos, 1984-88; pres. Greater Precinct 12 Neighborhood Assn., 1990-92; pres. Framingham Rep. Women's Club, 1990-92; co-founder Framington Condominium Coalition, 1992—. Mem. Soc. CPCU, Nat. Assn. Ins. Women, Mass. Assn. Ins. Women (treas. 1990-92, various coms. Middlesex and South Middlesex chpts., co-dir. South Middlesex chpt. 1986-88, bd. dirs. South Middlesex chpt. 1988-90, Woman of Yr. award 1980), Women's Rep. Club Mass., Middlesex Club. Roman Catholic. Home: 6 Prescott St Framingham MA 01701-7511 Office: Hoffman Ins Svcs 200 Linden St Wellesley MA 02181-7914

WEST, MARGARET LYNNE, computer science and mathematics educator; b. Biloxi, Miss., Sept. 13, 1950; d. George Theodore and Margaret Adriana (Leslie) Perkins; m. Adam J. Ortiz, July 4, 1973 (div. Jan. 1989); stepchildren: Margo, Mark, Daniel; m. William G. West, Dec. 23, 1989. BS, U. So. Miss., 1976, MEd, 1979; postgrad., U. Calif., Santa Barbara, 1988-90. Math. tchr. Harrison County Schs., Gulfport, Miss., 1976-79, Ocean Springs (Miss.) High Sch., 1979-81; math. tchr., dept. chair Mercy Cross High Sch., Biloxi, 1981-86; computer sci. tchr., dept. chair Biloxi Pub. Schs., 1986-92; computer sci./math. instr. Miss. Gulf Coast C.C.-Jefferson Davis Campus, Gulfport, 1992—; adj. faculty Embry-Riddle Aero. U., Keesler AFB, Miss., 1981-86, U. So. Miss.-Gulf Park Campus, Long Beach, 1986—; instr. Ctr. for Academically Talented and Gifted Youth, Johns Hopkins U., Redlands, Calif., 1990-91. Co-author (course curriculum) State Computer Lit. Course, 1991-92. Sunday Sch. tchr. Bapt. Ch., Biloxi, 1980—, ch. treas., pianist, 1992—; local/ch. choirs Community Chorus/Bapt. Ch., Biloxi, 1975—; mem. PTA. Recipient NSF fellowship, 1988-90, Summer Indsl. fellowship for tchrs. Naval Oceanographic Command, Miss. Gulf Coast Econ. Devel. Coun., and Johnson Controls World Svcs., Inc., 1992; nat. semi-finalist Tandy Corp.-Outstanding Tchr., 1990; named Star Tchr., State of Miss., 1986. Mem. Nat. Coun. Tchrs. Math., Miss. Coun. Tchrs. Math., Miss. Ednl. Computing Assn., Phi Delta Kappa, Delta Kappa Gamma. Republican. Home: 2098 Woodfield Ln Biloxi MS 39532-3349 Office: Miss Gulf Coast CC 2226 Switzer Rd Gulfport MS 39507-3824

WEST, MARSHA, elementary school educator; b. DeQueen, Ark., Sept. 1, 1950; d. Marshall T. and Mildred L. (Davis) Gore; m. Larry T. West, May 19, 1972; 1 child, Zachary. BS in Edn., So. State Coll., Magnolia, Ark., 1971; MEd, U. Ark., 1975; postgrad., Henderson State Coll., Arkadelphia, Ark., Purdue U.; specialist's degree, U. Ga., 1991. Cert. elem. and spl. edn. tchr., Tex., elem. tchr., early childhood, mid. sch. tchr., media specialist, Ga. Spl. edn. resource tchr. Gatesville (Tex.) Ind. Sch. Dist.; tchr. early childhood spl. edn. Bryan (Tex.) Ind. Sch. Dist.; elem. tchr. Tippecanoe Sch. Corp., Lafayette, Ind.; elem. tchr. Clarke County Sch. Dist., Athens, Ga., media specialist. Mem. ALA, NEA, Am. Assn. Sch. Librs., Internat. Reading Assn., Ga. Assn. Educators, Ga. Assn. Instrnl. Tech., Ga. Libr. Media Assn. (dist. V chair), N.E. Ga. Reading Coun., Clarke County Assn. Educators, Kappa Delta Pi.

WEST, MARTHA ULLMAN, writer; b. Pasadena, Calif., June 18, 1938; d. Allen and Sara (Bachrach) Ullman; m. Franklin C. West, June 22, 1963; 1 child, Alice Emily. BA, Barnard Coll., 1960. Visual arts writer, feature writer Manhattan East, N.Y.C., 1960-61; juvenile book editor William Morrow & Co., N.Y.C., 1961-63; advt. copywriter Lipman Wolfe; Meier & Frank, Portland, Oreg., 1965-68; tech. writer Follow Through, Portland, 1973-74, Head Start Tng., Portland, 1974-75; dance writer Dance Mag., N.Y.C., 1979—, The Oregonian, Portland, 1988—; dance and arts writer Willamette Week, Portland, 1984-88; site visitor Nat. Endowment Arts, Washington, 1993-95. Contbr. feature articles and revs. to profl. publs. Bd. dirs. Friends of Multnomah County Pub. Libr., Portland, 1974—, Oreg. Cultural Heritage Commn., Portland, 1994-95; mem. com. Multnomah County Dems., Portland, 1968-82. Mem. Dance Critics Assn. (co-chair bd. dirs. 1995-97), Oreg. Hist. Soc. Home and Office: 1237 SE 53d Ave Portland OR 97215

WEST, MARY ELIZABETH, psychiatric management professional; b. Spartanburg, S.C., Aug. 27, 1939; d. Thomas Benjamin and Virginia Milster (Smith) Anderson; m. William Duane West, Sept. 13, 1960; children: William Kevin, Walter Duane, Litia Allyn West Harrison, Thomas Anderson. Diploma in nursing, Ga. Bapt. Hosp., 1960; BS in Nursing Leadership, Tift Coll., 1966; MS in Counseling, U. Scranton, 1972; EdD, Nova U., 1979. RNC, Tenn.; cert. profl. counselor, Tenn., nurse adminstr. advanced. Staff nurse pub. health Fulton County Health Dept., Atlanta, 1960-61; instr. in nursing Macon (Ga.) Hosp. Sch. Nursing, 1965-66, Western Piedmont C.C., 1973-74; dir. nursing Tyler Meml. Hosp., Tunkhannock, Pa., 1967-70; assoc. dir. nursing Nesbitt Meml. Hosp., Kingston, Pa., 1971; assoc. adminstr. Home Health Svcs. Luzerne County, Wilkes-Barre, Pa., 1972; cons. nursing Hosp. Affiliates Internat., Nashville, 1974-76, v.p. nursing, 1976-78, v.p. quality assurance, 1978-80; v.p. nursing cons. svc. Advanced Mgmt. Sys., Nashville, 1981; sr. v.p. planning Hosp. Affiliates Devel. Corp., Nashville, 1982-83; v.p. ops. Winter Haven (Fla.) Hosp., 1986-90; pres. Hope Psychiat. Mgmt., Inc., Winter Haven, 1994—. Contbg. author: Political Action Handbook for Nurses, 1985 (Am. Jour. Nursing Book of Yr. 1986); co-author, editor manual Hosp. Affiliates International, 1978; contbr. articles to mags., chpt. to book. V.p. part time svcs. Winter Haven Hosp., 1987-90; insvc. tng. dir. Rotary Internat., Winter Haven, 1989-91; v.p. Winter Haven C. of C., 1988-90; pres. Polk County Nurse Exec. Orgn., Lakeland, Fla., 1989-90; bd. dirs. Women's Resource Ctr., Inc., Winter Haven, 1989-91; bd. dirs., founder Mothers Alone, Haines City, Fla., 1991—; nat. chair Sunhealth Nursing Coun., Charlotte, N.C., 1990; founder, bd. chmn. Hope Christian Counseling Inc., 1994; state bd. dirs., dir. profl. edn. Bapt. Nursing Fellowship, 1995—. Mem. ANA, Fla. Nursing Assn., Am. Orgn. Nurse Execs., Inner Wheel (v.p., treas., bd. dirs. 1992—), Theta Chi Omega. Republican. Baptist. Home: 3208 Lake Breeze Dr Haines City FL 33844 Office: HOPE Psychiat Mgmt Ste 5013 5665 Cypress Gardens Blvd Winter Haven FL 33884-2273

WEST, MAXINE MARILYN, psychologist; b. St. Thomas, Ont., Can., Apr. 25, 1945; came to U.S., 1945; d. James and Selma Laura (Khoury) Toms; m. Gordon James West, Jan. 8, 1966 (div. Nov. 1978); children: Gregory, Laura, Amy, Nicholas. BA, Oakland U., 1966; postgrad., Mpls. Community Coll., 1978; MA, St. Mary's Coll., Winona, Minn., 1982. Lic. psychologist, Minn. Chem. dependency counselor Chrysalis-A Ctr. for Women, Mpls., 1979-82; chem. dependency counselor Mpls., 1982-88, pvt. practice psychologist, 1988—. Author: Shame-Based Family Systems: The Assault on Esteem, 1991; co-author and producer: (video film) Shame: When it Happens to a Child, 1989; contbr. articles to Jour. of Couple Therapy. Mem. Am. Psychol. Assn. (assoc.). Office: 430 Oak Grove St Ste 203 A Minneapolis MN 55403-3234

WEST, ROBERTA BERTHA, writer; b. Saline County, Mo., Sept. 7, 1904; d. Robert and Amanda Melvina (Driver) Baur; m. Harold Clinton West, Aug. 27, 1932; children: Arle Faith W. Lohof, Lydia Ann (Lyda) F H. Hyde, Danna Rose F H. Burns. AB, William Jewell Coll., 1928; AM, U. Mo., 1930. Cert. tchr., Mo., Mont. Elem. and secondary sch. tchr. Mo. and Mont. Schs., 1922-47; supt. schs. Hogeland (Mont.) Schs., 1947-48, 55; prof. fgn. langs. Will Mayfield Coll., Marble Hill, Mo., 1930; columnist Quad County Star, Viburnum, Mo., 1982—; writer and researcher ch. history, 1964-91; cons. hist. com. Yellowstone Conf. Meth. Ch., 1971-84; compiler Mont. list of Meth. Mins. 1784-1984. Author: Northern Montana Methodist History, 3 vols., 1974, Faith, Hope and Love in the West, 1971; editor: Brother Van by Those Who Knew Him, 1975, reprinted, 1989,; also contbr. articles. Recipient 1st John M. Templeton prize, 1959. Mem. Alpha Zeta Pi. Democrat. Home: PO Box 583 Viburnum MO 65566-0583 Office: Quad County Star Viburnum MO 65566

WEST, SHARON M., public housing administrator; b. Buffalo, Feb. 8, 1948; d. William Eddy and Geraldine (Summers) W.; children: Lisa, Shontai. BA, SUNY, Buffalo, 1976. Legis. asst. Prince George County, Upper Marlborough, Md., 1978-80, N.Y. State Legislature, Albany, Buffalo, 1980-82; mgr. long range planning Niagara Frontier Transportation Auth., Buffalo, 1982-88; dep. commr. planning Erie County Dept. Environ. & Planning, Buffalo, 1988-95; exec. dir. Buffalo Mcpl. Housing Auth., 1995—. Sec. bd. dirs. United Way, Buffalo, 1988—, Geneva B. Savage Health Ctr., Buffalo, 1984—; trustee Erie C.C., Buffalo, 1982—. Kellogg Found. fellow, 1992-94. Democrat. Baptist. Office: BMHA 300 Perry St Buffalo NY 14204

WESTALL, SANDRA THORNTON, special education educator; b. Rochester, N.Y., Jan. 31, 1940; d. William Heldrith and Janice (King) Thonrton; m. Thomas Keith Westall, Jan. 10, 1965 (div. 1980); children: William Thornton, Robert Theodore. AS in Bus., So. Va. Coll. Women, 1962; BA in Early Childhood Edn., Mars Hill Coll., 1982; MA in Spl. Edn., Appalachian State U., 1989; MA in Behavioral Emotional Edn., Western Carolina U., 1990. Cert. tchr. spl. edn., learning disabilities, emotional handicapped, N.C., Fla. Tchr.'s asst. spl. edn. Mitchell County Sch., Spruce Pine, N.C., 1964-70; tchr. Pine Ridge Sch. for Learning Disabilities, Williston, Vt., summer 1985, 88, Summit Acad. for Learning Disabled Students, Waynesville, N.C., 1986-88; resource tchr. Ire B. Jones Elem. Sch. and Asheville Jr. High Sch., N.C., 1988-89; tchr. Irene Worthem Sch. for Severe/Profound Mentally Retarded, Asheville, 1989-90; resource tchr. G. Holmes Braddock High Sch., Miami, Fla., 1990-91, Kelsey L. Pharr Elem. Sch., Miami, 1991-94; tchr. severely emotionally disturbed Lakewood Elem. Sch., St. Petersburg, Fla., 1994—; night tchr. Nova U., Ft. Lauderdale, Fla., 1992—, Fla. Meml. Coll., Miami, 1992—; tutor, counselor Black Mountain (N.C.) Correctional Ctr. for Women, 1988-90; trainer behavior disorders No. Colo. U., Breckenridge, 1989, Willie M. Workshop, Asheville, 1989; condr. workshops on left and right brain teaching, 1980-87; speaker on learning disabled adults Harvard U., 1989; tchr. day camps for handicapped students, 1983, 84; advocate for learning disabled students and adults; del. Citizen Amb. Program field of learning disabilities, Diagnostic Ctr., various schs., Vilnius, Siauliai Pedagogical Inst., Dept. Spl. Pedagogics, Lithuania, Inst. Defectology, Russian Acad. Pedagogical, Moscow, City Coun., Inst. Econ. Problem Studies, St. Petersburg, Russia, 1993. Vol. Dade County Helpline and Dade County Schs. (in aid of Hurricane Andrew victims), swimming courses for ARC, 1980—; bd. dirs. N.C. Advocacy Ctr. for Children's Edn. and Parent Tng., 1986-90. Grantee Creative Learning for Behavior Handicapped Students, 1989; honoree ARC, 1980. Mem. Am. Coun. on Rural Spl. Edn., Assn. for Children and Adults with Learning Disabilities, The Orton Dyslexia Soc., Coun. for Exceptional Children, Coun. for Behavior Emotionally Handicapped Children. Episcopalian. Home: 751 Pinellas BayWay 205 Tierra Verde FL 33715 Office: Lakewood Elem Sch 4151 6th St S Saint Petersburg FL 33705

WESTBY, CAROL E., speech and language pathologist; b. Washington, Pa., Apr. 5, 1943; d. Louis and Ann (Yereb) Emrick. BA in English, Geneva Coll., 1965; MA in Speech Lang. Pathology, U. Iowa, 1968, PhD in Speech Lang. Pathology, 1971. Speech/lang. pathologist ARC, Troy, N.Y., 1971-73, Unity House, Troy, 1971-77; asst. prof. Albany (N.Y.) State U., 1973-77; lang. specialist programs for children U. N.Mex., Albuquerque, 1977-86, sr. rsch. assoc., 1986-94; assoc. prof. Wichita (Kans.) State U., 1994—; adv. bd. Project Ta-Kos, Albuquerque, 1991-94. Editorial bd. Topics in Lang. Disorders/Am. Jour. Speech Lang. Pathology; editor: Topics in Lang. Disorders; author: Analyzing Storytelling Skills, 1993. Recipient Disting. Svc. award Geneva Coll., Beaver Falls, Pa., 1989. Fellow Am. Speech, Lang. & Hearing Assn.; mem. N.Mex. Speech, Lang. & Hearing Assn. (pres. 1987-89, Hons. 1987). Home: 1808 Princeton Dr NE Albuquerque NM 87106-2530 Office: Wichita State Univ Wichita KS 67260

WESTERHAUS, CATHERINE K., social worker; b. Corydon, Ind., Oct. 13, 1910; d. Anthony Joseph and Permelia Ann (Mathes) Kannapel; m. George Henry Westerhaus, Apr. 15, 1950. BEd in Music, Kans. U., 1934; MSW, Loyola U., Chgo., 1949. Cert. Acad. Cert. Social Workers. Clin. social worker Friendly Acres Home of Aged, Newton, Kans.; county welfare dir., state adult svcs. supr. Newton-Harvey County, State of Kans.; vol. cert. social worker Newton. Project dir.: Memories of War Years, 1995, The War Years Including Veterans of Harvey County, Kansas, 1995; contbr. articles to profl. jours. With USNR, 1945-46. Named Kans. Social Worker of Yr., 1975. Mem. NASW (cert.), Kans. Soc. Cert. Social Work, Am. Legion (comdr. Wayne G. Austin post 1981-82). Home: 313 W Broadway St Newton KS 67114-2631

WESTERMAN, ROSEMARY MATZZIE, nurse, administrator; b. Sewickley, Pa., May 20, 1949; d. Joseph Edward and Martha (Aquino) Matzzie; m. Philip M. Westerman, Aug. 7, 1971. BSN, Duquesne U., 1971, MSEd, 1975. RN, Pa. Head nurse Dept. Vet. Affairs VA Med. Ctr., Pitts.; assoc. chief, nursing svc., edn. W. S. Middleton Meml. VA Hosp., Madison, Wis.; assoc. chief, nursing svc., edn. Dept. VA Affairs VA Med. Ctr., Chilicothe, assoc. chief nursing svc., long term. care; assoc. chief nurse VA Med. Ctr., Augusta, Ga.; chief nurse VA Med. Ctr., Muskogee, Okla. Active Literacy Vol. of Am. Mem. ANA (cert. nursing adminstrn. advanced), Assoc. Am. Coll. Health Care Execs., Okla. Orgn. Nurse Execs., Okla. Nurses Found., Nursing Orgn. of VA, Okla. Nurses Assn., VA Nurse Execs., Sigma Theta Tau. Home: 1409 E Concord St Broken Arrow OK 74012-9259

WESTFALL-HUEPENBECKER, SANDRA ANN, psychiatric nurse, consultant; b. Toledo, June 3, 1956; d. Billy Joe and Hilda Ann (Norman) Liggett; m. David Harley Westfall, Dec. 3, 1975 (div. Nov. 1987); m. Richard Clark Huepenbecker, May 18, 1993. ADN, U. Toledo C.C., 1987; BS in Health Care Adminstrn. magna cum laude, U. Toledo, 1995, postgrad., 1995—. RN, Ohio; LPN, Ohio. Staff nurse Lake Park Extend Care Facility, Sylvania, Ohio, 1984-87, house supr., 1987-90; psychiat. nurse supr. II Toledo Mental Health Ctr., 1987-92; med.-legal cons. Sylvania Consulting Svcs., 1992—. CPR instr., ARC, Toledo, 1989—. Mem. ANA, ABA, LPN Assn., Ohio Bar Assn., Women's Law Assn., Health Care Law Assn., Golden Key Honor Soc., Phi Kappa Phi, Delta Theta Phi. Republican. Home and Office: 6035 Glasgow Rd Sylvania OH 43560

WESTHEIMER, (KAROLA) RUTH SIEGEL, psychologist, television personality; b. Frankfurt, Fed. Republic Germany; came to U.S., 1956; m. Manfred Westheimer; children: Miriam, Joel. Grad. psychology, U. Paris Sorbonne; Master's degree, New Sch. for Social Research, N.Y.C., 1959; EdD, Columbia U., 1970. Research asst. Columbia U. Sch. Pub. Health, N.Y.C., 1967-70; assoc. prof. Lehman Coll., Bronx, N.Y., 1970-77; with Bklyn. Coll., West Point Milit. Acad.; counsellor, radio talk show hostess Sexually Speaking Sta. WYNY-FM, N.Y.C., 1980—; hostess TV series Good Sex, Dr. Ruth Show, Ask Dr. Ruth, 1987—; pvt. practice N.Y.C.; adj. assoc. prof. NYU; leader seminars for residents and interns in pediats. on adolescent sexuality Brookdale Hosp. Author: Dr. Ruth's Guide to Good Sex, 1983, First Love: A Young People's Guide to Sexual Information, 1985, Dr. Ruth's Guide for Married Lovers, 1986, (autobiography) All In a Lifetime, 1987, Sex and Morality: Who is Teaching Out Sex Standards?, 1988, Dr. Ruth's Guide to Erotic and Sensuous Pleasures, 1991, Dr. Ruth's Guide to Safer Sex, 1992, Dr. Ruth Talks to Kids, 1993, The Art of Arousal, 1993, Dr. Ruth's Encyclopedia of Sex, 1994, Heavenly Sex, 1995, Sex for Dummies, 1995, The Value of Family, 1996; co-author: (with Steven Kaplan) Surviving Salvation; contbr. articles to mags.; appeared in film A Woman or Two, 1986; appeared on TV show Quantum Leap, 1993, Play Boy Making Love Series (video), 1996, All New Dr. Ruth Show (nominated 5 times by Ace awards, Ace award for excellence in cable TV, 1988), What's Up, Dr. Ruth (gold medal Internat. Film and TV Festival for excellence in ednl. TV), You're on the Air with Dr. Ruth, Never Too Late, 1992—, Dr. Ruth's House, (calendar) Dr. Ruth's Good Sex Night-to-Night Calendar, 1993, 94, (boardgame) Dr. Ruth's Game of Good Sex; exec. prodr. documentary on Ethiopian Jews Surviving Salvation, 1991; columnist Ask Dr. Ruth. Pres. YMHA, Washington Heights. Recipient Mother of Yr. award Nat. Mother's Day Com., Liberty medal City of N.Y. Fellow N.Y. Acad. Medicine. Office: Pierre A Lehu Comms Connection 145 W 45th St Ste 1009 New York NY 10036*

WESTMORELAND, BARBARA FENN, neurologist, electroencephalographer, educator; b. N.Y.C., July 22, 1940; d. Robert Edward and Wanda Helen (Zabawski) Westmoreland. BS in Chemistry, Mary Washington Coll., 1961; MD, U. Va., 1965. Diplomate Am. Bd. Psychiatry and Neurology and certification of added qualification in clin. neurophysiology. Intern Vanderbilt Hosp., Nashville, 1965-66; resident in neurology U. Va. Hosp., Charlottesville, 1966-70; fellow in electroencephalography Mayo Clinic, Rochester, Minn., 1970-71, assoc. cons. neurology, 1971-73; asst. prof. neurology Mayo Med. Sch., Rochester, 1973-78, assoc. prof., 1978-85, prof., 1985—. Co-author: Medical Neurosciences, 1978, rev. edit., 1986, first author 3d edit., 1994. Mem. Am. Epilepsy Soc. (treas. 1978-80, pres. 1987-88), Am. EEG Soc. (sec. 1985-87, pres. 1991-92), Cen. Assn. Electroencephalographers (sec.-treas. 1976-78, pres. 1979-80, chair neurology resident in-svc. tng. exam 1994—), Mayo History of Medicine Soc. (pres. 1990-91), Sigma Xi (pres. chpt. 1987-88).

WESTON, FRANCINE EVANS, secondary education educator; b. Mt. Vernon, N.Y., Oct. 8, 1946; d. John Joseph and Frances (Fantino) Pisanielo. BA, Hunter Coll., 1968; MA, Lehman Coll., 1973; cert., Am. Acad. Dramatic Arts, N.Y.C., 1976; PhD, NYU, 1991. Cert. elem., secondary tchr., N.Y. Tchr. Yonkers (N.Y.) Bd. Edn., 1968—; aquatic dir. Woodlane Day Camp, Irvington-on-Hudson, N.Y., 1967-70, Yonkers Jewish Community Ctr., 1971-75; creative drama tchr. John Burroughs Jr. H.S., Yonkers, 1971-77; stage lighting designer Iona Summer Theatre Festival, New Rochelle, N.Y., 1980-81, Yonkers Male Glee Club, 1981-89, Roosevelt H.S., 1980—; rsch. specialist Scholarship Locating Svc., 1992-94, Yonkers Civil Def. Police Aux., 1994—; master electrician NYU Summer Mus. Theatre, 1979-80. Actress in numerous community theatre plays including A Touch of the Poet, 1979; dir. stage prodns. including I Remember Mama, 1973, The Man Who Came to Dinner, 1975; author: A Descriptive Comparison of Computerized Stage Lighting Memory Systems With Non-Computerized Systems, 1991, (short stories) A Hat for Louise, 1984, Old Memories: Beautiful and Otherwise, 1984; lit. editor: (story and poetry collection) Beautifully Old, 1984. Steering com. chairperson Roosevelt H.S.-Middle States Assn. of Schs. and Colls. Self-Evaluation, 1985-88; mem. Yonkers Civil Def. Police Aux., 1994—. Named Tchr. of Excellence, N.Y. State English Coun., 1990; recipient Monetary award for Teaching Excellence, Carter-Wallace Products, 1992, Educator of Excellence award N.Y. State English Coun., 1995; named to Arrid Tchrs. Honor Roll, 1992. Mem. U.S. Inst. for Theatre Tech., Nat. Coun. Tchrs. English, N.Y. State English Coun., N.Y. State United Tchrs. Assn., Yonkers Fedn. Tchrs., Port Chester Obedience Tng. Club, Inc., Kappa Delta Pi. Republican. Roman Catholic. Office: Roosevelt High Sch Tuckahoe Rd Yonkers NY 10710

WESTON, JANICE LEAH COLMER, librarian; b. Phila., Jan. 3, 1944; d. Robert Henry and Mildred Viola (Hale) Colmer; m. Stephen Paul Oksala, Aug. 21, 1965 (div. 1970); m. Leonard Charles Weston, Oct. 28, 1972. BA in History, U. Mich., 1966; MS in LS, Wayne State U., 1969; postgrad., Cath. U. Am., 1975, Brigham Young U., 1975. Cert. profl. libr., Va. Library clk. Edn. Libr., U. Mich., Ann Arbor, 1966-67; reference libr. John Tyler Community Coll., Chester, Va., 1969-70, Tech. Libr., Aberdeen Proving Ground, Md., 1971-72; br. libr. Chester Pub. Libr., 1969-70; libr. Gen. Equipment Test Activity, Ft. Lee, Va., 1970-71; chief libr. Army Ordnance Ctr. and Sch., Aberdeen Proving Ground, 1972-94; mem. job analysis task force Dept. Army, Washington, 1976; chmn. Aberdeen Proving Ground Media Svcs. Com., 1978, 83, 88. Author: Operating Procedures, 1988. Mem. James Buchanan Found., Lancaster, Pa., 1977—, Fulton Opera House Found., Lancaster, 1985—, Friends Libr. So. Lancaster County, Quarryville, Pa., 1985—; Humane League Friends, Lancaster, 1988—, Friends of Atglen Susquehanna Trail, 1994—, Friends of the Libr., Cocoa Beach, Fla., 1996—; mem. St. David's by the Sea Episcopal Ch., Cocoa Beach, 1996—. Mem. Spl. Librs. Assn., Ret. Officers Assn. Home: 25 Oak Ridge Dr Quarryville PA 17566-9284

WESTON, JOAN SPENCER, production director; b. Barton, Vt., Aug. 11, 1943; d. Rolfe Weston and Dorothy Lena (Spencer) Schoppe. BA magna cum laude, U. Mass., 1965. Tchr. high sch. Gorham (Maine) Schs., 1965-66; tchr. Sherwood Hall Sch., Mansfield, Eng., 1966-67, tchr. middle sch. Meden Sch., Warsop, Eng., 1967-68; dept. head high sch. Goffstown (N.H.) Schs., 1968-82; dir. circulation T.H.E. Jour., Acton, Mass., 1982-83; prodn. mgr. The Robb Report, Acton, 1983-87, prodn. dir., 1988; prodn. dir. New Age Pub. Inc., Watertown, Mass., 1993—. Mem. Boston Prodn. Mgrs. Group, Phi Beta Kappa. Office: New Age Jour 42 Pleasant St Watertown MA 02172-2316

WESTOVER, KATHLEEN MARJORIE, nurse anesthetist; b. Ware, Mass., May 14, 1943; d. Eldon Darius Westover and Doris Irene Danforth. Diploma, Dartmouth-Hitchcock Sch. Nursing, Hanover, N.H., 1964, cert. anesthesia, 1974; BA with honors, Stevens Coll., 1988. RN, N.H.; cert. RN anesthetist, N.H. RN Dartmouth-Hitchcock Hosp., Hanover, N.H., 1965-69, 71-72, Vis. Nurse Assn., Charlestown, N.H., 1969-71; RN anesthetist Springfield (Vt.) Hosp., 1974-77; chief RN anesthetist St. Luke's Hosp., Spokane, Wash., 1977-83; staff RN anesthetist Broward Gen. Med. Ctr., Ft. Lauderdale, Fla., 1983-84; solo RN anesthetist Weeks Meml. Hosp., Lancaster, N.H., 1984-88; RN anesthetist Lakes Region Anesthesiology, Laconia, N.H., 1988—. Mem. DAR (vice regent Mary Butler chpt. 1995—), Am. Assn. Nurse Anesthetists, N.H. Assn. Nurse Anesthetists (bd. dirs. 1989-92), N.H. Assn. Advanced RN Practitioners, New Eng. Assemby Nurse Anesthetists (treas. 1991-95). Office: Lakes Region Anesthesiology PO Box 1305 Laconia NH 03247

WESTPHAL, JAYNE STIRLING, vocal music educator; b. Salem, Ohio, Jan. 26, 1927; d. Richard Charles and Agnes Emily (Snyder) Stirling; m. Arlo Chevalier Westphal, June 9, 1951; 1 child, Greta Stirling Westphal-Friedman. B in Pub. Sch. Music, Mount Union Coll., Alliance, Ohio, 1947; postgrad., Ind. U., 1952-54. Vocal music tchr. Akron, Ohio, 1948-51, LaPorte, Ind., 1951-86. Mem. bd. Mainstreet, LaPorte, 1990-93; v.p. Symphony Orch., LaPorte, 1990-93; pres. LaPorte Hist. Reservation Rev. Bd., 1989-95. Mem. AAUW (pres. 1987-89, grant scholarship 1989), Delta Kappa Gamma. Baptist.

WESTROPE, MARTHA RANDOLPH, psychologist, consultant; b. Gaffney, S.C., May 19, 1922; d. Gordon Robert and Hannah (Brown) W.; 1 adopted child, Ashley Randolph. BS, Winthrop Coll., 1942; MA, U. N.C., 1944; PhD, State U. of Iowa, Iowa City, 1952. Lic. psychologist, S.C. Pvt. practice Greenville, S.C., 1960—, part-time pvt. practice, 1987—; part-time staff mem. Spartanburg (S.C.) Mental Health Clinic, 1971-73, Greenville Mental Health Ctr., 1974-85, Patrick B. Harris Psychiat. Hosp., Anderson, S.C., 1985-87; med. cons. S.C. Vocat. Rehab. Dept., Greenville, 1987-91, part-time med. cons., 1993—; cons. S.C. Parole Bd. for Psychol. Evaluation, S.C. Dept. Corrections, 1983-87. Mem. Am. Psychol. Assn., Southeastern Psychol. Assn., S.C. Psychol. Assn., Am. Assn. for Advancement of Psychology, Greenville County Mental Health Assn., Am. Group Psychotherapy Assn., Coun. for the Nat. Register of Health Svc. Providers in Psychology. Democrat. Presbyterian. Home: 11 Darien Way Greenville SC 29615-3236 Office: 506 Pettigru St Greenville SC 29601-3117

WESTWICK, CARMEN ROSE, nursing educator, consultant; b. Holstein, Iowa, Feb. 2, 1936; d. J. Alfred and Hazel C. (Lage) Armiger; m. Richard A. Westwick, Dec. 28, 1957; children: Timothy, Ann. BS in Nursing, U. Iowa, 1958; MS, U. Colo., 1960; PhD, Denver U., 1972. RN, Tenn. Instr. Sch. Nursing West Suburban Hosp., Oak Park, Ill., 1958-59, 60-62; nurse Navajo Presch., Carson's Trading Post, N.Mex., 1967; lectr. then prof. U. Colo., Denver, 1968-69, 72-77; program dir. Western Coun. on Higher Edn. in Nursing, Boulder, Colo., 1976-77; prof. nursing, dean U. N.Mex, Albuquerque, 1977-81, Boston U., 1982-85, S.D. State U., Brookings, 1988-91; NHC chair of excellence in nursing NHC, Murfreesboro, 1993—; exec. dir. N.H. Bd. Nursing, Concord, 1986-87; case reviewer Joint Underwriters Assn., Boston, 1983-92; mem. publs. and rsch. com. Aberdeen (S.D.) Area Indian Health Svc., 1989-91; manuscript reviewer Midwest Alliance in Nursing, Indpls., 1989-92, Holistic Nursing Jour.; mem. adv. coun. S.D. Office Rural Health, Pierre, 1989-91. Contbr. articles to profl. jours. Nurse trainee fellow Nursing div. Dept. Health and Human Svcs., 1959-60, Predoctoral fellow, 1969-72; Nat. Merit scholar, 1954-56. Fellow Am. Acad. Nursing; mem. Sigma Theta Tau (nat. 1st v.p. 1968, disting. lectr. 1996—), Phi Kappa Phi, Kappa Delta Phi. Lutheran. Office: Mid Tenn State U Dept Nursing Box 81 Murfreesboro TN 37132

WETHERALD, MICHELE WARHOLIC, lawyer; b. Lakewood, Ohio, June 17, 1954; d. Michael and Veronica (Walkuski) Warholic; m. Gary R. Wetherald, Nov. 26, 1987. AAB, Lorain County C.C., Elyria, Ohio, 1977; BA, Hiram Coll., 1980; JD, U. Akron, 1985. Bar: Ohio, 1986; U.S. Dist. Ct. (no. dist.) Ohio, 1987. Sec., dispatcher State Highway Patrol Ohio Turnpike Commn., Berea, Ohio, 1973-77; pers. and employee benefits rep. Terex Div. Gen. Motors Corp., Hudson, Ohio, 1978-83; labor relations rep. Lordstown Assembly Div. Gen. Motors Corp., Warren, Ohio, 1984-86; supr. labor relations and hourly employment Inland Div. Gen. Motors Corp., Livonia, Mich., 1986-87; staff atty. Hyatt Legal Svcs., Niles, Ohio, 1987-89; mng. atty. Hyatt Legal Svcs., Boardman, Ohio, 1990; assoc. Newman, Olson & Kerr, Youngstown, Ohio, 1990-95; human resources adminstr. W.Va. No. C.C., 1996—; instr. Hiram (Ohio) Coll. Mem. exec. bd. Hiram (Ohio) Coll. Alumni, 1990-93; mem. pub. affairs com., profl. connections, bd. trustees YMCA; mem. Cath. Svc. League; trustee, exec. com. Ursuline Ctr. Bd. Mem. ABA, AAUW (pres. Warren Ohio br., Ohio bd. and legal advocacy fund chair), Ohio State Bar Assn., Trumbull County Bar Assn., Mahoning County Bar Assn., The Pers. Assn. Roman Catholic. Home: 49376 S Park Cir Calcutta OH 43920-9530 Office: WVa No C C 1704 Market St Wheeling WV 26003

WETHERELL, CAROL LYNNETTE, program director; b. Terre Haute, Ind., Jan. 1, 1962; d. James Roland and Elizabeth Carol (Borders) Oxford; m. Donald Brent Wetherell, Aug. 19, 1989; children: Katherine Elizabeth, Samuel Robert. BS, Ind. State U., Terre Haute, 1984, MEd, 1996. Capt. U.S. Air Force Air Nat. Guard, Ind., 1984-85; sales mgr. Valley Environ., Terre Haute, 1985-86; substitute tchr. Vigo County Sch. Corp., Terre Haute, 1986-90; dir. constituent giving Rose-Hulman Inst. Technology, Terre Haute, 1990—; regional dir. Ind. Soc. of Fund Raising Execs., Terre Haute. Mem. bd. dirs. Life Line, Terre Haute, Marshall Parent Coop. Pre-Sch. Mem. Nat. Soc. Fund Raising Execs., Am. Prospect Rschrs., Coun. for Advancement and Support of Edn. Home: RR4 Box 210 Marshall IL 62441 Office: Rose-Hulman Inst Tech 5500 Wabash Ave Terre Haute IN 47803

WETHERINGTON, MARCIA MCALLISTER, secondary education educator; b. Augusta, Maine, July 22, 1946; d. Theodore Roosevelt and Hazel Roberta (Dawbin) McA.; m. William Leonard Wetherington Jr.; 1 child, William Leonard Wetherington III. BS, Farmington (Maine) State Coll., 1968; MEd, U. Ga., 1979, EdS, 1983. Cert. home econs. tchr., Fla., Ga. Home econs. tchr. Palm Springs Jr. H.S., Hialeah, Fla., 1968-70, 73-74; home econs. tchr. Horace Mann Jr. H.S., Miami Shores, Fla., 1970-73, Berkmar H.S., Lilburn, Ga., 1974-77, Abraham Baldwin Agrl. Coll., Tifton, Ga., 1977-78, Crisp County H.S., Cordele, Ga., 1978-89; occupational child care tchr. Tift County H.S., Tifton, 1989—; chmn. sch. climate com., sch. accreditation, Tift County H.S., 1993—. Mem. Hillcrest Neighbors, Tifton, 1981— (pres. 1986), choir, Sunday sch. tchr. Calvary Bapt. Ch., Tifton, 1979—. Named Dist. Tchr. of Yr., GHEA, Tifton, 1983, Crisp County H.S. Tchr. of Yr., Cordele, 1987-88. Mem. Profl. Assn. Ga. Educators. Republican. Baptist. Office: Tift County H S W 8th St Tifton GA 31794

WETSCH, PEGGY A., nursing informaticist, educator; b. San Diego; d. Harvey William Henry and Helen Catherine (Thorpe) Brink; m. Gearald M. Wetsch, June 26, 1971; children: Brian Gearald, Lynette Kirstiann Nicole. Diploma, Calif. Hosp. Sch. Nursing, 1971; BSN cum laude, Pepperdine U., 1980; MS in Nursing, Calif. State U., L.A., 1985. Cert. in nursing adminstrn., human resource devel. Clin. nurse Orange County Med. Ctr./U. Calif. Irvine Med. Ctr., Orange, Calif., 1971-75; pediatric head nurse U. Calif. Irvine Med. Ctr., 1975-79; clin. nurse educator Palm Harbor Gen./Med. Ctr. Garden Grove, Calif., 1980-81; dir. ednl. svcs. Med. Ctr. of Garden Grove, 1981-85; dir. edn. Mission Hosp. Regional Med. Ctr., Mission Viejo, Calif., 1986-92; coord. computer and learning resources L.A. Med. Ctr. Sch. Nursing, 1992-95; assoc. part time faculty Saddleback Coll., 1990-94; cons. ptnr. nur.SYS-Edn. systems Cons., 1995—; lectr. statewide nursing program Calif. State U., Dominguez Hills, 1986-92; ednl. cons. Author: (with others) Nursing Diagnosis: Guidelines to Planning Care, 1993, 2d edit., 1994, 3d edit., 1996; contbr. articles to profl. jours. Treas. Orange County Nursing Edn. Coun., 1986-87, 88-90, pres., 1987-88. Mem. ANA, NLN, Am. Nursing Informatics Assn. (pres.-elect 1996—, elections com. So. Calif. chpt. 1994, coord. continuing edn., conf. planning com.), Am. Soc. Health Edn. and Tng., N.am. Nursing Diagnosis Assn. (secondary reviewer Diagnostic Rev. 1989-90, expert adv. panel 1990-92, mem. diagnosis rev. com. 1992-96), Soc. Calif. Nursing Diagnosis Assn. (membership chmn. 1984-92, pres. 1992-94), Nat. Am. Mgmt. Assn. (charter L.A. County, U. So. Calif. Med. Ctr. chpt.), Spina Bifida Assn. Am., Phi Kappa Phi, Sigma Theta Tau (pres. Iota Eta chpt. 1990-92). Home: 1520 San Clemente Ln Corona CA 91720-7949

WETTERGREN, SANDRA MARIE, personnel consultant; b. Detroit, June 1, 1950; d. Romano and Catherine (Pessenda) Previdi; m. Frank Walter Wettergren, June 14, 1969 (div. Nov. 1988); children: Amanda, Matthew. AA, Macomb C.C., 1986. Cert. pers. cons. Nat. Assn. Pers. Svcs. Recruiter Henry Labus Pers., Detroit, 1985-93; office mgr. TempStaff, Inc., Birmingham, Mich., 1993-94; br. mgr., staffing specialist Contemporary Svcs., Inc., Troy, Mich., 1994—. Mem. Macomb chpt. Dem. Nat. Party, 1992—. Mem. NOW, Am. Profl. Women in Mortgages (edn. com. 1995-96), Mich. Mortgage Banker Assn. (membership com. 1995-96), Mich. Assn. Pers. Svcs. (3 sales awards 1995). Office: Contemporary Svcs Inc 2690 Crooks Rd Ste 111 Troy MI 48084

WETTERHAHN, KAREN ELIZABETH, chemistry educator; b. Plattsburgh, N.Y., Oct. 16, 1948; d. Gustave George and Mary Elizabeth (Thibault) W.; m. Leon H. Webb, June 19, 1982; children—Leon Ashley, Charlotte Elizabeth. B.S., St. Lawrence U., 1970; Ph.D., Columbia U., 1975. Chemist, Mearl Corp., Ossining, N.Y., 1970-71; research fellow Columbia U., N.Y.C., 1971-75, postdoctoral fellow, 1975-76; asst. prof. chemistry Dartmouth Coll., Hanover, N.H., 1976-82, assoc. prof., 1982-86, prof., 1986—, Albert Bradley 3rd Century prof. in the scis., 1996—; assoc. dean faculty scis., 1990-94, acting dean faculty, 1995. Contbr. articles to profl. jours. A.P. Sloan fellow, 1981. Mem. Am. Chem. Soc., Am. Assn. Cancer Research, AAAS, N.Y. Acad. Scis. Office: Dartmouth Coll Dept Chemistry 6128 Burke Lab Hanover NH 03755-3564

WETZEL, BETTY PREAT, writer; b. Roundup, Mont., Nov. 7, 1915; d. Alfred William and Rachel Preat (Johnston) Eiselein; m. Winston Warren Wetzel, June 5, 1940; children: Susan Hinman, Kurt, Gretchen Grafin von Rittberg, Rebecca. BA in Journalism, U. Mont., 1937. Columnist, reporter Roundup (Mont.) Rec.-Tribume, 1938-46; sec. SEATO Cholera Rsch. Lab. and Hosp., Dacca, Bangladesh, 1965-67; adminstrv. asst. to v.p. Wellesley (Mass.) U., 1969-73; dir. pub. rels. Oxfam-Am., Boston, 1973-77; book rev. editor Mont. Mag., Helena, 1989-91. Author: The Making of a Montanan, 1986, Missoula, The Town and The People, 1988, After You, Mark Twain, 1990; co-author: Older Women in the Outdoors, 1996. Bd. dirs. Flathead Lake Biol. Sta., Bigfork, Mont., 1980-86. Democrat. Home: 189 Pierce Ln PO Box 693 Bigfork MT 59911

WETZEL, JENNIFER LOUISE, accountant; b. Kinsley, Kans., Aug. 19, 1964; d. Robert W. and Thelma A. (Setzkorn) W. AA, Dodge City Cmty. Coll., Kans., 1984; BS, Emporia State U., 1986. Investor reporting clk. MetFirst Fin. Co., Overland Pk., Kans., 1986-87; acctg. clk. High Plains Pubs., Inc., Dodge City, Kans., 1987-90; acct. Servi-Tech, Inc., Dodge City, Kans., 1990—. Lutheran. Office: Servi-Tech Inc 1816 E Wyatt Earp Blvd Dodge City KS 67801

WETZEL, JODI (JOY LYNN WETZEL), history and women's studies educator; b. Salt Lake City, Apr. 5, 1943; d. Richard Coulam and Margaret Elaine (Openshaw) Wood; m. David Nevin Wetzel, June 12, 1967; children: Meredith (dec.), Richard Rawlins. BA in English, U. Utah, 1965, MA in English, 1967; PhD in Am. Studies, U. Minn., 1977. Instr. Am. studies and family social sci. U. Minn., 1973-77, asst. prof. Am. studies and women's studies, 1977-79, asst. to dir. Minn. Women's Ctr., 1973-75, asst. dir., 1975-79; dir. Women's Resource Ctrs. U. Denver, 1980-84, mem. adj. faculty history, 1981-84, dir. Am. studies program, dir. Women's Inst., 1983-84; dir. Women in Curriculum U. Maine, 1985-86, mem. coop. faculty sociology, social work and human devel., 1986; dir. Inst. Women's Studies and Svcs. Met. State Coll. Denver, 1986—, assoc. prof. history, 1986-89, prof. history, 1990—; speaker, presenter, cons. in field; vis. prof. Am. studies U. Colo., 1985. Co-author: Women's Studies: Thinking Women, 1993; co-editor: Readings Toward Composition, 2d edit., 1969; contbr. articles to profl. publs. Del. at-large Nat. Women's Meeting, Houston, 1977; bd. dirs. Rocky Mountain Women's Inst., 1981-84; treas. Colo. Women's Agenda, 1987-91. U. Utah Dept. English fellow, 1967; U. Minn. fellow, 1978-79; grantee NEH, 1973, NSF, 1981-83, Carnegie Corp., 1988; named to Outstanding Young Women of Am., 1979. Mem. Am. Hist. Assn., Nat. Assn. Women in Edn. (Hilda A. Davis Ednl. Leadership award 1996, Sr. Scholar), Am. Assn. for Higher Edn., Am. Studies Assn., Nat. Women's Studies Assn., Golden Key Nat. Honor Soc. (hon.), Alpha Lambda Delta, Phi Kappa Phi. Office: Met State Coll Denver Campus Box 36 PO Box 173362 Denver CO 80217-3362

WETZSTEIN, SANDRA LYNNE, elementary school educator; b. San Angelo, Tex., Mar. 28, 1944; d. Robert Hans and Arline Edwina (Milleville) Jensen; m. Merrell W. Wetzstein, July 17, 1966; children: Raechel, Joel, Rebecca. BA, Concordia Coll., River Forest, Ill., 1966; MEd, U. Okla., Norman, 1985. Cert. coop. learning trainer. Elem. tchr. St. Paul's Luth. Sch., West Point, Nebr., 1966-67; tchr. English Centro Cultural Brasil-Estados Unidos, Belem, Brazil, 1972-76; elem. tchr. St. Mary's Sch., Balboa, Republic Panama, 1981-82, Dept. Def. Dependent Sch., Howard AFB, Republic Panama, 1982-95, Curundu Mid. Sch., Republic of Panama, 1995—. Mem. ASCD, Nat. Coun. Math. Tchrs., Phi Delta Kappa. Home: PSC 07 Box 573 APO AA 34007

WEXLER, ANNE, government relations and public affairs consultant; b. N.Y.C., Feb. 10, 1930; d. Leon R. and Edith R. (Rau) Levy; m. Joseph Duffey, Sept. 17, 1974; children by previous marriage: David Wexler, Daniel Wexler. B.A., Skidmore Coll., 1951, LL.D. (hon.), 1978; D.Sc. in Bus. (hon.), Bryant Coll., 1978. Assoc. pub. Rolling Stone mag., 1974-76; personnel adviser Carter-Mondale transition planning group, 1976-77; dep. undersec. regional affairs Dept. Commerce, 1977-78; asst. to Pres. of U.S., Washington, 1978-81; pres. Wexler and Assocs., Washington, 1981-82; govt. relations and pub. affairs cons., chmn. Wexler, Reynolds, Harrison & Schule, Inc., Washington, 1981-90; vice chmn. Hill and Knowlton PA Worldwide, Washington, 1990-92; chmn. The Wexler Group, div. Hill & Knowlton, Washington, 1992—; bd. dirs. Alumax, Inc., NOVA, Nat. Park Found., New Eng. Electric System, Comcast Corp., Dreyfus Index Funds; mem. vis. com. J.F. Kennedy Sch. Govt., Harvard U. Mem. bd. advisors Carter Ctr., Emory U.; mem. bd. visitors U. Md. Sch. Pub. Affairs. Named Outstanding Alumna Skidmore Coll., 1972, recipient most disting. alumni award, 1984, Bryce Harlow award, 1989. Mem. Coun. on Fgn. Rels., Nat. Women's Forum. Jewish. Office: Wexler Group 1317 F St NW Ste 600 Washington DC 20004-1105

WEXLER, JACQUELINE GRENNAN (MRS. PAUL J. WEXLER), former association executive and college president; b. Sterling, Ill., Aug. 2, 1926; d. Edward W. and Florence (Dawson) Grennan; m. Paul J. Wexler, June 1, 1969; stepchildren: Wendy, Wayne. A.B., Webster Coll., 1948; M.A., U. Notre Dame, 1957; LL.D., Franklin and Marshall Coll., 1968, Phila. Coll. Textiles and Sci., 1987; D.H.L., Brandeis U., 1968; LL.D., Skidmore Coll., 1967, Smith Coll., 1975; HHD, U. Mich., 1967, U. Ohio, 1976; D.H.L., Carnegie Inst., 1966, Colo. Coll., 1967, U. Pa., 1979, U. South Fla., 1991; HHD (hon.), U. Hartford, 1987; DH, St. Ambrose Coll., 1981; DD, Lafayette Coll., 1990. Tchr. English and math. Loretto Acad., El Paso, Tex., 1951-54; tchr. English and math. Nerinx Hall, St. Louis, 1954-59; tchr. English Webster Coll., 1959-60, asst. to pres., 1959, v.p. devel., 1960, exec. v.p., 1962-65, pres., 1965-69; v.p., dir. internat. univ. studies Acad. for Ednl. Devel., N.Y.C., 1969; pres. Hunter Coll., City U. N.Y., 1969-79, Acad. Cons. Assoc., N.Y.C., 1982-90; ret., 1990; pres. NCCJ, 1982-90; writer, commentator, cons.; mem. Am. Council on Edn., Commn. on Internat. Edn., 1967; mem. adv. com. to dir. NIH, 1978-80; mem. exec. panel chief naval ops. U.S. Navy, 1978-81; bd. examiners Fgn. Service, Dept. State, 1981-83; mem. Pres.'s Adv. Panel on Research and Devel. in Edn., 1961-65; mem. Pres.'s Task Force on Urban Ednl. Opportunities, 1967. Author: Where I Am Going, 1968; contbr. articles to profl. jours. Trustee U. Pa. Recipient NYU Sch. Edn. Ann. award for creative leadership in edn., 1968, Elizabeth Cutter Morrow award YWCA, 1978, Abraham L. Sachar Silver medallion Brandeis U.'s Nat. Women's Com., 1988, The Albert Einstein award Am. Soc. Technion, 1989; named One of Six Outstanding Women of St. Louis Area St. Louis chpt. Theta Sigma Phi, 1963, Woman of Achievement in Edn. St. Louis Globe-Democrat, 1964, Woman of Accomplishment Harpers Bazaar, 1967, one of Am.'s Most Important 100 Women Ladies Home Jour., 1988; Kenyon lectr. Vassar Coll., 1967. Mem. Mo. Acad. Squires, Kappa Gamma Pi.

WEYER, ELIZABETH ANN, secondary school educator; b. Seattle, Oct. 6, 1968; d. John A. and Patricia (Yarno) R. BA in Edn., Pacific Luth. U., Tacoma, 1991. Cert. tchr., Wash. Swim coach Enumclaw (Wash.) H.S., 1992—, diving coach, 1992—, secondary tchr. math. and sociology, 1992—; mem./trainer Conflict Cons. Team, Enumclaw, 1992—; mem. Students/Tchrs. Against Racism, Enumclaw, 1992—; tchr. rsch. assoc. Battelle Labs., summer, 1995. Sci. and math project fellow U. Wash., 1995—. Mem. NEA, Nat. Coun. Tchrs. Math., Wash. Edn. Assn., Enumclaw Coaches Assn., U.S. Swimming, Wash. State Math. Coun. Office: Enumclaw HS 226 Semanski St Enumclaw WA 98022-2009

WEYHENMEYER, DIANA PARKER, oncology nurse; b. Springfield, Ill., July 13, 1953; d. Fredrick Williard Parker and Judith Joanne (Easley) Foster; m. Andrew Edward Remack, July 20, 1974 (div. 1985); children: Della, Jennifer; m. Charles Howard Weyhenmeyer, Jr., June 30, 1990. BSN, Sangamon State U., 1983, MA in Counseling, 1992. RN; cert. oncology nurse. Intermediary care staff nurse St. Johns Hosp., Springfield, Ill., 1976-80, staff nurse in hospice, 1980-81, critical care coord., 1981-86, oncology staff nurse, 1986-95; oncology clinic nurse St. Johns Pavilion, Springfield, 1995—; mem. St. John Pain Team, Springfield, 1990-95, Ill. Cancer Pain Initiative, Chgo., 1991-95. Grief facilitator Little Flower Ch., Springfield, 1984-86; pres. Rutledge Bd., 1986-87, Hyde Park Homeowners Assn., 1995; co-pres. Edn. Com., Springfield, 1991-95. Mem. Am. Counseling Assn., Oncology Nursing Soc. Republican. Roman Catholic. Home: 6 Delano Ln Springfield IL 62703-5312 Office: St Johns Hosp 301 N 8th St Springfield IL 62794-9248

WEYMOUTH, LISA ANN, microbiologist, educator; b. Washington, Jan. 11, 1946; d. Colin Crowell and Nellie Weymouth; divorced; 1 child, Kelani Katherine Larsen. BA in Zoology, Swarthmore Coll., 1967; PhD in Physiology, U. Pa., 1977. Cert. Am. Bd. Med. Microbiology. Postdoctoral assoc., fellow MIT, Cambridge, Mass., 1977-83; postdoctoral scholar dept. lab. medicine U. Calif., San Francisco, 1984-85; sr. rsch. assoc. dept. medicine New Eng. Deaconess Hosp., Boston, 1985-87; fellow dept. pathology Hartford (Conn.) Hosp., 1987-89; asst. prof. microbiology and immunology U. Rochester (N.Y.) Sch. Medicine and Dentistry, 1989-93, asst. dir. clin. microbiology lab., 1989-93; asst. prof. clin. pathology Med. Coll. Va./Va. Commonwealth U., Richmond, 1993—, assoc. dir. clin. microbiology lab., 1993-95, dir. clin. microbiology lab., 1995—; mem. bd. exam. com. Am. Bd. Med. Microbiology, Washington, 1994—; co-dir. Am. Acad. Microbiology Accredited Postdoctoral Tng. Program in Med. and Pub. Health Microbiology at Med. Coll. Va./VCU, Richmond, 1993-95, dir., 1995—; co-dir. Am. Acad. Microbiology Accredited Postdoctoral Tng. Program in Med. and Pub. Health Microbiology at U. Rochester Sch. Medicine, 1989-93. Author: (book chpt.) Genetic Engineering in Mammalian Cells, 1986, Cellular and Molecular Pathogenesis, 1996; editl. bd. Jour. Clin. Microbiology, 1996—; contbr. sci. articles to profl. jours. Predoctoral fellow U.S. Pub. Health Svc., 1970-75, postdoctoral fellow Helen Hay Whitney Found., 1977-80. Mem. Am. Soc. Microbiology (mem., councilor Va. br. 1996—, alt. councilor Va. br. 1994-96, mem. cen. N.Y. br., v.p.-elect cen. N.Y. br. 1993, councilor cen. N.Y. br. 1991-93), Am. Soc. Virology, Pan Am. Soc. for Clin. Virology, South Eastern Assn. for Clin. Microbiology. Office: Med Coll Va Dept Pathology Box 980210 403 N 13th St Richmond VA 23298-0210

WHALEN, DENISE LASCO, family therapist; b. Pottsville, Pa., Jan. 14, 1968; d. Philip John and Carol Ann (Kachelries) Lasco; m. Walter William Whalen, May 15, 1993. AAS in Bus. Adminstrn., Penn State U., 1987, B in Behavioral Sci., 1989; MA in Counseling Psychol., Kutztown U., 1994. Homeless svc. coord. Econ. Opportunity Cab., Pottsville, Pa., 1989; caseworker Sch. City Children & Youth, Pottsville, 1989-91; family therapist Turning Point, Pottsville, 1991—; ptnr. Heart & Sewl, Sch. Haven, Pa., 1994—; therapist Family Life Svcs., Topton, Pa., 1995—; mem. steering com. Cent. Chpt. Pa. Assn. Family Based Svcs., York, 1995. v.p. Sch. County Comm. Chorus Aux., 1994-95. Mem. ACA, Internat. Assn. Marriage & Family Counselors. Republican. Lutheran. Home: 103 Spruce St Minersville PA 17954 Office: Turning Point 16 S Centre St Pottsville PA 17901

WHALEN, LORETTA THERESA, religious educational administrator; b. Bklyn., May 21, 1940; d. William Michael and Loretta Margaret (Malone) Whalen; children: Ann Force, Margaret Force. RN, St. Vincent's Hosp., N.Y.C., 1960; BSN, U. Pa., 1965; MA in Edn., Fordham U., 1971; cert. in sociology religion, Louvain U., Belgium, 1974; PhD in Global Edn., The Union Grad. Sch., 1994. Staff nurse Holy Family Hosp., Atlanta, 1967-69; Latin Am. communication dir. Med. Mission Sisters, Maracaibo, Venezuela, 1969-71; intensive care nurse St. Vincent's Hosp., N.Y.C., 1971-72; mem. ministry team Med. Mission Sisters, various locations, 1972-74; dir. communications Med. Mission Sisters, Phila., 1974-77; asst. to exec. Interreligious Peace Colloquium, Washington, 1977; freelance writing, photography Ch. World Svc., N.Y.C., 1978-79; dir. Office Global Edn. Nat. Council Chs., N.Y.C., 1980—. Co-author: Make a World of Difference: Creative Activities for Global Learning, 1990, Tales of the Heart: Affective Approaches to Global Education, 1991; mem. editorial bd., rev. editor Connections Mag., 1984-87; contbr. articles to profl. jours. Mem. Peace and Justice Commn., Archdiocese of Balt., 1985-89. Mem. Amnesty Internat., Bread for the World, NOW, World Wildlife Fund, Greenpeace, Sigma Theta Tau. Democrat. Roman Catholic.

WHALEN, LUCILLE, academic administrator; b. Los Angeles, July 26, 1925; d. Edward Cleveland and Mary Lucille (Perrault) W. B.A. in English, Immaculate Heart Coll., Los Angeles, 1949; M.S.L.S., Catholic U. Am., 1955; D.L.S., Columbia U., 1965. Tchr. elem. and secondary parochial schs. Los Angeles, Long Beach, Calif., 1945-52; high sch. librarian Conaty Meml. High Sch., Los Angeles, 1950-52; reference/serials librarian, instr. in library sci. Immaculate Heart Coll., 1955-58; dean Immaculate Heart Coll. (Sch. Library Sci.), 1958-60, 65-70; assoc. dean, prof. SUNY, Albany, 1971-78, 84-87; prof. Sch. Info. Sci. and Policy SUNY, 1979-83; dean grad. programs, libr. Immaculate Heart Coll. Ctr., Los Angeles, 1987-90; ref. libr. (part-time) Glendale Community Coll., 1990—; dir. U.S. Office Edn. Instn. Author, editor: (with others) Reference Services in Archives, 1986. author: Human Rights: A Reference Handbook, 1989. Mem. ACLU, Common Cause, Amnesty Internat. Democrat. Roman Catholic. Home: 320 S Gramercy Pl Apt 101 Los Angeles CA 90020-4542 Office: Glendale Community Coll 1500 N Verdugo Rd Glendale CA 91208-2809

WHALEN, PATRICIA THERESE, marketing professional; b. Columbus, Ohio, June 26, 1955; d. Daniel Edward and Rose Eileen (Callahan) W. BA in English, Ohio State U., 1977; MS in Bus. Adminstrn., Ind. U., 1981; postgrad. in mass media, Mich. State U., 1994—. Sales promotion specialist Clark Components Div., Buchanan, Mich., 1978-81, supr., advt. and pub. rels., 1981-82; mgr. corp. comm. Clark Equipment Co., Buchanan, Mich., 1982-84; dir. govt. affairs Clark Equipment Co., South Bend, Ind., 1984-86; dir. pub. rels. COMSAT World Systems Div., Clarksburg, Md., 1986-87; dir. mktg. communications COMSAT World Systems Div., Washington, 1987-90; dir. mktg. COMSAT Mobile Comm., Washington, 1990-94; instr. dept. advt., mktg. cons. Miss. State U., 1995—; seminar speaker in field. Bd. dirs. Tri-county Pvt. Industry Coun., St. Joseph County, Mich., 1983-85, Jr. Achievement, Niles, Mich. and South Bend, Ind., 1982-86; chmn. Clark PAC Polit. Action Com., South Bend, 1984-86. Mem. Pub. Rels. Soc. Am. (tech. com. 1982—, Silver Anvil award 1982), Internat. Assn. Bus. Communicators, Bus. and Profl. Advertisers Assn., Soc. Satellite Profls. (bd. dirs. 1990-93). Roman Catholic. Home: 1747 Maple Ridge Rd # 13 Haslett MI 48840-8648

WHALEN-BLAAUWGEERS, HERMA-JOZÉ, financial analyst; b. Lichtenvoorde, Gelderland, The Netherlands, Dec. 14, 1944; arrived in U.S., 1988; d. Hermanus Jozeph Blaauwgeers and Henrica Everdina Dute; m. Helmut Gueth, Jan. 3, 1968 (div. May 1983); m. Frank Whalen, Mar. 29, 1988 (div. Dec. 1994); children: Mariëtte, Joerg-Peter. BA, Lyceum Fons Vitae, Amsterdam, 1964. Cert. translator, Fed. Govt. of The Netherlands, 1971. Dir. resource mgmt. U.S. Army, Schweinfurt, Germany, 1981-88; project mgr. ARS, Alexandria, Va., 1988-90; group mgr. internat. mktg. ARS, Alexandria, 1990-92; sr. ptnr. Herold & Assocs., Arlington, Va., 1992—; sr. fin. analyst IBES, Inc., Falls Church, Va., 1993—. Contbr. articles to European newspapers. pres. Club Der Jungen Hausfauen, Schweinfurt, 1971-75, Kind Im Krankenhaus, Schweinfurt, 1977-81; founder Legal Aid for Abused Women and Children, Arlington, 1994—. Mem. Nat. Assn. Women Bus. Owners (internat. chair Capital Area chpt. 1996—), Am. Soc. Mil. Comptrollers, Nat. Female Execs. Assn., Nat. Women's Political Caucus, Am. Assn. Univ. Women, Zonta Club of Alexandria (pres. 1995—), Zonta Internat. (mem. ad hoc com. domestic violence, 1996—). Roman Catholic.

WHALLEY-KILMER, JOANNE, actress; b. Manchester, England, Aug. 25, 1964; m. Val Kilmer. Actress (theater) Bows and Arrows, 1982, Rita, Sue, and Bob Too, 1982, The Genius, 1983, Kate, 1983, The Crimes of

Vautrin, 1983, The Pope's Wedding, 1984, Saved, 1984, As I Lay Dying, 1985, Women Beware Women, 1986, Three Sisters, 1987, What the Butler Saw, 1989 (Theatre World award 1989), (films) Pink Floyd-The Wall, 1982, Dance With a Stranger, 1985, The Good Father, 19886, No Surrender, 1986, Willow, 1988, Popielusko, (To Kill a Priest), 1989, Scandal, 1989, Kill Me Again, 1989, Navy SEALS, 1990, Crossing the Rapture, 1994, Trial By Jury, 1994, A Good Man in Africa, 1995 (TV) A Christmas Carol, 1984, A Kind of Loving, A Quiet Life, The Gentle Touch, Reilly, Save Your Kisses, Will You Love Me Tomorrow?, (TV mini-series) Edge of Darkness, 1986, The Singing Detective, 1988, Channel Crossings, 1988, Scarlett, 1994. Office: Creative Artists Agency 9830 Wilshire Blvd Beverly Hills CA 90212-1804*

WHAM, DOROTHY STONECIPHER, state legislator; b. Centralia, Ill., Jan. 5, 1925; d. Ernest Joseph and Vera Thelma (Shafer) Stonecipher; m. Robert S. Wham, Jan. 26, 1947; children: Nancy S. Wham Mitchell, Jeanne Wham Ryan, Robert S. II. BA, MacMurray Coll., 1946; MA, U. Ill., 1949; D of Pub. Adminstrn. (hon.), MacMurray Coll., 1992. Counsellor Student Counselling Bur. U. Ill., Urbana, 1946-49; state dir. ACTION program, Colo./Wyo. U.S. Govt., Denver, 1972-82; mem. Colo. Ho. of Reps., 1986-87; mem. Colo. Senate, 1987—, chair jud. com., 1988—; with capital devel. com., health, environ, welfare, instns., fin. appropriations, legal svcs. Mem. LWV, Civil Rights Commn. Denver, 1972-80; bd. dirs. Denver Com. on Mental Health, 1985-88, Denver Symphony, 1985-88. Mem. Am. Psychol. Assn., Colo. Mental Health Assn. (bd. dirs. 1986-88), Colo. Hemophilia Soc. Republican. Methodist. Lodge: Civitan. Home: 2790 S High St Denver CO 80210-6352 Office: State Capitol Rm 342 Denver CO 80203

WHARE, WANDA SNYDER, lawyer; b. Columbia, Pa., Nov. 5, 1959; d. William Sylvester and Dorothy Jacqueline (Luttman) W.; m. James Robert Snyder, Nov. 14, 1987; 1 child, Eric James. BA, Franklin & Marshall Coll., 1981; JD, Dickinson Sch. Law, 1984. Bar: Pa. 1984. Asst. counsel Pa. Dept. Labor and Industry, Harrisburg, 1984-87; assoc. Gibbel, Kraybill & Hess, Lancaster, Pa., 1987-89; corp. counsel Irex Corp., Lancaster, 1990—. Mem. parish-staff rels. com. 1st Meth. Ch., Lancaster, 1987-92, mem. com. on status and role of women, 1989-95, chair, 1992-95; chair commn. on status and role of women Ea. Pa. Conf. of United Meth. Ch., 1996—; mem., chair awareness subcom. Irex Continuous Improvement Coun. Democrat. Office: Irex Corp 120 N Lime St Lancaster PA 17602-2951

WHARTON, KAY KAROLE, special education educator; b. Butler, Pa., Nov. 19, 1943; d. Clarence Henry Jr. and Alberta Elizabeth (Yost) Gilkey; m. David Burton Wharton, Nov. 28, 1975 (dec. May 1987). BS in Edn., Geneva Coll., 1965. Cert. spl. edn. tchr., Md. Tchr. 2d grade Butler Area Sch., 1965-71; resource tchr. Queen Anne County Bd. of Edn., Centreville, Md., 1971—; facilitator sch. improvement team Centreville Mid. Sch., 1992-95. Music dir. Diocese of Easton (Md.) Mid. Convocation Episcopal Cursillo, Old St. Paul's, Kent, 1989-91, St. Paul's, Hillsboro, 1993—; Sunday sch. supt. primary dept. St. Mark's Luth. Ch., 1966-71, St. Paul's Episcopal Ch., 1985-87; program dir. Queen Anne's County chpt. Am. Cancer Soc., Centreville, 1981-85; mem. PTA; Episcopal lay min. Meridian Nursing Home, 1978—. Mem. NEA, Queen Anne County Edn. Assn., Md. State Tchrs. Assn., Coun. for Exceptional Children, Internat. Reading Assn., Upper Shore Reading Assn. (sec. 1985-91, 93—), Learning Disabled Am., Guardians Learning Disabled (sec. 1991-92), Smithsonian Assocs., Order Ea. Star (worthy matron Centreville 1977, sec. 1982-93), Nat. Geographic Soc., Town and Country Women's Club (pres. 1977, 79), Delta Kappa Gamma (Nu chpt. pres. 1992—, rsch. com. chairperson Alpha Beta State 1993-95, membership chairperson 1995—). Republican. Home: PO Box 237 Centreville MD 21617-0237 Office: Centreville Mid Sch 231 Ruthsburg Rd Centreville MD 21617-9702

WHARTON, LESLIE, lawyer; b. Phila., July 7, 1951. BA summa cum laude, Boston U., 1973; PhD, Princeton U., 1979; JD cum laude, Harvard U., 1984. Bar: Tex. 1984, U.S. Dist. Ct. (we. dist.) Tex. 1986. Teaching asst. Princeton U., N.J., 1978; editor Lafayette Papers Project, Ithaca, N.Y., 1978-79; instr. Suffolk U., Boston, 1979-80; asst. to v.p. acad. affairs R.I. Sch. Design, Providence, 1980-81, assoc. faculty, 1982-83; assoc. Matthews and Branscomb, San Antonio, 1984-87; assoc. Arnold & Porter, Washington, 1988-93, ptnr., 1993—; lctr. computer law, 1985-86. Author: Polity and the Good Public, 1980, Lafayette in the Age of American Revolution, Vol. 5; contbr. articles on computer law to profl. jours. Mem. ABA, Tex. Bar Assn., San Antonio Intellectual Property Law Assn. (treas. 1985—), Phi Beta Kappa. Office: Arnold & Porter Thurman Arnold Bldg 555 Twelfth St Washington DC 20004-1202*

WHARTON, MARGARET AGNES, artist; b. Portsmouth, Va., 1943. BS, U. Md., 1965; MFA, Sch. of Art Inst. Chgo., 1975. vis. artist Sch. of Art Inst. of Chgo., 1978, 89, 90, Columbia Coll., Chgo., 1994. One women shows include Phyllis Kind Gallery, Chgo., 1976, 80, 85, 88, 91, N.Y.C., 1977, 78, 79, 81, 83, 87, 90, Mus. Contemporary Art, Chgo, 1981-82, Laguna Gloria Art Mus., Austin, Tex., 1981-82, Zolla/Lieberman Gallery, Inc., Chgo., 1992, 94, Evanston Art Ctr., 1994; exhibited in group shows at The Cinn. Art Mus., 1988-90, U. Wis. Art Mus., Milw., 1991, The Chgo. Cultural Ctr., 1992, Rockford (Ill.) Art Mus., 1994, and numerous others; represented in permanent collections Am. Med. Assn., Art Inst. of Chgo., Dallas Mus., Seattle Art Mus., State Ill. Collection, Whitney Mus. Am. Art, and others; comms. include Mus. of Contemporary Art, Chgo., 1985, Chgo. Pub. Libr., West Lawn Branch, Chgo., 1986. Founding mem. Artemesia Cooperative Gallery, Chgo., Ill. Recipient NEA grant 1979, 88, 93, Visual Arts award, 1984.

WHATCOTT, MARSHA RASMUSSEN, elementary education educator; b. Fillmore, Utah, Mar. 29, 1941; d. William Hans and Evangelyn (Robison) Rasmussen; m. Robert LaGrand Whatcott, Sept. 14, 1961; children: Sherry, Cindy, Jay Robert, Justin William. Assoc., So. Utah State U., 1962; BS, Brigham Young U., 1968. Cert. tchr. early childhood, Utah. Tchr. 1st grade Provost Elem. Sch., Provo, Utah, 1968-84, tchr. kindergarten, 1991—, kindergarten tchr., 1984-91, tchr. 3d grade, 1991—, music specialist, 93-94, art specialist, 1984-85, math. specialist, 1988-89; music specialist Provost Elem., 1984-87, 91-92, 93-94, art specialist, 1984-85, math. specialist, 1988-89, sci. specialist, 1994—; del. Utah Edn. Assn., 1989-90; bldg. rep. Provo Edn. Assn., 1993-94, 94-95. Mem. polit. action com. Provo Sch. Dist., 1982, 90, mem. profl. devel. com. Bonniville Uniserve (Provo, Alpine and Nebo Sch. Dist.), 1994-95. Recipient Millard County Utah PTA scholarship, 1959-62, Golden Apple award Provo City PTA, 1984, Recognition Disting. Svc. in Edn. award Utah State Legis., 1992; named Outstanding Educator in Utah Legis. Dist. # 64, 1992. Mem. Utah Edn. Asn. (del. 1989-90), Provo Edn. Assn. (bldg. rep. 1993-94, 94-95), Bonneville Uniserve (profl. devel. com.). Mem. LDS Ch. Office: Provost Elem Sch 629 S 1000 E Provo UT 84606-5204

WHATLEY, JEANNETTE, lawyer, administrator; b. Harrisburg, Ark., Mar. 11, 1957; d. Robert Leo and Dorothy S. (Kimery) W. BA, Ark. State U., 1980; JD, U. Ark., 1985. Bar: Ark. 1985, Tenn. 1994. Staff atty. East Ark. Legal Svcs., Helena, Ark., 1985-88, Legal Svcs. of V.I., St. Thomas, 1990, Cen. Ark. Legal Svcs., Little Rock, 1988-92; adminstr. Housing Opportunities Corp., Memphis, 1994-96. Vol. Habitat for Humanity, 1996; educator Women's Project, Women's Unit, ADC, 1991-92. mem. legal panel ACLU of Ark., Little Rock, 1989-92; trainer Ark. Legal Svcs. Support, Little Rock, 1991; mem. juvenile justice com. Ark. Bar Assn., Little Rock, 1989-91. Democrat. Roman Catholic. Office: Housing Opportunities Corp # 800 147 Jefferson Ave Memphis TN 38103

WHAYNE, KATHERINE INGRAM, financial analyst; b. Columbus, Ohio, June 2, 1972; d. Thomas French and Eugenia MacDonald (Ingram) W. AB, Duke U., 1994. Asst. post office mgr. Hartland Swim and Racquet Club, Lexington, Ky., 1990, asst. swim coach, 1991; German au pair Coun. of Internat. Ednl. Exch., Röttenbach, Germany, 1992; intern Merrill Lynch, Lexington, 1993; corp. divsn. rsch. mgr. The Advisory Bd. Co., Washington, 1994—. Vol. Cmty. Kitchen, Durham, N.C., 1992-93; chair Broadway at Duke, Durham, 1993-94. Mem. Am. Guild of Organists, Japan-Am. Club, Delta Gamma. Democrat. Presbyterian.

WHEALEY, LOIS DEIMEL, humanities scholar; b. N.Y.C., June 20, 1932; d. Edgar Bertram Deimel and Lois Elizabeth (Hatch) Washburn; m. Robert Howard Whealey, July 2, 1954; children: Richard William, David John, Alice Ann Whealey Dediu. BA in History, Stanford U., 1951; MA in Edn., U. Mich., 1955; MA in Polit. Sci., Ohio U., 1975. Tchr. 5th grade Swayne Sch., Owyhee, Nev., 1952-53; tchr. 7th grade Ft. Knox (Ky.) Dependent's Sch., 1955-56; tchr. adult basic edn. USAF, Oxford, 1956-57; tchr. 6th grade Amerman Sch., Northville, Mich., 1957-58; tchr. 8th grade English, social studies Slauson Jr. High Sch., Ann Arbor, Mich., 1958-59; adminstrv. asst. humanities conf. Ohio U., Athens, 1974-76, 83; part-time instr. Ohio U., Athens, 1966-68, 75, VISTA with Rural Action, 1996—. Contbr. articles to profl. jours. Mem. Athens County Regional Planning Commn., 1974-78, treas., 1976-78; bd. dirs. Ohio Meadville Dist. Unitarian-Universalist Assn., 1975-81, Ohio Women Inc., 1995—; mem. Ohio coord. com. Internat. Women's Yr., 1977; v.p. Black Diamond Girl Scout Coun., 1980-86; chair New Day for Equal Rights Amendment, 1982; mem. Athens City Bd. Edn., 1984-90, v.p., 1984, pres., 1985; mem. Tri-County Vocat. Sch. Bd., Nelsonville, Ohio, 1984-90, v.p., 1988-89; mem. adv. com. Ohio River Valley Water Sanitation Commn., 1986-95; bd. dirs. Ohio Environ. Coun., 1984-90, sec., 1986-90; bd. dirs. Ohio Alliance for Environ., 1993—, Ohio Women, Inc., 1995—; coord. Southeast Ohio Collaborative on Women and Children, Ohio Dept. Edn., 1994—. Recipient Unsung UU award Ohio-Meadville Dist. Unitarian Universalist Assn., 1984, Thanks badge Black Diamond Girl Scout Coun., 1986, How to award Ednl. Press Assn. Am., 1990, Donna Chen Women's Equity award Ohio U., 1994; named Woman of Achievement, Black Diamond Girl Scout Coun., 1987. Mem. AAUW (pres. Athens br. 1969-70, 89-90, 93—, nat. pub. policy chair AAUW/Ohio 1995—), LWV (pres. 1975-77), Phi Lambda Theta (life). Democrat. Home: 14 Oak St Athens OH 45701-2605

WHEATLEY, BARNARESE P. (BONNIE WHEATLEY), health services consultant; b. New Iberia, La., Nov. 6, 1942; d. Ervin and Elizabeth (Pierce) Politte; m. Horace Wheatley, Oct. 9, 1967; children: Adrienne K., Alanna M. BS, Calif. State U., Hayward, 1989; MPH, San Jose State U., 1994. Project dir. breast cancer early detection program Summit Med. Ctr., Oakland, Calif., 1989-93; health svc. cons. Alameda County, Oakland, 1993—. Co-author: Wellness Perspective, 1993. Treas. Leadership Am., 1992-93; coord. Nat. Black Leadership No. Calif., 1992—; bd. dirs. Susan B. Komen Found., 1994—, Breast Cancer Action, 1994-96, Nat. Breast Cancer Coalition, 1993-96 ; adv. com. Cancer Info. Svc., 1993—; active Calif. Breast Cancer Rsch. Coun., Healthy City Fund Bd. Recipient Community Svcs. Outreach award Calif. Legislature, 1989, Outstanding Svc. award Nat. Assn. Bench and Bar Spouses, 1992, Reaching People Through Partnerships award, 1996. Mem. Women and Girls Against Tobacco (bd. dirs.). Democrat. Home: 42 La Salle Ave Piedmont CA 94611-3549 Office: Alameda County Med Ctr 1411 E 31st St Oakland CA 94602-1018

WHEATLEY, ELIZABETH ANN, academic administrator; b. Jamaica, N.Y., Apr. 6, 1946; d. John Francis and Emma Elizabeth (Dauber) Burkitt; m. Brian A. Hill, Sept. 23, 1967 (div. Aug. 1979); 1 child, Lisa; m. Edward Warren Wheatley, Oct. 26, 1980; children: Richard, Sarah. BS in Edn., St. John's U., N.Y.C., 1967; MS in Edn., CUNY, 1970. Cert. tchr. N.C., N.Y. Tchr. Pub. Sch. 147, Cambria Heights, N.Y., Winthrop Ave. Sch., Bellmore, N.Y., St. Pancras, Glendale, N.Y.; academic dean Gables Acad., Clearwater, Fla., Miami, Fla.; adminstr., mem. faculty East Carolina U., Greenville, N.C., 1986—; cons. in field. Editor: Technology and Teacher Conference, 1993; contbr. articles to profl. jours. Pres. E.B. Aycock Jr. High Sch. PTA, Greenville, 1982-84, Wahl-Coates Elem. Sch. PTA, Greenville, 1986-87. East Carolina U. grantee, 1992. Mem. Nat. Coun.Tchrs. English, Internat. Reading Assn., N.C. Assn. Devel. Studies, Assn. Tchr. Educators N.C., Greenville/Pitt Reading Assn., Orgn. Tchr. Educators of Reading, Phi Kappa Phi. Office: East Carolina U Sch Edn 5th St Greenville NC 27858

WHEATLEY, JOAN MERCEDESE, critical care nurse; b. Paoli, Ind., Jan. 13, 1947; d. Clayton James and Jessie Beatrice (Austin) Roberson; m. Curtis DeWayne Wheatley, June 5, 1965; children: Yvonne D. Burge, Lisa D. Maier, Nathan William. ADN, Olney Ctrl. Coll., 1986; BSN, So. Ill. U., Edwardsville, 1995. Cert. BLS, ACLS, pediat. advanced life support. Charge nurse Crestview Convalescent Ctr., Vincennes, Ind., 1986-87; gen. duty nurse Good Samaritan Hosp., Vincennes, 1987—, asst. head nurse, 1994—. Recipient Grace Sue Smith award, 1985, inducted into Sigma Theta Tau Internat., 1995. Mem. Nat. League Nursing. Home: 915 Cherry St Mount Carmel IL 62863

WHEATLEY, LUCILE ELIZABETH, civic worker; b. Corvallis, Oreg., Mar. 24, 1917; d. Paul Vestal and Mary Elizabeth (Davis) Maris; m. Melvin Ernest Wheatley, Jr., June 15, 1939; children: Paul Melvin, James Maris, John Sherwood (dec.). BA cum laude, Am. U., 1938. Cert. tchr., Va. Chmn. L.A. Portraits Am. Women, 1968-70. A founder Parents and Friends Lesbians and Gays, Denver, 1981, speaker, workshop leader, Colo. and Calif., 1981—; active LWV, Denver, 1973-84; active citizen protests at Rocky Flats Nuclear Plant, Denver, 1981, 82. Recipient Human Rights award Universal Fellowship Met. Cmty. Congregations, 1985, Peace and Justice award Ill. Sch. Theology, Denver, 1987, Nat. Affirmation award Calif.-Paciic Conf., United Meth. Ch., 1994, Nat. Affirmation award, 1994. Democrat. Home: 859-A Ronda Mendoza Laguna Hills CA 92653

WHEATLEY, SHARMAN B., art educator, artist; b. N.Y.C., Nov. 21, 1951; d. Norman Alexander and Marjorie Grace (Biggs) Johnson; m. Simon J. Wheatley, June 21, 1975; children: Gregory Drew, Justin West. BA in Art Edn., Wagner Coll., 1973; MA in Art Edn., Coll. of New Rochelle, 1979. Cert. art educator, N.Y.; provisional cert. art educator, Conn. Art educator for multi-handicapped students Bd. Coop. Edn. Svcs., New City, N.Y., 1973-75; art educator Ardsley Pub. Schs., N.Y., 1975-76; art and humanities educator The Ursuline Sch., New Rochelle, N.Y., 1976-83; owner, dir. of tour co. Big Apple Enrichment Tours, Larchmont, N.Y., 1981-83; libr. publicist Monroe Pub. Libr., Conn., 1987-88; newspaper editor Trumbull Times, Conn., 1988; art educator Trumbull Pub. Schs., Conn., 1989-91; theatrical prodr. Little Theatre Prodns., Wilton, Conn., 1993-96; art educator Wilton Pub. Schs., Conn., 1991—; summer crafts supr. Ardsley Pub. Schs., N.Y., 1971-79. Artist, illustrator cover design for Street Bagel mag., 1982; exhibited in group shows at Larchmont Libr., 1982, Union Trust Bank, Darien, Conn., 1983; cover illustrator Litton Pubs., N.Y.C., 1980. 1st v.p., treas., corr. sec. mem. parents coun. Monroe PTO, Conn., 1985—. Recipient 2d prize Darien Arts Coun., 1983, Adams Interior Design Ctr. award Darien Arts Coun., 1983. Mem. NEA, Conn. Edn. Assn., Met. Mus. Art, N.Y. Mus. Modern Art. Home: 44 Oakwood Dr Monroe CT 06468

WHEDON, MARGARET BRUNSSEN, television and radio producer; b. N.Y.C.; d. Henry and Anna Margaret (Nickel) Brunssen; m. G. Donald Whedon, 1942 (div. Sept. 1982); children: Karen Whedon Green, David Marshall. BA, U. Rochester, 1948; postgrad., CUNY-Hunter Coll., 1950. With ABC-TV and Radio News; asst. prodr. Coll. News Conf., 1952-60; prodr. This Week with David Brinkley, 1981-84. Prodr.: Issues and Answers, 1960-81, From the Capitol, ABC Radio, 1962-69; nres prodr. Pub. Affairs Satellite Sys., Inc., 1983—, Pubs at Pub. Affairs Satellite, Washington, 1986—; mem. Capitol Speakers, lectr., pub. speaker; commentator Flair Reports, 1962-64; music critic The Hill Rag; author: Always on Sunday, 1980, Dining in the Great Embassies, 1987. Recipient NCCJ award, 1968; nominee NATAS award, 1968. Mem. White House Corrs. Assn., Nat. Press Club, Am. Newspaper Women's Club (pres. 1983), Am. Women in Radio and TV, Radio-TV Corrs. Assn. Home: 4201 Cathedral Ave NW Apt 702E Washington DC 20016-4955

WHEELER, CATHY JO, government official; b. Birmingham, Ala., Feb. 14, 1954; d. Charles Edwin and Hazel Josephine (Hollis) W.; m. David Arthur Tate. BA, U. Montevallo, 1975; postgrad., U. Ala., 1982-84. With Social Security Adminstrn., Birmingham, 1975—, mgmt. analyst, 1991—, sr. employment devel. specialist, 1983-85, mgr. tech. tng. dept., 1985-91, mgmt. analyst, 1991—; v.p. Fed. Women's Program, Birmingham, 1984-85; treas., charter mem. Federally Employed Women, Birmingham, 1984-88. Alumni bd. dirs. U. Montevallo, Ala., 1991-94, v.p. fin., 1994—. Mem. ASTD (treas. 1987-88, pres. elect 1989, pres. 1990, asst. regional dir. 1991-92), Soc. Govt. Meeting Planners (chartered, v.p. 1989-90, sec. 1990-91), Jaycees (v.p. mgmt. devel. Hoover, Ala. chpt. 1988-89), Chi Omega Alumni Assn. (treas. 1991, advisor 1991—). Home: 4001 Fairchase Ln Birmingham AL 35244 Office: Social Security Adminstrn 2001 12th Ave N Birmingham AL 35285-0002

WHEELER, DENISE GRACE, nurse midwife; b. Des Moines, Mar. 16, 1955; d. Marion Warner and Doris Fae (Dinnin) W. ADN, Des Moines Area C.C., Ankeny, Iowa, 1975; BSN, St. Louis U., 1982; MS in Nursing Scis., U. Ill., 1983. Dir. Des Moines Birthplace, 1984-86; dir. nurse midwifery svcs., clin. faculty assoc. U. Ill., Chgo., 1986-89; dir. edn. Michael Reese Med. Ctr., Chgo., 1989-90; staff nurse midwife Ill. Masonic Med. Ctr., Chgo., 1989-90; nurse midwife Des Moines Ob-Gyn. Specialists, 1990-92; nurse midwife, mem. faculty Broadlawns Med. Ctr., Des Moines, 1992—; guest spkr. and women's groups, 1984—. Contbr. chpts. to books and articles to profl. jours. Bd. dirs. March of Dimes, Des Moines, 1984-86; mem. adv. bd. Birth Ctr. Task Force, Chgo., 1988-89. Grantee Mid Iowa Health Found., 1983, Iowa Dept. Pub. Health, 1994. Mem. ANA, ACOG, Iowa Nurses Assn., AWHONN (co-chair program com. 1991-92, regional workshop), Am. Coll. Nurse Midwives (cert., chpt. chair 1987-89, chair nat. bylaws com. 1990-93), Sigma Theta Tau. Office: Broadlawns Med Ctr 1801 Hickman Rd Des Moines IA 50314-1548

WHEELER, ELIZABETH FRANCES, education educator, primary school educator; b. Chgo., Mar. 18, 1909; d. Charles Roe and Maude Sanford (Peacock) W. BEd, Nat. Coll. Edn., 1936; MA, Northwestern U., 1951, PhD, 1965. Kindergarten & primary tchr. Highland Park (Ill.) Pub. Schs., 1929-32, Benton Harbor (Mich.) Pub. Schs., 1936-39; kindergarten tchr. Whitefish Bay (Wis.) Pub. Schs., 1939-53; nursery-kindergarten tchr. Campus Sch. Wis. State Coll., Milw., 1953-56; from asst. prof. to assoc. prof. curruculum & instrn. U. Wis., Milw., 1956-74, assoc. prof. emerita, 1974—; mem. gov. bd. U.S. Nat. Com. World Orgn. Early Childhood Edn., N.Y.C., 1968-70; pres. Nat. Assn. Edn. Young Children, Wasington, 1955-59, mem. adv. com. Wis. State Early Childhood Com., Madison, 1965-74. Contbr. articles to profl. jours. Bd. dirs. Day Care Svcs. Children, Milw., 1963-70, 75-92, pres., 1972-74; mem. nursing adv. com. Milw. Children's Hosp., 1965-70; elder, mem. various coms. Immanuel Presbyn. Ch., 1967—. Recipient Alumni Achievement award Nat. Coll. Edn., 1977. Mem. Delta Kappa Gamma (past pres. 1958—, advanced study scholar 1958), Pi Lambda Theta. Democrat.

WHEELER, JEANETTE NORRIS, entomologist; b. Newton, Iowa, May 21, 1918; d. David Ottis and Esther (Miles) Norris; widowed; 1 child, Ralph Allen. BA, U. N.D., 1939, MS, 1956, PhD, 1962. Tchr. Casselton (N.D.) High Sch., 1939-40; instr. U. N.D., Grand Forks, 1944-49, asst. prof., 1963-65, rsch. assoc., 1965-67; rsch. assoc. Desert Rsch. Inst., U. Nev., Reno, 1967-80, Fla. Collection of Arthropods, 1985—, Los Angeles County Natural History Mus., 1979—; rsch. assoc. Natural History Mus. L.A. County, Fla. Collection Arthropods. Co-author: The Ants of North Dakota, 1963, The Amphibians and Reptiles of North Dakota, 1966, Ants of Deep Canyon, Colorado, Desert, California, 1973, Ant Larvae: Review and Synthesis, 1976, The Ants of Nevada, 1986; contbr. over 100 articles to profl. jours. Recipient Sioux award U. N.D. Alumni Assn., 1989. Home: 3338 NE 58th Ave Silver Springs FL 34488-1867

WHEELER, JUDITH SUZANNE, educational counselor; b. Marion, Ala., Apr. 25, 1951; d. James Andrew and Marian Ella (Moody) W.; children: Carrie Suzanne Robertson, Casey Marian Robertson. BS in Edn., Auburn U., 1973; MEd in Guidance and Counseling, Livingston (Ala.) U., 1981, MEd in Libr.-Media Svcs., 1984; tchr. certification, U. Ala., Tuscaloosa, 1991, PhD, 1995. Cert. tchr. secondary sch. biology, sociology, elem. sch. libr. media svcs., adminstrn., guidance and counseling, Ala.; nat. cert. counselor Nat. Bd. Cert. Counselors, Inc.; lic. profl. counselor, Ala. Tchr. So. Acad., Greensboro, Ala., 1973-74, 81-83, libr., 1982-84; libr. West Blocton Elem. Sch., Centerville, Ala., 1984-87; program counselor Chpt. I Brookwood Elem. Sch., Tuscaloosa, Ala., 1987-90; grad. tchg. asst. Coll. Edn. U. Ala., Tuscaloosa, Ala., 1992-95; counselor Crestmont Elem. Sch., Northport, Ala., 1990—, coord. extended day program, 1994-95, resource tchr., adminstr., summer 1994; counselor pvt. practice, Tuscaloosa, Ala., 1995—; counselor Freshman Orientation Summer Program U. Ala., Tuscaloosa, 1990, 91, 92; spkr. workshops and seminars Brookwood Elem. Sch., Crestmont Elem. Sch., U. Ala. Contbr. articles to profl. jours. Tour Guide Warner Art Collection, Globe Security, Gulf States Paper Corp., Tuscaloosa, 1988-90. Thelma J.M. Smith scholar U. Ala., 1992, Isabella Hummel Graham scholar Univ. Women's Club, 1992. Mem. NEA, Am. Counseling Assn., Am. Sch. Counselor Assn., Ala. Counseling Assn., Ala. Sch. Counselor Assn., Ala. Assn. Psycho. Type, Ala. Assn. Play Therapy, Ala. Edn. Assn., Tuscaloosa County Edn. Assn., Tuscaloosa County Mental Health Assn., Chi Sigma Iota, Kappa Delta Pi, Alpha Kappa Delta. Home: 2962 Meadowlark Ln Northport AL 35476 Office: 2400 34th Ave Northport AL 35476

WHEELER, KATHERINE FRAZIER (KATE WHEELER), writer; b. Tulsa, July 27, 1955; d. Charles Bowen and Jan Nette (Moses) W. BA in English Fine Arts, Rice U., 1977; MA in Creative Writing, Stanford U., 1981. News reporter The Miami (Fla.) Herald, 1977-79; tchr. English composition Middlesex C.C., Lawrence, Mass., 1991; tchr. meditation Insight Meditation Soc., Barre, Mass., 1991—. Author: (short stories) Not Where I Started From, 1993; editor: (essays) In This Very Life, 1990; translator: (poems) Borrowed Time/Lo Esperady Lo Vivido, 1987; contg. editor: Tricycle Mag. Buddhist nun Mahasi Sasana Yeiktha, Rangoon, Burma, 1988; vol. Pet Share, Somerville (Mass.) Hosp., 1994. Recipient Pushcart Press prize, 1983-84, Best Am. Short Stories award Houghton Miflin, 1992, O'Henry award Doubleday, Inc., 1982, 93; nominee PEN/Faulkner award, 1994, Whiting Found. award, 1994; named one of Best 20 U.S. Novelists under 40, Granta Mmag., 1996; NEA grantee, 1994. Home: 72 Rev Nazareno Properzi Way Somerville MA 02143-3707

WHEELER, KATHERINE WELLS, state legislator; b. St. Louis, Feb. 8, 1940; d. Benjamin Harris and Katherine (Gladney) Wells; m. Douglas Lanphier Wheeler, June 13, 1964; children: Katherine Gladney, Lucille Lanphier. BA, Smith Coll., 1961; MA, Washington U., St. Louis, 1966. Founder auction N.H. Pub. TV, Durham, 1973-76; pub. mem. N.H. Pub. Broadcasting Coun., Durham, 1975-80; founding mem. bd. govs. N.H. Pub. TV, 1980-88; elected N.H. Ho. of Reps., Concord, 1988—; coord. internat. visitors program N.J. Coun. World Affairs, 1981-95. Bd. dirs. Planned Parenthood No. New England, 1989-95, Gt. Bay Sch. and Tng. Ctr., Newington, N.H., Devel. Svcs. Strafford County, Inc., 1991—; vice chairperson Strafford County Legis. Del., 1993-94; active Commn. on Health, Human Svcs. and Elderly Affairs N.H. Ho. of Reps., Concord, 1988. Named Woman of Yr., Union Leader Newspaper, 1984, Citizen of Yr., Homemakers of Strafford County, 1990, N.H. sect. NASW, 1993, Legislator of Yr., N.H. Nurses Assn., 1996, N.H. Acad. Pediat., 1996; recipient Elizabeth Campbell Outstanding Pub. TV Vol. award Nat. Friends Pub. Broadcasting, 1984, Meritorious Svc. award N.H. Women's Lobby, 1992, Dist. Contbn. award N.H. Psychol. Orgn., Inc., 1994, Cert. of Achievement for Outstanding Legis. Leadership N.H. Citizen Action, 1994. Mem. AAUW, LWV, Am. Assn. Ret. Persons, Order of Women Legislators, N.H. Smith Coll. Club (v.p. 1974-76, pres. 1976-78, v.p. class of 1961, 1991-96), N.H. Assn. Social Workers (Legislator of Yr. 1993), N.H. Psychol. Orgn. Inc. (Disting. Contbn. award 1994). Democrat. Mem. United Ch. of Christ. Home and Office: 27 Mill Rd Durham NH 03824-3006

WHEELER, M. CATHERINE, organization executive; b. Plainfield, N.J., May 31, 1942; d. William R. and Josephine S. (Ford) W. BA in Politics, Hollins Coll., 1964; MA in Theatre, U. Kans., 1966. Asst. mgr. South Shore Music Circus, Cohasset, Mass., 1967; pub. rels. asst. Trinity Square Repertory Co., Providence, 1967-68; co. mgr. Acad. Playhouse, Wilmette, Ill., 1968; adminstrv. asst. Am. U. Theatre, Washington, 1968-71; pub. rels. asst. Winterthur Mus. and Gardens, Wilmington, Del., 1972-76, dir. pub. rels., 1976-84; dir. Del. Tourism Office, Dover, 1984-93; pub. rels. coord. New Castle County Bd. of Realtors, Wilmington, 1994-95, dir. polit. affairs and comm., 1995—; pub. rels. cons. Historic Deerfield, Mass., 1983, Tourism Coun. Frederick County, Md., Bristol Riverside Theatre, Pa., 1994; bd. dirs. U.S. Travel Data Ctr., 1989-93. Editor Winterthur Newsletter, 1972-84. Mem. Del. Heritage Commn., 1984-93, Del. Coastal Heritage Greenways Coun., 1991-93. Mem. Nat. Coun. State Travel Dirs. (chmn. nominating com. 1987-89, chmn. edn. com. 1989-91, chmn. rsch. task force 1991-92), Travel Industry Assn. (bd. dirs. 1990-94, chmn. Mid-Atlantic U.S.A (1989-92). Office: New Castle Cty Bd Realtors 3615 Miller Rd Wilmington DE 19802-2523

WHEELER, SUSIE WEEMS, retired educator; b. Cassville, Ga., Feb. 24, 1917; d. Percy Weems and Cora (Smith) Weems-Canty; m. Dan W. Wheeler Sr., June 7, 1941; 1 child, Dan Jr. BS, Fort Valley (Ga.) State U., 1945; MEd, Atlanta U., 1947, EdD, 1978; postgrad., U. Ky., 1959-60; EdS, U. Ga., 1977. Tchr. Bartow County Schs., Cartersville (Ga.) City Schs., 1938-44, Jeanes supr., 1946-58; supr., curriculum dir. Paulding Sch. Sys.-Stephens Sch., Calhoun City, 1958-64; summer sch. tchr. Atlanta U., 1961-63; curriculum dir. Bartow County Schs., Cartersville, 1963-79; pres., co-owner Wheeler-Morris Svc. Ctr., 1990—; mem. Ga. Commn. on Student Fin., 1985-95. Coord. Noble Hill-Wheeler Meml. Ctr. Project, 1983—. Recipient Oscar W. Canty Cmty. Svc. award, 1991, Woman in History award Fedn. Bus. and Profl. Women, 1994-95. Mem. AAUW (v.p. membership 1989-91, Ga. Achievement award 1993), Ga. Assn. Curriculum and Supervision (pres.-elect 1973-74, pres. 1974-75, Johnnye V. Cox award 1975), Delta Sigma Theta (pres. Rome alumnae chpt. 1978-80, mem. nat. bd. 1984, planning com. 1988—, Dynamic Delta award 1967, 78), Ga. Jeanes Assn. (pres. 1968-70). Home: 105 Fite St Cartersville GA 30120-3410

WHEELER, VALERIE A. SYSLO, credit analyst; b. New Brunswick, N.J., Nov. 16, 1958; d. Joseph Jr. and Florence (Kulesa) Syslo; m. Ray J. Wheeler, Oct. 7, 1978. AAS in Acctg., Middlesex County Coll., 1979; BA in Acctg. and Econs., Rutgers U., 1993. Prodn. acctg. technician E. I. DuPont, Sayreville, N.J., 1981-86; import acctg. clk. Jeri-Jo Knitwear, Inc., Edison, N.J., 1986-87; cost acctg. clk. Neilson & Brainbridge, Edison, 1987-88; tax clk. Johnson & Johnson-CPI, Skillman, N.J., 1988-92; acct. mil. sales divsn., assoc. credit analyst Johnson & Johnson-CPI, New Brunswick, 1992—. Fundraising chair Rugters U. Coll., 1990-91. Mem. Inst. Mgmt. Accts., Univ. Coll. Governing Assn. Roman Catholic. Home: 12 Oxford Rd East Brunswick NJ 08816-4335

WHEELWRIGHT, IRENE NORA, computer program analyst; b. Wiesentheid, Bavaria, West Germany, Dec. 31, 1947; came to U.S., 1970; d. Heinz Werner and Gunda Hermine (Wagner) Scholz; m. George Wesley Neal, Nov. 14, 1970 (div. July 1992); children: Monique E., Geroge W.; m. Roger Warren Wheelwright, Dec. 1, 1995. BS, U. Md., 1978; MBA, Cen. Mich. U., 1981; Grad., U.S. Army War Coll., 1995. Claims examiner GSA, Washington, 1976-78, Judge Advocate-Gen., Aberdeen, Md., 1979-80; mgmt. analyst U.S. Army DCSRM, Frankfurt, Germany, 1982-83, U.S. Army, Ft. Belvoir, Va., 1983-84; inspector gen. HQ Dept. of Army/Pentagon, Washington, 1985-92; voting mem. ABCMR/Pentagon, Washington, 1989—; sr. analyst HQ Dept. of Army/ODCSOPS/Pentagon, 1992—; mem. women in mil. svc. com. Army-Mil. Pers./Pentagon, 1986—; EEO counselor HQDA/Pentagon, 1995—; architect/designer inspector: Gen. Corridor, Pentagon. Sp4 U.S. Army JAGC, 1973-75; 1st lt. U.S. Army AG, 1981-82, Pentagon; U.S. Army Res., 1981—. Decorated Meritorious Civil Svc. award, Meritorious Svc. medal. Mem. Mil. Comptroller Assn., Res. Officer Assn. Republican. Lutheran. Home: 4001 Pearlberry Ct Woodbridge VA 22193

WHELCHEL, BETTY ANNE, lawyer; b. Augusta, Ga., Dec. 22, 1956; d. John Davis and Charnell (Ramsey) W.; m. Douglas Charles Kruse, June 20, 1987. AB, U. Ga., 1978; JD, Harvard U., 1981. Bar: D.C. 1981, N.Y. 1984, gaikokuho-jimu-bengoshi (fgn. lawyer) Japan, 1988-89. Atty.-advisor U.S. Dept. Treasury, Washington, 1981-84; assoc. Shearman & Sterling, N.Y.C., 1984-87, 89-90, Tokyo, 1987-89; dep. chief counsel N.Y. br. Deutsche Bank AG, N.Y., 1990—; staff atty. Depository Instns. Deregulation Com., Washington, 1983-84. Mem. Am. Soc. Internat. Law, Assn. of the Bar of the City of N.Y. (com. on fgn. comparative law chmn. 1996), Harvard Law Sch. Assn. Office: Deutsche Bank AG 31 W 52nd St New York NY 10019-6118

WHIDDON, CAROL PRICE, writer, editor, consultant; b. Gadsden, Ala., Nov. 18, 1947; d. Curtis Ray and Vivian (Dooly) Price; m. John Earl Caulking, Jan. 18, 1969 (div. July 1987); m. Ronald Alton Whiddon, Apr. 13, 1988. Student, McNeese State U., 1966-68; BA in English, George Mason U., 1984. Flute instr. Lake Charles, La., 1966-68; flutist Lake Charles Civic Symphony, 1966-69, Beaumont (Tex.) Symphony, 1967-68; freelance editor The Washington Lit. Rev., 1983-84, ARC Hdqrs., Washington, 1984; writer, editor Jaycor, Vienna, Va., 1985-87; writer, editor Jaycor, Albuquerque, 1987-90, publs. mgr., 1990-91; writer, editor Proteus Corp., Albuquerque, 1991-92; owner Whiddon Editorial Svcs., Albuquerque, 1989—; mem. S.W. Writer's Workshop, 1991—. Co-author: The Spirit That Wants Me: A New Mexico Anthology, 1991; contbr. various articles to Albuquerque Woman and mil. dependent pubs. in Fed. Rpublic Germany. Bd. dirs. Channel 27-Pub. Access TV, 1991-93, exec. bd. sec., 1992, v.p., 1993; dep. mgr. Fed. Women's Program, Ansbach, Fed. Republic Germany, 1980-81; pres. Ansbach German-Am. Club, 1980-82; sec. Am. Women's Activities, Fed. Republic Germany, 1980-81, chairwoman, 1981-82. Recipient cert. of appreciation from Am. amb. to Germany Arthur T. Burns, 1982, medal of appreciation from comdr. 1st Armored Div., Ansbach, Germany, 1982. Mem. NAFE, Women in Comm. (newsletter editor 1989-90, 91-92, 94-95, v.p. 1990-91, pres.-elect 1992-93, pres. 1993-94, chair programs com. Nat. Profl. Conf. 1994), Soc. Tech. Comm. (membership dir. 1993-94), Nat. Assn. Desktop Pubs., Am. Mktg. Assn., Greater Albuquerque C. of C., N.Mex. Cactus Soc. (historian 1989-94, sec. 1991, newsletter editor 1992—, various show ribbons 1989-91). Republican. Home: 1129 Turner Dr NE Albuquerque NM 87123-1917

WHIGHAM, JEAN ANNE, banker; b. Sullivan, Ind., Apr. 14, 1948; d. Lloyd William and Mary Evelyn (Doane) Huffman; m. Ellis Glen Whigham, Apr. 16, 1966; children: Jeanie Renee, Teresa Ann. Degree, Am. Inst. Banking, 1991. From bookkeeper to compliance officer Poteau (Okla.) State Bank, 1979—. Bd. dirs. LeFlore County chpt. March of Dimes, Poteau, 1984-90. Democrat. Methodist. Home: 3204 Pleasant Valley Rd Poteau OK 74953 Office: Poteau State Bank 1409 N Broadway Poteau OK 74953

WHILDIN, LEONORA PORRECA, nurse midwife, nursing; b. Boston, Mass., Dec. 7, 1926; d. John and Anna (Annunziata) Porreca; m. William Miller Whildin; children: Susan Lee, Robert Miller, Walter Thomas. BS, Boston U., 1954; MS, Columbia U., 1971. RN, Mass., N.Y., N.J.; cert. nurse midwife, N.Y. Cadet nurse corps. Boston City Hosp., 1943-46, staff, asst. head nurse neurology, neurosurgery, 1946-48, scrub nurse neurosurgery, 1948-50; civilian nurse Dept. of Army, Bremerhaven, Germany, 1948; pub. health nurse Bklyn. Vis. Nurse Assn., 1954-56; instr. Helene Fulde Sch. of Practical Nursing, N.Y.C., 1956-57; pub. health nurse V.N.A. Morris Co., Morristown, N.J., 1967; instr. All Souls Hosp. Sch. of Nursing, Morristown, N.J., 1968-69; guest lectr. Seton Hall U., South Orange, N.J., 1978; del. Am. Nurses Assn, Mass., 1954; By-Laws Com. Am. Coll. Nurse Midwives, N.Y., 1972, By-Laws Com. Am. Coll. Nurse Midwives (N.J. chpt.), 1980; bd. mem. V.N.A. Morris Co., Morristown, N.J., 1977-78; v.p. bd. health, Randolph Twp., Randolph, N.J., 1972-74. Coun. woman Randolph Twp., 1972-78; mayor (1st woman mayor) Randolph Twp., 1977; dem. party county com., Morris Co., Morristown, N.J., 1972-96; dem. party state com., N.J., 1992—. Mem. APHA, ANA, LWV, Mass., N.Y., N.J. (bd. mem. 1964-66), Sigma Theta Tau. Democrat. Home: 82 Radtke Rd Randolph NJ 07869-3815

WHIPPLE, JUDITH ROY, book editor; b. N.Y.C., May 14, 1935; d. Edwin Paul and Elizabeth (Levis) Roy; m. William Whipple, Oct. 26, 1963. AB, Mount Holyoke Coll., 1957. Head libr. Am. Sch. Lima (Peru), S.A., 1957-59; asst. editor children's books G.P. Putnam's Sons, N.Y.C., 1959-62; assoc. editor W.W. Norton & Co., Inc., N.Y.C., 1962-68; editor Four Winds Press, 1968-75; editor-in-chief Scholastic Gen. Book Divsn., 1975-77; pub. Four Winds Press subs. Scholastic Inc., N.Y.C., 1977-82; pub., v.p. Macmillan Pub. Co., N.Y.C., 1982-89, exec. editor, 1989-94; editl. dir. Benchmark Books and Cavendish Children's Books, Tarrytown, N.Y., 1994—. Mem. PEN, Children's Book Coun. (pres. 1977, bd. dirs. 1970-79), Women's Nat. Book Assn., Soc. Children's Book Writers and Illustrators. Office: Marshall Cavendish Corp 99 White Plains Rd Tarrytown NY 10591-5502

WHITAKER, CAROL SUZANNE, small business owner; b. Chgo., Mar. 13, 1935; d. Frank D. and Suzanne D. (Kosko) Kettering; m. Ernest Leo Whitaker, May 3, 1953; children: Daniel A., William M., Laura L. Whitaker Stender. BA in Edn., Ariz. State U., 1967, MA in Edn., 1971. Tchr. Paradise Valley Schs., Phoenix, Ariz., 1967-83; owner Marco Polo Sch., Phoenix, 1989-90; herbalist, distbr. Nature's Sunshine, Provo, Utah, 1994—; shop owner Arachne's Web, Phoenix, 1994—. Choreographer original dances for amateur groups, 1958-83; newsletter coord. NOW, Phoenix/Scottsdale chpt., 1996. Office: Arachne's Web 15049 N 25 Pl Phoenix AZ 85032

WHITAKER, CYNTHIA ELLEN, nurse; b. Dearborn, Mich., June 15, 1948; d. John Harold and Marion Violet (Malmsten) Fields; m. Elbert Charles Whitaker, Sept. 7, 1968; children: Shannon Kaye, Kaycee Susan. ADN, Oakland C.C., Union Lake, Mich., 1982; BSN, U. Mich., 1985. Cert. case mgr. Nurse Wheelock Meml. Hosp., Goodrich, Mich., 1982-86; clin. nursing instr. Oakland C.C., Union Lake, Mich., 1985-86; rehab. nurse Continental Ins.-UAC, Southfield, Mich., 1987-88; med. mgmt. cons. Continental Rehab. Resources, Sacramento, 1988-89; pres. Rehab. Nursing Svcs., Sacramento, 1989—; CFO, v.p. Strategic Health Alliances, Inc., Sacramento, 1993—. Co-author: (book) Infectious Disease Handbook, 1981, (booklet) Standards of Practice for Case Management, 1995. Mem. adv. bd. grad. sch. nursing San Francisco State U., 1994—; mem. cmty. adv. bd. Mercy Healthcare Sacramento, 1993-95, Kentfield (Calif.) Rehab. Hosp., 1993—, North Valley Rehab. Hosp., Chico, Calif., 1991-93. Dean's Fellow Scholarship awardee U. Mich., 1986. Mem. ANA, Am. Assn. Legal Nurse Cons., Case Mgmt. Soc. Am. (co-founder No. Calif. chpt., affiliate dir. 1990-91, affiliate pres. 1992-93, nat. sec. 1995-96, nat. pres.-elect 1996—). Republican. Home: 1629 University Ave Sacramento CA 95825

WHITAKER, EILEEN MONAGHAN, artist; b. Holyoke, Mass., Nov. 22, 1911; d. Thomas F. and Mary (Doona) Monaghan; m. Frederic Whitaker. Ed., Mass. Coll. Art, Boston. Annual exhibits in nat. and regional watercolor shows; represented in permanent collections, Charles and Emma Frye Mus., Seattle, NAD, Hispanic Soc., N.Y.C., High Mus. Art, Atlanta, U. Mass., Norfolk (Va.) Mus., Springfield (Mass.) Mus. Art, Reading (Pa.) Art Mus., Nat. Acad. Design, U. Mass., Okla. Mus. Art, St. Lawrence U., Wichita State U., Retrospective show, Founders Gallery U. San Diego, 1988, invitational one-person show Charles and Emma Frye Art Mus., 1990; included in pvt. collections; featured in cover article of American Artist mag., Mar. 1987, in article Art of Calif. mag., July 1991; invitational Am. Realism Exhbn. Cir. Gallery, San Diego, 1992; author: Eileen Monaghan Whitaker Paints San Diego, 1986. Recipient numerous major awards, including Allied Artists Am., Am. Watercolor Soc., 1st prize Providence Water Color Club, Wong award Calif. Watercolor Soc., De Young award Soc. Western Artists, 1st award Springville (Utah) Mus., Ranger Fund purchase prize, Orbrig prize NAD, Walter Biggs Meml. award, 1987; silver medal Am. Watercolor Soc., Watercolor West; fellow Huntington Hartford Found., 1964. Academician NAD (William P. and Gertrude Schweitzer prize for excellence in watercolor 171st Annual Exbhn. 1996); mem. Am. Watercolor Soc. (Dolphin fellow), Watercolor West (hon.), San Diego Watercolor Soc. (hon.). Home and Studio: 1579 Alta La Jolla Dr La Jolla CA 92037-7101

WHITAKER, LINDA M., principal; b. Blue Island, Ill., Apr. 2, 1950; d. William Martin and Evelyn Cecilia (Klucznik) Locke; m. David George Whitaker, June 10, 1972. BS in Edn. magna cum laude, No. Ill. U., 1972, MS in Edn., 1975, C.A.S., 1985. Cert. adminstrv. type 75, secondary type 9, elem. type 3. Tchr. High Sch. Dist. 218, Oak Lawn, Ill.; dean Hazelgreen Sch., Sch. Dist. 126, Alsip, Ill.; elem. sch. prin., dist. curriculum coord. Worth (Ill.) Sch. Dist. 127. Contbr. articles to profl. jours. Recipient Govs. Master Tchr. award, 1984, PTA State Life Membership award, 1988. Mem. ASCD, Ill. ASCD, Nat. Assn. Elem. Sch. Prins., Ill. Prins. Assn., Nat. Coun. for Social Studies, Mortar Board, Delta Kappa Gamma (chpt. 1st v.p.), Kappa Delta Pi, Phi Alpha Theta.

WHITAKER, RUTH REED, retired newspaper editor; b. Blytheville, Ark., Dec. 13, 1936; d. Lawrence Neill and Ruth Shipton (Weidemeyer) Reed; m. Thomas Jefferson Whitaker, dec. 29, 1961; children: Steven Bryan, Alicia Morrow. BA, Hendrix Coll., 1958. Copywriter, weather person KTVE TV, El Dorado, Ark., 1958-59; nat. bridal cons. Treasure House, El Dorado, 1959; bridal cons. Pfeifers of Ark., Little Rock, 1959-60; dir. of continuity S. M. Brooks Advt. Agy., Little Rock, 1960-61; layout artist C. V. Mosby Co., St. Louis, 1961-62; editor, owner Razorback Am. Newspaper, Ft. Smith, Ark., 1979-81; ret., 1981. Host Crawford Conversations TV show; contbr. author indsl. catalog, 1979 (Addy award). State sec. Rep. Party of Ark., 1992-94; mem. Ben Geren Regional Park Commn., Sebastian County, Ark., 1984-89, pres., 1990; past pres. Jr. Civic League; mem. Ft. Smith Orchid Com.; mem. com. of 21 United Way; publicity chmn. Sebastian County Rep. Com., 1983-84; state press officer Reagan-Bush Campaign, 1984; exec. dir. Ark. Dole for Pres., 1995-96; pres. Women's Aux. Sebastian County Med. Soc., 1974; mem. Razorback Scholarship Fund; class agt. alumni fund Hendrix Coll., 1990, 91, 92; mem. Sparks Woman's Bd.; 1st vice chmn. 3d Dist. Rep. Party; state committeewoman Rep. Party Ark. Recipient Disting. Vol. Leadership award Nat. Found. March of Dimes, 1973, Appreciation award Ft. Smith Advt. Fedn., 1977, 78, Hon. Parents of Yr. award U. Ark., 1984, Recognition award United Cerebral Palsy, 1980. Mem. AAUW, Alden Soc. Am. (life), Ft. Smith C. of C., Ark. Nature Conservancy, Am. Legion Aux., Frontier Rschrs. Soc. (pres. 1995-96), Daus. Union Vets. Presbyterian. Home: PO Box 349 Cedarville AR 72932-0178

WHITAKER, SHIRLEY ANN, telecommunications company marketing executive; b. Asmara, Eritea, Ethiopia, Oct. 13, 1955; (parents Am. citizens); d. Calvin Randall and Ruth (Ganeles) Peck; m. John Marshall Whitaker, June 16, 1973; 1 child, Kathryn Ann. AA, Tacoma Community Coll., 1974; BA, Wash. State U., 1977, MBA, 1978. Planning adminstr. for econ. rsch. GTE NW, Everett, Wash., 1978-80; specialist in demand analysis western region GTE Svc. Corp., Los Gatos, Calif., 1980-81; fin. analyst GTE Svc. Corp., Stamford, Conn., 1981-83, staff specialist demand analysis and forecasting, 1983-84; group mgr. for rate devel. Nat. Exch. Carrier Assn., Whippany, N.J., 1984-87; mgr. pricing strategy and migration GTE Calif., Thousand Oaks, 1987-88; mgr. market forecasting GTE Telephone Ops. Hdqrs., Irving, Tex., 1989-90, dir. revenue analysis, 1990-92, dir. market rsch., 1992-93, dir. process re-engring., 1993-94; dir. network and resource mgmt., 1994—. Mem. Am. Mktg. Assn. (membership com. 1984), Beta Gamma Sigma, Phi Kappa Phi.

WHITAKER, SUSANNE KANIS, veterinary medical librarian; b. Clinton, Mass., Sept. 10, 1947; d. Harry and Elizabeth P. (Cantwell) Kanis; m. Daniel Brown Whitaker, Jan. 1, 1977. A.B. in Biology, Clark U., 1969; M.S. in Library Sci., Case Western Res. U., 1970. Regional reference librarian Yale Med. Library, New Haven, 1970-72; med. librarian Hartford Hosp., Conn., 1972-77; asst. librarian Cornell U., Ithaca, N.Y., 1977-78; vet. med. librarian Coll. Vet. Medicine, Cornell U., 1978—; sec. SUNY Council Head Librarians, 1981-83. Mem. Med. Libr. Assn. (sec.-treas. vet. med. librs. sect. 1983-84, chmn. 1984-85), Med. Libr. Assn. (upstate N.Y. and Ont. chpt.), Acad. Health Info. Profls. Home: 23 Wedgewood Dr Ithaca NY 14850 Office: Cornell U Coll Vet Medicine Flower-Sprecher Libr Ithaca NY 14853-6401

WHITAKER, VON BEST, nursing educator; b. New Bern, N.C.; d. Cleveland W. and Lillie (Bryant) Best; m. Roy Whitaker Jr., Aug. 9, 1981; 1 child, Roy Whitaker III. BS, Columbia Union Coll., 1972; MS, U. Md., 1974; MA, U. N.C., 1980, PhD, 1983. Lectr. U. N.C., Chapel Hill, 1981-82; asst. prof. U. Mo., Columbia, Mo., 1982-85; asst. prof. grad. sch. Boston Coll., Newton, Mass., 1985-86; asst. prof. U. Tex. Health Sci. Ctr., San Antonio, 1986-94; assoc. prof. Ga. So. U., Statesboro, 1994—; mem. cataract guideline panel Agy. for Health Care Policy Rsch., 1990-93; rsch. coord. glaucoma svc. Georgia Eye Inst., Savannah. Contbr. articles to profl. jours., chpts. to textbooks; presenter in field. Vol. to prevent blindness. Bush fellowship, 1979-81; recipient Cert. of Appreciation, Prevent Blindness South Tex., 1988, 89. Mem. ANA (cert. community health nurse), APHA, Am. Soc. Ophthalmic Nursing (chair rsch. com.), Assn. Black Faculty in Higher Edn., Nat. Black Nurses Assn., Sigma Theta Tau. Home: 1 Chelmsford Ln Savannah GA 31411

WHITAKER, WILMA NEUMAN, mathematics instructor; b. Chgo., Aug. 18, 1937; d. August P. and Wilma M. (Kaiser) Neuman; m. G.D. Whitaker, Mar. 28, 1970; children: Brett Allan Karlsen, Karen J. Whitaker Laflin, Mark D. Whitaker, David R. Whitaker. BA in Math., DePauw U., 1959; MEd in Math., Francis Marion Coll., 1988. Cert. secondary tchr., Ill., Mich., S.C.; cert. realtor Mich. High sch. math tchr. Dist. 209, Hillside, Ill., 1959-61, Dist. 214, Mt. Prospect, Ill., 1961-65; apprentice pharmacist Karlsen Pharmacy, Mt. Prospect, 1961-67; realtor Durbin Co., Clarkston, Mich., 1977-81; substitute tchr. Clarkston (Mich.) Community Schs., 1979-80; math instr. Florence (S.C.)-Darlington Tech. Coll., 1981-85, math dept. head, 1985-87, dean arts and scis., 1987-95, instr. math., 1995—. Stephen min. St. Lukes Luth. Ch., Florence, 1991—, coun., 1989-92, tchr., 1981—; founder, organizer Spring Cmty. Walk Along Rotary Beauty Trail, Florence, 1988, 89, 91. Named Faculty Mem. of Yr., Florence-Darlington Tech. Coll., 1987, Adminstr. of Yr., 1992, Exec. of Yr., Florence chpt. Profl. Secs. Internat., 1993. Mem. ASTD, AAUW, Am. Assn. Women in C.C.s, Am. Assn. C.C.s, S.C. Assn. Devel. Educators, S.C. Assn. Math. Tchrs. Two-Yr. Colls., S.C. Tech. Edn. Assn., S.C. Women in Higher Edn., Optimist Club of Florence (v.p. 1991-92, pres. 1992-93), Optimist Internat. (lt. gov. Zone 6 S.C. 1993-94, 95-96, gov.-elect S.C. dist. 1994-95, gov. 1995-96), Theta Sigma Phi, Delta Zeta. Office: Florence-Darlington Tech Coll PO Box 100548 Florence SC 29501-0548

WHITCOMB, CLAIRE, freelance writer; b. Orange, N.J., Aug. 17, 1955; d. John Philip and Helen (Hafemann) W.; m. Howard Klein, Dec. 26, 1993; 1 child, Jesse John Whitcomb Klein. BA, Bucknell U., 1977. Editl. asst. House & Garden, N.Y.C., 1977-80; sr. writer House Beautiful, N.Y.C., 1980-88; editl. dir. Victoria, N.Y.C., 1988-93; freelance writer N.Y.C., 1993—. Co-author: (with John Whitcomb) Oh Say Can You See, 1987, Great American Anecdotes, 1993. Mem. Am. Soc. Journalists and Authors.

WHITCOMB, VIRGINIA GOODBODY, medical technologist, educator; b. N.Y.C., Feb. 5, 1922; d. William Edward and Helen Edith-Agnes (Herb) Goodbody; m. Wayne Phillip Whitcomb, July 16, 1944 (dec. May 1976); children: Suzanne, William, Leslie, Patience. BS, Duke U., 1943; MS, So. Conn. State U., 1972. Cert. chemistry/math. tchr., Conn. Chem. analyst Burroughs Wellcome, Tuckahoe, N.Y., 1993-94; rsch./lab. instr. Coll. Medicine, U. Vt., Burlington, 1944-45; tchr. math. Derby (Conn.) H.S., 1971-72; lab. technologist Clin. Chem. Lab., Yale-New Haven Hosp., 1978-95. Deacon Orange (Conn.) Congl. Ch., 1980—. Republican. Home: 1075 Orange Center Rd Orange CT 06477

WHITE, ALICE ELIZABETH, physicist, researcher; b. Glen Ridge, N.J., Apr. 5, 1954; d. Alan David and Elizabeth Joyce (Jones) W.; m. Donald Paul Monroe, Oct. 13, 1990; children: Ellen Elizabeth White Monroe, Janet Clare White Monroe. BA in Physics, Middlebury (Vt.) Coll., 1976; MA in Physics, Harvard U., 1978, PhD in Physics, 1982. Postdoctoral mem. tech. staff AT&T Bell Labs., Murray Hill, N.J., 1982-84, mem. tech. staff, 1984-88, dept. head, 1988—. Contbr. over 100 articles to profl. pubs.; patentee in field. Recipient Alumni Achievement award Middlebury Coll., 1994. Fellow Am. Phys. Soc. (Maria Goeppert-Mayer award 1991); mem. Optical Soc. of Am., Materials Rsch. Soc., Phi Beta Kappa. Office: Bell Labs Lucent Technol Rm 2D328 PO Box 636 New Providence NJ 07974

WHITE, ANN HOSFORD, systems programmer; b. Cleve., Aug. 17, 1944; d. Harry William Hosford and Helen Elizabeth Hosford Bakken; m. David Russell White, June 27, 1968; children: Dennis Eric, Elizabeth Ann. BA in Math., Wells Coll., 1966. Programmer AT&T, White Plains, N.Y., 1966-68, Blue Cross N.E. Ohio, Cleve., 1968-69, Hanna Mining Co., Cleve., 1969-71, AC Nielsen, Dunedin, Fla., 1974-77; sys. programmer GE, Largo, Fla., 1977-92, Fla. Power Corp., St. Petersburg, 1992—. Softball coach, bd. dirs. Cross Bayou Little League, Largo, 1984-87. Mem. AAUW (programs v.p. 1993-95, treas. 1995-96). Office: Fla Power Corp PO Box 14042 Saint Petersburg FL 33711

WHITE, ANN WELLS, community activist; b. Kansas City, Mo., Mar. 16, 1927; d. William Gates and Annie Loretta (Morton) Wells; m. Norman E. White, Oct. 2, 1949 (div. Dec. 1977); children: Thomas Wells, Norman Lee. BJ, U. Mo., 1948. Asst. to pres. Cities in Schs., 1978-79. Lobbyist Common Cause, Atlanta, 1972-73; vol. Jimmy Carter's Peanut Brigade, 1976, Carter/Mondale campaign, 1980; bd. dirs., vice chair Atlanta Area Svcs. for the Blind, 1973-81; Gov.'s Commn. on the Status of Women, Atlanta, 1974-76; office mgr. Carter/Mondale Transition Office, Atlanta, 1976; chair evaluation com. United Way Met. Atlanta, 1980-90; bd. dirs. Mems. Guild, The High Mus. of Art, Atlanta, 1982-83, Hillside Hosp., Atlanta, 1989-94, Ga. Forum, Atlanta, 1988-91; bd. dirs. Planned Parenthood of Atlanta area, 1975-89, pres., 1978-81; bd. dirs. Planned Parenthood Fedn. Am., N.Y.C., 1980-86, chair ann. meeting, New Orleans, 1986; legis. chair, lobbyist Ga. Women's Polit. Caucus, 1984-90; convenor, founding chair Georgians for Choice, 1989. Democrat. Presbyterian. Home: Colony House 1237 145 Fifteenth St Atlanta GA 30309

WHITE, ANNE MACDONALD, resort chain executive; b. Summit, N.J., July 15, 1946; d. Charles Bruyn and Jane Sherman (Winans) W. BA, U. Pacific, 1969. Real estate saleswoman Valley Brokerage, Winter Park, Colo., 1979-80, King Realty, Sherman Oaks, Calif., 1980-82; mgr. advt. Winter Park ManiFest, 1982-84; sales mgr. The Inn at Silver Creek, Granby, Colo., 1984-85, Beaver Run Resort, Breckenridge, Colo., 1985-87; nat. sales mgr. Snowmass Resort Assn., Snowmass Village, Colo., 1987-90; sr. v.p. Preferred Resorts Internat., Aspen, Colo., 1990—. Recipient award for advt. excellence Colo. Press Assn., 1984. Home: Box 6316 Snowmass Village CO 81615 Office: Preferred Resorts Internat 715 W Main St Ste 201 Aspen CO 81611

WHITE, ANNETTE JONES, early childhood education administrator; b. Albany, Ga., Aug. 29, 1939; d. Paul Lawrence and Delores Christine (Berry) Jones; m. Frank Irvin White, Nov. 13, 1964; children: Melanie Francine, Sharmian Lynell. BA, Spelman Coll., 1964; MEd, Va. State U., 1980. Tchr. Flint Ave Child Devel. Ctr., Albany, 1966-67; tchr., supr. Flintside Child Devel. Ctr., Albany, 1967-68; tchr., dir. Albany Ga. Community Sch., 1968-69; tchr. Martin Luther King Community Ctr., Atlanta, 1975-77, The Appleton Sch., Atlanta, 1977-78; sec., proofreader The Atlanta Daily World, 1978-80; tchr. kindergarten Spelman Coll., Atlanta, 1981-88, dir. nursery and kindergarten, lectr. in edn., 1988—; cons., presenter child devel. assoc. program Morris Brown Coll., Atlanta, 1991; presenter ann. child care conf. Waycross (Ga.) Coll., 1993. Contbr. articles to profl. jours. Mem. Peace Action, Washington, 1990—, Children's Def. Action Coun., Washington, 1990—; mem. Native Am. Rights Fund, Am. Indian Rights Coun. Mem. AAUW, ASCD, Acad. Am. Poets, Assn. Childhood Edn. Internat., Nat. Asn. Edn. Young Children, Nat. Black Child Devel. Inst., Ga. Assn. Young Children (cons., presenter 1992), Nat. Coun. Negro Women, Atlanta Assn. Edn. Young Children, Sierra Club. Office: Spelman Coll Nursery-Kinder 350 Spelman Ln SW # 89 Atlanta GA 30314-4346

WHITE, BARBARA BOONE, artist, retired college instructor; b. Limestone, Tenn., Sept. 19, 1933; d. Ray Howard and Virginia Frances (Boone) W. BS, Kent State U., 1955; MA, Columbia U., 1964. Tchr. Cuyahoga Falls (Ohio) Schs., 1955-56; tchr. (art specialist) East Williston (N.Y.) Scbs., 1959-64; instr. art dept. Mott C.C., FLint, Mich., 1964-89. Recipient awards from art exhibitions, photography prints, metalsmithing, N.Y.C., Flint, Mich., Detroit, 1955-89. Mem. AAUW. Presbyterian. Home: 1836 Willow Brook Cir Flint MI 48507

WHITE, BEVERLY J., cytogeneticist; b. Seattle, Oct. 9, 1938. Grad., U. Wash., 1959, MD, 1963. Diplomate Nat. Bd. Med. Examiners, Am. Bd. Pediatrics, Am. Bd. Med. Genetics; lic physician and surgeon, Wash., Va. Rsch. trainee dept. anatomy Sch. Medicine U. Wash., Seattle, 1960-62, pediatric resident dept. pediatrics, 1967-69; rotating intern Phila. Gen. Hosp., 1963-64; rsch. fellow med. ob-gyn. unit Cardiovascular Rsch. Inst. U. Calif. Med. Ctr., San Francisco, 1964-65; staff fellow lab. biomed. scis. Nat. Inst. Child Health and Human Devel. NIH, Bethesda, Md., 1965-67, sr. staff fellow, attending physician lab. exptl. pathology Nat. Inst. Arthritis, Metabolism and Digestive Diseases, 1969-74, acting chief sect. cytogenetics, 1975-76, rsch. med. officer, attending physician sect. cytogenetics lab. cellular biology and genetics, 1974-86, dir. cytogenetics unit, interinstitute med. genetics program clin. ctr., 1987-95; dir. cytogenetics Corning Clin. Labs., Teterboro, N.J., 1995—; vis. scientist dept. pediat. divsn. genetics U. Wash. Sch. Medicine, 1983-84; intramural cons. NIH, 1975-95; cons. to assoc. editor Jour. Nat. Cancer Inst., 1976; mem. staff cons. dept. ob-gyn. Naval Hosp., Bethesda, 1988-89; lectr., presenter in field. Recipient Mosby Book award, 1963, Women of Excellence award U. Wash. and Seattle Profl. chpt. Women in Comm., 1963, Reuben award Am. Soc. for Study Sterility, 1963. Fellow Am. Coll. Med. Genetics (founding), Am. Acad. Pediatrics; mem.

AMA. Am. Soc. Human Genetics, Assn. Cytogenetic Technologists (program com. 1989). Home: 9916 Shrewsbury Ct Gaithersburg MD 20879 Office: Corning Clin Labs Dept Cytogenetics One Malcom Ave Teterboro NJ 07608-1070

WHITE, BONNIE HAVANA, retired federal agency official; b. Trammel, Va., Nov. 18, 1926; d. John Clark and Cordella (Burke) H.; m. Bonnie Havana Holbrook, Sept. 6, 1958; children: Jonnie, James, Sheila. BS, U. Md., 1988; postgrad., U. D.C., 1990. From libr. aide to examiner SEC, Washington, 1981-95, ret., 1995. Art docent Hirshborn Mus., 1990; art and history docent Nat. Mus. Am. History, 1992—; tutor, trainer D.C. Pub. Libr. Project for the Deaf, 1991. Mem. AAUW, U. Md. Alumni Assn. Republican. Presbyterian. Home: 704 Azalea Dr Rockville MD 20850-2015

WHITE, BONNIE YVONNE, management consultant, educator; b. Long Beach, Calif., Sept. 4, 1940; d. William Albert and Helen Iris (Harbaugh) W. BS, Brigham Young U., 1962, MS, 1965, EdD in Ednl. Adminstrn., 1976. Tchr., Wilson High Sch., Long Beach, Calif., 1962-63; grad. asst. Brigham Young U., Provo, Utah, 1963-65; instr., dir. West Valley Coll., Saratoga, Calif., 1965-76; instr., evening adminstr. Mission Coll., Santa Clara, Calif., 1976-80; dean gen. edn. Mendocino Coll., Ukiah, Calif., 1980-85; dean instrn. Porterville (Calif.) Coll., 1985-89, dean adminstrv. svc., 1989-93; rsch. assoc. SAGE Rsch. Internat., Orem, Utah, 1975—. Del. Tulare County Ctrl. Com. Rep. Party, 1993-94; pres. community adv. bd. Calif. Conservation Corps, 1989-93; v.p. Porterville Community Concerts, 1990-94; bd. dirs. United Way North Bay, Santa Rosa, Calif., 1980-85, St. Vincent de Paul, 1993—; mem. Calif. Commn. on Basic Skills, 1987-89, Calif. Commn. on Athletics, 1987-90. Mem. AAUW, Faculty Assn. Calif. Community Colls., Calif., Coun. Fine Arts Deans, Assn. Calif. Community Coll. Adminstrs. Assn. Calif. Community Coll. Adminstrs. Liberal Arts, Zonta (intern), Soroptimists (intern). Republican. Mormon.

WHITE, CHESLEY LYNNE, priest, therapist; b. Tyler, Tex., Oct. 23, 1945; d. Roy Chesley and Billie Hensley (Fielder) W. BA, Phillips U., 1968; M in Divinity, Ch. Divinity Sch. of Pacific, 1976. Ordained priest Ch. and Comty. of Mary Magdalene, the Apostle, 1977. Founder, priest, exec. dir. The Ch. and Comty. of Mary Magdalene, The Apostle, Oakland, Tyler, Calif. Tex, 1976—. Home and Office: Ch and Cmty Mary Magdalene Apostle PO Box 6273 Tyler TX 75711

WHITE, CHRISTINE, physical education educator; b. Taunton, Mass., Apr. 1, 1905; d. Peregrine Hastings and Sara (Lawrence) W. Cert., Boston Sch. Phys. Edn.; BS, Boston U., 1935, MEd, 1939. Instr. Winthrop Coll., Rock Hill, S.C., 1927-29; instr., asst. prof. The Woman's Coll. U. N.C., Greensboro, N.C., 1929-41; assoc. prof., head dept. physical edn. Meredith Coll., Raleigh, N.C., 1941-43; assoc. prof., prof. chair dept. physical edn. Wheaton Coll., Norton, Mass., 1943-70, prof. emerita, 1970—. co-editor Taunton Architecture: A Reflection of the City's History, 1981, 89. Chmn. Hist. Dist. Study Com., 1975-78, Recreation Commn., 1972-81; mem. Hist. Dist. Commn., 1979—, sec., 1979-86, acting chair, 1992-94; mem. Park and Recreation Commn., 1982—; bd. dirs. Star Theatre for the Arts, Inc., 1993—. Fellow AAHPERD; mem. AAUP (pres. Wheaton Coll. chpt. 1960-61), AAUW, LWV, Nat. Assn. Phys. Edn. in Higher Edn., Pi Lambda Theta. Home: 40 Highland Ter Taunton MA 02780-4729

WHITE, DONNA JO, accounting educator; b. Waco, Tex., Jan. 2, 1966; d. Weldon Clay and Joann (Richards) W.; married; three children. AAS, McLennan Community Coll., Waco, 1989; BBA, Baylor U., 1992, MBA, 1993; postgrad., U. Tex., Arlington, 1994-95. Tutor McLennan C.C., Waco, 1988-89; bookkeeper Assoc. Ct. Reporters, Waco, 1988-89; acctg. clk. Pattillo, Brown & Hill, CPAs, Waco, 1990; adminstrv. asst. honors program Baylor U., Waco, 1990-93; instr. acctg. Ctrl. Tex. Coll., 1994—; instr. mgmt. Tarleton State U., 1996—. Exec. bd. Woodway PTA, 1994-96; mem. exec. com. Cub Scouts Am., 1993-94; exec. bd. mem. Midway Coun. of PTAs, 1994-95. Recipient Student Scholar award Am. Assn. Cmty. and Jr. Colls. Mem. Phi Theta Kappa (reporter 1988-89, Student Scholar award, Outstanding Acctg. Student award 1988, Outstanding Svc. award 1989). Home: 3600 W Brookview Dr Waco TX 76710

WHITE, DURIE NEUMANN, federal agency administrator; b. Westerly, R.I., June 19, 1950; d. Reed Maurice Neumann and Alice M. (Victoria) Quinn; m. Donald L. White, Oct. 6, 1979; 6 stepchildren. BA, U. R.I., 1972. Supply clk. USAF/Europe, Mainz Kastel, Germany, 1972-73; adminstrv. asst. Pearson's Travel, Providence, 1973; contracting officer GSA, Washington, 1973-77; contract specialist AID, Washington, 1977-80; procurement analyst A/SDBU Dept. State, Washington, 1980-91, ops. dir. A/SDBU, 1991—; mem. Interagy. Small Bus. Dirs. Group, Washington, 1993—, White House Conf. on Small Bus., 1995. Roman Catholic. Office: Small/Disadvantaged Bus Dept State Rm 633 SA-6 Washington DC 20522-0602

WHITE, FAITH, sculptor; b. N.Y.C., Apr. 7, 1950; d. Edward and Faith-Hope (Green) Kahn. BA summa cum laude, L.I. U., 1971; studied woodcarving, with Nathaniel Burwash, Cambridge, Mass., 1976, with Joseph Wheelwright, Boston, 1977-94. Freelance sculptor Boston, 1971—, N.Y.C., 1995—; adminstrv. asst. to dean of students Grahm Jr. Coll., Boston, 1972-74; exec. sec. to New Eng. regional mgr. Bur. of Nat. Affairs, Inc., Boston, 1974-77; asst. to dir. New Eng. Aquarium, Boston, 1977-80, dir. pers., 1980-82; guest juror for travel grant Boston Visual Artists Union, 1994; show mgr. Sculpture and Large Works, The Copley Soc. of Boston, 1992; instr. woodcarving The Eliot Sch., Jamaica Plain, Mass., 1992-94; tchg. artist Very Spl. Arts program Mus. of Sci., Boston, 1992, 93; project coord. First Night, Boston, 1986, 87, 88; judge Sr. Panel Carving competition Belmont (Mass.) Hill Sch., 1985; docent Hands-On Sculpture show New Eng. Sculptors Assn. at Mus. of Sci., Boston, 1984. One-woman show at Mills Gallery, Boston, 1987; two-person invitational show at The Copley Soc. of Boston, 1994; other exhbns. include Boston Ctr. for Arts, 1984, 85, Boston Visual Artists Union Gallery, 1985, Concord Art Assn., 1985, Cambridge Art Assn., 1986, The Copley Soc. of Boston, 1984, 85, 88, 89, 91, 92, 93, 94, 95 (including holiday invitationals for award winners 1988, 91, 92), Fed. Res. Bank of Boston Gallery, 1989, with Copley Masters, 1984, Howard Yezerski Gallery, 1989, 90, 91, 92, 93, 94, 95, Libr. Ctr., Newport, Mass., 1990, Landau Gallery, Belmont Hill Sch., 1991, Attleboro (Mass.) Mus., 1992, Gallery NAGA, Boston, 1992, others; represented in permanent collection Sherrill House, Boston. Liaison between mission com. Trinity Ch., Boston and vol. program Sherrill House Nursing Home, 1987-94. Mem. Copley Soc. of Boston (Copley Master 1992), New Eng. Sculptors Assn. (bd. dirs., mem.-at-large 1985-86, 88-89), Nat. Sculpture Soc. Episcopalian. Studio: 115 E 34th St New York NY 10016-4629

WHITE, FLORENCE MAY, learning disabilities specialist; b. Ottawa, Kans., Sept. 1, 1936; d. O.C. Robert and Effie Lynne (Walker) Arnold; m. Donald L. White, June 1, 1958 (dec. Jan. 1996); children: Tab Vincent, Jacque Sue, Michelle May. BA, Ottawa U., 1958; MS, Kans. U., 1974; postgrad., Kans. U. Med. Ctr., 1975-76. Cert. reading specialist, learning disabilities specialist; cert. elem. and mid. sch. edn.: lang. arts, social studies, elem. curriculum. Classroom tchr. 2d grade Wellsville (Kans.) Elem., 1958-59; learning disabilities tchr. Olatha (Kans.) Spl. Edn. Coop., 1971-74; learning disabilities specialist, tchr. 7-9 Ottawa Mid. Sch., 1974-77; learning disabilities specialist, tchr. Paola Spl. Edn. Coop., Richmond, Kans., 1980-95; pub. rep., speaker on learning disabilities to civic groups and local orgns., 1972-75. Den mother Boy Scouts Am. and Brownies, Ottawa, 1968-70; chair state GOP women's polit. activities Rep. State Party, Topeka, 1964-67; chair scholarship contest DAR, Ottawa dist., 1984—; Sunday sch. tchr. Meth. Ch., Ottawa; crafts tchr. local 4-H, Ottawa; mem. Central Heights PTA (projects com. 1980-95); mem. Ottawa Arts Coun. State of Kans. scholar State Spl. Edn. Dept., 1976. Mem. Internat. Reading Assn., Kans. Reading Assn., Franklin County Reading Coun. (exec. bd. 1993-94, v.p., pres.-elect 1989-91, pres. 1991-92), Alpha Delta Kappa (projects com. 1988—, environment com., planning asst. to asst. pastor). Roman Catholic.

WHITE, IRENE, insurance complex case manager; b. Taumuning, Guam, Guam, Jan. 3, 1961; d. Antonio Gill and Irma Magdalena (Idrogo) Gill; m. William Paul Franck, Aug. 4, 1979 (div. July 1984); m. Richard Nelson White, May 12, 1989 (div. Dec. 1993). Cert. ins. adjuster, Tex. Ins. adjuster Gen. Accident Group, San Antonio, 1983-85, Crum & Forster Ins., San Antonio, 1985-89, Aetna Life & Casualty, San Antonio, 1979-83; adjuster, analyst, cons., complex case mgr. Aetna Life & Casualty, Dallas, 1989-96; complex case mgr. Travelers/Aetna Property Casualty Corp., Dallas, 1996—. Big sister Big Bros. and Sisters, San Antonio, 1987-89; vol. counselor March of Dimes, San Antonio, 1988-89. Republican. Roman Catholic. Office: Travelers/Aetna Property 2350 Lakeside Blvd Richardson TX 75082-4311

WHITE, JEAN TILLINGHAST, former state senator; b. Cambridge, Mass., Dec. 24, 1934; d. James Churchill Moulton and Clara Jean (Carter) Tillinghast; m. Peregrine White, June 6, 1970. B.A., Wellesley Coll., 1956. Supr., programmer Lumber Mut. Ins. Co., Cambridge, 1964-70; selectman, chmn. Town of Rindge (N.H.), 1975-80; clk. regulated revenues N.H. Ho. of Reps., Concord, 1978-80, vice chmn. regulated revenues, 1980-82; mem. N.H. Senate, 1982-88, chmn. fin. com.; v.p., treas. Perry White, Inc., Rindge, N.H., 1970—; dir. Peterborough Savings Bank (N.H.). Chmn., Rindge Friends of Library, 1972; pres. Nat. Order Women Legislators, 1990-91. Trustee Univ. System of N.H., 1989-92, Jaffrey/Rindge Sch. Bd., 1989—; commr. Cheshire County, 1995—. Republican. Unitarian. Office: Hampshire Rd Rindge NH 03461

WHITE, JENNIE KATHLEEN, artist, writer; b. Salem, Ohio, Nov. 30, 1952; d. Allan and Jane Watson (Fitzpatrick) W. BS cum laude, Duke U., Durham, N.C., 1974. Author and illustrator: The Komodo Dragon, 1982, J.K. White's Collection of Vases, 1984, Wheels of Fortune, 1986, My Mind, 1988, Washboard Road, 1990, In Search of the She Bear, 1992, The Weather Continues, 1993, Field Manual for Lots of Potential Ten Parlor But Lack of Focus Shooting Gallery, 1995. Recipient Golden Athena award for best short story Athens Film Festival, 1980Rosco award Sinking Creek Film Festival, 1981; grantee NEA, 1994, Mont. Arts Coun., 1995. Mem. Mont. Wilderness Assn.

WHITE, JENNIFER PHELPS, career services administrator; b. Palo Alto, Calif., Aug. 31, 1943; d. Delmer Frank and Luella Elizabeth (McHugh) Phelps; m. Charles Evan White, Oct. 29, 1965; children: George Kevin, Colleen Elizabeth. AA in Liberal Arts, Foothill Jr. Coll., 1964; BA in Sociology/Anthropology, U. N.Mex., 1967, MPA, 1987. Lic. profl. mental health counselor N.Mex. Counseling and Therapy Bd. Sales clk. Barron Park Pharmacy, Palo Alto, 1960-64; caseworker State of N.Mex., Albuquerque, 1968-70; info. sys. coord. City of Albuquerque, 1971-75; rsch. specialist Pub. Interest Rsch. Group, 1976-77; interviewer Sandia Market Rsch., 1980-81; acad. adviser, counselor U. N.Mex., 1981-88; rehab. specialist Intracorps, 1988-89; dir. career svcs. ctr. YWCA, 1989—; mem. staff adv. coun. U. N.Mex., Albuquerque, 1996; mem. women in transition Planning Commn. State of N.Mex., Albuquerque, 1990—; mem. career guidance project adv. com. Commn. on Status of Women, Albuquerque, 1993-95; employment cons. Genesis Project, Albuquerque, 1989-91. Chair women's affirmative action coun. City of Albuquerque, 1976-82; mem. steering com. Choice Pac, Albuquerque, 1984—; mem. affirmative action com. City of Albuquerque Human Rights Dept., 1995—. Named Outstanding N.Mex. Women, Office of Gov., State of N.Mex., 1994; recipient Grassroots Accomplishment award Nat. Coun. Negro Women, Las Mujeres de Lulac, 1994, Human Rights award City of Albuquerque, 1995. Mem. NOW (mem. Albuquerque and N.Mex. chpts., bd. dirs., pres., coord. 1975—, lobbyist N.Mex. State Legislature 1978-87), Nat. Abortion Rights Action League/Right to Choose (bd. dirs. 1980—), Career Devel. Assn., Women Work! Nat. Network (Svc. awards 1994, 95), Women's Housing Coalition (bd. dirs., pres., v.p. 1989—). Democrat. Home: 416 Montclaire SE Albuquerque NM 87108 Office: YWCA Career Svcs Ctr 7201 Paseo Del Norte NE Albuquerque NM 87113

WHITE, JILL CAROLYN, lawyer; b. Santa Barbara, Calif., Mar. 20, 1934; d. Douglas Cameron and Gladys Louise (Ashley) W.; m. Walter Otto Weyrauch, Mar. 17, 1973. BA, Occidental Coll., L.A., 1955; JD, U. Calif., Berkeley, 1972. Bar: Fla. 1974, Calif. 1975, D.C. 1981, U.S. Dist. Ct. (no. and mid. dists.) Fla., U.S. Ct. Appeals (5th and 11th cirs.), U.S. Supreme Ct. Staff mem. U.S. Dept. State, U.S. Embassy, Rio de Janeiro, Brazil, 1956-58; with psychol. rsch. units Inst. Human Devel., Inst. Personality Assessment and Rsch., U. Calif., Berkeley, 1961-68; adj. prof. U. Fla. Criminal Justice Program, Gainesville, Fla., 1976-78; pvt. practice immigration and nationality law Gainesville, 1976—; appointed mem. Fla. Bar Inaugural Immigration and Nationality Law Certification Com., 1994—, bd. cert. in immigration and nationality law, 1995—. Contbr. articles to profl. jours. Mem. ABA, Am. Immigration Lawyers Assn. (bd. dirs. Ctrl. Fla. chpt. 1985-94, 95—, chair Ctrl. Fla. chpt. 1988-89, co-chmn. So. Regional Liaison com. 1990-92, nat. bd. dirs. 1988-89), Fla. Assn. Women Lawyers (8th jud. cir. chpt.), Bar Assn. 8th Jud. Cir. Fla., Gainesville Area C. of C., Gainesville Area Innovation Network, Altrusa Club Gainesville. Democrat. Office: 2830 NW 41st St Ste C Gainesville FL 32606-6667

WHITE, JOAN MICHELSON, artist; b. Hartford, Conn., Jan. 4, 1936; d. William Allen and Mitzi (Lurie) Michelson; m. Harvey Marshall White, June 28, 1958; children: Randi Lynn, Andrew Steven. BA, Ctrl. Conn. State U., 1958; postgrad., Wesleyan U., 1980. Cert. tchr., Conn. One woman shows include Canton (Conn.) Gallery on the Green, 1977, Saltbox Gallery, West Hartford, Conn., 1986, Key Gallery, N.Y.C., 1982, Hartford Jewish Cmty. Ctr., 1980; mem. Hartford Art Sch. Aux.; mem. adv. bd. U. Hartford Joseloff Gallery. Group shows include Silvermine Guild New Eng. Exhbn., 1977, 79, Springfield (Mass.) Art League Nat. Exhbn., 1980, 83, 86, The Galleries, Wellesley, Mass., 1983, Stephen Haller Fine Arts, N.Y.C., 1987, 88, Penrose Gallery, Nantucket, Mass., 1984, Conn. Artists Showcase, Conn. Commn. on the Arts, Hartford, 1986, Provincetown (Mass.) Art Assn. and Mus., 1986, Old Lyme (Conn.) Art Works, 1985, Greene Gallery, Guilford, Conn., 1986, Signature Gallery, West Hartford, Conn., 1986-94, Allan Stone Gallery, N.Y.C., 1984, Shippee Gallery, N.Y.C., 1984, Heritage State Park Mus., Holyoke, Mass., 1988, Southern Conn. State U., New Haven, 1989, Farmington Valley Arts Ctr., Avon, Conn., 1992, John Slade Ely House, New Haven, 1993, Ute Stebich Gallery, Lenox, Mass., 1994, North Coast Collage Soc., Seattle, 1994. Mem. Conn. Watercolor Soc. (bd. dirs. 1980-82), West Hartford Ctr. for Visual Arts, Conn. Women Artists, Conn. Acad. Fine Arts. Home: 73 Avondale Rd West Hartford CT 06117-1108

WHITE, JOY MIEKO, communications executive; b. Yokohama, Japan, May 1, 1951; came to U.S., 1951; d. Frank Deforest and Wanda Mieko Mellen; m. George William White, June 5, 1948; 1 child, Karen. BA in Comms., Calif. State U., Fullerton, 1974, teaching cert., 1977; cert. bus. mgmt., Orange Coast Coll., 1981; cert. teaching, Community Coll., 1990. Cert. secondary tchr., Calif. Secondary tchr. Anaheim (Calif.) Union High Sch. Dist., 1977-80; tech. writer Pertec Computer Corp., Irvine, Calif., 1980-81; supr. large systems div. Burroughs, Mission Viejo, Calif., 1981-83; mgr. Lockheed div. CalComp, Anaheim, 1983-86; owner, pres. Communicator's Connection, Irvine, Calif., 1986-90; pres. Info Team, Inc., 1989—; adj. faculty, coord. tech. comm. program Golden West Coll., Huntington Beach, Calif., 1987-90; instr. U. Calif., Irvine, 1987-89, Calif. State U., Fullerton, 1988-91; condr. numerous workshops, profl. presentatious, 1982—; sec. Santa Ana Dist. chpt. U.S. SBA Assn. for Minority-Owned Bus., 1991-96. Active Performing Arts, Costa Mesa, 1986—; troop leader Girl Scouts U.S., 1995—, life mem., 1994—. Mem. NAFE, Soc. Tech. Comm. (sr., Orange County chpt. 1987, Mem. of Yr.), Soc. Profl. Journalists, Women in Comms. (pres. Orange County Profl. chpt. 1989-90), Nat. Assn. Women Bus. Owners, Rembrandts Wine Club (Yorba Linda), Girl Scouts U.S.A. (life). Democrat. Home: 21651 Vintage Way Lake Forest CA 92630-5760 Office: 22365 El Toro Rd # 265 Lake Forest CA 92630-5053

WHITE, JOYCE LOUISE, librarian; b. Phila., June 7, 1927; d. George William and Louisa (Adams) W. BA, U. Pa., 1949; MLS, Drexel U., 1963; MA in Religion, Episc. Sem. S.W., 1978. Head libr. Penniman Libr. Edn. U. Pa., Phila., 1960-76; archivist St. Francis Boys' Home, Salina, Kans., 1982-84; libr. Brown Mackie Coll., Salina, 1983-86; libr., dir. St. Thomas Theol. Sem., Denver, 1986-95; libr., dir. Archbishop Vehr Theol. Libr. Archdiocese of Denver, 1995-96. Author: Biographical and Historial Yarnall Library, 1979; asst. editor: Women Religious History Sources, 1983; contbr. articles to profl. jours. and chpts. to books. Vol. libr. St. John's Cath., Denver, 1993—. Mem. Ch. and Synagogue Libr. Assn. (life, founding, pres. 1969-70, exec. sec. 1970-72, exec. bd. 1967-76, ann. conf. chair 1996). Office: Archbishop Vehr Theol Libr 1300 S Steele St Denver CO 80210-2526

WHITE, JUDITH ANN, critical care nurse; b. Washington, Jan. 1, 1955; d. William Clayton and Marjorie Mae (Pace) W. AA, Prince George's Community Coll, 1975; BSN, U. Md., 1984; MSA, Cen. Mich. U., 1988. CCRN. Staff nurse intermediate care unit Greater S.E. Community Hosp., Washington, 1975-80, asst. head nurse, 1980-81, clin. nurse II, 1982-86, staff nurse ICU/CCU, 1986-88, clin. nurse II, 1988-89, clin. nurse III, 1989—; part-time staff devel. Ft. Washington Hosp., 1995. Mem. ANA, AACN.

WHITE, KAREN JEAN, artist; b. Coshocton, Ohio, Jan. 15, 1943; d. Patrick and Bonnie Jean (Porter) W.; m. W. Michael Shuster, Aug. 12, 1988. BFA, Ohio State U., 1969; postgrad., Met. State Coll., 1976-77, U. Colo., 1985. Tchr. Arapahoe C.C., 1988, U. No. Colo., 1990, Colo. Inst. Art, 1991, Colo. Art Tchrs. Conf., 1991; front range cmty. tchg. educator, 1996; co-founder Women's Art Gallery, Denver, 1995. Exhibited in numerous solo and group shows, including Denver Art Mus., 1974, Sandy Carson Gallery, Denver, 1987, Arvada (Colo.) Ctr. for Arts, 1987, Foothills Art Ctr., Golden, Colo., 1987, Emmanual Gallery, Denver, 1987, New Dawn Gallery, Edina, Minn., 1988, Contemporary Crafts Ctr., Denver, 1988, Core New Art Space, Denver, 1988, Boulder Ctr. for Visual Arts, 1989, Am. Craft Mus., Denver, 1989, Foothills Arts Ctr., 1990, Del Mano Gallery, L.A., 1989, Western Colo. Ctr. for Arts, Grand Junction, 1989, Grant St. Arts Ctr., Denver, 1989, Mariani Gallery, U. No. Colo., Greeley, 1989, Steamboat Springs (Colo.) Art Ctr., 1989, Technic Gallery, St. Paul, 1990, Banaker Gallery, Walnut Creek, Calif., 1990, Katie Gingress Gallery, Santa Fe, N.Mex., 1990, Gallery bel eTage, Basel, Switzerland, 1991, Internat. Gallery, San Diego, 1991, UMC Fine Arts Ctr., Boulder, Colo., 1992, Colo. Gallery of Arts, Littleton, 1992, J. Jevitts Ctr., N.Y.C., 1992, Emmanual Gallery, Denver, 1992, Nora Eccles Harrison Mus. Art, Utah, 1990, Loveland Art Mus., 1990, Bergen Mus. of Art, 1991, Nat. Libr., Royal Palace, Hungary, 1992, Mini Biennial Invitational, Olfstrom, Sweden, 1993, Concordia U., Que., Can., 1993, Musee du pays et Val de Charmeney, Switzerland, 1993, Nat. Assn. Women Artists, N.Y.C., 1994, Anna Blake Gallery, 1994, Mus. Papierfabrik Scheufen, Lenningen, Germany, 1995, others. Pres. Neighborhood Partnership Team, Denver, 1995-96; founder Clean Air Coalition, Denver, 1988, Broadway Corridor Arts Alliance, Denver, 1996. Pub. art grantee Neighborhood Cultures of Denver, 1995, Neighborhood Arts Program grantee Weed & Seed Dept. of Justice, Denver, 1995; recipient Juror's Choice award FIBER/texture, 1993, 1st prize Mannings Nat. Fibre Show, 1977, Colo. Lawyers for Arts Ann. Show, 1988. Mem. Nat. Assn. Women Artists, Internat. Assn. Hand Papermakers and Paper Artists. Democrat. Home and Studio: 282 Delaware St Denver CO 80223

WHITE, KAREN RUTH JONES, information systems executive; b. Ft. Meade, Md., Oct. 8, 1953; d. Frank L. Jones and Inge H. Lesser; m. M. Timothy Heath, Apr. 23, 1973 (div. Aug. 1976); m. Carl W. White, May 30, 1993. AS in electronic data processing, N.H. Tech. Inst., Concord, 1977; BS in MIS with high honors, Northeastern U., Boston, 1984; postgrad., Northeastern U. Programmer Chubb Life Ins. Co., Concord, Mass., 1977-79, Retailers Electronics Account Processing, Woburn, Mass., 1979-82; sr. programmer, analyst N.H. Ins. Group, Manchester, 1982-84; prin. systems analyst Wang Labs., Inc., Lowell, Mass., 1984-89; project mgr. TASC, Inc., Reading, Mass., 1989—. Bd. dirs. Brandywine Common Assn., Derry, N.H., 1991-94; mem. St. Paul's Sch. Advanced Studies Pgm Alumni Assn., Concord, N.H. With U.S. Army Res., 1974-84. Decorated Army Commendation medal, 1980. Mem. IEEE (computer soc., tech. com. in software engring., program chair 5th reengring. forum 1996, mem. exec. adv. bd. 1996—), Engring. Mgmt. Soc., Project Mgmt. Inst. (Mass. Bay chpt. program dir. 1992-93, project chair PMI '96 1994—), Sigma Epsilon Rho. Home: 10 Brandywine Common Derry NH 03038 Office: TASC 55 Walkers Brook Dr Reading MA 01867

WHITE, KATE, editor-in-chief. Former editor-in-chief Child mag.; editor-in-chief Working Woman mag., N.Y.C., 1989-91, McCall's mag, N.Y.C., 1991-94, Redbook, N.Y.C., 1994—. Office: Redbook Hearst Magazines 224 W 57th St New York NY 10019-3299*

WHITE, KATHLEEN MERRITT, geologist; b. Long Beach, Calif., Nov. 19, 1921; d. Edward Clendenning and Gladys Alice (Merritt) White; m. Alexander Kennedy Baird IV, Oct. 1, 1965 (dec. 1985); children: Pamela Roberts, Peter Madlem, Stephen Madlem, Mari Afify. Attended, Sch. Boston Mus. Fine Arts, 1939-40, Art Students League, 1940-42; BS in Geology, Pomona Coll., 1962; MS in Geochemistry, Claremont Grad. Sch., 1964. Rsch. asst. geology Pomona Coll., Claremont, Calif., 1962-66, rsch. assoc. geology, 1966-75; cons. geology Claremont, Calif., 1975-77; sr. scientist Jet Propulsion Lab./NASA, Pasadena, 1977-79, mem. tech. staff, 1979-86; ind. rschr. Claremont, 1986—; owner Kittie Tales, Claremont, 1992—. Contbr. Geosat Report, 1986; contbr. articles to profl. jours.; author, illustrator children's books. Grantee NASA, 1984, 85; Pomona Coll. scholar, 1963. Mem. Geol. Soc. Am. (invited paper 1994), Am. Geophys. Union, Pomona Coll. Alumni Assn. Republican. Home: 265 W 11th St Claremont CA 91711-3804

WHITE, KATHRYN CAMILLE, management consultant; b. Denville, N.J., Oct. 19, 1966; d. Leo Anthony and Rosanna (del Piero) W. BA in Econs., Johns Hopkins U., 1988. Market rsch. analyst Stouffer Harborplace Hotel, Balt., 1989-91, adminstr. transient sales, 1991-92; analyst HCIA Inc., Balt., 1992-95; mgmt. cons. HCIA Inc., Boston, 1995—. Mem., sec., bd. dirs. Hands on Balt., Inc., 1993-95. Mem. NOW.

WHITE, LARI, vocalist; b. Dunedin, Fla., May 13, 1965; m. Chuck Cannon, 1994. BA, U. Miami. Staff writer Ronnie Milsap's Pub. Co., Nashville, 1989-90; represented by RCA Records, 1993—; singer White Family Singers, 1969—; backup vocalist concert tour Rodney Crowell, 1991. Albums include Lead Me Not, 1993, Wishes, 1994; actress (TV pilot) XXX's and OOO's, 1994. Overall Winner, You Can Be a Star, Nashville Network, 1988; nominee Best New Female Vocalist award Acad. Country Music, 1994. Office: RCA Records One Music Circle N Nashville TN 37203 also: Carter Career Mgmt 1028 B 18th Ave S Nashville TN 37212*

WHITE, LESLIE MARY, epidemiologist; b. Huntington, N.Y., July 22, 1954; d. John B. and Inez M. (Montecalvo) W. BS, Mary Washington Coll., 1976; MPH, Johns Hopkins U., 1990; postgrad., U. Md., 1993-95. Microbiologist II Am. Type Culture Collection, Rockville, Md., 1980-83; analyst InterAm. Assocs., Rockville, Md., 1984-86; sr. assoc. Triton Corp., Washington, 1986-87; health analyst Row Scis., Inc., Rockville, 1987-88; rsch. analyst Nat. BioSystems, Rockville, 1988-90; sr. assoc. Clement Internat., Fairfax, Va., 1990-92; project dir. epidemiology Consultants in Epidemiology and Occupational Health, Washington, 1992-93; dir. epidemiology Scis. Internat., Inc., Alexandria, Va., 1993-94; pres. Epidemiology and Health Rsch., Inc., Bethesda, Md., 1994—, Dist. Nuskin/IDN Internat., Bethesda, 1996—. Mem. APHA, U.S. Tennis Assn.(umpire coun.), Soc. Epidemiologic Rsch., Soc. Occupl. and Environ. Health, Bethesda Country Club, Assn. Md. Tennis Ofcls. Home: 7401 Westlake Ter Apt 512 Bethesda MD 20817-6566 Office: Epidemiology and Health Rsch Inc 7401 Westlake Ter Apt 512 Bethesda MD 20817-6566

WHITE, LIBBY KRAMER, librarian; b. Boston, Sept. 30, 1934; d. Samuel and Ida (Drucker) Kramer; m. Gerald Milton White, June 6, 1956; children: Charles, Andrew, Judith White Cuttler, Abigail White D'Costa. BS in Social Sci., Simmons Coll., Boston, 1956; MLS, SUNY, Albany, 1972. Librarian Temple Israel, Albany, N.Y., 1966-73; bookmobile librarian Schenectady County Pub. Library, 1973, br. librarian, 1973-76, ref./YA librarian, 1976-85, ref./ethnic culture librarian, 1985—; chmn. Nat. Library Wk., Schenectady, 1985, 96. Book reviewer Sch. Libr. Jour., 1980—, Libr. Jour., 1989, Assn. Jewish Librs. Newsletter, 1994—.; cons. various encys., mags. Trustees Beth Israel Synagogue, Schenectady, 1986-94; resident advisor Summer Seminars in Judaic Studies, Skidmore Coll., Saratoga, N.Y., 1987—. Mem. N.Y. Library Assn., Hudson Mohawk Library Assn. (pres. 1989—). Jewish. Home: 1274 Hawthorne Rd Schenectady NY 12309-4609 Office: 99 Clinton St Schenectady NY 12305-2038

WHITE, LINDA DIANE, lawyer; b. N.Y.C., Apr. 1, 1952; d. Bernard and Elaine (Simons) Schwartz; m. Thomas M. White, Aug. 16, 1975; 1 child, Alexandra Nicole. AB, U. Pa., 1973; JD, Northwestern U., 1976. Bar: Ill. 1976. Assoc. Walsh, Case, Coale & Brown, Chgo., 1976-77, Greenberger & Kaufmann (merged into Katten, Muchin), Chgo., 1977-82; ptnr. Greenberger

& Kaufmann (merged into Katten, Muchin), 1982-85, Sonnenschein Nath & Rosenthal, Chgo., 1985—. Mem. ABA (real property fin. com., comml. leasing com., real property, probate and trust law sect. 1987—), Ill. Bar Assn., Chgo. Bar Assn., Internat. Assn. Corp. Real Estate Execs. Office: Sonnenschein Nath & Rosenthal 8000 Sears Tower 233 S Wacker Dr Chicago IL 60606-6306

WHITE, LORAY BETTY, public relations executive, writer, actress, producer; b. Houston, Nov. 27, 1934; d. Harold White and Joyce Mae (Jenkins) Mills; m. Sammy Davis Jr., 1957 (div. 1958); 1 child, Deborah R. DeHart. Student, UCLA, 1948-50, 90-91, Nichiren Shoshu Acad., 1988-92; AA in Bus., Sayer Bus. Sch., 1970; study div. mem. dept. L.A., Soka U., Japan, 1970-86. Editor entertainment writer L.A. Community New, 1970-81; exec. sec. guest rels. KNBC Prodns., Burbank, Calif., 1969-75; security specialist Xerox X10 Think Tank, L.A., 1975-80; exec. asst. Ralph Powell & Assocs., L.A., 1980-82; pres., owner, producer LBW & Assocs. Pub. Rels., L.A., 1980—; owner, producer, writer, host TV prodn. co. Pub. Pub. Rels., L.A., 1987—; dir., producer L.B.W. Prodn. "Yesterday, Today, Tomorrow, L.A., 1981—. Actress (film) Ten Commandments, 1956, (Broadway) Joy Ride; appeared in the following endorsements including Budweiser Beer, Old Gold Cigarettes, Salem Cigarettes, TV commls. including Cheer, Puffs Tissue, Coca Cola, Buffern, others; entertainment editor L.A. Community News, 1970-73; writer (column) Balance News, 1980-82. Vol. ARC, 1995. Recipient award ARC, 1955, 84, Cert. of Honor, Internat. Orgn. Soka Gakkai Internat. of Japan, Cmty. Vols. of Am. award, 1994; named Performer of Yr. Cardella Demillo, 1976-77. Mem. ARC (planning, mktg., prodn. event com. 1995), ULCA Alumni Assn., Lupus Found. Am. (So. Calif. chpt.), Nat. Fedn. Blind, Myohoji-Hokkeko Internat. Buddhist.

WHITE, MARCIA LYNNE, accountant; b. Jacksonville, Fla., Aug. 12, 1956; d. George William and Harriet Catherine (Tabb) Asinc; m. Joseph Anthony White (div. 1986). BSBA, Kennesaw State Coll., Marietta, Ga., 1981. Construction acct. Georgia-Pacific Corp., Atlanta, 1981-83, supr. payroll controls, 1983-84, gen. acctg. supr. HQ divsn., 1984-86, acctg. mgr. control bd. mktg., 1986-87, asst. contr. Doraville container, 1987-88, adminstrv. mgr. containerboard mktg., 1988-89, mktg. controller pulp & bleached bd. divsn., 1989-92, asst. to controller ops., 1992-93, sr. bus. analyst corp. plan & devel., 1993-95, sr. mgr. BPI, 1995—.

WHITE, MARGARET C., psychiatric nurse; b. Rochelle, Ill., Nov. 11, 1950; d. Lennie Otis and Vernia Imogene (Jacobs) Roland; m. Roy Roland White, Sept. 26, 1968; children: Mark Allen (dec.), Ryan Roy, Rory Roland. ADN, Sauk Valley Coll., 1975. Staff nurse Katherine Shaw Bethea Hosp., Dixon, Ill., 1975-79; dir. nursing Mapleside Manor Nursing Home, Amboy, Ill., 1979-80; sr. clinician Sinnissippi Ctrs., 1980-90; charge nurse Oakwood Hosp., 1990-94; utilization mgmt. United Behavioral Sys., 1994-96; dir. nursing Rosecrance on Harrison, 1996—. past pres. Lee Co., spec. bd., past mem. Dist. 271 Sch. Bd., past mem. Ops. Snowball, Inc. Mem. ANA (cert. psychiat. nurse, cert. alcohol drug counselor Ill.). Home: 1179 Inlet Rd Amboy IL 61310

WHITE, MARIE CALDERONE, public relations executive, sports broadcaster; b. White Plains, N.Y., Jan. 22; d. Philip and Mary (Rullo) Calderone; m. Raymond Joseph White, Oct. 8, 1960. BS cum laude, St. Lawrence U.; cert., Acad. Broadcasting Arts. Reg. Bus. Cert., self employed. Pub. rels. account exec. Sudler & Hennessey, N.Y.C., 1960-68; comml. copywriter, spokeswoman Sta. WVIP, Mt. Kisco, N.Y., 1969-71; sports broadcaster Sta. WGCH, Greenwich, Conn., 1973-76; owner, pres. MCW Enterprises, Chappaqua, N.Y., 1977—; pub. rels. dir. Sudler & Hennessey, N.Y.C., 1982—; broadcaster U.S. Open Golf, 1974, U.S. Open Tennis, 1974, Bergdorf-Goodman Gala, 1975; ednl. announcer Schloat Prodns., Inc., 1976. Editor-in-chief: (newsletter) S&H Highlights, 1982-94; patentee Stemware Rack, 1980. Dir./v.p. Stornowaye Assn., Chappaqua, N.Y., 1970-74; campaign co-chmn. N.Y. State Assemblyman, Chappaqua, 1972; exec. com. Sts. John & Mary Parish Coun., Chappaqua, 1972-74, fin. com., 1980 84; fashion adv. bd. B. Altman & Co., White Plains, N.Y., 1975. Mem. NAFE, Westchester Country Club, Twigs Orgn. of Northern Westchester Hosp Ctr. (publicity dir., exec. bd. mem.), Mount Kisco, N.Y., 1995-97. Republican. Roman Catholic. Home: 26 Stornowaye Chappaqua NY 10514-2323 Office: MCW Enterprises PO Box 216 Chappaqua NY 10514-0216

WHITE, MARJORIE MARY, elementary school educator; b. LaCrosse, Wis., May 10, 1944; d. Knute Emil and Florence Catherine (Frederich) Johnson; m. David James White, July 6, 1985; stepchildren: Christopher Howard, Wendy Marie White Ehert. BSE, Winona State U., 1966, MSEd, 1971. Cert. elem. tchr., Minn. Tchr. Lacrosse Cath. Schs., Wis., 1966-68, Winona County Schs., Dakota, Minn., 1968-72, Ind. Sch. Dist., Winona, Minn., 1972—. Mem. NEA, AAUW (treas. 1990-92), Minn. Edn. Assn., Winona Edn. Assn. (Faculty rep. 1970—, membership chmn. 1990—), Phi Delta Kappa (newsletter editor 1984-92, 94—, del. 1985-91, 94-96, v.p. membership 1989-91, Svc. Key award 1991). Democrat. Roman Catholic. Home: 705 W Wabasha St Winona MN 55987-2764 Office: Ind Sch Dist 861 654 Huff St Winona MN 55987-3320

WHITE, MARY LOU, fundraiser, writer, educator; b. Davenport, Iowa, Feb. 17, 1939; d. Edward Joseph and Madeleine (Levart) Briglia; m. Morton Bartho White, Dec. 6, 1965 (dec. Jan. 1973). Cert. d'etudes francaises, U. Grenoble, France, 1959; BA, Gettysburg Coll., 1960; postgrad., Sorbonne, Paris, 1961; MA, Middlebury Coll., 1962; MS, U. Bridgeport, 1972. Writer CIA, N.Y.C., 1962-64; tchr. French Miss Porter's Sch., Farmington, Conn., 1964-66; fundraiser N.Y. Philharm., N.Y.C., 1966-72; tchr. French Fairfield (Conn.) Country Day Sch., 1973-77, Greens Farms (Conn.) Acad., 1977-79; spl. events coord. N.Y. Philharm., N.Y.C., 1979-80; econ. devel. Broward C.C., Ft. Lauderdale, Fla., 1989-91; programming grants writer Broward Ctr. for the Performing Arts, Ft. Lauderdale, 1992—. Vol. Polit. Party, Ft. Lauderdale, 1990-93. Mem. Hereditary Register of U.S. Home: 888 Intracoastal Dr Fort Lauderdale FL 33304-3638

WHITE, MARY RUTH WATHEN, social services administrator; b. Athens, Tex., Dec. 27, 1927; d. Benedict Hudson and Sara Elizabeth (Evans) W.; m. Robert M. White, Nov. 10, 1946; children: Martha Elizabeth, Robert Miles, Jr., William Benedict, Mary Ruth, Jesse Wathen, Margaret Fay, Maureen Adele, Thomas Evan. BA, Stephen F. Austin State U., Nacogdoches, Tex., 1948. Chmn. Regional Drug Abuse Com., San Antonio, 1975-81, Met. Youth Council, San Antonio, 1976-78; state chmn. Citizens United for Rehab. Errants, San Antonio, 1978-91; sec. Bexar County Detention Ministries, San Antonio, 1979-88; chmn. Bexar County (Tex.) Jail Commn., 1980-82; chmn. com. on role of family in reducing recidivism Tex. Dept. Criminal Justice, Austin, 1985—; chmn. Met. Community Corrections Com., San Antonio, 1986-90; bd. dirs. Tex. Coalition for Juvenile Justice, 1975-93, Target 90 Youth Coordinating Coun., San Antonio, 1986-89; local chmn. vol. adv. bd. Tex. Youth Commn., 1986-87. Pres. San Antonio City Coun. PTA, 1976-78, Rep. Bus. Women Bexar County, San Antonio, 1984-86, North Urban Deanery, San Antonio Alliance Mental Illness, 1995-96, also legis. chmn.; bd. dirs. CURE, 1978-92; legis. chmn. Archdiocese of San Antonio Coun. Cath. Women; mem. allocation com. United Way, San Antonio, 1986-91. Named Today's Woman, San Antonio Light newspaper, 1985, Outstanding Rep. Woman, Rep. Bus. Women Bexar County, 1987; honoree Rep. Women Stars over Tex., 1992. Mem. Am. Corrections Assn., Assn. Criminal Justice Planners, LWV (pres. San Antonio chpt. 1984-86), Conservation Soc., Fedn. Women (bd. dirs. 1984-90), DAR (regent), Colonial Dames (pres.), Cath. Daus. Am. (profl. registered parliamentarian, past regent Ct. of St. Anthony), Tex. Cath. Daus. Am. (state legis. chair), San Antonio Alliance for Mentally Ill (pres. 1995—). Home: 701 E Sunshine Dr San Antonio TX 78228-2516 Office: 5372 Fredericksburg Rd Ste 114 San Antonio TX 78229-3559

WHITE, MARY WEFER, English educator; b. N.Y.C., Nov. 29, 1944; d. Harold T. and Helen (Brenia) Wefer; m. David L. White, July 26, 1968; 1 child, Geoffrey Aleksandr. BA in English, CUNY, 1966; MA in Secondary Edn., Hofstra U., 1968; MA in English Lit., Bucknell U., 1975. Elem. tchr. St. Joseph's Sch., Ronkonkoma, N.Y., 1966; tchr. English, Hauppauge (N.Y.) H.S., 1966-68, Joshua Barney Sch., Gaeta, Italy, 1968-69, Williamsport (Pa.) H.S., 1970-72; tchr. English and journalism Orange County H.S., Orange, Va., 1972-73; tchr. English and journalism Charlottesville (Va.) H.S., 1973-76, coord., 1976-78; assoc. prof. English, Lees-McRae Coll., Banner Elk, N.C., 1979—; faculty athletics rep./compliance coord. NAIA and NCAA; mem. eligibility com. dist. 26 Nat. Assn. Intercollegiate Athletics, 1993—; mem. exec. com. Carolinas Intercollegiate Athletic Conf., 1994-95; mem. eligibility com. Carolinas-Va. Athletic Conf., 1995—. Contbr. articles to profl. jours. Examiner bds. rev. troop 101 Boy Scouts Am., Blowing Rock, N.C., 1990—. Named Outstanding Educator, Phi Theta Kappa chpt. Lees-McRae Coll., 1982, 84, Edgar Tufts award for excellence in edn. Lees-McRae Coll., 1989; Malone fellow Nat. Coun. on U.S.-Arab Rels., 1993. Mem. Delta Kappa Gamma (pres. Alpha Gamma chpt. 1996—). Democrat. Home: Edgehill PO Box 152 Blowing Rock NC 28605 Office: Lees-McRae Coll English Dept Banner Elk NC 28604

WHITE, MICHELLE JO, economics educator; b. Washington, Dec. 3, 1945; d. Harry L. and Irene (Silverman) Rich; m. Roger Hall Gordon, July 25, 1982. AB, Harvard U., 1967; MSc in Econs., London Sch. Econs., 1968; PhD, Princeton U., 1973. Asst. prof. U. Pa., Phila., 1973-78; from assoc. prof. to prof. NYU, N.Y.C., 1978-83; prof. econs. U. Mich., Ann Arbor, 1984—; dir. PhD program in econs. U. Mich., 1992-94; vis. asst. prof. Yale U., New Haven, 1978; vis. prof. People's U., Beijing, 1986, U. Warsaw, 1990, U. Wis., Madison, 1991, U. Munich, Germany, 1992, Tilburg U., The Netherlands, 1993, 95, U. Chgo., 1993, Copenhagen Bus. Sch., 1995; cons. Pension Benefit Guaranty Corp., Washington, 1987; chmn. adv. com. dept. econs. Princeton U., 1988-90. Editor: The Non-profit Sector in a Three Sector Economy, 1981; contbr. numerous articles to profl. jours. Bd. dirs. Com. on Status of Women in Econs. Profession, 1984-86. Resources for Future fellow, 1972-73; grantee NSF, 1979, 82, 88, 91, 93, Sloan Found., 1984, Fund for Rsch. in Dispute Resolution, 1989; Fulbright scholar, Poland, 1990. Mem. Am. Econ. Assn., Am. Law and Econ. Assn. (bd. dirs. 1991-92), Am. Real Estate and Urban Econs. Assn. (bd. dirs. 1992-95), Social Scis. Rsch. Coun. (bd. dirs. 1994—), Midwest Econs. Assn. (1st v.p. 1996—). Office: Univ Mich Dept Economics 611 Tappan St Ann Arbor MI 48109-1220

WHITE, NANCY CAROLYN, publishing executive; b. Columbus, Ohio, Sept. 1, 1957; d. Thomas Edward and Joan Carolyn (Olsen) White; m. George Frank Bryant Jr., July 9, 1983 (div. 1993). AB, Sweet Briar Coll., 1979; student, Pratt Inst., 1983. Catalog prodn. staff Sotheby's, N.Y.C., 1981-84; mgr. traffic dept. Dancer, Fitzgerald, Sample Direct, N.Y.C., 1985; devel. officer Sarah Lawrence Coll., Bronxville, N.Y., 1986; pres. White-Bryant Fine Arts Consulting, Croton-on-Hudson, N.Y., 1986-88; assoc. pub., editor The Aircraft Bulletin, N.Y.C., 1988-89; mktg., creative dir., co-founder Interview Images Inc, Port Chester, N.Y., 1989-90; U.S. sales mgr. Cahner's Marine Pubs., Stamford, Conn., 1990; pubs. dir. Designer Showhouses Internat. Ltd., N.Y.C., 1991-92; founder, pres. Showhouse Publs. Inc., N.Y.C., 1992-95; nat. advt. mgr. Avenue Mag., 1996—. Pub. Showhouse mag., 1994-95. Pres., trustee Friends of Art, Sweet Brair Coll., 1985-95; chmn. Alzhaimer's Disease Brochure, 1985-86. Season champion Internat. One Design Yachts, Long Island Sound Fleet, 1990, '91, Yacht Racing Assn. Long Island Sound, 1991. Mem. Jr. League on Hudson (trustee 1987), The Coffeehouse, Am. Yacht Club, Alumnae Assn. Sweet Briar Coll. (trustee 1988-91).

WHITE, NANCY G., journalism educator; b. N.Y.C., Oct. 21, 1923; d. John C. and Mamie (Comparetto) Giunta; m. Paul Michael White, June 16, 1946; children: Paul Michael Jr., Nancy Melissa. BA, U. Tampa, 1944; MEd, U. Fla., 1954; Advanced Masters Degree, Fla. State U., 1956. Tchr. journalism, dir. student publs. Hillsborough High Sch., Tampa, Fla., 1952-55; tchr. journalism, newspaper advisor Chamberlain High Sch., Tampa, Fla., 1956-68; tchr. journalism, head English dept., newspaper advisor Plant High Sch., Tampa, Fla., 1968-69; prof. journalism, dir. student publs. Hillsborough C.C., Tampa, Fla., 1969—; chair profl. devel. Coll. Media Advisors, Inc., 1993-95, chair awards com., 1990-93, pub. rels. chair, 1988-90; mem. U. West Fla. Adv. Coun., Pensacola, 1984—; mem. State Dept. Edn. Common Course Numbering System Com., 1974—. Contbr. articles to profl. jours.; reporter Tallahassee Dem., 1955-57. Newsletter editor Ybor City Mus. Soc., Tampa, 1990-95; pres., newsletter editor Suncoast Aux. U.S. Submarine Vets. WWII, Tampa, 1986-92; mem., newsletter editor Tampa Women's Club, 1973—. Recipient Columbia U. Gold Key, Columbia Scholastic Press Assn., 1971, Disting. Svc. award Kappa Tau Alpha, 1984, Gold medallion Fla. Scholastic Press Assn., 1989, Disting. Newspaper Adviser award Coll. Media Advisers, 1983, also Disting. Mag. Adviser award, 1988; named to Acad. Hall of Fame, Fla. C.C. Activities Assn., 1995, Hall of Fame, Fla. C.C. Press Assn., 1991. Mem. Nat. C.C. Journalism Assn. (pres. 1992-94), Fla. C.C. Press Assn. (pres. 1971-73, Hall of Fame), Pan Am. Univ. Women (pres.-elect 1996), Fla. Scholastic Press Assn. (pres. 1954-57), Alpha Delta Kappa (pres. 1976-78), Phi Kappa Phi, Kappa Delta Pi, Sigma Delta Chi, Alpha Psi Omega. Democrat. Methodist. Home: 5105 Homer St W Tampa FL 33629 Office: Hillsborough C C 2001 14th St N Tampa FL 33605

WHITE, NANCY MARGARET, labor consultant, municipal official; b. Detroit, Mich., Apr. 12, 1938; d. Loraine E. and Margaret J. (Benson) Bancroft; m. Daryl L. White, May 12, 1962; children: Karen, Douglas. BS, Mich. State U., 1960; MA, Wayne State U., 1971. Tchr. Chagrin Falls (Ohio) Schs., 1960-62; tchr., counselor Fraser (Mich.) Pub. Schs., 1962-85; labor cons. Mich. Edn. Assn., Clinton Twp., Mich., 1985—; commr. Macomb County Bd. of Commrs., Mt. Clemens, Mich., 1992—. staff asst. Congressman Dave Bonior, Mt. Clemens, 1977; chair 12th congl. dist. Dem. com., Mt. Clemens, 1979-92; vice chair Macomb County Comty. Mental Health Bd., Mt. Clemens, 1983—; mem. United Way Comty. Svc. Bd., Detroit, 1990—; corr. sec., Mich. Dems., Lansing, 1993—. Office: MEA Local 1 37400 Garfield Clinton Township MI 48036

WHITE, PENNY J., judge; b. Kingsport, Tenn., May 3, 1956; d. C.A. and Alvira Emuogene (Bush) W.; m. Gary C. Shockley, Sept. 24, 1983. BS, East Tenn. State U., 1978; JD, U. Tenn., 1981; LLM, Georgetown U., 1987. Bar: Tenn. 1981, Md. 1983. Assoc. Richard Pectol & Assocs., Johnson City, Tenn., 1981-83; sole practice Johnson City, Tenn., 1985-94; assoc. justice Tenn. Supreme Ct., Nashville, 1994—; former judge Tenn. Cir. Ct., 1st jud. dist., Tenn. Ct. Criminal Appeals, eastern divsn.; bd. dirs. Family Violence Council, Johnson City. E. Barrett Prettyman fellow Georgetown Law Ctr., Washington, 1985-87. Mem. ABA, Assn. Trial Lawyers Am., Nat. Crime Def. Lawyers Assn., Tenn. Bar Assn., East Tenn. State U. Nat. Alumni Assn. (pres. 1985-86). Democrat. Home: 207 E Unaka Ave Johnson City TN 37601-4625 Office: Supreme Ct Bldg 401 7th Ave Nashville TN 37219*

WHITE, ROBERTA LEE, comptroller; b. Denver, Sept. 18, 1946; d. Harold Tindall and Araminta (Campbell) Bangs; m. Lewis Paul White, Jr., Jan. 23, 1973 (div. Sept. 1974). BA cum laude, Linfield Coll., 1976; postgrad., Lewis and Clark Coll. Office mgr. Multnomah County Auditor, Portland, Oreg., 1977-81; rsch. asst. Dan Goldy and Assocs., Portland, 1981-83; regional asst. Vocat. Rehab., Eugene, Oreg., 1983-85; internal auditor Multnomah County, Portland, 1985-89; cons. Portland, 1989-91; fin. analyst City of Portland, 1991-93; comptroller Wordsmith Svcs., Portland, 1993—; mem. Com. for Implementation of the ADA, Portland, 1991-93. Treas. Mary Wendy Roberts for Sec. of State, Portland, 1992, Re-Elect Mary Wendy Roberts, Portland, 1990, Elect Hank Miggins Com., 1994; mem. Oreg. Women's Polit. Caucus, Portland, 1982-85, City Club, Portland, 1978-81. Democrat. Mem. Disciples of Christ. Office: Wordsmith Svcs 1500 NE Irving Ste 350 Portland OR 97232

WHITE, RUTH BRYANT, media consultant, analyst, counselor, minister; b. Denver, May 6, 1955; d. Volleny Bryant Sr. and Ruth Ada (Washington) Smith; m. Steven Alan White, Nov. 21, 1980; children: Pershaun R., LeJeune B., LaVonda M. Ed. high sch., Denver. Ordained to ministry Christian Ch., 1988. With acctg. sect. U.S. Govt., Denver and L.A., 1972-81; remittance processor Auto Club So. Calif., L.A., 1981-84; with acctg. dept. various agys. L.A., 1984-91; sr. adminstrv. support specialist Infonet, L.A., 1991—; media cons. on interracial relationships. Author: Free Indeed: The Autobiography of an Interracial Couple, 1989; coordinating prodr. Hollywood Post Oscar Showcase, 1996; appeared on talk shows. V.p. A Place for Us, Gardena, Calif., 1984—. Mem. Assn. Multiethnic Ams. (charter, regional v.p. western U.S. 1991-93). Office: A Place for Us Nat PO Box 357 Gardena CA 90248-0357

WHITE, RUTH MELLBY, musician, writer; b. Thief River Falls, Minn., Aug. 26, 1908; d. Oscar Frederick and Louise Therese (Grindeland) Mellby; m. Edward Banker White, Jan. 10, 1942 (dec. April 1983); children: Katherine Louise, Edward Banker Jr., Jean Marie. BA, St. Olaf Coll., Northfield, Minn., 1929; MA, Columbia, N.Y., 1941. lectr. in field. Soloist: St. Celia's Soc., Columbia U. Chorus; pianist; choral dir.; lead part in Zeigfield's. Mem. Coll. Club, Harvard Womens Club (bd. dirs.), Scandinavian Forum, Browning Soc., Friends of Boston U. Libr., Sigma Alpha Iota (life). Lutheran.

WHITE, SALLY FOX, public relations director; b. Waxahachie, Tex.; d. Joseph Gilbert Fox and Nelia Alma (Carter) Fox Atkins; m. Joseph Andrew White, Dec. 25, 1947; 1 child, Clair Fox. Student, U. Mex., Mexico City, 1945; BJ with honors, U. Tex., 1946; postgrad., Scheil Sch. of Art, Chgo., 1954, Dallas Sch. Comml. Art, 1956, Va. Commonwealth U., 1967-68. Publicity chmn. United Fund, Richmond, Va.; admissions counselor William Woods Coll., Fulton, Mo.; feature writer, advt. mgr. Daily Texan; copywriter, layout artist, asst. to advt. mgr. Joske's, San Antonio; commentator, continuity writer Sta. KGKL, San Angelo, Tex.; advt. mgr. Meacham's, Ft. Worth; asst. to merchandising editor Ladies' Home Jour.; merchandising rep. Curtis Pubs.; free-lance fashion commentator, publicist, retail sales trainer Chgo., Dallas and New Orleans; mgr. retail promotion accounts The Merchandising Group, Inc., N.Y.C., 1950-67; fiber cons., publicist DuPont Textile Fiber div., N.Y.C., 1969-71; pub. rels. mgr. Neiman-Marcus, Atlanta, 1972—. Active Atlanta Hist. Soc., 1972—; mem. bd. dirs. YWCA, Atlanta, 1987, Sandy Springs Found., 1995—; adv. bd. Northside Hosp., 1993—; mem. Olympic Com. 1996 Olympics, pub. info. asst. 1994-96. Recipient Leadership award City of Atlanta, 1980, Gov.'s Art award in Bus. Embroiderers' Guild Am., 1987; named one of Outstanding Women of Atlanta, 1981. Mem. The Fashion Group Inc. (bd. dirs. 1980—), Women in Comm., Women's C. of C. (elected Leadership Atlanta 1980—), Atlanta Bot. Gardens Assocs, High Mus. Art, Sandy Springs Soc., Atlanta Preservation Ctr., Ctr. for Puppetry Arts (charter), Friends of Atlanta Zoo, Atlanta Press Club (charter), Women's Commerce Club (mem. adv. bd. 1988—), Ga. Hist. Trust, Hist. Med. Acad. (adv. bd. 1990—). Office: Neiman Marcus 3393 Peachtree Rd NE Atlanta GA 30326-1109

WHITE, SARAH JOWILLIARD, counselor; b. Oxford, N.C., Sept. 1, 1921; d. John Hiriam and Emma (Redfern) Isham; m. Hamilton B. Carson, Sept. 20, 1945 (div. 1968); 1 child, Lynne Denise. Honor student, Bennett Coll., 1939-42, Cornell U., 1979-82; BA, CCNY, 1973. Clk. N.Y. Dept. Law, N.Y.C., 1948-53; auditor U.S. Fed. Govt. Svc., N.Y.C., 1955-62; postal clk. U.S. Govt., Mt. Vernon, N.Y., 1963-66; prin. N.Y. State Dept. Labor, Mt. Vernon, 1966-88, ret., 1988; youth organizer N.Y. State Careerists Soc., Inc., N.Y.C., 1989—; youth and employment counselor Women in Community Svc., Nat. Coun. Negro Women, Manhattan sect., N.Y.C., 1983—. Vol. Advanced Vocation Edn. Day, Albany, N.Y., 1988; vol., coord. Decade of the Youth, N.Y.C., 1989, 90; corres. sec. Lower East Side United Neighbors, N.Y.C., 1989. Recipient Youth award, 1987, Recognition award, 1987, Internat. Assn. Pers. Employees Youth award, Plaque for Women in Cmty. Svcs., Outstanding Vol. Svc. award Gov. Mario Cuomo, 1994, Outstanding Vol. award, 1991, 92, Outstanding Vol. award Women in Cmty. Svc., 1994, Cert. Appreciation, 1995, Appreciation award South Bronx Job Alumni chpt., 1995, Nat. Coun. Negro Women Recognition award, 1996; named one of N.Y.'s Finest Vols. Women in Cmty. Svcs. Mag., 1994, Woman on the Move, Cable TV, 1994. Mem. NAFE, N.Y. Careerists Soc. (sec., Merit award 1988), Assn. U.S. Govt. Job Corps. (alumni recognition award 1995), Nat. Coun. Negro Women (chairperson, Achievement award 1988-90), Internat. Assn. Pers. Employees, Black Alumni CCNY (pub. rels. com., outstanding award 1989). Democrat. 7th Day Sabbath Keeper House of God.

WHITE, SUSIE MAE, school psychologist; b. Madison, Fla., Mar. 5, 1914; d. John Anderson and Lucy (Crawford) Williams; m. Daniel Elijah White, Oct. 20, 1938 (dec. Sept. 29, 1968). BS, Fla. Meml. Coll., St. Augustine, 1948; MEd, U. Md., 1953; postgrad., Mich. State U., 1955, Santa Fe Community Coll., 1988; Cert. Child Care Supervision, W.T. Loften Edn. Ctr., Gainesville, Fla., 1994. Elem. tchr. Grove Park (Fla.) Elem. Sch., 1943; tchr. Douglas High Sch., High Springs, Fla., 1944-55; sch. psychologist Alachua County Sch. Bd., Gainesville, Fla., 1956-69; coord. social svcs. Alachua County Sch. Bd., Gainesville, 1970; owner, dir. Mother Dear's Child Care Ctr., Gainesville, 1988—. Del. Bapt. World Alliance, Bapt. Conv. Fla., Tokyo, 1970; state dir. leadership Fla. Bapt. Gen. Conv., 1971-85. Recipient Cert. of Appreciation Fla. State Dept. Edn., Tallahassee, 1971, Appreciation for Disting. Svc. award Fla. Gen. Bapt. Conv., Miami, 1979, Hall of Fame award Martin Luther King Jr. Hall of Fame, 1994; The Susie Mae White scholarship fund established Mt. Sinai Congress Christian Edn., 1995. Mem. Nat. Ret. Tchrs. Assn., Alachua County Tchrs. Assn., Fla. Meml. Coll. Nat. Alumni Assn., AAUW, Heroines of Jerico, Masons. Democrat. Office: Child Care Ctr 811 NW 4th Pl Gainesville FL 32601-5049

WHITE, SYLVIA FRANCES, gerontology home care nurse, consultant; b. Dayton, Ohio, May 2, 1952; d. Arthur Francis and Eleanor Ida (Beach) Scarpelli; m. Alan Bruce White, Nov. 28, 1981. BSN, Loyola U., 1975; MPH, U. Ill., Chgo., 1984. Cert. gerontol. nurse; lic. nursing home adminstrn., Ill. Staff nurse Vis. Nurse Assn., Chgo., 1975-80, team leader, 1980-81, supr., 1981-83, dist. adminstr., 1984-86, mgr. North side, 1986-87, dir. patient svcs., 1987; dir. clin. svcs. Kimberly Quality Care, Evanston, Ill., 1987-89; pub. health nurse City of Evanston, Ill., 1989-90; geriatric nurse assoc. City of Evanston, 1990—; cons. surveyor Joint Commn. on Accreditation of Healthcare Orgns., Oakbrook Terrace, Ill., 1988—; vol. Hospice, literacy. Trainer The Arthritis Found., Chgo., 1991-92; mem. Panel Rev. State of Ill. Continuing Edn.; mem. profl. edn. com. Arthritis Found.; hospice vol. Mem. APHA, Ill. Pub. Health Assn., Ill. Home Health Coun., Ill. Alliance for Aging, Zonta, Arthritis Profl. Edn. Com., Nat. Assn. Home Care. Roman Catholic. Home: 222 Sunset Dr Wilmette IL 60091 Office: Evanston Health Dept 2100 Ridge Ave Evanston IL 60201-2796

WHITEAKER, RUTH CATHERINE, retired secondary education educator, counselor; b. Monte Vista, Colo., Mar. 3, 1907; d. Samuel sigel and Vina Catherine (Becraft) Heilman; m. George Henry Whiteaker, June 23, 1946. BA, U. Denver, 1930, MA, 1954; student, Columbia U., Ohio State, and others, 1933-66. cert. tchr. Tchr./drama coach Brighton (Colo.) High Sch., 1930-36; tchr. Meeker Jr. High Sch., Greeley, Colo., 1936-42; tchr. South High Sch., Denver, 1942-52, couselor, 1952-61; tchr. Thomas Jefferson High Sch., Denver, 1961-66; organizer first career day Greeley High Sch., 1939, Future Tchrs. Am. in Colo. High Schs. Colo. Edn. Assn., 1949-55; co-organizer Wyo. Future Tchrs. Am. Wyo. Edn. Assn., 1951; com. mem. Nat. Future Tchrs. Am. Adv. Bd., 1954. Author: (English speech units) Colo. English Guide, 1939, Denver K-12 Program, 1951; editor: (guidebook) South High Syllabus, 1952-60. Chmn. 50th reunion U. Denver Class 1930, 1980. Grantee U.S. Dept. Edn. and Ministry of Edn. Mex., Mexico City, 1945; recipient plaque Colo. Future Tchrs. Am., 1955, Student Nat. Edn. Assn., Colo., 1955; Yearbook dedication South Denver High Sch., 1958. Mem. AAUW, Bus. and Profl. Women's Club (pres. 1933, 38), Colo. Bus. and Profl. Women's Club (v.p. 1944), Columbia U. Women's Club Colo. (pres. 1975-77), Rep. Ladies Roundtable, Colo. Symphony Guild, PEO Sisterhood, Meth. Women's Assn., Terr. Daus., Columbia U. Alumni Club, Alpha Gamma Delta (regional sec.-treas. 1934-36, pres. 1936-40), Delta Kappa Gamma (v.p. Colo. chpt. 1959). Republican. Methodist. Home: 6930 E Girard Ave Apt 108 Denver CO 80224-2900

WHITEHEAD, BARBARA ANN, secondary school educator; b. Shreveport, La., Apr. 25, 1941; d. Clifton John and Leona Elizabeth (Lemoine) W. BA, McNeese State U., 1963, MEd, 1967; postgrad., Centenary Coll., 1982-83, La. Tech. U., 1983. Cert. secondary edn. tchr., La. Tchr. Calcasieu Parish Sch. System, Lake Charles, La., 1963-68, Caddo Parish Sch. System, Shreveport, 1968—; chair social studies dept. C.E. Byrd Math./Sci. Magnet High Sch., Shreveport, 1987—. Author: Teaching the Historical Origins of Nursery Rhymes and Folk Tales, 1982. Named La. Tchr. of Yr. DAR, 1983. Mem. NEA, La. Assn. Educators, Caddo Assn. Educators, Sigma Tau Delta. Roman Catholic. Office: CE Byrd Math Sci Magnet High Sch 3201 Line Ave Shreveport LA 71104-4241

WHITEHEAD, JULIETTE LORRAINE, retired sales manager, artist; b. Fall River, Mass., Feb. 16, 1928; d. Raymond and Laurette Marguerite

(Gagné) Talbot; m. Arthur Phillip Kirkwood, Jan. 4, 1947 (dec. July, 1993); children: Patricia Anne, Michael Raymond, Laura Beth; m. Walter Arthur Whitehead, Sept. 24, 1994. BFA in Painting, U. Mass., 1989. Unit mgr. Stanley Home Products, Westfield, Mass., 1948-50; dist. sales mgr. Avon, Rye, N.Y., 1961-85. One women shows at YWCA, New Bedford, Mass., 1991, 92, 95, 96, Wamsutta Club, New Bedford, 1993; group exhbns. include Bierstadt Art Gallery, New Bedford, 1989-96, (1st pl. photo award 1991, 92, 95, 1st pl. watercolor award 1996, hon mention photo award 1991, 95, 3d pl. acrylics award 1995, 2d pl. photo award 1995, first place mixed media award 1996), Taunton Art Assn., 1992-95 (hon. mention mixed media award 1995, hon. mention watercolor award 1995), Fairhaven Homecoming, 1991, 92, 95 (3d pl. oils award 1991, 3d pl. photo award 1992, 3d pl. photo and mixed media awards 1995), Friends of Dartmouth Librs. (3d pl. photo awards 1992, 95), First Night, New Bedford, 1995 (hon. mention acrylic award 1994), Fall River Art Assn. (2d pl. mixed media award 1994, 1st pl. photo award 1993). Recipient numerous art awards. Mem. Bierstadt Art Soc. (v.p. 1994-95.), Westport Art Group, Taunton Art Assn., Nat. Mus. Women in the Arts (charter mem.), Fall River Art Assn. Democrat. Roman Catholic. Home: 421 Pleasant St New Bedford MA 02740

WHITEHEAD, LUCY GRACE, health facility administrator; b. Jacksonville, Fla., Jan. 12, 1935; d. William Alexander and Hester Grace (Gray) Fisackerly; m. John Vernon Whitehead, Sept. 4, 1957; children: Marilyn Ruth, John Vernon Jr., James Andrew. BA, Fla. So. Coll., 1956; M of Christian Edn., Emory U., 1957; BSN, U. North Fla., 1990. RN, Fla. Staff nurse Venice (Fla.) Hosp., 1977, Med. Personnel Pool, Largo, Fla., 1978; charge nurse/nurse educator Gadsden Nursing Home, Quincy, Fla., 1979-85; primary nurse Meml. Regional Rehab. Hosp., Jacksonville, Fla., 1990-92; staff nurse, nurse mgr. Nassau Gen. Hosp., Fernandina Beach, Fla., 1992-94; clin. coord. Integrated Health Svcs., Ft. Pierce, Fla., 1994, dir. nursing, 1994-95. Mem. ANA, Fla. Nurses Assn., Order Ea. Star (worthy matron), Sigma Theta Tau. Methodist. Home: 1083 Tallavana Trail Havana FL 32333

WHITEHEAD, VALERIE HARAWAY, special education educator; b. Virginia Beach, Va., Oct. 24, 1966; d. Harris O'Neal Haraway and Genevieve Myrtle (Wall) Taylor; m. Michael Lewis Whitehead, Apr. 18, 1991; 1 child, Michael Chas. AS, Brunswick Coll., 1988; BEd cum laude, Ga. So. Coll., 1988; MEd, Ga. So. U., 1991, edn. specialist, 1993. Cert. learning disabilities, mental disabilities, gifted tchr. Learning disabilities tchr. Glynn County Middle Sch., Brunswick, Ga., 1988-92, Glyndale Elem. Sch., Brunswick, 1992—; student coun. advisor Glynn County Middle Sch., Brunswick, 1990-92, ptnrs. in edn. contact, 1991-92; staff devel. instr. Glynn County Schs. Sys., Brunswick, 1993—; spl. edn. lead tchr. Glyndale, 1996. Mem. NEA, Glynn County Assn. Educators (sec.), Phi Delta Kappa. Roman Catholic. Home: 115 Midway Cir Brunswick GA 31523-9604 Office: Glyndale Elem Sch 1785 Old Jesup Rd Brunswick GA 31523-1139

WHITEHILL, ANGELA ELIZABETH, artistic director; b. Leeds, Yorkshire, Eng., Oct. 21, 1938; came to U.S., 1952; became American citizen, Sept. 1995; d. Donald Paul and Audrey May (Clayforth) Warner; m. Norman James Whitehill, Dec. 16, 1928; children: Norman James III, Pamela Elizabeth. Student, Arts Ednl. Sch., London, 1955-59. With Corps de Ballet, Paris, 1958-59; dir. London Sch. Ballet, St. Thomas, V.I., 1960-63; asst. dir. Ocean County Ballet Co., Toms River, N.J., 1965-68; founder, dir. Shore Ballet Sch., Toms River, 1968-76; artistic dir. Shore Ballet Co., Toms River, 1971-76; artist in residence Castleton State Coll., Rutland, Vt., 1977-79; founder, artistic dir. Burklyn Ballet Theatre, Lyndonville, Vt., 1977—; vis. prof. Colby Sawyer Coll., New London, N.H., 1978-79; resident designer Atlanta Ballet Co., 1982-83; designer, pub. relations N.J. Ballet Co., Orange, 1983-85; artistic dir. Vt. Ballet Theatre, Burlington, 1985-94. choreographer Arensky dances, 1983, A Deux, 1984, 4 Plus 2, 1986, Twins From A Time Gone By, 1987; co-author: Parent's Book of Ballet, 1988, The Young Professional's Book of Ballet, 1990. Dir. Vt. Ballet Theatre Found. Recipient Francis Hopkins award Ocean County, N.J., 1976, Woman of Achievement award Vt. Woman, 1989, Author's award N.J. Inst. Tech., 1989. Mem. Vt. Council on the Arts, Nat. Assn. Regional Ballet. Quaker. Home: 218 Ocean Ave Burlington VT 05402-5069 also: PO Box 907 Island Heights NJ 08732 Office: Burklyn Ballet Theatre PO Box 5069 Burlington VT 05402-5069

WHITEHURST, MARY TARR, artist, poet, writer; b. Norfolk, Va., Nov. 20, 1923; d. Henry Bennitt and Martha Ida Tarr; m. Jerry Rutter Whitehurst, Dec. 24, 1943; children: Henry Armistead, Jeffrey Tarr, Martha W. Bryant. Student, Coll. William & Mary, 1940-42, Wytheville C.C., 1968, Sullins Coll., 1976-80, Va. Western C.C., 1988. Docent Mus. Fine Arts, Roanoke, Va., 1973-75; dir., endowing mem. Fine Arts Ctr. of New River Valley, Pulaski, Va., 1980-93; charter, endowing mem. Bristol Mus. Fine Arts, Va./Tenn., 1975-80; benefactor, mem. Arts Found. Radford U., Va., 1991—. One-woman shows include Mus. Fine Arts, Roanoke, Va., 1977, Emory & Henry Coll., Emory, Va., 1982, Radford U. Art Gallery, Va., 1991, Ashland Area Art Galery, Ky., 1993, Va. Polytech. Inst. & State U., Blacksburg, 1985—, New River C.C. Found., 1985—, Coll. William & Mary, Williamsburg, 1995. Endowing mem. Va. Polytech. Inst. & State U., Blacksburg, 1985—, New River C.C. Found., 1985—, Coll. William & Mary, Williamsburg, 1995. Recipient Clement Gueenberg award of distinction Mus. Fine Arts, Roanoke, 1976, Grumbacher Gold medal Soc. Water Color Artists, 1995; art dept. named in honor New River C.C., Dublin, Va., 1994. Mem. Catharine Lorillard Wolfe Art Club (Joyce Williams water color award 1985), Midwest Transparent Water Color Soc. (signature mem.), Va. Water Color Soc. (dir. 1994), Ala. Water Color Soc., Blacksburg Regional Artists Assn., Allied Artists (assoc.). Home: Painters Wood Rte 1 Box 356-E Draper VA 24324

WHITELAW, CHERYL REGENA, engineering and mathematics educator; b. Denver, Nov. 15, 1946; d. George H. and Susan (Matsumura) Sunada; m. Chandler Pratt Whitelaw, Dec. 21, 1968; children: Chery, Richard, Cindy, Bob, Randy, Brett Lynn. BSCE, Utah State U., 1969, MEngring., 1973; BS Math., So. Utah U., 1995. Pres., owner Regena, Cedar City, Utah, 1981-93; adj. instr. math. and engring. So. Utah U., Cedar City, 1992-94, instr. in computer sci., math. and engring., 1994—; substitute tchr. in math. and computers Iron County Sch. Dist., Cedar City, 1992-93; mem. State Networking Task Force-Librs., State of Utah, 1992-94. Author: Programmers Reference Guide to T1-99/4A, 1983, five others; contbr. articles to profl. jours. Bd. dirs. Cedar City Libr., 1987-95; del. White House Conf. on Librs. and Info. Svcs., 1991. Recipient Best Author award Fest-West, 1993. Home: 918 Cedar Knolls W Cedar City UT 84720-3631 Office: So Utah U Dept Math and Computer Sci Cedar City UT 84720

WHITELEY, SANDRA MARIE, librarian, editor; b. May 24, 1943; d. Samuel Smythe and Kathryn Marie (Voigt) Whiteley; m. R. Russell Maylone, Jan. 8, 1977; 1 child, Cybele Elizabeth. BA, Pa. State U., 1963; MLS, Columbia U., 1970; MA, U. Pa., 1975; postgrad., Northwestern U., 1985—. Tchr. Amerikan Kiz Koleji, Izmir, Turkey, 1967-69; reference libr. Yale U., New Haven, Conn., 1970-74; head reference dept. Northwestern U., Evanston, Ill., 1975-80; asst. editor Who's Who in Libr. and Info. ALA, Chgo., 1980-81, editor Reference Books Bull., 1985—; lectr. Grad. Libr. Sch. U. Chgo., 1982-83; assoc. exec. dir. Assn. Coll. and Rsch. Librs., Chgo., 1981-85. Author: Purchasing an Encyclopaedia, 5th edit., 1996, The American Library Association Guide to Information Access, 1994. Mem. ALA (various coms. 1977-81), Beta Phi Mu. Democrat. Congregationalist. Home: 1205 Noyes St Evanston IL 60201-2635 Office: ALA 50 E Huron St Chicago IL 60611-2729

WHITE-LIPSCOMB, CAROLYN, protective services official, social worker; b. N.Y.C., June 24, 1944; d. McKenzie and Bertha (Doe) Mack; m. Dewitt White, Apr. 3, 1977. BA, City Coll. N.Y., 1970; M in Social Work, Columbia U., 1972. Cert. tchr. N.Y., social worker N.Y., peace officer. Coll. counselor CUNY, Bayside, N.Y., 1972-75; sales, mktg. Xerox, N.Y.C., 1975-80; escort interpreter U.S. Dept. State, Washington, 1972-90; probation officer gang related intervention program Westchester County (N.Y.) Dept. Probation, White Plains, 1990—; owner, contractor C & D Update Interiors, Mt. Vernon, N.Y., 1980-90. Mem. Dem. Black Caucus, Mt. Vernon, 1995—; adv. bd. Cmty. Svc. Coun., 1993—. Mem. Columbia U. Alumni, Probation Officer Assn. Home: 115 Harborview Pl Mooresville NC 28115

WHITEMAN, CHERYL ANNE, nurse; b. Chgo., Jan. 10, 1951; d. George O. Timm and Margaret Timm Palicz; m. Thomas R. Whiteman, Jr., Sept. 15, 1973; children: Erica, Brandon. BSN, Emory U., 1973. RN, Fla.; cert. health care risk mgr. Hosp. bill auditor Equifax Svcs., Tampa, Fla., 1988-93; staff nurse, mgr. surg. ICU, St. Anthony's Hosp., St. Petersburg, Fla., 1973-87, hosp. bill auditor, 1993-95, risk mgr., 1995. Troop leader, cons. Suncoast coun. Girl Scouts U.S.A., 1984—. Mem. Sigma Theta Tau. Home: 3700 Shore Acres Blvd NE Saint Petersburg FL 33703 Office: St Anthony's Hosp 1200 7th Ave N Saint Petersburg FL 33705

WHITESIDE, CAROL GORDON, state official, former mayor; b. Chgo., Dec. 15, 1942; d. Paul George and Helen Louise (Barre) G.; m. John Gregory Whiteside, Aug. 15, 1964; children: Brian Paul, Derek James. BA, U. Calif., Davis, 1964. Pers. mgr. Emporium Capwell Co., Santa Rosa, 1964-67; pers. asst. Levi Strauss & Co., San Francisco, 1967-69; project leader Interdatum, San Francisco, 1983-88; with City Coun. Modesto, 1983-87; mayor City of Modesto, 1987-91; asst. sec. for intergovtl. rels. The Resources Agy., State of Calif., Sacramento, 1991-93; dir. intergovtl. affairs Gov.'s Office, Sacramento, 1993—. Trustee Modesto City Schs., 1979-83; nat. pres. Rep. Mayors and Local Ofcls., 1990. Named Outstanding Woman of Yr. Women's Commn., Stanislaus County, Calif., 1988, Woman of Yr., 27th Assembly Dist., 1991; Toll fellow Coun. of State Govts., 1996. Republican. Lutheran. Office: Governor's Office 1400 10th St Sacramento CA 95814-5502

WHITING, ANN HARRIET, retired computer service executive; b. Chgo., July 31, 1936; d. Thomas Brent and Florence Harriet (Beals) Legg Thorstensen; m. Louis D. Straubel, June 23, 1956 (div. 1974); children—Michael, Rick; m. 2d, Robert Alan Whiting, Apr. 19, 1980 (div. 1993). B.S., Mich. State U., 1962. Probation officer St. Joseph City Probate Ct., Centerville, Mich., 1960-62; police detective Kalamazoo Police Dept. (Mich.), 1962-77; security and safety supr. Indian River Meml. Hosp., Vero Beach, Fla., 1979-81; legal sec. state legislator R. Dale Patchett, Vero Beach, 1981-82; pres. Computer Creations By Ann, Inc., Vero Beach, 1982—. Mem. Republican Women Aware, Vero Beach; asst. polit. campaign mgr. R. Dale Patchett, Vero Beach, 1982. Mem. Internat. Assn. Women Police (life). Christian Scientist. Home: 1840 Maravilla Ave #806 Vero Beach FL 33901

WHITING, DEVORA JENKINS, community health nurse; b. Balt., June 14, 1942; d. Arthur B. Sr. and naomi (Battle) Jenkins; m. George W. Whiting, July 1, 1973; children: Tarik, Camille. Diploma, Helene Field Sch. of Nursing, Balt., 1965; BS, Morgan State U., 1972. RN, Md. Head nurse Provident Hosp., Balt., 1965-72; staff nurse pediatric ICU Johns Hopkins Hosp., Balt., 1966-68; community health nurse Dept. Pub. Health, Balt., 1968-73; community liaison nurse discharge planning women and children's health U. Md. Med. Systems, Balt., 1973-96, nurse case mgr. dept. medicine, divsn. clin. quality systems, 1996—; Resolve Through Sharing bereavement counselor. Named Outstanding Community Health Nurse, State of Md., 1985. Mem. ANA (cert. cmty. health nurse), Md. Perinatal Assn., Md. High Risk Infant Coun., Zeta Phi Beta (Zeta of Yr. award 1996), Chi Eta Sigma, Sigma Theta Tau. Home: 2318 Harlem Ave Baltimore MD 21216-4834

WHITING, JULIA DULANY, emergency physician; b. Seattle, Sept. 6, 1961; d. James Hudson and Luisa (Kreis) W.; m. John A. Malone, Apr. 9, 1994. BA, U. Va., 1983, MD, 1993. Intern and resident in emergency medicine Pitt County Meml. Hosp., Greenville, N.C., 1993-96; staff physician emergency dept. Martha Jefferson Hosp., 1996—; med. advisor Winterville (N.C.) Rescue Squad, 1993-96. EMT Charlottesville-Albermarle Rescue Squad, 1987-93; health educator Women's Health Ctr., Charlottesville, 1987-89. Mem. AMA, NOW, AAUW, Am. Med. Women's Assn., Am. Coll. Emergency Physicians, Am. Assn. Women Emergency Physicians, Emergency Medicine Residents' Assn. Episcopalian.

WHITING, LISA LORRAINE, video production educator, producer, director; b. Lansing, Mich., July 22, 1959; d. Lowell Stanton and Ruth Lorraine (Gregory) W. BS in Psychology, Mich. State U., 1981, BA in Telecommunication cum laude, 1984, MA in Telecommunication, 1988; AA in Dance magna cum laude, Lansing Community Coll., 1984. Video instr. dept. telecomms. Sta. WKAR-TV, Mich. State U., East Lansing, Mich., 1987—; producer, dir. (TV show) The Outreach Mass, East Lansing, 1984—. Mem. Jr. League of Lansing. Office: Mich State U Sta WKAR 508 Communication Arts Sci East Lansing MI 48824-1212

WHITKO, JEAN PHILLIPS, academic administrator; b. Dover, Del., Oct. 31, 1940; d. Albert Leroy and Helen (Busch) Phillips; m. Donald A. Whitko, July 1, 1972; children: Lenore Ann, Wayne P., Donna J., Sheri L. BS, U. Del., 1962; MEd, Pa. State U., 1968, postgrad., 1968-72. Cert. tchr., Del., Pa. Tchr. Newcastle (Del.) Spl. Sch. Dist., 1962-68; rsch. asst. Pa. State U., University Park, 1969, instr. edn., grad. asst., 1969-72; substitute tchr. Jerusalem Lutheran Nursery Sch. and Day Care, Schwenksville, Pa., 1983-85; supr. student teaching Pa. State U., 1988—; evaluator fed. title I and III projects Pa. Dept. Edn., Harrisburg, 1970-72. Officer Women's Civ. Club Schwenksville, 1972—; vol. tchr. Perkiomen Valley Schs., Schwenksville, 1976-86; bd. dirs. Jerusalem Lutheran Nursery Sch. and Day Care, 1983-85. Named Friend of Edn., Perkiomen Valley Edn. Assn., 1983; recipient Commendation from Gov. Richard Thornburg, 1985. Mem. ASCD, Pa. Assn. Colls. and Tchr. Educators. Home: 623 Main St Schwenksville PA 19473-1012 Office: Pa State Univ 179 Chambers Bldg University Park PA 16802-3205

WHITLEY, CLAUDIA GAY, middle school educator; b. Dallas, May 29, 1952; d. Joe Glenn and Clara Ruth Harris; m. Eddie Floyd Whitley, May 19, 1973; 1 child, Eddie Floyd Jr. BS in Edn., Stephen F. Austin State U., 1973, MEd, 1987. Cert. tchr.; cert. reading specialist. Spl. edn. tchr. Laneville (Tex.) Ind. Sch. Dist., 1973-74; state compensatory edn. math. tchr. Nacogdoches (Tex.) Ind. Sch. Dist., 1976-78; call faculty Stephen F. Austin State U., Nacogdoches, 1988-94; 7th grade reading tchr. Nacogdoches Ind. Sch. Dist., 1978-95, asst. prin., 1995—. Recipient Tchr. of Yr. award Daily Sentinel, Nacogdoches, 1992. Mem. Internat. Reading Assn., Tex. State Reading Assn., Tex. Mid. Sch. Assn., Assn. Supervision and Curriculum Devel., Tex. Assn. Secondary Sch. Prins., Stone Fort Reading Coun. (pres. 1990-92, treas. membership dir. 1992-94), Alpha Delta Kappa (sec. 1994-96). Methodist. Office: T J Rusk Mid Sch 411 N Mound St Nacogdoches TX 75961

WHITLEY, JOELLEN, library media specialist; b. El Paso, Tex., June 4, 1947; d. Joseph Talbird and Betsy Lou (Pixley) McCreary; m. Larry Wayne Whitley, June 28, 1969; children: Brent, Kristen. BS in Elem. Edn., U. Tex., El Paso, 1969; MA in Ednl. Libr. Media, U. Colo., Denver, 1986. Cert. tchr., Tex., Colo.; adminstrs. cert. U. Denver. Elem. sch. tchr. El Paso Pub. Schs., 1969-71; elem. sch. tchr. Jefferson County Pub. Schs., Denver, 1981-87, libr. media specialist, 1987—. Mem. Jefferson County Ednl. Media Specialists (pres. 1995-96), Delta Delta Delta (life, recording sec. alumni chpt). Home: 6927 S Saulsbury St Littleton CA 80123 Office: Colorow Elem Sch 6317 S Estes St Littleton CO 80123

WHITLEY, NANCY O'NEIL, retired radiology educator; b. Winston-Salem, N.C., Feb. 21, 1932; d. Norris Lawrence and Thelma Mae (Hardy) O'Neil; m. J.E. Whitley, Dec. 20, 1958; children—John O'Neil, Catherine Anne. Student, Duke U., 1950-53; M.D., Bowman Gray Sch. Medicine, 1957. Fellow in cardiology Bowman Gray Sch. Medicine, Winston-Salem, 1958-60; intern Jefferson Davis Hosp., Houston, 1957-58; resident in radiology Bowman Gray Sch. Medicine, 1966-69, instr., 1969-70, asst. prof., 1970-74, assoc. prof., 1974-78; prof. radiology U. Md. Sch. Medicine, Balt., 1978-92; prof. oncology U. Md. Cancer Ctr., Balt., 1988-92; prof. radiology Med. U. S.C., Charleston, 1992-94; ret., 1994. Author: (with J.E. Whitley) Angiopgraphy, Techniques and Procedures, 1971.

WHITLOCK, DENISE LUCILLE See DAVIS, DENISE WHITLOCK

WHITLOW, DONNA MAE, daycare and primary school administrator; b. Buffalo, S.D., May 23, 1933; d. Carl Axel and Esther Johanna (Wickman) Magnuson; married, June 13, 1953; children: Debra Diane Reasy, Cathleen Denise Corallo, Lisa Mae. Diploma, Eugene Bible Coll., 1956; BA in Religious Edn., Internat. Seminary, 1985, MA, 1986. Corp. sec. various orgns., 1953-56; asst. registrar, prof. child edn. Calif. Open Bible Inst., Pasadena, 1956-57; dir. religious edn. and music, sec. to gen. bd. Jamaica Open Bible Inst., 1958-59; dir. religious edn. and music, sec. to gen. bd.. prof. on staff, bus. mgr. Trinidad Open Bible Inst., 1960-65; asst. to full-charge bookkeeper Jennings Strouss Law Firm, 1966-68; dir. religious edn. and music., mem. gen. bd., assoc. pastor Biltmore Bible Ch., Phoenix, Ariz., 1967-93; founder, dir. Biltmore Bible Day Care & Kindergarten, Phoenix, 1977—; founder bible schs. in South Africa, Argentina, Ctrl. Am., Europe, Caribbean, Singapore. Author: How To Start a Daycare in the Local Church, 1986. Republican. Home: 2144 E Lamar Rd Phoenix AZ 85016-1147 Office: Biltmore Bible Ch 3330 E Camelback Rd Phoenix AZ 85018-2310

WHITMAN, CHRISTINE TODD, governor; b. Sept. 26, 1946; d. Webster Bray and Eleanor Schley Todd; m. John Whitman, 1974; children: Kate, Taylor. BA in Govt., Wheaton Coll., 1968. Former freeholder Somerset County, N.J.; former pres. State Bd. Pub. Utilities; host radio talk show Sta. WKXW, Trenton, N.J.; gov. State of N.J., 1994—; chmn. Com. for an Affordable N.J. Columnist newspapers. Bd. freeholders Somerset County, N.J., 1982-87; bd. pub. utilities, 1988-89; Rep. candidate for senator State of N.J., 1990. Office: State House CN 001 Office of Governor Trenton NJ 08625-0001*

WHITMAN, JOAN LYNN, learning center director; b. Ashland, Wis., Aug. 29, 1956; d. John Edward and Wilma Faye (Buss) Wrobleski; m. Kurt Edward Whitman, Apr. 28, 1979. BA, Northland Coll., 1979; MA, Cardinal Stritch Coll., 1987. Lic. secondary tchr., Wis. Tchr. social studies Nicolet H.S., Glendale, Wis., 1980-82; tchr. learning disabilities Brookfield (Wis.) East H.S., 1982-87, interim asst. prin., 1987-88, dir. learning ctr., 1988—; tchr. learning ctr. Nicolet H.S., Glendale, 1979-82; grad. tchr. Aurora U., Milw., 1989—; assessor Alverno Coll., Milw., 1995—; tchr. W.I. Ctr. for Gifted Learners, Glendale, 1996; tchr. grad. divsn. Cardinal Stritch Coll., 1996. vol. pet therapy Woodland Health Care, Brookfield, 1989—; vol. food basket, Milw. AIDS project, 1994—. Mem. AAUW (Outstanding Tchr. award 1989), Wis. Women's Alliance, Unified Voices (treas. 1993, bd. dirs. 1994). Home: 17685 Green Isle Ct Brookfield WI 53045 Office: Elmbrook Schs 3305 N Lilly Rd Brookfield WI 53005

WHITMAN, KATHY VELMA ROSE (ELK WOMAN WHITMAN), artist, sculptor, jeweler, painter, educator; b. Bismarck, N.D., Aug. 12, 1952; d. Carl Jr. and Edith Geneva (Lykken) W.; m. Robert Paul Luger, Feb. 21, 1971 (div. Jan. 1982); children: Shannon, Lakota, Cannupa, Palani; m. Dean P. Fox (div. 1985); 1 child, Otgadahe. Student, Standing Rock C.C., Ft. Yates, N.D., 1973-74, Sinte Gleska Coll., Rosebud, S.D., 1975-77, U. S.D., 1977, Ariz. State U., 1992-93. Instr. art Sinte Gleska Coll., 1975-77, Standing Rock C.C., 1977-78; co-mgr. Four Bears Motor Lodge, New Town, N.D., 1981-82; store owner Nux-Baga Lodge, New Town, 1982-85; artist-in-residence N.D. Coun. on Arts, Bismarck, 1983-84, bd. dirs., 1985; artist-in-residence Evanston Twp. H.S., Ill., 1996; cultural cons. movie prodn., Phoenix, Ariz., 1994. One woman shows include Mus. of Am. Indian, N.Y.C., 1983, Charleroi Internat. Fair, Belgium, 1984, Heard Mus., Phoenix, 1987-92, Phoenix Gallery, Nurnburg, Germany, 1990-96, Lovena Ohl Gallery, Phoenix, 1990-94, Phoenix Gallery, Coeur d'Alene, Idaho, 1992, Turquoise Tortoise Gallery, Tubac, Ariz., 1992-93, Yah-ta-hey Gallery, New London, Conn., 1992-93, Silver Sun Gallery, Santa Fe, N.Mex., 1992-96, Tribal Expessions Gallery, Arlington Heights, Ill., 1994-96, others; represented in permanent collections at Mus. of the Am. Indian, N.Y.C., Mesa (Ariz.) C.C. Bd. dirs. Ft. Berthold C.C., New Town, 1983-85; pres. Cannonball (N.D.) Pow-Wow Com., 1978; parent rep. Head Start, Ft. Yates, 1974. Recipient best craftsman spl. award Bullock's Indian Arts and Crafts, 1986, best of fine arts award No. Plains Tribal Arts, Sioux Falls, S.D., 1988, best of show award Pasadena Western Relic and Native Am. Show, 1991, 2 1st place awards Santa Fe Indian Market, 1993, 2 2nd place awards, 1994, 2 3rd place awards, 1994, 74th Ann. SWAIA Santa Fe Indian Mkt. 1st place award, 1995, 2d place award, 1995, 2 3rd place awards, 1995, 2 Honorable Mentions in sculpture N.Mex. State Fair, 1996. Mem. Indian Arts and Crafts Assn., S.W. Assn. on Indian Affairs (life, 1st and 2nd place awards Santa Fe Indian Market 1995, 2 3rd place awards 1995, 1st place and 2nd place awards Santa Fe Indian Market 1996). Home and Studio: 3401 E Paradise Dr Phoenix AZ 85028

WHITMAN, MARINA VON NEUMANN, economist; b. N.Y.C., Mar. 6, 1935; d. John and Mariette (Kovesi) von Neumann; m. Robert Freeman Whitman, June 23, 1956; children: Malcolm Russell, Laura Mariette. BA summa cum laude, Radcliffe Coll., 1956; MA, Columbia U., 1959, PhD, 1962; LHD (hon.), Russell Sage Coll., 1972, U. Mass., 1975, N.Y. Poly Inst., 1975, Baruch Coll., 1980; LLD (hon.), Cedar Crest Coll., 1973, Hobart and William Smith Coll., 1973, Coe Coll., 1975, Marietta Coll., 1976, Rollins Coll., 1976, Wilson Coll., 1977, Allegheny Coll., 1977, Amherst Coll., 1978, Ripon Coll., 1980, Mt. Holyoke Coll., 1980; LittD (hon.), Williams Coll., 1980, Lehigh U., 1981, Denison U., 1983, Claremont U., 1984, Notre Dame U., 1984, Eastern Mich. U., 1992 . Mem. faculty U. Pitts., 1962-79, prof. econs., 1971-73, disting. pub. svc. prof. econs., 1973-79; v.p., chief economist Gen. Motors Corp., N.Y.C., 1979-85, group exec. v.p. pub. affairs, 1985-92; disting. vis. prof. bus. adminstrn. & pub. policy U. Mich., Ann Arbor, 1992-94, prof. bus. adminstrn. and pub. policy, 1994—; mem. U.S. Price Commn., 1971-72, Coun. Econ. Advisers, Exec. Office of Pres., 1972-73; bd. dirs. Chase Manhattan Corp., ALCOA, Procter & Gamble Co., Browning-Ferris Industries, UNOCAL; mem. Trilateral Commn., 1973-84, 88-95; mem. Pres. Adv. Com. on Trade Policy and Negotiations, 1987-93; mem. tech. assessment adv. coun. U.S. Congress Office of Tech. Assessment, 1990-95, Dept. Treasury, from 1977; mem. Consultative Group on Internat. Econs. and Monetary Affairs, from 1979; trustee Nat. Bur. Econ. Rsch., 1993—. Bd. dirs. Inst. for Internat. Econs, 1986, Eurasia Found, 1992-95; bd. overseers Harvard U., 1972-78, mem. vis. com. Kennedy Sch., 1992—; trustee Princeton U., 1980-90. Fellow Earhart Found., 1959-60, AAUW, 1960-61, NSF, 1968-70, also Social Security Rsch. Coun.; recipient Columbia medal for excellence, 1973; George Washington award Am. Hungarian Found., 1975. Mem. Am. Econ. Assn. (exec. com. 1977-80), Am. Acad. Arts & Scis., Coun. Fgn. Rels. (dir. 1977-87), Phi Beta Kappa. Author: Government Risk-Sharing in Foreign Investment, 1965; International and Interregional Payments Adjustment, 1967; Economic Goals and Policy Instruments, 1970; Reflections of Interdependence: Issues for Economic Theory and U.S. Policy, 1979; also articles; bd. editors Am. Econ. Rev., 1974-77; mem. editorial bd. Fgn. Policy. Office: U Mich Sch Pub Policy 411 Lorch Hall Ann Arbor MI 48109-1220

WHITMORE, MENANDRA M., librarian; b. Ancash, Peru; d. Rafael and Jacinta (Moreno) Mosquera; m. Jacob L. Whitmore III, Jan. 7, 1965; children: Jacqueline Grace, Michelle Jacinta. Degree in social work, U. Catolica del Peru, 1967; MLS, U. P.R., 1974, Catholic U. Am., 1984. Social worker Cornell U., Vicos, Peru, 1960-62, Servicio de Extension Agricola del Peru, 1962-63, Am. Friends Svc. Com., Mex. and Peru, 1963-65; libr. Colegio Maria Auxiliadora, P.R., 1971, Country Day Sch., San Jose, Costa Rica, 1975-76, Colegio San Ignacio, P.R., 1976-77; dir. libs. Am. Coll. P.R., 1977-80; libr. Lib. Gov. Printing Office, 1981-84; chief acquisitions sect., mgr. Hispanic employment program Pentagon Lib., Washington, 1984—. Author: (all pub. under name Menandra Mosquera) Bibliography on Hypsipyla, 1976, Bibliography of Forestry of Puerto Rico, 1984, Useful Trees of Tropical North America, 1988. Recipient commendation Dept. Def., 1987-90. Mem. ALA, Soc. for Acquisition Latin Am. Libr. Materials, Reforma (treas. Washington chpt. 1988, pres. 1989-91, 95—, nat. ways and means chair 1991-92).

WHITNEY, ALISON See MOVIUS, ALISON WHITNEY BURTON

WHITNEY, LORI ANN, legislative staff member; b. Rhinelander, Wis., Feb. 20, 1968; d. Larry R. and Mary E. (Gaffney) W. BA in Spanish/Polit. Sci. cum laude, U. Wis., Eau Claire, 1990. Messenger Wis. State Assembly, Madison, 1991—. Fundraiser SECC, Madison, 1992—, mem., 1993—, NOW, Multiple Sclerosis Soc., 1993—; campaign vol. David Clarenbach and Tammy Baldwin, Madison, 1992, State Rep. Tammy Baldwin, 1994, 96, Fred Risser, 1996; mem. Amnesty Internat., 1991—, Madison chpt. Anti-Death Penalty Coord.; fundraiser, vol. Am. Diabetes Assn.; monthly donor Planned Parenthood Nat. Leadership Coun. Recipient Hopebuilder Habitat for Humanity award, 1995, 5 SECC Fundraising awards. Democrat. Home: 15 N Hancock St L-2 Madison WI 53703

WHITNEY, PHYLLIS AYAME, author; b. Yokohama, Japan, Sept. 9, 1903; d. Charles J. and Lillian (Mandeville) W.; m. George A. Garner, July 2, 1925; m. Lovell F. Jahnke, 1950 (dec. 1973). Grad., McKinley High Sch., Chgo., 1924. Instr. dancing San Antonio, 1 yr; tchr. juvenile fiction writing Northwestern U., 1945; children's book editor Chgo. Sun, 1942-46, Phila. Inquirer, 1947, 48; instr. juvenile fiction writing N.Y.U., 1947-58; leader juvenile fiction workshop Writers Conf., U. Colo., 1952, 54, 56. Author: A Place for Ann, 1941, A Star for Ginny, 1942, (vocat. fiction for teenage girls) A Window for Julie, 1943, (mystery novel for adults) Red Is for Murder, 1943, The Silver Inkwell, 1945, Willow Hill, 1947, Writing Juvenile Fiction, 1947, Ever After, 1948, Mystery of the Gulls, 1949, Linda's Homecoming, 1950, The Island of Dark Woods, 1951, Love Me, Love Me Not, 1952, Step to the Music, 1953, A Long Time Coming, 1954, Mystery of the Black Diamonds, 1954, The Quicksilver Pool, 1955, Mystery on the Isle of Skye, 1955, The Fire and The Gold (Jr. Lit. Guild), 1956, The Highest Dream (Jr. Lit. Guild), The Trembling Hills (Peoples Book Club), 1956, Skye Cameron, 1957, Mystery of the Green Cat (Jr. Lit. Guild), 1957, Secret of the Samurai Sword (Jr. Lit. Guild), 1958, The Moonflower, 1958, Creole Holiday, 1959, Thunder Heights, 1960, Blue Fire, 1961, Mystery of the Haunted Pool, 1961 (Edgar award Mystery Writers Am.), Secret of the Tiger's Eye, 1961, Window on the Square, 1962, Mystery of the Golden Horn, 1962, Seven Tears for Apollo, 1963, Mystery of the Hidden Hand, 1963 (Edgar award Mystery Writers Am. 1964), Black Amber, 1964, Secret of the Emerald Star, 1964, Sea Jade, 1965, Mystery of the Angry Idol, 1965, Columbella, 1966, Secret of the Spotted Shell, 1967, Mystery of the Strange Traveler, 1967, Silverhill, 1967, Hunter's Green, 1968, Secret of Goblin Glen, 1968, Mystery of the Crimson Ghost, 1969, Winter People, 1969, Secret of the Missing Footprint, 1970, Lost Island, 1970, The Vanishing Scarecrow, 1971, Listen for the Whisperer, 1971, Nobody Likes Trina, 1972, Snowfire, 1973, Mystery of the Scowling Boy, 1973, The Turquoise Mask, 1974, Spindrift, 1975, Secret of Haunted Mesa, 1975, The Golden Unicorn, 1976, Secret of the Stone Face, 1977, The Stone Bull, 1977, The Glass Flame, 1978, Domino, 1979, Poinciana, 1980, Vermilion, 1981, Guide to Fiction Writing, 1982, Emerald, 1983, Rainsong, 1984, Dream of Orchids, 1985, Flaming Tree, 1986, Silversword, 1987, Feather on the Moon, 1988, Rainbow in the Mist, 1989, The Singing Stones, 1990, Woman Without a Past, 1991, The Ebony Swan, 1992, Star Flight, 1993, Daughter of the Stars, 1994; sold first story to Chgo. Daily News; later wrote for pulp mags., became specialist in juvenile writing, now writing entirely in adult field. Pres. Authors Round Table, 1943, 44; pres. exec. bd. Fifth Annual Writers Conf., Northwestern U., 1944; spent first 15 years of life in Japan, China and P.I. (father in shipping and hotel bus.). Recipient Friends of Lit. award for contbns. to children's lit., 1974; Reynal and Hitchcock prize in Youth Today contest for book Willow Hill; Today's Woman award Coun. Cerebral Palsy Auxs., 1983, Agatha award Malice Domestic, 1990, Rita award Romance Writers Am., 1990, Lifetime award Romance Writers Am., 1990, Midland Authors award for a lifetime of literary achievement, 1995. Mem. Mystery Writers Am. (pres. 1975, Grandmaster award for lifetime achievement 1988), Am. Crime Writers League, Sisters in Crime, Authors League of Am.

WHITNEY, POLLY LOUISE, novelist; b. St. Louis, Oct. 22, 1948; d. Donald V. Seewoster and Margaret Eden (Head) Windsor; m. Michael R. Whitney, Oct. 25, 1969; children: Michael James, Elizabeth Daisy. BA, SUNY, New Paltz, 1982; MA, Yale U., 1984. Reporter New Haven Register, 1987-89; novelist St. Martin's Press, N.Y.C., 1994—; internet humorist Dorothyl, Kent State U., 1995-96. Author: Until Death, 1994 (Agatha award nominee 1995), Until the End of Time, 1995. Mem. Mystery Writers Am., Sisters in Crime. Democrat. Home: 8195-C Severn Dr Boca Raton FL 33433

WHITNEY, RUTH REINKE, magazine editor; b. Oshkosh, Wis., July 23, 1928; d. Leonard G. and Helen (Diestler) Reinke; m. Daniel A. Whitney, Nov. 19, 1949; 1 son, Philip. BA, Northwestern U., 1949. Copywriter edn. dept. circulation div. Time, Inc., 1949-53; editor-in-chief Better Living mag., 1953-56; assoc. editor Seventeen magazine, 1956-62, exec. editor, 1962-67; editor-in-chief Glamour mag., N.Y.C., 1967—. Recipient Nat. Mag. award gen. excellence, 1981, 91, Pub. Interest, 1992, Cosmetic Executive Women Achiever award, 1993, honor award Women's City Club N.Y.; honoree Gala 11 Birmingham, So. Coll., 1993. Mem. Fashion Group, Am. Soc. Mag. Editors (pres. 1975-77, exec. com. 1989-92), Women in Communication (Matrix award 1980), Women in Media, U.S. Info. Agy. (mag. and print com. 1989-93), Alpha Chi Omega. Office: Glamour Condé Nast Bldg 350 Madison Ave New York NY 10017-3704*

WHITSELL, HELEN JO, lumber executive; b. Portland, Oreg., July 20, 1938; d. Joseph William and Helen (Cornwell) Copeland; m. William A. Whitsell, Sept. 2, 1960; 2 children. BA, U. So. Calif., 1960. With Copeland Lumber Yard Inc., Portland, 1960—, pres., chief exec. officer, 1973-84, chmn., chief exec. officer, 1984—; bd. dirs. First Interstate Bank of Orgn. Office: Copeland Lumber Yards Inc 901 NE Glisan St Portland OR 97232-2730

WHITSON, FRANCES ELLEN, reading educator; b. Perryton, Tex., Dec. 16, 1947; d. Jack H. and Ruth Mary (King) W. BS, West Tex. State U., 1969, MEd, 1974. Cert. tchr., Tex. Elem. tchr. Perryton (Tex.) Ind. Sch. Dist., 1970-75; elem. tchr. Dumas (Tex.) Ind. Sch. Dist., 1975-92, tchr., leader reading recovery, 1993—. Mem. Reading Recovery Coun. N.Am., Internat. Reading Assn., Tex. Reading Assn., Classroom Tchrs. Assn., Assn. Tex. Profl. Educators (Delta Kappa Gamma (pres. Kappa Rho chpt. 1980-82). Methodist. Home: 1306 Bennett Dr Dumas TX 79029-5348 Office: Dumas Ind Sch Dist PO Box 615 Dumas TX 79029-0615

WHITSON, SANDRA JOYCE, antiques dealer; b. Balt., Apr. 4, 1948; d. Frank Gilson and Frances (Moore) W.; m. Ronald Edward Van Anda, Jan. 9, 1986. BA in Theology, Loyola Coll., Balt., 1980. Legal sec. Fedder & Garten, P.A., Balt., 1957-78; antiques dealer, Lititz, Pa., 1980—. Author: Figural Napkin Rings, 1995. Mem. Antique Toy Collectors Am. Democrat. Presbyterian. Home: PO Box 272 Lititz PA 17543

WHITSON, SARAH LEAH, lawyer; b. L.A., Jan. 2, 1967; d. Leroy Miles and Ashken A. (Haroutounian) W. BA in Polit. Sci. with highest honors, U. Calif., Berkeley, 1988, BA in Middle Ea. Studies with highest honors, 1988; JD cum laude, Harvard U., 1991; postgrad., Am. U, Cairo, 1986-87. Assoc. Cleary, Gottlieb, Steen & Hamilton, N.Y.C., 1992—. Contbr. articles to profl. jours. Gen. coun., adv. bd. mem. Ctr. for Econ. and Social Rights, N.Y.C., 1993—. Mem. ABA, Armenian Bar Assn. (chairperson Armenia programs com. 1995-96), Phi Beta Kappa. Democrat. Armenian Orthodox Christian. Office: Cleary Gottlieb Steen & Hamilton 1 Liberty Plz New York NY 10006

WHITTAKER, JUDITH ANN CAMERON, lawyer; b. N.Y.C., June 12, 1938; d. Thomas Macdonald and Mindel (Wallman) Cameron; m. Kent E. Whittaker, Jan. 30, 1960; children: Charles Evans II, Catherine Cameron. BA, Brown U., 1959; JD, U. Mo., 1963. Bar: Mo. 1963, U.S. Dist. Ct. (we. dist.) Mo. 1963, U.S. Ct. Appeals (8th cir.) 1965, U.S. Supreme Ct. 1980, D.C. 1987. Assoc. and ptnr. Sheffrey, Ryder & Skeer, Kansas City, Mo., 1963-72; asst. and assoc. gen. counsel, corp. v.p. legal Hallmark Cards, Inc., Kansas City, 1972—; dir., v.p., gen. counsel Univision Holdings, Inc., Kansas City, 1988-92; dir. MCI comms. Harmon Industries, 1993—; trustee Am. Arbitration Assn., 1996—. Trustee Brown U. Providence, 1977-83, U. Mo. Law Found., Kansas City, 1977-90; dir. Kansas City (Mo.) Indsl. Devel. Authority, 1981-84, Legal Aid Kansas City, 1971-77, De La Salle Sch., 1993—. Mem. Internat. Soc. Barristers. Episcopalian. Office: Hallmark Cards Dept 339 PO Box 419126 Kansas City MO 64141-6126

WHITTAKER, ROBBIE HERLINE, speech pathologist; b. Lake Charles, La., Jan. 7, 1957; d. Robert Ernest and Willa Bea (Hester) Herline; m. Dwayne F. Whittaker, Dec. 13, 1975 (div. Oct. 1992). BS, La. State U., 1980, MA, 1982. Cert. tchr., La. Speech pathologist Early Intervention Program, Baton Rouge, 1980-82; speech therapist/speech assessment cons. East Baton Rouge Parish Sch. Bd., 1982-96; speech/lang. pathologist Baton Rouge Speech and Hearing Found., 1992-96; owner Speech/Lang. Consulting Svcs., Leesville, La., 1996—. Mem. NEA, La. Edn. Assn., Am. Speech, Lang., Hearing Assn. (cert.). Office: Speech Lang Consulting Svcs 407-C N 5th St Leesville LA 71446

WHITTELL, POLLY (MARY) KAYE, editor, writer; b. Washington, Oct. 20; d. Alfred Whittell Jr. and Mary Halsey (Patchin) Hopper. BA in English, U. Calif., Berkeley; postgrad., Radcliffe Coll., Columbia U. Rschr. Nat. Rev. Mag., N.Y.C., 1970-71; asst. to presdl. speech writer The White House, Washington, 1971-72; asst. editor Travel Age Mag., Dunn & Bradstreet Publs., N.Y.C., 1973-75; copy editor Ski Mag. Skier's Guides, Times-Mirror Mags. and Am. Express, N.Y.C., 1975-76; asst. editor to sr. editor Hearst Mags., Motor Boating & Sailing Mag., N.Y.C., 1977—. Contbr. articles to nat. and internat. consumer mags. Mem. charity benefit com. Youth Counseling League, N.Y.C., 1975-85, and others; v.p. Knickerbocker Rep. Club, N.Y.C., 1979-80; elected mem. N.Y. Rep. County Com., N.Y.C., 1980-84. Mem. Boating Writers Internat. (award for environ. article 1995), Soc. Profl. Journalists, Social Register Assn., SandBar Beach Club (v.p. membership 1980-82). Episcopalian. Home: 240 Central Park S New York NY 10019-1413 Office: Motor Boating & Sailing Hearst Mags 250 W 55th St New York NY 10019

WHITTEN, BARBARA LU, physicist; b. Mpls., Sept. 26, 1946; d. Robert Arthur and Shirley Virginia (Palmer) W.; m. William Lowell Morgan, Jan. 1, 1982; children: Penelope Ariel Whitten Morgan, Jacob Lowell Whitten Morgan. BA, Carleton Coll., 1964; MA, U. Rochester, 1971, PhD, 1977. Instr. interdisciplinary studies Miami U., Oxford, Ohio, 1974-77; asst. prof. Miami U., Oxford, 1977-80; rsch. assoc. Rice U., Houston, 1980-81; physicist Lawrence Livermore (Calif.) Nat. Lab., 1981-87, cons., 1981-87; assoc. prof. physics Colo. Coll., Colorado Springs, 1987-94, prof., 1994—. Contbr. articles to profl. jours. Mem. Am. Phys. Soc., Am. Women in Sci. Office: Colo Coll Dept Physics 14 E Cache La Poudre St Colorado Springs CO 80903-3243

WHITTEN, MARY CARTER, secondary education educator, museum consultant; b. Lynchburg, Va., Nov. 12, 1963; d. Franklin Hardwell and Harriet Murrell (Jones) Whitten. BA in History, Agnes Scott Coll., Decatur, Ga., 1986; MEd in Social Scis., U. Ga., Athens, 1994. Cert. social sci. tchr., Ga., 1994. Edn. coord. Joel Chandler Harris Assn., Atlanta, 1986-87; edn. adminstr. Atlanta Hist. Soc., Inc., 1987-92; grad. asst. U. Ga. at Athens Edn. Initiative, 1992-94; secondary social sci. tchr. Atlanta Pub. Schs., 1994—; cons. Columbus (Ga.) Mus., 1988, co-chair North Ga. Mus. Educators, Atlanta, 1990-92. Vol. Ga. Spl. Olympics, Atlanta, 1990, 92, Athens Tutorial Program, 1994, Habitat for Humanity, 1995—, Atlanta Com. for the Olympic Games, 1996. Gov.'s intern, Ga. Mus. Art, 1993. Mem. Ga. Coun. for Social Scis., Kappa Delta Pi. Office: Henry W Grady High School 929 Charles Allen Dr Atlanta GA 30309

WHITTIER, GLORIA HERRICK, high school guidance counselor; b. Lewiston, Maine, Nov. 28, 1939; d. Lloyd Delbert and Gloria Nellie (Smith) Herrick; m. Glenn Harold Whittier, June 28, 1958; children: Erin Marie, Elin Coleen, Elisa Beth. BA with honors, U. Maine, Farmington, 1986; MS summa cum laude, U. So. Maine, Portland/Gorham, 1991. Cert. guidance counselor, Maine. Adminstrv. asst. Sch. Dept., Auburn, Maine, 1973-91; guidance dir., counselor Union 29, Poland, Maine, 1991—; chair Auburn Edn. Coun., 1973. Mem. Maine Sch. Counselors Assn., Poland Tchrs. Assn. (guidance chair 1991—), Order Eastern Star, Psi Chi, Phi Theta Kappa. Republican. Home: 36 Oxford St Auburn ME 04210-3726 Office: Poland Cmty Sch 1250 Maine St Poland ME 04274

WHITTLESEY, ANGELA TERI, children's counseler, consultant; b. Bellvue, Wash., Feb. 19, 1969; d. Terry Ugene and Dianne Nettie (Richmond) W. AA in Bus. Adminstrn., Cabrillo C.C., Aptis, Calif., 1990; BA in Child Devel., San Jose State U., 1994, postgrad., 1994—. Exec. sec. Automotive Mgmt. Group, Santa Cruz, Calif., 1987-92; adminstrv. asst. Ireland San Filippo & Co., San Jose, Calif., 1992-94; activities cons. Children's Shelter, San Jose, Calif., 1992-94, activities coord., 1994—, children's counselor, 1995—; cons. Children's Shelter Assn., San Jose, 1994—. Vol. Jr. League San Jose, 1995.

WHITTLESEY, JUDITH HOLLOWAY, public relations executive; b. Bartlesville, Okla., Dec. 28, 1942; d. Harry Haynes and Suzanne (Arnote) Holloway; m. Dennis Jeffrey Whittlesey, Aug. 3, 1968; children: Kristin Arnote, Kevin Jeffrey. BA, U. Okla., 1964; postgrad., Tulsa U., 1965, U. Va., 1971-72. Staff aide Office of the V.P. of U.S., Washington, 1979-81, Com. for Future of Am., Washington, 1981-82; dep. dir. scheduling and advance Mondale-Ferraro Campaign, Washington, 1982-84; dir. media rels. The Susan Davis Cos., Washington, 1986-87, v.p., 1987-88, exec. v.p., 1988—. Bd. dirs. Cultural Alliance of Greater Washington, 1983-93, Washington Project for the Arts, 1987-93, Levine Sch. Music, 1993—, Food Rsch. and Action Ctr., 1993—; mem. Decatur house coun. Chevy Chase Presbyn. Ch., Washington. Recipient numerous Mercury and Anvil awards. Office: Susan Davis Internat 1000 Vermont Ave NW Washington DC 20005

WHITWORTH, ELAINE ATKINS, counselor; b. Carrollton, Ga., June 16, 1945; d. Dewey D. and Estelle (Lovvorn) Atkins; m. William Lee Whitworth, June 11, 1966 (div. Apr. 1985); children: Kim, Lee. BS in Edn., West Ga. Coll., 1966, Ed. Specialist, 1993; BS in Psychology, Kennesaw State Coll., 1986; MSW, U. Ga., 1988. Cert. sch. counselor; lic. master social worker; lic. profl. counselor; nat. bd. cert. counselor. Practicum case mgr. Ga. Mental Health Inst., 1987-88, mental health technician, 1988-89; Devereaux therapist North Met. Counseling, Marietta, Ga., 1988-90; spl. edn. tchr. Cobb County Schs., Kennesaw, 1990; counselor New Dawn Counseling, Kennesaw, 1990—, Cobb County Schs., Acworth, Ga., 1991—. Vol. group leader Ga. Coun. on Child Abuse, Atlanta, 1994. Recipient hon. award Kennesaw Alumni Assn., 1987. Mem. Psi Chi. Democrat. Episcopalian. Office: New Dawn Counseling 2931 Lewis St Kennesaw GA 30144

WHITWORTH, KATHRYNNE ANN, professional golfer; b. Monahans, Tex., Sept. 27, 1939; d. Morris Clark and Dama Ann (Robinson) W. Student, Odessa (Tex.) Jr. Coll., 1958. Joined tour Ladies Profl. Golf Assn., 1959—; mem. adv. staff Walter Hagen Golf Co., Wilson Sporting Goods Co. Named to Hall of Fame Ladies Profl. Golf Assn., Tex. Sports Hall of Fame, Tex. Golf Hall of Fame, World Golf Hall of Fame; Capt. of Solheim Cup, 1990-92. Mem. Ladies Profl. Golf Assn. (sec. 1962-63, v.p. 1965, 73, 88, pres. 1967, 68, 71, 89, 1st mem. to win over $1,000,000). Office: care Ladies Profl Golf Assn 2570 Volusia Ave Daytona Beach FL 32114-1119

WHYTE-BANKS, HILA JANE, communication technician; b. St. Joseph, Mo., Oct. 21, 1949; d. Everett Louis and Janet Lee (Biggerstaff) Whyte; m. Henry Lee Clark, Feb. 19, 1980 (div. Mar. 1984); children: Haléa Lanay Clark, Heather Lynn Clark; m. Robert Banks Jr., Jan. 2, 1985; 1 child, Robert Banks III. Student, Tarkio Coll., 1967-69; BA, Calif. State U., San Diego, 1972. Mail aide U.S. Post Office, San Diego, 1970-72; order typist Pacific Bell, San Diego, 1972-74, staff clk., 1974-78, frame attendant, 1978-80, communication technician, 1980—; factory worker Whittaker Cable Corp., St. Joseph, summer 1969; illustrator, comedy writer, dramatic writer Reflections of Real Life, San Diego, 1990—. Author musical play, song. 0in. music Antioch Ch. of God in Christ, San Diego, 1976-86, Christian Compassion Ctr., San Diego, 1987—; singer Patrick White Singers, San Diego, 1982—; singer Cox Cable TV, Christian Compassion Ctr., San Diego, 1988—, corp. officer, sec.-treas., 1993-95. Scholar Tarkio Coll., 1967. Mem. Word of Faith Ch. Office: Reflections of Real Life PO Box 740422 San Diego CA 92174-0422

WIANT, SARAH KIRSTEN, law library administrator, educator; b. Waverly, Iowa, Nov. 20, 1946; s. James Allen and Eva (Jorgensen) W.; m. Robert E. Akins. BA, Western State Coll., 1968; MLS, U. North Tex., 1970; JD, Washington & Lee U., 1978. Asst. law librarian Tex. Tech U., 1970-72; asst. law librarian Washington & Lee U., 1972—, dir., 1978—, asst. prof. law, 1978-83, assoc. prof. law, 1984-92, prof. law, 1993—. Co-author: Copyright Handbook, 1984, Libraries and Copyright: A Guide to Copyright Law in the 1990s, 1994 Legal Research In the District of Columbia, Maryland and Virginia, 1995; contbr. chpts. to books; mem. adv. bd. Westlaw, 1990-93. Mem. ABA (com. on libraries 1987-93), Am. Assn. Law Libraries (program chmn. for ann. meeting 1987, copyright office rep.), Am. Law Sch. (chmn. sec. on librs. 1990-92, accreditation com. 1991-94), Spl. Libraries Assn. (chair copyright com. 1990—), Maritime Law Assn., U.S. Trademark Assn. Office: Washington & Lee U Law Libr Lewis Hall Lexington VA 24450

WIBKER, SUSAN GAYLE, lawyer; b. Shreveport, La., Apr. 8, 1952; d. Robert William and Audrey (Hill) W. BS, Northwestern State U., Natchitoches, La., 1974, MS, 1979; JD, U. Mich., 1991. Bar: Alaska 1992, D.C. 1993. Mental health counselor, Washington and, Alaska, 1979-88; asst. dist. atty. Dist. Atty.'s Office, Anchorage, 1991—. Home: 1440 E St Apt 1 Anchorage AK 99501 Office: Dist Atty's Office 310 K St Ste 600 Anchorage AK 99501

WICK, SISTER MARGARET, college administrator; b. Sibley, Iowa, June 30, 1942. BA in Sociology, Briar Cliff Coll., 1965; MA in Sociology, Loyola U., Chgo., 1971; PhD in Higher Edn., U. Denver, 1976. Instr. sociology Briar Cliff Coll., Sioux City, Iowa, 1966-71, dir. academic advising, 1971-72, v.p., acad. dean, 1972-74, 76-84, pres., 1987—; pres. Colls. of Mid-Am., 1985-87; bd. dirs. Boatmen's Bank, Sioux City. Bd. dirs. Mary J. Treglia Cmty. House, 1976-84, Marian Health Ctr., 1987—, Iowa Pub. TV, 1987-95. Mem. North Ctrl. Edn. Assn. (cons.-evaluator for accrediting teams 1980-84, 89—), Siouxland Initiative (adv. bd.), Assn. Cath. Colls. and Univs. (bd. dirs.), Quota Internat., Rotary. Home: 75 W Clifton Ave Apt 113 Sioux City IA 51104-2132 Office: Briar Cliff Coll Office of the President 3303 Rebecca St Sioux City IA 51104-2100

WICKER, JANET FRANCES, police officer; b. Aug. 19, 1955; d. Henry Joseph and Eleanor (Shutsy) Michalowski; divorced; 1 child, Scott. Assoc. in Police Sci., Lorain C.C., Elyria, Ohio, 1975. Cert. sr. operator breathalyzer; cert. instr. Ohio peace officer basic tng. program; cert. intoxilyzer calibration technician. Dispatcher Oberlin (Ohio) Police Dept., 1974-75; undercover narcotic agt. Met. Enforcement Group, Lorain, Ohio, 1976; security officer St. Joseph Hosp., Lorain, 1978-83, 85-87; police officer Milan (Ohio) Police Dept., 1983-88, Avon (Ohio) Police Dept., 1988—. DARE instr., 1989, 90, 91. Recipient Women of Distinction award Lake Erie Girl Scout Coun., 1992. Office: Avon Police Dept 36774 Detroit Rd Avon OH 44011

WICKER, MARIE PEACHEE, civic worker; b. Detroit, July 9, 1925; d. Charles Andrew and Bessie Louise (Sullivan) Peachee; m. Warren Jake Wicker, July 31, 1948; children: Beth Wicker Walters, Jane Fields Wicker-Miurin, Thomas Alton. BA, Westhampton Coll., 1946; MA, U. N.C., 1950. Test technician N.C. Merit System Coun., Durham, 1950-51; classification analyst N.C. Personnel Dept., Raleigh, 1951-52; engring. placement dir. N.C. State U., Raleigh, 1952-57. Author: You Can Make It Yourself, 1988, First Women of Orange County, N.C., 1994, 2d edit., 1995, A History of the Chapel Hill Woman's Club, 1910-1995, 1995. Chmn. Chapel Hill Recreation Commn., 1961-62; legis. chmn. N.C. Congress Parents and Tchrs., 1972-73; mem. Chapel Hill-Carrboro Bd. Edn., 1973-75, Historic Hillsborough (N.C.) Commn., 1987-93. Recipient Dist. Conservation award N.C. Wildlife Resources Commn., 1987. Mem. N.C. Fedn. Women's Clubs (dist. pres. 1984-86, dist. chmn. conservation dept. 1992-94, state chmn. conservation dept. 1992-94, sec.-treas. past dist. pres. club 1992-94, Sallie Southall Cotten scholarship com. 1994—), N.C. Coun. Women's Orgns. (bd. dirs. 1990, 1st v.p. 1992-93), Chapel Hill Women's Club (pres. 1985-87, 1st v.p. 1996-98), Orange County Commn. for Women. Democrat. Home: 1024 Highland Woods Rd Chapel Hill NC 27514-4410

WICKHAM, KATHLEEN WOODRUFF, educator; b. Wilson Boro, Pa., May 31, 1949; d. Ralph E. and Ann Mary (Korp) Woodruff; m. Peter Kuntz Wickham Jr., Sept. 30, 1978; children: Matthew Peter, Timothy Kuntz. BA, Glassboro State Coll., 1971; MA, Memphis State U., 1987. Reporter The Daily Advance, Dover, N.J., 1971-75, The Press, Atlantic City, N.J., 1975-77, The Star-Ledger, Newark, 1977-81; instr. U. Memphis, 1983—; presenter in field. Contbr. articles to newspapers, mags. and jours. Mem. adv. bd. Boling Ctr. Devel. Disabilities, U. Tenn., 1991-94. Mem. Nat. Headliner Club, Autism Soc. Am. (Memphis chpt. pres. 1988-89, v.p. 1987-88, sec. 1994-96, state conf. co-chair 1989, 92, 95, newsletter editor 1988-92, Tenn. state soc. pres. 1989-90, v.p. 1987-89, treas. 1993-95), Soc. Profl. Journalists, Investigative Reporters and Editors, Kappa Tau Alpha. Office: U Memphis Meeman Journalism Bldg Memphis TN 38152

WICKHAM-ST. GERMAIN, MARGARET EDNA, mass spectrometrist; b. Kansas City, Mo., June 7, 1956; d. Ronald Lee and Mary Ann (Nicholas) Wickham; m. Christopher Newman St. Germain, June 11, 1988; 1 child, Mark Anthony. BS in Chemistry, St. Mary Coll., Leavenworth, Kans., 1978; student, U. Mo., 1979-80, 1994—. Lab. technician VA Hosp., Kansas City, 1977; jr. chemist Midwest Rsch. Inst., Kansas City, 1978-80, jr. mass spectrometrist, 1980-81, asst. mass spectrometrist, 1981-85, assoc. mass spectrometrist, 1985-86, mass spectrometrist, 1986-90, sr. mass spectrometrist, 1990-94; owner Wickham Sci. Svcs., 1994—; chemist EPA Region 7, Kansas City, Kans., 1994—. Co-author: Priority Pollutants, 1983; author: Method Development for VOST Fractionator, 1994. Active Mid-Continent coun. Girl Scouts U.S., 1962—, St. Bernadette's Ch., Kansas City, 1986—. Mem. Am. Chem. Soc. (mem. nat. younger chemist com. 1988-91, chair memberships com. Kansas City chpt. 1979-80, sec. 1984, chair-elect 1985, chair 1986, past chair 1987, chair chemistry conf. 1989, founding mem. regional younger chemist com. 1990—, Chemagro Essay award 1977, 78), Am. Soc. for Mass Spectrometry, Soc. for Applied Spectroscopy, Air & Waste Mgmt. Assn., Kappa Gamma Pi (Excellence award 1978), Delta Epsilon Sigma (Excellence award 1978). Office: Wickham Sci Svcs 9102 E 50th Ter Kansas City MO 64133-2120

WICKIZER, CINDY LOUISE, elementary school educator; b. Pitts., Dec. 12, 1946; d. Charles Sr. and Gloria Geraldine (Cassidy) Zimmerman; m. Leon Leonard Wickizer, Mar. 21, 1971; 1 child, Charlyn Michelle. BS, Oreg. State U., 1968. Tchr. Enumclaw (Wash.) Sch. Dist., 1968—. Mem. NEA, Wash. Edn. Assn., Enumclaw Edn. Assn., Buckley C. of C., Wash. Contract Loggers Assn., Am. Rabbit Breeders Assn. (judge, chmn. scholarship found. 1986-87, pres. 1988-94, dist. dir. 1994-96, Disting. Svc. award 1987), Wash. State Rabbit Breeders Assn. (life, Pres.'s award 1983, 94, sec., dir., v.p. 1995—), Vancouver Island Rabbit Breeders Assn., Wash. State Rabbit and Cavy Shows Inc. (sec. 1994—), Evergreen Rabbit Assn. (sec., v.p., pres.), Alpha Gamma Delta. Home: 26513 112th St E Buckley WA 98321-9258

WICKIZER, MARY ALICE See BURGESS, MARY ALICE

WICKLINE, MARIAN ELIZABETH, former chemical librarian; b. St. Louis, Feb. 18, 1915; d. William Anderson and Grace B. (Gooding) W. BA, Mills Coll., 1935; postgrad., U. Calif., Berkeley, 1935-37. Tech. files asst. Shell Devel. Co., San Francisco, 1938-45; libr. western div. Dow Chem. Co., Pitts. and Walnut Creek, Calif., 1945-75; ret., 1975. Mem. Planning Commn., Danville, Calif., 1982-86, El Dorado County Libr. Commn., Placerville, Calif., 1989-92, policy adv. com. gen. plan, 1989-92; bd. dirs. Greenstone Country Cmty. Svcs. Dist., 1994—. Named Woman of Yr. San Ramon Valley C. of C., Danville, Calif., 1983. Mem. AAUW (Gift Honoree 1982, 84), Am. Chem. Soc., Spl. Libr. Assn. (pres. San Francisco Bay region chpt. 1973-74, chair chemistry divsn. 1970-71). Home: 5474 Comstock Rd Placerville CA 95667-8712

WICKWIRE, PATRICIA JOANNE NELLOR, psychologist, educator; b. Sioux City, Iowa; d. William McKinley and Clara Rose (Pautsch) Nellor; m. Robert James Wickwire, Sept. 7, 1957; 1 child, William James. BA cum laude, U. No. Iowa, 1951; MA, U. Iowa, 1959; PhD, U. Tex., Austin, 1971; postgrad. U. So. Calif., UCLA, Calif. State U., Long Beach, 1951-66. Tchr., Ricketts Ind. Schs., Iowa, 1946-48; tchr., counselor Waverly-Shell Rock Ind. Schs., Iowa, 1951-55; reading cons., head dormitory counselor U. Iowa, Iowa City, 1955-57; tchr., sch. psychologist, adminstr. S. Bay Union High Sch. Dist., Redondo Beach, Calif., 1962-82, dir. student svcs. and spl. edn.; cons. mgmt. and edn.; pres. Nellor Wickwire Group, 1981—; mem. exec. bd. Calif. Interagency Mental Health Coun., 1968-72, Beach Cities Symphony Assn., 1970-82; chmn. Friends of Dominguez Hills (Calif.), 1981-85. Lic. ednl. psychologist, marriage, family and child counselor, Calif.; pres. Calif. Women's Caucus, 1993-95. Mem. APA, AAUW (exec. bd., chpt. pres. 1962-72), Nat. Career Devel. Assn. (media chair 1992—), Am. Assn. Career Edn. (pres. 1991—), L.A. County Dirs. Pupil Svcs. (chmn. 1974-79), L.A. County Personnel and Guidance Assn. (pres. 1977-78), Assn. Calif. Sch. Adminstrs. (dir. 1977-81), L.A. County SW Bd. Dist. Adminstrs. for Spl. Edn. (chmn. 1976-81), Calif. Assn. Sch. Psychologists (bd. dirs. 1981-83), Am. Assn. Sch. Adminstrs., Calif. Assn. for Measurement and Evaluation in Guidance (dir.

1981, pres. 1984-85), ACA (chmn. Coun. Newsletter Editors 1989-91, mem. com. on women 1989-92, mem. com. on rsch. and knowledge, 1994—, chmn. 1995—, chmn. 1996—), Assn. Measurement and Eval. in Guidance (Western regional editor 1985-87, conv. chair 1986, editor 1987-90, exec. bd. dirs. 1987-91), Calif. Assn. Counseling and Devel. (exec. bd. 1984—, pres. 1988-89, jour. editor 1990—), Internat. Career Assn. Network (chair 1985—), Pi Lambda Theta, Alpha Phi Gamma, Psi Chi, Kappa Delta Pi, Sigma Alpha Iota. Contbr. articles in field to profl. jours. Office: Calif Assn Counseling 2555 E Chapman Ave Ste 201 Fullerton CA 92631

WIDENER, PERI ANN, business development executive; b. Wichita, Kans., May 1, 1956; d. Wayne Robert and LuAnne (Harris) W. BS, Wichita State U., 1978; MBA, Fla. Tech., 1992. Advt. intern Associated Advt., Wichita, 1978; pub. rels. asst. Fourth Nat. Bank, Wichita, 1978-79; mktg. communications rep. Boeing Co., Wichita, 1979-83, pub. rels. rep., Huntsville, Ala., 1983-85, pub. rels. mgr., 1985-92; sr. pub. rels. mgr. Boeing Mil. Airplanes, Seattle, 1992-95; bus. devel. mgr. Boeing Defense & Space Group, Washington, D.C., 1995—. mem. exec. devel. program Boeing Def. & Space Group, 1993—. Preston Huston scholar, Wichita State U., 1978; recipient Best Electronic Ad award Def. Electronics mag., 1982, Best Total Pub. Rels. Program award Huntsville Press Club, 1985, Huntsville Media awards, 1986, 87, 88, 89, 90, 91, Huntsville Advt. Fedn. Addys, 1988. Mem. Pub. Rels. Soc. Am. (Seattle chpt.), Women in Communications, Pub. Rels. Coun. Ala. (bd. dirs. 1985-92, state pres. 1992, officer Huntsville chpt. 1984-91, pres. No. Ala. chpt. 1989, Excellence award 1986-91, Achievement award 1986-91, Pres.'s award Huntsville chpt. 1985, State Practitioner of Yr. 1989, PRCA Medallion award excellence, numerous others), Internat. Assn. Bus. Communicators (D2 Silver Quills award 1985, 91, D6 Silver Quills 1993, 94), Pub. Rels. Soc. Am. (accredited 1989—), So. Pub. Rels. Fedn. (practitioner of yr. 1991, Excellence award 1986-91, Lantern award 1991), Huntsville-Madison County C. of C. (pub. rels. adv. com. 1987-92), Huntsville Press Club (bd. dirs. 1989-92), Sigma Delta Chi (pres.'s award 1991). Methodist. Office: The Boeing Co 1700 N Moore 20th Fl Arlington VA 22209

WIDER, DORINDA LEA, lawyer; b. Deer River, Minn., Mar. 16, 1952; d. Austin Albert and Betty Mae (Robertson) W. BA in History, Ft. Wright Coll. Holy Names, 1974; postgrad., U. Wash., 1979-81; JD, Hamline U., 1984. Bar: Minn. 1984, U.S. Fed. Ct. 1984. Staff atty. Legal Aid Soc. Mpls., 1984—. Active planning com. Am. Indian Rsch. and Policy Inst., Hamline U., St. Paul, 1992-93, Hamline Law Alumni of Color Coun., St. Paul, 1992-95, HUD Occupany Task Force, Washington, 1993-95; bd. mem. Nat. Legal Svcs. Homelessnes Task Force, Washington, 1993—, Minn. Housing Partnership, Mpls., 1995—. Recipient Disting. Svc. award Minn. Coalition for Homeless, Mpls., 1992. Mem. Hennepin County Bar Assn. Office: Legal Aid Soc Mpls 430 1st Ave N Ste 300 Minneapolis MN 55401

WIDLUS, HANNAH BEVERLY, lawyer; b. Montreal, Quebec, Can., Jan. 23, 1955; d. William Jayson and Martha (Klein) Widlus; m. Moses W. Gaynor, Dec. 20, 1986. BSBA cum laude, Miami U., Oxford, Ohio, 1976; JD with honors, George Washington U., 1979. Bar: Tex. 1979, N.Y. 1984, Ill. 1988, D.C. 1990. Assoc. Johnson & Gibbs (formerly Johnson, Swanson & Barbee), Dallas, 1979-82, Proskauer Rose Goetz & Mendelsohn, N.Y.C., 1982-83, Patterson, Belknap, Webb & Tyler, N.Y.C., 1983-86; assoc. Kirkland & Ellis, Chgo., 1987-88, ptnr., 1988-91; counsel benefits Waste Management, Inc., Oak Brook, Ill., 1991-94; assoc. D'Ancona & Pflaum, Chgo., 1994—; lectr. on pension and profit sharing plans, 1988-92; seminar on employment regulations in Ill., 1987-91, seminar on basic employee benefits, 1988-90, NYU 45th Ann. Inst. on Fed. Taxation, 1986, inst. for paralegal studies NYU Sch. Continuing Edn., 1984-86, tax seminar Dallas Gen. Agts. and Mgrs. Assn., 1980, 81, Corpus Christi chpt. Tex. Soc. CPAs, 1981, sect. taxation Dallas Bar Assn., 1980. Contbr. articles to profl. jours. Mem. ABA (sect. taxation), State Bar Tex., State Bar N.Y., Ill. Bar, D.C. Bar. Jewish.

WIDMANN, NANCY C., broadcast executive. Pres. radio divsn. CBS, N.Y.C., 1988—, sr. v.p. I-Mark syndication divsn., 1996—. Office: CBS Radio Networks 51 W 52d St New York NY 10019-2902*

WIDSETH, JANE CHRISTINA, psychologist, psychotherapist; b. Mpls., Oct. 14, 1942; d. Edwin Clarance and Janet Christine (Hart) W.; m. Robert Bruce Partridge II, Aug. 28, 1976; children: John Ditton Widseth Partridge, Carl Erik Widseth Partridge. BA, U. Minn., 1964; AM, Boston U., 1966, PhD, 1972. Lic. psychologist, Pa. Psychol. counselor Haverford (Pa.) Coll., 1970-72, dir. counseling, 1972-84, psychol. counselor, 1984—; vol. counselor Univ. Counseling Svcs., Cambridge, Eng., 1986; pvt. practice psychotherapy, Haverford, 1972—; bd. dirs. Phila. Ctr. for Psychoanalytic Edn., 1993—, pres., 1996—. Contbr. articles to profl. jours. Fellow Pa. Psychol. Assn.; mem. APA, Internat. Soc. for Study Dissociation, Phila. Soc. Clin. Psychologists, Phila. Soc. for Psychoanalytic Psychology (past pres.), Haverford Faculty Swimming Club (bd. dirs. 1988-92, treas. 1988-90), Phi Beta Kappa. Office: Haverford Coll Psychol Svcs Ctr Haverford PA 19041

WIEBENSON, DORA LOUISE, architectural historian, educator, author; b. Cleve., July 29, 1926; d. Edward Ralph and Jeannette (Rodier) W. BA, Vassar Coll., 1946; MArch, Harvard U., 1951; MA, NYU, 1958, PhD, 1964. Architect N.Y., 1951-66; lectr. Columbia U., 1966-68; assoc. prof. U. Md., 1968-72, prof., 1972-77; vis. prof. Cornell U., 1974; prof. U. Va., Charlottesville, 1977-92, prof. emerita, 1992—, chmn. div. archtl. history, 1977-79, assoc. fellow U. Va. Ctr. Advanced Studies, 1982-83; pres. Archtl. Publs., N.Y.C., 1982—. Editor: Marsyas XI: 1962-64, 1965, Essays in Honor of Walter Friedlaender, 1965; Architectural Theory and Practice from Alberti to Ledoux, 1982, rev., 1983, Spanish transl., 1988; Guide to Graduate Degree Programs in Architectural History, 1982, rev., 1984, 86, 88, 90; author: Sources of Greek Revival Architecture, 1969, Tony Garnier: The Cité Industrielle, 1969, Japanese transl., 1983, The Picturesque Garden in France, 1978, Mark J. Millard Architectural Collection, Vol. I: French Books: Sixteenth through Nineteenth Centuries, 1993; contbr. articles to profl. jours. Student fellow Inst. Fine Arts, 1961-62, 62-63; grantee Am. Philos. Soc., 1964-65, 70, Samuel H. Kress Found., 1966, Gen. Rsch. Fund, U. Md., 1969, 74, 76, NEH, 1972-73, Samuel H. Kress Found., 1972-73, Am. Coun. Learned Socs., 1976, 81, 85, Ctr. Advanced Studies, U. Va., 1980, 81, Graham Found. Advanced Studies Fine Arts, 1982, 93; fellow Yale Ctr. Brit. Art, 1983; sr. rsch. fellow NEH, 1986-87, Archtl. History Found., 1996. Mem. Soc. Archtl. Historians (bd. dirs. 1974-77, 80-83, chair edn. com. 1976-90), Coll. Art Assn., Am. Soc. Eighteenth Century (mem. exec. bd. 1991-94).

WIEBERS, DAWN RAE, secondary education educator; b. Viborg, S.D., Apr. 10, 1963; d. Dean A. and Carolina R. (Meyer) W. BS in Edn., Dakota State U., 1986. Cert. tchr., Kans. Tchr. Healy (Kans.) H.S., 1987-90, Peabody (Kans.) H.S., 1990-92, Otis (Kans.)-Bison H.S., 1992—; ind. devel. plan chairperson Otis, 1993—; quality performance accreditation chairperson Unified Sch. Dist. 403, Otis, 1993—. Active Jaycees, Bonner Springs, Kans., 1993. Mem. Otis-Bison Tchr. Assn. (sec.-treas. 1993—). Home: PO Box 335 Otis KS 67565-0335

WIECEK, BARBARA HARRIET, advertising executive; b. Chgo., Mar. 30, 1956; d. Stanley Joseph and Irene (Zagajewski) W. AA, Am. Acad. of Art, Chgo., 1977. Illustrator Clinton E. Frank Advt., Chgo., 1977-78, art dir., 1978-80, assoc. creative dir., 1980-84, v.p.; instr. Am. Acad. of Art, Chgo., 1977-80; assoc. creative dir. Tatham, Laird & Kudner, 1984—; ptnr. Tatham, Laird & Kudner, Chgo., 1986—, creative dir., 1987—, sr. ptnr., 1995—, exec. creative dir., 1996. Recipient Silver Awd. Internat. Film Festival of N.Y., 1981, Gold Awd. Internat. Film Festival of N.Y., 1981. Roman Catholic. Office: Tatham Euro RSCG 980 N Michigan Ave Chicago IL 60611-4501

WIEDEMANN, RAMONA DIANE, occupational therapist; b. Topeka, Kans., Oct. 1, 1962; d. John Daniel Fay and Sue Ann (Strotman) Fuller; m. William Newell Wiedemann, Aug. 9, 1986; children: William Jr., Meaghan, Nathaniel, Emily. BS in Occupl. Therapy, Tex. Woman's U., 1988. Occupl. therapist Healthcare Staff Resources, Dallas, 1988-91, Associated Rehab. Svcs., Greenville, Tex., 1991-96, 1st Rehab., Ft. Worth, 1996—. Mem. Am. Occupl. Therapy Assn. Republican. Methodist. Home: 210 Winding Creek Dr Highland Village TX 75067 Office: 1st Rehab 815 8th Ave Fort Worth TX 76104

WIEDENHOEFT, ANN MARIE, psychotherapist, consultant; b. Ladysmith, Wis., Feb. 16, 1938; d. Anton John and Josephine (Calmes) Schmirler; m. Gilbert John Wiedenhoeft, Nov. 29, 1958; children: Susan, Frances, Nicholas, Mathew. BSW, U. Wis., 1984; MA, St. Mary's Coll., 1987. Lic. clin. social worker, Minn. Group facilitator Family Svc., St. Paul, 1984-87, psychotherapist, 1987-90; pvt. practice St. Paul, 1990—; cons. Parents Anonymous Minn., St. Paul, 1985-87, 91, Capitol Community Ctr., St. Paul, 1987-90. Active Girl Scouts U.S., Stevens Point, Wis., 1966-70; mem. LWV, Madison, Wis., 1972-76; pres. PTA, Madison, 1972-75. Mem. NASW, Phi Eta Sigma.

WIEDERRICK, ALBERTA, district court clerk; b. Challis, Idaho, Jan. 24, 1940; d. S. Earl and Hazel H. (Santee) White; m. Robert A. Wiederrick, Oct. 29, 1960; children: Lori L. Holkan, Robert E., James D. Student, U. Idaho, Moscow, 1958-59; diploma in acctg., Grimms Bus. Coll., Pocatello, Idaho, 1959. Full charge bookkeeper Havemann Hardware, Salmon, Idaho, 1959-62; mem. temp. staff Kelly Girls, Tucson, Ariz., 1964-66; cashier Army-Air Force Exch., Shepard AFB, Tex., 1973; mem. staff acctg. office Army-Air Force Exch., Shepard AFB, 1973-74, supr. stockroom, 1974-76; dep. clk. Lemhi County Dist. Ct., Salmon, Idaho, 1978-82; clk. Lemhi County Dist. Ct., 1982—. Mem. Lemhi County Reps., 1982-96, Gov.'s Task Force Idaho Med. Assistance Program, Boise, 1993; elder, clk. of session Cmty. Presbyn. Ch., 1978-92; sec., treas. Youth Employment Program, 1995-96. Mem. Nat. Assn. County Rep. Officials, Nat. Assn. Counties (intergovtl. rels. steering com. 1985-96), Idaho Assn. Counties (bd. dirs., 1989-90, health and human svcs. com. 1985—), Idaho Assn. County Recorders and Clks. (pres., v.p., sec. 1987-90), Eagles (pres. 1979-81), Anna Rebekah, Rotary Club of Salmon (v.p.). Office: Lemhi County 206 Courthouse Dr Salmon ID 83467

WIEGAND, JULIE WILDS, gifted education educator; b. Galesburg, Ill., Apr. 14, 1954; d. John Wilson and Helen Arletta (Mitchell) Wilds; m. Michael Anthony Wiegand, Nov. 10, 1984; 1 child, Joseph Michael. BS, Ill. State U., 1975. Substitute tchr. Normal/Bloomington (Ill.) Schs., 1975-77; tchr. Immaculate Conception, Monmouth, Ill., 1977-79, CUSD #205, Galesburg, Ill., 1979—. Pres., sec., treas., parliamentarian Galesburg Jr. Woman's Club, 1980—; treas., sec. Ill. Fedn. of Women's Clubs, 1989-92. Mem. Galesburg Edn. Assn. (treas. 1981-85), Phi Delta Kappa (annual fund, rsch. rep. 1989-91). Democrat. Lutheran. Home: 1173 N Academy St Galesburg IL 61401-2646 Office: Gale Sch 1131 W Dayton St Galesburg IL 61401-1507

WIEGAND, SYLVIA MARGARET, mathematician, educator; b. Cape Town, South Africa, Mar. 8, 1945; came to U.S., 1949; d. Laurence Chisholm and Joan Elizabeth (Dunnett) Young; m. Roger Allan Wiegand, Aug. 27, 1966; children: David Chisholm, Andrea Elizabeth. AB, Bryn Mawr Coll., 1966; MA, U. Wash., 1967; PhD, U. Wis., Madison, 1972. Mem. faculty U. Nebr., Lincoln, 1967—, now prof. math.; vis. assoc. prof. U. Conn., Storrs, 1978-79, U. Wis., Madison, 1985-86; vis. prof. Purdue U., 1992-93. Editor Communications in Algebra jour., 1990, Rocky Mountain Jour. Math., 1991—; contbr. rsch. articles to profl. jours. Troop leader Lincoln area Girl Scouts U.S., 1988-92. Grantee NSF, 1985-88, 90-93, Vis. Professorship for Women, 1992, Nat. Security Agy.. Mem. AAUP, Am. Math. Soc. (mem.-at-large, coun.), Assn. Women in Math (pres.-elect 1995-96, pres. 1997-98), London Math. Soc., Math. Assn. Am. Office: U Nebr Dept Math Lincoln NE 68588-0323

WIELE, PATRICIA GIORDANO, interior decorator; b. Houston, Aug. 29, 1947; d. Conrad Joseph and Ellen Patricia (Condon) Schoppe; m. Natale Joseph Giordano, Apr. 17, 1971 (dec. Sept. 1989); children: Keith Joseph, Michael David, Ryan Peter, Todd Christopher. Student, U. Houston, 1965-67, NYU, 1969. Prin. Patricia S. Giordano Interiors, Ridgefield, Conn., 1975-94, Patricia G. Wiele Interiors, Los Gatos, Calif., 1994—; pub. speaker various floral design and horticulture workshops. Bd. dirs. Family and Children's Aid, Inc., Danbury, Conn., 1976-78, program and rev. and nominating coms., 1978, head pub. rels. com., 1978-79, pres. aux., 1976-79; v.p. Twin Homeowner's Assn., Ridgefield, Conn., 1978-79, chmn., founder area beautification, 1978; pres. East Ridge Mid. Sch. PTO, 1988-89, PTA, 1991-92. Recipient award of Excellence Fed. Garden Clubs Conn., 1984, Tricolor award Nat. Council State Garden Clubs, 1984, Aboreal award Nat. Council State Garden Clubs, 1984, Hort. Excellence award Nat. Council State Garden Clubs, 1984. Mem. Allied Bd. Trade, Caudatowa Garden Club (v.p. 1987-89, 90-91, pres. 1991-93). Republican. Roman Catholic.

WIEMERS, KATHY LYN, chemist; b. Kearney, Nebr., Jan. 24, 1969; d. Lesley LaVerne and Janice Rae (Merrick) Wiemers; m. Bernard Robert Oleksa, Jr., Feb. 14, 1992 (div. June 1994); 1 child, Philip M. BJ, U. Nebr., 1991; BS, U. Nebr., Kearney, 1995. Mgmt. trainee Enterprise Rent-A-Car, Lincoln, 1991-92; teaching asst. in chemistry U. Mo., Columbia, 1995—. Editor Nebr. Blueprint, 1987-90; contbr. articles to Daily Nebraskan, 1990-91. Sr. Enhancement Fellow in Chemistry, U. Mo., 1995. Mem. NAFE, NOW, Am. Chem. Soc. Office: Univ of Missouri 123 Chemistry Bldg Columbia MO 65211

WIENCEK-DAMAS, DEBORAH ANN, medical sales manager, nurse; b. Cleve., Oct. 10, 1954; d. Joseph Robert and Rita Marie (Sterby) Wiencek; m. Steven James Damas, July 6, 1973; children: Denise Marie, Joseph Andrew, Andrew James. RN, St. Alexis Sch. Nursing, Cleve., 1986. Nurse Parma (Ohio) Cmty. Hosp., 1986-88; med. sales cons. Support Systems Internat., Charleston, S.C., 1988-92; account sales mgr. Coram Healthcare, Denver, 1992—; mem. adv. bd. Support Systems Internat., 1990-91, field sales trainer, 1990. Mem. N.E. Ohio Case Mgmt. Network (co-chair planning and edn. com. 1995, seminar com. 1994—). Home: 6803 Thornton Dr Parma OH 44129

WIENECKE, JANA L., social worker; b. Hannibal, Mo., Mar. 3, 1966; d. Ronald L. Kolthoff and Joyce A. (Keithley) McPherson; m. Gorden Craig Wienecke, Sept. 26, 1992. BS, Southwest Bapt. U., 1988; MEd, U. Mo., St. Louis, 1995. Head resident counselor Youth In Need, St. Charles, Mo., 1988-92; social worker Mo. Bapt. Children's Home, Bridgeton, Mo., 1992—. Mem. Am. Counseling Assn. Baptist. Office: Mo Bapt Childrens Home 11300 St Charles Rock Rd Bridgeton MO 63044

WIENER, ANNABELLE, United Nations official; b. N.Y.C., Aug. 2, 1922; d. Philip and Bertha (Wrubel) Kalbfeld; ed. Hunter Coll.; married, Jan. 1, 1941; children: Marilyn Grunewald, Marjorie Petit, Mark. Chmn. UN Dept. Pub. Info., Nongovtl. Orgns. Exec. Com., spl. adviser to sec. gen. Internat. Women's Year Conf.; mem. exec. bd. Nongovtl. Orgns. Com. on Disarmament UN, UN Dept. Pub. Info's NGO Exec. Com.; bd. dirs. World Fedn. UN Assns., also founder, dir. art and philatelic program; bd. dirs. N.Y. chpt. UN Assn.-USA; bd. dirs., chmn. UN Day Programme, So. N.Y. State Div., v.p. North Shore chpt.; mem. UN Dept. Pub. Info.'s Non-Govtl. Orgn. Exec. Com.; mem., bd. dir. Non-Govtl. Orgn. for UNICEF at UN Hdqrs. Recipient Diplomatic World Bull. award for Distinction in politics and diplomacy and svc. to high ideals of UN, 1989; apptd. dep. sec.-gen. World Fedn. UN Assns., 1991. Mem. Am. Fedn. Arts, Mus. Modern Art, Musee Nat. Message Biblique Marc Chagall, Am. Philatelic Soc., UN Philatelic Soc., UN Assn. U.S., UNO Philatelie, Fed. Republic Germany. Address: Dep Sec-Gen World Fedn UN Assns DC1-1177 United Nations New York NY 10017

WIENER, VALERIE, communications executive; b. Las Vegas, Nev., Oct. 30, 1948; d. Louis Isaac Wiener and Tui Ava Knight. BJ, U. Mo., 1971, MA, 1972; MA, U. Ill., Springfield, 1974; postgrad., McGeorge Sch. Law, 1976-79. Producer TV show "Checkpoint" Sta. KOMU-TV, Columbia, Mo., 1972-73; v.p., owner Broadcast Assocs., Inc., Las Vegas, 1972-86; pub. affairs dir. First Ill. Cable TV, Springfield, 1973-74; editor Ill. State Register, Springfield, 1973-74; producer and talent "Nevada Realities" Sta. KLVX-TV, Las Vegas, 1974-75; account exec. Sta. KBMI (now KFMS), Las Vegas, 1975-79; nat. traffic dir. six radio stas., Las Vegas, Albuquerque and El Paso, Tex., 1979-80; exec. v.p., gen. mgr. Stas. KXKS and KKJY, Albuquerque, 1980-81; exec. adminstr. Stas. KSET AM/FM, KVEG, KFMS and KKJY, 1981-83; press sec. U.S. Congressman Harry Reid, Washington, 1983-87; adminstrv. asst Friends for Harry Reid, Nev., 1986; press sec. U.S. Senator Harry Reid, Washington, 1987-88; owner Wiener Comm. Group, Las Vegas, 1988—. Author: Power Communications: Positioning Yourself for High Visibility (Fortune Book Club main selection 1994), Gang Free: Friendship Choices for Today's Youth, 1995; contbg. writer The Pacesetter, ASAE's Comm. News. Sponsor Futures for Children, Las Vegas, Albuquerque, El Paso, 1979-83; mem. El Paso Exec. Women's Coun., 1981-83; mem. VIP bd. Easter Seals, El Paso, 1982; media chmn. Gov.'s Coun. Small Bus., 1989-93, Clark Coun. Sch. Dist. and Bus. Cmty. PAYBAC Spkrs. and Partnership Programs, 1989—; med. dir. 1990 Conf. on Women, Gov. of Nev.; media chmn. Congl. Awards Coun., 1989-93; vice chmn. Gov.'s Commn. on Postsecondary Edn., 1992—; bd. dirs. BBB So. Nev. Named Outstanding Vol., United Way, El Paso, 1983, SBA Nev. Small Bus. Media Adv. of Yr., 1992; recipient Woman of Achievement in Media award, 1992, Outstanding Achievement award Nat. Fedn. Press Women, 1991, Disting. Leader award Nat. Assn. for Cmty. Leadership, 1993, over 106 other comm. awards. Mem. Nev. Press Women (numerous 1st place media awards 1990—), Nat. Spkrs. Assn., Nat. Assn. Women Bus. Owners (media chmn., nat. rep. So. Nev. 1990-91, Nev. Adv. of Yr. award 1992), Dem. Press Secs. Assn., El Paso Assn. Radio Stas., U.S. Senate Staff Club, Las Vegas C. of C. (Circle of Excellence award 1993), Soc. Profl. Journalists. Democrat. Office: 1500 Foremaster Ln Ste 2 Las Vegas NV 89101-1103

WIER, PATRICIA ANN, publishing executive, consultant; b. Coal Hill, Ark., Nov. 10, 1937; d. Horace L. and Bridget B. (McMahon) Norton; m. Richard A. Wier, Feb. 24, 1962; 1 child, Rebecca Ann. B.A., U. Mo., Kansas City, 1964; M.B.A., U. Chgo., 1978. Computer programmer AT&T, 1960-62; lead programmer City of Kansas City, Mo., 1963-65; with Playboy Enterprises, Chgo., 1965-71; mgr. systems and programming Playboy Enterprises, 1971; with Ency. Britannica, Inc., Chgo., 1971—; v.p. mgmt. svcs. Ency. Britannica USA, 1975-83, exec. v.p. adminstrn., 1983-84; v.p. planning and devel. Ency. Britannica, Inc., 1985, pres. Compton's Learning Co. div., 1985; pres. Ency. Britannica (USA), 1986-91, Ency. Britannica N.A., 1991-92; exec. v.p. Ency. Britannica, Inc., 1986-94; pres. Ency. Britannica N.Am., 1991-94; mgmt. cons. pvt. practice, Chgo., 1994—; lectr. mktg. U. Chgo. Grad. Sch. Bus., 1995—; cons. pvt. practice, Chgo., 1994—; bd. dirs. NICOR, Inc., Golden Rule Ins., Alcas Corp., Hurley State Bank; mem. coun. Northwestern U. Assocs. Mem. fin. Coun. Archdiocese of Chgo., Coun. of Grad. Sch. of Bus. U. of Chgo. Mem. Direct Selling Assn. (bd. dirs. 1984-93, chmn. 1987-88, named to Hall of Fame 1991), Women's Coun. U. Mo. Kansas City (hon. life) Com. 200, The Chgo. Network. Roman Catholic. Office: Patricia A Wier Inc 175 E Delaware Pl Apt 8305 Chicago IL 60611-1732

WIESE, DOROTHY JEAN, business educator; b. Chgo., Sept. 20, 1940; d. Charles Ennis Chapman and Evelyn Catherine Flizikowski; m. Wallace Jon Wiese, Oct. 10, 1959; children: Elizabeth Jean Wiese Christensen, Jonathan Charles. BS in Edn., No. Ill. U., 1970, MS in Edn., 1976, EdD, 1994. Tchr. bus. Hampshire (Ill.) High Sch., 1970-78; prof. bus. Elgin (Ill.) C.C., 1978—; cons. Gould, Inc., Rolling Meadows, Ill., 1984; instr. vocat. practicum McDonald's Hamburger U., Ofcl. Airline Guides, Oak Brook, Ill., 1986; spkr. SIEC, Sweden and Austria, 1987-88, Czech Republic, 1995, North Ctrl. Bus. Edn. Assn./Wis. Bus. Edn. Assn. Conv., 1992, Chgo. Ara Bus. Edn. Assn., 1992, AAUW, Batavia and Geneva, 1993, Elgin, 1996; 1995 Internat. Bus. Inst. for Cmty. Coll. faculty Mich. State U., 1995. Presented paper 34th annual Adult Edn. Rsch. Conf., Pa. State U., 1993. Mem., sec. N.W. Kane County (Ill.) Airport Authority, 1987-94; bd. dirs. St. Joseph Hosp. Found., 1995—, mem. adv. bd. Cancer Wellness and Resource Ctr., 1995—; host family Am. Intercultural Student Exch., 1989-90; presenter women's seminar Trinity Luth. Ch., Roselle, Ill., 1992. Mem. AAUW, Am. Women of Internat. Understanding (bd. dirs.), Nat. Bus. Edn. Assn. (internat. task force), Internat. Soc. Bus. Edn. (North Ctrl. Bus. Edn. Assn. rep. 1989-90, rep.-elect 1996), Societe Internat. pour l'Ensignment Commercial, Ill. Bus. Edn. Assn., Ill. Vocat. Assn., Women in Mgmt. (spkr. No. Fox Valley chpt. 1996), Delta Pi Epsilon (past historian Alpha Phi chpt.), Kappa Delta Pi. Lutheran. Office: Elgin CC 1700 Spartan Dr Elgin IL 60123-7189

WIESE, NEVA, critical care nurse; b. Hunter, Kans., July 23, 1940; d. Amil H. and Minnie (Zemke) W. Diploma, Grace Hosp. Sch. Nursing, Hutchinson, Kans., 1962; BA in Social Sci., U. Denver, 1971; BSN, Met. State Coll., 1975; MS in Nursing, U. Colo., Denvr, 1978; postgrad., U. N.Mex., 1986—. RN, N.Mex.; CCRN. Cardiac ICU nurse U. N.Mex. Hosp., Albuquerque; coord. critical care edn. St. Vincent Hosp., Santa Fe, charge nurse CCU, clin. nurse III intensive and cardiac care. Recipient Mary Atherton Meml. award for clin. excellence St. Vincent Hosp., 1986. Mem. ANA (cert. med. surg. nurse), AACN (past pres., sec. N.Mex. chpt., Clin. Excellence award 1991), N.Mex. League Nursing (past v.p., bd. dirs., sec., membership com. 1992—).

WIESENBERG, JACQUELINE LEONARDI, medical lecturer; b. West Haven, Conn., May 4, 1928; d. Curzio and Filomena Olga (Turrinziani) Leonardi; m. Russel John Wiesenberg, Nov. 23; children: James Wynne, Deborann Donna. BA, SUNY, Buffalo, 1970, postgrad., 1970-73, 80—. Interviewer, examiner U.S. Dept. Labor, New Haven, 1948-52; sec. W.I. Clark Co., Hamden, Conn., 1952-55; acct. VA Hosp., West Haven, 1956-60; acct.-commissary U.S. Air Force Missle Site, Niagara Falls, N.Y., 1961-62; tchr. Buffalo City Schs., 1970-73, 79; acct. Erie County Social Svcs., Buffalo, 1971-73; lectr., 1973—. Contbr. articles to CAP, U.S. Air Force mag., 1954—. Capt., Nat. Found. March of Dimes, 1969—, com. mem. telethon, 1983-86; den mother Boy Scouts Am., 1961-68; chmn. Meals on Wheels, Town of Amherst, 1975-76; leader, travel chmn. Girl Scouts Am., 1968-77; mem. Nat. Congress Parents and Tchrs., 1957—; heart fund vol. Heart Assn., 1960-86; rep. Am. Diabetes Assn., 1994—, vol. Diabetes collection, 1994-95. Mem. AAUW, NAFE, Internat. Platform Assn., Nat. Parks and Conservation Assn., Am. Astrol. Assn., Nat. Arbor Day Found., Western N.Y. Conf. Aging, Nat. Geographic Soc., The Wilderness Soc., Nat. Trust for Hist. Preservation, The Nature Conservancy, Epsilon Delta Chi, Alpha Iota. Home: 14 Norman Pl Amherst NY 14226-4233

WIESENFELD, BESS GAZEVITZ, business executive, real estate developer; b. Elizabeth, N.J., May 6, 1915; d. Morris and Rebecca (Sokolov) Gazevitz; m. Benjamin Wiesenfeld, Oct. 23, 1938 (dec.); children: Myra Judith Wiesenfeld Lewis, Elaine Phyllis Wiesenfeld Livingston, Ira Bertram (dec.), Sarah Ann Wiesenfeld Wasserman. BFA, N.Y. Sch. Design, N.Y.C., 1982. Pres. Anasarca Corp., 1958—; real estate devel. Colonia, N.J., 1961—; interior designer, 1961—; chair Bess & Co., Phila., 1982—; pres. Carolier Lns., Inc., 1986—. Patron Met. Opera; mem. pres.'s coun. Norton Gallery and Sch. Art, Inc.; sustaining mem. N.J. Symphony Orch. Mem. AAUW, Nat. Trust for Hist. Preservation (assoc.), Am. Soc. Interior Designers (allied mem.), Met. Mus. Art, Mus. Modern Art, Smithsonian Instn., Victorian Soc. Preservation, N.J., Inc., Friends of Art Mus. of Princeton N.J., Friends of Music at Princeton. Republican. Jewish. Home: 374 New Dover Rd Colonia NJ 07067-2713 also: 2600 S Ocean Blvd Palm Beach FL 33480

WIESINGER, CAROLYN KAY, nurse; b. Leavenworth, Kans., Jan. 9, 1967; d. Leo Joseph and Jeanne Lou (Chambers) W.; 1 child, Willow Corine Marion. LPN, Ivy Tech. State Coll., Valparaiso, Ind., 1995, student, 1996—. Home health aide Porter County Vis. Nurses, Valparaiso, 1993-95; pvt. duty nurse, Chesterton, Ind., 1995—. Actor Cmty. Theatre Guild, 1989—. Mem. NOW. Democrat. Home: 61 East 600 North Valparaiso IN 46383

WIEST, DIANNE, actress; b. Kansas City, Mo., Mar. 28, 1948. Student, U. Md. Appeared in numerous plays including Ashes (off-Broadway), 1976, Leave It to Beaver is Dead, The Art of Dining (Obie award, 1979, Theatre World award 1983), Bonjour La Bonjour, Three Sisters, Serenading Louie (Obie award, 1983), Othello, After the Fall, Heartbreak House, Our Town, and Hunting Cockroaches, 1987, In the Summer House, 1993, Blue Light, 1994; appeared in films including It's My Turn, 1980, I'm Dancing as Fast as I Can, 1982, Independence Day, 1982, Footloose, 1984, Falling in Love, 1984, The Purple Rose of Cairo, 1985, Hannah and Her Sisters, 1986 (Acad. award for Best Supporting Actress 1987), Radio Days, 1987, Lost Boys, 1987, September, 1987, Bright Lights, Big City, 1988, Parenthood, 1989 (Acad. award nominee), Cookie, 1989, Edward Scissorhands, 1990, Little Man Tate, 1991, Cops and Robbersons, 1994, The Scout, 1994, Bullets Over Broadway, 1994 (Golden Globe award Best Supporting Actress-Drama 1995, Acad. award for Best Supporting Actress 1995), Drunks, 1995, The Birdcage, 1996; TV appearances include The Wall, 1982, The Face of Rage, 1983. *

WIGGERS, CHARLOTTE SUZANNE WARD, magazine editor; b. Cleve., Dec. 14, 1943; d. Raymond Paul and Irene Mary (Knapp) W.; m. John Houston Black, Feb. 1975 (div. 1980). AB, Smith Coll., 1966. Asst. editor The Hudson Rev., N.Y.C., 1966-76; assoc. editor The Print Collector's Newsletter, N.Y.C., 1977-79; copy editor Electronics mag., McGraw-Hill, N.Y.C., 1979-81; sr. copy editor Spectrum mag., N.Y.C., 1981-85; mng. editor Essence mag., N.Y.C., 1985—. Home: 50 W 85th St Apt 5 New York NY 10024-4572 Office: Essence Magazine 1500 Broadway New York NY 10036-4015

WIGGIN, JANICE J., music educator; b. McCalister, Okla., June 28, 1971; d. Eugene Calvin and Jeanice Nell (Reed) Caleb; m. James Vance Wiggin, Aug. 8, 1992; 1 child, Christian Andrew. B. in Music Edn., OPSU, 1993. Music tchr. grades 5-12 Springfield (Colo.) Pub. Schs., 1993—. Mem. Colo. Music Educators Assn. Democrat. Office: Springfield Pub Schs Dist RE-4 389 Tipton Springfield CO 81073

WIGGINS, GLORIA, nonprofit organization administrator, television producer; b. N.Y.C., Jan. 17, 1933; d. John and Gladys (Jones) Pruden; m. Albert Wiggins, Jan. 15, 1954 (dec. Aug. 1982); childrens: Michael, Teresa. BA, Richmons Coll., Staten Island, N.Y.; MA, SUNY, Albany. Project dir. Suffolk County Black History Assn., Smithtown, N.Y., 1982; pres., founder Zamanii Internat. Devel. Corp., Central Islip, N.Y., 1983—; chair, founder Ikeda Mandela Uhuru Cultural Ctr., Inc., Central Islip, 1991—; chair Univ. Sons & Daughters of Ethiopia, Deer Park, N.Y., 1990-91. Producer, artist: (pub. access TV) Celebration of Kwanzaa, 1993 (grant 1993); prodr.: (pub. access TV) Living Arts, 1994 (grant 1994), (exhibit) Adventure to the Homeland, 1995 (grant 1995), African Women/African Art, 1992 (grant 1992). Pres. Mariners Harbor Tenant Assn., Staten Island, 1968-70. Home: 248 Tree Ave Central Islip NY 11722

WIGGINS, JACQUELINE H., music education educator; b. N.Y.C., Dec. 11, 1950; d. Saul William and Elaine (Ellis) Held; m. Robert Andrew Wiggins, June 4, 1972; children: Jennifer Anne, Elizabeth Ann. BA, Queens Coll., 1972, MS, 1977; EdD, U. Ill., 1992. Cert. music tchr. K-12, N.Y. Music tchr. Lindenhurst Pub. Schs., N.Y., 1972-74, South Huntington Pub. Schs., N.Y., 1974-75, Elwood Pub. Schs., East Northport, N.Y., 1975-76, 82-83, L.I. Sch. for the Gifted, South Huntington, N.Y., 1981-82, Half Hollow Hills Sch. Dist., Dix Hills, N.Y., 1983-84, 85-94, Shoreham-Wading River Pub. Schs., Shoreham, N.Y., 1984-85; asst. prof. Oakland U., Rochester, Mich., 1994—; condr. All-Dist. Elem. Festival Chorus, Lindenhurst, N.Y., 1972, South Huntington Elem. Festival Chorus, 1975, guest accompanist, 1974, accompanist, 1976; guest condr. Festival Chorus "Salute to Music," Suffolk County Music Educators, Lindenhurst, 1975, Elem. Festival Chorus, Nassau County Music Educators Assn., 1990, Divsn. I Festival Chorus, Suffolk County Music Educators Assn., 1993, chair, 1989; guest condr. Young Artists Festival, Wateford Schs., 1995; choral clinical festival sponsored by Oakland Intermediate Schs., 1995; cons. tech. com. N.Y. State Sch. Music Assn., 1994—. Author: Composition in the Classroom: A Tool for Teaching, 1990, Synthesizers in the Elementary Music Classroom: An Integrated Approach, 1991; (book chpts.) L.I. Philharm. Arts in Edn. Program, 1988-89, The Best of MEJ: Elementary General Music, 1992, Toward Tomorrow: New Visions for General Music, 1995; contbr. articles to profl. jours. and papers to conf. procs. Mem. AAUW, AAUP, Internat. Soc. Music. Edn., Am. Ednl. Rsch. Assn., Music Educators Nat. Conf. (rsch. mem., mem. Soc. for Gen. Music, Soc. for Music Tchrs. Edn., creativity spl. rsch. interest group), Mich. Music Educators Assn. (bd. dirs., collegiate Music Educators Nat. Conf. adv. for Mich.), Mich. Sch. Vocal Music Assn., Mich. Sch. Band and Orch. Assn., Coll. Music Soc., Recorder Soc. L.I. (hon. life mem.). Office: Oakland U Rochester MI 48309

WIGGINS, MARY ANN WISE, small business owner, educator; b. Coushatta, La., Dec. 25, 1940; d. George Wilkinson and Maitland (Allums) Wise; m. Gerald D. Paul (div. Nov. 1977); children: John Barron, James Gordon, Brenda Michelle; m. Billy J. Wiggins, Oct. 3, 1981; children: Marshall Wade, Brian David, William Joshua, George Justin; stepchildren: Joseph James, Winona Gail. BA, Northwestern State U., Natchitoches, La., 1964, postgrad., 1994; postgrad., Weaterford Coll., 1967, North Tex. State U., 1968. Lic. ins. agt., real estate agt., La., pvt. pilot. Tchr. U.S. Army Schs., Nuremberg, Germany, 1964-66, Mineral Wells (Tex.) Ind. Sch. Dist., 1967-72; bookkeeper Wise Dept. Store, Coushatta, 1966-67; owner, mgr. Mary Ann's Furniture & Hardware, Coushatta, 1977—; tchr. Springville Mid. Sch., Coushatta, 1994-96, Red River Parish Alternative Sch., Coushatta, 1996—. Chmn. Am. Cancer Soc., Conway, Ark., 1972, Red River Parish United Way, Coushatta, 1985; treas., bd. dirs. Hall Summit United Meth. Ch. Recipient German-Am. hospitality award Orgn. German-Am. Women, Nuremberg, 1965. Mem. NEA, La. Assn. Educators, Red River Assn. Educators (v.p. 1994—), U.S. C. of C., Coushatta-Red River C. of C. (charter), Pi Kappa Sigma, Sigma Kappa. Democrat. Methodist. Home: Rt 5 Box 70 Hwy 71 S Coushatta LA 71019 Office: Mary Ann's Furniture & Hardware 1802 Ringgold Ave Coushatta LA 71019

WIGGINS, NANCY BOWEN, real estate broker, market research consultant; b. Richmond, Va., Oct. 9, 1948; d. William Roy and Mary Virginia (Colson) Bowen; m. Samuel Spence Saunders, Aug. 16, 1969 (div. 1977); m. Edwin Lindsey Wiggins, Jr., Apr. 16, 1983; children: Neal Bowen, Mark Edwin. AA, St. Mary's Coll., Raleigh, N.C., 1968; postgrad., Trinity U., 1968-69; BA, U.S. Internat. U., San Diego, 1970; MA, U. Tex., Arlington, 1975; postgrad., Tulane U., 1976-77. Bank teller Bank of Am., San Diego, 1971-72; lectr. U. Tex., Arlington, 1974-76; instr. Johnson C. Smith U., Charlotte, N.C., 1977-78; human svcs. planner Centralina Coun. of Govt., Charlotte, 1978-80; mktg. rsch. analyst First Union Nat. Bank, Charlotte, 1980-81; mktg. rep. Burroughs Corp., Charlotte, 1981-83; ptnr., mktg. researcher George Selden & Assocs., Charlotte, 1983-84; pres., broker Bowen Wiggins Co., Charlotte, 1984-92; pres. WRB, Inc. (merger Bowen Wiggins Co. and W. Roy Bowen Co., Inc.), Charlotte, 1992—; instr. U. N.C., Charlotte, 1984-85, 87-90, Winthrop U., Rock Hill, S.C., 1985-86, 91-92; bd. dirs. Roy Bowen, Inc., Frogmore, S.C., v.p., sec., 1990. Contbr. articles to profl. jours. Vice chmn. United Cerebral Palsy Coun., Charlotte, 1984; chmn. bd. dirs. Carriage House Condominium Assn., Charlotte, 1980-82; mem. Charlotte Mayor's Budget Adv. Com., 1980-81, Charlotte-Mecklenburg Planning Commn., 1994—, mem. planning com., 1994-95, zoning com., 1995-96; pres. Mecklenburg Dem. Women's Club, 1990; mem. state exec. com. N.C. Dem. Party, 1991-95; mem. Charlotte Women's Polit. Caucus, Mecklenburg County Solid Waste Adv. Bd., 1991-92, chmn. recycling com., 1991-94, re-appointed 1995-96. Mem. JCSU, Charlotte Region Comml. Bd. Realtors, N.C. Assn. Appraisers (bd. dirs., pres. 1989-90), Internat. Coun. Shopping Ctrs., Com. of 100 Friends, Multimillion Dollar Club, Tournament Players Club Piper Glen, Good Friends, Pi Sigma Alpha. Democrat. Episcopalian. Home: 6919 Seton House Ln Charlotte NC 28277 Office: Ste 300 501 N Church St Charlotte NC 28202

WIGGINS, PATRICIA BENNETT, mental health counselor; b. Pensacola, Fla., Oct. 9, 1946; d. Paul Buchanan and Alzada Eugenia (Trapp) Bennett; m. W.R. Wiggins, Aug. 19, 1967 (div. 1989); children: Mary, Deke, Susan. BS in Bus. Edn., East Carolina U., 1969; MEd in Counseling, Augusta Coll., 1993, EdS, 1995. Tchr. Pitt Tech. Inst., Greenville, N.C., 1968-69, Steven Decatur (Ill.) High Sch., 1969-70; substitute tchr. Columbia County, Augusta, Ga., 1990-92; probation officer Coun. Juvenile Ct. Judges, Augusta, 1992-93; affiliate counselor Concern Employee Assistance Program, Augusta, 1993-94; counselor Jesse Lewis, PhD, Augusta, 1994—; counselor Life Skills Counseling Ctr., Augusta, 1994—; group facilitator Magistrate Ct., Evans, Ga., 1995—, Juvenile Ct., Evans. Panel mem. Foster Care Rev. Panel, Evans, 1991—. Mem. ACA, Phi Kappa Phi. Republican. Presbyterian. Home: 3656 Bay Point Dr Augusta GA 30907 Office: Life Skills Counseling Ctr 1287-A Marks Church Rd Augusta GA 30909

WIGGINS-ROTHWELL, JEANINE ELLEN, artist; b. Jacksonville, Fla., Apr. 15, 1967; d. Otis K. Wiggins and Minnie Lois (Odem) Martin; m. John Joseph Rothwell, Jan. 2, 1993. Student, Fla. C.C., 1984, 85, U. Ga., 1985; BFA in Painting, U. Fla., 1995. Freelance illustrator Earth Art, Inc., Gainesville, Fla., 1990—; airbrush artist Shade Tree Creations, Inc., Gainesville, 1995, Cain Studios, Inc., Gainesville, 1994. Illustrator covers Horizons, 1995, Salamander, 1994, (Best in the West 1st pl. award 1984); painter set design Spunk, 1994. Donator art works and graphic illustrations Dance Alive, Gainesville, 1994, 95, Artitorium Coop. Gallery, Gainesville, 1988, 89, Greens of Alachua's Celebration of Diversity, Gainesville, 1994; artist, rep. of women's issues NOW, 1996. Coll. scholar Lions Club, 1984. Democrat. Home: 3131 NW 11th St Gainesville FL 32609-2156

WIGGINTON, CYNTHIA ANN, art director, graphic designer; b. Harrisburg, Pa., Mar. 29, 1962; d. William Barclay and Joanne Ethel (Kirk) W. BS in Textiles, U. Calif., Davis, 1985. Photographer's asst. Ray Moller Studios, London, 1986; editorial asst. Sokol & Berman Advt., San Francisco, 1987-89; art dir. ArtRock, San Francisco, 1989—. Musician/violinist CD/album Bedlam Rovers Frothing Green, 1990, Bedlam Rovers Wallow, 1992, The Doubters Plus Other Bands Ain't This Bliss With You and This, 1994, others; designer posters, including Led Zeppelin Hall of Fame Induction, 1995, Bob Dylan/Patti Smith Concert, 1995. Democrat. Home: 2400 8th Ave Oakland CA 94606 Office: ArtRock 1153 Mission St San Francisco CA 94606

WIGGS, RITA SUE, physical education educator, basketball coach; b. Fayetteville, N.C., May 25, 1953; d. Bobby Ray and Hazel Grey (Averitte) W. BS in Phys. Edn., U. N.C., Greensboro, 1975; MA in Edn., N.C. State U., 1980. Tchr., coach Cape Fear High Sch., Fayetteville, N.C., 1975-78, Westover Sr. High Sch., Fayetteville, 1977-78; grad. asst. N.C. State U., Raleigh, 1978-80, asst. basketball coach, 1980-85; head women's basketball coach Roane State Community Coll., Harriman, Tenn., 1985-86; asst. prof. phys. edn., head women's basketball coach Meth. Coll., Fayetteville, 1986—, asst. athletic dir., dir. sports info., 1986-91, dir. athletics, 1991—; chmn. women's basketball com. Dixie Intercollegiate Athletic Conf., Fayetteville, 1989-92. Liaison Adopt-A-Hwy., N.C., 1989-91. Named Coach of Yr., Dixie Intercollegiate Athletic Conf., 1989. Mem. Women's Basketball Coaches Assn. (ranking com. NCAA so. region divsn. III, 1988-96, Coach of Yr. selection com. NJCAA 1985-86, NCAA divsn. III women's basketball com. 1990-96)., chmn., 1993-96. Baptist. Office: Meth Coll 5400 Ramsey St Fayetteville NC 28311-1420

WIGHT, NANCY ELIZABETH, neonatologist; b. N.Y.C., Aug. 27, 1947; d. John Joseph and Gisela (Landers) Probst; m. Robert C.S. Wight, Oct. 1, 1988; 1 child, Robert C.S. II. Student, Cornell U., 1965-67; AB in Psychology, U. Calif., Berkeley, 1968; postgrad., George Washington U., 1971-72; MD, U. N.C., 1976. Diplomate Am. Bd. Pediatrics. Resident in pediatrics U. N.C., Chapel Hill, 1976-79; fellow in neonatal/perinatal medicine U. Calif., San Diego, 1979-81; clin. instr. Dept. of Pediatrics La. State U. Sch. of Medicine, Baton Rouge, 1982-86; neonatologist The Baton Rouge Neonatology Group, 1981-86; co-dir. neonatology, med. dir. respiratory therapy Woman's Hosp., Baton Rouge, 1981-85; med. dir. newborn svcs., neonatal respiratory therapy HCA West Side Hosp. Centennial Med. Ctr., Nashville, 1986-88; staff pediatrician, neonatologist Balboa Naval Hosp., San Diego, 1988-89; attending neonatologist Sharp Meml. Hosp., San Diego, 1990—, Children's Hosp.-San Diego, 1990—; asst. clin. prof. U. Calif. San Diego, 1991—; physician assoc. La Leche League. Contbr. articles to profl. jours. mem. exec. bd. Capital Area Plantation chpt. March of Dimes, Baton Rouge, 1981-86, chmn. health adv. com., 1982-86; mem. health com. Capital Area United Way, Baton Rouge, 1982-86; bd. mem. Baton Rouge Coun. for Child Protection, 1983-86, NICU Parents, Baton Rouge, 1981-86; mem. health adv. com. Nashville Area March of Dime, 1987-88. Recipient Am. Med. Women's Assn. award. Mem. AMA, Am. Acad. Pediatrics, Calif. Med. Assn., So. Med. Assn., San Diego County Med. Assn., Calif. Perinatal Assn., So. Perinatal Assn., Nat. Perinatal Assn., La. Perinatal Assn. (past 1st v.p. and pres.), Internat. Lactation Cons. Assn. (cert.), Hastings Soc. Home: 3226 Newell St San Diego CA 92106-1918 Office: Children's Assoc Med Group 8001 Frost St San Diego CA 92123-2746

WIGHTMAN, ANN, lawyer; b. Dayton, Ohio, July 29, 1958; d. William L. and Mary Ann (Lamb) W. AB, Ohio U., 1980; JD, Case Western Res. U., 1984. Bar: Ohio 1984, U.S. Dist. Ct. (so. dist.) Ohio 1984, U.S. Ct. Appeals (6th cir.) 1991, U.S. Ct. Appeals (7th cir.) 1992, U.S. Supreme Ct. 1993. Assoc. Smith & Schnacke, Dayton, 1984-89; sr. assoc. Faruki Gilliam & Ireland, Dayton, 1989-91, ptnr., 1991—; adj. prof. U. Dayton Sch. Law, 1988-93; chmn. Artemis House, Inc., Dayton, 1988-90, bd. dirs., 1985—; arbitrator Am. Arbitration Assn. Mem. Vol. Lawyer's Project, Dayton, 1988—; mem. Challenge 95 Task Force, Dayton, 1989-90, Up and Comer, Dayton, 1990; vol. arbitrator Montgomery County Common Pleas Ct., 1989—; bd. dirs. ACLU of Ohio Found., 1991-94; mem. Leadership, Dayton, 1992. Mem. ABA (trial and environ. sects.), Am. Arbitration Assn. (arbitrator), Ohio Bar Assn. (alternative dispute resolution com. 1990—), Dayton Bar Assn. (unauthorized practice com. 1990-93, com. on the judiciary 1993—), Phi Beta Kappa. Home: 240 W. Dixon Ave Dayton OH 45419 Office: Faruki Gilliam & Ireland 10 N Ludlow St Dayton OH 45402-1826

WIGHTMAN, LUDMILLA G. POPOVA, language educator, foreign educator, translator; b. Sofia, Bulgaria, Sept. 29, 1933; came to U.S., 1977; d. Genko Mateev and Liliana (Kusseva) Popov; m. Ivan Todorov Todorov, Aug. 13, 1957 (div. 1976); 1 child, Todor; m. Arthur Strong Wightman, Jan. 14, 1977. MS, U. Sofia, 1956. Cons. Nat. Libr., Sofia, 1956-58; rsch. assoc. Joint Inst. for Nuclear Rsch., Moscow, 1958-65; lectr. Russian Rutgers U., New Brunswick, N.J., 1969-70; editor Bulgarian Ency., Sofia, 1973-77; tchr. lang. Princeton (N.J.) Lang. Group, 1977—; libr. Firestone Libr., Princeton U., 1983-87. Translator: Introduction to Axiomatic Field Theory, 1975, New Eng. Rev., Bread Loaf Quar., 1987, Mr. Cogito, 1989, N.Y. Rev. Books, 1990, Poetry East, 1990-91, Literary Rev., 1992, Partisan Rev., 1996, Shifting Borders: East European Poetries of the Eighties, 1993. Home and Office: 16 Balsam Ln Princeton NJ 08540-5327

WIIG, ELISABETH HEMMERSAM, audiologist, educator; b. Esbjert, Denmark, May 22, 1935; came to U.S., 1957, naturalized, 1967; d. Svend Frederick and Ingeborg (Hemmersam) Nielsen; m. Karl Martin Wiig, June 10, 1958; children—Charlotte E., Erik D. B.A., Statsseminariet Emdrupborg, 1956; M.A., Western Res. U., 1960; Ph.D., Case Western Res. U., 1967; postgrad., U. Mich., 1967-68. Clin. audiologist Cleve. Hearing and Speech Center, 1959-60; instr. dept. phonetics Bergen (Norway) U., 1960-64; asst. prof., dir. aphasia rehab. program U. Mich., 1968-70; asst. prof. Boston U., 1970-73, asso. prof., chmn. dept., 1973-77, prof. dept. communication disorders, 1977-87, prof. emerita, 1987—; v.p. EDUCOM Assocs. Inc., 1992-93. Author: Language Disabilities in Children and Adolescents, 1976, Language Assessment and Intervention for the Learning Disabled, 1980, 84, CELF Screening Tests: Elementary and Secondary Levels, 1980, Clinical Evaluation of Language Fundamentals, rev. edit., 1987, Clinical Evaluation of Language Fundamentals 3, 1995, Test of Language Competence, 1985, expanded edit., 1989, Test of Word Knowledge, 1992, Clinical Evaluation of Language Fundamentals Preschool, 1992; editor: Human Communication Disorders: An Introduction, 1982, 86, 90, 94; contbr. articles to profl. jours. Recipient Metcalf Cup and Prize for excellence in teaching Boston U., 1967. Fellow Am. Speech and Hearing Assn. (cert. clin. competence in speech pathology and audiology); mem. Coun. for Learning Disabilities, Coun. for Exceptional Children, Internat. Assn. for Rsch. on Learning Disabilities, Am. Psychol. Soc. Address: 5211 Vicksburg Dr Arlington TX 76017-4941

WIITA, KATHRYN CARPENTER, public relations company executive; b. Casper, Wyo., Sept. 15, 1961; d. Hugh Lewis and Kathryn Estelle (Pepper) Carpenter; m. Thomas A. Wiita, Sept. 1, 1991. BS in Mass Communications, U. Utah, 1983. Mcht. rep. Tracy Collins Bank & Trust, Salt Lake City, 1983-84; communications specialist Arthur Young & Co., Salt Lake City, 1984-88; officer, dir. pub. rels. 1st Interstate Bank Utah, Salt Lake City, 1988-89; pres. KC Communications, Jackson, Wyo., 1989—; cons. Mountain West Venture Group, Salt Lake City, 1984-87, Catheter Tech. Inc., Salt Lake City, 1986-89, Sta. KTVX, Salt Lake City, 1986, Inter Therapy, Inc., Costa Mesa, Calif., 1990, Stop Gap, Santa Ana, Calif., Jackson Peak Outfitters, 1992—, M W Med., 1990—, Jacksoh Hole Cowboy Ski Challenge, 1994; mktg. cons.Wines & Spirits, 1992—. Mem. Pub. Rels. Soc. Am. (accredited; officer 1988-89), Pub. Rels. Soc. Am. Counselors Acad., Women in Comms. (officer 1988-89), Jr. League Orange County, Calif. Inc. (pub. rels. coord. 1991-92, dir. pub. rels. c992—), Kappa Kappa Gamma. Home and Office: 12010 SE 13th St Vancouver WA 98684

WILBER, LISA MARIE, design director; b. Walla Walla, Wash., June 11, 1966; d. David Thomas and Luella Jane (Farnsworth) W. BS in Archtl. Studies, Andrews U., 1989. Tech. aide The Boeing Co., Seattle, 1989-90, archtl. designer, 1990-95; dir. design B.L. Gertz & Assocs., Mt. Vernon, Wash., 1995—. V.p. Anacortes (Wash.) Cmty. Theatre, 1991-92, bd. mem., 1993-94. Recipient Pres.'s award Anacortes (Wash.) Cmty. Theatre, 1993. Mem. NOW, Internat. Conf. Bldg. Ofcls. Democrat. Seventh-Day Adventist. Home: 12221 Airport Rd C-308 Everett WA 98204 Office: B L Gertz & Assocs Ste A 1003 Cleveland Mount Vernon WA 98273

WILBURN, MARY NELSON, lawyer, writer; b. Balt., Feb. 18, 1932; d. David Alfred and Phoebe Blanche (Novotny) Nelson; m. Adolph Yarbrough Wilburn, Mar. 5, 1957; children: Adolph II, Jason David. AB cum laude, Howard U., 1952; MA, U. Wis., 1955, JD, 1975. Bar: Wis. 1975, U.S. Supreme Ct 1981. Lectr. U. Wis. Law Sch., 1975-77, 83, 84, 85; atty. Bur. Prisons, Dept. Justice, 1977-82, 90—; chmn. Wis. State Parole Bd., Madison, 1986-87; gen. counsel D.C. Bd. Parole, 1987-89; commr. The Commn. to Restructure the Interstate Compact, 1988-89; mgr. Bethune Mus.-Archives, Inc., 1990; mem. Wis. Sentencing Commn., 1986-87. Mem. Madison Met. Sch. Dist. Bd. Edn., 1975-77; assoc. mem. Schutz Am. Sch. Bd., Alexandria, Egypt, 1983-85; commr. Nat. Coun. of Negro Women Commn. on Edn., 1986—; treas. Women's Strategies for 21st Century, Inc.; judge NAACP ACT-SO Competition, 1994—; mentoring mem. Women of Washington, 1996; vol. One Ch. One Addict, 1995—; mem. bd. edn. Cath. Archdiocese of Washington, 1995—. Mem. Internat. Assn. Paroling Authorities (exec. v.p. 1987-89), Nat. Assn. Black Women Attorneys (pres. Rolark chpt. 1989-93), Fedn. Internat. de Abogadas, Howard U. Alumni Assn., Links, Inc., Leadership Greater Washington (bd. dirs. 1992-94, v.p. 1995—), Women of Washington, Coun. Black Catholics, Alpha Kappa Alpha. Office: 320 1st St NW Rm 437 Washington DC 20534-0002

WILCOX, MAUD, editor; b. N.Y.C., Feb. 14, 1923; d. Thor Fredrik and Gerda (Ysberg) Eckert; m. Edward T. Wilcox, Feb. 9, 1944; children: Thor (dec.), Bruce, Eric, Karen. A.B. summa cum laude, Smith Coll., 1944; A.M., Harvard U., 1945. Teaching fellow Harvard U., 1945-46, 48-51; instr. English Smith Coll., Northampton, Mass., 1947-48, Wellesley Coll., Mass., 1951-52; exec. editor Harvard U. Press, 1958-66, humanities editor, 1966-73, editor-in-chief, 1973-89, ret.; freelance editorial cons. Cambridge, 1989—; cons., panelist NEH, Washington, 1974-76, 82-84; cons. Radcliffe Pub. Course, 1991. Mem. MLA (com. scholarly edits. 1982-86), Assn. Am. Univ. Presses (chair com. admissions and standards 1976-77, v.p. 1978-79, chair program com. 1981-82), Phi Beta Kappa. Democrat. Episcopalian. Home and Office: 63 Francis Ave Cambridge MA 02138-1911

WILCOX, NANCY DIANE, nurse, administrator; b. Griffin, Ga., Oct. 28, 1951; d. Robert Wayne Birdwell and Eula F. (Maddox) Tatum; m. David Reed Wilcox, May 29, 1970; children: David Jr., Melanie, Bradley, Amy. AS, Panola Coll., 1971; lic. vocat. nurse, Kilgore Coll., 1990, ASN, 1993; BSN magna cum laude, U. Tex., Tyler, 1994. RN, Tex. Hemodialysis nurse Good Shepherd Hosp., Longview, Tex., 1990-91, critical care and telemetry nurse, 1993-94; staff nurse Roy H. Laird Hosp., Kilgore, 1991-93; case mgr. TLC Home Health Agy., Longview, 1994-95; owner, operator LifeCare Home Nursing, Inc., Kilgore, 1995—. Mem. ANA, Tex. Nurses Assn., Home Care Nurses Assn., Phi Theta Kappa, Alpha Chi, Sigma Theta Tau. Home: 1705 Oakwood Dr Kilgore TX 75662-8803

WILCOX, RHODA DAVIS, elementary education educator; b. Boyero, Colo., Nov. 4, 1918; d. Harold Francis and Louise Wilhelmina (Wilfert) Davis; m. Kenneth Edward Wilcox, Nov. 1945 (div. 1952); 1 child, Michele Ann. BA in Elem. Edn., U. No. Colo., 1941; postgrad., Colo. Coll., 1955-65. Life cert. tchr., Colo. Elem. tchr. Fruita (Colo.) Pub. Sch., 1938-40, Boise, Idaho, 1940-42; sec. civil service USAF, Ogden, Utah, 1942-43, Colorado Springs, Colo., 1943-44; sec. civil service hdqtrs. command USAF, Panama Canal Zone; sec. Tech. Libr., Eglin Field, Fla., 1945-46; elem. tchr. Colorado Springs Sch. Dist. 11, 1952-82, mem. curriculum devel. com., 1968-69; lectr. civic, profl. and edn. groups, Colo.; judge for Excellence in Literacy Coldwell Bankers Sch. Dist. 11, Colo. Coun. Internat. Reading. Assn. Author: Man on the Iron Horse, 1959, Colorado Slim and His Spectacklers, 1964, (with Jean Pierpoint) Changing Colorado (Social Studies), 1968-69, The Founding Fathers and Their Friends in Denver Posse of the Westerners Brand Bank, 1971, The Bells of Manitou, 1973, (with Len Froisland) In the Footsteps of the Founder, 1993. Mem. hist. adv. bd. State Colo., Denver, 1976; mem. Garden of the Gods master plan rev. com. City of Colorado Springs, 1987—; mem. cemetery adv. bd. City of Colorado Springs, 1988-91; mem. adv. bd. centennial com., 1971; mem. steering com. Spirit of Palmer Festival, 1986; judge Nat. Hist. Day, U. Colo., Colorado Springs, and Colo. Coll., Colorado Springs; hon. trustee Palmer Found., 1986—; mem. Am. the Beautiful Centennial Celebrations, Inc., 1992-93; active Friends of the Garden of the Gods, Friends of Winfield Scott Stratton, Friends of the Libr. Named Tchr. of the Yr., Colorado Springs Sch. Dist. 11, 1968. Mem. AAUW (Woman of Yr. 1987), Colo. Ret. Educators Assn., Colorado Springs Ret. Educators Assn., Helen Hunt Jackson Commemorative Coun., Women's Ednl. Soc. Colo. Coll. Home: 1620 E Cache La Poudre St Colorado Springs CO 80909-4612

WILCOXEN, JOAN HEEREN, fitness company executive; b. Flushing, N.Y., May 30, 1948; d. Paul Arnold and Helena Catherina (Laskowski) Heeren; m. Eddie Dean Wilcoxen, Dec. 31, 1981. BA, Long Island U., 1971; grad., Radford U. Karate Coll., 1994. Cert. referee AAU. Real estate broker Heeren Agy., Riverhead, N.Y., 1970-72; 2d v.p. Levitt House, Inc., Medford, N.Y., 1972-78; radio broadcaster Sta. KWHW Radio, Altus, Okla., 1979-84; exec. dir. Ironworks Family Gym and Heartland Health Club, Altus, Okla., 1984-94, Wilcoxen's Acad. of the Martial Arts, Altus, Okla., 1994—; lectr. martial arts; lectr. Shortgrass Arts and Humanities Coun., Altus, 1988—. Vol. United Way of Jackson County, Altus, 1989—, project co-chair, 1994; fundraiser Muscular Dystrophy Assn., Wichita Falls, Tex., 1987—; mem. Shortgrass Arts and Humanities Coun., 1988-93, Nat. Bd. Realtors, 1978-79; state coord., co-chair Sooner State Games Karate, Oklahoma City, 1989-93; bd. dirs. Am. Heart Assn. 1993-95; mem. Altus 2000 edn. task force. Named for civic leadership Okla. State U. Coop. Extension Svc., Altus, 1988, S.W. Bell Tel. Co., Altus, 1989, Rotary Club and March of Dimes, Altus, 1989, Jackson County Free Fair, Altus, 1988, 89; Okla. State AAU karate champion, 1990, black belt, Nat. AAU women's karate (sparring) champion, 1995. Mem. AAUW (v.p. Altus chpt. 1990, pres. 1992-93), Altus C. of C. (amb. 1989-90), Am. Bus. Women's Assn., Biz Tips Women's Assn. (v.p. 1989-90, pres. 1991-92), Am. Heart Assn. (bd. dirs. Altus chpt. 1994, pres. Jackson County divsn. 1996), Altus C. of C., Air Force Assn. Cmty. Ptnrs., Am. Ind. Karate Instrs. Assn. (instr. Christiansburg, Va. chpt. 1986—). Home: 1100 N Main St Altus OK 73521-3122 Office: Wilcoxen's Acad Martial Art Altus Plz Shopping Ctr 1100 N Main St # C5B Altus OK 73521-3122

WILCOXSON, CATHERINE ANN, science educator, consultant; b. Lemmon, S.D., Nov. 13, 1948; d. Alvin Herman and Myra V. (Eggers) Thies; m. Dale Arthur Wilcoxson, Dec. 13, 1969; children: Blaine, Erik. BS, Midland Luth. Coll., 1971; Masters, U. Nebr., Omaha, 1989; PhD, U. Nebr., 1994. Tchr. North Bend (Nebr.) Ctrl. Sch., 1971-78, Fremont (Nebr.) H.S., 1978-81, 84-92; project coord. N.E. Dept. Edn., Lincoln, 1993-95; assoc. prof. No. Ariz. U., Flagstaff, 1995—; cons. La. Dept. Edn., 1994, 95, Coun. Chief State Sch. Officers, Washington, 1994, 96, Ark. Dept. of Edn., 1996. Editor: N.E. Math/Science Frameworks, 1994, Guidelines for Teacher Preparation: Mathematics and Science, 1995. Recipient Master Tchr. award Midland Luth. Coll., 1993. Mem. ASCD, Nat. Sci. Tchrs. (manuscript reveiw com. Jour. Coll. Sci. Tchrs. 1995), Am. Ednl. Rsch. Assn., Nat. Assn. Biology Tchrs. (sec./treas. 1996—, Outstanding Biology Tchr. 1991, Excellence in Encouraging Equity award 1994), Phi Delta Kappa. Office: No Ariz Univ PO Box 5640 Flagstaff AZ 86011

WILCZYNSKI-ZOLLO, LAURIE ANN, nurse; b. Salem, Mass., July 14, 1966; d. Albert Joseph and Marion Shirley (Green) Wilczynski; m. Peter Nathaniel Zollo, Aug. 20, 1994. LPN, Essex Agrl. and Tech. Inst., Hathorne, Mass., 1984-85; ADN, North Shore C.C., Beverly, Mass., 1988; BSN, Salem State Coll., 1995, postgrad., 1995—. RN, Mass. Staff nurse Hogan Regional Ctr., Hathorne, Mass., 1985-89, Addison Gilbert Hosp., Gloucester, Mass., 1989-92, Saints Meml. Med. Ctr., Lowell, Mass., 1992-94, Holy Family Hosp., Methuen, Mass., 1994—. Recipient Rosalie Edwards Meml. scholarship, Addison Gilbert Hosp., 1992, Atlanticare scholarship Atlanticare Med. Ctr., Lynn, Mass., 1987, Peabody Vis. Nurses scholarship

Vis. Nurses Assn., Peabody, Mass., 1985. Mem. Mass. Nurse Assn., Sigma Theta Tau. Democrat. Home: 239 Maple St Danvers MA 01923

WILD, KATHRYN D., environmental educator, native California historian; b. Sept. 27, 1948; d. David Leon and Jean (Pearch) Ichelson; m. Norbert Craven Wild, Jr., July 22, 1982; children: Lani Jean, David Norbert. BA in History, U. Calif., Santa Barbara, 1970; PhD in Holistic Health Edn., U. for Humanistic Studies, 1987. Tutor Viejas Reservation, San Diego, 1973; tchr. Sultana Elem. Sch., Cucamonga, Calif., 1975-76, Herron Elem. Sch., North Las Vegas, Nev., 1976-77; exec. dir. Wild by Nature, Inc., San Diego, 1994—; also bd. dirs. Wild by Nature, Inc.; advisor, facilitator Children's Ecology Club, San Diego, 1990-96; mem. adv. bd. Spl. Species, Half Moon Bay, Calif., 1995-96; chair of nature learning ctr. Winterwood Park, San Diego, 1995—. Author, editor: Holistic Weight Management, 1986, Holistic Treatment of Candidiasis, 1986. Mem. exec. bd., chair environ. issues Mira Mesa Cmty. Planning Group, San Diego, 1993—. Recipient Nat. award Environ. Edn., 1993, grand prize Busch SeaWorld, Tampa, Fla., 1994, Environ. Ednl. grant Calif. State Dept. Environ. Edn., 1994; Wild by Nature day proclaimed by City of San Diego, 1994. Mem. NOW, NORML, Am. Indian Movement, Nat. Wildlife Fedn., Greenpeace, Haddasah, Calif. Indian Basketweavers Assn. Jewish Native Am. Office: Wild by Nature Inc 7275 Canyon Breeze San Diego CA 92126

WILD, SUSAN KURZWEG, insurance adjustor; b. New Orleans, Jan. 19, 1960; d. Charles Haynes and Elizabeth Louise (Gaudet) Kurzweg; m. Kyle Charles Wild, Sept. 5, 1987. BS, La. State U., 1983. Claims adjustor Aetna, New Orleans, 1983-87, 95—; claims supr. Aetna, St. Louis, 1987-90; claims supr. Aetna, New Orleans, 1990-92, svc. supervisor, 1992-95. Republican. Roman Catholic. Office: Aetna Life & Casualty P O Box 6001 Metairie LA 70009

WILDE, PATRICIA, artistic director; b. Ottawa, Ont., Can., July 16, 1928; m. George Bardyguine; children: Anya, Youri. Dancer Am. Concert Ballet, Marquis de Cuevas Ballet Internat., N.Y.C., 1944-45, Ballet Russe de Monte Carlo, N.Y.C., 1945-49, Roland Petit's Ballet Paris, Met. Ballet Britain, London, 1949-50; prin. ballerina N.Y.C. Ballet, 1950-65; dir. Harkness Sch. Ballet, N.Y.C., 1965-67; ballet mistress, tchr. Am. Ballet Theatre, N.Y.C., 1969-77; dir. Am. Ballet Theatre Sch., N.Y.C., 1977-82; artistic dir. Pitts. Ballet Theatre, 1982—; tchr. Am. Ballet Theatre, 1969-77, Joffrey scholarship program, N.Y.C. Ballet, 1968-69; established Sch. of Grand Theatre of Geneva, 1968-69; adjudicator Regional Ballet in Am. S.E. and S.W., 1969-82; choreographer N.Y. Philharmonic; guest tchr. various ballet cos. and colls.; trustee Dance U.S.A.; panelist Nat. Choreographic Project. Recipient Leadership award in Arts and Letters YWCA, 1990, Pitts. Woman of Yr. in Arts award, 1993. Office: Pitts Ballet Theatre 2900 Liberty Ave Pittsburgh PA 15201-1500

WILDER, CAROL ANN, painter, educator; b. Bakersfield, Calif., Dec. 22, 1942; d. Arthur Graves and Virginia Sawyer (Parker) W.; m. John Hart Polhemus, Apr. 6, 1963 (div. May 1975); children: Amy Polhemus Basting, John Hart Polhemus II. BFA, U. Utah, 1979; postgrad., U. Calif., Berkeley, 1992, U. Calif., Davis, 1995-96. Cert. profl. clear, art, Calif. Art tchr. Tamalpais H.S., Mill Valley, Calif., 1985-86, Tamalpais Cmty. Edn., Mill Valley, 1986-95, Lowell H.S., San Francisco, 1995, Calif. Acad. Scis., San Francisco, 1993-96; curator Marin Art and Garden Ctr., Ross, Calif., 1992; writer Calif. State Model Visual Arts Curriculum, Mill Valley, 1986-87; owner Coastal Murals, Mill Valley, 1993—. Murals, paintings and abstracts exhibited at Mill Valley Comty. Ch., 1973, 93, Mill Valley Arts Commn., 1986, 87, 88, Marin C.C. Dist., 1989, Marin Arts Coun., 1993, San Francisco State U., 1990, S.F.A.I., 1990. SEOG grantee U. Utah, 1975. Mem. Marin Arts Coun., Mus. Modern Art, Golden Gate Park Tennis Club. Democrat. Home and Office: Coastal Murals 1508 Madrone Ln Davis CA 95616

WILDER, CAROL LYNN, artist, art educator; b. Dallas, Dec. 6, 1949; d. Alvin Young and Jo Nell (McCabe) W.; m. Daniel Eugene Jennings, Dec., 1969 (div. 1972); 1 child, Trevor; m. Larry Gene Enge, Dec. 19, 1981; children: Amelia, Jora. BFA, East Tex. State U., 1977; MA, U. Dallas, 1980, MFA, 1981; student, Kent State U., summer 1977. Artist/supr. Neighborhood Walls Unltd., Dallas, 1979; instr.art sr. citizens' ctr., Irving, Tex., 1980; grad. asst., art history slide libr. U. Dallas, Irving, 1980-81; instr. art Children's Art and Ideas Found., Dallas, summers 1982,84; adj. art faculty Richland Coll., Dallas, 1982-85, North Lake Coll., Irving, 1989—; mural artist Dallas Can! Acad., 1995; group leader EF Ednl. Tours, Dallas, 1994—; vis. artist East Tex. State U., Commerce, El Centro Coll., Dallas, 1979, Eastfield Coll., Dallas, 1977. Solo exhbns. include Eastfield Coll. Gallery, 1977, Dallas Women's Ctr., 1978, Haggerty Art Ctr. U. Dallas, 1980, Clifford Gallery, 1981, Trinity Christian Acad., Addison, Tex., 1987, North Lake Coll. Gallery, Irving, 1990, Harleen & Allen Fine Art, San Francisco, 1991, 93-94, North Lake Coll. Gallery, Irving, 1996, GTE Corp. Gallery, Irving, 1996, Dallas Visual Art Ctr., 1996; group exhbns. include Alternative Mus., N.Y.C., 1983, Harleen & Allen Fine Art, San Francisco, 1989, Edith Baker Gallery, 1991, 92, 93, Beverly Gordon Gallery, 1991, North Lake Coll. Gallery, 1990, 91, Hewlett-Packard, Palo Alto, Calif., 1993, NLC Gallery, Dallas, 1994, City Hall Dallas, 1995—, Adkins/Hoover Gallery, Dallas, 1995—, Dallas Visual Arts Ctr., 1985, 94, 95, Galerie Art Present, Paris, 1995, Meyerson Symphony Ctr., Dallas, 1995, African Am. Mus., Dallas, 1995, Gallery One Compuserv Fine Art Forum (Best of Show), 1995, Irving Art Ctr., 1995, The Gallery, Dallas, 1995, NLC Gallery, Dallas, 1994, Mus. Fine Art, Santa Fe, 1996, Irving Art Ctr., 1996, numerous others; published artwork 1994 Ann. Report U. Dallas Alumni Assn., 1994; represented in various pub. collections in Calif. and Tex. Facilitator racial reconciliation seminar Bridging the Gap, Dallas, 1994. Recipient Purchase award African-Am. Mus., Dallas, 1995. Mem. ACACIA Arts Group, Interracial Family Social Alliance, Alpha Chi (Tex. Lambda chpt.)(life), Christians in Visual Arts. Office: N Lake Coll Visual and Performing Arts Divsn 5001 N MacArthur Blvd Irving TX 75038-3899

WILDER, ELAINE KATHRYN, university official; b. N.Y.C., Apr. 2, 1942; d. Edward Z. and Kathryn A. (Katsaras) Pichler; m. Edward H. Wilder, Jr., June 18, 1983; children: Kathryn Norris, Audrey Walker, David Walker. Grad. in respiratory therapy, Kennebec Valley Tech. Coll., Fairfield, Maine, 1983; AS in Gen. Studies, U. Maine, Augusta, 1995. Nat. cert. respiratory therapy technician. Physician and clinic asst. ARC, various locations, 1965-77; coord. archives Waterville (Maine) Pub. Libr., 1981; faculty asst., coord. tutoring svcs., tutor U. Maine, Augusta, 1984—; mem. adv. bd. Augusta Area Food Bank,1986—; mem. U. Maine Sys. Disabilities Network, Orono, 1994—; workshop presenter in field. Bd. dirs. St. Mark's Home, Augusta, 1984—, Belgrade Regional Health Ctr., Belgrade Lakes, Maine, 1995—; mem. planning bd. St. Mark's Home for Women, Augusta, 1994—; vol., mediator Consumer Fraud divsn. Atty. Gen.'s Office, State of Maine. Mem. Am. Assn. for Respiratory Care, Learning Disabilities Assn. Maine, Phi Theta Kappa. Office: U Maine 46 University Dr Augusta ME 04330

WILDER, ELEANOR MARIE (NORA ROBERTS WILDER), writer; b. Washington, Oct. 10, 1950; d. Bernard Edward Robertson and Eleanor Margaret Harris; m. Ronald Eugene Aufdem-Brinke, Aug. 17, 1968 (div. 1985); children: Daniel, Jason; m. Bruce Allen Wilder, July 6, 1985. Grad. high sch., Silver Spring, Md. Legal sec. Wheeler & Korpec, Silver Spring, 1966-68; sec. R&R Lighting, Silver Spring, 1972-75; writer, 1979—. Author: The Heart's Victory, 1982, Golden Medallion, 1982-89 (Rita award 1992), This Magic Moment, 1983, Untamed, 1983, A Matter of Choice, 1984, MacGregor Clan Series, 1985, Hot Ice, 1987, Brazen Virtue, 1988, O'Hurley Series, 1988, Sweet Revenge, 1989, Public Secrets, 1990, Genuine Lies, 1991, Carnal Innocence, 1991, Honest Illusions, 1992, Divine Evil, 1992, Private Scandals, 1993, Hidden Riches, 1994. First inductee Romance Writers of Am. Hall of Fame, 1986; recipient Waldenbooks award, 1985, 86, 88, 91, 92, 94, B. Dalton award, 1990, 91, 92. Mem. Washington Romance Writers, Romance Writers Am., Mystery Writers Am. Democrat. Roman Catholic. Avocations: dancing, reading, films.

WILDER, VALERIE, ballet company administrator; b. Pasadena, Calif., Aug. 5, 1947; d. Douglas Wilder and Helen Marie (Wilson) Morrill; m. Geoffrey Duer Perry, Nov. 24, 1973; children: Stuart Whittier, Sabina Woodman. Student, Butler U., Indpls., 1966-68, U. Toronto, 1969-75. Dancer Nat. Ballet Can., Toronto, 1970-78; ptnr. Perry & Wilder Inc., Toronto, 1976-83; artistic adminstr. Nat. Ballet Can., Toronto, 1983-86, assoc. artistic dir., 1986-87, co-artistic dir., 1987-89, assoc. dir., 1989-96, exec. dir., 1996—; adv. bd. Dancer Transition Ctr., Toronto, 1986—; dance adv. panel Can. Coun., 1984-89; dance adv. com. Ont. Arts. Coun., 1985-90. Bd. dirs. Toronto Arts Coun., 1990-94. Mem. Dance in Can. Assn., Can. Assn. Profl. Dance Orgns. (bd. dirs.). Office: Nat Ballet of Can, 157 King St E, Toronto, ON Canada M5C 1G9

WILDERMUTH, ANITA JEAN, elementary school educator; b. La Crosse, Wis., July 20, 1939; d. Arthur and Aleda Marie (Thompson) Thurin; m. Robert Berl Wildermuth, Aug. 15, 1970. BA, Luther Coll., 1961; MA in Tchg., Rockford Coll., 1977. Cert. tchr., Wis. Art tchr. Dodgeville (Wis.) Pub. Schs., 1961-62, Viroqua (Wis.) Pub. Schs., 1962-66, Beloit (Wis.) Sch. Dist., 1966—; supr. art Sch. Dist. Beloit, 1968—; owner Thurin Apts., Viroqua, Wis.; sec.-treas. Wildermuth Farms, Inc. EMT Turtle Fire Dept., Beloit, 1980—; mem. U. Wis. Ext. Homemakers, So. Wis. Interest Macintosh Computer Soc. Mem. NEA, Wis. Edn. Assn., Wis. Art Educators Assn., Nat. Art Educators Assn. (amb. to China for art edn. 1988), Nat. Farmers Orgn., Art League of Beloit, Altrusa. Home: 10001 S Clinton Corners Rd Clinton WI 53525-8308 Office: Sch Dist Beloit 1633 Keeler Ave Beloit WI 53511-4713

WILDING, DIANE, marketing, financial and information systems executive; b. Chicago Heights, Ill., Nov. 7, 1942; d. Michael Edward and Katherine Surian; m. Manfred Georg Wilding, May 7, 1975 (div. 1980). BSBA in Acctg. magna cum laude, No. Ill. U., 1963; postgrad., U. Chgo., 1972-74; cert. in German lang., Goethe Inst., Rothenburg, Germany, 1984; cert. in internat. bus. German, Goethe Inst., Atlanta, 1994. Lic. cosmetologist. Systems engr. IBM, Chgo., 1963-68; data processing mgr. Am. Res. Corp., Chgo., 1969-72; system rsch. and devel. project mgr. Continental Bank, Chgo., 1972-75; fin. industry mktg. rep. IBM Can., Ltd., Toronto, Ont., 1976-79; regional telecommunications mktg. exec. Control Data Corp., Atlanta, 1980-84; gen. mgr. The Plant Plant, Atlanta, 1985-92; IBM; sys. engr. IBM, Atlanta, 1993—; pioneer installer on-line Automatic Teller Machines, Pos Equipment. Author: The Canadian Payment System: An International Perspective, 1977. Mem. Chgo. Coun. on Fgn. Rels.; bd. dirs. Easter House Adoption Agy., Chgo., 1974-76. Mem. Internat. Brass Soc., Goethe Inst., Mensa. Clubs: Ponte Verde (Fla.); Royal Ont. Yacht, Libertyville Racquet. Home: 1948 Cobb Pky Apt 28J Smyrna GA 30080-2721

WILDMAN, IRIS J., law librarian, retired; b. Chgo., May 10, 1930; d. Isadore and Stella (Stark) W. BS, Northwestern U., Evanston, Ill., 1952; MLS, Case Western Res. U., 1954; JD, Santa Clara U., 1978. Asst. cataloger U. Chgo. Law Libr., 1952-53; cataloger Copyright Office/Libr. of Congress, 1954; law cataloger U.S. Army Libr./Pentagon, 1954-56; cataloger U.S. Dept. of Justice Libr., Washington, 1956-57; head tech. svcs. Ohio State U. Law Libr., Columbus, 1957-59, Skokie (Ill.) Pub. Libr., 1959-60; head cataloging and classification Northwestern U. Law Libr., Chgo., 1961-64; chief acquisitions and binding Yale Law Libr., New Haven, Conn., 1965-74; pub. svcs. libr. Stanford U. Law Libr., 1976-85; sr. reference libr. Robert Crown Law Libr. Stanford (Calif.) U., 1985-95; cons. Corp. Counsel, Govt., Washington D.C. Libr., 1957, U. P.R. Law Libr., 1968; faculty/dir. AALL Institutes on Cataloging, Classification and Acquisitions, 1966, 70, 73; libr./lectr. Stanford Law Sch., 1978-82, 85-93. Compiler: Federal Judges and Justices, 1987—; editor: Law Libraries in the U.S. and Can., 1958, Directory of Law Librs., 1964, 66; indexer: Index to Foreign Legal Periodicals, 1983—; contbr. articles to profl. jours. Mem. No. Calif. Assn. Law Librs. (v.p., pres. elect 1980-82), Am. Assn. Law Librs. Home: 1757 Pilgrim Ave Mountain View CA 94040-2363

WILDMAN, STEPHANIE MAY, law educator; b. N.Y.C., Apr. 10, 1949; d. Herman and Edith Wildman; m. Michael Tobriner; children: Becky, Ben. AB, Stanford U., 1970, JD, 1973. Bar: Calif. 1973. Clk. Hon. Charles M. MErrill U.S. Ct. Appeals (9th cir.), San Francisco, 1973-74; asst. prof. U. San Francisco, 1974-76; atty. pvt. practice, Berkeley, Calif., 1975-76; staff atty. CRLA, Santa Rosa, Calif., 1976-77; assoc. prof. law U. San Francisco, 1978-80, prof. law, 1980—; adj. prof. McGeorge Sch. Law, Sacramento, Calif., 1974-75; vis. prof. Stanford (Calif.) Law Sch., 1987, 88, U. Calif. Hastings Coll. Law, San Francisco, 1989-90, Santa Clara Sch. Law, 1994-95. Author: Privilege Revealed: How Invisible Preference Undermines America, 1996. Mem. Soc. Am. Law Tchrs. (bd. govs. 1989—, pres.-elect 1996). Office: U San Francisco Sch Law 2130 Fulton St San Francisco CA 94117-1080

WILE, JOAN, composer, lyricist, singer; b. Rochester, N.Y., July 17, 1931; d. Louis and Janet Louise (Wile) Meltzer; children: Ron Wasserman, Diana Wasserman McCloskey. BA, U. Chgo., 1952. Freelance compower, lyricist, singer, mus. book writer. Rec. artist Vanguard Records, 1954; singer Storyville, 1954, The Crystal Palace, 1957; mem. vocal-revue act The Neighbors performances include The Village Vanguard, Le Ruban Bleu, The Bon Soir and The Living Room ; singer, lyricist feature film The Happy Hooker, 1974; singer radio and TV jingles, movie sound tracks, supper clubs, hotels, TV music spls. and variety shows; lyricist, composer mus. Tobacco Road, 1974, Seven Ages of Woman, 1987 (named most promising new musical); writer, producer When They Turned on the Tap at the Watergate, The Truth Come Pourin' Out; lyricist songs for Romper Room, 1983; lyricist, composer, writer People is People, 1983; lyricist, composer script for children's albums for Golden and Peter Pan Records, others; lyricist, composer material in Julius Monk's Upstairs at the Downstairs, 1958; lyricist, composer, performer Nancy's Economic Plan, 1980; lyricist, composer Mothers and Daughters, 1984; lyricist, composer, author The Symposium, 1987; lyricist, composer From There to Here, 1987; writer Rhyme, Women and Song; lyricist, librettist, composer Museum of Natural Sex History, 1992. Organizer Women in Def. Eleanor Roosevelt, N.Y.C., 1989—. Runner-up Am. Song Festival, 1976. Mem. Dramatists Guild, SAG, Theatre Artists Workshop, AFTRA, ASCAP (Popular award 1970-88). Home and Office: 875 West End Ave Apt 5A New York NY 10025-4952

WILEY, BONNIE JEAN, journalism educator; b. Portland, Oreg.; d. Myron Eugene and Bonnie Jean (Galliher) W. BA, U. Wash., 1948; MS, Columbia U., 1957; PhD, So. Ill. U., 1965. Mng. editor Yakima (Wash.) Morning Herald; reporter, photographer Portland Oregonian; feature writer Seattle Times; war correspondent PTO AP; western feature editor AP, San Francisco; reporter Yakima Daily Republic; journalism tchr. U. Wash., Seattle, Cen. Wash. U., Ellensburg, U. Hawaii, Honolulu; mem. grad. faculty Bangkok U., Thailand, 1991; mem. faculty journalism program U. Hawaii, Honolulu, 1992—; Adminstr. Am. Samoa Coll., Pago Pago; news features advisor Xinhua News Agy., Beijing, Yunnan Normal U., Kumming, China, 1995. Mem. Women in Communications (Hawaii Headliner award 1985, Nat. Headliner award 1990), Theta Sigma Phi. Home: 1434 Punahou St Apt 1212 Honolulu HI 96822-4729

WILEY, JUDITH, association executive; b. London, Ont., Can., Feb. 24, 1947; children: Michael, Melissa, Marcia. With Amway of Can. Ltd., London, Ont., 1969-84; pres. YWCA of St. Thomas (Ont.)-Elgin, 1981-84, exec. dir., 1984-89; dir. internat. cooperation YWCA of Can., Toronto, 1989-91, CEO, 1991-96; pres. Can. Soc. Assn. Execs., Toronto, 1996—. Treas. Can. Congress Learning Opportunities for Women, 1989-91; bd. dirs., past chair Can. Coun. for Internat. Cooperation; mem. com. Five Days of Peace; bd. dirs. Seams Easy, High Street Recreation Complex, Elgin (Ont.) Gen Hosp., Elgin Family Violence Coordinating Ctr., Can. Physicians for Aid and Relief; founding mem. Gt. Lakes Women's Network for Peace; mem. campus adv. com. Fanshaw C.C. Mem. Can. Soc. Assn. Execs., Can. Assn. Women Execs. and Entrepreneurs, Bus. and Profl. Women's Club. Office: Can Soc Assn Execs, 40 University Ave Ste 1104, Toronto, ON Canada M5J 1T1

WILEY, MYRA, mental health nurse; b. Lexington, Ala., Jan. 20, 1938; d. Joseph Aaron and Annie Lura (Putnam) Haraway; m. Robert Harold Wiley, Sept. 17, 1960; children: Sonya, Robert, Marie. BSN, U. Ala., Huntsville, 1989. RN, Ala.; cert. in chem. dependency. Nursing asst., night-weekend coord. Upjohn Health Care, Huntsville, 1983-87; nursing asst. North Ala. Rehab. Hosp., Huntsville, 1987-89; staff nurse Humana Hosp., Huntsville, 1989-91; staff nurse counselor Bradford-Parkside, Madison, Ala., 1991-95; relief charge nurse for behavioral health Columbia Med. Ctr. of Huntsville (formerly Crestwood Hosp.), Huntsville, Ala., 1995—. Mem. ANA, Ala. State Nurses Assn., Madison County Nurses Assn, Nat. Consortium Chem. Dependency Nurses, Inc. Baptist.

WILFONG, BRENDA A., telecommunications executive; b. Ashland, Ohio, Jan. 2, 1963; d. Edward Eugene and Barbara Ann (Butterfield) Bush; m. Duane Hubert Wilfong, Oct. 22, 1984 (dec. Sept. 1994); children: Jessie Leona, Christina Elizabeth. BBA, Kent State U., 1989. Asst. editor Ohio dir. Harris Pub. Co., Twinsburg, Ohio, 1983-84; accounts payable clerk M. O'Neil's Co., Akron, Ohio, 1984-85; network mgmt. asst. Alltel Corp., Hudson, Ohio, 1985-86, treasury asst., 1986-87, assoc. analyst treasury, 1987-92, carrier svcs. coord., 1992-93; sr. staff asst. Alltel Corp., Twinsburg, 1993-95, adminstr. carrier svcs., 1995—; contracts adminstr. Alltel Corp., Hudson, Ohio, 1995—. Recipient Brownie Mother Vol. award Girl Scouts Am., Akron, 1994. Mem. Inst. Mgmt. Accts. (editor newsletter 1990-92, dir. ins. 1992-94). Baptist. Home: 1630 Goodyear Blvd Akron OH 44305-3505

WILFORD, BONNIE BAIRD, health policy specialist; b. Chgo., Jan. 11, 1946; d. George Martin and Ruth Eleanor (Anderson) Baird; m. David Edward Wilford, Oct. 2, 1967; children: Heather Lynn, Edward Baird. BA, Knox Coll., 1967; postgrad., Roosevelt U., 1969-71. Staff assoc. Am. Hosp. Assn., Chgo., 1967-70; mgr. plan devel. Blue Cross & Blue Shield Assn., Chgo., 1970-79; dir. dept. substance abuse AMA, Chgo., 1979-91, dir. divsn. clin. sci., 1988-91; ptnr. Wilford & Assocs., healthcare consultants, 1991—; exec. office of the Pres. The White House, 1991-92; cons. Pres.'s Commn. on Model State Drug Laws, 1993-94; dir. Pharm. Policy Project, George Washington U. Med. Ctr., Washington, 1992—. Author: Balancing the Response to Prescription Drug Abuse, 1990, Pharmaceutical Benefits for HIV/AIDS, 1996; editor Pharmaceutical Policy Rev., 1996—; contbr. articles to profl. jours. Recipient Outstanding Svc. award Fla. Task Force on Alcohol and Drug Abuse, 1986, Merit award State of Mo., 1985, Disting. Svc. award U.S. Dept. Health and Human Svcs., 1990. Mem. APHA, Internat. Narcotic Enforcement Officers Assn. (Award of Honor 1985), Assn. for Med. Edn. and Rsch. Substance Abuse, Informal Steering Com. Prescription Drug Abuse (bd. dirs.). Office: CHPR/George Washington U 2021 K St NW Ste 800 Washington DC 20006-1003

WILHELM, KATE (KATY GERTRUDE), author; b. Toledo, June 8, 1928; d. Jesse Thomas and Ann (McDowell) Meredith; m. Joseph B. Wilhelm, May 24, 1947 (div. 1962); children: Douglas, Richard; m. Damon Knight, Feb. 23, 1963; 1 child, Jonathan. PhD in Humanities(hon.), Mich. State U., 1996. Writer, 1956—; co-dir. Milford Sci. Fiction Writers Conf., 1963-76; lectr. Clarion Fantasy Workshop Mich. State U., 1968-94. Author: (novels) More Bitter Than Death, 1962, (with Theodore L. Thomas) The Clone, 1965, The Nevermore Affair, 1966, The Killer Thing, 1967, Let the Fire Fall, 1969, (with Theodore L. Thomas) The Year of the Cloud, 1970, Abyss: Two Novellas, 1971, Margaret and I, 1971, City of Cain, 1971, The Clewiston Test, 1976, Where Late the Sweet Birds Sang, 1976, Fault Lines, 1976, Somerset Dreams and Other Fictions, 1978, Juniper Time, 1979, (with Damon Knight) Better Than One, 1980, A Sense of Shadow, 1981, Listen, Listen, 1981, Oh! Susannah, 1982, Welcome Chaos, 1983, Huysman's Pets, 1986, (with R. Wilhelm) The Hills Are Dancing, 1986, The Hamlet Trap, 1987, Crazy Time, 1988, Dark Door, 1988, Smart House, 1989, Children of the Wind: Five Novellas, 1989, Cambio Bay, 1990, Sweet, Sweet Poison, 1990, Death Qualified, 1991, And the Angels Sing, 1992, Seven Kinds of Death, 1992, Naming the Flowers, 1992, Justice for Some, 1993, The Best Defense, 1994, A Flush of Shadows, 1995, Malice Prepense, 1996, (multimedia space fantasy) Axoltl, U. Oreg. Art Mus., 1979, (radio play) The Hindenburg Effect, 1985; editor: Nebula Award Stories #9, 1974, Clarion SF, 1976; contbr. short stories to anthologies and periodicals. Mem. PEN, Nat. Writers Union, Mystery Writers Am., Sci. Fiction Writers Am., Authors Guild. Address: 1645 Horn Ln Eugene OR 97404-2957

WILHELMI, MARY CHARLOTTE, education educator, college official; b. Williamsburg, Iowa, Oct. 2, 1928; d. Charles E. and Loretto (Judge) Harris; m. Sylvester Lee Wilhelmi, May 26, 1951; children: Theresa Ann, Sylvia Marie, Thomas Lee, Kathryn Lyn, Nancy Louise. BS, Iowa State U., 1950; MA in Edn., Va. Poly. Inst. and State U., 1973, cert. advanced grad. studies, 1978. Edn. coord. Nova Ctr. U. Va., Falls Church, 1969-73; asst. adminstr. Consortium for Continuing Higher Edn. George Mason U., Fairfax, Va., 1973-78; adminstr., asst. prof. George Mason U., Fairfax, 1978-83; dir. coll. rels. and devel., assoc. prof. No. Va. C.C., Annandale, 1983—; bd. dirs. No. Va. C.C. Ednl. Found., Inc., Annandale, 1984—; v.p. mktg. Fairfax (Va.) Symphony, 1995—; chmn. Health Systems Agy. No. Va., Fairfax; mem. George Mason U. Inst. for Ednl. Transformation. Edtl. bd. Va. Forum, 1990-93; contbr. articles to profl. jours. Bd. dirs. Fairfax County chpt. ARC, 1981-86, Va. Inst. Polit. Leadership, 1996—, Fairfax Com. of 100, 1986-88, 90—, Hospice No. Va., 1983-88, No. Va. Mental Health Inst., Fairfax County, 1978-81, Fairfax Profl. Women's Network, 1981, Arts oun. Fairfax County, 1989—; vice chmn. Va. Commonwealth U. Ctr. on Aging, Richmond, 1978—; mem. supt.'s adv. coun. Fairfax County Pub. Schs., 1974-86, No. Va. Press Club, 1978—; pres. Fairfax Ext. Leadership Coun., 1995; mem. Leadership Fairfax Class of 1992. Named Woman of Distinction, Soroptomists, Fairfax, 1988, Bus. Woman of Yr., Falls Church Bus. and Profl. Women's Group, 1993; fellow Va. Inst. Polit. Leadership, 1995. Mem. State Coun. Higher Edn. Va. (pub. affairs adv. com. 1985—), Greater Washington Bd. Trade, Fairfax County C. of C. (legis. affairs com. 1984—) Va. Women Lobbyists, 1991—, No. Va. Bus. Roundtable, Internat. Platform Assn., Phi Delta Kappa (10-Yr. Continuous Svc. award 1991), Kappa Delta Alumni No. Va., Psi Chi, Phi Kappa Phi. Roman Catholic. Home: 4902 Ravensworth Rd Annandale VA 22003-5552 Office: No Va CC 4001 Wakefield Chapel Rd Annandale VA 22003-3744

WILHOIT, CAROL DIANE, special education educator; b. Rockford, Ill., June 2, 1950; d. Iris May (Zeigler) Cleeton; m. Jerry Dean Wilhoit, Aug. 15, 1971; children: David, Heather, Hilary, Erin. BSE, N.E. Mo. State U., 1972; MS in Edn., 1991. Cert. spl. edn. tchr., Mo. Tchr. emotionally handicapped Clarence Cannon Elem., Elsberry, Mo., 1972-73; EMH tchr. Bowling Green (Mo.) Elem., 1973-77, Clopton High Sch., Clarksville, Mo., 1979-82; tchr. learning disabilities Eugene Field Elem., Hannibal, Mo., 1982—; active Accelerated Sch., chair curriculum cadre, intervention cadre, steering com., 1992-93, mem. parent involvement com., 1994; del. Northeast Dist. Tchrs. Assn. Assembly, 1994. Mem. state due process subcom., 1994; PL-94-142 adv. com., 1992—. Mem. Coun. Exceptional Children (pres. 1986-88, bd. dirs. Mo. chpt. 1986, 1988-91, organizer local chpt. 1988, awards chmn., chair profl. devel. subcom., chair registration com. 1991-92, chair membership com. Mark Twain chpt. 1991—, spring conf. session leader, del. to internat. coun. assembly 1992-93, spring conf. chair 1994, del. to internat. conf. 1995), Mo. State Tchrs. Assn. (del. to state assembly 1989-90, superintendent's com. 1989-91, dist. prof. devel. com. 1990—, mentor tchr. 1990-92, state spl. edn. monitoring com. 1991-92), Hannibal Cmty. Tchrs. Assn. (bldg. rep. exec. com. 1987—, v.p. 1988, pres. 1989), Learning Disabilities Assn. Office: Eugene Field Elem 1405 Pearl St Hannibal MO 63401-4151

WILK, PAULA RENEE See RENEE, PAULA

WILKEN, CLAUDIA ANN, judge; b. Mpls., Aug. 17, 1949; d. Claudius W. and Dolores Ann (Grass) W.; m. John M. True, 1984; 1 child, Peter Wilken True. BA with honors, Stanford U., 1971; JD, U. Calif., Berkeley, 1975. Bar: Calif. 1975, U.S. Dist. Ct. (no. dist.) Calif. 1975, U.S. Ct. Appeals (9th cir.) 1976, U.S. Supreme Ct. 1981. Asst. fed. pub. defender U.S. Dist. Ct. (no. dist.) Calif., San Francisco, 1975-78, U.S. magistrate judge, 1983-93, dist. judge, 1993—; ptnr. Wilkin & Leverett, Berkeley, Calif., 1978-84; adj. prof. U. Calif., Berkeley, 1978-84; prof. New Coll. Sch. Law, 1980-85; mem. jud. br. com. Jud. Conf. U.S.; mem. edn. com. Fed. Jud. Ctr. Magistrate Judges, 9th Cir. Magistrate Judges; chair 9th cir. Magistrates Conf., 1987-88. Mem. ABA (mem. jud. adminstrn. divsn.), Calif. State Bar Assn., Alameda County Bar Assn. (judge's membership), Fed. Magistrates Judges Assn. (sec.), Nat. Assn. Women Judges, Order of Coif, Phi Beta Kappa. Office: US Dist Ct No Dist 1301 Clay St Courtroom 2 Oakland CA 94612*

WILKENFELD, JUDITH DEBORAH, lawyer, legal advisor; b. Washington, Mar. 12, 1943; d. Harry Morris and Esther (Lipsez) Plotkin; m. Jonathan Wilkenfeld, July 26, 1964; children: Ari Micah, Daniela Lisa, Gilad Joseph. BA cum laude, Brown U., 1964; postgrad., George Washington U., 1964-66; JD summa cum laude, Ind. U., 1967. Bar: D.C., 1970, U.S.

Supreme Ct., 1975. Tchg. fellow Ind. U. Sch. Law, Bloomington, 1967-69; atty., affiliate Nat. Labor Rels. Bd., Washington, 1969-77; mem. faculty Hebrew U. Law Sch., Jerusalem, 1977-79; atty. Fed. Labor Rels. Authority, Washington, 1979-80; asst. dir., atty. Fed. Trade Commn., Washington, 1980-94; spl. advisor to commr. FDA, Rockville, Md., 1994—; bd. mem. editl. bd. Food, Drug Law Jour., Washington, 1991-95. Jewish. Home: 7542 14th St NW Washington DC 20012 Office: FDA 5600 Fishers Ln Rockville MD 20587

WILKENING, LAUREL LYNN, academic administrator, planetary scientist; b. Richland, Wash., Nov. 23, 1944; d. Marvin Hubert and Ruby Alma (Barks) W.; m. Godfrey Theodore Sill, May 18, 1974. BA, Reed Coll., 1966; PhD, U. Calif., San Diego, 1970. Asst. prof. to assoc. prof. U. Ariz., Tucson, 1973-80, dir. Lunar and Planetary Lab., head planetary scis., 1981-83, vice provost, prof. planetary scis., 1983-85, v.p. rsch., dean Grad. Coll., 1985-88; div. scientist NASA Hdqrs., Washington, 1980; prof. geol scis., adj. prof. astronomy, provost U. Washington, Seattle, 1988-93; chancellor U. Calif., Irvine, 1993—; dir. Seagate Tech., Inc., 1993—, Rsch. Corp., 1991—; vice chmn. Nat. Commn. on Space, Washington, 1984-86, Adv. Com. on the Future of U.S. Space Program, 1990; chair Space Policy Adv. Bd., Nat. Space Coun., 1991-92; co-chmn. primitive bodies mission study team NASA/European Space Agy., 1984-85; chmn. com. rendezvous sci. working group NASA, 1983-85; mem. panel on internat. cooperation and competition in space Congl. Office Tech. Assessment, 1982-83. Author: (monograph) Particle Track Studies and the Origin of Gas-Rich Meteorites, 1971; editor: Comets, 1982. U. Calif. Regents fellow, 1966-67; NASA trainee, 1967-70. Fellow Meteoritical Soc. (councilor 1976-80), Am. Assn. Advanced Sci.; mem. Am. Astron. Soc. (chmn. div. planetary scis. 1984-85), Am. Geophys. Union, AAAS, Planetary Soc. (dir. 1994—), Phi Beta Kappa. Democrat. Office: U Calif Chancellors Office 501 Adminstrn Bldg Irvine CA 92697-1900*

WILKER, PATRICIA YVONNE, project manger; b. Augusta, Ga., Sept. 25, 1948; d. Elias and Eula Mae (Adams) Becton; m. W. Ed Wilker, Aug. 14, 1971; children: Pamela Michelle, Erica Denise. BA, Paine Coll., 1970; M in Social Work, U. Ga., 1972. Sr. social worker Ga. Dept of Human Resources, Athens, 1972-78; svcs. cons. So. Bell Tel. Co., Athens, 1978-81, data sys. specialist, 1981-83; staff mgr. AT&T, Atlanta, 1983-85; training specialist AT&T, Parsippany, N.J., 1985-90; sys. cons. AT&T, Atlanta, 1990—; devel., presenter Self Esteem Program, bd. mem. Athens Comm. Coun. on Aging, 1994—, Family Counseling Svcs., 1994—. Regional dir. SE region Jack & Jill of Am. Inc., 1993-95. Mem. Delta Sigma Theta. Home: 135 Tamarack Dr Athens GA 30605

WILKERSON, ISABEL, journalist. With The N.Y. Times, N.Y.C.; bureau chief The N.Y. Times, Chgo. Bureau, Chgo., 1991-95; now sr. writer N.Y. Times, 1995. Recipient Pulitzer Prize for feature writing, 1994. Office: The New York Times 229 W 43rd St New York NY 10036*

WILKERSON, PATRICIA HELEN, director child development center; b. Victoria, Tex., Aug. 2, 1936; d. Milo Andrew and Gertrude H. (Nichols) Beeman; children: Cheryl Lynn, Susan Leigh, Debra Ann, Jon Craig. Student, U. Corpus Christi, 1954-56, Del Mar Coll., 1970-71-86-88. Tax clk. Nueces County Tax Assessor, Corpus Christi, Tex., 1956-57; corr. sec. Boy Scouts of Am. Gulf Coast Coun., Corpus Christi, 1957-58; elem. dir, nursery sch. coord. First Bapt. Ch., Corpus Christi, 1972-73, pre-K tchr., sec., 1975-85; dir. child devel. ctr. 2d Bapt. Ch., Corpus Christi, 1985—; ASSIST pre-sch. leader Corpus Christi Bapt. Assn., 1967—; conf. leader, cons. Bapt. Gen. Conv., Dallas, 1967—; mem. early childhood adv. bd., Del Mar Coll., Corpus Christi, 1981-86; mem. adv. com. Tex. Bapt. Weekday Assn., Dallas, 1995—, Gulf Coast Tng. coalition. Writer Presch. Sunday Sch. Curriculum, 1994-95, 95-96, Southern Bapt. Conv. Sunday sch. tchr., various Tex. Bapt. Chs., 1959—; presch. divsn. dir. Second Bapt. Ch., Corpus Christi, 1986—. Mem. Bay Area Assn. Edn. Young Children (sec. 1981-82, co-chair conf. 1991, Week of the Young Child chair 1995-96). Home: 4206 Walnut Hills Apt A Corpus Christi TX 78413 Office: 2nd Bapt Ch Child Devel Ctr 6901 S Staples Corpus Christi TX 78413

WILKERSON, RITA LYNN, special education educator, consultant; b. Crescent, Okla., Apr. 22; Mem. ASCD, Coun. for Exceptional Children, OARC, OACLD, Phi Delta Kappa, Kappa Delta Pi. BA, Cen. State U., Edmond, Okla., 1963; MEd, Cen. State U., 1969; postgrad., U. Okla., 1975. Elem. tchr. music Hillsdale (Okla.) Pub. Sch., 1963-64; jr. high sch. music and spl. edn. Okarche (Okla.) Pub. Sch., 1965-71; cons. Title III Project, Woodward, Okla., 1971-72; dir. Regional Edn. Svc. Ctr., Guymon, Okla., 1972-81; dir., psychologist Project W.O.R.K., Guymon, 1981-90; tchr. behavioral disorders Unified Sch. Dist. 480, Liberal, Kans., 1990—; sch. psychologist Hardesty (Okla.) Schs., 1994; cons. Optima (Okla.) Pub. Schs., 1990, Felt (Okla.) Pub. Schs., 1990, Texhoma (Okla.) Schs., 1994, Balko (Okla.) Pub. Schs., 1996; spl. edn. cons. Optima Pub. Schs., 1992—, Goodwell (Okla.) Pub. Schs., 1992—; diagnostician Tyrone, Okla. Pub. Schs., 1992-95; home svcs. provider Dept. Human Svcs., Guymon, 1990; active Kans. Dept. Social and Rehab. Svcs., 1993—; adj. tchr. Seward County C.C., 1994—. Grantee Cen. State U., 1968-69, Oklahoma City Dept. Edn., 1988-89. Mem. ASCD, NAFE, NEA (liberal Kans. chpt.), AAUW, Coun. Exceptional Children, Okla. Assn. Retarded Citizens, Okla. Assn. for Children with Learning Disabilities, Phi Delta Kappa. Republican. Home: 616 N Crumley St Guymon OK 73942-4341 Office: Unified Sch Dist 480 7th And Western Liberal KS 67901

WILKEY, DAPHNE LEIGH, answering service owner; b. Rome, Ga., June 27, 1969; d. Earl Wayne Sr. and Virginia Lela (Revis) W. Student, Wesleyan Coll., 1988-89, Christian Renewal Sch. of Theology & Missions, 1995. Owner Exec. Answering Svc., Brunswick, Ga., 1990—. sec., treas. Mayor's Com. Svcs. for Disabled, Brunswick, Ga., 1991—; founder Coastal Spinal Cord Injury Support Group, Brunswick, Ga., 1991—; contact Hadicap Parking Patrol, Brunswick, Ga., 1993—; singles ministry leader Christian Renewal Ch., Brunswick, Ga., 1995—; missionary Nicaragua, 1995, Mex., 1996. Recipient Cmty. Svc. award and 3rd runner-up Ms. Wheelchair U.S.A. Pageant, 1995. Mem. Women Bus. Owners (comm. chmn. 1989—). Republican. Office: Exec Answering Svc 4229 Norwich Ext Brunswick GA 31520

WILKEY, MARY HUFF, investor, writer, publisher; b. Dayton, Ohio, Sept. 30, 1940; d. Charles Joseph and Frances Rose (Wintersteen) Huff; divorced; children: Christopher Tyson, Charles Cory, Jennifer Jo. Student, Sinclair C.C., Dayton, 1979-85. Pvt. sec. Dare, Inc., Troy, Ohio, 1962-63; legal sec. Smith & Schnacke, Dayton, 1963-68; adminstrv. asst. U.S. Magistrate, Dayton, 1971-74; legal technician Coolidge, Wall, Womsley & Lombard Co., L.P.A., Dayton, 1968-75, 81-85, Lair & Owen, Dayton, 1979-81; owner, operator Village Mill Country Store, Tipp City, Ohio, 1987-88; owner, mgr. Happy Days Hotel, Franklin, Ohio, 1989—; pres., owner KSL Enterprises, Franklin, Ohio, 1988—. Author, pub. (directory) Your Personal Guide, 1988, 89, Why Many Christians Are Afflicted, 1994. Phone support vol. Operation Golden Ring, Dayton, 1984-85; vol. Sta. WPTD Pub. TV, Dayton, 1983-85. Mem. NAFE, Internat. Platform Assn., Greater Dayton Real Estate Investor Assn. Office: PO Box 854 Franklin OH 45005-0854

WILKINS, CAROL MARIE, communications executive; b. Lorain, Ohio, Aug. 24, 1954; d. Stanley Victor and Dorothy Elizabeth (Dhaemers) W. BA in Comm., Ohio Dominican Coll., 1972; MA in Comm., Ohio State U., 1976, postgrad. Cert. secondary tchr. Mgr. corp. com. ChemLawn Svcs. Corp., Columbus, Ohio, 1980-87; dir. sports mktg. Truesports Co., Hilliard, Ohio, 1987-89; dir. mktg. & pub. rels. Bobby Rahal, Dublin, Ohio, 1989-90; mgr. motor sports PPG Industries, Strongsville, Ohio, 1992-96; v.p. comm. Team Green Inc., Indpls., 1996—; bd. dirs. Championship Auto Racing Aux. Mem. Pub. Rels. Soc. Am. (Prism award Ctrl. Ohio chpt. 1987), Women in Comms. Roman Catholic. Home and Office: Team Green Inc 21228 Creekside Dr Strongsville OH 44136

WILKINS, CAROLINE HANKE, consumer agency administrator, political worker; b. Corpus Christi, Tex., May 12, 1937; d. Louis Allen and Jean Guckian Hanke; m. B. Hughel Wilkins, 1957; 1 child, Brian Hughel. Student, Tex. Coll. Arts and Industries, 1956-57, Tex. Tech. U., 1957-58; BA, U. Tex., 1961; MA magna cum laude, U. Ams., 1964. Instr. history Oreg. State U., 1967-68; adminstr. Consumer Svcs. divsn. State of Oreg., 1977-80, Wilkins Assoc., 1980—; mem. PFMC Salmon Adv. subpanel, 1982-86. Author: (with B. H. Wilkins) Implications of the U.S.-Mexican Water Treaty for Interregional Water Transfer, 1968. Dem. precinct committeewoman, Benton County, Oreg., 1964-90; publicity chmn. Benton County Gen. Election, 1964; chmn. Get-Out-the-Vote Com., Benton County, 1966; vice chmn.Benton County Dem. Ctrl. Com., 1966-70; vice chmn. 1st Congl. Dist., Oreg., 1966-68, chmn., 1969-74; mem. exec. com. Western States Dem. Conf., 1970-72; vice chmn. Dem. Nat. Com., 1972-77, mem. arrangements com., 1972, 76, mem. Dem. Charter Commn., 1973-74; mem. Dem. Nat. Com., 1972-77, 85-89, mem. size and composition com., 1987-89, rules com., 1988; mem. Oreg. Govt. Ethics Commn., 1974-76; del., mem. rules com. Dem. Nat. Conv., 1988; 1st v.p. Nat. Fedn. Dem. Women, 1983-85, pres., 1985-87, parliamentarian, 1993-95; mem. Kerr Libr. bd. Oreg. State U., 1989-95, pres., 1994-95; mem. Corvallis-Benton County Libr. Found., 1991—, sec., 1993, v.p., 1994, pres., 1995; bd. dirs. Oreg. chpt. U.S. Lighthouse Soc. Named Outstanding Mem., Nat. Fedn. Dem. Women, 1992. Mem. Nat. Assn. Consumer Agy. Adminstrs., Soc. Consumer Affairs Profls., Oreg. State U. Folk Club (pres. faculty wives 1989-90), Zonta (vice area bd. dirs. dist. 8 1992-94, area dir., bd. dist. 8 1994-96, bylaws and resolutions coord. 1996—). Office: 3311 NW Roosevelt Dr Corvallis OR 97330-1169

WILKINS, CAROLYN NOREEN, early childhood educator; b. Fall River, Mass., Apr. 29, 1967; d. Thomas K. Jr. and Barbara A. (Messier) Porter; m. James A. Wilkins III, Feb. 22, 1992; 1 child, Zachary. BS in Edn., Lesley Coll., 1989. Cert. in elem. edn., Fla. 4-6th grade tchr. Paul Coffee Sch., Westport, Mass., 1989-90; prekindergarten tchr. Tender Loving Child Care Ctr., New Bedford, Mass., 1990-92, My Sch. Learning Ctr., Stuart, Fla., 1992-94, St. Michael's Ind. Sch., Stuart, 1994-95; tchr. White City Elem. Sch., Ft. Pierce, Fla., 1995-96; pvt. tutor, Westport, Stuart, 1989-95. Grantee Fla. Coun. Ind. Schs., 1995-96, Fla. Power & Light Co. Democrat. Roman Catholic. Office: 905 W 2d St Fort Pierce FL 34982

WILKINS, JOSETTA EDWARDS, state representative; b. Little Rock, July 17, 1932; d. James Wesley and Laura Birdgette (Freeman) Edwards; m. Henry Wilkins III, Oct. 30, 1954 (dec.); children: Calvin Tyrone, Henry IV, Cassandra Felecia, Mark Reginald, Angela Juanita. BS, A.M. & N Coll., 1961; MEd, U. Ark., 1967; EdD, Okla. State U., 1987. Lic. counselor, Ark. Dep. dir. manpower tng. Ark. Coun./Farmer Workers, Little Rock, 1967-73; dir. cooperative edn. U. Ark., Pine Bluff, 1973-85, interim dir. univ. rels. and devel., 1987-88, assoc. prof., 1988—, prof. edn.; tchr. elem. Lincoln Sch. Dist., Star City, Ark., 1961-63; high sch. counselor Dollarway Pub. Sch. Dist., Pine Bluff, 1963-66; tchr. elem. Pitts. Pub. Schs., 1966-67; rehab. counselor State of Ark., Pine Bluff, 1967-69. Campaign mgr. senatorial race Edwards, Pine Bluff, 1988; sec. Mayor's Bi-Racial Coun., Pine Bluff, 1973, Comprehensive Health Care Jefferson County, Pine Bluff, 1973; rep. S.E. Ark. Health Systems Agy., 1975-85; pres. PTA Merrill High Sch., Pine Bluff, 1971; elected mem. Ho. of Reps., 1991; bd. dirs. Ptnrs. for a Better Pine Bluff; co-chair Dollarway Drug Adv. Coun.; active Wesley Found., Ark. Dem. Com., Jefferson County Juvenile Detention Commn., episcopacy com. United Meth. Ch., others. State of Ark. fellow, 1985. Mem. Nat. Assn. Tchr. Educators, Am. Assn. for Adult and Continuing Edn., Coop. Edn. Assn., Ark. Tchrs. Assn., Am. Assn. for Counseling and Devel., Ark. Assn. for Counseling Guidance and Devel., Ark. Personnel and Guidance Assn., Sorority Pub. Svc. Orgn., Delta Sigma Theta. Methodist. Home: 303 N Maple St Pine Bluff AR 71601-3346

WILKINS, RITA DENISE, researcher, multimedia design consultant; b. Detroit, June 21, 1951; d. William H. and Alice L. (Hayes) Smith. Student, George Peabody Coll., 1969-70, Cleveland (Tenn.) State Community Coll., 1973-75. Mgmt. coord., legal coord. Arlen Realty and Devel. Corp., Chattanooga, Tenn., 1973-76; asst. v.p., office mgr. Newburger Andes & Co., Atlanta, 1976-78, asst. v.p., project mgr., 1978-79; project mgr. Robinson-Humphrey, Atlanta, 1979-80; dept. head Office Properties Group Merrill Lynch Realty Comml. Svcs., Atlanta, 1980-83; acquisition devel. mgmt. rep. Cardinal Industries, Inc., Atlanta, 1983-86; pres., sr. cons. CPC/Foresite, Charleston, S.C., 1986—; guest lectr. Ga. State U. Contbr. articles to profl. jours. Mem. Indsl. Devel. Rsch. Coun. Office: CPC/Foresite 115 Dorris Ave Goodlettsville TN 37072-1306

WILKINS, SHEILA SCANLON, management consultant; b. Oakland, Calif., Sept. 23, 1936; d. Michael Joseph and Joan (Daly) Scanlon; m. Thomas Wayne Wilkins, Aug. 14, 1965; children: Mary, John, Kathleen. BMusic, AB Liberal Arts maxima cum laude, Holy Names Coll., Oakland, 1958, MA in Music, 1972; MA in Ednl. Adminstrn., St. Mary's Coll., Moraga, Calif., 1983. Cert. tchr., Calif.; cert. in human resources mgmt., human resources tng. and devel. Tchr., dir. student activities Vallejo (Calif.) Unified Sch. Dist., 1962-63; tchr. Berkeley (Calif.) Unified Sch. Dist., 1963-66; pub. rels. asst. Alta Bates Hosp., Berkeley, 1973-74; tchr., adminstr. Walnut Creek (Calif.) Sch. Dist., 1974-80; dist. tchg. Moraga Sch. Dist., 1980-83; tech. tng. adminstr. Crocker Nat. Bank, Walnut Creek, Calif., 1984-85; tng. officer Wells Fargo Bank, Concord, Calif., 1985-86; tng. mgr. Fab 3 Intel Corp, Livermore, Calif., 1986-91; orgn. cons. CIS ops. Intel Corp, Folsom, Calif., 1991-92; mgr. profl. devel. corp. edn. Intel Corp, Santa Clara, Calif., 1992-94; prin. The Wilkins Group, Walnut Creek, Calif., 1994—. Contbr. articles to profl. jours. Chair parent com. Boy Scouts Am., Concord, 1977-80; pres. Parents Club of St. Francis Sch., Concord, 1978-79; v.p. Parents Club of Carondelet High Sch., Concord, 1983-84. Mem. ASTD, Internat. Soc. for Performance Improvement (v.p. fin. 1988-89, pres. 1989-91), Inst. Mgmt. Cons. Home: 2182 Gill Port Ln Walnut Creek CA 94598-1150 Office: 712 Bancroft Rd Ste 250 Walnut Creek CA 94598-1531

WILKINS, SUSAN JACOBS, social services agency executive; b. N.Y.C., Oct. 30, 1950; d. Arnold and Harriet Sylvia (Poster) Jacobs; m. J. Ernest Wilkins III, Sept. 21, 1974; 1 child, Bree. BS in Exceptional and Elem. Edn., State Univ. Coll. at Buffalo, 1972. Cert. early childhood adminstr., Ariz. Lead tchr. Escondido (Calif.) Child Devel. Ctr., 1978-80; dir. child devel. programs Escondido YMCA, 1980-82; dir. Children's World, Phoenix, 1983; program coord. Assn. for Supportive Childcare, Tempe, Ariz., 1983-85; childcare licensing specialist Ariz. Dept. Health Svcs., Phoenix, 1985-86; asst. dir. child nutrition programs Ariz. Dept. Edn., Phoenix, 1986-89; mgr. child care policy Dept. Econ. Security, Phoenix, 1989-92; exec. dir. Assn. for Supportive Child Care, Tempe, 1992—; mem. Ariz. Child Care Adv. Com., Phoenix, 1992—; mem. child care adv. bd. Phoenix Coll., 1990, Mesa (Ariz.) C.C., 1993—; mem. Child Care Resource and Referral Coalition, Phoenix, 1992—. Co-author, editor: Standards of Excellence - Child Care Food Program, 1988. Founding mem. East Valley Moderates, Mesa, 1994—; mem. child care adv. bd. Sojourner Shelter for Abused Women, Phoenix, 1990—; mem. Coun. of United Way Agy. Execs., Phoenix, 1992—. Mem. Nat. Assn. for Edn. of Young Children, Nat. Assn. Childcare Resource and Referral Agys. (recognition for innovative programs 1993), Valley of the Sun Assn. for Edn. of Young Children (pres. 1994-96). Democrat. Office: Assn Supportive Child Care 4701 S Lakeshore Dr # 101 Tempe AZ 85282

WILKINSON, CHARLOTTE MCDOUGAL, counselor educator; b. Alexander City, Ala., Oct. 17, 1935; d. Joseph Elmo and Ruby Corrine (Ashworth) McDougal; children: Thomas George Jr., Joseph Mark. BA, Duke U., 1958; MEd, N.C. State U., 1978, EdD, 1990. English tchr. Raeford (N.C.) Elem. Sch.; social studies tchr. Southern High Sch., Durham, N.C., D.O.V.E. vocat. counselor; sch. counselor Jordan High Sch., Durham, Neal Middle Sch., Durham; assoc. prof. Winona (Minn.) State U. Contbr. articles to profl. jours. Recipient N.C. Sch. Counselor of Yr. award; scholar Duke U. Mem. ACA, Am. Sch. Counselor Assn., Am. Assn. Counselor Edn. and Supervision, Minn. Assn. for Counseling and Devel., Minn. Sch. Counselor Assn., Minn. Assn. for Counselor Edn. and Supervision, Phi Beta Kappa, Phi Kappa Phi, Dalta Kappa Gamma.

WILKINSON, DONNA MARIE, technical support engineer; b. Pasaic, N.J., June 3, 1959; d. Frederick Joseph and Claire T. (Perry) W. AA with high honors, Coll. DuPage, 1979; BA cum laude, U. S.C., 1980. Vol. Vols. Svc. Am., Green Bay, Wis., 1981; title/ins. clk. Assocs. Comml. Corp., Glen Ellyn, Ill., 1982-83, acctg. asst., 1983-86, ins. mgr., 1987-89; asst. survey dir. Nat. Opinion Rsch. Ctr. U. Chgo., Hyde Park, Ill., 1986-87; database adminstr. Miller, Mason & Dickenson, Chgo., 1989-90; bus. analyst Waste Mgmt., Oakbrook, Ill., 1990-94; lead tech. support engr. Planmium Tech., Inc., Oakbrook Terrace, Ill., 1994—. Vol. Bethlehem Ctr. Food Bank, Wheaton, Ill., 1993, Habitat for Humanity, DuPage County, 1995—; contbr., vol. Hesed House Homeless Shelter, Aurora, Ill., 1995—. Democrat. Roman Catholic.

WILKINSON, DORIS Y., medical sociology educator; b. Lexington, Ky., June 13, 1936; d. Howard Thomas and Regina Wilkinson. BA, U. Ky., 1958; MA, Case Western Res. U., 1960, PhD, 1968; MPH, Johns Hopkins U., 1985. Asst. prof. U. Ky., Lexington, 1968-70; assoc. prof., then prof. Macalester Coll., St. Paul, 1970-77; exec. assoc. Am. Sociol. Assn., Washington, 1977-80; prof. med. sociology Howard U., Washington, 1980-84; vis. prof. U. Va., 1984-85; prof. sociology U. Ky., Lexington, 1985—; chmn. panel women in sci. program NSF, Washington, 1976; rev. panelist Nat. Inst. Drug Abuse, Washington, 1978-79; mem. bd. sci. counselors Nat. Cancer Inst., Bethesda, Md., 1980-84; vis. scholar Harvard U., Cambridge, Mass., 1989-90, vis. prof., summers 1992, 93, 94; Rapoport vis. prof. social theory Smith Coll., summer 1995. Author: Wookbook for Introductory Sociology, 1968; editor: Black Revolt: Strategies of Protest, 1969; co-editor: The Black Male in America, 1977, Alternative Health Maintenance and Healing Systems, 1987, Race, Gender and the Life Cycle, 1991; social history photographic exhbn. "The African American Presence in Medicine" Harvard Med. Libr., 1991, Pearson Mus.- So. Ill. U. Med. Sch., 1992, N.J. Coll. Medicine and Dentistry, 1993, Louisville Mus. History and Sci., 1994, U. Cin. Med. Sch. Libr., 1994, Albert Einstein Coll. of Medicine, 1995; contbr. articles to profl. jours. Bd. overseers Case Western Res. U., Cleve., 1982-87. Recipient Pub. Humanities award U. Ky., 1990, Midway Coll. Women's History Month award, 1991, Gt. Tchr. award Nat. Alumni Assn. U. Ky., Disting. Scholar award Assn. Black Sociologists, 1993; inducted into Hall of Disting. Alumni, U. Ky., 1989; fellow Woodrow Wilson Found., 1959-61, Ford Found., 1989-90; grantee Social Sci. Rsch. Coun., 1975, Nat. Inst. Edn., 1978-80, Nat. Cancer Inst., 1986-88, Ky. Humanities Coun., 1988, Am. Coun. Learned Soc., 1989-90, NEH, 1991; Disting. Prof. in Coll. Arts and Scis., U. Ky., 1992-93. Mem. So. Sociol. Soc. (honors com. 1993-94), Am. Sociol. Assn. (exec. assoc., budget com. 1985-88, v.p. 1991-92, mem. coun. 1994—, Dubois-Johnson-Frazier award 1988), D.C. Sociol. Soc. (pres. 1982-83), Soc. for Study of Social Problems (v.p. 1984-85, pres. 1987-88), Ea. Sociol. Soc. (v.p. 1983-84, pres. 1992-93, I. Peter Gellman award 1987), Phi Beta Kappa (valedictorian), Alpha Kappa Delta. Unitarian.

WILKINSON, FRANCES CATHERINE, librarian, educator; b. Lake Charles, La., July 20, 1955; d. Derrell Fred and Catherine Frances (O'Toole) W.; div.; 1 child, Katrina Frances. BA in Communication with distinction, U. N.Mex., 1982, MPA, 1987; MLS, U. Ariz., 1990. Mktg. rsch. auditor Mktg. Rsch. N.Mex., Albuquerque, 1973-78; freelance photographer, 1974-75; libr. supr. gen. libr. U. N.Mex., Albuquerque, 1978-89, libr., asst. dept. head, 1989-90, libr., dept. head, 1990—; cons., trainer ergonomics univs. and govt. agys. across U.S., 1986—; bd. dirs. Friends of U. N.Mex. Librs., Aubuquerque, 1991-94; mediator Mediation Alliance, 1991-94. Contbr. articles to profl. jours. Counselor, advocate Albuquerque Rape Crisis Ctr., 1981-84. Mem. ALA (mem. com. 1990—), N.Am. Serials Interest Group (mem. com. 1994—), N.Mex. Libr. Assn., N.Mex. Preservation Alliance, (vice chair 1995—), Phi Kappa Phi (chpt. treas. 1991-92, chpt. pres. 1992-94), Pi Alpha Alpha. Home: PO Box 8102 Albuquerque NM 87198-8102 Office: U NMex Gen Libr Acquisitions and Serials Dept Albuquerque NM 87131

WILKINSON, JANET WORMAN, advertising and marketing consultant; b. Mpls., July 18, 1944; d. James Russell and Virginia Hale (Murty) Worman; m. Benjamin Delos Wilkinson, Jan. 7, 1967; children: David Delos, Steven Edward, John Douglas. BA, Wells Coll., 1966. With Met. Life Ins. Co., N.Y.C., 1966-67; elem. tchr. pub. schs., Parkersburg, W.Va. and Orange, Tex., 1968-69; on-air prin. WTAV-TV, Parkersburg, 1969-70; corp. communications educator Delmarva Power Co., Wilmington, Del., 1979-83; market mgr. W.L. Gore & Assocs., Inc., Elkton, Md., 1983-85; advt. coord., promotion mgr. Views Mag., Chadds Ford, Pa., 1985-86; cons. mktg. communications, 1986—; reading instr. Project ASSIST Inst., 1994; mem. Bus.-Industry Ednl. Consortium, Wilmington, 1981-83; chmn. steering com. NE Utilities Educators, 1981-83; tutor Dyslexic Children and Adults. Contbg. editor Lattice News, 1984-85; editor Retailer newsletter, 1984-85. Chmn. publicity Wilmington Flower Market, 1984-85, Wells Coll. Capital Campaign Fund, Wilmington, 1983-84, Wilmington Christmas Shop, 1973-81; loaned exec. United Way, Wilmington, 1985; bd. dirs. Girls Clubs Del., 1983-84; founder, developer Help Stop the Hurt child abuse awareness program, 1983; dir. Christian edn. Trinity Ch., Wilmington, 1982-88. Republican. Episcopalian. Avocations: sketching, watercolor, writing. Home and Office: 1001 Westover Rd Wilmington DE 19807-3016

WILKINSON, JEANNE CAROL, artist, educator; b. Duluth, Minn., Sept. 27, 1949; d. Gordon Eugene and Shirley Jean (Anderson) W.; m. Richard Earl Yonda, June 29, 1975 (div. April 1985); children: Aaron Mark, Andrew John; m. Frank Oscar Lind III, Mar. 24, 1993. Attended, U. Minn., Mpls., 1968-70; BA in Painting and Art Edn., U. Wis.-Stout, 1986; MFA in Painting, Pratt Inst., Bklyn., 1989. Organizer rural coop. truck farm Winding Rd. Farm, Boyceville, Wis., 1972-74; dairy farmer Nat. Farm Orgn., Boyceville, 1974-82; freelance artist Wis., 1981-86; exhbns. preparator N.Y. Pub. Library, N.Y.C., 1990-91; adminstrv. asst. Anita Shapolsky Gallery, N.Y.C., 1991-92; art history lectr. Kingsborough Cmty. Coll., CUNY, Bklyn., 1992—; adminstrv. asst. Estate of Artist Margery Edwards, N.Y.C., 1992—; art reviewer Cover Mag., N.Y. Review of Art, N.Y.C., 1993—, Review mag., N.Y.C., 1996—. Represented in numerous exhbns. including N.Y. County Lawyer's Assn., 1995, Dealer's Choice Art Initiatives, N.Y.C., 1995, Janos Gat Gallery, N.Y.C., 1994. Mem. Coll. Art Assn. Democrat. Home: 300 8th Ave Apt 4M Brooklyn NY 11215

WILKINSON, LINDA CORNELIA PAINTON, retired city official; b. Painton, Mo., Aug. 21, 1927; d. Herbert James and Bess Carmen (Cobb) Painton; m. A. Scott Wilkinson, July 20, 1957; children: Jean Mary Wilkinson Martinis, Ann Elizabeth. BS in Edn., S.E. Mo. State U., 1951; postgrad., U. N.Mex., 1961, 67. Cert. tchr., Mo. Tchr. pub. schs., Mo., 1945-53; adminstrv. asst. real estate dept. Gulf Oil Corp., N.Y.C., 1953-56; sec., adminstrv. asst. Bklyn. Law Sch., 1956-58; co-owner, mgr. Music Mart, Albuquerque, 1961-68; owner, mgr. rental properties, Albuquerque, 1968-86; chief dep. county clk. Valencia County, Los Lunas, N.Mex., 1986-89; adminstr. Harvey House Civic Ctr., City of Belen (N.Mex.), 1989-90. County commr., 1993—; mem. Valencia County Citizens Adv. Bd., 1985-90; sec., bd. dirs. Valencia County Hist. Soc., Belen, 1986-90; bd. dirs. Keep N.Mex. Beautiful, 1986-94, 1st v.p., acting pres., 1992, 93; bd. dirs. Shelter for Victims of Domestic Violence, Valencia County, 1988-94; elder Presbyn. Ch. U.S.A., 1991—. Home: 8 Meadowlake Ln Los Lunas NM 87031-9448

WILKINSON, LOUISE CHERRY, psychology educator, dean; b. Phila., May 15, 1948; m. Alex Cherry Wilkinson; 1 child, Jennifer Cherry. B.A. magna cum laude with honors, Oberlin Coll., 1970; Ed.M., Ed.D., Harvard U., 1974. Prof., chmn. dept. ednl. psychology U. Wis., Madison, 1976-85; prof., exec. officer Grad. Sch. Ph.D. Program CUNY, N.Y.C., 1984-86; prof. II, dean Grad. Sch. Edn. Rutgers U., 1986—; mem. nat. rev. bd. Nat. Inst. Edn., 1977, 85, 87; cons. Nat. Ctr. for Bilingual Rsch., 1982, 84, U.S. Dept. Edn., 1995-96; adv. bd. Nat. Reading Rsch. Ctr., 1992—. Co-author: Communicating for Learning, 1991; editor: Communicating in Classroom, 1982, Social Context of Instruction, 1984, Gender Influences in the Classroom; mem. editorial bds. and contbr. articles to profl. jours. Fellow Am. Psychol. Assn., Am. Psychol. Soc.; mem. Internat. Assn. for Study Child Lang., Am. Ednl. Rsch. Assn. (v.p. 1990-92, program chair 1997). Home: 3 Andrews Ln Princeton NJ 08540-7633 Office: Rutgers U Grad Sch Edn 10 Seminary Pl New Brunswick NJ 08901-1108

WILKINSON, REBECCA ELAINE, human resources systems analyst; b. Dallas, Nov. 11, 1960; d. John Cephas and Mary Magdeline (Rhea) Bishop; m. Billy Don Wilkinson, July 31, 1982; children: Eric Tyler, Kristen Rhea. BEd, U. Dallas, 1982, MBA, 1995. Human resources/payroll systems analyst IBM, Irving, Tex., 1982-85; equal opportunity coord. IBM, Irving, 1985-90; human resources data analyst IBM, Roanoke, Tex., 1990-94; systems analyst specialist Westinghouse Security Systems, Irving, 1994—. Mem. NOW, Greenpeace, Sigma Iota Epsilon. Democrat. Episcopalian.

WILKINSON, SIGNE, cartoonist; b. Phila.. BA in English, 1972. Reporter West Chester (Pa.) Daily Local News, Academy of Natural Scis.,

Phila.; freelance cartoonist Phila. and N.Y. publs.; cartoonist San Jose (Calif.) Mercury News, 1982-85, Phila. Daily News, 1985—. Assoc. editor Working Woman mag.; contbr. Organic Gardening mag., Univ. Barge Club News. Recipient Pulitzer Prize for editorial cartooning, 1992. Mem. Assn. Am. Editl. Cartoonists (pres. 1994-95). Office: Phila Daily News PO Box 8263 400 N Broad St Philadelphia PA 19101

WILKS, DEBBIE ARLENE, educator; b. Pasadena, Calif., Apr. 29, 1957; d. Donald Lee and Helen Arlene (Johnson) W. BA, U. No. Colo., 1979. Cert. tchr. (K-9), Kans., (K-6) Colo. Tchr. 4th grade, 2nd grade St. Francis (Kans.) Pub. Schs., St. Francis Elem., 1979-86; tchr. 3rd grade Wichita Pub. Sch. Riverside Cultural Arts and History Magnet Sch., Wichita, Kans., 1987—. Vol. Girl Scouts, Wichita, 1990-91, Big Bros./Big Sisters, Wichita, 1991-93. Grantee Wichita Bd. of Edn., 1990, 92. Mem. Internat. Reading Assn., Nat. Coun. of Tchrs. Math. Home: 7054 E Kellogg #G Wichita KS 67207 Office: Riverside Cultural Arts and History Magnet Sch 1001 Porter Wichita KS 67203

WILKS, DUFFY JEAN, counselor, educator; b. Spur, Tex., Feb. 15, 1936; d. Rub Lee Jay and Elizabeth Audeen (Simmons) Austin; m. children: Vicki, Juli, Randy, Rodney; m. W.B. Wilks, Oct. 22, 1986. BA in Psychology, Tex. Tech. U., 1981, MEd in Psychology, 1984, EdD in Ednl. Psychology, 1995. Cert. substance abuse counsleor; lic. profl. counselor, Tex.; lic. marriage and family therapist, Tex. Editor writer Floydada (Tex.) newspaper, 1972-80; probation officer Adult/Juvenile Probation, Lubbock, Tex., 1982-86; pvt. practice Horseshoe Bay, Tex., 1986—; instr. Western Tex. Coll., Snyder. Mem. ACA, Tex. Assn. Counseling and Devel. (editorial bd. jour. 1989-91, author revs., editor Disting. Svc. award 1991), Tex. Counseling Assn., Tex. C.C. Tchrs. Assn., Internat. Assn. for Addictions and Offender Counselors.

WILKS-OWENS, DIXIE RAE, state agency administrator; b. Oakland, Calif., Nov. 1, 1943; d. James D. Wilks and Pauline Ruth (Peoples) Biddulph; m. August Edward Slagle (div. 1974); children: Tonya Davina Slagle, Victor Scott Slagle; m. Howard Laverne Owens, Dec. 15, 1984. AA, Ohlone Coll., 1973; attended, U. Calif., Davis, 1993-94; cert. mgmt. effectiveness, U. So. Calif. Unemployment ins. specialist, employment and tng. generalist. Employment supr. Calif. Employment Devel. Dept., Sacramento, 1969-86, employment specialist, 1986-88, legis. analyst, 1988-90, legis. re-employment ctr. mgr., 1990-91, mktg. mgr., 1991-94, mgr. workforce preparation conf., 1994-96. Bd. dirs., membership chair Sacramento Women's Campaign Fund, 1993—. Mem. Internat. Assn. Pers. in Employment Security (mem. internat. rels. com. 1991, Calif. chpt. pres. 1992-94, bd. dirs. conf. planning bd. 1993-94, legis. chair 1995—). Democrat. Unitarian Universalist. Office: Calif Employment Devel Dept MIC 77 800 Capitol Mall Sacramento CA 95814

WILL, JANE ANNE, psychologist; b. Evansville, Ind., Feb. 6, 1945; d. Edwin Francis and Frances Elizabeth (Patry) W. BA in Edn., St. Benedict's Coll., Ferdinand, Ind., 1968; MA in Edn., MS in Clin. Psychology, U. Evansville, 1973, 1987; MA in Christian Spirituality, Creighton U., 1979; D Psychology, Fla. Tech., Melbourne, 1991. Lic. psychologist, Ind.; joined Sisters of St. Benedict, Inc., Roman Cath. Ch. Tchr. Ireland (Ind.) Jr. H.S., 1969-76, Meml. H.S., Evansville, Ind., 1976-77; dir. recruitment and tng. Sisters of St. Benedict, Inc., Ferdinand, Ind., 1978-84, cons. admissions bd., 1984—; tchr. Mater Dei H.S., Evansville, 1984-88; therapist Osceola Ctr., Kissimme, Fla., 1989-90, Charter Hosp., Kissimme, Fla., 1989-90; intern VA Med. Ctr., St. Louis, 1990-91; clin. psychologist St. Mary's Health Care Svcs., Evansville, 1991—; adj. prof. Bresica Coll., Owensboro, Ky., 1978-80, St. Mary's of the Woods Coll., Terre Haute, Ind., 1980-84. Author jour. Ind. Reading Quarterly, 1973. Bd. dirs. Nat. Formation Dirs., Washington, 1982-84; chairperson region VII Formation Conf., Mich. and Ind., 1982-84. Luise Whiting Bell scholar, 1986. Mem. APA, Ind. Psychol. Assn., Southwestern Ind. Psychol. Assn. (treas. 1992, sec. 1993, v.p. 1994, pres. 1995), Vanderburgh County Mental Health Assn. (bd. dirs. 1994—, v.p. 1996). Roman Catholic. Home: 725 Wedeking Ave Evansville IN 47711-3861

WILL, JOANNE MARIE, food and consumer services executive, communications consultant, writer; b. Mpls., Mar. 18, 1937; d. Lester John and Dorothea Amelia (Kuenzel) W. BS in Home Econs. and Journalism, Iowa State U., 1959. Food writer, editor food guide Chgo. Tribune, 1959-67; account supr., home econs. coordinator J. Walter Thompson Co., Chgo., 1967-73; assoc. food editor, then food editor Chgo. Tribune, 1973-81; dir. food and consumer services Hill and Knowlton, Inc., Chgo., 1981-87; dir., group mgr. food and consumer svcs. Selz/Seabolt Comms., Inc., Chgo. Mem. bd. govs. Iowa State U. Found., past mem. home econs. adv. bd.; past bd. dirs., officer Sr. Ctrs. Met. Chgo. Recipient Alumnae Recognition medal Iowa State U., 1994; named Outstanding Young Alumnus Iowa State U., 1968. Mem. Home Econs. in Bus., Am. Assn. Family and Consumer Scis. (Chgo. bus. sect.), Ill. Assn. Family and Consumer Scis., Chgo. Nutrition Assn. (pres.-elect 1993-94, pres. 1994-95), Am. Assn. Family and Consumer Scis., Ill. Assn. Family and Consumer Scis., Dames d'Escoffier (bd. dirs. Chgo. chpt., past v.p.).

WILL, SANDRA GAIL, controller; b. Windber, Pa., July 26, 1963; d. Gerald Ray and Dorothy Jane (Zimmerman) Mock; m. Robert Douglas Will, Jan. 26, 1985; children: Zachary Douglas, Laura Elizabeth. BS in Fin., Pa. State U., 1984. Fin. trainee Alcoa, Newburgh, Ind., 1985, project acct., 1985-87, product acct., 1988, sr. product acct., 1988-90, product acctg. supr., 1990-93; controller Alcoa, Ft. Meade, Fla., 1993-95, Leetsdale, Pa., 1995—. Mem. Inst. Mgmt. Accts. Office: Alcoa 99 W Park Rd Leetsdale PA 15056

WILLANS, JEAN STONE, religious organization executive; b. Hillsboro, Ohio, Oct. 3, 1924; d. Homer and Ella (Keys) Hammond; student San Diego Jr. Coll.; D.D. (hon.) Ch. of the East, 1996; m. Richard James Willans, Mar. 28, 1966; 1 dau., Suzanne Jeanne. Asst. to v.p. Family Loan Co., Miami, Fla., 1946-49; civilian supr. USAF, Washington, 1953-55; founder, dir. Blessed Trinity Soc., editor Trinity mag., Los Angeles, 1960-66; co-founder, exec. v.p., dir. Soc. of Stephen, Altadena, Calif., 1967—, exec. dir., Hong Kong, 1975-81; lectr. in field. Republican. Episcopalian. Author: The Acts of the Green Apples, 1974, rev. edit 1995; co-editor: Charisma in Hong Kong, 1970; Spiritual Songs, 1970; The People Who Walked in Darkness, 1977; The People Who Walked in Darkness II, 1992. Recipient Achievement award Nat. Assn. Pentecostal Women, 1964; monument erected in her honor Kowloon Walled City Park, Hong Kong Govt., 1996. Address: Soc of Stephen PO Box 6225 Altadena CA 91003-6225

WILLARD, NANCY MARGARET, writer, educator; b. Ann Arbor, Mich.; d. Hobart Hurd and Margaret (Sheppard) W.; m. Eric Lindbloom, Aug. 15, 1964; 1 child, James Anatole. B.A., U. Mich., 1958, Ph.D., 1963; M.A., Stanford U., 1960. Lectr. English Vassar Coll., Poughkeepsie, N.Y., 1965—. Author: (poems) In His Country: Poems, 1966; Skin of Grace, 1967; A New Herball: Poems, 1968, Testimony of the Invisible Man: William Carlos Williams, Francis Ponge, Rainer Maria Rilke, Pablo Neruda, 1970, Nineteen Masks for the Naked Poet: Poems, 1971, The Carpenter of the Sun: Poems, 1974, A Visit to William Blake's Inn: Poems for Innocent and Experienced Travelers, 1981 (Newbery Medal 1982), Household Tales of Moon and Water, 1983, Water Walker, 1989, The Ballad of Biddy Early, 1989; (short stories) The Lively Anatomy of God, 1968, Childhood of the Magician, 1973; (juveniles) Sailing to Cythera and Other Anatole Stories, 1974, All on a May Morning, 1975, The Snow Rabbit, 1975, Shoes Without Leather, 1976, T0e Well-Mannered Balloon, 1976, Night Story, 1986, Simple Pictures are Best, 1977, Stranger's Bread, 1977, The Highest Hit, 1978, Papa's Panda, 1979, The Island of the Grass King, 1979, The Marzipan Moon 1981, Uncle Terrible, 1982, (adult) Angel in the Parlor: Five Stories and Eight Essays, 1983, The Nightgown of the Sullen Moon, 1983, Night Story, 1986, The Voyage of the Ludgate Hill, 1987, The Mountains of Quilt, 1987, Firebrat, 1988; (novel) Things Invisible To See, 1984, Sister Water, 1993; (play) East of the Sun, West of the Moon, 1989, The High Rise Glorious Skittle Skat Roarious Sky Pie Angel Food Cake, 1991, A Nancy Willard Reader, 1991, Pish Posh said Hieronymus Bosch, 1991, Beauty and the Beast, 1992; illustrator: The Letter of John to James, Another Letter of John to James, 1982, The Octopus Who Wanted to Juggle (Robert Pack), 1990, (novel) Sister Water, 1993, (essays) Telling Time, 1993, (juvenile) A Starlit Somersault Downhill, 1993, (juvenile) The Sorcerer's Apprentice, 1993; author, illustrator: An Alphabet of Angels, 1994; (juvenile) Gutenberg's Gift, 1995; (poems, with Jane Yolen) Among Angels, 1995. Recipient Hopwood award, 1958, Devins Meml. award, 1967, John Newbery award, 1981, Empire State award, 1996; Woodrow Wilson fellow, 1960; NEA grantee, 1987. Mem. The Lewis Carroll Soc., The George MacDonald Soc. Office: Vassar Coll Dept English Raymond Ave Poughkeepsie NY 12601

WILLARD, SHIRLEY FAY, management executive; b. San Francisco, Nov. 7, 1933; d. James Lynn and Blanche Bernice (Miller) Cooper; m. Robert Edgar Willard, May 29, 1954; children: Laura Marie, John Judson. Student, Wash. State U., 1951-54; BA in Bus., Calif. State U., 1973. Mgmt. trainee Emporium, San Francisco, 1954-55; asst. buyer Filene's, Boston, 1955-58; pres. Calif. Legal Forms Svcs., Newport Beach, 1985—. Treas. Releaf Costa Mesa, Calif., 1994—. Office: Calif Legal Forms Svc Inc 1300 N Bristol # 100 Newport Beach CA 92660

WILLARDSON, KIMBERLY ANN CAREY, editor, writer, publisher; b. Akron, Ohio, May 8, 1959; d. James David and Concetta Marie (Bonanno) Carey; m. Roger Michael Willardson, Oct. 4, 1980; 1 child, Thomas Maxfield Carey Willardson. Student, Kent State U., 1978-79, Akron U., 1979-80; BA in English summa cum laude, Wright State U., 1983, MA in English, 1987. Teaching asst. Wright State U., Dayton, Ohio, 1983-84; assoc. editor Nexus Lit. Mag., Dayton, Ohio, 1982, editor, 1982-83; features editor The Daily Guardian Newspaper, Dayton, 1983; editorial asst. communications Wright State U., Dayton, 1985-88; freelance editor Dayton, 1986-88; editor The Vincent Bros. Rev. Mag., Fairborn and Dayton, Ohio, 1988—; pub. Vincent Bros. Pub., Dayton, 1988—; mem. adj. staff Antioch Writers Workshop, Yellow Springs, Ohio, 1990, fellow, 1991, 93. Author: (poems) Overcast at the Cat Dance Cafe, 1989, The Missy May Hopnoodle Saga (2d pl. Creative writing award Conf. Cin. Women 1990), Birch Violins (1st pl. poetry prize Conf. Cin. Women creative writing awards 1991), Violets for the Martyred Playwright, Heat Lightning, Waiting for the Vision Train; mem. bd. editors Fountain of Youth Literary Anthology, 1983-84. Regional organizer March of Dimes, Cuyahoga Falls, Ohio, 1977; canvasser Am. heart Assn., Fairborn, 1989-91; mem. SANE/FREEZE, Dayton Citizens for Global Security. Wright State U. scholar, 1982, 83, 84, 85; Ohio Arts Coun. grantee, 1989-95; Antioch Writers Workshop fellow, 1991, 93; Individual Artist grantee for fiction Ohio Arts Coun., 1994, Montgomery County Regional Arts and Cultural Dist., 1994. Roman Catholic. Home and Office: 4566 Northern Cir Riverside OH 45424

WILLE, LOIS JEAN, retired newspaper editor; b. Chgo., Sept. 19, 1931; d. Walter and Adele S. (Taege) Kroeber; m. Wayne M. Wille, June 6, 1954. B.S., Northwestern U., 1953, M.S., 1954; Litt.D. (hon.), Columbia Coll., Chgo., 1980, Northwestern U., 1990, Rosary Coll., 1990. Reporter Chgo. Daily News, 1958-74, nat. corr., 1975-76, assoc. editor charge editorial page, 1977; assoc. editor charge editorial and opinion pages Chgo. Sun-Times, 1978-83; assoc. editor editorial page Chgo. Tribune, 1984-87, editor editorial page, 1987-91, ret., 1991. Author: Forever Open, Clear and Free: the Historic Struggle for Chicago's Lakefront, 1972. Recipient Pulitzer prize for public svc., 1963, Pulitzer prize for editorial writing, 1989, William Allen White Found. award for excellence in editorial writing, 1978, numerous awards Chgo. Newspaper Guild, numerous awards Chgo. Headline Club, numerous awards Nat. Assn. Edn. Writers, numerous awards Ill. AP, numerous awards Ill. UPI. Home: 120 Charmont Dr Radford VA 24141-4205

WILLENBRINK, ROSE ANN, lawyer; b. Louisville, Ky., Apr. 20, 1950; d. J.L. Jr. and Mary Margaret (Williams) W. Student, U. Chgo., 1968-70; BA in Anthropology with highest honors, U. Louisville, 1973, JD, 1975. Bar: Ky. 1976, Ind. 1976, U.S. Dist. Ct. (we. dist.) Ky. 1976. Atty. Mapother & Mapother, Louisville, 1976-79; v.p., counsel Nat. City Bank, Louisville, 1980—. Mem. ABA, NAFE, Ky. Bar Assn., Louisville Bar Assn., Women Lawyers Assn., Conf. on Consumer Fin. Law, Corp. House Counsel Assn., Phi Kappa Phi. Home: 2356 Valley Vista Rd Louisville KY 40205-2002 Office: Nat City Bank 3700 Nat City Tower Louisville KY 40202

WILLENZ, JUNE ADELE, writer, public affairs executive, playwright, screenwriter. BS, MA, U. Mich., postgrad.; postgrad., New Sch. for Social Rsch. Instr. English, Montgomery Coll., Md.; exec. dir. Am. Vets. Com.; chair standing com. on women World Vet. Fedn.; conf. organizer Women In and After War, Bellagio, Italy, Rape in Armed Conflicts, Istanbul; lectr. USIA; spkr. vets. convs., NAAPC; radio and TV guest appearances; honored guest internat. vets. assns.; exec. dir. Am. Vets. Com., 1965; del. White House Conf. on Youth, White House Conf. Aging, mem. planning com. 5th and 6th legis. coms. World Vets. Author: Women Veterans: America's Forgotten Heroines, 1983; co-author: Gender Differences, 1991; editor, author: Dialogue on the Draft, 1967, Human Rights of the Man in Uniform, 1969; editor: AVC Bull.; presenter Am. Hist. Assn., Am. Polit. Sci. Assn.; contbr. articles to profl. publs. on vets., mil. women's internat. issues; columnist Stars and Stripes; contbr. articles to profl. jours. Mem. VA Adv. Com. on Women Vets., First Lady's Women's Conf. Cir., 1995—; mem. UN Decade for Women com., head of working group on refugee women; accredited rep. to UN; organizer Workshops on Refugee Women at UN; pub. mem. 19th Fgn. Officer Selection Bd. USIA; chmn. Task Force on Vets. and Mil. Affairs for Leadership Com. on Civil Rights; spkr. Nat. Urban League, Ctr. for Policy Rsch., Nat. League of Cities Vets. Program, advisor; co-chmn. Coordinating Com. on Voluntary Nat. Svc., organized nat. conf. Dialogue on Nat. Svc., 1989; chmn. subcom. on disabled vets. Pres. Com. Employment of People with Disabilities, 1995-96; mem. Inter-Univ. Seminar Armed Forces & Soc. Mem. Non Govtl. Orgn., Authors Guild, Dramatists Guild. Home: 6309 Bannockburn Dr Bethesda MD 20817-5403

WILLETT, ANNA HART, composer; b. Bartlesville, Ohio, June 18, 1931; d. Thomas Kellogg and Mary Kathryn (Feist) W.; m. Roger Garland Horn, Aug. 1956 (div. June 1962). B in Music Edn., Southwestern La. Inst., 1954; MA, La. State U., 1964, postgrad., 1976-87. Lifetime tchr. cert., La. Pub. sch. vocal music tchr. Iberville Parish, Plaquemine, La., 1954-55, Orleans Parish, New Orleans, 1966-71; elem. music pedagogy tchr. St. Mary's Dominican Coll., New Orleans, 1972. Composer: Dances for Solo Violin, 1981, Weaving Song, 1982, Entertainer's Song, 1983, Hercules Variations, 1986. Scholar Loyola U. of the South, New Orleans, 1972-73. Mem. AAUW. Episcopalian. Home: 2244 Ferndale Ave Baton Rouge LA 70808

WILLETT, ROSLYN LEONORE, public relations executive, food service consultant; b. N.Y.C., Oct. 18, 1924; d. Edward and Celia (Stickler) S.; m. Edward Willett (separated); 1 child, Jonathan Stanley. BA, Hunter Coll., N.Y.C., 1944; postgrad., Columbia U., 1944, CUNY, 1947-48, NYU, 1947-48, 52, New Sch., 1987-88. Dietitian YWCA, N.Y.C., 1944; tech. and patents libr. Stein Hall & Co., N.Y.C., 1944-46, food technologist tech. svcs. and devel. dept., 1946-48; editor McGraw-Hill, Inc., N.Y.C., 1949-50, Harcourt Brace Jovanovich, Inc., N.Y.C., 1950-54; pub. rels. writer Farley Manning Assocs., N.Y.C., 1954-58; cons. pub. rels. and food svc. Roslyn Willett Assocs., Inc., N.Y.C., 1959—; adj. prof. Hunter Coll., 1955-56, Polytech. Univ., N.Y., 1981-82; lectr. in field. Author: The Woman Executive in Woman in Sexist Society, 1971, short stories. chmn. Woman's Polit. Caucus, Inc., N.Y., N.J., Conn., 1971-73; v.p. Mid Hudson Arts and Sci. Ctr., Poughkeepsie, N.Y.; bd. dirs. Small Bus. Task Force, Assn. for Small Bus. and Professions, 1981-85, Regional Adv. Coun. Fed. SBA, 1976-78, Rhinebeck Chamber Music Soc., 1985-86, Will Inst. , New Paltz, 1980—. Mem. Pub. Rels. Soc. Am. (accredited), Food Svc. Cons. Soc. Internat., N.Y. Acad. Scis., Inst. Food Technologists, Paris Club. Home: Hunn's Lake Rd Stanfordville NY 12581 Office: 441 W End Ave New York NY 10024-5328

WILLEY, CHISTINA MARGARET ANNETTE, art educator; b. Denver, Jan. 17, 1953; d. Kenneth Wesley and Margaret Marie (Moore) W.; m. Russell Edward Greinke, June 25, 1994. BFA, U. Nebr., 1976; MFA, Syracuse U., 1986. Keyline artist Paul Norris & Assocs., Mission, Kans., 1977-78; illustrator, designer Tennis and Ski Warehouse, Kansas City, Mo., 1978-80; art dir. Fremerman Malcy Spivak & Rosenfield, Kansas City, 1980-81; designer Triad, Prairie Village, Kans., 1981-82; illustrator, designer, owner Chris Willey Illustrations, Kansas City, 1982-89; assoc. prof. art Ctrl. Mo. State U., Warrensburg, Mo., 1989—. Artist (cover illustration) White Roses, 1992 (Outstanding Cover award 1993); one woman shows include Fasone Garrett Advt. Agy., 1985, Maple Woods Cmty. Coll., 1986, Kansas City Gas Co., 1989, Commerce Plaza Bank, 1989, Ande-Leis Restaurant and Gallery, 1990, Ctrl. Mo. State U. Art Gallery, 1992; exhibited in group exhbns. at Master Eagle Gallery, N.Y., 1980, Bryant Bldg., 1986-89, Ctrl. Mo. State U., 1989, 90, 91, 93, 94, 95, 96, Art Ctr. Gallery, 1995, Glamorgan, Wales, 1995. Mem. Women's Coun., Ctrl. Mo. State U., 1991—. Mem. Kansas City Artists Coalition. Office: Ctrl Mo State U Art Dept 120 Warrensburg MO 64093

WILLEY, SUSAN GZEHOVIAK, journalist, educator; b. Grand Island, Nebr., Sept. 27, 1946; d. Louis Edward Gzehoviak and Emma Lillian Jezewski; divorced; children: Michael, David (dec.), Steven. BA in Comms., Coll. of St. Mary, Lincoln, Nebr., 1993; MA in Mass Comms., U. South Fla., 1995; postgrad., U. Mo., 1995—. Writer, reporter, columnist Natchez (Miss.) Democrat, 1976-88; religious edn. dir. St. Mary's Cath. Ch., Natchez, 1988-91; investigator Nebr. Equal Opportunity Com., Lincoln, 1991-93; religion writer Lincoln Jour.-Star, Lincoln, 1993, St. Petersburg (Fla.) Times, 1993-95; rsch. asst. U. South Fla., St. Petersburg, 1993-95, U. Mo., Columbia, 1995—; mem., acting pres. Mo. Mental Health Assn., Natchez, 1988-91, bd. dirs. Talk Line teen crisis line, founder, 1987-91. Contbr. articles and essays to profl. publs. Recipient Grand prize in coll. student writing competition Time mag., 1992; Stoody-West religion journalism fellow U. Meth. Comms., 1996, Poynter fellow, 1993-95; Scripps Howard scholar, 1992; funded rsch. assistantship, 1995. Home: #4 3800 E Cooper Dr Columbia MO 65201

WILLIAMS, ANN, elementary school educator; b. Royal Oak, Mich., July 7, 1946; d. Joseph James and Rose Alma (McMullen) Rodgers; m. Harold Spencer Williams, Mar. 3, 1972; children: Chad and Matt (twins). BS, Mercy Coll. of Detroit, 1968; MA in Curriculum, Instrn., Leadership, Oakland U., 1986. Cert. tchr. k-8, Mich. Tchr. Royal Oak (Mich.) Schs., 1968-88, 81—; tchr. Santa Cruz (Bolivia) Coop Sch., 1988-90, Graded Sch., Sao Paulo, Brazil, 1990-91; applicant tchr. in space program NASA, 1984; mem. Oakland County Tech. Edn. Program, Pontiac, Mich. 1994; Covey Tng. and Hunter Tng. program, Royal Oak, 1994. Office: Oak Ridge Sch 506 E 13 Mile Rd Royal Oak MI 48073-2836

WILLIAMS, ANN CLAIRE, federal judge; b. 1949; m. David J. Stewart. BS, Wayne State U., 1970; MA, U. Mich., 1972; JD, U. Notre Dame, 1975. Law clk. to hon. Robert A. Sprecher, 1975-76; asst. U.S. atty. U.S. Dist. Ct. (no. dist.) Ill., Chgo., 1976-85; faculty mem. Nat. Inst. for Trial Advocacy, 1979—; judge U.S. Dist. Ct. (no. dist.) Ill., Chgo., 1985—; chief Crime Drug Enforcement Task Froce North Ctrl. Region, 1983-85; chair ct. adminstrn. and case mgmt. com. Jud. Conf. U.S., 1993—. Trustee U. Chgo. Lab Sch.; sec. bd. trustees U. Notre Dame, Mus. Sci. and Industry. Mem. Fed. Bar Assn., Fed. Judges Assn. (treas.), Women's Bar Assn. of Ill. Office: US Dist Ct 219 S Dearborn St Chicago IL 60604-1702

WILLIAMS, ANN MEAGHER, retired hospital administrator; b. Hull, Mass., May 28, 1929; d. James Francis Meagher and Dorothy Frances (Antone) Mullins; m. Joseph Arthur Williams, May 15, 1954; children: James G., Mara A., A. Scott (dec.), Gordon M., Mark J., Antoinette M., Andrea M. BS, Chestnut Hill Coll., 1950; MS, Boston Coll., 1952. Radioisotope biologist Air Force Cambridge Rsch. Ctr., Bedford, Mass., 1952-55; asst. mgr. Roxbury Businessmen's Exch., Boston, 1956-66; owner, operator Chatterlane, Osterville, Mass., 1961-66; realtor James E. Murphy Inc., Hyannis, Mass., 1968-77; dir. community affairs Cape Cod Hosp., Hyannis, 1977-95; realtor Osterville, 1995—. Bd. dirs. Community Coun., Mid Cape, Mass., 1977-88, Cape Cod Mental Health Assn., 1977-82, Ctr. for Individual and Family Svcs., Mid Cape, 1982-87, Am. Cancer Soc., Mid Cape, 1981-96; mem. sch. com. Cape Cod Regional Tech. High Sch., 1978—, United Way of Cape Cod, 1988-89; chmn. fin. com. City of Barnstable, Mass., 1969-77. Named Woman of Yr. Bus./Profl. Women's Club, 1982; recipient Cert. Appreciation Am. Cancer Soc., 1983, 88, Pres. Recognition award United Way Cape Cod, 1989. Mem. Am. Soc. Hosp. Mktg. and Pub. Rels., New Eng. Hosp. Pub. Rels. Mktg. Assn., Southeastern Mass. Hosp. Pub. Rels. Assn., Nat. Assn. Hosp. Devel., Chestnut Hill Coll. Alumnae Assn., Rotary Club of Osterville (bd. dirs. 1992—, pres. 1996-97), Hyannis Area C. of C. (bd. dirs. 1993—). Roman Catholic. Home: 8 E Bay Rd Osterville MA 02655-1909 Office: Cape Cod Hosp 971 A Main St Osterville MA 02655

WILLIAMS, ANNA M., social worker; b. Ft. Meade, Md., Sept. 5, 1956; d. William Arthur and Jacqueline Rae (Hull) W. BSW, B in African Studies, U. Md., 1978; MSW, U. Pitts., 1981. Lic. social worker. Investigator child abuse Dept. Social Svcs., Balt., 1978-80; counselor, program coord., supr. girls unit Ward Home for Children, Pitts., 1981-86; mental health therapist Pace Sch., Pitts., 1986-89; program coord. Justice Resources Inc., Balt., 1989-94; therapist Union Meml. Hosp., Balt., 1993-94; v.p. resdl. svcs. Children's Home Wyoming Conf., Binghamton, N.Y., 1994-95; dir. Casey Family Svcs., Balt., 1996—; cons. Youth Advocacy Program, Balt., 1992-94. Bd. dirs. Ward Home for Children, Pitts., 1986-88, South Balt. Youth Ctr., 1993-94; speaker Meth. Women; adv. bd. WSKG Pub. Broadcasting, 1994—. Mem. NASW, Nat. Girls Caucus (charter), Kiwanis Internat., Alpha Kappa Alpha (Lambda Phi chpt.). Democrat. Office: Casey Family Svcs 1809 Ashland Ave Baltimore MD 21205

WILLIAMS, ANNE SHIPLEY, educator, consultant; b. Butte, Mont., Oct. 13, 1940; d. James Jefferson Shipley and Margaret Elizabeth Ralph Schreiner; m. James Rodney Williams, Nov. 28, 1964 (div. Feb. 1991); children: James Scott, Amanda Lee; m. Dennis Glen Brown, Oct. 3, 1991. BA in Sociology, BA in Philosophy, U. Mont., 1961, MA in Sociology, 1963; PhD in Devel. Sociology, Cornell U., 1977. Acting dir. interdisciplinary studies ctr. Mont. State U., Bozeman, 1972-75, asst. prof. sociology, 1971-78, assoc. prof., 1978-82, prof., 1982-91, acting dir. survey rsch. ctr., 1986-87, asst. dean Coll. Letters and Sci., 1985-87, dean Coll. Letters and Sci., 1987-91; dean grad. studies and sponsored rsch. West Chester (Pa.) U., 1991-95; rsch. prof., extension affairs assoc. Clarkson U., Potsdam, N.Y., 1995—; mem. adv. bd. Western Rural Devel. Ctr., Corvallis, Oreg., 1977-82; mem. task force on grad. edn. Pa. State Sys. Higher Edn., Harrisburg, 1991-92, others. Contbr. articles to profl. jours. Bd. dirs. Mus. of the Rockies, Bozeman, 1987-91. Recipient Family-Cmty. Leadership award Kellogg Found., 1984; Liberty-Hyde-Bailey rsch. awardee Cornell U., 1975-77; NSF grantee, 1971-75, FIPSE grantee, 1981-83. Mem. Rural Sociol. Soc. (mem. coun. 1975-77, treas. 1984-87), Clarkson Women's Club (hon. pres. 1995—). Home: 71 Pierrepont Ave Potsdam NY 13676 Office: Clarkson U Sch Liberal Studies Potsdam NY 13699

WILLIAMS, ANNIE DIGGS, educator, realty company executive; b. Geneva, Ala., Nov. 21; d. James Espy and Adell Gertrude (Bailey) Diggs; m. Marion Williams, June 17, 1967; children: Kellie Ann, Jason Alan. BS, Stillman Coll., 1965; MS, Ind. U., 1971. Tchr. biology William A. Wirt H.S., Gary, Ind., 1988—; CEO Lakeside Realty Co., Gary, Ind., 1977—; CEO, Lakeside Realty Co., Gary. Parliamentarian Voice of Pride, 1996; mem. Gary Pub. Libr., 1985-96. Mem. AAUW (com. chmn. Gary 1977), Nat. Assn. Parliamentarians, Alpha Pi Chi (chpt. pres. 1975), Zeta Phi Beta (chpt. pres. 1989-93, Ind. bd. dirs. 1994—, Disting. Pres. award 1991, Disting. Svc. awards 1994). Presbyterian. Office: Lakeside Realty Co 504 Broadway Ste 717 Gary IN 46402

WILLIAMS, BARBARA JEAN MAY, state official; b. Alphoretta, Ky., June 5, 1927; d. Andrew Jackson and Bess (Salisbury) May. A.B. in Spanish, Centre Coll., 1949; postgrad., Columbia U., 1957; M.S. in L.S., U. Ky., 1963. Librarian Midway Jr. Coll., 1960-62, Ky. Dept. Libraries, Frankfort, 1965-68; planning librarian Ky. Program Devel. Office, Frankfort, 1968-71, Ky. Exec. Dept. for Fin. and Adminstrn., Frankfort, 1972-76; asst. state librarian Ky. Dept. Libraries and Archives, Frankfort, 1976; state librarian Ky. Dept. Libraries and Archives, 1977-80; adminstr. Ky. suggestion system program Dept. Personnel, div. employee services State of Ky., Frankfort, 1980-91; retired; mem. Depository Library Council to Public Printer. Mem. ALA, Southeastern Libr. Assn., Ky. Libr. Assn. (sec. spl. libr. sect. 1976, chmn. sect. 1976), Chief Officers State Libr. Agys. (liaison com. office Edn. 1979-80), Assn. State Libr. Agys. (Index State Libr. Activities 1979-80), Coun. Planning Libr. (treas.), Ky. Coun. Archivists, Ky. Hist. Soc., J.B. Speed Mus. Guild, Dem. Woman's Club, Filson Club, La Jardinere Club, Garden Club. Episcopalian.

WILLIAMS, BARBARA JUNE, lawyer; b. Lansing, Mich., Jan. 6, 1948; d. Ben Allan and Virginia Jane (Searing) W.; m. John Paul Halvorsen, Oct. 21, 1971. AA, Stephens Coll., 1968; BA, U. Ill.-Champaign, 1970; JD, Rutgers

U., 1974. Bar: N.J. 1974, N.Y. 1981. Assoc., Bookbinder, Coulagori & Bookbinder, Burlington, N.J., 1974-76, Law Offices of Cyrus Bloom, Newark, 1976-78, Warren, Goldberg, Berman & Lubitz, Princeton, N.J., 1978-84; staff atty. Rutgers U. Sch. of Law, Newark, 1984-85; assoc. Strauss & Hall, Princeton, 1985-87; of counsel Weg & Myers, P.C., New York, 1987—. Assoc. editor Rutgers Camden Law Jour., 1973-74; contbr. articles to profl. jours. Mem. Nat. Sch. Bds. Assn. (bd. dir. nat. coun. sch. attys. 1981-86), ABA, N.J. Bar Assn. (dir. govt. law sect. 1981-84), Mercer County Bar Assn., Princeton Bar Assn., Assn. Trial Lawyers Am., NOW, Lawrence Arts Assn., Lawrence Twp. Home: 90 Denow Rd Trenton NJ 08648-2047

WILLIAMS, BETTYE JEAN, English educator; b. Pine Bluff, Ark., July 2, 1946; d. Eunice and Dorothy (Willingham) W. BA in English, Agrl. Meth. and Normal Coll., 1968; M of English, Pittsburg State U., 1970; DPhil in Am. Lit., Ind. U. Pa., 1993. Prof. English U. Ark., Pine Bluff, 1968-96, Ind. U. Pa., 1990-93, Pines Tech. Coll., Pine Bluff, 1995. NEH fellow, 1992-93. Mem. NAUW (pres. 1989-90), Nat. Assn. Advancement of Coll. People, Nat. Urban League, Nat. Lang. Assn., Coll. Lang. Assn., Sigma Tau Delta. Democrat. Baptist. Home: 2611 W 34th Apt 6-A Pine Bluff AR 71603

WILLIAMS, BRENDA LLEWELLYN, nursing administrator; b. Nashville, Sept. 19, 1955; d. Gilbert Ray and Doris Oleen (Dunaway) Llewellyn; m. Harold Raymond Williams, Sept. 3, 1983. BSN, U. Tenn., 1978. Cert. ins. rehab. specialist; cert. case mgr.; cert. registered rehab. nurse. Staff nurse Vanderbilt Children's Hosp., Nashville, 1979-80; nurse cons. Aetna Life & Casualty, Nashville, 1980-83; staff ICU nurse pediat. Med. Ctr. of Del., Wilmington, 1983-85; quality mgr. Baylor Coll. Medicine, Houston, 1985-86; quality assurance coord. St. Luke's Episcopal Hosp., Houston, 1986-90; mgr. quality control Care Mgmt. cons., Brentwood, Tenn., 1991—. Bd. dirs., sec. Humane Soc. Dickson County, Tenn., 1992-94; escort, vol. Planned Parenthood, Nashville, 1982, 83, 90, 91, Houston, 1990; mem. logistics com., subcom. chmn. Choice Coalition, Houston, 1990. Mem. Mid-South Workers Compensation Claims Assn. Democrat. Methodist. Office: Care Mgmt Cons Inc 111 Westwood Pl Brentwood TN 37024

WILLIAMS, CAMILLA, soprano, voice educator; b. Danville, Va.; d. Booker and Fannie (Cary) W.; m. Charles T. Beavers, Aug. 28, 1950. BS, Va. State Coll., 1941; postgrad., U. Pa., 1942; studies with, Mme. Marian Szekely-Freschl, 1943-44, 1952, Berkowitz and Cesare Sodero, 1944-46, Rose Dirman, 1948-52, Sergius Kagen, 1958-62; MusD (hon.), Va. State U., 1986, D. (hon.), 1985. Prof. voice Bronx Coll., N.Y.C., 1970, Bklyn. Coll., 1970-73, Queens Coll., N.Y.C., 1974, Ind. U., Bloomington, 1977—; 1st black prof. voice Cen. Conservatory Music, Beijing, People's Republic China, 1983. Created role of Madame Butterfly as 1st black contract singer, N.Y.C. Ctr., 1946, 1st Aida, 1948; 1st N.Y. performance of Mozart's Idomeneo with Little Orch. Soc., 1950; 1st Viennese performance Menotti's Saint of Bleecker Street, 1955; 1st N.Y. performance of Handel's Orlando, 1971; other roles include Nedda in Pagliacci, Mimi in La Boheme, Marguerite in Faust; major tours include Alaska, 1950, London, 1954, Am. Festival in Belgium, 1955, tour of 14 African countries for U.S. Dept. State, 1958-59, Israel, 1959, concert for Crown Prince of Japan as guest of Gen. Eisenhower, 1960, tour of Formosa, Australia, New Zealand, Korea, Japan, Philippines, Laos, South Vietnam, 1971, Poland, 1974; appearances with orchs. including Royal Philharm., Vienna Symphony, Berlin Philharm., Chgo. Symphony, Phila. Orch., BBC Orch., Stuttgart Orch., many others; contract with RCA Victor as exclusive Victor Red Seal rec. artist, 1944—. Recipient Marian Anderson award (1st winner), 1943, 44, Newspaper Guild award as First Lady of Am. Opera, 1947, Va. State Coll. 75th anniv. cert. of merit, 1957, NYU Presdl. Citation, 1959, Gold medal Emperor of Ethiopia and Key to City of Taiwan during Pres. Johnson's Cultural Exchange Program, 1962, Art, Culture and Civic Guild award, 1962, Negro Musician's Assn. plaque, 1963, Harlem Opera and World Fellowship Soc. award, 1963; named Disting. Virginian Gov. of Va., 1972; inducted Danville (Va.) Mus. Fine Arts and History Hall of Fame, 1974; Camilla Williams Park designated in her honor, Danville, 1974; honored by Ind. U. Sch. Music Black Music Students' Orgn., 1979; named to Hon. Order Ky. Cols., 1979; honored by Phila. Pro Arte Soc., 1982; Disting. award of Ctr. for Leadership and Devel., 1983; Taylor-Williams student residence hall at Va. State U. named in Billy Taylor's and her honor, 1985. Mem. NAACP (hon. life), Internat. Platform Assn., Alpha Kappa Alpha. Office: Ind U Sch Music Bloomington IN 47401

WILLIAMS, CAROL JORGENSEN, social work educator; b. New Brunswick, N.J., Aug. 12, 1944; d. Einar Arthur and Mildred Estelle (Clayton) Jorgensen; m. Oneal Alexander Williams, July 4, 1980. BA, Douglass Coll., 1966; MS in Computer Sci., Stevens Inst. Tech., 1986; MSW, Rutgers U., 1971, PhD in Social Policy, 1981. Child welfare worker Bur. Children's Svcs., Jersey City, 1966-67, Outagamie County Dept. Social Svcs., Appleton, Wis., 1967-69; supr. WIN N.J. Divsn. Youth and Family Svcs., New Brunswick, 1969-70; coord. Outreach Plainfield (N.J.) Pub. Libr., 1972-76; rsch. project dir. County and Mcpl. Govt. Study Commn., N.J. State Legislature, 1976-79; prof. social work Kean Coll. N.J., Union, 1979—; assessment liaison social work program Kean Coll. of N.J., Union, 1987—, dir. MSW program, 1995—; chmn. faculty senate gen. edn. com., Kean Coll. N.J., 1990-94, chmn. faculty senate ad hoc com. for 5-yr. review of gen. edn. program, 1991-93, mem. retention and tenure com. Sch. of Liberal Arts, 1988-94, vice chmn., 1992-94; cons. N.J. div. Youth and Family Svcs., 1979-93, Assn. for Children N.J., 1985-88; cons., evaluator Thomas A. Edison Coll., 1977—, emm. acad. coun. and others. Mem. NOW, Coun. on Social Work Edn. (com. on info. tech.), Nat. Assn. Social Workers (chpt. com. on nominating and leadership identification 1990-92, co-chmn. 1991-92), Kean Coll. Fedn. Tchrs., Assn. Baccalaureate Program Dirs. (mem. com. on info. tech.). Democrat. Clubs: Good Sam (Agoura, Calif.); Outdoor World (Bushkill, Pa.). Home: 32 Halstead Rd New Brunswick NJ 08901-1619 Office: Kean Coll of NJ Social Work Program Morris Ave Union NJ 07083-7117

WILLIAMS, CAROLE ANN, cytotechnologist; b. Duquesne, Pa., Apr. 14, 1934; d. Theodore Wylie and Dorothy Belle (Mehrmann) Williams; BS, Chatham Coll., 1956; postgrad. Case-Western Res. U., 1956-57; MS Calif. State U., 1989. Cytotechnologist, Clin. Path. Lab. of Paul Gross, Pitts., 1957-59; chief cytotechnologist, teaching supr. Presbyn. U. Hosp., Pitts., 1959-63; staff Pathology Lab. of Drs. Armanini & Wegner, Stockton, Calif., 1964; chief cytotechnologist, teaching supr. Hosp. of Good Samaritan, Los Angeles, 1964-89; dir. cytotechnology tng. program UCLA Med. Ctr., 1989—; conductor workshops in field. Mem. Am. Soc. Clin. Pathologists (cytotech. exam. com. bd. registry 1978, mem. bd. govs. 1990-95), Calif. Assn. Cytotechnologists (pres. 1967-68, 72-73), Internat. Acad. Cytology, Am. Soc. Cytopathology (Technologist of Yr. award 1981). Republican. Presbyterian. Home: 2460 Stoner Ave Los Angeles CA 90064-1326 Office: 10833 Le Conte Ave Los Angeles CA 90024

WILLIAMS, CAROLYN, school counselor; b. Barnwell, S.C., Nov. 17, 1949; d. Jessie Ashley and Harriett (Holmes) Odom; m. Melvin Lee Williams; children: Tarla, Melanie, Harriett. BS in Edn., Paine Coll., 1972; MEd, Augusta Coll., 1979, MEd in Counseling, 1992. Cert. sch. counselor, Ga. Tchr. Richmond County Bd. Edn., Augusta, Ga., 1973-94; counselor Columbia County Bd. Edn., Martinez, Ga., 1994—; assessor tchr. performance Ga. Dept. Edn., Augusta, 1983-90; mem. bias com. Ga. Assessment Divsn., Atlanta, 1993—. Chair Stevens Creek Guidance Com., 1994-96. Recipient 3d Pl. Coach award Math. Count Competitions, 1988, 89, Honors Tchrs. award NASA, 1988. Mem. ACA, Am. Sch. Counselors Assn., Ga. Sch. Counselors Assn., Profl. Orgn. Ga. Educators. Home: 3308 Sugar Mill Rd Augusta GA 30907

WILLIAMS, CAROLYN ELIZABETH, manufacturing executive; b. L.A., Jan. 24, 1943; d. George Kissam and Mary Eloise (Chamberlain) W.; m. Richard Terrill White, Apr. 9, 1972; children: Sarah Anne, William Daniel. BS, Ga. Inst. Tech., 1969; MM, Northwestern U., 1988. Saleswoman Ea. Airlines, Atlanta, Montreal (Can.) and Seattle, 1964-69; job analyst Allied Products Corp., Atlanta, 1969-70; mgr. Allied Products Corp., Frankfort, Mich., 1970-71; planning analyst, sr. planning analyst Allied Products Corp., Chgo., 1972-74, dir. planning, 1974-76, staff v.p. planning, 1976-79, v.p. planning and bus. research, 1979-86, v.p. corp. devel., chief planning officer, 1986-93; pres. White, Williams & Daniels, 1993—. Mem. adv. bd. Ga. Inst. Tech. Mem. Winnteka Yacht Club (dir. jr. sailing), Midwest Youth Sailing Assn. (bd. dirs., treas.).

WILLIAMS, CAROLYN WOODWORTH, retired elementary education educator, consultant; b. Binghamton, N.Y., Aug. 29, 1937; d. Charles Byron Woodworth and Dorothy Louise (Wheeler) Krum; m. James C. Williams, Mar. 29, 1958; children: Christopher, Lizette Macaluso, Matthew (dec.). BS in Elem. Edn., SUNY, Cortland, 1958; postgrad., SUNY, Geneseo, 1973-74, U. Vt., 1988; MS in Edn., SUNY, Brockport, 1989. Cert. tchr. K-6, N.Y. Elem. tchr. grade 6 Whitney Point (N.Y.) Ctrl. Sch., 1959-69; elem. tchr. grade 6 Palmyra (N.Y.)-Macedon Ctrl. Sch., 1969-71, elem. tchr. grade 4, 1971-79, 84-95, elem. tchr. grade 1, 1979-84, ret., 1995. Author, editor booklets. Active Women's Rep. Club, Binghamton, N.Y., 1959-67. Recipient Bring Local History Live into Classroom award Griffiss-McLouth Fund, 1993. Mem. ASCD, AAUW, N.Y. State United Tchrs., N.Y. State Hist. Soc., Wayne County Hist. Soc. (bicentennial history fair coord. 1989), Ea. Star (sister). Methodist. Home: 3304 Fallbrook Park Canandaigua NY 14424

WILLIAMS, CATHY LYNN, nurse; b. Galion, Ohio, Nov. 22, 1947; d. Ernest LeRoy and Wilma Eleanor (Fauth) Denton; m. Michael Earl Williams, July 14, 1979 (div. July 1984). ADN, Lorain County C.C., 1971. RN Ohio, Calif. Staff nurse U. Hosp., Cleve., 1971-75; critical care nurse, med. ICU Cedars-Sinai Med. Ctr., L.A., 1975-76; critical care nurse, surg. ICU Valley Med. Ctr., San Jose, Calif., 1976-80, Ohio State U. Hosp., Columbus, 1980-88; nurse utilization review Peer Review System, Columbus, 1988-91; case mgr. United Health Care, Columbus, 1991—. Vol. Children's Immunization Clinic. Home: 3412 Leighton Rd Upper Arlington OH 43221-1300

WILLIAMS, CHARLOTTE EDWINA, secondary school educator, real estate manager; b. Phila., Jan. 5, 1945; d. Charles Edward and Elaine Frances Lydia (Scott) Williams; m. Charles Ross, III, Jan. 19, 1971 (div. June 1985); 1 child, Amber Charlotte. BS, Cheyney (Pa.) State U., 1968; MEd, U. So. Miss., 1989; postgrad., Temple U., 1996—. Cert. secondary English tchr., sr. career tchr.; cert. secondary prin. Tchr. English Phila. Pub. Schs., 1968-69, 72-90, charter coord., 1990-91, tchr. English, 1991—; sys. engr. IBM Corp., Phila., 1969-72. Majority inspector Election Bd., Phila., 1982-90; treas. West Ctrl. Germantown Neighbors, Phila., 1995—; sec. Jack and Jill of Am., Inc., Phila., 1980-82. Mem. Phi Delta Kappa, Alpha Kappa Alpha.

WILLIAMS, CHARLOTTE EVELYN FORRESTER, civic worker; b. Kansas City, Mo., Aug. 7, 1905; d. John Dougal and Georgia (Lowerre) Forrester; student Kans. U., 1924-25; m. Walker Alonzo Williams, Sept. 25, 1926; children: Walker Forrester, John Haviland. Trustee, Detroit Grand Opera Assn., 1960-87, dir., 1955-60; chmn. Grinnell Opera Scholarship, 1958-66; founder, dir., chmn. adv. bd. Cranbrook Music Guild, Inc., 1952-59, life mem.; bd. dirs. Detroit Opera Theater, 1959-61, Severo Ballet, 1959-61; Detroit dist. chmn. Met. Opera Regional Auditions, 1958-66; Fla. Atlantic U. Found.; past pres. Friends of Caldwell Playhouse, Boca Raton. Mem. Debbie-Rand Meml. Svc. League (life), DAR, English-Speaking Union, Vol. League Fla. Atlantic U., PEO, Order Eastern Star. Home: 2679 S Ocean Blvd Apt 5C Boca Raton FL 33432-8353

WILLIAMS, CHERYL, educator; b. Neosho, Mo., July 7, 1957; d. Allen and Travestine Williams. BS in Math., East Tex. State U., 1978, postgrad., 1978-79; postgrad., Rose State Coll., 1980-81, Sheppard Tech. Tng. Ctr., 1980-81, U. Tex., 1996. Computer scientist Tinker AFB, Oklahoma City, 1980-81, Defense Comm. Agy., Washington, 1986; tchr. Parent Child Inc., San Antonio, 1989; asst. sec. Antioch Bapt. Ch., San Antonio, 1989-92; substitute tchr. San Antonio Ind. Sch. Dist., 1990-93; instrnl. asst. spl. edn. Northside Ind. Sch. Dist., San Antonio, 1995-96, asst. tchr., 1994-96; rep. West Telemarketing, 1996—; asst. mgr. Fashion Place, San Antonio, 1994-95. Counselor YMCA, San Antonio, 1989-91; active Girl Scouts U.S., 1964-86; mem. choir, asst. sec. area ch., 1972, tutor, 1970—, tchr. Sunday Sch., 1973—; mem. Dorcas Circle, Lupus Found. Am., Biomed. Rsch. U. Tex., 1995—; mem. Epilepsy Found. Am., Tex. Head Injury Assn., Nat. Head Injury Assn., Smithsonian Instn. Mem. NEA, Tex. Edn. Assn., Mu Alpha Theta.

WILLIAMS, CHRISTINE POWELL, motion picture editor; b. Asheville, N.C., Oct. 30, 1952; d. Carroll Warner and Dorothea Muriel Grace (Rockburne) W. BFA, U. N.Mex., 1975. Editor numerous motion pictures, 1988-94, including: Roy Lichtenstein Brushstrokes, Share the Magic, Protect Me From What I Want, Rocks With Wings, Dorothy Day, Design, Aids, The Journey is Home, Blackwood Productions/WARD West German TV; asst. film editor, 1979-93; Assault at West Point: The Trial of Johnson Wittikeiz, Sports Illustrated Swimsuit Special, The Quick and The Dead, The Trip to Bountiful, Zelig, A Midsummer Night Sex Comedy, Go Tell It On the Mountain, Lincoln and Seward, The Wash, The Fig Tree, Forever Lulu, Katherine-Anne Porter/The Eye of Memory, numerous others. Recipient Robert Rauchenberg scholarship, Skowhegan Sch. for Painting and Sculpture. Mem. Motion Picture Film and Video Tape Editors Union.

WILLIAMS, CYNTHIA ALEXANDER, organization development consultant, educator; b. Kansas City, Mo., Sept. 6, 1942; d. Barnett Ray and Mary Lucinda (Alexander) W.; m. Arthur lloyd Kelly, Oct. 25, 1961 (div.); children: Mary Lucinda, Thomas Lloyd II, Alison Williams. BS, Northwestern U., 1975; MS, U. San Francisco, 1978; PhD, Fielding Inst., 1986. Cert. marriage, family & child therapist. Pres. Integrated Human Systems, Santa Rosa, Calif., 1984-89; sr. cons. Pacific Gas & Electric, San Francisco, 1989-93; mgr. corp. change mgmt. Cinergy, Cin., 1994-95; regional dir. human & orgn. devel. Mercy Regional Health Sys., Cin., 1995—; cons. dept. social svcs., San Francisco, 1992-93. Bd. dirs. Canine Companions Independence, Santa Rosa, 1989-94. Mem. ASTD, Calif. Assn. Marriage & Child Therapists, Orgn. Devel. Network. Home: 1118 Belvedere St Cincinnati OH 45202

WILLIAMS, DELIA HARRIET, school counselor; b. Memphis, Oct. 4, 1961; d. Edmund Lewis Jr. amd Sue Gwendolyn (Garrison) W. BA, North Ga. Coll., 1984; MEd, U. Ga., 1991. Cert. early childhood tchr., Ga.; nat. cert. counselor, Ga. Kindergarten tchr. DeKalb (Ga.) County Pub. Schs., 1984-87; primary tchr. Gwinnett (Ga.) County Pub. Schs., 1987-93; sch. counselor GCPS, Gwinnett, Ga., 1993—; dir. Jr. DOK, Stone Mountain, Ga., 1985-86, 87-89. Coord. Meth. Ch. Recreation, Stone Mountain, 1984-90, DeKalb Volleyball Assn., Ga., 1985-87; mgmt. cons. Hopkins Elem., Lilburn, Ga., 1992—. Mem. ACA, Atlanta Lawn Tennis Assn., Alpha Gamma Delta.

WILLIAMS, DONNA LEE H., state agency adminstrator; b. Wilmington, Del., Nov. 13, 1960; d. Ronald Lee and Loretta M. (Simonson) H.; m. John R. Williams, Oct. 8, 1988. AA, Wesley Coll., 1979; BA in Govt., Coll. William and Mary, 1981; JD, Widener U., 1984. Atty. Prickett, Jones, Elliott, Kristol & Shnee, Dover, Del., 1983-87, Bayard Handelman & Murdock, Dover, 1987-92; ins. commr. State Del., Dover, 1993—. mem. Del. Bd. Accts., Dover. Mem. Nat. Assn. Ins. Commrs., Del. Bar Assn., Kent County Bar Assn. (past pres.), Women Bus. Leaders, Women's Rep. Club Dover (pres. 1985-87). Methodist. Office: Del Dept Ins PO Box 7007 841 Silver Lake Blvd Dover DE 19903-1507

WILLIAMS, DONNA RAE, dentist; b. Milw., Jan. 28, 1965; d. Irving Cardinal and Elvira Amelia (Felton) W. Registered Dental Hygienist, Howard U., Washington, 1986; DDS, U. Md., 1990. Dental hygienist Ft. Davis Dental Ctr., Washington, 1985-87, Dr. Linda Miles, Balt., 1986-88; owner, ptnr. Connor & Connor Dental Ctr., St. Thomas, U.S. Virgin Islands, 1990-94; owner Cmty. Dental Care Ctr., St. Thomas, V.I., 1990-94; spkr. Womens AIDS Conf., Dionne Warwick & Friends, St. Thomas, 1993; spkr. Health Fair, Harlem Succeeds, N.Y.C., 1995. Troop leader Girl Scouts, U.S. Virgin Islands, 1990-93; bd. dirs. Ahead, Inc., Rockville, Md., 1988—; mem. Harlem Succeeds, N.Y.C., 1995—; activities chairperson Positive Tree, Inc., U.S. Virgin Islands, 1990-93. Named Small Bus. Person of Yr. Small Bus. Assn., U.S. Virgin Islands, 1993. Mem. Nat. Dental Assn., Acad. Gen. Dentistry. Office: Cmty Dental Care 360 W 125th St Ste 7A New York NY 10027

WILLIAMS, DONNA REILLY, counselor, writer, consultant; b. Dauphin, Man., Can., Mar. 18, 1945; came to U.S., 1986; d. Allen Leslie and Mary Mabel (McNicol) Reilly; m. Clifford Neil Williams, May 31, 1966; children: Mary, Kevin, David, Laura. Diploma in Theol. Studies (distinction), Newman Theol. Coll., Edmonton, Alta., Can., 1985; MA in Pastoral Studies, Loyola Marymount U., L.A., 1990; postgrad., Marriage & Family Tng. Program, Seattle, 1996. Staff chaplain Edmonton Gen. Hosp., 1985-86; sr. theology tchr. Sacred Heart of Jesus H.S., L.A., 1987-88; pastoral min. Archdiocese of L.A., 1988-89; dir. support svcs. AIDS Healthcare Found., L.A., 1989-90; counselor, cons. Woodinville, Wash., 1991—; employee assistance program coord. Assoc. Cath. Cemeteries, Seattle, 1994—. Author: Grief Ministry: Helping Others Mourn, 1990, (children's) Morgan's Baby Sister, 1992, Our Family is Divorcing, 1996; contbr. articles to profl. jours. Mem. sr. citizen's action com. Beverly Hosp., Montebello, Calif., 1986-89. Fellow Am. Assn. Grief Counselors; mem. ACA, Am. Assn. Christian Counselors, Assn. for Death Edn. and Counseling (cert.), Internat. Assn. Marriage & Family Counselors, Assn. for Spiritual, Ethical and Religious Values in Counseling, Western Wash. Bereavement Specialists (v.p. 1990-91). Home and Office: 18327-147th Ct NE Woodinville WA 98072

WILLIAMS, DOROTHY STANDRIDGE, soft drink company official, civic worker; b. Powder Springs, Ga.; d. Robert Anderson and Bertie Mae (Elsberry) Standridge; m. Harold Thomas Barfield (div. 1967); 1 child, H. Gregory; m. J. Arden Williams (div. Dec. 1992). Student, DeKalb Coll., Atlanta, 1982-83, U. Laval, Que., 1996. Assoc. promotion mgr., promotion coord. Coca-Cola USA, Atlanta, 1978-83, promotions mgr., 1983-86; mgr. internat. promotion svcs. The Coca-Cola Co., Atlanta, 1986-90, mgr. global promotion svcs., 1990-94. Attaché Atlanta Conv. and Visitors Bur., 1992—; vol. Welcome South Ctr., Atlanta, 1995—; bd. advisors Life Coll. for Knowledge and Tng., 1995—; chmn. cmty. rels. com. Life Coll., 1995-96. Mem. Ga. Trust for Hist. Preservation, Atlanta High Mus. Art, Atlanta Bot. Gardens, Alliance Francaise.

WILLIAMS, EDNA ALETA THEADORA JOHNSTON, journalist; b. Halifax, N.S., Can., Sept. 19, 1923; d. Clarence Harvey and Edna May (Lewis) Johnston; m. Albert Murray Williams, Apr. 16, 1949 (dec.); children: Murleta, Norma, Martin, Charla, Kerrick, Renwick, Julia. Student, Maritime Bus. Coll., 1943. Typist Dept. Treasury (Navy), Halifax, 1944-49; with Bedford (N.S.) Mag., Halifax br., 1954-55, Presbyn. Office, New Glasgow, N.S., 1965-67, Thompson and Sutherland, New Glasgow, 1967-69; family editor, columnist and reporter New Glasgow Evening News, 1969-88, ret., 1988. Bapt. rep. Pictou County Coun. of Chs., 1978-82, sec., 1980-82; pres. ch. aux. 2d United Bapt. Ch., 1979-83, organist, 1970—, chorus dir. Men's Choir, 1980—, hon. mem. ch. aux., v.p., 1993—, tras. Ch.'s Men's Brotherhood, 1995—; organist St. James Anglican Ch., 1983-85, provincial organist, 1994—; organist St. Bee's Anglican Ch., 1996—; provincial pres. Women's Inst. of African United Bapt. Assn., 1983-86; mem. coun. Halifax YWCA; founding mem. Pictou County YM-YWCA, 1966—, bd. dirs., 1967-77, corr. sec., v.p., 1975-77, 1974-75; past pres., past provincial dir. Home and Sch.; provincial sec. African United Bapt. Assn. of Nova Scotia, 1988-90; sec. area IV Altantic United Bapt. Conv., 1989-93; past officer local interracial com.; bd. dirs. Big Bros./ Big Sisters, 1984-86, Pictou County United Way, 1983—, Palliative Care Aberdeen Hosp., 1985—, Black United Front; reference person media and religion Black History Month. Recipient Honor award United Way, 1993; honored by Pictou County Music Festival, 1994. Mem. N.S. Sr. Secretate. Mem. Can. Press Assn. Home: 230 Reservoir St, New Glasgow, NS Canada B2H 4K4 Office: Evening News, 352 East River Rd, Glasgow, NS Canada B2H 5E2

WILLIAMS, EDNA DORIS, retired educational administrator; b. Bronson, Iowa, July 26, 1908; d. Franklin James and Sarah Jane (Hunt) W. BA, U. No. Iowa, 1939; MA, U. Minn., 1947; postgrad., U. S.D., 1955-60, U. Iowa, 1957, 59, 60, U. Minn., 1951, 67, 69. Cert. adminstr., guidance counselor. Rural sch. tchr. Eurikia # 8, Sac County Rural Schs., Schaller, Iowa, 1929-30; tchr. grades 5 and 6 Bronson (Iowa) Consolidated Sch., 1931-38; normal tng. and English tchr. Rockwell City (Iowa) High Sch., 1939-44; history and debate tchr. Ames (Iowa) High Sch., 1944-47; dramatics and English tchr. East High, Sioux City (Iowa) Community Sch. Dist., 1947-51; dean of girls Central High, Sioux City Community Sch. Dist., 1951-52, East High, Sioux City Community Sch. Dist., 1952-67; asst. prin. East Sioux City Community Sch. Dist., 1967-72, asst. prin. North, 1972-73; cons., chmn. course of study in Am. history Iowa State Dept. Pub. Instrn., Des Moines, 1947-48; demonstration tchr. State Dept. Pub. Instrn., 1957; demonstration tchr. Woodbury County Supt., 1958; student coun. workshop adviser, mem. staff Iowa Assn. Student Couns., Cedar Falls, 1960-63; rep. of dist. Coll. Entrance Exam. Bd., 1950-73; advisor N.W. Coun. Student Coun., 1960-64; mem. exec. bd. N.W. Guidance Coun., 1965-66. Editor: (course book and handbook, high schs.) Ednl. Opportunities, 1968-69; author, editor: Food for Thought Yesterday Today and Tomorrow, 1987; author choral reading plays. Tax aide vol. IRS, Sioux City, 1979-86, 87-91; vol. Iowa Commn. for the Blind; chmn. of com. Sioux City Women's Club, pres. Sioux City Adminstrn. Club, 1957-58; circle chmn. United Meth. Women, 1978. Named one of 100 Counselors in U.S. Selected as a Guest, MIT, 1958, 1 of 30 Counselors as Guest of 6 Minn. Colls., 1966; recipient Cert. of Appreciation, Dir. Student Couns. in Iowa, 1963, Gov.'s Vol. award State of Iowa, 1989, Cert. Dedicated Svc. Am. Assn. Retired Persons, 1990. Mem. NEA (life), Iowa Assn. Women Deans and Counselors (state pres. 1961-62), Iowa State Edn. Assn. (life), Nat. Ret. Tchrs. Assn. (award from Iowa div., Cert. of Appreciation 1986), Sioux City Ret. Educators (life, pres. 1985-88), AAUW (life, treas. 1981-82, v.p. 1984-85, Cert. for Significant Svc. to Ednl. Found. 1981-82, 82-83, chair career women study group), Northern Iowa Alumni Assn., U. Minn. Alumni Assn. (life mem.). Methodist.

WILLIAMS, ELEANOR CLAFFIN (CLAFFY WILLIAMS), artist; b. Brookline, Mass., Jan. 31, 1916; d. Thomas Mack and Alice Morton (Osborn) Claflin; m. Thomas Blake Williams, Jan. 26, 1940; children: Thomas B. Jr., Susan Williams Dickie, Eleanor Williams Wright, Sandra M. Williams Weiss. Student, Sweet Briar Coll. art tchr.; lectr. on contemporary art. 0xhibited in various art shows including Copley Soc., Boston, 1974, 77, Chinese Cultural Inst., Boston, 1992, South Shore Art Ctr., Cohasset, Mass., 1996. Pres. bd. dirs. South Shore Art Ctr., Cohasset, Mass., 1985-87, mem. adv. bd., 1987—; dir. Prison Art Project, Boston, 1973-76; bd. dirs. Copley Soc., Boston, 1975-79.

WILLIAMS, ELEANOR JOYCE, government air traffic control specialist; b. College Station, Tex., Dec. 21, 1936; d. Robert Ira and Viola (Ford) Toliver; m. Tollie Williams, Dec. 30, 1955 (div. July 1978); children: Rodrick, Viola Williams Smith, Darryl, Eric, Dana Williams Jones, Sheila Williams Watkins, Kenneth. Student Prairie View A&M Coll., 1955-56, Anchorage Community Coll., 1964-65, U. Alaska-Anchorage, 1976. Clk./ stenographer FAA, Anchorage, 1965-66, adminstrv. clk., 1966-67, pers. staffing asst., 1967-68, air traffic control specialist, 1968-79, air traffic contr. supr., San Juan, P.R., 1979-80, Anchorage, 1983-85, airspace specialist, Atlanta, 1980-83 ; with FAA, Washington, 1985-87; area mgr. Kansas City Air Rt. Traffic Control Ctr., Olathe, Kans., 1987-89, asst. mgr. quality Assurance, 1989-91, supr. traffic mgmt., 1991, supr. system effectiveness section, 1991-93, asst. air traffic mgr., 1993-94, air traffic mgr. Cleve. Air Route Traffic Control Ctr., Oberlin, Ohio, 1994—, acting mgr. sys. mgmt. br., Des Plaines, Ill., 1995-96, mem. human resource reform team task force, Washington, 1996—. Sec. Fairview Neighborhood Coun., Anchorage, 1967-69; mem. Anchorage Bicentennial Commn., 1975-76; bd. dirs. Mt. Patmos Youth Dept., Decatur, Ga., 1981-82; mem. NAACP; del. to USSR Women in Mgmt., 1990; mem. citizens amb. program People to People Internat. Recipient Mary K. Goddard award Anchorage Fed. Exec. Assn. and Fed. Women's Program, 1985, Sec.'s award Dept. transp., 1985, Pres. VIP award, 1988, C. Alfred Anderson award, 1991, Disting. Svc. award Nat. Black Coalition of Fed. Aviation Employees, 1991, Paul K. Bohr award FAA, 1994, Nat. Performance Rev. Hammer award from V.P. Al Gore, 1996; A salute to Her Name in the Congl. Record 104th Congress, 1995. Mem. Nat. Assn Negro Bus. and Profl, Women (North to the Future club, charter pres. 1975-76), Blacks in Govt., Nat. Black Coalition of Fed. Aviation Employees (pres. cen. region chpt. 1987-92, Over Achievers award, 1987, Disting. Svc. award 1988), Profl. Women Contrs. Orgn., Air Traffic Contrs. Assn., Fed. Mgrs. Assn., Internat. Platform Assn., Women in Mgmt. (del. Soviet Union), Gamma Phi Delta. Democrat. Baptist. Avocations: singing; sewing. Home: 5770-D2 Great Northern Blvd North Olmsted OH 44070 Office: FAA 326 E Lorain St Oberlin OH 44074-1216

WILLIAMS, ELIZABETH EVENSON, writer; b. Sioux Falls, S.D., Sept. 25, 1940; d. A. Duane and Eleanor (Kelton) Evenson; m. Louis P. Williams Jr., Aug. 31, 1968; 1 child, Katherine. BS, S.D. State U., 1962; MA, U. Wis., 1964; postgrad., U. Minn., 1969-70; MA, S.D. State U., 1983, postgrad., 1992—. Dir. pubs. No. State Coll., Aberdeen, S.D., 1965-68; instr. journalism S.D. State U., Brookings, 1968-69, 85—; asst. editor Journalism Quar., Mpls., 1969-70; pub. info. specialist S.D. Com. on Humanities, Brookings, 1975-78; asst. and instr. speech dept. S.D. State U., Brookings, 1981-92; part-time dir. Women's Ctr., Brookings, 1988-90; reading series coord. S.D. Com. on Humanities, Brookings, 1986-91. Author: Emil Loriks: Builder of a New Economic Order, 1987, More Reflections of a Prairie Daughter, 1993; weekly columnist Brookings Daily Register, 1985-92, RFD News, 1992-95; contbr. articles to profl. jours. Vestry mem. St. Paul's Ch., Brookings, 1975-76, 84-86, 92—, sr. warden, 1995—; pres. LWV of S.D., 1985-89, treas., 1990-92. S.D. Humanities Com. grantee, 1984, 87, 90. Mem. Nat. Fedn. Press Women (1st place nat. writing contest 1977), Phi Kappa Phi, Pi Kappa Delta, Alpha Kappa Delta. Episcopalian. Home: 1103 3rd St Brookings SD 57006-2230 Office: SD State U Journalism Dept Brookings SD 57007

WILLIAMS, ELIZABETH YAHN, author, lecturer, lawyer; b. Columbus, Ohio, July 20, 1942; d. Wilbert Henry and Elizabeth Dulson (Brophy) Yahn. BA cum laude, Loyola Marymount U., 1964; secondary teaching credential, UCLA, 1965; JD, Loyola U., 1971. Cert. tchr. h.s. and jr. coll. law, English and history. Writer West Covina, Calif., 1964—; designer West Covina, 1966-68; tchr. jr./sr. h.s. L.A. City Schs., Santa Monica, Calif., 1964-65, La Puente (Calif.) H.S. Dist., 1965-67; legal intern, lawyer Garvey, Ingram, Baker & Uhler, Covina, Calif., 1969-72; lawyer, corp. counsel Avco Fin. Svcs., Inc., Newport Beach, Calif., 1972-74; sole practitioner and arbitrator Santa Ana, Calif., 1974-80, Newport Beach, 1980-87; mem. faculty continuing edn. State Bar of Calif., 1979; adj. prof. Western State U. Sch. Law, Fullerton, Calif., 1980; mem. fed. cts. com. Calif. State Bar, San Francisco, 1977-80. Author: (1-act plays) Acting-Out Acts, 1990, Grading Graciela, 1992, Boundaries in the Dirt, 1993; author, lyricist: (1-act children's musical) Peter and the Worry Wrens, 1995; contbr. articles to profl. jours.; panelist TV show Action Now, 1971; interviewee TV show Women, 1987; scriptwriter, dir. TV show Four/Four, 1994, (3-act adaptation) Saved in Sedona, 1995; scriptwriter, prodr., host TV show Guidelights to Success, 1996. Mem. alumni bd. Loyola-Marymount U., L.A., 1980-84; mem. adv. bd. Rancho Santiago Coll., Santa Ana, 1983-84; speaker Commn. on Status on Women, Santa Ana, 1979. Grantee Ford Found., 1964-65; French scholar Ohio State U., 1959, acad. scholar Loyola-Marymount U., 1960-64; Editor's Choice award, 1995, Telly award finalist, 1996; award Nat. Libr. of Poetry. Mem. Calif. Women Lawyers (co-founder, life, bd. dirs. 1975-76), Orange County Bar Assn. (faculty Orange County Coll. Trial Advocacy 1982, chmn. human and individual rights com. 1974-75, comml. law and bankruptcy com. 1978-79, corp. and bus. law sect. 1980-81), So. Calif. Book Writers and Illustrators, Phi Delta Delta, Phi Alpha Delta, Phi Theta Kappa (hon. life mem.). Address: PO Box 146 San Luis Rey CA 92068-0146

WILLIAMS, EMILY ALLEN, English language educator; b. Nottoway, Va., Aug. 14, 1955; d. Joseph Robert and Cornelia (Scott) Allen; m. Kenneth Jerome Williams, Feb. 29, 1992. BA, St. Paul's Coll., 1977; MA, Va. Commonwealth U., 1979; DAH, Clark Atlanta U., 1996. Instr. adult edn. Med. Coll. Va./Va. Commonwealth U., Richmond, 1977-79; instr. English Richmond Bus. Coll., 1979-80; regional grants coord. Va. Com. for Arts, Richmond, 1980-85; grants program coord. Ga. Coun. for Arts, Atlanta, 1986-87; grants dir. City of Atlanta Bur. Cultural Affairs, 1987-91; prof. English Clark Atlanta U., 1991-92, Morehouse Coll., Atlanta, 1992—, Spelman Coll., 1995—; adj. instr. English Reynolds C.C., Richmond, 1983-85; site reviewer NEA, Washington, 1990-91; panelist Nat. Black Arts Festival, Atlanta, 1991, Ga. Coun. Arts, Atlanta, 1987-90; cons. Fulton County Arts Coun., Atlanta, 1991-92, African Am. Philharmonic Orch., Atlanta, 1991-92. Contbr. numerous articles to profl. publs. Advisor student newspaper Morehouse Coll., 1992-93, grant com. chmn. English dept., 1992-93; speaker arts sem. Va. Commonwealth U., Richmond, 1982; cons. The APEX Mus., Atlanta, 1992-93. E. Bradlee Watson scholar, St. Paul's Coll., 1976. Mem. Popular Culture Assn., Coll. Lang. Assn., Delta Sigma Theta, Alpha Kappa Mu. Home: 6196 Spring Lake Walk Lithonia GA 30038-3467 Office: Morehouse Coll 830 Westview Dr SW Atlanta GA 30314-3773

WILLIAMS, ERIKA, company executive; b. La Paz, Bolivia, Mar. 28, 1947; came to U.S., 1965; BS, Boston U., 1974, MS, 1977; postgrad., MIT, 1978. Mgr. Amdahl Corp., Sunnyvale, Calif., 1978-82, dir., 1982-86, v.p., 1986—, corp. officer, 1990—, sr. v.p., gen. mgr., 1993-95; COO Sys. Integrators, Inc., Calif., 1995—; bd. dirs. Cin. Microwave. Fellow Silicon Valley chpt. Am. Leadership Forum, Los Altos Hills, Calif., 1991—; bd. dirs. Emergency Housing Consortium, San Jose, 1994-95. Office: PO Box 13626 1300 National Dr Sacramento CA 95853

WILLIAMS, GEORGANN HIBBARD, educational educator; b. Indpls., Dec. 3, 1961; d. George Lewis and Barbara Jane (Boyd) Hibbard; m. Collins Compton Williams, June 30, 1984; children: Anne, Caroline. AB cum laude, Duke U., 1984; MEd, U. N.C., Greensboro, 1988; EdD, N.C. State U., 1994. Admissions counselor Greensboro Coll., 1984-85, asst. dir. admissions, 1985-86, assoc. dir. admissions, 1986-88, acad. advisor, 1988-90, dir. admissions, 1988-91; rsch. asst. N.C. State U., Raleigh, 1991-93, teaching asst., 1994—; presenter various confs.; ednl. cons. Carolinas Assn. of Collegiate Registrars and Admissions Officers, 1987-89. Named to Outstanding Young Woman of Am., 1991; named Bus. Assoc. of Yr., Am. Bus. Women's Assn., Greensboro, 1988. Mem. Chi Omega, Phi Kappa Phi. Home: 5517 Netherby Ct Raleigh NC 27613-5722

WILLIAMS, GLADYS TUCKER, elementary school principal; b. Washington, May 15, 1943; d. Lee William and Cora Lena (Barksdale) Tucker; m. John Thomas Williams, June 6, 1964; children: Jon Trevor, Jamia Tiffani. BS, D.C. Tchrs. Coll., 1971; MA, George Washington U., 1981. From speech/lang. pathologist to prin. Prince Georges County Schs., Upper Marlboro, Md., 1971—. Pres. Largo (Md.) H.S. Choir Parents Assn., 1992-93; 2d v.p. Melwood Elem. Sch. PTA, Upper Marlboro, 1987-89. Mem. Nat. Assn. Elem. Prins. & Adminstrs., Assn. Sch.-Based Adminstrs. & Supervisors, Md. State Tchrs. Assn., Prince Georges County Tchrs. Assn., Alpha Delta Kappa, Delta Kappa Gamma (v.p. 1994-95). Office: James McHenry Elem Sch 8909 McHenry Ln Lanham MD 20706

WILLIAMS, GLORIA LOUISE, gifted and talented education educator; b. Greenville, S.C., Sept. 29, 1949; d. Harding and Gladys Louise (Burgess) Hendricks; children: Lisa, Philip. BA, Spelman Coll., 1971; MusB, Mich. State U., 1973; MS in Edn., Ind. U., 1979. Cert. elem. tchr., Ind. Dir. christian edn. Second Christian Ch., Indpls., 1975-77; staff devel. intern Indpls. Pub. Schs., 1977-78; tchr. elem. and mid. sch. Lawrence Twp. Schs., Indpls., 1980—; head human rels. com. Lawrence Twp. Sch., 1982-83. Part-time dir. children's ministry Light of the World Christian Ch., Indpls., 1984-89. Recipient Gloria and James Williams Day award Light of the World Christian Ch., 1989. Mem. Jack and Jill of Am., NAACP, Alpha Kappa Alpha. Office: MSD Lawrence Twp Sch 7601 E 56th St Indianapolis IN 46226-1310

WILLIAMS, GWENDOLYN JANICE, municipal or county official; b. Beufort, S.C., Oct. 29, 1955; d. Porter and Minnie Lee (Williams) Davis. AAS, Mercer County C. C., Trenton, N.J., 1978. Sub. tchr. Trenton Bd. of Edn., Trenton, 1978-80; file clerk divsn. of pension Dept. of Treasury, Trenton, 1984—; sheriff's officer Mercer County, N.J.; child placement review bd. advocate Mercer County Child Placement Review, Trenton, 1988-94. Mem. Nat. Polit. Congress of Black Women, Burlington, N.J., 1985-88, sr. citizen chair Urban League Guild of Met. Trenton, 1988— (pres. award 1989). Home: 327 Monmouth St Trenton NJ 08609

WILLIAMS, HARRIET CLARKE, retired academic administrator, artist; b. Bklyn., Sept. 5, 1922; d. Herbert Edward and Emma Clarke (Gibbs) W. AA, Bklyn. Coll., 1958; student, Art Career Sch., N.Y.C., 1960; cert., Hunter Coll., 1965, CPU Inst. Data Processing, 1967; student, Chineses Cultural Ctr., N.Y.C., 1973; hon. certs., St. Labre Sch./St. Joseph's, Ind. Sch., Mont., 1990. Adminstr. Baruch Coll., N.Y.C., 1959-85; mktg. researcher 1st Presbyn. Arts and Crafts Shop, Jamaica, N.Y., 1986-96; tutor in art St. John's U., Jamaica, 1986-96; founder, curator Internat. Art Gallery, Queens, N.Y., 1991—. Exhibited in group shows at Union Carbide Art Exhibit, N.Y.C., 1975, Queens Day Exhbn., N.Y.C., 1980, 1st Presbyn. Arts and Crafts Shop, N.Y.C., 1986, others; contbr. articles to profl. publs. Vol. reading tchr. Mabel Dean Vocat. High Sch., N.Y.C., 1965-67; mem. polit. action com. dist. council 37, N.Y.C., 1973-77; mem. negotiating team adminstrv. contracts, N.Y.C., 1975-78; mem. Com. To Save CCNY, 1976-77, Statue Liberty Ellis Island Found., Woodrow Wilson Internat. Ctr. Scholars, Wilson Ctr. Assocs., Washington, St. Labre Indian Sch., Ashland, Mont. Appreciation award Dist. Coun. 37, 1979; recipient Plaque Appreciation Svcs., Baruch Coll., Key award St. Joseph's Indian Sch., 1990, Key award in Edn. and Art, 1990, others. Mem. NAFE, AAUW, Women in Mil. Svc., Assn. Am. Indian Affairs, Nat. Mus. of Am. Indian, Artist Equity Assn. N.Y., Lakota Devel. Coun., Am. Film Inst., Bklyn. Coll. Alumni, Nat. Geographic Soc., Nat. Mus. Woman in the Arts, Statue of Liberty Ellis Island Found., Inc., Alliance of Queens Artists, U.S. Naval Inst., El Museo Del Barrio, Am. Mus. Natural History, Internat. Ctr. for Scholars-Wilson Ctr. Assocs., Arrow Club-St. Labre Indian Sch., Mus. of Television and Radio, Women in Military Meml. Found., Nat. Mus. of Am. Indian, U.S. Holocaust Mus., Navy Meml. (adv. coun.). Roman Catholic. Office: Baruch Coll 17 Lexington Ave New York NY 10010-5526

WILLIAMS, HELEN CLAYTON, university administrator; b. Williamsburg, Va., Jan. 19, 1947; d. Robert Lee and Edith Helen (Mundie) Clayton; m. Benjamin Guy Williams Jr., June 30, 1978. BA, Coll. of William and Mary, 1969, advanced degree in spl. edn., 1975, EdD, 1985; MEd, Va. Commonwealth U., 1975. Social studies instr. King William (Va.) Pub. Schs., 1969-71, York Acad., Shacklefords, Va., 1971-72; social skills/GED instr. Va. Correctional Ctr. for Women, Goochland, Va., 1973-76; chpt. I coord. Rehab. Sch. Authority, Richmond, Va., 1976-79, prin., 1979-87; dir. spl. edn. Dept. of Correctional Edn., Richmond, 1987-88, dir. spl. programs, 1988-93, dir. acad. programs, 1993-96, asst. supt. acad. programs, 1996—; pres. Ednl. Cons. Enterprise, Inc. Aylett, Va., 1992-95. Editor (strategic planning guide) State Agency Text, 1991. Vice chairperson King William County Sch. Bd., 1994-95, chairperson, 1993-94, bd. dirs. 1990-95. Mem. Correctional Edn. Assn. (dir. region II 1987), Va. Assn. of Correctional Educators (paliamentarian 1990, Pres. award 1994, Adinstr. of Yr. 1981, 84), Am. Correctional Assn. (assoc., book reviewer 1988). Home: PO Box 137 Aylett VA 23009 Office: Dept Correctional Edn James Monroe Bldg 7th Fl 101 N 14 St Richmond VA 23219

WILLIAMS, HELEN MARGARET, accountant; b. Fresno, Calif., Mar. 16, 1947; d. James Ray Jr. and Barbara (LaRue) Franklin; m. Phillip Dean Bangs, Apr. 16, 1977; children: Aluvia, Adevia, Rodney. AA in Home Economics, Sacramento City Coll., 1969, AA in Acctg., 1971; BS in Acctg. and Fin. cum laude, Calif. State U., Sacramento, 1988. Acct. tech. Sacramento Regional Transit Dist., 1974-87, revenue rm. contr., 1987-88, acct. I, 1988, acct. II, 1988—; editor employee newsletter Sacramento Regional Transit Dist., 1986-90. Past mother and worthy adv. Rainbow for Girls; past host parent Am. Field Svc., past chair host family selection com. Mem. NAFE, AAUW, Am. Soc. Women Accts. (chair scholarship com. 1992-94, chair pub. com. 1993-94, bd. dirs. 1993-96, sec. 1994-95, chair roster com. 1995-96, chair hospitality com. 1996—), Calif. State U.-Sacramento Alumni Assn., Order Ea. Star, Precious Moments Collectors Club (newsletter editor 1992—, treas. 1993-96). Office: PO Box 2110 Sacramento CA 95812-2110

WILLIAMS, HOLLY BETH, lawyer; b. Sherman, Tex., Sept. 13, 1967; d. John Michael and Janice Louise (Jenkins) W. BA in English and Polit. Sci., Rice U., 1989; JD, U. Tex., 1993, M Pub. Affairs, 1993. Bar: Tex. 1993, U.S. Ct. Appeals (5th cir.) 1995, U.S. Dist. Ct. (no. and we. dists.) Tex. 1995. Assoc. Kemp Smith Duncan & Hammond, Midland, Tex., 1993, Turner & Davis, Midland, 1994—. Mem. Leadership Midland, 1994-95. Mem. LWV (treas. 1994-95, pres. 1995—), Permian Basin Petroleum Assn. (mem. environ. com. 1995—, NEED com. 1996—), Tex. Assn. Def. Counsel, Jr. League of Midland. Home: 3218 Elma Dr Midland TX 79707 Office: Turner & Davis 400 W Illinois Ste 1400 Midland TX 79701

WILLIAMS, HOLLY THOMAS, business executive; b. Pitts., Dec. 24, 1931; d. Andrew Matthew and Elizabeth (Kuklinca) Thomas; m. Donald Evan Williams, May 14, 1961. AA cum laude, Keystone Jr. Coll., LaPlume, Pa., 1978; BS magna cum laude, U. Scranton, 1981. Dancer Arthur Murray Studios, Pitts., 1953-60; franchise owner Arthur Murray Studios, Scranton, Pa., 1960-80; mgr. Nutri/System Weight Loss Ctr., Scranton, 1984-85, franchise owner, 1985—. Fund raiser United Cerebral Palsy of Lackawanna County, Scranton, 1970-79, St. Joseph's Children's Hosp., Scranton, 1962-76; exec. sec. Foxhowe Assn., Buck Hill Falls, Pa., 1984-85. Mem. AAUW (bd. dirs. 1985-86, 94—), Scranton Club. Republican. Christian. Home: PO Box 151 Buck Hill Falls PA 18323-0151 also: 213 Karen Dr Scranton PA 18505-2207 Office: Nutri/System Weight Loss Ctr 216 Linden St Scranton PA 18503-1404

WILLIAMS, IDA JONES, consumer and home economics educator, writer; b. Coatesville, Pa., Dec. 1, 1911; d. William Oscar and Ida Ella (Ruth) Jones; m. Charles Nathaniel Williams, Mar. 17, 1940 (dec. July 1971). BS, Hampton Inst., 1935; MA, U. Conn., 1965; cert. recognition, Famous Writers Sch., Westport, Conn., 1976, 78. Cert. high sch. tchr., English, sci., home econs., Va., Pa. Sci. and home econs. tchr. Richmond County High Sch., Ivondale, Va., 1935-36; English and home econs. tchr. Northampton County High Sch., Chesaepeake, Va., 1936-40; consumer and home econs. tchr. Northampton County High Sch., Machipongo, Va., 1940-71, Northampton Jr. High Sch., Machipongo, 1971-76. Author: Starting Anew After Seventy, 1980 (plaque 1980), News and Views of Northampton County High Principals and Alumni, 1981; editor: Fifty Year Book 1935-1985 - Hampton Institute Class, 1985, Favorite Recipes of Ruth Family & Friends, 1986. V.p. Ea. Lit. Coun., Melfa, Va., 1987-89; mem. Ea. Shore Coll. Found., Inc.,Melfa, 1988-94; mem. Gov.'s Adv. Bd. on Aging, Richmond, Va., 1992-94; instr. Ladies Community Bible Class, 1976-80 (Plaque 1980); sec., treas., v.p. Hospice Support of Ea. Shore, 1980-94; mem. Northampton/Accomack Adv. Counc., 1992-94; marshall 28th anniv. commencement Ea. Shore Cmty. Coll., 1996. Recipient Nat. Sojourner Truth Meritorious Svc. award Nat. Assn. Negro Bus. and Profl. Women's Clubs, Gavel Ea. Shore Ret. Tchrs. Assn., 1994, Jefferson award Am. Inst. Pub. Svc., Wavy-TV-Bell Atlantic and Mattress Discounters, 1991, Gov.'s award for Vol. Excellence, 1994, Spl. Citation award AARP, 1996; named Home Econs. Tchr. of Yr., Am. Home Econs. Assn. and Family Cir., 1975. Mem. Progressive Women of Ea. Shore (pres. 1985-93, Gold Necklace 1993), C. of C., Univ. Women (v.p. Portsmouth br. 1985-87), Ea. Shore Ret. Tchrs. (pres. 1977-84), Dist. L Ret. Tchrs. (pres. 1989-91), Va. State Fedn. Colored Women's Club (pres. 1990-94, editor history com. 1996—), Am. Assn. Ret. Persons (Va. state legis. com. 1995—). Mem. Ch. of Christ. Home and Office: PO Box 236 14213 Lankford Hwy Eastville VA 23347-0236

WILLIAMS, JANE CROUCH, mental health counselor, social worker; b. Knoxville, Tenn., Apr. 23, 1931; d. Brockway and Elsie Irene (Wayland) Crouch; m. James Bowers Bell, June 27, 1950 (div. Sept. 1971); children: Steven Easterly Bell, Sharon Irene Bell Mann Trotter, Joseph Brockway Bell, Robert Wayland Bell; m. Don Roy Williams, Mar. 28, 1989. Student, U. Cin., 1949-50, Ft. Sanders Hosp. Sch. Nursing, 1950; BS in Social Work, U. Tenn., 1985. Office nurse Knoxville Surg. Group, 1955-82; therapist Overlook Health Ctr., Sevierville, Tenn., 1985-89; therapist, counselor Seymour (Tenn.) Family Physicians, 1985-89; coord. mental health day treatment Ridgeview Psychiat., Campbell County, Tenn., 1989-94; mental health counselor Wynn-Habersham Health, Campbell County, 1995—; rschr. Mountain Heritage Rsch., La Follette, Tenn., 1993—; rsch. cons. for family historians, 1955—. Author: Descendants of William Goddard of Sullivan County, Tennessee, 1994. Christian counselor Presbyn. Ch., La Follette, 1993—; elder 1st Presbyn. Ch., La Follette, 1993—; mem. divsn. reconciliation and compassion East Tenn. Presbytery, Knoxville, 1995-97; life mem. East Tenn. Hist. Soc., Knoxville, 1955—; Meml. Found. Germanna Colonies of Va., Culpeper, Va., 1981—. Mem. NSW, Nat. Geneal. Soc., Phi Kappa Phi, Phi Beta Kappa. Republican. Home: 1007 Ellison Rd La Follette TN 37766-3011 Office: Wynn Habersham Health Clin R # 3 Stinking Creek Rd La Follette TN 37766

WILLIAMS, JESSIE WILLMON, church worker, retired librarian; b. Boynton, Okla., Feb. 23, 1907; d. Thomas Woodard and Eliza Jane (Adams) Willmon; m. Austin Guest, Aug. 13, 1932 (div. 1945); m. Thomas Washington Williams, Dec. 12, 1946 (dec.). BA, East Tex. State U., 1930, MA, 1944. cert. English and Spanish tchr., Tex. Libr. Gladewater (Tex.) Pub. Libr., 1935-46; med. libr. VA Hosp., North Little Rock, Ark., 1946-58; base libr. Little Rock AFB, 1958-68; ret., 1968; lay worker 1st Bapt. Ch., Pecan Gap, Tex., 1988—. Mem. Delta Kappa Gamma, Phi Beta Kappa. Democrat. Mem. So. Bapt. Conv. Home: PO Box 43 Pecan Gap TX 75469-0043

WILLIAMS, JOANNE MOLITOR, elementary education educator; b. Medford, Wis., Oct. 25, 1935; d. Lawrence John and Marie Catherine (Bach) Molitor; m. Jack Dean Williams, Dec. 30, 1953; children: Patricia Varma, Ralph (Skip), L. Bradley. BS in Elem. Edn., U. Wis., Whitewater, 1971, MS in Elem. Edn., 1980; postgrad., U. Va., U. Colo. Cert. tchr. in elem. edn. and geography, Wis. Tchr. grades 4, 5 and 6 Lakewood Sch., Twin Lakes, Ill., 1971-82, 83—, tchr. 5th grade gifted, 1989-91; dir. Resources for Children, Milw., 1982-83; mem. textbook selection com. for reading, social studies, sci., lang.; mem. Lakewood Blue Ribbon Com., 1991, Lakewood Discipline Com., 1990-94; mem. Educators Consortium-Parkside, Kenosha, Wis., 1988—; co-developer Respect, Obedience, Attitude, Responsibility program for students with good behavior, 1990; mem. Social Studies Curriculum Com., 1990, Strategic Planning Com., 1994; mem. Kohl Scholarship Selection Com., 1990, 93; mem. Blue Ribbon Task Force Dept. Pub. Instrn., 1993. Audubon editor Chat, 1975, Slue Membersheet, 1988—. Phone bank organizer Friends of Channel 10/36 Milw., 1987, chair Walworth County portion of Fund Dr., 1989; mem. People for Am. Way, 1986—; mem. 1st Congl. Dist. Acad. Selection Bd., 1988-95; leader Badger coun. Girl Scouts U.S., 1960-82; mem. Walworth County Dem. Party, 1972—, vice chair 1989-91; host for congl. aide, 1988-93; county organizer presdl. campaign, 1980; vol. coord. assembly campaign, 1992, 94, 96; Statutory Party pollworker of Lake Geneva, 1984—; mem. Friends of Lake Geneva Libr., 1986—, Friends of Twin Lake/Randall Pub. Libr., 1992—, Assn. Preservation of Va. Antiquities; participant Rediscover Jamestown Archaeology Field Sch., 1994, Colonial Williamsburg Tchr. Inst., 1995. Recipient Youth Leader award Am. Legion, 1976, award VA Bloomfield Twp., 1977, Nat. Girl Scout award for community svc., 1976; Herbert Kohl fellow, 1990. Mem. AAUW, NEA (Twin Lakes del. to rep. assemblies, congl. contact team 1986-93, legis. com. 1995-96), Wis. Edn. Assn. (regional pub. rels. com. 1990-92), So. Lakes United Educators (pres. 1979-82, treas. 1982-84, pub. rels. chair 1986—, editor Membersheet, 1987—), Twin Lakes Edn. Assn. (local negotiator), Nat. Assn. Learning Disabled, State and Nat. Coun. Social Studies (curriculum writing team 1991), So. Lakes Reading Coun., Crow Canyon Archaeology Ctr., Sierra Club (coord. NEA Dump Watt campaign 1981, environ. Bill Rights campaign 1995), Nat. Audubon Soc., Lakeland Audubon Soc., Archael. Inst. Am., Tchr. Place and Parent Resources, Concerned Parents and Edn., Alpha Delta Kappa. Democrat. Home: 307 Water St Lake Geneva WI 53147-1521 Office: Lakewood Sch 1218 Wilmot Ave Twin Lakes WI 53181-9419

WILLIAMS, JOCELYN JONES, reading educator; b. Greenville, N.C., Sept. 24, 1948; d. William Edward and Elinor Suejette (Albritton) Jones; m. Robert Alexander Simpkins Jr., Sept. 7, 1969 (div. May 1972); m. Oscar James Williams Jr., July 12, 1985 (div. Mar. 1989). BS, Bennett Coll., 1970; MEd, N.C. Cen. U., 1988; MS, N.C. Agrl. & Tech. State U., 1992. Kindergarten/1st grade tchr. Greenville City Schs., 1970-74; elem./reading tchr. Orange County Schs., Hillsborough, N.C., 1974—; mem. N.C. Reading Recovery Adv. Bd., 1994—, Reading Recovery Coun. N.Am., 1994—. Mem. NEA, ASCD, Internat. Reading Assn., Nat. Assn. Edn. Young Children, N.C. Assn. Educators, Phi Delta Kappa, Alpha Kappa Alpha, Progressive Sertoma Club. Democrat. Baptist. Home: 47 Celtic Dr Durham NC 27703-2894

WILLIAMS, JUDITH LYNN, graphic artist; b. Evanston, Ill., Oct. 12, 1942; d. Allan Orville and Margaret Edith (Judson) W. BA in Tchg. of Spanish, U. Ill., 1964. Cert. secondary sch. tchr., Ill. Tchr. of English and Spanish Wheeling (Ill.) H.S., 1964-65; vocat. counselor State Dept. Pub. Aid, Chgo., 1966-67; English tchr. Libertyville (Ill.) H.S., 1967-71; graphic artist, editor Crandall, Pierce & Co., Northbrook, Ill., 1973-76; graphic artist BenGraphics & Forms (formerly ScanGraphics, Inc.), Elk Grove Village, Ill., 1977—. Contbr. poems to books. Recipient Editor's Choice award for outstanding achievement in poetry Nat. Libr. Poetry, 1994, 96, Pres.' award for lifelong excellence Nat. Authors Registry, 1995. Mem. Sigma Delta Pi. Home: 33187 N Sears Blvd Wildwood IL 60030

WILLIAMS, JULIE BELLE, psychiatric social worker; b. Algona, Iowa, July 29, 1950; d. George Howard and Leta Maribelle (Durschmidt) W. BA, U. Iowa, 1972, MSW, 1973. Lic. psychologist, ind. clin. social worker, marriage and family therapist, Minn.; lic. social worker, Iowa. Social worker Psychopathic Hosp., Iowa City, 1971-72; OEO counselor YOUR, Webster City, Iowa, 1972; social worker Child Devel. Clinic, Iowa City, 1973; therapist Mid-Eastern Iowa Community Mental Health Ctr., Iowa City, 1973; psychiat. social worker Mental Health Ctr. No. Iowa, Mason City, 1974-79, chief psychiat. social worker, 1979-80; asst. dir. Community Counseling Ctr., White Bear Lake, Minn., 1980-85, dir., 1985—; lectr., cons. in field. NIMH grantee, 1972-73. Mem. NASW (Acad. Cert. Social Workers, Qualified Clin. Social Workers, diplomate), NOW, Am. Orthopsychiat. Assn., Am. Assn. Sex Educators, Counselors and Therapists, Minn. Women Psychologists, Minn. Lic. Psychologists, Phi Beta Kappa. Democrat. Office: 1280 N Birch Lake Blvd White Bear Lake MN 55110

WILLIAMS, JULIE FORD, mutual fund specialist; b. Long Beach, Calif., Aug. 7, 1948; d. Julious Hunter and Bessie May (Wood) Ford; m. Walter Edward Williams, Oct. 20, 1984; 1 child, Andrew Ford. BA in Econs., Occidental Coll., 1970. Legal sec. Kadison, Pfaelzer, Woodard, Quinn & Rossi, L.A., 1970-71, 74-77; legal sec. Fried, Frank, Harris, Shriver & Jacobson, N.Y.C., 1971-72, Pallot, Poppell, Goodman & Shapo, Miami, Fla., 1973-74; adminstrv. asst. Capital Research-Mgmt., Los Angeles, 1978-82; corp. officer Cash Mgmt. Trust Am., 1982—, Bond Fund Am., 1982—, Tax-Exempt Bond Fund Am., 1982—, AMCAP Fund, 1984—, Am. Funds Income Series, 1985—, Am. Funds Tax-Exempt Series II, 1986—, Capital World Bond Fund, 1987—, Am. High-Income Trust, 1987—, Intermediate Bond Fund Am., 1987—, Tax-Exempt Money Fund Am., 1989—, U.S. Treasury Money Fund Am., 1991—, Fundamental Investors, 1992—, Ltd. Term Tax-Exempt Bond Fund Am., 1993—, Am. High-Income Mcpl. Bond Fund, 1994—; v.p. fund bus. mgmt. group Capital Rsch. Mgmt., 1986—. Pres.-elect Alumni Bd. Govs. Occidental Coll., 1994—. Democrat. Episcopalian. Office: Capital Rsch and Mgmt Co 333 S Hope St Los Angeles CA 90071-1406

WILLIAMS, KAREN HASTIE, lawyer, think tank executive; b. Washington, Sept. 30, 1944; d. William Henry and Beryl (Lockhart) Hastie; m. Wesley S. Williams, Jr.; children: Amanda Pedersen, Wesley Hastie, Bailey Lockhart. Cert., U. Neuchatel, Switzerland, 1965; BA, Bates Coll., 1966; MA, Tufts U., 1967; JD, Cath. U. Am., 1973. Bar: D.C. 1973. Staff asst. internat. gov. relations dept. Mobil Oil Corp., N.Y.C., 1967-69; staff asst. com. Dist. Columbia U.S. Senate, 1970, chief counsel com. on the budget, 1977-80; law clk. to judge Spottswood Robinson III U.S. Ct. Appeals (D.C. Cir.), Washington, 1973-74; law clk. to assoc. justice Thurgood Marshall U.S. Supreme Ct., Washington, 1974-75; assoc. Fried, Frank, Harris, Shriver & Kampelman, Washington, 1975-77, 1975-77; adminstr. Office Mgmt. and Budget, Washington, 1980-81; of counsel Crowell & Moring, Washington, 1982, ptnr., 1982—; Bd. dirs. Crestar Fin. Services Corp., Fannie Mae, Washington Gas Light Co., Continental Airlines, SunAmerica, Inc. Chair, trustee Greater Washington Research Ctr., chair. Mem. ABA (pub. contract law sect., past chair), Nat. Bar Assn., Washington Bar Assn., Nat. Contract Mgmt. Assn., NAACP (bd. dirs. legal defense fund). Office: Crowell & Moring Ste 1200W 1001 Pennsylvania Ave NW Washington DC 20004-2595

WILLIAMS, KAREN JOHNSON, federal judge; b. Orangeburg, S.C., Aug. 4, 1951; d. James G. Johnson and Marcia (Reynolds) Johnson Dantzler; m. Charles H. Williams, Dec. 27, 1968; children: Marian, Ashley, Charlie, David. BA, Columbia Coll., 1972; postgrad., U. S.C., 1973, JD cum laude, 1980. Bar: S.C. 1980, U.S. Dist. Ct. S.C. 1980, U.S. Ct. Appeals (4th cir.) 1981. Tchr. Irmo (S.C.) Mid. Sch., 1972-74, O-W High Sch., Orangeburg, 1974-76; assoc. Charles H. Williams P.A., Orangeburg, 1980-92; circuit judge U.S. Ct. Appeals (4th cir.), 1992—; mem. exec. bd. grievance commn. S.C. Supreme Ct., Columbia, 1983-92. Mem. child devel. bd. First Bapt. Ch.,

Orangeburg; bd. dirs. Orangeburg County Mental Retardation Bd., 1986-94, Orangeburg-Calhoun Hosp. Found.; bd. visitors Columbia Coll., 1988-92; dir. Reg. Med. Ctr. Hosp. Found., 1988-92; mem. adv. bd. Orangeburg-Calhoun Tech. Coll., 1987-92. Mem. ABA, Am. Judicature Soc., Fed. Judges Assn., S.C. Bar Assn., Orangeburg County Bar Assn. (co-chair Law Day 1981), S.C. Trial Lawyers Assn., Bus. and profl. Women Assn., Rotary, Order of Wig and Robe, Order of Coif. Home: 2503 Five Chop Rd Orangeburg SC 29115 Office: 1021 Middleton St Orangeburg SC 29115

WILLIAMS, KATHERINE BROWN, human services manager; b. Waco, Tex., Dec. 30, 1944; d. Robert Raymond and Katherine Warwick (Rust) Brown; m. Hollis R. Williams, Feb. 3, 1968; children: Daniell Brodie, Robert Hollis. BA, U. Ark., 1967; MPA, Seattle U., 1993. Supr. Neighborhood Study Ctr., Jacksonville, Little Rock, Ark., 1969-70; libr. Yazoo City (Miss.) Pub. Libr., 1972-73; receptionist Tillery and Lee Vets., Jackson, Miss., 1979-80; vol. dir. Brown Bag Program, Lake Charles, La., 1982-85, Mon. Lunch Program, Everett, Wash., 1986; coord. Partnerships Forum Human Svcs. Coun., Everett, 1988; from vol. youth program to campaign market mgr. United Way of Snohomish County, Everett, 1989-92; devel. officer Everett Gen. Hosp. and Med. Ctr., 1993; dir. endowment Everett Performing Arts Ctr., 1994-95; commr. Everett Youth Commn., 1994—; chair Ecology br. Everett Woman's Book Club, 1995-96; bd. dirs. Wash. chpt. Nat. Neurofibromatosis Found. Dep. to Grand Conv. of Episcopal Ch., 1985. Democrat. Episcopalian. Home: 3420 Kromer Ave Everett WA 98201

WILLIAMS, KATHRYN BLAKE, librarian; b. Lancaster, Pa., Mar. 20, 1923; d. Harry Leslie and Mary Kauffman (Strine) Blake; m. William George Williams Sr., June 1, 1945; children: Leslie Williams Aronson, William George Jr. BS in Edn., U. Pa., 1944; elem. cert., Shippensburg U., 1969, MLS, 1973. Home economist Pa. State Extension Svc., Carlisle, 1944-46; kindergarten tchr. Blind Assn. Harrisburg, Pa., 1955; asst. elem. tchr. Sweeney Day Sch., Harrisburg, 1955-57; week-day kindergarten tchr. Presbyn. Ch., Camp Hill, Pa., 1961-63; 1st grade tchr. West Shore Sch. System, Lemoyne, Pa., 1965-71; dir. Ralpho Twp. Pub. Libr., Elysburg, Pa., 1973-75; libr. Bloomsburg (Pa.) Univ. of Pa., 1979-80, Bloomsburg Hosp., 1980-81; mem. adv. coun. North Cen. Region Job Tng. of Pa., Ridgeway, 1991—; organizing dir. DuBois office, vista vol. Mid-State Literacy Coun., State College, Pa., 1987-88. Leader, day camp dir. Girl Scouts U.S., Harrisburg, 1957; field svc. coord. Am. Field Svc., Camp Hill, 1963-65; weekly radio panelist United Coun. of Chs., Harrisburg, 1963-65; vol. libr. DuBois (Pa.) Regional Med. Ctr., 1990—; story teller Bloomsburg Pub. Libr., 1974-83; commr. to gen. assembly Presbyn. Ch., 1983, elder, 1973—, deacon, 1994—, sec. of deacons, 1994—. Mem. AAUW (v.p. 1987-89), Pa. State Edn. Assn. (life), Friends of DuBois Pub. Libr. (pres. 1984-86), Presbyn. Women (resource coord. 1975-85, mission coord. 1992—). Home: 377 Treasure Lake Du Bois PA 15801-9008

WILLIAMS, KATHRYN SANDERS, elementary education administrator; b. Lexington, Ky., May 18, 1961; d. Gerald Louis and Donna Lee (Freeman) Sanders; m. R. Duane Williams, Jr., May 21, 1983; children: Bryan, Brad. BS in Elem. Edn., U. Louisville, 1983, M in Elem. Curriculum, 1990, rank I in ednl. adminstrn., 1995. Tchr. elem. sch. Indpls. Pub. Schs., 1984-85; tchr. mid. sch. Jefferson County Pub. Schs., Louisville, 1985-96; asst. prin. Mt. Washington (Ky.) Elem. Sch., 1996—. Vol. Talent Ctr. grantee, Louisville, 1990. Mem. ASCD, NEA, Ky. Assn. for Supervision and Curriculum Devel., Ky. Assn. Sch. Adminstrs., Ky. Edn. Assn., Nat. Assn. for Yr.-Round Edn. Democrat. Roman Catholic. Home: 4319 Saratoga Hill Rd Jeffersontown KY 40299-8306 Office: Mt Washington Elem Sch 9234 Hwy 44 E Mount Washington KY 40047

WILLIAMS, KEIRA LEE, city planning consultant; b. Stanford, Calif., Aug. 29, 1964; d. Russell David Jr. and Medill (Hanna) W. BA, U. Wash., 1986; MBA, U. Hawaii-Manoa, Honolulu, 1992. Intern Nat. Women's Health Network, Washington, 1987; staff asst. U.S. Senator Brock Adams, Washington, 1988-90; grad. asst. U. Hawaii, Honolulu, 1990-92; pvt. practice cons. in editing and market rsch. Honolulu and Palo Alto, 1992-93; exec. dir. Fort Bragg (Calif.) Main St., 1994-95; prin. City Works, San Francisco, 1995—. Editor Spleen, 1993-94. Active Caltrain Citizens Adv. Bd., San Mateo, Calif., 1993. Mem. Local Govt. Commn., Greenbelt Alliance, Hillary Rodham Clinton Fan Club (treas. San Francisco chpt. 1996). Office: City Works PO Box 2544 San Francisco CA 94126

WILLIAMS, KELLI D., elementary education educator; b. Tyler, Tex., Sept. 14, 1963; d. Otho Dale and Margie LaVerne (Henry) W. BA, Concordia Luth. U., 1992. Cert. elem., English and reading tchr., Tex. Libr. Round Rock (Tex.) Pub. Libr., 1984-89; tchr. C.D. Fulkes Mid. Sch., Round Rock, 1993—; student coun. exec. C.D. Fulkes Mid. Sch., 1993—; advisor Authentic Assessment Com., Round Rock, 1993—. Creator (class) P.A.T.H., 1993. Advisor Friends of Round Rock Libr., 1993-94. Recipient Acad. grant Concordia Luth. U., 1992. Mem. Nat. Coun. Tchrs. of English, Assn. Tex. Profl. Educators, Internat. Reading Assn., Sam Bass Theatre Assn.

WILLIAMS, LOIS, women's center administrator; b. Bessermer, Ala., Mar. 8, 1941; d. Jack and Louise (Clanton) W.; children: Keith, Raymond Elliott, Eddie, Patrice Inez. B in Bus. Adminstrn., Baker Coll., 1990. With Every Woman's Pl., Muskegon, Mich., 1981—, crisis ctr. mgr., 1994-96, crisis ctr. dir., 1996—. V.p. Mich. Coalition Against Domestic Violence, 1990-93, mem. coordinating com., 1994—; pres. Muskegon Fair Housing, 1992—; regional co-chair Women Matter, Muskegon, 1996; sec. Muskegon Br. NAACP, 1992—; food dir. Muskegon Summer Celebration, 1993—; youth advisor Urban League, Muskegon, 1992-94. Baptist. Office: Every Woman's Pl 1221 Laketon Ave Muskegon MI 49441

WILLIAMS, LOIS BAKER, educator secondary school and junior college; b. Ann Arbor, Mich., Feb. 7, 1940; d. James W. and Dixie (Johnson) Baker; m. James E. Williams, Jr., Dec. 23, 1958; children: James E. III, Lori Ann. AA, Freed-Hardeman Coll., 1959; BA, Harding U., 1961; MA, U. N. Ala., 1991. Cert. tchr. secondary sch. social studies, English. Tchr. Jackson (Mo.) Jr. H.S., 1961-62, Vogel Jr. H.S., Garden City, Mich., 1962-64, East Park Jr. H.S., Danville, Ill., 1971-74, Christian Acad. of Oak Cliff, Dallas, Tex., 1974-78, Hardin County H.S., Savannah, Tenn., 1978—; sponsor Jr. H.S. Cheerleaders Dallas, 1972-74, Student Coun., Dallas, 1974-78, History Club, Hardin County H.S., Savannah, Tenn., 1978-85; test adminstr. ACT at Hardin County H.S., 1985; mem. adj. faculty Jackson State C.C., 1994-95. Mem. Hardin County Republican Women., Savannah, 1986—. Mem. NEA, Tenn. Edn. Assn. (del. to RA 1996), Hardin County Edn. Assn., Nat. Coun. Social Studies, Delta Kappa Gamma (v.p. 1996). Republican. Mem. Ch. of Christ. Home: 105 Edwards Ct White House TN 37188 Office: Hardin County HS 615 Picwick Rd Savannah TN 38372

WILLIAMS, LORETTA JANICE, sociologist; b. Boston, Mass., Nov. 1, 1937; d. Leon Gerryfeld and Ira Janice (Graves) Lomax; children: Theos, Ken, Kyle McKinney. MA, SUNY, 1971, PhD, 1977. Assoc. prof. U. Mo., Columbia, 1974-81; dir. dept. social justice Unitarian Universalist Assn., Boston, 1980-89; faculty Women's Theol. Ctr., Boston, 1990-91; coord. Ch. Women United, N.Y.C., 1992-95; project dir. Chelsea/Dudley Partnership, Boston, 1995—; vis. assoc. prof. Brandeis U., Waltham, Mass., 1991-92; dir. Williams & Assocs., Boston, 1989—; cons. in field, 1989—. Author: Black Freemasonry & Middle Class Reality, 1977; contbr. articles to profl. jours. Bd. dirs. Racial Justice Working Group, N.Y.C., 1982—, Polit. Rsch. Assocs., Cambridge, Mass., 1992—, others. Office: BUSSW 264 Bay State Rd Boston MA 02215

WILLIAMS, LORI ELIZABETH, newspaper editor; b. Hammond, La., Aug. 18, 1957; d. Clinton Antoine and Eloise Cecilia (Cuevas) Guwang; m. John Barry Williams, Sept. 1, 1984; children: Walter Trace, August Burl. BJ, La. State U., 1979. Newspaper reporter Beaumont (Tex.) Enterprise, 1979-83, asst. city editor, 1983-84; gen. mgr. Miss. Bus. Newspaper, Jackson, 1985-88; editor Clear Lake Citizen, Houston, 1988—. Mem. Tex. Press Assn. (1st place Cmty. Svc. award 1992, editorial awards), Gulf Coast Newspaper Assn., Bay Area Profl. Communicators (bd. dirs., v.p. 1992). Home: 2021 Cortlandt St Houston TX 77008-2615 Office: Clear Lake Citizen 17511 El Camino Real Houston TX 77058-3073

WILLIAMS, LORRAINE ADELE, banking executive; b. Phila., Dec. 11, 1953; d. John S. Jr. and Ann B. (Riegler) Cicero; m. Stephen D. Williams, Nov. 9, 1974; children: Michele M., Stephen M. AS, Camden County Coll., Blackwood, N.J., 1989; BBA cum laude, Temple U., 1993. Teller Fidelity Mutual Savs. & Loan, Westmont, N.J., 1971-74, br. mgr., 1974-89; asst. v.p., br. mgr. Fidelity Mutual Savs. & Loan, Westmont, 1989-90, v.p., compliance officer, 1990-92; asst. v.p. ops. 1st Home Savs. Bank, Pennsville, N.J., 1992-93, asst. v.p., compliance and security officer, 1994—; mem. adv. bd. Vocat./Edn. Adv. Com., Pennsauken, N.J., 1983-85. Mem. Tri-State Assn. Criminal Investigators, South Jersey Fraud Prevention Network, Phi Theta Kappa. Office: 1st Home Savs Bank FSB PO Box 189 125 S Broadway Pennsville NJ 08070

WILLIAMS, LOUISE TAYLOR, assistant principal; b. Shreveport, La., Mar. 11, 1921; d. Bailey Taylor and Geneva (Arkansas) Jones; m. James Monroe Murphy, July 13, 1973 (dec. Sept. 1980); m. Andrew Jackson Williams, Aug. 6, 1987. BS, Tex. So. U., 1944; MS in Edn., Chgo. State U., 1972. Clin. lab. technician Houston Negro Hosp., 1943-44; med. rsch. asst. Michael Reese Hosp., Chgo., 1944-52; substitute tchr. Chgo. Pub. Sch., 1952-54; tchr. Chgo. Pub. Sch./Coleman Sch., 1954-63; tchr. 4th-6th grades Chgo. Pub. Sch./Neil Elem. Sch., 1954-63, acting asst. prin., 1971-73, asst. prin., 1973-85, ret., 1985; pres. Louise T. Williams Found., 1987—; tchr. 5th grade Pirie Elem. Sch., Chgo., summer 1962, Hookway, Chgo., summer 1966; team leader in-svc. program Sch. Community Reps. 5, summer 1967. Mem. adv. bd. Chatham-Avalon Mental Health Clinic, 1983—, St. Joachim Elem. Sch., 1987-92; bd. dirs. Chgo. State U., 1984-88, Ora Higgins Found., 1992-93, exec. bd., 1993—. Recipient Outstanding Svc. award Chgo. State U., 1988. Mem. AAUW (mem. at large 1994—), Women in the Arts, Coun. for Exceptional Children, West Chesterfield Community Block Club (social sec. Chgo. chpt. 1980—), Phi Delta Kappa. Roman Catholic.

WILLIAMS, LOVIE JEAN, elementary education educator; b. Kinston, N.C., Aug. 28; d. Robert Lee and Effie Mae (Hardy) W. BS, Mill. Coll. Edn., N.Y.C., 1973; MA, Columbia U., 1979, postgrad. Cert. tchr., N.Y. Instr. math. Coll. of New Rochelle, Bronx, N.Y.; tchr., asst. prin., prin. Christ Crusader Acad., N.Y.C.; elem. tchr. math. and sci. N.Y.C. Bd. Edn., Bklyn. Recipient Excellence in Teaching award, Rookie Tchr. award N.Y.C. Bd. Edn. Mem. ASCD, Elem. Sch. Sci. Assn., Math. Edn. through Mid. Grades, Delta Sigma Theta. Office: John Peter Zenger Elem Sch 502 Morris Ave Bronx NY 10451-5549

WILLIAMS, LULA AGNES, retired writer, retired educator; b. Bentonville, Ark., May 11, 1904; d. Thomas Andrew and Nellie Louella (Mason) Nichols; m. Esmond Leonidas Williams, June 12, 1927 (dec. Jan. 1961). BA, U. Ark., 1956. Cert. secondary tchr., cert. to teach English and social studies. Stenographer Benton County Hardware Co., Bentonville, Ark., 1922-25; tchr. country sch. Cross Lanes, Bentonville, 1925-26; stenographer-sec. Skelly Oil Co., El Dorado, Kans., 1926-27; asst. adminstr. Benton County Home, Bentonville, 1935-40; acting postmaster U.S. Post Office, Bentonville, 1944-45; tchr. Bentonville Schs., 1956-70; acting postmaster U.S. Post Office, Bentonville, 1961-62; writer Bentonville, 1985-88. Author, pub.: Hills Are for Climbing, 1988. Pres. Bates Meml. Hosp. Aux., 1972, Qui Vive, Gen. Fedn. Women's Clubs, Bentonville, 1973, Benton County Ret. Tchrs. Assn., 1976-77; worthy matron Order of Eastern Star, Bentonville, 1936. Named Woman of Yr., Bus. and Profl. Women's Club, Bentonville, 1981-82; recipient Svc. award AAUW, Bentonville, 1981, gift named in her honor AAUW 1987. Mem. Nat. Retired Tchrs. Assn. (life), Ark. Retired Tchrs. Assn. (life), U. Ark. Alumni Assn. (life). Democrat. Mem. Christian Ch. (Disciples of Christ). Home: 425 SE A St Bentonville AR 72712-5933

WILLIAMS, MADONNA JO, accountant; b. Traverse City, Mich., Mar. 24, 1945; d. Harold Augustus and Josephine Annabelle (Dreves) Barratt; m. Jerry J. Williams, Dec. 28, 1963; children: Jerry J. Jr., Scott T. AAS with honors, Northwestern Mich. Coll., 1983; BS in Acctg. with highest distinction, Ferris State U., 1984. CPA, Mich. Mem. taxpayer svc. staff IRS, Traverse City, 1971-73, staff acct. Seidman & Seidman, Traverse City, 1973-75; mem. staff, mgr. Fuller, Somero & Black, CPAs, Traverse City, 1975-85; ptnr. Black & Williams, CPAs, Traverse City, 1985—. Mem. AICPA, Am. Assn. CPAs (Elijah Watt Sells award 1984), Mich. Assn. CPAs (William A. Paton award 1984), Zonta Club Traverse City. Home: 8871 N Long Lake Rd Traverse City MI 49684-9622 Office: Black & Williams CPAs 3050 Sunset Ln Traverse City MI 49684-4672

WILLIAMS, MARGARET, federal official. Asst. to Pres., chief of staff to First Lady The White House, Washington, 1993—. Office: Office of the First Lady The White House 1600 Pennsylvania Ave NW Washington DC 20500

WILLIAMS, MARGARET LU WERTHA HIETT, nurse; b. Midland, Tex., Aug. 30, 1938; d. Cotter Craven and Mollie Jo (Tarter) Hiett; m. James Troy Lary, Nov. 16, 1960 (div. Jan. 1963); 1 child, James Cotter; m. Tuck Williams, Aug. 11, 1985. BS, Tex. Woman's U., 1960; MA, Tchrs. Coll., N.Y.C., 1964, EdM, 1974, doctoral studies, 1981; postgrad., U. Tex., 1991-92, U. Wis.; cert. completion, U. Wis., Scotland. Cert. clin. nurse specialist, advanced practice nurse; cert. psychiat./mental health nurse, nursing contuining edn. and staff devel. Nurse Midland Meml. Hosp., 1960-63; instr. Odessa (Tex.) Coll., 1963-67; dir. ADNP Laredo (Tex.) Jr. Coll., 1967-70; asst. prof. Pan Am. U., Edinburgh, Tex., 1970-72; rsch. asst. Tchrs. Coll., 1973-74; nursing practitioner St. Luke's Hosp., N.Y.C., 1975-79; sgt. Burns Security, Midland, 1979-81; with Area Builders, Odessa, 1981-83; field supr. We Care Home Health Agy., Midland, 1983-87; clin. educator, supr. Glenwood, A Psychiat. Hosp., Midland, 1987-92; dir. nursing Charter Healthcare Systems, Corpus Christi, Tex., 1992-93; RN III Brown Sch., San Marcos, Tex., 1993—; owner MTW Nursing Consultation, Lockhart, Tex., 1996—, Margaret Hiett Williams RN, CNS, Lockhart, Tex., 1996—; co-owner, operator MTW Med. Legal Cons.; adj. prof. Pace U., 1974-75, S.W. Tex. State U., 1995. Mem. Gov. Richards' Exec. Leadership Coun., 1991-95, re-election steering com., 1994. Recipient Isabelle Hampton-Robb award Nat. League for Nursing, 1976, Achievement award Community Leaders of Am., 1989, Ladies 1st of Midland, 1974. Mem. NAFE, ANA, Tex. Nurses Assn. (pres. dist. 21 1962-65, dist. 32 1970-72), Am. Psychiat. Nurses Assn., Parkland Meml. Hosp. Nurses Alumnae Assn., Tex. Women's U. Alumnae Assn., Midland H.S. Alumni, Bus. and Profl. Women's Club, Mensa, Lockhart Breakfast Lions Club. Democrat. Office: PO Box 324 Lockhart TX 78644

WILLIAMS, MARIAN LEAH, mathematics educator; b. Huntsville, Mo., Feb. 18, 1944; d. Leland A. and Vivian Berniece (Derigne) W. AA, Moberly Jr. Coll., 1964; BS in Edn., N.E. Mo. State U., 1966, MA, 1970. Cert. tchr., Mo. Math. tchr. North Shelby High Sch., Shelbyville, Mo., 1966-70; asst. prof. math. Hannibal-LaGrange (Mo.) Coll., 1970—. Active Southside Bapt. Ch., pianist, 1987—. Mem. Nat. Coun. Tchrs. Math., Mo. Coun. Tchrs. Math. Office: Hannibal-LaGrange Coll 2800 Palmyra Rd Hannibal MO 63401-1940

WILLIAMS, MARIE CLONEY, rehabilitation nurse administrator, business owner; b. Abilene, Tex., Oct. 20, 1944; d. Morton Earl and Emily Marie (Stepanek) Phillips; m. Richard Morgan Cloney, Aug. 25, 1965 (div. Nov., 1989); children: Kellen Frances, Shannon Cooper.; m. Clifford John Williams, Jr., May 17, 1992. BSN, U. N.C., 1966, MPH, 1967. RN, Pa.; cert. nurse adminstr. Rsch. assoc. U. N.C. Sch. of Pub. Health, Chapel Hill, N.C., 1967-68; head nurse Comty. Dr. Nursing Ctr., Manhasset, N.Y., 1968; staff nurse Hackettstown (N.J.), 1973-74; dir. nursing Welkind Neurol. Hosp., Chester, N.J., 1974-78; dir. nursing svcs. Healthbank Rehab. Ctr., Columbia, Pa., 1978-81; adminstr. for nursing svcs. Pa. State U.-Elizabethtown (Pa.) Rehab., 1981-83; assoc. adminstr. nursing svcs. Rehab. Hosp. York, Pa., 1983-85; adminstr., CEO Rehab. Hosp. York, 1985-88; v.p. ops. Rehab. Systems Co., Camp Hill, Pa., 1988-93; owner, ptnr. Interactive Health Co., Mechanicsburg, Pa., 1993—; mem. profl. adv. com. VNA of York, Pa., 1985-88; asst. sec., bd. dirs. York County Health Corp., York, 1986-88; bd. dirs. Mt. View Regional Rehab. Hosp., Morgantown, W. Va., 1990-92; owner, mgr., cons. Marie Williams Assocs., Mechanicsburg, Pa., 1993—. Contbr. articles to profl. jours. Com. mem. Country and Town Bapt. Ch., Mechanicsburg, Pa., 1989—. Mem. Assn. Rehab. Nurses, Ctrl. Pa. Tech. Coun., Am. Electronics Assn., Nat. Disting. Svc. Registry: Med. Rehab., Sigma Theta Tau, Delta Omicron. Republican. Home: 26 Cumberland Estates Dr Mechanicsburg PA 17055-1719 Office: Interactive Health Co 2415-A Old Gettysburg Rd Camp Hill PA 17011

WILLIAMS, MARSHA KAY, data processing executive; b. Norman, Okla., Oct. 26, 1963; d. Charles Michael and Marilyn Louise (Bauman) Williams; m. Dale Lee Carabetta, Dec. 13, 1981. BS in Computer Mgmt. & Sci., Metro. State Coll., Denver, 1996. Data processing supr. Rose Mfg. Co., Englewood, Colo., 1981-84, Mile High Equip. Co., Denver, 1984-88; mgr. info. tech. Ohmeda Monitoring Sys., Louisville, Colo., 1988—. Mem. info. tech. adv. bd. Warren Tech. Sch., 1994—. Mem. Bus. and Profl. Women's Assn. (Young Careerist 1991), Data Processing Mgmt. Assn. Home: 4700 Yates Ct Broomfield CO 80020 Office: Ohmeda Monitoring Systems 1315 W Century Dr Louisville CO 80027-9560

WILLIAMS, MARTHA ETHELYN, information science educator; b. Chgo., Sept. 21, 1934; d. Harold Milton and Alice Rosemond (Fox) W. B.A., Barat Coll., 1955; M.A., Loyola U., 1957. With IIT Rsch.Inst., Chgo., 1957-72, mgr. info. scis., 1962-72, mgr. computer search ctr., 1968-72; adj. assoc. prof. sci. info. Ill. Inst. Tech., Chgo., 1965-73, lectr. chemistry dept., 1968-70, rsch. prof. info. sci., coordinated sci. lab. Coll. engring.; also dir. info. retrieval research lab. U. Ill., Urbana, 1972—, prof. info. sci. grad. sch. of libr. info. sci., 1974—, affiliate, computer sci. dept., 1979—; chmn. large data base conf. Nat. Acad. Sci./NRC, 1974, mem. ad hoc panel on info. storage and retrieval, 1977, numerical data adv. bd., 1979-82, computer sci. and tech. bd., nat. rsch. network rev. com., 1987-88, chmn. utility sub-com., 1987-88; mem. task force on sci. info. activities NSF, 1977; U.S. rep. review com. for project on broad system of ordering, UNESCO, Hague, Netherlands, 1974; vice chmn. Gordon Rshc. Conf. on Sci. Info. Problems in Rsch., 1978, chmn., 1980; mem. panel on intellectual property rights in age of electronics and info. U.S. Congress, Office of Tech. Assessment; program chmn. Nat. Online Meeting, 1980—; cons. to numerous cos., govt. agys. and rsch. founds.; invited lectr. Commn. European Communities, Industrial R&D adv. com., Brussels, 1992. Editor in chief Computer-Readable Databases Directory and Data Sourcebook, 1976-89, founding editor, 1989-92; editor Ann. Rev. Info. Sci. and Tech., 1976—, Online Rev., 1979-92, Online and CDROM Rev., 1993—, procs. nat. online meeting, 1981—; contbg. editor column on databases to Bull. Am. Soc. Info. Sci., 1974-78; mem. editorial adv. bd. Database, 1978-88; mem. editorial bd. Info. Processing and Mgmt., 1982-89, The Reference Libr.; contbr. more than 200 articles to profl. jours. Trustee Engirng. Info., Inc., 1974-87, bd. dirs., 1976-91, chmn. bd. dirs., 1982-91, v.p., 1978-79, pres., 1980-81; regent Nat. Libr. Medicine, 1978-82, chmn. bd. regents, 1981; mem. task force on sci. info. activities NSF, 1977-78; mem. nat. adv. com. ACCESS ERIC, 1989-91. Recipient best paper of year award H. W. Wilson Co., 1975; NSF travel grantee Luxembourg, 1972; NSF travel grantee Honolulu, 1973; NSF travel grantee Tokyo, 1973; NSF travel grantee Mexico City, 1975; NSF travel grantee Scotland, 1976. Fellow AAAS (computers, info. and comm. mem.-at-large 1978-81, nominating com. 1983, 85), Inst. Info. Sci. (hon.); mem. NAS (joint com. with NRC on chem. info. 1971-73), Am. Chem. Soc., Am. Soc. Info. Sci. (councilor 1971-72, 87-89, chmn. networks com. 1973-74, spl. interest group of SDI 1974-75, pres.-elect 1986-87, pres. 1987-88, past pres., mem. planning com. 1988-89, publs. com. 1974—, chmn. 1989, mem. nominations com. 1989, chmn. budget and fin. com. 1987-89, award of merit 1984, Pioneer Info. Sci. award 1987, Watson Davis award 1995), Assn. for Computing Machinery (pub. bd. 1972-76), Assn. Sci. Info. Dissemination Ctrs. (v.p. 1971-73, pres. 1975-77), Internat. Fedn. for Documentation (U.S. nat. com.). Home: 2134 Sandra Ln Monticello IL 61856-9801 Office: U Ill 1308 W Main St Urbana IL 61801-2307

WILLIAMS, MARY ALICE BALDWIN, retired home economist, volunteer consultant; b. St. Louis, Mar. 24, 1928; d. Ulysses Grant and Irene (Jenkins) Gray; m. Earl Randolph Baldwin, June 28, 1952 (div. 1973); 1 child, Arlene Denise; m. Robert Williams Jr., Dec. 21, 1985. BS, Lincoln U., 1952; MA, Webster U., 1971; postgrad., Harris Stowe Tchrs. Coll., 1976-78, Cen. Mo. State U., 1979-80, U. Mo., 1981-82. Cert. home economist, Mo. Tchr. home econs. Cen. High Sch., Hayti, Mo., 1952-53, Cleve. Pub. Schs., 1953-56; tchr. elem. sch. St. Louis Pub. Schs., 1958-67, tchr. home econs., 1968-83, curriculum supr. home econs., 1984-93, cons. home econs. and character edn., 1993—; presenter workshops. Author curriculum materials in home econs. and character edn. Fund raising com. Annie Malone Children's Home, St. Louis, 1987-90; 75th anniversary com. YYWCA Phylliss Wheatley, St. Louis, 1988. Mem. Nat. Assn. Univ. Women (del. 1992), Am. Home Econs. Assn. (ethics com. 1990-92, population com. 1990-91), Mo. Home Econs. Assn. (tchr. rep. 1988-90), Am. Vocat. Assn., Mo. Vocat. Assn. (legis. com.), St. Louis Home Econs. Tchrs. Assn. (founder, adviser), Lincoln Univ. Alumni Assn. (chair founders day), Delta Sigma Theta. Home: 4910 Maffitt Pl Saint Louis MO 63113-1727

WILLIAMS, MARY ELEANOR NICOLE, writer; b. Atlanta, May 14, 1938; d. Edward King Merrell and Bernice I. (Pitts) Smith; m. Charlie Lloyd Williams, July 25, 1993; children: Mary Palmer, Susan Gober, Traci Cox. Student, Fla. Jr. Coll., 1974. Lic. real estate broker, Fla. Editor, writer, former owner Southwestern Advt. and Pub., Carrollton, Ga., 1991-94; freelance writer children's stories, 1992—. Author, editor: West Georgia Area Guide, 1991-93. Mem. Carroll County C. of C. Home: 103 Ferndale Rd Carrollton GA 30117-4312

WILLIAMS, MAUREEN ANNE, nursing educator; b. Jamaica, N.Y., May 7, 1963; m. Patrick Dewey Williams, June 12, 1983. BSN, Andrews U., 1986; MEd, U. Ga., 1992. RNC. Staff nurse urology Pawating Hosp., Niles, Mich., 1986, Bradley Meml. Hosp., Cleveland, Tenn., 1986-87; staff nurse/nurse mgr. St. Mary's Home Health Care Svcs., Athens, Ga., 1987-92; case mgr./clin. educator VNA of No. Va., Arlington, 1992—; adj. faculty No. Va. C.C., Alexandria and Woodbridge, 1992—, curriculum cons., 1994—. Youth leader/co-leader Silver Spring (Md.) Seventh-Day Adventist Ch., 1993—. Recipient Svc./Achievement/Leadership award Andrews U. Alumni, Berrien Springs, Mich., 1986; named to Outstanding Young Women of Am., 1987. Mem. Va. Nurses Assn., Home Health Nurses Assn., Nat. Nursing Staff Devel. Orgn., Sigma Theta Tau, Kappa Delta Pi. Home: 1916 Arcola Ave Silver Spring MD 20902 Office: VNA of No Va 2775 S Quincy St #200 Arlington VA 22206

WILLIAMS, NANCY LOUISE, health care facilities evaluator; b. Fremont, Ohio, Sept. 6, 1947; d. Dale Ronald and Helen Myrtle (Peterson) Shedenhelm; m. Eddie Lewis Williams, Dec. 10, 1971; 1 child, Nicole Lynn. Diploma, Clara Maass Meml. Hosp., 1968. RN, N.J. Staff nurse Clara Maass Meml. Hosp., Belleville, N.J., 1968, 69-72; acting head nurse Johns Hopkins Hosp., Balt., 1968-69; charge nurse East Orange (N.J.) Gen. Hosp., 1972-73; asst. head nurse Meml. Gen. Hosp., Union, N.J., 1973-76; staff nurse Hosp. Ctr. Orange (N.J.), 1976-82, Meml. Hosp. Burlington County, Mt. Holly, N.J., 1982-85; health care facilities evaluator N.J. Dept. Health, Trenton, N.J., 1985—. Democrat. Methodist. Home: 36 Eden Rock Ln Willingboro NJ 08046-2211 Office: NJ Dept Health 300 Whitehead Rd Trenton NJ 08625-0367

WILLIAMS, PAMELA STONE, technical writer; b. Atlanta, Dec. 20, 1963; d. Jonathan Stone Williams and Jane Jones (Knowlton) Formato. BA, Agnes Scott Coll., 1985. Sales clk. Wizard's Workshop, Boston, 1984-85; mgr. Applause! Applause!, Boston, 1985-86; shipping, receiving clk. Globe Corner Bookstore, Boston, 1986-88; adminstrv. asst. Mass. Coll. Pharmacy, Boston, 1988-89; tech. writer U. Mass., Lowell, 1989-91; freelance tech. writer, editor Lowell, 1991-93; tech. writer Cadec Systems, Inc., Londonderry, N.H., 1993—. Mem. Soc. Tech. Comm., Covenant of Goddess.

WILLIAMS, PATRICIA MARIE, middle school educator, art educator; b. Oak Park, Ill., Jan. 24, 1957; d. Norbert and Carol Estelle (Reum) Brown; m. Howard Glenn Hansen, June 3, 1989. BA in Elem. Edn., Coll. Saint Francis, Joliet, Ill., 1979. Group home counselor St. Joseph's Indian Sch., Chamberlain, S.D., 1980-82; art tchr., 1982-85; 1st grade tchr. Resurrection Elem. Sch., Chgo., 1985-87; asst. sr. recreation supr. Park Dist. of Oak Park, Oak Park, Ill., 1987-90; 6th grade tchr. J.C. Orozco Cmty. Acad., Chgo., 1990-91; 2nd grade tchr. George Leland Sch., Chgo., 1991-94; art and libr. tchr., 1994-96; math tchr. Emerson Mid. Sch., Oak Park, Ill., 1996—; arts and crafts instr. Playground and Recreation Commn., 1985-87, Park Dist. of Oak Park, 1982-87, River Forest (Ill.) Cmty. Ctr., 1986-87; math. tutor, proctor Triton Coll., River Grove, Ill., 1985-87; pottery instr. Park Dist. of Oak Park, 1991-96, Art Works, Oak Park, 1991-94. Vol. Mus. Sci. and Industry, Chgo., 1991-95, Six County Sr. Olympics, 1994-95, Chgo. Theater, 1993; presenter Young Artists Workshop, Oak Park Sch. Sys., 1994-96. Small grantee, 1991-95, Impact II Tchr. Mentor, 1993, Chgo. Found. for Edn. Mem. NSTA, Nat. Art Edn. Assn., Nat. Coun. Tchrs. Math., Nat. Coun. on Edn. for the Ceramic Arts, Ill. Art Edn. Assn. Home: 625 Thomas Ave Forest Park IL 60130-1965 Office: Emerson Sch 916 Washington Blvd Oak Park IL 60302

WILLIAMS, PAULETTE W., state agency administrator; b. Moulton, Ala., Oct. 21, 1944; d. Paul Price and Sallie Davis (Bass) Wiley; m. Robert Thomas Williams, Oct. 11, 1968; 1 child, Shannon Thomas. Student, Florence State Coll., 1963-64. Planning and ops. officer civil def Decatur (Ill.)/Morgan Co., 1964-74, planning and ops. officer emergency mgmt., 1975-77; planning and ops. officer, dep. dir. emergency mgmt. Mobile (Ala.) Co., 1977-89; emergency mgmt. area coord. I State of Ala., Clanton, 1989-95; dir. Ala. Emergency Mgmt. Agy., Clanton, 1994-95; observer nuc. power plant Dept. Def., Romania, 1994; mem. gov. cabinet State of Ala., Clanton, 1994-95. Mem. cmty. advisor coun. Occidental Chem. Co., Muscle Shoals, Ala., 1993—; mem. state disaster svcs. com. ARC, Ala., 1993—. Recipient Spl. Recognition award Ala. Police Acad., 1986, Appreciation cert. Mobile (Ala.) Police Acad., 1986, Outstanding Svc. and Dedication cert. and flag, 1988, Hon. Adm. cert. Mayor of Decatur, 1988, Outstanding Svc. and Contbns. Appreciation cert. Nat. Coordinating Coun. on Emergency Mgmt., 1988, Appreciation plaque Greater Mobile Indsl. Assn., 1989, Appreciation for Profl. Assistance plaque Kerr McGee Chem. Corp., 1989, Appreciation cert. State of Ala., 1989, Meritorious Svc. cert. City of Mobile, 1989, Appreciation for Help and Support plaque City of Mobile Police Dept. Hazardous Materials Unit, 1989, Outstanding Dedication and Svc. plaque Mobile County Local Emergency Planning Com., 1989, Appreciation cert. FEMA-Floods of 1990, 1990, Pub. Svc. award U.S. Dept. Commerce, NOAA, 1994. Mem. Ala. Emergency Mgmt. Coun. (pres., Sec.-treas. plaque 1986, Appreciation cert. 1986, Legis. Chmn. plaque 1987), Nat. Emergency Mgmt. Assn. (mem. recovery com.). Episcopal. Home: 2224 Marietta Ave Muscle Shoals AL 35661-2620 Office: Alabama Emergency Mgmt PO Drawer 2160 Clanton AL 35045

WILLIAMS, PENELOPE LAMSON, musician, recording company executive; b. Sanford, fla., Apr. 16, 1957; d. Volie Adkins and Constance Thomas (Lott) W. Freelance jazz musician, Atlanta, 1981—. Composer record album, 1991. Hope scholar Ga. State U., 1995. Mem. Internat. Assn. Jazz Educators, Am. Fedn. Musicians, Golden Key Honor Soc. Democrat.

WILLIAMS, PETRA SCHATZ, antiquarian; b. Poughkeepsie, N.Y., Sept. 2, 1913; d. Grover Henry and Mayme Nickerson (Bullock) Schatz; m. J. Calvert Williams, Nov. 26, 1946; children: Miranda, Frederica, Valerie. AB, Skidmore Coll., 1936; JD, Fordham U., 1940. Founder Fountain House, Phoenix, 1953, Fountain House East, Jeffersontown, Ky., 1966. Author: Flow Blue China, An Aid to Identification, 1971, Flow Blue China II, 1973, Flow Blue China and Mulberry Ware, 1975, Staffordshire Romantic Transfer Patterns, 1979, Staffordshire II Romantic Transfer Patterns, 1986. Past pres. Meml. Hosp. Aux., Phoenix, Heard Mus. Guild, Phoenix; bd. dirs. Ky. Humane Soc. Mem. Nat. Soc. Interior Designers (nat. dir. for Ariz. 1957-58, Ky. 1968, pres. Ky. 1967-68), DAR, Ky. Hist. Soc., Flow Blue Internat. Collectors Club (hon.). Mem. Soc. of Friends. Club: Filson. Address: PO Box 99298 Jeffersontown KY 40269-0298

WILLIAMS, PHYLLIS CUTFORTH, retired realtor; b. Moreland, Idaho, June 6, 1917; d. William Claude and Kathleen Jessie (Jenkins) Cutforth; m. Joseph Marsden Williams, Jan. 21, 1938 (dec. 1986); children: Joseph Marlis, Bonnie L. Williams Thompson, Nancy K. Williams Stewart, Marjorie Williams Karren, Douglas Claude, Thomas Marsden, Wendy K. Williams Clark, Shannon I. Williams Ostler. Grad., Ricks Coll., 1935. Lic. realtor, Idaho. Tchr. Grace (Idaho) Elem. Sch., 1935-38; realtor Williams Realty, Idaho Falls, Idaho, 1972-77; mem. Idaho Senate, Boise, 1977; owner, mgr. river property. Compiler: Idaho Legisladies Cookbook, Cookin' Together, 1981. With MicroFilm Ctr., LDS Ch. Mission, Salt Lake City, 1989-90; block chmn. March of Dimes Soc.; active Idaho State Legisladies Club, 1966-84, v.p., 1982-84. Republican. Home: 1950 Carmel Dr Idaho Falls ID 83402-3020

WILLIAMS, RHONDA LEE, counselor, mediator; b. Honolulu, Apr. 24, 1953; d. Richard C. and Watheta O. (O'Neal) Whitmore; m. Laurence Steven Rzepka, Aug. 7, 1976 (div. Aug. 1984); children: Richard Laurence; m. Bennie C. Williams, Aug. 12, 1989. BS, Kans. State U., 1975; MEd, U. Colo., 1986. Nat. cert. counselor; cert. counselor, Colo.; licensed profl. counselor, Colo. Tchr. phys. edn.grades K-12 Holly (Colo.) Sch. Dist., 1975-78, South Park Sch. Dist., Fairplay, Colo., 1978-83, Harrison Sch. Dist., Colorado Springs, Colo., 1984-86; counselor grades K-12 Ellicott (Colo.) Sch. Dist., 1986-87; counselor grades 6-9 Falcon (Colo.) Sch. Dist., 1987-92; counselor grades 6-8 Cherry Creek Sch. Dist., Aurora, Colo., 1992-95, Air Acad. Sch. Dist., Colorado Springs, Colo., 1995—; mem. consulting team Peer Concepts, 1988—; cons., presenter Colo. Dept. Edn., 1994—; presenter, adv. in field. Counselor SIDS Found., Colo., 1983—. Named Educator of the Year Colo. Bus. Assn., 1989. Mem. Am. Sch. Counselor Assn. (advocacy profl. rec. chair 1995—, prodr. video Role of Sch. Counselor 1995, Counselor of Yr. 1991, bd. dirs.), Colo. Sch. Counselor Assn. (v.p., pres. 1986—, prodr. video Role of Sch. Counselor 1995, Colo. Mid. Sch. Counselor of Yr. 1990), Colo. Counselor Assn. (bd. dirs. 1990-93, pres. 1990-93). Home: 18820 St Andrews Monument CO 80132 Office: Air Acad Sch Dist Challenger Middle Sch 10215 Lexington Dr Colorado Springs CO 80920

WILLIAMS, RUTH ELIZABETH (BETTY WILLIAMS), retired educator; b. Newport News, Va., July 31, 1938; d. Lloyd Haynes and Erma Ruth (Goodrich) W. BA, Mary Washington Coll., 1960; cert. d'etudes, Converse Coll., 1961, U. Oreg., 1962. Cert. tchr., Va. French tchr. York High Sch., York County Pub. Schs., Yorktown, Va., 1960-65; French resource tchr. Newport News Pub. Schs., 1966-74, tchr. French and photography, 1974-81, tchr. French, Spanish, German and Latin, 1981-91, ret., 1991; pres. Cresset Publs., Williamsburg, Va., 1977—; lectr. Sch. Edn., Coll. Williamand Mary, Williamsburg, 1962-65; French tchr., coord. fgn. langs. York County Pub. Schs., 1962-65; workshop leader dept. pub. instrn. State of Del., Dover, 1965; cons. Health de Rochemont Co., Boston, 1962-71. Driver Meals on Wheels, Williamsburg, 1989-90; contbr. Va. Spl. Olympics, Richmond, 1987—; charter mem. Capitol Soc. Colonial Williamsburg Found., Inc., 1994; mem. Colonial Williamsburg Assembly, Colonial Williamsburg Found., Inc.; mem. Altar Guild, Bruton Parish Ch., Williamsburg, 1960—. Grantee Nat. Def. Edn. Act, 1961, 1962. Mem. AAAU, Fgn. Lang. Assn. Va., AARP (ret. tchrs. divsn.), Heritage Soc., Mary Washington Coll. Alumni Assn., Va. Hist. Soc., Am. Assn. Tchrs. French, Mortar Bd., Women in the Arts, Alpha Phi Sigma, Phi Sigma Iota. Episcopalian. Home and Office: 471 Catesby Ln Williamsburg VA 23185-4732

WILLIAMS, RUTH H., business executive; b. Frankfurt, Germany, Dec. 22, 1956; d. E.J. and Elva N. (Soldate) Williams; m. Stephen P. Johnson, Aug. 20, 1993. BA in Psychology, Dominican Coll., San Rafael, Calif., 1978. Cost acct./account analyst Arrowhead Jewelry, San Rafael, 1982-84; customer svc. mgr. Team Design, Inc., Novato, Calif., 1984-86; gen. mgr. Natuzzi Americas, Inc., High Point, N.C., 1986-90, v.p. merchandising, 1990-92, exec. v.p., 1992—. Bd. dirs. Am. Cancer Soc., High Point, 1993-94. Office: Natuzzi Americas Inc PO Box 2438 High Point NC 27261

WILLIAMS, RUTH L., rehabilitation counselor, consultant; b. Dubois, Pa., July 28, 1945. Student, Massasoit C.C., Brockton, Mass., 1985, Empire State Coll.-SUNY, Saratoga Springs, 1992—. Nurses aid instr. Goddard Hosp., Brockton, 1963-72; counselor, cons. North Attleboro (Mass.) Rehab. Assoc., 1992-95; founder, dir. advocacy L.I.F.E. Orgn., Brockton, 1981-86; v.p. Abilities Unltd., Brockton, 1984-86; info. and referral vols. Stavros CIL, Amherst, Mass., 1990. Cmty. access monitor Mass. Office Disability, Boston, 1982—; mem. commn. disabilities, Brockton, 1984-96, North Attleborough, 1992—; arts and crafts dir. Sr. Citizen Ctr., East Bridgewater, Mass., 1990-91. Recipient Ednl. Scholarship grant Deaf Blind Multi-Disabled Unit Mass. Commn. for the Blind, 1992—. Mem. AAUW, Independence Assoc. Roman Catholic. Home: 111 Raymond Hall Dr North Attleboro MA 02760

WILLIAMS, RUTH LEE, clinical social worker; b. Dallas, June 24, 1944; d. Carl Woodley and Nancy Ruth (Gardner) W. BA, So. Meth. U., 1966; M Sci.in Social Work, U. Tex., Austin, 1969. Milieu coordinator Starr Commonwealth, Albion, Mich., 1969-73; clin. social worker Katherine Hamilton Mental Health Care, Terre Haute, Ind., 1973-74; clin. social worker, supr. Pikes Peak Mental Health Ctr., Colorado Springs, Colo., 1974-78; pvt. practice social work Colorado Springs, 1978—; pres. Hearthstone Inn, Inc., Colorado Springs, 1978—; practitioner Jin Shin Jyutsu, Colorado Springs, 1978—; pres., v.p. bd. dirs. Premier Care (formerly Colorado Springs Mental Health Care Providers Inc.), 1986-87, chmn. quality assurance com., 1987-89, v.p. bd. dirs., 1992-93. Author, editor: From the Kitchen of The Hearthstone Inn, 1981, 2d rev. edit., 1986, 3d rev. edit., 1992. Mem. Am. Bd. Examiners in Clin. Social Work (charter mem., cert.), Colo. Soc. Clin. Social Work (editor 1976), Nat. Assn. Soc. Workers (diplomate), Nat. Bd. Social Work Examiners (cert.), Nat. Assn. Ind. Innkeepers, So. Meth. U. Alumni Assn. (life). Home: 11555 Howells Rd Colorado Springs CO 80908-3735 Office: 536 E Uintah St Colorado Springs CO 80903-2515

WILLIAMS, SALLY, landscape designer; b. Kansas City, Mo., June 30, 1955; d. Douglas John and Margaret Ann (Paul) Williams; m. Siegfried Peter Duray-Bito, June 16, 1984; children: Cassie, Alana. BA, Metro State Coll., Denver, 1979. Bus. mgr. Muse, Denver, 1985-87; exec. dir. Colo. Fedn. of the Arts, Denver, 1987-88; owner Perennial Garden Planning, Littleton, Colo., 1992—. Advanced master gardener Arapahoe County Ext. Svc., Littleton, 1985—. Home and Office: Perennial Garden Planning 5000 Aspen Dr Littleton CO 80123

WILLIAMS, SANDRA CASTALDO, elementary school educator; b. Rahway, N.J., Sept. 19, 1941; d. Neil and Loretta Margaret (Gleason) Castaldo; m. Arthur Williams III, 1962; children: Arthur IV, Melinda S., Thomas N. Student, Syracuse U., 1959-61; AB, Kean Coll., 1969, MA magna cum laude, 1978. Cert. tchr. K-8, early childhood, N.J. Preschool tchr. St. Andrew's Nursery & Kindergarten, New Providence, N.J., 1973-82; kindergartern tchr. Walnut Ave. Sch. Cranford (N.J.) Sch. Dist., 1978-79; adjunct prof. Farleigh Dickinson Coll., Rutherford, Teaneck, N.J., 1983-86; tchr. 4th grade The Peck Sch., Morristown, N.J., 1986-89; dir. Summit Child Care Ctr., 1990-91; tchr. 1st grade Oak Knoll Sch. of Holy Child Jesus, Summit, N.J., 1992—, tchr. Confraternity of Christian Doctrine, 1995—; bd. dirs. Summit Child Care Ctr., 1970-71, cons., 1991; cert. instr. Jacki Soresen Aerobic Dancing, Inc., Summit, 1990, Westfield, 1992-95. Co-chair United Way, Summit, 1991; Eucharistic min. St. Teresa's Ch., Summit, 1994—. Mem. ASCD, Internat. Reading Assn., Phi Kappa Phi, Alpha Sigma Lambda, Kappa Kappa Gamma. Republican. Roman Catholic. Home: 8 Sunset Dr Summit NJ 07901-2323 Office: Oak Knoll Sch Holy Child Jesus 44 Blackburn Rd Summit NJ 07901-2408

WILLIAMS, SANDRA KELLER, postal service executive; b. Bethesda, Md., Oct. 3, 1944; d. Park Dudley and Julia Mildred (Hunter) Keller; m. Tommy Allen Williams, Dec. 24, 1970; children: Chris Allen, Wakenna, Barbara. BA, U. Colo., 1966; MBA, U. Mo., Kansas City, 1971; MS, Ga. Inst. Tech., 1973. Mathematician Colo. State U., Ft. Collins, 1966; sr. scientist Booz-Allen Applied Rsch., Kansas City, Mo., 1967-68; computer sci. instr. Mo. Western Coll., St. Joseph, 1968-71; systems planning analyst Decatur (Ga.) Fed. Savs. and Loan Assn., 1972-73; planning analyst Fed. Res. Bank, Atlanta, 1974-75; indsl. engr. so. region hdqrs. U.S. Postal Svc., Memphis, 1975-79; mat. mgr. quality control U.S. Postal Svc., Washington, 1979-86; dir. city ops. so. Md. div. U.S. Postal Svc., Capital Heights, 1986-87, dir., oper. supt. so. Md. div., 1987-88; postmaster U.S. Postal Svc., Reading, Pa., 1988—; cons. Personal Bus., St. Joseph, 1968-69; grad. teaching asst. Ga. Inst. Tech., Atlanta, 1971-73; adj. faculty Dekalb C.C., Clarkston, Ga., 1973-75, Memphis State U., 1976-78; owner Custom Florals, 1995—. Chmn. Combined Fed. Campaign, Reading, 1988-96, U.S. Postal Svc.-Berks County Savs. Bond Program, 1988-95, United Way's Govt. divsn., 1989-90; bd. dirs. YWCA, Reading and Berks County, treas., 1990, pres., 1991. Mem. Nat. League Postmasters (legis. officer 1988-91), Berks County Women's Network (bd. dirs. 1994-95, treas. 1995). Republican. Home: 1514 Hill Rd Reading PA 19602-1410

WILLIAMS, SHARRON ELAINE, gifted education specialist, legal consultant; b. Cin., July 6, 1951; d. Robert and Mary (Smith) Sawyer; 1 child, Wesley. BS, Kent State U., 1973; MS, Cleve. State U., 1988; JD, U. Akron, 1979. Tchr. Akron (Ohio) Pub. Schs., 1973-79; bus. law instr. Lorain (Ohio) Cmty. Coll., 1980; law clk. Roberty Sawyer, Cleve., 1981; gifted edn. tchr. Cleveland Heights (Ohio) Schs., 1983-88; resource tchr. Coventry Sch., Cleve., 1989-90; gifted edn. specialist Shaker Heights (Ohio) Schs., 1991—; workshop coord. Cleve. Alliance of Educators, 1994; Gestalt trainer Cleveland Heights Schs., 1990; instr. Gov.'s Summer Inst., Cleve., 1989; presenter in field. Contbg. author: Windows of Opportunity, 1994 (NCTM award 1994). Recipient grant Marth Holden Jennings Found., 1979, grant Shaker Heights Schs., 1994. Mem. Nat. Alliance of Black Educators, Heights Alliance of Black Educators, Delta Sigma Theta, Phi Delta Kappa (svc. coord. 1991—), Phi Alpha Delta. Office: Shaker Heights City Schs 17917 Lomond Blvd Shaker Heights OH 44122

WILLIAMS, SHIRLEY JEAN OOSTENBROEK AKERS, daycare provider, educator, writer; b. Kansas City, Kans., Feb. 18, 1931; d. James Ralph and Florence (Snodgrass) Akers; m. Raymond Gale Williams, Feb. 17, 1949; children: David Ray, James Ronald, Vickie Sue, Richard Gene, Randy Wayne. Tchr. Su-Z-Lu Ceramics, Kansas City, 1957-70, 78, 79; sch. bus. driver Argentine Transit Lines, Kansas City, 1959-69; ceramic tchr., owner Su-Z-Lu Ceramics, Tonganoxie, Kans., 1972-78; tchr. Ft. Leavenworth Army Post, Leavenworth, Kans., 1979-85; pres. Wagonettes Extension Homemakers Club, Forsyth, Mo., 1987-88; ceramic tchr. Crystal's Creations and Ceramic Shop, Drexel, Mo., 1996—; day-care provider for the elderly, 1990-93, 95—. Den mother Boy Scouts Am., Kansas City and Tonganoxie, 1955-66, instr., 1961; driver ARC, Kansas City, 1958-63, canteen chmn., campfire leader, 1961-64; contbr. Taney County Rep. newspaper, Forsyth, 1986-87, bd. dirs., 1987-91; mem. Univ.-Extension Coun. bd., 1988-91; vol., supt. ceramic divsn. Leavenworth County Fair, 1974-84; vol. tchr. Kester Found., 1956-57. Recipient 4-H Gold Clover, Taney County 4-H, 1987. Democrat. Home: PO Box 705 203 Willetta Drexel MO 64742-9110

WILLIAMS, SONIA KAY, secondary school educator; b. Duluth, Minn., Jan. 13, 1939; d. Allen Parke and Ruth Adelaide (Mitchell) Swayne; m. William Fedrick Williams, Mar. 26, 1960; children: Keith Douglass, Jennifer Gay. BMus, U. Tenn., Chattanooga, 1960; M in Secondary Tchg. of English, Statesboro U., 1975; edn. specialist, Valdosta State U., 1988. Tchr. North Chattanooga Jr. H.S., 1960-61; music tchr. Savannah (Ga.) Country Day Sch., 1968-72; English tchr. Appling County Jr. H.S., Baxley, Ga., 1972-74, Appling County Comprehensive H.S., Baxley, 1974—; accompanist Appling Applause, Baxley, 1978-92; drama tchr. Appling County H.S., 1990-92. Prodr. videotape Sonia's Signya's, 1991. Bd. dirs., Sunday sch. tchr. First United Meth. Ch., Baxley, 1980-94; pres. Friends of Libr., Baxley, 1990-92; bd. dirs. Appling Hist. Soc., Baxley, 1980-94; mem. Appling Heritage Com., Baxley, 1992-94. Named Star Tchr., Appling County C. of C., 1984. Mem. Nat. Coun. Tchrs. English, Appling County Assn. (pres. 1972-94), Ga. Assn. Educators (instrnl. and profl. devel. com. 1992—). Home: 1505 Torrance Rd Baxley GA 31513 Office: Appling County Comprehensive HS Blackshear Hwy Baxley GA 31513

WILLIAMS, SONJA D'ANNE, environmental consultant; b. Fort Worth, Feb. 15, 1965; d. Carroll Eugene and Ernestine Joy (Haney) W. BS, Texas Christian U., 1988; M. Sci. and Engring., So. Meth. U., 1996. Hydrologic asst. U.S. Geol. Survey, Fort Worth, 1985-86, hydrologic tech., 1986-89; project geologist ATEC Assocs, Inc., Dallas, 1990-92, project mgr., 1992-94, sr. project mgr., 1994-96; sr. project mgr. Leigh Engring., Inc., Dallas, 1996—. Com. leader, mem. Greater Dallas C. of C. Environ. Task Force, 1995-96. Mem. Assn. Ground Water Scientists & Engrs., Dallas Geol. Soc. Home: 6471 Axton Ln Dallas TX 75214 Office: Ste 408 8700 Stemmons Freeway Dallas TX 75247

WILLIAMS, SUE DARDEN, library director; b. Miami, Fla., Aug. 13, 1943; d. Archie Yelverton and Bobbie (Jones) Eagles; m. Richard Williams, Sept. 30, 1989. B.A., Barton Coll., Wilson, N.C., 1965; M.L.S., U. Tex., Austin, 1970. Cert. librarian, N.C., Va. Instr. Chowan Coll., Murfreesboro, N.C., 1966-68; libr.'s asst. Albemarle Regional Libr., Winston, N.C., 1968-69; br. libr. Multnomah County Pub. Libr., Portland, Oreg., 1971-72; asst. dir. Stanly County Pub. Libr., Albemarle, N.C., 1973-76; dir. Stanly County Pub. Libr., 1976-80; asst. dir. Norfolk (Va.) Pub. Libr., 1980-83; dir., 1983-94, Rockingham County Pub. Libr., Eden, N.C., 1996—. Mem. ALA (orientation com. 1990-92, chair 1991), Libr. Adminstrv. and Mgmt. Assn. (pub. rels. sec. 1985-87), Southeastern Libr. Assn. (staff devel. com. 1986-88, Rothrock award com. 1984-86, sec. pub. libr. sect. 1982-84), Va. Libr. Assn. (SELA rep. 1993-96, coun. 1984, 88-91, 93-96, ad hoc conf. guidelines com. 1985-86, chmn. conf. program 1984, awards and recognition com. 1983), Pub. Libr. Assn. (bd. dirs.-at-large Met. area 1986-89), Va. State Libr. (coop edn. com. 88-89). Home: 817A Carter St Eden NC 27288-5923 Office: Rockingham County Pub Libr 527 Boone Rd Eden NC 27288

WILLIAMS, SUSAN LEWIS, artist; b. Chgo., Feb. 10, 1938; d. Albert Lewis and Gertrude (Glasser) Zaus; m. Frank Williams, 1969 (div. 1976); 1 child, David. BA, Wis. U., 1960; MA, NYU, 1962; postgrad., Hunter Coll. co-founder A.I.R. Woman's Art Coop., N.Y.C., 1972. One woman shows include A.I.R. Gallery, N.Y.C., 1972, 74, Elaine Benson, N.Y.C., 1976; group shows include Milw. Arts Ctr., 1968, Mus. Contemporary Art, Chgo., 1968, Triennale, Milan, Italy, 1969, Witte Mus., San Antonio, 1969, Ann Leowanns Mus., Nova Scotia, 1970, City Ctr., N.Y.C., 1970, Nat. Gallery, Melbourne, Australia, 1971, Everson Mus., Syracuse, N.Y., 1971, Stedelijk Mus., Amsterdam, Netherlands, 1971, All Fla. Biennial, 1989, Coyote Annual Show, Chgo., 1994-95; contbr. articles to profl. jours. Home: 1735 N Paulina Loft #414 Chicago IL 60622

WILLIAMS, SUZANNE, pediatric cardiovascular nursing educator; b. Murray, Ky., Sept. 23, 1961; d. Clifton Eugene and Mary Helen (Lee) W. Diploma, Bapt. Meml. Hosp. Sch. Nursing, 1982; BSN, U. Ky., 1985; MSN, Vanderbilt U., 1989; student, 1996—. Staff nurse pediatric ICU U. Ky. Hosp., Lexington, 1982-86, divisional charge nurse pediatrics, 1988-89, pediatric clin. nurse specialist/case mgr., 1989-90; staff nurse pediatric ICU Vanderbilt U. Hosp., Nashville, 1986-87; pediatric cardiovascular case mgr. Med. U. of S.C., Charleston, 1990-94, clin. nurse V/nurse educator, 1994-96. Mem. AACN, ANA, Assn. for the Care of Children's Health (program planning com. 1990-92), Soc. Pediatric Cardiovascular Nurses, Sigma Theta Tau. Home: 412 Tinkerbell Rd Chapel Hill NC 27514

WILLIAMS, THELMA JEAN, social worker; b. Blytheville, Ark., Nov. 2, 1934; d. Willie Louis and Louise (Witherspoon) Morgan; m. Raymond Augustus Williams, Sr., July 22, 1955 (div. Jan. 1961); children: Ronald Duane, Derrick Lamont, Raymond Augustus Jr. BA, U. Mo., St. Louis, 1971; MPA, U. Mo., Kansas City, 1994. Caseworker Mo. Divsn. Welfare, St. Louis, 1959-69, casework supr., 1969-73; quality assurance specialist Dept. Health, Edn. and Welfare, Kansas City, Mo., 1973-74, program integrity specialist, 1974-82; supervisory quality control specialist Dept. Health Human Svcs., Kansas City, Mo., 1982-88, sr. quality control specialist, 1988-90, children and families program specialist, 1990—. Tutor Deramus Br. YMCA, Kansas City, 1994; mem. U. Mo. Coordinating Bd. on Diversity, 1995-96; mem. U. Mo. Minority Affairs Com., 1995-96; project leader Focus Kansas City, 1996; del. Citizen Ambassador Program, 1994-95. Recipient Pres.'s 1000 Points of Light award, 1991, Sec. Health and Human Svcs.' Disting. Vol. Svcs. award, 1991, Cert. of Appreciation Interagency Coun. on Homeless, 1992, Spl. Act of Svc., Dept. Health and Human Svcs. Dept., Family Support Administrn., 1989 (all Washington). Mem. ASPA, AAUW, People to People Internat. Methodist. Home: 803 West 48th St Kansas City MO 64112 Office: Dept Health Human Svcs Children & Families Admins 601 East 12th St Rm 276 Kansas City MO 64106

WILLIAMS, THRESIA WAYNE MATTHEWS, occupational health nurse; b. Moultrie, Ga., Oct. 20, 1945; d. James Wayne and Ola (Cone) Matthews; m. William Ensey Williams, Dec. 31, 1966; children: Darren Ensey, April Thresia Williams McIntosh. ADN, Abraham Baldwin Coll., Tifton, Ga., 1966. Nat. cert. occupational health nurse-specialist, Ga. Supr. Floyd Med. Ctr., Rome, Ga., 1967-71, 74-75; instr. Coosa Valley Vocat. H.S., Rome, 1972-73; med. dept. supr. Riegel Textile Corp., Trion, Ga., 1975-78, CBS Records, Carrollton, Ga., 1980-83, Carriage Industries, Inc., Calhoun, Ga., 1984-94, Galey & Lord, Inc., Shannon, Ga., 1994-96; COHN specialist, 1996—; specialist and spokesperson disaster health svcs. ARC, Rome, 1993—, chair disaster health svcs. cluster com., 1993—, mem. disaster action team, 1993—, vol. local, state and nat. disasters, 1991—, instr. HIV-AIDS, CPR/first aid, blood borne pathogens, freedom from smoking, 1996. Mem. Nat. Assn. Occupational Health Nurses, Am. Lung Assn. (Freedom from Smoking instr. 1996), Ga. Assn. Occupational Health Nurses (scholarship com. 1991—, chair com. 1994—, dir. 1995, proctor Atlanta 1994), N.W. Ga. Assn. Occupational Health Nurses (v.p. 1990-94, Ga. rep. 1993, 95, newsletter editor 1991-94), Jane Delano Soc. Methodist. Home: PO Box 86 208 Floyd Springs Rd Armuchee GA 30105 Office: Galey & Lord Inc PO Box 972 401 Burlington Dr Shannon GA 30172

WILLIAMS, TONDA, entrepreneur, consultant; b. N.Y.C., Nov. 21, 1949; d. William and Juanita (Rainey) W.; 1 child, Tywana. Student, Collegiate Inst., N.Y.C., 1975-78, C.W. Post Coll., 1981-83; BA in Bus. Mgmt., Am. Nat. U., Phoenix, 1983. Notary pub. N.Y. Asst. controller Acad. Ednl. Devel., N.Y.C., 1971-81; mgr. office Chapman-Apex Constrn. Co., Bayshore, N.Y., 1982-84; specialist computer RGM Liquid Waste Removal, Deerpark, N.Y., 1985-87; contr. LaMar Lighting Co., Freeport, N.Y., 1987—; owner, pres. Omni-Star, Bklyn., 1981—. Author: Tonda's Songs in Poetry, 1978, The Magic of Life, 1991; co-author: Computer Management of Liquid Waste Industry, 1986. Recipient Golden Poet award World of Poetry, 1992. Mem. Am. Mus. Natural History, Am. Soc. Notary Pubs. Home: 74 Cedar Dr Bay Shore NY 11706-2419

WILLIAMS, UNA JOYCE, psychiatric social worker; b. Youngstown, Ohio, June 24, 1934; d. Samuel Wilfred and Frances Josephine (Woods) Ellis; children: Wendy Louise, Christopher Ellis, Sharon Elizabeth. BA, U. Ala., 1957; MSW, Adelphi U., 1963. Diplomate CSW, Am. Bd. Examiners in Clin. Social Work, Internat. Acad. Behavioral Medicine, Counseling, Psychotherapy. Dir. Huntington Program for Sr. Citizens; psychiat. social worker-supr. N.Y. State Dept. Mental Hygiene, Suffolk Psychiat. Hosp., Central Islip; info.-referral counselor Mental Health Assn. Nassau County, Hempstead, N.Y.; therapist Madonna Heights Family Clinic, Dix Hills, N.Y.; med. and psychiat. social worker Northport (N.Y.) VA Med. Ctr., psychiat. social worker acute psychiat. treatment svs.; med. social worker dialysis svcs. Northport (N.Y.) Va. Med. Ctr.; cons. on programs for aging Luth. Social Svcs. Mt. N.Y., 1959, sr. citizens cons. Port Jefferson-L.I. Bd. Edn., 1963. Chmn. Huntington Twp. Com. Human Rels., 1970; sec. bd. trustess Unitarian Universalist Fellowship Huntington, 1984. Named Mem. of Yr. Germany Philetelic Soc. Mem. NASW (cert., diplomte), Am. Assn. Family Counselors and Mediators, Germany Philetelic Soc. (pres. chpt. 30, 1990). Home: 316 Lenox Rd Huntington Station NY 11746-2640

WILLIAMS, VANESSA, recording artist, actress; b. Millwood, N.Y., Mar. 18, 1963; m. Ramon Hervey II, 1988; children: Melanie, Jillian, Devin. Recording artist, 1988—. Stage appearances include: (Broadway) Kiss of the Spider Woman, 1994; film appearances include Pick-up Artist, 1987, Under the Gun, 1989, Another You, 1991, Harley Davidson and the Marlboro Man, 1991, Eraser, 1996; (TV films) Full Exposure: The Sex Tapes Scandal, 1989, Perry Mason: The Case of the Silenced Singer, 1990, Stompin' at the Savoy, 1992, Jacksons: An American Dream, 1992, Bye Bye Birdie, 1995, (TV mini series) Nothing Lasts Forever, 1995; (TV guest appearance) The Fresh Prince of Bel-Air, 1990; albums: The Right Stuff, 1988, The Comfort Zone, 1991, The Sweetest Days, 1994; # 1 hit single Save the Best for Last. Recipient 8 Grammy award nominations; named one of 50 Most Beautiful People, People Mag. Office: Mercury Records care Dawn Bridges 825 8th Ave New York NY 10019-7416*

WILLIAMS, VERONICA ANN, marketing and business consultant; b. Washington, Feb. 8, 1956; d. Vernon and Shirley Ann (Felton) W. BA, Brandeis U., 1977; MBA, Northwestern U., 1979. Systems mktg. rep. Control Data Corp., Chgo., 1979-81, mktg. rep., 1981-82; staff mgr. AT&T, Basking Ridge, N.J., 1982-84; nat. account exec. AT&T, N.Y.C., 1984-86; mgr. bus. planning AT&T, Berkeley Heights, N.J., 1986-87; product mgr.

AT&T, Morristown, N.J., 1987-88; dist. mgr. Unisoft Corp., N.Y.C., 1988-89; acct. mgr. Lotus Devel. Corp., N.Y.C., 1989-90; dir. bus. devel., 1990-91, Software Corp. of Am., Stamford, Conn., 1990-91; prin. and mng. dir. ACT, Inc., N.J., 1985—. Author: Wireless Computing Primer; contbr. articles to profl. jours. Mem. South Orange Planning Bd., 1985-87, South Orange Citizens Budget Adv. Com., 1983-87. Mem. Nat. Black MBA Assn. (fin. chmn. Chgo. br. 1979-81, Performance award 1981). Home: 541 Scotland Rd South Orange NJ 07079-3009 Office: ACT Inc PO Box 978 76 S Orange Ave Ste 4 South Orange NJ 07079

WILLIAMS, VIDA VERONICA, guidance counselor; b. Charleston, S.C., May 4, 1956; d. Timothy and Dotlee (Pendarvis) W. BA, Fisk U., 1978; MS in Edn., Queens Coll., 1986, postgrad., 1994-95. Cert. sch. counselor, spl. edn. tchr., N.Y. Job counselor Trident Work Experience, Charleston, 1980; spl. edn. tchr. Jr. High Sch. 158, Bayside, N.Y., 1983-86, Pub. Sch. 214, Bklyn., 1986-90; guidance counselor I.S. 171, 364, Pub. Sch. 214, Bklyn., 1990-95, I.S. 302, Bklyn., 1995—; co-dir. I.S. 302 Gospel Chorus, 1994-95; counselor Dist. 19 Bereavement, Bklyn., 1991-95; bd. dirs. Alpha Kappa Alpha Day Care Ctr., St. Albans, N.Y., 1992-94. Vol. Voter Registration, Jamaica, 1992, Increase the Peace Corps, N.Y.C., 1992, Feeding of 5,000, Jamaica, 1993, Victim Svcs., Bklyn., 1994-95; chair activities Harlem Dowling Foster Care, Jamaica, N.Y., 1995; active Allen A.M.E. Ch. Gospel Choir, 1994-95, Voices of Victory, 1994-95. Named one of Outstanding Young Women Am., 1980. Mem. Alpha Kappa Alpha. Home: 159-19 137th Ave Jamaica NY 11434 Office: IS 302 350 Linwood St Brooklyn NY 11208

WILLIAMS, VIVIAN LEWIE, college counselor; b. Columbia, S.C., Jan. 23, 1923; d. Lemuel Arthur Sr. and Ophelia V. (McDaniel) Lewie; m. Charles Warren Williams, Apr. 4, 1947 (div. Dec. 1967); children: Pamela Ann Williams-Coote, Charles Warren Jr. BA, Allen U., 1942; MA, U. Mich., 1946, postgrad., 1946, 48; MS, U. So. Calif., 1971, postgrad., 1971-72. Cert. marriage, family and child counselor, Calif.; cert. Calif. C.C. counselor. Asst. prof. psychology Tenn. State Agrl. and Indsl. U., Nashville, 1946-47; asst. prof. edn. Winston-Salem (N.C.) State U., 1947-50; asst. prof. edn., dir. tchr. edn. Allen U., Columbia, S.C., 1951-53; specialist reading, coord. lang. arts Charlotte (N.C.) Mecklenburg Schs., 1963-67, cons. comprehensive sch. improvement project, 1967-69; asst. prof. edn., psychology Johnson C. Smith U., Charlotte, 1967-69; counselor, team leader Centennial, U. So. Calif. Tchr. Corps, L.A., 1970-73; counselor Compton (Calif.) C.C., 1973—, adv. fgn. student, 1975-85; co-developer Hyde Park Estates and The Moors, Charlotte, N.C., 1960-63. Pres. bd. dirs. Charlotte Day Nursery, 1956-59; bd. dirs. Taylor St. USO, Columbia, S.C., 1951-53; sec. southwest region Nat. Alliance Family Life, 1973-74; sec. bd. dirs. NCCJ, Charlotte, 1959-62. Recipient Faculty Audit Program award Ford/Carnegie Found., Harvard U., Cambridge, Mass., 1968, Pub. Svc. Achievement award WSOC Broadcasting Co.; fellow U. Mich., 1946. Mem. NAACP (life, Golden Heritage mem. 1992), AAUW (life), NEA (life), Am. Fedn. Tchrs., Faculty Assn. Calif. C.C., Nat. Acad. Counselors and Family Therapists (life, clin. mem., pres. S.W. region 1989), C.C. Counselors Assn., The Links, Inc. (Harbor area chpt. historian 1985-87, chaplain 1990-94), Jack and Jill Am. (charter mem., organizer Charlotte chpt., pres. 1954-56), Women on Target, Calif. Tchrs. Assn., Delta Sigma Theta, Alpha Gamma Sigma (Golden Apple award 1981). Democrat. Methodist. Home: 6621 Caro St Paramount CA 90723-4755 Office: Compton Community Coll 1111 E Artesia Blvd Compton CA 90221-5314

WILLIAMS, WENDY BERNICE, elementary education educator; b. Milw., Sept. 26, 1965; d. Keith Roger and Nancy Ann (Zechel) W. BEd, U. Wis., Eau Claire, 1989; MEd in Curriculum and Instrn., U. Wis., Milw., 1994. Cert. in elem. edn., gifted and talented edn., Wis. Tchr. 5th grade Pewaukee (Wis.) Pub. Schs., 1990—; staff devel. rep. Waukesha County Sch.-to-Work Consortium, Waukesha, Wis., 1993-94. Recipient Innovative Tchg. award Waukesha County's Ptnrs. in Edn., 1995. Mem. Nat. Trust for Historic Preservation. Home: Apt 37 835 N Cass St Milwaukee WI 53202 Office: Pewaukee Pub Schs 140 Houle Cir Pewaukee WI 53072-3636

WILLIAMS, YVONNE G., corporate trainer; b. Waycross, Ga., Jan. 27, 1953; d. Alfred Hayward and Elizabeth Thomas; 1 child, Benjamin Nkrumah Williams. BA in Bus. Mgmt., Eckerd Coll., 1993; MA in Adult Edn., U. South Fla., 1995, postgrad. Mktg. rep. Xerox, Tampa, Fla., 1987-90, account exec., 1990-92, document mgmt. tng. rep., 1992-96; edn. specialist Xerox, Tampa, 1996—; adv. bd. PIMEG, St. Petersburg, Fla., 1995—. Active First Bapt. Instnl. Ch., St. Petersburg. Mem. NAACP, ASTD, Nat. Coun. Negro Women, Tamp Educators Sertoma Club, South Ctrl. Rotary, Phi Kappa Phi. Office: Xerox Corp 4200 W Cypress St Tampa FL 33706

WILLIAMS JONES, ELIZABETH, financial planner, business consultant; b. San Francisco, Jan. 16, 1948; d. John and Myrtle Mary (Thierry) W.; children: Brian, Jonathan; m. Archie W. Jones Jr. Cert. in bus., U. Calif., 1979. Cert. computers loan processing. Manpower coord., fed. programs U.S. Govt., San Francisco; patient svc. rep. Health Care Svc., Oakland, Calif.; ins. and real estate cons.; pres. Investments Unlimited, Oakland, EWJ & Assocs. Mktg. Firm; leisure svcs. commr. City of Pitts.; CEO Ultimate Vacations Inc. Mem. NAACP. Recipient Pub. Speaking award; European Investment fellow. Mem. AAUW, NAFE, Nat. Real Estate Owners Assn., Nat. Notary Assn., Order Ea. Star, Heroines Jericho, Daus. Isis, Toastmistress Club.

WILLIAMS-MONEGAIN, LOUISE JOEL, science educator, administrator; b. Chgo., June 13, 1941; d. Sylvester Emanuel Jr. and Carita Bell (Brown) Williams; m. Martin Monegain, Aug. 19, 1961; children: Michael Martin, Martin Marion II. BS, Shaw U., 1975; JD, Antioch Sch. of Law, Washington, 1979; cert. adminstrn., Roosevelt U., 1988; PhD, U. Ill., 1994. Tchr. Chgo. Archdiocese, 1968-73; assoc. dir. pub. affairs Warren Regional Planning Commn., Soul City, N.C., 1973-74; comm. specialist Coun. of the Great City Schs., Washington, 1974-76; lawyer Equal Employment Opportunity Commn., Washington, 1979-80; tchr. Olive Harvey City Coll., Chgo., 1981-83; mgr. Joy Travel Agt., Chgo., 1981-83; owner, pres. MJS Your Travel Agt., Chgo., 1983-86; sci. tchr. Chgo. Pub. Schs., 1986-91; program leader, evaluator Argonne (Ill.) Nat. Lab., 1991—; program leader, evaluation rep. Nat. Cancer Program, Accra and Jumasi, Ghana, West Africa, 1995. Vol. Art Inst., Chgo., 1994; green team adv. bd. Lincoln Park Zool. Soc., Chgo., 1992—. Scholarship State of Ill., 1987. Mem. ASCD, Am. Edn. Rsch. Assn., Nat. Sci. Tchrs. Assn., Assn. for Coll. and Univ. Women, Phi Delta Kappa. Office: Argonne Nat Lab 9700 Cass Ave Argonne IL 60439-4803

WILLIAMSON, DIANE MARIE, middle school educator; b. Detroit, May 11, 1961; d. Thomas Charles and Eileen Bernadine (Cody) Fischer; m. David Gary Williamson, July 13, 1985. BS in Spl. Edn., Wayne State U., 1985, MA in Ednl. Counseling, 1994. Facilitator, mgr. group homes Tungland Corp., Phoenix, 1985-90; resource, 7th grade sci. tchr. Littleton Sch. Dist., Cashion, Ariz., 1986-90; 8th grade sci. tchr. Cartwright Sch. Dist., Phoenix, 1990—; tchrs. adv. com. Salt River Project, Phoenix, 1994-96; facilitator Project Respect, 1995—. Tchr. resource grantee Salt River Project, 1994. Mem. Ariz. Edn. Assn, Cartwright Edn. Assn., Ariz. Assn. for Learning in and about the Environment, Nat. Sci. Tchrs. Assn., Ariz. Mining Assn. (minerals in soc. planning com. 1996—). Office: Desert Sands Jr HS 6308 W Campbell Ave Phoenix AZ 85033

WILLIAMSON, DONNA MARIA, pastoral counselor; b. Oswego, N.Y., Feb. 26, 1944; d. Donald Carl and Helen Mary (Saber) Townsley; m. Patrick H. Williamson, July 7, 1962; children: Kevin Patrick, Michael Brian, Timothy Daniel. Grad. pub. schs., Fulton, N.Y. Cert. in clin. pastoral edn., pastoral care, Onondaga Pastoral Counseling Ctr.; weight loss counselor. Chaplain Loretto Geriatric Ctr., Syracuse, 1981-82; hosp. chaplain St. Rose of Lima Parish, Syracuse, 1982-84, pastoral counselor, 1984—; weight loss counselor Nutri-System, Syracuse, 1988-91. Founding mem. Fulton Community Nursery Sch., 1967, Commn. on Women in Ch. and Society, Syracuse, 1984; mem. Alethea, Ctr. on Death and Dying, Inc., Syracuse, 1978, Syracuse Area Domestic Violence Coalition's Religious Task Force, 1994—. Mem. Menninger Found. Roman Catholic. Office: St Rose of Lima Parish 409 S Main St North Syracuse NY 13212

WILLIAMSON, JO ANN, psychologist; b. Wichita, Kans., Feb. 12, 1951; d. Howard T. Murray and Ferryl Arlene (Rumsey) Fleming; m. James Wallace Johnson, Apr. 5, 1984 (div. 1984); m. Michael R. Williamson, Dec. 21, 1990; children: Wesley, Wade. BA, U. Kans., 1973; MA in Psychology, U. Mo., 1974; PhD in Psychology, Auburn U., 1979. Lic. psychologist, Kans. Clin. asst. prof. Ohio State U., Columbus, 1979-80; asst. prof. Chgo. Med. Sch., 1980-81; psychologist U. Mo., Kansas City, 1981-82; psychologist II Rainbow Mental Health Ctr., Kansas City, 1982-83; pvt. practice Wichita, 1983-86; pres. Jo Ann Murray, Ph.D., P.A., Wichita, 1986-90; psychologist Iowa Meth. Hosp., Des Moines, 1989-90, Hutchinson (Kans.) Correctional Facility, 1990, Cedarvale, Wichita, 1991, Cowley County Mental Health, Winfield, Kans., 1991; mental health psychologist Cowley County, 1991-93; clin. dir. Cowley County Mental Health, 1993—. Contbr. articles to profl. jours. Mem. APA (div. clin. psychology).

WILLIAMSON, JOYCE JOAN, elementary education educator; b. Kendallville, Ind., Nov. 22, 1943; d. Gleason Robert and Martha Lenora (Eger) Williamson; m. Gordon James Grafton, June 3,1967 (div. Feb. 1975); 1 child, Erica Dawn Williamson. BS in Elem. Edn., Marion (Ind.) Coll., 1966; student, W.Va. U., Morgantown, 1973. Cert. in elem. edn., Ind. Tchr. 5th grade Oak Hill Sch. Dist., Swayzee, Ind., 1966-67; tchr. 4th grade Edison Local Schs., Hammondsville, Ohio, 1967-72, tchr. corrective reading, 1972-74, tchr. 3d grade, 1974-75, tchr. 4th grade, 1975—; mem. math. PPO and textbook com. Jefferson County Schs., Steubenville, Ohio, 1993-94, mem. health critical skills com., 1994-95. Chair children's coun. Finley Meth. Ch., Steubenville, 1990-93, jr. ch. tchr., 1990-93, primary Sunday sch. supt., 1988-93, adult Sunday sch. tchr., 1993-94. Mem. NEA, Ohio Edn. Assn., Edison Local Edn. Assn. Republican. Home: RD 1 Box 286 Toronto OH 43964

WILLIAMSON, MARILYN LAMMERT, English educator, university adminstrator; b. Chgo., Sept. 6, 1927; d. Raymond Ferdinand and Edith Louise (Eisenbies) Lammert; m. Robert M. Williamson, Oct. 28, 1950 (div. Apr. 1973); 1 child, Timothy L.; m. James H. McKay, Aug. 15, 1974. BA, Vassar Coll., 1949; MA, U. Wis., 1950; PhD, Duke U., 1956. Instr. Duke U., Durham, N.C., 1955-56, 58-59; lectr. N.C. State U., Raleigh, 1957-58, 61-62; asst. prof. Oakland U., Rochester, Mich., 1965-68, assoc. prof., 1968-72; prof. English Wayne State U., Detroit, 1972-90, Disting. prof. English, 1990—, chmn. dept. English, 1972-74, 81-83, assoc. dean Coll. Liberal Arts, 1974-79; dir. women's studies Wayne State U., 1976-87; dep. provost Wayne State U., Detroit, 1987-91, sr. v.p. for acad. affairs, provost, 1991-95; pres. Assn. Depts. English, 1976-77. Author: Infinite Variety, 1974, Patriarchy of Shakespeare's Comedies, 1986, British Women Writers 1650-1750, 1990; editor: Renaissance Studies, 1972, Female Poets of Great Britain, 1981; contbr. articles to profl. jours. Pres. LWV, Rochester, 1963-65. Recipient Detroit Disting. Svc. award, 1986, Faculty Recognition award Bd. Govs., Wayne State U., 1991; Bunting Inst. fellow, 1969-70, AAUW fellow, 1982-83, J.N. Keal fellow, 1985-86. Mem. MLA (exec. coun. 1977-80, mem. editorial bd. 1992-94), Renaissance Soc. Am., Coll. English Assn., Mich. Acad. (pres. 1978-79), Shakespeare Assn. Am., Mich. Coun. Humanities (chair 1991-93), Fed. State Humanitics Coun. (bd. dirs. 1994—). Democrat. Home: 2275 Oakway Dr West Bloomfield MI 48324-1855 Office: Wayne State Univ Dept of English Detroit MI 48202

WILLIAMSON, MARY DAWN, community development manager; b. Orangeburg, S.C., May 9, 1967; d. James Snyder and Mary Lou (Aultman) W. BS, U. S.C., 1985-89. Comty. devel. mgr. City of North Charleston, S.C., 1990—; mem. Comty. Housing Resource Bd., Charleston, 1990—, Coun. on Homelessness and Affordable Housing, Charleston, 1991—; bd. dirs. The N.E.W. Fund, Charleston. Mem. Nat. Comty. Devel. Assn., S.C. Comty. Devel. Assn. (bd. dirs., 2d v.p. 1996, 3-yr. scholar 1994-96). United Methodist. Home: 158 Riverbreeze Dr Charleston SC 29407 Office: City of North Charleston 4900 LaCross Rd North Charleston SC 29406

WILLIAMSON, MARY LOUISE, editor, reporter; b. Chgo., June 28, 1937; d. Lewis and Helen (Mathews) Miller; m. James Marion Williamson, Jan. 5, 1962; children: Carolyn, Peter Mathews, Margaret. BA in History, Western Coll. for Women, 1959. Info. clk. Internat. Bank for Reconstrn. and Devel., Washington, 1959-62; staff mem. Greenbelt (Md.) News Rev., 1962-72, editor, 1972—; com. sec. Prince Georges County Senators, Md. Legis. Session, 1984, 85, 86. Editor: Greenbelt: History of a New Town 1937-1987, 1987. Mem. 50th Anniversary Com., Greenbelt, 1985-87; publicity chair Greenbelt Coop. Nursery Sch., 1966-69, 70-72, pres. 1972; leader 4-H, Greenbelt, 1970s. Named Outstanding Citizen of Greenbelt, Greenbelt Labor Day Festival Com., 1985, Woman of Achievement in Prince George's County History, 1994; recipient Lion's Internat. medal of merit, 1990. Democrat. Unitarian. Home: 45-H Ridge Rd Greenbelt MD 20770 Office: Greenbelt News Rev Ste 100 15 Crescent Rd Greenbelt MD 20770

WILLIAMSON, MYRNA HENNRICH, retired army officer, lecturer, consultant; b. Gregory, S.D., Jan. 27, 1937; d. Walter Ferdinand and Alma Lillian (Rajewich) H. BS with highest honors, S.D. State U., 1960; MA, U. Okla., 1973; grad., U.S. Army Command and Gen. Staff Coll., 1977, Nat. War Coll., 1980. Commd. 2d lt. U.S. Army, 1960, advanced through grades to brig. gen., 1985; bn. comdr. Mil. Police Sch. U.S. Army, Fort McClellan, Ala., 1977-79; chief plans policy and service div. Jl 8th Army U.S. Army, Korea, 1980-81; chief mgmt. support Office Dep. Chief Staff for Research, Devel. and Acquisition U.S. Army, Washington, 1981-82; brigade comdr. U.S. Army, Fort Benjamin Harrison, Ind., 1983-84; comdg. gen. 3d ROTC Region U.S. Army, Fort Riley, Kans., 1984-87; dep. dir. mil. personnel mgmt. U.S. Army, Washington, 1987-89, ret., 1989; U.S. del. com. on women in NATO Forces, 1986-89. Pres., bd. dirs. S.D. State U. Found., 1988-96; bd. dirs. Women in Mil. Svc. to Am. Found.. Recipient Disting. Alumnus award S.D. State U., 1984. Mem. Internat. Platform Assn., Assn. U.S. Army (trustee), United Svcs. Automobile Assn. (bd. dirs.), The Internat. Alliance, Phi Kappa Phi.

WILLIAMSON, NORMA BETH, adult education educator; b. Hamilton, Tex., Nov. 2, 1939; d. Joseph Lawrence and Gladys (Wilkins) Drake; m. Stuart Williamson, Mar. 14, 1981. BA, Baylor U., 1962; MA, Tex. A&I U., 1969; postgrad., Tex. Tech. U., 1976-80, CIDOC, Cuernavaca, Mex., 1973, 75. Instr. English, Tex. Southmost Coll., Brownsville; lectr., Spanish; coll. prep. tchr. Tex. Dept. Corrections, 1995—; lectr. Spanish Sam Houston State U. Music chmn. Huntsville Unitarian Universalist Ch.; pres. S.W. Dist. Unitarian Universalist Assn., 1982-86. Mem. AAUW (pres. Huntsville br. 1995-96). Home: RR 1 Box 349 Bedias TX 77831-9625

WILLIAMSON, PAMELA POWELL, antiques dealer/appraiser, English educator; b. Heinsville, Ga., Feb. 28, 1953; d. Nathanial Thomas and Alice Jefers (Howell) Powell; m. Jerry Wayne Williamson, Mar. 5, 1983. BA in English, Appalachian State U., 1975; MA in English, N.C. State U., 1978. Editor Robert R. Nathan Assoc., Washington, 1978-80; sr. editor Ernst & Young, Washington, 1980-83; instr. Appalachian State U., Boone, N.C., 1983—; antiques dealer, appraiser Boone, N.C., 1985—; spkr. Women in Leadership, Boone, 1993. Editor Women Working in Watauga County, 1989. Chair Watauga County Coun. on Status of Women, 1994-96; founder, mem. 100 Women/State Polit. Action Group, Boone, 1993—; publicity chair Watauga County Dem. Party, Boone, 1995—. Mem. LWV (co-chair voter svc. 1994—), NOW (pres. Boone chpt. 1990—). Home: 2737 Hwy 421 S Boone NC 28607

WILLIAMSON, SARA HILLIARD, nursing administrator; b. Houston, Oct. 7, 1953; d. Harlan E. and Lucile (McQuary) Hilliard; m. Julien Holt Williamson, June 9, 1973; children: Rita, Walker. BSN, U. Tex., 1978, MSN, 1986. Cert. nursing adminstr., advanced; lic. nursing home adminstr. Mgmt. cons. Hilliard-Williamson Cons., Lakewood, Colo., 1989-90; dir. nursing Centennial Peaks Hosp., Louisville, 1990-92, asst. adminstr., 1992-93, assoc. adminstr., 1993-94; exec. dir. Esperanza House, Roswell, N.Mex., 1994; asst. v.p. Ea. N.Mex. Med. Ctr., Roswell, 1994—; bd. dirs. Esperanza House, Roswell. Ambassador family N.Mex. Mil. Inst., Roswell, 1994—; mem. Leadership Roswell, 1995—. Mem. Am. Orgn. Nurse Execs., N.Mex. Orgn. Nurse Execs. Democrat. Office: Ea NMex Med Ctr 405 W Country Club Rd Roswell NM 88201

WILLIAMS-STEINWENDER, KARIN MAE, artist; b. Santa Monica, Calif., Oct. 14, 1948; d. Marion Glen and Margaret Grace (Long) Williams; m. Helmut Adolf Ludwig Steinwender, Aug. 17, 1985. BA with hons., Calif. State U., Dominguez Hills, Carson, 1983. Cert. tchr. art-dance, Calif.; cert. hypnotist; cert. Shiat-su therapist; cert. Cecchetti Ballet instr. Chmn. bd. South Bay (Calif.) Ballet Co., 1977-78, choreographer, 1976-77; gallery coord. F.O.T.A., Hermosa Beach, Calif., 1978-79; ballet instr. Act III Acad., Redondo Beach, Calif., 1976-83; self-employed ballet instr. South Bay, 1972-93; artist, painter Calif., N.Y., Oreg., 1972—; ballet instr. Banks, Oreg., 1994, Pendleton, Oreg., 1995—; dir. Acad. Classical Ballet, Pendleton, 1996—; exhbns. include Art of 80's Gallery, Hermosa Beach, Calif., Barnsdale Mcpl. Gallery, L.A., Community galleries, South Bay, Calif., Ambiente', Redondo Beach, Calif., Everson Mus. exhbn., Syracuse, N.Y., Gallery Syracuse, 1972—; one-woman show Crackerjack Prodns.; interview and art filming South Bay News, Redondo Beach, Calif.; studio opening/exhbn., 1992. Author: Technique in Balance and Turning, 1985; writer, producer, choreographer (ballets) Woodcutter's Daughter, 1977, Power Plays, 1978; choreographer Midsummer Nights Dream, 1975, holiday and community programs, 1975-83. Vol. Rep. Party, Syracuse, 1988-89, Park Assn., Syracuse, 1990; mem. Rep. Women, Pendleton, 1996—. Recipient honor for one-man exhbn. Crackerjack TV Prodns., Redondo Beach, 1983. Mem. ASPCA, World Wildlife Fund, Rodale Inst., Arbor Day Found., Sierra Legal Fund, Nature Conservancy, Nat. Wildlife Fedn., Greenpeace, Wilderness Soc., Nat. Resources Def. Coun., Environ. Def. Fund, Rosicrucians, In Def. of Animals.

WILLIAMS-TIMS, LILLIE ALTHEA, distribution administrator, genealogist; b. Laurens, S.C., Aug. 17, 1951; d. Hunter Nathenial and Alma Sue Peal (hunter) W.; m. Benny Woodrow Tims, Sept. 1, 1973 (div. 1987); 1 child, Eltaro. Assoc. in Gen. Bus., Piedmont Tech. Coll., Greenwood, S.C., 1988. Weaver Delta Woodside Mills, Fountain Inn, S.C., 1981-87; seamstress, data entry clk. Josten's Cap and Gown, Laurens, 1987-88; supr. Wal-Mart Distbn. Ctr., Laurens, 1988—. Asst. supt. Flat Ruff Bapt. Ch. Sch., Laurens, 1989-91; pres. Young Woman Assn. for Flat Ruff Bapt. Ch., 1991—; founder, pres. African-Am. Hist. Found., Laurens. Mem. S.C. Geneal. Soc. (sec. Laurens chpt. 1992-95), S.C. African Am. Heritage Coun. (assoc.). Democrat. Home: 42 Chateau Arms Laurens SC 29360

WILLIAMS-WENNELL, KATHI, human resources officer; b. Danville, Pa., Sept. 22, 1955; d. Raymond Gerald and Julia Dolores (Higgins) Williams; m. Mark Kevin Wennell, Apr. 3, 1982; children: Ryan Christopher, Lauren Ashley. BA, Immaculata Coll., 1977; MEd, Pa. State U., State College, 1978. Cert. rehabilitation counselor, Pa. From project dir. to coord. devel. activities Community Interactions, Blue Bell, Pa., 1978-83; from mgmt. trainee to coord. coll. recruiting and rels. Meridian Bancorp, Inc., Reading, Pa., 1983-86, mgmt. recruiter, compensation analyst, 1986-88, 89-93, recruiter, 1993-96; cons. Chet Mosteller & Assocs., Reading, Pa., 1996—; cons. Norristown (Pa.) Life Ctr., 1981; instr. Immaculata (Pa.) Coll., 1981-83, Alvernia Coll., Reading, 1988-89. Meridian campaign coord. United Way Berks County, Reading, 1985. Named Recruiter of Yr. LaSalle U., Phila., 1986; recipient Excellence in Programming award Nat. Assn. Bank Women, Pa., 1986. Mem. Soc. Human Resources Mgmt. Republican. Roman Catholic. Home: 69 S Hampton Dr Wyomissing PA 19610-3108 Office: Meridian Bancorp Inc Meridian Ctr at Springridge 1 Meridian Blvd Wyomissing PA 19610-3200

WILLIE, CAROLJEAN, educational administrator; b. Bklyn., Mar. 26, 1948; d. Joseph John and margaret Lucille (Prenzel) W. BA in Sociology, Edgecliff Coll., Cin., 1971; MEd in Reading, Xavier U., Cin., 1983. Cert. tchr., Fla.; joined Sisters of Charity, Roman Cath. Ch., 1975. Jr. high tchr. Peace Corps, St. Lucia, Eastern Caribbean, 1972-74; elem. tchr., adminstrv. experience Archdiocese of Cin. Schs., St. Joseph Orphanage, Cin., 1974-79; sr. high tchr., teacher trainer Govt. St. Lucia, 1979-81; elem. tchr., secondary tchr. Archdiocese of Miami Schs., Fla., 1982-88; sr. high tchr. St. Catherine Indian Sch., Santa Fe, 1988-89; prin. Hope Rural Sch., Indiantown, Fla., 1989—; bd. mem. Dade Reading Coun., Miami, Fla., 1984-86, GCA Peace Edn. Found., 1986-88, Guatemala Tomorrow, Tequesta, Fla., 1994—; cons., guest speaker in field. Author: (play) Today's Catholic Teacher, 1994; contbr. articles to profl. jours. Named Peace Educator of Yr. Grace Contrino Abrams Peace Edn. Found, Miami, Fla., 1987; Centro de Idomas-Yucatan scholar, Mex., 1991, Fla. Internat. U. scholar, 1985, PhD fellow OBEMLA, U. Fla., Gainesville, 1993, 1st Pl. Photography award Soc. for Devel. Edn., 1994. Mem. ASCD (1st Pl. Photography award), Nat. Cath. Educators Assn., Internat. Reading Assn., Martin Reading Coun., Tchrs. English to Speakers of other Langs., Grace Contrino Abrams Peace Edn. Found. Office: Hope Rural School 15929 SW 150th St Indiantown FL 34956-3406

WILLINGER, RHONDA ZWERN, optometrist; b. Bklyn., Apr. 26, 1962; d. Jerome Max and Jeanette (Zwern) Willinger; m. Wayne Ken Chan, Aug. 26, 1990; 1 child, Jamie S. BS, U. Miami, 1983; OD with honors, New Eng. Coll. Optometry, 1987. Resident in optometry VA Med. Ctr., Bedford, Mass., 1987-88; pvt. practice, Burlington, Mass., 1988-89; pvt. practice specializing in contact lenses Framingham, Mass., 1989—. Scholar New Coll., U. South Fla., 1979-81; honors scholarship U. Miami, 1981-83. Mem. Am. Optometric Assn. (contact lens sect.), Mass. Soc. Optometrists. Home: 228 Lowell Ave Newton MA 02160-1830 Office: 659 Worcester Rd Framingham MA 01701-5308

WILLINGHAM, HELEN PITTARD, artist; b. Abbeville, S.C., July 10, 1921; d. Charles Edgar and Rachel Clifford (Pittard) Armour; m. Robert Marion Willingham, Nov. 25, 1945 (dec. Aug. 1994); 1 child, Robert Marion Jr. Student, U. Ga., 1939-40, LaGrange Coll., 1940-41. Tchr. art Washington (Ga.) H.S., 1952-69; book illustrator Willingham Art Studio, Washington, Ga., 1948-85, heraldry artist, 1948—, portrait and still life painter, 1948—. Exhibited in group shows at Augusta, Ga., 1964, Lake Lanier, Ga., 1968, 69, Thomaston, Ga., 1970, City of Washington (Ga.) Pub. Libr., 1993; represented in permanent collection at Augusta (Ga.) Mus. Mem. Women in the Arts, Augusta Art Assn. Republican. Presbyterian. Home: 102 Water St Washington GA 30673

WILLINGHAM, JEANNE MAGGART, dance educator, ballet company executive; b. Fresno, Calif., May 8, 1923; d. Harold F. and Gladys (Ellis) Maggart. student Tex. Woman's U., 1942; student profl. dancing schs., worldwide. dance tchr. Beaux Arts Dance Studio, Pampa, Tex., 1948—; artistic dir. Pampa Civic Ballet, 1972—. Mem. Tex. Arts and Humanities, Tex. Arts Alliance, Pampa C. of C. (fine arts com.), Pampa Fine Arts Assn. Office: Pampa Civic Ballet Beaux Arts Dance Studio 315 N Nelson St Pampa TX 79065-6013

WILLINGHAM, MARY MAXINE, fashion retailer; b. Childress, Tex., Sept. 12, 1928; d. Charles Bryan and Mary (Bohannon) McCollum; m. Welborn Kiefer Willingham, Aug. 14, 1950; children: Sharon, Douglas, Sheila. BA, Tex. Tech U., 1949. Interviewer Univ. Placement Svc., Tex. Tech U., Lubbock, 1964-69; owner, mgr., buyer Maxine's Accent, Lubbock, 1969—; speaker in field. Leader Campfire Girls, Lubbock, 1964-65; sec. Community Theatre, Lubbock, 1962-64. Named Outstanding Mcht., Fashion Retailor mag., 1971, Outstanding Retailer; recipient Golden Sun award Dallas Market, May 1985. Mem. Lubbock Symphony Guild, Ranch and Heritage Ctr. Club: Faculty Women's. Office: 16 Briercroft Shopping Ctr Lubbock TX 79412-3022

WILLIS, CONNIE (CONSTANCE E. WILLIS), author; b. 1945. Tchr. elem. and jr. high schs. Branford, Conn., 1967-69. Author: (short stories/novels) Letter from the Clearys (Nebula award 1982, Hugo award 1983), Lincoln's Dreams, 1987, Doomsday Book (Nebula award 1992, Hugo award 1993), Impossible Things, 1993, Uncharted Territory, 1994, Even the Queen (Nebula award 1992, Hugo award 1993), (novelette) Fire Watch (Nebula award 1982, Hugo award 1983), At the Rialto (Nebula award 1990), The Last of the Winnebagos (Nebula award 1988, Hugo award 1989), Death on the Nile (Hugo award 1994), (novel) Uncharted Territory, 1994, Remake, 1995, Bellwether, 1996; (with Cynthia Felice) Water Witch, 1982, Light Raid, 1989. Address: 1716 13th Ave Greeley CO 80631-5418

WILLIS, DAWN LOUISE, paralegal, small business owner; b. Johnstown, Pa., Sept. 11, 1959; d. Kenneth William and Dawn Louise (Joseph) Hagins; m. Marc Anthony Ross, Nov. 30, 1984 (div.); m. Jerry Wayne Willis, Dec. 16, 1989 (div.). Grad. high sch., Sacramento, Calif. Legal sec. Wilcoxen & Callahan, Sacramento, 1979-87, paralegal asst., 1987-88; legal adminstr. Law

Office Jack Vetter, Sacramento, 1989—; owner, mgr. Your Girl Friday Secretarial and Legal Support Svcs., Sacramento, 1991—. Vol. ARC, 1985. Mem. NAFE, Assn. Legal Adminstrs., Calif. Trial Lawyers Assn., Sacramento Legal Secs. Assn. Republican. Lutheran. Office: Law Office Jack Vetter 928 2nd St Ste 300 Sacramento CA 95814-2201

WILLIS, DOLLIE P., adult education educator; b. West Union, Ohio, Nov. 13, 1957; d. Arbra Edgar and Mallie Mae (Erwin) Plymail; m. Orland Willis, Aug. 14, 1983; children: Emerson, Thomas. Student, So. State Coll., Fincastle, Ohio, 1977; BS in Edn., Morehead (Ky.) State U., 1979; MEd, Coll. Mt. St. Joseph, Ohio, 1991. Cert. tchr. vocat. home econs., reading; cert. reading supr.; cert. Irlen screener. Substitute tchr. Ohio Valley Local Schs., West Union, 1983—, Highland County Schs., Hillsboro, Ohio, 1983—; pvt. tutor/owner Eclectic Reading Svc., Hillsboro, 1989—; tchr. jr. high sci. Lynchburg-Clay (Ohio) Schs., 1990-91, alternative classroom tchr., 1993—. Treas. Folsom (Ohio) United Meth. Ch., 1983—. Mem. ASCD, Ohio Reading Assn., Internat. Reading Assn. Republican. Home: 7360 Oakridge Rd Hillsboro OH 45133-9682

WILLIS, ELEANOR LAWSON, university official; b. Nashville, Sept. 15, 1936; d. Harry Alfred Jr. and Helen Russell (Howse) Lawson; m. Alvis Rux Rochelle, Aug. 25, 1956 (div. Mar. 1961); 1 child, Alfred Russell Willis; m. William Reese Willis Jr., Mar. 7, 1964 (div. June 1994); children: William Reese III, Brent Lawson. BA cum laude, Vanderbilt U., 1957. Host children's syndicated TV show Sta. WSIX-TV, Nashville, 1961-64; tchr. head start program Metro Pub. Sch., Nashville, 1965-67; co-investigator cognitive edn. curriculum project Peabody Coll., Nashville, 1979-81; dir., founder Heads Up Child Devel. Ctr., Inc., Nashville, 1973-87; dir. Tenn. Vols. for Gore for Pres. Campaign, Nashville, 1987-88; dir. devel. Vanderbilt Inst. Pub. Policy Studies, Vanderbilt U., Nashville, 1988—; mem. task force on child abuse Dept. Human Svcs., Nashville, 1976; mem. mental health ctr. adv. bd. Vanderbilt U., 1978-80, bd. dirs. Vanderbilt Child Devel. Ctr.; mem. instrumental enrichment adv. bd. Peabody/Vanderbilt U., 1981-82. Author: (with others) I Really Like Myself, 1973, I Wonder Where I Came From, 1973. Pres. Nashville Bar Aux., 1967-68, Nashville Symphony Guild, 1984-85, W.O. Smith Nashville Community Music Sch., 1987-89; founder, bd. mem. Rochelle Ctr., Nashville, 1968-96; vice chmn. Century III Com., Nashville, 1978-80; chmn. so. region Am. Symphony Orch. League Vol. Coun., Washington, 1984-86, Homecoming 1986 Steering Com., Nashville, 1985-86; mem. Cheekwood Fine Arts Ctr., Nahville City Ballet, Nashville Symphony Assn., Dem. Women of Davidson County; appointed Metro Arts Commn., 1992; exec. dir. Friends of Warner Park, 1994. Recipient Leadership Nashville award, 1982; Seven Leading Ladies award Nashville Mag., 1984; Eleanor Willis Day proclaimed by City of Nashville, 1987. Mem. Nashville C. of C., Tenn. Conservation League, Vanderbilt Alumni Assn. Presbyterian. Office: 50 Vaughn Rd Nashville TN 37221

WILLIS, JUDY ANN, lawyer; b. Hartford, Conn., July 7, 1949; d. Durward Joseph and Angeline Raphael (Riccardo) W. BA, Cen. Conn. State U., 1971; postgrad., U. Conn. Law Sch., 1976-77; JD, Boston Coll., 1979. Bar: Mass. 1979, U.S. Dist. Ct. Mass. 1980, Calif. 1990. Sr. atty. H.P. Hood Inc., Charleston, Mass., 1979-83; v.p. law Parker Bros., Beverly, Mass., 1983-89; sr. v.p. bus. affairs Mattel, Inc., El Segundo, Calif., 1989—. Bd. dirs. Children Affected by AIDS Found. Office: Mattel Inc 333 Continental Blvd El Segundo CA 90245-5032

WILLIS, KELLY, vocalist; b. Lawton, Okla., Sept. 1, 1968. Lead vocalist Kelly and the Fireballs, 1986, Radio Ranch, Austin, Tex., 1988-90; represented by MCA Records; progressive country vocalist. Albums include Well Travelled Love, 1990, Bang Bang, 1991, Kelly Willis, 1993. Nominee Best New Female Vocalist, Acad. Country Music, 1994. Office: MCA Records 1514 South St Nashville TN 37212 also: Mark Rothbaum & Assocs Inc 36 Mill Plain Rd # 406 Danbury CT 06811*

WILLIS, LAUREN ELIZABETH, lawyer; b. Greenville, S.C., Nov. 25, 1968; d. James Nelson Jr. and Barbara J. (Holmes) W. BA with high honors, Wesleyan U., 1990; JD with distinction, Stanford U., 1994. Bar: Md. 1995. Intern Sen. John F. Kerry, Washington, 1988; paralegal Soc. of Counsel, Seattle, 1990-91; rsch. asst. Stanford (Calif.) U., 1992-93, 93-94; summer assoc. White and Case, L.A., 1993; law clk. to solicitor gen. U.S. Dept. of Justice, 1994; law clk. to Judge Francis Murnaghan U.S. Ct. Appeals, Balt., 1994-95; assoc. Brown, Goldstein and Levy, Balt., 1995—; co-founder Pub. Interest Law Students Assn., Stanford Law Sch., 1991-92; mem. student jud. bd. Wesleyan U., 1987-88, 89-90. Book rev. editor: Stanford Law Rev., 1993-94. Summer coord. Domestic Violence Clinic, East Palo Alto Law Project, 1992; crisis counselor Sexual Assault Crisis Svc., Middletown, Conn., 1989-90. Recipient scholar award PEO, 1993-95, Matt Goldstein award Stanford Ctr. on Children and Families, 1993-94; Fgn. Lang. and Area Studies fellow Stanford U., 1994, Stanford Women Lawyers scholar Stanford Law Sch., 1992. Mem. ABA, Md. State Bar Assn., Order of Coif. Office: Brown Goldstein and Levy 300 Maryland Bar Ctr 520 W Fayette St Baltimore MD 21202

WILLIS, LOUISE FRANZEN, educator; b. Bridgeton, N.J., Feb. 23, 1926; d. John and Anna Marie (Japchen) Franzen; m. Lucien Howard Willis, June 7, 1947; children: John, Robyn Weston. Assoc., Hahnemann Sch. Med. Tech., Phila., 1946; BA, Glassboro (N.J.) State Coll., 1981; MA, Temple U., 1995. Tchr., writer Whitesbog Environ. Ctr., Browns Mills, N.J., 1980-85; tchr. Vo-Tech Sch., Sewell, N.J., 1985-86; tchr. sci. Lady Mercey Acad., Newfield, N.J., 1986-88, St. James H.S., Carneys Point, N.J., 1989-90; lab.mgr. Ron/Son Foods, Swedesboro, N.J., 1990-92; recycling coord., tchr. Harrison Twp., Mullica Hill, N.J., 1987-93; tchr. St. Catherine Elem., Clayton, N.J., 1990-93, Greenwich Sch., Gibbstown, N.J., 1994—; Cons., rschr. Alloway (N.J.) Landfill, 1987-89. Recipient scholarship Temple U., Phila., 1992. Mem. AAUW, NOW, Ext. Svc. Salem County, Embroiders Guild (com.), N.J. Environ. Edn., Biology Tchrs. Assn. N.J. Republican. Home: 112 Swedesboro Rd Monroeville NJ 08343

WILLIS, LOUISE MCKINNEY, retired petroleum company executive; b. Cooper, Tex., Nov. 12, 1924; d. Charles Martin and Birdie Floy (Griffin) McKinney; m. Glenn Harry Willis, May 7, 1948; children: Stephen Eric, Susan Renee, Mary Lynn, Glenda Ann. Student U. Okla., 1946-47. Instrument repair technician Tinker Field AFB, Okla., 1943-46; transit check clk. Fed. Res. Bank, Oklahoma City, 1948-50; sec. Southwestern Power Co., Tulsa, 1950-51, U.S. Govt. Agy., New Orleans, 1951-53; dist. mgr. World Book Encyclopedia, Dallas, 1972-78; v.p. Dor-Texan Petroleum, Inc., Dallas, 1980-87, ret., 1987. Mem. Dallas Opera Guild, 1984-85; pres. Dallas PTA, 1965-66, hon. life mem., 1975—; pres. St. Andrews Study Club, Dallas, 1968-69, 87-88; chmn. Cotillion Park Bd., Dallas, 1964-66. Mem. Dallas C. of C. Baptist. Clubs: Petroleum, Dallas Athletic. Lodge: Order of Rainbow Girls (chmn. bd. dirs. 1973-76).

WILLIS, NANCY JO, artist; b. Cin., Sept. 12, 1953; d. Robert Sidney and Suzanne E. (Gelsinger) W. BFA, U. Cin., 1976. Lecture series coord. Napa County Arts Coun., Napa, Calif., 1993—; visual stage designer Napa Valley Wine Auction, St. Helena, Calif., 1995, cmty. artists coord., 1994; curator Seven Days a Week Codorniu, Napa, 1994; coord. Arts and Culture Lecture Series, 1994, 95, prodr., 1994, 95, 96. One-person shows include Cuts Gallery, London, 1985, The Billboard at the Billboard Cafe, San Francisco, 1987, One Ten Powell St., San Francisco, 1988, The Hibernia Bank Bldg., San Francisco, 1988, Orient Express, San Francisco, 1989, Domaine Chandon, Yountville, Calif., 1990, 92, Auberge du Soleil, Rutherford, Calif., 1991, Codorniu Napa, 1992, Gordon Biersch, Palo Alto, Calif., 1993, Mumm Napa Valley, Rutherford, Calif., 1994, Napa Valley Wine Auction, 1995; exhibited in group shows at City Art Gallery, City Coll. San Francisco, 1988, Soco Gallery, Napa, 1990, 91, The Lowe Gallery, Atlanta, 1990, Cathedral facade, Grenoble, France, 1990, Gallery Concord, Calif., 1991, St Supery, St. Helena, Calif., 1992, Napa County Arts Coun., Open Studio, St. Helena, 1991, 92, 93, 94, Robert Mondavi Winery, Oakville, Calif., 1993, Codorniu Napa, 1994; represented in permanent collecions at Anthony Worrall-Thompson, Menage a Trois, London, Kaiser Steel, Oakland, Calif., Germaine Halas Design, Engelwood Cliffs, N.Y., Data Ctrl., San Francisco, Paine Webber, N.Y.C., Sheehan Hotel, San Francisco, Little City Antipasti Bar, San Francisco, Knickerbocker's Catering, Conner Peripherals, Silicon Valley, Calif., Pruneyard Inn, Campbell, Calif., Garden Court Inn, Palo Alto, Calif., Valley Sheet Metal, San Francisco, Domaine Chandon, Napa, Codorniu, Napa, Greenwood Ridge Winery, Philo, Calif., Markham Winery; also pvt. collections. Recipient Three Arts Coun. scholarship, 1975, 76. Mem. Arts Coun. Napa Valley (bd. dirs. 1993, 94, planning com. 1994, 95, mem. artsits adv. 1993, 94, 95).

WILLIS, NANCY JOE, elementary education educator; b. Smithville, Mo., Aug. 13, 1949; d. Joseph Andrew and Margaret (Buckley) W. BS, U. Mo., 1971, MA, 1975. Elem. sch. educator Independence (Mo.) Pub. Schs., 1971—. Mem. Internat. Reading Assn., Independence Nat. Edn. Assn. (sec. 1985-87, v.p. 1987-89, pres. 1989-90, profl. rights chair 1993—), PTA. Office: Santa Fe Trail Elem Sch 1301 S Windsor Independence MO 64055

WILLIS, SUSAN MARIE, education administrator; b. Johnson City, Tenn., May 20, 1952; d. Wesley T. and Edythe Marie (Parrott) W. BA, East Tenn. State U., 1974; MA, U. Tenn., 1979; PhD, Bowling Green State U., 1991. Grad. fellow Bowling Green (Ohio) State U., 1982-89; dean of student affairs St. Mary-of-the-Woods Coll., Terre Haute, Ind., 1989-90; dir. grad. studies Kutztown (Pa.) U. Pa., 1990—. Author: The College of Education at Bowling Green State University: A 75-Year History, 1986; contbr. articles to profl. jours. Named Outstanding Young Woman of Am., 1987. Mem. NOW, AAUW, Am. Assn. Higher Edn., Orgn. Am. Historians. Democrat. Home: 2050 Allen St Allentown PA 18104 Office: Kutztown U 112 Old Main Bldg Kutztown PA 19530

WILLIS, VALERIE ANN, hotel executive; b. L.A., Mar. 12, 1947; d. Hal Bradford and Doris Mae (Holsworth) W.; m. Michael Lance Neil (div. 1992); children: Sarah, Amy. BS, San Diego State U., 1968; cert. secondary tchr., U.S. Internat. U., 1970. Tchr. Sweetwater Union High Sch. Dist., Chula Vista, Calif., 1970-75; owner The Country Peddler, Coronado, Calif., 1979-87; owner, dir. retail ops. Ribbons & Roses, Coronado, 1988—; sr. v.p. Hotel Del Coronado, 1989—; mem., dir. C.C. Fashion Adv. Coun., San Diego, 1993—. Dir. Mainstreet, Ltd., Coronado, 1988-89; bd. dirs. C. of C., Coronado, 1993-94; apptd. mem. Bus. Area Adv. Com., Coronado, 1990-93. Recipient Tribute to Women in Industry, YWCA, San Diego, 1992. Mem. Rotary Internat. (bd. dirs. 1993-95). Republican. Methodist. Home: 3657 Kite St San Diego CA 92103 Office: Hotel Del Coronado 1500 Orange Ave Coronado CA 92118

WILLISCROFT, BEVERLY RUTH, lawyer; b. Conrad, Mont., Feb. 24, 1945; d. Paul A. and Gladys L. (Buck) W.; m. Kent J. Barcus, Oct. 1984. BA in Music, So. Calif. Coll., 1967; JD, John F. Kennedy U., 1977. Bar: Calif., 1977. Elem. tchr., Sunnyvale, Calif., 1968-72; legal sec., legal asst. various law firms, Bay Area, 1972-77; assoc. Neil D. Reid, Inc., San Francisco, 1977-79; sole practice, Concord, Calif., 1979—; exam. grader Calif. Bar, 1979—; real estate broker, 1980-88; tchr. real estate King Coll., Concord, 1979-80; lectr. in field; judge pro-tem Mcpl. Ct., 1981-93. Bd dirs. Contra Costa Musical Theatre, Inc., 1978-82, v.p. adminstrn., 1980-81, v.p. prodn., 1981-82; mem. community devel. adv. com. City of Concord, 1981-83, vice chmn., 1982-83, mem. status of women com., 1980-81, mem. redevel. adv. com., 1984-86, planning commnr. 1986-92, chmn., 1990; mem. exec. bd. Mt. Diablo coun. Boy Scouts Am., 1981-85; bd. dirs. Pregnancy Ctrs. Contra Costa County, 1991—, chmn., 1993—. Recipient award of merit Bus. and Profl. Women, Bay Valley Dist., 1981. Mem. Concord C. of C. (bd. dir., chmn. govt. affairs com. 1981-83, v.p. 1985-87, pres. 1988-89, Bus. Person of Yr. 1986), Calif. State Bar (chmn. adoptions subcom. north, 1994), Contra Costa County Bar Assn., Todos Santos Bus. and Profl. Women (co-founder, pres. 1983-84, pub. rels. chmn. 1982-83, Woman of Achievement 1980, 81), Soroptimists (fin. sec. 1980-81). Office: 3018 Willow Pass Rd Ste 205 Concord CA 94519-2570

WILLMAN, DOROTHY LEE, editor; b. Memphis; d. Walter Lee and Rubye (James) Whitehurst; m. Richard Bernard Willman, June 22, 1963; children: Richard Lee, Laura Anne Willman Williams, Fred Douglas, Tiffany Joyce. AA, Stephens Coll., 1963. Co-owner, mgr. Willman's Inc., Claremore, Okla., 1977-91; trends editor Claremore Progress daily newspaper, 1992—. Contbr. articles to popular mags. Orgnl. leader Rogers County 4-H Horse Club, Claremore, 1980-90; Stephen Ministry lay min. 1st United Meth. Ch., Claremore, 1992—. Home: 108 Valley W Claremore OK 74017

WILLNER, ANN RUTH, political scientist, educator; b. N.Y.C., Sept. 2, 1924; d. Norbert and Bella (Richman) W. B.A. cum laude, Hunter Coll., 1945; M.A., Yale U., 1946; Ph.D., U. Chgo., 1961. Lectr. U. Chgo., 1946-47, research assoc. Ctr. for Econ. Devel. and Cultural Change, 1954-56, 61-62; advisor on orgn. and tng. Indonesian Ministry for Fgn. Affairs, Jakarta, 1952-53; expert for small scale indsl. planning Indonesian Nat. Planning Bur., Jakarta, 1953-54; fgn. affairs analyst Congl. Reference Service, Library of Congress, 1960; asst. prof. polit. sci. Harpur Coll., Binghamton, N.Y., 1962-63; postdoctoral fellow polit. sci. and Southeast Asian studies Yale U., New Haven, 1963-64; research assoc. Ctr. Internat. Studies, Princeton U., 1964-69; assoc. prof. polit. sci. U. Kans., Lawrence, 1969-70, prof., 1970—; vis. prof. polit. sci. CUNY, 1975; cons. govt. agys. and pvt. industry. Polit. sci. editor: Ency. of the Social Scis., 1961; mem. editorial bd. Econ. Devel. and Cultural Change, 1954-57, Jour. Comparative Adminstrn., 1969-74, Comparative Politics, 1977—; author: The Neotraditional Accomodation to Political Independence, 1966, Charismatic Political Leadership: A Theory, 1968, The Spellbinders, 1984; also monographs, articles, chpts. to books. Grantee Rockefeller Found., 1965, Social Sci. Research and Am. Council Learned Socs., 1966. Mem. Am. Polit. Sci. Assn. (gov. council 1979-81). Home: 2112 Terrace Rd Lawrence KS 66049-2733

WILLNER, DOROTHY, anthropologist, educator; b. N.Y.C., Aug. 26, 1927; d. Norbert and Bella (Richman) W. Ph.B., U. Chgo., 1947, M.A., 1953, Ph.D., 1961; postgrad., Ecole Pratique des Hautes Etudes, U. Paris, France, 1953-54. Anthropologist Jewish Agy., Israel, 1955-58; tech. asst., adminstrn. expert in community devel. UN, Mexico, 1958; asst. prof. dept. sociology and anthropology U. Iowa, Iowa City, 1959-60; research assoc. U. Chgo., 1961-62; asst. prof. dept. sociology and anthropology U. N.C., Chapel Hill, 1962-63, Hunter Coll., N.Y.C., 1964-65; assoc. prof. dept. anthropology U. Kans., Lawrence, 1967-70; prof. U. Kans., 1970-90; professorial lectr. Johns Hopkins U. Sch. Advanced Internat. Studies, 1992. Author: Community Leadership, 1960, Nation-Building and Community in Israel, 1969. Contbr. numerous articles to profl. publs. Fellow Am. Anthrop. Assn., Soc. Applied Anthropology, Royal Anthrop. Inst.; mem. Cen. States Anthrop. Soc. (past pres.), Assn. Polit. and Legal Anthropology (past pres.). Home: 5480 Wisconsin Ave Bethesda MD 20815-3530

WILLOUGHBY, CHERYL LYNN, government agency executive; b. Lumberton, N.C., Feb. 19, 1957; m. Margelet Campbell. BA, Wake Forest U., 1979; MFA, U. Hawaii, 1983. Co-founder, dir. C2 Prodns., Honolulu, 1983-87; drama edn. instr. Bladen County Schs., Elizabethtown, N.C., 1987-88; ext. 4-H youth devel. specialist USDA/N.C. State U., Raleigh, 1989-95; sch. age specialist USDA/U.S. Army, Honolulu, 1995—; del. People to People Youth Theater Tour, People's Republic of China, 1992. Recipient Razor Walker award U. N.C.-Wilmington. Mem. ASCD, Ext. Specialists Assn., Nat. Storytelling Assn. Democrat. Baptist. Home: 4300 Waialae Ave #1801A Honolulu HI 96816 Office: US Army Pacific Attn APPE-CFA Fort Shafter HI 96858

WILLS, CORNELIA, research director; b. Eastaboga, Ala.; d. Willie Jr. and Rosa Lee (Elston) W. BS, Austin Peay State U., 1974; MEd, Tenn. State U., 1992, EdD, 1996. Adminstrv. sec. Tenn. State U., Nashville, 1974-77, 79-81; office mgr., adminstrv. asst. Fisk U., Nashville, 1981-84; gift acctg. coord. Meharry Med. Coll., Nashville, 1984-88; rsch. analyst Tenn. Bd. Regents, Nashville, 1988-89; dir. instnl. rsch. Mid. Tenn. State U., Murfreesboro, 1989—; cons. faculty rsch. com., strategic planning com. Mid. Tenn. State U., 1989—; mem. Exec. Com. for Instnl. Effectiveness, 1992—; mem. Com. for Performance Funding, 1992—. Mem. Am. Assn. Instnl. Rsch., So. Assn. for Instnl. Rsch., Tenn. Assn. Instnl. Rsch., Women in Higher Edn. in Tenn., Delta Sigma Theta, Phi Delta Kappa. Baptist. Office: Mid Tenn State U 153 Jones Hall PO Box 140 Murfreesboro TN 37132

WILLS, IRENE YOUNG, accountant; b. Wellington, Tex., Aug. 9, 1950; d. William Tiffin and Edith Irene (Lindsey) Young; m. James Randolph Ward, Aug. 22, 1970 (div. 1987); m. Donald Eugene Wills, June 17, 1988; children: James Tiffin Ward, Lindsey DeAnne Ward. BA, Tex. Christian U., 1972; MBA, Angelo State U., 1992. Sr. acct. Grogan & Dane, CPAs, San Angelo, Tex., 1985-91, GTE, San Angelo, 1991-93; cash mgr. USAA Buying Svc., San Antonio, 1993—; mem. supervisory com. 1st Cmty. Fed., San Angelo, 1988-89, bd. dirs., 1989-91, chmn. bd. dirs., 1991. Pres. Shannon Med. Aux., San Angelo, 1982; bd. dirs. Tom Green County Child Welfare Bd., San Angelo, 1980-83, San Angelo Cultural Affairs Coun., 1983-89; chmn. Regional Child Welfare Coun., San Angelo, 1983. Mem. San Antonio Treasury Mgmt. Assn., Treasury Mgmt. Assn. (cert. cash mgr.), Inst. Mgmt. Accts., Jr. League San Angelo. Home: 7517 Fair Oaks Pkwy Fair Oaks Ranch TX 78015 Office: USAA Buying Svc 9800 Fredricksburg Rd San Antonio TX 78288

WILLS, KATHERINE VASILIOS TSIOPOS, English language educator, biology researcher; b. St. Louis, Sept. 30, 1957; d. Vasilios and Kalliope (Stratos) Tsiopos. BA, Washington U., 1979; MA, Ind. U., 1990. Rsch. dir. U. Chgo. (Ill.) Gynecology, 1980-82, Northwestern U., Chgo., 1982-86; pres. Port of Nashville (Ind.) Inc., retailer of nautical items and antiques, 1986—; pub. reader various orgns.; adj. faculty dept. English Indian and Purdue Univs., Indpls., 1991—, rsch. asst. dept. biology Alzheimers and Parkinsons disease studies, 1991—. Contbr. articles and poetry to jours. Vol. Women's Writers' Conf., Chgo.; fundraiser Am. Bar Assn.; greeter World Congress on Equality and Freedom, St. Louis; student worker on dig for Am. Indian artifacts Tenn. River Archeol. Project; debutant Am. Hellenic Progressgive and Ednl. Assn. Recipient essay award Scholastic Mag., Inc., 1973, award for acad. excellence and community svc. Am. Hellenic Progessive and Ednl. Assn., A poetry award Wednesday Club of St. Louis, Mo., 1977, Roger Conant Hatch hon. mention for writing, Washington U., 1977. Mem. NAFE, Nat. Histotechnologie Soc., MLA, Assn. Writers and Poets, Conf. on Coll. Composition and Communication, Midwest Regional Conf., Nat. Coun. Tchrs. English Poets and Writers Inc. Greek Orthodox. Home: 7772 East Bellsville Rd Nashville IN 47448-9642 Office: IUPUI Dept English PO Box 806 Indianapolis IN

WILLS, LOIS ELAINE, relgious education educator; b. Dayton, Ohio, Feb. 26, 1939; d. Harold Otto and Marjorie Elizabeth (Schmidt) Wallen; m. David P. Wills, Sept. 26, 1960 (dec.); children: Marianne, Melody, Michele. Student, Coll. of Mount St. Joseph. Cert. catechist. Educator, substitute various schs., 1985-90; gallery dir. Studio San Giuseppe, Cin., 1987-90; curator Murdock Art and Antiques, Cin., 1990-92; mgr. Cin. Antique Mall, 1992-93; dir. religious edn. St. John the Bapt., Dover, Ind., 1993—. Group exhibits include Clermont County Libr., Batavia, Ohio, 1990, Murdock Gallery, Cin., 1990, Studio San Giuseppe, Mount St. Joseph Coll., Cin., 1990, Milford Libr., Cin., 1991; represented in pvt. collections. Mem. Youth Encouragement Svcs., Aurora, Ind., 1985—; active Dearborn Highland Arts Coun., Lawrenceburg, Ind., 1990-95; mem. Rev. Club, Lawrenceburg, 1985—. Home: 1286 Indian Woods Trail Lawrenceburg IN 47025 Office: 25740 State Route #1 Guilford IN 47022

WILLSON, MARY F., ecology researcher, educator; b. Madison, Wis., July 28, 1938; d. Gordon L. and Sarah (Loomans) W.; m. R.A. von Neumann, May 29, 1972 (dec.). B.A. with honors, Grinnell Coll., 1960; Ph.D., U. Wash., 1964. Asst. prof. U. Ill., Urbana, 1965-71, assoc. prof., 1971-76, prof. ecology, 1976-90; rsch. ecologist Forestry Scis. Lab., Juneau, Alaska, 1989—; prin. rsch. scientist, affiliate prof. biology Inst. Arctic Biology U. Alaska, Fairbanks; faculty assoc. divsn. biol. scis. U. Mont., Missoula. Author: Plant Reproductive Ecology, 1983, Vertebrate Natural History, 1984; co-author: Mate Choice in Plants, 1983. Fellow AAAS, Am. Ornithologists Union; mem. Soc. for Study Evolution, Am. Soc. Naturalists (hon. mem.), Ecol. Soc. Am., Brit. Ecol. Soc. Office: Forestry Scis Lab 2770 Sherwood Ln Juneau AK 99801-8545

WILMER, ANN, public relations executive; b. Waynesboro, Pa., Oct. 18, 1952; d. Vaughn Edward and Frances Laura (Hudson) W. BS in Journalism cum laude, U. Fla., 1975, cert. of East Asian studies, 1975; EdM, Salisbury State Coll., 1979. Pub. rels. dir. Delmarva Adv. Coun., Salisbury, Md., 1975-77; advt. mgr. Ahtes & Hanna Ptnrs., Inc., Salisbury, 1979-80; substitute tchr. Wicomico County Sch. Bd., Salisbury, 1979-82; instr. Wor Wic Tech. C.C., 1982-85; pub. affairs officer Md. Dept. State Planning, Balt., 1985-87; publs. adminstr. Md. Dept. Housing and Cmty. Devel., 1988; pub. affairs officer Md. Dept. Natural Resources, 1988—; freelance editor, religion writer and pub. rels. cons.; cons. editor Cmty. Arts Alliance of Md., 1995—, Friends of José Carreras Internat. Leukemia Found., Seattle, 1995—. Active Md. State Dem. Com., 1982-86; nat. committeewoman Young Dems. of Am., Md., 1984-86; mem. Preservation Trust of Wicomico, Inc., 1990-96, pres., 1991-95; trustee Salisbury Area Property Owners Assn., 1991-92. Named Outstanding Young Woman of the Yr., Salisbury Jaycees, 1982. Mem. Soc. Profl. Journalists (v.p. U. Fla. chpt. 1973-74, Pres. award 1975). Office: Capital Letters 408 N Division St Ste A Salisbury MD 21801

WILMES, BARBARA JOHNSON, special education and early childhood educator; b. St. Peter, Minn., Aug. 12, 1946; d. Arthur J. and Bernadine M. (Dadey) Johnson; children: Lyle B., Lee B., Bob L., Bernie Joy. BS, Mankato State Coll., 1969; MS, Mankato State U., 1988; PhD, U. Nebr., 1995. Cert. tchr. of trainable mentally handicapped, vocat. home econs., educable mentally handicapped. Tchr. home econs. LeCenter (Minn.) Pub. Sch., 1969-71; early childhood and spl. edn. cons. LeSueur County ARC, LeCenter, 1972-88; early childhood and early childhood spl. edn. tchr. Le Sueur County Devel. Achievement Ctr., Waterville, Minn., 1973-77; substitute tchr. LeCenter and Cleveland (Minn.) Schs., 1977-81; mgr. Wilmes Meats, LeCenter, 1981-88; instr. spl. edn. Tarko (Mo.) Coll., 1988-90; asst. prof. spl. edn. and early childhood edn. Peru (Nebr.) State Coll., 1990-95; asst. prof. early childhood and spl. edn. Ga. Southwestern Coll., Americus, 1995—; speaker, cons., v.p., pres. N.W. Mo. Learning, Tarkis, 1988-90; cons. Peru Day Care, 1990-94; evaluator Project Evenstart, 1995, 96. Chair S.E. Deanery of Cath. Women, S.E. Minn.; advocate LeSueur County Assn. for Retarded Citizens, LeCenter, 1973-88. Nebr. Edn. Assn. scholar, 1993-94, scholar Home Econs. Assn., 1987. Mem. Coun. for Exceptional Children, Nat. Assn. for Edn. of Young Children (advisor for affiliate 1994), Delta Kappa Gamma, Phi Delta Kappa. Home: 2002 Armory Dr Americus GA 31709 Office: Ga Southwestern U Divsn of Edn Americus GA 31709

WILMOT, BONNIE ANNE MCQUEEN, special education educator; b. Yerington, N.Y., June 4, 1970; d. David Dale and Patricia Linda (Tognoni) Gelmstedt; m. John Charles Wilmot. BS, U. Nev., 1992. Cert. elem. and spl. edn. tchr., Nev. Spl. edn. tchr. Swope Mid. Sch., Reno, 1993—; co-founder Parent and Sibling Support Group, Reno, 1994-95. V.p. Student Coun. fo Exceptional Children, U. Nev., Reno, 1990-92. Mem. AAUW, Nat. Tchrs. Assn., Golden Key Nat. Honor Soc., Phi Kappa Phi. Democrat. Presbyterian. Home: 2011 S 28th St Lincoln NE 68502-3208 Office: Swope Mid Sch 901 Keele Dr Reno NV 89509

WILMOT, LOUISE C., retired naval commander, charitable organization executive; b. Wayne, N.J., Dec. 31, 1942; d. W.J. Currie and Dorothy Murphy; m. James E. Wilmot. BA in History, Coll. St. Elizabeth, Convent Sta., N.J., 1964; student, Naval War Coll., Newport, R.I., 1977; M in Legis. Affairs, George Washington U., 1978. Commd. ensign USN, 1964; advanced through grades to rear adm., 1991; comm. watch officer, registered publs. custodian, women's barracks officer Naval Air Sta., Pensacola, Fla.; with NATO staff Allied Forces, So. Europe, 1966-68; officer recruiter Recruiting Area Seven, Dallas; Naval Senate liaison officer Office Legis. Affairs, Washington; head women's equal opportunity br. Bur. Naval Pers., 1974-76; exec. officer Navy Recruiting Dist., Montgomery, Ala., 1977-79; command of Navy Recruiting Dist., Omaha, 1979-82; dep. dir accession policy Asst. Sec. Def. for Manpower, Installations, and Logistics, Washington, 1982-85; comdr. Navy Recruiting Area Five, Gt. Lakes, Ill., 1985-87; exec. asst., Naval aide Asst. Sec. Navy for Manpower and Reserve Affairs, Washington, 1987-89; comdr. Naval Tng. Ctr., Orlando, Fla., 1989-91; vice chief Naval Edn. and Tng., Pensacola, 1991-93; comdr. Naval Base, Phila., 1993-94; ret. U.S. Navy, 1994; dep. exec. dir. Cath. Relief Svcs., Balt., 1994—. Decorated DSM, Def. Superior Svc. medal, Legion of Merit with 3 gold stars. Office: Cath Relief Svcs 209 W Fayette St Baltimore MD 21201-3443

WILMOTH, HELGA HOWARD, German language educator; b. Hamburg, Germany, July 9, 1932; came to U.S., 1959; d. Hans Rudolf and Gertrud Erna (Lietz) Ruebcke; m. Herbert A. Howard, Dec. 17, 1958 (dec. Mar.

1972); children: Pamela Sue Howard White, Kimberly Ann; m. James Noel Wilmoth, Sept. 1, 1973; children: Jonathan Noel, Penelope Lynn McVicar, K. Natalie. BA, Ball State U., 1963, MA, 1965. Cert. tchr. Grad. asst. Ball State U., Muncie, Ind., 1963-65; instr. German Auburn (Ala.) U., 1971-72; tchr. German Auburn H.S., 1980-96. Named one of 60 Tchrs. recognized in The Disney Channel and McDonald's Salute: The Am. Tchr. TV series, 1996, 97. Mem. Am. Assn. Tchrs. German (pres. Ala. chpt. 1994-96), Ala. Assn. Fgn. Lang. Tchrs., So. Conf. on Lang. Tchg. (Outstanding Fgn. Lagn. Tchr. award 1995). Lutheran. Home: 1233 E Samford Ave Auburn AL 36830 Office: Auburn H S 405 S Dean Rd Auburn AL 36830-6201

WILMOTH, MARGARET CHAMBERLAIN, oncology nurse, researcher; b. Columbus, Ohio, Apr. 9, 1953; d. Grover Harold Sr. and Juanita Rose (Hinkle) Chamberlain; m. Frank C. Wilmoth; children: Michael, John, Wendy, Jennifer. BSN, U. Md., Balt., 1975, MS, 1979; PhD, U. Pa., 1993. Nurse intern Med. Coll. Va., Richmond, 1975-76; clin. nurse U. Md. Hosp., Balt., 1976-79; instr. Coll. Nursing U. Del., Newark, 1979-84, asst. prof. Coll. Nursing, 1984-92; assoc. prof. Cen. Mo. State U., Warrensburg, 1993-95; rsch. asst. prof. U. Kans. Sch. Nursing, 1995-96. Contbr. articles to profl. jours. Vol. Am. Cancer Soc. Lt. col. Nurse Corps, USAR. Am. Cancer Soc. scholar, 1990-93. Mem. ANA, Nat. League Nursing, Kans. Nurses Assn., Oncology Nursing Soc. (coord. psychosocial spl. interest group 1995—, mem. rsch. com. 1990-92), Sigma Theta Tau.

WILNER, JUDITH, journalist; b. Framingham, Mass., Mar. 30, 1943; d. John C. and Marjorie E. (Devonshire) Earley; m. David Alan Wilner, Aug. 27, 1964 (div. Aug. 1968); 1 child, Erica Susan; m. Fred Karp, July 28, 1991; 1 child, Shai Shalom Karp. BA in Letters, U. Okla., 1964. Wire editor, copy editor The Norman (Okla.) Transcript, 1967-72; news editor Loveland (Colo.) Reporter-Herald, 1972-73; editor of editl. page The Albuquerque Tribune, 1974-76, city editor, 1974-76; copy editor The Denver Post, 1976-77, copy desk chief, 1977-80, mgr. editl. sys., 1980-84; dep. tech. editor N.Y. Times, 1984-86, tech. editor, 1986—; women's editor The Norman Transcript, 1964-66. Mem. Newspaper Assn. of Am. (tech. com., chmn. wire svc. guidelines com. 1992—).

WILNER, LOIS ANNETTE, retired speech and language pathologist; b. Newark, Jan. 15, 1935; d. Benjamin and Ida (Schwam) Friedman; m. Sherman Wilner, July 6, 1957 (dec. Apr. 1996); children: Bonnie Joy, Robert Steven. BS, Newark State Tchrs. Coll., 1953-57; MA, Newark State Coll., 1969-73. Tchr. 5th grade Maplewood-South Orange Bd. Edn., South Orange, N.J., 1957-58; permanent substitute Parsippany (N.J.)-Troy Hills Bd. Edn., 1967-68, speech and language pathologist, 1968-95, ret., 1995; cons., speech and lang. pathologist Ctr. for Communication Disorders, Livingston, N.J., 1987-89. Mem. AAUW, NEA, N.J. Edn. Assn., Morris County Edn. Assn., N.J. Speech-Hearing Assn., Morris County Speech-Hearing Assn. (libr. 1987-90), B'nai B'rith Women (Roseland, Livingston and Suburban Essex chpt. pres. 1985-88), Alpha Delta Kappa (pres. chpt. 1990-92, N.J. state scholarship chmn. 1992-94). Home: 7609 Island Breeze Ter Boynton Beach FL 33437

WILSON, ALICE BLAND, real estate consultant; b. Rainelle, W.Va., Apr. 1, 1938; d. Brady Floyd and Mildred Martha (George) Bland; m. Louis William Groves, Jr., Apr. 20, 1957 (div. 1981); children: Martha Rachel, Leonora Jayne; m. Glen Parten Wilson, Dec. 11, 1982. AB, W.Va. U., 1959, postgrad. in microbiology, 1975-78. Contract adminstr. Washington Plate Glass Co., Washington, 1979-80; mem. acctg. staff Forbes Co., Washington, 1981; customer relations rep. Stern's Co., Washington, 1982; real estate assoc. Prudential Preferred Properties, Washington, 1985—. Contbr. articles to Jour. Parasitology. Vol. coord. John Glenn for Pres. campaign, Washington, 1983-84; co-chmn. hospitality com. Women's Nat. Dem. Club, Washington, 1985—; mem. internat. adv. coun. ARC, Washington, 1985—; mem. exec. com. Nat. Symphony Orch., 1990—. Mem. Washington Assn. Realtors (mem. residential sales com. 1985—), Leading Edge Soc., Million Dollar Club. Avocations: flying, aerobatics, nature study. Home: Box 25297 Washington DC 20007 Office: Pardoe Real Estate Inc 2828 Pennsylvania Ave NW Washington DC 20007

WILSON, ALMA, state supreme court justice; b. Pauls Valley, Okla.; d. William R. and Anna L. (Schuppert) Bell; m. William A. Wilson, May 30, 1948 (dec. Mar. 1994); 1 child, Lee Anne. AB, U. Okla., 1939, JD, 1941, LLD (hon.), 1992. Bar: Okla. 1941. Sole practice Muskogee, Okla., 1941-43; sole practice Oklahoma City, 1943-47, Pauls Valley, 1948-69; judge Pauls Valley Mcpl. Ct., 1967-68; apptd. spl. judge Dist. Ct. 21, Norman, Okla., 1969-75, dist. judge, 1975-79; justice Okla. Supreme Ct., Oklahoma City, 1982—, now chief justice. Mem. alumni bd. dirs. U. Okla.; mem. Assistance League; trustee Okla. Meml. Union. Recipient Guy Brown award, 1974, Woman of Yr. award Norman Bus. and Profl. Women, 1975, Okla. Women's Hall of Fame award, 1983, Pioneer Woman award, 1985, Disting. Svc. Citation U. Okla., 1985. Mem. AAUW, Garvin County Bar Assn. (past pres.), Okla. Bar Assn. (co-chmn. law and citizenship edn. com.), Okla. Trial Lawyers Assn. (Appellate Judge of Yr. 1986, 89), Altrusa, Am. Legion Aux. Office: Okla Supreme Ct State Capitol Rm B2 Oklahoma City OK 73105*

WILSON, BETTY MAY, resort company executive; b. Moberly, Mo., Mar. 13, 1947; d. Arthur Bunyon and Martha Elizabeth (Denham) Stephens; m. Ralph Felix Martin, Aug. 22, 1970 (div. May 1982); m. Gerald Robert Wilson Sr., Mar. 3, 1984; stepchildren: Gerald Robert Jr., Heather Lynn, Jeffrey Michael. BS in Acctg. and Bus. Adminstrn., Colo. State U., 1969. CPA, Mo. Tax mgr. Arthur Andersen and Co., St. Louis, 1969-75; v.p., asst. sec., dir. taxes ITT Fin. Corp., St. Louis, 1975-95; v.p. taxes Caesars World, Inc., Las Vegas, Nev., 1995—; sr. v.p., bd. dirs. Lyndon Ins. Co., St. Louis, 1977-95, ITT Lyndon Life Ins. Co., ITT Lyndon Property Ins. Co., St. Louis, 1977-95. Mem. AICPA, Mo. Soc. CPAs (chmn. family issues com.), Nev. Soc. CPAs, Am. Fin. Svcs. Assn. (chmn. tax com. 1987-88), Tax Execs. Inst. Inc. (chair corp. tax mgmt. com. 1993-95, regional v.p. 1995-96, exec. com. 1995-96, bd. dirs. St. Louis chpt., past sec., past pres.), Mo. Girls Racing Assn. (pres. 1977-82). Baptist. Office: Caesars World Inc Ste 1600 3800 Howard Hughes Pkwy Las Vegas NV 89109

WILSON, BLENDA JACQUELINE, academic administrator; b. Woodbridge, N.J., Jan. 28, 1941; d. Horace and Margaret (Brogsdale) Wilson; m. Louis Fair Jr. AB, Cedar Crest Coll., 1962; AM, Seton Hall U., 1965; PhD, Boston Coll., 1979; DHL (hon.), Cedar Crest Coll., 1987, Loretto Heights Coll., 1988, Colo. Tech. Coll., 1988, U. Detroit, 1989; LLD (hon.), Rutgers U., 1989, Ea. Mich. U., 1990, Cambridge Coll., 1991, Schoolcraft Coll., 1992. Tchr. Woodbridge Twp. Pub. Schs., 1962-66; exec. dir. Middlesex County Econ. Opportunity Corp., New Brunswick, N.J., 1966-69; exec. asst. to pres. Rutgers U., New Brunswick, N.J., 1969-72; sr. assoc. dean Grad. Sch. Edn. Harvard U., Cambridge, Mass., 1972-82; v.p. effective sector mgmt. Ind. Sector, Washington, 1982-84; exec. dir. Colo. Commn. Higher Edn., Denver, 1984-88; chancellor and prof. pub. adminstrn. & edn. U. Mich., Dearborn, 1988-92; pres. Calif. State U., Northridge, 1992—; Am. del. U.S./U.K. Dialogue About Quality Judgments in Higher Edn.; adv. bd. Mich. Consolidated Gas Co., Stanford Inst. Higher Edn. Rsch., U. So. Col. Dist. 60 Nat. Alliance, Nat. Ctr. for Rsch. to Improve Postsecondary Teaching and Learning, 1988-90; bd. dirs. Alpha Capital Mgmt.; mem. higher edn. colloquium Am. Coun. Edn., vis. com. Divsn. Continuing Edn. in Faculty of Arts & Scis., Harvard Coll., Pew Forum on K-12 Edn. Reform in U.S.; trustee Children's TV Workshop. Dir. U. Detroit Jesuit High Sch., Northridge Hosp. Med. Ctr., Arab Cmty. Ctr. for Econ. and Social Svcs., Union Bank, J. Paul Getty Trust, James Irvine Found., Internat. Found. Edn. and Self-Help, Achievement Coun., L.A.; dir., vice chair Met. Affairs Corp.; exec. bd. Detroit area coun. Boy Scouts Am.; bd. dirs. Commonwealth Fund, Henry Ford Hosp.-Fairlane Ctr., Henry Ford Health System, Met. Ctr. for High Tech., United Way Southeastern Mich.; mem. Nat. Coalition 100 Black Women, Detroit, Race Rels. Coun. Met. Detroit, Women & Founds., Greater Detroit Interfaith Round Table NCCJ, Adv. Bd. Valley Cultural Ctr., Woodland Hills; trustee assoc. Boston Coll.; trustee emeritus Cambridge Coll.; trustee emeritus, bd. dirs. Found. Ctr.; trustee Henry Ford Mus. & Greenfield Village, Sammy Davis Jr. Nat. Liver Inst. Mem. AAUW, Assn. Governing Bds. (adv. coun. of pres.'s), Edn. Commn. of the States (student minority task force), Am. Assn. Higher Edn. (chair-elect), Am. Assn. State Colls. & Univs. (com. on policies & purposes, acad. leadership fellows selection com.), Assn. Black Profls. and Adminstrs., Assn. Black Women in Higher Edn., Women Execs. State Govt., Internat. Women's Forum, Mich. Women's Forum, Women's Econ. Club Detroit, Econ. Club, Rotary. Office: Calif State Univ Office of President 18111 Nordhoff St Northridge CA 91330-0001

WILSON, CAROL ANN, business manager; b. Hardtner, Kans., Dec. 29, 1942; d. Elmer C. and Dorothy B. (Joachims) Hartwig; m. Robert Carlisle Wilson; children: Kimberly Skinner, Stacey Hedges. BSEd, Northwestern Okla. State U., Alva, 1963; MS Sch Adminstrn., Ft. Hays (Kans.) State U., 1991. Cert. Kans. Sec. Northwestern Okla. State U., 1963-66; tchr. Unified Sch. Dist. # 507, Satanta, Kans., 1966-67, sec., 1967-81, clerk of bd., 1981-91; legal sec. Neubauer, Sharp, Liberal, Kans., 1991; ednl. fin. cons. Porter & Kreie, CPA, Ulysses, Kans., 1991-92; bus. mgr. Unified Sch. Dist. # 214, Ulysses, Kans., 1992—; ednl. cons. Unified Sch. Dist. # 214, Ulysses, 1991-92; liaison, cons. Satanta Rec. Com. Mem. bd. dirs. Satanta Recreation Commn.; mem. Youth Orgn. Club Civic Group, Satanta, Satanta C. of C., Satanta Arts Coun. Mem. AAUW, Kans. Assn. Sch. Bus. Officials, Assn. Sch. Bus. Officials. Republican. Lutheran. Home: 611 Santee Box 655 Satanta KS 67870 Office: Unified Sch Dist # 214 111 S Baughman St Ulysses KS 67880

WILSON, CAROLYN CAMPBELL, art historian; b. Bryn Mawr, Pa., Dec. 1, 1946; d. Robert North and Ruth (Spurlock) W.; m. Michael Ede Newmark, Aug. 28, 1976; children: Georgina Newmark, Serena Newmark, Diana Newmark. BA, Wellesley Coll., 1968; MA, NYU, 1970, diploma mus. tng. and connoisseurship, 1970, PhD, 1977. Lectr. Index of Christian Art Princeton (N.J.) U., 1975; lectr. U. Md., College Park, 1976-77; asst. curator of sculpture Nat. Gallery of Art, Washington, 1978-83; rsch. curator for Renaissance art Mus. Fine Arts, Houston, 1983-93; ind. scholar, 1994—; mem. collections com. Children's Mus., Houston, 1987-93. Author: Small Bronze Sculpture at the National Gallery of Art, 1983, Italian Paintings...Museum of Fine Arts, 1996. Grantee Ford Found., 1970-73, Kress Found., 1990, Getty Grants Program, 1988, Gladys Krieble Delmas Found., 1995. Mem. Coll. Art Assn., Renaissance Soc. Am., Midwest Art History Assn., Assn. Ind. Historians of Art, News on the Rialto, Wellesley Coll. Friends of Art. Home: 2222 Goldsmith St Houston TX 77030-1119

WILSON, CAROLYN RENEE, accountant; b. Grand Forks, N.D., Aug. 14, 1963; d. David Michael and Claudette Marie (Reinke) Ostlund; m. Thomas M. Stanley Jr., Aug. 3, 1985 (div. May 1989); m. Donald Tracy Wilson, Feb. 1, 1993; 1 child, Feirin Page. BSBA, U. Nebr., Omaha, 1990. Interrogator/debriefer U.S. Army, Ft. Monmouth, Nev., 1983-86; analyst Union Pacific Railroad, Omaha, 1990-92, mgr. supplier rels. and rsch., 1992-95, customer equipment mgr., 1995-96, asset mgr., 1996—. Departmental coord. United Way, Omaha, 1994-95; fundraiser YWCA, Omaha, 1991-92. With U.S. Army, 1983-86. Mem. NAFE, Fund for Effective Govt. Republican. Roman Catholic. Office: Union Pacific Railroad 1416 Dodge St Rm 500 Omaha NE 68179

WILSON, CAROLYN TAYLOR, librarian; b. Cookeville, Tenn., June 10, 1936; d. Herman Wilson and Flo (Donaldson) Taylor; m. Larry Kittrell Wilson, June 14, 1957 (dec.); children: Jennifer Wilson Rust, Elissa Anne Wilson. BA, David Lipscomb Coll., 1957; MLS, George Peabody Coll., 1976. Tchr. English Fulton County Sch. System, Atlanta, 1957-59; serials cataloger Vanderbilt U. Libr., Nashville, 1974-77; asst. libr. United Meth. Pub. House, Nashville, 1978-80; collection devel. libr. David Lipscomb U., Nashville, 1980—; cons. and rschr. in field; project dir. Tenn.'s Lit. Legacy for Tenn. Humanities Coun., 1994—, ALA grant, Frontier in Am. Culture, 1996-98. Rsch. asst. Handbook of Tennessee Labor History, 1987-89. Adv. bd. So. Festival of Books, Nashville, 1988-90, 90—, vol. coord., 1989, 90—; project dir. Women's Words (summer grant program) for Tenn. Humanities Coun., Tenn.'s Literary Legacy (summer grant program), 1994-96. Recipient Nat. Honor Soc. award Phi Alpha Theta, 1956, Internat. Honor Soc. award Beta Phi Mu, 1980, Frances Neel Cheney award Tenn. Libr. Assn., 1992; nominee Athena award, 1992; Growing Up Southern summer grantee, 1996—. Mem. ALA, Tenn. Hist. Soc., Tenn. Libr. Assn. (Frances Neel Cheney award 1992), Southeastern Libr. Assn. (chmn. outstanding S.E. author award com. 1991-92, chmn. So. Books competition 1992-94), Women's Nat. Book Assn. (pres., v.p., treas., awards chmn. 1980—), Tenn. Writers Alliance (bd. dirs. 1995—). Democrat. Office: David Lipscomb U Univ Libr # 317 Nashville TN 37204

WILSON, CASSANDRA, singer; b. Jackson, Miss., 1955. Albums include Point of View, 1986, Blue Skies, 1988, Days Aweigh, 1987, Jumpworld, 1990, She Who Weeps, 1991, Cassandra Wilson Live, 1992, Blue Light 'Till Dawn, 1993, Dance to the Drums Again, 1993, After the Beginning Again, 1994, New Moon Daughter, 1996. Office: c/o Blue Note Records 1290 Avenue of the Americas 35th Fl New York NY 10104*

WILSON, CATHERINE COOPER (KITTY WILSON), communications executive, writer; b. Dallas, Sept. 17, 1955; d. William Edward and Suzanne (Blessington) Cooper; m. James Alan Wilson, Oct.17, 1981; children: Nicholas James, Gregory Cooper. BA in Journalism, Tex. Tech U., 1977. Pub. rels. asst. Dallas Market Ctr., 1972-75, 77; pub. rels. coord. Herman Blum Engrs., Dallas, 1977-80, coord. new bus. devel., 1980; acct. exec. Helen Holmes & Assoc., Dallas, 1980; mktg. and pub. rels. coord. EDI Architects, Dallas, 1980-82; pres. Catherine Wilson Comm., Dallas, 1982—; owner, v.p. Wilson Creative, Inc., Dallas, 1988—. Contbr. articles to trade mags. Mem. membership com. North Tex. Commn., Dallas, 1979-81; mem. pub. rels. com., bldg. com. St. Rita Cath. Ch., Dallas, 1984-87. Mem. Greater Dallas Writers Assn. Roman Catholic. Home and Office: 6435 Sudbury Dr Dallas TX 75214-2435

WILSON, CATHERINE MARY, financial consultant; b. N.Y.C., Aug. 16, 1957; d. Daniel F. and Mary P. (Lowth) W.; m. Raymond A. Powers, May 26, 1985; children: Colin Wilson Powers, Alanna Wilson Powers. BS in Acctg., CUNY, 1979; MBA in Fin. and Mktg., Pace U., 1982; cert. in mgmt. acctg., Inst. Cert. Mgmt. Accts., 1988. Acct. Conrac Corp., Stamford, Conn., 1979-83; mktg. analyst Reader's Digest Assn., Pleasantville, N.Y., 1983, fin. analyst, 1984-85, mgr. accounts payable, 1985-88, mgr. corp. forecasting and fin. analysis, 1988-91, mgr. mktg. analysis, 1991-94; pres. Money Mastery Workshops, Inc., Thornwood, N.Y., 1994—. Mem. Nat. Assn. Accts., Toastmasters Internat. (treas. Pleasantville club 1989, 1st pl. award tri-state speech evaluation contest 1989).

WILSON, CHARLENE WILLA, industrial sales specialist; b. Jim Thoppe, Pa., Feb. 13, 1943; d. Charles Byron and Jennie Larue (Levis) Frehulfer; m. Arthur David Wilson, Oct. 13, 1962 (div. Dec. 1982); 1 child, Edward; m. Arthur David Wilson, Dec. 23, 1987. Student, E. Stroudsburg State Coll., Pa., 1961-62. Tchr. part-time Lourdesmont Sch., Clarks Green, Pa., 1973-81; seamstress Barbini Bridals, Scranton, Pa., 1981-82; credit corr. Tose Fowler, Inc., Scranton, 1982-84; sales rep. Challenge Industries, Inc., Sparta, N.J., 1984-85, asst. dist. mgr., 1985-86, product specialist, 1986-87, dist. sales mgr. for Pa. and N.Y., 1987-90; corp. liaison Challenge Industries, Inc., Sparta, 1990-92, key account exec., 1990-92; enroller Nat. Assn. for Self-employed, agt. PFL Life Ins. United Group Assocs., Irving, Tex., 1992-95; owner CW Wilson & Assocs., Union Dale, Pa., 1995—; Pa. del. White House Conf. on Bus. Author poems. Mem. Chinchilla (Pa.) Fire Co. Women's Aux., 1963-83; bd. dirs. Waverly, Pa. chpt. Abington Players, 1975-81. Mem. NAFE, VFW Women's Aux., VFW Elk Mountain Aux., Forest City Bus. and Profl. Women, Keynotes (sec. Clarks Summit chpt. 1969-77), Pa. Interscholastic Athletic Assn. (track and swimming ofcl. Lackawanna, Pa. chpt. 1975—), Susquehanna County C. of C. Republican. Episcopalian. Home and Office: RR 1 Box 117W Union Dale PA 18470-9747

WILSON, DONNA MAE, foreign language educator, administrator; b. Columbus, Ohio, Feb. 25, 1947; d. Everett John and Hazel Margaret (Bruck) Palmer; m. Steven L. Wilson, Nov. 16, 1968. BA, Ohio State U., 1973, MA, 1976; postgrad studies, U. Wash., Seattle Pacific U., 1980-93; cert., U. Salamanca, Spain, 1985. Tchg. assoc. Ohio State U., Columbus, 1974-76; lectr. U. Wash., Seattle, 1977-78; grants officer Seattle U., 1978-82; adj. prof. Shoreline Coll., Seattle, 1982-84; coord. fgn. langs., prof. Spanish Bellevue (Wash.) Coll., 1984-87; prof. Spanish Highline Coll., Des Moines, Wash., 1987—, chair fgn. lang. dept., 1990-94; chair arts and humanities Highline Coll., Des Moines, 1994—; bd. dirs. Wash. C.C.s, Olympia, 1991—; spkr. at lang. orgns., confs. regional and nat., 1985—. Editor: (book) Fronteras: En Contacto, 1992-93; (jours.) Modern Lang. Jour., 1991, 92, 94, Hispania, 1993; text editor D. C. Heath and Co., Harcourt, Brace and Jovanovich, Houghton Mifflin, Prentice Hall; contbr. articles to profl. jours., chpt. to book. Recipient cert. of excellence Phi Theta Kappa, 1990, Pathfinder award Phi Beta Kappa, 1995; fellowshp grant Coun. Internat. Edn. Exchange, Santiago, Chile, 1992. Mem. Am. Assn. Tchrs. of Spanish (v.p. Wash.), Am. Coun. Tchrs. of Fgn. Langs. (cert. oral proficiency), Assn. Dept of Fgn. Langs. (exec. bd. 1994—), Pacific N.W. Coun. Fgn. Langs., 1986—, Nat. Assn. Fgn. Lang. Suprs., Sigma Delta Mu. (nat. exec. sec. 1992—). Home: 8720 229th Pl SW Edmonds WA 98026-8438 Office: Highline Coll 240th & Pacific Hwy S Des Moines WA 98198

WILSON, DORIS H., volunteer; b. Akron, Ohio, Jan. 26, 1921; d. Charles Peter and Emma Clara (Howald) Huff; m. Angus Francis Wilson, June 14, 1952; children: Ann, Lea. BS, U. Akron, 1945; postgrad., Framingham State Coll., 1965, Salem State Coll., 1968. Adminstrv. asst. divsn. comml. engr. Ohio Bell Telephone Co., Akron, 1941-52; adminstr. Framingham Ctr. Kindergarten and Nursery Sch., 1965-68. Author: A History of Great Neck, Ipswich, 1984, 96. Vol. nurse's aide ARC, Akron, 1940s; mem. Gov.'s Coun. Civilian Def., Boston, 1960-66; co-founder, charter mem. Hospice at Home, Wayland, Weston, Natick, Sudbury, Mass., 1978; chmn. West Suburban Area Boston Symphony Orch. Coun. of Friends, 1978-81; docent The Great House at Castle Hill, Ipswich, 1984—, The Whipple House, Ipswich, 1985—; treas. Nuclear Freeze Coun., Ipswich, 1986-87; charter mem., bd. dirs. Aplastic Anemia Found. of Am. New Eng. region, Brookline, Mass., 1987-92; vol. office asst. Habitat for Humanity, St. Petersburg, Fla., 1988. Recipient Election Poll Officer citation Gov. of Mass., 1980. Mem. AAUW (charter mem., pres. Framingham-Wellesley Br., North Shore Br., grantee 1974), Boston Symphony Assn. of Vols., Peace Action, Ipswich Hist. Soc., Ipswich Woman's Club, Ipswich Bay Yacht Club (dir. 1981-82), Friends of Glen Magna (Danvers, Mass. dir. 1991-93), Wayland Woman's Club (hon. mem., pres.). Democrat. Roman Catholic. Home: 8 Bowdoin Rd Ipswich MA 01938

WILSON, DOROTHY FINLEY, educator; b. Albemarle County, Va., Nov. 1, 1920; d. William Walter and Melissa (Hoover) Finley; m. John Neville Wilson, Oct. 28, 1944; children: Melissa Wilson Atkinson, Elizabeth Wilson Alford, Kathleen Wilson Post. BS in Secondary Edn., James Madison U., 1943. Cert. secondary tchr., Va. Sec. to dir. pers. and employment Tenn. Eastman, Oak Ridge, 1943-44; exec. sec. ARC, Benton County, Washington, 1944-45; sec., bd. dirs. Hitchcock Rehab. Ctr., Aiken, S.C., 1958-70; reading tutor Aiken County Pub. Schs., 1970-85, instr., tutor tng., 1980-84; guardian ad litem Gov.'s Program for S.C., Aiken County, 1985-95. Mem. women's bd. Aiken 1st Presbyn. Ch., 1980, Sunday sch. tchr., moderator, 1952-95, Stephen min., 1995—; hon. life mem. Presbyn. Women; active Girl Scouts U.S., Aiken, 1953-68. Mem. Kappa Delta Pi. Democrat. Home: 1208 Abbeville Ave NW Aiken SC 29801

WILSON, ELEANOR VERNON, education educator; b. Boston, Apr. 7, 1940; d. Arthur Andrew and Hope (Jillson) Vernon; m. Richard Guy Wilson, Aug. 15, 1964; children: Kristina Forsyth, Abigail Elisabeth Victoria. AB, Brown U., 1962; EdM, Harvard U., 1963; PhD, U. Va., 1991. Elem. sch. tchr. Harrington Sch., Lexington, Mass., 1963-67, Spring St. Sch., Newport, R.I., 1963-67; asst. prof. edn. Ea. Mich. U., Ypsilanti, 1967-72, Iowa State U., Ames, 1973-76; elem. sch. tchr. Venable Sch., Charlottesville, Va., 1976-85; asst. prof. edn. U. Va., Charlottesville, 1991—; bd. dirs. Found. for Excellence, Charlottesville. Bd. mem. City Dem. Party, Charlottesville, 1985—. Mem. Am. Ednl. Rsch. Assn., Ea. Ednl. Rsch. Assn., Va. Edn. Assn. Democrat. Episcopalian. Home: 1860 Field Rd Charlottesville VA 22903 Office: U Va Curry Sch Edn 212 Ruffner Hall Charlottesville VA 22903

WILSON, ELIZABETH J(ANE), artist, educator; b. Phila., June 24, 1959. Attended, Corcoran Sch. Art, Washington, 1978-79; cert., Pa. Acad. Fine Arts, 1984. Represented by F.A.N. Gallery, Phila., Barbara Gillman Gallery, Miami, Fla., Bennett Galleries, Knoxville, Tenn., Rabbet Gallery, New Brunswick, N.J., Carspecker-Scott Gallery, Wilmington, Del.; assoc. adj. prof. Temple U., Phila., 1988-95; adj. prof. C.C. Phila., 1993, U. of Arts, Phila., 1994—; adj. asst. prof. Phila. Coll. Textiles and Sci., 1996. Solo shows include Pa. State U., Middletown, Pa., 1988, Gross McCleaf Gallery, Phila., 1990, 92, F.A.N. Gallery, Phila., 1994, 96; group shows include Marian Locks Gallery, Phila., 1985, So. Alleghenies Mus. Art, Loretto, Pa., 1986, First St. Gallery, N.Y.C., 1988, 95, Gallery East, East Hampton, N.Y., 1988, Gross McCleaf Gallery, 1989, Woodmere Art Mus., Phila., 1990, Phila. Mus. Art, 1990, Allentown (Pa.) Art Mus., 1992, Butler Inst. Am. Art, Youngstown, Ohio, 1993, Bennett Galleries, 1993, F.A.N. Gallery, 1993, Alexandria (La.) Mus., 1993, Mus. Am. Art at Pa. Acad. Fine Arts, 1994, Nat. Acad. Design, N.Y.C., and many others; permanent collections include West Allis Meml. Hosp., Milw., Johnson & Johnson, New Brunswick, E.I. DuPont de Nemours Co., Wilmington, Del., CCA Chicago Plz. Club, Bryn Mawr Coll., Bristol-Meyers Squibb Corp., Plainsboro, N.J., many others. Recipient First prize City of Camden Art Exhbn., 1988. Fellow Pa. Acad. Fine Arts (Catherine Gibbons Granger painting award 1993). Home: 126 Sumac St Philadelphia PA 19128

WILSON, ELIZABETH PEMBERTON LEWIS, primary school educator; b. Bryn Mawr, Pa., July 20, 1955; d. Thomas Arlington and Eleanor Mary (Troth) Lewis; m. Richard Wentworth Wilson, Jr., Apr. 19, 1980; 2 children. BA in Sociology and Fgn. Affairs, U. Va., 1977; MS in Sociology, Va. Commonwealth U., 1982; postgrad., Ga. State U. Counselor Commonwealth of Va. Employment Svcs., Culpeper, 1978; legis. aide to Rep. M. Caldwell Butler U.S. Ho. of Reps. 96th Congress, Washington, 1979-80; mgmt. cons. nat. and state policy Maximus, Inc., Washington, 1980-81; program adminstr. Dept. Housing Preservation & Devel., N.Y.C., 1981-82; budget coord., account mgmt. Ally & Gargano, Inc., N.Y.C., 1982, asst. account exec., 1982-83; staff adminstr. III MCI Telecomms., L.A., 1983-85, mgr. II sales and revenue support, 1985-86; lead tchr. sci. The Cathedral Presch., Atlanta, 1989-95, lead tchr. kindergarten, 1990—, asst. tchr. art, 1990-91; adj. prof. dept. social scis. J. Sargeant Reynolds C.C., Richmond, Va., 1977-79; trainer Tchr-in-Svc. courses, Atlanta, 1995—. Editor: The Bear Facts, 1987-89, The Shepherd's Watch, 1988-89. Leader Girl Scouts Am., Marietta, Ga., 1991-94; bullroast com. U. Va. Alumni Assn. Atlanta chpt., 1988-89, chairperson career forum schs. com. Atlanta chpt., 1990-92, bd. advisor Atlanta chpt., 1991-92; chairperson Childkind Project The Cathedral of St. Philip, Atlanta, 1993-94. Mem. AAUW, Am. Sociol. Assn., Ga. Presch. Assn. Episcopalian.

WILSON, EMILY HERRING, writer; b. West Point, Ga., June 11, 1939; d. Roy Clyde and Sarah O'Neal (Allen) Herring; m. Edwin G. Wilson, July 4, 1964; children: Edwin G. Jr., Sarah Elizabeth, Julie Cathleen. BA, U. N.C., Greensboro, 1961; MA, Wake Forest U., 1962. Instr. English, Wake Forest U., Winston-Salem, N.C., 1962-64, Salem Coll., Winston-Salem, 1964-65, 82-85; vis. writer Cornell U., Ithaca, N.Y., 1993. Author: (poetry) Balancing on Stones, 1975, Hope and Dignity, 1983. Chmn. People for Am. Way, N.C., 1990-92. Rsch. grantee NEH, 1979-81, grantee N.C. Arts Coun., 1992; fellow NacDowell Colony. Mem. Phi Beta Kappa. Democrat. Home: 3381 Timberlake Ln Winston Salem NC 27106

WILSON, ESTHER ELINORE, technical college educator; b. Uehling, Nebr., Nov. 4, 1921; d. Lorenz John and Dorothea Emma Rosena (Schmidt) Paulsen; m. Billy LeRoy Wilson, Nov. 14, 1919; 1 child, Frances Ann Wilson Dellar. BS, Morningside Coll., 1950; postgrad., U. Nebr., 1947-80, U. S.D., 1954-83; MS, U. Minn., 1963. Cert. postsecondary tchr., Iowa. Tchr. Irvington (Nebr.) Pub. Schs., 1942-44, Immanuel Luth. Schs., Wichita, Kans., 1944-45, Winnebago (Nebr.) Pub. Schs., 1946-50, Nat. Bus. Coll., Sioux City, Iowa, 1950-51; tchr., asst. prin. Liberty Consol. Sch., Merrill, Iowa, 1951-55; mktg. tchr. coord. South Sioux City (Nebr.) Community Schs., 1955-86; adj. faculty prof. adult basic edn. Western Iowa Tech. Coll., Sioux City, 1989-94; mgr. rental properties Sioux City, 1950—; real estate assoc. State Nat., Dakota City, Nebr., 1988-92, Century 21 Marketplace, Sioux City, 1987-88; advt. sales mgr. Auto Hotline, South Sioux City, 1986-87. Author: I Said I Would, 1995; contbg. author: Siouxland Anthology, 1995, Capturing Our Heritage. Vol. tchr. N.E. Nebr. C.C., South Sioux City, 1987-90; supt. St. Paul's Luth. Sunday Sch., Sioux City, 1972-76; treas. Hope Luth. Ch., 1989-95; SBA counselor SCORE, 1995—; co-pres. Friends of Libr., South Sioux City, 1986-88; fundraiser South Sioux City Pub. Libr.,

1984-85; pres. Am. Cancer Soc., Dakota County, Nebr., 1979-88; state pres. Nebr. Bus. Edn. Assn., 1979, Distributive Edn. Tchrs. Assn., 1980. Recipient Outstanding Svc. to State Orgns., Nebr. Vocat. Edn. Assn., 1976, Woman of the Yr. Am. Bus. Women Assn., 1972. Mem. Nebr. State Edn. Assn. (sec., treas., v.p., pres., Dedicated Svc. award 1986), NEA, South Sioux City Chamberettes (sec., v.p., pres. 1972-89), Am. Federated Women's Club (sec., v.p., pres.). Home and Office: 435 Dixon Path South Sioux City NE 68776

WILSON, FRANCES EDNA, protective services official; b. Keokuk, Iowa, Aug. 4, 1955; d. David Eugene and Anna Bell (Hootman) W. BA, St. Ambrose Coll., 1982; MA, Western Ill., 1990; cert. massage therapist, Shocks Ctr. for Edn., Moline, Ill., 1993. Lic. massage therapist, Iowa. Trainer, defensive tactics Davenport (Iowa) Police, 1990—, police corporal, 1985-94; police sgt. Iowa Assn. Women Police, Davenport, 1994—, apptd. recs. bur. comdr., 1996—, pres., 1989-92; cons., def. tactics Scott C.C., Bettendorf, Iowa, 1993—; owner Wilson Enterprises Ltd., Davenport, 1995—; spkr. workshops; guest spkr. Genesis Employee Assistance Program, 1996. Bd. dirs. Scott County Family YMCA, Davenport, 1990-95, instr., 1989—, The Family Connection, Ltd.; instr. Davenport Cmty. Adult Edn., 1991-94; mem. Iowa SAFE KIDS Coalition, 1992—; mem. First Presbyn. Ch., Davenport, 1986—, bd. deacons, 1995; vol. asst. Davenport Police Dept.'s Sgts. Planning Com. on Tng., 1991, K-9 Unit, 1990-94. Mem. Am. Soc. Law Enforcement Trainers, Law Enforcement Alliance Am., Am. Women Self Def. Assn., Iowa Assn. Women Police (pres. 1989-92, Officer of Yr. 1995), Iowa State Police Assn., Internat. Platform Assn., Internat. Assn. Women Police. Office: Davenport Police Dept 420 N Harrison St Davenport IA 52801-1310

WILSON, GERTRUDE ELIZABETH, medical and surgical nurse; b. San Antonio, June 25, 1937; d. Roy Roland and Hazel Lee (Grunewald) Brown; m. Edward Michael Wilson, Jan. 17, 1961; children: Sandra Kay, Clara Lee, Katherine Ann, Edward M. Jr. Student, S.W. Tex. State U., 1983, San Antonio Coll., 1992; ADN, Victoria Coll., 1994. RN, Tex. Office nurse, vol. Free Christian Clinic, Seguin, Tex., 1992-94; med. surg. nurse Guadalupe Valley Hosp., Seguin, Tex., 1994—; cmty. liaison officer Victoria Coll., Seguin Campus, 1992-94. Camp dir. Ch. of Latter Day Saints, San Antonio, 1979, pres. relief soc., 1985, Sun. sch. tchr., Seguin, 1994—; nurse alumni rep. Victoria Coll., Seguin, 1994—. Fellow ANA, Tex. Nurse Assn. LDS.

WILSON, JANICE ARLENE BURRELL, special education educator; b. Hamilton, Ind., Mar. 14, 1937; d. Marion Russell Burrell and Aileen Margaret (Wandell) Burrell-Dodds; m. Gerald Robert Wilson, Jan. 17, 1959; children: Robert Douglas, Amy Lucille. BS in Edn., Ball State U., 1958; MEd, Wayne State U., 1963. Tchr. of homebound Macomb Intermediate Sch. Dist., Mt. Clemens, Mich., 1958-65, rehab. counselor, 1969—, Project Find specialist, 1977-92; part-time instr. in tchr. edn. Wayne State U., Detroit, 1969-75. Recreation commr. City of Fraser, Mich., 1975-85; commr. Air Pollution Control Com., State of Mich., Lansing, 1985-92; councilwoman City of Fraser 1983-87, 1992-93, mayor pro tem, 1987-91; bd. dirs. Macomb Child Abuse Info. Coun., 1980-90; pres. Goodfellows, 1988—. Recipient Golden Nugget award Blue Water Coun. for Exceptional Children, 1988, Jane Scandary award for Excellence in Early Childhood Edn., 1992; named Handicapped Profl. Woman of the Yr., Pilot Club of South Macomb, 1982, Citizen of the Week Sta. WWJ, 1992. Mem. Amputee Golf Assn. (bd. dirs., state champion women's div. 1971, trophy 1971, 72, 73). Democrat. Office: Macomb Intermed Sch Dist 44001 Garfield Rd Clinton Township MI 48038-1100

WILSON, JANIS KAY, marketing executive; b. Anamosa, Iowa, Dec. 28, 1939; d. Clyde S. and Irma L. (Davis) W. B.F.A., Drake U., 1962. Copywriter, Chase Manhattan Bank, N.Y.C., 1962-66; presentation mgr. Newspaper Advt. Bur., N.Y.C., 1966-71; mktg./promotion mgr. Metromedia, N.Y.C., 1971-74; sr. promotion writer N.Y. Times, 1974-78; dir. mktg. svc. Crain Communications, N.Y.C., 1978-83; promotion dir., Standard Rate & Data Svc. div. Macmillan Pub., Wilmette, Ill., 1984-88, circulation dir., 1988-89; copy supr. The Bradford Exchange, Niles, Ill., 1989—. Mem. Direct Mktg. Assn. Republican. Roman Catholic. Home: 927 Suffolk Ct Libertyville IL 60048-5218 Office: The Bradford Exch 9333 N Milwaukee Ave Niles IL 60714-1303

WILSON, JEAN CAROL, art history educator; b. Point Pleasant, N.J., Aug. 4, 1950; d. A. Noel and Emma (Farr) W. BA, Am. U., 1972; MA, Johns Hopkins U., 1975, MEd, 1978, PhD, 1984. Rsch. asst. Ctr. for Advanced Study in Visual Arts, Washington, 1982-84; A.W. Mellon postdoctoral fellow in humanities Cornell U., Ithaca, N.Y., 1984-86; asst. prof. art history SUNY, Binghamton, 1986-94, assoc. prof. art history, 1995—. Contbr. articles to profl. publs. Grantee Samuel H. Kress Found., 1975, Adolf Katzenellenbogen Meml. Fund, 1976; Dorothy Miner fellow Balt. Bibliophiles, 1977, Gilman fellow Johns Hopkins U., 1974-78, 79-80, Robert H. and Clarice Smith fellow Nat. Gallery Art, 1978-79, Andrew Mellon fellow Cornell U., 1984-86, Am. Coun. Learned Socs., 1987, J. Paul Getty Grant Program, 1989-90. Mem. AAUW, Am. Hist. Assn., Am. Assn. Netherlandic Studies, Coll. Art Assn., Historians of Netherlandish Art, Medieval Acad. Am., Renaissance Soc. Am. Office: SUNY Dept Art History Binghamton NY 13902-6000

WILSON, JEAN L., retired state legislator; b. Phila., June 13, 1928; d. Horace and Catherine (Lennox) Terry; widowed; children: Sheryl J. Gordon, Denise T. Munn. BS in Edn., Pa. State U., 1949. Tchr. Columbia Inst., Phila., 1949-50, Wilkes Coll., Wilkes Barre, Pa., 1950-51; office mgr., exec. sec. Camden Fibre MIlls, Warminster, Pa., 1968-80; mem. Pa. Ho. of Reps., 1988-92. Active Bucks County Coun. Rep. Women, Doylestown V.I.A.; mem. bd. Bucks County Opportunity Coun., Bucks County chpt. Fox Chase Cancer Ctr. Home and Office: 12 Far View Rd Chalfont PA 18914-2511

WILSON, JEAN MARIE HALEY, civic worker; b. Dallas, Oct. 16, 1921; d. William Eldred and Helen Marie (Littlepage) Haley; BA, So. Meth. U., 1943; m. Edward Lewis Wilson, Jr., Mar. 19, 1943; children: Edward Lewis III, William Haley, Sarah. Bd. dirs. Dallas Symphony Orch. League, 1963-89, sec., 1964-68, 1st v.p., 1968-72, vice-chmn. spl. projects, 1977-78, rec. sec., 1984-85, 7th v.p., 1985-86, trustee, 1976-88, showhouse chmn., 1987, corresponding sec., 1987-88; v.p. activities, bd. dirs. Allegro Dallas, Inc., 1986-90; precinct chmn. Democratic Party, 1952-62; mem. Dallas County Dem. Exec. Com., 1952-62; bd. dirs. TACA (Com. for Fund Raising of the Arts), 1975-88; mem. Southwestern hospitality bd. Met. Opera; charter mem., bd. dirs., North Tex. Herb Club, 1974-78; mem. Grand Heritage Ball Com. of Old City Park, exec. com. 1992-94 exec. com. Les Femme du Monde-fundraising arm Dallas Coun. on World Affairs, 1992-95. Mem. Nat. Trust Hist. Preservation, Dallas Mus. Art/League, Decorative Arts Guild N. Tex., Herb Soc. Am. (life), Am. Hort. Soc., Pewter Collectors Club Am., Royal Hort. Soc., Le Circle Francaise of Dallas (hon. chmn. 1985-94), Herb Soc. of Old City Park, Kappa Alpha Theta. Methodist. Home: 3501 Lexington Ave Dallas TX 75205-3914 Office: 2909 Maple Ave Dallas TX 75201-1443

WILSON, JEANNETTE SOLOMON, retired elementary education educator; b. Columbus, Ga., Sept. 5, 1915; d. John C. and Mary L. (Parham) Solomon (adoptive parents, aunt and uncle); m. Harvie L. Wilson, Aug. 9, 1952; 1 child, Katrina M. Deese Turner. BS, Ft. Valley (Ga.) Coll., 1947; MS, Tuskegee (Ala.) Inst., 1951; postgrad., Syracuse U., 1961, U. Alaska, 1967. cert. elem. tchr. Elem. tchr. Muscogee County Sch. Dist., Columbus, 1939-53, 1954-60, 1969-71, home/hosp. tchr., 1971-75; elem. tchr. Am. Dependent Schs., Heilbronn, Fed. Republic Germany, 1953-54; ret., 1975; cons. in field. Active Girls Scouts Columbus chpt. Named one of Women of Achievement Girl Scouts, Inc., 1989; recipient Outstanding Svc. award Am. Cancer Soc., 1983-84. Mem. AAUW, The Links Club (one of the founders Columbus, Ga. chpt. 1964), Urban League, Nat. Coun. Negro Women, Tuskegee Alumni Assn., Mr. and Mrs. Club (sec. 1960-64), Matrons Club (Gracious Lady of Ga. 1988), Alpha Kappa Alpha.

WILSON, JUDITH FALTYSEK, development executive; b. Oak Park, Ill., Jan. 22, 1945; d. Paul Holmes and Mary Jane (Ward) Faltysek; m. Anthony Parks Wilson, Aug. 20, 1966; children: Catherine Holmes, Christopher Ward. BS, Northwestern U., 1967. Tchr. Ewing Twp. Schs., Trenton, N.J., 1967-70; cons. Bensinger, DuPont & Assoc., Chgo., 1981-90; assoc. dir. devel. Lawrenceville (N.J.) Sch., 1990-94; dir. of devel. Out-of-Door Acad., Sarasota, Calif., 1995. Bd. dirs., chmn. Jr. League of Chgo., 1976-81; bd. dirs., benefit chmn. Infant Welfare Soc. Chgo., 1978-86; mem. founders group Women in Devel., Princeton, N.J., 1992-95. Named Vol. of Yr. for drug edn. of parents Chgo. Mag., 1983. Mem. Nat. Soc. Fundraising Execs., Jr. League of San Francisco. Episcopalian. Home: 2900 Pacific Ave San Francisco CA 94115

WILSON, JUDY, insurance company executive. Sr. v.p. guaranteed investment contracts Protective Life Corp., Universal City, Calif., 1995—. Office: Protective Life Corp 10 Universal City Plz # 2401 Universal City CA 91608*

WILSON, KAREN LEE, museum director; b. Somerville, N.J., Apr. 2, 1949; d. Jon Milton and Laura Virginia (Van Dyke) W.; m. Paul Ernest Walker, 1980; 1 child, Jeremy Nathaniel. AB, Harvard U., 1971; MA, NYU, 1973, PhD, 1985. Rsch. assoc., dir. excavation at Mendes, Egypt Inst. Fine Arts, NYU, 1979-81; coord. exhbn. The Jewish Mus., N.Y.C., 1981-82, adminstrv. cataloguer, 1982-83, coord. curatorial affairs, 1984-86; curator Oriental Inst. Mus. U. Chgo., 1988-96, mus. dir., 1996—. Author, editor: Mendes, 1982; contbr. articles to profl. jours. Mem. Am. Oriental Soc., Am. Rsch. Ctr. in Egypt. Office: Oriental Institute Museum 1155 E 58th St Chicago IL 60637-1540

WILSON, KAREN MARGUERITE, singer, storyteller; b. N.Y.C., Aug. 13, 1952; d. William and Florine Susan (Riddick) W.; 1 child, Alissa Suzanne. BMus, N.C. Sch. Arts, Winston-Salem, 1972; MA, Columbia U., 1980. Classroom tchr. Computer Sch., N.Y.C., 1984-85; arts in edn. specialist N.Y.C. Bd. Edn., 1985-90; dir. edn. Bklyn. Children's Mus., 1990-91; site visitor Milw. Alternative and Partnerships Schs. Acad. for Ednl. Devel., N.Y.C., 1993—; assoc. Washington & Assocs., Bronx, 1994; music com., assoc. conductor Boricua Coll. Chorus, N.Y.C., 1994; choral music tchr. Fieldston Lower Sch., Riverdale, N.Y., 1991-94; storyteller-in-residence Elizabeth Morrow Sch., Englewood, N.J., 1992—; staff developer Educators for Social Responsibility, N.Y.C., 1992-94; nat. membership devel. specialist Girl Scouts U.S., N.Y.C., 1988-90; adj. prof. Mercy Coll., Bronx, 1989, 90. Adv. bd. Bronx (N.Y.) Creative Arts for Youth, 1990. Home: 3985 Saxon Ave Bronx NY 10463

WILSON, KATHRYN TERESE, food service director; b. Milw., Mar. 7, 1959; d. George Charles and Mary Kathryn (Fink) Schuld; m. Russel Harold Wilson, Dec. 21, 1985; children: Thomas Lawrence, James Charles. BS in Dietetics, U. Wis.-Stout, Menomonie, 1981, MS in Food Sci. and Nutrition, 1984. Lic. food svc. dir./adminstr. Resident housing-bldg. dir. U. Wis.-Stout, Menomonie, 1983-85, substitute teaching staff, 1984-85; asst. food svc. dir. Onalaska (Wis.) Pub. Schs., 1987-90; food svc. dir. West Salem (Wis.) Schs., 1990—; cons. outreach Wis. Dept. Pub. Instrn., Madison, 1993—. Recipient Silver Penguin award Nat. Frozen Food Assn., 1995-96; named Dir. of Yr., Wis. Sch. Food Svc., 1995-96; nutriton edn. grantee Wis. Dept. Pub. Instrn., Madison, 1992. Mem. Am. Sch. Food Svc. Assn. (legis. del. 1991-92, 93, 94, 95, midwest rep. dirs./suprs. com. 1995-98), Wis. Sch. Food Svc. Assn. (chpt. pres. 1991-93, v.p. 1992-93, pres.-elect 1993-94, state pres. 1994-95, legis. com., dist. rep. 1990-93, cons. program of excellence 1992—, legis. com. chair 1996-98, Gold awards 1991-93). Home: N2130 Sunset Ln Rt 2 La Crosse WI 54601

WILSON, KATHY H., principal; b. East Providence, R.I., Aug. 10, 1951; d. Marion A. and Rita (Castergine) Higdon; m. Paul O. Wilson, Dec. 21, 1974; children: Casey Rose, Fletcher Todd. BS in Edn., U. Mo., 1973, MA in Edn., 1976. Cert. in tchg., Mo. Social sci. rsch. analyst Dept. Labor, Washington, 1977-80; nat. pres. Nat. Women's Polit. Caucus, Washington, 1981-85; substitute tchr. Alexandria (Va.) City Pub. Schs., 1989-91; tchr. Resurrection Children's Ctr., Alexandria, Va., 1991-93; dir. Abracadabra Child Care & Devel. Ctr., Alexandria, Va., 1993—; model tchr. The Danny Chitwood Early Learning Ctr., Alexandria, Va., 1993, The Danny Chitwood Early Learning Inst. Family Child Care, Alexandria, 1992-93; jr. gt. books tchr. Maury & Lykes Crouch Elem. Schs., 1986-89. Contbr. articles to newspapers. Youth Soccer Coach Alexandria Soccer Assn., 1989-90; recording sec. PTA, gift wrap chmn.; chmn. All Night Grad. Party, T.C. William H.S., 1995—; mem. adv. bd. Nat. Womens Polit. Caucus; founder, bd. dirs. Nat. Rep. Coalition for Choice, Washington, 1989-91. Received award for one of Washington's Most Influential Washington Mag., 1985; named one of Am.'s 100 Most Important Women Ladies Home Jour. editl. bd., 1983. Mem. Nat. Assn. for the Edn. of Young Children, Alexandria Child Care Dirs. Assn. (co-chmn. 1995—). Republican. Baptist. Home: 1402 Orchard St Alexandria VA 22302 Office: Abracadabra Child Care & Devel Ctr 700 Commonwealth Ave Alexandria VA 22301

WILSON, LINDA, librarian; b. Rochester, Minn., Nov. 17, 1945; d. Eunice Gloria Irene Wilson. BA, U. Minn., Morris, 1967; MA, U. Minn., 1968. Libr. rsch. svcs. U. Calif., Riverside, 1968-69, head dept. phys. scis. catalog, 1969-71; city libr. Belle Glade (Fla). Mcpl. Libr., 1972-74; instr. part-time Palm Beach Jr. Coll., Belle Glade, 1973; head adult-young adult ext. Kern County Libr. Sys., Bakersfield, Calif., 1974-80; dir. dist. libr. Lake Agassiz Regional Libr. System, Crookston, Minn., 1980-85; supervising libr. San Diego County Libr., 1985-87; county libr. Merced (Calif.) County Libr., 1987-93; learning network mgr. Merced Coll., 1994-95; libr. dir. Monterey Park (Calif.) Bruggemeyer Meml. Libr., 1995—. Active Leadership Merced, 1987-88; mem. East Site Based Coordinating Coun., Merced, 1990-92, Merced Gen. Plan Citizens Adv. Com., 1992-95, Sister City Com., Merced, 1992-95, East L.A. Bus. and Profl. Women, 1996—, Monterey Pk. Rotary, 1996—. Recipient Libr. award Eagles Aux., 1984, Woman of Achievement award Commn. on the Status of Women, 1990, Libr. award Calif. Libr. Trustees and Commrs., 1990, Woman of Yr. award Merced Bus. and Profl. Women, 1987. Mem. ALA (sec. pub. libr. sys. sect. 1988-89), Calif. Libr. Assn. (sec. govt. rels. com. 1991-92, continuing edn. com. 1993-96), Minn. Libr. Assn. (pres. pub. libr. divsn. 1985), Merced County Mgmt. Coun. (pres. 1989), Merced Bus. and Profl. Women (pres. 1988-89). Democrat. Lutheran. Home: 1000 E Newmark Ave # 22 Monterey Park CA 91755

WILSON, LINDA SMITH, academic administrator; b. Washington, Nov. 10, 1936; d. Fred M. and Virginia D. (Thompson) Smith; m. Paul A. Wilson, Jan. 22, 1970; 1 dau. by previous marriage: Helen K. Whatley, a stepdau., Beth A. Wilson. B.A., Newcomb Coll., Tulane U., 1957; Ph.D., U. Wis., 1962; HLD (hon.), Tulane U., 1993; DLitt. (hon.), U. Md., 1993. Postdoctoral rsch. assoc. U. Md., College Park, 1962-64, rsch. asst. prof., 1964-67; vis. asst. prof. U. Mo.-St. Louis, 1967-68; asst. to vice chancellor for rsch., asst. vice chancellor for rsch., assoc. vice chancellor for rsch. Washington U., St. Louis, 1968-75; assoc. vice chancellor for rsch. U. Ill., Urbana, 1975-85; assoc. dean Grad. Coll., U. Ill., Urbana, 1978-85; v.p. for rsch. U. Mich., Ann Arbor, 1985-89; pres. Radcliffe Coll., Cambridge, Mass., 1989—; chmn. adv. com. office sci. and engrng. pers. NRC, 1990-96; mem. dir.'s adv. coun. NSF, Washington, 1980-89, adv. com. edn. and human resources, 1990-95; mem. Nat. Commn. on Rsch., Washington, 1978-80; mem. com. on govt.-univ. relationships NAS, 1981-83, mem. coun. for govt.-univ.-industry rsch. roundtable, 1984-89; mem. rsch. resources adv. coun. NIH, Bethesda, Md., 1978-82, energy rsch. adv. bd. DOE, 1987-90; mem. sci., tech. and states task force Carnegie Commn. on Sci., Tech. and Govt., 1991-92; trustee Com. on Econ. Devel., 1995—, overseer Mus. of Sci., Boston, 1992—. Author book chpts.; contbr. articles to profl. jours. Bd. govs. YMCA, Champaign-Urbana, Ill., 1980-83; mem. adv. bd. Nat. Coalition for Sci. and Tech., Washington, 1983-87; trustee Mass. Gen. Hosp., 1992—; dir. Citizen's Fin. Group, 1996—. Recipient Centennial award Newcomb Coll., 1986; named One of 100 Emerging Leaders Am. Coun. Edn. and Change, 1978. Fellow AAAS (bd. dirs. 1984-88); mem. NAS (coord. coun. for edn. 1991-93), Am. Chem. Soc. (bd. coun. com. on chemistry and pub. affairs 1978-80), Soc. Rsch. Adminstrs. (Disting. Contbn. to Rsch. Adminstrn. award 1984), Nat. Coun. Univ. Rsch. Adminstrs., Assn. for Biomed. Rsch. (bd. dirs. 1983-86), Inst. Medicine (mem. coun. 1986-89), Am. Coun. Edn. (commn. on women in higher edn. 1991-93, chair 1993), Phi Beta Kappa, Sigma Xi, Alpha Lambda Delta, Phi Delta Kappa, Phi Kappa Phi. Home: 76 Brattle St Cambridge MA 02138-3452 Office: Radcliffe Coll Office of Pres Fay House 10 Garden St Cambridge MA 02138

WILSON, LORRAINE M., medical and surgical nurse, nursing educator; b. Mich., Nov. 18, 1931; d. Bert and Frances Fern (White) McCarty; m. Harold A. Wilson, June 9, 1953; children: David Scott, Ann Elizabeth. Diploma in Nursing, Bronson Meth. Sch. Nursing, Kalamazoo, Mich., 1953; BS in Chemistry, Siena Heights Coll., 1969; MSN, U. Mich., 1972; PhD, Wayne State U., Detroit, 1985. RN, Mich. Staff nurse U. Mich. Med. Ctr., Ann Arbor, 1953-54, Herrick Meml. Hosp., Tecumseh, Mich., 1954-69; asst. prof. nursing U. Mich., Ann Arbor, 1972-78, Wayne State U., Detroit, 1978-79; assoc. prof. nursing Sch. of Nursing Oakland U., Rochester, Mich., 1986-89; prof. nursing Ea. Mich. U., Ypsilanti, Mich., 1989—; researcher in field; bd. advs. Profl. Fitness Systems, Warren, Mich., 1986—; cons. wellness and exercise program General Motors CPC Hdqs., Warren, 1986; cons. and faculty liaison nurse extern program in critical care Ea. Mich. U. Catherine McAuley Health Ctr., 1989—. Co-author: (with Sylvia Price) Pathophysiology: Clinical Concepts of Disease Processes, 5th edit., 1986; contbr. articles to profl. jours. Vol. Community Health Screening Drives, Tecumseh, 1960-70, leader Girl Scouts U.S., Tecumseh, 1960; sunday sch. tchr. Gloria Dei Luth. Ch., Tecumseh, 1960; mem. PTA. Grantee Mich. Heart Assn., 1984, 88, R.C. Mahon Found., 1988. Mem. ANA (various offices and com. chairs), Midwest Nursing Rsch. Soc. (v.p., sec.-treas., bd. dirs.), Mich. Nurses Assn. (del.), Nat. League Nursing, Nat. Orgn. Women, Sigma Theta Tau. Lutheran. Home: 1010 Red Mill Dr Tecumseh MI 49286-1145 Office: Ea Mich U 53 W Michigan Ave Ypsilanti MI 48197-5436

WILSON, LUCY LYNN WILLMARTH, postal service administrator; b. Russellville, Ala., May 18, 1953; d. Richard Bert and Alice Josephine (Gantt) Willmarth; m. Donald Wayne Wilson, Dec. 21, 1974; children: Beau Evan and Heath Edward (twins). BS in Home Econs., U. Ala., 1975; BS Ed. Sec. Biology/Psychology, Athens (Ala.) State Coll., 1996. Dietetic technician Athens (Ala.) Limestone Hosp., 1975-76, Med. Ctr. Hosp., Huntsville, Ala., 1976-78; kitchen supr. Lurleen B. Wallace Ctr., Decatur, Ala., 1979; food svc. dir. Limestone Nursing Hosp., Athens, 1980; city carrier U.S. Postal Svc., Huntsville, 1986; city carrier U.S. Postal Svc., Athens, 1986-88, distbn. clk., 1988—; officer in charge U.S. Postal Svc., Lester, Ala., 1992-93. Mem. Cowart Elem. Sch. PTA, Athens, 1985-91; clinic vol. Cowart Elem. Sch., 1985; team mother Dixie Youth Baseball, Athens, 1991; mem. Athens H.S. Athletic Boosters Club, 1994—. Recipient Good Citizenship award Civitan Club, Russellville, 1971. Mem. Nat. Assn. Postmasters of U.S. (assoc.), Ala. Sci. Tchrs. Assn., U. Ala. nat. Alumni Assn, MADD (Ala. chpt.), The Studebaker Drivers Club, Psi Chi. Home: 209 Cascade Dr Athens AL 35611-2215 Office: US Postal Svc 1110 W Market St Athens AL 35611-2466

WILSON, MARGO KAY, arts editor; b. Oshkosh, Wis., Dec. 11, 1949; d. Neil James and Elizabeth Mary (Bradford) W.; m. Michael Fredrick Kraft, June 25, 1970. BA in Journalism and Mass Comm., U. Wis., 1971; MA in Film and TV, UCLA, 1986. Publicity writer, dir. Campus Assistance Ctr. U. Wis., Madison, 1972-74; gen. assignment reporter The Chronicle-Jour., Thunder Bay, Ont., Can., 1974-75; feature writer Sunday Courier Press, Evansville, Ind., 1976; entertainment The Jour. Times, Racine, Wis., 1977-83; rsch. asst., tchg. asst. UCLA, 1983-86; freelance writer, editor, script reader L.A., 1986-90; copy editor, arts editor San Bernardino (Calif.) County Sun, 1990—; restaurant co-owner The Sanctuary, Racine, 1980-83. Author: (novel) On the Path of the Bear, 1996, also screenplays; freelance editor, 1990—. Mem. Soc. Profl. Journalists (nat. and Inland Empire chpt. bd. mem.), TV Critics Assn., Ind. Filmmaker's Assn. Office: The San Bernardino County Sun 399 N D St San Bernardino CA 92401

WILSON, MARJORIE PRICE, physician, medical commission executive. Student, Bryn Mawr Coll., 1942-45; M.D., U. Pitts., 1949. Intern U. Pitts. Med. Ctr. Hosps., 1949-50; resident Children's Hosp. U. Pitts., 1950-51, Jackson Meml. Hosp., U. Miami Sch. Medicine, 1954-56; chief residency and internship div. edn. svc. Office of Rsch. and Edn., VA, Washington, 1956, chief profl. tng. div., 1956-60, asst. dir. edn. svc., 1960; chief tng. br. Nat. Inst. Arthritis and Metabolic Disease NIH, Bethesda, Md., 1960-63, asst. to assoc. dir. for tng. Office of Dir., 1963-64, assoc. dir. program devel. OPPD, 1967-69, asst. dir. program planning and evaluation, 1969-70; assoc. dir. extramural programs Nat. Libr. Medicine, 1964-67; dir. dept. instl. devel. Assn. Am. Med. Colls., Washington, 1970-81; sr. assoc. dean U. Md. Sch. Medicine, Balt., 1981-86, vice dean, 1986-88, acting dean, 1984; pres., CEO, Ednl. Commn. Fgn. Med. Grads., Phila., 1988-95, emeritus, 1995—; mem. Inst. Medicine Nat. Acad. Scis.,1974—; bd. visitors U. Pitts. Sch. Medicine, 1974—; mem. Nat. Bd. Med. Examiners, 1980-87, 89—; mem. adv. bd. Fogarty Internat. Ctr., 1991—. Contbr. articles to profl. jours. Mem. adv. bd. Robert Wood Johnson Health Policy Fellowships, 1975-87; trustee Analytic Services, Inc., Falls Church, Va., 1976—. Fellow Am. Coll. Physician Execs., AAAS; mem. Assn. Am. Med. Colls., Am. Fedn. Clin. Research, IEEE. Office: Ste 475 2401 Pennsylvania Ave NW Washington DC 20037

WILSON, MARY CHRISTINA, history educator; b. Lakewood, Ohio, Aug. 15, 1950; d. William Draughn and Norma (Nelson) W.; m. Philip S. Khoury, Aug. 28, 1980. Student, Am. U. Beirut, Lebanon, 1970-71; AB, Oberlin Coll., 1972; PhD, Oxford U., 1983. Instr. history Wellesley (Mass.) Coll., 1982-83; vis. asst. prof. history NYU, N.Y.C., 1984-88; asst. prof. history U. Mass., Amherst, 1988-91, assoc. prof. history, 1991-96, prof. history, 1996—, dir. Middle Easter Studies Program, 1992-96, dir. grad. program dept. history, 1993-96; cons. MacArthur Found., Chgo., NEH, Washington, Social Sci. Rsch. Coun., N.Y.C. Author: King Abdullah, Britain and the Making of Jordan, 1987; co-editor: The Modern Middle East, 1993. Alumni fellow Oberlin Coll., 1982-83; Social Sci. Rsch. Coun. fellow, N.Y.C., 1984-85; fellow Bunting Inst., Radcliffe Coll., Cambridge, 1988-89, NEH, Washington, 1988-89, Inst. for Advanced Study of Humanities, U. Mass., Amherst, 1990. Mem. Am. Hist. Assn., Brit. Soc. for Middle Ea. Studies, Middle East Studies Assn. (nominating com. 1987, mem. editl. bd. bull. 1987-94, book rev. editor 1987-95). Office: History Dept Herter Hall U Mass Amherst MA 01003

WILSON, MARY ELIZABETH, physician, educator; b. Indpls., Nov. 19, 1942; d. Ralph Richard and Catheryn Rebecca (Kurtz) Lausch; m. Harvey Vernon Fineberg, May 16, 1975. AB, Ind. U., 1963; MD, U. Wis., 1971. Diplomate Am. Bd. Internal Medicine, Am. Bd. Infectious Diseases. Tchr. of French and English Marquette Sch., Madison, Wis., 1963-66; intern in medicine Beth Israel Hosp., Boston, 1971-72, resident in medicine, 1972-73, fellow in infectious diseases, 1973-75; physician Albert Schweitzer Hosp., Deschapelles, Haiti, 1974-75, Harvard Health Svcs., Cambridge, Mass., 1974-75; asst. physician Cambridge Hosp., 1975-78; hosp. epidemiologist Mt. Auburn Hosp., Cambridge, 1975-79, chief of infectious diseases, 1978—, dir. Travel Resource Ctr., 1996—; adv. com. immunization practices Ctrs. for Disease Control, Atlanta, 1988-92; acad. adv. com. Nat. Inst. Pub. Health, Mex., 1989-91; cons. Ford Found., 1988; instr. in medicine Harvard Med. Sch., Boston, 1975-93, asst. clin. prof., 1994—, assoc. Ctr. Health & Global Environ., 1996—; asst. prof. depts. epidemiology and population and internat. health Harvard Sch. Pub. Health, 1994—; lectr. Sultan Qaboos U., Oman, 1991; chair Woods Hole Workshop, Emerging Infectious Diseases, 1993. Author: A World Guide to Infections: Diseases, Distribution, Diagnosis, 1991; co-editor: (with Richard Levins and Andrew Spielman) Disease in Evolution: Global Changes and Emergence of Infectious Diseases, 1994; mem. editl. bd. Current Issues in Pub. Health; sect. editor, travel medicine & tropical diseases, editl. bd. Infectious Diseases in Clinical Practice. Mem. Cambridge Task Force on AIDS, 1987—, Earthwatch, Watertown, Mass., Cultural Survival, Inc., Cambridge; bd. dirs. Horizon Communications, West Cornwall, Conn., 1990. Recipient Lewis E. and Edith Phillips award U. Wis. Med. Sch., 1969, Cora M. and Edward Van Liere award, 1971, Mosby Scholarship Book award, 1971; scholar in residence Bellagio (Italy) Study Ctr., Rockefeller Found., 1996. Fellow ACP, Infectious Diseases Soc. Am., Royal Soc. Tropical Medicine and Hygiene; mem. Am. Soc. Microbiology, N.Y. Acad. Scis., Am. Soc. Tropical Medicine and Hygiene, Mass. Infectious Diseases Soc., Peabody Soc., Internat. Soc. Travel Medicine, Wilderness Med. Soc., Soc. for Vector Ecology, Internat. Union Against Tuberculosis and Lung Disease, Soc. for Epidemiol. Rsch., Sigma Sigma, Phi Sigma Iota, Alpha Omega Alpha. Office: Mt Auburn Hosp 330 Mount Auburn St Cambridge MA 02138-5502

WILSON, MARY ELLEN, retired project administrator; b. L.A., Aug. 7, 1927; d. Nels Efraim and Ellen (Matson) Lovemark; m. Richard Spencer Dyer, Mar. 6, 1952 (dec. July 1960); children: Robert Alan, Terry Ann; m. Edward LeRoy Wilson, Jan. 21, 1961 (dec. Jan. 1992); 1 child, Pamela

Susan; stepchildren: Scott Stanton, Jefferey Kevin Wilson. Expediter C F Braun & Co., Alhambra, Calif., 1947-53; project expediter The Ralph M. Parsons Co., Pasadena, Calif., 1977-79, project coord., 1979-83, project adminstr., 1984-89. Docent Scott Gallery, Huntington Libr., Pasadena, 1992—; publicity profl. Pasadena Rep. Women's Club, 1960s; pres. Pasadena Charity for Calif. Pediat. Ctr., L.A., 1955-60; First Lady, Pasadena Tournament of Roses, 1973-74. Republican. Home: # 5 727 S Orange Grove Pasadena CA 91105

WILSON, MARY L., psychiatric nurse; b. Detroit, Aug. 23, 1954; d. Percy Brown and Willie Margaret McClellan; m. Loyall Edward Wilson, Jr., Nov. 11, 1995; children: Anjeanetta, Anitra, Brandi. AAS magna cum laude, Southwestern Mich. Coll., 1993. RN Mich., Ind. RN Med. Personnel Pool, South Bend, Ind., 1991-95; charge nurse Lakeview Cmty. Hosp., PawPaw, Mich., 1993-95; sch. nurse South Bend (Ind.) Sch. corp., 1994-95; charge nurse Oakwood Hosp. Merriman Ctr., Westland, Mich., 1995—; nursing consultant Aetna, Southfield, Mich., 1995—; occupl. health nurse Interim Health Care, Lathrup Village, Mich., 1995—; Oakland Gen. Home Health Agy., Madison Heights, Mich. Mem. Phi Beta Kappa.

WILSON, MAUREEN O'NEILL, accountant; b. Shirley, Mass., Nov. 15, 1954; d. Charles Francis and Jacqueline Ann (Cameron) O'Neill; m. Paul Steven Wilson, Mar. 25, 1988; children: Cameron Mae Wilson, Steven Daniel Wilson. BS in Acctg., U. N.C., Charlotte, 1990. Planner Princeton Electronic Products, North Brunswick, N.J., 1974-80, Blonder-Tongue Labs., Old Bridge, N.J., 1980-82; officer mgr. Looseleaf Industries, South Plainfield, N.J., 1982-85; programmer, systems analyst Takatori Intech Corp., Charlotte, N.C., 1985-91; plant acctg. mgr. Jacobsen Divsn. of Textron, Charlotte, N.C., 1991—. Mem. ICMA (bd. dirs. 1989). Office: Jacobsen Divsn Textron PO Box 7708 11524 Wilmar Blvd Charlotte NC 28241

WILSON, MELINDA RICARDA, molecular biologist; b. La Jolla, Calif., Jan. 10, 1959; d. David Jordan and Wanda Mae (French) Wilson; m. Michael Frederick Daeschlein, Aug. 10, 1991; 1 child, Amber Mae. AAS, Pa. State U., 1980, BS in Microbiology, 1983; PhD in Animal Science, Mich. State U., 1993. Histochem. technician Pa. State U., State College, 1981-82, lab. asst., 1982-83; rsch. technician M.S. Hershey Med. Ctr., Hershey, Pa., 1983-85; devel. biologist Lederle Labs. (divsn. Am. Cyanamid), Pearl River, N.Y., 1985-88; grad. rsch. fellow Mich. State U., East Lansing, 1989-92, post-doctoral rsch. fellow, 1993-95, asst. prof., 1996—; workshop instr. Mich. State U., 1988-89. Contbr. articles to jours. Spiker Varsity Volleyball Team, Pa. State U., 1978-80; vol. ARC Flood Emergency, Harrisburg, Pa., 1972; treas. conf. Liberal Religious Youth, Pa., Del., Md., 1974-77; bd. dirs. Oliver La Grone Scholarship Fund, Harrisburg, 1984-85. Rsch. fellow Mich. State U., 1989, 90; named to Outstanding Young Women of Am., 1985; recipient varsity sports letters Pa. State U., York, 1978, 79, Health Svc. award NIH, 1993, 94. Mem. NAFE, AAUW, Nat. Mus. of Women in the Arts (charter), Am. Soc. Cell Biology, Pa. State Alumni Assn., Mich. State U. Animal Sci. Biotechnology Jour. Club (bd. dirs. 1988-91), Women in Cancer Rsch., Sigma Xi.

WILSON, MIRIAM GEISENDORFER, physician, educator; b. Yakima, Wash., Dec. 3, 1922; d. Emil and Frances Geisendorfer; m. Howard G. Wilson, June 21, 1947; children—Claire, Paula, Geoffrey, Nicola, Marla. B.S., U. Wash., Seattle, 1944, M.S., 1945; M.D., U. Calif., San Francisco, 1950. Mem. faculty U. So. Calif. Sch. Medicine, L.A., 1965—, prof. pediatrics, 1969—. Office: U So Calif Med Ctr 1129 N State St Los Angeles CA 90033-1069

WILSON, MIRIAM JANET WILLIAMS, publishing executive; b. London, Ont., Can., July 13, 1939; d. Ralph George and Lillian Conn Williams; m. Carson Winnette, Nov. 20, 1960 (div. 1971); children: Barrie Carson Winnette, Rebecca Lynn Winnette; m. Charles Lindsay Wilson, Dec. 14, 1973; 1 child, Charles William Wilson; stepchildren: Kenneth M., Carol Ann, Catherine S., Nancy L., Patrick L. Diploma in nursing, Glendale (Calif.) Sanitarium & Hosp., 1960. RN, Calif., Va., Ohio, Md., W.Va. Head nurse emergency and med. fls. Glendale Sanitarium and Hosp., 1960-65; psychometrist Harding Hosp., Worthington, Ohio, 1969-73; biofeedback specialist in assn. Dr. Randolph P. Johnston, Winchester, Va., 1980-84; dir. Stress Ctr. for Children and Adults, Shepherdstown, W.Va., 1985-87; pres. Rocky River Pubs., Shepherdstown, 1987—; lectr. ednl., profl. and civic groups, 1984—. Author: Help For Children, 6 edits., 1987-95, Stress Stoppers, 2 edits., 1987-89; contbr. articles to profl. pubis. Active Shepherdstown Women's Club, 1986-95. Mem. NAFE, Internat. Platform Assn., Am. Booksellers Assn., N.Y. Acad. Scis. Office: Rocky River Pubs PO Box 1679 Shepherdstown WV 25443-1679

WILSON, NANCY CAROL, office systems educator; b. Brighton, Tenn., July 11, 1940; d. John C. and Lillie Mai (Coates) W. BBA, Memphis State U., 1963, MEd, 1968. Cert. sec. tchr. bus. edn. Tchr. bus. Grand Junction, Tenn. H.S., 1962-64; tchr. 6th grade Munford (Tenn.) Elem. Sch., 1964-65; tchr. jr. high math. Munford (Tenn.) Jr. High, 1965-66; tchr. bus., dept. head Munford (Tenn.) H.S., 1966-71; asst. prof., program coord. office adminstrn. Hopkinsville (Ky.) Cmty. Coll., 1971 81, prof. office adminstrn., 1981 96, prof. office systems, 1996—. Mem. Nat. Bus. Edn. Assn. (Ky. mem. chmn. 1974-76, So. Bus. Edn. Assn. sec. 1979, mem. adminstrv. com. 1982, 85, vice chmn. basic bus. divsn. 1973, chmn. 1974, sec. 1982, chmn. secretarial divsn. 1975, chmn. cmty. and jr. coll. divsn. 1977), Ky. Bus. Edn. Assn. (pres.-elect 1973-74, pres. 74-75, past pres. 1975-76). Methodist. Home: 101 Talbert Dr Apt 1 Hopkinsville KY 42240

WILSON, NANCY JEANNE, laboratory director, medical technologist; b. Neptune, N.J., Apr. 17, 1951; d. Harry E. Sr. and Kathryn E. (O'Shea) W. BS, Monmouth Coll., 1975; MPA, Fairleigh Dickinson U., 1988. Clin. intern med. tech., staff med. technologist Riverview Med. Ctr., 1975; staff med. technologist Rush Clin. Labs., Red Bank, N.J., 1975; staff med. technologist Kimball Med. Ctr., Lakewood, N.J., 1975-76, clin. lab. supr., 1976-86; infection control practice Jersey Shore Med. Ctr., Neptune, N.J., 1990; dir. lab. and diagnostic svcs. Carrier Found., Belle Meade, N.J., 1991—. Mem. Am. Soc. Clin. Pathologists (diplomate lab. mgmt.), Am. Assn. Clin. Chemistry, Am. Soc. Microbiology, Clin. Lab. Mgmt. Assn., Am. Soc. Clinics Lab. Sci., Pi Alpha Alpha. Home: 42 Monument St Freehold NJ 07728 Office: Carrier Found Rt 601 PO Box 147 Belle Mead NJ 08502

WILSON, PAMELA AIRD, physician; b. Milw., May 13, 1947; d. Rushen Arnold and Marianna (Dickie) W.; m. Paul Quin, June 20, 1981. BS in Zoology, U. Md., 1969; MS in Physiology, U. Wis., 1971; MD, U. Md., Balt., 1976. Diplomate Am. Bd. Internal Medicine. Asst. prof. U. Wis., Madison, 1983-90, assoc. prof., 1990—. Bd. dirs. Wis. chpt. Am. Lung Assn. Office: 600 Highland Ave # H6 380 Madison WI 53792-0001

WILSON, PATRICIA ELSIE, librarian; b. East Orange, N.J., Dec. 9, 1940; d. Frank N. and Elsie V. (Carlson) W.; m. Richard L. Krajeski, Aug. 24, 1963 (div. Jan. 1981); children: Kathryn Wilson, Karyn Lanning. Student, Colby Coll., 1958-60; BA in Philosophy, Bloomfield (N.J.) Coll., 1963; M in Libr. and Info. Sci., La. State U., 1986. Serials asst. W.Va. U., Morgantown, 1980-85; asst. libr. Keystone Jr. Coll., La Plume, Pa., 1987-88; reference libr. Frostburg (Md.) State U., 1988—; co-chair dialog tng. com. U. Md., 1994—; spkr. Nat. Online Conf., N.Y.C., 1995. Contbr. articles to profl. jours., short story to Md. English Jour., 1995. Mem. Middle States Accrediting Steering Com., Frostburg, 1994—, Stage Left Theatre, Cumberland, Md., 1994—. Mem. ALA, Md. Libr. Assn., Coun. of the Alleghenies. Home: PO Box 332 Frostburg MD 21532 Office: Lewis J Ort Libr Frostburg State U Frostburg MD 21532

WILSON, PATRICIA POTTER, library science and reading educator, educational and library consultant; b. Jennings, La., May 3, 1946; d. Ralph Harold and Wilda Ruth (Smith) Potter; m. Wendell Merlin Wilson, Aug. 24, 1968. BS, La. State U., 1967; MS, U. Houston-Clear Lake, 1979; EdD, U. Houston, 1985. Cert. tchr., learning resources specialist (librarian), Tex. Tchr., England AFB (La.) Elem. Sch., 1967-68, Edward White Elem. Sch., Clear Creek Ind. Schs., Seabrook, Tex., 1972-77; librarian C.D. Landolt Elem. Sch., Friendswood, Tex., 1979-81; instr./lectr. children's lit. U. Houston 1983-86; with U. Houston/Clear Lake, 1984-87, asst. prof. libr. sci. and reading, 1988-94, assoc. prof. learning resources and reading edn., 1994—, mem. faculty senate, 1992-93; cons. Hermann Hosp., Baywood Hosp., 1986-87, Bedford Meadows Hosp., 1989-90, Wetcher Clinic, 1989; v.p., sec. Potter Farms, Inc., 1994—. Trustee, Freeman Meml. Library, Houston, 1982-87, v.p., 1985-86, pres., 1986-87; trustee Evelyn Meador Libr., 1993-94; adv. bd. Evelyn Meador Libr., 1994—; mem. adv. bd. Bay Area Soc. Prevention Cruelty Animals, 1994—; mem. Armand Bayou Nature Ctr., Houston, 1980—, bd. dirs. 1989-94; bd. dirs. Sta. KUHT-TV, 1984-87; mem. Bay Area Houston Symphony League. Editor A Rev. Sampler, 1985-86, 89-90; dir. Learning Resources Book Rev. Ctr., 1989-90. Author: HAPPENINGS: Developing Successful Programs for School Libraries, 1987, The Professional Collection for Elementary Educators, 1996; contbg. editor Tex. Library Jour., 1988-94; contbr. articles to profl. jours. Recipient Rsch. award Tex. State Reading Assn., 1993, Pres. award Tex. Coun. Tchrs. of English, Disting. Teaching award Enron Corp., 1996; grantee Tex. Libr. Assn., 1993. Mem. ALA, Am. Assn. Sch. Librarians, Internat. Reading Assn., Nat. Coun. Tchrs. English, (Books for You review com. 1985-88, Your Reading review com., 1993-96), Tex. Coun. Tchrs. English, Antarctican Soc., Phi Delta Kappa, Phi Kappa Phi. Methodist. Home: 629 Bay Vista Dr Seabrook TX 77586-3001 Office: U Houston Clear Lake 2700 Bay Area Blvd Houston TX 77058-1002

WILSON, PEGGY HENICAN, city official; b. New Orleans, June 24, 1937; d. C. Ellis and Elizabeth (Cleveland) Henican; m. Gordon Francis Wilson Jr., Dec. 10, 1932; children: Gordon, Alice, Peter, Carter. BA cum laude, Barat Coll., Lake Forest, Ill., 1959; postgrad., Tulane and Dominican Coll., 1960-75. Cert. tchr. Tchr. Mercy Acad., New Orleans, 1961-62, Acad. Sacred Heart, New Orleans, 1959-72; mgr. polit. campaigns Campaign Specialists, 1978-80; ptnr. Mason, Glickman, Wilson, New Orleans, 1981-82; owner Trolley Tours, 1975-85; pres. Peggy Wilson & Assocs., New Orleans, 1980-87; mem. City Coun., New Orleans, 1986—, pres., 1994—; chmn. fin. com. S&WB, mem. bd. liquidations. Author: Trolley Tours, 1982. Chmn. Alcoholic Beverage Control Bd., 1984-86; sec.-treas. Warehouse Dist. Devel. Assn., 1982-84, pres., 1984; bd. dirs. Carrollton-Hollygrove Community Ctr.; bd. dirs. YWCA, 1984-87; bd. dirs. City Park, New Orleans Mus. Art, Preservation Action; mem. mktg. com. City of New Orleans; mem. Cox Cable Com.; chmn. Hist. Dist. Landmarks Commn., 1981, 82; mem. bd., exec. com. St. George's Episcopal Sch., 1980-82; mem. Housing Task Force, 1978-80; mem. Police Chief Selection Com., 1978-79. Inst. Politics fellow Loyola U., 1978. Mem. Alliance for Good Govt., LWV, Upper St. Charles Civic Assn., Warehouse Dist. Devel. Assn., AARP. Office: Office City Council City Hall Rm 2E09 1300 Perdido St New Orleans LA 70112-2114

WILSON, PRISCILLA LYNN, home health administrator; b. Yuba City, Calif., Oct. 5, 1963; d. Robert Granville and Betty Alice (Gleffe) W. AS in Nursing, So. Coll. 7th-Day Adventist, Collegedale, Tenn., 1984, BS in Nursing, 1986; MS in Nursing, U. Calif., San Francisco, 1989. Cert. chemotherapy nurse, Ga.; cert. PICC line insertion, landmark insertion, Calif. Nurse oncology office mgr. Premier, Walnut Creek, Calif., 1989-90, nurse case mgr., 1990-91; nurse case mgr. Mt. Diablo Home Health, Concord, Calif., 1991; br. mgr. Care Home Health, Fairfield, Calif., 1991-92, infusion therapy coord. No. Calif., 1992-93; dir. home health Delta Pharm. Svcs., Carevan, Stockton, Calif., 1993; nurse case mgr. Delta Home Health & Hospice, Antioch, Calif., 1993-94, nursing supr., 1994, acting dir., 1994—; co-owner Cons. Assocs., Antioch, 1990-94. Contbr. articles to profl. jours. Infusion therapy instr. People to People Amb. Program, Spain, Portugal, Morocco, 1994. Mem. Oncology Nursing Soc., Intravenous Nursing Soc., Bay Area Venous Access Network. Seventh-day Adventist. Home: 5003 Brookhaven Way Antioch CA 94509-8401 Office: Delta Home Health & Hospice Lone Tree Way Antioch CA 94509

WILSON, REBECCA LYNN, lawyer; b. Glen Ellyn, Ill., July 22, 1965; d. Wayne Robert Wilson and Rosemary Phylis (Stoecklin) Maglio. BA, U. Wis., 1987; JD, William Mitchell Coll., 1990; cert. mediation, Lakewood (Minn.) C.C., 1994. Bar: Minn. 1990, U.S. Dist. Ct. Minn. 1992. Law clk., assoc. Jack S. Jaycox Law Offices, Bloomington, Minn., 1988-93; assoc. Steffens, Wilkerson & Lang, Edina, Minn., 1993, Wilkerson, Lang & Hegna, Bloomington, 1993-95, Wilkerson, Hegna & Walsten, Bloomington, 1996—. Mem. ABA, Minn. State Bar Assn., Hennepin County Bar Assn. Office: Wilkerson Hegna & Walsten Ste 1100 3800 W 80th St Bloomington MN 55431-4426

WILSON, RITA P., insurance company executive. Sr. v.p. corp. rels. Allstate Ins. Co., Northbrook, Ill. Office: Allstate Ins Co 2775 Sanders Rd Ste F8 Northbrook IL 60062-6127

WILSON, RUBY LEILA, nurse, educator; b. Punxsutawney, Pa., May 29, 1931; d. Clark H. and Alda E. (Armstrong) W. BS in Nursing Edn., U. Pitts., 1954; MSN, Case Western Res. U., 1959; EdD, Duke U., 1969. Staff nurse, asst. head nurse Allegheny Gen. Hosp., Pitts., 1951-52; night clin. instr., adminstrv. supr. Allegheny Gen. Hosp., 1951-55; staff nurse, asst. head nurse Fort Miley VA Hosp., San Francisco, 1957-58; instr. nursing Duke U. Sch. Nursing, Durham, N.C., 1955-57; asst. prof. med. surg. nursing Duke U. Sch. Nursing, 1959-66, assoc. in medicine, 1963-66, prof. nursing, 1971—, dean sch. nursing., 1971-84, asst. to chancellor for health affairs, 1984—; asst. prof. dept. community and family medicine Duke U. Sch. Medicine, 1971—; cons., vis. prof. Rockefeller Found., Thailand, 1968-71; vis. prof. Case Western Res. U., 1982-84; mem. Gov.'s Commn. on Health Care Reform in N.C., 1994. Contbr. articles to profl. jours. Active N.C. Med. Care Commn., Gov.'s Commn. on N.C. Health Care Reform, 1994—. Fellow Am. Acad. Nursing, Inst. Medicine; mem. ANA, Am. Assn. Colls. Nursing, Am. Assn. Higher Edn., Nat. League Nursing, Assn. for Acad. Health Ctrs. (mem. inst. planning com.), Women's Forum N.C. (bd. dirs. 1984-88, 95—), N.C. Found. for Nursing (pres. 1990-94). Office: Duke U Med Ctr PO Box 3243 Durham NC 27715-3243

WILSON, SANDRA LEE, school nurse; b. Akron, Ohio, Sept. 27, 1950; d. Earl Buel and Erma Wilma (Stephens) Stalnaker; m. Daniel Lee Wilson, Dec. 19, 1970; children: Daniel Lee, Matthew David. Diploma, Akron Gen. Hosp. Sch. Nursing, 1968-71; BSH, Ohio U., 1980; MEd, Kent State U., 1985. Surgical nurse Akron (Ohio) Gen. Hosp., 1971-72, Green Cross Gen. Hosp., Cuyahoga Falls, Ohio, 1972-74; staff nurse St. Thomas Hosp., Akron, Ohio, 1974-75; staff devel. Riverside Meth. Hosp., Columbus, Ohio, 1975-78; sch. nurse Logan Elem. Schs., Circleville, Ohio, 1978-81; staff devel. Canton (Ohio) Autlman, 1981; sch. nurse Canton (Ohio) City Schs., 1982-86, Lakewood (Ohio) City Schs., 1986-87, Beachwood (Ohio) City Schs., 1987—; clin. faculty Kent State U., Ohio, 1984, 87—, Cuyahoga C.C., Cleve., 1989—, Case Western Reserve U., Cleve., 1988—; preceptor Cleve. State U., 1993—. Contbr. articles to profl. jours. Healthy Learner Legis. chairperson Ohio Assn. Sch. Nurses, 1985-94; Lake Local Sch. Sch. bd. mem. Uniontown, Ohio, 1982-84; legis. liason Nat. Sch. Bds. Assn. Washington, 1983-84; Spl. Edn. Com. Ohio Fedn. of Tchrs., Columbus, Ohio, 1993; task force mem. Ohio Bd. Nursing, Columbus, Ohio, 1992-93. Recipient Betty Dobkins scholarship, Ohio, 1968, Membership Excellence award Nat. Assn. Sch. Nurses, Maine, 1986; grantee Ohio Dept. Health, 1990-92. Mem. NEA, DEA, PTA, Ohio Assn. Sch. Nurses, Nat. Assn. Sch. Nurses, Ohio Fedn. Tchrs., Am. Fedn. Tchrs., Am. Sch. Health Assn., Nat. Preservation, Ohio U. Women's Club, Shaker Heights Hockey Assn., N.E. Ohio Sch. Nurses, Kent State Alumni, Phi Kappa Phi, Sigma Theta Tau. Republican. Home: 2877 Torrington Rd Shaker Heights OH 44122 Office: Beachwood Schools 2860 Richmond Rd Beachwood OH 44122-2333

WILSON, SHANICE, vocalist; b. Pitts., 1974. Represented by Motown Record Co. Vocalist, TV comml. (with Ella Fitzgerald) Kentucky Fried Chicken, 1982; stage productions include Get Happy, L.A., 1985; TV appearances include Tonight Show, 1992, Ebony/Jet Showcase, 1992, Welcome Freshman, 1993; albums include Discovery, 1988, Inner Child, 1992, 21...Ways to Grow, 1994. Winner first place Star Search, 1985. Office: Motown Record Co 5750 Wilshire Blvd Ste 300 Los Angeles CA 90036-3697*

WILSON, SHERRY DENISE, speech and language pathologist; b. Rutherford, N.C., Jan. 10, 1963; d. Morris William and Betty Jean (Hudgins) Wilson. AA, Isothermal Community Coll., 1981; BS, Cen. Mo. State U., 1985, MS, 1988. Lic. speech-lang. pathologist, N.C. Speech pathologist DePaul Hosp. Home Health, Cheyenne, Wyo., 1987, 89; coord. handicap svcs., staff speech-lang. pathologist Laramie County Head Start, Cheyenne, 1987-89; speech pathologist, supr., coord., dir. inclusive pre-sch. Ednl. Svcs. Unit # 13, Scottsbluff, 1989-95, project dir. The Early Intervention Demonstration Project, 1991-95; dir. rehab. svc. Brentwood Hills Nursing Ctr. (Beverly Enterprises), Asheville, N.C., 1995—; planning region chair Interagy. coord. Coun. Presch. Spl. Edn., Scottsbluff, Nebr., 1989-93, mem. 1993-95; mem. health adv. bd. Head Start, Gering, Nebr., 1989-91; cons. trainer in field. Founding mem. S.E. Wyo. AIDS Project, Cheyenne, 1989; Odyssey of the Mind coach Gering Jr. H.S., 1989-93; project dir., mem. exec. bd. Cmty. Devel. Coalition, 1994. Named Outstanding Speech Pathologist of Yr., Sigma Alpha Eta, 1985, Two Thousand Notable Am. Women, 1992, 96. Mem. NEA, Am. Speech-Lang.-Hearing Assn. (cert. clin. competence 1989—, Cert. Excellence 1993), Nebr. State Edn. Assn., Coun. for Exceptional Children (early childhood divsn.). Office: Brentwood Hills Nursing Ctr Asheville NC 28804

WILSON, SHERYL A., pharmacist; b. Nashville, Apr. 6, 1957; d. Robert Lewis and Norma Anne (Cox) W. BS in Biology, David Lipscomb U., 1979; BS in Pharmacy, Auburn U., 1985. Lic. pharmacist, Tenn. Student extern/intern East Alabama Med. Ctr., Opelika, Ala., 1982-86; staff pharmacist Metro Nashville Gen. Hosp., 1987-95, PharmaThera, Inc., Nashville, 1995—. Flutist Nashville Community Concert Band, 1973—; preschool tchr. Donelson Ch. of Christ, 1988—. Mem. Am. Pharm. Assn., Am. Soc. Health Sys. Pharmacists, Am. Soc. Parenteral and Enteral Nutrition, Tenn. Soc. Hosp. Pharmacists, Nashville Area Pharmacists Assn. Democrat. Home: 1439 Mcgavock Pike Nashville TN 37216-3231 Office: PharmaThera Inc 1410 Donelson Pike Ste B-3 Nashville TN 37217

WILSON, SHERYL J., state agency administrator; b. Shelton, Wash., May 23, 1936; d. Kenneth F. and Bernice (Angell) Sturdevant; m. Daniel I. Stuckey, Sept. 8, 1956 (div. June 1967); children: Mark, Ann, David, Noni; m. Donald R. Wilson, Aug. 9, 1968. Student, Wash. State U., 1954-57; BA, Evergreen State Coll., 1985. Rsch. analyst Wash. Pub. Pension Commn., Olympia, 1967-75; budget analyst Wash. State Senate, Olympia, 1975-80; retirement and ins. officer U. Wash., Seattle, 1980-83; asst. dir. Wash. Dept. Retirement Sys., Olympia, 1983-89, dir., 1993—; exec. dir. Oreg. Pub. Employees Retirement Sys., Portland, 1989-93; mem. exec. com. Nat. Coun. Tchr. Retirement, Astin, 1992—, mem. com. on deferred compensation, 1995—; pres., mem. exec. com. Nat. Preretirement Edn. Assn., 1985-91; chair Wash. State Investment Bd., Olympia, 1995—; mem. steering com. cert. employee benefit specialist program U. Wash., 1983—; mem. vis. com. U. Wash. Ext., 1996—. Chair Interagy. Com. Status of Women, Olympia, 1987-88. Mem. Nat. Assn. State Retirement Adminstrs. (legis. com. 1989—), Women in Pub. Adminstrn. (founder Oreg. chpt. 1990), Govt. Fin. Officers (retirement and benefits adminstrn. com. 1992—), Zonta Internat.

WILSON, SKEETER J. H., real estate sales executive; b. Pineville, La., Aug. 25, 1952; d. Gary Lee and Patricia Eleanor (Smart) Thomsen; m. Patrick Bing Renquist, Mar., 1971 (div. 1976); 1 child, Moon Ivy; m. Michael James Wilson, Feb. 12, 1977; 1 child, Shannon Michelle. Grad. high sch., Holdrege, Neb., 1970. Office mgr. So. New Eng. Eggs, Ledyard, Conn., 1970-73; asst. mgr. Topps & Trowsers, Denver, 1974-76; head teller Boeing Credit Union, Seattle, 1976-78; accounts clk. Stanley Structures, Denver, 1981-84; sales mgr. Sheraton Graystone Castle, Denver, 1985-87; dir. sales Ramada Hotel Denver/Boulder, 1987—; mem. Adams County (Colo.) Pvt. Industry Coun., 1988-94. Tchr. Jr. Achievement, Denver, 1989—, pvt. industry coun. chair, 1992-93; tchr. Northglenn (Colo.) High Sch., 1989—, mem. mktg. adv. com.; chair Metro North Polit. Action Com., Denver, 1989-90; chair Com. to Re-elect Mayor Carpenter, Thornton, 1988; mem. zoning bd. appeals City of Thornton, 1990-95. Mem. Rocky Mountain Bus. Travelers Assn., Soc. Govt. Mktg. Planners, Colo. Ramada Mgrs. Assn. (sec. 1989-90), Metro C. of C. (amb., chair 1988-90, vice chair membership and mktg. 1991, 92, fin. com. 1992, Leadership award 1985-86, Bus. Woman of Yr. award 1988, 91), Women of the Moose. Office: ReMax N W 12000 Pecos St Denver CO 80234-2074

WILSON, STEPHANIE RENAE, district attorney; b. Seattle, Nov. 29, 1968; d. Garry and Diane (Page) W. BA, Scripps Coll., Claremont, Calif., 1990; JD, Southwestern U., L.A., 1993. Bar: Calif. 1993. Dep. dist. atty. L.A. County Dist Atty., 1994—. Vol. tchr. Project Lead, Compton, Calif., 1995. Named Outstanding Woman Law Grad. Nat. Assn. Women Lawyers, 1993. Office: LA County Dist Atty 200 W Compton Blvd 7th Fl Compton CA 90212

WILSON, SUSAN BERNADETTE, psychologist; b. Pitts., May 3, 1954; d. Booker Talifero and Edna Jean (Marconi) W.; m. John C. Scott Jr., Feb. 1975 (div.); children: Sharmel D., Justin. BS cum laude, U. Pitts., 1974, MS, 1981, PhD, 1985. Lic. clin. psychologist, Mo. Teaching asst., fellow U. Pitts., 1979-81; intern VA Med. Ctr., Pitts., 1983-84; staff psychologist, fellow Menninger Found., Topeka, 1984-89; clin. dir. Crittenton Kansas City (Mo.) Clinic, 1989-90; asst. prof. Med. Sch. U. Mo., Kansas City, 1990—; cons. The Kaufmann Found., Kansas City, 1990; mem. faculty Karl Menninger Sch. Psychiatry, Topeka, 1986-89; asst. prof. Sch. Medicine, U. Mo., Kansas City, 1990—. Creator workshop: Being the Best You Can Be: A Psychoeducational Program for an Urban Workforce, 1989. Commr. Mayor's Commn. on Human Rights, Kansas City, 1992—; regional adv. com. Dept. Mental Health, Alcohol and Drug Abuse, 1992. Provost Devel. Fund fellow U. Pitts., 1977-79. Mem. Am. Psychol. Assn., Am. Group Psychotherapy, Jack and Jill of Am., Delta Sigma Theta. Democrat. Roman Catholic. Home: 7223 E 134th Cir Grandview MO 64030-3343 Office: Crittenton Kansas City 10918 Elm Ave Kansas City MO 64134-4108

WILSON, TERESA ANN, maternal/newborn nurse; b. Iowa City, Sept. 1, 1950; d. Robert Reginald and Patricia Mary (McMahon) W. B of Gen. Studies, U. Iowa, 1972, BSN, 1983; MS in Maternal Newborn Nursing, U. Ariz., 1990. RN, Ariz., Iowa. Staff nurse maternity ward U. Iowa Hosps./Clinics, Iowa City, 1983-85; nurse level III Carondelet St. Joseph's Hosp., Tucson, 1985-94; clin. mgr. labor delivery recovery postpartum Carondelet St. Mary's Hosp., Tucson, 1994-96, nurse level IV, 1996—; instr. childbirth and parenting Carondelet St. Joseph's Hosp., Tucson, 1986-93; project dir., rsch. specialist U. Ariz. Coll. Nursing, Tucson, 1991-92, clin. instr., 1993; nurse level III, Tucson Med. Ctr., 1992-94; cons. Ariz. Dept. Health Svcs., Office of Women & Children's Health, 1996—. Mem. cmty. svcs. com. So. Ariz. March of Dimes, 1990-96, cmty. adv. bd. The Parent Connection Inc., 1992—; health educator El Rio Health Ctr., Tucson, 1992-95; adv. bd. trainer Woman to Woman Cmty. Prenatal Action Team, 1994-95. Mem. Pima County Health Mothers Health Babies Coalition (sec. 1991-96), Assn. Women's Health, Obstetrics and Neonatal Nursing (chpt. coord. 1991-94), Tucson-Almaty Health Care Coalition, Sigma Theta Tau. Office: Carondelet St Mary's Hosp 1601 W St Mary's Rd Tucson AZ 85745

WILSON, TISH, children's services administrator; b. San Diego, Feb. 27, 1950; d. Kelley Frank and Evelyn Jewel (Parr) Scott; m. David Alexander Stephenson, Apr. 17, 1983; children: Wes, Dwight. BS, San Diego State U., 1973; MS, Utah State U., 1976. Tchr. Neighborhood Assoc./Head Start, San Diego, 1970-72, San Diego Unified Schs., 1972-73; instr. Utah State U., Logan, 1973-78; edn. coord. Ute Indian Tribe, Ft. Duchesne, Utah, 1975-78; edn. specialist Community Devel. Inst., Kansas City, Mo., 1978-79; exec. dir. Community Devel. Inst., Albuquerque, 1979-88; divsn. head early childhood multicultural edn. program Santa Fe C.C., 1988-95; systems devel. dir. Presbyn. Med. Svcs., Santa Fe, 1995—; bd. dirs. Community Devel. Inst., Albuquerque, Work Systems by Design, Kansas City, Twisted Pine Nursery, Inc., Santa Fe; validator Acad. of Early Childhood Programs, Washington, 1984—; rep. Cun. for Early Childhood Profl. Recognition, Washington, 1978—. Mem. City of Santa Fe Children & Youth Commn., 1990-92; task force mem. State of N.M., House Meml., Santa Fe, 1989-95, Senate Joint Meml., 1996—. Recipient Gov.'s Outstanding N.Mex. Women award, 1995. Mem. Nat. Assn. for the Edn. of Young Children, N.Mex. Head Start Assn. Democrat. Office: Presbyn Med Svcs PO Box 2267 1422 Paseo De Peralta Santa Fe NM 87504

WILSON, VICTORIA JANE SIMPSON, former nurse, farmer; b. Floresville, Tex., Nov. 30, 1952; d. Joseph Eugene and Eva Gertrude (Ferguson) Simpson; m. Richard Royce Wilson, May 15, 1976; children: Sarah Beth, Nathan Lawrence. BSN, U. Cen. Ark., 1977; MS in Nursing, Northwestern State U., 1981. Charge nurse surg. St. Vincent Infirmary,

Little Rock; staff nurse ICU La. State U. Med. Ctr., Shreveport, La.; patient edn. coord. White River Med. Ctr., Batesville, Ark.; co-owner, chief exec. officer Health Plus, Stuttgart, Ark.; co-owner, mgr. Wilson & Son Fish Farm. Mem. Catfish Farmers Am. (bd. dirs.), Catfish Farmers Ark., Sigma Theta Tau. Home and Office: Rt 1 PO Box 310 Humphrey AR 72073-0310

WILSON, WENDY MELGARD, elementary and special education educator; b. Fargo, N.D., Jan. 13, 1952; d. Howard A. Melgard and Grace B. (Alphson) Watkins; m. Henry Milton Wilson II, July 31, 1982; children: Andrew J., Aaron C. BA/BS in Edn., U. N.D., 1972-77; postgrad., Drake U., 1984-86, Simpson Coll., 1992-94. Secondary spl. edn. tchr. Ctrl. Decatur Community Schs., Leon, Iowa, 1978-80; work experience instr. Green Valley AEA, Creston, Iowa, 1980-82; elem. spl. edn. tchr. Stuart (Iowa) Menlo Community Schs., 1983-86; elem. spl. edn. tchr. Greenfield (Iowa) Community Schs., 1986-93, kindergarten tchr., 1993—; pres., bd. dirs. Little Lambs Presch., Greenfield, 1991-92; sec., v.p. bd. Sunshine Daycare Ctr., Greenfield, 1987-90; co-chairperson S.W. Iowa Very Spl. Art Festival, Creston, 1981; innkeeper, co-owner Wilson Home Bed & Breakfast, 1986-95. com. mem. Greenfield Tourism Com., 1988-94; mem. Greenfield Mother's Club, 1987—, sec., 1991; mem. Adair County Meml. Hosp. Aux., 1987—. Mem. NEA, PEO, Greenfield Edn. Assn. (pres., v.p., com. ch. 1989-91), Nat. Assn. for Educating Young Children, Iowa State Edn. Assn., Iowa Bed and Breakfast Innkeepers Assn. (sec. 1990-92), Greenfield C. of C., Winterset C. of C., Greenfield Bus. Women, Iowa Aviation Preservation Soc. Home: PO Box 93 Greenfield IA 50849-9757

WILSON-WEBB, NANCY LOU, adult educational administrator; b. Maypearl, Tex., Jan. 20, 1932; d. Madison Grady and Mary Nancy Pearson (Haney) Wilson; m. John Crawford Webb, July 29, 1972. BS magna cum laude, Abilene (Tex.) Christian U., 1953; MEd with high honors, Tex. Christian U., 1985. Cert. tchr., adult edn. dir., Tex. Tchr. elem. grades Ft. Worth Ind. Sch. Dist., 1953-67, tchr., 1970-73; dir. adult edn. consortium for 38 sch. dists. Tex. Edn. Agy., 1973—; pres. Nat. Commn. on Adult Basic Edn., 1994-95; pres. Tex. Adult Edn. Adminstrn., 1994; apptd. mem. Tex. State Literacy Coun., 1987—, Tex. State Sch. Bd. Commn., 1994-95; exec. bd. Tex. Coun. Co-op Dirs., 1989—. Cons. to textbook: On Your Mark?, 1994. Pres. Jr. Womans Club, Ft. Worth, 1969, Fine Arts Guild, Tex. Christian U., Ft. Worth, 1970-72, Ft. Worth Womens Civic Club Coun., 1970; active Exec. Libr. Bd., Ft. Worth, 1990—; apptd. bd. dirs. Literacy Plus in North Tex., 1988, Greater Ft. Worth Literacy Coun.; commr. Ed-16 Task Forces Tex. Edn. Agy., 1985-92; literacy bd. dirs. Friends of Libr., 1967—, Opera Guild Ft. Worth, 1965—, Johnson County (Tex.) Corrs. Bd. Recipient Bevy award Jr. Womans Club, 1968, Proclamation Commrs. Ct. Outstanding 40 Yr. Literacy Svc. to Tarrant County, 1994, Tarrant County Woman of Yr. award, 1995, Outstanding Leadership award Ft. Worth ISD Sch. Bd., 1995; named one of Most Outstanding Educators in U.S. Nat. Assn. Adult Edn., 1983, Most Outstanding Woman Edn., City of Ft. Worth, 1991, others; named to Tex. Hall of Fame for Women, 1991; scholar Germany, 1983. Mem. NEA, DAR (Nat. Most Outstanding Literacy award 1992, Leadership Literacy award 1985-87, 89, 94), AAUW, Am. Assn. Adult and Continuing Edn. (v.p. 1987-89, chair 1993 internat. conv. 1992) Tex. Assn. Adult and Continuing Edn. (pres. 1985-86, Most Outstanding Adult Adminstr. in Tex. 1984), Tex. Coun. Adult Edn. Dirs. (pres.), Coun. World Affairs (bd. dirs. 1980-92), Am. Bus. Womens Assn., Ft. Worth C. of C., Lecture Found., Internat. Reading Assn. (Literacy Challenge award 1991), Ft. Worth Adminstrv. Assn., Zonta, Ft. Worth Garden Club, Womans Club Ft. Worth, Petroleum Club, Carousel Dance Assn., Optimist Club (Ft. Worth), Met. Dinner and Dance Club, Ridglea County Club, Crescent Club, Phi Beta Kappa, Alpha Delta Kappa (Nat. Literacy award), Phi Delta Kappa. Democrat. Mem. Church of Christ. Home: 3716 Fox Hollow St Fort Worth TX 76109-2616 Office: 100 N University Dr Fort Worth TX 76107-1360

WILSTED, JOY, elementary education educator, reading specialist, parenting consultant; b. St. Marys, Pa., Aug. 12, 1935; d. Wayne and Carrie (Neiger) Furman; m. Richard William Wilsted, Feb. 14, 1982; 2 children. BA, Fla. Atlantic U., 1970; MS in Edn., Old Dominion U., Norfolk, Va., 1975. Cert. reading specialist, elem. tchr., Mo.; cert. permanent tchr., N.Y. Tchr. creative dramatics Hillsboro Country Day Sch., Pompano Beach, Fla., 1966-68; tchr. PTA Kindergarten, Boca Raton, Fla., 1968-69; tchr. creative dramatics Wee-Wisdom Montessori Sch., Delray Beach, Fla., 1969-70; elem. tchr. Birmingham (Mich.) Pub. Schs., 1970-72; classroom and reading resource tchr. Chesapeake (Va.) Pub. Schs., 1972-79; reading coord. Harrisonville (Mo.) Pub. Schs., 1979-81; Chpt. I reading tchr., reading improvement tchr. North Kansas City Pub. Schs., Kansas City, Mo., 1981-96; instr. continuing edn. U. Mo., Kansas City, 1980-87, Ottawa U., Overland Park, Kans., 1990—; cons. Young Authors' Conf., Oakland U., Rochester, Mich., 1971; coord. fine arts Alpha Phi Alpha Tutorial Project, Chesapeake, 1973-75; presenter Chpt. I Summer Inst., Tech. Asistance Ctr., Mo., 1984; cons. on parenting Reading Success Unltd., Gallatin, Mo., 1987—; mem. adv. bd. Parents & Children Together, Ind. U. Family Literacy Ctr., Bloomington, 1990-93; keynote speaker ann conf. Nat. Coalition of Chapter I Parents. Author: Dramatics for Self-Expression, 1967, Now Johnny CAN Learn to Read, 1987, Reading Songs and Poems of Joy, 1987, Character-Building Poems for Young People. Mem. Internat. Reading Assn. (mem. coun., pres. local coun. 1986-88, state chmn. parents and reading com. 1988-89, mem. nat. parents and reading com. 1989-92, keynote spkr. IRA Conf. Inst. 1990, local coun., Literacy award 1989). Office: Reading SUCCESS Unltd PO Box 215 Gallatin MO 64640-0215

WIMBERLY, EVELYN LOUISE RUSSELL, nursing coordinator; b. Tallutah, La., Feb. 7, 1941; d. Luther Franklin and Marion Gertrude (Martin) Russell; m. William Lary Wimberly, Mar. 29, 1963; children: Collin, Holly, Allison. BSN, Northwestern State U., 1963; MSN, Northwestern State U. La., 1994. Head nurse Hanna Hosp., Coushatta, La.; dir. nurses Sr. Citizen Ctrs., Coushatta; evening supr. Riverside Med. Ctr., Bossier City, La.; house supr. La. State U. Hosp., Shreveport, coord. nursing quality improvement and policy and procedure. Mem. ANA, La. Nurses Assn., Sigma Theta Tau (Beta Chi chpt.). Home: PO Box 145 Hall Summit LA 71034-0145

WIMMER, MAUREEN KATHRYN, chemical engineer; b. Quakertown, Pa., Oct. 25, 1969; d. Ronald Homer and Jane (Astheimer) W. BSChemE, Lehigh U., 1992. Engring. intern Gen. Chem., Claymont, Del., 1991; process control engr. Johnson Matthey CSD, Wayne, Pa., 1992-94, washcoat engr., 1994—. Mem. AIChE. Republican. Lutheran. Home: 123 Roskeen Ct Phoenixville PA 19460

WIN, KHIN SWE, anesthesiologist; b. Rangoon, Burma, Sept. 27, 1934; came to U.S., 1962; d. U Mg and Daw Aye (Kyin) Maung; m. M. Shein Win, May 28, 1959; children: Tha Shein, Thwe Shein, Maw Shein, Thet Shein, Htoo Shein. Intermediate of Sci. Degree, U. Rangoon, 1954, MB, BS, 1962. Intern Waltham (Mass.) Hosp., 1962-63; resident anesthesiology Boston City Hosp., 1963-65; fellow pediatric anesthesiology New Eng. Med. Ctr. Hosps., Boston, 1965-66; fellow anesthesiology Martin Luther King Jr. Gen. Hosp., L.A., 1978-79; pvt. practice anesthesiology Apple Valley, Calif., 1984—; asst. prof. anesthesiology Martin Luther King Jr./Charles R. Drew Med. Ctr., L.A., 1979-84. Republican. Buddhist. Home: 13850 Pamlico Rd Apple Valley CA 92307-5400 Office: St Mary Desert Valley Hosp Dept Anesthesiology 18300 Us Highway 18 Apple Valley CA 92307-2206

WINANS, ANNA JANE, dietitian; b. Freeport, Ill., June 13, 1939; d. Leo Dale and Gwendolyn Jane White; m. Roger Eugene Winans, Aug. 26, 1967; children: Robert, Jonathan. BS in Dietetics, Iowa State U., 1962. Registered dietitian. Clin. dietitian VA Hosp., Madison, Wis., 1963-67; coord. U. Wis. Hosp., Madison, 1967-69; instr. nutrition Madison Gen. Hosp., 1969-75, Madison Area Coll., 1976-81; nutritionist Women, Infants and Children Nutrition Program, USDA, Fremont, Nebr., 1981—; nutrition cons. area health care facilities, Wis., 1976-81, Nebr., 1985—; food svc. auditor, 1995—. Sec. Chapel Hill Pool Bd., Elkhorn, Nebr., 1987-89; bd. dirs. Homeowner's Assn., Elkhorn, 1989-93; active Elkhorn Woman's Club, 1982—; pres. Elkhorn Libr. Bd., 1989-91, 94. Mem. Am. Dietetic Assn. (registered), Nebr. Dietetic Assn., Omaha Dietetic Assn., PEO, Omicron Nu, Psi Chi. Methodist. Home: 910 S 218th St Elkhorn NE 68022-1938 Office: WIC 626 N D St Fremont NE 68025-5054

WINBUSH, ANGELA, singer, producer; b. St. Louis; m. Ronald Isley. Student, Howard U. Singer Stevie Wonder's Wonderlove, 1970's, René & Angela, 1980, solo recording career, 1987—; co-prodr. Isley Bros., 1987—; founder Angela Winbush Prodns., 1990—; toured U.S., England, Japan with Isley Bros.; writer, arranger, producer for Janet Jackson, Sheena Easton, Stephanie Mills, Lalah Hathaway, others. Albums include The Real Thing, 1989, Angela Winbush, 1994. Office: Elektra Entertainment 75 Rockefeller Plz New York NY 10019*

WINBY, MARY BERNADETTE, marketing executive; b. N.Y.C., Sept. 16, 1958; d. John Joseph and Theresa Eunice (Schoeffler) Vasile; m. Allan Gerard Winby, July 21, 1990. BSBA, St. John's U., Jamaica, N.Y., 1980. V.p. mktg. IBM Mid-Hudson Employees Fed. Credit Union, Kingston, N.Y., 1989-92; officer, dir. mktg. Mid-Hudson Savings Bank, FSB, 1992-94; pres., owner The Mktg. Analysts, Patterson, N.Y., 1994—; pres., owner Freelance Advt. Co., Poughkeepsie, N.Y., 1982-88; cons., tchr. in field. Office: The Mktg Analysts Hampshire Ctr Rte 311 Patterson NY 12563

WINCE-SMITH, DEBORAH L., federal agency administrator; m. Michael B. Smith; 2 children. Grad. magna cum laude, Vassar Coll., 1972; Master's, Cambridge (Eng.) U., 1974. Former program mgr. internat. programs NSF; asst. dir. internat. affairs and global competitiveness Office of Sci. and Tech. Policy The White House, 1984-89; asst. sec. tech. policy Dept. Commerce, Washington, 1989-93; sr. fellow Coun. on Competitiveness, Washington, 1993—; sr. fellow Congl. Econ. Leadership Inst., Washington, 1993—. Office: Coun on Competitiveness 1401 H St NW Ste 650 Washington DC 20005

WINCHELL, MARGARET WEBSTER ST. CLAIR, realtor; b. Clinton, Tenn., Jan. 26, 1923; d. Robert Love and Mayme Jane (Warwick) Webster; student Denison U., 1940, Miami U., Oxford (Ohio), 1947, 48; m. Charles M. Winchell, June 7, 1941; children—David Alan (dec.), Margaret Winchell Boyle; m. 2d, Robert George Sterrett, July 15, 1977 (dec. 1982). Saleswoman Fred K.A. Schmidt & Shirmer real estate, Cin., 1960-66, Cline Realtors, Cin., 1966-70; owner, broker Winchell's Showplace Realtors, Cin., 1972—; ins. agt. United Liberty Life Ins. Co., 1966—, dist. mgr., 1967-70, 77-82, regional mgr., 1982—; stockbroker Waddell & Reed, Columbus, Ohio, 1972—, Security Counselors; ins. broker, 1984, gen. agent; dir. Fin. Consultants, 1984, 85, 86, 87, owner; instr. evening coll. Treas., v.p. Parents without Partners, 1969, sec., 1968; pres. PTA; dir. Children's Bible Fellowship Ohio, 1953-76; dir. Child Evangelism Cin.; nat. speaker Child Evangelism Fellowship and Nat. Sunday Sch. Convs., 1955-57; pres. Christian Solos, 1974, Hamilton Fairfield Singles; chaplain Bethesda N. Hosp.; leader singles groups Hyde Park Community United Meth. Ch.; dir. Financial Cons., Sr. Ctr. Dance Leader and Coord. Mem. Nat. Assn. Real Estate Bds. West Shell Realtors (v.p.), Womens Council Real Estate Bd. (treas.). Clubs: Alfonta, Travel go go, Guys and Gals Singles (founder, 1st pres.), Hamilton Singles (pres.). Home and Office: 8221 Margaret Ln Cincinnati OH 45242-5309

WINDHAM, PATRICIA WOOD, community college official; b. Andalusia, Ala., Oct. 9, 1946; d. John Edwin and Sarah Roberta (Cochran) W.; m. Bernard Moore, Dec. 28, 1974; children: Cynthia Lynn, Phillip Bernard, Jonathan Patrick. BS, Birmingham-So. Coll., 1969; MS, Fla. State U., 1971; PhD, 1994. Statistician II, Fla. Dept. Labor and Employment Security, Tallahassee, 1972-74; statistician III, Fla. Dept. Environ. Regulation, Tallahassee, 1974-76; rsch. asst. Fla. Dept. Adminstrn., Tallahassee, 1976, fed. programs analyst, 1976-77; rsch. assoc. Fla. Dept. Edn., Tallahassee, 1977-84; instnl. rsch. adminstr. Tallahassee Community Coll., 1984-96; edn. policy dir. edn. effectiveness and rsch. Fla. Dept. Edn., Tallahassee, 1996—; mem. Edn. Equity Act. Adv. Group, Tallahassee, 1987-92, MIS Adv. TAsk Froce, Tallahassee, 1989-91. Contbr. articles to profl. jours. Mem. AAUW (br. program v.p. 1994-96, br. pres. 1996—), Assn. for Instnl. Rsch., Am. Assn. for Higher Edn., Fla. Assn. for Instnl. Rsch. (sec.-treas. 1989-91, pres.-elect 1991-92, pres. 1992-93), Southeastern Assn. for c.C. Rsch. (pres.-elect 1993-94, pres. 1994-95). Democrat. Mem. United Ch. Christ. Office: State Bd Cmty Coll 1340 Turlington Bldg 325 West Gaines St Tallahassee FL 32399-0400

WINDROW, KATHY, artist, educator; b. Dallas, Mar. 17, 1953; d. Robert David and Mary Frances (Taylor) W.; m. Jess Ryland Galloway, Oct. 23, 1982. BFA summa cum laude, So. Meth. U., 1984, MFA, 1986, MA, 1993. Co-owner Appalachian Hang Gliding Sch. & Great Outdoors, Louisville, 1974-78; adj. instr. art, art history Eastfield Coll., Mesquite, Tex., 1986-92, prof. art, 1992—, co-chair art dept., 1995—; instr. art, art history continuing edn. So. Meth. U., Dallas, 1987—, asst. dir. SMU in Italy, 1991—; lectr. art history U. Tex., Tyler, 1991; assoc. mus. educator Dallas Mus. Art, 1988-91, curatorial rsch. asst., 1992; cons. Intercultura, Fort Worth, 1990—; project illustrator excavations in Tuscany So. Meth. U., 1995—; lectr. in field. Set designer: Small Craft Warnings, 1995, Faust, 1995, The Bargain, 1996; exhbns. include So. Meth. U., 1984, 500 X Gallery, 1984, Clifford Gallery, Dallas, 1984, Tex. Christian U., Fort Worth, 1986, Crescent Gallery, Dallas, 1988, Lamar U., Beaumont, Tex., 1992, Durango (Colo.) Arts Ctr., 1992, Warehouse Living Arts Ctr., Corsicana, Tex., 1992, Hickory St. Gallery, Dallas, 1993, Tex. Biennial, Dallas, 1993, Elizabeth Baker Gallery, Dallas, 1994, Pesterzsébeti Mus., Budapest, Hungary, 1994-95, Bath House Cultural Ctr., Dallas, 1994, Lubbock (Tex.) Fine Arts Ctr., 1994, Trammell Crow Ctr., Dallas, 1994, Harwood Ctr. Gallery, Albuquerque, 1994, Craighead-Green Gallery, Dallas, 1995, Dallas Visual Art Ctr., 1995, L.A. Thompson Gallery, Dallas, 1996, others; represented in permanent collections at So. Meth. U., Ariz. State U., pvt. collections. Founder, coord. Art Outreach Program Eastfield Coll., 1996—. Haakon rsch. grantee Meadows Sch. Grad. Studies, 1984—. Mem. Tex. Fine Arts Assn., Dallas Zen Ctr. (bd. trustees), Albuquerque United Artists, Womens Caucus Arts, Coll. Art Assn.. Democrat. Buddhist. Office: Eastfield Coll 3737 Motley Dr Mesquite TX 75150

WINDSOR, AGATHA SYLVIA, state trooper; b. Dothan, Ala., July 20, 1958; d. Harold and Agnes Louise (Miller) Windsor. BS, Troy State U., 1979, MS in Criminal Justice, 1980; MS in Counseling and Human Devel., Troy State U. Montgomery, 1992. Cert. Peace Officers Standard Tng. Commn., State of Ala. State trooper Ala. Dept. Pub. Safety, Montgomery, 1980—. Adviser Explorer scouts Boy Scouts Am., Montgomery, 1987-92; mem. Coun. of Substance Abuse, Montgomery, 1995—; ch. tour guide Dexter King Meml. Bapt. Ch., Montgomery, 1989-93. Named Outstanding Young Law Enforcement Officer, Decatur Jaycees, 1983, named to Congress of Outstanding Alabamians, 1983; named Outstanding Law Enforcement Officer, Altrusa Club, Decatur, 1984; recipient Nellie B. Mobley traffic safety award, 1995. Mem. Ala. State Troopers Assn., Ctrl. State Troopers Assn., Alpha Kappa (pres. 1978-82). Baptist. Home: 811 Deatsville Hwy Apt A10 Millbrook AL 36054

WINDSOR, JOAN RUTH, author, professional counselor; b. Rahway, N.J., Dec. 26, 1934; d. Thomas Clifford and Ruth L. (Labar) Laurent; m. James Clayton Windsor, June 22, 1957; children: James Laurent, Robin Joan Windsor Rice. BA in French, Coll. William and Mary, 1956, MEd in Counseling and Guidance, 1969. Lic. profl. counselor, Va. Tchr. 4th grade Rahway (N.J.) Sch. System, 1956-57, Rochester (N.Y.) Sch. System, 1957-58; edn. diagnostician Coll. William and Mary, Williamsburg, Va., 1968-70, Child Devel. Clinic, Hampton, Va., 1968-72; learning devel. counselor Personal Devel. Inst., Newport News, Va., 1972-75, personal devel. counselor, 1975-88; owner mgr., counselor Personal Devel. Inst., Williamsburg, Va., 1988—; continuing edn. instr. Coll. William & Mary, Williamsburg, 1994-95; presenter med. rsch. Jungian Analysts, Memphis, Tenn., 1995, Internat. Parapsychol. Assn., Durham, N.C., 1995. Author: (books) The Inner Eye, 1986, Dreams and Healing, 1988, Passages of Light, 1991; also articles. Grantee: Pvt. Grant, Williamsburg, Va., 1992. Mem. ACA. Office: Personal Devel Inst PO Box 1056 Williamsburg VA 23187

WINE-BANKS, JILL SUSAN, lawyer; b. Chgo., May 5, 1943; d. Bert S. and Sylvia Dawn (Simon) Wine; m. Ian David Volner, Aug. 21, 1965; m. Michael A. Banks, Jan. 12, 1980. BS, U. Ill.-Champaign-Urbana, 1964; JD, Columbia U., 1968; LLD (hon.), Hood Coll., 1975. Bar: N.Y. 1969, U.S. Ct. Appeals (4th cir.) 1969, U.S. Ct. Appeals (6th and 9th cirs.) 1973, U.S. Supreme Ct. 1974, D.C. 1976, Ill. 1980. Asst. press. and pub. rels. dir. Assembly of Captive European Nations, N.Y.C., 1965-66; trial atty. criminal div. organized crime and racketeering sect. and labor racketeering sect. U.S. Dept. Justice, 1969-73; asst. spl. prosecutor Watergate Spl. Prosecutor's Office, 1973-75; lectr. law seminar on trial practice Columbia U. Sch. Law, N.Y.C., 1975-77; assoc. Fried, Frank, Harris, Shriver & Kampelman, Washington, 1975-77; gen. counsel Dept. Army, Pentagon, Washington, 1977-79; ptnr. Jenner & Block, Chgo., 1980-84; solicitor gen. State of Ill. Office of Atty. Gen., 1984-86, dep. atty. gen., 1986-87; exec. v.p., chief oper. officer ABA, Chgo., 1987-90; pvt. practice law, 1990-92; bd. dirs. Cenvill Devel. Corp., 1991-92; v.p. Motorola Internat. Network Ventures Inc. and dir. strategic transaction and alliance group Network Ventures Divsn., Motorola, 1992—; mem. EEC disting. vis. program European Parliament, 1987; bd. dirs. Cenvill Devel. Corp., 1991-92; chmn. bd. dirs. St. Petersburg Telecom, Russia, 1994—, Omni Capital Ptnrs., Inc., 1994—; mem. bd. assocs. program for the study of cultural values & ethics U. Ill. Recipient Spl. Achievement award U.S. Dept. Justice, 1972, Meritorious award, 1973, Cert. Outstanding Svc., 1975; decoration for Disting. Civilian Svc., Dept. Army, 1979; named Disting. Visitor to European Econ. Community. Mem. Internat. Women's Forum, The Chgo. Network, Econ. Club. Address: 425 N Martingale Rd Ste 18 Schaumburg IL 60173-2219

WINEBRENNER, BETH ANN, social worker, college student affairs specialist; b. South Bend, Ind., Feb. 25, 1950; d. Jack Joseph and Marina Louise (Hudson) W.; m. Louis Attila Pierre Balázs, May 27, 1984. BS, Ball State U., 1972; MSW, Ind. U., Indpls., 1978; MS, Purdue U., 1991. Cert. clin. social worker; lic. sch. social worker. Case worker Clay County Dept. Pub. Welfare, Brazil, Ind., 1973, Monroe County Dept. Pub. Welfare, Bloomington, Ind., 1973-76; med. social worker Bloomington Hosp., 1978-79; assessment counselor Employment Devel. Systems, Inc., Frankfort, Ind., 1979-88; fin. planner Waddell & Reed, Inc., Lafayette, Ind., 1988-90; case worker Family Svcs. Inc., Lafayette, Ind., 1989-90; med. social worker Vis. Nurse Home Health Svc., Lafayette area, 1992; spl. asst. to dir. internat. student svcs. Purdue U., West Lafayette, Ind., 1992-93; program mgr./psychotherapist partial hospitalization program Charter Hosp. Lafayette, 1993-94, psychotherapist adolescent outpatient program, 1994—; asst. exec. dir. Lion and Lamb Journeys, Inc., West Lafayette, 1995—; tchr. Hong Kong Coll. Langs., Kowloon, summer 1977; asst. to v.p. Ind. Hosp. Assn., Indpls., summer 1978. Chmn. Com. Human Rights in USSR of Greater Lafayette, 1982-91; mem. Speaker's Corps Mayor's Commn. on Status of Women, Columbus, Ind., 1972, Internat. Awareness Task Force Greater Lafayette, 1991. Mem. ACA, NASW (student rep. to state bd. 1977), Assn. Specialists in Group Work, Am. Coll. Counseling Assn., Acad. Cert. Social Workers, Pi Gamma Mu, Kappa Delta Pi. Democrat. Roman Catholic. Home: 218 Trace Two West Lafayette IN 47906-1869

WINFREY, OPRAH, television talk show host, actress, producer; b. Kosciusko, Miss., Jan. 29, 1954; d. Vernon Winfrey and Vernita Lee. BA in Speech and Drama, Tenn. State U. News reporter Sta. WVOL Radio, Nashville, 1971-72; reporter, news anchorperson Sta. WTVF-TV, Nashville, 1973-76; news anchorperson Sta. WJZ-TV, Balt., 1976-77, host morning talk show People Are Talking, 1977-83; host talk show A.M. Chgo. Sta. WLS-TV, 1984; host The Oprah Winfrey Show, Chgo., 1985—; nationally syndicated, 1986—; host series of celebrity interview spls. Oprah: Behind the Scenes, 1992—; owner, prodr. Harpo Prodns., 1986—. Appeared in films The Color Purple, 1985 (nominated Acad. award and Golden Globe award), Native Son, 1986, Throw Momma From the Train, 1988, Listen Up: The Lives of Quincy Jones, 1990; prodr., actress ABC-TV mini-series The Women of Brewster Place, 1989, also series Brewster Place, 1990, movie There Are No Children Here, 1993; exec. prodr. (ABC Movie of the Week) Overexposed, 1992; host, supervising prodr. celebrity interview series Oprah: Behind the Scenes, 1992, ABC Afterschool. Spls., 1991-93; host, exec. prodr. Michael Jackson Talks...to Oprah-90 Prime-Time Minutes with the King of Pop, 1993. Recipient Woman of Achievement award NOW, 1986, Emmy award for Best Daytime Talk Show Host, 1987, 91, 92, 94, 95, America's Hope award, 1990, Industry Achievement award Broadcast Promotion Mktg. Execs./Broadcast Design Assn., 1991, Image awards NAACP, 1989, 90, 91, 92, Entertainer of the Yr. award NAACP, 1989, CEBA awards, 1989, 90, 91, George Foster Peabody's Individual Achievement award, Gold Medal award IRTS; named Broadcaster of Yr. Internat. Radio and TV Soc., 1988; recognized as one of America's 25 Most Influential People, Time mag. Office: Harpo Prodns 110 N Carpenter St Chicago IL 60607-2101

WING, ADRIEN KATHERINE, law educator; b. Oceanside, Calif., Aug. 7, 1956; d. John Ellison and Katherine (Pruitt) Wing; children: Che-Cabral, Nolan Felipe. A.B. magna cum laude, Princeton U., 1978; M.A., UCLA, 1979; J.D., Stanford Law Sch., 1982. Bar: N.Y. 1983, U.S. Dist. Ct. (so. and ea. dists.) N.Y. 1983, U.S. Ct. Appeals (5th and 9th cirs.). Assoc. Curtis, Mallet-Prevost, Colt & Mosle, N.Y.C., 1982-86, Rabinowitz, Boudin, Standard, Krinsky & Lieberman, 1986-87; assoc. prof. law U. Iowa, Iowa City, 1987-93, prof. law, 1993—; mem. alumni council Princeton U., 1983-85, trustee Class of '78 Alumni Found., 1984-87, v.p. Princeton Class of 1978 Alumni, 1993—; mem. bd. visitors Stanford Law Sch., 1993-96. Mem. bd. editors Am. Jour. Comp. Law, 1993—. Mem. ABA (exec. com. young lawyers sect. 1985-87), Nat. Conf. Black Lawyers (UN rep., chmn. internat. affairs sect. 1982-95), Internat. Assn. Dem. Lawyers (UN rep. 1984-87), Am. Soc. Internat. Law (exec. council 1986-89, group chair S. Africa 1996—, nom. com. 1991, 93), Black Alumni of Princeton U. (bd. dirs. 1982-87), Transafrica Scholars Forum Coun. (bd. dirs 1993—), Iowa City Foreign Rels. Coun. (bd. dirs. 1989-94), Iowa Peace Inst. (bd. dirs. 1993-95), Council on Fgn. Rels., Internat. Third World Legal Studies Assn. (bd. dirs. 1996—). Democrat. Avocations: photography, jogging, writing, poetry. Office: U Iowa Sch Law Boyd Law Bldg Iowa City IA 52242

WING, ELIZABETH SCHWARZ, museum curator, educator; b. Cambridge, Mass., Mar. 5, 1932; d. Henry F. and Maria Lisa Schwarz; m. James E. Wing, Apr. 18, 1957; children: Mary Elizabeth Wing-Berman, Stephen R. BA, Mt. Holyoke Coll., 1955; MS, U. Fla., 1957, PhD, 1962. Interim asst. curator Fla. Mus. Natural History, U. Fla., Gainesville, 1961-69, asst. curator, 1969-73, assoc. curator, 1973-78, curator, 1978—; U. Fla., Fla. Mus. Natural History, Gainesville, 1990-92; U.S. rep. Internat. Congress Archaeozoology, 1981—. Author: (with A.B. Brown) Paleonutrition, 1979; editor (with J.C. Wheeler) Economic Prehistory of the Central Andes, 1988; contbr. articles to profl. jours. Recipient Fryxell award Soc. Am. Archaeology, 1996; NSF grantee, 1961-64, 68-73, 79-80, 84-85, 89-91, 95-96. Mem. Soc. Ethnobiology (pres. 1989-91, trustee 1991—). Office: U Fla Fla Mus Natural History PO Box 117800 Museum Rd Gainesville FL 32611-7800

WINGARD, JENNIFER MARIE, association director; b. Coldwater, Mich., Apr. 15, 1946; d. Harry Edward and Charlotte Elizabeth (Miller) W.; m. Eugene Augustine Conti, Oct. 12, 1968; children: Aidan Keally, Marcus Bradley. BA in Sociology, Ea. Mich. U., 1971; M of Pub. Policy, George Washington U., 1986. Program dir. Orange County Hunger Com., N.C., 1978-79; field staff, lobbyist NOW, N.C., 1978-81; spl. asst. to the pres., dir. NOW, Washington, 1981-83; adminstr. asst., legis. asst. U.S. House, Congresswoman Katie Hall, Washington, 1983-84; staff dir. U.S. House, Subcom. on Census and Population, Washington, 1984-85; dir. assoc. dir. Nat. Assn. of State U. and Land-Grant Colls., Washington, 1985—. Vol. VISTA, Ky., 1966; v.p. N.C. NOW, 1977-79; registrar, election judge Eno Precint, N.C., 1976-79; vice chair, mem. Orange County Com. on the Status of Women, N.C., 1977-80; chair Dem. Precinct 7-11, Montgomery County, Md., 1981—; mem. PTA, 1977-92; mem., chair Women's Studies Endowment, 1985-88, 93—. Recipient Congl. fellow Women's Rsch. and Edn. Inst., 1983-84. Mem. AAUW. Home: 4613 De Russey Pkwy Chevy Chase MD 20815 Office: Nat Assn of State Univs and Land-Grant Colls One DuPont Circle Ste 710 Washington DC 20036

WININGER, CAROL SIGNORELLI, mental health counselor, elementary educator; b. New Orleans, Feb. 10, 1954; d. John James and Etta (Stansbury) Signorelli; m. Bryant Eugene Wininger, Apr. 29, 1983; children: Amy, Derek, Melanie. BA, U. New Orleans, 1981, MEd, 1995. Tchr. St. Catherine of Sienna, Metairie, La., 1981-82, St. Ann Sch., Metairie, 1982-96; mental health counselor R.A.G.S., Metairie, 1994—, Bockrath Mental Health Counseling, Metairie, 1995—; lectr. in field. Mem. ACA, La. Counseling Assn., Phi Delta Kappa, Chi Sigma Iota. Republican. Roman

Catholic. Home: 4841 Loveland St Metairie LA 70006 Office: Bockrath Mental Health Coun 3515 N Arnoult Rd Metairie LA 70002

WINKELMAN, MARY LYNN, middle school educator; b. May 22, 1950; children: Candice, Joseph. Student, U. Wis., 1968-70, BS, 1975. Cert. tchr. 1-8, Wis. 6th grade tchr. St. Williams Sch., Waukesha, Wis., 1979-90; 7th grade tchr. Waukesha Cath. Sch. Sys., St. Joseph's Middle Sch., Waukesha, 1990—. Mem. Phi Kappa Phi. Office: Waukesha Cath Sch Sys St Josephs 822 N East Ave Waukesha WI 53186-4808

WINKLE, SHARON LOUISE, library administrator; b. Cin., Nov. 29, 1950; d. John F. and Marguerite T. (Platt) W.; m. Clifford J. Smith, June 16, 1979. BS, Findlay Coll., 1972; MLS, U. Ky., 1973; MPA, U. Denver, 1984. Libr. Findlay (Ohio)-Hancock County Pub. Libr., 1973-74; deputy dir. Sandusky (Ohio) Libr., 1974-76, dir., 1976-79; libr. dir. Englewood (Colo.) Pub. Libr., 1979-89; dir. libr. and recreation svcs. City of Engelwood, 1989-90; libr. dir. Mead Pub. Libr., Sheboygan, Wis., 1991—. Ohio State U. scholar, 1972; named Mktg. Student of Yr., Findlay Coll., 1972, Outstanding MPA Student U. Denver, 1984, Woman of Yr. Englewood Bus and Profl. Women, 1989. Mem. ALA, Wis. Libr. Assn., Sheboygan Rotary, Altrusa Club Sheboygan, Sheboygan C. of C. Home: 1810 N 5th St Sheboygan WI 53081-2840 Office: Mead Pub Library 710 N 8th St Sheboygan WI 53081-4505

WINKLER, AGNIESZKA M., advertising agency executive; b. Rome, Italy, Feb. 22, 1946; came to U.S., 1953, naturalized, 1959; d. Wojciech A. and Halina Z. (Owsiany) W.; children from previous marriage: children: Renata G. Ritcheson, Dana C Sworakowski.; m. Arthur K. Lund. BA, Coll. Holy Name, 1967; MA, San Jose State U., 1971; MBA, U. Santa Clara, 1981. Teaching asst., San Jose State U., 1968-70; cons. to ea. European bus., Palo Alto, Calif., 1970-72; pres./founder Commart Communications, Palo Alto, 1973-84; pres./founder, chmn. bd. Winkler McManus, Santa Clara, Calif., 1984—; bd. dirs. Supercuts, Inc., Reno Air. Trustee Santa Clara U., 1991—; trustee O'Connor Found., 1987-93, mem. exec. com., 1988—, mem. Capital Campaign steering com., 1989; mem. nat. adv. bd. Comprehensive Health Enhancement Support System, 1991—; mem. mgmt. west com. A.A.A.A. Agy., 1991—; project dir. Poland Free Enterprise Plan, 1989-92; mem. adv. bd. Normandy France Bus. Devel., 1989-92; mem. bd. regents Holy Names Coll., 1987—; bd. dirs. San Jose Mus. Art, 1987; mem. San Jose Symphony, Gold Baton, 1986; mem. nat. adv. com. CHESS, 1991—; dir. Bay Area Coun., 1994—. Recipient CLIO award in Advt., Addy award and numerous others; named to 100 Best Women in Advt., Ad Age, 1988, Best Woman in Advt., AdWeek and McCall's Mag., 1993. Mem. Family Svc. Assn. (trustee 1980-82), Am. Assn. Advt. Agys. (agy. mgmt. west com. 1991), Bus. Profl. Advt. Assn., Polish Am. Congress, San Jose Advt. Club, San Francisco Ad Club, Beta Gamma Sigma (hon.), Pi Gamma Mu, Pi Delta Phi (Lester-Tinneman award 1966, Bill Raskob Found. grantee 1965). Office: Winkler McManus 150 Spear St Fl 16 San Francisco CA 94105-1535

WINKLER, DOLORES EUGENIA, retired hospital administrator; b. Milw., Aug. 10, 1929; d. Charles Peter and Eugenia Anne (Zamka) Kowalski; m. Donald James Winkler, Aug. 18, 1951; 1 child, David John. Grad., Milw. Bus. Inst., 1949. Acct. Curative Rehab. Ctr., Milw., 1949-60; staff acct. West Allis (Wis.) Meml. Hosp., 1968-70, chief acct., 1970-78, reimbursement analyst, 1978-85, dir. budgets and reimbursement, 1985-95; ret., 1995; mem. adv. coun./fin. com. Tau Home Health Care Agy., Milw., 1981-83. Mem. Healthcare Fin. Mgmt. Assn. (pres. 1989-90, Follmer Bronze award 1980, Reeves Silver award 1986, Muncie Gold award 1989, medal of honor 1993), Inst. Mgmt. Accts. (pres. 1983-84, nat. dir. 1986-88, pres. Mid Am. Regional Coun. 1988-89, award of excellence 1989), Beta Chi Rho (pres. 1948). Home: 12805 W Honey Ln New Berlin WI 53151-2652

WINKLER, JOANN MARY, secondary school educator; b. Savanna, Ill., Dec. 17, 1955; d. Donald Edgar and Genevieve Eleanor (Withhart) Winkler; m. Russell Arthur Ehlers, May 25, 1990. BS in Art Edn., No. Ill. U., 1979; MA in Art Edn., N.E. Mo. State U., 1984. Tchr. art, chmn. dept. art Clinton (Iowa) H.S., 1979—; Coll. for Kids instr. Area Edn. Agy. #9, Clinton, summers, 1986—, Davenport, summers, 1987—; instr. St. Ambrose U., Clinton, 1990, Mt. St. Clare Coll., Clinton, 1993—. Costume designer Utah Mus. Theatre, "Two by Two," 1987; exhibited in group shows at Clinton Art Assn., 1990-93. Judge Art in the Park, Clinton, 1988, 93; co. mgr. Utah Mus. Theager, Ogden, 1987; founding bd. dirs. Art's Alive, Clinton, 1985-86; bd. dirs. Gateway Contemporary Ballet, Clinton, 1987-89; founding com. mem. Louis Sullivan's Van Allen Bldg. Jr. Mus., Clinton, 1991-93. Recipient Gold Key Group award Clinton Sch. Bd., 1990, Gold Key Individual award, 1989; R.I. Sch. Design scholar, 1989, Alliance for Ind. Colls. of Art scholar, summers 1988. Mem. NEA, Ill. Art Edn. Assn., Chgo. Art Inst., Clinton Art Assn., Art Educators of Iowa, Nat. Art Edn. Assn., PEO. Home: 722 Melrose Ct Clinton IA 52732-5508 Office: Clinton High Sch 817 8th Ave S Clinton IA 52732-5616

WINLAND, DENISE LYNN, physician; b. Elizabeth, N.J., Aug. 9, 1951; d. James Edward and Audrey Anna (Hansen) W.; m. Charles F. Francke III, May 30, 1982; children: Shannon W. Francke, Eric W. Francke. BS with honors, Rutgers U., 1973; M in Phys. Therapy with honors, Baylor U., 1975; MD, U. Louisville, 1982. Resident in psychiatry U. Louisville, 1982-83, 90-93, staff physician student health svc., 1983-89; pvt. practice psychiatry Louisville, 1993—; emergency room physician North Clark Community Hosp., Charlestown, Ind., 1983-87; physician Immediate Care Ctrs., Louisville, 1983-86. With U.S. Army, 1974-77, lt. col. Res., 1977—. Teagle Found. scholar, 1978-82; named Outstanding Young Women Am., 1983, 84. Mem. AMA, APA, Ky. Psychiat. Assn., Ky. Med. Assn., Jefferson County Med. Assn., Res. Officers Assn., Am. Med. Women's Assn. Democrat. Mem. Unity Christian Ch. Home: 1103 Holly Springs Dr Louisville KY 40242-7762 Office: 2120 Newburg Rd Louisville KY 40205-1867

WINN, JULIE, state representative; b. Tucson, Ariz., Sept. 6, 1956; d. George Richard and Mary Kay (Behnke) W. AS, U. Maine, BS, MBA. Mem. Maine Ho. of Reps., Augusta, 1993—. Home: 139 Merryman Rd Glenburn ME 04401 Office: Maine House of Reps State House Sta 2 Augusta ME 04333*

WINNER, KARIN, newspaper editor. Editor San Diego Union-Tribune. Office: Copley Press Inc 350 Camino De La Reina San Diego CA 92108-3003

WINNER, LESLIE JANE, state legislator, lawyer; b. Asheville, N.C., Oct. 24, 1950; d. Harry and Julienne (Marder) W.; m. Kenneth L. Schorr, Dec. 20, 1987; 1 child, Lilian I. AB, Brown U., 1972; JD, Northeastern U., Boston, 1976. Bar; N.C. 1976, U.S. Dist. Ct. (we. dist.) N.C. 1976, U.S. Ct. Appeals (4th cir.) 1976, U.S. Dist. Ct. (ea. and mid. dists.) 1981, U.S. Supreme Ct. 1985. Clk. to presiding judge U.S. Dist. Ct., Charlotte, N.C., 1976-77; mng. atty. Legal Services of So. Piedmont, Charlotte, 1977-81; ptnr. Ferguson, Stein, Watt, Wallas, Adkins and Gresham, P.A., Charlotte, 1981-92; mem. N.C. Senate, Raleigh, 1993—; mem. adv. com. U.S. Ct. Appeals (4th cir.), N.C. rep., 1989-95. Pres. N.C. Women's Employment Law Ctr., 1989-90; past chmn. Mecklenburg County Dispute Resolution Ctr., Charlotte, 1985-86; coun. mem. So. Regional Coun., Atlanta, 1989-94; trustee Temple Israel, Charlotte, 1988-89; pres. Elizabeth Cmty. Assn., Charlotte, 1980-81. Mem. N.C. Assn. Women Attys. (pres. 1982-83, pub. svc. award 1985), N.C. Acad. Trial Lawyers (legis. com.), N.C. Bar Assn. (litigation sect. coun.), Mecklenburg County Bar Assn. (grievance com.). Democrat. Jewish. Office: NC Senate Legis Office Bldg Rm 409 Raleigh NC 27611-2808

WINNER, SONYA D., lawyer; b. Mountain Home AFB, Idaho, May 13, 1957. BA with honors, Mich. State U., 1979; JD magna cum laude, Harvard U., 1982. Bar: D.C. 1983. Law clk. to Judge Louis F. Oberdorfer U.S. Dist. Ct. for D.C., 1982-83; ptnr. Covington & Burling, Washington. Mem. Harvard Law Rev. 1980-82; co-author: Clean Air Deskbook, 1992. Office: Covington & Burling PO Box 7566 1201 Pennsylvania Ave NW Washington DC 20044-7566*

WINNINGHAM, MARE, actress; b. Phoenix, May 16, 1959. Appeared in (TV movies and miniseries): The Thorn Birds, 1983, Special Olympics/A Special Kind of Love, 1978, Amber Waves, 1980 (Emmy award 1980), The Women's Room, 1980, Off the Minnesota Strip, 1980, A Few Days in Weasel Creek, 1981, Freedom, 1981, Missing Children: A Mother's Story, 1982, Helen Keller: The Miracle Continues, 1984, Single Bars, Single Women, 1984, Love is Never Silent, 1985 (Emmy award nomination 1986), Who Is Julia?, 1986, A Winner Never Quits, 1986, Eye on the Sparrow, 1991, God Bless the Child, 1988, Love and Lies, Crossing to Freedom, Fatal Exposure, 1991, She Stood Alone, Those Secrets, Intruders, 1992, Better Off Dead, 1994, Betrayed by Love, Letter to My Killer; appeared in (films): One Trick Pony, 1980, Threshold, 1983, St. Elmo's Fire, 1985, Nobody's Fool, 1986, Shy People, 1987, Made in Heaven, 1987, Miracle Mile, 1988, Turner and Hooch, 1989, Hard Promises, 1992, Teresa's Tattoo, Wyatt Earp, 1994, Georgia, 1995 (Acad. award nomination best supporting actress 1995); sang title song in (film) Freedom, 1981; singer (solo album) What Might Be, 1992, Red and Brown, 1996. Office: care William Morris Agy 151 El Camino Beverly Hills CA 90212*

WINOGRAD, AUDREY LESSER, advertising executive; b. N.Y.C., Oct. 6, 1933; d. Jack J. and Theresa Lorraine (Elkind) Lesser; m. Melvin H. Winograd, Apr. 29, 1956; 1 child, Hope Elise. BA, U. Conn., 1953. Asst. advt. mgr. T. Baumritter Co., Inc., N.Y.C., 1953-54; asst. dir. pub. rels. and creative merchandising Kirby, Block & Co., Inc., N.Y.C., 1954-56; divsn. mdse. mgr., dir. advt. and sales promotion Winograd's Dept. Store, Inc., Point Pleasant, N.J., 1956-73, v.p., 1960-73, exec. v.p., 1973-86; pres. AMW Assocs., Ocean Twp., N.J., 1976—. Editor bus. newsletters. Bd. dirs. Temple Beth Am, Lakewood, N.J., 1970-72. Mem. NAFE, Jersey Pub. Rels. and Advt. Assn. (past pres., bd. dirs.), Retail Advt. and Mktg. Assn. Internat., Monmouth Ocean Devel. Coun., Monmouth County Bus. Assn. (bd. dirs. 1985—, pres. 1988-90, Woman of Yr. 1992-93, Person of Yr. 1995), N.J. Assn. Women Bus. Owners, Am. Soc. Advt. and Promotion, Ocean C. of C. (bd. dirs. 1994—, award 1993, 94), Retail Advt. Conf. (Career Achievements & Contbns. to Soc. award 1993), Soc. Prevention Cruelty to Animals, Animal Protection Inst. Am., Human Soc., United Animal Nation U.S., Internat. Fund Animal Welfare, World Wildlife Fund, Friends of Animals, Animal Protection Inst., Defenders of Wildlife, Nat. Humane Edn. Soc. Office: AMW Assocs 10 Pine Ln Ocean NJ 07712-7242

WINOGRAD, SESSILE SARAH, psychotherapist, consultant; b. Providence, June 18, 1928; d. Benjamin and Freda (Shaulson) Mayberg; m. Seymore Winograd, May 27, 1956; children: Yeuhda Leib, Jeffrey Asher. BA in Psychology summa cum laude, U. R.I., 1974, cert. in drug counseling, 1976; MS, Barry U., 1979. Diplomate Am. Bd. Med. Psychotherapists; lic. mental health counselor; nat. cert. counselor; cert. clin. mental health counselor. Field interviewer Brown U., Providence, 1968-69, med. coder, 1969-71; student counselor continuing edn. for women U. R.I. Ext., Providence, 1970-74; student counselor The Talmudic Coll. Fla., Miami Beach, 1979-84; drug counselor Aleph Inst., Miami Beach, 1979-86; dir. social svcs. Jewish Outreach Project Greater Miami, Inc., Miami, Fla., 1992-93; coord. cancer activities Ctr. for Psychol. Growth, Miami, 1992—; coord. women's cancer recovery program family workshop Miami Heart Inst., Miami Beach, 1992-94; pvt. practice Miami Beach, 1979—, Bklyn., 1994—; cons. Reaching Out for Emergency Help, Brookline, Mass., 1980—, Caring and Sharing, Bklyn., 1984—; lectr. and workshop presenter in field, 1985—; mem. instnl. rev. bd. Guidelines, Inc., Miami, 1991—. Author: Get Help, Get Positive, Get Well: The Aggressive Approach to Cancer Therapy, A Resource Book, 1992, (chpt.) Times of Challenge, 1988. Vice pres. Beth Yeshaye Charities of Miami, Miami Beach, 1980—; cons. Jewish Community Coun. for Russian Immigrants, Miami Beach, 1988—; bd. dirs. Jewish Outreach of Greater Miami, Inc., Miami Beach, 1991—; mem. Neshei Chabad Miami Beach, 1981—. Recipient Pulitzer prize nomination, 1992; named to Barry U. Alumni Hall of Fame, 1994. Mem. ACA, Am. Mental Health Counselor Assn., Gestault-in-Action, Alumni Assn. Barry U., Phi Kappa Phi. Home and Office: 900 Bay Dr Apt 627 Miami FL 33141-5631

WINSHIP, JO See BUFFALO, JO

WINSLOW, ANNE BRANAN, artist; b. Waynesboro, Ga., July 28, 1920; d. Walter Augustus and Rubie (Griffin) Branan; m. James Addison Winslow Jr., May 8, 1943; children: Lu Anne, Jan Renee. BS in Fine Art, Queens Coll., Charlotte, N.C., 1941; postgrad., U. South Fla., 1974-75. One-woman shows include Dunedin (Fla.) Art Ctr., 1980, Tampa (Fla.) Originals Gallery, 1982, Pub. Libr., St. Petersburg, Fla., 1982, Lee Scarfone Gallery, 1983, 84, Studio 1212, Clearwater, Fla., 1983, 87, 90, Gallery 600, Largo, Fla., 1986, Gallery of State Capitol, Tallahassee, 1987, Berghoff Gallery, Clearwater, 1988, 92, Anderson-Marsh Gallery, St. Petersburg, 1989, 92, Loveland (Colo.) Mus., 1990, Gallery at City Hall of Tampa, 1990, Lawrence Charles Gallery, Tampa, 1993, Gallery Contemporanea, Jacksonville, Fla., 1994; painting, oil painting, Fla. Series II, Images II, 1980, Amagedon, 1974, Eastern Series III, 1984, original handpulled serigraphs, 1991, 92. Mem. Studio 1212, Fla. Artist Group, Mus. Women in Arts, Fla. Printmakers Soc., Generator Gallery (founding). Republican. Home and Studio: 5224 W Neptune Way Tampa FL 33609-3639

WINSLOW, FRANCES EDWARDS, city official; b. Phila., Sept. 12, 1948; d. Harry Donaldson and Anna Louise (McColgan) E.; m. David Allen Winslow, June 6, 1970; children: Frances Lavinia, David Allen Jr. BA, Drew U., 1969, MA, 1971; M Urban Planning, NYU, 1974, PhD, 1978; cert. hazardous material mgmt., U. Calif., Irvine. Adminstrv. asst. Borough of Florham Park, N.J., 1970-73; instr. Kean Coll., Union, N.J., 1973-75; adminstrv. analyst Irvine (Calif.) Police Dept., 1984-86; coord. emergency svcs. City of Irvine, 1986-91; dir. emergency svcs. City of San Jose, Calif., 1991—; instr. U. Calif., Irvine Extension; commr. Calif. Seismic Safety Commn., 1991-95, Calif. Hosp. Bldg. Safety Bd., 1994-95. Editor NCEER Workshop Procs., 1990, 92; contbr. chpts. in books and articles to profl. jours. Vice pres. San Diego Chaplain's Wives, 1976-79; treas. Girl Scouts U.S.A., Yokohama, Japan, 1980-81; treas. Camp Pendleton Officer's Wives Club, 1982-83, pres., 1983-84; vice chmn. curriculum ARC Disaster Acad., 1989-90, chmn., 1991; mem. community disaster preparedness com. ARC, 1992—; del. Nat. Coordinating Com. on Emergency Mgmt., 1990—. Recipient Vol. Svc. award Navy Relief Soc., 1984; Lasker Found. fellow, 1972; named one of Women of Distinction, Soroptimist Internat., 1991. Mem. ASPA (program chmn. Orange County 1984-85, chmn. criminal justice sect. award com. 1988-92, Santa Clara County bd. dirs., co-chmn. mini-conf. 1993, sec. 1994-95, pres. 1995—, bd. mem. Sect. Emergency Mgmt., Nat. Policy Com., nat. membership chair 1996—), Am. Planning Assn. (regional conf. planning com. 1989-90), Internat. City Mgrs. Assn., Assn. Environ. Profls., Assn. Police Planning and Res. Officers (past sec., v.p. Orange County 1984-90), Creekers Club (pres. 1985-88), San Jose Mgmt. Assn. (bd. dirs.), Calif. Emergency Svcs. Assn. (conf. program com. 1992, 95). Republican. Methodist. Home: 20405 Via Volante Cupertino CA 95014-6318 Office: City of San Jose 855 N San Pedro St # 404 San Jose CA 95110-1718

WINSTEAD, ELISABETH WEAVER, poet, writer, English language educator; b. Nashville, July 31, 1926; d. Charles Preston and Carrie Lawrence (Hadley) Weaver; m. George Alvis Winstead, July 18, 1945. BA, Vanderbilt U., 1946; MA, Peabody Coll. Vanderbilt U., 1947; postgrad., Trevecca Nazarene, 1975-79, Vanderbilt U., 1980-83. Cert. tchr. of lang. arts, bus. edn., social sci., English, Tenn., Va., Ind., Idaho, Ariz. Head bus. edn. dept. La Crosse (Ind.) High Sch., 1947-48, Franklin (Tenn.) High Sch., 1952-54, Belmont Coll., Nashville, 1954-56; with English dept. Boise (Idaho) High Sch., 1948-49; critical analyst Dept. Commerce, Washington, 1949-50; with bus. edn. dept. Averitt Coll., Danville, Va., 1950-52; elem. and high sch. tchr. Met. Nashville Schs., 1956-85; cons. Model Tchr. Program, Nashville Met. Sch., 1958-68, mem. faculty adv. coun., 1970-79, mem. profl. devel. coun., 1980-84. Author: Social Studies Curriculum Guide, 1970, Metro Beautiful Programs, 1976, Metro PTA School History, 1980; contbr. poetry to anthologies and popular mags. Chmn. TB Seal Drive, Franklin, 1956-60, March of Dimes Fund Drive, Nashville, 1982-84, Red Cross Blood Drive, Nashville, 1984-86; capt. Heart Fund Drive, Nashville, 1979-81. Recipient Tchr. Appreciation awrd Sta. WKDA, 1970, Galaxy of Stars award Nashville Met. Schs., 1982, Ednl. Appreciation award City of Nashville, 1983, Commendation for pub. svc. Tenn. Legislature, 1994; named to Honorable Order of Ky. Cols., 1988. Mem. NEA, Am. Childhood Edn. Internat., Tenn. Hist. Soc., Wisdom Soc., Kappa Delta Pi, Pi Omega Pi, Pi Gamma Mu. Baptist. Home: 3819 Gallatin Rd Nashville TN 37216-2609

WINSTEAD, JOY, journalist, consultant; b. Washington, May 31, 1934; d. Purnell Judson and Mellie Richardson (Winstead) W.; m. David Boyd Propert, Jul. 28, 1956 (div. June 1980); children: Kathleen Joy, David Bruce. BA in pol. sci., U. Richmond, 1955. Reporter Richmond (Va.) Times-Dispatch, 1955-56; staff writer, pub. rels. U. Pa., Phila., 1956-58; dir. publicity Children's Hosp., Washington, 1958-59; staff writer Richmond News Leader, 1972-77; features editor Columbia (S.C.) Record, 1977-81; asst. editor lifestyles Richmond Times-Dispatch, 1981-83, fashion editor, 1983-92; coord. pub. rels. Sci. Mus. Va., Richmond, 1992-93; dir. communications Medical Soc. Va., Richmond, 1993—; guest lectr. U. Richmond, Va. Commonwealth U., U. S.C.; book reviewer Richmond Times-Dispatch. Contbg. author: Richmond Reader; contbg. editor: A Gem of a Coll. History of Westhampton Coll.; author (introduction): University of Richmond, A Portrait. Co-chmn. alumni weekend U. Richmond, 1968, chmn. alumnae fund, 1989, chmn. lectr. series, 1992-94, mem. 75th Anniversary Com. Recipient 1st pl. award for spl. articles Nat. Fedn. Press Women, 1975, Va. Press Women, 1975, 95, Va. Press Assn., 1978. Mem. Soc. Profl. Journalists (bd. dirs. 1975), Va. Press Women (hospitality chmn. 1993), Soc. Profl. Journalists Found. (bd. dirs. 1987-91), Va. Assn. Med. Soc. Execs. (assoc.), Am. Assn. Med. Soc. Execs., Richmond Pub. Rels. Assn., Fashion Editors and Reporters Assn. (bd. dirs. 1985-91, nominating com. chmn. 1991). Presbyterian. Home: 109 N Crenshaw Ave Richmond VA 23221-2705 Office: Medical Soc Va 4205 Dover Rd Richmond VA 23221-3267

WINSTEAD, LOIS MCIVER, mayor, real estate broker; b. Gulf, N.C.; d. John McMillan McIver and Lillian Dunlap; divorced; children: Barden, Kate M., Alexander M. BA in English Lit./Edn., U. N.C., 1953. Lic. real estate broker, N.C. Owner real estate office; mayor Roxboro City, N.C., 1993—; coord. devel. and promotion of state agy. to attract film industry to N.C.; part-time tchr. English, history N.C. pub. schs.; pers. officer N.C. Pers. Dept.; adminstr. city zoning laws; mem. Person County Econ. Devel. Corp. Organizer, condr. fund raising and campaign programs for spl. interest groups; co-dir. planning/operation bi-county Lake Authority and pub. pk.; mem. Roxboro City Bd. Adjustment, Person County Sch. Bd., 1974-82, Person-Caswell Lake Authority Bd., 1987-96, vice-chairperson; bd. dirs. N.C. Dept. Natural Resources and Comty. Devel., 1976-79, N.C. League Municipalities; Women in Mcpl. Govt., pres., mem. FAIR com.; Person County Party chairperson N.C. Dem. Party, mem. N.C. state com., del. nat. conv., 1972, 80, 88; exec. bd. dirs. Kerr-Tar Coun. Govt., 1993—, Roxboro Uptown Devel. Corp., 1994, 95; mem. Person County Hist. Soc., N.C. Symphony and N.C. Art Mus., Person County United Way, Person County Arts Coun.; bd. trustees Louisburg (N.C.) Coll.; mem. crime prevention and pub. safety com. Nat. League Cities; adult Sunday sch. tchr. Long Meml. United Meth. Ch., Roxboro, mem. adminstrv. bd., lay mem. N.C. ann. conf. Mem. Roxboro Rsch. Club (lit. mem.), Roxboro Woman's Club. Home: 219 S Lamar St Roxboro NC 27573

WINSTON, JANET MARGARET, real estate professional, civic volunteer; b. Binghamton, N.Y., Sept. 30, 1937; d. Cornelius Adrian and Vera Helene (Strohman) Salie; m. Edmund Joseph Winston, Nov. 29, 1958 (dec. July 1981); children: Mark Edmund, Deborah Ann. Student, SUNY, 1955-57, Bliss Coll., 1978. Sales assoc. HER Realtors, Worthington, Ohio, 1979—. Dist. chair women's div. Community Chest ARC, Kalamazoo, 1970; docent Indpls. Mus. Art, 1975, Columbus (Ohio) Mus. Art, 1976—, beaux art mem. , 1976-87; docent Chinese Son of Heaven Exhibit, 1989, mus. fund drive 1986-87, '89—; trustee Worthington Resource Ctr., 1979-84, v.p. 1984, chair youth employment svcs. 1980-83; trustee, sec. Worthington Hills Civic Assn., 1986-89. Mem. Columbus Bd. Realtors (pub. rels. com. 1980, 83, 86, 88, sales adv. com. 1987, svcs. task force 1989), Nat. Assn. Realtors, Ohio Assn. Realtors (Pres.'s Sales Club, the Dozen Nat. Sales award), Worthington C. of C., Worthington Hills Country Club, Worthington Hills Women's Club, Worthington Hills Garden Club (bd. dirs. 1989). Republican. Episcopalian. Home: 8036 Golfview Ct Columbus OH 43235-1230 Office: HER Realtors 6902 N High St Worthington OH 43085-2510

WINSTON, JUDITH ANN, lawyer; b. Atlantic City, Nov. 23, 1943; d. Edward Carlton and Margaret Ann (Goodman) Marianno; B.A. magna cum laude, Howard U., Washington, 1966; J.D., Georgetown U., 1977; m. Michael Russell Winston, Aug. 10, 1963; children: Lisa Marie, Cynthia Eileen. Dir. EEO Project, Council Great City Schs., Washington, 1971-74; legal asst. Lawyers Com. for Civil Rights Under Law, Washington, 1975-77; admitted to D.C. bar, 1977, U.S. Supreme Ct. bar; spl. asst. to dir. Office for Civil Rights, HEW, Washington, 1977-79; exec. asst., legal counsel to chair U.S. EEO Commn., Washington, 1979-80; asst. gen. counsel U.S. Dept. Edn., 1980-86; dep. dir. Lawyers Com. for Civil Rights Under Law, 1986-88; dep. dir. pub. policy Women's Legal Def. Fund, Washington, 1988-90, chair employment discrimination com., 1979-88; ednl. cons., 1974-77; asst. prof. law Washington Coll. Law of Am. U., 1990-93. assoc. prof. law, 1993-95; gen. counsel U.S. Dept. Edn., Washington, 1993—. Pres. bd. dirs. Higher Achievement Program. Fellow ABA Found.; mem. ACLU (pres. Nat. Capital Area, bd. dirs.), Fed. Bar Assn. (chair gen. counsels sect. 1993—), D.C. Bar Assn., Washington Council Lawyers, Washington Bar Assn., Nat. Bar Assn., Lawyers' Com. for Civil Rights Under Law (treas., bd. dirs.), Links Inc., Alpha Kappa Alpha, Phi Beta Kappa, Delta Theta Phi. Democrat. Episcopalian. Author: Desegregating Schools in the Great Cities: Philadelphia, 1970, Chronicle of a Decade 1961-1970, 1970, Desegregating Urban Schools: Educational Equality/Quality, 1970; contbr. articles to profl. jours. Home: 1371 Kalmia Rd NW Washington DC 20012-1444 Office: Dept Edn 600 Independence Ave SW Washington DC 20202-0004

WINSTON, KRISHNA RICARDA, foreign language professional; b. Greenfield, Mass., June 7, 1944; d. Richard and Clara (Brussel) W.; 1 child, Danielle Billingsley. BA, Smith Coll., 1965; MPhil, Yale U., 1969, PhD, 1974. Instr. Wesleyan U., Middletown, Conn., 1970-74, asst. prof., 1974-77; assoc. prof. Wesleyan U., Middletown, 1977-84, prof., 1984—, acting dean, 1993-94; coord. Mellon Minority Undergrad. Program, 1993—. Author: O. v. Horváth: Close Readings of Six Plays, 1975; translator: O. Schlemmer, Letters and Diaries, 1972, S. Lenz, The Heritage, 1981, G. Grass, Two States, One Nation, 1990, C. Hein, The Distant Lover, 1989, G. Mann, Reminiscences and Reflections, 1990, W. v. Goethe, Wilhelm Meister's Journeyman Years, 1989, C. v. Krockow, The Hour of the Women, 1991, E. Heller, With the Next Man Everything Will be Different, 1992, R.W. Fassbinder, The Anarchy of the Imagination, 1992, G. Reuth, Goebbels, 1994, E. Lappin, editor, Jewish Voices, German Words, 1994, P. Handke, Essay on the Jukebox, 1994. Vol. Planned Parenthood, Middletown, 1972-77; mem. Recycling Task Force, Middletown, 1986-87; chmn. Resource Recycling Adv. Coun., Middletown, 1989—. Recipient Schlegel-Tieck prize for translation, 1994; German Acad. Exch. Svc. fellow. Mem. MLA, NEMLA, Soc. for Exile Studies, Am. Lit. Translators' Assn., Am. Assn. Tchrs. German, PEN, Phi Beta Kappa (pres. Wesleyan chpt. 1987-90). Home: 655 Bow Ln Middletown CT 06457-4808 Office: Wesleyan Univ German Studies Dept Middletown CT 06459

WINTER, DEBRA, accountant; b. Allentown, Pa., May 4, 1969; d. Constantine A. and Constance (Albanese) DeAngelo; m. Andrew Anthony Winter, June 4, 1994; 1 stepchild, Kyle Winter. BBA, Kutztown U., 1991. CPA, Pa. Acct. Campbell, Rappold & Yurasits, Allentown, Pa., 1991-94; acctg. mgr. Customs Paper Group, Inc., Alpha, N.J., 1994—. Fellow Pa. Inst. CPAs, AICPAS, Inst. Mgmt. Accts. Home: 2644 Northwood Ave Easton PA 18045

WINTER, MILDRED M., educational administrator. BA summa cum laude, Harris Tchrs. Coll.; MEd, U. Mo.; postgrad., Harvard U., U. Cin. Exec. dir. Parents As Tchrs. Nat. Ctr. Inc., St. Louis; tchr., cons., Mo., 1962-68; developer, dir. Ferguson-Florissant Parent-Child Early Edn. Program, Mo., 1969-72; first dir. early childhood edn. Mo. Dept. Elem. and Secondary Edn., 1972-84; sr. lectr. dept. elem. and early childhood edn. U. Mo., St. Louis; cons. in field. Contbr. articles to profl. jours. Named Outstanding Leader in Field of Edn., Mo. House of Reps., 1982, Outstanding Educator and Adv. for Young Children, Mo. Gov. Christopher S. Bond, 1984, Pioneer in Edn., State Bd. Edn., Mo. Dept. Edn., 1991, St. Louis Woman of Achievement in Edn., 1992; cited for Pioneering Leadership in Edn. Resolution, Mo. Senate, 1995; recipient Outstanding Svc. award Assn. Edn. of Young Children, 1984, Vol. Accreditation Leadership award, 1993, Spl. award Nat. Soc. Behavioral Pediat., 1992, Charles A. Dana Pioneering Achievements Health and Edn. Inst. Medicine award NAS, 1995.

Office: Parents As Tchrs Nat Ctr Inc 10176 Corporate Sq Dr Ste 230 Saint Louis MO 63132*

WINTER, RUTH GROSMAN (MRS. ARTHUR WINTER), journalist; b. Newark, May 29, 1930; d. Robert Delmas and Rose (Rich) Grosman; m. Arthur Winter, June 16, 1955; children: Robin, Craig, Grant. B.A., Upsala Coll., 1951; MS, Pace U., 1989. With Houston Press, 1955-56; gen. assignment Newark Star Ledger, 1951-55, sci. editor, 1956-69; columnist L.A. Times Syndicate, 1973-78, Register and Tribune, syndicate, 1981-85; contbr. to consumer mags.; instr. St. Peters Coll., Jersey City.; vis. lectr. mag. writing Rutgers U. Author: Poisons in Your Food, rev. edits., 1971, 91, How to Reduce Your Medical Bills, 1970, A Consumer's Dictionary of Food Additives, 1972, 3d rev. edit. 1994, Vitamin E, The Miracle Worker, 1972, So You Have Sinus Trouble, 1973, Ageless Aging, 1973, So You Have a Pain in the Neck, 1974, A Consumer's Dictionary of Cosmetic Ingredients, 1974, 4th rev. edit., 1994, Don't Panic, 1975, The Fragile Bond: Marriage in the 70's, 1976, Triumph Over Tension, 1976 (N.J. Press Women's Book award), Scent Talks Among Animals, 1977, Cancer Causing Agents: A Preventive Guide, 1979, The Great Self-Improvement Sourcebook, 1980, The Scientific Case Against Smoking, 1980, People's Guide to Allergies and Allergens, 1984, A Consumer's Guide to Medicines in Food, 1995; co-author: The Lean Line One Month Lighter Program, 1985, Thin Kids Program, 1985, Build Your Brain Power, 1986, Eat Right: Be Bright, 1988, A Consumer's Dictionary of Medicines: Prescription, Over-the-Counter and Hebral, 1994, Super Soy,: The Miracle Bean, 1996. Recipient award of merit ADA, 1966, Cecil award Arthritis Found., 1967, Am. Soc. Anesthesiologists award, 1969, Arthritis Found. award, 1978; named Alumnus of Year Upsala Coll., 1971, Woman of Year N.J. Daily Newspaper Women, 1971, Woman of Achievement Millburn Short Hills Profl. and Bus. Women's Assn., 1991. Mem. Soc. Mag. Writers, Authors League, Nat. Assn. Sci. Writers, Am. Med. Writers Assn. (Eric Martin Meml. award), N.J. Daily Newspaper Women (awards news series 1958, 70, named Woman of Achievement 1971, 83), Am. Soc. Journalists and Authors (pres. 1977-78, spl. service award 1983), N.J. Press Women (pres. 1982-84). Home and Office: 44 Holly Dr Short Hills NJ 07078-1318

WINTERER-SCHULZ, BARBARA JEAN, art designer, author; b. Manchester, N.H., Apr. 1, 1938; d. John Edward and Elizabeth Virginia Grace; m. Allen George Winterer, Mar. 30, 1959 (div. 1977); children: Audrey Lyn Winterer, Amy Jo Winterer DeNoble; m. James Robert Schulz, May 28, 1983. AA, Mesa (Ariz.) C.C., 1980; BS summa cum laude, U. Md., Heidelberg, Germany, 1996. Art designer Morningstar Art Design Studio, Cortez, Colo., 1988—. Contbr. articles to newspapers and jours. Ofcl. U.S. reporter at World Eskimo Indian Olympics, Faribanks, Alaska, 1994. Recipient Humanitarian award Phila. Inst. Human Potential, 1972, Chancellor of Germany award for acad. achievement, 1986. Mem. Am. Landscape Contractors Assn., Alpha Sigma Lambda, Phi Theta Kappa. Office: Morningstar Art Design Studio 201 W Downey Ave Cortez CO 81321

WINTERGERST, ANN CHARLOTTE, language educator; b. Memmingen, Bavaria, Germany, Mar. 11, 1950; came to U.S., 1958; d. Martin and Charlotte Frieda (Denk) W. BA summa cum laude, St. John's U., 1972; MA, Columbia U., 1978, EdM, 1981, EdD, 1989. Teaching fellow U. Pa., Phila., 1972-73; lang. arts tchr. Our Lady Miraculous Medal Sch., Ridgewood, N.Y., 1973-81; assoc. tchr. Columbia U., N.Y.C., 1978-82; asst. prof. St. John's U., Queens, N.Y., 1981-86, 92-93, dir. ESL, 1986-91, assoc. prof., 1993—; leader, pres. N.Y. State Coun. Langs., 1988-90; cons. Ednl. Testing Svc., Oakland, Calif., 1989—, Bd. Regents N.Y. State, Albany, 1992-95, St. Martin's Press, N.Y.C., 1993-95, United Nations, N.Y.C., 1994-95. Author: Second-Language Classroom Interaction, 1994; editor: Focus on Self-Study, 1995; contbr. articles to profl. jours. Mem. Dem. Nat. Com., Washington, 1990—; pres. N.Y. State TESOL, 1995-96; higher edn. chair Internat. TESOL, 1993-94. Democrat. Roman Catholic. Home: 70-15 71st Pl Glendale NY 11385 Office: St Johns Univ Dept Fgn Langs Jamaica NY 11439

WINTERHALTER, DOLORES AUGUST (DEE WINTERHALTER), art educator; b. Pitts., Mar. 22, 1928; d. Joseph Peter and Helen August; m. Paul Joseph Winterhalter, June 21, 1947 (dec.); children: Noreen, Audrey, Mark; m. Marvin Bernard Hoeing, Mar. 26, 1988 (div. Dec. 1994). Student, Yokohama, Japan, 1963-64, Paris, 1968-70. Cert. tchr. Japanese Flower Arranging, Kamakuri Wood Carving. Tchr. YWCA, Greenwich, Conn., 1978-84, Friends of the Arts and Scis., Sarasota, Fla., 1992—; lectr. Sarasota Art Assn., 1984—; tchr., workshop presenter, Bangkok, 1971; mem. staff Hilton Leech Art Studio and Gallery, Sarasota; events chmn. State of Fla. Watercolor Exhbn., Sarasota, 1995; cultural exch. tchr. univs., fine arts acads., China; mem., tchr. Venice Art Ctr., Sarasota, 1996-97, Hilton Leech Tchr., Sarasota, 1996. Exhbns. Xiam, China, 1994; numerous works in watercolor, ink, oriental brushwork; paintings in numerous corp. collections. Pres., Am. Women's Club, Genoa, Italy, 1962; participant to help raise money for scholarships Collectors and Creators Tour of Fine ARts Soc. of Sarasota, 1994. Recipient numerous awards Old Greenwich (Conn.) Art Assn., 1971-84, Sarasota, 1985, Collectors and Creators Tour award Fine Arts Soc. Sarasota, 1994; named Artist of Yr., Fine Arts Soc. Sarasota, 1994. Mem. Nat. League Am. Pen Women (pres. Sarasota br. 1994—), Suncoast Fla. Watercolor Soc. (life), Fla. Watercolor Soc., Long Boat Key Art Assn., Sarasota Art Assn., Sumi-e Soc. Am., Nat. League Am. PEN Women (pres. 1994-96). Democrat. Roman Catholic. Home and Office: 4027 Westbourne Cir Sarasota FL 34238

WINTERMUTE, MARJORIE MCLEAN, architect, educator; b. Great Falls, Mont., Sept. 15, 1919; d. Allan Edward and Gladys Pearl (Pelton) McLean; m. Charles Richard Wintermute, June 14, 1947 (div.); children: Lynne Wintermute, Lane. BA, U. Oreg., 1941; postgrad. Portland State U., 1969-72. Registered architect, Oreg. Archtl. draftsman Def. Projects, Portland and San Francisco, 1941-43; architect Pietro Belluschi, Portland, 1943-47; free-lance architect, Portland, 1948—; architect-in-residence Edn. Service Dist., Portland, 1978-91, ret.; instr. Portland State U., 1973—; architect-in-residence Dept. Def. Dependents Sch., Asian Region Hdqrs. Japan, 1981-83; with Upshur Group Collaborative, 1976-87; architect-in-residence program coord. Oreg. Arts Commn., 1987—, AIA; leader archtl. tours to Europe, 1969, 71, 73, Greece and Turkey, 1989, 91. Author: Students, Structures, Spaces, 1983, Blueprints: A Built Environment Education Program, 1984, Architecture As A Basic Curriculum Builder, 1987-90; editor: Pitter Patter (Gold medal 1965), 1960-69. Prin. archtl. works include comml. and residential bldgs. and restoration and mus. installation Timberline Lodge, Oreg., 1983, 2d Timberline Restoration project, 1993. Bd. dirs. Oreg. Heart Assn., Portland, 1960-70, pres. 1968-69; bd. dirs. Friends of Timberline, Creative Arts Community, pres. 1993—; program devel. cons. Am. Heritage Assn., Lake Oswego, Oreg., 1969-83, Mt. Angel Abbey, St. Benedict, Oreg., 1970-73; bd. dirs., com. chmn. Environ. Edn. Assn., Portland, 1978-85. Recipient Disting. Citizen award Environ. Edn. Assn., 1983; role model award area coun. Girl Scouts, 1994; Woman of Achievement award Inst. Profl. and Managerial Women, 1984; Woman of Distinction award Women in Arch., 1993, named Disting. Citizen Portland Hist. Landmarks Commn., 1988, fellowship in The Am. Inst. of Architects, 1978. Fellow AIA (pub. edn. com. 1970-80, chair 1972-73); mem. Women's Archtl. League (bd. dirs., com. chmn. 1980—), Fashion Group Internat. (facilitator 1983-84), Ednl. Futures Inc. (Western rep. 1978-83), Oreg. State Dept. Edn. (adv. bd. 1980-83). Republican. Presbyterian. Home: 6740 SW Canyon Ln # 1 Portland OR 97225-3606

WINTER-NEIGHBORS, GWEN CAROLE, special education educator, art educator; b. Greenville, S.C., July 14, 1938; d. James Edward and Evelyn (Lee) Walters; m. David M. Winter Jr., Aug., 1963 (dec. Feb. 1982); children: Robin Carole Winter, Charles G. McCuen; m. Thomas Frederick Neighbors, Mar. 24, 1989. BA in Edn. & Art, Furman U., 1960, MA in Psychology, 1967; cert. in guidance/pers., Clemson U., 1981; EdD in Youth & Mid. Childhood Edn., Nova Southeastern U., 1988; postgrad., U. S.C., Spartanburg, 1981-89; cert. clear specialist instruction, Calif. State U., Northridge, 1991; art edn. cert., Calif. State U., L.A., 1990—; postgrad., Glendale U., 1996—. Cert. tchr. art, elem. edn., psychology, secondary guidance, S.C. Tchr. 7th grade Greenville Jr. H.S., 1960-63; art tchr. Wade Hampton H.S., Greenville, 1963-67; prin. adult edn. Woodmont H.S., Piedmont, S.C., 1983-85, Mauldin H.S., Greenville and Mauldin, S.C., 1981; tchr. ednl. psychology edn. dept. Allen U., Columbia, S.C., 1969; activity therapist edn. dept. S.C. Dept. of Corrections, Columbia, 1973-76; art specialist gifted edn. Westcliffe Elem. Sch., Greenville, 1976-89; tchr. self-contained spl. day class Elysian Heights Elem. Sch., Echo Park and L.A., Calif., 1989-91; art tchr. medh. drawing Sch. Dist. Greenville County Blue Ridge Mid. Sch., Greer, S.C., 1991-95; participant nat. conf. U.S. Dept. Edn./So. Bell, Columbia, 1989; com. mem. nat. exec. com. Nova Southeastern U., 1988-89. Illustrator: Mozart Book, 1988; author: (drama) Let's Sing a Song About America, 1988 (1st pl. Nat. Music award 1990). Life mem. Rep. Presdl. Task Force, 1970—; mem. voter registration com. Lexington County Rep. Party, 1970-80; grand jury participant 13th Jud. Ct. Sys., Greenville, 1987-88, guardian ad litem, 1988-89. Tchr. Incentive grantee Sch. Dist. Greenville County, 1986-88, Project Earth grantee Bell South, 1988-89, 94-95, Edn. Improvement Act/Nat. Dissimination Network grantee S.C. State Dept. Edn., 1987-88, Targett 2,000 Arts in Curricular grantee S.C. Dept. Edn., 1994-95, Alliance grantee Bus. Cmty. Greenville, 1992-95, Greer Art Rsch. grantee, 1993-94, S.C. Govs. Sch. Study grantee, 1994, Edn. Improvement Act Competitive Tchr. grantee S.C. Dept. Edn., 1994-95, Alliance Grand grant, 1995-96. Mem. NEA, ABA (student orgn.), Nat. Art Edn. Assn., Nat. Mus. Women in Arts, S.C. Arts Alliance, S.C. Art Edn. Assn., Phi Delta Kappa (com. mem. 1976-90), Upstate IBM-PC Users Group. Baptist/Lutheran. Home: 26 Charterhouse Ave Piedmont SC 29673-9139 Office: Neighbors Enterprises 3075 Foothill Blvd Apt 138 La Crescenta CA 91214-2742

WINTERS, BARBARA JO, musician; b. Salt Lake City; d. Louis McClain and Gwendolyn (Bradley) W. AB cum laude, UCLA, 1960, postgrad., 1961; postgrad., Yale, 1960. Mem. oboe sect. L.A. Philharm., 1961-94, prin. oboist, 1972-94; ret.; clinician oboe, English horn, Oboe d'amore. Recs. movie, TV sound tracks. Home: 3529 Coldwater Canyon Ave Studio City CA 91604-4060 Office: 135 N Grand Ave Los Angeles CA 90012-3013

WINTERS, CYNTHIA SAINTSING, middle school education educator; b. Winston-Salem, N.C., Oct. 14, 1969; d. Estus Benniewayne and JoAnne Meredith Saintsing; m. Jeffrey Mark Winters, Jan. 1, 1994; 1 child, John Estus. BA, U. N.C., Greensboro, 1991. Econ., govt. tchr. So. Vance H.S., Henderson, N.C., 1991-92; spl. edn. tchr. South Davidson H.S., Thomasville, N.C., 1992; 8th grade tchr. Brown Mid. Sch., Thomasville, 1992-94, 6th grade tchr., 1994—, social studies dept. chair, 1995—. Ch. youth leader Unity United Meth. Ch., Thomasville, 1992-95. Mem. N.C. Edn. Assn., N.C. Geography Alliance, Phi Beta Kappa. Republican. Home: 201 Hasty School Rd Thomasville NC 27360

WINTERS, JANET LEWIS, writer; b. Chgo., Aug. 17, 1899; d. Edwin Herbert and Elizabeth (Taylor) Lewis; m. Yvor Winters, June 22, 1926; children: Joanna, Daniel. PhB, U. Chgo., 1920. Writer, 1934—; vis. lectr. Stanford U., Palo Alto, Calif., 1969-70, U. Calif., Berkeley, winter 1979; vis. artist Dierassi Found., Woodside, Calif., Yaddo, Saratoga Springs, N.Y., 1979. Author: (novels) Invasion, 1932, The Wife of Martin Guerre, 1941, The Trial of Sören Quist, 1947, The Ghost of Monsieur Scarron, 1959, also 3 books of poetry and 5 librettos. Guggenheim fellow, France, 1951. Mem. NAACP. Home: 143 W Portola Ave Los Altos CA 94022-1211

WINTERS, JUDY ELIZABETH, alternative education educator; b. Cumming, Ga., Oct. 25, 1970; d. Jerry Clark and Margie Mae (Sosebee) Nichols; m. Jeff Michael Winters, Jan. 8, 1992. BA in Edn., Piedmont Coll., 1991. Tchr. alternative sch. Dawson County Bd. Edn., Dawsonville, Ga., 1993—; head softball coach Dawson H.S., Dawsonville, 1994—. Home: Rt 1 Box 1650 Dawsonville GA 30534 Office: Dawson County Crossroads PO Box 828 Dawsonville GA 30534

WINTERS, LAUREL ANN, artist; b. Alexandria, Va., Nov. 7, 1950; d. Robert Thomas and Marilou (Thomas) W.; m. William S. Jordan III, Mar. 17, 1984; children: William S. IV, Robert Thomas. Student, Radford (Va.) U., 1969-71; BFA with honors, Va. Commonwealth U., Richmond, 1980, MFA, 1982. Mgmt. analyst HUD, Washington, 1976-78, 84-85; curator women's perspectives show women's studies dept. U. Akron, Ohio, 1993-96, instr. continuing edn. dept., 1993, 94, 96, 1994, 95, 96; instr. pastels Firelands Assn. Visual Arts, Oberlin, Ohio; lectr. women artists, 1991—. One person shows include Chowan Coll., Murfreesboro, N.C., 1982, Mt. Vernon Coll., Washington, 1984, Second St. Gallery, Charlottesville, Va., 1983; group shows include Okla. Art Ctr., Oklahoma City, 1981, Wustum Mus., Racine, Wis., 1986, Matrix Gallery, Sacramento, 1990, Trumbull Art Gallery, Warren, Ohio, 1991, 93-95; permanent collections include Fed. Res. Bank, Richmond, Hospice No. Va., Arlington, Rails-to-Rails Conservancy, Washington, U. Akron, Unitarian Universalist Ch., Akron. Cultural arts chair King Sch. PTA, Akron, 1993-96; mem., past bd. mem., scholarship chair Faculty Women's Club, U. Akron, 1986—; bd. dirs. YWCA Summit County, 1996—. Recipient scholarship Altrusa Club, Richmond, Va., 1982. Mem. Artists of Rubber City (bd. dirs. 1990—), Women's Caucus for Art, New Orgn. for Visual Arts. Democrat. Universalist. Office: Laurel Winters Studio 188 N Highland Ave Akron OH 44303

WINTERS, NOLA FRANCES, food company executive; b. Achilles, Kans., Aug. 27, 1925; d. Edward Earl and Mary Ruby (Mikesell) Ginther; divorced. Student, U. Kans., 1943-45; BA, U. Colo., 1972. Exec. sec. Holly Sugar Corp., Colorado Springs, Colo., 1953-66, asst. sec., 1966-84, dir. corp. rels., asst. sec., 1981-84, dir. corp. and pub. rels., asst. sec., 1984-90; asst. sec. HSC Export Corp., Colorado Springs, 1980-90, Imperial Holly Corp., Colorado Springs, 1988-90. Mem. Phi Beta Kappa. Republican. Methodist.

WINTER-SWITZ, CHERYL DONNA, travel company executive; b. Jacksonville, Fla., Dec. 6, 1947; d. Jacqueline Marie (Carroll) Winter; m. Frank C. Snedaker, June 24, 1974 (div. May 1976); m. Robert William Switz, July 1, 1981. AA, City Coll. of San Francisco, 1986; BS, Golden Gate U., 1990, MBA, 1992. Bookkeeper, agt. McQuade Tours, Ft. Lauderdale, Fla., 1967-69; mgr. Boca Raton (Fla.) Travel, 1969-76; owner, mgr. Ocean Travel, Boca Raton, 1976-79; ind. contractor Far Horizons Travel, Boca Raton, 1979-80; mgr. Tara/BPF Travel, San Francisco, 1981-84; mgr. travel. dept. Ernst & Whinney/Lifeco Travel, San Francisco, 1984-86; travel cons. Siemer & Hand Travel, San Francisco, 1989—; instr. Golden Gate U., 1986—, U. San Francisco. Mem. Amateur Trapshooting Assn., Hotel and Restaurant Mgmt. Club. Republican. Episcopalian. Home: 642 Brussels St San Francisco CA 94134-1902 Office: Siemer & Hand Travel 101 California St Ste 1750 San Francisco CA 94111-5862

WINTHROP, ELIZABETH AMORY, horse trainer; b. N.Y.C., Dec. 14, 1931; d. Robert and Theodora (Ayer) W.; m. Francis E. Baker, June 16, 1949 (div. 1953); m. Malcolm P. Ripley, Apr. 21, 1958 (div. 1974). Student, Bradford Jr. Coll., 1952, Columbia U., 1956. Registered horseshow judge. Horse trainer Morley Farms, Millbrook, N.Y., 1955-67; humane investigator Dutchess and Putnam Counties, 1969-86, peace officer; humane investigator, 1969-86. Bd. dirs. Fund for Animals, N.Y.C., 1974—, N.Y. State Humane Assn., New Paltz, N.Y., 1975—; pres. Winley Found., N.Y.C., 1967—; registered judge Am. Horseshow Assn., N.Y.C., 1966-88; mem. gen. adv. bd. Am. Inst. Life Threatening Illness and Loss, 1992—. Mem. Defenders of Wildlife (life), Nat. Audubon Soc. (life), Wild Horse Organized Assistance (life), World Wildlife Fund, African Wildlife Found., Human Soc. U.S., Nat. Inst. Social Scis., English Speaking Union, New Eng. Soc., Animal Welfare Inst., New Eng. Anti-Vivisection Soc. (life), Am. Horse Show Assn. (life), Colony Club, Lansdowne Club (London), Mashomech Club, Sharon Country Club, River Club, Thursday Evening Club, Regency Whist Club, Doubles. Episcopalian. Home: RR 1 Box 40 Millbrook NY 12545-9720

WINTOUR, ANNA, editor; b. Eng., Nov. 3, 1949; came to U.S., 1976; d. Charles and Elinor W.; m. David Shaffer, Sept. 1984; children: Charles, Kate. Student, Queens Coll., 1963-67. Deputy fashion editor Harper's and Queen Mag., London, 1970-76; fashion editor Harper's Bazaar, New York, 1976-77; fashion and beauty editor Viva Mag., New York, 1977-78; contbg. editor fashion and style Savvy Mag., New York, 1980-81; sr. editor N.Y. Mag., 1981-83; creative dir. U.S. Vogue, N.Y., 1983-86; editor-in-chief British Vogue, London, 1986-87, House and Garden, N.Y., 1987-88, Vogue, N.Y., 1988—. Office: Vogue Mag Conde Nast Bldg 350 Madison Ave New York NY 10017-3704*

WINTRESS, KAREN KILPATRICK, reinsurance company executive; b. Hartford, Conn., Sept. 13, 1949; d. Kran Russell Kilpatrick and Carolyn Ogden (Wilson) Hayes; m. James Douglas Wintress, Sept. 24, 1983; children: Kristina Erin, Douglass Russell. BS in Psychology, Ursinus Coll., 1971; MBA in Mgmt., Golden Gate U., 1976. Mktg. analyst Travelers Ins. Co., Hartford, 1971; forms analyst Crocker Nat. Bank, San Francisco, 1972-73; sr. rsch. analyst Bechtel Corp., San Francisco, 1973-78; mgr. internat. ins. ops. Aetna Life & Casualty, Hartford, 1979-86; asst. v.p. tech. transfer Am. Re-Ins. Co., Princeton, N.J., 1986—; exec. dir. Bldg. Environ. Edn. Solutions, Princeton, 1995—. Recipient Pub. Edn. award N.J. chpt. Am. Planning Assn., 1995, Mercer County Planning Bd., 1996, Edn. award Granville Acad., 1996. Fellow Leadership N.J. Home: 27 Summit Rd Belle Mead NJ 08502 Office: Am Re-Ins Co 685 College Rd E Princeton NJ 08543

WINTZ, MARILYN BELLE, elementary education educator; b. Aspen, Colo., Feb. 14, 1940; d. Fred Arthur and Mary Alta (Sturm) Cook; m. Rodney G. Wintz, June 16, 1963; children: Marilee, Shirrae. BA, U. No. Colo., 1962; MA, Adams State Coll., 1990; postgrad., Denver U., 1992—. Cert. administr., Colo. Tchr. El Paso Sch. Dist. 11, Colorado Springs, Colo., 1962-63, Creede (Colo.) Sch. Dist. 1, 1963—; ranch mgr. Wason Ranch Corp., Creede, 1963—. Named Tchr. of Yr., Creede Sch. Dist. 1, San Luis Valley Bd. of Coop. Ednl. Svcs. Mem. Nat. Coun. Tchrs. Math., Assn. for Curriculum and Devel., Internat. Reading Assn., Colo. Coun. Internat. Reading. Home: Wason Ranch Creede CO 81130 Office: Lamb Elem Sch La Garita Ave Creede CO 81130

WINZELER, JUDITH KAY, foundation administrator; b. Canton, Ohio, Dec. 17, 1942; d. Charles and Pauline Doris (Werstler) Wenzlawski; m. Robert Lee Winzeler, Nov. 4, 1961; children: Elizabeth Ann, Alice Louise Winzeler Smith. BA, U. Nev., 1971, MA, 1981. Instr. anthropology Western Nev. C.C., Reno, 1976-77; program developer Nev. Humanities Com., Reno, 1977-78, asst. dir., 1978-80, assoc. dir., 1980-84, exec. dir., 1984—; panelist NEH, 1991; mem. Hilliard Found. Com., Reno, 1984—; mem. program com. Fedn. of State Humanities Couns., Washington, 1989; mem. selections com. Grace A. Griffen Chair in History, Reno, 1992. Mem. Nev. Commn. on Bicentennial of U.S. Constn., 1985-91; pres. Luth. Ch. of Good Shepherd, Reno, 1987-89; mem. nominating com. Evang. Luth. Ch. Am., Sierra Synod, Oakland, Calif., 1991-94; bd. dirs., officer Reno/Sparks Metro Min., Reno, 1987—; active Nev. Hist. Soc., Nev. State Mus., Nev. Mus. Art, Western Folklife Ctr., Friends of Washoe County Libr. Mem. Asian Pacific Assn. of No. Nev., Sierra Art Found., Reno Rotary Club, Nev. Corral, Westerners Internat. Home: 1579 Belford Rd Reno NV 89509-3907 Office: Nev Humanities Com 1034 N Sierra St Reno NV 89503-3721

WINZER, P.J., lawyer; b. Shreveport, La., June 7, 1947; d. C.W. Winzer and Pearlene Hall Winzer Tobin. BA in Polit. Sci., So. U., Baton Rouge, 1968; JD, UCLA, 1971. Bar: Bar: Calif. 1972, U.S. Supreme Ct. 1986. Staff atty. Office of Gen. Counsel, U.S. HEW, Washington, 1971-80; asst. spl. counsel U.S. Office of Spl. Counsel Merit Systems Protection Bd., Dallas, 1980-82; regional dir. U.S. Merit Systems Protection Bd., Falls Church, Va., 1982—. Mem. Fed. Bar Assn., Calif. Bar Assn., Fed. Cir. Bar Assn., Delta Sigma Theta. Office: US Merit System Protection 5203 Leesburg Pike Ste 1109 Falls Church VA 22041-3401

WIRTHS, CLAUDINE GIBSON, psychologist, author; b. Covington, Ga., May 9, 1926; d. Count Dillon and Julia (Thompson) Gibson; m. Theodore William Wirths, Dec. 28, 1945; children: William M., David G. AB, U. Ky., 1946, MA, 1948; MEd, Am. U., 1979. Program dir. N.C. League for Crippled Children, Chapel Hill, 1948-49; research psychologist Savannah River Urbanization Studies, Aiken, S.C., 1950-52; research psychologist, cons. various pub. and pvt. agys., S.C., D.C., Md., Bermuda, 1953-79; spl. edn. tchr. Montgomery Pub. Schs., Gaithersburg, Md., 1979-80, coordinator learning ctr., 1980-84; adj. faculty Frederick (Md.) Community Coll., 1985—. Author: (with Williams) Lives Through the Years, 1968, (with Bowman-Kruhm) I Hate School, 1986 (Best Book award ALA 1987), I Need A Job, 1988, Where's My Other Sock?, 1989, Are You My Type?, 1992, How to Get Up When Schoolwork Gets You Down, 1993, Time to Be series, 1994, Upgrade, 1995; contbr. articles to profl. jours. and popular press. Vice chair Def. Adv. Com. Women in Service, Washington, 1960-63, adv. com. Seneca Pk., Montgomery County, 1970-79; adv. bd. Sec. Nat. Resources, Md., 1976-79. Named Outstanding Citizen of County, Aiken, 1954; recipient award Montgomery County Environ. Trust, 1973, 1st pl. award for feature story, Md., D.C., Del. Press Assn., 1980. Mem. Soc. Children's Book Writers, Assn. Children with Learning Disabilities, Phi Beta Kappa. Episcopalian. Home and Office: PO Box 335 Braddock Heights MD 21714-0335

WIRTSHAFTER, EDITH B., physical education educator, administrator; b. Cleve., Jan. 31, 1956; d. Don M. and Mina B. (Bialosky) W. BS in Phys. Edn., Western Mich. U., 1978; MA in Athletic Adminstrn., Ctrl. Mich. U., 1994. Sports and lesiure coord. City of Kalamazoo, Mich., 1980-86; sports dir. Mich. Spl. Olympics, Mt. Pleasant, 1986-90, assoc. dir., 1990-93; regional mgr. Mich. Spl. Olympics, Kalamazoo, 1993—; tchr. asst. Dale Carnegie Leadership, Saginaw, Mich., 1993. Mem. S.W. Mich. Soccer Assn. (v.p. 1995—). Democrat. Jewish. Home: 246 Dunbarton Ct Kalamazoo MI 49006 Office: Mich Spl Olympics 133 W Cedar Kalamazoo MI 49007

WISCH, PATRICIA BOGIN, psychologist, mediator; b. Phila., Apr. 17, 1932; d. Barney M. and Dora (Schultzberg) Bogin; m. Herbert H. Wisch, Dec. 7, 1952 (dec. Sept. 1979); children: Judith C., Benjamin J., Elizabeth S., David R.; m. William L. Yancey, July 4, 1985. BS in Edn., Temple U., 1970, MEd, 1972, EdD, 1975. Lic. psychologist, Pa. Dir. Inst. of Awareness of YM-YWHA, Phila., 1975-83; prof. Antioch U., Phila., 1983-88; pvt. practice psychologist Phila., 1976—; dir. Mediation Svcs., Phila., 1981—. Bd. mem. Action AIDS, Phila., 1988. Mem. NOW, APA, Pa. Psychol. Assn., Soc. for Profls. in Dispute Resolution, Acad. Family Mediators, B'nai Brith Internat. Jewish. Home: 2419 Fairmount Ave Philadelphia PA 19130

WISE, MAUREEN KAMEN, public relations executive, editor, educator; b. Los Angeles, Mar. 26, 1946; d. Murray Morton and Rosalyn Estelle (Horowitz) Kamen; m. Murray Jay Wise, Aug. 7, 1966; children: Stephanie Lauren Deutchman, Tracey Meredith Wise. BS, Elmira Coll., 1966; MS, Iona Coll., 1993. Cert. elem. and lang. tchr., N.Y. Tchr. elem. Horseheads (N.Y.) Cen. Sch. Dist., 1966-67, East Ramapo Sch. Dist., Spring Valley, N.Y., 1967-69, 91-92, Pearl River (N.Y.) Ctrl. Sch. Dist., 1994-96; dir. pub. rels. United Jewish Appeal of Rockland, Spring Valley, N.Y., 1971-86; publicity coordinator recreation dept. Town of Ramapo, Suffern, N.Y., 1973; community resources dir. Planned Parenthood of Rockland, West Nyack, N.Y., 1979-82; owner, pres. Wise Promotions, Spring Valley, 1981-91; pub. relations dir. Women's League for Conservative Judaism, N.Y.C., 1985-91; bd. dirs. United Jewish Appeal of Rockland, Rockland City, N.Y., 1976-91; mem. chancellor's com. Jewish Theol. Sem., N.Y.C., 1987; founding mem., v.p. Rockland County Tourism Bd., Suffern, 1983-85. Mng. editor Women's League Outlook mag., 1985-91; editor newspaper The Rockland Jewish Reporter, 1995—; producer, dir. multimedia presentations, theatrical prodns. Mem. citizens adv. com. Rockland County, 1984; mem. Pomona Jewish Ctr. Recipient Woman of Achievement award, J.T. Sem. Torah Fund Campaign, 1986, Disting. Service award Rockland County, 1984. Mem. Rockland Women's Network (In Celebration of Women award for achievement in bus. 1984), Westchester-Rockland Women's League (past chmn. pub. rels.), Elmwood Playhouse, Hadassah, Phi Delta Kappa. Democrat. Home: 24 Fairway Oval Spring Valley NY 10977-1723

WISE, RAYE MCGILBERY, accountant, artist; b. Zavalla, Tex., Jan. 23, 1920; d. Angus and Gladys (Sanders) McGilbery; m. James Edward Wise, Jul. 23, 1937 (dec. 1990); children: Herman Angus, Paul Timothy. Student, S.F.A. U., 1958. Acct. Mathews, Miller and W.W. Mathews, Co., San Augustine, Tex., 1956-95. Mem. Women in the Arts, Hist. Soc. of San Augustine County Tex., Hist. Soc. of Angelina County Tex., Order of the Ea. Star.

WISE, SANDRA CASBER, lawyer. BA, Macalester Coll., 1969; JD, U. Minn., 1972. Bar: Minn. 1972, D.C., 1986, W.Va., 1987. Legis asst. to Rep. Martha Keys, Washington, 1977-78; asst. to asst. to the pres. for women's issues Sara Weddington, The White Ho., Washington, 1979; staff sub-com. on pub. assistance Ho. Com. on Ways and Means, Washington, 1980, staff sub-com. on health, 1981-85; atty. White, Fine and Verville, 1986; staff dir.

sub-com. on social security Ho. Com. on Ways and Means, Washington, 1987-94, minority counsel subcom. on social security, 1995—. Office: House Com on Ways & Means 1106 Longworth House Office Bldg Washington DC 20515

WISE, SUSAN TAMSBERG, management and communications consultant, speaker; b. Memphis, Nov. 16, 1945; d. Joseph Lane and Mable Rosa (Koth) Tamsberg; m. Roy Thomas Wise, June 29, 1968; children: Kristin Rebecca, Mary Catherine. BA in Math., Columbia (S.C.) Coll., 1967; M in Edn., Ga. State U., Atlanta, 1986. Tchr. high sch. math. various pub. schs., N.C., S.C., and Ga., 1967-73; instr. Cen. Piedmont Community Coll., Charlotte, N.C., 1979; devel. dir. Classique, Inc., Kannapolis, N.C., 1979-81; asst. v.p. First Nat. Bank of Atlanta, 1981-87; Ga. dir. The Exec. Speaker, Inc., Atlanta, 1987-90; pres. TrimTime, Inc., Atlanta, 1988—, Wise Consulting Inc., Atlanta, 1990—; speaker Girl Scouts USA, Jr. League, numerous med. assns., Atlanta and S.E. area, 1985—. Tng. cons. Jr. League of Atlanta, 1988-89; bd. dirs. Incarnation Luth. Ch., Atlanta, 1984; mem. ch. coun., bd. dirs, Luth. Ch. of the Redeemer. Mem. ASTD (v.p., bd. dirs., Leadership award 1987), Kappa Delta Pi. Republican.

WISEHART, MARY RUTH, academic administrator; b. Myrtle, Mo., Nov. 2, 1932; d. William Henry and Ora (Harbison) W. BA, Free Will Baptist Bible Coll., 1955; BA, George Peabody Coll. Tchrs., 1959, MA, 1960, PhD, 1976. Tchr. Free Will Bapt. Bible Coll., Nashville, 1956-60, chmn. English dept., 1961-85; exec. sec.-treas. Free Will Bapt. Women Nat. Active for Christ, 1985—. Author: Sparks Into Flame, 1985; contbr. poetry to jours. Mem. Nat. Coun. Tchrs. English, Christian Mgmt. Assn., Religious Conf. Mgmt. Assn., Scribbler's Club. Avocations: photography, music, drama. Office: Women Nat Active for Christ Free Will Bapt PO Box 5002 Antioch TN 37011-5002

WISEMAN, GLORIA DIANA, medical educator, physician; b. N.Y.C.. BS, CCNY, 1977; MD, Columbia U., 1981. Diplomate Nat. Bd. Medical Examiners. Intern and resident in pediatrics NYU Med. Ctr., 1981-84, teaching asst., 1983-84; neonatal-perinatal medicine fellow Babies' Hosp. Columbia U., 1984-86, asst. pediatrician Babies' Hosp., 1984-86, staff assoc., 1984-86; instr. U. Medicine and Dentistry of N.J.-N.J. Med. Sch., 1986-87, asst. prof. clin. pediatrics, 1987-88; neonatology/pediatric attending physician U. Hosp. N.J., 1986-88; rsch. fellow in allergy and immunology Albert Einstein Coll. Medicine, Bronx, N.Y., 1988-91; fellow in allergy and immunology Weiler Hosp. of Albert Einstein Coll. Medicine, Bronx, 1988-91; dir. neonatal-perinatal medicine Englewood (N.J.) Hosp., 1991-96, Holy Name Hosp., N.J., 1996—; asst. attending physician divsn. perinatal medicine Babies' and Children's Hosp. of N.Y., N.Y.C., 1991-96; attending physician divsn. perinatal medicine Columbia-Presbyn. Med. Ctr., N.Y.C., 1996—; divsn. bd. of inquiry faculty of medicine Columbina U., 1978-80; com. of admissions U.M.D.N.J.-N.J. Med. Sch., 1986-88; crit. care com. intensive care nursery U. Hosp. N.J., 1986-88; perinatal morbidity rate mortality com. Englewood Hosp., 1991—, co-chmn. perinatal policy com., 1991-96, pharmacy and therapeutics com., 1992—, future devel. com., 1992-96, ob-gyn. quality improvement com., 1995—, chmn. neonatal intensive care quality assurance com., 1993—; co-chmn. neonatal clin. stds. com., 1994—, level of care design com., 1995-96; asst. attending pediatrician divsn. newborn medicine Mt. Sinai Hosp., 1991-96; asst. prof. pediatrics Mt. Sinai Sch. Medicine/CUNY, 1991-96. Contbr. articles to profl. jours. Recipient Internat. Cultural Diploma of Honor Order Internat. Ambassadors, Internat. Order of Merit Women's Inner Circle of Achievement. Fellow Am. Acad. Pediatrics; mem. AMA (Physician's Recognition awards (2), Am. Acad. Allergy and Immunology, Clin. Immunology Soc., Joint Coun. Allergy and Immunology, N.Y. Perinatal Soc., Babies' Hosp. Alumni Assn., NYU Pediatric Alumni Assn., P&S Columbia U. Alumni Assn., Alumni Orgn. City Coll., Phi Beta Kappa (Gamma chpt.). Office: Holy Name Hosp 718 Teaneck Rd Teaneck NJ 07666

WISHARD, DELLA MAE, state legislator; b. Bison, S.D., Oct. 21, 1934; d. Ervin E. and Alma J. (Albertson) Preszler; m. Glenn L. Wishard, Oct. 18, 1953; children: Glenda Lee, Pamela A., Glen Ervin. Grad. high sch., Bison. Mem. S.D. Ho. of Reps., Pierre, 1984—. Columnist County Farm Bur., 1970—. Committeewoman state Rep. Cen. Com., Perkins County, S.D., 1980-84. Mem. Am. Legis. Exch. Coun. (state coord. 1985-91, state chmn. 1991—), Fed. Rep. Women (chmn. Perkins County chpt. 1978-84), S.D. Farm Bur. (state officer 1982). Lutheran. Home and Office: HC 1 Box 139 Prairie City SD 57649-9714

WISHERT, JO ANN CHAPPELL, elementary and secondary education educator; b. Carroll County, Va., July 10, 1951; d. Joseph Lenox and Helen Alata (Wagoner) Chappell; m. Clarence Hinnant Wishert, Jr., June 10, 1987; 1 child, Kelly Marie. BA, Oral Roberts U., 1974; MS, Radford U., 1977; Degree in Advanced Postgrad Studies, Va. Poly. Inst. and State U., 1981; postgrad., U. S.C., Spartanburg, 1990. Cert. elem. music supr., Va., elem. and secondary music tchr., S.C., music tchr., ednl. specialist, N.C. Head start tchr. Rooftop of Va., Galax, 1975; elem. music tchr. Carroll County Pub. Schs., Hillsville, 1975-78; grad. asst., supr., course advisor Coll. Edn., Va. Poly. Inst. and State U., Blacksburg, 1975-81, pregrad. interviewer placement svcs., 1981-83; music dir. Heritage Acad., Charlotte, N.C., 1984-85, fine arts specialist, 1985-86; choral dir. Chester County Schs., Chester, S.C., 1986—; fine arts chairperson Chester H.S., 1995-96, chmn.; guest condr. workshop Patrick County Schs., Stuart, Va., 1980; liaison for Chester County Schs. to S.C. Gov.'s Sch. for Arts, 1990-91. Soloist PTL TV Network, Charlotte, 1984-85. Guest spkr. on battered women and marital abuse to chs. and workshops; entertainer; co-dir. Chester City Schs. Choral Festival; active Arts Coun. Chester County, 1988—, S.C. Arts Alliance and Arts Advocacy, Winthrop Consortium for the Arts; mem. steering com. Chester H.S., 1995-96. Named Tchr. of the Yr., Chester Sr. H.S., 1989, Chester County Schs., 1991, Educator of Yr., Chester County C. of C., 1992, Tchr. of the Week, The Herald, 1995. Mem. ASCD, AAUW (mem. bylaws com. Chester br. 1987—, sec. 1988-89, fine arts chmn. 1995—), Music Educators Nat. Conf., S.C. Music Educators Assn. (del. pub. rels. network Chester County Schs. 1991), S.C. Edn. Assn., Am. Ednl. Rsch. Assn., Am. Assn. Choral Dirs., Chester County Edn. Assn., Nat. Assn. Secondary Music Edn. (team evaluator divsn. tchr. edn. cert. 1989, 91—), State So. Assn. Schs. and Colls. (mem. evaluation team, mem. steering com.), All U.S.A. Chorus Student Group (alumni), 4-H Club (life), Phi Delta Kappa. Republican. Baptist. Home: 1122 Virginia Dare Dr Rock Hill SC 29730-9669

WISHNICK, MARCIA MARGOLIS, pediatrician, geneticist, educator; b. N.Y.C., Oct. 10, 1938; d. Hyman and Tillie (Stoller) Margolis; m. Stanley Wishnick, June 12, 1960; 1 child, Elizabeth Anne. BA, Barnard Coll., 1960; PhD, NYU, 1970, MD, 1974. Diplomate Am. Bd. Pediatrics, Nat. Bd. Med. Examiners. Rsch. technician Lederle Labs./Am. Cyanamid, Pearl River, N.Y., 1960-66; postdoctoral fellow N.Y. Pub. Health Lab., N.Y.C., 1970-71; resident in pediatrics NYU-Bellevue Med. Ctr., N.Y.C., 1974-77, asst. prof. pediatrics, 1977-82; clin. assoc. prof. pediatrics Bellevue Med. Ctr. NYU Med. Ctr., N.Y.C., 1982-87; clin. prof. pediatrics NYU-Bellevue Med. Ctr., N.Y.C., 1987—; pvt. practice, N.Y.C., 1977—. Contbr. articles to profl. jours. Fellow Am. Acad. Pediatrics; mem. AMA, N.Y. Pediatric Soc., N.Y. Med. Soc., N.Y. Women's Med. Assn. Office: 157 E 81st St New York NY 10028-1844

WISKOSKI, SUSAN SAGE, business educator; b. Rockledge, Fla., Dec. 5, 1931; d. Wilfred Jesse and Dorothy Florence (Cordiner) Sage; m. John Wiskoski, Aug. 16, 1950 (div. July 1979); children: Scott, John, Stanley, Ursula. BS in Bus. Edn., So. Vt. Coll., 1979; MA in Women's Studies, Vt. Coll., 1996. Owner, operator Chef Shop, Bennington, Vt., 1954-56, Chef Sandwich Shop, Bennington, 1958-66, Shirkshire Restaurant, Bennington, 1967-79; mgr. Kirkside Motor Lodge, Bennington, 1975-83; paraprofl. edn. S.W. Vt. Supervisory Union, Bennington, 1979-81; bus. tchr. S.W. Vt. Career Devel. Ctr., Bennington, 1981-96. Advisor women's issues group Mt. Anthony Union H.S., Bennington, 1994-95; bd. dirs. Cooper-Kelly Scholarship Fund, Vt. Girls Scout Coun., Burlington, Vt., 1987-88; county PAC coord. Vt. Nat. Edn. Assn., Bennington, 1986-87. Mem. NOW, NEA, Vt. Bus. and Profl. Women pres. 1990-91), Bennington Bus. and Profl. Women (Woman of Yr. 1993), Olden Women's League, So. Vt. Coll. Alumni (bd. dirs. 1992-96). Democrat. Congregationalist. Home: 225 Park St Bennington VT 05201

WISMER, PATRICIA ANN, secondary education educator; b. York, Pa., Mar. 23, 1936; d. John Bernhardt and Frances Elizabeth Loreen Marie (Fry) Feiser; m. Lawrence Howard Wismer, Aug. 4, 1961. BA in English, Mt. Holyoke Coll., 1958; MA in Speech/Drama, U. Wis., 1960; postgrad., U. Oreg., 1962, Calif. State U., Chico, 1963-64, U. So. Calif., 1973-74. Tchr., co-dir. drama program William Penn Sr. High Sch., York, 1960-61; instr. English, dir. drama York Jr. Coll., 1961-62; assoc. church editor San Francisco Examiner, 1962-63; reporter, publicist News Bur. Calif. State U., Chico, 1963-64; chmn. English Dept. Chico Sr. H.S., 1966-96; mentor tchr. Chico Sr. High Sch., Chico Unified Sch. Dist., 1983-93; judge writing awards Nat. Coun. Tchr. English, 1970—; cons. No. Calif. Writing Project, 1977—; curriculum cons., freelance writer and photographer, 1996—. Mem. Educators for Social Responsibility, Calif. Assn. for Gifted, Upper Calif. Coun. Tchrs. English (bd. dirs. 1966-85, pres. 1970-71), Calif. Assn. Tchrs. English, Nat. Coun. Tchrs. English, NEA, Calif. Tchrs. Assn., Chico Unified Tchrs. Assn. Democrat. Lutheran. Home: 623 Arcadian Ave Chico CA 95926-4504 Office: PO Box 1250 Cannon Beach OR 97110

WISNER, LINDA ANN, advertising agency executive, publishing company executive, interior designer; b. Sidney, N.Y., Apr. 28, 1951; d. Herbert and Ruth W. B.A. in Theatre and Art, Macalester Coll., 1973, postgrad. in journalism, 1974; postgrad. in graphic design Mpls. Coll. Art and Design, 1973-74; postgrad. in advtg. and mktg. U. Minn., 1974. Designer, publs. asst. Macalester Coll., St. Paul, 1973-76; designer Stretch & Sew Inc., Eugene, Oreg., 1976-78; free-lance designer, Eugene, 1978-79; owner, creative dir. Wisner Assocs., Eugene, 1979-87, Portland, 1987—, Interludes, Eugene, 1981—; ptnr. Instant Interiors, Eugene, 1979-88; design dir. Palmer/Pletsch Assocs., 1988—, v.p., 1992—; chmn. Bus. Images Exhibit, Eugene, 1983. Author: Creative Serging for the Home, 1991 (Best Sewing Book award 1991); designer/author, editor booklet series: Instant Interiors, 1979-83 (Woodie award 1980-83); designer, illustrator: Palmer/Pletsch Sewing Books, 1981—. Ambassador, City of Eugene, 1985-87; apptd. commr. design commn. City of Portland, 1995; bd. dirs. Maude Kerns Art Ctr., Eugene, 1984-85, Oreg. Repertory Theatre, 1986-87, Oreg. Sales and Mktg. Exec., 1986; bd. dirs Portland Culinary Alliance, 1989—, pres., 1992-93. Nat. Merit scholar Macalester Coll., 1969. Mem. Designers' Forum (pres. 1983-84, Designer of Yr. 1983), Sales and Mktg. Execs., Graphic Artists Guild, Exec. Bus. Women (pres. 1983-84), Mid Oreg. Ad Club (numerous certs. and trophy 1980-85), Eugene C. of C. (M.V.P. Leadership Program award 1986), Sullivan's Gulch Neighborhood Assn. (chairperson land use planning com., 1993—, bd. dirs 1990—). Avocations: design, soft sculpture, gardening, catering.

WISNESKI, MARY JO ELIZABETH, reading specialist, educator; b. Saginaw, Mich., Dec. 18, 1938; d. Walter Frank and Hedwig Josephine (Borowicz) W. BS, Cen. Mich. U., 1961; MS, So. Ill. U., 1969; EdD, U. No. Colo., 1979; postdoctoral, U. Calif., Berkeley, 1980-81. Cert. elem. educator, elem. adminstr., reading specialist, Calif.; reading recovery tchr. Elem. educator various schs., 1960-75; instr. U. No. Colo., Greeley, 1976-78, 79; reading specialist Vacaville (Calif.) Unified Sch. Dist., 1980—; lectr. San Francisco State U., 1983-86; prof. Chapman Coll., Travis AFB, Calif., 1986-90; med. transcriptionist, office mgr. collections, 1991-94; cons. in field. Author: Clifford Books Teacher Manual, 1991, Reading Recovery Position Paper, 1995. Vol. ARC, Travis Air Mus., Travis AFB; bd. dirs. Polish Arts and Culture Found., San Francisco, 1988-91, Vistula Dancers; mem. Reading Del. to Vietnam, People-to-People Internat. Amb. Program, 1995. Recipient Tchr. in Space Certificate NASA, 1986, Outstanding Tchr. Commendation Dept. of Defense, 1973. Mem. AAUW, Nat. Women's Polit. Caucus, Nat. Reading Conf., Internat. Reading Assn., Western Coll. Reading Assn., Calif. Profs. Reading (v.p., treas.), Calif. Edn. Assn., Solano County Reading Assn. (pres., v.p., sec.), Lowiczanie Folk Dance Ensemble (pres. pro tem, treas.), Polish Am. Congress, Phi Delta Kappa, Phi Kappa Phi, Kappa Delta Pi, Pi Lambda Theta. Home: 314 Creekview Ct Vacaville CA 95688-5318

WISNIEWSKI, HELENA STASIA, telecommunications and information systems company executive, mathematician; b. Englewood, N.J., Dec. 8, 1949; d. Julius George and Katherine Rose (Godlewski) W.; m. Phillip B. Chesson, Jan. 1, 1978; 1 child, Alexis Wisniewski-Chesson. BS in Maths., William Patterson Coll., 1971; MS in Maths., Stevens Inst. Tech., 1973; PhD in Maths., CUNY, 1980. Cert. secondary tchr., N.J. Prof. computer and decision scis. Seton Hall U., South Orange, N.J., 1980-81, dept. chair, 1981-82, dir. div. rsch., 1983-84; prof. maths. Rochester (N.Y.) Inst. Tech., 1982-83; project officer CIA, Washington, 1984-85; founding dir. maths. program Def. Advanced Rsch. Projects Agy., Washington, 1985-88; corp. dir.hdqrs. Lockheed Corp., Calabasas, Calif., 1988-92; v.p. VITA, Arlington, Va., 1992-93; dir. advanced program devel. Titan Corp., Reston, Va., 1993-94, v.p. advanced programs, 1995—; rev. panel Computational Fluid Dynamics Office of the Under Sec. Def., Washington, 1987-88; chair adv. bd. So. Ill. U. Neuro-Engr. Rsch. Ctr., Carbondale, Ill., 1990—; founding bd. dirs. Calif. Coalition for Maths., 1991—. Founding editor: Technology Acceleration, 1991—; editl. bd. Jour. Applied Numerical Maths., 1987-91; co-chair Lockheed Horizons editl. bd., 1991-92; editor SPIE Proceedings, Springer Verlag, vol. 1771; contbr. articles to jour. SPIE, Visiual Info. Processing, Chaoes & Comm., NATO ASI Series-Springer Verlag, Transactions of the Am. Math. Soc., Internat. Symposium Dynamical Systems, Proceedings Rio de Janiero, Springer Verlag. Sci. fair judge Westlake High Sch., Westlake Village, Calif., 1990; organizer career exploration program Calabasas High Sch., 1990; mem. math. coun. L.A. Ednl. Partnership, 1991. Recipient Teaching Excellence award Va. Poly. Inst. and State U., 1976, Spl. Achievement award, CIA 1986, Spl. Recognition award DARPA, 1988, Dedicated Svc. award George Washington U. Adv. Bd., 1995. Mem. AIAA (sr.), N.Y. Acad. Scis., Soc. Indsl. and Applied Maths., Security Affairs Support Assn., Armed Forces Comm. & Electronics Assn., Lockheed Mgmt. Assn. (v.p. 1989-90, pres. 1990-91, adv. bd. George Washington U. 1995—, Recognition of Extraordinary Leadership, Mgmt. & Svc. Honor award 1992), Pi Mu Epsilon, Kappa Delta Pi. Office: Titan Corp 1900 Campus Commons Dr Ste 400 Reston VA 22091

WISSLER-THOMAS, CARRIE, professional society administrator, artist; b. Ephrata, Pa., Nov. 2, 1946; d. Robert Uibel and Grace Urbane (Nicholas) Wissler; m. James Richard Gamber, June 12, 1968 (div. 1972); m. Scott Kerry Thomas, Mar. 3, 1972; 1 child, Dylan Crayton Llewellyn. BA, Hood Coll., 1968; MS, Temple U., 1986. Copywriter WGSA Radio, Ephrata, Pa., 1970-71, William Assocs., Harrisburg, Pa., 1977; correspondent Art Matters of Phila., Harrisburg, 1984-86; art columnist Pennsylvania Beacon, Harrisburg, 1983-85; writer Strictly Business, Harrisburg, 1985-86; painting instr. Art Assn. of Harrisburg, 1980-86; freelance artist Harrisburg, 1968—; exec. dir., pres. Art Assn. of Harrisburg, 1986—; mem. exhbn. panel Harrisburg City Govt. Ctr., 1983-89; mem. art adv. panel Harrisburg Area C.C., 1985—; mem. gallery com. Univ. Ctr. at Harrisburg, 1988—; chmn. Easter Seals Art Show by Disabled Artists, Harrisburg, 1983-86; trustee Pa. Sch. Art and Design, 1989—; mem. Harrisburg Multi-Cultural Coalition, 1992—; chmn. Harrisburg Gallery Walk, 1989—; bd. dirs. Historic Harrisburg Assn., 1992—; pres. Allied Arts Affiliates Coun., 1993-95. Prin. work includes Broadway Babies oil painting, 1982 (Grumbacher Gold Medallion 1982); over 30 solo exhibitions. Mem. Hist. Soc. Cocalico Valley, Ephrata, 1982—, Dauphin County Hist. Soc., Harrisburg, 1986—; minority inspector Paxtang Election Bd., Harrisburg, 1977-79; mem. ACLU, Pa., 1988—; bd. dirs. Historic Harrisburg Assn., 1992—. Recipient Women Who Work award Communications and the Arts Pomeroy's, 1985, Disting. Svc. to Arts award Harrisburg Community Theatre, 1991. Mem. Pa. Soc. Assn. Execs., Am. Coun. on Arts, Art Assn. Harrisburg (pres. 1980-84), Rotary. Democrat. Anglican. Home and Studio: 2721 N 2nd St Harrisburg PA 17110-1205 Office: Art Assn of Harrisburg 21 N Front St Harrisburg PA 17101-1606

WISSMANN, CAROL RENEÉ, sales executive; b. Berkeley, Calif., July 9, 1946; d. Conrad Clayton and Carol Elizabeth (Ward) W. BA, Whittier Coll., 1968; Montessori Diploma, Coll. Notre Dame, Belmont, 1970. Dist. mgr. U.S. C. of C., Washington; div. mgr. Classified Yellow Pages Inc., Cookeville, Tenn., 1986; pres. The BelleMann Corp., Gig Harbor, Wash., 1988—; cons., spkr. sales, telemarketing, customer svc.; instr. St. Martin's Coll., Tacoma C.C. Republican. Home and Office: Ste E 305 5114 Point Fosdick Dr NW Gig Harbor WA 98335-1717

WISWALL, MAUREEN LERAE, adoption consultant; b. Cedar Rapids, Iowa, Mar. 13, 1942; d. Marvin L. and Valena M. (Elmore) Stoner; m. John P. Wiswall, June 26, 1965; children: Courtney, Matthew, Kyle, Kristin, Kara. BS, W.Va. U., 1965; postgrad., Seton Hall U., 1965. Cert. tchr., N.J. Tchr. Parsippany (N.J.) High Sch., 1965-66; adoption resource cons. Boonton, N.J., 1978—. Bd. dirs. Amigos de las Americas, Montclair, N.J., 1989—; v.p. Wilson Sch. Bd. Trustees, Mountain Lakes, N.J., 1980—, sec., 1994-95, co-chair Art '92 com., 1980-91, chair, 1992, chair Art '93 com., 1993, Art '94 com., 1994. Home and Office: 209 Old Beach Glen Rd Boonton NJ 07005-9501

WITCHER, PHYLLIS HERRMANN, secondary education educator; b. Wilmington, Del., Feb. 23, 1938; d. Carl Victor and Ruth Naomi (Ice) Herrmann; m. Murray H. Witcher, Apr. 8, 1961 (div. 1992); children: David, Stephanie Witcher Stewart. BS, U. Del., 1960; MEd, West Chester U., 1982. Cert. secondary tchr., Pa. Tchr. pub. schs. Pa., Tenn., Del., 1974—; textile analyst Sears Roebuck Labs., Chgo., 1977-79; ind. admissions counselor Coll. Selection Svcs., Chadds Ford, Pa., 1983—; bd. dirs. Unionville-Chadds Ford Sch. Dist., 1986-91, Chester County Intermediate Unit, Exton, Pa., 1988-91. Author, speaker No-Fault Div., 1990. Bd. dirs. Mental Health Assn. in Del., Wilmington, 1985-93; past pres. Del. Symphony League, Wilmington, 1985; founder, pres. Protecting Marriage, Inc., Chadds Ford, 1991. Recipient Giraffe Project Nat. Commendation, 1994. Republican. Roman Catholic. Home: 22 Mountainview Tr Chadds Ford PA 19317-9182 Office: Protecting Marriage Inc 22 Mountainview Trl Chadds Ford PA 19317-9182

WITH, GERDA BECKER, artist; b. Hamburg, Germany, Mar. 4, 1910; came to U.S., 1939; d. Ludwig and Martha (De Bruycker) Becker; m. Karl E. With, July 17, 1939 (dec. Dec. 1980); children: Christopher B., Nela W. Dwyer. M in Decorative Arts, Charlottenburg, Berlin, 1938. One woman shows include Otis Art Inst., Mus. St. Barbara, also pvt. galleries throughout Europe and U.S., 1958—; illustrator: (book) The Man Who Stole the Word "Beautiful", 1991, others. Home: 3045 Kelton Ave Los Angeles CA 90034-3021

WITHAEGER, ROSEMARY ANNE, civic volunteer, flight attendant; b. Chgo., Oct. 2; d. Edwin Louis and Marjorie Louise (Montgomery) W. Degree in nursing, Cook County Hosp. Sch. Nursing, 1973. RN, Ill. Staff nurse Cook County Hosp., Chgo., 1973-76; charge nurse, staff nurse Northwest Community Hosp., Arlington Heights, Ill., 1976-83; flight attendant Northwest Airlines, Mpls., 1980—; model and product spokesperson, Chgo., 1970-93. Vol., chmn. transitional living programs Ctr. for Abused Children, Chgo., 1986-90; vol. Columbus-Maryville Children's Ctr., Chgo., Cabrini Alive Rehab., Chgo.; vol. RN Camp Action, 1991-93, Chgo. Lung Assn.; bd. dirs. Fourth Presbyn. Ch. Ctr. for Whole Life, 1993, deacon, 1996—. Recipient Vol. award Transitional Living Programs, 1988. Mem. Chgo. Coun. Fgn. Rels., Alliance Francaise de Chgo., Chgo. Health and Tennis Club. Presbyterian. Home: 663 W Barry Ave Apt K Chicago IL 60657-4504 Office: Northwest Airlines 2700 Lone Oak Pky Eagan MN 55121-1546

WITHAM, CAROL ANN, elementary education educator; b. Dover, N.H., Dec. 23, 1946; d. Walter S. and Beatrice F. (Spencer) Prescott; children from previous marriage: Christopher A. Gosselin, Keith A. Gosselin, Kevin A. Gosselin; m. Kenneth F. Witham, May 1, 1993. BA, U. N.H., 1968; MEd, Notre Dame Coll., Manchester, N.H., 1984. Cert. elem. tchr., N.H. Tchr. Underhill Sch., Hooksett, N.H., 1968-72, Auburn (N.H.) Village Sch., 1977—; instr. Notre Dame Coll., 1984—. Author: Games, A N.H. Learning Experience, 1984. Mem. DAR, NEA (sec. 1990, chmn. 1991, regional treas. 1992—), Granite State Reading Coun., Auburn Edn. Assn. (pres. 1991-93, treas. 1993-95), Phi Delta Kappa. Home: PO Box 432 Northwood NH 03261-0432 Office: Auburn Village Sch Eaton Rd Auburn NH 03032

WITHERINGTON, JENNIFER LEE, sales and marketing executive; b. Albuquerque, Sept. 8, 1960; d. Terrence Lee and Pamela Ann (Hoerter) W. BA in Polit. Sci., James Madison U., 1982. Asst. press sec. U.S. Senate, Washington, 1983-85; nat. sales mgr. Madison Hotels, Washington, 1986-88; dir. sales Madison Air Charter Svcs., Washington, 1987-88; nat. sales mgr. Ritz-Carlton Hotels, Palm Springs, Calif., 1988-90; dir. sales and mktg. Cappa and Graham, Inc., San Francisco, 1990-95; gen. mgr. USA Hosts, San Francisco, 1995—; spkr. in field. Contbr. articles to profl. jours. Vol. San Francisco Emergency Rescue Team, Yerba Buena Ctr. for Arts. Mem. Am. Soc. Assn. Execs., Profl. Conv. Mgmt. Assn., Hospitality Sales and Mktg. Assn. Internat. (pres. San Francisco chpt. 1994—), Meeting Profls. Internat. Republican. Roman Catholic. Home: 1565 Green St Apt 304 San Francisco CA 94123-5129 Office: USA Hosts 177 Post St Ste 550 San Francisco CA 94108

WITHERS, DINAH LEA, special education educator; b. Amarillo, Tex., Mar. 14, 1953; d. John Eugene and Janelle (Williamson) W. BA in Spl. Edn., Ariz. State U., 1992. Cert. spl. edn. tchr., Ariz., Calif.; cert. child devel. credential. Kindergarten tchr., asst. dir., dir. Palo Alto Presch., Mesa, Ariz., 1978-84; tchr. Kachina County Day Sch., Phoenix, 1984-85; tchr. aide to handicapped Parkway Sch., Mesa, 1986; classroom aide to phys. handicapped Manzano H.S., Albuquerque, 1986-87; classroom aide/driver in head trauma classroom Devereaux Ctr., Scottsdale, Ariz., 1987-88; tchr. Tesseract Sch., Paradise Valley, Ariz., 1988-91; residential care technician Tempe Ctr. for Habilitation, Tempe, Ariz., 1991; residential staff, tchr. Victory House Discovery Ctr., Mesa, 1991; spl. edn. tchr. cross categorical Roosevelt Sch. Dist., Phoenix, 1992-93; spl. edn. tchr. San Leandor (Calif.) Unified Sch. Dist., 1993—; master tchr. San Leandro Unified Sch. Dist., 1994—. Grantee Kiwanis Club, 1993, Community Edn. Fund., 1994. Mem. Coun. for Exceptional Children, Golden Key Nat. Honor Soc., Phi Kappa Phi.

WITHERSPOON, HILDA, artist, television producer; b. Istanbul, Turkey, Oct. 4, 1935; came to U.S., 1974, naturalized; d. Hagop and Mari (Avakian) Ekmekciyan; m. Robert Witherspoon, Jan. 2, 1967; 1 child, Eric Bentley. Diploma, Notre Dame de Sion, Istanbul, 1957, U. Paris, 1967; postgrad., Corcoran Sch. of Art, 1990. Armenian tchr. St. Mary's Cultural Ctr., 1968-78; pres. Hilda's Right, Washington, 1982—, Studio Gallery, Washington, 1989; French tchr. St. Albans Sch., Washington, 1991-92; art tchr. Sacred Heart Sch., Washington, 1991-92, Zagorsk (Russia) Elem. Sch., 1992; TV prodr. The Art of Living program Fairfax County Access Cable, Fairfax, Va., 1995—; represented by Alla Rogers Gallery, Georgetown. One-woman shows include Armenian Cultural Ctr., Washington, 1987, Studio Gallery, Washington, 1988, 89, Gensler and Assocs., Washington, 1990, 91, Alla Rogers Gallery, 1990, 91, Astrea, Washington, 1991, Tula (Russia) Art Mus., 1992, Ctrl. Artists House, Moscow, 1992, Armenian Libr. and Mus. of Am., Watertown, Mass., 1993, World Bank, Washington, 1995, Roche Bobois, 1994, Embassy of France, Washington, 1995; exhibited in group shows at Fairfax County Art Show, 1982, Touchstone Gallery, Washington, 1986, Arts Club of Washington, 1986, Foundry Gallery, Washington, 1986, 88, 91, Whitewalls Gallery, Corcoran Sch. of Art, Washington, 1987, 1988, Arts Club of Washington, 1987, Inst. Policy Studies, Washington, 1987, R St. Gallery, Washington, 1987, Omni Hotel, Washington, 1987, Park Place Cafe, Washington, 1987, Arnold and Porter, Washington, 1987, Studio Gallery, Washington, 1987, 88, 89, United Meth. Ch., Washington, 1987, Corcoran Sch. of Art, Washington, 1987, 88, Stables Art Ctr., Washington, 1988, Gt. Falls Arts Ctr., Va., 1988, Martin Luther King Libr., Washington, 1988, Art Barn, Washington, 1989, Katchadourian Gallery, Saddlebrook, N.J., 1990, Corcoran Connection Gallery, Washington, 1991, Mayor's Art Gallery, Washington, 1991, Carnegie Libr., Washington, 1991, No. Va. C.C., Annandale, 1992, Congl. Offices, Washington, 1992, 93, New Eng. Fine Arts Inst. Exhibit, Woburn, Mass., 1993, Dante Alighieri Soc. Mass., Cambridge, 1993, Open Studio, Washington, 1993, 1054 Galleries, Washington, 1993, NIH, Bethesda, Md., 1993, Universal North, Washington, many others. Recipient Cmty. Residences award, 1996, Cmty. Edn. award, 1996. Armenian Apostolic. Home: Apt 5 2101 Connecticut Ave NW Washington DC 20008

WITHROW, LUCILLE MONNOT, nursing home administrator; b. Alliance, Ohio, July 28, 1923; d. Charles Edward Monnot and Freda Aldine (Guy) Monnot Cameron; m. Alvin Robert Withrow, June 6, 1945 (dec. 1984); children: Cindi Withrow Johnson, Nancy Withrow Townley, Sharon Withrow Hodgkins, Wendel Alvin. AA in Health Adminstrn., Eastfield Coll., 1976. Lic. nursing home adminstr., Tex.; cert. nursing home ombudsman. Held various clerical positions Dallas, 1950-72; office mgr., asst. adminstr. Christian Care Ctr. Nursing Home, Mesquite, Tex., 1972-76; head adminstr. Christian Care Ctr. Nursing Home and Retirement Complex, Mesquite, 1976-91; nursing home ombudsman Tex. Dept. Aging and Tex. Dept. Health, Dallas, 1991-93; legal asst. Law Offices of Wendel A. Withrow, Carrollton, Tex., 1993—; mem. con. on geriatric curriculum devel. Eastfield Coll., Mesquite, 1979, 87; mem. ombudsman adv. com. Sr. Citizens Greater Dallas; nursing home cons.; notary pub., 1995—. Vol. Dallas Arboretum and Bot. Soc., Dallas Summer Musicals Guild; mem. Ombudsman adv. com. Sr. Citizens of Greater Dallas, Health Svcs. Speakers Bur.; charter mem. Stage Show Prodns. Recipient Volunteerism awards Tex. Atty. Gen., 1987, Tex. Gov., 1992. Mem. Tex. Assn. Homes for Aging, Am. Assn. Homes for Aging, Health Svcs. Speakers Bur., White Rock Kiwanis. Republican. Mem. Ch. of Christ. Home: 11344 Lippitt Ave Dallas TX 75218-1922 Office: Law Office of W A Withrow 1120 Metrocrest Dr Ste 200 Carrollton TX 75006-5787

WITHROW, MARY ELLEN, treasurer of United States; b. Marion, Ohio, Oct. 2, 1930; d. Clyde Welsh and Mildred (Stump) Hinamon; m. Norman David Withrow, Sept. 4, 1948; children: Linda Rizzo, Leslie Legge, Norma, Rebecca. Mem. Elgin Local Bd. Edn., Marion, Ohio, 1969-73, pres., 1972; safety programs dir. ARC, Marion, 1968-72; dep. registrar State of Ohio, Marion, 1972-75; dep. county auditor Marion County, Ohio, 1975-77, county treas., 1977-83; treas. State of Ohio, Columbus, 1983-94; treas. of the U.S. Dept. Treasury, Washington, 1994—; chmn. Ohio Bd. Deposits, 1983—, Anthony Commn. on Pub. Fin. Mem. exec. com. Ohio Dem. Com., mem. exec. com. women's caucus; mem. Dem. Nat. Com.; mem. Met. Women's Ctr.; pres. Marion County Dem. Club, 1976; participant Harvard U. Strategic Leadership Conf., 1990.; mem. Dem. Leadership Coun. Recipient Donald L. Scantlebury Meml. award, 1991, Women of Achievement award YWCA of Met. Columbus, 1993, Outstanding Govt. Svc. award Am. Numis. Assn., 1995; inducted Ohio Women's Hall of Fame, 1986; named Outstanding Elected Dem. Woman Holding Pub. Office, Nat. Fedn. Dem. Women, 1987, Advocate of Yr., SBA, 1988, Most Valuable State Pub. Ofcl., City and State newspaper, 1990; Women Execs. in State Govt. fellow Harvard U., 1987. Mem. LWV (dem. leadership coun.), State Assn. County Treas. (legis. com. 1979-83, treas. 1982), Nat. Assn. State Treas. (pres. 1992, Jesse Unruh award 1993, chair long range planning com., mem. exec. com.), Nat. Assn. State Auditors Comtps. and Treas. (pres. 1990, strategic planning com., intergov. rels. com., chair state and mcpl. bonds com.), Coun. State Govts. (exec. com., internat. affairs com., orgnl. planning and coord. com., strategic planning task force), Women Execs. in State Govt. (chair fund devel. com.). Club: Bus. and Profl. Women's. Office: Dept Treasury 1500 Pennsylvania Ave NW Washington DC 20005-1007

WITHROW-GALLANTER, SHERRIE ANNE, construction and audio company executive; b. Sacramento, Mar. 10, 1960; d. Jim and Ilene (James) Withrow; m. Michael Paul Gallanter, Jan. 7, 1990. Student, Diablo Valley Community Coll., Pleasant Hill, Calif., 1977-81, Tarrant County Jr. Coll., Ft. Worth, 1982-83, Coll. of Marin, Kentfield, Calif., 1988, Merritt Coll., Oakland, Calif., 1990; AA in Bus. Adminstrn. and Mgmt., St. Louis Community Coll., Florissant, Mo., 1981. Internal cashier AAA Automobile Club Mo., St. Louis, 1977-79; receiving clk. Dayton-Hudson Target Stores, Florissant and Ft. Worth, 1979-81; supr. credit and collection World Svc. Life Ins. Co., Ft. Worth, 1982-83; bank br. balancer, data processing div. Tex. Am. Bank Svcs., Inc., Ft. Worth, 1984-85; asst. to contr. Positive Video-Post Prodn., Orinda, Calif., 1985-87; with contractor's desk adminstrn. dept. Shell Oil Co., Martinez, Calif., 1987-88; asst. to chief fin. officer J.T. Thorpe & Son, Inc., Richmond, Calif., 1988-89; founder, gen. ptnr. HomeVisions Constrn. Svcs., El Sobrante, Calif., 1989—, AudioVisions Sound Co., El Sobrante, 1990—, AV Electric, El Sobrante, 1994—; audio engr., cons. and project fin. cons. various constrn. cos., No. Calif., 1988—. Fundraiser Sr. Citizen Subsidized Housing Complex, Martinez, 1987, 88. David L. Underwood scholar Florissant Valley (St. Louis) C.C., 1980-81. Mem. NAFE, Internat. Platform Assn., Phi Theta Kappa. Democrat. Office: Visions Group/AV Cos PO Box 20368 El Sobrante CA 94820-0368

WITKIN, BELLE RUTH, writer, former speech and English language educator; b. Seattle, June 1, 1917; d. Samuel and Lena (Eichenwald) Clayman; m. Joseph Jacob Witkin, Jan. 8, 1944; 1 child, Sheryl Marie Killman. BA in English, U. Puget Sound, 1939; MA in Speech Edn., U. Wash., 1952, PhD in Speech Pathology and Audiology, 1962. Life teaching credential, Wash., Calif., adminstrv. credential, Calif. H.s. tchr. in English, speech and journalism Gig Harbor (Wash.) H.S., 1940-43; writer, aircraft inspector, office mgr. County Health Dept., Tex., Fla.; newspaper feature reporter, insp. Boeing Co., Wash., 1943-46; speech comm. instr., lectr. U. Wash., Seattle, 1948-60; speech cons. King County Supt. of Schs., Seattle, 1960-66; dir. PACE Ctr. Alameda County, Hayward, Calif., 1966-77; speech lectr. San Jose (Calif.) State U., 1976-77; rschr., adminstr. Alameda County Office of Edn., Hayward, Calif., 1966-80; writer Renton, Wash., 1981—; vis. scholar U. Wash., Seattle, 1990—. Author: (book) Assessing Needs in Educational and Social Programs, 1984; co-author: (book) Planning and Conducting Needs Assessments: A Practical Guide, 1995; contbr. chpts. to books. Northwest regional adv. bd. Anti-Defamation League, Seattle, 1955-66, exec. coun., 1964-65; mem. LWV, South King County, 1982—, Citizens Edn. Ctr., Seattle, 1982—. Named to Order of the Rose, Beta Sigma Phi, 1955, Hall of Fame, Internat. Listening Assn., 1992; recipient ERIC award Toastmasters Internat., 1966. Mem. Internat. Listening Assn. (chair rsch. task force 1986-92, rsch. award 1996), Am. Speech-Lang.-Hearing Assn., Am. Evaluation Assn., Am. Ednl. Rsch. Assn., Speech Comm. Assn., Internat. Soc. for Ednl. Planning (exec. bd. 1975-77), Calif. Assn. for Program Evaluation (pres. 1979-80), Wash. State Speech Assn. (pres. 1964-65), N.W. Comm. Assn. Home and Office: 201 Union Ave SE #132 Renton WA 98059

WITKIN, EVELYN MAISEL, geneticist; b. N.Y.C., Mar. 9, 1921; d. Joseph and Mary (Levin) Maisel; m. Herman A. Witkin, July 9, 1943 (dec. July 1979); children—Joseph, Andrew. AB, NYU, 1941; MA, Columbia U., 1943, PhD, 1947; DSc honoris causa, N.Y. Med. Coll., 1978, Rutgers U., 1995. Mem. staff genetics dept. Carnegie Inst., Washington, 1950-55; mem. faculty State U. N.Y. Downstate Med. Center, Bklyn., 1955-71; prof. medicine State U. N.Y. Downstate Med. Center, 1968-71; prof. biol. scis. Douglass Coll., Rutgers U., 1971-79, Barbara McClintock prof. genetics, 1979-83; Barbara McClintock prof. genetics Waksman Inst. Microbiology, 1983-91; Barbara McClintock prof. emerita Waksman Inst. Microbiology, Rutgers U., 1991—. Author articles; mem. editorial bds. profl. jours. Postdoctoral fellow Am. Cancer Soc., 1947-49; fellow Carnegie Instn., 1957; Selman A. Waksman lectr., 1960; Phi Beta Kappa vis. scholar, 1980-81; grantee NIH, 1956-89; recipient Prix Charles Leopold Mayer French Acad. Scis., 1977, Lindback award, 1979. Fellow AAAS, Am. Acad. Microbiology; mem. NAS, Am. Acad. Arts and Scis., Environ. Mutagen Soc., Am. Genetics Soc., Am. Soc. Microbiology. Home: 1 Firestone Ct Princeton NJ 08540-5220 Office: Rutgers U Waksman Inst Microbiology Piscataway NJ 08854

WITKIN, MILDRED HOPE FISHER, psychotherapist, educator; b. N.Y.C.; d. Samuel and Sadie (Goldschmidt) Fisher; children: Georgia Hope, Roy Thomas, Laurie Phillips, Kimberly, Nicole, Scott, Joshua, Jennifer; m. Jorge Radovic, Aug. 26, 1983. AB, Hunter Coll., MA, Columbia U., 1968; PhD, NYU, 1973. Diplomate Am. Bd. Sexology, Am. Bd. Sexuality; cert. supr. Head counselor Camp White Lake, Camp Emanuel, Long Beach, N.J.; tchr. econs., polit. sci. Hunter Coll. High Sch.; dir., group leader follow-up program Jewish Vacation Assn., N.Y.C.; investigator N.Y.C. Housing Authority; psychol. counselor Montclair State Coll., Upper Montclair, N.J., 1967-68; mem., lectr. Creative Problem-Solving Inst., U. Buffalo, 1968; psychol. counselor Fairleigh Dickinson U., Teaneck, N.J., 1968, dir. Counseling Center, 1969-74; pvt. practice psychotherapy, N.Y.C., also Westport, Conn.; sr. faculty supr., family therapist and psychotherapist Payne Whitney Psychiat. Clinic, N.Y. Hosp., 1973—; clin. asst. prof. dept. psychiatry Cornell U. Med. Coll., 1974—; assoc. dir. sex therapy and edn. program Cornell-N.Y. Hosp. Med. Ctr., 1974—; sr. cons. Kaplan Inst. for Evaluation and Treatment of Sexual Disorders, 1981—; supr. master's and doctoral candidates, NYU, 1975-82; pvt. practice psychotherapy and sex therapy, N.Y.C., also Westport, Conn.; cons. counselor edn. tng. programs N.Y.C. Bd. Edn., 1971-75; cons. Health Info. Systems, 1972-79; vis. prof. numerous colls. and univs.; chmn. sci. com. 1st Internat. Symposium on Female Sexuality, Buenos Aires, 1984. Exhibited in group shows at Scarsdale (N.Y.) Art Show, 1959, Red Shutter Art Studio, Long Beach, 1968. Edn. legislation chmn. PTA, Yonkers, 1955; publicity chmn. United Jewish Appeal, Scarsdale, 1959-65; Scarsdale chmn. mothers com. Boy Scouts Am., 1961-64; mem. Morrow Assn. on Correction N.J., 1969-91; bd. dirs. Girl Scouts of Am. Recipient Bronze medal for svcs. Hunter Coll.; United Jewish Appeal plaque, 1962; Founders Day award N.Y. U., 1973, citation N.Y. Hosp./Cornell U. Med. Ctr., 1990. Fellow Internat. Coun. Sex Edn. and Parenthood of Am. U., Am. Acad. Clin. Sexologists; mem. AAUW, APA, ACA, Assn. Counseling Supervision, Am. Coll. Personnel Assn., Internat. Assn. Marriage and Family Counselors, Am. Coll. Sexuality (cert.), Women's Med. Assn. N.Y.C., N.Y. Acad. Sci., Am. Coll. Pers. Assn. (nat. mem. commn. II 1973-76), Nat. Assn. Women Deans and Counselors, Am. Assn. Sex Educators, Counselors and Therapists (regional bd., nat. accreditation bd., cert. internat. supr.), Soc. for Sci. Study Sex Therapy and Rsch., Eastern Assn. Sex Therapists, Am. Assn. Marriage and Family Counselors, N.J. Assn. Marriage and Family Counselors, Ackerman Family Inst., Am. Personnel and Guidance Assn., Am., N.Y., N.J. psychol. assns., Creative Edn. Found., Am. Assn. Higher Edn., Assn. Counselor Supervision and Edn., Profl. Women's Caucus, LWV, Am. Assn. counseling and Devel., Am. Women's Med. Assn., Nat. Coun. on Women in Medicine, Argentine Soc. Human Sexuality (hon.), Am. Assn. Sexology (diplomate), Conn. Assn. Marriage and Family Therapy, Pi Lambda Theta, Kappa Delta Pi, Alpha Chi Alpha. Author: 45-And Single Again, 1985, Single Again, 1994; contbr. articles to profl. jours. and textbooks; lectr. internat. and nat. workshops, radio and TV. Home: 9 Sturges Commons Westport CT 06880-2832 Office: 35 Park Ave New York NY 10016-3838

WITMAN-GLENN, LAURA KATHLEEN, bookkeeper, writer; b. Pottstown, Pa., Mar. 4, 1957; d. William Tedford and Kathleen (Nieman) Witman; m. David Dale Roripaugh, Oct. 11, 1985 (div.); life ptnr. Marjorie Lorraine Witman-Glenn, Aug. 18, 1989; 1 child, Scotty Levengood Witman-Glenn. Degree in Actg. magna cum laude, Adelphi Bus. Coll., San Bernardino, Calif., 1985. Cert. acctg. bookkeeper. Silent alarm monitor, payroll acct. Comml. Security Alliance, San Bernardino, Calif., 1985—. Author: The Sun, 1994; (poetry) World of Poetry, 1990, National Library of Poetry, 1992, Sparrowgrass, 1993; (short story) Antivivesection Soc., 1993, Animal Voice, 1994. Mem. O.C.D. Found., PETA. Democrat. Home: 488 W 17th St San Bernardino CA 92405-4423

WITMER, DIANE F., communication educator; b. Pasadena, Jan. 20, 1945; d. Stanley Lamar and Mary Evelyn Witmer; m. Robert D. Joyce (div. 1987); 1 child, David William Penkoff. AA, Golden West Coll., Huntington Beach, Calif., 1977; BS in BA, U. LaVerne (Calif.), 1980; MS in Sys. Mgmt., U. So. Calif., L.A., 1989; MA in Communication Arts, U. So. Calif., 1993, PhD in Orgnl. Comm., 1994. Dir. pub. rels. Weight Watchers, Santa Ana, Calif., 1980-84; dir. comm. March of Dimes, Costa Mesa, Calif., 1986-90; prin. Penkoff Comm. Resources, L.A., 1990-92; instr. Calif. State U., Fullerton, 1990-94; asst. lectr. comm. arts and scis. U. So. Calif., University Park, 1991-94; asst. prof. Purdue U., West Lafayette, Ind., 1994—. Editor, The Paper Weight, 1981-84. Chmn. award com. March of Dimes, Costa Mesa, nat. vol., 1980—, also chair speakers bur. Sagemore divsn., mem. exec. com. Mem. Pub. Rels. Soc. Am. (accredited mem.), U. So. Calif. Alumni Assn., Indpls. Symphony Chorus.

WITSCHI, EMILY, art educator; b. Detroit, May 25, 1957; d. Ralph William and Elizabeth (Toler) Witschi; children: Jason Daniel, Jason Joseph. BFA, Lake Erie Coll., Painesville, Ohio, 1979. Cert. tchr. visual arts K-12. Pottery instr. City of Pontiac, Mich., 1975-79; youth art instr. Willoughby (Ohio) Sch. Fine Art, 1979-80; human resources staff May Co., Mentor and Cleve., Ohio, 1980-93; art dir. Fairmont Fine Arts Ctr., Russel, Ohio, 1994—; art tchr. Cuyahoga Heights (Ohio) Bd. Edn., 1993—; gallery dir. Fairmont Fine Art Ctr., 1995—; artist Three Streams Pottery, Chesterland, Ohio,1995—. Group shows (pottery) include Four Coll. Invitational Art Show, 1977, Willoughby Regional Art Show, 1978, Womansart Show, 1979, Elise Newman Gallery, 1995. Advisor student coun. Cuyahoga Heights H.S., 1993-95; vol. demonstrating pottery various schs. N.E. Ohio. Mem. Clay Arts Guild, Art Educators Assn., Psi Beta. Republican. Home: 8977 Cedar Rd Chesterland OH 44026-3574

WITT, ANNE CLEINO, musician, education educator; b. Winston-Salem, N.C., May 14, 1945; d. Edward Henry and Elizabeth Anne (White) Cleino; m. Robert Ernest Witt, Nov. 23, 1977; children: Peter Ivy, Karen Ivy. BS in Music Edn., U. Ala., 1967; MMus, U. Tex., 1974, PhD in Music Edn., 1983. Choral dir. Lee H.S., Huntsville, Ala., 1967-70; profl. cellist Austin (Tex.) Symphony Orch., 1974-95; pvt. cello tchr. Austin, 1990-93; orch. dir. and string tchr. Lamar Mid. Sch. and McCallum H.S., Austin, 1974-80, 83-90; lectr. edn. U. Tex., Austin, 1990-93; dir. U. Tex. String Project, Austin, 1993-95; clinician conv. sessions, insvc. tng., 1980—. Author: Recruiting for the School Orchestra, 1984, 2d edit. 1987; editor: Teaching Stringed Instruments, 1991, Strategies for Teaching Strings and Orchestra, 1996. Mem. Am. String Tchrs. Assn. (past pres., Citation for Exceptional Leadership and Merit 1988, 96, nat. pres. 1992-94), Tex. Orch. Dirs. Assn. (pres. 1991-92), Music Educators Nat. Conf. (life), Tex. Music Educators Assn., Suzuki Assn. of Americas. Episcopalian. Home: 2329 Table Rock Arlington TX 76006 Office: Univ of Texas School of Music Arlington TX 76019

WITT, CAROL A., lawyer; b. Fremont, Ohio, Nov. 27, 1947; Student, Bowling Green State U., 1965-68; B.S., Suffolk U., 1973, J.D. cum laude, 1977. Bar: Mass. 1977, U.S. Dist. Ct. Mass. 1978, U.S. Tax Ct. 1978, U.S. Dist. Ct. Vt. 1982. Assoc., Louison & Cohen, P.C., Brockton, Mass., 1977-79; ptnr. Louison, Witt & Hensley, P.C., Brockton, 1979-83; mng. ptnr. Louison & Witt, P.C., Brockton, 1983-96, Law Office of Carol A. Witt, Nantucket, 1996—. Fellow Am. Acad. Matrimonial Lawyers; mem. ABA, ATLA, Mass. Bar Assn. (civil litigation sect. coun. 1984-87, family law section coun. chair 1990-92), Mass. Bar Found. (trustee 1995—), Mass. Continuing Legal Edn., Inc. (trustee 1994—), Plymouth County Bar Assn., Mass. Acad. Trial Attys., Women's Bar Assn. Home: 14 S Mill St Nantucket MA 02554 Office: PO Box 308 Nantucket MA 02554

WITT, CATHERINE LEWIS, neonatal nurse practitioner, writer; b. Burlington, Iowa, Nov. 21, 1957; d. Rodney Darrell and Neola Ann (Wharton) Lewis; m. John Robert Witt, Mar. 31, 1984; children: Jeffrey Lewis, Jennifer Diane. BSN, U. No. Colo., 1980; MSN, U. Colo., 1987. Cert. neonatal nurse practitioner. Staff nurse St. Joseph's Hosp., Denver, 1980-85; neonatal nurse practitioner Denver Children's Hosp., 1986-88; coord. neonatal nurse practitioner and neonatal transport Presbyn.-St. Luke's Med. Ctr., Denver, 1988—. Column editor Neonatal Network; contbr. chpts. to books. Troop leader Girl Scouts U.S. Mem. Nat. Assn. Neonatal Nurses (co-chair program com. 1992-94), Nat. Certification Corp. (test. com. 1994—). Democrat. Episcopalian. Home: 17586 E Dickinson Pl Aurora CO 80013 Office: Presbyn-St Luke's Med Ctr 1719 E 19th Ave Denver CO 81102

WITT, SANDRA SMITH, federal agency official; b. Rockwood, Tenn., Aug. 27, 1944; d. William Perry and Imogene C. Smith; children: Whitney, Christian. Student, U. Chattanooga, 1966-67; AS in Nuclear Technology, Chattanooga State Tech. Coll., 1976; BS in Physics, U. Tenn., 1978; MS in Engring. Sci., U. Tenn. Space Inst., 1982. Cert. nuclear equipment qualification engr., Ala. Tech. writer, editor Tenn. Blue Cross-Blue Shield, Chattanooga, 1966-68; supr. editing dept. Corp. Law Firm, Chattanooga, 1968-77; asst. physics lab. U. Tenn., Chattanooga, 1977-78; oil field engr. Schlumberger Co., Houston, 1978; research assoc. U. Tenn. Space Inst., Tullahoma, Tenn., 1979-81; sr. project engr. Wyle Labs., Huntsville, Ala., 1981-82; sr. engr., br. chief U.S. Dept. Energy, Aiken, S.C., 1983-91; engr. mgr. Martin Marietta Energy Sys., 1991-95; engring. mgr. Lockheed Martin Energy Rsch. Corp., 1996—. Recipient spl. svc. award Dept. Energy, 1986, 87, 90, career award Nat. Bus. and Profl. Women, 1977; Diuguid fellow, 1976. Mem. NAFE, Am. Nuclear Soc., Phi Theta Kappa (past v.p.), Sigma Pi Sigma.

WITTACKER, KATHERINE MICHELE, judge. Justice Calif. Supreme Ct. Office: 303 2d St Fl 8 South Tower San Francisco CA 94107*

WITTEMAN, CHERYL ANN, accountant; b. Atlanta, Oct. 7, 1953; d. Van Zandt and Gloria Adelia (Wilkins) W. BS in Math., U. Ga., 1975; MBA in Acctg., Ga. State U., 1981. CPA, Ga.; CMA, Ga. Acct. Cheryl's Closet, Doraville, Ga., 1975-78; mgr. Radio Shack, Norcross, Ga., 1976-77; sr. auditor Lockheed Martin, Marietta, Ga., 1978—. Vol. Cherokee County Humane Soc., Woodstock, Ga., 1992—, Hands on Atlanta, 1994,Christmas Trees Around the World, Atlanta, 1994. Mem. Inst. Mgmt. Accts. (dir. mem. acquisition 1986-87, dir. membership attendance 1987-88). Presbyterian. Home: 1648 Gun Creek Cir Woodstock GA 30188 Office: Lockheed Martin 86 S Cobb Dr Marietta GA 30063

WITTICH, BRENDA JUNE, religious organization executive, minister; b. Muncie, Ind., Dec. 19, 1946; d. Plano Brentie and Norma June (Huggins) Gossett; m. Chester Edward Wittich, Dec. 24, 1980; 1 child, September Leigh Noonan. Lic., Morris Pratt Inst. Assn., 1979, postgrad., 1983-86. Ordained minister Nat. Spiritualist Assn. of Churches, 1986. Pastor Fifth Spiritualist Ch., St. Louis, 1988—. Co-author, editor: National Spiritualist Association Churches Public Relations Handbook, 1992; co-author booklet: Spiritualism - Pathway of Light, 1992; contbr. articles to Nat. Spiritualist Mag. Mem. St. Louis Pub. Sch. Clergy Leaders Forum, 1991-92, Tchrs. for Nat. Spiritualist Assn. of Chs. Ednl. Ctr.-Psychology and Parlimentary Procedures. Mem. Nat. Hemlock Soc., Nat. Spiritualist Assn. of Chs. (trustee 1990-92, supt. pub. rels. 1990-94, v.p. bd. trustees 1992-94, pres. bd. trustees 1994), Inst. Noetic Scis. Home: 3903 Connecticut St Saint Louis MO 63116-3905 Office: Nat Spiritualist Assn Chs 13 Cottage Row PO Box 217 Lily Dale NY 14752

WIZEN, SARABETH MARGOLIS, stockbroker; b. Ypsilanti, Mich., May 11, 1950; d. Isidor and Ada (Eglovitch) Margolis; m. Sidney K. Wizen, July 27, 1975. BA, Mich. State U., 1972; MA, Eastern Mich. U., 1974. Adminstr. Faulkner Dawkins & Sullivan, N.Y.C., 1976-77, Dean Witter Reynolds, N.Y.C., 1977-79; adminstrv. salesman Cowen & Co., N.Y.C., 1979; v.p., dir. ops. Brookehill Equities, Inc., N.Y.C., 1979-87, prin., pres., chief exec. officer, 1987—; prin., exec. v.p. Brookehill Ptnrs., Inc., N.Y.C., 1987—; apptd. to NASD Bd. Arbitrators, 1996. Mem. Fin. Womens Assn. N.Y. (bd. dirs. 1989-95), Women's Econ. Roundtable, Met. Mus. Art, Securities Industry Assn., Mich. State U. Alumni Assn., Eastern Mich. U. Alumni Assn., Alpha Epsilon Phi Alumni Assn. Office: Brookehill Equities Inc 545 Madison Ave New York NY 10022-4219

WLODY, GINGER SCHAFER, healthcare administrator, critical care nurse; b. Bklyn.; d. Samuel and Bertha (Ressler) Schafer; m. Sanford Wlody; children: Laura Anne, Randall Lee. BSN, U. Mich., 1960; MS in Nursing, Ariz. State U., 1976; EdD in Instnl. Mgmt., Pepperdine U., 1993; postgrad., Sorbonne U., Paris, 1994. RN, Calif., Ariz.;. Evening charge nurse Comanche County Meml. Hosp., Lawton, Okla., 1962-63; recovery rm. staff nurse/team leader Good Samaritan Med. Ctr., Phoenix, 1970-75; clin. supr. surg. nursing svc. VA Med. Ctr., Phoenix, 1976-81, critical care/cardiovascular clin. nurse, 1981-86; critical care clin. nurse specialist VA Med. Ctr., L.A., 1986-87; nursing quality assurance dir. VA Med. Ctr., L.A., 1987-90; quality assurance/utilization rev. coord. VA Med. Ctr., L.A., 1990-91, quality mgmt. dir., 1991-92, asst. chief quality mgmt. svc., 1992-95, chief quality mgmt. svc., 1995—; adj. faculty mem. Ariz. State U. Coll. Nursing, Tempe, 1984-86; chmn. peer rev. program Nurse Profl. Standards Bd., 1988-90; asst. clin. prof. Sch. Nursing UCLA, 1986—; lectr. various internat. and nat. confs. Editor: Managing Clinical Practice in Critical Care Nursing, 1994; guest editor Ethical Principles in AACN's Clin. Issues in Critical Care Nursing, 1994; ethics editor Critical Care Nurse, 1995—; contbr. articles to profl. jours.; developed Wlody Model for Addressing Ethical Issues in Nursing. Named Ariz. Nurse of Yr., 1985, Nursing Model of Yr., Dimensions of Critical Care Nursing Jour., 1990; recipient Norma Shoemaker award for critical care excellence, 1994. Fellow Coll. Critical Care Medicine; mem. AACN (cert. critical care nurse, bd. dirs. 1983-86, mem. ethics com.), Soc. Critical Care Medicine (mem. nat. coun. 1995—). Office: West LA VA Med Ctr 11301 Wilshire Blvd Los Angeles CA 90073

WOBBLETON, JUDY KAREN, artist, educator; b. Williamston, N.C., Aug. 31, 1947; d. Lloyd Thomas and Lillian Edith (Hudson) Letchworth; m. Albert Virgil Wobbleton Jr., Apr. 7, 1968; children: Olivia Elizabeth, Virgil Alan. Clk. Beaufort County Hosp., Washington, N.C., 1965-68; ins. supr. Mercy Hosp., Sacramento, 1968-72; adminstrv. asst. hosp. svcs. Fairbanks (Alaska) Meml. Hosp., 1972-75; basketry artist Williamston, 1983—; instr. basketry N.C. Basketmakers, 1984-94, Wayne C.C., Goldsboro, N.C., 1986-91, Wayne County Arts Coun., Goldsboro, 1990-91; co-founder N.C. Basketmakers, 1984. Contbg. artist: The Basket Book, 1988, Basketmaker's Baskets, 1990, Craft Works in The Home, 1990. Troop leader Girl Scouts U.S., Goldsboro, 1983-88, svc. unit mgr., 1987-91; active Roanoke Arts & Crafts Guild, 1991-96. Recipient 2d Pl. award Wilson Arts Coun., 1987, 3d Pl. award Martin County Arts Coun., 1992. Mem. N.C. Basketmakers Assn. (hon., co-founder 1984, bd. dirs. 1984-94, membership chmn. 1984-87, pres. 1990-94, conv. rev. com. 1994-96), Goldweavers Basketry Guild (hon.). Home and Office: Baskets By Judy 1325 Oakview Rd Williamston NC 27892

WOGAMAN, DIERDRE ELIZABETH ATKINSON, pipeline operator, real estate agent; b. Fort Belvoir, Va., July 8, 1953; d. Robert Wharton Atkinson and Pamela Marchant Perkins Atkinson Frederick; m. Donald Ray Wogaman, May 13, 1995. AA, Bucks County C. C., 1973. Owner Ran Dea Trucking, New Hope, Pa., 1973-78; truck driver Matlack, Inc., Pensauken, N.J., 1978-79, Shell Oil Co., Willow Grove, Pa., 1979-81; pipeline operator Shell Pipe Line Corp., Columbus, Ohio, 1981-84, BP Oil Pipeline Co., Columbus, Ohio, 1994—; owner ASP Properties, Columbus, Ohio, 1985—; real estate agent Century 21, Dublin, Ohio, 1990—; realtor Century 21, Ohio, 1993. Mem. Guild RSZ First Cmty. Ch., vol. Franklin County Children's Svcs. Mem. Am. Horse Show Assn., Ohio Horseman's Coun., Ctrl. Ohio Combined Training Assn., Mid Ohio Dressage Assn., Columbus Bd. of Realtors. Home: 5982 Banzoli Way Galloway OH 43119-8807 Office: Century 21 Brockmeyer & Assoc 5841 Karric Square Dr Dublin OH 43017

WOHL, LAURIE, artist; b. Washington, Dec. 17, 1942; d. Elmer Philip and Betty T. Wohl; m. Stephen J. Schulhofer, May 28, 1975; children: Samuel A. Schulhofer-Wohl, Jonah B. Schulhofer-Wohl. BA, Sarah Lawrence Coll., 1965; LLB, Columbia U., 1968. Bar: N.Y. 1968. Clk. to Hon. Charles Metzner U.S. Dist. Ct. (so. dist.) N.Y., 1968-69; assoc. Debevoise, Plimpton, N.Y.C., 1969-71; asst. prof. U. Nairobi, Kenya, 1971-72, Northeastern U. Law Sch., Boston, 1972-73, U. Pa. Law Sch., Phila., 1973-75; artist, 1976—; reporter com. on lawyers' role in securities transactions N.Y. City Bar Assn., 1975-76; lectr. in field. One-person shows include ARC Gallery, 1987, 89, 92, C.G. Jung Inst., Evanston, Ill., 1988, Two Ill. Ctr., Chgo., 1990, Barrington (Ill.) Area Arts Coun. Gallery, 1990, Carole Jones Gallery, Chgo., 1994, 95, 96, Cuneo Mus., Vernon Hills, Ill., 1995, Cath. Theol. Union, 1996; exhibited in group shows Galerie Taub, Phila., 1984, Univ. City Arts League, Phila., 1985, ARC on Tour, 1986-87, Countryside Art Ctr., Arlington Heights, Ill., 1987, Galerie Ten, Rockford, Ill., 1988, ARC Gallery, 1988, 91, 93, 94, Around the Coyote, Chgo., 1990, 91, Cross Currents Gallery, Chgo., 1991, 4th Presbyn. Ch., Chgo., 1992, No. Ind. Arts Assn., Munster, 1991, Schneider Gallery, Chgo., 1992, Tonalli Gallery, Centro Cultural Ollin Yolliztli, Mexico City, 1992, Rush-Presbyn.-St. Lukes Med. Ctr. Chgo., 1992, R.H. Love Contemporary, Chgo., 1993, Seebeck Gallery, Kenosha, Wis., 1993, Old Courthouse Art Ctr., Woodstock, Ill., 1994, Chgo. Sch. Profl. Psychology, Chgo., 1994, Arts Ctr., Iowa City, 1994, Billy Graham Ctr. Mus., Wheaton (Ill.) Coll., 1995, 2d Presbyn. Ch., Chgo., 1995, Guilford (Conn.) Handcraft Ctr., 1995, Cuneo Mus., Am. Craft Mus., N.Y.C., 1995, Gen. Media Fine Arts Exec. Gallery, N.Y.C., 1995; represented in mus. and pub. collections Am. Craft Mus., N.Y.C., Kenosha Hosp. Chapel; represented in pvt. collections throughout U.S. and abroad. Mem. Textile Soc. Am., ARC Gallery (affiliate, bd. dirs. 1989-93). Home and Studio: 1030 E 50th St Chicago IL 60615

WOHL, ROBYN, artist; b. West Orange, N.J., June 28, 1954; d. Irving and Muriel W. BFA, Pratt Inst., N.Y.C., 1976; student, Studio & Forum Stage Design, N.Y.C., 1980. Display dir. Gucci Shops, N.Y.C., 1977-85; mfr. greeting cards On the Range Studio, N.Y.C., 1993-96; licensor of images Nobleworks Greeting Cards, Hoboken, N.J., 1995-96. Office: On the Range Studio Planetarium Station PO Box 95 New York NY 10024-0095

WOHLAUER, GABRIELE ELISABETH M., chemist; b. Berlin, Germany, Jan. 3, 1925; came to U.S., 1949; d. Hans and Helena (Riedl) W. MS in Music, Musikhochschule, Hamburg, Germany, 1948; AB in Chemistry, Hunter Coll., 1952; MS in Phys. Chemistry, Iowa State U., 1956; MS in Libr. Sci., Geneseo State U. Coll., 1976. Supr. libr. Shell Devel. Co., Emeryville, Calif., 1956-72; rsch. libr. Eastman Kodak Co., Rochester, N.Y.,

1972-76, patent searcher, 1976-91, patent specialist, 1991—. Co-editor: German Chemical Abbreviations, 1962; contbr. articles to profl. jours. Mem. Am. Chem. Soc. Office: Eastman Kodak Co 1700 Dewey Ave Rochester NY 14650-1915

WOHLEBER, LYNNE FARR, archivist, librarian; b. Pitts., Mar. 16, 1939; d. Donald Elmer and Helen Rose (Lula) F.; m. David Louis Wohleber, Oct. 14, 1972 (div. Sept. 1989); 1 child, Jeffrey David. AB, Allegheny, 1961; MLS, U. Pitts., 1991. Comms. sec. Aluminum Co. of Am., Pitts., 1968-73; shop mgr. The Thread Shed, Pitts., 1986-90; libr. Coun. Am. Embroiderer's Libr., Carnegie, Pa., 1985-93; archivist Episcopal Diocese of Pitts., 1989—; libr. Bower Hill Cmty. Ch., 1996—; cons. Calvary Episcopal Ch. Archives, Pitts., 1992-93, Bapt. Home Libr., Mt. Lebanon, 1994, First United Meth. Ch. Archives, Pitts., 1995; bldg. archives workshop instr. 1995; bd. dirs. Marag Publs. Coord. presch. program Am. Lung Assn., Pitts., 1977-87; capt., ward chair Am. Cancer Soc., Pitts., 1978-84; mem. newsletter editor Mendelssohn Choir of Pitts., 1973-87; cub scout den leader Boy Scouts Am., Mt. Lebanon, Pa., 1983-84. Mem. Soc. Am. Archivists, Mid-Atlantic Regional Archives Conf. (co-chair spl. events 1992, pubs. com. 1996—), Nat. Episcopal Historians and Archivists (Pitts. coord. for 1997 Episcopal Tri-History Conf., bd. dirs. 1996-97), Pitts. Curators Coalition, Women's Episcopal History Project, Beta Phi Mu. Republican. Presbyterian and Episcopalian. Home: 110 Skylark Cir Pittsburgh PA 15234 Office: Episcopal Diocese of Pitts 325 Oliver Ave Pittsburgh PA 15222-2403

WOHLGELERNTER, BETH, organization executive; b. N.Y.C., Jan. 30, 1956; d. Maurice Nathaniel and Esther Rachel (Feinerman) W. BA, Barnard Coll., 1977. Exec. aide to pres. Barnard Coll., N.Y.C., 1977-80; spl. asst. to pres. The Commonwealth Fund, N.Y.C., 1980-81; asst. to chief exec. officer/pres. Mary McFadden, Inc., N.Y.C., 1981-84; exec. adminstr. The Donna Karan Co., N.Y.C., 1984-90; exec. dir. Hadassah, The Women's Zionist Orgn. Am., Inc., N.Y.C., 1990—; comm. adv. coun. AT&T, 1992—. Bd. dirs., v.p. N.Am. Conf. on Ethiopian Jewry, N.Y.C., 1981-85, bd. advisors, 1985—; bd. govs. Lincoln Sq. Synagogue, N.Y.C., 1988-94, bd. trustees, 1994—; bd. trustees United Israel Appeal, 1991—. Office: Hadassah The Women's Zionist Orgn Am Inc 50 W 58th St New York NY 10019-2500*

WOHLSTADTER, ELLEN JOAN, entrepreneur; b. Bklyn., Feb. 25, 1954; d. Joseph Neitlich and Evelyn Goldberg; m. David Alan Wohlstadter, Aug. 1982; children: Jason, Natalie. Prodn. dir. RSO Records, L.A., 1978-82; mktg. dir. Audio Environments Inc., L.A., 1982-85; CEO, pres. Discovery Music, Van Nuys, Calif., 1985-95, Power Play, Sherman Oaks, Calif., 1995—; cons. West End Kids, Sherman Oaks, 1994-95. Mem. AAUW, NAFE, Nat. Assn. Women Bus. Owners. Office: Power Play 4130 Greenbush Ave Sherman Oaks CA 91423

WOHLTMANN, HULDA JUSTINE, pediatric endocrinologist, diabetologist; b. Charleston, S.C., Apr. 10, 1923; d. John Diedrich and Emma Lucia (Mohrmann) W. B.S., Coll. Charleston, 1944; M.D., Med. U. S.C., 1949. Diplomate Am. Bd. Pediatrics. Intern Louisville Gen. Hosp., 1949-50; resident in pediatrics St. Louis Children's Hosp., 1950-53; mem. faculty Washington U. Sch. Medicine, St. Louis, 1953-65, instr., 1953-58, asst. prof., 1958-65, postdoctoral fellow biochemistry, 1961-63; assoc. prof. pediatrics, head pediatric endocrinology Med. U. S.C., Charleston, 1965-70, prof., 1970-90, prof. emeritus, 1990—. Bd. dirs. Franke Home, Charleston, 1975—, treas., 1989-91; mem. adv. bd. for ethics ctr. Newberry (S.C.) Coll., 1989—; trustee Luth. Theol. So. Sem., 1991—. Mem. Am. Pediatric Soc., Ambulatory Pediatric Assn., Endocrine Soc., Am. Diabetes Assn., Am. Acad. Pediatrics, Am. Fedn. Clin. Rsch., Midwest Soc. Pediatric Rsch., So. Soc. Pediatric Rsch., S.C. Diabetes Assn. (bd. dirs. 1970-86, pres. 1970-73, 84-85, v.p., 1982-83, Profl Svc. award 1977), Lawson Wilkins Endocrine Soc., Sugar Club. Lutheran. Contbr. articles to sci. jours. Home: # 3 46th Ave Isle of Palms SC 29451-2607

WOJTOWECZ, REITA MARYE, corporate secretary; b. Ballston Spa, N.Y., Sept. 8, 1929; d. Gilbert Gordon and Florence Mae (Reckner) Ingraham; m. Walter Wojtowecz, May 1, 1948 (dec. Aug. 1978); children: Carol Buckley, Gary, Bonnie Richards, Jeanne Honadel, Walter M., Ronald, Timothy. Grad. h.s., Ballston Spa. Stenographer Joseph Romano, Atty., Ballston Spa; stenographer GE Co., Schenectady, N.Y., 1946-48, sec., 1950-53; sec. Espey Mfg. and Electronics Corp., Saratoga Springs, N.Y., 1962-79, security officer, pers. mgr., 1979-92, corp. sec., 1992—; mem. C. of C. Pers. Coun., Saratoga Springs, 1979—. Mem. Nat. Orgn. for Women. Office: Espey Mfg and Elec Corp 1 New St Saratoga Springs NY 12866

WOLANCZYK, ROXANNE, artist, sculptor; b. Southampton, N.Y., Oct. 1, 1971; d. John Peter Wolanczyk and Linda Louise Hill. BFA with honors, Pratt Inst., 1994. Exhibited subway installations, N.Y.C., 1993, redlight dist., Amsterdam, The Netherlands, 1993, Steuben Gallery, Bklyn., 1994, Queensborough C.C. Gallery, CUNY, Bayside, 1995, Here Gallery, N.Y.C., 1995-96, PS 122 Gallery, 1996, Bronx Mus., 1996. Mem. Soc. of Friends. Home and Studio: 614 E 9th St New York NY 10009

WOLANIN, SOPHIE MAE, civic worker, tutor, scholar, lecturer; b. Alton, Ill., June 11, 1915; d. Stephen and Mary (Fijalka) W. Student Pa. State Coll., 1943-44; cert. secretarial sci. U. S.C., 1946, BSBA cum laude, 1948; PhD (hon.), Colo. State Christian Coll., 1972. Clk., stenographer, sec. Mercer County (Pa.) Tax Collector's Office, Sharon, 1932-34; receptionist, social sec., nurse-technician to doctor, N.Y.C., 1934-37; coil winder, assembler Westinghouse Electric Corp., Sharon, 1937-39, duplicator operator, typist, stenographer, 1939-44, confidential sec., Pitts., 1949-54; exec. sec., charter mem. Westinghouse Credit Corp., Pitts., 1954-72, hdqrs. sr. sec., 1972-80, reporter WCC News, 1967-68, asst. editor, 1968-71, asso. editor, 1971-76; student office sec. to dean U. S.C. Sch. Commerce, 1944-46, instr. math., bus. adminstrn., secretarial sci., 1946-48. Publicity and pub. relations chmn., corr. sec. South Oakland Rehab. Council, 1967-69; U. S.C. official del. Univ. Pitts. 200th Anniversary Bicentennial Convocation, 1986; mem. nat. adv. bd. Am. Security Council; mem. Friends Winston Churchill Meml. and Library, Westminster Coll., Fulton, Mo.; active U. S.C. Ednl. Found. Fellow; charter mem. Rep. Presdl. Task Force, trustee; sustaining mem. Rep. Nat. Com.; permanent mem. Nat. Rep. Senatorial Com.; patron Inst. Community Service (life), U. S.C. Alumni Assn. (Pa. state fund chmn. 1967-68, pres. council 1972-76, ofcl. del. rep. inauguration Bethany Coll. pres. 1973); mem. Allegheny County Scholarship Assn. (life), Allegheny County League Women voters, AAUW (life), Internat. Fedn. U. Women, N.E. Historic Geneal. Soc. (life), Hypatian Lit. Soc. (hon.), Acad. Polit. Sci. (Columbia) (life), Bus. and Profl. Women's Club Pitts. (bd. dirs. 1963-80, editor Bull. 1963-65, treas. 1965-66, historian 1969-70, pub. relations 1971-76, Woman of Year 1972), Met. Opera Guild, Nat. Arbor Day Found., Kosciuszko Found. (assoc.), World Literary Acad., Missionary Assn. Mary Immaculate Nat. Shrine of Our Lady of Snows; charter mem. Nat. Mus. Women in Arts, Statue Liberty Ellis Island Found. Inc., Shenago Conservancy (life); supporting mem. Nat. Woman's Hall of Fame; Recipient numerous prizes Allegheny County Fair, 1951-56; citation Congl. Record, 1969; medal of Merit, Pres. Reagan, 1982; named WPIC Sweetheart-of-the-Day Mercer County's Info. and Entertainment Radio Sta. 790, 1991. Fellow Internat. Inst. Community Service (founder); mem. World Inst. Achievement (rep.), Liturgical Conf. N. Am. (life), Westinghouse Vet. Employees Assn., Nat. Soc. Lit. and Arts, Early Am. Soc., Am. Acad. Social and Polit. Sci., Societe Commemorative de Femmes Celebres, Nat. Trust Historic Preservation, Am. Counselors Soc. (life), Am. Mus. Natural History (asso.), Nat. Hist. Soc. (founding mem.), Anglo-Am. Hist. Soc. (charter), Nat. Assn. Exec. Secs., Internat. Platform Assn., Smithsonian Assos., Asso. Nat. Archives, Nat., Pa., Fed. bus. and profl. women's clubs, Mercer County Hist. Soc. (life), Am. Bible Soc., Polish Am. Numismatic Assn., Polonus Philatelic Soc., UN Assn. U.S., Polish Inst. Arts and Scis. Am. Inc. (assoc.), N.Y. Acad. Scis. (assoc.), Am. Council Polish Cultural Clubs Inc. Roman Catholic (mem. St. Paul Cathedral Altar Soc., patron organ recitals). Clubs: Jonathan Maxcy of U. S.C. (charter); Univ. Catholic of Pitts.; Key of Pa., Fedn. Bus. and Profl. Women (hon.); Coll. (hon.) (Sharon). Contbr. articles to newspapers. Home: 5223 Smith Stewart Rd Girard OH 44420-1341

WOLCOTT-MOORE, LINDA, fine art photography dealer; b. Washington, Aug. 28, 1942; d. Leon Oliver and Marion (Post) Wolcott; m. Michael Telford Moore (div. 1975); children: Robin Lee, Carey Lynn. BA, U. Calif., 1962; JD, Santa Barbara Coll., 1986. Bar: Calif. 1987. Dir. Lawyer Referral Svc., Santa Barbara, Calif., 1975-80; cons. Calif. State Senate, Sacramento, 1980-82; legal rsch. paralegal Santa Barbara, 1982-87, atty., 1987-90; dir. The Halsted Gallery West, San Francisco, 1989-91; owner Linda Wolcott-Moore FIne Art, Mill Valley, Calif., 1991—; dir. Environ. Def. Ctr., Santa Barbara, 1987-88, cons. Photo Law Reform Group, San Francisco, 1990-92. Vol. Frank Egger for Marin County Appraiser, Dotty Lemieux dor Supr., Goleta Water bd. Campaigns. Mem. Citizens Planning Assoc., San Francisco Mus. of Modern Art. Democrat.

WOLF, ANNE K., sales and marketing manager; b. Carlisle, Eng., July 16, 1959; came to U.S., 1963; d. John and Maureen Diamond Killen; m. Jeffrey William Wolf, Dec. 9, 1989; children: Megan Anne, William Jeffrey. BA, Calif. State U., Long Beach, 1982. Asst. br. mgr. Orange Micro, Anaheim, Calif., 1982-83, br. mgr., 1983, internat. sales mgr., 1983-84, mktg. mgr., 1984-85; sales rep. Sperry Corp., Orange, Calif., 1985-86; account mgr. UNISYS (formerly Sperry Corp.), L.A., 1986-88; mgr. strategic programs Hughes Aircraft Corp., L.A., 1988-89; edn. devel. mgr. Apple Computer, Inc., Newport Beach, Calif., 1989-92; nat. higher edn. market mgr. Apple Computer, Inc., Irvine, Calif., 1992; market devel. exec. Apple Computer, Inc., Phoenix, Ariz., 1992-94; nat. sales mgr. Apple Computer, Inc., Phoenix, 1994-96, edn. divsn. mktg. mgr., 1996—. Vol. Youth Motivation Task Force, L.A., 1988—, Make-A-Wish Found., L.A., 1987—, Jr. Achievement, 1996—; mem. Commn. on Child Pornography and Obscenity, L.A., 1988; chairperson Fiesta Bowl Parade, 1993-96. Mem. Gamma Phi Beta (advisor 1984-85). Office: Apple Computer Inc 2425 E Camelback Rd Ste 1100 Phoenix AZ 85016-4237

WOLF, CAROL SUE, medical association administrator, writer; b. Buffalo, Mar. 18, 1941; d. Paul A. and Charlotte Voas; m. Richard A. Wolf, Nov. 14, 1959; children: Richard P., Kenneth W. Supr. outpatient dept., bus. office Children's Hosp., Buffalo, 1966-77; adminstr. Highgate Med. Group PC, Williamsville, N.Y., 1977-93, dir. devel., 1993—; owner, mgr. Metcalf/Wolf Enterprises, Williamsville, 1990-95. Author: Journey into Prayer, 1995; contbr. articles to profl. jours. V.p. Coun. Chs., Buffalo, 1994-95, dir., 1990-94; chair evangelism & outreach Niagara Bapt. Assn., Buffalo, 1990-95. Mem. Med. Group Mgrs. Assn., NAFE. Home: 182 Presidio Pl Williamsville NY 14221 Office: Highgate Med Group PC 1150 Youngs Rd Williamsville NY 14221

WOLF, CONSTANCE SLOGGATT, art educator; b. Merrick, N.Y., June 25, 1959; d. Arthur Hastings Sloggatt and Dorothea Mae (Green) Sloggatt-Rush; m. Charles Robert Wolf. BFA in Painting, Pratt Inst., 1982; MFA in Painting, L.I. U., 1987; studies in edn., art and computers, 1990—. Asst. tchr. Usdan Ctr. for Performing & Creative Arts, Wheatley Heights, N.Y., summer 1986; asst. painting tchr. L.I. U., Greenvale, N.Y., 1985-87; asst. to dir. Fine Arts Mus. L.I., Hempstead, N.Y., 1987-89; art instr. Huntington (N.Y.) Twp. Art League, summer 1991, 94, 95; secondary art tchr. Northport (N.Y.)-East Northport Sch. Dist., 1991—; presenter conf. N.Y. State Art Tchrs. Assn., 1994; coord. ednl. resource Women Artists Visual Resource Collection, 1994-95, Student Portfolio on Laser Disc, 1994-95, Portfolio on CD ROM. One woman show Northport (N.Y.) Cmty. Gallery, 1994; two-person shows include Alfred Van Loen Gallery, Huntington, 1996; represented in numerous pvt. collections. Sponsor, co-sponsor Nat. Art Honor Soc., Northport H.S., 1992-93, 93-94, 94-95, 95-96, 96—; instr. religious edn. Old First Ch., Huntington, 1990-91. Recipient mini grant Western Suffolk Tchrs. Ctr., 1994-95. Mem. NOW, Nat. Art Edn. Assn., Nat. Mus. for Women in Arts, Huntington Twp. Art League (instr.), N.Y. State Art Tchrs. Assn., Girls, Inc. Office: Northport-E Northport Sch D Art Dept Laurel Hill Rd Northport NY 11768

WOLF, JUDITH LOUISE, artist, educator; b. N.Y.C., Apr. 23, 1968; d. Ira Kenneth and Lynn Rachel (Zweigenthal) W.; m. Justin Stuart David, June 13, 1993. BA, Haverford Coll., 1990; MFA, Md. Inst. Coll. Art, 1993. Mus. instr. Kidspace Mus., Pasadena, Calif., 1993, Skirball Mus., L.A., 1993, L.A. County Mus. Art, 1993-94; art tchr. L.A. Music and Art Sch., 1993-94, Meadow Oak Sch., Callabasas, Calif., 1994-95. Solo shows 101 Wooster St. Gallery, N.Y.C., 1994, Bryant Gallery, Roslyn, N.Y., 1994; group shows Colors of Jerusalem Gallery, Israel, 1996, U. Judaism, L.A., 1995, Sch. 33 Art Ctr., Balt., 1995. Democrat. Jewish. Home: 12 Rugby Rd Roslyn Heights NY 11577

WOLF, LAURA CATHERINE, photographer; b. N.Y.C., Sept. 23, 1967; d. John Curtis and Nancy Gay (Albert) W. BFA, Md. Ins. Coll. of Art, 1989; postgrad., Parson's Sch. of Design, 1995-96. Cibarchrome mural printer Duggal Color Projects Inc., N.Y.C.; intern Manhattan Plz. Environ. Program, N.Y.C.; asst. Robert Vance Blosser Studio, N.Y.C., Christopher Gallo Photography, N.Y.C. Photographer (photo essay) The Nature Conservancy, 1995, (ann. report) The Baltimore Zoo, 1991; exhbn.: The Pier Show III, 1995. Coord. Poplar St. Garden., Bklyn., 1995. Mem. Bklyn. Waterfront Artist's Coalition. Democrat. Unitarian. Home and Office: 87 State St Brooklyn NY 11201

WOLF, LESLEY SARA, lawyer; b. N.Y.C., Jan. 15, 1953; d. Herbert and Ardelle (Brush) W.; m. Dhiya El-Saden; children: Jordan, Evan. BA, Sarah Lawrence Coll., 1975; JD, U. Va., 1978. Bar: Calif. 1978. Assoc. Gibson, Dunn & Crutcher, L.A., 1978-86, ptnr., 1987—. Bd. dirs. L.A. Arts Coun., 1990-91, Franciscan Health Ctr., 1992-94. Office: Gibson Dunn & Crutcher 333 S Grand Ave Los Angeles CA 90071-1504

WOLF, LINDA, advertising executive. Exec. v.p. new bus., dir. worldwide Leo Burnett Co., Inc., Chgo. Office: Leo Burnett Co Inc 35 W Wacker Dr Chicago IL 60601*

WOLF, LINDA LOU, education educator, college administrator; b. Oskaloosa, Iowa, Apr. 29, 1946; d. Hugh and Mary Evelyn (Lane) Walker; m. Gerald Lee Wolf, Dec. 23, 1967; children: Maud Suzanne, Jenny Lin Wolf Edmundson. BA in Home Econs., William Penn Coll., 1968; MS in Child and Family Devel., U.Mo., 1970; PhD in Higher Edn., Iowa State U., 1993. Presch. tchr. U. Mo. Sch. of Higher Edn., Columbia, Mo., 1968-69, Happiness Is Preschool, Solon, Iowa, 1977-79; coord. tchr. Good Time Preschool/Day Care, Oskaloosa, Iowa, 1979-82; instr. internat. advisor William Penn Coll., Oskaloosa, 1982-89, from asst. prof. to assoc. prof. and internat. advisor, 1989—; mem. early childhood edn. adv. coun. Southern Prairie Area Edn. Agy., Ottumwa, Iowa, 1993-95, William Penn Coll. rep. Assn. Internat. Educators, Region IV, 1984—. Contbr. numerous articles and poems to Global I. (newsletter). V.p., pres. Oskiowa People to People, Oskaloosa, Iowa, 1992-96; chairperson Sister City Com., Oskaloosa, 1993—; chairperson edn. com. Iowa/Cherkassy O. Sister State, 1996-97. Mem. Iowa Global Edn. Assn. (steering com. 1986—, treas. 1993—), Alpha Chi, Phi Beta Delta, Phi Kappa Chi. Democrat. Mem. Ch. of Disciples of Christ. Office: William Penn Coll 201 Trueblood Ave Oskaloosa IA 52577

WOLF, MARY CAHN, YMCA association volunteer; b. Chgo., Apr. 1, 1929; d. Morton David and Elizabeth (Hofeller) Cahn; m. Stephen Louis Wolf, Jan. 29, 1955; 1 child, Matthew Stephen. BA, Rockford Coll., 1951. Bd. dirs. YWCA, N.Y.C., 1966-73; nat. bd. dirs. YWCA U.S.A., 1973-85, asst. treas. nat. bd. dirs., 1976-79, 1st v.p. nat. bd. dirs., 1982-85, del. triennial convs., 1967-85; vis. del. World YWCA Coun., Singapore, 1983; UN NGO rep. World YWCA, 1985—. N.Y. State Dem. commiteewoman, 1960-64; mem. The Mt. Sinai Hosp. Aux. Bd, 1970—, pres., 1976-81; founding mem., pres. Playwrights Horizons, N.Y.C., 1974-76; active World Svc. Coun., 1980—; vol. NGO Forum, Decade Women, Nairobi, 1985; trustee Mt. Sinai Hosp., 1976-81; bd. dirs. New Alternatives Children, N.Y., 1982—. Named hon. mem. nat. bd. dirs. YWCA U.S.A., 1991. Mem. Cosmopolitan Club, Women's City Club. Reform Jewish.

WOLF, MICHELE ANN, academic enrichment educator; b. Rochester, N.Y., July 24, 1967; d. Alan Lee and Ruth (Haggstrom) Nobel; m. Jonathan Scott Wolf, Oct. 13, 1990. B in Comm./English, SUNY, Geneseo, 1989; Cert. in Elem. Edn., Medaille Coll., 1993; postgrad. in Edn./English, Buffalo State Coll., 1995—. Cert. elem. tchr., N.Y. Mktg. rep. Waste Stream Tech., Buffalo, 1989-90; claims rep. S.H. Gow & Co., Inc., Buffalo, 1990-93; acad. enrichment, gifted and talented tchr. Iroquois Ctrl. Sch., Elma, N.Y., 1993-96; tchr. third grade Iroquois Ctrl. Sch., Elma, 1996—; mem. Gifted Adv. Coun., Buffalo/Lockport, 1993-96; mem. Dist. Assessment Com. ICS, Elma, 1993-94; participant Creative Problem Solving Inst., Buffalo, 1994-96; me. Creative Edn. Found., 1994—. Home: 302 Oakwood Ave East Aurora NY 14052 Office: Iroquois Central Sch Dist 2111 Girdle Rd Elma NY 14059

WOLF, REVA JUNE, art historian; b. Denver, June 17, 1956; d. Abraham and Ruth (Smith) W. BA summa cum laude, Brandeis U., 1978; MA, NYU, 1981, PhD, 1987. Gallery lectr., course instr. Mus. Modern Art, N.Y.C., 1984-88; lectr. SUNY, Purchase, 1987-88; asst. prof. fine arts Boston Coll., Chestnut Hill, Mass., 1988-95; Mellon Faculty Fellow Harvard U., Cambridge, Mass., 1990-91; asst. prof. of art history SUNY, New Paltz, N.Y., 1996—; vis. fellow Yale Ctr. for Brit. Art, New Haven, 1989, mem. and NEH fellow, Inst. for Advanced Study, Princeton, 1995-96. Author: (book/exhibit/catalogue) Goya and the Satirical Print, 1991 (NEA grant 1990-91); contbr. articles, essays, books revs. to profl. publs. Grantee: faculty resh. incentive grant, Boston Coll., 1989, teaching grant, 1993; named J. Clawson Mills fellow, Met. Mus. Art, N.Y.C., 1985-86. Mem. MLA, Am. Soc. Eighteenth Century Studies, Am. Soc. Hispanic Art Hist. Studies, Coll. Art Assn. Am. Office: SUNY Art History Dept New Paltz NY 12561

WOLF, SARA HEVIA, art librarian; b. Havana, Cuba, Jan. 15, 1936; came to U.S., 1961; d. Policarpo and Manuela (Ruiz) Hevia; m. Luis A. Wolf, Sept. 23, 1960; 1 child, Sara Caroline. B in Bus., Havana Bus. U., 1956. Libr. asst. N.C. State U., Raleigh, 1963-65; cataloguer Ctrl. Piedmont C.C., Charlotte, N.C., 1970-71; libr. Mint Mus. Art, Charlotte, N.C., 1972—. Bd. dirs. YMCA, Charlotte, 1985-87; co-chair All Nations Festival, Inc., Charlotte, 1977-78; pres. Cath. Hispanic Ctr., Charlotte, 1981-82, editor Spanish Newsletter, 1972-75, chair Internat. Cultural Festival, 1973-76; steering com. Latin-Am. Week, Charlotte, 1993. Mem. Art Librs. Soc., N.Am. (mem. George Wittenborn Meml. Book Awards com. 1992, chair nominating com. S.E. chpt. 1987, chair Mary Ellen Lo Presti Publ. Awards com. S.E. chpt. 1989, v.p., pres.-elect S.E. chpt. 1990, pres. S.E. chpt. 1991), Metrolina Libr. Assn. (exec. bd. 1988), L.Am. Women's Assn. (pres. 1994-96), L.Am. Coalition. Office: Mint Mus of Art 2730 Randolph Rd Charlotte NC 28207-2012

WOLF, SHARON ANN, psychotherapist; b. Dallas, May 13, 1951; d. Frank Allan and Ursula (Mohnblatt) W.; 1 child, Allan. BA in Psychology, New Eng. Coll., 1973; MA in Counseling Psychology, Antioch Grad. Sch., 1976; PhD in Clin. Psychology, Union Grad. Sch., 1989. Behavioral spl. ednl. planner Philbrook Children's Learning Ctr., Concord, N.H., 1972; asst. to spl. edn. cons. N.H. Hosp., Concord, 1972-73; spl. edn. planner Rochester (N.H.) Child Devel. Ctr., 1973; counseling practicum Morrill Sch., Concord, N.H., 1973; counseling practicum Contoocook Valley Mental Health Ctr., Henniker, N.H., 1973-74, counseling psychology intern, 1974-76; lab. instr. New Eng. Coll., Henniker, 1973; ednl. and guidance counselor asst. Hillsboro (N.H.)-Deering Sch. Dist., 1973-74; pediatric psychology intern parent-infant devel. program Ctrl. N.H. C.M.H. Ctr., Concord, 1986-87; assoc. psychologist Easter Seal Rehab. Ctr., Manchester, N.H., 1976-80, Ctrl. N.H. Community Mental Health Svcs., Concord, 1980-88; intern forensic psychology Concord Dist. Ct., 1987-88; pvt. practice Northfield, N.H., 1988—; psychol. cons. children and youth program Twin Rivers Counseling Ctr., Franklin, N.H. 1980-83, therapist, 1984-86; therapist Ctrl. N.H. Comm. Mental Health Ctr., 1980-83, Parent-Infant Devel. Program, Concord, N.H., 1983-88. Fellow Am. Orthopsychiat. Assn.; mem. Am. Assn. Suicidology, Am. Assn. Counseling and Devel., New England Coun. on Crime and Delinquency, N.H. Assn. of the Deaf, N.H. Registry of Interpreters for the Deaf. Office: PO Box 253 Tilton NH 03276-0253

WOLF, SUSAN LEE MILLER, sexuality educator; b. San Bernardino, Calif., July 11, 1960; d. Edwin Foster and Dorothy Marion (McIntosh) Miller; m. Paul Milton Wolf, June 5, 1982; children: Christina, Noelle, Heather. BA in Psychology, U. Md., 1985; MS Edn. in Counseling, SUNY, Plattsburgh, 1990. Tutor migrant program North Country Tutorial Program, Plattsburgh, N.Y., 1986-87; workshop leader resume/interview Atwater, Calif., 1991-92; instr., counselor, coord. Merced (Calif.) Coll., 1989-92; sexuality educator Project SIGHT Teenage Pregnancy Prevention, Northfield, Minn., 1994—; editor pamphlets Life Skills Edn., Northfield, 1995. Mem. AAUW. Office: Project SIGHT 1001 Division St Northfield MN 55057

WOLFE, BRENDA L., psychologist; b. Montreal, Can., Oct. 5, 1956; came to U.S., 1980; d. Joseph and Mania (Tisch) Lichtenstein; m. Kenneth E. Wolfe; children: Alissa Jennifer, Emily Jeanne. BA, McGill U., 1980; MA, U. Calif., Santa Barbara, 1982, PhD, 1985. Teaching assoc. U. Calif., Santa Barbara, 1980-85; mgr. project and curriculum prodn. Edn. Systems Corp., San Diego, 1985-86; sr. project mgr. Jostens Learning Corp., San Diego, 1986-89; dir. rsch. Jenny Craig, Inc., San Diego, 1989-94; pres. Self Mgmt. Systems, Inc., Rio Rancho, 1994—. Co-author: Jenny Craig's What Have You Got to Lose?, 1992, The Lifestyle Counselor's Guide to Weight Control, 1995; columnist The Albuquerque Tribune, 1994—; contbr. numerous articles to profl. jours. Scholar Western Psychol. Assn., 1982, 83, McGill U. faculty scholar, 1979; First Class Honors, 1980. Mem. APA, Assn. Advancement Behavior Therapy (chmn. obesity and eating disorders spl. interest group), Western Psychol. Assn., Sci. Rsch. Soc., Soc. Behavioral Medicine, Sigma Xi. Office: Am Health Pub PO Box 44582 Rio Rancho NM 87174

WOLFE, CONNIE J., biology educator; b. Niceville, Fla., June 13, 1965; d. James William and Jean Almeda (Miller) W.; m. Ignacio Saul Sedeño Arcos, Oct. 11, 1992. BS in Biology, Cedar Crest Coll., 1987; PhD in Marine Biology, U. Calif., San Diego, 1994. Manuscript editor On-Line-Edit, Cardiff by the Sea, Calif., 1993-94; lectr. San Diego State U., 1994; asst. prof. biology Westmont Coll., Santa Barbara, Calif., 1994—. Contbr. articles to profl. jours. Ednl. liaison Santa Barbara Channel Aquarium Com., 1995-96; vol. funding panel United Way, Santa Barbara, 1996. Scholar Allen Found., 1983-87, ABC Found., 1991. Mem. Am. Soc. Microbiology, Molecular Biology and Evolution Assn., Beta Beta Beta. Office: Westmont Coll 955 La Paz Rd Santa Barbara CA 93108

WOLFE, DEBORAH CANNON PARTRIDGE, government education consultant; b. Cranford, N.J.; d. David Wadsworth and Gertrude (Moody) Cannon; 1 son, Roy Partridge. BS, N.J. State Coll., 1937; MA, EdD, Tchrs. Coll., Columbia U.; postgrad., Vassar Coll., U. Pa., Union Theol. Sem., Jewish Sem. Am.; hon. doctorates, Seton Hall U., 1963, Coll. New Rochelle, 1963, Morris Brown U., 1964, Glassboro/Rowan Coll., 1965, Bloomfield Coll., 1988, Monmouth Coll., 1988, William Paterson Coll., 1988; LLD (hon.), Kean Coll., 1981; LHD (hon.), Stockton State Coll., 1982; LLD (hon.), Jersey City State Coll., 1987, Centenary Coll., William Paterson Coll., 1989, Tuskegee U., 1989, Glassboro State Coll., 1985, Tuskegee U., 1989, St. Peter's Coll., 1989, Rider Coll., 1989, Georgian Court Coll., 1990; DSc (hon.), Stevens Inst. Tech., 1991; LLD (hon.), Rutgers U., 1992, Thomas Edison Coll., 1992; DSc, U. Med. and Dentistry N.J., 1989. Former prin., tchr. pub. schs. Cranford, also Tuskegee, Ala.; faculty Tuskegee Inst., Grambling Coll., NYU, Fordham U., U. Mich., Tex. Coll., Columbia U.; supervision and adminstrn. curriculum devel., social studies U. Ill., summers; prof. edn., affirmative action officer Queens Coll.; prof. edn. and children's lit. Wayne State U.; edn. chief U.S. Ho. of Reps. Com. on Edn. and Labor, 1962—; Fulbright prof. Am. lit. NYU; U.S. rep. 1st World Conf. on Women in Politics; chair non-govtl. reps. to UN (NGO/DPI exec. com.), 1983—; editl. cons. Macmillan Pub. Co.; cons. Ency. Brit.; adv. bd. Ednl. Testing Svc.; mem. State Bd. Edn., 1964-94; chairperson N.J. Bd. Higher Edn., 1967-94; mem. nat. adv. panel on vocat. edn. HEW; mem. citizen's adv. com. to Bd. Edn., Cranford; mem. Citizen's Adv. Com. on Youth Fitness, Pres.'s Adv. Com. on Youth Fitness, White House Conf. Edn., 1955, White House Conf. Aging, 1960, White House Conf. Civil Rights, 1966, White House Conf. on Children, 1970, Adv. Coun. for Innovations in Edn.; v.p. Nat. Alliance for Safer Cities; cons. Vista Corps, OEO; vis. scholar Princeton Theol. Sem., 1989—; active Human Rels. Coun., N.J., 1994—; vis. prof. U. Ill., U. N.C., Wayne State U.; theologian-in-residence Duke U.; mem. trustee bd. Sci. Svc.; mem. N.J. Commn. on Holocaust Edn., 1996. Contbr. articles to ednl. publs. Bd. dirs. Cranford Welfare Assn., Cmty. Ctr., 1st Bapt. Ch., Cranford Cmty. Ctr. Migratory Laborers, Hurlock, Md.; trustee Sci. Svc., Seton Hall U., bd. regents; mem. Pub. Broadcasting Authority, N.J. Commn. on Holocaust, 1996—, Tuskegee U. Alumni, 1995, N.J. Conv. of Progressive Baptists, 1995; sec. Kappa Delta Pi Ednl. Found.; mem. adv. com. Elizabeth and Arthur Schlesinger Libr., Radcliffe Coll., trustee Edn. Devel. Ctr., 1965—; assoc. min. 1st Bapt. Ch.; chair Human Rels. Commn., 1995. Recipient Woman of Yr. award Delta Beta Zeta, Woman of Yr. award Morgan State Coll., Medal of Honor, DAR, 1990, Disting. Svc. medal Nat. Top Ladies of Distinction, 1991, Disting. Svc. award nat. Assn. State Bds. Edn., 1992, 94, Disting. Svc. to Edn. award N.J. Commn. on Status of Women, 1993, Svc. to Children award N.J. Assn. Sch. Psychologists, 1993, Disting. Medal award U. Medicine and Dentistry N.J., Union Coll., citation N.J. State Coun. on Vocat. Edn., 1994, citation N.J. State Bd. Edn., 1994, Svc. award for 50 Yrs., Cranford Bd. Edn., 1995, Women Who Count award Zonta Internat., 1996, Minister's Appreciation award Progressive Nat. Baptist Convention, 1996, Edn. award Tuskegee U. Alumni, 1996. Mem. NEA (life), ASCD (rev. coun.), AAAS (chmn. tchr. edn. com.), LWV, NCCJ, AAUW (nat. edn. chmn.), AAUP, NAACP (Medal of Honor 1994), Coun. Nat. Orgns. Children and Youth, Am. Coun. Human Rights (v.p.), Nat. Panhellenic Coun. (dir.), Nat. Assn. Negro Bus. and Profl. Women (chmn. spkrs. bur., Nat. Achievement award 1958), Nat. Assn. Black Educators (pres.), N.Y. Tchrs. Assn., Am. Tchrs. Assn., Fellowship So. Churchmen, Internat. Reading Assn., Comparative Edn. Soc., Am. Acad. Polit. and Social Sci., Internat. Assn. Childhood Edn., Nat. Soc. Study Edn., An. Edn. (commn. fed. rels.), Nat. Alliance Black Educators (pres.), Internat. Platform Assn., Ch. Women United (UN rep., mem. exec. com.), UN Assn.-U.S.A. (exec. com.), N.J. Fedn. Colored Women's Clubs, Delta Kappa Gamma (chmn. world fellowship com.), Kappa Delta Pi (chmn. ritual com., mem. ednl. found., 1980—, laureate 1990, scholarship named in her honor, citation 1994, Pres.'s award 1996), Pi Lambda Theta, Zeta Phi Beta (internat. pres. 1954, chmn. edn. found. 1974—, Monore Twp., N.J. chair human rels. commn., Achievement award Atlantic region). Home: 326 Nantuckett Ln Jamesburg NJ 08831-1704 Office: NJ State Bd Higher Edn 20 W State St Trenton NJ 08608-1206

WOLFE, ELLEN DARLENE, librarian, elementary school educator; b. Mattoon, Ill., Dec. 16, 1952; d. Floyd Dale and Irma Jane (Hensley) Robinson; m. Walter Ray Wolfe, Mar. 12, 1994; children: Gregory David, William Scott, Joseph Dean, Brian Matthew, Joshua Paul. BS, Ind. State U., 1987. Cert. elem. educator, Ill. Reading tchr. Marshall (Ill.) Community Dist. 2, 1987-91; law libr. Robinson (Ill.) Correctional Ctr., 1991-94; libr. Palestine (Ill.) Cmty. Unit Sch. Dist. # 3, 1994—; libr. City of Marshall, 1986—; dir. summer camp Clark County Handicapped Assn., Marshall, 1988—; law libr. Robinson Correctional Ctr., 1991. Coord. Jr. youth group St. Mary's Cath. Ch. Mem. Correctional Edn. Assn., Home Ext. Club, Kappa Delta Pi, Phi Delta Kappa. Roman Catholic. Home: 18993 E River Rd Palestine IL 62451-9705 Office: Robinson Correctional Ctr PO Box 1000 Robinson IL 62454-0919

WOLFE, HARRIET MUNRETT, lawyer; b. Mt. Vernon, N.Y., Aug. 18, 1953; d. Lester John Francis Jr. and Olga Harriet (Miller) Munrett; m. Charles Briant Wolfe, Sept. 10, 1983. BA, U. Conn., 1975; postgrad., Oxford U. (Eng.), 1976; JD, Pepperdine U., 1978. Bar: Conn. 1979. Assoc. legal counsel, asst. sec. Citytrust, Bridgeport, Conn., 1979-90; v.p., sr. counsel, asst. sec. legal dept. Shawmut Bank Conn., N.A., Hartford, 1990—; mem. govt. rels. com. Electronic Funds Transfer Assn., Washington, 1983—. Mem. Conn. Bar Assn. (mem. legis. com. banking law sect.), ABA, Conn. Bankers Assn. (trust legis. com.), Guilford Flotilla Coast Guard Aux., U.S. Sailing Assn., Phi Alpha Delta Internat. (Frank E. Gray award 1978, Shepherd chpt. Outstanding Student award 1977-78). Home: 26 Farm View Dr Madison CT 06443-1631 Office: Shawmut Bank Conn NA 777 Main St Hartford CT 06115-2000

WOLFE, JANICE KAY, oncological nurse; b. Cedar Rapids, Iowa, Sept. 13, 1942; d. Francis Demerlin Brown and Lora Elizabeth Miller; m. Lincoln Louis Marburger Jr., Oct. 4, 1960 (dec. Aug. 18, 1972); children: Rhonda, Lora, Helen Phillip, Carmen; m. Clifford G. Wolfe, Apr. 11, 1992. Diploma in nursing, Kirkwood Coll., 1977, ADN, 1982. RN, Iowa, Ariz. Supr. staff nurses Long Term Care Ctr., Marion, Iowa, 1977-79; staff nurse ICU Mercy Hosp., Cedar Rapids, 1979-80; hematology/oncology nurse U. Iowa Hosp. and Clinics, Iowa City, 1982-92; clin. nurse Indian Health Svc., USPHS, Winslow, Ariz., 1992—, HIV-AIDS coord. and counselor, 1994—. Lutheran. Home: 210 Papago Blvd Winslow AZ 86047-2024

WOLFE, JEAN ELIZABETH, medical illustrator, artist; b. Newark, Oct. 3, 1925; d. Arthur Howard and Ethel (Harper) Wolfe; BS, Russell Sage Coll., 1947; student Pratt Inst., 1949-50; grad. diploma U. Rochester Sch. Medicine and Dentistry, 1955; postgrad. (W.B. Saunders fellow), U. Pa., 1955-56, U. Pa., 1980, 95; MFA in Painting, U. Pa., 1973, MA (hon.), 1973. Cert. Med. Illustrator. Exhibitor, Pratt Inst. Galleries, Bklyn., 1958, N.Y. Med. Coll., 1958, Assn. Med. Illustrators, 1961-86, 90, AMA, N.Y.C., 1965, Phila., 1965, A.C.S., Atlantic City, 1965, Rsch. Study Club L.A., 1966, Phila. Art Alliance, 1967, 73, U. Pa. Alumni Ophthal. Assn., 1967-68, N.J. Med. Soc., 1968, Cayuga Mus. History and Art, 1968, Pensacola Art Ctr., 1969, FAA Aero. Center, Oklahoma City, 1970, Scheie Eye Inst., 1972-75, Assn. Med. Illustrators Traveling Salon, 1978, Moore Coll. Art, 1985, Mus. of Am. Illustration Soc. of Illustrators, 1986, Mutter Mus., Phila. Coll. of Physicians, 1990-92, Axis Gallery, 1992; represented in permanent collections Archives of Med. Visual Resources, Francis A. Countway Med. Libr., Harvard Univ., Mutter Mus., Phila. Coll. Physicians; collection of work donated by Scheie Eye Inst., memoirs and papers housed in The Arthur and Elizabeth Schlesinger Libr. on the History of Women in Am., Radcliffe Coll.; contbg. illustrator Adler's Textbook Ophthalmology, 8th edit., 1969; illustrations in med. books, jours., pharm. house pubs.; instr. Pembroke Coll. Brown U., 1947-49; dept. head Kimberley Sch., Upper Montclair, N.J., 1950-52; freelance med. illustration Studio N.Y. Med. Coll., 1956-60; instr. Pratt Inst., 1958-59; med. artist in ophthalmology, 1960-61, asst. instr. in med. illustration in ophthalmology, 1961-62, instr. in med. illustration in ophthalmology, 1962-65; assoc. in med. illustration U. Pa. Sch. Medicine, 1965-72, tenured sole artist in the hist. of the sch. of medicine, rsch. asst. prof. med. art in ophthalmology, 1972-85, rsch. asst. prof. emeritus, 1985—; independent studio (fine art) painting and med. illustration, 1985—; guest lectr. Johns Hopkins Med. Sch., 1973, NIH; guest artist USAF, Air Force Acad. and NORAD, 1971. Recipient Merit certificate AMA; Appreciation certificate ACS; 1st prize Pensacola Art Ctr., Am. Heart Assn., 1969, Gold medal Graphic Arts Soc. of Del. Valley, 1973. Fellow Assn. Med. Illustrators (emeritus); mem. Assn. Med. Illustrators (Ralph Sweet, Tom Jones awards, gov. 1970—, chmn. nominating com. 1972-73, vice chmn. bd. govs. 1973-74, chmn. bd. 1974-75, selection com., Lifetime Achievement award 1989—, adv. coun. Vesalius Trust 1990—), Soc. Illustrators (cert. merit 1986), Coll. Art Assn., Women's Caucus for Art, Faculty Club of U. Pa. Address: 55 Frazer Rd Beech 222 Malvern PA 19355-1976 also: Scheie Eye Inst 51 N 39th St Philadelphia PA 19104

WOLFE, LISA ANN, accountant; b. New Kensington, Pa., Sept. 29, 1962; d. Otis Lawrence and Lois Ann (Smouse) Wolfe. BS, Ind. U. Pa., 1983; MBA, Duquesne U., 1992. Investor rels. adminstr. Allegheny Power Svc. Corp., Greensburg, Pa., 1984-95, N.Y.C., 1995—. Vol. Am. Cancer Soc. Mem. Assn. Mgmt. Info. Systems, Zeta Tau Alpha (v.p. Ind. U. Pa. chpt. 1982-83). Republican. Home: 420 Spring Run Dr Monroeville PA 15146 Office: Allegheny Power Svc Corp 800 Cabin Hill Dr Greensburg PA 15601

WOLFE, LISA HELENE, psychologist; b. Phila., Jan. 15, 1959; d. Stuart and Barbara Joyce (Blumenburg) W. BA, U. Pa., 1981; AM, Harvard U., 1985, PhD, 1989. Lic. psychologist. Teaching fellow Harvard U., 1983-88; psychology intern Mass. Mental Health Ctr., Boston, 1988-89; psychology fellow N.Y. Hosp./Cornell Med. Ctr., White Plains, 1989-91; sr. staff psychologist Met. Hosp., N.Y.C., 1991; staff psychologist Ctr. for Women's Devel.-HRI Hosp., Brookline, Mass., 1992-95; supr. The Trauma Ctr. at Human Resource Inst., Brookline, 1995—; pvt. practice psychology, 1992—. Author: (with others) (book chpt.) The Cognitive Rehabilitation of Learning Disabilities, 1987. Mem. adv. bd. Women's Supported Housing and Empowerment Inc. Mem. APA (divsns. 30, 39), Am. Assn. Applied and Preventive Psychology, Pi Gamma Mu.

WOLFE, MARGARET RIPLEY, historian, educator, consultant; b. Kingsport, Tenn., Feb. 3, 1947; d. Clarence Estill and Gertrude Blessing Ripley; m. David Earley Wolfe, Dec. 17, 1966; 1 child, Stephanie Ripley. BS magna cum laude, East Tenn. State U., 1967, MA, 1969; PhD, U. Ky., 1974. Instr. history East Tenn. State U., 1969-73, asst. prof., 1973-77, assoc. prof., 1977-80, prof., 1980—. Author: Lucius Polk Brown and Progressive Food and Drug Control, Tennessee and New York City, 1908-1920, 1978, An Industrial History of Hawkins County, Tennessee, 1983, Kingsport, Tennessee: A Planned American City, 1987, Daughters of Canaan: A Saga of Southern Women, 1995; contbg. author to books, also introductions to books; contbr. articles to profl. jours. Mem. Tenn. Com. for Humanities, 1983-85, exec. coun. mem., 1984-85; mem. Women's Symphony Com., Kingsport, 1990-95; exec. com. Tenn. Commemorative Woman's Suffrage Commn., 1994-95; mem. state rev. bd. Tenn. Hist. Commn., 1995—. Haggin fellow U. Ky., 1972-73; recipient Disting. Faculty award East Tenn. State U., 1977; East Tenn. State U. Found. rsch. award, 1979, Alumni cert. merit, 1984. Mem. AAUP, ACLU (exec. com. Tenn. 1991-92), NOW, Tenn. State Employees Assn., Am. Studies Assn. (John Hope Franklin Prize com. 1992), Am. Hist. Assn., Orgn. Am. Historians, So. Assn. Women Historians (pres. 1983-84, exec. com. 1984-86), So. Hist. Assn. (com. on the status of women 1987, program com. 1988, interim chair of program com. 1988, mem. com. 1993, 94, 95, nominating com. 1994, chair nominating com. 1995), Smithsonian Assocs., Tenn. Hist. Soc. (editorial bd., 1995—), Coordinating Com. for Women in Hist. Profession, East Tenn. Hist. Soc. (mem. editorial bd. Jour. East Tenn. History), Phi Kappa Phi. Office: ETSU/UT at Kingsport Kingsport TN 37660 also: East Tenn State U Dept History Johnson City TN 37614

WOLFE, NATALIE SUE, real estate broker; b. Springfield, Mo., Feb. 13, 1954; d. Gerald Halbert Lowther and Patti Jean (Byers) Winget; m. Jeffrey Mark Wolfe, Nov. 25, 1976; children: Wendy, Brad, Alexis. BS, U. Mo., 1976. V.p. CB Comml. Real Estate Svcs., Inc., Kansas City, Mo., 1978—. Mem. adv. bd. mktg. dept. U. Mo. Bus. Sch., Columbia, 1985—. Mem. Soc. Indsl. and Comml. Office Brokers (former v.p.), Met. Kansas City Bd. Realtors (v.p., treas., pres., v.p. comm. divsn., Top Achiever in Comml. Sales 1989, Salesperson of Yr. 1990), Kappa Alpha Theta Alumnae. Office: CB Comml Real Estate Group Inc 3100 Broadway Ste 1102 Kansas City MO 64111

WOLFE, PAMELA KLINE, history educator; b. Richmond, Va., Dec. 14, 1957; d. Paul Miller and Betty (Halterman) Kline; m. Robert Edward Wolfe, Apr. 5, 1980; children: Matthew Chambers, Hannah Elizabeth. BA French/ Secondary Edn. summa cum laude, Bridgewater (Va.) Coll., 1979; postgrad., U. Strasbourg, France, 1978; MA, U. Md., 1983. Cert. in French and history edn. Tchr. French Yeshiva of Greater Washington, Silver Spring, Md., 1980—, tchr. history, 1983—, chmn. social studies dept., 1987—; judge Nat. Peace Essay Contest, Nat. Inst. Peace, Washington, 1992—; grader AP test Coll. Bds./AP, Princeton, N.J., 1996—; coach geography bee Yeshiva Team, Silver spring, 1993—, coach citizen bee, 1993-95. Dist. organizer Neighborhood Watch, Silver Spring, 1994-95; mem. Piney Br. Elem. Sch. PTA, 1992—, Eastern Mid. Sch. PTA, 1995—. George C. Marshall fellow, 1976. Mem. Phi Alpha Theta. Democrat. Office: Yeshiva of Greater Wash 1910 University Blvd W Silver Spring MD 20902

WOLFE, VERDA NELL, pension consultant, financial planner; b. Sulphur Springs, Tex., Jan. 31, 1927; d. Marvin Alvin and Winnie Davis (Bass) Hamiter; m. James Braddy Wolfe, May 3, 1947; children: James Gordon, William Gregory, Charles Gary. Student, Baylor U., 1948-52, Tex. Tech U., 1974-76. CLU, CFP; cert. pension cons. Estate analyst Estate Fin. Planning Svc., Lubbock, Tex., 1973-76, Planning Cons., Lubbock, 1977-81; pres. DDRW Fin. Svcs., Lubbock, 1982-85, Pension Concepts and Administration, Lubbock, 1986—. Mem. Am. Soc. CLU and ChFC (chpt. pres. 1988-89), Inst. Cert. Fin. Planners, Am. Soc. Pension Actuaries and Cons. Home: 2125 57th St Lubbock TX 79412-2625 Office: Pension Concepts & Adminstn 2811A 74th St Lubbock TX 79423-1437

WOLFERT, RUTH, Gestalt therapist; b. N.Y.C., Nov. 10, 1933; d. Ira and Helen (Herschdorfer) W. BS summa cum laude, Columbia U., 1967, postgrad., 1966-68. Pvt. practice N.Y.C., 1972—; dir. Action Groups, N.Y.C., 1974-76, Gestalt Groups, N.Y.C., 1976—, Chrysalis, N.Y.C., 1996—; mem. faculty, mem. coordinating bd. Women's Interart Ctr., N.Y.C., 1971-75, also bd. dirs.; presenter Stockton (N.J.) State Coll., 1974-75; mem. faculty Inst. for Experiential Learning and Devel., 1988-92, Woodstock U., 1989-91, Gestalt Inst., Atlanta, 1989—; presenter in field. Contbg. author: (booklet) A Consumer's Guide to Non-Sexist Therapy, 1978. Mem. Assn. Humanist Psychology (bd. dirs. ea. regional network 1981-87, pres. 1985-87), N.Y. Inst. Gestalt Therapy (trainer 1979—, chair workshops program 1979-83, co-chair conf. 1983-85, brochure com. 1987-95, interim exec. com. 1988-90, conf. com. 1989-91, v.p. 1993-95), Assn. Transpersonal Psychology (co-chair N.Y. discussion group 1991-92), Assn. Advancement Gestalt Therapy (bd. dirs. 1993—, co-chair Women's Issues in Gestalt Therapy interest group 1993—, conf. com. 1993—). Office: 200 E 32nd St New York NY 10016-6306

WOLFF, CYNTHIA GRIFFIN, humanities educator, author; b. St. Louis, Aug. 20, 1936; d. James Thomas and Eunice (Heyn) Griffin; m. Robert Paul Wolff, June 9, 1962 (div. 1986); children—Patrick Gideon, Tobias Barrington; m. Nicholas J. White, May 21, 1988. B.A., Radcliffe Coll., 1958; Ph.D., Harvard U., 1965. Asst. prof. English Manhattanville Coll., Purchase, N.Y., 1968-70; asst. prof. English U. Mass., Amherst, 1971-74, assoc. prof., 1974-76, prof., 1976-80; prof. humanities MIT, Cambridge, 1980-85, Class of 1922 prof. lit. and writing, 1985—; mem. exec. com. for Am. lit. MLA, 1979-81; mem. selection bd. Literary Classics Am., 1981—; mem. exec. bd. for fgn. grants Am. Council Learned Socs., 1981-84. Author: (literary criticism) Samuel Richardson, 1972, (literary biography) A Feast of Words: The Triumph of Edith Wharton, 1977, 2d edit., 1995, Emily Dickinson, 1986; bd. editors Am. Quar., 1979-84. AAUW grantee, 1964-65; NEH grantee, 1975-76, 1983-84; Am. Council Learned Socs. grantee, 1984-85. Mem. Am. Studies Assn. Home: 416 Commonwealth Ave Apt 619 Boston MA 02215-2812 Office: MIT Dept Humanities 14N-226 Cambridge MA 02139

WOLFF, DEBORAH H(OROWITZ), lawyer; b. Phila., Apr. 6, 1940; d. Samuel and Anne (Manstein) Horowitz; m. Morris H. Wolff, May 15, 1966 (div.); children: Michelle Lynn, Lesley Anne; m. Walter Allan Levy, June 7, 1987. BS, U. Pa., 1962, MS, 1966; postgrad., Sophia U., Tokyo, 1968; JD, Villanova U., 1979; LLM, 1988. Tchr. Overbrook High Sch., Phila., 1962-68; homebound tchr. Lower Merior Twp., Montgomery County, 1968-71; asst. dean U. Pa., Phila., 1975-76; law clk. Stassen, Kostos and Mason, Phila., 1977-78; assoc. Spencer, Sherr, Moses and Zuckerman, Norristown, Pa., 1980-81; ptnr. Wolff Assocs., 1981—; lectr. law and estate planning, Phila., 1980—; Recipient 3d Ann. Community Svc. award Phila. Mayor's Com. for Women, 1984; named Pa. Heroine of Month, Ladies Home Jour., July 1984. Founder Take a Brother Program; bd. dirs. Germantown Jewish Ctr.; high sch. sponsor World Affairs Club, Phila., 1962-68; mem. exec. com., sec. bd. Crime Prevention Assn., Phila., 1965—; bd. dirs. U. Pa. Alumnae Bd., Phila., 1965—, pres. bd. dirs., 1993—, v.p. organized classes, bd. crime prevention; chmn. urban conf. Boys Club Am., 1987; active Hahnaman Brain Tumor Rsch. Bd. Mem. ABA, Pa. Bar Assn., Assn. Trial Lawyers Am., Phila. Bar Assn., Montgomery County Bar Assn., Phila. Women's Network, Bus. Women's Network (pres., bd. dirs.), Crime Prevention Assn. (sec. bd. dirs., v.p. bd. dirs.), Cosmopolitan Club (membership com. Phila.), Lions Club (chmn., pres., bd. dirs., 2nd v.p.). Home and Office: 422 W Mermaid Ln Philadelphia PA 19118-4204

WOLFF, ELEANOR BLUNK, actress; b. Bklyn., July 10, 1931; d. Sol and Bessie (Schultz) Blunk; m. William Howard Wolff, June 19, 1955; children: Ellen Jill, Rebecca Louise. BA in Edn., Speech and Theatre, Bklyn. Coll., 1972, MS in Spl. Edn., 1975; postgrad., Adelphi U., 1980-81. Cert. tchr., N.Y. Fashion model Garment Ctr., N.Y.C., 1949-50; sec. to v.p. out-of-town/export sales Liebmann Breweries Inc., Bklyn., 1950-58; tchr. N.Y.C. Bd. Edn., Bklyn., 1971-76; sec. to dir. environ. programs, pub. affairs officers, speakers bur. project leader Power Authority State of N.Y., N.Y.C., 1976-85; tchr. Hewlett-Woodmere (N.Y.) Sch. Dist., 1986-89; instr. adult edn. County of Nassau, N.Y., 1986—; actress/model, N.Y.C., 1992—. V.p. program devel. for youth ctr. Wavecrest Gardens Community Assn., Far Rockaway, N.Y., 1959-63; teen leader Far Rockaway Jewish Ctr. Youth Coun., 1965-68; pres. Parents Assn. P.S. 215Q, Far Rockaway, 1966-67; tutor N.Y. C. Bd. Edn. Sch. Vol. Program, Far Rockaway, 1969-71; chair civic affairs Dem. Club, Far Rockaway, 1961-63; committeewoman Dem. Ctrl. Com., Queens County, N.Y., 1963-64; v.p. membership, mem. constn. com. Nassau County Dem. Women's Caucus, 1988, 89; awards com. Bklyn Coll. Named Mother of Yr. Congregation Shaaray Tefila, Far Rockaway, 1968; recipient Merit award Wavecrest Gardens Community Assn., 1960, Theater Arts Trophy for disting. svc. Bklyn. Coll. Alumni, 1992. Mem. AFTRA, SAG, Nassau Assn. Cmty./ Continuing Edn., Alumni Assn. Bklyn. Coll. (life). Home: 29 Princeton Ave Hewlett NY 11557-1521

WOLFF, FRANCES MINKIN, librarian; b. Springfield, Mo., Mar. 31, 1943; d. Arthur and Lena (Minkin) Rosen; m. Larry Rottmann, Dec. 24, 1965 (div. Dec. 1994); 1 child, Leroy Rottmann. BS, U. Mo., 1964, MEd, 1965, MLS, 1987. Cert. sch. libr., Mo. Tchr. English St. Louis Pub. Schs., 1965-67, Springfield (Mo.) Pub. Schs., 1968-70; tchr. substitute Albuquerque Pub. Schs., 1970-73; owner Packrat's Nest, Madrid, N.Mex., 1974-78; dir. project Intermountain Cultural Ctr. and Mus., Weiser, Idaho, 1979-80; libr. assoc. Duane G. Libr. Southwest Mo. State U., Springfield, 1981—. Singer/ songwriter (cassette) Finally Time to Sing, 1992, Come On In to My House, 1995; creator, writer, dir. (video) Spirit of Pioneer Women, 1993, Silver Telly, 1994; writer, dir., producer (video) Give the Ballot to the Mothers: Songs of the Suffragists, 1996; contbr. articles to profl. jours. Recipient Mirror Scholar Spkrs. Bur. Mo. Humanities Coun., 1993-96. Mem. ALA, AAUW (grantee 1996), LWV (activity bd. 1995-96, grantee 1996), Popular Culture Assn. Home: 1160 S Maryland Springfield MO 65807 Office: Southwest Mo State U Duane G Meyer Libr Springfield MO 65804

WOLFF, GRACE SUSAN, pediatrician; b. Rome, N.Y.. MD, Med. Coll. Wis., 1965. Diplomate Am. Bd. Pediatrics, Am. Bd. Cardiovascular Diseases. Intern St. Vincents Hosp., N.Y.C., 1965-66; resident Columbia-Presbyn Med. Ctr., N.Y.C., 1967-69; fellow in pediatrics and cardiology Childrens Hosp., Boston, 1969-71; pediatrician U. Miami (Fla.) -Jackson Meml. Hosp.; prof. U. Miami. Mem. Am. Assn. Pediatricians, Am. Coll. Cardiology, Am. Hosp. Assn. Office: U Miami-Jackson Meml Hosp PO Box 016960-R76 Miami FL 33101*

WOLFF, LISA ANN, cultural arts coordinator; b. Wilmington, Del., Feb. 20, 1967; d. Albert Stanley and Eleanor Dorothea (Scherry) Kula; m. Allen Dietz Wolff, Oct. 23, 1993. BS, Elon Coll., 1989. Coord. cultural arts Burlington (N.C.) Recreation and Parks, 1989—; region V vice chair N.C. Recreation and Parks Soc., Raleigh, 1994-96; sec., pub. rels. Burlington/Ala. Spl. Olympics, 1992—. Author: (recreation column) Times-News, Burlington, 1995—. Chairwoman Suicide & Crisis, Burlington, 1995—, United Way campaign, Burlington, 1993; co-chair Leadership Alamance, Burlington, 1995-96; bd. dirs. Burlington Downtown Corp., 1996. Recipient Algernon Sydney Sullivan award Elon Coll., 1989. Democrat. Roman Catholic. Office: Burlington Recreation Parks PO Box 1358 Burlington NC 27215-1358

WOLFF, MARGARET ELAINE, writer, trainer; b. Detroit, Feb. 25, 1946; d. Morris Harry and Regina Rachel (Schiller) Gross; m. Jonathan Wolff, Apr. 6, 1980; children: Julie Gidion-Smith, Janey Gidion. BA in Art Therapy, Immaculate Heart Coll., L.A., 1979; MA in Leadership, Human Behavior, Nat. U., San Diego, 1993. Cert. in psychosynthesis. Freelance writer Encinitas, Calif., 1980—; comty. edn. cons. Scripps Health, La Jolla, Calif., 1990—; tng. cons. Personal Resource Sys., Inc., Empact, San Diego City Schs., YMCA, Children's Creative Workshops, ARC, etc., 1985—. Author: Kids' After School Activity Book, 1983; contbr. articles, stories, interviews, columns, essays to popular publs., 1984—. Bd. dirs. Madonna House, 1980-81, No. County Prep Sch., 1983-84; mem. bd. Rainbow Gardens Sch., 1980-89. Recipient Nat. Univ. Leadership award PEO, So. Calif., 1992. Mem. Inst. Noetic Scis., Nat. Assn. Exec. Women, Self Realization Fellowship. Home and Office: PO Box 230360 Encinitas CA 92023

WOLFF, SIDNEY CARNE, astronomer, observatory administrator; b. Sioux City, Iowa, June 6, 1941; d. George Albert and Ethel (Smith) Carne; m. Richard J. Wolff, Aug. 29, 1962. BA, Carleton Coll., 1962, DSc (hon.), 1985; PhD, U. Calif., Berkeley, 1966. Postgrad. research fellow Lick Obs. Santa Cruz, Calif., 1969; asst. astronomer U. Hawaii, Honolulu, 1967-71, assoc. astronomer, 1971-76; astronomer, assoc. dir. Inst. Astronomy, Honolulu, 1976-83, acting dir., 1983-84; dir. Kitt Peak Nat. Obs., Tucson, 1984-87, Nat. Optical Astronomy Observatories, 1987—; dir. Gemini Project Gemini 8-Meter Telescopes Project, 1992-94. Author: The A-Type Stars--Problems and Perspectives, 1983, (with others) Exploration of the Universe, 1987, Realm of the Universe, 1988, Frontiers of Astronomy, 1990; contbr. articles to profl. jours. Trustee Carleton Coll., 1989—. Rsch. fellow Lick Obs. Santa Cruz, Calif., 1967; recipient Nat. Meritorious Svc. award NSF, 1994. Mem. Astron. Soc. Pacific (pres. 1984-86, bd. dirs. 1979-85), Am. Astron. Soc. (coun. 1983-86, pres.-elect 1991, pres. 1992-94). Office: Nat Optical Astronomy Obs PO Box 26732 950 N Cherry Ave Tucson AZ 85719-4933

WOLFF, VIRGINIA EUWER, writer, secondary education educator; b. Portland, Oreg., Aug. 25, 1937; d. Eugene Courtney and Florence Evelyn (Craven) Euwer; m. Art Wolff, July 19, 1959 (div. July 1976); children: Anthony Richard, Juliet Dianne. AB, Smith Coll., 1959; postgrad., Goddard Coll., Warren Wilson Coll., L.I. U., Portland State U., Lewis & Clark Coll. Cert. tchr., Oreg. Tchr. The Miquon Sch., Phila., 1968-72, The Fiedel Sch., Glen Cove, N.Y., 1972-75, Hood River Valley (Oreg.) H.S., 1976-86, Mt. Hood Acad., Govt. Camp, Oreg., 1986—; 2d violinist Quartet con brio, Portland, 1989—, Parnassius Quartet, Portland, 1996. Author: Probably Still Nick Swansen, 1988, The Mozart Season, 1991, Make Lemonade, 1993. Violinist Mid-Columbia Sinfonietta, Hood River, 1976—, Oreg. Sinfonietta, Portland, 1988—. Recipient Young Adult Book award Internat. Reading Assn., 1989, PEN U.S.A. Ctr. West, 1989, Best Young Adult Book of Yr. award Mich. Libr. Assn., 1993, Child Study Children's Book award Bank Street Coll., 1994, Oreg. Book award Oreg. Lit. Arts, 1994. Mem. Soc. Children's Book Writers/Illustrators (Golden Kite 1994), Chamber Music Soc. Oreg. Office: Curtis Brown Ltd care Marilyn E Marlow 10 Astor Pl New York NY 10003-6935

WOLFGANG, BONNIE ARLENE, musician, bassoonist; b. Caribou, Maine, Sept. 29, 1944; d. Ralph Edison and Arlene Alta (Obetz) W.; m. Eugene Alexander Pridonoff, July 3, 1965 (div. Sept. 1977); children: George Randall, Anton Alexander, Stephan Eugene. MusB, Curtis Inst. Music, Phila., 1967. Soloist Phila. Orch., 1966; soloist with various orchs. U.S., Cen. Am., 1966-75; prin. bassoonist Phoenix Symphony, 1976—, with Woodwind Quintet, 1986—. Home: 9448 N 106th St Scottsdale AZ 85258-6056

WOLF-LOCKETT, ADRIENNE, university administrator; b. Stamford, Conn., Dec. 27, 1947; d. Raymond Goldberg and Eva (Freedman) Gilbert; m. Robert S. Lockett, July 26, 1986. BA, U. Wis., 1969; MA, Humboldt State U., 1976; PhD, Sierra U., 1990. Cert. C.C. tchr., Calif. Exec. dir. Easter Seal Soc., Eureka, Calif., 1971-74; svcs. dir. Big Bros./Big Sisters, Eureka, 1972-77; staff psychologist Humboldt State U., Arcata, Calif., 1977-94; counseling dir. SUNY, Morrisville, 1994—; adj. faculty mem. Coll. of the Redwoods, Eureka, 1976-78; adj. faculty mem. Humboldt State U., 1977-94, chair task force on acquaintance rape, 1987-92; chair Madison County Mental Health Com., N.Y., 1995—. Co-author: Understanding and Preventing Acquaintance Rape, 1993, also rsch. papers in field. Pres., bd. dirs. Audubon Soc., Eureka, 1978-86; pres. Northcoast Environ. Ctr., ARcata, 1986-89; bd. dirs. Planned Parenthood, Eureka, 1987-89; mem. com. Am. Field Svc., Eureka, 1992-94. Recipient State Merit award State of Calif., 1984, award Andrée Wagner Peace Trust Fund, 1993, Margaret Sanger award Planned Parenthood, 1994; fellow Inst. for Culturally Dem. Edn., 1993-94. Mem. Am. Coll. Pers. Assn., Assn. for Women in Psychology, New Eng. Psychol. Assn., Western Psychol. Assn. Office: SUNY Morrisville Counseling Svc Morrisville NY 13408

WOLFMAN, BRUNETTA REID, education educator; b. Clarksdale, Miss., Sept. 4, 1931; d. Willie Orlando and Belle Victoria (Allen) Reid Griffin; m. Burton Wolfman, Oct. 4, 1952; children: Andrea, Jeffrey. BA, U. Calif., Berkeley, 1957, MA, 1968, PhD, 1971; DHL (hon.), Boston U., 1983; DP (hon.), Northeastern U., 1983; DL (hon.), Regis Coll., 1984, Stonehill Coll., 1985; DHL, Suffolk U., 1985; DET (hon.), Wentworth Inst., 1987; AA (hon.), Roxbury Community Coll., 1988. Asst. dean faculty Dartmouth Coll., Hanover, N.H., 1972-74; asst. v.p. acad. affairs U. Mass., Boston, 1974-76; acad. dean Wheelock Coll., Boston, 1976-78; cons. Arthur D. Little,

Cambridge, Mass., 1978; dir. policy planning Dept. Edn., Boston, 1978-82; pres. Roxbury C.C., Boston, 1983-88, ACE sr. assoc., 1988-94, NAWE sr. assoc., 1994—; assoc. v.p. acad. affairs George Washington U., Washington, 1989-92, prof. edn., 1992-96, prof. edn. emeritus, 1996—; pres. bd. dirs. Literacy Vols. of Capitol Region; mem. comm. com. bd., pub. rels. com. LVA, Inc.; bd. dirs. Am. Coun. Edn., Harvard Cmty. Health Plan. Author: Roles, 1983; contbr. articles to profl. jours. Bd. overseers Wellesley (Mass.) Coll., 1981; bd. dirs. Boston-Fenway Program, 1977, Freedom House, Boston, 1983, Boston Pvt. Industry Coun., 1983, NCCJ, Boston, 1983, co-chmn.; bd. overseers Boston Symphony Orch.; trustee Mus. Fine Arts, Boston; councilor Coun. on Edn. for Pub. Health. Recipient Freedom award NAACP No. Calif., 1971, Amelia Earhart award Women's Edn. and Indsl. Union, Boston, 1983; Sr. scholar Nat. Assn. Women in Edn. Mem. Am. Sociol. Assn., Assn. Black Women in Higher Edn., D.C. Sociol. Soc., Greater Boston C. of C. (edn. com. 1982), Cosmos Club (Washington), Pi Lambda Theta, Alpha Kappa Alpha (Humanitarian award 1984), Phi Delta Kappa. Home: 657 Commercial St Provincetown MA 02657

WOLFORD, NANCY LOU, medical and surgical nurse; b. Cumberland, Md., Feb. 22, 1956; d. Charles Leo and Shirley Lou (Weicht) Westfall; m. Harry Edward Wolford, Aug. 20, 1977; 1 child, James. AA in Nursing, Allegany C.C., 1977. RN, Md.; cert. in med.-surg. nursing. Staff nurse in emergency dept. Frostburg (Md.) Community Hosp., 1978-88; staff nurse med. surg. unit Frostburg Hosp., Inc., 1988-95; staff nurse oncology/med.-surg. unit Meml. Hosp. and Med. Ctr., Cumberland, Md., 1995—; ind. beauty cons. Mary Kay Cosmetics, Inc., 1993—. Recipient Congl. scholarship Md. State Sen., 1974-77. Mem. AAUW, Nat. League Nurses, Order of Ea. Star. Republican. Methodist. Home: 412 Park St Frostburg MD 21532-1511 Office: Meml Hosp and Med Ctr Memorial Ave Cumberland MD 21502

WOLFSKILL, MARY MARGARET, archivist; b. Ft. Benning, Ga., June 10, 1946; d. Clifford Lawrence and Margaret W. BS in History, Radford Coll., 1968; MA in Mgmt., Ctrl. Mich. U., 1979; MS in Women's Studies, George Washington U., 1980. Cert. archivist. Reference libr. Manuscript Divsn. Libr. of Congress, Washington, 1968-70, archivist, presdl. papers, 1970-71, archives specialist preparation sect., 1971-84, asst. head reference libr., 1984-88, head reference svcs., 1988—. Contbr. articles to profl. jours. Mem. Soc. Am. Archivists, Mid-Atlantic Regional Archives Conf. Democrat. Roman Catholic. Office: Libr Congress Manuscript Divsn Washington DC 20540

WOLFZAHN, ANNABELLE FORSMITH, psychologist; b. N.Y.C., Jan. 23, 1932; d. Paul Phillip and Addie (Glassman) Forsmith; m. Herbert Eytan Wolfzahn, Feb. 4, 1956; children: Risa Wolfzahn Herskowitz, Felice, Orna. BA, Hunter Coll., 1953; MA in Counseling Psychology, Manhattan Coll., 1971; PhD in Clin. and Community Psychology, Union Inst., 1979. Cert. sch. psychologist, sch. counselor, N.Y. Counselor for handicapped children Bklyn. Tuberculosis Assn., 1952; social worker Child Placement Svcs., N.Y.C., 1953-58; fellow in social and community psychiatry Albert Einstein Coll. Medicine, 1977-79; intern Bronx (N.Y.) Devel. Svcs., 1977-79; intern head trauma program Rusk Inst., NYU Med. Ctr., 1979; psychologist Creedmore Psychiat. Ctr., 1980-82, Harlem Valley Psychiat. Ctr., 1982-87; clin. coord. of group homes Green Chimneys Children's Svcs., 1987-88; with Ulpan Akiva and Assaf Harofeh Med. Ctr., Tel Aviv U., Israel, 1988-89; nursing home cons., psychotherapist Bklyn. Ctr. for Psychotherapy, 1989-91; pres., coord. Westchester chpt. Vols. for Israel, 1992—; freelance psychologist, counselor, 1994—; mem. workshops in field; mem. staff Mother-Child Home Program of White Plains, N.Y., 1975-76; counselor with multiple sclerosis victims and their families. Contbr. articles to profl. pubis. Vol. Vols. for Israel, 1988, 91-92, founder, pres., coord. Westchester Region chpt., 1993—; mem. archaeol. dig Bet Shaan, Israel. Recipient Vol. award White Plains Hosp., 1974-76, John C. Klein Meml. Writing award Newspaper Inst. Am., 1965; Alvin Johnson scholar, 1953. Mem. APA, Westchester County Psychol. Assn., N.Y. Neuropsychology Assn., Am. Mental Health Affiliates of Israel, N.Y. Acad. Scis., Nat. Coun. Jewish Women, Am. Orthopsychiat. Assn. Home and Office: 34 Springdale Rd Scarsdale NY 10583-7329

WOLIN, FLORENCE B., special education educator; b. Norfolk, Va., Apr. 19, 1944; d. George Clifford and Florence Rhoda (Benham) Bishop; m. Ronald M. Wolin, Aug. 16, 1968 (div.); 1 child, Karl Jonathan. AB, Coll. William and Mary, 1966, MEd, 1968. Cert. tchr. spl. edn., learning disabilities, emotionally disturbed, reading, elem. edn. 1-7. Tchr. first grade Robert E. Lee Elem. Sch., Hampton, Va., 1967-68, Jefferson Elem. Sch., Holden, Mass., 1968-70; tchr., reading specialist Congressional Elem. Sch., Rockville, Md., 1970-71; tchr., LD LD Ctr., Chesapeake, Va., 1975-77; tchr. LD/reading Western Br. Jr. High, Chesapeake, 1979-87; tchr., LD/ED Chesapeake Alt. Sch., 1987-88; tchr. ED Western Br. High, Chesapeake, 1988-91; tchr., spl. edn. Tidewater Detention Home, Chesapeake, 1991—; profl. cons. Chesapeake Pub. Schs. Recertification Courses for Tchrs., 1993—. Editor: Spl. Edit. newsletter, 1993-94. Mem. com. Comm. Am. Disability Act, Portsmouth, Va., 1992—. Mem. Correctional Edn. Assn., NEA, Va. Edn. Assn., Chesapeake Edn. Assn. (bldg. rep. 1991-96). Methodist. Home: 3516 Shoreline Dr Portsmouth VA 23703-4032

WOLL, SUZANNE RENEE, export/import manager; b. San Francisco, Nov. 20, 1962. BSBA, U. Calif., Berkeley, 1984. Dir. imports Mex. Circa Corp., San Francisco, 1985-92; dir. internat. sales and mktg. Ribco Mfg. Inc., San Francisco, 1993—; mem. mktg. adv. com. Glamour Mag., Mademoiselle Mag.; cons. to various cos. in exporting, mfg., importing. Mem. Ocean Plz. Assn. (bd. dirs., sec. 1995—), U. Calif. Berkeley Alumni Club. Address: 45 Meriam Dr San Rafael CA 94903

WOLLERSHEIM, JANET PUCCINELLI, psychology educator; b. Anaconda, Mont., July 24, 1936; d. Nello J. and Inez Marie (Ungaretti) Puccinelli; m. David E. Wollersheim, Aug. 1, 1959 (div. June 1972); children: Danette Marie, Tod Neil; m. Daniel J. Smith, July 17, 1976. AB, Gonzaga U., 1958; MA, St. Louis U., 1960; PhD, U. Ill., 1968. Lic. psychologist, Mont. Asst. prof. psychology, asst. dir. testing and counseling ctr. U. Mo., 1968-71; prof. psychology U. Mont., Missoula, 1971—, dir. chin. psychology, 1980-87; chair Mont. Bd. Psychologists, 1977-78; cons. Mont. State Prison, 1971-85, Trapper Creek Job Corps, 1973—; pvt. practice, Missoula, 1971—. Author numerous rsch. articles. Bd. dirs. Crisis Ctr., Missoula, 1972-73; mem. profl. adv. bd. Head Start, Missoula, 1972-79. Recipient Disting. scholar award U. Montana, 1991. Fellow Am. Psychol. Assn. (bd. dirs. div. clin. psychology 1990-92); mem. Rocky Mountain Psychol. Assn. (pres. 1983-84), Nat. Council Univ. Dirs. Clin. Psychology (bd. dirs., 1982-88). Roman Catholic. Catholic. Home: 105 Greenwood Ln Missoula MT 59803-2401 Office: 900 N Orange St Ste 201 Missoula MT 59802-2998

WOLOSHCHUK, CANDACE DIXON, elementary school educator, artist, consultant; b. Joliet, Ill., Jan. 11, 1947; d. Harold Russell and Beatrice Diane (Johnson) Dixon; m. Christopher Ralph Jose, Mar. 1, 1969 (div. Sept. 1982); children: Amy Russell, Jennifer Seavey; m. Thomas Woloshchuk, Dec. 23, 1988; stepchildren: Michael, Debbie, Paul, John. BA in Art, Salem Coll., 1969; postgrad., Merrimac Coll., 1969; MA in Art Edn., U. Hartford, 1977; postgrad., Fitchburg State Coll., 1994. Cert. tchr., Mass., Conn. Art dir. Fred D. Wish Sch., Hartford, Conn., 1969-71; art tchr. Timothy Edwards Jr. H.S., South Windsor, Conn., 1971-72; art coord. Hebron (Conn.) Elem. Sch., Gilead Hill Sch., 1974-78; art tchr. Longmeadow (Mass.) Pub. Schs., 1978-82, Agawan (Mass.) Pub. Schs., 1982-85; visual arts coord. Wilbraham (Mass.) Mid. Sch., 1985—; pres., owner Scholarships Unltd., Monson, Mass., 1992-94; mem. tchr.-trainer program U. Hartford, 1974-78; enrichment, art tchr. Elms Coll., 1988-93. One-women show Garrett Gallery, 1981; group shows include Spencer Arts Ctr., 1993, Craft Adventure Expo '93, 1993 (2nd and 3rd pl. awards), Craft Expo '92, 1992 (2nd pl. award), Wilbraham Pub. Libr., 1992, 93, 94. Chairwomen, mem. Wilbraham Arts Lottery Coun., 1987-88. Recipient Outstanding Visual and Performing Arts Edn. award, Mass. Alliance for Arts Edn., 1988, gold award Am. Sch. Food Svc. Assn., 1987. Mem. ASCD, NAFE, Nat. Art Edn. Assn., Mass. Art Edn. Assn., Mass. Tchrs. Assn., Wilbraham Tchrs. Assn., Am. Craft Coun. Republican. Office: Wilbraham Mid Sch 466 Stony Hill Rd Wilbraham MA 01095-1574

WOLOSZYK, HOLLY ARLENE, microbiologist; b. Chgo., Jan. 19, 1960; d. Leonard Benedict and Dorothy Elaine (Wegehenkel) W. BS, U. Ill., 1982. Quality control technician G.D. Searle Pharm., Mount Prospect, Ill., 1982-83, Am. Hosp. Supply, McGaw Park, Ill., 1983-84; sr. technician rsch. and devel. G.D. Searle, Skokie, Ill., 1984-86, microbiologist rsch. and devel., 1986-87, supr. microbiology svcs. rsch. and devel., 1987-89; sr. microbiologist Intermedics, Inc., Freeport, Tex., 1989-92; microbiologist Eli Lilly and Co., Indpls., 1992—. Mem. Am. Soc. Microbiology. Home: # 3018 3843 Kessler Blvd N Dr Indianapolis IN 46228 Office: Eli Lilly and Co Lilly Corp Ctr Indianapolis IN 46285

WOLOTKIEWICZ, MARIAN M., museum official; b. Camden, N.J., Apr. 22, 1954; d. Edward J. and Rita J. Wolotkiewicz; m. Paul J. Sagan, Mar. 31, 1984 (div. Aug. 1, 1994). AB in Polit. Sci., Mount Holyoke Coll., 1976; JD, Suffolk U., 1979. Manuscript editor Little, Brown & Co., Boston, 1979-84; freelance editor, 1984-88; freelance writer Camp Dresser & McKee Inc., 1985-87; dir. pub. info. Regis Coll., Weston, Mass., 1988-90; assoc. dir. planned giving Clark U., Worcester, Mass., 1990-93; dir. gift planning & policy Mus. Fine Arts, Boston, 1993-94; pvt. practice cons. Boston, 1994—; various writing, editing and communications activities for Mass. Bar Assn., 1978-83, Womens Bar Assn., 1979-83; freelance editor for publishers including Little, Brown & Co., Artech Ho., Ballinger, Butterworth, 1984-88. Chmn. adv. com. Stow (Mass.) Cable TV, 1983-94; active fundraising Mass. Assn. Womens Lawyers charity auction, 1984, Mt. Holyoke Coll., 1986—; notary pub. State of Mass. Mem. Phi Delta Phi.

WOLOVITZ, VIVIAN TOBY, fine arts educator, artist; b. Phila., Dec. 24, 1950; d. Harry and Ann Muriel (Blank) W.; m. Michael Slotznick, Feb. 23, 1986; children: Molly, William. BFA, Tyler Sch. of Art, 1972; MFA, Md. Inst. Coll. of Art, 1978. Vis. asst. prof., artist-in-residence Grand Valley State Coll., Allendale, Mich., 1978-79; asst. prof. fine arts Moore Coll. of Art and Design, Phila., 1980—; numerous acad. related activities Moore Coll. of Art, 1980—, chair dept. fine arts, 1996—. Exhibited in solo and groups shows nat. and abroad including Stephen Haller Gallery, N.Y.C., Albers Gallery, Memphis, Jessica Berwind Gallery, Phila. Recipient Ind. Artist grant Pa. Coun. for Arts, 1995. Home: 1020 Little Shiloh Rd West Chester PA 19382 Office: Moore Coll Art and Design 20th and Race Sts Philadelphia PA 19103

WOLTER, VIRGINIA LYNN, librarian; b. Flint, Mich., Nov. 5, 1962; d. James Herbert and Elizabeth Jane (Yeatter) W. BA in Anthropology, U. Mich., Flint, 1988; M.Info. and Libr. Studies, U. Mich., Ann Arbor, 1990. Libr./vol. Art Danforth Coop Libr., Ann Arbor, 1990; ref. libr. Toledo-Lucas County Pub. Libr., Toledo, 1991—. Mem. Look at Tech. for Libr. Sys. Tech. Standing Com., Toledo, 1995—; mem. People for the Am. Way, 1995—, Rails to Trails Conservation, 1996—. Mem. ALA (social responsibility roundtable), ACLU, Nature Conservancy, Soc. for Creative Anachronisms, Ohio Libr. Coun., Ohio Libr. Assn. (intellectual freedom com. 1992-94). Unitarian Universalist. Office: Holland Branch Library 1032 S McCord Rd Holland OH 43528

WOLTERING, MARGARET MAE, secondary school educational consultant; b. Trenton, Ohio, July 24, 1913; d. David Lindy and Nellie Stevenson; m. Elmer Charles Woltering, Apr. 9, 1938 (dec. Oct. 1994); 1 child, Eugene Anthony. Student, Mercy Sch. Nursing, Hamilton, Ohio, 1931-34; BS, Miami U., 1962, MEd, 1968, postgrad., 1975. RN, Ohio; cert. tchr., curriculum supr., Ohio. Pub. health nurse Ohio State Dept. Health, Butler County, 1936-49; supr. Swedish Hosp., Seattle, 1944-45; various h.s. teaching positions Cin., 1968-78; ednl. cons. Ohio, 1981-94; cons., Ohio, 1981—; ednl. cons. specializing in curriculum devel., 1980—; book reviewer Friends of Libr., 1991-93. Author: The National Library of Poetry Anthology, 1996, spelling book, 1981; contbr. poetry to anthology. Chmn. Hosp. Svc. for Children, Hamilton, 1981-85; lectr. Sr. Citizens Ctr., 1992-93; chmn. vol. tutorial program Hamilton High Sch., 1989-93, Audubon Tutorial Program, 1994-96. Mem. AAUW, Toastmasters. Democrat. Roman Catholic.

WOLTZ, MARY LYNN MONACO, management consultant; b. Columbus, Ohio, Mar. 11, 1951; d. Frank Guy and Mary Catherine (Montenaro) Monaco; m. James David Woltz, June 19, 1971; children: Joseph David, Bethany Anne. Student, Ohio State U., 1969-71. Tchr. Career Acad., Columbus, Ohio, 1971-72; supr., mgmt. Battelle Meml. Inst., Columbus, Ohio, 1973—; pub. spkr. schs., bus., clubs. and profl. orgns., Ohio, 1981; dir. mktg. The General's Books. Amb. Assn. World Affairs, Columbus, 1968; co-chmn. United Way, Columbus, 1976; committeewoman Ohio Crime Prevention Assn., Columbus, 1988; mem. founding bd. Ohio Crime Prevention Found., Columbus, 1989—; founding mem., pres. Parents Support Group, 1990-94; cons. Lao Mai Assn., Columbus, 1981-85. Named Ohio Crime Practitioner of the Yr., 1988; recipient Nat. Crime Prevention award Nat. Crime Prevention Coalition, Washington, 1988, Spotlight award Nat. Crime Prevention Coalition and Am. Dist. Telegraph, 1993. Mem. Am. Soc. Indsl. Security (sec. 1992-93, mem. exec. bd. 1993-94). Roman Catholic. Office: Battelle Meml Inst 505 King Ave Columbus OH 43201-2696

WOLYNIES, EVELYN See GRADO-WOLYNIES, EVELYN

WOMACK, JUANITA RAE, library information specialist; b. L.A., Mar. 5, 1937; d. Daris D. and Zona Eileen (Michael) Newman; m. Robert B. Womack, Dec. 8, 1962; children: David D., W. Dan, Eric S. BS, State U. Iowa, 1959; MA, U. Colo. Denver, 1980, U. No. Colo., 1993. Bus. edn. tchr. Denver Pub. Schs., 1959-62; sub. tchr. Englewood, Littleton, Colo., 1979-83; libr. media specialist Cheltenham Elem. Sch., Denver, 1982-83, Kendallvue Elem., Morrison, Colo., 1984-85, Belmar Elem. Sch., Lakewood, Colo., 1985-86, Kyffin Elem., Golden, Colo., 1986-89, Lasley Elem. Sch., Lakewood, Colo., 1989-96. Mem. NEA, Colo. Ednl. Media Assn., Internat. Reading Assn., Jefferson County Ednl. Media, Jefferson County Ednl. Assn., Colo. Edn. Assn., Delta Kappa Gamma, Phi Delta Kappa, Winnebago Users Group. Home: 6935 S Ogden Ct Littleton CO 80122-1370 Office: Lasley Elem Sch 1401 S Kendall St Lakewood CO 80232-5748

WOMACK, NANCY HARMON, academic administrator; b. Forest City, N.C., Jan. 23, 1940; d. Ralph L. and Grace (Campbell) Harmon; m. Russell W. Womack, June 8, 1962; children: Angela Caroline, Alice Lorraine. BS in Edn., Western Carolina U., 1962; MA in English, U. Cen. Fla., 1975; PhD in English, U. S.C., 1993. English tchr. Titusville (Fla.) H.S., 1969-75; English tchr., then transfer divsn. dean Isothermal C.C., Spindale, N.C., 1976—. Editor The Mentor, 1994. Bd. dirs., violist Little Symphony of Rutherford County, 1992—. Office: Isothermal CC PO Box 803 Spindale NC 28160-0803

WONG, BETTY MELINDA ARK FUNG, entrepreneur; b. Kowloon, Hong Kong, June 20, 1959; d. Ark Sam and Ying Fung Wong. BS, NYU, 1980; MBA, Columbia U., 1982. Product mgr. Internat. Playtex, N.Y.C., 1983-86, Fleischmann Distilling Co., N.Y.C., 1986-87; brand mgr. Ferrero USA Inc., N.Y.C., 1987-90; cons., mng. dir. New Markets and Horizons Inc., N.Y.C., 1990-95; COO, exec. v.p. Corp. Comm. Mktg. Group Inc., N.Y.C., 1990-95; CEO, pres. CEO Global Resources Inc., N.Y.C., 1995—; advisor Columbia Bus. Sch. Alumni Assn., N.Y.C., 1994—; dir. Asian Fin. Soc., N.Y.C., 1995—. Adv. bd. mem. ARC-N.Y.-Mktg. Group, N.Y.C., 1993; dir. Graham-Windham Svcs. for Families and Children, N.Y.C., 1995—. Recipient scholarship Bus. and Profl. Women's Assn. N.Y., 1977, Minority Leadership award Johnson & Johnson, 1980-82. Mem. NAFE, Am. Women Econ. Devel. Corp., Women in Comms. (mem. N.Y. strategic planning com. 1992-94). Office: CEO Global Resources Inc 245 E 87th St New York NY 10128

WONG, GWENDOLYN NGIT HOW JIM, banking executive; b. Chgo., Oct. 9, 1952; d. Vernon K. S. and Yun Soong (Chock) Jim; m. Carey R. Wong, Nov. 10, 1979; children: Jacquelyn C., Brandon R. BEd in Secondary Math., U. Hawaii, 1974; MA in Secondary Math., Columbia U., 1975; postgrad., St. John's U., N.Y.C., 1975-77; MBA, U. San Francisco, 1979. Tng. and devel. analyst and instr. Chase Manhattan Bank, N.Y.C., 1975-77; human resources profl. Crocker Nat. Bank, San Francisco, 1978-82, with credit rev. dept. contrs. divsn., 1982-85; comml. lender Calif. middle market Wells Fargo Bank/Crocker Nat. Bank, Palo Alto and San Mateo, Calif., 1985-88; mgr. credit dept. San Francisco (Calif.) internat. br. Algemene Bank Nederland N.V., 1988-90; sr. v.p., mgr. credit control and rsch. The Indsl. Bank of Japan, Ltd. San Francisco (Calif.) Agy., 1990—. Treas. United Way of Bay Area; bd. dirs. United Nonprofits Ops., San Francisco Bay coun. Girl Scouts, v.p., legis. liaison, coun. trainer, internat. applicants selection com., chair Tri-City Assn., 1991-92, troop leader; bd. dirs. San Francisco Sch. Vols.; chair, founding bd. dirs. Multicultural Initiative, 1991—; mem. US/China Women's Issues Conf. & NGO Forum, Beijing, White House Briefing, Interagy. Coun. Women. Mem. AAUW (nat. com., San Mateo br., bd. dirs. 1989-90, 94—, v.p. program, newsletter editor, cmty. programs com., chair couples gourmet interest group, others), Fin. Women's Assn., Assn. Jr. Leagues Internat. Inc. (1st v.p., exec. com. 1993-95, bd. dirs. 1992-95), Jr. League San Francisco, Inc. (adv. mem. bd. dirs. 1992-95, treas. 1990-91, exec. com., bd. dirs. 1990-91, endowment fund com. 1992, others).

WONG, MAY ANN, bank officer; b. Lompoc, Calif., Aug. 14, 1962; d. Ning Hoy and Rosa Kung (Chi) W. BA with honors, U. Calif., Santa Cruz, 1984; cert. bus. adminstrn., U. Calif., Berkeley, 1992. Asst. mgr. Rice Bowl Restaurant, Lompoc, 1976-84; letters of credit processor Bank of Orient, San Francisco, 1984-88, fed. funds trader, 1989-92, asst. ops. officer, 1992-96, account officer, 1996—. Mem. U. Calif.-Santa Cruz Bay Area Alumni Assn. (pres. 1992-95). Home: 358 25th Ave San Francisco CA 94121

WONG, MONA, programmer analyst; b. Taipei, Republic of China, 1964; d. Dan and Dorra (Shih) Wang. Student, U. Calif., San Diego. Tech. support clk. Palo Alto (Calif.) Main Library, 1981-85; database adminstr. Westminster Software Inc., Palo Alto, 1983-85; computer assisted design adminstr. Pacific Monolithics, Sunnyvale, Calif., 1985-89; programmer analyst Salk Inst., LaJolla, Calif., 1989-93, U. Calif., San Diego, 1994—; cons., MIP Microcomputer Inc., Sunnyvale, 1987. Author user manual Word 3.0, Sidekick, 1988. Vol. Palo Alto Wildlife Rescue Inc., 1984-86, San Francisco Vol. Ctr., 1985-89; watch capt. Palo Alto Neighborhood Watch Program, 1986—; dir. Animal Alternatives, 1990—.

WONG, NANCY L., dermatologist; b. Chung King, China, Aug. 23, 1943; came to U.S., 1947; d. Alice (Lee) Wong; m. Robert Lipshutz; children: Seth, Alison, David. BS magna cum laude, Pa. State U., 1963; MS in Physics, Columbia U., 1965; MD, Jefferson Med. Coll., Phila., 1971. Diplomate Am. Bd. Dermatology. Intern Wilmington Med. Ctr., 1972; resident Jackson Meml. Hosp., Miami, Mount Sinai Med. Ctr., Miami, 1977; physician Kaiser Med. Ctr., Redwood City, Calif., 1987—. Woodrow Wilson fellow 1960-61, NSF fellow, 1963-64, AEC fellow, 1963-64. Fellow Am. Acad. Dermatology. Office: 910 Maple St Redwood City CA 94063-2034

WONG, SANDRA, mathematics educator; b. The Dalles, Oreg., Dec. 28, 1954; d. Shung and Yuk Chu (Li) W. BS in Gen. Sci., Oreg. State U., 1977; MST in Math., Portland State U., 1984. Cert. tchr., Oreg., advanced math. tchr., Oreg. Math. tchr., dept. head Wasco County Union H.S., 1977—; adj. faculty mem. dept. math. Columbia Gorge C.C., The Dalles, 1993-95; co-advisor student league Wasco County Union H.S., 1977—, acad. award, 1987-90, 91—, mem. sch. adv. com., 1991—. Participant March of Dimes Walkathon, The Dalles, 1994, Hood River, 1995, 96, The Dalles Christian Sch. All Car Rd. Rally, The Dalles, 1992, 93. Mem. NEA, Nat. Coun. Tchrs. Math., Oreg. Edn. Assn., Oreg. Coun. Tchrs. Math., Wasco County Union High Edn. Assn. (sec./treas. 1977-96), S. Wasco Edn. Assn. (treas. 1996—), Kappa Delta Pi. Office: Wasco County Union HS 4th and Lloyd Maupin OR 97037

WONG-LIANG, EIRENE MING, psychologist; b. Nassau, Bahamas, Nov. 20, 1961; came to U.S., 1969; d. Menyu and Lim Ming (Chow) Wong; m. Danqing Liang. BA, Trinity U., San Antonio, 1984; PhD, Calif. Sch. Profl. Psychology, 1992. Crisis counselor United Way Crisis Hotline, San Antonio, 1983; lab. asst. Trinity U., 1983; counselor Bayer County Women's Ctr., San Antonio, 1984, Turning Point Juvenile Diversion Project, Garden Grove, Calif., 1985-86; psychol. trainee Wolters Elem. Sch., Fresno, 1987, San Luis Obispo (Calif.) Youth Day Treatment, 1987-88, Calif. Sch. Profl. Psychology Svc. Ctr., Fresno, 1988-89; staff psychologist 314th Med. Ctr., Little Rock, Ark., 1989-93; pvt. practice, clin. psychologist Houston, 1993—. Mem. APA, Am. Soc. Clin. Hypnosis, Nat. Register Health Svc. Providers in Psychology, Tex. Psychol. Assn., Houston Psychol. Assn., Houston Assn. Clin. Hypnosis (charter, exec.), Psi Chi, Zeta Chi (charter, Trinity U. chpt.). Office: 10101 Southwest Fwy Ste 445 Houston TX 77074-1112

WONYCOTT, KYTLE MARIE, school system administrator; b. New Orleans, Oct. 6, 1967; d. John Michael and Ann Lee (Swanner) W. BBA, So. Meth. U., 1989; MS, Northwestern U., 1991; MEd, U. New Orleans, 1993. Dir. 3 and 4 yr. old summer program C.L. Ganus Sch., New Orleans, summer 1987-88; rsch. asst. So. Meth. U., Dallas, 1987-89, Northwestern U., Evanston, Ill., 1989-91; grad. asst. U. New Orleans Children's Ctr., 1991-93, adminstrv. asst., 1993—; gifted math. tchr. Orleans Parish Pub. Schs., New Orleans, 1993-95; dir. admission Trinity Episcopal Sch., New Orleans, 1995—; pvt. tutor, 1982-92; chmn. student assistance team, mem. faculty cabinet, coord. acad. games Warren Easton H.S., New Orleans, 1994-95; supr. afternoon kindergarten enrichment extended day program, staff nursery. Recipient scholarship Northwestern U., 1989-91, grant State of La., 1994. Mem. Am. Ednl. Rsch. Assn., Nat. Soc. for Study of Edn., Leadership for Edn. Adminstrn. Doctoral Support U. New Orleans, Phi Delta Kappa. Office: Trinity Episcipal Sch 1315 Jackson Ave New Orleans LA 70130

WOO, MARIE, artist; b. Seattle, Wash., Apr. 3, 1928; d. L.N. and J. (Chiu) W.; m. Harvey Levine, Nov. 1959; children: Ian Levine, Leslie Raymond. BA, Univ. Wash., 1951; MFA, Cranbrook Acad. Art, 1956; postgrad., Alfred Univ., 1957, Calif. Coll. Arts & Crafts, 1952. Instr. ceramics Henry Ford Cmty. Coll., Dearborn, Mich., 1984-85, Wayne State Univ., Detroit, 1983, CCS Coll. Art & Design, Detroit, 1984-90, Univ. Mich., Ann Arbor, Mich., 1956-59, 71, 85, Univ. Wash., Seattle, 1964-65, Chula Longkorn Univ., Bangkok, Thailand, 1965-68; vis. artist Univ. Tenn., Knoxville, 1996, Kent State Univ., Kent, Ohio, 1993, Kalamazoo (Mich.) Inst. Art, 1994; lectr. Heibei Tchrs. Univ., Shijazhunag, Helbel, China, 1995. Represented in permanent collections including Comerica Bank Corp., Alfred Ceramic Mus., Detroit Inst. Art Mus., Leningrad Mukhina Inst. of Art, Cranbrook Acad. Art Mus., Everson Mus., Smithsonian Mus., Mott Found., City Nat. Bank. Bd. trustee mem. Pewabic Pottlery, Detroit, 1981-96. Recipient Arts Found. Mich. for Outstanding Achievement in the Arts award, 1991, Individual Arts award Mich. Coun. for the Arts, 1987, travel grant Horace Rackham Rsch., 1960. Home: 6666 Bloomfield Ln West Bloomfield MI 48322

WOOD, ANDREÉ ROBITAILLE, archaeologist, researcher; b. Chgo., Feb. 10, 1929; d. Andrew George and Alice Marie (Fortier) Robitaille; m. Richard Lawrence Wood, Jan. 14, 1956; children: Mary Wood Molo, Matthew William Wood, Melissa Irene Wood, Elizabeth Wood Wesel, John Andrew Wood. BA, No. Ill. Univ., DeKalb, 1977, MA, 1982. Freelance archaeologist, 1981-84; rsch. asst. Prehistoric Project Oriental Inst., Univ. Chgo., Ill., 1984—; rsch., discovery, removal and analysis of ancient blood Çayönü-Ergani, Turkey.

WOOD, BARBARA ANN, retail company executive; b. Uniontown, Pa., July 9, 1954; d. George E. Jr. and Mary Anne (Vidovic) W. BS in Health, Phys. Edn. and Recreation, Slippery Rock State Coll., 1976; MEd in Elem. Phys. Edn., U. Maine, 1978. Loss control rep. CIGNA Ins., Allentown, Pa., Manchester, N.H., 1979-85; distbn. picker L.L. Bean, Inc., Freeport, Maine, 1985-86, indsl. engr., 1986-90, coord. total quality, 1990-91, mgr. distbn., 1991—. Mem. Portland (Maine) City Coun., 1988-91; bd. dirs. Metro Transit Dist., Portland, 1988—, Maine Lesbian and Gay Polit. Alliance, 1985—; spokesperson Equal Protection Portland, 1992. Recipient Woman in Industry award YWCA Greater Portland, 1991. Democrat. Office: LL Bean Inc Casco Distbn Ctr Freeport ME 04033

WOOD, BARBARA LOUISE CHAMPION, state legislator; b. Swampscott, Mass., Jan. 10, 1924; d. John Duncan and Eva Louise (Moore) Champion; m. Newall Arthur Wood, June 12, 1948; children: Gary Duncan, Craig Newall, Brian Scott, Dennis Michael, Joan Wood Unger. Diploma in Nursing, Mary Hitchcock Meml. Hosp. Sch. Nursing, Hanover, N.H., 1945; student, Simmons Coll., 1947-48. RN. Rep., mem. ho. edn. com. Vt. Gen. Assembly, Montpelier, 1981-94, vice chmn. edn. com., 1983-87; trustee Vt. State Colls., Waterbury, 1986-90, Gifford Meml. Hosp., Randolph, Vt.,

1986-95; commr., Vt. rep. Edn. Commn. of the States, Denver, 1981-86. Sch. dir. Bethel Sch. Bd., Vt., 1963-85; mem.-at-large Vt. Sch. Bds. Assn., Montpelier, 1982-85. Served to 2d lt. U.S. Army, 1945-46. Mem. Am. Legion, Vis. Nurse Alliance Vt.-N.H. (bd. dirs. 1991—). Republican. Congregationalist. Clubs: Bethel Woman's (pres. 1976-78); Vt. Fedn. Women's Clubs (dist. pres. 1978-80). Home: Woodland Rd Bethel VT 05032 Office: Vt House of Reps State House Montpelier VT 05602

WOOD, BETTY EGGLESTON, retired librarian, civic worker; b. Marshalltown, Iowa, June 1, 1930; d. Russell W. and Wilma L. (Hanna) Eggleston; m. John R. Wood, Aug. 20, 1953 (dec. Oct. 1990); children: Sarah, James, Elizabeth. BA, U. No. Iowa, 1952. Cert. speech clinician, Iowa. Speech clinician various orgns., Iowa, 1952-85; libr. Conrad (Iowa) Pub. Libr., 1988-90; ret., 1990. Vol. numerous orgns., 1991—; vol. 3 hospices, 1993—; pres. bd. Conrad City Mus., 1994—; mem. Conrad Park Bd., 1994—; pres. Iowa Ethical Culture Ch., 1995. Mem. Mensa, Intertel. Democrat. Home: 403 S Main St Conrad IA 50621

WOOD, CHRISTIE ANN, stained glass artist; b. Texas City, Tex., Dec. 6, 1955; d. Clarence Jefferson and Mary Ellen (Standley) W. BME, U. North Tex., 1978. Asst. ops. mgr. North Tex. State U. Computer Ctr., Denton, 1980-81, programmer, 1981; computer sci. tchr. La. Sch. Professions, Shreveport, 1981-82; computer analyst Bossier Parrish Sch. Bd., Bossier City, La., 1982-84; sr. mktg. support Unisys Corp., Dallas, 1984-87; mktg. mgr. Unisys Corp. WHQ, Blue Bell, Pa., 1987-91; product devel. mgr. Unisys Corp., Blue Bell, Pa., 1991-93; software devel. project leader Paramount Packaging, Chalfont, Pa., 1993-96; owner Art Glass Ensembles, Inc., North Wales, Pa., 1996—; awards chmn. Data Processing Mgmt. Assn., Dallas, 1985. Editor: The LINC Systems Appraoch, 1989, The LINC Systems Approach 3.0, 1992, The LINC Systems Approach 4.0, 1995; composer cantata. Flutist Shreveport Symphony Orch., 1981-84, Canterbury Chamber Consort, 1989-91, Ensemble Pro Musica, 1991—, Voces Novae et Antiquae, 1995—; bd. dirs. Nehemiah's Way, 1992-93; chmn. St. Peter's Evang. Luth. Ch., 1993-95. Recipient Exemplary Action award Burroughs Corp., 1985. Mem. Ensemble Pro Musica, Pa. Guild Craftsmen, Internat. Guild Glass Artists (contbg. editor 1995—). Democrat.

WOOD, CORY SHECTER, advertising consultant; b. Cheverly, Md.; d. William Morris and Sandra Louise (Styron) Shecter; m. William Allen Wood V, Feb. 14, 1995. BA, Va. Tech. U., 1990. Advt. cons. Datanational, Chantilly, Va., 1993—; sales leadership coun. Datanational/Volt, 1994—. Charity ball com. Fairfax (Va.) Hosp. HIV Svcs., 1995-96. Mem. AAUW, Am. Women in the Arts, Va. Tech. Alumni Assn., Belle Haven Country Club, Chi Omega. Republican. Episcopalian. Home: 507 Colecroft Ct Alexandria VA 22314 Office: Datanational 3800 Concorde Pkwy #500 Chantilly VA 22021

WOOD, DIANE PAMELA, judge; b. Plainfield, N.J., July 4, 1950; d. Kenneth Reed and Lucille (Padmore) Wood; m. Dennis James Hutchinson, Sept. 2, 1978; children: Kathryn, David, Jane. BA, U. Tex.-Austin, 1971, JD, 1975. Bar: Tex. 1975, D.C. 1978. Law clk. U.S. Ct. Appeals (5th cir.), 1975-76, U.S. Supreme Ct., 1976-77; atty.-advisor U.S. Dept. State, Washington, 1977-78; assoc. law firm Covington & Burling, Washington, 1978-80; asst. prof. law Georgetown U. Law Ctr., Washington, 1980-81, U. Chgo., 1981-88, prof. law, 1988-95, assoc. dean, 1989-92, Harold J. and Marion F. Green prof. internat. legal studies, 1990-95, sr. lectr. in law, 1995—; spl. cons. antitrust divsn. internat. guide U.S. Dept. Justice, 1986-87, dep. asst. atty. gen. antitrust divsn., 1993-95; cir. judge U.S. Ct. Appeals (7th cir.), 1995—. Contbr. articles to profl. jours. Bd. dirs. Hyde-Park-Kenwood Cmty. Health Ctr., 1983-85. Mem. ABA (sec. antitrust and internat. law, chmn. internat. law sect. BIT com., co-chmn. internat. antitrust com., ILP coun. 1989-91, internat. legal scholar officer 1991-93, chmn., antitrust sec. subcom. on internat. unfair trade, vice-chair, sec. internat. antitrust com. 1991, standing com. on law and nat. security 1991-93), Am. Soc. Internat. Law, Am. Law Inst., Internat. Acad. Comparative Law. Democrat.

WOOD, EMILY CHURCHILL, gifted and talented education educator; b. Summit, N.J., Apr. 11, 1925; d. Arthur Burdett and Ruth Vail (Pierson) Churchill; m. Philip Warren Wood, June 22, 1946; children: Martha, Arthur, Warren, Benjamin. BA, Smith Coll., 1946; MA in Teaching, Manhattanville Coll., 1971; postgrad., U. Tulsa, 1974-79, Langston U., 1990-92. Cert. tchr. social studies, learning disabilities, elem. edn., econs., Am. history, world history. Tchr. Miss Fines Sch., Princeton, N.J., 1946-47, Hallen Ctr. for Edn., Portchester, N.Y., 1973-74, Town and Country Sch., Tulsa, Okla., 1974-79, Tulsa Pub. Schs., 1979—, Tulsa Jr. Coll., 1990-92, 94; adv. bd. Great Expectations Educators, Tulsa, 1985—; leader colloquia bill of rights Arts and Humanities Coun., Tulsa, 1989; mem. literacy task force Tulsa 2000 Edn. Com., 1990-92; chmn. internat. student exch. Eisenhower Internat. Sch., Tulsa, 1992-94. Author: (with others) Visual Arts in China, 1988, Applauding Our Constitution, 1989, The Bill of Rights: Who Guarantees What, 1993; contbr. articles to profl. jours. Dir. Smith Coll. Alumnae, Northampton, Mass., 1956-59; leader, founder Am. Field Svc., Tulsa, 1982-84; pres., v.p. Booker T. Washington H.S. PTA, Tulsa, 1985; campaign mgr. auditors race Dem. Party, Tulsa, 1988, 92, 94; bd. dirs., nominations chair Sister Cities Internat., Tulsa, 1992—. Named Tulsa Tchr. of Yr. Tulsa Classroom Tchrs. Assn., 1988, Nat. Elem. Tchr. of Yr., Nat. Bar Aux., 1992; recipient Elem. Medal of Excellence, Okla. Found. for Excellence, 1990, Valley Forge Tchrs. medal Freedoms Found., 1992, Paragon award Tulsa Commn. on Status of Women, 1996. Mem. Nat. Coun. Social Studies (religion program com. 1984—), DAR, Okla. Edn. Assn., Okla. Coun. Social Studies (pres. 1995, tchr. of yr. 1984), Okla. Bar Assn. (law related com. 1988—, tchr. of yr. 1990), Okla. Coun. Econ. Edn. (state and nat. awards 1981, 89, 92), Kent Place Alumnae Assn. (disting. alumna award 1992). Home: 3622 S Yorktown Pl Tulsa OK 74105-3452

WOOD, GLADYS BLANCHE, retired secondary education educator, journalist; b. Sanborn, N.D., Aug. 12, 1921; d. Charles Kershaw and Mina Blanche (Kee) Crowther; m. Newell Edwin Wood, June 13, 1943 (dec. 1990); children: Terry N., Lani, Brian R., Kevin C.; m. F.L. Stutzman, Nov. 30, 1991. BA in Journalism, U. Minn., 1943; MA in Mass Comm., San Jose State U., 1972. Cert. secondary tchr., Calif. Reporter St. Paul Pioneer-Dispatch, 1943-45; editor J.C. Penney Co., N.Y.C., 1945-46; tchr. English and journalism Willow Glen H.S., San Jose, Calif., 1968-87; freelance writer, photographer, 1947—; cons. in field. Named Secondary Journalism Tchr. of Yr. Calif. Newpaper Pubs. Assn., 1977. Mem. AAUW, Soc. Profl. Journalists, Journalism Edn. Assn., Calif. Tchrs. English, Calif. Ret. Tchrs. Assn., Women in Comm., Santa Clara County Med. Assn. Aux., Friends of Libr., Delta Kappa Gamma, Alpha Omicron Pi. Republican. Methodist. Home: 14161 Douglass Ln Saratoga CA 95070-5535

WOOD, JACALYN KAY, education educator, educational consultant; b. Columbus, Ohio, May 25, 1949; d. Carleston John and Grace Anna (Schumacher) W. BA, Georgetown Coll., 1971; MS, Ohio State U., 1976; PhD, Miami U., 1981. Elem. tchr. Bethel-Tate Schs., Ohio, 1971-73, Columbus Christian Sch., 1973-74, Franklin (Ohio) Schs., 1974-79; teaching fellow Miami U., Oxford, Ohio, 1979-81; cons. intermediate grades Erie County Schs., Sandusky, Ohio, 1981-89, presenter, tchr. insvc. tng. Mem. coun. Sta. WVIZ-TV, 1981-88; assoc. prof. Ashland U., Elyria, Ohio, 1989, dir. elem. edn., 1989—; mem. Lorain County 20/20, mem. strategic planning bd., 1992—; mem. Leadership Lorain County, 1994—; mem. exec. com. Perkins Community Schs., 1981-85; mem. community adv. bd. Sandusky Vols. Am., 1985-89, Sandusky Sec. Bank, 1987-88, vol. Firelands Community Hosp., 1986-87; active Leadership Lorain County, 1994—. Mem. AAUW, ASCD, Am. Businesswomen's Assn. (local pres. 1985), Internat. Reading Assn., Ohio Sch. Suprs. Assn. (regional pres. 1986, state pres. 1986-87), Phi Delta Kappa (local sec. 1985, 86, v.p. 1991-93, pres. 1993—), Phi Kappa Phi, Kappa Delta Pi (local adv. 1989-91). Baptist. Home: 35873 Westminster Ave N Ridgeville OH 44039-1380 Office: Ashland U at LCCC 1005 Abbe Rd N Elyria OH 44035-1613

WOOD, JANE SEMPLE, editor, writer; b. Easton, Pa., June 23, 1940; d. Royer Daniel and Wilhelmina Annette (Weichel) Semple; m. James MacPherson Wood, Sept. 8, 1961; children: James MacPherson Jr., Robert Semple. BA in Journalism, U. Calif., Berkeley, 1961. Reporter San Jose (Calif.) Mercury News, 1962; asst. dir. pub. rels. Nat. Symphony Orch., Washington, 1963-65; free-lance writer and editor Adoption Listing Svc. of Ohio, Cleve., 1976; freelance writer and editor AIA, Cleve., 1977; free-lance writer and editor City of Bedford Heights, Ohio, 1980-81; free-lance writer and editor City of Shaker Heights, Ohio, 1979-80, pub. info. officer, dir. publs., 1980-85, 92—; founding editor Shaker mag., Shaker Heights, Ohio, 1983—; free-lance writer Exec. Living, Cleve., 1990-91; contbg. editor Corp. Cleve., 1991-92; pub. rels. cons. Cable TV Com., Shaker Heights, 1978-85, Oak Park Exch. Congress, Shaker Heights, 1981. Vol. editor, columnist Friends of Shaker Sq., Cleve., 1979-82; vol. pub. rels. com. Cleve. Ballet, 1980, Cleve. Orch., 1983; vol. contbg. editor Univ. Hosps., Cleve., 1990-92. Recipient Grand award City Hall Digest, 1983, 85, 87, Excellence in Journalism award Soc. Profl. Journalists, 1988, 92, 95, Woman of Profl. Excellence award Cleve. YWCA, 1986, Ace award of Merit, 1991, Hon. mention Blue Pencil Competition of Nat. Assn. Govt. Communicators, 1993. Mem. Press Club of Cleve., Cleve. Internat. Vol. Orgn., U. Calif. Alumni Assn. (permanent class sec. 1961). Office: Shaker Mag 3400 Lee Rd Cleveland OH 44120-3408

WOOD, JANICE, educator; b. Cleve., Apr. 7, 1943; d. Molly Amos; m. Lowell David Wood, Nov. 25, 1965; children: Joel, Courtney. AB, Cedarville Coll., 1961; BS, Ctrl. State U., 1961, MA, 1965; PhD, Fla. State U., 1974. Assoc. prof. U. North Fla., Jacksonville, 1974—; mem. grad. faculty U. Fla., 1986—; pres. faculty Coll. Edn. and Human Svcs., 1994-96; cons. and presenter in field. Author: Helping Students with Homework, 1987; contbr. articles to profl. jours. Pres. Jacksonville chpt. Children's Internat. Summer Village, 1993, village planner, 1992; chair United Way Northeast Fla. Allocations, 1988, 89, 90; mem. Duval County Interagy. Coun. 1992—, J. Allen Axson Elem. Sch. Adv. Coun., 1992, Comm. Svcs. Spl. Needs Children, 1989—, JCCI Study Team, 1987; sec. bd. dirs. Hubbard House, 1985. Recipient EVE award, 1982. Mem. Nat. Assn. for Edn. of Young Children, Fla. Assn. Children Under Six, North Fla. Assn. Children Under Six, Southern Assn. Children Under Six, Assn. Childhood Edn. Internat. Office: U North Fla 4567 Saint Johns Bluff Rd S Jacksonville FL 32224-2646

WOOD, JEANNINE KAY, state official; b. Dalton, Nebr., Apr. 22, 1944; d. Grover L. and Elsie M. (Winkelman) Sanders; m. Charles S. Wood, Dec. 7, 1968; children: Craig C., Wendi L. Wood Armstrong. Exec. sec. Idaho Hosp. Assn., Boise, 1966-71; com. sec. Idaho State Senate, Boise, 1976-81, jour. clk., 1981-85, asst. to sec. of senate, 1985-91, sec. of senate, 1991—; pvt. practice typing svc. Boise, 1979-86. Mem. Am. Soc. Legis. Clks. and Secs. (vice chmn. legis. adminstr. com.), Nat. Assn. Parliamentarians, Idaho Assn. Parliamentarians. Methodist. Home: 3505 S Linder Meridian ID 83642 Office: Idaho State Capitol PO Box 83720 Boise ID 83720-0081

WOOD, JO NELL, curriculum facilitator; b. Aurora, Mo., Apr. 11, 1951; d. Edwin Harold and Ona Marie (McNatt) Buchanan; m. Michael C. Wood, Aug. 10, 1973; children: AManda Dawn, Joshua Michael. BS in Edn., Southwest Mo. State U., 1973, MS in Edn., 1976; postgrad., U. Mo., 1988—. Tchr. Green County R-8, Rogersville, Mo., 1974-77, Aurora (Mo.) Schs., 1977-83; tchr. Springfield (Mo.) Schs., 1983-89, curriculum specialist, 1989-92, curriculum facilitator, 1992—; cons. in field. Mem. Springfield Area Arts Coun.; bd. dirs. Springfield Area coun. Boy Scouts Am., 1994—, pack sec., 1986-89; leader Campfire, Springfield, 1982-86. Mem. ASCD, NCTE, NASSP, Internat. Reading Assn., Phi Delta Kappa, Delta Kappa Gamma. Methodist. Home: 2326 E Shady Glen Springfield MO 65804 Office: Springfield Pub Schs 1418 E Pythian Springfield MO 65802

WOOD, JUDITH G., nurse; b. Hays, Kans., Nov. 28, 1948; d. Rudolph Anton Ardith and Martha Johannah (Kerth) Nelson; m. Ron D. Wood, Apr. 17, 1991; children: Cassandra Louise Blackwill Armbruster, Terrence Wayne Blackwill. ADN, Barton County C.C., Great Bend, Kans., 1987; BS, Ft. Hays State U., 1991, Family Nurse Practitioner Cert., 1993, MS, 1994. RN, advanced nurse practitioner, Kans. RN Hadley Regional Med. Ctr., Hays, Kans., 1987-88, Ellis (Kans.) Good Samaritan Ctr., 1988, Kans. Neurol. Inst., Topeka, Kans., 1988, Hadley Regional Med. Ctr., Hays, 1989-90; charge RN Larned (Kans.) State Hosp., 1988-89, St. John's Hosp., Salina, Kans., 1991-92, Meadow Brook Manor, Sedgwick, Kans., 1992; advanced RN practitioner Great Bend (Kans.) Children's Clinic, 1994, Cardinal Med. Clinic, Hoisington, Kans., 1994-95; asst. prof. of nursing Fort Hays (Kans.) State U., 1995—. Recipient Family Nurse Practitioner scholarship Wagner Trust, Hays, 1992. Mem. ANA. Democrat. Lutheran. Home: 3502 Canal Blvd Apt B Hays KS 67601 Office: Fort Hays State U Dept of Nursing Stroup Hall 167 Hays KS 67601

WOOD, KAREN MARIE, elementary education educator; b. Machias, Maine, Jan. 2, 1954; d. Douglas George and Rita Marie (Gagnon) W. BS in Liberal Arts, U. Maine, 1977, MEd, 1991. Cert. tchr. K-8, cert. literary specialist K-12, Maine. Resource tchr./gifted program MSAD #77, East Machias, 1979-86, 3rd grade tchr., 1980-89, 4th grade tchr., 1989—; chess coach MSAD #77, 1980—; dist. design team SAD 77, East Machias, 1994—; tchr. Summit Conf.; participant Learning Results State Maine; presenter in field. Mem. ASCD, Maine Tchrs. Assn., Internat. Reading Assn., Maine Reading Assn. Democrat. Roman Catholic. Home: 12 Hudson Blvd Machias ME 04654-9708

WOOD, KATHLEEN MARIE, physical therapist; b. Scranton, Pa., Nov. 18, 1968; d. Michael Joseph and Faye Ann (Hocker) Kostelnik; m. Robert Nevin Wood, Sept. 16, 1995. BS in Phys. Therapy, Beaver Coll., 1990. Phys. therapist Mercy Hosp., Scranton, 1990—; home health phys. therapist Mercy Hosp., Scranton, 1994—, quality assurance, 1994—. Mem. Altrusa Club Scranton (sec. 1993). Roman Catholic. Home: 105 2nd St Dalton PA 18414 Office: Mercy Hosp 746 Jefferson Ave Scranton PA 18501

WOOD, KATHLEEN RING, speech and communications educator; b. Morristown, N.J., June 27, 1946. BS in Elem. Edn., West Chester U., 1975; MA in Speech Comm./Pub. Rels. Mgmt., U. Houston, 1982, postgrad., 1989-96; studied with David Sloat, Houston Grand Opera, 1991-94. Asst. tchr. Twin Springs Farm Nursery and Kindergarten, Ambler, Pa., 1970; substitute tchr. St. Luke's Sch., Glenside, Pa., 1971; tchr. St. Rose of Lima Sch., North Wales, Pa., 1971-72, Bailey Elem. Sch., Pasadena, Tex., 1988-89; caseworker Montgomery County Bd. Assistance, Norristown, Pa., 1972-80; adminstrv. asst. Montgomery County Drug and Alcohol Program, Norristown, 1979-80; prodn. coord. Channel 8/KUHT-TV, Houston, 1981; prodn. coord., officer mgr., press asst. David W. Frederickson and Co., Channel 39/KHTV, Houston, 1981; dir. Columbia Cable Comms., Inc., Rosenberg, Tex., 1983; prodn. coord. Storer Cable Comms., Inc., Houston, 1982-85; instr. San Jacinto Coll. South, Houston, 1989—; adj. instr. speech comm. U. Houston-Downtown, 1986—, San Jacinto Coll., South and North, Houston, 1986-89, U. Houston-Clear Lake, 1987-91, Galveston (Tex.) Coll., 1988, North Harris County Coll., 1987-88, Houston C.C., 1986-87; adj. instr. comm. Alvin (Tex.) C.C., 1986-87, 96; instr. "Kids Coll." San Jacinto Coll., South, 1993-94; spkr., cons., lectr. in field; judge various forensics festivals and speech tournaments. Mem. Gulf Coast Intercollegiate Consortium Literary Arts Com. for South Campus, San Jacinto Coll., 1989—, mem. libr. resources com. 1989-94, mem. dist. textbook selection com. 1989—; mem. Pasadena Little Theatre, 1984—; pub. rels. dir., pres. exec. bd. Theatre Network of Houston, 1985-88; cultural arts dir. exec. bd. Clear Brook H.S. PTA, 1990-92; mem. Vol. in Pub. Schs., Houston Ind. Sch. Dist., 1982-85; mem. steering com., media cons. Houston Bus. Com. for Edn. Excellence, 1984-86; mem. Internat. Soc. Poets, 1995—. Recipient Cert. of Appreciation Am. Heart Assn., USMC, Leukemia Assn., Boy Scouts Am., Vols. in Pub. Schs., Letter of Commendation Fire Marshal of Houston, DePelchin Children's Ctr., Escape Ctr. of Houston, Spirit of San Jacinto award, 1990-96; named Hon. Sheriff's Dep., Harris County, 1981. Mem. ASCD, San Jacinto Coll. Dist. Spkrs. Bur., Tex. C.C. Tchrs. Assn., Harris County Sheriff's Assn. (assoc.), DAV Assn., Tex. State Troopers Assn., Houston Police Patrolmen's Union Assn., U. Houston Alumni Assn., U. Houston Cmty. Alumni Assn., U. Houston Women's Studies.

WOOD, KATHY RENÉ, psychotherapist; b. Ardmore, Okla., Sept. 12, 1951; d. Thomas A. and Helen Jayne (Miller) Patterson; 1 child, Karleen René Bapiste. BA in Liberal Arts/Psychology, Okla. City U.; MS in Counseling Psychology, So. Nazarene U., 1995. Group facilitator Parents Assistance Ctr., Oklahoma City, 1980-94; reach out counselor Oklahoma County Crisis Intervention Ctr. Okla. Dept. Mental Health, Oklahoma City, 1994; psychotherapist, case mgr. Integris/Willow View Mental Health Sys., Oklahoma City, 1994—; adv. Passageway Ctr. for Abused Women, Oklahoma City, 1991-92. Mem. APA, Psi Chi. Office: Integris/Willow View Mental Health Sys 5501 N Portland Oklahoma City OK 73112

WOOD, KIMBA M., judge; b. Port Townsend, Wash., Jan. 2, 1944. BA cum laude, Conn. Coll., 1965; MSc, London Sch. Econs., 1966; JD, Harvard U., 1969. Bar: U.S. Dist. Ct. D.C. 1969, U.S. Ct. Appeals D.C. 1969, N.Y. 1972, U.S. Dist. Ct. (ea. and so. dists.) N.Y. 1974, U.S. Ct. Appeals (2d cir.) 1975, U.S. Supreme Ct. 1980, U.S. Dist. Ct. (we. dist.) N.Y. 1981. Assoc. Steptoe & Johnson, Washington, 1969-70; with Office Spl. Counsel, OEO Legal Svcs., Washington, 1970-71; assoc., then ptnr. LeBoeuf, Lamb, Leiby & MacRae, N.Y.C., 1971-88; judge, U.S. Dist. Ct. (so. dist.) N.Y., N.Y.C., 1988—. Mem. ABA (chmn. civil practice, procedure com. 1982-85, mem. coun. 1985-88, jud. rep. 1989-91), N.Y. State Bar Assn. (chmn. antitrust sect. 1983-84), Fed. Bar Coun. (trustee from 1978, v.p., 1984-85), Am. Law Inst. Office: US Dist Ct US Courthouse 500 Pearl St New York NY 10007

WOOD, LARRY (MARY LAIRD), journalist, author, university educator, public relations executive, environmental consultant; b. Sandpoint, Idaho; d. Edward Hayes and Alice (McNeel) Small; children: Mary, Marcia, Barry. BA summa cum laude, U. Wash., 1939, MA summa cum laude, with highest honors, 1940; postgrad., Stanford U., 1941-42, U. Calif., Berkeley, 1946-47; cert. in photography, U. Calif., Berkeley, 1971; postgrad. journalism, U. Wis., 1971-72, U. Minn., 1971-72, U. Ga., 1972-73; postgrad. in art, architecture and marine biology, U. Calif., Santa Cruz, 1974-76, Stanford Hopkins Marine Sta., Santa Cruz, 1977-80. Lifetime secondary and jr. coll. teaching cert., Wash., Calif. Feature writer and columnist Oakland Tribune and San Francisco Chronicle, Calif., 1939—; archtl. and environ. feature and travel writer and columnist San Jose (Calif.) Mercury News (Knight Ridder), 1972-90; teaching fellow Stanford U., 1940-43; dir. pub. rels. 2-counties, 53-parks East Bay Regional Park Dist., No. Calif., 1948-68; pres. Larry Wood Pub. Rels., 1946—; prof. (tenure) pub. rels., mag. writing, journalism, investigative reporting San Diego State U., 1974, 75; disting. vis. prof. journalism San Jose State U., 1976; assoc. prof. journalism Calif. State U., Hayward, 1978; prof. sci. and environ. journalism U. Calif. Berkeley Ext. grad. divsn., 1979—; press del. nat. convs. Am. Geophys. Union Internat. Conf., 1986—, AAAS, 1989—, Nat. Park Svc. VIP Press Tour, Yellowstone after the fire, 1989—, Nat. Assn. Sci. Writers, 1989—, George Washington U./Am. Assn. Neurol. Surgeons Sci. Writers Conf., 1990, Am. Inst. Biol. Scis. Conf., 1990, Nat. Conf. Sci. Writers, Am. Heart Assn., 1995, Internat. Cardiologists Symposium for Med./Sci. Writers, 1995, Annenberg Program Electronic Media Symposium, Washington, 1995; EPA del. to USSR and Ea. Europe; expert witness on edn., pub. rels., journalism and copyright; cons. sci. writers interne project Stanford U., 1989—; spl. media guest Sigma Xi, 1990—; mem. numerous spl. press corps; selected White House Spl. Media, 1993—; selected mem. Duke U. 14th Ann. Sci. Reporters Conf., 1995; internat. press guest Can. Consulate Gen. Dateline Can., 1995, French Govt. Tourist Office, 1996-97, Ministerio delle Risorse Agricole Alimentari e Forestali and Assocs. Conf., 1995; appeared in TV documentary Larry Wood Covers Visit of Queen Elizabeth II. Contbr. over 5,000 articles on various topics for newspapers, nat. mags., nat. and internat. newspaper syndicates including L.A. Times-Mirror Syndicate, Washington Post, Phila. Inquirer, Chgo. Tribune, Miami Herald, Oakland Tribune, Seattle Times, San Francisco Chronicle, Parade, San Jose Mercury News (Nat. Headliner award), Christian Sci. Monitor, L.A. Times/Christian Monitor Worldwide News Syndicate, Washington Post, Phila. Inquirer, Hawaiian Airlines In Paradise and other in-flight mags., MonitoRadio, Sports Illus., Life, Mechanix Illus., Popular Mechanics, Parents (contbg. editor), House Beautiful, Am. Home (awards 1988, 89), Archl. Digest, Better Homes and Gardens, Sunset, Architectural Digest, National Geographic World, Travel & Leisure, Chevron USA/Odyssey (Calif. Pub.'s award 1984), Xerox Edn. Publs., Europe's Linguapress, PSA Mag., Off Duty, Oceans, Sea Frontiers, AAA Westways, AAA Motorland, Travelin', others. Significant works include home and garden columnist and editor, 5-part series Pacific Coast Ports, 5-part series Railroads of the West, series Immigration, Youth Gangs, Endangered Species, Calif. Lighthouse Chain, Elkhorn Slough Nat. Estuarine Res., Ebey's Landing Nat. Hist. Res., Calif. Water Wars, BLM's Adopt a Horse Program, Mt. St. Helen's Eruption, Loma Prieta Earthquake, Oakland Firestorm, Missing Children, Calif. Prison Reform, Columbia Alaska's Receding Glacier, Calif. Underwater Parks, and many others; author: Wonderful U.S.A.: A State-by-State Guide to Its Natural Resources, 1989; co-author over 21 books including: McGraw-Hill English for Social Living, 1944, Fawcett Boating Books, 1956-66, Fodor's San Francisco, Fodor's California, 1982-89, Charles Merrill Focus on Life Science, Focus on Physical Science, Focus on Earth Science, 1983, 87, Earth Science, 1987; contbr. Earth Science 1987; 8 works selected for use by Europe's Woltors-Nordoff-Longman English Language Texts, U.K., Netherlands, 1988; author: (with others) anthology West Winds, 1989; reviewer Charles Merrill texts, 1983-84; book reviewer Profl. Communicator, 1987—; selected writings in permanent collections Oakland Pub. Libr., U. Wash. Main Libr.; environ. works included in Dept. Edn. State of Md. textbook; contbr., author Journalism Quar.; author script PBS/AAA America series, 1992; contbg. editor: Parents. Nat. chmn. travel writing contest for U.S. univ. journalism students Assn. for Edn. in Journalism/Soc. Am. Travel Writers, 1979-83; judge writing contest for Nat. Assn. Real Estate Editors, 1982—; press del. 1st Internat. Symposium Volcanism and Aviation Safety, 1991, Coun. for Advancement of Sci. Writing, 1977—, Rockefeller Media Seminar Feeding the World-Protecting the Earth, 1992, Global Conf. on Mercury as Pollutant, 1992, Earth Summit Global Forum, Rio de Janeiro, 1992; invited Nat. Park Svc. Nat. Conf. Sci. Writers, 1985, Postmaster Gen.'s 1992 Stamps, 1991, Internat. Geophys. Union Conf., 1982-95, The Conf. Bd., 1995, Corp. Comm. Conf., Calif. Inst. Tech.'s Media and Sci. Seminar, 1995-96, EPA and Dept. Energy Tech. Conf., 1992, Am. Soc. Photogrammetry and Remote Sensing Internat. Conv. Mapping Global change, 1992, N.Y. Mus. Modern Art Matisse Retrospective Press Rev., 1992, celebration 150th anniversary Oreg. Trail, 1993, Coun. Advancement Sci. Writing, 1993-96, Sigma Xi Nat. Conf., 1988-96, Nat. Sci. Writers Confs., 1996, PRSA Travel and Tourism Conf., 1993, Internat. Conf. Environment, 1994, 95, Quality Life Europe, Prague, 1994, Calif. Sesquicentennial, 1996, 14th Ann. Sci. Writers Conf., 1996, Picasso Retrospective, 1996, many others; mem. Gov.'s Conf. Tourism N.C., 1993, 94, 95, Calif., 1976—, Fla., 1987—; press guest 14 U.S. states and 12 fgn. countries' Depts. Tourism, 1986-96. Recipient numerous awards, honors, citations, speaking engagements, including induction into Broadway Hall of Fame, U. Wash., 1984, Broadway Disting. Alumnus award, 1995; citations for environ. writing Nat. Park Svc., U.S. Forest Svc., Bur. Land Mgmt., Oakland Mus. Assn., Oakland C. of C., Chevron USA, USN plaque and citation, best mag. articles citation Calif. Pubs. Assn., 1984; co-recipient award for best Sunday newspaper mag. Nat. Headliners, citation for archtl. features Oakland Mus., 1983; honoree for achievements in journalism Nat. Mortar Bd., 1988, 89; selected as one of 10 V.I.P. press for Yellowstone Nat. Park field trip on "Let Burn" rsch., 1989; named one of Calif.'s top 40 contemporary authors for writings on Calif. underwater parks, 1989, nat. honoree Social Issues Resources Series, 1987; invited V.I.P. press, spl. press guest numerous events worldwide. Mem. Am. Bd. Forensic Examiners, Calif. Acad. Scis., San Francisco Press Club, Nat. Press Club, Pub. Rels. Soc. Am. (charter mem. travel, tourism, environment and edn. divs.), Nat. Sch. Pub. Rels. Assn., Environ. Cons. N.Am., Am. Assn. Edn. in Journalism and Comm. (exec. bd. nat. mag. div. 1978, panel chmn. 1979, 80, author Journalism Quar. jour.), Women in Comm. (nat. bd. officer 1975-77, book reviewer Prof. Communicator), Soc. Profl. Journalists (nat. bd. for hist. sites 1980—), Nat. Press Photographers Assn. (hon. life, cons. Bay Area interne project 1989—, honoree 1995), Investigative Reporters and Editors (charter), Bay Area Advt. and Mktg. Assn., Nat. Assn. Sci. Writers, Calif. Writers Club (state bd., Berkeley bd. 1989—, honoree ann. conv. Asilomar, Calif. 1990), Am. Assn. Med. Writers, Internat. Assn. Bus. Communicators, Soc. Environ. Journalists (charter), Am. Film Inst., Am. Heritage Found. (citation 1986, 87, 88), Soc. Am. Travel Writers, Internat. Oceanographic Found., Oceanic Soc., Calif. Acad. Environ. News Writers, Seattle Advt. and Sales Club (former officer), Nature Conservancy, Smithsonian Audubon Soc., Nat. Wildlife Fedn., Nat. Parks and Conservation Assn., Calif. State Parks Found., Calif. Environ. Leadership Roundtable, Fine Arts Mus., San Francisco, Seattle Jr. Advt. Club (charter), U. Wash. Comm. Alumni (Sch. Comm. alumni, life, charter mem. ocean scis. alumni, Disting. Alumni 1987), U. Calif., Berkeley Alumni (life, v.p., scholarship chmn. 1975-81), Stanford Alumni (life), Mortar Board Alumnae Assn. (life, honoree 1988, 89), Am. Mgmt. Assn., Nat. Soc. Environ. Journalists (charter), Calif. Environ. Leadership Roundtable, Phi Beta Kappa (v.p., bd. dirs. Calif. Alumni Assn., statewide chmn. scholarship awards 1975-81), Purple and Gold Soc. (planning com., charter, 1995—), Pi Lambda Theta, Theta Sigma Phi. Home: Piedmont Pines 6161 Castle Dr Oakland CA 94611-2737

WOOD, LISA GAYE, civil engineering design company executive; b. Tampa, Fla., Dec. 12, 1957; d. James W. and Sylvia (Rosello) W.; m. Robert Howell, Mar. 13, 1976 (div. Nov. 1979); 1 child, Kyle A. Howell. With svc. dept. Sears, Tampa, 1975-80; with drafting dept. Heidt & Assocs., Tampa, 1980-83, Landmark Engring., Tampa, 1983-85; permit coord. Genesis Profl. Svcs., Lutz, Fla., 1985-89; sec.-treas. Premiere Engring., Inc., Tampa, 1989—. Notary pub., Tampa, 1989-97. Mem. NAFE, Tampa Bay C. of C. (N.W. coun.), Tampa Bay Snow Skiers, Carrollwood Area Bus. Assn. (chair holiday tree lighting event 1993), Gaither High Sch. Booster Club (boys baseball liaison 1995—). Office: Premiere Engring Inc 7605-A Gunn Hwy Tampa FL 33625

WOOD, MARCIA J., sales executive; b. Montego Bay, Jamaica, Aug. 27, 1960. Assoc. in Bus. Mgmt. with honors, Borough of Manhattan C.C., 1993; BA, NYU, 1995; MA, Columbia U., 1996. Lic. cosmetologist. Sec. Cunard Line, N.Y.C., 1984-85, sales rep., 1985-89, adminstrv. asst., 1989-91, asst. to sr. v.p. sales, 1991—. Mem. Fundraising Com. for Econ. Redevel. of Jamaica; mem. adv. bd. bus. mgmt. dept. Borough of Manhattan C.C., 1992. Etta Kallman scholar, 1994. Mem. Phi Theta Kappa. Home: 616 E 18th St Apt 3D Brooklyn NY 11226

WOOD, MARGARET GRAY, dermatologist, educator; b. Jamaica, N.Y., May 23, 1918; d. C.W. Bromley and B. Eleanor (Niblack) Gray; m. Alfred Conard Wood, Mar. 24, 1950; children: M. Diana Wood, Deirdre Wood-Harper, Moira Dorothy Wood. BA, U. ALa., Tuscaloosa, 1941; MD, Woman's Med. Coll. Pa., 1948; D in Med. Scis. (hon.), Med. Coll. Pa., 1990, emeritus prof. medicine, 1993. Diplomate Am. Bd. Dermatology, Am. Bd. Dermatopathology. Intern Phila. Gen. Hosp., 1948-50; resident U. Pa. Hosp., 1950-53; instr. dept. dermatology U. Pa. Sch. Medicine, Phila., 1952-53, assoc., 1953-67, asst. prof., 1967-71, assoc. prof., 1971-75, clin. prof., 1975-80, prof. and chmn. dept. dermatology, 1980-82, prof., 1988-92, prof. emeritus, 1989—; assoc. prof. grad. Sch. Medicine U. Pa., Phila., 1957-71, cons. Sch. Dental Medicine, Sch. Vet. Medicine U. Pa., Phila.; asst. prof. Med. Coll. Pa., Phila., 1957-93, prof. emeritus, 1993—, vice chmn. bd. dirs. 1984—; vice chmn. bd. dirs. Med. Coll. Hosps., Phila., 1991—, Hahnemann U. Hosp., 1993—; mem. exec. com. Am. Med. Women's Hosp. Svc. Com., Washington, 1970—; dir. Alleghany Health Systems, Pitts., 1987-91, Alleghany Health Edn. and Rsch. Found., 1991-94; bd. dirs. St. Christophers Hosp. for Children, Alleghany U. Pitts., Alleghany Hosp. Systems. Author (with others) 4 books; contbr. numerous articles to med. jours. Recipient Rose Hershfeld award Women's Dermatology Soc., 1989. Mem. AMA, Internat. Dermatology Assn., Internat. Dermatopathology Assn., Phila. Dermatology Soc. (pres. 1978-79), Alpha Omega Alpha. Republican. Episcopalian.

WOOD, MARIAN STARR, publishing company executive; b. N.Y.C., Mar. 30, 1938; d. Edward James and Betty (Starr) Markow; m. Anthony Stuart Wood, Mar. 21, 1963. B.A., Barnard Coll., 1959; postgrad., Columbia U., 1959-64. Teaching asst., lectr. Columbia U., N.Y.C., 1960-64; editor Praeger Pubs., N.Y.C., 1965-71; sr. editor Henry Holt & Co., N.Y.C., 1972-81, exec. editor, 1981-96; assoc. pub. Marian Wood Books, 1996—.

WOOD, MARION LONGMORE, educator, nurse; b. New Bedford, Mass., May 16, 1927; d. Harold Thomas and Martha Longmore; m. Floyd T. Wood (dec.); 1 child, Monica. BSN magna cum laude, Adelphi U., Garden City, N.Y., 1948; BS in Edn., Rutgers U., 1960; postgrad., NYU, 1960. Sch. nurse Levittown, N.Y., 1952-58; tchr. Edison (N.J.) Sch. Sys., 1958, Dade County, Miami, Fla., 1963—. Named Tchr. of Yr., Dade County Sch. Sys., 1994. Mem. Delta Gamma.

WOOD, MARISA LEIGH, librarian; b. Fresno, Calif., June 20, 1969; d. Roger Lee and Madelon Karel (Montgomery) W. BA cum laude, Pacific Luth. U., 1991; MA, Wash. State U., 1993; M of Libr., U. Wash., 1995. Cert. libr., Wash. Interlibr. loan asst. Wash. State U., Pullman, 1992-93; resource sharing asst. U. Wash., Seattle, 1993-95, reference intern, 1995; record retention profl. Ben Bridge Jeweler, Seattle, 1995—. Vol. Nat. Archives br., Seattle, 1994; vol. archival aide Ballard Libr., Seattle, 1996—. Pres.'s scholar Pacific Luth. U., 1987-91; Koon Family fellow U. Wash. Libr. Sch., 1993. Mem. NOW, Planned Parenthood. Democrat. Unitarian. Office: care Ben Bridge Jeweler Ste 200 2901 Third Ave Seattle WA 98121

WOOD, MARTHA OAKWELL, obstetrical and gynecological nurse practitioner; b. Chester, Pa., Apr. 19, 1941; d. Albert Edward Jr. and Gertrude Cecelia (Morgan) Warburton; m. Lawrence Dakin Wood, Nov. 22, 1957; children: Lawrence Dakin Jr., Thomas C., Elizabeth W., Michael L., Kathryn M., Scott G. BSN, Neumann coll., 1981; MSN, U. Pa., 1987. RN, Pa. Staff nurse Sacred Heart Med. ctr., Chester, Pa., 1981-84, Crozer-Chester Med. Ctr., 1984-88; clin. instr. obstetrics Neumann Coll., Aston, Pa., 1988, adj. faculty, 1991; instr. maternal-child health Chester County Hosp. Sch. Nursing, West Chester, Pa., 1989-90; adj. clin. instr. Widener U., Chester, 1991; staff devel. specialist Episcopal Hosp., Phila., 1992-93; ob.-gyn. nurse practitioner Camcare Health Corp., Camden, N.J., 1993—, nurse mgr., 1994—; supr. women and children nursing Bryn Mawr (Pa.) Hosp., 1988-89; perinatal nursing support Home Care Obstetrics, Bryn Mawr, 1991-93; manuscript reviewer Lippincott Pub. Co., Phila.; lectr. in field. Educator women's health Women's Assn. for Women's Alternatives, Wawa, Pa., 1990-91; big sister Del. County Pregnancy Ctr.; deaconess North Chester Bapt. Ch., 1991-94. Mem. Pa. Perinatal Assn., Acad. Nurse Practitioners, Assn. Reproductive Health Profls., Assn. Women's Health, Obstetrics, Neonatal Nurses, Sigma Theta Tau (Delta Tau chpt.). Baptist. Home: 103 W Mowry St Chester PA 19013-5023 Office: Camcare Health Corp 3 Cooper Plz Rm 104 Camden NJ 08103-1438

WOOD, NANCY ELIZABETH, psychologist, educator; d. Donald Sterret and Orne Louise (Erwin) W. B.S., Ohio U., 1943, M.A., 1947; Ph.D., Northwestern U., Evanston, Ill., 1952. Prof. Case-Western Res. U., Cleve., 1952-60; specialist, expert Dept. HEW, Washington, 1960-62; chief of research Pub. Health, Washington, 1962-64; prof. U. So. Calif., Los Angeles, 1965—; learning disabilities cons., 1960-70; assoc. dir. Cleve. Hearing and Speech Ctr., 1952-60; dir. licensing program Brit. Nat. Trust, London. Author: Language Disorders, 1964, Language Development, 1970, Verbal Learning, 1975 (monograph) Auditory Disorders, 1978, Levity, 1980, Stoneskipping, 1989, Bird Cage, 1994. Pres. faculty senate U. So. Calif., 1987-88. Recipient Outstanding Faculty award Trojan Fourth Estate, 1982, Pres.' Svc. award U. So. Calif., 1992. Fellow Am. Speech and Hearing Assn. (elected, legis. council 1965-68), Am. Psychol. Assn. (cert.), AAAS; mem. Internat. Assn. of Scientists. Republican. Methodist. Office: U So Calif University Park Los Angeles CA 90089

WOOD, PAULA DAVIDSON, lawyer; b. Oklahoma City, Dec. 20, 1952; d. Paul James and Anna Mae (Ferrero) Davidson; m. Andrew E. Wood; children: Michael Paul, John Roland. BS, Okla. State U., 1976; JD, Oklahoma City U., 1982. Bar: Okla. 1983, U.S. Dist. Ct. (we. dist.) Okla. 1983, U.S. Supreme Ct. 1995; cert. pub. mgr. Pvt. practice Oklahoma City, 1984-85; ptnr. Davidson & Wood, Oklahoma City, 1985-87; child support enforcement counsel Okla. Dept. Human Svcs., Oklahoma City, 1987-92, child support adminstr. (IV-D dir.), 1992—; adj. instr. Tech. Inst. Okla. State U., Oklahoma City, 1985. Articles editor Oklahoma City U. Law Rev., 1982. Mem. Okla. Bar Assn. (sec. family law sect. 1987, Golden Gavel award 1987), Nat. Child Support Enforcement Assn. (bd. dirs. 1995), Okla. Child Support Enforcement Assn., S.W. Regional Child Assn. State Child Support Enforcement Adminstrs., Western Interstate Child Support Enforcement Coun. (sec. 1995). Republican. Roman Catholic. Office: Okla Dept Human Svcs PO Box 53552 Oklahoma City OK 73152-3552

WOOD, ROBERTA SUSAN, foreign service officer; b. Clarksdale, Miss., Oct. 4, 1948; d. Robert Larkin and Dorothy Eloise (Shelton) Wood. BA with distinction, Rhodes Coll., Memphis, 1970; postgrad. Nat. U. Cuyo, Mendoza, Argentina, 1970-71; MPA, Harvard U., 1980. Joined U.S. Fgn. Svc., 1972; svc. in Manila, Philippines, Naples and Turin, Italy, and Port-au-Prince, Haiti; mgmt. analyst Dept. State, Washington, 1980-84; U.S. consul gen., Jakarta, Indonesia, 1984-87, NATO Def. Coll., Rome, 1987-88; U.S. consul gen. Marseilles, France, 1988-91, Montreal, Que., Can., 1991-94; min., dep. chief of mission US Embassy, Quito, Ecuador, 1994-95; mem. U.S. Commn. Immigration Reform, Washington, 1995—. Fulbright scholar, 1970-71. Home: 4315 N 19th St Arlington VA 22207 Office: 2430 E St NW South Bldg Washington DC 20037

WOOD, RUBY FERN, writer, retired elementary educator; b. Strauss, Kans., Aug. 17, 1922; d. John Elijah and Mildred Floy (Cole) Morrow; m. Leonard Edgar Wood, Oct. 18, 1942; children: Michael Wood, Sherry Wood Ruddell, Toni Wood Treaster. BS in Elem. Edn., Pittsburg (Kans.) State U., 1961, MS in Elem. Edn., 1965. Cert. tchr. elem. edn., secondary English, reading, lit., social studies, psychology, Kans. Tchr. grades 1-8 Cunningham Sch., Labette County, Kans., 1939-41, Centennial Sch., Montgomery County, Kans., 1941-42, Overfield Sch., Montgomery County, 1942-43, Foster Sch., Montgomery County, 1946-47, Racob-Wetzel Sch., Montgomery County, 1955-58; elem. tchr. Cherryvale (Kans.) Unified Sch. Dist. 447, 1961-87; pres. Cherryvale Tchrs. Assn., 1971-72; mem. selection panel Master Tchrs. Kans., Emporia, 1983-85. Author: (biography) Pop and Bud, 1981, (hist. fiction) The Benders-Keepers of the Devil's Inn, 1992; editor: 10-Year History of the SWC Region of AAUW, 1986, (anthology) Memories of a Country School, 1989; editor, contbg. author: Southeast Kansas: Land of Discovery, 1993. Coord. Heritage 200 Day, Cherryvale, 1976; guest White House briefing, Washington, 1984; coord. spl. exhibits Cherryvale Mus., 1980—. Recipient 1st prize Tulsa Professionalism in Writing Conf., 1991. Mem. AAUW (Kans. pres. 1983-85), Kans. Authors Club (pres. 3d dist. 1989-93, state pres. 1995—, 1st prize Eisenhower theme 1990), Kans. Coun. Women, Phi Theta Kappa. Democrat. Methodist. Home: RR 2 Box 114 Cherryvale KS 67335-9726

WOOD, RUTH DIEHM, artist, design consultant; b. Cleve., July 31, 1916; d. Ellis Raymond and Frances Helen (Peshek) Diehm; m. Kenneth Anderson Wood, Sept. 14, 1937. Student, Spencerian Bus. Coll., 1935-36, John Huntington Inst., 1936, Cleve. Inst. Art, 1934-37, 45. Legal sec. Klein, Diehm & Farber, Attys., Cleve., 1936-37; freelance graphic designer Bailey Meter Co., Wickliffe, Ohio, 1967; interior design cons., lectr. One-woman shows include Artist & Craftsmen Assn., Cleve., 1949, Art Colony, Cleve., 1953, Women's City Club, Cleve., 1955, Cleve. Inst. Art Alumni, 1954, Malvina Freedson Gallery, Lakewood, Ohio, 1965, Intown Club, Cleve., 1953, Studio Inn, Painesville, Ohio, 1955, Little Gallery, Chesterland, Ohio, 1961, Hospitality Inn, Willoughby, Ohio, 1965, Coll. Club Cleve., 1965, Lakeland Community Coll., Mentor, Ohio, 1979, Holden Arboretum, Mentor, 1981, Fairmount Fine Arts Ctr., Russell, Ohio, 1992; represented in 12 nat. juried shows, 28 regional and local mus., many pvt. collections. Recipient 1st prize Oil Still Life, Cleve. Mus. Art, 1945, Grumbacher Merit award Lakeland Fla. Internat., 1952, Artistic Achievement award Gates Mills, 1973, numerous other awards; certs. of award in Nyumon and Shoden, Ikenobo Sch. Floral Art, Kyoto, Japan. Mem. Cleve. Inst. Art Alumni, Artists and Craftsmen, Geauga Artists, Women in the Arts. Republican. Mem. Seventh-Day Adventist. Home and Studio: Kenwood Designers 11950 Sperry Rd Chesterland OH 44026-2225

WOOD, RUTH LUNDGREN WILLIAMSON See LUNDGREN, RUTH WILLIAMSON WOOD

WOOD, SANDRA SUE, counselor; b. Merced, Calif., Mar. 9, 1952; d. David L. and Betty Jean (Ingle) Tucker. AA, Merced Jr. Coll., 1982, BA, Stanislaus U., 1991, pupil pers. credential, 1994, MA in Edn. and Counseling, 1996; tchg. credential, Chapman U., 1992. Tutor Merced Coll., 1977-79; tchr. Acts Christian Sch., Merced, 1979-85, 89-90, adminstr., 1985-89; tchr. reading intervention Merced City Schs., 1991-93, counselor, 1993—. Mem. APA. Pentecostal.

WOOD, SHARON, mountaineer; b. Halifax, N.S., Can., May 18, 1957; d. Stan and Peggy Wood. LLD (hon.), U. Calgary, 1987. Climbed peaks Mt. McKinley (Alaska), Mt. Logan (Can.), Mt. Aconcagua (Argentina), Mt. Makalu (Himalayas), Mt. Everest (Himalayas, 1st N.Am. woman to climb); Can. Light Everest Expedition, 1986; lectr. in field. Recipient Tenzing Norgay Trophy, 1987. Address: Box 1482, Canmore, AB Canada T0L 0M0

WOOD, VIRGINIA ANN, educator; b. Petoskey, Mich., June 24, 1936; d. William Nelson and Mildred Alice (Cope) Reed; m. Frederick Lee Wood, Sept. 28, 1970 (dec. Apr. 1971); 1 child, Frederick Lee. BS, Ferris State U., 1957. Tchr. Reese (Mich.) Schs., 1957-59, Utica (Mich.) Schs., 1963-64, Richmond (Mich.) Cmty. Schs., 1959-63, 64—; coach Sci. Olympiad, Richmond H.S., 1984—. Contbr. software revs. to Sci. Tchr. mag., 1987. Trustee Pub. Libr. Bd., 1980—; mem. Richmond Cmty. Theatre, 1965-71; organist United Ch. of Christ. NSF grantee in chemistry and project physics, 1962-68. Mem. NEA, Nat. Sci. Tchrs. Assn., Mich. Edn. Assn., Mich. Sci. Tchrs. Assn. (sec., bd. dirs. 1961-70), Richmond Edn. Assn. (pres. 1966-67, sec. 1984-94), Alpha Delta Kappa (pres. 1968-70). Republican. Home: 70109 Karen St Richmond MI 48062-1098 Office: Richmond High Sch 35320 Division Rd Richmond MI 48062-1378

WOOD, VIVIAN POATES, mezzo soprano, educator, author; b. Washington, Aug. 19, 1923; d. Harold Poates and Mildred Georgette (Patterson) W.; studies with Walter Anderson, Antioch Coll., 1953-55, Denise Restout, Saint-Leu-La-Fôret, France and Lakeville, Conn., 1960-62, 64-70, Paul A. Pisk, 1968-71, Paul Ulanowsky, N.Y.C., 1958-68, Elemer Nagy, 1965-68, Vyautas Marijosius, 1967-68; MusB Hartt Coll. Music, 1968; postgrad. (fellow) Yale U., 1968; MusM (fellow), Washington U., St. Louis, 1971, PhD (fellow), 1973. Debut in recital series Internat. Jeunesse Musicals Arts Festival, 1953, solo fellowship Boston Symphony Orch., Berkshire Music Ctr., Tanglewood, 1964, St. Louis Symphony Orch., 1969, Washington Orch., 1949, Bach Cantata Series Berkshire Chamber Orch., 1964, Yale Symphony Orch., 1968; appearances in U.S. and European recitals, oratorios, operas, radio and TV, 1953-68; appeared as soloist in Internat. Harpsichord Festival, Westminister Choir Coll., Princeton, N.J., 1973; appeared as soloist in meml. concert, Landowska Ctr., Lakeville, 1969; prof. voice U. So. Miss., Hattiesburg, 1971—, asst. dean Coll. Fine Arts, 1974-76, acting dean, 1976-77; guest prof. Hochschule für Musik, Munich, 1978-79; prof. Italian Internat. Studies Program, Rome, 1986; Miss. coord. Alliance for Arts Edn., Kennedy Ctr. Performing Arts, 1974—; mem. Miss. Gov.'s Adv. Panel for Gifted and Talented Children, 1974—; mem. 1st Miss. Gov.'s Conf. on the Arts, 1974—; bd. dirs. Miss. Opera Assn. Author: Polenc's Songs: An Analysis of Style, 1971. Recipient Young Am. Artists Concert award N.Y.C., 1955; Wanda Landowska fellow, 1968-72. Mem. Miss. Music Tchrs. Assn., Nat. Assn. Tchrs. of Singing, Music Tchrs. Nat. Assn., Am. Musicology Soc., Golden Key, Mu Phi Epsilon, Delta Kappa Gamma, Tau Beta Kappa (hon.), Pi Kappa Lambda. Democrat. Episcopalian. Avocation: sailing. Office: U So Miss Sch Music South Pt # 8264 Hattiesburg MS 39406-9539

WOOD, WENDY DEBORAH, filmmaker; b. N.Y.C., Oct. 4, 1940; d. John Meyer and Marion Emily (Peters) W.; m. William Dismore Chapple, Dec. 7, 1963; 1 child, Samuel Eliot. BA cum laude, Vassar Coll., 1962; MA, Stanford U., 1964. Teaching asst. Stanford U., 1962-64; photographer, film editor Bristol (Eng.) U., 1964-66, asst. dir. Internat. Conf. Film Schs., 1966; rsch. asst. biology dept. U. Conn., Storrs, 1970-72; sr. media specialist Aetna Life & Casualty Co., Hartford, Conn., 1972-89; media writer, prodr., dir. U. Conn. Ctr. for Media and Tech., Storrs, 1989—; pres. Chapple Films, Inc., 1972—. Films include: Yankee Craftsman, 1972; Alcoholism, Industry's Costly Hangover, 1974; Draggerman's Haul, 1975; Flight Without Wings, 1977; Auto Insurance Affordability (2 awards), 1981; Where Rivers Run to the Sea (award), 1981; Our Town is Burning Down (6 awards), 1982; Wellness at the Worksite, 1984 (4 awards); Welcome to the Aetna Institute, 1985 (4 awards); Aenhance, 1989 (3 awards). Mem. peer rev. com. Conn. Commn. Higher Edn, 1992—. Recipient CINE Golden Eagle award Council on Internat. Non-theatrical Events, 1972, 76, 84, 1st Place award Indsl. Photography, 1974, cert. Outstanding Creativity U.S. TV Commls. Festival, 1974, EFLA award Am. Film Festival, 1974, 76, Dir's. Choice award Sinking Creek Film Festival, 1975, award Columbus Film Festival, 1975, award Excellence Life Ins. Advtrs. Assn., 1975, Silver Screen award U.S. Indsl. Film Festival, 1976, 81, 1st place award Conn. Film Festival, 1977, 1st prize Nat. Outdoor Travel Film Festival, 1978, 1st pl. Houston Film Festival, 1982, CINE Golden Eagle, 1982, 84, award Am. Film Festival, 1982, N.Y. Film Festival, 1982, 83, Silver CINDY award Assn. Visual Communicators, 1985, others. Bd. dirs. Windham Regional Arts Council, 1987, 88, 89; mem. jury N.Y. Internat. Video and Film Festival. Mem. Info. Film Producers Am. (nat. dir., pres. chpt. 1981-82, Cindy award 1971, 72, 81, 82, 85, 87), Internat. Quorum Motion Picture Producers, Audio Visual Communicators (pres. Conn. chpt. 1985, treas. 1988). Democrat. Quaker. Home: 604 Phoenixville Rd Chaplin CT 06235-2211 Office: U Conn Media Ctr # U-1 Storrs CT 06269

WOODARD, CAROL JANE, educational consultant; b. Buffalo, Jan. 19, 1929; d. Harold August and Violet Maybelle (Landsittel) Young; m. Ralph Arthur Woodard, Aug. 19, 1950; children: Camaron Jane, Carsen Jane, Cooper Ralph. BA, Hartwick Coll., 1950; MA, Syracuse U., 1952; PhD, SUNY, Buffalo, 1972; LHD (hon.), Hartwick Coll., 1991; postgrad., Bank St. Coll., Harvard U. Cert. tchr., N.Y. State. Tchr. Orchard Park, N.Y., 1950-51, Danville, Ind., 1951-52, Akron, N.Y., 1952-54; dir. Garden Nursery Sch., Williamsville, N.Y., 1955-65; tchr. Amherst (N.Y.) Coop. Nursery Sch., 1967-69; asst. prof. early childhood edn. SUNY, Buffalo, 1969-72; lab. demonstration tchr. and student teaching supr. SUNY, 1969-76, assoc. prof., 1972-79, prof., 1979-88, prof. emeritus, 1988—; co-dir. Consultants in Early Childhood, 1988—; cons. Lutheran Ch. Am., Villa Maria Coll., Buffalo Pub. Schs., Buffalo Mus. Sci., Headstart Tng. Programs, Erie Community Coll., N.Y. State Dept. Edn., numerous workshops.; cons. sch. systems, indsl. firms, pubs., civic orgns. in child devel.; vis. prof. The Netherlands and East China Univ., Shanghai, People's Republic of China; sci. trainer The Wright Group, 1995. Author 7 books for young children, 2 textbooks in field; co-author: Physical Science in Early Childhood, 1987; co-author nat. curriculum for ch. sch. for 3-yr.-olds; author: (booklet) You Can Help Your Baby Learn; author/coord. TAKE CARE child protection project, 1987; contbr. chpts. to books, articles to profl. jours. Trustee Hartwick Coll., Oneonta, N.Y., 1978-87; cons. EPIC Birth to Three Program, 1992; design cons. indoor playground Noah's Ark Jewish Ctr., Buffalo, 1992; Sites Project coord. Buffalo Pub. Schs., 1994-96; student tchg. supervisor SUNY, Fredonia, 1994—. Mem. Nat. Assn. Edn. Young Children, Early Childhood Edn. Council Western N.Y., Assn. Childhood Edn. Internat., Phi Delta Kappa, Pi Lambda Theta. Home: 1776 Sweet Rd East Aurora NY 14052-3028

WOODARD, CLARA VERONICA, nursing home official; b. Bayonne, N.J.; d. William George and Lula (Langston) Yelverton; m. John Henry Woodard; children: John Michael, Stephen Jay. Grad., Bayonne Hosp. Sch. Nursing, 1951, Manhattan Sch. Radiology, 1953, NYU-Bellevue Med. Ctr., 1955, Valencia Community Coll., Orlando, Fla. RN, N.J., Fla. Head nurse Bayonne Hosp., 1949-50; office nurse Dr. D.G. Morris, Bayonne, 1951-52; pvt. duty nurse Christ Hosp and Bayonne Hosp., 1954-58; tchr. kindergarten, Nuremburg, Fed. Republic Germany, 1972-73; ICU-CCU nurse Holy Spirit Hosp., Camp Hill, Pa., 1973-74; head nurse Orlando Gen. Hosp., 1974-76, house supr., 1976-78; dir. nurses Winter Park (Fla.) Care Ctr., 1980-83; Medicare coord. Pinar Terrace Manor, Orlando, 1987-92, clin. instr., 1992—, house supr., nurse mgr. Alzheimer unit, 1993—; instr. Valencia Coll., Orlando, Fla. Named Employee of Yr. and Employee of Month, Orlando Gen. Hosp., 1980, Employee of Month, Winter Park Care Ctr., 1983. Mem. NAFE, Nat. League Negro Women. Democrat. Roman Catholic. Home: 2931 De Brocy Way Winter Park FL 32792-4505 Office: Pinar Terrace Manor 7950 Lake Underhill Rd Orlando FL 32822-8229

WOODARD, DOROTHY MARIE, insurance broker; b. Houston, Feb. 7, 1932; d. Gerald Edgar and Bessie Katherine (Crain) Floeck; student N.Mex. State U., 1950; m. Jack W. Woodard, June 19, 1950 (dec.); m. Norman W. Libby, July 19, 1982 (dec. Dec. 1991). Ptnr. Western Oil Co., Tucumcari, N.Mex., 1950—; owner, mgr. Woodard & Co., Las Cruces, N.Mex., 1959-67; agt., dist. mgr. United Nations Ins. Co., Denver, 1968-74; agt. Western Nat. Life Ins. Co., Amarillo, Tex., 1976—. Exec. dir. Tucumcari Indsl. Commn., 1979—; dir. Bravo Dome Study Com., 1979—; owner Libby Cattle Co., Libby Ranch Co.; regional bd. dirs. N.Mex., Eastern Plains Council Govts., 1979—. Mem. NAFE, Tucumcari C. of C., Mesa Country Club. Home: PO Box 823 Tucumcari NM 88401-0823

WOODARD, LISA BETH, legal assistant, ballet dancer; b. Syracuse, N.Y., June 1, 1966; d. Richard Charles and Elizabeth Dorothy (Vanderpool) W. BA in Psychology, Am. History, William Smith Coll., 1988. Rsch. asst. Alumni House Hobart & William Smith Colls., Geneva, N.Y., 1985-88; case clk. Morrison & Foerster, San Francisco, 1987, legal asst., 1988-90; legal asst. Milberg, Weiss, Bershad Hynes & Lerach, San Diego, 1990-96, Milberg, Weiss, Bershad Haynes & Lerach, San Francisco, 1996—; ballet dancer Mirabilé Ballet Co., Lemon Grove, Calif., 1994-96. Performed with Boston Ballet, with mems. of Pitts. Ballet, Am. Ballet Theatre, Nat. Ballet Can.; co-editor B.C. Scoop newspaper, 1989-90. Bd. dirs. Cmty. Arts Adv. Coun., Lemon Grove, 1995-96; admissions vol., 1988 class agt. William Smith Coll., 1988—. Mem. San Diego Assn. Legal Assts. Office: Milberg Weiss Bershad Hynes 10th Fl 222 Kearney St San Francisco CA 94122

WOODARD, NINA ELIZABETH, banker; b. L.A., Apr. 3, 1947; d. Alexander Rhodes and Harriette Jane (Power) Mathews; divorced; children: Regina M., James D. Grad. Pacific Coast Banking Sch., 1987; BS in mgmt., Calif. Coast U., 1993; postgrad., Ctr. for Creative Leadership, 1994. Lifetime cert. sr. profl. in human resources. Dental asst. Donald R. Shire DDS, L.A., 1965-66; with Security Pacific Nat. Bank, Marina Del Rey, Calif., 1968-69; with First Interstate Bank, Casper, Wyo., 1971—, adminstr. asst. personnel, 1975-78, asst. v.p., asst. mgr. pers., 1978-82, v.p., dir. mktg. and pers., 1982-84, v.p., mgr. human resources, 1984-88; v.p., mgr. employee rels. First Interstate Bank Ltd., L.A., 1988-93, v.p. mgr. employee rels. Americas Region, Standard Charter Bank, 1993—, sr. v.p., 1995; instr. mktg. Am. Inst. Banking, 1983, Casper Coll., 1982. Mem. Civil Svc. Commn., City of Casper, 1983-88; bd. dirs. YMCA, 1984-87, Downtown Devel. Assn.; pres. Downtown Casper Assn. Named Bus. Woman of Yr., Bus. and Profl. Women, 1982, Young Career Woman, 1975. Mem. Nat. Assn. Bank Women, Bus. and Profl. Women (dist. dir.), Am. Soc. Pers. Adminstrn. (regional v.p., state coun. Wyo. 1987-88), Pers. and Indsl. Rels. Assn. (chmn. govt. affairs com. 1989-90, Fast Track award 1991, Pres.'s Achievement award 1993, conf. chmn. 1991, 92, dist. vice chair 1992, dist. chair 1993, 2d v.p. 1994), Fin. Women Internat. (Wyo. state chair 1986, regional edn. and tng. chair 1987, dist. coord. L.A. 1993, L.A. group chair 1994), Soc. Human Resource Mgmt. (area I v.p. 1996), St. Patrick's Parish Religious Edn. (instr. 1991-92, parish coun. 1993-94). Republican. Roman Catholic.

WOODEN, REBA FAYE BOYD, guidance counselor; b. Washington, Ind., Sept. 21, 1940; d. Lester E. and Opal M. (Burch) Boyd; m. N. Nuel Wooden, Jr., Dec. 23, 1962 (div. 1993); children: Jeffrey Nuel, Cynthia Faye. BA, U. Indpls., 1962; MS, Butler U., 1968, Ind. U., 1990. Cert. tchr., counselor, Ind. Tchr. Mooresville (Ind.) High Sch., 1962-66; tchr. Perry Meridian High Sch., Indpls., 1974-92, counselor, 1992—; part-time instr. Ind. U.-Purdue U. at Indpls., 1994-95. Named Outstanding High Sch. Psychology tchr. APA, 1987. Mem. NEA, Ind. State Tchrs. Assn., Perry Edn. Assn. Methodist. Home: 113 Severn Dr Greenwood IN 46142-1880 Office: Perry Meridian High Sch 401 W Meridian School Rd Indianapolis IN 46217-4215

WOODFORD, BETSY CLARK, public relations professional, consultant; b. Pasadena, Calif., Feb. 2, 1954; d. Robert Spears and Eleanor LaRose (Clark) W.; children: Scott Wesley Hatch, Emily Woodford Hatch. BS, Calif. State U., L.A., 1976; postgrad., U. So. Calif., L.A. Geophysicist Unocal, L.A., 1978-86; freelance writer Arcadia, Calif., 1980-86; pub. rels. writer Calif. Inst. Tech., Pasadena, 1989—; rschr. on pub. rels. for nonprofit and self-employed, Arcadia, Calif., 1995; bd. dirs. Caltech Women's Ctr., Pasadena, seminar leader, 1995. Columnist Quilting Today, 1985-87. Svc. unit mgr. Mt. Wilson Vista coun. Girl Scouts U.S., leader, 1991-95, comms. cons., 1995, dir. pride-bldg. events, 1992-95; leader Boy Scouts Am., Arcadia, 1989-90; writer, prodr. awards show Camino Grove PTA, 1989-95; life mem. Calif. State PTA, 1994. Recipient Cmty. Svc. award Girl Scouts-Mt. Wilson Vista Coun., 1992, 95; grantee Berger Found., 1991. Republican. Office: Pub Rels 1-71 Calif Inst Tech Pasadena CA 91125

WOODFORD, MARY IMOGENE STEELE, secondary school educator; b. Balt., Jan. 7, 1919; d. Percy Howard and Mary Imogene (Waring) Steele; m. Hackley Elbridge Woodford, June 7, 1940; children: Peggy, John, Joan, Barbara. BA, Howard U., 1940; MA, U. Chgo., 1960. Tchr. Benton Harbor (Mich.) Schs., 1960-70; tchr. Jr. and Sr. H.S., Pasadena, Calif., 1971-75, L.A., 1975-84. Bd. dirs. Girl Scouts of U.S., Benton Harbor, Mich., 1947-50; mem. Ys Neighbors, YWCA, Benton Harbor, 1947-70. Recipient scholarship Lotta Crabtree Estate, Wayland, Boston 1936; named Mother of Yr. Mem. AAUW, Tuskegee Airmen Inc. (membership chair 1995, 96), The Links, Inc. (Mothr of Yr. 1994). Democrat. Presbyterian. Home: 16071 Avenida Lamego San Diego CA 92128

WOODHULL, NANCY JANE, foundation executive; b. Perth Amboy, N.J., Mar. 1, 1945; d. Harold and May (Post) Cromwell; m. William Douglass Watson, Sept. 24, 1976; 1 child, Tennessee Jane. Student, Trenton State Tchrs. Coll., 1963-64. Dept. editor News Tribune, Woodbridge, N.J., 1964-73; reporter Detroit Free Press, 1973-75; mng. editor Times-Union, Rochester, N.Y., 1975-80, Democrat & Chronicle, Rochester, 1980-82; mng. editor USA Today, Arlington, Va., 1982-83, sr. editor, 1983-87; pres. Gannett New Media, Washington, 1986-90, Gannett News Svc., Washington, 1988-90; exec. v.p., editor-in-chief So. Living Mags., Birmingham, Ala., 1990-92; pres. Nancy Woodhull & Assoc., Inc., Washington and Pittsford, N.Y., 1991-96; scholar-in-residence U. Rochester, N.Y., 1992-96; chmn. bd. Peabody Radio and TV awards; trustee The Freedom Forum, 1989-96; co-chair Women, Men & Media, Washington, 1989—; mem. adv. bd. New Direction For News U. Mo., 1989—; mem., pres. Nat. Women's Hall of Fame, Seneca Falls, N.Y., 1990-96, chair adv. bd., 1996—; mem. adv. bd. Knight Ctr. for Specialized Journalism U. Md., 1993—; vice chair Internat. Women's Media Found., Washington, 1996—; exec. dir. Media Studies Ctr., N.Y., 1996—; sr. v.p. The Freedom Forum, Arlington, Va., 1996—. Office: Media Studies Ctr 580 Madison Ave New York NY 10022

WOODHULL, PATRICIA ANN, artist; b. Gary, Ind., Nov. 24, 1924; d. John Joseph and Georgia Mildred (Voorhis) Harding; m. Bradley Allen Woodhull, May 8, 1948; children: Leslie, Marcia, Clarisse. BS in Clothing Design, Purdue U., 1946; life teaching credential, Calif. State U., Fullerton, 1978. Social worker County Dept. Lake County and Bartholomew County, Gary and Columbus, Ind., 1946-50; home demonstrator Pub. Svc. Co. Ind., Columbus, 1950-53; substitute tchr. Fullerton (Calif.) H.S. Dist., 1968-73; children's art and drama tchr. Fullerton Cmty. Svcs., 1973-85; children's pvt. art tchr. Fullerton, 1990-93; art tchr. Montessori Sch., Fullerton, 1990-91; art/drama tchr. creative arts program Fullerton Pub. Schs., 1972-89; founder, dir. Players Improv Theatre Group, Fullerton, Calif. One woman shows include Fullerton City Libr., 1992, William Carlos Gallery, Fullerton , 1992, 93, Whittier (Calif.) City Hall, 1993, Muckinthaler Ctr., Fullerton, 1993, Brookhurst Ctr., Anaheim, 1993, Whitier Libr. Show, 1994; exhibited in group shows at Whittier Art Gallery, 1991, Hillcrest Art Show, Creative Arts Ctr., Burbank, Calif., 1991, Bidge Gallery City Hall, L.A., 1992, The Art Store, Fullerton, 1992, Women Painters West, 1993, New England Fine Arts Inst., Boston, 1993; represented in pvt. collections. Recipient Spl. award Orange County Fair, Costa Mesa (Calif.) County Fair, 1985; 3rd pl. award Hillcrest Whittier (Calif.) Show, 1990, 2nd award West Coast Collage Show, Lancaster, Calif., 1989, Evelyn Nunn Miller award Women Painters West, Torrance, Calif., 1994. Mem. Nat. League Am. Pen Women (pres. Orange County 1993), Women Painters West, Pan Hellenic Orange County (pres. 1994), Alpha Chi Omega (pres. local chpt. 1993). Republican. Home: 1519 E Harmony Ln Fullerton CA 92631-2015

WOODRING, MARGARET DALEY, architect, planner; b. N.Y.C., Mar. 29, 1933; d. Joseph Michael and Mary (Barron) Daley; m. Francis Woodring, Oct. 25, 1954 (div. 1962); m. Robert Bell, Dec. 20, 1971; children: Ward, Lissa, Gabrielle, Phaedra. Student, NYU, 1959-60; BArch, Columbia U., 1966; MArch, Princeton U., 1971. Registered architect; cert. planner. Architect, planner various firms, N.Y.C.; environ. design specialist Rutgers U., New Brunswick, N.J., 1966-68; programming cons. Davis & Brody, N.Y.C., 1968-71; planning cons. William H. Liskamm, San Francisco, 1971-74; mgr. planning Met. Transp. Commn., Oakland, Calif., 1974-81; dir. Internat. Program for Housing and Urban Devel. Ofcls. Ctr. for Environ. Design Rsch. U. Calif., Berkeley, 1981-89; prin. Woodring & Assocs., San Rafael, Calif., 1989—; adj. lectr. dept. architecture U. Calif., Berkeley, 1974-84; founder New Horizons Savs. Assn., San Rafael, 1977-79; cons. U.S. Agy. for Internat. Devel., Washington, 1981-89; mem. jury Nat. Endowment Arts, others. Chair Bicentennial Com., San Rafael, 1976; bd. dirs. Displaced Homemakers Ctr., Oakland, 1981-84; pres. Environ Design Found., San Francisco, 1984-90. William Kinne Travel fellow Columbia U., 1965-66; Richard King Mellon fellow Princeton U., 1968-70. Mem. AIA (chair urban design com. San Francisco chpt. 1980-81), Am. Inst. Cert. Planners, Urban Land Inst., Soc. for Internat. Devel. (pres. San Francisco chpt. 1980-83), World Affairs Coun., Internat. World Congress on Land Policy. Home: 226 Magnolia Ave San Rafael CA 94901-2244 Office: Woodring & Assocs 938 B St San Rafael CA 94901-3005

WOODRUFF, DEBRA A., occupational health nurse; b. Salem, Ill., Dec. 22, 1952; d. Merle D. and Georgia Lee (Johnson) Anderson; m. Thomas E. Howarth, June 16, 1973 (div. Sept. 1979; 1 child, Michael T. Diploma in Practical Nursing, Vo-Tech Teche Area, New Iberia, La., 1972; ADN, Miss. Delta Jr. Coll., Moorhead, 1975. LPN, La.; cert. occupl. health nurse. LPN in ICU Iberia Gen. Hosp., New Iberia, 1972-73, head nurse ICU, 1979-81; charge nurse infection control Bolivar County Hosp., Cleveland, Miss., 1973-79, dir. long-term care, 1981-89; sr. indsl. nurse Baxter Healthcare Corp., Cleveland, 1989—. Mem. Am. Assn. Occupl. Health Nurses, Miss. Assn. Occupl. Health Nurses. Republican. Baptist. Office: Baxter Healthcare Corp 911 N Davis Ave Cleveland MS 38732-2106

WOODRUFF, DOLORES ANNE, business educator, accountant; b. Woodward, Okla., Feb. 15, 1953; d. Robert Ian and Rose Marie Smith; m. Danny Wade Woodruff, Dec. 17, 1977; children: Tyler Wade, Chase Bradon, Paige Nicole. BBA, U. Okla., 1975; tchg. cert., Northwestern Okla. State U., 1989. Auditor Haskins & Sells, Tulsa, 1976-77; acct., sec. H & H Oilfield Svcs., Woodward, Okla., 1979-84; acct. D W Enterprises, Woodward, 1978—; bus. tchr. Woodward H.S., 1990—; clubs sponsor Woodward H.S., 1990—, com. mem., 1990—; mem. tech. com. Woodward Pub. Schs., 1996; v.p. Woodward H.S. Alumni, 1982, 86. Mem. parish coun. St. Peter's Cath. Ch., 1996—; mem. Cedar Heights PTA, Woodward, 1986-95, pres., 1987-88. Mem. NEA, Okla. Bus. Edn. Assn., Okla. Edn. Assn., Alpha Gamma (pres., sec., treas., social chmn. 1979—). Office: Woodward H S 13th and Downs Woodward OK 73801

WOODRUFF, FAY, paleoceanographer, geological researcher; b. Boston, Jan. 23, 1944; d. Lorande Mitchell and Anne (Fay) W.; m. Alexander Whitehill Clowes, May 20, 1972 (div. Oct. 1974); m. Robert G. Douglas, Jan. 27, 1980; children: Ellen, Katerina. RN, Mass. Gen. Hosp. Sch. Nursing, Boston, 1965; BA, Boston U., 1971; MS, U. So. Calif., 1979. Rsch. assoc. U. So. Calif., L.A., 1978-81, rsch. faculty, 1981-96; keynote spkr. 4th Internat. Symposium on Benthic Foraminifera, Sendai, Japan, 1990. Contbg. author: Geological Society of America Memoir, 1985; contbr. articles to profl. jours. Life mem. The Nature Conservancy, Washington, 1992; bd. dirs. Friends of Friendship Park, 1995-96. NSF grantee, 1986-88, 88-91, 91-94. Mem. Am. Geophys. Union, Geol. Soc. Am., Internat. Union Geol. Scis. (internat. commn. on stratigraphy, subcommn. on Neogene stratigaphy 1991-92), Soc. Woman Geographers (sec. So. Calif. chpt. 1990-96), Soc. Econ. Paleontologists and Minerologists (sec., editor N.Am. Micropaleontology sect. 1988-90), Oceanography Soc. (chpt. mem.), Sigma Xi. Episcopalian. Office: U So Calif Dept Geol Scis Los Angeles CA 90089-0740

WOODRUFF, JUDY CARLINE, broadcast journalist; b. Tulsa, Nov. 20, 1946; d. William Henry and Anna Lee (Payne) W.; m. Albert R. Hunt, Jr., Apr. 5, 1980; children: Jeffrey Woodruff, Benjamin Woodruff, Lauren Ann Lee. Student, Meredith Coll., 1964-66; B.A., Duke U., 1968. News announcer, reporter Sta. WAGA-TV, Atlanta, 1970-75; news corr. NBC News, Atlanta, 1975-76; White House corr. NBC News, Washington, 1977-83; anchor Frontline, PBS documentary series, 1983-90; corr. MacNeil-Lehrer News Hour, PBS, Washington, 1983-93; anchor and sr. corr. CNN, Washington, 1993—; mem. bd. advisors Henry Grady Sch. Journalism, U. Ga., 1979-82; bd. visitors Wake Forest U., 1982-89; mem. bd. advisors Benton Fellowship in Broadcast Journalism, U. Chgo., 1984-90, Knight Fellowship in Journalism, Stanford U., 1985—; trustee Duke U., 1985—; founding bd. dirs. Internat. Women's Media Found., 1989—. Author: This is Judy Woodruff at the White House, 1982. Mem. Commn. on Women's Health, The Commonwealth Fund. Recipient award Leadership Atlanta, Class of 1974, Atlanta chpt. Women in Comms., 1975, Edward Weintal award for excellence in fgn. policy reporting, 1987, Joan Shorenstein Barone award for series on def. issues, 1987, Helen Bernstein award for excellence in journalism N.Y. Pub. Libr., 1989, Pres.'s award Nat. Women's Hall of Fame, 1994, CableAce award for best newscaster, 1995, Allen H. Neuharth award for excellence in journalism, 1995. Mem. NATAS (Atlanta chpt. Emmy award 1975), White House Corrs. Assn. Office: Cable News Network 820 1st St NE Washington DC 20002-4243

WOODRUFF, KATHRYN ELAINE, English educator; b. Ft. Stockton, Tex., Oct. 12, 1940; d. James Arthur and Catherine H. (Stevens) Borron; m. Thomas Charles Woodruff, May 18, 1969; children: Robert Borron, David Borron. BA, Our Lady of the Lake U., San Antonio, 1963; MFA, U. Alaska, 1969; PhD, U. Denver, 1987. Cert. tchr., Tex. English and journalism tchr. Owensboro (Ky.) Cath. High Sch., 1963-64, Grand Junction (Colo.) Dist. 12, 1964-66; English tchr. Monroe High Sch., Fairbanks, Alaska, 1966-67; teaching asst. U. Alaska, Fairbanks, 1967-69, instr., 1969-70; instr. U. Colo., Boulder, 1979, Denver, 1988-89; instr. Regis Coll., Denver, 1987-89; asst. prof. Econs. Inst., Boulder, 1990-93; asst. prof. English Colo. Christian U., Lakewood, 1994—; tchr. Upward Bound, Fairbanks, 1968; instr. ethnic and women writers course U. Colo., Denver, 1986-93; mem. Assoc. Writing Programs; soprano Boulder Chorale, Cantabile Singers. Author: (poetry) Before the Burning, 1994; poetry readings in Colo., Tex. and Paris. Friend Chautauqua Music Festival, Boulder, 1985—; dir. 12th Annual Arts Festival, Fairbanks, 1969. Named one of Outstanding Young Women Am., 1966. Mem. AAUW, MLA, Soc. Internat. Devel. UN Assn., Tchrs. English to Speakers of Other Langs., Colo. Tchrs. English to Speakers of Other Langs. Democrat. Mem. Christian Ch. Office: Colo Christian U 180 S Garrison St Lakewood CO 80226-7499

WOODRUFF, MARSHA CHOATE, lawyer; b. Searcy, Ark., Dec. 23, 1953; d. Oscar Lee and Marliss Faye Choate; m. Ronald G. Woodruff, Nov. 11, 1979; children: Logan, Leigh. BA, U. Ark., 1975, JD, 1978. Bar: Ark.; ordained elder First United Presbyn., 1988. Sec. Bill Clinton, Fayetteville, Ark., 1975-76, U. Ark. Athletic Dept., Fayetteville, 1976-78; instr. U. Ark., Fayetteville, 1979-90; pvt. practice Berling & Fayetteville, Fayetteville, 1978-81, Pearson Woodruff and Evans, Fayetteville, 1981-89, Woodruff Law Firm, Fayetteville, 1989—. Bd. dirs. Vera Lloyd Home, Monticello, Ark., 1990—; del. Ark. Dem. Conv., Little Rock, 1992, 96. Mem. Ark. Bar Assn. (ho. of dels. 1995—), Wash. County Bar Assn., Am. Trial Lawyers Assn., Ark. Trial Lawyers Assn. Democrat. Presbyterian. Office: Woodruff Law Firm PO Box 1866 34 E Center Fayetteville AR 72702

WOODRUFF, WANDA LEA, elementary education educator; b. Woodward, Okla., May 2, 1937; d. Milton Casper and Ruth Arlene (Bradshaw) Shuck; m. William Jennings Woodruff, Aug. 18, 1962; children: Teresa Kaye, Bruce Alan, Neal Wayne. BS, Northwestern State U., 1959; MA in Edn., Olivet Nazarene U., 1973. Cert. K-8th grade tchr. 2d grade tchr. Anthony (Kans.) Pub. Schs., 1959-60, transition class tchr., 1960-61, 1st grade tchr., 1961-62; 5th grade tchr. Versailles (Ky.) Pub. Schs., 1962-63; 1st grade tchr. Bradley (Ill.) Elem. Schs., 1968-93; presch. vol. Concern Ctr., Bartlesville, Okla., 1994—. Com. chmn. Bus. and Profl. Women, Anthony, 1959-62; sec. com. PTA, Anthony, 1959-63, Bradley (Ill.) PTA, 1968-93. Recipient grant for edn. First of Am. Bank, 1991-92, 92-93. Mem. Bartlesville Pilot Club Internat. (edn./patriotism chairperson 1994-95, dir. 1995-96, mem. com. Spl. Olympics 1995-96, pres-elect 1996—). Home: 2373 Mountain Dr Bartlesville OK 74003-6926

WOODRUM, PATRICIA ANN, librarian; b. Hutchinson, Kans., Oct. 11, 1941; d. Donald Jewell and Ruby Pauline (Shuman) Hoffman; m. Clayton Eugene Woodrum, Mar. 31, 1962; 1 child, Clayton Eugene, II. BA, Kans. State Coll., Pittsburg, 1963; MLS, U. Okla., 1966. Br. libr. Tulsa City-County Libr. System, 1964-65, head brs., 1965-66, head reference dept., 1966-67, chief extension, chief pub. svc., 1967-73, asst. dir., 1973-76, exec. dir., 1976—; bd. dirs. Local Am. Bank Tulsa. Mem. editorial bd. Jour. of Library Administration. Active Friends of Tulsa Libr., Leadership Tulsa Alumni; regent UCT/RSC, Tulsa. Recipient Disting. Libr. award Okla. Libr. Assn., 1982, Leadership Tulsa Paragon award, 1987, Women in Comm. Newsmaker award, 1989, Outstanding Alumnus award U. Okla. Sch. Libr. Info. Studies, 1989, Headliner award Tulsa Press Club, 1996; inducted into Tulsa City-County Libr. Hall of Fame, 1989, Okla. Womens Hall of Fame, 1993, Mem. ALA, Pub. Libr. Assn. (pres. 1993-94), Okla. Libr. Assn. (pres. 1978-79, Disting. Libr. award 1982, Meritorious Svc. award 1996), Tulsa C. of C. Democrat. Episcopalian. Office: Tulsa City-County Libr 400 Civic Ctr Tulsa OK 74103-3857

WOODS, BARBARA A. SHELL, psychotherapist; b. Banner Elk, N.C., June 11, 1939; d. Oscar Ketron and Mamie Maruja (Perry) Shell; m. James Wesley Woods, May 7, 1966; children: Jonathan Scott, Eric Jason. BS in Bus. Mgmt., East Tenn. State U., 1961; MA in Counseling and Devel., George Mason U., 1983, postgrad., 1985-88. Cert. clin. mental health counselor, mediator, Va.; nat. cert. counselor, nat. cert. career counselor; lic. profl. counselor, Va. Office asst. vet. affairs East Tenn. State U., Johnson City, 1958-61; sec. purchasing dept. U. Tenn., Knoxville, 1961-62; social worker I and II Tenn. Welfare Dept., Knoxville, 1962-66; daycare coord. Econ. Opportunity of Atlanta, 1966-67; child welfare worker Forsyth County Dept. of Welfare, Winston Salem, N.C., 1967-68; dir., tchr. Woodland Pre-Sch., Alexandria, Va., 1975-78; pers. mgmt. Woodward & Lothrup, Tyson's Corner, Va., 1983; career coord. Nat. Bd. for Cert. Counselors, Alexandria, 1984; counselor, trainer The Women's Ctr. of Northern Va., Vienna, Va., 1985-90; counseling dir. The Women's Health Connection, Vienna, 1990-92; trainer, counselor City of Falls Ch. Youth At Risk Program, Falls Church, 1993-94; dir./owner Change & Growth Consulting, Tyson's Corner and Woodbridge, Va., 1984—. Zoning chairperson West Springfield (Va.) Civic Assn., 1980-82; citizen mem. Fairfax County Citizens Planning Task Force, Springfield, 1979-82. Scholarship Am. Legion, 1957. Mem. ACA, No. Va. Chpt. clin. Counselors (chairperson 1990-92, Appreciation award 1992), Va. Clin. Counselor (regional rep. 1990-92), Nat. EAP Assn. (sec. 1989-90), Met. Area Career/Life Planning Network (founder, Appreciation award 1985), Va. Counselors Assn. Methodist. Office: Change and Growth Cons 1334 G St Woodbridge VA 22191-1603

WOODS, BERNICE IRENE, graphics specialist, small business owner; b. Bristol, Tenn., Feb. 15, 1956; d. Walter Edward Jr. and Mary Jane (Fleenor) Guinn; m. Robert Millard Morton, June 9, 1977 (div. Aug. 1985); m. Onzie Gene Woods, Oct. 4, 1990; 1 child, Stacey Renée Woods. AS in Legal Secretarial, Bristol Comml. Coll., 1977; BS in Bus. Adminstrn. cum laude, Bristol Coll., 1984. Legal sec. Penn, Stuart, Eskridge & Jones, Abingdon, Va., 1976; office mgr., legal sec. Jim Bates, Esq., Blountville, Tenn., 1977-78; graphics specialist Eastman Chem. Co., Kingsport, Tenn., 1978—; owner Enchanted Woods, Kingsport, Tenn., 1995—. Designer T-shirts, displays, brochures Northeast Tenn. chpt. Am. Chem. Soc., Kingsport, 1993-96; contbr. articles to profl. jours. Vol. United Way Greater Kingsport, 1988-89, Johnson City (Tenn.) Suzuki Assn., 1994—, Am. Heart Assn., 1996; bd. dirs., entertainment dir. Sonrise Emmaus Cmty, Kingsport, 1994-95; mem. Miller-Perry PTA, 1996—; Art Fair Com. mem., 1996—; chairperson Suzuki Sch. Music Fundraising com., 1996—. Mem. Profl. Picture Framers Assn., Crossings Golf Assn., Suzuki Assn. Am. Home: 405 Heatherview Ct Kingsport TN 37663 Office: Eastman Chem Co PO Box 1972 Kingsport TN 37662

WOODS, CYNDY JONES, junior high educator, researcher; b. Phoenix, Oct. 26, 1954; d. Glenn Billy and Helen Marie (Harrison) Jones; m. Clifford R. Woods, Apr. 3, 1975; children: Sean, Kathleen, Connor. AA in English, St. John's Coll., 1974; BA in English, Ariz. State U., 1992, M in Secondary Edn., 1994. Cert. secondary tchr., c.c. instr., Ariz. Tchr. grades 6-8 John R. Davis Sch., Phoenix, 1993; tchr. grade 7 Thomas J. Pappas Sch., Phoenix, 1994—; adj. faculty English and lit. Rio Salado C.C., 1995—; treas. Martin Luther Sch. Bd., Phoenix, 1985-89; presenter in field. Contbr. poetry to anthologies Dance on the Horizons, 1993, The Sound of Poetry: Best Poems of 1995, Across the Universe, 1996; contbr. articles to profl. jours. Mem. St. Francis Xavier Sch. Bd., Phoenix, 1995; v.p. City/County Child Care Bd., Phoenix, 1988-92; youth group advisor Mt. Calvary Luth. Ch., Phoenix, 1988-96. Mem. Ariz. Edn. Assn., Brophy Coll. Prep. Mother's Guild, Xavier Coll. Prep. Mother's Guild. Democrat. Home: P O Box 27575 Phoenix AZ 85061 Office: Thomas J Pappas Sch 413 N 7th Ave Phoenix AZ 85007

WOODS, DARLENE JUDITH, counselor; b. Mankato, Minn., Sept. 1, 1945; d. David Edmund and Hilda Elizabeth (Hanel) W.; children: Grant David King, Graham Arnold King, Crystal Grace King, Ginger Elizabeth Graham. BS, Mankato State U., 1993, MS, 1996. Career counselor grad. asst. Mankato (Minn.) State U., 1993-95; career counselor intern St. Olaf Coll., Northfield, Minn., 1995-96; career counselor Gustavus Adolphus Coll., St. Peter, Minn., 1995-96. Participant Adopt-A-Hwy., Mankato, 1995; donor Sharing Tree, Mankato, 1995. Keith La Vake scholar Counseling and Student Pers., Mankato State U., 1995. Mem. ACA, Nat. Employment Counselors Assn., Career Devel. Counseling Assn., Am. Assn. Christian Counselors, Minn. Assn. for Counseling and Devel., Minn. Career Devel. Assn.

WOODS, DONNA SUE, education educator, reading consultant, state agency administrator; b. Springhill, La., Jan. 15, 1954; children: Klaten A., Matthew M., Laura E., Gabriele E. BA, La. Tech U., 1975; MEd, La. State U., 1983; EdD, Okla. State U., 1992. Cert. English, social studies, gifted edn. tchr., La.; cert. English, gifted edn. and reading tchr., Okla. Tchr. English, Grawood (La.) Christian Schs., 1979-80; tchr. spl. edn. Bossier Parish Sch. Bd., Benton, La., 1981-83, curriculum developer, 1990; tchr. gifted Curtis Elem. Sch., Bossier City, La., 1983-88; tchr. lang. arts Elm Grove (La.) Jr. High Sch., 1988-90; teaching asst., univ. rep. Okla. entry yr. assistance Okla. State U., Stillwater, 1990-92, co-dir., instr. 13th ann. reading workshop, 1991, instr. Coll. Vet. Medicine, 1991, developer, dir. student tchr. seminar, 1992; asst. prof. Coll. Edn. Northwestern Okla. State U., Alva, 1992-95; dir. reading and literacy Okla. State Dept. Edn., Oklahoma City, 1995—; adj. instr. Oklahoma City C.C., 1991-92, U. Okla., 1995—; dir. Okla. Nat. Young Readers' Day, 1994, 95-96; presenter in field. Tutor YWCA, Shreveport, La., 1975; supt. youth Sun. schs. 1st Presbyn. Ch., Edmond, Okla., 1991, youth choir dir., 1994—, youth handbells dir., 1995—. Named Favorite Tchr. of Yr., Bossier C. of C., 1987; Centennial scholar Okla. State U. Coll. Edn. Alumni Assn., 1992. Mem. Internat. Reading Assn. (conf. presenter 1996), Okla. Reading Assn. (conf. presenter 1993—), Okla. Early Childhood Tchrs. Assn. (conf. presenter 1991), Alpha Upsilon Alpha (faculty sponsor 1994-95), Kappa Delta Pi, Phi Delta Kappa. Republican. Home: 777 E 15th St #160 Edmond OK 73013

WOODS, DORRIS STUBBS, health sciences consultant; b. Magee, Miss., Nov. 20, 1938; d. Leo and Ethelene (McLaurin) Stubbsa; m. Burton Leon Woods, Aug. 21, 1965; children: April, Brian, Brannon. BS in Nursing and Psychology, Ind. U.; M Nursing, UCLA, 1978, UCLA, 1987; MS in Counseling, Calif. State U., L.A., 1985; PhD, Claremont Grad. Sch., 1990; BS in Humanities (hon.), SUNY, Albany, 1995. RN, Calif. Adminstrv. supr. Children's Meml. Hosp., Chgo., 1961-64; unit coord. Bloomington (Ind.) Hosp., 1964-66; head nurse Brotman Med. Ctr., Culver City, Calif., 1966-69; presch. dir. Woods' Early Enrichment Ctr., L.A., 1969-78; instr. Hamilton H.S., L.A., 1978-79, L.A. C.C., 1980-89; assoc. prof. L.A. Pierce Coll., Woodland Hills, Calif., 1989-95; prof. health scis. Calif. State U., Northridge, 1995—; cons. Kaiser Counseling and Learning Ctr., L.A, 1985—; dir. tech. prep. program L.A. Pierce Coll., 1992-94; founder, CEO Parent Involvement in Edn., L.A., 1996—; prin. investigator adolescent suicide study Ednl. Testing Svc. Conf. on Adolescence, 1990. Author: (poetry) Spirit of the Age, 1996 (award); contbr. articles to jours. Mem. cmty. adv. bd. Santa Monica, 1991—, mentor Successful Young Women program, 1996—; precinct officer Registrar of Voters, L.A., 1992-94; mentor Women in Cmty. Svc. program L.A. Job Corp. Ctr., L.A., 1996. Grad. fellow Claremont Grad. Sch., 1988, UCLA postdoctoral fellow, 1990-91. Mem. NAFE, AAUW, UCLA Alumni Assn., Phi Lambda Theta. Democrat. Methodist. Home: 1431 Stradella Rd Los Angeles CA 90077 Office: Woods' Ednl Svcs PO Box 2239 Los Angeles CA 90049

WOODS, ELEANOR C., music educator; b. Stamford, Conn., Oct. 30, 1939; d. Richard and Anna Marie (Feldtmose) Cunliffe; m. David R. Woods, Aug. 18, 1962; children: Richard, Laurie. BA, Smith Coll., 1961; MAT, Yale U., 1962. String tchr., music tchr. Kariat Jr. High Sch., Spring Valley, N.Y., 1962-65; musich tchr. Flint Hill Sch., Fairfax, Va., 1966-68; violin tchr. Am. U. Prep, Washington, 1972; pvt. instr. Washington, 1972—; violin tchr. Nat. Cathedral Sch., St. Albans, Washington, 1988—. Named Tchr. of Yr., Am. String Tchrs. Assn. of Md., 1993. Mem. Md. State Music Tchrs. Assn. (chmn., judge of competitions 1976—), Wash. Music Tchrs. Assn. (judge of competitions 1976—), Suzuki Assn. Am., Suzuki Assn. Greater Washington Area.

WOODS, GWENDOLYN ANNETTE, retired secondary education educator; b. Jacksonville, Ill., May 31, 1920; d. Robert L. and Genevieve L. (Dorsey) Brim; m. Mervin R. Woods, Aug. 20, 1943; children:Roger, Kristine Woods Camphouse, Kerry David, Loraine Woods Berquist. BA, Ill. Coll., Jacksonville, 1942. Cert. secondary tchr., Ill. Tchr. math., Latin, and phys. edn. Franklin (Ill.) High Sch., 1942-46; tchr. math., Latin, and French Perry (Ill.) High Sch., 1946-95. Leader Perry 4-H Stitchers, 1949—. Honored Citizen, Perry Pioneer Day Com., 1991. Mem. NEA, Nat. Coun. Math. Tchrs. , Ill. Edn. Assn., Perry PTA (past officer), Perry PTO, Am. Legion Aux. (past officer), Perry Garden Club (officer), DAR (regent Nancy Ross chpt. 1995—). Home: Box 65 201 N William Perry IL 62362

WOODS, HARRIETT RUTH, retired political organization president; b. Cleve., June 2, 1927; d. Armin and Ruth (Wise) Friedman; student U. Chgo., 1945; B.A., U. Mich., 1949; LLD (hon.) Webster U., 1988; m. James B. Woods, Jan. 2, 1953; children: Christopher, Peter, Andrew. Reporter, Chgo. Herald-Am., 1948, St. Louis Globe-Democrat, 1949-51; producer Star. KPLR-TV, St. Louis, 1964-74; moderator, writer Sta. KETC-TV, St. Louis, 1962-64; council mem. University City, Mo., 1967-74; mem. Mo. Hwy. Commn., 1974, Mo. Transp. Commn., 1974-76; mem. Mo. Senate, 1976-84, lt. gov. State of Mo., 1985-89; pres. Inst. for Policy Leadership, U. Mo., St. Louis, 1989-91; pres. Nat. Women's Polit. Caucus, 1991-95; dir. Federal Home Loan Mortgage Corp., 1995—; fellow inst. politics J.F. Kennedy Sch. Govt., Harvard U., 1988. Bd. dirs. LWV of Mo., 1963, Nat. League of Cities, 1972-74; Dem. nominee for U.S. Senate, 1982, 86. Jewish. Office: 1211 Connecticut Ave NW Washington DC 20036-2701

WOODS, JENNIFER LYNN, real estate broker, investments broker; b. Baytown, Tex., June 13, 1958. BS in Interior Architecture, U. Tex., 1982. Architect, space planner Trammell Crow Co., Austin, Tex., 1982-83; project architect, space planner Interior Cons., Inc., Austin, Tex., 1983-85; mktg. dir. Tipton Group of Tex., Dallas, 1985-86; nat. mktg. dir. Atlantic Pacific Realty & Investment Corp., San Antonio, Tex., 1986-88; archtl. programmer 3D/Internat., San Antonio, Tex., 1988-89; account exec. San Antonio Bus. Jour., Tex., 1990-92; sr. comml. assoc. Bradfield Comml., San Antonio, Tex., 1993-95; sr. assoc. Dominion Adv. Group, Inc., San Antonio, Tex., 1995—. Mem. Rep. Nat. Com., 1984—. Mem. Corporate Real Estate Svcs. Alliance, San Antonio Real Estate Coun., Urban Land Inst. (cert. comml. investment mem.), Real Estate Fin. Exec. Assn., Comml. Investment Real Estate Inst., Comml. Investment Divsn. (bd. govs.), San Antonio North C. of C., San Antonio Greater C. of C. Methodist. Office: Dominion Adv Group Inc 9862 Lorene # 115 San Antonio TX 78216

WOODS, MELISSA DIANNE, secondary education educator; b. Bellamy, Ala., July 14, 1957; d. Franklin Roosevelt and Willie Meaner (Smith) Evans; m. Fred Leon Woods, Feb. 17, 1994; children: Tamara, Kranse, Dakarai. AA, Mary Holmes Coll., 1977; BA, Talladega (Ala.) Coll., 1979. Receptionist Best Western Inn, Livingston, Ala., 1980-94; asst. libr. Ruby Pickens Tartt Pub. Libr., Livingston, 1983-93; tchr. Sumter Country Sch. System, Livingston, 1993—; advisor N. Sumter Jr. H.S. 4H Club, Panola, Ala., 1993-95, Honor Soc., 1994-95. Mem. Nat. Assn. Student Activity Advisors, Reston, Va. Baptist. Home: Rte 2 Box 115 Boligee AL 35443 Office: North Sumter Jr HS PO Box 98 Panola AL 35442

WOODS, MERILYN BARON, psychologist, consultant; b. Bklyn., July 8, 1927; d. David Theodore and Helen (Mintz) Baron; m. John Galloway Woods, Sept. 15, 1948; children: Anne Helen, Elizabeth Ruth. BS, Cornell U., 1948; MEd, Temple U., 1957; PhD, Bryn Mawr Coll., 1968. Lic. psychologist, Pa. Rsch. asst. psychiatry Temple U., Phila., 1958-59, instr., counselor students, 1960-64; clin. psychologist Gloucester County Guidance Ctr., Woodbury, N.J., 1959-60; seminar coord. Bryn Mawr Coll., 1966-67, lectr., 1968-70, asst. prof., 1970-73; dir. counseling and placement Jewish Employment and Vocat. Svc., 1973-75; assoc. dean students Rider Coll.,

1975-77; dir. student svcs., clin. asst. prof. mental health scis. Hahnemann Med. U., Phila., 1978-83; dir. Ctr. for Pers. and Profl. Devel. Pa. Coll. Optometry, Phila., 1983-93; pvt. practice psychologist Phila., 1983-86; pres. pvt. practice, 1986—. Mem., pres. bd. mgrs. Sr. Employment and Ednl. Svc., Phila., 1983-95; bd. dirs. Awbury Arboretum Assn., 1986—; mem. Mayor's Sci. and Tech. Adv. Coun. divsn. Urban Affairs City of Phila., 1973-76. Tuition scholar Bryn Mawr Coll. Fellow Nat. Vocat. Guidance Assn., Pa. Psychol. Assn., Behavior Therapy and Rsch. Soc. (clin.); mem. APA, Ea. Psychol. Assn., Am. Counseling Assn., Am. Coll. Pers. Assn., Phila. Soc. Clin. Psychologists (bd. dirs. 1981-91), Cornell Alumni Club of Phila. (co-chair 1989-91).

WOODS, PHYLLIS MICHALIK, elementary school educator; b. New Orleans, Sept. 12, 1937; d. Philip John and Thelma Alice (Carey) Michalik; 1 child, Tara Lynn Woods. BA, Southeastern La. U., 1967. Cert. speech and English tchr., libr. sci., La. Tchr. speech, English and drama St. Charles Parish Pub. Schs., Luling, La., elem. tchr., secondary tchr. remedial reading, Chpt. I reading specialist; Wicat tchr. coord.; tchr. cons. St. Charles parish writing project La. State U. Writing Project. Author: Egbert, the Egret, Angel Without Wings; songwriter; contbr. articles and poems to River Parish Guide, St. Charles Herald. Sch. rep. United Fund, St. Charles Parish Reading Assn.; parish com. mem. Young Authors, Tchrs. Who Write; active 4-H. Mem. ASCD, Internat. Reading Assn., St. Charles Parish Reading Coun., Newspaper in Edn. (chmn., historian), La. Assn. Newspapers in Edn. (state com.).

WOODS, ROSE MARY, former presidential assistant, consultant; b. Sebring, Ohio, Dec. 26, 1917; d. Thomas M. and Mary (Maley) W. Ed. high sch.; L.D.H., Pfeiffer Coll., 1971. With Royal China, Inc., Sebring, 1935-43, Office Censorship, 1943-45, Internat. Tng. Adminstrn., 1945-47, Herter Com. Fgn. Aid, 1947, Fgn. Service Ednl. Found., 1947-51; sec. to senator, then v.p. Nixon, 1951-61; asst. Mr. Nixon with firm Adams, Duque & Hazeltine, Los Angeles, 1961-63, firm Nixon, Mudge, Rose, Guthrie, Alexander & Mitchell, N.Y.C., 1963-68; exec. asst. to former Pres. Nixon, 1969-75; now consultant. Named 1 of 10 Women of Year Los Angeles Times, 1961, 1 of 75 Most Important Women in Am. Ladies Home Jour., 1971. Home: 1194 W Cambridge St Alliance OH 44601-2169

WOODS, SANDRA KAY, manufacturing executive; b. Loveland, Colo., Oct. 11, 1944; d. Ivan H. and Florence L. (Betz) Harris; m. Gary A. Woods, June 11, 1967; children: Stephanie Michelle, Michael Harris. BA, U. Colo., 1966, MA, 1967. Personnel mgmt. specialist CSC, Denver, 1967; asst. to regional dir. HEW, Denver, 1968-69; urban renewal rep. HUD, Denver, 1970-73, dir. program analysis, 1974-75, asst. regional dir. community planning and devel., 1976-77, regional dir. fair housing, 1978-79; mgr. ea. facility project Adolph Coors Co., Golden Colo., 1980, dir. real estate, 1981, v.p. chief environ. health and safety officer, 1982—. pres. Industries for Jefferson County (Colo.), 1985. Mem. Exec. Exchange, The White House, 1980; bd. dirs. Golden Local Devel. Corp. (Colo.), 1981-82; fundraising dir. Coll. Arts and Scis., U. Colo., Boulder, 1982-89, U. Colo. Found.; mem. exec. bd. NCCJ, Denver, 1982-94; v.p. Women in Bus., Inc., Denver, 1982-83; mem. steering com. 1984 Yr. for All Denver Women, 1983-84; mem. 10th dist. Denver br. Fed. Reserve Bd., 1990—, chmn. bd., 1995—; bd. dirs Nat. Jewish Hosp. 1994—. Named one of Outstanding Young Women Am., U.S. Jaycees, 1974, 78, Fifty Women to Watch, Businessweek, 1987, 92, Woman of Achievement YWCA, 1988. Chmn. Greater Denver Corp., 1991—. Mem. Indsl. Devel. Resources Council (bd. dirs. 1986-89), Am. Mgmt. Assn., Denver C. of C. (bd. dirs. 1988—, Disting. Young Exec. award 1974, mem. Leadership Denver, 1976-77), Colo. Women's Forum, Nat. Assn. Office and Indsl. Park Developers (sec. 1988, treas. 1989), Committee of 200 (v.p. 1994-95), Phi Beta Kappa, Pi Alpha Alpha. Republican. Presbyterian. Club: PEO (Loveland, Colo.). Office: Coors Brewing Co BC 320 Golden CO 80401

WOODS, SUSANNE, educator, academic administrator; b. Honolulu, May 12, 1943; d. Samuel Ernest and Gertrude (Cullom) W. BA in Polit. Sci., UCLA, 1964, MA in English, 1965; PhD in English and Comparative Lit., Columbia U., 1970; MA (hon.), Brown U., 1978. Staff Senator Daniel K. Inouye, 1963; asst. editor Rand Corp., Calif., 1963-65; instr. Ventura Coll., Calif., 1965-66; lectr. CUNY, 1967-69; asst. prof. U. Hawaii, 1969-72; asst. prof. English Brown U., Providence, 1972-77, assoc. prof., 1977-83, prof., 1983-93, dir. grad. studies, 1986-88, assoc. dean faculty, 1987-90; v.p., dean Franklin and Marshall Coll., Lancaster, Pa., 1991-95, prof. English, 1991—; vis. assoc. prof. U. Calif., 1981-82; chair exec. bd. NEH-Brown Women Writers Project, 1988—. Author: Natural Emphasis, 1984; gen. editor: Women Writers in English, 1350-1850, 1992—; editor: The Poetry of Aemilia Lanyer, 1993; contbr. numerous articles to profl. jours. and scholarly books; reviewer for various profl. jours., including Renaissance Quar., Jour. of English and Germanic Philology; reader for PMLA Jour., SEL Jour., also others; editorial bd. Hunting Libr. Quar., 1987-90, Ben Jonson Jour., Duquesne U. Press. Pres. Cultural Coun. of Lancaster County, 1993-95, bd. dirs., 1990-95; bd. dirs. Lancaster Gen. Hosp. Found., 1992-95; active various polit. campaigns, 1960-64, 68-76, 84, 92. Bronson fellow, 1976, Huntington Library, 1979-80, 81, Clark Library, 1981, Huntington-NEH, 1984-85, Woodrow Wilson Found., 1968-70. Mem. Am. Council Edn. (R.I. women's coord. 1988-90), MLA (chmn. div. 17th Century English lit. 1982), N.E. MLA (chmn. English Renaissance sect. 1978, Milton sect. 1983), Am. Assn. Higher Edn., Nat. Women's Studies Assn., Renaissance Soc. Am., Milton Soc. (exec. com. 1987-89), Lyrica Soc. (pres. 1987-90), Alpha Gamma Delta. Democrat. Episcopalian. Office: Coll of Wooster Office of President Wooster OH 44691

WOODSIDE, LISA NICOLE, academic administrator; b. Portland, Oreg., Sept. 7, 1944; d. Lee and Emma (Wenstrom) W. Student Reed Coll., 1962-65; MA, U. Chgo., 1968; PhD, Bryn Mawr Coll., 1972; cert. Harvard U. Inst. for Ednl. Mgmt., 1979; MA, West Chester U., 1994. Mem. dean's staff Bryn Mawr Coll., 1970-72; asst. prof. Widener U., Chester, Pa., 1972-77, assoc. prof. humanities, 1978-83, asst. dean student services, 1972-76, assoc. dean, 1976-79, dean, 1979-83; acad. dean, prof. of humanities Holy Family Coll., Phila., 1983—, v.p., dean acad. affairs, prof. humanities, 1990—; cons. State N.J. Edn. Dept., 1990; accreditor Commn. on Higher Edn., Middle States Assn., 1977-83, 94. Co-author: New Age Spirituality: An Assessment. City commr. for community rels. Chester, 1980-83; mem. Adult Edn. Council Phila. Am. Assn. Papyrology grantee Bryn Mawr Coll.; S. Maude Kaemmerling fellow Bryn Mawr Coll. Mem. Am. Assn. Higher Edn., Coun. Ind. Colls., Eastern Assn. Coll. Deans, Pa. Assn. Colls. and Tchr. Educators, AAUW (univ. rep. 1975-83), Nat. Assn. Women in C. of C., Am. Psychol. Assn., Transpersonal Assn., Audubon Soc., Del. Valley Orienteering, Phi Eta Sigma, Alpha Sigma Lambda, Psi Chi. Home: 360 Saybrook Ln # A Media PA 19086-6761 Office: Holy Family Coll Torresdale Philadelphia PA 19114

WOODSON, GAYLE ELLEN, otolaryngologist; b. Galveston, Tex., June 9, 1950; d. Clinton Eldon and Nancy Jean (Stephens) W.; m. Kevin Thomas Robbins; children: Nicholas, Gregory, Sarah. BA, Rice U., 1972; MD, Baylor Coll. Medicine, 1975. Diplomate Am. Bd. Otolaryngology (bd. dirs.). Fellow Baylor Coll. Medicine, Houston, 1976, Inst. Laryngology & Otology, London, 1981-82; asst. prof. Baylor Coll. Medicine, 1982-87; asst. attending Harris County Hosp. Dist., Houston, 1982-86; with courtesy staff Saint Luke's Episcopal Hosp., Houston, 1982-87; assoc. attending The Methodist Hosp., Houston, 1982-87; asst. prof. U. Calif. Med. Sch., San Diego, 1987-89; chief otolaryngology VA Med. Ctr., San Diego, 1987-92; assoc. prof. U. Calif. Sch. Med., San Diego, 1989-92; prof. otolaryngology U. Tenn., Memphis, 1993—; mem. staff Bapt. Meml. Hosps., Meth. Hosps., Le Bonheur Children's Hosp.; numerous presentations and lectures in field. Contbr. numerous articles and abstracts to med. jours., also videotapes. Fellow ACS (bd. govs.), Royal Coll. Surgeons, Soc. Univ. Otolaryngologists (exec. coun.), Am. Soc. Head and Neck Surgery, Am. Laryngol. Assn., Triological Soc.; mem. AMA, Am. Acad. Otolaryngology-Head and Neck Surgery (bd. dirs.), Am. Med. Women's Assn. (pres. Memphis br.), Soc. Head and Neck Oncologists Eng., Am. Physiol. Soc., Assn. Women Surgeons, Am. Bd. Otolaryngology (bd. dirs., residency rev. com. for otolaryngology), Am. Soc. of Head and Neck Surgeons (coun.). Office: U Tenn Dept Oto/HNS 956 Court B2-10 Memphis TN 38163

WOODSON-HOWARD, MARLENE ERDLEY, former state legislator; b. Ford City, Pa., Mar. 8, 1937; d. James and Susie (Lettrich) Erdley; m. Francis M. Howard; children: George Woodson, Bert Woodson, Robert Woodson, Daniel Woodson, David Woodson. BS, Ind. U. of Pa., 1958; MA, U. South Fla., 1968; EdD, Nova U., 1981. Prof. math. Manatee Community Coll., 1970-82, dir., Inst. Advancement, 1982-86; exec. dir. Manatee Community Coll. Foundation, 1982-86; pres. Pegasus Enterprises, Inc., 1986—; state senator Fla., 1986-90. Candidate for gov. of Fla., 1990; pres. New Coll. Libr. Assn.; past pres. Manatee Symphony. Mem. Women Owners Network, Sarasota C. of C., Sarasota Tiger Bay Club, Kiwanis (bd. dirs.). Republican. Roman Catholic. Home: 12 Tidy Island Blvd Bradenton FL 34210-3301

WOODSWORTH, ANNE, university dean, librarian; b. Fredericia, Denmark, Feb. 10, 1941; d. Thorvald Ernst and Roma Yrsa (Jensen) Lindner; 1 child, Yrsa Anne. BFA, U. Man., Can., 1962; BLS, U. Toronto, Ont., Can., 1964, MLS, 1969; PhD, U. Pitts., 1987. Edn. libr. U. Man., 1964-65; reference libr. Winnipeg Pub. Library, 1965-67; reference libr. sci. and medicine dept. U. Toronto, 1967-68; med. librarian Toronto Western Hosp., 1969-70; research asst. to chief librarian U. Toronto, 1970-71, head reference dept., 1971-74; personnel dir. Toronto Pub. Library, 1975-78; dir. librs. York U., Toronto, 1978-83; assoc. provost for librs. U. Pitts., 1983-88, assoc. prof., 1988-91; dean Palmer Sch. Libr. and Info. Sci. L.I. U., 1991—; pres. Anne Lindner Ltd., 1974-83; bd. dirs. Population Rsch. Found., Toronto, 1980-83, Ctr. for Rsch. Libraries, 1987-88; mem. rsch. libraries adv. coun. OCLC, 1984-87. Author: The Alternative Press in Canada, 1972, Leadership and Research Libraries, 1988, Patterns and Options for Managing Information Technology on Campus, 1990, Library Cooperation and Networks, 1991, Managing the Economics of Leasing and Contracting Out Information Services, 1993, Reinvesting in the Information Job Family, 1993, The Future of Education for Librarianship: Looking Forward from the Past, 1994. Dir. Sr. Fellows Inst., 1995—; trustee L.I. Librs. Resources Coun., 1993-96. Can. Coun. grantee, 1974, Ont. Arts Coun. grantee, 1974, Coun. on Libr. Resources grantee, 1986, 88, 91, 93; UCLA sr. fellow, 1985. Mem. ALA (com. on accreditation 1990-94, councillor 1993—), Can. Assn. Rsch. Librs. (pres. 1981-83), Assn. Rsch. Librs. (bd. dirs. 1981-84, v.p. 1984-85, pres. 1985-86), Assn. Coll. and Rsch. Librs. (chmn. K.G. Saur award com. 1991-93), Assn. for Libr. and Info. Sci. Edn., N.Y. Libr. Assn., Internat. Soc., Am. Soc. Info. Sci., Archons of Colophon. Office: LI U CW Post Campus Brookville NY 11548

WOODWARD, DEBORAH, elementary educator; b. Balt., Oct. 5, 1953; d. Charles Franklin and Helen Lyle (Clinebell) Woodward; 1 child, Kortney Rae Howes. BS in Criminal Justice, U. Ctrl. Fla., 1974; MS in Criminal Justice, Rollins Coll., 1982; MA in Edn., U. Ctrl. Fla., 1988, postgrad., 1994—. Law enforcement officer City Police Dept., Titusville, Fla., 1973-76; tchr. elem. sch. Brevard County Sch. Bd., Titusville, Fla., 1988—; criminal justice advisor, Titusville, 1987—. Author: The Ladybug and the Rainbow, 1994. Mem. Young Dems., Brevard County, 1976—, Literaty League, Brevard County, 1988—, Girl Scouts Am., 1980—, troop advisor. With USAF, 1976-87. Mem. AAUW, ASCD, Nat. Assn. Edn. Young Children, Nat. Coun. Tchrs. Math., Brevard Fedn. Tchrs., U. Cen. Fla. Alumni Assn., ZTA Alumni Assn. Methodist. Home: 995 Dawn Dr Titusville FL 32796

WOODWARD, ISABEL AVILA, educational writer, foreign language educator; b. Key West, Fla., Mar. 14, 1906; d. Alfredo and Isabel (Lopez) Avila; student Fla. State Coll. for Women, 1925, A.B. in Edn., 1938; cert. in teaching Spanish, U. Miami, 1961; summer study U. Fla., Eckerd Coll.; postgrad. St. Lawrence U., U. Miami; m. Clyde B. Woodward, June 6, 1944 (dec.); children: Joy Avis Ball, Greer Isabel Woodward Sucke. Tchr., Key West, 1927-42, remedial reading cons., 1941-42; reading tchr., asst. reading lab. and clinic St. Lawrence U., summer 1941; Spanish translator U.S. Office of Censorship, Miami, 1943; tchr. Central Beach Elem. Sch., Miami Beach, Fla., 1943-44, Silver Bluff Elem. Sch., 1943-50, Henry West Lab. Sch., Coral Gables, Fla., 1955-57, Dade Demonstration Sch., Miami, 1957-61; author 125 sch. radio lessons for teaching Spanish, Dade County Elem. Schs., 1961; tchr. Spanish Workshop for Fla.; speaker poetry and short story writing, 1977; guest lectr. on writing the short story Fla. Inst. Tech., Jensen Beach, 1981; guest lectr. Circle Bay Yacht Club, Stuart, Fla., 1995; freelance writer; contbr. to Listen Mag., Sunshine Mag., Lookout Mag., Christian Sci. Monitor, Miami Herald, Three/Four, Child Life, Wee Wisdom, Fla. Wildlife, Young World; sponsor Port St. Lucie Jr. Woman's Club, 1983. Recipient Honoris Causa award Alpha Delta Kappa, 1972-74, award Contra Costa Times, Calif., 1985, 1st prize for short story in nat. Ark. writers conf. contest, 1992; named one of 5 Outstanding Fla. Tchrs., 1972-74. Mem. Nat. League Am. Pen Women (1st v.p. Greater Miami br. 1974-76, historian 1978—, librarian 1978—, awards for writing 1973, 74, 77, 1st and 3d place state writing awards for adult and juvenile fiction 1983, state 1st prize short story 1985), AAUW, Alpha Delta Kappa, Psi Psi Psi. Address: Apt 6-301 1950 SW Palm City Rd Stuart FL 34994

WOODWARD, MARY LOU, retired elementary education educator; b. Vandalia, Mo., Sept. 9, 1931; d. Carl Wesley and Katy Jane (Williams) Lovelace; m. A. Leon Woodward, Aug. 17, 1954; children: Charles Leon, Paul Louis, Robert Lee, William Lawrence. BA, N.E. Mo. U., 1954; MA, Washington U., St. Louis, 1980. Lifetime tchg. cert. in elem. and secondary edn. Tchr. elem. edn. Vandalia Pub. Schs., 1950-52, Berkeley (Mo.) Pub. Schs., 1954-55, St. Louis Pub. Schs., 1959-95, mem. St. Louis tchrs. ret. com., ad hoc com. St. Louis Pub. Schs. Retirement Sys., 1988-95; cons. affective domain, presenter workshops for Title I Ctr., Insvc. Ctr., 1976-79; cons. spl. projects St. Louis Pub. Schs., 1979-82. Mem. Grand Oak Hill Neighborhood Assn., 1959—, pub. newsletter, 1960-75; block co-chmn. Operation Brightside, 1970-95; mem., spokesperson Mo. State Found., Columbia, 1990-2001; mem. Concerned Citizens Against Govt. Waste, Nat. Right to Work, Mo. Bot. Gardens, St. Louis Art Mus., St. Louis Zoo, Mo. Hist. Soc., St. Louis Sci. Ctr., St. Louis Geneal. Soc. Mem. Mo. State Tchrs. Assn. (state exec. bd. 1984-90, pres. local chpt. 1992-94, pres.-elect local chpt. 1990-92, pub. newsletter 1972-92, Outstanding Educator of Yr. 1994), Ret. Tchrs. St. Louis, Am. Assn. Ret. Persons. Home: 4158 Arsenal Saint Louis MO 63116

WOODWARD, NANCY HATCH, English language educator; b. Omaha, Sept. 11, 1954; d. Harold Howard Hatch Jr. and Molly Jean Huston; m. Michael Vaughan Woodward; children: Natalie Kaye Hatch Woodward, Vanessa Hatch Woodward. BA, U. Tenn., Chattanooga, 1992, MA, 1994. Cert. childbirth educator. Asst. adminstr. Athens (Ga.) Neighborhood Health Ctr., 1978-79; bus. mgr. Buccaneer Broadcasting/WHBO Radio, Tampa, Fla., 1981-84; asst. to exec. v.p. Human Resource Mgmt./Jarvis Walker Group, Tampa, 1984-86; dir. religious edn. Unitarian Universalist Ch., Chattanooga, 1988-91; adj. instr. English dept. U. Tenn., Chattanooga, 1993-94, 95—; tchr. English Girl's Prep. Sch., Chattanooga, 1994-95; edn. outreach coord. Planned Parenthood, Chattanooga, 1995—; nat. v.p. CPM, Inc., Syracuse, N.Y., 1988-91; mem. provost task force on sexual harassment U. Tenn., 1993-94, mem. women studies com., 1991-93; guest lectr. Chatham (Va.) Hall, 1987, McCallie Sch., Chattanooga, 1988, 89, 90, U. Tenn., Chattanooga, 1989, 90, 91, Chattanooga Sch. for Arts and Scis., 1991, Chattanooga Sch. for Liberal Arts, 1992. Contbr. articles, poems, short story to profl. publs. Leader Girl Scouts U.S., Tampa and Chattanooga, 1984-89; treas. Com. to Elect Pete Melcher, Chattanooga, 1990; tutor Youth Devel. Ctr., Athens, 1974; counselor Rape Crisis Line, Athens, 1978-79.

WOODWARD, NICOLE GIRVIN, elementary school educator; b. Owensboro, Ky., Mar. 1, 1946; d. Edward and Nina (Hopper) Girvin; m. Byron Monroe Woodward, Nov. 15, 1969; children: Wesley, Ryan. BS in Elem. Edn., Vanderbilt U., 1968; MEd, Western Ky. U., 1978, postgrad., 1984. Cert. reading specialist; cert. tchr., Ky. Tchr. Robert E. Lee Elem. Sch., Owensboro, 1968-69, Amelia Earhart Elem. Sch., Hialeah, Fla., 1970, West Louisville Elem. Sch., Davies County, Ky., 1970-77, F. T. Burns Mid. Sch., Davies County, Ky., 1977-95; Giants team leader F.T. Burns Mid. Sch., Davies County, Ky., 1993-95; team leader, lang. arts curriculum leader College View Mid. Sch., 1995—; chair lang. arts com. Davies County Schs., Owensboro, 1994-95; textbook rev. com. Ky. Dept. Edn., Lexington, 1992; presenter NEA, 1986, World Congress of Reading, London, Eng., 1986, Brisbane, Australia, 1988. Bd. dirs. H.L. Neblett Cmty. Ctr., Owensboro, 1988-91; mem. allocations com. United Way, Owensboro, 1990-91. Recipient Mem. of Yr. award Owensboro Reading Assn., 1990. Mem. Ky. Mid. Sch. Assn. (bd. dirs. 1988—), Ky. Reading Assn. (bd. dirs. 1991—, pres. 1986-87), Alpha Delta Kappa. Democrat. Methodist. Home: 1639 Lee Ct Owensboro KY 42301-0557 Office: Coll View Mid Sch 5061 New Hartford Rd Owensboro KY 42303

WOODWARD, SUSAN ELLEN, economist, federal official; b. Loma Linda, Calif., June 14, 1949; d. Frank Colwin and Dollie Dorothy (O'Kane) W.; 1. child, Sonja Stenger Weissman; m. Robert E. Hall, July 20, 1996. BA in Econs., UCLA, 1970, PhD in Mgmt./Fin., 1978. Instr. U. Wash., Seattle, 1975, U. Toronto, 1975-77, UCLA, 1976-83, 84-85, U. Calif., Santa Barbara, 1977-79, U. Rochester (N.Y.), 1983-84; sr. staff economist Coun. Econ. Advisers, Washington, 1985-87; dep. asst. sec., chief economist HUD, Washington, 1987-92; chief economist SEC, Washington, 1992-95; with Cornerstone Rsch., Menlo Park, Calif., 1996—. Mem. Am. Econ. Assn. (editor 1983-87), Am. Fin. Assn. Home: 2122 California St NW # 252 Washington DC 20008-1803 also: 1682 Oak Ave Menlo Park CA 94025 Office: Cornerstone Rsch 1000 El Camino Real Menlo Park CA 94025

WOODY, CAROL CLAYMAN, data processing executive; b. Bristol, Va., May 20, 1949; d. George Neal and Ida Mae (Nelms) Clayman; B.S. in Math., Coll. William and Mary, Williamsburg, Va., 1971; M.B.A. with distinction (IBM Corp. fellow 1978, Stephen Bufton Meml. Ednl. Found. grantee, 1978-79), Babcock Sch., Wake Forest U., 1979; m. Robert William Woody, Aug. 19, 1972. Programmer trainee GSA, 1971-72; systems engr. Citizens Fidelity Bank & Trust Co., Louisville, 1972-75; programmer/analyst-tng. coordinator Blue Bell, Inc., Greensboro, N.C., 1975-79; supr. programming and tech. services J.E. Baker Co., York, Pa., 1979-82, fin. design supr. bus. systems Lycoming div. AVCO, Stratford, Conn., 1982-83; project mgr. Yale U., 1984—; co-owner Sign of the Sycamore, antiques; mem. Data Processing Standards Bd., 1977, CICS/VS Adv. Council, 1975; speaker Nat. Fuse Conf., 1989, Aion expert systems nat. conf., 1990, bus. sch. Coll. William & Mary, 1994. Mem. Am. Bus. Woman's Assn. (chpt. v.p. 1978-79; Merit award 1978), Nat. Assn. Female Execs. (founder shoreline network 1993), Assn. for System Mgmt., Delta Omicron (alumni pres. 1973-75, regional chmn. 1979-82). Republican. Presbyterian. Author various manuals, contbr. article to profl. jour. Home: PO Box 1450 Guilford CT 06437-0550 Office: PO Box 208276 175 Whitney Ave New Haven CT 06511-7209

WOOLERY-ANTILL, MYRA JO, pediatric clinical nurse specialist; b. Balt., Jan. 20, 1959; d. James Elmer and Myra Eileen (Hoover) Woolery; m. Forrest Dewer Antill, Feb. 14, 1982. BSN, U. Md., Balt., 1981; M of Nursing, U. Wash., 1986. Cert. pediatric oncology nurse, PALS. Clin. nurse Johns Hopkins Hosp., Balt., 1981-84; pediatric home care nurse Staff Builders, Balt., 1984; rsch. asst. U. Wash., Seattle, 1985; staff nurse Swedish Med. Ctr., Seattle, 1986-87; clin. nurse specialist NIH, Bethesda, Md., 1987—. Contbr. chpts. to books; contbr. articles to profl. newsletters and jours. Vol., planning com. Camp Goodtimes, Seattle, 1985-87; nurse Camp Fantastic, Front Royal, Va., 1991, 94, 95, 96, Camp Sunshine, Front Royal, 1994. Named one of Outstanding Young Women in Am., 1986; Am. Cancer Soc. scholar, 1985-86. Mem. Assn. Pediatric Oncology Nurses (cert., practice chair 1991-93, mem. FDA working group 1991-94, Pres.' Cert. of Appreciation 1993, hon. bd. mem. Nat. Capitol chpt. 1988-89, sec. 1989-91, pres. 1991-95), Assn. for Care of Children's Health, Oncology Nurses Assn., Sigma Theta Tau. Home: 5638 Carville Ave Baltimore MD 21227-3927 Office: NIH 9000 Rockville Pike Bethesda MD 20892-0001

WOOLEVER, GAIL WALUK, elementary school educator, artist; b. Auburn, Ind., Apr. 26, 1952; d. Edward and Dorothy Mae (Rieke) Waluk; m. Stephen J. Woolever, July 18, 1981; 1 child, Zachary. BA, Valparaiso U., 1974; MS, Ind. U., 1979. Cert. permanent tchr., Ind. Art tchr. Kankakee Valley Sch. Corp., Wheatfield, Ind., 1974 . One-woman show includes Munce Art Ctr., 1988; group show includes studio show, 1990; designer 8 sets of stained glass windows, 1993-95, logo design for sch., 1992; owner 1700 North Arts & Craft, Wheatfield. Den leader Cub Scouts, DeMotte, Ind., 1989-94; Sunday sch. tchr. jr. high Demotte United Meth., 1993—, jr. high youth leader, 1995—; sec. Little League, Wheatfield, Ind., 1994-95. Mem. NEA, Nat. Art Edn. Assn., Ind. State Tchrs. Assn., Prairie Arts Coun., Hobart Arts League. Home: 3219 W 1700 N Wheatfield IN 46392 Office: Wheatfield Elem Sch PO Box 158 Wheatfield IN 46392

WOOLF, AMY KASPAR, librarian, storyteller; b. Peoria, Ill., June 7, 1954; d. Edgar Armand and Gwendolyn Eleanor (Mackenzie) Kaspar; m. William Randolph Woolf, Oct. 7, 1978; children: Katherine Michele, Sarah Elizabeth. BA magna cum laude, Bradley U., 1976; MS in LS, U. Ill., 1977. Children's libr. Wichita (Kans.) Pub. Libr., 1978-86; head libr. Botanica, The Wichita Gardens, 1987-96; storyteller Wichita Pub. Schs., 1986-96. Mem. Wichita Area Libr. Assn., Coun. on Bot. and Horticultural Librs. Office: Botanica The Wichita Gardens 701 Amidon Wichita KS 67203

WOOLLEY, CATHERINE (JANE THAYER), writer; b. Chgo., Aug. 11, 1904; d. Edward Mott and Anna L. (Thayer) W. AB, UCLA, 1927. Advt. copywriter Am. Radiator Co., N.Y.C., 1927-31; freelance writer, 1931-33; copywriter, editor house organ Am. Radiator & Standard San. Corp., N.Y.C., 1933-40; desk editor Archtl. Record, 1940-42; prodn. editor SAE Jour., N.Y.C., 1942-43; pub. relations writer NAM, N.Y.C., 1943-47; condr. workshop on juvenile writing Truro Ctr. for Arts, 1977, 78, 92, Cape Cod Writers Conf., 1990, 91, 92; instr. writing for juveniles Cape Cod Writers Conf., 1965, 66, 92. Author: juvenile books (under name Catherine Woolley) I Like Trains, 1944, rev., 1965, Two Hundred Pennies, 1947, Ginnie and Geneva, 1948, paperback edit., 1988, David's Railroad, 1949, Schoolroom Zoo, 1950, Railroad Cowboy, 1951, Ginnie Joins In, 1951, David's Hundred Dollars, 1952, Lunch for Lennie, 1952 (pub. as L'Incontentabile Gigi in Italy), The Little Car That Wanted a Garage, 1952, The Animal Train and Other Stories, 1953, Holiday on Wheels, 1953, Ginnie and the New Girl, 1954, Ellie's Problem Dog, 1955, A Room for Cathy, 1956, Ginnie and the Mystery House, 1957, Miss Cathy Leonard, 1958, David's Campaign Buttons, 1959, Ginnie and the Mystery Doll, 1960, Cathy Leonard Calling, 1961, paperback edit., 1988, Look Alive, Libby!, 1962, Ginnie and Her Juniors, 1963, Cathy's Little Sister, 1964, paperback edit., 1988, Libby Looks for a Spy, 1965, The Shiny Red Rubber Boots, 1965, Ginnie and the Cooking Contest, 1966, paperback 1979, Ginnie and the Wedding Bells, 1967, Chris in Trouble, 1968, Ginnie and the Mystery Cat, 1969, Libby's Uninvited Guest, 1970, Cathy and the Beautiful People, 1971, Cathy Uncovers a Secret, 1972, Ginnie and the Mystery Light, 1973, Libby Shadows a Lady, 1974, Ginnie and Geneva Cookbook, 1975, adult book Writing for Children, 1990, paperback, 1990; (under name Jane Thayer) The Horse with the Easter Bonnet, 1953, The Popcorn Dragon, 1953, rev. edit. 1989, Where's Andy?, 1954, Mrs. Perrywinkle's Pets, 1955, Sandy and the Seventeen Balloons, 1955, The Chicken in the Tunnel, 1956, The Outside Cat, 1957, English edit., 1958, 83, Charley and the New Car, 1957, Funny Stories To Read Aloud, 1958, Andy Wouldn't Talk, 1958, The Puppy Who Wanted a Boy, 1958, rev., 1986, paperback edition, 1988, French translation Le Petit Chien Qui Voulait Un Garcon, 1991, The Second-Story Giraffe, 1959, Little Monkey, 1959, Andy and His Fine Friends, 1960, The Pussy Who Went To the Moon, 1960, English edit., 1961, A Little Dog Called Kitty, 1961, English edit., 1962, 75, The Blueberry Pie Elf, 1961, English edit., 1962, revised edit., 1994, Spanish edit., 1995, Andy's Square Blue Animal, 1962, Gus Was a Friendly Ghost, 1962, English edit., 1971, Japanese edit., 1982, A Drink for Little Red Diker, 1963, Andy and the Runaway Horse, 1963, A House for Mrs. Hopper; the Cat that Wanted to Go Home, 1963, Quiet on Account of Dinosaur, 1964, English edit., 1965, 74, paperback edit., 1988, Emerald Enjoyed the Moonlight, 1964, English edit., 1965, The Bunny in the Honeysuckle Patch, 1965, English edit., 1966, Part-Time Dog, 1965, English edit. 1966, The Light Hearted Wolf, 1966, What's a Ghost Going to Do?, 1966, English edit. 1972, Japanese edit., 1982, The Cat that Joined the Club, 1967, English edit. 1968, Rockets Don't Go To Chicago, Andy, 1967, A Contrary Little Quail, 1968, Little Mr. Greenthumb, 1968, English edit., 1969, Andy and Mr. Cunningham, 1969, Curious, Furious Chipmunk, 1969, I'm Not a Cat, Said Emerald, 1970, English edit. 1971, Gus Was A Christmas Ghost, 1970, English edit. 1973, Japanese edit., 1982, Mr. Turtle's Magic Glasses, 1971, Timothy And Madam Mouse, 1971, English edit., 1972, Gus And The Baby Ghost, 1972, English edit. 1973, Japanese edit., 1982, The Little House, 1972, Andy and the Wild Worm, 1973, Gus Was a Mexican Ghost, 1974, English edit. 1975, Japanese edit., 1982, I Don't Believe in Elves, 1975, The Mouse on the Fourteenth Floor, 1977, Gus Was a Gorgeous Ghost, 1978, English edit., 1979, Where Is Squirrel?, 1979, Try Your Hand, 1980, Applebaums Have a Robot, 1980, Clever Raccoon, 1981,

Gus Was a Real Dumb Ghost, 1982, Gus Loved His Happy Home, 1989; contbr. stories to juvenile anthologies in U.S., Great Britain, France, Germany, and Holland, sch. readers, juvenile mags. Trustee Truro Pub. Libraries, 1974-84; Mem. Passaic (N.J.) Bd. Edn., 1953-56, Passaic Redevel. Agy., 1952-53; pres. Passaic LWV, 1949-52. Named mem. N.J. Literary Hall of Fame, 1987; recipient Phantom Friends Lifetime Achievement award, 1992. Mem. Authors League Am., Friends of Truro Libraries, Truro Hist. Soc., Amnesty Internat. U.S.A., Kenilworth Soc. Democrat. Home: PO Box 71 Truro MA 02666-0071

WOOLLEY, DONNA PEARL, timber, lumber company executive; b. Drain, Oreg., Jan. 3, 1926; d. Chester A. and Mona B. (Cheever) Rydell; m. Harold Woolley, Dec. 27, 1952 (dec. Sept. 1970); children: Daniel, Debra, Donald. Diploma, Drain High Sch. Sec. No. Life Ins. Co., Eugene, Oreg., 1943-44; sec., bookkeeper D & W Lumber Co., Sutherlin, Oreg., 1944, Woolley Logging Co. & Earl Harris Lumber Co., Drain, 1944-70; pres. Woolley Logging Co., 1970—, Smith River Lumber Co., 1970—, Mt. Baldy Mill, 1970-81, Drain Plywood Co., 1970-81, Woolley Enterprises, Inc., Drain, 1973—, Eagle's View Mgmt. Co., Inc., Eugene, 1981—. Bd. dirs. Oreg. Cmty. Found., Portland, Oreg., 1990—, Wildlife Safari, Winston, Oreg., 1986; trustee emeritus U. Oreg. Found., Eugene, 1979—; trustee Linfield Coll. Found., McMinnville, Oreg., 1990—; v.p. Oreg. Trail coun. Boy Scouts Am., Eugene, 1981—; exec. dir. World Forestry Ctr., Portland, 1991—. Recipient Pioneer award U. Oreg., 1982, Econ. and Social Devel. award Soroptimist Club, 1991. Mem. Oreg. Women's Forum, Pacific Internat. Trapshooting Assn., Amateur Trapshooting Assn., Eugene C. of C. (bd. dirs. 1989-92), Arlington Club, Town Club (bd. dirs., pres.), Sunnydale Grange, Cottage Grove/Eugene Rod & Gun Club. Republican. Office: Eagle's View Mgmt Co Inc 1399 Franklin Blvd Eugene OR 97403-1979

WOOLLEY, JEAN GIBSON, dean; b. L.A., Oct. 13, 1939; d. Robert Everett and Marie Laura (Butler) G.; m. William Jon Woolley, July 29, 1961; children: William Allen, Pamela Jean, Stephen Douglas, Jennifer Lynn. BA, U. Colo., 1961; MS, Ind. U., 1966. Cert. supr./coord., curriculum specialist, English and social studies tchr., Wis. Tchr. grade 4 Plaza Elem. Sch., Virginia Beach, Va., 1961-63, East Elem. Sch., Martinsville, Ind., 1963-64; comm./social sci. inst. educator Moraine Park Tech. Coll., Fond du Lac, Wis., 1976-81; curriculum planner Moraine Park, Fond du Lac, 1981-86, dean gen. edn./instrnl. support, 1986—; mem. gen. edn. task force Wis. tech. Coll. Sys., Madison, 1989-94, mem. bd. gen. edn. deans, 1986—, chmn., 1996—. Chpt. advisor Alpha Delta Pi at Ripon (Wis.) Coll., 1969-75, 89-95; Sunday sch. tchr., liturgist at local ch., Ripon, 1986—. Recipient Excellence in Vocat. Adminstrn. award Moraine Park Vocat. Assn., 1986, 94. Methodist. Home: 611 Hillside Terr Ripon WI 54971 Office: Moraine Park Tech Coll 235 N National Ave Fond Du Lac WI 54935

WOOLLEY, MARGARET ANNE (MARGOT WOOLLEY), architect; b. Bangor, Maine, Feb. 4, 1946; d. George Walter and Anne Geneva (Collins) W.; m. Gerard F. Vasisko, June 22, 1985. BA, Vassar Coll., 1969; MArch, Columbia U., 1974. Registered architect, N.Y. Urban designer Mayor's Office Lower Manhattan Devel., 1974-76, Mayor's Office Devel., N.Y.C., 1976-78; project mgr. Office Econ. Devel., N.Y.C., 1978-81, dep. dir. design and engring., 1981-83; dep. dir. design N.Y.C. Pub. Devel. Corp., 1983-85, asst. v.p. design, 1985-86, v.p. design, 1986-91; v.p. design N.Y.C. Econ. Devel. Corp., 1991-94; dep. program dir. corrections program unit N.Y.C. Dept. Design and Constrn., 1996—; mem. N.Y. State Licensing Bd. Architecture, 1994—; mem. archtl. registration examination com. Nat. Coun. Archtl. Registration Bds., 1995—. Mem. assoc. bd. regents L.I. Coll. Hosp., Bklyn., 1982-93, mem. planning and devel. com., 1983-93; pres. assoc. bd. regents, 1988-89. William Kinne Fellows scholar, 1973. Mem. AIA (bd. dirs. N.Y.C. chpt. 1988-90, nat. pub. architects steering com. 1993—), N.Y. State Assn. Architects (bd. dirs. 1990-92), Heights Casino Club, Vassar Club, Jr. League. Home: 135 Willow St Brooklyn NY 11201-2255

WOOLLS, ESTHER BLANCHE, library science educator; b. Louisville, Mar. 30, 1935; d. Arthur William and Esther Lennie (Smith) Sutton; m. Donald Paul Woolls, Oct. 21, 1953 (div. Nov. 1982); 1 son, Arthur Paul. AB in Fine Arts, Ind. U., 1958, MA in Libr. Sci., 1962, PhD in Libr. Sci., 1973. Elem. libr. Hammond Pub. Schs., Ind., 1958-65, libr. coord., 1965-67; libr. coord. Roswell Ind. Schs., N.Mex., 1967-70; prof. libr. sci. U. Pitts., 1973—; exec. dir. Beta Phi Mu, 1981-95. Author: The School Library Media Manager, 1995, So You're Going to Run a Library, 1995, Ideas for School Library Media Centers, 1996; editor: Continuing Professional Education and IFLA: Past, Present, and a Vision for the Future, 1993. Fulbright scholar, 1995-96; recipient disting. svc. award Pa. Sch. Librs. Assn., 1993. Mem. ALA (mem. coun. 1985-89, 91-94, 95—), Am. Assn. Sch. Librs. (bd. dirs. 1983-88, pres. 1993-94), Pa. Learning Resources Assn. (pres. 1984-85), Internat. Assn. Sch. Librs. (bd. dirs. 1991—), Internat. Fedn. Libr. Assns. (mem. standing com. sch. librs. sect. 1991—, editor continuing profl. edn. roundtable newsletter). Office: U Pitts Sch Libr and Info Sci Pittsburgh PA 15260

WOOLSEY, LYNN, congresswoman; b. Seattle, Nov. 3, 1937. BA, U. San Francisco, 1980. Mem. 103rd-104th Congresses from 6th Calif. dist., 1993—; mem. Ho. Reps. coms. on budget, & econ. & ednl. opportunity. Office: US House of Reps 439 Cannon Bldg Washington DC 20515-0003*

WOOTEN-BRYANT, HELEN CATHERINE, principal; b. Houston, Feb. 24, 1940; d. Johnny Clement and Roberta (Glenn) Steward. BS in Elem. Edn., Prairie View A&M U., 1962, MEd in Adminstrn. and Supervision, 1966. Cert. elem. tchr. Tchr. Chgo. Bd. Edn., 1962-83; asst. prin. Vanderpoel Magnet Sch. Humanities, Chgo., 1984—. Communion minister St. James Cath. Ch. Mem. Nat. Women of Achievement (pres. Chgo. chpt. 1988—, Excellence award 1988), Chgo. Asst. Prin. Assn., Prairie View A&M U. Alumni Assn. (founder, pres. Chgo. chpt., 1987—), Sigma Gamma Rho (pres. 1981-83, chairwoman cen. regional nominating com. 1982-84, chairwoman polit. action com. 1985—, Karrie Regional award 1980, Outstanding Pres. award Chgo. Alumnae chpt., 1987, Fred Hampton Inst. award 1990). Republican. Roman Catholic. Office: Vanderpoel Magnet Sch Humanities 9510 S Prospect Ave Chicago IL 60643-1220

WOOTTON, BROOKII E., executive assistant; b. Uvalde, Tex., Mar. 4, 1965; d. Charles K. and Leona Agnus (Farley) W.; m. John J. Ferguson Jr.; 1 child, J. Grey Ferguson. BS, SW Tex. State U., 1988. Operator test floor Motorola, Austin, Tex., 1987-88; stockbroker's asst. Shearson Lehman Hutton, Austin, 1988-89; instr. office adminstrn. Devine (Tex.) Ind. Sch. Dist., 1989-91; asst. to chief exec. officer Turbeco, Inc., Houston, 1991—; rep. for Turbeco, Inc. N.W. C. of C. Active community and charitable orgns.; sponsor cheerleading and twirling; judge, contest dir. Am. Twirling Festival. Mem. NEA, NAFE, AAUW, VOTAT, Bus. Profls. Am. Club (sponsor), Tex. Tchrs. Assn., Tex. Bus. Educators Assn., Devine Educators Assn. (v.p.), N.W. Houston C. of C. (rep.), Jr. League N.W. Harris County, Tex. Computer Edn. Assn., Golden Key Nat. Alumni Soc., Order of Omega, Phi Theta Kappa, Alpha Phi, Phi Upsilon Omicron. Office: 7030 Empire Central Dr Houston TX 77040

WORDEN, ELIZABETH ANN, artist, comedy writer, singer; b. Karnes City, Tex., Nov. 8, 1954; d. Alan Walker and Mary Paralee (Long) W. BS in Comms., U. Tex., 1977. Disc jockey, newsperson KMMK Radio, McKinney, Tex., 1978, KPBC Radio, Irving, Tex., 1979-80, KDNT Radio, Denton, Tex., 1980-81, KJIM Radio, Ft. Worth, 1981-82, KPBC Radio, Irving, 1983, KRYS Radio, Corpus Christi, Tex., 1984; owner Worden Industries, Corpus Christi, Tex. Executed paintings for Am. Embassy, Bogota, Colombia; one-woman shows include Art Ctr., Corpus Christi, 1990; exhibited in group shows at Tex. A&M, corpus Christi, 1986, 92, Galeria Chapparal, Corpus Christi, 1988, New Eng. Fine Art Inst., Boston, 1993, Am. Embassy, Bogota; paintings in pvt. collections throughout the country. Mem. Art Ctr. Corpus Christi. Mem. Tex. Fine Arts Assn., Nat. Assn. Fine Artists. Home and Office: Worden Industries 3842 Brookhill Dr Corpus Christi TX 78410-4404

WORDEN, KATHARINE COLE, sculptor; b. N.Y.C., May 4, 1925; d. Philip Gillette and Katharine (Pyle) Cole; m. Frederic G. Worden, Jan. 8, 1944; children: Rick, Dwight, Philip, Barbara, Katharine. Student Potters Sch., Tucson, 1940-42, Sarah Lawrence Coll., 1942-44. Sculptor; works exhibited Royce Galleries, Galerie Francoise Besnard (Paris), Cooling Gallery (London), Galerie Schumacher (Munich), Selected Artists Gallery, N.Y.C., Art Inst. Boston, Reid Gallery, Nashville, Weiner Gallery, N.Y.C., Boston Athanaeum, House of Humor and Satire, Gabrovo, Bulgaria, 1983, Newport Bay Club, 1984; pvt. collections Grand Palais (Paris), Dakar and Bathurst, Africa; dir. Stride Rite Corp., 1980-85; occupational therapist psychopathic ward Los Angeles County Gen. Hosp., 1953-57; Headstart vol., Watts, Calif., 1965-67; tchr. sculpture Watts Towers Art Center, 1967-69; participant White House Women Doers Luncheon meeting, 1968; dir. Cambridgeport Problem Center, Cambridge, Mass., 1969-71; mem. Jud. Nominating Commn., 1976-79; bd. overseers Boston Mus. Fine Arts, 1980-83; bd. govs. Newport Seamens Ch. Inst., 1989-91; trustee Comm. Rsch., Miami, Fla., 1960-69, chmn. bd., 1966-69; trustee Newport Art Mus., 1984-86, 92-94, Jamestown Cmty. Theatre, 1994—, Newport Health Found., 1986-91, Hawthorne Sea Fund, 1990-93; bd. dirs. Boston Center for Arts, 1976-80, Child and Family Svcs. of Newport County, 1983-90, 91—. Mem. Common Cause (Mass. adv. bd. 1971-72, dir. 1974-75), Mass. Civil Liberties Union (exec. bd. 1973-74, dir. 1976-77). Home: 24 Fort Wetherill Rd Jamestown RI 02835-2908

WORDSMAN, ELIZABETH SCHMITT, senior manager print production; b. Milw., Mar. 1, 1955; d. Paul E. and Dorothy A. (Rehmer) Schmitt; m. Arthur Wordsman, Dec. 29, 1986. BFA, Boston U., 1981. Advt. mgr. Brills Inc., Milw., 1983-85; prodn. mgr. in tng. Allied Graphics Arts, N.Y.C., 1985-87; acct. supr. Bel-Aire Assoc., N.Y.C., 1987-88; cons. Bloomingdale's, N.Y.C., 1988-89; sales promotion prodn. dir. Lord & Taylor, N.Y.C., 1989-95; sr. mgr. print purchasing and prodn. Avon Products, N.Y.C., 1995—; judge Gravure Assn. of Am. Golden Cylinder awards, 1996. Recipient Gold Ink award Printing & Pub. Exec., 1992, 93, 96, Rose Achievement award Lord & Taylor, 1993. Mem. Direct Mktg. Assn., Gravure Assn. of Am. Office: Avon Products 9 W 57th St 23rd Fl New York NY 10019

WORGAFTIK, SUSAN CAROL, social worker; b. Bronx, N.Y., Feb. 13, 1946; d. Alex and Rose (Rosen) W. BA, U. Conn., 1968; MA, Columbia U., 1969; M in Social Svcs., Boston U., 1976. Cert. social worker, Mass. Coord. interagy. rels. Divsn. Alcoholism Commonwealth of Mass., Boston, 1976-77; mgr., planner contracts Federated Dorchester (Mass.) Neighborhood Houses, 1977-89; adminstr. Local 26 Trust Funds Greater Boston Hotel Employees, 1989-92; dir. cmty.-wide programs Federated Dorchester Neighborhood Houses, 1992—; mem. delegation Lessons Without Borders, Jamaica, 1995. Bd. dirs. Bowdoin St.-Geneva Ave. Main Sts., Dorchester, com. chair, 1995—; mem. adv. bd. Roxbury (Mass.) Cmty. Coll. Prep, 1995—, Safe Neighborhood Initiative, Dorchester, 1993—. Mem. NASW. Office: Federated Dorchester Neighborhood Houses 90 Cushing Ave Fl 3 Dorchester MA 02125

WORK, JANE MAGRUDER, professional society administrator; b. Owensboro, Ky., Mar. 30, 1927; d. Orion Noel and Willie May (Stallings) Magruder; m. William Work, Nov. 26, 1960; children: Paul MacGregor, Jeffrey William. BA, Furman U., 1947; MA, U. Wis., 1948; PhD, Ohio State U., 1959. Dir. radio U. South Miss., Hattisburg, 1948-51; pub. relations assoc. Ohio Fuel Gas Co./Columbia Gas, Columbus, 1952-62; adj. prof. communications Pace U., N.Y.C., 1963-75; dir. speechmodule ERIC, Washington, 1975-76; mgr. orgn. liaison, dir. legis. analysis Nat. Assn. Mfgs., Washington, 1977-84, asst. v.p. legis. analysis, 1984-87, v.p. legis. analysis, 1987-93, v.p. mem. comm., 1993—; adv. bd. public affairs NYU Grad. Bus. Sch., 1983-87; adv. bd. Proedn. Mag., 1984-87; cons. IBM, Xerox, 1963-77. Contbr. articles to profl. jours. Transition team Consumer Product Safety Commn., Washington, 1979-80; mem., chmn. No. Va. Pvt. Industry Council, Fairfax County, 1979-85; co-chair Va. Gov.'s Employment & Tng. Task Force, Richmond, 1983; active in other civic activities. Named to Acad. Women Achievers YWCA, 1987. Mem. Future Homemakers of Am. (bd. dirs. 1985-88), Issue Mgmt. Assn. (bd. dirs. 1985-88), Nat. Assn. Industry-Edn. Coop. (bd. dirs. 1983—), Am. Soc. Assn. Execs. (rsch. adv. com. 1989—), Speech Communication Assn. (sect. chmn. 1980-82), The Planning Forum (bd. dirs. Capital chpt. 1990-93), World Future Soc. (steering network 1993 Gen. Assembly), Alpha Psi Omega (hon.), Pi Kappa Delta (hon.). Republican. Presbyterian. Home: 6245 Cheryl Dr Falls Church VA 22044-1809 Office: Nat Assn Mfrs Ste 1500 1331 Pennsylvania Ave NW Washington DC 20004-1790

WORKMAN, KAYLEEN MARIE, special education educator; b. Paola, Kans., Aug. 25, 1947; d. Ralph I. and Pearl Marie (Shults) Platz; m. John Edward Workman, Aug. 10, 1980; children: Andrew Ray, Craig Michael. BS in Edn., Emporia State U., 1969, MS in Edn., 1983. Tchr. English/speech Lincoln (Kans.) High Sch., 1969-70, substitute tchr., 1970-71; substitute tchr. Hudson (Wis.) Sch. Dist., 1971-72; tchrs. aide learning disabilities Park Forest South (Ill) Jr. High Sch., 1977-78; learning disabilities/English instr. George York Sch., Osawatomie, Kans., 1978—; supr. Loose Ends Clown Troop, 1988-91; presenter in field. Author of poems. Com. mem., sec. Cub Scouts, Osawatomie, 1987-88, com. mem. Boy Scouts Am., 1988-91, sec., 1990-91; forensics judge Osawatomie H.S. Forensics Team, 1991-92; hunter's safety instr. Osawatomie Sportsman's Club, 1982-86; mem. Osawatomie Cmty. Band, 1990-92. Mem. Osawatomie-NEA (v.p. 1982-83, 93-94, pres. 1983-84, 94-95, sec. 1986), Kans.-NEA (Sunflower uniserv adminstrv. bd. 1985, Sunflower uniserv coord. coun.), Learning Disabilities Assn., Delta Kappa Gamma. Office: York Sch at Osawatomie St Hosp PO Box 500 Osawatomie KS 66064-0500

WORKMAN, MARGARET LEE, state supreme court justice; b. May 22, 1947; d. Frank Eugene and Mary Emma (Thomas) W.; m. Edward T. Gardner III; children: Lindsay Elizabeth, Christopher Workman, Edward Earnshaw. AB in Polit. Sci., W.Va. U., 1969, JD, 1974. Bar: W.Va. 1974. Asst. counsel to majority, pub. works com. U.S. Senate, Washington, 1974-75; law clk. 13th jud. cir., W.Va. Ct., Charleston, 1975-76, judge, 1981-88; pvt. practice Charleston, 1976-81; justice W.Va. Supreme Ct. Appeals, Charleston, 1989—, chief justice, 1993. Advance person for Rosalyn Carter, Carter Presdl. Campaign, Atlanta, 1976. Democrat. Episcopalian. Office: State Supreme Ct 317 State Capitol Charleston WV 25305-0001

WORLEY, KAREN BOYD, psychologist; b. Hot Springs, Ark., Apr. 23, 1952; d. Wayne Johnson and Lou (Hull) Boyd; m. Timothy Riker, Sept. 22, 1979; children: Travis, Tyler, Kaitlin, Kelsey. BA, Okla. State U., 1974; PhD, Tex. Tech. U., 1983. Lic. psychologist, Ark. Rsch. asst. Rsch. and Tng. Ctr. for Mentally Retarded Tex. Tech. U., Lubbock, 1974-77, teaching asst., 1977-78; psychology intern Kansas City (Mo.) VA Med. Ctr., 1978-79; psychologist Johnson County Mental Health Ctr., Shawnee Mission, Kans., 1979-81; pvt. practice Pleasant Valley Clinic, Little Rock, 1982—; asst. prof. dept. pediatrics U. of Ark. for Med. Scis., 1991—; mem. Gov.'s Task Force on Child Abuse in Arks., 1983-85, Pulaski County Child Abuse Task Force, 1985, Pulaski County Family Svcs. Rev. Com., 1986-87, Com. to Rev. Investigation Procedures Ark. Children and Family Svcs., 1986, Child Sexual Abuse Network, 1988-93; bd. dirs. Ark. Child Sexual Abuse Edn. Commn., 1985-91, Suspected Child Abuse and Neglect, 1986-92, Ark. Commn. on Child Abuse, Rape and Domestic Violence, 1991—, Victims of Crime Act Bd., 1992—; cons. Mother's Support Group, Parent Ctr., Little Rock, 1983-92. Contbr. articles to profl. publs. Mem. APA, Ark. Psychol. Assn., Nat. Register Health Svc. Providers in Psychology (coun.), Am. Profl. Soc. on Abuse of Children, Assn. for Treatment of Sexual Abusers, Phi Kappa Phi. Methodist. Office: Family Treatment Program 1120 Marshall St Little Rock AR 72202-4600 also: Pleasant Valley Clinic 12361 Hinson Rd North Little Rock AR 72113

WORLEY, VIRGINIA KING, microbiologist; b. Pitts., Apr. 15, 1925; d. Wilbert Frederick and Helena Anna (Blotter) King; m. Carl Milton Worley, Apr. 14, 1945 (div. Dec. 1963); children: Mark, Seth, Paul, Marianne. BS in Microbiology, U. Pitts., 1946; M in Music Edn., Duquesne U., 1991. Part-time organist, choir dir. various chs., Pitts., 1944-85; environ. health sanitarian Allegheny County Health Dept., Pitts., 1969-87; music min. St. Peter Roman Catholic Ch., Pitts., 1985-94; dir. therapeutic music programs various schs. and chs., Pitts., 1990—; gen. music. tchr., 1990—; music min. Good Shepherd Luth. Ch., Pitts., 1994—; pvt. tutor piano and pipe organ, 1955—. Musician Choral divsn. Tuesday Musical Club, 1995; bd. dirs. Freedom House Enterprises, 1979—, music outreach Sisters St. Francis, 1993—; founder Greater Pitts. Women's Ctr. and Shelter, 1975, Greater Pitts. Cmty. Food Bank, 1980; mem. Ctrl. Northside Citizen's Coun., Pitts., 1993—, Manchester Citizens' Corp., Pitts., 1983—. Grantee various founds., 1990—. Mem. AAUW, Am. Guild Organists (bd. dirs. 1994-95), Nat. Orgn. Parish Musicians, Nat. Mus. Women Arts, Pitts. Assn. Arts Edn. and Therapy, Choristers Guild. Democrat. Home: 1413 Faulsey Way Pittsburgh PA 15233

WORMAN, LINDA KAY, nursing administrator; b. Buffalo, N.Y., Sept. 28, 1959; d. Robert Kindig and Winifred (Hostetter) W. BSN, Emory U., 1980; MPH, U. N.C., 1986. RN; cert. lactation cons.; cert. advanced nursing adminstr. Staff nurse SICU U. Hosp., Cleve., 1980-81; staff nurse labor and delivery Med. Ctr., Columbus, Ga., 1981; dep. prin. tutor Macha (Africa) Mission Hosp., 1981-85; staff nurse neurosci. ICU Duke U. Hosp., Durham, N.C., 1985-86; nurse mgr. maternal-child Woodland (Calif.) Meml. Hosp., 1986-88; nurse mgr. obstetrics Pa. State U. Hosp., Hershey, 1988-94; v.p. nursing svcs. Jersey Shore (Pa.) Hosp., 1994—. Rape and domestic violence crisis vol. Harrisburg YWCA, 1992-94. Mem. Am. Orgn. of Nurse Execs., Pa. Perinatal Assn. (bd. dirs. 1989-94). Home: 8 Spruce Dr Lock Haven PA 17745-1037 Office: Jersey Shore Hosp 1020 Thompson St Jersey Shore PA 17740

WORNER, THERESA MARIE, physician; b. Breckenridge, Minn., Feb. 19, 1948; d. William Daniel and Elizabeth (Stelten) W.; m. Martin Herbst, Mar. 24, 1979. AB, St. Theresa Coll., 1970; MD, U. Minn., 1974. Diplomate Am. Bd. Internal Medicine. Rotating intern Kings County Hosp., Bklyn., 1974-75, resident medicine, 1975-77; fellow VA Med. Ctr., Bronx, N.Y., 1977-78; chief med. sect. Alcoholism treatment program VA Med. Ctr., Bronx, 1978-87; asst. prof. medicine Mt. Sinai Sch. Medicine, N.Y.C., 1984-87; mem. faculty Postgrad. Ctr., 1985-90; physician in charge alcoholism svcs. L.I. Coll. Hosp., Bkyn., 1987-92; assoc. prof. clin. medicine SUNY, Health Sci. Ctr., Bkyn., 1988—; dir. rsch. 32BJ Health Fund, 1992—; clin. assoc. prof. Pub. Health Cornell U. Med. Coll., 1996—; pres./founder Alcohol. Info, 1995; advisor Patient Care Mag., 1984—; cons. REA, 1996—. Referee Hepatology, 1986, Jour. Study Alcohol, 1984—, Substance Abuse, 1992—, Alcoholism: Clinical and Exptl. Rsch., 1992—, Drug and Alcohol Dependence, 1993—, Drug Therapy, 1994—, Addiction, 1996—; contbr. numerous articles to profl. jours. Active Bronx Bot. Garden, Mus. Modern Art, Met. Mus. Art, Mus. Natural History, Bklyn. Mus. Art, Turtle Bay Civic Assn., Bklyn. Lyric Opera, Empire State Opera, Amato Opera. Grantee Child Welfare Adminstrn., 1991, 92, 93; recipient Physicians Recognition award AMA, 1984, 89, 91, 96, Cert. of Merit Govt. Employees Ins. Co., 1986, PACT Intern Site award, 1991, 92. Fellow ACP; mem. AAAS, Am. Med. Soc. on Alcoholism and Other Drug Dependence, Am. Soc. Internal Medicine, Am. Assn. for Study Liver Diseases (Travel award 1978), N.Y. Acad. Scis., Rsch. Soc. on Alcoholism, Internat. Soc. Biologic Rsch. in Alcoholism. Home: 322 E 50th St New York NY 10022-7902 Office: Rsch Dept 32BJ Health Fund 13th fl 101 Ave of Americas New York NY 10013

WORONOV, MARY, actress, writer; b. Bklyn., Dec. 8, 1946; d. Victor D. and Carol W.; m. Ted Gershuny, 1969 (div.); m. Ted Whitehead, 1979. Student, Cornell Univ. Actress (films) The Chelsea Girls, 1967, Death Race 2000, 1975, Rock 'n' Roll High School, 1979, Eating Raoul, 1982, Black Widow, 1987, Warlock, 1989, (TV series) Logan's Run, 1977, Sledge Hammer!, 1987, (TV movie) Challenge of a Lifetime, 1985, (TV special) Cheech and Chong's Get Out of My Room, 1985, (stage prodns.) Kitchenette, 1968, Boom Boom Room, 1974; author: Wake for the Angels: Paintings and Stories, 1994, Swimming Underground: My Years in the Warhol Factory, 1995. *

WORRELL, CYNTHIA CELESTE, school nurse; b. Des Moines, Feb. 13, 1948; d. Ralph E. and Mary (Nading) W.; children: Steven F. Durand II, Sonya R. Bellson. BSN, Ariz. State U., 1977, MS, 1983; postgrad. in law, Newport U.; PhD in Health Svcs., Walden U. RN, Ariz. Adminstrv. nurse mgr. Humana Hosp.; charge nurse med./surg. floor Humana Hosp. Desert Valley, Phoenix; staff nurse Staff Builders, Phoenix; sch. nurse Creighton Sch. Dist., Phoenix, 1978-81, Scottsdle Sch. Dist., 1986—; instr. nursing dept. U. Phoenix, 1990—; mem. comprehensive sch. health essential skills adv. com. Ariz. Dept. Edn. Allstate Found. scholar. Mem. NEA, Am. Holistic Nurses Assn., Ariz. Sch. Nurses Assn., Sch. Nurse Orgn. Ariz. (del.), Ariz. Edn. Assn., Scottsdale Edn. Assn. (exec. bd.).

WORRELL, CYNTHIA LEE, bank executive; b. Moncton, N.B., Can., May 27, 1957; came to U.S., 1979; d. Ronald William and Audrey Helen (Crothers) Jones; m. Geoffrey H. Worrell, Sept. 1, 1979; children: Lindsay Andrea, Geoffrey Andrew, Ashley Taylor. Student, U. New Brunswick, Fredericton, 1979. Lic. real estate broker, Mass., Pa., Calif. Instr. New Brunswick C.C., Fredericton, N.B., Can., 1978-79, Massasoit C.C., Brockton, Mass., 1981-82, Brockton Cmty. Schs., 1981-82; regional mgr. and instr. Worldwide Ednl. Services, Clifton, N.J.; procedures and documentation analyst Capital Blue Cross, Harrisburg, Pa., 1985; v.p., br. mgr. Comfed Mortgage Co., Inc., Mass., 1985-90; sr. residential loan officer Bank of Am., Santa Clara, Calif., 1990-92; regional sales mgr., asst. v.p. Shearson Lehman Mortgage, San Jose, Calif., 1992-93; br. mgr. Cypress Fin., San Jose, 1993-94, PNC Mortgage Corp. Am., San Jose, 1994—; program dir. worldwide Ednl. Svcs., Taunton, Mass., 1995; area prodn. mgr. Plymouth Mortgage Co., Foxborough, Mass., 1995-96, Ameriquest Mortgage, Hingham, Mass., 1996—; guest spkr. numerous trade shows, real estate bd. seminars, cmty. workshops; instr. mortgage banking Calif. State U., Hayward, 1994—; mem. adv. bd., instr., outside cons. Calif. State U. Ext. divsn., 1993-95; cert. trainer Carlson Learning Co., 1993—. Mem. editl. bd. Mortgage Originator, 1995; contbr. articles to profl. jours. Vol. Handi Kids, Bridgewater, Mass., 1985-90, Fremont/Newark YMCA youth basketball and soccer; mem. Forest Park PTA, Self-Def. Inst. Tae Kwon Do Club; donor Berwick Boys Club. Named to IBC 200 Women of Achievement, 1991-92, ABI 2000 Notable Women, 1991-92,ABI Personalities of Am., 1992, Internat. Order of Merit, 1992, The World Found. of Successful Women, 1992, Outstanding Young Women in Am., 1984, 88. Mem. NAFE, Mass. Mortgage Bankers Assn., Data Entry Mgmt. Assn., Middleboro C. of C., Wareham Bus. and Profl. Women's Club, Taunton Area C. of C., Toastmasters, Women's Coun. of Realtors, Bristol County C. of C. Republican. Home: 7 Kingwood St Wareham MA 02571-2828 Office: Ameriquest Mortgage 99 Derby St Ste 201 Hingham MA 02043

WORTH, IRENE, actress; b. Nebr., June 23, 1916. B.Edn., U. Calif. at Los Angeles, 1937; pupil, Elsie Fogarty, London, 1944-45. Formerly tchr. Debut as Fenella in: Escape Me Never, N.Y.C., 1942; Broadway debut as Cecily Harden in: The Two Mrs. Carrolls, 1943; London debut in The Time of Your Life, 1946; following roles, mostly on London stage, include Anabelle Jones in Love Goes to Press, 1946; Ilona Szabo in: The Play's The Thing, 1947; as Eileen Perry in: Edward my Son, 1948; as Lady Fortrose in: Home is Tomorrow, 1948; as Mary Dalton in: Native Son, 1948; title role in: Lucrece, 1948; as Olivia Raines in: Champagne for Delilah, 1949; as Celia Coplestone in: The Cocktail Party, 1949, 50; various roles with Old Vic Repertory Co., London, including Desdemona in Othello; Helena in Midsummer Night's Dream and Lady Macbeth in Macbeth; also Catherine de Vausselles in: The Other Heart, tour to S. Africa, 1952; as Portia in: The Merchant of Venice, 1953; found. mem. Shakespeare Festival Theatre, Stratford, Ont., Can., 1953; as Helena in: All's Well That Ends Well; Queen Margaret in: Richard III, London; appeared as Frances Farrar in: A Day by the Sea, 1953-54; leading role in: The Queen and the Rebels, 1955, Hotel Paradiso, 1956; as Mary Stuart, 1957, The Potting Shed, 1958; Albertine Prine in: Toys in the Attic, 1960 (Page One award); mem., Royal Shakespeare Co., 1962-64; including world tour King Lear, 1964; star: Tiny Alice, N.Y.C., 1964, Aldwych, 1970; Noel Coward trilogy Shadows of the Evening; Hilde in: A Song at Twilight; Anna-Mary in: Come into the Garden Maud (Evening Standard award); Hesione Hushabye in: Heartbreak House (Variety Club Gt. Britain award 1967); Jocasta in: Oedipus, 1968; Hedda in: Hedda Gabler, 1970; with internat. Co., Theatre Research, Paris and Iran, 1971; leading role in: Notes on a Love Affair, 1972; Mme. Arkadina in: The Seagull, 1973; Gertrude in: Hamlet; Mrs. Alving in: Ghosts, 1974; Princess Kosmonopolis in: Sweet Bird of Youth, 1975-76 (Jefferson award, Tony award); Lina in: Misalliance, 1976; Mme. Ranevskaya in: The Cherry Orchard, 1977 (Drama Desk award); Kate in: Old Times, 1977, After the Season, 1978, Happy Days, 1979, Eyewitness, 1980, Coriolanus, 1988, Lost In Yonkers, (Tony award, 1991), Valentina in The Bay at Nice-Royal Nat. Theatre, 1986, Irene Worth's Edith Wharton on tour, 1994 "A Weeks

Worth" Almeida Theatre, 1996, Melbourne Festival, 1996; films include; role of Leonie in: Orders to Kill, 1958 (Brit. Film Acad. award), The Scapegoat, 1958, King Lear, 1970, Nicholas and Alexandra, 1971, Rich Kids, 1979, Eyewitness, 1981, Death Trap, 1982, Fast Forward, 1985, Lost in Yonkers, 1993, also numerous radio, TV appearances, Eng., Can., U.S., including; Stella in: The Lake; Ellida Wangel in: The Lady from the Sea (Daily Mail Nat. TV award), also Candida, Duchess of Malfi, Antigone, Prince Orestes, Variations on a Theme, The Way of the World, The Displaced Person; (with Brit. Broadcasting Co.) Coriolanus, 1984; poetry recitals, recs.; (recipient Whitbread Anglo-Am. award outstanding actress 1967). Decorated comdr. Brit. Empire (hon.). Address: Internat Creative Mgmt care Sam Cohn 40 W 57th St Fl 6 New York NY 10019-4001

WORTH, MARY PAGE, mayor; b. Balt., Jan. 23, 1924; d. Christian Allen and Margaret Pennington (Holbein) Schwarzwaelder; m. William James Worth, Nov. 4, 1947 (dec. May 1986); children: Margaret Page, William Allen, John David III. Student, Ladycliff Coll., Highland Falls, N.Y., 1941-42, Abbott Sch. Art, Washington, 1942-44. Selectman Town of Searsport, Maine, 1973-75; mayor City of Belfast, Maine, 1986—; recreation chmn. Town of Searsport, 1970-72. Del. Rep. State Conv., Maine, 1970-94; pres. Searsport Reps., 1974-76; active ARC Overseas Assn., 1976—; pres. Searsport C. of C., 1976-79; mem. exec. bd. Waldo County Com. for Social Action, Belfast, 1986—; mem. Abnacki coun. Girl Scouts U.S.; tutor Literacy Vols. Am.; recreation specialist ARC, Camp Haugen, Japan, 1946-47; bd. dirs. RSVP-Walto County, Heat Start Waldo County; vol. tchr. Sch. for Blind, Cholon, Republic Vietnam, 1959-61, Am. Sch. at Saigon, Republic Vietnam, 1959-61; club dir. USAF Spl. Svcs., Ft. Meyer, Va., 1962-63, U.S. Army Spl. Svcs., Ft. Belvoir, Va., 1963-64; mem. Congresswoman Olympia Snow's Mpcl. Adv. Bd.; town chair Rep. Party; mem. adv. Belfast History Project. Mem. DAR (officer Maine 1986—), Internat. Platform Assn., Ret. Officers Assn. (life), 11th Airborne Assn./511th Parachute Infantry Regiment Korea War Vets. Assn., Waldo County Humane Soc. (pres. 1990—), Waldo County Law Enforcement (v.p. 1990—), VFW Aux., Am. Legion Aux., Belfast Garden Club (parliamentarian 1984—), Rotary (bd. govs. com. Maine St. '90). Home: 5 Seaside Dr Belfast ME 04915-1432 Office: City of Belfast Mayor's Office 71 Church St Belfast ME 04915-1705

WORTHAM, DEBORAH LYNNE, school system director, principal; b. Chgo., May 13, 1949; d. Leon Cabot and Bessie (Summers) Smith; m. Chester Hopes Wortham, Jan. 29, 1972; children: Shelley Sharon, Chester Hopes III. BS, U. Wis., 1972; MS, Morgan State U., 1981. Tchr., reading tchr., support tchr. Balt. City Pub. Schs., 1972-87, asst. prin., 1988-90, prin. Samuel Coleridge Taylor Sch., 1990-94, dir. efficacy, 1994—; program facilitator Balt. Schs.-Johns Hopkins U., 1987-88; dean of edn. Higher Dimensions Learning Ctr., Balt., 1985—. Author: Teaching by Signs and Wonders, 1992. Recipient Mayor's Citation for Volunteerism, Balt., 1982, Am. Best Elem. Sch. for Significant Improvement award Redbook Mag., 1993, 95; cited Administrator's Class Act, Channel ll TV, Balt., 1991. Mem. ASCD, Phi Delta Kappa, Alpha Kappa Alpha. Democrat. Pentecostal. Office: Balt City Pub Schs Bd Edn 200 E North Ave Baltimore MD 21202-5910

WORTHAM, MAXINE ALLINE, early childhood education executive director; b. Jackson, Tenn., June 23, 1947; d. Wilie and Alline (Hayes) W. BS, Lane Coll., 1968; MS, Ill. State U., 1973, PhD, 1985. Adminstrv. endorsement and superintendency. Math/sci. tchr. Roosevelt & Trewyn Sch., Peoria, Ill., 1968-72; spl. edn. tchr. Lincoln Elem., Peoria, 1973-76, tchr. grade 6, 1976-78; dean of students Manual H.S., Peoria, 1978-86; adminstrv. asst. Blaine Sumner Middle Sch., Peoria, 1986-87; prin. Glen Oak Primary, Peoria, 1987-88; dir. pers. Peoria (Ill.) Pub. Schs., 1988-89, exec. dir. pers., 1989-91, exec. dir. primary schs., 1991-92; pres. bd. Ill. Assn. Sch., Coll. and Univ. Staff, 1992-93. Author: The Constitutionality of the Illinois Public Schools Finance System, 1985. Pres. bd. dirs. Tri-County Urban League, Peoria, 1983-84; fellow Edn. Policy Fellowship Program, 1985-86; mem. adv. bd. Peoria (Ill.) Pub. Libr., 1986-89, Salvation Army, Peoria, 1987-93, Ctrl. Ill. Light Co., Peoria, 1991-94; bd. mem. Peoria (Ill.) Assn. Retarded Citizen, 1994—; pres. Tri-Urban League Guild; steward Ward Chapel African Meth. Episc. Ch. Recipient Martin Luther King Jr. Leadership award Southside Pastors Assn., Peoria, 1989, Profl. award YWCA, Peoria, 1989; named Outstanding Young Women in Am., 1983. Mem. Alpha Kappa Alpha, Delta Kappa Gamma (v.p.), Phi Delta Kappa, Rotary. Methodist. Home: 6908 N Michele Ln Peoria IL 61614-2625 Office: Peoria Pub Schs 3202 N Wisconsin Ave Peoria IL 61603-1260

WORTHEY, CAROL, composer; b. Worcester, Mass., Mar. 1, 1943; d. Bernard Krieger and Edith Lilian (Cramer) Symonds; m. Eugene Worthey III, June 1969 (div. 1980); 1 child, Megan; m. Raymond Edward Korns, Sept. 21, 1980. BA in Music Composition, Columbia U., 1965; grad., Dick Grove Sch. Music., L.A., 1979; grad. filmscoring prog., UCLA, 1978; music studies with Darius Milhaud, Walter Piston, Elliot Carter, Vincent Persichetti, Grant Beglarian, Karl Korte, Otto Luening, Eddy Lawrence Manson, Dick Grove; studied, RISD, 1948-54, Columbia U., 1965. Sr. composer, arranger Celebrity Ctr. Internat. Choir, Hollywood, Calif., 1985—. Composer, arranger The Hollywood Chorale; composer ballets Athena, 1963, The Barren, 1965; composer, lyricist, librettist full-length musical The Envelope Please, 1988; composer piano works performed in France, Italy, Germany, Can., U.S. and Eng. by Mario Feninger, 1982; composer Pastorale performed in Mex., 1994, Neighborhood of the Heart, 1994, (choir) Unquenchable Light, 1993; composer film score The Special Visitor, 1992; compositions performed at Aspen Music Festival, 1963, Carnegie Hall, 1954, Dorothy Chandler Pavilion, 1986-89; appeared as singer-songwriter on L.A. Songwriter's Showcase, 1977; arranger Merv Griffin Show, 1981, The Night Before Christmas, L.A. Children's Theatre, 1988-91, Capistrano Valley Symphony, 1994, Very Old Merry Old Christmas, Dorothy Chandler Pavillion, 1994, Judge, 1994; author: Treasury of Holiday Magic, 1992, (poems) The Lonely Wanderer Comes Home, 1994; art work exhibited RISD, 1952, Folk and Craft Mus., L.A., 1975, 1st Internat. Art Exhibit Celebrity Ctr. Pavillion, 1992; cable TV show: Neighborhood of the Heart, 1995, 96. Vol. performer various childcare ctrs., old folks homes, etc.; judge Composer's Competition, Inner City Cultural Ctr., 1995. Recipient Silver Poet award World of Poetry, 1987, 2nd place winner, 1st BarComposers and Songwriters Competition for "Fanfare for Joy & Wedding March", 1990, Golden Poet award World of Poetry, 1992. Mem. Nat. Assn. Composers, USA, Broadcast Music Inc., Nat. Acad. Songwriters, Songwriters and Composers Assn., Toastmasters Internat., Film Adv. Bd. Jewish.

WORTHING, CAROL MARIE, minister; b. Duluth, Minn., Dec. 27, 1934; d. Truman James and Helga Maria (Bolander) W.; children: Gregory Alan Beatty, Graydon Ernest Beatty. BS, U. Minn., 1965; Master of Divinity, Northwestern Theol. Seminary, 1982; D of Ministry, Grad. Theol. Found., Notre Dame, Ind., 1988; MBA in Ch. Mgmt., Grad. Theol. Found., Donaldson, Ind., 1993. Secondary educator Ind. (Minn.) Sch. Dist., 1965-78; teaching fellow U. Minn., 1968-70; contract counselor Luth. Social Svc., Duluth, 1976-78; media cons. Luth. Media Svcs., St. Paul, 1978-80; asst. pastor Messiah Luth. Ch., Fargo, N.D., 1982-83; vice pastor Messiah Luth. Ch., Fargo, 1983-84; assoc. editor Luth. Ch. Am. Ptnrs., Phila., 1982-84; editorial assoc. Luth. Ptnrs. Evang. Luth. Ch. Am., Phila. and Mpls., 1984—; parish pastor Resurrection Luth. Ch., Pierre, S.D., 1984-89; assoc. pastor Bethlehem Luth. Ch., Cedar Falls, Iowa, 1989-90; exec. dir. Ill. Conf. Chs., Springfield, 1990-96, Tex. Conf. of Chs., 1996—; mem. pub. rels. and interpretation com. Red River Valley Synod, Fargo, 1984-86, mem. ch. devel., Pierre, 1986-87; mem. mgmt. com. office comm. Luth. Ch. in Am., N.Y.C., Phila., 1984-88; mem. mission ptnrs. S.D. Synod, 1988, chmn. assembly resolutions com., 1988; mem. pre-assembly planning com., ecumenics com., chmn. resolutions com. N.E. Iowa Synod, 1989-90; mem. ch. and society com., 1990-96; ecumenical com., 1995-96; Luth. Ecumenical Rep. Network, 1995-96; Cen. and So. Ill. Synod,; nat. edn. cons. Am. Film Inst., Washington, 1967-70; chaplain state legis. bodies, Pierre, 1984-89. Author: Cinematics and English, 1967, Peer Counseling, 1977, Tischrede Lexegete, 1986, 88, 90, Way of the Cross, Way of Justice Walk, 1987, Introducing Collaboration as a Leadership Stance and Style in an Established Statewide Conference of Churches, 1993. Co-facilitator Parents of Retarded Children, 1985; bd. dirs. Countryside Hospice, 1985; cons. to adminstrv. bd. Mo. Shores Women's Ctr., 1986. Mem. NAFE, Nat. Assn. Ecumenical Staff (chair of site selection com. 1991-92, chair of scholarship com. 1993-94, mem. profl. devel. com. 1993-94, chair program planning com. 1996, bd. dirs. 1995-96), Pierre-Ft. Pierre Ministerium (v.p. 1986-87, pres. 1987-88). Democrat. Home: 3816 S Lamar Blvd #3816 Austin TX 78704 Office: Tex Conf Chs 6633 Hwy 290 E Ste 200 Austin TX 78723-1157

WORTHINGTON, JANET EVANS, academic director, English language educator; b. Springfield, Ill., Jan. 30, 1942; d. Orville Ray and Helen May (Tuxhorn) Evans; m. Gary H. Worthington; children: Rachael Allene, Evan Edmund, Adam Nicholas Karl. Student, Blackburn Coll., 1960-62; BA in English Lang. and Lit., U. Chgo., 1965; MA in English, U. Iowa, 1969; PhD in English Edn., Fla. State U., 1977; postgrad., W. Va. Inst. Tech., 1981-82, Rensselaer Poly. Inst., 1984. Teaching. fellow Fla. State U., Tallahassee, 1971-72, grad. assistant, 1972-73; coord. lang. arts rsch. Piedmont Schs. Project, Greer, S.C., 1973-76; English instr. Woodrow Wilson High Sch., Beckley, W.Va., 1976-77; Reading specialist, adj. instr. in English W. Va. Inst. Tech., Montgomery, W.Va., 1977-78; asst. prof. W.Va. Inst. Tech., Montgomery, 1979-82, assoc. prof., 1983-87, prof. English, 1987-88; dir. W.Va. Inst. Tech., Oak Hill, 1988-90; tech. writing program coord. Community and Tech. Coll. W.Va. Inst. Tech., Montgomery, 1983-88; dir. continuing edn. Nicholls State U., Thibodaux, La., 1990—; tech. writing cons., various bus., 1986—, Dept. of Mines, State of W.Va., 1980-81; reading cons. Dept of Mines, 1980-81, Mt. Hope (W.Va.) High Sch., 1980-81, Reading Tchrs. Study Group, Kanawha County, W.Va., 1981-83; project mgr. Dept. of Mines, State of W.Va., 1981-83, Dept. of Nat. Resources, State of W.Va., 1984-85; involved in curriculum devel. for various depts., W.Va. Inst. Tech., 1973-90, Raleigh County Schs., Beckley, W.Va., Piedmont Schs. Project, Greer, S.C., English and reading instr. Upward Bound Program, W.Va. Inst. Tech., 1980-85; adj. instr. W.Va. Coll. Grad. Studies, 1979, 81, 83. Author (with William Burns): Practical Robotics: Systems, Interfacing, and Applications, 1986, (with A.B. Somers): Candles and Mirrors: Response Guides for Teaching Novels and Plays in Grades Six through Twelve, 1984, Response Guides for Teaching Children's Books, 1979; editorial bd.: W.Va. Community Coll. Jour.; reviewer: Macmillan Pub. Co. texts, 1985; editor: Diamond Shamrock, 1985; co-producer, host (TV series): About the Author; contbr. numerous articles to profl. jours.; participated in numerous presentations. Mem. W.Va. Community Coll. Assn.; bd.dirs., Curtain Callers, 1979-89, Fayette Fine Arts Coun., 1986-87; promotions chair, W.Va. Children's Book award com., 1984-85. Mem. AAUW (recording sec. 1983-85, pres. 1985—), Assn. for Tchrs. of Tech. Writing, Nat. Assn. for Devel. Edn., Soc. for Tech. Comm. Home: 112 E Garden Dr Thibodaux LA 70301-3750 Office: Nicholls State U Continuing Edn PO Box 2011 Thibodaux LA 70310

WORTHINGTON, MARY ANN, chemist, educator; b. Springfield, Mass., Apr. 21, 1936; d. Chester Raymond and Marian Louise (Davis) Cooper; m. David Gibbs Worthington, Oct. 4, 1958; children: Bradford Scott, Judith Ann, Jan Leslie. BS, U. Mass., 1957, MA in Teaching, 1958. Sr. tech. aide Bell Telephone Labs., Murray Hill, N.J., 1958-60; instr. U. Bridgeport (Conn.), 1960-78; staff chemist Handy & Harman, Fairfield, Conn., 1978-96, lab. mgr., 1996—. Patentee in field. Chmn. Greater Bridgeport Crop Hunger Walk, 1976-83; pres. Stepney PTO, 1969-70, United Meth. Women, Trumbull, Conn., 1974-75; vice chmn. Monroe Rep. Town Com., 1969-70. Recipient Salute to Women award YWCA, 1983, Ecumenical Ministry award Bridgeport Coun. of Chs., 1984. Mem. ASTM (subcommittee chmn. 1986—), AAUW, Soc. for Applied Spectroscopy. Office: Handy & Harman 1770 Kings Hwy Fairfield CT 06430-5317

WORTMANN, DOROTHY WOODWARD, physician; b. Easton, Pa., Mar. 14, 1945; d. Robert Simpson III and Esther (Thomas) Woodward; m. Robert Lewis Wortmann, June 14, 1969; children: Jonathan Thomas, William Lewis. BA, Mount Holyoke Coll., 1967; MD, U. Kans. Sch. Medicine, 1971. Diplomate Am. Bd. Pediatrics, subspecialty pediat. rheumatology. Clin. instr. pediatrics Med. Coll. Wis., Milw., 1979-80, instr. pediatrics, 1980-82, asst. prof. pediatrics, 1982-92; assoc. clin. prof. pediatrics East Carolina U. Sch. Medicine, Greenville, N.C., 1993—; med. dir. rheumatology Children's Hosp. Wis., Milw., 1980-92. chair for juvenile arthritis and mem. pub. and patient svcs. com. Arthritis Found., Milw., 1981-92; med. adv. bd. Lupus Found., Milw., 1983-92. Recipient Disting. Svc. award Arthritis Found., 1991. Fellow Am. Acad. Pediatrics (mem. exec. coun. for rheumatology 1993—), Am. Coll. Rheumatology (mem. sect. pediat. rheumatology); mem. N.C. Med. Soc. Office: East Carolina U Sch Medicine Dept Pediatrics Brody Med Scis Bldg Greenville NC 27858

WOS, CAROL ELAINE, small business owner; b. Bremerton, Wash., Apr. 21, 1957; d. Standley Ralph and Janet Estele (Galber) Stocker; m. George Joseph Wos; children: Samuel Harrison, Bridget Monique. BS in Chem., Wash. State U., 1979. Mfg. engr. Internat. Bus. Machines, E. Fishkill, N.Y., 1979-80; process devel. engr. Sperry Corp., Eagan, Minn., 1980-83; sr. process devel. engr. Cray Rsch. Inc., Chippewa Falls, Wis., 1983-90, mem. cleanroom design and constrn. team, 1991-92, bump/tab process engr., 1993-94; owner, mgr. The Nature of Things, Eau Claire, Wis., 1995—. Bd. dirs. Eau Claire Regional Arts Coun.

WOS, JOANNA H., fiction writer; b. Buffalo, Dec. 12, 1951; d. Peter and Maria (Dziegala) W.; m. Ray W. Gonyea, June 1984; 1 child, Thomas J. BA, U. Pitts., 1973; MA, Boston U., 1975. Curator Octagon Mus., Washington, 1982-84; mus. program asst. Inst. Mus. Svcs., Washington, 1984; devel. cons. N.Y. State Mus., Albany, 1985; devel. dir. Albany Inst. History & Art, 1987-89; devel. coord. Jr. Mus., Troy, N.Y., 1990-91; program asst. N.Y. State Writers Inst., Albany, 1989-91; writers series coord. Santa Fe (N.Mex.) Literary Ctr., 1991-93; program coord. Hudson Valley Writers Ctr., North Tarrytown, N.Y., 1994-95; tchg. asst. Sycamore Sch., Indpls., 1995—; judge Children's Creative Writing Opportunity 1989, Albany; freelance editor Western States Arts Fedn., Santa Fe, 1992-93; editl. asst. 13th Moon mag., 1991. Contbr. short stories to anthologies including Flash Fiction, Loss of the Groundnote, also numerous lit. mags. including The Malahat Rev., Quarterly West. Mem. Writers Ctr. Indpls., PEN. Democrat. Unitarian. Home: 8148 Lieber Rd Indianapolis IN 46260

WOSK, MIRIAM, artist; b. Vancouver, B.C., Can., Aug. 17, 1947; d. Morris J. and Dena W.; m. Stephen Gunther, Feb. 6, 1988; 1 child, Adam. Student, U. B.C., Can., 1966; AAS, Fashion Inst. Tech., N.Y.C., 1969; postgrad., Sch. Visual Arts, New Sch. Social Rsch., N.Y.C., 1969-74. lectr. Fashion Inst. Tech., N.Y.C., Sch. Visual Arts, N.Y.C., Art Ctr. Sch. Design, Pasadena, Calif., Woman's Bldg. Graphic Ctr., L.A., Otis Parsons Sch. Design, L.A., Ctr. Early Edn., L.A., Crossroads Sch., Santa Monica, Calif.; freelance illustrator mags. including 1st cover of Ms., Mademoiselle, N.Y. Times, Esquire, Vogue, N.Y. Mag., Viva, McCalls, Saturday Rev., Sesame St., New West, Psychology Today; curator group show The Inner Lives of Women: Psyche, Spirit and Soul, Spring St. Gallery, L.A., 1996. One woman shows include Transam. Ctr., L.A., 1983, L'Express Brasserie, L.A., 1987, West Beach, L.A., 1988, Wilshire Pacific Bldg., L.A., 1990, Robert Berman Gallery, Santa Monica, Calif., 1991, Drago, Santa Monica, 1992, Jazz, Pacific Design Ctr., West Hollywood, Calif., 1995; exhibited in group shows at Harkness House Gallery, N.Y.C., 1978, Steps into Space, L.A., 1979-80, Dist. 1199 Cultural Ctr. Inc., N.Y., 1981, Smithsonian Inst., Washington, 1981, China Club, L.A., 1981, Biltmore Hotel, L.A., 1982, Transam. Pyramid, San Francisco, 1983, Barnsdall Art Gallery, L.A., 1983, Functional Art Gallery, L.A., 1985, One Market Plaza, San Francisco, 1986, Laforet Mus., Tokyo, 1986, Art et Industrie Gallery, N.Y.C., 1986, Otis Parsons Sch. Design, L.A., 1987, B1 Gallery, Santa Monica, 1987, Katharina Rich Perlow Gallery, N.Y.C., 1988, Deborah Schiller Hadl Art, Culver City, Calif., 1988, L.A., 1993, Sam Francis Studio, Santa Monica, 1988, Gallery Functional Art, Santa Monica, 1989, 91, Art Store Gallery, L.A., Santa Monica, 1990, Santa Monica Mus. Art, 1990, Getty Mus., Malibu, Calif., 1990, James Corcoran Gallery, Santa Monica, 1990, Joan Robey Gallery, Denver, 1992, Cultural Ctr., Eureka, Calif. State U., Long Beach, 1992, Pacific Design Ctr., L.A., 1992, U. Art Mus., Long Beach, 1992, L.A. County Mus. Art, 1992, 96, Helander Gallery, Palm Beach, Fla., 1993, Spring Street Gallery, L.A., 1994, 96, Anderson Ranch Art Ctr., Aspen, Colo., 1995; pub. in nat. and internat. mags., books and newspapers. Recipient Merit award Art Dirs. Club N.Y., cert. of merit Soc. Illustrators, cert. excellence Am. Inst. Graphic Artists; named guest editor Maedmoiselle Mag.

WOYSKI, MARGARET SKILLMAN, retired geology educator; b. West Chester, Pa., July 26, 1921; d. Willis Rowland and Clara Louise (Howson) Skillman; m. Mark M. Woyski, June 19, 1948; children: Nancy Elizabeth, William Bruno, Ronald David, Wendelin Jane. BA in Chemistry, Wellesley (Mass.) Coll., 1943; MS in Geology, U. Minn., 1945, PhD in Geology, 1946. Geologist Mo. Geol. Survey and Water Resources, Rolla, 1946-48; instr. U. Wis., Madison, 1948-52; lectr. Calif. State U., Long Beach, 1963-67; lectr. to prof. Calif. State U., Fullerton, 1966-91, assoc. dean Sch. Natural Sci. and Math., 1981-91, emeritus prof., 1991—. Contbr. articles to profl. jours.; author lab. manuals; editor 4 guidebooks. Fellow Geol. Soc. Am. (program chmn. 1982); mem. South Coast Geol. Soc. (hon. pres. 1974), Mineral Soc. Am. Home: 1843 Kashlan Rd La Habra CA 90631-8423

WOZNIAK, DEBRA GAIL, lawyer; b. Rockford, Ill., Oct. 3, 1954; d. Richard Michael and Evalyn Louise Wozniak. BA, U. Nebr., 1976, JD, 1979. Bar: Nebr. 1980, Iowa 1980, Ill. 1982. CPCU. Asst. legal counsel Iowa Ho. of Reps., Des Moines, 1980-81; mng. atty. Rapp & Gilliam, Des Moines, 1981; from asst. counsel to counsel and asst. dir. Alliance of Am. Insurers, Schaumburg, Ill., 1981-87; from asst. counsel to counsel StateFarm Ins. Cos., Bloomington, Ill., 1987—. Mem. Nebr. Bar Assn., Iowa Bar Assn. Office: State Farm Ins Cos One State Farm Plz Bloomington IL 61710

WOZNIAK, ELLEN T., banker; b. Elmira, N.Y., Feb. 15, 1958; d. Edward F. and Theresa M. (Gourley) C.; m. Timothy M. Wozniak, June 16, 1995. BSBA, SUNY, Oswego, 1980; MBA, Rochester Inst. Tech., 1987. Teller to asst. br. mgr. to credit analyst to br. mgr. First Nat. Bank of Rochester, N.Y., 1980-87; br. mgr., fin. analyst to retail fin. mgr. Rochester Cmty. Savs. Bank, 1987—; various bd. dirs. Inst. of Mgmt. Accts., Rochester, 1992—. Fin. mgr. Lifespan, Rochester, 1993—. Office: Rochester Cmty Savs Bank 40 Franklin St Rochester NY 14604

WOZNIAK, JOYCE MARIE, sales executive; b. Detroit, Aug. 3, 1955; d. Edmund Frank and Bernice (Liske) W. BA, Mich. State U., 1976; MA, Nat. U., San Diego, 1988; postgrad., U.S. Internat. U., 1989-90. Probation officer San Diego County Probation, 1979-81; prodn. engr. Tuesday Prodns., Inc., San Diego, 1981-85; nat. sales mgr. Advance Rec. Products, San Diego, 1986-88; acct. exec. Joyce Enterprises, San Diego, 1986-95; sales exec. Audio-Video Supply Inc., San Diego, 1988—. Producer (video) Loving Yourself, 1987, southwest cable access program, 1986-95; registered marriage, family and child counselor-intern, Calif., 1989. Active Zool. Soc. San Diego. Mem. NAFE, Art Glass Assn. So. Calif., Calif. Assn. Marriage and Family Therapists, Internat. TV Assn. (treas. San Diego chpt. 1990-91), Nat. Acad. TV Arts and Scis.

WRAY, GAIL MILLER, government agency administrator, environmentalist; b. Milw., Feb. 23, 1939; d. Frederic C. Miller and Adele E. (Kanaley) O'Shaughnessy; children: Jennifer, Edward, Hillary. BA in Polit. Sci., Trinity Coll., Washington, 1961; spl. degree, Montessori Soc., Chgo., 1963. Office mgr., asst. plant mgr. Americology Can Co., 1978-81; recycling dir. Village of Shorewood, Wis., 1981-89; recycling coord. U.S. EPA, Washington, 1989-91; chair Presidential Coun. on Fed. Recycling and Procurement Policy, Washington, 1991-94; apptd. by gov. Wis. as exec. dir. Wis. Recycling Market Devel. Bd., 1994—. Polit. affairs chair Jr. League of Am., 1976-77; founder Shorewood (Wis.) Conservation Com., 1980; chair LWV Nat. Resources Portfolio, 1987-86, pres. Greater Milw. LWV, 1980-82; mem. program com. Pub. Policy Forum, Milw., 1985-89; founder and pres. Associated Recyclers of Wis., 1987-89; bd. dirs. Midwest Recycling Coalition. Recipient Cert. Appreciation Am. Field Svc. Internat./Inter-cultural., People on the Move award, Milw. Bus. Jour., 1988, Nat. Govs. Assn. Recognition award, 1990; Named to Most Interesting People, Milw. Mag., 1990. Mem. Worldwide Women in the Environment (chair EPA Forum 1989-94, bd. dirs.), Friends of UN Environment Program, Nat. Recycling Coalition (market devel. com.). Roman Catholic. Home: 12144 N Ridge Rd Mequon WI 53092-1025

WRAY, GERALDINE SMITHERMAN (JERRY WRAY), artist; b. Shreveport, La., Dec. 15, 1925; d. David Ewart and Mary Virginia (Hoss) Smitherman; m. George Downing Wray, June 24, 1947; children: Mary Virginia Hill, Deanie Galloway, George D. Wray III, Nancy Armistead. BFA with honors, Newcomb Art Sch., Tulane U., 1946. One woman shows include Don Batman Gallery, Kansas City, Mo., 1982, Gallery II, Baton Rouge, 1985, McNeese Coll., Lake Charles, La., 1987, Dragonfly Gallery, Shreveport, La., 1987, Barnwell Garden and Art Ctr., Shreveport, 1988, 95, Southdown Mus., Houma, La., 1989, La. State U., Shreveport, 1991, WTN Radio Station, Shreveport, 1993, The Cambridge Club, Shreveport, 1993, Centerary Coll., 1993, Northwestern State U., Natchitoches, La., 1995, Goddard Mus., Ardmore, Okla., 1996, Art Buyers Caravan, Atlanta, 1996, Lockhaven (Pa.) U., 1996, Billingsley Gallery, Pensacola, Fla., 1996; Group shows include Waddell's Gallery, Shreveport, 1990, 91, Water Works Gallery, Dallas, 1990, Southwestern Watercolor Show, 1991 (D'Arches award), Masur Mus. Exhibition (honorable mention 91, 92), 1991, 92, Bossier Art Ctr., Bossier City, La., 1992, Irving Art Assn. (honorable mention), 1992, Leon Loard Gallery, Montgomery, Ala., 1993, Ward-Nasse Gallery, N.Y.C., 1993, Soc. Experimental Artists Internat. (1st. place, honorable mention), 1993, Palmer Gallery, Hot Springs, Ark., 1994, Art Expo, N.Y.C., 1996, Carson Gallery, Dallas, Billingsley Gallery, Pensacola, Fla., 1996, Hummingbird Gallery, Ft. Worth, Tex., Casa D'Arte, Shreveport, La., Lock Haven U., Pa., 1996, Casa D'Arte, Shreveport, 1996, Art Buyers Caravan, Atlanta, 1996. Art chmn. Jr. League, Shreveport, 1955-60; bd. dirs. Holiday-in-Dixie Cotillion, Shreveport, 1974-76. Mem. Nat. Watercolor Soc. (signature mem. 1994, 96), Southwestern Watercolor Soc. (signature mem. 1991), La. Watercolor Soc. (signature mem. 1990), La. Artists Inc. (elected mem.). Episcopalian. Home: 573 Spring Lake Dr Shreveport LA 71106-4603

WREGE, JULIA BOUCHELLE, tennis professional, physical education educator; b. Charleston, W.Va., Apr. 11, 1944; d. Dallas Payne and Mary Louise (Hagan) Bouchelle; m. Douglas Ewart Wrege, July 13, 1968; children: Dallas Ewart, Shannon Bouchelle. B.S. in Physics, Ga. Inst. Tech., 1965, M.S. in Physics, 1967. Systems analyst GE Apollo Systems, Daytona Beach, Fla., 1967-68; med. scientist Space Instruments Research, Atlanta, 1968-70; head tennis profl. Riverside Tennis Club, Atlanta, 1971-72, Am. Adventures, Roswell, Ga., 1972-75, Hampton Farms Tennis Club, Marietta, Ga., 1975-79; head women's tennis coach Ga. Inst. Tech., Atlanta, Ga., 1979-86, 91-92; v.p. Sirius Software, Inc., 1988—; instr. physics So. Coll. Tech., 1990—; stadium chmn., umpire, referee USTA, Atlanta, 1977—. Author: Tournament Manual, 1977, 3d edit., 1989; co-developer software TMS Tennis Tournament, 1989. Pres. Dickerson Mid. Sch. Parent-Tchr.-Student Assn., Marietta, Ga., 1982-85. Named Umpire of Yr., Ga. Tennis Assn., 1978, So. Tennis Assn., 1978; Ga. Tennis Coach of Yr., Assn. Intercollegiate Athletics for Women-Ga. Tennis Coaches Assn., 1981, 82, 83. Mem. U.S. Profl. Tennis Assn. (pres. 1980), U.S. Tennis Assn., Intercollegiate Tennis Coaches Assn., Ga. Tennis Assn. (pres. 1976-81, 94—, v.p. 1974-76, 91-92), Atlanta Lawn Tennis Assn., Atlanta Profl. Tennis Assn., Alpha Xi Delta, Sigma Pi Sigma. Republican. Episcopalian. Home: 1366 Little Willeo Rd Marietta GA 30068-2135

WRENN, RUTHANNE BLOYD, gifted and talented mathematics educator; b. Houston, Sept. 22, 1952; d. Ted and C. Ruth (Carson) Bloyd; m. Robert Lee Wrenn, Aug. 5, 1978. BA, Stephen F. Austin State U., 1974; MA in Math. Edn., U. Houston, Clear Lake, 1980; doctoral studies, U. North Tex., Denton, 1993—. Cert. secondary edn. educator in English, math., sociology, Tex. Tchr. math. Friendswood (Tex.) Ind. Sch. Dist., 1977-78, Columbia-Brazoria Ind. Sch. Dist., West Columbia, Tex., 1978-94, Cypress Fairbanks Ind. Sch. Dist., Houston, 1984-85, Birdville Ind. Sch. Dist., N. Richland Hills, Tex., 1985-89, Jasper (Tex.) Ind. Sch. Dist., 1989-90; tchr. gifted and talented math. Grapevine (Tex.)-Colleyville Ind. Sch. Dist., 1990—; advisor Colleyville Mid. Sch. Nat. Jr. Honor Soc., Colleyville, Tex., 1991—, coord. Acad. Pentathlon, 1992—, coach CMS Math./Sci. Club, 1990—, mentor tchr., 1991—. Colleyville mid. sch. liaison to Colleyville C. of C., 1994—. Recipient Colleyville Mid. Sch. Tchr. of Yr. award, 1994, Grapevine-Colleyville Ind. Sch. Dist. Tchr. of Yr., Grapevine C. of C., 1994. Mem. ASCD, Nat. Coun. Tchrs. Math., Phi Delta Kappa, Delta Kappa Pi. Baptist. Home: 98 Regents Park Ct Bedford TX 76022 Office: Colleyville Mid Sch 1100 Bogart Colleyville TX 76034

WRIGHT, BARBARA EVELYN, microbiologist; b. Pasadena, Calif., Apr. 6, 1926; d. Gilbert Munger Wright and Leta Luella (Brown) Deery. AB,

Stanford U., 1947, MA, 1948, PhD, 1951. Biologist NIH, Bethesda, Md., 1953-61; assoc. biochemist Mass. Gen. Hosp., Boston, 1961-69; asst. prof. microbiology Harvard Med. Sch., Boston, 1966-75, assoc. prof., 1975-82; rsch. dir. Boston Biomed. Rsch. Inst., 1967-82; rsch. prof. divsn. biol. scis. U. Mont., Missoula, 1982—; dir. Stella Duncan Rsch. Inst., Missoula, 1982—; cons. Miles Lab., Elkhart, Ind., 1980-84. Author: Critical Variables in Differentiation, 1973; editor: Control Mechanisms in Respiration and Fermentation, 1963; contbr. articles to profl. jours. Grantee NIH, NSF, 1991-96. Mem. AAAS (pres. Pacific divsn. 1984-85), Am. Soc. for Microbiology (Nat. Found. for Microbiology lectr. 1970, divsnl. lectr. 1978), Am. Soc. Biol. Chemists. Home: 1550 Trotting Horse Ln Missoula MT 59801-9220 Office: U Mont DBS Missoula MT 59812

WRIGHT, BETH SEGAL, art historian, educator; b. N.Y.C., July 23, 1949; d. Ben and Ella (Litvack) Segal; m. Woodring Erik J. Wright, Sept. 5, 1971; children: Benjamin, Joshua. AB cum laude, Brandeis U., 1970; MA, U. Calif., Berkeley, 1972, PhD, 1978. Instr. Mountain View Coll., Dallas, 1978-82; lectr. U. Tex., Dallas, 1980-81, Tex. Christian U., Ft. Worth, 1981; asst. prof. U. Tex., Arlington, 1984-88, assoc. prof., 1988—; adj. and vis. asst. prof. art history U. Tex., Arlington, 1981-84. Contbr. articles to Art Bull., Arts Mag., Nouvelles de l'Estampe, others. Kress Found. hon. traveling fellow, 1975-76; NEH Travel to Collections grantee, Paris, 1987, 93; U. Tex. Arlington Rsch. Enhancement grantee, Paris, 1990, 93, Coll. Art Assoc. Meiss grant, 1996. Mem. Société de l'Histoire de l'Art Française (contbr. articles to bull.), Am. Soc. for 18th-Century Studies, Coll. Art Assn., Midwest Art History Soc. (bd. dirs. 1990-93).

WRIGHT, CAROLE DEAN, reading specialist; b. Mt. Clemens, Mich., Aug. 18, 1943; d. Edward Lawrence and Alice Agnes (Roshinski) Hundt; m. David John Wright, Dec. 20, 1964 (div. Sept. 1984); 1 child, Amy Elizabeth. BA, Mich. State U., 1964, MA, 1967. Reading specialist Holt (Mich.) Pub. Schs., 1965-70, Ypsilanti (Mich.) Pub. Schs., 1970-71, Aurora (Colo.) Pub. Schs., 1972—; pres. Aurora Edn. Assn., 1978-80, Colo. Edn. Assn., Denver, 1982; mem. adv. com. Nat. Assessment of Ednl. Progress, Denver, 1975; chair unit accreditation bd. Nat. Coun. Accreditation of Tchr. Edn., Washington, 1990—; trustee Pub. Employees Retirement Assn. Colo., 1993—. Contbg. author to Idea's for Children's Literature, 1976. Mem. Colo. Commn. on Tchr. Edn. and Accreditation, Denver, 1976-82; vice chair Gov.'s Chpt. 2 Adv. Com., Denver, 1987-93. Named Outstanding Educator, Fed. Programs Adminstr. Coun. U.S. Dept. Edn., 1991. Mem. NEA (bd. dirs. 1984-87), Internat. Reading Assn., Colo. Edn. Assn. (v.p. 1980-81, 83-84, pres. 1982), Phi Delta Kappa. Home: 2268 Clermont St Denver CO 80207-3740

WRIGHT, CONNIE SUE, special education educator; b. Nampa, Idaho, Aug. 26, 1943; d. Ruel Andrew and Renabel Carol (Graham) Farwell; m. Roger R. Wright, July 5, 1968; 1 child, Jodi C. BA, N.W. Nazarene Coll., 1967; MA in Spl. Edn., Boise State U., 1990. Cert. elem. tchr. grades kindergarten through 8th, cert. spl. edn. tchr. grades kindergarten through 12th, Idaho. Tchr. 3rd and 4th grades Vallivue Sch. Dist. 139, Caldwell, Idaho, 1967-69; tchr. 2nd grade Nampa Sch. Dist. 131, 1969-70; tchr. 3rd grade Caldwell Sch. Dist. 132, 1970-73; tchr. spl. edn. grades kindergarten through 3rd Hubbard Elem. Sch., Kuna (Idaho) Joint Sch. Dist. 3, 1985-92; tchr. adolescents CPC Intermountain Hosp. of Boise, 1992-93; tchr. spl. edn. Pioneer Elem. Sch., Meridian, Idaho, 1993—; mem. Internat. Edn. Conf. Between Russia and U.S., 1994. Libr. Horizon's Reading Coun., 1990-91. Named Tchr. Yr. Pioneer Elem. Sch., 1994-95. Mem. Coun. for Exceptional Children, Coun. for Learning Disabilities, Internat. Reading Assn. (Idaho coun.), Delta Kappa Gamma Soc. Internat. (Omicron chpt.).

WRIGHT, ELLEN FLORENCE, education consultant; b. Seattle, Aug. 29, 1939; d. Edwin Sherman and Mildred (Redfield) W.; children: Michael Stanley Tetelman, Margaret Elaine. BA in English and Speech, U. Calif., L.A., 1962; MA in Edn., Stanford U., 1965, postgrad., 1970-74. Gen. adminstrv. credential, Calif.; C.C. credential; tchg. credential grades 7-12. Prin. Piedmont (Calif.) H.S., 1978-79; dir. devel. Packard Children's Hosp., Palo Alto, Calif., 1983-85; exec. dir. Peninsula Ctr. for Blind and Visually Impaired, Palo Alto, 1987-90; dir. devel. The Nueva Sch., Hillsborough, Calif., 1990-92; owner Ellen Wright Consulting Co., Menlo Park, Calif., 1992—; mem. Calif. Post Secondary Edn. Commn., Sacramento, 1994—; mem. Western Interstate Commn. for Higher Edn., 1995—; bd. dirs. Alumni Cons. Team Stanford U. Sch. Bus.; bd. dirs. Children's Health Coun., Palo Alto, Garfield Charter Sch.; mem. Com. for Establishment of Academia Content & Performance Standards, 1996—. Mem. Lincoln Club No. Calif., Phi Delta Kappa. Republican. Office: Bldg 3 Ste 140 3000 Sandhill Rd Menlo Park CA 94025

WRIGHT, ESTHER ESTELLE, educational consultant; b. N.Y.C., Mar. 9, 1941; d. Hyman Weiser and Sophie (Salinas) Gray; m. Edward Rosenblueth, July 11, 1964 (div. Apr. 1982); 1 child, Stephen. BA, San Francisco State U., 1962, MA, 1963. Tchr. Alhambra (Calif.) City Schs., 1964-65, Hayward (Calif.) Pub. Schs., 1965-67; tchr. San Francisco Unified Schs., 1967-76, program cons., 1976-92; tchr. trainer, lectr. San Francisco State U., 1989—; ednl. cons. Teaching From the Heart, San Francisco, 1988—; bd. dirs. Calif. Coun. Self Esteem, Davis. Author: Good Morning Class-I Love You, 1988, Loving Discipline A to Z, 1994. Mem. Calif. Learning Disability Assn. (v.p. 1993-94, bd. dirs. 1992-94), San Francisco Learning Disability Assn. (pres. 1989-92), Phi Delta Kappa. Democrat. Jewish. Office: Teaching From the Heart PO Box 460818 San Francisco CA 94146-0818

WRIGHT, ETHEL, secondary education educator; b. Apr. 5, 1947; m. James A. Wright, Sept. 26, 1969; children: Cassandra, Hannibal, Omari. BS in English, Alcorn State U., Lorman, Miss., 1970; MS in Edn., Butler U., Indpls., 1975. Tchr. Simmons H.S., Arcola, Miss., 1970-71; tchr. English Indpls. Pub. Schs., 1971—; mem. textbook adoption com. Indpls. Pub. Schs., 1979, liaison for Tchrs. Ctr., mem. film preview com. Clk., Democratic Com., Indpls. Recipient ABCD award Indpls. Pub. Schs., 1985, 92; Gregg and Reed scholar Indpls. Pub. Schs. Mem. NEA, Indpls. Edn. Assn.

WRIGHT, FAITH-DORIAN, artist; b. Bklyn., Feb. 9, 1934; d. Abraham and Molly (Janoff) J.; children: Jordan Merritt, Igrid-beth. BS, NYU, 1955, MA, 1958; postgrad., Pratt and Parsons Sch. of Design. Works exhibited in Kathryn Markel Gallery, N.Y.C., 1981, 92, Cumberland Gallery, Nashville, 1981, 92, Barbara Gillman Gallery, Miami, 1982, Hand and Hand Gallery, 1985, 86, Suzanne Gross, Phila., 1986, 87, Gallery Four, Alexandria, Va., 1986, 87, 88, Henri Gallery, Washington, 1986, 87, 88, 89. 90. 91. 92. 93. 94, Benton Gallery, Southampton, 1986, 87, 88, 89, 91, 92, 93, King Stephen Mus., Hungary, 1987, Nat. Gallery Women in the Arts, 1987, 88, 90, 91, 92, Ruth Volid Gallery, Chgo., 1990, James Gallery, Pitts., 1990, Aart Vark Gallery, Phila., 1990, Merrill Chase Gallery, Chgo., 1990, 91, 92, Guild Hall Mus., East Hampton, N.Y., 1991, Joy Berman Gallery, Phila., 1992, Ctr. for Book Arts, N.Y.C., 1992, Barnard-Biederman Fine Arts, N.Y.C., 1994, Arlene Bujese Gallery, East Hampton, 1994, 95, 96, Stoney Brook U., 1994, Harper Collins Exhbn. Space, 1995, Ctr. for Book Arts, 1996; permanent collections Nat. Postal Art Mus., Ottawa, Can., Nat. Inst. Design, Ahmedabad, India, Fine Arts Acad., New Delhi, India, Mus. Modern Art, N.Y.C., Nat. Mus. Women in the Arts, Washington, D.C., Israel Mus., Jerusalem, Brenau Coll., Grainsville, Ga. Blue Cross, Blue Shield, Phila., Mc Donald's, Oakbrook, Ill., The Hyatt Collection, Chgo., Guild Hall Mus.; contbr. critical essays to various periodicals. Mem. Women in Arts, Women's Caucus for Arts, Artists Equity, Visitation Bd. of Met. Mus.-Rockefeller Connection. Address: 300 E 74th St New York NY 10021-3712

WRIGHT, FREDDIE TUCKER, business owner; b. Marion, Ala., Mar. 21, 1921; d. Fulton Compton and Daisy Lula (Kynerd) Tucker; m. Orrin Hughitt Wright, Feb. 2, 1946; children: Edith, Barbara, Anne, Marian. RN, St. Margaret's Hosp., Montgomery, Ala., 1942. Pvt. duty nurse Selma (Ala.) Bapt. Hosp., 1942; nurse USNR, 1943-46; head nurse pediatric ward Polk Gen. Hosp., Bartow, Fla., 1962-65; co-owner Conctracting & Investing Co., Bartow, Fla., 1965—. Author, compilor: History of the First Presbyterian Church, 1982. Pres. Floral Ave. PTA, Bartow, 1959-60, Bartow H.S. PTA, 1963-64; mem. City Libr. bd., Bartow, 1976-79. Mem. DAR (chpt. regent 1970-74, dist. dir. 1972-73, state chmn. 1988-92), Polk County Hist. Assn. (editor 1981—), Bartow Garden Club. Democrat. Presbyterian. Home: 1215 S Orange Ave Bartow FL 33830

WRIGHT, GIOVANNA, quality consultant; b. St. Louis, July 21, 1948; d. Edward Lehman and Giovanna (De Simone) Finn; m. Riley Richard Pope, Nov. 22, 1969 (div. July 1978); m. Isaac Wilson Wright Jr., Nov. 12, 1988. BSBA, Washington U., 1974; MA in Pub. Adminstrn., Syracuse U., 1992. Pk. technician Nat. Pk. Svc., St. Louis, 1970-71; tax auditor IRS, St. Louis, 1971-76, pers. specialist, 1976-80; pers. officer IRS, Milw., 1980-83; adminstrv. officer IRS, Birmingham, Ala., 1983-90, quality cons., 1990-95; quality coord. IRS, Milw., 1995—; cons. The Wright Stuff, Birmingham, 1994-95; mem. bus. adv. bd. for quality inst. Jacksonville (Ala.) State Coll., 1994; adj. instr. U. Ala., Birmingham, 1991, 93. Bd. dirs. LWV, Birmingham, 1984-86, Singles South Civitan, Birmingham, 1983-86; pres. Soc. Govt. Meeting Planners, Birmingham, 1988; coun. on ministries Valley United Meth., Birmingham, 1994-95. Mem. Am. Soc. Quality Control (sr. mem., cert. quality auditor, bd. dirs. 1994-95), NAFE, NOW, Assn. for Improvement of Minorities. Office: IRS 310 W Wisconsin Ave Milwaukee WI 53203

WRIGHT, GLADYS STONE, music educator, composer, writer; b. Wasco, Oreg., Mar. 8, 1925; d. Murvel Stuart and Daisy Violet (Warren) Stone; m. Alfred George Wright, June 28, 1953. BS, U. Oreg., 1948, MS, 1953. Dir. bands Elmira (Oreg.) U-4 High Sch., 1948-53, Otterbein (Ind.) High Sch., 1954-61, Klondike High Sch., West Lafayette, Ind., 1962-70, Harrison High Sch., West Lafayette, 1970-84; organizer, condr. Musical Friendship Tours, Cen. Am., 1967-79; v.p., condr. U.S. Collegiate Wind Band, 1975—; bd. dirs. John Philip Sousa Found. 1984—; chmn. Sudler Cup, 1986—, Sudler Flag, 1982; pres. Internat. Music Tours, 1984—, Key to the City, Taxco, Mex., 1975. Editor: Woman Conductor, 1986—; composer: marches Big Bowl and Trumpets and Tabards, 1987; contbg. editor: Informusica (Spain). Bd. dirs. N. Am. Wildlife Park, Battleground, Ind. 1985. Recipient Medal of the order John Philip Sousa Found., 1988, Star of Order, 1991; 1st woman guest conductor U.S. Navy Band, Washington D.C., 1961, Goldman Band, N.Y.C., 1958, Kneller Hall Band, London, 1975, Tri-State Music Festival Massed Orch., Band, Choir, 1985; elected to Women Bd. Dirs. Hall of Fame of Disting. Women Conductor, 1994. Mem. Am. Bandmasters Assn. (bd. dirs. 1993, 1st woman mem.), Women Band Dirs. Nat. Assn. (founding pres. 1967, sec. 1985, recipient Silver Baton 1974, Golden Rose 1990, Hall of Fame 1995), Am. Sch. Band Dirs. Assn., Nat. Band Assn. (Citation excellence 1970), Tippecanoe Arts Fedn. (bd. dirs. 1986-90), Tippecanoe Fife and Drum Corps. (bd. dirs. 1984), Daughters of Am. Revolution, Col. Dames-Pre Quitanen Chpt., New England Women, Tau Beta Sigma (Outstanding Svc. to Music award 1970), Phi Beta Mu (1st hon. women mem. 1972), North Am. Wildlife Park (bd dirs, 1990—).

WRIGHT, HANNAH CHRISTINE, social worker; b. Houlton, Maine, Jan. 21, 1951; d. Charles Putnam and Carol Maxine (Gardner) Osborne; m. Kerry Allan Stevens, Jan. 1, 1981 (div. Oct. 1989); 1 child, Nathan Allan. BA in Sociology, U. Maine, 1973; basic police cert., Maine Criminal Justice Acad., 1974. Juvenile officer Waterville Police Dept., 1974-78; youth outreach project dir. YMCA, Waterville, 1979; child welfare caseworker Dept. of Human Svcs., Skowhegan, Maine, 1980-81; victim/witness advocate Office of the Dist. Atty., Skowhegan, 1983-85; child welfare caseworker Dept. of Human Svcs., Skowhegan, 1985-88; institutional abuse program specialist Dept. of Human Svcs., Augusta, Maine, 1988-91; child welfare caseworker Dept. of Family and Children Svcs., Atlanta, 1991-94; sch. social worker Maine Sch. Adminstrv. Dist. #74, North Anson, Maine, 1994—; trainer, presenter Maine Criminal Justice Acad., Waterville, 1975-77, 84; adv. bd. Crisis and Counseling Ctr., Waterville, 1976-78, Crisis Stabilization Unit, Skowhegan, 1984-85, Youth and Family Svcs., Skowhegan, 1986-88; criminal justice adv. com. North Kennebec Regional Planning Com., 1979; presenter and spkr. in field. Foster Parent adv. com. Dept. of Human Svcs., Augusta, 1988; pre-trial intervention com. Cmty. Justice Project, Waterville, 1975; task force mem. Gov.'s Task Force, Augusta, 1976-77, 84-85. Named Police Officer of the Yr. Greater Waterville Area Exch. Club, 1975. Mem. ACA, MENSA, Am. Cancer Soc. Mem. LDS Ch. Office: MSAD #74 PO Box 159 North Anson ME 04958

WRIGHT, HELEN KENNEDY, professional association administrator, publisher, editor, librarian; b. Indpls., Sept. 23, 1927; d. William Henry and Ida Louise (Crosby) Kennedy; m. Samuel A. Wright, Sept. 5, 1970; 1 child, Carl F. Prince II (dec.). BA, Butler U., 1945, MS, 1950; MS, Columbia U., 1952. Reference libr. N.Y. Pub. Libr., N.Y.C., 1952-53, Bklyn. Pub. Libr., 1953-54; reference libr., cataloger U. Utah, 1954-57; libr. Chgo. Pub. Libr.; asst. dir. pub. dept. ALA, Chgo., 1958-62, editor Reference Books Bull., 1962-85, asst. dir. for new product planning, pub. svcs., 1985—, dir. office for libr. outreach svcs., 1987-90, mng. editor yearbook, 1988—. Contbr. to Ency. of Careers, Ency. of Libr. and Info. Sci., New Book of Knowledge Ency., Bulletin of Bibliography, New Golden Book Ency. Recipient Louis Shores/Oryx Pr. award, 1991. Mem. Phi Kappa Phi, Kappa Delta Pi, Sigma Gamma Rho. Roman Catholic. Home: 1138 W 111th St Chicago IL 60643-4508 Office: ALA 50 E Huron St Chicago IL 60611-2729

WRIGHT, JANET SCRITSMIER, investment consultant; b. Pomona, Calif., May 21, 1960; d. Jerome Lorenzo and Mildred Joan (Lloyd) Scritsmier; children—Justin Michael, Corey Gray, Cody James. Student Calif. State Poly. U., 1978-79. Vice pres. sales E.L.A. Co., Industry, Calif., 1979-84; investment cons. Cameron Properties Inc., Covina, Calif., 1980—. Asst. instr. Dale Carnegie Sales Course, 1981-82, Human Relations, 1983. Republican. Mormon. Home: 436 N Washington Ave Glendora CA 91741-2560

WRIGHT, JEAN NORMAN, elementary education educator; b. Norristown, Pa., June 20, 1931; d. John Rich and Mildred (Hitchcock) Norman; m. John A. Wright (dec. Mar. 1979); children: Lori Wright Lutter, Larry. BA cum laude, Cedar Crest Coll., Allentown, Pa., 1953. Cert. tchr., Pa. Elem. tchr. Upson Sch., Euclid, Ohio, 1953-55; tchr. art and music Schuylkill Elem. Sch., Phoenixville, Pa., 1965-70, elem. tchr., 1970—. Mem. alumni bd. dirs. Cedar Crest Coll., 1980-84; mem. Phoenixville Community Concert Bd., 1986—. Mem. NEA, Pa. Edn. Assn., Cedar Crest Coll. Alumnae Club (pres. 1962-64), Delta Kappa Gamma (pres. 1990-92). Republican. Presbyterian. Office: Schuylkill Elem Sch Whitehorse Rd Phoenixville PA 19460

WRIGHT, JEANNE ELIZABETH JASON, advertising executive; b. Washington, June 24, 1934; d. Robert Stewart and Elizabeth (Gaddis) Jason; m. Benjamin Hickman Wright, Oct. 30, 1965; stepchildren: Benjamin (dec.), Deborah, David, Patricia. B.A., Radcliffe Coll., 1956; M.A., U. Chgo., 1958. Psychiat. social worker Lake County Mental Health Clinic, Gary, Ind., Psychiat. and Psychosomatic Inst., Michael Reese Hosp., Chgo., Jewish Child Care Assn., N.Y.C., 1958-70; gen. mgr. Black Media, Inc. (advt. rep. co.), N.Y.C., 1970-74; pres. Black Media, Inc. (advt. rep. co.), 1974-75; pres., exec. editor, syndicator weekly editorial features Black Resources, Inc., N.Y.C., 1975—. Mem. planning com. First Black Power Conf., Newark, 1966, Second Black Power Conf., Phila., 1967, First Internat. Black Cultural & Bus. Expn., N.Y.C., 1971; nat. bd. dirs. Afro-Am. Family & Community Svcs., Inc., Chgo., 1971-75; founding coun. mem. Nat. Assault on Illiteracy Program, 1980—; pres. Metro-N.Y. chpt. Nat. Assn. Media Women, Inc., 1986-89. Recipient Pres.' award Nat. Assn. Black Women Attys., 1977, 2d ann. Freedom's Jour. award Journalism Students and Faculty of U. D.C. Dept. Communicative and Performing Arts, 1979, Communication award Harlem Svc. Ctr., ARC, 1988, Spl. award Beta Omicron chpt. Phi Delta Kappa, 1982; named Disting. Black Woman in Industry, Nat. Coun. Negro Women, 1981. Mem. AAAS, Nat. Assn. Social Workers, Acad. Cert. Social Workers, Nat. Assn. Media Women (pres. Met. N.Y. chpt. 1986-89, Nat. Media Woman of Yr. award 1984, 86, Founders award 1986), Newswomen's Club N.Y., U. Chgo. Alumni Assn., NAACP, Radcliffe Club, Harvard Club, Alpha Kappa Alpha. Democrat. Office: 231 W 29th St Ste 1205 New York NY 10001-5209 Home and Office: 1800 NW 187th St Opa Locka FL 33056

WRIGHT, JENIFER VAUSE, accountant, controller; b. Las Vegas, Nov. 24, 1957; d. Earl Wayne Vause and Mae (Brockbank) Inskeep; m. Douglas Keith Rothe, Feb. 17, 1977 (div. Oct. 15, 1979); m. A. Thomas Wright IV, Feb. 14, 1981; children: Lane Marie, Desiree. BA in Gen. Studies, Clark County C.C., Las Vegas, 1989; BS in Bus. Adminstrn., U. Nev., Las Vegas, 1992. CPA, Nev. Bookkeeper, receptionist Roberts Realty, Las Vegas, Nev., 1971-73; teller Valley Bank of Nev., Las Vegas, 1973-75; supr. Avis Rent-A-Car, Las Vegas, 1975-79; acct. Caesar's Palace Hotel and Casino, Las Vegas, 1979-85; fin. controller Nevada Palace Hotel & Casino, Las Vegas, 1985-93; sr. acct. Deloitte & Touche, Las Vegas, 1993-95; controller Fitzgerald's Casino/Hotel, Las Vegas, 1995—; cons. acctg. Physician's Inst. Therapeutic Massage, Las Vegas, 1995—. Recipient Outstanding Acctg. Student award U. Nev. Las Vegas Alumni Assn., 1991; Student Achievement award Wall St. Jour., 1992. Mem. AICPA, Nev. Soc. CPAs, Internat. Assn. Hospitality Accts., So. Nev. Golf Assn. for Bus. Women (treas.), U. Nev. Las Vegas Alumni Assn., Delta Sigma Pi, Alpha Kappa Psi. Office: Fitzgerald's Casino Hotel 301 Fremont St Las Vegas NV 89101 Home: 188 Reed Ln Henderson NV 89014

WRIGHT, JUDITH MARGARET, law librarian, educator; b. Jackson, Tenn., Aug. 16, 1944; d. Joseph Clarence and Mary Catherine (Key) Wright; m. Mark A. Johnson, Apr. 17, 1976; children—Paul, Michael. B.S., Memphis State U., 1966; M.A., U. Chgo., 1971; J.D., DePaul U., 1980. Bar: Ill. 1980. Librarian Oceanway Sch., Jacksonville, Fla., 1966-67; program dir. ARC, South Vietnam, 1967-68; documents and reference librarian D'Angelo Law Library, U. Chgo., 1970-74, reference librarian, 1974-77, dir., lectr. in law, 1980—; mem. adv. bd. Legal Reference Svcs. Quar., 1981—. Mem. ABA, Am. Assn. Law Libraries, Chgo. Assn. Law Libraries. Democrat. Methodist. Home: 5525 S Harper Ave Chicago IL 60637-1829

WRIGHT, JUDITH RAE, retired accountant; b. Paoli, Ind., Feb. 16, 1929; d. Samuel Earl and Bernice Louise (Lomax) Hudelson; m. James Edward Walters, July 11, 1947 (div. June 1971); children: Jamie Jo, Jennifer Rae; m. 2d, George Ralph Wright, Feb. 20, 1972 (dec. Apr. 1977). Student Northwood Inst., West Baden, Ind., 1968-69, Ind.-U.-Purdue U., Indpls., 1972-77. Acct., Ind. Hwy. Commn., Indpls., 1969-75, Ind. Dept. Correction, Indpls., 1975-76, Ind. Dept. Pub. Welfare, Indpls., 1976-78, Ind. Office Social Services, Indpls., 1978-79; acct. supr. Ind. Dept. Pub. Welfare, Indpls., 1979-92, ret. 1992. Recipient Gov.'s Spl. Achievement award, 1992; Mem. Assn. Govt. Accts., Am. Legion Aux., Order of the Eastern Star, Kappa Kappa Kappa. Republican. Mem. First Christian Ch.

WRIGHT, KATIE HARPER, educational administrator, journalist; b. Crawfordsville, Ark., Oct. 5, 1923; d. James Hale and Connie Mary (Locke) Harper; BA, U. Ill., 1944; MEd, 1959; EdD, St. Louis U., 1979; m. Marvin Wright, Mar. 21, 1952; 1 dau., Virginia K. Jordan. Elem. and spl. edn. tchr. East St. Louis (Ill.) Pub. Schs., 1944-65, dir. Dist. 189 Instructional Materials Program, 1965-71, dir. spl. edn. Dists. 188, 189, 1971-77, asst. supt. programs, 1977-79; interim supt. East St. Louis Sch. Dist. 189, 1993-94; adj. faculty Harris/Stowe State Coll., 1980; mem. staff St. Louis U., 1989—; interim supt. Dist. 189 Schs., 1994—; cons. to numerous workshops, seminars in field; mem. study tour People's Republic of China, 1984. Mem. Ill. Commn. on Children, 1973-85, East St. Louis Bd. Election Commrs.; pres. bd. dirs. St. Clair County Mental Health Center, 1970-72, 87— (award 1992); bd. dirs. River Bluff coun. Girl Scouts U.S., 1979—, nat. bd. dirs., 1981-84; bd. dirs. United Way, 1979—, Urban League, 1979—, Provident Counseling Ctr., 1995—; pres. bd. trustees East St. Louis Pub. Library, 1972-77; pres., bd. dirs. St. Clair County Mental Health Ctrs., 1987; adv. bd. Magna Bank; charter mem. Coalition of 100 Black Women; mem. coordinating council ethnic affairs Synod of Mid-Am., Presbyn. Ch. U.S.A; charter mem. Metro East Links Group; charter mem. Gateway chpt. The Links, Inc.; Ill. Minority/Female Bus. Coun., 1991—; mem. State of Ill. Corrections Sch. Bd. Author: Delta Sigma Theta/East St. Louis Chapter History, 1992. Recipient Lamp of Learning award East St. Louis Jr. Wednesday Club, 1965, Outstanding Working Woman award Downtown St. Louis, Inc., 1967, Ill. State citation for ednl. document Love is Not Enough, 1974, Delta Sigma Theta citation for document Good Works, 1979, Girl Scout Thanks badge, 1982, award Nat. Coun. Negro Women, 1983, Community Svc. award Met. East Bar Assn., 1983, Journalist award Sigma Gamma Rho, Spelman Coll. Alumni award, 1990, A World of Difference award, 1990, 91, Edn. award St. Louis YWCA, 1991, SIU-E-Kimmel award, 1991, St. Clair County Mental Health award, 1992, Gateway East Metropolitan Ministry Dr. M.L. King award, 1993, Nat. Coun. Negro Women Black Women Leader of the Year, 1995, Disting. Alumni award U. Ill., 1996; named Woman of Achievement, St. Louis Globe Democrat, 1974, Outstanding Adminstr. So. region Ill. Office Edn., 1975, Woman of Yr. in Edn. St. Clair County YWCA, 1987, Nat. Top Lady of the Yr., 1988; named to Vashon High Sch. Hall of Fame, 1989, Citizen Ambassador, South Africa, 1996. Mem. Am. Libraries Trustees Assn. (regional v.p. 1978-79, 92, nat. sec. 1979-80), Ill. Commn. on Children, Mensa, Council for Exceptional Children, Top Ladies of Distinction (pres. 1987-91, nat. editor 1991—, journalism award 1992, Media award 1992), Delta Sigma Theta (chpt. pres. 1960-62), Kappa Delta Pi (pres. So. Ill. U. chpt. 1973-74), Phi Delta Kappa (Service Key award 1984, chpt. pres. 1984-85), Iota Phi Lambda, Pi Lambda Theta (chpt. pres. 1985-87). Republican. Presbyterian. Club: East St. Louis Women's (pres. 1973-75). Contbr. articles to profl. jours.; feature writer St. Louis Argus Newspaper, 1979—. Home: 733 N 40th St East Saint Louis IL 62205-2138

WRIGHT, L. KATHLENE, physical education educator; b. Harrisburg, Pa., Nov. 16, 1961; d. H. Eugene Wright and Lorelle L. (Zacharias) Vowler. AS, Harcum Jr. Coll., Bryn Mawr, Pa., 1981; BS, West Chester U., 1987; MEd, Pa. State U., 1996. Cert. athletic trainer. Vet. asst. New Bolton Ctr. U. Pa., Kennett Square, 1981-83; athletic trainer Milpitas (Calif.) Phys. Therapy, 1987-88, Chester County Sports P.T., West Chester, Pa., 1988-89; athletic dir. Harcum Coll., Bryn Mawr, Pa., 1989—; athletic trainer Immaculata (Pa.) Coll., 1989—; speaker in field. Athletic trainer U.S. Women's Lacrosse Squad, 1990—. Mem. AAHPERD, U.S. Women's Lacrosse Assn. (head athletic trainer nat. lacrosse tournament 1994), Nat. Athletic Trainer's Assn., Pa. Athletic Trainer's Soc., Ea. Athletic Trainer's Assn. Methodist. Home: 1086 W King Rd # C115 Malvern PA 19355-1975

WRIGHT, LAURALI R. (BUNNY WRIGHT), writer; b. Saskatoon, Sask., Can., June 5, 1939; d. Sidney Victor and Evelyn Jane (Barber) Appleby; m. John Herbert Wright, Jan. 6, 1962 (separated 1986); children: Victoria Kathleen, Johnna Margaret. Student, Carleton U., 1958-59, U. B.C., 1960, 62-63, U. Calgary, 1970-71, Banff Sch. Fine Arts, 1976; MA, Simon Fraser U., Burnaby, B.C., Can., 1995. Reporter Saskatoon Star-Phoenix, 1968-69, Calgary Albertan, 1969-70; reporter, columnist Calgary Herald, 1970-76, 1970-76, asst. city editor, 1976-77; freelance writer Calgary, 1977—. Author: (novels) Neighbours, 1979 (New Alta. novelist award Alta Culture and Multiculturalism 1978), The Favorite, 1982, Among Friends, 1984, The Suspect, 1985 (Edgar Allen Poe award Mystery Writers Am. 1986), Sleep While I Sing, 1986, Love in the Temperate Zone, 1988, A Chill Rain in January, 1989 (Arthur Ellis award Crime Writers Can. 1990), Fall From Grace, 1991, Prized Possessions, 1993, A Touch of Panic, 1994, Mother Love, 1995. Mem. Writers Union Can., Authors' Guild of U.S., Internat. P.E.N., Mystery Writers of Am., Authors League Am., Periodical Writers Assn. Can., Writers Fedn. B.C. Office: Virginia Barber Lit Agy Inc 101 Fifth Ave New York NY 10003-1008

WRIGHT, LILYAN BOYD, physical education educator; b. Upland, Pa., May 11, 1920; d. Albert Verlenden and Mabel (Warburton) Boyd; B.S., Temple U., 1942, M.Ed., 1946; Ed.D., Rutgers U., 1972; m. Richard P. Wright, Oct. 23, 1942; 1 child, Nicki Wright Vanek. Tchr. health and phys. edn. Woodbury (N.J.) High Sch., 1942-43, Glen-Nor High Sch., Glenolden, Pa., 1944-46, Chester (Pa.) High Sch., 1946-54; chmn. women's dept. health and phys. edn. Union (N.J.) High Sch., 1954-61; with Trenton State Coll., 1961-90, head women's program health and phys. edn., 1967-77, chmn. dept. health, phys. edn. and recreation, 1977-86, adj. faculty mem. 1990-92, prof. emeritus, 1991—; mem. N.J. State Com. Div. Girls and Women's Sports, 1958-80; chmn. New Atlantic Field Hockey Sectional Umpiring, 1981-85; chmn. New Atlantic Field Hockey Assn., 1985-90; with recreation after sch. program Newport Counseling Ctr., 1992-93. Active Chester United Fund; water safety, first aid instr.; vestry Ch. Epiphany, Newport, N.H., 1992—, sr. warden, 1995—; vestry St. Luke's Episcopal Ch., 1988-91; trustee Olive Pettis Libr., Goshen, 1992—; dist. ednl. improvement team for Goshen-Lempster Sch. Dist., 1995—. ARC Scholarship in her honor N.J. Athletic Assn. Girls, 1971; named to Hall of Fame, Temple U., 1976. Recipient U.S. Field Hockey Assn. award, 1989, named Nat. Honorary Field Hockey Umpire. Mem. AAHPERD (chmn. Eastern Dist. Assn. Div. Girls and Women's Sports, sec. to council for services Eastern dist. 1979-80, chmn. 1980-81, chmn. com. on aging and adult devel. of ea. dist. 1993—, N.J. rep. to council for convs. 1984-85, Honor Fellow award 1986), N.J. AHPER (pres. 1974-75, past pres. 1975-76, v.p. phys. edn. div., parliamentarian

1990—, Disting. Service and Leadership award 1969, 93, Honor Fellow award 1977, Presdl. Citation award 1993, 95, Disting. Leadership award 1994), N.J. Women's Lacrosse Assn. (umpiring chmn. 1972-76), Nat. Assn. Phys. Edn. in Higher Edn., Eastern Assn. Phys. Edn. Coll. Women, North Jersey, Ctrl. Jersey bds. women's ofcls., Am., Pa. (v.p. 1953-54), Chester (pres. 1949-54) fedns. tchrs., U.S. Field Hockey Assn. (exec. com., chair honorary umpire award com. 1992), North Jersey Field Hockey Assn. (past pres.), N.H. Field Hockey Umpires' Assn., No. New Eng. Lacrosse Officials Bd., U.S. Women's LaCrosse Assn. (Honorary and Emeritus Umpiring Rating award), Kappa Delta Epsilon, Delta Psi Kappa (past pres. Phila. alumni chpt.), Kappa Delta Pi. Home: PO Box 239 Goshen NH 03752

WRIGHT, LINDA JEAN, manufacturing company executive; b. Chgo., Dec. 14, 1949; d. Eugene F. and Rosemary Margaret (Kiley) Kemph; m. Kelly W. Wright, Jr., Feb. 1979 (div. 1984); m. Samuel Neuwirth Klewans, Aug. 28, 1986 (div. 1991). Student Loretto Heights Coll., 1967-69, U. Ill., 1970-71. Asst. to v.p. Busey 1st Nat. Bank, Urbana, 1969-72; spa mgr., supr. sales tng. Venus and Apollo Health Club, San Antonio, 1973-76; owner Plant Shop, San Antonio, 1976-77; with Enterprise Bank, Falls Church, Va., 1977-84, comml. lending officer, 1978-84, sr. v.p., 1979-84, corp. sec. of bd. dirs., 1980-84; pres., CEO Fairfax Savs. Bank, 1984-87, Bankstar, N.A. (formerly Bank 2000 of Reston, N.A.), 1988-90; v.p. Ryan-McGinn Inc., Arlington, Va., 1991-95; v.p. Bethlehem Corp., 1995—; bd. dirs. INOVA Inst. Rsch. and Edn., 1990-94. Apptd. pub. ofcl., chmn. Va. Small Bus. Fin. Authority, Richmond, 1984-88; trustee Inova Health System, 1992-95; mem. exec. com. Fairfax-Falls Ch., United Way, United Way Capital Area, Washington, 1984-85; Fairfax County Spl. Task Force, 1986; bd. dirs. Fairfax Com. of 100, 1993-95; mem., bd. dirs. Hospice No. Va., Arlington, 1985-86, chmn. No. Va. Local Devel. Corp., 1986; mem. oper. bd. Fairfax Hosp., 1987-94; pres. No. Va. Transp. Alliance, 1987-92; bd. dirs. Va. Found. for Rsch. and Econ. Edn., 1989-91, No. Va. coun. Am. Heart Assn., 1989-94. Mem. Fairfax County C. of C. (dir., v.p., pres. 1987-88), Nat. Assn. Bank Women (chmn. No. Va. group 1980-81), Fairfax Hunt Club, Tower Club (bd. govs. 1989-95). Roman Catholic. Avocations: aviation, fox hunting.

WRIGHT, LISA KATHRYN, rehabilitation counselor; b. Houston, Feb. 26, 1966; d. Larry Joe Shook and Janel Blalock. AA, Tarran County Jr. Coll., Hurst, Tex., 1986; BA, Stephen F. Austin State U., 1988; MS, Univ. Tex., 1991. Rehabilitation counselor LW Assocs., Dallas, 1990-92, High Plains Baptist Hosp., Amarillo, Tex., 1992—. Recipient Most Likely to Succeed award Zeta Tau Alpha, 1988. Mem. Nat. Rehabilitation Assn., Nat. Rehabilitation Counseling Assn., Tex. Rehabilitation Assn. Home: 5638 River Rd Amarillo TX 79108 Office: FIRSTCARE-Amarillo Medicine & Rehabilitation 320 S Polk Ste 900 Amarillo TX 79101

WRIGHT, MAE A., engineering and emergency management specialist; b. Northampton, Mass., Nov. 14, 1956; d. Lawrence Sheperd and Caroline Mary (La Rose) Wright; m. Frederick Wright Damerow, Aug. 7, 1981 (div. 1991). BSME, Worcester Poly. Inst., 1980. Assoc. engr. nuclear safety Westinghouse Electric Corp., Monroeville, Pa., 1978-80, engr. nuclear safety, 1980, shift tech. advisor Salem nuclear plant, 1980-81, engr. info. program, 1981-84, sr. engr. info. program, 1984, mgr. info. program, 1984-86, mgr. bus. rels., 1987-88; mgr. community rels. West Valley (N.Y.) Demonstration Project, 1988—, mgr. community rels. and total quality, 1990-91, mgr. ops. support, 1991—; speaker Campus Am., nationwide, 1979-81; bd. dirs. Energy Source Edn. Coun., Washington, 1987, pres. bd. dirs., 1988-90; mem. mgmt. com. Electric Info. Coun., N.D., 1987-89; mem. program com. U.S. Com. for Energy Awareness, Washington, 1987-89; mem. publs. subcom. U.S. Coun. for Energy Awareness, 1988-89.

WRIGHT, MARCIA LOUISE, information systems professional; b. Ocala, Fla., Oct. 29, 1952; d. Abner Wendell and Margaret J. (Glattli) W. BS in Math. with honors, U. Fla., 1974; postgrad., Fla. Internat. U., 1977-79. Programmer/analyst IBM, Research Triangle Park, N.C., 1974, Lee-Vac Enterprises, Morgan City, L.A., 1975-76, sr. programmer/analyst Deltona Corp., Miami, Fla., 1976-79; v.p., ptnr. S.E.D.I.P., Ft. Lauderdale, Fla., 1979-81; exec. dir. info. sys. Alamo Rent A Car, Inc., Ft. Lauderdale, 1981—; mem. DIS forum U. Fla., Gainesville, 1989-95; mem. mgmt. adv. bd. ViaSoft, Phoenix, 1993-95; mem. MIS adv. bd. Fla. State Univ. Sys., 1989—. Chair Alumnae Leadership Broward Found. Cmty. Focus Group, Ft. Lauderdale, 1994-96, mem. family finders project, 1993-94; mem. IS Softball Team, 1981-95; mem. Mus. Art, Ft. Lauderdale, 1991-95. Fla. Regents scholar, 1970-72, Fla. Tchrs. scholar, 1970-74. Mem. NAFE. Democrat. Baptist.

WRIGHT, MARIE ANNE, management information systems educator; b. Albany, N.Y., Oct. 21, 1953; d. Arthur Irving and Ethel (Knickerbocker) W. BS, U. Mass., Boston, 1981; MBA, Clarkson U., 1984; PhD, U. Mass., Amherst, 1989. Systems analyst St. Lawrence U., Canton, N.Y., 1983-84; instr. Bentley Coll., Waltham, Mass., 1984-85; computer cons. Amherst (Mass.) Police Dept., 1986-88; asst. prof. Elms Coll., Chicopee, Mass., 1986-89; assoc. prof. Western Conn. State U., Danbury, 1990—; cons. Ctr. for Human Devel., Springfield, Mass., 1986-87, Early Childhood Ctr., 1986-87. Contbr. articles to profl. jours. and mags. Recipient Teaching Assistantship, U. Mass., 1985, Rsch. Assistantship, 1986; Grad. Assistantship, Clarkson U., Potsdam, N.Y., 1982, MIS award U. Mass., 1981. Mem. AAUW, IEEE, Assn. Computing Machinery, Math. Assn. Am., Comm. Security Assn., Nat. Computer Security Assn., Info. Sys. Security Assn., Assn. Women in Math., Boston Computer Soc., Beta Gamma Sigma. Democrat. Office: Western Conn State U MIS Dept Danbury CT 06810

WRIGHT, MILDRED ANNE (MILLY WRIGHT), conservator, researcher; b. Athens, Ala., Sept. 9, 1939; d. Thomas Howard and Anne Louise (Ashworth) Speegle; m. William Paul Wright, Nov. 20, 1965; children: Paul Howard, William Neal. BS in Physics, U. Ala., Tuscaloosa, 1963. Rschr. in acoustics Wyle Labs., Huntsville, Ala., 1963-64; tchr. physics, English Huntsville H.S., 1964-67; ptnr. Flying Carpet Oriental Rugs, Florence, Ala., 1974—; adj. mem. faculty U. North Ala., Florence, 1988, lectr. Inst. for Learning in Retirement, 1991—. Columnist Times Daily, 1992—; photojournalist, writer River Views Mag., 1993—; contbr. articles to profl. jours. (1st pl. award 1986, 87). Pianist, organist Edgemont Meth. Ch., Florence, 1987-90 (Outstanding Svc. award 1990); mem. steering com. Melton Hollow Nature Ctr., Florence, 1990—, Design Ala., Florence, 1991, River Heritage Discovery Campt, 1993—; mem. River Heritage Com., Florence, 1991—; accompanist Shoals Boy Choir, Muscle Shoals, Ala., 1992-93; bd. dirs. Heritage Preservation, Inc., 1989—, Capital award, 1992, pres., 1990-92, 96—, treas., 1995-96, Tenn. Valley Hist. Soc., pres., 1991-95, Ala. Preservation Alliance, treas., 1993—, Florence Main Street program, 1992-94, Maud Lindsay Free Kindergarten, Frank Lloyd Wright Rosenbaum House Found., Inc., 1992—, Gen. Joseph Wheeler Home Found., 1994—, treas. 1995—, newsletter editor, 1995—; sec. Friends of the Ala. Archives, 1995—; mem. adv. coun. Human Environ. Scis. Dept.; mem. Coby Hall steering com. U. North Ala., 1992—, Kennedy-Douglas Ctr. Arts; adv. bd. Cahala of Ala., 1996—; adv. bd. Waterloo Mus., 1995—, Florence Children's Mus., 1995—; exhibit chmn. Tenn. Valley Art Assn., 1996—. Recipient Disting. Svc. award Ala. Hist. Commn., 1991, Merit award Ala. Preservation Alliance, 1995. Mem. Ala. Writers' Conclave (Creative Works award 1986, 87), Ala. Hist. Assn., Ala. Archeol. Soc., Natchez Trace Geneal. Soc., Colbert County Hist. Landmarks Found., Nat. Trust for Hist. Preservation, Tennessee Valley Art Assn. (exhibit chmn. 1995—), La Grange Living History Assn., Trail of Tears Assn., Firenze Club (past pres., pres. 1996—), Optimist Club, Sigma Pi Sigma. Home: PO Box 279 Florence AL 35631-0279

WRIGHT, NANCY JANE, English language educator; b. Springfield, Ill., Feb. 28, 1939; d. William Joseph and Elizabeth (Walton) Lucasey; m. Arthur Lee Wright, Aug. 21, 1960; 1 child, John Arthur. BS magna cum laude, Western Ill. U., 1961; MS summa cum laude, So. Ill. U., 1963; PhD, Tex. A&M U., 1975. Tchg. asst. So. Ill. U., Carbondale, 1961-62; instr. Ferris State Coll., Big Rapids, Mich., 1962-65, Christian Coll., Columbia, Mo., 1965-70; tchg. asst. then instr. Tex. A&M U., College Station, 1971-76; instr. lit. Blinn Coll., Bryan, Tex., 1977—; mem. Am. Disabilities Task Force, Blinn Coll., Bryan, 1994—, mem. curriculum com., 1993-94, acad. advisor coord., 1995—; workshop leader. Co-author: How to Prepare for the Tasp, 1991, 2d edit., 1994. Vol. instr. LIFT Program, Dallas, 1970-71; dir. music, pianist/accompanist First Christian Ch., Bryan. Mem. Blinn Coll. Profl. Assn. (founding pres.), Nat. Coun. Tchrs. English, Tex. Jr. Coll. Tchrs. Assn. Republican. Mem. Disciples of Christ Ch. Home: 1008 Holt St College Station TX 77840-2621

WRIGHT, PHYLLIS CAROL, physical education educator; b. Fairmont, W.Va., Sept. 23, 1944; d. Fred Charles and Margaret (Worley) Smay; m. Harold David Wright, Apr. 23, 1966; children: Susan Elizabeth Wright Foley, Jill Allison Wright Walters. BS cum laude, Fairmont State Coll., 1966. Cert. tchr. elem. phys. edn., secondary health, Va. Tchr. phys. edn. Warren County Schs., Front Royal, Va., 1969—; lectr. in field. Author: (games) Great Activities Publications, 1993, 94. Bd. dirs., v.p. and telethon chmn. Am. Cancer Soc., 1995-96. Mem. Va. Edn. Assn., Warren County Edn. Assn. (pres. 1981-83), No. Shenandoah Valley Alumnae (life), Skyline Uniserv (sec. 1994-95), Sigma Sigma Sigma. Home: PO Box 478 Front Royal VA 22630 Office: Jeffries Elementary Sch 320 E Criser Rd Front Royal VA 22630

WRIGHT, ROBIN, actress; b. Dallas, Apr. 8, 1966; d. Fred Wright; children: Dylan Frances, Hopper Jack; m. Sean Penn, Apr. 27, 1996. Television appearances include The Yellow Rose, 1983-84, Santa Barbara, 1984-87 (Emmy awards Best Ingenue in a Daytime Drama series 1985-87); films include Hollywood Vice Squad, 1986, The Princess Bride, 1987, State of Grace, 1990, Denial, 1991, The Playboys, 1992, Toys, 1992, Forrest Gump, 1994, The Crossing Guard, 1995, Moll Flanders, 1995, Loved, 1996. Office: Care CAA 9830 Wilshire Blvd Beverly Hills CA 90212*

WRIGHT, ROSALIE MULLER, newspaper and magazine editor; b. Newark, June 20, 1942; d. Charles and Angela (Fortunata) Muller; m. Lynn Wright, Jan. 13, 1962; children: James Anthony Meador, Geoffrey Shepard. BA in English, Temple U., 1965. Mng. editor Suburban Life mag., Orange, N.J., 1960-62; assoc. editor Phila. mag., 1962-64, mng. editor, 1969-73; founding editor Womensports mag., San Mateo, Calif., 1973-75; editor scene sect. San Francisco Examiner, 1975-77; exec. editor New West mag., San Francisco and Beverly Hills, Calif., 1977-81; features and Sunday editor San Francisco Chronicle, 1981-87, asst. mng. editor features, 1987-96; v.p. and editor-in-chief Sunset Mag, Menlo Park, Calif., 1996—; tchr. mag. writing U. Calif., Berkeley, 1975-76; participant pub. procedures course Stanford U., 1977-79; chmn. mag. judges at conf. Coun. Advancement and Support of Edn., 1980, judge, 1984. Contbr. numerous mag. articles, critiques, revs., Compton's Ency. Mem. Am. Assn. Sunday and Feature Editors (treas. 1984, sec. 1985, 1st v.p. 1986, pres. 1987), Am. Newspaper Pubs. Assn. (pub. task force on minorities in newspaper bus. 1988-89, Chronicle minority recruiter 1987-94), Internat. Women's Forum, Women's Forum West (bd. dirs. 1993—, sec. 1994). Office: Sunset Magazine 80 Willow Rd Menlo Park CA 94025

WRIGHT, SHEILA PHELAN, education educator, university official; b. Bristol, Conn., Apr. 27, 1941; d. John Fenton and Helen (Breene) Phelan; m. Robert Curtis Wright (div. 1976); children: Robert, Christian; m. Roscoe Earl Hill, Aug. 26, 1995. BA in English magna cum laude, U. Hartford, MA in Lit., 1976, MEd in Reading, 1978; PhD in Higher Edn., U. Conn., 1988. Tchr. English, Watkinson Sch., 1975-76; instr. composition and lit. and ESL, U. Hartford, Conn., 1976-82, lectr. humanities, 1982-86, assoc. prof., 1986-90; dir., chmn. all-univ. curriculum U. Hartford, 1990-93; assoc. prof. edn. U. Denver, 1993—, vice provost for undergrad. studies and campus life, 1993—, cons., spkr. women mentoring women, 1996; co-dir. gen. edn. project Strong Founds., 1991-93; seminar participant NYU, 1990, Spelman Coll., 1992; presenter in field. Author: (with P. Russman) Changing Bodies, Changing Goals: Youth Soccer Stories, 1984; contbr. articles to profl. jours. Former vol. Glastonbury (Conn.) Dm. Com.; fundraiser Glastonbury United Soccer, 1984-88. Grantee Greater Hartford Consortium, 1991-92. Mem. Assn. Am. Colls. and Univs., Am. Assn. Higher Edn., Am. Coun. on Edn., Coun. on Undergrad. Rsch., Assn. for Advancement Core Curriculum, Profl. and Orgnl. Devel. Network, Nat. Assn. Humanities Educators, Nat. Women's Studies Assn., Nat. Collegiate Athletic Conf., Colo. Assn. for Women in Highr Edn. Home: 420 Adams St Unit D Denver CO 80206 Office: U Denver University Ave Denver CO 80208

WRIGHT, SUSAN WEBBER, judge; b. Texarkana, Ark., Aug. 22, 1948; d. Thomas Edward and Betty Jane (Gary) Webber; m. Robert Ross Wright, III, May 21, 1983; 1 child, Robin Elizabeth. BA, Randolph-Macon Woman's Coll., 1970; MPA, U. Ark., 1972, JD with high honors, 1975. Bar: Ark. 1975. Law clk. U.S. Ct. Appeals 8th Circuit, 1975-76; asst. prof. law U. Ark.-Little Rock, 1976-78, assoc. prof., 1978-83, prof., 1983-90, asst. dean, 1976-78; dist. judge U.S. Dist. Ct. (ea. dist.) Ark., Little Rock, 1990—; vis. assoc. prof. Ohio State U., Columbus, 1981, La. State U., Baton Rouge, 1982-83; mem. adv. com. U.S. Ct. Appeals 8th Circuit, St. Louis, 1983-88. Author: (with R. Wright) Land Use in a Nutshell, 1978, 2d edit., 1985; editor-in-chief Ark. Law Rev., 1975; contbr. articles to profl. jours. Mem. ABA, Ark. Bar Assn., Pulaski County Bar Assn., Ark. Assn. Women Lawyers (v.p. 1977-78). Episcopalian. Office: US Courthouse 600 W Capitol Ave Ste 302 Little Rock AR 72201-3323

WRIGHT, TARA JEAN, guidance counselor; b. S.I., N.Y., July 21, 1968; d. James and Eileen (Darragh) W. BS in Elem. Edn., We. Conn. State U., 1990, MS in Sch. Counseling, 1995. Cert. sch. counselor, N.Y., K-t tchr., N.Y. Elem. tchr. North Salem (N.Y.) Schs., 1991-94; guidance counselor Dover (N.Y.) Jr./Sr. H.S., 1994-95, Webutuck H.S., Amenia, N.Y., 1995—. Mem. ACA, Am. Sch. Counseling Assn. Home: 10 West Ridge Rd Brewster NY 10509

WRIGHT, TENA RENÉE, educational administrator; b. N.Y.C., Oct. 25, 1947; d. William and Norma (Pincus) Brown; m. Charles Edward Wright, May 23, 1970; children: Alyssa Pamela, Aaron Jacob. BS of Edn., SUNY, Buffalo, 1969, MS of Edn., 1972. Permanent cert. secondary edn. biology, N.Y., cert. sci. K-12, N.J., cert supr., N.J. Tchr. Buffalo Bd. Edn., 1969-78; editor Macmillan Pub. Co., N.Y.C., 1981-84; lab. technician N.Y. State Inst. for Basic Rsch., S.I., 1984-86; tchr. Linden (N.J.) Bd. of Edn., 1986-93; supr. Hillsborough (N.J.) Bd. of Edn., 1993—; adj. faculty Rutgers U., New Brunswick, N.J., 1990—; trainer, cons. Rutgers Family Sci., New Brunswick, 1989—; trainer Gt. Expectations in Math. and Sci., Berkeley, Calif., 1990—. Editor: Family Science Manual, 1993. Named to Honor Roll of Tchrs., Assn. Sci./Tech. Ctrs., 1990; grantee N.J. Statewide Sys. Initiative, 1995. Mem. AAUW, NOW, Nat. Sci. Tchrs. Assn. (Ohaus award for innovations in elem. sci. tchg. 1991), N.J. Sci. Suprs. Assn., N.J. Sci. Tchrs. Assn. Office: Hillsborough Twp Bd Edn 555 Amwell Rd Neshanic Station NJ 08853

WRISTON, KATHRYN DINEEN, lawyer, business executive; b. Syracuse, N.Y.; d. Robert Emmet and Carolyn (Bareham) Dineen; m. Walter B. Wriston, Mar. 14, 1968; 1 stepchild. Student, U. Geneva, 1958-59; BA cum laude, Smith Coll., 1960; LLB, U. Mich., 1963. Bar: N.Y.1964, U.S. Ct. Appeals (2nd cir.) 1964, U.S. Supreme Ct. 1968. Assoc. Shearman & Sterling, N.Y.C., 1963-68; bd. dirs. Northwestern Mut. Life Ins. Co., mem. ins. products and mktg. com., 1986-89, mem. audit com., 1989—, mem. investment and fin. policy com., 1989—; bd. dirs. Santa Fe Energy Resources, Inc., mem. audit com., 1990—, chmn., 1990-93, 95—, mem. nominating com., 1990—; trustee Fin. Acctg. Found., 1992—, mem. selection com., 1992-95, mem. audit com., 1992—, chmn., 1993-96, chmn. devel. com., 1996—, mem. fin. com., 1994—, mem. exec. com., 1996—; mem. task force on timely fin. reporting guidanace Fin. Acctg. Stds. Bd., 1982-83, mem. bd. agenda adv. com., 1981-85, mem. process and structure com., 1981-85, chmn., 1983-85; mem. exec. com. CPR Inst. for Dispute Resolution, 1994—; bd. dirs. Waccamaw Corp., mem. adult stkoption, comp. coms.; bd. dirs. The Stanley Works, mem. public policy and fin. and pension coms., 1996—. Mem. vis. com. U. Mich. Law Sch., 1973—; trustee Fordham U., Bronx, N.Y., 1971-77, 78-81, vice chmn. bd. trustees, 1980-81, mem. student affairs com., 1971-77, chmn., 1974-77, mem. faculty affairs com., 1978-81, mem. grievance com., 1971-77, 78-81, mem. com. on law sch., 1978-81; mem. ea. region selection panel Pres. Commn. on White House Fellowships, 1981-83, chmn., 1982-83; mem. bus. com. Nat. Ctr. for State Cts., 1982-88; bd. overseers Rand Inst. for Civil Justice, 1985-93; trustee John A. Hartford Found., 1991—, mem. grant com., 1991—, vice chmn., 1992—, mem. evaluation com., 1991—, mem. audit com., 1992—, chmn., 1993—; active Gov. Wilson's N.Y. Little Hoover Commn., 1974. Mem. ABA, Nat. Assn. Accts., Practicing Law Inst. (exec. 1976—, mem. programs and publs. com., chmn. 1979—, mem. membership com. 1976—, chmn. 1977-79, mem. nominating com. 1978, 81-85, mem. bar rev. courses 1978-79, mem. fin. com. 1989—, mem. Am. Law Inst./ABA subcom. on Am. law network 1989-91), Fin. Women's Assn. N.Y., N.Y. County Lawyers Assn. (legal aid com. 1972-76), N.Y. State Bar Assn., Assn. Bar City N.Y.

WROBLE, LISA ANN, writer, educator; b. Dearborn, Mich., June 17, 1963; d. Robert Frank and Ruth Marie (Schiller) W. Diploma, Inst. Children's Lit., 1983; BA, Ea. Mich. U., Ypsilanti, 1985. Cert. ESL tchr. Asst. editor cmty. rels. Vets. Adminstrn., Ann Arbor, Mich., 1983-85; prodn. coord. Cmty. Crier Newspaper/COMMA Graphics, Plymouth, Mich., 1985-86; proofreader Valassis Inserts, Livonia, Mich., 1986-89; tech. writer Nat. TechTeam, Dearborn, Mich., 1989-90; freelance writer Plymouth, 1990—; part-time publicist Garden City (Mich.) Osteopathic Hosp., 1990-91; creative writing instr. Cmty. Edn. Plymouth (Mich.)-Canton Schs., 1992-93. Contbg. editor Metroparent, 1991-93; contbg. tech. writer Facilities Planning News, 1993—; book reviewer The ALAN Rev., 1993—; contbr. essays and sects. to reference books. Tutor Cmty. Literacy Coun., Plymouth, 1989-93; vol. spkr. in schs. Recipient Reading Tutor award Cmty. Literacy Coun., 1991, 92, 93. Mem. Soc. Childrens Book Writers and Illustrators (adv. com. Mich. chpt. 1993-94), Nat. Writers Assn. (vol. critiquer 1989-93), Childrens Lit. Assn., Livonia Writers Group. Republican. Roman Catholic.

WROBLESKI, JEANNE PAULINE, lawyer; b. Phila., Feb. 14, 1942; d. Edward Joseph and Pauline (Popelak) W.; m. Robert J. Klein, Dec. 3, 1979. BA, Immaculata Coll., 1964; MA, U. Pa., 1966; JD, Temple U., 1975. Bar: Pa. 1975. Pvt. practice law, Phila., 1975—; ptnr. Kohn, Swift & Graf, P.C., Phila.; lectr. on bus. law Wharton Sch., Phila. Mem. Commn. on Women and the Legal Profession, 1986-89; v.p. Center City Residents' Assn. Eisenhower Citizen Amb. del. to Soviet Union. Bd. dirs. South St. Dance Co., Women in Transition; bd. dirs., mem. exec. com. Temple Law Alumni; del. to Moscow con. on law and econ. coop., 1990; del. to jud. conf. for 3d cir. U.S. Ct. Appeals, 1991; mediator U.S. Dist. Ct. (ea. dist.) Pa., 1996. Rhea Liebman scholar, 1974. Mem. AAUW, ABA, Pa. Bar Assn., Phila. Bar Assn. (chmn. women's rights com. 1986, com. on jud. selection and reform 1986-87, chmn. appellate cts. com. 1992, bus. cts. task force), Pa. Acad. Fine Arts, Nat. Mus. Women in the Arts, Am. Judicature Soc., Jagiellonian Law Soc., Alpha Psi Omega, Lambda Iota Tau. Democrat. Clubs: Lawyers, Founders, Peale, Penn. Office: Kohn Swift & Graf PC 2400 One Reading Ctr 1101 Market St Philadelphia PA 19107-2934

WRUCK, MICHELLE MINGINO, pediatric nurse practitioner; b. Mastic, N.Y., Dec. 14, 1957; d. Michael A. and Vivian (Marrazzo) Mingino; m. Ernest R. Wruck, Oct. 14, 1979; children: Kristanya, Alexander. RN, Beth Israel Hosp., 1978; BS, St. Joseph's Coll., 1989; MS, SUNY, Stony Brook, 1993. Staff nurse pediatrics/pediatric ICU SUNY, Stony Brook, 1980-86, clin. coord. outpatient transfusion clinic, 1988-90; dir. nursing Infants and Children's Health Svcs., Middle Island, N.Y., 1990-93; PNP, Suffolk County Dept. Health, Hauppauge, N.Y., 1993-94, SUNY, Stony Brook, 1994—; chmn. nursing panel discussion Thalassemia Internat. Fedn. Conf. and N.Y. Acad. Scis. Conf., 1990; vol. insvc. educator battered women's shelter, 1985; guest lectr. in field, 1980—. Mem. Coalition Nurse Practitioners L.I., N.Y. State Nurses Assn. (bd. dirs. dist. # 19 1990-93), Sigma Theta Tau. Home: 8 Drew Dr Eastport NY 11941-1335

WRUCKE-NELSON, ANN C., elementary school educator; b. Mankato, Minn., Nov. 5, 1939; d. G.F. and Dorothy (Thomas) Wrucke; children: Chris, Dor-Ella. BS, Mankato State U., 1961; MLA, So. Meth. U., 1974; postgrad., U. Minn., 1963, Tex. Woman's U.; EdD in Early Childhood Edn., Tex. Woman's U., 1992. Cert. elem., kindergarten, bilingual-ESL, history tchr., Tex. Tchr. Rochester (Minn.) Pub. Schs., Christ the King Sch., Dallas; dir., tchr. Norway Christian Presch., Dallas; Every Student Learns Lang. program kindergarten tchr. Dallas Ind. Sch. Dist.; tchr. summer session Tex. Woman's U., 1991; presenter in field. Producer video: A Year of Language Learning, 1990. Sunday sch. tchr. Holy Trinity Ch. Recipient Tchr. of Yr. award, 1989, Tex. TESOL scholarship, 1994; Bill Martin Literacy Conf. scholar; named ESL Tchr. of Yr., 1991. Mem. Assn. for Childhood Edn. Internat., So. Assn. on Children Under Six, Tchrs. English to Speakers Other Lang., Tex. Tchrs. English to Speakers Other Lang., Dallas Assn. for Edn. of Young Child.

WRYNN, GAIL SUSAN, elementary educator; b. N.Y.C., Jan. 25, 1956; d. Leo and Angela (Bavaro) Beccaro; m. James Wrynn, Sept. 17, 1978 (div. 1986). BS in Psychology, Fordham U., 1978; MS in Edn., Coll. New Rochelle, 1993. Cert. tchr., adminstrn. and supervision, N.Y. Tchr. Immaculate Heart Acad., Washington Twp., N.J., 1981-86; head tchr. Mosholu Montefiore, N.Y.C., 1986-87; tchr. N.Y.C. Bd. Edn., 1988—; mentor tchr. N.Y.C. Bd. Edn., Bronx, 1988—. Active learning grantee Chase Manhattan Bank, 1993-94. Mem. United Fedn. Tchrs. Democrat. Home: 97 Lee Ave Yonkers NY 10705 Office: NYC Bd Edn 2545 Gunther Ave Bronx NY 10705

WU, NAN FAION, pediatrician; b. Malaysia, July 13, 1943; came to U.S., 1969; m. Chia F. Wu, June 22, 1969; children: Edwin, Karen. MD, Nat. Taiwan U., 1969. Diplomate Am. Bd. Pediatrics. Intern Atlantic City Med. Ctr., 1969-70; resident in pediatrics Martland Hosp. U. Medicine and Dentistry of N.J., N.J. Med. Sch., Newark, 1970-73; pvt. practice pediatrics West Orange, N.J. Fellow Am. Acad. Pediatrics. Office: 35 Park Ave West Orange NJ 07052-5526

WU, PATTI T., lawyer; b. N.Y.C., Aug. 30, 1953. BA, SUNY, Stony Brook, 1974; JD, NYU, 1981, LLM in Taxation, 1986. Bar: N.Y. 1982. Ptnr. Brown & Wood, N.Y.C. Office: Brown & Wood One World Trade Ctr New York NY 10048-0557*

WU, YING CHU LIN SUSAN, engineering company executive, engineer; b. Beijing, June 23, 1932; came to U.S., 1957; d. Chi-yu and K.C. (Kung) Lin; m. Jain-Ming Wu, June 13, 1959; children: Ernest H., Albert H., Karen H. BSME, Nat. Taiwan U., 1955; MS in Aero. Engring., Ohio State U., 1959; PhD in Aeros., Calif. Inst. Tech., 1963. Sr. engr. Elecro-Optical Systems, Inc., Pasadena, Calif., 1963-65; asst. prof. aero. engring. U. Tenn. Space Inst., Tullahoma, 1965-67, assoc. prof., 1967-73, prof., 1973-88; adminstr. Energy Conversion R&D Programs, Tullahoma, 1981-88; pres., chief exec. officer ERC, Inc., Tullahoma, 1987—; presdl. appointee adv. bd. Nat. Air and Space Mus., Smithsonian Inst., 1993—. Contbr. over 90 articles to profl. jours. Mem. Better Sch. Task Force, Tullahoma, 1985-86; founding mem. Tullahoma Edn. Found. for Excellence; trustee Rochester Inst. Tech., 1992-94; mem. adv. com. NASA Aeronautics, 1994—. Recipient Chancellor's Rsch. award U. Tenn., 1978, Outstanding Educator of Am. award, 1973, 75; Amelia Earhart fellow, 1958, 59, 62, Plasmadynamics and Laser-saward Am. Inst. of Aeronautics and Astronautics, 1994. Fellow ASME, AIAA (assoc., chmn. Tenn. sect., H.H. Arnold award 1984, Plasmodynamics and Lasers award 1994); mem. Soc. Women Engrs. (life mem., achievement award 1985), Rotary, Sigma Xi (chmn. U. Tenn. Space Inst. club). Office: ERC Inc PO Box 417 Tullahoma TN 37388-0417 Address: 111 Lakewood Dr Tullahoma TN 37388

WUDUNN, SHERYL, journalist, correspondent; b. N.Y.C., Nov. 16, 1959; d. David and Alice (Mark) W.; m. Nicholas D. Kristof, Oct. 8, 1988. BA, Cornell U., Ithaca, N.Y., 1981; MBA, Harvard U., 1986; MPA, Princeton U., 1988. Lending officer Bankers Trust Co., N.Y.C., 1981-84; intern reporter Wall St. Jour., L.A., 1986; bus. reporter South China Morning Post, Hong Kong, 1987; corr. N.Y. Times, Beijing, 1989-93, Tokyo, 1995—. Coauthor: China Wakes, 1994. Recipient Pulitzer Prize for fgn. reporting, 1990, George Polk award L.I. U., N.Y., 1990, Hal Boyle award Overseas Press Club, 1990. Office: NY Times Asahi Shumbun Bldg, 3-2 Tsukiji 5-chome, Chuo-ku Tokyo 104-11, Japan Office: NY Times 229 W 43rd St New York NY 10036-3913

WUEBBELS, THERESA ELIZABETH, visual art educator; b. Breese, Ill., Nov. 8, 1950; d. Wilson Theodore and Selma Maria (Haake) W. BA, Notre Dame Coll., St. Louis, 1972; postgrad., Boston Coll., 1976-79, Pembroke State U., 1988. Teaching nun Sch. Sisters of Notre Dame, St. Louis, 1969-80; art tchr. Cathedral Sch., Belleville, Ill., 1972-76, Sacred Heart Sch., Fort Madison, Iowa, 1976-80; missionary sister Little Sisters of Jesus, 1980-87; art tchr. Balden County Schs., Clarkton, N.C., 1989—; visual art tchrs. coord. Bladen County Schs., Elizabethtown, N.C., 1991—. Coord. Celebration of the Arts Festival for Bladen County, 1992—; task force mem. founding Clarkton Sch. Discovery, Clarkton, N.C., 1993-94. Named Tchr. of Yr. Clarkton Sch. of Discovery, 1992-93, 93-94, 94-95. Mem. N.C. Art Edn. Assn., Nat. Art Edn. Assn., Visual Art Guild. Roman Catholic. Home: 653 Poe Elkins Rd Clarkton NC 28433-7243 Office: Clarkton Sch Discovery PO Box 127 Clarkton NC 28433-0127

WUJCIAK, SANDRA CRISCUOLO, personnel executive; b. Newark, Nov. 26, 1949; d. Salvatore Michael Criscuolo and Maria (Agliata) Ventura; m. Alfred J. Wujciak Jr., Oct. 11, 1969; children: Kimberly, Joseph. Student, Morris County Coll., 1979-81. Parental cons. Lake Dr. Sch. Hearing Impaired, Mountain Lakes, N.J., 1975-83; mktg. rep. Accts. On Call, Livingston, N.J., 1981-84, Edison, N.J., 1984-85; br. mgr. Accts. On Call, Edison, 1985-87; area mgr. Accts. On Call, Edison, Princeton, N.J., Mpls., 1987-88; area v.p. Accts. On Call, Edison, Princeton, Atlanta, Cin., Miami, Fla., Mpls., 1988-90, Mpls., Edison, Princeton, N.J., 1990—; area v.p. Accts. on Call, Edison, Princeton, 1988—. Pres. ad hoc com. Dodge Tract, Parsippany, N.J., 1979-80. Mem. N.J. Assn. Pers. Cons., Rockaway River Country Club (Denville, N.J.). Republican. Roman Catholic.

WULF, SHARON ANN, management consultant; b. New Bedford, Mass., Aug 23, 1954; d. Daniel Thomas and Norma Dorothy (McCabe) Vieira; m. Stanley A. Wulf, 1983. BS in Acctg. cum laude, Providence Coll., 1976; MBA, Northeastern U., 1977; PhD, Columbia Pacific U., 1984. Staff acct., intern Laventhol & Horwath, Providence, 1977; jr. fin. analyst Polaroid Corp., Waltham, Mass., 1977-78, fin. analyst, Freetown, Mass., 1978-79, Cambridge, 1979-81; sr. fin. cons., mktg. strategic planner Digital Equipment Corp., Stow, Mass., 1981-82, Maynard, Mass., 1982-83, mgr. fin. devel. program, 1983-84, strategic fin. cons. engring. div., 1984-86, group mgr. planning and strategic ops., Hudson, Mass., 1986-87, group mgr. strategic bus. planning, 1987-89, mktg. planning mgr. Digital Equipment Corp., Marlboro, 1989-90, new ventures bus. devel. mgr., 1990-92; lectr. in fin. acctg. Southeastern Mass. U., 1979-81; adj. prof. acctg., mgmt. and fin., Northeastern U., Boston, 1980—; exec. com. enterprise forum MIT, 1987-92; prin. Work Systems Assocs., Inc., Marlborough, Mass., 1992-93; pres. Enterprise Systems, Framingham, Mass., 1993—; instr. Nat. Tech. U., 1991—; bd. advisors Spaceball Tech., Inc., Lowell, Mass., Terasys, Inc.; cons. in field. Chairperson pub. support and fund raising ARC, New Bedford, Mass., 1974-84; bd. dirs. Vets. Outreach Ctr., Metrowest, Framingham, Mass., 1989-93; v.p. MIT Leadership Found., Cambridge, Mass., 1991-93; mem. exec. com. MIT Enterprise Forum, also co-chair stant up clinics, 1986-92. Mem. Black Alumni of MIT (bd. advisors 1989-92), Univ. Coll. Faculty Soc., Phi Sigma Tau. Home: 902 Salem End Rd Framingham MA 01701-5532 Office: Enterprise Systems 1257 Worcester Rd Ste 301 Framingham MA 01701-5217

WULFF, JULIE BADER, quality professional; b. St. Louis, May 17, 1963; d. Frederick Raymond and Eileen Elizabeth (Thompson) Bader; m. Robert Joseph Wulff, Nov. 11, 1995. BSChemE, U. Mo., 1985; MBA, U. Mo., St. Louis, 1996. Process engr. Procter & Gamble Paper Co., Cape Girardeau, Mo., 1985-89; making prodn. mgr. Procter & Gamble Mfg. Co., St. Louis, 1989-91, reliability dept. mgr., 1991-94, quality dept. mgr., 1994—. Tutor St. Louis Literary Coun., 1991-93; bd. dirs. Jr. C. of C., St. Louis, 1994-95. Enterprise Leasing scholar Enterprise Leasing, U. Mo., St. Louis, 1995. Mem. Phi Kappa Phi.

WUNDER, HAROLDENE FOWLER, accounting educator; b. Greenville, S.C., Nov. 16, 1944; d. Harold Eugene Fowler and Sarah Ann (Chaffin) Crooks. BS, U. Md., 1971; M Acctg., U. S.C., 1975, PhD, 1978. CPA, Ohio. Vis. asst. prof. U. S.C., Columbia, 1977-78; asst. prof. U. Pa., Phila., 1978-81; vis. asst. prof. U. N.C., Chapel Hill, 1981-82; asst. prof. U. Mass., Boston, 1982-86; vis. assoc. prof. Suffolk U., Boston, 1986-87; assoc. prof. U. Toledo, 1987-93; prof. acctg. Calif. State U., Sacramento, 1993—. Contbr. articles to acad. and profl. publs. George Olson fellow, 1975. Mem. NAFE, AICPA, Calif. Soc. CPAs, Am. Acctg. Assn., Am. Taxation Assn., Nat. Tax Assn., Beta Gamma Sigma. Office: Calif State U Sch Bus Adminstrn Sacramento CA 95819-6088

WUNDERMAN, JAN DARCOURT, artist; b. Winipeg, Man., Can., Jan. 22, 1921; d. Rene Paul and Georgette Marie (Guionet) Darcourt; m. Frank Joseph Malina, 1938 (div. 1945); m. Lester Wunderman (div. 1967); children: Marc, George, Karen Renee. BFA, Otis Art Inst., L.A., 1942. One man show Easthampton Guild Hall, L.I., 1977; represented in numerous permanent pub., corp. and pvt. collections including Zimmerli Mus., Nat. Assn. of Women Artists, Rutgers U., 1994. Recipient Ohashi award Pan Pacific Exhbn., Tokyo and Osaka, 1962, Emily Lowe award 1965, J.J. Akston Found. prize, 1965, Canaday Meml. prize, 1979, Marian De Solo Mendes prize, 1981, Charles Horman Meml. prize, 1983, Amelia Peabody award Nat. Assn. Women, 1991, Grumbacher Gold medal of honor, 1992, Doris Kreindler award 1992. Mem. Nat. Assn. Women Artists (medal of honor 1966, Marcia Brady Tucker award 1965, E. Holzinger prize 1966, Jane C. Stanley prize 1977, Marge Greenblatt award 1990, Amelia Peabody award 1991), Am. Soc. Contemporary Artists (corr. sec. 1977-78, Bocour award 1980, Elizabeth Erlanger Meml. award 1990, Kreindler award 1992), Contemporary Artists Guild (rep. by Denise Bibro Fine Art N.Y.C.). Studio: 41 Union Sq W Rm 516 New York NY 10003-3208

WUNNICKE, BROOKE, lawyer; b. Dallas, May 9, 1918; d. Rudolph von Falkenstein and Lulu Lenore Brooke; m. James M. Wunnicke, Apr. 11, 1940; (dec. 1977); 1 child, Diane B. BA, Stanford U., 1939; JD, U. Colo., 1945. Bar: Wyo. 1946, U.S. Dist. Ct. Wyo. 1947, U.S. Supreme Ct. 1958, Colo. 1969. Pvt. practice law, 1946-56; ptnr. Williams & Wunnicke, Cheyenne, Wyo., 1956-69; of counsel Calkins, Kramer, Grimshaw & Harring, Denver, 1969-73; chief appellate dep. atty. Dist. Atty's Office, Denver, 1973-86; of counsel Hall & Evans L.L.C., Denver, 1986—; adj. prof. law U. Denver Coll. of Law, 1978—; lectr. Internat. Practicum Inst. Denver, 1978—; panelist Judicial Resolutions. Author: Ethics Compliance for Business Lawyers, 1987; co-author: Standby Letters of Credit, 1989, supplement, 1995, Corporate Financial Risk Management, 1992, Legal Opinion Letters Formbook, 1994, UCP 500 and Standby Letters of Credit-Special Report, 1994, Supplement, 1995, Standby and Commercial Letters of Credit, 1996; columnist Letters of Credit Report; contbr. articles to profl. jours. Pres. Laramie County Bar Assn., Cheyenne, Wy., 1967-68; Dir. Cheyenne C. of C., Cheyenne, Wy., 1965-68. Recipient awards for Outstanding Svc., Colo. Dist. Attys. Coun., 1979, 82, 86, Disting. Alumni award U. Colo. Sch. of Law, 1986, 93, Lathrop Trailblazer award Colo. Women's Bar Assn., 1992. Fellow Colo. Bar Found. (hon.); mem. ABA, Wyo. State Bar, Denver Bar Assn. (trustee 1977-80), Colo. Bar Assn., Am. Arbitration Assn. (nat. panel, regional panel large complex cases), William E. Doyle Inn of Ct. (hon.), Order of Coif, Phi Beta Kappa. Republican. Episcopalian. Office: Hall & Evans L L C 1200 17th St Denver CO 80202-5800

WUNSCH, KATHRYN SUTHERLAND, lawyer; b. Tipton, Mo., Jan. 30, 1935; d. Lewis Benjamin and Norene Marie (Wolf) Sutherland; m. Charles Martin Wunsch, Dec. 22, 1956 (div. May 1988); children: Debra Kay, Laura Ellen. AB, Ind. U., 1958, JD summa cum laude, 1977; postgrad., Stanford (Calif.) U., 1977. Bar: Calif. 1977, U.S. Dist. Ct. (no. dist.) Calif. 1977. Assoc. Hunt and Hunt, San Francisco, 1977-89; ptnr. Wunsch and George, San Francisco, 1989-93; founder Kathryn Wunsch and Assoc. Counsel, San Francisco, 1993—. Articles editor Ind. U. Law Rev., 1975-76. Mem. ABA, Calif. Bar Assn. (bus. law prof., real property and trusts sect.), San Mateo County Bar Assn., Calif. Acad. Scis., Nat. Assn. Women Bus. Owners (pres. San Francisco chpt. 1992-93), San Francisco Opera Guild, City Club, Phi Beta Kappa (v.p. no. calif. 1995—), Psi Chi. Republican. Office: Ste 3320 701 Welch Rd Palo Alto CA 94304

WURTZ, BETTY LOU, retired educator; b. Dayton, Ohio, June 13, 1925; d. Herbert Eugene and Pauline Edith (Elwell) Cashner; m. Conrad R. Wurtz, Aug. 29, 1948; children: Patricia, Richard, Douglas, Gary, Stewart. BA, U. Iowa, 1949; MS in Tchg., Drake U., 1970. Reservation agt. Am. Airlines, Indpls., 1946-48; dir., tchr. Kingerhaus Day Care, Des Moines, 1970-72, Temple Shalom Nursery Sch., Auburn, Maine, 1973-85; supr. Maine State Foster Grandparents, Pownal, 1985-92; tutor Auburn Sch. Sys., 1992-94, ret., 1994. Chair Women's Internat. League for Peace and Freedom, Des Moines, 1968-70; workshop facilitator on conflict resolution Am. Friends Svc. Com., Portland, 1978-90; co-chair Maine Assn. for Edn. of Young Children, Portland, 1978-79, Educators for Social Responsibility, So. Maine, 1985-93; chair conflict resolution com. Peace Action Maine, Portland, 1992-94. Unitarian. Home: 19 Megquier Rd New Gloucester ME 04260

WUSSOW, HELEN MAE, university administrator, English educator; b. Fargo, N.D., Sept. 1, 1960; d. Richard Herman and Eleanor Mae (Dolezal) W. BA in English and Humanities, Moorhead State U., 1982; MPhil in English, U. Oxford, Eng., 1984, DPhil in English, 1989. Asst. to pres. Moorhead (Minn.) State U., 1988-89; assoc. prof. English U. Memphis, 1989—, interim dir. univ. honors program, 1996, interim asst. vice provost for acad. affairs, 1995—. Editor: A Dialogue of Voices, 1994, New Essays on Virginia Woolf, 1995, The Hours, 1996; contbr.: Twentieth Century Literature, Jour. Modern Lit., Women and Language; assoc. editor Woolf Studies Ann., N.Y.C., 1993—, River City, Memphis, 1993—. Recipient Travel to Collection awards NEH, 1992, Overseas Student Rsch. award Brit. Govt., U. Oxford, 1982-84. Mem. MLA, Midwest MLA, Virginia Woolf Soc., D. H. Lawrence Soc. N.Am. Office: U Memphis 323 Administration Bldg Memphis TN 38152

WUSTENBERG, WENDY WIBERG, public affairs specialist, consultant; b. Faribault, Minn., Sept. 30, 1958; d. George Lyman and Ruth Elizabeth (Morris) Wiberg; m. William Wustenberg, Nov. 11, 1989; children: Russell Morris, Lauren Ruth. BA in Journalism, U. Minn., 1977-83. Dir. comms., press sec. Office Gov. Quie, St. Paul, 1980-83; sr. prodr. news and pub. affairs Twin Cities Pub. TV, St. Paul, 1983-88; chief of staff Minn. House Reps., St. Paul, 1990; CFO, mng. ptnr. Issue Strategies Group, St. Paul, 1988-92; cons. Wustenberg and Assocs., Farmington, MN, 1992—; trustee Farmington Sch. Bd., 1993—; dir. Cmty. Action Coun., Apple Valley, Minn., 1991-93; pres. SOAR, Inc., Rosemount, Minn., 1990—; adj. prof. Metro. State U., St. Paul, 1986—; lobbyist State of Minn., St. Paul, 1992—. Author: Families and Sexuality, 1983; creative dir.: (avt. campaign) Environmental Trust Fund, 1988 (Assn. Trends award 1988); contbr. articles to profl. jours. Minn. exec. dir. Bush/Quayle Campaign, Bloomington, 1992; instr. Courage Ctr. Alpine Skiers, Welch, Minn., 1988; trustee The Carpenter Found. and Carpenter Nature Ctr., 1995—. Recipient Nat. Promotion award Corp. for Pub. Broadcasting, Washington, 1986, 87, Local Documentary and Outreach award, 1987, J.C. Penney award U. Mo. Journalism Sch., 1987; finalist TV Acad. awards Nat. Acad. TV Arts and Scis., N.Y.C., 1986; named Adult Educator of Yr., Mo. Valley Assn. Adult Edn., 1986; named Disting. Alumni, U. Minn., 1994. Mem. Minn. Sch. Bds. Assn. (del.), Minn. Alumni Assn., Order Eastern Star. Republican.

WUTTKE, LORIE A., gallery owner, graphic designer; b. Elkhorn, Wis., Dec. 21, 1968; d. Roger G. and Karen J. (Sundberg) W. BS in Art, BS in Comms., U. Wis., 1991. Paste up artist Success Bus. Industries, Milw., 1991-92; freelancer in design Milw., 1992-93; graphic designer Abco Dealers, Inc., Milw., 1993; dir. pubs. R&J Med. Supply, Milw., 1993-94; graphic designer Design Ptnrs., Inc., Racine, Wis., 1994-95; owner Fritz Gallery, St. Charles, Ill., 1995—; freelancer in design St. Charles, Ill., 1995—. Exhibited in group show at Becca Gallery, Berlin, Wis., 1993-96, Norris Art Gallery, St. Charles, Ill., 1996. Mem. U. Wis. Alumni Assn. Republican. Lutheran. Home: PO Box 522 Saint Charles IL 60174

WYATT, DORIS FAY CHAPMAN, English language educator; b. Del Rio, Tex., July 12, 1935; d. Cecil Cornelius and Lola Wade (Veazey) Chapman; m. Jimmy Trueman Wyatt, June 2, 1956 (div. Nov. 1977); children: Abra Natasha Smith, Kent Colin Wyatt, Garrett Bret Wyatt. BS in Edn., S.W. Tex. State U., 1956; MA in English, U. North Tex., 1969; MA in Counseling, East Tenn. State U., 1983. Cert. profl. tchr. career ladder III, Tenn.; cert. marriage and family therapist. Elem. tchr. Clover Pk. Pub. Schs., Tacoma, 1957-58; jr. high reading tchr. Levelland (Tex.) Pub. Schs., 1964-67; tchr. English Denton (Tex.) Pub. Schs., 1967-70; tchr. reading & English Vets. Upward Bound, East Tenn. State U., Johnson City, 1981-87; tchr. English Johnson City (Tenn.) Pub. Schs., 1970—; beauty cons. Mary Kay Cosmetics, Johnson City, 1971-95; adj. faculty mem. Tusculum Coll., Greeneville, Tenn., 1993—; pine plantation owner. Area dir. People-to-People Student Ambassador Program, Washington County, Tenn., 1975-94, tchr.-leader, Johnson City, 1974-84. Named to Nat. Dean's list, 1982-83. Mem. NEA, AAUW, Johnson City Edn. Assn. (pres., bd. dirs. 1989-90), Tenn. Edn. Assn., Nat. Coun. Tchrs. English, Alpha Delta Kappa (pres. 1994-96), Phi Kappa Phi. Democrat. Methodist. Home: 1805 Sundale Rd Johnson City TN 37604-3023 Office: Johnson City Pub Schs Sci Hill High Sch John Exum Pky Johnson City TN 37604-4553

WYATT, EDITH ELIZABETH, elementary education educator; b. San Diego, Aug. 13, 1914; d. Jesse Wellington and Elizabeth (Fultz) Carne; m. Lee Ora Wyatt, Mar. 30, 1947 (dec. Jan. 1966); children: Glenn Stanley (dec.), David Allen. BA, San Diego State Coll., 1936. Elem. tchr. Nat. Sch. Dist., National City, Calif., 1938-76. Sec. San Diego County Parks Soc., 1986—; librarian Congl. Ch. Women's Fellowship, Chula Vista, Calif., 1980—; active Boy Scouts Am, 1959—. Recipient Who award San Diego County Tchrs. Assn., 1968, Silver Fawn award Boy Scouts Am. Mem. AAUW (sec. 1978-80, pub. rels. 1985—), Calif. Ret. Tchrs. Assn. (scholarship com. 1985-90, 92-95, treas. 1996—), Starlite Hiking Club (sec.-treas. 1979—). Home: 165 E Millan St Chula Vista CA 91910-6255

WYATT, LENORE, civic worker; b. N.Y.C., June 12, 1929; d. Benedict S. Rosenfeld and Ora (Copel) Kanner; m. Bernard D. Copeland, May 17, 1953 (dec. March 1968); children: Harry (dec.), Robert (dec.); m. C. Wyatt Unger, Mar. 26, 1969 (dec. Feb. 1992); 1 child, Amy Unger; m. F. Lowry Wyatt, Sept. 12, 1992. Student, Mills Coll., 1946-48; BA, Stanford U., 1950, MA, 1952; postgrad., NYU, 1952-53. Instr. Stanford U., Palo Alto, Calif., 1952, Hunter Coll., N.Y.C., 1952-53, Calif. State U., Sacramento, 1956-60, U. Calif., Davis, 1965-69; property mgr. Unger, Demas & Markakis, Sacramento, 1974-83; former actress and model. Pres. Sacramento Opera Assn., 1972-73; treas. Sacramento Children's Home, 1990-92, v.p., 1992—; former mem. bd. dirs. Sutter Hosp. Aux., Sutter Hosp. Med. Rsch. Found., Sacramento Symphony League, Temple B'nai Israel Sisterhood, Sacramento chpt. Hadassah, Sacramento Children's Home Guild; active Sacramento Opera Assn., Crocker Soc. of Crocker Art Gallery, Sacramento Symphony Assn., Sacramento Reportory Theater Assn.; founding mem. Tacoma Communities Art Sch.; mem. Temple Beth El of Tacoma. Mem. Joint Adventure Investment Club, Am. Contract Bridge League, Sacramento Pioneer Assn., Stanford U. Alumni Assn. (past bd. dirs. Sacramento) Sutter Club, Kandahar Ski Club, Sutter Lawn Tennis Club, DelPaso Country CLub (capt. women's golf 1983), Tacoma Country and Golf Club, Maui Country Club, Wash. Athletic Club, Tacoma Club. Republican. Jewish.

WYATT, SUSAN ALLISON, computer programmer; b. Alexandria, Va., Feb. 3, 1960; d. Richard Howard and Margaret Mary (Eveleth) Allison; m. Gary Joe Buttram, Aug. 7, 1979 (div. Feb. 1985); children: Jason Michael, Chad Tyler; m. Thomas Stuart Wyatt, Jr., Sept. 22, 1990. B.Computer Sci. summa cum laude, Mary Washington Coll., 1987. Computer sci. co-op NSWC, Dahlgren, Va., 1984-86, computer scientist, 1986-88; sr. applications programmer Verifone, Fairfax, Va., 1988-92, software cons., 1992-93; sr. programmer/analyst Computer Power Inc., Jacksonville, Fla., 1993-94, team leader internchange connections, 1994-95; sr. programmer/analyst System Innovators, Jacksonville, 1995; sys. adminstr. VTC First Coast, Jacksonville, 1995—; contract programmer Konetix, Boulder, Colo., 1993—. Vol. Wolfson's Children's Hosp., 1994—. Mem. Phi Beta Kappa. Home: 4157 Stacey Rd Jacksonville Beach FL 32250

WYCHE, MARGUERITE RAMAGE, realtor; b. Birmingham, Ala., May 30, 1950; d. Raymond Crawford and Marguerite Getaz (Taylor) Ramage; m. Madison Baker Wyche III, Aug. 7, 1971; children: Madison Baker IV, James Ramage. BA cum laude, Vanderbilt U., 1972. Lic. broker, S.C., also cert. real estate specialist, grad. Real Estate Inst. Real estate agt. Slappey Realty Co., Albany, Ga., 1973-76, McCutcheon Co., Greenville, S.C., 1973-76; real estate agt. Furman Co., Greenville, 1985-87, broker's assoc., 1987-95; v.p., broker in charge The Furman Co. Residential LLC, Greenville, 1995—; v.p. The Furman Co. Residential LLC, 1996. Bd. dirs. Christ Ch. Episcopal Sch., Greenville, 1979-82, 86-89, chmn. bd. visitors, 1992-93; bd. dirs., cmty. v.p. Jr. League of Greenville, 1983, state pub. affairs chair S.C. Jr. League, 1984; mem. Greenville Cmty. Planning Coun., 1983; bd. dirs., chmn. long range planning com. Meals on Wheels, Greenville, 1990-93; mem. Palmetto Soc.-United Way of Greenville, 1992—; mem. elves workshop com. Children's Hosp., Greenville, 1992-93; mem. Greenville Tech. Found. Bd., 1995—, Met. Arts Coun., 1996—, Endowment Corp. Christ Ch., 1996—, Mayor's Task Force, 1996—. Mem. Greenville Bd. Realtors, Million Dollar Club (life), Vanderbilt Alumni Assn., Christ Ch. Episcopal Sch. Alumni Assn. (pres., bd. dirs. 1980-81), Mortar Board, Delta Delta Delta. Republican. Episcopalian. Home: 134 Rockingham Rd Greenville SC 29607-3621 Office: The Furman Co 252 S Pleasantburg Dr Ste 100 Greenville SC 29607-2547

WYERS, MELISSA L., non profit administrator; b. Denver, Oct. 2, 1965. BA, Emory U., 1988; MA, U. Md., 1995, postgrad. Spl. events mgr. Emory U., Atlanta, 1988-89; adult edn. program developer USAID Peace Corps, Morocco, 1989-91; spl. program coord. Common Cause, Washington, 1991-95; dir. program devel. Immigrant and Refugee Svcs. of Am., Washington, 1996—; tchr., trainer U.S. Peace Corps, Morocco, 1990; ESL instr. Sacred Heart Acad., Washington, 1991-93. Office: IRSA 1717 Massachusetts Ave Washington DC 20036

WYESS, PAMELA MARIE, police officer; b. Detroit, Sept. 25, 1962; d. Henry Albert and Marie Teresa (Delich) W.; m. Sidney Raymond Moen, Jan. 14, 1995. BA in Comms., U. Mich., 1984; MS in Adminstrn., Madonna U., 1996. Comms. operator Ann Arbor (Mich.) Police Dept., 1984-87, police officer, 1987-92, staff sgt., 1992-96, lt., 1996—; co-owner Network Tng. Group, Saline, Mich., 1996—. Literacy tutor Washtenaw Literacy, Ypsilanti, Mich., 1992. Mem. NAFE, Women Bus. Owners Southeastern Mich., So. Police Inst. Alumni Assn. Home: 6463 Robison Ln Saline MI 48176 Office: Ann Arbor Police Dept 100 N 5th Ave Ann Arbor MI 48107

WYLAN, BARBARA, artist; b. Providence, 1933; divorced; children: Andrea, Brock. BFA, R.I. Sch. of Design, Providence, 1955; studied with Donald Stoltenberg, Claude Croney, Murray Wentworth, Ruth Wynn, Charles Movalli, Dong Kingman. Tchr. watercolor workshops; juror various exhbns. 25 one-person shows; exhibited widely in more than 100 group shows including Watercolor USA (Springfield award 1982), Nat. Soc. Painters in Casein and Acrylic 38th Ann., Nat. Arts club, N.Y.C. (Dr. David Solowax award 1991); works owned by numerous pvt., corp. and instnl. collectors including Fine Arts Mus. of the South.; represented by Market Barn Gallery, Falmouth, The Spectrum of Am. Artists and Craftsmen, Brewster, Hyannis, Nantucket, Newport, West Palm Beach. Mem. Nat. Soc. Painters in Casein and Acrylic (elected mem.), Watercolor USA Honor Soc., New Eng. Watercolor Soc., Copley Soc. Boston.

WYMAN, L. PILAR, indexer; b. Beirut, Nov. 14, 1964; d. Samuel Haynes and Laura Pilar (Garzon) W.; m. Peter John McMenamin, Nov. 4, 1991; children: Leith Maria, Hugh Haynes. BA, St. John's Coll., 1986. Typist Editl. Svcs., Annapolis, Md., 1983-86, assoc. indexer, 1989-93; chief indexer Wyman Indexing, Annapolis, 1990—. Author: (booklet) Indexing FAQ, 1994; contbr. articles, letters, and indexes to profl. publs. Minority grad. fellow NSF, 1987. Mem. Soc. for Tech. Comm., Women's Nat. Book Assn., Am. Med. Writers Assn., Am. Soc. Indexers (chair Washington chpt. 1995-96). Democrat. Episcopalian. Office: Wyman Indexing 1240L Gemini Dr Annapolis MD 21403

WYMAN, NANCY S., state legislator; b. Bklyn., Apr. 21, 1946; d. Arthur and Ann (Rosenzweig) Schmukler; m. Ronald Michael Wyman, Sept. 11, 1966; children: Stacey, Meryl. Student, L.I. Coll. Hosp., 1966. X-ray technician Bapt. Hosp., Miami, Fla., 1966-67, Baird Orthopedics, Miami, 1967-70, Rockville (Conn.) Orthopedics, 1975-83; legis. aide State of Conn., Hartford, 1983-87, state rep., 1987-94; state comptroller, 1995—. Named Legislator of Yr., Nat. Abortion Rights Reproductive Rights Action League, 1990, Arts Commn., 1992, Coun. Small Towns, 1992; recipient Friend of Edn. award Conn. Edn. Assn., 1990. Democrat. Jewish. Home: 18 Pilgrim Dr Tolland CT 06084-2906

WYNE, MARGARET MARY, sales representative; b. Seattle, Feb. 16, 1965; d. Wilbert Michael and Anne (Godefroy) W. BA in Sociology, U. Wash., 1987. Asst. mgr. Crown Books, Seattle, 1987-89, mgr., 1989-91; mgr. Benjamin Books, Seattle, 1991; sales rep. Penguin USA, Inc., Seattle, 1991—. mem. Snoqualmie Pass Ski Patrol, Wash., 1980—, jr. advisor, 1984-94; regional jr. advisor Ski Patrol, Wash., 1987-91. Home: 5558 29th Ave NE Seattle WA 98105-5520

WYNETTE, TAMMY, singer; b. Red Bay, Ala., May 5, 1942; d. William Hollis Pugh; m. George Jones, Sept. 1968 (div.); m. George Richey, 1978; children: Gwen, Jackie, Tina. Former beauty operator. Rec. artist Epic Records, 1967—; regular appearances on Grand Ole Opry; tours U.S., Can., Europe; recs. include: Womanhood, Stand By Your Man, 1975, Run Woman Run, 1970, Woman to Woman, 1974, Womanhood, 1978, Crying In The Rain, 1981, Sometimes When We Touch, 1985, From the Bottom of my Heart, 1986, Higher Ground, 1987, Next To You, 1989, Heart Over Mind, 1990, Best Loved Hits, 1991, (with others) Tears of Fire: The 25th Anniversary Collection, 1992; author autobiography Stand By Your Man, 1982; TV appearances include: (TV movie) Stand by Your Man, 1981; host The Acad. Country Music's 20th. Anniversary Reunion, 1986, The 25th Ann. Acad. Country Music Awards, 1990, The Legends of Country Music, 1994; films include From Nashville with Music, 1969. Named Female Vocalist of Year Country Music Assn., 1968, 69, 70. *

WYNN, KARLA WRAY, artist, agricultural products company executive; b. Idaho Falls, Idaho, Oct. 1, 1943; d. Wiliam and Elma (McCowin) Lott; m. Russell D. Wynn, June 7, 1963 (div. 1996); children: Joseph, Jeffrey, Andrea. Student, Coll. of Holy Names, 1962-63, Providence Coll. Nursing, 1962-63; BFA, Idaho State U., 1989; postgrad., Alfred U., 1993. Co-owner R.D. Wynn Farms, American Falls, Idaho, 1963-96, office mgr., 1975-84; co-owner Redi-Gro Fertilizer Co., American Falls, 1970-96, office mgr., 1980-84; pres. Lakeside Farms, Inc. (name now Redi-Gro Fertilizer Inc.), American Falls, 1975-96; artist, 1990—; owner Blue Heron, Pocatello, Idaho, 1991-96. Watercolor paintings and ceramic clay sculptures exhibited at various art shows and galleries. Buddhist.

WYNN, LINDA DELOIS THOMPSON, public administrator, educator, researcher; b. Nashville, July 22, 1948; D. George Edward and Frances Delois (Coleman) T.; m. Ronald Eugene Wynn, Dec. 19, 1970. BS in History, Tenn. State U., 1969, MS in History, 1971, MPA, 1980. Social worker Met. Health Dept., 1971-73; grants mgmt. officer Tenn. Hist. Commn., State of Tenn., Nashville, 1974-82, adminstv. svcs. asst. II, 1982-89, asst. dir. state programs, 1989—; adj. instr. African-Am. history Fisk U., 1991-92, 94—, lectr. Baynard Ruskin seminar; lectr. Saturday Acad. for Tchg. and Learning African-Am. History, U. Toledo, 1992; lectr. Extended Summer Tchrs. Inst., Tenn. State U.-NEH, 1981-82, cons. grant on constrn., 1986—; mem. legis task force com. on African-Am. history in Tenn. pub. schs., 1990; mem. doscementary adv. panel Electrovision/for African-Am. history in Tenn.; cons. Tenn. Dept. Edn., 1992—; mayoral appointee history com. City of Nashville. Contbr. profiles to: Notable Black American Women, 1992, book II, 1996, Epic Lives: One Hundred Women Who Made a Difference, 1993, A Bicentennial Tribute to Tennessee Women, 1796-1996; co-editor: Profiles of African-Americans in Tennessee History, 1996; contbr. to Bicentennial edit. Tenn. Hist. Quar., 1996; contbr. articles to profl. publs. Founding mem. Local Conf. on Afro-Am. Culture and History; mem. Tenn. Treasures rev. com. Tenn. State Mus., 1993; mem. adv. coun. World War II Tenn. Maneuvers Commn., 1993; copy cons. Tenn. Dept. Tourism, 1993; lectr. Cohn Adult Learning Ctr., 1993—; mem. planning com., co-chairperson Conf. on Tenn. Women's History, 1993—; panelist book festival Dyersburg State C.C., 1993; mem. documentary adv. panel Electrovision/S. Ctrl. Bell/Tennessee Valley Authority, 1993; bd. dirs. Friends of Mill Creek Graveyard, 1994—; mem. Southeastern African-Am. Regional Archives Planning Com., Rosenwald Schs. Conf. Planning Com. (MTSU Ctr. for Historic Preservation), adv. panel A Bicentennial Tribute to Tenn. Women; cons. to Sec. of State's Office for the Bicentennial Issue of the Tenn. Blue Book; apptd. to Tenn. Commemorative Woman's Sufferage Commn., Nashville's History Com. Named Outstanding Young Woman Am., 1975, 82; recipient cert. appreciation Nat. Alliance Bus., 1975, 82, plaque Spruce St. Bapt. Ch., 1975, 82. Mem. ASPA (Tenn. chpt), So. Hist. Assn., Tenn. Hist. Soc. (co-chair Mid. Tenn., vol. discussion leader Tenn. bicentennial celebration conf. 1989, adv. bd. for minority concerns 1990, lectr.), NAACP (Nashville chpt. history and tours com. Nat. Conv. 1992), Orgn. of African Am. Ch. Historians, Southern Baptist Hist. Assn., Southern Assn. for Women Historians. Office: Tenn Hist Commn 2941 Lebanon Rd Nashville TN 37214-2508

WYNNE, LINDA MARIE, administrative assistant, artist; b. N.Y.C., Nov. 10, 1950; d. Thomas Lauren Flake and Sally (Gullotti) Gaudiosi; m. Michael Francis Wynne, Jan. 9, 1973 (div. Apr. 1985); 1 child, Michael Thomas. AA, Borough of Manhattan C.C., 1972. Stock person S&A Stores, Queens, N.Y., 1966-69; part-time bookkeeper Bohack Corp., Queens, N.Y., 1970-72; sr. teller, tng. specialist Union Dime Savs. Bank, N.Y.C., 1973-77; adminstrv. asst. Eagle Elec. Mfg., N.Y.C., 1983-84, Castle Oil Corp., Harrison, N.Y., 1985-91, Prisma Group, N.Y.C., 1992-93, Misco Enterprises, N.Y.C., 1994-95, Concord Comm., Woodside, N.Y., 1995—. Exhibited in group shows at Oliver Art Studio, 1979-89, The Emerging Collector, 1987, All Queens Women, 1991, Cultural Environ., 1991; exhibited in outdoor shows at Big Six Towers, 1983, Friends of the Mineola Libr., 1983-89, Joseph Bulova Sch., 1990, 40th St. Festival, 1991, The Sunnyside Found. Fall Festival, 1988-91, Sunnyside Gardens Cmty. Assn. Inc., 1989, 90, 91, Gateway, 1988-91, Bowne Park, 1991, 93, 94, Queens Bot. Garden, 1990, 91, Floral Park Art League, 1991, Mineola's Performing Art Weekend, 1988-91, Alliance of Queens Artists, 1991, Washington Square Outdoor Art Exhibit, 1988, 89, 90.

WYNNS, JILL PERCIVAL, child advocate, educator; b. Bayshore, N.Y., Oct. 7, 1947; d. James and Nora (Lourie) Percival; m. George Samuel Wynns, Dec. 31, 1991; children: Justin, Emily, Evan. BA, Hofstra U., 1969. Costume shop mgr. Am. Conservatory Theatre, San Francisco, 1969-72; designer, costume shop mgr. San Francisco Opera, 1974-78; mem. sch. bd. San Francisco Unified Sch. Dist., 1993—; network coord. Children & Families Action Network, Hayward, Calif., 1994—; polit. cons. Wynns/Kauffman Assocs., San Francisco, 1988-92. Pres. San Francisco Parents' Lobby, 1986-92; chairperson Bernal Heights East Slope Design Rev. Bd., San Francisco, 1987-90; active Nat. Women's Polit. Caucus, 1991—. Mem. AAUW, Calif. Sch. Bds. Assn. (dir. 1996—), Assn. Calif. Urban Sch. Dists. (pres. 1994-96), Calif. Elected Womens Assn. Democrat. Home: 124 Brewster St San Francisco CA 94110

WYNSTRA, NANCY ANN, lawyer; b. Seattle, June 25, 1941; d. Walter S. and Gaile E. (Cogley) W. BA cum laude, Whitman Coll., 1963; LLB cum laude, Columbia U., 1966. Bar: Wash. 1966, D.C. 1969, Ill. 1979, Pa. 1984. With appellate sect., civil div. U.S. Dept. Justice, Washington, 1966-67; TV corr.-legal news Stas. WRC, NBC and Stas. WTOP, CBS, Washington, 1967-68; spl. asst. Corp. Counsel, Washington, 1968-70; dir. planning and rsch. D.C. Superior Ct., Washington, 1970-78; spl. advisor White House Spl. Action Office for Drug Abuse Prevention, Washington, 1973-74; fellow Drug Abuse Coun., 1974-75; gen. counsel Michael Reese Hosp. and Med. Ctr., Chgo., 1978-83; exec. v.p., gen. counsel Allegheny Health Edn. and Rsch. Found., Pitts., 1983—; pres., chief exec. officer Allegheny Health Svcs. Provider's Ins. Co., 1989—; assoc. prof. Sch. of Urban and Pub. Affairs Carnegie Mellon U., 1985—, Med. Coll. Pa., 1991—; cons. to various drug abuse programs, 1971-78; bd. overseers Whitman Coll., 1993—. Mem. ABA, Nat. Health Lawyers Assn. (bd. dirs. 1985-91, chair publs. com. 1989-91, audit com. 1991-92, treas. 1992-93, 95-96, exec. com. 1992—, edn. fund com., 1992-93, mem. nominating com. 1992-93, sec. 1993-95, treas. 1995-96, pres.-elect 1996—), Am. Soc. Hosp. Attys., others. Presbyterian. Author: Fundamentals of Health Law; contbr. articles to profl. jours. Office: Allegheny Health Edn & Rsch Found 120 5th Ave Ste 2900 Pittsburgh PA 15222-3001

WYRICK, PRISCILLA BLAKENEY, microbiologist; b. Greensboro, N.C., Apr. 28, 1940; d. Carnie Lee and Prestine (Blakeney) W. BS in Med. Tech., U. N.C., Chapel Hill, 1962; MS in Bacteriology, U. N.C., 1967, PhD in Bacteriology, 1971. Technologist Clin. Microbiology Lab., N.C. Meml. Hosp., Chapel Hill, 1962-64; asst. supr. Clin. Microbiology Lab., N.C. Meml. Hosp., 1964-65, supr., 1965-66; sci. staff fellow Nat. Inst. Med. Rsch., Mill Hill, London, 1971-73; asst. prof. dept. microbiology U. N.C. Sch. Medicine, Chapel Hill, 1973-79; assoc. prof. U. N.C. Sch. Medicine, 1979-88, prof., 1988—. Grantee, NIH. Mem. Am. Acad. Microbiology, Am. Soc. Microbiology (pres. N.C. br. 1981-82, chmn. div. gen. med. microbiology 1981-82), AAAS, Soc. Infectious Diseases, Sigma Xi. Office: U NC Sch Medicine CB 7290 816 FLOB Chapel Hill NC 27599

WYSE, BONITA W(ENSINK), nutrition educator, researcher; b. Lorain, Ohio, Oct. 2, 1945; d. Norbert B. and Ruth B.(DeChant) Wensink. BS, Notre Dame of Ohio, 1967; MS, Mich. State U., 1970; PhD, Colo. State U., 1977. Registered dietitian. Clin. dietitian St. Lawrence Hosp., Lansing, Mich., 1968-69; instr. nutrition Utah State U., Logan, 1970-73, asst. prof., 1973-77, assoc. prof., dir. coordinated undergrad. med. dietetics program, 1977-81, prof., 1981—, acting dean Coll. Family Life, 1984-86, dean, 1986—; bd. dirs. Gerber Products Co., Fremont, Mich.; cons. Met. Life Found., N.Y.C., 1983-86; mem. adv. bd. Heart, Blood, Lung Inst., NIH, Bethesda, Md., 1984-87. Author: Nutritional Quality Index of Foods, 1979; contbr. articles to profl. jours. Bd. dirs. Citizens Against Phys. and Sexual Abuse, Logan, 1984. Recipient Outstanding Alumna award Dept. Food Sci. and Nutrition, Mich. State U., 1982. Mem. Am. Dietetic Assn. (council on research 1982-87, bd. dirs. 1984-87, Frances E. Fischer Meml. Nutrition Lectr., 1984), Utah Dietetic Assn. (pres. 1976-77), Am. Inst. Nutrition, Am. Home Econs. Assn. (Borden award for research 1981). Republican. Roman Catholic. Office: Utah State U Dean's Office Family Life Logan UT 84322-2900

WYSE, LOIS, advertising executive, author; b. Cleve., 1928; d. Roy B. Wohlgemuth and Rose (Schwartz) Weisman; m. Marc Wyse (div. 1980); m. Lee Guber (dec. 1988). Pres. Wyse Advt. Inc., N.Y.C., 1951—; bd. dirs. Consol. Natural Gas, Pitts.; ptnr. City & Co. Author 56 books; contbg. editor Good Housekeeping; syndicated columnist Wyse Words. Trustee Beth Israel Med. Ctr., N.Y.C. Mem. Woman's Forum (bd. dirs.), PEN. Office: Wyse Advt Inc 24 Public Sq Cleveland OH 44113-2201*

WYSHAK, JEANNE GRACE, photographer; b. L.A., Feb. 28, 1965; d. Robert Habeeb and Lillian Mary (Worthing) W. BA, U. Calif., Berkeley, 1987; MA, U. Mich., 1992. Curatorial researcher Art Inst. Chgo., 1987-89; instr. art history U. Mich., Ann Arbor, 1991-94. painter & photographer, 1988—. Home: 166 State St Apt 14 Brooklyn NY 11201-5613

WYSOCK, SANDRA LOU, insurance executive; b. Olewein, Iowa, July 14, 1946; d. Robert H. and Bonnie Lou (Antwine) Bassett; m. George D. Wysock, Apr. 1, 1967; children: Matthew G., Nathan A. BA in Sociology, U. Iowa, 1970. CPCU. Claims examiner Time Ins., Milw., 1970-71, Bankers Life of Des Moines, Milw., 1971-73; ins. agt. Am. Family Group, Lannon, Wis., 1975-77; personal lines underwriter Am. Family Group, Milw., 1977-88; personal lines supr. Am. Family Group, Peoria, Ill., 1988-91, br. underwriting mgr., 1991-93; area underwriting mgr. Am. Family Group, Madison, Wis., 1993—. Bus. sponsor Inroads. Mem. Soc. CPCU, Am. Soc. CLU (student mem.). Office: Am Family Group 6000 American Pky Madison WI 53717

WYSS, CYNTHIA JANE, newspaper bureau chief; b. Woodstock, Ill., Mar. 30, 1962; d. Harry Howard and Jane Mary (Henley) Weiss; m. Jeffrey Allen Naber, June 5, 1988 (div. Sept. 1993); 1 child, Chance Allen Naber. BS, So. Ill. U., 1985. Beat reporter Sunday Courier and Press, Evansville, Ind., 1985-86; crime reporter Del. State News, Dover, 1987-88, feature writer, 1988-89; assoc. editor Profl. Roofing, Rosemont, Ill., 1990-91; beat reporter Northwest Herald, McHenry, Ill., 1991-93; feature writer Northwest Herald, Crystal Lake, Ill., 1993-94; bur. chief Northwest Herald, McHenry, 1994—; freelance writer Northwest Herald, Crystal Lake, 1989-90; participating author Young Author's Conf., Kent Coun. for Reading, Dover, 1989. Bd. dirs. Big Bros./Big Sisters, McHenry County, 1994-96; mem. McHenry County Citizens for Choice, 1991—. Recipient 3d place Feature award AP, 1993, 3d place Investigative or In-depth Reporting, Ill. Press Assn., 1994, 3d place Editl. Excellence Investigative In-depth Reporting, AP, 1995, 2d place best column Suburban Newspaper Assoc., 1995. Mem. So. Ill. Univ. Alumnae Assn. Democrat. Home: 4307 Shamrock Ln # 3A McHenry IL 60050 Office: Northwest Herald 4005F Kane Ave McHenry IL 60050

WYSS, NORMA ROSE TOPPING, counselor, supervisor, educator, writer; b. Wautoma, Wis., Jan. 7, 1919; d. Eugene Leonard Topping and Sylvia Maude (Attoe-Dumond) Topping Schubert; m. Werner Oscar Wyss; children: Werner Oscar II (dec.), Christine Camille (dec.), Melanie Rose (dec.), Sylvia Ann (dec.). Diploma, Waushara Normal, 1939; BA in Elem. Edn., Fla. State U., 1949, MS, 1960; postgrad., U. Md., 1964; PhD in Social Change and Counselling, Walden U., 1986; grad., Inst. Children's Lit., West Redding, Conn., 1993. Cert. employment counselor and supr. Tchr. Hoeft Sch., Berlin, Wis., 1939-40, Escambia County Sch. Bd., Pensacola, Fla., 1946-66; area I counselor supr. Fla. State Dept. of Labor, Pensacola and Tallahassee, 1966-79; freelance writer N.Y.C., 1986-90; field interviewer Arbitron, Laurel, Md., 1985-88; counselor Career Mgmt. Specialists, 1994-95. Author: Core Counseling: The Christian Faith and the Helping Relationship: A Paradigm of Social Change, 1990; children's short stories. Communicant mem., usher, greeter, cantor, pre-marriage counselor, good shepherd o-chmn. Luth. Ch. of the Resurrection, Pensacola, Fla. Mem. Am. Counseling Assn., Nat. Assn. Ret. Tchrs., Escambia Educators (life), Fla. Ret. Educators (life), DAR (treas. Pensacola chpt. 1988-90, Alpha Delta Kappa (1st pres. Fla. Alpha chpt. 1953), Kappa Delta Pi. Democrat. Office: 4602 Petra Circle Pensacola FL 32526-1132

WYZYKOWSKI, MARSHA ELAINE, consultant, trainer; b. Portsmouth, Ohio, Apr. 21, 1949; d. Alton McClelland and Alice Marie (Delabar) Wamsley; m. Brent C. Smith, Nov. 8, 1974 (div. Oct. 1982); children; David Alan, Trish Jabrina; m. Peter John Wyzykowski, Aug. 14, 1993; 1 stepchild, Stephen James. BBA in Accounting cum laude, Ohio U., 1974, BS in Edn., 1976; postgrad. in taxation, U. Akron, 1975-76; MA in Corp. and Orgnl. Comm., Western Ky. U., 1990. CPA, CMA. Spl. projects auditor/Orient Chase Manhattan Bank, Agana, Guam, 1971-74; pvt. practice cons. and trainer Smith and Assocs., Akron, Ohio/Bowling Green, Ky., 1974—; organized rsch. acct. U. Akron, 1974-76; adj. prof. Western Ky. U., Bowling Green, 1990—, Lindsey Wilson Coll., Scottsville/Columbia, Ky., 1991—. Mem. AICPA, Inst. Mgmt. Accts. (nat. bd. mem. and dir. 1993—, REAP instr. 1994—), Inst. Cert. Mgmt. Accts., Nat. Assn. Women Bus. Owners (v.p. fin. 1996—), Networking Union, Internat. Spkrs. Network, South Cen. Ky. Inst. Mgmt. Acct. (v.p. comm. 1996—, Mem. of Yr. 1976), Tenn. Valley Coun.-IMA (pres. 1996—), Bowling Green C. of C., KC Ladies Aux. Roman Catholic. Office: Smith and Assocs 1615 Curling Way Bowling Green KY 42104-4509

XENARIOS, SUSAN JANE, health facility administrator; b. Englewood, N.J., Aug. 8, 1946; d. George Rodger Preston and Mildred Anders; m. Giorgos Xenarios, Nov. 8, 1974; 1 child, Elena. BA in Sociology, Fairleigh Dickinson U., 1968; MS, MSW, Columbia U., 1982. Caseworker welfare/income maintenance ctr. N.Y.C. Dept. Social Svcs., 1968-71, caseworker special svcs. for children, 1971-76; social worker emergency dept. St. Luke's Roosevelt Hosp. Ctr., N.Y.C., 1976-82, social worker rape intervention program, 1983-87, dir. rape intervention program, crime victims assessment program, 1987-96, dir. crime victims treatment ctr., 1996—; pvt. practice N.Y.C., 1988—; field instr., adj. prof. Columbia U. Sch. Social Work, N.Y. U. Grad. Sch. Creative Arts and Rehab., Columbia U. Coll. Physicians and Surgeons, 1986-94. Contbr. articles to profl. jours. Mem. adv. coun. N.Y. State Crime Victims Bd., 1987-93, 95; vice chairperson N.Y. State Dept. Health Rape Crisis Adv. Bd., 1987—; exec. com. mem., vice chair N.Y.C. Task Force Against Sexual Assault, 1987-90; co-chairperson N.Y. State Downstate Coalition for Crime Victims, 1990—; exec. bd. mem., steering com. N.Y.C. Balkan Rape Crisis Response Team, 1993—; vice chair N.Y. State Health Dept., 1995, 96; bd. dirs. N.Y.C. Rape Crisis Consortium, 1994—, N.Y.C. Interagy. Task Force on Domestic Violence, 1995—, N.Y. State Adv. Bd., N.Y. State Office of Mental Health and Rape Crisis Programs, 1996—. Recipient Citation of Merit, Mayor of N.Y., 1987, Eleanor Roosevelt Cmty. Svc. award Gov. of State of N.Y., 1988, Pres.'s Voluntary Action award Pres. George Bush, 1989, Susan B. Anthony award NOW, N.Y.C., 1993, Citation for exemplary svc. Nat. Victim Ctr., 1995. Mem. NASW, Nat. Assn. Orthopsychiatry, Nat. Coalition Against Sexual Assault, Nat. Coalition Against Domestic Violence, N.Y. State Coalition Against Sexual Assault, N.Y. State Coalition Against Domestic Violence, N.Y. Women's Agenda (domestic violence com. 1994—). Democrat. Home: 505 West End Ave New York NY 10024 Office: St Lukes Roosevelt Crime Victims Treatment Ctr 411 W 114 St # 6D New York NY 10025

XENICK, ANGELIQUE KATHERINE, school counselor; b. Tampa, Fla., Dec. 13, 1970; d. George and Cynthia Elizabeth (Kladis) X. BS, U. Fla., 1992, MEd, EdS, 1995. Cert. counselor, U.S., Fla. Mental health technician Northside Psychiat. Ctr., Tampa, 1992; sch. counselor Oak Ridge H.S., Orlando, Fla., 1995—; teaching supr. U. Fla., Gainesville, 1994; freshman, jr. varsity cheerleading sponsor Oak Ridge H.S., 1996—. Vol. Interface Youth Runaway Shelter, Gainesville, 1992. Paul W. Fitzgerald Meml. scholar U. Fla., 1995. Mem. Am. Counseling Assn., Am. Sch. Counseling Assn., Fla. Sch. Counseling Assn., Fla. Counseling Assn., Orange County Counseling Assn., Chi Sigma Iota. Address: Apt 913 2200 Metropolitan Way Orlando FL 32839

XIONG, JEAN Z., artist, consultant; b. Beijing, China, Nov. 1, 1953; came to U.S., 1983; d. Xian-Li and Zhang Yao (Zhu) Xiong; m. Charles C. Feng, Apr. 12, 1989. Grad., Shu Zhou (China) Inst., 1977; MFA, Acad Art Coll., San Francisco, 1986. Freelance artist/instr. Beijing, 1978-81; design artist First Impressions Advt., Reno, 1986; computer artist Visual Dynamics, San Francisco, 1988-89, Mediagenic, Menlo Park, 1989-91; leader artist Tecmagik Inc., Redwood City, Calif., 1992-94; computer artist Electronic Arts, San Mateo, Calif., 1995—; cons. entertainment software devel., Calif., 1991-92, 94-95; artist Electronic Arts, San Mateo, 1995—. One-woman shows San Francisco, 1984, 85, Monterey, Calif., 1984; exhbns. in Hong Kong, China, 1979, 80, 81. Recipient prize of Excellence Nat. Youth Artist Assn., 1980, Artist Assn., Hong Kong, 1981; scholar Acad. Art Coll., 1983-86. Mem. Mus. Modern Art, Tradtional Chinese Inst. (Beijing). Office: 2000 DeAnza Blvd San Mateo CA 94402

YABLONSKI, JANICE BETH, museum administrator; b. Cooperstown, N.Y., July 20, 1967; d. Edward Stanley Yablonski and Matilda Ann Lenk. BA in Am. History, Barnard Coll., 1989; MA in Am. Studies, Columbia U., 1992. Asst. to mgr. spl. publs. dept. The Met. Mus. Art, N.Y.C., 1989-91, asst. mgr. adminstrn., spl. publs. dept., 1993-96, assoc. mgr. for adminstrn., spl. publs. dept., 1996—. Mem. Am. Assn. Mus. Office: The Met Mus Art Spec Publs 6 E 82nd St New York NY 10028

YABLONSKY, TERRI LYNN, medical writer; b. Mpls., Feb. 26, 1963; d. Joseph M. and Sharleen (Blinder) Y. BA in Psychology summa cum laude, U. Minn., 1985, MA in Sci. Writing, 1987. Staff reporter Am. Jewish World newspaper, Mpls., 1987-89; comm. specialist Ethix Midwest, Mpls., 1989-91; sr. comms. specialist Jostens, Inc., Mpls., 1991-93; features editor for Lab. Medicine Am. Soc. Clin. Pathologists, Chgo., 1994—. Contbr. articles to profl. jours. Mem. Women in Comms. Jewish. Home: 222 E Pearson Chicago IL 60611 Office: Am Soc Clin Pathologists 2100 W Harrison St Chicago IL 60612

YACONETTI, DIANNE MARY, business executive; b. Chgo., Dec. 16, 1946; d. Anthony and Dora Marie (Mazzoni) Pontillo. Student, Mallinckrodt Coll., 1984-85; Advanced Mgmt. Program, Harvard U., 1990. Various positions Brunswick Corp., Skokie, Ill., 1964-80, mgr. legal support services, 1980-83, asst. sec., 1984-86, corp. sec., 1986-88, v.p. adminstrn., corp. sec., 1988—; bd. dirs. The Lambs, Libertyville, Ill. Mem. Am. Soc. Corp. Secs. Roman Catholic. Office: Brunswick Corp 1 N Field Ct Lake Forest IL 60045-4811

YACOVONE, ELLEN ELAINE, banker; b. Ithaca, N.Y., Aug. 4, 1951; d. Wilfred Elliott and Charlotte Frances (Fox) Drew; m. Richard Daniel Yacovone, June 2, 1979; stepchildren: Christopher Daniel, Kimberly Marie. Student Broome Community Coll., 1973-80; cert. Inst. Fin. Edn., Chgo., 1974. Sec. to exec. v.p. Ithaca Savs., N.Y., summer 1968; mortgage clk. Citizens Savs. Bank, 1968-69; with Lincoln Bank, Van Nuys, Calif., 1970-71; asst. bookkeeper Henry's Jewelers, Binghamton, N.Y., 1971-74; teller, br. supt., br. mgr. First Fed. Savs., Binghamton, N.Y., 1974-82, v.p., cen. regional sales mgr., 1982-86, dist. sales mgr., 1986-88; br. mgr. Great Western Bank, Pensacola, Fla., 1988-89, v.p., regional mgr. San Diego east region, 1989-95; br. v.p. Gateway Ctr., San Diego, 1995—, North Park, 1996—; owner, operator EYE Shirts, 1995—. Mem. Gov.'s Commn. on Domestic Violence, Albany, N.Y., 1983-87; bd. dirs. S.O.S. Shelter, Inc., Endicott, N.Y., 1979-88, pres., 1982-83, treas., 1985-86; vol. United Way of Broome County, Binghamton, 1976-88, Sta. WSKG Pub. TV, Conklin, N.Y., 1974-88; mem. Found. State U. Ctr. at Binghamton; bd. dirs. Interfaith Shelter Network, San Diego, 1992—, Schs. of Success and the San Diego Innovative Presch. Project, 1995—, San Diego Urban League, 1995—, Black Econ. Task Force, 1995—. Named Woman of Achievement, Broome County Status of Women Coun., 1981. Mem. Triple Cities Bus. and Profl. Women (pres. 1979-81, young careerist award 1977), Sales and Mktg. Execs., Broome County C. of C., Broome County Bankers Assn. (bd. dirs. 1979-88, pres. 1983-84), Inst. Fin. Edn. (bd. dirs. 1976-88, pres. 1984-85, winner N.Y. State speech contest 1984), The Catfish Club. Republican. Methodist. Avocations: exercise, hand painting wearables and wood, wood working, gardening, needlecrafts. Home: 602 Myra Ave Chula Vista CA 91910-6230 Office: Great Western Bank 3921 30th St San Diego CA 92104

YAKIMOVICZ, ANN DENISE, landscape architect, distance learning designer; b. Tampa, Fla., Dec. 19, 1950; d. Frank George and Blanche (Gach) Y. AA, Rogue Community Coll., 1978; BSLA cum laude, Tex. A&M U., 1986; MS, 1993, PhD, 1995. Lic. Landscape Architect, Pa., Tex. Landscape designer Huth Engrs. Inc., Lancaster, Pa., 1986-88; project mgr. Rettew Assocs., Inc., Mechanicsburg, Pa., 1989-90, H. Edward Black and Assocs., Harrisburg, Pa., 1990-92; prin. Biodynamix, Jonestown, Tex., 1992—; product design/devel. coord. Quantum Cons. Internat. Inc., Austin, Tex.; prin. 21st Century Learning Systems, 1996—. Contbr. articles to profl. jours., 1985—; designer numerous landscape architecture projects, 1986—. Active Friends of Libr., Mechanicsburg, 1989-91; precinct chair Cumberland County Reps., Mechanicsburg, 1990-92; vice chair Planning and Zoning Commn., City of Jonestown. Mem. Am. Soc. Landscape Architects (sec.-treas. chpt. 1989-91, cert. of merit 1986), Web Soc., Am. Ednl. Rsch. Assn., Travis County Rep. Club, Phi Kappa Phi. Home: 18404 E Lake Terr Dr Jonestown TX 78645

YALMAN, ANN, judge; b. Boston, June 9, 1948; d. Richard George and Joan (Osterman) Y. BA, Antioch Coll., 1970; JD, NYU, 1973. Trial atty. Fla. Rural Legal Svcs., Immokalee, Fla., 1973-74; staff atty. EEO, Atlanta, 1974-76; pvt. practice Santa Fe, N.Mex., 1976—; part time U.S. magstrate, N. Mex., 1988-96. Commr. Met. Water Bd., Santa Fe, 1986-88. Mem. N.Mex. Bar Assn. (commr. Santa Fe chpt. 1983-86). Home: 441 Calle La Paz Santa Fe NM 87501-2821 Office: 304 Catron St Santa Fe NM 87501-1806

YALOW, ROSALYN SUSSMAN, medical physicist; b. N.Y.C., N.Y., July 19, 1921; d. Simon and Clara (Zipper) Sussman; m. A. Aaron Yalow, June 6, 1943; children: Benjamin, Elanna. A.B., Hunter Coll., 1941; M.S., U. Ill., Urbana, 1942, Ph.D., 1945; D.Sc. (hon.), U. Ill., Chgo., 1974, Phila. Coll. Pharmacy and Sci., 1976, N.Y. Med. Coll., 1976, Med. Coll. Wis., Milw., 1977, Yeshiva U., 1977, Southampton (N.Y.) Coll., 1978, Bucknell U., 1978, Princeton U., 1978, Jersey City State Coll., 1979, Med. Coll. Pa., 1979, Manhattan Coll., 1979, U. Vt., 1980, U. Hartford, 1980, Rutgers U., 1980, Rensselaer Poly. Inst., 1980, Colgate U., 1981, U. So. Calif., 1981, Clarkson Coll., 1982, U. Miami, 1983, Washington U., St. Louis, 1983, Adelphi U., 1983, U. Alta. (Can.), 1983, SUNY, 1984, Tel Aviv U., 1985, Claremont (Calif.) U., 1986, Mills Coll., Oakland, Calif., 1986, Cedar Crest Coll., Allentown, Pa., 1988, Drew U., Madison, N.J., 1988, Lehigh U., 1988; L.H.D. (hon.), Hunter Coll., 1978; DSc. (hon.), San Francisco State U., 1989, Technion-Israel Inst. Tech., Haifa, 1989; DSc (hon.), Med. Coll. Ohio Toledo, 1991; L.H.D. (hon.), Sacred Heart U., Conn., 1978, St. Michael's Coll., Winooski Park, Vt., 1979, Johns Hopkins U., 1979, Coll. St. Rose, 1988, Spertus Coll. Judaica, Chgo., 1988; D. honoris causa, U. Rosario, Argentina, 1980, U. Ghent, Belgium, 1984; D. Humanities and Letters (hon.), Columbia U., 1984; DSc (hon.), Fairleigh Dickinson U., 1992, Conn. Coll., 1992, Smith Coll., Northampton, Mass., 1994, Union Coll., Schenectady, 1994. Diplomate: Am. Bd. Scis. Lectr., asst. prof. physics Hunter Coll., 1946-50; physicist, asst. chief radioisotope service VA Hosp., Bronx, N.Y., 1950-70, chief nuclear medicine, 1970-80, acting chief radioisotope service, 1968-70, sr. med. investigator emeritus; research prof. Mt. Sinai Sch. Medicine, CUNY, 1968-74, Disting. Service prof., 1974-79, Solomon A. Berson Disting. prof.-at-large, 1986—; Disting. prof.-at-large Albert Einstein Coll. Medicine, Yeshiva U., 1979-85, prof. emeritus, 1986—; chmn. dept. clin. scis. Montefiore Med. Ctr., Bronx, 1980-85; cons. Lenox Hill Hosp., N.Y.C., 1956-62, WHO, Bombay, 1978; sec. U.S. Nat. Com. on Med. Physics, 1963-67; mem. nat. com. Radiation Protection, Subcom. 13, 1957; mem. Pres.'s Study Group on Careers for Women, 1966-72; sr. med. investigator VA, 1972-92, sr. med. investigator emeritus, 1992—. Co-editor: Hormone and Metabolic Research, 1973-79; editorial adv. council: Acta Diabetologica Latina, 1975-77, Ency. Universalis, 1978—; editorial bd.: Mt. Sinai Jour. Medicine, 1976-79, Diabetes, 1976, Endocrinology, 1967-72; contbr. numerous articles to profl. jours. Bd. dirs. N.Y. Diabetes Assn., 1974. Recipient VA William S. Middleton Med. Research award, 1960; Eli Lilly award Am. Diabetes Assn., 1961; Van Slyke award N.Y. met. sect. Am. Assn. Clin. Chemists, 1968; award A.C.P., 1971; Dickson prize U. Pitts., 1971; Howard Taylor Ricketts award U. Chgo., 1971; Gairdner Found. Internat. award, 1971; Commemorative medallion Am. Diabetes Assn., 1972; Bernstein award Med. Soc. State N.Y., 1974; Boehringer-Mannheim Corp. award Am. Assn. Clin. Chemists, 1975; Sci. Achievement award AMA, 1975; Exceptional Service award VA, 1975; A. Cressy Morrison award N.Y. Acad. Scis., 1975; sustaining membership award Assn. Mil. Surgeons, 1975; Distinguished Achievement award Modern Medicine, 1976; Albert Lasker Basic Med. Research award, 1976; La Madonnina Internat. prize Milan, 1977; Golden Plate award Am. Acad. Achievement, 1977; Nobel prize for physiology/medicine, 1977; citation of esteem St. John's U., 1979; G. von Hevesy medal, 1978; Rosalyn S. Yalow Research and Devel. award established Am. Diabetes Assn., 1978; Banting medal, 1978; Torch of Learning award Am. Friends Hebrew U., 1978; Virchow gold medal Virchow-Pirquet Med. Soc., 1978; Gratum Genus Humanum gold medal World Fedn. Nuclear Medicine or Biology, 1978; Jacobi medallion Asso. Alumni Mt. Sinai Sch. Medicine, 1978; Jubilee medal Coll. of New Rochelle, 1978; VA Exceptional Service award, 1978; Fed. Woman's award, 1961; Harvey lectr., 1966; Am. Gastroenterol. Assn. Meml. lectr., 1972; Joslin lectr. New Eng. Diabetes Assn., 1972; Franklin I. Harris Meml. lectr., 1973; 1st Hagedorn Meml. lectr. Acta Endocrinologica Congress, 1973; Sarasota Med. award for achievement and excellence, 1979; gold medal Phi Lambda Kappa, 1980; Achievement in Life award Ency. Brit., 1980; Theobald Smith award, 1982; Pres.'s Cabinet award U. Detroit, 1982; John and Samuel Bard award in medicine and sci. Bard Coll., 1982; Disting. Research award Dallas Assn. Retarded Citizens, 1982, Nat. Medal Sci., 1988; Abram L. Sachar Silver Medallion Brandeis U., Waltham, Mass., 1989, Disting. Scientist of Yr. award ARCS, N.Y.C., 1989, Golden Scroll award The Jewish Advocate, Boston, 1989, spl. award Clin. Ligand Assay Soc., Washington, 1988, numerous others. Fellow N.Y. Acad. Scis. (chmn. biophysics div. 1964-65), Am. Coll. Radiology (asso. in physics), Clin. Soc. N.Y. Diabetes Assn.; mem. Nat. Acad. Scis., Am. Acad. Arts and Scis., Am. Phys. Soc., Radiation Research Soc., Am. Assn. Physicists in Medicine, Biophys. Soc., Soc. Nuclear Medicine, Endocrine Soc. (Koch award 1972, pres. 1978), Am. Physiol. Soc., (hon.) Harvey Soc., (hon.) Med. Assn. Argentina, (hon.) Diabetes Soc. Argentina, (hon.) Am. Coll. Nuclear Physicians, (hon.) The N.Y. Acad. Medicine, (hon.) Am. Gastroent. Assn., (hon.) N.Y. Roentgen Soc., (hon.) Soc. Nuclear Medicine, Phi Beta Kappa, Sigma Xi, Sigma Pi Sigma, Pi Mu Epsilon, Sigma Delta Epsilon, Tau Beta Pi. Office: VA Hosp 130 W Kingsbridge Rd Bronx NY 10468-3992*

YAMAGUCHI, KRISTI TSUYA, ice skater; b. Hayward, Calif., July 12, 1971; d. Jim and Carole (Doi) Y. Gold medalist, Figure Skating Albertville Olympic Games, 1992; U.S. Skating champion, 1992, World Skating champion, 1991, 1992, World Junior champion, 1988, world profl. figure skating champion, 1994. Recipient Women First award YWCA, 1993. Address: U.S. Figure Skating Assn. 20 1st St Colorado Springs CO 80906-3624*

YAMPOLSKY, PHYLLIS, artist; b. Phila.; d. Louis Jacob Yampolsky and Bassia Yampolsky Green; m. Peter Forakis, June 12, 1959 (div. 1964); children: Gia, Joseph Peter. Student, Phila. Mus. Sch. Arts, 1950-52, Instituto Allende, San Miguel de Allende, Mex., 1954-55, Ecole Beaux Arts, Fontainbleau, France, 1956, Hans Hofmann Atelier, N.Y.C., 1956-58. Founder, dir., tchr. Workshop Yampolsky, N.Y.C., 1956-66; art instr. 92d St. YMHA, N.Y.C., 1958-60; founder, dir. Hall of Issues, N.Y.C., 1960-61; 1st artist-in-residence N.Y.C., 1966-67; creator, dir. Portrait of Ten Towns N.Y. State Coun. Arts, 1967-70; founder, officer Northeast Windham Coun. Arts, Vt., 1978-79; instr. Vt. Acad., Saxton's River, 1979-81, Vt. C.C., Springfield, 1979-81; co-founder, instr. New Vt. Sch. Arts, 1981; founder, pres. Ind. Friends McCarren Pk., Inc., N.Y.C., 1988-96; cons. Model Cities, Columbus, Ohio, 1968, Province Ont. Coun. Arts, 1968-70, Phila. Bicentennial Commn., Smithsonian Inst. Bicentennial Travelling Festival Kit; cons., panelist, performance artists Arcosanti, Ariz., 1977-78, 80, 81; facilitator NEA, 1970-75; cons., organizer, program dir. Habitat II CBO Host Com., N.Y.C., 1995-96; spl. events dir. Youth Pavilion, San Antonio, 1968; writer art curriculum Marylerose Acad., Albany, 1969, Bennett Coll., 1970; presenter Habitat II, UN conf., Istanbul, Turkey, 1996. One woman shows include Phila. Art Alliance, 1953, Judson Gallery, N.Y.C., 1960, 62, Walker Gallery, N.Y.C., 1974, Kulicke Gallery, N.Y.C., 1975, Graham Gallery, N.Y.C., 1977, O.K. Harris and Susan Caldwell Galleries, N.Y.C., 1978, Stryke Gallery, N.Y.C., Windam Coll., Vt., 1978, Marlboro Coll., Vt., 1981, A Place Apart, N.Y.C., 1984, City Bank Gallery, Bklyn., 1986, Loft Lawyers, N.Y.C., 1987, 479 Gallery, N.Y.C., 1996; group shows include Park Place Gallery, N.Y.C., Brata Gallery, Cornell U., Dallas Mus. Fine Arts, Mus. Erotic Art, San Francisco, Mus. Erotic Art, Stockholm, Whitney Mus., Weisner Gallery, N.Y.C., City Without Walls Gallery, Newark, Green Gallery, N.Y.C., Leo Castelli Gallery, N.Y.C., Allan Stone Gallery, N.Y.C., Franklin Furnace, N.Y.C., Dorsky Gallery, N.Y.C., Bklyn. Terminal Show, N.Y.C., Food Stamp Gallery, N.Y.C., ABC No Rio, N.Y.C., Blue Mountain Gallery, N.Y.C., Boriqua Coll., N.Y.C., Phila. Mus. Art, Holland-Goldowsky, Chgo., Peter David, Mpls., Mc Nay Inst., San Antonio, Tex.; represented in pvt. collections; designer Am. Town Hall Wall Sys. used in Robert Kennedy Presdl. Primary, 1968, Clinton Presdl. Campaign and Inaugural Festivities, UN Women's Conf., Beijing, 1995, UN 50th Celebration, N.Y.C., 1995, V.P. Gore's Reinvention Revolution Conf., Washington, 1996, also numerous others. Recipient Hoving Happenings award N.Y. State Coun. Arts, 1967, Cue Mag., 1967, Betsy Barlow Rogers award Ind. Friends McCarren Pk., 1995; Ecole Beaux Arts scholar, Hans Hofmann Atelier scholar; grantee Ind. Friends McCarren Pk., J.M. Kaplan Fund, Andy Warhol Found., N.Y. Found., Vincent Astor Found., Citizen's Com. N.Y.C. Inc., 1990-95.

YAN, HAIPING, theatre and comparative literature educator; b. Shanghai, July 4, 1959; d. Ciqing and Xionlan (Chen) Y.; m. Zhigang Yang, Aug. 26, 1961. BA, Fudan U., Shanghai, 1982; MA, Cornell U., 1987, PhD, 1990. Instr., artistic dir. Shanghai Yang-pu Children's Performing Arts Ctr., 1973-78; asst. prof. Chinese Lit. Fudan U., 1982-84; tchg. asst. modern langs. and linguistics Cornell U., 1984-85, tchg. asst. Asian studies, 1988-89, vis. prof. East Asian studies, 1990-91; vist. asst. prof. theatre and East Asian studies Oberlin Coll., 1991-92, vis. asst. prof. theatre and comparative lit., 1992-94; asst. prof. theatre U. Colo., Boulder, 1994—; lectr. in field. Contbr. articles to profl. jours. Recipient 1st prize for excellence in drama Soc. Chinese Dramatists and Ministry of Culture of People's Republic of China, 1980-81, Sage scholarship Cornell U., 1983-84, Martin M. McVoy, Jr. Trust scholarship Cornell U., 1984-85, 85-86, 86-87, 87-88, Larry E. Gubb scholarship Cornell U., 1988, Cornell U. China-Japan Mellon grant, 1988, Rsch. grant U. Colo., 1994, Rsch. Travel award U. Colo., 1995, grant U. Colo., 1995. Mem. MLA, Assn. of Theatre in Higher Edn., Assn. Asian Studies, Chinese Dramatists' Assn. (China), Chinese Writers' Assn. (China), Telluride Assn. (student 1985-86, 86-87, 87-88, faculty 1989-90). Home: 33 S Boulder Cir # 315 Boulder CO 80303 Office: Univ Colo Boulder Dept Theatre and Dance C132 Univ Theatre Box 261 Boulder CO 80309-0261

YAN, SAU-CHI BETTY, biochemist; b. Hong Kong, Nov. 25, 1954; d. Ming Yan and Choo-Chen Woo; m. Victor J. Chen, Feb. 29, 1980; 1 child, Heidi I. BS, Ctrl. Mo. State U., 1975; PhD, Iowa State U., 1980. Postdoctoral fellow St. Paul-Ramsey Med. Ctr., 1980-82; postdoctoral fellow med. sch. U. Tex., Houston, 1982-84; sr. biochemist Eli Lilly & Co., Indpls., 1985-88, sr. scientist, 1989-93, sr. rsch. scientist, 1993—. Patentee in field; contbr. articles to profl. jours. Bd. dirs. A Children's Habitat, Indpls., 1994. Mem. AAAS, Am. Soc. Biochemistry, Molecular Biology, Protein Soc., Soc. Chinese Bioscientists Am. Office: Eli Lilly & Co 307 W Mccarty St # Dc1543 Indianapolis IN 46225-1235

YANAGITANI, ELIZABETH, optometrist; b. Ogden, Utah, Nov. 24, 1953; d. Katsuyoshi and Yaeko (Watanabe) Y. AS, Weber State Coll., Ogden, Utah, 1974; BA magna cum laude, U. Utah, 1976; OD, Pacific U., Forest Grove, Oreg., 1980. Externship Tripler Army Med Ctr., Schofield Barracks, Hawaii, 1979; staff optometrist Gen. Med., San Diego, 1984-89, San Ysidro Health Ctr., Calif., 1985-87, 91—, Logan Heights Family Health Ctr., San Diego, 1989-91; assoc. of pvt. office Chula Vista, Calif., 1985—; asst. instr. Am. Bus. Coll., San Diego, 1982. Recipient Gates Meml. award Nat. Eye Rsch. Found., 1980; scholar Weber State Coll., 1972-73, U. Utah, 1975, Project award Beta Sigma Kappa, 1980. Mem. San Diego County Optometric Soc. (v.p. 1985), Calif. Optometric Soc. (del. to leadership conf. 1985), Achievement Through Vision/COVD (pres. 1990), Phi Kappa Phi.

YANCEY, ELEANOR GARRETT, retired crisis intervention clinician; b. Ga., Oct. 24, 1933; adopted d. Overton LaVerne Garrett; m. Robert Grady Yancey, Nov. 10, 1961 (div. Apr. 1968); children: Katherine La Verne, David Shawn. Student, High Mus. Art Inst., 1952-53, Ga. State U., 1953-55, 78; BA, La Grange Coll., 1958. Social worker, case worker Fulton County Dept. Family and Children's Svcs., Atlanta, 1957-61; asst. tchr. Atlanta (Ga.) Bd. Edn., 1973-85; mental health crisis intervention clinician Dekalb County Bd. Health, Decatur, 1985-95, acting dir. crisis intervention, 1988-90; ret., 1995. Performed summer stock, 1969-70. Performed with Rogers & Co., 1969, 70; band booster pres. Henry Grady High Sch., Atlanta, 1977-78, v.p. PTA, 1978-79; pres. PTA Morningside Elem. Sch., Atlanta, 1977; grand juror Dekalb County, Decatur, 1983; active Sesquicentennial Celebration of Ala. Statehood. Mem. Kappa Kappa Iota (Lambda chpt. state pres. 1987-88, Eta pres. local chpt. 1992—). Democrat. Home: 3425 Regalwoods Dr Doraville GA 30340-4019

YANERO, LISA JOYCE, medical and surgical nurse; b. Clarksburg, W.Va., May 13, 1970; d. Franklin Allen and Etheldean Joyce (Poe) Y. AS, Fairmont State Coll., 1991, BS in Psychology, 1994. Cert. med./surg. nurse. RN Monongalia Gen. Hosp., Morgantown, W.Va., 1991—, charge nurse, 1994-95. Mem. ANA, The Am. Mmgt. Assn., W.Va. Nurses Assn., Pi Gamma Mu. Methodist. Office: Monongalia Gen Hosp 1200 JD Anderson Dr Morgantown WV 26505

YANKEE, PATRICIA ELAINE, judicial assistant; b. Flint, Mich., Jan. 18, 1955; d. Lloyd Perry and Bonnie Theresa (Knapp) Gleason; m. Lanny G. Yankee, Feb. 1, 1975; children: Steven Lloyd, Shaun Patrick. Student, Delta Coll., 1995—. Legal sec. Legal Svcs. of Eastern Mich., Bay City, 1973-80; legal sec./asst. Pergande, Shaw, Spector & Wenzloff P.C., Bay City, 1980-84; jud. asst. U.S. Bankruptcy Ct., Bay City, 1984—. Club leader Trail Blazers 4-H Club, Linwood, Mich., 1989—. Mem. Assn. Bankruptcy Jud. Assts. Roman Catholic. Office: US Bankruptcy Ct 111 1st St Bay City MI 48708

YANKOWITZ, SUSAN, writer, playwright; b. Newark; m. Herbert Leibowitz, May 3, 1978; 1 child. BA, Sarah Lawrence Coll.; MFA, Yale U. Author plays: Slaughterhouse Play, 1971, Boxes, 1973, Portrait of a Scientist (screenplay), 1974, Terminal, 1975, Alarms, 1988, A Knife in the Heart, 1991, Night Sky, 1992, Under the Skin, 1996, Slain in the Spirit, 1996, 1969 Terminal 1996, 1996, various unpublished stage plays, screenplays, teleplays; author (novels): Silent Witness, 1976-77, Taking the Fall, excerpt from novel, 1989, Night Sky, Samuel French, 1992, Night Sky, in Playwriting Women, 1993; contbr. to short fiction, monologues, essays in Gnosis, Solo, Heresies, Interview with Contemporary Women Playwrights, others. Recipient Vernon Rice Drama desk award for most promising playwright, 1969; Joseph Levine Screenwriting fellow, 1968, Guggenheim Found., 1975, MacDowell Colony Residency fellow, 1975, 84, 87, 90, McKnight fellow, 1990, NEA Creative Writing fellowship, 1995; grantee Rockefeller Found., 1973, 74, Creative Writing fellowship, 1979, U.S.-Japan Fellowship, 1984, Nat. Endowment for the Arts, 1989, TCG, 1990. Mem. New Dramatists, PEN, Dramatists Guild, Authors Guild. Office: Mary Harden Agent 850 7th Ave #405 New York NY 10019

YANNUZZI, ELAINE VICTORIA, food and home products executive; b. Summit, N.J.; d. Emil and Alice (Vance) Y. BA, Seton Hall U., 1968. Pres. Expression Unltd., Warren, N.J., 1971-89; pvt. practice cons. pub. industry and small bus. Bedminster, N.J., 1989—; presenter seminar N.Y. Food and Wine Show, Splty. Food Show; lectr. NYU, Rutgers U.; moderator Am. Women's Econ. Devel., N.Y.C., 1985-87; spkr. Women Bus. Owners N.J., Princeton, 1986. Author: Gift Wrapping Food, 1985; editorial advisor Fancy Food mag., 1985—; editorial cons. Family Circle Gt. Ideas mag., 1987-89. Named Entrepreneur of Yr. N.J. Living mag., 1983, Woman of Yr. NYU, 1986. Mem. Roundtable for Women (bd. dirs. 1986-89, Pacesetter award 1985), Nat. Assn. for Splty. Food Trade (steering com. 1986). Home and Office: 612 Timberbrooke Dr Bedminster NJ 07921-2106

YARBOROUGH, VALERIE ANN AMINA, voiceover artist, admissions officer; b. Washington, July 24, 1956; d. Baxter Austin Shirley and Virginia Dare (Dunston) Y. BA in Comm. and BA in Sociology, The Am. U., 1978. FCC 3rd Class Radio Operator Cert. Radio announcer WUST, WYCB Religious Radio, Washington, 1979-85; pub. svc. dir. WGIV Radio, Charlotte, N.C., 1980-81; vocalist, exec. dir. RDA Nuptial Notes, Unltd., Washington, 1985—; pub. rels. dir. Atiya Performing Arts, Inc., Suitland, Md., 1989-92; sr. admissions officer Ft. Washington (Md.) Med. Ctr., 1991—; owner, voiceover artist Televoyce Sys., Washington, 1991—; cons. Running on Faith Prodns., Washington, 1996. Editor, voiceover artist (CD recording) God Reigns, 1996. Named Outstanding Student, Am. U. Chpt. NAACP, 1978. Mem. SAG, Women in the Arts. Eckankar. Home: 20 Chesapeake St SE #7C Washington DC 20032-2828

YARBROUGH, DENA COX, retired special education educator; b. Gorman, Tex., June 20, 1933; d. William Thomas and Imogene (Dunlap) Cox; m. James Edgar Yarbrough, June 20, 1950. BA, Nicholls State U., 1964, MEd, 1971, postgrad., 1978. Supr. profl. pers., prin. schs., elem. tchr. Terrebonne Parish Sch. Bd., Houma, La., 1964-79, dir. spl. edn. svcs., 1980-91; ret., 1991. Bd. dirs. Terrebonne Literacy Coun., Dulac Community Ctr.; mem. adv. bd. Terrebonne Guidance Ctr. Mem. Terrebonne Retired Tchrs. Assn., Coun. for Exceptional Children, La. Mental Health Assn., La. Retired Tchrs. Assn., Alcohol and Drug Abuse Coun. for South La., Phi Delta Kappa. Democrat. Methodist. Home: 303 Westview Dr Houma LA 70364-2537

YARBROUGH, MARILYN VIRGINIA, lawyer, educator; b. Bowling Green, Ky., Aug. 31, 1945; d. William Ottoway Yarbrough and Merca Lee (Hardin) Toole; m. Walter James Ainsworth, Sept. 3, 1967 (div. Oct. 1980); children: Carmen Virginia, Carla Renee; m. David A. Didion, Dec. 31, 1987. BA, Va. State U., 1966; JD, UCLA, 1973. Bar: Calif. 1973, Kans. 1982. Instr. Boston Coll. Law Sch., Newton, Mass., 1975-76; prof. law U. Kans., Lawrence, 1976-87, assoc. vice chancellor, 1983-87; prof. Law Sch. U. Tenn., Knoxville, 1987-93; dean Law Sch U. Tenn., Knoxville, 1987-91; William J. Maier Jr. chair law W.Va. U., Morgantown, 1991-92; prof. U. N.C. Law Sch., Chapel Hill, 1992—, assoc. provost, 1994—. Editor in chief Black Law Jour. 1972-73; contbr. articles to profl. jours. Bd. dirs. Knox County Endl. Enrichment Fund, Knoxville, 1989-92, Knoxville Housing Partnership, 1989-92, United Way of Knoxville, 1990-92; trustee Law Sch. Admission Coun., pres., 1986-88; trustee Webb Sch. of Knoxville, 1988-91, Kenyon Coll.; mem. Pulitzer Prize Bd., 1990—. Mem. ABA (reporter Am. Law Inst.-ABA com. continuing profl. edn. 1988-90, sect. legal edn. and admissions to bar 1989-94), Poynter Inst. for Media Studies (adv. bd. 1984-90, bd. dirs. 1990-92). Democrat. Mem. United Ch. of Christ. Home: PO Box 9221 Chapel Hill NC 27515-9221

YARBROUGH, MARTHA CORNELIA, music educator; b. Waycross, Ga., Feb. 8, 1940; d. Henry Elliott and Jessie (Sirmans) Y.; B.M.E., Stetson U., 1962; M.M.E., Fla. State U., 1968, Ph.D., 1973. Choral dir. Ware County High Sch., Waycross, Ga., 1962-64, Glynn Acad., Brunswick, Ga., 1964-70; asst. choral dir. Fla. State U., 1970-72; cons. in music Muscogee County Sch. Dist., Columbus, Ga., 1972-73; cons. in tchr. edn. Psycho-Edno. Cons., Inc., Tallahassee, 1972-73; asst. prof. music edn., dir. univs. choruses and oratorio soc. Syracuse U., 1973-76, assoc. prof. music edn., 1976-83, prof., 1983-86, acting asst. dean Coll. Visual and Performing Arts, 1980-82, acting dir. Sch. Music, 1980-82, chmn. music edn., 1982-86; prof. music La. State U., Baton Rouge, 1986—, coordinator music, edn., 1986—, Haymon prof. of Music, 1995—; artist in residence Sch. Music U. Ala., Tuscaloosa, 1989-90. Chair exec. com. Music Edn. Rsch. Coun., 1992-94. Mem. Music Educators Nat. Conf. (sr. rschr. award, 1996), N.Y. State Sch. Music Assn., Am. Ednl. Research Assn., Soc. Research Music Edn. (mem. exec. com. 1988-90, program chair 1990-92, chair, 1992-94), AAUP, Pi Kappa Lambda, Phi Beta, Kappa Delta Pi. Co-author: Competency-Based Music Education, 1980; mem. editorial com. Jour. Research in Music Edn.; contbr. articles to profl. jours., chpts. in books. Office: Sch Music La State U Baton Rouge LA 70803

YARBROUGH, SONJA DIANNE, marketing and public relations professional; b. Trenton, Fla., June 6, 1948; d. George Charlie and Dorothy Mae (Carver) Y. BA in English, U. Fla., 1971; MS in Pub. Rels., Boston U., 1980. Pub. rels. asst. Digital Equipment Corp., Maynard, Mass., 1979; interim editor, rsch. asst. Rehab. Rsch. Inst., Gainesville, Fla., 1980-81; bus. mgr. Dental Specialty Practice, Atlanta, 1982-84; asst. account exec. Grizzard Advt., Atlanta, 1984-86; pub. rels. mktg. cons. Atlanta, 1987-88; account exec. Northlake Typography, Atlanta, 1988-89, TypoGraphics Atlanta, 1989-90; mktg. coord. Future Aviation Profls., Atlanta, 1990-93; pub. rels./mktg. cons. Atlanta, 1993-94; pub. rels. dir. Tech. Coll. of the Lowcountry, Beaufort, S.C., 1994—. Scholarship in Communications Boston U., 1979; recipient Bernice McCullar award Exemplary Leadership, 1990-91. Mem. Women in Communications, Inc. (co-chairperson ACE Competition 1989-90, publicity guide 1989-90, v.p. programs 1990-91, pres. 1992-93, past pres. 1993-94). Democrat. Home: 3125 W University Ave Gainesville FL 32607-2575 Office: 100 S Ribaut Rd PO Box 1288 Beaufort SC 29901

YARD, MOLLY, social activist; d. James Maxon and Mabelle Merriam (Hickcox) Y.; m. Sylvester Garrett; 3 children. AB, Swarthmore Coll., 1933, Hon. LLD, 1988. Chmn. Am. Student Union; active in Dem. party politics, Pa. and Calif., 1940s and 50s; active in civil rights movement, Pa., 1960s and 70s; staff mem. VISTA, 1960s; active NOW, from 1970s, polit. dir., 1985-87, pres., 1987-91. *

YARDLEY, ROSEMARY ROBERTS, journalist, columnist; b. Albertville, Ala., Apr. 1, 1938; d. James Bailey Jr. and Mildred (Smith) Roberts; m. Jonathan Yardley, June 14, 1961 (div. 1975); children: James B., William W. II; m. Donald Arthur Boulton, Apr. 30, 1988. BA, U. N.C., 1960; MA, U. N.C., Greensboro, 1978. Staff writer The Charlotte (N.C.) Observer, 1960-61; editorial asst. The N.Y. Times, N.Y.C., 1962-64; staff writer The Greensboro (N.C.) News and Record, 1974-78, editorial writer, 1978-88, editorial columnist, 1988—; mem. faculty English dept. U. N.C., Greensboro, 1990—. Contbr. articles, book revs. to various publs. Bd. dirs. Weatherspoon Art Mus. U. N.C., Greensboro, 1986—, U. N.C. Journalism Found., 1985-93, Weatherspoon Art Found., 1989—, Friends U. Libr., Greensboro, 1994—, Ea. Music Festival, Greensboro, 1984-88; bd. dirs. English Speaking Union, Greensboro, 1995—. Recipient 2d prize N.C. Press Assn., 1976, 1st prize 1987, 2d prize 1995; John S. Knight fellow Stanford U., 1980-81; Bosch Found. travel fellow, 1990, Atlantik Bruke Found. travel fellow, 1988. Democrat. Presbyterian. Home: 223 Elmwood Dr Greensboro NC 27408-5829 Office: The Greensboro News and Record 200 E Market St Greensboro NC 27401-2910

YARED, LINDA S., mechanical engineer; b. East Grand Rapids, Mich., July 31, 1952; d. Fozee S. and Penny (Bassler) Y. BS in Mech. Engring., U. Md., 1987. Sr. tech. rep. Xerox Corp., Rosslyn, Va., 1979-84; sr. engr. Mack Trucks, Allentown, Pa., 1987-90, Allied Signal Braking Systems, South Bend, Ind., 1990-95; project engr. Tri/Mark Corp., New Hampton, Iowa, 1995—. Patentee in field. Mem. ASME, NOW (treas. 1994), Soc. Automotive Engrs. (sec. 1988-90), Soc. Women Engrs. Office: Tri/Mark Corp Indsl Park New Hampton IA 50659

YARES, RIVA, art dealer, writer, publishing executive; b. Tel-Aviv, Aug. 17, 1940; d. Fishel and Sala (Singer) Kilstok; single; children: Dennis, Shelli Yares Poulos. BA in Art and Psychology, U. Jerusalem. Art dealer Riva Yares Gallery, Scottsdale, Ariz., 1963—, Santa Fe, N.Mex., 1990—; Art dealer Riva Yares Sculpture Pk., Ariz., 1985—; pres. Pueblo Arts & Real Estate, Scottsdale, Ariz., 1970—. Author various books on artists. Recipient Archtl. award City of Scottsdale, 1972. Mem. Charter 100. Office: Riva Yares Gallery 3625 Bishop Ln Scottsdale AZ 85251

YARYAN, RUBY BELL, psychologist; b. Toledo, Apr. 28, 1938; d. John Sturges and Susan (Bell) Y.; m. John Frederick Buenz, Jr., Dec. 15, 1962 (div. 1968). AB, Stanford U., 1960; PhD, U. London, 1968. Lic. clin. psychologist; diplomate Am. Bd. Psychology. Rsch. dir., univ. radio and tv U. Calif., San Francisco, 1968-70; dir. delinquency com. U.S. Dep. Justice, Washington, 1970-73; evaluation dir. Office of Criminal Justice Planning, Sacramento, Calif., 1973-76; CAO project mgr. San Diego (Calif.) County, 1977-92; dir. devel. svcs. Childhelp USA, Woodland Hills, Calif., 1992-94; rsch. coord. Neuropsychiat. Inst. and Hosp. UCLA, 1986-87; exec. dir. Centinela Child Guidance Clinic, Inglewood, Calif., 1987-89; clin. dir. Nat. Found. Emotionally Handicapped, North Hills, Calif., 1990-93; pvt. practice Beverly Hills, Calif., 1973—; psychologist Sr. Psychology Svcs., North L.A. County, 1994—; cons. White House Conf. Children, Washington, 1970; mem. Nat. Adv. Com. Criminal Justice Standards and Goals, Washington, 1973; clin. affiliation UCLA Med. Ctr. Contbr. articles to profl. jours.; chpts. to books and monographs in field. Chair Human Svcs. Commn., City of West Hollywood, Calif., 1986; first vice-chair United Way/Western Region, L.A., 1988; mem. planning-allocations-rsch. coun. United Way, San Diego, 1980-82. Grantee numerous fed., state and local govt. orgns. Mem. Am. Psychol. Assn., Western Psychol. Assn., Calif. Psychol. Assn., Am. Orthopsychiat. Assn., Am. Profl. Soc. on Abuse of Children, Phi Beta Kappa. Episcopalian. Office: 337 S Beverly Dr Ste 107 Beverly Hills CA 90212-4307

YASUI, LARAINE SUE, elementary education educator; b. Hilo, Hawaii, May 8, 1943; d. Kongo and Sue (Hokada) Kimura; m. Roger S. Yasui, Sept. 18, 1965; children: Yvette Leiko, Ryan S. BEd, U. Hawaii, 1965, MEd, 1967. Tchr. 5th and 6th grades Pearl City (Hawaii) Elem. Sch., 1967-79; tchr. 4th grade/Chpt. I Honowai Elem. Sch., Waipahu, Hawaii, 1979-89; Chpt. I tchr. Pohakea Elem. Sch., Ewa Beach, Hawaii, 1989—. Pres. precinct State Dem. Party, Pearl City, 1994. Recipient Chpt. I Excellence award U.S. Dept. Edn., 1989. Mem. Hawaii State Tchrs. Assn., Internat. Reading Assn. (chmn. chpt. 1987-95), Am. Bus. Women's Assn. (chpt. pres. 1988, Woman of Yr. 1988). Congregationalist. Home: 1654 Kaleilani St Pearl City HI 96782-2044

YATES, BRENDA H. CARROLL, secondary school educator; b. Carrolltown, Ga., Sept. 16, 1949; d. Buford Bledsoe and Lovie Beatrice (Thaxton) Holmes; m. Kenneth Wayne Carroll, Aug. 23, 1969 (div. Aug. 1984); children: Kenneth W. Jr., Samuel Mark; m. Gwendolyn Ray Yates, Dec. 10, 1987. BA in Secondary Edn. Social Studies, West Ga. Coll., 1970, MEd in Secondary Edn. English, 1974, EdS in Secondary Edn. English, 1988. Cert. tchr., Ga. Social studies and lang. arts tchr. Rockmart (Ga.) H.S., 1970-78; lang. arts tchr., dept. head Douglas County Comprehensive H.S., Douglasville, Ga., 1978—; adj. instr. Mercr U., Lithia Springs, Ga., 1990-95. Named Star Tchr., State of Ga., 1994. Mem. NEA, Ga. Assn. Educators. Democrat. Baptist. Home: 4978 Pebblebrook Dr Douglasville GA 30135-4520 Office: Douglas County Comp HS 8705 Campbellton St Douglasville GA 30134-2202

YATES, ELIZABETH (MRS. WILLIAM MCGREAL), author, editor; b. Buffalo, Dec. 6, 1905; d. Harry and Mary (Duffy) Y.; m. William McGreal, Nov. 6, 1929. Grad., Franklin Sch., Buffalo, Oaksmere, Mamaroneck, N.Y.; student, London (Eng.); Litt.D. (hon.), Aurora Coll., 1965, Ripon Coll., 1970, Rivier Coll.; L.H.D. (hon.), Eastern Bapt. Coll., 1966, U. N.H., 1967, New Eng. Coll., 1972, Franklin Pierce Coll., 1981. Staff mem. U. Conn., U. Ind., U. Colo., U. N.H. writers confs., 1948—; staff mem. Christian Writers and Editors Conf., Green Lake, Wis., 1957—; Mem. gov.'s State Library Commn. Author: High Holiday, 1938, Hans and Frieda, 1938, Gathered Grace, 1939, Climbing Higher, 1939, Quest in the Northland, 1940, Haven for the Brave, 1941, Under the Little Fir, 1941, Around the Year in Iceland, 1942, Patterns on the Wall, 1942, Mountain Born, 1943, Wind of Spring, 1944, The Young Traveller in the U.S.A, 1946, Nearby, 1947, Once in the Year, 1947, Beloved Bondage, 1948, Amos Fortune, Free Man, 1950, Guardian Heart, 1950, Children of the Bible, 1950, Brave Interval, 1952, A Place For Peter, 1952, Hue and Cry, 1953, Rainbow Round the World, 1954 (Jane Addams children's book award Women's Internat. League for Peace and Freedom 1955), Prudence Crandall, Woman of Courage, 1955, The Carey Girl, 1956, Pebble in a Pool, The Widening Circles of Dorothy Canfield Fisher's Life, 1958 (reissued as The Lady from Vermont 1971), The Lighted Heart, 1960, The Next Fine Day, 1961, Someday You'll Write, 1962, Sam's Secret Journal, 1963, Carolina's Courage, 1963, Howard Thurman, Portrait of a Practical Dreamer, 1964, Up the Golden Stair, 1966, Is There a Doctor in the Barn, 1966, With Pipe, Paddle and Song, 1968, New Hampshire, 1969, On that Night, 1969, Sarah Whitcher's Story, 1971, Skeezer, Dog with a Mission, 1972, The Road Through Sandwich Notch, 1973, We, The People, 1974, A Book of Hours, 1976, Call It Zest, 1977, The Seventh One, 1978, My Diary, My World, 1981, Silver Lining, 1981; My Widening World, 1983, One Writer's Way, 1984, Sound Friendships, 1987; Editor: Piskey Folk, 1941, Doll Who Came Alive, 1941, 72, Joseph, 1947, The White Ring, 1949, The Christmas Story, 1949, Your Prayers and Mine, 1954, Sir Gibbie, 1962; Contbr. book revs., articles, essays, interviews to periodicals. Trustee Town Library, Peterborough, N.H.; bd. dirs. N.H. Assn. for Blind. Recipient N.Y. Herald Tribune Spring Festival award, 1943, 50; Newbery medal, 1951; William Allen White award, 1953; Sarah Josepha Hale award, 1970; N.H. Gov.'s award of distinction, 1982. Mem. Delta Kappa Gamma. Address: Box 295 149 E Side Dr Concord NH 03301-5475

YATES, ELLA GAINES, library consultant; b. Atlanta, June 14, 1927; d. Fred Douglas and Laura (Moore) Gaines; m. Joseph L. Sydnor (dec.); 1 child, Jerri Gaines Sydnor Lee; m. Clayton R. Yates (dec.). A.B., Spelman Coll., Atlanta, 1949; M.S. in L.S, Atlanta U., 1951; J.D., Atlanta Law Sch., 1979. Asst. br. librarian Bklyn. Pub. Library, 1951-54; head children's dept. Orange (N.J.) Pub. Library, 1956-59; br. librarian E. Orange (N.J.) Pub. Library, 1960-69; med. librarian Orange Meml. Hosp., 1967-69; asst. dir. Montclair (N.J.) Pub. Library, 1970-72; asst. dir. Atlanta-Fulton Pub. Library, 1972-76, dir., 1976-81; dir. learning resource ctr. Seattle Opportunities Industrialization Ctr., 1982-84; asst. dir. adminstrn. Friendship Force, Atlanta, 1984-86; state librarian Commonwealth of Va., 1986-90; library cons. Price Waterhouse, 1991; adv. bd. Library of Congress Center for the Book, 1977-85; cons. in field; vis. lectr. U. Wash., Seattle, 1981-83; mem. Va. Records Adv. Bd., 1986-90; mem. Nagara Exec. Bd., 1987-91. Contbr. to profl. jours. Vice chmn. N.J. Women's Coun. on Human Rels., 1957-59; chmn. Friends Fulton County Jail, 1973-81; bd. dirs. United Cerebral Palsy Greater Atlanta, Inc., 1979-81 Coalition Against Censorship, Washington, 1981-84, YMCA Met. Atlanta, 1979-81, Exec. Women's Network, 1979-82, Freedom To Read Found., 1979-85, Va. Black History Mus., Richmond, 1990-91; sec., exec. dir. Va. Libr. Found. Bd., 1986-90. Recipient meritorious svc. award Atlanta U., 1977, Phoenix award City of Atlanta, 1980, Serwa award Nat. Coalition 100 Black Women, 1989, Black Caucus award, 1989, disting. svc. award Clark-Atlanta U., 1991, ednl. support svc. award Tuskegee Airmen, 1993; named profl. woman of yr. NAACP N.J., 1972, outstanding chum of yr., 1976; named outstanding alumni Spelman Coll., 1977, named to alumni hall of fame, 1995. Mem. ALA (exec. bd. 1977-83, commn. freedom of access to info.), NAACP, Southeastern Libr. Assn., Nat. Assn. Govt. Archives and Records Adminstrn. (exec. bd. 1987-91), Delta Sigma Theta. Baptist. Home and Office: 1171 Oriole Dr SW Atlanta GA 30311-2424

YATES, ELSIE VICTORIA, retired secondary English educator; b. Newport, R.I., Dec. 16, 1916; d. Andrew James and Rachel Agnes (Sousa) Tabb; m. George Herman Yates, July 12, 1941 (div. Apr. 1981); children: Serena, George Jr., Michael, Elsie French, David. AB in English and History, Va. Union U., 1938; postgrad., U. R.I., 1968-73, Salve Regina U., 1968-73. Life cert. in secondary English and reading specialist, R.I. Reading specialist grades 7 and 8 title I Newport (R.I.) Sch., 1971-74, secondary English educator, 1975-87; ret., 1987. Mem. adult com. Young Life, Newport, 1981-93; active Newport (R.I.) Substance Abuse Force, 1989-93; chmn. multicultural curriculum com. New Visions for Newport (R.I.) Schs., 1991-94; mem. edn. com. Swinburne Sch., Newport, 1992-94. Recipient Outstanding Ednl. Contbn. Under Title I award U.S. Office Edn., Bur. Sch. Sys., 1976, Presdl. citation Nat. Edn. Assn. R.I., 1987, Appreciation for Svc. award Cmty. Bapt. Ch., Newport, 1988, Outstanding Svc.

award in field of edn. to the youth in cmty. Queen Esther Chpt. 2, Newport, 1992. Mem. R.I. Ret. Tchrs. Assn., Newport Ret. Tchrs. Assn. Baptist. Home: 8 Bayside Vlg Apt A Newport RI 02840-1321

YATES, ISABEL MCCANTS, city council member; b. Winnsboro, S.C., Oct. 1, 1924; d. Charles Spencer and Isabel Elliott (Gooding) McCants; m. Eugene Wilson Yates, June 30, 1948; children: Eugene W., Mackie Yates Hempel, Carolyn Yates Cunningham, Elliott Glenn. BA, U. S.C., 1944; MA, Ohio State U., 1945; postgrad., U. Ky., 1964-78. English tchr. Spartanburg (S.C.) H.S., 1945-46; English instr. U. S.C., Columbia, 1946-48, Newberry (S.C.) Coll., 1948-49; ptnr. retail dress shop Track Two, Midway, Ky., 1973-78; sec., ptnr. Merit Tours and Convention Planning, Lexington, Ky., 1981-90; 4th dist. coun. mem. Lexington-Fayette Urban County Govt., 1992—. Contbr. articles to profl. jours. Bd. vice chmn. Lexington Philharm. Soc., 1974-75; bd. chmn. Environ. Commn., Lexington, 1980-82, Lexington Directives, 1985-87, Arts and Heritage Festival, Lexington, 1989-90, U. Ky. Ctr. on Aging Found., Lexington, 1989-92; v.p. Nat. Am. Mothers, Inc., Am. Mothers, Inc., Waldorf Astoria, N.Y., 1989-91; chair devel. coun. Midway (Ky.) Coll., 1991-93. Named Ky. Mother of Yr., Ky. Mother's Assn., Elizabethtown, Ky., 1981, Outstanding Women of Lexington Chpt. Beta Sigma Phi, 1984, Outstanding Vol. Fund Raiser, Nat. Soc. Fund-Raising Execs., 1990; recipient Woman of Achievement award YWCA, Lexington, 1989, Campaign Cabinet award United Way, Lexington, 1989. Mem. Ky. Ednl. TV (adv. bd.), Lexington Jr. League (adv. bd.), Lexington Arts and Cultural Coun. (co-chair fund raising 1992-95), Friends of McConnell Springs (mem., founder, bd. chair 1993-96), New Century Lexington (bd. mem. 1995-96). Democrat. Methodist. Home: 717 Malabu Dr Lexington KY 40502 Office: Lexington-Fayette Urban County Govt 200 East Main Lexington KY 40507

YATES, LINDA SNOW, communications executive; b. St. Louis, July 20, 1938; d. Robert Anthony Jerrue and June Alberta (Crowder) Armstrong; m. Charles Russell Snow, Nov. 26, 1958 (div. 1979); children: Cathryn Louise, Christopher Armstrong, Heather Highstone, Sean Webster; m. Alan Porter Yates, July 22, 1983. BBA, Auburn U., 1973, MEd, 1975, postgrad. Cert. profl. sec. Div. head placement div. Solutions Group, Atlanta, 1981-83; employment coord. Fulton Fed. Savs., Atlanta, 1983-84; owner, recruiter Data One, Inc., Atlanta, 1984-85; ops. mgr. Talent Tree Temporaries, Atlanta, 1985-87; legal asst., sec. Rice & Keene, Atlanta, 1987-90; legal word processing asst. Kilpatrick & Cody, Atlanta, 1990-94; pres., owner Power Comm., Hilton Head, S.C., 1994—; adj. instr. DeKalb C.C., Atlanta, 1980-84, Mercer U., Atlanta, 1981-82; instr. bus. So. Union State Jr. Coll., Valley, Ala., 1974-75; legal sec. Swift, Currie, McGhee & Hiers, Atlanta, 1979-80, Samford, Torbert, Denson & Horsley, Opelika, Ala., 1969-71. Columnist Neon News Flash, 1995. Mem. Paralegal Assn. Beaufort County (charter mem., sec. 1993-94), Women Bus. Owners, Nat. Assn. Pers. Cons., Internat. Soc. Poets (Disting. mem., Internat. Poet of Merit 1996), Phi Delta Kappa. Republican. Episcopalian. Home: 234 Tennis Villas Fripp Island SC 29920 also: PO Box 2441 Cashiers NC 28717 Office: 33 Office Park Rd 4A-127 Hilton Head Island SC 29928-4612

YATES, MADONNA MOORE, journalist, columnist; b. Oklahoma City, Apr. 27, 1938; d. Chester K. and Grace H. (Andrews) Moore; m. Donald L. Yates, June 8, 1956 (dec. Dec. 1991); children: David Carlyle, Donita Ruth Yates Fox. Cert. in nursing, U. Okla., 1959; BS, St. Mary-of-Woods (Ind.) Coll., 1978. RN, Ind., Jamaica. Missionary nurse Christian Missionary Fellowship, Addis Ababa, Ethiopia, 1963-65, Kano (Nigeria) Eye Hosp., from 1966; weekly religion columnist Terre Haute (Ind.) Tribune-Star, 1984-91; med. group missions corr. Christian Med. & Dental Soc., Richardson, Tex., 1988-95; resource devel. dir. Med. Ministry Internat., Richardson, 1995—. Author: Million-Dollar Vacations, 1984; contbr. numerous articles to religious publs. Mem. ecumenical affairs com. Greater Terre Haute Ch. Fedn., 1978-88; docent Sheldon Swope Art Mus., Terre Haute, 1978-83; mem. bd. advisors Habit for Humanity Internat., 1978—. Recipient award in religion Terre Haute C. of C., 1985, Humanitarian award NAACP, 1990, Lifetime Achievement award Optimist Club, 1991; named One of 75 Outstanding Women, Girl Scouts U.S.A., 1987. Mem. Religion Newswriter's Assn. Presbyterian. Office: Med Ministry Internat 50 Business Pky Ste B Richardson TX 75081

YATES, MARGERY GORDON, elementary education educator; b. Walton, N.Y., July 3, 1910; d. McClellan Gordon and Marcia Beulah (Ramsdell) Gordon-Strahl; m. James McKendree Yates, Aug. 11, 1933; 1 child, Sally. BS, U. Houston, 1943, MS, 1948; MA, Stanford U., 1952. Tchr. Baldwin (N.Y.) Sch. Dist., 1928-34, Houston Sch. Dist., 1943-48; supr. primary edn. Watsonville (Calif.) Sch. Dist., 1948-53; edn. cons. San Mateo County Office Edn., Redwood City, Calif., 1953-58; supr. primary edn. Jefferson Elem. Sch. Dist., Daly City, Calif., 1958-65; tchr. Hillsborough (Calif.) Sch. Dist., 1965-75; instr. U. Houston, 1956, San Jose State Coll., 1957. Mem. AAUW (edn. area rep. 1987-88, 89-90, 91-92, 92-93, 93-94, Fellowship award honoree 1991), Burlingame Music Club (pres. 1992-93, 93-94), Commonwealth Club Calif., Alpha Delta Kappa (corr. sec. Calif. state bd. 1981-82, Gamma Beta chpt. pres. 1971-74, treas. 1985-89, 94—). Republican. Mem. Ch. Christian Sci. Home: 2731 Summit Dr Burlingame CA 94010-6039

YATES, PATRICIA ENGLAND, employment company executive; b. Sparta, Tenn., Sept. 18, 1958; d. Edsel and Gladys Mary (Garland) England; m. Dennis Eugene Yates, Nov. 30, 1990. BS in Home Econs., Tenn. Tech. U., 1982. Purchasing sec. Porelon, Inc., Cookeville, Tenn., 1982-87; buyer purchasing dept. Tenn. Tech. U., Cookeville, Tenn., 1987-88; dir. pers. J & S Constrn. Co., Inc., Cookeville, 1988-93; placement coord. Holland Employment (formerly Putnam Employment Svc. Inc.), Cookeville, 1993-95; svc. specialist Hamilton-Ryker Co., Shelbyville, Tenn., 1995—; dir. projects Nat. and Internat. Issues Rsch., Sparta, Tenn., 1982—. Mem. Nat. Exch. Club, Profl. Secs. Internat., Bus. and Profl. Women's Orgn. (treas. 1990, 2d v.p. 1992, Finalist Young Careerist 1994), U.C. Soc. Resource Mgmt. (treas. 1993), Internat. Platform Assn. Office: The Hamilton-Ryker Co 100 Public Square Shelbyville TN 37160

YATES, RENEE HARRIS, economist; b. Oct. 20, 1950; d. Marion and Betty Jane (Edgenton) Harris; m. Earl W. Yates, Sept. 6, 1980 (div. July 1991); 1 child, Clinton Harris Yates. BA, Western Coll. for Women, 1972; MA in Internat. Studies, Johns Hopkins U., 1974. Project devel. officer U.S. Agy. for Internat. Devel., Washington, 1975-81; internat. economist U.S. Treasury Dept./Office Sec. of Internat. Affairs, Washington, 1981-87; pres. World Trade Assocs., Inc., Washington, 1987—; pres. InterFuture, N.Y.C., 1984-87. Mem. TransAfrica, Washington, 1991. Mem. Thursday Luncheon Group. Office: World Trade Assoc Inc 7320 Carroll Ave Takoma Park MD 20912-4514

YATVIN, JOANNE INA, school superintendent; b. Newark, Apr. 17, 1931; d. John and Mary Edna (Cohen) Goldberg; m. Milton Brian Yatvin, June 8, 1952; children: Alan, Bruce, Lillian, Richard. Ba, Douglass Coll., 1952; MA, Rutgers U., 1962; PhD, U. Wis., 1974. Cert. sch. adminstr. Tchr. Hamburg (N.J.) Pub. Schs., 1952-53, New Brunswick (N.J.) Pub. Schs., 1953-55, Mayaguez (P.R.) Schs., 1958-59, Milltown (N.J.) Pub. Schs., 1959-62, East Brunswick (N.J.) Pub. Schs., 1962-63; tchr., prin. Madison (Wis.) Met. Sch. Dist., 1963-88; supt. Cottrell Sch. Dist., Boring, Oreg., 1988—; adv. bd. mem. Big Books Mag., 1990-91; cons. various sch. dists. Author: Learning Language Through Communication, 1986, (monograph) A Whole Language Program for a Whole School, 1991; contbr. chpts. in books and articles to profl. jours. Recipient Excellence in Print award Washington Edpress, 1987, Disting. Elem. Edn. Alumni award U. Wis., 1988; named Elem. Prin. of Yr. Wis. Dept. Edn., 1985, Wis. State Reading Assn., 1985. Mem. ASCD, Internat. Reading Assn., Nat. Coun. Tchrs. English (chair com. on ctrs. excellence 1986-89), Nat. Middle Sch. Assn., Oreg. Reading Assn., Oreg. Coun. Tchrs. English, Phi Delta Kappa. Home: 5226 SW Northwood Ave Portland OR 97201-2832 Office: Cottrell Sch Dist 36225 SE Proctor Rd Boring OR 97009-9719

YAVITZ, JUDITH A., lawyer; b. New Rochelle, N.Y., Apr. 3. BA cum laude, Colgate U., 1978; JD, Columbia U. Bar: N.Y. 1982, U.S. Dist. Ct. (so., ea., we., no. dists.) N.Y. 1982. Ptnr. Anderson Kill Olick & Oshinsky, N.Y.C. Contbr. articles to profl. jours. Mem. ABA, Assn. of Bar of City of N.Y., N.Y. County Lawyers Assn. (tort law com. 1993). Office: Anderson Kill Olick & Oshinsky 1251 Ave of the Americas New York NY 10020-1182*

YAWORSKI, JOANN, reading skills educator; b. Phillipsburg, N.J., Oct. 11, 1956; d. Michael and Cecilia (Ruchala) Y. BA, Pa. State U., 1977; MEd, Millersville U., 1982; postgrad., U. Houston, 1984, Lehigh U., 1988-90; PhD, SUNY, Albany, 1996. Cert. tchr. Russian lang., Russian area studies, reading specialist, elem edn., Tex., N.J., Pa., N.Y. Reading tutor Ephrata (Pa.) Sr. H.S., 1980-81; tchr. Am. History/World Cultures Linden Hall Sch., Lititz, Pa., 1981-82; tchr., Russian lang. Spring Branch Sch. Dist., Houston, Tex., 1982-85; dir. devel. reading Green Mountain Coll., Poultney, Vt., 1989-95; tchg. asst. dept. reading U. Albany (N.Y.), SUNY, 1995-96; ind. reading cons., 1996—; reading cons. Sundance Pub. Co., 1996—; presenter 28th and 29th ann. confs. Coll. Reading and Learning Assn. Mem. U.S. Figure Skating Assn. Democrat. Roman Catholic. Home: 81 Lake Ave #6 Saratoga Springs NY 12866

YAX, ELLEN MARIE, photographer finisher; b. Boonton, N.J., Nov. 26, 1962; d. Bernard Joseph and Theresa Lorretta (Evans) Merchak; m. Thomas Alan Yax, Sept. 24, 1988. Cert. achievement, Gemini Sch. Art and Design, 1987. Driver Hertz-Rent-a-Car, Romulus, Mich., 1981-89; sign painter Sign Specialties, Allen Park, Mich., 1988; photography finisher N.Am. Photo, Livonia, Mich., 1989—. Vol. St. Hilary's Ch., Redford, Mich., 1992—; mem. St. Hilary's Rosary Altar Soc., 1994—. Roman Catholic. Office: 27451 Schoolcraft Livonia MI 48150

YBARRA, KATHRYN WATROUS, systems engineer; b. Middletown, Conn., Aug. 7, 1943; d. Claude Philip Jr. and C. Lyle (Crook) Watrous; m. Norman L. Adams (div.); children: Cynthia Anne Leonard, Suzette Mae Gross, Daniel Joseph Adams; m. Raul M. Ybarra, Dec. 11, 1976; stepchildren: Esther Ingram, Yolanda Ybarra, Lisa Ybarra. BA in Computer Sci., U. Tex., 1985. Scientific programmer Tracor, Inc., Austin, 1978-86; tech. staff engr. Honeywell, Inc. Comml. Avionics, Phoenix, 1986—. Mem. Friends of Phoenix Libr., v.p. Juniper chpt., 1996. Mem. RTCA (spl. com. # 147, Traffic Alert and Collision Avoidance Sys. II, chair requirements working group 1991—, leadership citation 1995). Roman Catholic. Home: 3360 W Phelps Rd Phoenix AZ 85023

YEAGER, ANDREA WHEATON, editor; b. Baytown, Tex., Apr. 17, 1951; d. Virgil Jerry Jr. and Billy Ruth (Leslie) Wheaton; m. Danny Rhea Bowen, Feb. 21, 1976 (div. Sept. 1985); m. Hubert Allen Yeager Jr., Dec. 21, 1985; 1 child, Elyssa Mae. BA in Teaching, Sam Houston State U., Huntsville, Tex., 1973. Assoc. editor The Houstonian, Sam Houston State U., Huntsville, Tex., 1970-73; reporter The Orange (Tex.) Leader, 1973-74, lifestyle editor, 1974-78; editor The Suburbia Reporter, Houston, 1978-79; copy editor The Houston Chronicle, 1979-81, features copy desk chief, 1981-85; copy editor The Sun Herald, Biloxi, Miss., 1986-88, features editor, 1988-91, mng. editor, 1991—. Crisis vol. Gulf Coast Women's Ctr., Biloxi, 1991—; bd. dirs. Am. Heart Assn., Gulfport, 1990-92, Boys & Girls Clubs of Gulf Coast, Biloxi, Crimestoppers, Internat. Tng. in Comm.; mem. Leadership Gulf Coast Class, 1991-92, class rep., 1995—; pres. Altrusa Internat. of Biloxi, 1993—; mem. nutrition adv. bd. Gulfport Sch. Dist./Am. Cancer Soc., 1993—. Mem. La.-Miss. AP Mng. Editors (pres. 1995-96), Harrison County Home Econs. Coun. (v.p. 1991—), Miss. Press Assn., Pub. Rels. Assn. Miss., Gayfers Career Club. Republican. Baptist. Home: 12297 Windward Dr Gulfport MS 39503-5501 Office: The Sun Herald 205 Debuys Rd Gulfport MS 39507-2838

YEAGER, CAROLINE HALE, radiologist, consultant; b. Little Rock, Sept. 5, 1946; d. George Glenn and Crenor Burnelle (Hale) Y.; m. William Berg Singer, July 8, 1978; children: Adina Atkinson Singer, Sarah Rose Singer. BA, Ind. U., Bloomington, 1968; MD, Ind. U., Indpls., 1971. Diplomate Am. Bd. Radiology; med. lic. State of Calif. Intern Good Samaritan Hosp., Los Angeles, 1971-72; resident in radiology King Drew Med. Ctr. UCLA, Los Angeles, 1972-76; dir. radiology Hubert Humphrey Health Ctr., Los Angeles, 1976-77; asst. prof. radiology UCLA, Los Angeles, 1977-84; asst. prof. radiology King Drew Med. Ctr. UCLA, Los Angeles, 1977-85, dir. ultrasound, 1977-84; ptnr. pvt. practice Beverly Breast Ctr., Beverly Hills, Calif., 1984-87; cons. Clarity Communications, Pasadena, Calif., 1981—; pvt. practice radiology Claude Humphrey Health Ctr., 1991-93; dir. sonograms and mammograms Rancho Los Amigos Med. Ctr., 1993-94; trustee Assn. Teaching Physicians, L.A., 1976-81; cons. King Drew Med. Ctr., 1984, Gibraltar Savs., 1987, Cal Fed. Inc., 1986, Medical Faculty At Home Professions, 1989—, Mobil Diagnostics, 1991-92, Xerox Corp., 1990-91, Frozen Leopard, Inc., 1990-91. Author: (with others) Infectious Disease, 1978, Anatomy and Physiology for Medical Transcriptionists, 1992; contbr. articles to profl. jours. Trustee U. Synagogue, Los Angeles, 1975-79; mem. Friends of Pasadena Playhouse, 1987-90. Grantee for innovative tng. Nat. Fund for Med. Edn., 1980-81. Mem. Am. Inst. Ultrasound in Medicine, L.A. Radiology Soc. (ultrasound sect.), Nat. Soc. Performance and Instrn. (chmn. conf. Database 1991, publs. L.A. chpt. 1990, info. systems L.A. chpt. 1991, dir. adminstrn. L.A. chpt. 1992, Outstanding Achievement in Performance Improvement award L.A. chpt. 1990, bd. dirs. 1990-93, Pres. award for Outstanding Chpt. 1992, v.p. programs 1993), Stanford Profl. Women L.A. Jewish. Home and Office: 3520 Yorkshire Rd Pasadena CA 91107-5440

YEAGER, ELIZABETH ANNE, education educator; b. Tuscaloosa, Ala., Nov. 10, 1960; d. John Fritz Yeager Jr. and Suzanne (Jackson) Crump; m. James Willard Morris III, Dec. 18, 1993. BA cum laude, U. Ala., 1983; MAT in History, Ga. State U., 1990; postgrad., U. Tex., 1984-86. Master's level social studies composite grades 7-12, gifted endorsement grades K-12, Ga.; lifetime provisional social studies composite grades 7-12, Tex. Rsch. assoc./tchg. asst. Ctr. for Mexican Am. Studies, U. Tex., Austin, 1984-87; social studies tchr. Northside H.S., Atlanta, 1987-89, Peachtree Jr. H.S., Atlanta, 1989-92; English tchr. Charles U. Med. Sch., Hradec Kralove, Czech Republic, 1992; tchg. asst. dept. curriculum and instrn. U. Tex., Austin, 1992-95; asst. prof. instrn. and curriculum U. Fla., 1995—; charter faculty, instr. Tex. Gov.'s Sch., Austin, summers 1986, 87, 88; cons. in curriculum Cable News Network, Atlanta, 1990-93; cons. Stanley Found., Muscatine, Iowa, 1993; reviewer various jours., 1993-94. Editl. asst. Jour. Curriculum and Supervision, 1993; contbr. articles to profl. jours. Vol. various polit. campaigns, Atlanta and Austin, 1988—; contbr., mem. U. Ala. Alumni Assn., Tuscaloosa, 1989—, Habitat for Humanity, Austin, 1994, Laguna Gloria Art Mus., Austin, 1994; vol. driver Meals on Wheels/United Way, Austin, 1993—. Recipient Louise Berman Curriculum award Friends of Louise Berman, 1994, Outstanding Dissertation award ASCD, 1995-96. Mem. Am. Ednl. Rsch. Assn. (Spencer/AERA Doc. Rsch. fellow 1994-95), Nat. Coun. for Social Studies, Soc. for Study Curriculum History, Midwest History Edn. Soc., Pi Lambda Theta, Kappa Delta Pi (pres. Delta chpt. 1993-95, Caswell Doctoral Rsch. scholar 1993-94), Phi Beta Kappa.

YEAGER, LILLIAN ELIZABETH, nurse educator; b. Bainbridge, Ga., Dec. 23, 1943; d. Earnest and Lottie (Brown) Martin; m. Thomas Stephen Yeager, May 26, 1973 (dec. Oct. 1993); 1 child, Michelle. BSN, Tuskegee U., 1964; MSN, Wayne State U., 1972. RN, Ky., Ind., Mich. Staff/charge nurse John Andrew Hosp., Tuskegee Institute,, Ala., 1964-65; instr. nursing Tuskegee U., 1965-69; sr. instr. Harper Hosp. Sch. Nursing, Detroit, 1969-73; staff nurse Met. Hosp., Detroit, 1970-72; asst. prof. nursing Ind. U. Southeast, New Albany, 1973-79, assoc. prof. nursing, 1979—, acting asst. dean Sch. of Nursing, 1990-91; cons. nursing process VA Med. Ctr., Louisville, Ky., 1987-88; cons. clin. recognition Floyd Meml. Hosp., New Albany, 1989-90. Prodr., presenter (video) Patient Education, 1993. Mem. fertilization overview com. Alliant Hosps., Louisville, 1982-95; bd. dirs. Frazier Rehab. Ctr., Louisville, 1981—; mem. Louisville Urban League, 1992—; mem. dept. evangelism Dicoese of Ky.-Episcopal, Louisville, 1992—. Recipient VA Appreciation award VA Med. Ctr., Louisville, 1986, FACET Excellence in Teaching award Office of Pres., Ind. U., 1990, Outstanding Contbns. to Nursing award Jefferson C.C., Louisville, 1992, Univ. Svc. award Coun. Nursing Faculty Ind. U. Sch. Nursing, 1993. Mem. ANA, Ind. State Nurses Assn. (1st v.p. 1986-88, 95—, treas. 1988-92), N.Am. Nursing Diagnosis Assn., Kyanna Black Nurses Assn., Sigma Theta Tau, Chi Eta Phi, Delta Sigma Theta. Democrat. Home: 4604 Lincoln Rd Louisville KY 40220-1069 Office: Ind U Sch Nursing Southeast Campus 4201 Grant Line Rd New Albany IN 47150-2158

YEAW, MARION ESTHER, retired nurse; b. Chgo., June 13, 1926; d. Clarence Yates and Olga Sophia (Gorling) Y. BSN, U. Mich., 1949; MEd, Mills Coll., Oakland, Calif., 1965. Cert. tchr. in nursing, Calif. Staff nurse U. Mich. Hosp., Ann Arbor, 1949-51; instr. pediatric nursing Kaiser Found. Sch. Nursing, Oakland, 1951-76, 1976-78; instr. pediatric nursing Contra Costa Community Coll., San Pablo, Calif., 1976-78, Merritt C.C., Oakland, Calif.; dir. staff devel. Waters Edge Inc., Alameda, Calif., 1978-89; retired, 1989. Mem. AAUW, Bus. and Profl. Women's Club (Woman of Achievement award 1988), Alumnae Assn. U. Mich. Sch. Nursing, Mills Coll. Alumni Assn. Lutheran. Home: 1601 Broadway # 6 Alameda CA 94501-3050

YEAZELL, RUTH BERNARD, English language educator; b. N.Y.C., Apr. 4, 1947; d. Walter and Annabelle (Reich) Bernard; m. Stephen C. Yeazell, Aug. 14, 1969 (div. 1980). BA with high honors, Swarthmore Coll., 1967; MPhil (Woodrow Wilson fellow), Yale U., 1970, PhD, 1971. Asst. prof. English Boston U., 1971-74, UCLA, 1975-77, assoc. prof., 1977-80, prof., 1980-91, Yale U, 1991—, dir. grad. studies, 1993—, Chace family prof., 1995—. Author: Language and Knowledge in the Late Novels of Henry James, 1976, Death and Letters of Alice James, 1981, Fictions of Modesty: Women and Courtship in the English Novel, 1991; assoc. editor Nineteenth-Century Fiction, 1977-80; editor: Sex, Politics, and Science in the 19th Century Novel, 1986, Henry James: A Collection of Critical Essays, 1994. Woodrow Wilson fellow, 1967-68, Guggenheim fellow, 1979-80, NEH fellow, 1988-89, Pres.'s Rsch. fellow U. Calif., 1988-89. Mem. MLA (exec. coun. 1985-88), English Inst. (supervising com. 1983-86). Office: Yale U Dept English New Haven CT 06524

YECKE, CHERI PIERSON, educational reform advocate, columnist, author; b. St. Paul, Feb. 5, 1955; d. Leo Sylvester and Marceline Mae (Intihar) Pierson; m. Dennis Joseph Yecke, Dec. 22, 1973; children: Anastasia, Tiffany. BA, U. Hawaii, 1975; MST, U. Wis., River Falls, 1984; postgrad., U. Va. Cert. tchr. history, social studies, English, grades 7-12, Va., Wis., Minn. Tchr. U. Va., Charlottesville, grad. asst., 1993-96; ednl. cons. Minn./Va., 1991—; mem. Champion Sch. Commn., Richmond, 1994-96; apptd. mem. State Bd. Edn., 1995—. Mem. ASCD, Nat. Assn. for Gifted Children, Am. Ednl. Rsch. Assn., Va. Assn. for Edn. of the Gifted. Republican. Home: 19 Brixham Ct Stafford VA 22554-7667

YEE, JANICE, dentist; b. N.Y.C., July 20, 1963; d. Jimmy and Yuen-Hing (Chin) Y. BS, Fordham U., 1985; DMD, Tufts U., 1989. Assoc. dentist Dr. Robert Guen, Brookline, Mass., 1989-92; sr. dentist Pub. Health Svc.-ZUNI, N.Mex., 1992-94; clin. prof. Sch. Dental Medicine Tufts U., Boston, 1990-92; clin. prof. N.Y.U. Dental Sch., N.Y.C., 1993; pvt. practice East Patchogue, N.Y., 1994—. Bd. dirs. YMCA, Boston, 1992. Lt. USPHS, 1993-94. Mem. ADA. Office: 250 Yaphank Rd Ste 4 East Patchogue NY 11772

YEGGY-DAVIS, GERALDINE MARIE, elementary reading and special education educator; b. Riverside, Iowa, July 25, 1922; d. Henry Clair and Mary Maurine (Bigley) Yeggy; m. Henry Louis Davis, Dec. 28, 1976. BA, Marycrest Teikyo U., Davenport, Iowa, 1947; MA, U. Detroit, 1970; postgrad., UCLA; Ednl. Specialist degree, Western Ill. U., 1976; PhD in Reading Edn., La Salle U., 1995. Cert. permanent tchr., ednl. adminstr., reading specialist, learning disabilities, Iowa. Primary tchr. numerous sch. systems, including, Davenport, Ottumwa, Iowa, Ft. Madison, Des Moines, Mpls., Rock Island, Ill.; reading specialist, primary tchr. Chpt. I, Davenport Community Schs.; tchr. spl. edn. Child Devel., Inc., Milan, Ill.; pres. Child Devel. Inc., Milan, Ill.; administrator C.O.P.E. Tutoring Sch., Milan, Ill.; workshop presenter curriculum of perceptual/conceptual experiences program; adminstr. C.O.P.E. tutorial sch. for primary children with learning disabilities, Milan, Ill. Contbr. numerous publs. for children. Bd. dirs. Quad-Cities Spl. Persons Encounter Christ (S.P.E.C.); active Illowa Dog Trainers. Recipient Ind. U. Sch. Project award for Effective Teaching of Reading, 1983, Golden Apple award Scott County, 1991; fellow Wall St. Jour., 1964. Mem. NEA, ASCD, Nat. Coun. Tchrs. Math., Internat. Reading Assn., Ill. State Edn. Assn., Iowa Reading Assn., Miss. River Band Reading Assn., Nat. Learning Disabilities Assn., Ill. Learning Disabilities Assn., Early Childhood Edn. Assn. Home: 509 33rd Ave W Milan IL 61264-3753 Office: COPE Tutoring Sch Annex Bldg 3 12 W First St Milan IL 61264

YELLIN, JEAN FAGAN, English educator; b. Lansing, Mich., Sept. 19, 1930; d. Peter and Sarah (Robinson) Fagan; m. Edward L. Yellin; children: Peter, Lisa Mitchell-Yellin, Michael.; BA, Roosevelt U., 1951; MA, U. Ill., 1963, PhD, 1969. From asst. prof. to disting. prof. Pace U., N.Y.C., 1969—; vis. prof. Harvard U., Cambridge, Mass., 1994-95; review panelist NEH, 1989, 90; adv. bd. Afro-Am. Novel Project, 1987—, Black Periodical Lit. Project, 1982—. Author: The Intricate Knot: Black Figures in American Literature, 1972, Women and Sisters: The Anti-Slavery Feminists in American Culture, 1990 (Pulitzer nomination); editor: Incidents in the Life of a Slave Girl, 1987; co-editor: The Abolitionist Sisterhood: Antislavery and Women's Political Culture, 1994; contbr. articles to profl. jours. NEH fellow, 1974-75, 87, 95-96, AAUW fellow, 1967-68, 81-82, Smithsonian Instn. fellow, 1978-79. Mem. MLA, Am. Studies Assn., Collegium for African-Am. Studies, Soc. for the Study of Multi-Ethnic Literature of the U.S., 19th Century Am. Women Writers Study Group. Home: 41 Main St Box 568 Golden's Bridge NY 10526 Office: Dept English Pace U Pace Plz New York NY 10038

YELLIN, JUDITH, electrologist; b. Balt., Feb. 21; d. Jack and Sarah (Grebow) Levin; m. Sidney Yellin, Jan. 1; children: David, Paul, Tamar. Student U. Md., Catonsville Community Coll. Mgr. credit dept. Lincoln Co., Balt.; office mgr. Seaview Constrn. Co.; owner, operator Yellin Telephone Soliciting Agy.; mgr. Liberty Antique Shop; owner, mgr. Judith Yellin Electrology, 1973—; creator jewelry; chief examiner Md. State Bd. Electrology, 1978-81; designer jewelry. Poet: New American Poetry Anthology, 1988, Great Poems of the Western World, Vol. II, 1990. Mem. Am. Electrolysis Assn., Md. Assn. Profl. Electrologists. Avocations: travel, reading, collecting Haitian, art deco, nouveau art and jewelry, poetry, inventing. Home: 6232 Blackstone Ave Baltimore MD 21209-3909 Office: Judith Yellin Electrology 1401 Reisterstown Rd Baltimore MD 21208-3807

YENDES, NANCY KELLEY, lawyer; b. South Bend, Ind., Sept. 24, 1954; d. Dale Edgar and Ester Juanita (Stockham) Kelley; m. Carl Stephen Yendes, Aug. 7, 1983. BS, Cen. Mo. State U., 1976; JD, U. Mo., Columbia, 1979. Bar: Mo. 1979, U.S. Dist. Ct. (we. dist.) Mo. 1979, U.S. Ct. Appeals (8th cir.) 1981, U.S. Supreme Ct. 1989. Hearing officer Mo. State Tax Commn., Jefferson City, 1979-80; asst. atty. gen. State of Mo., Jefferson City, 1980-84, 86-89; asst. counsel Mo. Dept. Social Services, Springfield, 1984-85; asst. city atty. Springfield, Mo., 1989—. Bd. dirs. Salvation Army. Mem. ABA (forum com.), Mo. Bar Assn. (com. on delivery of legal services, subcom. rights of handicapped), Springfield Met. Bar, Nat. Inst. for Trial Advocacy, Mo. Nat. Assn. Telecomm. Officers (bd. dirs.). Methodist. Office: 840 Boonville Ave Springfield MO 65802

YENSON, EVELYN P., lottery official; b. Johannesburg, Republic of South Africa, Dec. 20, 1944; came to U.S., 1963; d. T. and P.F. Yenson; children: Megan Y. Sun, Elliot H. Sun. BA, Coll. New Rochelle, 1967; MA, U. Wis., Milw., 1968. Planner/evaluator Seattle Pub. Schs., 1971-73; dir. planning divsn., various other positions Dept. Cmty. Devel., Seattle, 1973-83; planning dir. Seattle Ctr., 1983-84; pvt. practice as cons. Seattle, 1984-85; dir., dep. commr. Expo '86, Vancouver, B.C., Can., 1985-86; dir. Wash. State Lottery, Olympia, 1987—; presenter in field. Mem. Mcpl. League Bd., Seattle, 1991-92; bd. dirs. Seattle Arts Commn., 1989-93, Camp Brotherhood, Seattle, 1994—, treas., 1995; bd. dirs. Leadership Tomorrow; sec. bd. dirs. Sunhill, Inc., Seattle. Mem. N.Am. Assn. State and Provincial Lotteries (pres. 1991-93, past pres.), Intertoto (bd. dirs.). Roman Catholic. Home: 2350 34th Ave S Seattle WA 98144-5554 Office: Wash State Lottery PO Box 43001 Olympia WA 98504-3001

YEREMSKY, ELIZABETH ANN, accountant; b. Fairview, Pa., Nov. 2, 1938; d. Paul Gerald and Eva (Gobla) Lebert; m. Anthony Robert Yeremsky, Sept. 30, 1967 (dec. Aug. 1992); 1 child, Heather Ann. BS, Coll. Misericordia, 1960; MBA, U. Scranton, 1963; postgrad., Marywood Coll., 1993—. CPA, Pa. Staff auditor Albert B. Melone, P.A., Pittston, Pa., 1959-74; chief internal auditor Keystone Automotive Warehouse, Exeter, Pa.,

1974—; instr. Coll. Misericordia, Dallas, Pa., 1962-86, Luz County C.c., Nanticoke, Pa., 1986—. Mem. AICPA, Pa. Inst. CPA, Am. Inst. Internal Auditors, Pittston C. of C. (bd. dirs. 1995—). Roman Catholic. Home: 74 Carroll St Pittston PA 18640-2638 Office: Keystone Automotive 44 Tunkhannock Ave Exeter PA 18643

YERKES, SUSAN GAMBLE, newspaper columnist; b. Evanston, Ill., Sept. 5, 1959; d. Charles Tyson and Darthea (Campbell) Higgins. BA in Liberal Arts (hon.), U. Austin, 1974; MA in Mass Comms., Wichita State U., 1976. Pub. affairs dir. anchor KAKE-TV, Wichita, Kans., 1977-81; freelance writer pub. rels. YS Comms. Global, 1981-84; metro columnist San Antonio Light, 1986-93; lifestyle columnist S.A. Express News, San Antonio, 1993—; radio TV host WOAI-AM, San Antonio, 1993—; nat. assn. broadcast editls., Boston, 1978-81. Recipient 1st Place Column Writing Nat. Press Women, 1988. Mem. Internat. Women's Forum, Women in Comm., Pub. Rel. Soc. Am., Phi Beta Kappa. Episcopalian. Home: 7711 Broadway # 29B San Antonio TX 78209 Office: San Antonio Express News Ave E 3rd St San Antonio TX 78205

YERXA, JANE ANNE, artist; b. Wichita, Kans., July 3, 1933; d. Laurence Alan and Mary Jane (Nation) Figge; m. Jay Allen Yerxa, June 23, 1956; children: Jeffrey Todd, James Jay, Jonathan Alan. BA in Fine Arts and Comml. Arts, U. Kans., 1955. Fashion artist Wichita (Kans.) Beacon, 1955-56; freelance fashion artist Fall River, Mass., 1956-57; freelance artist agrl. extension dept. Wash. State U., Pullman, 1959; pub. rels. coord. Spokane (Wash.) Symphony, 1972; docent Expo '76 Gallery, Spokane. Represented in pvt. collections in Kans., Tex., N.Mex., Ariz., Calif., Utah, and Wash. Vol. Spokane Art Sch., 1973-83, Corbin Art Ctr., Spokane, 1989-90. Mem. DAR, Artist's Trust (Seattle), Riverridge Fine Arts Assn. (v.p. 1994-95, pres. 1984, 85, 1st place watercolors 1986), Stanek House Art Ctr. (charter mem.), Bible Study Fellowship, Gamma Alpha Chi, Alpha Delta Pi.

YESLOW, ROSEMARIE, real estate professional; b. Detroit; d. Karl E. and Madeline E. (Paret) Norberg; widowed; children: Bradford (dec.), Tod, Eric (dec.), Mark. Student, U. Miami, 1947-49; AA in Journalism, Broward Jr. Coll., 1972; student, Fla. Atlantic U., 1973-75; grad., Realtor Inst., 1995. Ins. agt. Wittenstein Ins. Agy., Hollywood, Fla., 1965-75; owner, operator The Karl Motel/Apartments, Hallandale, Fla., 1980—; realtor/assoc. The Keyes Co., Hollywood, 1990-93; realtor, assoc. Ebby Halliday Real Estate, Dallas, 1993—; real estate investor, Hollywood, 1960—. Contbr. articles to profl. jours. Edn. v.p. Nat. Coun. Jewish Women, Hollywood, 1960-66; unit and dept. chmn. LWV, Ft. Lauderdale, Fla., 1960-72; edn. chmn. Dem. Exec. Com., Broward County, Fla., 1976-78; mem. planning and zoning bd. City of Hallandale, 1988-92. Recipient Sch. Bell award Fla. Edn. Assn., 1966. Mem. Nat. Assn. Realtors, Hollywood Bd. Realtors, Hallandale Adult Cmty. Ctr. (adv. com., Cert. of Appreciation 1989), Hallandale Citizens United, Hallandale C. of C. (bd. dirs. 1987-92, Small Bus. Person of Yr. award 1990), Sierra Club. Democrat. Jewish. Home: 4247 Throckmorton St Dallas TX 75219-2206 Office: Ebby Halliday Real Estate 8333 Douglas Ave Ste 100 Dallas TX 75225-5811

YETMAN, LEITH ELEANOR, academic administrator; b. Kellits, Clarendon, Jamaica, West Indies; came to U.S., 1967; d. 2nd child of 12 children of Percival Augustus and Grace Elizabeth (Anderson) Y.; m. Noel W. Miller, Apr. 8, 1961 (div. 1977); children: Donovan, Jo-Ann, Kirk, Lori-Anne; adopted children: LaFara, Samantha, Brandon Ryan. Attended, Bethlehem Teachers Coll., St. Elizabeth, Jamaica, 1960; BSC, Baruch Coll., 1976; MA, Columbia U., 1978. Cert. tchr., N.Y. Legal sec. various law firms, N.Y.C., 1969-76; instr. Taylor Bus. Inst., N.Y.C., 1977-79; founder, pres., dir. N.Y. Inst. Bus. Tech., N.Y.C., 1981—. Founder Grace Inst. Bus. Tech., Bklyn., 1996. Recipient Outstanding Achievement award Baruch Coll. Alumni Assn., 1989; Leith E. Yetman Day proclaimed June 1, 1994 by Manhattan Borough Pres. Mem. Better Bus. Bur. N.Y.C. Office: NY Inst Bus Tech 401 Park Ave S New York NY 10016-8808

YETTO, LYNETTE M., English educator; b. Kane, Pa.. BA in Theatre, Pa. State U., 1977; BS in Speech/Comm./Theatre, Clarion U., 1978. English tchr. Morrisville (Pa.) Sch. Dist., 1978-95, tchr. of gifted, 1986-95, drama advisor, 1978-84, 92-95, gym night advisor, 1986-89, pub. info. liason, 1985-88; instr. Tomato Patch Theatre Workshop, Trenton, N.J., 1981; English tchr. Ctrl. Bucks Sch. Dist., Chalfont, Pa., 1995—; participant Phila. Mus. Art: Visual Arts as Sources of Teaching program, 1990. V.p. Bucks County Theatre Co. Recipient Salute to Teaching award Pa. Acad. for Profession Teaching, 1990. Mem. NEA, ASCD, Pa. State Edn. Assn. Democrat. Office: Ctrl Bucks Sch Dist Unami Mid Sch 164 S Moyer Rd Chalfont PA 18914

YEVICK, JEAN EVELYN, mortgage broker; b. Pitts., Oct. 26; d. William Frank and Yolanda Rofina (Morosetti) Y. Student in chemistry, U. Pitts., 1960-68. Adminstr., nurse Office of Mayer Green, Pitts., 1960-64; tech. dir. U. Pitts. Med. Sch., 1964-83; allergy specialist Brentwood Med. Group, Pitts., 1965—; office mgr., owner Overland Fin. Network, Pitts., 1984—; pres. Am. Congress of Real Estate, Pitts., 1982-83, 84-90. Author (audio tapes, books) Recycling Cash, 1983, It's Time to Start, 1986, Money Secrets Made Easy, 1990. Mem. Mayor's Task Force bd., Pitts., 1994—. Mem. Real Estate Leadership Assn. Am. (treas. 1989-91, sec. 1991-92, pres. 1987-88), Western Pa. Real Estate Investors Assn. (pres. 1994—). Office: Overland Fin Network Inc 106 Southern Ave Pittsburgh PA 15211

YGLESIAS, AUDRY HILL, foreign language educator; b. Hammond, La., Feb. 3, 1942; d. Thomas William and Ida Mary (Savoy) Hill; m. Bernard Doris Yglesias, Oct. 5, 1962; children: Craig Benton, Maria Colina. BFA, Miss. State U. Women, 1969; MA in Edn., La. State U., 1982, specialist degree curriculum and instrn., 1996. Tchr. Gulfview Elem. Sch., Lakeshore, Miss., 1972-73; tchr., curriculum advisor Costa Rica Acad., San José, 1974-75; prin. tchr., reading specialist, diagnostician Millerville Acad., Baton Rouge, 1976-91; elem. sch. tchr. E.B.R. Parish Cath. Schs., Greenwell Springs, La., 1991; tchr. fgn. lang., reading Livingston Parish Schs., Denham Springs, La., 1991-95; content stds. writing team leader State Dept. Edn., Baton Rouge, 1995—; mem. task force State Dept. Edn., Baton Rouge, 1995—. Contbr. children's stories, poetry, and articles to profl. publs. Vol. Orleans Parish Pub. Schs., New Orleans, 1971-72. Philosophy fellow MSCW. Mem. AATSP, LFLTA, Internat. Reading Assn., Nat. Network for Early Lang. Learning. Office: Southside Jr High and 7th Ward Elem Hwy 16 Denham Springs LA 70726

YIANNIAS, NANCY MAGAS, municipal official; b. Kalamazoo, Feb. 1, 1936; d. George A. and Irene (Callas) Magas; m. Andrew Chris Yiannias, Oct. 20, 1968; 1 child, Chris Andrew. BA, Western Mich. U., 1957; MPH, U. Mich., 1963. Registered sanitarian, Ill. Health educator Stickney Pub. Health Dist., Burbank, Ill., 1966-72, Chgo. Heart Assn., 1972-73; health coord. Village of Elk Grove, Ill., 1974—. Bd. counselors Alexian Bros. Med. Ctr., Elk Grove Village, 1977-93. Mem. Am. Pub. Health Assn., Ill. Pub. Health Assn. (sec. 1981), Soc. Pub. Health Educators, Ill. Soc. Pub. Health Educators (program planning com. 1966), Ill. Environ. Health Assn., N.W. Suburban Access to Care Assn. Home: 1521 Manor Ln Park Ridge IL 60068-1541 Office: Elk Grove Village Dept Health 901 Wellington Ave Elk Grove Village IL 60007

YIH, MAE DUNN, state legislator; b. Shanghai, China, May 24, 1928; d. Chung Woo and Fung Wen (Feng) Dunn; m. Stephen W.H. Yih, 1953; children: Donald, Daniel. BA, Barnard Coll., 1951; postgrad. Columbia U., 1951-52. Asst. to bursar Barnard Coll., N.Y.C., 1952-54; mem. Oreg. Ho. of Reps. from 36th dist., 1977-83, Oreg. Senate from 19th dist., 1983—. Mem. Clover Ridge Elem. Sch. Bd., Albany, Oreg., from 1969-78, Albany Union H.S. Bd., from 1975-79, Joint Legis. Ways and Means Com., Senate Transp. Com., 1995, senate pres. pro-tempore, 1993. Episcopalian. Home: 34465 Yih Ln NE Albany OR 97321-9557

YILMAZCETIN, MURIEL JEAN, human resources and outplacement consultant; b. Bklyn., Nov. 9, 1946; d. Jerry Isaac and Blossom (Markowitz) Negrie; m. Neal Savitt, Apr. 29, 1967 (div. Jan. 1973); children: Gary, Jason, Matthew Keysor; m. Sevket Yilmazcetin, Apr. 4, 1982 (div. Aug. 1993). BA in Anthropology, Calif. State U., Northridge, 1968; MA in Applied Psychology, U. Santa Monica, 1991. Mgr. pers. and adminstrn. Kontron Electronics, Inc., Mountain View, Calif., 1980-86; corp. mgr. human resources Kabi Vitrum, Inc., Almeda, Calif., 1986-88, Nova Pharm. Corp., Balt., 1988-90; human resources cons., owner, pres. Mentor, Inc., Severna Park, Md., 1990-93; v.p. Exec. Asst. Search, Balt., 1992-92; v.p. outplacement divsn. Dinte Resources, Inc., McLean, Va., 1992-96; pres. Mentor, Inc., 1996—; com. chmn., v.p. No. Calif. Tech. Pers. Com., Sunnyvale, 1985-86; com. mem. Entrepreneur's Exch., Inc., Annapolis, Md., 1990-93. Pres. Turkish Am. Assn. Calif., San Francisco, 1987-89; com. mem. Alliance for Drug Free Am., Annapolis, 1990-93, Anne Arundel County Trade Coun., Arnold, Md., 1990-91; com. chmn., bd. dirs. Greater Severna Park Coun., 1991-94. Mem. Soc. Human Resource Mgmt. (No. Va. chpt. 1995—), Am. Bus. Women (com. chmn. 1991, v.p. 1992), Dulles Soc. Human Resource Mgmt. (dir. 1996, treas. 1994-96), Severna Park C. of C. (com. 1990-94), Toastmasters (sec. Dundalk, Md. 1990-91), Women in Technology, Tower Club (mem. coun. 1996). Home: 7619 Greenbrook Dr Greenbelt MD 20770 Office: 7529 Greenbelt Rd # 100 Greenbelt MD 20770

YIN, BEATRICE WEI-TZE, medical researcher; b. Taipei, Taiwan, Mar. 9, 1959; came to U.S., 1970; d. Chuan Keun and Ming Hsien (Huang) Y. BS, CUNY, Flushing, 1982, MS, 1988. Rsch. asst. Meml. Sloan-Kettering Cancer Ctr., N.Y.C., 1982—. Inventor Monoclonal antibodies to human gastrointestinal cancers, 1992. Office: Meml Sloan Kettering Cancer Ctr 1275 York Ave New York NY 10021-6007

YITTS, ROSE MARIE, nursery school executive; b. Bridgeport, Conn., Apr. 29, 1942; m. Richard Francis Yitts, Dec. 28, 1963; children: Anthony Michael, Jennifer Lisa, Heather Michelle. BS, So. Conn. State Coll., 1963; MS, So. Conn. State U., 1983. Tchr. Trumbull (Conn.) Bd. Edn., 1963-69; substitute tchr. Seymour (Conn.) and Oxford (Conn.) Bd. Edn., 1970-79; tchr. aide spl. edn. Oxford (Conn.) Bd. Edn., 1979-82; dir., founding ptnr., pres. and treas. Strawberry Tyme Nursery Sch. and Day Care Ctr. Ltd., Seymour, 1983—. Corr. sec. student senate So. Conn. State Coll., 1963; den leader, com. chmn. Boy Scouts Am., Seymour, 1973-77; troop leader Girl Scouts U.S., Seymour, 1978-80; chair fundraisers, coach George J. Hummel Little League, Seymour, 1982-86, 1st woman pres., 1987-88, player agt., 1990; tchr., spl. edn. curriculum developer Ch. of Good Shepherd, mem. parish coun., 1984-86; corr. sec. Seymour Libr., bd. dirs., 1983-89; elected mem. Republican Town Com., 1996. Recipient award of merit, honorable mention, Golden Poet award World of Poetry, 1987, Editor's Choice award Nat. Libr. Poetry, 1994, 95. Mem. Nat. Assn. for Edn. Young Children, Oxford Bus. Assn. (membership com. 1993-95, Republican town com.), Woman's Coll. Club, Internat. Soc. Poets, Trumbull Edn. Assn. (corr. sec.), Chi Delta Sigma (founder, past pres.). Republican.

YNTEMA, MARY KATHERINE, retired mathematics educator; b. Urbana, Ill., Jan. 20, 1928; d. Leonard Francis and M. Jean (Busey) Y. BA in Math., Swarthmore Coll., 1950; MA in Math., U. Ill., 1961, PhD in Math., 1965. Tchr., secondary math. Am. Coll. for Girls, Istanbul, Turkey, 1950-54, Columbus (Ohio) Sch. for Girls, 1954-57; computer programmer MIT Lincoln Lab., Lexington, Mass., 1957-58; tchr., secondary math Roundup (Mont.) High Sch., 1959-60; asst. prof. math U. Ill., Chgo., 1965-67; asst. prof. computer sci. Pa. State U., University Park, 1967-71; assoc. prof. to prof. math. Sangamon State U., Springfield, Ill., 1971-91; ret., 1991.

YOCHELSON, BONNIE ELLEN, museum curator, art historian; b. Buffalo, Nov. 6, 1952; d. Samuel and Kathryn (Mersey) Y.; m. Paul Lewis Shechtman, Sept. 3, 1972; children: Emily, Anna. BA in History, Swarthmore Coll., 1974; MA, NYU, 1979, PhD, 1985. Asst. curator dept. prints and drawings Nat. Gallery Art, Washington, 1979-81; lectr. dept. art history U. Pa.q, Phila., 1985-87; curator prints and photographs Mus. of the City of N.Y., 1987-91, cons. curator, 1991—; faculty M of Photography program Sch. Visual Arts, N.Y.C., 1988—; adj. assoc. prof. dept. art history NYU, 1987. Mem. Coll. Art Assn.

YOCHEM, BARBARA JUNE, sales executive, lecturer; b. Knox, Ind., Aug. 22, 1945; d. Harley Albert and Rosie (King) Runyan; m. Donald A. Yochem (div. 1979); 1 child, Morgan Lee; m. Don Heard, Dec. 12, 1987. Grad. high school, Knox, Ind., 1963. Sales rep. Hunter Woodworks, Carson, Calif., 1979-84, sales mgr., 1984-87; sales rep. Comml. Lumber and Pallet, Industry, Calif., 1987-92; owner By By Prodns., Glendora, Calif., 1976—. Author: Barbara Yochem's Inner Shooting; contbr. articles to profl. jours. Head coach NRA Jr. Olympic Shooting Camp, 1989-94; foster parent, 1992-94. Recipient U.S. Bronze medal U.S. Olympic Com., 1976, World Bronze medal U.S Olympic Com., 1980; nominated Calif. Trapshooting Hall of Fame, 1994. Address: By By Prodns PO Box 7363 Mesa AZ 58216

YOCHIM, SUSAN LAUREL, psychologist; b. Oak Park, Ill., July 20, 1952; d. John Joseph and Ida Helene (Besler) Shea-Szczepaniak; m. Scott Albert Yochim; children: Jonathan, Allison. BSE cum laude, Northern Ill. U., 1974; postgrad., U. Chgo., 1976; MA in sch. psychology, Govs. State U., 1979. Elem. tchr. Forest Ridge Sch. Dist. 142, Oak Forest, Ill., 1974-79; sch. psychologist Atwood Heights Sch. Dist. 125, Oak Lawn, Ill., 1980-90, Downers Grove (Ill.) Sch. Dist. 58, 1990—. Author: Melvin and the Mysterious Moot, 1974 (unpublished). Mem. Oak Brook (Ill.) Civic Assn., 1988—, Brook Forest Homeowners Assn., Oak Brook, 1988—; soccer coach Am. Youth Soccer Assn., Oak Brook, 1989-90; food days coord. Brook Forest PTA, Oak Brook, 1991-92, room mother, 1988—, leader Great Books, 1994; mem. Oak Brook Caucus, 1994-95; mem. Butler sch. dist. 53 bd. edn., 1995—. Mem. NEA, NASP, AAUW (bd. dirs., officer 1990-92, newsletter editor 1990-92), Ill. Edn. Assn., Ill. Sch. Psychologists Assn., Oak Brook Women's Club (bd. dirs., officer 1989—, newsletter editor 1989-90, membership sec. 1990-92, v.p. activities 1992-93, pres. 1993-95), Infant Welfare Soc. Chgo. (Oak Brook chpt. 1992—). Lutheran. Home: 27 Concord Dr Oak Brook IL 60521-1735

YOCKEL, CHRISTINA ANN, elementary education educator; b. Glen Ridge, N.J., Mar. 14, 1944; d. Lewis Phillip and Ina Christina (MacKinnon) Conner; John Roger Yockel, Dec. 3, 1966; children: Timothy James, Maggie Lou, Allison Rachel. BA, W.Va. Wesleyan, 1966; postgrad., Rutgers U., 1991, Seton Hall U., 1992, St. Peter's Coll., Jersey City, 1993. 1st grade tchr. West Orange (N.J.) Pub. Schs., 1966; 5th and 2nd grade tchr. Miss. Pub. Schs., Harrison County, 1967-68; head tchr. Project Head Start, Smyrna, Tenn., 1968-69; pre-kindergarten tchr. YMCA, Scotch Plains, N.J., 1972-74; 1st and 2nd grade tchr. The Linn Hill Sch., Westfield, N.J., 1986-89; tchr. Sylvan Learning Ctr., Mountainside, N.J., 1987-91; 1st grade tchr. Irvington (N.J.) Pub. Schs., 1990-95; 2d grade tchr. Dunellen (N.J.) Pub. Schs., 1995—; v.p., sec. Westfield (N.J.) Adult Sch. Bd. Trustees. V.p., sec. Westfield (N.J.) Parent-Tchr. Coun., 1983-85; residential chairperson United Fund, Westfield, 1983; v.p. Svc. League, Westfield; deacon Presbyn. Ch., Westfield; membership chmn. Irvington-Florence Ave. PTA, 1992-94. Named Nat. Outstanding Reading Tchr., Nat. Reading Rsch. Ctr., U. Md.; Gov.'s Tchr. Recognition award N.J. Gov., Trenton, 1994. Mem. N.J. Edn. Assn., Irvington Edn. Assn., Coll. Woman's Club. Home: 129 Woodland Ave Westfield NJ 07090-1814 Office: Florence Ave Sch 1334 Springfield Ave Irvington NJ 07111-1916

YOCUM, RHODA FAY, medical and surgical nurse, nursing educator, consultant; b. Troy, Ohio, June 29, 1950; d. George David and Isabell Ellen (Snyder) Y. Diploma in Nursing, Miami Valley Hosp., Dayton, Ohio, 1971; BS, George Mason U., Fairfax, Va., 1979; MSN, Med. Coll. Ga., Augusta, 1980; AA in Photography, Ohio Inst. Photography, Dayton, 1988. Clin. nurse Dettmer Gen. Hosp., Troy, Ohio, 1971-76, Naval Hosp., Quantico, Va., 1976-78; edn. charge nurse, clin. nurse Newport, R.I., 1980-83; dir. Inservice Edn. Moberly (Mo.) Regional Med. Ctr., 1984-85; part time clin. nurse Naval Hosp., Patuxent River, Md., 1986-88; head branch clinic Naval Med. Clinic, Key West, Fla., 1988-91; spl. project coord. Wayne Meml. Hosp., Jesup, Ga., 1991-92; staff nurse Gallup (N.Mex.) Indian Health Svc., 1992, VA at WPAFB, Dayton, Ohio, 1992-96; cons. 1994, educator, 1995 Awareness Prodns., Tipp City, Ohio. Author: Documentation Skill for Quality Patient Care, 1993; contbr. articles to profl. jours. Lt. comdr. USN, 1976—. Recipient honorable mention Rear Adm. Hall award for nursing publ. USN Nurse Corps, 1993. Mem. ANA, Ohio Nurses Assn. (bd. dirs. Dist. 10), Nursing Entrepreneur Assembly. Methodist. Office: Awareness Prodns PO Box 85 Tipp City OH 45371-0085

YODER, ANNA A., elementary school educator; b. Beach City, Ohio, Sept. 5, 1934; d. Abram J. and Barbara D. (Miller) Y. BS, Ea. Mennonite Coll., 1966; MEd, Frostburg State Coll., 1974. Cert. elem. tchr., Ohio, recreational leader. Tchr. Garrett County Schs., Oakland, Md., 1966-70; prin. elem. sch. Garrett County Schs., 1970-74; tchr. E. Holmes Local Schs., Berlin, Ohio, 1974—; chairperson edn. com. German Culture Mus., Berlin, Ohio, 1987-90; cons. bilingual edn. E. Holmes Local Schs., Berlin, Ohio, 1982—. Supporting mem. German Culture Mus., Berlin, Ohio, 1983—; mem. Killbuck (Ohio) Valley mus., 1988—, Holmes County Hist. Soc., Millersburg, Ohio, 1989—; life mem. Mennonite Info. Ctr., Berlin, Ohio, 1985—; sustaining mem. The Wilderness Ctr., Wilmot, Ohio, 1974—. Jennings scholar Martha Holden Jennings Found., 1983-84; Silver Poet award World of Poetry, 1986. Mem. AAUW (v.p. Holmes County chpt. 1994), Creative Arts Soc. (sec.-treas. 1987-89), Delta Kappa Gamma (sec. Beta Iota chpt. 1987-90, pres. 1990-92). Mennonite. Home: 5229 State Route 39 Millersburg OH 44654-8408

YODER, ELIZABETH JANE, neuroscience researcher; b. Champaign, Ill., Jan. 23, 1968; d. Chris and Donnalee (Blair) Y. BS in Exercise Sci., Ariz. State U., 1990; MS in Neurosci., U. Calif., San Diego, 1992, PhD in Neurosci., 1996. Lab. asst. in zoology Ariz. State U., Tempe, 1989-90; summer rsch. fellow Barrow Neurol. Inst., Phoenix, 1990; grad. student rschr. Sch. of Medicine U. Calif., San Diego, 1990-96; postgrad. rschr. Sch. of Medicine UCLA, 1996—; student rep. admissions, exec., advancement, dept. coms. neurosci. grad. program U. Calif., San Diego, 1991-95. Mem. Sierra Club, San Diego, 1991-95. Mem. AAAS, Grad. Women in Sci., Am. Assn. Women in Sci., Women in Neurosci., Soc. for Neurosci., Ariz. State U. Alumni Assn., Serotonin Club. Democrat.

YODER, MARIANNE ELOISE, software developer, consultant; b. Phoenix, Ariz.; d. William Amber and Maryanne King; m. William Ernest Yoder, Dec. 26, 1977. BSN, U. San Francisco, 1972; MS, U. Ariz., 1982, PhD, 1989. RN, Ariz. Nurse U.S. Navy, 1971-80, 91; grad. teaching asst. U. Ariz., Tucson, 1980-82, faculty, 1982-85, grad. rsch. assoc., 1985-90; faculty, dir. coll. health profl. Computer Learning Ctr. No. Ariz. U., Flagstaff, Ariz., 1990-92; software developer Flagstaff, Ariz., 1992—; chair Ariz. state commn. nursing rsch., 1992-96; chair of PILOT group, Assn. Devel. of Computer-Based Instructional Systems, Columbus, Ohio, 1990-92. Author: Software Integration Plan Introduction to Nursing Diagnosis, 1992, 2nd edit., 1993, contbg. author: Computer Applications in Nursing Education and Practice, 1993; contbr. articles to profl. jours. Vol. Flagstaff Pub. Libr., 1993-96. Recipient Pioneer in Nursing Edn. Informatics award Nurse Educator's Microworld & Fuld, 1994, Meritorious Tchg. Asst. award U. Ariz. Found., 1987. Mem. NLN (exec. bd 1993-97), N.Y. Acad. of Scis., WEB Soc., Ariz. Statewide Coun. on Nursing, Sigma Xi, Sigma Theta Tau (treas. 1970-71), Pi Lambda Theta. Home and Office: 631 Roundup Rd Carson City NV 89701

YODER, MARY JANE WARWICK, psychotherapist; b. Corryton, Tenn., Nov. 20, 1933; d. Harry Alonzo and Mary Luzelle (Furches) Warwick; m. Edwin Milton Yoder, Jr., Nov. 1, 1958; children: Anne Daphne, Edwin Warwick. BA, U. N.C., Chapel Hill, 1956; MFA, U. N.C., Greensboro, 1969; MSW, Va. Commonwealth U., 1987; cert. individual psychotherapy, Smith Coll., 1991. Lic. ind. clin. social worker, D.C.; lic. clin. social worker, Va. Editorial asst. Harper & Bros., N.Y.C., 1956-57; flight attendant Pan Am. Airlines, N.Y.C., 1957-59; adj. faculty mem. in ballet Guilford Coll., Greensboro, 1961-64; ballet tchr., adminstr. Jane Yoder Sch. of Ballet, Greensboro, 1964-75; homilitics listener Va. Theol. Sem., Alexandria, 1978-80; social worker, dance therapist Woodbine Nursing Ctr., Alexandria, 1983-87; staff psychotherapist D.C. Inst. Mental Health, 1987-92; pvt. practice Capitol Hill Ctr. Individual and Family Therapy, 1992—. Ballet and book critic Greensboro Daily News, 1961-75. Dancer, choreographer Greensboro Civic Ballet, 1961-75. Mem. Nat. Assn. Social Workers, Greater Washington Soc. for Clin. Social Work, Inc., Washington Sch. Psychiatry, Washington Soc. for Jungian Psychology, Jungian Venture, Army-Navy Country Club. Episcopalian. Office: Capitol Hill Ctr Individual and Family Therapy 530 7th St SE Washington DC 20003-2768

YODER, PATRICIA DOHERTY, public relations executive; b. Pitts., Oct. 30, 1939; d. John Addison and Camella Grace (Conti) Doherty; children: Shari Lynn, Wendy Ann. BA, Duquesne U., 1961. Press sec. U.S. Ho. of Reps., 1965-69; dir. office of pub. info. City of Ft. Wayne, 1973-76; asst. mgr. pub. and corp. communications Mellon Bank N.A., Pitts., 1977-79; v.p. pub. affairs Am. Waterways Operators Inc., Washington, 1980-83; sr. v.p., gen. mgr. 1983-86, exec. v.p., dir. internat. banking, 1989-91, Hill and Knowlton Inc., Pitts.; sr. v.p. corp. and pub. affairs PNC Bank, Pitts., 1987-89; v.p., mgr. corp. pub. rels. and advt. GE Capital, Stamford, Conn., 1991-95; corp. v.p. pub. affairs and comm. GTE Corp., Stamford, 1995—. Trustee Shadyside Hosp., Pressley Ridge Sch., Pitts., Ellis Sch.; bd. dirs. Children's Mus., Civic Light Opera, Pitts. Ballet Theatre, Stamford, (Conn.) Symphony; mem. communications bd. visitors U. Pitts. Recipient Outstanding Woman Bus. & Industry, 1988, Disting. Alumna award Duquesne U., 1996. Mem. Pitts. Field Club, Duquesne Club, Indian Harbor Yacht Club, Century Club of Disting. Duquesne U. Alumni. Roman Catholic. Home: 13 Brownhouse Rd Old Greenwich CT 06870-1502 Office: One Stamford Forum Stamford CT 06904

YODER WISE, PATRICIA SNYDER, nurse, educator; b. Wadsworth, Ohio, July 2, 1941; d. Belford Grant and Leona Cora (Mohler) Snyder; m. Robert Thomas Wise, Feb. 17, 1973; children: Doreen Ellen, Deborah Ann. BSN, Ohio State U., 1963; MSN, Wayne State U., 1968; EdD, Tex. Tech U., 1984. Cert. gerontol. nurse and nursing adminstr., RN, Tex., Ohio. Rsch. asst. Wayne State U., Detroit, 1968; ednl. dir. Ohio Nurses' Assn., Columbus, 1968-72; asst. dir. nursing Mt. Clemens (Mich.) Gen. Hosp., 1972-73; assoc. prof., head of nursing Ferris State Coll., Big Rapids, Mich., 1975-77; asst. prof., assoc. prof., dir. continuing edn. U. Colo., Denver, 1977-79; assoc. dean, assoc. prof. Sch. Nursing, Tex. Tech U. Health Scis. Ctr., Lubbock, 1979-86, assoc. dean, prof., 1986-87, interim assoc. dean grad. program, 1986-89, exec. assoc. dean, prof. nursing, 1989-92, interim dean, prof., 1992-93; dean, prof. Sch. Nursing, 1993—; prin. p.t. Wylan Assocs., Lubbock, 1989—; mem. acad. adv. panel on nursing Health and Scis. Network, 1983-92, Nurses Coalition, 1982-92; bd. dirs. RN Polit. Action Com., 1989-93. Editor Jour. Continuing Edn. in Nursing, 1986—. Named Woman of Excellence in Medicine, YWCA, 1996; recipient Book of the Yr. award Am. Jour. Nursing, 1996. Fellow Am. Acad. Nursing; mem. ANA (site visitor continuing edn. 1982-88), Tex. Nurses Assn. (bd. dirs. 1989-93, pres. dist. 18 1987-89, pres. 1995—), Coun. Continuing Edn., Am. Nurses Found. (Tchg. Excellence award 1968), Tex. Nurses Found. (pres. 1992-95), Sigma Theta Tau (grantee). Home: 3713 95th St Lubbock TX 79423-3811

YOGEV, SARA, psychologist; b. Tel Aviv, May 23, 1946; came to U.S., 1975; d. Israel and Cila (Fink) Frankel; m. Ram Yogev, Oct. 2, 1967; children: Eldad, Shelly, Tomer. BA, Hebrew U., 1965-69, MA, 1970-73; PhD, Northwestern U., Evanston, Ill., 1976-79. Cert. clin. psychologist, Ill. Clin. experience dist. sch. psychologist Office Edn. and Culture, Jerusalem, Israel, 1968-71; intern. Beer Yaakov Psychiatric Hosp., Israel, 1971-72; asst. dir. Dept. Psychology, Hebrew U., Jerusalem, Israel, 1972-73; psychotherapist Mental Health Ctr., Hebrew U., Jerusalem, Israel; clin. psychologist Inst. Psychoanalysis, Jerusalem, Israel, 1973-75; psychotherapist, supr. Youth and Family Services, Ill., 1977-80; pvt. practice psychology Skokie, Ill., 1981—; academic experience instr. counseling psychology, 1977-79, asst. prof., Northwestern U., 1979-82, research psychologist at the rank asst. prof., 1983-86, visiting scholar, Ctr. Urban Affairs and Policy Research, 1987. Contbr. articles to profl. jours. and books. Mem. American Assn. for Marriage and Family Therapy, American Psychological Assn., Nat. Register Health Service. Jewish. Office: # 32 5225 Old Orchard Rd Skokie IL 60077-1027

YOHN, SHARON A., manufacturing executive; b. Altoona, Pa., Mar. 1, 1952. AS in Retail cum laude, Harcum Jr. Coll. (Pa.), 1972; BSBA, Villanova U., 1976. V.p. legal dept. Items Internat., Inc., Altoona, Pa., 1987-95, v.p., 1995—. Active ch. choir and choral soc. Republican. Methodist. Office: Items Internat Inc 1540 E Pleasant Valley Blvd Altoona PA 16602-7224

YONUSAITIS, LINDA SUSAN, educator, environmentalist; b. Bklyn., Dec. 23, 1954; d. Edward Joseph and Dorothy Virginia (Brestlin) Y. Student, Nassau Community Coll., 1973-75; BA in Child Study and Spl. Edn., St. Joseph's Coll., Brentwood, L.I., N.Y., 1977; MS in Deaf Edn. with Speech Pathology/Audiology/Edn. Emphasis, Adelphi U., 1986. Cert. early childhood, elem., spl. edn., multihandicapped, deaf/hearing impaired tchr., N.Y., C.E.D., early childhood, elem., multihandicapped profl. cert. for teaching the hearing impaired, Coun. on Edn. Deaf, Washington. Naturalist, instr. outdoor and environ. edn. Caumsett State Park and various ctrs., L.I., N.Y., 1978-84; direct care resident counselor, instr. EPIC House Hicksville of Epilepsy Found., L.I., 1981-87; substitute tchr. spl. edn., multihandicapped Rosemary Kennedy Ctr., Wantagh, L.I., N.Y., 1979-81, 87-90; tutor/cons. elem., secondary study skills, spl. edn., deaf and hearing impaired, Wantagh, 1978, 81, 84-86, 88, 90—; home instrn., spl. edn. biol. and earth sci., tutor, Creative Tutoring Inc., L.I., 1989; subs. tchr. deaf edn., early intervention and programs for hearing impaired Nassau Bd. Coop. Ednl. Svcs., Wantagh, Merrick and North Merrick, L.I., 1985-90; tchr. various extended yr. summer programs for multihandicapped James E. Allen Learning Ctr. Melville-Bd. Coop. Ednl. Svcs. III, 1983, elem. sci. tchr. physically disabled, mentally handicapped (with hearing impaired and language delayed) Nassau Bd. Coop. Ednl. Svcs., L.I., 1987, 89. Author: College Study Guide in Anatomy and Physiology on Speech/Hearing/Vocal Mechanism Questions and Answers, Methods Guide to Young Adult Meetings in Special Education: A Series of Applied Christian Living Skills, 1980-90; contbg. author treatment modality studies of Office of Mental Retardation and Devel. Disabilities, Horticulture Therapy: Organic Gardening, 1983; founder Good Guys newsletter Let's Communicate, 1988; editor-in-chief: Reflections Yearbook; rsch. on hyperactivity-drugs vs. diet, otitis media with ctrl. auditory processing disorders, lang. delay and Landau-Kleffner Syndrome; contbr. articles to profl. jours. Vol. fund raiser United Cerebral Palsy Assn. Nassau County, 1969-81, Forest City Community Assn., Wantagh, 1973-80; tutor Elem. Remedial Reading Club Parochial Sch., Deer Pk., 1976; spl. edn. tchr. St. Frances de Chantal Religious Edn. Program, Wantagh, 1979-82; dir. and spl. edn. instr. and program developer: Young Adult Evening Meetings, The Good Guys-Spl. Guides, Wantagh, Diocese of Rockville Ctr., L.I., 1982-92; horticulture and organic gardening program developer Community Based Intermediate Care Facility, EPIC House, 1982-86; participant various antinuclear rallies Shoreham, L.I., and N.Y.C., 1979; land protection petitioner for Mill Pond Wantagh, Bellmore; preservation advocate Suffolk County Farm and Edn. Ctr., Riverhead, L.I., 1989; rschr. to promote Horticulture Therapy, 1991-92. Recipient rsch. assistantship Dept. Speech Arts & Communicative Disorders, Adelphi U., 1984-85, scholarship Grad. Sch. Arts & Scis., 1984, Honorable Mention Interdisciplinary Team Excellence Nat. Epilepsy Found. Am. to EPIC House, 1982. Mem. MADD, AAUW, AAUW Environ. Network, Am. Assn. on Mental Retardation, Am. Hort. Therapy Assn., N.Am. Assn. for Environ. Edn., N.Am. Conf. on Christianity and Ecology, N.Y. State Outdoor Edn. Assn., Bicultural Exch., Conv. of Am. Instrs. of the Deaf, Talking Over and Understanding Children with Handicaps, Endometriosis Assn., Nat. Coun. Therapy and Rehab. through Horticulture, Nature Conservancy, Women's Sports Found., Sierra Club, Forest City Community Assn., Support Our Country's Mil.

YOOST, BARBARA LYNN, critical care nurse, educator; b. Warren, Ohio, Mar. 11, 1955; d. Willard R. and Vivian C. (Wood) Richards; m. Charles D. Yoost, Dec. 27, 1974; children: Timothy R., Stephen M. BSN, Kent State U., 1977, MSN, 1994. Staff nurse ICU Akron (Ohio) Gen. Med. Ctr., 1977-84; per diem nurse Western Reserve Care Sys., Youngstown, Ohio, 1986-92; instr. nursing Kent (Ohio) State U., 1979-84; assoc. prof. nursing North Ctrl. Tech. Coll., Mansfield, Ohio, 1993—. Treas. Liberty Ednl. Endowment, Inc., Youngstown, 1989-92; mem. E. Ohio Conf. United Meth. Women, 1974—, Commn. on Pastoral Care and Counseling, Canton, Ohio, 1988-94. Mem. NAFE, Kent State U. Sch. Nursing Alumni Assn. (pres. 1981-82), Ohio Orgn. Assoc. Degree Nursing, Sigma Theta Tau (Linnea E. Henderson award 1994), Colony Club. Home: 1445 Royal Oak Dr Mansfield OH 44906-3522 Office: N Ctrl Tech Coll 2441 Kenwood Cir Mansfield OH 44906-1546

YORBURG, BETTY (MRS. LEON YORBURG), sociology educator; b. Chgo., Aug. 27, 1926; d. Max and Hannah (Bernstein) Gitelman; m. Leon Yorburg, June 23, 1946; children: Harriet, Robert. PhB, U. Chgo., 1945, MA, 1948; PhD, New Sch. Social Rsch., 1968. Instr., Coll. New Rochelle, 1966-67; lectr. City Coll. and Grad. Center, City U. N.Y., 1967-69, asst. prof., 1969-73, assoc. prof. sociology dept., 1973-77, prof., 1978—; rsch. asst. Prof. Clifford Shaw, Chgo. Area Project, 1946-47. Author: Utopia and Reality, 1969, The Changing Family, 1973, Sexual Identity: Sex Roles and Social Change, 1974, The New Women, 1976, Introduction to Sociology, 1982, Families and Societies, 1983, Family Relationships, 1993, Sociological Reality, 1995. Mem. AAAS, Am. Sociol. Assn., Ea. Sociol. Assn., Am. Coun. Family Rels., N.Y. Acad. Scis. Home: 20 Earley St Bronx NY 10464-1512 Office: CCNY Sociology Dept 138th Convent Ave New York NY 10031-9127

YORK, ELIZABETH FAIR, music therapy educator; b. Spartanburg, S.C., Dec. 21, 1949; d. James Pinckney York and Betty Fair (Campbell) Howard. MusB, U. Ga., 1974; MusM, U. Miami, 1993, PhD, 1995. Registered, bd. cert. music therapist Cert. Bd. for Music Therapists. Music educator Glenrose Hosp. Sch., Edmonton, Alta., Can., 1974-75; music therapist Ga. Mental Health Inst., Atlanta, 1977-80, 81-85; activity dir. South DeKalb Mental Health Ctr., Atlanta, 1980-81; music therapist Star, Inc., Atlanta, 1988-89, VA Med. Ctr., Miami, Fla., 1991-92; coord. arts programming Spl. Audiences, Inc., Atlanta, 1988-90; grad. tchg. asst. U. Miami, Coral Gables, Fla., 1990-95; asst. prof. Utah State U., Logan, 1995—; lectr. Ga. State U., Atlanta, 1989, Augusta (Ga.) Coll., 1989; trainer, staff devel. Ga. Mental Health Inst., Atlanta, 1984-85; adv. bd. Bear River House, Logan, Utah, 1995—. Contbr. articles to profl. jours.; composer: (rec.) Transformations, 1983 (Nat. Assn. Ind. Record Distbrs. award 1985). Artist in edn. Ga. Coun. for Arts, Atlanta, 1988-91; artist in residence Fulton County Arts Coun., Atlanta, 1989-90; artist/facilitator DeKalb Coun. for Arts, Atlanta, 1989. Adminstrn. on Aging grantee/rsch. asst., 1995, grad. rsch. grantee Ctr. Adult Devel. and Aging, 1990, Meet the Composer grantee So. Arts Fedn., 1989. Mem. Nat. Assn. for Music Therapy, (mem., mem. chair S.E. region 1974-95, mem. Western region 1995—), Pi Kappa Lambda. Democrat. Unitarian. Office: Utah State U Music Therapy Program Logan UT 84322-4015

YORK, GLADYS DOUGHTY, minister; b. Fall River, Mass., May 30, 1911; d. Wilbert Howe and Nellie Mae (Alexander) Doughty; m. Neal Farwell York, June 18, 1939 (dec. Jan. 1974); 1 child, Ruth Edna. BA, Jackson Coll., 1932; BD, Andover Newton Theological Sc., 1935. Ordained to ministry United Ch. of Christ, 1935. Min. First Congl. Ch., North Yarmouth, Maine, 1935-67, Danville (Maine) Union Ch., 1950-58, Princeton, Waite-Talmage, and Grand Lake Stream Chs., 1967-76, Highland Lake Congl. Ch., Westbrook, Maine, 1976-81, East Windham (Maine) Union Ch., 1977—. Author: GDNFY: Both a License Number and a Statement of Faith, 1990. Recipient Disting. Ministry award Alumni Assn. Andover Newton Theological Sch., 1986. Mem. New Eng. Mins. Assn., Internat. Assn. Women Mins. Home and Office: 21 Gray Rd North Yarmouth ME 04097

YORK, KAREN SUE, artist; b. Wichita, Kans., Sept. 19, 1955; d. Jack Shannon and Pat Sue (Sittel) Compton; m. Kevin Blaine Hardin, June 1977 (div. 1981); 1 child, Kate; m. Robert Sterling York, Sept. 19, 1981. BFA, Tex. Woman's U., 1995. Jr. art dir. Ackerman, Inc., Tulsa, Okla., 1975-77, Fred Davis & Assocs., Tulsa, 1977-78; graphic designer Tulsa, 1978-82; art dir. Advantage Advt., Tulsa, 1982-83; entertainment mgr. Tulsa, Houston, Denton, Tex., 1983-95; art dir. Internat. Jugglers Assn., 1982-84. One-woman show includes Tex. Woman's U., 1995. Recipient Ben Keith award North Tex. Art League, 1995. Mem. Phi Kappa Phi (Acad. Excellence award 1994, 95), Gamma Beta Phi, Alpha Chi. Home: 3534 Burks Ct Bloomington IN 47401

YORK, MELBA CRANFORD, secondary and special education educator; b. Enigma, Ga., July 7, 1941; d. Demetrius and Rutha Mae (Stone) Cranford; m. Thomas Alton York, Oct. 23, 1959; children: Natalie, Anita. AS in Home Econs., Abraham Baldwin Agrl. Coll., Tifton, Ga., 1976; BS in Child Devel./Mental Retardation, U. Ga., 1978; MEd in Interrelated Spl. Edn., Albany (Ga.) State Coll., 1986. Cert. tchr. mental retardation and interrelated spl. edn., Ga. Tchr. 1st grade Brunswick (Ga.) Christian Acad., 1978-79; elem. spl. edn. tchr. Glynn County Bd. Edn., Brunswick, 1979-80; secondary spl. edn. tchr. Tift County Bd. Edn., Tifton, 1980—. Named Tchr. of Yr., Matt Wilson Mid. Sch., Tifton, 1982. Mem. NEA, Ga. Assn. Educators, Tift Assn. Educators (sec. 1981-82, treas. 1982-83, publicity chair 1987-88, pres.-elect 1991-92, pres. 1992-93). Office: Tift County HS W 8th St Tifton GA 31794

YORK, SHIRLEY MARIE, artist; b. Aurora, Ill., Aug. 25, 1923; d. John Frederick and Beulah Mary (Noack) Vockrodt; m. Herman Maxwell Grimwood, 1947 (div. Feb. 1959); children: Sherry Lynn, Jon Frederick; m. John Garth York, June 12, 1959. Student, Chgo. Art Inst., 1943, U. Chgo., 1944; BAF, U. N.Mex., 1945; student, Inst. of Fine Arts, Mexico City, 1960. Mosaic glass artist; worked with archtl. firms in Tex. and Okla. Artist: Italian glass mosaics, 1960-78; commd. artist in Tex., Okla., Ill., N.Y., Costa Rica, Mexico; represented in pvt. collections in U.S., Mexico and Europe. Recipient purchase award N.Mex. Arts Divsn., Office of Cultural Affairs, Santa Fe, 1995. Mem. AAUW.

YORKE, MARIANNE, lawyer, real estate executive; b. Ridley Park, Pa., Nov. 4, 1948; d. Joseph George and Catherine Veronica (Friel) Y. BA, West Chester U., 1971; JD, Temple U., 1980; MS, U. Pa., 1987. M in Corp. Real Estate, Internat. Assn. Corp. Real Estate Execs. Bar: Pa. 1981, N.Y. 1992. Mgr. CIGNA Corp., Phila., 1982-85, asst. dir., Phila., 1985-89; v.p. Chase Manhattan Bank, N.Y.C., 1989-92; real estate dir. Johnson & Johnson, 1992—; real estate atty. Garfinkel & Volpicelli, Phila., 1980-82; prin., mng. ptnr. Yorke/Eisenman, Real Estate, Phila., 1976-89, prin., mng. ptnr. Yorke/Mac Lachlin Real Estate, Phila, 1989—; lectr. Women in the Arts, 1982-90; guest speaker Wharton Sch. Bus. Class of 1989, U. Pa., grad. sch. arts and scis. Class of 1990. Contbr. articles to profl. jours. Solicitor Pa. Ballet, Phila., 1983-90, United Way, Phila., 1983-90; mem. steering com. U. Pa., 1986-90, dir. alumni assn., 1987-90; mem. adv. com. for econ. devel. Luth. Settlement House Adv, 1986-88; bd. dirs. Hamilton Townhouse Assn., Phila., 1988-90, chmn. ins. com., 1989-90, 718 Broadway, Inc., N.Y.C., 1990-94, Johnson Health Care Svcs. Recipient Live for Life award Johnson Health Mgmt., 1995. Mem. ABA (forum on constrn. 1982-90), Pa. Bar Assn. (condominium and zoning coms. 1982-90), Assn. of Bar of City of N.Y. (sects. on internat. law and real property law 1992-94), Phila. Bar Assn., Phila. Women Real Estate Attys., Nat. Assn. Corp. Real Estate Execs. (internat. coun. 1984—, comml. coun. 1984—), Internat. Atty's Roundtable, Women's Law Caucus, Phi Alpha Delta. Independent. Roman Catholic. Office: Johnson & Johnson World Headquarters Ste 7135 1 Johnson & Johnson Plz New Brunswick NJ 08933

YOSHIKI-KOVINICK, MARIAN TSUGIE, author; b. L.A., Feb. 17, 1941; d. Eddie Junichi and Teruko Ruth (Kawamoto) Yoshiki; m. Philip Peter Kovinick, June 17, 1973. BA, U. So. Calif., 1963; MA, Azusa Pacific U., 1980. Tchr. Pasadena (Calif.) Unified Sch. Dist., 1964-66, Centinela Valley Union H.S. Dist., Lawndale, Calif., 1966-83; freelance writer, rschr. L.A., 1983—. Rschr., cons. for various exhbns.: The Woman Artist in the American West, 1976, California Light, 1990, Guy Rose, American Impressionist, 1995; rschr. for books: Elsie Palmer Payne, 1990, American Scene Painting, 1991; transcriber: Oral History of American Artists, Archives of American Art, Smithsonian Instn., 1995—. Democrat. Home and Office: 4735 Don Ricardo Dr Los Angeles CA 90008

YOSHIUCHI, ELLEN HAVEN, childbirth educator; b. Newark, Apr. 15, 1949; d. Michael Joseph and Adeline V. (Lindblom) Haven; m. Takeshi Yoshiuchi, Dec. 1, 1973; children: Teri Takumi, Niki Noboru. BA summa cum laude, CUNY, 1980; M Profl. Studies in Human Rels., N.Y. Inst. Tech., 1991. Cert. bereavement svcs. counselor. Pvt. practice childbirth edn., 1983-89; program asst. parent/family edn. St. Luke's/Roosevelt Hosp. Ctr., N.Y.C., 1989-93, mem. faculty parent/family edn. program, 1990—; mem. faculty Family Ctr. at Riverdale Neighborhood House, Bronx, N.Y., 1991—; mem. perinatal bereavement com. St. Luke's/Roosevelt Hosp. Ctr., N.Y.C., 1989—;. Editor ASPO/N.Y.C. News, 1983-86; contbr. articles to profl. jours. Fellow Am. Coll. Childbirth Educators; mem. ACA, Internat. Childbirth Edn. Assn., Assn. Specialists in Group Work, N.Y. State Perinatal Assn., Am. Soc. for Psychoprophylaxis in Obstetrics/Lamaze (cert. tchr., pres. N.Y.C. chpt. 1987-91, nominating com. 1991-93, dir. ednl. program 1991-93).

YOST, BERNICE, detective agency owner; b. Houston; d. Kenneth Wayne and Georgia (Sampson) Cox; m. Matthew Yost. Student, L.A. Trade Tech, 1968-70, Compton Coll., 1974-76, Ariz. State U., 1983-85. Staff acct. Moultrie, Liggens, Terrel CPA's, L.A., 1969-71; spl. agt. IRS, L.A., 1972-79; supervisory spl. agt. IRS, Phoenix, 1979-91; program mgr. IRS, Washington, 1991-93; owner, operator Yost Detective Agy., Silver Spring, Md., 1994—. Recipient Albert Gallatin award for merit, 1993. Mem. Nat. Orgn. of Black Law Enforcement Execs. Democrat. Baptist.

YOST, ELLEN G. (ELLEN YOST LAFILI), lawyer; b. Buffalo, May 30, 1945; d. Irwin Arthur and Sylvia Ruth Ginsberg; m. Louis Lafili; children: Elizabeth Anne, Peter Andrew, Benjamin Lewis Yost. AB, Mt. Holyoke Coll., 1966; JD, SUNY, Buffalo, 1983. Bar: N.Y., U.S. Dist. Ct. (we. dist.) N.Y. 1984. Assoc. Jaeckle, Fleischmann & Mugel, Buffalo, 1983-89, Saperston & Day, P.C., Buffalo, 1989—; ptnr. Griffith & Yost, Buffalo, 1991—. Pres. Buffalo Coun. on World Affairs, 1987-89; bd. dirs. Buffalo World Trade Assn., 1988-90, Legal Svcs. for Elderly, Disabled, Disadvantaged, 1984—. Mem. ABA (co-chair Can. law com. of internat. law and practice sect. 1990-94, vice chair immigration and nationality law com. 1994—, co-chair 1995—, co-chair task force N.Am. Free Trade Agreement 1991-94), N.Y. State Bar Assn. (chmn. U.S. Can. law com. 1987-89, mem. exec. com. internat. law and practice sect. 1987-89, sec. commn. in internat. trade and transactions 1984-87), Am. Immigration Lawyers' Assn. Jewish. Office: Griffith & Yost Ste 1320 Key Center 50 Fountain Plz Buffalo NY 14202-2212

YOST, KELLY LOU, pianist; b. Boise, Idaho, Aug. 10, 1940; d. Roy Daniel and Helen Roberta (Kingsbury) Frizzelle; m. Nicholas Peter Bond, Dec. 27, 1961 (div. 1973); 1 child, Brook Bernard; m. Samuel Joseph Yost, June 16, 1984. BA in Music, U. Idaho, 1962; postgrad., U. So. Calif., 1965-69. Pvt. tchr. classical piano Twin Falls, Idaho, 1962-88; rec. artist, co-owner ind. record label Channel Prodns., Twin Falls, 1986—; soloist U. Idaho Symphony Orch., Moscow, 1962; pianist, keyboardist Magic Valley Symphony Orch., Twin Falls, 1985, 86; touring guest piano soloist Vandaleer Concert Choir, Moscow, 1961. Recorded record albums: Piano Reflections, 1987, Quiet Colors, 1991, Roses and Solitude, 1996. Mem. NARAS, Nat. Assn. Ind. Record Distbrs., Music Tchrs. Nat. Assn., Idaho Music Tchrs. Assn. (sec. 1981-82), Magic Valley Cmty. Concert Assn. (bd. dirs. 1964-87), Phi Beta Kappa, Kappa Kappa Gamma (Alumnae Achievement award 1996). Office: Channel Prodns PO Box 454 Twin Falls ID 83303-0454

YOST, NANCY RUNYON, artist, designer, art educator; b. Eaton, Ohio, July 16, 1933; d. Stanley Everett and Treva (Geeting) Runyon; m. Kenneth John Yost, Aug. 17, 1952 (div. Dec. 1962); 1 child, Debra Colleen Yost Mayne. BS in Art Edn., Miami U., Oxford, Ohio, 1966, MEd in Art, 1970. Cert. profl. permanent tchr., Ohio. Sec. N.Am. Aircraft, Columbus, Ohio, 1957; sec. Miami U., Oxford, 1957-61, textile instr., 1978; textile instr. Living Arts Ctr., Dayton, Ohio, 1972-73; coord. art, music and phys. edn. Stewart Jr. High Sch., Oxford, 1981-86; art instr. Talawanda Sch. System, Oxford, 1965-90, dist. coord., 1986-90; owner, creator Allegro Adornments Bus., 1988—; postgrad. Sem. Charles Jeffrey, Cleve., Inst. Art, Miami U., 1973, David Van Dommelen Penn State at U. Tenn., 1975, Bill Helwig, N.Y., 1975, Nik Krevitsky, N.Y., 1976, Tom Shafer, Columbus, Ohio, 1982; mem. curriculum coun. Talawanda Sch. Dist., 1982—; rep. Amway Corp., 1980-81, World Book Co., Chgo., 1986-88; lectr. Miami U., 1986; invited workshop speaker, presenter Nat. Art Edn. Assn. Conv., Phoenix, 1992. Contbg. artist: Wall Hangings, 1971, Knotting, 1973; One-woman exhibit at Creative Fibers Studio, Buffalo, 1974; exhibited group show Dayton Art Inst., Invitational Fiber Artists Am., Ball State U., 1974, Christkindl Markt, Canton Art Inst. 1994 (hon. mention); designer Oxford Bicentennial Calender, 1976; guest jewelry designer Saks 5th Avenue. Supr. Community Artworks, 1986; mem. adv. bd. Miami U. Summer Theatre, 1991-93; mem. spl. events planning com. Miami U. Art Mus., 1993—. Recipient Winner Most Creative Costume Ohio Mart, 1992, 93, First Pl. awards Community Photo Contest, 3d Pl. and Hon. Mention award Oxford Audubon Photo Show, 1994, 1st Pl. 3D Design, Greater Hamilton Art Exhibit at Fitton Ctr, Cash award ribbon and Purchase award Wyo. Art Show, 1996. Mem. Southwestern Art Edn. Assn., Ohio Art Edn. Assn., Ohio Edn. Assn., Talawanda Edn. Assn., Ohio Designer Craftsmen, Ohio Arts and Crafts Guild, Oxford Arts Club, Kappa Delta Pi. Home and Studio: 6674 Fairfield Rd Oxford OH 45056-9707

YOTHER, MICHELE, publisher; b. Atlanta, Aug. 25, 1965; d. Carole (Spence) Marsh; m. Michael B. Yother, Mar. 17, 1990; 1 child, Christina Michele. BA in acctg. cum laude, Ga. State U., 1990. Asst. v.p. Bank Am., Atlanta, 1986-90; pres. Gallopade Pub. Group, Atlanta, 1990—; pres. Carole Marsh Family Interactive Multimedia, 1993—. Pub. over 2500 children's books, computer disks and activities. Equifax Bus. scholar Ga. State U., 1989. Mem. Women's Nat. Book Assn. (bd. dirs. 1994-95), Bank Am. Club (pres. 1989), Golden Key. Methodist. Home: 359 Milledge Ave SE Atlanta GA 30312-3238 Office: Gallopade Pub Group 359 Milledge Ave SE Ste 100 Atlanta GA 30312-3238

YOTHERS, WENDY LOU, artist, silversmith; b. Grand Rapids, Mich., May 21, 1952; d. Lee W. and Winona (Largen) Y.; 1 child, Douglas Emory Olds. BFA cum laude, U. Mich., 1974; cert., Nat. Coll. Goldsmithing, Lahti, Finland, 1984; MFA (Mgh) with distinction, Guldsmedehojiskolen, Copenhagen, 1987. Teaching asst. Tex. Tech. U., Lubbock, 1979-81; lectr. Nat. Coll. Goldsmithing, Lahti, 1982-84; silversmith specializing in restoration, prototype making and prodn. smithing Tiffany & Co., N.Y.C. and Parsipany, N.J., 1993—; silversmith specializing in restoration, prototype making and prodn. smithing Kirk Stieff & Co., Balt., 1988, prototype, model maker, 1989-92. Author: (textbook) Enameling, 1984; exhibited in group shows at Tex. Tech. Mus., Lubbock, 1980, Nat. Inst. Arts and Handcraft, Lahti, 1982, Mus. Applied Art, Hensinki, 1984, Bella Ctr., Copenhagen, 1986, Galleri Metal, Copenhagen, 1986, Gallery Fgn. Ministry, Houses Parliament, Copenhagen, 1986, Galleri Hummeluhre, Jutland, Denmark, 1986, Hotel Sheraton, Goteborg, Sweden, 1986, Frantz Hingelberg Gallery, Arhus, Denmark, 1987, Petur Tryggvi Hjalmarsson Gallery, Reykjavik, Iceland, 1987, Musee des Arts Decoratifs, Paris, 1987-88, Mus. Applied Art, Copenhagen, 1987, Soc. Am. Silversmiths and Soc. Arts and Crafts, Boston, 1990, Soc. Arts and Crafts, 1991, Pritam & Eames, East Hampton, N.Y., 1992, Nat. Mus. Ornamental Metalwork, Memphis, 1992, Worcester (Mass.) Ctr. Crafts, 1992, Nat. Ornamental Metal Mus., Memphis, 1993, Lunt's Design Ctr. Gallery, 1996, Yashiva U. Gallery, 1996, Shreve, Crump and Lowe Bicentennial Exhbn., 1996. Grad. rsch. grantee Tex. Tech. U., Lubbock, 1979-80; Rotary Internat. grad. fellow, 1981-82; recipient Cultural award Am. Women's Club, Denmark, 1986, Direcktor Ib Henrickson's Fond stipend, 1985-87. Fellow Soc. Am. Silversmiths. Roman Catholic. Home: 90 Oakwood Village #3 Flanders NJ 07836 Office: Tiffany & Co 801 Jefferson Rd Parsippany NJ 07054-3710

YOUNG, ALICE, lawyer; b. Washington, Apr. 7, 1950; d. John and Elizabeth (Jen) Y.; m. Thomas L. Shortall, Sept. 22, 1984; children: Amanda, Stephen. AB magna cum laude, Yale U., 1971; JD, Harvard U., 1974. Bar: N.Y. 1975. Assoc. Coudert Bros., N.Y.C., 1974-81; mng. ptnr. Graham & James, N.Y.C., 1981-87; ptnr. Milbank, Tweed, Hadley & McCloy, N.Y.C., 1987-93; ptnr., chair Asia Pacific Practice (U.S.) Kaye, Scholer, Fierman, Hays & Handler, N.Y.C., 1994—; mem. Coun. on Fgn. Rels., 1977—. Contbr. articles to profl. jours. Trustee Aspen (Colo.) Inst., 1988—, Pan-Asian Repertory Theatre, N.Y.C., 1987-90, Lingnan Found., N.Y.C., 1984-91, Asia/Pacific Coun. of The Nature Conservancy, 1995 ; mem. bus. com. Met. Mus. Art, N.Y.C., 1989-94, Nat. Com. on U.S.-China Rels., 1993—, U.S.-China Bus. Coun., 1993—, Com. of 100, 1993—, dir. 1995—; mem. bd. overseers visitation com. to Law Sch., Harvard U., 1994—, chair subcom. on grad. program Harvard U., 1996. Named one of 40 Under 40 Crain's Bus., N.Y.C., 1989; Bates fellow Yale U., 1970, NDFL fellow Harvard U., 1967-68; recipient Star award N.Y. Women's Agenda, 1992. Mem. ABA, N.Y. State Bar Assn. (fgn. investment com.), Assn. Bar City N.Y. (spl. com. on rels. with Japanese bar, Union Internat. des Avocats), Nat. Asian Pacific Am. Bar Assn., Asian Am. Bar Assn. N.Y., Harvard Law Sch. Assn. N.Y.C. (trustee 1990-94), Japan Soc. (sec. 1989—), Asia Soc. (pres.'s coun. 1984—). Office: Kaye Scholer Fierman Hays & Handler 425 Park Ave New York NY 10022-3598

YOUNG, ALINE PATRICE, controller; b. Sacramento, Nov. 8, 1957; d. Rene Francis and Patricia May (Taylor) LeFevre; m. Patrick Charles Young, Sept. 6, 1976 (div. Oct. 1979); 1 child, Daniel Alan Young. AA, Fullerton Coll., 1979; BA, Calif State U., Fullerton, 1981; MBA, Pepperdine U., 1988. Mgmt. devel. program Gen. Electric Credit, Anaheim, Calif., 1981-83; credit mgr. Kwikset/Emhart, Anaheim, Calif., 1983-88, Avery Dennison, Azusa, Calif., 1988-90; contr., fin. mgr. Avery Dennison, Monrovia, Calif., 1990-92, site mgr., contr., 1992-95; mgr. continuous bus. change Allied Signal Inc., Torrance, Calif., 1995—. Chairperson Vision 95 Lutheran High Sch., Orange, Calif., 1993. Mem. Am. Mgmt. Assn., Inst. Mgmt. Accts. Republican. Lutheran. Office: Allied Signal Aerospace M/Stor 38-2 2525 W 190th St Torrance CA 90504

YOUNG, AMY ELIZABETH, television producer; b. Wareham, Mass., Apr. 2, 1971; d. George William and Valerie Helen (Stinson) Y. BA, Stonehill Coll., North Easton, Mass., 1993; MA, Emerson Coll., Boston, 1995. Prodr., dir., co-writer Yea Prodns., Wareham, 1993—; prodr., dir., writer Continental Cablevision, Marion, Mass., 1994. Prodr. (documentary) Stellwagen Bank-An Investment for the Future, 1995; prodr., dir. (Cable TV show) Kidsquest, 1994; contbr. poetry and prose to Cairn-Stonehill Coll. Lit. Mag., 1990-93. Recipient Harvard Book award, Boston, 1988, Brown Book award, 1988, Comm. fellowship Gen. Fedn. Women's Clubs Mass., 1993. Mem. Lambda Epsilon Sigma. Home and Office: 167 High St Wareham MA 02571

YOUNG, ANDREA C., communications executive; b. Rochester, N.Y., June 21, 1952; d. Vito Anthony and Mary Christine (Ruta) Calzone; m. Dennis Young, Jan. 4, 1989. BA in Music, Psychology, SUNY, Oswego, 1974. Media buyer Grey Advt., Los Angeles, 1976-77; media dir. Pickwick Internat., Los Angeles, 1977-79; regional coordinator MCA Distbg., Inc., Los Angeles, 1979-80; dir. Franklin Music div. Young Entertainment, Atlanta, 1980-84; v.p. Young Systems, Ltd., Atlanta, 1984-90, pres., 1990—. Mem. Nat. Assn. Rec. Merchandisers (assoc.). Address: PO Box 88569 Atlanta GA 30356-8569 Home: 5018 Hidden Branches Cir Atlanta GA 30338-4019 Office: Young Systems Ltd 6185 Buford Hwy Ste C100 Norcross GA 30071-2303

YOUNG, ANN ELIZABETH O'QUINN, historian, educator; b. Waycross, Ga.; d. James Foster and Pearl Elizabeth (Sasser) O'Quinn; student Shorter Coll.; BA, MA, U. Ga., PhD, 1965; m. Robert William Young, Aug. 18, 1968; children: Abigail Ann, Leslie Lynn. Asst. prof. history Kearney (Nebr.) State Coll. (name now U. Nebr. at Kearney 1991), 1965-69, assoc. prof., 1969-72, prof., 1972—; participant Inst. on Islam, Middle East and World Politics, U. Mich., summer 1984, Coun. on Internat. Ednl. Exch., London, 1990, NEH Seminar NYU, 1993, mem. faculty senate, 1985—, sec. 1993-94, pres., 1995-96. Mem. NEA, PEO, Phi Alpha Theta, Delta Kappa Gamma (chpt. pres. 1978-79), Phi Mu. Republican. Presbyterian. Contbg. author Dictionary of Georgia Biography; contbr. articles to profl. revs. Office: U Nebr at Kearney Dept History Kearney NE 68849-1285

YOUNG, ARLEEN C., education educator; b. Laurens, S.C., Sept. 9, 1962; d. Walter Richard Douglas and Sarah Ethel (Philson) Y. BS in Social Studies, Presbyn. Coll., Clinton, S.C., 1984; MEd in Reading Edn., U. S.C., 1990, postgrad., 1993—. Cert. in secondary social studies, mid. sch. social studies, reading, S.C. Tchr. Greenwood (S.C.) H.S., 1985-87, Laurens Dist. 55 H.S., 1987-88; tchr. reading Woodruff (S.C.) Jr. H.S., 1989; instr., student tchr. supr. U. S.C., Spartanburg, 1989-93; mem. minority affairs coun. Presbyn. Coll., 1991—. James A. Morris fellow U.S.C., 1993—; Holmes scholar, 1993—. Mem. ASCD, Nat. Coun. Tchrs. English, Internat. Reading Assn., Kappa Delta Pi, Phi Delta Kappa. Home: 314 Green St Laurens SC 29360-3411 Office: U SC Coll of Edn Columbia SC 29208

YOUNG, ARLEEN MCLAWHON, elementary school educator; b. Washington, Oct. 21, 1947; d. Arthur and Hebe (Amy) McLawhon; m. Drew

MacKenzie Young II, Aug. 29, 1970; children: Drew, Amy, Caitlin. BA, William Woods Coll., Fulton, Mo., 1969; MEd, U. Mo., 1970. Tchr. 3d grade Dwight Sch., Englewood, N.J., 1971-72; tchr. 1st and 2d grades Buckley Sch., N.Y.C., 1972-75; reading resource tchr. Trinity Luth. Sch., Wahiawa, Hawaii, 1975-76, Bradley Sch., Ft. Leavenworth, Kans., 1987-88; tchr. 1st grade Pope sch., Ft. Bragg, N.C., 1989-94; tchr. evaluator Ft. Bragg Schs., 1994—. Named Outstanding Elem. Math Tchr. of Yr. award Ft. Bragg Schs. and N.C. Coun. Tchrs. Math., 1994. Mem. Internat. Reading Assn., N.C. Reading Assn. (tchr. exemplary reading program award 1993), Cross Creek Reading Coun., N.C. Sci. Tchrs. Assn., N.C. Coun. Tchrs. Math. Office: Fort Bragg Schools PO Box 70089 Fort Bragg NC 28307-0089

YOUNG, CAROL ANN (CASEY YOUNG), information systems consultant; b. Teaneck, N.J., Aug. 7, 1951; d. Stephen John and Mildred Olga (Weideman) Martin; m. Chester Frederick D'Elia, May 10, 1980 (div. 1983); 1 child, Antonio Preston; m. Stanley Warren Young, Jr., June 10, 1985; 1 child, Jesse Stephen. BA in Theatre, Montclair State U., 1973; MA in Theatre, U. Mich., 1975. Assoc. instr. Eastern Mont. Coll., Billings, 1975-76; tchr. English Browning (Mont.) Jr. High, 1976-79; project adminstr. ITT, N.Y.C., 1980-82; info. ctr. adminstr. Selective Ins., Branchville, N.J., 1982-86; data base adminstr. AT&T, Parsippany, N.J., 1986-90, United Parcel Svc., Mahwah, N.J., 1991-94; prin. cons. RYC, Inc., Key Biscayne, Fla., 1994—. Contbr. articles to profl. jours. Leader, den mother, com. mem. Cub Scouts, Milford, Pa., 1989—. Mem. Internat. DB2 Users Group (v.p. bd. dirs. 1994—, chairperson planning 1995-96, Best User Spkr. 1992). Democrat. Episcopal. Address: 108 Cardiff Ct Santa Cruz CA 95060

YOUNG, CYNTHIA MYERS, artist; b. Ravenna, Ohio, May 20, 1933; d. Robert Glen Myers and Edith Freeman (Myers) Schultz; m. Alfred Avery Young, Nov. 26, 1955; 1 child, Meredith Coe Young Barritz. Student, RISD, 1954; BA, Conn. Coll. for Women, 1955; postgrad., U. Hawaii, 1963; MFA, George Washington U., 1979. Adj. faculty North Va. C.C., Alexandria, 1980-94, Annandale, 1993-95, Merrymount Coll., McLean, Va., 1989; bd. mem. D.C. chpt. Artists' Equity, 1989—, Touchstone Gallery, D.C., 1990—, Eye Wash Artists Newsletter, D.C., 1992-93; juror Potomac (Md.) Watercolor Soc., The Art Ctr., Springfield, Va., Falls Ch. (Va.) Cmty. Ctr., McLean Art Guild; artist-in-residence Nat. Pk. Svc., Washington, Art Found., La Napoule, France, Ctr. for Internat. Studies, Collegio Colombo, Viareggio, Italy, Va. Ctr. for the Creative Arts, Lynchburg, Va. One-person show Touchstone Gallery, Washington, 1995;. Chairperson Cmty. for Creative Non-Violence Shelter for the Homeless (Mitch Snyder), collected 50 artworks for homeless shelter, Washington, 1989. Recipient David Lloyd Kreeger Painting award George Washington U., Washington, Graphics award Art Inst., San Diego, Saul Alexander award Found. Purchase award, Charleston, Dudley B. Cooper award, Norfolk; fellow Va. Ctr. for the Creative Arts. Home: 6903 South Ridge Dr Mc Lean VA 22101

YOUNG, DARLENE, post office executive; b. Chicago Heights, Ill., Aug. 31, 1954; d. Jeff Sr. and Ruther Lee (Prince) Y. BA in Sociology, Lawrence U., 1976; postgrad., Bloomfield Coll., 1993; cert. in materials mgmt., Bloomfield (N.J) Coll., 1994. Dir. youth devel. Newark Inst.-Urban Programs, 1977-78; vocat. counselor Newark Comprehensive Manpower Rehab. Project Drug Abusers, 1979-80; supr. distbn. ops. U.S. Postal Svc., Newark, 1980-94, 1994—. Mem. NAFE, Am. Soc. Quality Control, Nat. Assn. Postal Suprs. Home: 51 Clifton Ave Newark NJ 07104-1880

YOUNG, DONA DAVIS GAGLIANO, lawyer, insurance executive; b. Bklyn., Jan. 8, 1954; d. Vincent Joseph and Shirley Elizabeth (Davis) Gagliano; m. Roland F. Young III, Aug. 18, 1979; children: Meghan Davis, Wesley Davis, Taylor Davis. BA and MA in Polit. Sci., Drew U., 1976; JD, U. Conn., 1980. Bar: Conn. 1980, U.S. Dist. Ct. Conn. 1980. With Phoenix Home Life Ins. Co., Hartford, Conn., 1980—, ast. v.p. reinsurance adminstrn., 1983-85; 2d v.p., ins. counsel Phoenix Mut. Life Ins. Co., Hartford, Conn., 1985-87, v.p. and asst. gen. counsel, 1987-89; sr. v.p. and gen. counsel Phoenix Home Life Mut. Ins. Co., Hartford, 1989-94; exec. v.p. individual sales and mktg., gen. counsel Phoenix Home Life Mut. Ins. Co., 1994-95, exec. v.p. individual ins. and gen. counsel, 1995—; trustee Hartford Coll. Women; bd. dirs. LIMRA Internat., Sonoco Products Co. Mem. fin. com. Asylum Hill Congl. Ch. Mem. ABA, Am. Coun. of Life Ins. (com. on risk classification 1985-88, legis. com. 1989—), Am. Soc. Corp. Secs., Assn. Life Ins. Counsel (bd. govs.), Hartford County Bar Assn., Conn. Bar Assn. Republican. Congregationalist. Office: Phoenix Home Life Mut Ins 1 American Row Hartford CT 06103-2833

YOUNG, EDNA MAE OAR, artist, designer; b. Colden, N.Y., Sept. 10, 1944; d. Arnold Evan and Helen (Hambleton) Oar; m. Leon Ray Young, June 25, 1982 (div. Feb. 1993); 1 child, Leah J.; m. George David Jung, Nov. 10, 1962; children: Gerhard H., Susan G., Gregory G. Grad., Griffith Inst., 1962. Owner, propr., buyer Colden (N.Y.) Country Store, 1965-77; owner, operator Edna's Antiques, Hamburg, N.Y., 1977-82; designer, co-owner, mktg. mgr., photographer Shadowdancer, Inc., Angelica, N.Y., 1983-893; freelance artist-designer Angelica, 1993-94; sole owner, designer, mgr. Edna Oar Young, Co., Angelica, 1994—. Chair decoration com. scholarship rev. bd. Alfred (N.Y.) U., 1992-96. Mem. Women's Assn. Profl. Writers, Masons-Eastern Star. Republican. Office: Edna Oar Young Co 21 W Main St Angelica NY 14709

YOUNG, EILEEN M., music educator; b. Pottsville, Pa., Jan. 20, 1964; d. Russell C. and Mary E. Lowthert. BS in Music Edn., Messiah Coll., 1986; MMus, U. N.C., Greensboro, 1988, DMus, 1994; MMus, N.C. Sch. of Arts, 1995. Cert. tchr., N.C., Pa. Woodwinds tchr. Moore Music Studios, Greensboro, N.C., 1991—; prof. clarinet and saxophone Catawba Coll., Salisbury, N.C., 1992-95; prof. bass clarinet N.C. Sch. of Arts, Winston-Salem, N.C., 1994—; prin. bass clarinetist N.C. Symphony, 1994—. Prin. clarinetist Salisbury (N.C.) Symphony, 1991—; prin. bass clarinet Winston-Salem (N.C.) Symphony, 1992—; clarinetist, founding mem. Bolton Woodwind Quintet, Winston-Salem, 1994—. Sec. Winston-Salem Symphony Orch., 1994—. Emerging artist grantee Greensboro Arts Coun., 1991. Mem. Chamber Music Am., Internat. Clarinet Soc., Pi Kappa Lamda. Democrat. Office: Moore Music Studios Greensboro NC 27401

YOUNG, ELEANOR LOUISE, retired senior staff nurse; b. Cambridge, Mass., Oct. 10, 1930; d. Allison Homer and Florence May (Sheppard) Jones; m. Joseph Moses, May 6, 1951; children: Catherine, Joseph, Terence, Nora. Student, Mass. Gen. Hosp., Boston, 1949-51; ADS, Massasoit C.C., Brockton, Mass., 1972. Registered nurse, Mass., 1972. RN CCU South Shore Hosp., Weymouth, Mass., 1972-80, sr. staff nurse CCU, 1980-95; retired, 1995; pacemaker instr., 1985-89, quality mgmt. 1988-94, South Shore Hosp., Weymouth, Mass. Mem. Am. Heart Assn., South Shore RN Assn., Alpha Nu Omega.

YOUNG, ELIZABETH LOUISE, bank officer, artist; b. South Bend, Ind., Apr. 5, 1958; d. Carl J. and Loretta H. (Niedbalski) Kot; m. William Roger Young (div. Jan. 1986). BA, Ft. Lewis Coll., 1992. Mgr. Wendy's Hallmark, Show Low, Ariz., 1980-83; br. ops. specialist First Interstate Bank, 1985-89; mgr. Oak Ridge Sports Ctr., Pagosa Springs, Colo., 1989-90; teller supr. Norwest Bank, Durango, Colo., 1994—. Mem. Durango Arts Ctr. Home: 1942 County Rd 513 Ingacio CO 81137

YOUNG, ESTELLE IRENE, dermatologist; b. N.Y.C., Nov. 2, 1945; d. Sidney D. and Blanche (Krosney) Young. BA magna cum laude, Mt. Holyoke Coll., 1963; MD, Downstate Med. Ctr., 1971. Intern, Lenox Hill Hosp., N.Y.C., 1971-72, resident in medicine, 1972-73; resident in dermatology Columbia Presbyn. Hosp., N.Y.C., 1973-74, NYU Med. Ctr., 1974-75, Boston U. Hosp., 1975-76; asst. dermatologist Harvard U. Health Services, Cambridge, Mass., 1975-76; assoc. staff mem. dermatology Boston U. Med. Ctr., 1976-77; practice medicine specializing in dermatology, Petersburg, Va., 1976—; mem. staff Poplar Springs Hosp., 1976—, Southside Regional Med. Ctr. (formerly Petersburg Gen. Hosp.), 1976—, Cen. State Hosp., 1984—; clin. instr. dept. dermatology Med. Coll. Va., 1976—, asst. clinic prof., 1988-94, assoc. clin. prof., 1994—; sec. med. staff Petersburg Gen. Hosp., 1982—. Fellow Am. Acad. Dermatology; mem. Va. Med. Soc., Va. Dermatology Soc., Tidewater Dermatology Soc. (pres. 1982-83), Physicians for Social Responsiblity Soc., Tidewater Physicians for Social Responsibility (pres. 1990—), Internat. Physicians for Prevention of Nuclear War, Southside Va. Med. Soc., Sigma Xi. Contbr. articles to profl. jours. Home: 2319 Monument Ave Richmond VA 23220-2603 Office: 612A S Sycamore St Petersburg VA 23803-5828

YOUNG, FREDDIE GILLIAM, educational administrator; b. Miami, Fla., Nov. 1, 1939; d. Thomas and Myrtle (Gibson) Gilliam. BS, Fla. A&M U., 1961; MS, Hunter Coll., 1970; postgrad., U. Ghana, 1970; EdD, Nova U., 1990; cert. Prin.'s Exec. Tng. Program, Dade County Pub. Schs. Cert. supervision and adminstrn., African studies, elem. and jr. coll. Tchr. Collier County Pub. Schs., Naples, Fla., N.Y.C. Pub. Schs., Bronx, N.Y.; tchr. Dade County Pub. Schs., Miami, prin.; adj. lead prof. Nova U.; presenter Am. Assn. Ethnic Studies Conf., Fla. Atlantic U., 1991, Assn. Carribean Studies Cairo, 1993, Georgetown, Guyana, 1994. Del. 19th congl. dist. Dem. conv., 1988; mem. Am. Jewish Com. Named Most Outstanding Black Woman, S. Fla., Women's C. of C., Educator of Yr. Zeta Phi Beta; recipient 50 outstanding svc. awards Prin. Ctr. Harvard U. Sch. Edn., 1989, Metro Dade County commendation for dedicated svc.; finalist for Adminstr. of Yr., 1991, DCAA. Mem. AAUW, ASCD, Am. Jewish Com., Nat. Alliance Black Educators, S. Fla. Exec. Educators, Leadership Miami, Miami Alliance Black Educators, Dade County Adminstrs. Assn. (chair), Fla. Reading Assn., Dade Reading Coun., Fla. A&M U. Alumni Assn. (pres. Miami-Dade chpt.), Nova U. Alumni Assn. (sec. Miami chpt.), Phi Delta Kappa. Home: 12390 SW 144th Ter Miami FL 33186-7419

YOUNG, GLADYS EVELYN LAMBETH, physician, air force officer; b. Vernon, Tex., Nov. 6, 1948; d. Otha Banks and Tena Ruth (Adams) Lambeth; m. James Arthur Bryan, June, 1971 (div. Dec. 1974); m. Herbert Lee Young, Dec. 31, 1974; 1 child, Otha Benjamin. BSc in Biology magna cum laude, Midwestern U., 1970; MD, U. Tex., 1974. Instr. ACLS, ATLS, pre-hosp. trauma life support, EMT. Resident So. Ill. U. Sch. Med.-Carbondale Doctors Meml. Hosp., 1974-75; commd. 1st lt. USAF, 1975, advanced through grades to col., 1993, gen. med. officer, chief primary care, Altus AFB (Okla.) Hosp., 1975-77, emergency physician, Duncan (Okla.) Regional Hosp., 1977-79; flight surgeon active reserves 507 TAC Clinic USAF, Tinker AFB, Okla., 1977-79; chief AMIC Clinic GS-11, Reynolds Army Hosp. USAF, Malmstrom AFB, Mont., 1982-84; emergency physician, Columbus Hosp. USAF, Great Falls, Mont., 1981-83; chief aerospace medicine, Hosp. Malmstrom USAF, 1982-84; emergency physician, Jackson County Meml. Hosp. USAF, Altus, 1984-87; chief aeromed. svcs., Hosp. Altus USAF, 1984-87, chief hosp. svcs., Hosp. Altus, 1986-87; dir. base med. svcs. USAF, Suwon AFB, Korea, 1987-88; chief aerospace medicine, 43 Med. Group/SGP USAF, Malmstrom AFB, 1988-94, comdr. 341 AERMS 341 Med. Group, 1994—; mem. 1611th Aeromed. Evacuation Squadron, provisional, Desert Storm USAF, King Khalid Mil. City, Saudi Arabia, 1991; comdr. 1610 med. squadron provisional, Restore Hope USAF, Caro West AB, Egypt, 1993. Field dir. med. team Great Centennial Trail Drive, 1989. Decorated Meritorious Svc. medal with oak leaf cluster, Nat. Def. medal, South West Asia 1st device, Outstanding Unit 4 device with valor, Liberation of Kuwait medal. Mem. Am. Acad. Family Physicians (cert., fellow 1980), Order of Eastern Star, VFW (life). Republican. Baptist. Office: 341 AMS/SGPoup Malmstrom A F B MT 59402

YOUNG, HELEN MARSHALL, dietitian; b. Christiansburg, Va., Aug. 13, 1943; d. Lewis Elemander and Lela Wanda (Lester) Marshall; m. Phillip Lee Young, June 11, 1965 (div. July 1985); 1 child, Deidre Anne. BS in Home Econs. Edn., Radford U., 1965; MS in Human Nutrition & Foods, Va. Polytech. Inst. & State U., 1974. Lic. dietitian/nutritionist. Home econs. tchr. Christiansburg (Va.) H.S., 1965-67, William Byrd H.S., Vinton, Va., 1967-76; asst. chief clin. dietitian St. Mary's Hosp., West Palm Beach, Fla., 1977-79; assoc. dir. food svc. JFK Med. Ctr., Lake Worth, Fla., 1979-85; food svc. dir. Palms West Hosp., Loxahatchee, Fla., 1985-88; adminstrv. dietitian Al Fanateer Hosp., Jubail, Saudi Arabia, 1988-89; lectr., internship dir. King Saud U., Riyadh, Saudi Arabia, 1989-90; food svc. dir. Dhahran Health Ctr., Saudi Arabia, 1990-93; nutrition svcs. specialist Morrison's Health Care Inc., Orlando, Fla., 1994-95; dir. food svc. Our Lady of Lake Regional Med. Ctr., Baton Rouge, 1995—. Recipient Outstanding Alumna award Va. Polytech. Inst. & State U., 1983. Mem. Am. Dietetic Assn. (registered dietitian 1977), Fla. Dietetic Assn. (chmn. quality assurance, chmn. ann. meeting, Fla. outstanding dietitian award 1983), Palm Beach Dietetic Assn. (pres.-elect, pres., rec. sec., diet therapy chmn. legis. com.). Republican. Home: 17451 Chasefield Ave Baton Rouge LA 70817

YOUNG, JACQUELINE EURN HAI, state legislator; b. Honolulu, May 20, 1934; d. Paul Bai and Martha (Cho) Y.; m. Harry Valentine Daniels, Dec. 25, 1954 (div. 1978); children: Paula, Harry, Nani, Laura; m. Everett Kleinjans, June 4, 1988. BS in Speech Pathology, Audiology, U. Hawaii, 1969; MS in Edn., Spl. Edn., Old Dominion U., 1972; advanced cert., Loyola Coll., 1977; PhD in Communication, Women's Studies, Union Inst., 1989. Dir. dept. speech and hearing Md. Sch. for the Blind, Balt., 1975-77; dir. deaf-blind project Easter Seal Soc. Oahu, Hawaii, 1977-78; project dir. equal ednl. opportunity programs Hawaii State Dept. Edn., Honolulu, 1978-85, state ednl. specialist, 1978-90; state rep. dist. 20 Hawaii State Legislature, Honolulu, 1990-92, state rep. dist. 51, 1992-94; vice-speaker Hawaii Ho. of Reps., Honolulu; apptd. to U.S. Dept. Def. Adv. Commn. on Women in the Svc.; cons. spl. edn. U.S. Dept. Edn., dept. edn. Guam, Am. Samoa, Ponape, Palau, Marshall Islands, 1977-85; cons. to orgns. on issues relating to workplace diversity; adj. prof. commn., anthopology, mgmt. Hawaii Pacific U. TV producer. 1st v.p. Nat. Women's Polit. Caucus, 1988-90; chair Hawaii Women's Polit. Caucus, 1987-89; bd. dirs. YWCA Oahu, Kalihi Palama Immigrant Svc. Ctr., Hawaii Dem. Movement, Family Peace Ctr.; appointee Honolulu County Com. on the Status of Women, 1986-87; mem. Adv. Coun. on Family Violence. Recipient OUtstanding Woman Leader award YWCA of Oahu, 1994, Pres.'s award Union Inst., 1993, Fellow of the Pacific award Hawaii-Pacific U., 1993, Headliner award Honolulu chpt. Women in Commn., 1993. Mem. Soroptimist Internat. (Kailua chpt.), Orgn. Women Leaders, Kailua C. of C., Korean C. of C., Kook Min Hur, Sierra Club, Korean Univ. Club. Home: 212 Luika Pl Kailua HI 96734-3237

YOUNG, JANET CHERYL, electrical engineer; b. Roanoke, Va., Oct. 3, 1960; d. Don Gordon and Barbara Hill (Mumpower) Y. BS in Physics, U. Tenn., Chattanooga, 1982; MSEE, Va. Tech. Inst., 1991. Engr. Sci. Applications Internat. Corp., Springfield, Va., 1982-91, UTC Svc. Corp., Washington, 1991-93; LCC, LLC, Arlington, Va., 1993—. Active in World Peace Mission Foundry United Meth. Ch., Washington, 1984, Community Band, Vienna, Va., 1985; vol. Shakespeare Theatre Co., 1996—. Mem. IEEE (mem. Electromagnetic Compatibility Soc. 1987—, Comm. Soc. 1992—). Methodist. Home: 4044 Chetham Way Lake Ridge VA 22192-5079 Office: LCC LLC 2300 Clarendon Blvd Ste 800 Arlington VA 22201-3367

YOUNG, JANET MARIE, counselor, educator; b. Wake, N.C., June 27, 1946; d. Calvin and Eloise Young; divorced; 1 child, Janelle Eloise. BA in Social Sci., Bennett Coll., 1968; MA in Guidance Counseling, N.C. Ctrl. U., 1979; EdD in Student Pers., N.C. State U., 1990. Nat. cert. counselor; lic. practicing counselor, N.C.; cert. psychotherapist. Tchr. Halifax County Sch. Sys., Enfield, N.C., 1968-71, Chapel Hill (N.C.) Carborro Sch. Dist., 1971-80; counselor, instr. N.C. Ctrl. U., Durham, 1980-92, counselor, 1992—; career counselor Talent Search, Raleigh, N.C., 1991-92; interim assoc. dir. health careers N.C. Ctrl. U., Durham, 1992, adj. asst. prof., 1992—; psychotherapist Edwards Hayes & Assocs., Raleigh, 1993—; counselor cons. Raleigh Employee Assistance Program, 1993—. Facilitator Chronic Pain Support Group, Raleigh, 1989-91; participant Beyond Breast Cancer, Raleigh, 1993-95; vol. Project Direct, Raleigh, 1995-96. Mem. ACA, Am. Coll. Counseling Assn., Assn. Multicultural Counseling & Devel., Assn. Religious & Value Issues In Counseling. Democrat. Baptist. Home: 2245 Sheffield Rd Raleigh NC 27610 Office: Counseling Ctr NC Ctrl U PO Box 19688 Durham NC 27707

YOUNG, JEANNETTE COCHRAN, corporate planner, reporter, analyst; b. Franklin, Ind., Mar. 12, 1953; d. Charles Morris and Marjorie Elizabeth (Rohrbaugh) Cochran; m. William Alan Young, Aug. 18, 1979 (div. 1994); children: Kathryn Elizabeth, Stephen Robert. BA, De Pauw U., 1975; MBA, U. Pa., 1977. Fin. analyst Eli Lilly & Co., Indpls., 1977-79; sr. fin. analyst Samsonite, Denver, 1980, Honeywell Test Instruments divsn., Denver, 1980-82; prin. analyst Fluor Corp., Sugar Land, Tex., 1982-86; sr. fin. analyst Caterpillar, Joliet, Ill., 1989-90, Texaco Chem. Co., Houston, 1990-93; coord. planning, budget Texaco, Inc., Houston, 1993—. Mem. ARC, Arapahoe County, Colo., 1982; vol. United Way ofTex. Gulf Coast, 1996. Office: Texaco 1111 Bagby Houston TX 77002 also: Texaco PO Box 4325 Houston TX 77210-4325

YOUNG, JOAN CRAWFORD, advertising executive; b. Hobbs, N.Mex., July 30, 1931; d. William Bill and Ora Maydelle (Boone) Crawford; m. Herchelle B. Young, Nov. 23, 1971 (div.). BA, Hardin Simmons U., 1952; postgrad. Tex. Tech. U., 1953-54. Reporter, Lubbock (Tex.) Avalanche-Jour., 1952-54; promotion dir. Sta. KCBD-TV, Lubbock, 1954-62; account exec. Ward Hicks Advt., Albuquerque, 1962-70; v.p. Mellekas & Assocs., Advt., Albuquerque, 1970-78; pres. J. Young Advt., Albuquerque, 1978—. Bd. dirs. N.Mex. Symphony Orch., 1970-73, United Way of Greater Albuquerque, 1985-89; bd. trustees N.Mex. Children's Found., 1994-96. Recipient Silver medal N.Mex. Advt. Fedn., 1977. Mem. N.Mex. Advt. Fedn. (bd. dirs. 1975-76), Am. Advt. Fedn., Greater Albuquerque C. of C. (bd. dirs. 1984), Albuquerque Petroleum Club (membership chmn. 1992-93, bd. dirs. 1993—, sec. 1994-95, v.p. 1995—). Republican. Author: (with Louise Allen and Audre Lipscomb) Radio and TV Continuity Writing, 1962. Home: 1638 Tierra Del Rio NW Albuquerque NM 87107 also: 500 Marquette NW Albuquerque NM 87102

YOUNG, JOANN ELIZABETH, veterinarian; b. Ware, Mass., July 2, 1953; D. Gordon Charles and Barbara Ann (Robinson) Y.; m. Jerome Peter Lang, May 24, 1986. AAS, SUNY, 1973; BSN, Boston U., 1985; DVM, Wash. State U., 1994. Lic. Vet. Wash., Mont., Maine. Vet. tech. Westboro (Mass.) Animal Hosp., 1973-78, Berkshire Vet. Hosp., Pittsfield, Mass., 1979-82; admitting officer U. Mass. Med. Ctr., Worcester, Mass., 1978-79; RN Ruidoso (N. Mex.) Hondo Valley Hosp., 1985-86, Group Health Ctrl. Hosp., Seattle, 1986-87, SE Wash. Home Health and Hospice, Pullman, 1988-90; vet. Colfax (Wash.) Vet. Hosp., 1994—. Mem. AVMA, Wash. State Vet. Med. Assn. Democrat. Roman Catholic. Home: 302 Old Moscow Rd Pullman WA 99163 Office: Colfax Vet Hosp N 1715 Oak St Colfax WA 99111

YOUNG, JULIA FRANCES, graphic designer; b. Rochester, N.Y., Oct. 9, 1934; d. Gustaf and Carolyn Myra (Skinner) Anderson; m. Jim Young, June 19, 1955; 1 child, Jennifer. AB, Little Rock Jr. Coll., 1954; BA, U. Ark., 1956. Graphic designer Emporium/Capwell Co., Oakland, Calif., 1958-62, Lesher Comms., Walnut Creek, Calif., 1970-90; owner, designer Julia Young Advt., Lafayette, Calif., 1990—. Mem. Contra Costa County Graphic Artists Assn., Lafayette Langeac Soc., Lafayette C. of C. Republican. Presbyterian. Office: Julia Young Advt 3658 Mt Diablo Blvd Ste 159 Lafayette CA 94549

YOUNG, KATHERINE ANN, education educator; b. Castleford, Idaho, Apr. 9, 1941; d. Ross and Norna (Scully) Stoner; m. Virgil Monroe Young, Dec. 20, 1964; 1 child, Susan Annette. BS in Elem. Edn., U. Idaho, 1965; MEd, Ea. Washington U., 1969; EdD, Utah State U., 1980. Cert. advanced elem. tchr., Idaho. Tchr. spl. edn. Coeur d'Alene (Idaho) Sch. Dist., 1965-66; tchr. elem. grades Coeur d' Aleue (Idaho) Sch. Dist., 1966-67, Boise (Idaho) Sch. Dist., 1967-88; assoc. prof. edn. Boise State U., 1988-93, prof., 1993—; dir. Alliance of Idaho Geographers/Nat. Geographic Soc., 1993—. Co-author: (resource book) The Story of Idaho Author's, 1977, The Story of Idaho Guide and Resource Book, 1993; author: The Utah Activity Book, 1980, Constructing Buildings, Bridges, and Minds, 1993; cons., contbr. (nat. edn. jour.) Learning, 1991—. Named Idaho Tchr. of Yr., State Dept. of Edn., Boise, 1983; invited to luncheon at White House, Pres. Ronald Reagan, Washington, 1983; Recipient Outstanding Young Educator award Boise Jaycees, 1983; profiled in Idaho Centennial pub., 1990; travel to Japan grantee Rocky Mountain Region Japan Project, 1990. Mem. ASCD, Nat. Coun. for Social Studies, Idaho Law Found., Alliance Idaho Geographers (state coord.). Office: Boise State U Dept Tchr Edn 1910 University Dr Boise ID 83725-0001

YOUNG, KATHERINE TRATEBAS, occupational health nurse; b. Valparaiso, Ind., Aug. 31, 1962; d. Russell Lewis and Edith May (Downs) Tratebas; m. Jeffrey Alan Young, Oct. 22, 1988 (div. July 1994). Diploma, St. Elizabeth's Hosp., 1984; BSN, Ind. U., 1987; MS in Occupational/Safety Mgmt., Ind. State U., 1996. RN Ind. Nurse II adult burn care Wishard Meml. HOsp., Indpls., 1984-88; occupational health nurse Meth. Occupational Health Ctrs., Indpls., 1988-92, Cmty Occupational Health Ctrs., Indpls., 1992-93; occupational health nurse Delta Faucet Co., Greensburg, Ind., 1993-95, mgr. corp. health and safety, 1995—. Named Medique Pharms. Unique Leader, State of Ind., 1994. Mem. Am. Assn. Occupational Health Nurses, Ind. Assn. Occupational Health Nurses (program chair 1988-92, corr. sec. 1990—, membership sec. 1990—), Ind. Acad. Occupational Health Nurses, Mid-Ind. Assn. Occupational Health Nursing (pres. 1995—). Home: 8823 Crestview Dr Indianapolis IN 46240-1934 Office: Delta Faucet Co 55 E 111th St Indianapolis IN 46280

YOUNG, KATHLEEN ANNE, environmental engineer; b. Pompton Plains, N.J., Apr. 5, 1966; d. William Vincent and Lois Mae (Hazel) G. BS in Mech. Engring., U. Rochester, 1988, MS in Biomed. Engring., 1989. Cert. in biomed. engring. Mech. technician U. Rochester (N.Y.) Lab. for Laser Energetics, 1986-87; teaching asst. dept. mech. engring. U. Rochester, 1988-89; nuclear/environ. engr. U.S. Dept. Energy, Schenectady, 1989-92; environ. engr. Dames & Moore Cons., Dallas, 1992-94; sr. project adminstr. Central & Southwest Svcs., Inc., 1994—; Job Fair rep. U.S. Dept. Energy, 1989. Folk music soloist St. Mary's Ch., Schenectady, 1985-91; mem. Big Bros./Big Sisters, Rochester, 1985; vol. Ellis Hosp., Schenectady, 1992. Rochester scholar, 1984-88. Mem. ASME (officer 1994—), Soc. Women Engrs. (activity chairperson 1986-87), Air & Water Mgmt. Assn. (officer 1994—), U. Rochester Alumni Assn. (com. mem. 1991—), Toastmasters (crime watch capt.). Republican. Roman Catholic. Home: 1907 Golden Trl Carrollton TX 75010-4521 Office: Central & SW Svc Inc 1616 Woodall Rodgers Fwy P O Box 660164 Dallas TX 75266-0164

YOUNG, KAY LYNN, dance educator, small business owner; b. Decatur, Tex., Aug. 7, 1955; d. Cecil V. and Evelyn Jane (Cohron) Y. BS in Dance Edn., U. North Tex., 1977, MS in Dance Edn., 1981. Freelance instr. Dallas, 1977—; owner, dir. Kay Lynn's Studio of Dance, Carrollton, Tex., 1982—; choreographer, dir. in field. Hostess (cable TV) Kay Lynn's Aerobics, 1985-87, Dallas Dance News, 1989—. Member Metrocrest C. of C., Carrollton, 1982-87, Farmers Branch C. of C., 1985—; mentor Carrollton Farmers Branch; key communicator Carrollton Farmers Branch Ind. Sch. Dist., 1982—. Named one of Outstanding Young Women of Am., 1983. Mem. AAUW (ednl. v.p. 1983-84, cultural v.p. 1987-88, membership v.p. 1991-93), Dallas Dance Coun. (social v.p. 1988-91, bd. dirs.), Nat. Assn. Dance and Affiliate Artists (sec., treas. 1988-91). Baptist. Home and Office: 3009 Lavita Ln Farmers Branch TX 75234

YOUNG, LAURA, dance educator, choreographer; b. Boston, Aug. 5, 1947; d. James Vincent and Adelaide Janet (Coupal) Y.; m. Anthony Charles Catanzaro, Sept. 26, 1970 (div. Nov. 1981); m. Christopher Edward Mehl, Aug. 23, 1987. Grad. high sch., Cohasset, Mass. Dancer Met. Opera Ballet, N.Y.C., 1971-73; dancer Boston Ballet Co., 1963-65, prin. dancer, 1965-71, 73-89, ballet mistress, 1989-91; guest tchr. Dance Tchrs. Club Boston, 1978-82, Dance Masters Assn., 1979, 90, 92, 93, Walnut Hill Sch., Natick, Mass., 1984-87, 90-91; asst. dir. Boston Ballet II, 1984-86, tchr., dir., 1986-96, dir. summer dance program, 1986-94; 1st hon. mem. Dance Masters Assn., Chpt. 5, 1992; mem. faculty Boston Conservatory, 1990-94; prin. Boston Ballet Sch., 1993—. Choreographer (ballets) Occasional Waltzes, 1984, Albinoni Suite, 1986, Champ Dances, 1987, A Place of Sound and Mind, 1988, Deadlock, 1989, Rumpelstiltskin, 1989. Recipient Leadership award Greater Boston C. of C., 1987; named Disting. Bostonian, Boston's 350th Jubilee Com., 1980. Mem. Am. Guild Mus. Artists, Dance Masters Am. (hon.). Office: Boston Ballet Co 19 Clarendon St Boston MA 02116-6107

YOUNG, LAURA CHILDREE, nursing administrator; b. Ozark, Ala., May 20, 1948; d. Lawrence Clifton and Evelyn Marie (Chapman) Childree; m. David Edward Young, Dec. 4, 1976; 1 child, John Mark. BSN, U. Ala., Birmingham, 1970; MSN, 1983. Lic. RN Ala., Tex., Ga. Charge nurse, inservice dir., house supr. Jackson Hosp. and Clinic, Montgomery, Ala., 1970-73, 74; team leader, inservice Mercy Hosp., Birmingham, Ala., 1973; ICU supr., dir. nursing Elmore County Hosp., Wetumpka, Ala., 1974-76; head nurse nursery St. Margaret's Hosp., Montgomery, Ala., 1976; critical care clinician N.E. Ala. Regional Med. Ctr., Anniston, Ala., 1977-78; head nurse CVSU, critical care clinician St. Margaret's Hosp., Montgomery, Ala., 1978-81; unit mgr., dir. med. nursing Brookwood Med. Ctr., Birmingham, Ala., 1981-83; pt. care coord., dir. critical care Bapt. Montclair Med. Ctr., Birmingham, Ala., 1983-85; asst. adminstr. Bay Med. Ctr., Panama City, Fla., 1985-88; v.p. nursing Harris Meth. Health Sys., Bedford, Tex., 1988-94; v.p. patient care svcs. Phoebe Putney Meml. Hosp., 1994—; adj. faculty U. Tex., Arlington, 1989-94, Auburn U., Montgomery, Ala., 1980-81; mem. adv. bd. for lic. cert., Montgomery, Ala., 1978-83; mem. adv. bd. Darton Coll., Ga. Southwestern Adv. Bd., Albany, Ga., 1994—, Albany State Coll., 1994—. Co-author: (with A. Hayne) Nursing Administration: From Concepts to Practice, 1988; contbr. articles to profl. jours. Bd. dirs. Circle T Girl Scouts Coun., Ft. Worth, Tex., 1991-93; mem. AIDS Coord. Coun. Tarrant County, Tex., 1992; grad. Leadership Colleyville, Tex., 1993. Named Outstanding Nurse Educator Ala. State Nurses Assn., 1981, Hall of Fame Robert E. Lee H.S., Montgomery, Ala., 1994, scholarship Nurses-Harris Meth. HEB, Bedford, Tex., 1990. Mem. ANA, AACN, Am. Orgn. of Nurse Execs., Am. Hosp. Assn., Nat. Assn. Women's Healthcare. Office: Phoebe Putney Meml Hosp 417 3rd Ave Albany GA 31703

YOUNG, LAURA ELIZABETH, artist; b. Glen Ridge, N.J., Apr. 1, 1941; d. Thomas Edward and Charlotte Elizabeth (Post) Y.; m. James Andrew Murphy, Jun. 15, 1963 (div. 1985); children: Kevin Thomas, Timothy James.; m. Thomas Raymond Aprile, May 20, 1995. BA, Skiomore Coll., 1963; MA, Montclair State Coll., 1978; MFA, Rutgers U., 1983. Cert. Fine Arts and English, K-12 tchr., N.J. Adj. faculty Fine Arts Dept. Kean Coll., Union, N.J., 1983-84, Montclair (N.J.) State Coll., 1983-92, Long Island U., Bklyn., 1994; cons., workshop leader The Lincoln Ctr. Inst., N.Y.C., 1983—; lectr. Mus. Modern Art, N.Y.C., 1990—; visual arts cons., workshop leader The Nashville Inst. for the Arts, 1992—, Lincoln Ctr. Inst., Columbia Tchrs. Coll., N.Y.C., 1994—. One person shows: Interior Space Design, N.Y.C., 1991, Manhattenville Coll., N.Y., 1993; two person show: Colgate U., Hamilton, N.Y., 1995. Grantee fellow in painting N.J. State Coun. on the Arts, Trenton, 1985; Intermedia Performance grantee Sch. Fine and Performing Arts, Montclair, 1992; Pollock Krasner Found. grantee, 1994. Democrat. Home: 127 Grand Avenue Ct Iowa City IA 52240

YOUNG, LOIS CATHERINE WILLIAMS, poet, former reading specialist; b. Wakeman, Ohio, Mar. 10, 1930; d. William McKinley and Leona Catherine (Woods) Williams; m. William Walton Young; children: Ralph, Catherine, William. BS, NYU, 1957; MS, Hofstra U., 1962, profl. diploma, 1967, EdD, 1981; M Pub. Adminstrn., Fla. Internat. U., 1988. Cert. tchr., sch. supr., N.Y., pub. mgmt., Fla. Tchr. Copiaque (N.Y.) Schs., 1957-59; research assoc. Columbia and Hofstra Univs., Hempstead, N.Y., 1964-69; tchr. Half Hollow Hills Pub. Schs., Dix Hills, N.Y., 1970-72; instr. Conn. Coll., New London, 1972-73; tchr., supr., reading coordinator Hempstead (N.Y.) Pub. Schs., 1975-85; cons. South African project AID Fla. Meml. Coll., Miami, Fla., 1987-88; clinician Hofstra U., Hempstead, 1962-64; tchr. trainer Amityville (N.Y.) Pub. Schs., 1965, Hofstra Univ., 1982; key speaker Internat. Reading Assn., N.Y., Calif., Caribbean Islands, 1982-86. Author numerous poems. Sec. Nassau County (N.Y.) chpt. Jack and Jill of Am., 1960-62; pres. PTA, Uniondale, N.Y., 1962-68; active Boy Scouts Am., Uniondale, N.Y., 1963-65; bd. dirs. Miami chpt. UN Assn./USA, 1987-92, 1st v.p. 1989-91, Broward Fort Lauderdale chpt., 1993—; active multilateral project, 1987-90; contbr. Procs. South African Project, 1987. Recipient Lifetime Membership award PTA, 1964, rsch. grant N.Y. State Fed. Programs, 1978, Laurel Wreath award Doctoral Assn. of N.Y. Educators, 1982, Cert. of award UN Assn./USA, 1987, 88, Outstanding Achievement award Fla. Internat. U., 1988, Golden Poet award World of Poetry, 1990, 91; fellow Fla. Internat. U., 1987. Mem. Internat. Soc. Poets (life, lifetime adv. panel 1993—, award, Nat. Libr. of Poetry award 1994, 95, Poetry Today 1996), Fla. Internat. U. Alumni Assn., NYU Alumni Assn. (bd. dirs. 1983-90, 2d v.p. 1986-87), Hofstra U. Alumni Assn., Tuskegee Airmen, Inc., Weston (Fla.) Toastmasters Club (charter), Toastmasters Internat., Kappa Delta Pi, Alpha Kappa Alpha, Theta Iota Omega (global affairs com. 1984-86), Phi Delta Kappa. Home: 7187 Crystal Lake Dr W Palm Beach FL 33411

YOUNG, LORETTA ANN, accountant; b. Reading, Pa., Dec. 2, 1962; d. Milton and Delois Jean (Ridley) Y. BS, Towson State U., 1985. CPA. Auditor Irving Burton Assocs., Inc., Washington, 1984-88; tax technician Gen. Bus. Svcs., Germantown, Md., 1989; auditor Montgomery County Govt., Rockville, Md., 1989-90; dir. membership devel. Nat. Forum for Black Pub. Adminstrs., Washington, 1990-91; sr. acct.-analyst Cox & Assocs. CPAs, P.C., Hyattsville, Md., 1992; mgr. ops. LKA Computer Cons., Inc., Hyattsville, 1992-94; sr. auditor Office Specialists, Inc., Washington, 1994—. Mem. NAFE, Mid Atlantic Notary Assn. Home: 763 Quince Orchard Blvd Apt 24 Gaithersburg MD 20878-1661 Office: 1025 Connecticut Ave NW Ste 419 Washington DC 20036-5405

YOUNG, LUCY CLEAVER, physician; b. Wheeling, W.Va., Aug. 8, 1943. B.S. in Chemistry, Wheaton Coll. (Ill.), 1965; M.D., Ohio State U., 1969. Diplomate Am. Bd. Family Practice, Bd. of Ins. Medicine. Rotating intern Riverside Meth. Hosp., Columbus, Ohio, 1969-70; resident Trumbull Meml. Hosp., Warren, Ohio, 1970-71; practice medicine specializing in family practice, West Chicago, Ill., 1971-73, Paw Paw and Mendota, Ill., 1973-78; co-founder and med. dir. Wholistic Health Ctr. of Mendota, 1976-78; asst. med. dir. Met. Life Ins. Co., Gt. Lakes Head Office, Aurora, Ill., 1979-80; med. dir. Commonwealth Life Ins. Co., Louisville, 1980-85; assoc. prof. U. Ill. Abraham Lincoln Sch. Medicine, 1976-79; faculty monitor MacNeal Meml. Hosp. Family Practice Ctr. (Ill.), 1979-80; faculty preceptor U. Louisville Family Practice Dept., 1981-85; Locum Tenens Family Practice for Kron Med. Corp. of Chapel Hill, N.C., 1986-89; physician Red Bird Mission & Med. Ctr., Beverly, Ky., 1989-90; family practice floater Ochsner Clinic satellites, New Orleans, 1990—; clin. faculty preceptor La. State U. Sch. Medicine, 1992—; mem. staffs Central DuPage Hosp., Winfield, Ill., 1971-73, Mendota Community Hosp., 1973-80. Vol. Red Bird Med. Ctr., 1985—. Fellow Am. Acad. Family Practice; mem. Christian Med. and Dental Soc. (del. to House 1995—). Home: PO Box 0730 Madisonville LA 70447-0730 Office: Ochsner Clinic 1514 Jefferson Hwy New Orleans LA 70121-2429

YOUNG, MARGARET ALETHA MCMULLEN (MRS. HERBERT WILSON YOUNG), social worker; b. Vossburg, Miss., June 13, 1916; d. Grady Garland and Virgie Aletha (Moore) McMullen; BA cum laude, Columbia Bible Coll., 1949; grad. Massey Bus. Coll., 1958; MSW, Fla. State U., 1965; postgrad. Jacksonville U., 1961-62, Tulane U., 1967; m. Herbert Wilson Young, Aug. 19, 1959. Dir. Christian edn. Eau Claire Presbyn. Ch., Columbia, S.C., 1946-51; tchr. Massey Bus. Coll., Jacksonville, Fla., 1954-57, office mgr., 1957-59; social worker, unit supr. Fla. div. Family Svcs., St. Petersburg, 1960-66, dist. casework supr., 1966-71; social worker, project supr., program supr. Project Playpen, Inc., 1971-81, pres. bd., 1982-83, cons., 1986-89; pvt. practice family counselor, 1982—; mem. coun. Child Devel. Ctr., 1983-89; mem. transitional housing com., Religious Community Svcs., 1984-90. Mem. Acad. Cert. Social Workers, Nat. Assn. Social Workers (pres. Tampa Bay chpt. 1973-74), Fla. Assn. for Health and Social Services (pres. chpt. 1971), Nature Conservancy, Eta Beta Rho. Democrat. Presbyn. Rotary Ann (pres. 1970-71). Home: Presbyterian Home CMR 13 201 W 9th North St Summerville SC 29483-6721

YOUNG, MARGARET BUCKNER, civic worker, author; b. Campbellsville, Ky.; d. Frank W. and Eva (Carter) Buckner; m. Whitney M. Young, Jr., Jan. 2, 1944 (dec. Mar. 1971); children: Marcia Elaine, Lauren Lee. BA, Ky. State Coll., 1942, MA, U. Minn., 1946. Instr. Ky. State Coll., 1942-44; instr. edn. and psychology Spelman Coll., Atlanta, 1957-60; dir. emeritus N.Y. Life Ins. Co.; alt. del. UN Gen. Assembly, 1973. Mem. pub. policy com. Advt. Coun. Trustee emerita Lincoln Ctr. for Performing Arts; chmn. Whitney M. Young, Jr. Meml. Found., 1971-92; trustee Met. Mus. Art, 1976-90; bd. govs. UN Assn., 1975-82; bd. visitors U.S. Mil. Acad., 1978-80; dir. Philip Morris Cos., 1972-91. Author: The First Book of American Negroes, 1966, The Picture Life of Martin Luther King, Jr., 1968, The Picture Life of Ralph J. Bunche, 1968, Black American Leaders-Watts, 1969, The Picture Life of Thurgood Marshall, 1970, pub. affairs pamphlet.

YOUNG, MARGARET CHONG, elementary education educator; b. Honolulu, May 8, 1924; d. Henry Hon Chin and Daisy Kyau (Tong) Chong; m. Alfred Y.K. Young, Feb. 21, 1948; children: Robert S.W., Richard S.K., Linda S.K. EdB, 5th yr. cert., U. Hawaii, 1945. Cert. tchr., Hawaii. Tchr. Waipahu (Hawaii) Elem. Sch., Manoa Housing Sch., Hawaii Dept. Edn., Honolulu, Pauoa Elem. Sch., Honolulu. Author: And They Also Came, History of Chinese Christian Association, Hawaii's People From China; contbr. numerous articles to profl. jours. Ch. sch. tchr., supt. United Ch. Christ-Judd St. Grantee San Francisco State Coll. Mem. NEA, Hawaii State Tchrs. Assn., Hawaii Congress of Parents and Tchrs. (hon. life mem.), Kappa Kappa Iota (Disting. Educator award 1986-87), Delta Kappa Gamma (internat.).

YOUNG, MARILYN RAE, former school system adminstrative secretary, mayor; b. Muskegon, Mich., Dec. 29, 1934; d. Albert Henry Cribley and Mildred Ida (Johnson) Raby; m. Peter John Young, May 21, 1955; children: Pamela Lynn Young-Walker, Lane Allen. Grad. high sch., Calumet City, Ill., 1952. Dep. pub. fiduciary Yuma County, Ariz., 1979-83; adminstrv. sec. Yuma Sch. Dist. One, 1983-95; councilman City of Yuma, 1990-93, mayor, 1993—. Pres. bd. dirs. Behavioral Health Svcs. of Yuma, 1979-90; vice chmn. Yuma Planning and Zoning Commn., 1985-89; v.p. bd. dirs. Children's Village, Yuma, 1983-89; lay leader Trinity United Meth. Ch., 1986—; grad. Yuma Leadership Inc., 1985, treas. bd. dirs., 1986-89; participant Ariz. Women's Town Hall, 1989, various Yuma County Town Halls, 1987-93; adv. bd. mem. Friends of KAWC; chmn. Yuma Pub. Safety Police Bd., 1990—, Yuma Fire Pub. Safety Bd., 1990—, Yuma Youth Leadership Com., 1991-95; mem. allocation panel United Way, 1991-93; charter mem. Friends of Roxaboxen; active H.S. Ad Hoc Com., 1991—; exec. bd. mem. Yuma Met. Planning Orgn., 1990—, Western Ariz. Coun. of Govts., 1990—; corp. bd. dirs. Greater Yuma Econ. Devel., 1990-95; hon. chmn. Yuma County San Luis Rio Colo. Commn., 1990—; mem. Nat. League of Cities FAIR Com., 1990—, Binational Border Health Task Force, 1990—, resolution com. League of Ariz. Cities and Towns, 1990—, mem. com. U.S. Conf. of Mayors, 1990—. Mem. Yuma County C. of C. (mem. mil. affairs com. 1988-90). Home: 1288 W 18th St Yuma AZ 85364-5313 Office: City of Yuma 180 W 1st St Yuma AZ 85364-1407

YOUNG, MARY ELIZABETH, history educator; b. Utica, N.Y., Dec. 16, 1929; d. Clarence Whitford and Mary Tippit Y. B.A., Oberlin Coll., 1950; Ph.D. (Robert Shalkenbach Found. grantee, Ezra Cornell fellow), Cornell U., 1955. Instr. dept. history Ohio State U., Columbus, 1955-58; asst. prof. Ohio State U., 1958-63, assoc. prof., 1963-69, prof., 1969-73; prof. history U. Rochester, N.Y., 1973—; cons. in field. Author: Redskins, Ruffleshirts, and Rednecks: Indian Allotments in Alabama and Mississippi, 1830-1860, 1961; co-editor, contbr.: The Frontier in Americal Development: Essays in Honor of Paul Wallace Gates, 1969. Recipient Pelzer award Miss. Valley Hist. Assn., 1955, Award Am. Studies Assn., 1982, Ray A. Billington award, 1982; Social Sci. Research Council grantee, 1968-69. Mem. Am. Hist. Assn., Orgn. Am. Historians, Am. Studies Assn., Am. Soc. Ethnic History, Soc. for Historians of the Early Am. Republic, Am. Antiquarian Soc. Home: 2230 Clover St Rochester NY 14618-4124 Office: U Rochester Dept History Rochester NY 14627

YOUNG, MICHELLE DIANE, editor; b. Norman, Okla., Dec. 18, 1966; d. Gerald Wayne Wuest and Diane Lee (Osborn) Giddings; m. Derek Allen Young, June 3, 1990. AA in Sociology and Polit. Sci., Southwestern U., 1989; MEd in Bilingual Spl. Edn., U. Tex., 1993, postgrad., 1993—. Legal aide, librarian J. Neill Wilkerson, Atty., Georgetown, Tex., 1983-89; tchr. English Surat Thani (Thailand) Poly. Coll., 1990-91; rsch. asst. bilingual spl. edn.program U. Tex., Austin, 1991-93, tchg. asst. dept. spl. edn., 1993, acad. asst. continuing edn., 1994; rsch. dir. Effective Border Schs. R & D Inst., Austin and other cities, 1994-95; instr. English as ESL, St. Edward's U., Austin, 1992; mng. editor Internat. Jour. Qualitative Studies in Edn., Austin, 1995-96; proposal reviewer Am. Assn. Sch. Prins., Denver, 1995; mem. adv. bd. grad. adv. com., Austin, 1994-95. Capt. USNG, 1986-96. Mem. Am. Edn. Rsch. Assn. (divsn. A rep.), Women in Edn. (chairwoman), Ednl. Policy Students Assn. (pres.), Ednl. Aminstrn. Students Assn. (co-pres.), Soc. Study of Symbolic Interaction, Soc. Study Edn. Home: 1624 W 6th St Apt L Austin TX 78703 Office: U Tex Coll Edn SZB 310 Austin TX 78712-1291

YOUNG, OLIVIA KNOWLES, retired librarian; b. Benton, Ark., Sept. 3, 1922; d. Wesley Taylor and Med Belle (Crawford) Knowles; m. Calvin B. Young, Oct. 6, 1951; 1 child, Brigham Taylor. BA, Tenn. Tech. U., 1942; BS in Libr. Sci., George Peabody Coll. for Tchrs., 1946. Head periodicals and documents dept. Peabody Coll. Library, Nashville, 1946-49; area librarian U.S. Army, Austria, 1949-51; librarian Cairo Pub. Library, Ga., 1955-57, Caney Fork Regional Library, Sparta, Tenn., 1957-58; chief librarian Fort Stewart Ft. Stewart (Ga.) U.S. Army, 1959-63; dir. Watauga Regional Library, Johnson City, Tenn., 1963-70; dir. devel. and extension Tenn. State Library and Archives, Nashville, 1971-82, state librarian and archivist, 1982-85; ret., 1985. Mem. Tenn. Library Assn. (treas. 1970, Honor award 1985), Southeastern Library Assn., ALA, Boone Tree Library Assn. (pres. 1968). Methodist. Club: Altrusa (sec. 1967). Home: PO Box 160444 San Antonio TX 78280-2644

YOUNG, PAULA B., home health nurse, administrator; b. Oakland City, Ind., Mar. 15, 1956; d. Clemmer P. and Wilma E. (McKinney) Beasley; m. L. Gregory Young, May 29, 1976; children: Sara E., Emily S. BSN, U. Evansville, 1979. RN, Ind. ICU staff RN Welborn Bapt. Hosp., Evansville, Ind., 1979-81; staff RN ARC, Evansville, Ind., 1983-85; asst. dir. nursing Cristopher East Living Ctr., Evansville, Ind., 1985-87; staff RN Wirth Osteo. Hosp., Oakland City, 1988-89, Ptnrs. Home Health, Evansville, 1990-91, Riverfront Home Health, Vincennes, 1991-93; adminstr., owner, pres., CEO New Horizons Home Health, Inc., Boonville, Ind., 1993—, also bd. dirs., mem. adv. com., 1993—. Mem. Ind. Assn. Home Care (voting mem., quality improvement com. 1994-95, legis. com. 1995—), Ind. Home Care Network (bd. dirs.). Office: New Horizons Home Health Inc 1120 S 8th St Boonville IN 47660

YOUNG, REBECCA MARY CONRAD, state legislator; b. Clairton, Pa., Feb. 28, 1934; d. Walter Emerson and Harriet Averill (Colcord) Conrad; m. Merwin Crawford Young, Aug. 17, 1957; children: Eve, Louise, Estelle, Emily. BA, U. Mich., 1955; MA in Teaching, Harvard U., 1963; JD, U. Wis., 1983. Bar: Wis. 1983. Commr. State Hwy. Commn., Madison, Wis., 1974-76; dep. sec. Wis. Dept. of Adminstrn., Madison, 1976-77; assoc. Wadsack, Julian & Lawton, Madison, 1983-84; elected rep. Wis. State Assembly, Madison, 1985—. Translator: Katanga Secession, 1966. Supr. Dane County Bd., Madison, 1970-74; mem. Madison Sch. Bd., 1979-85. Recipient Wis. Register Deeds Assn. Cert. of Appreciation for Leadership, 1995, Wis. NOW Feminist of Yr. award, 1996. Mem. LWV. Democrat. Home: 639 Crandall St Madison WI 53711-1836 Office: State Legislature-Assembly PO Box 8953 Madison WI 53708-8953

YOUNG, RUTH WHITELAW, educator, researcher; b. Durban, Natal, South Africa, June 10, 1966; came to US, 1987; d. David Peter and Adrienne Myrna (Roux) W.; m. Luke Titus Young, July 3, 1993. BA in Music Edn., U. Witwaters and Johannesburg, South Africa, 1987; MEd, Olivet Nazarene U., 1989; PhD, U. Ill., 1995. Cert. tchr., South Africa. Piano tchr. pvt. practice Johannesburg, South Africa and Kankakee, Ill., 1985-90; instr. English dept. Olivet Nazarene U., Kankakee, Ill., 1989-90; supr. tchg. techniques lab. U. Ill., Champaign, Ill., 1990-91; tchg. asst. English dept. U. Ill., Champaign, 1991-93, instr. Summer bridge program, 1992, asst. researcher Ctr. Instrnl. Rsch. and Curriculum Evaluation, 1992; writing instr.parallel studies Austin (Tex.) C. C., 1994-95. Contbr. article to profl. jour. Evaluator Laguna Gloria Art Mus., Austin, 1994-95, vol. intern, docent, 1993-95. Mem. Am. Ednl. Rsch. Assn., Assn. Supervision and Curriculum Devel., Nat. Art Edn. Assn. Home: 1211 Paint Brush Tr Cedar Park TX 78613

YOUNG, SHERRY ANN, medical and surgical nurse; b. Louisville, Ky., Aug. 6, 1954; d. Noble Robert and Bonnie Mae (Turner) Shadowens; m. Otto Marion Young, Jr., Nov. 21, 1970; children: Stephanie Rachel, Jonathon Paul. Diploma, Jefferson Vocat. Sch., 1981; ADN, Jefferson C.C., 1993. Med. asst. Drs. Moore & Petty, Louisville, 1981-91; med.-surg. nurse Audubon Regional Med. Ctr., Louisville, 1991—; dialysis nurse Biomedical Applications of Louisville, 1996—. Home: 1025 Reasor Ave Louisville KY 40217-1503 Office: Audubon Regional Med Ctr One Audubon Plaza Dr Louisville KY 40217

YOUNG, SHIRLEY, automotive industry executive, strategic marketing consultant; b. Shanghai, China, May 25, 1935; d. Clarence and Juliana (Koo) Y.; divorced; children: David W., William C., Douglas H.L. Hsieh. B.A. in Econs., Wellesley Coll., 1955; postgrad., NYU, 1956-57; Dr. Letters (hon.), Russell Sage Coll., 1982. Rsch. assoc. Alfred Politz Rsch., N.Y.C., 1955-57; research mgr. Hudson Paper Corp., N.Y.C., 1957-59; rsch. assoc. Grey Advt. Inc., N.Y.C., 1959-69, dir. mktg. and rsch., 1969-71, exec. v.p., mem. agy. policy com., 1971-79, exec. v.p. mktg., planning and strategy devel., 1980-83; pres. Grey Strategic Mktg. Inc., N.Y.C., 1983-88, chmn., 1988-90; v.p. consumer market devel. Gen. Motors, Detroit, 1988-96, v.p. strategic devel. China, 1996—; mem. bus. adv. coun. U.S. State Dept. Aid; bd. dirs. Promus Corp., Bell Atlantic, Phila.; vice chmn. nominating com. N.Y. Stock Exch., 1980-81; cons., bd. dirs. dayton Hudson Corp., 1987—. Chmn. Com. 100, Chinese Am. Leadership Resource; bd. dirs. United Way of Tri-State, N.Y.C., 1981, Catalyst, 1980-86, Am. Pub. Radio, Detroit Symphony Orch., Interlochen Corp. Coun.; trustee Founders Soc. of Detroit Inst. Art, Wellesley Coll.; mem. Com. of 200; bd. dirs. Assocs. Harvard Bus. Sch.; bd. dirs. Jr. Achievement, Inc., 1993—; mem. bus. adv. coun. U.S. AID; trustee Wellesley Coll.; mem. Citizen's Adv. Coun. U. Mich., Dearborn; bd. dirs. WTVS/Channel 56, Detroit Symphony Orch. Named Advt. Woman of Yr., Am. Advt. Fedn., 1974, Woman of Achievement, Am. Parkinson Disease Assn., 1980, Outstanding Corp. Dir., Catalyst, 1981; recipient WEAL Award in Advt., 1982, Alumna Achievement award Wellesley Coll., 1986, Alumna of Yr. award Chinese Am. Planning Coun., 1987. Mem. Advt. Research Found., Am. Assn. Advt. Agencies, Am. Mktg. Assn., Phi Beta Kappa. Office: GM Corp GM Bldg 14-117 3044 W Grand Blvd Detroit MI 48202-3091*

YOUNG, SONIA WINER, public relations director, educator; b. Chattanooga, Tenn., Aug. 20, 1934; d. Meyer D. and Rose (Demby) Winer; m. Melvin A. Young, Feb. 24, 1957; 1 child, Melanie Anne. BA, Sophie Newcomb Coll., 1956; M in Ednl. Psychology, U. Tenn.-Chattanooga, 1966. Cert. speech and hearing specialist Am. Speech and Hearing Assn. Speech therapist Chattanooga-Hamilton County Speech and Hearing Ctr., 1961-66, ednl. psychology, 1966-78; staff psychologist Chattanooga Testing and Counseling Services, 1978-80; ins. rep. Mut. Benefit Life Ins. Co., Chattanooga, 1980-84; columnist Chattanooga Times, 1982-84; cmty. affairs reporter Sta. WRCB-TV, Chattanooga, 1983-84; pub. relations and promotions dir. Purple Ladies, Inc., Chattanooga, 1984—; cons. psychology Ga. Dept. Human Resources, also Cheerhaven Sch., Dalton, 1970-78; adj. prof. psychology U. Tenn.-Chattanooga, 1971-80, adj. prof. dept. theatre and speech, 1988—; pres. Speak Out; bd. dirs. M. Young Comm., Vol. Ctr., 1995—, Arthritis Found., 1995—; spl. projects dir. Chattanooga State Technical C.C., 1995—. Contbg. editor Chattanooga Life and Leisure Mag. Pres. Chattanooga Opera Guild, 1973-74, Chattanooga Opera Assn., 1979-80; bd. dirs., sec. Chattanooga-Hamilton County Bicentennial Libr., 1977-79; pres. Little Theatre of Chattanooga, 1984-90, bd. dirs., 1974—; v.p. Girls Club, Chattanooga, 1979-80; bd. dirs. March of Dimes, 1988, Chattanooga Symphony Guild, Mizpah Congregation, Chattanooga Area Literacy Council, Chattanooga Cares, 1993—, Tourist Devel. Agy., 1990—; mem. alumni council U. Tenn.-Chattanooga; mem. selection com. Leadership Chattanooga, 1984-86; sec. Allied Arts Greater Chattanooga, 1978-80, residential campaign chmn., 1985; bd. dirs. Chattanooga Ctr. for the Dance, Ptnrs. for Acad. Excellence, 1987—, Chattanooga Mental Health Assn., 1988; chmn. March of Dimes Mother's March, 1988, One of a Kind-the Arts Against AIDS-Chattanooga Cares, 1993, 94; co-chair Am. Heart Assn. Gala, 1994, chmn., 1995; chair Little Theatre Capital Campaign, 1995. Recipient Disting. Citizens award City of Chattanooga, 1975, Steakley award Little Theatre Chattanooga, 1982, Pres. award, 1991, 92, Vol. of Yr., 1995, Woman of Distinction award Am. Lung Assn., 1995, Vol. of Yr. award, 1995, Vol. of Yr. award Chattanooga Cares, 1995. Mem. Phi Beta Kappa (pres. Chattanooga chpt. 1978-79). Jewish. Home: 1025 River Hills Cir Chattanooga TN 37415-5611 Office: U Tenn Theatre & Speech Dept 615 Mccallie Ave Chattanooga TN 37403-2504

YOUNG, TERI ANN BUTLER, pharmacist; b. Littlefield, Tex., Aug. 22, 1958; d. Doyle Wayne and Bettie May (Lair) Butler; m. James Oren Young, Aug. 1, 1981; children: Andrew Wayne, Aaron Lee. BS in Pharmacy, Southwestern Okla. State U., 1981. Staff pharmacist St. Mary of Plains Hosp., Lubbock, Tex., 1981-84; staff pharmacist West Tex. Hosp., Lubbock, 1984-85, asst. dir. pharmacy, 1985-86; pharmacist cons. for nursing homes Billy D. Davis & Assocs., Lubbock, 1986—; relief pharmacist Prescription Lab., Med. Pharmacy and Foster Infusion Care, Lubbock, 1987-89; staff pharmacist Univ. Med. Ctr., 1990—, diabetic teaching pharmacist, 1995—; relief pharmacist West Tex. Hosp., 1986-91, Highland Hosp., 1990—, Med. Infusion Technology, 1992—. Mem. Lubbock Area Soc. of Hosp. Pharmacists (sec., treas. 1982-83), Lubbock Area Pharm. Assn., West Tex. Pharm. Assn., Am. Soc. Hosp. Pharmacists, Pilot Internat., Lubbock Genealogical Soc. Republican. Baptist. Lodge: Eastern Star. Home: 7410 Toledo Ave Lubbock TX 79424-2214 Office: Univ Med Ctr 602 Indiana Ave Lubbock TX 79415-3364

YOUNG, TOMMIE MORTON, social psychology educator, writer; b. Nashville. BA cum laude, Tenn. State U., 1951; MLS, George Peabody Coll. for Tchrs., 1955; PhD, Duke U., 1977; postgrad. U. Okla., 1967, U. Nebr., 1968. Coord., Young Adult Program, Lucy Thurman br. YWCA, 1951-52; instr. edn. Tenn. State U., Nashville, 1956-59; instr., coord. media program Prairie View Coll. (Tex.), 1959-61; asst. prof. edn., assoc. prof. English, dir. IMC Ctr., U. Ark.-Pine Bluff, 1965-69; asst. prof. English and edn., dir. learning lab., N.C. Central U., Durham, 1969-74; prof., dir./chairperson libr. media svcs. and dept. ednl. media, dir. Afro-Am. Family Project, N.C. Agrl. and Tech. State U., Greensboro, 1975—; adj. prof. langs., lit. and philosophy, dir. schs. history project Tenn. State U., Nashville, 1994—; dir. workshops, grants; pres., dir. Ednl. Cons. Svcs. Author: Afro American Genealogy Sourcebook, 1987, Oral Histories of Former All-Black Public Schools, 1991, After School Programs for At-Risk Youth and Their Families, 1994, Sable Scenes, 1996; contbr. poem to Poetry: American Heritage; contbr. rsch. papers, articles to profl. jours. Nat. chmn. Com. to Re-Elect the Pres.; past sec. Fedn. Colored Women's Clubs; bd. dirs. Southwestern div. ARC, Nashville area, 1994—, dir. Volun-Teens; chairperson learning resources com. Task Force Durham Day Care Assn.; bd. dirs., chairperson schs. div. Durham County Unit Am. Cancer Soc.; past mem. adv. bd., bd. dirs. YMCA, Atlanta; chair Guilford County Commn. on Needs of Children; bd. advisors NIH, N.C. Coun. of the Arts; mem. Guilford County Involvement Coun.; chmn. N.C. adv. com. U.S. Civil Rights Com.; mem. exec. planning com. Greensboro. Recipient awards ARC, 1968, 73, NAACP, 1973, HEW, 1978, U.S. Commn. on Civil Rights, 1982; named Disting. Alumni Tenn. State U., 1994. Mem. AAUW (honor award 1983, pres. Greensboro br., chairperson internat. rels. com.), ALA (divsn. coll. and rsch. librs., past chair), NAACP (life, 1st v.p. Durham br., exec. bd. Greensboro br., dir. parent edn./child advocacy program, Woman of Yr. 1992), NEA, Assn. Childhood Ednl. Internat., Comparative and Internat. Edn. Assn., Archives Assoc., Internat. Platform Assn., Nat. Hist. Soc., Greensboro Jr. League (community adv. bd. 1991—), African Am. Gen. Soc. Tenn. (founder 1994), Zeta Phi Beta (chairperson polit. action com. eastern region, nat. grammateus, Polit. and Civic Svc. award 1974, Outstanding Social-Polit. Svc. award 1982, Woman of Yr. 1977), Commn. on Status of Women (Woman of Achievement 1991), Phi Kappa Phi (Disting. State U. Alumni award 1994, Disting Alumni NAFEO award, 1995, Carl Rowan-Oprah Winfrey lectr. Tenn. State U., 1995, Excellence in Journalism award SPJ, 1995, info. officer 1996). Home: PO Box 17684 Nashville TN 37217-0684

YOUNGBLOOD, DEBORAH S., lawyer; b. Fairview, Okla., July 29, 1954; d. G. Dean and Beatrice J. (Hiebert) White. BS with honors, Okla. State U., 1976, MA with honors, 1979; JD cum laude, Boston Coll. Law Sch., 1991; MPH in Health Care Mgmt., Harvard U., 1992. Judicial law clk. Colo. Supreme Ct., 1992-94; assoc. atty. Patton Boggs, L.L.P., 1994—. Mem. Colo. Bar Assn., N.Mex. Bar Assn., Minoru Yasui Am. Inns of Ct. (exec. coun. 1995—), Phi Kappa Phi.

YOUNGBLOOD, ELAINE MICHELE, lawyer; b. Schenectady, N.Y., Jan. 9, 1944; d. Roy W. and Mary Louise (Read) Ortoleva; m. William Gerald Youngblood, Feb. 14, 1970; children: Flagg Khristian, Megan Michele. BA, Wake Forest Coll., 1965; JD, Albany Law Sch., 1969. Bar: Tex. 1970, U.S. Dist. Ct. (no. dist.) Tex. 1971, U.S. Dist. Ct. (so. dist.) Tex. 1972, Tenn. 1978, U.S. Dist. Ct. (mid. dist.) Tenn. 1978. Assoc. Fanning & Harper,

Dallas, 1969, Crocker & Murphy, Dallas, 1970-71, McClure & Burch, Houston, 1972-75, Brown, Bradshaw & Plummer, Houston, 1975-76; ptnr. Seligmann & Youngblood, Nashville, 1977-88; atty. Law Offices of Elaine M. Youngblood, Nashville, 1988-94; of counsel Ortale, Kelley Herbert & Crawford, 1994—. Mem. Com. for Women in Govt., Dallas, 1969-71, Law Day com. of Dallas Bar Assn., 1970-71. Mem. ABA, Tex. Bar Assn., Tenn. Bar Assn., Nashville Bar Assn. (fee dispute com. 1990—, vice chmn. 1996, CLE com. 1996), Tenn. Trial Lawyers Assn., Nat. Assn. Women Lawyers, Phi Beta Pi. Republican. Episcopalian. Club: Cable of Nashville (charter). Address: PO Box 198985 200 Fourth Ave N Fl 3 Noel Pl Nashville TN 37219-8985

YOUNGBLOOD, PEGGY ELAINE, organist; b. New Orleans, May 24, 1922; d. Henry Otto and Jessie Edna (Pierce) Hearn; m. Stephen Gilbert Youngblood, 1941 (dec. 1996); 1 child, Mark. Student, Southwestern La. Coll., 1945; BS, Mary Washington Coll., Fredericksburg, Va., 1945-46; postgrad., Southwestern Sem., Ft. Worth, 1951. Tchr. pub. schs., Natchitoches, La., 1946-47, Cloutierville and Ghoram, La., 1952-53; profl. accompanist Northwestern La. U., Natchitoches, 1948-49, Southwestern Sem. Music Sch., 1955-61; choir dir. Poplar Springs Drive Bapt. Ch., Meridian, Miss., 1950-51; accompanist Oglethorpe U., Atlanta, 1963-65, Emory U., Atlanta; accompanist, soloist 2d Ponce de Leon Bapt. Ch., Atlanta, 1961-89; organist Northside Park Bapt. Ch., Atlanta, 1989—. Mem. Robert Shaw Chorus Repertory Opera Co., Atlanta, 1989—. Home: 3428 Regalwoods Dr Atlanta GA 30340 Office: Northside Park Bapt Ch 1877 Howell Mill Rd Atlanta GA 30318

YOUNGER, JUDITH TESS, lawyer, educator; b. N.Y.C., Dec. 20, 1933; d. Sidney and Kate (Greenbaum) Weintraub; m. Irving Younger, Jan. 21, 1955; children: Rebecca, Abigail M. B.S., Cornell U., 1954; J.D., NYU, 1958; LL.D. (hon.), Hofstra U., 1974. Bar: N.Y. 1958, U.S. Supreme Ct 1962, D.C. 1983, Minn. 1985. Law clk. to judge U.S. Dist. Ct., 1958-60; asso. firm Chadbourne, Parke, Whiteside & Wolff, N.Y.C., 1960-62; mem. firm Younger and Younger, and (successors), 1962-67; adj. asst. prof. N.Y. U. Sch. Law, 1967-69; asst. atty. gen. State of N.Y., 1969-70; assoc. prof. Hofstra U. Sch. Law, 1970-72, prof., assoc. dean, 1972-74; dean, prof. Syracuse Coll. Law, 1974-75; dep. dean, prof. law Cornell Law Sch., 1975-78, prof. law, 1975-85; vis. prof. U. Minn. Law Sch., Mpls., 1984-85, prof., 1985—; of counsel Popham, Haik, Schnobrich & Kaufman, Ltd., Mpls., 1989-95; cons. NOW, 1972-74, Suffolk County for Revision of Its Real Property Tax Act, 1972-73; mem. N.Y. Gov.'s Panel To Screen Candidates of Ct. of Claims Judges, 1973-74; mem. Minn. Lawyers' Profl. Responsibility Bd., 1991-93. Contbr. articles to profl. jours. Trustee Cornell U., 1973-78. Mem. ABA (council legal edn. 1975-79), Am. Law Inst. (adv. restatement property 1982-84), AAUP (v.p. Cornell U. chpt. 1978-79), N.Y. State Bar Assn., Assn. of Bar of City of N.Y., Minn. Bar Assn. Home: 3520 W Calhoun Pky Minneapolis MN 55416-4657 Office: U Minn Law Sch Minneapolis MN 55455

YOUNG LIVELY, SANDRA LEE, nurse; b. Rockport, Ind., Dec. 31, 1943; d. William Cody and Flora Juanita (Carver) Thorpe; m. Kenneth Leon Doom, May 4, 1962 (div. 1975); children: Patricia, Anita, Elizabeth, Melissa, Kenny. AS, Vincennes U., 1979, student, U. So. Ind., 1987—. Nursing aide, nurse Forest Del Nursing Home, Princeton, Ind., 1975-80; charge nurse Welborn Bapt. Hosp., Evansville, Ind., 1979-80, 82-83; staff nurse Longview Regional Hosp., Tex., 1980-82; dir. home health Roy H. Laird Meml. Hosp., Kilgore, Tex., 1984-86; med. post-coronary nurse Mercy Hosp., Owensboro, Ky., 1987, Dept. of Corrections charge nurse, Branchville Tng. Ctr., Tell City, Ind, 1987-90; charge nurse dept. mental health Evansville (Ind.) State Hosp., 1990—; staff nurse, asst. dir. Leisure Lodge Home Health, Overton, Tex., 1983-84. Grantee Roy H. Laird Meml. Hosp., 1986. Mem. NAFE, Menniger Found., Vincennes U. Alumni Assn., Internat. Platform Assn. Avocations: writing, research, cake decorating, house plants. Home: 614 Gilmer Rd Apt 251 Longview TX 75604 Office: Evansville State Hosp 3400 Lincoln Ave Evansville IN 47714-0147

YOUNKER, NANCY ELAINE, elementary school educator; b. Chambersburg, Pa., Oct. 17, 1948; d. Bruce O. and A. Virginia (Shutt) Bivens; m. Carl Thurman Younker, Nov. 22, 1969; children: Susan R. Younker, Carri L. BS, Shippensburg U., 1969, MEd, 1974. Elem. sch. tchr. Ctrl. Fulton Sch. Dist., McConnellsburg, Pa., 1969—; mem. supt.'s adv. com. Ctrl. Fulton Sch. Dist., McConnellsburg, 1990-94. Bd. dirs. Fulton County Med. Ctr. Mem. NEA, ASCD, Pa. Edn. Assn., Pa. Coun. Math. Tchrs., Beta Sigma Phi (past pres., v.p. Gamma Phi chpt., preceptor). Democrat. Presbyterian. Home: HCR 81 Box 114 Big Cove Tannery PA 17212 Office: 151 Cherry St Mc Connellsburg PA 17233

YOUNKINS, ROSE BUD, nurse; b. Orangebury, S.C., July 15, 1937; d. Leon Boneparte and Genova (McMichael) Parker; married; children: Sharon, Debra, Emanuel, David. BA in Psychology, Chgo. State U., 1986, MS in Edn., 1993. cert. pharmacology, Ill.; lic. nurse Chgo Bd. Health. Psychiat. nurse Ill. Psychiat. Inst., Chgo., 1959-66; nurse ob-gyn nursery Presbyn. St. Luke's Hosp., Chgo., 1966-67; staff nurse Michael Reese Hosp., Chgo., 1966-77; pvt. duty nurse Nursefinders, Elmwood Park, Ill., 1980—; home nurse United Health Care, Des Plaines, Ill., 1983-84. dir. ch. Girl Scouts Am., Chgo., 1972-75; asst. precinct capt. City of Chog. 21st ward hdqrs., 1976; Rep. judge Bd. of Election, Chgo., 1981. Mem. Chgo. State U. Alumni Assn. Club: 93d Block (Chgo. asst. chmn. 1984—). Office: Nursefinders Agy 7334 W North Ave Chicago IL 60635-4235

YOUNKMAN, JANE MIKESELL, historian, small business owner; b. Bellefontaine, Ohio, Jan. 13, 1936; d. Hobart Ludlow and Helene Marie (Foust) Mikesell; m. David Alan Younkman, June 7, 1958; children: Derek Alan, Jonathan Mikel. BFA, Ohio State U., 1958. Tchg. cert. Elem. tchr. Tallmadge (Ohio) City Schs., 1959-64; art tchr. Akron (Ohio) Art Mus., 1963; elem. tchr. Columbus (Ohio) Pub. Schs., 1964-67; vol. educator St. Agatha Sch., Bridgeville, Pa., 1973-76; owner, operator The Pioneer House, West Liberty, Ohio, 1984—. Mem. sch. adv. bd. West Liberty (Ohio) Schs., 1980-85; bd. mem. Logan County Conv./Tourism, Bellefontaine, 1985-96. Mem. AAUW, Soroptimist Internat. Republican. Methodist. Home: PO Box 705 West Liberty OH 43357 Office: The Pioneer House 10245 Township Rd #47 West Liberty OH 43357

YOUREE, BEVERLY B., library science educator; b. Jackson, Tenn., Mar. 29, 1948; d. Beverly Durward and Rebecca Wade B.; m. Mack Moore Youree, May 26, 1973; 1 child, Roderick Buford. BA, Union U., 1969; MLS, Peabody Coll., 1970; EdD, Vanderbilt U., 1984. Reserves circulation libr. Mid. Tenn. State U., Murfreesboro, 1970-74, instr. libr. sci., 1974—, mem. faculty senate, 1984-90, sec.-treas., 1987-88; chmn. vis. coms. So. Assn. Evaluation Teams, 1989—; pres. Concerned Faculty and Adminstrv. Women, 1986-90. Contbr. articles to profl. jours. State founder, coord. Tenn. Exhibitors' and Media Profls. Tour; mem. adv. bd. John Wiley & Sons Pub. Co., 1991—; active Middle Tenn. State U.; mem. faculty senate, 1984-90, sec.-treas., 1987-88, mem. univ. libr. com., 1981-83, sec. 1981-82; mem. ad hoc com. on edn., curriculum svc. and facilities, 1975-76; mem. faculty senate legis. com., 1980-83, sec. 81-83; mem. non-instructional assignment semester com., 1988-90, sec. 88-89, chair 89-90; mem. com. on status of women, 1988-94; mem. grad. coun., 1988-90; active So. Assn. Evaluation Teams, chair vis. coms., 1989, 90, 91, 92, 93, 94; pres. Concerned Faculty and Adminstrv. Women, 1986-90; chmn. Commn. on Status of Women, 1994—. Mem. ALA (mem. state liaison to young adult svcs. divsn. 1988—, mem. outstanding theatre for the college bound list revision com. 1988), NEA, Tenn. Libr. Assn. (chair libr. edn. sect. 1979-80, 88-89, chair vol. state book award com. 1980—, co-chair exhibits for state conv. 1985—, Frances Neal Cheney award 1993), Southeastern Libr. Assn. (sec. sch. libr. sect. 1986-88, chair-elect sch. libr. sect. 1988-90, chair, 1990-92, co-chair exhibits for conv. 1988-90, 90-92), Tenn. Edn. Assn. (sec. higher edn. dept. 1989-93, pres. 1993-95, mem. instructional and prof. devel. commn. 1991-94, past pres. and sec. Middle Tenn. State U. chpt.), Tenn. Assn. Sch. Librs., Middle Tenn. Edn. Assn., Assembly Literature for Adolescents, Soc. Sch. Librs. Internat. (mem. legis. task force 1988-89), Kappa Delta Pi (mem. nominating com. mem. 1991-92, mem. Theta Omicron chpt., treas, 1981—, assoc. counselor 1983-86, counselor 1987-94, Svc. to Edn. award), Phi Delta Kappa. Democrat. So. Baptist. Home: 3567 Castlewood Dr Murfreesboro TN 37129-4605 Office: Middle Tenn State U Dept Ednl Leadership PO Box 184 Murfreesboro TN 37132-0184

YOUSEF, MONA LEE, psychotherapist; b. N.Y.C., May 16, 1964; d. Mohamed Moawad and Myra (Schansinger) Y. BS in Human Devel. and Family Studies, Cornell U., 1986; MSW, NYU, 1991. Cert. social worker, HIV counselor, N.Y. Coord. People with AIDS buddy program Home Care Am., N.Y.C., 1987-88; rsch. asst. Gay Men's Health Crisis, N.Y.C., 1988; caseworker AIDS assessment program Gouverneur Hosp., N.Y.C., 1989; support group facilitator Body Positive, N.Y.C., 1989-92; clin. social worker mental health clinic Lower Eastside Svc. Ctr., N.Y.C., 1991-93; clin. social worker alcoholism outpatient dept. Manhattan Bowery Corp., N.Y.C., 1993-95; psychotherapist Counseling Ctr., Morris Heights Health Ctr., Bronx, N.Y., 1995—; pvt. practice psychotherapy, N.Y.C., 1993—. Contbg. writer PWA Coalition Newsline. Participant AIDS walk Gay Men's Health Crisis, N.Y.C. Mem. NASW, Acad. Cert. Social Workers, Am. Assn. Grief Counselors, N.Y. State Soc. for Clin. Social Work, Assn. for Death Edn. and Counseling, Stuyvesant H.S. Alumni Assn., Psi Chi (life). Democrat. Office: 168 Fifth Ave Ste 2N New York NY 10010

YOUSUFF, SARAH SAFIA, physician; b. Binghampton, N.Y., Dec. 8, 1960; d. Mohamed and Razia (Sivaramasastry) Y.; m. Donald John Sudy, Aug. 7, 1993. BA in Zoology, U. Tex., Austin, 1982; MD, U. Tex., 1988. Diplomate Am. Bd. Anesthesiology, Am. Bd. Pain Medicine. Fellow in med. mgmt. U. N.C., Chapel Hill, 1992-93; resident in anesthesiology U. Wash., Seattle, 1988-92; staff anesthesiologist Krön Med., Research Triangle Park, N.C., 1992-94; med. dir. dept. anesthesiology Southwest Hosp., Little Rock, Ark., 1994-96; pres. Southwest Anesthesia Assocs., Little Rock, 1994-95; ptnr. Pain Cons. Ark., 1995—; dir. Southwest Pain Mgmt. Clinic, Little Rock, 1995—. capt. USAR, 1990—. Mem. AMA, Am. Soc. Anesthesiology, Am. Coll. Physician Execs., Ark. Med. Soc., Pulaski County Med. Soc., Internat. Spinal Injection Soc., Internat. Assn. for Study of Pain, Am. Acad. of Pain Medicine, Am. Soc. of Regional Anesthesia. Home: 18 Edenfield Cv Little Rock AR 72212-2667 Office: Southwest Pain Mgmt Clinic 11401 Interstate 30 Little Rock AR 72209

YOZELL, SALLY J., federal agency administrator; b. Boston; d. Peter S. and Jeanne (Wolfe) Y. BA in Polit. Sci., U. Vt., 1982; MPA, Harvard U., 1993. Staff asst. to Rep. Robert F. Drinan, 1980; field dir. Jim Guest for U.S. Senate Campaign, 1982; local staff coord. Mass. Office of Lt. Gov., 1983; legis. affairs specialist Mass. Office Fedn. and State Rels., 1984; minority staff dir. Subcom. on Handicapped, Senate Com. on Labor and Human Resources, 1984-86; sr. legis. asst. for environ. and energy issues, dep. legis. dir. to Sen. John Kerry Washington, 1987-92; dir. Office Legis. Affairs for Nat. Oceanic and Atmospheric Adminstrn. U.S. Dept. Commerce, Washington, 1993-96, dep. asst. sec. for oceans and atmosphere, 1996—. Office: US Dept Commerce 14th St & Constitution Ave NW Washington DC 20230

YRIGOLLEN, ANGELICA TORRES, hospital administrator, consultant; b. San Vicente Banderillas, San Luis Potosi, Mex., Sept. 19, 1964; came to U.S., 1974; d. Armando and Eloiza (Pinal) Torres; m. Benjamin F. Yrigollen, Nov. 24, 1990. BSN, Dallas Bapt. U., 1988; MSN, Tex. Woman's U., 1996. Lic. vocat. nurse; CCRN, ACLS, BLS. Staff nurse, lic. vocat. nurse Dallas Family Hosp., 1984-89; staff nurse RN CCU Presbyn. Hosp., Dallas, 1988-93, cardiology case mgr., 1993-95, clin. nurse CCU, 1995-96, cmty. nurse educator and coord., 1996—; mem. maternal child health adv. bd. Southwestern Med. Sch., Dallas, 1993-94. Counselor, interviewer Oakliff Christian Chs. Emergency Aid, Dallas, 1989-93; mem. cmty. adv. bd. Greiner Mid. Sch., Dallas, 1990-93; chairwoman social concerns el Buen Samaritano United Meth. Ch., Dallas, 1990—; coord. youth enrichment program Ctr. Cmty. Devel., Dallas, 1992-94. Recipient Excellence in Nursing award Presbyn. Hosp. of Dallas, 1992; named one of Great 100 Nurses of 1993, Tex. Nursing Assn. and Dallas-Ft. Worth Hosps.; Edith Cavaill Nursing scholar, 1983-88; Ladders in Nursing Careers scholar, 1994-95. Mem. AACN, Hispanic Nursing Assn. (mem. local/nat. chpt.). Methodist. Home: 7344 Walling Ln Dallas TX 75231 Office: Presbyn Hosp 8200 Walnut Hill Ln Dallas TX 75231-4402

YU, ELEANOR NGAN-LING, advertising company executive; b. Hong Kong, July 28, 1958; d. Seong Yoon and Esther (Lam) Chan. Student, Oxford U., 1976; BA with honors, U. Ottawa, 1979; MBA, Golden Gate U., 1986. Copywriter, intern Ogilvy & Mather, Ottawa, Can.; asst. account exec. DDB, N.Y.C.; account exec. JWT, N.Y.C.; account supr. Mktg. Group, Phila.; chief exec. officer, pres. AdLand, San Francisco. Mem. com. San Francisco Grandprix Assn., 1988; bd. dirs. Chinatown Youth Ctr., San Francisco, 1986, United Way, San Francisco, 1986, San Francisco C. of C., 1995, Internat. Assn. Advt. Agys., 1995, Asian Am. Arts Found., 1995; mem. San Francisco Econ. Vitality Com., 1994; bd. overseers U. Calif., San Francisco Med./Nursing Sch.; bd. trustees Fielding Inst., 1996; bd. advisors Nat. Asian and Pacific Am. Coalition. Named Entrepreneur of Yr. SBA, 1995, Alumnus of Yr. Golden Gate U., 1995. Mem. NAFE, Asian Bus. Assn. (pres. 1985-86), Pacific Affairs Council (chmn. 1988—), San Francisco C. of C. (mem. bd. dirs. 1994), Golden Gate U. Alumni Assn. (bd. dirs. 1986—), Inter Assn. of Advt. Agy's. Office: AdLand & AdLand Worldwide Penthouse Suites 2728 Hyde St at Beach San Francisco CA 94109

YU, JULIE HUNG-HSUA, marketing educator; b. Taipei, Republic of China, Nov. 22, 1954; came to U.S., 1959; d. Wei-Wen and Yueh-Hsin (Wang) Y.; m. Holger Gossmann, Feb. 1989; 1 child, Hans-Trevor. BA in Biol. Sci., U. Mo., 1975, MSEE in Biomed. Engring., 1977, MBA in Mktg., 1981, PhD in Mktg., 1983. Rsch. asst. U. Mo., Columbia, 1975-81, grad. instr., 1981-82; asst. prof. mktg. Wake Forest U., Winston-Salem, N.C., 1983-84, Hofstra U., Hempstead, N.Y., 1984-86, U. Hawaii at Manoa, Honolulu, 1986-88; assoc. prof. Chinese U. Hong Kong, 1988—; rsch. cons. Mktg. Metrics, N.J., 1985-86. Mem. Am. Mktg. Assn. (doctoral consortium fellow 1982), Acad. Internat. Bus., Mu Kappa Tau. Office: Chinese U Hong Kong, Dept Mktg, Sha Tin Hong Kong

YU, KATHERINE KIT, internist; b. Beijing, Jan. 19, 1960; came to the U.S., 1974; BS, UCLA, 1983; MD, U. Calif., San Francisco, 1987. Intern and resident UCLA-San Fernando Valley Program, 1987-90; cons. specialist Olive-View-UCLA Med. Ctr., Sylmar, 1990-91; Kenamar fellow UCLA, 1991; physician specialist Olive-View-UCLA Med. Ctr., Sylmar, 1991—; asst. clin. prof. UCLA Sch. Medicine, 1991—. Mem. ACP. Office: Olive View UCLA Med Ctr 14445 Olive View Dr Sylmar CA 91342

YUE, AGNES KAU-WAH, otolaryngologist; b. Shanghai, Peoples Republic China, Dec. 1, 1947; came to U.S., 1967; d. Chen Kia and Nee Yuan (Ying0 ; m. Gerald Kumata, Sept. 25, 1982; children: Julie, Allison Benjamin. BA, Wellesley Coll., 1970; MD, Med. Coll. Pa., 1974; postgrad., Yale U., 1974-78. Intern Yale-New Haven Hosp., 1974-75, resident, 1975-78; fellow U. Tex. M.D. Anderson Cancer Ctr., Houston, 1978-79; asst. prof. U. Wash., Seattle, 1979-82; physician Pacific Med. Ctr., Seattle, 1979-90; pvt. practice Seattle, 1991—. Fellow Am. Acad. Otolaryngology, Am. Coll. Surgeons; mem. Northwest Acad. Otolaryngology. Office: 1801 NW Market St Ste 410 Seattle WA 98107-3909

YUEN, JANET, financial analyst; b. Hong Kong, Aug. 10, 1958; came to U.S., 1969; d. Chun Kong and Chi Ying (Wong) Y. BS, U. Calif., Berkeley, 1980; MBA, U. Pa. Wharton Sch. of Bus., 1985. Chartered Fin. Analyst. Fin. mgr. Analor Inc., N.Y.C., 1980-82; sr. acct. Marine Midland Bank, N.Y.C., 1982-83; treasury analyst Goldman Sachs & Co., N.Y.C., summer 1984; sr. fin. analyst Bank of Am., San Francisco, 1985-87, Citicorp/Citibank, N.Y.C., 1987-89; asst. v.p., bank analyst Chem. Banking Corp., N.Y.C., 1989-93, Thomson Bankwatch, N.Y.C., 1993-94; analyst Lipper Analytical Svcs., Inc., N.Y.C., 1994—; part-time lectr. dept. fin., law and taxation NYU Sch. Continuing Edn., 1995—; bd. dirs. N.Y. State Coun. on Econ. Edn. N.Y.C. coord. N.Y.C. exhbn. art show Artists to End Hunger, Inc., 1987-91. Recipient Citation of Honor Young Careerist, Bus. and Profl. Women Inc., N.Y. League, N.Y.C., 1988; nominated Internat. Woman of Yr., 1992-93. Mem. AAUW (treas. 1982-83), Fin. Women's Assn. (coll. intern liaison 1988—), N.Y. Soc. Security Analysts (chair program com. 1995—), Assn. Investment Mgmt. and Rsch., Calif. Alumni Assn., Toastmasters. Home: 300 E 46th St Apt 9K New York NY 10017-3013 Office: Lipper Analytical Svcs Inc 74 Trinity Pl New York NY 10006

YUN, MICHELLE WONHE, librarian; b. Seoul, South Korea, July 18, 1936; d. Tchi-Chang and Jinsil Virginia (Sohn) Y.; m. Myungsoo Chun, Aug. 22, 1955 (div. Mar. 1963); m. Yoon-Choo Kim, June 15, 1968 (div. Dec. 1972). Student, Purdue U., 1955-57; BA magna cum laude, U. Pitts., 1974; MLS, Columbia U., 1977. Registered profl. libr., N.Y. Gen. libr. asst. East Asian Librs. Columbia U., N.Y.C., 1975-77; English instr. Korean Lang. Sch., N.Y.C., 1978-79; translator, synopsis writer Asian Bilingual Curriculum Devel. Ctr., Seton Hall U., N.J., 1979-82; journalist Korean East Asian Daily News, N.Y.C., 1981-82; translator, lang. officer, analyst U.S. Dept. of Army, 1982-95; ret., 1995. Vol. Friends of Librs. of Montgomery County, Md., 1995—; mem. Friends of Book Arts Press, Columbia U., 1977—; mem. Montgomery chpt. ARC, 1995. Colby Coll. dean grantee, 1955. Mem. NAFE, Internat. Women's Assn. World Peace, Alumni Assn. U. Pitts., Alumni Assn. Columbia U., Alumni Assn. Kyongki Girls H.S. Home: Apt # 427 8775-M Centre Park Dr Silver Spring MD 20902

YUNGMEYER OLSON, JANE ELIZABETH, conservationist; b. Henrietta, Okla., Feb. 27, 1957; d. Harold Ross and Sally C. (Sumpter) Yungmeyer; m. James S. Olson, Oct. 21, 1994; 1 child, Iris Mary. BS with honors, U. Wyo., 1984. Pesticide applicators cert., Wyo. Bartender Fireside Lounge, Gallery Saloon, Conner Lounge, Laramie, Wyo., 1977-82; laborer, saw operator Big Horn Lumber Co., Laramie, 1978-79; lead forestry technician USDA Forest Svc., Douglas, Wyo., summer 1984; range technician USDA Forest Svc., Laramie, summer 1985, summer 1986, summer 1987; rsch. technician zoology dept. U. Wyo., Cody, winters 1986-87; soil conservationist USDA Soil Conservation Svc., Pinedale, Wyo., 1987-88; wetland coord. USDA Soil Conservation Svc., Greybull, Wyo., 1989-90; dist. conservationist USDA Soil Conservation Svc., Sandpoint, Idaho, 1990-91, Lander, Wyo., 1991-94; com. mem. Equal Opportunity Com., Soil Conservation Svc., Casper, Wyo., 1989-90. Mem. NOW, Soc. for Range Mgmt. Home: 4000 Argonaut Ave Boise ID 83709

YUNKER, PENELOPE JANE, accountancy educator; b. Derby, Eng., Dec. 3, 1945; d. Frederic L. and Margaret (Harrison) Castiau; m. James A. Yunker, Sept. 6, 1966. B in Bus., Western Ill. U., 1975, M in Acct., 1976; PhD in Bus. Adminstrn., St. Louis U., 1981. CPA, Ill. Instr. Western Ill. U., Macomb, 1976-78, asst. prof., 1979-84, assoc. prof., 1984-91, prof., acctg. dept. chair, 1986; mem. adv. bd. Midwest Bus. Adminstrn. Assn., 1985-91; v.p., program chair Midwest Acctg. Soc., 1986-87, pres., 1987-88. Contbr. articles to profl. jours. Recipient Price Waterhouse fellowship St. Louis U., 1978-79, Grad. assistantship St. Louis U., 1978-79. Mem. Am. Acctg. Assn. (bd. mem., treas. adminstrs. acctg. programs group 1990-92, accreditation com. 1990-91), Ill. CPA Soc. (subcom. on non-recruited schs. 1986-89, com. on rels. with acctg. educators 1986-90, chair rsch. grant subcom. 1989-89, com. on grants, scholarships and fin. aids 1990-91), Phi Kappa Phi, Beta Alpha Psi (faculty v.p. Zeta Beta chpt. 1982-88, nat. councilor region 3 1988-90, internat. task force 1991-92, dir. nat. & internat. programs 1992-96, pres. 1996—). Home: 75 Richmond Rd Macomb IL 61455-9327 Office: Western Ill U Dept Acctg 418 Stipes Hall Macomb IL 61455

YURCHENCO, HENRIETTA WEISS, ethnomusicologist, writer; b. New Haven, Mar. 22, 1916; d. Edward and Rebecca (Bernblum) Weiss; m. Basil Yurchenco, June 1936 (div. 1955); 1 child, Peter; m. Irving Levine, 1965 (div. 1979). Student, Yale U., 1935-36; student piano scholarship, Mannes Coll. Music, 1936-38. Radio producer WNYC, WBAI, others, 1939-69; writer, critic, tchr., folk music editor Am. Record Guide and Musical Am., 1959-70; prof. music Coll. City N.Y., 1962-86, Bklyn. Coll., 1966-69, New Sch. for Social Research, 1961-68; co-dir. project for study of women in music, Grad. Ctr. CUNY. Author: A Fiesta of Folk Songs From Spain and Latin America, 1967, A Mighty Hard Road: A Biography of Woody Guthrie, 1970, !Hablamos! Puerto Ricans Speak, 1971; contbr. articles to profl. jours.; 11 field recs. from Mexico, P.R., John's Island, S.C., Guatemala, Ecuador, Morocco, issued by Libr. Congress, Folkways, Nonesuch, Folkways/Smithsonian Global Village; collections in Libr. Congress, Discoteca Hebrew U., Jerusalem, Arais Montana Inst., Madrid, Inst. Nacional Indigenista, Mexico City. Recipient grants-in-aid Am. Philos. Soc., 1954, 56, 57, 65, 67, 89, grants-in-aid CUNY Faculty Research Fund, 1970, 83, 87; NEH grantee, 1984. Mem. Internat. Council Traditional Music (com. on women's studies), Soc. Ethnomusicology, Soc. Asian Music, Sonneck Soc., Internat. Assn. Study of Popular Music, Am. Musicologists Soc. Home: 360 W 22nd St New York NY 10011-2600 Office: 139th St And Convent Ave New York NY 10031

YUSPEH-HIDALGO, DENISE ANNE, juvenile writer, editor; b. N.Y.C., Apr. 29, 1959; d. Michel H. and Sonia E. (Nejame) Yuspeh; children: Ariel S. Hidalgo, Jason D. Hidalgo. Internat. baccalaureate, UN Internat. Sch., N.Y.C., 1977; BA, Yale U., 1981. Editor-in-chief Children's Express, N.Y.C., 1974-77; personal asst. John Guare, N.Y.C., 1978-79; stage mgr. Little Theatre, L.A., 1979-80; author, co-lyricist Sweet Pickles, N.Y.C., 1981-82; activity book author Scholastic, Marvel mags., N.Y.C., 1983-84; textbook author MacMillan, Prentice-Hall, N.Y.C., 1985-87; co. adminstr. Deja Vu/Barry Martin, N.Y.C., 1988-90; personal asst. Marvin Hamlisch, N.Y.C., 1991—; script supr. ABC/CAP cities, N.Y.C., 1994—; script reader Learning Corp. of Am., N.Y.C., 1981-82. Author, editor; Sweet Pickles 16 vol. dictionary, 1982; author: (sch. activity packages) Health is Harmony, 1992-93, Tales to Tell, Going Places, 1991-92, Poetry & Rhyme Time, Lots of Laughs, 1990-91, Summer Starters, Following Directions, 1985-86; co-author, lyricist: (albums) Loving Lion Looks at Love, 1983, also several musical albums; asst. prodr. Secondari Prodns., Ltd., N.Y.C., 1981-82; singer for N.Y. Renaissance Festival, Sterling Forest, N.Y., 1987, French Conservatory Choir of Carnegie Hall, 1995-96. Recipient hon. mention Nat. Arts Club Pastel show, N.Y.C., 1975. Mem. ASCAP, NAFE, Dramatists' Guild. Home and Office: 2211 Broadway 10L New York NY 10024

YUTZEY, SUSAN DYKES, school librarian; b. Hackensack, N.J., Nov. 23, 1949; d. Norman M. Jr. and Constance (Harrington) Dykes; m. John A. Yutzey, Sept. 2, 1978; 1 child, Elizabeth Frost. BA, Muskingum Coll., 1971; MA, Bowling Green State U., 1973; PhD, Ohio State U., 1988; MLS, Kent State U., 1995. Residence hall dir. Muskingum Coll., New Concord, Ohio, 1971-72; residence hall dir. Otterbein Coll., Westerville, Ohio, 1972-73, dir. off-campus programs, 1972-75, admissions counselor, 1973-75; asst. to sec. Coll. Arts and Scis. Ohio State U., Columbus, 1981-85, acad. counselor, staff asst., 1988-95; libr. Bishop Watterson H.S., Columbus, 1995—; mem. exec. bd. Women in Devel., Ohio State U., 1993-94. Contbr. articles to profl. jours.; reviewer Linworth Pub., Inc. Vol. Friends of Upper Arlington Libr., Columbus, 1992—; mem. evangelism and new mem. bd. North Congregational United Ch. of Christ, 1996—. Mem. Ohio Ednl. Libr. Media Assn., Am. Bus. Women's Assn. (pres. Buckeye chpt. 1994-95, Woman of Yr. award 1994), Phi Beta Delta, Phi Kappa Phi, Phi Delta Kappa. Home: 1254 Norwell Dr Columbus OH 43220-3957 Office: Bishop Watterson HS 99 E Cooke Rd Columbus OH 43214

ZABEL, VIVIAN ELLOUISE, secondary education educator; b. Randolph AFB, Tex., July 28, 1943; d. Raymond Louis and Dolly Veneta (Lyles) Gilbert; m. Robert Lee Zabel, Feb. 18, 1962; children: René Lynne, Robert Lee Jr., Randel Louis, Regina Louise. BA in English and Speech, Panhandle State U., 1977; postgrad., U. Cen. Okla., 1987-92. Cert. tchr., Okla. Tchr. English, drama, speech, debate Buffalo (Okla.) High Sch., 1977-79; tchr. English, drama, speech Schulter (Okla.) High Sch., 1979-80; tchr. English Morris (Okla.) High Sch., 1980-81; tchr. speech, drama, debate Okla. Christian Schs., Edmond, 1981-82; tchr. English, drama, debate, speech/debate coach Braman (Okla.) High Sch., 1982-83; debate coach Pawhuska (Okla.) High Sch., 1983-84; tchr. English, French, drama, speech and debate coach Luther (Okla.) High Sch., 1984-95; tchr. debate, forensics, yearbook, newspaper, English, competitive speech Deer Creek H.S., Edmond, Okla., 1995—; dir. drama Nazarene Youth Impace Team, Collinsville, Okla., 1979-81; tchr. h.s. Sun. sch. class Edmond Ch. of Nazarene, 1991—; mem. cmty.-sch. rels. com. Luther Pub. Schs., 1991-92, supt.'s adv. com., 1992—. Editor Potpourri mag., 1975-77; author poetry, short stories. Adult supr. Texas County 4-H, Adams, Okla., 1975-77; double diamond coach NFL; adjudicator and tournament dir. qualifying OSSAA Tournaments. Recipient Disting. Svc. award NFL, 1994. Mem. Nat. Debate Coaches Assn., Nat. Fedn. Interscholastic Speech and Debate Assn., Okla. Speech Theatre Communications Assn., Okla. Coun. Tchrs. Engl. Republican. Nazarene. Home: 2912 Rankin Ter Edmond OK 73013-5344 Office: Deer Creek HS Rte 1 Box 139 Edmond OK 73003

ZABILKA, ANITA LOUISE, guidance counselor; b. Charleston, Ill., Apr. 16, 1937; d. Kenneth E. and Margaret Eloise (Rigg) Hughes; m. Bruce Zachary Shaeffer, June 4, 1956 (div. Mar. 1970); children: Robert Bruce, Douglas Kent, Laura Elizabeth; m. Anthony Joseph Zabilka, July 28, 1974; children: Anthony, Fred. BS in Edn., Ea. Ill. U., Charleston, 1971, MS in Guidance and Counseling, 1975. Profl. cert. in guidance, Fla. Tchr. Bryan Jr. H.S., Elmhurst, Ill., 1971-78; tchr., counselor Monsignor Edward Pace H.S., Miami, Fla., 1978-93, St. Paul's Cath. Ch., Leesburg, Fla., 1993—. Fellow mem. Property Owners Assn. Villages of Lady Lake, 1993—. Mem. Am. Sch. Counselor Assn., Am. Guidance Assn., Fla. Assn. Sci. Tchrs., Ill. Club. Republican. Home: 907 Orchid St Lady Lake FL 32159 Office: St Pauls Cath Ch 1330 Sunshine Ave Leesburg FL 34748

ZABLOCKI, ELAINE, writer; b. Bklyn., June 13, 1942; d. Harry and Anne Finkelstein; m. Benjamin D. Zablocki; 1 child, Abraham M. BA with honors, Swarthmore Coll., 1963. Adminstr. Takilma (Oreg.) Clinic, 1973-80; freelance writer, polit. cons. Oreg., 1981-82; com. adminstr. Oreg. Senate Com. on Human Svcs. and Aging, Salem, 1983; newsletter mgr. New Options, Inc., Washington, 1983-85; writer Craver, Mathews, Smith & Co., Falls Church, Va., 1985-86; freelance writer specializing in healthcare Corona Comms., Arlington, Va., 1986—. Author: Changing Physician Practice Patterns, 1995—; editor Physician Mgr. Newsletter; contbg. editor The Quality Letter for Healthcare Leaders, 1994—; contbr. numerous articles to profl. publs.

ZABLOCKI, TERRY SMITH, educator, mediator; b. Pitts., June 6, 1953; d. George and Lois (Bouson) Dewey; divorced; children: Pam, John. BS in Comms., West Chester (Pa.) U., 1975. Cert. secondary tchr. Mediator Discovery Mediation, San Antonio, 1993—; tchr. San Antonio Ct. Reporting Inst., 1992—; pvt. investigator Narcotics Cons., Inc., San Antonio, 1994—; tchr. Northside ISD, 1994—, also sch. bd. trustee. Mem. Soc. Profls. in Dispute Resolution, PTA (pres. Scobecc Elem. 1993-94). Address: 7606 Lynn Anne St San Antonio TX 78240-3614

ZACCONE, SUZANNE MARIA, sales executive; b. Chgo., Oct. 23, 1957; d. Dominic Robert and Lorretta F. (Urban) Z. Grad. high sch., Downers Grove, Ill. Sales sec. Brookeridge Realty, Downers Grove, 1975-76; sales cons. Kafka Estates Inc., Downers Grove, 1975-76; adminstrv. asst. Chem. Dist., Inc., Oak Brook, Ill., 1976-77; sales rep., mgr. Anographics Corp., Burr Ridge, Ill., 1977-85; pres., owner Graphic Solutions, Inc., Burr Ridge, 1985—. Recipient Supplier Mem. award Internat. Bottled Water Assn., 1987-88, Supplier award for excellence, 1990, Adminstrs. award for excellence U.S. SBA, 1990, Eugene Singer award for best managed co. in small bus. category Graphic Solutions, 1992, Top Performer Supplied award Cutler Hammer Westinghouse Divsn., 1993, 94, Blue Chip Enterprise Initiative award, 1994; named Supplied of Yr. Through Preferred Supplied, Gen. Binding Corp., 1988. Mem. NAFE, Tag and Label Mfrs. Inst. (chmn. pub. rels. and mktg. com., bd. dirs. Best Managed Co. award 1993, 1st place award in U.S. for screen printing 1994, 95), Women Entrepreneurs DuPage County (past pres.), Inst. Packaging Profls., Women in Packaging (exec. bd.), World Label Assn. (1st pl. in world championship 1994, 95). Office: Graphic Solutions Inc 150 Shore Dr Hinsdale IL 60521-5819

ZACEK, JANE SHAPIRO, dean; b. N.Y.C., Nov. 10, 1938; d. Charles and Dorothy (Gintzler) Perlberg; m. Alan Shapiro, 1961; children: Leslie, Peter; m. Joseph Frederick Zacek, 1979. BA in Polit. Sci. with honors, Cornell U., 1960; cert. Russian Inst., MA in Polit. Sci., Columbia U., 1962, PhD in Polit. Sci., 1967; diploma nat. security affairs, The Nat. War Coll., 1979. Prof. polit. sci. Manhattanville Coll., Purchase, N.Y., 1965-78; prof. nat. security affairs The Nat. War Coll., Washington, 1978-80; divsn. mgmt./confidential affairs Gov.'s Office of Employee Rels., Albany, N.Y., 1980-86; dir. mgmt. resource project Gov.'s Office and Rockefeller Inst., Albany, 1986-89; sr. project dir. Rockefeller Inst. Govt. SUNY, Albany, 1989-91; pvt. rsch. and orgnl. cons. Albany, 1991-93; assoc. dean and dir. grad. studies Union Coll., Schenectady, N.Y., 1993—; rsch. cons. Yankelovich, Skelly, White, N.Y.C., 1976-78; adj. prof. polit. sci. SUNY, Albany, 1983, 90-93. Author, compiler: Governing the Empire State: An Insider's Guide, 1988; editor: The Gorbachev Generation: Issues in Soviet Foreign Policy, 1988, The Gorbachev Generation: Issues in Soviet Democracy, 1989; co-editor: Communist Systems in Comparative Perspective, 1974, Change and Adaptation in Soviet and East Politics, 1976, Politics and Participation under Communist Rule, 1983, Reform and Transformation in Communist Systems, 1991, Establishing Democratic Rule: The Reemergence of Local Governments in Post-Authoritarian Systems, 1993; contbr. chpts. to books and articles to profl. jours. Pres. Women's Equity Action League, N.Y., 1991—; bd. dirs., v.p. YWCA of Albany, N.Y., 1991-94; bd. dirs. Albany (N.Y.-Russia) Tula Alliance, 1994—, Red Cross-Heritage Valley chpt., 1994—. Mem. Phi Beta Kappa. Home: 104 Manning Blvd Albany NY 12203 Office: Union Coll Grad Studies Fero House Schenectady NY 12308

ZACHARY, ROBIN BETH, art director; b. L.I., N.Y., Aug. 29, 1960; d. Eugene and Maxine Zachary. BA, SUNY, Binghamton, 1982. Assoc. art dir. Better Health and Living Mag., N.Y.C., 1985-88; art dir. Expecting Mag., N.Y.C., 1988-91; prin. Robin Zachary Design, N.Y.C., 1991—; art dir. Fragrance Found., 1986-95. Art. dir. Am. Cheerleader mag., 1994-95. Recipient Ad Directions award Art Direction Mag., 1988. Office: 208 W 23 St Ste 1409 New York NY 10011

ZACHER, VALERIE IRENE, interior designer; b. Woodland, Calif., Dec. 12, 1942; d. Albert Richard and Laura Ruth (Mast) Z.; m. William Robert Wallace, June 14, 1964 (div. Oct. 1968); 1 child, Jason Zachery Wallace. BA in Polit. Sci., Stanford U., 1964; AS in Interior Design, West Valley Coll., 1982; cert. TESL, U. Calif. Santa Cruz, Santa Clara, 1994. Owner, operator Artefactorage, Fresno, Calif., 1968-77; owner, designer Viz a Viz, Los Gatos, Calif., 1978-82; facilities project mgr. Nat. Semiconductor, Santa Clara, Calif., 1982-85; project supr. Mervyns, Hayward, Calif., 1985-86; interior designer, project mgr. Charles Schwab & Co., San Francisco, 1986-87; small bus. advisor US Peace Corps, Gaborone, Botswana, 1987-89, Swedish Coop. Ctr., Gaborone, 1989-90; English tchr. YCC Am. Club, Yokohama, Japan, 1992-93; interior design cons. Los Gatos, 1993—; design/facilities cons. Octel Comm. Corp., Milpitas, Calif., 1994—; interior designer Am. Cancer Soc. Designers Showcase, 1994, 95, 96. Home and Office: 16721 Madrone Ave Los Gatos CA 95030-4120

ZACHER, VALERIE MARIE, art educator; b. Duluth, Minn.; d. Patrick Moore and Mary Jane (Younge) Langston; m. William John Zacher, Aug. 30, 1941; children: Michael William, Steven Patrick. Degree, State Tchrs. Coll.; student, Duluth Art Inst.; postgrad., U. Md. Docent Basil's Art Gallery, Duluth, Minn., 1956-58; instr. Sketch Pad Studio, Duluth, 1958—, Vocat. Inst. Tech., 1962-68, Latchkey Program, St. Petersburg, Fla., 1985-90; art specialist YMCA, St. Petersburg, 1990-95; adult instr. recreation dept. Gulfport, Fla., 1994-96; instr. adult edn. painting class Yankee Trailer Park, Largo, Fla., 1991-96. Pres. Suntan Art Ctr., St. Petersburg; steering com. Pinellas Art Coun.; active with physically and mentally challenged children Adult Edn. Program; active PTA, Duluth. Recipient Outstanding Achievement award, 1990; named Vol. of Yr., St. Mary's Hosp., 1960. Mem. AAUW, Nat. Mus. Women in Arts, Mus. Fine Art, Smithsonian Instn. Lutheran.

ZACHERT, MARTHA JANE, retired librarian; b. York, Pa., Feb. 7, 1920; d. Paul Rodes and Elizabeth Agnes (Lau) Koontz; m. Edward G. Zachert, Aug. 25, 1946; 1 child, Lillian Elizabeth. AB, Lebanon Valley Coll., 1941; MLS, Emory U., 1953; DLS, Columbia U., 1968. Asst. Enoch Pratt Free Library, Balt., 1941-46; head librarian Wood Research Inst., Atlanta, 1947; sch. librarian DeKalb (Ga.) County Schs., 1950-52; head librarian, prof. history of pharmacy So. Coll. Pharmacy, Mercer U., Atlanta, 1952-63; instr. Ga. State Coll., 1962-63, Emory U., summers 1955-59, 1956-57, 59-60; mem. faculty Library Sch., Fla. State U., 1963-78, prof., 1973-78; prof. Coll. Librarianship U. S.C., Columbia, 1973-74, 78-84; vis. fellow Brit. Library, 1980; cons. So. Regional Med. Library, Emory U., 1976-77, Nat. Library Medicine, 1977, others. Assoc. editor: Jour. Library History, 1966-71, 73-76; mng. editor, 1971-73; cons. editor: Jour. Library Adminstrn., 1979-86; contbr. numerous articles to profl. jours. Fellow Med. Libr. Assn.; mem. ALA, Spl. Librs. Assn. (past pres. Fla. chpt., spl. citation 1977, Hall of Fame 1985), Southwestern Libr. Assn. (Hall of Fame 1985), Am. Printing History Assn., Beta Phi Mu (pres. 1974-75). Home and Office: 2018 W Randolph Cir Tallahassee FL 32312-3349

ZACHERT, VIRGINIA, psychologist, educator; b. Jacksonville, Ala., Mar. 1, 1920; d. R.E. and Cora H. (Massee) Z. Student, Norman Jr. Coll., 1937; AB, Ga. State Woman's Coll., 1940; MA, Emory U., 1947; PhD, Purdue U., 1949. Diplomate: Am. Bd. Profl. Psychologists. Statistician Davison-Paxon Co., Atlanta, 1941-44; research psychologist Mil. Contracts, Auburn Research Found., Ala. Poly. Inst.; indsl. and research psychologist Sturm & O'Brien (cons. engrs.), 1958-59; research project dir. Western Design, Biloxi, Miss., 1960-61; self-employed cons. psychologist Norman Park, Ga., 1961-71, Good Hope, Ga., 1971—; rsch. assoc. med. edn. Med. Coll. Ga., Augusta, 1963-65, assoc. prof., 1965-70, rsch. prof., 1970-84, rsch. prof. emeritus, 1984—, chief learning materials divsn., 1973-84, faculty senate, 1976-84, acad. coun., 1976-82, pres. acad. coun., 1983, sec., 1978; mem. Ga. Bd. Examiners Psychologists, 1974-79, v.p., 1977, pres. 1978; adv. bd. Comdr. Gen. ATC USAF, 1967-70; cons. Ga. Silver Haired Legislature, 1980-86, senator, 1987-93, pres. protem, 1987-88, pres., 1989-93, rep., spkr. protem, 1993—; govs. appointee Ga. Coun. on Aging, 1988-96; U.S. Senate mem. Fed. Coun. on the Aging, 1990-93; senator appointee White House Conf. on Aging, 1995. Author: (with P.L. Wilds) Essentials of Gynecology-Oncology, 1967, Applications of Gynecology-Oncology, 1967. Del. White House Conf. on Aging, 1981, 95. Served as aerologist USN, 1944-46;aviation psychologist USAF, 1949-54. Fellow AAAS, Am. Psychol. Assn.; mem. AAUP (chpt. pres. 1977-80), Sigma Xi. (chpt. pres. 1980-81). Baptist. Home: 1126 Highland Ave Augusta GA 30904-4628 Office: Med Coll Ga Dept Ob-Gyn Augusta GA 30912

ZACKER, THEADORA MARCIA, sculptor, educator; b. N.Y.C., Nov. 8, 1939; d. Dave and Sara (Satwick) Snow; m. Joseph Zacker, Aug. 24, 1958; 1 child, Cherie. Student, Rockland Ctr. for Arts, West Nyack, N.Y., 1976-82, Old Church Cultural Ctr., Demerest, N.J., 1982-86, Art Ctr. No. N.J., New Milford, 1982-86, Hana Geber Studio, Yonkers, N.Y., 1982-86, Rockland C.C., Suffern, N.Y., 1985, County Art Ctr., White Plains, N.Y., 1985. Tchr. sculpture, Pomona, N.Y., 1986—; tchr. Pomona Cultural Ctr., 1994-96, Children's Mus., Nyack, N.Y., 1996—; founding mem., v.p. Piermont (N.Y.) Flywheel Gallery, 1992—; juror East Ramapo Sch. Dist., 1992-94, Young Adult Ctr., Rockland County Mental Health Ctr., 1993-95, Nat. Assn. Women Artists, 1992—; juror and curator for Salute to Women in the Arts, 1996—. One-woman shows Finklestein Libr., Spring Valley, N.Y., 1985, Rockland C.C., 1986, 95, Gallery at Valley Cottage (N.Y.) Libr., 1986, 92, Mag Gallery, Larchmont, N.Y., 1990, Lumen Winter Gallery, New Rochelle, N.Y., 1991, Piermont Flywheel Gallery, 1993, 94-96; exhibited in group shows Stone Sculpture Soc. N.Y., Blue Hill Gallery, Pearl River, Carlyle Gallery, N.Y.C., Nabisco Gallery, East Hanover, N.J., Ringwood (N.J.) Gallery, Art Ctr. No. N.J., Pearl River Libr. Gallery, Schoharie County Arts Coun., Schoharie, N.Y., Broome Street Gallery, N.Y.C., Westbeth Gallery, N.Y.C., Catherine Lorillard Wolfe Art Club, Mari Gallery, Mamaroneck, N.Y., Silvermine Guild Arts Ctr., New Canaan, Conn., ARC Gallery, Chgo., Wildcliff Ctr. for Arts, New Rochelle, N.Y., C.W. Post College, Brookeville, N.Y., Ramapo Coll. Art Gallery, Mahwah, N.J., Paterson (N.J.) Mus., John Harms Gallery, Englewood, N.J., numerous others; represented in pvt. and corp. collections; commd. by Arts Coun. Rockland, March of Dimes, Am. Cancer Soc. Recipient Aanna Hyaatt Huntington bronze medal for sculpture Catherine Lorillard Wolfe Art Club, 1986, Tallix award Pen and Brush Exhbn., Dermot Gale award for sculpture, Adolph Grant award for sculpture New Rochelle Art Assn., 1st prize Cmty. Arts Assn., Ridgewood, Argos Art Foundry Casting awad, 1st prize for sculpture Mid-Rockland Arts Festival, 1st prize Ringwood Manor Assn., silver award for sculpture Putnm Arts Coun. Mem. Nat. Assn. Women Artists (sculpture juror 1992—, Elizabeth Morse Genius Found. award 1990), Am. Soc. Contemporary Artists, Knickerbocker Artists, Allied Artists Am., Salute to Women in Arts (1st prize for excellence in sculpture), Nat. Mus. Women in Arts (founding), U.S. Holocaust Meml. Mus. (founding), N.Y. Artists Equity Assn., Stone Sculpture Soc. N.Y., Sculpture Affiliates Arts Ctr. No. N.J., Rockland Ctr. for Holocaust Studies, Arts Coun. Rockland, Assn. Craftsmen and Artists (1st prize for sculpture 1990), Hopper House, Rockland Ctr. for Arts, Mamaroneck Artists Guild (Barbara Bisgeyer most innovate sculpture awad). Home and Studio: 7 Wavey Willow Ln Pomona NY 10970

ZADOROZNY, ELIZABETH, elementary education educator, writer; b. St. John, Kans., Dec. 23, 1945; d. O.R. and Nell (Pitts) Johnson; m. Allen A. Zadorozny, Aug. 21, 1966; children: Lisa, Scott, Mark. BS, Northwestern Okla. State U., 1968, MS, 1973. Cert. elem. tchr., Okla. 4th grade tchr. Woodward (Okla.) Pub. Schs., 1968-69; phys. edn. tchr. K-6 Dept. Def., Mannheim, Germany, 1969-70; tchr. grades 4-6 Woodward Pub. Schs., 1970—; presenter 1991 Soviet/Am. Sci. Conf., Moscow State U., Nat. Sci. Tchrs. Conv., Houston, Boston, Kansas City, Anaheim, Phila., St. Louis, 1990-96. Author: Pearls Hands-on Science, 1990, Emeralds Hands-on-Science, 1993. Bd. dirs. Okla. Sci. Tchrs., 1991-93; chair City of Woodward Park Bd.; mem. Woodward Arts and Theater Coun. (Best Supporting Patron award); bd. dirs. Kids Incorporated. Christa McAuliffe fellow, U.S. Dept. Edn., 1990; recipient Presl. award NSF, 1991, medal of excellence Found. for Excellence, State of Okla., 1996; finalist Okla. State Tchr. of Yr., 1995. Mem. NEA, NSTA, Children's Book Coun. (book rev. panel 1992-95), Kappa Kappa Iota. Home: 1604 Hillcrest Woodward OK 73801 Office: Woodward Middle Sch Box 592 Woodward OK 73802

ZAFFIRINI, JUDITH, state senator; b. Laredo, Tex., Feb. 13, 1946; d. George and Nieves Pappas; m. Carlos Zaffirini, 1965; 1 child, Carlos Jr. BS, U. Tex., 1967, MA, 1970, PhD, 1978. Committeewoman Tex. State Dem. Exec. Com., 1978-84; mem. Tex. State Senate, 1987—; del. Dem. Nat. Conv., 1980, 84. Bd. dirs., dir. pub. relations Laredo Civic Music Assn., 1968—. Recipient Medal of Excellence Nat. League United Latin Am. Citizens, 1987, Jose Maria Morelos y Pavon Medal of Merit for leadership in strengthening U.S.-Mex. rels., 1987, George Washington Medal of Excellence for Individual Achievement Freedoms Found. at Valley Forge, 1988; named to Nat. Hispanic Hall of Fame, 1987; named Woman of Achievement Tex. Press Women, 1980. Democrat. Roman Catholic. Home: PO Box 627 Laredo TX 78042-0627 Office: 1407 Washington St Laredo TX 78040-4411

ZAGON, LAURIE, artist, writer, color consultant; b. N.Y.C., Feb. 4, 1950; d. Jerome and Janet (Rabinowitz) Z.; m. Joseph Sorrentino, Dec. 21, 1991. BFA, Md. Inst. Coll. Art, 1971; MFA, Syracuse U., 1973. Asst. prof. Art CUNY, N.Y.C., 1973-87; color cons. Fieldcrest/Cannon, N.Y.C., 1987-88; nat. speaker Am. Soc. Interior Designers, Washington, 1993—; color, art therapist, Flagstaff, Ariz., 1996, Big Brothers/Big Sisters No. Ariz., 1996. Illustrator (book) It's Never Too Late to Have a Happy Childhood, 1989; one-woman shows include The Nat. Arts Club, N.Y.C., 1989, Gallery 1757, Laguna Beach, Calif., 1991; group exhibits include John Szoke Gallery, N.Y.C., Helio Galleries, N.Y.C., CUNY Abstract Show of Shanghai, China, 1986, L.A. Mcpl. Gallery, 1993, Phoenix Airport Galleries, 1996; co-author: Power of Color, 1995. Color/art therapist for AIDS Children, L.A. Childrens Hosp., 1994; color/art therapist for recovering addicts Capo by the Sea, Dana Point, Calif., 1991, Martin Luther Hosp., Anaheim, 1990. Mem. Nat. Symposium on Healthcare Design (speaker). Home and Office: 1107 Fair Oaks Ave #147 South Pasadena CA 91030

ZAHM, MARY HESS, psychotherapist, educator; b. Omaha, Nebr., Oct. 31, 1945; d. Marvin A. and Kathleen A. (Moore) Hess; m. Dennis Lee Zahm, Aug. 10, 1968; children: Jennifer R., Benjamin J., Christopher D., Matthew A. and Micah J. (twins). BA in Secondary Edn., Oakland U., Rochester, Mich., 1968, MA in Clinical Psychology, 1973; postgrad., Walden U., 1996—. Ltd. lic. psychologist, Mich.; lic. prof. counselor, Wis. Psychologist Oakland County Child Adolescent Clinic, Pontiac, Mich., 1973-78, Medrano Clinic, Farmington Hills, Mich., 1977-84, Whaley Children's Ctr., Flint, Mich., 1978-84, Psychoeducational Clinic, Grand Blanc, Mich., 1985-87; therapist Luth. Social Svcs., Washburn, Wis., 1989—; tchr. St. Louis Ch., 1987—; tchr. parenting classes Luth. Social Svcs., Washburn, Wis., 1990—; bd. dirs. New Perspectives, Wis. Indianhead Tech. Coll., Ashland, Wis., 1991—. Author: Did You Say Two Babies?, 1986. Co-pres. Adult Child Planning Comm., Washburn, Wis., 1988; pres. Mother of Twins Orgn., Clarkston, Mich., 1984-86; dir. religious edn. St. Louis Ch., Washburn, 1989—. Mem. ACA. Roman Catholic. Office: Luth Social Svcs 320 Superior Ave Washburn WI 54891

ZAHN, PAULA, newscaster; b. Feb. 24, 1956; m. Richard Cohen; 1 child, Haley. With Sta. WHDH, Boston, 1983-85; anchor, reporter Sta. KCBS, L.A., 1985-87; co-anchor World News Now ABC News, N.Y.C., 1987-90; co-anchor CBS This Morning CBS News, N.Y.C., 1990—; contbr. CBS news mag. 48 Hours; co-host CBS broadcast Winter Olympics, Albertville, France, 1992. Office: CBS News CBS This Morning 524 W 57th St New York NY 10019-2902*

ZAHNER, DOROTHY SIMKIN, elementary education educator; b. Chengdu, Szechuan, China, May 1; came to U.S. in the 1930s; d. Robert Louis and Margaret Isadore (Timberlake) Simkin; divorced; children: Mary de Avilan, Robert Louis. BA in Sociology, Whittier Coll.; MLS, U. So. Calif., L.A. Cert. tchr. Calif., Ariz. Tchr. L.A. and Pasadena (Calif.) Schs., 1969-93; dir., owner Betty Ingram Sch., North Hollywood, Calif., 1976-79; dir. Foothill Nursery Sch., La Crescenta, Calif., 1970s; tchr. L.A. Unified Sch. Dist.; guest tchr. Washington Unified Sch. Dist., Phoenix, 1994—. Author: (poetry) Yucca Poetry Workshop, 1993-94, Treasured Poems of America, 1993, others. Bd. dirs. Ariz. Tenants Assn., Phoenix, 1994, 95; vol. Am. Friends Svc. Com., Phila., Calif., 1985—, Common Cause, L.A., 1990, Dem. Candidates, L.A. and Phoenix. Recipient award for a poem, Ariz. State Poetry Soc., Phoenix, 1995. Mem. Phoenix Poetry Soc. (com. mem.), Alameda Writers Group.

ZAHNER, MARY ANNE, art educator; b. Dover, Ohio, Mar. 30, 1938; d. Alfred James and Anna Elizabeth (Stewart) Riggle; m. Gordon Dean Zahner, Aug. 27, 1960 (dec. Mar. 1967); 1 child, Anne Colette; m. John Charles Opalek, Aug. 21, 1982. BFA, Ohio U., 1960, MA, 1969; PhD, Ohio State U., 1987. Cert. tchr., Ohio. Instr. art Springfield Twp. Schs., Akron, Ohio, 1960-61, Logan (Ohio) High Sch., 1961-62; instr. art Dover High Sch., 1967-68, chair art dept., 1969-71; teaching asst. Ohio State U., Columbus, 1980-82; from instr. art edn. to asst. prof. U. Dayton, 1971-80, asst. prof., 1982-91, assoc. prof., 1991—; mem. faculty rights, governance and svc. com. U. Dayton, 1992-93, mem. arts series com., 1995—; reviewer Harcourt, Brace, 1993-94. Author: (chpt.) The History of ARt Education: Proceedings from the Second Pa. State Conference, 1989; group exhibn. includes Westpeth Gallery, N.Y., 1995. Sec. Kettering (Ohio) Arts Coun., 1990, mem., 1988—; mem. discretionary support com. Miami Valley Arts Coun., Dayton, 1992; coord. 3d congl. art contest sponsored by Tony P. Hall, Dayton, 1993, 94, 95. Recipient Best of Show award Canton Art Inst., 1969, Inst. Faculty award The Ohio Partnership for the Visual Arts, 1989. Fellow Ohio Art Edn. Assn. (mem. editl. bd. Ohio Art Edn. Jour. 1986—, editor newsletter Artline 1988, workshop coord. 1992, cons. tchr. insvc. for Dayton Pub. Schs. 1995, Outstanding Art Tchr. western dist. 1992); mem. ASCD, Nat. Art Edn. Assn., Assn. Tchr. Educators, Ohio Alliance for Arts Edn. (bd. dirs.), Univ. Coun. for Art Edn., Phi Delta Kappa, Phi Kappa Phi, Delta Kappa Gamma. Democrat. Presbyterian. Home: 4429 Wilmington Pike Kettering OH 45440-1934 Office: U Dayton 114 Rike Ctr Dayton OH 45489-1690

ZAHOUDANIS, DEMETRIA ELENE, marketing executive; b. Torrance, Calif., Sept. 8, 1969; d. John and Sandra (Wood) Z. AA, Am. Coll. Switzerland, Leysin, 1989; BA in Internat. Affairs, Econs., Am. U. of Paris, 1991. Exec. asst. L.F. Properties, Gardena, Calif., 1991-92; sales cons. Ruesch Internat., Washington, L.A., 1993-94; dir. mktg. RJR Fashion Fabrics, Gardena, 1994—. Mem. Am. Mktg. Assn., Am. Mgmt. Assn., Am. Craft Coun. Republican. Greek Orthodox. Home: 744 Kingman Ave Santa Monica CA 90402 Office: RJR Fashion Fabrics 13748 S Gramercy Gardena CA 90249

ZAHRLY, JANICE HONEA, management educator; b. Ft. Payne, Ala., Sept. 27, 1943; d. John Wiley and Lillian (McKown) Honea. BA, U. Fla., 1964; MBA, U. Ctrl. Fla., 1980; PhD, U. Fla., 1984. Tchr. Hope Mills (N.C.) H.S., 1964-65, Satellite Beach (Fla.) H.S., 1965-69; realtor-assoc. WD Webb Realty, Melbourne, Fla., 1969-70; realtor Aero Realty, Melbourne, 1970-72, Albert J. Tuttle, Realtor, Melbourne, 1972-74; mktg. mgr. Cypress Woods Devel., Orlando, Fla., 1974-76; regional campaign mgr. Pres. Ford Com., 1976; ednl. researcher Peace Corps, Korea, 1976-78; rsch. analyst, tech. writer Rsch. Sys. Inc., Orlando, 1979-80; rsch. asst., lectr. U. Fla., Gainesville, 1980-84; asst. prof. Wayne State U., Detroit, 1984-89; assoc. prof. Old Dominion U., Norfolk, Va., 1989-94, U. N.D., Grand Forks, 1994—; mem. Melbourne Bd. Realtors, 1969-76, orientation chair, 1972, pub. rels. chair, 1973, civic affairs chair, 1973, grievance com., 1975; cons. Wayne County Retarded Persons Assn., Detroit, 1985, Gov.'s Conf. on Women Entrepreneurs, Mich., 1986, Oakland County AAUW Conf. on Women, Mich., 1987, 88, Coll. Bus. and Pub. Adminstrn. Inst. of Mgmt., Old Dominion U., Norfolk, 1990, U.S. Army Corps Engrs., Norfolk, 1990; presenter in field. Contbr. chpts. to books, articles to profl. jours. and procs. Vol. Tidewater AIDS Crisis Task Force, Norfolk, 1990-93, bd. dirs., 1990-92, v.p., 1991, rec. sec., 1992; mem. occupational adv. com. Brevard County Mental Health Ctr., Fla., 1973-74; mem. Brevard County Libr. Bd., 1973-74; bd. dirs. Fla. Dist. 12 Mental Health Bd., 1973-74, sec. 1973-74; bd. dirs. Alachua County Crisis Ctr., Gainesville, 1982-84, chair, 1983-84; vol. Open Door, Detroit, 1986-89; bd. dirs. United Way Grand Forks area, 1996—. Recipient Best Paper award Midwest Soc. for Human Resources/Indsl. Rels., 1989; rsch. fellow Fed. Mogul Corp., 1987-88, rsch. grantee Wayne State U., 1985-89, Old Dominion U., 1990, U. N.D., 1995, 96. Mem. AAUW (bd. dirs. 1974-75), Acad. Mgmt., Assn. for Rsch. on Nonprofit Orgns./Vols., So. Mgmt. Assn., Hampton Rds. Gator Club (co-founder, treas. 1989-91), Alpha Omicron Pi (bd. dirs. alumnae chpt. 1969-73, v.p. 1969-73). Home: 3424 Cherry St Apt A1 Grand Forks ND 58201-7692

ZAHUMENY, JANET MAE, secondary education educator; b. Rahway, N.J., Mar. 23, 1945; d. Richard Evans and Elsie Mae (Walling) Franklin; m. Edward Zahumeny, Dec. 21, 1966 (div. 1987); 1 child, Carole Ann. BA, Newark State Coll., 1967; MEd, William Paterson Coll., 1990; MA, Kean Coll., 1994. Cert. secondary tchr., N.J. Math. tchr. Hunterdon Cen. High Sch., Flemington, N.J., 1967-68; math., computer tchr. Roselle Park (N.J.) High Sch., 1968—; instr. computers Roselle Park Adult Sch., 1987-88; instr. computer tech. William Paterson Coll., 1992—, U. Calif., Berkeley, 1995—; cons. Gray's Appraisal, Cranford, N.J., 1987; textbook editor Prentice Hall, 1989; computer group asst. Bell Labs., Whippany, N.J., summers 1972-73; chmn. Dist. Computer Study Com., 1988; in svc. tchr. tng, 1988—, 8th grade computer coord., 1988-89; mem. Mid. States Evaluation Team, 1972, 82, 85; liason com. RPHS, 1985—, cooperating tchr. Kean Coll., 1990—, Montclair State U.; adminstrv. asst. to v.p. Alpha Wire, summer 1991—; participant Computing Inst., 1983, Woodrow Wilson Inst., 1991, NSF Inst., 1991; mem. Key Curriculum Press Profl. Devel. Team, 1993—. Mem. Web Site editl. bd. William Paterson Coll. Inst. for Tech. in Math. Active Cranford PTA, Roselle Park PTSA; advisor Roselle Park Web Site Editl. Bd. Named Outstanding Acad. Tchr., Cittone Inst., Edison, N.H., 1988, Outstanding Tchr., N.J. Gov.'s Recognition Program, 1989, Outstanding Computer/Math. Tchr. Tandy Techs., 1991; recipient Grad. Scholarship Kean Coll., Union, N.J., 1992, Computer Grant award 1993, Presdl. award for excellence in math. tchg., 1994, 95. Mem. NEA, Nat. Coun. Tchrs. Math., Assn. Math. Tchrs. N.J., N.J. Edn. Assn., Roselle Park Edn. Assn., N.J. Assn. for Ednl. Tech., WPC Inst. for Tech. in Math., Mensa, Kean Coll. Alumni Assn., William Paterson Coll. Alumni Assn., Pi Lambda Theta, Kappa Delta Pi, Phi Kappa Phi. Office: Roselle Park High Sch 185 W Webster Ave Roselle Park NJ 07204

ZAIDI, EMILY LOUISE, retired elementary school educator; b. Hoquiam, Wash., Apr. 20, 1924; d. Burdick Newton and Emily Caroline (Williams) Johnston; m. M. Baqar Abbas Zaidi, June 12, 1949 (dec. Dec. 1983). BA in Edn. and Social Studies, Ea. Wash. State U., 1948; MEd, U. Wash., 1964, EdD, 1974. Tchr. 4th grade Hoquiam Schs., 1948-49; tchr. grades 5-6 Lake Washington Sch. Dist., Kirkland, Wash., 1949-51; tchr. grades 2-3 Port Angeles (Wash.) Schs., 1951-54; tchr. grade 2 Seattle Schs., 1954-55; tchr., reading specialist Northshore sch. Dist., Bothell, Wash., 1955-69, Sacramento City Schs., 1969-87; ret.; mem. Calif. State Instructional Materials Panel, Sacramento, 1975. Mem. Sacramento Opera Assn., 1986—, Sacramento Ballet Assn., 1987—, Sacramento Symphony Assn., 1985—. Fulbright Commn. Exchange Tchr., 1961-62. Mem. Reading Club, Comstock Club. Democrat. Home: 4230 N River Way Sacramento CA 95864-6055

ZAJICEK, FAITH ELAINE, secondary education educator; b. Cameron, Tex., Jan. 24, 1953; d. Floris Kennith and Mary Lou (Meeck) Springer; m.

Jimmy Gene Zajicek, June 7, 1974; children: Kenny James, Lauren Elizabeth, Michael Jeffrey. BE, U. Mary Hardin Baylor, Belton, Tex., 1989. Cert. secondary tchr., Tex. Tchr. Temple (Tex.) H.S., 1990-94; tchr. Rogers (Tex.) Jr. H.S. and H.S., 1994—; mem. Strategy II Action Team, Temple H.S., 1990, Site Based Mgmt. for Rogers H.S., 1994-95. Editl. cons.: (textbook) Discovering Drawing, 1994. Contbr. articles to profl. jours. Author: (poem) River of Dreams (Nat. Libr. of Poetry), 1994. Dir. religious edn. St. Joseph's Cath. Ch., Burlington, Tex., 1987; tchr. religious edn. Ctrl. Tex. area, 1981-94; treas. St. Matthew's Cath. Chapel, Rogers, Tex., 1991-94. Recipient Tchr. Edn. Com. Merit award U. Mary Hardin Baylor, 1990. Mem. Tex. Art Educators Assn., Assn. of Tex. Profl. Educators, Tex. A&M Mothers Club. Home: PO Box 691 Rogers TX 76569-0691 Office: Rogers H S High St Rogers TX 76569

ZAJICEK, IVA MARIE, educator; b. Hastings, Nebr., June 19, 1925; d. Harold Loper and Laura Jean (Evans) Foreman; m. Jerome Robert Zajicek, Sept. 10, 1944; children: James Craig, Ashley Marie. BSc, U. Nebr., 1959, ME, 1960, EdD, 1978. Tchr. pub. schs. York, Nebr., 1956-57, Ceresco, Nebr., 1957-58; art/libr. pub. schs. Los Alamos, N.Mex., 1960-64; edn. advisor, Advance Tchrs. Coll. Ohio U./U.S.A.I.D./Nigeria Project, Kano, 1964-68; elem. edn. advisor Washington County Elem. Schs., Title III, Marietta, Ohio, 1968-70; prin. Fort Frye Schs., Beverly, Ohio, 1970-71; prof. Marietta (Ohio) Coll., 1971-81; edn. advisor Botswana U. Ohio U./U.S.A.I.D., Gaborone, Botswana, 1981-85; edn. advisor U. Swaziland/Ohio U., Mbabane, Swaziland, 1985-87; cons. in field. Mem. Nat. Soc. DAR, PEO. Republican. Methodist. Home: 4281 S Royal Lytham Ct Green Valley AZ 85614-5636

ZAJICEK, LYNN ENGELBRECHT, educational administrator; b. Newport News, Va., Mar. 25, 1950; d. Herbert Charles and Lois (Kohler) Engelbrecht; m. Jon M. Zajicek, June 6, 1970; children: Carlye Lynn, Kate Elizabeth. BA, Kearney State Coll., 1971; MEd, U. Nebr., 1973, EdS, 1988. Cert. profl. adminstr./supr., Nebr. Tchr. Lincoln (Nebr.) Pub. Schs., 1971-73; instr. U.S. Army PREP Program, Crailsheim, Fed. Republic of Germany, 1974-76; subs. tchr. Grand Island (Nebr.) Pub. Schs., 1976-77; mgr., owner rental property Grand Island, 1978—; asst. on survey project U. Nebr., Lincoln, 1987-88; adminstr., ednl. diagnostician Nebr. Ctr. for Evaluation of Devel. and Learning, Inc., Grand Island, 1988—; bd. dirs. Reorganized Mark V Mortgage Corp. Bd. mem. PTA, Grand Island, 1980—; supt. Bible Sch. St. Stephen's Ch., Grand Island, 1984-85; mem. Christian edn. com. St. Stephen's, 1985—, subcom. for adult and continuing edn. of strategic planning com. Grand Island Pub. Schs., 1987; coach Odyssey of the Mind Grand Island Pub. Schs., 1986—; active in heart and cancer funds in Grand Island; bd. dirs. Episc. Ch. Women; candidate cmpaign mgr. Rep. Women, 1978; bd. dirs., exec. com. Marque of Nebr., 1989—. Recipient Gen. Arnold scholarship USAF, 1967. Mem. AAUW, Assn. Supervision and Curriculum Devel., Nat. Assn. Secondary Sch. Prins., Nebr. Coun. Sch. Adminstrs., Nebr. Assn. Elem. Sch. Prins., Nebr. Dental Assn. Aux. (numerous offices including pres. 1981-82), Hall County Dental Aux. (sec., treas. 1976—), St. Francis Med. Aux., Nebr. Assn. for Children and Adults with Learning Disabilities, Phi Delta Kappa, Pi Delta Phi, Alpha Mu Gamma, Sigma Tau Delta, Xi Phi. Home: 1618 S Harrison St Grand Island NE 68803-6359 Office: Nebr Ctr for Evaluation of Devel and Learning Inc 2121 N Webb Rd Ste 305 Grand Island NE 68803-1751

ZAK, ROSALIE SARAH, elementary education educator; b. New Brunswick, N.J., May 18, 1946; d. Ralph Nathan and Annie M. (Ruperto) Greer; m. Daniel John Zak, July 6, 1974; children: Daniel John Jr., Stacie Anne. BA, Trenton State Coll., 1968, MEd in Spl. Edn., 1974. Tchr. Piscataway (N.J.) Twp. Bd. Edn., 1968-74, Salem (N.J.) Bd. Edn., 1974-75, Lower Alloways Creek Bd. Edn., Salem, 1984—; presenter, tchr. Family Connections, 1993—. Former mem. Woodstown (N.J.) Zoning Bd.; former leader Brownies and Girl Scouts U.S.A., Woodstown; vol. Literacy Vols. Am., Salem County, 1993—. Mem. NEA, AAUW (past v.p. membership, program v.p. 1995-97, chmn. Ednl. Found. 1993—), N.J. Edn. Assn., Lower Alloways Creek (treas.), N.J. Assn. Kindergarden Educators, Salem County Assn. Kindergarten Educators (v.p. 1994-96, past treas. and sec.). Home: 13 Wynnwood St Woodstown NJ 08098

ZAK-DANCE, CAROL CAMILLE, human communication educator; b. Milw., Nov. 26, 1950; d. Joseph T. and Alice M. (Tatera) Zak; m. Frank E.X. Dance, July 4, 1974; children: Zachary, Gabriel, Caleb, Catherine. BA, U. Wis., Milw., 1972; MA, U. Denver, 1976, PhD, 1979. Instr. Arapahoe Cmty. Coll., Littleton, Colo., 1976-82, Regis U., Denver, 1983-85; lectr. U. Denver-The Women's Coll., 1984—; adj. faculty U. Denver-Univ. Coll., 1984—; v.p. Human Comm. Cons., Denver, 1976—; guest spkr. numerous schs. and orgns. Editl. asst. Comm. Edn., Washington, 1980, editl. bd., 1985-86; author: Public Speaking, 1986, Speaking Your Mind, 1994, 2d edit., 1996; contbr. articles to profl. jours. Adv. bd. Gove Cmty. Sch., Denver, 1983-89; vol. St. Vincent de Paul Sch., Denver, 1984—, Regis Jesuit H.S., Aurora, 1994—; vol. recreation soccer coach South Ctrl. Denver Soccer, 1986—. Mem. AAUW, Speech Comm. Assn. (divsn. sec. 1983-84). Office: Womens Coll/U Denver Montview and Quebec Park Hill Campus Denver CO 80237

ZAKHEIM, BARBARA JANE, international business company consulting executive; b. London, Jan. 31, 1953; d. David Sloma and Sarah Frances (Leifer) Portnoi; m. Dov Solomon Zakheim, Aug. 20, 1972 (div. 1990); children: Keith Samuel, Roger Israel, Scott Elisha; m. Ronald Kleinfeldt, Dec. 13, 1992. BA, Oxford U., Eng., 1974, MA, 1978. Economist Maxima Corp., Silver Spring, Md., 1979, U.S. Dept. Energy, Washington, 1979-80; sr. project analyst Applied Mgmt. Scis., Silver Spring, 1980-83, staff assoc., 1983-85; prin. analyst NUS Corp., Gaithersburg, Md., 1985-87, cons. analyst, 1987-89; pres. Keith R. Scott Assocs., Inc., 1989—, African Treasures, Inc., 1990-93; dir. policy and econ. studies Sanford, Cohen & Assocs., Inc., 1993-96, v.p. policy divsn., 1996—; U.S. rep. Coll. Petroleum Studies, Oxford, 1984-93; N.Am. rep. Twirltrade Internat. Ltd., London, 1985—; mem. adv. com. on women in bus. Theodore Roosevelt Nat. Bank, Washington, 1991-92; profl. team mem. Venture Ptnrs. Internat., Inc., N.Y.C., 1990-94. Contbr. articles to profl. jours. Bd. dirs. SE Hebrew Congregation, Silver Spring, 1977-78. Mem. Nat. Assn. Environ. Profls. Republican. Home and Office: 11247 Watermill Ln Silver Spring MD 20902-3439

ZALE, ELIZABETH ANNE (LIZ ZALE), management consultant; b. Rochester, N.Y., Apr. 3, 1968; d. Robert Joseph and Signe Ruth (Sebo) Z. BA, Middlebury Coll., 1990; student, Simmons Grad. Sch. Mgmt., 1993-94. Prodn. specialist Houghton Mifflin Co., Boston, 1990-91, prodn. coord., 1991-93, prodn. supr., 1993-94; project mgr. IMAGE Inc., N.Y.C., 1994-96. Mem. bd. NetGALA, N.Y., 1995; co-chair, founder MiddGALA, Middlebury, Vt., 1993-96; commr. Cambridge (Mass.) Commn. on Status of Women, 1993-94; mem., rschr. Feminist Majority Found., Washington, 1991-93. Mem. Publishing Triangle. Democrat. Office: IMAGE Inc 45 E 30th St New York NY 10016

ZALESKI, JEAN, artist; b. Birkirkara, Malta; d. John M. and Carolina (Micallef) Busuttil; children: Jeffrey, Philip, Susan. Student, Art Students League, N.Y.C., 1955-58, New Sch., N.Y.C., 1967-69, Moore Coll. Art, Phila., 1970-71, Parsons Sch. Design, N.Y.C., 1974-75, Pratt Inst., N.Y.C., 1976-77. Dir. art Studio 733, Great Neck, N.Y., 1963-67; sr. art instr. Hussian Coll. Art, Phila., 1970-71; dir. Naples (Italy) Art Studio, 1972-74; corp. sec. Women in The Arts, N.Y.C., 1974-75, exec. coord., 1976-78; adj. lectr. Bklyn. Coll., 1974-75, Hofstra U., 1977-82, Cooper Union, 1986—. One-woman shows include: Adelphi U., 1975, Women in Arts Gallery, N.Y.C., 1975, Il Gabbiano Gallery, Naples, 1973, Wallnuts Gallery, Phila., 1971, Neikrug Gallery, N.Y.C., 1970, Alonzo Gallery, N.Y.C., 1979, 80, Va. Ctr. for Creative Arts, Sweet Briar, 1981, Hodgell Galleries, Sarasota, Fla., 1982, 83, Elaine Starkman Gallery, N.Y.C., 1986, Romano Gallery, Barnegat Light, N.J., 1987, 88, Citicorp Ctr., N.Y.C., 1988-89, Z Gallery, N.Y.C., 1991, Sweet Briar Coll., Va., 1993, Trinity Coll., Hartford, 1996; group exhbns. include Art U.S.A., N.Y.C., 1969, Internat. Art Exhbn., Cannes, France, 1969, Frick Mus., Pitts., 1970, NAD, N.Y.C., 1970-71, Phila. Mus. Art, 1971, Am. Women Artists, Palazzo Vecchio, Florence, 1972, Internat. Women's Arts Festival, Milan, Italy, 1973 (Gold medal), Bklyn. Mus., 1975, Sweet Briar Coll., 1977, CUNY, 1978, Va. Ctr., 1988, Mus. Hudson Highlands, 1982, Pace U. Gallery, N.Y.C., 1982, Bayly Mus., Charlottesville, Va., 1986, Allbright Knox Mus., Buffalo, 1986, E. Starkman Gallery, N.Y.C., 1987, Nabisco, 1989, Queens Coll., N.Y., 1991-92, Mus. City of N.Y., 1993; author: Winged Spirits, 1995; co-author COW/LINES, 1983; represented in permanent collections N.Y. Pub. Library, Met. Mus. Art, Va. Ctr. for Creative Arts, Nat. Mus. Women in Arts, Mus. of City of N.Y., Nat. Mus. Malta; vis. artist, critic various colls. and univs., 1976—. Ragdale fellow, 1986—, Va. Ctr. for Creative Arts fellow, 1976-96, Tyrone Guthrie Ctr. fellow, 1991; grantee NEA, 1982, Artists Space, 1988; recipient Susan B. Anthony award NOW, 1986. Mem. Artists Equity, Women in the Arts, Manhattan Pl. Health Club. Democrat. Roman Catholic.

ZALINSKY, SANDRA H. ORLOFSKY, school counselor; b. Elizabeth, N.J., July 11, 1959; d. Marion E. (Carrajat) Orlofsky; m. Thomas J. Zalinsky, Apr. 12, 1985. BA in Math. & Sci. Edn., Glassboro State Coll., 1981; MA in Adminstrn., Jersey City State Coll., 1985, MA in Counseling, 1990; EdD in Child & Youth Studies, Nova Southeastern U., 1994. Nat. cert. counselor; master addictions counselor. Sr. cam counselor Brick (N.J.) Recreation Dept., 1978-81; tchr. high sch. math. and sci. Brick (N.J.) Twp. Bd. Edn., 1981-88; counselor, cons. pvt. agys., Ocean County, N.J., 1978-81; counselor high sch. Brick Twp. Bd. Edn., 1988—; dept. head guidance Brick Twp. H.S., 1985—; speaker in field. Mem. ASCD (nat. cert. counselor), N.J. Counseling Assn., N.J. Sch. Counselors Assn., N.J. Edn. Assn. (sch. rep. 1981—), Skippers Cove Yacht Club, Phi Delta Kappa. Home: 20 Davey Jones Way Waretown NJ 08758-2106 Office: Brick Twp Bd Edn 101 Hendrickson Ave Brick NJ 08724-2574

ZALKIND, SUSAN, stonecarver; b. Fall River, Mass., Dec. 15, 1947; d. Charles Sumner and Sylvia Dorothy (Goldman) Z.; m. Paul Adams Hawkins, Apr. 7, 1976; children: Zaliah Kahlil Zalkind-Hawkins, Amber Serene Zalkind-Hawkins. BA, Boston U., 1969; MEd, Northeastern U., 1972. Exec. trainee Filene's Dept. Store, Boston, 1969-70; child care worker New Eng. Home for Little Wanderers, Boston, 1970; social worker Cambridge (Mass.) Welfare Office, 1970; cmty. devel. worker Solomon Mental Health Ctr., Lowell, Mass., 1972-74; profl. stonecarver, 1976—. One-person show: Tiffany & Co., Beverly Hills, Calif., 1991; numerous group shows, including Am. Gem Trade Assn., Tucson, Ariz., 1995. Home: PO Box 531 Camp Verde AZ 86322

ZALLA, LINDA HELEN, artist; b. Detroit, Oct. 29, 1941; d. David and Rose (Schulman) Rubenstein; children: Lisa, Steven. BS in Art, Wayne State U., Detroit, 1963; postgrad., Ctr. for Creative Studies, Detroit, 1963. Cert. tchr. Art tchr. Detroit Schs., 1963-64, Livona (Mich.) Schs., 1964-66, Jewish Cmty. Ctr., West Bloomfield, Mich., 1980-90; art dir. Jewish Assn. Residential Care, West Bloomfield, 1990—; spl. advisor bd. trustees Channel 56 Art Auction, Detroit, 1989-90. Featured Cable TV artist Am. Watercolor Linda Zalla, 1986—, Woman on the Move, 1991—; represented in permanent collection City Hall, Livonia, Mich. Bd. mem. sisterhood Congregation Sharrey Zedek, Southfield, Mich., 1965—, head cultural commn., 1984-92. Recipient Woman in Arts award, Wis., 1986, award Mich. Fine Arts Competition, 1989, Jurors award Woman's Caucus Arts, Mich., 1990. Mem. Nat. Mus. Women Artists, Soc. Woman Painters, Bloomfield Art Assn., Soc. Detroit Inst. Arts, Wayne State U. Alumni. Home and Studio: 4787 S Chipping Glen Bloomfield Hills MI 48302

ZALOZNIK, ARLENE JOYCE, oncologist, military officer; b. Pitts., Jan. 30, 1948; d. Ernest and Frances Elizabeth (Augustin) Z. BS, Carlow Coll., 1969; MS, Duquesne U., 1972; MD, Med. Coll. PA, 1976. Diplomate Am. Bd. Internal Medicine, Am. Bd. Oncology. Commd. U.S. Army, 1976, advanced through grades to col.; intern then resident in hematology and oncology Madigan Army Med. Ctr., Tacoma, 1976-77; fellow in hematology and oncology Fitzsimons Army Med. Ctr., Aurora, Colo., 1979-81, staff oncology, 1981-82, asst. chief med. oncology, 1982-84, chief hematology and oncology, 1984-86; chief hematology and oncology Brooke Army Med. Ctr., Ft. Sam Houston, Tex., 1986—; clin. instr. dept. medicine U. Colo. Health Sci. Ctr., 1982-86. Contbr. articles to books and profl. jours. and publs. Active profl. edn. com. Aurora-Adams Unit Am. Cancer Soc., 1983-86, pres., 1983-86, also active Colo. div., 1984-86. Fellow ACP; mem. AMA, Am. Coll. Physician Execs., Am. Soc. Clin. Oncology, Assn. Mil. Surgeons. Home: 13703 Fairway Hedges San Antonio TX 78217 Office: HQ MEDCOM 2050 Worth Rd Fort Sam Houston TX 78234 also: US MEDCOM Fort Sam Houston TX 78234

ZALUCHA, PEGGY FLORA, artist; b. Peoria, Ill., Sept. 18, 1948; d. John H. and Betty R. (T.) Flora; m. L. Anthony Zalucha, Apr. 3, 1971. BFA, Ill. Wesleyan U., 1972; completion cert., Zhejiang Acad. Fine Arts, Hangzhou, China, 1992. Artist Zalucha Studio, Mt. Horeb, Wis., 1973—; workshop tchr. Zalucha Studio, Mt. Horeb, 1980—; chmn. bd. dirs. Hagerty Bros. Co., East Peoria, Ill., Contract Distbn., Inc., Peoria; art show judge in field, 1986—; advisor, selection chair Ctr. Gallery/Non-Profit Co-op, Madison, Wis., 1982-83; advisor Wis. Painters & Sculptors, Madison, 1985—. Dane County Cultural Affairs Commn., Madison, 1988-90, Wis. Arts Bd., Madison, 1989. One-woman show Center Gallery, Madison, Wis., 1982, Valperine Gallery, Madison, 1984, 85, 87, 88, 93, Horwich Gallery, Chgo., 1985, 87, Gingrass Gallery Fine Art, Milw., 1987, Lakeview Mus. Arts and Scis., Peoria, Ill., 1990, Neville Mus. Brown County, Green Bay, Wis., 1991, Wis. Acad. Arts and Scis., Madison, 1991; exhibited in numerous group shows, including Salmagundi Art Club, N.Y.C., 1982, Nat. Arts Club, N.Y.C., 1982, George W.V. Smith Art Mus., Springfield, Mass., 1982, 84, 90, Pitts. Watercolor Soc., 1983, 84, Nat. Arts Club, N.Y.C., 1983, 89, 92, 94, Birmingham (Ala.) Mus. Art, 1984, 88, West Bend (Wis.) Gallery Art, 1986, U. Ky. Art Mus., Lexington, 1989, Parkersburg (W.Va.) Art Ctr., 1990, Madison Art Ctr., 1990, Springfield (Mo.) Art Mus., 1987, 88, 91, Zhejiang Acad. Fine Art, Hangzhou, China, 1992, Salmagundi Club, N.Y.C., 1989, 90, 92, 93, Butler Inst. Am. Art, Youngstown, Ohio, 1982, 93, Foothills Art Ctr., Golden, Colo., 1985, 88, 89, 92, 94, Poway (Calif.) Ctr. for Performing Arts, 1987, 94, 95, Wustum Mus. Art, Racine, Wis., 1981, 83, 84-89, 92, 92, 94, 95, Neville Pub. Mus., Green Bay, 1986-91, 94-96, NAD, N.Y.C., 1994, 95. Ex-officio advisor Peoria Area Cmty. Found., 1995. Recipient Best of Show awards Watercolor Wis., 1988, 94, Flora 94-Chgo. Botanical Gardens, 1994. Mem. Nat. Watercolor Soc. (Best of Show 1988), Am. Watercolor Soc., Midwest Watercolor Soc. (Shapiro Meml. award 1995), Rocky Mountain Watercolor Soc., Nat. Soc. Painters in Casein and Acrylic. Office: Hagerty Bros Co PO Box 1500 East Peoria IL 61655

ZAMBONI, HELEN ATTENA, lawyer; b. Tuxedo, N.Y., Oct. 29, 1951; d. Frank Joseph and Janet Edwards (Johnson) Z.; m. Steve I. Rosen, Jan. 2, 1982. BA cum laude, Mount Holyoke Coll., 1973; JD cum laude, Syracuse U. Coll. of Law, 1977. Title officer Ticor Title Guarantee, Rochester, N.Y., 1977-79; assoc. atty. Underberg & Kessler, Rochester, 1980-82, Phillips, Lytle, Hitchcock et al, Rochester, 1982-83; corp. atty. Frontier Corp., Rochester, 1983-84; sr. corp. atty. Rochester Telephone, Rochester, 1984-85, mng. atty., 1985-93, acting gen. counsel, 1993-94, corp. counsel, 1994-96; pres. internat. ops., 1996—. Dir. YMCA of Greater Rochester, 1986—, Career Devel. Svcs., 1992—; mem. capital campaign com. Syracuse U. Coll. of Law, 1994—. Home: 25 Spring St Avon NY 14414-1330 Office: Frontier Corp 180 S Clinton Ave Rochester NY 14646-0007

ZAMORA, MARJORIE DIXON, retired political science educator; b. Farm Randolph, N.Y., Nov. 8, 1933; d. Wendell Hadley and Jessie (Mercer) Dixon; m. Cornelio Raul Zamora, Dec. 20, 1969; 1 child, Daniel Cornelio. BA, Earlham Coll., 1956; MA, U. Ill., 1968; postgrad., U. Ill., Chgo., 1989—. Tchr. Ridge, Sch., Godsman Sch., Stenson Sch., various cities, 1956-62; with U.S. Peace Corps, tchr. Palmares High Sch., Costa Rica, 1963-64; reporter Lerner Newspaper, Chgo., 1965; dormitory counselor U. Ill., Urbana, 1966-68, 86; instr. Chgo. City Coll., 1968-69; prof. polit. sci. Moraine Valley C.C., Palos Hills, Ill., 1969-94, prof. emeritus, 1994—; researcher, Univ. Ill., Chgo., 1985-88. Contbr. articles on Costa Rican polit. bus. cycle and economy, land reform to various publs. in U.S., Cen. Am. Campaign dir. Polit. State Legis., 1974-76. Mem. AAUW, Western Springs Bank and Orch. Assn. (pres. 1990-91), Am. Assn. Retired Persons, State Cmty. Coll. Retirees Assn., Kiwanis (LaGrange, Ill.). Mem. Soc. of Friends. Home: 3820 Lawn Ave Western Springs IL 60558-1141

ZANCHETTI, PAMELA JOAN, elementary education educator; b. Milw., Jan. 25, 1950; d. Joseph William and Jane Florence (Gorski) Hess; m. Mark Anthony Zanchetti, Mar. 17, 1973; children: Christina, Nicole. BS in Edn., U. Wis., Whitewater, 1972. Primary tchr. St. Roman Sch., Milw., 1972-74; elem. tchr. St. Kilian Sch., Hartford, Wis., 1974-81, 86—; mem. English Lang. Arts Reading Com., Hartford, 1986-93, Washington County Reading Coun., West Bend, Wis., 1990-93, Washington County Young Writers, West Bend, 1991-92. Mem. ASCD, Wis. State Reading Assn., Wis. Cath. Edn. Assn. Roman Catholic. Home: N844 Franklin Rd Oconomowoc WI 53066-9527 Office: St Kilian Sch 245 High St Hartford WI 53027-1119

ZANDER, GAILLIENNE GLASHOW, psychologist; b. Bklyn., Apr. 7, 1932; d. Saul and Anna (Karasik) G.; m. A.J. Zander, Aug. 5, 1952; children: Elizabeth L., Caroline M., Catherine A. MusB, U. Wis., 1953, MS, 1970; PhD, Marquette U., 1984. Diplomate Am. Bd. Forensic Examiners. Music tchr. Wis. Sch. Systems, 1953-65; psychol. asst. Vernon Psychol. Labs., Chgo., 1965-70; psychologist Milw. Pub. Schs., 1970-92, CESA 19, Kenosha, Wis., 1977-78; pvt. practice psychology Milw., 1980—. Fellow Am. Orthopsychiat. Assn.; mem. APA, Wis. Psychol. Assn., Psychologists Assn. in Milw. Pub. Schs. (rep., v.p., pres.), Am. Acad. Pain Mgmt. (diplomate). Home: 13750 Carson Ct Brookfield WI 53005-4989 also: Cooper Resource Ctr 20860 Watertown Rd Waukesha WI 53186-1872

ZANDER, JANET ADELE, psychiatrist; b. Miles City, Mont., Feb. 19, 1950; d. Adelbert William and Valborg Constance (Buckneberg) Z.; m. Mark Richard Ellenberger, Sept. 16, 1979; 1 child, Evan David Zander Ellenberger. BA, St. Olaf Coll., 1972; MD, U. Minn., 1976. Diplomate Am. Bd. Psychiatry and Neurology. Resident in psychiatry U. Minn., Mpls., 1976-79, fellow in psychiatry, 1979-80, asst. prof. psychiatry, 1981—; staff psychiatrist St. Paul (Minn.) Ramsey Med. Ctr., 1980—, dir. edn. in psychiatry, 1980—, dir. inpatient psychiatry, 1986—; vice chair Dept. Psychiatry St. Paul Ramsey Med. Ctr., 1991-96; bd. dirs. Perry Assurance. Contbr. research articles to sci. jours. Sec. Concentus Musicus Bd. Dirs., St. Paul, 1981-89; mem. property com. St. Clement's Episcopal Ch., St. Paul, 1985. Mem. Am. Psychiat. Assn., Am. Med. Women's Assn., Minn. Psychiat. Soc. (ethics com. 1985-87, women's com. 1985-87, coun. 1994-96), Minn. Med. Assn., Ramsey County Med. Soc. (bd. dirs. 1994—). Democrat. Home: 230 Crestway Ln West Saint Paul MN 55118-4424 Office: St Paul Ramsey Med Ctr 640 Jackson St Saint Paul MN 55101-2502

ZANDERS, PATTIE BALDWIN, computer specialist; b. Conway, S.C., July 2, 1951; d. Jesse Odell and Clara Bell (Etheredge) Baldwin; m. Melvin Zanders, July 8, 1983; 1 child, Monya Loleta Baldwin. BS, S.C. State Coll., 1974. Computer programmer Liberty Mut. Assurance Co., Boston, 1974-75; head bookkeeper Southview Apts., Oxon Hill, Md., 1976-77; community vol. Aiken County, Aiken, S.C., 1975; vol. tutor Univ. Yr. for Action, VISTA, Elloree, S.C., 1973-74; computer programmer Naval Communication Unit, Cheltenham, Md., 1977-78; computer analyst Bur. Alcohol Tobacco and Firearms, Washington, 1978-82, Fin. Mgmt. Svc. U.S. Dept. Treasury, Washington, 1982—. Vol. aide Kapitol Day Care, Capitol Heights, 1991-92. Democrat. Home: 4104 Byers St Capitol Hts MD 20743-5724 Office: US Dept Treasury Fin Mgmt Svc 3700 E West Hwy Rm 900B Hyattsville MD 20782-2015

ZANDY, JANET, language and literature educator; b. Hoboken, N.J., Oct. 30, 1945; d. Charles Francis and Mildred (Parisi) Ballotta; m. William J. Zandy, June 12, 1970; children: Victor, Anna. BA, Montclair State U., 1967; MA, U. Rochester, 1973; PhD, SUNY, Buffalo, 1996. Tchr. Glen Rock (N.J.) H.S., 1967-69; tchg. asst. Purdue U., Lafayette, Ind., 1969-70; adj. assoc. prof. English Monroe C.C., Rochester, 1972-87; asst. prof. lang. and lit. Rochester (N.Y.) Inst. Tech., 1989—. Editor: Calling Home: Working Class Women's Writings, 1990, Liberating Memory, 1995; editor Working Class Studies Women's Studies Quar., 1995; contbr. articles and essays to profl. jours. Recipient Tchr. for Multicultural Excellence award N.Y. State English Coun., 1990. Mem. MLA, Am. Studies Assn., Nat. Coun. Tchrs. English, Soc. for Study of Multi-Ethnic Lit. of U.S., Oral History Assn. Home: 580 Hillside Ave Rochester NY 14610 Office: RIT Coll Liberal Arts 92 Lomb Memorial Dr Rochester NY 14623-5604

ZANESKI, ANNE MARLA, marketing executive; b. Boston, Apr. 6, 1960; d. Chester Edward and Mary Nancy (Blume) Z. BA in Polit. Sci., Wellesley Coll., 1982. Paralegal Howard, Rice, Nemerovski, Canady, Robertson & Falk, San Francisco, 1983-86, Wilson, Sonsini, Goodrich & Rosati, Palo Alto, Calif., 1986-87; healthcare mktg., 1987—, mktg. and FDA regulatory cons. to biosci. cos., 1990-91; mktg. and ops. exec. Parenteral Alimentation Providers Assn., Emeryville, Calif., 1991-96. Editor profl. newsletter P.A.P.A. Pen, 1991-96; contbr. articles to profl. jours. Mem. Kosciuszko Found., 1978—, Jr. League, 1986—; mem. Young Reps., 1988—; bd. dirs., profl. mem. coun. Fine Arts Mus. of San Francisco, 1991-93. Republican. Roman Catholic.

ZANJANI, SALLY, political science educator, author; b. San Francisco, Nov. 21, 1937; d. George and Sallie Maria (Ruperti) Springmeyer; m. Esmail D. Zanjani, May 31, 1963. BA magna cum laude, NYU, 1964, MA, 1967, PhD, 1974. Adj. prof. polit. sci. U. Nev., Reno, 1975—; project dir. Jack Longstreet Country, touring art exhibit, Nev., 1990-92; advisor hist. documentaries Sta. KNPB-TV, Reno, 1991-93. Author: The Unspiked Rail, 1981, Jack Longstreet, 1988, Goldfield, 1992 (award Westerners Internat. 1992), Ghost Dance Winter and Other Tales of the Frontier, 1994; co-author: The Ignoble Conspiracy, 1986; contbr. articles to hist. jours. Mem. Western Writers Am., Mining History Assn. (exec. coun. 1994-96), Phi Beta Kappa. Democrat. Office: U Nev Polit Sci Dept Reno NV 89557

ZANUCK, LILI FINI, film director, producer; b. Leominster, Mass., Apr. 2, 1954; m. Richard Zanuck, Sept. 23, 1978; children: Virginia, Janet, Harrison, Dean. Rsch. asst. World Bank, Washington, 1970-78; office mgr. Carnation Co., L.A., 1977-78; rsch. and devel. Zanuck-Brown Co., 1978-89; co-founder, co-owner Zanuck Co., 1989—. Co-prodr.: (films) Cocoon, 1985, Driving Miss Daisy, 1989 (Academy Award 1989), Rich in Love, 1993; dir.: (film) Rush, 1991. Office: The Saul Zaentz Co Film Ctr 2600 10th St Berkeley CA 94710-2522*

ZARATE, ANN GAIRING, academic administrator, lawyer; b. Oak Park, Ill., Oct. 28, 1959; d. Donald Albert and Beverly Jean (Eppink) Gairing; m. Eugene Anthony Zarate, Oct. 5, 1985; children: Anthony Michael, Melissa Ann. BA in Comm. magna cum laude, Tulane U., 1982; JD, Cleve. State U., 1985. Bar: Ohio. Atty. Seymour Gross, Assoc., Cleve., 1985; adminstr. endowment trusts Case Western Res. U., Cleve., 1986-91; dir. devel. Salvation Army, Cleve., 1991-92; exec. dir. and asst. v.p. univ. advancement U. North Ala. Found., Florence, 1992—. Mem. Jr. women's com. Cleve. Playhouse, 1989-92. Mem. AAUW, Leadership Shoals/Shoals C. of C., Florence Rotary Club, Alpha Lambda Delta. Office: Univ North Ala Found PO Box 5059 Florence AL 35630

ZARK, JENNA J., playwright, freelance writer; b. Bklyn., Aug. 17, 1954; d. Max and Faye (Greenberg) Z.; m. Mitchell David Kowitz, Sept. 2, 1979 (div. June 1993); 1 child, Joshua Gabriel; m. Peter Bullard Budd, Oct. 8, 1995. BS cum laude, Emerson Coll., 1976. Staff and freelance writer Scholastic mag., N.Y.C., 1987-91; playwright Circle Repertory Theatre, N.Y.C., 1994; playwright Illusion Theatre, Mpls., 1994—, co-author new commn., 1995-96; grants writer Melpomene Inst., St. Paul. Author: (plays) Burnt House, 1990 (James Chambers award 1990), A Body of Water, 1994 (produced by Circle Repertory Co.), also several children's plays; co-author: Bridges of Stone, Fresh Ink series, Illusion Theater. Artists fellow Ind. Arts Commn., 1980, Minn. Arts Bd., 1994; advancement grantee McKnight Found., Minn., 1994. Mem. AFTRA, Dramatists Guild, Women in Comm., Chgo. Dramatists Workshop (playwright), Playwrights Ctr. (core.). Jewish.

ZARKY, KAREN JANE, newspaper editor; b. St. Louis, Jan. 20, 1948; d. Herbert Lee Lawrence and Alice Ruth (Harrison) Lawrence Robison; m. Robert Gerald McCoy, Feb. 15, 1964 (div. Feb. 1982); 1 child, Karen; m. A.A. Zarky, Aug. 29, 1986. BA, Maryville Coll., St. Louis, 1988. Asst. to dir. fin. Clayton Mark Corp., Chgo., 1966-68; office mgr. A.R. Musical Enterprises, Columbus, Ind., 1969-75; owner, pres. Antique Galleries Inc., Louisville, 1975-81; sales mgr. Rainbow Graphics and Displays, St. Louis, 1981-87; editor, pres. Senior Circuit, Inc., St. Louis, 1987—; tchr. St. Louis Community Coll., 1987-89. Bd. dirs. Greeley Community Ctr., St. Louis, 1988—; mem. reorgn. com. United Way, St. Louis, 1988—; sec. Housing

Options Provided for the Elderly, 1991—; v.p. mktg. and comm. Women's Consortium, 1993. Mem. Nat. Assn. Women Bus. Owners, Women in Comm., Internat. Assn. Bus. Communicators, Mo. Press Women (pres. Gateway chpt. 1993—), Mid-Am. Mature Pubs. Assn. (sec.-treas.).

ZAROSINSKI, CATHERINE JO, physical therapist; b. Klamath Falls, Oreg., May 2, 1951; d. Theodore Joseph and Helen La Vonne (Eckert) Z. BS, So. Oreg. Coll., 1973; MS in Phys. Therapy, Tex. Woman's U., Denton, 1975. Lic. phys. therapist, Oreg. Supr., clin. edn. coord. St. Vincent Hosp., Portland, Oreg., 1976-84; pvt. practice West Hills Phys. Therapy Clinic, Portland, 1984-95; clinic dir. Pacific Rehab. and Sports Medicine, Portland, 1995—. Mem. Am. Phys. Therapy Assn. (com. on chpts. 1991-93, coun. on chpt. pres. 1988-92), Oreg. Phys. Therapy Assn. (sec. 1985-87, pres. 1988-92, legis. com. 1979). Democrat. Office: West Hills Phys Therapy 9450 SW Barnes Rd # 215 Portland OR 97225

ZARRETT, MARY ANN, mental health professional, educator, consultant; b. Big Clifty, Ky., July 8, 1949; d. Julius Forest and Gladys Mae (Hawkins) Duvall; m. Robert Warren Zarrett, Dec. 27, 1969 (div. Aug. 1983); children: Rob Warren, Elizabeth Duvall. BSN, U. Ky., 1971; MS in Counseling, Ctrl. Mo. State U., 1977; MA in Human and Orgnl. Devel., The Fielding Inst., 1994, PhD in Human and Orgnl. Systems, 1996. RN, N.D.; nat. cert. counselor. Rsch., cataloging and circulation asst. U. Ky. Med. Ctr. Library, Lexington, 1969-71; nurse aide Taylor Manor Nursing Home, Versailles, Ky., 1970; self-employed Burlington, Vt., 1971-74; per diem nurse psychiat. ward St. Luke's Hosp., Fargo, N.D., 1988-92; counselor, instr. Moorhead State U., Fargo, 1985-89, asst. prof., 1990—, dir. tng. Counseling Ctr., 1987-90, outreach coord., 1989-90, affirmative action officer, 1992; cons. Minn. Army N.G. through Met. State U., 1987; cons. Pathways/U.S. West, 1990—; orgnl. cons., 1990—. Adv. bd. mem. Compassionate Friends Fargo, N.D., 1986—; chmn. music Plymouth Congregational Ch., Fargo, 1986-88; chmn. Fargo Clinic Art Gallery, 1982-84. Mem. ACA, Minn. Assn. Specialists in Group Work, Am. Mental Health Counselors Assn., Nat. Orgnl. Devel. Network, Phi Kappa Phi. Republican. Congregationalist. Office: Moorhead State U Counseling Ctr Moorhead MN 56560

ZARZOUR, ROBIN ANN, special education educator; b. Parma, Ohio, Apr. 14, 1964; d. Robert Halim and Rosalie Frances (Ezzie) Z. AAS in Early Childhood Edn., Cuyahoga C.C., 1985; BS in Spl. Edn., Cleve. State U., 1990, MA in Early Childhood Spl. Edn., 1993. Early childhood spl. edn. aide Middleburg Spl. Presch., Middleburg Heights, Ohio, 1983-86; counselor Camp Sunshine, Parma, Ohio, 1986-88; early childhood spl. religious tchr. St. Charles, Parma, Ohio, 1988-89; early childhood spl. edn. tchr. Parma City Sch. System, 1990—. Mem. Cleve. Assn. Mid. Ea. Orgn., 1992—. Recipient Tchr. of Yr. award Cuyahoga Spl. Edn. Svc. Ctr., 1993—. Mem. Coun. for Exception Children, Parma Edn. Assn. (union bldg. rep. 1992—). Democrat. Roman Catholic.

ZARZYCKI, LISA MESTDAGH, bank executive, independent sales consultant; b. Detroit, June 12, 1966; d. Ronald P. and Elizabeth L. Mestdagh; ;m. Dale Adam Zarzycki, May 12, 1989; children: Joseph Michael, Jacob Adam, Luke Ronald. BA, U. Mich., 1988. Asst. supr. Standard Fed. Bank, Troy, Mich., 1987-88, investigator, loss prevention, 1988—, asst. v.p., asst. dept. mgr. corporate security, 1994—; independent beauty cons. Mary Kay Cosmetics, Clinton Twp., Mich., 1996—. Mem. North Oakland Loss Prevention Assn., Detroit Loss Prevention Assn. Republican. Roman Catholic. Office: Standard Federal Bank 2600 W Big Beaver Rd Troy MI 48084

ZASLAVSKY, CLAUDIA, mathematics education consultant, author; b. N.Y.C., Jan. 12, 1917; d. Morris and Olga (Reisman) Cogan; m. Sam Zaslavsky, July 19, 1941; children: Thomas, Alan. BA, Hunter Coll., 1937; MA, U. Mich., 1938; postgrad., Columbia U., 1974-78. Cert. secondary math. tchr., N.Y. Cost acct. Block Drug Co., Jersey City, 1938-42; jr. engr. Remington Arms, Ilion, N.Y., 1942-43; music tchr. various music schs., N.Y.C., 1954-59; tchr. math., chair dept. New Rochelle (N.Y.) Acad., 1959-65; tchr. math. Woodlands H.S., Hartsdale, N.Y., 1965-77; adj. asst. prof. math. Coll. New Rochelle, 1979-81; math textbook cons. Macmillan/McGraw-Hill and other pub. cos., N.Y.C., 1992, 96; math. edn. cons. U. Alaska, Fairbanks, 1993-94; mem. task force on multiculturalism and gender Nat. Coun. Tchrs. Math., Reston, Va., 1993-94; condr. workshops and seminars on multicultural math., 1970—. Author: Africa Counts: Number and Pattern in African Culture, 1973, Fear of Math, 1994, The Multicultural Math Classroom, 1996, others; contbr. articles to profl. jours. and books. Trustee Davis-Putter Scholarship Fund, 1982—; bd. dirs. Girls Inc. "Eureka" Program, N.Y., 1992-95; Educators for Social Responsibility, N.Y., 1984—; adv. bd. Educators Against Racism and Apartheid, N.Y., 1986-94. NSF grantee, 1960-70. Mem. AAUW, Internat. Study Group on Ethnomath., Am. Fedn. Tchrs., Authors Guild, Nat. Coun. Tchrs. Math., N.Y. State Coun. Tchrs. Math., Women's Internat. League for Peace and Freedom.

ZASTROW, PATRICIA MARCELLA HABLE, artist; b. Bloomer, Wis., Apr. 13, 1937; d. William and Marcella Katherine (Grill) Hable; m. Milfred Norman Zastrow, June 14, 1958; 1 child, Sara. BS, Stout State U., 1960. Cert. tchr., Wis. Home econs. tchr. Shawano (Wis.) Pub. Schs., 1960; tchr. home econs., consumer and family sci. Madison (Wis.) Pub. Schs., 1962-92; pvt. practice surface design artist and fiber arts PZ Fiber Arts, Sun Prairie, Wis., 1988—; active mentorship program Sun Prairie (Wis.) Pub. Schs., 1992-93. Charter mem., mus. bd. Sun Prairie (Wis.) Hist. Libr. and Mus., 1970-73. Mem. Nat. Surface Design Assn., Wis. Surface Design Assn. Home: 167 North St Sun Prairie WI 53590

ZATZ, ARLINE, writer, photographer; b. Bklyn., May 2, 1937; m. Joel Leon Zatz, Nov. 4, 1956; children: Robert Jay, David Alan. BA in Journalism, Rutgers U., 1977. Consumer affairs officer Borough of Highland Park, N.J., 1970-72; asst. coord. N.J. Div. Consumer Affairs, Newark, 1972-75; writer, photographer A-Z Publs., Metuchen, N.J., 1977—. Author: 25 Bicycle Tours in New Jersey, 1988, New Jersey's Special Places, rev. edition 1994 (Best Book N.J. Press Women, Nat. Assn. Press Women), Best Hikes with children in New Jersey, 1992; contbr. articles to profl. jours. Bd. dirs. YMCA, Metuchen, 1984-86. Mem. Nat. Assn. Press Women, N.J. Press Women, Outdoor Writers Assn. Am., Author's Guild Am. Home: 77 Woodside Ave Metuchen NJ 08840-1629 Office: A-Z Publs 77 Woodside Ave Metuchen NJ 08840-1629

ZAUDERER, NAOMI BETH, union organizer; b. Columbus, Ohio, June 5, 1967; d. Philip Zauderer and Eve Jean (Sweet) Struve; m. Kevin Hughes Monroe, June 20, 1987 (div. Jan. 1995). BA in Govt., Coll. William and Mary, 1988; MA in Polit. Sci., U. Calif., Berkeley, 1990, postgrad., 1994. Grad. student instr. U. Calif., Berkeley, 1990-94; grad. student rschr. Emma Goldman Papers Project, Berkeley, 1995; v.p. Assn. Grad. Student Employees Local, Berkeley, 1993-94, pres., 1994-95; faculty asst. Columbia Law Sch., N.Y.C., 1995-96. Contbr. articles to profl. jours. Pardee fellowship U. Calif., 1989-90. Mem. UAW, Nat. Writers Union, Phi Beta Kappa. Democrat. Home: 208 W 23rd St Apt 1614 New York NY 10011 Office: Nat Writers Union Nat Office E 113 University Pl Fl 6 New York NY 10003

ZAVORA, MARGARET S., chiropractor, kinesiologist; b. Waynesburg, Pa., Aug. 5, 1952; d. Casimer Paul and June Margaret (Harvey) Z. BA in Psychology with honors, W.Va. U., 1974, MA in Counseling & Guidance with honors, 1980; DC with honors, Palmer Coll. Chiropractic, 1987. Cert. chiropractor, Pa.; cert. phys. therapist, Pa.; cert. applied kinesiology Internat. Coll. of Applied Kinesiology. Assoc. chiropractor Pitts., 1988-92; prin., chiropractor Zavora Chiropractic Ctr., Pitts., Pa., 1992—; presenter on applied kinesiology. Mem. NAFE, Nat. Assn. Women Bus. Owners, Acad. Clin. Close Encounter Therapists, Program for Extraordinary Experience Rsch., Pitts. Friends of Tibet, Bethel Park C. of C., Warrior Trail Assn. of Greene County, Mensa. $D Women Bus. Owners, Mensa. Office: Zavora Chiropractic Ctr Ste 700 1121 Boyce Rd Pittsburgh PA 15241

ZAYDON, JEMILLE ANN, English language and communications educator, school system administrator; b. Peckville, Pa., Feb. 21; d. Joseph and Catherine Ann (Hazzouri) Z.; student Barry Coll. for Women; BS, Marywood Coll.; MS in Edn., Wilkes Coll., 1978; doctoral candidate Temple U. Tchr. St. Hugh Elem. Sch., Coconut Grove, Fla., Allapattah Elem. Sch., Miami, Columbus Elem. Sch., Westfield, N.J.; communications instr. Keystone Job Corps, Drums, Pa., 1966-73; vol. instr. Keystone Rehab. Ctr., Scranton, Pa., 1970-71; curriculum cons. for mentally retarded, Vienna, Austria, 1974; prof. English and reading Lackawanna Jr. Coll., Scranton, 1974—, head dept. English, speech and reading, 1976—, chmn. dept. arts, humanities and social studies, 1977—; adj. prof. English, U. Scranton, 1980—; communications instr. Lackawanna County Vocat. Tech. Sch., 1974—. Supr. recreation program, Hazleton, Pa., summer 1968; founder, adviser Keystone Kourier, 1967-69. Sec. Fedn. Youth, William W. Scranton; coord. annual Christmas for Mentally Retarded Keystone City Residence, Scranton, 1975—; supr. students Heart Fund campaign, 1968-71; developer program mentally retarded Allied Svcs. for Handicapped Scranton, 1973; Class rep. Marywood Coll. Fund Dr., 1978; gen., 1980—; faculty coord. Am. Cancer Soc., 1990—; active ARC, March of Dimes, Heart Fund, Leukemia and United Fund drives, also Sickle Cell Anemia Found. Bd. dirs. Michael F. Harrity Meml. Fund.; mem. exec. bd. Northeastern Pa. Environ. Council, also co-chmn. public edn. and funding. Recipient Faculty Mem. of Yr. award, Job Corps, 1969, Humanitarian award, 1980, Outstanding Educators award, 1992, Educators award Dade County, 1973, 75; named Tchr. of Yr., 1973, Tchr. We Will Never Forget, Dade County Allpattah Elem. Students, 1991, Northeast Woman by Scranton Sunday Times, 1993; Service scholar, Barry Coll., 1958. Mem. Nat. Edn. Assn., Pa. State Edn. Assn., Beta Lambda Tau, Sigma Tau Delta, Theta Chi Beta (charter pres.), Lambda Iota Tau (life). Democrat. Roman Catholic (instr. Confraternity Christian Doctrine). Editor Lebanese Am. Jour., 1957-63. Home: 608 N Main Ave Scranton PA 18504-1870

ZBIEGIEN, ANDREA, educator, consultant, educational administrator; b. Berea, Ohio, May 12, 1944; d. Leopold and Anna Meri (Voskovich) Z. BS in Edn., St. John Coll., 1969; MS in Edn., John Carroll U., 1973; MDiv, Grad. Theol. Union, 1986, D of Ministry, 1988. Tchr. jr. high sch. Diocese of Cleve., 1964-76, instr. dept. religious edn., 1971-82, dir. religious edn., 1976-82; diocesan dir. religious edn. Diocese of Toledo, 1982-87; instr. Dept. Christian Formation Diocese of Savannah, Ga., 1987—; dir. religious edn. Diocese of Savannah, 1987—; substitute tchr., Cleve., also Brunswick, Ga., 1976—; cons. Benziger Pub. co., Ohio, 1971-78, Our Sunday Visitor Pubs., 1978-90, Silver, Burdett & Ginn, Savannah, Charleston, St. Augustine, 1988—; adj. prof. St. John U. Grad. Theol. Sem., summers 1978—. Author: RCIA: Parish Team Formation, 1987; producer, author: (videos) RCIA: Parish Team Formation, 1987; contbr. articles to profl. jours. Facilitator Bishop's Task Force Action for a Change, Cleve., 1969-72; advocate, facilitator Systematic Techniques of Effective Parenting, Huron County, Ohio, 1982-87; advocate Commn. on Children and Youth, Glynn County, Ga., 1989—; vol. Medicine for World's Poor. Recipient scholarship KC, Cleve., 1961-69. Mem. AAUW, ASCD, YWCA, Nat. Assn. of Pastoral Coords. and Dirs., Nat. Cath. Edn. Assn., Sisters for Christian Cmty., Ind. Order of Foresters, Golden Isles Fiberarts Guild. Home: 707A Newcastle St Brunswick GA 31520-8012 Office: SFX Christian Formation Ctr 1116 Richmond St Brunswick GA 31520

ZECK, LINDA ANN, elementary education educator; b. Camden, N.J., Nov. 6, 1966; d. Ronald E. Sr. and Patricia Ann (Cwik) Z. BA, Glassboro (N.J.) State Coll., 1989; M in Student Pers. Svcs., Rowan Coll. of N.J., 1996. Cert. elem. tchr., N.J. Elem. tchr. Birches Sch., Turnersville, N.J., 1989—. Author, performer: (video) The Friendly Letter, 1994. Mem. Pentecostal Faith. Home: Landing Rd Clarksboro NJ 08020 Office: Birches Sch 416 Westminster Blvd Turnersville NJ 08012-1625

ZEEMAN, JOAN JAVITS, writer, inventor; b. N.Y.C., Aug. 17, 1928; d. Benjamin Abraham and Lily (Braxton) Javits; m. John Huibert Zeeman III, Mar. 20, 1954; children: Jonathan Huibert, Andrea Zeeman Deane, Eloise Zeeman Scharff, Phoebe Zeemon Fitch, Merrily Margaret. BA, Vassar Coll., 1949; MEd, U. Vt., 1976. Pub. relations exec. Benjamin Sonnenberg, N.Y.C., 1949-51; freelance writer, 1952—. Trustee Theatreworks (formerly Performing Arts Repertory Theatre), N.Y.C., 1953-83, Profl. Childrens Sch., N.Y.C., 1980-89, Palm Beach Sch. Arts Found., 1993—, Fla. Theatrical Assn., 1994—. Author: The Compleat Child, 1964. Lyricist musical plays: Young Abe Lincoln, 1961; Hotel Passionato, 1965; Author, lyricist: Young Columbus, 1992; song lyricist: Santa Baby, 1953. Patentee Alphocube. Mem. ASCAP, Dramatists Guild, Gilbert and Sullivan Soc., Vassar Club (sec. 1978-84, v.p. 1984-86) (Westchester, N.Y.). Home: 230 Palmo Way Palm Beach FL 33480-3135

ZEFF, OPHELIA HOPE, lawyer; b. Oak Park, Ill., Aug. 19, 1934; d. Bernard Allen and Esther (Levinsohn) Gurvis; m. David Zeff, Dec. 29, 1957 (div. 1983); children: Sally Lyn Zeff Propper, Betsy Zeff Russell, Ellen, Adam; m. John Canterbury Davis, Sept. 18, 1987. BA, Calif. State U., 1956; JD, U. Pacific, 1975. Bar: Calif. 1975. Reporter Placerville (Calif.) Mountain Dem., 1956-57, Salinas Californian, 1957-59; corr. Modesto (Calif.) Bee, 1962-64; atty. ALRB, Sacramento, 1975-76, Yolo County Counsel, Woodland, Calif., 1976-78, Law Office of O.H. Zeff, Woodland, 1978-85; employee rels. officer Yolo County, 1985-87; ptnr. Littler, Mendelson, Fastiff, Tichy & Mathiason, Sacramento, 1987—. Mem. Vallejo (Calif.) Sch. Bd., 1971-74, pres., 1974; mem. Woodland Libr. Bd., 1982; v.p. LWV, Vallejo, 1972; mem. LWV, Sacramento, 1987—. Recipient Am. Jurisprudence Lawyer Coop. Pub., 1974. Mem. Sacramento County Bar, Sacramento Women Lawyers, Indsl. Rels. Assn. No. Calif., Traynor Soc. (life). Democrat. Jewish. Office: Littler Mendelson Fastiff Tichy & Mathiason 400 Capitol Mall Fl 16 Sacramento CA 95814-4407

ZEHAGEN, BONNIE LEE, city official; b. Ogdensburg, N.Y., May 30, 1947; d. James Rodger and Violet (Robinson) Cuthbert; m. Clayton Edward ZeHagen, June 23, 1974 (div.); 1 child, Bonnie-Marie. AA, St. Petersburg Jr. Coll., 1967. Cert. mcpl. clk. Sec. bldg. and pub. works City of Treasure Island, Fla., 1967-73, bd. coord., 1974-78, dep. city clk., 1978—. Mem. Sunset Beach Civic Assn., Treasure Island, 1967-89. Mem. Internat. Inst. Mcpl. Clks., Fla. Assn. City Clks., Treasure Island Hist. Soc. Inc. (pres. 1989-91), Pinellas County Clks. Assn. Republican. Congregationalist. Office: City of Treasure Island 120 108th Ave Treasure Island FL 33706-4702

ZEHRING, KAREN, information executive; b. Washington, Dec. 5, 1945; d. Robert William Zehring and Gretchen (Lorenz) Proos; m. George Lang, 1970 (div. 1979); m. Peter Frank Davis, June 10 1979 (div. 1995); children: Jesse, Antonia. BA, U. Denver, 1967; postgrad., Yale U., 1967-68. Assoc. pub. mktg. and sales Instl. Investor Systems, Inc., N.Y.C., 1968-74; co-owner, co-creator Café des Artistes Restaurant, N.Y.C., 1975-79; owner, pub. The Corp. Fin. Letter, N.Y.C., 1976-78; group dir. planning and devel. Bus. Week mag., N.Y.C., 1977-78; owner, pub., exec. editor Corp. Fin. Sourcebook The Corp. Fin. Bluebook, N.Y.C., 1979-84; chmn., pres., pub., editor-in-chief Corp. Fin. mag., N.Y.C., 1986-90; cons. Karen Zehring & Assocs., Castine, Maine, 1990-94; mng. ptnr. Creative Devel. Ptnrs., N.Y.C., 1995—; founder The Fin. Learning Ctr., 1995—. Mem. The Women's Forum, Am. Soc. Mag. Editors, Vt., N.H. Direct Mktg. Assn. Unitarian. Office: 100 W 57th St New York NY 10019-3327

ZEHRING, PEGGY JOSEPHINE, artist; b. Hutchinson, Kans., Jan. 4, 1941; d. Phillip E. and Bernice (Ashley) Johnson; m. R. David Zehring, July 27, 1963; children: Lisa, Geoff. BS, U. Kans., 1963; BA, U. Ill., 1977. Instr. Bellevue (Wash.) C.C., 1979-93, Sch. Visual Concepts, Seattle, 1985-86, Seattle Ctrl. C.C., 1987—, North Seattle C.C., 1987—, Coupeville (Wash.) Art Ctr., 1993—; juror and lectr. Eastside Assn. Fine Art, Mercer Island Visual Arts League, Nat. League Am. Artists & Pen Women; lectr. Women Painters of Washington, Bellevue Art Mus., N.W. Watercolor Soc. One-woman shows include King County Arts Commn., Seattle, Blake Gallery, Seattle, Bellevue (Wash.) C.C., PACCAR, Bellevue, Pacific N.W. Bell, Seattle, U. Ill., Chgo.; exhibited in group shows at COCA Annual, Seattle, Seattle Art Mus. Sales & Rental Gallery, LewAllen Fine Art, Santa Fe, Bellevue Art Mus., Diablo Valley Coll., Elizabeth Prince Gallery, Prescott, Ariz.; represented in selected collections City of Lynnwood, Wash., Pacific NW Bell, PACCAR, Delitte, Haskins & Sells, Opti-Copy, Kansas City, Harper & Assocs., Bellevue and numerous other pvt. collections. Recipient First Place award Ariz. Internat., Snowgrass Art Inst., Cashmere, Wash., Kans. State Fair, Hutchinson, Honorable Mention award W. Wash. State Fair; named finalist Pierce County Libr. Project, Gig Harbor, Wash. Home: 832 31st Ave S Seattle WA 98144 also: PO Box 967 La Veta CO 81055

ZEIBERG, MONA CAROL, lawyer; b. Bronx, N.Y., May 23, 1961; d. Seymour Lawrence and Marilyn Sonia (Wolfson) Z. BA, Am. U., 1983; JD, Emory U., 1986. Bar: Ga. 1986, D.C. 1991. Law clk. Office Adminstrv. Law Judges, U.S. Dept. Labor, 1986-88; sr. counsel labor and employment law Litigation Ctr., U.S. C. of C., Washington, 1988—. Mem. Fed. Bar Assn., Am. Corp. Counsel Assn. Office: US C of C 1615 H St NW Washington DC 20062-0001

ZEIDER, SUSAN KAY, insurance claims administrator; b. Vancouver, Wash., July 6, 1952; d. Russell William and Martha (Pierson) Z. BA in History, Willamette U., 1974; MA in History, U. N.D., 1978. ChFC; CLU; cert. sr. claims law assoc. Am. Edn. Inst. Sales rep. Met. Life Ins., Grand Forks, N.D., 1977; asst. office mgr. Acacia Mutual Life Ins., Portland, Oreg., 1978-79; claims rep. Farmers Ins. Group, Portland and Vancouver, 1979-81; br. claims supr. Farmers Ins. Group, Vancouver, 1981-84, regional property claims mgr., 1984-86; br. claims mgr. Farmers Ins. Group, Medford, Oreg., 1986-90; human resources mgr. Farmers Ins. Group, L.A., 1990-91, claims customer rels. and legis. mgr., 1991—; pres. Ins. Women Jackson County, Oreg., 1988. Vol. March of Dimes Walk Am., Simi Valley, 1990—, Simi Valley (Calif.) Cultural Arts Ctr., 1995—; pres. Sycamore Ridge Homeowners Assn., Simi Valley, 1993. Recipient Assn. Achievement award Am. Assn. Mng. Gen. Agts., 1994. Mem. Am. Inst. for CPCU/Ins. Inst. Am. (CPCU, assoc. in claims 1982, assoc. in ins. svc. 1995, IR 201 adv. panel 1995—), Nat. Assn. Ins. Women (cert. profl. ins. woman 1988, legis. adv. panel 1994—, profl. scholarship chair edn. found. 1995, v.p. Region VIII 1996—, Claims Woman of Yr. Region IX 1988, Claims Profl. of Yr. Region VIII 1992, Claims Profl. of Yr. 1992, Ins. Profl. of Yr. Region VIII 1996), Soc. CPCU (regulatory and legis. sect. com. 1993-95), Soc. CLU/ChFc, Internat. Assn. Arson Investigators (dir. Oreg. state chpt. 1983-90, Exemplary Mem. award Oreg. state chpt. 1988), Ins. Women of L.A. (Ins. Woman of Yr. 1992), Ins. Women of Portland Oreg., Tucson Assn. Ins. Women.

ZEIDNER, LISA ALISON, novelist, poet, educator; b. Washington, Mar. 27, 1955; d. Joseph and Dorothy (Gould) Zeidner; m. John Lafont, May 8, 1988; 1 child, Nicolas. BA, Carnegie-Mellon U., 1977; MA, Johns Hopkins U., 1978. Prof. dept. English Rutgers U., Camden, N.J., 1979—. Author (novels): Limited Partnerships, 1989, Alexandra Freed, 1983, Customs, 1981; author (vols. of poetry): Pocket Sundial, 1989, Talking Cure, 1981. Home: 108 Chestnut St Haddonfield NJ 08033

ZEIGER GILLESPIE, CHRISTINE MARIE, school program administrator, educator; b. Harrisburg, Pa., Feb. 2, 1945; d. Dale Lebo and Christiana Joan (Disanto) Zeiger; m. John Richard Gillespie, Jr., Aug. 17, 1968 (div. Feb. 1996); children: Jennifer Marie, Laura Leigh. BS in Edn., West Chester U., 1967, MEd in Edn., 1981. Cert. reading specialist, elem. edn. tchr. Elem. tchr. Harrisburg Sch. Dist., 1967-68, Westminster (Colo.) Sch. Dist., 1968-70; substitute tchr. Delaware County Schs., Pa., 1974-78; Title I reading specialist Ridley Sch. Dist., Folsom, Pa., 1979-81; reading specialist Benchmark Sch., Media, Pa., 1981-82; Title I reading specialist Delaware County Schs., 1982—; Even Start program coord. Delaware County Ind. Unified # 25, 1992—; cons. Ednl. Consulting Svcs., Wallingford, Pa., 1990—; conf. presentor Pa. Dept. Edn., Harrisburg, 1990, Del. Dept. Edn., Great Oak, 1992, Pa. State U., University Park, 1995. Leader Girl Scouts Am., Delaware County, 1978-82; Dimensions in Art coord. Wallingford-Swarthmore Sch. Dist., Pa., 1981-84; mem., vol. Jr. League Phila., 1984—; fundraiser, vol. Crozer Chester Med. Ctr., Upland, Pa., 1985-91. Mem. IRA, PASCD, ASCD, NCTE, DVRA, KSRA, NAEYC. Republican. Office: Delaware County Intermediate Unit # 25 6th and Olive St Media PA 19063

ZEIGLER, PAMELA LYNN, food scientist, microbiologist; b. Fridley, Minn., July 30, 1970; d. Thomas Wayne and Victoria Elizabeth (Anderson) Z. BS, N.D. State U., 1992; MS, U. Minn., 1995. Lab. asst. sci. dept. N.D. State U., Fargo, 1990-92; quality control tech. Faribault (Minn.) Foods, 1991, 92; R & D tech. Northwestern Foods, St. Paul, 1993-94; QA/QC mgr. Fairest Foods, Baldwin, Wis., 1995—. Vol. Pet Haven, Mpls., 1994-95, Red Cross, Woodville, Wis., 1995. Mem. Internat. Food Technologists, Gamma Sigma Delta. Home: 2476 C Cobble Hill Alcove Woodbury MN 55125 Office: Fairest Foods 1030 6th Ave Baldwin WI 54002

ZEIGLER, VICKI LYNN, pediatrics nurse; b. Hampton, S.C., May 26, 1961; d. Richard Jackson and Miriam Banner (Smith) Z.; m. Paul Crawford Gillette, Feb. 1, 1992. BSN, Med. U. of S.C., 1982, MSN, 1991. RN, S.C.; cert. spl. competency in cardiac pacing for non-physicians N.Am. Soc. Pacing and Electrophysiology. Staff nurse pediatrics Med. U. S.C., Charleston, 1983-85, nurse clinician pediatric cardiology, 1985-91, pediatric arrhythmia/pacemaker case mgr., 1992-94, pediatric arrhythmia nurse specialist, 1994-96; pediat. arrhythmia case mgr. Cook Children's Med. Ctr., Ft. Worth, 1996—; BLS instr. Am. Heart Assn., Columbia, S.C. Contbr. articles to profl. jours. Recipient Young Investigator award Sigma Theta Tau. Mem. AACN, Assn. for Care of Children's Health, North Am. Soc. of Pacing and Electrophysiology, Am. Heart Assn. Coun. of Cardiovascular Nursing, Sigma Theta Tau. Republican. Office: Cook Childrens Med Ctr Cardiology Dept 801 7th Ave Fort Worth TX 76104-2796

ZEILER, ALETA REDMOND, educational consultant; b. Winston Salem, N.C., May 4, 1960; d. Dewey Carter and Willa Belle (Johnson) Redmond; m. John Zeiler, Nov. 22, 1986. BS in Indsl. Rels./Psychology, U. N.C., 1982, MEd, 1984. Guidance counselor Johnston County Schs., Smithfield, N.C., 1984-86; cons. Prescription Learning, Atlanta, 1987-88, lead cons., 1988-90; cons. edn. Jostens Learning, N.C., S.C., 1990-92; sr. cons. edn. Jostens Learning, N.C., 1992-95. Whittaker scholar U. N.C, Chapel Hill, 1979-82. Mem. ASTD, ASCD, N.C. Counselors Assn. Home: 1111 Pinelake Dr Hartsville SC 29550 Office: Jostens Learning Ste 200 100 Hartsfield Ctr Pkwy Atlanta GA 30354

ZEILIG, NANCY MEEKS, magazine editor; b. Nashville, Apr. 28, 1943; d. Edward Harvey and Nancy Evelyn (Self) Meeks; m. Lanny Kenneth Fielder, Aug. 20, 1964 (div. Dec. 1970); m. Charles Elliot Zeilig, Jan. 6, 1974 (div. Dec. 1989); 1 child, Sasha Rebecca. BA, Birmingham-So. Coll., 1964; postgrad., Vanderbilt U., 1971-73. Editorial asst. Reuben H. Donnelley, N.Y.C., 1969-70; asst. editor Vanderbilt U., Nashville, 1970-74; editor U. Minn., St. Paul, 1975; asst. editor McGraw-Hill Inc., Mpls., 1975-76; mng. editor Denver mag., 1976-80; editor Jour. Am. Water Works Assn., Denver, 1981—. Editor, co-pub.: WomanSource, 1982, rev. edit., 1984; contbr. articles to consumer mags. Co-chair arts adv. com. Denver Sch. of the Arts, 1994-96. Office: Jour Am Water Works Assn 6666 W Quincy Ave Denver CO 80235-3011

ZEILINGER, ELNA RAE, elementary educator, gifted-talented education educator; b. Tempe, Ariz., Mar. 24, 1937; d. Clayborn Eddie and Ruby Elna (Laird) Simpson; m. Philip Thomas Zeilinger, June 13, 1970; children: Shari, Chris. BA in Edn., Ariz. State U., 1958, MA in Edn., 1966, EdS, 1980. Bookkeeper First Nat. Bank of Tempe, 1955-56; with registrar's office Ariz. State U., 1956-58; piano tchr., recreation dir. City of Tempe; tchr. Thew Sch., Tempe, 1958-61; elem. tchr. Mitchell Sch., Tempe, 1962-74, intern prin., 1976, personnel intern, 1977; specialist gifted edn. Tempe Elem. Schs., Tempe, 1977-86; elem. tchr. Holdeman Sch., Tempe, 1986-89; tchr. grades 1-12 and adult reading, lang. arts, English Zeilinger Tutoring Svc., 1991—; grad. asst. ednl. adminstrn., Iota Workshop coordinator Ariz. State U., 1978; presenter Ariz. Gifted Conf., 1978-81; condr. survey of gifted programs, 1980; reporter public relations Tempe Sch. Dist., 1978-80, Access com. for gifted programs, 1981-83. Author: Leadership Role of the Principal in Gifted Programs: A Handbook, 1980; Classified Personnel Handbook, 1977, also reports, monographs and paintings. Mem. Tempe Hist. Assn., liaison, 1975; mem. Tempe Art League; mem. freedom train com. Ariz. Bicentennial Commn., 1975-76; bd. dirs. Maple Property Owners Assn., 1994—. Named Outstanding Leader in Elem. and Secondary Schs., 1976' Ariz. Cattle Growers scholar, 1954-55; Elks scholar, 1954-55; recipient Judges award Tempe Art League, 1970, Best of Show, Scottsdale Art League, 1976. Democrat. Congregationalist.

ZEISEL, GLORIA, real estate company executive; b. Braddock, Pa., June 21, 1920; d. Max and Rachel (Kaufman) Sperling; m. Henry Israel Zeisel, Feb. 1, 1942; children: Cheryl Z. Kramer, Elliot, Howard, Debra Moed. Student, Bklyn. Coll. Pres., founder Adolph Schreiber Sch., Monsey, N.Y., 1954-95; sec., treas., dir. HiTech Mfg. Co., N.J., 1992—; sec., treas., dir. Real Estate Cos., N.Y., N.J., Fla., 1975—. Founder, life mem. Cmty. Synagogue Monsey, 1954—; founder, bd. trustees Holocaust Ctr., Spring Valley, N.Y., 1988—; bd. govs. Good Samaritan Hosp., Nyack, N.Y., co-chmn. showcase, 1994; vol. United Jewish Fund. Recipient Outstanding Citizen of Jewish Cmty. Ramapo Town Bd., 1994. Mem. Amit Women Nat. Orgn. (life), Brandies Women Nat. Orgn. (life), Israel Bond Orgn. (bd. dirs., bd. trustees). Home: 18 Hilltop Pl Monsey NY 10952

ZEIT, RUTH MAE, foundation administrator; b. N.Y.C., May 13, 1945; d. Albert Joseph and Gertrude (Goldberg) Janover; children: Rachael Miriam, Rebecca Madeleine. BA, U. Pa., 1967, postgrad., 1969-70; postgrad., Temple U., 1967-69. Teaching fellow Temple U., Phila., 1967-69, U. Pa., Phila., 1969-70; dir. piano music studio Phila., 1969—; pres. Lupus Found. Del. Valley, Ardmore, Pa., 1983—; Mem. Winner's Ball com. Lupus Found. of Del. Valley, Ardmore, 1986-87, presiding officer, bd. dirs., med. adv. bd., 1983—, prin. organizer Ednl. Symposia, 1983—, prin. organizer patient support groups, 1983—; organizer Lupus Loop Fundraising Marathon Walk/Run; lectr. Prin. coordinator Lupus Found. of Del. Valley Newsletter, 1983—. Liaison with Phila. Mayor Ed Rendell, liaison between Julius Erving and Children's Hosp. of Phila.; coord. Julius Erving Lupus Rsch. Fund; target chmn. Undergrad. Admissions Secondary Sch. Com., U. Pa. Mem. Am. Coll. of Musicians, Sigma Delta Gamma, Music Tchrs. Nat. Assn., Pa. Music Tchrs. Assn. Democrat. Jewish. Home: 1640 Oakwood Dr Apt W-122 Narberth PA 19072-1232 Office: Lupus Found Delaware Valley 44 W Lancaster Ave Ardmore PA 19003-1339

ZEKMAN, TERRI MARGARET, graphic designer; b. Chgo., Sept. 13, 1950; d. Theodore Nathan and Lois (Bernstein) Z.; m. Alan Daniels, Apr. 12, 1980; children: Jesse Logan, Dakota Caitlin. BFA, Washington U., St. Louis, 1971; postgrad, Art Inst. Chgo., 1974-75. Graphic designer (on retainer) greeting cards and related products Recycled Paper Products Co., Chgo., 1970—, Jillson Roberts, Inc., Calif.; apprenticed graphic designer Helmuth, Obata & Kassabaum, St. Louis, 1970-71; graphic designer Container Corp., Chgo., 1971; graphic designer, art dir., photographer Cuerden Advt. Design, Denver, 1971-74; art dir. D'Arcy, McManus & Masius Advt., Chgo., 1975-76; freelance graphic designer Chgo., 1976-77; art dir. Garfield Linn Advt., Chgo., 1977-78; graphic designer Keiser Design Group, Van Noy & Co., Los Angeles, 1978-79; owner and operator graphic design studio Los Angeles, 1979—. Recipient cert. of merit St. Louis Outdoor Poster Contest, 1970, Denver Art Dirs. Club, 1973.

ZELBY, RACHEL, realtor; b. Sosnowiec, Poland, May 6, 1930; came to U.S., 1955; d. Herschel Kupfermintz and Sarah Rosenblatt; m. Leon W. Zelby, Dec. 28, 1954; children: Laurie Susan, Andrew Stephen. Student, U. Pa., 1955, Realtors' Inst., Norman, Okla., 1974; grad., Realtors Inst., Oklahoma City, 1978. Lic. realtor, broker, Okla.; cert. residential specialist, Okla. Realtor, broker, ptnr. Realty World Norman Heritage, 1973-81; realtor, broker Century 21 Parker Real Estate, Norman, 1981—, residential specialist, 1986—. Mem. Jr. Svc. League, Norman, 1980—; charter mem. Assistance League Norman, 1970—; bd. dirs. Juvenile Svcs., Inc., Norman, 1975-76; bd. viss. Coll. Fine Arts U. Okla., 1992—. Mem. Nat. Assn. Realtors, Norman Bd. Realtors, Women's Coun. Realtors (treas. 1985), U. Okla. Women's Assn. (past pres.), Norman C. of C., LWV. Home: 1009 Whispering Pines Dr Norman OK 73072-6912 Office: Century 21 Parker Real Estate 319 W Main St Norman OK 73069-1312

ZELENY, MARJORIE PFEIFFER (MRS. CHARLES ELLINGSON ZELENY), psychologist; b. Balt., Mar. 31, 1924; d. Lloyd Armitage and Mable (Willian) Pfeiffer; BA, U. Md., 1947; MS, U. Ill., 1949, postgrad., 1951-54; m. Charles Ellingson Zeleny, Dec. 11, 1950 (dec.); children: Ann Douglas, Charles Timberlake. Vocational counseling psychologist VA, Balt., 1947-48; asst. U. Ill. at Urbana, 1948-50, research asso. Bur. Research, 1952-53; chief psychologist dept. neurology and psychiatry Ohio State U. Coll. Medicine, Columbus, 1950-51; research psychologist, cons., Tucson, Washington, 1954—. Mem. Am., D.C. psychol. assns., AAAS, Southeastern Psychol Assn., DAR, Nat. Soc. Daus. Colonial Wars, Nat. Soc. Colonial Dames XVII Century, Nat. Soc. Descendants of Early Quakers, Nat. Soc. Daus. of Am. Colonists, Nat. Soc. Dames of Ct. of Honor, Nat. Soc. U.S. Daus. of 1812, Mortar Bd., Delta Delta Delta, Sigma Delta Epsilon, Psi Chi, Sigma Tau Epsilon. Roman Catholic. Home: 6825 Wemberly Way Mc Lean VA 22101-1534

ZELEZNAK, SHIRLEY ANNE, psychotherapist; b. Ft. Dodge, Iowa; d. Melvin Peter and Illiah Mary (Olson) Hood; m. Donald John Zeleznak, June 14, 1969; children: Kristine Anne, Ryan John. BA, Briar Cliff Coll., 1967; MS in Clin. and Ednl. Psychology and Counseling, Winona State U., 1972. Cert. hypnotherapist, psychotherapist. Secondary tchr. Rochester, Minn., 1969-74; secondary tchr./counselor Mankato, Minn., 1974-77; task force dir. Heart Assn., Mankato, 1978-82; mental health counselor Scottsdale, Ariz., 1985—; tchr. Maricopa County C.C., Scottsdale, 1986-89; motivational speaker, Mankato, 1974-84; sch. cons. Paradise Valley/Scottsdale Sch. Dist., 1987—; bd. dirs. Home Base, Phoenix; psychotherapist St. Maria Goretti Ch., Scottsdale, 1986—; crisis intervention counselor, police dept., Phoenix, 1993—. Author: Series for Junior High Students, 1981 (books), 1982-83 (software programs). Chef A'La Heart, Minn. Heart Assn., Mankato, 1979-81; motivational speaker Gang Awareness, Scottsdale, 1992—. Recipient Appreciation award Minn. Heart Assn., 1981. Mem. Mental Health Counselors, Nat. Ctr. for Learning Disabilities, Am. Counseling Assn., Phoenix Scottish Rite Found., Inst. for Developmental and Behavioral Neurology. Roman Catholic.

ZELLER, SHIRLEY EVELYN, manufacturing executive; b. Linton, N.D., Sept. 21, 1937; d. Gordon Towne and Evelyn (Green) Ward; m. William V. Zeller, Aug. 10, 1957; children: Greg Alan, William Lee, Timothy Neil. AA in Gen. Bus., Gen. Studies, Jackson (Mich.) C.C., 1983; BA in Mgmt. of Human Resources, Spring Arbor (Mich.) Coll., 1984. Sec. Consumers Power Co., Jackson, 1959-66; sec., bus. mgr. Gisler, Howell & Simms, Kansas City, Mo., 1966-67; exec. sec. Commonwealth Assocs., Jackson, 1967-71, Hayes Albion Industries, Jackson, 1971-75; supr. external auditing Gilbert/Commonweath, Jackson, 1975-89; mgr. quality assurance Constrn. Technologies, Jackson, 1989-90; sr. quality assurance engr. Mactec, San Diego, 1990-91; mgr. compliance mgmt. Westinghouse Idaho Nuclear Co., Idaho Falls, Idaho, 1991-94; mgr. quality Lockheed Idaho Technologies Co., Idaho Falls, 1994—. Commr. Mich. Transp. Commn., Lansing, 1985-91; candidate for state senate, 1986. Recipient Athena award Oldsmobile and C. of C., Jackson, Profl. Achievement award Spring Arbor Coll. Alumni, 1991, Susan B. Anthony award Jackson Y Ctr.; named Alumnae of the Yr. Jackson C.C. Mem. LWV (nat. nominating com. 1996—), Bus. and Profl. Women (Mich. pres. 1983-84, nat. legis. com. 1989-92, Idaho pres. 1996), Jackson C. of C. (chair legis. com. 1988-91). Home: 962-C McKinley Ave Pocatello ID 83201 Office: Lockheed Martin Idaho Tech PO Box 1625 Idaho Falls ID 83415-0316

ZELLICK, SANDRA ZELDA, psychotherapist; b. Everett, Mass., Oct. 26, 1936; d. Louis Herman and Lillian Ethel (Brown) Z.; m. Norman W. Beberman, Aug. 25, 1957 (div. Feb. 1985); children: Ellen, Julie, David, Laura. BA, Brandeis U., 1957; MEd, Harvard U., 1958; MBA, Western New Eng. Coll., 1980; MS, Nova U., 1988, PhD, 1993. Lic. mental health counselor; cert. family mediator Fla. Supreme Ct., cert. hypnotherapist. Tchr. Newton (Mass.) Pub. Sch., 1957-58; rschr. Harvard U., Cambridge, Mass., 1958-59; sys. engr. IBM Corp., Balt., 1959-60; psychotherapist Family Counseling Ctr., Sarasota, 1987-89; family therapist Family Therapist Assocs., Nova U., Ft. Lauderdale, Fla., 1990-92, The Inst. for Family Therapy, Miami, Fla., 1992-95; psychotherapist in pvt. practice, Venice, Fla., 1995—. Mem. APA, ACA, Am. Assn. Marriage and Family Therapists, Fla. Soc. Psychotherapists. Democrat. Jewish. Home: 1091 Covert Rd South Venice FL 34293

ZELON, LAURIE DEE, lawyer; b. Durham, N.C., Nov. 15, 1952; d. Irving and Doris Miriam (Baker) Z.; m. David L. George, Dec. 30, 1979; children: Jeremy, Daniel. BA in English with distinction, Cornell U., 1974; JD, Harvard U., 1977. Bar: Calif. 1977, U.S. Ct. Appeals (9th cir.) 1978, U.S. Supreme Ct. 1989. Assoc. Beardsley, Hufstedler & Kemble, L.A., 1977-81; assoc. Hufstedler, Miller, Carlson & Beardsley, L.A., 1981-82, ptnr., 1983-88; ptnr. Hufstedler, Miller, Kaus & Beardsley, L.A., 1988-90, Hufstedler, Kaus & Ettinger, L.A., 1990-91, Morrison & Foerster, L.A., 1991—. Editor-in-chief: Harvard Civil Rights-Civil Liberties Law Rev., 1976-77. Vol. atty. ACLU of So. Calif., L.A., 1977—; bd. dirs. N.Y. Civil Liberties Union, 1973-74. Mem. ABA (chmn. young lawyers divsn. pro bono project 1981-83, delivery and pro bono projects com. 1983-85, subgrant competition-subgrant monitoring project 1985-86, chair standing com. on lawyers pub. svc. responsibility 1987-90, chair law firm pro bono project 1989-91, standing com. legal aid and indigent defendants 1991—, chair 1993—), Calif. Bar Assn., L.A. County Bar Assn. (trustee 1989-91, v.p. 1992-93, sr. v.p. 1993-94, pres.-elect 1994-95, pres. 1995-96, fed. cts. and practices com. 1984-93, vice chmn. 1987-88, chmn. 1988-89, chmn. judiciary com. 1991-92, chair real estate litigation subsect. 1991-92), Women Lawyers Assn. L.A., Calif. Women Lawyers Assn. Democrat. Office: Morrison & Foerster 555 W 5th St Ste 3500 Los Angeles CA 90013-1080

ZEMANS, FRANCES KAHN, legal association executive; b. Chgo., May 1, 1943; married; 3 children. BA in zoology, U. Mich., 1965; MA in polit. sci., Northwestern U., 1966, PhD in Polit. Sci., 1972. Instr. dept. politics Lake Forest (Ill.) Coll., 1973-74; instr. dept. polit. sci. Northwestern U., Evaston, Ill., 1974-75; asst. prof. depts. edn. and polit. sci. U. Chgo., 1975-80; dir. edn., rsch. Am. Judicature Soc., Chgo., 1983-85, asst. exec. dir. programs, 1985-87, exec. v.p., dir., 1987—; cons. ABA, 1980; mem. task force on judicial conduct and ethics of spl. commn. on administrn. of justice in Cook County, 1985-88; vis. lectr. Northwestern U., Chgo., 1986; bd. dirs. Cook County Criminal Justice Project, 1987-90; adjudication working group Bureau Justice Assistance, U.S. Dept. Justice, Washington, 1987, 88; mem. task force gender bias in courts, State of Ill., 1988-90;mem. Ill. Judicial Inquiry Bd., 1988-92. Contbr. articles to profl. jours.; mem. editorial bd. Justice System Journal, 1986-90; presenter in field. Bd. dirs. ACLU, Ill., 1978-87; mem. Police Bd. City of Chgo., 1980-87, chair budget com., office of profl. standards com., rules and regulations revision com.; mem. Chgo. crime survey planning com. Chgo. Community Trust, 1984-86, bd. dirs. govt. assistance project, 1990—; bd. visitors So. Meth. U. Sch. Law, 1987-90. Scholar ABF, 1974-83. Mem. Am. Polit. Sci. Assn., Law and Soc. Assn. (trustee 1980-83). Office: Am Judicature Soc 180 N Michigan Ave Chicago IL 60601-7401

ZEMBLE, PHYLLIS LAZARUS, municipal official, consultant, artist; b. Phila., May 28, 1943; d. Nathan Leon and Tillie (Cohen) Lazarus; children: Michael Scott, David Benjamin, Karen Stephanie, Richard Jonathan, Robert Marc. BS in Fine Arts and Art Edn., Phila. Coll. Art, 1964; BArch, Temple U., 1983, MBA, 1988. Art tchr. Sch. Bd. Phila., 1964-66; artist, arch. Lower Merion Township, Pa., 1973-91, commr., 1992—; dir. mktg. Gocial & Co., Jenkintown, Pa., 1994-95. Pres. Montgomery County Assn. First Class Twps., Penn Valley, Pa., 1995-96; v.p. Ea. Assn. First Class Twp. Commrs., Boothwyn, Pa., 1995-96; v.p., bd. dirs. Lower Merion Libr. Sys., 1993, 95-96; mem. exec. com. Pa. State Assn. First Class Twp. Commrs., Harrisburg, 1994-96; mem. drought task force Montgomery County Office of Emergency Preparedness, Eagleville, Pa., 1995; Comcast newsmaker CNN Headline News, Montgomery County/Phila. area, 1996. Mem. Alpha Lambda Delta. Democrat. Jewish. Home and Office: Montgomery County Assn 1st Class Townships 923 Hagys Ford Rd Penn Valley PA 19072

ZEMM, SANDRA PHYLLIS, lawyer; b. Chgo., Aug. 18, 1947; d. Walter Stanley and Bernice Phyllis (Churas) Z. BS, U. Ill., 1969; JD, Fla. State U., 1974. Bar: Ill. 1975, Fla. 1975. With fin. dept. Sinclair Oil, Chgo., 1969-70; indsl. rels. advisor Conco Inc., Mendota, Ill., 1970-72; assoc. Seyfarth, Shaw, Fairweather & Geraldson, Chgo., 1975-82, ptnr., 1982—. Bd. dirs. Chgo. Residential Inc., 1993—, pres., 1994-96; mem. Art Inst. Round Table, Chgo., 1993-94. Mem. Ill. State Bar Assn., Fla. State Bar Assn., Univ. Club Chgo. (bd. dirs. 1991-94). Office: Seyfarth Shaw 55 E Monroe St Chicago IL 60603-5702

ZENO, JO ANN, sales executive; b. Akron, Ohio, Sept. 25, 1952; d. Ross and Mary Francis (Gerbec) Z. BA in French and Edn., BS in Spanish, U. Akron, 1975. Tchr. French, Spanish S.E. Local, Ravenna, Ohio, 1975-77, Akron Pub. Schs., 1977-80; sales rep. Xerox Corp., Akron, Cleve., 1980-83; cert. stapling technician U.S. Surg. Corp., Norwalk, Conn., 1983-88; rep. cardiovascular surg. products Medtronic Inc., 1988-95; sales rep. Karl Storz Endoscopy-Am. Inc., Culver City, Calif., 1995—. Home: 2895 Spring Meadow Ct Indianapolis IN 46268

ZERMAN, MAXINE LORAINE, mathematics and science braille consultant; b. Menomonie, Wis., Oct. 18, 1927; d. James and Celia May (Dunahee) Beaver; m. R. P. Allan, Feb. 11, 1945 (div. Aug. 1956); children: Darlene, David (dec.), Daniel; m. Arnold Elwood Zerman, Oct. 29, 1967 (dec. Nov. 1993); stepchildren: Patricia, Gary, Karen (dec.). Student, Milw. Conservatory of Music, 1950-51. Cert. literary braille, math. and sci. braille, math. and sci. braille proofreading. Math. and sci. braille advisor Libr. of Congress/Nat. Libr. Svc. for the Blind and Physically Handicapped, Washington, 1986-96; cons. All Braillists, 1985-96. Contbr. articles to profl. jours. Named Innovator of the Yr., Fla. Assn. Educators and Rehabilitators, 1991. Mem. Nat. Braille Assn. (math. chmn. 1985-88), Visual Aid Vols. Fla. (pres. 1989-91, editor newsletter 1988-90), Sarasota County Braille Transcribers (pres. 1991-95). Home and Office: 2526 Wisteria St Sarasota FL 34239-4001
Died Sept. 3, 1996.

ZERNIAL, SUSAN CAROL, education educator; b. L.A., July 2, 1948; d. Gus Edward and Gladys Elizabeth (Hale) Z. BA, Calif. State U., Long Beach, 1973; MA, Calif. State U., 1975; EdD, U. San Francisco, 1992. Cert secondary and elementary tchr.; libr. credential. Libr. Clovis (Calif.) Unified Schs., 1975-78; media specialist Anaheim (Calif.) Union High Sch. Dist., 1975; libr. Benicia (Calif.) Unified Sch. Dist., 1978-80; tchr. Atascadero (Calif.) Unified Schs., 1985-93; adj. prof. Edn. Adams State Coll., Alamosa, Colo., 1993—; acquisitions editor Librs. Unltd./Tchrs. Ideas Press, Englewood, Colo. Recipient Scholarship, Calif. Assn. Sch. Librs., 1974. Mem. ASCD, Am. Rsch. Assn., Phi Delta Kappa. Home: 8547 E Arapahoe Rd # J-152 Englewood CO 80112-1430

ZETTER, LOIS C., personal manager; b. Boston, Jan. 6, 1939; d. Oscar and Pauline (Krasnov) Z.; m. Walter S. Unterseher, Sept. 25, 1988. BA in Theatre Arts cum laude, Brandeis U., 1960. Prin. LeMond/Zetter Mgmt. Inc., L.A., Carson City, Nev., 1971—. Appeared in plays Fiddler on the Roof, How To Succeed in Business Without Really Trying, Ben Bagley's Cole Porter Revue; assoc. prodr. (film) Moment By Moment; co-prodr. (TV series) Cover Up, Dads; prodn. cons. (films) Grease, Blow Out, Urban Cowboy; managed careers of John Travolta, Patrick Swayze, Katherine Helmond, Mickey Rourke, Mark Harmon, etc. Donor Aid for AIDS, Brandeis U., Friendly Hand Found., The Pacific Ctr., Gaucher Disease Found. Recipient Spirit award Brandeis U., 1995. Mem. Acad. TV Arts and Scis., Conf. Personal Mgrs., Women in Film. Office: LeMond/Zetter Mgmt Inc 5570 Old Hwy 395 N Carson City NV 89704

ZEVNIK-SAWATZKY, DONNA DEE, litigation coordinator; b. Tulsa, Dec. 15, 1946; d. Robert Joseph Z. and Dorothy Dee (Robertson) Zink; m. Kenneth Sawatzky, May 30, 1965; children: K. Brian, Kaira D. Student, U. Ctrl. Okla., 1977, Okla. State U., 1984. Cert. AIDS educator, State of Okla. Sec. Farmers Ins. Co., Oklahoma City, 1974-80; office mgr. S.A.F.E., Inc., Oklahoma City, 1980-83; jr. acct. Southeast Exploration Corp., Oklahoma City, 1983-84; acct. Young Bros., Inc., Oklahoma City, 1984-88, The Denman Co., Inc., Oklahoma City, 1988-89; litigation coord. ACLU Okla., Oklahoma City, 1994—; bd. dirs. ACLU Okla., treas., 1994—. Author and illustrator: That Place--Otherwhere, 1994, Something for Otherwhere, 1995; author: At Our House, 1979-83; columnist Putnam City-N.W. News, Warr Acres, Okla., 1979-83; designer stage sets Miss Warr Acres Pageant, 1971-88. Bd. dirs. Miss War Acres Pageant, Oklahoma City, 1984-88, Warr Acres C. of C., 1981-85; treas. ACLU of Okla., 1994—, bd. dirs., 1995—; child welfare advocate Okla. State Dept. Human Svcs., Oklahoma City, 1987-89; coord. AIDS clinic Triangle Assn., Oklahoma City, 1994—. Named Honorary Mayor of Warr Acres, 1971, Super Citizen, 1973, Outstanding Vol. Okla. State Dept. Human Svcs., 1988; recipient Svc. award Warr Acres C. of C., 1979, Legis. Commendation State of Okla., 1988, numerous Okla. Newspaper Column of Month awards Okla. Press Assn., Oklahoma City, 1981-82. Mem. Amnesty Internat., The Interfaith Alliance, Pflag, Human Rights Campaign. Republican. Methodist. Office: 3012 N Lee Ste A Oklahoma City OK 73103

ZEVON, SUSAN JANE, editor; b. N.Y.C., July 23, 1944; d. Louis and Rhea (Alter) Z. BA, Smith Coll., 1966. Asst. editor trends and environments House & Garden, N.Y.C., 1970-80; account supr. Jessica Dee Communications, N.Y.C., 1981-84; editor architecture House Beautiful, N.Y.C., 1985—. Author: Inside Architecture, 1996, (with others) Decorating On The Cheap, 1984. Mem. Archtl. League N.Y., Smith Coll. N.Y. Club (v.p. 1987-88, pres. 1988-89). Office: House Beautiful 1700 Broadway New York NY 10019-5905

ZEWE, JUDITH LYNN, human resources professional; b. Monongahela, Pa., May 2, 1947; d. Norman Edward and Martha Ellen (Harkins) Kenny; m. Dennis Dale Zewe, Aug. 17, 1964; children: Dennis Dale Jr., Donna Lynn. BA in Mgmt., Mercyhurst Coll., 1979; cert. of mgmt., U. Colo., Denver, 1982, postgrad.; MS in Mgmt., Regis U., 1995. Dir. pers. Mercyhurst Coll., Erie, Pa., 1975-79; compensation mgr. Community Coll. of Denver System, 1979-83, dir. employee rels., 1983-85; founder, pres., career cons. Lynn Dale & Co., Southfield, Mich., 1985-88; dir. pers., affirmative action Colo. Sch. Mines, Golden, 1988-93; dir. human resources Arapahoe C.C., Littleton, Colo., 1993—; compensation cons. Colo. Bd. Community Colls., 1981. Author: Successful Job Search Strategies. Vol. Make-a-Wish Found. Colo., 1990—, Children's Hosp. Denver, 1990—. Named Outstanding Vol. Make-a-Wish Found. Colo., 1991. Mem. Coll. and Univ. Pers. Assn. (nat. benefits coun. 1983-84, bd. dirs. S.W. region, human resource devel. adv. bd. 1995—), Colo. Higher Edn. Affirmative Action Adminstrs., Coll. and Univ. PErs. Assn. Colo. (pres. 1992-93). Home: 10244 Owens St Broomfield CO 80021-6656 Office: Arapahoe C C 2500 W College Dr Littleton CO 80160-9002

ZGONC, JANICE ANN, technical information specialist; b. Greensburg, Pa., Apr. 8, 1956; d. Joseph and Jennie (Yaniszeski) Z. BA, Edinboro U. of Pa., 1979. Tech. info. specialist Dept. of Def., Washington, 1983—. With U.S. Army, 1974-76. Mem. NAFE, Capital PC Users Group, Assn. Old Crows, Data Processing Mgmt. Assn., Armed Forces Communication and Electronics Assn. Home: 1304 S Thomas St Arlington VA 22204-3671

ZHANG, XIAO-FENG, power system engineer, researcher; b. Sichuan, Peoples Republic of China, Aug. 8, 1951; came to U.S., 1988; d. Yong-Qing and Lan (Li) Z.; m. Paul McEntire, June 22, 1996; 1 child, John. BS in EE, Taiyuan Engring. Inst., Shanxi, 1976; MS in EE, Electric Power Rsch. Inst., 1983. Power engr. Jinchong Dist. Power Bur., Shanxi, 1976-80; power system engr. EPRI, Beijing, 1983-88, Systems Control, Palo Alto, Calif., 1988-89; sr. power engr. Empros Systems Internat., Plymouth, Minn., 1989-93; cons. Pacific Gas & Elec. Co., San Ramon, Calif., 1993-94; sr. engr. ABB Systems Control, Santa Clara, Calif., 1995—. Contbr. articles to profl. jours. Recipient 1st prize EPRI of China, 1985, 2d prize Ministry of Electric Power, Beijing, 1986, 3d prize Chinese Nat. Com., 1987. Mem. Power Engring. Soc. IEEE (sr.), Computer Soc. IEEE. Home: 1523 Johnson Ave San Jose CA 95129 Office: ABB Systems Control 2550 Walsh Ave Santa Clara CA 95051

ZHAO, JIA, lawyer; b. Shanghai, Sept. 23, 1940. BA, Beijing Fgn. Langs. Inst., 1963; JD, Harvard U., 1983. Bar: Ill. 1985, D.C. 1986. Ptnr. Baker & McKenzie, Chgo. Mem. ABA, D.C. Bar, Chgo. Bar Assn., Beijing Fgn. Econ. Law Assn. Office: Baker & McKenzie 1 Prudential Plz 130 E Randolph Chicago IL 60601*

ZHAO, LI, fine arts company executive, teacher, consultant; b. Tianjin, China, Mar. 16, 1958; came to U.S., 1984; d. Robert Yunnian Chao and Qizhen Cao; m. Shiyi Zhang, Aug., 1984 (div. 1987); m. Kenneth Lloyd Schoolland, Aug. 8, 1988 (div. 1994); 1 child, Kenli Dulcinea. BA, Foreign Lang. Inst., Tianjin, China, 1983; MA, U. Minn., 1987; Mgmt. Sci. (Japanese), Japan-Am. Inst. Mgmt. Sci., Honolulu, 1988; MS in Japanes Bus. Study, Chaminade U., Honolulu, 1988. Steel mill worker Guang Xi, China, 1969-78; tchr. Liu-Zhou Steel Mill High Sch., Guang Xi, 1978; translator, researcher China Dept. Transp., Beijing, 1983-84; teaching asst. U. Minn., Mpls., 1985-87; intern trainee Tobu Dept. Store, Tokyo, Japan, 1988; pres. Schoolland Internat., 1988—; sales mgr. trainee Duty Free Shops, Honolulu, 1989-92; gen. mgr. Double-Eye Hawaii, Honolulu, 1989-92, 1989—; gen. mgr. Tianjin Victor Entertainment Co. Ltd., Tianjin, China, 1994—. Editor: (newsletters) Double-Eye News, 1989-92, Libertarian Party Hawaii News, 1991-93. Chmn. membership com. U.S.-China People's Friendship Assn., 1988-89; mem. legis. com. Small Bus. Hawaii; bd. dirs. Libertarian Party Hawaii, 1992. Recipient Model Citizen award Mpls. Police Dept., 1992; named Outstanding Grad. Student, U. Minn., 1992. Mem. Am. Mktg. Assn. (bd. dirs.), Am. Soc. Interior Designers, Sales and Mktg. Execs. of Honolulu, Honolulu Japanese C. of C. (chair com.), Honolulu Acad. Art, Japan-Am. Assn. Hawaii, Assn. Hawaii Artists (corr. sec.), Chinese C. of C. Honolulu.

ZHENG, LISA LIQING, computer programmer; b. Xian, China, May 11, 1966; came to U.S., 1990; d. Youzhong Zheng and Siuping Huang. BSEE, Huazhong U. Sci. & Tech., 1988; MSEE, Purdue U., 1992. Asst. engr. Inst. Electronics Chinese Acad. Scis., Beijing, 1988-90; electronics engr., systems programmer Computer Graphics, Corp., Indpls., 1992-94; programmer Bertelsmann Music Group, Inc., Indpls., 1994—. Office: Bertlesmann Music Group Inc 6550 E 30th St Indianapolis IN 46219-1102

ZHENG, MAGGIE (XIAOCI), materials scientist, vacuum coating specialist; b. Shanghai, Apr. 21, 1949; came to U.S., 1986; d. George and Helen (Chou) Cheng; 1 child, Dee. BS in Physics, Qutu Normal U., Shangdong, China, 1981; MSEE, U. Sci. and Tech. China, Beijing, 1984; MS in Materials Sci., U. Wis., 1988, PhD in Materials Sci., 1991. Lectr. Tsinghua U., Beijing, 1984-86; assoc. scientist United Techs., East Hartford, Conn., 1991-92; staff scientist Engineered Coatings, Inc., Rocky Hill, Conn., 1992-93; materials and coating process engr. Chromalloy Turbine Techs., Middletown, N.Y., 1993-94; engr. GE Power Generation, Schenectady, N.Y., 1995—; rsch. asst. U. Wis., Madison, 1986-91. Contbr. articles in profl. publs.; patentee in field. Mem. NAFE, Am. Metal Soc., Minerals, Metals and Materials Soc. Office: GE Power Generation Bldg 55 Rm 103 River Rd Schenectady NY 12365

ZHORNE, WENDY KELLER, literary agency executive, speaker; b. Chgo., Oct. 2, 1964; d. Alexander Robert and Carol Ruth (Wheeler) Keller; m. Jeff E. Zhorne, Sept. 9, 1984 (div. June 1994); children: Jeremy Winston (dec.), Amelia Louise (dec.), Sophia Rose. Student, Yavapai C.C., 1980-81, Ariz. State U., 1981-83. Features editor The Ruff-Riter, Prescott, Ariz., 1981-82; drama critic State Press, Tempe, Ariz., 1982-83; assoc. editor Pointe mag., Tempe, 1982-83, La Gaceta de L.A., 1983-84; reporter Knight-Ridder Media, Arcadia, Calif., 1984; assoc. agt. The Writers' Assocs., Sun Valley, Calif., 1988; pres. Forthwrite Lit. Agy., Pasadena, Calif., 1989—, pub. cons., 1990—; lectr. to numerous clubs and confs. internationally, 1989—; presenter on overcoming obstacles to various orgns. nationally, 1994—. Author: Children's Craft Ideas, 1991, Nature Crafts for Kids, 1996; contbr. numerous articles to various publs. Literacy counselor, Calif. Recipient Mary C. Brown award Ariz. Press Women, 1981. Mem. Women's Nat. Book Assn., Pubs. Mktg. Assn., Nat. Spkrs. Assn. (content compatible adv. com.). Office: Forthwrite Lit Agy Ste 327 3579 E Foothill Blvd Pasadena CA 91107

ZIAKA-VASILEIADOU, ZOE DIMITRIOS, chemical engineer; b. Larissa, Thessalia, Greece, Apr. 15, 1963; came to U.S., 1988; d. Dimitrios J. and Melpomeni D. (Sakellariou) Z.; m. Savvas P. Vasileiadis, Feb. 17, 1985; 1 child, Eugenia-Melina. Diploma in Chem. Engring., Aristotle U. Thessaloniki, Greece, 1987; MS in Chem. Engring., Syracuse U., 1990; PhD in Chem. Engring., U. So. Calif., 1994. Registered profl. engr., European Cmty. Scholar chem. engring. Aristotle U. Thessaloniki, 1982-87; rschr. chem. lab. Exxon Corp., Thessaloniki, 1984, engring. mgr., 1986; fellow Norwegian Ednl. Coun., 1988; scholar Ctr. Indsl. Devel., Greece, 1987-88; rsch. assoc., scholar Syracuse (N.Y.) U., 1988-90; rsch. assoc., fellow U. So. Calif., L.A., 1990-94, lectr., 1995; practical trainee Internat. Assn. Exch. Student Engring., Finland, 1985, Israel, 1986; patentee in field. Contbr. articles to AIChE Jour., Chem. Engring. Sci., Jour. Membrane Sci., Separation Sci. and Tech., 5th World Congress Chem. Engring., Chem. Engring. Commn. NATO fellow Greek Govt., Thessaloniki, 1987-88, AXIOS Found. for Worthiness fellow, Torrance, Calif., 1994, CRESPE, COGPS-U. So. Calif. fellow, L.A., 1992, 93, 94. Mem. AIChE, Materials Rsch. Soc.,

N.Am. Catalysis Soc., Greek Inst. Chem. Engrs., Internat. Platform Assn. Orthodox Christian. Home: 1179 W 37th St Apt D Los Angeles CA 90007

ZICHEK, SHANNON ELAINE, secondary school educator; b. Lincoln, Nebr., May 29, 1944; d. Melvin Eddie and Dorothy Virginia (Patrick) Z. AA, York (Nebr.) Coll., 1965; BA, U. Nebr., Kearney, 1968; postgrad., U. Okla., Edmond, 1970, 71, 72, 73, 74, 75, U. Nebr., Kearney, 1980, 81, 82, 89, 92. Tchr. history and English, NW High Sch., Grand Island, Nebr., 1948—. Republican. Christian. Home: 2730 N North Rd Grand Island NE 68803-1143

ZIEGLER, CHRISTINE BERNADETTE, psychology educator, consultant; b. Syracuse, N.Y., Mar. 22, 1951; d. Salvatore and Beverlie (Hopkins) Capozzi; m. Steven Jon Ziegler, Jan. 7,1979;1 child. Justin. Bs, SUNY, Brockport, 1978; MS, Syracuse U., 1980, PhD, 1982. Adj. asst. prof. SUNY, Cortland, N.Y., 1983-86, Syracuse (N.Y.) U., 1984-86, LeMoyne Coll., Syracuse, 1986-87; rsch. cons. Syracuse (N.Y.) U., 1982-86; assoc. prof. Kennesaw (Ga.) State Coll., 1987—; dean continuing edn. East Cobb Mid. Sch.; parent facilitator Ga. Coun. Child Abuse, Atlanta, 1990—; cons. Dissertation Rsch. UGA, Atlanta; cons. aggression reduction tng. N.W. Regional Hosp., Rome, Ga.; presenter numerous profl. confs. in field. Reviewer for Teaching of Psychology Jour., Jour. Undergrad. Rsch.; contbr. articles to profl. jours. Mem. Juvenile Ct. Panel, Health Children's Initiative; mem. sch. adv. com., Marietta, Ga., 1989, mem. sch. bond com., 1989. Recipient fellowship Syracuse U., 1982. Mem. APA, AAAS, NAS, Ga. Psychol. Assn., Southeastern Psychol. Assn., Soc. Philosophy and Psychology, Soc. for Rsch. in Child Devel., Psychology Club (advisor), Blue Key (chpt. v.p.). Home: 1408 Dewberry Trl Marietta GA 30062-4013 Office: Kennesaw State College 3455 Steve Frey Rd Kennesaw GA 30144

ZIEGLER, DELORES, mezzo-soprano; b. Decatur, Ga.; children: Katie, Adam. Grad., Maryville Coll.; postgrad., U. Tenn. Operatic roles include Dorabella in Cosi Fan Tutti, Octavian in Der Rosenkavalier, Dulcinee in Don Quichotte, Cherubino in Le Nozze di Figaro, Rosina in Barber of Seville, Romeo, in I Capuleti e i Montecchi (first singer to sing the role of Romeo in Moscow and San Francisco), Idamante in Idomeneo, Charlotte in Werther, Adalgisa in Norma, Sextus in La Clemenza di Tito; performances with Atlanta Symphony, Bonn Theater der Stadt, Theater der Stadt Koln, La Scala Opera, Paris Opera, Bolshoi Opera, Moscow, Vienna Stattsopera, Phila. Orch., Met. Opera; recs. include Dorabella in Cosi Fan Tutte, EMI, Mozart Requiem, Mozart Great Mass, Atlanta Symphony, Mahler's 8th Symphony Telark Records, Beethoven 9th Symphony, Phila. Orch., EMI, Bach B Minor Mass, Teldek records, Margared in Le Roi d'ys, Erato Disque, title role in Bertoni's Orfeo, Frequenz records, Mozart's Kronenmesse, Deutsch Grammaphon; debut as Dorabella in Cosi fan Tutti, Lyric Opera Chgo., first Carmen at Atlanta Opera; debut at N.Y. Met. as Siebel in Faust, 1990. Office: care Lynda Kay 2702 Crestworth Ln Buford GA 30519-6483 Office: Côté Artists Mngmt Inc 157 W 57th St Ste 803 New York NY 10019-2210

ZIEGLER, JAN, writer, media consultant; b. Hartford, Conn., Oct. 18, 1953; d. Richard T. and Margaret (Whinnem) Z. BA cum laude, U. Conn., 1975. Reporter, photographer, features editor The Norwich (Conn.) Bulletin, 1975-78; reporter UPI, Hartford, Conn., 1978-79; sci. writer, broadcast writer, New England weekend editor UPI, Boston, 1979-82; editor fgn. desk UPI, N.Y.C., 1982-83; sci. writer UPI, Washington, 1983-87, sci. editor, 1987-88; free-lance writer, media cons. Washington, 1989—; cons. nat. vaccine program USPHS; cons. White Ho. report to UNICEF on child health, Nat. Rsch. Coun. report on sharing lab resources, 1993. Contbr. Omni, National Geographic, The Scientist, Mirabella. Bd. dirs. Cleve. Park Hist. Soc., Washington, 1986-87. Mem. Women in Film and Video. Office: 2724 Ordway St NW Apt 2 Washington DC 20008-5047

ZIEL, DONNA RAE, university administrator; b. Santa Barbara, Calif., Sept. 12, 1943; d. Raymond Joseph and Emma Josephine (Osner) Gilbreth; m. Theodore Brian Ziel, Sept. 8, 1962 (div. Jan. 1975); children: Laura Ann, Brian Patrick. BA with distinction, San Jose State U., 1973, MA in Asian History, 1979. Deptl. sec. San Jose State U., 1973-76, liberal studies advisor, 1976-89, dir. Student Advisement Ctr. Salinas, 1979-89, assoc. dir. Monterey County campus, 1989-92, assoc. dir. student outreach and recruitment, 1992—. Creator, exec. dir. teleconf. series: Live! from San Jose State, 1993—. Commr. Women's Commn., Santa Cruz County, Calif., 1984-89, co-chair, 1985-86; pres. Industry Edn. Coun., Monterey County, 1990-91; participant NGO Forum Fourth UN Conf. Women, Beijing, 1995; Calif. state contact UN Women's Conf. One Yr. Later nat. teleconf., 1996. Sourisseau Acad. grantee, 1975; Calif. State U. Adminstrv. Fellows Program fellow, 1980-81. Mem. Nat. Assn. Student Pers. Adminstrs., Nat. Assn. Acad. Advisors, Nat. Assn. Coll. Admissions Counselors, Western Assn. Coll. Admission Counselors, Western Assn. Women Historians, Calif. Advocates for Re-entry Edn. (pres.-elect 1996—), Calif. Women in Higher Edn. (pres. 1980-81), San Jose State U. Alumni Assn. (founder, bd. dirs. 1992—), Phi Kappa Phi (Disting. Svc. award 1992). Office: San Jose State Univ One Washington Sq San Jose CA 95192-0011

ZIELINKSI, BETH BABICH, marketing consultant; b. Columbus, Ohio, Nov. 29, 1947; d. Robert and Marilyn B.; m. Thomas Zielinski, June 11, 1989. B.A. in Psychology, Ohio State U., 1969; M.Internat.Mgmt., Am. Grad. Sch. Internat. Mgmt., 1977. Counselor, cons. Ohio Bur. Employment Services, 1969-73; propr. retail art gallery, Toronto, Ont., Can., 1973-75; mktg. and advt. mgr. Ellio's Frozen Pizza div. Purex, Inc., 1977-78; mktg. mgr. The Drop Shop Ltd., cable TV installation parts, Roselle, N.J., 1978-80; product mgr. cheese and butter products mfg. div. Atlantic & Pacific Tea Co. Inc., Montvale, N.J., 1980-82; mktg. mgr. pies and pie shells Mrs. Smith's Frozen Foods Co., Pottstown, Pa., 1982-83; product mgr. Respond Communications Software Software Synergy, New Rochelle, N.Y., 1984-85; mktg. mgr. Eventide, Inc., Little Ferry, N.J., 1986-92; sr. ptnr. Strategic Directions Inc., Burr Ridge, Ill., 1992—. mem. research com. Alzheimer's Disease Soc., 1980-81; founding mem. singles div. United Jewish Appeal, Fort Lee, N.J., 1978. Recipient Outstanding Creativity award Am. Dairy Assn., 1981. Mem. Nat. Assn. Female Execs., Am. Grad. Sch. Internat. Mgmt. Alumni Assn., Mensa, Phi Alpha Theta.

ZIENTARA, SUZANNAH DOCKSTADER, insurance company executive; b. Wichita, Kans., Oct. 1, 1945; d. Ralph Walter and Patricia Ann (Harvey) Dockstader; m. Larry Henry Zientara, Oct. 18, 1975; 1 child, Jillian Sue Zientara Cox. Student, U. Kans., 1963-64; BS in Bus. Edn., Ft. Hays State U., 1968; MEd in Secondary Guidance and Counseling, U. Mo., St. Louis, 1973. CLU. Sec. to supt. Wichita Pub. Schs., 1968-69; tchr. bus. edn. Wichita Heights High Sch., 1969-71, Lindbergh High Sch., St. Louis, 1971-72, Holman Jr. High Sch., St. Louis, 1972-75; guidance counselor Pattonville Heights Jr. High Sch., St. Louis, 1975-79; tchr. data processing Lawrence (Kans.) High Sch., 1979-85; ins. agt. State Farm Ins. Cos., Lawrence, 1985-90; agy. mgr. State Farm Ins. Cos., Tulsa, 1990-95; agy. field exec. State Farm Ins. Cos., Topeka, 1995—; mem. Regional Mgr. Coun., Tulsa, 1992-93; participant Purdue Profl. Mgmt. Inst., West Lafayette, Ind., 1993. Author: Introduction to Data Processing, 1983. Mem. Williams Edn. Fund, U. Kans. Named Outstanding Young Woman of Am., 1974. Mem. Am. Soc. CLU's and ChFC's, USTA, Am. Ski Assn., Topeka C. of C., U. Kans. Alumni Assn., PEO, Shawnee Country Club, Mortar Bd., Pi Omega Pi. Republican. Episcopalian. Home: 3637 SW Kings Forest Rd Topeka KS 66610 Office: State Farm Ins Cos 2930 Wanamaker Dr Ste 6 Topeka KS 66614

ZIEVE, CHARLOTTE R., research scientist; b. Chgo., Sept. 17, 1926; d. Charles and Bessie Cantor; m. Edward Robert Zieve, June 15, 1947; children: Andrew, Gary, Peter, Wendy, Kathie. BS, U. Ill., 1947; MS, U. Wis., Milw., 1975; PhD, U. Wis., 1986. Chemist Farmers Chem. Co., Kalamazoo, 1947-48, Marquette Med. Sch., Milw., 1948-49; lectr. U. Wis., Milw., 1982-87; lectr. U. Wis., Madison, 1986-94, asst. scientist, 1990—; rep. UN conf. Inst. for Environ. Studies, Cairo, 1994. contbr. articles and papers to profl. jours. and procs. Bd. dirs. Planned Parenthood, Milw., 1978-84, Future Milw., 1980; gov. commn. State of Wis., Madison, 1980. Mem. Nat. Audubon Soc. (treas. 1978-82, rep. UN conf. Beijing 1995—), Wis. Audubon Soc. (treas. 1978-82, Citizens Activist award 1978), Sigma Xi. Democrat. Jewish. Home: PO Box 267 Elkhart Lake WI 53020

ZIGRAY, DEBRA RENEE, elementary school educator; b. Brownsville, Pa., June 2, 1959; d. Tony Sr. and Iona Gertrude (Smith) Iacconi; m. m. Jeffrey John Zigray, Aug. 29, 1981; 1 child, Ethan John. BS, California (Pa.) State Coll., 1980; MA, W.Va. U., 1989. 1st grade tchr. Tunnelton (W.Va.)-Denver Elem., 1981-82, 2nd grade tchr., 1982-83, 3rd grade tchr., 1983-85; 4th grade tchr. Kingwood (W.Va.) Elem., 1985—; cheerleader coach Varsity Coach for Ctrl. Preston Sr. H.S., Kingwood, 1985-91; competition dir. Jr. H.S. Cheerleader Competition, Preston County, 1987—; student coun. advisor Kingwood Elem., 1994—; editor sch. newspaper Kingwood Elem. Gazette, 1990—. Pub. affairs chmn. Kingwood Jr. Women's Club, 1990-94, corr. sec., 1996—; youth league cheerleader coord. Preston County Youth League, 1994—; children's ct. advisor Preston County Buckwheat Festival, 1993—. Mem. Internat. Reading Coun., W.Va. State Reading Coun., Preston County Reading Coun. (pres. 1994—), Nat. Youth Sports Coaches Assn. Democrat. Home: Box B13 123 Western Dr Kingwood WV 26537 Office: Kingwood Elem 207 S Price St Kingwood WV 26537

ZIKMUD, BARBARA BROWN, seminary president, religious studies educator; m. Joseph Zikmund II, Aug. 26, 1961; 1 child. BA, Beloit Coll., 1961; BD, Duke U., 1964, PhD, 1969; DDiv, Doane Coll., 1984, Chgo. Theol. Sem., 1985, Ursinus Coll., 1989. Ordained to ministry United Ch. of Christ, 1964. Dir. studies, prof. Chgo. Theol. Sem.; prof., dean faculty Pacific Sch. Religion, Berkeley, Calif., 1981-90; pres., prof. Am. religious studies Hartford (Conn.) Sem., 1990—; mem. program on theol. edn. World Coun. Chs., 1984-89; mem. interfaith rels. commn. Nat. Coun. Chs. of Christ; vis. scholar Schlesinger Women's History Libr., Racliffe Coll., Cambridge, Mass.; bd. dirs. Mechanics Savs. Bank. Author: Discovering the Church, 1983, Hidden Histories in the United Church of Christ, 2 vols., 1984, 87; series editor: Living Theological Heritage of the United Church of Christ; mem. editl. bd. Mid-Stream, Jour. Ecumenical Studies; contbr. numerous articles to religion jours. Elector Wadsworth Atheneum; corporator St. Francis Hosp., Hartford Hosp. Named Disting. Alumna Duke Div. Sch., 1994. Fellow Am. Leadership Forum; mem. Assn. Theol. Schs. in U.S. and Can. (past pres., mem. coms.), World Conf. Assns. Theol. Ednl. Instns. (sec.-treas. 1992-96, pres. 1996—), Am. Soc. Ch. History (pres. 1996—), Greater Hartford C. of C. (bd. dirs.). Office: Hartford Sem 77 Sherman St Hartford CT 06105-2260

ZIKMUND, BARBARA BROWN, minister, seminary president, church history educator; b. Ann Arbor, Mich., Oct. 16, 1939; d. Henry Daniels and Helen (Langworthy) Brown; m. Joseph Zikmund II, Aug. 26, 1961; 1 child, Brian Joseph. BA, Beloit Coll., 1961; BDiv, Duke U., 1964, PhD, 1969; D in Div (hon.), Doane Coll., 1984, Chgo. Theol. Sem., 1985, Ursinus Coll., 1989. Ordained to ministry United Ch. of Christ, 1964. Instr. Albright Coll., Reading, Pa., 1966-67, Temple U., Phila., 1967-68, Ursinus Coll., Collegeville, Pa., 1968-69; asst. prof. religion studies Albion Coll., Mich., 1970-75; asst. prof. ch. history, dir. studies Chgo. Theol. Sem., 1975-80; dean and assoc. prof. ch. history Pacific Sch. Religion, Berkeley, Calif., 1981-85, dean and prof. ch. history, 1985-90; pres. Hartford (Conn.) Sem., 1990—; chmn. United Ch. of Christ Hist. Coun., 1983-85, mem. coun. for ecumenism, 1983-89; mem. Nat. Coun. Chs. Commn. on Faith and Order, 1979-87, World Coun. of Chs. Programme Theol. Edn., 1984-91, Nat. Coun. Chs. Working Group on Inter-Faith Rels., 1992—, World Orgn. Confs. Theol. Instns., sec. treas. 1992—; bd. dirs. Mechanics Savings Bank. Author: Discovering the Church, 1983; editor: Hidden Histories in the UCC, 1984, vol. 2, 1987; (with Manschreck) American Religious Experiment, 1976; mem. editorial bd. Jour. Ecumenical Studies, 1987—, Mid-Stream, 1991—; contbr. articles to profl. jours. Mem. City Coun., Albion, Mich., 1972-75; elector Wadsworth Atheneum, 1994—, corporator St. Francis Hosp., 1994—; pres. Greater Hartford Consortium for Higher Edn., 1994—. Woodrow Wilson fellow, 1964-66; NEH grantee, 1974-75; vis. scholar Schlesinger Libr. Women's History, Radcliffe Coll., 1988-89. Mem. Assn. Theol. Schs. (v.p. 1984-86, pres. 1986-88, issues implementation grantee 1983-84), Am. Soc. Ch. History (council 1983-85, pres. elect 1995—), Internat. Assn. Women Ministers (v.p. 1977-79), AAUW (v.p. 1973-75), Greater Hartford C. of C. (bd. dirs. 1992-95). Democrat. Office: Hartford Sem Office of Pres 77 Sherman St Hartford CT 06105-2260

ZILL, ANNE BRODERICK, foundation executive; b. Phila., Nov. 25, 1941; d. John Daniel and Mary Lynna (Flynn) Broderick; children: Katherine and Persephone, Oriana Valentina, Lydia Daniel Dennett, Nicholas II, Leland Dennett. BA in Govt., Barnard Coll., 1963; MA in Journalism, Am. Univ., 1970. Nat news prodr. Nat. Edn. Radio, Washington, 1969-71; congrl. fellow Am. Polit. Sci. Assn., Washington, 1972-73; project staff mem. Ralph Nader Congress Project Study, Washington, 1972; rep. Stewart R. Mott Charitable Trust, 1973—; founder Women's Campaign Fund, Washington, 1974; co-founder, pres. Fund Constitutional Govt., Washington, 1974—; co-founder Ctr. Consentual Democracy, Maine, 1991; founding cons., bd. dirs. Maine Women's Fund, 1989—; Washington rep. Women's Environ. and Devel. Orgn., 1994; project cons. china Strategic Inst., Washington, 1995—, Inter-Am. Devel. Bank Creator Women's Leadership Fund for LAC. Contbr. articles to profl. jours. Adv. bd. mem. U. New Eng., 1992—, Women's Program for Ethics in Action. Congl. fellow Am. Polit. Sci. Found., 1992. Mem. Internat. Ctr. (bd. dirs. 1978—). Home: 1734 P St NW Washington DC 20036 Office: Fund Constitutional 900 121 Constitution Ave NE Washington DC 20002

ZILLMAN, LINDA G., art gallery owner; b. Chgo., Mar. 27, 1945; d. Robert Marvin and Violette Lucille (Rosemerkel) Goforth; m. Donald Norman Zillman, June 8, 1968. BA, U. Wis., 1967; MA, Ariz. State U., 1980. Specialist Office of Planning and Analysis U. Wis., Madison, 1967-69; tech. writer San Diego County Dept. Edn., San Diego, 1969-70; asst. internat. student advisor Ariz. State U., Tempe, 1974-78; dissertation editor U. Utah, Salt Lake City, 1982-89; owner Meander Gallery, Portland, Maine, 1989—; v.p. Maine Arts, Inc., Portland, 1995-96, bd. dirs., 1993-96. Author: Sir William Newton, Miniature Painter and Photographer, 1785-1869, 1986. Co-moderator Williston-West Ch., Portland, 1993-95. Mem. Greater Portland Landmarks. Home and Office: 40 Pleasant St Portland ME 04101

ZIMMERMAN, CAROLE LEE, public relations professional; b. Roxboro, N.C., Aug. 28, 1948; d. Ray Richard and Annie Theresa (O'Briant) Z.; m. Richard A. Hoehn, Oct. 26, 1991; 1 child, Kristin Nicole Sizemore. BS in Edn., Fla. State U., 1970; publs. specialist cert., George Washington U., 1980; MA in Pub. Comm., Am. U., 1993. Tchr. Gadsden County Pub. Schs., Quincy, Fla., 1971-72, Am. schs., Kaiserslautern and Darmstadt, Germany, 1974-76; editor, writer USLICO Corp., Arlington, Va., 1980-84; dir. communications Bread for the World, Washington, 1984-95; dir. comms. com. Nat. Inst. for Environment, Washington, 1995—. vol. homeless women's shelter Luther Pl. Meml. Ch., Washington, 1983—. Mem. Am. Soc. Assn. Execs., Pub. Rels. Soc. Am., Washington Women in Comms. (bd. dirs. 1996—), Washington Women in Pub. Rels. Democrat. Lutheran. Office: Com Nat Inst Environment 1725 K St NW Washington DC 20006-1401

ZIMMERMAN, DIANE LEENHEER, law educator, lawyer; b. Newton, N.J., Apr. 16, 1941; d. Adrian and Mildred Eleanor (Booth) Leenheer; m. Earl A. Zimmerman, Sept. 24, 1960 (div. Aug. 1982); m. 2d, Cavin P. Leeman, Feb. 18, 1984. BA, Beaver Coll., Glenside, Pa., 1963; JD, Columbia U., 1976. Bar: N.Y. 1977, U.S. Supreme Ct. 1983. Reporter, Newsweek mag., N.Y.C., 1963-71; spl. features writer N.Y. Daily News, N.Y.C., 1971-73; law clk. U.S. Dist. Ct. (ea. dist.) N.Y., Bklyn., 1976-77; asst. prof. law NYU, N.Y.C., 1977-80, assoc. prof., 1980-82, prof., 1982—; mem. faculty Practicing Law Inst., N.Y.C., 1979, 84, 90, 92, 94; of counsel Skadden, Arps, Slate, Meagher & Flom. Author: Fed. Ct. Reporter Gender Fairness in Second Cir., 1994—; articles and book rev. editor Columbia Law Rev., 1975-76. Mem. working group on women, censorship and pornography Nat. Coalition Against Censorship. Recipient citation of merit Columbia U. Sch. Journalism, 1972; Kent scholar and Stone scholar, 1973-76; Disting. Lee vis. prof. Coll. William and Mary, 1994. Mem. ABA (vice chmn. tort liability study com. tort and ins. sect. 1986-87, chair 1st amendment rights com. 1989-94), Am. Law Inst., Assn. of Bar of City of N.Y. (chairperson com. civil rights 1981-83), Copyright Soc. USA (trustee 1988-91). Office: NYU Sch Law 40 Washington Sq S New York NY 10012-1005

ZIMMERMAN, DORIS LUCILE, chemist; b. L.A., July 30, 1942; d. Walter Merritt and Letta Minnie (Reese) Briggs; m. Christopher Scott Zimmerman, June 5, 1964; children: Susan Christina, David Scott, Brian Allan. BS in Chemistry, Carnegie Mellon U., 1964; MS in Chemistry, Youngstown State U., 1989, MS in Materials Engring., 1992; postgrad., Kent (Ohio) State U. High sch. tchr. Ohio County Schs., Vienna and Campbell, 1983-87; sr. chemist Konwal, Warren, Ohio, 1988-91; limited faculty mem. Kent (Ohio) State U., 1991-95; temp. full-time instr. dept. chemistry Edinboro U. Pa., 1995—; substitute tchr. County Schs. of Ohio, Warren, 1972-82; tutor, 1965—. Instr. water safety ARC, Warren, 1965—; chmn. Trumbull Mobile Meals, Warren, 1977-92, Pink Thumb Garden Club, Warren, 1965—. Recipient Svc. award ARC, 1981, Trumbull Mobile Meals, 1985. Mem. Materials Info. Soc., Soc. for the Advancement of Material and Process Engring., Am. Chem. Soc. (sec. 1985-90, chmn. elect 1990, chmn. 1991, alternate councilor 1992—, Commendation award 1990), Carnegie Mellon Alumni Assn. (admissions councilor, Svc. award 1981), Phi Lambda Upsilon, Phi Kappa Phi, Sigma Xi. Republican. Methodist. Home and Office: 1390 Waverly Dr NW Warren OH 44483-1718

ZIMMERMAN, HELENE LORETTA, business educator; b. Rochester, N.Y., Feb. 26, 1933; d. Henry Charles and Loretta Catherine (Hobert) Z. BS, SUNY, Albany, 1953, MS, 1959; PhD, U. N.D., 1969. Cert. records mgr. Bus. tchr., chmn. bus. dept. Williamson (N.Y.) Cen. Sch., 1953-69; asst. prof. U. Ky., Lexington, 1969-70; assoc. prof. bus. Cen. Mich. U., Mt. Pleasant, 1970-74, prof., 1974—. Author General Business, 1977; contbg. author to records mgmt. text book, 1987. Sec. Isabella County Christmas Outreach, Mt. Pleasant, 1983—. Mem. Assn. Records Mgmt. and Adminstrn., Inst. Cert. Records Mgrs. (sec. 1985-89, exam. devel. com. 1993—), Internat. Soc. Bus. Edn. (internat. v.p. English speaking nations 1986-88), Nat. Bus. Edn. Assn., Mich. Bus. Edn. Assn. (bd. dirs. 1985-90, 95—, pres. 1988-89), AAUW (pres. 1984-86), Delta Kappa Gamma (state pres. 1987-89, internat. fin. com. 1990-94). Office: Ctrl Mich U Grawn # 337 Mount Pleasant MI 48859

ZIMMERMAN, JEAN, lawyer; b. Berkeley, Calif., Dec. 3, 1947; d. Donald Scheel Zimmerman and Phebe Jean (Reed) Doan; m. Gilson Berryman Gray III, Nov. 25, 1982; children: Charles Donald Buffum and Catherine Elisabeth Phebe (twins); stepchildren: Alison Travis, Laura Rebecca, Gilson Berryman. BSBA, U. Md., 1970; JD, Emory U., 1975. Bar: Ga. 1975, D.C. 1976, N.Y. 1980. Asst. mgr. investments FNMA, Washington, 1970-73; assoc. counsel Fuqua Industries Inc., Atlanta, 1976-79; assoc. Sage Gray Todd & Sims, N.Y.C., 1979-84; assoc. counsel J. Henry Schroder Bank & Trust Co., N.Y.C., 1984-85, asst. gen. counsel, 1986, assoc. gen. counsel, 1987; assoc. gen. counsel, asst. sec. IBJ Schroder Bank & Trust Co., N.Y.C., 1988-90, chief counsel, sec., 1991-93, sr. v.p., gen. counsel, sec., 1993—; asst. sec. IBJ Schroder Leasing Corp., N.Y.C., 1987-90, bd. dirs., sec., 1991—; asst. sec. IBJ Schroder Banking Corp., N.Y.C., 1989-90, chief counsel, sec., 1991-93; asst. sec. IBJ Schroder Internat. Bank, Miami, Fla., 1989-90, sec., 1991—; asst. sec. IBJS Capital Corp., N.Y.C., 1988-90, sec., 1991—; sec. Bonaght Corp., N.Y.C., 1991—; chief legal officer, sec. Execution Svcs., Inc., N.Y.C., 1991-93. Founder, officer ERA Ga., Atlanta, 1977-79; bd. dirs. Ct. Apptd. Spl. Advs., 1988-94. Named one of Outstanding Atlantans, 1978-79. Mem. ABA, Assn. of Bar of City of N.Y., Ga. Assn. Women Lawyers (bd. dirs. 1977-79), Am. Soc. Corp. Secs., Inc., LWV, DAR. Republican. Office: IBJ Schroder Bank & Trust Co 1 State St New York NY 10004-1505

ZIMMERMAN, JO ANN, health services and educational consultant, former lieutenant governor; b. Van Buren County, Iowa, Dec. 24, 1936; d. Russell and Hazel (Ward) McIntosh; m. A. Tom Zimmerman, Aug. 26, 1956; children: Andrew, Lisa, Don and Ron (twins), Beth. Diploma, Broadlawns Sch. of Nursing, Des Moines, 1958; BA with honors, Drake U., 1973; postgrad., Iowa State U., 1973-75. RN, Iowa. Asst. head nurse maternity dept. Broadlawns Med. Ctr., Des Moines, 1958-59, weekend supr. nursing svcs., 1960-61, supr. maternity dept., 1966-68; instr. maternity nursing Broadlawns Sch. Nursing, 1968-71; health planner, community rels. assoc. Iowa Health Systems Agy., Des Moines, 1978-82; mem. Iowa Ho. Reps., 1982-86; lt. gov., Senate pres. State of Iowa, 1987-91; cons. health svcs., grant writing and continuing edn. Zimmerman & Assocs., Des Moines, 1991-95; dir. patient care svcs. Nursing Svcs. of Iowa, 1996—; ops. dir. Medlink Svcs., Inc., Des Moines, 1992-96; dir. nurses Nursing Svcs. of Iowa, 1996—. Contbr. articles to profl. jours. Mem. advanced registered nurse practioner task force on cert. nurse mid-wives Iowa Bd. Nursing, 1980-81, Waukee, Polk County, Iowa Health Edn. Coord. Coun., Iowa Women's Polit. Caucus, Dallas County Women's Polit. Caucus; chmn. Des Moines Area Maternity Nursing Conf. Group, 1969-70, task force on sch. health svcs. Iowa Dept. Health, 1982, task force health edn. Iowa Dept. Pub. Instruction, 1979, adv. com. health edn. assessment tool, 1980-81, Nat. Lt. Govs., chair com. on Agrl. and Rural Devel., 1989; Dallas County Dem. Cen. Com., 1972-84; bd. dirs. Waukee Cmty. Sch. Bd., 1976-79, pres. 1978-79; bd. dirs. Iowa PTA, 1979-83, chairperson Health Com., 1980-84; mem. steering com. ERA, Iowa, 1991-92; founder Dem. Activist Women's Network (DAWN), 1992. Mem. ANA, LWV (health chmn. mct. Des Moines chpt.), Iowa Nurses Assn., Iowa League for Nursing (bd. dirs. 1979-83), Family Centered Childbirth Edn. Assn. (childbirth instr., advisor), Iowa Cattleman's Assn., Am. Lung Assn. (bd. dirs. Iowa 1988-92), Dem. Activist Women's Network (founder 1992). Mem. Christian Ch. Office: Zimmerman & Assocs 7630 Ashworth Rd West Des Moines IA 50266-5859

ZIMMERMAN, JUDITH ROSE, elementary art educator; b. Youngstown, Ohio, Jan. 17, 1945; d. Emery and Josephine Leona (Terlecki) Ference; m. William Carl Zimmerman, Jr., Nov 27, 1965; children: Shawn, William III. BFA in Art Edn., Kent State U., 1977, MEd in Curriculum and Instruction, 1992. Cert. art tchr., Ohio. Elem. art tchr. Sandy Valley Sch. Dist., Magnolia, Ohio, 1977—; instr. art Massillon (Ohio) Art Mus. Adv. com. Edn. Enhancement Partnership Coun., Canton, Ohio, 1992; active Little Art Gallery, 1992, Massillon Art Mus. Mem. NEA, Nat. Art Edn. Assn., Ohio Edn. Assn., Ohio Art Edn. Assn. (chairperson east cen. divsn. 1985-90, elem. divsn. 1989-91, Art Educator of Yr. 1983, Featured Art Tchr. of Month 1990), Ohio Alliance for Art Edn., Canton Art Inst. (Art Educator of Yr. 1992), Phi Delta Kappa (newsletter editor McKinley chpt.). Roman Catholic. Home: 802 Lucille Ave SW North Canton OH 44720-2820 Office: Sandy Valley Sch Dist RR 2 Magnolia OH 44643-9802

ZIMMERMAN, KATHLEEN MARIE, artist; b. Floral Park, N.Y., Apr. 24, 1923; d. Harold G. and Evelyn M. (Andrade) Z.; m. Ralph S. Iwamoto, Nov. 23, 1963. Student, Art Students League, N.Y.C., 1942-44, Nat. Acad. Sch. Fine Arts, N.Y.C., 1944-47, 50-54. tchr. drawing and painting Midtown Sch. Art, N.Y.C., 1947-52. Illustrator: (with Ralph S. Iwamoto) Diet for a Small Planet, 1971; one woman shows include Westbeth Gallery, N.Y.C., 1973, 74, St. Mary's Coll., St. Mary's City, Md., 1990; exhibited in group shows at Woodstock Art Gallery, N.Y., 1945, Nat. Arts Club, N.Y.C., 1948-56, 84, Emily Lowe Award Show, 1951, Contemporary Arts Gallery, N.Y.C., 1952, 60, Allied Artists Ann., N.Y.C., 1956, 78, 80-91, 93, Art USA, 1958, Village Art Ctr., 1956-61, ACA Gallery, 1958, 59, Studio Gallery, 1957-60, City Center Gallery, 1960, Janet Nessler Gallery, N.Y.C., 1961, Silvermine Guild, Conn., 1962, Pioneer Gallery, Cooperstown, N.Y., 1962, 63, Audubon Artists Anns., N.Y.C., (various shows) 1963-95, NAD, (15 shows) 1969-95, Nat. Assn. Women Artists Anns., N.Y.C., 1957-85, 87-94, Women Artists Award Winners Show, N.Y.C., 1974, Am. Watercolor Soc., N.Y.C., 1975-78, 80, Cheyenne (Wyo.) Western Galleries, 1975, 76, 77, Edward-Dean Mus., Cherry Valley, Calif., 1975, 76, 77, Frye Mus., Seattle, 1975, 76, 77, Boise Gallery Art, 1975, Central Wyo. Mus. Art, 1975, 76, Willamette U., 1975, Yellowstone Art Ctr., Billings, Mont., 1975, Utah State U., 1975, Applewood Art Gallery, Colo., 1976, Charleston Art Gallery, W.Va., 1976, Kent State U., 1976, Cin. Art Club, 1976, Martello Mus., Key West, Fla., 1976, Buecker Gallery, N.Y.C., 1976, Anchorage Fine Arts Mus., 1976, Davis and Long Gallery, N.Y.C., 1977, Butler Inst. Am. Art, 1978, Washington Square East Gallery, NYU, 1979, Internat. Festival Women Artists, Copenhagen, 1980, City Gallery, N.Y.C., 1981, Bergen Community Mus., Paramus, N.J., 1983, Kenkeleba Gallery, N.Y.C., 1985, Adelphi Univ., Garden City, N.Y., 1987, Lotos Club, N.Y.C., 1987, Temperance Hall Gallery, Bellport, N.Y., 1987, Monmouth Mus., Lincroft, N.J., 1987, Marbella Gallery, N.Y.C., 1989, Knickerbocker Artists, 1990, Brownstone Gallery, N.Y.C., 1993, Viridian Gallery, N.Y.C., 1995, Sundance Gallery, Bridgehampton, N.Y., 1996; represented in permanent collections, Butler Inst. Am. Art, Youngstown, Ohio, Sheldon Swope Art Gallery, Terre Haute, Ind., Lauren Rogers Mus. Art, Laurel, Miss., U. Wyo. Art Mus., Laramie, U. Miami Lowe Art Mus., Coral Gables, Fla., N.C. Mus. Art, Raleigh, Swarthmore Coll., Pa., Erie Art Ctr. (Pa.), Nat. Acad. Design, N.Y.C.;

bibiography James Mellow, N.Y. Times Art Review, 1973, Hilton Kramer, N.Y. Times Review, 1977; contbr. bibliography to Gerald F. Brommer's The Art of Collage, 1978, Christopher Schink's Mastering Color & Design in Watercolor, 1981, John and Joan Digby's The Collage Handbook, 1985, David Ferry's "Painting Without a Brush", 1992, Gerald F. Brommer's Collage Techniques, 1994. John F. and Anna Lee Stacey scholar, 1954. Mem. NAD (Henry Ward Ranger Fund purchase prize 1976, 82, cert. of merit 1980, L.G. Sawyer prize 1988, Ogden Pleissner Meml. award 1991, William A. Paton prize 1993), Audubon Artists (John Wenger Meml. award 1978, Ralph Fabri medal 1981, J&E Liskin Meml. award 1987, Dick Blick award 1994), Am. Watercolor Soc. (Barse Miller Meml. award 1976), Nat. Assn. Women Artists (14 prizes 1957—), Allied Artists Am. (silver medal 1981, 91, Jane Peterson award 1985, Creative Watercolor prize 1989), N.Y. Artists Equity Assn. (Dr. Maury Leibovitz award 1985). Home: 463 West St Apt 1110A New York NY 10014-2040

ZIMMERMAN, LINDA, author, editor; b. Chgo., Sept. 30, 1946; d. Louis Joseph and Sydell Muriel (Lakowitz) Z.; m. Gerry Goffin (div.). Student, Roosevelt U., 1963-65, Santa Monica Coll., 1981-83. Prodn. asst. films, asst. video editor various features, 1970-81; freelance photographer, 1979-86, freelance writer, 1983—; editor, pub. The Food Yellow Pages, L.A., 1987-91; contbg. editor Food Arts mag., L.A.; creative svcs. dir. El Cholo Restaurants, L.A.; instr. food journalism UCLA and various colls.; speaker radio and TV; specialist food and restaurants L.A., So. Calif. real estate, 1979—. Author: Puddings, Custards and Flans, 1990, (with Peggy Mellody) Cobblers, Crumbles and Crisps, 1991, (with Gerri Gilliland) Grills & Greens, 1993, Chicken Soup, 1994; contbr. articles to mags. and newspapers. Mem. AFTRA, Internat. Assn. Cooking Profls., Calif. Assn. Realtors, Women's Culinary Alliance (bd. dirs. 1988-92), So. Calif. Culinary Guild (bd. dirs.), N.Y.C. Authors Guild, Ciao Italia (hon., ednl. bd.).

ZIMMERMAN, LYDIA, public health nurse; b. McMinnville, Oreg., Jan. 12, 1929; d. Frederick H. and Anna Katarina (Beisel) Koch; m. Howard C. Zimmerman, July 14, 1956; children: Sylvia, Angela, Joan, Garth. Diploma in nursing, Emanuel Hosp. Sch. Nursing, Portland, Oreg., 1949; BSN, U. Wash., 1953; cert. sch. nurse practitioner, UCLA, 1977. RN, Calif.; cert. pub. health nurse; cert. family life educator, sch. nurse. Asst. supr., head nurse surg. Emanuel Hosp., Portland, Oreg., 1949-50; coll. nurse Linfield Coll., McMinnville, Oreg., 1951-52; public health nurse I, sch. nurse, counselor high sch. Lane County Health Dept., Eugene, Oreg., 1953-57, staff nurse, asst. supr. maternal-child, mental health, 1958-63; public health nurse Lucas County Health Dept., Toledo, Ohio, 1967-69; private nurse Shafter, Calif., 1972-74; sch. nurse Rosedale Sch. Dist., Bakersfield, Calif., 1974-76, Beardsley Sch. Dist., Bakersfield, Calif., 1974-80, Panama-Buena Vista Union Sch. Dist., Bakersfield, Calif., 1974—; lctr. Bakersfield Coll., Calif. State Coll., Bakersfield. Mem. APHA, NEA, AAUW, Am. Acad. Nurse Practitioners, Calif. Tchrs. Assn., Nat. Assn. Sch. Nurses (Calif. rep. 1986-87, 87-88), Calif. Sch. Nurses Orgn., Kern County Sch. Nurses Orgn. (co-founder, pres. 1981-83, 91-92), Sex Info. and Edn. Coun. U.S., Nat. Coun. on Family Rels., Ctr. Sci. in Pub. Interest, Calif. Assn. Neurologically Handicapped Children, Assn. Children with Learning Disabilities, Learning Disabilities Assn. Am. (co-founder, pres. Kern County chpt. 1972-74, 76-78, 88—), Am. Hist. Soc. Germans from Russia, Sigma Theta Tau Internat. Congregationalist.

ZIMMERMAN, PAULA, writer; b. N.Y.C., Feb. 26, 1949; 1 child, Alicia Zimmerman Hofstetter. Student, Ind. U., 1967-69, NYU, 1973-75. Head pub. rels. Shiki's Restaurant, N.Y.C., 1993; copywriter Broadway Theatre Inst., N.Y.C., 1995-96; writer Rsch. Assocs., Jersey City, 1995-96. Author: What Should I Do About Bruce?, 1993, (screenplay) Vinnie's Omega, 1994, (poem in cassette) Sunday Night Local, 1994 (Editor's Choice award Nat. Libr. Poetry); co-author: (play) Historical Recreation of Union Square - Day of N.Y., 1994, Dreamers, Schemers, and Disbelievers, 1996; contbr. poetry to literary mag. Chmn. N.Y.C. Bd. Elections, 1991-96; pub. rels. asst. Ind. Feature Project, N.Y.C., 1994-96; tenant rep. Holland House, N.Y.C., 1996; mem. Met. Coun. on Housing, 1986—, Fund for Feminist Majority, 1989—. Recipient Essence of Best award Street News, N.Y.C., 1990, mayor's letter of commendation City of N.Y.C., 1992, letter of commendation McNeil-Lehrer journalist Roger Rosenblatt, 1994. Mem. Internat. Coll. Astrology (scholar 1994), Soka Gakkai Internat. (study cert., grup chief 1994—). Buddhist. Address: care Jo Sea Prodns PO Box 455 New York NY 10025

ZIMMERMAN, SARA ANN, counselor; b. Springfield, Ohio, June 15, 1943; d. Harry L. and Martha J. (Beltz) Young; m. Douglas Kent Zimmerman, Nov. 12, 1966; children: Douglas K. Jr., Jon M. BSN, Ohio State U., 1965; MS, SUNY, Buffalo, 1976; EdS, James Madison U., 1986. Lic. profl. counselor, Va.; RN, Va. Staff nurse Ohio State U. Hosp., Columbus, 1965-66; pub. health nurse Columbus Health Dept., 1966-68; staff nurse (charge nurse) Ravenna (Ohio) Meml. Hosp., 1970-71; instr., co-dir. Coll. "H" SUNY, Buffalo, 1972-74; instr. D'Youville Coll. Nursing, Buffalo, 1973-75, James Madison U., Harrisonburg, Va., 1975-77; asst. prof. nursing Ea. Mennonite Coll., 1977-84; clin. dir. Arlington Treatment Ctr., 1984-85; lic. profl. counselor Shenandoah Valley Sex Offenders Treatment Program, 1985—; child and family therapist cons. Valley Comty. Mental Health Svcs., 1985-86, child and family therapist, 1986-91; lic. profl. counselor Shenandoah Counseling Assocs., 1989-94; pvt. practice as lic. profl. counselor, 1994—; part-time staff nurse Camelot Hall Nursing Home, Harrisonburg, 1975-78. Big stster Big Bros./Big Sisters, Staunton, Va., 1995—; pvt. practice rep. Cmty. Mgmt. and Planning Team, Staunton, 1995; mem. Teen Pregnancy Prevention Coalition, Staunton and Waynesboro, 1995; mem., past chair Staunton/Augusta County Child Sexual Abuse Team, 1995. Mem. ACA, Am. Mental Health Counselors Assn., Assn. of Treatment of Sexual Abusers (clin. mem.), Cen. Valley Counselors Assn., Clin. Counselors Assn. Va., Play Therapy Assn. Home: PO Box 971 Verona VA 24482 Office: Ste B-3 511 Thornrose Ave Staunton VA 24401

ZIMMERMANN, POLLY GERBER, emergency nurse; b. Orrville, Ohio, Apr. 6, 1954; d. Vernon Lee and Paula Mae (Hemple) Gerber; m. Rudolf Zimmermann, May 14, 1988. Diploma in nursing, Aultman Hosp. Sch. Nursing, Canton, Ohio, 1977; BSN, DePaul U., 1982; MBA, North Park Coll., 1995, MSN, 1996. RN, Ill.; cert. emergency nurse; cert. ACLS, PALS, ENPC, TNCC, NALS, trauma nurse specialist, instr. ENPC, breath alcohol technician. Staff nurse med.-surg. Columbus Hosp., Chgo., 1977-80, asst. head nurse, 1980-81, staff nurse neonatal ICU, 1981-82, staff nurse emergency dept., 1983—, clin. nurse dir. emergency dept., 1990-92; staff nurse emergency dept. and occupational health Swedish Covenant Hosp., Chgo., 1992—; assoc. nurse Am. Airlines; part-time psychiat. nurse Chgo. Lakeshore Hosp., 1983-84; part-time staff triage nurse Michael Reese HMO, 1986-90; presenter in field. Contbg. editor, mgr. Ask and Answer, sect. editor Jour. Emergency Nursing; contbr. chpt. to book, articles to Jour. Emergency Nursing, Nursing 95, others. Commonwealth Fund Exec. Nurse fellow Commonwealth Fund, 1993. Mem. ANA, AACCN (clin. inquiry grantee), Am. Soc. Quality Control, Am. Orgn. for Nurse Execs., Am. Assn. Occupational Health Nurses, Emergency Nurses Assn. (CEN test examiner, mem. clin. practice for cert. 1993—, del. and spkr. sci. assembly, Gary Sparger Meml. scholar 1994, ENF leadership Grad. Nursing Edn. scholar 1994), Sigma Theta Tau (Grace Peterson scholar 1994, sec. 1995-96, pres.-elect 1996-98), Delta Epsilon Sigma. Republican. Home: 4200 N Francisco Ave Chicago IL 60618-2610

ZIMMERMANN, SUSANNE WIEBKE, family physician; b. Neptune, N.J., Feb. 21, 1963; d. Rudolf and Annelene (Wohlert) Z. BA, Rutgers U., 1985; MD, U. Medicine and Densitry N.J., Piscataway, 1989. Diplomate Am. Bd. Family Practice. Pvt. practice, Freehold, N.J, 1992—. Mem. AMA, Am. Acad. Family Physicians. Lutheran. Office: Monmouth Family Med Group 500 Candlewood Commons Howell NJ 07731

ZIMNY, MARILYN LUCILE, anatomist, educator; b. Chgo., Dec. 12, 1927; d. John and Lucile Ruth (Andryske) Z. BA, U. Ill., 1948; MS, Loyola U., Chgo., 1951, PhD, 1954. Asst. prof. anatomy La. State U. Med. Ctr., New Orleans, 1954-59, assoc. prof., 1959-64, prof., 1964-75, prof., acting head, 1975-76, prof., head, 1976—, acting dean sch. grad. studies, 1989-90, dean sch. grad. studies and vice-chancellor for academic affairs, 1990—; vis. prof. anatomy U. Costa Rica Sch. Medicine, 1961, 62; chmn. La. Edn. Quality Support Fund Planning Com., State of La., Bd. Regents, 1993—; mem. So. Regional Edn. Bd., Regional Consortium of State higher Edn. Health Affairs Ofcls., 1993—. Grantee, NIH, 1958-72, 88-89, Arthritis Found., 1969-72, Schlieder Ednl. Found., 1972-75, Frost Found., 1975-78, NSF, 1982-83. Mem. AAAS, Am. Assn. Anatomists (mem. exec. com. 1981-85, program sec. 1990-94), Am. Physiol. Soc., Assn. Anatomy Chmn. (pres. 1983), Electron Microscopic Soc. Am., Am. Assn. Dental Schs. (sect. anat. scis.), Assn. Rsch. in Vision and Ophthalmology, Am./Internat. Assn. Dental Rsch., Omicron Kappa Upsilon, Alpha Omega Alpha. Home: 3330 Esplanade Ave New Orleans LA 70119-3132 Office: La State U Med Ctr Resource Ctr New Orleans LA 70112

ZINAMAN, HELAINE MADELEINE, gifted and talented education educator; b. N.Y.C., Sept. 11, 1951; d. Harold Joseph and Charlotte (Orenstein) Z. BA, Am. U., 1973; MEd, U. Md., 1979. Spl. edn. resource tchr. John Eager Howard Elem. Sch., Capitol Heights, Md., 1973-85; coord. talented and gifted program Glenarden Woods TAG Magnet, Lanham, Md., 1985-96; coord. Owens Rd. Math., Sci. and Tech. Sch., Oxon Hill, Md., 1992-93, Walker Mill Mid. Sch., Capital Heights, Md., 1993-94; pvt. tutor, Washington, 1982-85, 92—; talented and gifted specialist Talented and Gifted Office, Capitol Heights, 1996—; tchr. overview course GED, Bladensburg, Md., 1983; instr. creative thinking Prince George's Community Coll., Largo, Md., 1983, 85; instr. Thinktank, U. Md., College Park, 1989—; mem. Math., Sci. and Tech. Network, 1989; writer curriculum for gifted children, 94, 95. Asst. editor Sci. Bowl, 1990-92. Judge Md. State Odyssey of the Mind Competition; talent on "Count on Us" Cable TV Math. Show. Washington Post grantee, 1989, 95; recipient Bowie Excellence in Edn. award, 1991. Mem. Nat. Assn. for Gifted Children, Assn. for Supervision and Curriculum Devel., Md. State Tchrs. Assn., Nat. Educators Assn., Prince Georges County Educators Assn. Democrat. Jewish. Home: 4222 38th St NW Washington DC 20016-3006 Office: Glenarden Woods Elem Glenarden Pky Lanham Seabrook MD 20706

ZINAMAN, NAN, retail executive; b. N.Y.C.; d. H. James and Patricia (Jacobs) S.; m. Stephen Eric Messinger, Sept. 25, 1977 (div. May 1994); 1 child, Sara; m. Steven R. Zinaman, Oct. 22, 1994. Student, Ohio U., 1972. Buyer Saks Fifth Ave, N.Y.C., 1972-76, Bloomingdales, N.Y.C., 1976-86; pres., owner Shenanigans of Chappaqua (N.Y.) Inc., 1986—.

ZINECKER, TRICIA JOLENE, elementary school educator; b. Springfield, Mo., Aug. 3, 1966; d. Chesley Junior Wiggins and Jacquelyn Kay (Hamilton) Hamilton; m. James Paul Zinecker, Aug. 11, 1990. MusB, Drury Coll., 1988; MusM, Northwestern U., 1989. Cert. elem. tchr., Mo., Tex. Music tchr. Collins Intermediate Jr. H.S., The Woodlands, Tex., 1990—; soprano soloist, Tex., 1990—; pvt. voice tchr., Spring, Tex., 1990—. Mem. Nat. Assn. Tchrs. of Singing, Tex. Music Educators Assn. (elem. honor choir dir. 1994), Tex. Choral Dir. Assn., Sigma Alpha Iota, Kappa Delta Pi. Democratic. Episcopalian. Office: Collins Intermediate 6020 Shadowbend The Woodlands TX 77381

ZINNES, HARRIET FICH, poet, retired English educator, writer, literary and art critic; b. Boston; d. Assir and Sarah (Goldberg) Fich; m. Irving I. Zinnes, Sept. 24, 1943 (dec. 1979); children: Clifford, Alice. BA cum laude, CUNY, 1939, MA, 1944; PhD, NYU, 1953. Editor publs. divsn. Raritan (N.J.) Arsenal, 1942-43; assoc. editor Harper's Bazaar, N.Y.C., 1944-46; tutor Hunter Coll. CUNY, N.Y.C., 1946-49; asst. prof. Queens Coll. CUNY, Flushing, 1949-53, assoc. prof., 1962-78, full prof., 1978-89, prof. emerita, 1989—; lectr. in English Rutgers U., New Brunswick, N.J., 1961-62; vis. prof. Am. lit. U. Geneva, 1968. Author: Waiting and Other Poems, 1964, An Eye for an I, 1966, I Wanted to See Something Flying, 1976, Entropisms, 1978, Book of Ten, 1981, Lover: Short Stories, 1989, Book of Twenty, 1992, My, Haven't the Flowers Been?, 1995; editor: Ezra Pound and the Visual Arts, 1980; translator Blood and Feathers: Selected Poems of Jacques Prevert, 1988, rev. edit., 1993; author of poems. MacDowell Art Colony fellow, 1972, 73, 74, 77, MADDO fellow, 1978, 81, Va. Ctr. for Creative Arts fellow, 1975, 76, 81, 82, 84, 86, 88, 89, 90, 91, 92, 93, Djerassi Found. resident fellow, 1990; Am. Coun. Learned Soc. grantee, 1978, CUNY summer grantee, 1979, 81, 86. Fellow Poets Editors & Novelists, Nat. Book Critics Circle, Acad. Am. Poets, Internat. Assn. Art Critics, Poetry Soc. Am.; mem. Phi Beta Kappa. Home: 25 West 54 St New York NY 10019 Office: Dept English Queens Coll Flushing NY 11367

ZINS, MARTHA LEE, elementary education educator, media specialist; b. Mankato, Minn., Dec. 14, 1945; d. Hubert Joseph and Rose Marie (Johannes) Z. BA in History, Mankato State U., 1966, BA in English, 1967; MLS, Western Mich. U., 1971; postgrad., U. Minn. Tchr. history Worthington (Minn.) High Sch., 1966-67; sch. media generalist Hopkins (Minn.) West Jr. High Sch., 1967-83, Curren Elem. Sch., Hopkins, 1986—; mem. Hopkins Dist. Tech. Com., 1986—; co-chair Hopkins Elem. Sci. Com., 1991—. Contbr. articles to profl. jours.; presenter and speaker at confs. Pres. Saddlewood Patio Homes Assn. Inc., Minnetonka, 1991-95, bd. dirs., 1987—; mem. various gov.'s task forces; del. Ngo Forum 95, Beijing; mem. WILPF's Internat. Peace Train (Helsinki to Beijing), 1995; mem. Metronet Adv. Com., 1994-96. Mem. NEA (bd. dirs. 1976-77, 91—, Woman Educator of Yr. 1975), ALA, ACLU, Minn. Edn. Assn. (bd. dirs. 1975-86, 91—, v.p. 1977-83, pres. 1983-86, Human Rels. award 1979), Minn. Civil Liberties Union (bd. dirs. 1982-95), State of Minn. Tchrs. Retirment Assn. (bd. dirs. 1989—), Minn. Ednl. Media Orgn. (co-founder, v.p. 1990), Delta Kappa Gamma (Beta Beta chpt., co-founder, chpt. treas.), Beta Phi Mu, Phi Alpha Theta. Mem. Dem. Farm Labor Party. Roman Catholic. Home: 17509 Saddlewood Ln Minnetonka MN 55345-2663 Office: Curren Sch Dept Media 1600 Mainstreet Hopkins MN 55343-7409

ZINSER, ELISABETH ANN, academic administrator; b. Meadville, Pa., Feb. 20, 1940; d. Merle and Fae Zinser. BS, Stanford U., 1964; MS, U. Calif., San Francisco, 1966, MIT, 1982; PhD, U. Calif., Berkeley, 1972. Nurse VA Hosp., Palo Alto, Calif., 1964-65, San Francisco, 1969-70; instr. Sch. Nursing U. Calif., San Francisco, 1966-69; pre-doctoral fellow Nat. Inst. Health, Edn. and Welfare, 1971-72; adminstr. Sch. Medicine U. Wash., Seattle, 1972-75, Coun. Higher Edn., State of Ky., 1975-77; prof., dean. Coll. Nursing U. N.D., Grand Forks, 1977-83; vice chancellor acad. affairs U. N.C., Greensboro, 1983-89; pres. Gallaudet U., Washington, 1988, U. Idaho, Moscow, 1989-95; chancellor U. Ky., Lexington, 1995—; bd. dirs. Am. Coun. Edn., Washington; cons. Boeing Aircraft Co., Seattle; chmn. commn. on outreach and tech. transfer; bd. dirs. Nat. Assn. State Univs. and Land Grant Colls. Primary author: (with others) Contemporary Issues in Higher Education, 1985, Higher Education Research, 1988. Bd. dirs. Humana Hosp., Greensboro, 1986-88; v.p., bd. dirs. Ea. Music Festival, Greensboro, 1987-89; trustee N.C. Coun. Econ. Edn., 1985-89, Greensboro Day Sch., 1987-89. Leadership fellow Bush Found., 1981-82. Mem. Am. Assn. Higher Edn., Assn. Am. Colls. (Coun. Liberal Learning), Am. Assn. Univ. Adminstrs., AAUP, AAUW, Pi Lambda Theta, Sigma Theta Tau. Office: U Ky 111 Adminstrn Bldg Lexington KY 40502

ZION-SHELTON, OLGA-JEAN, school counselor; b. Omaha, Aug. 10, 1957; d. Howard Kenton and Doris Jean (Harkness) Z. Student, U. Minn., 1975-77; BA, Adams State U., Alamosa, Colo., 1980; MS, Emporia (Kans.) State U., 1987. Cert. in counseling and lang. arts, Colo. Tchr. speech Upward Bound, Alamosa, 1980; tchr. English Wyandotte High Sch., Kansas City, Kans., 1980-81; tchr. English and speech Bishop Ward High Sch., Kansas City, 1984-86; grad. asst. Emporia State U., 1986-87; counselor Winfield (Kans.) High Sch., 1987-88, Perry (Kans.)-Lecompton High Sch., 1988-91, Clear Creek High Sch., Idaho Springs, Colo., 1991-93, Heritage High Sch., Littleton, Colo., 1993-96, Elbert (Colo.) Schs., 1996—; instr. psychology Highland (Kans.) Community Coll., 1989. Editor newsletter for Kans. Sch. Counselors Assn., 1988-91. Grantee in field. Mem. Am. Counselors Assn., Am. Sch. Counselors Assn., Rocky Mountain Soc. Adlerian Psychology (pres. 1993), Kans. Assn. Counseling and Devel. (bd. dirs. 1990-91), Kans. Sch. Counselors Assn. (pub. rels. chmn. 1988-89, pres. 1990-91), Colo. Sch. Counselors Assn. (grants chmn. 1994-95). Democrat. Roman Catholic. Home: 8041 Eagleview Dr Littleton CO 80125

ZIPPORAH, ZENA, artist; b. Phila., Jan. 18, 1942; d. Jess and Sylvia (Ruttenberg) Pinsky; m. Joseph Krall, Aug. 6, 1960 (div. May 1975); children: Roy, Jennifer, Sarah; m. Myron Israel Kaplan, Feb. 10, 1980. BA, SUNY, Buffalo, 1965; MA, Case Western Res. U., 1970; postgrad., Cleve. Inst. Art, 1985. Tchr. Ohio Arts Coun., 1970-75, resident various schs., 1975-80. Solo exhbns. include McDonough Mus. Arts, Youngstown, Ohio, 1992, Zanesville (Ohio) Ctr. Arts; group shows include Allan Stone Gallery, N.Y.C., 1990, Granary Books, N.Y.C., 1991, Cleve. Mus. Art, 1993, Dru Arstark Gallery, N.Y.C., 1996, A.I.R. Gallery, N.Y.C., 1996, others; represented in pvt. collections N.Y. Pub. Library, Doubleday and Co., N.Y., others; numerous one-woman and juried exhibits, 1984—. Home: 3544 Fairmount Blvd Shaker Heights OH 44118

ZIPPRODT, PATRICIA, costume designer. B.A., Wellesley Coll.; student, Art Inst. Chgo., Art Students League N.Y., Fashion Inst. Tech. Asst. to various theatre designers; lectr., condr. master classes Yale U., Harvard U., others; vis. lectr. theatre arts NYU; prof. theatre arts Brandeis U., 1985-93; founding mem. Nat. Theater for the Deaf. Designer: (Broadway mus.) Fiddler on the Roof, 1964 (Tony award 1964), Cabaret, 1966 (Tony award 1966), Zorba, 1968 (Drama Desk award 1968), 1776, 1969 (Drama Desk award 1969, Joseph P. Maharam award 1970), Pippin, 1972 (Drama Desk award 1973), Mack and Mable, 1974, Chicago, 1975, King of Hearts, 1978, Alice in Wonderland, 1982 (Joseph P. Maharam award 1983), Smile, 1983, The Accidental Death of an Anarchist, 1984, Sweet Charity, 1985 (Tony award 1986), Big Deal, 1986, Shogun: The Musical, 1990 (Drama Desk award 1990, Joseph P. Maharam award 1990), My Fair Lady, 1993; (Broadway plays) A Period of Adjustment, 1962, Little Foxes, 1967, Plaza Suite, 1968, Scratch, 1971, All God's Chillun' Got Wings, 1975, Poor Murderer, 1976, Kingdoms, 1981, Fools, 1981, Brighton Beach Memoirs, 1983, The Glass Menagerie, 1983, Macbeth, 1988, Cat on a Hot Tin Roof, 1989, My Favorite Year, 1992; (off-Broadway plays) Our Town, 1960, The Balcony, 1960, Camino Real, 1961, Oh Dad Poor Dad Etc., 1962, A Man's a Man, 1963, The Blacks, 1962; (Guthrie Theatre) Waiting for Godot, 1973, Don Juan, 1982 (Joseph P. Maharam award 1983), The Bacchae, 1987; (Nat. Actors Theatre) The Crucible, 1991-92, Hotel Paradiso, 1991-92, The Master Builder, 1991-92, Little Hotel On The Side, 1992, School for Scandal, 1994, Picasso At The Lapin Agile, 1995; (Boston Opera) Madam Butterfly, 1962, Hippolyte E Aricie, 1966, The Rise and Fall of the City of Mahagonny, 1972; (New York City Opera) Katerina Ismailova, 1967, The Flaming Angel, 1968, Naughty Marietta, 1978; (Guggenheim Mus., N.Y.C.) The Mother of Us All, 1972; (Julliard Opera) Lord Byron, 1973; (Met. Opera) Tannhaüser, 1977, The Barber of Seville, 1982; (Am. Repertory Theatre, Cambridge, Mass.) The Fall of the House of Usher, 1988; (Am. Ballet Theatre) Les Noces, 1969, The Leaves are Fading, 1975, Estuary, 1982, Coppélia, 1991; (New York City Ballet) Watermill, 1972, Dybbuk Variations, 1974, The Sleeping Beauty, 1991; (Houston Ballet) Helgi Tommasen, 1985; (Ballet Hispanico) Cada Noche Tango Jnez de Castro Tres Cantos, 1988; (films) The Graduate, 1967; (television spls.) Anne Bancroft Spl., CBS, 1970, June Moon, WNET, 1973, The Glass Menagerie, ABC, 1973, Alice in Wonderland, WNET, 1983, Chrysler Skating, 1992; (nat. tours) Bette Midler, 1976, Ben Vereen, 1983; designer, advisor: The Seagull (St. Petersburg, Russia), Anna Christie (Beijing, China); exhibitor design sketches Wright-Hepburn, London, 1966, Capicorn Gallery, N.Y.C., 1968, Mus. City N.Y., 1972, U. Calif.-San Diego, 1974, Toneelmuseum, Amsterdam, The Netherlands, 1975, U.S. Internat. Theatre Inst. traveling exhibit, 1974-78, N.Y. City Ballet, 1994. Recipient award for spl. costumes NATAS, 1970, spl. award New Eng. Conf., 1973, Ritter award Fashion Inst. Tech., 1977, Disting. Career award S.E. Theatre Conf., 1985; inductee Theater Hal of Fame, 1992. Mem. United Scenic Artists, Costume Designers Guild, Motion Picture Acad. Arts and Scis. Address: 29 King St New York NY 10014-4966

ZIRBEL, ESTHER LUISE, astronomy educator, researcher; b. Istanbul, Turkey, Aug. 3, 1961; came to U.S., 1986; d. Richard Edgar Zirbel and Gerda Luise (Koprivc) Paulus. BSc with honors, Newcastle U., Newcastle upon Tyne, Eng., 1982; MSc, Sussex U., Brighton, Eng., 1985; MPhil, Yale U., 1989, PhD, 1993. Geophysicist Merlin Geophys., Woking, Surrey, Eng., 1982-83; rsch. asst. Landessteinwarte, Heidelberg, Germany, 1984-85, Raman Inst., Bangalore, India, 1986; postdoctoral fellow Space Telescope Inst., Balt., 1993-95; asst. prof. astronomy Haverford (Pa.) Coll., 1995—. Recipient Tinsley award, 1992; scholar German Acad. Exch. Svc., scholar Newcastle U., 1980-82, Sci. and Engring. Rsch. Coun., 1983-84, Yale U., 1986-93; travel grants to various confs. Mem. AAUW, Am. Astron. Soc., Astron. Assn. Paciic. Office: Haverford Coll Astronomy Dept 370 Lancaster Ave Haverford PA 19041

ZIRBES, MARY KENNETH, social justice ministry coordinator; b. Melrose, Minn., Sept. 4, 1926; d. Joseph Louis and Clara Bernadine (Petermeier) Z. BA in History and Edn., Coll. St. Catherine, 1960; MA in Applied Theology, Sch. Applied Theology, Berkeley, Calif., 1976. Joined Order of St. Francis, Roman Cath. Ch., 1945. Tchr. Pub. Grade Sch., St. Nicholas, Minn., 1947-52; prin. Holy Spirit Grade Sch., St. Cloud, Minn., 1953-59, St. Mary's Jr. High Sch., Morris, Minn., 1960-62; coord. Franciscan Mission Team, Peru, South America, 1962-67, Franciscan Missions, Little Falls, Minn., 1967-70; dir. St. Richard's Social Ministry, Richfield, Minn., 1971-80, Parish Community Devel., St. Paul, Mpls., Minn., 1980-85; councillor gen. Franciscan Sisters of Little Falls, 1960-62, 67-70; asst. dir. Renew-Archdiocese of St. Paul-Mpls., 1986-89; coord. Parish Social Justice Ministry-Archdiocese of St. Paul-Mpls., 1990-93; minister Franciscan Assocs., 1993—; leader of team on evangelical life Franciscan Sisters of Little Falls, 1994—; co-developer Assn. of Pastoral Ministers, Mpls., St. Paul, 1979-81, Compañeros/Sister Parishes-Minn. and Nicaragua, 1984-89, Minn. Interfaith Ecology Coalition, 1989-92. Author: Parish Social Ministry, 1985, (manual) Acting for Justice, 1992. Organizer Twin Cities Orgn., Mpls., 1979-80; bd. dirs. Franciscan Sisters Health Care, Inc., Little Falls, 1990-93, Rice-Marion Residents Assn., St. Paul, 1991-92. Named Outstanding chair Assn. Pastoral Ministers, 1981; recipient Five Yrs. of Outstanding Svc. award Companeros, 1989. Mem. Assn. Pastoral Ministers (chair 1979), Amnesty Internat., Voices for Justice-Legis. Lobby, Audubon Soc., Network, Minn. Interfaith Ecology Coalition, Franciscan Sisters of Little Falls. Office: Franciscan Sisters 116-8th Ave SE Little Falls MN 56345

ZISKIN, LAURA, film producer. Co-founder Frogwood Films. Films include: (assoc. prodr.) Eyes of Laura Mars, 1978; (prodr.) Murphy's Romance, 1985, No Way Out, 1987, D.O.A., 1988, Everybody's An American, 1988, The Rescue, 1988, What About Bob?, 1991, The Doctor, 1991, Hero, 1992; (exec. prodr.) Pretty Woman, 1990; producer: To Die For, 1995. •

ZLAMANY, BRENDA LOUISE, artist; b. N.Y.C., Dec. 21, 1959; d. Carl and Bette (Gugliotti) Zlamany. Student, Yale Coll. before Coll. Prog., New Haven, 1976-77; BA, Wesleyan U., 1981; student, S.W. Hayter's Atelier 17, Paris, 1981, Tyler Sch. Art, Rome, 1981, Skowhegan Sch. Painting Sculpt, Maine, 1984. Commissioned portrait of Jeffrey Dahmer, N.Y. Times Mag., 1995, portrait of Dr. Martini, Martini Libr., Meml. Sloan-Kettering Cancer Ctr., 1995. Group shows include Yale U., New Haven, 1977, UCLA, 1981, Pier C, Hoboken, N.J., 1982, BACA, Bklyn., 1982, 85, 88, City Without Walls, Newark, 1982, Jack Tilton Gallery, N.Y.C., 1983, 84, 90, Rhona Hoffman Gallery, Chgo., 1983, Public Image Gallery, N.Y.C., 1983, Cayman Gallery, N.Y.C., 1983, Four Walls, Hoboken, 1984, White Columns, N.Y.C., 1987, 90, Hudson River Mus., Yonkers, N.Y., 1989, 91, Rosa Esman Gallery, N.Y.C., 1990, Epoche Gallery, Bklyn., 1990, Althea Viafora Gallery, N.Y.C., 1990, Edith C. Blum Art Inst., N.Y.C., 1990, N.Y. Hist. Soc., N.Y.C., 1991, E.M. Donahue Gallery, N.Y.C., 1991, 92, 93, Art in General, N.Y.C., 1991, Artists' Space, N.Y.C., 1992, Scott Alan Gallery, N.Y.C., 1992, Robischon Gallery, Denver, 1992, Stiebel Modern, N.Y.C., 1992, 93, MVNC Gallery, Mount Vernon, Ohio, 1993, Cavin-Morris Gallery, N.Y.C., 1993, Blum Helman Gallery, N.Y.C., 1993, Sabine Wachters Fine Arts, Brussels, 1993, , 95, Littlejohn/Sternau Gallery, N.Y.C., 1994, Art Miami'94 Internat. Art Exhbn., O'Hara Gallery, N .Y.C., 1994, Stux Gallery, N.Y.C., 1994, Allez les Filles, Columbus, Ohio, 1995, James Graham and Sons, N.Y.C., 1995, 96, Neuberger Mus. of Art, Purchase, N.Y., 1995, Zoller Gallery, University Park, Pa., 1995, U. Mass., Amherst, 1995, Silverstein Gallery, N.Y.C., 1996; one-woman shows include Wesleyan U., Middletown, Conn., 1981, Hallwalls Contemporary Art Ctr., Buffalo, N.Y., 1989, E.M. Donahue Gallery, 1991, 92, 94, Sabine Wachters Fine Arts, 1993, 95, Galerie Quintessens, Utrecht, The Netherlands, 1994, Jessica Fredricks Gallery, N.Y.C., 1996. Recipient grants CETA Arts, 1978, 79, MacDowell Colony, 1986, 92, 95, Ucross Found., Wyo., 1987, Millay Colony, Steepletop, N.Y., 1988, Triangle Artists' Workshop, Pine Plains, N.Y., 1990; Johnston Trust scholar, 1977-81, Jerome Found. fellow, 1981-82, Vermont Studio Colony fellow, 1987, N.Y. Found. for the Arts fellow in painting, 1994.

ZNACHKO, BRENDA VANOVER, lawyer; b. Sumter, S.C., Mar. 26, 1961; d. Andy Martin and Aggie (Taylor) Vanover; m. Michael Joseph Znachko, May 20, 1985. BS, U. So. Miss., 1984; JD, U. Miss., 1987; LLM in Taxation, U. Fla., 1989. Bar: La. 1987, Fla. 1989, Miss. 1988. Assoc. Phelps & Dunbar, New Orleans, 1987-89; tax atty. Annis Mitchell, Tampa, Fla., 1989-92; ptnr., tax atty. Eaton and Cottrell, P.A., Gulfport, Miss., 1992—. Contbr. articles to legal jour. and newspaper. Lt. (j.g.) USNR, 1984—. Mem. ABA, Miss. Bar Assn., La. Bar Assn., Fla. Bar Assn. Home: 2666 Broadwater Dr Gulfport MS 39507 Office: Eaton and Cottrell PA 1310 25th Ave Gulfport MS 39501

ZOBEL, JAN ARLEEN, tax consultant; b. San Francisco, Feb. 8, 1947; d. Jerome Fremont and Louise Maxine (Purwin) Z. BA, Whittier Coll., 1968; MA, U. Chgo., 1970. Tchr. Chgo. Pub. Schs., 1969-70, San Francisco Pub. Schs., 1971-78; editor, pub. People's Yellow Pages, San Francisco, 1971-81; pvt. practice tax cons. San Francisco, Oakland, 1978—; tchr. community coll. dist., San Francisco, 1986-91; tax lectr. U. Hawaii, 1989—, U. Calif., San Francisco State U., Marin C.C. Author: Minding Her Own Business: The Self-Employed Woman's Guide to Taxes and Recordkeeping, 1997; editor People's Yellow Pages, 1971-81 (cert. of honor San Francisco Bd. Suprs. 1974), Where the Child Things Are, 1977-80. Com. mem. Bay Area Career Women's Fund. Named Acct. Adv. of Yr., SBA, 1987; presented Key to City of Buffalo, 1970. Mem. Nat. Assn. Enrolled Agts., Calif. Assn. Enrolled Agts., Nat. Assn. Tax Preparers, Bay Area Career Women. Home: 3045 Holyrood Dr Oakland CA 94611-2541 Office: 1197 Valencia St San Francisco CA 94110-3026

ZOBEL, LOUISE PURWIN, author, educator, lecturer, writing consultant; b. Laredo, Tex., Jan. 10, 1922; d. Leo Max and Ethel Catherine (Levy) Purwin; m. Jerome Fremont Zobel, Nov. 14, 1943; children: Lenore Zobel Harris, Janice A., Robert E., Audrey Zobel Dollinger. BA cum laude, Stanford U., 1943, MA, 1976. Cert. adult edn. and community coll. tchr., Calif. Freelance mag. writer and author Palo Alto, Calif., 1942—; writer, editor, broadcastor UP Bur., San Francisco, 1943; lectr. on writing, history, travel No. Calif., 1964—; lectr., Calif. campuses, other colls. and univs., 1969—; writing cons. to pvt. clients, 1969—; editorial asst. Assn. Coll. Unions Internat., Palo Alto, 1972-73; acting asst. prof. journalism San Jose State U., 1976; keynote speaker, seminar leader, prin. speaker at nat. confs. Author: (books) The Travel Writer's Handbook, 1980, (paperback), 1982, 83, 84, 85, rev. edits., 1992, 94; author, narrator (90 minute cassette) Let's Have Fun in Japan, 1982; contbr. articles to anthologies, nat. mags. and newspapers; writer advertorials. Bd. dirs., publicity chair Friends of Palo Alto Libr., 1985—; officer Santa Clara County Med. Aux., Esther Clark Aux., others; past pres. PTA. Recipient award for excellence in journalism Sigma Delta Chi, 1943, awards Writers Digest, 1967-75, 94, Armed Forces Writers League, 1972, Nat. Writers Club, 1976. Mem. Am. Soc. Journalists and Authors, Travel Journalists Guild, Internat. Food, Wine and Travel Writers Assn., Pacific Asia Travel Assn., Calif. Writers Club (v.p. 1988-89), AAUW (v.p. 1955-57, Nat. writing award 1969), Stanford Alumni Assn., Phi Beta Kappa. Home and Office: 23350 Sereno Ct Unit 30 Cupertino CA 95014-6543

ZOBEL, RYA WEICKERT, federal judge; b. Germany, Dec. 18, 1931. A.B., Radcliffe Coll., 1953; LL.B., Harvard U., 1956. Bar: Mass. 1956, U.S. Dist. Ct., Mass., 1956, U.S. Ct. Appeals (1st cir.) 1967. Assoc. Hill & Barlow, Boston, 1967-73; assoc. Goodwin, Procter & Hoar, Boston, 1973-76, ptnr., 1976-79; U.S. dist. judge of Mass. Boston, 1979—; dir. Fed. Jud. Ctr., Washington, 1994—. Mem. ABA, Boston Bar Assn., Am. Bar Found., Mass. Bar Assn., Am. Law Inst. Office: Fed Judicial Ctr Thurgood Marshall Fed Bldg One Columbus Cir NE Washington DC 20002

ZOCH, NINA BETH, principal; b. Houston, Feb. 13, 1949; d. Louis Grey and Bobbie Nell (Sloan) Stansel; m. Howard Gene Zoch, Feb. 25, 1973 (div. Dec. 30, 1987); 1 child, Rachel Elizabeth. AA, San Jacinto Coll., 1969; BA, U. Tex., 1971, MEd, 1974. Tchr., dept. head Seabrook (Tex.) Ind. Sch. Dist., Intermediate Sch. in Clear Creek Ind. Sch. Dist., 1972-83; tchr. Clear Lake H.S., Houston, 1983-94, asst. prin., 1994—; trustee La Porte (Tex.) Ind. Sch. Dist., 1991-96; mem. La Porte Edn. Found., 1994-96. Greater Houston Area Writing Project fellow, 1986; named vol. of yr. E.A. Smith YMCA, Webster, 1991. Mem. NEA, AAUW. Democrat. Lutheran. Home: 725 Purdue Deer Park TX 77536 Office: Clear Lake HS 2929 Bay Area Blvd Houston TX 77062

ZOELLER, JUDITH BEEBE, elementary school educator; b. Ridgewood, N.J., Aug. 2, 1957; d. Joseph R. and Judy K. (Garland) Beebe; children: Catherine J. Bell, Samantha A. Bell; m. Geoffrey Warren Zoeller, June 26, 1993. BA in Elem. Edn., Georgian Ct. Coll., 1979; MEd, East Stroudsburg U., 1995. Cert. tchr., N.J. Day camp counselor, dir. day camp Engle Sch., Sparta, N.J., 1971-81; tchr. Our Lady of Mt. Carmel, Newport News, Va., 1981-83, St. Columba Sch., Oxon Hills, Md., 1983-84, Sparta (N.J.) Alpine Sch., 1989—; mem. insvc. facilitator Mimosa Publ., Sparta, 1991—, conf. attendee, Gwingana, Australia, summer 1991; honors tchr. NASA/NEWEST, summer 1996. Asst. leader, treas. Girl Scouts USA, Sparta, 1990-95. Recipient Gov.'s Tchr. Recognition award N.J. Dept. Edn., 1993-94. Mem. Nat. Coun. Tchrs. Math., N.J. Ednl. Assn., Sparta Edn. Assn. Roman Catholic. Home: 74 Hunters Ln Sparta NJ 07871-2556 Office: Sparta Alpine Sch 151 Andover Rd Sparta NJ 07871-1006

ZOGOPOULOS, GLORIA, fundraising executive; b. Franklin, N.H., Apr. 18, 1943; d. Edward Alcide and Marieanne Blanche (Pelletier) LaPlante; m. M. Stephen Zogopoulos, Feb. 18, 1969; 1 child, Michael Stephen. AA in Mgmt. and Mgmt. Info. Sys., Merrimack Valley Coll., 1980; BA in Humanities summa cum laude, U. N.H., 1983. Program dir. N.H. Charitable Fund, Concord, N.H., 1969-79; office adminstr. Devine, Millimet, Branch, Manchester, N.H., 1983-86; asst. to pres. Easter Seal Soc., Manchester, 1986-88, coord. pub. rels., 1988-91; dir. mem. rels. N.H. Pub. Radio, Concord, 1991—. Bd. dirs. N.H. Humanities Coun., Concord, 1977-79, chmn. nominating com., 1978-79, N.H. Lung Assn., Manchester, 1980-83, Employment Connection Specialists, Inc., Manchester, 1993-94; mem. venture grant allocations com. United Way of Manchester, 1984-89. Mem. Continuing Edn. in Fund Raising. Office: NH Pub Radio 207 N Main St Concord NH 03301

ZOHLMAN, SUSAN KANN, interior designer; b. Pitts., Mar. 5, 1947; d. Gilbert Sanes and Elise W. (Kann) Goldman; m. Robert Stephen Zohlman, Aug. 30, 1969; children: Andrew Sanes, Zachary Alan. BA, U. Wis., 1969. Interior designer Paraphernalia, Santa Rosa, Calif., 1982—; coord. Jewish program Friendship Cir., Santa Rosa, Calif., 1985-91; adminstr. No. Bay Nephrology, Santa Rosa, Calif., 1985—. Bd. dirs. Congregation Beth Ami, Santa Rosa, 1984-90, Planned Parenthood, San Raphael, 1991-95; pres.-elect So. County Med. Assn. Alliance, So. County, Calif., 1996—. Democrat. Jewish. Home: 3490 Ridgeview Dr Santa Rosa CA 95404

ZOHN, DEBORAH SUE, music educator; b. Paterson, N.J., Mar. 21, 1956; d. Ludwig J. and Lucille (Auerbach) Crane; m. Lawrence Keith Zohn, Apr. 12, 1986. Student, Carnegie-Mellon U., 1974; BA, Glassboro (N.J.) State U., 1977; MA, NYU, 1980. Cert. tchr., N.J., Pa.; cert. aerobics instr. Am. Coun. on Exercise. Music tchr. Bloomfield (N.J.) Pub. Schs., 1977-89, Parkland Sch. Dist., Allentown, Pa., 1989—; condr. Bloomfield Music Festival, 1989; condr. jr. high regional chorus N.J. Mus. Educators Assn., 1980; mus. dir. Glassboro Summer Theatre, 1977, Coleridge Summer Camp, Bklyn., 1987-88, Camp Wyoda, Ely, Vt., 1976. Choral arranger Liberty Tree, 1976; composer Overture to Eternity, Lines From Off the Sea, Petrified City, Strings, Come Live With Me and Be My Love, Two Familiar Tunes, Alleluia, Thirteen Ways of Looking at a Blackbird, The Seasons, The White Dress, Agnus Dei, Sonate, My November Guest, Benediction, Lullaby for Daddy, The Answer to My Dreams, Why Must You Change, Jake, The Seasons of My Love, Waking Up Alone, Leaving for Rhode Island, Playing Games With You, You Are My Life, It's Understood, I Can't Write This Love Song, The Night We Fall in Love, Isn't It Nice to be Home Again, Happy New Year. Vol. piano player Devon House, Allentown, Pa., 1990-91, Phoebe Home, 1995—. Named Outstanding Educator Jaycees, 1991; Delta Kappa Gamma grantee, 1976. Mem. NEA, Pa. State Edn. Assn., Am. Coun. on Exercies, Parkland Edn. Assn., Camerata Singers (bd. dirs. 1994—). Jewish. Office: Troxell Jr HS 2219 N Cedar Crest Blvd Allentown PA 18104

ZOLBER, KATHLEEN KEEN, nutrition educator; b. Walla Walla, Wash., Dec. 9, 1916; d. Wildie H. and Alice (Johnson) Keen; m. Melvin L. Zolber, Sept. 19, 1937. BS in Foods and Nutrition, Walla Walla Coll., 1941; MA, Wash. State U., 1961; PhD, U. Wis., 1968. Registered dietitian. Dir. food service Walla Walla Coll., 1941-50, mgr. coll. store, 1951-59, asst. prof. food and nutrition, 1959-62, assoc. prof., 1962-64; assoc. prof. nutrition Loma Linda (Calif.) U., 1964-72, prof. nutrition, 1973-91, dir. dietetic edn., 1967-84, dir. dietetics Med. Ctr., 1972-84, dir. nutrition program, 1984-91; retired. Mead Johnson grantee, 1965-67; recipient Alumna of Yr. award Walla Walla Coll., 1977; Delores Nyhus award Calif. Dietetic Assn., 1978. Mem. Am. Dietetic Assn. (pres. 1982-83, Copher award 1992), Am. Pub. Health Assn., AAUP, Omicron Nu, Delta Omega. Home: PO Box 981 Loma Linda CA 92354-0981

ZOLL, MIRIAM HANNAH, activist, writer; b. Boston, Oct. 1, 1962; d. Nathan Hyman and Jacqueline Harper (Bonney) Z. BS in Journalism and Psychology, U. Mass., 1984. Dep. dir. comm. Earth Day, N.Y.C., 1990; spl. projects cons. Gay Men's Health Crisis, 1990-93; co-prodr., dir. comm. Take Our Daughters to Work, Ms. Found. for Women, 1992-94; nat. program cons. Northeastern U., 1994-95; media cons. Internat. Women's Conf., 1995; nat. project mgr. Girls Inc., 1995-96; program dir. Youth Vote '96 Harvard Univ. Conf., 1996; mem. advance team Nat. Dem. Conv., 1992, Clinton-Gore Inaugural Com., 1993; logistician Nat. Dem. Inst., Malawi, Ctrl. Africa, 1994; nat. advisor God Bless the Child Films, Boston, 1995-96; adv. bd. mem. Girls Re-Cast TV, N.Y.C.; lectr. Inst. Politics, Kennedy Sch. Govt., Harvard U., 1996; trainer Ctr. Study Sport in Soc., Northeastern U. Contbr. articles to profl. jours. Advisor Mentors in Violence Prevention (MVP) Project, 1994-96. Home: PO Box 1014 Brookline Village MA 02147

ZOLLAR, CAROLYN CATHERINE, lawyer; b. Evanston, Ill., July 5, 1947; d. Maurice Adam and Alice S. (Kelm) Z. BA, Smith Coll., Northampton, Mass., 1969; MA, Columbia U., 1970; JD, Am. U., Washington, 1976. Bar: D.C., Va. Legis. asst. Congressman William Anderson U.S. Ho. of Reps., Washington, 1970-72; planning cons. Nat. Inst. Edn., Washington, 1972, legal asst., 1973, asst. for govt. and external rels., 1973-75; assoc. Joe W. Fleming II, P.C., Washington, 1975-82; gen. counsel Nat. Assn. Rehab. Facilities, Washington, 1982-86, gen. counsel, dir. med. rehab., 1986-94; gen. counsel, v.p. policy Am. Rehab. Assn., Washington, 1994—; sec. Am. Rehab. Svcs., Inc., Washington, 1988-94; bd. adv. Ind. Living Mag., N.Y.C., 1988—; mem. Joint Commn. Accreditation Health Care Orgns. Task Force on Rehab. Svcs., 1988. Contbr. articles to profl. jours. Sec. bd. dirs. Rock Creek Found., Silver Spring, Md., 1983-90, Affiliated Sante Group, 1993—; chair Nat. Rehab. Caucus, 1991—. Recipient legis. achievement award Nat. Assn. Rehab. Facilities, 1981, legis. advocacy award U. Buffalo, 1993, pub. svc. award Am. Acad. Phys. Medicine and Rehab., 1994. Mem. Am. Soc. Assn. Execs., Nat. Health Lawyers Assn., Va. Bar Assn., D.C. Bar, Women in Govt. Rels. Episcopalian. Office: Am Rehab Assn 1910 Association Dr Reston VA 20191

ZOLLAR, JAWOLE WILLA JO, art association administrator; b. Kansas City, Kans., Dec. 21, 1950; d. Alfred Jr. and Dorothy Delores Zollar; 1 child, Elizabeth Herron. BA in Dance, U. Mo., Kansas City, 1975; MFA in Dance, Fla. State U., 1979. Faculty Fla. State U., Tallahassee, 1977-80; artistic dir. Urban Bush Women, N.Y.C., 1984—. Recipient N.Y. Dance and Performance award, 1992; named Outstanding Alumni U. Mo.-Kansas City, 1993; Mankato State U. Worlds of Thought Resident scholar, 1994; Nat. Endowment of Arts Choreography fellow, 1992, 93, 94. Mem. Dance U.S.A., Assn. of Am. Cultures, Internat. Assn. of Blacks in Dance. Address: 339 15th St Brooklyn NY 11215 Office: Urban Bush Women 225 Lafayette St Ste 201 New York NY 10012 also: care IMG Artists 22 E 71st St New York NY 10021-4911*

ZOLLAR, NIKKI MICHELE, state agency administrator; b. Chgo., June 18, 1956; d. Lowell M. and Doris J. (Lowe) Z.; m. William A. Von Hoene, Jr., June 18, 1983; children: William Lowell Von Hoene, Branden Tracey. BA, Johns Hopkins U., 1977; JD, Georgetown U., 1980. Fed. jud. law clk. U.S. Dist. Ct. (no. dist.) Ill., Chgo., 1980-81; assoc. Lafontant, Wilkins, Jones & Ware, Chgo., 1981-83, Kirkland & Ellis, Chgo., 1983-85; chmn., sec. Chgo. Bd. Election Commrs., 1987-90; dir. Ill. Dept. Profl. Regulation, Chgo., 1991—. Trustee Cmty. Youth Creative Learning Experience; mem. women's coun. Chgo. Hear Assn.; mem. Chgo. com. Solidarity with So. Africa; mem. women's bd. Jackson Park Hosp. (award); active Chgo. Urban League, Nat. Coalition of 100 Black Women. Recipient outstanding achievement award YWCA, Washington Park YMCA, youth svc. bd. Beatrice Caffrey Found., David C. Hilliard award Chgo. Bar Assn., 1988-89, Kizzy award Revlon Corp./Kizzy Scholarship Fund, African Am. Women's Achievement award Columbia Coll., Martin Luther King Jr. award for dedicated leadership Boy Scouts Am., outstanding young profl. award Chgo. Urban Profls., svc. and leadership award United Negro Coll. Fund, outstanding achievement cert. Ill. State Atty. Appellate Svc. Commn., African Am. history maker award Gov. Jim Edgar; named one of 100 outstanding black bus. and profl. women in U.S. Dollars and Sense mag. Mem. Ill. Women in Govt., Women Execs. in State Govt., Alpha Gamma Pi. Mem. United Ch. of Christ. Office: Ill Dept Profl Regulation 320 W Washington St Springfield IL 62786

ZOLOTOW, CHARLOTTE SHAPIRO, author, editor; b. Norfolk, Va., June 26, 1915; d. Louis J. and Ella F. (Bernstein) Shapiro; m. Maurice Zolotow, Apr. 14, 1938 (div. 1969); children: Stephen, Ellen. Student, U. Wis., 1933-36. Editor children's book dept. Harper & Row, N.Y.C., 1938-44; sr. editor Harper & Row, 1962-70; v.p., assoc. pub. Harper Jr. Books, 1976-81; editorial cons., editorial dir. Charlotte Zolotow Books, 1982-90; pub. emerita, advisor Harper Collins Children's Books, 1991—; tchr. U. Colo. Writers Conf. on Children's Books, U. Ind. Writers Conf.; also lectr. children's books. Author: The Park Book, 1944, Big Brother, 1960, The Sky Was Blue, 1963, The Magic Words, 1952, Indian Indian, 1952, The Bunny Who Found Easter, 1959, In My Garden, 1960, But Not Billy, 1947, 2d edit, 1983, Not a Little Monkey, 1957, 2d edit., 1989, The Man With The Purple Eyes, 1961, Mr. Rabbit and the Lovely Present, 1962, The White Marble, 1963, A Rose, A Bridge and A Wild Black Horse, 1964, 2d edit., 1987, Someday, 1965, When I Have a Little Girl, 1965, If It Weren't for You, 1966, 2d edit., 1987, Big Sister, Little Sister, 1966, All That Sunlight, 1967, When I Have A Son, 1967, My Friend John, 1968, Summer Is, 1968, Some Things Go Together, 1969, The Hating Book, 1969, The New Friend, 1969, River Winding, 1970, 79, Lateef and His World, 1970, Yani and His World, 1970, You and Me, 1971, Wake Up and Goodnight, 1971, William's Doll, 1972, Hold My Hand, 1972, 2d edit., 1987, The Beautiful Christmas Tree, 1972, Janie, 1973, My Grandson Lew, 1974, The Summer Night, 1974, 3d edit. 1991, The Unfriendly Book, 1975, It's Not Fair, 1976, 2d edit., 1987, Someone New, 1978, Say It, 1980, If You Listen, 1980, 2d edit. 1987, The New Friend, 1981, One Step, Two ..., 1981, The Song, 1982, I Know a Lady, 1984, Timothy Too!, 1986, Everything Glistens, Everything Sings, 1987, I Like to be Little, 1987, The Poodle Who Barked at the Wind, 1987, The Quiet Mother and the Noisy Little Boy, 1988, Something's Going to Happen, 1988, This Quiet Lady, 1992, The Seashore Book, 1992, Snippets, 1992, The Moon Was the Best, 1993, Peter and the Pigeons, 1993, others; compiler An Overpraised Season, Early Sorrow. Recipient Harper Gold award for editorial excellence, 1974, Kerlan award U. Minn., 1986, Corp. award for children's books Lit. Market Pl., 1990, Silver medallion U. So. Miss., 1990, Tribute for Far Reaching Contbn. to Children's Lit., ALA, 1991. Mem. PEN, Authors League. Home: 29 Elm Pl Hastings Hudson NY 10706-1703 Office: 10 E 53d St New York NY 10022-5244

ZONA, PAULA KRISTINE, elementary education educator; b. Houston, Mar. 9, 1971; d. Warren Paul and Donna Sharon (Vise) Pieplow; m. Jason Edward Zona, Nov. 27, 1993. BS in Edn., Tex. Tech. U., 1992. Tchr. 3d grade Roscoe Wilson Elem. Sch., Lubbock, Tex., 1993—. Mem. Tex. Classroom Tchrs. Assn., Golden Key. Republican. Lutheran.

ZONDLER, JOYCE EVELYN, kindergarten educator; b. Jersey City, N.J., June 28, 1952; d. Vincent Roger and Marta (Gruber) Hohmann; m. Kenneth P. Zondler, June 20, 1976 (div.). BA, Jersey City State Coll., 1974, MA, 1981. Cert. elem., early childhood tchr., N.J. Kindergarten tchr. Robert Fulton Sch., North Bergen, N.J., 1974—; mem. curriculum rev. coms. for math. and sci. North Bergen Schs., 1993—, for lang. arts, 1992-93, mem. report card rev. com. Mem. exec. bd. Fulton Sch. PTA, 1976-86, sec., 1978-80, v.p. 1980-82, treas. 1982-86. Recipient Gov.'s Recognition award, 1991. Mem. North Bergen Edn. Assn. (sec. 1989-91, v.p. 1991-93, pres. 1993—). Democrat. Roman Catholic. Office: Robert Fulton Sch 7407 Hudson Ave North Bergen NJ 07047-5607

ZOOK, THERESA FUETTERER, gemologist, consultant; b. Barberton, Ohio, Mar. 12, 1919; d. Charles Theodore and Ethel May (Knisely) Fuetterer; m. Donovan Quay Zook, June 21, 1941; children: Theodore Alan, Jacqueline Deborah Zook Cochran. AB, Ohio U., 1941; MA in Pub. Adminstrn., Am. U., 1946. Adminstrv. intern Nat. Inst. Pub. Affairs, Washington, 1941-42; mgmt. intern U.S. Dept. Agr., Washington, 1941-42; adminstrv. analyst Office Emergency Mgmt., Washington, 1942-43, Office Price Adminstrn., Washington, 1943-45; founder Zook and Zook Cons., Arlington, Va., 1945-47; tchr. ancient history and U.S. govt. Fairfax County (Va.) Pub. Schs., 1963-64; founder, pres. Associated Gem Consulting Lab., Alexandria, 1974—, Alpha Gate Crafts Ltd., Alexandria, 1977—; color cons. Internat. Com. on Color in Gems, Bangkok, Thailand, 1983. Author: Directory of Selected Color Resources Annotated Guide, 1982, Reunion of Descendants of David and Magdalena (Blough) Zook, 1983, Basic Machine Knitting, 1979; contbr. articles to profl. jours. Bd. dirs. Am. Embassy Com. on Edn., Montevideo, Uruguay, 1962; co-founder Workshop of Arts, Santiago, Chile, 1958; mem. Nat. Trust for Hist. Preservation, Nat. Mus. Women in Arts, Nat. Mus. Am. Indian, Am. Horticulture Soc., Textile Mus. Fellow Gemmological Assn. of Gt. Britain (diplomate); mem. AAUW, DAR, Nat. Geneal. Soc., Inter-Soc. Color Coun. (chmn. com. color in gemstones 1982-84, Appreciation cert. 1984), Accredited Gemological Assn. (co-founder, v.p.). Home: PO Box 6310 Alexandria VA 22306-0310

ZOON, KATHRYN EGLOFF, biochemist; b. Yonkers, N.Y., Nov. 6, 1948; d. August R. and Violet T. (Pollock) Egloff; BS, Rensselaer Poly. Inst., 1970; PhD Johns Hopkins U., 1975; m. Robert A. Zoon, Aug. 22, 1970; children: Christine K, Jennifer R. Interferon rsch. fellow NIH, Bethesda, Md., 1975-77, staff fellow, 1977-79, sr. staff fellow, 1979-80; sr. staff fellow div. biochem. biophysics Bur. Biologics, FDA, Bethesda, 1980-83; rsch. chemist divsn. biochem. biophysics, 1983-84, rsch. chemist divsn. virology, 1984-88, rsch. chemist div. cytokine biology, Ctr. for Biologics Evaluation and Rsch., FDA, 1988—, div. dir., 1989-92; dir. Ctr. for Biologics Evaluation and Rsch., 1992—; lectr. NIH, 1994, Reigelman Lectureship, 1994. N.Y. State Regents fellow, 1970; Person of the Yr. award Biopharm, 1992, 95, Pub. Svc. award Genetic Engring. News, 1994; Presdl. Meritorious Exec. Rank award, 1994. Mem. Am. Soc. Biochemistry and Molecular Biology, Internat. Soc. Interferon Rsch., Internat. Soc. Cytokine Rsch. Roman Catholic. Contbr. numerous articles on research in biol. chemistry to sci. jours.; sect. editor Jour. Interferon Research, 1980—. Office: CBER 1401 Rockville Pike Rockville MD 20852-1428

ZOSH, LILLIAN E., biologist; b. Wilkes-Barre, Pa., Feb. 26, 1924; d. John Witt and Florence (Crawford) Hawkins. BS, Coll. Misericordia; MS, Loyola U., Balt.; PhD in Counseling Psychology, Bucknell U.; postgrad., St. Johns U. Biology tchr. Harford County Bd. of Edn., Bel Air, Md., 1964-72, 1972-88; profl. counselor and sch. counselor pvt. practice Dayton, Ohio, 1989—. Mem. Counselor and Social Worker Bd. (counselor 1988-95).

ZOTOS, KAREN ANN, healthcare administrator; b. Poughkeepsie, N.Y., July 28, 1967; d. Edward Charles Jr. and Janet Elizabeth Ehrlich; m. Pete Alexander Zotos, Oct. 23, 1993; 1 child, Maxwell Pete. BA, Columbia Univ., 1989. Provider rels. rep. The Prudential, Dallas, 1991-93; network developer Anthem Health Sys., Dallas, 1993-94; contract mgr. UT Southwestern, Dallas, 1994; profl. svcs. trainer Heritage S.W. Med. Group, Irving, Tex., 1994-95; sr. provider rels. rep. Metra Health Care Plan, Dallas, 1995—; cons. North Tex. Podiatry Network, Dallas, 1994, 96. Mem. Jr. League Dallas, Med. Group Mgmt. Assn., Slipper Club of Dallas, Kappa Alpha Theta Alumnae. Presbyterian. Home: 6706 Bob-O-Link Dallas TX 75214

ZOUBAREFF, OLGA KATARINA (KATHY BAREOFF), adminstrative assistant; b. Hassalt, Belgium; d. Vladimir F. and Kataryna (Sarcov) Z. Student in Film Acting, John Robert Powers Sch.; BA in Polit. Sci., Wayne State U.; postgrad., Ann Parsley Sch. Dance, Clinton Twp., Mich., 1990-95, Mary Skiba Sch. Dance, 1995—; A in Gen. Studies, Drama, Macomb Community Coll.; fitness and nutrition cert., Internat. Corr. Schs. Ctr., Detroit; voice studies, Ctr. for Creative Studies, Detroit, 1994—; drama studies, Wayne State U., 1994—. Acct./adminstrv. asst. Univ. Orthopaedic Assocs. Detroit, P.C., 1990—; mem. Charles J. Givens Orgn., 1991-96; actress, dancer, fashion, TV comml. and photgraphic model/film screen extra. Model, Renaissance Ctr. Fashion Panel, Detroit, 1989-91; rsch. bd. advisors Am. Biog. Inst.; mem. Internat. Biog. Centre Adv. Coun., 1992. Home: 38579 Delta Dr Clinton Township MI 48036-1711 Office: Univ Orthopaedic Assocs Detroit PC 4707 Saint Antoine St Detroit MI 48201-1427

ZSCHAU, MARILYN, singer; b. Chgo., Feb. 9, 1944; d. Edwin Arthur Eugene and Helen Elizabeth (Kelly) Z. BA in Radio, T.V., Motion Pictures, U. N.C.; ed. Juilliard Sch. Music, opera theatre with Christopher West, voice with Florence Page Kimball, also studied with John Lester. Toured with Met. Nat. Co., 1965-66, debut, Vienna Volksoper, in Die Tote Stadt, 1967, Vienna Staatsoper, in Ariadne auf Naxos, 1971; with N.Y.C. Opera from 1978; debut Met. Opera, in La Boheme, 1985, La Scala, in Die Frau ohne Schatten, 1986, Royal Opera, Covent Garden; has toured and sung in many countries. Office: Janice Mayer & Assocs 201 W 54th St Ste 1C New York NY 10019

ZUBER, NORMA KEEN, career counselor, educator; b. Iuka, Miss., Sept. 27, 1934; d. William Harrington and Mary (Hebert) Keen; m. William Frederick Zuber, Sept. 14, 1958; children: William Frederick Jr., Michael, Kimberly, Karen. BS in Nursing, U. Southwestern La., 1956; MS in Counselling, Calif. Luth. U., 1984. Nat. cert. counselor, nat. cert. career counselor. Intensive care nurse Ochsner Found. Hosp., New Orleans, 1956-59; career devel. counselor BFC Counseling Ctr., Ventura, Calif., 1984-87; founder, prin., counselor Career & Life Planning-Norma Zuber & Assocs., Ventura, 1987—; instr. adult continuing edn. Ventura C.C., 1987—; instr. Calif. State U., Northridge, 1988-89; instr. U. Calif. Santa Barbara, Antioch U.; mem. adv. coun. on tchr. edn. Calif. Luth. U., Thousand Oaks, 1984-87; mem. adv. bd. for development of profl. career counseling cert. program U. Calif., San Diego, 1991—. Co-author: The Nuts and Bolts of Career Counseling: Setting Up and Succeeding in Private Practice, 1992. Chmn. bd. dirs. women's ministries Missionary Ch., Ventura, 1987-90. Recipient profl. contbn. award H.B. McDaniel Found.-Stanford U. Sch. Edn., 1988, Govt. Rels. Com. Cert. of Appreciation, Am. Assn. for Counseling and Devel. Mem. NAFE, ACA, Nat. Career Devel. Assn., Calif. Assn. Couseling and Devel. (chmn. legis. task force 1987-89, So. Calif. coord. area cons. for Calif. Career Devel. Assn. 1990, Jim Saum govt. rels. award 1989), Internat. Platform Assn., Nat. Career Devel. Assn. (western regional trustee 1995—), Calif. Career Devel. Assn. (bd. dirs. 1985-91, membership dir. 1991-92, pres. 1992-93, Leadership and Professionaliam award 1988, 89), Calif. Career Conf. (program chair 1993), Ventura County Profl. Women's Network (dir. membership 1990-91), Calif. Registry Profl. Counselors and Paraprofls. (chmn. bd. dirs. 1990—). Republican. Home: 927 Sentinel Ct Ventura CA 93003-1202 Office: Career and Life Planning Norma Zuber and Assocs 3585 Maple St Ste 237 Ventura CA 93003-3508

ZUCCO, RONDA KAY, addictions program manager; b. Peoria, Ill., Apr. 3, 1960; d. Richard Leon Zucco. BA, So. Ill. U., 1981. Cert. addictions profl.; internat. cert. alcohol and drug counselor. Counselor Spl. Supportive Svcs., So. Ill. U., Carbondale, 1981-83; substance abuse counselor Interventions, Chgo., 1984-86; addictions counselor Parkside at BroMenn, Bloomington, Ill., 1986-89; dir. continuing care/sr. counselor Fla. Hosp. (formerly Parkside), Orlando, Fla., 1989-95, cmty. rels. rep. Ctr. for Psychiatry, 1995; addictions program mgr. Charter Behavioral Health Sys., Kissimmee, Fla., 1995—; tng. instr. for group facilitation Parkside/Fla. Hosp., 1989-95; presenter seminars in field, bd. dirs. Ill. Cert. Bd. Addiction Profls., Bloomington, 1986-89. Vol. ARC, Cardondale, 1978-81, crisis hotline Jackson County Cmty. Mental Health Ctr., Cardondale, 1981, Alliance for the Mentally Ill Greater Orlando, 1995—, Coalition for the Homeless, Orlando, 1995—; active AIDS Spkr.'s BUr., BroMenn Healthcare, Bloomington, Ill., 1986-89. State of Ill. Gen. Assembly scholar, 1977-81. Mem. Am. Mktg. Assn., Am. Assn. for Counseling and Devel., Am. Mental Health Counselors

Assn., Fla. Alcohol and Drug Abuse Assn., Fla. Prevention Assn., Nat. Businesswomen's Leadership Assn., C. of C. Greater Orlando, Kappa Delta Pi, Chi Sigma Iota. Home: 10600 Bloomfield Dr Apt 311 Orlando FL 32825

ZUCHELLI, LISA MARIE, environmental policy specialist, researcher; b. Charlottesville, Va., June 3, 1956; d. Artley Joseph Zuchelli and Hazel (Bryant) Houston. BA in Comm., George Mason U., 1993, MS in Biology, 1995. Registered environ. profl., Nat. Registry Environ. Profls. Environ. policy specialist Logistics Mgmt. Inst., McLean, Va., 1994—. Co-author (software manual) STC Publs. Database Software, 1993; contbr. articles to profl. jours. Vol. 2d grade tchr. ESL Program, Arlington (Va.) Schs., 1990-91. Mem. Soc. Environ. Mgmt. and Tech., SW Va. Solid Waste Mgmt., Phi Theta Kappa, Lambda Pi Eta.

ZUCHOWSKI, BEVERLY JEAN, chemistry educator; b. Toledo, Ohio, Jan. 11, 1950; d. Frank I. and Esther C. (Steinke) Patronik; m. Mark G. Zuchowski, May 21, 1971; children: Caroline H., Mark J., Gregory S., Beverly A. BS in Edn., Bowling Green State U., 1974, MAT in Chemistry, 1989. Cert. tchr. physics, chemistry and math. 7-12, Ohio. Instr. chemistry and physics Eastwood Schs., Luckey, Ohio, 1974-77, Perrysburg (Ohio) Pub. Schs., 1978-88, Owens Tech. Coll., Perrysburg, 1981-88; grad. asst. Bowling Green (Ohio) State U., 1988-89; chemistry instr. Perrysburg Pub. Schs., 1989—; mem. Ohio Dept. Edn. Sci. Proficiency Content Com., 1995—; tchr. intern Ctr. of Sci. and Industry, Columbus, Ohio, 1987; mem. Rossford (Ohio) Bd. Edn., 1988—; tchr. chaperone, Young Exptl. Scientist, Columbus, 1988—, Women in Sci., Bowling Green, 1989—. Mem. Rossford (Ohio) Bd. Edn., 1988—, v.p., 1991-92; mem. Penta County Vocat. Sch. Bd. Edn., 1994-95; leader Girl Scouts U.S., Rossford, 1978—; precinct worker Wood County Bd. of Elections, 1982-87. Mem. NEA, Ohio Edn. Assn., Nat. Sci. Tchrs. Assn., Ohio Coun. Tchrs. Math., Ohio Acad. Sci., Sch. Edn. Coun. Ohio, Perrysburg Edn. Assn. (treas. 1981), Rossford Community Svc. League (sec. 1992), Ohio Womens Caucus, Rossford Lions Club (charter), Toledo Mothers of Twins Club, Penta County Vocational Sch. Bd. of Edn. Democrat. Lutheran. Home: 3 Riverside Dr Rossford OH 43460 Office: Perrysburg High Sch 550 E South Boundary St Perrysburg OH 43551-2501

ZUCK, WYNONA COLLEEN, editor; b. Kansas City, Mo., Sept. 30, 1939; d. Earl Albert and Bertha (Drake) Howell; m. James Daniel Bardwell (div. 1967); 1 child, John Albert; m. Willard Alonzo Zuck; step-children: Cathy, Dawn, Sherrie, Linda. AA, Longview Community Coll. Paste-up artist Western Auto, Kansas City, Mo., 1957-60; keyline artist Trainor, Christianson & Barclay, Kansas City, 1960-61, Art, Inc., Kansas City, 1961-62, Nat. Bellas Hess, N. Kansas City, Mo., 1965-69, Unity Sch. Christianity, 1969-72; assoc. editor Wee Wisdom, Unity Village, Mo., 1972, editor, 1977-85; assoc. editor Daily Word, Unity Village, 1985, editor, 1985—; mem. editorial adv. com. Unity Sch., Unity Village, 1986—. Mem. Phi Theta Kappa. Office: Daily World 1901 NW Blue Pkwy Unity Village MO 64065-0001

ZUCKER, BARBARA J., artist; b. Abington, Pa., Oct. 5, 1943; d. Martin J. Herbert and Jean Elizabeth (McCormick) Martin; m. F. Donald Zucker, Apr. 4, 1964. BA, Ursinus Coll., 1966; postgrad., Acad. Fine Arts, Florence, Italy, 1968-69; MEd, Temple U., 1971. One-woman shows include Bucknell U., Lewisburg, Pa., 1975, Phila. Art Alliance, 1975, Multiple Choice Gallery, Blue Bell, Pa., 1976, Ursinus Coll., 1977, 81, Muhlenberg Coll., Allentown, Pa., 1979, Gwynedd-Mercy Coll., Gwynedd Valley, Pa., 1982, Glassboro (N.J.) State Coll., 1984, Gallery 1st Bapt. Ch. in Am., Providence, 1985, Univ. Gallery, St. Joseph's U., Phila., 1989, The Berman Mus. Art, Phila., 1990, Moravian Coll., Bethlehem, Pa., 1992, Phila. Mus. Art, 1993, Widener U. Mus., Chester, Pa., 1994, Ocean Wood Gallery, Birch Harbor, Maine, 1995, Gloucester Country Coll., Sewell, N.J., 1996. Recipient Best of Show award Perkiomen Valley Art Ctr., 1993, 95, Open House Gallery award for excellence in water color, 1994, award in memory Ethel Sokolove, 1995. Mem. Artists Equity Assn. (pres. Phila. chpt. 1993-94, exhibition chair 1993—, bd. dirs. 1992—, Golden Svc. award 1994), Phila. Water Color Club, Nat. League Am. Pen Women. Home and Studio: 10 Delphi Rd Schwenksville PA 19473

ZUCKER, JEAN MAXSON, nurse; b. Dunmore, Pa., Aug. 9, 1925; d. Earl L. and Florence M. (Cromwell) Maxson; R.N., Kings County Hosp. Center, 1948; cert. gerontol. nurse; children—Lawrence F., Pamela J., Diane K. Pvt. duty nurse various locations, N.Y., N.J., 1959-64; indsl. nurse Bendix Corp., Eatontown, N.J., 1955; asst. head nurse Point Pleasant Hosp., N.J., 1964-66; head nurse intensive and coronary care unit VA Hosp., Ft. Howard, Md., 1974-78; clin. nurse USPHS Hosp., Balt., 1978-81; nursing supr. VA Hosp. Center, Ft. Howard, 1981-94; clin. nurse VAMC, Ft. Howard, 1994—; tchr. in field. Mem. Am., Md. nurses assns., Am. Assn. Critical Care Nurses, NOW. Democrat. Methodist.

ZUCKER, MARJORIE BASS, medical researcher, hematologist; b. N.Y.C., June 10, 1919; d. Murray H. and Agnes (Naumburg) Bass; m. Howard D. Zucker, June 25, 1938; children: Andrew A., Ellen Zucker Harrison, Joan, Barbara Zucker-Pinchoff. AB, Vassar Coll., 1939; postgrad., Columbia Coll. Medicine, 1943-45; PhD, Columbia U., 1944. Rsch. asst. Coll. Physicians and Surgeons Columbia U., N.Y.C., 1944-49; asst. to assoc. prof. physiology Coll. of Dentistry NYU, 1949-54; assoc. mem. Sloan Kettering Inst., N.Y.C., 1955-63; asst. rsch. dir. ARC Rsch. Lab NYU Med. Ctr., N.Y.C., 1963-70, assoc. prof. pathology, 1963-71, prof. pathology, 1971-92, prof. emeritus, 1992—; mem. various rev. coms. NIH, Bethesda, Md., 1971-85. Co-author: The Physiology of Blood Platelets, 1965; co-patentee composition containing platelet factor 4, 1988; contbr. numerous articles to prof. jours. Recipient award N.Y. Met. chpt. Am. Women in Sci., 1986. Mem. Internat. Soc. Thrombosis (mem. coun., Marian Barnhart Lecture award 1989), Soc. for Exptl. Biology and Medicine (pres. 1983-85), Choice in Dying (dir., v.p. 1990). Democrat. Address: 333 Central Park W New York NY 10025-7145

ZUCKER-FRANKLIN, DOROTHEA, medical scientist, educator; b. Berlin, Aug. 9, 1930; came to U.S., 1949; d. Julian and Gertrude (Feige) Zucker; m. Edward C. Franklin, May 15, 1956 (dec. 1982); 1 child, Deborah Julie. BA, Hunter Coll., 1952; MD, N.Y. Med. Coll., 1956. Diplomate Am. Bd. Internal Medicine. Intern Phila. Gen. Hosp., 1956-57; resident in internal medicine Montefiore Hosp., N.Y.C., 1957-59, postdoctoral fellow in hematology, 1959-61; with Med. Sch. NYU, N.Y.C., 1962—, prof. Med. Sch., 1974—, dir. lab., 1966—; asst. attending physician Montefiore Hosp., 1961-65; assoc. attending physician Univ. Hosp., 1968-74, attending physician, 1974—; assoc. attending physician Bellevue Hosp., 1968-74, attending physician, 1974—; cons. physician Manhattan (N.Y.) VA Hosp., 1970—, PHS Agy. for Healthcare Policy and Rsch., 1992—; sci. adv. bd., rev. panel Israel Cancer Rsch. Fund, 1982—; mem. U.S.-Israel Binat. Sci. Found., 1980—; bd. dirs. Henry M. and Lillian Stratton Found., Inc., 1987—; AID related Rsch. Rev. Com. NIHLB, 1986-90; mem. allergy immunol. com. NIH, 1974-80, pathological tng. com. NIH, 1971-74, Health Resource Coun., N.Y.C., 1971-74, blood products com. FDA, 1981-87. Mem. editl. bd. Blood, 1973-76, 80-86, Jour. Reticuloendothelial Soc., 1964-74, 80—, Am. Jour. Pathology, 1979—, Blood Cells, 1980—, Ultrastructural Pathology, 1979, Am. Jour. Medicine, 1981—, Hematology Oncology, 1982—, Jour. Immunology, 1986—; author: (with others) The Physiology and Pathology of Leukocytes, 1962, Atlas of Blood Cells, Function and Pathology, 1981, 2d edit., 1989, Amyloidosis, 1990; contbr. 250 articles to sci. publs., and 10 chpts. to med. textbooks. Recipient Career Devel. award NIH, 1965-70; NIH rsch. grantee, 1970—; postdoctoral fellow in electromicroscopy NYU, 1962-63. Fellow N.Y. Acad. Scis.; mem. Inst. Medicine NAS, Am. Fedn. Clin. Rsch., Am. Soc. Clin. Investigation, Am. Assn. Physicians, Am. Soc. Hematology (pres. 1995, chairperson subcom. on leukocyte physiology 1977, chairperson subcom. on immunohematology 1984, exec. coun. 1985—, advanced learning resources com. 1987—), Soc. Exptl. Biology and Medicine, Am. Soc. Exptl. Biology, Am. Soc. Immunologists, Am. Soc. Cell Biology, Reticuloendothelial Soc. (pres. program and nominating coms. 1984-85), N.Y. Soc. Electron Microscopists (pres. 1962, 84-85), N.Y. Soc. for Study of Blood. Office: NYU Med Ctr 550 1st Ave New York NY 10016-6481

ZUCKERMAN, KAREN MARSHA, lawyer; b. Bklyn., Dec. 3, 1947; d. Jacob Eli and Pearl Lee (Cantor) Z.; 1 child, Maxwell Zuckerman-Fisher. BA, Rider Coll., 1969; MA, Hofstra U., 1978; JD, U. Houston, 1984. Bar: Tex. 1984, U.S. Dist. Ct. (so. dist.) Tex. 1985, U.S. Ct. Appeals (5th cir.) 1988. Tchr. Massapequa (N.Y.) High Sch., 1969-75; program analyst N.Y. State Dept. Mental Hygiene, Albany, 1975-79; field rep. pub. employees fedn. N.Y. State, Albany, 1979-80; program dir. sch. pub. health U. Tex., Houston, 1980-81; law intern to dist. judge U.S. Dist. Ct. (so. dist.) Tex., Houston, 1984; ptnr. Liddell, Sapp, Zivley, Hill & LaBoon, Houston, 1991-93; of counsel McFall, Sherwood & Sheehy, Houston, 1994-95; pres., CEO Profl. Fee Oversight Ptnrs., Inc., Houston, 1995—; adj. prof. law U. Houston, 1986, 87; participant People to People/Citizen Amb. Program to USSR, 1988. Mem. ABA, Am. Corp. Counsel Assn., State Bar Tex. Democrat. Jewish. Office: Profl Fee Oversight Ptnrs Inc Two Houston Ctr 909 Fannin St Houston TX 77010

ZUCKERMAN, MARJORIE EVELYN, lawyer; b. Bklyn., Mar. 10, 1929; d. Herman and Adelaide (Lemlein) Wohl; m. George R. Zuckerman, Sept. 22, 1955; children: Marcia Lynn, Steven Alan. BA, Bklyn. Coll., 1948; MA, Adlephi U., Garden City, N.Y., 1971; JD, Touro Law Sch., Huntington, N.Y., 1989. Bar: N.Y. 1989; cert. tchr. English, grades 9-12. Asst. county atty. Suffolk County atty., Hauppauge, N.Y., 1989-91; pvt. practice Bay Shore, N.Y., 1991-94; ptnr. Zuckerman & Zuckerman, Bay Shore, 1994—; officer Suffolk Acad. Law, Hauppauge, 1995—. Recipient Pro Bono award Suffolk County Bar Assn., 1994. Office: Zuckerman & Zuckerman 134 4th Ave Bay Shore NY 11706

ZUCKMAN, JILL B., reporter; b. Washington, July 6, 1965; d. Harvey Lyle and Charlotte (Snyder) Z. BA, Brown U., 1987. Reporter The Milw. Jour., 1987-89, Congrl. Quar., Washington, 1989-94, The Boston Globe, Washington, 1994—; bd. dirs. Brown Alumni Monthly, Providence, R.I. Office: The Boston Globe 1130 Connecticut Ave NW Washington DC 20036

ZUICK, DIANE MARTINA, elementary education educator; b. Gary, Ind., May 19, 1951; d. Arnold and Matilda (Chaimovitz) Herskovic; m. Norman Robert Zuick, Aug. 12, 1973; children: Scott, Amy. BS in Edn., Ind. U., 1972, MS in Edn., 1974. Tchr. 5th grade George L. Myers Sch., Portage, Ind., 1972-73, tchr. 3d grade, 1973-83, tchr. 1st grade, 1983-90, tchr. 2d grade, 1990—; mem. prime time com. Portage Twp. Schs., 1991—, mem. reading curriculum com., 1987-88, mem. devel. com., 1983-85; mem. adv. K'ton Ton Pre-Sch., Highland, Ind., 1984-86. Chair sch. bd. Congregation Beth Israel, Hammond, Ind., 1993-95, mem. sch. bd., 1992-95, mem. exec. bd., 1994—; mem. B'nai B'rith, Hammond, 1993—, mem. dist. bd. govs., 1995—. Recipient Ind. Dept. Instrn. Prime Time award, 1988, 89; Portage Twp. Schs. grantee, 1993, 94. Mem. NEA, Ind. State Tchrs. Assn., Portage Assn. Tchrs., Tchrs. Applying Whole Langs., Internat. Reading Assn., Ind. U. Alumni Assn. Home: 58 Cedar Ln Schererville IN 46375-1107 Office: Portage Twp Schs 6240 US Highway 6 Portage IN 46368-5057

ZUKAS, PATRICIA LYDIA, artist, chef; b. Brooklyn, N.Y., Jan. 1, 1948; d. Thomas Joseph and Margaret (Feuerstein) Z.; 1 child, Christopher Minchin. AAin Mgmt. Theater, Dance, Nassau C.C., N.Y., 1971; BS in Interdisciplinary Fine Arts, Empire State Coll., 1976; MFA, Md. Inst., 1979. Cert. whole foods chef. Grad. asst. to Irving Kriesberg Empire State Coll., N.Y., 1971-72; supr. art dept. Little Mecca Youth Ctr., Long Island, N.Y., 1974-75; instr., vis. artist Ctr. Creative Studies Coll. Art and Design, Detroit, 1979-80; art instr. Metro. Coll. U. New Orleans, 1981; group counselor, art therapist Young Adult Inst., N.Y.C., 1981-82; art instr. Leisure Edn. Evergreen State Coll., Olympia, Wash., 1983-84; guest lectr. Gross Point Artists Assn., Detroit, 1979. One woman exhibns. include U. New Orleans, 1981, Ctrl. Hall Artists, N.Y.C., 1983; group exhibns. include Westbeth Gallery, N.Y.C., 1975, SUNY Old Westbury, 1974-75, 76, SUNY Albany, 1977, Marion Sarach Dance Co., N.Y.C., 1977, Mount Royal Sch. Painting Decker Gallery, Balt., 1979, Md. Acad. Scis., Balt., 1979, Marchand-Parson Gallery, Shelter Is., N.Y., 1979, Ctr. Creative Studies Coll. Art. and Design, Detroit, 1979, 80, Gertrude Stein Gallery, New Orleans, 1981, Scheurich Gallery, New Orleans, 1981, Ctrl. Hall Artists, N.Y.C., 1983, U. Wash., Seattle, 1985, Seattle Women's Gym, 1985, Pratt Fine Art Ctr., Seattle, 1985, Husted Gallery, 1986, Silvermine Gallery, New Canaan, Conn., 1992, Willow St. Gallery, Washington, 1992, 93, A. Salon/Willow St. Gallery, Washington, 1993, E St., Washington, 1993, Gallery 76,Wenatchee, Wash., 1995, Confluence Gallery, Twisp, Wash., 1995, 96; dance perfomance The Sannyas Theatre Am. Renaissance Theater, N.Y.C., 1982; featured in We'Moon, 1993. Founding mem. Poumonok Movement Co., Sea Cliff, N.Y., 1976; founder, pres. Seattle chpt. Women's Caucus for Art, 1984; del. nat. adv. bd. Women's Caucus for Art, Phila., 1986-88. Grantee Artist Space, N.Y.C, 1975; recipient cash award Most Exptl. Painting Women's Caucus for the Arts, 1981; recognition Nat. Mus. Women inthe Arts, 1994. Fellow Vermont Studio Ctr. Buddhist.

ZULAUF, MADELINE RUTH, civilian military employee, photographer; b. Neptune, N.J., Oct. 9, 1948; d. Everett Minor and Mary Elizabeth (Williams) Slocum; m. Bateston Franklin Stoddard, Jr., Apr. 2, 1967 (div. July 1972); children: Michael, Mary Beth; m. Sander William Zulauf, May 26, 1979. AA, County Coll. of Morris, 1976; BA, Montclair State U., 1978. Photographer U.S. Army Rsch., Devel. & Engring. Ctr., Picatinny Arsenal, N.J., 1979-84, TV prodr., dir., 1984-87, visual info. specialist, 1987—; cons. phototech. program County Coll. of Morris, Randolph, N.J., 1983-88, mem. student co-op adv. bd., 1989-94; pres. federally employed women U.S. Army Rsch., Devel. & Engring. Ctr., Picatinny Arsenal, 1984-85, chairperson fed. women's program, 1987-89. Photographer: (mag.) Horns of Plenty, 1989, (book) Above the River, 1990. Photographer Jersey Battered Women's Shelter, Morristown, N.J., 1985-88. Recipient Humanitarian award Equal Opportunity Office, 1984. Mem. Acad. Am. Poets, Internat. Ctr. Photography. Episcopalian. Home: 3 Braemar Ct Andover NJ 07821 Office: US Army Rsch Devel & Engring Ctr B-1 Dover NJ 07801

ZULCH, JOAN CAROLYN, retired medical publishing company executive, consultant; b. Great Neck, N.Y., Apr. 10, 1931; d. Walter Howard and Edna Ruth (Howard) Z. B.S. in Biology, Allegheny Coll., 1952; postgrad., Hunter Coll., 1954. Med. sec. E.R. Squibb & Sons, N.Y.C., 1952; with Macmillan Pub. Co., N.Y.C., 1952-88, editorial asst. med. dept., 1952-56, asst. editor med. dept., 1956-58, editor med. dept., 1958-61, med. editor coll. and profl. div., 1961-75, sr. editor medicine, coll. and profl. div., 1975-78, exec. editor med. books, profl. books div., 1978-79, editor-in-chief, 1979-80, asst. v.p., editor-in-chief profl. books div., 1980-82; v.p., pub. med., nursing, health sci. dept. Macmillan Pub. Co., 1982-85, v.p., pub. med. books, sci., tech., med. dept., 1985-88, cons. med. pub., 1989—. Recipient Best Illustrated Med. Book award Assn. Med. Illustrators, 1977, Outstanding Book in Health Sci. award Assn. Am. Pubs., 1982. Mem. AAAS, AAUW, Post Libr. Assn., L.I.U. (rec. sec. 1990-93, exec. coun. 1990—), Friends of Locust Valley Libr. (pres. 1991-93, 94-96, treas. 1993-94, 96—), Alpha Gamma Delta, Delta Sigma Rho. Republican. Home and Office: 36 Wood Ln Lattingtown PO Box 547 Locust Valley NY 11560-0547

ZULLO, CHRISTINE PATRICIA, nurse; b. Jamaica, N.Y., Jan. 12, 1951; d. Thomas Vincent and Beatrice Elsie (Stumpf) Marblo; m. Douglas Anthony Zullo, Mar. 25, 1972; children: Brian, David, Aimee, Jeffrey. BSN, Molloy Coll., 1972. RN, N.Y. Staff nurse Albert Einstein Hosp., Bronx, N.Y., 1972-73; pub. health nurse Vis. Nurse Svc. of N.Y., Flushing, N.Y., 1973-74, Vis. Nurse Assn. of L.I., Garden City, N.Y., 1974—. Co-pres. Herricks Athletic Booster Assn., New Hyde Park, N.Y., 1994-96; co-treas. USAF Acad. Parents Club of L.I., 1994-96. Home: 41 Yorkshire Rd New Hyde Park NY 11040 Office: Vis Nurse Assn LI 100 Garden City Plaza Garden City NY 11530

ZUMO, BILLIE THOMAS, biologist; b. Cheyenne, Wyo., Sept. 25, 1936; d. Thomas Elias and Katherine A. (Pappas); m. Charles Vincent, Aug. 21, 1959; 1 child, Thomas J. BA, U. Wyo., Laramie, 1958; MA, U. No.Colo., Greeley, 1963. Cert. tchr. Tchr. Carey Jr. H.S., Cheyenne, 1958-61, 61-63; English language tchr. McCormick Jr. H.S., Cheyenne, 1961; biology tchr. Laramie County C.C., Cheyenne; tchr. Central H.S., Cheyenne, 1963; exec. bd. Sch. Dist. curriculum adv., 1982-85; chmn. sci. dept., 1990—; mem. faculty adv. com. Central High Sch., 1988—, mem. prin. screening com., 1990-91. Football statis. Cen. Football Team, Cheyenne, 1976—; lay mem. rsch. com. of the Pharmacy Theraputics Com., 1985; judge sch. dist. sci. fair, Cheyenne, 1987-88; ch. choir dir., Cheyenne. Recipient Disting. Svc. award Sts. Constandine and Helen Orthodox Ch., 1979, Disting. Svc. award as choir dir. Archbishop Iakovos, N.Y., 1988. Mem. Nat. Assn. Biology Tchrs. (state rep. 1992—), NEA, Cheyenne Tchrs. Edn. Assn., Wyo. Edn. Assn., Nat. Forum of Greek Orthodox Musicians, Ladies Philoptochos Soc. of Denver Diocese (treas. 1989-93, 1st v.p. 1993-95, pres. 1995—), AAUW, Phi Delta Kappa. Democrat. Eastern Greek Orthodox. Home: 900 Ranger Dr Cheyenne WY 82009-2535 Office: Cen High Sch 5500 Education Dr Cheyenne WY 82009-4008

ZUMPANO, MARYANN, administrative assistant; b. Woodside, N.Y., Mar. 12, 1936; d. Anthony Joseph and Katherine (Viano) De Nicola; m. Anthony William Zumpano; children: Toni, Kathryn, William, Nicholas. B of Profl. Studies, SUNY, 1990; cert. pc specialist, SUNY, Stony Brook, 1996. Engring. asst. McClave Engring., Smithtown, N.Y., 1983—; student adv. asst. Empire State Coll., N.Y., 1989-90; regional office asst. state edn. dept. SARA, Hauppaug, N.Y., 1990—; student asst. info. sessions Empire State Coll., Hauppauge, 1995—. Trustee, pres., v.p. Smithtown (N.Y.) Sch. Bd., 1978-93; trustee Western Suffolk BOCES, Dix Hills, N.Y., 1995—; adv. for handicapped children Smithtown SEPTA, 1975—. Recipient Outstanding Cmty. Svc. award Smithtown Sch. Adminstrs., 1985, Letter of Recognition award Gov. M. Cuomo, N.Y., 1993, U.S. Rep. G. Hochbreuckner, 1993. Mem. NOW, Nat. Womens Polit. Caucus. Home: 10 Hill Rd Saint James NY 11780

ZUMPE, DORIS, ethologist, researcher, educator; b. Berlin, May 18, 1940; came to U.S., 1972; d. Herman Frank and Eva (Wagner) Z. BSc, U. London, 1961, PhD, 1970. Asst. to K.Z. Lorenz, Max-Planck-Inst. für Verhaltensphysiologie, Seewiesen, Fed. Republic Germany, 1961-64; rsch. asst. and assoc., lectr. Inst. Psychiatry, U. London, 1965-72; rsch. assoc. Emory U. Sch. Medicine, Atlanta, 1972-74, asst. prof. psychiatry (ethology), 1974-77, assoc. prof., 1977-87, prof., 1987—; reviewer NSF, 7 sci. jours. Contbr. over 140 articles to profl. jours. NIMH grantee, 1971—. Mem. AAAS, Internat. Soc. Psychoneuroendocrinology, Internat. Primatological Soc., Internat. Soc. for Human Ethology, Soc. for Study of Reprodn., Am. Soc. Primatologists, N.Y. Acad. Scis., Earl Music Am., Viola da Gamba Soc. Am. Office: Emory U Sch Medicine Dept Psychiatry Atlanta GA 30322

ZUMWALD, TERESA MARIE, communications specialist; b. Cin., Aug. 12, 1963; d. Jerome Anthony Armbruster and Eileen Mae Bachus; m. Joseph Frank Zumwald, Jr., Oct. 10, 1987; children: Sierra Marie, Sheridan Marija, Marin Kellie. BA in Journalism, Ohio State U., 1985. Writer, copyeditor Med. Econs. Co., Oradell, N.J., 1984; reporter, copyeditor Univ. Comms. Ohio State U., Columbus, 1984-85; comms. specialist Woolpert, Dayton, Ohio, 1985-89; owner, comms. specialist Zumwald & Co., Englewood, Ohio, 1989—. Author: For the Love of Dayton, 1995 (awards of merit Women in Comms. and Internat. Assn. Bus. Comms., 1996); co-author: Metropolitan Dayton: Flying High, 1993; editor mng. program mag. U.S. Air and Trade Show souvenir program, 1992-95, trade, 1992, 94 (best program award 1992, 93). Vol. Children's Med. Ctr., Dayton, 1985-86. Mem. Women in Comms. (chairperson Vanguard award 1987-88, publicity chair regional conf. 1991-92, newsletter editor 1989-90, sec. 1990-92, awards of merit 1990-91, 93, 95-96, Woman of Achievement award 1992), Internat. Assn. Bus. Communicators (best news writing award 1990, award of merit for feature writing, 1996). Office: Zumwald & Co PO Box 206 Englewood OH 45322

ZUNK, DOLORES, secretary; b. Hooker, Okla., Apr. 21, 1930; d. Allen Walker and Hazel Pearl (Rollins) Loughridge; m. Robert Arnold Zunk, Mar. 26, 1950; children: Vickie Sue, Kathy Lynn, Steven Wayne, Beckie Gayle. Attended, Salt City Bus. Coll., Hutchinson, Kans., 1948-49. Meat clk., bookkeeper Hooker (Okla.) Locker, 1970-78; bookkeeper, sec. Tumbleweed Lock & Key Trophy & Engraving, Hooker, 1978—. Mem. DAR (rec. sec. High Plains chpt. 1989-92, vice regent 1993-95, regent 1995—), First Families of Brown County, Ohio, First Families of Twin Territories, Soc. of Descendants of W.Va. Pioneers. Democrat. Disciples of Christ. Home: PO Box 130-805 N Jefferson Hooker OK 73945-0130

ZUNKER, SHARON JIENELL, commercial expediters company executive; b. Charleston, W.Va., July 28, 1943; d. Clifford W. and Iva A. (Neeley) Kenneway; m. Anthony F. Zunker, Sept. 19, 1980; children: Tibor Kreiter, Melissa J., Anthony F. Jr. Diploma, Sprayberry High Sch., 1963. Various clerical positions N.Y. and Ga.; mgr. Winn Dixie, Ft. Lauderdale, Fla., 1973-76; owner, operator Union 76 Svc. Sta., Manistee, Mich., 1980-82; pres., owner Am. Comml. Expediters, Pompano Beach, Fla., 1988—; sec.-treas. Atlanta Envelope Co., 1962-64. Mem. Am. Legion, Odd Fellows, Rosecrucions, Internat. Platform Assn. U.S. C. of C., Smithsonian. Republican. Home: 6250 SW 6th St Pompano Beach FL 33068-1709 Office: Am Comml Expediters 1852 NW 21st St Pompano Beach FL 33069-1306

ZUPKUS, ELLEN CICCONE, clinical psychologist, consultant; b. Passaic, N.J., Oct. 28, 1954; d. Joseph Condoluro and Emma (Gash) Ciccone; m. Edward Walter Zupkus Jr., July 29, 1984; children: Maureen, Erin, Emily, Lauren. BA, Kean Coll. N.J., 1976; MA, Seton Hall U., 1978, PhD, 1985. Cert. sch. psychologist N.J.; Nat. cert sch. psychologist, group psychotherapist; lic. psychologist, N.J., N.Y. Adj. instr. Seton Hall U., South Orange, N.J., 1979-84; chairperson child study team Bergen County Spl. Svcs. Sch. Dist., Paramus, N.J., 1983-85; pvt. practice Holmdel, N.J., 1985—; adj. instr. Rider Coll., Lawrenceville, N.J., 1986; prin. clin. psychologist Marlboro (N.J.) Psychiat. Hosp., 1986-88; cons. psychologist Arthur Brisbane Child Treatment Ctr., Farmingdale, N.J., 1988-89; adj. instr. Monmouth Coll., West Long Branch, N.J., 1989; cons. psychologist Cedar Grove (N.J.) Residential Ctr., 1989—; cons. psychologist Adult Diagnostic and Treatment Ctr., Avenel, N.J., 1980-82; clin. psychologist Woodbridge Child Diagnostic Ctr., Avenel, 1980-83; presenter workshop on Million Adolescent Personality Inventories, 1989, Internat. Play Therapy Conf., The Netherlands, 1996. Author: (with others) Conference on the Millon Inventories, 1987; contbr. articles to profl. jours. Mem. Monmouth County Sexual Abuse Coalition, Monmouth County Child Sexual Abuse Com., Nat. Audubon Soc., Nat. Wildlife Fedn., Vienna, Va. Mem. APA (assoc.), N.J. Psychol. Assn., N.J. Assn. Sch. Psychologists, Monmouth Ocean County Psychol. Assn., Seton Hall U. Sch. Psychology Assn. (pres. 1981), N.J. Network for Treatment Sex Offenders, Am. Coll. Forensic Examiners. Office: 702 N Beers St Holmdel NJ 07733-1510

ZURAW, KATHLEEN ANN, special education and physical education educator; b. Bay City, Mich., Sept. 29, 1960; d. John Luke and Clara Josephine (Kilian) Z. AA with high honors, Delta Community Coll., 1980; BS with high honors, Mich. State U., 1984, MA, 1987. Cert. spl. edn., mentally impaired phys. edn. grade K-12, adaptive phys. edn. tchr., Mich. Summer water safety instr. Camp Midicha, Columbia, Mich., 1982, Bay Cliff Health Camp, Big Bay, Mich., 1983; summer spl. edn. tchr. Jefferson Orthopedic Sch., Honolulu, 1984, 85, 86, Ingham Intermediate Sch. Dist., Mason, Mich., 1987; spl. edn. tchr. Bay Arenac Intermediate Sch. Dist., Bay City, 1985-87, Berrien County Intermediate Sch. Dist., Berrien Springs, Mich., 1987—; mem. citizen amb program fitness delegation People's Republic China, 1991. Area 17 coach Mich. Spl. Olympics, Berrien Springs, 1987—; mem. YMCA, St. Joseph, Mich., 1987—, Y-Ptnrs., 1989, Coun. Exceptional Children; participant Citizen Ambassador Delegation to People's Republic of China, 1991. Mem. Am. Alliance Health, Phys. Edn., Recreation and Dance, Phi Theta Kappa, Phi Kappa Phi, Phi Delta Kappa. Roman Catholic. Home: 7306 W S Saginaw Rd Bay City MI 48706

ZURBUCHEN, SUSAN JANE, arts consultant; b. Madison, Wis., June 28, 1949; d. Herbert August and Ruth Helen (Pfaffenbach) Z. BA in Speech and Theatre, Lakeland Coll., Sheboygan, Wis., 1970; MA in Theatre Arts, U. Minn., 1972. Regional coordinator Office Criminal Justice Programs, Traverse City, Mich., 1976-77; bus. mgr. Old Town Playhouse, Traverse City, 1978-81; dir. adminstrn. Ind. Arts Commn., Indpls., 1982-85; arts cons. 10th Pan Am. Games, Indpls., 1985-87; mem. faculty arts adminstrn. and theatre Butler U., Indpls., 1988—; mng. dir. Indpls. Children's Choir, 1994—. Bd. dirs. Criminal Justice Adv. Council, Traverse City, 1976-82; pres. bd. dirs Women's Resource Ctr., Traverse City, 1977-80; bd. dirs. Very Spl. Arts Ind., 1989-92, Fiesta Indpls., Ind. Assembly Local Arts Agys., 1995—. Mem. LWV (bd. dirs. 1981-82), Am. Theatre Assn. Mem. United Ch. of Christ.

ZUSSY, NANCY LOUISE, librarian; b. Tampa, Fla., Mar. 4, 1947; d. John David and Patsy Ruth (Stone) Roche; m. R. Mark Allen, Dec. 20, 1986. BA in Edn., U. Fla., 1969; MLS, U. So. Fla., 1977, MS in Pub. Mgmt., 1980. Cert. librarian, Wash. Ednl. evaluator State of Ga., Atlanta,

1969-70; media specialist DeKalb County Schs., Decatur, Ga., 1970-71; researcher Ga. State Libr., Atlanta, 1971; asst. to dir. reference Clearwater (Fla.) Pub. Libr., 1972-78, dir. librs., 1978-81; dep. state libr. Wash. State Libr., Olympia, 1981-86, state libr., 1986—; chmn. Consortium Automated Librs., Olympia, 1982—; cons. various pub. librs., Wash., 1981—; exec. officer Wash. Libr. Network, 1986-90; v.p. WLN (non-profit orgn.), 1990-93. Contbr. articles to profl. jours. Treas. Thurston-Mason Community Mental Health Bd., Olympia, 1983-85, bd. dir., 1982-85; mem. race com. Seafair Hydroplane Race, Seattle, 1986—, mem. milk carton derby team, 1994—. Mem. ALA, Assn. Specialized and Coop. Libr. Agys. (legis. com. 1983-86, chmn. 1985-87, vice chmn. state libr. agys. sect. 1985-86, chmn. 1986-87, chmn. govt. affairs com. Libr. Adminstrn. and Mgmt. Assn., 1986-87), Freedom To Read Found. (bd. dirs. 1987-91), Chief Officers of State Libr. Agys. (bd. dirs.-at-large 1987-90, v.p., pres.-elect 1990-92, pres. 1992-94), Wash. Libr. Assn. (co-founder legis. planning com. 1982—, fed. rels. coord. 1984—), Fla. Libr. Assn. (legis. and planning com. 1978-81), Pacific N.W. Libr. Assn., Rotary (bd. dirs. 1995—), Phi Kappa Phi, Phi Beta Mu. Home: 904 E Bay Dr NE # 404B Olympia WA 98506-3970 Office: Wash State Libr PO Box 42460 Olympia WA 98504-2460

ZUTTER-BROCK, PAMELA JEAN, secondary school educator; b. Lima, Peru, Feb. 8, 1951; d. Louis Eric and Georgia Nell (Carpenter) Zutter; m. Carrol Bruce Brock, June 11, 1978; 1 child, Eric David. BA English, McKendree Coll., 1969-73; degree in Spanish and French, So. Ill. U., Edwardsville, 1973-74. Tchr. and chair French, Spanish, English Wright City (Mo.) High Sch., 1974-83; tchr. Francis Howell H.S., St. Charles, Mo., 1983—; fgn. lang. chair Francis Howell High Sch., St. Charles, Mo., 1987—; sponsor Spanish Club, St. Charles; pres. Community Tchrs. Assn., Wright City, 1980-81. New mem. followup First United Meth. Ch., St. Charles, 1992, 93, 94, bd. mem., 1985-87; mem. Rennaisance, St. Charles, 1993-96. Mem. Am. Assn. Tchrs. Spanish and Portuguese, Fgn. Lang. Tchrs. Assn. Greater St. Louis. Methodist. Home: 175 Quail Run Dr Defiance MO 63341

ZWEIFEL, KARYN KAY, author; b. McAlester, Okla., Jan. 24, 1962; d. Jack I. and Kay L. (Wallace) Zweifel; m. Douglas G. Turner, Jr., Apr. 27, 1985; 1 child, Kathryn. Student, Ala. Sch. Fine Arts, Birmingham, 1975-79, LaGrange (Ga.) Coll., 1979; BA, U. Ala., Birmingham, 1983. Copywriter Direct Comm., Birmingham, 1983. Author: Southern Vampires, 1995, Covered Bridge Ghost Stories, 1995, Dog-gone Ghost Stories, 1996, The Contractor's Book of Excuses, 1996. Vol. various polit. campaigns, Birmingham, 1980—; mem. Ala. Arise, Montgomery, 1992—, Birmingham Clinic Def. Team, 1994—; chair com. St. Andrew's Presch., 1993-96. Recipient Young Adult Libr. Svcs. award ALA, 1996. Mem. NOW. Episcopalian.

ZWILICH, ELLEN TAAFFE, composer; b. Miami, Fla., Apr. 30, 1939; d. Edward Porter and Ruth (Howard) Taaffe; m. Joseph Zwilich, June 22, 1969 (dec. June 1979). MusB, Fla. State U., 1960, MusM, 1962; D Mus. Arts, Juilliard Sch., 1975; studies with Roger Sessions and Elliott Carter; MusD (hon.), Oberlin Coll., 1987, Converse Coll., 1994; LHD (hon.), Manhattanville Coll., 1991, Marymount Manhattan Coll., 1994, N.Y. New Sch., Mannes, 1995. composer in residence Santa Fe Chamber Music Festival, 1990, Am. Acad. Rome, 1990; first Composer's Chair, Carnegie Hall, 1995. Premiere, Symposium for Orch., Pierre Boulez, N.Y.C., 1975, Chamber Symphony and Passages, Boston Musica Viva, Richard Pittman, 1979, 82. Symphony 1, Gunther Schuller, Am. Composers Orch., 1982; violinist Am. Symphony, N.Y.C., 1965-73; composer: Sonata in Three Movements, 1973-74; String Quartet, 1974; Clarino Quartet, 1977; Chamber Symphony, 1979; Passages (for Soprano and Chamber Ensemble), 1981; String Trio, 1982; Symphony 1:3 Movements for Orch., 1982 (Grammy nomination New World Records, 1987); Divertimento, 1983; Einsame Nacht, 1971; Emlekezet, 1978; Im Nebel, 1972; Passages for Soprano and Orch., 1982; Trompeten, 1974; Fantasy for Harpsichord, 1983; Intrada, 1983; Prologue and Variations, 1983; Double Quartet for Strings, Chamber Music Soc. of Lincoln Ctr., 1984; Celebration for Orch., Indpls. Symphony, John Nelson, 1984; Symphony #2 (Cello Symphony) San Francisco Symphony, Edo De Waart, 1985, Symphony #2 Louisville Orch. recording, L.L. Smith (Grammy nomination 1991); Concerto Grosso 1985, Handel Festival Orch., Steven Simon, 1986; Concerto for Piano and Orch., Detroit Symphony, Gunther Herbig, Marc-André Hamelin, 1986; Images for 2 Pianos and Orch., Nat. Symphony Orch., F. Machetti, 1987; Tanzspiel, Peter Martins N.Y.C. Ballet, 1987; Praeludium Boston chpt. AGO, 1987; Trio for piano, violin and cello; Kalichstein, Laredo, Robinson trio, 1987; Symbolon, Zubin Mehta and the N.Y. Philharm., Leningrad and Moscow (USSR), N.Y.C. (Koussevitsky Internat. Rec. award nominee 1990), 1988; concerto for trombone and orch. J. Friedman, Sir Georg Solti, Chgo. Symphony, 1989, concerto for trombone and orch. Christian Lindberg, James De Priest, Malmö Symphony, concerto for flute and orch. D.A. Dwyer, Seija Ozawa, Boston Symphony, 1990, quintet for clarinet and string quartet David Schiffrin, Chamber Music N.W., 1990; concerto for oboe and orch. John Mack, Christoph von Dohnanyi, Cleve. Orch., 1991; concerto for bass trombone strings, timpani and cymbals Chgo. Symphony Orch. Ch. Vernon, Daniel Barenboim, 1991; concerto for violin, violoncello and orch. Jaime Laredo, Sharon Robinson, Louisville Orch., L. Smith, 1991; Immigrant Voices Peter Leonard, St. Lukes Orch., N.Y. Internat. Festival ot the Arts Chorus, Ellis Island, 1991, concerto for flute and orch., D.A. Dwyer, J. Sedares, London Symphony Orch., 1992, Symphony #3 (Grammy nominee 1993), J. Ling, N.Y. Philharmonic, 1993, concerto for bassoon and orch., Nancy Goeres, Lorin Maazel, Pitts. Symphony, 1993, concerto for horn and string Orch., David Jolley, Rochester Philharm., L.L. Smith., 1993, Fantasy for Orch., JoAnn Falletta, Long Beach Symphony Orch., 1994, American Concerto, 1994, A Simple Magnificat, 1994; New World Records: Music By Ellen Taaffe Zwilich; N.Y. Philharm. conducted by Zubin Mehta. Recipient Elizabeth Sprague Coolidge Chamber Music prize, 1974, Gold medal G.B. Viotti, Vercelli, Italy, 1975, citation Ernst von Dohnanyi, 1981, Pulitzer prize, 1983, Composers award Lancaster Symphony Orch., Arturo Toscanini Music Critics award, 1987, Alfred I. DuPont award, 1991; Martha Baird Rockefeller Fund rec. grantee, 1977, 79, 82, Guggenheim fellow, 1981. Mem. AAAL, Am. Fedn. Musicians (hon. life), Am. Music Ctr. (bd. dirs., v.p. 1982-84), Am. Composers Orch. (bd. dirs.), Am. Acad. Arts and Letters (Acad. award 1984, elected 1992), MacDowell Colony (bd. dirs.), Fla. Artists Hall of Fame, Carnegie Hall Composer's Chair. Home: 600 W 246th St Bronx NY 10471-3611 Office: care Music Assocs Am 224 King St Englewood NJ 07631-3026

ZYLANOFF, PHILLIPA LOUISE, anesthesiologist; b. Indpls., Feb. 2, 1943; d. Joseph David Zylanoff and Phillipa (Schreiber) Moore; divorced; children: Gwendolynn, Ann, Daniel, Aliza, Tamar. BS, Calif. State U., Hayward, 1966; MD, Med. Coll. Pa., 1972. Diplomate Am. Bd. Anesthesiology. Asst. prof. U. Calif., Davis, 1977-79; staff anesthesiologist New Iberia (La.) Parish Hosp., 1979-81; pvt. practice anesthesiology Moorehead, Ky., 1981-84; asst. prof. U. S. Ala., Mobile, 1985-87; dir. anesthesiology Randolph Hosp., Asheboro, N.C., 1987-90; pvt. practice anesthesiology Detroit, 1990—. Contbr. articles to profl. jours. Course dir. Mich. affiliate Am. Heart Assn. Mem. AMA, Mich. Soc. Anesthesiologists, Mich. State Med. Soc., Wayne County Med. Soc. (peer review com. 1991-93), Soc. Cardiovascular Anesthesiologists (presenter 1987). Republican. Jewish. Home: 17311 Beechwood Ave Franklin MI 48025-5523

ZYROFF, ELLEN SLOTOROFF, information scientist, classicist, educator; b. Atlantic City, N.J., Aug. 1, 1946; d. Joseph George and Sylvia Beverly (Roth) Slotoroff; m. Jack Zyroff, June 21, 1970; children: Dena Rachel, David Aaron. AB, Barnard Coll., 1968; MA, The Johns Hopkins U., 1969, PhD, 1971; MS, Columbia U., 1973. Instr. The Johns Hopkins U., Balt., 1970-71, Yeshiva U., N.Y.C., 1971-72; Bklyn Coll., 1971-72; libr., instr. U. Calif., 1979, 81, 91, San Diego State U., 1981-85, 94; prof. San Diego Mesa Coll., 1981—; dir. The Reference Desk Rsch. Svcs., La Jolla, Calif., 1983—; prin. libr. San Diego County Libr., 1985—; v.p. Archaeol. Soc. Am., Balt., 1970-71. Author: The Author's Apostrophe in Epic from Homer Through Lucan, 1971, Cooperative Library Instruction for Maximum Benefit, 1989; contbr. articles to profl. jours. Pres. Women's Am. ORT, San Diego, 1979-81. Mem. ALA (chair divsn. coms. 1982—), Am. Philol. Assn., Calif. Libr. Assn. (elected to assembly 1993-95, 96—), Am. Soc. Info. Sci., Am. Classical League, Libr. Congress Cataloging in Publ. Adv. Group, Toastmasters, Beta Phi Mu. Office: PO Box 12122 La Jolla CA 92039-2122